About this book

International GAAP® 2017 has been fully revised and updated in order to:

- Include a new chapter on the new leases standard IFRS 16 (*Leases*). This is a joint standard issued by the IASB and FASB which is likely to affect all entities in all industries, and will result in more assets and liabilities being recognised on the Statement of Financial Position.
- Explore the implementation issues arising as entities plan for the future adoption of IFRS 9 (*Financial Instruments*) and IFRS 15 (*Revenue from Contracts with Customers*), including those referred to the IFRS Transition Resource Group for Impairment of Financial Instruments and the Joint Transition Resource Group for Revenue Recognition.
- Address amended standards and new interpretations issued since the preparation of the 2016 edition.
- Explain the many other initiatives that are currently being discussed by the IASB and by the IFRS Interpretations Committee and the potential consequential changes to accounting requirements. In particular, projects on insurance contracts and the conceptual framework for financial reporting may all result in significant changes to current accounting practice.
- Provide insight on the many issues relating to the practical application of IFRS, based on the extensive experience of the book's authors in dealing with recent day-to-day issues.

The book is published in three volumes. The 54 chapters – listed on pages ix to xi – are split between the three volumes as follows:

- Volume 1 - Chapters 1 to 23,
- Volume 2 - Chapters 24 to 41,
- Volume 3 - Chapters 42 to 55.

Each chapter includes a detailed list of contents and list of illustrative examples.

Each of the three volumes contains the following indexes covering all three volumes:

- an index of extracts from financial statements,
- an index of references to standards and interpretations,
- a general index.

Preface

The IASB reported earlier this year that 122 of the 147 jurisdictions they have researched require the use of IFRS for all or most listed companies and financial institutions, and a further 13 jurisdictions permit the use of IFRS. Several large economies like China, India and Japan do not require IFRS for all or most of their listed companies, but they have made considerable progress to move towards or to converge with IFRS. While it is unlikely that the United States will adopt IFRS in the near term, there are more than 500 foreign IFRS reporters with a significant market capitalisation listed on US markets and many US investors are familiar with IFRS-based financial statements. Global financial reporting is now in a position where there are essentially only two global-scale systems of financial reporting – IFRS and US GAAP.

In 2016, the IASB completed its project on lease accounting and made considerable efforts to provide implementation and adoption support regarding the new revenue recognition and financial instruments standards.

The publication of IFRS 16 – *Leases*, which is effective from 1 January 2019 onwards, marks the completion of the IASB's long-running project on lease accounting. The main objective of the new standard – to bring most lease obligations that are currently not recognised, on to the balance sheet – is converged with the FASB's objective. However, certain requirements for the recognition, measurement, presentation and disclosure of leases by lessees and lessors differ. IFRS 16 is more complex than its predecessor, IAS 17 – *Leases*, and is giving rise to implementation questions that the IASB will need to address in a timely manner.

IFRS 9 – *Financial Instruments* – and IFRS 15 – *Revenue from Contracts with Customers*, which are effective from 1 January 2018, introduce important improvements and fill major gaps in the existing literature. The joint IASB/FASB transition resource group for revenue recognition (TRG) and the IASB's transition resource group for impairment of financial instruments have provided valuable forums for identifying interpretation questions that inevitably arise when entities implement complex accounting standards. In April 2016, the IASB published amendments that improve the guidance in IFRS 15 and address some issues that the TRG discussed. These amendments and the many interpretations and emerging practices regarding the new standards have been included in this edition of *International GAAP* and will help companies that are implementing these standards.

In the past year, the IASB has worked on its projects on insurance contracts and the conceptual framework. The work on insurance contracts, the IASB's longest running project, is crucial because as Hans Hoogervorst noted in comments to the European

Parliament: '[i]nsurance is an extremely important business with substantial systemic risks. These risks are currently amplified by the current environment of persistently low interest rates. ... There is no real global standard and there is a wide variety of practices around the world. Some of these standards provide information that is clearly wrong.' In February 2016, the Board concluded that it had completed all the necessary due process steps and instructed the staff to commence the drafting process. A final standard is now expected to be published in the first half of 2017. In order to address the complex interaction between IFRS 9 and the insurance contracts project, the IASB published, in September 2016, amendments to IFRS 4 – *Insurance Contracts.* These amendments provide certain reliefs to insurers that are intended to mitigate the impact of applying IFRS 9 until the new insurance contracts standard becomes effective.

The IASB is redeliberating its revised conceptual framework based on the comments received in response to the exposure draft *Conceptual Framework for Financial Reporting.* Some of the most challenging areas being discussed are measurement, the distinction between debt and equity, and the role of profit and loss versus other comprehensive income. While it is hard to make progress on such major conceptual issues, these are nevertheless the areas that will be most important to constituents. The IASB expects to publish the revised conceptual framework in the first half of 2017.

The IASB has recently been considering its priorities for the period from 2016 to 2020, based on the feedback it received in response to its request for views *2015 Agenda Consultation.* The IASB's new work programme can be broken down into the following main categories, each of which contains a number of projects:

- *Standard-setting and relating projects* – conceptual framework, disclosure initiative: materiality practice statement, insurance contracts, and rate-regulated activities;
- *Implementation and other activities* – implementation and adoption support activities, post-implementation reviews, and a public consultation on small and medium-sized entities;
- *Active research agenda* – principles of disclosure, primary financial statements, financial instruments with characteristics of equity, goodwill and impairment, dynamic risk management, and business combinations under common control; and
- *Research pipeline* – equity method of accounting, extractive activities, pollutant pricing mechanisms, provisions, contingent liabilities and contingent assets (review of IAS 37), variable and contingent consideration, and feasibility studies (on small and medium-sized entities, post-employment benefits that depend on asset returns, and high inflation).

We believe that these are important areas of accounting where the IASB will be able to make meaningful improvements in financial reporting. In particular, the IASB is addressing the needs of users and preparers of financial statements by focussing on better communication (by way of better disclosures and presentation), implementation and adoption support, and post-implementation reviews of existing standards.

We think that it is important for the IASB to consider carefully the scope of a new project before starting the development of a new standard. This is to avoid scope-creep and projects taking longer than necessary to complete. In addition, the decision to undertake a major project should not automatically lead to the decision not to address urgent practical issues affecting the same area of accounting. In our view, such a situation might warrant two projects: one to solve the existing practical issue; and one to address the more fundamental and conceptual issues.

The IFRS Foundation Trustees identified, in the 2015 review of the organisation, the consistency of application and implementation of IFRS as one of the IFRS Foundation's primary strategic goals. They correctly see this in a holistic manner as requiring: clear drafting of standards; guidance that is consistent with a principle-based approach to standard setting; a responsive approach towards requests for interpretations; close co-operation with enforcers and educational efforts.

We believe the IASB should take its time in the final drafting stages of a standard, i.e. between the final redeliberations and the issuance of the standard, thereby ensuring that the drafting of the standard is clear and unambiguous. Drafting accounting standards for a worldwide audience involves a particular level of complexity because constituents interpret the wording in the context of their own experience and background. In addition, the operability of a standard enhances its quality to a large degree and we believe that the benefits of spending more time on this during the drafting phase outweigh the costs of doing so.

The consistent application of IFRS remains essential to its credibility. We believe that *International GAAP*, now in its twelfth edition, plays an important role in ensuring consistent application. Our team of authors and reviewers hails from all parts of the world, and includes not only our global technical experts but also senior client-facing staff. This gives us an in-depth knowledge of practice in many different countries and industry sectors, enabling us to go beyond mere recitation of the requirements of standards to explaining their application in many varied situations.

We are deeply indebted to many of our colleagues within the global organisation of EY for their selfless assistance and support in the publication of this book. It has been a truly international effort, with valuable contributions from EY people around the globe.

Our thanks go particularly to those who reviewed, edited and assisted in the preparation of drafts, most notably: John Alton, Mark Barton, Silke Blaschke, Jason Bond, Brian Byrne, Larissa Clark, Tony Clifford, Muriel Courel, Tai Danmola, Jackson Day, Alison Dobbie, Chantelle Duffy, Charles Feeney, Lisa Filomia-Atkas, Josh Forgione, Peter Gittens, Lindsay Gotsman, Laure Guégan, Paul Hebditch, Jennifer Hillenmeyer, Deborah Jones, Guy Jones, Akashi Kohno, Steinar Kvifte, Vincent de La Bachelerie, Martin Lee, Twan van Limpt, Meredith Lloyd, Michiel van der Lof, James Luke, Mark Mahar, Robert McCracken, Joseph McGrath, Ellie Morris, John O'Grady, Eric Ohlund, Gerard van Santen, Cyra Sharma, Rachel Simons, Alison Spivey, Paul Sutcliffe, Leo van der Tas, Evangelia Tsakiroglou, Hans van der Veen, Emma VanEmon, Jana Wahrisch, Arne Weber, Chris White and Luci Wright.

Our thanks also go to everyone who directly or indirectly contributed to the book's creation, including the following members of the Financial Reporting Group in the UK: Denise Brand, Rob Carrington, Larissa Connor, Anna Costigan, Diego Fernandez, Prahalad Halgeri, Parbin Khatun, Maria Kingston, Andrea Maylor, Bunmi Oluitan, Anna Pickup and Claire Taylor.

We also thank Jeremy Gugenheim for his assistance with the production technology throughout the period of writing.

London,	*Martin Beyersdorff*	*Jane Hurworth*	*Margaret Pankhurst*
October 2016	*Mike Bonham*	*Praveen Jindal*	*Tina Patel*
	Linzi Carr	*Ted Jones*	*Alexandra Poddubnaya*
	Victor Chan	*Bernd Kremp*	*Michael Pratt*
	Wei Li Chan	*Dean Lockhart*	*Tim Rogerson*
	Angela Covic	*Thomas Luescher*	*Serene Seah-Tan*
	Mike Davies	*Sharon MacIntyre*	*Anna Sirocka*
	Pieter Dekker	*Takahiro Makino*	*Charlene Teo*
	Julie Dempers	*Amanda Marrion*	*Michael Varila*
	Tim Denton	*Steve Martin*	*Tracey Waring*
	Dennis Deysel	*Emily Moll*	*Jane Watson*
	Dennis Esterhuizen	*Richard Moore*	

Lists of chapters

Volume 1

The lists of chapters in volumes 2 and 3 follow overleaf.

Volume 2

The list of chapters in volume 3 follows overleaf.

Volume 3

Abbreviations

The following abbreviations are used in this book:

Professional and regulatory bodies:

AASB	Australian Accounting Standards Board
AcSB	Accounting Standards Board of Canada
AICPA	American Institute of Certified Public Accountants
AOSSG	Asian-Oceanian Standard-Setters Group
APB	Accounting Principles Board (of the AICPA, predecessor of the FASB)
ARC	Accounting Regulatory Committee of representatives of EU Member States
ASAF	Accounting Standards Advisory Forum
ASB	Accounting Standards Board in the UK
ASBJ	Accounting Standards Board of Japan
ASU	Accounting Standards Update
CASC	China Accounting Standards Committee
CESR	Committee of European Securities Regulators, an independent committee whose members comprised senior representatives from EU securities regulators (replaced by ESMA)
CICA	Canadian Institute of Chartered Accountants
EC	European Commission
ECB	European Central Bank
ECOFIN	The Economic and Financial Affairs Council
EDTF	Enhanced Disclosure Task Force of the (FSB)
EFRAG	European Financial Reporting Advisory Group
EITF	Emerging Issues Task Force in the US
EPRA	European Public Real Estate Association
ESMA	European Securities and Markets Authority (see CESR)
EU	European Union
FAF	Financial Accounting Foundation
FASB	Financial Accounting Standards Board in the US

FCAG	Financial Crisis Advisory Group
FEE	Federation of European Accountants
FSB	Financial Stability Board (successor to the FSF)
FSF	Financial Stability Forum
G4+1	The (now disbanded) group of four plus 1, actually with six members, that comprised an informal 'think tank' of staff from the standard setters from Australia, Canada, New Zealand, UK, and USA, plus the IASC
G7	The Group of Seven Finance Ministers (successor to G8)
G8	The Group of Eight Finance Ministers
G20	The Group of Twenty Finance Ministers and Central Bank Governors
GPPC	Global Public Policy Committee of the six largest accounting networks
HKICPA	Hong Kong Institute of Certified Public Accountants
ICAI	Institute of Chartered Accountants of India
IASB	International Accounting Standards Board
IASC	International Accounting Standards Committee. The former Board of the IASC was the predecessor of the IASB
IASCF	International Accounting Standards Committee Foundation (predecessor of the IFRS Foundation)
ICAEW	Institute of Chartered Accountants in England and Wales
ICAS	Institute of Chartered Accountants of Scotland
IFAC	International Federation of Accountants
IFASS	International Forum of Accounting Standard Setters
IFRIC	The IFRS Interpretations Committee (formerly the International Financial Reporting Interpretations Committee) of the IASB
IGC	Implementation Guidance Committee on IAS 39 (now disbanded)
IOSCO	International Organisation of Securities Commissions
IPSASB	International Public Sector Accounting Standards Board
IPTF	International Practices Task Force (a task force of the SEC Regulations Committee)
ISDA	International Swaps and Derivatives Association
IVSC	International Valuation Standards Council
KASB	Korea Accounting Standards Board
RICS	Royal Institution of Chartered Surveyors
SAC	Standards Advisory Council, predecessor of the IFRS Advisory Council which provides advice to the IASB on a wide range of issues
SEC	Securities and Exchange Commission (the US securities regulator)
SIC	Standing Interpretations Committee of the IASC (replaced by IFRIC)

TEG	Technical Expert Group, an advisor to the European Commission
TRG	Joint Transition Resource Group for Revenue Recognition

Accounting related terms:

ADS	American Depositary Shares
AFS	Available-for-sale investment
ARB	Accounting Research Bulletins (issued by the AICPA)
ARS	Accounting Research Studies (issued by the APB)
ASC	Accounting Standards Codification®. The single source of authoritative US GAAP recognised by the FASB, to be applied to non-governmental entities for interim and accounting periods ending after 15 September 2009
ASU	Accounting Standards Update
CCIRS	Cross Currency Interest Rate Swap
CDO	Collateralised Debt Obligation
CGU	Cash-generating Unit
CU	Currency Unit
DD&A	Depreciation, Depletion and Amortisation
DPF	Discretionary Participation Feature
E&E	Exploration and Evaluation
EBIT	Earnings Before Interest and Taxes
EBITDA	Earnings Before Interest, Taxes, Depreciation and Amortisation
EIR	Effective Interest Rate
EPS	Earnings per Share
FAS	Financial Accounting Standards (issued by the FASB). Superseded by Accounting Standards Codification® (ASC)
FC	Foreign currency
FICE	Financial Instruments with the Characteristics of Equity
FIFO	First-In, First-Out basis of valuation
FRS	Financial Reporting Standard (issued by the ASB)
FTA	First-time Adoption
FVLCD	Fair value less costs of disposal
FVLCS	Fair value less costs to sell (following the issue of IFRS 13, generally replaced by FVLCD)
GAAP	Generally accepted accounting practice (as it applies under IFRS), or generally accepted accounting principles (as it applies to the US)
HTM	Held-to-maturity investment

IAS	International Accounting Standard (issued by the former board of the IASC)
IBNR	Incurred but not reported claims
IFRS	International Financial Reporting Standard (issued by the IASB)
IGC Q&A	Implementation guidance to the original version of IAS 39 (issued by the IGC)
IPO	Initial Public Offering
IPR&D	In-process Research and Development
IPSAS	International Public Sector Accounting Standard
IRR	Internal Rate of Return
IRS	Interest Rate Swap
JA	Joint Arrangement
JCA	Jointly Controlled Asset
JCE	Jointly Controlled Entity
JCO	Jointly Controlled Operation
JO	Joint Operation
JV	Joint Venture
LAT	Liability Adequacy Test
LC	Local Currency
LIBOR	London Inter Bank Offered Rate
LIFO	Last-In, First-Out basis of valuation
NCI	Non-controlling Interest
NBV	Net Book Value
NPV	Net Present Value
NRV	Net Realisable Value
OCI	Other Comprehensive Income
PP&E	Property, Plant and Equipment
R&D	Research and Development
SCA	Service Concession Arrangement
SE	Structured Entity
SFAC	Statement of Financial Accounting Concepts (issued by the FASB as part of its conceptual framework project)
SFAS	Statement of Financial Accounting Standards (issued by the FASB). Superseded by Accounting Standards Codification® (ASC)
SME	Small or medium-sized entity
SPE	Special Purpose Entity
SV	Separate Vehicle

TSR	Total Shareholder Return
VIU	Value In Use
WACC	Weighted Average Cost of Capital

References to IFRSs, IASs, Interpretations and supporting documentation:

AG	Application Guidance
AV	Alternative View
B, BCZ	Basis for Conclusions on IASs
BC	Basis for Conclusions on IFRSs and IASs
DI	Draft Interpretation
DO	Dissenting Opinion
DP	Discussion Paper
ED	Exposure Draft
IE	Illustrative Examples on IFRSs and IASs
IG	Implementation Guidance
IN	Introduction to IFRSs and IASs
PIR	Post-implementation Review

Authoritative literature

The content of this book takes into account all accounting standards and other relevant rules issued up to September 2016. Consequently, it covers the IASB's *Conceptual Framework for Financial Reporting* and authoritative literature listed below.

References in the main text of each chapter to the pronouncements below are generally to the versions of those pronouncements as approved and expected to be included in the Blue Book edition of the Bound Volume 2017 International Financial Reporting Standards – IFRS – Consolidated without early application – Official pronouncements applicable on 1 January 2017, to be published by the IASB.

References to those pronouncements below which have an effective date after 1 January 2017 (such as IFRS 9 – *Financial Instruments*) are to the versions of those pronouncements as denoted by the ISBN references noted below. These are expected to be included in the Red Book edition of the Bound Volume 2017 International Financial Reporting Standards – IFRS – Official pronouncements issued at 1 January 2017, to be published by the IASB.

References in the main text to pronouncements that applied only to periods beginning before 1 January 2017 are generally denoted by the last version of the Blue Book edition of the Bound Volume in which they were included. For example, IFRS 3 (2007) refers to IFRS 3 – *Business Combinations*, which was included in the Blue Book edition of the Bound Volume 2007 International Financial Reporting Standards – IFRS – Consolidated without early application – Official pronouncements applicable on 1 January 2007.

US GAAP accounting standards are organised within a comprehensive FASB Accounting Standards Codification®, which is now the single source of authoritative US GAAP recognised by the FASB to be applied to non-governmental entities and has been applied in this publication.

† The standards and interpretations marked with a dagger have been withdrawn or superseded.

IASB Framework

The Conceptual Framework for Financial Reporting

International Financial Reporting Standards (2017 Bound Volume)

IFRS 1	First-time Adoption of International Financial Reporting Standards
IFRS 2	Share-based Payment
IFRS 3	Business Combinations
IFRS 4	Insurance Contracts
IFRS 5	Non-current Assets Held for Sale and Discontinued Operations

IFRS 6	Exploration for and Evaluation of Mineral Resources
IFRS 7	Financial Instruments: Disclosures
IFRS 8	Operating Segments
IFRS 10	Consolidated Financial Statements
IFRS 11	Joint Arrangements
IFRS 12	Disclosure of Interests in Other Entities
IFRS 13	Fair Value Measurement
IFRS 14	Regulatory Deferral Accounts

International Financial Reporting Standards (mandatory after 1 January 2017)

IFRS 9	Financial Instruments	ISBN 978-1-909704-47-3
IFRS 15	Revenue from Contracts with Customers	ISBN 978-1-909704-33-6
IFRS 16	Leases	ISBN 978-1-911040-03-3

International Accounting Standards (2017 Bound Volume)

IAS 1	Presentation of Financial Statements
IAS 2	Inventories
IAS 7	Statement of Cash Flows
IAS 8	Accounting Policies, Changes in Accounting Estimates and Errors
IAS 10	Events after the Reporting Period
IAS 11	Construction Contracts
IAS 12	Income Taxes
IAS 16	Property, Plant and Equipment
IAS 17	Leases
IAS 18	Revenue
IAS 19	Employee Benefits
IAS 20	Accounting for Government Grants and Disclosure of Government Assistance
IAS 21	The Effects of Changes in Foreign Exchange Rates
IAS 23	Borrowing Costs
IAS 24	Related Party Disclosures
IAS 26	Accounting and Reporting by Retirement Benefit Plans
IAS 27	Separate Financial Statements
IAS 28	Investments in Associates and Joint Ventures
IAS 29	Financial Reporting in Hyperinflationary Economies
IAS 32	Financial Instruments: Presentation
IAS 33	Earnings per Share
IAS 34	Interim Financial Reporting
IAS 36	Impairment of Assets
IAS 37	Provisions, Contingent Liabilities and Contingent Assets
IAS 38	Intangible Assets
IAS 39	Financial Instruments: Recognition and Measurement
IAS 40	Investment Property
IAS 41	Agriculture

IFRS Interpretations Committee Interpretations

IFRIC 1	Changes in Existing Decommissioning, Restoration and Similar Liabilities
IFRIC 2	Members' Shares in Co-operative Entities and Similar Instruments
† IFRIC 3	Emission Rights
IFRIC 4	Determining whether an Arrangement contains a Lease
IFRIC 5	Rights to Interests arising from Decommissioning, Restoration and Environmental Rehabilitation Funds
IFRIC 6	Liabilities arising from Participating in a Specific Market – Waste Electrical and Electronic Equipment
IFRIC 7	Applying the Restatement Approach under IAS 29 Financial Reporting in Hyperinflationary Economies
IFRIC 9	Reassessment of Embedded Derivatives
IFRIC 10	Interim Financial Reporting and Impairment
IFRIC 12	Service Concession Arrangements
IFRIC 13	Customer Loyalty Programmes
IFRIC 14	IAS 19 – The Limit on a Defined Benefit Asset, Minimum Funding Requirements and their Interaction
IFRIC 15	Agreements for the Construction of Real Estate
IFRIC 16	Hedges of a Net Investment in a Foreign Operation
IFRIC 17	Distributions of Non-cash Assets to Owners
IFRIC 18	Transfer of Assets from Customers
IFRIC 19	Extinguishing Financial Liabilities with Equity Instruments
IFRIC 20	Stripping Costs in the Production Phase of a Surface Mine
IFRIC 21	Levies

Standing Interpretations Committee Interpretations

SIC-7	Introduction of the Euro
SIC-10	Government Assistance – No Specific Relation to Operating Activities
SIC-15	Operating Leases – Incentives
SIC-25	Income Taxes – Changes in the Tax Status of an Entity or its Shareholders
SIC-27	Evaluating the Substance of Transactions Involving the Legal Form of a Lease
SIC-29	Service Concession Arrangements: Disclosures
SIC-31	Revenue – Barter Transactions Involving Advertising Services
SIC-32	Intangible Assets – Web Site Costs

IASB Exposure Drafts

ED/2013/7	Insurance Contracts
ED/2014/4	Measuring Quoted Investments in Subsidiaries, Joint Ventures and Associates at Fair Value (Proposed amendments to IFRS 10, IFRS 12, IAS 27, IAS 28 and IAS 36 and Illustrative Examples for IFRS 13)
ED/2015/1	Classification of Liabilities (Proposed amendments to IAS 1)
ED/2015/3	Conceptual Framework for Financial Reporting
ED/2015/4	Updating References to the Conceptual Framework (Proposed amendments to IFRS 2, IFRS 3, IFRS 4, IFRS 6, IAS 1, IAS 8, IAS 34, SIC-27 and SIC-32)

ED/2015/5	Remeasurement on a Plan Amendment, Curtailment or Settlement/Availability of a Refund from a Defined Benefit Plan (Proposed amendments to IAS 19 and IFRIC 14)
ED/2015/7	Effective Date of Amendments to IFRS 10 and IAS 28
ED/2015/9	Transfers of Investment Property (Proposed amendments to IAS 40)
ED/2016/1	Definition of a Business and Accounting for Previously Held Interests (Proposed amendments to IFRS 3 and IFRS 11)

IFRS Interpretations Committee Exposure Drafts

DI/2012/2	Put Options Written on Non-controlling Interests	ISBN 978-1-907877-61-2
DI/2015/1	Uncertainty over Income Tax Treatments	ISBN 978-1-909704-99-2
DI/2015/2	Foreign Currency Transactions and Advance Consideration	ISBN 978-1-909704-98-5

IASB Discussion Papers

DP/2014/1	Accounting for Dynamic Risk Management: a Portfolio Revaluation Approach to Macro Hedging	ISBN 978-1-909704-39-8
DP/2014/2	Reporting the Financial Effects of Rate Regulation	ISBN 978-1-909704-58-9

Other IASB publications

IFRS for SMEs	International Financial Reporting Standard (IFRS) for Small and Medium-sized Entities (SMEs)	ISBN 978-1-911040-07-1

Chapter 42 Financial instruments: Introduction

Chapter 42 Financial instruments: Introduction

1 STANDARDS APPLYING TO FINANCIAL INSTRUMENTS

The IASB's accounting requirements for financial instruments are regarded by many as some of the more difficult to understand. There are many likely reasons for this, including the fact that it is such a broad topic encompassing some of the more complex contracts entities enter into. In addition, the requirements have been subject to a process of almost continual change over the last fifteen years or so and are dealt with in a number of different standards and other pronouncements.

The following are the standards which deal primarily with the accounting for financial instruments:

- IAS 32 – *Financial Instruments: Presentation;*
- IAS 39 – *Financial Instruments: Recognition and Measurement;*
- IFRS 7 – *Financial Instruments: Disclosures;* and
- IFRS 9 – *Financial Instruments.*

In addition a number of interpretations address the requirements of these standards, including:

- IFRIC 2 – *Members' Shares in Co-operative Entities and Similar Instruments;*
- IFRIC 9 – *Reassessment of Embedded Derivatives;*
- IFRIC 10 – *Interim Financial Reporting and Impairment;*
- IFRIC 16 – *Hedges of a Net Investment in a Foreign Operation;* and
- IFRIC 19 – *Extinguishing Financial Liabilities with Equity Instruments.*

Information about the development of the standards is set out at 1.1 to 1.4 below.

1.1 IAS 32

The original version of IAS 32 – *Financial Instruments: Disclosure and Presentation* – was published in March 1995. The presentation requirements of the standard were subject to significant review during 2002 and 2003 as part of the IASB's improvements project and a revised standard was published in December 2003. IFRS 7, which was published in August 2005, superseded the disclosure requirements in IAS 32 and the title of the latter standard was changed to reflect this. In February 2008, the IASB amended IAS 32 to change the classification of certain puttable financial instruments and instruments of limited life entities from liabilities to equity. Further amendments to IAS 32, designed to clarify its requirements for offsetting (or netting) of financial instruments, were issued in December 2011 and numerous other amendments have been made throughout the life of the standard.

The IASB recognises that the classification of financial instruments as liabilities or equity in accordance with IAS 32 presents many challenges. Consequently, it is working on a research project exploring whether the requirements in IAS 32 could be improved. In addition, it is looking at what improvements could be made to the presentation and disclosure requirements for financial instruments with characteristics of equity. The next formal step in this project is likely to be the publication of a discussion paper, possibly during 2017.

1.2 IAS 39

IAS 39 was originally published in March 1999. Its origins could be found in US GAAP and at a high level there were only limited differences between the two systems. The IASC adopted a similar 'mixed attribute' model, i.e. some financial instruments were measured by reference to their historical cost and some by reference to their fair value and the main ideas embodied in IAS 39 were:

- derivatives (including some embedded within other contracts) were measured at fair value;
- many financial assets were also measured at fair value;
- non-derivative liabilities were measured at amortised cost;
- hedge accounting rules were established such that:
  - the methods of hedge accounting were defined in a way that severely curtailed existing practices in many countries;
  - hedges were tested for effectiveness; and
  - ineffectiveness was reported in profit or loss; and
- certain fair value gains and losses could be reported initially in equity before being recycled into profit or loss at a later date.

By dealing with most aspects of virtually all financial instruments, it was the longest, and by far the most complex, standard issued by the IASC. The IASC saw a consequent need to help preparers, auditors and users to understand the practical implications of IAS 39. They did this by establishing a process whereby guidance in the form of Questions and Answers (Q&A) was developed and over 200 final Q&A were published. IAS 39, like IAS 32, was subject to significant review during 2002 and 2003 as part of the IASB's improvements project and a revised standard, incorporating most of the Q&A as implementation guidance, was published in December 2003.

Many other changes have been made to IAS 39 since its original publication. These include amendments in March 2004 allowing the use of hedge accounting for certain portfolio (or macro) hedges of interest rate risk and more in June 2005 restricting the ability of entities to designate financial instruments at fair value through profit or loss. Another notable change was made during the financial crisis in October 2008, allowing entities to reclassify certain financial assets thereby reducing the use of fair value accounting (see Chapter 46 at 6).

More recently, the publication of IFRS 9 will, when applied, result in most of the requirements of IAS 39 being superseded or carried forward to IFRS 9. However, as noted at 1.4 below, entities may continue to apply some or all the hedge accounting requirements of IAS 39 even after applying IFRS 9.

1.3 IFRS 7

A project principally focused on revising the then IAS 30 – *Disclosures in the Financial Statements of Banks and Similar Financial Institutions* – evolved into a comprehensive review of all disclosure requirements related to financial instruments. This resulted in the publication of IFRS 7 in August 2005, superseding IAS 30 and the disclosure requirements in IAS 32.

IFRS 7 has been subject to a number of amendments since publication. The requirements relating to liquidity risk were improved in the light of experience gained in the financial crisis; disclosures about transfers of financial assets were enhanced following an aborted attempt to revise the requirements addressing derecognition of financial assets in IAS 39; and more information about offsetting and netting agreements is now required. IFRS 9, when applied, also makes a significant number of amendments and additions to IFRS 7.

1.4 IFRS 9

In April 2009, during the financial crisis, the IASB committed itself to a comprehensive review of IAS 39. The IASB's plan split this project into the following three phases, each of which would result in the publication of requirements replacing the corresponding parts of IAS 39:

- classification of financial assets and financial liabilities;
- impairment and the effective interest method; and
- hedge accounting.

Originally, the IASB had proposed a simplified accounting model under which all financial instruments would be measured either at amortised cost or at fair value through profit or loss. Subsequently, additional categories of financial asset were introduced allowing certain investments in debt and equity instruments to be measured at fair value with most changes in value recognised in other comprehensive income. For debt instruments, those gains and losses are subsequently recycled to profit or loss on derecognition. In addition, the accounting for financial liabilities was eventually left much the same as in IAS 39, although the IASB introduced a requirement to recognise in other comprehensive income (rather than profit or loss) gains or losses on most financial liabilities designated at fair value through profit or loss to the extent they represent changes in the instrument's credit risk. The requirements of these parts of IFRS 9 are primarily covered in Chapters 47 and 50.

During the financial crisis, a number of commentators criticised the requirements of IAS 39 for unnecessarily delaying the recognition of impairments. IAS 39 uses a so called 'incurred loss' approach whereby impairments are not recognised until there is objective evidence of the impairment having occurred. The requirements in IFRS 9 are better described as an 'expected loss' approach. In almost all circumstances, applying IFRS 9 will result in the recognition of an impairment expense sooner than would have been the case under IAS 39. Consequently, at any point in time, an entity will have accumulated a higher impairment provision (and report a lower amount of equity) than would have arisen from applying IAS 39. This part of IFRS 9 is covered in Chapter 50 at 5.

The hedge accounting phase of the project was designed to simplify hedge accounting, expand the relationships for which hedge accounting could be applied and align the accounting requirements more closely with entities' risk management practices. IFRS 9 does not itself address portfolio hedge accounting and, viewed in isolation, is much less accommodating than IAS 39. However, IFRS 9 does allow for the continued application of the portfolio fair value hedge accounting requirements of IAS 39 alongside its more general hedge accounting requirements. In addition, entities wishing to use the portfolio cash flow hedge accounting guidance in IAS 39 can continue applying the entirety of IAS 39's hedge accounting requirements but without applying any of the hedge accounting requirements of IFRS 9.

The IASB has a separate research project which aims to eliminate any need for this continued application of IAS 39 (and also the so-called EU 'carve-out' – see 2 below). A discussion paper, *Accounting for Dynamic Risk Management: a Portfolio Revaluation Approach to Macro Hedging*, was published in April 2014, but the IASB has since concluded it is not yet in a position to develop its proposals into an exposure draft. Instead, the likely next step will be the publication of another discussion paper, the timing of which is uncertain and will not be before 2017. The hedge accounting requirements of IFRS 9 are covered in Chapter 53 and those of IAS 39 in Chapter 52.

The first version of IFRS 9 was published in November 2009 and significant amendments followed in October 2010 and November 2013 before it was finally completed in July 2014. Adoption of IFRS 9 is required for periods commencing on or after 1 January 2018.

A number of constituents have identified adverse accounting consequences that might arise from insurers applying IFRS 9 before a replacement for IFRS 4 – *Insurance Contracts.* The IASB has responded by developing amendments to IFRS 4 allowing certain insurers to adopt IFRS 9 at a later date as well as offering other reliefs if they do adopt IFRS 9. Further information about these changes is included in Chapter 55 at 11.

During the development of IFRS 9, the IASB worked closely with its counterparts at the FASB with the aim of aligning as far as possible the financial reporting requirements for financial instruments in accordance with IFRS and US GAAP. The measurement of fair values under the two bodies of GAAP is to a large extent the same and in June 2016 the FASB published a new standard requiring impairment of financial assets to be based on expected losses, although it is somewhat different to the approach in IFRS 9. Important differences also remain in the area of hedge accounting and there are significant differences in other areas including the approaches to classifying and measuring financial assets and to offsetting financial assets and financial liabilities.

1.5 Structure and objectives of the standards

The main text of the standards is supplemented by application guidance (which is an integral part of each standard).[1] IAS 32, IAS 39 and IFRS 9 are each supplemented by illustrative examples and IAS 39, IFRS 7 and IFRS 9 by implementation guidance. These examples and implementation guidance accompany, but are not part of, the standards.[2]

The objective of IAS 32 is to establish principles for presenting financial instruments as liabilities or equity and for offsetting financial assets and financial liabilities *[IAS 32.2]* whilst for IAS 39 (until IFRS 9 is applied) it is to establish principles for recognising and measuring financial assets, financial liabilities and some contracts to buy or sell non-financial items. *[IAS 39.1]*. The objective of IFRS 9 is to establish principles for the financial reporting of financial assets and financial liabilities that will present relevant and useful information to users of financial statements for their assessment of the amounts, timing and uncertainty of the entity's future cash flows. *[IFRS 9.1.1]*. The objective of IFRS 7 is to require entities to provide disclosures in their financial statements that enable users to evaluate:

(a) the significance of financial instruments for the entity's financial position and performance; and

(b) the nature and extent of risks arising from financial instruments to which the entity is exposed during the period and at the reporting date, and how the entity manages those risks. *[IFRS 7.1]*.

2 ADOPTION OF IFRS IN THE EUROPEAN UNION

An endorsement mechanism has been implemented whereby only those standards and interpretations that have been adopted for application within the EU may be applied in financial statements prepared in accordance with the 'IAS Regulation'. The role of this mechanism is not to reformulate or replace IFRSs, but to oversee the adoption of new standards and interpretations, intervening only when they contain material deficiencies or have failed to cater for features specific to the EU economic or legal environments. Given the number of constituents within the EU, the potential for non-endorsement in practice provides a degree of additional leverage over the work of the IASB.

IAS 39 as endorsed for use in the EU is currently different in one important respect from the version published by the IASB. Certain text has been removed (commonly known as a 'carve-out') so that, essentially, the EU version allows the use of macro-hedge accounting in situations that the full version of IAS 39 does not.[3] The European Commission has continued to emphasise the need for the IASB and representatives of European banks to find an appropriate technical solution to allow the removal of the carve-out as rapidly as possible.[4] However, there have been only limited signs of progress on this issue and IFRS 9 will not remove the reasons for the carve-out (see 1.4 above).

Originally IFRS 9 was scheduled for fast-track endorsement so that banks could apply the first version in their 2009 financial statements. However, these plans were withdrawn and the process postponed, pending completion of the entire standard. At the time of writing, it had been suggested that endorsement could well occur by the end of 2016, especially given the IASB's concessions for certain insurers (see 1.4 above), but until that happens European companies are prohibited from adopting IFRS 9 in financial statements prepared in accordance with the IAS Regulation.

3 HOW FINANCIAL INSTRUMENTS ARE DEALT WITH IN CHAPTERS 42 TO 54

The subject matter of this and the next twelve chapters is the recognition, measurement, presentation and disclosure of financial instruments as addressed in IAS 32, IAS 39, IFRS 7 and, where applied, IFRS 9. The topics covered by each, are as follows:

Chapter 42 – *Introduction*

- standards dealing with financial instruments
- European adoption

Chapter 43 – *Definitions and scope*

- key definitions
- scope and exceptions

Chapter 44 – *Derivatives and embedded derivatives*

- the defining characteristics of derivatives
- derivatives embedded within other contracts
- linked and separate transactions and 'synthetic' instruments

Chapter 45 – *Financial liabilities and equity*

- the classification of financial instruments by their issuer as financial liabilities or equity
- contracts settled by the delivery of equity instruments
- compound financial instruments (i.e. those containing both a liability and an equity component from the issuer's perspective)
- settlement of financial liabilities with equity instruments
- accounting for interest, dividends gains and losses
- treasury shares (i.e. shares held by their issuer)

Chapter 46 – *Classification (IAS 39)*

- determining the measurement category of financial assets and financial liabilities

Chapter 47 – *Classification (IFRS 9)*

- determining the measurement category of financial assets and financial liabilities

Chapter 48 – *Recognition and initial measurement*

- recognition
- initial measurement

Chapter 49 – *Subsequent measurement (IAS 39)*

- subsequent measurement and recognition of gains and losses
- amortised cost and the effective interest method
- impairment of financial assets
- the effect of foreign currencies

Chapter 50 – *Subsequent measurement (IFRS 9)*

- subsequent measurement and recognition of gains and losses
- amortised cost and the effective interest method
- impairment of financial assets
- the effect of foreign currencies

Chapter 51 – *Derecognition*

- derecognition of financial assets
- derecognition of financial liabilities

Chapter 52 – *Hedge accounting (IAS 39)*

- hedging instruments and hedged items
- types of hedging relationships
- accounting for effective hedges
- qualifying conditions for hedge accounting
- portfolio (or macro) hedging

Chapter 53 – *Hedge accounting (IFRS 9)*

- hedging instruments and hedged items
- qualifying conditions for hedge accounting
- other changes from IAS 39

Chapter 54 – *Presentation and disclosure*

- disclosure requirements of IFRS 7
- presentation of financial instruments and related transactions, gains and losses in the financial statements.

References

1 IAS 32, Application Guidance, para. before para. AG1, IAS 39, Application guidance, para. before para. AG1, IFRS 7, *Financial Instruments: Disclosure,* Appendix B, Application guidance, para. after main heading, IFRS 9, *Financial Instruments,* Appendix B, Application guidance, para. after main heading.

2 IAS 32, Illustrative Examples, para. after main heading, IAS 39, Illustrative Example, para. after main heading and Guidance on Implementing, para. before main heading Section A, IFRS 7, Guidance on implementing, para. after main heading and IFRS 9, Illustrative Example, para. after main heading and Guidance on Implementing, para. before main heading Section B.

3 Press Release IP/04/1385, *Accounting standards: Commission endorses IAS 39,* European Commission, 19 November 2004.

4 Press Release IP/05/1423, *Accounting standards: Commission endorses 'IAS 39 Fair Value Option',* European Commission, 15 November 2005.

Chapter 43 Financial instruments: Definitions and scope

List of examples

Chapter 43 Financial instruments: Definitions and scope

1 INTRODUCTION

In many cases it will be clear whether an asset, liability, equity share or other similar instrument should be accounted for in accordance with one or more of the relevant standards that apply to financial instruments. However, at the margins, determining whether these IFRSs should be applied is not so easy.

Firstly, one needs to determine whether the definition of a financial instrument is met; secondly, not all financial instruments are within the scope of each of these IFRSs – some are within the scope of other standards and some are not within the scope of any standard; and finally, certain contracts that do not meet the definition of a financial instrument are within the scope of some of these standards.

This chapter addresses these issues in three main sections covering the following broad areas:

- application of the definitions used in IFRS, i.e. determining what a financial instrument actually is (see 2 below);
- determining which financial instruments are within the scope of which standards (see 3 below); and
- assessing whether a non-financial contract is to be accounted for as if it were a financial instrument (see 4 below).

IFRS 9 – *Financial Instruments* – was finalised by the IASB in July 2014. It is effective for periods beginning on or after 1 January 2018 and will replace substantially all of the requirements relating to the recognition and measurement of financial instruments in IAS 39 – *Financial Instruments: Recognition and Measurement.* Where IFRS 9 changes the definitions or its scope is different to IAS 39, this is noted in the relevant part of this chapter.

2 WHAT IS A FINANCIAL INSTRUMENT?

2.1 Definitions

The main terms used in the standards that apply to financial instruments are defined in IAS 32 – *Financial Instruments: Presentation* – as follows:

A *financial instrument* is any contract that gives rise to a financial asset of one entity and a financial liability or equity instrument of another entity.

A *financial asset* is any asset that is:

(a) cash;

(b) an equity instrument of another entity;

(c) a contractual right:

- (i) to receive cash or another financial asset from another entity; or
- (ii) to exchange financial assets or financial liabilities with another entity under conditions that are potentially favourable to the entity; or

(d) a contract that will or may be settled in the entity's own equity instruments and is:

- (i) a non-derivative for which the entity is or may be obliged to receive a variable number of the entity's own equity instruments; or
- (ii) a derivative that will or may be settled other than by the exchange of a fixed amount of cash or another financial asset for a fixed number of the entity's own equity instruments. For this purpose the entity's own equity instruments do not include certain puttable and similar financial instruments classified by exception as equity instruments (see Chapter 45 at 4.6) or instruments that are themselves contracts for the future receipt or delivery of the entity's own equity instruments.

A *financial liability* is any liability that is:

(a) a contractual obligation:

- (i) to deliver cash or another financial asset to another entity; or
- (ii) to exchange financial assets or financial liabilities with another entity under conditions that are potentially unfavourable to the entity; or

(b) a contract that will or may be settled in the entity's own equity instruments and is:

- (i) a non-derivative for which the entity is or may be obliged to deliver a variable number of the entity's own equity instruments; or
- (ii) a derivative that will or may be settled other than by the exchange of a fixed amount of cash or another financial asset for a fixed number of the entity's own equity instruments. For this purpose the entity's own equity instruments do not include certain puttable and similar financial instruments classified by exception as equity instruments, or instruments that are themselves contracts for the future receipt or delivery of the entity's own equity instruments.

An *equity instrument* is any contract that evidences a residual interest in the assets of an entity after deducting all of its liabilities. *[IAS 32.11]*.

For the purpose of these definitions, 'entity' includes individuals, partnerships, incorporated bodies, trusts and government agencies. *[IAS 32.14]*.

2.2 Applying the definitions

2.2.1 *The need for a contract*

The terms 'contract' and 'contractual' are important to the definitions and refer to 'an agreement between two or more parties that has clear economic consequences that the parties have little, if any, discretion to avoid, usually because the agreement is enforceable by law'. Such contracts may take a variety of forms and need not be in writing. *[IAS 32.13]*.

The Interpretations Committee examined the question of what constitutes a contract in the context of gaming transactions. This is because, in some jurisdictions, a wager does not give rise to a contract that is enforceable under local contract law. The Interpretations Committee staff noted that a gaming transaction constitutes an agreement between two or more parties that has clear economic consequences for both. Furthermore, in most countries, gambling is heavily regulated and only parties acting within a regulated framework are licensed to operate gaming institutions, so that such entities cannot realistically fail to pay out on a good wager and therefore the gaming institution will have little or no discretion as to whether it pays out on the bet. Consequently, the Interpretations Committee agreed that a wager should be treated as a contract.[1]

Whilst this seems an entirely plausible analysis in context, it is a little difficult to reconcile with the conclusions of the Interpretations Committee and the IASB concerning the existence (or otherwise) of a contractual obligation to make payments on certain preference shares and similar securities. In those cases, terms of an instrument that effectively force the issuer to transfer cash or other financial assets to the holder although not legally required to do so (often referred to as 'economic compulsion'), are not taken into account (see Chapter 45 at 4.5.6).

A contractual right or contractual obligation to receive, deliver or exchange financial instruments is itself a financial instrument. A chain of contractual rights or contractual obligations meets the definition of a financial instrument if it will ultimately lead to the receipt or payment of cash or to the acquisition or issue of an equity instrument. *[IAS 32.AG7]*.

Assets and liabilities relating to non-contractual arrangements that arise as a result of statutory requirements imposed by governments, such as income taxes or levies are not financial liabilities or financial assets because they are not contractual. *[IAS 32.AG12]*. Accounting for income taxes is dealt with in more detail in another standard, IAS 12 – *Income Taxes* (see Chapter 31), while levies are covered by IFRIC 21 – *Levies* (see Chapter 28).

Similarly, constructive obligations as defined in IAS 37 – *Provisions, Contingent Liabilities and Contingent Assets* (see Chapter 28 at 3.1.1) do not arise from contracts and are therefore not financial liabilities. *[IAS 32.AG12]*.

2.2.2 *Simple financial instruments*

Currency (or cash) is a financial asset because it represents the medium of exchange and is therefore the basis on which all transactions are measured and recognised in financial statements. A deposit of cash with a bank or similar financial institution is a financial asset because it represents the contractual right of the depositor to obtain cash from the institution or to draw a cheque or similar instrument against the balance in favour of a creditor in payment of a financial liability. *[IAS 32.AG3]*.

The following common financial instruments give rise to financial assets representing a contractual right to receive cash in the future and corresponding financial liabilities representing a contractual obligation to deliver cash in the future:

(a) trade accounts receivable and payable;

(b) notes receivable and payable;

(c) loans receivable and payable; and

(d) bonds receivable and payable.

In each case, one party's contractual right to receive (or obligation to pay) cash is matched by the other party's corresponding obligation to pay (or right to receive). *[IAS 32.AG4]*.

Another type of financial instrument is one for which the economic benefit to be received or given up is a financial asset other than cash. For example, a note payable in government bonds gives the holder the contractual right to receive, and the issuer the contractual obligation to deliver, government bonds, not cash. The bonds are financial assets because they represent obligations of the issuing government to pay cash. The note is, therefore, a financial asset of the note holder and a financial liability of the note issuer. *[IAS 32.AG5]*.

Perpetual debt instruments (such as perpetual bonds, debentures and capital notes) normally provide the holder with the contractual right to receive payments on account of interest at fixed dates extending indefinitely, either with no right to receive a return of principal or a right to a return of principal under terms that make it very unlikely or very far in the future. For example, an entity may issue a financial instrument requiring it to make annual payments in perpetuity equal to a stated interest rate of 8% applied to a stated par or principal amount of $1,000. Assuming 8% is the market rate of interest for the instrument when issued, the issuer assumes a contractual obligation to make a stream of future interest payments having a net present value (or fair value) of $1,000 on initial recognition. The holder and issuer of the instrument have a financial asset and a financial liability, respectively. *[IAS 32.AG6]*.

2.2.3 Contingent rights and obligations

The ability to exercise a contractual right or the requirement to satisfy a contractual obligation may be absolute (as in the examples at 2.2.2 above), or it may be contingent on the occurrence of a future event. A contingent right or obligation, e.g. to receive or deliver cash, meets the definition of a financial asset or a financial liability. *[IAS 32.AG8]*.

For example, a financial guarantee is a contractual right of the lender to receive cash from the guarantor, and a corresponding contractual obligation of the guarantor to pay the lender, if the borrower defaults. The contractual right and obligation exist because of a past transaction or event (the assumption of the guarantee), even though the lender's ability to exercise its right and the requirement for the guarantor to perform under its obligation are both contingent on a future act of default by the borrower. *[IAS 32.AG8]*.

However, even though contingent rights and obligations can meet the definition of a financial instrument, they are not always recognised in the financial statements as such. For example, contingent rights and obligations may be insurance contracts within the scope of IFRS 4 – *Insurance Contracts* (see Chapter 55 at 3.3) or may otherwise be excluded from the scope of IAS 39 or IFRS 9, when applied (see 3 below). *[IAS 32.AG8]*.

2.2.4 Leases

A lease typically creates an entitlement of the lessor to receive, and an obligation of the lessee to make, a stream of payments that are substantially the same as blended payments of principal and interest under a loan agreement. The lessor accounts for its investment in the amount receivable under a finance lease rather than the underlying asset itself. Accordingly, a lessor regards a finance lease as a financial instrument. *[IAS 32.AG9]*. The lessee accounts for its obligation to make payments to the lessor (in addition to the leased asset) and also regards it as a financial instrument.

In contrast, a lessor does not recognise its entitlement to receive lease payments under an operating lease. The lessor continues to account for the underlying asset itself rather than any amount receivable in the future under the contract. Accordingly, a lessor does not regard an operating lease as a financial instrument, except as regards individual payments currently due and payable by the lessee. *[IAS 32.AG9]*.

Similarly, a lessee does not recognise its obligation to make lease payments under an operating lease under IAS 17 – *Leases*, and does not regard an operating lease as a financial instrument, except as regards individual payments currently due and payable to the lessor. However, when applied, IFRS 16 – *Leases* – requires a lessee to recognise a lease liability, with corresponding right-of-use asset, at the commencement date at the present value of the lease payments that are not paid at that date. *[IFRS 16.22, 26]*. Accordingly, under IFRS 16, a lessee regards a lease as giving rise to a financial liability. Nevertheless, as discussed in more detail at 3.2 below, financial instruments arising from leases are not always accounted for under IAS 39 or IFRS 9.

The standards do not explicitly address whether an accrued liability (or receivable) under an operating lease meets the definition of a financial liability (or financial asset) before the due date for payment. However, the guidance on accounting for service concession arrangements (see 2.2.6 below) suggests that such accruals should be considered financial instruments.

2.2.5 Non-financial assets and liabilities and contracts thereon

Physical assets (such as inventories, property, plant and equipment), right-of-use assets and intangible assets (such as patents and trademarks) are not financial assets. Control of such physical assets, right-of-use assets and intangible assets creates an opportunity to generate an inflow of cash or another financial asset, but it does not give rise to a present right to receive cash or another financial asset. *[IAS 32.AG10]*. For example, whilst gold bullion is highly liquid (and perhaps more liquid than many financial instruments), it gives no contractual right to receive cash or another financial asset, and so is therefore a commodity, not a financial asset. *[IAS 39.B.1, IFRS 9.B.1]*.

Assets such as prepaid expenses, for which the future economic benefit is the receipt of goods or services rather than the right to receive cash or another financial asset, are not financial assets. Similarly, items such as deferred revenue and most warranty obligations are not financial liabilities because the outflow of economic benefits associated with them is the delivery of goods and services rather than a contractual obligation to pay cash or another financial asset. *[IAS 32.AG11]*.

Contracts to buy or sell non-financial items do not meet the definition of a financial instrument because the contractual right of one party to receive a non-financial asset or service and the corresponding obligation of the other party do not establish a present right or obligation of either party to receive, deliver or exchange a financial asset. For example, contracts that provide for settlement only by the receipt or delivery of a non-financial item (e.g. an option, future or forward contract on silver and many similar commodity contracts) are not financial instruments. However, as set out at 4 below, certain contracts to buy or sell non-financial items that can be settled net or by exchanging financial instruments, or in which the non-financial item is readily convertible into cash are included within the scope of IAS 32, IAS 39 and IFRS 9, essentially because they exhibit similar characteristics to financial instruments. *[IAS 32.AG20]*.

In some industries, e.g. brewing and heating gas, entities distribute their products in returnable containers. Often, these entities will collect a cash deposit for each container delivered which they have an obligation to refund on return of the container. The Interpretations Committee found itself in November 2007 addressing the classification of these obligations, in particular whether they met the definition of a financial instrument.[2] It is easy to jump to the conclusion (as the Interpretations Committee did initially)[3] that such an arrangement represents a contract to exchange a non-financial item (the container) for cash and is therefore outside the scope of IAS 39. However, the Interpretations Committee recognised that this analysis holds true only if, in accounting terms, the container ceases to be an asset of the entity when the sale is made, i.e. it is derecognised. If the container is not derecognised, the entity cannot be regarded as receiving the non-financial asset because the accounting treatment regards the entity as retaining the asset. Instead, the deposit simply represents an obligation to transfer cash and is therefore a financial liability.[4]

Some contracts are commodity-linked, but do not involve settlement through the physical receipt or delivery of a commodity. Instead they specify settlement through cash payments that are determined according to a formula in the contract. For example, the principal amount of a bond may be calculated by applying the market price of oil prevailing at the maturity of the bond to a fixed quantity of oil, but is settled only in cash. Such a contract constitutes a financial instrument. *[IAS 32.AG22]*.

Financial instruments also include contracts that give rise to a non-financial asset or non-financial liability in addition to a financial asset or financial liability. Such arrangements often give one party an option to exchange a financial asset for a non-financial asset. For example, an oil-linked bond may give the holder the right to receive a stream of fixed periodic interest payments and a fixed amount of cash on maturity, with the option to exchange the principal amount for a fixed quantity of oil. The desirability of exercising this option will vary over time depending on the fair value of oil relative to the exchange ratio of cash for oil (the exchange price) inherent in the bond, but the intentions of the bondholder do not affect the substance of the component assets. The financial asset of the holder and the financial liability of the issuer make the bond a financial instrument, regardless of the other types of assets and liabilities also created. *[IAS 32.AG23]*.

2.2.6 Payments for goods and services

Where payment on a contract involving the receipt or delivery of physical assets is deferred past the date of transfer of the asset, a financial instrument arises at the date of delivery. In other words, the sale or purchase of goods on trade credit gives rise to a financial asset (a trade receivable) and a financial liability (a trade payable) when the goods are transferred. *[IAS 32.AG21]*. This is the case even if an invoice is not issued at the time of delivery.

IAS 32 does not explain whether the same logic should apply to the delivery of other, less tangible, non-financial items, e.g. construction or other services. IFRIC 12 – *Service Concession Arrangements* – provides guidance on how operators of service concessions over public infrastructure assets should account for these arrangements. Where an operator obtains an unconditional contractual right to receive cash from the grantor in exchange for construction or other services, the accrued revenue represents a financial asset. This is the case even if payment is not due immediately and even if it is contingent on the operator ensuring that the underlying infrastructure meets specified quality or efficiency requirements (see Chapter 27 at 4.2). *[IFRIC 12.16]*.

However, should the same logic apply to the delivery of construction or other services where the revenue earned is accounted for under IAS 11 – *Construction Contracts* – or IAS 18 – *Revenue*? In these cases it is not entirely clear whether amounts recoverable on contracts or other accrued revenue that is not currently due and payable should be considered a financial asset. Whilst the guidance on accounting for service concession arrangements suggests that these assets should be regarded as financial instruments, the standards are not clear on this, at least in cases where future performance is necessary before a payment becomes due.

In July 2008 the Interpretations Committee considered a similar issue, namely the question of when trail commissions paid by an investment manager to a financial advisor should be recognised as revenue (or a liability) if no further services are to be provided. Typically, an advisor will continue to receive payments from the manager whose products were recommended by them, provided the client does not withdraw or redeem the invested funds. Similar arrangements are common in many other industries, for example telecommunications where the retailer of a mobile telephone and related contract will often receive commissions from the network operator based on the customer's telephone usage.

The Interpretations Committee staff was clear in its analysis that the advisor's contingent right to receive uncertain amounts of cash from the investment manager represented a financial asset that should be recognised as revenue immediately. Similarly, it concluded that the fund should recognise a financial liability. The staff noted, in particular, that payments do not need to be certain or fixed in amount for a financial instrument to exist.[5] However, the Interpretations Committee decided not to take the issue onto its agenda, noting the complexity of the issue, the pervasive effect of any conclusions reached and that there was diversity in practice. This diversity was, it said, caused in part by the difficulty in determining whether the entity is required to provide any future service in return for the commission, considering all relevant circumstances, and also by the fact that IAS 18 and IAS 39 or IFRS 9 have different recognition criteria and views differ on which is the relevant standard.[6]

IAS 11 and IAS 18 are replaced by IFRS 15 – *Revenue from Contracts with Customers* – with effect from 1 January 2018. Rights and obligations within the scope of IFRS 15 are not accounted for as financial instruments, other than unconditional rights to consideration in exchanges for goods and services transferred to the customer that IFRS 15 specifies as accounted for in accordance with IAS 39 or IFRS 9 (see Chapter 30 at 9.1). *[IAS 39.2(k), IFRS 9.2.1(j), IFRS 15.108]*. This will provide a degree more clarity about the accounting to be followed by a supplier of goods or services. Furthermore, the consequential amendments to IFRIC 12 brought in by IFRS 15 align the IFRIC 12 guidance with IFRS 15.

2.2.7 Equity instruments

Equity instruments include non-puttable ordinary shares, some puttable and similar instruments, some types of preference shares and warrants or written call options that allow the holder to subscribe for or purchase a fixed number of non-puttable ordinary shares in the issuing entity, in exchange for a fixed amount of cash or another financial asset. *[IAS 32.AG13]*. The definition of equity instruments is considered in more detail in Chapter 45 at 3.

2.2.8 Derivative financial instruments

In addition to primary instruments such as receivables, payables and equity instruments, financial instruments also include derivatives such as financial options, futures and forwards, interest rate swaps and currency swaps. Derivatives normally transfer one or more of the financial risks inherent in an underlying primary instrument between the contracting parties without any need to transfer the underlying instruments themselves (either at inception of the contract or even, where cash settled, on termination). *[IAS 32.AG15, AG16]*.

There are important accounting consequences for financial instruments that are considered to be derivatives, and the defining characteristics of derivatives are covered in more detail in Chapter 44 at 2.

As noted at 2.2.5 above, certain derivative contracts on non-financial items are included within the scope of IAS 32 and IAS 39, even though they are not, strictly, financial instruments as defined. These contracts are covered in more detail at 4 below.

On inception, the terms of a derivative financial instrument generally give one party a contractual right (or obligation) to exchange financial assets or financial liabilities with another party under conditions that are potentially favourable (or unfavourable). Some instruments embody both a right and an obligation to make an exchange and, as prices in financial markets change, those terms may become either favourable or unfavourable. *[IAS 32.AG16]*.

A put or call option to exchange financial assets or financial liabilities gives the holder a right to obtain potential future economic benefits associated with changes in the fair value of the underlying instrument. Conversely, the writer of an option assumes an obligation to forgo such potential future economic benefits or bear potential losses associated with the underlying instrument. The contractual right (or obligation) of the holder (or writer) meets the definition of a financial asset (or liability). The financial instrument underlying an option contract may be any financial asset, including shares in other entities and interest-bearing instruments. An option may require the writer to issue a debt instrument, rather than transfer a financial asset, but the instrument underlying the option would constitute a financial asset of the holder if the option were exercised. The option-holder's right (or writer's obligation) to exchange the financial asset under potentially favourable (or unfavourable) conditions is distinct from the underlying financial asset to be exchanged upon exercise of the option. The nature of the holder's right and of the writer's obligation (which characterises such contracts as a financial instrument) are not affected by the likelihood that the option will be exercised. *[IAS 32.AG17]*.

Another common type of derivative is a forward contract. For example, consider a contract in which two parties (the seller and the purchaser) promise in six months' time to exchange $1,000 cash (the purchaser will pay cash) for $1,000 face amount of fixed rate government bonds (the seller will deliver the bonds). During those six months, both parties have a contractual right and a contractual obligation to exchange financial instruments (cash in exchange for bonds). If the market price of the government bonds rises above $1,000, the conditions will be favourable to the purchaser and unfavourable to the seller, and *vice versa* if the market price falls below $1,000. The purchaser has a contractual right (a financial asset) similar to the right under a call option held and a contractual obligation (a financial liability) similar to the obligation under a put option written. The seller has a contractual right (a financial asset) similar to the right under a put option held and a contractual obligation (a financial liability) similar to the obligation under a call option written. As with options, these contractual rights and obligations constitute financial assets and financial liabilities separate and distinct from the underlying financial instruments (the bonds and cash to be exchanged). Both parties to a forward contract have an obligation to perform at the agreed time, whereas performance under an option contract occurs only if and when the holder of the option chooses to exercise it. *[IAS 32.AG18]*.

Many other types of derivative also embody a right or obligation to make a future exchange, including interest rate and currency swaps, interest rate caps, collars and floors, loan commitments, note issuance facilities and letters of credit. An interest rate swap contract may be viewed as a variation of a forward contract in which the parties agree to make a series of future exchanges of cash amounts, one amount calculated with reference to a floating interest rate and the other with reference to a fixed interest rate. Futures contracts are another variation of forward contracts, differing primarily in that the contracts are standardised and traded on an exchange. *[IAS 32.AG19]*.

2.2.9 Dividends payable

As part of its project to provide authoritative accounting guidance for non-cash distributions (see Chapter 8 at 2.4.2), the Interpretations Committee found itself debating the seemingly simple question of how to account for a declared but unpaid cash dividend (or, more accurately, which standard applies to such a liability). Although there are clear indicators within IFRS that an obligation to pay a cash dividend is a financial liability,[7] the Interpretations Committee originally proposed that IAS 37 should be applied to all dividend obligations,[8] a decision that appeared to have been made more on the grounds of expediency rather than using any robust technical analysis. By the time IFRIC 17 – *Distributions of Non-cash Assets to Owners* – was published in November 2008, the Interpretations Committee had modified its position slightly. Aside from those standards dealing with the measurement of liabilities that are clearly not relevant (e.g. IAS 12), they considered that others, except IAS 37 and IAS 39, were simply not applicable because they addressed liabilities arising only from exchange transactions, whereas IFRIC 17 was developed to deal with non-reciprocal distributions. *[IFRIC 17.BC22]*. Finally, IFRIC 17 simply specifies the accounting treatment to be applied to distributions without linking to any individual standard. *[IFRIC 17.BC27]*. The Interpretations Committee concluded that it was not appropriate to conclude that all dividends payable are to be regarded as financial liabilities.

3 SCOPE

IAS 32, IAS 39, IFRS 7 – *Financial Instruments: Disclosures* – and IFRS 9 apply to the financial statements of all entities that are prepared in accordance with International Financial Reporting Standards. *[IAS 32.4, IAS 39.2, IFRS 7.3, IFRS 9.2.1]*. In other words there are no exclusions from the presentation, recognition, measurement, or even the disclosure requirements, of these standards, even for entities that do not have publicly traded securities or those that are subsidiaries of other entities.

The standards do not, however, apply to all of an entity's financial instruments, some of which are excluded from their scope, for example, insurance contracts (see Chapter 55). These exceptions are considered in more detail below. Conversely, certain contracts over non-financial items that behave in a similar way to financial instruments but do not actually fall within the definition – essentially some commodity contracts – are included within the scope of the standards and these are considered at 4 below.

3.1 Subsidiaries, associates, joint ventures and similar investments

Most interests in subsidiaries, associates, and joint ventures that are consolidated or equity accounted in consolidated financial statements are outside the scope of IAS 32, IAS 39, IFRS 7 and IFRS 9. However, such instruments should be accounted for in accordance with IAS 39 or IFRS 9 and disclosed in accordance with IFRS 7 in the following situations: *[IAS 32.4(a), IAS 39.2(a), IFRS 7.3(a), IFRS 9.2.1(a)]*

- in separate financial statements of the parent or investor if the entity chooses not to account for those investments at cost (see Chapter 8 at 2); *[IAS 27.10, IAS 27.11, IAS 28.44]*
- when investments in an associate or a joint venture held by a venture capital organisation, mutual fund, unit trust or similar entity are classified as financial instruments at fair value through profit or loss on initial recognition (see Chapter 11 at 5.3 and Chapter 46 at 2.2.2). *[IAS 28.18]*. When an entity has an investment in an associate, a portion of which is held indirectly through a venture capital organisation, mutual fund, unit trust or similar entity including an investment-linked insurance fund, the entity may elect to measure that portion of the investment in the associate at fair value through profit or loss regardless of whether the venture capital organisation, mutual fund, unit trust or similar entity has significant influence over that portion of the investment. If the election is made, the equity method should be applied to any remaining portion of the investment; *[IAS 28.19]* and
- an investment in a subsidiary by an investment entity that is measured at fair value through profit or loss using the investment entity exception (see Chapter 6 at 2.3.3). *[IFRS 10.31]*.

In January 2013, the Interpretations Committee concluded that impairments of investments in subsidiaries, associates and joint ventures accounted for at cost in the separate financial statements of the investor are dealt with by IAS 36 – *Impairment of Assets* – not IAS 39.[9]

In May 2016, the Interpretations Committee discussed the interaction between IFRS 9 and IAS 28 – *Investments in Associates and Joint Ventures* – regarding the measurement of long-term interests in an associate or a joint venture that, in substance, form part of the net investment in the associate or joint venture, but to which the equity method is not applied. The discussion was framed in the context of IFRS 9 but a similar analysis would apply under IAS 39. In a tentative agenda decision, the Interpretations Committee observed the following:

- an entity should account for long-term interests in accordance with IFRS 9, including the impairment requirements in IFRS 9;
- in allocating any losses of the associate or joint venture applying the requirements of IAS 28, the entity should include the carrying amount of those long-term interests (determined applying IFRS 9) as part of the net investment to which losses are allocated;
- then the entity should assess the net investment, of which the long-term interests are a part, for impairment in accordance with IAS 28, not IFRS 9; and
- if an entity allocates losses or recognises impairment charges when applying IAS 28, they should be ignored when accounting for long-term interests under IFRS 9 in subsequent periods.

However, the Interpretations Committee observed diversity in practice for accounting for long-term interests and so tentatively decided to develop a draft Interpretation explaining how to account for long-term interests (see Chapter 11 at 8.1).[10]

IAS 32, IAS 39, IFRS 7 and IFRS 9 apply to most derivatives on interests in subsidiaries, associates and joint ventures, irrespective of how the investment is otherwise accounted for. However, IAS 39 and IFRS 9 do not apply to instruments containing potential voting rights that, in substance, give access to the economic benefits arising from an ownership interest which is consolidated or equity accounted (see Chapter 7 at 2.2, Chapter 11 at 4.3 and Chapter 12 at 4.2.2). *[IFRS 10.B91]*.

From the perspective of an entity issuing derivatives, the requirements of IAS 39, IFRS 9 and IFRS 7 do not apply if such derivatives meet the definition of an equity instrument of the entity. *[IAS 32.4(a), IAS 39.2(a), IFRS 7.3(a), IFRS 9.2.1(a)]*. For example, a written call option allowing the holder to acquire a subsidiary's shares that can be settled only by delivering a fixed number of those shares in exchange for a fixed amount of cash might meet the definition of equity in the group's consolidated financial statements (see 3.6 below and Chapter 45 at 5.1).

Sometimes an entity will make a strategic investment in the equity of another party. These are often made with the intention of establishing or maintaining a long-term operating relationship with the investee. Unless they are equity accounted as associates or joint ventures, these investments are within the scope of IAS 39 and IFRS 9. *[IAS 39.AG3, IFRS 9.B2.3]*.

3.2 Leases

Whilst all rights and obligations under leases that represent financial instruments and to which IAS 17 or IFRS 16 applies (see Chapters 24 and 25) are within the scope of IAS 32 and IFRS 7, they are only within the scope of IAS 39 and IFRS 9 to the following extent:

- lease receivables and lease liabilities are subject to the derecognition provisions of IAS 39 and IFRS 9 (see Chapter 51);
- lease receivables are subject to the 'incurred loss' impairment provisions of IAS 39 (see Chapter 49 at 4) or the 'expected credit loss' requirements of IFRS 9 (see Chapter 50 at 5); and
- the relevant provisions of IAS 39 and IFRS 9 apply to derivatives embedded within leases (see Chapter 44 at 4 to 7).

Otherwise the applicable standard is IAS 17 or IFRS 16, not IAS 39 or IFRS 9. *[IAS 39.2(b), IFRS 9.2.1(b)]*.

3.3 Insurance contracts

Although insurance contracts often satisfy the definition of a financial instrument, in general they have not, historically, been accounted for as such. In fact the IASB has been conducting a project on accounting for insurance contracts for a number of years and the first standard on the topic, IFRS 4 (which is discussed in detail in Chapter 55), was published in March 2004.

An insurance contract is defined in IFRS 4 as one under which one party (the insurer) accepts significant insurance risk from another party (the policyholder) by agreeing to compensate the policyholder if a specified uncertain future event (the insured event) adversely affects the policyholder. Insurance risk is defined as risk, other than financial risk, transferred from the holder of a contract to the issuer. Financial risk is defined as the risk of a possible future change in one or more of a specified interest rate, financial instrument price, commodity price, foreign exchange rate, index of prices or rates, credit rating or credit index or other variable, provided in the case of a non-financial variable that the variable is not specific to a party to the contract. *[IFRS 4 Appendix A]*. In many cases it will be quite clear whether a contract is an insurance contract or not, although this will not always be the case and IFRS 4 contains several pages of guidance on this definition (see Chapter 55 at 3). *[IFRS 4 Appendix B]*.

Insurance contracts, as defined, are generally outside the scope of IAS 32, IAS 39, IFRS 7 and IFRS 9. *[IAS 32.4(d), IAS 39.2(e), IFRS 7.3(d), IFRS 9.2.1(e)]*. IAS 39 and IFRS 9 do, however, apply to derivatives that are embedded in insurance contracts if the derivative itself is not within the scope of IFRS 4. *[IFRS 4.7, IAS 39.2(e), IFRS 9.2.1(e)]*. IAS 32 and IFRS 7 apply to derivatives embedded in insurance contracts if IAS 39 or IFRS 9 requires them to be accounted for separately. *[IAS 32.4(d), IFRS 7.3(d)]*. Finally, financial guarantee contracts, which meet the definition of an insurance contract if the risk transferred is significant, are normally accounted for by the issuer under IAS 39 and IFRS 9 and disclosed in accordance with IFRS 7 (see 3.4 below). *[IAS 39.AG4(a), IFRS 9.B2.5(a)]*.

The application guidance makes it clear that insurers' financial instruments that are not within the scope of IFRS 4 should be accounted for under IAS 39 or IFRS 9. *[IAS 39.AG3A, IFRS 9.B2.4]*.

3.3.1 Weather derivatives

Contracts which require a payment based on climatic variables (often referred to as 'weather derivatives') or on geological or other physical variables are within the scope of IAS 39 or IFRS 9 unless they meet the definition of an insurance contract. *[IAS 39.AG1, IFRS 9.B2.1]*. Generic or standardised contracts will rarely meet the definition of insurance contracts because the variable is unlikely to be specific to either party to the contract. *[IFRS 4.B18(l), IFRS 4.B19(g)]*. This is illustrated in the following example.

Example 43.1: Rainfall contract – derivative financial instrument or insurance contract?

Company E has contracted to lease a stall at an open-air event from which it plans to sell goods to people attending the event. The event will be held at a village approximately 100 km from Capital City.

Because E is concerned that poor weather may deter people from attending the event, it enters into a contract with Financial Institution K, the terms of which are that, in return for a premium paid by E on inception of the contract, K will pay a fixed amount of money to E if, during the day of the event, it rains for more than three hours at the meteorological station in the centre of Capital City.

The non-financial variable in the contract, i.e. rainfall at the meteorological station, is not specific to E. Particularly, E will only suffer loss as a result of rainfall at the village, not at Capital City. Also, because the potential payment to be received is for a fixed amount, it might not be possible to demonstrate that E has suffered a loss for which it has been compensated. Therefore, E should account for the contract as a financial instrument under IAS 39 or IFRS 9.

3.3.2 *Contracts with discretionary participation features*

Financial instruments (normally taking the form of life insurance policies) which contain what are called discretionary participation features, essentially rights of the holder to receive additional benefits whose amount or timing is, contractually, at the discretion of the issuer, are accounted for under IFRS 4. *[IFRS 4 Appendix A]*. Accordingly, IAS 39 and the parts of IAS 32 dealing with the distinction between financial liabilities and equity instruments (see Chapter 45 at 3 to 7) do not apply to such contracts, although the disclosure requirements of IFRS 7 do apply. *[IAS 32.4(e), IAS 39.2(e), IFRS 9.2.1(e), IFRS 4.2(b), IFRS 7.3]*.

IAS 39 and IFRS 9 do, however, apply to derivatives that are embedded in contracts containing discretionary participation features if the derivative itself is not within the scope of IFRS 4. *[IAS 39.2(e), IFRS 9.2.1(e)]*.

3.4 Financial guarantee contracts

Where a contract meets the definition of a financial guarantee contract (see 3.4.1 below) the issuer is normally required to apply specific accounting requirements within IAS 39 or IFRS 9, which are different from those applying to other financial liabilities – essentially the contract is measured at fair value on initial recognition and this amount is amortised to profit or loss provided it is not considered probable that the guarantee will be called (see Chapter 49 at 2.8 and Chapter 50 at 2.8). There are exceptions to this general requirement and these are dealt with at 3.4.2 below.

3.4.1 *Definition of a financial guarantee contract*

A financial guarantee contract is defined as a contract that requires the issuer to make specified payments to reimburse the holder for a loss it incurs because a specified debtor fails to make payment when due in accordance with the original or modified terms of a debt instrument. *[IAS 39.9, IFRS 4 Appendix A, IFRS 9 Appendix A]*.

3.4.1.A Reimbursement for loss incurred

Some credit-related guarantees (or letters of credit, credit derivative default contracts or credit insurance contracts) do not, as a precondition for payment, require that the holder is exposed to, and has incurred a loss on, the failure of the debtor to make payments on the guaranteed asset when due. An example of such a guarantee is one that requires payments in response to changes in a specified credit rating or credit index. Such guarantees are not financial guarantee contracts, as defined in IAS 39 and IFRS 9, and are not insurance contracts, as defined in IFRS 4. Rather, they are derivatives and accordingly fall within the scope of IAS 39 and IFRS 9. *[IAS 39.AG4(b), IFRS 9.B2.5(b), IFRS 4.B19(f)]*.

When a debtor defaults on a guaranteed loan a significant time period may elapse prior to full and final legal settlement of the loss. Because of this, certain credit protection contracts provide for the guarantor to make a payment at a fixed point after the default event using the best estimate of loss at the time. Such payments typically terminate the credit protection contract with no party having any further claim under it whilst ownership of the loan remains with the guaranteed party. In situations like this, if the final loss on the debtor exceeds the amount estimated on payment of the guarantee, the guaranteed party will suffer an overall financial loss; conversely, the guaranteed party may receive a payment under the guarantee but eventually suffer a smaller loss on the loan. Therefore such a contract will often not meet the essence of the definition of a financial guarantee. However, if the payment is designed to be a reasonable estimate of the loss actually incurred, such a feature (which is common in many conventional insurance contracts) will sometimes allow the contract to be classified as a financial guarantee contract. This will particularly be the case if such payments are agreed by both parties in order to settle the financial guarantee, as opposed to being specified as part of the original contract.

Also, such a contract should meet the definition of a guarantee if it was structured in either of the following ways:

- the contract requires the guarantor to purchase the defaulted loan for its nominal amount; or
- on settlement of the final loss, the contract provides for a further payment between the guarantor and guaranteed party for any difference between that amount and the initial loss estimate that was paid.

3.4.1.B Debt instrument

Although the term 'debt instrument' is used extensively as a fundamental part of the definition of a 'financial guarantee contract', it is not defined within IAS 32, IAS 39, IFRS 9, IFRS 4 or IFRS 7. The term will typically be considered to include trade debts, overdrafts and other borrowings including mortgage loans and certain debt securities.

However, entities often provide guarantees of other items and analysing these in the context of IAS 39, IFRS 9 and IFRS 4 is not always straightforward. Consider, for example, a guarantee of a lessor's receipts under a lease. In substance, a finance lease gives rise to a loan agreement (see 2.2.4 above) and it therefore seems clear that a guarantee of payments on such a lease should be considered a financial guarantee contract.

From the perspective of the guarantor, a guarantee of a non-cancellable operating lease will give rise to a substantially similar exposure, i.e. credit risk of the lessee. Moreover, individual payments currently due and payable are recognised as financial (debt) instruments. Therefore, such guarantees would seem to meet the definition of a financial guarantee at least insofar as they relate to payments currently due and payable. It may be argued that the remainder of the contract (normally the majority) fails to meet the definition because it provides a guarantee of *future* debt instruments. However, the standard does not explicitly require the debt instrument to be accounted for as a financial instrument that is currently due and we believe a guarantee of a lessor's receipts under an operating lease could also be argued to meet the definition of a financial guarantee contract.

Where it is accepted that such a guarantee is not a financial guarantee contract, one must still examine how the related obligations should be accounted for – the contract is, after all, a financial instrument. The possibilities are a derivative financial instrument (accounted for at fair value through profit or loss under IAS 39 and IFRS 9) or an insurance contract (accounted for under IFRS 4 – commonly resulting only in disclosure of a contingent liability, assuming payment is not considered probable). The analysis depends on whether the risk transferred by the guarantee is considered financial risk or insurance risk (see 3.3 above). Credit risk sits on the cusp of the relevant definitions making the judgement a marginal one, although we believe that in many situations the arguments for treatment as an insurance contract will be credible. Of course for this to be the case the guarantee must only compensate the holder for loss in the event of default.

Other types of guarantee can add further complications – for example guarantees of pension plan contributions to funded defined benefit schemes. Where such a guarantee is in respect of discrete identifiable payments, the analysis above for operating leases seems equally applicable. However, the terms of such a guarantee might have the effect that the guaranteed amount depends on the performance of the assets within the scheme. In these cases, the guarantee seems to give rise to a transfer of financial risk (i.e. the value of the asset) in addition to credit risk, which might lend support for its treatment as a derivative.

3.4.1.C Form and existence of contract

The application guidance to IAS 39 and IFRS 9 emphasises that, whilst financial guarantee contracts may have various legal forms (such as guarantees, some types of letters of credit, credit default contracts or insurance contracts), their accounting treatment does not depend on their legal form. *[IAS 39.AG4, IFRS 9.B2.5]*.

In some cases guarantees arise, directly or indirectly, as a result of the operation of statute or regulation. In such situations, it is necessary to examine whether the arrangement gives rise to a contract as that term is used in IAS 32. For example, in some jurisdictions, a subsidiary may avoid filing its financial statements or having them audited if its parent and fellow subsidiaries guarantee its liabilities by entering into a deed of cross guarantee. In other jurisdictions similar relief is granted if group companies elect to make a statutory declaration of guarantee. In the first situation it would seem appropriate for the issuer to regard the deed as a contract and hence any guarantee made under it would be within the scope of IAS 39 or IFRS 9. The statutory nature of the declaration in the second situation makes the analysis more difficult. Although the substance of the arrangement is little different from the first situation, statutory obligations are not financial liabilities and are therefore outside the scope of IAS 39 or IFRS 9.

3.4.2 Issuers of financial guarantee contracts

In general, issuers of financial guarantees contracts should apply IAS 32, IAS 39, IFRS 9 and IFRS 7 to those contracts even though they meet the definition of an insurance contract in IFRS 4 if the risk transferred is significant. *[IAS 39.AG4(a), IFRS 9.B2.5(a)]*. However, if an entity has previously asserted explicitly that it regards such contracts as insurance contracts and has used accounting applicable to insurance contracts, the issuer may elect to apply either IAS 39/IFRS 9 or IFRS 4 (see Chapter 55 at 2.2.3.D). That election may be made contract by contract, but the election for each contract is irrevocable. *[IAS 32.4(d), IAS 39.2(e), IFRS 4.4(d), IFRS 7.3(d), IFRS 9.2.1(e)]*. This concession does not extend to contracts that are similar to financial guarantee contracts but are actually derivative financial instruments (see 3.4.1.A above).

The IASB was concerned that entities other than credit insurers could elect to apply IFRS 4 to financial guarantee contracts and consequently (if their accounting policies permitted) recognise no liability on inception. Consequently, it imposed the restrictions outlined in the previous paragraph. *[IAS 39.BC23A, IFRS 9.BCZ2.12]*. The application guidance contains further information on these restrictions where it is explained that assertions that an issuer regards contracts as insurance contracts are typically found throughout the issuer's communications with customers and regulators, contracts, business documentation as well as in their financial statements. Furthermore, insurance contracts are often subject to accounting requirements that are distinct from the requirements for other types of transaction, such as contracts issued by banks or commercial companies. In such cases, an issuer's financial statements would typically include a statement that the issuer had used those accounting requirements, i.e. ones normally applied to insurance contracts. *[IAS 39.AG4A, IFRS 9.B2.6]*. Nevertheless, other companies do consider it appropriate to apply IFRS 4 rather than IAS 39 or IFRS 9 to these contracts. Rolls Royce discloses the following accounting policy in respect of guarantees that it provides.

Extract 43.1: Rolls-Royce Holdings plc (2015)

NOTES TO THE CONSOLIDATED FINANCIAL STATEMENTS [extract]

1. **Accounting policies** [extract]
Sales financing support [extract]

In connection with the sale of its products, the Group will, on occasion, provide financing support for its customers. These arrangements fall into two categories: credit-based guarantees and asset-value guarantees. In accordance with the requirements of IAS 39 and IFRS 4 *Insurance Contracts*, credit-based guarantees are treated as insurance contracts. The Group considers asset-value guarantees to be non-financial liabilities and accordingly these are also treated as insurance contracts.

The IASB is addressing the question of how to account for financial guarantee contracts in its project on insurance contracts. At the time of writing, the IASB has proposed that insurers will continue to be given a similar accounting policy choice (see Chapter 55 at 12.3).[11]

Accounting for the revenue associated with financial guarantee contracts issued in connection with the sale of goods is dealt with under IAS 18 or IFRS 15 (see Chapter 29 and Chapter 30). *[IAS 39.AG4(c), IFRS 9.B2.5(c)]*.

3.4.3 Holders of financial guarantee contracts

Financial guarantee contracts held are not within the scope of IAS 39 or IFRS 9 because they are insurance contracts (see 3.3 above). *[IAS 39.IN6]*. Nor does IFRS 4 apply to insurance contracts that an entity holds (other than reinsurance contracts). *[IFRS 4.4(f)]*. Accordingly, as explained in the guidance on implementing IFRS 4, the holder of a financial guarantee contract will need to develop its accounting policy in accordance with the 'hierarchy' in IAS 8 – *Accounting Policies, Changes in Accounting Estimates and Errors*. The IAS 8 hierarchy specifies criteria to use if no IFRS applies specifically (see Chapter 3 at 4). *[IFRS 4.IG2 Example 1.11]*.

In selecting their policy, entities may initially look to the requirements of IAS 37 dealing with contingent assets (see Chapter 28 at 3.2.2), at least as far as recoveries under the contract are concerned. However, applying IAS 37 will not always be appropriate, as discussed in Chapter 49 at 4.2.2 in the context of loan impairments. In certain situations it may also be possible for the holder of a financial guarantee contract to account for it as an asset at fair value through profit or loss. This might be considered appropriate if it was acquired subsequent to the initial recognition of a guaranteed asset that had itself been classified as at fair value through profit or loss.

3.4.4 Financial guarantee contracts between entities under common control

The IASB was asked to provide an exemption from the measurement requirements of IAS 39 for guarantees issued between parents and their subsidiaries, between entities under common control and by a parent or subsidiary on behalf of a subsidiary or a parent (a similar exemption is available under US GAAP). It was argued that the requirement to recognise these financial guarantee contracts in separate or individual financial statements would cause costs disproportionate to the likely benefits, given that intragroup transactions are eliminated on consolidation. However, to avoid the omission of material liabilities from separate or individual financial statements, the IASB decided not to create such an exemption. *[IAS 39.BC23C, IFRS 9.BCZ2.14]*.

Therefore, for example, where a parent guarantees the borrowings of a subsidiary, the guarantee should be accounted for as a standalone instrument in the parent's separate financial statements. However, for the purposes of the parent's consolidated financial statements, such guarantees are normally considered an integral part of the terms of the borrowing (see Chapter 45 at 4.8) and therefore should not be accounted for independently of the borrowing. *[IAS 32.AG29]*.

3.5 Loan commitments

Loan commitments are firm commitments to provide credit under pre-specified terms and conditions. *[IAS 39.BC15, IFRS 9.BCZ2.2]*. The term can include arrangements such as offers to individuals in respect of residential mortgage loans as well as committed borrowing facilities granted to a corporate entity.

Although they meet the definition of a derivative financial instrument (see 2.2.8 above and Chapter 44 at 2), a pragmatic decision has been taken by the IASB to simplify the accounting for holders and issuers of many loan commitments. *[IAS 39.BC16, IFRS 9.BCZ2.3]*. Accordingly, loan commitments that cannot be settled net – in practice, most loan commitments – may be excluded from most of the scope of IAS 39 and IFRS 9. They are, however, subject to the IAS 39 and IFRS 9 derecognition provisions (see Chapter 51 at 6) and are included within the scope of IFRS 7. *[IAS 39.2(h), IFRS 7.4]*. Some loan commitments, however, are within the scope of IAS 39 and IFRS 9, namely: *[IAS 39.2(h), 4, IFRS 9.2.1(g)]*

- those that are designated as financial liabilities at fair value through profit or loss (this may be appropriate if the associated risk exposures are managed on a fair value basis or because designation eliminates an accounting mismatch – see Chapter 46 at 2.2.1); *[IAS 39.4(a), IAS 39.BC17, IFRS 9.2.3(a)]*
- commitments that can be settled net in cash or by delivering or issuing another financial instrument; *[IAS 39.4(b), IAS 39.BC18, IFRS 9.2.3(b)]* and
- all those within the same class where the entity has a past practice of selling the assets resulting from its loan commitments shortly after origination. The IASB sees this as achieving net settlement. *[IAS 39.4(a), IAS 39.BC18, IFRS 9.2.3(a)]*.

In addition, commitments to provide a loan at a below-market interest rate are also within the scope of IAS 39 and IFRS 9. *[IAS 39.4(c), IFRS 9.2.3(c)]*. For these loan commitments, the standards contain specific measurement requirements which are different from those applying to other financial liabilities. Under IAS 39 they are measured at fair value on initial recognition and this amount is amortised to profit or loss, provided it is not considered an onerous contract (see Chapter 49 at 2.8 and Chapter 50 at 2.8). IFRS 9 also requires the commitments to be measured at fair value on initial recognition and subsequently amortised to profit or loss but requires the expected credit loss allowance to be used if higher and does not take into account whether there is an onerous contract or not. *[IAS 39.47(d), IFRS 9.4.2.1(d)]*. The reason for this accounting treatment is that the IASB was concerned that liabilities resulting from such commitments might not be recognised in the statement of financial position because, often, no cash consideration is received. *[IAS 39.BC20]*.

Entities applying IFRS 9 that have issued loan commitments which are not otherwise within the scope of the standard should apply the impairment requirements of IFRS 9 to those loan commitments. *[IFRS 9.2.1(g)]*.

In respect of commitments that can be settled net in cash IAS 39 and IFRS 9 contain only limited guidance on what 'net settlement' means. Clearly a fixed interest rate loan commitment that gives the lender and/or the borrower an explicit right to settle the value of the contract (taking into account changes in interest rates etc.) in cash or by delivery or issuing another financial instrument would be considered a form of net settlement and therefore a derivative. However, paying out a loan in instalments (for example, a mortgage construction loan where instalments are paid out in line with the progress of construction) is not regarded as net settlement. *[IAS 39.4(b)]*.

As a matter of fact, most loan commitments could be settled net if both parties agreed, essentially by renegotiating the terms of the contract. Of more relevance is the question of whether one party has the practical ability to settle net, e.g. because the terms of the contract allow net settlement or by the use of some market mechanism.

Where the entity has a past practice of selling the assets shortly after origination, no guidance is given on what is meant by a class (although the basis for conclusions makes it clear that an entity can have more than one). *[IAS 39.BC19, IFRS 9.BCZ2.6]*. Therefore, an assessment will need to be made based on individual circumstances.

Example 43.2: Identifying classes of loan commitment

A banking group has two main operating subsidiaries, one in country A and the other in country B. Although they share common functions (e.g. information systems) the two subsidiaries' operations are clearly distinct.

Both subsidiaries originate similar loans under loan commitments. In country A there is an active and liquid market for the assets resulting from loan commitments issued in that country. The subsidiary operating in that country has a past practice of disposing of such assets in this market shortly after origination. There is no such market in country B.

The fact that one subsidiary has a past practice of settling its loan commitments net (as the term is used in the standard) would not normally mean that the loan commitments issued in country B are required to be classified as at fair value through profit or loss.

The above example is relatively straightforward – in some circumstances it may be more difficult to define the class. However, there is no reason why an individual entity (say a subsidiary of a group) cannot have two or more classes of loan commitment, e.g. where they result in the origination of different types of asset that are clearly managed separately.

An issuer of loan commitments applying IAS 39 is required to apply IAS 37 if they are not subject to the requirements of IAS 39. *[IAS 39.2(h)]*. Particularly, a provision should be established if a loan commitment becomes an onerous contract as defined in that standard (see Chapter 28 at 6.2). HSBC has disclosed the following accounting policy in respect of onerous loan commitments.

Extract 43.2: HSBC Holdings plc (2015)

Notes on the Financial Statements [extract]

1. Basis of preparation and significant accounting policies [extract]

(i) Loans and advances to banks and customers [extract]

HSBC may commit to underwrite loans on fixed contractual terms for specified periods of time. [...]. When HSBC intends to hold the loan, a provision on the loan commitment is only recorded where it is probable that HSBC will incur a loss.

Entities applying IFRS 9 would, instead of the requirements of IAS 37, apply the impairment provisions of IFRS 9. *[IFRS 9.5.5.1]*.

Any associated entitlement to fees should be accounted for in accordance with IAS 18 or IFRS 15, IAS 39 or IFRS 9 (see Chapter 29, Chapter 30, Chapter 48 at 3 and Chapter 49 at 3 respectively). No accounting requirements are specified for holders of loan commitments, but they will normally be accounted for as executory contracts – essentially, this means that fees payable will be recognised as an expense in a manner that is appropriate to the terms of the commitment. Any resulting borrowing will obviously be accounted for as a financial liability under IAS 39 or IFRS 9.

Although much of the discussion has focused on loan commitments as options to provide credit, *[IAS 39.BC15, IFRS 9.BCZ2.2]*, we believe it can be appropriate to apply the exclusion from IAS 39 or IFRS 9 to non-optional commitments to provide credit, provided the necessary conditions above are met.

The exclusion is available only for contracts to provide credit. Normally, therefore, it will be applicable only where there is a commitment to lend funds, and certainly not for all contracts that may result in the subsequent recognition of an asset or liability that is accounted for at amortised cost. Consider, for example, a contract between entities A and B that gives B the right to sell to A a transferable (but unquoted) debt security issued by entity C that B currently owns. Even if, on subsequent acquisition, A will classify the debt security within loans and receivables (see Chapter 46 at 4), the contract would not generally be considered a loan commitment as it does not involve A providing credit to B.

3.6 Equity instruments

3.6.1 Equity instruments issued

Financial instruments (including options and warrants) that are issued by the reporting entity and meet the definition of equity instruments in IAS 32 (see 2.1 above and Chapter 45 at 3 and 4) are outside the scope of IAS 39 and IFRS 9. *[IAS 39.2(d), IFRS 9.2.1(d)]*.

In principle, IFRS 7 applies to issued equity instruments except for those that are derivatives based on interests in subsidiaries, associates or joint ventures (see 3.1 above). *[IFRS 7.3(a)]*. However, this is of largely academic interest because IFRS 7 specifies no disclosure requirements for issued equity instruments.

In fact, the scope of IFRS 7 for these types of instrument is even more curious. Firstly, it is explained that derivatives over subsidiaries, associates and joint ventures that are equity instruments from the point of view of the issuer are excluded from the scope of IFRS 7 because equity instruments are not remeasured and hence do not expose the issuer to statement of financial position and income statement risk. Also, the disclosures about the significance of financial instruments for financial position and performance are not considered relevant for equity instruments. *[IFRS 7.BC8]*. Given the reasons quoted, it is not entirely clear why the IASB did not exclude all instruments meeting the definition of equity in IAS 32 from the scope of IFRS 7, e.g. non-puttable ordinary shares issued by the reporting entity. Secondly, it is very difficult to see how a derivative over a reporting entity's associate or joint venture could ever meet the definition of equity from the perspective of the reporting entity.

3.6.2 Equity instruments held

From the point of view of the holder, equity instruments are within the scope of IAS 39, IFRS 7 and IFRS 9 (unless they meet the exception at 3.1 above). *[IAS 39.2(d), IFRS 9.2.1(d)]*.

3.7 Business combinations

3.7.1 Contingent consideration in a business combination

3.7.1.A Payable by an acquirer

For business combinations accounted for under IFRS 3 – *Business Combinations*, contingent consideration that meets the definition of a financial instrument will be measured at fair value, with any resulting gain or loss recognised either in profit or loss or in other comprehensive income, in accordance with IAS 39 and IFRS 9 (see Chapter 9 at 7.1). *[IFRS 3.58(b)(i)]*.

Further, contingent consideration arising from an acquiree's prior business combination that an acquirer assumes in its subsequent acquisition of the acquiree does not meet the definition of contingent consideration in the acquirer's business combination. Rather, it is one of the identifiable liabilities assumed in the subsequent acquisition. Therefore, to the extent that such arrangements are financial instruments, they are within the scope of IAS 32, IAS 39, IFRS 9 and IFRS 7.[12]

3.7.1.B Receivable by a vendor

IAS 39 does not go on to explain whether the vendor should be accounting for the contingent consideration in accordance with its provisions.

In most cases the vendor will have a contractual right to receive cash or another financial asset from the purchaser and, therefore, it is hard to avoid the conclusion that the contingent consideration meets the definition of a financial asset and hence is within the scope of IAS 39 and IFRS 9, not IAS 37. IFRS 10 – *Consolidated Financial Statements* – requires consideration received on the loss of control of an entity or business to be measured at fair value, which is consistent with the treatment required by IAS 39 and IFRS 9.

3.7.2 Contracts between an acquirer and a vendor in a business combination

IAS 39 and IFRS 9 do not apply to forward contracts between an acquirer and a selling shareholder to buy or sell an acquiree that will result in a business combination at a future acquisition date. In order to qualify for this scope exclusion, the term of the forward contract should not exceed a reasonable period normally necessary to obtain any required approvals and to complete the transaction, for example to accommodate the completion of necessary regulatory and legal processes. *[IAS 39.2(g), BC24A, IFRS 9.2.1(f), BCZ2.39]*.

It applies only when completion of the business combination is not dependent on further actions of either party. Option contracts allow one party to control the occurrence or non-occurrence of future events depending on whether the option is exercised. Consequently, option contracts that on exercise will result in the reporting entity obtaining control of another entity are within the scope of IAS 39, whether or not they are currently exercisable. *[IAS 39.BC24B, BC24C, IFRS 9.BCZ2.40, BCZ2.41]*.

It was suggested that 'in-substance' or 'synthetic' forward contracts, e.g. the combination of a written put and purchased call where the strike prices, exercise dates and notional amounts are equal, or a deeply in- or out-of-the-money option, should be excluded from the scope of IAS 39 and by implication IFRS 9. However, the IASB staff did not agree with the notion that synthetic forward contracts (which do provide optionality to one or both parties) are substantially identical to forward contracts (which commit both parties). The IASB staff accepted that in normal financial instrument transactions, the economics of a synthetic forward will be favourable to one party to the contract and should therefore result in its exercise, but a similar assumption does not necessarily hold true in business combination transactions because one party may choose not to exercise the option due to other factors. Therefore, it is not possible to assert that the contracts will always result in a business combination.[13]

The acquisition of an interest in an associate represents the acquisition of a financial instrument, not an acquisition of a business. Therefore the scope exclusion should not be applied by analogy to contracts to acquire investments in associates and similar transactions. *[IAS 39.BC24D, IFRS 9.BCZ2.42]*.

Another related issue is the treatment of contracts, whether options or forwards, to purchase an entity that owns a single asset such as a ship or building which does not constitute a business. The reason a contract for a business combination is normally considered to be a financial instrument seems to be because it is a contract to purchase equity instruments. Consequently, a contract to purchase all of the shares in a single asset company would also meet the definition of a financial instrument, yet on the face of it such a contract would not be excluded from the scope of IAS 39 if the asset did not represent a business. The IASB staff disagreed with this analysis and argued that such a contract should be analysed as a contract to purchase the underlying asset which would normally be outside the scope of IAS 39 or IFRS 9.[14] Although forward contracts between an acquirer and a vendor in a business combination are scoped out of IAS 39 and hence are not accounted for as derivatives, they are still within the scope of IFRS 7.

3.8 Contingent pricing of property, plant and equipment and intangible assets

IAS 32 (as currently worded) is clear that the purchase of goods on credit gives rise to a financial liability when the goods are delivered (see 2.2.6 above) and that a contingent obligation to deliver cash meets the definition of a financial liability (see 2.2.3 above). Consequently, it would seem that a financial liability arises on the outright purchase of an item of property, plant and equipment or an intangible asset, where the purchase contract requires the subsequent payment of contingent consideration, for example amounts based on the performance of the asset. Further, because there is no exemption from applying IAS 39 or IFRS 9 to such contracts, one might expect that such a liability would be accounted for in accordance with IAS 39 or IFRS 9, i.e. any measurement changes to that liability would flow through the statement of profit or loss. This would be consistent with the accounting treatment for contingent consideration arising from a business combination under IFRS 3 (see 3.7.1.A above).

However, in practice, contracts can be more complex than suggested in the previous paragraph and often give rise to situations where the purchaser can influence or control the crystallisation of the contingent payments, e.g. where the contingent payments take the form of sales-based royalties. These complexities can raise broader questions about the nature of the obligations and, like for trail commissions (see 2.2.6 above), the appropriate accounting standard to apply. In March 2016, the Interpretations Committee determined that this issue is too broad for it to address within the confines of existing IFRS Standards. Consequently, the Interpretations Committee decided not to add this issue to its agenda.

The Interpretations Committee had discussed this issue a number of times. Initially the discussions focused on purchases of individual assets but they were later widened to cover contingent payments made under service concessions. The Interpretations Committee could not reach a consensus on whether the purchaser should recognise a liability at the date of purchasing the asset for variable payments that depend on its future activity or, instead, should recognise such a liability only when the related activity occurs. It was also unable to reach a consensus on how the purchaser should measure a liability for such variable payments. It considered the proposed definition of a liability in the May 2015 Exposure Draft – *The Conceptual Framework for Financial Reporting* – as well as the deliberations of the Board on its project on leases. The Interpretations Committee observed that the Board did not conclude on whether variable payments linked to future performance or use of the underlying asset meet the definition of a liability at commencement of a lease or, instead, meet that definition only at the time that the related performance or use occurs. In addition, it noted that there are questions about the accounting for variable payments subsequent to the purchase of the asset. Accordingly, it concluded that the Board should address the accounting for variable payments comprehensively.[15] This issue is discussed in more detail in Chapter 17 at 4.5, Chapter 18 at 4.1.9 and Chapter 41 at 8.4.1.

Where contingent consideration arises in the event of a sale, there is some uncertainty as to the accounting for the disposal of single assets held within a corporate entity. IFRS 10 applies when accounting for the loss of control of a subsidiary, but, from a group perspective, the entity is disposing of an asset that is within the scope of IAS 16 – *Property, Plant and Equipment*. It is therefore unclear, where a single asset held within a subsidiary is disposed of by selling the shares in the subsidiary, whether IAS 16 (and, thereby, the requirements of IFRS 15) or IFRS 10 should be applied. Depending on which standard is applied to the disposal, the accounting outcome could be very different when contingent consideration is involved. When IAS 16 is applied, an entity measures the disposal proceeds in accordance with IFRS 15. IFRS 15 requires that variable consideration (which includes contingent consideration) be estimated, using one of two methods, but requires that the amount of the estimate included within the transaction price be constrained to avoid significant reversals in future periods (see Chapter 30). In contrast, as noted at 3.7.1.B above, IFRS 10 requires consideration received on the loss of control of a subsidiary to be measured at fair value. *[IFRS 10.B98(b)(i)]*.

3.9 Employee benefit plans and share-based payment

Employers' rights and obligations under employee benefit plans, which are dealt with under IAS 19 – *Employee Benefits* – are excluded from the scope of IAS 32, IAS 39, IFRS 7 and IFRS 9. *[IAS 32.4(b), IAS 39.2(c), IFRS 7.3(b), IFRS 9.2.1(c)]*. The Interpretations Committee noted that IAS 19 indicates that employee benefit plans include a wide range of formal and informal arrangements and concluded it was clear that the exclusion of employee benefit plans from IAS 32 (and by implication IAS 39, IFRS 7 and IFRS 9) includes all employee benefits covered by IAS 19, for example a liability for long service leave.[16]

Similarly, most financial instruments, contracts and obligations arising from share-based payment transactions, which are dealt with under IFRS 2 – *Share-based Payment* – are also excluded. However, IAS 32, IAS 39, IFRS 7 and IFRS 9 do apply to contracts to buy or sell non-financial items in share-based transactions that can be settled net (as that term is used in this context) unless they are considered to be 'normal' sales and purchases (see 4 below). *[IAS 32.4(f)(i), IAS 39.2(i), IFRS 7.3(e), IFRS 9.2.1(h)]*. For example, a contract to purchase a fixed quantity of oil in exchange for issuing of a fixed number of shares that could be settled net would be excluded from the scope of IAS 32, IAS 39, IFRS 7 and IFRS 9 only if it qualified as a 'normal' purchase (which would be unlikely).

In addition, IAS 32 applies to treasury shares (see Chapter 45 at 9) that are purchased, sold, issued or cancelled in connection with employee share option plans, employee share purchase plans, and all other share-based payment arrangements. *[IAS 32.4(f)(ii)]*.

3.10 Reimbursement rights in respect of provisions

Most reimbursement rights in respect of provisions arise from insurance contracts and are therefore outside the scope of IAS 39 as set out at 3.3 above. The scope of IAS 39 and IFRS 9 is also restricted so as not to apply to other financial instruments that are rights to payments to reimburse the entity for expenditure it is required to make to settle a liability that it has recognised as a provision in accordance with IAS 37 in the current or an earlier period. *[IAS 39.2(j), IFRS 9.2.1(i)]*.

However, a residual interest in a decommissioning or similar fund that extends beyond a right to reimbursement, such as a contractual right to distributions once all the decommissioning has been completed or on winding up the fund, may be an equity instrument within the scope of IAS 39 and IFRS 9. *[IFRIC 5.5]*.

3.11 Disposal groups classified as held for sale and discontinued operations

The disclosure requirements in IFRS 7 will not apply to financial instruments within a disposal group classified as held for sale or within a discontinued operation, except for disclosures about the measurement of those assets and liabilities (see Chapter 54 at 4) if such disclosures are not already provided in other notes to the financial statements. *[IFRS 5.5B]*. However, additional disclosures about such assets (or disposal groups) may be necessary to comply with the general requirements of IAS 1 – *Presentation of Financial Statements* – particularly for financial statements to achieve a fair presentation and to disclose information about assumptions made and the sources of estimation uncertainty (see Chapter 3 at 4.1.1.A and 5.2.1 respectively). *[IAS 1.15, 125, IFRS 5.5B]*.

3.12 Indemnification assets

IFRS 3 specifies the accounting treatment for 'indemnification assets', a term that is not defined but is described as follows:

> 'The seller in a business combination may contractually indemnify the acquirer for the outcome of a contingency or uncertainty related to all or part of a specific asset or liability. For example, the seller may indemnify the acquirer against losses above a specified amount on a liability arising from a particular contingency; in other words, the seller will guarantee that the acquirer's liability will not exceed a specified amount. As a result, the acquirer obtains an indemnification asset.' *[IFRS 3.27]*.

An indemnification asset will normally meet the definition of a financial asset within IAS 32. In some situations the asset might be considered a right under an insurance contract (see 3.3 above) and in others it could be seen as similar to a reimbursement right (see 3.10 above). However, there will be cases where these assets are, strictly, within the scope of IAS 39 or IFRS 9, creating something of a tension with IFRS 3. This appears to be nothing more than an oversight and, in our view, entities should apply the more specific requirements of IFRS 3 when accounting for these assets which are covered in more detail in Chapter 9 at 5.6.4.

4 CONTRACTS TO BUY OR SELL COMMODITIES AND OTHER NON-FINANCIAL ITEMS

Contracts to buy or sell non-financial items do not generally meet the definition of a financial instrument (see 2.2.5 above). However, many such contracts are standardised in form and traded on organised markets in much the same way as some derivative financial instruments. The application guidance explains that a commodity futures contract, for example, may be bought and sold readily for cash because it is listed for trading on an exchange and may change hands many times. *[IAS 32.AG20]*. In fact, this is not strictly true because such contracts are bilateral agreements that cannot be transferred in this way. Rather, the contract would normally be 'closed out' (rather than sold) by entering into an offsetting agreement with the original counterparty or with the exchange on which it is traded.

The ability to buy or sell such a contract for cash, the ease with which it may be bought or sold (or, more correctly, closed out), and the possibility of negotiating a cash settlement of the obligation to receive or deliver the commodity, do not alter the fundamental character of the contract in a way that creates a financial instrument. The buying and selling parties are, in effect, trading the underlying commodity or other asset. However, the IASB is of the view that there are many circumstances where they should be accounted for as if they were financial instruments. *[IAS 32.AG20]*.

Accordingly, the provisions of IAS 32, IAS 39, IFRS 7 and IFRS 9 are normally applied to those contracts to buy or sell non-financial items that can be settled net in cash or another financial instrument or by exchanging financial instruments or in which the non-financial instrument is readily convertible to cash, effectively as if the contracts were financial instruments (see 4.1 below). However, there is an exception for what are commonly termed 'normal' purchases and sales or 'own use' contracts (these are considered in more detail at 4.2 below). *[IAS 32.8, IAS 39.5, IFRS 9.2.4, IFRS 7.5]*.

Typically the non-financial item will be a commodity, but this is not necessarily the case. For example, an emission right, which is an intangible asset (see Chapter 17 at 11.2), is a non-financial item. Therefore, these requirements would apply equally to contracts for the purchase or sale of emission rights if they could be settled net. These requirements will also be appropriate for determining whether certain commodity leases are within the scope of IAS 39 and IFRS 9. Commodity leases generally do not fall within the scope of IAS 17 or IFRS 16 as they do not relate to a specific or identified asset.

4.1 Contracts that may be settled net

IAS 39 and IFRS 9 explain that there are various ways in which a contract to buy or sell a non-financial item can be settled net, including when: *[IAS 32.9, IAS 39.6, BC24, IFRS 9.2.6, BCZ2.18]*

(a) the terms of the contract permit either party to settle it net;

(b) the ability to settle the contract net is not explicit in its terms, but the entity has a practice of settling similar contracts (see 4.2.1 below) net (whether with the counterparty, by entering into offsetting contracts or by selling the contract before its exercise or lapse);

(c) for similar contracts (see 4.2.2 below), the entity has a practice of taking delivery of the underlying and selling it within a short period after delivery for the purpose of generating a profit from short-term fluctuations in price or dealer's margin; and

(d) the non-financial item that is the subject of the contract is readily convertible to cash (see below).

There is no further guidance in IAS 39 or IFRS 9 explaining what is meant by 'readily convertible to cash'. Typically, a non-financial item would be considered readily convertible to cash if it consists of largely fungible units and quoted spot prices are available in an active market that can absorb the quantity held by the entity without significantly affecting the price.

Whether there exists an active market for a non-financial item, particularly a physical one such as a commodity, will depend on its quality, location or other characteristics such as size or weight. For example, if a commodity is actively traded in London, this may have the effect that the same commodity located in, say, Rotterdam is considered readily convertible to cash as well as if it was located in London. However, if it were located in Siberia it might not be considered readily convertible to cash if more than a little effort were required (often because of transportation needs) for it to be readily sold.

Like loan commitments, most contracts could as a matter of fact be settled net if both parties agreed to renegotiate terms. Again we do not believe the IASB intended the possibility of such renegotiations to be considered in determining whether or not such contracts may be settled net. Of more relevance is the question of whether one party has the practical ability to settle net, e.g. in accordance with the terms of the contract or by the use of some market mechanism.

4.2 Normal sales and purchases (or own use contracts)

As indicated at 4 above, the provisions of IAS 32, IAS 39, IFRS 9 and IFRS 7 are not to be applied to those contracts to buy or sell non-financial items that can be settled net if they were entered into and continue to be held for the purpose of the receipt or delivery of the non-financial item in accordance with the entity's expected purchase, sale or usage requirements (a 'normal' purchase or sale). *[IAS 32.8, IAS 39.5, IFRS 7.5, IFRS 9.2.4]*. When such a contract meets the criteria to be classified as own use, an entity cannot normally choose to apply IAS 39 or IFRS 9 to it. However, an entity applying IFRS 9 may in certain circumstances be able to designate such a contract at fair value through profit or loss (see 4.2.6 below). Further, some entities currently consider it appropriate to designate such contracts at fair value though profit or loss under IAS 39 if they contain substantive embedded derivatives – see Chapter 46 at 2.2.3. It should be noted that this is a two-part test, i.e. in order to qualify as a normal purchase or sale, the contract needs to both (a) have been entered into, and (b) continue to be held, for that purpose. Consequently, a reclassification of an instrument can be only one way. For example, if a contract that was originally entered into for the purpose of delivery ceases to be held for that purpose at a later date, it should subsequently be accounted for as a financial instrument under IAS 39 or IFRS 9. Conversely, where an entity holds a contract that was not originally held for the purpose of delivery and was accounted for under IAS 39 or IFRS 9, but subsequently its intentions change such that it is expected to be settled by delivery, the contract remains within the scope of IAS 39 or IFRS 9.

The IASB views the practice of settling net or taking delivery of the underlying and selling it within a short period after delivery as an indication that the contracts are not normal purchases or sales. Therefore, contracts to which (b) or (c) at 4.1 above apply cannot be subject to the normal purchase or sale exception. Other contracts that can be settled net are evaluated to determine whether this exception can actually apply. *[IAS 32.9, IAS 39.6, BC24, IFRS 9.2.6, BCZ2.18]*.

The implications of this requirement are considered further at 4.2.1 and 4.2.2 below.

The implementation guidance illustrates the application of the exception as follows: *[IAS 39.A.1, IFRS 9.A.1]*

Example 43.3: Determining whether a copper forward is within the scope of IAS 39 and IFRS 9

Company XYZ enters into a fixed-price forward contract to purchase 1,000 kg of copper in accordance with its expected usage requirements. The contract permits XYZ to take physical delivery of the copper at the end of twelve months, or to pay or receive a net settlement in cash, based on the change in fair value of copper.

The contract is a derivative instrument because there is no initial net investment, the contract is based on the price of copper, and it is to be settled at a future date. However, if XYZ intends to settle the contract by taking delivery and has no history of settling similar contracts net in cash, or of taking delivery of the copper and selling it within a short period after delivery for the purpose of generating a profit from short-term fluctuations in price or dealer's margin, the contract is accounted for as an executory contract rather than as a derivative.

Sometimes a market design or process imposes a structure or intermediary that prevents the producer of a non-financial item from physically delivering it to the customer. For example, a gold miner may produce gold bars (dore) that are physically delivered to a mint for refining and, whilst remaining at the mint, the gold could be credited to either the producer's or a counterparty's 'gold account'. Where the producer enters into a contract for the sale of gold which is settled by allocating gold to the counterparty's gold account, this may constitute 'delivery' as that term is used in the standard. Accordingly, a contract that is expected to be settled in this way could potentially be considered a normal sale (although of course it would need to meet all the other requirements). However, if the gold is credited to the producer's account and the sale contract was settled net in cash, this would not constitute delivery. In these circumstances, treating the contract as a normal sale would, in effect, link a non-deliverable contract entered into with a customer with a transaction to buy or sell through an intermediary as a single synthetic arrangement, contrary to the general requirements on linking contracts discussed in Chapter 44 at 8.[17]

4.2.1 Net settlement of similar contracts

If the terms of a contract do not explicitly provide for net settlement but an entity has a practice of settling similar contracts net, that contract should be considered as capable of being settled net (see 4.1 above). Net settlement could be achieved either by entering into offsetting contracts with the original counterparty or by selling the contract before its maturity. In these circumstances the contract cannot be considered a normal sale or purchase and is accounted for in accordance with IAS 39 or IFRS 9 (see 4.1 above). *[IAS 32.9, IAS 39.6, BC24, IFRS 9.2.4, BCZ2.18]*.

The standard contains no further guidance on what degree of past practice would be necessary to prevent an entity from treating similar contracts as own use. We do not believe that any net settlement automatically taints an entity's ability to apply the own use exception, for example where an entity is required to close out a number of contracts as a result of an exceptional disruption arising from external events at a production facility. However, judgement will always need to be applied based on the facts and circumstances of each individual case.

Read literally, the reference to 'similar contracts' could be particularly troublesome. For example, it is common for entities in, say, the energy sector to have a trading arm that is managed completely separately from their other operations. These trading operations commonly trade in contracts on non-financial assets, the terms of which are similar, if not identical, to those used by the entity's other operations for the purpose of physical supply. Accordingly, the standard might suggest that the normal purchase or sale exemption is unavailable to any entity that has a trading operation. However, we believe that a more appropriate interpretation is that contracts should be 'similar' as to their purpose within the business (e.g. for trading or for physical supply) not just as to their contractual terms.

4.2.2 Commodity broker-traders and similar entities

IAS 39 and IFRS 9 contain no further guidance on what degree of net settlement (or trading) is necessary to make the normal sale or purchase exemption inapplicable, but in many cases it will be reasonably clear. For example, in our view, the presumption must be that contracts entered into by a commodity broker-trader that measures its inventories at fair value less costs to sell in accordance with IAS 2 – *Inventories* (see Chapter 22 at 2) falls within the scope of IAS 39 and IFRS 9. However, there will be situations that are much less clear-cut and the application of judgement will be necessary. Factors to consider in making this assessment might include:

- how the entity manages the business and intends to profit from the contract;
- whether value is added by linking parties which are normal buyers and sellers in the value chain;
- whether the entity takes price risk;
- how the contract is settled; and
- the entity's customer base.

Again the reference in the standard to 'similar contracts' in this context may be troublesome for certain entities. However, as noted at 4.2.1 above, we believe contracts should be 'similar' as to their purpose within the business (e.g. for trading or for physical supply) not just as to their contractual terms.

4.2.3 Written options that can be settled net

The IASB does not believe that a written option to buy or sell a non-financial item that can be settled net can be regarded as being for the purpose of receipt or delivery in accordance with the entity's expected sale or usage requirements. Essentially, this is because the entity cannot control whether or not the purchase or sale will take place. Accordingly, IAS 32, IAS 39, IFRS 7 and IFRS 9 apply to written options that can be settled net according to the terms of the contract or where the underlying non-financial item is readily convertible to cash (see (a) and (d) at 4.1 above). *[IAS 32.10, IAS 39.7, BC24, IFRS 9.2.7, BCZ2.18]*.

Example 43.4: Determining whether a put option on an office building is within the scope of IAS 39 and IFRS 9

Company XYZ owns an office building. It enters into a put option with an investor, which expires in five years and permits it to put the building to the investor for £150 million. The current value of the building is £175 million. The option, if exercised, may be settled through physical delivery or net cash, at XYZ's option.

XYZ's accounting depends on its intention and past practice for settlement. Although the contract meets the definition of a derivative, XYZ does not account for it as a derivative if it intends to settle the contract by delivering the building in the event of exercise and there is no past practice of settling net.

The investor, however, cannot conclude that the option was entered into to meet its expected purchase, sale, or usage requirements because it does not have the ability to require delivery. The contract may be settled net and is a written option. Regardless of past practices, its intention does not affect whether settlement is by delivery or in cash. Accordingly, the investor accounts for the contract as a derivative. As noted in Chapter 44 at 2 and in Chapter 46 at 2, this will involve remeasuring the derivative to its fair value each reporting period with any associated gains and losses recognised in profit or loss.

However, if the contract were a forward contract rather than an option, required physical delivery and the investor had no past practice of settling net (either in cash or by way of taking delivery and subsequently selling within a short period), the contract would not be accounted for as a derivative. *[IAS 39.A.2, IFRS 9.A.2]*.

4.2.4 Electricity and similar 'end-user' contracts

There have been problems in determining whether or not IAS 32, IAS 39, IFRS 7 and IFRS 9 apply to contracts to sell non-financial items (for example electricity or natural gas) to 'end-users' such as retail customers. The non-financial items will often be considered readily convertible to cash (see 4.1 above), at least by the supplier. Accordingly, contracts to supply such items might be considered contracts that can be settled net.

Furthermore, end-user contracts often enable the customer to purchase as much of the non-financial item as needed at a given price to satisfy its usage requirements, i.e. the supplier does not have the contractual right to control whether or not the sale will take place. This might suggest that, from the perspective of the supplier, the contract is a written option with the consequence that it could not regard it as meeting the normal sale and purchase exemption (see 4.2.3 above).

However, many argued that this was not necessarily the case, particularly in the following circumstances:

- the non-financial item is an essential item for the customer;
- the customer does not have access to a market where the non-financial item can be resold;
- the non-financial item is not easily stored in any significant amounts by the customer; and
- the supplier is the sole provider of the non-financial item for a certain period of time.

In circumstances such as these, the apparent optionality within the contract is not exercisable by the retail customer in any economic sense. The customer will purchase volumes required whether the terms in the contract are advantageous or not and would not have the practical ability to sell any excess amounts purchased. Such a contract can have both a positive value and a negative value for the supplier when compared with market conditions and therefore fails to exhibit one of the key characteristics of an option, i.e. that it has only a positive value for the holder (the customer) and only a negative value for the writer (the supplier). In many respects the positive value stems from an intangible, rather than financial, aspect of the contract, being the likelihood that the customer will exercise the option. Accordingly, it was often argued that such contracts should not be considered written options (and therefore not within the scope of IAS 39 or IFRS 9).

Even if contracts such as these are considered to be within the scope of IAS 39 or IFRS 9, it is common for the supplier to have the ability to increase the price charged at relatively short notice. Also, the customer may be able to cancel the contract without penalty and switch to another supplier. Features such as these are likely to reduce any fair value that the contract can have.

Only a small number of energy suppliers appeared to regard these contracts as falling within the scope of IAS 39 or IFRS 9, The Interpretations Committee noted that the guidance already explains what constitutes a written option, essentially confirming that in this context a written option arises where a supplier does not have the contractual right to control whether or not a sale will take place.[18]

The Interpretations Committee also noted that 'in many situations these contracts are not capable of net cash settlement' and 'would not be ... within the scope of IAS 39'. No detailed explanation was provided of why the ability of the supplier to readily realise the non-financial item for cash does not enable it to settle the contract net (as that term is used in IAS 39).[19] However, we understand the reason underlying the comment to be the inability of the counterparty to realise the non-financial item (and hence the contract) for cash. This establishes a useful principle that may be applied in similar situations, i.e. a contract is not capable of net settlement if the contract is an option and the option holder cannot readily realise the non-financial item for cash.

4.2.5 Other contracts containing volume flexibility

It is not uncommon for other sales contracts, such as those with large industrial customers, to contain volume flexibility features. For example, a supplier might enter into a contract requiring it to deliver, say, 100,000 units at a given price as well as giving the counterparty the option to purchase a further 20,000 units at the same price. The customer might well have access to markets for the non-financial item and, following the guidance of the Interpretations Committee, the supplier might consider such a contract to be within the scope of IAS 39 or IFRS 9 as it contains a written option.

However, the supplier could split the contract into two separate components for accounting purposes: a forward contract to supply 100,000 units (which may qualify as a normal sale) and a written option to supply 20,000 units (which would not). Arguments put forward include:

- the parties could easily have entered into two separate contracts, a forward contract and a written option; and
- it is appropriate to analogise to the requirements for embedded derivatives and separate a written option from the normal forward sale or purchase contract because it is not closely related (see Chapter 44 at 4 to 7).

In our view, entities may apply either of these interpretations as an accounting policy choice. The Interpretations Committee was asked to consider the appropriate treatment of such contracts and the initial view of the staff was that such contracts could not be split into two accounting units. However, after performing further research, the Interpretations Committee recognised that significant diversity exists in practice and decided not to address the issue because the IASB would consider the scope of IAS 39, including the guidance about contracts to buy or sell non-financial items, as part of the project to replace that standard.[20] However, IFRS 9 does not address these scope issues except for the application of the fair value option to non-financial items referred to at 4.2.6 below.

4.2.6 Fair value option in IFRS 9

Own use contracts are accounted for as normal sales or purchase contracts (i.e. executory contracts), with the idea that any fair value change of the contract is not relevant given that the contract is used for the entity's own use. However, participants in several industries often enter into similar contracts both for own use and for trading purposes and manage all the contracts together with derivatives on a fair value basis (so as to manage the fair value risk to close to nil). In such a situation, own use accounting leads to an accounting mismatch, as the fair value change of the derivatives and the trading positions cannot be offset against fair value changes of the own use contracts.

To eliminate the accounting mismatch, an entity could apply hedge accounting by designating own use contracts as hedged items in a fair value hedge relationship. However, hedge accounting in these circumstances is administratively burdensome and often produces less meaningful results than fair value accounting. Furthermore, entities enter into large volumes of commodity contracts and, within the large volume of contracts, some positions may naturally offset each other. An entity would therefore typically hedge on a net basis. *[IFRS 9.BCZ2.24]*.

IFRS 9, however, introduces a fair value option for own use contracts. At inception of a contract, an entity may make an irrevocable designation to measure an own use contract at fair value through profit or loss (the 'fair value option') even if it was entered into for the purpose of the receipt or delivery of a non-financial item in accordance with the entity's expected purchase, sale or usage requirement. However, such designation is only allowed if it eliminates or significantly reduces an accounting mismatch that would otherwise arise from not recognising that contract because it is excluded from the scope of IFRS 9. *[IFRS 9.2.5]*.

On transition to IFRS 9, entities can apply the fair value option on an 'all-or-nothing' basis for similar types of (already existing) own use contracts (see Chapter 53 at 10.2). *[IFRS 9.7.2.14A]*.[21]

References

1 Information for Observers (May 2007 IFRIC meeting), *Gaming Transactions*, IASB, May 2007, paras. 25 to 27 and *IFRIC Update*, July 2007.
2 Information for Observers (November 2007 IFRIC Meeting), *Deposits on returnable containers (Agenda Paper 7B)*, IASB, November 2007, paras. 1 and 2.
3 *IFRIC Update*, November 2007.
4 *IFRIC Update*, May 2008.
5 Information for Observers (July 2008 IFRIC meeting), *Accounting for Trailing Commission (Agenda Paper 6B)*, IASB, July 2008, paras. 6 and 7.
6 *IFRIC Update*, September 2008.
7 For example, IAS 32, paras. 13 and AG13 and IAS 39, para. F.2.7.
8 IFRIC D23, *Distributions of Non-cash Assets to Owners*, IASB, January 2008, paras. 9 to 11.
9 *IFRIC Update*, January 2013.
10 *IFRIC Update*, May 2016.
11 *Exposure Draft, Insurance Contracts,* IASB, June 2013, 7(f).
12 *IASB Update*, June 2009.
13 Information for Observers (March 2009 IASB meeting), *IAS 39 Financial Instruments: Recognition and Measurement – Scope exemption for business combination contracts (IAS 39.2(g)) (Agenda Paper 10C)*, IASB, March 2009, paras. 13 and 15.
14 Information for Observers (March 2009 IASB meeting), *IAS 39 Financial Instruments: Recognition and Measurement – Scope exemption for business combination contracts (IAS 39.2(g)) (Agenda Paper 10C)*, IASB, March 2009, paras. 9 and 10.
15 *IFRIC Update*, March 2016.
16 *IFRIC Update*, November 2005.
17 *IFRIC Update*, August 2005.
18 *IFRIC Update*, March 2007 and Information for Observers (January 2007 IFRIC meeting), *IAS 39 Financial Instruments: Recognition and Measurement – Written options in retail energy contracts (Agenda Paper 14(iv))*, IASB, January 2007, paras. 9 to 11.
19 *IFRIC Update*, March 2007 and Information for Observers (January 2007 IFRIC meeting), *IAS 39 Financial Instruments: Recognition and Measurement – Written options in retail energy contracts (Agenda Paper 14(iv))*, IASB, January 2007, para. 15.
20 *IFRIC Update*, March 2010.
21 *IASB Update*, January 2013.

Chapter 44 Financial instruments: Derivatives and embedded derivatives

List of examples

Chapter 44 Financial instruments: Derivatives and embedded derivatives

1 INTRODUCTION

Under IAS 39 – *Financial Instruments: Recognition and Measurement* – and IFRS 9 – *Financial Instruments*, the question of whether an instrument is a derivative or not is an important one for accounting purposes. Derivatives are normally recorded in the statement of financial position at fair value with any changes in value reported in profit or loss (see Chapter 46 at 2.1 and Chapter 47 at 2 and 3), although there are some exceptions, e.g. derivatives that are designated in certain effective hedge relationships.

For many financial instruments, it will be reasonably clear whether or not they are derivatives, but there will be more marginal cases. Accordingly, the term derivative is formally defined within IAS 39 and IFRS 9, and this definition, together with examples of derivatives, is considered further at 2 and 3 below.

IAS 39 and IFRS 9 also contain the concept of an embedded derivative which is described as a component of a hybrid or combined instrument that also includes a non-derivative host contract. In certain circumstances embedded derivatives are required to be accounted for separately as if they were freestanding derivatives. The IASB introduced this concept because it believes that entities should not be able to circumvent the accounting requirements for derivatives merely by embedding a derivative in a non-derivative financial instrument or other non-financial contract, e.g. by placing a commodity forward in a debt instrument. In other words, it is chiefly an anti-abuse measure designed to enforce 'derivative accounting' on those derivatives that are 'hidden' in other contracts. *[IAS 39.BC37, IFRS 9.BCZ4.92]*. Embedded derivatives, and the situations in which they are required to be accounted for separately, are considered in more detail at 4 to 7 below. Under IFRS 9 the concept of embedded derivatives applies to financial liabilities and non-financial items only. Embedded derivatives are not separated from financial assets within the scope of IFRS 9 and the requirements of IFRS 9 are applied to the hybrid contract as a whole.

In addition to assessing when a financial instrument or other contract should be accounted for as if it were two contracts, we consider at 8 below situations when two financial instruments should be accounted for as if they were one, together with the question of linkage (for financial reporting purposes) of transactions more generally.

This chapter does not deal with valuation of derivative financial instruments. Chapter 14 outlines the requirements of IFRS 13 – *Fair Value Measurement*, a standard that defines fair value and provides principles-based guidance on how to measure fair value under IFRS. Additional guidance affecting the valuation of derivatives can be found in Chapter 52 at 5.3.4.A ('Discount rates for calculating the fair value of derivatives') and at 5.3.4.B ('Currency basis risk in cross-currency interest rate swaps').

2 DEFINITION OF A DERIVATIVE

A derivative is a financial instrument or other contract within the scope of IAS 39 or IFRS 9 (see Chapter 43 at 2 and 3) with all of the following characteristics:

(a) its value changes in response to the change in a specified interest rate, financial instrument price, commodity price, foreign exchange rate, index of prices or rates, credit rating or credit index, or other variable, provided in the case of a non-financial variable that the variable is not specific to a party to the contract (sometimes called the 'underlying');

(b) it requires no initial net investment, or an initial net investment that is smaller than would be required for other types of contracts that would be expected to have a similar response to changes in market factors; and

(c) it is settled at a future date. *[IAS 39.9, IFRS 9 Appendix A]*.

These three defining characteristics are considered further below.

2.1 Changes in value in response to changes in underlying

2.1.1 Notional amounts

A derivative usually has a notional amount, such as an amount of currency, number of shares or units of weight or volume, but does not require the holder or writer to invest or receive the notional amount at inception.

Example 44.1: Notional amount of a derivative

Company XYZ, whose functional currency is the US dollar, has placed an order with a company in France for delivery in six month time. The price to be paid in six month time is €2,000,000. To hedge the exposure to currency risk, XYZ enters into a contract with an investment bank to convert US dollars to euros at a fixed exchange rate. The contract requires the investment bank to remit €2,000,000 in exchange for US dollars at a fixed exchange rate of 1.65 (US$3,300,000). The notional amount of the contract in euros terms is €2,000,000.

However, while a derivative usually has a notional amount, this is not always the case: a derivative could require a fixed payment or payment of an amount that can change (but not proportionally with a change in the underlying) as a result of some future event that is unrelated to a notional amount. For example, a contract that requires a fixed payment of €1,000 if six-month LIBOR increases by 100 basis points is a derivative, even though a notional amount is not specified (at least not in the conventional sense). *[IAS 39.AG9, IFRS 9.BA.1]*. A further example is shown below.

Example 44.2: Derivative containing no notional amount

XYZ enters into a contract that requires payment of $1,000 if ABC's share price increases by $5 or more during a six-month period; XYZ will receive $1,000 if the share price decreases by $5 or more during the same six-month period; no payment will be made if the price swing is less than $5 up or down.

The settlement amount changes with an underlying, ABC's share price, although there is no notional amount to determine the settlement amount. Instead, there is a payment provision that is based on changes in the underlying. Provided all the other characteristics of a derivative are present, which they are in this case, such an instrument is a derivative.[1]

2.1.2 Underlying variables

It follows from the definition (see 2 above) that a derivative will always have at least one underlying variable. The following underlying variables are referred to in the standard, but this is not an exhaustive list (we have provided an example for each of the underlyings):

- specified interest rate (e.g. LIBOR);
- financial instrument price (e.g. the share price of an entity);
- commodity price (e.g. the price of a barrel of oil);
- foreign exchange rate (e.g. the £/$ spot rate);
- index of prices or rates (e.g. Consumer Price Index);
- credit rating (e.g. Fitch);
- credit index (e.g. AAA rated corporate bond index); and
- non-financial variable (e.g. index of earthquake losses or of temperatures).

The application guidance explains that a contract to receive a royalty, often in exchange for the use of certain property that is not exchange-traded, where the payment is based on the volume of related sales or service revenues and accounted for under IAS 18 – *Revenue* – or IFRS 15 – *Revenue from Contracts with Customers* (see Chapter 29 at 3.12 and Chapter 30 at 8.5) is not accounted for as a derivative. *[IAS 39.AG2, IFRS 9.B2.2]*.

Derivatives that are based on sales volume are not necessarily excluded from the scope of IAS 39 (IFRS 9), especially where there is another (financial) underlying, as set out in the next example.

Example 44.3: Derivative containing two underlyings

Company XYZ, whose functional currency is the US dollar, sells products in France denominated in euros. XYZ enters into a contract with an investment bank to convert euros to US dollars at a fixed exchange rate. The contract requires XYZ to remit euros based on its sales volume in France in exchange for US dollars at a fixed exchange rate of 1.00.

The contract has two underlying variables, the foreign exchange rate and the volume of sales, no initial net investment, and a payment provision. Therefore, as the implementation guidance explains, it is a derivative. *[IAS 39.B.8, IFRS 9.B.8]*.

However, contracts that are linked to variables that might be considered non-financial, such as an entity's revenue, can sometimes cause particular interpretative problems.

2.1.3 Non-financial variables specific to one party to the contract

The definition of a derivative (see 2 above) refers to underlyings that are non-financial variables specific to one party to the contract. This reference was introduced by IFRS 4 – *Insurance Contracts* – to help determine whether or not a financial instrument is an insurance contract (see Chapter 43 at 3.3). An insurance contract is likely to contain such an underlying, for example the occurrence or non-occurrence of a fire that damages or destroys an asset of a party to the contract. Non-financial variables that are not specific to one party to the contract might include an index of earthquake losses in a particular region or an index of temperatures in a particular city. *[IAS 39.AG12A, IFRS 9.BA.5]*. Those based on climatic variables are sometimes referred to as 'weather derivatives'. *[IAS 39.AG1, IFRS 9.B2.1]*.

A change in the fair value of a non-financial asset is specific to the owner if the fair value reflects not only changes in market prices for such assets (a financial variable) but also the condition of the specific non-financial asset held (a non-financial variable). For example, if a guarantee of the residual value of a specific car exposes the guarantor to the risk of changes in the car's physical condition, the change in that residual value is specific to the owner of the car, and so would not be a derivative. *[IAS 39.AG12A, IFRS 9.BA.5]*.

Contracts with non-financial variables arise in the gaming industry where a gaming institution takes a position against a customer (rather than providing services to manage the organisation of games between two or more parties). For example, a customer will pay a stake to a bookmaker such that the bookmaker is contractually obliged to pay the customer a specified amount in the event that the bet is a winning one, e.g. if the specified horse wins a given race. The underlying variable (the outcome of the race) is clearly non-financial in nature, but it is unlikely to be specific to either party to the contract. Accordingly such contracts will typically be derivative financial instruments.[2]

It is not clear whether the reference to non-financial variables specific to one party to the contract means that all instruments with such an underlying would fail to meet the definition of a derivative or only those contracts that are insurance contracts, for which the reference was originally introduced. Until the standard is clarified, in our view, a legitimate case can be made for either view.

The Interpretations Committee considered this issue in the context of contracts indexed to an entity's revenue or EBITDA and initially came to a tentative conclusion that the exclusion was not restricted to insurance contracts.[3] However, that conclusion was later withdrawn and the Interpretations Committee referred the issue to the IASB, recommending that the standard be amended to limit the exclusion to insurance contracts.[4]

The IASB confirmed that it had intended the exclusion to apply only to contracts that are within the scope of IFRS 4[5] and in October 2007 proposed amendments to IAS 39 to reflect this view.[6] However, the proposed amendments would have resulted in a significant change to current practice with many contracts being brought into the scope of IAS 39 and inappropriately accounted for at fair value, for example:

- lease contracts with payments based on performance measures specific to the lessee;
- pharmaceutical contracts with payments based on the success rate of that drug;
- mobile phone service provider arrangements with distributors remunerated on the basis of the length of contract term agreed with the end customer;
- technology licensing agreements with payments due to the licensor based on production volumes; and
- some service concession arrangements.

In effect, entities would be required to place a fair value on their own business risk or future profit streams. The IASB staff concluded that further research into possible implications was needed and that this should be included as a separate project for a major amendment of IAS 39.[7] In October 2008, the IASB decided not to proceed with the proposed amendment in the annual improvements process, but would consider addressing the issue in a future project.[8] The existing definition of a derivative (see 2 above) was incorporated in IFRS 9 without alteration, leaving the issue unaddressed.

A further issue arises in that it is not always clear whether a variable is non-financial. This is illustrated in the following example (in this case the underlying is associated with an embedded feature which might or might not meet the definition of a derivative).

Example 44.4: Borrowing with coupons linked to revenue

Company F, a manufacturing entity, issues a debt instrument for its par value of €10m. It is repayable in ten years' time at par and an annual coupon is payable that comprises two elements: a fixed amount of 2.5% of the par value and a variable amount equating to 0.01% of F's annual revenues. Company F does not designate the instrument at fair value through profit or loss.

It is assumed that if F had instead issued a more conventional fixed rate borrowing for the same amount with the same maturity it would have been required to pay an annual coupon of 4% of the par value. Therefore, on the face of it, the debt contains an embedded feature that represents a swap with an initial fair value of zero whereby F receives a fixed amount annually (1.5% of €10m) and pays a variable amount annually (0.01% of its revenues). The question is now whether this feature represents an embedded derivative that should be separated from the host contact and accounted for separately; see embedded derivative guidance at 4 below.

It is very hard to argue that the economic characteristics and risks of this embedded feature are closely related to the debt instrument and the variable (F's revenue) is clearly specific to F. The key issue is whether F's revenue is a financial or non-financial variable and therefore whether the embedded feature meets the definition of a derivative.

It is not only contracts with payments based on revenue that can cause such problems. Some contracts may require payments based on other measures taken or derived from an entity's financial statements such as EBITDA. The Interpretations Committee considered this matter in July 2006 and concluded there was a lack of clarity within IAS 39, believed it would be unable to reach a consensus on a timely basis and tentatively decided not to address it further.[9] In January 2007, the Interpretations Committee decided to withdraw its earlier conclusion and referred the matter to the IASB.[10] However, the IASB eventually decided not to amend IAS 39 to deal with this issue.

Whilst it is tempting to regard an entity's revenue and EBITDA as financial variables, they are driven by a number of different factors many of which are clearly non-financial in nature, for example the general business risks faced by the entity.

Chapter 44

In addition, many of the drivers of EBITDA and revenue will be specific to that business, for example the location of the business, the nature of its goods or services and management actions.

Two companies that have faced this issue in practice are Gaz de France and Renault. They have issued liabilities on which coupons are linked to 'value added' (a measure of profit previously reported under French GAAP), revenue and net profit. As can be seen in the following extracts, Gaz de France, in accounting for the entire instrument at amortised cost, appears to view 'value added' as a non-financial variable, whereas Renault clearly states that its revenue-linked and net profit-linked features are considered embedded derivatives.

Extract 44.1: Gaz de France S.A. (2007)

NOTES (TO THE CONSOLIDATED FINANCIAL STATEMENTS) [extract]

A – ACCOUNTING PRINCIPLES AND EVALUATION METHODS [extract]

2 – 22.3 Loans and receivables [extract]

Gaz de France issued irredeemable securities in 1985 and 1986 as authorized by French law 83.1 of January 1, 1983, and by Law 85.695 of July 11, 1985. These securities are assessed at their amortized cost. As they do not meet the criteria of an equity instrument, they are classified as debt/financial liabilities.

Return

The return of irredeemable securities, subject to a limit of between 85% and 130% of the average bond interest rate, comprises a fixed portion equal to 63% of the French Average Bond Rate ("TMO" in the French acronym) and a variable portion calculated on the basis of the growth in Gaz de France's "value added" in the previous year (or that of the consolidated group, Group share only, if this is more favourable).

The return on irredeemable securities according to the effective interest method is treated as a borrowing cost in interest expense.

Extract 44.2: Renault SA (2015)

NOTES TO THE CONSOLIDATED FINANCIAL STATEMENT [extract]

2 – ACCOUNTING POLICIES AND SCOPE OF CONSOLIDATION [extract]

W – Financial liabilities of the Automotive segment and sales financing debts [extract]

Redeemable shares [extract]

In accordance with IAS 39, the Group considers that the variable interest on redeemable shares is an embedded derivative ...

23 – Financial liabilities and sales financing debts [extract]

Redeemable shares [extract]

The redeemable shares issued in October 1983 and April 1984 by Renault SA are subordinated perpetual shares. They earn a minimum annual return of 9% comprising a 6.75% fixed portion and a variable portion that depends on consolidated revenues and is calculated based on identical Group structure and methods. [...]

The return on Diac redeemable shares issued in 1985 comprises a fixed portion equal to the Annual Monetary Rate, and a variable portion calculated by multiplying an amount equal to 40% of the Annual Monetary Rate by the rate of increase in net consolidated profit of the Diac sub-group compared to the prior year.

In 2009 the Interpretations Committee was asked to consider the accounting treatment for an instrument that contains participation rights by which the instrument holder shares in the net income and losses of the issuer. However, the Interpretations Committee considered the issue without reconsidering the assumptions described in the request, including one that the financial liability did not contain any embedded derivatives.[11] In other words, the Interpretations Committee implicitly accepted that such a feature need not be separated but did not indicate that separation was necessarily prohibited.

In practice, we believe that an entity may make an accounting policy choice as to whether the entity's revenue, EBITDA or other measures taken or derived from the entity's financial statements, are financial or non-financial variables. Once an entity elects a particular policy, it must consistently apply that approach to all similar transactions.

2.2 Initial net investment

The second key characteristic of a derivative is that it has no initial net investment, or one that is smaller than would be required for other types of contracts that would be expected to have a similar response to changes in market factors (see 2 above). *[IAS 39.9, IFRS 9 Appendix A].*

An option contract meets the definition because the premium is less than the investment that would be required to obtain the underlying financial instrument to which the option is linked. *[IAS 39.AG11, IFRS 9.BA.3].*

The implementation guidance to the original standard suggested that the purchase of a deep in the money call option would fail to satisfy the original 'little net investment' test if the premium paid was equal *or close to* the amount required to invest in the underlying instrument.[12] However, the implementation guidance on which Example 44.8 below is based explains that a contract is not a derivative if the initial net investment *approximates* the amount that an entity otherwise would be required to invest. *[IAS 39.B.9, IFRS 9.B.9].* Currency swaps sometimes require an exchange of different currencies of equal value at inception. This does not mean that they would not meet the definition a derivative, i.e. no initial net investment or an initial investment that is smaller than would be required for other types of contracts that would be expected to have a similar response to changes in market factors, as the following example demonstrates.

Example 44.5: Currency swap – initial exchange of principal

Company A and Company B enter into a five year fixed-for-fixed currency swap on euros and US dollars. The current spot exchange rate is €1 = US$1. The five year interest rate in the US is 8%, while the five year interest rate in Europe is 6%. On initiation of the swap, A pays €2,000 to B, which in return pays US$2,000 to A. During the swap's life, A and B make periodic interest payments to each other without netting. B pays 6% per year on the €2,000 it has received (€120 per year), while A pays 8% per year on the US$2,000 it has received (US$160 per year). On termination of the swap, the two parties again exchange the original principal amounts.

The currency swap is a derivative financial instrument since the contract involves a zero initial *net* investment (an exchange of one currency for another of equal fair values), it has an underlying, and it will be settled at a future date. *[IAS 39.AG11, IFRS 9.BA.3].*

The following examples illustrate how to assess the initial net investment characteristic in various prepaid derivatives – these can provide guidance when assessing whether what appears to be a non-derivative instrument is actually a derivative.

Example 44.6: Prepaid interest rate swap (prepaid fixed leg)

Company S enters into a €1,000 notional amount five year pay-fixed, receive-variable interest rate swap. The interest rate of the variable part of the swap resets on a quarterly basis to three month LIBOR. The interest rate of the fixed part of the swap is 10% per annum. At inception of the swap S prepays its fixed obligation of €500 (€1,000 × 10% × 5 years), discounted using market interest rates, while retaining the right to receive the LIBOR-based interest payments on the €1,000 over the life of the swap.

The initial net investment in the swap is significantly less than the notional amount on which the variable payments under the variable leg will be calculated and therefore requires an initial net investment that is smaller than would be required for other types of contracts that would be expected to have a similar response to changes in market conditions, such as a variable rate bond. It therefore fulfils the 'no initial net investment or an initial investment that is smaller than would be required for other types of contracts that would be expected to have similar response to change in market factors' criterion. Even though S has no future performance obligation, the ultimate settlement of the contract is at a future date and its value changes in response to changes in LIBOR. Accordingly, it is a derivative. *[IAS 39.B.4, IFRS 9.B.4]*.

Example 44.7: Prepaid interest rate swap (prepaid floating leg)

Instead of the transactions in Example 44.6, Company S enters into a €1,000 notional amount five year pay-variable, receive-fixed interest rate swap. The variable leg of the swap resets on a quarterly basis to three month LIBOR. The fixed interest payments under the swap are calculated as 10% of the notional amount, i.e. €100 per year. By agreement with the counterparty, S prepays and discharges its obligation under the variable leg of the swap at inception by paying a fixed amount determined according to current market rates, while retaining the right to receive the fixed interest payments of €100 per year.

The cash inflows under the contract are equivalent to those of a financial instrument with a fixed annuity stream since S knows it will receive €100 per year over the life of the swap. Therefore, all else being equal, the initial investment in the contract should equal that of other financial instruments consisting of fixed annuities. Thus, the initial net investment in the pay-variable, receive-fixed interest rate swap is equal to the investment required in a non-derivative contract that has a similar response to changes in market conditions. For this reason, the instrument does not exhibit characteristic 'no initial net investment or an initial investment that is smaller than would be required for other types of contracts that would be expected to have similar response to changes in market factors' requirement and is therefore not a derivative. *[IAS 39.B.5, IFRS 9.B.5]*.

The conclusions in Examples 44.6 and 44.7 above are fundamentally different for what, on the face of it, appear to be very similar transactions. The key difference is that in Example 44.7 all possible cash flow variances are eliminated and, consequently, the resulting cash flows exhibit the characteristics of a simple non-derivative instrument, i.e. an amortising loan.

Example 44.8: Prepaid forward purchase of shares

Company S also enters into a forward contract to purchase 100 shares in T in one year. The current share price is €50 per share and the one year forward price €55. S is required to prepay the forward contract at inception with a €5,000 payment.

The initial investment in the forward contract of €5,000 is less than the notional amount applied to the underlying, 100 shares at the forward price of €55 per share, i.e. €5,500. However, the initial net investment approximates the investment that would be required for other types of contracts that would be expected to have a similar response to changes in market factors because T's shares could be purchased at inception for the same price of €50. Accordingly, the prepaid forward does not exhibit characteristic 'no initial net investment or an initial investment that is smaller than would be required for other types of contracts that would be expected to have similar response to changes in market factors' criterion and is therefore not a derivative. *[IAS 39.B.9, IFRS 9.B.9]*.

Many derivative instruments, such as futures contracts and exchange traded written options, require margin payments. The implementation guidance explains that a margin payment is not part of the initial net investment in a derivative, but is a form of collateral for the counterparty or clearing-house and may take the form of cash, securities, or other specified assets, typically liquid assets. Consequently, they are separate assets that are accounted for separately. *[IAS 39.B.10, IFRS 9.B.10]*. However, while accounted for separately, the margin call and the derivative would be presented net in the statement of financial position if the offsetting requirements of IAS 32 – *Financial Instruments: Presentation* – are met (see Chapter 54 at 7.4). In some jurisdictions, depending on the precise terms of the related contracts, margin payments may actually represent a partial settlement of a derivative.

2.3 Future settlement

The third characteristic is that settlement takes place at a future date. Sometimes, a contract will require gross cash settlement. However, as illustrated in the next example, it makes no difference whether the future settlements are gross or net.

Example 44.9: Interest rate swap – gross or net settlement

Company ABC is considering entering into an interest rate swap with a counterparty, XYZ. The proposed terms are that ABC pays a fixed rate of 8% and receives a variable amount based on three month LIBOR, reset on a quarterly basis; the fixed and variable amounts are determined based on a €1,000 notional amount; ABC and XYZ do not exchange the notional amount and ABC pays or receives a net cash amount each quarter based on the difference between 8% and three month LIBOR. Alternatively, settlement may be on a gross basis.

The contract meets the definition of a derivative regardless of whether there is net or gross settlement because its value changes in response to changes in an underlying variable (LIBOR), there is no initial net investment and settlements occur at future dates – it makes no difference whether ABC and XYZ actually make the interest payments to each other (gross settlement) or settle on a net basis. *[IAS 39.B.3, IFRS 9.B.3]*.

The definition of a derivative also includes contracts that are settled gross by delivery of the underlying item, e.g. a forward contract to purchase a fixed rate debt instrument. An entity may have a contract to buy or sell a non-financial item that can be settled net, e.g. a contract to buy or sell a commodity at a fixed price at a future date; if that contract is within the scope of IAS 39 or IFRS 9 (see Chapter 43 at 4), then the question of whether or not it meets the definition of a derivative will be assessed in the same way as for a financial instrument that may be settled gross. *[IAS 39.AG10, IFRS 9.BA.2]*.

Expiry of an option at its maturity is a form of settlement even though there is no additional exchange of consideration. Therefore, even if an option is not expected to be exercised, e.g. because it is significantly 'out of the money', it can still be a derivative. *[IAS 39.B.7, IFRS 9.B.7]*. Such an option will have some value, albeit small, because it still offers the opportunity for gain if it becomes 'in the money' before expiry even if such a possibility is remote – the more remote the possibility, the lower its value.

3 EXAMPLES OF DERIVATIVES

3.1 Common derivatives

The following table provides examples of contracts that normally qualify as derivatives. The list is not exhaustive – any contract that has an underlying may be a derivative. Moreover, as set out in Chapter 43 at 3, even if an instrument meets the definition of a derivative, it may not fall within the scope of IAS 39 or IFRS 9.

Type of contract	*Main underlying variable*
Interest rate swap	Interest rates
Currency swap (foreign exchange swap)	Currency rates
Commodity swap	Commodity prices
Equity swap	Equity prices (equity of another entity)
Credit swap	Credit rating, credit index, or credit price
Total return swap	Total fair value of the reference asset and interest rates
Purchased or written bond option (call or put)	Interest rates
Purchased or written currency option (call or put)	Currency rates
Purchased or written commodity option (call or put)	Commodity prices
Purchased or written stock option (call or put)	Equity prices (equity of another entity)
Interest rate futures linked to government debt (treasury futures)	Interest rates
Currency futures	Currency rates
Commodity futures	Commodity prices
Interest rate forward linked to government debt (treasury forward)	Interest rates
Currency forward	Currency rates
Commodity forward	Commodity prices
Equity forward	Equity prices (equity of another entity) *[IAS 39.B.2, IFRS 9.B.2]*

3.2 In-substance derivatives

The implementation guidance explains that the accounting should follow the substance of arrangements. In particular, non-derivative transactions should be aggregated and treated as a derivative when, in substance, the transactions result in a derivative. Indicators of this would include:

- they are entered into at the same time and in contemplation of one another;
- they have the same counterparty;
- they relate to the same risk; and
- there is no apparent economic need or substantive business purpose for structuring the transactions separately that could not also have been accomplished in a single transaction. *[IAS 39.B.6, IFRS 9.B.6]*.

The application of this guidance is illustrated in the following example.

Example 44.10: In-substance derivative – offsetting loans

Company A makes a five year fixed rate loan to Company B, while at the same time B makes a five year variable rate loan for the same amount to A. There are no transfers of principal at inception of the two loans, since A and B have a netting agreement.

The combined contractual effect of the loans is the equivalent of an interest rate swap arrangement, i.e. there is an underlying variable, no initial net investment, and future settlement. This meets the definition of a derivative.

This would be the case even if there was no netting agreement, because the definition of a derivative instrument does not require net settlement (see Example 44.9 at 2.3 above). *[IAS 39.B.6, IFRS 9.B.6]*.

The analysis above would be equally applicable if the loans were in different currencies – such an arrangement could synthesise a cross-currency interest rate swap and should be accounted for as a derivative if that is its substance.

3.3 Regular way contracts

A regular way purchase or sale is a purchase or sale of a financial asset under a contract whose terms require delivery of the asset within the time frame established generally by regulation or convention in the marketplace concerned. *[IAS 39.9, IFRS 9 Appendix A]*. Such contracts give rise to a fixed price commitment between trade date and settlement date that meets the definition of a derivative. However, because of the short duration of the commitments, they are not accounted for as derivatives but in accordance with special accounting rules. These requirements are discussed in Chapter 48 at 2.2. *[IAS 39.AG12, IFRS 9.BA.4]*.

4 EMBEDDED DERIVATIVES

An embedded derivative is a component of a hybrid or combined instrument that also includes a non-derivative host contract; it has the effect that some of the cash flows of the combined instrument vary in a similar way to a stand-alone derivative. In other words, it causes some or all of the cash flows, that otherwise would be required by the contract, to be modified according to a specified interest rate, financial instrument price, commodity price, foreign exchange rate, index of prices or rates, credit rating or credit index, or other underlying variable (provided in the case of a non-financial variable that the variable is not specific to a party to the contract). *[IAS 39.10, IFRS 9.4.3.1]*.

Common examples of contracts that can contain embedded derivatives include non-derivative financial instruments (especially debt instruments), leases, insurance contracts as well as contracts for the supply of goods or services. In fact, they may occur in all sorts of unsuspected locations.

Under IFRS 9 the concept of embedded derivatives applies to only financial liabilities and non-financial items. Embedded derivatives are not separated from financial assets within the scope of IFRS 9 and the requirements of IFRS 9 are applied to the hybrid contract as a whole. *[IFRS 9.4.3.2]*.

Normal sale or purchase contracts (see Chapter 43 at 4) can also contain embedded derivatives. This is an important difference from US GAAP, under which a contract for the sale or purchase of a non-financial item, that can be settled net, cannot be treated as a normal sale or purchase at all if it contains an embedded pricing feature, that is not clearly and closely related to the host contract – instead the whole contract would be accounted for as a derivative.

In the basis for conclusions to IAS 39 and IFRS 9, the IASB asserts that, in principle, *all* embedded derivatives that are not measured at fair value with gains and losses recognised in profit or loss ought to be accounted for separately, but explains that, as a practical expedient, they should not be where they are regarded as 'closely related' to their host contracts. In those cases, it is believed less likely that the derivative was embedded to achieve a desired accounting result. *[IAS 39.BC37, IFRS 9.BCZ4.92]*.

Accordingly, only where all of the following conditions are met should an embedded derivative be separated from the host contract and accounted for separately:

(a) the economic characteristics and risks of the embedded derivative are not closely related to the economic characteristics and risks of the host contract;

(b) a separate instrument with the same terms as the embedded derivative would meet the definition of a derivative; and

(c) the hybrid (combined) instrument is not measured at fair value with changes in fair value recognised in profit or loss. *[IAS 39.11, IFRS 9.4.3.3]*.

If any of these conditions are not met, the embedded derivative should not be accounted for separately, *[IAS 39.11, AG33, IFRS 9.4.3.3, IFRS 9.B4.3.8]*, i.e. an entity is prohibited from separating an embedded derivative that is closely related to its host contract. The process is similar, although not identical, to that applied when separating the equity element of a compound instrument by the issuer under IAS 32 (see Chapter 45 at 6). The assessment of the closely related criterion should be made when the entity first becomes a party to a contract or in other words on initial recognition of the contract (see 7 below). *[IFRIC 9.7, IFRS 9.B4.3.1, B4.3.11]*.

The accounting treatment for a separated embedded derivative is the same as for a standalone derivative. Such an instrument (actually, in this case, a component of an instrument) will normally be recorded in the statement of financial position at fair value with all changes in value being recognised in profit or loss (see 1 above, Chapter 46 at 2.1 and Chapter 47 at 2 and 3), although there are some exceptions, e.g. embedded derivatives may be designated as a hedging instrument in an effective hedge relationship in the same way as standalone derivatives (see Chapter 52 at 2.1.1).

A derivative that is attached to a financial instrument but is contractually transferable independently of that instrument, or has a different counterparty from that instrument, is not an embedded derivative, but a separate financial instrument. *[IAS 39.10, IFRS 9.4.3.1]*.

Where the embedded derivative's fair value cannot be determined reliably on the basis of its terms and conditions (for example if it is based on an equity instrument, that does not have a quoted price in an active market for an identical instrument, i.e. a Level 1 input), it may be determined indirectly as the difference between hybrid (combined) instrument and the host instrument, if their fair values can be determined. *[IAS 39.13, IFRS 9.4.3.7]*. If an entity is unable to measure an embedded derivative that is required to be separated from its host, either on acquisition or subsequently, the entire contract is designated at fair value through profit or loss. *[IAS 39.12, IAS 39.C.11, IFRS 9.4.3.6]*.

It is important to note that the requirement to separate an embedded derivative from a host contract applies to all parties to a contract e.g. the issuer of a debt instrument and the holder of the debt instrument. However, the parties might reach different accounting treatments when applying the guidance in the standard. From the issuer's perspective, the conversion option in a convertible debt instrument denominated in the functional currency of the issuer would be classified as an equity instrument, assuming it meets the conditions for classification as equity under IAS 32 (see Chapter 45), and is therefore excluded from the scope of IAS 39 or IFRS 9. From the holder's perspective under IAS 39 the conversion option is not closely related to the host debt instrument and therefore needs to be separated from the host contract (see 5.1.8 below).

Chapter 44

5 EMBEDDED DERIVATIVES: THE MEANING OF 'CLOSELY RELATED'

The standard does not define what is meant by 'closely related'. Instead, it illustrates what was intended by providing a series of situations where the embedded derivative is, or is not, regarded as closely related to the host. Making this determination can prove very challenging, not least because the illustrations do not always seem to be consistent with each other. This guidance is considered in the remainder of this subsection.

5.1 Financial instrument hosts

Where a host contract has no stated or predetermined maturity and represents a residual interest in the net assets of an entity, its economic characteristics and risks are those of an equity instrument – therefore, an embedded derivative would need to possess equity characteristics related to the same entity to be regarded as closely related. More commonly, if the host is not an equity instrument and meets the definition of a financial instrument, then its economic characteristics and risks are those of a debt instrument. *[IAS 39.AG27, IFRS 9.B4.3.2]*. The application of these principles to debt hosts is considered at 5.1.1 to 5.1.8 below and to equity hosts at 5.1.10 below; instruments that may be debt or equity hosts are considered at 5.1.9 below.

5.1.1 Foreign currency monetary items

A monetary item denominated in a currency other than an entity's functional currency is accounted for under IAS 21 – *The Effects of Changes in Foreign Exchange Rates* – with foreign currency gains and losses recognised in profit or loss. The embedded foreign currency derivative is considered closely related to the debt host and is not separated. In other words it would not be considered a functional currency monetary item and a foreign currency forward contract. This also applies where the embedded derivative in a host debt instrument provides a stream either of principal or of interest payments denominated in a foreign currency (e.g. a dual currency bond). *[IAS 39.AG33(c), IFRS 9.B4.3.8(c)]*.

5.1.2 Interest rate indices

Many debt instruments contain embedded interest rate indices that can change the amount of interest that would otherwise be paid or received. One of the simplest examples would be a floating rate loan whereby interest is paid quarterly based on three month LIBOR. More complex examples might include the following:

- inverse floater – coupons are paid at a fixed rate minus LIBOR;
- levered inverse floater – as above but a multiplier greater than 1.0 is applied to the resulting coupon;
- delevered floater – coupons lag overall movements in a specified rate, e.g. coupons equal a proportion of the ten year constant maturity treasuries rate plus a fixed premium; or
- range floater – interest is paid at a fixed rate but only for each day in a given period that LIBOR is within a stated range.

In such cases the embedded derivative is closely related to the host debt instrument unless:

(a) the combined instrument can be settled in such a way that the holder would not recover substantially all of its recognised investment; or

(b) the embedded derivative could at least double the holder's initial rate of return on the host contract *and* could result in a rate of return that is at least twice what the market return would be for a contract with the same terms as the host contract (often referred to as the 'double-double test'). *[IAS 39.AG33(a), IFRS 9.B4.3.8(a)]*.

If a holder is permitted, but not required, to settle the combined instrument in a manner such that it does not recover substantially all of its recognised investment, e.g. puttable debt, condition (a) is not satisfied and the embedded derivative is not separated. *[IAS 39.C.10, IFRS 9.C.10]*. The standard does not define 'substantially all' and therefore judgement will need to be applied, considering all relevant facts and circumstances.

To meet condition (b), the embedded derivative must be able to double the initial return *and* result in a rate of return that is at least twice what would be expected for a similar contract at the time it takes effect. If it meets only one part of this condition, but not the other, the derivative is regarded as closely related to the host. Due to the requirement 'could result in a rate of return that is at least twice what the market return would be for a contract with the same terms as the host contract', the derivative embedded in a simple variable rate loan would be considered closely related to the host because the variable rate at any specific time would be a market rate.

As with all embedded derivatives, the assessment of condition (a) and (b) above is made when the entity becomes party to the contract on the basis of market conditions existing at that time (see 4 above). Important to note is, the assessment is based on the

possibility of the holder not recovering its recognised investment or doubling its initial return and obtaining twice the then-market return. The likelihood of this happening is ignored in making the assessment. Therefore, even if the likelihood of this happening is low, the embedded derivative has to be separated from the host contract. The valuation of the embedded derivative would however consider the low probability of this happening, possibly resulting in a relatively low fair value at inception.

An example where the holder would not recover substantially all of its recognised investment would be a bond which becomes immediately repayable if LIBOR increases above a certain threshold, at an amount significantly lower than its issue price. A further example is set out below.

Example 44.11: Leveraged inverse floater – not recovering substantially all of the initial investment

Company A invests in a leveraged inverse floater loan note for its par value of US$20m. Interest is payable annually and is calculated as 10% minus 2 times three month LIBOR. At the time company A invests in the loan note, three month LIBOR is 3%, giving an initial return of 4%. There is no floor imposed on the interest rate and the rate could therefore be negative if LIBOR increases above 5%. In such a case, company A would need to pay interest on its investment, which would leave it unable to recover substantially all of its recognised investment. The embedded derivative is therefore not closely related to the host contract and will be accounted for separately.

An example of condition (b) above, the 'double-double test', is set out below.

Example 44.12: Leveraged inverse floater – 'double-double test'

Assume the same fact pattern as in Example 44.11, except that there is a floor imposed on the coupon rate so that rate could not be negative. In such a case, company A would recover substantially all of its recognised investment, meaning that no embedded derivative needs to be separated based on condition (a) above. However, before company A could conclude on whether or not an embedded derivative needs to be recognised separately, it would need to evaluate condition (b) above. The first step is to assess whether there is a possible scenario in which the initial return of the investor would at least double. If LIBOR falls to 1% or to below 1%, say 0.5%, then the interest rate on the loan note would be 9%, which is more than double the investor's initial rate of return of 4%. The first part of the condition under (b) above is therefore fulfilled.

The question is now whether 9% is twice the market return for a contract with the same terms as the host contract. With LIBOR being 0.5% this will most likely be the case, leaving both parts of condition (b) above fulfilled. The embedded derivative is therefore not closely related to the host contract and will be accounted for separately. If however, it is concluded that 9% is not twice the market return for a contract with the same terms as the host contract, then only one part of the condition under (b) above would be fulfilled and the embedded feature would be considered closely related to the host with no requirement to record it separately.

5.1.3 Term extension and similar call, put and prepayment options in debt instruments

The application guidance explains that a call, put or prepayment option embedded in a host debt instrument is closely related to the host instrument if, on each exercise date, the option's exercise price is approximately equal to the debt instrument's amortised cost or the exercise price reimburses the lender for an amount up to the approximate present value of lost interest for the remaining term of the host contract; otherwise it is not regarded as closely related. *[IAS 39.AG30(g), IFRS 9.B4.3.5(e)]*. There is no elaboration on what is meant by the term 'approximately equal' and so judgement will need to be applied.

It also says that an option or automatic provision to extend the remaining term to maturity of a debt instrument is not closely related to the host unless, at the time of the extension, there is a concurrent adjustment to the approximate current market rate of interest. *[IAS 39.AG30(c), IFRS 9.B4.3.5(b)]*. The current market rate of interest would take into consideration the credit risk of the issuer. Taken in isolation, the above two paragraphs appear reasonably straightforward to apply. However, in some situations, they are contradictory as set out in the following example.

Example 44.13: Extension and prepayment options

Company Z borrows €1,000 from Bank A on which it is required to pay €50 per annum interest. Under the terms of the borrowing agreement, Z is required to repay €1,000 in three years' time unless, at repayment date, it exercises an option to extend the term of the borrowing for a further two years. If this option is exercised €50 interest per annum is payable for the additional term.

Company Z also borrows €1,000 from Bank B on which it is required to pay €50 per annum interest. Under the terms of this borrowing agreement, Z is required to repay €1,000 in five years' time unless, at the end of three years, it exercises an option to redeem the borrowing for €1,000.

It can be seen that in all practical respects these two instruments are identical – the only difference is the way in which the terms of the embedded options are expressed. In the first case the guidance indicates that the (term extension) option is not closely related to the debt as there is no concurrent adjustment to market interest rates. However, in the second case the (prepayment) option *is* considered closely related provided the amortised cost of the liability would be approximately €1,000, the exercise price of the settlement option, at the end of year three (which it should be).

As set out at 6.2 below, an embedded option-based derivative should be separated from its host contract on the basis of the stated terms of the option feature. However, in situations similar to the one described above, there is significant diversity in practice and we are aware of at least two ways in which entities have dealt with this contradiction in practice. Some entities have looked to the wording in the contract so that what is described as an extension option (or a prepayment option) is evaluated in accordance with the guidance for extension options (or prepayment options). Other entities have determined the most likely outcome of the hybrid instrument based on conditions at initial recognition and the alternative outcome is regarded as the 'option'. Under this latter approach, if Company Z in the example above considered it was likely to repay its loans from Bank A and Bank B after three years, both loans would be regarded as having a two-year extension option. The first approach is based on the contractual terms, while the second approach is substance-based.

Another complication is that, viewed as a separate instrument, a term extension option is effectively a loan commitment. As loan commitments are generally outside the scope of IAS 39 (see Chapter 43 at 3), some would argue they do not meet the definition of a derivative (see 2 above). Accordingly, when embedded in a host debt instrument, a loan commitment would not be separated as an embedded derivative or, alternatively, would be separated and accounted for as a loan commitment.[13]

The Interpretations Committee discussed both of the above contradictions in March 2012, noting significant diversity in practice and recommended that the IASB consider this issue when it redeliberated the classification and measurement requirements of financial liabilities under IFRS 9. The Committee decided that if the Board did not address this issue as part of its redeliberations, then the Committee would revisit this issue and consider whether guidance should be provided to clarify the accounting for the issuer of a fixed-rate-debt instrument that includes a term-extending option.[14] This issue remains unaddressed in IFRS 9 with no indication from the Interpretations Committee about bringing it back onto its agenda. Preparers of financial statements are therefore left to apply their own judgement considering all the facts and circumstances.

For put, call and prepayment options, there is a further complication that the determination as to whether or not the option is closely related depends on the amortised cost of the instrument. It is not clear whether this reference is to the amortised cost of the host instrument, on the assumption that the option is separated, or to the amortised cost of the entire instrument on the assumption that the option is not separated. As can be seen in Chapter 49 at 3.2 and Chapter 50 at 3.2, the existence of such options can affect the amortised cost, especially for a portfolio of instruments. Although one trade body has published guidance explaining that where early repayment fees are included in the calculation of effective interest, the prepayment option is likely to be closely related to the loan,[15] entities are largely left to apply their own judgement to assess which appears the most appropriate in the specific circumstances.

Prepayment options are also considered closely related to the host debt instrument if the exercise price reimburses the lender for an amount up to the approximate present value of lost interest for the remaining term of the host contract. For these purposes, lost interest is the product of the principal amount prepaid multiplied by the interest rate differential, i.e. the excess of the effective interest rate of the host contract over the effective interest rate that the entity would receive at the prepayment date if it reinvested the principal amount prepaid in a similar contract for the remaining term of the host contract. *[IAS 39.AG30(g)(ii), IFRS 9.B4.3.5(e)(ii)]*. In other words, in order for the prepayment option to be considered closely related to the host, the exercise price of the prepayment option would need to compensate the lender for loss of interest by reducing the economic loss from that which would be incurred on reinvestment. *[IAS 39.BC40C, IFRS 9.BCZ4.97]*.

From the perspective of the issuer of a convertible debt instrument with an embedded call or put option, the assessment of whether the option is closely related to the host debt instrument is made before separating the equity element in accordance with IAS 32. *[IAS 39.AG30(g), IFRS 9.B4.3.5(e)]*. This provides a specific relaxation from the general guidance on prepayment options above because, for accounting purposes, separate accounting for the equity component results in a discount on recognition of the liability component (see Chapter 45 at 6.2), which means that the amortised cost and exercise price are unlikely to approximate to each other for much of the term of the instrument.

An embedded prepayment option in an interest-only or principal-only strip is regarded as closely related to the host contract provided the host contract (i) initially resulted from separating the right to receive contractual cash flows of a financial instrument that, in and of itself, did not contain an embedded derivative, and (ii) does not contain any terms not present in the original host debt contract. *[IAS 39.AG33(e), IFRS 9.B4.3.8(e)]*. Again this is a specific relaxation from the general guidance on prepayment options above.

If an entity issues a debt instrument and the holder writes a call option on the debt instrument to a third party, the issuer regards the call option as extending the term to maturity of the debt instrument, provided it can be required to participate in or facilitate the remarketing of the debt instrument as a result of the call option being exercised. *[IAS 39.AG30(c), IFRS 9.B4.3.5(b)]*. Such a component is presumably considered to represent part of a hybrid financial instrument contract rather than a separate instrument in its own right (see 4 above).

5.1.4 Interest rate floors and caps

An embedded floor or cap on the interest rate on a debt instrument is closely related to the host debt instrument, provided the cap is at or above the market rate of interest, and the floor is at or below the market rate of interest, when the instrument is issued (in other words it needs to be at- or out-of-the-money), and the cap or floor is not leveraged in relation to the host instrument. *[IAS 39.AG33(b), IFRS 9.B4.3.8(b)]*.

The standard does not clarify what is meant by 'market rate of interest', or whether the cap (floor) should be considered as a single derivative or a series of caplets (floorlets) to be evaluated separately. Where the cap (floor) is at a constant amount throughout the term of the debt, historically entities have often compared the cap (floor) rate with the current spot floating rate at inception of the contract to determine whether the embedded derivative is closely related. However, in the current extremely low, or negative, interest rate environment of many economies, floors are more commonly being set at higher rates than current spot rates. As a result, entities are starting to evaluate whether more sophisticated approaches to evaluate these features are more appropriate, e.g. by comparing the average forward rate over the life of the bond with the floor rate or by comparing the forward rate at each interest reset date with each floorlet rate. We do not believe it is necessary for both a cap *and* a floor to be present to be considered closely related. For example, a cap (or floor) on the coupon paid on a debt instrument without a corresponding floor (or cap) could be regarded as closely related to the host, provided it was above (or below) the market rate of interest on origination.

The Interpretations Committee was asked, in January 2016, to clarify the application of the embedded derivatives requirements in a negative interest rate environment. The Interpretations Committee observed that:

- neither IAS 39.AG33(b) nor IFRS 9.B4.3.8(b) distinguishes between positive and negative interest rate environments. As such an interest rate floor in a negative interest rate environment should be treated in the same way as in a positive interest rate environment;
- when applying paragraph IAS 39.AG33(b) or IFRS 9B4.3.8(b) in a positive or negative interest rate environment, an entity should compare the overall interest rate floor (i.e. benchmark interest rate referenced in the contract plus contractual spreads and if applicable any premiums, discounts or other elements that would be relevant to the calculation of the effective interest rate) for the hybrid contract to the market rate of interest for a similar contract without the interest rate floor (i.e. the host contract); and
- the appropriate market rate of interest for the host contract should be determined by considering the specific forms of the host contract and the relevant spreads (including credit spreads) appropriate for the transaction. They also noted that the term 'market rate of interest is linked to the concept of fair value as defined in IFRS 13 and is described in IAS 39 as the rate of interest 'for

a similar instrument (similar to currency, term, type of interest and other factors) with a similar credit rating'. *[IAS 39.AG64].*

The Interpretations Committee determined that neither an Interpretation nor an amendment to a Standard was necessary and did not add this issue to its agenda.[16]

In practice entities perform the assessment of whether a cap or floor is 'at or below market interest' by either considering the cap or floor as a single instrument and applying the current swap rate, or by considering the component caplets and floorlets making up the overall cap or floor using the forward rate for the payment date of each particular caplet or floorlet.

Where, in making the assessment on the cap or floor as a single instrument, an entity determines that the cap or floor is not closely related, then the whole embedded cap or floor is accounted for as a single non-closely related embedded derivative at fair value through profit or loss.

5.1.5 Inflation-linked debt instruments

It is quite common for some entities (and governments) to issue inflation-linked debt instruments, i.e. where interest and/or principal payments are linked to, say, a consumer price index. The only guidance in IAS 39 and IFRS 9 relating to embedded inflation-linked features is provided in the context of leases (see 5.3.2 below). If that guidance is accepted as applying to finance leases, it should also apply to debt instruments because finance leases result in assets and liabilities that are, in substance, no different to debt instruments (see Chapter 43 at 2.2.4). Further, in much finance theory, either real (applied to current prices) or nominal (applied to inflation adjusted prices) interest rates are used, suggesting a strong link between inflation and interest rates. Finally, a government or central bank will generally raise short-term interest rates as inflation rises and reduce rates as inflation recedes, which also suggests a close relationship between the two.

Therefore, we believe it would often be appropriate to treat the embedded derivative in inflation-linked debt as similar to an interest rate index and refer to the guidance at 5.1.2 above to determine whether the index is regarded as closely related to the debt. Typically, the index will be closely related to the debt where it is based on inflation in an economic environment in which the bond is issued/denominated, it is not significantly leveraged in relation to the debt and there is a sufficiently low risk of the investor not recovering its initial investment (only sometimes do such instruments provide an absolute guarantee that the principal will not be lost, although this situation will normally only arise if, over the life of the instrument, cumulative inflation is negative). However, some may argue that even if there is a very small risk of the initial investment not being recovered, the embedded derivative should be separated.

The staff of the Interpretations Committee has expressed a view that it would be appropriate to treat the embedded derivative in inflation-linked debt as closely related in economic environments where interest rates are mainly set so as to meet inflation targets, as evidenced by strong long-run correlation between nominal interest rates and inflation. In such jurisdictions they considered the characteristics and risks of the inflation embedded derivative to be closely related to the host debt contract.[17] Further, in debating the application of the effective interest method to such instruments (see Chapter 49 at 3.6 and Chapter 50 at 3.5) they have implicitly acknowledged that these instruments do not necessarily contain embedded derivatives requiring separation.

5.1.6 Commodity- and equity-linked interest and principal payments

Equity-indexed or commodity-indexed interest or principal payments embedded in a host debt instrument, i.e. where the amount of interest or principal is indexed to the value of an equity instrument or commodity (e.g. gold), are not closely related to the host debt instrument because the risks inherent in the embedded derivative are dissimilar to those of the host. *[IAS 39.AC30(d)-(e), IFRS 9.B4.3.5(c)-(d)]*. This is illustrated in the following example.

Example 44.14: Bond linked to commodity price

A mining company issues a ten year debt instrument for its par value of US$15m. Interest is payable annually and consists of guaranteed interest of 5% per annum and contingent interest of 0.5% if the price of commodity A increases above US$300 in the relevant year, 1% if the price of commodity A increases above US$400 in the relevant year or 1.5% if the price of commodity A increases above US$500 in the relevant year. The mining company could have issued the bond without the contingent interest rate feature at a rate of 6%.

The commodity price feature is a swap contract to receive 1% fixed interest and pay a variable amount of interest depending on the price of commodity A. This feature is not closely related to the debt host contract and therefore must be separated as an embedded derivative.

Another example of such an instrument is given in Example 46.1 in Chapter 46 at 3.1.

A common type of transaction is where refiners of commodities enter into purchase contracts for mineral ores, whereby the price is adjusted subsequent to delivery, based on the quoted market price of the refined commodity extracted from the ore. These arrangements, often called provisionally-priced contracts, can provide the refiner with a hedge of the fair value of its inventories and/or related sales proceeds which vary depending on subsequent changes in quoted commodity prices. Like the debt instruments noted above, any payable (or receivable) recognised at the time of delivery will contain an embedded commodity derivative. BHP Billiton supplies products on these terms and explains its accounting policy as follows.

Extract 44.3: BHP Billiton (2015)

Financial Statements [extract]

43 Significant accounting policies [extract]

(d) Sales revenue [extract]

For certain commodities, the sales price is determined on a provisional basis at the date of sale and adjustments to the sales price subsequently occurs based on movements in quoted market or contractual prices up to the date of final pricing. The period between provisional invoicing and final pricing is typically between 60 and 120 days. Revenue on provisionally priced sales is recognised based on the estimated fair value of the total consideration receivable. The revenue adjustment mechanism embedded within provisionally priced sales arrangements has the character of a commodity derivative. Accordingly, the fair value of the final sales price adjustment is re-estimated continuously and changes in fair value are recognised as an adjustment to revenue. In all cases, fair value is estimated by reference to forward market prices.

However, it would not normally be regarded as necessary to account separately for such an embedded derivative prior to delivery of the non-financial item. This is because, until delivery occurs, the contract is considered executory and the pricing feature would be considered closely related to the commodity being delivered (see 5.2.2 below).

5.1.7 Credit-linked notes

Credit derivatives are sometimes embedded in a host debt instrument whereby one party (the 'beneficiary') transfers the credit risk of a particular reference asset, which it may not own, to another party (the 'guarantor'). Such credit derivatives allow the guarantor to assume the credit risk associated with the reference asset without directly owning it.

Whilst the economic characteristics of a debt instrument will include credit risk, should the embedded derivative be a credit derivative linked to the credit standing of an entity other than the issuer, it would not normally be regarded as closely related to the host debt instrument if the issuer were not required, through the terms of the financial instrument, to own the reference asset. *[IAS 39.AG30(h), IFRS 9.B4.3.5(f)]*.

For example, an entity (commonly a structured entity) may issue various tranches of debt instruments that are referenced to a group of assets, such as a portfolio of bonds, mortgages or trade receivables, and the credit exposure from those assets is allocated to the debt instruments using a so called 'waterfall' feature. The waterfall feature itself does not normally result in the separation of an embedded credit derivative; it is the location or ownership of the reference assets that is most important to the assessment.[18] If the entity is required to hold the reference assets, the credit risk embedded in the debt instruments is considered closely related. However, if the issuer of the debt instruments held a credit derivative over the reference assets rather than the assets themselves, the embedded credit derivative would not be regarded as closely related.

Bradford and Bingley has separately accounted for derivatives embedded within a number of its collateralised debt obligation investments as explained below.

Extract 44.4: Bradford and Bingley plc (2007)

Notes to the Financial Statements [extract]

1. Principal accounting policies [extract]

(n) Derivative financial instruments and hedge accounting [extract]

The Group recognises that its holding of synthetic CDOs (where the SPV Issuing the CDO contains a credit derivative) contains an embedded derivative if the CDO's originator does not hold the reference assets on its balance sheet or if the sponsor of the CDO is not required to hold the reference assets on its own balance sheet. Consequently, the fair value of the credit derivative contract is separated from the host synthetic CDO with changes in its fair value recognised within 'fair value movements'.

5.1.8 Convertible and exchangeable debt instruments

An equity conversion feature, embedded in a convertible debt instrument, is not closely related to the host debt instrument from the perspective of the holder of the instrument (from the issuer's perspective, the equity conversion option is often an equity instrument and excluded from the scope of IAS 39 – see Chapter 45 at 6.2). *[IAS 39.AG30(f), C.3]*.

Where IFRS 9 is applied, the embedded derivative is not separated from financial assets within the scope of the standard and the requirements of the standard are applied to the hybrid contract as a whole. *[IFRS 9.4.3.2]*.

In some instances, venture capital entities provide subordinated loans on terms that entitled them to receive shares if and when the borrowing entity lists its shares on a stock exchange, as illustrated in the following example.

Example 44.15: Equity kicker

A venture capital investor, Company V, provides a subordinated loan to Company A and agrees that in addition to interest and repayment of principal, if A lists its shares on a stock exchange, V will be entitled to receive shares in A free of charge or at a very low price (an 'equity kicker'). As a result of this feature, interest on the loan is lower than it would otherwise be. The loan is not measured at fair value with changes in fair value recognised in profit or loss.

The economic characteristics and risks of an equity return are not closely related to those of the host debt instrument. The equity kicker meets the definition of a derivative because it has a value that changes in response to the change in the price of A's shares, requires only a relatively small initial net investment, and is settled at a future date. It does not matter that the right to receive shares is contingent upon the borrower's future listing *[IAS 39.C.4, IFRS 9.C.4]* (although the probability of this event occurring will influence the fair value of the embedded derivative).

Similarly, the derivative embedded in a bond that is convertible (or exchangeable) into equity shares of a third party will not be closely related to the host debt instrument – in this case, either from the point of view of the holder or of the issuer.

5.1.9 Puttable instruments

Another example of a hybrid contract is a financial instrument that gives the holder a right to put it back to the issuer in exchange for an amount that varies on the basis of the change in an equity or commodity price or index (a 'puttable instrument'). Where the host is a debt instrument, the embedded derivative, the indexed principal payment, cannot be regarded as closely related to that debt instrument. Because the principal payment can increase and decrease, the embedded derivative is a non-option derivative whose value is indexed to the underlying variable (see 6.1 below). *[IAS 39.AG30(a), AG31, IFRS 9.B4.3.5(a), B4.3.6]*.

From the perspective of the issuer of a puttable instrument, that can be put back at any time for cash equal to a proportionate share of the net asset value of an entity (such as units of an open-ended mutual fund or some unit-linked investment products), the effect of the issuer separating an embedded derivative and accounting for each component is to measure the combined instrument at the redemption amount, that would be payable at the end of the reporting period, if the holder were to exercise its right to put the instrument back to the issuer. *[IAS 39.AG32, IFRS 9.B4.3.7]*.

IAS 39 is not entirely clear whether a similar treatment should apply to the holder of such an instrument. If it did, it would mean that all changes in the fair value of an entity's investment in a unit trust would be recognised in profit or loss, even if it were classified as available-for-sale. However, to the extent that anyone has a residual interest in the net assets of a unit trust, it is the unit-holders. Consequently, a more intuitive view of the investment might be as an equity instrument host with an embedded put option, exercisable at net asset value. Further, because net asset value will approximate fair value, the embedded derivative would have little or no value. A related issue has been considered by the Interpretations Committee, namely the treatment by the holder of instruments, that are puttable at an amount other than fair value (for example a proportion of the book value of net assets determined under IFRS or local GAAP) but which otherwise have characteristics and risks that are similar to an equity instrument, such as discretionary distributions. Although the Interpretations Committee did not take the issue onto its agenda, it indicated that the requirement for the issuer to apply IAS 32 and the holder to apply IAS 39 means that their respective accounting treatments need not necessarily be symmetrical.

Accordingly, it may be appropriate for the holder to regard the host as an equity, not debt, instrument. Of course, in this case, the put option would have a non-zero fair value and should be accounted for separately as an embedded derivative.[19]

Further support for this can be found in the definition of loans and receivables: IAS 39 explains that an interest in a pool of assets that are not loans or receivables (such as an interest in a mutual fund) is not considered to be a loan or receivable (see Chapter 46 at 4). *[IAS 39.9]*. This also suggests the host might validly be considered an equity instrument from the point of view of the holder.

Therefore, we believe entities can account for unit trust and similar investments under IAS 39 as available-for-sale equity investments whilst recognising fair value gains and losses in equity. Where IFRS 9 is applied, the requirements of the standard are applied to the instrument as a whole, resulting in such investments in puttable instruments being recognised at fair value through profit or loss in their entirety. *[IFRS 9.4.3.2]*.

5.1.10 Callable equity instruments

An equity instrument containing an embedded call option enabling the issuer to reacquire that equity instrument at a specified price is not closely related to the host equity instrument from the perspective of the holder under IAS 39. *[IAS 39.AG30(b)]*.

Where IFRS 9 is applied, embedded derivatives are not separated from financial assets within the scope of the standard and the requirements of IFRS 9 are applied to the hybrid contract as a whole. *[IFRS 9.4.3.2]*.

5.2 Contracts for the sale of goods or services

5.2.1 Foreign currency derivatives

An embedded foreign currency derivative in a contract that is not a financial instrument is closely related to the host contract provided it is not leveraged, does not contain an option feature and requires payments denominated in one of the following currencies:

(i) the functional currency of any substantial party to the contract – see 5.2.1.A below;

(ii) the currency in which the price of the related good or service that is acquired or delivered is routinely denominated in commercial transactions around the world (such as the US dollar for crude oil transactions) – see 5.2.1.B below; or

(iii) a currency that is commonly used in contracts to purchase or sell non-financial items in the economic environment in which the transaction takes place (e.g. a relatively stable and liquid currency that is commonly used in local business transactions or external trade) – see 5.2.1.C below.

Therefore, in such cases the embedded foreign currency derivative is not accounted for separately from the host contract. *[IAS 39.AG33(d), IFRS 9.B4.3.8(d)]*. An example would be a contract for the purchase or sale of a non-financial item, where the price is denominated in a foreign currency that meets one of the three criteria outlined above.

5.2.1.A Functional currency of counterparty

In principle, the assessment of exception (i) above is straightforward. In practice, however, the functional currency of the counterparty to a contract will not always be known with certainty and, in some cases, can be a somewhat subjective assessment even for the counterparty's management (assuming the counterparty is a corporate entity) – see Chapter 15 at 4. Consequently, entities will need to demonstrate they have taken appropriate steps to make a reasonable judgement as to their counterparties' functional currencies. Where available, a counterparty's financial statements will provide evidence of its functional currency. Otherwise, it would often be appropriate to assume that an entity operating in a single country has that country's currency as its functional currency, although if there were indicators to the contrary these would have to be taken into account.

Another practical problem that arises in applying this exception is identifying which parties to a contract are 'substantial'. Neither IAS 39 nor IFRS 9 provide any further guidance, but it is generally considered that such a party should be one that is acting as principal to the contract. Therefore if, as part of a contract, a parent provides a performance guarantee in respect of services to be provided by its operating subsidiary, the parent may be seen to be the substantial party to the contract and not the subsidiary, where the subsidiary is acting as an agent. However, if the guarantee is not expected to be called upon, the parent would not normally be considered a substantial party to the contract. Particular care is necessary when assessing a contract under which one party subcontracts an element of the work to another entity under common control, say a fellow subsidiary with a different functional currency, although in most cases it will only be the primary contractor that is considered a substantial party.

5.2.1.B Routinely denominated in commercial transactions

For the purposes of exception (ii) above, the currency must be used for similar transactions all around the world, not just in one local area. For example, if cross-border transactions in natural gas in North America are routinely denominated in US dollars and such transactions are routinely denominated in euros in Europe, neither the US dollar nor the euro is a currency in which the good or service is routinely denominated in international commerce. *[IAS 39.C.9, IFRS 9.C.9]*. Accordingly, the number of items to which this will apply will be limited – in practice it will be mainly commodities that are traded in, say, US dollars throughout much of the world. Examples include crude oil, jet fuel, certain base metals (including aluminium, copper and nickel) and some precious metals (including gold, silver and platinum). One other notable item might be wide-bodied aircraft where it appears that Boeing and Airbus, the two major manufacturers, routinely denominate sales in US dollars.

In September 2014 the Interpretations Committee received a request relating to the routinely denominated criterion. They were asked to consider whether a licensing agreement denominated in a currency, in which commercial transactions of that type were routinely denominated around the world, held an embedded foreign currency derivative that was closely related to the economic characteristics of the host contract.[20]

The Interpretations Committee noted that the issue related to a contract for a specific type of item and observed that an assessment of routinely denominated criterion is based on evidence of whether or not such commercial transactions are denominated in that currency all around the world and not merely in one local area. They further observed that the assessment of the routinely denominated criterion is a question of fact and is based on an assessment of available evidence.

5.2.1.C Commonly used currencies

The IASB noted that the requirement to separate embedded foreign currency derivatives may be burdensome for entities that operate in economies in which business contracts denominated in a foreign currency are common. For example, entities domiciled in small countries may find it convenient to denominate business contracts with entities from other small countries in an internationally liquid currency (such as the US dollar, euro or yen) rather than the local currency of any party to the transaction. Also, an entity operating in a hyperinflationary economy may use a price list in a hard currency to protect against inflation, for example an entity that has a foreign operation in a hyperinflationary economy that denominates local contracts in the functional currency of the parent. *[IAS 39.BC39, IFRS 9.BCZ4.94]*.

Unfortunately, however, the assessment of whether or not a particular currency meets this requirement in a particular situation has not been straightforward in practice and this question reached the attention of the Interpretations Committee in May 2007. After debating the matter in four consecutive meetings and initially deciding not to deal with the topic because any guidance it could provide would be more in the nature of application guidance, it asked the IASB to amend IAS 39 to clarify the wording and meaning of the standard.[21]

During its debates, the Interpretations Committee did note that entities should:[22]

- Identify where the transaction takes place.

  This is not as straightforward as it might seem. For example, consider a Polish company that manufactures components in Poland and exports them to a third party in the Czech Republic. Should the sale of components be regarded as a transaction occurring in Poland or in the Czech Republic?[23] It is likely that the Polish company would regard it as occurring in Poland and the Czech entity in the Czech Republic, but this is not entirely beyond debate; and

- Identify currencies that are commonly used in the economic environment in which the transaction takes place.

  Entities need to address what the population of transactions in the economic environment is. Some might suggest that transactions to which (i) or (ii) above apply should be excluded, although this is not a view shared by the staff of the Interpretations Committee which considered that all transactions should be included.[24]

  Entities should also consider what an economic environment is. The guidance, on which Example 44.16 below is based, implies that a country could be an economic environment. The references to local business transactions and to external trade in (iii) above suggest that other examples of economic environment are the external trade or internal trade environment of the country in which the transaction takes place. The question remains as to whether there could be other economic environments, for example the luxury goods market in a country. Depending on the view taken, a different treatment could arise.[25] In considering the issue subsequently, the IASB staff noted their understanding that all of these views (and possibly more, such as the internal or external trade of a specific company) were being applied in practice.[26]

The Interpretations Committee had also been asked to provide guidance on how to interpret the term 'common', but understandably was reluctant to do so.[27] The IASB staff noted that there is no guidance as to the quantum of transactions or value that would need to be denominated in a foreign currency to conclude that the currency was commonly used and that a related matter is whether 'common' should be considered in the context of a particular entity, of an industry, or of a country.[28]

The IASB staff noted other related interpretive questions raised by constituents including the following:[29]

- What evidence does an entity require to support the notion that the use of a currency is common?
- Does the reporting entity need to investigate published statistics?
- If the reporting entity has to look for statistics, what percentage of business needs to be conducted in that currency to assert that use of the currency is common?
- Whether the consideration that a currency is commonly used should exclude from the population set those transactions falling under (i) or (ii) above.

They concluded that there are a variety of views on the appropriate interpretation of this guidance and, consequently, that there is significant diversity in practice.[30]

In response to this analysis, the IASB decided to amend IAS 39 as part of its second annual improvements process, which resulted in proposed amendments being published in August 2008. It was noted that the guidance is intended to prohibit the separation of embedded foreign currency derivatives if the embedded derivatives are 'integral' to the contractual arrangement. This is likely to be the case if the foreign currency has one or more of the characteristics of a functional currency set out in paragraph 9 of IAS 21 (see Chapter 15 at 4.1). Accordingly, it was proposed that IAS 39 be amended to state that a currency that has one or more of those characteristics is integral to the contract.[31]

The IASB indicated that under these proposals, contracts denominated in the following foreign currencies would likely be considered integral to the contractual arrangement:[32]

- the functional currency of any substantial party to that contract;
- the currency in which the price of the related good or service that is acquired or delivered is routinely denominated in commercial transactions around the world (such as the US dollar for crude oil transactions);
- a local currency of any substantial party to that contract;
- a liquid international currency used by parties domiciled in small countries, as a convenient means of exchange;
- a hard currency used by an entity operating in a hyperinflationary economy to protect against inflation; and
- a foreign currency commonly used in local business transactions, for example when monetary amounts are viewed by the general population not in terms of the local currency but in terms of another related currency.

Aside from the examples in the first two bullets noted above, which follow from the exceptions discussed at 5.2.1.A and 5.2.1.B above, it was unclear to us why most of the other examples would follow from the proposed amendment to the standard. A number of concerns were raised by respondents to the exposure draft and in January 2009 it was concluded that this amendment could not be completed in time for inclusion in the second annual improvements process so redeliberations were deferred.[33] In June 2009 the IASB stated that it remained committed to making such an amendment and indicated that an exposure draft of revised proposals may be published later in the year.[34] However, in January 2010 the Interpretations Committee formally removed the issue from the annual improvements project in the light of the IASB's accelerated project to replace IAS 39.[35] The guidance in IAS 39 in respect of that matter was incorporated in IFRS 9 without alteration, leaving the issue unaddressed.

5.2.1.D Examples and other practical issues

The application of the guidance above is illustrated in the examples below.

Example 44.16: Oil contract denominated in Swiss francs

A Norwegian company agrees to sell oil to a company in France. The oil contract is denominated in Swiss francs, although oil contracts are routinely denominated in US dollars in international commerce and Norwegian krone are commonly used in contracts to purchase or sell non-financial items in Norway. Neither company carries out any significant activities in Swiss francs.

The Norwegian company should regard the supply contract as a host contract with an embedded foreign currency forward to purchase Swiss francs. The French company should regard it as a host contract with an embedded foreign currency forward to sell Swiss francs. *[IAS 39.C.7, IFRS 9.C.7]*.

The implementation guidance on which this example is based does not state in which currency the host contract should be denominated (this will also be the currency of the second leg of the embedded forward contract). The currency should be chosen so that the host does not contain an embedded derivative requiring separation. In theory, therefore, it could be Norwegian krone or euro (the functional currencies of the parties to the contract) or US dollars (the currency in which oil contracts are routinely denominated in international commerce). Typically, however, an entity will use its own functional currency to define the terms of the host contract and embedded derivative.

A second issue arises where the terms of the contract require delivery and payment on different dates. For example, assume the contract was entered into on 1 January, with delivery scheduled for 30 June and payment required by 30 September. Should the embedded derivative be considered a six-month forward contract maturing on 30 June, or a nine-month forward contract maturing on 30 September? Conceptually at least, the latter approach seems more satisfactory, for example because it does not introduce into the notional terms cash flows at a point in time (i.e. on delivery) when none exist in the combined contract. In practice, however, the former approach is used far more often and is not without technical merit. For example, it avoids the recognition of an embedded foreign currency derivative between the delivery and payment dates on what would be a foreign currency denominated monetary item, something that is prohibited by IAS 39 and IFRS 9 (see 5.1.1 above).

Example 44.17: Oil contract, denominated in US dollars and containing a leveraged foreign exchange payment

Company A, whose functional currency is the euro, enters into a contract with Company B, whose functional currency is the Norwegian Krone, to purchase oil in six months for US$1,000. The host oil contract will be settled by making and taking delivery in the normal course of business and is not accounted for as a financial instrument because it qualifies as a normal sale or contract (see Chapter 43 at 4). The oil contract includes a leveraged foreign exchange provision whereby the parties, in addition to the provision of, and payment for, oil will exchange an amount equal to the fluctuation in the exchange rate of the US dollar and Norwegian Krone applied to a notional amount of US$100,000.

The payment of US$1,000 under the host oil contract can be viewed as a foreign currency derivative because the dollar is neither Company A nor B's functional currency. However, it would not be separated as the US dollar is the currency in which crude oil transactions are routinely denominated in international commerce.

The leveraged foreign exchange provision is in addition to the required payment for the oil transaction. It is unrelated to the host oil contract and is therefore separated and accounted for as an embedded derivative. *[IAS 39.C.8, IFRS 9.C.8]*.

In practice, all but the simplest contracts will contain other terms and features that can often make it much more difficult to isolate the precise terms of the embedded foreign currency derivative (and the host). For example, a clause may allow a purchaser to terminate the contract in return for making a specified compensation payment to the supplier – the standard offers little guidance as to whether such a feature should be included within the terms of the host, of the embedded foreign currency derivative or, possibly, of both. Other problematic terms can include options to defer the specified delivery date and options to order additional goods or services.

5.2.2 Inputs, ingredients, substitutes and other proxy pricing mechanisms

It is common for the pricing of contracts for the supply of goods, services or other non-financial items to be determined by reference to the price of inputs to, ingredients used to generate, or substitutes for the non-financial item, especially where the non-financial item is not itself quoted in an active market. For example, a provider of call centre services may determine that a large proportion of the costs of providing the service will be employee costs in a particular country. Accordingly, it may seek to link the price in a long-term contract to supply its services to the relevant wage index, effectively to provide an economic hedge of its exposure to changes in employee costs. Similarly, the producer of goods may index the price of its product to the market value of commodities that are used in the production process.

The standard contains little or no detailed guidance for determining whether or not such pricing features should be considered closely related to the host contract. However, the general requirement of the standard to assess the economic characteristics and risks would suggest that where a good link to the inputs can be established, such features will normally be considered closely related to the host, unless they were significantly leveraged.

Other proxy pricing mechanisms may arise in long-term supply agreements for commodities where there is no active market in the commodity. For example, in the 1980s, when natural gas first started to be extracted from the North Sea in significant volumes, there was no active market for that gas and thus no market price on which to base the price of long-term contracts. Because of this, suppliers and customers were willing to enter into such contracts where the price was indexed to the market price of other commodities such as crude oil that could potentially be used as a substitute for gas. For contracts entered into before the development of an active gas market, such features would normally be considered closely related, especially if similar pricing mechanisms were commonly used by other participants in the market.

Where there is an active market price for the non-financial items being supplied under the contract, different considerations apply. The use of the proxy pricing mechanism is a strong indication that the entity has entered into a speculative position and we would not normally consider such features to be closely related to the host. The separation of these types of embedded derivatives can be seen in the following extract from BP's financial statements.

Extract 44.5: BP p.l.c. (2014)

Notes on financial statements [extract]
28. Derivative financial instruments [extract]
Embedded derivatives [extract]

The group is a party to certain natural gas contracts containing embedded derivatives. Prior to the development of an active gas trading market, UK gas contracts were priced using a basket of available price indices, primarily relating to oil products, power and inflation. After the development of an active UK gas market, certain contracts were entered into or renegotiated using pricing formulae not directly related to gas prices, for example, oil product and power prices. In these circumstances, pricing formulae have been determined to be derivatives, embedded within the overall contractual arrangements that are not clearly and closely related to the underlying commodity. The resulting fair value relating to these contracts is recognized on the balance sheet with gains or losses recognized in the income statement.

5.2.3 *Inflation-linked features*

Apart from that related to leases (see 5.3.2 below), there is no reference in the guidance to contracts containing payments that are linked to inflation. Many types of contracts contain inflation-linked payments and it would appear sensible to apply the guidance in respect of leases to these contracts. Consider, for example, a long-term agreement to supply services under which payments increase by reference to a general price index and are not leveraged in any way. In cases such as this, the embedded inflation-linked derivative would normally be considered closely related to the host, provided the index related to a measure of inflation in an appropriate economic environment, such as the one in which the services were being supplied.

5.2.4 *Floors and caps*

Similar to debt instruments (see 5.1.4 above), provisions within a contract to purchase or sell an asset (e.g. a commodity) that establishes a cap and a floor on the price to be paid or received for the asset are closely related to the host contract if both the cap and floor were out-of-the-money at inception and are not leveraged. *[IAS 39.AG33(b), IFRS 9.B4.3.8(b)]*.

5.2.5 *Fund performance fees*

In the investment management industry, it is common for a fund manager to receive a fee based on the performance of the assets managed in addition to a base fee. For example, if a fund's net asset value increases over its accounting year, the manager may be entitled to a percentage of that increase. The contract for providing investment management services to the fund clearly contains an embedded derivative (the underlying is the value of the fund's assets). However, whilst not addressed explicitly in the standard, we would normally consider it appropriate to regard such features as closely related to the host contract.

5.3 Leases

5.3.1 *Foreign currency derivatives*

A finance lease payable or receivable is accounted for as a financial instrument, albeit one that is not subject to all of the measurement requirements of IAS 39 or IFRS 9 (see Chapter 43 at 2.2.4). Therefore, a finance lease denominated in a foreign currency will not generally be considered to contain an embedded foreign currency derivative requiring separation, because the payable or receivable is a monetary item within the scope of IAS 21.

However, an operating lease is accounted for as an executory contract. Accordingly, where the lease payments are denominated in a foreign currency, the analysis at 5.2.1.A is applicable and it may be necessary to separate an embedded derivative. See Example 44.18 at 6.1 below for an example of a foreign exchange currency derivative requiring separation from a (hybrid) lease contract.

5.3.2 *Inflation-linked features*

An embedded derivative in a lease is considered closely related to the host if it is an inflation-related index such as an index of lease payments to a consumer price index, provided that the lease is not leveraged and the index relates to inflation in the entity's own economic environment. *[IAS 39.AG33(f)(i), IFRS 9.B4.3.8(f)(i)].*

5.3.3 *Contingent rentals based on related sales*

Where a lease requires contingent rentals based on related sales, that embedded derivative is considered to be closely related to the host lease. *[IAS 39.AG33(f)(ii), IFRS 9.B4.3.8(f)(ii)].*

5.3.4 *Contingent rentals based on variable interest rates*

If a derivative embedded within a lease arises from contingent rentals based on variable interest rates, it is considered closely related. *[IAS 39.AG33(f)(iii), IFRS 9.B4.3.8(f)(iii)].*

5.4 Insurance contracts

The guidance at 5.1.2 to 5.1.4, 5.1.6 and 5.2.1 above also applies to insurance contracts. IFRS 4 added two further illustrations to IAS 39 and IFRS 9 that deal primarily with insurance contracts.

A unit-linking feature embedded in a host financial instrument, or host insurance contract, is closely related to the host if the unit-denominated payments are measured at current unit values that reflect the fair values of the assets of the fund. A unit-linking feature is a contractual term that requires payments denominated in units of an internal or external investment fund. *[IAS 39.AG33(g), IFRS 9.B4.3.8(g)].*

A derivative embedded in an insurance contract is closely related to the host if the embedded derivative and host are so interdependent that the embedded derivative cannot be measured separately, i.e. without considering the host contract. *[IAS 39.AG33(h), IFRS 9.B4.3.8(h)]*.

Derivatives embedded within insurance contracts are covered in more detail in Chapter 55 at 4.

6 IDENTIFYING THE TERMS OF EMBEDDED DERIVATIVES AND HOST CONTRACTS

The IASB has provided only limited guidance on determining the terms of a separated embedded derivative and host contract. Accordingly, entities may find this aspect of the embedded derivative requirements particularly difficult to implement. In addition to the guidance set out below, Examples 44.16 and 44.17 above also identify the terms of an embedded derivative requiring separation.

6.1 Embedded non-option derivatives

IAS 39 and IFRS 9 do not define the term 'non-option derivative' but suggests that it includes forwards, swaps and similar contracts. An embedded derivative of this type should be separated from its host contract on the basis of its stated or implied substantive terms, so as to result in it having a fair value of zero at initial recognition. *[IAS 39.AG28, IFRS 9.B4.3.3]*.

The IASB has provided implementation guidance on separating non-option derivatives in the situation where the host is a debt instrument. It is explained that, in the absence of implied or stated terms, judgement will be necessary to identify the terms of the host (e.g. whether it should be a fixed rate, variable rate or zero coupon instrument) and the embedded derivative. However, an embedded derivative that is not already clearly present in the hybrid should not be separated, i.e. a cash flow that does not exist cannot be created. *[IAS 39.C.1, IFRS 9.C.1]*.

For example, if a five year debt instrument has fixed annual interest payments of £40 and a principal payment at maturity of £1,000 multiplied by the change in an equity price index, it would be inappropriate to identify a floating rate host and an embedded equity swap that has an offsetting floating rate leg. The host should be a fixed rate debt instrument that pays £40 annually because there are no floating interest rate cash flows in the hybrid instrument. *[IAS 39.C.1, IFRS 9.C.1]*.

Further, as noted above, the terms of the embedded derivative should be determined so that it has a fair value of zero on inception of the hybrid instrument. It is explained that if an embedded non-option derivative could be separated on other terms, a single hybrid instrument could be decomposed into an infinite variety of combinations of host debt instruments and embedded derivatives. This might be achieved, for example, by separating embedded derivatives with terms that create leverage, asymmetry or some other risk exposure not already present in the hybrid instrument. *[IAS 39.C.1, IFRS 9.C.1]*.

Finally, it is explained that the terms of the embedded derivative should be identified based on the conditions existing when the financial instrument was issued, *[IAS 39.C.1, IFRS 9.C.1]*, or following the application of IFRIC 9 – *Reassessment of Embedded Derivatives* – (see 7.1 below) or the IFRS 9 equivalent guidance, when a contract is required to be reassessed.

The following example illustrates how a foreign currency derivative embedded in a (hybrid) lease contract, that is not closely related, could be separated.

Example 44.18: Separation of embedded derivative from lease

Company X has Indian Rupees (INR) as its functional currency. On 1 January 2016 Company X entered into a nine month lease over an item of PP&E which required payments of US$100,000 on 31 March 2016, 30 June 2016 and 30 September 2016. The functional currency of the lessor is not US dollars; the price of such leases is not routinely denominated in US dollars and US dollars is not a currency that is commonly used in the economic environment in which the lease took place (see 5.3.1 above). Accordingly the embedded foreign currency derivative is not closely related to the lease.

On 1 January 2016 the spot exchange rate was 40 and the forward exchange rates for settlement on 31 March 2016, 30 June 2016 and 30 September 2016 were 41, 42 and 43 respectively. The terms of the embedded derivative could be determined as follows:

31 March 2016	Pay US$100,000	Receive INR4,100,000
30 June 2016	Pay US$100,000	Receive INR4,200,000
30 September 2016	Pay US$100,000	Receive INR4,300,000

Given the terms of the embedded derivative above, the host contract will be a nine month lease over the same PP&E as the hybrid lease contract, commencing 1 January 2016 and with scheduled payments of INR 4,100,000, INR 4,200,000 and INR 4,300,000 on 31 March 2016, 30 June 2016 and 30 September 2016. It can be seen that this host after separation of the foreign currency derivative, an INR denominated lease, does not contain an embedded derivative requiring separation and the combined terms of the two components sum to the terms of the hybrid contract. IAS 17 – *Leases* – will be applicable to this lease (see Chapter 24).

6.2 Embedded option-based derivative

As for non-option derivatives, IAS 39 and IFRS 9 do not define the term 'option-based derivative' but suggests that it includes puts, calls, caps, floors and swaptions. An embedded derivative of this type should be separated from its host contract on the basis of the stated terms of the option feature. *[IAS 39.AG28, IFRS 9.B4.3.3]*.

The implementation guidance explains that the economic nature of an option-based derivative is fundamentally different from a non-option derivative and depends critically on the strike price (or strike rate) specified for the option feature in the hybrid instrument. Therefore, the separation of such a derivative should be based on the stated terms of the option feature documented in the hybrid instrument. Consequently, in contrast to the position for non-option derivatives (see 6.1 above), an embedded option-based derivative would not normally have a fair value of zero. *[IAS 39.C.2, IFRS 9.C.2]*.

In fact, if the terms of an embedded option-based derivative were identified so as to result in it having a fair value of zero, the implied strike price would generally result in the option being infinitely out-of-the-money, i.e. it would have a zero probability of the option feature being exercised. However, since the probability of the option feature in a hybrid instrument being exercised generally is not zero, this would be inconsistent with the likely economic behaviour of the hybrid. *[IAS 39.C.2, IFRS 9.C.2]*.

Similarly, if the terms were identified so as to achieve an intrinsic value of zero, the strike price would equal the price of the underlying at initial recognition. In this case, the fair value of the option would consist only of time value. However, this may also be inconsistent with the likely economic behaviour of the hybrid, including the probability of the option feature being exercised, unless the agreed strike price was indeed equal to the price of the underlying at initial recognition. *[IAS 39.C.2, IFRS 9.C.2]*.

6.3 Nature of a financial instrument host

If a contract consists of equity- and debt-like features, it must be determined whether the host contract is debt or equity. The classification of the host will form the basis for the 'closely related' assessment and therefore will drive whether embedded derivative features need to be separated from the host contract. For some hybrid instruments this assessment will be straightforward, for others a significant amount of judgement might be required.

Consistent with the 'closely related' assessment (see 5 above), it is suggested that, where a financial instrument contains an embedded derivative, the host should be considered as a debt instrument 'if the hybrid instrument has a stated maturity, i.e. it does not meet the definition of an equity instrument'. *[IAS 39.C.5]*.

The implementation guidance illustrates this by way of an example, the substance of which is reproduced below.

Example 44.19: Equity-linked debt

Company A purchases a five year 'debt' instrument issued by Company B with a principal of £1,000, indexed to Company C's share price. At maturity, A will receive the principal plus or minus the change in the fair value of 100 of C's shares and no interest payments are made before maturity. On the date of acquisition, the purchase price is £1,000 and C's share price is £12. A classifies the instrument as available-for-sale.

The instrument is a hybrid instrument with an embedded derivative because of the equity-indexed principal and the host is a debt instrument (see above). The host is a zero coupon debt paying £1,200 at maturity. The embedded non-option derivative (a forward contract to purchase 100 shares of C for an amount equal to the forward price of C's shares at inception of the arrangement) is separated and will have an initial fair value of zero. *[IAS 39.C.5]*.

A financial instrument can give rise to a residual interest in the net assets of an entity, even though IAS 32 prevents the issuing entity from classifying the instrument as equity. Where such an instrument contains an embedded derivative that requires separation, it may be appropriate to classify the host as equity rather than debt from the holder's perspective. This will commonly be the case for an investment in a unit trust (see 5.1.9 above) and may be appropriate for some structured investments which can, in substance, give rise to a residual interest in the net assets of an entity.

The treatment by the holder of equity-like instruments (say ordinary shares) that are puttable at an amount other than fair value (for example a proportion of the book value of net assets determined under IFRS or local GAAP) was discussed by the Interpretations Committee. Whilst deciding not to issue application guidance, it noted the approach the holder (as opposed to the issuer) of such a financial instrument should take as follows:[36]

- Step 1 – identify embedded derivatives;
- Step 2 – determine whether the remaining instrument (i.e. the host) is a debt or an equity instrument; and
- Step 3 – determine whether the characteristics and risks of any identified embedded derivatives are closely related to those of its host contract.

Therefore, the holder would first identify the put option as an embedded derivative (the right to exchange the underlying equity instrument for a variable amount of cash); secondly it would identify the remainder as an equity instrument; and finally determine that the two were not closely related.[37]

Host contracts that are financial instruments should be accounted for under IAS 39. Otherwise, they are accounted for in accordance with other appropriate standards. This does not necessarily mean that the embedded derivative and host should be presented separately (or together) on the face of the financial statements (see Chapter 54 at 7.4.3). *[IAS 39.11, IFRS 9.4.3.4]*.

Where IFRS 9 is applied, the question whether the host is a debt or equity instrument is, from the perspective of the holder of the instrument, of no relevance because embedded derivatives are not separated from financial assets within the scope of the standard and the requirements of the standard are applied to the hybrid contract as a whole. *[IFRS 9.4.3.2]*.

How challenging and judgemental the identification of the host contract and the subsequent classification as debt or equity can be, is evidenced by a request received by the Interpretations Committee, to clarify the classification by the holder of a hybrid financial instrument with a revolving maturity option, an early settlement option and a suspension of interest payments option (all at the option of the issuer). The request was discussed during the March 2014 and July 2014 meetings. Specifically, the question raised was whether the host instrument should be classified as equity or as a debt instrument under IAS 39.[38]

The main features of the instrument under consideration were:

- A 30 year maturity.
- Interest feature:
  - fixed rate (government bond plus a spread);
  - the spread is stepped up after the start of the early settlement option;
  - the benchmark interest is reset every 10 years.
- Options of the issuer:
  - revolving maturity option every 30 years (option to extend the maturity every 30 years);
  - early settlement option after 10 years;
  - suspension of interest payment option in the event that dividends on ordinary shares are not distributed.

The issuer explained in its submission that if the host contract is classified before identifying any embedded derivatives, then the host could be classified as an equity instrument. This is because the instrument represents the residual interest in the net assets of the issuer, has no stated maturity and accordingly meets the definition of an equity instrument in IAS 32. On the other hand, if the host is to be classified after identifying embedded derivative features, then the host would be classified as a debt instrument. This is because it can be only regarded as equity under the assumption that the issuer will not exercise the early settlement option but will certainly exercise the revolving maturity option and this assumption may be inconsistent with the market participant's or investor's view. The Interpretations Committee observed that the issue is not widespread and noted that the financial instrument described in the submission is specific and it would not be appropriate to provide guidance on this particular issue and therefore decided not to add this issue to its agenda.

6.4 Multiple embedded derivatives

Generally, multiple embedded derivatives in a single instrument should be treated as a single compound embedded derivative. However, embedded derivatives that are classified as equity are accounted for separately from those classified as assets or liabilities (see Chapter 45 at 6). In addition, derivatives embedded in a single instrument that relate to different risk exposures and are readily separable and independent of each other, should be accounted for separately from each other. *[IAS 39.AG29, IFRS 9.B4.3.4]*.

For example, if a debt instrument has a principal amount related to an equity index and that amount doubles if the equity index exceeds a certain level, it is not appropriate to separate both a forward and an option on the equity index because those derivative features relate to the same risk exposure. Instead, the forward and option elements are treated as a single compound embedded derivative. For the same reason, an embedded floor or cap on interest rates should not be separated into a series of 'floorlets' or 'caplets' (i.e. single interest rate options).[39]

If a hybrid instrument contains both a put option and a written call option that require separation, e.g. callable debt with a put to the holder, those options are treated as a single embedded derivative because they are not independent of each other. Furthermore, if an investor holds callable convertible debt, which can be called by the issuer, for which separation of the call option is required, it is not appropriate to separate an equity conversion option and a written call option on the debt instrument separately because the two embedded derivative features should not be valued independently of each other.[40]

On the other hand, if a hybrid debt instrument contains, for example, two options that give the holder a right to choose both the interest rate index on which interest payments are determined and the currency in which the principal is repaid, those two options may qualify for separation as two separate embedded derivatives since they relate to different risk exposures and are readily separable and independent of each other.[41]

7 REASSESSMENT OF EMBEDDED DERIVATIVES

It is clear that, on initial recognition, a contract should be reviewed to assess whether it contains one or more embedded derivatives requiring separation. However, IAS 39 is largely silent on whether this initial assessment should be revisited throughout the life of the contract. *[IFRIC 9.BC3, IFRS 9.BCZ4.99]*.

Consider, for example, an entity that enters into a purchase contract denominated in US dollars. If, at the time the contract is entered into, US dollars are commonly used in the economic environment in which the transaction takes place, the contract will not contain an embedded foreign currency derivative requiring separation. Subsequently, however, the economic environment may change such that transactions are now commonly denominated in euros, rather than US dollars. Countries joining the European Union may encounter just such a scenario.

Clearly, in this situation, an embedded foreign currency derivative would be separated from any new US dollar denominated purchase contracts, assuming they would not otherwise be considered closely related. However, should the entity separately account for derivatives embedded within its existing US dollar denominated contracts that were outstanding prior to the change in the market?

Conversely, the entity may have identified, and separately accounted for, embedded foreign currency derivatives in contracts denominated in euros that were entered into before the economic environment changed. Does the change in economic circumstances mean that the embedded derivative should now be considered closely related and not separately accounted for as a derivative? *[IFRIC 9.BC4, BC5, IFRS 9.BCZ4.100-101]*.

In practice, there appeared to be differing views developing on this issue. Therefore, without further guidance, the IFRIC considered it quite possible that inconsistent practice would develop. *[IFRIC 9.BC3]*. Accordingly it decided to take the issue onto its agenda and, in March 2006, published IFRIC 9. Note that IFRS 9 supersedes IFRIC 9 upon adoption. However, the IASB incorporated into IFRS 9 the main requirements previously set out in IFRIC 9.

7.1 IFRIC 9

IFRIC 9 and the equivalent guidance in IFRS 9 confirm that entities should assess whether an embedded derivative is required to be separated from the host contract and accounted for as a derivative when the entity first becomes a party to the contract and explains that subsequent reassessment is generally prohibited. *[IFRIC 9.7, IFRS 9.B4.3.11]*.

There are two exceptions under IAS 39 and one exception under IFRS 9 to this prohibition:

(a) where there is a change in the terms of a contract that significantly modifies the cash flows that otherwise would be required under it, in which case an assessment is required by both Standards.

In order to determine whether a modification to cash flows is significant, an entity should consider the extent to which the expected future cash flows associated with the embedded derivative, the host contract or both have changed and whether the change is significant relative to the previously expected cash flows on the contract; *[IFRIC 9.7, IFRS 9.B4.3.11]* and

(b) a reclassification of a financial asset out of the fair value through profit or loss category under IAS 39 (see Chapter 46 at 6.1.1), in which case an assessment is also required. *[IFRIC 9.7]*.

In this case, the assessment of whether an embedded derivative is required to be accounted for separately from the host contract should be made on the basis of the circumstances that existed on the later date of:

(i) when the entity first became a party to the contract; and

(ii) a change in the terms of the contract that significantly modified the cash flows that otherwise would have been required.

For the purpose of this assessment, the fact that the financial asset had previously been classified at fair value through profit or loss (condition (c) at 4 above) does not mean an embedded derivative should not be separated.

If an entity is unable to make this assessment or is unable to measure separately the embedded derivative, reclassification is prohibited and the hybrid (combined) contract should remain classified as at fair value through profit or loss in its entirety. *[IFRIC 9.7A, IAS 39.12]*.

7.2 Acquisition of contracts

IAS 39 and IFRS 9 require an entity to assess whether an embedded derivative needs to be separated from the host contract and accounted for as a derivative when it first becomes a party to that contract. Therefore, if an entity purchases a contract that contains an embedded derivative, it assesses whether the embedded derivative needs to be separated and accounted for as a derivative on the basis of conditions at the date it acquires it, not the date the original contract was established. *[IFRIC 9.BC10, IFRS 9.BCZ4.106]*.

For example, consider an entity that purchases a debt instrument containing an embedded prepayment, put or call option some time after it was issued. In this case, the assessment of whether the exercise price of the option is approximately equal to the instrument's amortised cost (see 5.1.3 above) will be based on the amortised cost of the acquirer (taking into account any premium or discount paid as a result of changes in value since origination), not that of the issuer or original holder.

7.3 Business combinations

From the point of view of a consolidated entity, the acquisition of a contract within a business combination accounted for using the acquisition method under IFRS 3 – *Business Combinations* – is hardly different from the acquisition of a contract in general. Consequently, an assessment of the acquiree's contracts should be made on the date of acquisition as if the contracts themselves had been acquired. *[IFRS 3.15, 16(c)]*.

Neither IFRIC 9, IFRS 3, nor the guidance on reassessment of embedded derivatives in IFRS 9 applies to a combination of entities or businesses under common control or the formation of a joint venture. *[IFRIC 9.5, IFRS 3.2, IFRS 9.B4.3.12]*. However, in our view, if the acquisition method is applied to such arrangements, the requirements set out in IFRS 3 should be followed.

7.4 Remeasurement issues arising from reassessment

IFRIC 9 and IFRS 9 do not address remeasurement issues arising from a reassessment of embedded derivatives. *[IFRIC 9.4]*. One of the reasons cited by the Interpretations Committee for prohibiting reassessment in general was the difficulty in determining the accounting treatment following a reassessment, which is explained in the following terms.

Assume that an entity, when it first became party to a contract, separately recognised a host asset, say a loan or receivable, and an embedded derivative liability. If the entity were required to reassess whether the embedded derivative was to be accounted for separately and if the entity concluded some time after becoming a party to the contract that the derivative was no longer required to be separated, then questions of recognition and measurement would arise. In the above circumstances, the entity could: *[IFRIC 9.BC9, IFRS 9.BCZ4.105]*

(a) remove the derivative from its statement of financial position and recognise in profit or loss a corresponding gain or loss. This would lead to recognition of a gain or loss even though there had been no transaction and no change in the value of the total contract or its components;

(b) leave the derivative as a separate item in the statement of financial position. The issue would then arise as to when the item is to be removed from the statement of financial position. Should it be amortised (and, if so, how would the amortisation affect the effective interest rate of the asset), or should it be derecognised only when the asset is derecognised?

(c) combine the derivative (which is recognised at fair value) with the asset (which is recognised at amortised cost). This would alter both the carrying amount of the asset and its effective interest rate even though there had been no change in the economics of the whole contract. In some cases, it could also result in a negative effective interest rate.

IFRIC 9 states that subsequent reassessment is appropriate only when there has been a change in the terms of the contract that 'significantly' modifies the cash flows, accordingly the above issues are not expected to arise. *[IFRIC 9.BC9, IFRS 9.BCZ4.105]*.

8 LINKED AND SEPARATE TRANSACTIONS AND 'SYNTHETIC' INSTRUMENTS

A derivative that is attached to a financial instrument, but is contractually transferable independently of that instrument, or has a different counterparty from that instrument, is not an embedded derivative, but a separate financial instrument. *[IAS 39.10, IFRS 9.4.3.1]*. This is also the case where a synthetic instrument is created by using derivatives to 'alter' the nature of a non-derivative instrument, as illustrated in the following example:

Example 44.20: Investment in synthetic fixed-rate debt

Company A acquires a five year floating rate debt instrument issued by Company B. At the same time, it enters into a five year pay-variable, receive-fixed interest rate swap with Bank C. A considers the combination of the two instruments to be a synthetic fixed rate bond and, since it has the positive intent and ability to hold them to maturity, wants to classify them as a held-to-maturity investment (see Chapter 46 at 3).

Embedded derivatives are terms and conditions that are *included in* non-derivative host contracts and it is generally inappropriate to treat two or more separate financial instruments as a single combined, or synthetic, instrument. Each of the financial instruments has its own terms and conditions and may be transferred or settled separately. Therefore, the debt instrument and the swap must be classified separately. *[IAS 39.C.6, IFRS 9.C.6]*.

It is asserted that these transactions differ from those discussed at 3.2 above because those had no substance apart from the resulting interest rate swap. *[IAS 39.C.6, IFRS 9.C.6]*. Although some might argue that the substance of the two transactions above is the resulting synthetic fixed rate debt instrument, this interpretation is clearly not allowed under the standard.

Interestingly, the guidance does not address a much more common situation whereby a company both borrows from, and transacts a related derivative with, the same counterparty – typically the borrowing will be floating rate and the derivative a perfectly matched pay-fixed, receive-floating interest rate swap.

In fact, the subject of linking transactions for accounting purposes is a difficult one, especially in the context of financial instruments. The IASB's *Conceptual Framework* specifies that transactions should be reported in accordance with their substance and economic reality and not merely their legal form, *[Framework.4.6]*, and linking transactions can be seen as dealing with the question of how to interpret this principle.

IAS 32, IAS 39 and IFRS 9 deal with the subject in a piecemeal way. For example, in addition to the synthetic instrument illustration above:

- two or more non-derivative contracts that are, 'in substance', no more than a single derivative are treated as a single derivative (see 3.2 above);
- derivatives that are 'attached' to a non-derivative financial instrument may sometimes be regarded as part of a single combined instrument (see 4 above);
- in classifying an instrument in consolidated financial statements as equity or a financial liability, all terms and conditions agreed between members of the group and holders of the instrument are considered (see Chapter 45 at 4.8);
- if a loan is guaranteed by a third party, the expected credit loss determined in accordance with IFRS 9 should be calculated based on the combined credit risk of the guarantor and the guaranteed party if the guarantee is 'integral' to the contractual terms of the loan (see Chapter 50 at 5.4.7). IAS 39 is less clear on this point, although it is implied that in certain circumstances guarantees should be considered an integral part of the guaranteed loan; *[IAS 39.IG.E4.1]* and
- determining the appropriate accounting treatment for a transaction that involves the transfer of some or all rights associated with financial assets, without the sale of the assets themselves, inevitably involves linking separate contracts to assess whether the transaction results in derecognition of the assets. For example, there might be one contract defining the continued ownership of the asset and another obliging the owner to transfer the rights associated with the asset to a third party (see Chapter 48 at 3, Chapter 49 at 2, Chapter 50 at 2 and Chapter 51 at 3 and 4).

The Interpretations Committee first considered the subject of linkage in 2002 and has, in the past, made certain recommendations to the IASB. In fact, the requirement to take account of linked terms when classifying instruments as debt or equity in consolidated financial statements was introduced into IAS 32 in December 2003 following the Interpretations Committee's deliberations. In spite of agreeing proposed indicators for when transactions should be linked, and proposed guidance on accounting for linked transactions, these have never been published as an interpretation or standard.[42]

In August 2013 the Interpretations Committee received a request to clarify whether three different transactions should be accounted for separately or be aggregated and treated as a single derivative. The Committee decided not to add this issue to its agenda but noted that in order to determine whether to aggregate and account for the three transactions as a single derivative, reference should be made to B.6 (see 3.2 above) and C.6 (see Example 44.20 above) of the Implementation Guidance to IAS 39 and paragraph AG39 of IAS 32. The Interpretations Committee noted that the application of the guidance in paragraph B.6 of IAS 39 requires judgement and that the indicators in that paragraph may help an entity to determine the substance of the transaction, but that the presence or absence of any single specific indicator alone may not be conclusive.[43]

Consequently, in considering the borrowing and swap situation above, we are left principally with the guidance in IAS 39 and IFRS 9. It is likely that the swap and the loan have their own terms and conditions and may be transferred or settled independently of each other. Therefore, the principles in Example 44.20 above would suggest separate accounting for the two instruments. Applying the guidance at 3.2 above (aggregating non-derivative transactions and treating them as a derivative) would also suggest separate accounting in most cases. Even though the instruments are transacted with the same counterparty, there will normally be a substantive business purpose for transacting the instruments separately.

It seems clear that in situations involving two separate legal contracts, in most cases, the two instruments will be regarded as separate for accounting purposes. However, in certain situations the linkage between those contracts (normally itself contractual) may be such that for accounting purposes those contracts cannot be regarded as existing independently of each other.

References

1 IGC Q&A 10-6.
2 *IFRIC Update*, July 2007.
3 *IFRIC Update*, July 2006.
4 *IFRIC Update*, January 2007.
5 *IASB Update*, February 2007.
6 Exposure Draft, *Improvements to International Financial Reporting Standards*, IASB, October 2007.
7 Information for Observers (20 February 2008 IASB meeting), *ED Annual improvements process – Comment analysis: Summary of preliminary analysis and project plan*, IASB, February 2008, Appendix 2.
8 *IASB Update*, October 2008.
9 *IFRIC Update*, July 2006.
10 *IFRIC Update*, January 2007.

11 *IFRIC Update*, May 2009.
12 IGC Q&A 10-10.
13 Staff paper, *Term-extending options in fixed rate debt instruments*, IFRS Interpretations Committee, March 2012.
14 *IFRIC Update*, March 2012.
15 *Implementation of International Accounting Standards*, British Bankers' Association, July 2004, para. 10.
16 *IFRIC Update*, January 2016.
17 Information for Observers of March 2006 IFRIC meeting, *Hedging Inflation Risk (Agenda Paper 12)*, IASB, March 2006, para. 32.
18 Information for Observers (December 2008 IASB meeting), *Clarification of accounting for investments in collateralised debt obligations (Agenda Paper 6E)*, IASB, December 2008 and *Q&As on accounting for some collateralised debts obligations (CDOs) – prepared by staff of the IASB*, IASB, February 2009.
19 *IFRIC Update*, January 2007 and Information for Observers (November 2006 IFRIC meeting), *Financial Instruments puttable at an amount other than Fair Value (Agenda Paper 12(ii))*, IASB, November 2006.
20 *IFRIC Update,* September 2014.
21 *IFRIC Update*, May 2007, July 2007, September 2007 and November 2007.
22 *IFRIC Update*, May 2007.
23 Information for Observers (May 2007 IFRIC meeting), *IAS 39: Financial Instruments: Recognition and Measurement AG33(d)(iii) of IAS 39 (Agenda Paper 11(v))*, IASB, May 2007, paras. 12 to 14.
24 Information for Observers, paras. 18 to 19.
25 Information for Observers, paras. 20 to 28.
26 Information for Observers (December 2007 IASB meeting), *Application of paragraph AG33(d)(iii) – Bifurcation of embedded foreign currency derivative (Agenda Paper 3C)*, IASB, December 2007, para. 11.
27 Information for Observers (May 2007 IFRIC meeting), *IAS 39: Financial Instruments: Recognition and Measurement AG33(d)(iii) of IAS 39 (Agenda Paper 11(v))*, IASB, May 2007, para. 44.
28 Information for Observers (December 2007 IASB meeting), *Application of paragraph AG33(d)(iii) – Bifurcation of embedded foreign currency derivative (Agenda Paper 3C)*, IASB, December 2007, paras. 12 and 13.
29 Information for Observers, para. 14.
30 Information for Observers, para. 15.
31 Information for Observers, Appendix 1, *IASB Update*, December 2007 and Exposure Draft, *Improvements to IFRSs*, IASB, August 2008, IAS 39, para. AG33(d)(iii).
32 Exposure Draft, *Improvements to IFRSs*, IASB, August 2008, IAS 39, para. BC19.
33 *IASB Update*, January 2009 and Information for Observers (January 2009 IASB Meeting), *Annual Improvements 2009 – Comment Analysis, (Agenda Paper 6A)*, IASB, January 2009, para. 11(c) and Appendix 2.
34 *IASB Update*, June 2009 and IASB Staff Paper (June 2009 IASB Meeting), *Financial Instruments: Recognition and Measurement – Sweep Issues (Agenda Paper 3G)*, IASB, January 2009, paras. 10, 11 and 14.
35 *IFRIC Update*, January 2010.
36 Information for Observers (November 2006 IFRIC meeting), *Financial Instruments puttable at an amount other than Fair Value (Agenda Paper 12(ii)*), IASB, November 2006, para. 29.
37 Information for Observers, paras. 30 to 41.
38 *IFRIC Update*, March 2014.
39 IGC Q&A 23-8.
40 IGC Q&A 23-8.
41 IGC Q&A 23-8.
42 *IFRIC Update*, April 2002, July 2002 and February 2003 and *IASB Update*, October 2002.
43 *IFRIC Update*, March 2014.

Chapter 45 Financial instruments: Financial liabilities and equity

List of examples

Chapter 45 Financial instruments: Financial liabilities and equity

1 INTRODUCTION

1.1 Background

The accounting treatment of liabilities (such as loans or bonds) and equity instruments (such as shares, stock or warrants) by their issuer was not historically regarded as presenting significant problems. Essentially the accounting was dictated by the legal form of the instrument, since the traditional distinction between equity and liabilities is clear. The issue of equity creates an ownership interest in a company, remunerated by dividends, which are accounted for as a distribution of retained profit, not a charge made in arriving at the result for a particular period. Liabilities, such as loan finance, on the other hand, are remunerated by interest, which is charged to profit or loss as an expense. In general, lenders rank before shareholders in priority of claims over the assets of the company, although in practice there may also be differential rights between different categories of lenders and classes of shareholders. The two forms of finance often have different tax implications, both for the investor and the investee.

In economic terms, however, the distinction between share and loan capital can be far less clear-cut than the legal categorisation would suggest. For example, a redeemable preference share could be considered to be, in substance, much more like a liability than equity. Conversely, many would argue that a bond which can never be repaid but which will be mandatorily converted into ordinary shares deserves to be thought of as being more in the nature of equity than of debt, even before conversion has occurred. The ambiguous economic nature of such instruments has encouraged the development of a number of complex forms of finance which exhibit characteristics of both equity and debt. The 'holy grail' is generally to devise an instrument regarded as a liability by the tax authorities (such that the costs of servicing it are tax-deductible) but treated as equity for accounting and/or regulatory purposes (so that the instrument is not considered as a component of net borrowings).

The accounting classification of an instrument as a liability or equity is much more than a matter of allocation – i.e. where particular amounts are shown in the financial statements. The increasing requirement of IFRS for certain liabilities, in particular derivatives, to be carried at fair value means that the classification of an item as a liability can introduce significant volatility into reported results, that would not arise if the item were classified as an equity instrument. This is due to the fact that changes in the fair value of an equity instrument are not recognised in the financial statements. *[IAS 32.36]*.

Moreover, the extent to which an entity funds its operations through debt or equity is regarded as highly significant not only by investors, but also by other users of financial statements such as regulators and tax authorities. This means that the question of whether a particular instrument is a liability or equity raises issues of much greater and wider sensitivity than the mere matter of financial statement classification.

1.2 Development of IFRS on classification of liabilities and equity

Under IFRS, the classification of items as liabilities or equity is dealt with mainly in IAS 32 – *Financial Instruments: Presentation* – with some cross-reference to IAS 39 – *Financial Instruments: Recognition and Measurement* – or, where applicable, IFRS 9 – *Financial Instruments.*

IAS 32 was originally issued in March 1995 and subsequently amended in 1998 and 2000 as the result of the issue of, and subsequent changes to, IAS 39. However, in December 2003, the previous version of IAS 32 was withdrawn and superseded by a new version, which has itself been amended by subsequent new pronouncements, most notably IFRS 7 – *Financial Instruments: Disclosures* (see Chapter 54) and the amendment to IAS 32 – *Puttable Financial Instruments and Obligations Arising on Liquidation.*

The main text of IAS 32 is supplemented by application guidance (which is an integral part of the standard),[1] and by illustrative examples (which accompany, but are not part of, the standard).[2]

The Interpretations Committee has issued two interpretations of IAS 32 discussed in this chapter:

- IFRIC 2 – *Members' Shares in Co-operative Entities and Similar Instruments* (see 4.6.6 below); and
- IFRIC 19 – *Extinguishing Financial Liabilities with Equity Instruments* (see 7 below).

A joint attempt of the IASB and the FASB to develop a new model, in which classification of an instrument was based on whether the instrument would be settled with assets or with equity instruments of the issuer, was suspended in October 2010 due to significant challenges raised by a small group of external reviewers of a draft exposure draft.

In May 2015 the IASB published Exposure Draft ED/2015/3 – *Conceptual Framework for Financial Reporting.* Amongst other topics this proposes to refine the definition of assets and liabilities (see Chapter 2 at 3.3). The exposure draft proposes to define a

liability as an entity's present obligation to transfer an economic resource as a result of a past event if the entity has no practical ability to avoid the transfer. The amount of the transfer is determined by reference to benefits that the entity has received, or activities that it has conducted, in the past. The exposure draft retains the existing definition of equity – that it is the residual interest in the assets of an entity after deducting all its liabilities.

In October 2014 the IASB also resumed the *Financial Instruments with Characteristics of Equity Research Project* to explore further how to distinguish liabilities from equity claims. The project is at an early stage with the IASB considering various aspects of the definition, presentation and disclosure of liabilities and equity.

2 OBJECTIVE AND SCOPE

2.1 Objective

The objective of IAS 32 is 'to establish principles for presenting financial instruments as liabilities or equity and for offsetting financial assets and financial liabilities.' *[IAS 32.2]*. The standard, and its associated IFRIC interpretations, address:

- the classification of financial instruments, by their issuer, into financial assets, financial liabilities and equity instruments (see 3 to 6 below);
- settling a financial liability with an equity instrument (see 7 below);
- the classification of interest, dividends, losses and gains (see 8 below);
- treasury shares – i.e. an entity's own equity instruments held by the entity (see 9 below);
- forward contracts or options for the receipt or delivery of the entity's own equity instruments (see 11 below); and
- the circumstances in which financial assets and financial liabilities should be offset (see Chapter 54 at 7.4.1).

The principles in IAS 32 complement the principles for recognising and measuring financial assets and financial liabilities in IAS 39, or where applicable IFRS 9, and for disclosing information about them in IFRS 7. *[IAS 32.3]*.

2.2 Scope

The scope of IAS 32 is discussed in detail in Chapter 43 at 3.

3 DEFINITIONS

The following definitions in IAS 32 are relevant to the issues discussed in this chapter. Further general discussion on the meaning and implications of the definitions may be found in Chapter 43 at 2.

A *financial instrument* is any contract that gives rise to a financial asset of one entity and a financial liability or equity instrument of another entity. *[IAS 32.11]*.

A *financial asset* is any asset that is:

(a) cash;

(b) an equity instrument of another entity;

(c) a contractual right:

  (i) to receive cash or another financial asset from another entity; or

  (ii) to exchange financial assets or financial liabilities with another entity under conditions that are potentially favourable to the entity; or

(d) a contract that will or may be settled in the entity's own equity instruments and is:

  (i) a non-derivative for which the entity is or may be obliged to receive a variable number of the entity's own equity instruments; or

  (ii) a derivative that will or may be settled other than by the exchange of a fixed amount of cash or another financial asset for a fixed number of the entity's own equity instruments. For this purpose the entity's own equity instruments do not include:

    - puttable financial instruments classified as equity instruments in accordance with paragraphs 16A and 16B of the standard (see 4.6.2 below),
    - instruments that impose on the entity an obligation to deliver to another party a *pro rata* share of the net assets of the entity only on liquidation and are classified as equity in accordance with paragraphs 16C and 16D of the standard (see 4.6.3 below), or
    - instruments that are contracts for the future receipt or delivery of the entity's own equity instruments. *[IAS 32.11]*.

A *financial liability* is any liability that is:

(a) a contractual obligation:

  (i) to deliver cash or another financial asset to another entity; or

  (ii) to exchange financial assets or financial liabilities with another entity under conditions that are potentially unfavourable to the entity; or

(b) a contract that will or may be settled in the entity's own equity instruments and is:

  (i) a non-derivative for which the entity is or may be obliged to deliver a variable number of the entity's own equity instruments; or

  (ii) a derivative that will or may be settled other than by the exchange of a fixed amount of cash or another financial asset for a fixed number of the entity's own equity instruments. For this purpose, rights, options or warrants to acquire a fixed number of the entity's own equity instruments for a fixed amount of any currency are equity instruments if the entity offers the rights, options or warrants *pro rata* to all of its existing owners of the same class of its own non-derivative equity instruments. Also, for these purposes the entity's own equity instruments do not include:

- puttable financial instruments classified as equity instruments in accordance with paragraphs 16A and 16B of the standard (see 4.6.2 below);
- instruments that impose on the entity an obligation to deliver to another party a *pro rata* share of the net assets of the entity only on liquidation and are classified as equity in accordance with paragraphs 16C and 16D of the standard (see 4.6.3 below); or
- instruments that are contracts for the future receipt or delivery of the entity's own equity instruments. *[IAS 32.11]*.

As an exception to the general definition of a financial liability, an instrument that meets the definition of a financial liability is nevertheless classified as an equity instrument if it has all the features and meets the conditions in paragraphs 16A or 16B (see 4.6.2 below) or paragraphs 16C and 16D of the standard (see 4.6.3 below). *[IAS 32.11]*.

A *puttable instrument* is a financial instrument that gives the holder the right to put the instrument back to the issuer for cash or another financial asset or is automatically put back to the issuer on the occurrence of an uncertain future event or the death or retirement of the holder. *[IAS 32.11]*.

An *equity instrument* is any contract that evidences a residual interest in the assets of an entity after deducting all of its liabilities. *[IAS 32.11]*.

A *derivative* is a financial instrument or other contract within the scope of IAS 39 (see Chapter 44 at 2) with all three of the following characteristics:

- its value changes in response to the change in a specified interest rate, financial instrument price, commodity price, foreign exchange rate, index of prices or rates, credit rating or credit index, or other variable, provided in the case of a non-financial variable that the variable is not specific to a party of the contract (sometimes called the 'underlying');
- it requires no initial net investment or an initial net investment that is smaller than would be required for other types of contracts that would be expected to have a similar response to changes in market factors; and
- it is settled at a future date. *[IAS 39.9]*.

Fair value is the price that would be received to sell an asset or paid to transfer a liability in an orderly transaction between market participants at the measurement date. *[IAS 32.11]*. This is the same definition as used in IFRS 13 – *Fair Value Measurement* (see Chapter 14 at 3).

In these definitions (and throughout IAS 32 and the discussion in this chapter):

- *Contract* and *contractual* refer to an agreement between two or more parties that has clear economic consequences that the parties have little, if any, discretion to avoid, usually because the agreement is enforceable by law. Contracts, and thus financial instruments, may take a variety of forms and need not be in writing. *[IAS 32.13]*.
- *Entity* includes individuals, partnerships, incorporated bodies, trusts and government agencies. *[IAS 32.14]*.

4 CLASSIFICATION OF INSTRUMENTS

The most important issue dealt with by IAS 32 is the classification of financial instruments (or their components) by their issuer as financial liabilities, financial assets or equity instruments, including non-controlling interests. The rule in IAS 32 for classification of items as financial liabilities or equity is essentially simple. An issuer of a financial instrument must classify the instrument (or its component parts) on initial recognition as a financial liability, a financial asset or an equity instrument in accordance with the substance of the contractual arrangement and the definitions of a financial liability, a financial asset and an equity instrument (see 3 above). *[IAS 32.15]*. The application of this principle in practice, however, is often far from straightforward.

IAS 32 considers the question of whether a transaction is a financial liability or an equity instrument at two levels. First it examines whether an individual instrument (or class of instruments) issued by the entity is a financial liability or equity. This is principally discussed in this Section, although some of the provisions discussed at 5 and 6 below may also be relevant.

Second, where an entity settles a transaction using instruments issued by it that, when considered in isolation, would be classified as equity, IAS 32 requires the entity to consider whether the transaction considered as a whole is in fact a financial liability. This will typically be the case where a transaction is settled by issuing a variable number of equity instruments equal to an agreed value. This is principally discussed at 5 and 6 below, although some of the provisions discussed in this Section 4 may also be relevant.

The appropriate classification is made on initial recognition of the instrument and, in general, not changed subsequently (see 4.9 below on reclassification of instruments).

4.1 Definition of equity instrument

Application of the basic definitions in IAS 32 means that an instrument is an equity instrument only if both the following conditions are met:

- The instrument includes no contractual obligation either:
  - to deliver cash or another financial asset to another entity; or
  - to exchange financial assets or financial liabilities with another entity under conditions that are potentially unfavourable to the issuer.
- If the instrument will, or may, be settled in the issuer's own equity instruments, it is either:
  - a non-derivative that includes no contractual obligation for the issuer to deliver a variable number of its own equity instruments; or
  - a derivative that will be settled only by the issuer exchanging a fixed amount of cash or another financial asset for a fixed number of its own equity instruments. For this purpose the issuer's own equity instruments do not include instruments that have all the features and meet the conditions described in paragraphs 16A and 16B (see 4.6.2 below) or paragraphs 16C and 16D (see 4.6.3 below) of IAS 32 or instruments that are contracts for the future receipt or delivery of the issuer's own equity instruments. *[IAS 32.16]*.

As a pragmatic exception to these basic criteria, an instrument that would otherwise meet the definition of a financial liability is nevertheless classified as an equity instrument if it is either:

- a puttable instrument with all the features, and meeting the conditions described, in paragraphs 16A and 16B of IAS 32 (see 4.6.2 below); or
- an instrument entitling the holder to a pro-rata share of assets on a liquidation with all the features, and meeting all the conditions, described in paragraphs 16C and 16D of IAS 32. *[IAS 32.16]*. This is discussed further at 4.6.3 below.

Broadly speaking, apart from this exemption, an instrument can only be classified as equity under IAS 32 if the issuer has an unconditional right to avoid delivering cash or another financial instrument (see 4.2 below) or, if it is settled through own equity instruments, it is for an exchange of a fixed amount of cash for a fixed number of the entity's own equity instruments. In all other cases it would be classified as a financial liability.

4.2 Contractual obligation to deliver cash or other financial assets

It is apparent from 4.1 above that a critical feature in differentiating a financial liability from an equity instrument is the existence of a contractual obligation of one party to the financial instrument (the issuer) either:

- to deliver cash or another financial asset to the other party (the holder); or
- to exchange financial assets or financial liabilities with the holder under conditions that are potentially unfavourable to the issuer. *[IAS 32.17]*.

IAS 32 focuses on the contractual rights and obligations arising from the terms of an instrument, rather than on the probability of those rights and obligations leading to an outflow of cash or other resources from the entity, as would be the case for a provision accounted for under IAS 37 – *Provisions, Contingent Liabilities and Contingent Assets* (see Chapter 28). Thus, IAS 32 may well:

- classify as equity: an instrument that is virtually certain to result in regular cash payments by the entity; but
- treat as a liability: an instrument which:
  - gives its holder a right to receive cash rather than equity which no rational holder would exercise; or
  - exposes the issuer to a liability to repay the instrument contingent on an external event so remote that no liability would be recognised if IAS 37 rather than IAS 32 were the applicable standard.

The holder of an equity instrument (e.g. a non-puttable share) is entitled to receive a *pro rata* share of any dividends or other distributions of equity that are made. However, since the issuer does not have a contractual obligation to make such distributions (because it cannot be required to deliver cash or another financial asset to another party), the instrument is not a financial liability of the issuer. *[IAS 32.17]*. The price or value of such an instrument may well reflect a general expectation by market participants that distributions will be made on a regular basis, but, under IAS 32, the absence of a contractual obligation requires the instrument to be classified as equity.

IAS 32 requires the issuer of a financial instrument to classify a financial instrument by reference to its substance rather than its legal form, although it is conceded that substance and form are 'commonly', but not always, the same. Typical examples of instruments that are equity in legal form but liabilities in substance are certain types of preference share (see 4.5 below) and certain units in open-ended funds, unit trusts and similar entities (see 4.6 below). *[IAS 32.18]*. Conversely, a number of entities have issued instruments which behave in most practical respects as perpetual (or even redeemable) debt, but which IAS 32 requires to be classified as equity (see 4.5 below). IAS 32 further clarifies that a financial instrument is an equity instrument, and not a financial liability, not merely if the issuer has no legal obligation to deliver cash or other financial assets to the holder at the reporting date, but only if it has an unconditional right to avoid doing so in all future circumstances other than an unforeseen liquidation. Thus, a financial instrument (other than one classified as equity under the exceptions discussed at 4.6 below) is classified as a financial liability even if:

- the issuer's ability to discharge its obligations under the instrument is restricted (e.g. by a lack of funds, the need to obtain regulatory approval to make payments on the instrument, or a shortfall of distributable profits, or other statutory restriction); *[IAS 32.19, AG25]* or
- the holder has to perform some action (e.g. formally exercise a redemption right) in order for the issuer to become obliged to transfer cash or other financial assets. *[IAS 32.19]*.

In September 2015 the Interpretations Committee considered the classification of a prepaid card and how the unspent balance on such a card would be accounted for. The Interpretations Committee specifically considered a prepaid card with the following features:

- no expiry date;
- cannot be refunded, redeemed or exchanged for cash;
- redeemable only for goods and services;
- redeemable only at selected merchants which could include the entity;
- upon redemption by the cardholder at a merchant, the entity has a contractual obligation to pay cash to the merchant;
- no back-end fees, e.g. the balance on the prepaid card does not reduce unless spent by the cardholder; and
- is not issued as part of a customer loyalty programme.

The Interpretations Committee observed that the liability of the entity for the prepaid card meets the definition of a financial liability, because the entity has a contractual obligation to deliver cash to the merchants on behalf of the cardholder, conditional upon the cardholder using the prepaid card to buy goods or services and the entity does not have an unconditional right to avoid delivering cash to settle this contractual obligation. The Interpretations Committee decided that even if redemption with the entity is a possibility, the entity's obligation is still a financial liability. This is because the entity does not have an unconditional right to avoid delivering cash when the cardholder redeems the prepaid card at a third party merchant.[3]

Following the receipt of responses to the draft agenda decision, the Interpretations Committee, in March 2016, limited the fact pattern to where the card could only be redeemed at specified third-party merchants and not at the entity itself but otherwise did not change its conclusion.

The Interpretations Committee determined that neither an Interpretation nor an amendment to a Standard was necessary.[4]

One of the key consequences of this decision is that if the card gives rise to a financial liability then the unspent balance on the card cannot be derecognised. Any unredeemed portion of the card will continue to be recognised as a liability in perpetuity as financial liabilities can only be derecognised when extinguished. *[IAS 39.39]*. It is also of note that the balances on such cards are regarded as financial liabilities even though they do not meet the strict IAS 32 definition of a financial instrument, as the balance on the prepaid card will not constitute a financial asset in the hands of the cardholder.

4.2.1 *Relationship between an entity and its members*

The unconditional right of the entity to avoid delivering cash or another financial asset in settlement of an obligation is crucial in differentiating a financial liability from an equity instrument. In our view, the role of the entity's shareholders is critical in determining the classification of financial instruments when the shareholders can decide whether the entity delivers cash or another financial asset. It is therefore important to understand the relationship between the entity and its members. Shareholders can make decisions as part of the corporate governance decision making process of the entity (generally exercised in a general meeting), or separate from the entity's corporate governance decision making process in their capacity as holders of particular instruments.

In some entities, the right to declare dividends and/or redeem capital is reserved for the members of the entity in general meeting, as a matter either of the entity's own constitution or of general legislation in the jurisdiction concerned. The effect of such a right may be that the members can require payment of a dividend irrespective of the wishes of management. Even where management has the right to prevent a payment declared by the members, the members will generally have the right to appoint the management, and can therefore appoint management that will not oppose an equity distribution declared by the members.

This raises the question whether an entity whose members have such rights should classify all its distributable retained earnings as a liability, on the grounds that the members could require earnings to be distributed as dividend, or capital to be repaid, at any time. In our view this is not appropriate, since an action reserved to the entity's shareholders in general meeting, is effectively an action of the entity itself. It is therefore at the discretion of the entity itself (as represented by the members in general meeting) that retained earnings are paid out as a dividend. Accordingly, in our view, such earnings are classified as equity, and not as a financial liability, until they become a legal liability of the entity.

If on the other hand, decisions by the shareholders are not made as part of the entity's corporate governance decision making process, but made in their capacity as holders of particular instruments, it is our view that the shareholders should be considered to be separate from the entity. The entity therefore would not have an unconditional right to avoid delivering cash or another financial asset and would have to classify the financial instrument as a financial liability.

This issue was brought to the Interpretations Committee in January 2010. The Interpretations Committee identified that diversity may exist in practice in assessing whether an entity has an unconditional right to avoid delivering cash if the contractual obligation is at the ultimate discretion of the issuer's shareholders, and consequently whether a financial instrument should be classified as a financial liability or equity. However, the Interpretations Committee concluded that the Board's then current project on financial instruments with characteristics of equity was expected to address the distinction between equity and non-equity instruments on a timely basis, and that the Interpretations Committee would therefore not add this to its agenda.[5] In October 2010 the project was suspended but was restarted in October 2014 (see 12 below).

4.2.2 Implied contractual obligation to deliver cash or other financial assets

A financial instrument that does not explicitly establish a contractual obligation to deliver cash or another financial asset may nevertheless establish an obligation indirectly through its terms and conditions. *[IAS 32.20]*.

IAS 32.20 provides two examples:

(a) A financial instrument may contain a non-financial obligation that must be settled if, and only if, the entity fails to make distributions or to redeem the instrument. If the entity can avoid a transfer of cash or another financial asset only by settling the non-financial obligation, the financial instrument is a financial liability.

(b) A financial instrument is a financial liability if it provides that on settlement the entity will deliver either:
   i. cash or another financial asset; or
   ii. its own shares whose value is determined to exceed substantially the value of cash or other financial asset.

Although the entity does not have an explicit contractual obligation to deliver cash or another financial asset, the value of the share settlement alternative is such that the entity will settle in cash. *[IAS 32.20]*.

The basic requirement of IAS 32.20 is for an entity to recognise a financial liability when it can only avoid using cash to settle an obligation by transferring a financial asset or a non-financial asset, in other words settlement of the obligation cannot be avoided in any other way. Then, given that the entity's own shares are not an asset, subparagraph (b)(ii) avoids a potential loophole: if the value of the shares would exceed the amount of cash that would be required to settle the liability, the entity will be economically compelled to settle the cash amount and hence, has a financial liability.

This accounting treatment was illustrated by a question put to the Interpretations Committee in 2015[6]. They considered an arrangement whereby an entity received cash from a government to fund a research and development project. The cash was repayable to the government only if the entity decided to exploit and commercialise the results of the project. If the project was not commercially exploited the entity was obliged to transfer the rights to the research to the government.

The Interpretations Committee observed in May 2016[7] that, in this case, the cash receipt gave rise to a financial liability. In reaching their conclusion the Interpretations Committee took the view that the entity could avoid transferring cash only by settling the obligation with a non-financial instrument (the rights to the research). The Interpretations Committee further noted that the cash received from the government does not meet the definition of a forgivable loan in IAS 20 – *Accounting for Government Grants and Disclosure of Government Assistance* – as the government does not undertake to waive repayment of the loan but requires settlement in cash or by transfer of the rights to research. However they also noted that the entity would be required at initial recognition to assess whether the cash received from the government is something other than a financial instrument, for example the difference between the cash received and the fair value of the financial liability may represent a government grant that should be accounted for in accordance with IAS 20.

This last sentence implies that where the fair value of the alternative settlement option is less than fair value of the cash settlement option, IAS 32.20 only requires a financial liability to be recorded to the extent of the fair value of the alternative settlement option. But, in this example, the Interpretations Committee did not discuss what the fair value of the research and development might be. The Interpretations Committee's discussion demonstrates that where entities receive loans with alternative repayment conditions involving settlement with a non-financial asset, judgement will be necessary in assessing the substance of the settlement requirements and determining the value at inception of the non-financial asset.

4.3 Contingent settlement provisions

Some financial instruments may require the entity to deliver cash or another financial asset, or otherwise to settle it in such a way that it would be classified as a financial liability, in the event of the occurrence or non-occurrence of uncertain future events (or on the outcome of uncertain circumstances), that are beyond the control of both the issuer and the holder of the instrument. These might include:

- a change in a stock market index or a consumer price index;
- changes in interest rates;
- changes in tax law; or
- the issuer's future revenues, net income or debt-to-equity ratio. *[IAS 32.25]*.

IAS 32 provides that, since the issuer of such an instrument does not have the unconditional right to avoid delivering cash or another financial asset (or otherwise to settle it in such a way that it would be a financial liability), the instrument is a financial liability of the issuer unless:

- the part of the contingent settlement provision that could require settlement in cash or another financial asset (or otherwise in such a way that it would be a financial liability) is not genuine (see 4.3.1 below);

- the issuer can be required to settle the obligation in cash or another financial asset (or otherwise to settle it in such a way that it would be a financial liability) only in the event of liquidation of the issuer (see 4.3.2 below); or
- the instrument is classified as equity under the exceptions discussed at 4.6 below. *[IAS 32.25]*.

Whether or not the contingency is within the control of the issuer is therefore an important consideration when classifying financial instruments with contingent settlement provisions as either financial liabilities or equity (see 4.3.4 below).

It is interesting that 'future revenues, net income or debt-to-equity ratio' are given as examples of contingencies beyond the control of both the issuer and the holder of the instrument, since, in some cases, these matters are within the control of the entity. For example, if a payment under a financial instrument is contingent upon revenue rising above a certain level, the entity could avoid the payment by ceasing to trade before revenue reaches that level. Indeed, IAS 37 argues that certain expenses (such as legally required maintenance costs) that an entity is certain to incur if it continues to trade are not liabilities until they become legally due, because the entity could avoid them by ceasing to trade by that date. As in 4.2.2 above, the analysis in IAS 32 appears to be relying on the concept of 'economic compulsion' (i.e. the entity would not rationally cease its activities merely in order to avoid making a contingent payment), even though this does not feature in the definition of 'contingent liability' in IAS 37, or indeed in the classification of many instruments under IAS 32.

4.3.1 Contingencies that are 'not genuine'

A requirement to settle an instrument in cash or another financial asset (or otherwise in such a way that it would be a financial liability) is not genuine (see 4.3 above) if the requirement would arise 'only on the occurrence of an event that is extremely rare, highly abnormal and very unlikely to occur'. *[IAS 32.AG28]*.

Similarly, if the terms of an instrument provide for its settlement in a fixed number of the entity's equity instruments, but there are circumstances, beyond the entity's control, in which such settlement may be contractually precluded, and settlement in cash or other assets required instead, those circumstances can be ignored if there is 'no genuine possibility' that they will occur. In other words, the instrument continues to be regarded as an equity instrument and not as a financial liability. *[IAS 32.AG28]*.

Guidance in IAS 32 on the meaning of 'not genuine' in this context is unfortunately restricted to the thesaurus of synonyms ('extremely rare, highly abnormal and very unlikely to occur') above. It is, however, helpful to consider the changes made when in 2003 SIC-5 – *Classification of Financial Instruments – Contingent Settlement Provisions*[8] – was withdrawn, and its substance incorporated in these provisions of IAS 32. SIC-5 had previously required redemption terms to be ignored if they were 'remote'. Examples given by SIC-5 were where the issue of shares is contingent merely on formal approval by the authorities, or where cash settlement is triggered by an index reaching an 'extreme' level relative to its level at the time of initial recognition of the instrument.[9]

IAS 32 deliberately did not reproduce the reference to, or the examples of, 'remote' events in SIC-5. In the Basis for Conclusions to IAS 32 the IASB states that it does not believe it is appropriate to disregard events that are merely 'remote'. *[IAS 32.BC17]*. Thus it is clear that, under the revised version of IAS 32, it is not appropriate to disregard a redemption term that is triggered only when an index reaches an extreme level. This suggests that it is not open to an entity to argue (for example) that a bond that is redeemed in cash only if the entity's share price falls below, or fails to reach, a certain level can be treated as an equity instrument on the grounds that there is no genuine possibility that the share price will perform in that way.

In general, terms are included in a contract for an economic purpose and therefore are genuine. The current reference in IAS 32 to terms that are 'not genuine' is presumably intended to deal with clauses inserted into the terms of financial instruments for some legal or tax reason (e.g. so as to make conversion technically 'conditional' rather than mandatory) but having no real economic purpose or consequence.

An example of a clause that has caused some debate on this point is a 'regulatory change' clause, generally found in the terms of capital instruments issued by financial institutions such as banks and insurance companies. Such entities are generally required by local regulators to maintain certain minimum levels of equity or highly subordinated debt (generally referred to as regulatory capital) in order to be allowed to do business.

A 'regulatory change' clause will typically require an instrument which, at the date of issue, is classified as regulatory capital to be repaid in the event that it ceases to be so classified. The practice so far of the regulators in many markets has been to make changes to a regulatory classification with prospective effect only, such that any instruments already in issue continue to be regarded as regulatory capital even though they would not be under the new rules.

This has led some to question whether a 'regulatory change' clause can be regarded as a contingent settlement provision which is 'not genuine'.[10] This is ultimately a matter for the judgement of entities and their auditors in the context of the relevant regulatory environment(s). This judgement has not been made easier by the greater unpredictability of the markets (and therefore of regulators' responses to it) since the last financial crisis.

4.3.2 *Liabilities that arise only on liquidation*

As noted in 4.3 above, IAS 32 provides that a contingent settlement provision that comes into play only on liquidation of the issuer may be ignored in determining whether or not a financial instrument is a financial liability. IAS 32 refers specifically to 'liquidation'. In other words, if an instrument provides for redemption on the occurrence of events that are a possible precursor of liquidation (e.g. extreme insolvency, the financial statements not being prepared on a going concern basis, or the entity being placed under the protection of Chapter 11 of the United States Bankruptcy Code) but falling short of formal liquidation, the instrument must be treated as a financial liability. Also where liquidation is in the control of the holder, the instrument will be a liability as this exception only applies to contingencies beyond the control of both the issuer and the holder.

4.3.3 Liabilities that arise only on a change of control

A number of entities have issued instruments on terms that require the issuing entity to transfer cash or other financial assets only in the event of a change in control of the issuing entity. This raises the question of whether such an event is outside the control of the issuing entity, with the effect than any instrument containing such a provision would be classified as a liability to the extent of any obligations arising on a change of control.

This issue is far from straightforward. As noted at 4.2.1 above, it is our view that, where the power to make a decision is reserved for the members of an entity in general meeting, for the purposes of such a decision, the members and the entity are one and the same. Therefore, we consider that any change of control requiring the approval of the members in general meeting should be regarded as within the control of the entity. Conversely, in our view, a change of control is not within the control of the entity where it can be effected by one or more individual shareholders without reference to the members in general meeting, for example where a shareholder holding 40% of the ordinary equity sells its shares to another party already owning 30%.

However, we recognise that such a distinction is not as clear-cut as might at first sight appear, and indeed in some situations may give rise to what could be regarded as a purely form-based distinction, as illustrated by Example 45.1 below.

Example 45.1: Change of control

X plc is owned by:

- two wealthy individuals A and B, who own, respectively, 48% and 42% of X's equity, together with
- a number of private individuals with small shareholdings totalling 10% of the equity.

In practical terms, if A and B agree that B will sell his shares to A, thus giving A a 90% controlling stake in the entity, it makes very little difference whether this is achieved by a private sale treaty between A and B or a general meeting of the company (at which A and B would be able to cast 90% of available votes in favour of the transaction).

In a situation such as that in Example 45.1 it would seem strange to say that a sale by private treaty is not within the control of X plc, but a sale agreed in general meeting is, when in either case all that matters is the intentions of A and B.

In our view, this is an area on which it would be useful for the IASB or the Interpretations Committee to issue guidance. It may be that such guidance would need to be based on 'rules' rather than principles.

4.3.4 Some typical contingent settlement provisions

The matrix below gives a number of contingent settlement provisions that we have encountered in practice – some common, some rather esoteric – together with our view as to whether they should be regarded as outside the control of the reporting entity. If a contingent settlement provision is regarded as outside the control of the issuing entity, the instrument will be classified as a liability by the issuer. If a contingent settlement provision is regarded as within the control of the reporting entity, the instrument will be classified as equity, provided that it has no other features requiring its classification as a liability and that the contingent settlement event is also outside the control of the holder.

Contingent settlement event	Within the issuer's control?
Issuer makes a distribution on ordinary shares.	Yes. Dividends on ordinary shares are discretionary (see also 4.2 above).
Upon the successful takeover of the issuer (i.e. a 'control event').	It depends. See 4.3.3 above.
Event of default under any of the issuer's debt facilities.	No.
Appointment of a receiver, administrator, entering a scheme of arrangement, or compromise agreement with creditors.	No. Whether this leads to the instrument being classified as equity or liability will depend on the respective requirements in each jurisdiction. In cases when these events do not necessarily result in liquidation of the issuer, this leads to classification as a liability, due to the requirement to ignore settlement provisions arising only on liquidation (see 4.3.2 above).
Upon commencement of proceedings for the winding up of the issuer.	No, but this does not lead to classification as a liability due to the requirement to ignore settlement provisions arising only on liquidation (see 4.3.2 above).
Incurring a fine exceeding a given amount, or commencement of an investigation of the issuer by, a government agency or a financial regulator.	No.
A change in accounting, taxation, or regulatory regime which is expected to adversely affect the financial position of the issuer.	No.
Suspension of listing of the issuer's shares from trading on the stock exchange for more than a certain number of days.	Probably not, but it will depend on the jurisdiction and whether the reasons for suspension are always within the control of the entity.
Commencement of war or armed conflict.	No.
Issue of a subordinated security that ranks equally or in priority to the securities.	Yes.
Issue of an IPO prospectus prior to the conversion date.	Yes.
Execution of an effective IPO.	No. The execution of a successful IPO is not within the control of the issuer.
Disposal of all or substantially all of the issuer's business undertaking or assets.	Yes.
Change in credit rating of the issuer.	No.

4.4 Examples of equity instruments

4.4.1 Issued instruments

Under the criteria above, equity instruments under IAS 32 will include non-puttable common (ordinary) shares and some types of preference share (see 4.5 below). *[IAS 32.AG13]*.

Whilst non-puttable shares are typically equity, an issuer of non-puttable ordinary shares nevertheless assumes a liability when it formally acts to make a distribution and becomes legally obliged to the shareholders to do so. This may be the case following the declaration of a dividend, or when, on a winding up, any assets remaining after discharging the entity's liabilities become distributable to shareholders. *[IAS 32.AG13]*. For example, if an entity has issued €100 million of equity instruments on which it declares a dividend of €2 million, it recognises a liability of only €2 million. Whether or not a liability arises on declaration of a dividend will depend on local legislation or the terms of the instruments or both.

IAS 32 also treats as equity instruments some puttable instruments (see 4.6.2 below) and some instruments that impose an obligation on the issuer to deliver a *pro rata* share of net assets only on liquidation (see 4.6.3 below) that would otherwise be classified as financial liabilities. However, a contract that is required to be settled by the entity receiving or delivering either of these types of 'deemed' equity instrument is a financial asset or financial liability, even when it involves the exchange of a fixed amount of cash or other financial assets for a fixed number of such instruments. *[IAS 32.22A, AG13]*.

4.4.2 Contracts to issue equity instruments

A contract settled using equity instruments is not necessarily itself regarded as an equity instrument. The classification of contracts settled using issued equity instruments is discussed further at 5 below.

Warrants or written call options that allow the holder to subscribe for or purchase a fixed number of non-puttable common (ordinary) shares in the issuing entity in exchange for a fixed amount of cash or another financial asset, or the fixed stated principal of a bond, are classified as equity instruments. *[IAS 32.22, AG13]*. The meaning of a 'fixed' amount of cash is not as self-evident as it might appear and is discussed further at 5.2.3 below. The meaning of the 'fixed stated principal' of a bond is discussed further at 6.3.2.A below.

Conversely, an instrument is a financial liability (or financial asset) of the issuer if it gives the holder the right to obtain:

- a variable number of non-puttable common (ordinary) shares in the issuing entity in exchange for a fixed amount of cash or another financial asset; *[IAS 32.21]* or
- a fixed number of non-puttable common (ordinary) shares in the issuing entity in exchange for a variable amount of cash or another financial asset. *[IAS 32.24]*.

An obligation for the entity to issue or purchase a fixed number of its own equity instruments in exchange for a fixed amount of cash or another financial asset is classified as an equity instrument of the entity. However, if such a contract contains an obligation – or even a potential obligation – for the entity to pay cash or another financial asset, it gives rise to a liability for the present value of the redemption amount (which results in a reduction of equity, not an expense – see 5.3 below). *[IAS 32.23, AG13]*.

A purchased call option or other similar contract acquired by an entity that gives it the right to reacquire a fixed number of its own equity instruments in exchange for delivering a fixed amount of cash or another financial asset is not a financial asset of the entity. Rather, it is classified as an equity instrument, and any consideration paid for such a contract is therefore deducted from equity (see 11.2.1 below). *[IAS 32.22, AG14]*. This requirement refers only to contracts which require the entity to settle gross (i.e. the entity pays cash in exchange for its own shares). Contracts which can be net settled (i.e. the party for whom the contract is loss-making delivers cash or shares equal to the fair value of the contract to the other party) are generally treated as financial assets or financial liabilities. This is discussed in more detail at 11 below.

4.5 Preference shares and similar instruments

Whilst some of the discussion below (and the guidance in IAS 32) is, for convenience, framed in terms of 'preference shares', it should be applied equally to any financial instrument, however described, with similar characteristics. In practice, many such instruments are not described as shares (possibly to avoid weakening any argument that, for fiscal purposes, they are tax-deductible debt rather than non-deductible equity).

Preference shares may be issued with various rights. In determining whether a preference share is a financial liability or an equity instrument, IAS 32 requires an issuer to assess the particular rights attaching to the share to determine whether it exhibits the fundamental characteristic of a financial liability. *[IAS 32.AG25]*.

IAS 32 does this in part by drawing a distinction between:

- instruments mandatorily redeemable or redeemable at the holder's option (see 4.5.1 below); and
- other instruments – i.e. those redeemable only at the issuer's option or not redeemable (see 4.5.2 to 4.5.4 below).

4.5.1 Instruments redeemable mandatorily or at the holder's option

A preference share (or other instrument) that:

- provides for mandatory redemption by the issuer for a fixed or determinable amount at a fixed or determinable future date; or
- gives the holder the right to require the issuer to redeem the instrument at or after a particular date for a fixed or determinable amount,

contains a financial liability, since the issuer has an obligation, or potential obligation, to transfer cash or other financial assets to the holder. This obligation is not negated by the potential inability of an issuer to redeem a preference share when contractually required to do so, whether because of a lack of funds, a statutory restriction or insufficient profits or reserves. *[IAS 32.18(a), AG25]*.

It is more correct to say (in the words of the application guidance) that an instrument 'contains' a financial liability than to say (as the main body of the standard does) that it 'is' a financial liability. For example, if a preference share is issued on terms that it is redeemable at the holder's option but dividends are paid entirely at the issuer's discretion, it is only the amount payable on redemption that is a liability. This would lead to a 'split accounting' treatment (see 6 below), whereby, at issue, the net present value of the amount payable on redemption would be classified as a liability and the balance of the issue proceeds as equity. *[IAS 32.AG37]*.

Non-discretionary dividends, on the other hand, establish an additional liability component. In such a case there is a contractual obligation to pay cash in respect of both the redemption of the principal and the required dividend payments up to the redemption of the instrument. The liability would be recognised at an amount equal to the present value of both the redemption amount and the non-discretionary dividends. Assuming that the dividends were set at market rate, which is generally the case, this would typically result in an overall liability classification of the whole instrument. While dividend payments might be set at a fixed percentage of the nominal value, this does not need to be the case. Any non-discretionary obligation to pay dividends creates a liability that needs to be recorded on initial recognition of the instrument. If an entity has an obligation that is non-discretionary, for example to pay out a percentage of it profits, then that gives rise to a financial liability (see Chapter 44 at 2.1.3 for discussions around embedded derivatives and non-financial variables specific to one party to the contract).

4.5.2 Instruments redeemable only at the issuer's option or not redeemable

A preference share (or other instrument) redeemable in cash only at the option of the issuer does not satisfy the definition of a financial liability in IAS 32, because the issuer does not have a present or future obligation to transfer financial assets to the shareholders. In this case, redemption of the shares is solely at the discretion of the issuer. An obligation may arise, however, when the issuer of the shares exercises its option, usually by formally notifying the shareholders of an intention to redeem the shares. *[IAS 32.AG25]*.

Likewise, where preference shares are non-redeemable, there is clearly no financial liability in respect of the 'principal' amount of the shares. In reality there may be little distinction between shares redeemable at the issuer's option and non-redeemable shares, given that in many jurisdictions an entity can 'repurchase' its 'irredeemable' shares subject to no greater restrictions than would apply to a 'redemption' of 'redeemable' shares.

Ultimately, the classification of preference shares redeemable only at the issuer's option or not redeemable according to their terms must be determined by the other rights that attach to them. IAS 32 requires the classification to be based on an assessment of the substance of the contractual arrangements and the definitions of a financial liability and an equity instrument. *[IAS 32.AG26]*.

If the share does establish a contractual right to a dividend, subject only to restrictions on payment of dividends in the relevant jurisdiction, it contains a financial liability in respect of the dividends. This would lead to a 'split accounting' treatment (see 6 below), whereby the net present value of the right to receive dividends would be shown as a liability and the balance of the issue proceeds as equity. Where the dividends are set at a market rate at the date of issue, it is likely that the issue proceeds would be equivalent to the fair value (at the date of issue) of dividends payable in perpetuity, so that the entire proceeds would be classified as a financial liability.

However, when redemption of the preference shares and distributions to holders of the preference shares, whether cumulative or non-cumulative, are at the discretion of the issuer, the shares are equity instruments. The classification of preference share distributions as an equity component or a financial liability component is not affected by, for example:

- a history of making distributions;
- an intention to make distributions in the future;
- a possible negative impact on the price of ordinary shares of the issuer if distributions are not made (because of restrictions on paying dividends on the ordinary shares if dividends are not paid on the preference shares – see 4.5.3 below);
- the amount of the issuer's reserves;
- an issuer's expectation of a profit or loss for a period; or
- an ability or inability of the issuer to influence the amount of its profit or loss for the period. *[IAS 32.AG26]*.

The treatment of non-redeemable preference shares or other instruments with preferred rights under IAS 32 is a particularly difficult issue, since such shares often inhabit the border territory between financial liabilities and equity instruments. However, the starting point is that a non-redeemable preference share whose dividend rights are simply that a dividend (whether of a fixed, capped or discretionary amount) will be paid at the issuing entity's sole discretion, is equivalent to an ordinary equity share and therefore appropriately characterised as equity.

4.5.3 Instruments with a 'dividend blocker' or a 'dividend pusher' clause

4.5.3.A Instruments with a 'dividend blocker'

A number of entities have issued non-redeemable instruments (or instruments redeemable only at the issuer's option) with the following broad terms:

- a discretionary annual coupon or dividend will be paid up to a capped maximum amount; and
- unless a full discretionary coupon or dividend is paid to holders of the instrument, no dividend can be paid to ordinary shareholders.

This restriction on dividend payments to ordinary shareholders is colloquially referred to as a 'dividend blocker' clause. Because payments of annual coupons or dividends are at the discretion of the issuer and the instrument is non-redeemable, the issuer has an unconditional right to avoid delivering cash or another financial asset. This is not negated by the fact that the issuer cannot pay dividends to ordinary shareholders if no coupon or dividend is paid to the holder of the instruments. The instrument is therefore classified as equity in its entirety.

The economic reality is that many entities that issue such instruments are able to do so at a cost not significantly higher than that of callable perpetual debt. This indicates that the financial markets regard 'dividend blocker' clauses as providing investors with reasonable security of receiving their 'discretionary' coupon or dividend, given the adverse economic consequences for the entity of not paying it (if sufficiently solvent to do so), namely:

- the disaffection of ordinary shareholders who could not receive any dividends; and
- the fact that the entity would find it very difficult to raise any similar finance again.

These factors could admit an argument that such instruments are equivalent to perpetual debt, which give rise to a financial liability of the issuer (see 4.7 below), in all respects, except that the holder has no right to sue for non-payment of the discretionary dividend. However, the analysis in IAS 32 is based on the implicit counter-argument that the position of a holder of an instrument, all payments on which are discretionary, is equivalent to that of an ordinary shareholder. Ordinary shares do not cease to be equity instruments simply because an entity that failed to pay dividends to its ordinary shareholders, when clearly able to do so, would be subject to adverse economic pressures from those shareholders, and might find it very difficult to raise additional share capital.

However it is worth noting that, as mentioned in 1.2 above, the Exposure Draft ED/2015/3 – *Conceptual Framework for Financial Reporting* – includes a proposed new definition of liability as a present obligation of an entity to transfer an economic resource as a result of past events where the entity has no practical ability to avoid the transfer. If adopted, this definition could result in instruments with 'dividend blockers' being classified as financial liabilities on the grounds that the entity has no practical ability to avoid the transfer.

Aviva has issued instruments with 'dividend blocker' clauses that are accounted for as equity instruments (see, in particular, the final sentences of the extract).

Extract 45.1: Aviva plc (2015)

Notes to the consolidated financial statements [extract]

34 Direct capital instruments and tier 1 notes [extract]

Notional amount	**2015 £m**	2014 £m
5.9021% £500 million direct capital instrument – issued November 2004	**500**	500
Direct capital instrument	**500**	500
8.25% US $650 million fixed rate tier 1 notes – issued May 2012	**392**	392
6.875% £210 million STICS – issued November 2013 (note 38)	**231**	–
Total tier 1 notes	**623**	392
	1,123	892

> The direct capital instrument (the DCI) were issued on 25 November 2004 and qualifies as Innovative Tier 1 capital, as defined by the PRA in GENPRU Annex 1 'Capital Resources' as at 31 December 2015. The DCI has no fixed redemption date but the Company may, at its sole option, redeem all (but not part) of the principal amount on 27 July 2020, at which date the interest rate changes to a variable rate, or on any respective coupon payment date thereafter. [...]
>
> No interest will accrue on any deferred coupon on the DCI or FxdRNs. Interest will accrue on deferred coupons on the STICS at the then current rate of interest on the STICS.
>
> Deferred coupons on DCI, FxdRNs and the STICS will be satisfied by the issue and sale of ordinary shares in the Company at their prevailing market value, to a sum as near as practicable to (and at least equal to) the relevant deferred coupons. In the event of any coupon deferral, the Company will not declare or pay any dividend on its ordinary or preference share capital. These instruments have been treated as equity. Please refer to accounting policy AE.

4.5.3.B Instruments with a 'dividend pusher'

A variation of the financial instrument discussed under 4.5.3.A above is one with a so called 'dividend pusher' clause which, in practice, often comes with the following broad terms:

- a discretionary annual coupon or dividend will be paid up to a capped maximum amount;
- payment of the annual coupon or dividend is required if the entity pays dividends to ordinary shareholders; and
- the instrument is non-redeemable (or redeemable only at the issuer's option).

The annual coupons or dividends are at the discretion of the issuer and the instrument is non-redeemable, indicating an unconditional right of the issuer to avoid delivering cash or another financial asset to the holder of the instrument. Whether the 'dividend pusher' clause introduces a contractual obligation to deliver cash or another financial asset depends on whether the payments of dividends to ordinary shareholders (referenced in the dividend pusher clause) are themselves discretionary. In general, payments of dividends to ordinary shareholders are at the discretion of the issuer of those shares. The 'dividend pusher' clause therefore does not introduce a contractual obligation, meaning that the issuer has an unconditional right to avoid delivering cash or another financial asset. Thus the instrument is classified as equity in its entirety.

4.5.4 Perpetual instruments with a 'step-up' clause

Some perpetual instruments are issued on terms that they are not required to be redeemed. However, if they are not redeemed on or before a given future date, any coupon or dividend paid after that date is increased, usually to a level that would give rise to a cost of finance higher than the entity would normally expect to incur. This effectively compels the issuer to redeem the instrument before the increase occurs. A provision for such an increase in the coupon or dividend is colloquially referred to as a 'step-up' clause. A 'step-up' clause is often combined with a 'dividend-blocker' or 'dividend pusher' clause (see 4.5.3.A and 4.5.3.B above).

Paragraph 22 of the version of IAS 32 in issue before its revision in December 2003 (see 1.2 above) specifically addressed 'step-up' clauses as follows:

> 'A preferred share that does not provide for mandatory redemption or redemption at the option of the holder may have a contractually provided accelerating dividend such that, within the foreseeable future, the dividend yield is scheduled to be so high that the issuer would be economically compelled to redeem the instrument.'[11]

The Basis for Conclusions to the current version of IAS 32 indicates that this example was removed because it was insufficiently clear, but there was no intention to alter the general principle of IAS 32 that an instrument that does not explicitly establish an obligation to deliver cash or other financial assets may establish an obligation indirectly through its terms and conditions (see 4.2.3 above). *[IAS 32.BC9]*.

This has led some to suggest that any instrument with a 'step-up' clause contains a financial liability. In our view, however, this is to misunderstand the reason for the IASB's decision to delete the old paragraph 22. The 'confusion' caused by the paragraph was that the existence of a step-up clause is in fact irrelevant to the analysis required by IAS 32. If an instrument, whether redeemable or not, contains a contractual obligation to pay a coupon or dividend, it is a liability, irrespective of the 'step-up' clause. However, if the coupon or dividend, both before and after the step-up date, is wholly discretionary, then the instrument is, absent other contractual terms that make it a liability, an equity instrument, again irrespective of the step-up clause (see 4.5.1 and 4.5.2 above).

This analysis was confirmed by the Interpretations Committee in March 2006 in its discussion of the classification of an instrument that included a 'step-up' dividend clause that would increase the dividend at a pre-determined date in the future. The Interpretations Committee agreed that this instrument included no contractual obligation ever to pay the dividends or to call the instrument and that therefore it should be classified as equity under IAS 32.[12]

4.5.5 Relative subordination

Some have argued that instruments with 'dividend-blocker', 'dividend-pusher' or 'step-up' clauses (see 4.5.3 and 4.5.4 above) do not meet the definition of an equity instrument. Those that take this view point out that paragraph 11 of IAS 32 defines an equity instrument as 'any contract that evidences a residual interest in the assets of an entity after deducting all of its liabilities' (see 3 above) – whereas many instruments of the type described in 4.5.3 and 4.5.4 above are typically entitled only to a return of the amount originally subscribed on a winding up, rather than to any 'residual interest' in the assets. However, such an instrument does not meet the definition of a liability either, for all the reasons set out above.

Moreover, as noted at 4.1 above, IAS 32 paragraph 16 indicates that, in applying the definition in paragraph 11, an entity concludes that an instrument is equity if and only if the criteria in paragraph 16 are met. In other words, an instrument is equity if it satisfies the criteria of paragraph 16, whatever construction might be placed on paragraph 11.

In March 2006, the Interpretations Committee considered various issues relating to the classification of instruments under IAS 32, and agreed that IAS 32 was clear that the relative subordination on liquidation of a financial instrument was not relevant to its classification under IAS 32, even where the instrument ranks above an instrument classified as a liability.[13] This supports the view that an instrument can be classified as equity even if there are restrictions on participation by its holder in a liquidation or on winding up.

However, in February 2008, the IASB issued an amendment to IAS 32 (see 1.2 above) which, in very specific circumstances, requires the relative subordination of an instrument to be taken into account in determining its classification as debt or equity (see 4.6 below).

4.5.6 Economic compulsion

The discussion in 4.5.1 to 4.5.5 above illustrates that, while IAS 32 requires the issuer of a financial instrument to classify a financial instrument by reference to its substance rather than its legal form, in reality the substance is determined, if not by the legal *form*, then certainly by the precise legal *rights* of the holder of the financial instrument concerned. Ultimately, the key determinant of whether an instrument is a financial liability or an equity instrument of the issuer is whether the terms of the instrument give the holder a contractual right to receive cash or other financial assets which can be sued for at law, subject only to restrictions outside the terms of the instrument (e.g. statutory dividend controls).

By contrast, terms of an instrument that effectively force the issuer to transfer cash or other financial assets to the holder although not legally required to do so (often referred to as 'economic compulsion'), are not taken into account.

In response to a submission for a possible agenda item, in March 2006 the Interpretations Committee discussed the role of contractual and economic obligations in the classification of financial instruments under IAS 32.

The Interpretations Committee agreed that IAS 32 is clear that, in order for an instrument to be classified as a liability, a contractual obligation must be established (either explicitly or indirectly) through the terms and conditions of the instrument. Economic compulsion, by itself, would not result in a financial instrument being classified as a liability.

The Interpretations Committee also noted that IAS 32 restricts the role of 'substance' to consideration of the contractual terms of an instrument, and that anything outside the contractual terms is not considered for the purpose of assessing whether an instrument should be classified as a liability under IAS 32.[14]

4.5.7 'Linked' instruments

An entity may issue an instrument (the 'base' instrument) that requires a payment to be made if, and only if, a payment is made on another instrument issued by the entity (the 'linked' instrument). An example of such an instrument would be a perpetual instrument with a 'dividend blocker' clause (see 4.5.3.A above), on which the issuing entity is required to pay a coupon only if it pays a dividend to ordinary shareholders. Absent other terms requiring the perpetual instrument to be classified as a liability, it is classified as equity on the basis that the event that triggers a contractual obligation to make a payment (i.e. payment of an ordinary dividend) is itself not a contractual obligation.

If, however, where payments on the linked instrument are contractually mandatory (such that the linked instrument contains a liability), it is obvious that the base instrument must also contain a liability. This is due to the fact that, in this case, the event that triggers a contractual obligation to make a payment on the base instrument (i.e. a payment on the linked instrument) is a contractual obligation that the issuing entity cannot avoid. This analysis was confirmed by the Interpretations Committee in March 2006 following discussion of linked instruments with similar terms to these.[15]

This issue had arisen in practice in the context that the linked instrument was often very small and callable by the issuer, but on terms that required its classification as a liability under IAS 32. This would allow the issuer, with no real difficulty, to redeem the linked instrument at will and thus convert the base instrument from a liability to equity at any time. This had led some to argue that only the linked instrument should be classified as a liability.

4.5.8 'Change of control', 'taxation change' and 'regulatory change' clauses

A number of entities have issued instruments with 'dividend blocker', 'dividend pusher' and 'step-up' clauses (see 4.5.3 and 4.5.4 above), which would otherwise have been treated as equity by IAS 32, but have wished to account for them as liabilities, perhaps because they can then be hedged in a way that allows hedge accounting to be applied (see 10 below). Methods of achieving this have included the use of a *de minimis* linked liability instrument, or the inclusion of a clause requiring the repayment of the instrument in the event of a change of control. This raises the question of whether a change of control is within the control of the entity (such that the instrument is equity) or not (such that the instrument is debt), which is discussed in more detail at 4.3.3 above.

Another common method of converting an instrument that would otherwise be classified by IAS 32 as equity into debt is to add a clause requiring repayment of the instrument in the event of a fiscal or regulatory change (that in reality may be a remote possibility) – see 4.3.1 above.

4.6 Puttable instruments and instruments repayable only on liquidation

4.6.1 The issue

A 'puttable instrument' is essentially a financial instrument that gives the holder the right to put the instrument back to the issuer for cash or another financial asset (see 3 above). Prior to its amendment in February 2008 (see 1.2 above), IAS 32 classified any puttable instrument as a financial liability, including instruments the legal form of which gives the holder a right to a residual interest in the assets of the issuer.

This classification produced what some regarded as an inappropriate result in the financial statements of entities such as open-ended mutual funds, unit trusts, partnerships and some co-operative entities. Such entities often provide their unit holders or members with a right to redeem their interests in the issuer at any time for cash. Under IAS 32, prior to the February 2008 amendment, an entity whose holders had such rights might report net assets of nil, or even negative net assets, since what would, in normal usage, have been regarded as its 'equity' (i.e. assets less external borrowings) was classified as a financial liability.

For example, the owners of some co-operatives and professional partnerships are entitled to have their ownership interests repurchased at fair value. However, such entities typically do not reflect that fair value in their financial statements, because a significant part of the value may be represented by property accounted for at cost rather than fair value or by internally generated goodwill which cannot be recognised in financial statements prepared under IFRS.

Clearly, if such an entity were to recognise a liability for the right of its owners to be bought out at fair value, it would show net liabilities, which would increase (creating accounting losses) the more the fair value of the entity increases, and decrease (creating accounting profits) the more the fair value decreases. Moreover, any distributions to the owners of such entities would be shown as a charge to, rather than a distribution of, profit.

Similar concerns were raised in relation to limited-life entities. In some jurisdictions, certain types of entity are required to be wound up after a certain period of time, either automatically, or unless the members resolve otherwise. Some entities may also have a limited life under their own governing charter, or equivalent document. For example:

- a collective investment fund might be required to be liquidated on, say, the tenth anniversary of its foundation; or
- a partnership might be required to be dissolved on the death or retirement of a partner.

Such an entity arguably had no equity under IAS 32 prior to the February 2008 amendment, since its limited life imposes an obligation, outside the entity's control, to distribute all its assets. Again, some questioned whether it was very meaningful to show such an entity as having no equity.

In order to deal with these concerns, IAS 32 was amended in February 2008. In the meantime, the Interpretations Committee had published IFRIC 2 which addresses the narrower issue of the classification of certain types of puttable instrument typically issued by co-operative entities (see 4.6.6 below).

The effect of the amended standard is that certain narrowly-defined categories of puttable instruments (see 4.6.2 below) and instruments repayable on a pre-determined liquidation (see 4.6.3 below) are classified as equity, notwithstanding that they have features that would otherwise require their classification as financial liabilities.

Moreover, as discussed further at 4.6.5 below, one of the criteria for classifying such an instrument as equity, is that it is the most subordinated instrument issued by the reporting entity. This represents a significant, and controversial, departure from the normal approach of IAS 32 that the classification of an instrument should be determined only by reference to the contractual terms of that instrument, rather than those of other instruments in issue. This may mean that two entities may classify an identical instrument differently, if it is the most subordinated instrument of one entity but not of the other. It may also mean that the same entity may classify the same instrument differently at different reporting dates.

It was essentially these departures from the normal requirements of IAS 32 that led two members of the IASB (Mary Barth and Robert Garnett) to dissent from the amendment. In their view, it is not based on a clear principle, but comprises 'several paragraphs of detailed rules crafted to achieve a desired accounting result ... [and] ... to minimise structuring opportunities'.[16]

Where the exceptions in 4.6.2 and 4.6.3 below do not apply, IAS 32 takes the view that the effect of the holder's option to put the instrument back to the issuer for cash or another financial asset is that the puttable instrument meets the definition of a financial liability, *[IAS 32.18(b)]*, (see 3 above).

The IASB believes that the accounting treatment required by IAS 32 for instruments not subject to the exceptions in 4.6.2 and 4.6.3 below is appropriate, but points out that the classification of members' interests in such entities as a financial liability does not preclude:

- the use of captions such as 'net asset value attributable to unitholders' and 'change in net asset value attributable to unitholders' on the face of the financial statements of an entity that has no equity capital (such as some mutual funds and unit trusts); or
- the use of additional disclosure to show that total members' interests comprise items such as reserves that meet the definition of equity and puttable instruments that do not. *[IAS 32.18(b), BC7-BC8]*.

The illustrative examples appended to IAS 32 give specimen disclosures to be used in such cases – see Chapter 54 at 7.4.

4.6.2 Puttable instruments

As noted above, a puttable financial instrument includes a contractual obligation for the issuer to repurchase or redeem that instrument for cash or another financial asset on exercise of the put. IAS 32 classifies a puttable instrument as an equity instrument if it has all of the following features: *[IAS 32.16A-16B]*

(a) It entitles the holder to a *pro rata* share of the entity's net assets in the event of the entity's liquidation. The entity's net assets are those assets that remain after deducting all other claims on its assets. A *pro rata* share is determined by:
   - (i) dividing the entity's net assets on liquidation into units of equal amount; and
   - (ii) multiplying that amount by the number of the units held by the financial instrument holder.

(b) The instrument is in the class of instruments that is subordinate to all other classes of instruments. To be in such a class the instrument:
   - (i) has no priority over other claims to the assets of the entity on liquidation; and
   - (ii) does not need to be converted into another instrument before it is in the class of instruments that is subordinate to all other classes of instruments.

(c) All financial instruments in the class of instruments that is subordinate to all other classes of instruments have identical features. For example, they must all be puttable, and the formula or other method used to calculate the repurchase or redemption price is the same for all instruments in that class.

(d) Apart from the contractual obligation for the issuer to repurchase or redeem the instrument for cash or another financial asset, the instrument does not include any contractual obligation to deliver cash or another financial asset to another entity, or to exchange financial assets or financial liabilities with another entity under conditions that are potentially unfavourable to the entity, and it is not a contract that will or may be settled in the entity's own equity instruments as set out in subparagraph (b) of the definition of a financial liability (see 3 above).

(e) The total expected cash flows attributable to the instrument over the life of the instrument are based substantially on the profit or loss, the change in the recognised net assets, or the change in the fair value of the recognised and unrecognised net assets of the entity over the life of the instrument (excluding any effects of the instrument). *[IAS 32.16A]*. Profit or loss and the change in recognised net assets must be determined in accordance with relevant IFRSs. *[IAS 32.AG14E]*.

(f) In addition to the instrument having all the features in (a) to (e) above, the issuer must have no other financial instrument or contract that has:

  (i) total cash flows based substantially on the profit or loss, the change in the recognised net assets or the change in the fair value of the recognised and unrecognised net assets of the entity (excluding any effects of such instrument or contract); and

  (ii) the effect of substantially restricting or fixing the residual return to the puttable instrument holders.

  In applying this condition, the entity should not consider non-financial contracts with a holder of an instrument described in (a) to (e) above that have contractual terms and conditions that are similar to the contractual terms and conditions of an equivalent contract that might occur between a non-instrument holder and the issuing entity. If the entity cannot determine that this condition is met, it should not classify the puttable instrument as an equity instrument. *[IAS 32.16B]*.

Some of these criteria raise issues of interpretation, which are addressed at 4.6.4 below.

4.6.3 *Instruments entitling the holder to a pro rata share of net assets only on liquidation*

Some financial instruments include a contractual obligation for the issuing entity to deliver to another entity a *pro rata* share of its net assets only on liquidation. The obligation arises because liquidation either is certain to occur and outside the control of the entity (for example, a limited life entity) or is uncertain to occur but is at the option of the instrument holder. IAS 32 classifies such an instrument as an equity instrument if it has all of the following features: *[IAS 32.16C-16D]*

(a) It entitles the holder to a *pro rata* share of the entity's net assets in the event of the entity's liquidation. The entity's net assets are those assets that remain after deducting all other claims on its assets. A *pro rata* share is determined by:
   (i) dividing the net assets of the entity on liquidation into units of equal amount; and
   (ii) multiplying that amount by the number of the units held by the financial instrument holder.

(b) The instrument is in the class of instruments that is subordinate to all other classes of instruments. To be in such a class the instrument:
   (i) has no priority over other claims to the assets of the entity on liquidation; and
   (ii) does not need to be converted into another instrument before it is in the class of instruments that is subordinate to all other classes of instruments.

(c) All financial instruments in the class of instruments that is subordinate to all other classes of instruments must have an identical contractual obligation for the issuing entity to deliver a *pro rata* share of its net assets on liquidation. *[IAS 32.16C]*.

(d) In addition to the instrument having all the features in (a) to (c) above, the issuer must have no other financial instrument or contract that has:
   (i) total cash flows based substantially on the profit or loss, the change in the recognised net assets or the change in the fair value of the recognised and unrecognised net assets of the entity (excluding any effects of such instrument or contract); and
   (ii) the effect of substantially restricting or fixing the residual return to the instrument holders.

   For the purposes of applying this condition, the entity should not consider non-financial contracts with a holder of an instrument described in (a) to (c) above that have contractual terms and conditions that are similar to the contractual terms and conditions of an equivalent contract that might occur between a non-instrument holder and the issuing entity. If the entity cannot determine that this condition is met, it should not classify the instrument as an equity instrument. *[IAS 32.16D]*.

Some of these criteria raise some issues of interpretation, which are addressed at 4.6.4 below.

Some of the criteria for classifying as equity financial instruments that entitle the holder to a *pro rata* share of assets only on liquidation are similar to those (in 4.6.2 above) for classifying certain puttable instruments as equity. The difference between these criteria and those for puttable instruments are:

- there is no requirement for there to be no contractual obligations other than those arising on liquidation;
- there is no requirement to consider the expected total cash flows throughout the life of the instrument; and
- the only feature that must be identical among the instruments in the class is the obligation for the issuing entity to deliver to the holder a *pro rata* share of its net assets on liquidation.

The reason for the more relaxed criteria in this case is that the IASB took the view that, given that the only obligation in this case arises on liquidation, there was no need to consider obligations other than those on liquidation. However, the IASB notes that, if an instrument does contain other obligations, these may need to be accounted for separately under IAS 32. *[IAS 32.BC67]*.

4.6.4 Clarification of the exemptions in 4.6.2 and 4.6.3 above

The conditions for treating certain types of puttable instruments (see 4.6.2 above) and instruments repaying a *pro rata* share of net assets on liquidation (see 4.6.3 above) as equity are complex. IAS 32 provides some clarification in respect of the following matters:

- instruments issued by a subsidiary (see 4.6.4.A below);
- determining the level of subordination of an instrument (see condition (b) under 4.6.2 and 4.6.3 above), (see 4.6.4.B below);
- the meaning of 'no obligation to deliver cash or another financial asset' (see condition (d) under 4.6.2 above) in respect of instruments with a requirement to distribute a minimum proportion of profit to shareholders (see 4.6.4.D below);
- other instruments that substantially fix or restrict the residual return to the holder of an instrument (see condition (f)(ii) in 4.6.2 above and condition (d)(ii) in 4.6.3 above), (see 4.6.4.E below); and
- transactions entered into by an instrument holder other than as owner of the entity (see 4.6.4.F below).

One matter on which IAS 32 does not provide further clarification is the meaning of 'identical features' (see condition (c) under 4.6.2 above). This is dealt with in 4.6.4.C below.

Chapter 45

4.6.4.A Instruments issued by a subsidiary

A subsidiary may issue an instrument that falls to be classified as equity in its separate financial statements under one of the exceptions summarised in 4.6.2 and 4.6.3 above. However, in the consolidated financial statements of the subsidiary's parent such an instrument is not recorded as a non-controlling interest, but as a financial liability. *[IAS 32.AG29A]*. This reflects the fact that the exceptions in 4.6.2 and 4.6.3 above are both subject to the condition that the instrument concerned is the most subordinated instrument issued by the reporting entity. The IASB took the view that a non-controlling interest, by its nature, can never be regarded as the residual ownership interest in the consolidated financial statements. *[IAS 32.BC68]*.

4.6.4.B Relative subordination of the instrument

The exceptions in 4.6.2 and 4.6.3 above are both subject to the criterion – condition (b) – that the instrument concerned is the most subordinated instrument issued by the reporting entity. As noted at 4.6.1 above, this represents a departure from the normal principle of IAS 32 that the classification of an issued instrument as a financial liability or equity should be determined by reference only to the contractual terms of that instrument.

In order to determine whether an instrument is in the most subordinate class, the entity calculates the instrument's claim on a liquidation as at the date when it classifies the instrument. The entity reassesses the classification if there is a change in relevant circumstances (for example, if it issues or redeems another financial instrument). *[IAS 32.AG14B]*. This is discussed further at 4.6.5 below.

An instrument that has a preferential right on liquidation of the entity is not regarded as an instrument with an entitlement to a *pro rata* share of the net assets of the entity. An example might be an instrument that entitles the holder to a fixed dividend on liquidation, in addition to a share of the entity's net assets, when other instruments in the subordinate class with a right to a *pro rata* share of the net assets of the entity do not have the same right on liquidation. *[IAS 32.AG14C]*.

If an entity has only one class of financial instruments, that class is treated as if it were subordinate to all other classes. *[IAS 32.AG14D]*.

In our view, the test of whether the instrument is the most subordinated has to be applied according to the legal rights of the various classes of instrument, even where what is legally the most subordinated instrument in issue is entitled to the return of only a nominal sum on liquidation which may be dwarfed by the entitlement of other classes of shares.

It should be noted, however, that the requirement for a puttable instrument to be in the most subordinate class of instruments issued by an entity does not preclude other, non-puttable, instruments from being classified as equity at the same time. In an agenda decision issued in March 2009, the Interpretations Committee noted that a financial instrument is first classified as a liability or equity instrument in accordance with the general requirements of IAS 32. That classification is not affected by the existence of puttable instruments.[17] Thus, for example, founders' shares in an investment fund, which are entitled only to the return of their par value on liquidation, would be classified as equity even if less subordinate than a class of puttable shares which also qualify for equity classification. Conversely, if the founders' shares were the most subordinate instruments, the puttable shares would have to be classified as liabilities.

4.6.4.C Meaning of 'identical features'

Condition (c) under 4.6.2 above requires that 'all financial instruments in the class of instruments that is subordinate to all other classes of instruments have identical features. For example, they must all be puttable, and the formula or other method used to calculate the repurchase or redemption price is the same for all instruments in that class'. The word 'identical' does not normally need much further explanation in the English language. Nevertheless, some have questioned how literally the word must be interpreted in this case.

Consider, for example, an investment fund that issues several types of puttable shares, each equally subordinate, having identical redemption and dividend rights, but different minimum subscription thresholds and subscription fees. Do all these instruments have identical features for the purpose of this exemption? In our view the condition referred to above is primarily designed to ensure that the redemption rights of the shares do not differ. Accordingly, terms that take effect before the shares are issued (as in the example above), or are not financial, should not cause instruments to fail the 'identical features' test. Examples of features which are not financial might include rights to information or management powers. In our opinion, instruments with different features of this kind will not necessarily fail the 'identical features' test, provided such features do not have the potential to impact the redemption rights of the instruments.

4.6.4.D No obligation to deliver cash or another financial asset

One of the conditions for classifying a financial instrument as equity under 4.6.2 above is that the instrument does not include any contractual obligation to deliver cash or another financial asset to another entity, or to exchange financial assets or financial liabilities with another entity under conditions that are potentially unfavourable to the entity.

Some entities, particularly ones with limited lives, are required by their constitution to distribute a minimum proportion of profits to shareholders or partners each year. Subject to the matters discussed at 4.2 above, such a requirement will normally result in the puttable instrument being considered a liability. It might be argued, firstly, that no obligation arises in these circumstances until profits are made, and secondly that such distributions only represent advance payments of the residual interest in the entity and so are consistent with equity classification. However, the IASB discussed this issue while developing the 2008 amendment and concluded that a contractual obligation existed, the measurement of which was uncertain. Nevertheless, the IASB declined to provide further guidance on this issue as they considered that it would have implications for other projects.

In May 2010 the Interpretations Committee considered a request to clarify whether puttable income trust units, that include contractual provisions to make distributions on a pro-rata basis, can be classified as equity. The submission to the Interpretations Committee argued that such pro-rata obligations should not prevent the instrument from being classified as equity, by analogy to the *Classification of Rights Issues* amendment to IAS 32 (October 2009). The Interpretations Committee decided not to propose any amendment to IAS 32 to deal with this issue, making it fairly clear in the process that they did not believe such an instrument would qualify to be classified as equity.

4.6.4.E Instruments that substantially fix or restrict the residual return to the holder of an instrument

A condition for classifying a financial instrument as equity under 4.6.2 or 4.6.3 above is that the issuing entity has no other financial instrument or contract that has:

- total cash flows based substantially on the profit or loss, the change in the recognised net assets or the change in the fair value of the recognised and unrecognised net assets of the entity; and
- the effect of substantially restricting or fixing the residual return.

IAS 32 notes that the following instruments, when entered into on normal commercial terms with unrelated parties, are unlikely to prevent instruments that otherwise meet the criteria in 4.6.2 or 4.6.3 above from being classified as equity:

- instruments with total cash flows substantially based on specific assets of the entity;
- instruments with total cash flows based on a percentage of revenue;
- contracts designed to reward individual employees for services rendered to the entity; and
- contracts requiring the payment of an insignificant percentage of profit for services rendered or goods provided. *[IAS 32.AG14J]*.

4.6.4.F Transactions entered into by an instrument holder other than as owner of the entity

IAS 32 observes that the holder of a financial instrument subject to one of the exceptions in 4.6.2 or 4.6.3 above may enter into transactions with the entity in a role other than that of an owner. For example, an instrument holder also may be an employee of the entity. IAS 32 requires that only the cash flows and the contractual terms and conditions of the instrument that relate to the instrument holder as an owner of the entity be considered when assessing whether the instrument should be classified as equity under conditions (a) to (e) in 4.6.2 above or conditions (a) to (c) in 4.6.3 above. *[IAS 32.AG14F]*.

An example might be a limited partnership that has limited and general partners. Some general partners may provide a guarantee to the entity and be remunerated for providing that guarantee. In such situations, the guarantee and the associated cash flows relate to the instrument holders in their role as guarantors and not in their roles as owners of the entity. Therefore, such a guarantee and the associated cash flows would not result in the general partners being considered subordinate to the limited partners, and would be disregarded when assessing whether the contractual terms of the limited partnership instruments and the general partnership instruments are identical. *[IAS 32.AG14G]*.

Another example might be a profit or loss sharing arrangement that allocates profit or loss to the instrument holders on the basis of services rendered or business generated during the current and previous years. Such arrangements are regarded as transactions with instrument holders in their role as non-owners and should not be considered when assessing the criteria in conditions (a) to (e) in 4.6.2 above or conditions (a) to (c) in 4.6.3 above. By contrast, profit or loss sharing arrangements, that allocate profit or loss to instrument holders based on the nominal amount of their instruments relative to others in the class, represent transactions with the instrument holders in their roles as owners and should be considered when assessing the criteria in conditions (a) to (e) in 4.6.2 above or conditions (a) to (c) in 4.6.3 above. *[IAS 32.AG14H]*.

IAS 32 notes that, in order for a transaction with an owner to be assessed as being undertaken in that person's capacity as a non-owner, the cash flows and contractual terms and conditions of the transaction must be similar to those of an equivalent transaction that might occur between a non-instrument holder and the issuing entity. *[IAS 32.AG14I]*.

4.6.5 Reclassification of puttable instruments and instruments imposing an obligation only on liquidation

As noted in 4.6.4.B above, IAS 32 requires the entity to continually reassess the classification of such an instrument. The entity classifies a financial instrument as an equity instrument from the date on which it has all the features and meets the conditions set out in 4.6.2 or 4.6.3 above, and reclassifies the instrument from the date on which it ceases to have all those features or meet all those conditions.

For example, if an entity redeems all its issued non-puttable instruments, any puttable instruments that remain outstanding and that have all of the features and meet all the conditions in 4.6.2 above, are reclassified as equity instruments from the date of redemption of the non-puttable instruments. *[IAS 32.16E]*.

Where an instrument, previously classified as an equity instrument, is reclassified as a financial liability, the financial liability is measured at fair value at the date of reclassification, with any difference between the carrying value of the equity instrument and the fair value of the financial liability at the date of reclassification being recognised in equity. *[IAS 32.16F(a)]*.

Where an instrument, previously classified as a financial liability, is reclassified as an equity instrument, the equity instrument is measured at the carrying value of the financial liability at the date of reclassification. *[IAS 32.16F(b)]*.

4.6.6 IFRIC 2

The issue that ultimately led to the publication of IFRIC 2 was the appropriate accounting treatment for the members' contributed capital of a co-operative entity, the members of which are entitled to ask for the return of their investment. However, the scope of IFRIC 2 is not confined to co-operative entities, and extends to any entity whose members may ask for a return of their capital. *[IFRIC 2.1-4]*.

IFRIC 2 states that the contractual right of the holder of a financial instrument to request redemption does not, in itself, require that financial instrument to be classified as a financial liability. Rather, the entity must consider all of the terms and conditions of the financial instrument in determining its classification as a financial liability or equity. Those terms and conditions include relevant local laws, regulations and the entity's governing charter in effect at the date of classification, but not expected future amendments to those laws, regulations or charter. *[IFRIC 2.5]*.

Accordingly, IFRIC 2 provides that an instrument, that would be classified as equity if the holder did not have the right to request redemption, should be classified as an equity instrument where:

- the entity has the unconditional right to refuse redemption;
- local law, regulation or the entity's governing charter imposes an unconditional prohibition on redemption; or
- the members' shares meet the criteria in 4.6.2 or 4.6.3 above for classification as equity. *[IFRIC 2.6-8]*.

IFRIC 2 distinguishes between those prohibitions on redemption in local law, regulation or the entity's governing charter that are 'unconditional' (i.e. they apply at any time) and those which prohibit redemption only when certain conditions – such as liquidity constraints – are met or not met. Prohibitions that apply only in certain circumstances are ignored and therefore would not result in equity classification. *[IFRIC 2.8]*. This is consistent with the fact that under IAS 32 the classification of an instrument as debt or equity is not influenced by considerations of liquidity (see 4.2 above).

In some cases, there may be a partial prohibition on redemption. For example, redemption may be prohibited where its effect would be to reduce the number of members' shares or the amount of paid-in capital below a certain minimum. In such cases, only the amount subject to a prohibition on redemption is treated as equity, unless:

- the entity has the unconditional right to refuse redemption as described above; or
- the members' shares meet the criteria in 4.6.2 or 4.6.3 above for classification as equity.

If the minimum number of members' shares or amount of paid-in capital changes, an appropriate transfer is made between financial liabilities and equity. *[IFRIC 2.9]*.

Any financial liability for the redemption of instruments not classified as equity is measured at fair value. In the case of members' shares with a redemption feature, the entity measures the fair value of the financial liability for redemption at no less than the maximum amount payable under the redemption provisions of its governing charter or applicable law, discounted from the first date that the amount could be required to be paid. *[IFRIC 2.10]*.

In accordance with the general provisions of IAS 32 regarding interest and dividends (see 8 below), distributions to holders of equity instruments are recognised directly in equity, net of any income tax benefits. Interest, dividends and other returns relating to financial instruments classified as financial liabilities are expenses, regardless of whether those amounts paid are legally characterised as dividends, interest or otherwise. *[IFRIC 2.11]*.

IFRIC 2 clarifies that, where members act as customers of the entity (for example, where it is a bank and members have current or deposit accounts or similar contracts with the bank), such accounts and contracts are financial liabilities of the entity. *[IFRIC 2.6]*.

4.7 Perpetual debt

'Perpetual debt' instruments are those that provide the holder with the contractual right to receive payments on account of interest at fixed dates extending into the indefinite future, either with no right to receive a return of principal or a right to a return of principal under terms that make it very unlikely or very far in the future. However, this does not mean that 'perpetual debt' is to be classified as equity, since the issue proceeds will typically represent the net present value of the liability for interest payments.

For example, an entity may issue a financial instrument requiring it to make annual payments in perpetuity equal to a stated interest rate of 8% applied to a stated par or principal amount of €1 million. Assuming 8% to be the market rate of interest for the instrument when issued, the issuer assumes a contractual obligation to make a stream of future interest payments having a fair value (present value) of €1 million. Thus perpetual debt gives rise to a financial liability of the issuer. *[IAS 32.AG6]*.

4.8 Differences of classification between consolidated and single entity financial statements

4.8.1 Consolidated financial statements

In consolidated financial statements, IAS 32 requires an entity to present non-controlling interests (i.e. the interests of other parties in the equity and income of its subsidiaries) within equity, in accordance with IAS 1 – *Presentation of Financial Statements* (see Chapter 3 at 3.1.5) and IFRS 10 – *Consolidated Financial Statements* (see Chapter 7 at 4 and Chapter 9 at 8). *[IAS 32.AG29]*.

When classifying a financial instrument (or a component of it) in consolidated financial statements, an entity must consider all the terms and conditions agreed between all members of the group and the holders of the instrument in determining whether the group as a whole has an obligation to deliver cash or another financial asset in respect of the instrument or to settle it in a manner that results in its classification as a financial liability. *[IAS 32.AG29]*.

For example, a subsidiary in a group may issue a financial instrument and a parent or other group entity may then agree additional terms directly with the holders of the instrument so as to guarantee some or all of the payments to be made under the instrument. The effect of this is that the subsidiary may have discretion over distributions or redemption, but the group as a whole does not. *[IAS 32.AG29]*.

Accordingly, the subsidiary may appropriately classify the instrument without regard to these additional terms in its individual financial statements. For the purposes of the consolidated financial statements, however, the effect of the other agreements between members of the group and the holders of the instrument is to create an obligation or settlement provision, so that the instrument (or the component of it that is subject to the obligation) is classified as a financial liability. *[IAS 32.AG29]*.

Thus it is quite possible for a financial instrument to be classified as an equity instrument in the financial statements of the issuing subsidiary but as a financial liability in the financial statements of the group.

4.8.2 Single entity financial statements

The converse of the discussion in 4.8.1 above is that it is not uncommon for instruments that are classified as equity in the consolidated financial statements to give rise to liabilities and embedded derivatives in the financial statements of individual members of the group.

This is because a group wishing to raise finance for its operations will generally do so through a group entity specialising in finance-raising, which will then on-lend the proceeds of the finance raised to the relevant operating subsidiaries. The terms of the intragroup on-lending transactions will often be such that finance which constitutes equity from the perspective of group as a whole may be a liability in the individual financial statements of the finance-raising entity itself.

For example, the finance-raising entity might issue an irredeemable instrument with a 'dividend blocker' clause (see 4.5.3.A above), under the terms of which that entity is not required to make any payments to the holder unless the ultimate parent entity of the group pays a dividend to ordinary shareholders. Absent any other terms requiring its classification, in whole or in part, as a liability under IAS 32, the instrument will be treated as equity in the consolidated financial statements, since payments under the instrument are contingent on an event within the control of the group (payment of a dividend by the parent entity). In the finance-raising entity's single entity financial statements, however, the instrument should be classified as a liability, because the subsidiary cannot control the dividend policy of its parent and could therefore be forced to make payments to the holder of the instrument as a consequence of its parent entity paying a dividend.

Another common example is that a group may issue a convertible bond which is actually structured as a series of transactions along the following lines:

- a finance-raising subsidiary issues a bond, giving the holder a right to receive fixed, non-discretionary interest payments, which converts into preference shares of that subsidiary; and
- at the time that this conversion occurs, the parent entity is required to acquire the preference shares of the subsidiary from the holder (i.e. the previous bondholder) in exchange for equity of the parent.

Absent any other terms requiring classification as a liability under IAS 32, the instrument will be treated as a compound instrument, consisting of a liability and an equity component (see 6 below) in the consolidated financial statements. The instrument as a whole might be classified as a liability in the subsidiaries financial statements, if (for example) the preference shares issued on conversion by the subsidiary have terms that require them to be classified as a liability by IAS 32. In that case, the subsidiary will have issued an instrument that the holder can exchange either for cash or for a debt instrument.

From the subsidiary's perspective, therefore, there is no equity component to the instrument and the overall instrument would be classified as a liability that, under the general rules of IAS 39, must be recorded at fair value on initial recognition, which will typically be lower than the proceeds received. This is because the pricing of the instrument as a whole considers the conversion option that the holder receives, so that the interest is typically paid at a rate below the rate that would apply to a liability without a conversion option. In other words, the holder of the instrument 'pays' for the conversion option through a reduced entitlement to interest.

The group accounts reflect the difference between the proceeds of issue and the fair value of the liability component as the equity component (see 6 below). In the financial statements of the issuing subsidiary, the most appropriate accounting treatment, in our view, would be to treat this difference as an equity contribution by the parent, reflecting the fact that the subsidiary can borrow on a reduced interest basis due to the conversion option issued by the parent. Moreover, in the period prior to conversion, the parent is required to account for its contingent forward contract to acquire the preference shares in the finance company.

4.9 Reclassification of instruments

It happens from time to time that the terms of a financial instrument are modified in such a way that an instrument that was an equity instrument at the original date of issue would be classified as a financial liability if issued at the date of modification, or *vice versa*. Alternatively, the terms of the instrument may remain unaltered, but external circumstances may change. For example,

- an instrument might have been issued subject to a contingent settlement provision (see 4.3 above) that, at the date of issue, was within the control of the issuer, but ceases to be so at a later date,
- an instrument might have been issued subject to a contingent settlement provision (see 4.3 above) that, at the date of issue, was not considered genuine, but becomes so at a later date, or
- an instrument might have been issued requiring interest payments to be made when contractually mandatory interest payments are made on another instrument issued by the entity, the 'linked' instrument (see 4.5.7 above), but this linked instrument is later repaid by the entity.

Such situations raise the question of whether such changes of terms or circumstances should lead to reclassification of the instruments affected in the financial statements and, if so, how the reclassification should be accounted for.

4.9.1 Change of terms

IAS 32 gives no guidance as to whether reclassification is required, permitted or prohibited. The requirement of IAS 32 paragraph 15 that an instrument be classified 'on initial recognition' (see 4 above) could be read as implying that classification occurs only on initial recognition and is not subsequently revisited.

However, we do not consider this an appropriate analysis. A change in the terms of an instrument is equivalent to the issue of a new instrument in settlement of the original instrument. Such an exchange transaction would be accounted for by derecognising the settled instrument and recognising (and classifying as a financial liability or equity) the new replacement instrument. This analysis has been confirmed by an agenda decision of the Interpretations Committee (see 4.9.1.A below). In our view, it would be inappropriate to apply a different accounting treatment to a change in the terms of the original instrument which has the same economic result.

4.9.1.A Equity instrument to financial liability

At its meeting in November 2006, the Interpretations Committee considered a situation in which an amendment to the contractual terms of an equity instrument resulted in the instrument being classified as a financial liability. Two issues were discussed:

- the measurement of the financial liability at the date of the amendment to the terms; and
- the treatment of any difference between the carrying amount of the previously recognised equity instrument and the amount of the financial liability recognised.

The Interpretations Committee decided not to add this issue to its agenda because, in its view, the accounting treatment is clear. The financial liability is initially recognised at fair value under the general provisions of IAS 39 (see Chapter 48 at 3). Any difference between the carrying amount of the liability and that of the previously recognised equity instrument is recognised is equity in accordance with the general principle of IAS 32 (see 8 below) that no gain or loss is recognised in profit or loss on the purchase, sale, issue or cancellation of an entity's own equity instruments.[18]

4.9.1.B Financial liability to equity instrument

In the converse situation where the terms of a financial liability are changed such that the instrument then meets the definition of an equity instrument, we believe, as above, that the instrument should be reclassified to equity. That situation is analogous to a debt-for-equity swap as discussed at 7 below and, therefore, should be accounted for in accordance with IFRIC 19, where that interpretation applies. The most likely situation in which IFRIC 19 would not apply would be in a transaction with shareholders in their capacity as shareholders, as discussed at 7.3 below.

4.9.2 Change of circumstances

The nature and risk profile of a financial instrument may change as a result of a change in circumstances. Such a change may occur simply as the result of the passage of time. For example, in 2015 an entity might issue a bond mandatorily convertible at the end of 2018. The conversion terms are that the holder will receive a number of the issuer's equity shares, being the lower of 100 shares or a number of shares determined according to a formula based on the share price at 31 December 2015.

At the date of issue, this instrument is a financial liability since it involves an obligation to deliver a variable number of equity instruments. At 31 December 2015, however, the number of shares to be delivered on conversion can be determined and becomes fixed. Accordingly, if considered as at 31 December 2015 and later, the instrument is an equity instrument (absent any other terms requiring its continued classification as financial liability).

In our view, the liability component of the bond representing the obligation to deliver a variable number of equity instruments on 31 December 2018 expires on 31 December 2015. This liability component must therefore be derecognised (see Chapter 51 at 6), to be replaced with an equity component (see the discussion at 7 below of the appropriate accounting treatment in such circumstances).

Changes of circumstances for reasons other than the passage of time are more challenging. For example, an entity might issue a convertible bond denominated in its functional currency at that time. Such a bond would have an equity component (see 6 below). Subsequently, the entity's functional currency changes but the bond remains outstanding, now denominated in a currency other than the entity's functional currency. If a bond with these terms were issued after the change in functional currency, it would be classified in its entirety as a financial liability, since the principal of the bond would not be a 'fixed' amount by reference to the entity's functional currency (see 5.2.3 below). This raises the question of whether the equity component of the bond should be reclassified as a financial liability on the change in functional currency.

In our view, there are arguments both for and against reclassification. As the arguments for reclassification are to some extent a rebuttal of those against reclassification, we discuss the latter first.

4.9.2.A Arguments against reclassification

The principal arguments against reclassification are:

(a) The requirement of paragraph 15 of IAS 32 to classify an instrument as a financial liability or equity 'on initial recognition' (see 4 above) could be read as implying that such classification occurs only on initial recognition and is not subsequently revisited.

(b) Paragraphs IG35 and IG36 of the implementation guidance to IFRS 1 – *First-time Adoption of International Financial Reporting Standards* – require a compound instrument to be analysed into its components, based on the substance of the contractual arrangement, as at the date on which the instrument first satisfied the recognition criteria in IAS 32. Changes to the terms of the instrument after that date are taken into account on first-time adoption, but changes in circumstances are not.

    This could be construed as establishing a more general principle that changes in the terms of instruments should be accounted for but changes in circumstances should not.

(c) IFRIC 9 – *Reassessment of Embedded Derivatives* (see Chapter 44 at 7.1) clarifies that the assessment required by IAS 39 of whether or not an embedded derivative is required to be separated from its host contract is undertaken when the entity first becomes party to the contract, and is not revisited in the light of any subsequently changing circumstances. IFRIC 9 gives a change in functional currency as a specific example of a change in circumstance that does not lead to a reassessment.

(d) IFRIC 2 and the provisions of IAS 32 requiring certain types of puttable and redeemable instrument to be classified as equity (see 4.6 above) each require accounting recognition to be given to some changes in the classification of a financial instrument as the result of changing circumstances. This implies that, absent such specific guidance, the 'default' position would be that there should be no accounting consequences, an inference reinforced by the requirement that the provisions of IAS 32 requiring certain types of puttable and redeemable instrument to be classified as equity must not be applied by analogy to other transactions.

4.9.2.B Arguments for reclassification

The principal arguments in favour of reclassification are:

(a) The definitions of financial liability and equity both use the present tense, implying that the definitions are to be applied at each reporting date, absent any more specific provision against doing so.

    This is consistent with our view that some transactions falling within the scope of IFRS 2 – *Share-based Payment* – should be reclassified from equity-settled to cash-settled and *vice versa* in the light of changing circumstances (see Chapter 32 at 10.2.3). However, it could be argued that such an analogy is inappropriate given the significant differences between the definitions of equity and financial liability in IAS 32 and those of equity-settled and cash-settled share-based payment transaction in IFRS 2 (see 5.1.1 below).

(b) The provisions of IFRS 1 referred to in (b) under 4.9.2.A above are contained in implementation guidance, which is not part of the standard. Moreover, it refers only to compound financial instruments, and appears to be implicitly addressing changes in market interest rates that might alter the arithmetical split of the instrument into its financial liability and equity components (see 6 below), rather than more general changes in circumstances.

(c) The fact that IFRIC 9 (see (c) under 4.9.2.A above) was issued after IFRS 1, and again addresses a specific issue, indicates that a general prohibition on reassessment should not be inferred from IFRS 1. Had the Interpretations Committee wished to clarify that this was the case, they could easily have done so in IFRIC 9, which, moreover, is stated as being an interpretation of IAS 39, IFRS 1 and IFRS 3 – *Business Combinations* – not IAS 32.

However, it is equally difficult to argue that there is an implied 'default' requirement for reclassification, given the specific requirement for reclassification of certain puttable and redeemable instruments on a change in circumstances referred to in (d) in 4.9.2.A above.

What emerges from the analysis above is a lack of definitive general guidance as to whether reclassification of an instrument is permitted, required or prohibited. Accordingly, we believe that in some circumstances, such as a change in the entity's functional currency, the entity may choose, as a matter of accounting policy, either to reclassify or not to reclassify an instrument following that change of circumstances which, had it occurred before initial recognition of the instrument, would have changed its classification. The policy adopted should, in our view, be followed consistently in respect of all changes of circumstances of a similar nature.

However, some changes in circumstances can be more fundamental to the nature of the contract. For example the change in circumstances could lead to the instruments delivered under a contract ceasing to be equity instruments of the reporting entity. This situation could arise where a parent had entered into a derivative involving delivery of the equity instruments of a subsidiary and subsequently loses control of that subsidiary. Here the former subsidiary's equity instruments would now represent financial assets rather than non-controlling interests (equity) of the group. In these circumstances, it may be more difficult to argue that not reclassifying the derivative contract is appropriate.

5 CONTRACTS SETTLED BY DELIVERY OF THE ENTITY'S OWN EQUITY INSTRUMENTS

This Section deals with contracts, other than those within the scope of IFRS 2 (see Chapter 32), settled in equity instruments issued by the settler. Throughout the discussion in Section 5, 'equity instrument(s)' excludes certain puttable and redeemable instruments classified as equity under the exceptions discussed at 4.6.2 and 4.6.3 above (any contract involving the receipt or delivery of such instruments is a financial asset or liability – see 4.1 above).

In order for an instrument to be classified as an equity instrument under IAS 32, it is not sufficient that it involves the reporting entity delivering or receiving its own equity (as opposed to cash or another financial asset). The number of equity instruments delivered, and the consideration for them, must be fixed – the so called 'fixed for fixed' requirement. Contracts that will be settled other than by delivery of a fixed number of shares for a fixed amount of cash do not generally meet the definition of equity. The IASB considered that to treat any transaction settled in the entity's own shares as an equity instrument would not deal adequately with transactions in which an entity is using its own shares as 'currency' – for example, where it has an obligation to pay a fixed or determinable amount that is settled in a variable number of its own shares. *[IAS 32.BC21]*. In such transactions the counterparty bears no share price risk, and is therefore not in the same position as a 'true' equity shareholder.

Where such a contract is not classified as an equity instrument by IAS 32, it will be accounted for in accordance with the general provisions of IAS 39 or, where applicable, IFRS 9 as either a financial liability or a derivative.

Broadly speaking:

- a non-derivative contract involving the issue of a fixed number of own equity instruments is an equity instrument (see 5.1 below);
- a non-derivative contract involving the issue of a variable number of own equity instruments is a financial liability (see 5.2.1 below);
- a derivative contract involving the sale or purchase of a fixed number of own equity instruments for a fixed amount of cash or other financial assets is an equity instrument (see 5.1 below);
- a derivative contract for the purchase by an entity of its own equity instruments, even if for a fixed amount of cash or other financial assets (and therefore an equity instrument) may give rise to a financial liability in respect of the cash or other financial assets to be paid. However, the initial recognition of the liability results in a reduction in equity and not in an expense (see 5.3 below). In other words, whilst there is a liability to pay cash under the contract, the contract itself is an equity instrument (and is therefore not subject to periodic remeasurement to fair value);
- a derivative contract involving the delivery or receipt of:
  - a fixed number of own equity instruments for a variable amount of cash or other financial assets;
  - a variable number of own equity instruments for a variable amount of cash or other financial assets; or
  - an amount of cash or own equity instruments with a fair value equivalent to the difference between a fixed number of own equity instruments and a fixed amount of cash or other financial assets (i.e. a net-settled derivative contract),

  is a financial asset or financial liability (see 5.2 below); and
- a derivative financial instrument with settlement options is a financial asset or liability, unless all possible settlement options would result in classification as equity (see 5.2.8 below).

There are some difficulties of interpretation surrounding the treatment of certain contracts to issue equity (see 5.4 below).

In undertaking the analysis required by IAS 32, it is sometimes helpful, where the detailed guidance in the standard is not entirely clear, to consider whether the instrument or contract under discussion exposes the holder or the issuer to the risk of movements in the fair value of the issuer's equity. If the holder is at risk to the same degree as equity investors in the entity, it is likely that the instrument or contract should be classified as equity. If, however, the entity bears the risk of movements in the fair value of the entity's equity, or the holder bears some risk, but less than that borne by equity investors in the entity, it is likely that the contract should be classified, at least in part, as a liability.

5.1 Contracts accounted for as equity instruments

A contract that will be settled by the entity delivering or receiving a fixed number of its own equity instruments in exchange for a fixed amount of cash (see 5 above) or another financial asset is an equity instrument, although a liability may be recorded for any cash payable, by the entity on settlement of the contract. An example would be an issued share option that gives the counterparty a right to buy a fixed number of the entity's shares for a fixed price or for a fixed stated principal amount of a bond (see 6.3.2.A below). *[IAS 32.22]*.

The fair value of such a contract may change due to variations in market interest rates and the share price. However, provided that such changes in fair value do not affect the amount of cash or other financial assets to be paid or received, or the number of equity instruments to be received or delivered, on settlement of the contract, the contract is an equity instrument and accounted for as such. *[IAS 32.22]*.

Any consideration received (such as the premium received for a written option or warrant on the entity's own shares) is added directly to equity. Any consideration paid (such as the premium paid for a purchased option) is deducted directly from equity. Changes in the fair value of an equity instrument are not recognised in financial statements. *[IAS 32.22, AG27(a)]*. This is consistent with the treatment of equity under the *Conceptual Framework* (and as defined in IAS 32 – see 3 above) as a residual after deducting total liabilities from total assets rather than an item 'in its own right'.

IAS 32 requires some types of puttable instruments (see 4.6.2 above) and instruments that impose an obligation to deliver a *pro rata* share of net assets only on liquidation (see 4.6.3 above) to be treated as equity instruments. However, a contract that is required to be settled by the entity receiving or delivering either of these types of equity instrument is a financial asset or financial liability, even when it involves the exchange of a fixed amount of cash or other financial assets for a fixed number of such instruments. *[IAS 32.22A, AG13]*.

5.1.1 Comparison with IFRS 2 – Share-based Payment

The approach in IAS 32 differs from that in IFRS 2. IFRS 2 essentially treats any transaction that falls within its scope and can be settled only in shares (or other equity instruments) as an equity instrument, regardless of whether the number of shares to be delivered is fixed or variable (see Chapter 32 at 1.4.1). The two standards also differ as regards to:

- the classification of financial instruments that can be settled at the issuer's option in either equity instruments or cash (or other financial assets). Broadly, IFRS 2 requires the classification to be based on the likely outcome, whereas IAS 32 focuses on the strict legal obligations imposed by the contract; and
- the definition of equity instrument. IFRS 2 refers to the exchange of a 'fixed or determinable' amount of cash, whereas IAS 32 refers to the exchange of a 'fixed' amount of cash. This means that written options to issue own equity with a foreign currency strike price are typically equity instruments under IFRS 2, but financial assets or liabilities under IAS 32, subject to the limited exception for short-term rights issues (see 5.2.3.A below).

The IASB offers some (pragmatic rather than conceptual) explanation for these differences in the Basis for Conclusions to IFRS 2. First, it is argued that to apply IAS 32 to share option plans would mean that a variable share option plan (i.e. one where the number of shares varied according to performance) would give rise to more volatile (and typically greater) cost than a fixed plan (i.e. one where the number of shares to be awarded is fixed from the start), even if the same number of shares was ultimately delivered under each plan, which would have 'undesirable consequences'. *[IFRS 2.BC109]*. This serves only to beg the question of why it is not equally 'undesirable' for the same result to arise in accounting for share-settled contracts within the scope of IAS 32 rather than IFRS 2. Second, it is noted that this is just one of several inconsistencies between IFRS 2 and IAS 32 which will be addressed in the round as part of the IASB's review of accounting for debt and equity. *[IFRS 2.BC110]*. As discussed further at 12 below, this review remains somewhat more distant than was probably envisaged when IFRS 2 was issued in 2004.

5.1.2 *Number of equity instruments issued adjusted for capital restructuring or other event*

Entities, particularly larger listed companies, routinely restructure their equity capital. This may take many forms, including:

- structural changes in the issuer's ordinary shares (such as a share split, a share consolidation or a reclassification of the outstanding ordinary shares of the issuer);
- a repurchase of shares;
- a distribution of reserves or premiums, by way of extraordinary dividend;
- a payment of a dividend, or extraordinary dividend, in shares; or
- a bonus share or rights issue to existing shareholders.

Accordingly, contracts for the purchase or delivery of an entity's own equity often provide that the number of shares specified in the contract is modified in the event of such a restructuring. This provides protection to both the holder of the contract and to existing shareholders, by ensuring that their relative rights remain the same before and after the restructuring. For example, an entity with shares with a nominal (par) value of €1 might enter into an agreement that requires it to issue '100 shares'. If, before execution of that agreement, the entity has split each €1 share into ten €0.10 shares, it must issue 1,000, not 100, shares in order to give effect to the intention of the contract.

Such adjustment formulae are most commonly seen in the terms of convertible instruments (see 6 below for convertible instrument classification), so that the number of shares into which the bonds eventually convert will take account of any capital restructuring between issue and conversion of the bond, with the broad intention of putting the holders of the bond in the same position with respect to other equity holders before and after the restructuring. In addition, the terms of many convertible instruments provide for similar adjustment upon the occurrence of other actions or events which would affect the position of the convertible bondholders relative to other equity holders. Such actions or events may include, for example:

- the payment of ordinary dividends;
- an issue of equity at less than current market value;
- the repurchase of equity at more than current market value;
- the issue of further convertible securities at less than fair market value; or
- the acquisition of assets in exchange for equity at more than fair market value.

This raises the question of whether a contract with any such terms can be classified as equity under IAS 32, since the number of shares ultimately issued on conversion is not fixed at the outset, but may vary depending on whether a restructuring or other event occurs before conversion. In our view, an adjustment to the number of equity instruments issued in such circumstances should not be considered to result in the issue of a variable number of shares, where its purpose is to ensure that the bondholder's equity interest is not diluted or augmented. In other words, if the adjustment attempts to put the holders of the instruments into the same economic position relative to ordinary shareholders after the restructuring as they were in before the restructuring, then the fixed for fixed criterion is still met. We consider that the potential dilution or augmentation in the bondholder's equity interest which is to be adjusted for should be determined in comparison to the effect of the event on the other equity holders in aggregate. Thus, if shares are issued to new shareholders at a discount, the dilution suffered by the bondholders should be calculated by reference to the total number of shares in existence following the new issue.

The effect of such an adjustment is that the risks and rewards of the bondholder are more closely aligned to those of a holder of ordinary shares. IAS 32 generally treats contracts involving a variable number of equity instruments as a financial liability because the effect of the variability is that the counterparty is not exposed to any movement in the fair value of the equity instruments between the inception and execution of the contract. In this case, however, the variability is introduced so as to ensure that the counterparty remains exposed to any movement in the fair value of the equity instruments, and maintains the same interest in the equity relative to other shareholders.

The same question arises in circumstances where a convertible bond is convertible into a fixed percentage of equity. This is discussed at 6.6.6 below.

However not all convertible securities with adjustable conversion ratios can be classified as equity. Where a convertible security has a contractual feature for the conversion ratio to be adjusted down to the lower price of any later issue in the underlying shares, the instrument will fail equity classification. The modification feature is not fixed for fixed and therefore the conversion option is a financial liability. *[IAS 32.11(b)(ii)]*. As such it is an embedded derivative of a debt host rather than an equity component. The entity's ability to control the non-fixed for fixed settlement is not relevant to the assessment as a derivative instrument that gives either party the choice over settlement is a financial asset or liability unless all of the settlement alternatives would result in it being an equity instrument. *[IAS 32.26]*. The conversion option will therefore be treated as a derivative liability.

The Interpretations Committee considered a number of 'fixed for fixed' issues raised by constituents at its November 2009 meeting. However, the Interpretations Committee concluded that the Board's project *Financial Instruments with Characteristics of Equity* was expected to address issues relating to the fixed for fixed condition, and that the Interpretations Committee would therefore not add this to its agenda. As discussed further at 12 below, work on this project was suspended between October 2010 and October 2014, but has now restarted.

5.1.3 Stepped up exercise price

Another type of adjustment which is commonly found is where an entity issues subscription shares that have a stepped exercise price, which is fixed at inception and increases with the passage of time. Such subscription shares are typically issued as bonus shares on a *pro rata* basis to existing shareholders and give the holder the right (but not the obligation) to subscribe for a certain number of ordinary shares, at a certain price and at a certain time in the future. Our view is that subscription shares that have a stepped exercise price meet the 'fixed for fixed' condition only if the exercise prices are fixed at inception and for the entire term of the instrument, such that at any point in time the exercise price is pre-determined at the issuance of the subscription shares. If the exercise price per share is linked to an index of any kind, the 'fixed for fixed' condition is not met and the contract to issue the shares would not be classified as an equity instrument.

5.1.4 Exchange of fixed amounts of equity (equity for equity)

As discussed above, IAS 32 requires a contract settled in own equity to be classified as equity if, *inter alia*, it involves the exchange of a fixed amount of cash (or other financial assets) for a fixed amount of equity. This begs the question of how to classify a contract that provides for the exchange of a fixed amount of one class of the entity's equity for a fixed amount of another class. Examples might be:

- a warrant allowing the holder of a preference share classified as equity (see 4.5 above) to exchange it for an ordinary equity share; or
- in consolidated financial statements, an option for a shareholder of a partly-owned subsidiary (classified within equity in the consolidated financial statements) to exchange a fixed number of shares in the subsidiary for a fixed number of shares in the parent.

One view might be that, as such a contract does not fall within the definition of an 'equity instrument' in accordance with IAS 32 it must therefore be accounted for as a derivative. The contrary view would be that the contract is so clearly an equity instrument that it should be accounted for as such. Those who hold this view would argue that the absence of any reference to such 'fixed equity for fixed equity' contracts in IAS 32 does not reflect a conscious decision by the IASB, but rather indicates that the IASB never considered such contracts at all.

A third view might be that the analysis may depend upon the specific terms of the equity instruments. For example, if the equity instrument being exchanged has debt-like features (e.g. it pays regular, but discretionary, coupons), and is denominated in the same currency as the entity's functional currency, the contract would be classified as equity, but if it were denominated in a different currency, the contact would, for the reasons discussed at 5.2.2 below, be classified as a derivative.

5.2 Contracts accounted for as financial assets or financial liabilities

5.2.1 Variable number of equity instruments

An entity may have a contractual right or obligation to receive or deliver a number of its own shares or other equity instruments that varies so that the fair value of the entity's own equity instruments to be received or delivered equals the amount of the contractual right or obligation.

The right or obligation may be for:

- a fixed amount – e.g. as many shares as are worth £100; or
- an amount that fluctuates in part or in full in response to changes in a variable other than the market price of the entity's own equity instruments, such as movements in interest rates, commodity prices, or the price of a financial instrument – e.g. as many shares as are worth:
  - 100 ounces of gold;
  - £100 plus interest at LIBOR plus 200 basis points;
  - 100 government bonds; or
  - 100 shares in a particular entity.

Such a contract is a financial asset or liability. Even though the contract must, or may, be settled through receipt or delivery of the entity's own equity instruments, the number of own equity instruments required to settle the contract will vary. The contract will therefore not fulfil the requirements of an equity instrument, and is therefore a financial asset or financial liability. *[IAS 32.21, AG27(d)]*.

5.2.2 Fixed number of equity instruments for variable consideration

A contract that will be settled by the entity delivering or receiving a fixed number of its own equity instruments in exchange for a variable amount of cash or another financial asset is a financial asset or financial liability. An example is a contract for the entity to deliver 100 of its own equity instruments in return for an amount of cash calculated to equal the value of 100 ounces of gold, *[IAS 32.24]*, or 100 specified government bonds. As discussed at 5.2.3 below, it would also include a contract for the entity to deliver 100 of its own equity instruments in return for a fixed amount of cash denominated in a currency other than its own functional currency.

5.2.3 Fixed amount of cash (or other financial assets) denominated in a currency other than the entity's functional currency

Some contracts require an entity to issue a fixed number of equity instruments in exchange for a fixed amount of cash denominated in a currency other than the entity's functional currency. Such contracts raise a problem of interpretation illustrated by the example in paragraph 24 of IAS 32 (referred to in 5.2.1 above) of a contract being a financial asset or financial liability where the reporting entity is required 'to deliver 100 of its own equity instruments in return for an amount of cash calculated to equal the value of 100 ounces of gold'. If one substitutes '100 US dollars' for '100 ounces of gold', the latent problem becomes apparent.

Suppose a UK entity (with the pound sterling as its functional currency) issues a £100 bond convertible into a fixed number of its equity shares. As discussed in more detail at 6 below, IAS 32 requires this to be accounted for by splitting it into a liability component (the obligation to pay interest and repay principal) and an equity component (the holder's right to convert into equity). In this case the equity component is the right to convert the fixed stated £100 principal of the bond (see 6.3.2.A below) into a fixed number of shares.

Suppose instead, however, that the UK entity (with the pound sterling as its functional currency) issues a 100 US dollar bond convertible into a fixed number of its shares. The conversion feature effectively gives the bondholder the right to acquire a fixed number of shares for a fixed stated principal (see 6.3.2.A below) of $100 – is this a 'fixed amount' of cash, or is it to be regarded as being just as variable, in terms of its conversion into the functional currency of the pound sterling, as 100 ounces of gold?

If the conclusion is that $100 is a fixed amount of cash, the conversion right is accounted for as an equity component of the bond – in other words a value is assigned to it on initial recognition and it is not subsequently remeasured (see 6.2.1 below). If, on the other hand, the conclusion is that $100 is not a fixed amount of cash, then the conversion right (as an embedded derivative not regarded by IAS 39 as closely related to the host contract – see Chapter 44 at 4) is accounted for as a separate derivative financial liability, introducing potentially significant volatility into the financial statements.

There is no obvious answer to this. A contention that the $100 is a 'fixed amount' of cash is hard to reconcile with the fact that a contract to issue shares for 'as many pounds sterling as are worth $100' would clearly involve the issue of a fixed number of shares for a variable amount of cash and would therefore not be an equity instrument.

The Interpretations Committee considered this issue at its meeting in April 2005. The Committee noted that although this matter was not directly addressed in IAS 32, it was clear that, when the question is considered in conjunction with guidance in other Standards, particularly IAS 39, any obligation denominated in a foreign currency represents a variable amount of cash. Consequently, the Committee concluded that a contract settled by an entity delivering a fixed number of its own equity instruments in exchange for a fixed amount of foreign currency should be classified as a liability.[19]

5.2.3.A Rights issues with a price fixed in a currency other than the entity's functional currency

In July 2009, as a result of a recommendation from the Interpretations Committee, the IASB reconsidered this matter in the specific context of rights issues (options to purchase additional shares at a fixed price) where the price is denominated in a currency other than the entity's functional currency. The IASB was advised that the Interpretations Committee's conclusion was being applied to rights issues, with the result that the rights were being accounted for as derivative liabilities with changes in fair value being recognised in profit or loss. HSBC explained that such accounting would result in the recognition of a loss of $4.7 billion in the first quarter of 2009.

Extract 45.2: HSBC Holdings plc (2009)

Interim Management Statement Q1 2009 [extract]
Accounting impact of HSBC's Rights Issue [extract]

On 2 March 2009, HSBC announced a 5 for 12 Rights Issue of 5,060 million new ordinary shares at 254 pence per share, which was authorised by the shareholders in a general meeting on 19 March 2009. The offer period commenced on 20 March 2009, and closed for acceptance on 3 April 2009. Under IFRSs, the offer of rights is treated as a derivative because substantially all of the issue was denominated in currencies other than the Company's functional currency of US dollars, and accordingly HSBC was not able to demonstrate that it was issuing a fixed number of shares for a fixed amount of US dollars, which is the criterion under IFRSs for HSBC to account for the offer of rights in shareholders' equity. The derivative liability was measured at inception of the offer as the difference between the share price at that date and the rights price, with a corresponding debit to shareholders' equity. The revaluation of this derivative liability over the offer period, arising from an increase in the share price, has resulted in the recognition of a loss in the income statement of US$4.7 billion. The derivative liability expired on acceptance of the offer, and the closing balance was credited to shareholders' equity. Accordingly, there is no overall impact on the Group's shareholders' equity, capital position or distributable reserves.

Consequently, in October 2009, the IASB made a limited amendment to IAS 32 so as to require a rights issue granted *pro rata* to an entity's existing shareholders for a fixed amount of cash to be classified as equity, regardless of the currency in which the exercise price is denominated. *[IAS 32.11]*.

This amendment does not apply to other instruments that grant the holder the right to purchase the entity's own equity instruments, such as the conversion feature in a convertible bond. It also does not apply to long-dated foreign currency rights issues, which are therefore classified as financial liabilities if the strike price is denominated in a foreign currency. The reason for the restricted scope of the amendment is that the IASB countenanced an exception to the 'fixed for fixed' concept in IAS 32 for short-dated rights issues only because the rights are distributed *pro rata* to existing shareholders, and can therefore be seen as a transaction with owners in their capacity as such. *[IAS 32BC4I]*. The IASB does not consider long-dated transactions as primarily transactions with owners in their capacity as owners. *[IAS 32.BC4K]*.

5.2.4 Instrument with equity settlement alternative of significantly higher value than cash settlement alternative

A financial instrument is also a financial liability if it provides that on settlement the entity will deliver either:

(a) cash or another financial asset; or

(b) a number of its own shares whose value is determined to exceed substantially the value of the cash or other financial asset.

IAS 32 explains that, although the entity does not have an explicit contractual obligation to deliver cash or another financial asset, the value of the share settlement alternative is such that the entity will settle in cash. In any event, the holder has in substance been guaranteed receipt of an amount that is at least equal to the cash settlement option. *[IAS 32.20]*.

5.2.5 Fixed number of equity instruments with variable value

A contract is a financial asset or financial liability if it is to be settled in a fixed number of shares, the value of which will be varied (e.g. by modification of the rights attaching to them) so as to be equal to a fixed amount or an amount based on changes in an underlying variable. *[IAS 32.AG27(d)]*.

5.2.6 Fixed amount of cash determined by reference to share price

An entity might enter into an option or forward contract to sell a fixed number of equity shares for a fixed price, where the price is determined by reference to the share price. For example, it might contract to sell 100 shares for £10 each if the share price is between £0 and £10, and for £15 each if the price is higher than £10. Considered as a whole, the contract provides for the exchange of a fixed number of equity instruments for a variable amount of cash, and is therefore a derivative financial liability.

5.2.7 Net-settled contracts over own equity

The value of a contract over an entity's own equity instruments at the date of settlement is the difference between the value of the fixed number of equity instruments to be delivered by one party and the fixed amount of cash (or other financial assets) to be delivered by the other party. If such a contract allows for net settlement, it can then be settled by a transfer (of cash, other financial assets, or the entity's own equity) of a fair value equal to this difference. It is inherent in the general definition of an equity instrument in IAS 32 that a contract settled by a single net payment (generally referred to as net cash-settled or net equity-settled as the case may be) is a financial asset or financial liability and not an equity instrument. This is notwithstanding the fact that an economically equivalent contract settled gross (i.e. by physical delivery of the equity instruments in exchange for cash or other financial assets) would be treated as an equity instrument.

5.2.8 Derivative financial instruments with settlement options

A derivative financial instrument may have settlement options, whereby it gives one or other party a choice over how it is settled (e.g. the issuer or the holder can choose settlement net in cash, net in shares, or by exchanging shares for cash). A derivative that gives one party a choice of settlement options is required to be treated as a financial asset or a financial liability, unless all possible settlement alternatives would result in it being an equity instrument. *[IAS 32.26]*. An example of a derivative financial instrument with a settlement option that is a financial liability is a share option that the issuer can decide to settle net in cash or by exchanging its own shares for cash. *[IAS 32.27]*.

These provisions will apply mostly to contracts involving the sale or purchase by an entity of its own equity instruments. However, they will also be relevant to those contracts to buy or sell a non-financial item in exchange for the entity's own equity instruments that are within the scope of IAS 32 (rather than IFRS 2) because they can be settled either by delivery of the non-financial item or net in cash or another financial instrument. Such contracts are financial assets or financial liabilities and not equity instruments. *[IAS 32.27]*.

5.3 Liabilities arising from gross-settled contracts for the purchase of the entity's own equity instruments

The following discussion in 5.3 relates only to contracts that must be settled by the counterparty delivering equity instruments (other than those classified as such under the exceptions discussed at 4.6 above) and the entity paying cash (gross-settled contracts). Contracts which can be settled net (i.e. by payment of the difference between the fair value, at the time of settlement, of the equity instruments and that of the consideration given) are accounted for as financial assets or financial liabilities *[IAS 32.AG27(c)]* (see 5.2.8 above and 11 below).

IAS 32 requires some types of puttable instruments (see 4.6.2 above) and instruments that impose an obligation to deliver a *pro rata* share of net assets only on liquidation (see 4.6.3 above) to be treated as equity instruments. However, a contract that is required to be settled by the entity receiving or delivering either of these types of equity instrument is a financial asset or financial liability, even when it involves the exchange of a fixed amount of cash or other financial assets for a fixed number of such instruments. *[IAS 32.22A, AG27]*.

Entering into a gross-settled contract for the purchase of own equity instruments gives rise to a financial liability in respect of the obligation to pay the purchase or redemption price, *[IAS 32.23, AG27(a)-(b)]*, (but resulting, on initial recognition, in a reduction of equity rather than an expense). This treatment is intended to reflect the idea that a forward contract or written option to repurchase an equity share gives rise to a liability similar to that contained within a redeemable share (see 4.5 above). *[IAS 32.BC12]*.

This is the case even if:

- the contract is an equity instrument;
- the contract is a written put option (i.e. a contract that gives the counterparty the right to require the entity to buy its own shares) rather than a forward contract (i.e. a firm commitment by the entity to purchase its own shares); or
- the number of shares subject to the contract is not fixed. *[IAS 32.23, AG27(a)-(b)]*.

The final bullet point above might refer to a put option written by the entity whereby the counterparty can require the entity to purchase between 1,000 and 5,000 of its own equity shares at €2 per share. In other words, the entity cannot avoid recognising a liability for the contract on the argument that it does not know exactly how many of its own shares it will be compelled to purchase.

When such a liability first arises it must be recognised, in accordance with IAS 39, at its fair value, i.e. the net present value of the redemption amount. Subsequently, the financial liability is measured in accordance with IAS 39 or, where applicable, IFRS 9 (see Chapter 48). *[IAS 32.23, AG27(b)]*. IAS 32 offers no guidance as to how this is to be calculated when, as might be the case with respect to a written put option such as that described in the previous paragraph, the number of shares to be purchased and/or the date of purchase is not known.

In our view, it would be consistent with the requirement of IFRS 13 that liabilities with a demand feature such as a demand bank deposit should be measured at the amount payable on demand, *[IFRS 13.47]*, (see Chapter 14 at 11.5) to adopt a 'worst case' approach. In other words, it should be assumed that the purchase will take place on the earliest possible date for the maximum number of shares. This is also consistent with IAS 32's emphasis, in the general discussion of the differences between liabilities and equity instruments, on a liability arising except to the extent that an entity has an 'unconditional' right to avoid delivering cash or other financial assets (see 4.2 above).

The treatment proposed in the previous paragraph would lead to a different accounting treatment for written 'American' put options (i.e. those that can be exercised at any time during a period ending on a future date) and written 'European' put options (i.e. those that can be exercised only at a given future date). In the case of an American option, a liability would be recorded immediately for the full potential liability. In the case of a European option, a liability would be recorded for the net present value of the full potential liability, on which interest would be accrued until the date of potential exercise. If this interpretation is correct, it has the effect that:

- a gross-settled written American put option that is an equity instrument has no effect on profit or loss (because the full amount payable on settlement would be charged to equity on inception of the contract); but
- a gross-settled European put option that is an equity instrument does affect profit or loss (because the net present value of the amount payable on settlement would be charged to equity on inception of the contract and accrued to the full settlement amount through profit or loss).

If the contract expires without delivery of the shares, the carrying amount of the financial liability is reclassified to equity. This has the rather curious effect that a share purchase contract that expires unexercised (and therefore has no impact on the entity's net assets, other than the receipt or payment of the option premium) can nevertheless give rise to a loss to the extent that interest has been recognised on the liability between initial recognition and its transfer to equity (see Example 45.20 at 11.3.2 below).

5.3.1 Contracts to purchase own equity during 'closed' or 'prohibited' periods

Financial markets often impose restrictions on an entity trading in its own listed securities for a given period (sometimes referred to as a 'closed' or 'prohibited' period) in the run-up to the announcement of its financial results for a period. However, an entity may well wish to continue to purchase its own listed equity throughout the closed period, for example as part of an ongoing share-buyback programme.

One method of achieving this may be for the entity, in advance of the closed period, to enter into a contract with a counterparty (such as a broker) whereby the counterparty purchases shares in the entity, which the entity is then obliged to acquire from the counterparty. Such a contract will give rise to a financial liability for the entity from the day on which it is entered into. As discussed above, this would initially be recorded at the net present value of the amount to be paid, with the unwinding of the discount on that liability recorded as a finance charge in profit or loss.

In addition, if the contract is for the purchase of a fixed number of shares for their market price (as opposed to the exchange of a fixed amount of cash for as many shares as are worth that amount), it will be necessary to remeasure the liability to reflect movements in the share price.

5.3.2 Contracts to acquire non-controlling interests

IFRS 10 requires non-controlling interests to be shown within equity in consolidated financial statements (see Chapter 7 at 4.3). Accordingly, the requirements of IAS 32 relating to contracts over own equity instruments also generally apply, in consolidated financial statements, to forward contracts and put and call options over non-controlling interests.

This analysis was confirmed by the Interpretations Committee in November 2006, when it considered a request to clarify the accounting treatment of contracts to acquire non-controlling interests that are put in place at the time of a business combination. It is arguable that such contracts are more appropriately accounted for under the provisions of IFRS 3 relating to deferred consideration. It may also be the case that such contracts have the effect that, while there is a non-controlling interest as a matter of law, the relevant subsidiary is nevertheless regarded by IFRS 10 as wholly-owned, in which case the acquirer also recognises a financial liability for the price payable to the non-controlling interest. A further discussion of these issues may be found in Chapter 7 at 5.

The Interpretations Committee agreed that there was likely to be divergence in practice in how the related equity is classified, but did not believe that it could reach a consensus on this matter on a timely basis. Accordingly, the Interpretations Committee decided not to add this item to its agenda.

However, the Interpretations Committee noted that the requirements of IAS 32 relating to the purchase of own equity apply to the purchase of a minority interest. After initial recognition any liability, to which IFRS 3 is not being applied, will be accounted for in accordance with IAS 39. The parent will reclassify the liability to equity if a put expires unexercised.[20] Whilst this comment was made in the context of the original version of IFRS 3 (issued in 2004), it would be equally applicable where the current version (issued in 2008) is applied.

5.3.2.A Put options over non-controlling interests – Interpretations Committee and IASB developments

The accounting for put options over non-controlling interest has been the subject of much debate over the years. For a summary of the Interpretations Committee and IASB developments on this issue see Chapter 7 at 5.5.

5.4 Gross-settled contracts for the sale or issue of the entity's own equity instruments

The following discussion in 5.4 relates only to contracts which must be settled by the entity delivering its own equity instruments (other than those classified as such under the exceptions discussed at 4.6 above) and the counterparty paying cash (gross-settled contracts). Contracts which can be settled net (i.e. by payment of the difference between the fair value, at the time of purchase, of the shares and that of the consideration given) are accounted as financial assets or financial liabilities (see 5.2.7). *[IAS 32.AG27(c)]*.

IAS 32 requires some types of puttable instruments (see 4.6.2 above) and instruments that impose an obligation to deliver a *pro rata* share of net assets only on liquidation (see 4.6.3 above) to be treated as equity instruments. However, a contract that is required to be settled by the entity receiving or delivering either of these types of equity instrument is a financial asset or financial liability, even when it involves the exchange of a fixed amount of cash or other financial assets for a fixed number of such instruments. *[IAS 32.22A, AG27]*.

If an entity enters into a gross-settled contract to sell its own equity instruments, the contract is economically the 'mirror image' of a contract for the purchase of own equity. However, there is no provision in IAS 32 that the contract gives rise to a financial asset in respect of the cash to be received from the counterparty, as compared to the specific provision that a contract to purchase own equity gives rise to a financial liability in respect of the cash to be paid to the counterparty (see 5.3 above). Consequently, it appears that such contracts give rise to no accounting entries until settlement. This analysis is confirmed by an illustrative example to IAS 32 (see Example 45.16 at 11.1.2 below).

Contracts for the sale or issue of own equity arise in situations such as those in Examples 45.2 and 45.3 below.

Example 45.2: Share issue payable in fixed instalments

A government intends to privatise a nationalised industry with a functional currency of euro through an initial public offering (IPO) at €5 per share. In order to encourage widespread share ownership, the terms of the issue are that shares are issued on 1 January 2016, but subscribers to the IPO are required to pay only €3 per share on 1 January 2016 followed by two further instalments of €1 per share on 1 January 2017 and 1 January 2018.

Example 45.3: Right to call for additional equity capital

A start-up technology entity with a functional currency of UK pounds sterling is unsure of its working capital requirements for the first few years of its operations. It therefore enters into an agreement with its major shareholders whereby it can require those shareholders to contribute an additional £2 per share at any time during the next seven years.

One view might be that the situation in Example 45.2 is not a contract for the future issue of equity – the share has already been issued, and so it would be quite appropriate to record a receivable for the deferred subscription payments. The accounting standard *IFRS for Small and Medium-Sized Entities* indicates that a receivable should be recognised only for shares that have been issued, but that such a receivable should be recognised as a deduction from equity, not as an asset.[21] The standard states that this proposal is derived from IAS 32[22] – an assertion difficult to reconcile with the discussion above. Interestingly, an early IASB staff draft of the exposure draft of *IFRS for Small and Medium-Sized Entities* (as made available on the IASB's website as at September 2006) admitted, with perhaps unintended candour, that this treatment is 'not in any standard'![23] In our view, current IFRS requires any receivable recognised in respect of an issued share to be shown as an asset.

On the other hand, it is clear from IAS 32 that no receivable would be recognised if the arrangement provided for the entity actually to issue further shares (*pro rata* to the shares initially issued) for €1 on 1 January 2017 and 1 January 2018.

6 COMPOUND FINANCIAL INSTRUMENTS

6.1 Background

While many financial instruments are either a liability or equity in their entirety, that is not true for all financial instruments issued by an entity. Some, referred to as compound instruments in IAS 32, contain both elements. A compound financial instrument is a non-derivative financial instrument that, from the issuer's perspective, contains both a liability and an equity component. *[IAS 32.28, AG30]*. Examples include:

- A bond, in the same currency as the functional currency of the issuing entity, convertible into a fixed number of equity instruments, which effectively comprises:
  - a financial liability (the issuer's obligation to pay interest and, potentially, to redeem the bond in cash); and
  - an equity instrument (the holder's right to call for shares of the issuer).

  IAS 32 states that the economic effect of issuing such an instrument is substantially the same as simultaneously issuing a debt instrument with an early settlement provision and warrants to purchase ordinary shares, or issuing a debt instrument with detachable share purchase warrants. *[IAS 32.29]*. However, this analysis is questionable in the sense that, if a company did issue such instruments separately, it is extremely unlikely that one would lapse as the result of the exercise of the other (as happens on the conversion or redemption of a convertible bond);
- A mandatorily redeemable preference share with dividends paid at the issuer's discretion, which effectively comprises:
  - a financial liability (the issuer's obligation to redeem the shares in cash); and
  - an equity instrument (the holder's right to receive dividends if declared). *[IAS 32.AG37]*.

IAS 32 requires the issuer of a non-derivative financial instrument to evaluate the terms of the financial instrument to determine whether it contains both a liability and an equity component. This evaluation is based on the contractual terms of the financial instruments, the substance of the arrangement and the definition of a financial liability, financial asset and an equity instrument. If such components are identified, they must be accounted for separately as financial liabilities, financial assets or equity, *[IAS 32.28]*, and the liability and equity components shown separately in the statement of financial position. *[IAS 32.29]*.

This treatment, commonly referred to as 'split accounting', is discussed in more detail in 6.2 to 6.6 below. For simplicity, the discussion below (like that in IAS 32 itself) is framed in terms of convertible bonds, by far the most common form of compound financial instrument, but is equally applicable to other types of compound instrument, such as preference shares with different contractual terms in respect of dividends and re-payments of principal (see 4.5 above).

6.1.1 *Treatment by holder and issuer contrasted*

'Split accounting' is to be applied only by the issuer of a compound financial instrument. The accounting treatment by the holder is dealt with in IAS 39 or, where applicable, IFRS 9 and is significantly different. *[IAS 32.AC30]*. In particular:

- In the issuer's financial statements, under IAS 32:
  - on initial recognition of the instrument, the fair value of the liability component is calculated first and the equity component is treated as a residual; and
  - the equity component is never remeasured after initial recognition.
- In the holder's financial statements, under IAS 39 (see Chapter 44 at 4 and Chapter 48 at 2 and 3):
  - on initial recognition of the instrument, the conversion option is a derivative financial asset, the fair value of which is calculated first, with the loan treated as a residual amount; and
  - the derivative financial asset is likely to be constantly remeasured at fair value.
- In the holder's financial statements, under IFRS 9:
  - the instrument fails the criteria for measurement at amortised cost (in particular the 'contractual cash flow characteristics test') and is therefore carried at fair value through profit or loss (see Chapter 47 at 6).

6.2 Initial recognition – 'split accounting'

On initial recognition of a compound instrument such as a convertible bond, IAS 32 requires the issuer to:

(a) identify the various components of the instrument;

(b) determine the fair value of the liability component (see below); and

(c) determine the equity component as a residual amount, essentially the issue proceeds of the instrument less the liability component determined in (b) above.

The liability component of a convertible bond should be measured first, at the fair value of a similar liability that does not have an associated equity conversion feature, but including any embedded non-equity derivative features, such as an issuer's or holder's right to require early redemption of the bond, if any such terms are included.

In practical terms, this will be done by determining the net present value of all potential contractually determined future cash flows under the instrument, discounted at the rate of interest applied by the market at the time of issue to instruments of comparable credit status and providing substantially the same cash flows, on the same terms, but without the conversion option. The fair value of any embedded non-equity derivative features is then determined and 'included in the liability component' – see, however, the further discussion of this point at 6.4.2 below. *[IAS 32.31]*.

Thereafter the liability component is accounted for in accordance with the requirements of IAS 39, or – where applicable – IFRS 9, for the measurement of financial liabilities (see Chapter 48). *[IAS 32.31-32]*.

IAS 32 notes that:

- the equity component of a convertible bond is an embedded option to convert the liability into equity of the issuer;
- the fair value of the option comprises its time value and its intrinsic value, if any; and
- this option has value on initial recognition even when it is out of the money. *[IAS 32.AG31(b)]*.

However, not all these features are directly relevant to the accounting treatment, since the equity component is not (other than by coincidence) recorded at its fair value. Instead, in accordance with the general definition of equity as a residual, the equity component of the bond is simply the difference between the fair value of the compound instrument (total issue proceeds of the bond) and the liability component as determined above. Because of this 'residual' treatment, IAS 32 does not address the issue of how, or whether, the issue proceeds are to be allocated where more than one equity component is identified. It is important to note, that the equity component will not be remeasured subsequently.

The methodology of 'split-accounting' in IAS 32 has the effect that the sum of the carrying amounts assigned to the liability and equity components on initial recognition is always equal to the fair value that would be ascribed to the instrument as a whole. No gain or loss arises from the initial recognition of the separate components of the instrument. *[IAS 32.31]*.

This treatment is illustrated in Examples 45.4 and 45.8 below. *[IAS 32.IE34-36]*.

Example 45.4: Convertible bond – basic 'split accounting

An entity, whose functional currency is the Euro, issues 2,000 convertible bonds. The bonds have a three-year term, and are issued at par with a face value of €1,000 per bond, giving total proceeds of €2,000,000. Interest is payable annually in arrears at a nominal annual interest rate of 6% (i.e. €120,000 per annum). Each bond is convertible at any time up to maturity into 250 ordinary shares. When the bonds are issued, the prevailing market interest rate for similar debt without conversion options is 9% per annum. The entity incurs issue costs of €100,000.

The economic components of this instrument are:

- a liability component, being a discounted fixed rate debt, perhaps with an imputed holder's put option (due to the holder's right to convert at any time), and
- an equity component, representing the holder's right to convert at any time before maturity. In effect this is a written call option (from the issuer's perspective) on American terms (i.e. it can be exercised at any time until maturity of the bond).

The practical problem with this analysis is that it is not clear what is the strike price of the holder's options to put the debt and call for shares, specifically whether it is the €2,000,000 face value of the bonds or the discounted amount at which they are recorded until maturity. Perhaps for this reason, IAS 32 does not require the true fair values of these components to be calculated.

Instead the liability component is measured first at the net present value of the maximum potential cash payments that the issuer could be required to make. The difference between the proceeds of the bond issue and the calculated fair value of the liability is assigned to the equity component. The net present value (NPV) of the liability component is calculated as €1,848,122, using a discount rate of 9%, the market interest rate for similar bonds having no conversion rights, as shown.

Year	Cash flow	€	Discount factor (at 9%)	NPV of cash flow €
1	Interest	120,000	1/1.09	110,092
2	Interest	120,000	$1/1.09^2$	101,001
3	Interest and principal	2,120,000	$1/1.09^3$	1,637,029
			Total liability component	1,848,122
			Total equity component (balance)	151,878
			Total proceeds	2,000,000

It is next necessary to deal with the issue costs of €100,000. In accordance with the requirements of IAS 32 for such costs (see 8.1 below), these would be allocated to the liability and equity components on a *pro rata* basis. This would give the following allocation of the net issue proceeds.

	Liability component €	Equity component €	Total €
Gross proceeds (allocated as above)	1,848,122	151,878	2,000,000
Issue costs (allocated *pro rata* to gross proceeds)	(92,406)	(7,594)	(100,000)
Net proceeds	1,755,716	144,284	1,900,000

The €144,284 credited to equity is not subsequently remeasured (see 6.2.1 below). On the assumption that the liability is not classified as at fair value through profit or loss, the €1,755,716 liability component would be accounted for under the effective interest rate method. It should be borne in mind that, after taking account of the issue costs, the effective interest rate is not the 9% used to determine the gross value of the liability component, but 10.998%, as shown below.

Year	Liability b/f €	Interest at 10.998% €	Cash paid €	Liability c/f €
1	1,755,716	193,094	(120,000)	1,828,810
2	1,828,810	201,134	(120,000)	1,909,944
3	1,909,944	210,056	(2,120,000)	–
	Total finance cost	604,284		

The total finance cost can be proved as follows:

	€
Cash interest	360,000
Gross issue proceeds originally allocated to equity component	151,878
Issue costs allocated to liability component	92,406
	604,284

Chapter 45

6.2.1 Accounting for the equity component

On initial recognition of a compound financial instrument, the equity component (i.e. the €144,284 identified in Example 45.4 above) is credited direct to equity and is not subsequently remeasured. IAS 32 does not prescribe:

- whether the credit should be to a separate component of equity (although a transitional provision relating to the February 2008 amendment of IAS 32 suggests that there is such a requirement); or
- if the entity chooses to treat it as such, how it should be described.

This ensures that there is no conflict between, on the one hand, the basic requirement of IAS 32 that there should be a credit in equity and, on the other, the legal requirements of various jurisdictions as to exactly how that credit should be allocated within equity.

After initial recognition, the classification of the liability and equity components of a convertible instrument is not revised, for example as a result of a change in the likelihood that a conversion option will be exercised, even when exercise of the option may appear to have become economically advantageous to some holders. IAS 32 points out that holders may not always act in the way that might be expected because, for example, the tax consequences resulting from conversion may differ among holders. Furthermore, the likelihood of conversion will change from time to time. The entity's contractual obligation to make future payments remains outstanding until it is extinguished through conversion, maturity of the instrument or some other transaction. *[IAS 32.30]*.

The amount originally credited to equity is subsequently neither remeasured nor reclassified to profit or loss. Thus, as illustrated by Example 43.5 above, the effective interest rate shown in profit or loss for a simple convertible bond will be equivalent to the rate that would have been paid for non-convertible debt. In effect, the dilution of shareholder value represented by the embedded conversion right is shown as an interest expense.

However, on conversion of a convertible instrument, it may be appropriate to transfer the equity component within equity (see 6.3.1 below).

6.2.2 Temporary differences arising from split accounting

In many jurisdictions it is only the cash interest paid, and sometimes also the issue costs, that are deductible for tax purposes, rather than the full amount of the finance cost charged under IAS 32. Moreover, some of these costs may be deductible in periods different from those in which they are recognised in the financial statements. These factors will give rise to temporary differences between the carrying value of the liability component of the bond and its tax base, giving rise to deferred tax required to be accounted for under IAS 12 – *Income Taxes* (see Chapter 31, particularly at 6.1.2 and 7.2.8).

6.3 Conversion, early repurchase and modification

6.3.1 Conversion at maturity

On conversion of a convertible instrument at maturity, IAS 32 requires the entity to derecognise the liability component and recognise it as equity. There is no gain or loss on conversion at maturity. *[IAS 32.AC32]*.

Thus, for example, if the bond in Example 45.4 above were converted at maturity, the accounting entry required by IAS 32 would be:

	€	€
Liability	2,000,000	
Equity		2,000,000

The precise allocation of the credit to equity (e.g. as between share capital, additional paid-in capital, share premium, other reserves and so on) would be a matter of local legislation. In addition, IAS 32 permits the €144,284 originally allocated to the equity component in Example 45.4 above to be reallocated within equity. *[IAS 32.AG32].*

6.3.2 *Conversion before maturity*

6.3.2.A *'Fixed stated principal' of a bond*

The consideration given for the issue of equity instruments on conversion of a bond is the discharge by the holder of the issuer from the liability to pay any further interest or principal payments on the bond. If conversion can take place only at maturity, the amount of the liability transferred to equity on conversion will always (as in Example 45.4 at 6.2 above) be €2,000,000. Hence, the conversion right involves the delivery of a fixed number of shares for the waiver of the right to receive a fixed amount of cash and so is clearly an equity instrument.

However, the bond in Example 45.4 allows conversion at some point before the full term. Therefore, conversion might occur at the end of year 2, when the carrying value of the bonds would have been accreted to only €1,909,944. Hence, the carrying amount of the liability that is forgiven on conversion can vary depending on when conversion occurs. This begs the question as to whether the conversion right now involves the delivery of a fixed number of shares for the waiver of the right to receive a *variable* amount of cash, suggesting that it is no longer an equity instrument.

It is for this reason, in our view, that IAS 32 defines as an equity instrument one that involves the exchange of a fixed number of shares for the 'fixed stated principal' rather than the 'carrying amount' of a bond. *[IAS 32.22].* In other words, IAS 32 regards the 'fixed stated principal' of the bond in Example 45.4 as a constant €2,000,000. The intention is to clarify that the variation in the carrying amount of the bond during its term does not preclude the conversion right from being classified as an equity instrument.

6.3.2.B *Accounting treatment*

IAS 32 refers to the treatment summarised in 6.3.1 above being applied on conversion 'at maturity'. This begs the question of the treatment required if a holder converts prior to maturity (as would have been possible under the terms of the bond in Example 45.4).

As noted in 6.3.2.A above, IAS 32 concludes that the equity component of the bond is an equity instrument on the grounds that it represents the holder's right to call for a fixed number of shares for fixed consideration, in the form of the 'fixed stated principal' of the bond.

It could be argued that the logical implication of this is that, on a holder's early conversion of the bond in Example 45.4 above, the issuer should immediately recognise a finance cost for the difference between the then carrying amount of the liability component of the bond and the fixed stated principal of €2,000,000. This would create a liability of €2,000,000 immediately before conversion, so as to acknowledge that the strike price under the holder's call option is the waiver of the right to receive a fixed stated principal of €2,000,000, rather than whatever the carrying value of the bond happens to be at the time.

However, we take the view, supported by general practice, that all that is required is to transfer to equity the carrying value of the liability at the date of conversion, as calculated after accrual of finance costs on a continuous basis, rather than at the amount shown in the most recently published financial statements. In such a case, the consideration for the issue of equity instruments is the release, by the bondholder, of the issuer from its liability to make future contractual payments under the bond, measured at the net present value of those payments.

IFRIC 19 (which generally applies to debt for equity swaps) does not apply to the conversion of a convertible instrument in accordance with its original terms (see 7 below).

6.3.2.C Treatment of embedded derivatives on conversion

IAS 32 does not specifically address the treatment of any separated non-equity embedded derivatives outstanding at the time of conversion. The issue of principle is that, when a holder exercises its right to convert, it is effectively requiring the issuer to issue equity in consideration for the bondholder ceding its rights. These may include any right to receive future payments of principal and/or interest or to require early repayment of the bond. It seems entirely appropriate that any amounts carried in respect of such rights, including those reflected in the carrying amount of separated embedded derivatives, should be transferred to equity on conversion.

Where, however, conversion has the effect of removing an issuer's right (for example, to compel early redemption or conversion), this could be seen as a loss to the issuer rather than as consideration given by the holder for an issue of equity. In our view, however, the loss of such a right by the issuer on conversion by the holder simply represents a reduction in the proceeds received for the issue of equity, and should therefore by accounted for as a charge to equity (see also 8.1 below).

6.3.3 Early redemption or repurchase

It is not uncommon for the issuer of a convertible bond to redeem or repurchase it before the end of its full term, either through exercise of rights inherent in the bond, such as an embedded issuer call option, or through subsequent negotiation with bondholders.

IAS 32 contains guidance for the accounting treatment of an early redemption or repurchase of compound instruments following a tender offer to bondholders (see 6.3.3.A below).

It is not entirely clear whether this guidance applies only to redemption pursuant to a subsequent negotiation with bondholders, or whether it also applies where redemption occurs through exercise of a right inherent in the original terms of the bond. We therefore believe an entity has an accounting policy choice if redemption is based on a right inherent in original terms of the bond, such as an embedded issuer call option at par that was allocated to the liability component and considered to be clearly and closely related to the host contract (see 6.3.3.B below).

6.3.3.A Early repurchase through negotiation with bondholders

When an entity extinguishes a convertible instrument before maturity through an early redemption or repurchase in which the original conversion privileges are unchanged, IAS 32 requires the entity to allocate the consideration paid and any transaction costs for the repurchase or redemption to the liability and equity components of the instrument at the date of the transaction. *[IAS 32.AG33]*.

It is not entirely clear what is meant by a 'redemption or repurchase in which the original conversion privileges are unchanged'. However, we assume that it is intended to imply that the repurchase must occur without modification of the original terms of the compound instrument, and at a price representing a fair value for the instrument on its original terms. A repurchase based on a modification of the original terms of the instrument, or at a price implying a modification of them, should presumably be dealt with according to the provisions of IAS 32 for the modification of a compound instrument (see 6.3.4 below) or those in IAS 39 for the exchange and modification of debt (see Chapter 51 at 6.2).

The method used for allocating the consideration paid and transaction costs to the separate components should be consistent with that used in the original allocation to the separate components of the proceeds received by the entity when the convertible instrument was issued (see 6.2 above). *[IAS 32.AG33]*.

The issuer is therefore required to:

- determine the fair value of the liability component and allocate this part of the purchase price to the liability component;
- allocate the remainder of the purchase price to the equity component; and
- allocate the transaction costs between the liability and equity component on a *pro rata* basis.

Once this allocation of the consideration has been made:

- the difference between the consideration allocated to the liability component and the carrying amount of the liability is recognised in profit or loss; and
- the amount of consideration relating to the equity component is recognised in equity. *[IAS 32.AG34]*.

The treatment of a negotiated repurchase at fair value of a convertible instrument is illustrated by Example 45.5 below, which is based on an illustrative example in IAS 32. *[IAS 32.IE39-46]*.

Example 45.5: Early repurchase of convertible instrument

For simplicity this example:

- assumes that at inception the face amount of the instrument was equal to the carrying amount of its liability and equity components in the financial statements – i.e. there was no premium or discount on issue; and
- ignores transaction costs and tax.

On 1 January 2012, an entity issued a convertible bond with a face value of €100 million maturing on 31 December 2021, at which point the holder may opt for repayment of €100 million or conversion into 4 million shares. Interest is paid half-yearly in arrears at a nominal annual interest rate of 10% (i.e. €5m per half year). At the date of issue, the entity could have issued non-convertible debt with a ten-year term bearing interest at 11%. On issue, the carrying amount of the bond was allocated as follows:

	€m
Present value of the principal – €100m payable at the end of ten years[1]	34.3
Present value of the interest – 20 6-monthly payments of €5m[2]	59.7
Total liability component	94.0
Equity component (balance)	6.0
Proceeds of the bond issue	100.0

The amounts above are discounted using a semi-annual rate of 5.5% (11%/2) as follows:

1 $€100m/1.055^{20}$

2 $€5m \times (1/1.055 + 1/1.055^{2} + 1/1.055^{3} + ... 1/1.055^{20})$

On 1 January 2017, the entity makes a tender offer to the holder of the bond to repurchase the bond at its then fair value of €170 million, which the holder accepts. At the date of repurchase, the entity could have issued non-convertible debt with a five-year term with interest payable half-yearly in arrears at an annual coupon interest rate of 8%.

At the time of repurchase, the carrying amount of the liability component of the bond, discounted at the original semi-annual rate of 5.5% is as follows.

	€m
Present value of the principal – €100m payable at the end of five years[1]	58.5
Present value of the interest – 10 6-monthly payments of €5m[2]	37.7
Carrying value of liability component	96.2

1 $€100m/1.055^{10}$

2 $€5m \times (1/1.055 + 1/1.055^{2} + 1/1.055^{3} + ... 1/1.055^{10})$

The fair value of the liability component of the bond, discounted at the current semi-annual rate of 4% (8%/2) is as follows.

	€m
Present value of the principal – €100m payable at the end of five years[1]	67.6
Present value of the interest – 10 6-monthly payments of €5m[2]	40.5
Fair value of liability component	108.1

1 $€100m/1.04^{10}$

2 $€5m \times (1/1.04 + 1/1.04^{2} + 1/1.04^{3} + ...1/1.04^{10})$

The fair value calculation indicates that, of the repurchase price of €170 million, €108.1 million is to be treated as redeeming the liability component of the bond, and the balance of €61.9 million as redeeming the equity component. This gives rise to the accounting entry:

	€m	€m
Liability component of bond	96.2	
Equity	61.9	
Debt settlement expense (profit or loss)	11.9	
Cash		170.0

The debt settlement expense represents the difference between the carrying value of the debt component (€96.2m) and its fair value (€108.1m).

Any costs of the repurchase would have been allocated between profit or loss and equity in proportion to the fair value of the liability and equity components at the time of redemption.

6.3.3.B *Early repurchase through exercising an embedded call option*

It is not entirely clear whether the guidance in 6.3.3.A above applies only on early redemption or repurchase to a subsequent negotiation with bondholders, or whether it also applies where redemption occurs through exercise of rights inherent in the terms of the bond (for example an issuer call option at par allocated to the liability component and considered to be clearly and closely related to the host contract).

One way of accounting for such redemptions would be by applying the accounting treatment as discussed under 6.3.3.A above.

If, however, this early repayment option was determined, on initial recognition of the convertible bond, to be clearly and closely related to the liability host contract (see 6.4.2.A below), then it might be argued that the general measurement rules of IAS 39 apply. In such a case the liability (including the embedded call option) would be measured at amortised cost (assuming that it was not designated at fair value through profit or loss on initial recognition). Accounting under the amortised cost method is based on an effective interest rate, calculated initially based on expected future cash flows. Any change in those expected cash flows is reflected in the carrying amount of the financial instrument, by computing the present value of the revised estimated future cash flows at the instrument's original effective interest rate, with any difference from the previous amortised cost carrying amount recorded in profit or loss. *[IAS 39.AG8]*.

A change in the expected repayment date would therefore require the amortised cost of the financial liability component to be remeasured. This treatment has the effect that the overall repayment amount at par is allocated to the liability portion of the compound instrument.

6.3.4 Modification

An entity may amend the terms of a convertible instrument to induce early conversion, for example by offering a more favourable conversion ratio or paying other additional consideration in the event of conversion before a specified date. The difference, at the date the terms are amended, between:

- the fair value of the consideration the holder receives on conversion of the instrument under the revised terms; and
- the fair value of the consideration the holder would have received under the original terms,

is recognised as a loss in profit or loss. *[IAS 32.AG35]*. IAS 32 illustrates this treatment, as shown in Example 45.6 below. *[IAS 32.IE47-50]*.

Example 45.6: Modification of terms of bond to induce early conversion

Suppose that the entity in Example 45.5 at 6.3.3.A above wished, on 1 January 2017, to induce the bondholder to convert the bond early. The original terms of the bond allowed for conversion into 4 million shares. The entity offers the bondholder the right to convert into 5 million shares during the period 1 January to29 February 2017. The market value of the entity's shares is €40 per share.

The enhanced conversion terms offer the bondholder the right to receive an additional 1 million shares. Accordingly, the entity recognises a cost of €40m (1m shares × share price €40/share) in profit or loss.

Chapter 45

6.4 The components of a compound instrument

6.4.1 *Determining the components of a compound instrument*

The most difficult aspect of 'split accounting' is often the initial assessment of whether the instrument consists of different components and if it does, what the various components of the instrument actually are. In the examples above, it is fairly clear that the instruments consist of different components and what the various components are. However, in some instruments the analysis is far from straightforward, as illustrated by Example 45.7 below.

Example 45.7: Analysis of compound financial instrument into components

An entity issues a bond for €100, paying an annual cash coupon of 5% on the issue price and mandatorily convertible after five years on the following terms. If, at the date of conversion, the entity's share price is €1.25 or higher, the holder will receive 80 shares. If the entity's share price is €1.00 or lower, the holder will receive 100 shares. If the entity's share price is in the range €1.00 to €1.25, the holder will receive such number of shares (between 80 and 100) as have a fair value of €100.

Any analysis must begin by determining whether the bond as whole is a non-derivative instrument. This is the case, since the issuing entity receives full consideration for its issue. The next step is to assess whether the instrument consists of different components and, if it does, to break the instrument down into these components so as to identify any equity components in the whole.

The difficulty of this assessment is evidenced by two requests received by the Interpretations Committee to address the accounting for two instruments with substantially the same features as the one in Example 45.7 above but with an additional early settlement option for the issuer, to settle the instrument at any time by delivering a maximum (fixed) number of shares (see 6.6.3.A below).[24] While the request focused only on the additional early settlement option, and not on the classification of the 'basic' instrument (an instrument with the features described in Example 45.7 above), the accounting treatment of the 'basic instrument' was added to the Interpretations Committee's agenda. It was discussed during the January 2014 and May 2014 Interpretations Committee meetings.[25]

Four alternative views with significantly different accounting outcomes, ranging from classifying the whole financial instrument as a financial liability to various combinations of financial liabilities, equity instruments and/or derivative financial liabilities, were considered by the Interpretations Committee. In the end the Interpretations Committee noted that:

- the issuer's obligation to deliver a variable number of the entity's own equity instruments is a non-derivative that meets the definition of a financial liability in paragraph 11(b)(i) of IAS 32 in its entirety (see 3 and 4.1 above); and
- the definition of a liability in IAS 32 does not have any limits or thresholds regarding the degree of variability that is required.

Therefore, the contractual substance of the instrument is a single obligation to deliver a variable number of equity instruments at maturity, with the variation based on the value of those equity instruments. The Interpretations Committee noted further that such a single obligation to deliver a variable number of own equity instruments cannot be subdivided into components for the purposes of evaluating whether the instrument contains a component that meets the definition of equity. Even though the number of equity instruments to be delivered is limited and guaranteed by the cap and the floor, the overall number of equity instruments that the issuer is obliged to deliver is not fixed and therefore the entire obligation meets the definition of a financial liability.

The Interpretations Committee noted that the cap and the floor are embedded derivative features, whose values change in response to the price of the issuer's equity shares. Therefore, assuming that the issuer has not elected to designate the entire instrument under the fair value option, the issuer must separate those features and account for the embedded derivative features separately from the host liability contract, at fair value through profit or loss in accordance with IAS 39 (or IFRS 9) (see Chapter 44 at 4 and 5).

The fact that the issue was submitted to the Interpretations Committee in the first place together with the fact that four possible accounting views were drawn up under the guidance of IAS 32, evidences how difficult and judgemental any analysis of increasingly complex instruments can be under the provisions of IAS 32.

6.4.2 *Compound instruments with embedded derivatives*

As noted above, in order to qualify for split accounting, a financial instrument, when considered as a whole, must be a non-derivative instrument. However, one or more of its identified components may well be embedded derivatives. Indeed, the conversion right in any convertible bond represents a holder's call option whereby the entity can be required to issue a fixed number of shares for a fixed consideration (the 'fixed stated principal' of the bond – see 6.3.2.A above), which is accordingly identified as an equity component.

A bond may well contain other (non-equity) derivatives, such as options for either the issuer or the holder to require early repayment or conversion or to extend the period until conversion. The detailed guidance in IAS 32 requires 'the fair value of any embedded non-equity derivative features to be determined and included in the liability component' when split accounting is applied (see 6.2 above). *[IAS 32.31]*. They are then subject to the normal requirement of IAS 39 for embedded derivatives to be accounted for separately if they are not considered to be closely related to the host contract (see Chapter 44 at 4).

The issuer of a compound financial instrument with other embedded derivatives is therefore required to go through the following steps:

- First step: determine the fair value of the liability component that does not have an associated equity conversion feature but including any embedded non-equity derivatives features;
- Second step: determine the equity component as a residual amount by deducting the fair value of the liability component, including any embedded non-equity derivative features, from the fair value of the compound instrument (essentially its issue proceeds); and
- Third step: assess whether the embedded non-equity derivative features are closely related to the host liability component. Any not closely related embedded non-equity derivative features are accounted for separately and therefore separated from the host liability component (see Chapter 44 at 4 and 5).

Note, on initial recognition, the sum of the initial carrying amounts of the various components, determined as indicated above, must equal the overall fair value of the compound instrument.

The separation of the liability and equity components of a compound financial instrument with multiple embedded derivative features is demonstrated in Example 45.8 below which is based on an illustrative example in IAS 32. *[IAS 32.IE37-38]*.

6.4.2.A Issuer call option – 'closely related' embedded derivatives

Example 45.8: Convertible bond – split accounting with multiple embedded derivative features

The proceeds received on the issue of a convertible bond, callable at par, are £60 million, which equals the nominal amount of the convertible bond. The value of a similar bond without a call or equity conversion option is £57 million. Based on an option-pricing model, it is determined that the value to the entity of the embedded call feature in a similar bond without an equity conversion option is £2 million. In this case, the value is allocated to the liability component so as to reduce the liability component to £55 million (£57m – £2m) and the value allocated to the equity component is £5 million (£60m – £55m). Because IAS 39 requires the embedded derivative assessment to be done before separating the equity component and the call option is at par, the option is considered to be clearly and closely related and therefore not separated from the liability host contract.

Where (as is often the case) a convertible bond is callable at par, the call option would not be a separable derivative. IAS 39 and IFRS 9 states that a call option is generally closely related to the host debt contract if the exercise price is approximately equal to the amortised cost of the host on each exercise (which would not, *prima facie* be the case). However, as an exemption to the general rule, IAS 39 (or, where applicable, IFRS 9) requires this assessment to be made in respect of any embedded call, put or prepayment option in a convertible bond before separating the equity component. *[IAS 39.AG30(g), IFRS 9.B4.3.5(e)]*. This has the effect that an issuer's call over a convertible bond at par is effectively deemed to be equal to amortised cost for the duration of the instrument. This is discussed further in Chapter 44 at 5.

6.4.2.B Issuer call option – 'not closely related' embedded derivatives

If a non-equity embedded derivative is considered not to be closely related to the host contract then it should be accounted for separately. If, in Example 45.8 above, the issuer call option were at an amount that was not approximately equal to amortised cost, and not intended to reimburse the approximate present value of lost interest (see Chapter 44 at 5), say at par plus £5 million, then the call option would not be considered clearly and closely related and therefore should be accounted for separately. The issuer in Example 45.8 would therefore record a derivative financial asset at its fair value of £2 million, assuming it would have the same fair value as in Example 45.8, a liability component of £57 million and an equity component of £5 million. The call option would subsequently be remeasured at fair value through profit or loss.

There are cases where over-enthusiastic trawling for embedded derivatives may dredge up results so counter-intuitive that it is hard to believe that they were really intended by the IASB, as illustrated by Example 45.9 below.

Example 45.9: Foreign currency denominated equity instrument with issuer's redemption right

An entity with a functional currency of pounds sterling issues a euro-denominated capital instrument for €145 million (equivalent to £100 million at the date of issue). Coupons on the instrument are paid entirely at the entity's discretion. The entity has the right, but not the obligation, in certain circumstances to redeem the instrument (in Euros) for an amount equal to the original issue proceeds.

Taken as a whole, this is an equity instrument, because it gives rise to no obligation to transfer cash or other financial assets to the holder. However, the issuer's right to redeem, if considered in isolation is not an equity instrument, but a financial asset (a call option over own equity), since it is a derivative involving the purchase of a fixed number of equity instruments for €145 million which, although fixed in euros, is variable when translated into sterling. Suppose that the fair value of the call option, at the date of issue was £15 million.

This analysis would result in the following accounting entry on issue of the instrument:

	£m	£m
Cash	100	
Call option (statement of financial position)	15	
Equity		115

In our view, it would be inappropriate to show an increase in net assets of £115 million, when the only real transaction has been the raising of £100 million of equity for cash. In this particular case, this treatment is, in our view, not required since paragraph 28 of IAS 32 requires split accounting to be applied only where an instrument is determined to contain 'both a liability and an equity component'. In this case, there is no liability component, since the embedded derivative that has potentially been identified is, and can only ever be, an asset; accordingly, 'split accounting' is not required.

Chapter 45

6.5 Other issues

The following issues discussed earlier in this chapter are of particular relevance to convertible bonds:

- the Interpretations Committee's conclusion that a fixed amount of cash denominated in a currency other than the entity's functional currency is not a 'fixed amount' of cash (see 5.2.3 above and 6.6.4 and 6.6.4.A below); and
- the treatment of instruments settled with equity instruments the number of which varies to reflect major capital restructurings before settlement (see 5.1.2 above).

These and other issues noted at various points above reinforce an increasing concern that the 'split accounting' rules in IAS 32 are implicitly based on a bond with terms much more straightforward than those of many – if not most – bonds currently in issue. See 12 below for possible future developments.

6.6 Common forms of convertible bonds

6.6.1 *Functional currency bond convertible into a fixed number of shares*

The most common form of convertible bond, a functional currency bond convertible into a fixed number of own equity instruments at the discretion of the holder, is discussed in Example 45.4 at 6.2 above.

6.6.2 Contingent convertible bond

A contingent convertible bond is a bond that is convertible, at the option of the holder, only on the occurrence of a contingent event outside of the control of the holder or the issuer. If the contingent event occurs then the holder has the option, but not the obligation, to convert. If the contingent event does not occur, then the bond will be settled in cash at maturity.

The fact that conversion is only contingent does not mean the instrument has no equity component. If, on occurrence of the contingent event, exercise of the conversion option would result in the exchange of a fixed number of the issuer's own equity instruments for a fixed amount of cash (in the functional currency of the issuing entity), the conversion option would meet the definition of an equity instrument under IAS 32 and the overall instrument would be treated as a compound instrument.

6.6.3 Mandatorily convertible bond

A mandatorily convertible bond is an instrument that, at a certain time in the future, converts into shares of the issuing entity, rather than the conversion being at the option of either the holder or the issuer of the bond. The classification of a mandatorily convertible bond on initial recognition as debt or equity depends on:

- how the convertible bond will be settled; and
- whether the issuer is required to pay interest up to the point of conversion.

If the fixed stated principal will be settled through delivery of a fixed number of the issuer's own shares, and the principal of the convertible bond is in the same currency as the functional currency of the issuing entity, then this feature of the bond is an equity instrument and accounted for as such (see 4.1 and 5.2.3 above). If interest on the bond is payable only at the discretion of the entity, then there is no liability component, and the entire bond is classified as an equity instrument. If, however, the entity is required to pay interest, the obligation to pay interest establishes a liability component, which is measured at the present value of the required interest payments.

If settlement can only occur through the delivery of a variable number of the issuer's own shares, calculated so that the fair value of these shares issued equals the principal amount (see 5.2.1 above), and the entity is required to pay interest then the entire bond is classified as a financial liability.

Example 45.10: Mandatorily convertible bond classified as equity

An entity, with a functional currency of Euro, issues 2,000 convertible bonds with a nominal value of €1,000 per bond, giving total proceeds of €2,000,000. The bonds have a three-year term, and interest is payable, at the discretion of the entity, annually in arrears at a nominal annual interest rate of 6% (i.e. €120,000 per annum). At maturity of the bond each bond converts into 250 ordinary shares. Because the conversion option meets the definition of an equity instrument and payment of interest is at the discretion of the entity, the entire instrument is classified as an equity instrument. The entity records the following accounting entry.

	€	€
Cash	2,000,000	
Equity		2,000,000

Example 45.11: Mandatorily convertible bond classified as a compound instrument

Assume the same fact pattern as in Example 45.10 above, except that the entity has an obligation to pay interest annually in arrears at a nominal annual interest rate of 6% (i.e. €120,000 per annum). The obligation to pay interest over three years represents a liability of the issuing entity at the net present value, using a discount rate of 9%, which is the market interest rate.

Year	Cash flow	€	Discount factor (at 9%)	NPV of cash flow €
1	Interest	120,000	1/1.09	110,092
2	Interest	120,000	$1/1.09^2$	101,001
3	Interest	120,000	$1/1.09^3$	92,662
			Total liability component	303,755
			Total equity component (balance)	1,696,245
			Total proceeds	2,000,000

The entity records the following accounting entry.

	€	€
Cash	2,000,000	
Equity		1,696,245
Liability		303,755

6.6.3.A Bond which is mandatorily convertible into a variable number of shares with an option for the issuer to settle early for a maximum number of shares

At its meeting in July 2013, the Interpretations Committee considered the IAS 32 classification for a financial instrument that is mandatorily convertible into a variable number of shares, subject to a cap and floor, but with an issuer option to settle by delivering the maximum (fixed) number of shares.[26] This is a financial instrument with essentially the same features as the one described in Example 45.7 above, but with an additional option for the issuer to settle the instrument at any time before maturity (see 6.4.1 above for IAS 32 classification considerations for the 'basic financial instrument', ignoring the early settlement option). If the issuer chooses to exercise its early settlement option, it must deliver the maximum number of shares specified in the contract (e.g. 100 shares in Example 45.7 and pay in cash all of the interest that would have been payable if the instrument had remained outstanding until its maturity date (a so called 'make-whole provision').

Applying the IAS 32 definitions of a financial liability and of an equity instrument to such a financial instrument would result in accounting for it as a compound instrument (i.e. a financial instrument consisting of an equity element and a financial liability element). IAS 32 states that a non-derivative financial instrument is an equity instrument if the instrument will be settled in the issuer's own equity instruments and includes no contractual obligation for the issuer to deliver a variable number of its own equity instruments. *[IAS 32.11(b)(i)]*. With the early settlement option, the issuer has the right to avoid delivering a variable number of shares. A portion of the financial instrument would therefore meet the definition of equity and would be accounted for as such. The interest payments on the instrument, on the other hand, impose a contractual obligation on the issuer to deliver cash in all cases and therefore meet the definition of a financial liability and would be accounted for as such.

However, this analysis ignores the fact that in exercising the early settlement option, the issuer must deliver at an earlier time a potentially greater number of its own shares, plus all the interest in cash which would have been payable over the instrument's life. The issuer can avoid delivering a variable number of its own shares but only by giving away a potentially larger amount of economic value. The question asked of the Interpretations Committee was whether such an early settlement option should be considered when classifying the financial instrument under IAS 32.

In its analysis, the Interpretations Committee noted that the definitions of financial asset, financial liability and equity instrument in IAS 32 are based on the financial instrument's contractual rights and contractual obligations.[27] However, IAS 32 requires the issuer of a financial instrument to classify the instrument in accordance with the substance of the contractual arrangement. *[IAS 32.15]*. An issuer cannot assume that a financial instrument (or any component) meets the definition of an equity instrument simply because the issuer has the contractual right to settle the financial instrument by delivering a fixed number of equity instruments. The issuer would need to consider whether the early settlement option is substantive and, if it was concluded that it lacks substance, then it should be ignored for the classification assessment of the instrument.

It was noted that the guidance in paragraph 20(b) of IAS 32 is relevant because it provides an example of a situation in which one of an instrument's settlement alternatives is excluded from the classification assessment. Specifically, the example in that paragraph describes an instrument that the issuer will settle by delivering either cash or its own shares, and states that one of the settlement alternatives should be excluded from the classification assessment in some circumstances (see 5.2.4 above).

To determine whether the early settlement option is substantive, the issuer would need to understand whether there are actual economic or business reasons that would lead the issuer to exercise the option. In making that assessment, the issuer could consider whether the instrument would have been priced differently if the issuer's early settlement option had not been included in the contractual terms. The Interpretations Committee also noted that factors such as the term of the instrument, the width of the range between the cap and the floor, the issuer's share price and the volatility of the share price could be relevant to the assessment of whether the issuer's early settlement option is substantive. For example, the early settlement option may be less likely to have substance – especially if the instrument is short-lived – if the range between the cap and the floor is wide and the current share price would equate to the delivery of a number of shares that is close to the floor. That is because the issuer may have to deliver significantly more shares to settle early than it may otherwise be obliged to deliver at maturity. The Interpretations Committee considered that in light of its analysis of the existing IFRS requirements, it would not add this issue to its agenda.

6.6.3.B *Bond which is mandatorily convertible into a variable number of shares upon a contingent 'non-viability' event*

Since the financial crisis, regulators have been looking to strengthen the capital base of financial institutions, particularly in the banking sector. Rising requirements for capital adequacy have resulted in banks looking into new forms of capital instruments. One form of such capital instruments are financial instruments that convert into a variable number of the issuer's own ordinary shares if the institution breaches a minimum regulatory requirement. This type of contingent event is called a 'non-viability' event.

While the exact terms of these instruments vary in practice, they do generally come with the following key features:

- no stated maturity but the issuer can call the instrument for the par amount of cash;
- while the instrument has a stated interest rate (e.g. 5%), payment of interest is at the discretion of the issuer; and
- if the issuer breaches a minimum regulatory requirement (e.g. 'Tier 1 Capital ratio'), the instrument mandatorily converts into a variable number of the issuer's own ordinary shares. The number of shares delivered would depend on the current share price, i.e. the issuer must deliver as many shares as are worth the par amount of the instrument at conversion.

In July 2013 the Interpretations Committee considered a request to clarify the accounting for such instruments.[28] In its tentative agenda decision, the Committee noted that the instrument is a compound instrument that is composed of the following two components:

- a liability component, which reflects the issuer's obligation to deliver a variable number of its own equity instruments if the contingent non-viability event occurs; and
- an equity component, which reflects the issuer's discretion to pay interest.

To measure the liability component, the Interpretations Committee noted that the issuer must consider the fact that the contingent non-viability event could occur immediately because it is beyond the control of the issuer. Hence the liability component must be measured at the full amount that the issuer could be required to pay immediately. The equity component would be measured as a residual and thus would be measured at zero, because the instrument is issued at par and the value of the variable number of shares that will be delivered on conversion is equal to that fixed par amount.

The Interpretations Committee received 12 comment letters on the tentative agenda decision, many accepting that the Interpretation Committee's view is one way of analysing the financial instrument under IAS 32, but generally expressing the view that the relevant guidance in IAS 32 is unclear and that equally valid arguments could be made for other views. For instance, one view discussed at the time was that, when measuring the liability component, the issuer should consider the expected timing of the contingent non-viability event occurring and discount the liability accordingly. Therefore, if the issuer believed that the contingency would not occur in the near-term, the liability component would be recognised at an amount of less than par. The comments provided focused in particular on (a) the measurement of the liability component and (b) whether interest paid on the instrument, if any, would need to be recognised in equity or as interest in profit or loss. Based on the comments received, the Interpretations Committee decided, after further discussions in its January 2014 meeting, not to add this issue to its agenda and noted that the scope of the issues raised in the submission was too broad to be addressed in an efficient manner.[29] There is therefore the potential for diversity in practice until this issue is clarified by the IASB. This is illustrated by the following example:

Example 45.12 Convertible bond mandatorily convertible upon 'non-viability' event

A bank issues €100 million of contingent convertible bonds. The bonds notionally pay fixed interest of 7% annually however interest payments are at the sole discretion of the issuer providing that no dividend is paid on the ordinary shares of the issuer. The bonds are perpetual, but the issuer has the right to call the shares after five years and on every succeeding fifth anniversary thereafter.

The instrument is immediately converted into ordinary shares with a fair value equal to the par value of the bonds upon either:

- the bank's fully loaded Common Equity Tier 1 (CET 1) ratio falling below 7%; or
- the local regulator declaring a non-viability event.

The instrument has both debt features, such as the contingent settlement provision which requires settlement in a variable number of shares upon a non-viability event, and equity features, such as the perpetual nature of the instrument and the discretionary interest payments. As discussed above there are a number of views that could be taken on how to classify this instrument.

Based on the Interpretations Committee's discussion, the view could be taken that the bonds are a compound instrument and that because the contingent settlement provision might be activated immediately, a liability for the par amount of the bond should be recorded. The equity component of the instrument representing the discretionary interest payments would therefore have no value.

However this could be viewed as odd given that there is usually no expectation that a trigger event will occur when the instrument is first issued. As such it might be considered to be more reasonable to estimate when a trigger event is most likely to occur and calculate the liability component on that basis with the residual amount being classified as equity.

There is a further argument that the whole instrument falls within the definition of a liability rather than a compound instrument as the entity may be required to deliver a variable number of shares for a non-derivative instrument. *[IAS 32.11(b)(i)]*.

The conversion trigger itself is not a separable embedded derivative as redemption at amortised cost is regarded as being closely related to the host contract. This is the case even if the debt and equity components of the instrument are separated, as the evaluation of the embedded derivative has to be performed prior to the separation of the equity component. *[IAS 39.AG30(g)]*.

Similarly the call option exercisable to extend the term of the instrument is not a separable embedded derivative as the option is at par and so is also closely related.

Any discretionary interest payments would be classified depending on whether the host is classified as a liability, in which case the payments would be interest, or as a compound instrument, in which case payments would be dividends.

A further complication arises with the recent introduction of bank resolution regimes, such as the European Union's Banking Recovery and Resolution Directive (BRRD). These regimes subject certain financial instruments to bail-in, where banking regulators have the power to write down an instrument or convert it into another CET 1 instrument at their discretion.

As the right to convert the instrument is at the option of the regulator and not the issuer it is arguable that the instrument cannot be classified as equity. The exception for settlement in case of liquidation (see 4.3.2 above) does not apply here as the regulator is likely to invoke the resolution tool well before liquidation occurs. Also IFRIC 2 specifies that local law and regulations in effect at the classification date together with the terms contained in the instrument's documentation constitute the terms and conditions of the instrument. *[IFRIC 2.BC10]*.

The main conclusion to be drawn from examples such as these is that the provisions of IAS 32, which were originally drafted in the mid-1990s to deal with 'traditional' convertible instruments, are not always adequate for dealing with the increasingly complex range of instruments available in the financial markets.

6.6.4 *Foreign currency convertible bond*

If an entity issues a bond in a currency other than its functional currency, the conversion option will not meet the definition of equity in IAS 32, even if the bond is convertible into a fixed number of shares. This is because a fixed amount of foreign currency (a currency different to the functional currency of the bond) is not a fixed amount of cash (see 5.2.3 above). A foreign currency convertible bond is therefore classified as a financial liability under IAS 32, and then measured under the requirements of IAS 39. An equity conversion option embedded in a financial liability is not considered by IAS 39 to be clearly and closely related to the host contract, and should be accounted for as a separate derivative financial instrument measured at fair value through profit or loss.

6.6.4.A *Instrument issued by foreign subsidiary convertible into equity of parent*

The Interpretations Committee's conclusion that (other than in the context of certain rights issues – see 5.2.3.A above) a fixed amount of cash denominated in a currency other than the entity's functional currency is not a 'fixed amount' of cash (see 5.2.3 above) leads to the rather counter-intuitive result that the classification of certain instruments in consolidated financial statements depends on the functional currency of the issuing entity.

If, in the example in 5.2.3 above, the UK entity's US subsidiary (with a functional currency of US dollars) issued the same $100 bond convertible into its own equity, convertible in turn into the UK parent's equity, the conversion right would (from the perspective of the US subsidiary) involve the issue of a fixed number of shares for a fixed amount of cash and thus be an equity instrument. Moreover, this classification would not change on consolidation since IFRS has no concept of a group functional currency (see Chapter 15).

The Interpretations Committee discussed this issue at its meetings in July and November 2006. Specifically, it was asked to consider whether the fixed stated principal of the convertible instrument exchanged for equity of the parent on conversion can be considered 'fixed' if it is denominated in the functional currency of either the issuer of the exchangeable financial instruments (i.e. the US subsidiary in the example above) or the issuer of the equity instruments (i.e. the UK parent in the example).

The Interpretations Committee noted that a group does not have a functional currency. It therefore discussed whether it should add a project to its agenda to address which currency should be the reference point in determining whether the embedded conversion options are denominated in a foreign currency. The Interpretations Committee believed that the issue was sufficiently narrow that it was not expected to have widespread relevance in practice. The Interpretations Committee, therefore, decided not to take the issue onto its agenda.[30]

In our view, given the absence of specific guidance, an entity may, as a matter of accounting policy, determine the classification, in its consolidated financial statements, of an instrument issued by a subsidiary by reference either to that subsidiary's own functional currency or to the functional currency of the parent into whose equity the bond is convertible.

The effect of this policy choice will be that, where the debt is denominated in a currency other than the designated reference functional currency, the consolidated financial statements contain no equity component. This policy, and its consequences under IAS 32, must be applied consistently, as illustrated by Example 45.13 below.

Example 45.13: Convertible bond issued by a subsidiary with a functional currency different to that of the parent

Suppose that a UK entity with a functional currency of the pound sterling (GBP) has a US trading subsidiary with a functional currency of the US dollar (USD). The US subsidiary issues a bond convertible, at the holder's option, into equity of the UK parent.

If the parent's functional currency (GBP) is the reference currency, the accounting treatment of the holder's conversion right in the consolidated financial statements will be as follows:

- if the fixed stated principal of the bond is denominated in GBP: equity (stated principal of bond is fixed by reference to GBP); but
- if the fixed stated principal of the bond is denominated in a currency other than GBP: derivative (stated principal of bond is variable by reference to GBP).

If, however, the subsidiary's functional currency (USD) is the reference currency, a converse analysis applies, and the accounting treatment of the holder's conversion right in the consolidated financial statements will be as follows:

- if the fixed stated principal of the bond is denominated in USD: equity (stated principal of bond is fixed by reference to USD); but
- if the fixed stated principal of the bond is denominated in a currency other than USD: derivative (stated principal of bond is variable by reference to USD).

It may be that the Interpretations Committee's reluctance to issue guidance on this matter was influenced by the more subtle point that, in most cases, the issuing entity will not be, as in Example 45.13 above, a trading subsidiary, but rather a subsidiary created only for the purposes of the bond issue. IAS 21 – *The Effects of Changes in Foreign Exchange Rates* – suggests that the functional currency of such a 'single transaction' entity is the same as that of the parent for whose equity the bond will be exchanged, irrespective of the currency in which the bond is denominated (see Chapter 15 at 4). In short, the

Interpretations Committee was perhaps hinting that the real problem may be the misapplication of IAS 21 in the financial statements of the issuing subsidiary rather than the interpretation of IAS 32.

6.6.5 *Convertibles with cash settlement at the option of the issuer*

As discussed as 5.2.8 above, IAS 32 requires a derivative with two or more settlement options to be treated as a financial asset or a financial liability unless all possible settlement alternatives would result in it being an equity instrument. Many convertible bonds currently in issue contain a provision whereby, if the holder exercises its conversion option, the issuer may instead pay cash equal to the fair value of the shares that it would otherwise have been required to deliver. This is to allow for unforeseen circumstances, such as an inability to issue the necessary number of shares to effect conversion at the appropriate time.

Where a bond has such a term, the conversion right is a derivative (in effect, a written call option over the issuer's own shares) which may potentially be settled in cash, such that there is a settlement alternative that does not result in it being an equity instrument. This means that the 'equity component' of a bond with an issuer cash settlement option is not in fact an equity instrument, but a financial liability. The financial reporting implication of this is that the conversion right must be accounted for as a derivative at fair value, with changes in value included in profit or loss – in other words the financial statements will reflect gains and losses based on the movement of the reporting entity's own share price.

6.6.6 *Bond convertible into fixed percentage of equity*

The terms of a convertible bond may allow conversion into a fixed percentage of outstanding shares of the issuer at the time of the conversion, so that the absolute number of shares to be issued is not fixed and is not known until conversion occurs. This raises the question of whether such a clause violates the 'fixed for fixed' criterion, or whether it can be seen as an anti-dilutive mechanism to keep the holder in the same economic position relative to other shareholders at all times (similarly to bonds whose conversion ratio is adjusted for changes in share capital, as discussed under 5.1.2 above).

Our view is that such a conversion option cannot normally be classified as equity, because the entity's capital structure could change in ways that put the convertible bond holder into a better economic position relative to other shareholders.

7 SETTLEMENT OF FINANCIAL LIABILITY WITH EQUITY INSTRUMENT

Neither IAS 32 nor IAS 39 specifically addresses the accounting treatment to be adopted where an entity issues non-convertible debt, but subsequently enters into an agreement with the debt holder to discharge all or part of the liability in exchange for an issue of equity. These transactions, which are sometimes referred to as 'debt for equity swaps', most often occur when the entity is in financial difficulties and became widespread, particularly among highly leveraged entities, following the financial crisis.

The Interpretations Committee noted that divergent accounting treatments for such transactions were being applied and decided to address this by developing an interpretation. As a result, IFRIC 19 was published in November 2009. *[IFRIC 19.1]*.

7.1 Scope and effective date of IFRIC 19

IFRIC 19 addresses the accounting by an entity when the terms of a financial liability are renegotiated and result in the entity issuing equity instruments to a creditor to extinguish all or part of the financial liability. It does not address the accounting by the creditor. *[IFRIC 19.2]*.

Further, the interpretation does not apply to transactions in situations where: *[IFRIC 19.3]*

- the creditor is also a direct or indirect shareholder and is acting in its capacity as a direct or indirect existing shareholder (see 7.3 below);
- the creditor and the entity are controlled by the same party or parties before and after the transaction and the substance of the transaction includes an equity distribution by, or contribution to, the entity (see 7.3 below); or
- the extinguishment of the financial liability by issuing equity shares is in accordance with the original terms of the financial liability. This will most commonly arise on conversion of a convertible bond that has been subject to 'split accounting', the accounting for which is covered at 6 above.

7.2 Requirements of IFRIC 19

Equity instruments issued to a creditor to extinguish all or part of a financial liability are treated as consideration paid and should normally be measured at their fair value at the date of extinguishment. However, if that fair value cannot be reliably measured, the equity instruments should be measured to reflect the fair value of the financial liability extinguished. The difference between the carrying amount of the financial liability and the consideration paid (including the equity instruments issued) should be recognised in profit or loss and should be disclosed separately. *[IFRIC 19.5-7, 9, 11]*.

These requirements are illustrated in the following simple example.

Example 45.14 Discharge of liability for fresh issue of equity

During 2010 an entity issued £100 million bonds due to be repaid in 2020. By 2017 the entity is in some financial difficulty and reaches an agreement with the holders of the bonds whereby they will accept equity shares in the entity in full and final settlement of all amounts due under the bonds. On the date the agreement concludes, the carrying amount of the bonds is £99 million and the fair value of the equity shares issued is £60 million.

In this situation the entity would measure the equity instruments issued at their fair value of £60 million and recognise a profit on extinguishment of £39 million [£99 million – £60 million].

Debt for equity swaps often take place in situations when the terms of the financial liability such as covenants are breached and the liability has become, or will become, repayable on demand. Normally, the fair value of a financial liability with a demand feature is required by IFRS 13 to be measured at no less than the amount payable on demand, discounted from the first date that the amount could be required to be paid (see Chapter 14 at 11.5). However, in the IASB's view, the fact that a debt for equity swap has occurred indicates that the demand feature is no longer substantive. Consequently, where the fair value of the equity instruments issued is based on the fair value of the liability extinguished, this particular aspect of IFRS 13 is not applied. *[IFRIC 19.7, BC22]*.

If only part of the financial liability is extinguished, some of the consideration paid might relate to a modification of the terms of the liability that remains outstanding. If so, the consideration paid should be allocated between the part of the liability extinguished and the part of the liability that remains outstanding. All relevant facts and circumstances relating to the transaction should be considered in making this allocation. *[IFRIC 19.8]*. Any consideration so allocated forms part of the assessment of whether the terms of that remaining liability have been substantially modified. If the remaining liability has been substantially modified, the modification should be accounted for as an extinguishment of the original liability and the recognition of a new liability in accordance with IAS 39 (see Chapter 51 at 6.2). *[IFRIC 19.10]*.

7.3 Debt for equity swaps with shareholders

As noted at 7.1 above, a debt for equity swap is outside the scope of IFRIC 19 when the creditor is a shareholder acting in its capacity as such, or where the entity and the creditor are under common control and the substance of the transaction includes a distribution by, or capital contribution to, the entity.

In our view, such transactions may be accounted for either in a manner similar to that required by IFRIC 19 or by recording the equity instruments issued at the carrying amount of the financial liability extinguished so that no profit or loss is recognised. This latter method was in fact commonly applied to debt for equity swaps before the publication of IFRIC 19.

8 INTEREST, DIVIDENDS, GAINS AND LOSSES

The basic principle of IAS 32 is that inflows and outflows of cash (and other assets) associated with equity instruments are recognised in equity and the net impact of inflows and outflows of cash (and other assets) associated with financial liabilities is ultimately recognised in profit or loss. Accordingly, IAS 32 requires:

- interest, dividends, losses and gains relating to a financial instrument or a component that is a financial liability to be recognised as income or expense in profit or loss;
- distributions to holders of an equity instrument to be debited directly to equity; and
- the transaction costs of an equity transaction to be accounted for as a deduction from equity, other than the costs of issuing an equity instrument that are directly attributable to the acquisition of a business (which are accounted for under IFRS 3 – see Chapter 9). *[IAS 32.35]*.

The treatment of the costs and gains associated with instruments is determined by their classification in the financial statements under IAS 32, and not by their legal form. Thus dividends paid on shares classified as financial liabilities (see 4.5 above) will be recognised as an expense in profit or loss, not as an appropriation of equity.

The basic principle summarised above also applies to compound instruments and requires any payments in relation to the equity component to be recorded in equity and any payments in relation to the liability component to be recorded in profit or loss. (As discussed at 6.6.3.B above, it is not clear whether this basic principle also applies when the full amount of the issuance proceeds of a compound instrument is allocated to the liability.) A mandatorily redeemable preference share with dividends paid at the discretion of the entity results in the classification of a liability equal to the net present value of the redemption amount and an equity classification equal to the excess of the proceeds over the liability component (the net present value of the redemption amount) (see 4.5.1 above). Because the redemption obligation is classified as a liability, the unwinding of the discount on this component is recorded and classified as an interest expense. Any dividends paid, on the other hand, relate to the equity component and are therefore recorded as a distribution of profit. *[IAS 32.AG37]*.

Gains and losses associated with redemptions or refinancings of financial liabilities are recognised in profit or loss, whereas redemptions or refinancings of equity instruments are recognised as changes in equity. *[IAS 32.36]*.

Similarly, gains and losses related to changes in the carrying amount of a financial liability are recognised as income or expense in profit or loss, even when they relate to an instrument that includes a right to the residual interest in the assets of the entity in exchange for cash or another financial asset (see 4.6 above). However, IAS 32 notes that IAS 1 requires any gain or loss arising from the remeasurement of such an instrument to be shown separately in the statement of comprehensive income, where it is relevant in explaining the entity's performance. *[IAS 32.41]*.

Changes in the fair value of an instrument that meets the definition of an equity instrument are not recognised in the financial statements. *[IAS 32.36]*.

IAS 32 permits dividends classified as an expense (i.e. because they relate to an instrument, or component of an instrument, that is legally a share but classified as a financial liability under IAS 32) to be presented in the statement of comprehensive income or separate income statement (if presented), either with interest on other liabilities or as a separate item. The standard notes that, in some circumstances, separate disclosure is desirable, because of the differences between interest and dividends with respect to matters such as tax deductibility. Disclosure of interest and dividends is required by IAS 1 (see Chapter 3) and IFRS 7 (see Chapter 54). *[IAS 32.40]*.

8.1 Transaction costs of equity transactions

An entity typically incurs various costs in issuing or acquiring its own equity instruments, such as registration and other regulatory fees, amounts paid to legal, accounting and other professional advisers, printing costs and stamp duties. The transaction costs of an equity transaction are accounted for as a deduction from equity, but only to the extent they are *incremental costs directly attributable* to the equity transaction that otherwise would have been avoided. The costs of an equity transaction that is abandoned are recognised as an expense. *[IAS 32.37]*.

IAS 32 requires that only the costs of 'issuing or acquiring' equity are recognised in equity. Accordingly, it seems clear that the costs of listing shares already in issue should not be set off against equity, but recognised as an expense.

The standard also requires that transaction costs that relate jointly to more than one transaction (for example, costs of a concurrent offering of some shares and a stock exchange listing of other shares) are allocated to those transactions using a basis of allocation that is rational and consistent with similar transactions. *[IAS 32.38]*. In its agenda decision of September 2008, the Interpretations Committee declined to provide further guidance on the extent of the transaction costs to be accounted for as a deduction from equity and how to allocate costs that relate jointly to more than one transaction, believing existing guidance to be adequate.

However, the Interpretations Committee noted that the terms 'incremental' and 'directly attributable' are used with similar but not identical meanings in many Standards and Interpretations, leading to diversity in practice. It therefore recommended that the IASB develop common definitions for both terms to be added to the Glossary as part of the annual improvements process.[31] However, the IASB did not propose any such amendments in the next exposure draft published in August 2009.

It may well be that, in an initial public offering ('IPO'), for example, an entity simultaneously lists its existing equity and additional newly-issued equity. In that situation the total costs of the IPO should, in our view, be allocated between the newly issued shares and the existing shares on a rational basis (e.g. by reference to the ratio of the number of new shares to the number of total shares), with only the proportion relating to the issue of new shares being deducted from equity.

Transaction costs that relate to the issue of a compound financial instrument are allocated to the liability and equity components of the instrument in proportion to the allocation of proceeds (see Example 45.4 at 6.2 above). *[IAS 32.37]*.

IAS 32 does not specifically address the treatment of transaction costs incurred to acquire a non-controlling interest in a subsidiary, or dispose of such an interest without loss of control in the consolidated financial statements of the parent entity. IFRS 10 indicates that 'changes in a parent's ownership interest in a subsidiary that do not result in the parent losing control of the subsidiary are equity transactions'. *[IFRS 10.23]*. Accordingly, we believe that the costs of such transactions should be deducted from equity in accordance with the principles described above.

IAS 32 and IFRS 10 do not specify whether such costs should be allocated to the parent's equity or to the non-controlling interest, to the extent it is still reflected in the statement of financial position. In our view, this is a matter of choice based on the facts and circumstances surrounding the transaction, and any local legal requirements. On any subsequent disposal of the subsidiary involving loss of control, the transaction costs previously recognised in equity should not be reclassified from equity to profit or loss, since they represent transactions with owners in their capacity as owners rather than components of other comprehensive income. *[IAS 1.106, 109]*.

The amount of transaction costs accounted for as a deduction from equity in the period is required to be disclosed separately under IAS 1 (see Chapter 3 at 3.3) and IFRS 7 (see Chapter 54 at 7.3).

8.2 Tax effects of equity transactions

As originally issued, IAS 32 required distributions to shareholders and transaction costs of equity instruments to be shown net of any tax benefit. *Annual Improvements to IFRSs 2009-2011 Cycle* issued in May 2012 amended IAS 32 so as to remove the reference to income tax benefit from IAS 32. This means that all tax effects of equity transactions are allocated in accordance with the general principles of IAS 12.

Unfortunately, it is not entirely clear how IAS 12 requires the tax effects of certain equity transactions to be dealt with and different views can be taken whether tax benefits in respect of distributions are to be recognised in equity or profit or loss (see Chapter 31 at 10.3.5).

9 TREASURY SHARES

Treasury shares are shares issued by an entity that are held by the entity. *[IAS 32.33]*. In consolidated financial statements, this will include shares issued by any group entity that are held by that entity or by any other members of the consolidated group. They will also include shares held by an employee benefit trust that is consolidated or treated as an extension of the reporting entity. Treasury shares will generally not include shares in a group entity held by any associates or the entity's pension fund. However, IAS 1 requires disclosure of own shares held by subsidiaries or associates, *[IAS 1.79(a)(vi)]*, and IAS 19 – *Employee Benefits* – requires disclosure of own shares held by defined benefit plans. *[IAS 19.143]*. Holdings of treasury shares may arise in a number of ways. For example:

- The entity holds the shares as the result of a direct transaction, such as a market purchase, or a buy-back of shares from shareholders as a whole, or a particular group of shareholders.
- The entity is in the financial services sector with a market-making operation that buys and sells its own shares along with those of other listed entities in the normal course of business, or holds them in order to 'hedge' issued derivatives.
- In consolidated financial statements:
  - the shares were purchased by another entity which subsequently became a subsidiary of the reporting entity, either through acquisition or changes in financial reporting requirements; or
  - the shares have been purchased by an entity that is a consolidated SPE of the reporting entity.

The circumstances in which an entity is permitted to hold treasury shares are a matter for legislation in the jurisdiction concerned.

Treasury shares do not include own shares held by an entity on behalf of others, such as when a financial institution holds its own equity on behalf of a client. In such cases, there is an agency relationship and as a result those holdings are not included in the entity's statement of financial position, either as assets or as a deduction from equity. *[IAS 32.AG36]*.

If an entity reacquires its own equity instruments, IAS 32 requires those instruments to be deducted from equity. They are not recognised as financial assets, regardless of the reason for which they are reacquired. No gain or loss is recognised in profit or loss on the purchase, sale, issue or cancellation of an entity's own equity instruments. Accordingly, any consideration paid or received in connection with treasury shares must be recognised directly in equity. *[IAS 32.33, AG36]*.

IAS 1 requires the amount of treasury shares to be disclosed separately either on the face of the statement of financial position or in the notes (see Chapter 3 at 3.1.6). In addition, IAS 32 requires an entity to make disclosure in accordance with IAS 24 – *Related Party Disclosures* – if the entity reacquires its own equity instruments from related parties (see Chapter 37 at 2.5). *[IAS 32.34]*.

As in the case of the requirements for the treatment of the equity component of a compound financial instrument (see 6 above), IAS 32 does not prescribe precisely what components of equity should be adjusted as the result of a treasury share transaction. This may have been to ensure that there was no conflict between, on the one hand, the basic requirement of IAS 32 that there should be an adjustment to equity and, on the other hand, the legal requirements of various jurisdictions as to exactly how that adjustment should be allocated within equity.

9.1 Transactions in own shares not at fair value

The requirement of IAS 32 that no profits or losses should ever be recognised on transactions in own equity instruments differs from the approach taken in IFRS 2. If an employee share award is characterised as an equity instrument under IFRS 2 (a 'share-settled' award) and settled in cash (or other assets) at more than its fair value, the excess of the consideration over the fair value is recognised as an expense (see Chapter 32).

It is not clear whether or not the IASB specifically considered transactions in own equity other than at fair value in the context of IAS 32, particularly since the relevant provisions of IAS 32 essentially reproduce requirements previously contained in SIC-16 – *Share Capital – Reacquired Own Equity Instruments (Treasury Shares)* – which was implicitly addressing market purchases and sales at fair value. In other words, the provision can be seen merely as clarifying that, if an entity buys one of its own shares in the market for £10 which it later reissues in the market at £12 or £7, it has not made, respectively, a profit of £2 or a loss of £3.

This is slightly different to the situation where an entity purchases an equity instrument for more than its fair value – i.e. if the original purchase had been for £11 when the market price was £10. Such a transaction could occur, for example where the entity wishes to rid itself of a troublesome shareholder or group of shareholders. In this case, the entity might have to offer a premium specific to the holder over and above the 'true' fair value of the equity instruments concerned. There could be an argument that such a transaction does not fall within the type of transaction envisaged by the rules for treasury shares, such that the holder-specific premium should be accounted for in profit or loss, not equity. Alternatively, it might be argued that, in the specific circumstances, the amount paid is the fair value of the particular shares concerned.

A transaction in which the entity issues shares (or reissues treasury shares) for cash or other assets with a fair value lower than the fair value of the shares would *prima facie* fall within the scope of IFRS 2, requiring the shortfall to be accounted for under IFRS 2 (see Chapter 32 at 2.2.2.C).

10 'HEDGING' OF INSTRUMENTS CLASSIFIED AS EQUITY

A consequence of the requirement, discussed in 4.5.2 to 4.5.6 above, to treat discretionary instruments with certain debt-like characteristics as equity is that the issuer will not be able to adopt hedge accounting in respect of any instrument taken out as a hedge of the instrument (e.g. a receive fixed, pay floating interest rate swap taken out to hedge a fixed rate discretionary dividend on non-redeemable shares). This is because IAS 39 does not recognise a hedge of own equity as a valid hedging relationship (see Chapter 52 and 53).

Accordingly, if an issuer of an equity instrument bearing a fixed-rate discretionary coupon or dividend enters into an interest rate swap to hedge its cash outflows, the swap will be accounted for under the normal rules for derivatives not forming part of a hedging relationship – i.e. at fair value with all value changes recognised in profit or loss (see Chapters 46, 47 and 48). Although, economically speaking, any such gains and losses are offset by equal gains and losses (due to interest rate movements) on the shares, the latter, like all movements in the fair value of own equity, are ignored for financial reporting purposes under IFRS.

11 DERIVATIVES OVER OWN EQUITY INSTRUMENTS

IAS 32 provides a number of detailed examples of the accounting treatment required, under the provisions of revised IAS 32 and IAS 39, to be adopted by an entity for derivative contracts over its own equity instruments. Examples are given of each of the main possible permutations, namely:

- a forward purchase (see 11.1.1 below);
- a forward sale (see 11.1.2 below);
- a purchased call option (see 11.2.1 below);
- a written call option (see 11.2.2 below);
- a purchased put option (see 11.3.1 below); and
- a written put option (see 11.3.2 below).

All such contracts can be either:

(a) net cash-settled (i.e. the contract provides that the parties will compare the fair value of the shares to be delivered by the seller to the amount of cash payable by the buyer and make a cash payment between themselves for the difference);

(b) net share-settled (i.e. the contract provides that the parties will compare the fair value of the shares to be delivered by the seller to the amount of cash payable by the buyer and make a transfer between themselves of as many of the entity's shares as have a fair value equal to the difference);

(c) gross settled (i.e. the contract provides that the seller will deliver shares to the buyer in exchange for cash); or

(d) subject to various settlement options, whereby the manner of settlement is not predetermined, and instead one or other party can choose the manner of settlement (i.e. gross, net cash or net shares).

The examples consider the above settlement options in turn for the main possible permutations of derivatives over own equity instruments.

All derivative contracts over own equity, where settlement is not exclusively by an exchange of a fixed number of shares for a fixed amount of cash, do not meet the definition of equity instruments in IAS 32 and are, in general, treated as derivative financial assets or liabilities (see 5.2.8 above). IAS 39, or where applicable IFRS 9, requires such contracts to be accounted for at fair value through profit or loss (see Chapter 48). Exemption to this rule applies to forward purchases and written put options with an option to settle gross (see 11.1.1 and 11.3.2 below).

11.1 Forward contracts

11.1.1 Forward purchase

In a forward purchase transaction, the entity and a counterparty agree that on a given future date the counterparty will sell a given number of the entity's shares to the entity. Such a contract is illustrated in Example 45.15 below. *[IAS 32.IE2-6]*.

Example 45.15 Forward purchase of shares

The reporting entity (A), which has a functional currency of Euro and a year end of 31 December, and another party (B) enter into a forward contract for the purchase of A's shares by A, for which the following are the major assumptions.

Contract date	1 February 2017
Maturity date	31 January 2018
Fixed forward price to be paid on 31 January 2018	€104
Present value of forward price on 1 February 2017	€100
Number of shares under contract	1,000
Market price per share on 1 February 2017	€100
Market price per share on 31 December 2017	€110
Market price per share on 31 January 2018	€106
Fair value of forward to A on 1 February 2017	€0
Fair value of forward to A on 31 December 2017	€6,300
Fair value of forward to A on 31 January 2018	€2,000

For simplicity, it is assumed that no dividends are paid on the underlying shares (i.e. the 'carry return' is zero) so that the present value of the forward price equals the spot price when the fair value of the forward contract is zero. The fair value of the forward has been computed as the difference between the market share price and the present value of the fixed forward price. At settlement date this is €2,000 representing 1,000 shares at €2, being the difference between the market price of €106 and the contract price of €104.

A Net cash settlement

If the contract is entered into as net cash-settled on 1 February 2017, settlement on 31 January 2018 will take the form of receipt or delivery by A of a cash payment for the difference between the fair value of 1,000 of A's own shares, at 31 January 2018, and €104,000 (i.e. 1,000 shares at the forward price of €104 per share). Since IAS 32 classifies such contracts as derivative financial assets or liabilities (see 11 and 5.2.7 above), which are carried at fair value through profit or loss under IAS 39 (IFRS 9), A records the following accounting entries:

	€	€
1 February 2017		
No entry is required because the fair value of the contract is zero at inception and no cash is paid or received		
31 December 2017		
Forward contract (statement of financial position)	6,300	
Gain on forward (profit or loss)		6,300
To record movement in fair value of forward from zero to €6,300		
31 January 2018		
Loss on forward (profit or loss)	4,300	
Forward contract (statement of financial position)		4,300
To record movement in fair value of forward from €6,300 to €2,000		
Cash	2,000	
Forward contract (statement of financial position)		2,000
To record settlement of forward by payment of €2,000 by B to A		

B Net share settlement

If the contract is entered into as net share-settled on 1 February 2017, settlement on 31 January 2018 will take the form of receipt or delivery by A of as many of A's shares as have a fair value equal to the difference between the fair value, at 31 January 2018, of 1,000 of A's own shares and €104,000 (i.e. 1,000 shares at the forward price of €104 per share). Because IAS 32 classifies such contracts as derivative financial assets or liabilities (see 11 and 5.2.7 above), which are carried at fair value through profit or loss under IAS 39 (or IFRS 9), A records the following accounting entries:

	€	€
1 February 2017		
No entry is required because the fair value of the contract is zero at inception and no cash is paid or received		
31 December 2017		
Forward contract (statement of financial position)	6,300	
Gain on forward (profit or loss)		6,300
To record movement in fair value of forward from zero to €6,300		
31 January 2018		
Loss on forward (profit or loss)	4,300	
Forward contract (statement of financial position)		4,300
To record movement in fair value of forward from €6,300 to €2,000		
Equity	2,000	
Forward contract (statement of financial position)		2,000
To record net settlement of forward by transfer of €2,000 worth of A's shares (€2000/106=18.9 shares) by B to A. This is shown as a deduction from equity in accordance with IAS 32's requirements for treasury shares (see 9 above).		

C Gross settlement

If the contract is entered into as gross-settled on 1 February 2017, settlement on 31 January 2018 will take the form of receipt of 1,000 own shares by A in exchange for a payment of €104,000 to B. IAS 32 classifies this derivative contract as an equity instrument giving rise to a financial liability for the present value of the purchase price amount payable in one year's time (see 5.3 above). On the assumption that A accounts for this liability under the effective interest method in IAS 39 (or IFRS 9), A records the following accounting entries:

	€	€
1 February 2017		
Equity	100,000	
Liability for forward contract (statement of financial position)		100,000
To record net present value of liability on forward contract		
31 December 2017		
Interest expense	3,660	
Liability for forward contract (statement of financial position)		3,660
To accrue interest, under the effective interest rate method, on the liability to settle forward contract		
31 January 2018		
Interest expense	340	
Liability for forward contract (statement of financial position)		340
To accrue further interest, under the effective interest rate method, on the liability to settle forward contract		
Liability for forward contract (statement of financial position)	104,000	
Cash		104,000
To record settlement of the liability in cash		

D Settlement options

If there are settlement options (such as net in cash, net in shares or by an exchange of a fixed amount of cash for a fixed number of shares), the forward contract is a financial asset or a financial liability – see 5.2.7 above. The contract does not meet the definition of an equity instrument, because it can be settled otherwise than by delivery of a fixed amount of cash for a fixed number of equity instruments. If one of the settlement alternatives is gross settlement by an exchange of cash for shares, A recognises a liability for the obligation to deliver cash. Otherwise, A accounts for the forward contract as a derivative.

The implementation guidance to IAS 32 states that A should recognise a liability 'if one of the settlement alternatives is to exchange cash for shares'. As drafted, this applies whether the choice of settlement rests with A or B. This seems curious since, where A has the choice of settlement, there would be no obligation for A to settle gross. We assume that the example is written on the presumption that the choice of settlement would normally rest with the counterparty rather than the entity. Paragraph 23 in the main body of the standard is clear that an equity contract gives rise to a liability for the purchase price of the shares only where there is an obligation for the entity to purchase its own equity. Accordingly, in our view, where the choice of settlement rests only with the entity, it is acceptable to record no liability, and to account for the contract as a derivative.

11.1.2 Forward sale

In a forward sale transaction, the entity and a counterparty agree that on a given future date the entity will sell (or issue) a given number of the entity's shares to the counterparty. Such a contract is illustrated in Example 45.16 below. *[IAS 32.IE7-11]*.

Example 45.16 Forward sale of shares

The reporting entity (A), which has a functional currency of Euro and a year end of 31 December, and another party (B) enter into a forward contract for the purchase of A's shares by B, for which the following are the major assumptions.

Contract date	1 February 2017
Maturity date	31 January 2018
Fixed forward price to be paid on 31 January 2018	€104
Present value of forward price on 1 February 2017	€100
Number of shares under contract	1,000
Market price per share on 1 February 2017	€100
Market price per share on 31 December 2017	€110
Market price per share on 31 January 2018	€106
Fair value of forward to A on 1 February 2017	€0
Fair value of forward to A on 31 December 2017	€(6,300)
Fair value of forward to A on 31 January 2018	€(2,000)

For simplicity, it is assumed that no dividends are paid on the underlying shares (i.e. the 'carry return' is zero) so that the present value of the forward price equals the spot price when the fair value of the forward contract is zero. The fair value of the forward has been computed as the difference between the market share price and the present value of the fixed forward price. At settlement date this is negative €2,000 representing 1,000 shares at €2, being the difference between the market price of €106 and the contract price of €104.

A Net cash settlement

If the contract is entered into as net cash-settled on 1 February 2017, settlement on 31 January 2018 will take the form of receipt or delivery by A of a cash payment for the difference between the fair value of 1,000 of A's own shares, at 31 January 2018, and €104,000 (i.e. 1,000 shares at the forward price of €104 per share). Since IAS 32 classifies such contracts as derivative financial assets or liabilities (see 11 and 5.2.7 above), which are carried at fair value through profit or loss under IAS 39 (or IFRS 9), A records the following accounting entries:

	€	€
1 February 2017		
No entry is required because the fair value of the contract is zero at inception and no cash is paid or received.		
31 December 2017		
Loss on forward (profit or loss)	6,300	
Forward contract (statement of financial position)		6,300
To record movement in fair value of forward from zero to €(6,300)		
31 January 2018		
Forward contract (statement of financial position)	4,300	
Gain on forward (profit or loss)		4,300
To record movement in fair value of forward from €(6,300) to €(2,000)		

Forward contract (statement of financial position)	2,000	
Cash		2,000
To record net settlement of forward by payment of €2,000 cash by A to B		

B Net share settlement

If the contract is entered into as net share-settled on 1 February 2017, settlement on 31 January 2018 will take the form of receipt or delivery by A of a payment of as many of A's shares as have a fair value equal to the difference between the fair value, at 31 January 2018, of 1,000 of A's own shares and €104,000 (i.e. 1,000 shares at the forward price of €104 per share). As IAS 32 classifies such contracts as derivative financial assets or liabilities (see 11 and 5.2.7 above), which are carried at fair value through profit or loss under IAS 39 (or IFRS 9), A records the following accounting entries:

	€	€
1 February 2017		
No entry is required because the fair value of the contract is zero at inception		
31 December 2017		
Loss on forward (profit or loss)	6,300	
Forward contract (statement of financial position)		6,300
To record movement in fair value of forward from zero to €(6,300)		
31 January 2018		
Forward contract (statement of financial position)	4,300	
Gain on forward (profit or loss)		4,300
To record movement in fair value of forward from €(6,300) to €(2,000)		
Forward contract (statement of financial position)	2,000	
Equity		2,000
To record net settlement of forward by delivery of €2,000 worth of A's shares to B (€2000/106=18.9 shares)		

C Gross settlement

If the contract is entered into as gross-settled on 1 February 2017, settlement on 31 January 2018 will take the form of delivery of 1,000 own shares by A to B in exchange for a payment of €104,000. IAS 32 classifies this derivative contract as an equity instrument (see 5.4 above) and therefore no entries are recorded other than on settlement on the contract. While a forward sale is economically a 'mirror' of a forward purchase and both are classified as equity instruments, the accounting impact is different. A forward sale does not result in any accounting entries until the shares are finally issued/delivered, while a forward purchase establishes an obligation to pay the settlement amount and therefore meets the definition of a financial liability which needs to be recorded upon entering the contract (see part C of Example 45.15 above).

	€	€
31 January 2018		
Cash	104,000	
Equity		104,000
To record settlement of forward contract through delivery of 1,000 shares for the payment of €104,000		

Chapter 45

D Settlement options

If there are settlement options (such as net in cash, net in shares or by an exchange of cash and shares), the forward contract is a financial asset or a financial liability – see 5.2.8 above. A accounts for the forward contract as a derivative (as in A and B above), with the accounting entry made on settlement determined by the manner of settlement (i.e. equity or cash).

11.1.3 'Back-to-back' forward contracts

The accounting treatment in 11.1.1 and 11.1.2 above produces rather strange results when applied to 'back-to-back' forward contracts, such as might be entered into by a financial institution with two different clients. Example 45.17 below illustrates the point.

Example 45.17 'Back-to-back' forward contracts

Suppose that a bank entered into the forward purchase contract in Example 45.15 above with a client and laid off its risk by entering into the reciprocal forward sale contract in Example 45.16 above with a second client. If both contracts are required to be settled gross, the overall effect of the accounting entries required to be made by the bank (assuming that the bank was the reporting entity in Examples 45.15 and 45.16 can be summarised as set out below. Note that these are not the actual entries that would be made, but the arithmetical sum of all the entries:

	€	€
Profit or loss (interest expense on liability for purchase contract)	4,000	
Equity (€104,000 on sale less €100,000 on purchase)		4,000

If the purchase contract is required to be settled gross, but the sale contract net in cash, the required accounting entries (again, not the actual entries, but the arithmetical sum of all the entries) can be summarised as:

	€	€
Profit or loss (loss on sale contract €2,000 plus interest on liability for purchase contract €4,000)	6,000	
Equity (purchase contract)	100,000	
Cash (€104,000 on purchase, €2,000 on sale)		106,000

If the purchase contract is required to be settled net in cash, but the sale contract gross, the required accounting entries (again, not the actual entries, but the arithmetical sum of all the entries) can be summarised as:

	€	€
Cash (€104,000 in on sale, €2,000 in on purchase)	106,000	
Profit or loss (gain on purchase contract)		2,000
Equity (sale contract)		104,000

If both contracts are net settled, no net gain or loss arises.

Some might argue that this exposes a flaw in the requirements of IAS 32. Self-evidently, these contracts are matched and should therefore, if both run to term, give rise to no economic profit or loss, irrespective of how they are settled. However, IAS 32 requires three different results to be shown depending on whether both contracts are settled gross, or one gross and the other net. This is less understandable in the case where both contracts are settled gross. However, in cases where one contract is settled net and that contract gives rise to an initial receipt or payment of cash, then some difference is bound to occur due to interest effects.

11.2 Call options

11.2.1 Purchased call option

In a purchased call option, the entity pays a counterparty for the right, but not the obligation, to purchase a given number of its own equity instruments from the counterparty for a fixed price at a future date. The accounting for such a contract is illustrated in Example 45.18 below. *[IAS 32.IE12-16]*.

Example 45.18 Purchased call option on shares

The reporting entity (A), which has a functional currency of Euro and a year end of 31 December, purchases a call option over its own shares from another party (B), for which the following are the major assumptions.

Contract date	1 February 2017
Exercise date (European terms – i.e. can be exercised only on maturity)	31 January 2018
Fixed exercise price to be paid on 31 January 2018	€102
Number of shares under contract	1,000
Market price per share on 1 February 2017	€100
Market price per share on 31 December 2017	€104
Market price per share on 31 January 2018	€104
Fair value of option to A on 1 February 2017	€5,000
Fair value of option to A on 31 December 2017	€3,000
Fair value of option to A on 31 January 2018	€2,000

The fair value of the option would be computed using an option pricing model and would be a function of a number of factors, principally the market value of the shares, the exercise price, and the time value of money.

A Net cash settlement

If the contract is entered into as net cash-settled on 1 February 2017, then A can, on the exercise date 31 January 2018, require B to make a cash payment to A for the excess, if any, of the fair value of 1,000 of A's own shares, as of 31 January 2018, over €102,000 (i.e. 1,000 shares at the option price of €102 per share). Since IAS 32 classifies such contracts as derivative financial assets (see 11 and 5.2.7 above), which are carried at fair value through profit or loss under IAS 39 (or IFRS 9), A records the following accounting entries:

1 February 2017	€	€
Call option asset	5,000	
Cash		5,000

Payment of option premium (equal to fair value of option) to B

31 December 2017		
Loss on option (profit or loss)	2,000	
Call option asset		2,000

To record movement in fair value of option from €5,000 to €3,000

31 January 2018	€	€
Loss on option (profit or loss)	1,000	
Call option asset		1,000
To record movement in fair value of option from €3,000 to €2,000		
Cash	2,000	
Call option asset		2,000
To record net settlement of option by payment of €2,000 cash by B to A		

B Net share settlement

If the contract is entered into as net share-settled on 1 February 2017, then A can, on the exercise date 31 January 2018, require B to deliver to A as many of A's own shares as have a fair value equal to any excess of 1,000 of A's own shares fair value, as of 31 January 2018 over €102,000 (i.e. 1,000 shares at the option price of €102 per share). Since IAS 32 classifies such contracts as derivative financial assets (see 11 and 5.2.7 above), which are carried at fair value through profit or loss under IAS 39 (or IFRS 9), A records the following accounting entries.

1 February 2017	€	€
Call option asset	5,000	
Cash		5,000
Payment of option premium (equal to fair value of option) to B		
31 December 2017		
Loss on option (profit or loss)	2,000	
Call option asset		2,000
To record movement in fair value of option from €5,000 to €3,000		
31 January 2018		
Loss on option (profit or loss)	1,000	
Call option asset		1,000
To record movement in fair value of option €3,000 to €2,000		
Equity	2,000	
Call option asset		2,000
To record net settlement of option by transfer of €2,000 worth of A's shares by B to A. This is shown as a deduction from equity in accordance with IAS 32's requirements for treasury shares (see 9 above).		

C Gross settlement

If the contract is entered into as gross-settled, on 1 February 2017, then A can, on the exercise date 31 January 2018, require B to deliver 1,000 of A's shares in return for a payment by A of €102,000. IAS 32 classifies such a derivative contract as an equity instrument (see 5.4 above); therefore no entries are recorded, other than to record the cash flows arising under the contract:

1 February 2017	€	€
Equity	5,000	
Cash		5,000
Payment of option premium (equal to fair value of option) to B		

31 January 2018	€	€
Equity	102,000	
Cash		102,000

To record gross settlement of option by payment of €102,000 cash to B in exchange for 1,000 own shares.

If the option had lapsed unexercised, because the market price of A's shares had fallen below €102 as at 31 January 2018, the €5,000 premium would remain in equity, even though it is, from an economic perspective, clearly a loss rather than an amount paid to repurchase A's own shares. This is because IFRS regards any holder of an instrument classified as equity under IAS 32 as an 'owner'.

In contrast to the treatment of a gross-settled forward purchase (see 11.1.1 above) and a gross-settled written put option (see 11.3.2 below), which also require a gross outflow of cash on settlement, there is no requirement to record a liability at the outset of the contract on which interest is accrued during the period of the contract. This is because:

- in a gross-settled forward purchase or written put option, the entity can be required to make a payment of cash, but
- in a purchased call option, there is no liability, since the entity has no obligation to exercise its right to call for the shares even if the option is 'in the money' and it is in the entity's interest to do so.

D Settlement options

If there are different settlement options (such as net in cash, net in shares or by an exchange of cash and shares), the option is a financial asset. A accounts for the forward contract as a derivative (as in A and B above), with the accounting entry made on settlement determined by the manner of settlement (i.e. equity or cash).

11.2.2 Written call option

In a written call option, the entity receives a payment from a counterparty for granting to the counterparty the right, but not the obligation, to purchase a given number of the entity's own equity instruments from the entity for a fixed price at a future date. The accounting for such a contract is illustrated in Example 45.19 below. *[IAS 32.IE17-21].*

Example 45.19: Written call option on shares

The reporting entity (A), which has a functional currency of Euro and a year end of 31 December, writes a call option over its own shares with another party (B), for which the following are the major assumptions.

Contract date	1 February 2017
Exercise date (European terms – i.e. can be exercised only on maturity)	31 January 2018
Fixed exercise price to be paid on 31 January 2018	€102
Number of shares under contract	1,000
Market price per share on 1 February 2017	€100
Market price per share on 31 December 2017	€104
Market price per share on 31 January 2018	€104
Fair value of option to A on 1 February 2017	€(5,000)
Fair value of option to A on 31 December 2017	€(3,000)
Fair value of option to A on 31 January 2018	€(2,000)

The fair value of the option would be computed using an option pricing model and would be a function of a number of factors, principally the market value of the shares, the exercise price, and the time value of money.

A Net cash settlement

If the contract is entered into as net cash-settled on 1 February 2017, then B can, on the exercise date 31 January 2018, require A to make a cash payment to B for the excess, if any, of the fair value of 1,000 of A's own shares, as of 31 January 2018, over €102,000 (i.e. 1,000 shares at the option price of €102 per share). Since IAS 32 classifies such contracts as derivative financial liabilities (see 11 and 5.2.7 above), which are carried at fair value through profit or loss under IAS 39 (or IFRS 9), A records the following accounting entries:

	€	€
1 February 2017		
Cash	5,000	
Call option liability		5,000
Receipt of option premium (equal to fair value of option) from B		
31 December 2017		
Call option liability	2,000	
Gain on option (profit or loss)		2,000
To record movement in fair value of option from €(5,000) to €(3,000)		
31 January 2018		
Call option liability	1,000	
Gain on option (profit or loss)		1,000
To record movement in fair value of option from €(3,000) to €(2,000)		
Call option liability	2,000	
Cash		2,000
To record net settlement of option by payment of €2,000 cash to B		

B Net share settlement

If the contract is entered into as net share-settled on 1 February 2017, then B can, on the exercise date 31 January 2018, require A to deliver to B as many of A's own shares as have a fair value equal to any excess of 1,000 of A's own shares, as of 31 January 2018, over €102,000 (i.e. 1000 shares at the option price of €102 per share). Since IAS 32 classifies such contracts as derivative financial liabilities (see 11 and 5.2.7 above), which are carried at fair value through profit or loss under IAS 39 (or IFRS 9), A records the following accounting entries.

	€	€
1 February 2017		
Cash	5,000	
Call option liability		5,000
Receipt of option premium (equal to fair value of option) from B		
31 December 2017		
Call option liability	2,000	
Gain on option (profit or loss)		2,000
To record movement in fair value of option from €(5,000) to €(3,000)		

31 January 2018	1,000	
Call option liability Gain on option (profit or loss)		1,000
To record movement in fair value of option from €(3,000) to €(2,000)		
Call option liability Equity	2,000	2,000
To record net settlement of option by issue of €2,000 worth of A's shares to B		

C Gross settlement

If the contract is entered into as gross-settled, on 1 February 2017, then B can, on the exercise date 31 January 2018, require A to deliver 1,000 of A's shares in return for a payment by B of €102,000. IAS 32 classifies this derivative contract as an equity instrument (see 5.4 above); therefore no entries are recorded, other than to record the cash flows arising under the contract:

	€	€
1 February 2017		
Cash Equity	5,000	5,000
Receipt of option premium (equal to fair value of option) to B		
31 January 2018		
Cash Equity	102,000	102,000
To record gross settlement of option by receipt of €102,000 cash from B in exchange for 1,000 of A's own shares.		

If the option had lapsed unexercised, because the market price of A's shares had fallen below €102 as at 31 January 2017, the €5,000 premium would remain in equity, even though it is, from an economic perspective, clearly a gain rather than an amount received from an owner. This is because IFRS regards any holder of an instrument classified as equity under IAS 32 as an 'owner'.

D Settlement options

If there are different settlement options (such as net in cash, net in shares or by an exchange of cash and shares), the option is a financial liability. A accounts for the forward contract as a derivative (as in A and B above), with the accounting entry made on settlement determined by the manner of settlement (i.e. equity or cash).

11.3 Put options

11.3.1 Purchased put option

In a purchased put option, the entity makes a payment to a counterparty for the right, but not the obligation, to require the counterparty to purchase a given number of the entity's own equity instruments from the entity for a fixed price at a future date. The accounting for such a contract is illustrated in Example 45.20 below. *[IAS 32.IE22-26]*.

Chapter 45

Example 45.20: Purchased put option on shares

The reporting entity (A), which has a functional currency of Euro and a year end of 31 December, purchases a put option over its own shares from another party (B), for which the following are the major assumptions.

Contract date	1 February 2017
Exercise date (European terms – i.e. can be exercised only on maturity)	31 January 2018
Fixed exercise price to be paid on 31 January 2018	€98
Number of shares under contract	1,000
Market price per share on 1 February 2017	€100
Market price per share on 31 December 2017	€95
Market price per share on 31 January 2018	€95
Fair value of option to A on 1 February 2017	€5,000
Fair value of option to A on 31 December 2017	€4,000
Fair value of option to A on 31 January 2018	€3,000

The fair value of the option would be computed using an option pricing model and would be a function of number of factors, principally the market value of the shares, the exercise price, and the time value of money.

A Net cash settlement

If the contract is entered into as net cash-settled on 1 February 2017, then A can, on the exercise date 31 January 2018, require B to make a cash payment to A for the excess, if any, of €98,000 (i.e. 1,000 shares at the option price of €98 per share) over the fair value of 1,000 of A's own shares, as of 31 January 2018. Because IAS 32 classifies such contracts as derivative financial liabilities (see 11 and 5.2.7 above), which are carried at fair value through profit or loss under IAS 39 (or IFRS 9), A records the following accounting entries.

	€	€
1 February 2017		
Put option asset	5,000	
Cash		5,000
Payment of option premium (equal to fair value of option) to B		
31 December 2017		
Loss on option (profit or loss)	1,000	
Put option asset		1,000
To record movement in fair value of option from €5,000 to €4,000		
31 January 2018		
Loss on option (profit or loss)	1,000	
Put option asset		1,000
To record movement in fair value of option from €4,000 to €3,000		
Cash	3,000	
Put option asset		3,000
To record net settlement of option by receipt of €3,000 cash from B		

B Net share settlement

If the contract is entered into as net share-settled on 1 February 2017, then A can, on the exercise date 31 January 2018, require B to deliver to A as many of A's own shares as have a fair value equal to any excess of €98,000 (i.e. 1,000 shares at the option price of €98 per share) over the fair value of 1,000 of A's own shares, as of 31 January 2018. Because IAS 32 classifies such contracts as derivative financial assets (see 11 and 5.2.7 above), which are carried at fair value through profit or loss under IAS 39 (or IFRS 9), A records the following accounting entries.

	€	€
1 February 2017		
Put option asset	5,000	
Cash		5,000
Payment of option premium (equal to fair value of option) to B		
31 December 2017		
Loss on option (profit or loss)	1,000	
Put option asset		1,000
To record movement in fair value of option from €5,000 to €4,000		
31 January 2018		
Loss on option (profit or loss)	1,000	
Put option asset		1,000
To record movement in fair value of option from €4,000 to €3,000		
Equity	3,000	
Put option asset		3,000
To record net settlement of option by receipt of €3,000 worth of A's shares from B. This is shown as a deduction from equity in accordance with IAS 32's requirements for treasury shares (see 9 above).		

C Gross settlement

If the contract is entered into as gross-settled, on 1 February 2017, then A can, on the exercise date 31 January 2018, require B to take delivery 1,000 of A's shares in return for a payment by B of €98,000. IAS 32 classifies this derivative contract as an equity instrument (see 5.4 above); therefore no entries are recorded, other than to record the cash flows arising under the contract:

	€	€
1 February 2017		
Equity	5,000	
Cash		5,000
Payment of option premium (equal to fair value of option) to B		
31 January 2018		
Cash	98,000	
Equity		98,000
To record gross settlement of option by delivery of 1,000 own shares to B in exchange for €98,000.		

If the option had lapsed unexercised, because the market price of A's shares had risen above €98 as at 31 January 2018, the €5,000 premium would remain in equity, even though it is, from an economic perspective, clearly a loss rather than an amount paid to repurchase A's own shares.

Chapter 45

D Settlement options

If there are different settlement options (such as net in cash, net in shares or by an exchange of cash and shares), the option is a financial asset. A accounts for the forward contract as a derivative (as in A and B above), with the accounting entry made on settlement determined by the manner of settlement (i.e. equity or cash).

11.3.2 Written put option

In a written put option, the entity receives a payment from a counterparty for granting to the counterparty the right, but not the obligation, to sell a given number of the entity's own equity instruments to the entity for a fixed price at a future date. The accounting for such a contract is illustrated in Example 45.21 below. *[IAS 32.IE27-31]*.

Example 45.21: Written put option on own shares

The reporting entity (A), which has a functional currency of Euros and a year end of 31 December, writes a put option over its own shares with another party (B), for which the following are the major assumptions.

Contract date	1 February 2017
Exercise date (European terms – i.e. can be exercised only on maturity)	31 January 2018
Fixed exercise price to be paid on 31 January 2018	€98
Number of shares under contract	1,000
Market price per share on 1 February 2017	€100
Market price per share on 31 December 2017	€95
Market price per share on 31 January 2018	€95
Fair value of option to A on 1 February 2017	€(5,000)
Fair value of option to A on 31 December 2017	€(4,000)
Fair value of option to A on 31 January 2018	€(3,000)

The fair value of the option would be computed using an option pricing model and would be a function of a number of factors, principally the market value of the shares, the exercise price, and the time value of money.

A Net cash settlement

If the contract is entered into as net cash-settled on 1 February 2017, then B can, on the exercise date 31 January 2018, require A to make a cash payment to B for the excess, if any, of €98,000 (i.e. 1,000 shares at the option price of €98 per share) over the fair value of 1,000 of A's own shares, as of 31 January 2018. Because IAS 32 classifies such contracts as derivative financial liabilities (see 11 and 5.2.7 above), which are carried at fair value through profit or loss under IAS 39 (or IFRS 9), A records the following accounting entries.

	€	€
1 February 2017		
Cash	5,000	
Put option liability		5,000
Receipt of option premium (equal to fair value of option) from B		
31 December 2017		
Put option liability	1,000	
Gain on option (profit or loss)		1,000
To record movement in fair value of option from €(5,000) to €(4,000)		

31 January 2018

	€	€
Put option liability	1,000	
Gain on option (profit or loss)		1,000

To record movement in fair value of option from €(4,000) to €(3,000)

	€	€
Put option liability	3,000	
Cash		3,000

To record net settlement of option by payment of €3,000 cash to B

B Net share settlement

If the contract is entered into as net share-settled on 1 February 2017, then B can, on the exercise date 31 January 2018, require A to deliver to B as many of A's own shares as have a fair value equal to any excess of €98,000 (i.e. 1,000 shares at the option price of €98 per share) over the fair value of 1,000 of A's own shares, as of 31 January 2018. Because IAS 32 classifies such contracts as derivative financial assets (see 11 and 5.2.7 above), which are carried at fair value through profit or loss under IAS 39 (or IFRS 9), A records the following accounting entries.

	€	€
1 February 2017		
Cash	5,000	
Put option liability		5,000

Receipt of option premium (equal to fair value of option) from B

	€	€
31 December 2017		
Put option liability	1,000	
Gain on option (profit or loss)		1,000

To record movement in fair value of option from €(5,000) to €(4,000)

	€	€
31 January 2018		
Put option liability	1,000	
Gain on option (profit or loss)		1,000

To record movement in fair value of option from €(4,000) to €(3,000)

	€	€
Put option liability	3,000	
Equity		3,000

To record net settlement of option by issue of €3,000 worth of own shares to B

C Gross settlement

If the contract is entered into as gross-settled on 1 February 2017, then B can, on the exercise date 31 January 2018, require A to take delivery of 1,000 of A's own shares in return for a payment by A of €98,000. IAS 32 classifies this derivative contract as an equity instrument giving rise to a financial liability for the present value of the purchase price amount payable in one year's time (see 5.3 above). On the assumption that A accounts for this liability under the effective interest method in IAS 39 (or IFRS 9), A records the following accounting entries.

	€	€
1 February 2017		
Cash	5,000	
Equity		5,000

Receipt of option premium (equal to fair value of option) from B

Chapter 45

	€	€
Equity	95,000	
Liability (net present value of €98,000 potentially payable under option)		95,000

Recording of potential liability to settle option

31 December 2017

Interest (profit or loss)	2,750	
Liability		2,750

To accrue interest, under the effective interest rate method, on the liability

31 January 2018

Interest expense (profit or loss)	250	
Liability		250

To accrue further interest, under the effective interest rate method, on the liability

Liability	98,000	
Cash		98,000

To record gross settlement of option by delivery of by B of 1,000 shares in A in exchange for €98,000

If the option had lapsed unexercised, because the market price of A's shares had risen above €98 as at 31 January 2018, the premium of €5,000 would remain in equity and the liability of €98,000 would be reclassified to equity. The economic consequence is clearly that A has made a profit of €5,000 – the premium that it received from B, for which it has ultimately had to give nothing in return. However the overall effect of the treatment that would be required by IAS 32 can be summarised as follows:

	€	€
Cash	5,000	
Profit or loss (interest on potential liability to pay cash)	3,000	
Equity (€98,000 carrying amount of liability transferred at date of lapse less €90,000 debited on 1 February 2016)		8,000

To record a loss on a transaction that makes a profit might seem a distortion of economic reality; but in this case is a consequence of applying the *Conceptual Framework*.

D Settlement options

If there are different settlement options (such as net in cash, net in shares or by an exchange of cash and shares), the option is a financial liability. A accounts for the forward contract as a derivative (as in A and B above), with the accounting entry made on settlement determined by the manner of settlement (i.e. equity or cash). If one of the settlement alternatives is to exchange cash for shares, A recognises a liability for the obligation to deliver cash (as in C above). Otherwise, Entity A accounts for the put option as a derivative liability.

The implementation guidance to IAS 32 states that A should recognise a liability 'if one of the settlement alternatives is to exchange cash for shares'. *[IAS 32.IE31]*. As drafted, this applies whether the choice of settlement rests with A or B. This seems curious since, where A has the choice of settlement, there would be no obligation for A to settle gross. We assume that the example is written on the presumption that the choice of settlement of an option would normally rest with the buyer rather than the writer of the option. Paragraph 23 in the main body of the standard is clear that an equity contract gives rise to a liability for the purchase price of the shares only where there is an obligation for the entity to purchase its own equity (see 5.3 above). Accordingly, in our view, where the choice of settlement rests only with the entity, it is acceptable to record no liability, and to account for the contract as a derivative.

12 POSSIBLE FUTURE DEVELOPMENTS

An increasing number of commentators have begun to question whether the current criteria used to distinguish equity from financial liabilities, both under IFRS and US GAAP, are entirely satisfactory. In an agenda paper for the IASB board meeting in January 2007, the IASB staff highlighted the following broad categories of implementation issue arising from IAS 32:

- *Issues arising from specific rules in the standard*

  The specific provisions in IAS 32 were written with particular types of capital instrument in mind. Where these rules are applied to instruments that differ from those for which they were written, the result may be a classification of an item as debt or equity that does not faithfully represent the underlying instrument.

- *Counter-intuitive results*

  The classification of an instrument under IAS 32 can produce results that conflict with the generally-held perception of how the instrument should be faithfully represented. An example is the treatment of certain puttable instruments, which was the subject of the amendment to IAS 32 in February 2008 discussed at 4.6.2 and 4.6.3 above.

- *Conflicts with the conceptual framework*

  Some provisions of IAS 32 conflict with the IASB's own conceptual framework. For example, IAS 32 requires some contracts over the entity's own equity, which are to be executed at a future date, to be accounted for as if they had been executed on inception of the contract. This contrasts with the required treatment under IFRS of nearly all other executory contracts, such as purchase orders and contracts of employment, for which no liability is recorded, except to the extent that the contract is onerous.

The IASB staff noted that the first of these issues could potentially be resolved by a more principles-based revision to the drafting of IAS 32, whilst the other two issues raised more fundamental questions about the whole approach of the standard.[32]

The Memorandum of Understanding published by the IASB and the FASB in February 2006 set as one of its goals for 2008 'to have issued one or more due process documents relating to a proposed standard' on the distinction between liabilities and equity. The IASB fulfilled that commitment by publishing a discussion paper in February 2008. Following receipt of comments on the discussion paper, the IASB and the FASB ('the Boards') began further deliberations and developed a draft exposure draft. In May 2010 this was distributed to a small group of external reviewers, who raised significant challenges. The reviewers felt that the proposed approach lacked clear principles, and could produce inconsistent results when applied to broadly similar instruments. In particular, many reviewers felt that the 'specified for specified' criterion was unclear and just as prone to interpretative difficulties as the 'fixed for fixed' criterion in IAS 32.

At a joint meeting in October 2010, the Boards suspended the project, acknowledging that they did not have the time necessary to deliberate the key issues. In October 2014 the IASB decided to resume the *Financial Instruments with Characteristics of Equity*

Research Project (FICE), to explore further how to distinguish liabilities from equity claims. The relaunched project is at an early stage, however it has been agreed that the project will be based on IAS 32 rather than starting completely afresh. It will consider presenting changes in the recorded value of certain arrangements in other comprehensive income instead of profit or loss, along with classification issues and how disclosures can be improved.

In May 2015 the IASB published Exposure Draft ED/2015/3 – *Conceptual Framework for Financial Reporting*. Amongst other topics this proposes to refine the definition of assets and liabilities and to develop principles and guidance to help support the classification of assets, liabilities and equity whilst retaining the existing definition of equity. The proposed definition of liability is discussed in Chapter 2 at 3.3. However it is worth noting that the proposed definition of liability as a present obligation of the entity to transfer an economic resource as a result of a past event if the entity has no practical ability to avoid the transfer may, if incorporated into FICE, result in instruments with 'dividend blocker' arrangements being classified as financial liabilities rather than equity (see 4.5.3 above).

References

1 IAS 32, Application Guidance, para. after main heading.
2 IAS 32, Illustrative Examples, para. after main heading.
3 *IFRIC Update*, September 2015.
4 *IFRIC Update*, March 2016.
5 *IFRIC Update*, January 2010.
6 *IFRIC Update*, November 2015.
7 *IFRIC Update*, May 2016.
8 SIC-5, *Classification of Financial Instruments – Contingent Settlement Provisions*, SIC, May 1998 (superseded December 2003).
9 SIC-5, para. 9.
10 *Agenda item 12B*, Information for Observers, IASB meeting, January 2007, para. 39.
11 IAS 32, (pre-2003 version – issued March 1995 and revised December 1998 and October 2000), para. 22.
12 *IFRIC Update*, March 2006.
13 *IFRIC Update*, March 2006.
14 *IFRIC Update*, March 2006.
15 *IFRIC Update*, March 2006.
16 *Amendments to IAS 32 Financial Instruments: Presentation and IAS 1 Presentation of Financial Statements – Puttable Instruments and Obligations Arising on Liquidation*, IASB, February 2008, paras. DO1-DO6.
17 *IFRIC Update*, March 2009.
18 *IFRIC Update*, November 2006.
19 *IFRIC Update*, April 2005.
20 *IFRIC Update*, November 2006.
21 *IFRS for Small and Medium-Sized Entities*, IASB, July 2009, para. 21.2.
22 IFRS for SMEs, Derivation Table.
23 IASB staff draft of proposed exposure draft *International Financial Reporting Standard for Small and Medium-Sized Entities* (as made available on the IASB's website as at September 2006) paras. 22.2-22.4.
24 *IFRIC Update*, July 2013.
25 *IFRIC Update*, May 2014 and January 2014.
26 *IFRIC Update*, July 2013.
27 *IFRIC Update*, January 2014.
28 *IFRIC Update*, July 2013.
29 *IFRIC Update*, January 2014.
30 *IFRIC Update*, July 2006.
31 *IFRIC Update*, September 2008.
32 *Overview of IAS 32 (Agenda paper 12B)*, Information for Observers, IASB meeting, January 2007, para. 48.

Chapter 46 Financial instruments: Classification (IAS 39)

List of examples

Chapter 46 Financial instruments: Classification (IAS 39)

1 INTRODUCTION

Under IAS 39 – *Financial Instruments: Recognition and Measurement* – the accounting treatment of a particular financial instrument (e.g. whether it is carried at historical cost, fair value or some other amount and whether any remeasurement gains are reported immediately in profit or loss or in other comprehensive income) will depend to some extent on some or all of the following factors:

- the purpose for which it is held, for example trading, long-term investment or hedging;
- its contractual characteristics, for example whether it is a derivative, an equity security or a debt instrument;
- whether the instrument is listed on an exchange;
- the industry in which the reporting entity operates; and
- an accounting policy or similar choice of the reporting entity.

Four categories of financial asset are set out in IAS 39. In summary, the definitions of these are as follows: *[IAS 39.9]*

- *Financial assets at fair value through profit or loss* – financial assets that are either designated as such on initial recognition or defined as held for trading (see 2.1 below);
- *Held-to-maturity investments* – non-derivative financial assets with fixed or determinable payments and fixed maturity, other than loans and receivables, for which there is a positive intention and ability to hold to maturity and which have not been designated 'at fair value through profit or loss' or as 'available-for-sale';
- *Loans and receivables* – non-derivative financial assets with fixed or determinable payments that are not quoted in an active market, do not qualify as 'trading' assets, have not been designated 'at fair value through profit or loss' or as 'available-for-sale'; and

- *Available-for-sale financial assets* – non-derivative financial assets that are designated as 'available-for-sale' or are not classified as 'loans and receivables', 'held-to-maturity investments' or 'at fair value through profit or loss'.

There are also two main categories of financial liabilities dealt with: *[IAS 39.9]*

- *Financial liabilities at fair value through profit or loss* – financial liabilities that are either designated as such on initial recognition or classified as *held for trading*; and
- *Other financial liabilities* – not explicitly defined, but are those that are neither held for trading nor designated 'at fair value through profit or loss'.

In addition, IAS 39 specifies the accounting treatment for liabilities arising from certain financial guarantee contracts (see Chapter 43 at 3.4 and Chapter 49 at 2.8) and commitments to provide loans at below market rates of interest (see Chapter 43 at 3.5 and Chapter 49 at 2.8).

The definitions summarised above are covered in more detail in the remainder of this chapter.

2 ASSETS AND LIABILITIES AT FAIR VALUE THROUGH PROFIT OR LOSS

This category comprises instruments that are defined as 'held for trading' (including derivatives which are not designated effective hedging instruments) and those that are designated as at fair value through profit or loss – often referred to as those to which the 'fair value option' is applied. Whilst trading instruments are encompassed within this category, they are not a separate category. *[IAS 39.BC81]*. Contingent consideration that is payable (or receivable) in respect of a business combination is also included within this category where it meets the definition of a financial liability (or financial asset). *[IFRS 3.58]*.

Designation under the fair value option must take place on initial recognition of the instrument (subject to certain exemptions on first-time adoption of IFRS – see Chapter 5 at 5.11.2) and may not be revoked subsequently, i.e. a designated instrument will be included in this category from when it is first recognised until it is derecognised.

It will come as no surprise that the basic accounting requirement for all instruments included in this category is that they are recorded on the statement of financial position at fair value and any changes in value are reported in profit or loss (see Chapter 49 at 2.1).

2.1 Assets and liabilities held for trading

Assets and liabilities held for trading are defined as those that:

- are acquired or incurred principally for the purpose of sale or repurchase in the near term;
- on initial recognition are part of a portfolio of identified financial instruments that are managed together and for which there is evidence of a recent actual pattern of short-term profit-taking; or

- are derivatives (except for those that are financial guarantee contracts – see Chapter 43 at 3.4 – or are designated effective hedging instruments – see Chapter 52 at 2.1.1). The definition of a derivative is covered in Chapter 44 at 2. *[IAS 39.9]*.

It follows that if an entity originates a loan with an intention of syndicating it, but fails to find sufficient commitments from other participants and tries to sell the surplus loan amount to other parties in the near term rather than holding it for the foreseeable future (a failed loan syndication), the surplus loan amount should be classified as held for trading.[1]

It is explained that trading generally reflects active and frequent buying and selling, and financial instruments held for trading are normally used with the objective of generating a profit from short-term fluctuations in price or a dealer's margin. *[IAS 39.AG14]*. This is obviously not always true because, for example, many derivatives will be held for hedging or risk management purposes yet by default they are included in this category (unless the entity chooses to designate them as hedges and is successful in achieving hedge accounting as set out in Chapter 52 at 5).

In addition to derivatives that are not accounted for as hedging instruments, financial liabilities held for trading include:

(a) obligations to deliver financial assets borrowed by a short seller (i.e. an entity that sells financial assets it has borrowed and does not yet own);

(b) financial liabilities that are incurred with an intention to repurchase them in the near term, such as quoted debt instruments that the issuer may buy back in the near term depending on changes in fair value; and

(c) financial liabilities that are part of a portfolio of identified financial instruments that are managed together and for which there is evidence of a recent pattern of short-term profit-taking. *[IAS 39.AG15]*.

However, the fact that a liability is used merely to fund trading activities does not in itself make that liability one that is held for trading. *[IAS 39.AG15]*.

The term 'portfolio' is not explicitly defined in IAS 39, but the context in which it is used suggests that a portfolio is a collection of financial assets or financial liabilities that are managed as part of the same group. If there is evidence of a recent actual pattern of short-term profit taking on financial instruments included in such a portfolio, those financial instruments qualify as held for trading even though an individual financial instrument may, in fact, be held for a longer period of time. *[IAS 39.B.11]*.

Evidence of a recent actual pattern of short-term profit taking may be established based on an evaluation of management intentions and past practice, including the level of turnover in the portfolio, whether performance is measured based on short-term profits and the average holding period (e.g. see Example 46.5 at 5 below).

2.2 Instruments designated at fair value through profit or loss

One of the reasons for the fair value option is to simplify the application of IAS 39 by mitigating some of the anomalies that result from its mixed model approach. For example, it eliminates:

- the need for hedge accounting for hedges of fair value exposures when there are natural offsets, and thereby eliminates the related burden of designating hedges, tracking and analysing hedge effectiveness;
- the burden of separating embedded derivatives; and
- problems arising from a mixed-measurement model where financial assets are measured at fair value and related financial liabilities are measured at amortised cost.

In particular, it eliminates volatility in profit or loss and equity that results when matched positions of financial assets and financial liabilities are not measured consistently. It also de-emphasises interpretative issues around whether a financial instrument should be classified as held for trading. *[IAS 39.BC74A]*.

An entity may designate a financial asset or financial liability at fair value through profit or loss only in either of the following circumstances: (a) when doing so results in more relevant information, because either:

- it eliminates or significantly reduces a measurement or recognition inconsistency (sometimes referred to as 'an accounting mismatch') that would otherwise arise; or
- a group of financial assets, financial liabilities or both is managed and its performance is evaluated on a fair value basis;

or (b) if it contains an embedded derivative that meets particular conditions. These are discussed further at 2.2.1 to 2.2.3 below.

Investments in unquoted equity instruments that do not have a quoted market price in an active market, and whose fair value cannot be reliably measured, cannot be designated at fair value through profit or loss. *[IAS 39.9, 11A, AG4B]*.

The decision to designate a financial asset or financial liability as at fair value through profit or loss is similar to an accounting policy choice (although, unlike an accounting policy choice, it is not required in all cases to be applied consistently to all similar transactions). In other words, an entity can freely choose, when the relevant criteria are met, which of its financial assets and liabilities are to be designated without having to designate all similar instruments. *[IAS 39.AG4C]*. However, an entity that designates a financial instrument as at fair value through profit or loss on the basis that it is part of a group of financial instruments that is managed and its performance is evaluated on a fair value basis should also designate all *eligible* financial instruments within that same group. New instruments that will become part of that group should also be designated at fair value through profit or loss. A similar, but separate, group of financial instruments does not need to be designated at fair value profit or loss in a similar manner.

As noted earlier, the designation of a financial instrument at fair value through profit or loss must take place on initial recognition of the instrument (subject to certain exemptions on first-time adoption of IFRS – see Chapter 5 at 5.11.2) and may not be revoked subsequently. Accordingly, when making the designation decision, reporting entities, which use the designation in lieu of hedge accounting, need to make the decision about whether or not to economically hedge the instrument on or before the time of acquisition or issuance, and also evaluate whether they intend to economically hedge the instrument until derecognition. Designating a financial instrument under the fair value option is likely to lead to unnecessary earnings volatility if the economic hedge is not intended to last until derecognition.

The fair value option cannot be applied to a portion or component of a financial instrument, e.g. changes in the fair value of a debt instrument attributable to one risk such as changes in a benchmark interest rate, but not credit risk. Further, it cannot be applied to proportions of an instrument. However, if an entity simultaneously issues two or more identical financial instruments, it is not precluded from designating only some of those instruments as being subject to the fair value option (e.g. if doing so achieves a significant reduction in an accounting mismatch). Therefore, if an entity issued a bond totalling US$100 million in the form of 100 certificates each of US$1 million, the entity could designate 10 specified certificates if to do so would meet at least one of the criteria noted above. *[IAS 39.BC85, BC86, BC86A]*.

2.2.1 Designation eliminates or significantly reduces a measurement or recognition inconsistency (accounting mismatch) that would otherwise arise

The notion of an accounting mismatch necessarily involves two propositions. First, that an entity has particular assets and liabilities that are measured, or on which gains and losses are recognised, on different bases; second, that there is a perceived economic relationship between those assets and liabilities. *[IAS 39.9, BC75]*.

For example, a financial asset might otherwise be classified as available-for-sale (with most changes in fair value recognised directly in equity) and a liability that is considered related would be measured at amortised cost (with changes in fair value not recognised). In such circumstances, the entity may conclude that its financial statements would provide more relevant information if both the asset and the liability were classified as at fair value through profit or loss. *[IAS 39.AG4D]*. It should be noted in this case that it does not matter that there is unlikely to be a significant accounting mismatch in profit or loss – the fact that the mismatch arises only in the statement of financial position does not prevent the use of the fair value option.

IAS 39 gives the following examples of situations in which designation at fair value through profit or loss might eliminate or significantly reduce an accounting mismatch and produce more relevant information: *[IAS 39.AG4E, AG4F]*

(a) An entity has liabilities whose cash flows are contractually based on the performance of assets that would otherwise be classified as available for sale. For example, an insurer may have liabilities containing a discretionary participation feature that pay benefits based on realised and/or unrealised investment returns of a specified pool of the insurer's assets. If the measurement of those liabilities reflects current market prices, classifying the assets as at fair value through profit or loss means that changes in the fair value of the financial assets are recognised in profit or loss in the same period as related changes in the value of the liabilities.

(b) An entity has liabilities under insurance contracts whose measurement incorporates current information (as permitted by IFRS 4 – *Insurance Contracts*), and financial assets it considers related that would otherwise be classified as available for sale or measured at amortised cost.

(c) An entity has financial assets, financial liabilities or both that share a risk, such as interest rate risk, that gives rise to opposite changes in fair value that tend to offset each other. However, only some of the instruments would be measured at fair value through profit or loss (i.e. derivatives or those classified as held for trading). It may also be the case that the requirements for hedge accounting are not met, for example because the requirements for effectiveness are not met (see Chapter 52 at 5.3).

(d) An entity has financial assets, financial liabilities or both that share a risk, such as interest rate risk, that gives rise to opposite changes in fair value that tend to offset each other and the entity does not qualify for hedge accounting because none of the instruments is a derivative. Furthermore, in the absence of hedge accounting there is a significant inconsistency in the recognition of gains and losses. For example:

    (i) the entity has financed a portfolio of fixed rate assets that would otherwise be classified as available-for-sale with fixed rate debentures, the changes in the fair value of which tend to offset each other. Reporting both the assets and the debentures at fair value through profit or loss corrects the inconsistency that would otherwise arise from measuring the assets at fair value with changes reported in equity and the debentures at amortised cost; or

    (ii) the entity has financed a specified group of loans by issuing traded bonds, the changes in the fair value of which tend to offset each other. If, in addition, the entity regularly buys and sells the bonds but rarely, if ever, buys and sells the loans, reporting both the loans and the bonds at fair value through profit or loss eliminates the inconsistency in the timing of recognition of gains and losses that would otherwise result from measuring them both at amortised cost and recognising a gain or loss each time a bond is repurchased.

For practical purposes, an entity need not acquire all the assets and incur all the liabilities giving rise to the measurement or recognition inconsistency at exactly the same time. A reasonable delay is permitted provided that each transaction is designated as at fair value through profit or loss at its initial recognition and, at that time, any remaining transactions are expected to occur. *[IAS 39.AG4F]*.

It is emphasised that it would not be acceptable to designate only some of the financial assets and financial liabilities giving rise to the inconsistency as at fair value through profit or loss if to do so would not eliminate or significantly reduce the inconsistency and would therefore not result in more relevant information. However, it would be acceptable to designate only some of a number of similar financial assets or similar financial liabilities if doing so does achieve a significant reduction (and possibly a greater reduction than other allowable designations) in the inconsistency. *[IAS 39.AG4G]*.

For example, assume an entity has a number of similar financial liabilities totalling €100 and a number of similar financial assets totalling €50, but these are measured on a different basis. The entity may significantly reduce the measurement inconsistency by designating at initial recognition all of the assets but only some of the liabilities (for example, individual liabilities with a combined total of €45) as at fair value through profit or loss. However, because designation as at fair value through profit or loss can be applied only to the whole of a financial instrument, the entity in this example must designate one or more liabilities in their entirety. It could not designate either a component of a liability (e.g. changes in value attributable to only one risk, such as changes in a benchmark interest rate) or a proportion (i.e. percentage) of a liability. *[IAS 39.AG4G]*.

The standard does not provide detailed prescriptive guidance about when the fair value option could be applied to eliminate an accounting mismatch. Therefore an entity is not required to demonstrate that particular assets and liabilities are managed together, that a management strategy is effective in reducing risk, e.g. by performing effectiveness tests similar to those required for hedge accounting, or that other ways of overcoming the inconsistency are unavailable. Rather, the IASB concluded that financial reporting was best served by providing entities with the opportunity to eliminate perceived accounting mismatches whenever that results in more relevant information. *[IAS 39.BC75A, BC75B]*.

Although not explicitly stated, one of the items giving rise to the mismatch may, at least in principle, be non-financial. For example, investment properties accounted for using the fair value model in IAS 40 – *Investment Property* (see Chapter 19 at 6) are commonly financed with fixed rate borrowings and if it were possible to demonstrate a sufficiently high correlation between the values of these items, the borrowings could be designated as at fair value through profit or loss. However, the value of a property will depend to some extent on rent, location, maintenance and other factors which can make it difficult to do this. Nevertheless, CESR has reported that, based on the specific evidence available in a particular case, one of its enforcement agencies has accepted this treatment.[2]

2.2.2 A group of financial assets, financial liabilities or both is managed and its performance is evaluated on a fair value basis

The second situation in which the fair value option may be used is where a group of financial assets, financial liabilities or both is managed, and its performance evaluated, on a fair value basis. In order to meet this condition, it is necessary for the group of instruments to be managed in accordance with a documented risk management or investment strategy and for information, prepared on a fair value basis, about the group of instruments to be provided internally to the entity's key management personnel (as defined in IAS 24 – *Related Party Disclosures* – see Chapter 37 at 2.2.1.D), for example the entity's board of directors and chief executive officer. *[IAS 39.9]*.

It is explained that if an entity manages and evaluates the performance of a group of financial assets, financial liabilities or both in such a way, measuring that group at fair value through profit or loss results in more relevant information. The focus in this instance is on the way the entity manages and evaluates performance, rather than on the nature of its financial instruments. *[IAS 39.AG4H]*. Accordingly, subject to the requirement of designation at initial recognition, an entity that designates financial instruments as at fair value through profit or loss on the basis of this condition should so designate all eligible financial instruments that are managed and evaluated together. *[IAS 39.AG4J]*.

An entity's documentation of its strategy need not be extensive (e.g. it need not be in the level of detail required for hedge accounting) but should be sufficient to demonstrate that using the fair value option is consistent with the entity's risk management or investment strategy. Such documentation is not required for each individual item, but may be on a portfolio basis. The IASB notes that in many cases, the entity's existing documentation, as approved by its key management personnel, should be sufficient for this purpose. For example, if the performance management system for a department (as approved by the entity's key management personnel) clearly demonstrates that its performance is evaluated on a total return basis, no further documentation is required. *[IAS 39.AG4K, BC76B]*.

The IASB made it clear in its basis for conclusions that in looking to an entity's documented risk management or investment strategy, it makes no judgement on what an entity's strategy should be. However, the IASB believes that users, in making economic decisions, would find useful a description both of the chosen strategy and of how designation at fair value through profit or loss is consistent with that strategy. Accordingly, IFRS 7 – *Financial Instruments: Disclosures* – requires these to be disclosed (see Chapter 54 at 4.1). *[IAS 39.BC76B]*.

The following examples show when this condition could be met. In all cases, an entity may use this condition to designate financial assets or financial liabilities as at fair value through profit or loss only if it meets the principle above:

(a) The entity (or component of an entity) is a venture capital organisation, mutual fund, unit trust or similar entity whose business is investing in financial assets with a view to profiting from their total return in the form of interest or dividends and changes in fair value. IAS 28 – *Investments in Associates and Joint Ventures* – allows investments in associates and joint ventures to be measured at fair value through profit or loss in accordance with IAS 39. Such an entity may apply the same accounting policy to other investments managed on a total return basis but over which its influence is insufficient for them to be within the scope of IAS 28.

(b) The entity has financial assets and financial liabilities that share one or more risks and those risks are managed and evaluated on a fair value basis in accordance with a documented policy of asset and liability management. An example could be an entity that has issued 'structured products' containing multiple embedded derivatives and manages the resulting risks on a fair value basis using a mix of derivative and non-derivative financial instruments. A similar example could be an entity that originates fixed interest rate loans and manages the resulting benchmark interest rate risk using a mix of derivative and non-derivative financial instruments.

(c) The entity is an insurer that holds a portfolio of financial assets, manages that portfolio so as to maximise its total return (i.e. interest or dividends and changes in fair value) and evaluates its performance on that basis. The portfolio may be held to back specific liabilities, equity or both. If the portfolio is held to back specific liabilities, this condition may be met for the assets regardless of whether the insurer also manages and evaluates the liabilities on a fair value basis. It may also be met when the insurer's objective is to maximise total return on the assets over the longer term even if amounts paid to holders of participating contracts depend on other factors such as the amount of gains realised in a shorter period (e.g. a year) or are subject to the insurer's discretion. *[IAS 39.AG4I]*.

2.2.3 *Instruments containing embedded derivatives*

If a contract contains one or more embedded derivatives, an entity may designate the entire hybrid (or combined) contract as a financial asset or financial liability at fair value through profit or loss unless:

(a) the embedded derivative(s) does not significantly modify the cash flows that otherwise would be required by the contract; or

(b) it is clear with little or no analysis when a similar hybrid (combined) instrument is first considered that separation of the embedded derivative(s) is prohibited, such as a prepayment option embedded in a loan that permits the holder to prepay the loan for approximately its amortised cost. *[IAS 39.11A]*.

As discussed in Chapter 44 at 4 to 6, when an entity becomes a party to a hybrid (combined) instrument that contains one or more embedded derivatives, it is required to identify any such embedded derivative, assess whether it is required to be separated from the host contract and, if so, measure it at fair value at initial recognition and subsequently. These requirements can be more complex, or result in less reliable measures, than measuring the entire instrument at fair value through profit or loss. For that reason the entire instrument is normally permitted to be designated as at fair value through profit or loss. *[IAS 39.AG33A]*.

Such designation may be used whether the entity is required to, or prohibited from, separating the embedded derivative from the host contract, except for those situations in (a) or (b) above – this is because doing so would not reduce complexity or increase reliability. *[IAS 39.AG33B]*.

Little further guidance is given on what instruments might fall within (a) and (b). The basis for conclusions explains that, at one extreme, the terms of a prepayment option in an ordinary residential mortgage is likely to mean that the fair value option is unavailable to such a mortgage (unless it met one of the conditions in 2.2.1 and 2.2.2 above). At the other, it is likely to be available for 'structured products' that contain several embedded derivatives which are typically hedged with derivatives that offset all (or nearly all) of the risks they contain irrespective of the accounting treatment applied to the embedded derivatives. *[IAS 39.BC77A, BC77B]*.

Essentially, the IASB explains, the standard seeks to strike a balance between reducing the costs of complying with the embedded derivatives provisions and the need to respond to concerns expressed regarding possible inappropriate use of the fair value option. Allowing the fair value option to be used for any instrument with an embedded derivative would make other restrictions on the use of the option ineffective, because many financial instruments include an embedded derivative. In contrast, limiting the use of the fair value option to situations in which the embedded derivative must otherwise be separated would not significantly reduce the costs of compliance and could result in less reliable measures being included in the financial statements. *[IAS 39.BC78]*.

Taken at face value, IAS 39 might allow the fair value option to be applied to any contract containing a substantive embedded derivative, such as a lease accounted for under IAS 17 – *Leases* – or a pension arrangement accounted for under IAS 19 – *Employee Benefits*. In May 2007, the Interpretations Committee tentatively concluded that it could be applied only to a contract that would otherwise be within the scope of IAS 39.[3] However, the Interpretations Committee did not finalise its conclusion as it had become apparent that a number of entities had taken a different view, at least as regards commodity contracts that qualify as normal purchases or sales (see Chapter 43 at 4). After much discussion the Interpretations Committee, in November 2007, referred the matter to the IASB.[4]

As part of its second annual improvements process the IASB, in August 2008, proposed to amend IAS 39 so that the fair value option could be applied only to financial instruments within the scope of IAS 39.[5] However, a number of concerns were raised by respondents and, in January 2009, the IASB concluded this amendment could not be completed in time, redeliberations were deferred and in January 2010 the Interpretations Committee decided to remove the issue from the annual improvements project given the IASB's accelerated project to replace IAS 39.[6]

It would be unusual for entities to apply the fair value option to non-financial contracts containing embedded derivatives. In our experience, the one exception to this is in respect of contracts to buy or sell a non-financial item (such as a commodity) that can be settled net but are not within the scope of IAS 39 because they are considered 'normal' sale or purchase contracts (see Chapter 43 at 4). Where such contracts contain a substantive embedded derivative, some entities do designate such contracts as at fair value through profit or loss.

3 HELD-TO-MATURITY INVESTMENTS

As noted at 1 above, the held-to-maturity category comprises non-derivative financial assets with fixed or determinable payments and fixed maturity, other than loans and receivables, for which there is a positive intention and ability to hold to maturity and which have not been designated at fair value through profit or loss or as available-for-sale. *[IAS 39.9]*.

This category is viewed as an exception to be used only in limited circumstances. *[IAS 39.AG20]*. Consequently, its use is restricted by a number of detailed conditions, largely designed to test whether there is a genuine intention and ability to hold such investments to maturity. To further restrict the use of this category, hedge accounting cannot be used if interest rate or prepayment risk associated with held-to-maturity investments is hedged, *[IAS 39.79]*, for example by using a pay-fixed, receive-floating rate interest rate swap to hedge an investment that pays a fixed rate of interest (see Chapter 52 at 2.2.6). The reason for this is that designation of an investment as held to maturity requires an intention to hold to maturity regardless of changes in the fair value or cash flows due to changes in interest rates.

In theory, investments are not *designated* as held-to-maturity – they *must* be included in this category if they meet the appropriate conditions. In practice, however, because it is relatively easy for an entity to selectively fail any of the conditions, it is in effect a voluntary classification.

3.1 Instruments that may or may not be classified as held-to-maturity

Only assets with fixed or determinable payments and fixed maturity can be included in this category (see 1 and 3 above). Most equity instruments cannot be held to maturity because they have an indefinite life (such as ordinary shares) or because the amounts the holder may receive can vary in a manner that is not predetermined (such as share options, warrants and rights). A debt instrument with a variable interest rate generally can satisfy this condition. *[IAS 39.AG17].*

A perpetual debt instrument on which interest payments are made for an indefinite period cannot be classified as held-to-maturity because there is no maturity date. *[IAS 39.AG17].* However, there is no reason why what is in legal form a perpetual debt instrument but requires fixed or determinable payments for only a limited period cannot be classified as held-to-maturity. In effect, the instrument matures at the date of the last contractual payment and the amount invested is recovered through fixed or determinable payments and the rights in liquidation have no fair value (see Example 49.14 in Chapter 49 at 3.4).

A financial asset that is callable by the issuer satisfies the criteria for a held-to-maturity investment if the holder intends, and is able, to hold it until it is called, or until maturity, and if the holder would recover substantially all of its carrying amount. The call option, if exercised, simply accelerates the investment's maturity. However, if the investment is callable on a basis that the holder would not recover substantially all of its carrying amount, it cannot be classified as held-to-maturity. Any premium paid and capitalised transaction costs should be considered in determining whether the carrying amount would be substantially recovered. *[IAS 39.AG18].*

A financial asset that is puttable (the holder has the right to require the issuer to repay or redeem the instrument before maturity) cannot be classified as held-to-maturity. Paying for a put feature is considered inconsistent with expressing an intention of holding such an instrument to maturity. *[IAS 39.AG19].*

The reference to 'fixed or determinable payments and fixed maturity' in the definition means a contractual arrangement that defines the amounts and dates of payments to the holder, such as interest and principal payments. The likelihood of default is not a consideration in qualifying for this category, provided there is an intention and ability, considering the credit condition existing at the acquisition date, to hold the investment to maturity. Even if there is a significant risk of non-payment of interest and principal, for example a bond with a very low credit rating, the contractual payments on the bond may well be fixed or determinable. *[IAS 39.AG17].*

Investments in funds where the payout in dividends and on liquidation is based on the performance of the fund would not satisfy the conditions for this category. Similarly, investments in subordinated notes for which the payout is dependent on residual cash flows would normally not satisfy the conditions for this category.

Where a combined instrument contains a host contract and an embedded derivative (see Chapter 44 at 4), the host may be classified as held-to-maturity if it has fixed or determinable payments and no other conditions are breached. This is illustrated in the following examples.

Example 46.1: Note with index-linked principal

Company A purchases a five year interest free equity-index-linked note, with an original issue price of €10, for its market price of €12. At maturity, the note requires payment of the original issue price of €10 plus a supplemental redemption amount that depends on whether a specified stock price index exceeds a predetermined level at the maturity date. If the stock index does not exceed the predetermined level, no supplemental redemption amount is paid. If it does, the supplemental redemption amount equals the product of €1.15 and the difference between the level of the stock index at maturity and original issuance divided by the level at original issuance. A has the positive intention and ability to hold the note to maturity.

The note can be classified as a held-to-maturity investment because it has a fixed payment of €10 and fixed maturity and there is the positive intention and ability to hold it to maturity. However, the equity index feature is a call option not closely related to the debt host which must be separated as an embedded derivative (see Chapter 44 at 5.1.6). The purchase price (initial fair value) of €12 is allocated between the host debt instrument and the embedded derivative – the latter will have a non-zero fair value because it is an option-based derivative. *[IAS 39.B.13]*.

Example 46.2: Note with index-linked interest

Subsequently, A purchases a note with a fixed payment at a fixed maturity date and interest payments that are indexed to the price of a commodity or equity. There is an intention and ability to hold the note to maturity.

Again the note can be classified as held-to-maturity because it has a fixed payment and fixed maturity. However, the commodity-indexed or equity-indexed interest payments result in an embedded derivative that is separated and accounted for as a derivative. *[IAS 39.B.14]*.

It is possible for the terms of the embedded derivative to breach other conditions for classifying the host as held-to-maturity. For example, an investment in a convertible bond that can be converted *before* maturity generally cannot be classified as held-to-maturity. The embedded conversion feature allows the investor to settle the host investment before maturity and, as noted above, paying for such a conversion feature would be inconsistent with an intention to hold the host to maturity. *[IAS 39.C.3]*.

3.2 Positive intention and ability to hold to maturity

An entity should assess its intention and ability to hold these instruments to maturity when they are initially acquired and also at the end of each subsequent reporting period. *[IAS 39.AG25]*.

If any one of the following criteria is met, a positive intention to hold an investment to maturity is deemed not to exist (and the asset cannot be classified as such):

- the intention to hold the investment is for only an undefined period;
- the holder stands ready to sell the financial asset in response to changes in market interest rates or risks, liquidity needs, changes in the availability of and the yield on alternative investments, changes in financing sources and terms, or changes in foreign currency risk (although this does not apply to situations that are non-recurring and could not have been reasonably anticipated); or
- the issuer has a right to settle the financial asset at an amount significantly below its amortised cost. *[IAS 39.AG16]*.

Further, an investor is deemed not to have a demonstrated ability to hold an investment to maturity if:

- it does not have the financial resources available to continue to finance the investment until maturity; or
- it is subject to an existing legal or other constraint that could frustrate its intention to hold the financial asset to maturity (although an issuer's call option does not necessarily frustrate this intention – see 3.1 above). *[IAS 39.AG23]*.

The intention and ability to hold debt instruments to maturity is not necessarily constrained if those instruments have been pledged as collateral or are subject to a repurchase or securities lending agreements. However, an entity would not have the positive intention and ability to hold the debt instruments until maturity if it did not expect to be able to maintain or recover access to the instruments. *[IAS 39.B.18]*.

The standard also suggests that circumstances other than those described above can indicate that an entity does not have a positive intention or ability to hold an investment to maturity, *[IAS 39.AG24]*, but gives no indication of what these other circumstances might be.

3.3 The tainting provisions

When an entity's actions cast doubt on its intention or ability to hold such investments to maturity, the use of amortised cost for held-to-maturity assets is precluded for 'a reasonable period of time'. *[IAS 39.AG20]*. Consequently, no investment should be classified as held-to-maturity if, during either the current financial year or the two preceding financial years, the reporting entity has sold or reclassified more than an insignificant (in relation to the total) amount of such investments before maturity other than by those effected:

(a) close enough to maturity or call date (e.g. less than three months before maturity) so that changes in the market rate of interest did not have a significant effect on the investment's fair value;

(b) after substantially all of the investment's original principal had been collected through scheduled payments or prepayments; or

(c) due to an isolated non-recurring event that is beyond the holder's control and could not have been reasonably anticipated by the holder. *[IAS 39.9]*.

Therefore, if an entity makes any 'not insignificant' sale or reclassification of a held-to-maturity investment that does not fall within (a) to (c) above, the entire remaining portfolio of such investments will have to be reclassified as available-for-sale (see 5 and 6.3 below) and will be remeasured to fair value for at least the following two financial years. The nature of this 'punishment' is unique within accounting standards and has become known as the 'tainting' or, by rugby followers, the 'sin-bin' provisions.

The standard neither defines nor provides further guidance on how 'an insignificant amount' should be interpreted. Accordingly, reporting entities should make the assessment based on the facts and circumstances in each particular situation.

The guidance to the original version of IAS 39 explained that conditions (a) and (b) relate to situations in which an entity is expected to be indifferent whether to hold or sell a financial asset because movements in interest rates after substantially all of the original principal has been collected or when the instrument is close to maturity will not have a significant impact on its fair value. Accordingly, such a sale should not affect profit or loss and no price volatility would be expected during the remaining period to maturity.

It went on to say that if a financial asset is sold less than three months prior to maturity, that would generally qualify for this exception because the impact on the instrument's fair value of a difference between the stated interest rate and the market rate would generally be small for an instrument that matures in three months relative to an instrument that matures in several years. If sold after 90% or more of its original principal has been collected through scheduled payments or prepayments, condition (b) would generally be met. However, if only, say, 10% of the original principal has been collected, then that condition is clearly not met.[7]

The conditions must be applied to all held-to-maturity investments in aggregate and not to separate sub-categories of such assets (e.g. US dollar and euro denominated investments). *[IAS 39.B.20]*. In consolidated financial statements they must be applied to all investments classified as held-to-maturity in those financial statements, even if they are held by different entities within the group, in different countries or in different legal or economic environments. *[IAS 39.B.21]*.

Example 46.3: Application of tainting provisions

On a number of occasions during 2014, B, a company with a calendar year-end, sold certain securities from its held-to-maturity portfolio to realise a large appreciation in their value. The value of the securities sold, in relation to the total carrying amount of the portfolio, was considered to be insignificant with respect to the individual sale transactions.

However, the cumulative amount of sales was considered significant and raised doubts over B's intention to hold new investments to maturity. Therefore the application of the tainting provisions meant that the rest of the held-to-maturity portfolio was reclassified to available-for-sale during 2014. B was also prohibited from reclassifying any new investments as held-to-maturity during 2015 and 2016 (i.e. two full years). Accordingly, the earliest date B could subsequently use the held-to-maturity classification is 1 January 2017.

A 'disaster scenario' that is only remotely possible, such as a run on a bank or a similar situation affecting an insurer, is not anticipated in deciding whether there is positive intention and ability to hold an investment to maturity. *[IAS 39.AG21]*. Consequently, a sale triggered by such a scenario would not contradict the reporting entity's intention to hold a financial asset to maturity.

The standard also explains that sales before maturity may satisfy condition (c) above 'an isolated non-recurring event that is beyond the holder's control and could not have been reasonably anticipated' – and therefore not trigger the tainting provisions – if they are attributable to:

- a significant deterioration in the issuer's creditworthiness (see 3.3.1 below);
- a change in tax law that eliminates or significantly reduces the tax-exempt status of interest on the held-to-maturity investment, but not a change in tax law that revises the marginal tax rates applicable to interest income;
- a major business combination or major disposition, such as the sale of a segment, that necessitates the sale or transfer of held-to-maturity investments to maintain the holder's existing interest rate risk position or credit risk policy. Although the business combination itself is an event within the holder's control, the changes to its investment portfolio to maintain its interest rate risk position or credit risk policy may be consequential rather than anticipated;
- a change in statutory or regulatory requirements significantly modifying either what constitutes a permissible investment or the maximum level of particular types of investments, thereby causing disposal of a held-to-maturity investment;
- a significant increase in the industry's regulatory capital requirements that causes a downsizing by selling held-to-maturity investments; or
- a significant increase in the risk weights of held-to-maturity investments used for regulatory risk-based capital purposes. *[IAS 39.AG22]*.

3.3.1 Deterioration in issuer's creditworthiness

A sale following a downgrade in a credit rating by an external rating agency would not necessarily raise a question about the entity's intention to hold other investments to maturity if the downgrade provides evidence of a significant deterioration in the issuer's creditworthiness judged by reference to the credit rating at initial recognition. *[IAS 39.AG22]*. However, the rating downgrade must not have been reasonably anticipated when the investment was classified as held-to-maturity. A credit downgrade of a notch within a class or from one rating class to the immediately lower rating class could often be regarded as reasonably anticipated. *[IAS 39.B.15]*.

Similarly, where internal ratings are used for assessing exposures, changes in those ratings may help to identify issuers for which there has been a significant deterioration in creditworthiness, provided the approach to assigning ratings and changes therein give a consistent, reliable and objective measure of the credit quality of the issuers. *[IAS 39.AG22]*.

In our view, there should be a clear link between the downgrade and the sale for it to meet condition (c) at 3.3 above. If an extended period of time has elapsed between the two events, this will call into question whether the sale is actually due to the credit downgrade.

If there is evidence that a financial asset is impaired (see Chapter 49 at 4), for example a rating downgrade in combination with other information, the deterioration in creditworthiness is often regarded as significant. *[IAS 39.AG22, B.15]*.

Following the European sovereign debt crisis, a number of entities have considered disposing of certain of their held-to-maturity investments, particularly bonds issued by the weaker eurozone governments. The requirements above apply equally to government bonds as they do to other held-to-maturity investments.

In situations where a reporting entity decides to sell some, but not all, instruments issued by a single issuer who has subsequently suffered a significant deterioration in creditworthiness, significant judgement is required to assess whether the entity's intention and ability to hold some investments remains demonstrable.

3.3.2 Major business combinations or disposals

The implementation guidance makes it clear that condition (c) at 3.3 above does not extend to an unsolicited tender offer on economically favourable terms. *[IAS 39.B.19]*.

3.3.3 Significant changes in statutory or regulatory requirements

Sales of held-to-maturity investments in response to an unanticipated significant increase by the regulator in the *industry's* capital requirements may not necessarily raise a question about the intention to hold other investments to maturity. However, in some countries, regulators may set *entity-specific* capital requirements based on an assessment of the risk in that particular entity. In such scenarios, it will normally be difficult to demonstrate that the regulator's decision could not have been reasonably anticipated by the particular reporting entity. Consequently, any sales in response to the regulator's action *will* raise doubt over the intention to hold other financial assets to maturity unless it can be demonstrated that the sales fulfil condition (c) at 3.3 above. In other words, they should result from an increase in capital requirements which is an isolated non-recurring event that is beyond the entity's control and could not have been reasonably anticipated. *[IAS 39.B.17]*.

3.3.4 Change of management

A change in management is not identified as an exception and the guidance explains that sales in response to such a change would call into question the intention to hold investments to maturity. *[IAS 39.B.16]*.

Example 46.4: Change of management

A company has a portfolio of financial assets that is classified as held-to-maturity. In the current period, at the direction of the board of directors, the senior management team has been replaced. The new management wishes to sell a portion of the held-to-maturity financial assets in order to carry out an expansion strategy designated and approved by the board.

Although the previous management team had been in place since the company's formation and had never before undergone a major restructuring, the sale nevertheless calls into question the company's intention to hold remaining held-to-maturity financial assets to maturity and the company may be prohibited from using the held-to-maturity classification if the amounts involved are not insignificant. *[IAS 39.B.16]*.

4 LOANS AND RECEIVABLES

As noted at 1 above, the loans and receivables category comprises non-derivative financial assets with fixed or determinable payments that are not quoted in an active market, do not qualify as 'trading' assets, have not been designated at fair value through profit or loss or as available-for-sale. In addition, the category cannot include financial assets for which the holder may not recover substantially all of its initial investment for reasons other than the issuer's credit deterioration. *[IAS 39.9]*.

For most entities this category includes trade receivables, other debtors and bank deposits; for banks and similar financial institutions it will constitute a significant proportion of their non-trading assets, in particular loans and advances to customers. *[IAS 39.AG26]*.

A loan asset need not be originated by the entity. For example, if an entity purchases a portfolio of loans they may be included within this category if they meet the relevant conditions. *[IAS 39.BC28]*.

An asset with terms such that the holder may not recover substantially all of its initial investment (other than because of credit deterioration), for example a fixed rate interest-only strip created in a securitisation and subject to prepayment risk, should not be classified within loans and receivables. The IASB believes such instruments should be recorded at fair value, *[IAS 39.9, BC29]*, probably because that value can be more volatile than that of other loans and receivables.

As noted above, instruments 'quoted in an active market' are prohibited from being included within this category and must therefore be included in one of the other three categories of financial asset. *[IAS 39.9]*. 'Quoted in an active market' means that prices are readily available in a market accessible by the reporting entity, where orderly transactions take place with sufficient frequency and volume to provide pricing information on an ongoing basis. Such quoted prices would normally be representative of fair value because they are based on current information that reflects market participants' assumptions. *[IFRS 13 Appendix A, 15-20, B34]*.

Provided there is no intention to sell the instrument immediately or in the short term, where a bank makes a term deposit with a central or other bank it is classified within loans and receivables even if the proof of deposit is negotiable, i.e. the deposit is capable of being sold. If there was such an intention to sell, the deposit would be a trading asset. *[IAS 39.B.23]*.

Non-derivative instruments that have the legal form of equities, such as preference shares, but which under IAS 32 – *Financial Instruments: Presentation* – would be classified as liabilities in the financial statements of the issuer and have fixed or determinable payments and fixed maturity (see Chapter 45 at 4.2) can potentially be classified within loans and receivables, provided the instrument is not quoted in an active market and the definition is otherwise met. However if, under IAS 32, an instrument would be classified as equity in the financial statements of the issuer, it could not be classified within loans and receivables by the holder. *[IAS 39.B.22]*.

The standard explains that an interest acquired in a pool of assets that are not loans or receivables (for example, an interest in a mutual fund or a similar fund) is not a loan or receivable. *[IAS 39.9]*. We believe this was added to clarify the treatment of investments in mutual funds, unit trusts and similar funds – this issue is dealt with in more detail in Chapter 44 at 5.1.9.

The principal difference between loans and receivables and held-to-maturity investments is that loans and receivables are not subject to the tainting provisions (see 3.3 above). Consequently, loans and receivables that are not held for trading may be measured at amortised cost even if an entity does not have the positive intention and ability to hold the loan asset until maturity. *[IAS 39.BC25]*. However, if financial assets classified as loans and receivables are subsequently sold within a short period after origination, it may call into question whether the newly originated or acquired assets are held for trading and should therefore be measured at fair value through profit or loss. Financial assets that do not meet the definition of loans and receivables, e.g. because they are quoted in an active market, may be classified as held-to-maturity investments if they meet the relevant conditions. *[IAS 39.AG26]*. However, it is important to recognise another major difference between the two classes of instrument, namely the significant restrictions on applying hedge accounting when the hedged item is a held-to-maturity investment (see Chapter 52 at 2.2.6).

On initial recognition a financial asset that would otherwise be classified as a loan or receivable may, at the entity's discretion, be designated as available-for-sale, or potentially designated at fair value through profit or loss under the fair value option, if the relevant criteria are met (see 5 below and 2.2 above respectively). *[IAS 39.9]*.

5 AVAILABLE-FOR-SALE ASSETS

Unless designated into this category (see 4 above), a financial asset is classified as available-for-sale if it does not properly belong in one of the three other categories of financial assets – at fair value through profit or loss, held-to-maturity or loans and receivables. In many respects available-for-sale is a 'default' classification.

This category normally includes equity and quoted debt securities not classified or designated at fair value through profit or loss, other than quoted debt securities held-to-maturity.

The main interpretative issue an entity is likely to experience in respect of this classification is whether a portfolio of investments can properly be regarded as available-for-sale rather than trading. The implementation guidance provides the following example to assist in making this judgement.

Example 46.5: Portfolio balancing

Company A has an investment portfolio of debt and equity instruments. The documented portfolio management guidelines specify that the equity exposure of the portfolio should be limited to between 30% and 50% of total portfolio value. The investment manager of the portfolio is authorised to balance the portfolio within the designated guidelines by buying and selling equity and debt instruments. The instruments should be classified as trading or available-for-sale depending on Company A's intent and past practice.

If the portfolio manager is authorised to buy and sell instruments to balance the risks in a portfolio, but there is no intention to trade and there is no past practice of trading for short-term profit, the instruments can be classified as available-for-sale. If instruments are bought and sold to generate short-term profits, the financial instruments in the portfolio should be classified as held for trading. *[IAS 39.B.12]*.

6 RECLASSIFICATIONS

This section deals with the situations in which financial instruments should or may be reclassified from one category to another. Accounting for the subsequent measurement of reclassified instruments is dealt with in Chapter 49 at 2.7 and the related disclosure requirements are covered in Chapter 54 at 4.4.5.

6.1 Reclassifications to or from fair value through profit or loss

To impose discipline on an entity's ability to designate items at fair value through profit or loss, financial instruments cannot generally be reclassified into or out of this category subsequent to initial recognition. *[IAS 39.50, BC73]*.

Accordingly, if an entity starts to trade (as set out at 2.1 above) a portfolio of, say, available-for-sale investments all newly acquired investments will be classified as trading, but the legacy investments will continue to be classified as available-for-sale. *[IAS 39.50]*.

However, there are a limited number of exceptions to this prohibition which are discussed below.

6.1.1 Reclassifications from held for trading

IAS 39 allows a non-derivative financial asset classified as held for trading to be reclassified out of the fair value through profit or loss category, in certain circumstances. Such a reclassification is conditional on the asset no longer being held for the purpose of sale in the near term (notwithstanding that it may have been acquired or incurred principally for this purpose) and is subject to further conditions which are considered at 6.1.1.A and 6.1.1.B below. *[IAS 39.50(c)]*. Derivatives and financial instruments designated at fair value through profit or loss on initial recognition may not be reclassified. *[IAS 39.50(a), (b)]*.

Hybrid (combined) financial assets reclassified out of the held for trading classification are required to be reassessed for bifurcation into a host contract and an embedded derivative upon reclassification (see Chapter 44 at 7.1). *[IFRIC 9.7]*.

Any such reclassification of a financial asset can now take effect only from the date when the reclassification is made. *[IAS 39.103H, 103I]*. In other words, a reclassification from the held for trading classification cannot be applied retrospectively.

6.1.1.A Reclassifications to loans and receivables

In order to be reclassified to loans and receivables, a financial asset meeting the condition described at 6.1.1 above would need to have met the definition of loans and receivables (if the financial asset had not been required to be classified as held for trading at initial recognition) and at the date of reclassification the reporting entity should have the intention and ability to hold it for the foreseeable future or until maturity. *[IAS 39.50D]*.

As set out at 1 and 4 above, a financial asset that is quoted in an active market does not meet the definition of loans and receivables. It is not clear whether an asset would need to have met the definition of loans and receivables at the date of (a) initial recognition, or (b) reclassification, in order to qualify for reclassification. This can make a significant difference because, for example, the turbulence in the financial markets in the second half of 2008 meant that many financial assets had ceased to be quoted in an active market (which was the period many entities were seeking to reclassify them). In our opinion, both interpretations are acceptable as an accounting policy choice, and both have been seen in practice. The interpretation chosen should be applied consistently to all similar reclassifications. The following extracts show that HSBC selected the first approach and Deutsche Bank the second.

Extract 46.1: HSBC Holdings plc (2012)

Notes on the Financial Statements [extract]

2 Summary of significant accounting policies [extract]

(e) Reclassification of financial assets [extract]

Non-derivative financial assets (other than those designated at fair value through profit or loss upon initial recognition) may be reclassified out of the fair value through profit or loss category in the following circumstances:

– financial assets that would have met the definition of loans and receivables at initial recognition (if the financial asset had not been required to be classified as held for trading) may be reclassified out of the fair value through profit or loss category if there is the intention and ability to hold the financial asset for the foreseeable future or until maturity; and

– financial assets (except financial assets that would have met the definition of loans and receivables at initial recognition) may be reclassified out of the fair value through profit or loss category and into another category in rare circumstances.

Extract 46.2: Deutsche Bank Aktiengesellschaft (2012)

Notes to the Consolidated Financial Statements [extract]

01 – Significant Accounting Policies [extract]

Financial Assets and Liabilities [extract]

Reclassification of Financial Assets [extract]

The Group may reclassify certain financial assets out of the financial assets at fair value through profit or loss classification (trading assets) and the AFS classification into the loans classification. For assets to be reclassified there must be a clear change in management intent with respect to the assets since initial recognition and the financial asset must meet the definition of a loan at the reclassification date. Additionally, there must be an intent and ability to hold the asset for the foreseeable future at the reclassification date. There is no single specific period that defines foreseeable future. Rather, it is a matter requiring management judgment. In exercising this judgment, the Group established the following minimum requirements for what constitutes foreseeable future. At the time of reclassification,

– there must be no intent to dispose of the asset through sale or securitization within one year and no internal or external requirement that would restrict the Group's ability to hold or require sale; and
– the business plan going forward should not be to profit from short-term movements in price.

Financial assets proposed for reclassification which meet these criteria are considered based on the facts and circumstances of each financial asset under consideration. A positive management assertion is required after taking into account the ability and plausibility to execute the strategy to hold.

In addition to the above criteria the Group also requires that persuasive evidence exists to assert that the expected repayment of the asset exceeds the estimated fair value and the returns on the asset will be optimized by holding it for the foreseeable future.

Foreseeable future is not a defined term and it may vary in duration depending on circumstances. Consequently, entities will need to apply judgement whenever considering such a reclassification. In our view, it would be acceptable to use twelve months as a guide. This approach has been used by a number of banks as illustrated in the following extract from RBS and Extract 46.2 above from Deutsche Bank.

Extract 46.3: The Royal Bank of Scotland Group plc (2012)

Accounting policies [extract]

15. Financial assets [extract]

Reclassifications – held-for-trading and available-for-sale financial assets that meet the definition of loans and receivables (non-derivative financial assets with fixed or determinable payments that are not quoted in an active market) may be reclassified to loans and receivables if the Group has the intention and ability to hold the financial asset for the foreseeable future or until maturity. The Group typically regards the foreseeable future as twelve months from the date of reclassification. Additionally, held-for-trading financial assets that do not meet the definition of loans and receivables may, in rare circumstances, be transferred to available-for-sale financial assets or to held-to-maturity investments.

An entity cannot normally assert it intends to hold a financial asset for the foreseeable future unless it has an expectation that it will not consider any offers to sell. In our opinion, an entity prepared to sell a financial asset on receipt of a reasonable offer does not have an intention to hold it for the foreseeable future.

A reporting entity assesses its intention to hold a financial asset for the foreseeable future at the date of potential reclassification and ordinarily it does not need to revisit this. However, an entity may subsequently change its intentions towards a reclassified financial asset and dispose of it. In these circumstances, one would need to examine carefully the circumstances surrounding the sale to determine whether the original reclassification was appropriate, especially if the sale took place a relatively short time after reclassification. Such disposals may cast doubt about an entity's assertion that it has the intention to hold for the foreseeable future other assets that it wishes to reclassify. Nevertheless, such disposals do not necessarily mean the reclassification represents an accounting error.

6.1.1.B Reclassifications in rare circumstances

In addition to those reclassifications from held for trading to loans and receivables discussed at 6.1.1.A above, an entity may, in rare circumstances, reclassify non-derivative financial assets meeting the condition described at 6.1.1 above as available-for-sale financial assets or held-to-maturity investments. *[IAS 39.50B]*. These assets can include investments in equity instruments and debt instruments that are quoted in an active market.

The standard does not expand on what is meant by rare circumstances and entities will need to exercise judgement in determining what they consider them to be. However, the IASB noted that rare circumstances arise from a single event that is unusual and highly unlikely to recur in the near term. *[IAS 39.BC104D]*. Furthermore, an October 2008 press release stated that the deterioration of the world's financial markets that had occurred during the third quarter of 2008 was a possible example and quoted the IASB's Chairman as referring to 'the rare circumstances of the current credit crisis' which provided some context for entities making this judgement.[8]

6.1.2 Re-designation and de-designation of derivatives as hedging instruments

Entities are not prohibited from (a) designating a derivative as a hedging instrument in a cash flow hedge or hedge of a net investment if it was previously classified as trading nor (b) revoking the designation of an effective cash flow hedge or hedge of a net investment involving a derivative – these are not regarded as reclassifications. *[IAS 39.50A]*.

6.1.3 Changes in accounting policy for insurance contracts

When an insurer changes its accounting policies for insurance liabilities, it is permitted (but not required) to change its accounting policy for some or all of its financial assets and reclassify them as at fair value through profit or loss (see Chapter 55 at 8.4). *[IFRS 4.45]*. IAS 39 makes it clear that this change in accounting policy is not a prohibited reclassification. *[IAS 39.50A]*.

6.2 Reclassifications between available-for-sale financial assets and loans and receivables

A financial asset classified as available-for-sale that would have met the definition of loans and receivables (if it had not been designated as available for sale) may be reclassified to loans and receivables if the entity has the intention and ability to hold the financial asset for the foreseeable future or until maturity. *[IAS 39.50E]*. Any such reclassification of a financial asset can now take effect only from the date when the reclassification is made. *[IAS 39.103H, 103I]*. In other words, reclassifications cannot be applied retrospectively.

Similar to the situation for reclassifications from held for trading to loans and receivables (see 6.1.1.A above), it is not clear whether an asset would need to have met the definition of loans and receivables at the date of (a) initial recognition, or (b) reclassification in order to qualify for reclassification. Again, either interpretation is, in our opinion, an acceptable accounting policy choice. The interpretation chosen should be applied consistently to all similar reclassifications. In contrast to the position taken on reclassifications from held for trading, one of CESR's enforcement agencies has accepted reclassifications from available-for-sale based on an assessment at the date of reclassification.[9]

IAS 39 neither requires nor prohibits reclassification of financial assets from loans and receivables to available-for-sale financial assets, for example if a debt instrument becomes quoted in an active market after initial recognition (or after reclassification to loans and receivables) and the market is expected to remain active. In our opinion, it is acceptable, although not required, for an entity to adopt an accounting policy of reclassifying such instruments as available-for-sale in these circumstances, provided the policy is applied consistently. Of course, this would require the reporting entity to continually monitor the existence or otherwise of an active market for its financial assets.

6.3 Reclassifications between held-to-maturity investments and available for sale financial assets

Reclassifications between held-to-maturity investments and available-for-sale assets are permitted. An investment will be reclassified as available-for-sale if, as a result of a change in intention or ability, it fails to meet the requirements for classification as held-to-maturity. *[IAS 39.51]*. If the tainting provisions (see 3.3 above) are triggered, any remaining held-to-maturity investments should also be reclassified as available-for-sale. *[IAS 39.52]*. Similarly, if, as a result of a change in intention or ability or because the tainting period has passed, it becomes appropriate to regard an available-for-sale asset as held-to-maturity, it should be reclassified accordingly. *[IAS 39.54]*.

6.4 Prohibited reclassifications

As noted in 6.1.1 above, derivatives and financial instruments designated at fair value through profit or loss may not be reclassified. Further, reclassifying any financial instrument into the fair value through profit or loss category after initial recognition is prohibited. *[IAS 39.50]*. Despite this, paragraph 12 of IAS 39 appears to allow for one exception when an entity is unable to separately measure a separated embedded derivative from its host contract at the end of a subsequent financial reporting period. In such a scenario the standard requires the reporting entity to designate the entire hybrid (combined) contract as at fair value through profit or loss.

Reclassifications of financial liabilities are not allowed. *[IAS 39.50]*. This prohibition extends to loan commitments classified at fair value through profit or loss because they will either be derivatives or will be financial liabilities designated at fair value through profit or loss.

7 CLASSIFICATION OF FINANCIAL INSTRUMENTS IN A BUSINESS COMBINATION

From the perspective of an acquirer applying the acquisition method of accounting to a business combination, IFRS 3 – *Business Combinations* – views the business combination as giving rise to the initial recognition by the acquirer of the acquiree's financial instruments. *[IFRS 3.15, 16(a)]*. Therefore all financial instruments should be classified by reference to the acquirer's circumstances and intention towards those financial instruments and any designation made when the business combination occurs. In other words, an entity classifies the acquired financial instruments at the acquisition date (i.e. the moment of initial recognition from the acquirer's perspective) by applying the classification requirements, without regards to how they were previously classified by the acquiree.

In rare cases, the pooling of interests method may be used for a business combination, for example in a transaction involving entities under common control (see Chapter 10 at 3.1 and 3.3). In such cases the basis of preparation involves an assumption that the acquired entities were always part of the same reporting entity and therefore it would be appropriate to look to the classification of the financial instruments in the financial statements of the acquired entity.

8 FUTURE DEVELOPMENTS

IAS 39 will be superseded by IFRS 9 – *Financial Instruments* – which is effective for periods commencing on or after 1 January 2018. Classification of financial instruments in accordance with IFRS 9 is covered in Chapter 47.

References

1 *IFRIC Update*, May 2009.
2 *2nd extract from EECS's database of enforcement decisions*, CESR, December 2007, Decision Ref. EECS/1207-06.
3 *IFRIC Update*, May 2007.
4 *IFRIC Update*, July 2007, September 2007 and November 2007.
5 Exposure Draft, *Improvements to IFRSs*, IASB, August 2008, IAS 39, para. 11A.
6 *IASB Update*, January 2009, Information for Observers (January 2009 IASB Meeting), *Annual Improvements 2009 – Comment Analysis, (Agenda Paper 6A)*, IASB, January 2009, para. 11(c) and Appendix 2, and *IFRIC Update*, January 2010.
7 IGC Q&A 83-1.
8 Press Release, *IASB amendments permit reclassification of financial instruments*, IASB, October 2008.
9 *5th extract from EECS's database of enforcement decisions*, CESR, March 2009, Decision Ref. EECS/0209-01.

Chapter 47 Financial instruments: Classification (IFRS 9)

List of examples

Chapter 47 Financial instruments: Classification (IFRS 9)

1 INTRODUCTION

On 24 July 2014, the International Accounting Standards Board (the IASB or the Board) published the consolidated version of IFRS 9 – *Financial Instruments* (IFRS 9 or the standard) including the revised classification requirements for financial assets. Classification determines how financial instruments are accounted for in the financial statements and, in particular, how they are measured on an ongoing basis.

The more principle-based approach of IFRS 9 will require careful use of judgment in its application. Some fact patterns have no simple and distinct outcome and we highlight in this chapter the factors that need to be considered in arriving at a conclusion. Further issues and questions are likely to be raised during the course of implementation.

2 CLASSIFYING FINANCIAL ASSETS: AN OVERVIEW

IFRS 9 has the following measurement categories for financial assets:

- Debt instruments at amortised cost.
- Debt instruments at fair value through other comprehensive income with cumulative gains and losses reclassified to profit or loss upon derecognition.
- Debt instruments, derivatives and equity instruments at fair value through profit or loss.
- Equity instruments designated as measured at fair value through other comprehensive income with gains and losses remaining in other comprehensive income, i.e. without recycling to profit or loss upon derecognition.

Apart from some options which are described in more detail at 7 and 8 below, the classification is based on both the entity's business model for managing the financial assets and the contractual cash flow characteristics of the financial assets. *[IFRS 9.4.1.1]*. The synopsis below illustrates the thought process on which the classification of financial assets is based:

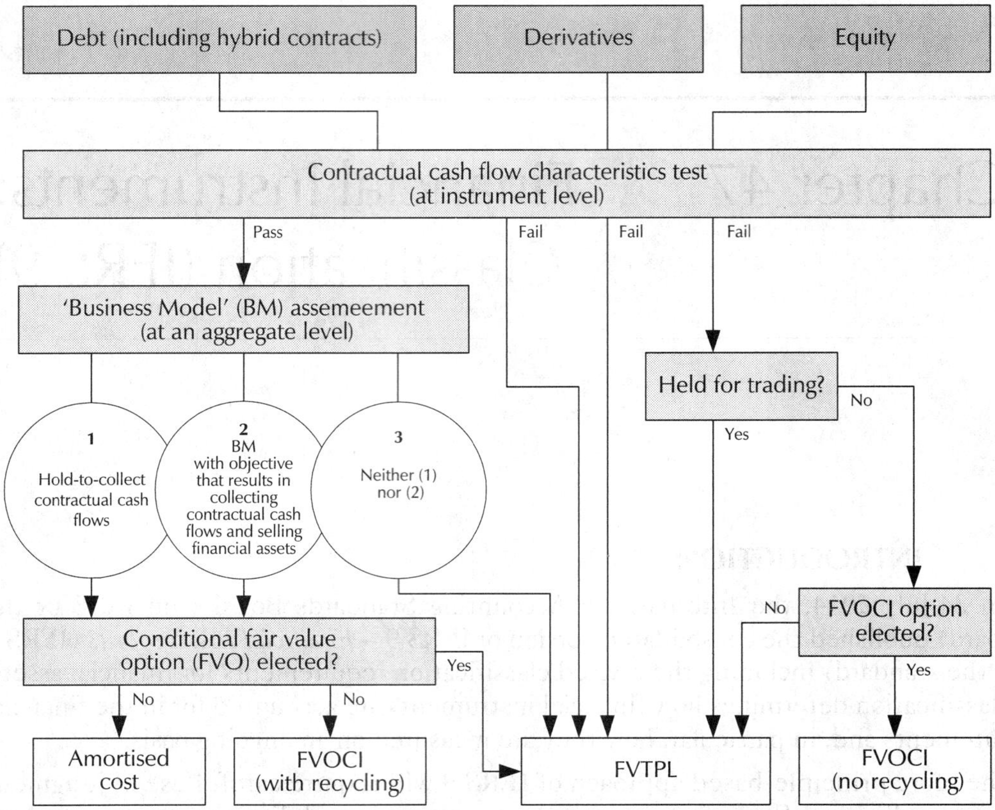

The following matrix summarises the outcome of the thought process depicted in the synopsis above:

		Contractual cash flow characteristics test	
		Pass	**Fail**
Business model	Held within a business model whose objective is to hold financial assets in order to collect contractual cash flows	Amortised cost	FVTPL[1]
	Held within a business model whose objective is achieved by both collecting contractual cash flows and selling financial assets	FVOCI[2] (debt)	FVTPL
	Financial assets which are neither held at amortised cost nor at fair value through other comprehensive income	FVTPL	FVTPL
Options	Conditional fair value option is elected	FVTPL	n/a[3]
	Option elected to present changes in fair value of an equity instrument not held for trading in OCI	n/a[4]	FVOCI (equity)

1 Fair value through profit or loss
2 Fair value through other comprehensive income

3 Financial assets which fail the contractual cash flow characteristics test are measured at fair value through profit or loss

4 Only debt instruments can pass the contractual cash flow characteristics test. The fair value through other comprehensive income option only applies to equity instruments and does not apply to those instruments

Measurement is covered in Chapter 50, particularly at 2.1 (financial assets measured at fair value through profit or loss), 2.2 (equity investments designated at fair value through other comprehensive income), 2.3 (debt instruments measured at fair value through other comprehensive income) and 2.4 (financial assets measured at amortised cost). This includes the effective interest method and expected credit loss impairment model for financial assets measured at amortised cost and fair value through other comprehensive income. Fair value is determined in accordance with IFRS 13 – *Fair Value Measurement* – see Chapter 14.

2.1 Debt instruments

A debt instrument is normally measured at amortised cost if both of the following conditions are met: *[IFRS 9.4.1.2]*

(a) the asset is held within a business model whose objective is to hold assets in order to collect contractual cash flows; and

(b) the contractual terms of the financial asset give rise on specified dates to cash flows that are solely payments of principal and interest on the principal amount outstanding.

A debt instrument is normally measured at fair value through other comprehensive income if both of the following conditions are met: *[IFRS 9.4.1.2A]*

(a) the asset is held within a business model in which assets are managed to achieve a particular objective by both collecting contractual cash flows and selling financial assets; and

(b) the contractual terms of the financial asset give rise on specified dates to cash flows that are solely payments of principal and interest on the principal amount outstanding.

The application of these conditions (the 'business model' assessment and 'contractual cash flow characteristics' test) is covered in more detail at 5 and 6 below, respectively.

The above requirements should be applied to an entire financial asset, even if it contains an embedded derivative. *[IFRS 9.4.3.2]*. That is, in contrast with the requirements of IAS 39 – *Financial Instruments: Recognition and Measurement*, a derivative embedded within a hybrid (combined) contract containing a financial asset host should not be accounted for separately.

The application of these requirements to debt instruments means that, apart from the exceptions described in section 6.4 below, only relatively simple 'plain vanilla' debt instruments qualify to be measured at amortised cost or at fair value through other comprehensive income. Debt instruments that are neither measured at amortised cost nor at fair value though other comprehensive income are measured at fair value through profit or loss. *[IFRS 9.4.1.4]*. As will be shown at 5.4 below, this includes instruments that are held for trading (see 4 below).

Notwithstanding the criteria for debt instruments to be classified at amortised cost or at fair value through other comprehensive income, as described above, an entity may irrevocably designate a debt instrument as measured at fair value through profit or loss at initial recognition. This is allowed if doing so eliminates or significantly reduces a measurement or recognition inconsistency (sometimes referred to as an 'accounting mismatch'). Such mismatches would otherwise arise from measuring assets or liabilities or recognising the gains and losses on them on different bases. *[IFRS 9.4.1.5]*. This is covered further at 7 below.

In its Basis for Conclusions, the IASB noted that the fair value through other comprehensive income measurement category is intended for debt instruments for which both amortised cost information and fair value information are relevant and useful. This will be the case if their performance is affected by both the collection of contractual cash flows and the realisation of fair values through sales. *[IFRS 9.BC4.150]*.

The fair value through other comprehensive income measurement category may also help some insurers achieve consistency of measurement for assets held to back insurance liabilities under the new IFRS 4 – *Insurance Contracts* – insurance contracts model. It should also help to address concerns raised by preparers who expect to sell financial assets in greater volume than would be consistent with a business model whose objective is to hold financial assets to collect contractual cash flows and would, without this category, have to record such assets at fair value through profit or loss.

The fair value through other comprehensive income category differs from the available-for-sale category in IAS 39 in several aspects. First, the available-for-sale category for debt instruments was essentially a residual classification and an unrestricted election. The fair value through other comprehensive income classification under IFRS 9 reflects a business model evidenced by facts and circumstances and is neither a residual classification nor an election. Second, financial assets measured at fair value through other comprehensive income will be subject to the same impairment model as those measured at amortised cost. Accordingly, although the assets are recorded at fair value, the profit or loss treatment will be the same as for an amortised cost asset, with the difference between amortised cost and fair value recorded in other comprehensive income. Third, only relatively simple debt instruments will qualify for measurement at fair value through other comprehensive income as they will also need to pass the contractual cash flow characteristics test.

2.2 Equity instruments and derivatives

Equity instruments and derivatives are normally measured at fair value through profit or loss. *[IFRS 9.5.7.1]*. However, on initial recognition, an entity may make an irrevocable election (on an instrument-by-instrument basis) to present in other comprehensive income subsequent changes in the fair value of an investment in an equity instrument within the scope of IFRS 9. This option applies to instruments that are neither held for trading (see 4 below) nor contingent consideration recognised by an acquirer in a business combination to which IFRS 3 – *Business Combinations* – applies. *[IFRS 9.5.7.1(b), 5.7.5]*. For the purpose of this election, the term equity instrument uses the definition in IAS 32 – *Financial Instruments: Presentation*. The use of this election is covered further at 8 below.

Although most gains and losses on investments in equity instruments designated at fair value through other comprehensive income will be recognised in other comprehensive income, dividends will normally be recognised in profit or loss. *[IFRS 9.5.7.6]*. However, the IASB noted that dividends could sometimes represent a return of investment instead of a return on investment. Consequently, the IASB decided that dividends that clearly represent a recovery of part of the cost of the investment are not recognised in profit or loss. *[IFRS 9.BC5.25(a)]*. Meanwhile, gains or losses recognised in other comprehensive income are never reclassified from equity to profit or loss on derecognition of the asset, and consequently, there is no need to review such investments for possible impairment.

Determining when a dividend does or does not clearly represent a recovery of cost could prove somewhat judgemental in practice, especially as the standard contains no further explanatory guidance. Also, because it is an exception to a principle, it could open up the possibility of structuring transactions to convert fair value gains into dividends through the use of intermediate holding vehicles. However, in the IASB's view, those structuring opportunities would be limited because an entity with the ability to control or significantly influence the dividend policy of the investee would not account for those investments in accordance with IFRS 9. Furthermore the IASB require disclosures that would allow the user to compare the dividends recognised in profit or loss and other fair value changes easily. *[IFRS 9.BC5.25(a)]*.

3 CLASSIFYING FINANCIAL LIABILITIES

The classification of financial liabilities does not follow the approach used for the classification of financial assets; rather it remains broadly the same as under IAS 39. Financial liabilities are measured either at fair value through profit or loss or at amortised cost.

In addition, IFRS 9 specifies the accounting treatment for liabilities arising from certain financial guarantee contracts (see Chapter 43 at 3.4 and Chapter 50 at 2.8) and commitments to provide loans at below market rates of interest (see Chapter 43 at 3.5 and Chapter 50 at 2.8).

Financial liabilities are measured at fair value through profit or loss when they meet the definition of held for trading (see 4 below), *[IFRS 9 Appendix A]*, or when they are designated as such on initial recognition (see 7 below). Designation at fair value through profit or loss is permitted when either: *[IFRS 9.4.2.2]*

(a) it eliminates or significantly reduces a measurement or recognition inconsistency (sometimes referred to as an 'accounting mismatch'). Such mismatches would otherwise arise from measuring assets or liabilities or recognising the gains and losses on them on different bases;

(b) a group of financial liabilities or financial assets and financial liabilities is managed and its performance is evaluated on a fair value basis in accordance with a documented risk management or investment strategy, and information is provided internally on that basis to the entity's key management personnel (as defined in IAS 24 – *Related Party Disclosures* – see Chapter 37 at 2.2.1.D); or

(c) a financial liability contains one or more embedded derivatives that meet certain conditions. *[IFRS 9.4.3.5]*.

However, for financial liabilities designated as at fair value through profit or loss, the element of gains or losses attributable to changes in credit risk should normally be recognised in other comprehensive income with the remainder recognised in profit or loss. *[IFRS 9.5.7.7]*. These amounts recognised in other comprehensive income are not recycled to profit or loss if the liability is ever repurchased. However if this treatment creates or enlarges an accounting mismatch in profit or loss the entity shall present all gains and losses on that liability (including the effects of changes in credit risk) in profit or loss *[IFRS 9.5.7.8]*. The guidance indicates that an economic relationship is required in these cases. In other words the liability's own credit risk must be offset by changes in the fair value of the other instrument. If there is no economic relationship between the liability's own credit risk and the fair value of the other instrument then the gains and losses arising from the changes in credit risk cannot be recognised in profit or loss. 'Economic relationship' is not defined in the standard but the IASB noted that the relationship need not be contractual, *[IFRS 9.BC5.41]*, and that such a relationship does not arise by coincidence. *[IFRS 9.BC5.40]*. However, judging from the example given in the standard it would seem that the IASB would not expect this to be very common. *[IFRS 9.B5.7.10]*. The standard also requires increased disclosure about an entity's methodology for making determinations about potential mismatches. This is discussed in further detail in Chapter 50 at 2.1.

All other financial liabilities are generally classified as subsequently measured at amortised cost using the effective interest method. *[IFRS 9.4.2.1]*.

The definition of held for trading is dealt with at 4 below and designation at fair value through profit or loss is covered further at 7 below.

In contrast to the treatment for hybrid contracts with financial assets hosts, derivatives embedded within a financial liability host within the scope of IFRS 9 will often be separately accounted for, in the same manner as under IAS 39. That is, they must be separated if they are not closely related to the host contract, they meet the definition of a derivative, and the hybrid contract is not measured at fair value through profit or loss (see Chapter 44 at 4). Where an embedded derivative is separated from a financial liability host, the requirements of IFRS 9 dealing with classification of financial instruments should be applied separately to each of the host liability and the embedded derivative.

4 FINANCIAL ASSETS AND FINANCIAL LIABILITIES HELD FOR TRADING

The fact that a financial instrument is held for trading is important for its classification. For financial assets that are debt instruments, held for trading is a business model objective that results in measurement at fair value through profit or loss, as indicated at 2.1 above and further covered in more detail at 5.4 below. Whether or not an asset is held for trading is also relevant for the option to designate an equity instrument as measured at fair value through other comprehensive income (see 2.2 above). Similar to financial assets, if a financial liability is held for trading it is classified as measured at fair value through profit or loss (see 3 above).

Financial assets and liabilities held for trading are defined as those that: *[IFRS 9 Appendix A]*

- are acquired or incurred principally for the purpose of sale or repurchase in the near term;
- on initial recognition are part of a portfolio of identified financial instruments that are managed together and for which there is evidence of a recent actual pattern of short-term profit-taking; or
- are derivatives (except for those that are financial guarantee contracts – see Chapter 43 at 3.4 – or are designated effective hedging instruments – see Chapter 52 at 2.1.1 and Chapter 53 at 4).

It follows from the definition that if an entity originates a loan with an intention of syndicating it, the amount of the loan to be syndicated should be classified as held for trading, even if the bank fails to find sufficient commitments from other participants (a so-called 'failed' loan syndication).

The term 'portfolio' in the definition of held for trading is not explicitly defined in IFRS 9, but the context in which it is used suggests that a portfolio is a group of financial assets and/or financial liabilities that are managed as part of that group. If there is evidence of a recent actual pattern of short-term profit taking on financial instruments included in such a portfolio, those financial instruments qualify as held for trading even though an individual financial instrument may, in fact, be held for a longer period of time. *[IFRS 9.IG B.11].*

A financial asset or liability held for trading will always be measured at fair value through profit or loss.

Trading generally reflects active and frequent buying and selling, and financial instruments held for trading are normally used with the objective of generating a profit from short-term fluctuations in price or a dealer's margin. *[IFRS 9.BA.6].*

In addition to derivatives that are not accounted for as hedging instruments, financial liabilities held for trading include:

(a) obligations to deliver financial assets borrowed by a short seller (i.e. an entity that sells financial assets it has borrowed and does not yet own);

(b) financial liabilities that are incurred with an intention to repurchase them in the near term, such as quoted debt instruments that the issuer may buy back in the near term depending on changes in fair value; and

(c) financial liabilities that are part of a portfolio of identified financial instruments that are managed together and for which there is evidence of a recent pattern of short-term profit-taking. *[IFRS 9.BA.7].* However, the fact that a liability is used merely to fund trading activities does not in itself make that liability one that is held for trading. *[IFRS 9.BA.8].*

Chapter 47

5 FINANCIAL ASSETS: THE 'BUSINESS MODEL' ASSESSMENT

The business model assessment is one of the two steps to classify financial assets. An entity's business model reflects how it manages its financial assets in order to generate cash flows; its business model determines whether cash flows will result from collecting contractual cash flows, selling the financial assets or both. This assessment is performed on the basis of scenarios that the entity reasonably expects to occur. This means, the assessment excludes so-called 'worst case' or 'stress case' scenarios. For example, if an entity expects that it will sell a particular portfolio of financial assets only in a stress case scenario, this would not affect the entity's assessment of the business model for those assets if the entity does not reasonably expect it to occur. *[IFRS 9.B4.1.2A]*.

If cash flows are realised in a way that is different from the entity's expectations at the date that the entity assessed the business model (for example, if the entity sells more or fewer financial assets than it expected when it classified the assets), this does not give rise to a prior period error in the entity's financial statements (as defined in IAS 8 – *Accounting Policies, Changes in Accounting Estimates and Errors* – see Chapter 3 at 4.6) nor does it change the classification of the remaining financial assets held in that business model (i.e. those assets that the entity recognised in prior periods and still holds), as long as the entity considered all relevant and objective information that was available at the time that it made the business model assessment. However, when an entity assesses the business model for newly originated or newly purchased financial assets, it must consider information about how cash flows were realised in the past, along with all other relevant information. This means that there is no 'tainting' concept, as in the treatment of held to maturity financial assets under IAS 39, but if there is a change in the way that cash flows are realised then this will affect the classification of new assets when first recognised in the future. (See also 9 below for guidance on reclassifications.) *[IFRS 9.B4.1.2A]*.

An entity's business model for managing the financial assets is a matter of fact and typically observable through particular activities that the entity undertakes to achieve its objectives. An entity will need to use judgment when it assesses its business model for managing financial assets and that assessment is not determined by a single factor or activity. Rather, the entity must consider all relevant and objective evidence that is available at the date of the assessment. Such relevant and objective evidence includes, but is not limited to: *[IFRS 9.B4.1.2B]*

(a) how the performance of the business model and the financial assets held within that business model are evaluated and reported to the entity's key management personnel;

(b) the risks that affect the performance of the business model (and the financial assets held within) and, in particular, the way those risks are managed; and

(c) how managers of the business are compensated (for example, whether the compensation is based on the fair value of the assets managed or the contractual cash flows collected).

In addition to these three forms of evidence, in most circumstances the expected frequency, value and timing of sales are important aspects of the assessment. These are covered in more detail in 5.2.1 below.

5.1 The level at which the business model assessment is applied

The business model assessment should be performed on the basis of the entity's business model as determined by the entity's key management personnel (as defined in IAS 24 – see Chapter 37 at 2.2.1.D). *[IFRS 9.B4.1.1]*.

An entity's business model is determined at a level that reflects how groups of financial assets are managed together to achieve a particular business objective. This does not need to be the reporting entity level. The entity's business model does not depend on management's intentions for an individual instrument. Accordingly, this condition is not an instrument-by-instrument approach to classification and should be determined on a higher level of aggregation. However, a single entity may have more than one business model for managing its financial instruments (for example, one portfolio that it manages in order to collect contractual cash flows and another portfolio that it manages in order to trade to realise fair value changes). *[IFRS 9.B4.1.2]*.

Similarly, in some circumstances, it may be appropriate to split a portfolio of financial assets into sub-portfolios to reflect how an entity manages them. *[IFRS 9.B4.1.2]*. Those portfolios would be split and treated as separate portfolios, provided the assets belonging to each sub-portfolio are defined. A sub-portfolio approach would not be appropriate in cases where an entity is not able to define which assets would be held to collect contractual cash flows and which assets would potentially be sold. It is clear that judgement will need to be applied when determining the level of aggregation to which the business model assessment should be applied. Splitting a portfolio into two sub-portfolios might allow an entity to achieve amortised cost accounting for most of the assets within the portfolio, even if it is required to sell a certain volume of assets. The entity could define the assets it intends (or is required) to sell as one sub-portfolio while it defines the assets it intends to keep as another.

5.2 Hold to collect contractual cash flows

A financial asset which is held within a business model whose objective is to hold assets in order to collect contractual cash flows is measured at amortised cost (provided the asset also meets the contractual cash flow characteristics test). *[IFRS 9.4.1.2]*. An entity manages such assets to realise cash flows by collecting contractual payments over the life of the instrument instead of managing the overall return on the portfolio by both holding and selling assets. *[IFRS 9.B4.1.2C]*.

5.2.1 Impact of sales on the assessment

In determining whether cash flows are going to be realised by collecting the financial assets' contractual cash flows, it is necessary to consider the frequency, value and timing of sales in prior periods, whether the sales were of assets close to their maturity, the reasons for those sales, and expectations about future sales activity. However, the standard states that sales, in themselves, do not determine the business model and therefore cannot be considered in isolation. It goes on to say that, instead, information about past sales and expectations about future sales provide evidence related to how the entity's stated objective for managing the financial assets is achieved and, specifically, how cash flows are realised. An entity must consider information about past sales within the context of the reasons for those sales and the conditions that existed at that time as compared to current conditions. *[IFRS 9.B4.1.2C]*.

The standard is slightly cryptic concerning the role of sales. When it says that 'sales in themselves do not determine the business model', the emphasis seems to be on past sales. Given the guidance in the standard, the magnitude and frequency of sales is certainly very important evidence in determining an entity's business models. However, the key point is that the standard requires the consideration of *expected* future sales while past sales are of relevance only as a source of evidence. Unlike the held-to-maturity classification under IAS 39, there is no concept of tainting, whereby assets are reclassified if sales activity differs from what was originally expected.

Although the objective of an entity's business model may be to hold financial assets in order to collect contractual cash flows, the entity need not hold all of those instruments until maturity. Thus an entity's business model can be to hold financial assets to collect contractual cash flows even when some sales of financial assets occur or are expected to occur in the future. *[IFRS 9.B4.1.3]*.

The following scenarios might be consistent with a hold to collect business model:

- The business model may be to hold assets to collect contractual cash flows even if the entity sells financial assets when there is an increase in the assets' credit risk. To determine whether there has been an increase in the assets' credit risk, the entity considers reasonable and supportable information, including forward looking information. Irrespective of their frequency and value, sales due to an increase in the assets' credit risk are not inconsistent with a business model whose objective is to hold financial assets to collect contractual cash flows because the credit quality of financial assets is relevant to the entity's ability to collect contractual cash flows. Credit risk management activities that are aimed at mitigating potential credit losses due to credit deterioration are integral to such a business model. Selling a financial asset because it no longer meets the credit criteria specified in the entity's documented investment policy is an example of a sale that has occurred due to an increase in credit risk. However, in the absence of such a policy, the entity may be able to demonstrate in other ways that the sale occurred due to an increase in credit risk. *[IFRS 9.B4.1.3A]*.
- Sales that occur for other reasons, such as sales made to manage credit concentration risk (without an increase in the assets' credit risk), may also be consistent with a business model whose objective is to hold financial assets in order to collect contractual cash flows. However, such sales are likely to be consistent with a business model whose objective is to hold financial assets in order to collect contractual cash flows only if those sales are infrequent (even if significant in value) or insignificant in value both individually and in aggregate (even if frequent). *[IFRS 9.B4.1.3B]*.
- In addition, sales may be consistent with the objective of holding financial assets in order to collect contractual cash flows if the sales are made close to the maturity of the financial assets and the proceeds from the sales approximate the collection of the remaining contractual cash flows. *[IFRS 9.B4.1.3B]*. How an entity defines 'close' and 'approximate' will be a matter of judgment.

If more than an infrequent number of sales are made out of a portfolio and those sales are more than insignificant in value (either individually or in aggregate), the entity needs to assess whether and how such sales are consistent with an objective of collecting contractual cash flows. An increase in the frequency or value of sales in a particular period is not necessarily inconsistent with an objective to hold financial assets in order to collect contractual cash flows, if an entity can explain the reasons for those sales and demonstrate why those sales do not reflect a change in the entity's business model and, hence, sales will in future be lower in frequency or value. *[IFRS 9.B4.1.3B]*. This assessment is about expectations and not about intent. For instance, the fact that it is not the entity's objective to realise fair value gains or losses is not sufficient in itself to be able to conclude that measurement at amortised cost is appropriate.

Furthermore, whether a third party (such as a banking regulator in the case of some liquidity portfolios held by banks) imposes the requirement to sell the financial assets, or that activity is at the entity's discretion, is not relevant to the business model assessment. *[IFRS 9.B4.1.3B]*.

In contrast, if an entity manages a portfolio of financial assets with the objective of realising cash flows through the sale of the assets, the assets would not be held under a hold to collect business model. For example, an entity might actively manage a portfolio of assets in order to realise fair value changes arising from changes in credit spreads and yield curves. In this case, the entity's business model is not to hold those assets to collect the contractual cash flows. Rather, the entity's objective results in active buying and selling with the entity managing the instruments to realise fair value gains.

IFRS 9 does not explain how 'infrequent' and 'insignificant in value' should be interpreted in practice. Overall, those thresholds could lead to diversity in application, although it is an area where we expect that consensus and best practices will emerge over time.

The overarching principle is whether the entity's key management personnel have made a decision that, collecting contractual cash flows but not selling financial assets is integral to achieving the objective of the business model. *[IFRS 9.B4.1.2C, B4.1.4A]*. Under that objective, an entity will not normally expect that sales will be more than infrequent and more than insignificant in value.

Many organisations hold portfolios of financial assets for liquidity purposes. Assets in those portfolios are regularly sold because sales are required by a regulator to demonstrate liquidity, because the entity needs to cover everyday liquidity needs or because the entity tries to maximise the yield of the portfolio. It follows that such portfolios (except those that may be sold only in stress case scenarios) would probably not be measured at amortised cost (see also 5.5 below).

With reference to measuring 'insignificant in value', the standard refers to more than an infrequent number of such sales being made out of a portfolio. *[IFRS 9.B4.1.3B]*. The reference point to measuring 'insignificant in value' could therefore be considered to be the portfolio, particularly as it is the portfolio that is subject to the business model assessment. Also, the standard is not explicit as to whether any test of insignificance should be performed period by period, or by taking into account sales over the entire life of the portfolio. However, if a period by period approach were to be used, the determination of whether sales are insignificant in value would depend on the length of the period, which means that two entities with identical portfolios but with different lengths of the reporting period would arrive at different assessments. Further, if a bank holds a portfolio of bonds with an average maturity of 20 years, sales of, say, 5% each year would mean that a considerable portion of the portfolio will have been sold before it matures, which would not seem to be consistent with a business model of holding to collect. Therefore applying the average life of the portfolio would seem to be more relevant than applying the reporting period.

Another approach would be to assess whether the value is insignificant in the light of whether the business model is suitable for applying an internal rate of return accounting approach, that is, whether amortised cost information is a relevant representation of the cash flows from the portfolio.

It will be important to observe what practices emerge as the standard is implemented.

5.2.2 *Transferred financial assets that are not derecognised*

There are a number of circumstances where an entity may sell a financial asset but those assets will remain on the selling entity's statement of financial position. For example, a bank may enter into a 'repo' transaction whereby it sells a debt security and at the same time agrees to repurchase it at a fixed price. Similarly, a manufacturer may sell trade receivables as part of a factoring programme and provide a guarantee to the buyer to compensate it for any defaults by the debtors. In each case, the seller retains substantially all risks and rewards of the assets and the financial assets would not be derecognised in line with the requirements of IFRS 9.

The inevitable question that arises in these circumstances is whether these transactions should be regarded as sales when applying the business model assessment. In this context, IFRS 9 contains in example 3 of paragraph B4.1.4 only one passing reference to derecognition, but it does suggest that it is the accounting treatment and not the legal form of a transaction that determines whether the entity has ceased to hold an asset to collect contractual cash flows. Application of such an approach would give an intuitively correct answer for repo transactions, in which the seller is required to repurchase the asset at an agreed future date and price, and which are, in substance, secured financing transactions rather than sales. However, as the IASB did not provide the basis for the treatment in the example quoted above, it is not clear if accounting derecognition should always be the basis for the assessment. For instance, if a loan is sold under an agreement by which the seller will indemnify the purchaser for any credit losses (for instance if it is factored with recourse) and so the asset is not derecognised, it is not clear whether there has been a sale for the purposes of the IFRS 9 business model assessment, given that the transferor will never retake possession of the asset. We therefore believe that, except for repos, an entity has an accounting policy choice of whether it considers the legal form of the sale or the economic substance of the transaction when analysing sales within a portfolio.

5.3 Hold to collect contractual cash flows and selling financial assets

The fair value through other comprehensive income measurement category is a mandatory category for portfolios of financial assets that are held within a business model whose objective is achieved by both collecting contractual cash flows and selling financial assets (provided the asset also meets the contractual cash flow test). *[IFRS 9.4.1.2A]*.

In this type of business model, the entity's key management personnel have made a decision that both collecting contractual cash flows and selling are fundamental to achieving the objective of the business model. There are various objectives that may be consistent with this type of business model. For example, the objective of the business model may be to manage everyday liquidity needs, to maintain a particular interest yield profile or to match the duration of the financial assets to the duration of the liabilities that those assets are funding. To achieve these objectives, the entity will both collect contractual cash flows and sell the financial assets. *[IFRS 9.B4.1.4A]*.

Compared to the business model with an objective to hold financial assets to collect contractual cash flows, this business model will typically involve greater frequency and value of sales. This is because selling financial assets is integral to achieving the business model's objective rather than only incidental to it. There is no threshold for the frequency or value of sales that can or must occur in this business model. *[IFRS 9.B4.1.4B]*.

As set out in the standard, the fair value through other comprehensive income is a defined category and is neither a residual nor an election. However, in practice, entities may identify those debt instruments which are held to collect contractual cash flows (see 5.2 above), those which are held for trading, those managed on a fair value basis (see 5.4 below) and those for which the entity applies the fair value option to avoid a measurement mismatch, (see 7.1 below), and then measure the remaining debt instruments at fair value through other comprehensive income. As a consequence, the fair value through other comprehensive income category might, in effect, be used as a residual, just because it is far easier to articulate business models that would be classified at amortised cost or at fair value through profit or loss.

5.4 Other business models

IFRS 9 requires financial assets to be measured at fair value through profit or loss if they are not held within either a business model whose objective is to hold assets to collect contractual cash flows or within a business model whose objective is achieved by both collecting contractual cash flows and selling financial assets. A business model that results in measurement at fair value through profit or loss is where the financial assets are held for trading (see section 4 above). Another is where the financial assets are managed on a fair value basis (see Example 47.14 below).

When the standard explains what it means by a portfolio of financial assets that is managed and whose performance is evaluated on a fair value basis it refers to the requirements for designating financial liabilities as measured at fair value through profit or loss. *[IFRS 9.B4.1.6]*. In order to be considered to be managed on a fair value basis, the portfolio needs to be managed in accordance with a documented risk management or investment strategy and for information, prepared on a fair value basis, about the group of instruments to be provided internally to the entity's key management personnel (this is as defined in IAS 24 see Chapter 37 at 2.2.1.D), for example the entity's board of directors and chief executive officer. *[IFRS 9.4.2.2(b)]*. Further, it is explained that if an entity manages and evaluates the performance of a group of financial assets, measuring that group at fair value through profit or loss results in more relevant information. *[IFRS 9B4.1.33]*. Documentation of the entity's strategy need not be extensive but should be sufficient to demonstrate that the classification at fair value through profit or loss is consistent with the entity's risk management or investment strategy. *[IFRS 9B4.1.36]*.

In each case, the entity manages the financial assets with the objective of realising cash flows through the sale of the assets. The entity makes decisions based on the assets' fair values and manages the assets to realise those fair values. As a consequence, the entity's objective will typically result in active buying and selling. Even though the entity will collect contractual cash flows while it holds financial assets in the fair value through profit or loss category, this is only incidental and not integral to achieving the business model's objective. *[IFRS 9.B4.1.5, B4.1.6]*.

5.5 Applying the business model test in practice

The application of the business model test is illustrated through a number of examples.

Example 47.1: The level at which the business model assessment should be applied

A global banking group operates two business lines, retail banking and investment banking. These businesses both operate in the same five locations by means of separate subsidiaries. Each subsidiary has its own Board of Directors that is responsible for carrying out the strategic objectives as set by the group's Board of Directors.

The financial assets held by the investment banking business are measured at fair value through profit or loss in line with the group's strategy, which defines the business model, to actively trade these financial assets. Within the retail banking business, four of the five subsidiaries hold debt securities in line with the group's objective to collect contractual cash flows. However, the fifth subsidiary holds a portfolio of debt securities that it expects to sell before maturity. These assets are not held for trading, but individual assets are sold if the portfolio manager believes he or she can reinvest the funds in assets with a higher yield. As a result, a more than infrequent number of sales that are significant in value are anticipated for this portfolio and it is unlikely that this portfolio would meet the amortised cost criteria if it were assessed on its own.

The bank will need to exercise judgement to determine the appropriate level at which to assess its business model(s). Hence, different conclusions are possible depending on the facts and circumstances.

This does not mean that the bank has an accounting policy choice, but it is, rather, a matter of fact that can be observed by the way the organisation is structured and managed. In many organisations, key management personnel may determine the overall strategy and then delegate their authority for executing the strategy to others. The combination of the overall strategy and the effect of the delegated authority are among the factors that can be considered in the determination of business models.

In the specified fact pattern, the determining factor is whether the fifth subsidiary is managed independently from the other four subsidiaries (and performance is assessed and management is compensated accordingly). If it is separately managed, the number of business models is three (i.e. investment banking, one business model for the first four subsidiaries and a third business model for the fifth subsidiary). If not, the number of business models is two (i.e. one for retail banking and one for investment banking). In the case of two business models, all of the debt securities held by the retail banking business would be accounted for at fair value through other comprehensive income, unless the sales activity of the fifth subsidiary is not significant to the bank.

Example 47.2: Splitting portfolios

Entity A has debt instruments worth CU100, comprising notes with maturities of three to five years. Until the adoption of IFRS 9, all of these debt instruments were classified as available-for-sale under IAS 39. CU10 of the portfolio is sold and reinvested at least once a year, while the remaining CU90 investments are typically held to near their maturity. First, the entity needs to use judgement to determine whether it has:

(a) Two business models: (i) CU90 debt instruments held to near their maturity; and (ii) CU10 debt instruments which are actively bought and sold, provided those assets can be separately identified, or

(b) One business model applied to the overall portfolio of CU100 debt investments

If scenario (a) above is considered more appropriate, the entity could achieve amortised cost classification for a majority of the debt instruments and would probably need to account for the remaining debt instruments at fair value through profit or loss or fair value through other comprehensive income. This is more likely to be the case where there is clearly a different management objective for the two groups of assets and their performance is measured, and management is compensated, accordingly.

Alternatively, if scenario (b) is considered more appropriate, the entity needs to determine whether the level of expected sales and repurchases is more than infrequent and is significant in value, requiring the whole portfolio to be measured at fair value through profit or loss or fair value through other comprehensive income (see 5.2.1 above). Whether the assets are required to be measured at fair value through profit or loss instead of fair value through other comprehensive income depends on whether the portfolio is managed on a fair value basis and fair value information is primarily used to assess asset's performance and to make decisions.

Example 47.3: Credit risk management activities

An entity holds investments to collect their contractual cash flows. The funding needs of the entity are predictable and the maturity of its financial assets is matched to its estimated funding needs.

The entity performs credit risk management activities with the objective of maintaining the credit risk of the portfolio within defined risk limits. In the past, sales have typically occurred when the financial assets' credit risk has increased such that the assets no longer meet the entity's documented investment policy.

Reports to key management personnel focus on the credit quality of the financial assets and the contractual return. The entity also monitors fair values of the financial assets, among other information.

Irrespective of their frequency and value, sales due to an increase in the assets' credit risk are not inconsistent with a business model whose objective is to hold financial assets to collect contractual cash flows, because the credit quality of financial assets is relevant to the entity's ability to collect contractual cash flows.

Credit risk management activities that are aimed at avoiding potential credit losses due to credit deterioration are integral to such a business model. Selling a financial asset because it no longer meets the credit criteria specified in the entity's documented investment policy is an example of a sale that has occurred due to an increase in credit risk. However, this conclusion cannot be extended to sales to avoid excessive credit concentration (see also Example 47.4 below).

Although the entity considers, among other information, the financial assets' fair values from a liquidity perspective (i.e. the cash amount that would be realised if the entity needs to sell assets), the entity's objective is to hold the financial assets in order to collect the contractual cash flows.

Therefore, under the fact pattern specified, the entity will still be able to measure the portfolio at amortised cost.

In the absence of a documented investment or similar policy, the entity may be able to demonstrate in other ways that a sale only occurred due to an increase in credit risk. *[IFRS 9.B4.1.4 Example 1]*.

Example 47.4: Sales to manage concentration risk

An entity sells financial assets to manage the concentration of the entity's credit risk to a particular obligor, country or industrial sector, without an increase in the assets' credit risk.

Such sales may be consistent with a business model whose objective is to hold financial assets in order to collect contractual cash flows, but only to the extent that they are infrequent (even if significant in value) or insignificant in value both individually and in aggregate (even if frequent). That means such sales are treated no differently than sales for any other reason. Thus, such sales are more likely to be consistent with a business model whose objective is to hold financial assets in order to collect contractual cash flows and to sell financial assets. *[IFRS 9.B4.1.3B].*

Example 47.5: Credit-impaired financial assets in a hold to collect business model

An entity's business model is to purchase portfolios of financial assets, such as loans. Those portfolios may or may not include financial assets that are credit-impaired, that is, there have already been one or more events that have had a detrimental impact on future cash flows. If payment on the loans is not made on a timely basis, the entity attempts to realise the contractual cash flows through various means – for example, by making contact with the debtor by mail, telephone or other methods. The entity's objective is to collect contractual cash flows and the entity does not manage any of the loans in this portfolio with an objective of realising cash flows by selling them.

The objective of the entity's business model is to hold the financial assets in order to collect the contractual cash flows. *IFRS 9.B4.1.4 Example 2].*

Example 47.6: Hedging activities in a hold to collect business model

A bank holds a portfolio of variable rate loans and enters into interest rate swaps to change the interest rate on particular loans in the portfolio from a floating interest rate to a fixed interest rate.

The fact that the entity has entered into derivatives to modify the cash flows of the portfolio does not in itself change the entity's business model. *[IFRS 9.B4.1.4 Example 2].*

Example 47.7: Securitisation

An entity has a business model with the objective of originating loans to customers and subsequently to sell those loans to a securitisation vehicle. The securitisation vehicle issues instruments to investors. The originating entity controls the securitisation vehicle and thus consolidates it. The securitisation vehicle collects the contractual cash flows from the loans and passes them on to its investors.

It is assumed for the purposes of this example that the loans continue to be recognised in the consolidated statement of financial position because they are recognised by the securitisation vehicle.

The consolidated group originated the loans with the objective of holding them to collect the contractual cash flows and, therefore, measures them at amortised cost. The same conclusion may be drawn if the securitisation vehicle is not consolidated but the originating entity is unable to derecognise the assets (see 5.2.2 above).

However, the originating entity has an objective of realising cash flows on the loan portfolio by selling the loans to the securitisation vehicle, so for the purposes of its separate financial statements it would not be considered to be managing this portfolio in order to collect the contractual cash flows, but to sell them. The loans would probably need to be recorded at fair value through profit or loss as long as they continue to be recognised. *[IFRS 9.B4.1.4 Example 3].*

Example 47.8: Liquidity portfolio for stress case scenarios

A financial institution holds financial assets to meet liquidity needs in a 'stress case' scenario (e.g. a run on the bank's deposits). The entity does not anticipate selling these assets except in such a scenario. The entity monitors the credit quality of the financial assets and its objective in managing the financial assets is to collect the contractual cash flows. The entity evaluates the performance of the assets on the basis of interest revenue earned and credit losses realised.

However, the entity also monitors the fair value of the financial assets from a liquidity perspective to ensure that the cash amount that would be realised if the entity needed to sell the assets in a stress case scenario would be sufficient to meet the entity's liquidity needs. Periodically, the entity makes sales that are insignificant in value to demonstrate liquidity.

The objective of the entity's business model is to hold the financial assets to collect contractual cash flows.

The analysis would not change even if during a previous stress case scenario the entity made sales that were significant in value in order to meet its liquidity needs. Similarly, recurring sales activity that is insignificant in value is not inconsistent with holding financial assets to collect contractual cash flows.

However, the assessment would change if the entity periodically sells debt instruments that are significant in value to demonstrate liquidity, or if the entity sells the debt instruments to cover everyday liquidity needs. See Examples 47.9 and 47.10 below. *[IFRS 9.B4.1.4 Example 4]*.

Example 47.9: Anticipated capital expenditure

A non-financial entity anticipates capital expenditure in a few years. The entity invests its excess cash in short-term and long-term financial assets so that it can fund the expenditure when the need arises. Many of the financial assets have contractual lives that exceed the entity's anticipated investment period. Therefore the entity will need to sell some of the assets before maturity to meet those funding needs.

The objective of the business model is achieved by both collecting contractual cash flows and selling financial assets.

In contrast, consider an entity that anticipates a cash outflow in five years to fund capital expenditures and invests excess cash in short-term financial assets. When the investments mature, the entity reinvests the cash into new short-term financial assets. The entity maintains this strategy until the funds are needed, at which time the entity uses the proceeds from the maturing financial assets to fund the capital expenditures. Only insignificant sales occur before maturity (unless there is an increase in credit risk). The objective of such a business model is to hold financial assets in order to collect contractual cash flows. *[IFRS 9.B4.1.4C Example 5]*.

Example 47.10: Liquidity portfolio for every day liquidity needs

A financial institution holds financial assets to meet its everyday liquidity needs. In the past, this has resulted in frequent sales activity and such sales have been significant in value. This activity is expected to continue in the future as everyday liquidity needs can rarely be forecast with any accuracy.

The objective of the business model is meeting everyday liquidity needs. The entity achieves those objectives by both collecting contractual cash flows and selling financial assets. This means that both collecting contractual cash flows and selling financial assets are integral to achieving the business model's objective and the financial assets are measured at fair value through other comprehensive income. The frequent and significant sales activity does not mean that the portfolio is held for trading because under the business model objective above, assets are not sold with the intention of short-term profit taking. *[IFRS 9.B4.1.4 Example 4]*.

Example 47.11: Opportunistic portfolio management

A financial institution holds a portfolio of financial assets. The entity actively manages the return on the portfolio on an opportunistic basis trying to increase the return, without a clear intention of holding the financial assets to collect contractual cash flows (although it might end up holding the assets if no other investment opportunities arise). That return consists of collecting contractual payments as well as gains and losses from the sale of financial assets.

As a result, the entity holds financial assets to collect contractual cash flows and sells financial assets to reinvest in higher yielding financial assets. In the past, this strategy has resulted in frequent sales activity and such sales have been significant in value. It is expected that the sales activity will continue in the future.

The entity achieves the objective stated above by both collecting contractual cash flows and selling financial assets. Both collecting contractual cash flows and selling financial assets are integral to achieving the business model's objective and, thus, the financial assets are measured at fair value through other comprehensive income. *[IFRS 9.B4.1.4C Example 6]*.

In some cases, entities may manage a portfolio to manage its yield. In such cases, the portfolio manager may be remunerated based on the overall yield of the portfolio and fair value gains or losses may not be considered in his or her remuneration. Furthermore, management's documented strategy and defined key performance indicators may emphasise optimising long-term yield rather than fair value gains or losses and accordingly, the entity's management reporting focuses on yield rather than fair value of the debt instruments within the portfolio. However, in our view, the fact that it is not the entity's objective to realise fair value gains or losses is not sufficient in itself to be able to conclude that measurement at amortised cost is appropriate as the business model objective is not only holding financial assets to collect contractual cash flows but also results in sales which are more than infrequent and significant in value. Thus, such a portfolio would be measured at fair value through other comprehensive income.

Example 47.12: Replication portfolios

Fact pattern 1: Insurance company

An insurer holds financial assets in order to fund insurance contract liabilities. The insurer uses the proceeds from the contractual cash flows on the financial assets to settle insurance contract liabilities as they come due. To ensure that the contractual cash flows from the financial assets are sufficient to settle those liabilities, the insurer undertakes significant buying and selling activity on a regular basis to rebalance its portfolio of assets and to meet cash flow needs as they arise.

The objective of the business model is to fund the insurance contract liabilities. To achieve this objective, the entity collects contractual cash flows as they come due and sells financial assets to maintain the desired profile of the asset portfolio. Thus, both collecting contractual cash flows and selling financial assets are integral to achieving the business model's objective and it follows that the financial assets are measured at fair value through other comprehensive income. *[IFRS 9.B4.1.4C Example 7]*.

Fact pattern 2: Bank

A bank allocates investments into maturity bands to match the expected duration of customers' time deposits. The invested assets have a similar maturity profile and amount to the corresponding deposits. The target ratio of assets to deposits for each maturity band has pre-determined minimum and maximum levels. For example, if the ratio exceeds the maximum level because of an unexpected withdrawal of deposits, the bank will sell some assets to reduce the ratio. The choice of assets to be sold would be based on those that would generate the highest profit or incur the lowest loss.

Meanwhile, new assets will be acquired when necessary (i.e. when the ratio of assets to deposits falls below the pre-determined minimum level). The expected repayment profile of the deposits would be updated on a quarterly basis, based on changes in customer behaviour. Under IAS 39, these assets were classified as available-for-sale and there has been no history of active trading.

The question is whether adjusting the assets/deposits ratio by selling assets to correspond with a change in the expected repayment profile of the deposits would mean that the business model is inconsistent with the objective of holding to collect the contractual cash flows. In these circumstances, an analogy can be drawn to the insurance company above.

If the bank has a good track record of forecasting its deposit repayments, so that sales are expected to be infrequent, it is possible that the objective of the business model is to hold the investments to collect contractual cash flows. But, if significant sales take place each year, it is likely to be difficult to rationalise such practice with this objective. Due consideration will also need to be given to the magnitude of sales and the reasons for the sales.

Example 47.13: Loans that are to be sub-participated

An entity originates loans so that it holds part of the portfolio to maturity, but 'sub-participates' a portion of the loans to other banks, so that it transfers substantially all the risks and rewards and so achieves derecognition. The question arises whether, for the purposes of application of IFRS 9, the entity has one business model or two.

The entity could consider the activities of lending to hold and lending to sell or sub-participate as two separate business models, requiring different skills and processes. Whilst the financial assets resulting from the former would typically qualify for amortised cost measurement, those from the latter would probably not and would, therefore, most likely need to be measured at fair value through profit or loss. This split approach is likely to be acceptable as long as the entity is able to forecast with reasonable confidence that it will indeed hold the assets (or the proportion of a group of identical assets) that it determines to be measured at amortised cost.

If a loan is assessed, in part, to be sold or sub-participated, this raises the additional issue of whether a single financial asset can be classified into two separate business models. As it is already common under IAS 39 for loans to be classified in part as held for trading and in part at amortised cost, it is likely that this practice will continue under IFRS 9.

In some cases, an entity may fail to achieve the intended disposal, having previously classified a portion of a loan at fair value through profit or loss because of the intention to sell.

The standard requires classification to be determined in accordance with the business model applicable at the point of initial recognition of the asset. In this example, the fact that the entity fails to achieve an intended disposal does not trigger a reclassification in accordance with the standard as the threshold for reclassification is a very high hurdle. Therefore, loans or portions of loans that the entity fails to dispose of would continue to be recorded at fair value through profit or loss.

Example 47.14: Portfolio managed on a fair value basis

An entity manages a portfolio and measures its performance on a fair value basis and makes decisions based on the fair value of the financial assets. Such an objective typically results in frequent sales and purchases of financial assets.

A portfolio of financial assets that is managed and whose performance is evaluated on a fair value basis is neither held to collect contractual cash flows nor held both to collect contractual cash flows and to sell financial assets. In addition, a portfolio of financial assets that meets the definition of held for trading is not held to collect contractual cash flows or held both to collect contractual cash flows and to sell financial assets. The entity is primarily focused on fair value information and uses that information to assess the assets' performance and to make decisions.

Even though the entity will collect contractual cash flows while it holds financial assets in the fair value through profit or loss category, this is only incidental and not integral to achieving the business model's objective. Consequently, such portfolios of financial assets must be measured at fair value through profit or loss.

6 CHARACTERISTICS OF THE CONTRACTUAL CASH FLOWS OF THE INSTRUMENT

The assessment of the characteristics of a financial asset's contractual cash flows aims to identify whether they are 'solely payments of principal and interest on the principal amount outstanding'. Hence, the assessment is colloquially referred to as the 'SPPI test'.

The contractual cash flow characteristics test is designed to screen out financial assets on which the application of the effective interest method either is not viable from a pure mechanical standpoint or does not provide useful information about the uncertainty, timing and amount of the financial asset's contractual cash flows.

Because the effective interest method is essentially an allocation mechanism that spreads interest revenue or expense over time, amortised cost is only appropriate for simple cash flows that have low variability such as those of traditional unleveraged loans and receivables, and 'plain vanilla' debt instruments. Accordingly, the contractual cash flow characteristics test is based on the premise that it is only when the variability in the contractual cash flows arises to maintain the holder's return in line with a 'basic lending arrangement' that the application of effective interest method provides useful information. *[IFRS 9.BC4.23,158, 171, 172]*.

In this context, the term 'basic lending arrangement' is used broadly to capture both originated and acquired financial assets, the lender or the holder of which is looking to earn a return that compensates primarily for the time value of money and credit risk.

However, such an arrangement can also include other elements that provide consideration for other basic lending risks such as liquidity risks, costs associated with holding the financial asset for a period of time (e.g. servicing or administrative costs) and a profit margin. *[IFRS 9.B4.1.7A, BC4.182(b)]*.

In contrast, contractual terms that introduce a more than *de minimis* exposure (see section 6.4.1 below) to risks or volatility in the contractual cash flows that is unrelated to a basic lending arrangement, such as exposure to changes in equity prices or commodity prices, do not give rise to contractual cash flows that are solely payments of principal and interest on the principal amount outstanding. *[IFRS 9.B4.1.7A, B4.1.18]*.

The IASB noted that it believes that amortised cost would provide relevant and useful information as long as the contractual cash flows do not introduce risks or volatility that are inconsistent with a basic lending arrangement. *[IFRS 9.BC4.180]*.

The following sections cover the main aspects of the contractual cash flow characteristics test, starting with the meaning of the terms 'principal' and 'interest' in sections 6.1 and 6.2, and discusses instruments that normally pass the test at 6.3. So called 'modified' contractual cash flows and their effect on the contractual cash flow characteristics test are dealt with in section 6.4. Contractually linked instruments are separately covered in section 6.5.

6.1 The meaning of 'principal'

'Principal' is not a defined term in IFRS 9. However, the standard states that, for the purposes of applying the contractual cash flow characteristics test, the principal is 'the fair value of the asset at initial recognition' and that it may change over the life of the financial asset (for example, if there are repayments of principal). *[IFRS 9.4.1.3(a), B4.1.7B]*.

The IASB believes that this usage reflects the economics of the financial asset from the perspective of the current holder; in other words, the entity would assess the contractual cash flow characteristics by comparing the contractual cash flows to the amount that it actually invested. *[IFRS 9.BC4.182(a)]*.

For example: Entity A issued a bond with a contractually stated principal of CU1,000. The bond was originally issued at CU990. Because interest rates have risen sharply since the bond was originally issued, Entity B, the current holder of the bond, acquired the bond in the secondary market for CU975. From the perspective of entity B, the principal amount is CU975.

The principal is, therefore, not necessarily the contractual par amount, nor (when the holder has acquired the asset subsequent to its origination) is it necessarily the amount that was advanced to the debtor when the instrument was originally issued.

The description of 'principal' as the fair value of an instrument on initial recognition avoids a concern that any financial asset acquired or issued at a substantial discount would be leveraged and hence would not have economic characteristics of interest.

A clear understanding of what the standard means by 'principal' is also necessary for the appropriate and consistent application of the contractual cash flow characteristics test to prepayable financial assets (see section 6.4.4 below).

6.2 The meaning of 'interest'

IFRS 9 states that the most significant elements of interest within a basic lending arrangement are typically the consideration for the time value of money and credit risk. In addition, interest may also include consideration for other basic lending risks (for example, liquidity risk) and costs (for example, administrative costs) associated with holding the financial asset for a particular period of time. Furthermore, interest may include a profit margin that is consistent with a basic lending arrangement.

In extreme economic circumstances, interest can be negative if, for example, the holder of a financial asset effectively pays a fee for the safekeeping of its money for a particular period of time and that fee exceeds the consideration the holder receives for the time value of money, credit risk and other basic lending risks and costs.

Contractual terms that introduce exposure to risks or volatility in the contractual cash flows that is unrelated to a basic lending arrangement, such as exposure to changes in equity prices or commodity prices, do not give rise to contractual cash flows that are solely payments of principal and interest on the principal amount outstanding. An originated or a purchased financial asset can be a basic lending arrangement irrespective of whether it is a loan in its legal form. *[IFRS 9.4.1.3(b), B4.1.7A]*.

The IASB notes that the assessment of interest focuses on what the entity is being compensated for (i.e. whether the entity is receiving consideration for basic lending risks, costs and a profit margin or is being compensated for something else), instead of how much the entity receives for a particular element. For example, the Board acknowledges that different entities may price the credit risk element differently. *[IFRS 9.BC4.182(b)]*. Although two entities may receive different amounts for the same element of interest, e.g. credit risk, they could both conclude that their consideration for credit risk is appropriate within a basic lending arrangement.

Time value of money is the element of interest that provides consideration for only the passage of time. That is, the time value of money element does not provide consideration for other risks or costs associated with holding the financial asset. To make this assessment, an entity applies judgement and considers relevant factors such as the currency in which the financial asset is denominated, and the period for which the interest rate is set. *[IFRS 9.B4.1.9A]*.

The IASB also notes that, as a general proposition, the market in which the transaction occurs is relevant to the assessment of the time value of money element. For example, in Europe, it is common to reference interest rates to LIBOR and in the United States it is common to reference interest rates to the prime rate. However, a particular interest rate does not necessarily reflect consideration for only the time value of money merely because that rate is considered 'normal' in a particular market. For example, if an interest rate is reset every year but the reference rate is always a 15-year rate, it would be difficult for an entity to conclude that such a rate provides consideration for only the passage of time, even if such pricing is commonly used in that particular market. Accordingly the IASB believes that an entity must apply judgement to conclude whether the stated time value of money element meets the objective of providing consideration for only the passage of time. *[IFRS 9.BC4.178]*.

It could be argued that the standard is not entirely clear as to the status of benchmark rates such as LIBOR. For such rates, the consideration for credit risk is neither fixed, nor varies over time to reflect the specific credit risk of the obligor, but instead varies to reflect the credit risks associated with a class of borrowers. However, this seems to be a purist approach and given that LIBOR is widely used as a benchmark rate in capital markets and is cited in the standard as an example of a rate that would satisfy the criteria of the contractual cash flow characteristics test, it would seem that this is not an issue.

Interest may include profit margin that is consistent with a basic lending arrangement. But elements that introduce exposure to risks or variability in the contractual cash flows that are unrelated to lending (such as exposure to equity or commodity price risk) are not consistent with a basic lending arrangement. The IASB also noted that the assessment of interest focusses on what the entity is being compensated for e.g. basic lending risk or something else, rather than how much the entity receives *[IFRS 9.BC4.182(b)]*.

6.3 Contractual features that normally pass the test

The most common instruments that normally pass the test are plain vanilla debt instruments which are acquired at par, have a fixed maturity and pay interest that is fixed at inception. Instruments that pay variable interest also normally pass the test, although further consideration is required in that case (see 6.4.4 below).

There are several features that are common in many financial assets and which would not usually cause the contractual cash flow characteristics test to be failed. This section describes some of those features and instruments that are normally unproblematic but also highlights cases that might result in an asset failing the contractual cash flow characteristics test. Section 6.4 below describes features that are more complex and need more consideration.

6.3.1 Conventional subordination features

In many lending transaction the instrument is ranked relative to amounts owed by the borrower to its other creditors. An instrument that is subordinated to other instruments may be considered to have contractual cash flows that are payments of principal and interest on the principal amount outstanding if the debtor's non-payment arises only on a breach of contract and the holder has a contractual right to unpaid amounts of principal and interest on the principal amount outstanding even in the event of the debtor's bankruptcy.

For example, a trade receivable that ranks its creditor as a general creditor would qualify as having payments of principal and interest on the principal amount outstanding. This is the case even if the debtor has issued loans that are collateralised, which in the event of bankruptcy would give that loan holder priority over the claims of the general creditor in respect of the collateral but does not affect the contractual right of the general creditor to unpaid principal and other amounts due. *[IFRS 9.B4.1.19]*.

On the other hand, if the subordination feature limits the contractual cash flows in any other way or introduces any kind of leverage, the instrument would fail the contractual cash flow characteristics test.

6.3.2 *Full recourse loans secured by collateral*

The fact that a full recourse loan is collateralised does not in itself affect the analysis of whether the contractual cash flows are solely payments of principal and interest on the principal amount outstanding. *[IFRS 9.B4.1.13 Instrument D]*. However, a full recourse loan may, in substance, be non-recourse if the borrower has limited other assets, in which case an entity would need to assess the particular underlying assets (i.e. the collateral) to determine whether or not the contractual cash flows of the loan are payments of principal and interest on the principal amount outstanding. *[IFRS 9.B4.1.17]*. The contractual cash flows may be limited to the value of the collateral which is most likely inconsistent with payments representing principal and interest in which case the loan fails the contractual cash flow characteristics test (see also Example 47.22 below).

6.3.3 *Bonds with a capped or floored interest rate*

Some bonds may have a stated maturity date but pay a variable market interest rate that is subject to a cap or a floor. The contractual cash flows of such instrument could be seen as being an instrument that has a fixed interest rate and an instrument that has a variable interest rate.

These both represent payments of principal and interest on the principal amount outstanding as long as the interest reflects consideration for the time value of money, for the credit risk associated with the instrument during the term of the instrument and for other basic lending risks and costs, as well as a profit margin.

Therefore, such an instrument can have cash flows that are solely payments of principal and interest on the principal amount outstanding. A feature such as an interest rate cap or floor may reduce cash flow variability by setting a limit on a variable interest rate or increase the cash flow variability because a fixed rate becomes variable. *[IFRS 9.B4.1.13 Instrument C]*. If there is no leverage and no mismatch of term with respect to interest then the instrument should pass the contractual cash flows characteristics test.

There is no requirement to determine whether or not the cap or floor is in the money on initial recognition, as is required by the test in IAS 39 to assess whether there is a separable embedded derivative.

Caps and floors will generally pass the contractual cash flows test without further analysis, apart from some instruments, namely those with features that create leverage. These 'exotic' instruments would require detailed assessment and judgement. An instrument with a floor which is deeply in the money at origination is not seen as a problem for passing the contractual cash flows characteristics test.

We assume that a variable rate debt instrument that is subject to both a cap and a floor (known as a collar) would also satisfy the contractual cash flow characteristics test for the same reasons.

In many jurisdictions interest rates on loans are capped by law to a multiple of an absolute interest or index rate. Whereas a capped interest rate meets the contractual cash flow characteristic test when the interest reflects the time value of money as discussed above, in some cases the cap is referenced to a multiple of an index rate, so it can be argued that the cap introduces leverage into the instrument. However it can also be argued that the feature is not intended to introduce leverage into the market but to protect consumers, as a cap it will only reduce interest rates and does not introduce volatility such as exposure to changes in equity prices or commodity prices. IFRS 9 also permits interest rates that are regulated to meet the contractual cash flow characteristic test if the interest rate represents consideration that is broadly consistent with the passage of time. *[IFRS 9.B4.1.9E]*. If the cap is introduced by the regulator to protect consumers by providing an estimate of the fair market interest rate it could be considered to represent consideration for the passage of time (see 6.4.3 below).

6.3.4 Lender has discretion to change the interest rate

In some instances, the lender may have the right to unilaterally adjust the interest rates of its loans in accordance with its own business policy. However, should the borrower disagree with the new rate, it has the right to terminate the contract and prepay the loan at par.

Such a feature does not *per se* result in the loans failing the contractual cash flow characteristic test. However, whether the loan passes the test depends on facts and circumstances which require assessment on a case-by-case basis, specifically whether interest represents considerations for the time value of money, credit risk and other basic lending risk and costs, as well as a profit margin. Aspects relevant to this assessment may include but are not limited to:

- whether this feature represents common lending practice in the jurisdiction or not; and
- whether the change in interest rate applies to all similar loans, including new loans and the ones in issue, or only to one or certain individual borrowers (this excludes changes in interest rates due to changes in the credit spread of the borrower).

Note that in practice the bank is likely to be restricted as to how much it can increase the interest rate, since if it is too high the borrower will be motivated to prepay and the bank is unlikely to remain competitive.

6.3.5 Unleveraged inflation-linked bonds

For some financial instruments, payments of principal and interest on the principal amount outstanding are linked to an inflation index of the currency in which the instrument is issued. The inflation link is not leveraged and the principal is protected. Linking payments of principal and interest on the principal amount outstanding to an unleveraged inflation index resets the time value of money to a current level. In other words, the interest rate on the instrument reflects 'real' interest. Thus, the interest amounts are consideration for the time value of money on the principal amount outstanding.

The reason that the principal has to be protected is that the holder might not get repaid the principal amount (if, for instance inflation is less than anticipated, the instrument would fail the contractual cash flow characteristics test).

However, if the interest payments were indexed to another variable such as the debtor's performance (e.g. the debtor's net income) or an equity index, the contractual cash flows are not payments of principal and interest on the principal amount outstanding (unless it can be demonstrated that the indexing to the debtor's performance results in an adjustment that only compensates the holder for changes in the credit risk of the instrument, such that contractual cash flows will represent only payments for principal and interest). That is because the contractual cash flows reflect a return that is inconsistent with a basic lending arrangement (see 6 above). *[IFRS 9.B4.1.13 Instrument A]*.

Example 47.15: Unleveraged inflation linked bond

Entity A invests in euro-denominated bonds with a fixed maturity issued by Entity B. Interest on the bond is linked directly to the inflation index of Eurozone Country C, which is Entity B's principal place of business. The question arises whether Entity A can measure the euro bonds at amortised cost or fair value through other comprehensive income given that interest is not linked to the inflation index of the entire Eurozone area.

The bond is denominated in euros and Eurozone Country C is part of the Eurozone, therefore, we consider the inflation link to be acceptable. The inflation index reflects the inflation rate of the currency in which the bond is issued since it is the inflation index of Entity B's economic environment, and the euro is the currency for that economic environment.

By linking the inflation index to the inflation rate of Eurozone Country C, Entity B is reflecting 'real' interest for the economic environment in which it operates. Hence, in these circumstances, Entity A may regard the interest as consideration for the time of value of money and credit risk associated with the principal amount outstanding on the bond.

6.4 Contractual features that may affect the classification

Sometimes, contractual provisions may affect the cash flows of an instrument such that they do not give rise to only a straightforward repayment of principal and interest. An entity is required to carefully assess those features in order to conclude whether or not the instrument passes the contractual cash flow characteristics test. It is important to note that the standard grants an exception for all features that are non-genuine or have only a *de minimis* impact, and can be disregarded when making the assessment (see 6.4.1 below).

Furthermore, the standard allows the time value of money element of interest to be what is referred to as 'modified' but only when the resulting cash flows could not be significantly different from an instrument that has an unmodified time value of money element (see 6.4.2 below). It also allows regulated interest rates as long as they provide consideration that is broadly consistent with the passage of time and do not introduce risks that are inconsistent with a basic lending arrangement (see 6.4.3 below).

An instrument may have other features that change the timing or amount of contractual cash flows which need to be assessed whether they represent payments of principal and interest on the principal outstanding. Examples of such features are variable interest rates, interest rates that step up, prepayment and extension options (see 6.4.4 below).

Lastly, there are features that most likely result in an instrument failing the contractual cash flow characteristics test because they introduce cash flow volatility caused by risks that are inconsistent with a basic lending arrangement (see 6.4.5).

6.4.1 *De minimis and non-genuine features*

A contractual cash flow characteristic does not affect the classification of the financial asset if it could have only a *de minimis* effect on the contractual cash flows of the financial asset.

In addition, if a contractual cash flow characteristic could have an effect on the contractual cash flows that is more than *de minimis* (either in a single reporting period or cumulatively) but that cash flow characteristic is not genuine, it does not affect the classification of a financial asset. A cash flow characteristic is not genuine if it affects the instrument's contractual cash flows only on the occurrence of an event that is extremely rare, highly abnormal and very unlikely to occur. *[IFRS 9.B4.1.18].*

Although the '*de minimis*' and 'non-genuine' thresholds are a high hurdle, allowing entities to disregard such features will result in more debt instruments qualifying for the amortised cost or fair value through other comprehensive income measurement categories than in previous versions of IFRS 9. The terms will need to be interpreted by preparers in analysing the impact of the clarified contractual cash flow characteristics test on the debt instruments they hold.

6.4.1.A De minimis features

The standard does not prescribe whether a qualitative or a quantitative analysis should be performed to determine whether a feature is *de minimis* or not. While *de minimis* is not defined in IFRS 9, one dictionary definition is 'too trivial to merit consideration'. Implicit in this definition is that if an entity has to consider whether an impact is *de minimis*, whether quantitatively or qualitatively, would imply that it is not.

The *de minimis* threshold concerns the magnitude of the possible effects of the contractual cash flow characteristic. To be considered *de minimis*, the impact of the feature on the cash flows of the financial asset must be expected to be *de minimis* in each reporting period and cumulatively over the life of the financial asset.

6.4.1.B Non-genuine features

Non-genuine features, as used in this context, are contingent features. A cash flow characteristic is not genuine if it affects the instrument's contractual cash flows only on the occurrence of an event that is extremely rare, highly abnormal and very unlikely to occur. This means, although the feature can potentially lead to cash flows which are not solely payments of principal and interest, and those cash flows may even be significant, the instrument would still qualify for amortised cost or fair value through other comprehensive income measurement, depending on the business model. (See also Chapter 45 at 4.3.1).

In our view, terms are included in a contract for an economic purpose and therefore are, in general, genuine. The threshold 'not genuine' is presumably intended to deal with clauses inserted into the terms of financial instruments for some legal or tax reason but having no real economic purpose or consequence.

An example of a clause that has caused some debate in the context of IAS 32.AG28 which uses the term non-genuine is a 'regulatory change' clause, generally found in the terms of capital instruments issued by financial institutions such as banks and insurance companies. Such entities are generally required by local regulators to maintain certain minimum levels of equity or highly subordinated debt (generally referred to as regulatory capital) in order to be allowed to do business.

A 'regulatory change' clause will typically require an instrument which, at the date of issue, is classified as regulatory capital to be repaid in the event that it ceases to be so classified. The practice so far of the regulators in many markets has been to make changes to a regulatory classification with prospective effect only, such that any instruments already in issue continue to be regarded as regulatory capital even though they would not be under the new rules.

This has led some to question whether a 'regulatory change' clause can be regarded as a contingent settlement provision which is 'not genuine'. This is ultimately a matter for the judgement of entities in the context of the relevant regulatory environment(s). This judgement has not been made easier by the greater unpredictability of the markets (and therefore of regulators' responses to it) in the recent financial crisis. However, as the clause was inserted to provide regulators with flexibility in their actions, even if they do not normally exercise that flexibility, it would be difficult to argue that it is 'non-genuine'.

Disregarding non-genuine features also means that the classification requirements of IFRS 9 cannot be overridden by introducing a contractual non-genuine cash flow characteristic in order to achieve a specific accounting outcome.

6.4.2 *Contractual features that modify the consideration for the time value of money*

In some cases, the time value of money element may be what the standard describes as 'modified' and so 'imperfect'. It cites, as an example, instances where the tenor of the interest rate does not correspond with the frequency with which it resets. In such cases, an entity must assess the modification to determine whether the contractual cash flows represent solely payments of principal and interest on the principal outstanding. In some circumstances, the entity may be able to make that determination by performing a qualitative assessment whereas, in other circumstances, it may be necessary to perform a quantitative analysis. *[IFRS 9.B4.1.9B]*.

The objective of a quantitative assessment is to determine whether or not the contractual (undiscounted) cash flows could be significantly different from the (undiscounted) cash flows that would arise if the time value of money element was not modified (referred to as 'the benchmark' cash flows).

For example, if the financial asset under assessment contains a variable interest rate that is reset every month to a one-year interest rate, the entity compares that financial asset to a financial instrument with identical contractual terms and credit risk, except the variable interest rate is reset monthly to a one-month interest rate. If the modified time value of money element could result in contractual (undiscounted) cash flows that are significantly different from the (undiscounted) benchmark cash flows, the financial asset fails the contractual cash flow characteristics test. To make this determination, the entity must consider the effect of the modified time value of money element in each reporting period and cumulatively over the life of the financial instrument. The reason for the interest rate being set this way is not relevant to the analysis. If it is clear, with little or no analysis, whether the contractual (undiscounted) cash flows on the financial asset under the assessment could (or could not) be significantly different from the (undiscounted) benchmark cash flows, an entity need not perform a detailed assessment. *[IFRS 9.B4.1.9C]*. 'Significantly different' is not defined in IFRS 9 and is a matter for management judgement.

The following table lists examples of modifications of the consideration for the time value of money which possibly meet the contractual cash flow characteristics test, depending on the outcome of the assessment described above.

Example 47.16: Examples of a modified time value of money component

	Modification	Fact pattern
1	Average interest rate	The stated coupon on a debt instrument is referenced to an average of benchmark interest rates for a specified period. For example, 3-month Euribor rate determined as an average of 3-month rates during the previous quarter.
2	Lagging interest rate	The stated interest rate is referenced to lagging interest rates. For example, 6-month Euribor rate set for a 6 month period, but where the rate is fixed 2 months before the start of the interest period.
3	Tenor mismatch	The stated interest rate is reset to a reference interest rate but the frequency of reset does not match the tenor of the reference rate. For example, the interest rate on a retail mortgage is reset semi-annually based on three-month Libor.
4	Combination of the above	The stated interest rate is reset monthly to an average 12-month reference rate. The interest rate is fixed based on the average rate one month before the start of the interest period.

Time value of money does not include credit risk, so it is important to exclude it from the assessment. The standard suggests this is done by comparing the instrument with a benchmark instrument with the same credit risk, but presumably the comparison could be against an instrument with a different credit risk, as long as the effect of the difference can be excluded. *[IFRS 9.B4.1.9C]*.

When assessing a modified time value of money element, an entity must consider factors that could affect future contractual cash flows. In making the assessment, it must consider every interest rate scenario that is reasonably possible instead of every scenario that could possibly arise. This requirement is illustrated in Example 47.18 below.

If an entity concludes that the contractual (undiscounted) cash flows could be significantly different from the (undiscounted) benchmark cash flows, the financial asset does not pass the contractual cash flow characteristics test and therefore cannot be measured at amortised cost or fair value through other comprehensive income. *[IFRS 9.B4.1.9D]*.

The following examples illustrate instruments with a modified time value of money element and how the benchmark test is applied to them.

Example 47.17: Interest rate period selected at the discretion of the borrower

An entity holds an instrument that is a variable interest rate instrument with a stated maturity date that permits the borrower to choose the market interest rate on an ongoing basis. For example, at each interest rate reset date, the borrower can choose to pay three-month LIBOR for a three-month term or one-month LIBOR for a one-month term.

The contractual cash flows are solely payments of principal and interest on the principal amount outstanding as long as the interest paid over the life of the instrument reflects consideration for basic lending risks and costs as well as a profit margin. Basic lending risks and costs include consideration for the time value of money, for the credit risk associated with the instrument and for other basic lending risks and costs. The fact that the LIBOR interest rate is reset during the life of the instrument does not in itself disqualify the instrument.

However, if the borrower is able to choose to pay a one-month interest rate that is reset every three months, the interest rate is reset with a frequency that does not match the tenor of the interest rate. Therefore the time value of money element is modified. That is because the interest payable in each period is disconnected from the interest period.

In such cases, the entity must qualitatively or quantitatively assess the contractual cash flows against the cash flows of a benchmark instrument to determine whether the mismatch between the two sets of cash flows could be significantly different. The benchmark instrument is identical in all respects except that the tenor of the interest rate matches the interest period. If the analysis results in the conclusion that the two sets of cash flows could be significantly different, payments would not represent principal and interest on the principal amount outstanding.

The same analysis would apply if the borrower is able to choose between the lender's various published interest rates (e.g. the borrower can choose between the lender's published one-month variable interest rate and the lender's published three-month variable interest rate). *[IFRS 9.B4.1.13 Instrument B]*.

Example 47.18: Five-year constant maturity bond

Some bonds pay what is called a constant maturity interest rate. For example, an instrument with an original five-year maturity may pay a variable rate that is reset semi-annually but always reflects a five year rate. In such cases, the time value of money element is modified. The entity must determine whether the instrument's cash flows could be significantly different from those on a bond with a similar maturity, credit risk and interest rate reset frequency, but that that pays a semi-annual rate of interest.

In making this assessment, the entity cannot conclude that the contractual cash flows are solely payments of principal and interest on the principal amount outstanding, simply because the interest rate curve at the time of the assessment is such that the difference between a five-year interest rate and a semi-annual interest rate is not significant. Rather, the entity must also consider whether the relationship between the five-year interest rate and the semi-annual interest rate could change over the life of the instrument such that the contractual (undiscounted) cash flows over the life of the instrument could be significantly different from the (undiscounted) benchmark cash flows. *[IFRS 9.B4.1.9D]*.

In this example, if the entity considers future developments, it is unlikely that it can conclude that the contractual cash flows could not be significantly different from the benchmark cash flows, considering the magnitude of the mismatch between the interest rate tenor and reset frequency. The bond will always pay a five year rate even though, except at the outset, this exceeds the instrument's remaining life. Therefore, the instrument is not likely to meet the contractual cash flow characteristics test.

6.4.3 *Regulated interest rates*

In some jurisdictions, the government or a regulatory authority sets interest rates. For example, such government regulation of interest rates may be part of a broad macroeconomic policy or it may be introduced to encourage entities to invest in a particular sector of the economy. In some of these cases, the objective of the time value of money element is not to provide consideration for only the passage of time. However, the Board notes that the rates are set for public policy reasons and thus are not subject to structuring to achieve a particular accounting result. *[IFRS 9.BC4.180]*. Consequently, as a concession, a regulated interest rate is considered by the IASB to serve as a proxy for the time value of money element for the purpose of applying the contractual cash flow characteristics test if that regulated interest rate:

- provides consideration that is broadly consistent with the passage of time; and
- does not provide exposure to risks or volatility in the contractual cash flows that are inconsistent with a basic lending arrangement. *[IFRS 9.B4.1.9E]*.

As the standard does not establish criteria to determine whether a regulated rate provides consideration that is 'broadly consistent' with the passage of time, consensus needs to be established on how this concession is applied in practice. However, in the Basis for Conclusions, the board implies that the particular instrument described in the following example would satisfy the two criteria above.

Example 47.19: Regulated interest rates –'Livret A'

In France the interest rate on 'Livret A' savings products issued by retail banks is determined by the central bank and the government according to a formula that reflects protection against inflation and an adequate remuneration to provide incentive for investment. The legislation requires a particular portion of the amounts collected by the retail banks to be lent to a governmental agency that uses the proceeds for social programmes. The IASB noted that the time value element of interest on these accounts may not provide consideration for only the passage of time; however the IASB believes that amortised cost would provide relevant and useful information as long as the contractual cash flows do not introduce risks or volatility that are inconsistent with a basic lending arrangement. *[IFRS 9.BC4.180]*.

6.4.4 Other contractual features that change the timing or amount of contractual cash flows

Some financial assets contain contractual provisions that change the timing or amount of contractual cash flows. For example, the asset may be prepaid before maturity or its term may be extended. In such cases, the entity must determine whether the contractual cash flows that could arise over the life of the instrument due to those contractual provisions are solely payments of principal and interest on the principal amount outstanding.

To make this determination, the entity must assess the contractual cash flows that could arise both before, and after, the change in contractual cash flows. The entity may also need to assess the nature of any contingent event (i.e. the trigger) that would change the timing or amount of contractual cash flows. While the nature of the contingent event in itself is not a determinative factor in assessing whether the contractual cash flows are solely payments of principal and interest, it may be an indicator.

For example, compare a financial instrument with an interest rate that is reset to a higher rate if the debtor misses a particular number of payments to a financial instrument with an interest rate that is reset to a higher rate if a specified equity index reaches a particular level. It is more likely in the former case that the contractual cash flows over the life of the instrument will be solely payments of principal and interest on the principal amount outstanding, because of the relationship between missed payments and an increase in credit risk. In contrast, in the latter case, the contingent event introduces equity price risk which is not a basic lending risk. *[IFRS 9.B4.1.10]*.

The following are examples of contractual terms that result in contractual cash flows that are solely payments of principal and interest on the principal amount outstanding: *[IFRS 9.B4.1.11]*

(a) a variable interest rate that is consideration for the time value of money and for the credit risk associated with the principal amount outstanding during a particular period of time (the consideration for credit risk may be determined at initial recognition only, and so may be fixed) and other basic lending risks and costs, as well as a profit margin (which are also likely to be fixed);

(b) a contractual term that permits the issuer (i.e. the debtor) to prepay a debt instrument or permits the holder (i.e. the creditor) to put a debt instrument back to the issuer before maturity and the prepayment amount substantially represents unpaid amounts of principal and interest on the principal amount outstanding, which may include reasonable additional compensation for the early termination of the contract; and

(c) a contractual term that permits the issuer or holder to extend the contractual term of a debt instrument (i.e. an extension option) and the terms of the extension option result in contractual cash flows during the extension period that are solely payments of principal and interest on the principal amount outstanding, which may include reasonable additional compensation for the extension of the contract.

Unfortunately, neither the standard itself nor the Basis for Conclusions specify what the IASB meant by 'reasonable additional compensation'. It seems reasonable to include direct or indirect costs attributable to early termination or extension, ranging from costs for the additional paper work to costs for adjusting a bank's hedging relationships. Penalties, imposed by the lender on the borrower with the aim of reducing the lender's interest rate risk and discouraging the borrower from prepaying the debt, could also, in certain circumstances, be considered to be reasonable additional compensation. This would be dependent on facts and circumstances such as whether the penalty clause was genuine and the expectation of whether the penalty would be triggered. If the borrower is not expected to exercise the prepayment option, as it would involve the payment of a significant penalty, except in extremely rare or highly abnormal situations then the penalty feature would not be genuine and the asset would pass the contractual cash flows test. *[IFRS 9.B4.1.18]*.

It should be noted that as the standard refers to the prepayment amount including reasonable additional compensation, it would appear, as worded, that the standard requires the lender rather than the borrower to be compensated. As such, amounts that compensate the lender would usually be considered solely payments of principal and interest on the principal amount outstanding, whereas terms that effectively compensate the borrower would not (see Example 47.29 below). An example of this would be a symmetrical break clause where the lender could be liable to compensate the borrower. Therefore, any compensation paid by the lender would seem to need to be floored at par plus accrued interest to pass the contractual cash flow characteristics test, otherwise the lender might not get the principal and interest back. Whether this is what the standard would require is something that could be usefully clarified by the Interpretations Committee or the Board.

The compensation for lost interest in case of early termination requires more judgment. If a borrower prepays because market interest rates have fallen, the bank may only be able to invest the prepaid amount at the new lower market rate. Therefore, the bank might charge the customer the present value of the interest differential between the original rate of the loan and the new market rate for the original remaining maturity of the loan. In addition, the bank may not be able to immediately reinvest the money and has to deposit it on its account with the central bank where it earns only little or no interest (or in some jurisdiction even incurs negative interest). Reasonable additional compensation might include compensation for lost interest for this period as well. However, this period may only include a limited number of days and certainly not the original remaining maturity of the loan.

The strict application of the definition of principal in 6.1 above would mean that debt instruments originated or acquired at a premium or discount, and which are prepayable at par, have to be measured at fair value through profit or loss. This is because, if the issuer prepays, the holder may receive a gain that is less than or in excess of a basic lending return. The IASB, however, decided to provide a narrow scope exception. Financial assets originated or acquired at a premium or discount that would otherwise have cash flows that are principal and interest, except for the effect of a prepayment option, are deemed to meet the above conditions, but only so long as: *[IFRS 9.B4.1.12]*

(a) the prepayment amount substantially represents the contractual par amount and accrued (but unpaid) interest, which may include reasonable additional compensation for the early termination of the contract; and

(b) the fair value of the prepayment feature on initial recognition of the financial asset is insignificant.

The conditions described above apply regardless of whether (i) the prepayment provision is exercisable by the issuer or by the holder; (ii) the prepayment provision is voluntary or mandatory; or (iii) the prepayment feature is contingent.

Because the prepayment amount may include reasonable additional compensation for the early termination of the contract, the treatment of prepayment options under IFRS 9 is different from that under IAS 39. Under the latter, a prepayment feature is considered 'closely related' (and so is not treated as an embedded derivative that is required to be separated) only if it is prepayable at approximately the amortised cost.

Notwithstanding the above, this exception would allow some financial assets that otherwise do not have contractual cash flows that are solely payments of principal and interest to be measured at amortised cost or fair value through other comprehensive income (subject to the assessment of the business model in which they are held). In particular, the IASB observed that this exception will apply to many purchased credit-impaired financial assets with contractual prepayment features. If such an asset was purchased at a deep discount, the contractual cash flows would not be solely payments of principal and interest if, contractually, the asset could be repaid immediately at the par amount. However, that contractual prepayment feature would have an insignificant fair value if it is very unlikely that prepayment will occur. *[IFRS 9.BC4.193]*.

Prepayment might be very unlikely because the debtor of a credit-impaired financial asset might not have the ability to prepay the financial asset.

Similarly, the IASB observed that this exception will apply to some prepayable financial assets that are originated at below-market interest rates. For example, this scenario may arise when an entity sells an item (for example, an automobile) and, as a marketing incentive, provides financing to the customer at an interest rate that is below the prevailing market rate. At initial recognition the entity would measure the financial asset at fair value and, as a result of the below-market interest rate, the fair value would be at a discount to the contractual par amount. The IASB observed that in that case a contractual prepayment feature would likely have an insignificant fair value because it is unlikely that the customer will choose to prepay; in particular, because the interest rate is below-market and thus the financing is advantageous. *[IFRS 9.BC4.194]*.

For instruments that are initially recognised at a discount, the fair value of the prepayment option will usually be insignificant, because the discount is a function of either an increased credit risk of the borrower (as in the first example above) or a below-market interest rate (as in the second example), and in each case the prepayment option is unlikely to be exercised and so will have little fair value. For instruments that are initially recognised at a premium, because the coupon rate is above the current market rate, the application of this guidance is more difficult. While the prepayment option will likely have a more than insignificant fair value, this will usually also be reflected in the fair value at which the asset is acquired. For instance, an investor is unlikely to pay above par for a bond that pays an above market rate of interest if it can be prepaid at par at any time. It would seem that in order for the prepayment option to be relevant for the asset's classification, it would need to be constrained. An example would be a bond that pays an above market rate of interest, with a remaining maturity of five years and that can be prepaid but only after three years. Hence the bond will have an initial fair value greater than par due to the above market rate for the first three years, while the prepayment option will have a significant fair value since it is expected to be exercised in three years' time.

In contrast, an instrument which is prepayable at fair value does not fall under the exception stated above. For such an instrument, the prepayment feature does not only affect the time value of money component. If the fair value of the instrument were to be below par on prepayment due to an increase in interest rates, then the lender may receive less than the instrument's amortised cost and is not *reimbursed* for the present value of lost interest, since the effective interest rate is less than the market rate. The return of such an instrument could therefore be different from a basic lending return. Such a prepayment feature has to be assessed similar to other features which could lead to a cash flow that is neither principal nor interest. See Example 47.29 at 6.4.5 below.

An additional issue might arise for variable rate instruments acquired at a significant discount or premium. For example, a variable rate asset acquired at a deep discount includes some leverage (see section 6.4.5 below) because the variable interest is based on the nominal amount whereas the principal is the fair value on initial recognition by the acquirer. Such an instrument would appear to fail the contractual cash flow characteristics test. However, it is unclear if this was the IASB's intention.

The following examples illustrate further instruments with contractual features that modify the timing and amount of contractual cash flows such that the instruments pass the contractual cash flow characteristics test. Some examples include possible changes to the fact pattern which may change that assessment.

Example 47.20: Debt covenants

A loan agreement contains a covenant whereby the contractual spread above the benchmark rate will increase if the borrower's earnings before interest, tax, depreciation and amortisation (EBITDA) or its debt-to-equity ratio deteriorate by a specified amount by a specified date.

Whether this instrument passes the contractual cash flow characteristics test depends on the specific terms. The loan would pass the contractual cash flow characteristics test if the covenant serves to compensate the lender for taking on a higher credit or liquidity risks.

However, if the covenant results in more than just credit or liquidity protection, or provides for an increase in the rate of return which is not considered appropriate under a basic lending arrangement, the instrument will fail the test. For example, an increase in interest rate to reflect an increase in EBITDA would not satisfy the criteria.

Example 47.21: Auction Rate Securities (ARSs)

ARSs have long-term maturity dates but their interest rate resets more frequently based on the outcome of an auction. As a result of the auction process, the interest rates are short-term and the instruments are treated like short-term investments.

In the event that an auction fails (i.e. there are insufficient buyers of the bond to establish a new rate), the rate resets to a penalty rate. The penalty rate is established at inception and does not necessarily reflect the market rate when the auction fails. It is often intended to compensate the holder for the instrument's lack of liquidity as demonstrated by the auction failure. The auction process for many such securities failed during the financial crisis.

The classification at initial recognition should be based on the contractual terms over the life of the instrument. Although the presumption on acquisition may have been that the auctions were not expected to fail, the potential penalty rate should still be taken into account in the assessment of the instrument's characteristics at initial recognition. If the penalty rate could be considered to compensate the holder for the longer-term credit risk of the instrument following the auction failure as a result of a reduction in market liquidity, it may be possible that the penalty rate reflects interest. However, as such instruments usually have multiple issues with different penalty rates, each different case would need to be carefully evaluated before a conclusion could be reached.

6.4.5 Contractual features that normally do not represent payments of principal and interest

In some cases, financial assets may have contractual cash flows that are not solely payments of principal and interest. *[IFRS 9.B4.1.14]*. Unless such a feature is *de minimis* or non-genuine, the instrument would fail the contractual cash flow characteristics test. *[IFRS 9.B4.1.18]*. Examples of such instruments with contractual cash flows that may not represent solely payments of principal and interest include instruments subject to leverage and instruments that represent investments in particular assets or cash flows.

Leverage is a contractual cash flow characteristic of some financial assets. It increases the variability of the contractual cash flows with the result that they do not have the economic characteristics of just principal and interest. Stand-alone option, forward and swap contracts are examples of financial assets that include such leverage. Thus, such contracts fail the contractual cash flow characteristics test and cannot be measured at amortised cost or fair value through other comprehensive income. *[IFRS 9.B4.1.9]*.

However a variable rate asset at a deep discount will not normally fail the contractual cash flow characteristics test. When the IASB deliberated the meaning of principal in September 2013 they did not distinguish between fixed and variable rate assets and do not seem to have intended a variable rate plain vanilla instrument to fail the contractual cash flow characteristics test. Moreover, a variable rate asset which is acquired or originated at a deep discount will normally be a purchased or originated credit impaired asset. As such, the effective interest rate used will be the credit-adjusted effective interest rate. In these cases the borrower will usually be unable to pay any increases in rates and any decrease in rates would result in the borrower repaying more principal. Either way, the loan is essentially fixed rate and, therefore not leveraged, so will not fail the contractual cash flow characteristic test.

A financial asset may have contractual cash flows that are described as principal and interest but those cash flows do not, in economic substance, represent the payment of principal and interest on the principal amount outstanding. *[IFRS 9.B4.1.15]*. For example, under some contractual arrangements, a creditor's claim is limited to specified assets of the debtor or the cash flows from specified assets (described in the standard as a 'non-recourse' financial asset). Another example given in the standard is contractual terms stipulating that the financial asset's cash flows increase as more automobiles use a particular toll road. Those contractual cash flows are inconsistent with a basic lending arrangement. *[IFRS 9.B4.1.16]*. As a result, the instrument would not pass the contractual cash flow characteristics test unless such a feature is *de minimis* or non-genuine. *[IFRS 9.B4.1.18]*.

However, the fact that a financial asset is non-recourse does not in itself necessarily preclude the financial asset from passing the contractual cash flow characteristics test (see also section 6.3.2 above). Furthermore, conventional subordination features do not preclude an asset from passing the test (see 6.3.1 above).

The following examples illustrate instruments which normally fail the contractual cash flow characteristics test because their cash flows are not solely payments of principal and interest on the principal amount outstanding.

Chapter 47

Example 47.22: Non-recourse loans

Under some contractual arrangements, a creditor's claim is limited to specified assets of the debtor or the cash flows from specified assets (described in the standard as a 'non-recourse' financial asset). *[IFRS 9.B4.1.16]*. In such cases, the contractual cash flows may reflect a return that is inconsistent with a basic lending arrangement; e.g. if the contractual terms stipulate that the financial asset's return effectively varies on the basis of the performance of an underlying asset, the contractual cash flows do not represent the payment of principal and interest on the principal amount outstanding.

However, the fact that a financial asset is non-recourse does not in itself necessarily preclude the financial asset from passing the contractual cash flow characteristics test. In such situations, the creditor is required to assess ('look through to') the particular underlying assets or cash flows to determine whether the contractual cash flows of the financial asset being classified are payments of principal and interest on the principal amount outstanding. If the terms of the financial asset give rise to any other cash flows or limit the cash flows in a manner inconsistent with payments representing principal and interest, the financial asset fails the contractual cash flow characteristics test. Whether the underlying assets are financial assets or non-financial assets does not in itself affect this assessment. *[IFRS 9.B4.1.17]*.

Non-recourse loans need careful consideration and many instruments that are non-recourse will fail the test. The following examples illustrate how the guidance above might be applied to non-recourse instruments that are common in practice and under which circumstances those instruments pass the contractual cash flow characteristics test:

(a) Project finance loans

Where a loan is given for the construction and maintenance of a toll road and the payments of cash flows to the lender are reduced or cancelled if less than a certain number of vehicles travel on that road, the loan is unlikely to pass the contractual cash flow characteristics test. Similarly, a loan with cash flows specifically referenced to the performance of an underlying business will not pass the test.

In other cases, where there is no such reference and there is adequate equity in the project to absorb losses before affecting the ability to meet payments on the loan, it may well pass the contractual cash flow characteristics test.

(b) Loans to a special purpose entity (SPE)

Where a loan is provided to an SPE that funds the acquisition of other assets, whether that loan passes the contractual cash flow characteristics test will depend on the specific circumstances of the arrangement.

If the assets of the SPE are all debt instruments which would themselves pass the contractual cash flow characteristics test, the loan to the SPE might well pass it too. Further, if, the SPE uses the loan from the entity to fund investments in assets which will not themselves pass the contractual cash flow characteristics test, such as equity securities or non-financial assets, but the SPE has sufficient equity to cover the losses on its investments, the loan may again pass the contractual cash flow characteristics test. However, if the loan is the only source of finance to the SPE so that it absorbs any losses from the equity securities, it would not pass the contractual cash flow characteristics test. Whether the loan is legally non-recourse does not matter in this scenario because the SPE has limited other assets to which the lender can have recourse. Therefore the SPE must have adequate equity for the interest to represent compensation for basic lending risk.

(c) Mortgages

There are many different types of mortgage loans and some are structured so that in the event of default the lender has legal recourse only to the property provided as collateral and not to the borrower. This type of arrangement is common in some states of the USA. Other mortgages may, in substance, be non-recourse if the borrower has limited other assets.

In general, we do not believe that IFRS 9 was intended to require all normal collateralised loans such as mortgages to be accounted for at fair value through profit or loss. Consequently, if a loan is granted at a rate of interest that compensates the lender for the time value of money and for the credit risk associated with the principal amount, it would in our view usually pass the contractual cash flow characteristics test, whether or not it is legally non-recourse.

However, at inception, if the expected repayment of a loan is primarily driven by future movements in the value of the collateral so that the loan is, in substance, an investment in the real estate market, then measurement at amortised cost or fair value through other comprehensive income classification would most likely be inappropriate.

The contractual cash flow characteristics are assessed at initial recognition of the asset. If at initial recognition the asset is full recourse there is no need to reassess whether there is any change thereafter.

Other loans could also be considered to be in substance non-recourse if the borrower has limited resources with which to repay the loan. Under certain circumstances impaired loans backed by collateral could also be considered to be non-recourse in substance, such as if the lender could only recover the loan by realising the collateral. This would in substance be similar to the lender buying the collateral directly.

Where an SPE issues non-recourse notes and uses the funding to buy an asset which is pledged as collateral for the non-recourse notes, the question arises as to how to assess whether 'a creditor's claim is limited to specified assets of the debtor or the cash flow from specified assets' and whether 'the terms of the financial asset give rise to any other cash flows or limit the cash flows in a manner inconsistent with payments representing principal and interest'. In these cases the question revolves around whether the SPE has adequate equity such that interest represents compensation for the basic lending risks rather than asset risks.

Example 47.23: Dual currency instruments

For some financial assets the interest payments are denominated in a currency that is different from the principal of the financial asset. IFRS 9 requires the assessment of 'whether contractual cash flows are solely payments of principal and interest on the principal outstanding for the currency in which the financial asset is denominated'. *[IFRS 9.B4.1.8]*.

This implies that any instrument in which interest is calculated based on a principal amount other than that payable on maturity will not pass the contractual cash flow characteristics test. For instance, if *variable* interest payments are computed based on a fixed principal amount in another currency, e.g. US dollars, although repayment of the principal is in sterling, the financial asset is not considered to have cash flows that are solely payments of principal and interest.

However, there may be instances where interest is denominated in a currency that is different from the principal currency, but the contractual cash flows could possibly constitute solely payments of principal and interest. For example, the principal amount of the bond is denominated (and redeemed at a fixed maturity) in Canadian dollars (CAD). Interest payments are fixed in Indian Rupees (INR) at inception based on the market interest rates and foreign exchange spot and forward rates at that time.

While not explicit in the standard, in our view, if the bond can be separated into two components that, on their own, would meet the contractual cash flow characteristics test, then the combined instrument would do so. That is, if the bond can be viewed as the combination of a zero-coupon bond denominated in CAD and a stream of fixed payments denominated in INR, and if both instruments can be analysed as a stream of cash flows that are solely payments of principal and interest, then the sum of the two would do so as well.

The defining criterion is the fact that the interest payments have been fixed at inception and there is no exposure to changes in cash flows in the currency of denomination of the cash flows.

Example 47.24: Convertible debt

An entity holds a bond that is convertible into equity instruments of the issuer.

The holder would analyse the convertible bond in its entirety, since IFRS 9 does not separate embedded derivatives from financial assets.

The contractual cash flows are not payments of principal and interest on the principal amount outstanding because they reflect a return that is inconsistent with a basic lending arrangement (see 6 above) i.e. the return is also linked to the value of the equity of the issuer. *[IFRS 9.B4.1.14 Instrument F]*.

The assessment would change if the issuer were to use its own shares as 'currency'. That is, if the bond is convertible into a variable number of shares with a fair value equal to unpaid amounts of principal and interest on the principal amount outstanding. In this case, the bond might satisfy the contractual cash flow characteristics test and would be derecognised on conversion. However, such conversion features are often capped because, otherwise, the issuer could be required to deliver a potentially unlimited amount of shares. The existence of such a cap, if genuine, would result in the failure of the test.

Example 47.25: Inverse floater

An entity holds a loan that pays an inverse floating interest rate (i.e. the interest rate has an inverse relationship to market interest rates, such as 6% minus 2 times LIBOR).

The contractual cash flows are not solely payments of principal and interest on the principal amount outstanding because an inverse floating rate does not represent consideration for the time value of money. *[IFRS 9.B4.1.14 Instrument G]*.

Example 47.26: Perpetual instruments with potentially deferrable coupons

An entity holds a perpetual instrument but the issuer may call the instrument at any time, paying the holder the par amount plus accrued interest due.

The instrument pays interest but payment of interest cannot be made unless the issuer is able to remain solvent immediately afterwards. There are two scenarios.

Scenario a) interest is accrued on the deferred amounts.

The contractual cash flows could be payments of principal and interest on the principal amount outstanding.

An example in the standard states that the fact that the instrument is perpetual does not in itself mean that the contractual cash flows are not payments of principal and interest on the principal amount outstanding. In effect, a perpetual instrument has continuous (multiple) extension options. Such options may result in contractual cash flows that are payments of principal and interest on the principal amount outstanding if interest payments are mandatory and must be paid in perpetuity.

Some may find it strange that the instrument is deemed to satisfy the contractual cash flow characteristics test even though the principal will never actually be paid. Also, the fact that the instrument is callable does not mean that the contractual cash flows are not payments of principal and interest on the principal amount outstanding, unless it is callable at an amount that does not substantially reflect payment of outstanding principal and interest on that principal amount outstanding. Even if the callable amount includes an amount that reasonably compensates the holder for the early termination of the instrument, the contractual cash flows could be payments of principal and interest on the principal amount outstanding. (See section 6.4.4 above).

Scenario a) deferred interest does not accrue additional interest.

The contractual cash flows are not payments of principal and interest on the principal amount outstanding. This is because the issuer may be required to defer interest payments and additional interest does not accrue on those deferred interest amounts. As a result, interest amounts are not consideration for the time value of money on the principal amount outstanding.

Note that, in this example, the holder is not entitled to assess whether it is probable that interest may ever be deferred. As long as the feature is genuine, the deferral of interest must be taken into account in assessing whether interest amounts are consideration for the time value of money on the principal outstanding. *[IFRS 9.B4.1.14 Instrument H]*.

Example 47.27: Write-down or conversion imposed by regulator

Scenario a) the provision is not a contractual feature

A regulated bank issues an instrument with a stated maturity date. The instrument pays a fixed interest rate and all contractual cash flows are non-discretionary.

However, the issuer is subject to legislation that permits or requires a national resolution authority to impose losses on holders of particular instruments, including the above mentioned instrument, in particular circumstances. For example, the national resolution authority has the power to write down the par amount of such an instrument or to convert it into a fixed number of the issuer's ordinary shares if the national resolution authority determines that the issuer is having severe financial difficulties, needs additional regulatory capital or is failing.

The holder would analyse the contractual terms of the financial instrument to determine whether they give rise to cash flows that are solely payments of principal and interest on the principal amount outstanding and thus are consistent with a basic lending arrangement.

According to the standard, this analysis would not consider the write-down or conversion that arise only as a result of the national resolution authority's power under statutory law to impose losses on the holders of such an instrument. That is because that power is not a contractual term of the financial instrument.

Although this example makes use of a principle that is widely applied, we note that it is not consistent with the position taken in IFRIC 2 – *Members' Shares in Co-operative Entities and Similar Instruments*, which requires an entity to include 'relevant local laws, regulations and the entity's governing charter in effect at the date of classification' when classifying a financial instrument as a liability or equity.

Scenario b) the provision is a contractual feature

The contractual terms of the financial instrument permit or require the issuer or another entity to impose losses on the holder (e.g. by writing down the par amount or by converting the instrument into a fixed number of the issuer's ordinary shares), if the issuer fails to meet particular regulatory capital requirements (a non-viability event).

Provided the 'non-viability' provision is genuine, which will normally be the case, the instrument will fail the contractual cash flow characteristics test even if the probability is remote that such a loss will be imposed. *[IFRS 9.B4.1.13 Instrument E]*.

Note that payments that arise as a result of a regulator's statutory power and that are either only referenced or not mentioned in the contractual terms of the instrument are not considered in the analysis of the contractual payment features of the instrument.

Example 47.28: Multiple of a benchmark interest rate

An entity holds an instrument for which the interest rate is quoted as a multiple of a benchmark interest rate (e.g. 2 times 3-month EURIBOR for a 3-month term).

Such features introduce leverage and the standard is explicit that leverage increases the variability of the contractual cash flows, resulting in them not having the economic characteristics of interest. As a result, such instruments would need to be measured at fair value through profit or loss. *[IFRS 9.B4.1.9]*.

Example 47.29: Fixed rate bond prepayable by the issuer at fair value

A company acquires a bond which requires the issuer to pay a fixed rate of interest and repay the principal on a fixed date. However, the issuer has the right to prepay (or call) the bond before maturity, although the amount the issuer must pay is the fair value of the bond at the time of prepayment, i.e. the fair value of the contractual interest and principal payments that remain outstanding at the point of exercise. For example, if the bond has a term of five years and the call option is exercised at the end of the second year, the fair value would be calculated by discounting the principal and interest payments due over the remaining three years at the current market interest rate for a three-year bond with similar characteristics.

The exercise price represents the fair value of unpaid amounts of principal and interest on the principal amount outstanding at the date of exercise, albeit discounted at the current market interest rate rather than the original market interest rate.

The fact that the exercise price is the fair value could be interpreted as providing reasonable additional compensation to the holder for early termination in a scenario, although this holds true only where the market rate has fallen since the issue of the bond. If interest rates rise, the holder will not receive additional compensation for early termination and will receive less than the principal amount. In these circumstances, due to the negative compensation, the bond holder would not be receiving principal and interest.

In cases where the prepayment amount is set so that there is a 'floor' equal to the par amount, i.e. the prepayment amount received by the holder cannot be less than the par amount of the bond, the prepayment amount could possibly be regarded as representing unpaid amounts of principal and interest.

Example 47.30: Investment in open-ended money market or debt funds

In an open-ended fund, new investors are accepted by the fund after inception and existing investors have the option of leaving the fund at any time. The price at which new entrants invest in the fund or leavers exit the fund is normally based on the fair value of the fund's assets. Given that investors enter and exit the fund at a price based on fair value, the cash flows of an investment in such a fund are not solely payments of principal and interest.

In addition, such investments would not normally qualify for the option for equity instruments, to present gains and losses in other comprehensive income, as they do not normally meet the definition of an equity instrument from the perspective of the fund (i.e. the issuer). See also 8 below.

6.4.6 *Loan commitments*

Where a loan commitment is granted long periods may elapse before the commitment is drawn down. The question therefore arises as to whether the drawdown of loans under an irrevocable loan commitment should be assessed for classification based on when the loan commitment came into being or when the loan was actually drawn down.

IFRS 9 requires that an entity shall recognise a financial asset in its statement of financial position when the entity becomes party to the contractual provisions of the instrument. When an entity first recognises a financial asset it shall classify it in accordance with IFRS 9. *[IFRS 9.3.1.1]*. As the issuer of the irrevocable loan commitment becomes a party to the entire contractual cash flows of the loan at grant date it could be argued that any drawdowns could be treated as continuations of the original facility and that any loans drawn down should be classified on the basis of the criteria applying at the date of the origination of the loan commitment. Such an interpretation is consistent with how the time value of money on loan commitments are calculated under the expected credit loss method, 'a financial asset that is recognised following a draw down on a loan commitment shall be treated as a continuation of that commitment instead of as a new financial instrument'. *[IFRS 9.B5.5.47]*.

However if a long period elapses between the origination of the irrevocable loan commitment and draw down it is possible that conditions affecting the assessment of classification might have changed considerably, for instance where a bank grants a loan commitment to an SPE and the SPE has sufficient equity at the date the commitment is originated but does not at the time the loan is drawn down. This is something that could be usefully clarified by the Interpretations Committee or the Board.

6.5 Contractually linked instruments

In some types of transactions, an entity may prioritise payments to the holders of financial assets using multiple contractually linked instruments that create concentrations of credit risk (known as tranches). Each tranche has a subordination ranking that specifies the order in which any cash flows generated by the issuer are allocated to the tranche. In such situations, the holders of a tranche have the right to payments of principal and interest on the principal amount outstanding only if the issuer generates sufficient cash flows to satisfy higher ranking tranches. *[IFRS 9.B4.1.20]*. As this guidance should be applied to 'multiple contractually linked instruments' an investment in a single tranche securitisation would not be assessed under this test.

Also the Basis for Conclusions refers to classic waterfall structures with different tranches, rather than a single tranche. *[IFRS 9.BC4.26]*.

These types of arrangements can concentrate credit risk into certain tranches of a structure. Essentially such investments contained leveraged credit risk and accordingly, the IASB believes that measuring such investments at amortised cost or fair value through other comprehensive income may be inappropriate in certain circumstances. Where a structure has in issue only a single tranche, it may be more appropriate to view an investment in that tranche as a non-recourse loan (see 6.4.5 above) rather than a contractually linked instrument.

In multi-tranche transactions that concentrate credit risk in the way described above, a tranche is considered to have cash flow characteristics that are payments of principal and interest on the principal amount outstanding only if the following three criteria are met: *[IFRS 9.B4.1.21]*

(a) the contractual terms of the tranche being assessed for classification (without looking through to the underlying pool of financial instruments) give rise to cash flows that are solely payments of principal and interest on the principal amount outstanding (e.g. the interest rate on the tranche is not linked to a commodity index);

(b) the underlying pool of financial instruments must contain one or more instruments that have contractual cash flows that are solely payments of principal and interest on the principal amount outstanding (the primary instruments) and any other instruments in the underlying pool must either: *[IFRS 9.B4.1.23-25]*

  (i) reduce the cash flow variability of the primary instruments in the pool and, when combined with the primary instruments in the pool, result in cash flows that are solely payments of principal and interest on the principal amount outstanding; or

  (ii) align the cash flows of the tranches with the cash flows of the underlying primary instruments in the pool to address differences in and only in:

  - whether the interest rate is fixed or floating;
  - the currency in which the cash flows are denominated, including inflation in that currency; or
  - the timing of the cash flows.

  For these purposes, when identifying the underlying pool of financial instruments, the holder should 'look through' the structure until it can identify an underlying pool of instruments that are creating (rather than passing through) the cash flows. *[IFRS 9.B4.1.22]*.

(c) the exposure to credit risk in the underlying pool of financial instruments inherent in the tranche is equal to, or lower than, the exposure to credit risk of all of the underlying pool of instruments (for example, the credit rating of the tranche is equal to or higher than the credit rating that would apply to a single borrowing that funded the underlying pool).

If the holder cannot assess whether a financial asset meets criteria (a) to (c) above at initial recognition, the tranche must be measured at fair value through profit or loss. *[IFRS 9.B4.1.26]*.

IFRS 9 implies that the underlying pool should consist of financial instruments. *[IFRS 9.B4.1.21(b)]*. Contractually linked instruments referencing a pool of non-financial instruments that do not meet the contractual cash flow characteristics test cannot be classified at amortised cost. However, a non-recourse financial asset could pass the contractual cash flow test depending on whether the underlying assets or cash-flows meet the contractual cash flow criteria. This is the case whether the underlying assets are financial assets or non-financial assets. *[IFRS 9.B4.1.17]*. The question therefore arises as to whether the guidance concerning non-recourse requirements (see 6.4.5 above) can be applied to contractually linked instruments.

The standard would suggest that the guidance for contractually linked instruments applies to all contractually linked instruments without exception. The scope of contractually linked instruments is based on the nature of the instruments issued not on the nature of the pool of assets underlying the instrument.

Furthermore, in a structure where an SPE issues contractually linked notes referenced to a non-recourse note issued by another SPE referencing a pool of non-financial assets, IFRS guidance would require the entity holding the instrument to look through all contractually linked instruments.

Because of the way the standard is written it would appear that the outcome of the contractual cash flow characteristics assessment will depend on the form of the arrangement. Arrangements which involve using multiple contractually linked instruments would be assessed under the contractually linked instruments requirements while arrangements with non-recourse features but without multiple tranches would be assessed under the non-recourse requirements. It seems strange that, for instance, a non-recourse financial asset whose cash flows depend on vehicles using a toll road would be required to be assessed under the non-recourse requirement if structured as a single instrument but, if structured into tranches, would be assessed differently under the contractually linked instrument criteria.

In practice it may be difficult for the holder to perform the look-through test because the underlying reference assets of a collateralised debt obligation (CDO) may not all have been acquired at the time of investment. In such circumstances, the holder will need to consider, amongst other things, the intended objectives of the CDO as well as the manager's investment mandate before determining whether the investment qualifies for measurement at amortised cost or fair value through other comprehensive income. If after this consideration the holder is able to conclude that all the underlying reference assets of the CDO will always have contractual cash flows that are solely payments of principal and interest on the principal amount outstanding, the interest in the CDO can qualify for measurement at amortised cost or fair value through other comprehensive income. Otherwise, the investment in the CDO must be accounted for at fair value through profit or loss because it fails the contractual cash flow characteristics test, unless the effect is *de minimis*.

If the underlying pool of instruments can change after initial recognition in a way that does not meet conditions (a) and (b) above, the tranche must be measured at fair value through profit or loss. However, if the underlying pool includes instruments that are collateralised by assets that do not meet the conditions above (as will often be the case), the ability to take possession of such assets is disregarded for the purposes of applying this paragraph, unless (which will be rare) the entity acquired the tranche with the intention of controlling the collateral. *[IFRS 9.B4.1.26]*.

The IASB noted that a key principle underlying the contractual cash flow provisions for contractually linked instruments was that an entity should not be disadvantaged simply by holding an asset indirectly if the underlying asset has cash flows that are solely principal and interest, and the holding is not subject to more-than-insignificant leverage or a concentration of credit risk relative to the underlying assets.

Accordingly, the IASB clarified that a tranche may have contractual cash flows that are solely payments of principal and interest even if the tranche is prepayable in the event that the underlying pool of financial instruments is prepaid. The Board noted that because the underlying pool of assets must have contractual cash flows that are solely payments of principal and interest, then, by extension, any prepayment features in those underlying financial assets are also required to be solely payments of principal and interest. *[IFRS 9.BC4.206(a)]*.

The Board's clarification that a prepayment feature in the underlying pool of assets does not necessarily prevent a tranche from meeting the contractual cash flow characteristics test is helpful. But, unless the underlying pool can only be acquired at origination, it may be very difficult to 'look through' to the underlying pool to determine if its prepayment features would themselves be solely payments of principal and interest. This is because the information will often not be available to determine whether the assets were acquired at a premium or discount, and whether the fair value of any prepayment feature was insignificant on acquisition (see 6.4.4 above).

While some contractually linked instruments may pass the contractual cash flow characteristics test and consequently may be measured at amortised cost or fair value through other comprehensive income, the contractual cash flows of the individual tranches are normally based on a pre-defined waterfall structure (i.e. principal and interest are first paid on the most senior tranche and then successively paid on more junior tranches). Accordingly, one could argue that more junior tranches could never suffer a credit loss because the contractually defined cash flows under the waterfall structure are always equal to the cash flows that an entity expects to receive, and so would never be regarded as impaired. This is, because Appendix A of IFRS 9 defines 'credit loss' as 'the difference between all contractual cash flows that are due to an entity in accordance with the contract and all the cash flows that the entity expects to receive, discounted at the original effective interest rate'.

However, consistent with treating these assets as having passed the contractual cash flow characteristics test, we believe that the impairment requirements of IFRS 9 (see Chapter 50 at 5) apply to such tranches if they are measured at amortised cost or fair value through other comprehensive income. Instead of the cash flows determined under the waterfall structure, an entity needs to consider deemed principal and interest payments as contractual cash flows when calculating expected credit losses. In many cases, when a bank sets up an SPE to securitise assets and issue notes, the bank will also provide a liquidity facility to the SPE to ensure that interest and principle on the notes can be paid on time regardless of the timing of the cash flows of the underlying assets. In these cases the liquidity facility is not considered to be a tranche of the contractually linked instrument even if it is included in the liquidity waterfall structure of the arrangement e.g. it is given a place in the subordination ranking of the tranches. The characteristics of the liquidity feature are sufficiently different from the notes. If the liquidity feature does not have features that would fail the contractual cash flow characteristics test then it would be treated as a short term loan.

6.5.1 Assessing the characteristics of the underlying pool

For the purposes of criterion (b) at 6.5 above, the underlying pool may contain financial instruments such as interest rate swaps. In order for these instruments not to preclude the use of amortised cost or fair value through other comprehensive income accounting for holders of a tranche, they must reduce the variability of cash flows, or align the cash flows of the tranches with the cash flows of the underlying pool of the primary instruments. Accordingly, an underlying pool that contains government bonds and an instrument that swaps government credit risk for (riskier) corporate credit risk would not have cash flows that represent solely principal and interest on the principal amount outstanding. *[IFRS 9.BC4.35(d)]*.

If the underlying pool of financial instruments contained a purchased credit default swap, this would not prejudice the use of amortised cost or fair value through other comprehensive income accounting provided it paid out only to compensate for the loss of principal and interest, although in practice it is far more common for underlying pools to contain written rather than purchased credit default swaps. As a consequence, it may well be possible to obtain amortised cost or fair value through other comprehensive income accounting treatment for the more senior investments in 'cash' CDOs, i.e. those where the underlying pool comprises the reference debt instruments. However, tranches of 'synthetic' CDOs for which the risk exposure of the tranches is generated by derivatives, would not pass the contractual characteristics test.

6.5.2 Assessing the exposure to credit risk in the tranche held

IFRS 9 does not prescribe a method for comparing the exposure to credit risk in the tranche held to that of the underlying pool of financial instruments.

For the more senior and junior tranches, it may become obvious with relatively little analysis whether the tranche is more or less risky than the underlying assets. In some cases, it might be possible to compare the credit rating allocated to the tranche as compared with that for the underlying pool of financial instruments, provided they are all rated.

However, in some circumstances involving complex securitisation structures, a more detailed assessment may be required. For example, it might be appropriate to prepare an analysis that involves developing various credit loss scenarios for the underlying pool of financial instruments, computing the probability weighted outcomes of those scenarios, determining the probability weighted effect on the tranche held, and comparing the relative variability of the tranche held with that of the underlying assets, which is shown in the following example.

Example 47.31: Assessing the exposure to credit risk in the tranche held

Bank A is the sponsor of a securitisation vehicle (the SPE) and holds the junior notes issued by the SPE. The SPE's assets consist of a portfolio of residential mortgages that were originated and transferred to the SPE by Bank A. The SPE does not hold any derivatives. A number of other banks invest in the mezzanine, senior and super senior tranches of notes issued by the SPE. None of the banks has any further involvement with the SPE and all banks have assessed that the SPE is not required to be consolidated in their respective financial statements. The total notional amount of mortgage assets and notes issued is CU 1,000.

The following table shows a range of expected credit losses for the portfolio of mortgages as at inception and the estimated probability that those scenarios will occur.

	Loss	Estimated probability of loss	Estimated weighted average loss
	CU	%	CU
Scenario I	40	10%	4
Scenario II	70	25%	18
Scenario III	110	30%	33
Scenario IV	180	25%	45
Scenario V	230	10%	23
Weighted average loss expectancy			**123**

The probability weighted expected losses of the underlying assets represent therefore 12.3%.

The following table illustrates how an entity may compare the credit risk of the tranche with that of the underlying pool of financial instruments:

Tranche		Super senior	Senior	Mezzanine	Junior	**Total**
Notional amount (A)		630	200	90	80	**1,000**
	Probability	Probability weighted expected losses of the tranches*				
Scenario I	10%	–	–	–	4	**4**
Scenario II	25%	–	–	–	18	**18**
Scenario III	30%	–	–	9	24	**33**
Scenario IV	25%	–	2	23	20	**45**
Scenario V	10%	–	6	9	8	**23**
Expected loss by tranche (B)		–	8	41	74	**123**
Expected loss % by tranche (B)/(A)		0.0%	4.0%	45.6%	92.5%	**12.3%**
Credit risk of tranche is less than the credit risk of the underlying assets?		Yes	Yes	No	No	
Tranche passes the contractual cash flow characteristic test		Yes	Yes	No	No	

* For each scenario, expected losses are first allocated to the junior tranches and progressively to the more senior tranches until all expected losses are absorbed. For example, in Scenario IV, the loss of CU180 would be absorbed by the Junior tranche (CU 80), mezzanine tranche (CU 90) and senior tranche (CU 10). The probability weight of 25% for Scenario IV is then applied to the expected losses allocated to each tranche.

The junior notes have an expected loss which is, in percentage terms, greater than the overall expected loss on the underlying portfolio. Therefore, these notes must be accounted for at fair value through profit or loss. Similarly, the mezzanine notes have a greater expected loss than the underlying pool and would not pass the contractual cash flow characteristics test.

The expected losses on the senior notes and the super senior notes are lower than the overall expected loss on the underlying pool of instruments and may qualify for amortised cost or fair value through other comprehensive income treatment, provided all other IFRS 9 requirements are met and the instruments are not held for trading.

In this example, it might have been possible to come to the same conclusion without a numerical calculation for the junior and super senior tranches, but the technique is helpful to determine the treatment of the intermediary notes. In practice, it may also be necessary to apply judgment through a qualitative assessment of specific facts and circumstances.

7 DESIGNATION AT FAIR VALUE THROUGH PROFIT OR LOSS

Financial assets or financial liabilities may be designated as measured at fair value through profit or loss at initial recognition if doing so eliminates or significantly reduces a measurement or recognition inconsistency (sometimes referred to as an 'accounting mismatch') that would otherwise arise. *[IFRS 9.4.1.5, 4.2.2(a)]*.

Financial liabilities may also be designated at fair value through profit or loss where a group of financial liabilities or financial assets and financial liabilities is managed and its performance is evaluated on a fair value basis. *[IFRS 9.4.2.2(b)]*. Financial assets that are managed on a fair value basis will always be classified at fair value through profit or loss (see 5.4 above), hence, a designation option is not needed.

Designation at fair value through profit or loss in the two situations described above is permitted provided doing so results in the financial statements presenting more relevant information. *[IFRS 9.B4.1.27]*. Such a designation can be made only at initial recognition and cannot be revoked subsequently.

In addition, a hybrid contract with a host that is not an asset within the scope of IFRS 9 that contains one or more embedded derivatives meeting particular conditions may be designated, in its entirety, at fair value through profit or loss. *[IFRS 9.4.3.5]*. These conditions are discussed in detail at 7.3 below.

The decision to designate a financial asset or financial liability as measured at fair value through profit or loss is similar to an accounting policy choice, although, unlike an accounting policy choice, it is not required in all cases to be applied consistently to all similar transactions. However, for a group of financial assets and financial liabilities that is managed and its performance is evaluated on a fair value basis, all eligible financial liabilities that are managed together should be designated. *[IFRS 9.B4.1.35]*. When an entity has such a choice, IAS 8 requires the chosen policy to result in the financial statements providing reliable and more relevant information about the effects of transactions, other events and conditions on the entity's financial position, financial performance or cash flows. For example, in designating a financial liability at fair value through profit or loss, an entity needs to demonstrate that it falls within at least one of the circumstances set out above. *[IFRS 9.B4.1.28]*.

The fair value option cannot be applied to a portion or component of a financial instrument, e.g. changes in the fair value of a debt instrument attributable to one risk such as changes in a benchmark interest rate, but not credit risk. Further, it cannot be applied to proportions of an instrument. However, if an entity simultaneously issues two or more identical financial instruments, it is not precluded from designating only some of those instruments as being subject to the fair value option (e.g. if doing so achieves a significant reduction in an accounting mismatch). Therefore, if an entity issued a bond totalling US$100 million in the form of 100 certificates each of US$1 million, the entity could designate 10 specified certificates if to do so would meet at least one of the criteria noted above. *[IFRS 9.BCZ4.74-76]*.

The conditions in which financial instruments may be designated at fair value through profit or loss are discussed further at 7.1 to 7.3 below.

7.1 Designation eliminates or significantly reduces a measurement or recognition inconsistency (accounting mismatch) that would otherwise arise

The notion of an accounting mismatch necessarily involves two propositions. First, that an entity has particular assets and liabilities that are measured, or on which gains and losses are recognised, on different bases; and second, that there is a perceived economic relationship between those assets and liabilities. *[IFRS 9.BCZ4.61]*.

For example, absent any designation, a financial asset might be classified as subsequently measured at fair value and a liability the entity considers related would be subsequently measured at amortised cost (with changes in fair value not recognised). In such circumstances, an entity may conclude that its financial statements would provide more relevant information if both the asset and the liability were measured as at fair value through profit or loss. *[IFRS 9.B4.1.29]*.

IFRS 9 gives the following examples of situations in which designation of a financial asset or financial liability as measured at fair value through profit or loss might eliminate or significantly reduce an accounting mismatch and produce more relevant information: *[IFRS 9.B4.1.30]*

(a) an entity has liabilities under insurance contracts whose measurement incorporates current information (as permitted by IFRS 4), and financial assets it considers related that would otherwise be measured at fair value through other comprehensive income or amortised cost;

(b) an entity has financial assets, financial liabilities or both that share a risk, such as interest rate risk, that gives rise to changes in fair value that tend to offset each other. However, only some of the instruments would be measured at fair value through profit or loss (e.g. derivatives or those classified as held for trading). It may also be the case that the requirements for hedge accounting are not met, for example because the requirements for effectiveness are not met;

(c) an entity has financial assets, financial liabilities or both that share a risk, such as interest rate risk, that gives rise to changes in fair value that tend to offset each other and the entity does not use hedge accounting. This could be for different reasons, for example, because items giving rise to the accounting mismatch would not qualify for hedge accounting or because the entity does not want to use hedge accounting because of operational complexity. Furthermore, in the absence of hedge accounting there is a significant inconsistency in the recognition of gains and losses. For example, the entity has financed a specified group of loans by issuing traded bonds, the changes in the fair value of which tend to offset each other. If, in addition, the entity regularly buys and sells the bonds but rarely, if ever, buys and sells the loans, reporting both the loans and the bonds at fair value through profit or loss eliminates the inconsistency in the timing of recognition of gains and losses that would otherwise result from measuring them both at amortised cost and recognising a gain or loss each time a bond is repurchased.

For practical purposes, an entity need not acquire all the assets and incur all the liabilities giving rise to the measurement or recognition inconsistency at exactly the same time. A reasonable delay is permitted provided that each transaction is designated as at fair value through profit or loss at its initial recognition and, at that time, any remaining transactions are expected to occur. *[IFRS 9.B4.1.31]*.

It would not be acceptable to designate only some of the financial assets giving rise to the inconsistency as at fair value through profit or loss if to do so would not eliminate or significantly reduce the inconsistency and would therefore not result in more relevant information. However, it would be acceptable to designate only some of a number of similar financial assets if doing so does achieve a significant reduction (and possibly a greater reduction than other allowable designations) in the inconsistency. *[IFRS 9.B4.1.32]*.

For example, assume an entity has a number of similar financial assets totalling €100 and a number of similar financial liabilities totalling €50, but these are measured on a different basis. The entity may significantly reduce the measurement inconsistency by designating at initial recognition all of the liabilities but only some of the assets (for example, individual assets with a combined total of €45) as at fair value through profit or loss. However, because designation as at fair value through profit or loss can be applied only to the whole of a financial instrument, the entity in this example must designate one or more assets in their entirety. It could not designate either a component of an asset (e.g. changes in value attributable to only one risk, such as changes in a benchmark interest rate) or a proportion (i.e. percentage) of an asset. *[IFRS 9.B4.1.32]*.

7.2 A group of financial liabilities or financial assets and financial liabilities is managed and its performance is evaluated on a fair value basis

The second situation in which the fair value option may be used (for financial liabilities) is where a group of financial liabilities or financial assets and financial liabilities is managed, and its performance evaluated, on a fair value basis. In order to meet this condition, it is necessary for the group of instruments to be managed in accordance with a documented risk management or investment strategy and for information, prepared on a fair value basis, about the group of instruments to be provided internally to the entity's key management personnel (as defined in IAS 24 – see Chapter 37 at 2.2.1.D), for example the entity's board of directors and chief executive officer. *[IFRS 9.4.2.2(b)]*.

If an entity manages and evaluates the performance of a group of financial liabilities or financial assets and financial liabilities in such a way, measuring that group at fair value through profit or loss results in more relevant information. The focus in this instance is on the way the entity manages and evaluates performance, rather than on the nature of its financial instruments. *[IFRS 9.B4.1.33]*. Accordingly, subject to the requirement of designation at initial recognition, an entity that designates financial instruments as at fair value through profit or loss on the basis of this condition should so designate all eligible financial instruments that are managed and evaluated together. *[IFRS 9.B4.1.35]*.

An entity may designate financial liabilities as at fair value through profit or loss if it has financial assets and financial liabilities that share one or more risks and those risks are managed and evaluated on a fair value basis in accordance with a documented policy of asset and liability management. For example, the entity may issue 'structured products' containing multiple embedded derivatives and manage the resulting risks on a fair value basis using a mix of derivative and non-derivative financial instruments. *[IFRS 9.B4.1.34]*.

An entity's documentation of its strategy need not be extensive (e.g. it need not be in the level of detail required for hedge accounting) but should be sufficient to demonstrate that using the fair value option is consistent with the entity's risk management or investment strategy. Such documentation is not required for each individual item, but may be on a portfolio basis. The IASB notes that in many cases, the entity's existing documentation, as approved by its key management personnel, should be sufficient for this purpose. For example, if the performance management system for a department (as approved by the entity's key management personnel) clearly demonstrates that its performance is evaluated on a total return basis, no further documentation is required. *[IFRS 9.B4.1.36]*.

The IASB made it clear in its basis for conclusions that in looking to an entity's documented risk management or investment strategy, it makes no judgement on what an entity's strategy should be. However, the IASB believes that users, in making economic decisions, would find useful a description both of the chosen strategy and of how designation at fair value through profit or loss is consistent with that strategy. Accordingly, IFRS 7 – *Financial Instruments: Disclosures* – requires these to be disclosed (see Chapter 54 at 4.1). *[IFRS 9.BCZ4.66]*.

7.3 Hybrid contracts with a host that is not a financial asset within the scope of IFRS 9

If a contract contains one or more embedded derivatives, and the host is not a financial asset within the scope of IFRS 9, an entity may designate the entire hybrid contract as at fair value through profit or loss unless:

(a) the embedded derivative does not significantly modify the cash flows that otherwise would be required by the contract; or

(b) it is clear with little or no analysis when a similar hybrid (combined) instrument is first considered that separation of the embedded derivative(s) is prohibited, such as a prepayment option embedded in a loan that permits the holder to prepay the loan for approximately its amortised cost. *[IFRS 9.4.3.5]*.

As discussed in Chapter 44 at 4 to 6, when an entity becomes a party to a hybrid financial instrument that contains one or more embedded derivatives and the host is not a financial asset within the scope of IFRS 9, the entity is required to identify any such embedded derivative, assess whether it is required to be separated from the host contract and, if so, measure it at fair value at initial recognition and subsequently. These requirements can be more complex, or result in less reliable measures, than measuring the entire instrument at fair value through profit or loss. For that reason the entire instrument is normally permitted to be designated as at fair value through profit or loss. *[IFRS 9.B4.3.9]*.

Such designation may be used whether the entity is required to, or prohibited from, separating the embedded derivative from the host contract, except for those situations in (a) or (b) above – this is because doing so would not reduce complexity or increase reliability. *[IFRS 9.B4.3.10]*.

Little further guidance is given on what instruments might fall within (a) and (b) above. The basis for conclusions explains that, at one extreme, the terms of a prepayment option in an ordinary residential mortgage is likely to mean that the fair value option is unavailable to such a mortgage (unless it met one of the conditions in 7.1 and 7.2 above). At the other, it is likely to be available for 'structured products' that contain several embedded derivatives which are typically hedged with derivatives that offset all (or nearly all) of the risks they contain irrespective of the accounting treatment applied to the embedded derivatives. *[IFRS 9.BCZ4.68-70]*.

Essentially, the IASB explains, the standard seeks to strike a balance between reducing the costs of complying with the embedded derivatives provisions and the need to respond to concerns expressed regarding possible inappropriate use of the fair value option. Allowing the fair value option to be used for any instrument with an embedded derivative would make other restrictions on the use of the option ineffective, because many financial instruments include an embedded derivative. In contrast, limiting the use of the fair value option to situations in which the embedded derivative must otherwise be separated would not significantly reduce the costs of compliance and could result in less reliable measures being included in the financial statements. *[IFRS 9.BCZ4.70]*.

8 DESIGNATION OF NON-DERIVATIVE EQUITY INVESTMENTS AT FAIR VALUE THROUGH OTHER COMPREHENSIVE INCOME

An entity may acquire an investment in an equity instrument that is not held for trading. At initial recognition, the entity may make an irrevocable election (on an instrument-by-instrument basis) to present in other comprehensive income subsequent changes in the fair value of such an investment. *[IFRS 9.5.7.5, B5.7.1]*. For this purpose, the term equity instrument uses the definition in IAS 32, application of which for issuers is dealt with in detail in Chapter 45.

In particular circumstances a puttable instrument (or an instrument that imposes on the entity an obligation to deliver to another party a *pro rata* share of the net assets of the entity only on liquidation) is classified by the issuer as if it were an equity instrument. This is by virtue of an exception to the general definitions of financial liabilities and equity instruments. However, such instruments do not actually meet the definition of an equity instrument and therefore the related asset cannot be designated at fair value through other comprehensive income by the holder. *[IFRS 9.BC5.21]*.

Under IFRS 9 and IAS 39, all derivatives are deemed to be held for trading. Consequently, this election cannot be applied to a derivative such as a warrant that is classified as equity by the issuer. However, it could be applied to investments in preference shares, 'dividend stoppers' and similar instruments (see Chapter 45 at 4.5) provided they are classified as equity by the issuer.

The IASB had originally intended this accounting treatment to be available only for those equity instruments that represented a 'strategic investment'. These might include investments held for non-contractual benefits rather than primarily for increases in the value of the investment, for example where there is a requirement to hold such an investment if an entity sells its products in a particular country. However, the Board concluded that it would be difficult, and perhaps impossible, to develop a clear and robust principle that would identify investments that are different enough to justify a different presentation requirement and abandoned this restriction. *[IFRS 9.BC5.25(c)]*.

The subsequent measurement of instruments designated in this way, including recognition of dividends, is summarised at 2 above and covered in detail in Chapter 50, particularly at 2.2.

The example below illustrates the requirements for the designation of a non-derivative equity investment at fair value through other comprehensive income, specifically, the requirement that the instrument meets the definition of an equity instrument in accordance with IAS 32.

Example 47.32: Callable, perpetual 'Tier 1' debt instrument

Consider the example where entity A invests in a perpetual Tier 1 debt instrument, which is redeemable at the option of the issuer (entity B). The instrument carries a fixed coupon that is deferred if entity B does not pay a dividend to its ordinary shareholders. If a coupon is not paid it will not accrue additional interest. The instrument does not have a maturity date, however, the coupon steps up to a higher level 20 years after issue and entity B has the right to purchase the instrument after that date for its nominal amount and any unpaid interest.

Under IFRS 9, such an instrument would not be eligible for amortised cost accounting by the holder. However, given that Entity B does not have a contractual obligation to pay cash, the instrument will qualify for classification at fair value through other comprehensive income, as it meets the definition of equity from the perspective of the issuer in accordance with IAS 32.

IFRS 7 requires disclosure of the fair value at the reporting date of each investment in equity instruments designated as fair value through other comprehensive income. The standard is specific that this is required for each such investment, if material. If an entity designated investments in equity instruments to be measured at fair value through other comprehensive income, it shall identify those investments and disclose, among other information, the fair value for each such investment at the end of the reporting period. *[IFRS 7.11A]*.

The disclosure requirement may be onerous if an entity makes significant use of the fair value through other comprehensive income option and this may act as a disincentive for its use, so entities will need to be careful when making the choices available within the standard. A further question is whether it is necessary to provide disclosures at length if each individual instrument is immaterial. We believe that the concept of materiality will need to be applied, such that the disclosures required are provided separately for investments that are themselves material and aggregated disclosures may suffice for immaterial items.

9 RECLASSIFICATION OF FINANCIAL ASSETS

In certain rare circumstances, non-derivative debt assets are required to be reclassified between the amortised cost, fair value through other comprehensive income and fair value through profit or loss categories. More specifically, when (and only when) an entity changes its business model for managing financial assets, it should reclassify all affected financial assets in accordance with the requirements set out at 5 above. *[IFRS 9.4.4.1]*. The reclassification should be applied prospectively from the 'reclassification date', *[IFRS 9.5.6.1]*, which is defined as:

> 'The first day of the first reporting period following the change in business model that results in an entity reclassifying financial assets.' *[IFRS 9 Appendix A]*.

Accordingly, any previously recognised gains, losses or interest should not be restated. *[IFRS 9.5.6.1]*.

In our view, the reference to reporting period includes interim periods for which the entity prepares an interim report. For example, an entity with a reporting date of 31 December might determine that there is a change in its business model in August 2016. If the entity prepares and publishes quarterly reports in accordance with IAS 34 – *Interim Financial Reporting*, the reclassification date would be 1 October 2016. However, if the entity prepares only half-yearly interim reports or no interim reports at all, the reclassification date would be 1 January 2017.

Changes in the business model for managing financial assets are expected to be very infrequent. They must be determined by an entity's senior management as a result of external or internal changes and must be significant to the entity's operations and demonstrable to external parties. Accordingly, a change in the objective of an entity's business model will occur only when an entity either begins or ceases to carry on an activity that is significant to its operations, and generally that will be the case only when the entity has acquired or disposed of a business line. Examples of a change in business model include the following: *[IFRS 9.B4.4.1]*

(a) An entity has a portfolio of commercial loans that it holds to sell in the short term. The entity acquires a company that manages commercial loans and has a business model that holds the loans in order to collect the contractual cash flows. The portfolio of commercial loans is no longer for sale, and the portfolio is now managed together with the acquired commercial loans and all are held to collect the contractual cash flows.

(b) A financial services firm decides to shut down its retail mortgage business. That business no longer accepts new business and the financial services firm is actively marketing its mortgage loan portfolio for sale.

A change in the objective of an entity's business model must be effected before the reclassification date. For example, if a financial services firm decides on 15 February to shut down its retail mortgage business and hence must reclassify all affected financial assets on 1 April (i.e. the first day of the entity's next reporting period, assuming it reports quarterly), the entity must not accept new retail mortgage business or otherwise engage in activities consistent with its former business model after 15 February. *[IFRS 9.B4.4.2]*.

The following are not considered to be changes in business model: *[IFRS 9.B4.4.3]*

(a) a change in intention related to particular financial assets (even in circumstances of significant changes in market conditions);

(b) a temporary disappearance of a particular market for financial assets; and

(c) a transfer of financial assets between parts of the entity with different business models.

Example 47.33: Change in the way a portfolio is managed

An entity's business model objective for a portfolio meets the criteria for amortised cost measurement but, subsequently, the entity changes the way it manages the assets.

Having determined that the objective for a portfolio originally met the business model test to be classified at amortised cost, if the entity subsequently changes the way it manages the assets (which results in a more than an infrequent number of sales), so that the business model would no longer qualify for amortised cost accounting, the question of how the entity should measure the existing assets and any newly acquired assets then arises.

Although more than an infrequent number of sales have occurred, unless there has been a fundamental change in the entity's business model, the requirements of the standard regarding reclassification are unlikely to be triggered. Changes in the business model for managing financial assets that trigger reclassification of financial assets must be significant to the entity's operations and demonstrable to external parties. They are expected to be very infrequent.

Assuming that the assets are not reclassified, it is likely that the entity will have to divide the portfolio into two sub-portfolios going forward – one for the old assets and one for any new assets acquired.

Financial assets previously held will remain at amortised cost. New financial assets acquired will be measured at fair value through profit or loss or at fair value through other comprehensive income. Whether the assets are measured at fair value through profit or loss or at fair value through other comprehensive income depends on the business model and the characteristics of the assets.

Unlike a change in business model, the contractual terms of a financial asset are known at initial recognition. However, the contractual cash flows may vary over that asset's life based on its original contractual terms. Because an entity classifies a financial asset at initial recognition on the basis of the contractual terms over the life of the instrument, reclassification on the basis of a financial asset's contractual cash flows is not permitted, unless the asset is sufficiently modified that it is derecognised. *[IFRS 9.BC4.117]*.

For instance, no reclassification is permitted or required if the conversion option of a convertible bond lapses. If, however, a convertible bond is converted into shares, the shares represent a new financial asset to be recognised by the entity. The entity would then need to determine the classification category for the new equity investment.

A related question to the above is to what extent the contractual cash flow characteristics test influences the test of whether a financial asset is sufficiently modified such that it is derecognised. It has been suggested that a modification which would result in the asset failing the contractual cash flow characteristics test is a 'substantial modification' that would result in derecognition of the asset (see also Chapter 51 at 3.4). That is because an asset that is measured at fair value through profit or loss is substantially different to an asset measured at amortised cost or fair value through other comprehensive income.

Nevertheless, whether or not a modified asset would still meet the contractual cash flow characteristics test or not could be a helpful indicator for the derecognition assessment.

10 EFFECTIVE DATE AND TRANSITION

This section covers the requirements that are applicable when an entity, which had not previously applied the November 2009 (IFRS 9(2009)), October 2010 or November 2013 version of IFRS 9, applies the final version.

Previous versions of IFRS 9 are no longer available for early adoption. Consequently, the requirements that are applicable in those situations are not covered in this publication, but are described in earlier editions.

10.1 Effective date

IFRS 9 is mandatorily applicable for periods beginning on or after 1 January 2018. Early application is permitted, although early application may be subject to approval or endorsement by the local jurisdiction. If the standard is applied early that fact should be disclosed. *[IFRS 9.7.1.1]*.

IFRS 9 allows an entity to early apply the 'own credit' requirements for non-derivative financial liabilities available for early application before the remainder of the standard is applied. These provisions require an entity to present in other comprehensive income the fair value gains and losses attributable to changes in the entity's own credit risk for non-derivative financial liabilities designated as measured at fair value through profit or loss (see Chapter 50 at 2.1). This would mean that, before the mandatory effective date of IFRS 9, entities could elect to change only their accounting policy for own credit risk while continuing to account for their financial instruments in accordance with IAS 39. If an entity chooses to early apply only those provisions, it shall disclose that fact and provide on an ongoing basis the related disclosures (see Chapter 54 at 8.1). *[IFRS 9.7.1.2]*.

10.2 Transition provisions

IFRS 9 contains a general requirement that it should be applied retrospectively, although it also specifies a number of exceptions which are considered in the rest of this section. *[IFRS 9.7.2.1]*. The transition to IFRS 9 also requires additional disclosures which are described in Chapter 54 at 8.1.

10.2.1 Date of initial application

A number of the transition provisions refer to the 'date of initial application'. This is the date when an entity first applies the requirements of IFRS 9, which is the beginning of the period in which it first reports under IFRS 9, not the earliest period for which comparative figures are amended. *[IFRS 9.7.2.2].*

10.2.2 Applying the 'business model' assessment

Entities should make the business model assessment (see section 5 above) on the basis of the facts and circumstances that exist at the date of initial application. The resulting classification should be applied retrospectively, irrespective of the entity's business model in prior reporting periods. *[IFRS 9.7.2.3].* For these purposes, an entity should determine whether financial assets meet the definition of held for trading as if they had been acquired at the date of initial application. *[IFRS 9.B7.2.1].*

The following examples illustrate two practical issues which an entity may need to consider when applying the business model assessment at the date of initial application of IFRS 9.

Example 47.34: Loans previously reclassified from trading under IAS 39

At the date of initial application of IFRS 9, a bank holds a portfolio of loans that it intends to sell as soon as possible, but is currently unable to do so due to illiquidity in the market. The bank had taken advantage of the October 2008 amendments to IAS 39 and because it had the intention and ability to hold the assets for the foreseeable future had reclassified this portfolio from trading to loans and receivables.

An entity applying IFRS 9 for the first time should apply the business model assessment at the date of initial application. Given management's intention to sell the assets as soon as possible, the presumption would be that the portfolio should be classified as at fair value through profit or loss. It does not matter that the bank may have to hold the portfolio for the foreseeable future due to the market's illiquidity. The standard is clear that the entity's objective should be to hold the assets to collect the contractual cash flows to qualify for amortised cost classification. Such a portfolio would not meet the fair value through other comprehensive income criteria either if the intention is to sell all of the financial assets in the near term.

Example 47.35: Loans held within a business intended for disposal

An international bank has a variety of businesses each of which is managed separately. Before the date of initial application of IFRS 9, the bank makes a strategic decision to dispose of its auto finance business, which originates loans. The portfolio of loans is held under a business model whose objective is to collect their contractual cash flows. The bank intends to dispose of the entire business, including personnel, IT systems and buildings, and not merely a portfolio of loans.

There is no 'right' answer in respect of these facts and circumstances. Arguments can be articulated to support either classification of the loans at amortised cost or at fair value through profit or loss.

Proponents of amortised cost classification would argue that, at the date of initial application, even though the bank intends to sell the business at some point in the future, the loans are still held within a business model whose objective is to hold them to collect their contractual cash flows. That objective continues regardless of whether the bank intends or is able to sell the business. In addition, some of the loans may be fully collected even before the business is sold. Therefore, based on facts and circumstances at the date of initial application, the loans are considered to be held within a business model whose objective is to hold them to collect their contractual cash flows.

On the other hand, proponents of the fair value through profit or loss classification would argue that on the date of initial application, the expectation is that the bank will dispose of the loans rather than hold them to collect their contractual cash flows. Therefore, from the bank's perspective, the loans are no longer held within a business model whose objective is to hold assets to collect their contractual cash flows.

Due to the diversity in views and the fact that this is a prevailing issue as a result of both regulatory and government initiatives to require banks to dispose of non-core business activities or selected businesses, this is an area where further guidance from the IASB or Interpretations Committee would be welcome.

10.2.3 Applying the contractual cash flow characteristics test

For existing IFRS reporters, there are no transition provisions relating to the application of the contractual cash flow characteristics test. Accordingly, the contractual cash flow characteristics of an asset should be assessed based on conditions at the date of initial recognition, not at the date of initial application. This is likely to have the most effect when assessing contractually linked instruments (see 6.5 above) because their characteristics may have changed significantly between the date of initial recognition and the date of initial application.

At the date of initial application, it may be impracticable (as defined in IAS 8) for an entity to assess a modified time value of money element as described in section 6.4.2 above on the basis of the facts and circumstances that existed at the initial recognition of the financial asset. In such instances, the entity must assess the contractual cash flow characteristics of that financial asset on the basis of the facts and circumstances that existed at the initial recognition of the financial asset. This is done without taking into account the requirements related to the modification of the time value of money element as set out in section 6.4.2 above. *[IFRS 9.7.2.4]*. This means that, in such cases, the entity would apply the assessment of the asset's contractual cash flows characteristics as set out in the original requirements issued in IFRS 9 (2009); i.e. without the notion of a modified economic relationship. *[IFRS 9.BC7.55]*. As a result, the asset would most likely be classified as measured at fair value though profit or loss.

At the date of initial application, it may be impracticable (as defined in IAS 8) for an entity to assess whether the fair value of a prepayment feature was insignificant, as described in section 6.4.4 above, on the basis of the facts and circumstances that existed at the initial recognition of the financial asset. If this is the case, an entity shall assess the contractual cash flow characteristics of that financial asset on the basis of the facts and circumstances that existed at the initial recognition of the financial asset. The entity would not take into account the exception for prepayment features. *[IFRS 9.7.2.5]*. This means that the asset would be classified as measured at fair value though profit or loss.

For contractually linked instruments, on initial application of the standard, the look-through assessment should be performed as at the date that the reporting entity (i.e. the investor in the tranche) initially recognised the contractually linked instrument. It is inappropriate to make the risk assessment based on the circumstances existing either at the date that the arrangement was first established or the date of initial application of IFRS 9.

The situation is slightly different for first-time adopters of IFRS, who are required to apply the contractual cash flow characteristics test to previously acquired assets on the basis of the facts and circumstances that exist at the date of transition to IFRSs (or the beginning of the first IFRS reporting period for entities that choose not to apply IFRS 9 in comparative periods). *[IFRS 1.B8, E1]*.

10.2.4 Making and revoking designations

On application of IFRS 9, entities are required to revisit designations previously made in accordance with IAS 39 and are given an opportunity to make designations in accordance with IFRS 9. More specifically, at the date of initial application:

(a) any previous designation of a financial asset as measured at fair value through profit or loss may be revoked in any case, but must be revoked if such designation does not, or no longer eliminates or significantly reduces an accounting mismatch;

(b) a financial asset or a financial liability may be designated as measured at fair value through profit or loss if such designation would now eliminate or significantly reduce an accounting mismatch;

(c) any previous designation of a financial liability as measured at fair value through profit or loss that was made on the basis that it eliminated or significantly reduced an accounting mismatch may be revoked in any case, but must be revoked if such designation no longer eliminates or significantly reduces an accounting mismatch; and

(d) any investment in a non-derivative equity instrument that is not held for trading may be designated as at fair value through other comprehensive income.

It should be noted that it is not possible to change the previous designation of a financial liability to being measured at fair value through profit or loss on the grounds that it is now managed on a fair value basis.

Such designations and revocations should be made on the basis of the facts and circumstances that exist at the date of initial application and that classification should be applied retrospectively. *[IFRS 9.7.2.8-10]*. For the purposes of (d), an entity should determine whether equity investments meet the definition of held for trading as if they had been acquired at the date of initial application. *[IFRS 9.B7.2.1]*.

At the date of initial application, an entity shall determine whether the own credit requirements of IFRS 9 would create or enlarge an accounting mismatch in profit or loss on the basis of the facts and circumstances that exist at the date of initial application. Those requirements shall be applied retrospectively on the basis of that determination. *[IFRS 9.7.2.14]*.

10.2.5 Restatement of comparatives

Notwithstanding the general requirement to apply the standard retrospectively, an entity that adopts the classification and measurement requirements of IFRS 9 (which include the requirements related to amortised cost measurement for financial assets and expected credit losses as described in Chapter 50) shall provide the disclosures set out in IFRS 7 as described in Chapter 54 at 8.1, but need not restate prior periods. An entity may restate prior periods if, and only if, it is possible without the use of hindsight. *[IFRS 9.7.2.15]*.

Where prior periods are not restated, any difference between the previous reported carrying amounts and the new carrying amounts of financial assets and liabilities at the beginning of the annual reporting period that includes the date of initial application should be recognised in the opening retained earnings (or other component of equity, as appropriate) of the annual reporting period that includes the date of initial application. However, if an entity restates prior periods, the restated financial statements must reflect all of the requirements in IFRS 9. *[IFRS 9.7.2.15]*.

Where interim financial reports are prepared in accordance with IAS 34, the requirements in IFRS 9 need not be applied to interim periods prior to the date of initial application, if it is impracticable to do so. *[IFRS 9.7.2.16]*.

Entities adopting IFRS 9 in 2015 and onwards are required to provide additional disclosures showing the changes, as at the date of initial application, in the classification of financial assets and financial liabilities upon transition from the classification and measurement requirements of IAS 39 to those of IFRS 9. These disclosures are required even if an entity chooses to restate the comparative figures for the effect of applying IFRS 9 (see Chapter 54 at 8.1).

10.2.6 Financial instruments derecognised prior to the date of initial application

If an entity decides to restate prior periods or chooses to apply IFRS 9 from other than the beginning of an annual reporting period, it should not apply the standard to financial assets or financial liabilities that have already been derecognised at the date of initial application. *[IFRS 9.7.2.1]*. In other words, following the application of IFRS 9, to the extent those financial assets or financial liabilities were held during any period presented prior to the date of initial application, they will be accounted for under IAS 39.

When the reporting entity elects to restate comparative information or, for example, chooses to apply IFRS 9 from the beginning of an interim reporting period, the effect of derecognition could potentially be confusing for users of the financial statements, Therefore, it may require careful explanation. This is because the information for reporting periods prior to the date of initial application would be prepared on a mixed basis, partially under IFRS 9 (for those financial instruments not derecognised before that date) and partially under IAS 39 (for those financial instruments which have been derecognised prior to that date), reducing the consistency of the information provided.

10.2.7 Transition adjustments and measurement of financial assets and liabilities

10.2.7.A Hybrid financial assets

A hybrid financial asset that is measured at fair value through profit or loss in accordance with IFRS 9, may previously have been accounted for as a host financial asset and a separate embedded derivative in accordance with IAS 39. In these circumstances, if the entity restates prior periods and the fair value of the hybrid contract had not been determined in those comparative reporting periods, at the end of each comparative reporting period the fair value of the hybrid contract is deemed to be the sum of the fair values of the components (i.e. the non-derivative host and the embedded derivative). *[IFRS 9.7.2.6]*.

At the date of initial application, any difference between the fair value of the entire hybrid contract at the date of initial application and the sum of the fair values of the components of the hybrid contract at the date of initial application should be recognised in the opening retained earnings (or other component of equity, as appropriate) of the reporting period of initial application. *[IFRS 9.7.2.7]*.

IFRS 9 abolishes the separation of embedded derivatives from financial assets required by IAS 39. Under IFRS 9, most financial assets with separable embedded derivatives would be required to be classified in their entirety as at fair value through profit or loss. For example, a loan might contain a profit participation feature that provides the lender with an additional return based on a share of profits of the borrower. However, in some cases, it might be possible to renegotiate the transaction as two separate instruments before the transition to IFRS 9 – one instrument being a loan, the host instrument (which could be recorded at amortised cost or fair value through other comprehensive income) and the other being the profit-sharing derivative (to be recorded at fair value through profit or loss). This would only be possible, we believe, if after the renegotiation, the two new instruments are in substance separate financial instruments. Indicators that this is the case would include:

- each instrument can be closed out or transferred separately, which will be a test of commercial practicality as well as legal possibility; or
- there are no clauses that have the effect that the cash flows on one instrument will affect those on the other, except for typical master netting arrangements.

The case for recognising the contracts as two separate financial instruments would be strengthened if the two new contracts were entered into at prevailing market prices, so that the original compound instrument is derecognised under IAS 39 and a gain or loss is recognised when the two new instruments are first recorded at their fair values.

10.2.7.B Financial assets and liabilities measured at amortised cost

It may be impracticable to apply retrospectively the effective interest method to a financial asset or liability that is measured at amortised cost on transition to IFRS 9, e.g. if it was previously classified at fair value through profit or loss. In those circumstances, the fair value of the financial asset or liability at the end of each comparative period should be treated as its gross carrying amount or amortised cost, respectively. Also, the fair value of the financial asset or financial liability at the date of initial application should be treated as its new gross carrying amount or amortised cost, respectively, at that date. *[IFRS 9.7.2.11]*.

Aside from this exception, the effective interest method should be applied retrospectively. This means that for any financial asset reclassified in accordance with the October 2008 amendments to IAS 39, for example from trading to loans and receivables or available-for-sale, the effective interest method should be applied based on the original cost of the asset, not the amounts determined on reclassification. This is because retrospective application means that an entity presents its financial statements as if it had always applied IFRS 9. However, the standard does not have the same reclassification requirements as IAS 39. Hence, the entity has to go back to the date of initial recognition of the financial instrument in order to determine the accounting treatment.

10.2.7.C Unquoted equity investments

An investment in an unquoted equity instrument (or a derivative that is linked to and must be settled by delivery of such an unquoted equity instrument) might previously have been measured at cost in accordance with IAS 39. In those circumstances the instrument should be measured at fair value at the date of initial application of IFRS 9. Any difference between the previous carrying amount and fair value should be recognised in the opening retained earnings (or other component of equity, as appropriate) of the reporting period that includes the date of initial application. *[IFRS 9.7.2.12-13]*. This means that that previous periods cannot be restated. The Board explains that this is because as an entity would not have previously determined the fair value of an investment in an unquoted equity instrument and it will not now have the necessary information to determine fair value retrospectively without using hindsight. *[IFRS 9.BC7.15]*.

Chapter 48 Financial instruments: Recognition and initial measurement

List of examples

Chapter 48 Financial instruments: Recognition and initial measurement

1 INTRODUCTION

The introduction to Chapter 42 provides a general background to the development of accounting for financial instruments. Chapter 43 deals with what qualifies as financial assets and financial liabilities and other contracts that are treated as if they were financial instruments.

This chapter deals with the question of when financial instruments should be recognised in financial statements and their initial measurement under IAS 39 – *Financial Instruments: Recognition and Measurement*, or IFRS 9 – *Financial Instruments* – when applied.

Initial measurement is normally based on the fair value of an instrument and most, but not all, of the detailed requirements of IFRS governing fair values are dealt with in IFRS 13 – *Fair Value Measurement* – which is covered in Chapter 14. IAS 39 (IFRS 9) also contains some requirements addressing fair value measurements of financial instruments and these are covered at 3.2 below.

2 RECOGNITION (IAS 39 AND IFRS 9)

2.1 General requirements

IAS 39 and, when applied, IFRS 9, provide that an entity must recognise a financial asset or a financial liability on its statement of financial position when, and only when, the entity becomes a party to the contractual provisions of the instrument. *[IAS 39.14, IFRS 9.3.1.1]*. Before that, the entity does not have contractual rights or contractual obligations. Hence, there is no financial asset or a financial liability, as defined in IAS 32 – *Financial Instruments: Presentation*, to recognise. IAS 39 (IFRS 9) provides a practical exception to the application of this general principle for 'regular way' purchases of financial assets (see 2.2 below). IAS 39 (IFRS 9) gives the following examples of the more general application of this principle.

2.1.1 Receivables and payables

Unconditional receivables and payables are recognised as assets or liabilities when the entity becomes a party to the contract and, as a consequence, has a legal right to receive or a legal obligation to pay cash. *[IAS 39.AG35(a), IFRS 9.B3.1.2(a)]*.

2.1.2 Firm commitments to purchase or sell goods or services

Under IFRS, assets to be acquired and liabilities to be incurred as a result of a firm commitment to purchase or sell goods or services are generally not recognised until at least one of the parties has performed under the agreement. For example, an entity that receives a firm order for goods or services does not generally recognise an asset for the consideration receivable (and the entity that places the order does not generally recognise a liability for the consideration to be paid) at the time of the commitment, but instead delays recognition until the ordered goods or services have been shipped, delivered or rendered. *[IAS 39.AG35(b), IFRS 9.B3.1.2(b)]*.

This accounting applies on the assumption that the firm commitment to buy or sell non-financial items is not treated as if it were a derivative (see Chapter 43 at 4) nor designated as a hedged item in a fair value hedge (see Chapter 52 at 4.1 and Chapter 53 at 8). Where the firm commitment is treated as a derivative or designated as a hedged item in a fair value hedge, it would be recognised as an asset or liability before delivery.

2.1.3 Forward contracts

A forward contract is a contract which obliges one party to the contract to buy, and the other party to sell, the asset that is the subject of the contract for a fixed price at a future date.

A forward contract within the scope of IAS 39 (IFRS 9) is recognised as an asset or a liability at commitment date, rather than on settlement. When an entity becomes a party to a forward contract, the fair values of the right and obligation are often equal, so that the net fair value of the forward at inception is zero. If the net fair value of the right and obligation is not zero, the contract is recognised as an asset or liability. *[IAS 39.AG35(c), IFRS 9.B3.1.2(c)]*.

2.1.4 Option contracts

An option contract is a contract which gives one party to the contract the right, but not the obligation, to buy from, or sell to, the other party to the contract the asset that is the subject of the contract for a fixed price at a future date (or during a period of time). An option giving the right to buy an asset is referred to as a 'call' option and one giving the right to sell as a 'put' option. An option is referred to as a 'bought' or 'purchased' option from the perspective of the party with the right to buy or sell (the 'holder') and as a 'written' option from the perspective of the party with the potential obligation to buy or sell. An option is referred to as 'in the money' when it would be in the holder's interest to exercise it and as 'out of the money' when it would not be in the holder's interest to exercise it.

Under IAS 39 (IFRS 9) an option is:

- 'deeply in the money' when it is so far in the money that it is highly unlikely to go out of the money before expiry; *[IAS 39.AG40(d), IFRS 9.B3.2.5(d)]* and
- 'deeply out of the money' when it is so far out of the money that it is highly unlikely to become in the money before expiry. *[IAS 39.AG39(c), IFRS 9.B3.2.4(c)]*.

IAS 39 does not elaborate on what it means by 'highly unlikely' in this context, although the implementation guidance clarifies that 'highly probable' (in the context of a 'highly probable forecast transaction' subject to a hedge) indicates a much greater likelihood of happening than the term 'more likely than not'. *[IAS 39.F.3.7]*.

Option contracts that are within the scope of IAS 39 (IFRS 9) are recognised as assets or liabilities when the holder or writer becomes a party to the contract. *[IAS 39.AG35(d), IFRS 9.B3.1.2(d)]*.

2.1.5 *Planned future transactions (forecast transactions)*

Planned future transactions, no matter how likely, are not assets and liabilities because the entity has not become a party to a contract. They are therefore not recognised under IAS 39 (IFRS 9). *[IAS 39.AG35(e), IFRS 9.B3.1.2(e)]*. However, transactions that have been entered into as a hedge of certain 'highly probable' future transactions are recognised under IAS 39 (IFRS 9) – this raises the issue of the accounting treatment of any gains or losses arising on such hedging transactions (see Chapter 52 at 4.2 and Chapter 53 at 8).

2.1.6 *Treatment by transferee of transfers of financial assets not qualifying for derecognition by transferor (symmetry of recognition and derecognition of transferred assets)*

IAS 39 (IFRS 9) states that, where a financial asset is transferred from one party to another in circumstances where the transferor does not derecognise the asset, the transferee should not recognise the transferred asset. Instead, the transferee derecognises the cash or other consideration paid and recognises a receivable from the transferor. If the transferor has both a right and an obligation to reacquire control of the entire transferred asset for a fixed amount (such as under a repurchase agreement – see Chapter 51 at 4.1), the transferee may account for its receivable as a loan or receivable. *[IAS 39.AG34, AG50, IFRS 9.B3.1.1, B3.2.15]*.

Underlying this requirement appears to be a concern that more than one party cannot satisfy the criteria in IAS 39 (IFRS 9) for recognition of the same financial asset at the same time. In fact, however, this principle may not hold in all circumstances, since it is common for the same assets to be simultaneously recognised by more than one entity – for example if the transferor adopts settlement date accounting and the transferee trade date accounting (see 2.2 below).

Chapter 48

2.2 'Regular way' transactions

A *regular way purchase or sale* is defined as a purchase or sale of a financial asset under a contract whose terms require delivery of the asset within the time frame established generally by regulation or convention in the marketplace concerned. *[IAS 39.9, IFRS 9 Appendix A]*. A contract that can be settled by net settlement (i.e. payment or receipt of cash or other financial assets equivalent to the change in value of the contract) is not a regular way transaction, but a derivative accounted for in accordance with the requirements of IAS 39 (IFRS 9) in respect of derivatives (see Chapter 49 at 2.1 and Chapter 50 at 2.1). *[IAS 39.AG54, IFRS 9.B3.1.4]*.

Many financial markets provide a mechanism whereby all transactions in certain financial instruments (particularly quoted equities and bonds) entered into on a particular date are settled a fixed number of days after that date. The date on which the agreement is entered into is called the 'trade date' and the date on which it is settled by delivery of the assets that are the subject of the agreement is called the 'settlement date'. *[IAS 39.AG55, 56, IFRS 9.B3.1.5, B3.1.6]*.

One effect of this system is that, while legal title to the assets that are the subject of the transaction passes only on or after settlement date, the buyer is effectively exposed to the risks and rewards of ownership of the assets from trade date. For example, suppose that an entity enters into a contract to purchase a financial asset and later, but before settlement date, decides that it no longer requires that asset and therefore enters into a second contract to sell the asset immediately after it is received. The price of the second contract will be influenced, *inter alia*, by movements in the market value of the asset between the trade date of the first contract and that of the second, so that the entity will make a gain or incur a loss just as if it had actually owned the asset in that period.

Absent any special provisions, the accounting analysis for such transactions under IAS 39 (IFRS 9) would be that, between trade date and settlement date, an entity has a forward contract to purchase an asset (see 2.1.3 above) which, in common with all derivatives, should be recorded at fair value, with all changes in fair value recognised in profit or loss (see Chapter 49 at 2.1 and Chapter 50 at 2.1), unless the special rules for hedge accounting apply (see Chapters 52 and 53). This would not only be somewhat onerous but would also have the effect that changes in a financial asset's fair value between trade date and settlement date would be recognised in profit or loss, even though the asset itself is not measured at fair value through profit or loss.

To avoid this, IAS 39 (IFRS 9) permits assets subject to regular way transactions to be recognised, or derecognised, either as at the trade date ('trade date accounting') or as at the settlement date ('settlement date accounting'). *[IAS 39.38, IAS 39.AG55, AG56, IFRS 9.B3.1.3, B3.1.5, B3.1.6]*. Whichever method is used, it is applied consistently and symmetrically (i.e. to acquisitions and disposals) to each of the main categories of financial asset identified by IAS 39 – i.e. held for trading, designated at fair value through profit or loss, held-to-maturity, loans and receivables and available-for-sale (see Chapter 46) *[IAS 39.AG53]* – or, when applied, by IFRS 9 – i.e. *mandatorily* measured at amortised cost, at fair value through other comprehensive income (FVOCI) or at fair value through profit or loss or *designated* as measured at fair value through profit or loss or at FVOCI (equity investments only) (see Chapter 47). *[IFRS 9.B3.1.3]*.

The above requirements apply only to transactions in financial assets. IAS 39 does not contain any specific requirements about trade date accounting and settlement date accounting for transactions in financial instruments that are classified as financial liabilities. Therefore, the general recognition and derecognition requirements for financial liabilities in IAS 39 (IFRS 9) normally apply. *[IAS 39.B.32, IFRS 9.B.32]*. Therefore, financial liabilities are normally recognised on the date the entity 'becomes a party to the contractual provisions of the instrument' (see 2.1 above) and are derecognised only when they are extinguished, i.e. when the obligation specified in the contract is discharged, cancelled or expires (see Chapter 51 at 6).

In January 2007, the IFRS Interpretations Committee addressed the accounting for short sales of securities when the transaction terms require delivery of the securities within the time frame established generally by regulation or convention in the marketplace concerned.

Constituents explained that in practice, many entities apply trade date accounting to such transactions. Specifically, industry practice recognised the short sales as financial liabilities at fair value with changes in fair value recognised in profit or loss. Profit or loss would be the same as if short sales were accounted for as derivatives, but the securities are presented differently on the statement of financial position. Those constituents argued that a short sale is created by a transaction in a financial asset and hence the implementation guidance noted in the previous paragraph is not relevant.

The Committee acknowledged that requiring entities to account for short positions as derivatives may create considerable practical problems for their accounting systems and controls with little, if any, improvement to the quality of financial information presented. For these reasons, and because there is little diversity in practice, the Committee decided not to take the issue onto its agenda and thus industry practice remains prevalent.[1]

2.2.1 *Trade date accounting*

As noted above, the trade date is the date on which an entity commits itself to purchase or sell an asset. Trade date accounting requires:

(a) in respect of an asset to be bought: recognition on the trade date of the asset and the liability to pay for it, which means that during the period between trade date and settlement date, the entity accounts for the asset as if it already owned it; and

(b) in respect of an asset to be sold: derecognition on the trade date of the asset, together with recognition of any gain or loss on disposal and the recognition of a receivable from the buyer for payment.

IAS 39 (IFRS 9) notes that, generally, interest does not start to accrue on the asset and corresponding liability until the settlement date when title passes. *[IAS 39.AG55, IFRS 9.B3.1.5]*.

2.2.2 *Settlement date accounting*

As noted above, the settlement date is the date that an asset is delivered to or by an entity. Settlement date accounting requires:

(a) in respect of an asset to be bought: the recognition of the asset on the settlement date (i.e. the date it is received by the entity). Any change in the fair value of the asset to be received during the period between the trade date and the settlement date is accounted for in the same way as the acquired asset. In other words: *[IAS 39.57, IAS 39.AG56, IFRS 9.5.7.4, IFRS 9.B3.1.6]*

- for assets carried at cost or amortised cost, the change in fair value is not recognised (other than impairment losses);
- for assets classified as financial assets at fair value through profit or loss, the change in fair value is recognised in profit or loss; and
- for available-for-sale assets (IAS 39) and financial assets measured at FVOCI (IFRS 9), the change in fair value is recognised in other comprehensive income (OCI).

(b) in respect of an asset to be sold: derecognition of the asset, recognition of any gain or loss on disposal and the recognition of a receivable from the buyer for payment on the settlement date (i.e. the date it is delivered by the entity). *[IAS 39.AG56, IFRS 9.B3.1.6]*. A change in the fair value of the asset between trade

Chapter 48

date and settlement date is not recorded in the financial statements because the seller's right to changes in the fair value ceases on the trade date. *[IAS 39.D.2.2, IFRS 9.D.2.2]*.

2.2.3 *Illustrative examples*

Examples 48.1 and 48.2 below (which are based on those in the implementation guidance appended to IAS 39 (IFRS 9)) illustrate the application of trade date and settlement date accounting to the various categories of financial asset identified by IAS 39 (IFRS 9). *[IAS 39.D.2.1, D.2.2, IFRS 9.D.2.1, D.2.2]*. The accounting treatment for these categories of asset is discussed in more detail in Chapter 46 and Chapter 47.

Example 48.1: Trade date and settlement date accounting – regular way purchase

On 29 December 2017 (trade date), an entity commits itself to purchase a financial asset for €1,000, which is its fair value on trade date. On 31 December 2017 (financial year-end) and on 4 January 2018 (settlement date) the fair value of the asset is €1,002 and €1,003, respectively. The accounting entries required to be recorded for the transaction will depend on how it is classified and whether trade date or settlement date accounting is used, as shown in the tables below:

A Financial asset accounted for at amortised cost

	Trade date accounting			*Settlement date accounting*		
		€	€		€	€
29 December 2017						
	Financial asset	1,000				
	Liability to counterparty		1,000			
	To record purchase of asset and liability thereof			*No accounting entries*		
31 December 2017						
	No accounting entries			*No accounting entries*		
4 January 2018						
	Liability to counterparty	1,000		Financial asset	1,000	
	Cash		1,000	Cash		1,000
	To record settlement of liability			*To record purchase of asset*		

B Financial asset accounted for at fair value through profit or loss

	Trade date accounting			*Settlement date accounting*		
		€	€		€	€
29 December 2017						
	Financial asset	1,000				
	Liability to counterparty		1,000			
	To record purchase of asset and liability thereof			*No accounting entries*		
31 December 2017						
	Financial Asset	2		Receivable	2	
	Income statement		2	Income statement		2
	To record change in fair value of asset			*To record change in fair value of contract*		

	€	€		€	€
4 January 2018					
Liability to counterparty	1,000		Financial asset	1,003	
Cash		1,000	Cash		1,000
Financial asset	1		Receivable		2
Income statement		1	Income statement		1
To record settlement of liability and change in fair value of asset			*To record purchase of asset, change in fair value and settlement of contract*		

C Debt instrument measured at fair value through other comprehensive income *

Trade date accounting	€	€	*Settlement date accounting*	€	€
29 December 2017					
Financial asset	1,000				
Liability to counterparty		1,000			
To record purchase of asset and liability thereof			*No accounting entries*		
31 December 2017					
Financial Asset	2		Receivable	2	
OCI		2	OCI		2
To record change in fair value of asset			*To record change in fair value of contract*		
4 January 2018					
Liability to counterparty	1,000		Financial asset	1,003	
Cash		1,000	Cash		1,000
Financial asset	1		Receivable		2
OCI		1	OCI		1
To record settlement of liability and change in fair value of asset			*To record purchase of asset, change in fair value and settlement of contract*		

* The same analysis will apply to financial assets accounted for as available-for-sale under IAS 39 and equity investments measured at FVOCI under IFRS 9.

As illustrated above, for a regular way purchase, the key difference between trade date and settlement date accounting is the timing of recognition of a financial asset. Regardless of the method used, the impact on profit or loss, OCI and net assets is the same.

Chapter 48

Example 48.2: Trade date and settlement date accounting – regular way sale

On 29 December 2017 (trade date) an entity enters into a contract to sell a financial asset for its then current fair value of €1,010. The asset was acquired one year earlier for €1,000 and its amortised cost is €1,000. On 31 December 2017 (financial year-end), the fair value of the asset is €1,012. On 4 January 2018 (settlement date), the fair value is €1,013. The amounts to be recorded will depend on how the asset is classified and whether trade date or settlement date accounting is used as shown in the tables below (any interest that might have accrued on the asset is disregarded).

A change in the fair value of a financial asset that is sold on a regular way basis is not recorded in the financial statements between trade date and settlement date, even if the entity applies settlement date accounting, because the seller's right to changes in the fair value ceases on the trade date.

A Financial asset accounted for at amortised cost

Trade date accounting	€	€	*Settlement date accounting*	€	€
Before 29 December 2017 (cumulative net entries)					
Financial asset	1,000		Financial asset	1,000	
Cash		1,000	Cash		1,000
To record acquisition of the asset a year earlier			*To record acquisition of the asset a year earlier*		
29 December 2017					
Receivable from counterparty	1,010				
Financial asset		1,000			
Gain on disposal (income statement)		10			
To record disposal of asset			*No accounting entries*		
4 January 2018					
Cash	1,010		Cash	1,010	
Receivable from counterparty		1,010	Financial asset		1,000
			Gain on disposal (income statement)		10
To record settlement of sale contract			*To record disposal of asset*		

B Financial asset accounted for at fair value through profit or loss

Trade date accounting	€	€	*Settlement date accounting*	€	€
Before 29 December 2017 (cumulative net entries)					
Financial asset	1,010		Financial asset	1,010	
Cash		1,000	Cash		1,000
Income statement		10	Income statement		10
To record acquisition and net change in fair value up to date			*To record acquisition and net change in fair value up to date*		
29 December 2017					
Receivable from counterparty	1,010				
Financial asset		1,010			
To record disposal of asset			*No accounting entries*		
4 January 2018					
Cash	1,010		Cash	1,010	
Receivable from counterparty		1,010	Financial asset		1,010
To record settlement of sale contract			*To record disposal of asset*		

C Debt instrument measured at fair value through other comprehensive income *

	Trade date accounting	€	€	Settlement date accounting	€	€
Before 29 December 2017 (cumulative net entries)						
	Financial asset	1,010		Financial asset	1,010	
	Cash		1,000	Cash		1,000
	OCI		10	OCI		10

	Trade date accounting	€	€	Settlement date accounting	€	€
29 December 2017						
	Receivable from counterparty	1,010				
	Financial asset		1,010			
**	OCI	10				
	Gain on sale (income statement)		10			
	To record disposal of asset			*No accounting entries*		
4 January 2018						
	Cash	1,010		Cash	1,010	
	Receivable from counterparty		1,010	Financial asset		1,010
**				OCI	10	
				Gain on sale (income statement)		10
	To record settlement of sale contract			*To record disposal of asset*		

* The same analysis will apply to financial assets accounted for as available-for-sale under IAS 39 and equity investments measured at FVOCI under IFRS 9, except that for the latter, IFRS 9 does not permit 'recycling' (i.e. transfers) of cumulative gains and losses from OCI to profit or loss. However, an entity may transfer the cumulative gains and losses within equity (e.g. from accumulated OCI to retained earnings).

** The transfers from OCI to profit or loss (retained earnings) represent the 'recycling' of cumulative gains and losses required by IFRS 9 on disposal of a debt instrument accounted for at FVOCI (see Chapter 50 at 2.3) (or an available-for-sale asset under IAS 39 (see Chapter 49 at 2.4)). Disposal is regarded as occurring on trade date when trade date accounting applies and on settlement date when settlement date accounting applies.

As illustrated above, for a regular way sale, the key differences between trade date and settlement date accounting relate to the timing of derecognition of a financial asset and the timing of recognition of any gain or loss arising from the disposal of the financial asset.

2.2.3.A Exchanges of non-cash financial assets

The implementation guidance to IAS 39 (IFRS 9) addresses the situation in which an entity enters into a regular way transaction whereby it commits to sell a non-cash financial asset in exchange for another non-cash financial asset.

This raises the question of whether, if the entity applies settlement date accounting to the asset to be delivered, it should recognise any change in the fair value of the financial asset to be received arising between trade date and settlement date. A further issue is that the asset being bought may be in a category of asset to which trade date accounting is applied.

The implementation guidance essentially requires the buying and selling legs of the exchange transaction to be accounted for independently, as illustrated by the following example *[IAS 39.D.2.3, IFRS 9.D.2.3]*.

Example 48.3: Trade date and settlement date accounting – exchange of non-cash financial assets

On 29 December 2017 (trade date), an entity enters into a contract to sell Note Receivable A, which is carried at amortised cost, in exchange for Bond B, which will be classified as held for trading and measured at fair value. Both assets have a fair value of €1,010 on 29 December 2017, while the amortised cost of Note Receivable A is €1,000. The entity uses settlement date accounting for loans and receivables and trade date accounting for assets held for trading.

On 31 December 2017 (financial year-end), the fair value of Note Receivable A is €1,012 and the fair value of Bond B is €1,009. On 4 January 2018 (settlement date), the fair value of Note Receivable A is €1,013 and the fair value of Bond B is €1,007.

The following entries are made:

	€	€
29 December 2017		
Bond B	1,010	
Liability to counterparty		1,010
To record purchase of Bond B (trade date accounting)		
31 December 2017		
Loss on Bond B (income statement)	1	
Bond B		1
To record change in fair value of Bond B		
4 January 2018		
Liability to counterparty	1,010	
Note Receivable A		1,000
Gain on disposal (income statement)		10
To record disposal of receivable A (settlement date accounting)		
Loss on Bond B (income statement)	2	
Bond B		2
To record change in fair value of Bond B		

The simultaneous recognition, between 29 December and 4 January, of both the asset being bought and the asset being given in consideration may seem counter-intuitive. However, it is no different from the accounting treatment of any purchase of goods for credit which results, in the period between delivery of, and payment for, the goods, in the simultaneous recognition of the goods, the liability to pay the supplier and the cash that will be used to do so.

3 INITIAL MEASUREMENT (IAS 39 AND IFRS 9)

3.1 General requirements

On initial recognition, financial assets and financial liabilities at fair value through profit or loss are normally measured at their fair value on the date they are initially recognised. The initial measurement of other financial instruments is also based on their fair value, but adjusted in respect of any transaction costs that are incremental and directly attributable to the acquisition or issue of the instrument. *[IAS 39.43]*. Where IFRS 15 – *Revenue from Contracts with Customers* – is applied, IAS 39 and IFRS 9 specifically exclude from this requirement trade receivables that do not have a significant financing component. Such trade receivables should be measured at initial recognition at their transaction price net of transaction costs as defined by IFRS 15. *[IAS 39.43, 44A, IFRS 9.5.1.1, 5.1.3]*.

3.2 Initial fair value and 'day 1' profits

IAS 39 (IFRS 9) and IFRS 13 acknowledge that the best evidence of the fair value of a financial instrument on initial recognition is normally the transaction price (i.e. the fair value of the consideration given or received), although this will not necessarily be the case in all circumstances (see Chapter 14 at 13.1.1). *[IAS 39.AG64, IFRS 9.B5.1.1, IFRS 13.58]*. Although, IFRS 13 specifies how to measure fair value, IAS 39 (IFRS 9) contains restrictions on recognising differences between the transaction price and the initial fair value as measured under IFRS 13, often called day 1 profits, which apply in addition to the requirements of IFRS 13 (see Chapter 14 at 13.2). *[IFRS 13.60, BC138]*.

If an entity determines that the fair value on initial recognition differs from the transaction price, the difference is recognised as a gain or loss only if the fair value is based on a quoted price in an active market for an identical asset or liability (i.e. a Level 1 input) or based on a valuation technique that uses only data from observable markets. Otherwise, the difference is deferred and recognised as a gain or loss only to the extent that it arises from a change in a factor (including time) that market participants would take into account when pricing the asset or liability. *[IAS 39.43A, AG76, IFRS 9.5.1.1A, B5.1.2A]*. The subsequent measurement and the subsequent recognition of gains and losses should be consistent with the requirements of IAS 39 (IFRS 9) that are covered in detail in Chapter 49 and Chapter 50. *[IAS 39.AG76A, IFRS 9.B5.2.2A]*.

Therefore, entities that trade in financial instruments are prevented from immediately recognising a profit on the initial recognition of many financial instruments that are not quoted in active markets. Consequently, locked-in profits will emerge over the life of the financial instruments, although precisely how they should emerge is not at all clear. The IASB was asked to clarify that straight-line amortisation was an appropriate method of recognising the day 1 profits but decided not to do so. Somewhat unhelpfully, it stated (without further explanation) that although straight-line amortisation may be an appropriate method in some cases, it will not be appropriate in others. *[IAS 39.BC222(v)(ii)]*.

3.2.1 Interest-free and low-interest long-term loans

As noted in 3.2 above, the fair value of a financial instrument on initial recognition is normally the transaction price. IAS 39 (IFRS 9) explains further that if part of the consideration given or received was for something other than the financial instrument, the entity should measure the fair value of the financial instrument in accordance with IFRS 13. For example, the fair value of a long-term loan or receivable that carries no interest could be estimated as the present value of all future cash receipts discounted using the prevailing market rate(s) of interest for instruments that are similar as to currency, term, type of interest rate, credit risk and other factors. Any additional amount advanced is an expense or a reduction of income unless it qualifies for recognition as some other type of asset. IFRS 13 requires the application of a similar approach in such circumstances. *[IAS 39.AG64, IFRS 9.B5.1.1, IFRS 13.60]*. For example, an entity may provide an interest free loan to a supplier in order to receive a discount on goods or services purchased in the future and the difference between the fair value and the amount advanced might well be recognised as an asset, for example under IAS 38 – *Intangible Assets* – if the entity obtains a contractual right to the discounted supplies.

Similar issues often arise from transactions between entities under common control. In fact, IFRS 13 suggests a related party transaction may indicate that the transaction price is not the same as the fair value of an asset or liability (see Chapter 14 at 13.3). For example, parents sometimes lend money to subsidiaries on an interest-free or low-interest basis where the loan is not repayable on demand. Where, in its separate financial statements, the parent (or subsidiary) is required to record a receivable (or payable) on initial recognition at a fair value that is lower than cost, the additional consideration will normally represent an additional investment in the subsidiary (or equity contribution from the parent).

Another example is a loan received from a government that has a below-market rate of interest which should be recognised and initially measured at fair value in accordance with IAS 39 (IFRS 9). The benefit of the below-market rate loan, i.e. the excess of the consideration received over the initial carrying amount of the loan, should be accounted for as a government grant. *[IAS 20.10A]*. The treatment of government grants is discussed further in Chapter 26.

If a financial instrument is recognised where the terms are 'off-market' (i.e. the consideration given or received does not equal the instrument's fair value) but instead a fee is paid or received in compensation, the instrument should be recognised at its fair value that includes an adjustment for the fee received or paid. *[IAS 39.AG65, IFRS 9.B5.1.2]*.

Example 48.4: Off-market loan with origination fee

Bank J lends $1,000 to Company K. The loan carries interest at 5% and is repayable in full in five years' time, even though the market rate for similar loans is 8%. To compensate J for the below market rate of interest, K pays J an origination fee of $120. There are no other directly related payments by either party.

The loan is recorded at its fair value of $880 (in this example, assumed to be the net present value of $50 interest payable annually for five years and $1,000 principal repaid after five years, all discounted at 8%). This equals the net amount of cash exchanged ($1,000 loan less $120 origination fee) and hence no gain or loss is recognised on initial recognition of the loan.

Example 48.4 has been extrapolated from the example in IAS 39.AG65 and IFRS 9.B5.1.2.

Applying the requirements of IAS 39 (IFRS 9) to the simple fact pattern provided by the IASB is a relatively straightforward exercise. In practice, however, it may be more difficult to identify those fees that are required by IAS 39 (IFRS 9) to be treated as part of the financial instrument and those that should be dealt with in another way, for example under IAS 18 – *Revenue* (IFRS 15). In particular it may be difficult to determine the extent to which fees associated with a financial instrument that is not quoted in an active market represent compensation for off-market terms or for the genuine provision of services.

3.2.2 Measurement of financial instruments following modification of contractual terms that leads to initial recognition of a new instrument

An entity may agree (with the holder or the issuer) to modify the terms of an instrument that it already recognises in its financial statements as a financial asset, a financial liability or an equity instrument. In such a scenario, an entity needs to consider whether the modification of the terms triggers derecognition of the existing instrument and recognition of a new instrument (see Chapter 51 at 3.4.1). If so, the new instrument would be initially measured at fair value in accordance with the general requirements discussed at 3.1 above.

For example, when the contractual terms of an issued equity instrument are modified such that it is subsequently reclassified as a financial liability, it should be measured at its fair value on the date it is initially recognised *as a financial liability*, with any difference between this amount and the amount recorded in equity being taken to equity. This follows IAS 32 which prohibits the recognition of gains or losses on the purchase, issue, or cancellation of an entity's own equity instrument.[2]

Example 48.5: Changes in the contractual terms of an existing equity instrument

On 1 January 2016, Company L issues a fixed rate cumulative perpetual instrument with a face value of £10 million at par. Dividends on the instrument are cumulative but discretionary and therefore it is initially classified as equity. On 1 January 2017, L adds a new clause to the instrument so that if L is subject to a change of control, L will be required to redeem the instrument at an amount equal to the face value plus any accumulated unpaid dividends. This results in a reclassification of the instrument from equity to liability. The fair value of the instrument on 1 January 2017 is £12 million.

Upon reclassification, L should recognise the financial liability at its then fair value of £12 million and the difference of £2 million is recognised in equity (e.g. retained earnings).

The accounting for a modification of a financial asset (or financial liability) that results in the recognition of a new financial asset (or financial liability) is dealt with in more detail in Chapter 51 at 3.4 and 6.2.

3.2.3 Financial guarantee contracts and off-market loan commitments

The requirement to measure financial instruments at fair value on initial recognition also applies to issued financial guarantee contracts that are within the scope of IAS 39 (IFRS 9) as well as to commitments to provide a loan at a below-market interest rate (see Chapter 43 at 3.4 and 3.5).

When issued to an unrelated party in a stand-alone arm's length transaction, the fair value of a financial guarantee contract at inception is likely to equal the premium received, unless there is evidence to the contrary. *[IAS 39.AG4(a)]*. There is likely to be such evidence where, say, a parent provided to a bank a financial guarantee in respect of its subsidiary's borrowings and charged no fee.

When an off-market loan is provided to an entity's subsidiary (see 3.2.1 above), a 'spare debit' arises in the separate financial statements of the parent as a result of the recognition of the loan at fair value. The same situation can arise when a parent provides a subsidiary with an off-market loan commitment. Again, it is normally appropriate to treat this difference as an additional cost of investment in the subsidiary (and as an equity contribution from the parent in the accounts of the subsidiary).

3.2.4 Loans and receivables acquired in a business combination

Consistent with IAS 39 (IFRS 9) and IFRS 13, IFRS 3 – *Business Combinations* – requires financial assets acquired in a business combination to be measured by the acquirer on initial recognition at their fair value. *[IFRS 3.18, IFRS 3.36]*.

IFRS 3 contains application guidance explaining that an acquirer should not recognise a separate valuation allowance (i.e. bad debt provision) in respect of loans and receivables for contractual cash flows that are deemed to be uncollectible at the acquisition date. This is because the effects of uncertainty about future cash flows are included in the fair value measure (see Chapter 9 at 5.5.5 and Chapter 50 at 5.6.3). *[IFRS 3.B41]*.

3.3 Transaction costs

As noted at 3.1 above, the initial carrying amount of an instrument that is not classified at fair value through profit or loss should be adjusted for transaction costs. Consequently, these costs are included in the calculation of the effective interest rate, in effect reducing (increasing) the amount of interest income (expense) recognised over the life of the instrument (for interest-bearing items) or affecting the amount of profit or loss on disposal or impairment (for investments in equity securities). For available-for-sale instruments or financial instruments that are measured at fair value through other comprehensive income, transaction costs are recognised in other comprehensive income as part of the change in fair value at the next remeasurement. *[IAS 39.IG E.1.1, IFRS 9.IG E.1.1]*. Transaction costs relating to the acquisition or incurrence of financial instruments at fair value through profit or loss are recognised in profit or loss as they are incurred.

Transaction costs are defined as incremental costs that are directly attributable to the acquisition, issue or disposal of a financial asset or liability. An incremental cost is one that would not have been incurred had the financial instrument not been acquired, issued or disposed of. *[IAS 39.9, IFRS 9 Appendix A]*. Expenses that would be incurred on the subsequent transfer or disposal of a financial instrument are not transaction costs. *[IAS 39.E.1.1, IFRS 9.E.1.1]*.

Example 48.6: Transaction costs – initial measurement

Company A acquires an equity security that will be classified as available-for-sale (or, if IFRS 9 is applied, measured at fair value through other comprehensive income). The security has a fair value of £100 and this is the amount A is required to pay. In addition, A also pays a purchase commission of £2. If the asset was to be sold, a sales commission of £3 would be payable.

The initial measurement of the asset is £102, i.e. the sum of its initial fair value and the purchase commission. The commission payable on sale is not considered for this purpose. *[IAS 39.AG67, IFRS 9.B5.2.2]*. If A had a reporting date immediately after the purchase of this security it would measure the security at £100 and recognise a loss of £2 in other comprehensive income.

Transaction costs include fees and commissions paid to agents (including employees acting as selling agents), advisers, brokers, and dealers. They also include levies by regulatory agencies and securities exchanges, transfer taxes and duties. Debt premiums or discounts, financing costs and allocations of internal administrative or holding costs are not transaction costs. *[IAS 39.AG13, IFRS 9.B5.4.8]*.

Treating internal costs as transaction costs could open up a number of possibilities for abuse by allowing entities to defer expenses inappropriately. However, it is made clear that internal costs should be treated as transaction costs only if they are incremental and directly attributable to the acquisition, issue or disposal of a financial asset or financial liability. *[IAS 39.BC222(d)]*. Therefore, it will be rare for internal costs (other than, say, commissions paid to sales staff in respect of a product sold that results in the origination or issuance of a financial instrument) to be treated as transaction costs.

3.4 Embedded derivatives and financial instrument hosts

In Chapter 44 at 6, it was explained that, in accordance with IAS 39 for financial assets and financial liabilities and as required by IFRS 9 for financial liabilities, the terms of an embedded derivative that is required to be separated and the associated host should be determined so that the derivative is initially recorded at its fair value and the host as the residual (at least for an optional derivative – a non-option embedded derivative will have a fair value and initial carrying amount of zero). *[IAS 39.AG28, IFRS 9.B4.3.3]*. Separation does not apply to embedded derivatives with financial asset hosts under IFRS 9.

The standard does not clarify what it is that entities are meant to be determining the residual of. In two separate instances, the implementation guidance suggests that a host financial instrument should be recognised as the residual of the *purchase price* after adjusting for the fair value of the embedded derivative. *[IAS 39.C.3, C.5]*. This does not correctly reflect the requirements of IAS 39 (IFRS 9) (which require measurement to be based on the instrument's fair value, not its purchase price – see 3.1 above) but this could be seen as little more than an oversight on the part of the IASB. We suspect the IASB's most likely intention was that the host should initially be measured based on the residual of the *fair value* of the hybrid instrument (which, admittedly, will normally equal its purchase price) adjusted for any transaction costs and also after adjusting for the fair value of the embedded derivative.

3.5 Regular way transactions

When settlement date accounting is used for 'regular way' transactions (see 2.2.2 above) and those transactions result in the recognition of assets that are subsequently measured at amortised cost or (very rarely) at cost, there is an exception to the general requirement to measure the asset on initial recognition at its fair value (see 3.1 above).

In such circumstances, rather than being initially measured by reference to their fair value on the date they are first recognised, i.e. settlement date, these financial instruments are initially measured by reference to their fair value on the trade date. *[IAS 39.44, IFRS 9.5.1.2]*.

Chapter 48

In practice, the difference will rarely be significant because of the short time scale involved between trade date and settlement date. It is because of this short duration that regular way transactions are not recognised as derivative financial instruments, but accounted for as set out at 2.2 above. *[IAS 39.AG12, IFRS 9.BA.4]*.

3.6 Assets and liabilities arising from loan commitments

Loan commitments are a form of derivative financial instrument, although for pragmatic reasons the IASB decided that certain loan commitments could be excluded from the recognition requirements of IAS 39 (IFRS 9) (see Chapter 43 at 3.5).

IAS 39 requires an issuer of loan commitments not within the scope of the recognition requirements of the Standard to apply IAS 37 – *Provisions, Contingent Liabilities and Contingent Assets* – to such loan commitments (see Chapter 28). *[IAS 39.2(h)]*. However, IFRS 9 requires an issuer to apply the impairment rules of IFRS 9 (see Chapter 50) to such loan commitments. *[IFRS 9.2.1(g)]*.

The exclusion of loan commitments from the recognition requirements creates a degree of confusion over how assets and liabilities arising from such arrangements should be measured on initial recognition, as illustrated in the following example.

Example 48.7: Drawdown under a committed borrowing facility (IAS 39)

Company H obtains from Bank Q a committed facility allowing it to borrow up to €10,000 at any time over the following five years, provided certain covenants specified in the facility agreement are not breached. Interest on any drawdowns is payable at LIBOR plus a fixed margin, representing Q's initial assessment of H's credit risk. Any such borrowings can be repaid at any time at the option of H, but must be repaid by the end of five years unless the facility is renegotiated and extended. They also become repayable immediately in the event that H breaches the covenants. For the purposes of this illustration, any other amounts payable by H to Q (such as non-utilisation fees) have been ignored.

Both H and Q choose to exclude the commitment from the requirements of IAS 39 and any asset or liability arising from drawdowns under the facility will be classified within loans and receivables by Q and within other liabilities by H. Q applies IAS 37 and assesses whether the facility is an onerous contract (e.g. by assessing the probability of H's default following a future drawdown). If it were, Q would recognise a provision.

After one year, no drawdowns have been made and H's credit risk has increased (although it has not breached any of the covenants, there is no expectation of default and there are no other reasons to consider it an onerous contract as defined in IAS 37). As a result of this change in credit risk, the fair value of the facility is, say, €200 (positive value to H, negative value to Q). Because the commitment is not recognised under IAS 39 and because it is not onerous, nothing is recognised in the accounts of either Q or H in respect of the facility.

Shortly afterwards H draws down the maximum €10,000 available under the facility. Because of the change in credit risk the drawdown results in the recognition of an asset (liability) by Q (H) that has a fair value at that date of, say, €9,800.

The €200 difference between the €9,800 fair value of the financial instrument created and the €10,000 cash transferred effectively represents the change in fair value of the commitment arising from the change in H's credit risk.

Should Q (H) initially measure the resulting asset (liability) at its €9,800 fair value or at €10,000, being the amount of cash actually exchanged? If it is recognised at €9,800, how is the 'spare' €200 accounted for, particularly does Q (H) recognise it as a loss (profit)?

The general requirement noted at 3.1 above would imply that the asset (liability) should initially be measured at €9,800. Consequently a loss (profit) of €200 would be recognised – this is because the spare €200 does not represent any other asset or liability arising from the transaction.

However, the Basis for Conclusions on IAS 39 (IFRS 9), explains that the effect of the loan commitment exception is that, consistent with the likely measurement basis of the resulting loan, the fair value of these commitments from changes in market interest rates or credit spreads will not be recognised or measured. *[IAS 39.BC16, IFRS 9.BCZ2.3]*. This is exactly what the 'spare' €200 represents so, in accordance with the underlying rationale and objective of allowing loan commitments to be excluded from the scope of IAS 39 (IFRS 9), it seems appropriate to initially measure the asset or liability arising in this case at €10,000.

Such treatment is also consistent with that for similar assets arising from regular way transactions recognised using settlement date accounting (see 3.5 above). This is relevant because the IASB introduced the loan commitment exception as a result of issues identified by the IGC and the only solution the IGC could identify at the time involved treating loan commitments as regular way transactions and using settlement date accounting.[3]

If, in the above example, Q (H) accounted for the loan commitment at fair value through profit or loss this issue would not arise. At the time the loan was drawn down the commitment would have already been recognised as a €200 liability (asset) and an equivalent loss (profit) would have been recorded in profit or loss. The loan would then be recognised at its fair value of €9,800 and the €200 balance of the cash movement over this amount would be treated as the settlement of the loan commitment liability (asset previously recognised). Therefore, no further gain or loss would need to be recognised at this point. Until the loan is recognised, the same mechanics apply for IAS 39 and IFRS 9. Under both standards, the loan is recognised at its fair value, but after that, it is subject to either the impairment rules of IAS 39 or the impairment rules of IFRS 9. The latter require recording of the 12-month or lifetime expected loss at the first reporting date after the loan is recognised (see Chapter 50).

References

1 *IFRIC Update*, January 2007.
2 *IFRIC Update*, November 2006.
3 IAS 39 Implementation Guidance Committee (IGC), Q&A 30-1, July 2001.

Chapter 49 Financial instruments: Subsequent measurement (IAS 39)

List of examples

Chapter 49 Financial instruments: Subsequent measurement (IAS 39)

1 INTRODUCTION

Chapter 48 deals with when financial instruments should be recognised in financial statements and their initial measurement.

For entities continuing to apply IAS 39 – *Financial Instruments: Recognition and Measurement* – rather than IFRS 9 – *Financial Instruments*, this chapter deals with the subsequent measurement requirements of the standard. This includes the requirements relating to amortised cost and the effective interest method, impairment, and foreign currency considerations. The related question of when a previously recognised financial instrument should be derecognised from financial statements is dealt with in Chapter 51.

Most, but not all, of the detailed requirements of IFRS governing the measurement of fair values are dealt with in IFRS 13 – *Fair Value Measurement* – which is covered in Chapter 14. IAS 39 also contains some requirements addressing fair value measurements of financial instruments and these are covered at 2.6 below.

2 SUBSEQUENT MEASUREMENT AND RECOGNITION OF GAINS AND LOSSES

As set out in Chapter 46, IAS 39 requires financial assets to be classified into one of the following four categories: *[IAS 39.45]*

- at fair value through profit or loss;
- held-to-maturity investments;
- loans and receivables; and
- available-for-sale assets.

Financial liabilities that are within the scope of IAS 39 are classified either at fair value through profit or loss or as other financial liabilities.

Following the initial recognition of financial assets and financial liabilities, their subsequent accounting treatment depends principally on the classification of the instrument, although there are a small number of exceptions. *[IAS 39.46, 47]*. These requirements are summarised in the following table and are considered in more detail in the remainder of this section.

Classification	Instrument type	Statement of financial position	Fair value gains and losses	Interest and dividends	Impairment	Foreign exchange
At fair value through profit or loss (including derivatives that are not designated in effective hedges)	Debt, Equity or Derivative	Fair value	Profit or loss*	Profit or loss*	Profit or loss* (assets)	Profit or loss*
	Equity or equity derivative: not reliably measurable	Cost	–	Profit or loss: dividends receivable	Profit or loss (assets)	–
Held-to-maturity investments	Debt	Amortised cost	–	Profit or loss: effective interest rate	Profit or loss	Profit or loss
Loans and receivables	Debt	Amortised cost	–	Profit or loss: effective interest rate	Profit or loss	Profit or loss
Available-for-sale assets	Debt	Fair value	Other comprehensive income†	Profit or loss: effective interest rate	Profit or loss	Profit or loss
	Equity	Fair value	Other comprehensive income†	Profit or loss: dividends receivable	Profit or loss	Other comprehensive income†
	Equity: not reliably measurable	Cost	–	Profit or loss: dividends receivable	Profit or loss	–
Other financial liabilities	Debt	Amortised cost	–	Profit or loss: effective interest rate	–	Profit or loss

* Little guidance is given on how gains and losses should be disaggregated – see Chapter 54 at 7.1.1.
† Reclassified from equity to profit or loss on disposal or impairment.

In addition, IAS 39 sets out the accounting treatment for certain financial guarantee contracts (see Chapter 43 at 3.4) and commitments to provide a loan at a below market interest rate (see Chapter 43 at 3.5).

2.1 Financial assets and financial liabilities at fair value through profit or loss

After initial recognition, financial assets and financial liabilities that are classified at fair value through profit or loss (including derivatives that are not designated in effective hedging relationships) should, in general, be measured at fair value, with no deduction for sale or disposal costs. Associated gains and losses are recognised in profit or loss. *[IAS 39.46, 55(a)]*.

Investments in equity instruments whose fair value cannot be reliably measured and derivatives that are linked to, and must be settled by delivery of, such instruments (see 2.6 below) are measured at cost less (for assets) any impairment (see 4.4 below). *[IAS 39.46(c), 47(a)]*. If a reliable measure of fair value subsequently becomes available, the instrument should be remeasured at that fair value, and the gain or loss recognised in profit or loss. *[IAS 39.53]*. If a reliable measure ceases to be available, it should thereafter be measured at 'cost', which is deemed to be the fair value carrying amount on that date. *[IAS 39.54]*.

The standard points out that if the fair value of a financial asset falls below zero it becomes a financial liability (assuming it is measured at fair value). *[IAS 39.AG66]*. The only real alternative would be treatment as a negative asset which would not be sensible. Although not explained in the standard, if the fair value of a financial liability becomes positive it is safe to assume that it becomes a financial asset not a negative liability.

2.2 Held-to-maturity investments

The basic requirement for held-to-maturity investments is that they are measured at amortised cost using the effective interest method, although they are also subject to review for impairment. *[IAS 39.46(b)]*. Gains and losses are recognised in profit or loss when the instrument is derecognised or impaired, as well as through the amortisation process. *[IAS 39.56]*.

The effective interest method of accounting is dealt with at 3 below and the impairment requirements of IAS 39 at 4 below.

2.3 Loans and receivables

Loans and receivables are also measured at amortised cost using the effective interest method and are subject to review for impairment with gains and losses recognised in profit or loss when the instrument is derecognised or impaired, as well as through the amortisation process. *[IAS 39.46(a), 56]*. However, in contrast to the treatment for held-to-maturity investments, this method of accounting applies to *all* loans and receivables without regard to whether they are intended to be held until maturity. *[IAS 39.AG68]*.

2.4 Available-for-sale assets

Accounting for available-for-sale assets is slightly more complex. They should, in general, be measured at fair value, with no deduction for sale or disposal costs. *[IAS 39.46]*. Gains and losses arising from changes in fair value (after adjusting for interest accruals, dividends receivable and foreign exchange gains and losses on monetary items) are initially recognised in other comprehensive income. When an asset is derecognised, often by way of sale, or is impaired, the cumulative gain or loss recognised in other comprehensive income is reclassified from equity to profit or loss. *[IAS 39.55(b)]*.

For example, consider an equity security that is purchased for its fair value of €100, has a fair value of €120 at the end of the year and is sold subsequent to the year-end for €130. In the first year a gain of €20 is recognised in other comprehensive income as a result of remeasuring the security at its fair value. In the second year a profit of €30 is recognised in profit or loss. This profit of €30 effectively represents the €10 difference between the proceeds received (€130) and the previous carrying amount of the asset (€120) and the reclassification of the €20 gain from equity. However, the implementation guidance to IAS 1 – *Presentation of Financial Statements* – illustrates that, in principle, the asset should continue to be remeasured at its fair value until the time of disposal. Therefore in the second year a gain of €10 should be recognised in other comprehensive income followed by a reclassification from equity to profit or loss of €30. *[IAS 1.IG7-9]*.

Where appropriate, interest receivable on available-for-sale assets is recognised in profit or loss using the effective interest method (see 3 below), and dividends receivable are recognised in profit or loss when a right to receive payment is established (see Chapter 29 at 3.12). Impairment and foreign currency retranslation are covered in more detail at 4 and 5 below respectively. *[IAS 39.55(b)]*. However, it should be remembered that foreign exchange gains and losses arising on monetary available-for-sale assets, such as investments in debt securities, should normally be recognised in profit or loss, not in other comprehensive income (the only exceptions being if it is designated as the hedging instrument in a cash flow hedge or hedge of a net investment – see Chapter 52).

The accounting requirements for available-for-sale assets are further illustrated in the examples below.

Example 49.1: Gain or loss on available-for-sale shares in takeover target

Company S holds a small number of shares in Company T. The shares are classified as available-for-sale. On 20 December 2017, the fair value of the shares is $120 and the cumulative gain recognised in other comprehensive income is $20. On the same day, Company U, a large public company, acquires T. As a result, S receives shares in U in exchange for those it had in T of equal fair value.

The transaction qualifies for derecognition (see Chapter 51), therefore the cumulative gain of $20 that has been recognised in other comprehensive income should now be reclassified to profit or loss. *[IAS 39.E.3.1]*.

Example 49.2: Available-for-sale asset – determination of interest

A company acquires a zero coupon bond at the end of 2016 for £760, its fair value, which matures at the beginning of 2020 at £1,000. It is classified as an available-for-sale asset and, accordingly, associated fair value gains and losses are recognised in other comprehensive income. Its fair value at the end of 2017, 2018 and 2019 is £850, £950 and £1,000 respectively and it can be determined that the effective interest rate is 9.6% (the effective interest method is discussed in more detail at 3 below).

Therefore, ignoring the application of IFRS 9 in 2018, the financial statements would include the accounting entries set out in the following table (amortised cost is memorandum information used to determine interest).

Year	Amortised cost at start of year £		Interest – profit or loss £		Gains and losses – other comprehensive income £		Cash flow £	Fair value B/S £
2016	–		–		–		–	760
2017	760		73	*[=760 × 9.6%]*	17	*[=850 – {760 + 73}]*	–	850
2018	833	*[=760 + 73]*	80	*[=833 × 9.6%]*	20	*[=950 – {850 + 80}]*	–	950
2019	913	*[=833 + 80]*	87	*[=913 × 9.6%]*	(37)	*[=1,000 – {950 + 87}]*	–	1,000
2020	1,000	*[=913 + 87]*	–		–		1,000	–

The standard does not specify the cost formula to be used for fungible (i.e. substitutable) available-for-sale assets (or, indeed, for any other fungible financial instrument), for example equity shares issued by a single entity that are identical except perhaps for a serial number or similar identifier. This is in contrast to, say, IAS 2 – *Inventories* – which specifies the use of a weighted average cost or FIFO (first-in, first-out) basis in most circumstances. *[IAS 2.25]*.

On a theoretical level, an asset-by-asset approach is arguably the most technically pure. This would, for example, prevent the offsetting of an impairment arising on one asset against an unrealised gain on another. However, it could also allow entities to manipulate their earnings. For example, when selling an asset an entity could choose to sell one with a low (or high) cost base in order to maximise (minimise) the profit on disposal. In practice, average cost bases are typically used (perhaps applied to individual portfolios within the entity), although others may be acceptable provided they are applied consistently (e.g. both to disposals and impairment).

The financial statements of UBS disclose that it uses an average cost method.

Extract 49.1: UBS Group AG (2015)

Notes to the UBS Group AG consolidated financial statements [extract]

Note 1 Summary of significant accounting policies [extract]

9) Financial investments classified as available-for-sale [extract]

Financial investments that are classified as available-for-sale are recognized initially at fair value less transaction costs and are measured subsequently at fair value. Unrealized gains and losses are reported in *Other comprehensive income* within *Equity*, net of applicable income taxes, until such investments are sold, collected or otherwise disposed of, or until any such investment is determined to be impaired. [...]

On disposal of an investment, any related accumulated unrealized gains or losses included in *Equity* are reclassified to the income statement and reported in *Other income.* Gains or losses on disposal are determined using the average cost method.

Available-for-sale equity investments whose fair value cannot be reliably measured (see 2.6 below) are measured at cost less any impairment (see 4.4 below). *[IAS 39.46(c)]*. If a reliable measure of fair value subsequently becomes available, the asset should be remeasured at that fair value, and the gain or loss recognised in other comprehensive income (provided it is not impaired). *[IAS 39.53, 55(b)]*. If a reliable measure ceases to be available, it should thereafter be measured at 'cost', which is deemed to be the fair value carrying amount on that date. Any gain or loss previously recognised in other comprehensive income should remain in equity until the asset has been sold, otherwise disposed of or impaired, at which time it should be reclassified to profit or loss. *[IAS 39.54(b)]*.

2.5 Other financial liabilities

Other financial liabilities, as that term is used in Chapter 46, are measured at amortised cost using the effective interest method with gains and losses recognised in profit or loss when the instrument is derecognised as well as through the amortisation process. *[IAS 39.47, 56]*.

2.6 Unquoted equity instruments and related derivatives

IAS 39 has special accounting requirements for certain equity instruments that do not have a quoted market price in an active market and derivatives that are linked to, and must be settled by delivery of, such unquoted equity instruments. Specifically, they should be measured at cost, less impairment, if their fair value cannot be reliably measured (this guidance does not replace, but rather supplements, the fair value requirements in IFRS 13).

The fair value of these instruments is deemed to be reliably measurable if: *[IAS 39.AG80]*

- the variability in the range of reasonable fair value estimates is not significant for that instrument; or
- the probabilities of the various estimates within the range can be reasonably assessed and used in estimating fair value.

IAS 39 explains that there are many situations in which the variability in the range of reasonable fair value estimates of such investments is likely not to be significant and that, normally, it is possible to estimate the fair value of a financial asset that has been acquired from a third party. However, if the range of reasonable fair value estimates is significant and the probabilities of the various estimates cannot be reasonably assessed, such instruments are precluded from fair value measurement. *[IAS 39.AG81]*.

It is not stated explicitly that the fair value of any other type of financial instrument is deemed to be reliably measurable, although in our view, it should be. There was such a statement in the original standard[1] and the original implementation guidance contained the following example to illustrate the point.

Example 49.3: Complex stand-alone derivative – no unquoted equity underlying

Company Z acquires a complex stand-alone derivative that is based on several underlying variables, including commodity prices, interest rates, and credit indices. There is no active market or other price quotation for the derivative and no active markets for some of its underlying variables.

The presumption that the derivative's fair value can be reliably determined cannot be overcome because it is not linked to, or required to be settled by delivery of, an unquoted equity instrument. It cannot, therefore, be carried at cost.[2]

However, the Interpretations Committee has addressed this in the context of certain principal-to-principal derivatives designed to fix the price of supply of electricity. Here, valuation issues include the fact that the derivative can have a variable notional amount (often depending on one party's usage requirements) and that the term of the derivative may extend well beyond the period for which there is any observable market data. The Interpretations Committee confirmed that the only exception in IAS 39 from the requirement to fair value derivatives after initial recognition relates to instruments that are linked to, and must be settled by delivery of, unquoted equity instruments.[3]

Where a financial instrument contains an embedded derivative whose fair value cannot be reliably measured (see Chapter 44 at 4) the relaxation may apply to the hybrid (or combined) contract in its entirety if it contains a link to an unquoted equity instrument and the equity component of the hybrid instrument is sufficiently significant to preclude the reliable estimation of the fair value of the hybrid contract. The following example illustrates this situation.

Example 49.4: Embedded derivative cannot be reliably measured

A company enters into a contract containing an embedded derivative that requires separation. However, the derivative cannot be reliably measured because it will be settled by delivery of an unquoted equity instrument whose fair value cannot be reliably measured. An example of such an instrument might be a convertible bond issued by a company whose shares are unquoted.

The entire combined contract is designated as a financial instrument at fair value through profit or loss (see Chapter 44 at 4). If the fair value of the combined instrument can be reliably measured, it is measured at fair value. However, the equity component of the combined instrument may be sufficiently significant to preclude the reliable estimation of its fair value. In this case, the combined contract is measured at cost less impairment. *[IAS 39.C.11]*.[4]

2.7 Reclassifications of financial assets

As set out in Chapter 46 at 6, the standard restricts the scope for reclassifying instruments between the main categories, except in certain circumstances. This section deals with the measurement of financial instruments subsequent to their reclassification.

2.7.1 Reclassifications from held-for-trading

The circumstances in which a financial asset may be reclassified out of the held for trading category are discussed in Chapter 46 at 6.1.1. The financial asset should be reclassified at its fair value on the date of reclassification and this fair value becomes its new cost or amortised cost, as applicable. Any gain or loss previously recognised in profit or loss should not be reversed. *[IAS 39.50C, 50F]*. If an embedded derivative is required to be separated from the reclassified financial asset (see Chapter 44 at 7.1), the initial carrying amount of the non-derivative host financial asset will be the fair value of the hybrid instrument at the date of reclassification adjusted by the fair value of the embedded derivative.

Thereafter, the appropriate measurement requirements within IAS 39 should be applied to the asset based on its new classification. For example, financial assets reclassified as loans and receivables will be measured at amortised cost using the effective interest method. However, where the effective interest method is applied, there is one difference in the way revisions to estimated cash flows are dealt with – this difference is discussed at 3.2.2 below.

2.7.2 Reclassifications from available-for-sale to loans and receivables

The circumstances in which a financial asset may be reclassified from the available-for-sale category to loans and receivables are discussed in Chapter 46 at 6.2. The financial asset should be reclassified at its fair value on the date of reclassification and this fair value becomes its new amortised cost. *[IAS 39.50F]*. Thereafter, the financial asset will be measured at amortised cost using the effective interest method. However, similar to financial assets transferred out of the held for trading category (see 2.7.1 above), there is a difference in the way the effective interest method should be applied – see 3.2.2 below.

Any gain or loss previously recognised in other comprehensive income prior to reclassification should be amortised over the remaining life of the investment using the effective interest method. Similarly, any difference between the new amortised cost and maturity amount should be amortised, akin to the amortisation of a premium or discount. If the asset subsequently becomes impaired, any gain or loss remaining in equity should be reclassified to profit or loss. *[IAS 39.50F, 54]*. Further, to ensure the appropriate amount is reclassified from equity to profit or loss, the amount related to the impairment of the financial asset will normally need to be assessed on an individual basis, as it was prior to reclassification, as well as on a collective basis where appropriate.

2.7.3 *Reclassifications between held-to-maturity investments and available-for-sale financial assets*

Where a held-to-maturity investment is reclassified as available-for-sale (for example as a result of triggering the 'tainting' provisions – see Chapter 46 at 3.3), the asset should be remeasured to fair value and any associated gain or loss recognised in other comprehensive income. *[IAS 39.51, 52]*.

If an available-for-sale asset is reclassified as held-to-maturity, the fair value carrying amount of the financial asset on that date becomes its new amortised cost. Any previous gain or loss on that asset that has been recognised in other comprehensive income should be amortised over the remaining life of the investment using the effective interest method. Any difference between the new amortised cost and maturity amount should be similarly amortised, akin to the amortisation of a premium or discount. *[IAS 39.54(a)]*.

Example 49.5: Debt instrument reclassified as held-to-maturity

Company Y acquires a debt instrument that it classifies as available-for-sale. The purchase price equals the fair value of the instrument, £110. Its terms are such that it pays a fixed coupon for ten years and a principal payment of £100. Subsequently, when the fair value of the instrument is £120, a gain of £12 has been recognised in other comprehensive income, and £2 of the initial cost has been amortised to profit or loss, Y reclassifies the debt instrument as held-to-maturity.

The £120 fair value carrying amount becomes the new amortised cost of the instrument thereby giving rise to an effective premium of £20 that is amortised over the remaining term to maturity using the effective interest method. In addition, the £12 gain within equity is also amortised to profit or loss over the remaining period to maturity.

In effect, interest income should be broadly the same as if the instrument had not been reclassified (or had always been classified as held-to-maturity).

If the asset subsequently becomes impaired, any gain or loss remaining in equity should be reclassified to profit or loss. *[IAS 39.54(a)]*.

2.8 Financial guarantees and commitments to provide a loan at a below-market interest rate

Financial guarantees issued and commitments made to provide a loan at a below-market interest rate should be measured on initial recognition at their (negative) fair value and subsequently at the higher of:

- the amount recognised under IAS 37 – *Provisions, Contingent Liabilities and Contingent Assets* (Chapter 28); and
- the amount initially recognised less, where appropriate, cumulative amortisation recognised in accordance with IAS 18 – *Revenue* (or, when adopted, the principles of IFRS 15 – *Revenue from Contracts with Customers*) (Chapters 29 and 30).

This assumes that the instrument is not classified at fair value through profit or loss (in which case 2.1 above applies) and, in the case of a financial guarantee contract, it does not arise from a 'failed derecognition' transaction (see 2.9.3 below). *[IAS 39.47(c), 47(d), AG4(a)]*.

In assessing whether a provision should be recognised for financial guarantee contracts, entities need to determine whether groups of similar contracts should be assessed on an individual or a portfolio basis. IAS 37 itself explains that the measurement of a provision involving a large population of items should be determined on a portfolio basis using an expected value method *[IAS 37.39]* (a treatment the IASB has previously implied could be adopted for guarantees)[5] and in our experience some form of portfolio approach is commonly adopted in practice. However, the FASB published requirements applying to insurers writing financial guarantee contracts, which require provisions to be recognised and measured on a contract-by-contract basis.[6] In our view, selection of an accounting policy that is consistent with US GAAP rather than applying a portfolio approach could also be appropriate.

2.9 Exceptions to the general principles

2.9.1 Hedging relationships

Financial assets and financial liabilities that are designated as hedged items are subject to measurement under the hedge accounting requirements of IAS 39 *[IAS 39.46, 47, 56]* and these can over-ride the general accounting requirements discussed above. Also, financial instruments may be designated as hedging instruments (in hedges of foreign currency risk), which can affect whether exchange gains and losses are recognised in profit or loss or in other comprehensive income. *[IAS 39.72, 95, 102]*. Hedge accounting is covered in Chapter 52.

2.9.2 Regular way transactions

Where settlement date accounting is used for regular way transactions (see Chapter 48 at 2.2.2), any change in the fair value of the asset to be received arising between trade date and settlement date is not recognised for those assets that will be measured at cost or amortised cost. For assets that will be recorded at fair value, such changes in value are recognised:

- in profit or loss for assets to be classified at fair value through profit or loss; and
- in other comprehensive income (except for impairments and certain foreign exchange gains and losses as above) for available-for-sale assets. *[IAS 39.55, 57]*.

On disposal, changes in value of such assets between trade date and settlement date are not recognised because the right to changes in fair value ceases on the trade date. *[IAS 39.D.2.2]*. This is illustrated in Chapter 48 at 2.2.3.

2.9.3 Liabilities arising from 'failed derecognition' transactions

There are special requirements for financial liabilities (including financial guarantee contracts) that arise when transfers of financial assets do not qualify for derecognition, or are accounted for using the continuing involvement approach. *[IAS 39.47(b)]*. These are dealt with in Chapter 51 at 5.3.

3 AMORTISED COST AND THE EFFECTIVE INTEREST METHOD

IAS 39 contains three key definitions relating to this method of accounting, which are set out below.

The *amortised cost* of a financial instrument is defined as the amount at which it was measured at initial recognition minus principal repayments, plus or minus the cumulative amortisation using the 'effective interest method' of any difference between that initial amount and the maturity amount, and minus any loss allowance. The *effective interest method* is a method of calculating the amortised cost of a financial instrument (or group of instruments) and of allocating the interest income or expense over the relevant period. *[IAS 39.9]*.

The *effective interest rate* is the rate that exactly discounts estimated future cash payments or receipts over the expected life of the instrument or, when appropriate, a shorter period, to the instrument's net carrying amount. The calculation of the effective interest rate should include all fees and points paid or received between the contracting parties to the extent they are an integral part of the effective interest rate. The definition refers to IAS 18 for further guidance on what should and should not be considered integral (see Chapter 29 at 5.2.3.A). The calculation should also include transaction costs, and all other premiums or discounts, but not the effect of future credit losses. *[IAS 39.9]*. Transaction costs expected to be incurred on transfer or disposal of a financial instrument are not included in the measurement of the financial instrument. *[IAS 39.E.1.1]*.

It is important to note that the effective interest rate is normally based on estimated, not contractual, cash flows and there is a presumption that the cash flows and the expected life of a group of similar financial instruments can be estimated reliably. However, in those rare cases when it is not possible to estimate reliably the cash flows or the expected life of a financial instrument (or group of instruments), the contractual cash flows over the full contractual term of the financial instrument (or group of instruments) should be used. *[IAS 39.9]*.

For consistency with the estimated cash flows approach, the effective interest rate should be calculated over the expected life of the instrument or, when applicable, a shorter period. Generally, the expected life of the instrument should be used although a shorter period is used if this is the period to which the fee, transaction costs, discount or premium relates. This will be the case when the related variable (e.g. interest rates) is re-priced to market rates before the expected maturity of the instrument. In such a case, the appropriate amortisation period is the period to the next such re-pricing date. *[IAS 39.9, AG6, BC35]*. The application of this requirement is considered in more detail at 3.3 and 3.6 below.

As set out in Chapter 45 at 6, an issued compound financial instrument such as a convertible bond is accounted for as a financial liability component and an equity component. In accounting for the financial liability at amortised cost, the expected cash flows should be those of the liability component only and the estimate should not take account of the bond being converted.

3.1 Fixed interest, fixed term instruments

The effective interest method is most easily applied to instruments that have fixed payments and a fixed term. The following examples (as well as Example 49.2 at 2.4 above) illustrate this.

Example 49.6: Effective interest method – amortisation of premium or discount on acquisition

At the end of 2014, a company purchases a debt instrument with five years remaining to maturity for its fair value of US$1,000 (including transaction costs). The instrument has a principal amount of US$1,250 and carries fixed interest of 4.7% payable annually (US$1,250 × 4.7% = US$59 per year). In order to allocate interest receipts and the initial discount over the term of the instrument at a constant rate on the carrying amount, it can be shown that interest needs to be accrued at the rate of 10% annually. The table below provides information about the amortised cost, interest income, and cash flows of the debt instrument in each reporting period (ignoring the application of IFRS 9 in 2018).[7] *[IAS 39.B.26]*.

Year	*(a)* Amortised cost at start of year (US$)	*(b = a × 10%)* Interest income (US$)	*(c)* Cash flows (US$)	*(d = a + b – c)* Amortised cost at end of year (US$)
2015	1,000	100	59	1,041
2016	1,041	104	59	1,086
2017	1,086	109	59	1,136
2018	1,136	113	59	1,190
2019	1,190	119	1,250 + 59	–

Example 49.7: Effective interest method – stepped interest rates

On 1 January 2015, Company A acquires a debt instrument for its fair value of £1,250 (including transaction costs). The principal amount is £1,250 which is repayable on 31 December 2019. The rate of interest is specified in the debt agreement as a percentage of the principal amount as follows: 6% in 2015 (£75), 8% in 2016 (£100), 10% in 2017 (£125), 12% in 2018 (£150) and 16.4% in 2019 (£205). It can be shown that the interest rate that exactly discounts the stream of future cash payments to maturity is 10%. In each period, the amortised cost at the beginning of the period is multiplied by the effective interest rate of 10% and added to the amortised cost. Any cash payments in the period are deducted from the resulting balance. Accordingly, ignoring the application of IFRS 9 in 2018, the amortised cost, interest income and cash flows of the debt instrument in each period are as follows:

Year	*(a)* Amortised cost at start of year (£)	*(b = a × 10%)* Interest income (£)	*(c)* Cash flows (£)	*(d = a + b – c)* Amortised cost at end of year (£)
2015	1,250	125	75	1,300
2016	1,300	130	100	1,330
2017	1,330	133	125	1,338
2018	1,338	134	150	1,322
2019	1,322	133	1,250 + 205	–

It can be seen that, although the instrument is issued for £1,250 and has a maturity amount of £1,250, its amortised cost does not equal £1,250 at each reporting date. *[IAS 39.B.27]*.

Methods for determining the effective interest rate for a given set of cash flows (as in the examples above) include simple trial and error techniques as well as more methodical iterative algorithms. Alternatively, many spreadsheet applications contain 'goal-seek' or similar functions that can also be used to derive effective interest rates.

3.2 Prepayment, call and similar options

When calculating the effective interest rate, all contractual terms of the financial instrument, for example prepayment, call and similar options, should be considered. *[IAS 39.9]*. The following simple example illustrates how this principle is applied.

Example 49.8: Effective interest rate – embedded prepayment options

Bank ABC originates 1,000 ten year loans of £10,000 with 10% stated interest. Prepayments are probable and it is possible to reasonably estimate their timing and amount. ABC determines that the effective interest rate including loan origination fees received by ABC is 10.2% based on the *contractual* payment terms of the loans as the fees received reduce the initial carrying amount.

However, if the *expected* prepayments were considered, the effective interest rate would be 10.4% since the difference between the initial amount and maturity amount is amortised over a shorter period.

The effective interest rate that should be used by ABC for this portfolio is 10.4%.[8]

3.2.1 Revisions to estimated cash flows

The standard contains an explanation of how changes to estimates of payments or receipts (e.g. because of a reassessment of the extent to which prepayments will occur) should be dealt with.

When estimates change, the carrying amount of the financial instrument (or group of instruments) should be adjusted to reflect actual and revised estimated cash flows. More precisely, the carrying amount should be calculated by computing the present value of estimated future cash flows at the instrument's original effective interest rate or, if the instrument has been designated as the hedged item in a fair value hedge, the revised effective interest rate. Any consequent adjustment should be recognised immediately in profit or loss. *[IAS 39.AG8]*.

The IASB considers this approach to have the practical advantage that it does not require recalculation of the effective interest rate, i.e. an entity simply recognises the remaining cash flows at the original rate. Consequently, a possible conflict with the requirement to discount estimated cash flows using the original effective interest rate when assessing impairment is avoided. *[IAS 39.BC36]*.

This requirement is illustrated in the following example taken from the implementation guidance.

Example 49.9: Effective interest method – revision of estimates

At the end of 2014, a company purchases in a quoted market a debt instrument with the same terms as the instrument in Example 49.6 at 3.1 above, except that the contract also specifies that the borrower has an option to prepay the instrument and that no penalty will be charged for prepayment (i.e. any prepayment will be made at the principal amount of US$1,250 or a proportion thereof).

At inception, there is an expectation that the borrower will not prepay and so the information about the instrument's effective interest rate, amortised cost, interest income and cash flows in each reporting period would be the same as that in Example 49.6.

On the first day of 2017, the investor revises its estimate of cash flows. It now expects that 50% of the principal will be prepaid at the end of 2017 and the remaining 50% at the end of 2019. Therefore, the opening balance of the debt instrument in 2017 is adjusted to an amount calculated by discounting the amounts expected to be received in 2017 and subsequent years using the original effective interest rate (10%). This results in a revised balance of US$1,138. The adjustment of US$52 (US$1,138 – US$1,086) is recorded in profit or loss in 2017.

The table below provides information about the amortised cost, interest income and cash flows as they would be adjusted taking into account this change in estimate (and ignoring the application of IFRS 9 in 2018).

Year	*(a)* Amortised cost at start of year (US$)	*(b = a × 10%)* Interest and similar income* (US$)	*(c)* Cash flows (US$)	*(d = a + b – c)* Amortised cost at end of year (US$)
2015	1,000	100	59	1,041
2016	1,041	104	59	1,086
2017	1,086	114 + 52	625 + 59	568
2018	568	57	30	595
2019	595	60	625 + 30	–

*the standard and related guidance do not state whether the catch-up adjustment (US$52 in 2017 in this case) should be classified as interest income or as some other income or expense, but simply states that the adjustment is recognised in profit or loss as income or expense.

This amortised cost calculation would be applicable whether the instruments were classified as held-to-maturity or available-for-sale. *[IAS 39.B.26]*.

3.2.2 *Special requirements for financial assets reclassified in accordance with IAS 39*

Special rules apply to the application of the effective interest method where a financial asset is reclassified into the loans and receivables category in accordance with IAS 39 (see 2.7.1 and 2.7.2 above and Chapter 46 at 6.1 and 6.2). In such cases, where the estimates of future cash receipts are subsequently increased as a result of their increased recoverability, the effect of that increase should be recognised as an adjustment to the effective interest rate from the date of the change in estimate rather than as an adjustment to the carrying amount of the asset at the date of the change in estimate. *[IAS 39.AG8]*.

3.2.3 *Interaction with the requirements for embedded derivatives*

As set out in Chapter 44 at 5.1, certain debt instruments containing terms such as prepayment options are required by IAS 39 to be accounted for as two separate contracts, i.e. a host debt instrument and an embedded derivative. Although not explained in the standard, the terms accounted for separately as an embedded derivative should not be taken into account in applying the effective interest method to the host. If a prepayment option, say, were accounted for as an embedded derivative at fair value, it would effectively be accounted for twice if it was also taken into account in determining the effective interest rate of the host.

In Example 49.9 above, which is based on the implementation guidance to IAS 39, it is not clear why the prepayment option has *not* been separately accounted for as an embedded derivative. The exercise price is US$1,250 and the option may be exercised at any time, yet the amortised cost is initially only US$1,000. Therefore, unless these two figures were considered approximately equal, the option would not be regarded as closely related to the host under IAS 39 (see Chapter 44 at 5). We find it hard to believe that the IASB considers two numbers, one of which is 25% larger than the other, to be approximately equal. More likely, the requirements regarding embedded derivatives were overlooked when developing the above example as it is intended, primarily, to illustrate the accounting requirements when estimates of cash flows are revised.

This actually raises other questions with regards to the issue of whether prepayment and similar options should be regarded as closely related to the host instrument. In assessing whether the exercise price is approximately equal to the amortised cost at each exercise date, should one consider the amortised cost of the hybrid on the assumption the option is regarded as closely related, or the amortised cost of the host on the assumption that it is not? This conundrum is illustrated in the following simple example (which also provides further illustrations of the application of the effective interest method to instruments containing prepayment options).

Example 49.10: Embedded prepayment option

Company P borrows €1,000 on terms that require it to pay annual fixed rate coupons of €80 and €1,000 principal at the end of ten years. The terms of the instrument also allow P to redeem the debt after seven years by paying the principal of €1,000 and a penalty of €100.

The debt instrument can be considered to comprise the following two components:

- a host debt instrument requiring ten annual payments of €80 followed by a €1,000 payment of principal; and
- an embedded prepayment option, exercisable only at the end of seven years with an exercise price of €1,100.

If, at inception, the prepayment option was expected *not* to be exercised, the effective interest rate of the *hybrid* would be 8%. This is the rate that would discount the expected cash flows of €80 per year for ten years plus €1,000 at the end of ten years to the initial carrying amount of €1,000. The table below provides information about the amortised cost, interest income and cash flows using this assumption.

Year	*(a)* Amortised cost at start of year (€)	*(b = a × 8%)* Interest and similar income (€)	*(c)* Cash flows (€)	*(d = a + b – c)* Amortised cost at end of year (€)
1	1,000	80	80	1,000
2	1,000	80	80	1,000
3	1,000	80	80	1,000
4	1,000	80	80	1,000
5	1,000	80	80	1,000
6	1,000	80	80	1,000
7	1,000	80	80	1,000
8	1,000	80	80	1,000
9	1,000	80	80	1,000
10	1,000	80	80 + 1,000	–

However if, at the outset, the option *was* expected to be exercised, the effective interest rate of the *hybrid* would be 9.08% as this is the rate that discounts the expected cash flows of €80 per year for seven years, plus €1,100 at the end of seven years, to the initial carrying amount of €1,000. The table below provides information about the amortised cost, interest income and cash flows using this alternative assumption.

Year	*(a)* Amortised cost at start of year (€)	*(b = a × 9.08%)* Interest and similar income (€)	*(c)* Cash flows (€)	*(d = a + b – c)* Amortised cost at end of year (€)
1	1,000	91	80	1,011
2	1,011	92	80	1,023
3	1,023	93	80	1,036
4	1,036	94	80	1,050
5	1,050	95	80	1,065
6	1,065	97	80	1,082
7	1,082	98	80 + 1,100	–

On the face of it, therefore, comparing the amortised cost of the hybrid with the exercise price of the option at the date it could be exercised suggests the prepayment option might be considered closely related if it was likely to be exercised but not if exercise was unlikely.

However, even this is not the whole story. If the option (on inception) was not expected to be exercised, but at a later date exercise became likely, the amortised cost carrying amount would be revised so that it represented the expected future cash flows discounted at the original effective interest rate. For example, if at the end of Year 5, it became likely that the option would be exercised, the carrying amount would be revised so that it represented €80 discounted for one year at 8% plus €1,180 discounted for two years at 8% – in other words, €1,086 rather than €1,065. The difference of €21 would be recognised in profit or loss immediately and the amortised cost carrying amount would subsequently accrete so that it represented the final cash outflow (option exercise price of €1,100 plus coupon of €80) at the end of Year 7. So even in this situation there is an argument to suggest that the prepayment option should not be separated as the exercise price will always equal the amortised cost (at least to the extent that the option is expected to be exercised).

If the assessment was performed based on the amortised cost of the *host*, the initial fair value of the prepayment option is needed to determine the initial carrying amount of the host (see Chapter 48 at 3.4). From P's perspective it will have a positive fair value and for the purpose of this example this is assumed to be €50. Therefore, the initial value of the host will be €1,050 (€1,000 + €50). The effective interest rate of the host can be demonstrated to be 7.28% and the amortised cost each year would be as follows:

Year	*(a)* Amortised cost at start of year (€)	*(b = a × 7.28%)* Interest and similar income (€)	*(c)* Cash flows (€)	*(d = a + b – c)* Amortised cost at end of year (€)
1	1,050	76	80	1,046
2	1,046	76	80	1,042
3	1,042	76	80	1,038
4	1,038	76	80	1,034
5	1,034	75	80	1,029
6	1,029	75	80	1,024
7	1,024	75	80	1,019
8	1,019	74	80	1,013
9	1,013	74	80	1,007
10	1,007	73	80 + 1,000	–

In this case, the amortised cost at the date the option can be exercised is €1,019. Comparing this with the exercise price of €1,100 suggests the option may not be considered closely related in this case.

In fact if this analysis were applied to prepayment options for which there was no associated penalty (i.e. the instrument would always be redeemed at its principal amount), separating the embedded derivative in this way would artificially create a difference between the amortised cost of the *host* and the exercise price. However, we are entirely unconvinced it would be appropriate to separate an embedded derivative from such a simple instrument.

Unfortunately, the standard is silent on these issues and preparers of accounts will be required to exercise judgement as to the most appropriate method to use in their individual circumstances, although as noted in Chapter 44 at 5.1.3, one trade body has published guidance explaining that where early repayment fees are included in the calculation of effective interest, the prepayment option is likely to be closely related to the loan.[9]

3.3 Floating rate instruments

When estimating cash flows for a floating rate instrument, application of the basic requirements discussed at 3 above could produce some surprising results, as shown in the following example.

Example 49.11: Effective interest method – variable rate loan

At the start of July 2016, Company G originates a floating rate debt instrument. Its fair value is equal to its principal amount of $1,000 and no transaction costs are incurred. The instrument pays, in arrears at the end of June, a variable rate coupon, determined by reference to 12 month LIBOR at the start of each previous July. It has a term of five years and is repayable at its principal amount at the end of June 2021.

On origination, 12 month LIBOR is 5% and this establishes the first payment, to be made in June 2017, at $50. Based on a market-derived yield curve, G estimates that the subsequent floating rate payments will be $60, $70, $80 and $90 (yield curve rises steeply). It can be demonstrated that the interest rate that exactly discounts these estimated coupon payments and the $1,000 principal at maturity to the current carrying amount of $1,000 is 6.87% (the definition does not acknowledge the possibility of more than one effective interest rate that would be reflective of a yield curve that is not flat).

In this situation, recognising interest at 6.87% in the first year would seem entirely counter-intuitive and is inconsistent with traditional notions of interest recognition for floating rate instruments. Nevertheless, there are some who believe, at least in principle, that such an approach is technically correct, even if it is not applied widely in practice.

The standard does contain additional guidance for applying the effective interest method to floating rate instruments. Normally, the effective interest rate remains constant over the life of an instrument. However, for floating rate instruments, it is stated that periodic re-estimation of cash flows to reflect movements in market interest rates *does* alter the effective interest rate. The standard goes on to explain that where such an instrument is initially recognised at an amount equal to the principal repayable on maturity, re-estimating the future interest payments normally has no significant effect on the carrying amount of the instrument. *[IAS 39.AG7]*.

Typically this has been interpreted to mean that entities should simply account for periodic floating rate payments on an accruals basis in the period to which they relate. However, those that believe entities should forecast all future cash flows argue that this means that the calculated effective interest rate (6.87% in Example 49.11 above) is applied until estimated future cash flows are revised, at which point a new effective interest rate is calculated based on the revised cash flow expectations and the current carrying amount.

Whilst payments, receipts, discounts and premiums included in the effective interest method calculation are normally amortised over the expected life of the instrument, there may be situations when they are amortised over a shorter period (see 3 above). This will be the case when the variable to which they relate reprices to market rates before the instrument's expected maturity. In such cases, the appropriate amortisation period is to the next re-pricing date.

For example, if a premium or discount on a floating rate instrument reflects interest that has accrued since interest was last paid, or changes in market rates since the floating interest rate was reset to market rates, it will be amortised to the next date when the interest rate is reset to market rates. This is because the premium or discount relates to the period to the next interest reset date because, at that date, the variable to which the premium or discount relates (i.e. the interest rate) is reset to market rates. If, however, it results from a change in the credit spread over the floating rate specified in the instrument, or other variables that are not reset to market rates, it is amortised over the expected life of the instrument. *[IAS 39.AG6]*.

The following examples illustrate the requirements of applying a discount arising on acquisition of a debt instrument resulting from (a) a credit downgrade and (b) accrued interest.

Example 49.12: Effective interest method – amortisation of discount arising from credit downgrade

A twenty year bond is issued at £100, has a principal amount of £100, and requires quarterly interest payments equal to current three month LIBOR plus 1% over the life of the instrument. The interest rate reflects the market-based required rate of return associated with the bond issue at issuance. Subsequent to issuance, the credit quality of the bond deteriorates resulting in a rating downgrade. It therefore trades at a discount, although there is no objective evidence of impairment. Company A purchases the bond for £95 and classifies it as held-to-maturity.

The discount of £5 is amortised to income over the period to the maturity of the bond and not to the next date interest rate payments are reset as it results from a change in credit spreads.[10]

Example 49.13: Effective interest method – amortisation of discount arising from accrued interest

At the start of November 2016, Company P acquires the bond issued by Company G in Example 49.11 above – current interest rates have not changed since the end of July 2016 and G's credit risk has not changed since origination so P pays $1,017.

The premium of $17 paid by P relates to interest accrued since the last reset date and so is amortised to income over the period to the next re-pricing date, June 2017; further, the $50 cash flow received at the end of June 2017 is also 'amortised' over this period.

Consequently, for the eight months ended June 2017, P will record interest of $33 ($50 – $17), which is also the approximate equivalent of eight months interest at current rates (5%) earned on P's initial investment.

This treatment is consistent with the requirements of IAS 18 that apply when unpaid interest has accrued before the acquisition of an interest-bearing investment. In such cases, it is explained (in more traditional terms) that the subsequent receipt of interest should be allocated between pre-acquisition and post-acquisition periods and only the post-acquisition portion should be recognised as revenue. *[IAS 18.32]*. In fact for many floating rate instruments, it will often be appropriate to apply a simplistic method of accounting – for example, by amortising transaction costs on a straight line basis over the life of the instrument combined with a simple time apportionment approach to the floating rate coupons.

3.4 Perpetual debt instruments

The fact that an instrument is perpetual does not change how amortised cost is calculated. The present value of the perpetual stream of future cash payments is discounted at the effective interest rate, resulting in an amortised cost that equals the principal amount in each period. *[IAS 39.B.24]*.

However, in cases where interest is only paid over a limited amount of time, some or all of the interest payments are, from an economic perspective, repayments of the principal amount as illustrated in the following example. *[IAS 39.B.25]*.

Example 49.14: Amortised cost – perpetual debt with interest payments over a limited amount of time

On 1 January 2017, Company A subscribes £1,000 for a debt instrument which yields 25% interest for the first five years and 0% in subsequent periods and is classified as a loan. It can be determined that the effective yield is 7.9% and the amortised cost, ignoring the application of IFRS 9 in 2018, is shown in the table below.[11]

Year	*(a)* Amortised cost at start of year (£)	*(b = a × 7.9%)* Interest income (£)	*(c)* Cash flows (£)	*(d = a + b – c)* Amortised cost at end of year (£)
2017	1,000	79	250	829
2018	829	66	250	645
2019	645	51	250	446
2020	446	36	250	232
2021	232	18	250	–
2021	–	–	–	–

3.5 Acquisition of credit impaired debt instruments

In some cases, financial assets are acquired at a deep discount that reflects incurred credit losses. IAS 39 requires such incurred (but not expected or future) credit losses to be included in the estimated cash flows when computing the effective interest rate. This is illustrated in the following example. *[IAS 39.AG5]*.

Example 49.15: Purchase of impaired debt

On 1 January 2010, Company D issued a debt instrument that required it to pay an annual coupon of €800 in arrears and to repay the principal of €10,000 on 31 December 2020. By 2016, D was in financial difficulties and was unable to pay the coupon due on 31 December 2016. On 1 January 2017, Company V estimated that the holder could expect to receive a single payment of €4,000 at the end of 2018 and acquired the debt instrument at an arm's length price of €3,000.

It can be shown that using the contractual cash flows (including the €800 overdue) gives rise to an effective interest rate of 70.1% (the net present value of €800 now and annually thereafter until 2020 and €10,000 receivable at the end of 2020 is €3,000 when discounted at 70.1%). However, because the debt instrument is clearly credit impaired, V should calculate the effective interest rate using the estimated cash flows on the instrument. In this case, the effective interest rate is 15.5% (the net present value of €4,000 receivable in two years is €3,000 when discounted at 15.5%).

All things being equal, interest income of €464 (€3,000 × 15.5%) would be recognised on the instrument during 2017 and its carrying amount at the end of the year would be €3,464 (€3,000 + €464). However if at the end of the year the cash flow expected to be generated by the instrument had increased to €4,250 (still to be received at the end of 2018), an adjustment to the asset would be made as set out at 3.2.1 above. Accordingly, its carrying amount would be increased to €3,681 (€4,250 discounted over one year at 15.5%) and a further €217 income would be recognised in profit or loss. Of course, there would need to be a substantive and supportable basis for revising the cash flow estimates.

In the above example, let us say at the time of acquisition of the debt instrument, Company V forecasts that it has to incur collection costs of €200. These forecast collection costs would not normally be included in the estimated future cash flows when computing the effective interest rate of the acquired impaired debt instrument, since they should be treated as expenses when incurred rather than as a reduction in interest income. However, given that the standard requires incurred credit losses to be included in the estimated cash flows when computing the effective interest rate for financial assets acquired at a deep discount with incurred credit losses and paragraph AG84 requires the calculation of the present value of the estimated future cash flows of a collateralised financial asset to reflect 'the cash flows that may result from foreclosure less costs for obtaining and selling the collateral', it would follow that costs associated with obtaining and selling collateral should normally be included in the estimated future cash flows when computing the effective interest rate for an acquired impaired debt instrument (see 4.2.2 below).

3.6 Inflation-linked debt

As noted in Chapter 44 at 5.1.5, the issuance of debt instruments whose cash flows are linked to changes in an inflation index is quite common and, typically, the embedded derivative representing the variability in cash flows is treated as closely related to the host instrument. Consequently, entities that hold or issue these instruments must apply the effective interest method to determine the amount of interest to be recognised in profit or loss each period (assuming the instrument is not classified at fair value through profit or loss).

In May 2008, the Interpretations Committee was asked to consider a request for guidance on this issue. Three ways of applying the effective interest method that were being used in practice were included in the request. These are summarised in the following example.[12]

Example 49.16: Application of the effective interest method to inflation-linked debt instruments[13]

On 1 January 2016, Company A issues a debt instrument for $100,000 that is linked to the local Consumer Prices Index ('CPI'). The terms of the instrument require it to be repaid in full after five years at an amount equal to $100,000 adjusted by the cumulative change in the CPI over those five years. Interest on the loan is paid at each year end at an amount equal to 5% of the principal ($100,000) adjusted by the cumulative change in the CPI from issuance of the instrument.

The following table sets out the expected annual inflation rates on issuance of the instrument and one year later:

	Expected annual inflation rates	
	At start of 2016	*At start of 2017*
2016	0.7%	
2017	2.6%	1.4%
2018	2.8%	1.9%
2019	2.8%	3.5%
2020	2.8%	3.5%

During 2016 actual inflation is 1.2%.

Method 1 – application of IAS 39.AG8 (the 'AG8 approach')

This approach follows the requirements set out at 3.2.1 above. Therefore, the effective interest rate is established on 1 January 2016 based on expected cash flows at that time:

Date: end of	*Expected cash flow ($)*	*Calculation*
2016	5,035	=5,000 × 1.007
2017	5,166	=5,000 × 1.007 × 1.026
2018	5,311	=5,000 × 1.007 × 1.026 × 1.028
2019	5,459	=5,000 × 1.007 × 1.026 × 1.028 × 1.028
2020	117,854	=105,000 × 1.007 × 1.026 × 1.028 × 1.028 × 1.028

It can be demonstrated that these expected cash flows produce an effective interest rate of 7.4075%, i.e. the net present value of these cash flows, discounted at 7.4075%, equals $100,000.

During 2016, A applies the effective interest rate to the financial liability to recognise a finance charge of $7,408 ($100,000 × 7.4075%), increasing the carrying amount of the financial liability to $107,408 ($100,000 + $7,408). At the end of the year A pays cash interest of $5,060 ($5,000 × 101.2%) reducing the liability to $102,348 ($107,408 – $5,060). In addition, A must adjust the carrying amount of the financial liability so that it equals the net present value of expected future cash flows discounted at the original expected interest rate.

The expected future cash flows are now as follows:

Date: end of	*Cash flow ($)*	*Calculation*
2017	5,131	=5,000 × 1.012 × 1.014
2018	5,228	=5,000 × 1.012 × 1.014 × 1.019
2019	5,411	=5,000 × 1.012 × 1.014 × 1.019 × 1.035
2020	117,615	=105,000 × 1.012 × 1.014 × 1.019 × 1.035 × 1.035

The net present value of these cash flows discounted at 7.4075% is $102,050. Therefore A reduces its finance charge by $298 ($102,050 – $102,348) so that the total finance charge for 2016 is $7,110 ($7,408 – $298).

Method 2 – application of IAS 39.AG7 using forecast future cash flows (the 'AG7 approach')

This approach is referred to at 3.3 above.

The initial effective interest rate is calculated and applied in the same way as Method 1. However, no adjustment is made to the carrying amount of the financial liability at the end of 2016 ($102,348) or to the finance charge for 2016 ($7,408) as a result of A, at the start of 2017, revising its expectations about inflation over the remaining term of the instrument.

Instead, a revised effective interest rate is calculated at the start of 2017 using the revised forecast cash flows (shown above under Method 1, i.e. $5,131 at the end of 2017, $5,228 at the end of 2018, $5,411 at the end of 2019 and $117,615 at the end of 2020) and the current carrying amount ($102,348). It can be demonstrated that this produces a revised effective interest rate of 7.3237%, i.e. the net present value of those cash flows, discounted at 7.3237% equals $102,348.

Applying this revised rate prospectively in 2017 (and assuming estimates of future inflation are not revised again until the start of 2018) there will be a finance charge for 2017 of $7,496 ($102,348 × 7.3237%).

Method 3 – application of IAS 39.AG6-AG7 without forecasting future cash flows

This method is based on the traditional method of accounting for floating rate debt instruments and is commonly used under other bodies of GAAP. Rather than taking account of expectations of future inflation it takes account of inflation only during the reporting period.

Therefore, in 2016, A would recognise a finance charge of $5,060 as a result of accruing the variable interest payment in respect of 2016. In addition, the actual inflation experienced during 2016 increases the amount of principal that will be paid from \$100,000 to \$101,200 (\$100,000 × 1.012%). This increase, i.e. \$1,200, is effectively a premium to be paid on the redemption of the financial liability. Paragraph AG6 of IAS 39 explains that a premium should normally be amortised over the expected life of an instrument. However, it goes on to explain that a shorter period should be used if this is the period to which the premium relates. *[IAS 39.AG6]*. In this case, the premium clearly relates to 2016 as it arises from inflation during that year and so it is appropriately amortised in that year.

Consequently, the total finance charge for 2016 using this method would be \$6,260 (\$5,060 + \$1,200).

In analysing the submission, it initially appeared as if the Interpretations Committee staff completely rejected Method 3. The submission argued that Method 3 was justified by reference to IAS 29 – *Financial Reporting in Hyperinflationary Economies*. The staff concluded (quite correctly) that it was inappropriate to apply IAS 29 because that standard applies only to the financial statements of an entity whose functional currency is the currency of a hyperinflationary economy and instead the guidance in IAS 39 should be applied.[14]

However, the Interpretations Committee noted that paragraphs AG6 to AG8 of IAS 39 provide the relevant application guidance and that judgement is required to determine whether an instrument is floating rate and within the scope of paragraph AG7 or is within the scope of paragraph AG8.[15] Further, it was noted that IAS 39 is unclear as to whether future expectations about interest rates (and presumably, therefore, inflation) should be taken into account when applying paragraph AG7.[16] Consequently, in our view, all three methods noted in the example comply with the current requirements of IAS 39. This view is consistent with the opinion of one national standard-setter that operates in a jurisdiction where such instruments are extremely common.[17]

3.7 Other, more complex, instruments

The application of the effective interest method to instruments with unusual embedded derivatives that are deemed closely related to the host, or other embedded features that are not accounted for separately, is not always straightforward or intuitive. Specifically it is not always clear how to deal with changes in the estimated cash flows of the instrument and in any given situation one needs to assess which of the approaches set out at 3.2.1 above (changes in cash flows generally, or the 'AG8' approach) and 3.3 above (specific requirements for floating rate instruments, or the 'AG7' approach) is more appropriate.

Consider an entity that issues a debt instrument for its par value of €10m which is repayable in ten years' time and on which an annual coupon is payable comprising two elements: a fixed amount of 2.5% of the par value and a variable amount equating to 0.01% of the entity's annual revenues. The instrument is not designated at fair value through profit or loss and it is judged that the embedded feature is not a derivative as outlined in Example 43.4 in Chapter 44.

The AG7 approach and the AG8 approach could give rise to significantly different accounting treatments. In the latter case, the issuer would need to estimate the amount of payments to be made over the life of the bond (which will depend on its estimated revenues for the next ten years) in order to determine the effective interest rate to be applied. Any changes to these estimates would result in a catch-up adjustment to profit or loss and the carrying amount of the bond which, potentially, could give rise to significant volatility. In the former case the annual coupon would simply be accrued each year and changes in estimated revenues of future periods would have no impact on the accounting treatment until the applicable year.

In 2009, the Interpretations Committee was asked to consider the accounting treatment for an instrument with similar terms. However, it considered the issue without reconsidering the assumptions described in the request, namely that the financial liability (a) did not contain any embedded derivatives, (b) was measured at amortised cost using the effective interest method, and (c) did not meet the definition of a floating rate instrument.[18] In other words, whilst clearly indicating that the AG8 approach was acceptable, it did not explicitly preclude the use of the AG7 approach. In this situation we believe that it would often be appropriate to apply the AG8 approach, principally because the entity's revenue does not represent a floating rate that changes to reflect movements in market rates of interest, although as covered at 3.6 above, judgement is required to determine which approach is appropriate.[19]

For other instruments, the decision as to which approach to use is even less clear. For example, as set out at 3.6 above, it can be argued that simple inflation-linked bonds are similar enough to floating rate instruments to apply the AG7 approach. However, this approach would not extend to more exotic instruments, for example to an 'inverse floater' where coupons on an otherwise simple debt instrument are paid at a fixed rate minus LIBOR (subject to a floor of zero), even though re-estimation of cash flows will only reflect movements in market interest rates.

In other cases, it might be considered appropriate to apply a combination of both approaches if, for example, an instrument contains both fixed and floating rate features.

4 IMPAIRMENT

Although the impairment requirements of IAS 39 are less complex than those of IFRS 9, they may appear somewhat over-engineered for what is a relatively simple subject for many entities, i.e. making appropriate provisions for bad and doubtful debts. The reason for this complexity is that IAS 39 is designed for use by all entities, including financial institutions for which impairment losses are often highly material. Accordingly, the IASB has tried to lay down clear guidelines as to when impairment losses should (and should not) be recognised in order to ensure that a consistent approach is taken both from period to period for individual entities and from entity to entity.

4.1 Impairment reviews

All financial assets, except for those measured at fair value through profit or loss, are subject to review for impairment. *[IAS 39.46]*. Assessments should be made at the end of each reporting period as to whether there is any objective evidence that a financial asset or group of assets is impaired. If such evidence exists, the requirements set out at 4.2, 4.3 or 4.4 below should be followed to determine the amount of any impairment loss. *[IAS 39.58]*.

A financial asset or a group of assets is impaired (and impairment losses are determined) if, and only if, there is objective evidence of impairment as a result of one or more events that occurred after initial recognition (a 'loss event') and that loss event (or events) has an impact on the estimated future cash flows of the financial asset or group of assets that can be reliably estimated. *[IAS 39.59]*.

Therefore, an entity should recognise an impairment loss on a group of loans even if the loss expectation since initial recognition of the loans has not changed, provided it could be estimated reliably, based on past history, that loss events have occurred after initial recognition, but before the reporting date.[20]

It may not be possible to identify a single, discrete event that caused the impairment; rather, the combined effect of several events may have caused the impairment. However, losses expected as a result of future events, no matter how likely, are not recognised. *[IAS 39.59]*. Therefore, an impairment loss is not permitted to be recognised at the time an asset is originated (i.e. before a loss event can have occurred) as illustrated in the following example. *[IAS 39.E.4.2]*.

Example 49.17: Immediate recognition of impairment

Bank B lends $1,000 to Customer M. Based on historical experience, B expects that 1% of the principal amount of loans given will not be collected, but an immediate impairment loss of $10 cannot be recognised. *[IAS 39.E.4.2]*.

4.1.1 Examples of loss events

Objective evidence that a financial asset or group of assets is impaired includes observable data that comes to the attention of the holder about the following loss events:

- significant financial difficulty of the issuer or obligor;
- breach of contract, such as a default or delinquency in interest or principal payments;
- the lender, for economic or legal reasons relating to the borrower's financial difficulty, granting to the borrower a concession that would not otherwise be considered;
- it becoming probable that the borrower will enter bankruptcy or other financial reorganisation;
- the disappearance of an active market for that asset because of financial difficulties (but not simply because the asset is no longer publicly traded *[IAS 39.60]*); or
- observable data indicating that there is a measurable decrease in the estimated future cash flows from a group of financial assets since initial recognition, although the decrease cannot yet be identified with the individual assets in the group, including:
  - adverse changes in the payment status of borrowers in the group (e.g. an increased number of delayed payments or an increased number of credit card borrowers who have reached their credit limit and are paying the minimum monthly amount); or
  - national or local economic conditions that correlate with defaults on the assets in the group (e.g. an increase in the unemployment rate in the geographical area of the borrowers, a decrease in property prices for mortgages in the relevant area, a decrease in oil prices for loan assets to oil producers, or adverse changes in industry conditions that affect the borrowers in the group). *[IAS 39.59]*.

A downgrade of an entity's credit rating is not, of itself, evidence of impairment, although it may be when considered with other available information. *[IAS 39.60]*. Other factors that would be considered in determining whether an impairment loss has been incurred include information about the debtors' or issuers' liquidity, solvency and business and financial risk exposures, levels of and trends in delinquencies for similar financial assets, national and local economic trends and conditions, and the fair value of collateral and guarantees. *[IAS 39.E.4.1]*. A decline in the fair value of a financial asset below its cost or amortised cost is not necessarily evidence of impairment – for example, the fair value of a debt instrument may decline only from an increase in the risk-free interest rate. *[IAS 39.60, E.4.10]*. Therefore, it is possible that an 'available-for-sale reserve' within equity can be negative.

4.1.2 Loss events related to investments in equity instruments

The standard explains that the following are objective evidence of impairment of an equity investment:

- information about significant changes with an adverse effect that have taken place in the technological, market, economic or legal environment in which the issuer operates, and indicates that the cost of the investment in the equity instrument may not be recovered; and
- a significant or prolonged decline in the fair value of an investment in such an instrument below its cost (see 4.1.3 below). *[IAS 39.61]*.

These triggers apply in addition to those specified at 4.1.1 above, which focus on the assessment of impairment in debt instruments. *[IAS 39.BC107]*.

4.1.3 Significant or prolonged declines in fair value

The meaning of the terms 'significant' and 'prolonged' is not defined or explained further. In March 2009, the Interpretations Committee received a request to provide guidance on the conceptual meaning of these terms as a result of considerable diversity in practice, sometimes driven by regulatory guidance issued in various jurisdictions.[21] The Interpretations Committee decided not to take the issue onto its agenda, but took the unusual step of outlining inappropriate applications of IAS 39 in recognising impairment on available-for-sale equity instruments,[22] including the following:[23]

- the standard cannot be read to require the decline in value to be both significant *and* prolonged. Thus, either a significant *or* a prolonged decline is sufficient to require the recognition of an impairment loss (although there is obviously some interaction between the notions of 'significant' and 'prolonged');[24]
- because IAS 39 states that a significant or prolonged decline in the fair value of an investment in an equity instrument below its cost is objective evidence of impairment, when such a decline exists, recognition of an impairment loss is required. Therefore, it is not possible to consider such a decline as only an indicator of possible impairment;[25]
- the fact that a decline in the value of an investment is in line with the overall level of decline in the relevant market does not mean that it can be concluded that the investment is not impaired;

- the existence of a significant or prolonged decline cannot be overcome by forecasts of an expected recovery of market values, regardless of their expected timing. Consequently, an anticipated market recovery is not relevant to the assessment of 'significant or prolonged'.

  To illustrate why such a recovery should not be anticipated, the Japanese Nikkei index reached its peak at 38,900 in December 1989, trended downwards to a low of 8,000 in March 2003, had a brief recovery to 17,900 in May 2007 and in May 2009 when it stood at 8,100, had not exceeded 20,000 since March 2000.[26]

  The Interpretations Committee was specifically asked to address whether an actual recovery in the fair value of an investment, after the end of the reporting period but before the financial statements were approved, could be taken into account. The Interpretations Committee staff noted that the impairment assessment was to be made at the end of the reporting period and noted that IAS 10 – *Events after the Reporting Period* – states that a decline in the fair value of an investment after the year end does not normally relate to the condition of the investment at the end of the reporting period. In the light of this they were clearly of the view that such a recovery was not relevant.[27] Ultimately, however, the Interpretations Committee did not state that it was inappropriate to take account of actual recoveries; and
- significant or prolonged declines must be assessed in the functional currency of the entity holding the instrument because that is how any impairment loss is determined – i.e. it is inappropriate to make the assessment in the foreign currency in which the equity investment is denominated.

  The Interpretations Committee was asked whether an impairment assessment made by a subsidiary in its functional currency should be reassessed when the financial statements of the subsidiary are translated to another currency (which could result in the reversal of an impairment recognised at the subsidiary level or *vice versa*). However, such a reassessment would not comply with the general requirements of IAS 21 – *The Effects of Changes in Foreign Exchange Rates.*[28]

The matters above are examples only and they are unlikely to be an exhaustive list of all the inconsistencies in the way the standard is applied that might exist in practice.

The determination of what constitutes a significant or prolonged decline is a matter of fact that requires the application of judgement. This is true even though an entity may develop internal guidance to assist it in applying that judgement consistently.[29] In fact more than one judgement may be necessary. For example, an entity may decide which criteria it uses to categorise investments by similar risk profiles, e.g. by geography, industry or price volatility. An entity may then decide which criteria are relevant for each category of investments to identify individual equity investments that require further analysis, e.g. any quantitative thresholds of percentage or duration of decline. These criteria should then be applied consistently in order to conclude whether or not the decline in fair value is significant or prolonged.[30]

Each equity investment is unique and should be evaluated individually. Accordingly the use only of 'bright line' tests is inappropriate. However, in our view, a decline of less than 10% would not normally be considered significant but, depending on the circumstances, it could be difficult to argue that a decline of more than 20% is not significant (although for a less liquid investment that has historically been particularly volatile, it may be possible to make a case for a larger decline, say 30%, not being significant). Similarly, whilst a decline that had persisted for less than six months would not normally be considered prolonged, we consider that a decline that had persisted for more than twelve months would typically be seen as prolonged.

When impairments of available-for-sale equity investments are material or potentially material it is appropriate to explain the judgements made in determining the existence of objective evidence and the amounts of impairment (see Chapter 3 at 5.1.1.B and Chapter 54 at 4.1).[31] Allianz provides the following disclosure indicating the quantitative thresholds it uses.

Extract 49.2: Allianz SE (2015)

Notes to the Consolidated Financial Statements [extract]

2. Summary of significant accounting policies [extract]

Impairments [extract]

An available-for-sale equity security is considered to be impaired if there is objective evidence that the cost may not be recovered. Objective evidence that the cost may not be recovered, in addition to qualitative impairment criteria, includes a significant or prolonged decline in the fair value below cost. The Allianz Group's policy considers a decline to be significant if the fair value is below the weighted average cost by more than 20%. A decline is considered to be prolonged if the fair value is below the weighted average cost for a period of more than nine months. If an available-for-sale equity security is impaired, any further declines in the fair value at subsequent reporting dates are recognized as impairments. Therefore, at each reporting period, for an equity security that was determined to be impaired, additional impairments are recognized for the difference between the fair value and the original cost basis, less any previously recognized impairment. Reversals of impairments of available-for-sale equity securities are not recorded through the income statement but recycled out of other comprehensive income when sold.

4.2 Financial assets carried at amortised cost

4.2.1 Individual and collective assessments

The standard requires that impairment assessments should be performed as follows:

- for assets that are individually significant, assessment should be made on an individual basis;
- other assets may also be assessed individually, although such an assessment is not necessarily required;
- assets that have been individually assessed, but for which there is no objective evidence of impairment, should be included within a group of assets with similar credit risk characteristics and collectively assessed for impairment;
- assets that are individually assessed for impairment and for which an impairment loss is (or continues to be) recognised cannot be subject to a collective impairment assessment; and
- any other assets, i.e. those that have not been individually assessed, should also be the subject of a collective assessment. *[IAS 39.64]*.

The above requirements might be read as allowing an asset that is not individually significant, but known to be impaired, to be included in a collective assessment thereby avoiding the recognition of a loss if, say, the fair value of other assets in the group exceed their amortised cost. However, the implementation guidance clearly states that if an entity knows that an individual financial asset carried at amortised cost is impaired, the impairment loss should be recognised. *[IAS 39.E.4.7]*.

The ability to include individual assets that have been reviewed for impairment in a collective assessment is a controversial one and two IASB members cited this as a reason for them voting against publication of the standard. *[IAS 39.DO2, DO4, DO7]*. The Basis for Conclusions contains an extensive discussion of the arguments for and against the proposal, *[IAS 39.BC108, BC121]*, but it is essentially a question of whether or not one believes a loan can actually be impaired even if a review has not identified it as such.

If, in performing an individual review, the lender had access to all relevant information about the loan and the borrower, it might seem quite reasonable to conclude that there is no need to perform an additional collective review. However, in practice, not all information is going to be readily available on a timely basis, and any individual assessment is likely to be incomplete. Therefore, in our view, it is entirely appropriate to require an additional collective review.

4.2.2 Measurement – general requirements

If there is objective evidence that an impairment loss has been incurred on loans and receivables or held-to-maturity investments, that loss should be measured as the difference between the asset's carrying amount and the present value of estimated future cash flows. Those cash flows, which should exclude future credit losses that have not been incurred, should be discounted at the original effective interest rate of the financial asset, i.e. the effective interest rate computed at initial recognition. *[IAS 39.63]*. The original effective interest rate is used because discounting at the current market interest rate would, in effect, impose fair-value measurement on assets that would otherwise be measured at amortised cost. *[IAS 39.AG84]*.

The standard allows the carrying amount of an impaired asset to be reduced, either directly or through use of an allowance account, but emphasises that the loss should always be recognised in profit or loss. *[IAS 39.63]*.

If the terms of an instrument are renegotiated or otherwise modified because of the borrower's financial difficulties and assuming that this is not regarded as an event that leads to derecognition of the original asset (see Chapter 51 at 3.4), impairment should be measured using the original effective interest rate.

For variable rate assets, the discount rate for measuring the impairment loss is the current effective interest rate(s) determined under the contract. As a practical expedient, impairment may be measured based on an instrument's fair value using an observable market price. *[IAS 39.AG84]*. In the original standard, this concession was allowed only for floating rate assets,[32] but it may now be used for fixed rate assets too. There is little conceptual merit in this, but it aligns IAS 39 more closely with US GAAP. *[IAS 39.BC221(f)]*. If an entity applies this practical expedient, then the IFRS 13 fair value measurement and disclosure requirements would apply.

The implementation guidance makes it clear that recognition of impairment losses in excess of those that are determined based on objective evidence (either at an individual asset or collective group level) is not permitted. *[IAS 39.E.4.6]*.

These basic principles are illustrated in the following example.

Example 49.18: Impairment – changes in amount or timing of payments

A bank is concerned that, because of financial difficulties, five customers, Companies A to E, will not be able to make all principal and interest payments due on originated loans in a timely manner. It negotiates a restructuring of the loans and expects the customers will meet their restructured obligations. The restructured terms are as follows:

- A will pay the full principal amount of the original loan five years after the original due date, but none of the interest due under the original terms;
- B will pay the full principal amount of the original loan on the original due date, but none of the interest due under the original terms;
- C will pay the full principal amount of the original loan on the original due date but with interest at a lower interest rate than the interest rate inherent in the original loan;
- D will pay the full principal amount of the original loan five years after the original due date and all interest accrued during the original loan term, but no interest for the extended term; and
- E will pay the full principal amount of the original loan five years after the original due date and all interest, including interest on all outstanding amounts for both the original term of the loan and the extended term.

An impairment loss has been incurred if there is objective evidence of impairment – this is assumed to be the case here because of the customers' financial difficulties. The amount of the impairment loss for a loan measured at amortised cost is the difference between the loan's carrying amount and the present value of future principal and interest payments, discounted at the loan's original effective interest rate.

For A to D, the present value of the future principal and interest payments discounted at the loan's original effective interest rate will be lower than the carrying amount of the loan. Therefore an impairment loss is recognised in those cases. For E, even though the timing of payments has changed, the bank will receive interest on interest, so that the present value of the future principal and interest payments, discounted at the loan's original effective interest rate, will equal the carrying amount of the loan. Therefore, there is no impairment loss. However, this fact pattern is unlikely given Company E's financial difficulties. *[IAS 39.E.4.3]*.

Accounting for and disclosure of banks' forbearance practices has become a common area of scrutiny by financial reporting regulators in the wake of the financial crisis. Please refer to Chapter 54 at 5.2.2.C for more details.

Consistent with the initial measurement requirements, cash flows relating to short-term receivables are not discounted if the effect of discounting is immaterial. *[IAS 39.AG84]*. This does not mean that such instruments are not, as a matter of principle, discounted, as illustrated in the following example.

Example 49.19: Impairment of short-term receivable

A construction company, K, agrees to build a new stadium for a professional football club, L. The project takes approximately six months and payment of €10 million is due six weeks after completion. On completion, K has recognised revenue and a corresponding receivable of €10 million because the effect of discounting at the current annualised rate of 5% is immaterial.

Shortly after completion, it becomes apparent that L is in financial difficulties and is unlikely to be able to settle the €10 million debt. In order to avoid formal insolvency proceedings, L attempts to restructure its financial obligations and offers to pay K €1 million per year for the next 10 years. Because it believes this arrangement appears to offer the best prospects for the recovery of its debt, K accepts.

On the face of it (and assuming no defaults on the rescheduled debt are expected), it might be argued that K need not recognise an impairment loss because it will receive all of the money owed and the debt's original effective interest rate was 0%. However, the original receivable was, in principle, discounted – it is just that the effects of discounting were not reflected in the financial statements as they were not material. Therefore, the effect of discounting the rescheduled payments at 5% per annum (approximately €2.28 million) should be recognised as an impairment loss.

It is common practice for commercial companies to determine bad debt provisions on accounts receivable using a provisioning matrix or similar formula based on the number of days a loan or debt is overdue, e.g. 0% if less than 90 days, 20% if 90 to 180 days, 50% if 180 to 365 days and 100% if more than 365 days overdue. This will be acceptable only if the formula can be demonstrated to produce an estimate sufficiently close to one determined under the methodology specified in IAS 39. *[IAS 39.E.4.5]*.

In measuring the impairment of a collateralised or secured loan, the cash flows used should reflect those that may result from foreclosure less costs for obtaining and selling the collateral, whether or not foreclosure is probable. *[IAS 39.AG84]*. The collateral itself should not be recognised as a separate asset unless it meets the recognition criteria for an asset in another standard. *[IAS 39.E.4.8]*.

To a lender, guarantees provided by a third (sometimes related) party such as a parent, other shareholder or fellow subsidiary, are little different to collateral – they provide a source of funds in the event that the debtor defaults. In the original implementation guidance it was made clear that guarantees should be taken into account in determining the amount of an impairment loss.[33] However, as noted in Chapter 44 at 8 and in Chapter 50 at 5.4.7, it is less clear under the existing version of IAS 39 whether a particular guarantee should be treated for accounting purposes as an integral part of the loan or as a separate financial instrument.

If the guarantee is considered a separate financial instrument it is likely to satisfy the definition of an insurance contract in IFRS 4 – *Insurance Contracts* – but will be excluded from the scope of that standard because it is a direct insurance contract held by the insured (who is not a cedant). *[IFRS 4.4(f)]*. (A cedant is an insurer that is the policyholder under a reinsurance contract.) If the guarantee satisfies the definition of an insurance contract in IFRS 4 it is outside the scope of IAS 39 *[IAS 39.2(e)]* irrespective of whether it is within the scope of IFRS 4 (see Chapter 43 at 3.3 and 3.4). Therefore it might be considered hard to avoid the conclusion that the guarantee is a contingent asset within the scope of IAS 37 because it is not 'covered' by another standard *[IAS 37.1(c), 37.5(e)]* (see Chapter 28 at 2.2.1.B).

What this would mean is that the guarantee could only be recognised as an asset when it is 'virtually certain' that a recovery will be made. In conceptual terms this is a more onerous test than that for recognising an impairment loss on the associated loan asset. Therefore, it might seem necessary to recognise an impairment loss on the asset (that would be fully recovered under the guarantee) but without being able to recognise an offsetting recovery from the guarantee.

There is more than one counter-argument to this analysis. Even if it is considered that IAS 37 should apply to the guarantee, some might argue that it is more appropriate to characterise it as a 'reimbursement' in respect of the impairment loss, rather than as a standalone contingent asset. As set out in Chapter 28 at 4.5, a reimbursement is recognised as an asset when it is virtually certain that the reimbursement will be received if the obligation for which a provision has been established is settled. By analogy, therefore, the guarantee would be recognised as an asset to the extent it is virtually certain a recovery could be made if the lender suffered the impairment loss on the loan.

However, IFRS 4 explains that the holder of a financial guarantee contract will normally need to develop its accounting policy in accordance with the 'hierarchy' in IAS 8 – *Accounting Policies, Changes in Accounting Estimates and Errors* (see Chapter 43 at 3.4.3 and Chapter 3 at 4.3), *[IFRS 4.IG2 Example 1.11]*, suggesting an entity does not automatically apply IAS 37 and could adopt a policy that aligns more closely the recognition of impairment losses and associated recoveries under the guarantee.

4.2.3 Measurement – detailed requirements

The standard contains a significant amount of detailed application guidance on the processes to be used for the assessment and calculation of impairment losses within groups of financial assets carried at amortised cost. In practice, this will be of limited relevance to entities that are determining a bad debt provision in respect of a portfolio of short-term trade receivables. However, for banks and other financial institutions with significant portfolios of loans and receivables, these detailed requirements will be highly relevant and could have a major impact on the way that loan impairments are assessed. This guidance might also be more relevant for entities providing goods or services on deferred settlement terms, such as retailers operating their own store-cards.

The guidance explains that the process for estimating impairment should consider all credit exposures, not only those of low credit quality. For example, if an internal credit grading system is used, all credit grades should be considered, not only those reflecting severe credit deterioration. *[IAS 39.AG85]*. In other words, the possibility of impairment existing in a portfolio of high quality assets that contain a low risk of default should not be ignored.

Whatever process is used to estimate an impairment loss, it may produce either a single amount or a range of possible amounts. In the latter case, the best estimate within the range should be recognised as the impairment loss. This estimate should take into account all relevant information about known conditions that existed at the end of the reporting period. The standard cross-refers to IAS 37 for guidance on selecting the best estimate in a range of possible outcomes (see Chapter 28 at 4.1). *[IAS 39.AG86]*.

When performing a collective evaluation of impairment, assets should be grouped on the basis of similar credit risk characteristics that are indicative of the debtors' ability to settle according to the contractual terms of the instruments concerned. For example, this may be done on the basis of a credit risk evaluation or grading process that considers some or all of the following characteristics depending on their relevance: asset type, industry, geographical location, collateral type, past-due status as well as other factors. *[IAS 39.AG87]*.

It is stated that loss probabilities and other loss statistics differ at a group level between (a) assets that have been individually evaluated for impairment and found not to be impaired, and (b) assets that have not been individually evaluated for impairment, with the result that a different amount of impairment may be required. *[IAS 39.AG87]*. In practice, the extent of the difference in approach to these groups will depend on the quality of the individual assessments – i.e. the less detailed or accurate the individual assessment is, the less the loss probabilities for assets in (a) and in (b) should differ.

Further, it is explained that if an entity does not have a group of assets with similar risk characteristics, it should not make any additional assessment over and above that performed at an individual level. *[IAS 39.AG87]*. It is this situation that the two dissenting IASB members found hard to accept. If one entity owned 50% of a loan asset for which there was no evidence of impairment when assessed on an individual basis, but it owned no similar assets, then it would recognise no impairment loss. However, if another entity owned the other 50% of the loan asset and also owned a number of similar assets, that entity may end up recognising an impairment loss in respect of its identical asset. *[IAS 39.DO4]*.

This anomaly may be rationalised in a number of ways. For example, if a company owned only one significant asset, rather than a group of similar assets, it is quite likely to assess impairment of that asset in a more detailed manner than a company with a group of similar assets. Also, this situation is not dissimilar to the treatment of warranty claims under IAS 37. If there was a small probability, say 1%, of a warranty claim arising on each sale made, a company that had sold one unit would not normally recognise a provision. However, a company that had sold thousands of identical units would almost certainly recognise a provision.

It is explained that impairment losses recognised on a group basis represent an interim step pending the identification of impairment losses on individual assets in the group. Accordingly, as soon as information is available that specifically identifies losses on individually impaired assets, those assets should be removed from the group. *[IAS 39.AG88]*.

Estimates of future cash flows for a group of financial assets should be based on historical loss experience for assets with credit risk characteristics similar to those in the group. Entities that have no, or insufficient, entity-specific loss experience, should use peer group experience for comparable groups of assets. Historical loss experience should be adjusted on the basis of current observable data to reflect the effects of current conditions that did not affect the period on which the historical loss experience is based, and to remove the effects of conditions in the historical period that do not exist currently. Estimates of changes in future cash flows should reflect, and be directionally consistent with, changes in related observable data from period to period (such as changes in unemployment rates, property prices, commodity prices, payment status or other factors that are indicative of incurred losses in the group and their magnitude). The methodology and assumptions used for estimating future cash flows should be reviewed regularly to reduce any differences between loss estimates and actual loss experience. *[IAS 39.AG89]*.

As an example of this approach, historical experience may demonstrate that one of the main causes of default on credit card loans is the death of the borrower. Although the death rate may be unchanged since the previous year, some of the group of borrowers could have died in the year. This would indicate that an impairment loss has occurred, even if it was not possible to identify which specific borrowers had died at the year-end, and it would be appropriate for an impairment loss to be recognised for these 'incurred but not reported' losses. However, it would not be appropriate to recognise an impairment loss for deaths that are expected to occur in a future period. In that case the necessary loss event (the death of the borrower) has not yet occurred. *[IAS 39.AG90]*.

When using historical loss rates in estimating future cash flows, it is important that information about historical loss rates is applied to groups that are defined in a manner consistent with the groups for which the historical loss rates were observed. Therefore, the method used should enable each group to be associated with information about past loss experience in groups of assets with similar credit risk characteristics and relevant observable data that reflect current conditions. *[IAS 39.AG91]*.

Formula-based approaches or statistical methods may be used to determine impairment losses in a group of financial assets (e.g. for smaller balance loans) as long as they are consistent with the general requirements of the standard. Therefore any model used should incorporate the effect of the time value of money, consider the cash flows for all of the remaining life of an asset (not only the next year), consider the age of the loans within the portfolio and not give rise to an impairment loss on initial recognition. *[IAS 39.AG92]*.

Sometimes, the observable data required to estimate an impairment loss may be limited or no longer fully relevant to current circumstances, for example when a borrower is in financial difficulties and there is little available historical data relating to similar borrowers. In such cases, judgement and experience should be used to estimate the amount of any impairment loss and to adjust observable data for a group of financial assets to reflect current circumstances. The fact that an impairment loss is difficult to measure is not a reason for not recognising a loss that has been incurred. The use of reasonable estimates is an essential part of the preparation of financial statements and does not undermine their reliability. *[IAS 39.62]*.

4.2.4 *Impairment of assets subject to hedges*

When a loan asset with fixed interest rate payments is hedged against the exposure to interest rate risk by a receive-variable, pay-fixed interest rate swap, the carrying amount of the asset will include an adjustment for fair value changes attributable to movements in interest rates (see Chapter 52 at 4.1). As a result, in accounting for the asset, the original effective interest rate and amortised cost of the asset are adjusted to take into account these recognised fair value changes and the adjusted effective interest rate is calculated using the adjusted carrying amount of the asset. *[IAS 39.E.4.4]*.

Any impairment loss on such a hedged asset should be calculated after taking account of the adjustments noted above. In other words, it will be the difference between the carrying amount of the asset *after* adjustment for fair value changes attributable to the risk being hedged and the expected future cash flows of the loan discounted at the *adjusted* effective interest rate. *[IAS 39.E.4.4]*.

When a loan is included in a portfolio hedge of interest rate risk (see Chapter 52 at 6) the change in the fair value of the hedged portfolio should be allocated to the loans (or groups of similar loans) being assessed for impairment on a systematic and rational basis. *[IAS 39.E.4.4]*.

4.2.5 *Reversal of impairment losses*

If, in a subsequent period, the amount of the impairment or bad debt loss decreases and the decrease can be objectively related to an event occurring after the write-down (such as an improvement in the debtor's credit rating), the previously recognised impairment loss should be reversed, either directly or by adjusting an allowance account. The reversal should not result in a carrying amount of the asset that exceeds what its amortised cost would have been at the date of reversal, had the impairment not been recognised. The amount of the reversal should be recognised in profit or loss. *[IAS 39.65]*.

4.3 Available-for-sale assets measured at fair value

4.3.1 *Recognition of impairment*

When a decline in the fair value of an available-for-sale asset has been recognised in other comprehensive income and there is objective evidence that the asset is impaired (see 4.1 above), the cumulative loss within equity should be reclassified to profit or loss even though the asset has not been derecognised. *[IAS 39.67]*.

The amount of the loss that should be reclassified is the difference between the acquisition cost of the asset (net of any principal repayment and amortisation for assets measured using the effective interest method) and current fair value, less any impairment loss on that asset previously recognised in profit or loss. *[IAS 39.68]*.

For debt instruments, this requirement is not uncontroversial. Unlike an impairment loss on an equivalent asset measured at amortised cost, the amount recognised in profit or loss is measured by reference to the fair value of the asset. This will include the effects of changes in interest rates and credit or liquidity spreads, whereas the impairment loss for, say, a loan or receivable, will reflect only the present value of the expected cash loss.

For non-monetary assets, such as equity instruments, the cumulative net loss included within equity will include any portion attributable to foreign currency changes. It follows that this element of the loss should also be reclassified to profit or loss if the asset becomes impaired. *[IAS 39.E.4.9]*.

4.3.2 *Impairment of available-for-sale equity instruments subject to fair value hedges*

In assessing the impairment of available-for-sale equity instruments, IAS 39 requires an entity to use the 'cost' of the instrument as the basis to determine whether there has been a significant or prolonged decline in fair value. *[IAS 39.61]*. Similarly, in recognising the impairment loss, the entity would reclassify the amount of the loss within equity to profit or loss based on the difference between the 'acquisition cost' and current fair value, less any amount already recognised in profit or loss (see 4.3.1 above). *[IAS 39.68]*.

However, for an equity instrument that was previously subject to a fair value hedge and the hedge was subsequently terminated, it would make sense for the entity to adjust the 'cost' basis when assessing whether there has been a significant or prolonged decline in fair value. For example, an equity investment that was bought at a price of £100 and hedged for fair value decline to £80 (where the hedge was subsequently terminated), then the assessment of whether there is an impairment loss and subsequent calculation of that loss should be based on £80 rather than the original cost of £100.

The adjustment to the cost basis for impairment purposes is consistent with the guidance on assessing impairment for inventories and fixed interest rate loans subject to fair value hedges (see 4.2.4 above). *[IAS 39.E.4.4, F.3.6]*.

4.3.3 Reversals of impairment

If, in a subsequent period, the fair value of an available-for-sale *debt* instrument increases, and the increase can be objectively related to an event occurring after the loss was recognised in profit or loss, the impairment loss should be reversed and recognised in profit or loss. *[IAS 39.70]*. Judgement is required to determine whether a recovery in the fair value of an available-for-sale debt security relates to an event that occurred after the loss was recognised. Questions arise as to what to do when the fair value partially recovers or when there is evidence of an improvement in the credit quality of the debt instrument but the entity cannot determine that there is no longer any objective evidence of impairment. In these circumstances, we believe policy choices need to be made. This is illustrated in the following example:

Example 49.20: Increase in the fair value of an impaired available-for-sale debt investment

An entity purchased a debt instrument, which it designated as available-for-sale with a cost of £100. In year two, the fair value of the instrument decreased to £70 and the entity concluded that the instrument was impaired and consequently recognised an impairment loss of £30. In year three, the fair value of the instrument increases to £95.

Scenario 1 – The entity can determine that there is no longer any objective evidence of impairment. That is, the credit event triggering the impairment reverses in its entirety.

Scenario 2 – The entity cannot determine that there is no longer any objective evidence of impairment (that is, the credit event triggering the impairment did not entirely reverse) however, it can determine that the credit quality of the instrument improved compared to the situation when the instrument was impaired.

In both scenarios, the entity might have reversed a small part of the impairment loss through the application of the higher effective interest rate determined at the time the instrument was impaired. This effect is ignored in the conclusion below.

An entity can only reverse through profit or loss an increase in the fair value of an available-for-sale debt instrument that occurs subsequent to impairment if there is an actual improvement in the credit quality of the instrument. If there is no improvement in the credit quality, the entity recognises the increase in fair value in other comprehensive income (OCI). Judgement is required to determine whether the credit event triggering the impairment reversed in its entirety (i.e. there is no longer any objective evidence of impairment) or whether there is only some improvement in credit quality.

Scenario 1 – If there is no longer objective evidence of impairment, such that the event reversed in its entirety, we believe the entity has an accounting policy choice, which it must apply consistently:

The entity can recognise in profit or loss a reversal of impairment of £30 and recognise a loss of £5 in OCI or it can recognise in profit or loss a reversal of impairment of £25.

Scenario 2 – If there is some evidence of improvement in credit quality, but the credit event did not reverse, the entity has an accounting policy choice, which it must apply consistently:

The entity can recognise in profit or loss a reversal of impairment of £25. Alternatively, the entity could choose not to recognise any reversal of impairment in profit or loss, until the event reverses in its entirety. Therefore, the entity recognises an increase in fair value in OCI (of £25).

However, in the case of *equity* instruments, impairments cannot be reversed through profit or loss. *[IAS 39.69]*.

The Basis for Conclusions includes an explanation for the difference in treatment. In particular, in the context of the reversal of impairments on available-for-sale debt securities, it is noted that:

- the reversal of impairment losses of non-financial assets (e.g. inventories, property, plant and equipment and intangible assets) is required if circumstances change;
- the treatment provides consistency with the requirement to reverse impairment losses on loans and receivables and on assets classified as held-to-maturity; and
- determining an increase in fair value attributable to an improvement in credit standing is more objectively determinable than for equity instruments. *[IAS 39.BC128]*.

The IASB could not find an acceptable way to distinguish reversals of impairment losses from other increases in fair value of available-for-sale equity instruments. Therefore, it decided that precluding such reversals for equity instruments was the only appropriate solution, even though a number of other approaches were considered. *[IAS 39.BC130]*. In the end, this approach probably seemed most expedient as it is comparable to US GAAP under which reversals of impairment losses on equity instruments are not permitted. *[IAS 39.BC221(g)]*. One IASB member formally disagreed with the approach adopted, not because he considered it appropriate to reverse an impairment loss but because he would have preferred all losses below original cost on equity instruments to be recognised as impairments, *[IAS 39.DO13]*, i.e. in profit or loss.

4.3.4 Further declines in the fair value of impaired equity instruments

The question has arisen as to what the accounting treatment should be if, following an impairment, the fair value of an available-for-sale equity instrument declines further. This is illustrated in the following example.

Example 49.21: Decline in the fair value of an impaired available-for-sale equity investment

Company A acquired 100 shares in Company X on 1 January 2016, for their fair value of €10,000. On 31 December 2016, A's year end, the fair value of the shares in X had fallen to €6,000 and A concluded the shares were impaired. Accordingly, in its 2016 financial statements, A recognised an impairment loss of €4,000 in profit or loss.

On 31 December 2017, the fair value of the shares in X had fallen a little further to €5,900. In its 2017 financial statements, should A automatically regard the loss of €100 as a further impairment (to be recognised in profit or loss) or should it regard it as a normal revaluation to be recognised in other comprehensive income?

The implementation guidance to the standard suggests that any further declines in the fair value of an impaired available-for-sale equity instrument should be recognised in profit or loss, although only in the context of explaining the treatment of portions of fair value movements arising from foreign currency changes. *[IAS 39.E.4.9]*.

However, perhaps because the accounting treatment is said to be comparable to US GAAP (see 4.3.3 above), some considered that, once impaired, the asset acquired a new 'cost base' equal to the fair value at the date of impairment. Consequently, the €100 decline in fair value would be assessed for impairment as if the asset had been acquired on 31 December 2016 for €6,000. This approach would not necessarily result in the €100 being characterised as an impairment loss.

The Interpretations Committee has addressed this issue and took the view that impairments do not establish a new cost basis. Therefore, for an equity instrument for which a prior impairment loss has been recognised, in applying the indicators discussed at 4.1 above, 'significant' should be evaluated against the original cost at initial recognition and 'prolonged' should be evaluated against the period in which the fair value of the investment has been below original cost at initial recognition.[34] Consequently, any further decline in fair value, whatever its cause, should be recognised in profit or loss. Extract 49.2 at 4.1.3 above (Allianz) contains an accounting policy that explicitly addresses this requirement.

4.3.5 Timing of impairment tests and interaction with interim reporting

The standard does not discuss how frequently an available-for-sale equity instrument should be assessed for impairment, only that it should be done 'at the end of each reporting period'. *[IAS 39.58]*. It might seem sensible to perform such reviews at the end of both interim and annual periods. However, this could give rise to what some see as anomalous results.

Consider, for example, an entity that purchases an equity share for €100 at the start of its reporting period. If the fair value of the share had fallen to €60 at the end of the half-year, it is very likely to conclude that the share had become impaired. Consequently, a €40 loss would be recognised in profit or loss. However, if the share price had recovered to €100 by the end of the full financial year, should this loss be reversed? IAS 34 – *Interim Financial Reporting* – states that '... the frequency of an entity's reporting (annual, half-yearly, or quarterly) shall not affect the measurement of its annual results.' *[IAS 34.28]*. This might suggest that the impairment loss recognised at the half-year could be reversed at the year-end.

On the other hand, the guidance that accompanies IAS 34 states that the same impairment testing, recognition, and reversal criteria that would be applied at the year-end should be applied at an interim date. *[IAS 34.B36]*. Further, the accounting requirements of IAS 39 are generally applied on a continuous basis and it might be argued that ignoring losses between the end of reporting periods (whatever their frequency) fails to apply properly the requirements of the standard.

This is an issue that has reached the Interpretations Committee's agenda. Early on in their deliberations it was made clear that the Interpretations Committee did not support an approach that would require entities to review for impairment on a continuous basis, leaving the apparent conflicts within IAS 34 and between IAS 34 and IAS 39 to be dealt with.[35]

In July 2006, the Interpretations Committee published an interpretation, IFRIC 10 – *Interim Financial Reporting and Impairment* – setting out how to resolve the conflicts. The Interpretations Committee took the view that the more specific requirements in IAS 39 should take precedence and, therefore, that impairments of available-for-sale equity instruments recognised in an interim period should not be reversed. *[IFRIC 10.8, BC9]*. IFRIC 10 also deals with a similar conflict in the treatment of goodwill impairments but it contains a prohibition on extending by analogy its consensus to other areas of potential conflict between IAS 34 and other standards. *[IFRIC 10.9]*.

4.4 Financial assets carried at cost in accordance with IAS 39

As set out at 2.1 and 2.4 above, unquoted equity instruments and derivative assets that are linked to and must be settled by delivery of such instruments whose fair value cannot be reliably measured, are measured at cost.

If there is objective evidence that an impairment loss has been incurred on such an asset, the amount of the impairment loss is measured as the difference between the carrying amount of the financial asset and the present value of estimated future cash flows, discounted at the current market rate of return for a similar financial asset. *[IAS 39.66]*. This requirement applies equally to financial assets classified as at fair value through profit or loss and to available-for-sale financial assets.

Consistent with the treatment for available-for-sale equity securities measured at fair value, any such impairment losses may not be reversed. *[IAS 39.66]*. The requirements of IFRIC 10 apply to these assets as well as to available-for-sale assets measured at fair value. *[IFRIC 10.6]*.

4.5 Interest income after impairment recognition

Once a financial asset, or group of similar assets, has been written down as a result of an impairment loss, interest income is thereafter recognised based on the rate of interest that was used to discount the future cash flows for the purpose of measuring the impairment loss. *[IAS 39.AG93]*.

It is not clear how this requirement should be applied to a fixed interest rate debt instrument that is measured at amortised cost and has been written down to its fair value (rather than its net present value using the original effective interest rate of the instrument – see 4.2.2 above). Using an appropriate long-term interest rate at the date of the impairment would seem consistent with the measurement basis adopted, although this is not strictly in accordance with the standard.

5 FOREIGN CURRENCIES

5.1 Foreign currency instruments

The provisions of IAS 21 apply to transactions involving financial instruments in just the same way as they do for other transactions, although the manner in which certain hedges are accounted for can over-ride its general requirements.

Consequently, the statement of financial position measurement of a foreign currency financial instrument is determined as follows:

- firstly, it is recorded and measured in the foreign currency in which it is denominated, whether it is carried at fair value, cost, or amortised cost;
- secondly, that amount is retranslated to the entity's functional currency using:
  - closing rate, for all monetary items (e.g. a debt security) and for non-monetary items (e.g. an equity share) carried at fair value; or
  - a historical rate, for non-monetary items carried at cost because their fair value cannot be reliably measured.

Therefore, for a foreign currency denominated monetary asset carried at amortised cost, amortised cost is calculated in the currency in which it is denominated. That foreign currency amount is then retranslated into the entity's functional currency at the closing rate.

As an exception, if the non-monetary financial instrument carried at cost (for example, unquoted equity instruments) is designated as a hedged item in a fair value hedge of foreign currency exposure, it is remeasured for changes in foreign currency rates even if it would otherwise have been recognised using a historical rate (see Chapter 52 at 4.1).

The reporting of changes in the carrying amount of a financial instrument in profit or loss or in other comprehensive income depends on a number of factors, including whether it is an exchange difference or other change in carrying amount, whether the instrument is a monetary or non-monetary item and whether it is designated as part of a foreign currency cash flow hedge or hedge of a net investment.

Profit and loss items associated with financial instruments, e.g. dividends receivable, interest payable or receivable and impairments, are recorded at the spot rate ruling when they arise (although average rates may be used when they represent an appropriate approximation to spot rates throughout the period). Exchange differences arising on retranslating monetary items are generally recognised in profit or loss, although they may be recognised in other comprehensive income for instruments designated as hedges of future foreign currency transactions or net investments in foreign entities (see Chapter 52 at 4.2 and 4.3). All other fair value changes (e.g. the change in value of a debt instrument as a result of interest rate movements) are recognised in profit or loss if the instrument is classified at fair value through profit or loss, or other comprehensive income if it is available-for-sale.

In cases where some portion of the change in carrying amount is recognised in profit or loss and some in other comprehensive income, e.g. if the fair value of a bond has increased in foreign currency and decreased in the functional currency, those two components cannot be offset for the purposes of determining gains or losses that should be recognised in profit or loss and other comprehensive income. *[IAS 39.AG83, E.3.4].*

These principles are illustrated in the following example.

Example 49.22: Available-for-sale foreign currency debt security

On 31 December 2014, Company A, whose functional currency is the euro, acquires a dollar bond for its fair value of $1,000. The bond is the same as the one in Example 49.6 at 3.1 above, i.e. it has five years to maturity and a $1,250 principal, carries fixed interest of 4.7% paid annually ($1,250 × 4.7% = $59 per year), and has an effective interest rate of 10%.

A classifies the bond as available-for-sale. The exchange rate is $1 to €1.50 and the carrying amount of the bond is €1,500 ($1,000 × 1.50).

	€	€
Bond	1,500	
Cash		1,500

On 31 December 2015, the dollar has appreciated and the exchange rate is $1 to €2.00. The fair value of the bond is $1,060 and therefore its carrying amount is €2,120 ($1,060 × 2.00). Its amortised cost is $1,041 (or €2,082 = $1,041 × 2.00) and the cumulative gain or loss to be included in other comprehensive income is the difference between its fair value and amortised cost, i.e. a gain of €38 (€2,120 – €2,082; or, alternatively, [$1,060 – $1,041] × 2.00).

Interest received on the bond on 31 December 2015 is \$59 (or €118 = \$59 × 2.00). Interest income determined in accordance with the effective interest method is \$100 (\$1,000 × 10%) of which \$41 (\$100 – \$59) is the accretion of the initial discount.

It is assumed that the average exchange rate during the year is \$1 to €1.75 and that the use of an average exchange rate provides a reliable approximation of the spot rates applicable to the accrual of interest during the year. Therefore, reported interest income is €175 (\$100 × 1.75) including accretion of the initial discount of €72 (\$41 × 1.75).

The exchange difference recognised in profit or loss is €525, which comprises three elements: a €500 gain from the retranslation of the initial amortised cost (\$1,000 × [2.00 – 1.50]); a €15 gain from the retranslation of interest income received (\$59 × [2.00 – 1.75]) and a €10 gain on the retranslation of the interest income accreted (\$41 × [2.00 – 1.75]).

	€	€
Bond	620	
Cash	118	
Interest income (P&L)		175
Exchange gain (P&L)		525
Fair value change (equity)		38

On 31 December 2016, the dollar has appreciated further and the exchange rate is \$1 to €2.50. The fair value of the bond is \$1,070 and therefore its carrying amount is €2,675 (\$1,070 × 2.50). Its amortised cost is \$1,086 (or €2,715 = \$1,086 × 2.50) and the cumulative gain or loss to be included in other comprehensive income is the difference between its fair value and the amortised cost, i.e. a loss of €40 (€2,675 – €2,715; or, alternatively, [\$1,070 – \$1,086] × 2.50). Therefore, there is a debit to other comprehensive income equal to the change in the difference during 2016 of €78 (€40 + €38).

Interest received on the bond on 31 December 2016 is \$59 (or €148 = \$59 × 2.50). Interest income determined in accordance with the effective interest method is \$104 (\$1,041 × 10%), of which \$45 (\$104 – \$59) is the accretion of the initial discount.

Using the same assumptions as in the previous year, interest income is €234 (\$104 × 2.25) including accretion of the initial discount of €101 (\$45 × 2.25).

The exchange difference recognised in profit or loss is €547, which again comprises three elements: a €521 gain from the retranslation of the opening amortised cost (\$1,041 × [2.50 – 2.00]); a €15 gain from the retranslation of interest income received (\$59 × [2.50 – 2.25]) and an €11 gain on the retranslation of the interest income accreted (\$45 × [2.50 – 2.25]). *[IAS 39.E.3.2]*.

	€	€
Bond	555	
Cash	148	
Fair value change (equity)	78	
Interest income (P&L)		234
Exchange gain (P&L)		547

It is worth repeating that the treatment would be different for available-for-sale equity instruments. Under IAS 21, these are not considered monetary items and exchange differences would form part of the change in the fair value of the instrument, which would be recognised in other comprehensive income.

5.2 Foreign entities

IAS 39 does not amend application of the net investment method of accounting for foreign entities set out in IAS 21 (see Chapter 15 at 6). Therefore, for the purpose of preparing its own accounts for inclusion in consolidated accounts, a foreign entity that is part of a group applies the principles at 5.1 above by reference to its own functional currency. Consequently, the treatment of gains and losses on, say, trading assets held by a foreign entity should follow the treatment in the example below.

Example 49.23: Interaction of IAS 21 and IAS 39 – foreign currency debt investment

Company A is domiciled in the US and its functional currency and presentation currency is the US dollar. A has a UK domiciled subsidiary, B, whose functional currency is sterling. B is the owner of a debt instrument which is held for trading and is therefore carried at fair value.

In B's financial statements for 2016, the fair value and carrying amount of the debt instrument is £100. In A's consolidated financial statements, the asset is translated into US dollars at the spot exchange rate applicable at the end of the reporting period, say 2.0, and the carrying amount is US$200 (£100 × 2.0).

At the end of 2017, the fair value of the debt instrument has increased to £110. B reports the trading asset at £110 in its statement of financial position and recognises a fair value gain of £10 in profit or loss. During the year, the spot exchange rate has increased from 2.0 to 3.0 resulting in an increase in the fair value of the instrument from US$200 to US$330 (£110 × 3.0). Therefore, A reports the trading asset at US$330 in its consolidated financial statements.

Since B is classified as a foreign entity, A translates B's statement of comprehensive income 'at the exchange rates at the dates of the transactions'. Since the fair value gain has accrued through the year, A uses the average rate of 2.5 (= [3.0 + 2.0] ÷ 2) as a practical approximation. Therefore, while the fair value of the trading asset has increased by US$130 (US$330 – US$200), A recognises only US$25 (£10 × 2.5) of this increase in profit or loss. The resulting exchange difference, i.e. the remaining increase in the fair value of the debt instrument of US$105 (US$130 – US$25), is recognised in other comprehensive income until the disposal of the net investment in the foreign entity. *[IAS 39.E.3.3].*

References

1 *IAS 39.70 (2000).*
2 *IGC Q&A 70-1.*
3 *IFRIC Update*, November 2006.
4 The implementation guidance says the entire combined contract should be treated as held for trading (not designated at fair value through profit or loss). This reflects an earlier version of IAS 39 as the implementation guidance was not updated to reflect a subsequent amendment.
5 *Exposure Draft, Proposed Amendments to IAS 39 and IFRS 4, Financial Guarantee Contracts and Credit Insurance, IASB, July 2004, BC18(a).*
6 *ASC 944-20-15-69, Financial Guarantee Insurance Contracts, FASB.*
7 *IGC Q&A 73-1.*
8 *IGC Q&A 10-19.*
9 *Implementation of International Accounting Standards*, British Bankers' Association, July 2004, 10.
10 *IGC Q&A 76-1.*
11 Based on the example in IAS 39.B.25.
12 *IFRIC Update*, July 2008.
13 Information for Observers (May 2008 IFRIC meeting), *Application of the Effective Interest Rate Method*, IASB, May 2008, Appendix.
14 Information for Observers, 6.
15 *IFRIC Update*, July 2008.
16 Information for Observers (July 2008 IFRIC meeting), *Application of the Effective Interest Rate Method*, IASB, July 2008, 4.
17 Position Paper, *IAS 39 – Financial Instruments: Recognition and Measurement – assets and liabilities linked to an inflation index which are not measured at fair value (continuation to the paper published in February 2008)*, Israel Accounting Standards Board, August 2008.
18 *IFRIC Update*, May 2009.
19 *IFRIC Update*, July 2008.
20 *IFRIC Update*, October 2004.
21 Staff Paper (May 2009 IFRIC Meeting), *IAS 39 Financial Instruments: Recognition and Measurement – Meaning of 'significant or prolonged' (Agenda reference 10)*, IASB, May 2009, 2 and 5.
22 *IASB Update*, July 2009.

23 *IFRIC Update*, July 2009.
24 Staff Paper (May 2009 IFRIC Meeting), 33.
25 Staff Paper (May 2009 IFRIC Meeting), 24.
26 Staff Paper (May 2009 IFRIC Meeting), 25.
27 Staff Paper (July 2009 IFRIC Meeting), *IAS 39 Financial Instruments: Recognition and Measurement – Meaning of 'significant or prolonged' (Agenda reference 21)*, IASB, July 2009, 15 to 18.
28 Staff Paper (July 2009 IFRIC Meeting), 19 to 28.
29 *IFRIC Update*, July 2009.
30 Staff Paper (July 2009 IFRIC Meeting), 11 to 14.
31 *IFRIC Update*, July 2009.
32 *IGC Q&A 113-3.*
33 *IGC Q&A 113-1.*
34 *IFRIC Update*, June 2005.
35 *IFRIC Update*, August 2005.

Chapter 50 Financial instruments: Subsequent measurement (IFRS 9)

List of examples

Chapter 50 Financial instruments: Subsequent measurement (IFRS 9)

1 INTRODUCTION

The introduction to Chapter 42 provides a general background to the development of accounting for financial instruments. Chapter 43 deals with what qualify as financial assets and financial liabilities and other contracts that are treated as if they were financial instruments, and Chapter 46 discusses the classification of financial instruments under IFRS 9 – *Financial Instruments*. Chapter 48 deals with the question of when financial instruments should be recognised in financial statements and their initial measurement. The related question of when a previously recognised financial instrument should be derecognised from the financial statements is dealt with in Chapter 51. Hedge accounting under IFRS 9 is dealt with in Chapter 53 and the presentation and disclosure of financial instruments are covered in Chapter 54.

This chapter discusses the subsequent measurement of financial instruments under IFRS 9, including the requirements relating to amortised cost, the effective interest method, foreign currency revaluation, impairment. It also discusses the effective date and the transition requirements of IFRS 9.

Most, but not all, of the detailed requirements of IFRS governing the measurement of fair values are dealt with in IFRS 13 – *Fair Value Measurement* – which is covered in Chapter 14. IFRS 9 also contains some requirements addressing fair value measurements of financial instruments and these are covered at 2.6 below.

2 SUBSEQUENT MEASUREMENT AND RECOGNITION OF GAINS AND LOSSES

As explained in Chapter 47 at 2, following the application of IFRS 9, financial assets and financial liabilities are classified into one of the following measurement categories: *[IFRS 9.4.1.1]*

- debt instruments at amortised cost;
- debt instruments at fair value through other comprehensive income (with cumulative gains and losses reclassified to profit or loss upon derecognition);
- debt instruments, derivatives and equity instruments at fair value through profit or loss;
- equity instruments designated as measured at fair value through other comprehensive income (with gains and losses remaining in other comprehensive income, without recycling); or
- financial liabilities either at fair value through profit or loss or at amortised cost.

Following the initial recognition of financial assets and financial liabilities, their subsequent accounting treatment depends principally on the classification of the instrument, although there are a small number of exceptions. These requirements are summarised in the following table and are considered in more detail in the remainder of this section.

Classification	Instrument type	Statement of financial position	Fair value gains and losses	Interest and dividends	Impairment	Foreign exchange
Fair value through profit or loss (including derivatives not designated in effective hedges)	Debt, Equity or Derivative	Fair value	Profit or loss*†	Profit or loss*	–	Profit or loss
Equity investments at fair value through other comprehensive income	Equity	Fair value	Other comprehensive income‡	Profit or loss: dividends receivable	–	Other comprehensive income‡
Debt financial assets at fair value through other comprehensive income	Debt	Fair value	Other comprehensive income and recycled to profit or loss when derecognised	Profit or loss: using an effective interest rate	Profit or loss	Profit or loss
Financial assets and liabilities at amortised cost	Debt	Amortised cost	–	Profit or loss: using an effective interest rate	Profit or loss (assets)	Profit or loss

* Little guidance is given on how gains and losses should be disaggregated – see Chapter 54 at 7.1.1.

† The gain or loss on a financial liability attributable to changes in its credit risk is sometimes recognised in other comprehensive income – see 2.1.1 and 6.2.3 below.

‡ These gains and losses are not reclassified from equity to profit or loss, even on disposal.

In addition, IFRS 9 sets out the accounting treatment for certain financial guarantee contracts (see Chapter 43 at 3.4) and commitments to provide a loan at a below market interest rate (see Chapter 43 at 3.5).

2.1 Financial assets and financial liabilities measured at fair value through profit or loss

After initial recognition, financial assets and financial liabilities that are classified as fair value through profit or loss (including derivatives that are not designated in effective hedging relationships) are measured at fair value, with no deduction for sale or disposal costs (see Chapter 47 at 2, 5.4 and 7). *[IFRS 9.5.2.1, 5.3.1, 5.7.1]*.

The standard helpfully points out that if the fair value of a financial asset falls below zero it becomes a financial liability (assuming it is measured at fair value). *[IFRS 9.B5.2.1]*. The standard does not explain what happens if the fair value of a financial liability becomes positive, but it is safe to assume that it becomes a financial asset and not a negative liability.

Gains and losses arising from remeasuring a financial asset or financial liability at fair value should normally be recognised in profit or loss. *[IFRS 9.5.7.1]*. However, there is an exception for most non-derivative financial liabilities that are *designated* as measured at fair value through profit or loss. For these liabilities the element of the gain or loss attributable to changes in credit risk (see 2.1.1 and 6.2.3 below) should normally be recognised in other comprehensive income (with the remainder recognised in profit or loss). *[IFRS 9.5.7.7, B5.7.8]*. These amounts presented in other comprehensive income should not be subsequently transferred to profit or loss. However, the cumulative gain or loss may be transferred within equity. *[IFRS 9.B5.7.9]*.

This exception does not apply to loan commitments or financial guarantee contracts, nor does it apply if it would create or enlarge an accounting mismatch in profit or loss (see 2.1.2 below). *[IFRS 9.5.7.8, 5.7.9]*. In these cases, all changes in the fair value of the liability (including the effects of changes in the credit risk) should be recognised in profit or loss. *[IFRS 9.B5.7.8]*.

2.1.1 Liabilities at fair value through profit or loss: calculating the gain or loss attributable to changes in credit risk

IFRS 7 – *Financial Instruments: Disclosures* – defines credit risk as 'the risk that one party to a financial instrument will cause a financial loss for the other party by failing to discharge an obligation', which is also part of non-performance risk as defined in IFRS 13 (see Chapter 14 at 11.3). *[IFRS 7 Appendix A]*. The change in fair value of a financial liability that is attributable to credit risk relates to the risk that the issuer will fail to pay that particular liability. It may not solely relate to the creditworthiness of the issuer but may be influenced by other factors, such as collateral.

For example, if an entity issues a collateralised liability and a non-collateralised liability that are otherwise identical, the credit risk of those two liabilities will be different, even though they are issued by the same entity. The credit risk on the collateralised liability will be less than the credit risk of the non-collateralised liability. In fact, the credit risk for a collateralised liability may be close to zero. *[IFRS 9.B5.7.13]*. It is important to distinguish between what the standard refers to as credit risk and what the sections which address impairment refer to as the risk of default, since the latter does not include the benefit of collateral.

For these purposes, credit risk is different from asset-specific performance risk. Asset-specific performance risk is not related to the risk that an entity will fail to discharge a particular obligation but rather it is related to the risk that a single asset or a group of assets will perform poorly (or not at all). *[IFRS 9.B5.7.14]*. For example, consider: *[IFRS 9.B5.7.15]*

(a) a liability with a unit-linking feature whereby the amount due to investors is contractually determined on the basis of the performance of specified assets. The effect of that unit-linking feature on the fair value of the liability is asset-specific performance risk, not credit risk;

(b) a liability issued by a structured entity with the following characteristics:
- the structured entity is legally isolated so the assets in the structured entity are ring-fenced solely for the benefit of its investors, even in the event of bankruptcy;
- the structured entity enters into no other transactions and the assets in the SPE cannot be hypothecated; and
- amounts are due to the structured entity's investors only if the ring-fenced assets generate cash flows.

Thus, changes in the fair value of the liability primarily reflect changes in the fair value of the assets. The effect of the performance of the assets on the fair value of the liability is asset-specific performance risk, not credit risk.

Unless an alternative method more faithfully represents the change in fair value of a financial liability that is attributable to credit risk, this amount should be determined as the amount of change in the fair value of the liability that is not attributable to changes in market conditions that give rise to market risk. *[IFRS 9.B5.7.16]*. Changes in market conditions that give rise to market risk include changes in a benchmark interest rate, the price of another entity's financial instrument, a commodity price, foreign exchange rate or index of prices or rates. *[IFRS 9.B5.7.17]*.

If the only significant relevant changes in market conditions for a financial liability are changes in an observed (benchmark) interest rate, the amount to be recognised in other comprehensive income can be estimated as follows: *[IFRS 9.B5.7.18]*

(a) first, the liability's internal rate of return at the start of the period is computed using the fair value and contractual cash flows at that time and from this is deducted the observed (benchmark) interest rate at the start of the period, to arrive at an instrument specific component of the internal rate of return;

(b) next, the present value of the cash flows associated with the liability is calculated using the liability's contractual cash flows at the end of the period and a discount rate equal to the sum of the observed (benchmark) interest rate at the end of the period and the instrument-specific component of the internal rate of return at the start of the period as determined in (a); and

(c) the difference between the fair value of the liability at the end of the period and the amount determined in (b) is the change in fair value that is not attributable to changes in the observed (benchmark) interest rate and this is the amount to be presented in other comprehensive income.

This method is illustrated in the following example. *[IFRS 9.IE1-IE5].*

Example 50.1: Estimating the change in fair value of an instrument attributable to its credit risk

On 1 January 2017, Company J issues a 10-year bond with a par value of €150,000 and an annual fixed coupon rate of 8%, which is consistent with market rates for bonds with similar characteristics. J uses LIBOR as its observable (benchmark) interest rate. At the date of inception of the bond, LIBOR is 5%. At the end of the first year:

- LIBOR has decreased to 4.75%; and
- the fair value of the bond is €153,811 which is consistent with an interest rate of 7.6% [i.e. the remaining cash flows on the bond, €12,000 per year for nine years and €150,000 at the end of nine years, discounted at 7.6% equals €153,811].

J assumes a flat yield curve, that all changes in interest rates result from a parallel shift in the yield curve, and that the changes in LIBOR are the only relevant changes in market conditions.

The amount of change in the fair value of the bond that is not attributable to changes in market conditions that give rise to market risk is estimated as follows:

Step (a)

The bond's internal rate of return at the start of the period is 8%. Because the observed (benchmark) interest rate (LIBOR) is 5%, the instrument-specific component of the internal rate of return is 3%.

Step (b)

The contractual cash flows of the instrument at the end of the period are:

- interest: €12,000 [€150,000 × 8%] per year for each of years 2017 to 2026.
- principal: €150,000 in 2025.

The discount rate to be used to calculate the present value of the bond is thus 7.75%, which is the 4.75% end of period LIBOR rate, plus the 3% instrument-specific component calculated as at the start of the period, which gives a notional present value of €152,367 [$€12,000 \times (1 - 1.0775^{-9}) / 0.0775) + €150,000 \times 1.0775^{-9}$], on the assumption that there has been no change in the instrument-specific component.

Step (c)

The market price of the liability at the end of the period (which will reflect the real instrument-specific component at the end of the period within the 7.6% yield) is €153,811, therefore J should disclose €1,444 [€153,811 – €152,367] as the increase in fair value of the bond that is not attributable to changes in market conditions that give rise to market risk.

This method assumes that changes in fair value other than those arising from changes in the instrument's credit risk or from changes in observed (benchmark) interest rates are not significant. It would not be appropriate to use this method if changes in fair value arising from other factors are significant. In such cases, an alternative method should be used that more faithfully measures the effects of changes in the liability's credit risk. For example, if the instrument in the example contained an embedded derivative, the change in fair value of the embedded derivative should be excluded in determining the amount to be presented in other comprehensive income. *[IFRS 9.B5.7.19, B5.7.16(b)].*

The above method will produce an amount which includes any changes in the liquidity spread charged by market participants, since such changes are not considered to be attributable to changes in market conditions that give rise to market risk. This method is applied in practice as the effect of a liquidity spread cannot normally be isolated from that of the credit spread.

As with all estimates of fair value, the measurement method used for determining the portion of the change in the liability's fair value that is attributable to changes in its credit risk should make maximum use of market inputs. *[IFRS 9.B5.7.20]*.

2.1.2 Liabilities at fair value through profit or loss: assessing whether an accounting mismatch is created or enlarged

If a financial liability is designated as at fair value through profit or loss, it must be determined whether presenting in other comprehensive income the effects of changes in the liability's credit risk would create or enlarge an accounting mismatch in profit or loss. An accounting mismatch would be created or enlarged if this treatment would result in a greater mismatch in profit or loss than if those amounts were presented in profit or loss. *[IFRS 9.B5.7.5]*.

In making that determination, an assessment should be made as to whether the effects of changes in the liability's credit risk are expected to be offset in profit or loss by a change in the fair value of another financial instrument measured at fair value through profit or loss. Such an expectation should be based on an economic relationship between the characteristics of the liability and the characteristics of the other financial instrument. *[IFRS 9.B5.7.6]*.

The determination should be made at initial recognition and is not reassessed. For practical purposes, all of the assets and liabilities giving rise to an accounting mismatch need not be entered into at exactly the same time – a reasonable delay is permitted provided that any remaining transactions are expected to occur. An entity's methodology for making this determination should be applied consistently for similar types of transactions. IFRS 7 requires an entity to provide qualitative disclosures in the notes to the financial statements about its methodology for making that determination – see Chapter 54 at 4.4.2.B. *[IFRS 9.B5.7.7]*.

The following example describes a situation in which an accounting mismatch would be created in profit or loss if the effects of changes in the credit risk of the liability were presented in other comprehensive income. *[IFRS 9.B5.7.10]*.

Example 50.2: Liabilities at fair value through profit or loss: accounting mismatch in profit or loss

A mortgage bank provides loans to customers and funds those loans by selling bonds with matching characteristics (e.g. amount outstanding, repayment profile, term and currency) in the market. The contractual terms of the loans permit the mortgage customer to prepay its loan (i.e. satisfy its obligation to the bank) by buying the corresponding bond at fair value in the market and delivering that bond to the mortgage bank.

As a result of that contractual prepayment right, if the credit quality of the bond worsens (and, thus, the fair value of the mortgage bank's liability decreases), the fair value of the mortgage bank's loan asset also decreases. The change in the fair value of the asset reflects the mortgage customer's contractual right to prepay the mortgage loan by buying the underlying bond at fair value (which, in this example, has decreased) and delivering the bond to the mortgage bank. Therefore, the effects of changes in the credit risk of the liability (the bond) will be offset in profit or loss by a corresponding change in the fair value of a financial asset (the loan).

If the effects of changes in the liability's credit risk were presented in other comprehensive income there would be an accounting mismatch in profit or loss. Therefore, the mortgage bank is required to present all changes in fair value of the liability (including the effects of changes in the liability's credit risk) in profit or loss.

In the example above, there is a contractual linkage between the effects of changes in the credit risk of the liability and changes in the fair value of the financial asset (i.e. as a result of the mortgage customer's contractual right to prepay the loan by buying the bond at fair value and delivering the bond to the mortgage bank). However, an accounting mismatch may also occur in the absence of a contractual linkage. *[IFRS 9.B5.7.11]*.

An accounting mismatch is not caused solely by the measurement method that an entity uses to determine the effects of changes in a liability's credit risk. For instance, if changes in a liability's credit risk are not isolated from changes in liquidity risk, such a mismatch is caused by measurement imprecision and not the offsetting relationship. An accounting mismatch in profit or loss would arise only when the effects of changes in the liability's credit risk (as defined in IFRS 7 – see 2.1.1 above) are expected to be offset by changes in the fair value of another financial instrument. *[IFRS 9.B5.7.12]*.

The following example illustrates another situation in which an accounting mismatch is not due to an economic relationship (in the sense intended by the IASB) between the movement in the fair value of the financial assets and the movement in the fair value of the financial liabilities related to the liabilities' own credit risk.

Example 50.3: Liabilities at fair value through profit or loss: no accounting mismatch in profit or loss

A bank issues structured products (consisting of a host debt contract and one or more embedded derivatives) in the market. These financial liabilities are designated as at fair value through profit or loss because they are managed on a fair value basis.

The bank invests the funds received in highly rated bonds, which are also designated as at fair value through profit or loss, and derivatives whose terms mirror those of the embedded derivatives in the structured products.

In periods when market credit spreads are volatile, it is expected that the effect of changes in credit spreads on the fair value of the structured products will be mainly compensated for by the effect of an offsetting credit spread movements on the bonds. This is because the credit quality of the bank is similar to the credit quality of the highly rated bonds in which the bank has invested.

Unlike Example 50.2 above, there is no direct link between the bank's own credit risk of the structured financial liabilities and the credit risk of the financial assets. The credit quality of the financial assets may be similar to that of the financial liabilities and these may move in a correlated manner as they are affected by similar movements in the general price of credit and other market risks, but the fair value of the financial assets will not move directly in response to changes in the bank's own credit risk.

Therefore, the requirements for an economic relationship are not met and all fair value changes attributable to changes in the credit risk of the financial liabilities should be taken to other comprehensive income.

2.2 Investments in equity investments designated at fair value through other comprehensive income

After initial recognition, investments in equity instruments not held for trading that are designated as measured at fair value through other comprehensive income (see Chapter 47 at 2.2) should be measured at fair value, with no deduction for sale or disposal costs. With the exception of dividends received, the associated gains and losses (including any related foreign exchange component) should be recognised in other comprehensive income. Amounts presented in other comprehensive income should not be subsequently transferred to profit or loss, although the cumulative gain or loss may be transferred within equity. *[IFRS 9.5.2.1, 5.7.5, B5.7.1, B5.7.3]*.

Dividends from such investments should be recognised in profit or loss when the right to receive payment is probable and can be measured reliably unless the dividend clearly represents a recovery of part of the cost of the investment. *[IFRS 9.5.7.1A, 5.7.6, B5.7.1]*. Determining when a dividend does or does not clearly represent a recovery of cost could prove somewhat judgmental in practice, especially as the standard contains no further explanatory guidance.

2.3 Debt instruments measured at fair value through other comprehensive income

For financial assets that are debt instruments measured at fair value through other comprehensive income (see Chapter 47 at 2.1), the IASB decided that both amortised cost and fair value information are relevant because debt instruments held by entities in this measurement category are held for both the collection of contractual cash flows and the realisation of fair values. *[IFRS 9.4.1.2A, BC4.150]*.

After initial recognition, investments in debt instruments that are classified as measured at fair value through other comprehensive income are measured at fair value in the statement of financial position (with no deduction for sale or disposal costs) and amortised cost information is presented in profit or loss. *[IFRS 9.5.7.10, 5.7.11]*.

Subsequent measurement of debt instruments at fair value through other comprehensive income involves the following: *[IFRS 9.5.7.1(d), 5.7.10, B5.7.1A]*

(a) impairment gains and losses (see 5 below) are derived using the same methodology that is applied to financial assets measured at amortised cost and are recognised in profit or loss; *[IFRS 9.5.2.2, 5.5.2]*

(b) foreign exchange gains and losses (see 4 below) are calculated based on the amortised cost of the debt instruments and are recognised in profit or loss; *[IFRS 9.B5.7.2, B5.7.2A]*

(c) interest revenue is calculated using the effective interest method (see 3 below) and is recognised in profit or loss; *[IFRS 9.5.4.1]*

(d) other fair value gains and losses are recognised in other comprehensive income; *[IFRS 9.5.7.10, B5.7.1A]*

(e) when debt instruments are modified (see 5.7 below), the modification gains or losses are recognised in profit or loss;[1] *[IFRS 9.5.7.10, 5.7.11, 5.4.3]* and

(f) when the debt instruments are derecognised, the cumulative gains or losses previously recognised in other comprehensive income are reclassified (i.e. recycled) from equity to profit or loss as a reclassification adjustment. *[IFRS 9. 5.7.10, B5.7.1A]*.

It follows that the amount recognised in other comprehensive income is the difference between the total change in fair value and the amounts recognised in profit or loss (excluding any amounts received in cash, e.g. the coupon on a bond).

2.4 Financial assets measured at amortised cost

Financial assets that are measured at amortised cost require the use of the effective interest method and are subject to the IFRS 9 impairment rules. *[IFRS 9.5.2.1, 5.2.2]*. Gains and losses are recognised in profit or loss when the instrument is derecognised or impaired, as well as through the amortisation process. *[IFRS 9.5.7.2]*. The effective interest method of accounting is dealt with at 3 below, foreign currency retranslation is discussed at 4 below and impairment is addressed in 5 below.

2.5 Financial liabilities measured at amortised cost

Liabilities that are measured at amortised cost require the use of the effective interest method with gains or losses recognised in profit or loss when the instrument is derecognised as well as through the amortisation process. *[IFRS 9.5.3.1, 5.7.2]*. The effective interest method of accounting is dealt with at 3 below and foreign currency retranslation is discussed at 4 below.

2.6 Unquoted equity instruments and related derivatives

In contrast to the position in IAS 39 – *Financial Instruments: Recognition and Measurement*, IFRS 9 requires all investments in equity instruments and contracts on those instruments to be measured at fair value (see Chapter 14). However, it is recognised that in limited circumstances, cost may be an appropriate estimate of fair value. That may be the case if insufficient more recent information is available to determine fair value, or if there is a wide range of possible fair value measurements and cost represents the best estimate of fair value within that range. *[IFRS 9.B5.2.3]*.

Such guidance was provided to alleviate some of the concerns expressed by constituents and also, to replace the IAS 39 cost exception that was not brought forward to IFRS 9. IAS 39 contained an exception from fair value measurement for investments in equity instruments (and some derivatives linked to those investments) that do not have a quoted price in an active market and whose fair value cannot be reliably measured. Those equity investments were required to be measured at cost less impairment, if any. *[IFRS 9.BC5.13, BC5.16, BC5.18]*.

Indicators that cost might not be representative of fair value include: *[IFRS 9.B5.2.4]*

(a) a significant change in the performance of the investee compared with budgets, plans or milestones;

(b) changes in expectation that the investee's technical product milestones will be achieved;

(c) a significant change in the market for the investee's equity or its products or potential products;

(d) a significant change in the global economy or the economic environment in which the investee operates;

(e) a significant change in the performance of comparable entities, or in the valuations implied by the overall market;

(f) internal matters of the investee such as fraud, commercial disputes, litigation, changes in management or strategy; and

(g) evidence from external transactions in the investee's equity, either by the investee (such as a fresh issue of equity), or by transfers of equity instruments between third parties.

This list is not intended to be exhaustive. All information about the performance and operations of the investee that becomes available after the date of initial recognition should be used and to the extent that any such relevant factors exist, they may indicate that cost might not be representative of fair value. In such cases, fair value should be estimated. *[IFRS 9.B5.4.16]*.

For the avoidance of doubt, IFRS 9 emphasises that cost is never the best estimate of fair value for investments in quoted equity instruments (or contracts on quoted equity instruments). *[IFRS 9.B5.4.17]*.

2.7 Reclassifications of financial assets

In certain situations financial assets classified as measured at fair value through profit or loss should be reclassified as measured at amortised cost and *vice versa*. The situations in which a reclassification might arise are considered in more detail in Chapter 47 at 9.

The reclassification should be applied prospectively from the reclassification date which is defined as 'the first day of the first reporting period following the change in business model that results in an entity reclassifying financial assets'. *[IFRS 9.5.6.1, Appendix A]*.

Accordingly, any previously recognised gains, losses (including impairment gains and losses) or interest should not be restated. *[IFRS 9.5.6.1]*. For example, when a financial asset is reclassified so that it is measured at fair value, its fair value is determined at the reclassification date. Any gain or loss arising from a difference between the previous carrying amount and fair value should be recognised in profit or loss of the current period without restating prior periods. *[IFRS 9.5.6.2]*. Accordingly, when a financial asset is reclassified so that it is measured at amortised cost, its fair value at the reclassification date becomes its new gross carrying amount. *[IFRS 9.5.6.3]*.

2.8 Financial guarantees and commitments to provide a loan at a below-market interest rate

Financial guarantees issued and commitments made to provide a loan at a below-market interest rate should be measured on initial recognition at their (negative) fair value and subsequently at the higher of:

- the amount of the loss allowance determined in accordance with the impairment requirements of IFRS 9 (see 5 below); and
- the amount initially recognised less, where appropriate, cumulative amortisation recognised in accordance with IAS 18 – *Revenue* (or when adopted the principles of IFRS 15 – *Revenue from Contracts with Customers*) (see Chapters 29 and 30).

This assumes that the instrument is not classified at fair value through profit or loss (in which case the requirements considered at 2.1 above apply) and, in the case of a financial guarantee contract, does not arise from a failed derecognition transaction (see 2.9.3 below). *[IFRS 9.4.2.1(a), 9.4.2.1(c), 4.2.1(d)]*.

For financial guarantees, there have been discussions by the ITG on how the timing of future premiums to be received affects the measurement of the expected credit loss (ECL) allowance and this is discussed further at 5.1.5 and 5.10 below.

2.9 Exceptions to the general principles

2.9.1 Hedging relationships

Financial assets and financial liabilities that are designated as hedged items are subject to measurement under the hedge accounting requirements of IFRS 9, or IAS 39 if the entity chooses as its accounting policy to continue to apply the hedge accounting requirements of IAS 39. *[IFRS 9.5.2.3, 5.3.2, 5.7.3, 7.2.21]*.

Also, derivatives and non-derivative debt financial instruments may be designated as hedging instruments which can affect whether fair value or foreign exchange gains and losses are recognised in profit or loss or in other comprehensive income. *[IFRS 9.B5.7.2]*. Hedge accounting is covered in Chapters 52 and 53.

2.9.2 Regular way transactions

IFRS 9 requires an entity to recognise a financial asset in its statement of financial position when, and only when, the entity becomes party to the contractual provisions of the instrument and to derecognise a financial asset when, and only when, the contractual rights to the cash flows from the financial asset expire (see Chapter 48 at 2.1). *[IFRS 9.3.1.1, 3.2.3]*. In other words, IFRS 9 requires a financial asset to be recognised or derecognised on a trade date basis, i.e. the date that an entity commits itself to purchase or sell an asset. *[IFRS 9.B3.1.5]*. However, the standard permits financial assets subject to so called 'regular way transactions' to be recognised, or derecognised, either as at the trade date or as at the settlement date (see Chapter 48 at 2.2). *[IFRS 9.3.1.2, B3.1.3, B3.1.5, B3.1.6]*. Whichever method is used, it is applied consistently and symmetrically (i.e. to acquisitions and disposals) to each of the main categories of financial asset identified by IFRS 9, i.e. *mandatorily* measured at amortised cost, at fair value through other comprehensive income or at fair value through profit or loss or *designated* as measured at fair value through profit or loss or at fair value through other comprehensive income (equity investments only) (see Chapter 48 at 2.2). *[IFRS 9.B3.1.3]*.

Where settlement date accounting is used for regular way transactions, any change in the fair value of the asset to be received arising between trade date and settlement date is not recognised for those assets that will be measured at amortised cost. For assets that will be recorded at fair value, such changes in value are recognised: *[IFRS 9.5.7.4, B3.1.6]*

- in profit or loss for assets to be classified as measured at fair value through profit or loss; and
- in other comprehensive income for investments in equity instruments to be designated as measured at fair value through other comprehensive income.

For financial assets measured at amortised cost or at fair value through other comprehensive income, IFRS 9 requires entities to use the trade date as the date of initial recognition for the purposes of applying the impairment requirements. *[IFRS 9.5.7.4]*.

This means that entities that use settlement date accounting may have to recognise a loss allowance for financial assets which they have purchased but not yet recognised and, correspondingly, no loss allowance for assets that they have sold but not yet derecognised (see 5.6.2 below).

On disposal, changes in value of such assets between trade date and settlement date are not recognised because the right to changes in fair value ceases on the trade date. *[IFRS 9.D.2.2]*. This is illustrated in Chapter 48 at 2.2.3.

2.9.3 Liabilities arising from failed derecognition transactions

There are special requirements for financial liabilities (including financial guarantee contracts) that arise when transfers of financial assets do not qualify for derecognition, or are accounted for using the continuing involvement approach. *[IFRS 9.4.2.1(b)]*. These are dealt with in Chapter 51 at 5.3.

3 AMORTISED COST AND THE EFFECTIVE INTEREST METHOD

The amortised cost measurement requirements, including the calculation of effective interest rates under IFRS 9, are the same as under IAS 39, although the terminology has changed. IFRS 9 contains three key definitions relating to this method of accounting, which are set out below: *[IFRS 9 Appendix A]*

- The *amortised cost* is the amount at which the financial asset or financial liability is measured at initial recognition minus any principal repayments, plus or minus the cumulative amortisation using the effective interest method of any difference between that initial amount and the maturity amount and, for financial assets, adjusted for any loss allowance.
- The *gross carrying amount* is the amortised cost of a financial asset before adjusting for any loss allowance.
- The *effective interest method* is the method that is used in the calculation of the amortised cost of a financial asset or a financial liability and in the allocation and recognition of the interest revenue or interest expense in profit or loss over the relevant period. *[IFRS 9 Appendix A]*.

The *effective interest rate* (EIR) is the rate that exactly discounts estimated future cash payments or receipts through the expected life of the financial asset or financial liability to the *gross carrying amount* of a financial asset or to the amortised cost of a financial liability. *[IFRS 9.5.4.1, IFRS 9 Appendix A]*. When calculating the EIR, an entity should estimate the expected cash flows by considering all the contractual terms of the financial instrument (e.g. prepayment, extension, call and similar options). The calculation includes all fees and points paid or received between parties to the contract that are an integral part of the EIR, transaction costs, and all other premiums or discounts. *[IFRS 9 Appendix A]*.

Guidance related to what elements should and should not be considered integral is also included in IFRS 9. Fees that are an integral part of the EIR of a financial instrument are treated as an adjustment to the EIR, unless the financial instrument is measured at fair value, with the change in fair value being recognised in profit or loss.

In those cases, the fees are recognised as revenue or expense when the instrument is initially recognised. *[IFRS 9.B5.4.1]*.

Fees that are an integral part of the EIR of a financial instrument include:

- origination fees received on the creation or acquisition of a financial asset. Such fees may include compensation for activities such as evaluating the borrower's financial condition, evaluating and recording guarantees, collateral and other security arrangements, negotiating the terms of the instrument, preparing and processing documents and closing the transaction. These fees are an integral part of generating an involvement with the resulting financial instrument;
- commitment fees received to originate a loan when the loan commitment is not measured at fair value through profit or loss and it is probable that the entity will enter into a specific lending arrangement. These fees are regarded as compensation for an ongoing involvement with the acquisition of a financial instrument. If the commitment expires without the entity making the loan, the fee is recognised as revenue on expiry; and
- origination fees paid on issuing financial liabilities measured at amortised cost. These fees are an integral part of generating an involvement with a financial liability. An entity distinguishes fees and costs that are an integral part of the EIR for the financial liability from origination fees and transaction costs relating to the right to provide services, such as investment management services. *[IFRS 9.B5.4.2]*.

Fees that are not an integral part of the EIR of a financial instrument and are accounted for in accordance with IFRS 15 include:

- fees charged for servicing a loan;
- commitment fees to originate a loan when the loan commitment is not measured at fair value through profit or loss and it is unlikely that a specific lending arrangement will be entered into; and
- loan syndication fees received to arrange a loan and the entity does not retain part of the loan package for itself (or retains a part at the same EIR for comparable risk as other participants). *[IFRS 9. B5.4.3]*.

Except for purchased or originated financial assets that are credit-impaired on initial recognition, ECLs are not considered in the calculation of the EIR. This is because the recognition of ECLs is decoupled from the recognition of interest revenue (see 5.3.1 below). *[IFRS 9 Appendix A, BCZ5.67]*.

For a purchased or originated credit-impaired financial asset (see 5.3.3 below), the *credit-adjusted effective interest rate* is applied when calculating the interest revenue and it is the rate that exactly discounts the estimated future cash payments or receipts through the expected life of the financial asset to the amortised cost of a financial asset. An entity is required to include the initial ECLs in the estimated cash flows when calculating the credit-adjusted EIR for such assets. *[IFRS 9.5.4.1, B5.4.7, Appendix A]*.

However, this does not mean that a credit-adjusted EIR should be applied solely because the financial asset has high credit risk at initial recognition. The application guidance explains that a financial asset is only considered credit-impaired at initial recognition when the credit risk is very high or, in the case of a purchase, it is acquired at a deep discount. *[IFRS 9.B5.4.7]*.

It is important to note that the EIR is normally based on estimated, not contractual, cash flows and there is a presumption that the cash flows and the expected life of a group of similar financial instruments can be estimated reliably. However, in those rare cases when it is not possible to estimate reliably the cash flows or the expected life of a financial instrument (or group of instruments), the contractual cash flows over the full contractual term of the financial instrument (or group of instruments) should be used. *[IFRS 9 Appendix A]*. During the development of IAS 39, the IASB considered whether the EIR for all financial instruments should be calculated on the basis of *estimated* cash flows, or whether *contractual* cash flows should be used for individual financial instruments with the use of estimated cash flows being restricted to groups of financial instruments. The position adopted was chosen because the IASB believes it achieves consistent application of the effective interest method throughout the standard. *[IFRS 9.BCZ5.65]*.

When applying the effective interest method, an entity generally amortises any fees, points paid or received, transaction costs and other premiums or discounts that are included in the calculation of the EIR over the expected life of the financial instrument. However, a shorter period is used if this is the period to which the fees, points paid or received, transaction costs, premiums or discounts relate. This will be the case when the related variable (e.g. interest rates) to which the fees, points paid or received, transaction costs, premiums or discounts relate is repriced to market rates before the expected maturity of the instrument. In such a case, the appropriate amortisation period is the period to the next such repricing date. *[IFRS 9.B5.4.4, BCZ5.70]*. For example, if a premium or discount on a floating-rate financial instrument reflects the interest that has accrued on that financial instrument since the interest was last paid, or changes in the market rates since the floating interest rate was reset to the market rates, it will be amortised to the next date when the floating interest is reset to market rates. This is because the premium or discount relates to the period to the next interest reset date because, at that date, the variable to which the premium or discount relates (i.e. interest rates) is reset to the market rates. If, however, the premium or discount results from a change in the credit spread over the floating rate specified in the financial instrument, or other variables that are not reset to the market rates, it is amortised over the expected life of the financial instrument. *IFRS 9.B5.4.4]*.

For floating-rate financial assets and floating-rate financial liabilities, periodic re-estimation of cash flows to reflect the movements in the market rates of interest alters the EIR. If a floating-rate financial asset or a floating-rate financial liability is recognised initially at an amount equal to the principal receivable or payable on maturity, re-estimating the future interest payments normally has no significant effect on the carrying amount of the asset or the liability. *IFRS 9.B5.4.5]*. The application of the effective interest method to floating rate instruments and inflation-linked debt is considered in more detail at 3.3 and 3.5 below.

As set out in Chapter 45 at 6, an issued compound financial instrument such as a convertible bond is accounted for as a financial liability component and an equity component. In accounting for the financial liability at amortised cost, the expected cash flows should be those of the liability component only and the estimate should not take account of the bond being converted.

3.1 Fixed interest, fixed term instruments

The effective interest method is most easily applied to instruments that have fixed payments and a fixed term. The following examples, adapted from the Implementation Guidance to the standard, illustrate this. *IFRS 9.IC.B.26, IC.B.27].*

Example 50.4: Effective interest method – amortisation of premium or discount on acquisition

At the start of 2017, a company purchases a debt instrument with five years remaining to maturity for its fair value of US$1,000 (including transaction costs). The instrument has a principal amount of US$1,250 and carries fixed interest of 4.7% payable annually (US$1,250 × 4.7% = US$59 per year). In order to allocate interest receipts and the initial discount over the term of the instrument at a constant rate on the carrying amount, it can be shown that interest needs to be accrued at the rate of 10% annually. The table below provides information about the gross carrying amount, interest income, and cash flows of the debt instrument in each reporting period.[2] *[IFRS 9.B.26].*

Year	*(a)* Gross carrying amount at the start of the year (US$)	*(b = a × 10%)* Interest income (US$)	*(c)* Cash flows (US$)	*(d = a + b – c)* Gross carrying amount at the end of the year (US$)
2017	1,000	100	59	1,041
2018	1,041	104	59	1,086
2019	1,086	109	59	1,136
2020	1,136	113	59	1,190
2021	1,190	119	1,250 + 59	–

Example 50.5: Effective interest method – stepped interest rates

On 1 January 2017, Company A acquires a debt instrument for its fair value of £1,250 (including transaction costs). The principal amount is £1,250 which is repayable on 31 December 2021. The rate of interest is specified in the debt agreement as a percentage of the principal amount as follows: 6% in 2017 (£75), 8% in 2018 (£100), 10% in 2019 (£125), 12% in 2020 (£150) and 16.4% in 2021 (£205). It can be shown that the interest rate that exactly discounts the stream of future cash payments to maturity is 10%. In each period, the amortised cost at the beginning of the period is multiplied by the EIR of 10% and added to the gross carrying amount. Any cash payments in the period are deducted from the resulting balance. Accordingly, the gross carrying amount, interest income and cash flows of the debt instrument in each period are as follows:

Year	*(a)* Gross carrying amount at the start of the year (£)	*(b = a × 10%)* Interest income (£)	*(c)* Cash flows (£)	*(d = a + b – c)* Gross carrying amount at the end of the year (£)
2017	1,250	125	75	1,300
2018	1,300	130	100	1,330
2019	1,330	133	125	1,338
2020	1,338	134	150	1,322
2021	1,322	133	1,250 + 205	–

It can be seen that, although the instrument is issued for £1,250 and has a maturity amount of £1,250, its gross carrying amount does not equal £1,250 at each reporting date. *[IFRS 9.IC.B.27].*

Methods for determining the EIR for a given set of cash flows (as in the examples above) include simple trial and error techniques as well as more methodical iterative algorithms. Alternatively, many spreadsheet applications contain goal-seek or similar functions that can also be used to derive EIRs.

3.2 Prepayment, call and similar options

When calculating the EIR, all contractual terms of the financial instrument, for example prepayment, call and similar options, should be considered. *[IFRS 9 Appendix A]*. (This assumes that the presence of such contractual terms do not cause the contractual cash flow characteristics test to fail, i.e. the contractual terms of the debt instrument give rise on specified dates to cash flows that are solely payments of principal and interest on the principal amount outstanding (see Chapter 47 at 2 and 6)). The following simple example illustrates how this principle is applied.

Example 50.6: Effective interest rate – embedded prepayment options

Bank ABC originates 1,000 ten year loans of £10,000 with 10% stated interest, prepayable at par. Prepayments are probable and it is possible to reasonably estimate their timing and amount. ABC determines that the EIR including loan origination fees received by ABC is 10.2% based on the *contractual* payment terms of the loans as the fees received reduce the initial carrying amount.

However, if the *expected* prepayments were considered, the EIR would be 10.4% since the difference between the initial amount and maturity amount is amortised over a shorter period.

The EIR that should be used by ABC for this portfolio is 10.4%.[3]

3.2.1 *Revisions to estimated cash flows*

The standard contains an explanation of how changes to estimates of payments or receipts (e.g. because of a reassessment of the extent to which prepayments will occur) should be dealt with.

When there is a change in estimates of payments or receipts, excluding changes in estimates of ECLs, the gross carrying amount of the financial asset or amortised cost of a financial liability (or group of instruments) should be adjusted to reflect actual and revised estimated cash flows. More precisely, the gross carrying amount of the financial asset or amortised cost of the financial liability should be re-calculated by computing the present value of estimated future contractual cash flows that are discounted at the financial instrument's original EIR (or if the instrument has been designated as the hedged item in a fair value hedge, the revised EIR). Any consequent adjustment should be recognised immediately in profit or loss. *[IFRS 9.B5.4.6]*. This is equivalent to the IAS 39 approach set out in paragraph AG8 (see Chapter 49 at 3.2).

The revision of estimates is illustrated in the following example adapted from the Implementation Guidance to the standard. *[IFRS 9.IG.B.26]*.

Example 50.7: Effective interest method – revision of estimates

At the start of 2017, a company purchases in a quoted market a debt instrument with the same terms as the instrument in Example 50.4 at 3.1 above, except that the contract also specifies that the borrower has an option to prepay the instrument and that no penalty will be charged for prepayment (i.e. any prepayment will be made at the principal amount of US$1,250 or a proportion thereof).

At inception, there is an expectation that the borrower will not prepay and so the information about the instrument's EIR, gross carrying amount, interest income and cash flows in each reporting period would be the same as that in Example 50.4.

On the first day of 2019, the investor revises its estimate of cash flows. It now expects that 50% of the principal will be prepaid at the end of 2019 and the remaining 50% at the end of 2021. Therefore, the opening balance of the debt instrument in 2019 is adjusted to an amount calculated by discounting the amounts expected to be received in 2019 and subsequent years using the original EIR (10%). This results in a revised balance of US$1,138. The adjustment of US$52 (US$1,138 – US$1,086) is recorded in profit or loss in 2019.

The table below provides information about the gross carrying amount, interest income and cash flows as they would be adjusted taking into account this change in estimate.

	(a)	*(b = a × 10%)*	*(c)*	*(d = a + b – c)*
Year	Gross carrying amount at start of year (US$)	Interest and similar income* (US$)	Cash flows (US$)	Gross carrying amount at end of year (US$)
2017	1,000	100	59	1,041
2018	1,041	104	59	1,086
2019	1,086 + 52	114	625 + 59	568
2020	568	57	30	595
2021	595	60	625 + 30	–

*the standard and related guidance do not state whether the catch-up adjustment (US$52 in 2019 in this case) should be classified as interest income or as some other income or expense, simply that it should be recognised in profit or loss.

This above calculation would be applicable whether the instruments were classified as measured at amortised cost or FVOCI under IFRS 9.

This example assumes that the prepayment option does not cause the debt instrument to fail to comply with the amortised cost classification criteria. For this to be the case, the fair value of the prepayment feature on initial recognition would have to be insignificant. *[IFRS 9.4.1.2(b), B4.1.12]*.

3.2.2 Interaction with the requirements for embedded derivatives

If a hybrid contract contains a host that is a liability within the scope of IFRS 9, any embedded derivative (e.g. a prepayment option) that is required to be separated from the host must be accounted for as a derivative (see Chapter 44 at 4 and 5). *[IFRS 9.4.3.3]*. Once separated, the embedded derivative should not be taken into account in applying the effective interest method of the host.

Another issue is whether prepayment and similar options should be regarded as closely related to the host instrument. In assessing whether the exercise price is approximately equal to the amortised cost at each exercise date, should one consider the amortised cost of the hybrid that would reflect the entity's original expectations regarding the future exercise of the prepayment option, or potential revised estimates applying the catch up method to the amortised cost? This question is illustrated in the following simple example (which also provides further illustrations of the application of the effective interest method to instruments containing prepayment options).

Example 50.8: Embedded prepayment option

Company P borrows €1,000 on terms that require it to pay annual fixed rate coupons of €80 and €1,000 principal at the end of ten years. The terms of the instrument also allow P to redeem the debt after seven years by paying the principal of €1,000 and a penalty of €100.

The debt instrument can be considered to comprise the following two components:

- a host debt instrument requiring ten annual payments of €80 followed by a €1,000 payment of principal; and
- an embedded prepayment option, exercisable only at the end of seven years with an exercise price of €1,100.

If, at inception, the prepayment option was expected *not* to be exercised, the EIR of the *hybrid* would be 8%. This is the rate that would discount the expected cash flows of €80 per year for ten years plus €1,000 at the end of ten years to the initial carrying amount of €1,000. The table below provides information about the amortised cost, interest income and cash flows using this assumption.

Year	*(a)* Gross carrying amount at the start of the year (€)	*(b = a × 8%)* Interest and similar income (€)	*(c)* Cash flows (€)	*(d = a + b – c)* Gross carrying amount at the end of the year (€)
1	1,000	80	80	1,000
2	1,000	80	80	1,000
3	1,000	80	80	1,000
4	1,000	80	80	1,000
5	1,000	80	80	1,000
6	1,000	80	80	1,000
7	1,000	80	80	1,000
8	1,000	80	80	1,000
9	1,000	80	80	1,000
10	1,000	80	80 + 1,000	–

However if, at the outset, the option *was* expected to be exercised, the EIR of the *hybrid* would be 9.08% as this is the rate that discounts the expected cash flows of €80 per year for seven years, plus €1,100 at the end of seven years, to the initial carrying amount of €1,000. The table below provides information about the amortised cost, interest income and cash flows using this alternative assumption.

Year	*(a)* Gross carrying amount at the start of the year (€)	*(b = a × 9.08%)* Interest and similar income (€)	*(c)* Cash flows (€)	*(d = a + b – c)* Gross carrying amount at the end of the year (€)
1	1,000	91	80	1,011
2	1,011	92	80	1,023
3	1,023	93	80	1,036
4	1,036	94	80	1,050
5	1,050	95	80	1,065
6	1,065	97	80	1,082
7	1,082	98	80 + 1,100	–

On the face of it, therefore, comparing the amortised cost of the hybrid with the exercise price of the option at the date it could be exercised suggests the prepayment option might be considered closely related if it was likely to be exercised but not if exercise was unlikely.

However, even this is not the whole story. If the option (on inception) was not expected to be exercised, but at a later date exercise became likely, the amortised cost carrying amount would be revised so that it represented the expected future cash flows discounted at the original EIR. For example, if at the end of Year 5, it became likely that the option would be exercised, the carrying amount would be revised so that it represented €80 discounted for one year at 8% plus €1,180 discounted for two years at 8% – in other words, €1,086 rather than €1,065. The difference of €21 would be recognised in profit or loss immediately and the amortised cost carrying amount would subsequently accrete so that it represented the final cash outflow (option exercise price of €1,100 plus coupon of €80) at the end of Year 7. So even in this situation there is an argument to suggest that the prepayment option should not be separated as the exercise price will always equal the amortised cost (at least to the extent that the option is expected to be exercised).

Unfortunately, the standard is silent on these issues and preparers of accounts will be required to exercise judgement as to the most appropriate method to use in their individual circumstances.

3.3 Floating rate instruments

For floating rate instruments, the periodic re-estimation of cash flows to reflect the movements in the market interest rates alters the EIR. The standard goes on to explain that where a floating-rate financial asset or a floating-rate financial liability is initially recognised at an amount equal to the principal receivable or repayable on maturity, re-estimating the future interest payments normally has no significant effect on the carrying amount of the asset or the liability. *[IFRS 9.B5.4.5]*. This is equivalent to the IAS 39 approach set out in paragraph AG7 (see Chapter 49 at 3.3). This is normally interpreted to mean that entities should simply account for periodic floating rate payments on an accrual basis in the period they are earned. An alternative treatment would consist in calculating the EIR based on a market-derived yield curve applicable for the entire life of the instrument. Applying this alternative approach, the calculated EIR is applied until estimated future cash flows are revised, at which point a new EIR is calculated based on the revised cash flow expectations and the current carrying amount. This more complicated treatment is illustrated in the following example (in which it is assumed that the instrument meets the criteria for measurement at amortised cost under IFRS 9).

Example 50.9: Effective interest method – variable rate loan

At the start of July 2017, Company G originates a floating rate debt instrument. Its fair value is equal to its principal amount of $1,000 and no transaction costs are incurred. The instrument pays, in arrears at the end of June, a variable rate coupon, determined by reference to 12 month LIBOR at the start of each previous July. It has a term of five years and is repayable at its principal amount at the end of June 2021.

On origination, 12 month LIBOR is 5% and this establishes the first payment, to be made in June 2017, at $50. Based on a market-derived yield curve, G estimates that the subsequent floating rate payments will be $60, $70, $80 and $90 (the yield curve rises steeply). It can be demonstrated that the interest rate that exactly discounts these estimated coupon payments and the $1,000 principal at maturity to the current carrying amount of $1,000 is 6.87%.

Even if it is not applied widely in practice (and the effect may often not be material), such an approach seems technically correct. This was also confirmed by the IFRIC discussion on inflation-linked instruments in May 2008 (see 3.5 below).

Payments, receipts, discounts and premiums included in the effective interest method calculation are normally amortised over the expected life of the instrument and it will often be acceptable to amortise transaction costs on a straight line basis over the life of the instrument on a basis of materiality.

However, there may be situations when discounts or premiums are amortised over a shorter period (see 3 above). This will be the case when the variable to which they relate reprices to market rates before the instrument's expected maturity. In such cases, the appropriate amortisation period is to the next repricing date.

For example, if a premium or discount on a floating rate instrument reflects interest that has accrued since interest was last paid, or changes in market rates since the floating interest rate was reset to market rates, it will be amortised to the next date when the interest rate is reset to market rates. This is because the premium or discount relates to the period to the next interest reset date because, at that date, the variable to which the premium or discount relates (i.e. the interest rate) is reset to market rates. If, however, the premium or discount results from a change in the credit spread over the floating rate specified in the financial instrument, or other variables that are not reset to market rates, it is amortised over the expected life of the instrument. *[IFRS 9.B5.4.4]*.

The following examples illustrate the requirements of applying a discount arising on acquisition of a debt instrument resulting from (a) a credit downgrade and (b) accrued interest.

Example 50.10: Effective interest method – amortisation of discount arising from credit downgrade

A twenty year bond is issued at £100, has a principal amount of £100, and requires quarterly interest payments equal to current three month LIBOR plus 1% over the life of the instrument. The interest rate reflects the market-based required rate of return associated with the bond issue at issuance. Subsequent to issuance, the credit quality of the bond deteriorates resulting in a rating downgrade. It therefore trades at a discount, although it is assessed not to be credit-impaired (see 5.3.1 below). Company A purchases the bond for £95 and classifies it as measured at amortised cost.

The discount of £5 is amortised to income over the period to the maturity of the bond and not to the next date interest rate payments are reset as it results from a change in credit spreads.[4] This is because it relates to an adjustment for credit quality which is not a variable that reprices to market rates before the expected maturity.

Example 50.11: Effective interest method – amortisation of discount arising from accrued interest

At the start of November 2016, Company P acquires the bond issued by Company G in Example 50.8 above – current interest rates have not changed since the end of July 2016 and G's credit risk has not changed since origination so P pays $1,017.

The premium of $17 paid by P relates to interest accrued since the last reset date and so is amortised to income over the period to the next repricing date, June 2017; further, the $50 cash flow received at the end of June 2017 is also amortised over this period.

Consequently, for the eight months ended June 2017, P will record interest of $33 ($50 – $17), which is also the approximate equivalent of eight months interest at current rates (5%) earned on P's initial investment.

This treatment is consistent with the requirements of IAS 18 that apply when unpaid interest has accrued before the acquisition of an interest-bearing investment. In such cases, it is explained (in more traditional terms) that the subsequent receipt of interest should be allocated between pre-acquisition and post-acquisition periods and only the post-acquisition portion should be recognised as revenue. *[IAS 18.32]*. This guidance was not included in IFRS 15 or as a consequential amendment to IFRS 9 as a result of the issuance of IFRS 15. However, it is expected that practice will not change.

3.4 Perpetual debt instruments

The fact that an instrument is perpetual does not change how the gross carrying amount is calculated. The present value of the perpetual stream of future cash payments, discounted at the EIR, equals the gross carrying amount in each period. *[IFRS 9.IG.B.24]*.

However, in cases where interest is only paid over a limited amount of time, some or all of the interest payments are, from an economic perspective, repayments of the gross carrying amount, as illustrated in the following example. *[IFRS 9.B.25]*.

Example 50.12: Amortised cost – perpetual debt with interest payments over a limited amount of time

On 1 January 2017, Company A subscribes £1,000 for a debt instrument which yields 25% interest for the first five years and 0% in subsequent periods. The instrument is classified as measured at amortised cost. It can be determined that the effective yield is 7.9% and the gross carrying amount is shown in the table below.[5]

	(a)	*(b = a × 7.9%)*	*(c)*	*(d = a + b – c)*
	Gross carrying amount at the start of the year	Interest income	Cash flows	Gross carrying amount at the end of the year
Year	(£)	(£)	(£)	(£)
2017	1,000	79	250	829
2018	829	66	250	645
2019	645	51	250	446
2020	446	36	250	232
2021	232	18	250	–
2022	–	–	–	–

3.5 Inflation-linked debt

As noted in Chapter 44 at 5.1.5, the issue of debt instruments whose cash flows are linked to changes in an inflation index is quite common. Under IAS 39, the embedded derivative representing the variability in cash flows is often treated as closely related to the host instrument and this practice is expected to continue for financial liabilities under IFRS 9. IFRS 9 will also often allow inflation-linked financial assets to satisfy the criteria to be recorded at amortised cost, as shown in Example 46.11 in Chapter 46. Entities that record these instruments at amortised cost must apply the effective interest method to determine the amount of interest to be recognised in profit or loss each period. In May 2008, the Interpretations Committee was asked to consider a request for guidance on this issue. Three ways of applying the effective interest method that were being used in practice were included in the request. These are summarised in the following example that has been revised to reflect the requirements in IFRS 9 instead of IAS 39.[6]

Example 50.13: Application of the effective interest method to inflation-linked debt instruments[7]

On 1 January 2017, Company A issues a debt instrument for $100,000 that is linked to the local Consumer Prices Index (CPI). The terms of the instrument require it to be repaid in full after five years at an amount equal to $100,000 adjusted by the cumulative change in the CPI over those five years. Interest on the loan is paid at each year end at an amount equal to 5% of the principal ($100,000) adjusted by the cumulative change in the CPI from issuance of the instrument. For IFRS 9 purposes, it is assumed that the debt instrument is not held for trading or designated at fair value through profit or loss and thereby, the debt instrument is classified as subsequently measured at amortised cost.

The following table sets out the expected annual inflation rates on issuance of the instrument and one year later:

	Expected annual inflation rates	
	At start of 2017	*At start of 2018*
2017	0.7%	
2018	2.6%	1.4%
2019	2.8%	1.9%
2020	2.8%	3.5%
2021	2.8%	3.5%

During 2017 actual inflation is 1.2%.

Method 1 – application of IFRS 9.B5.4.6 (or the IAS 39 AG8 approach)

This approach follows the requirements set out at 3.2.1 above. Therefore, the EIR is established on 1 January 2017 based on expected cash flows at that time:

Date: end of	*Expected cash flow ($)*	*Calculation*
2017	5,035	=5,000 × 1.007
2018	5,166	=5,000 × 1.007 × 1.026
2019	5,311	=5,000 × 1.007 × 1.026 × 1.028
2020	5,459	=5,000 × 1.007 × 1.026 × 1.028 × 1.028
2021	117,854	=105,000 × 1.007 × 1.026 × 1.028 × 1.028 × 1.028

It can be demonstrated that these expected cash flows produce an EIR of 7.4075%, i.e. the net present value of these cash flows, discounted at 7.4075%, equals $100,000.

During 2017, A applies the EIR to the financial liability to recognise a finance charge of $7,408 ($100,000 × 7.4075%), increasing the carrying amount of the financial liability to $107,408 ($100,000 + $7,408). At the end of the year A pays cash interest of $5,060 ($5,000 × 101.2%) reducing the liability to $102,348 ($107,408 – $5,060). In addition, A must adjust the carrying amount of the financial liability so that it equals the net present value of expected future cash flows discounted at the original expected interest rate. The expected future cash flows are now as follows:

Date: end of	*Cash flow ($)*	*Calculation*
2018	5,131	=5,000 × 1.012 × 1.014
2019	5,228	=5,000 × 1.012 × 1.014 × 1.019
2020	5,411	=5,000 × 1.012 × 1.014 × 1.019 × 1.035
2021	117,615	=105,000 × 1.012 × 1.014 × 1.019 × 1.035 × 1.035

The net present value of these cash flows discounted at 7.4075% is $102,050. Therefore A reduces its finance charge by $298 ($102,050 – $102,348) so that the total finance charge for 2017 is $7,110 ($7,408 – $298).

Method 2 – application of IFRS 9.B5.4.5 using forecast future cash flows (or the IAS 39 AG7 approach)

This approach is referred to at 3.3 above for simple floating-rate instruments.

The initial EIR is calculated and applied in the same way as Method 1. However, no adjustment is made to the carrying amount of the financial liability at the end of 2017 ($102,348) or to the finance charge for 2016 ($7,408) as a result of A, at the start of 2018, revising its expectations about inflation over the remaining term of the instrument.

Instead, a revised EIR is calculated at the start of 2018 using the revised forecast cash flows (shown above under Method 1, i.e. $5,131 at the end of 2018, $5,228 at the end of 2018, $5,411 at the end of 2020 and $117,615 at the end of 2021) and the current carrying amount ($102,348). It can be demonstrated that this produces a revised EIR of 7.3237%, i.e. the net present value of those cash flows, discounted at 7.3237% equals $102,348.

Applying this revised rate prospectively in 2018 (and assuming estimates of future inflation are not revised again until the start of 2019) there will be a finance charge for 2018 of $7,496 ($102,348 × 7.3237%).

Method 3 – application of IFRS 9 B5.4.4-5 without forecasting future cash flows

This method is based on the traditional method of accounting for floating rate debt instruments and is commonly used under other bodies of GAAP. Rather than taking account of expectations of future inflation it takes account of inflation only during the reporting period.

Therefore, in 2017, A would recognise a finance charge of $5,060 as a result of accruing the variable interest payment in respect of 2017. In addition, the actual inflation experienced during 2017 increases the amount of principal that will be paid from $100,000 to $101,200 ($100,000 × 1.012%). This increase, i.e. $1,200, is effectively a premium to be paid on the redemption of the financial liability. Paragraph B5.4.4 of IFRS 9 explains that a premium should normally be amortised over the expected life of an instrument. However, it goes on to explain that a shorter period should be used if this is the period to which the premium relates. *[IFRS 9.B5.4.4]*. In this case, the premium clearly relates to 2017 as it arises from inflation during that year and so it is appropriately amortised in that year.

Consequently, the total finance charge for 2017 using this method would be $6,260 ($5,060 + $1,200).

In analysing the submission, it initially appeared as if the Interpretations Committee staff completely rejected Method 3. The submission argued that Method 3 was justified by reference to IAS 29 – *Financial Reporting in Hyperinflationary Economies*. The staff concluded (quite correctly) that it was inappropriate to apply IAS 29 because that standard applies only to the financial statements of an entity whose functional currency is the currency of a hyperinflationary economy and instead the guidance in IAS 39 should be applied.[8]

However, in their final rejection notice the Interpretations Committee noted that paragraphs AG6 to AG8 of IAS 39 provide the relevant application guidance and that judgement is required to determine whether an instrument is floating rate and within the scope of paragraph AG7 or is within the scope of paragraph AG8.[9] Further, it was noted that IAS 39 is unclear as to whether future expectations about interest rates (and presumably, therefore, inflation) should be taken into account when applying paragraph AG7.[10] Consequently, in our view, all three methods noted in the example comply with the current requirements of IAS 39 and therefore, since the requirements are unchanged, of IFRS 9. This view is consistent with the opinion of one national standard-setter that operates in a jurisdiction where such instruments are extremely common.[11]

3.6 More complex financial liabilities

The application of the effective interest method to instruments with unusual embedded derivatives that are deemed closely related to the host, or other embedded features that are not accounted for separately, is not always straightforward or intuitive. Specifically it is not always clear how to deal with changes in the estimated cash flows of the instrument and in any given situation one needs to assess which of the approaches set out above is more appropriate:

- the general requirements for changes in cash flows set out in paragraph B5.4.6 of IFRS 9, equivalent to the IAS 39 AG8 approach (see 3.2.1 above); and
- specific requirements for floating rate instruments under paragraph B5.4.5 of IFRS 9, equivalent to the IAS 39 AG7 approach (see 3.3 above).

Consider an entity that issues a debt instrument for its par value of €10m which is repayable in ten years' time on which an annual coupon is payable comprising two elements: a fixed amount of 2.5% of the par value and a variable amount equating to 0.01% of the entity's annual revenues. The instrument is not designated at fair value through profit or loss and it is judged that the embedded feature is not a derivative as outlined in Example 44.3 in Chapter 44.

The requirements under paragraphs B5.4.5 and B5.4.6 of IFRS 9 could give rise to significantly different accounting treatments. In the latter case, the issuer would need to estimate the amount of payments to be made over the life of the bond (which will depend on its estimated revenues for the next ten years) in order to determine the EIR to be applied. Any changes to these estimates would result in a catch-up adjustment to profit or loss and the carrying amount of the bond which, potentially, could give rise to significant volatility. In the former case the annual coupon would simply be accrued each year and changes in estimated revenues of future periods would have no impact on the accounting treatment until the applicable year.

In 2009, the Interpretations Committee was asked for guidance on how an issuer should account for a financial liability that contains participation rights by which the instrument holder shares in the net income and losses of the issuer. The holder receives a percentage of the issuer's net income and is allocated a proportional share of the issuer's losses. Losses are applied to the nominal value of the instrument to be repaid on maturity. Losses allocated to the holder in one period can be offset by profits in subsequent periods. The submission was asking how the issuer should account for such instruments in periods in which the issuer records a loss and allocates a portion of that loss to the participating financial instruments. Two possible views were submitted to IFRIC:

- In one view the requirements in paragraph AG8 of IAS 39 (equivalent to paragraph B5.4.6 of IFRS 9) do not apply. Rather, the requirements for derecognition should be applied and a gain equal to the allocated loss should be recognized in the current period (with an offsetting reduction in the carrying amount of the instrument).
- In a second view, the requirements in paragraph AG8 (equivalent to paragraph B5.4.6 of IFRS 9) apply. Current period losses are one factor that the issuer would consider when it evaluates whether it needs to revise its estimated future cash flows and adjust the carrying amount of the participating financial instrument.

The IFRIC noted that paragraphs AG6 and AG8 of IAS 39 (equivalent to paragraphs B5.4.4. to B5.4.6 of IFRS 9) provide the relevant application guidance for measuring financial liabilities at amortised cost using the EIR method. The IFRIC also noted that it is inappropriate to analogise to the derecognition guidance in IAS 39 because the liability has not been extinguished. Therefore, a gain equal to the allocated loss should not be recognized in the current period. Rather, current period losses should be considered together with further expectations when evaluating the need to revise its estimated future cash flows and adjust the carrying amount of the participating financial instrument.

It should be noted that the IFRIC considered the issue without reconsidering the assumptions described in the request, namely that the financial liability (a) did not contain any embedded derivatives, (b) was measured at amortised cost using the effective interest method, and (c) did not meet the definition of a floating rate instrument.[12] In other words, whilst clearly indicating that the B5.4.6 approach was acceptable, it did not explicitly preclude the use of the B5.4.5 approach. In this situation, we believe that it would often be appropriate to apply the requirements under paragraph B5.4.6 of IFRS 9, principally because the entity's revenue does not represent a floating rate that changes to reflect movements in market rates of interest. However, as covered at 3.5 above, judgement is required to determine which approach is appropriate.[13]

There are some financial instruments for which re-estimation of cash flows will only reflect movements in market interest rates but for which use of B5.4.5 would not be appropriate. An example would be an 'inverse floater', on which coupons on are paid at a fixed rate *minus* LIBOR (subject to a floor of zero).

For some financial instruments, it might be considered appropriate to apply a combination of both the B5.5.5 and B5.4.6 approaches. An example might be, for instance, a prepayable floating rate liability on which transaction costs have been incurred and that have been included in the EIR.

4 FOREIGN CURRENCIES

4.1 Foreign currency instruments

The provisions of IAS 21 – *The Effects of Changes in Foreign Exchange Rates* –apply to transactions involving financial instruments in just the same way as they do for other transactions, although the manner in which certain hedges are accounted for can override its general requirements.

Consequently, the statement of financial position measurement of a foreign currency financial instrument is determined as follows:

- firstly, it is recorded and measured in the foreign currency in which it is denominated, whether it is carried at fair value, cost, or amortised cost;
- secondly, that amount is retranslated to the entity's functional currency using the closing rate. *[IAS 21.23]*.

Profit and loss items associated with financial instruments, e.g. dividends receivable, interest payable or receivable and impairments, are recorded at the spot rate ruling when they arise (although average rates may be used when they represent an appropriate approximation to spot rates throughout the period).

The reporting of exchange differences in profit or loss or in other comprehensive income depends on whether the instrument is a monetary or non-monetary item and whether it is designated as part of a foreign currency cash flow hedge or hedge of a net investment.

Foreign exchange differences arising on retranslating monetary items, including debt instruments measured at fair value through other comprehensive income, are generally recognised in profit or loss. However, those exchange differences may be recognised in other comprehensive income for instruments designated as a hedging instrument in a cash flow hedge, a hedge of a net investment in a foreign operation or a fair value hedge of an equity instrument for which an entity has elected to present changes in fair value in other comprehensive income (see 2.2 above and Chapter 53). *[IFRS 9.B5.7.2, B5.7.2A]*.

In cases where some portion of the change in carrying amount is recognised in profit or loss and some in other comprehensive income, e.g. if the amortised cost of a foreign currency bond measured at fair value through other comprehensive income has increased in foreign currency (resulting in a gain in profit or loss) but its fair value has increased in foreign currency, those two components cannot be offset for the purposes of determining gains or losses that should be recognised in profit or loss or in other comprehensive income. *[IFRS 9.B5.7.2, 5.7.2A, E.3.4]*.

The Board developed the example below to illustrate the separation of the currency component for a financial asset that is measured at fair value through other comprehensive income in accordance with paragraph 4.1.2A of IFRS 9. Presumably to simplify the example, they ignored the need to record expected credit losses. *[IFRS 9.IG.E.3.2]*. A more complex illustration, including expected credit losses is included as Example 50.35 at 5.8 below.

Example 50.14: Foreign currency debt security measured at fair value through other comprehensive income (separation of currency component)

On 31 December 2016, Company A, whose functional currency is the euro, acquires a dollar bond for its fair value of $1,000. The bond is the same as the one in Example 50.4 at 3.1 above, i.e. it has five years to maturity and a $1,250 principal, carries fixed interest of 4.7% paid annually ($1,250 × 4.7% = $59 per year), and has an effective interest rate of 10%.

A classifies the bond as subsequently measured at fair value through other comprehensive income in accordance with paragraph 4.1.2A of IFRS 9, and thus recognises gains and losses in other comprehensive income. The exchange rate is $1 to €1.50 and the carrying amount of the bond is €1,500 ($1,000 × 1.50).

	€	€
Bond	1,500	
Cash		1,500

On 31 December 2017, the dollar has appreciated and the exchange rate is $1 to €2.00. The fair value of the bond is $1,060 and therefore its carrying amount is €2,120 ($1,060 × 2.00). Its amortised cost is $1,041 (or €2,082 = $1,041 × 2.00) and the cumulative gain or loss to be included in other

comprehensive income is the difference between its fair value and amortised cost, i.e. a gain of €38 (€2,120 – €2,082; or, alternatively, [$1,060 – $1,041] × 2.00).

Interest received on the bond on 31 December 2017 is $59 (or €118 = $59 × 2.00). Interest revenue determined in accordance with the effective interest method is $100 ($1,000 × 10%) of which $41 ($100 – $59) is the accretion of the initial discount.

It is assumed that the average exchange rate during the year is $1 to €1.75 and that the use of an average exchange rate provides a reliable approximation of the spot rates applicable to the accrual of interest during the year. Therefore, reported interest revenue is €175 ($100 × 1.75) including accretion of the initial discount of €72 ($41 × 1.75).

The exchange difference recognised in profit or loss is €525, which comprises three elements: a €500 gain from the retranslation of the initial amortised cost ($1,000 × [2.00 – 1.50]); a €15 gain from the retranslation of interest revenue received ($59 × [2.00 – 1.75]) and a €10 gain on the retranslation of the interest revenue accreted ($41 × [2.00 – 1.75]).

	€	€
Bond	620	
Cash	118	
Interest revenue (P&L)		175
Exchange gain (P&L)		525
Fair value change in other comprehensive income (equity)		38

On 31 December 2018, the dollar has appreciated further and the exchange rate is $1 to €2.50. The fair value of the bond is $1,070 and therefore its carrying amount is €2,675 ($1,070 × 2.50). Its amortised cost is $1,086 (or €2,715 = $1,086 × 2.50) and the cumulative gain or loss to be included in other comprehensive income is the difference between its fair value and the amortised cost, i.e. a loss of €40 (€2,675 – €2,715; or, alternatively, [$1,070 – $1,086] × 2.50). Therefore, there is a debit to other comprehensive income equal to the change in the difference during 2018 of €78 (€40 + €38).

Interest received on the bond on 31 December 2018 is $59 (or €148 = $59 × 2.50). Interest revenue determined in accordance with the effective interest method is $104 ($1,041 × 10%), of which $45 ($104 – $59) is the accretion of the initial discount.

Using the same assumptions as in the previous year, interest income is €234 ($104 × 2.25) including accretion of the initial discount of €101 ($45 × 2.25).

The exchange difference recognised in profit or loss is €547, which again comprises three elements: a €521 gain from the retranslation of the opening amortised cost ($1,041 × [2.50 – 2.00]); a €15 gain from the retranslation of interest income received ($59 × [2.50 – 2.25]) and an €11 gain on the retranslation of the interest income accreted ($45 × [2.50 – 2.25]). *[IAS 39.E.3.2]*.

	€	€
Bond	555	
Cash	148	
Fair value change in other comprehensive income (equity)	78	
Interest revenue (P&L)		234
Exchange gain (P&L)		547

It is worth repeating that the treatment would be different for equity instruments measured at fair value through other comprehensive income. Under IAS 21, these are not considered monetary items and exchange differences would form part of the change in the fair value of the instrument, which would be recognised in other comprehensive income with no recycling.

4.2 Foreign entities

IFRS 9 does not amend application of the net investment method of accounting for foreign entities set out in IAS 21 (see Chapter 15 at 6). Therefore, for the purpose of preparing its own accounts for inclusion in consolidated accounts, a foreign entity that is part of a group applies the principles at 4.1 above by reference to its own functional currency. Consequently, the treatment of gains and losses on, say, trading assets held by a foreign entity should follow the treatment in the example below, adapted from the Implementation Guidance of IFRS 9. *[IFRS 9.IG.E.3.3]*.

Example 50.15: Interaction of IAS 21 and IFRS 9 – foreign currency debt investment

Company A is domiciled in the US and its functional currency and presentation currency is the US dollar. A has a UK domiciled subsidiary, B, whose functional currency is sterling. B is the owner of a debt instrument which is held for trading and is therefore carried at fair value through profit or loss in accordance with IFRS 9.

In B's financial statements for 2016, the fair value and carrying amount of the debt instrument is £100. In A's consolidated financial statements, the asset is translated into US dollars at the spot exchange rate applicable at the end of the reporting period, say 2.0, and the carrying amount is US$200 (£100 × 2.0).

At the end of 2017, the fair value of the debt instrument has increased to £110. B reports the trading asset at £110 in its statement of financial position and recognises a fair value gain of £10 in profit or loss. During the year, the spot exchange rate has increased from 2.0 to 3.0 resulting in an increase in the fair value of the instrument from US$200 to US$330 (£110 × 3.0). Therefore, A reports the trading asset at US$330 in its consolidated financial statements.

Since B is classified as a foreign entity, A translates B's statement of comprehensive income 'at the exchange rates at the dates of the transactions'. Since the fair value gain has accrued through the year, A uses the average rate of 2.5 (= [3.0 + 2.0] ÷ 2) as a practical approximation. Therefore, while the fair value of the trading asset has increased by US$130 (US$330 – US$200), A recognises only US$25 (£10 × 2.5) of this increase in profit or loss. The resulting exchange difference, i.e. the remaining increase in the fair value of the debt instrument of US$105 (US$130 – US$25), is recognised in other comprehensive income until the disposal of the net investment in the foreign entity.

5 IMPAIRMENT

5.1 Introduction

The IASB has sought to address a key concern that arose as a result of the financial crisis that the incurred loss model in IAS 39 contributed to the delayed recognition of credit losses. To do so, it has introduced a forward-looking expected credit loss ('ECL') model in IFRS 9. The ECL requirements and application guidance in the standard are accompanied by 14 Illustrative Examples.

This section discusses the new ECL model as set out in IFRS 9. This section also briefly describes the new credit risk disclosures in relation to the ECL model as set out in IFRS 7 (see 5.13 below). A more detailed discussion of the disclosure requirements can be found in Chapter 54 at 5.2.3.

5.1.1 Brief history and background of the impairment project

During the financial crisis, the delayed recognition of credit losses that are associated with loans and other financial instruments was identified as a weakness in existing accounting standards. This is primarily due to the fact that the current impairment requirements under IAS 39 are based on an incurred loss model, i.e. credit losses are not recognised until a credit loss event occurs. Since losses are rarely incurred evenly over the lives of loans, there is a mismatch in the timing of the recognition of the credit spread inherent in the interest charged on the loans over their lives and any impairment losses that only get recognised at a later date. A further identified weakness was the complexity of different entities using different approaches to calculate impairment.

As part of the joint approach by the IASB and the FASB to deal with the financial reporting issues arising from the financial crisis, the boards set up the Financial Crisis Advisory Group (FCAG) in October 2008 to consider how improvements in financial reporting could help to enhance investor confidence in financial markets. Not long after, the leaders of the Group of 20 (also known as the G20) published a report *Declaration on Strengthening the Financial System* in April 2009 that called on the accounting standard setters to reduce the complexity of accounting standards for financial instruments and to strengthen accounting recognition of loan-loss provisions by incorporating a broader range of credit information.[14]

In July 2009, the FCAG presented its report to the IASB and the FASB about the standard-setting implications of the global financial crisis. Consistent with the G20's recommendations, the FCAG also recommended both the IASB and the FASB to explore alternatives to the incurred loss model for loan loss provisioning that used more forward-looking information.[15]

In June 2009, the IASB published a request for information – *Impairment of Financial Assets: Expected Cash Flow Approach* – on the feasibility of an expected loss model for the impairment of financial assets. Following this, the IASB issued an Exposure Draft – *Financial Instruments: Amortised Cost and Impairment* – in November 2009, that proposed an impairment model based on expected losses rather than on incurred losses, for all financial assets recorded at amortised cost. In this approach, the initial ECLs were to be recognised over the life of a financial asset, by including them in the computation of the EIR when the asset was first recognised. This would build an allowance for credit losses over the life of a financial asset and so match the recognition of credit losses with that of the credit spread implicit in the interest charged. Subsequent changes in credit loss expectations would be reflected in catch-up adjustments to profit or loss based on the original EIR. Because the proposals were much more closely linked to credit risk management concepts, the IASB acknowledged that this would represent a fundamental change from how entities currently operate (i.e. typically, entities operate their accounting and credit risk management systems separately). Consequently, the IASB established a panel of credit risk experts, the Expert Advisory Panel (EAP), to provide input to the project. *[IFRS 9.BC5.87]*.

Comments received on the 2009 Exposure Draft and during the IASB's outreach activities indicated that constituents were generally supportive of a model that distinguished between the effect of initial estimates of ECLs and subsequent changes in those estimates. However, they were also concerned about the operational difficulties in implementing the model proposed. These included: *[IFRS 9.BC5.89]*

- estimating the full expected cash flows for all financial instruments;
- applying a credit-adjusted EIR to those cash flow estimates; and
- maintaining information about the initial estimate of ECLs.

Also, the proposals would not have been easy to apply to portfolios of loans managed on a collective basis, in particular, open portfolios to which new financial instruments are added over time, and concerns were expressed about the volatility of reported profit or loss arising from the catch up adjustments.

To address these operational challenges and as suggested by the EAP, the IASB decided to decouple the measurement and allocation of initial ECLs from the determination of the EIR (except for purchased or originated credit-impaired financial assets). Therefore, the financial asset and the loss allowance would be measured separately, using an original EIR that is not adjusted for initial ECLs. Such an approach would help address the operational challenges raised and allow entities to leverage their existing accounting and credit risk management systems and so reduce the extent of the necessary integration between these systems. *[IFRS 9.BC5.92]*.

By decoupling ECLs from the EIR, an entity must measure the present value of ECLs using the original EIR. This presents a dilemma, because measuring ECLs using such a rate double-counts the ECLs that were priced into the financial asset at initial recognition. In other words, because the fair value of the loan at original recognition already reflects the ECLs, to provide for the ECLs as an additional allowance would be to double count these losses. Hence, the IASB concluded that it was not appropriate to recognise lifetime ECLs on initial recognition. In order to address the operational challenges while trying to reduce the effect of double-counting as well as to replicate (very approximately) the outcome of the 2009 Exposure Draft, the IASB decided to pursue a dual-measurement model that would require an entity to recognise: *[IFRS 9.BC5.93]*

- a portion of the lifetime ECLs from initial recognition as a proxy for recognising the initial ECLs over the life of the financial asset; and
- the lifetime ECLs when credit risk had increased since initial recognition (i.e. when the recognition of only a portion of the lifetime ECLs would no longer be appropriate because the entity has suffered a significant economic loss).

It is worth noting that any approach that seeks to approximate the outcomes of the model in the 2009 Exposure Draft, without the associated operational challenges, will include a recognition threshold for lifetime ECLs. This gives rise to what has been referred to as a cliff effect, i.e. the significant increase in allowance that represents the difference between the portion that was recognised previously and the lifetime ECLs. *[IFRS 9.BC5.95]*.

Subsequently, the IASB and FASB spent a considerable amount of time and effort developing a converged impairment model. In January 2011, the IASB issued with the FASB a Supplementary Document – *Financial Instruments: Impairment* – reflecting a joint approach that proposed a two-tier loss allowance: *[IFRS 9.BC5.96]*

- for the good book, an entity would recognise the higher of a time-proportionate allowance (i.e. the lifetime ECLs over the weighted average life of the portfolio of assets) or ECLs for the 'foreseeable future'; and
- for the bad book, an entity would recognise lifetime ECLs on those financial assets when the collectability of contractual cash flows had become so uncertain that the entity's credit risk management objective had changed from receiving the regular payments to recovery of all, or a portion of, the asset.

However, this approach received only limited support, because respondents were concerned about the operational difficulties in performing the dual calculation for the good book, that it also lacked conceptual merit and, potentially, would provide confusing information to users of financial statements. Moreover, concerns were also raised as to how 'foreseeable future' should be interpreted and applied.

Many constituents emphasised the importance of achieving convergence and this encouraged the IASB and FASB to attempt to develop another joint alternative approach. In May 2011, the boards decided to develop jointly an expected credit loss model that would reflect the general pattern of increases in the credit risk of financial instruments, the so-called three-bucket model. *[IFRS 9.BC5.111]*.

However, due to concerns raised by the FASB's constituents about the model's complexity, the FASB decided to develop an alternative expected credit loss model. In December 2012, the FASB issued a proposed accounting standard update, *Financial Instruments Credit Losses (Subtopic 825-15)*, that would require an entity to recognise a loss allowance for ECLs from initial recognition at an amount equal to lifetime ECLs (see 5.1.4 below). *[IFRS 9.BC5.112]*.

In March 2013, the IASB published a new Exposure Draft – *Financial Instruments: Expected Credit Losses*, based on proposals that grew out of the joint project with the FASB. The 2013 Exposure Draft proposed that entities should recognise a loss allowance or provision at an amount equal to 12-month credit losses for those financial instruments that had not yet seen a significant increase in credit risk since initial recognition, and lifetime ECLs once there had been a significant increase in credit risk. This new model was designed to:

- ensure a more timely recognition of ECLs than the existing incurred loss model;
- distinguish between financial instruments that have significantly deteriorated in credit quality and those that have not; and
- better approximate the economic ECLs.[16]

This two-step model was designed to approximate the build-up of the allowance as proposed in the 2009 Exposure Draft, but involving less operational complexity. Figure 50.1 below illustrates the stepped profile of the new model, shown by the solid line, compared to the steady increase shown by the black dotted line proposed in the 2009 Exposure Draft (based on the original ECL assumptions and assuming no subsequent revisions of this estimate). It shows that the two step model first overstates the allowance (compared to the method set out in the 2009 Exposure Draft), then understates it as the credit quality deteriorates, and then overstates it once again, as soon as the deterioration is significant.

Figure 50.1 Accounting for expected credit losses – 2009 ED versus IFRS 9[17]

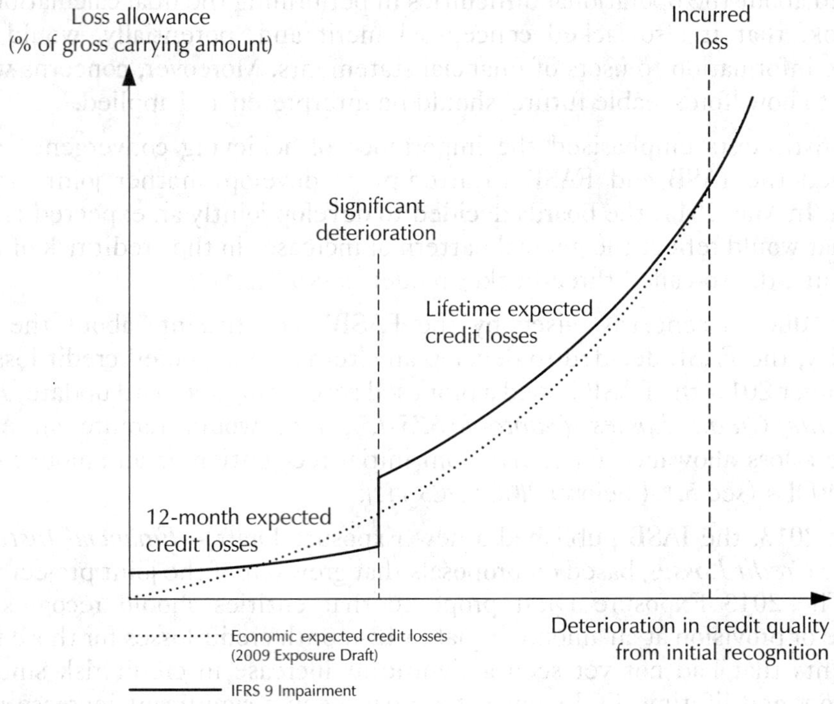

Feedback received on the IASB's 2013 Exposure Draft and the FASB's 2012 Proposed Update was considered at the joint board meetings. In general, non-US constituents preferred the IASB's proposals whilst the US constituents preferred the FASB's proposals. These differences in views arose in large part because of differences in the starting point of how preparers apply US GAAP for loss allowances from that for most IFRS preparers, while the interaction between the role of prudential regulators and calculation of loss allowances is historically stronger in the US. *[IFRS 9.BC5.116]*.

Many respondents urged the IASB to finalise the proposals in the 2013 Exposure Draft as soon as possible, even if convergence could not be achieved, in order to improve the accounting for the impairment of financial assets in IFRSs. *[IFRS 9.BC5.114]*. The IASB re-deliberated particular aspects of the 2013 Exposure Draft proposals, with the aim of providing further clarifications and additional guidance to help entities implement the proposed requirements. The IASB finalised the impairment requirements and issued them in July 2014, as part of the final version of IFRS 9.

The IASB has set up an IFRS Transition Resource Group for Impairment of Financial Instruments (ITG) (see 5.1.5 below) and has published a webcast on forward-looking information and multiple scenarios (see 5.4.4 below). Also, the Basel Committee has provided guidance aimed primarily at internationally active banks on the implementation of the IFRS 9 impairment model (see 5.1.6 and 5.6.1 below), the Global Public Policy Committee has published guidance to help those charged with governance to identify the elements of a high-quality implementation of IFRS 9 impairment by banks (see 5.6.2 below) and the Canadian Office of the Superintendent of Financial Institutions (OSFI) has issued a local guideline about credit risk management and its expectations for IFRS 9 implementation, largely based on the Basel Committee's Guidance on accounting for ECLs (see 5.1.6 below). The European Banking Authority has issued a Consultation Paper as well that seeks further input from stakeholders (see 5.6.1 below). Given the development of consensus on the part of preparers, auditors and other stakeholders, many of the views that we express in this chapter must inevitably be regarded as tentative.

5.1.2 Overview of IFRS 9 impairment requirements

The new impairment requirements in IFRS 9 are based on an ECL model and replace the IAS 39 incurred loss model. The ECL model applies to debt instruments (such as bank deposits, loans, debt securities and trade receivables) recorded at amortised cost or at fair value through other comprehensive income, plus lease receivables and contract assets. Loan commitments and financial guarantee contracts that are not measured at fair value through profit or loss are also included in the scope of the new ECL model.

Conceptually, an impairment model is a necessary complement to an accounting model for financial assets that is based on the concept of realisation. For financial assets in the scope of the impairment model, the recognition of revenue follows the effective interest method, and gains and losses relating to changes in their fair value are generally only recognised in profit or loss when the financial asset is derecognised, when that gain or loss is realised. In order to avoid delaying the recognition of impairment losses, those accounting models are complemented by an impairment model that anticipates impairment losses by recognising them before they are realised. The new impairment model of IFRS 9 does this on the basis of ECLs, which means impairment losses are anticipated earlier than under the incurred loss impairment model of IAS 39. The accounting models for financial assets in IFRS 9 that are not based on the concept of realisation, i.e. those measured at fair value through profit or loss or at fair value through other comprehensive income without recycling (under the presentation choice for fair value changes of some investments in equity instruments, see Chapter 47 at 8 and 2.2 above) do not involve any separate impairment accounting. Those measurement categories implicitly include impairment losses in the fair value changes that are recognised immediately (and without any later reclassification entries between other comprehensive income and profit or loss when they are realised).

The guiding principle of the ECL model is to reflect the general pattern of deterioration or improvement in the credit quality of financial instruments. The ECL approach has been commonly referred to as the three-bucket approach, although IFRS 9 does not use this term. Figure 50.2 below summarises the general approach in recognising either 12-month or lifetime ECLs.

Figure 50.2 General approach

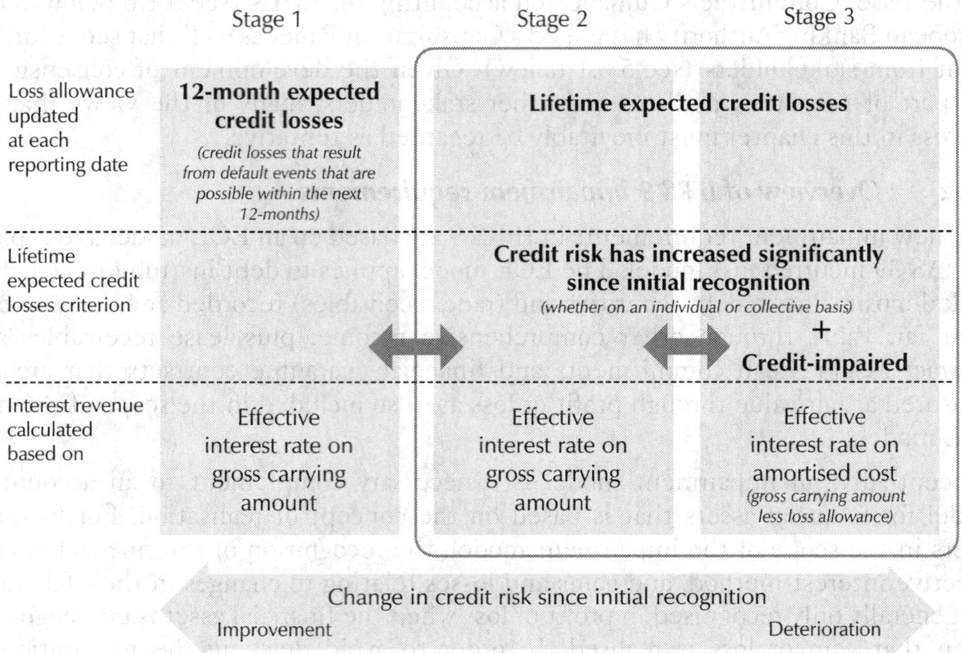

The amount of ECLs recognised as a loss allowance or provision depends on the extent of credit deterioration since initial recognition. Under the general approach (see 5.3.1 below), there are two measurement bases:

- 12-month ECLs (stage 1), which apply to all items as long as there is no significant deterioration in credit risk; and
- lifetime ECLs (stages 2 and 3), which apply when a significant increase in credit risk has occurred on an individual or collective basis.

When assessing significant increases in credit risk, there are a number of operational simplifications available, such as the low credit risk simplification (see 5.5.4 below).

Stages 2 and 3 differ in how interest revenue is recognised. Under stage 2 (as under stage 1), there is a full decoupling between interest recognition and impairment, and interest revenue is calculated on the gross carrying amount. Under stage 3 (when a credit event has occurred, defined similarly to an incurred credit loss under IAS 39), interest revenue is calculated on the amortised cost (i.e. the gross carrying amount adjusted for the impairment allowance).

The following example illustrates how the ECL allowance changes when a loan moves from stage 1 to stage 3.

Example 50.16: Expected credit loss allowance in stages 1, 2 and 3 under the general approach

On 31 December 2015, Bank A originates a 10 year bullet loan with a gross carrying amount of $1,000,000, with interest being due at the end of each year and the principal due on maturity. There are no transaction costs and the loan contracts include no options (for example, prepayment or call options), premiums or discounts, points paid, or other fees.

At origination, the loan is in stage 1 and a corresponding 12-month ECL allowance is recognised in the year ending 31 December 2017.

On 31 December 2018, the loan has shown signs of significant deterioration in credit quality and Bank A moves the loan to stage 2. A corresponding lifetime ECL allowance is recognised. In the following year, the loan defaults and is moved to stage 3.

The ECL allowance in each stage is shown below and the detailed calculation is illustrated in Example 50.18 at 5.4.2 below.

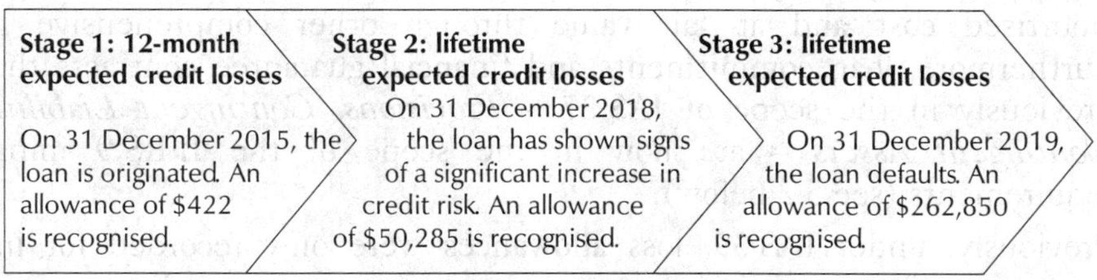

There are two alternatives to the general approach:

- the simplified approach, that is either required or available as a policy choice for trade receivables, contract assets and lease receivables (see 5.3.2 below); and
- the credit-adjusted effective interest rate approach, for purchased or originated credit-impaired financial assets (see 5.3.3 below).

ECLs are an estimate of credit losses over the life of a financial instrument and when measuring ECLs (see 5.4 below), an entity needs to take into account:

- the probability-weighted outcome (see 5.4.4 below), as ECLs should not be simply either a best or a worst-case scenario, but should instead reflect the possibility that a credit loss occurs and the possibility that no credit loss occurs. Following discussion at the ITG, this is understood to include a need to consider multiple economic scenarios (see 5.5.6 below);
- the time value of money (see 5.4.5 below); and
- reasonable and supportable information that is available without undue cost or effort at the reporting date about past events, current conditions and forecasts of future economic conditions (see 5.4.8 below).

The ECL requirements must be adopted with the other IFRS 9 requirements from 1 January 2018, with early application permitted if the other IFRS 9 requirements are adopted at the same time.

5.1.3 Key changes from the IAS 39 impairment requirements and the main implications of these changes

The new IFRS 9 impairment requirements eliminate the IAS 39 threshold for the recognition of credit losses, i.e. it is no longer necessary for a credit event to have occurred before credit losses are recognised. Instead, an entity always accounts for ECLs, and updates the loss allowance for changes in these ECLs at each reporting date to reflect changes in credit risk since initial recognition. Consequently, the holder of the financial asset needs to take into account more timely and forward-looking information in order to provide users of financial statements with useful information about the ECLs on financial instruments that are in the scope of these impairment requirements.

The main implications for both financial and non-financial entities are as follows:

- The scope of the impairment requirements is now much broader. Previously, under IAS 39, there were different impairment models for financial assets measured at amortised cost and available-for-sale financial assets. Under IFRS 9, there is a single impairment model for all debt instruments measured at amortised cost and at fair value through other comprehensive income. Furthermore, loan commitments and financial guarantee contracts that were previously in the scope of IAS 37 – *Provisions, Contingent Liabilities and Contingent Assets* – are now in the scope of the IFRS 9 impairment requirements (see 5.2 below).
- Previously, under IAS 39, loss allowances were only recorded for impaired exposures. The new impairment requirements result in earlier recognition of credit losses, by necessitating a 12-month ECL allowance for all credit exposures not measured at fair value through profit or loss. In addition, there will be a larger allowance for all credit exposures that have significantly deteriorated (as compared to the recognition of incurred losses under IAS 39 today). While credit exposures in stage 3, as illustrated in Figure 50.2 above, are similar to those deemed by IAS 39 to have suffered individual incurred losses, credit exposure in stages 1 and 2 will essentially replace those exposures measured under IAS 39's collective approach.
- The ECL model is more forward-looking than the IAS 39 impairment model. This is because holders of financial assets are not only required to consider historical information that is adjusted to reflect the effects of current conditions and information that provides objective evidence that financial assets are impaired in relation to incurred losses, but they are now required to consider reasonable and supportable information that includes forecasts of future economic conditions including, where relevant, multiple scenarios, when calculating ECLs, on an individual and collective basis.
- The application of the new IFRS 9 impairment requirements is expected to increase the credit loss allowances (with a corresponding reduction in equity on first-time adoption) of many entities, particularly banks and similar financial institutions. However, the increase in the loss allowance will vary by entity, depending on its portfolio and current practices. Entities with shorter term and higher quality financial instruments are likely to be less significantly affected. Similarly, financial institutions

with unsecured retail loans are more likely to be affected to a greater extent than those with collateralised loans such as mortgages.

- Moreover, the focus on expected losses will possibly result in higher volatility in the ECL amounts charged to profit or loss, especially for financial institutions. The level of loss allowances will increase as economic conditions are forecast to deteriorate and will decrease as economic conditions are forecast to become more favourable. This effect may be increased by the need to consider the effect of multiple macroeconomic scenarios (see 5.4.4 below). This may be further compounded by the significant increase in the loss allowance when financial instruments move between 12-month and lifetime ECLs and *vice versa*.
- The need to incorporate forward-looking information, including establishing multiple macroeconomic scenarios, determining the probability of their occurrence and assessing how changes in macroeconomic factors will affect ECLs, means that the application of the standard will require considerable judgement. Also, the increased level of judgement required in making the ECL calculation may mean that it will be difficult to compare the reported results of different entities. However, the more detailed disclosures (compared with those required to complement IAS 39) that require entities to explain their inputs, assumptions and techniques used in estimating ECLs requirements, should provide greater transparency over entities' credit risk and provisioning processes. The Enhanced Disclosures Task Force, established in 2012 by the Financial Stability Board to recommend best practice market risk disclosures, has published guidance to promote greater transparency and comparability about the application of the ECL model (see Chapter 54 at 9.2).
- In financial institutions, finance and credit risk management systems and processes will have to be better connected than today because of the necessary alignment between risk and accounting in the new model. Risk models and data will have to be more extensively used to make the assessments and calculations required for accounting purposes, which are both a major change from IAS 39 and a key challenge.
- In addition, financial institutions will need to fully understand the complex interactions between the IFRS 9 and regulatory capital requirements in relation to credit losses. At the time of writing, these have yet to be determined by the Basel Committee. In many cases, it is expected that the new IFRS 9 ECL requirements will result in a reduction in the regulatory capital of financial institutions.
- For corporates, the ECL model will most likely not cause a major increase in allowances for short-term trade receivables because of their short term nature. Moreover, the standard includes practical expedients, in particular the use of a provision matrix, which should help in measuring the loss allowance for short-term trade receivables. *[IFRS 9.B5.5.35]*. However, the model may give rise to challenges for the measurement of long-term trade receivables, bank deposits and debt securities which are measured at amortised cost or at fair value through other comprehensive income. For example, a corporate that has a large portfolio of debt securities that are currently held as available-for-sale under IAS 39, is likely to classify its holdings as measured at fair value through other comprehensive income if the contractual cash flow characteristics and business model test are met (see Chapter 47 at 5 and 6). For these securities, the corporate would be required to recognise a loss allowance

based on 12-month ECLs even for debt securities that are highly rated (e.g. AAA- or AA-rated bonds).

- Given that the IFRS 9 impairment requirements apply to lease receivables and that the IASB in its project to replace IAS 17 – *Leases* – decided to eliminate the distinction between finance and operating leases, there was a concern that this could give rise to significant ECL allowances for those that are currently classified as operating leases. However, the IASB, in finalising IFRS 16 – *Leases*, decided not to require a similar treatment for lessors as for lessees, so that they will not need to record financial assets for operating leases. With this change in the final standard, the effect of the IFRS 9 impairment requirements for many lessors has been significantly reduced. As the requirement under IFRS 9 is to take into account only those cash flows used to measure the receivable, there is no need to make a provision against future cash flows that are not yet recognised in the statement of financial position. As a result, the new impairment requirements will have a greater impact on lessors of those that are currently classed as finance leases, particularly if they opt to apply the simplified approach (see 5.3.2 below). In those situations, the effect would be to recognise a potentially significant allowance based on the lifetime ECLs of the lease. However, the lessor's 'loan' is in substance collateralised by the leased asset, which will reduce the ECLs.

5.1.4 Key differences from the FASB's standard

On 16 June 2016, the FASB issued an Accounting Standard Update (ASU), *Financial Instruments – Credit Losses (Topic 326)*, that aims to address the same fundamental issue that the IASB's ECL model (in IFRS 9) addresses, namely the delayed recognition of credit losses resulting from the incurred credit loss model. It is therefore also an ECL model but it is not the same. The most significant differences between the FASB's and the IASB's ECL models are, as follows:

- The FASB's ECL model will not be applied to debt securities measured at fair value through other comprehensive income (i.e. available for sale securities under US GAAP). Rather, for these securities, the FASB's existing other-than-temporary impairment model will be modified to require an allowance to recognise estimated credit losses rather than a direct write-down, among other things.
- The FASB's ECLs will be calculated based on the losses expected over the remaining contractual life of an asset, considering the effect of prepayments. An allowance for lifetime ECLs will be required when the loan is initially recognised instead of 12-month ECLs. As a result, the FASB's model does not require an entity to assess whether there has been a significant deterioration in credit quality, in contrast to the assessment required by IFRS 9. This is similar to the IFRS 9 simplified approach (see 5.3.2 below).
- The FASB's standard is less prescriptive about how ECLs should be measured, in particular, probability weighted outcomes are not required to be considered. On the other hand, the consideration of multiple scenarios should be compatible with the FASB's model.
- For purchased credit-impaired assets defined as 'acquired individual financial assets (or acquired groups of financial assets with shared risk characteristics) that, as of the

date of acquisition, have experienced a more-than-insignificant deterioration in credit quality since origination, as determined by an acquirer's assessment', the FASB's model will require an entity to increase the purchase price by the allowance for ECLs upon acquisition. In doing so, the FASB model will gross-up the asset's carrying amount by the ECLs existing upon acquisition, but also recognise a corresponding credit loss allowance, thereby resulting in a net carrying amount equal to the purchase price (see 5.3.3 below for the accounting treatment of credit-impaired assets under IFRS 9).

- There is no exception for revolving credit facilities (e.g. commitments connected with overdrafts and credit cards) under the FASB's model (see 5.11 below for the IFRS 9 treatment) and therefore, no impairment allowance is required if the commitment is legally revocable without any conditions5.4.3.

The FASB standard has tiered effective dates, starting in 2020 for calendar-year reporting public business entities that meet the definition of a U.S. Securities and Exchange Commission (SEC) filer. Early adoption is permitted for all entities but this cannot be before 2019 for calendar-year entities.

5.1.5 The IFRS Transition Resource Group for Impairment of Financial Instruments (ITG)

The IASB has set up an ITG that aims to:

- provide a public discussion forum to support stakeholders on implementation issues arising from the new impairment requirements that could create diversity in practice; and
- inform the IASB about the implementation issues, which will help the IASB determine what action, if any, will be needed to address them.[18]

However, the ITG will not issue any guidance.

Members of the ITG include financial statement preparers and auditors from various geographical locations with expertise, skills or practical knowledge on credit risk management and accounting for impairment. Board members and observers from the Basel Committee on Banking Supervision and the International Organisation of Securities Commissions also attend the meetings.

The ITG agenda papers are prepared by the IASB staff and are made public before the meetings. The staff also provides ITG meeting summaries which are not authoritative. Both the staff papers and the meeting summaries represent educational reading on the issues submitted.

Following its inaugural meeting in December 2014 to discuss its operating procedures, the ITG met on 22 April 2015 to discuss eight implementation issues raised by stakeholders. These included:[19]

- when applying the impairment requirements at the reporting date, whether and how to incorporate events and forecasts, that occur after economic forecasts have been made but before the reporting date and between the reporting period end and the date of signing the financial statements (see 5.4.8.C below);

- whether the impairment requirements in IFRS 9 must also be applied to other commitments to extend credit, in particular, a commitment (on inception of a finance lease) to commence a finance lease at a date in the future and a commitment by a retailer through the issue of a store account to provide a customer with credit when the customer buys goods or services from the retailer in the future (see 5.10 below);
- whether there is a requirement to measure ECLs at dates other than the reporting date, namely the date of derecognition and the date of initial recognition (see 5.6.3 below);
- whether an entity should consider the ability to recover cash flows through an integral financial guarantee contract when assessing whether there has been a significant increase in the credit risk of the guaranteed debt instrument since initial recognition (see 5.5.1 below);
- the maximum period to consider when measuring ECLs on a portfolio of mortgage loans that have a stated maturity of 6 months, but contain a contractual feature whereby the term is automatically extended every 6 months subject to the lender's non-objection (see 5.4.3 below);
- the maximum period to consider when measuring ECLs for revolving credit facilities and the determination of the date of initial recognition of the revolving facilities for the purposes of assessing them for significant increases in credit risk (see 5.11 below);
- whether the measurement of ECLs for financial guarantee contracts issued should consider future premium receipts due from the holder and, if so, how (see 5.10 below); and
- the measurement of ECLs in respect of a modified financial asset, the calculation of the modification gain or loss and subsequent requirement to measure ECLs on the modified financial asset as well as the appropriate presentation and disclosure (see 5.7 below).

On 16 September 2015, the ITG held its third meeting to discuss six implementation issues raised by stakeholders. These included:[20]

- how to identify a significant increase in credit risk for a portfolio of retail loans when identical pricing and contractual terms are applied to customers across broad credit quality bands (see 5.5.2 below);
- the possibility of using behavioural indicators of credit risk for the purpose of the assessment of significant increases in credit risk since initial recognition (see 5.5.2 below);
- when assessing for significant increases in credit risk, whether an entity would be required to perform an annual review to determine whether circumstances still support the use of the 12-month risk of a default occurring as an approximation of changes in the lifetime risk of a default occurring (see 5.5.4.C below);
- when measuring ECLs for revolving credit facilities, how an entity should estimate future drawdowns on undrawn lines of credit when an entity has a

history of allowing customers to exceed their contractually set credit limits on overdrafts and other revolving credit facilities (see 5.11 below);

- at what level should forward-looking information be incorporated – at the level of the entity or on a portfolio-by-portfolio basis (see 5.4.8.C below); and
- how to determine what is reasonable and supportable forward-looking information and how to treat shock events with material, but uncertain, economic consequences (see 5.4.8.C below).

On 11 December 2015, the ITG held its fourth meeting to discuss eleven implementation issues raised by stakeholders. These included:[21]

- what was meant by the 'current EIR' when an entity recognises interest revenue in each period based on the actual floating rate applicable to that period (see 5.4.5 below);
- what was meant by 'part of the contractual terms', specifically whether a credit enhancement must be an explicit term of the related asset's contract in order for it to be taken into account in the measurement of ECLs, or whether other credit enhancements that are not recognised separately can also be taken into account (see 5.4.7 below);
- whether cash flows that are expected to be recovered from the sale on default of a loan could be included in the measurement of ECLs (see 5.4.7 below);
- application of the revolving credit facilities exception set out in paragraph 5.5.20 of IFRS 9 to multi-purpose facilities (see 5.11 below);
- how future drawdowns should be estimated for charge cards when measuring ECLs if there is no specified credit limit in the contract (see 5.11 below);
- how an entity should determine the starting-point and the ending-point of the maximum period to consider when measuring ECLs for revolving credit facilities (see 5.11 below);
- when measuring ECLs, whether an entity can use a single forward-looking economic scenario or whether an entity needs to incorporate multiple forward-looking scenarios, and if so how (see 5.4.4 below);
- when assessing significant increases in credit risk, whether an entity can use a single forward-looking economic scenario or whether the entity needs to incorporate multiple forward-looking scenarios, and if so how (see 5.5.6 below);
- whether there is a requirement to assess significant increases in credit risk for financial assets with a maturity of 12 months or less (see 5.5 below);
- how to measure the gross carrying amount and loss allowance for credit impaired financial assets that are not purchased or originated credit-impaired and that are measured at amortised cost (see 5.4.5 below); and
- whether an entity is required to present the loss allowance for financial assets measured at amortised cost (or trade receivables, contract assets or lease receivables) separately in the statement of financial position (see 5.12.1 below).

Although no further meetings have been planned, the group has not been disbanded and stakeholders may continue to submit potential implementation issues following the submission guidelines. Further meetings will be convened if warranted.

The FASB (see 5.1.4 above) has also set up its own Transition Resource Group (TRG) for credit losses and its discussions may prove relevant to the application of IFRS 9 in areas where the two ECL models are similar.

5.1.6 *Other guidance on expected credit losses*

In December 2015, the Basel Committee on Banking Supervision issued its *Guidance on accounting for expected credit losses*, which sets out supervisory expectations regarding sound credit risk practices associated with implementing and applying an ECL accounting framework. This is discussed at 5.6.1 below and we anticipate that jurisdictions may adapt the Basel guidance into its own regulations. In June 2016, the Canadian Office of the Superintendent of Financial Institutions (OSFI) issued local guidance in a new guideline *IFRS 9 Financial Instruments and Disclosures* and at the time of writing this publication, the European Banking Authority has issued a consultation paper to this effect (see 5.6.1 below).

On 17 June 2016, the Global Public Policy Committee of representatives of the six largest accounting networks ('the GPPC') published *The implementation of IFRS 9 impairment by banks – Considerations for those charged with governance of systemically important banks* ('the GPPC guidance') to promote the implementation of accounting for ECLs to a high standard. It aims to help those charged with governance to evaluate management's progress during the implementation and transition phase (see 5.6.2 below).

5.2 Scope

IFRS 9 requires an entity to recognise a loss allowance for ECLs on: *[IFRS 9.5.5.1]*

- financial assets that are debt instruments such as loans, debt securities, bank balances and deposits and trade receivables (see 5.9 below) that are measured at amortised cost; *[IFRS 9.4.1.2]*
- financial assets that are debt instruments measured at fair value through other comprehensive income (see 5.8 below); *[IFRS 9.4.1.2A]*
- lease receivables under IAS 17, and finance lease receivables (i.e. net investments in finance leases) and operating lease receivables under IFRS 16 (when applied) (see 5.9 below, Chapter 24 and Chapter 25);
- contract assets under IFRS 15 (see 5.9 below and Chapter 30). IFRS 15 defines a contract asset as an entity's right to consideration in exchange for goods or services that the entity has transferred to a customer when that right is conditioned on something other than the passage of time (for example, the entity's future performance); *[IFRS 15 Appendix A, IFRS 9 Appendix A]*
- loan commitments that are not measured at fair value through profit or loss under IFRS 9 (see 5.10 and 5.11 below). The scope excludes loan commitments designated as financial liabilities at fair value through profit and loss and loan commitments that can be settled net in cash or by delivering or issuing another financial instrument; *[IFRS 9.2.1(g), 2.3, 4.2.1(a), 4.2.1(d)]* and
- financial guarantee contracts that are not measured at fair value through profit or loss under IFRS 9 (see 5.10 below).

5.3 Approaches

In applying the IFRS 9 impairment requirements, an entity needs to follow one of the approaches below:

- the general approach (see 5.3.1 below);
- the simplified approach (see 5.3.2 below); or
- the purchased or originated credit-impaired approach (see 5.3.3 below).

Figure 50.3 below, based on a diagram from the standard, summarises the process steps in recognising and measuring ECLs.

Figure 50.3 Application of the impairment requirements at a reporting date

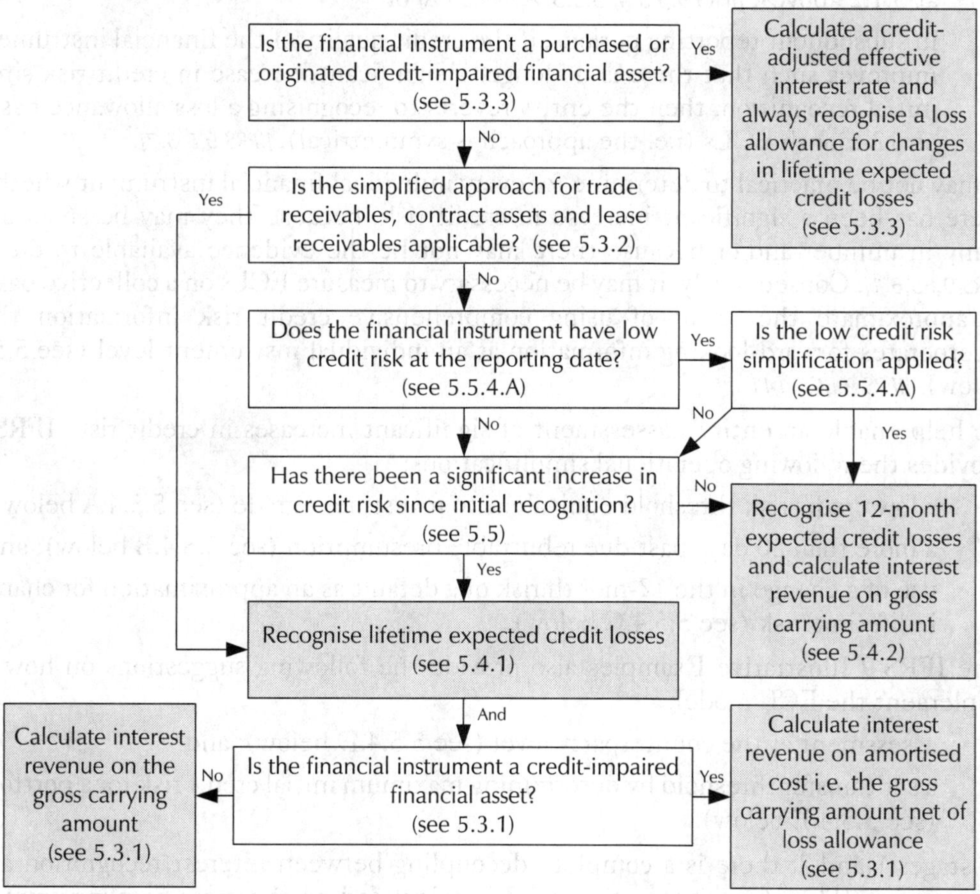

5.3.1 General approach

Under the general approach, at each reporting date, an entity recognises a loss allowance based on either 12-month ECLs or lifetime ECLs, depending on whether there has been a significant increase in credit risk on the financial instrument since initial recognition. *[IFRS 9.5.5.3, 5.5.5]*. The changes in the loss allowance balance are recognised in profit or loss as an impairment gain or loss. *[IFRS 9.5.5.8, Appendix A]*.

Essentially, an entity must make the following assessment at each reporting date:

- for credit exposures where there have not been significant increases in credit risk since initial recognition, an entity is required to provide for 12-month ECLs, i.e. the portion of lifetime ECLs that represent the ECLs that result from default events that are possible within the 12-months after the reporting date (stage 1 in Figure 50.2 at 5.1.2 above); *[IFRS 9.5.5.3, Appendix A]*
- for credit exposures where there have been significant increases in credit risk since initial recognition on an individual or collective basis, a loss allowance is required for lifetime ECLs, i.e. ECLs that result from all possible default events over the expected life of a financial instrument (stages 2 and 3 in Figure 50.2 at 5.1.2 above); *[IFRS 9.5.5.4, 5.5.5, Appendix A]* or
- in subsequent reporting periods, if the credit quality of the financial instrument improves such that there is no longer a significant increase in credit risk since initial recognition, then the entity reverts to recognising a loss allowance based on 12-month ECLs (i.e. the approach is symmetrical). *[IFRS 9.5.5.7]*.

It may not be practical to determine for every individual financial instrument whether there has been a significant increase in credit risk, because they may be small and many in number and/or because there may not be the evidence available to do so. *[IFRS 9.B5.5.1]*. Consequently, it may be necessary to measure ECLs on a collective basis, to approximate the result of using comprehensive credit risk information that incorporates forward-looking information at an individual instrument level (see 5.5.5 below). *[IFRS 9.BC5.141]*.

To help enable an entity's assessment of significant increases in credit risk, IFRS 9 provides the following operational simplifications:

- a low credit risk threshold equivalent to investment grade (see 5.5.4.A below);
- a more than 30 days past due rebuttable presumption (see 5.5.4.B below); and
- use of a change in the 12-month risk of a default as an approximation for change in lifetime risk (see 5.5.4.C below).

The IFRS 9 Illustrative Examples also provide the following suggestions on how to implement the ECL model:

- assessment at the counterparty level (see 5.5.4.D below); and
- a set transfer threshold by determining maximum initial credit risk for a portfolio (see 5.5.4.E below).

In stages 1 and 2, there is a complete decoupling between interest recognition and impairment. Therefore, interest revenue is calculated on the gross carrying amount (without deducting the loss allowance). If a financial asset subsequently becomes credit-impaired (stage 3 in Figure 50.2 at 5.1.2 above), an entity is required to calculate the interest revenue by applying the EIR in subsequent reporting periods to the amortised cost of the financial asset (i.e. the gross carrying amount net of loss allowance) rather than the gross carrying amount. *[IFRS 9.5.4.1, Appendix A]*. Financial assets are assessed as credit-impaired using substantially the same criteria as for the impairment assessment of an individual asset under IAS 39 (see 5.4.7 below). *[IAS 39.59, IFRS 9 Appendix A]*.

A financial asset is credit-impaired when one or more events that have a detrimental impact on the estimated future cash flows of that financial asset have occurred. Evidence that a financial asset is impaired includes observable data about such events. IFRS 9 provides a list of events that are substantially the same as the IAS 39 loss events for an individual asset assessment: *[IFRS 9 Appendix A]*

- significant financial difficulty of the issuer or the borrower;
- a breach of contract, such as a default or past due event;
- the lender(s) of the borrower, for economic or contractual reasons relating to the borrower's financial difficulty, having granted to the borrower a concession(s) that the lender(s) would not otherwise consider;
- it is becoming probable that the borrower will enter bankruptcy or other financial reorganisation;
- the disappearance of an active market for that financial asset because of financial difficulties; or
- the purchase or origination of a financial asset at a deep discount that reflects the incurred credit losses.

It may not be possible for an entity to identify a single discrete event. Instead, the combined effect of several events may have caused the financial asset to become credit-impaired. *[IFRS 9 Appendix A]*.

In subsequent reporting periods, if the credit quality of the financial asset improves so that the financial asset is no longer credit-impaired and the improvement can be related objectively to the occurrence of an event (such as an improvement in the borrower's credit rating), then the entity should once again calculate the interest revenue by applying the EIR to the gross carrying amount of the financial asset. *[IFRS 9.5.4.2]*.

When the entity has no reasonable expectations of recovering the financial asset, then the gross carrying amount of the financial asset should be directly reduced in its entirety. A write-off constitutes a derecognition event (see 5.12.1.A below).

5.3.2 *Simplified approach*

The simplified approach does not require an entity to track the changes in credit risk, but instead requires the entity to recognise a loss allowance based on lifetime ECLs at each reporting date. *[IFRS 9.5.5.15]*.

An entity is required to apply the simplified approach for trade receivables or contract assets that result from transactions within the scope of IFRS 15 and that do not contain a significant financing component, or when the entity applies the practical expedient for contracts that have a maturity of one year or less, in accordance with IFRS 15 (see Chapter 30). *[IFRS 9.5.5.15(a)(i)]*. Paragraphs 60-65 of IFRS 15 provide the requirements for determining the existence of a significant financing component in the contract, including the use of the practical expedient for contracts that are one year or less.

A contract asset is defined as an entity's right to consideration in exchange for goods or services that the entity has transferred to a customer when that right is conditioned on something other than the passage of time (for example, the entity's future performance). *[IFRS 15 Appendix A]*. IFRS 15 describes contracts with a significant financing component as those for which the agreed timing of payment provides the customer or the entity with a significant benefit of financing on the transfer of goods or services to the customer and hence, in determining the transaction price, an entity is required to adjust the promised amount of consideration for the effects of the time value of money. *[IFRS 15.60]*. However, if the entity expects at contract inception that the period between when the entity transfers a promised good or service to a customer and when the customer pays for that good or service will be one year or less, as a practical expedient, an entity need not adjust the promised amount of consideration for the effects of a significant financing component. *[IFRS 15.63]*.

Application of the simplified approach to trade receivables and contract assets that do not contain a significant financing component intuitively makes sense. In particular, for trade receivables and contract assets that are due in 12-months or less, the 12-month ECLs are the same as the lifetime ECLs.

However, an entity has a policy choice to apply either the simplified approach or the general approach for the following: *[IFRS 9.5.5.16]*:

- all trade receivables or contract assets that result from transactions within the scope of IFRS 15, and that contain a significant financing component in accordance with IFRS 15. The policy choice may be applied separately to trade receivables and contract assets (see 5.9.1 below and Chapter 30); *[IFRS 9.5.5.15(a)(ii)]* and
- all lease receivables that result from transactions that are within the scope of IAS 17 and IFRS 16 (when applied). The policy choice may be applied separately to finance and operating lease receivables (see 5.9.2 below, Chapter 24 and Chapter 25). *[IFRS 9.5.5.15(b)]*.

The IASB noted that offering this policy choice would reduce comparability. However, the IASB believes it would alleviate some of the practical concerns of tracking changes in credit risk for entities that do not have sophisticated credit risk management systems. *[IFRS 9. BC5.225]*.

5.3.3 *Purchased or originated credit-impaired financial assets*

On initial recognition of a financial asset, an entity is required to determine whether the asset is credit-impaired. The criteria are set out at 5.3.1 above. *[IFRS 9.5.5.3, 5.5.5, 5.5.13]*.

A financial asset may be purchased credit-impaired because it has already met the criteria. Such an asset is likely to be acquired at a deep discount. However, this does not mean that an entity is required to apply the credit-adjusted EIR to a financial asset solely because the financial asset has a high credit risk at initial recognition, if it has not yet met those criteria. *[IFRS 9.B5.4.7]*.

In some unusual circumstances, it may be possible that an entity originates a credit-impaired financial asset, for example following a substantial modification of a distressed financial asset that resulted in the derecognition of the original financial asset (see 5.7 below). *[IFRS 9.B5.5.26]*.

Consider an example of a bank originating a loan of €100,000 with interest of 30% per annum charged over the term of the loan, payable in monthly amortising instalments. The bank's customer has a high credit risk on origination and the bank expects a large portion of this type of customer to pay late or fail to pay some or all of their instalment payments. Although the loan is of high credit risk (which is supported by the high interest rate), none of the loss events listed above *have occurred* and the loan was not the result of a substantial modification and derecognition of a distressed debt, hence, the bank should assess the loan not to be credit-impaired on origination.

For financial assets that are considered to be credit-impaired on purchase or origination, the EIR (see 3 above) is calculated taking into account the initial lifetime ECLs in the estimated cash flows. *[IFRS 9.B5.4.7, Appendix A, BC5.214, BC5.217]*. This accounting treatment is the same as that under IAS 39 for similar assets. *[IAS 39.AG5]*. It is also consistent with the original method for measuring impairment proposed in the 2009 Exposure Draft.

Consequently, no allowance is recorded for 12-month ECLs for financial assets that are credit-impaired on initial recognition. The rationale for not recording a 12-month ECL allowance for these assets is that the losses are already reflected in the fair values at which they are initially recognised. The same logic could be applied to all the other financial assets which are not credit-impaired, arguing that they, too, are initially recognised at a fair value that reflects expectations of future losses. The distinction is made because the double-counting of 12-month ECLs on initial recognition would be too large for assets with such a high credit risk, and the exclusion of initial ECLs from the computation of the EIR would lead to a distortion that would be too significant to be acceptable.

For financial assets that were credit-impaired on purchase or origination, the credit-adjusted EIR is also used subsequently to discount the ECLs. In subsequent reporting periods an entity is required to recognise:

- in the statement of financial position, the cumulative changes in lifetime ECLs since initial recognition, discounted at the credit-impaired EIR (see 5.4.5 below), as a loss allowance; *[IFRS 9.5.5.13, B5.5.45]* and
- in profit or loss, the amount of any change in lifetime ECLs as an impairment gain or loss. An impairment gain is recognised if favourable changes result in the lifetime ECLs estimate becoming lower than the original estimate that was incorporated in the estimated cash flows on initial recognition when calculating the credit-adjusted EIR. *[IFRS 9.5.5.14]*.

For favourable changes that result in a lower lifetime ECLs than the original estimate on initial recognition, IFRS 9 does not provide guidance on where in the statement of financial position the debit entry should be booked. In our view, the impairment gain should be recognised as a direct adjustment to the gross carrying amount. This is supported by paragraph B5.4.6 as, for purchased or originated credit-impaired financial assets, the ECLs are included in the estimated cash flows when calculating the credit-adjusted EIR and hence, the changes in estimates of ECLs should adjust the gross carrying amount of the financial asset. An alternative treatment would be to recognise a negative loss allowance which would reflect the favourable changes in lifetime ECLs.

Along with the other credit risk disclosures requirements (see 5.13 below and Chapter 54 at 5.2.3), the holder is required to explain how it has determined that assets are credit-impaired (including the inputs, assumptions and estimation techniques used). It is also required to disclose the total amount of undiscounted ECLs at initial recognition for financial assets initially recognised during the reporting period that were purchased or originated credit-impaired. *[IFRS 7.35H(c)]*.

The accounting treatment for a purchased credit-impaired financial asset is illustrated in the following example.

Example 50.17: Calculation of the credit-adjusted effective interest rate and recognition of a loss allowance for a purchased credit-impaired financial asset

On 1 January 2011, Company D issued a bond that required it to pay an annual coupon of €800 in arrears and to repay the principal of €10,000 on 31 December 2020. By 2016, Company D was in significant financial difficulties and was unable to pay the coupon due on 31 December 2016. On 1 January 2017, Company V estimates that the holder could expect to receive a single payment of €4,000 at the end of 2018. It acquires the bond at an arm's length price of €3,000. Company V determines that the debt instrument is credit-impaired on initial recognition, because of evidence of significant financial difficulty of Company D and because the debt instrument was purchased at a deep discount.

It can be shown that using the contractual cash flows (including the €800 overdue) gives rise to an EIR of 70.1% (the net present value of €800 now and annually thereafter until 2020 and €10,000 receivable at the end of 2020 equals €3,000 when discounted at 70.1%). However, because the bond is credit-impaired, V should calculate the EIR using the estimated cash flows of the instrument. In this case, the EIR is 15.5% (the net present value of €4,000 receivable in two years equals €3,000 when discounted at 15.5%).

All things being equal, interest income of €464 (€3,000 × 15.5%) would be recognised on the instrument during 2017 and its carrying amount at the end of the year would be €3,464 (€3,000 + €464). However if at the end of the year, based on reasonable and supportable evidence, the cash flow expected to be received on the instrument had increased to, say, €4,250 (still to be received at the end of 2018), an adjustment would be made to the asset's amortised cost. Accordingly, its carrying amount would be increased to €3,681 (€4,250 discounted over one year at 15.5%) and an impairment gain of €217 would be recognised in profit or loss.

5.4 Measurement of expected credit losses

The standard defines credit loss as the difference between all contractual cash flows that are due to an entity in accordance with the contract and all the cash flows that the entity expects to receive (i.e. all cash shortfalls), discounted at the original EIR (or credit-adjusted EIR for purchased or originated credit-impaired financial assets). When estimating the cash flows, an entity is required to consider: *[IFRS 9 Appendix A]*

- all contractual terms of the financial instrument (including prepayment, extension, call and similar options) over the expected life (see 5.4.3 below) of the financial instrument. The maximum period to consider when measuring ECLs is the maximum contractual period (including extension options) over which the entity is exposed to credit risk (with an exception for revolving facilities); and
- cash flows from the sale of collateral held (see 5.4.7 below) or other credit enhancements that are integral to the contractual terms.

Also, the standard goes on to define ECLs as 'the weighted average of credit losses with the respective risks of a default occurring as the weights'. *[IFRS 9 Appendix A]*.

The standard does not prescribe specific approaches to estimate ECLs, but stresses that that the approach used must reflect the following: *[IFRS 9.5.5.17]*

- an unbiased and probability-weighted amount that is determined by evaluating a range of possible outcomes (see 5.4.4 below);
- the time value of money (see 5.4.5 below); and
- reasonable and supportable information that is available without undue cost or effort at the reporting date about past events, current conditions and forecasts of future economic conditions (see 5.4.8 below).

5.4.1 Lifetime expected credit losses

IFRS 9 defines lifetime ECLs as the ECLs that result from all possible default events over the expected life of a financial instrument (i.e. an entity needs to estimate the risk of a default occurring on the financial instrument during its expected life). *[IFRS 9 Appendix A, B5.5.43]*. The expected life considered for the measurement of lifetime ECLs cannot be longer than the maximum contractual period (including extension options) over which the entity is exposed to credit risk. However, there is an exception for revolving facilities (see 5.11 below).

ECLs should be estimated based on the present value of all cash shortfalls over the remaining expected life of the financial asset, i.e. the difference between: *[IFRS 9.B5.5.29]*

- the contractual cash flows that are due to an entity under the contract; and
- the cash flows that the holder expects to receive.

As ECLs take into account both the amount and the timing of payments, a credit loss arises even if the holder expects to receive all the contractual payments due, but at a later date. *[IFRS 9.B5.5.28]*.

When estimating lifetime ECLs for undrawn loan commitments (see 5.10 below), the provider of the commitment needs to:

- estimate the expected portion of the loan commitment that will be drawn down over the expected life of the loan commitment. Except for revolving facilities (see 5.11 below), the expected life will be capped at the maximum contractual period, including extension options, over which the entity is exposed to credit risk (see 5.4.2 below for 12-month ECLs); *[IFRS 9.B5.5.31]* and
- calculate the present value of cash shortfalls between the contractual cash flows that are due to the entity if the holder of the loan commitment draws down that expected portion of the loan and the cash flows that the entity expects to receive if that expected portion of the loan is drawn down. *[IFRS 9.B5.5.30]*.

For a financial guarantee contract (see 5.10 below), the guarantor is required to make payments only in the event of a default by the debtor in accordance with the terms of the instrument that is guaranteed. Accordingly, the estimate of lifetime ECLs would be based on the present value of the expected payments to reimburse the holder for a credit loss that it incurs less any amounts that the guarantor expects to receive from the holder, the debtor or any other party. If an asset is fully guaranteed, the ECL estimate for the financial guarantee contract would be the same as the estimated cash shortfall estimate for the asset subject to the guarantee. *[IFRS 9.B5.5.32]*.

5.4.2 12-month expected credit losses

The 12-month ECLs is defined as a portion of the lifetime ECLs that represent the ECLs that result from default events on a financial instrument that are possible within the 12 months after the reporting date. *[IFRS 9 Appendix A]*. The standard explains further that the 12-month ECLs are a portion of the lifetime ECLs that will result if a default occurs in the 12 months after the reporting date (or a shorter period if the expected life of a financial instrument is less than 12 months), weighted by the probability of that default occurring. *[IFRS 9.B5.5.43]*.

Because the calculation is based on the probability of default (PD), the standard emphasises that the 12-month ECL is not the lifetime ECL that an entity will incur on financial instruments that it *predicts* will default in the next 12 months (i.e. for which the PD over the next 12 months is greater than 50%). For instance, the PD might be only 25%, in which case this should be used to calculate 12-month ECLs, even though it is not probable that the asset will default. Also, the 12-month ECLs are not the cash shortfalls that are predicted over only the next 12 months. For an asset defaulting in the next 12 months, the lifetime ECLs that need to be included in the calculation will normally be significantly greater than just the cash flows that were contractually due in the next 12 months.

For undrawn loan commitments (see 5.10 below), an entity's estimate of 12-month ECLs should be based on its expectations of the portion of the loan commitment that will be drawn down within 12 months of the reporting date. *[IFRS 9.B5.5.31]*.

As already mentioned at 5.1.2 above, the IASB believes that the 12-month ECLs serve as a proxy for the recognition of initial ECLs over time, as proposed in the 2009 Exposure Draft, and they mitigate the systematic overstatement of interest revenue that is recognised under IAS 39. *[IFRS 9.BC5.135]*. This practical approximation was necessary as a result of the decision to decouple the measurement and allocation of initial ECLs from the determination of the EIR following the re-deliberations of the 2009 Exposure Draft. *IFRS 9.BC5.199]*.

The stage 1, 12-month allowance overstates the necessary allowance for each financial instrument after initial recognition. However, this is offset by the fact that the allowance is not further increased (except for changes in the 12-month ECLs) until the instrument's credit risk has significantly increased and it is transferred to stage 2. For a portfolio of instruments, with various origination dates, the overall provision may (very approximately) be a similar size as might be achieved using a more conceptually robust approach. Although there is no conceptual justification for an allowance based on 12-month ECLs, it was designed to be a pragmatic solution to achieve an appropriate balance between faithfully representing the underlying economics of a transaction and the cost of implementation.

How accurate a proxy the 12-month and lifetime ECL model is for a more conceptually pure approach will depend on the nature of the portfolio. Also, the effect of recording a 12-month ECL in the first reporting period that a financial instrument is recognised will not have a significant effect on reported income if the portfolio is stable in size from one period to the next. The 12-month ECL allowance may, however, significantly reduce the reported income for entities which are expanding the size of their portfolio.

Although the choice of 12 months is arbitrary, it is the same time horizon as used for the more advanced bank regulatory capital calculation under the Basel framework.[22] The definition of 12-month ECLs is similar to the Basel Committee's definition of ECL, although the modelling requirements differ significantly.[23] The 12-month requirement under IFRS 9 will always differ from that computed for regulatory capital purposes, as the IFRS 9 measure is a point-in-time estimate, reflecting currently forecast economic conditions (see 5.4.8.C below), while the Basel regulatory figure is based on through-the-cycle assumptions of default and conservative estimates of losses given default. However, banks that use an advanced approach to calculate their capital requirements should be able to use their existing systems and methodologies as a starting point and make the necessary adjustments to flex the calculation to comply with IFRS 9.

Following from Example 50.14 at 5.1.2 above, calculations of the 12-month and lifetime ECLs are illustrated below.

Example 50.18: 12-month and lifetime expected credit loss measurement based on a PD approach

On 31 December 2015, Bank A originates a 10 year bullet loan with a gross carrying amount of $1,000,000, with interest being due at the end of each year and the principal due at maturity. In line with IFRS 9, Bank A must recognize an impairment allowance for the ECLs, considering current and forward looking credit risk information.

The ECLs are a probability-weighted estimate of the present value of estimated cash shortfalls – i.e. the weighted average of credit losses, with the respective risks of a default occurring used as the weights. For this purpose, the following parameters must be estimated:

- Probability of Default ('PD') – Estimate of the likelihood of default over a given time horizon (e.g. from t_{i-1} to t_i). A default may only happen at a t_i horizon if the facility has not been previously derecognized and is still in the portfolio. An early exit ('EE') may occur in case of default unless the facility reverts to performing without significant modification of the contractual terms. The marginal probability of default for the period t_{i-1} to t_i is then adjusted from the probability that an early exit occurred during the previous periods:

  $$PD_{t_i} \times \prod_{j=1}^{j=i-1}(1 - EE_{t_j})$$

  We note that, for simplicity, Bank A may decide to model EE within the PD component.
- Loss Given Default ('LGD') – Estimate of the loss arising in case a default occurs at a given time (e.g. t_i). It is based on the difference between the contractual cash flows due and those that the lender would expect to receive, including from the realization of any collateral. It is usually expressed as a percentage of the EAD.
- Exposure at Default ('EAD') – Estimate of the exposure at a future default date, taking into account expected changes in the exposure after the reporting date, including repayments of principal and interest, whether scheduled by contract or otherwise, expected drawdowns on committed facilities, and accrued interest from missed payments.
- Discount Rate ('r') – Rate used to discount an expected loss to a present value at the reporting date.

Based on these parameters, an ECL can be computed for any horizon – typically for each due date of an exposure. The computation formula can be expressed as follow:

$$\mathrm{ECL}_{t_n} = \sum_{t_i=t_1}^{t_i=t_n} \frac{PD_{t_i} \times \prod_{j=1}^{j=i-1}(1 - EE_{t_j}) \times LGD_{t_i} \times EAD_{t_i}}{(1 + r_i)^{t_i}}$$

Where:

i	= each future payment
ti	= maturity of the payment i
tn	= horizon considered (either 12-month or lifetime)

Stage 1: 12-month ECLs of $422

At origination, the loan is in stage 1. Thus a corresponding 12-month ECL allowance is recognised, i.e. the portion of the lifetime ECLs that result from default events that are possible within 12-months after the reporting date.

Based on statistical and qualitative information, Bank A has computed the following ECL parameters at origination.

As interest is paid on a yearly basis, ECLs are calculated using annual periods.

Each year EAD equals the outstanding principal plus accrued interest due at the end of the year. This bullet loan does not allow any prepayment, therefore the EAD is constant.

The effective interest rate of the loan is assumed to be the contractual rate, which is 3%.

Bank A sets EE = $PD_{n-1} \times 0.8$, on the basis that a proportion of the loans which default are expected to cure and will once again be at risk of default.

Based on provided guarantees and collateral, LGD is estimated at 25% of EAD, whatever the date of default.

Year	EAD	Dis-counting rate	Cumulative PD @ origination	Marginal PD	Cumulative EE t–1 @ origination	LGD	Marginal ECL	
2015	1,000,000							
2016	1,030,000	3%	0.17%	0.17%	0.00%	25%	**$422**	**12m ECL**
2017	1,030,000	3%	0.49%	0.32%	0.14%	25%	$775	
2018	1,030,000	3%	0.86%	0.37%	0.39%	25%	$877	
2019	1,030,000	3%	1.38%	0.53%	0.69%	25%	$1,196	
2020	1,030,000	3%	1.84%	0.47%	1.11%	25%	$1,027	
2021	1,030,000	3%	2.37%	0.54%	1.47%	25%	$1,141	
2022	1,030,000	3%	2.85%	0.49%	1.90%	25%	$1,014	
2023	1,030,000	3%	3.30%	0.46%	2.28%	25%	$912	
2024	1,030,000	3%	3.84%	0.56%	2.64%	25%	$1,073	
2025	1,030,000	3%	4.50%	0.69%	3.07%	25%	$1,280	
							$9,718	**Lifetime ECL**

$$\text{Marginal PD}_i = 1 - \frac{1 - \text{Cum PD}_i}{1 - \text{Cum PD}_{i-1}}$$

$$\text{Marginal ECL}_i = \frac{PD_i \times Cum\ EE_{i-1} \times LGD_i \times EAD_i}{(1 + r_i)^i}$$

Stage 2: lifetime ELCs of $50,285

On 31 December 2018 – 3 years after origination, the loan shows signs of significant deterioration in credit quality based on the creditworthiness of the obligor and forward looking information, and Bank A moves it to stage 2. Example 50.25 below shows the calculation underlying this assessment.

Consistent with the significant increase in credit risk, the PD of the obligor has increased. In consequence, the probability of an early exist has also increased, because of the higher level of default. For the purposes of this example, we assume that there are no significant fluctuations in collateral values and the LGD remains constant.

Year	EAD	Dis-counting rate	Cumulative PD	Marginal PD	Cumulative EE t–1	LGD	Marginal ECL	
2018	1,000,000		0.00%					
2019	1,030,000	3%	1.40%	1.40%	0.00%	25%	**$3,495**	**12m ECL**
2020	1,030,000	3%	3.87%	2.51%	1.12%	25%	$6,017	
2021	1,030,000	3%	8.82%	5.15%	3.10%	25%	$11,756	
2022	1,030,000	3%	12.84%	4.40%	7.06%	25%	$9,366	
2023	1,030,000	3%	16.04%	3.67%	10.27%	25%	$7,322	
2024	1,030,000	3%	18.98%	3.50%	12.83%	25%	$6,585	
2025	1,030,000	3%	21.60%	3.23%	15.18%	25%	$5,745	
							$50,285	**Lifetime ECL**

Stage 3: lifetime ECLs of $262,850

In the following year, on 31 December 2019, the obligor does not pay the amount due. Based on credit information available, it is already considered to be in default and is moved to stage 3 – credit impaired. At this time, the exposure is $1,030,000.

Once a facility becomes credit-impaired, impairment must still represent ECLs. Therefore, it must be probability-based. At the reporting date, Bank A updates the appraisal value of the collateral and considers 3 probable scenarios:

- **Scenario 1 – Cure**: the obligor eventually pays past dues and the loan reverts to performing. In this case, ECL corresponds to lifetime losses expected from loans that have recently defaulted. Based on its historical data and using the methodology described above, Bank A expects an ECL of $130,000.
- **Scenario 2 – Restructure**: Bank A comes to a restructuring agreement with the obligor. After 6 months of negotiation, the loan is written off and a new loan is initiated with a net present value of $800,000.
- **Scenario 3 – Liquidation:** The loan is written off and the bank starts the collection of the contractual collateral. Bank A expects to sell the collateral within a year and to collect $700,000 net of recovery costs.

The ECL of each scenario can be calculated as follows:

$$\mathrm{ECL} = \mathrm{EAD} - \sum_{t_i = t_1}^{t_i = t_n} \frac{\mathrm{CF}_{t_i} - \mathrm{RC}_{t_i}}{(1 + r_i)^{t_i}}$$

Where:

CF = expected future cash flows
RC = expected recovery costs

Probable scenarios	Probability	EAD	Discounting rate	Expected net future cash flows	Expected recovery time	ECL of each scenario	Weighted ECL
Scenario 1: Cure	20%	1,030,000	3%	900,000	0.0	$130,000	$26,000
Scenario 2: Restructure	40%	1,030,000	3%	800,000	0.5	$241,737	$96,695
Scenario 3: Liquidation	40%	1,030,000	3%	700,000	1.0	$350,388	$140,155
Weighted average ECL						Lifetime ECL	$262,850
						% of EAD:	26%

$$\text{ECL} = \text{EAD} - \frac{\text{Exp. net future CF}}{(1+\text{r})^{\text{exp recovery time}}}$$

From observation of emerging practices, most sophisticated banks are intending to develop their IFRS 9 solutions by adjusting and extending their existing Basel models. This is true for all types of component models: PD, LGD and EAD. This is perhaps unsurprising given the historical investment large banks have made in their Basel models, and the fact that IFRS 9 shares fundamental similarities in expected loss modelling. But, for many banks, creating lifetime estimates and altering models to satisfy the complex and detailed IFRS 9 requirements will still require significant work.

5.4.2.A Definition of default

Default is not defined for the purposes of determining the risk of a default occurring. Because it is defined differently by different institutions (for instance, 30, 90 or 180 days past due), the IASB was concerned that defining default could result in a definition that is inconsistent with that applied internally for credit risk management. In particular, since default is the anchor point used to measure probabilities of default and losses given default in Basel modelling, requiring a different definition would require building a whole different set of models for accounting purposes. Therefore, the standard requires an entity to apply a definition of default that is consistent with how it is defined for normal credit risk management practices, consistently from one period to another. It follows that an entity might have to use different default definitions for different types of financial instruments. However, the standard stresses that an entity needs to consider qualitative indicators of default when appropriate in addition to days past due, such as breaches of covenant. *[IFRS 9.B5.5.37]*.

ECL calculations were not originally expected by the IASB to change as a result of differences in the definition of default, because of the counterbalancing interaction between the way an entity defines default and the credit losses that arise as a result of that definition of default. *[IFRS 9.BC5.248]*. (For instance, if an entity uses a shorter delinquency period of 30 days past due instead of 60 days past due, the associated LGD will be correspondingly smaller as it is to be expected that more debtors that are 30 days past due will in due course recover). However, the notion of default is fundamental to the application of the model, particularly because it affects the subset of the population that is subject to the 12-month ECLs measure. *[IFRS 9.BC5.249]*.

The standard restricts diversity resulting from this effect by establishing a rebuttable presumption that default does not occur later than when a financial asset is 90 days past due. This presumption may be rebutted only if an entity has reasonable and supportable information to support an alternative default criterion. *[IFRS 9.B5.5.37, BC5.252]*.

A 90 day default definition would also be consistent with that used by banks for the advanced Basel II regulatory capital calculations (with a few exceptions). We observe that most banks intend to align their regulatory and accounting definitions of default. This generally means aligning the number of days past due trigger to 90 days under IFRS 9, with some exceptions for certain portfolios such as mortgages for which the regulatory definition may allow longer delinquency periods. (For these portfolios, not all banks who use the longer periods have yet decided whether to rebut the 90 DPD presumption or not). Most banks also intend to align the accounting definition of credit impaired for transfer to stage 3 with the definition of default.

5.4.2.B *Measurement of 12-month expected credit losses based on a loss rate approach*

Not every entity calculates a separate risk of a default occurring and an LGD, but instead uses a loss rate approach. Using this approach, the entity develops loss-rate statistics on the basis of the amount written off over the life of the financial assets. It must then adjust these historical credit loss trends for current conditions and expectations about the future. The following Illustrative Example 9 from IFRS 9 is designed to illustrate how an entity measures 12-month ECLs using a loss rate approach. *[IFRS 9 IC Example 9, IE53-IE57]*.

Example 50.19: 12-month expected credit loss measurement based on a loss rate approach

Bank A originates 2,000 bullet loans with a total gross carrying amount of $500,000. Bank A segments its portfolio into borrower groups (Groups X and Y) on the basis of shared credit risk characteristics at initial recognition. Group X comprises 1,000 loans with a gross carrying amount per client of $200, for a total gross carrying amount of $200,000. Group Y comprises 1,000 loans with a gross carrying amount per client of $300, for a total gross carrying amount of $300,000. There are no transaction costs and the loan contracts include no options (for example, prepayment or call options), premiums or discounts, points paid, or other fees.

Bank A measures ECLs on the basis of a loss rate approach for Groups X and Y. In order to develop its loss rates, Bank A considers samples of its own historical default and loss experience for those types of loans. In addition, Bank A considers forward-looking information, and updates its historical information for current economic conditions as well as reasonable and supportable forecasts of future economic conditions. Historically, for a population of 1,000 loans in each group, Group X's loss rates are 0.3 per cent, based on four defaults, and historical loss rates for Group Y are 0.15 per cent, based on two defaults.

	Number of clients in sample	Estimated per client gross carrying amount at default	Total estimated gross carrying amount at default	Historic per annum average defaults	Estimated total gross carrying amount at default	Present value of observed loss (a)	Loss rate
Group	A	B	C = A × B	D	E = B × D	F	G = F ÷ C
X	1,000	$200	$200,000	4	$800	$600	0.3%
Y	1,000	$300	$300,000	2	$600	$450	0.15%

(a) ECLs should be discounted using the EIR. However, for purposes of this example, the present value of the observed loss is assumed. *[IFRS 9.5.5.17(b)]*.

At the reporting date, Bank A expects an increase in defaults over the next 12 months compared to the historical rate. As a result, Bank A estimates five defaults in the next 12 months for loans in Group X and three for loans in Group Y. It estimates that the present value of the observed credit loss per client will remain consistent with the historical loss per client.

On the basis of the expected life of the loans, Bank A determines that the expected increase in defaults does not represent a significant increase in credit risk since initial recognition for the portfolios. On the basis of its forecasts, Bank A measures the loss allowance at an amount equal to 12-month ECLs on the 1,000 loans in each group amounting to $750 and $675 respectively. This equates to a loss rate in the first year of 0.375 per cent for Group X and 0.225 per cent for Group Y.

	Number of clients in sample	Estimated per client gross carrying amount at default	Total estimated gross carrying amount at default	Expected defaults	Estimated total gross carrying amount at default	Present value of observed loss	Loss rate
Group	A	B	C = A × B	D	E = B × D	F	G = F ÷ C
X	1,000	$200	$200,000	5	$1,000	$750	0.375%
Y	1,000	$300	$300,000	3	$900	$675	0.225%

Bank A uses the loss rates of 0.375 per cent and 0.225 per cent respectively to estimate 12-month ECLs on new loans in Group X and Group Y originated during the year and for which credit risk has not increased significantly since initial recognition.

The example above illustrates that under the loss rate approach, an entity would compute its loss rates by segmenting its portfolio into appropriate groupings (or sub-portfolios) based on shared credit risk characteristics and then updating its historical loss information with more forward-looking information. The loss rate was derived simply by computing the ratio between the present value of observed losses (the numerator) and the gross carrying amount of the loans (the denominator). Note that, although it does not require an explicit risk of a default occurring, there has to be an estimate of the number of defaults in order to determine whether there has been a significant increase in credit risk (see 5.5 below). Hence application will require any entities that intend to use this approach to track the incidence of default.

ECLs should be discounted at the EIR. However, in this example, the present value of the observed loss is just assumed. This is an additional area of complexity that entities will have to take into account when trying to build upon their existing loss rate approaches.

5.4.3 *Expected life versus contractual period*

Lifetime ECLs are defined as the ECLs that result from all possible default events over the *expected life* of a financial instrument. *[IFRS 9 Appendix A]*. This is consistent with the requirement that an entity should assess whether the credit risk on a financial instrument has increased significantly since initial recognition by using the change in the risk of a default occurring over the *expected life* of the financial instrument. *[IFRS 9.5.5.9]*.

An entity must therefore estimate cash flows and the instrument's life by considering all contractual terms of the financial instrument (for example, prepayment, extension, call and similar options). There is a presumption that the expected life of a financial instrument can be estimated reliably. In those rare cases when it is not possible to reliably estimate the expected life of a financial instrument, the entity shall use the remaining contractual term of the financial instrument. *[IFRS 9 Appendix A, B5.5.51]*.

However, the maximum period to consider when measuring ECLs should be the maximum contractual period (including extension options) over which the entity is exposed to credit risk and not a longer period, even if that longer period is consistent with business practice. *[IFRS 9.5.5.19]*. Although an exception to this principle has been added for revolving facilities (see 5.11 below), the IASB remains of the view that the contractual period over which an entity is committed to provide credit (or a shorter period considering prepayments) is the correct conceptual outcome. The IASB noted that most loan commitments will expire at a specified date, and if an entity decides to renew or extend its commitment to extend credit, it will be a new instrument for which the entity has the opportunity to revise the terms and conditions. *[IFRS 9.BC5.260]*.

This means that extension options should only be reflected in the measurement of ECLs as long as this does not extend the horizon beyond the maximum contractual period over which the entity is exposed to credit risk. Extension options at the discretion of the lender should therefore be excluded from the measurement of ECLs. Similarly, a lender's ability to require prepayment limits the horizon over which it is exposed to credit risk. The first prepayment date at the discretion of the lender should therefore represent the maximum period to be reflected in the expected loss calculation.

When assessing the impact of extension options at the discretion of the borrower, an entity should estimate both the probability of exercise of the extension option as well as the portion of the loan that will be extended (if the extension option can be exercised for a portion of the loan only). This is consistent with how lifetime expected losses must be assessed for loan commitments where an entity's estimate of ECLs must be consistent with its expectations of drawdowns on that loan commitment. Although the standard is not explicit on this point, the effect of extension options would be best modelled not by estimating an average life of the facility but by estimating the EAD each year over the maximum lifetime. This is because use of an average life would not reflect losses expected to occur beyond the average life. *[IFRS 9.B.5.5.31]*.

Expected prepayments at the discretion of borrowers should also be reflected in the measurement of ECLs. As with extension options, an entity should estimate both the probability of exercise of the prepayment option as well as the portion of the loan that will be prepaid (if the prepayment option can be exercised for a portion of the loan only). As with extension options, the standard does not specify whether prepayment patterns should be reflected through an amortising EAD over the maximum contractual period of the financial instruments or, rather, by shortening the horizon over which to measure ECLs to the average life of the financial instruments. Similar to the treatment of extension options, described above, in our view it is more appropriate to adjust the EAD for the facility each year over the maximum lifetime. We consider this a more transparent way of incorporating product features and potential impacts of different macroeconomic scenarios that can, for example, affect pre-payment patterns and customers' ability to re-finance.

Another degree of complexity in assessing expected prepayments and extensions arises if one considers that the behaviour of borrowers is affected by their creditworthiness. This means that prepayment and extension patterns should probably be estimated separately for stage 1 and stage 2 assets. This may represent a significant challenge, as making such estimates would require distinct historical observations for each of the stage 1 and 2 populations, which are unlikely to be available given that these populations were never identified in the past. Prepayment assumptions for stage 2 assets would need to factor in the probabilities that some may subsequently default and some may cure. A further complication is that expected prepayment and extension behaviour may vary with changes in the macroeconomic outlook.

The standard is clear that, for loan commitments and financial guarantee contracts, the time horizon to measure ECLs is the maximum contractual period over which an entity has a present contractual obligation to extend credit. *[IFRS 9.B5.5.38]*. However, for revolving credit facilities (e.g. credit cards and overdrafts) that include both a loan and an undrawn commitment component, that do not have a fixed term or repayment structure and usually have a short contractual cancellation period (for example, one day), this period is extended beyond the maximum contractual period and includes the period over which the entity is exposed to credit risk and ECLs would not be mitigated by credit risk management actions (see 5.11 below). *[IFRS 9.5.5.20, B5.5.39, B5.5.40]*.

At its April 2015 meeting, the ITG discussed, how to determine the maximum period for measuring ECLs, by reference to the following example.[24]

Example 50.20: Determining the maximum contractual period when measuring expected credit losses

Bank A manages a portfolio of variable rate mortgages on a collective basis. The mortgage loans are issued to retail customers in Country X with the following terms:

- the stated maturity is 6 months with an automatic extension feature whereby, unless the borrower or lender take action to terminate the loan at the stated maturity date, the loan automatically extends for the following 6 months;
- the interest rate is fixed for each 6-month period at the beginning of the period. The interest rate is reset to the current market interest rate on the extension date; and
- the lender's right to refuse an extension is unrestricted.

It is assumed that the mortgage loans meet the criteria for amortised cost measurement under paragraph 4.1.2 of IFRS 9.

In practice, borrowers are generally expected not to elect to terminate their loans on the stated maturity date, because moving the mortgage to another bank, or applying for a new product, generally involves an administrative burden and has little or no economic benefit for the borrower.

Furthermore, Bank A does not complete regular credit file reviews for individual loans and as a result does not usually cancel the loans unless it receives information about an adverse credit event in respect of a particular borrower. On the basis of historical evidence, such loans extend many times and can last for up to 30 years.

The ITG noted that:

- IFRS 9 is clear that the maximum period to consider when measuring ECLs in this example would be restricted to 6 months, because this is the maximum contractual period over which the lender is exposed to credit risk, i.e. the period until the lender can next object to an extension. *[IFRS 9.B5.5.19]*.
- The standard requires that extension options must be considered when determining the maximum contractual period, but does not specify whether these are lender or borrower extension options. However, if the extension option is within the control of the lender, the lender cannot be forced to continue extending credit and therefore such an option cannot be considered as lengthening the maximum period of exposure to credit risk. Conversely, if a borrower holds an extension option that could force the lender to continue extending credit, this would have the effect of lengthening that maximum contractual period of credit exposure.
- The maximum contractual period over which the entity is exposed to credit risk should be determined in accordance with the substantive contractual terms of the financial instrument. To further illustrate this point, a situation in which a lender is legally prevented from exercising a contractual right should be seen as distinct from a situation in which a lender chooses not to exercise a contractual right for practical or operational reasons.
- In the example presented, the facility is not of a revolving nature and the borrower does not have any such flexibility regarding drawdowns. Consequently, it would not be appropriate to analogise the 6-month mortgage loan to a revolving credit facility that has been fully drawn at the reporting date. Hence, the example falls outside the narrow scope exception for revolving credit facilities (e.g. credit cards and overdraft facilities) in which the maximum period to consider when measuring ECLs is over the period that the entity is exposed to credit risk and ECLs would not be mitigated by credit risk management actions, even if that period extends beyond the maximum contractual period (see 5.11 below). *[IFRS 9.B5.5.20]*.
- Consequently, it was acknowledged that there may be a disconnect between the accounting and credit risk management view in some situations (e.g. an entity may choose to continue extending credit to a long-standing customer despite being in a position to reduce or remove the exposure). See further discussion on the application of the revolving credit facilities exception to multi-purpose facilities (see 5.11 below).

For demand deposits that have no fixed maturity and can be withdrawn by the holder on very short notice (e.g. one day) (assuming there is no contractual or legal constraint that could prevent the holder from withdrawing its cash at any time), the period used by the holder of such demand deposits to estimate ECLs would be limited to the contractual notice period, i.e. one day. This is the maximum contractual period over which the holder is exposed to credit risk. In accordance with paragraph 5.5.19 of IFRS 9, extension periods at the option of the holder are excluded in estimating the maximum contractual period because the holder can unilaterally choose not to extend credit and thus can limit the period over which it is exposed to credit risk. Furthermore, demand deposits do not fall under the revolving credit facility exception in IFRS 9.5.5.20 as they do not comprise an undrawn element.

5.4.4 Probability-weighted outcome

ECLs must reflect an unbiased and probability-weighted estimate of credit losses over the expected life of the financial instrument (i.e. the weighted average of credit losses with the respective risks of a default occurring as the weights). *[IFRS 9.5.5.17(a), Appendix A, B5.5.28].*

The standard makes it clear that when measuring ECLs, in order to derive an unbiased and probability-weighted amount, an entity needs to evaluate a range of possible outcomes. *IFRS 9.5.5.17(a)].* This involves identifying possible scenarios that specify:

a) the amount and timing of the cash flows for particular outcomes; and
b) the estimated probability of these outcomes.

Although an entity does not need to identify every possible scenario, it will need to take into account the possibility that a credit loss occurs, no matter how low that probability is. *[IFRS 9.5.5.18].* This is not the same as a single estimate of the worst-case or best-case scenario, or the most likely outcome (i.e. when there is a low risk or probability of a default (PD) with high loss outcomes, the most likely outcome could be no credit loss even though an allowance would be required based on probability-weighted cash flows). *[IFRS 9.B5.5.41].* It is worthwhile noting that it is implicit that the sum of the weighted probabilities will be equal to one. A simple example of application of a probability-weighted calculation is shown in Example 50.18.

Without taking into account multiple economic scenarios (see below) calculating a probability-weighted amount may not require a complex analysis or a detailed simulation of a large number of scenarios and the standard suggests that relatively simple modelling may be sufficient. For instance, the average credit losses of a large group of financial instruments with shared risk characteristics may be a reasonable estimate of the probability-weighted amount. In other situations, the identification of scenarios that specify the amount and timing of the cash flows for particular outcomes and the estimated probability of those outcomes will probably be needed. In those situations, the ECLs shall reflect at least two outcomes in accordance with paragraph 5.5.18 of IFRS 9. *[IFRS 9.B5.5.42].*

At the December 2015 ITG meeting the question was asked as to whether the use of multiple scenarios referred to in the standard relates only to what might happen to particular assets given a single forward-looking economic scenario (i.e. default or no default), or whether application of the standard requires an entity to use multiple forward-looking economic scenarios, and if so how.

The ITG members noted that the measurement of ECLs is required to reflect an unbiased and probability-weighted amount that is determined by evaluating a range of possible outcomes. Consequently, when there is a non-linear relationship between the different forward-looking scenarios and their associated credit losses, using a single forward-looking economic scenario would not meet this objective. In such cases, more than one forward-looking economic scenario would need to be used in the measurement of ECLs.[25] For each scenario the associated ECLs would need to be multiplied by the weighting allocated to that scenario.

The ITG also discussed the use of multiple economic scenarios to assess whether exposures should be measured using lifetime economic losses (see 5.5 below). It was noted by the ITG that if the same variable is relevant for determining significant increase in credit risk and for measuring ECLs, the same forward-looking scenarios should be used for both.

The ITG discussed a particular example in which there are considered to be three possible economic scenarios.[26] This is illustrated in the example below.

Example 50.21: Incorporating single versus multiple forward-looking scenarios when measuring expected credit losses

Scenario	Future unemployment	Likelihood of occurrence	ECLs
(a)	4%	20%	£30
(b)	5%	50%	£70
(c)	6%	30%	£170

Use of a single central economic scenario based on the most likely outcome of 5 per cent unemployment, i.e. scenario (b), would give rise to an ECL of £70. However, using a probability-weighted range of scenarios, the ECL would be £92 ((£30 × 0.2) + (£70 × 0.5) + (£170 × 0.3)). Consequently, the ITG observed that in this example, using a single central forward-looking economic scenario would not result in an unbiased and probability-weighted amount in accordance with the standard.

The ITG were concerned about the distribution of possible losses often being 'non-linear', in that the increase in losses associated with those economic scenarios that are worse than the central forecast will be greater than the reduction in losses associated with those scenarios that are more benign. To use statistical terminology, the distribution is skewed. Depending on how it is calculated, a single scenario gives the mode of this distribution (i.e. the most likely outcome) or the median (the central forecast). In contrast, the standard requires the use of the mean (i.e. a probability-weighted estimation) (see Figure 50.4 below).

Figure 50.4 Distribution of losses

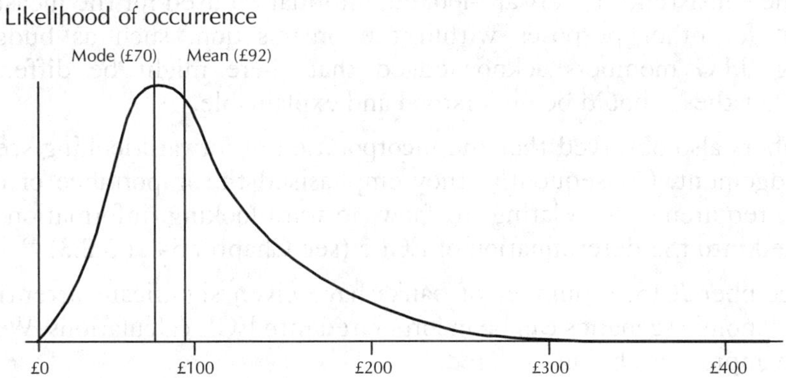

At the ITG meeting, it was noted that there are a number of possible approaches that might be used to incorporate multiple economic approaches. IFRS 9 does not prescribe any particular method of measuring ECLs and the measurement should reflect an entity's own view. What the standard does require is that the expected losses must reflect:

(a) an unbiased and probability-weighted amount that is determined using a range of possible outcomes; and

(b) reasonable and supportable information that is available without undue cost or effort at the reporting date.

With respect to reasonable and supportable information, ITG members made the following observations:

(a) although IFRS 9 does not specifically require an entity to consider external information, an entity should consider information from a variety of sources in order to ensure that the information used is reasonable and supportable;

(b) the information considered could vary depending on the facts and circumstances including the level of sophistication of the entity, geographical region and the particular features of the portfolio; and

(c) while entities are not expected to consider every possible scenario, the scenarios considered should reflect a representative sample of possible outcomes.[27]

ITG members recognised that materiality considerations would need to be taken into account.

In an IASB webcast on 25 July 2016, it was noted that, having considered:

(a) whether the effect of non-linearity is material;

(b) whether the entity has a reasonable and supportable basis for this multiple scenario analysis; and

(c) whether the application is possible without undue cost or effort;

a conclusion may sometimes be reached that it is not necessary to actually *use* multiple scenarios to apply the impairment requirements in IFRS 9. However, multiple scenarios must always be considered.

At the December 2015 ITG meeting, the ITG also noted that consideration should be given to the consistency of forward-looking information used for the measurement of ECLs and for other purposes within the organisation, such as budgeting and forecasting. ITG members acknowledged that there might be differences, but observed that these should be understood and explainable.

ITG members also observed that the incorporation of forward-looking scenarios will require judgement. Consequently, they emphasised the importance of the IFRS 7 disclosure requirements relating to how forward-looking information has been incorporated into the determination of ECLs (see Chapter 54 at 5.2.3).[28]

Since December 2015, a number of banks have given significant attention to how multiple economic scenarios can be incorporated into ECL calculations. We have seen three main approaches being explored:

(a) Probability weighted scenarios. This is similar to the method discussed at the ITG meeting in December 2015 and illustrated in Example 50.21 above. It involves establishing a number of scenarios (we have seen varying numbers between two and five), estimating the losses that would arise in those scenarios and allocating a weighting to each scenario. Unlike Example 50.21 above, these do not normally model economic variables such as unemployment rates in isolation – to do so, would also require complex modelling of the correlations between those variables – but, instead, each scenario is normally a coherent combination of economic variables. For example, a scenario relevant to mortgage loans might include assumptions about unemployment, interest rates and house prices. This approach is transparent, but it may be difficult to assign the weightings to each scenario, requiring judgement as well as experience of the past. While selecting scenarios and respective weights, we expect banks to take into consideration the entire distribution of macroeconomic scenarios and select points (i.e. scenarios) from that distribution, with their respective weights representing the area of the distribution represented by the scenario. We would expect that the mean of the selected scenarios and weights is similar to that of the entire distribution.

(b) The second approach is to calculate ECLs based on a central forward-looking scenario and to adjust the outcome where necessary by a factor to reflect the non-linearity of the loss distribution. In practice it may be that a method similar to (a) will need to be used in order to calculate this factor – so that it is not a very different approach. However, some banks view the merits of this approach as being less mechanistic and allowing more room for judgement. At the time of writing, various ways are being examined as to when and how to calculate this adjustment.

(c) Monte Carlo simulation. This method seeks to calculate the expected losses associated with the entire distribution of possible scenarios, around the bank's central economic forecast. It has the advantage that it does not require the bank to formulate specific scenarios or assign weightings to them, but the simulation is dependent on assumptions that may not be transparent to either users or preparers, so that this solution can seem a 'black box'. It is also very demanding as to the volume of data that has to be manipulated and it is not how most banks manage credit risk today.

The effect of multiple scenarios will affect not just the probability of default but also the losses given default. For instance, for property-based lending it will be necessary to forecast the value of collateral associated with each economic scenario that is modelled. A consequence of this is that there may be a need to record an ECL allowance for an asset that, based on the central forecast of future collateral values, is fully collateralised. (Also, as a result, the loss allowance for a stage 3 asset may be higher than for an impaired asset under IAS 39).

The use of multiple scenarios may also have an effect on the estimated EAD.

A number of other observations can be made about the use of multiple scenarios:

(a) Whatever approach is used to calculate the effect of non-linearity, it will be necessary for banks to communicate the result of the calculation in a manner which can be understood by readers of the financial statements. One possible approach would be for banks to report the losses associated with the central forecast and then, separately, the effect of the consideration of other scenarios. This would allow banks to communicate the amounts they expect to lose and would permit comparison between banks of the effect of the adjustment for non-linearity, even if the banks use different methods to make the calculation.

(b) It would seem that the effects of non-linearity depend on the countries in which banks operate and the economic characteristics of those countries. For instance, the effect of alternative scenarios of interest rates and unemployment may be greater in countries where there is more of a 'boom and bust' economic cycle. The size of the effect is also dependent on origination practices and the particular lending products – variable rate loans being more sensitive to interest rates than fixed rate ones, while defaults on credit cards are more affected by unemployment rates. In some cases the issue is seen as most relevant for exposures to a particular economic variable, a topical example being lending to companies involved in the oil industry. In this example, banks might model a number of scenarios as to how oil prices could evolve. A similar approach may be relevant for non-banks with similar exposures through long term construction contracts or leasing activities.

(c) It should be stressed that the ITG discussion highlighted the importance of calculating the effect of non-linearity using only reasonable and supportable information, implying that if the information is not available than there is a limit to what can be done. However, banks will need to take into account their regulators' expectations (see 5.1.6 and 5.6.1 for Basel Committee guidance).

The process of forecasting future economic conditions is discussed further in 5.4.8.C.

5.4.5 Time value of money

An entity needs to consider the time value of money when measuring ECLs, by discounting the estimated losses to the reporting date using a rate that approximates the EIR of the asset (see 3 above). *[IFRS 9.5.5.17, B5.5.44]*. This has two components:

- Discounting recoveries to the date of default, hence 'a credit loss arises even if the entity expects to be paid in full but later than when contractually due'. *[IFRS 9.B5.5.28]*.
- Discounting losses from the date of default to the reporting date. This is needed because the gross amortised cost of the asset is based on the contractual cash flows discounted at the EIR, and so not to discount cash flows that are now not expected to be received would overstate the loss.

Of these two components, the first is typically included by banks in their calculation of the LGD (although not necessarily using the EIR). However the second will also need to be calculated to comply with the standard.

The discount rate is calculated as follows:

- for a fixed-rate financial asset, entities are required to determine or approximate the EIR on the initial recognition of the financial asset, while for a floating-rate financial asset, entities are required to use the current EIR; *[IFRS 9.B5.5.44]*
- for a purchased or originated credit-impaired financial asset (see 5.3.3 above), entities are required to discount ECLs using the credit-adjusted EIR determined on the initial recognition of the financial asset; *[IFRS 9.B5.5.45]*
- for a loan commitment (see 5.10 below), entities are required to use the EIR of the asset that will result once the commitment is drawn down. This would give rise to a consistent rate for a credit facility that includes both a loan

(i.e. a financial asset) and an undrawn commitment (i.e. a loan commitment). If the EIR of the resulting asset is not determinable, then entities are required to use the current risk-free rate (i.e. the discount rate that reflects the current market assessment of the time value of money). This should be adjusted for risks specific to the cash flows, but only if the cash flows have not already been adjusted for these risks, in order to avoid double counting; *[IFRS 9.B5.5.47, B5.5.48]*

- for financial guarantee contracts (see 5.10 below) entities are required to use the current risk-free rate adjusted for risks specific to the cash flows, again to the extent that those cash flows have not already been adjusted for the risks; *[IFRS 9.B5.5.48]* and
- for lease receivables (see 5.9.2 below), entities are required to discount the ECLs using the same discount rate used in the measurement of the lease receivables in accordance with IAS 17 or IFRS 16 (when applied). *[IFRS 9.B5.5.46]*.

In relation to the guidance in paragraphs B5.5.47 and 48 on loan commitments when the EIR on the resulting asset is not determinable and for financial guarantee contracts, we make the following observations:

- Although it is not clear in the standard, any adjustment for the risks specific to the cash flows would be a *reduction* of the risk free rate, not an increase. This would be consistent with the approach applied to provisions in IAS 37 and as was made clear in the staff paper presented to the Board when this treatment was discussed in December 2013.
- For loan commitments when the EIR on the resulting asset is not determinable, this approach provides a prudent calculation of ECLs, given that it is likely that the entity which enters into the commitment will receive a credit spread on the loan if it is drawn down. It is in a much better position than the issuer of a financial guarantee contract, who will receive no credit spread should it be required to pay out on the guarantee.
- The idea that the rate should be adjusted only if the cash flows have not already been adjusted for the risks may not be easy to apply in practice. This is because the cash flows should have already been estimated with regard to any non-linearities in the distribution of losses (see 5.4.4) and so will already have been partly adjusted for risk. It may not be easy to calculate the necessary adjustment to reflect a market assessment of the remaining risks.

It is rare that customers just fail to pay amounts when due. In most cases, default also involves payments being paid late, while default can lead to the acceleration of payment of amounts that are not contractually due until a later date. Therefore, modelling losses involves modelling the timing of payments when default occurs and different patterns of timing of recoverable cash flows, such as the time it takes to foreclose on and sell collateral and complete bankruptcy proceedings, before the ECLs can be discounted back to the reporting date.

The standard and its Illustrative Examples are silent on how the calculation should be made. In Illustrative Example 9 the present value of the observed loss is assumed and in Illustrative Example 8, a footnote states that, '[b]ecause the LGD represents a percentage of the present value of the gross carrying amount, this example does not illustrate the time value of money'. One approach would be to model various scenarios as to how cash is collected once the loan has defaulted, and probability-weight the discounted cash flows of these various scenarios.

LGD data available from Basel models should include a discounting factor and sometimes this may be different from the rate required by IFRS 9. Furthermore, the discount rate used in Basel models only covers the period between default and subsequent recoveries. Therefore, entities will have to find ways to adjust their LGDs to reflect the discounting effect required by the standard (i.e. based on a rate that approximates the EIR and over the entire period from recoveries back to the reporting date). Given the requirement to use an approximation to the EIR, entities will need to work out how to determine a rate that is sufficiently accurate. One of the challenges is to interpret how much flexibility is afforded by the term 'approximation'.

At its meeting in December 2015, the ITG also discussed what was meant by the current EIR when an entity recognises interest revenue in each period based on the actual floating rate applicable to that period. The ITG first noted that the definition of the EIR in IFRS 9 was carried forward essentially unchanged from the definition within IAS 39. Consequently, similarly to IAS 39, IFRS 9 does not specify whether an entity should use the current interest rate at the reporting date or the projected interest rates derived from the current yield curve as at the reporting date. There should be consistency between the rate used to recognise interest revenue, the rate used to project future cash flows (including cash shortfalls) and the rate used to discount those cash flows (see 3 above).

5.4.6 Interaction between expected credit losses calculations and fair value hedge accounting

Another operational difficulty arises from the interplay between the new impairment model and fair value hedge accounting. For financial assets designated in a hedge, because the fair value hedge adjustment is a part of the carrying value of the financial asset that is hedged, the measurement of the loss allowance should presumably take that adjustment into account. In other words, the fair value hedge adjustment changes the carrying amount that is assessed for impairment, which is achieved by adjusting the EIR used to measure the impairment allowance.

This requirement was previously illustrated by the implementation guidance of IAS 39. This pointed out that the fair value hedge adjustment would be included in the carrying amount that is subject to the impairment requirements. Otherwise, for an asset in the scope of the impairment requirements, a part of its carrying amount would not have a loss allowance or the loss allowance would be overstated (in case of a negative fair value hedge adjustment). This guidance states that the effect of fair value hedge accounting is to adjust the EIR, which affects the rate used to discount expected future cash flows. This guidance has not been carried forward to IFRS 9 but it would appear to be equally relevant. *[IAS 39.E.4.4]*.

The interaction between fair value hedge accounting and impairment is more complex under the new impairment model of IFRS 9 because:

- Under IAS 39 an entity can often avoid the difficulty of measuring impairment losses on the financial assets it includes in the designation of a fair value hedge by designating only higher quality assets, which do not have any associated incurred losses under IAS 39.
- In contrast, under the new impairment model of IFRS 9, all financial assets in the scope of the impairment requirements, whether recorded at amortised cost or at fair value through other comprehensive income, require the measurement of a loss allowance, even if they are high quality assets and have not deteriorated.
- IFRS 9 allows expected losses to be discounted by a rate that approximates to the EIR. This approximation would presumably need to take account of the effect of fair value hedge accounting.
- For portfolio hedging strategies it may not be possible to allocate fair value hedge adjustments to individual assets, so it would be necessary for entities to determine a basis of allocation of such hedges to those assets subject to a 12-month loss allowance and those for which lifetime ECLs are provided for. This is likely to be feasible only for groups of assets with similar credit characteristics, including maturities and EIRs. Even for micro hedges of individual assets it may be difficult to link the hedge accounting and impairment processes to calculate the consequences of hedge accounting for impairment.

The complexity of combining the ECL impairment model and fair value hedge accounting is illustrated by Example 50.35 at 5.8 below.

5.4.7 *Credit enhancements: collateral and financial guarantees*

Although credit enhancements such as collateral and guarantees play only a limited role in assessing whether there has been a significant increase in credit risk (see 5.5.1 below), they do affect the measurement of ECLs. For example, for a mortgage loan, even if an entity determines that there has been a significant increase in credit risk on the loan since initial recognition, if the expected proceeds from the collateral (i.e. the mortgaged property) exceeds the amount loaned, then the entity may have nil ECLs, and hence an allowance of zero.

In measuring the ECLs and hence the expected cash shortfalls for a collateralised financial instrument, an entity should include the cash flows from the realisation of the collateral and other credit enhancements that are: *[IFRS 9.B5.5.55]*

- part of the contractual terms; and
- not recognised separately by the entity.

As is the case in IAS 39, the standard specifies that the estimate of cash flows from collateral should include the effect of a foreclosure, regardless of whether foreclosure is probable, and the resulting cash flows from foreclosure on the collateral less the costs of obtaining and selling the collateral, taking into account the amount and timing of these cash flows. *[IFRS 9.B5.5.55]*. The wording does not mean that the entity is required to assume that recovery will be through foreclosure only, but rather that the entity should calculate the cash flows arising from the various ways that the asset may be recovered, only some of which may involve foreclosure, and to probability-weight these different scenarios (see Example 50.18 at 5.4.2 above).

Although the standard does not refer to fair value when determining the valuation of the collateral, in practice, an entity is likely to estimate the cash flows from the realisation of the collateral, based on the fair value of the collateral. In the case of illiquid collateral, such as real estate, adjustments will probably need to be made for expected changes in the fair value, depending on the economic conditions at the estimated date of selling the collateral.

Also, as in IAS 39, any collateral obtained as a result of foreclosure is not recognised as an asset that is separate from the collateralised financial instrument unless it meets the relevant recognition criteria for an asset in IFRS 9 or other standards. *[IFRS 9.B5.5.55]*.

If a loan is guaranteed by a third party as part of its contractual terms, it should carry an allowance for ECLs based on the combined credit risk of the guarantor and the guaranteed party by reflecting the effect of the guarantee in the measurement of losses expected on default.

A challenge is interpreting what constitutes 'part of the contractual terms'. This was addressed by the ITG at its meeting in December 2015, specifically whether the credit enhancement must be an explicit term of the related asset's contract in order for it to be taken into account in the measurement of ECLs, or whether other credit enhancements that are not recognised separately can also be taken into account. The ITG noted that:

- The definition of credit losses states that, when estimating cash flows, an entity shall include cash flows from the sale of collateral held or other credit enhancements that are *integral* to the contractual terms. Consequently, credit enhancements included in the measurement of ECLs should not be limited to those that are explicitly part of the contractual terms.
- An entity would be required to apply its judgement in assessing what is meant by 'integral to the contractual terms' and in making that assessment, an entity should consider all relevant facts and circumstances. Also, an entity must not include cash flows from credit enhancements in the measurement of ECLs if the credit enhancement is accounted for separately. This was particularly important in order to avoid double counting.
- IFRS 7 requires disclosures to enable users of financial statements to understand the effect of collateral and other credit enhancements on the amounts arising from ECLs (see 5.13 below and Chapter 54 at 5.2.3).

Although not reflected in the official minutes of the ITG meeting, the IASB members highlighted during the course of the discussion that similar assessment of (i) 'integral' features and (ii) separate recognition for credit enhancements are required under IAS 39 and that there was no intention to alter the treatment when drafting IFRS 9. Currently, because there is no equivalent guidance in IAS 39 similar to paragraph B5.5.55 in IFRS 9, there is some diversity in practice as to how collateral is taken into account in loan loss impairment calculations. In practice, most banks incorporate the guarantees as part of their measurement of losses given default, in line with the reference to 'the fair value of guarantees' in the IAS 39 Implementation Guidance E.4.1.

The ITG also emphasised that paragraph B5.5.55 of IFRS 9 was drafted only with the intention to caution against double counting those credit enhancements that are already recognised separately, and was not intended to limit the inclusion of credit enhancements that were previously included in IAS 39 allowances for loan losses.

However, the ITG discussion does not fully answer the question of how to interpret when a financial guarantee is 'integral to the contractual terms' when it is not mentioned in the contractual terms of the loan.

It seems reasonably clear that a credit default swap on a loan entered into by the lender to mitigate its credit risk on the loan, would not normally be classed as integral to a loan's contractual terms. The second criteria mentioned in B5.5.55 is that the credit enhancement should not be recognised separately and separate accounting for a derivative is clearly required by IFRS 9. Also, payment under a credit default swap does not normally require the holder of the instrument to have suffered the credit loss referenced by the swap. As a result, cash flows from a credit default swap that is accounted for as a derivative would not be included in the measurement of ECLs of the associated loan.

For a financial guarantee (as defined in IFRS 9), one view is that it is integral to the contractual terms of a loan only if it is, at least implicitly, part of the contractual terms of the loan. Examples of an implicit contractual linkage might include:

- Inseparability: The financial guarantee is inseparable from the loan contract, i.e. the loan cannot be transferred without the guarantee.
- Local laws and regulations: Credit enhancements required by local laws and regulations that govern the loan contract but that are not specifically in the contract itself. For example, in some jurisdictions legislation requires that lenders must take out financial guarantee contracts that contain little or no down payment in respect of certain loans.
- Business purpose: The guarantee and the loan have been contracted in contemplation of one another, i.e. the loan would not have been contracted without the guarantee.
- Market convention: The exposure and the financial guarantee are traded as a package in the market.

Another view might be that any contract that meets the definition of a financial guarantee under IFRS 9 can be considered 'integral to the contractual terms' of the guaranteed loan. As the loan is explicitly referenced to in the contractual terms of the financial guarantee and it is required that the lender incurs a credit loss on the loan to be reimbursed, there is a clear contractual linkage that ensures that any credit loss incurred on the loan will be compensated by the financial guarantee and no compensation will arise on the financial guarantee unless a credit loss is actually incurred by the lender on the guaranteed loan.

Although it is not clear as to when a financial guarantee contract would be regarded as 'integral', this is probably not of major importance for the accounting by the lender. A financial guarantee contract is likely to satisfy the definition of an insurance contract in IFRS 4 – *Insurance Contracts* – but will be excluded from the scope of IFRS 4 because it is a direct insurance contract held by the insured who is not a cedant (i.e. an insurer that is the policyholder under a reinsurance contract). *[IFRS 4.4(f)]*. If the guarantee satisfies the definition of an insurance contract in IFRS 4 it is outside the scope of IAS 39 irrespective of whether it is within the scope of IFRS 4. *[IAS 39.2(e)]*. IFRS 4 points to paragraphs 10 to 12 of IAS 8 – *Accounting Policies, Changes in Accounting Estimates and Errors* – which apply to situations where no IFRS specifically applies to a transaction, i.e. the holder of a financial guarantee contract will normally need to develop its accounting policy in accordance with the hierarchy in IAS 8. *[IFRS 4 IG2 Example 1.11]*.

Applying the IAS 8 hierarchy, one possibility would be to look to IAS 37 and treat the guarantee as a right to a reimbursement in respect of the impairment loss. IAS 37 permits a reimbursement of a liability to be recognised as an asset when it is virtually certain that the reimbursement will be received if the obligation for which a provision has been established is settled. In this instance the guarantee would be recognised as an asset to the extent it is virtually certain a recovery could be made if the lender were to suffer the impairment loss on the loan. The amount recognised for the reimbursement may not exceed the amount of the provision. *[IAS 37.53]*. Using this approach, the overall expense for the lender will be the same as if the guarantee was included in the measurement of ECLs, but it would be presented as an asset rather than as a reduction of the impairment allowance.

At its meeting in December 2015, the ITG also discussed whether cash flows that are expected to be recovered from the sale on default of a loan could be included in the measurement of ECLs. ITG members noted that:

- Such cash flows should be included in the measurement of ECLs if:
  - (a) selling the loan is one of the recovery methods that the entity expected to pursue in a default scenario;
  - (b) the entity is neither legally nor practically prevented from realising the loan using that recovery method; and
  - (c) the entity has reasonable and supportable information upon which to base its expectations and assumptions.
- In order to support an entity's expectation that loan sales would be used as a recovery method in a default scenario, an entity's past practice would be an important consideration. However future expectations, which may differ from past practice, would also need to be considered. With respect to the amount of recovery proceeds to be included in the measurement of ECLs, an entity should consider relevant market related information relating to loan sale prices.
- In these circumstances, the inclusion of recovery sale proceeds in the measurement of ECLs would be appropriate for financial instruments in all stages; stage 1, 2 and 3 (see 5.3.1 above). This is because when measuring ECLs, IFRS 9 requires an entity to consider possible default scenarios for financial instruments in all three stages.
- Expected sale proceeds would only be relevant when considering the possibility that a credit loss occurs (i.e. in a default scenario) and would not be relevant when considering the possibility that no credit loss occurs (i.e. in a performing scenario). For example if, in the case of a particular loan, an entity concluded that there was a 10 per cent probability of default occurring, it would only be when considering the outcome of this default scenario that expected sale proceeds would be considered. If, in that default scenario, the entity expected to recover 30 per cent of the contractual cash flows of the loan through sale proceeds but only 25 per cent through continuing to hold, then the LGD would be 70 per cent rather than 75 per cent. In addition, the expected sale proceeds should be net of selling costs.

There have also been some discussions in practice on whether financial assets that are considered to be in default (e.g. because payments are more than 90 days past due) but that are fully collateralised (so that there is no ECL) would qualify as credit-impaired and therefore have to be transferred to stage 3 (see 5.3.1 above). Although the definition of credit-impaired refers to 'a detrimental impact on the estimated future cash flows', it is not clear whether this should be read to include any recoveries from the realisation of collateral and IFRS 9 has no explicit requirements to consider collateral when assessing credit-impaired financial assets.

There are some strong arguments in favour of aligning the criteria for transferring an asset to stage 3 with those for assessing whether it is in default. First, IFRS 9 bases significant deterioration on risk of a default occurring and it would therefore seem inconsistent (and potentially confusing for users) if the value of collateral is considered for stage 3 allocation. Also, if collateral value were to influence the stage 3 allocation, this could result in some instability between stage 2 and 3, as exposures would potentially go back and forth depending on the collateral value.

Aligning stage 3 with the default status affects the scope of instruments to which the purchased or originated credit-impaired approach must be applied (see 5.3 above). However, for any exposure which is fully collateralised and where the expected loss is zero, classification as a purchased or originated credit-impaired financial asset, or classification between stage 1, 2 or 3 does not affect the accounting. If the expected loss is zero, it will not affect the EIR calculation.

Also, IFRS 7 requires a quantitative disclosure about the collateral held as security and other credit enhancements (e.g. quantification of the extent to which collateral and other credit enhancements mitigate credit risk) for financial assets that are credit-impaired at the reporting date. *[IFRS 7,35K(c)]*. Furthermore, IFRS 7 requires a narrative description of collateral held as security and other credit enhancements, including information about financial instruments for which an entity has not recognised a loss allowance because of the collateral. *[IFRS 7,35K(b)]*. As already noted in 5.4.4 above, it will be less likely for a financial asset with an existing objective evidence of impairment under IAS 39 to have no impairment amount under IFRS 9 due to the use of several probability-weighted scenarios. In addition, as discussed at 5.4.5 above, even if all the contractual cash flows are expected to be recovered, there is likely to be a loss if any of these cash flows will be recovered at a date other than the contractual payment dates of the instrument.

5.4.8 Reasonable and supportable information

IFRS 9 requires an entity to consider reasonable and supportable information that is available without undue cost or effort at the reporting date about past events, current conditions and forecasts of future economic conditions and that is relevant to the estimate of ECLs, including the effect of expected prepayments. *[IFRS 9.5.5.17(c), B5.5.51]*.

5.4.8.A Undue cost or effort

The term undue cost or effort is not defined in the standard, although it is clear from the guidance that information available for financial reporting purposes is considered to be available without undue cost or effort. *[IFRS 9.B5.5.49]*.

Beyond that, although the standard explains that entities are not required to undertake an exhaustive search for information, it does include, as examples of relevant information, data from risk management systems, as described in section 5.4.8.B below.

What is available without undue cost or effort would be an area subject to management judgement in assessing the costs and associated benefits. This is consistent with the Q&A (non-mandatory guidance) provided by the SME (small and medium-sized entities) Implementation Group in relation to the application of undue cost or effort when implementing IFRSs for SMEs.[29] The Q&A explains that application of a requirement would result in undue cost or effort if the cost or effort is excessive in comparison to the benefits that the users of the financial statements would receive from having the information. If the reporting entity is a bank, there would presumably be a higher hurdle to determine what credit risk information would require undue cost or effort, compared to a reporter that is not a bank, given that the benefit to users of its financial statements would be also expected to be higher. It is an issue on which the Basel Committee has issued guidance (see 5.6.1 below).

5.4.8.B Sources of information

The standard states that the information used should include factors that are specific to the borrower, general economic conditions and an assessment of both the current as well as the forecast direction of conditions at the reporting date. Entities may use various sources of data, both internal (entity-specific) data and external data that includes internal historical credit loss experience, internal ratings, credit loss experience of other entities for comparable financial instruments, and external ratings, reports and statistics. Entities that have no, or insufficient, sources of entity-specific data may use peer group experience for the comparable financial instrument (or groups of financial instruments). *[IFRS 9.B5.5.51]*.

Although the ECLs reflect an entity's own expectations of credit losses, an entity should also consider observable market information about the credit risk of particular financial instruments. *[IFRS 9.B5.5.54]*. Therefore, although entities with in-house economic teams will inevitably want to use their internal economic forecasts, while loss estimation models will be built based on historical data, they should not ignore external market data.

5.4.8.C Information about past events, current conditions and forecasts of future economic conditions

One of the significant changes from the IAS 39 impairment requirements is that entities are not only required to use historical information (e.g. their credit loss experience) that is adjusted to reflect the effects of current conditions, but they are also required to consider how forecasts of future conditions would affect their historical data. Section 5.4.4 above contains a discussion of how this process needs to consider the existence of non-linearity in how expected losses will change with varying economic conditions and the need to assess multiple economic scenarios. This section explores some of the other challenges in forecasting future conditions and the consequent ECLs.

The degree of judgement that is required to estimate ECLs depends on the availability of detailed information. An entity is not required to incorporate detailed forecasts of future conditions over the entire expected life of a financial instrument. The standard notes that as the forecast horizon increases, the availability of detailed information decreases and the degree of judgement required to estimate ECLs increases. Therefore, an entity is not required to perform a detailed estimate for periods that are far in the future and may extrapolate projections from available, more detailed information. *[IFRS 9.B5.5.50]*.

The application guidance suggests that entities may often be able to assume that economic conditions revert to their long-term average, beyond a horizon for which they can be reliably forecast. There are at least two methods of how this might be done: either by reverting to the average immediately beyond the forecast horizon, or by adjusting the forecast data to the long-term average over a few years. The latter would, perhaps, more effectively make use of all reasonable and supportable information.

Historical information should be used as a starting point from which adjustments are made to estimate ECLs on the basis of reasonable and supportable information that incorporates both current and forward-looking information: *[IFRS 9.B5.5.52]*

- in most cases, adjustments would be needed to incorporate these effects that were not present in the past or to remove these effects that are not relevant for the future; and
- in some cases, unadjusted historical information may be the best estimate, depending on the nature of the historical information and when it was calculated, compared to circumstances at the reporting date and the characteristics of the financial instrument being considered. But it should not be assumed to be appropriate in all circumstances. *[IFRS 9.BC5.281]*.

Additionally, when considering whether historical credit losses should be adjusted, an entity will need to consider various items, including:

- whether the historical data captures ECLs that are through-the-cycle (i.e. estimates based on historical credit loss events and experience over the entire economic cycle) or point-in-time (i.e. estimates based on information, circumstances and events at the reporting date); and
- the period of time over which its historical data has been captured and the corresponding economic conditions represented in that history. The historical data period may reflect unusually benign or harsh conditions unless it is long enough. While products, customers and lending behaviours all change over time; and when using historical credit loss experience, it is important that information about historical credit losses is applied to groups that are defined in a manner that is consistent with the groups for which the historical credit losses were observed.

The estimates of changes in ECLs should be directionally consistent with changes in related observable data from period to period (i.e. consistent with trends observed on payment status and macroeconomic data such as changes in unemployment rates, property prices, and commodity prices). Also, in order to reduce the differences between an entity's estimates and actual credit loss experience, the estimates of ECLs should be back-tested and re-calibrated, i.e. an entity should regularly review its inputs, assumptions, methodology and estimation techniques used as well as its groupings of sub-portfolios with shared credit risk characteristics (see 5.5.5 below).

Back testing will be considerably more challenging for forecasts over several years than may be the case for just the 12-month risk of default, because detailed information may not be available over the forecast horizon and the degree of judgement increases as the forecast horizon increases. *[IFRS 9.B5.5.52, B5.5.53]*. Also, economic forecasts are usually wrong, as reality is much more complex than can ever be effectively modelled. Therefore it is probably not a useful exercise to back test macroeconomic assumptions against what actually transpires, but it is useful to back test whether, for a given macroeconomic scenario, credit losses increased or decreased as expected.

In estimating ECLs, entities must consider how to bridge the gap between historical loss experience and current expectations. Estimating future economic conditions is only the first step of the exercise; having decided what will happen to macroeconomic factors such as interest rates, house prices, unemployment and GDP growth, entities then need to decide how they translate into ECLs. This will need to reflect how such changes in factors affected defaults in the past. However, it is possible that the forecast combination of factors may have never been seen historically together.

We observe that banks are also trying to align IFRS 9 to their existing risk management practices. Many banks intend to leverage and align their regulatory capital calculation and stress testing frameworks for their IFRS 9 calculations. This manifests itself in many of the individual decisions that banks are making as part of their development of IFRS 9 methodologies (e.g. definitions of default and alignment to stress testing). It is likely that regulators and standard-setters will concur with this approach. Basel PDs are used as a starting point and there is a need for a different calibration for IFRS 9, in order to transform a Basel PD into an unbiased point in time metric and include forward looking expectations. Stress testing resources, previously working almost exclusively with capital issues, will likely play a major role in calculating lifetime ECLs, although the scenarios modelled for IFRS 9 will not be stressed. However, estimating losses (especially given the need to consider multiple scenarios) will still be challenging for many entities.

The ITG has discussed several aspects of the forecast of ECLs (see 5.1.5 above). In April 2015, the ITG debated whether and how to incorporate events and new information about forecasts of future economic conditions that occur after the ECLs have been estimated. Due to operational practicality, entities may perform their ECL calculations before the reporting period end in order to publish their financial statements in a timely manner (e.g. forecasts of future economic conditions developed in November may be used as the basis for determining the ECLs at the reporting date as at 31 December). Further information may then become available after the period end. The ITG noted that:

- If new information becomes available before the reporting date, subject to materiality considerations in accordance with IAS 8, an entity is required to take into consideration this information in the assessment of significant increases in credit risk and the measurement of ECLs at the reporting date.
- IFRS 9 does not specifically require new information that becomes available after the reporting date to be reflected in the measurement of ECLs at the reporting date. If new information becomes available between the reporting date and the date the financial statements are authorised for issue, an entity needs to apply judgement, based on the specific facts and circumstances, to determine whether it is an adjusting or non-adjusting event in accordance with IAS 10 – *Events after the Reporting Period* (see Chapter 36). Similarly, materiality considerations apply in accordance with IAS 8.
- ECLs are similar in nature to the measurement of fair value at the reporting date, in that movements in fair value after the reporting date are generally not reflected in the measurement of fair value at the reporting date. *[IAS 10.11]*. For example, a change in interest rates or the outcome of a public vote after the reporting date would not normally be regarded as adjusting events for the ECL calculation.
- However, ECLs are a probability-weighted estimate of credit losses at the reporting date (see 5.4.4 above). Accordingly, the determination of ECLs should take into consideration relevant possible future scenarios based on a range of expectations at the reporting date, using the information available at that date. Hence, the probabilities attached to future expected movements in interest rates and expected outcomes of a future public vote based on information available at the reporting date would be reflected in the determination of ECLs at that date.
- Entities need robust processes and appropriate governance procedures for incorporating information, including forecasts of future economic conditions, to ensure transparent and consistent application of the impairment requirements in IFRS 9. This includes processes for updating ECLs for new information that becomes available after the initial modelling has taken place up until the reporting date.

At its meeting on 16 September 2015, the ITG examined two further questions about the use of forward-looking information:[30]

- the level at which forward-looking information should be incorporated – whether at the level of the entity or on a portfolio-by-portfolio basis; *[IFRS 9 B5.5.16, B5.5.51]* and
- how to determine what is reasonable and supportable forward-looking information and how to treat shock events with material, but uncertain, economic consequences, such as an independence referendum. The same considerations could apply to events such as the UK 'Brexit' vote or natural disasters. *[IFRS 9 B5.5.49-54]*.

With respect to the first issue, the ITG members confirmed that forward-looking information should be relevant for the particular financial instrument or group of financial instruments to which the impairment requirements are being applied. Different factors may be relevant to different financial instruments and, accordingly, the relevance of particular items of information may vary between financial instruments, depending on the specific drivers of credit risk. For example, this is highlighted in Illustrative Example 5 to IFRS 9 (see Example 50.30 below), in which expectations about future levels of unemployment in a specific industry and specific region are only relevant to a sub-portfolio of mortgage loans in which the borrowers work in that industry in that specific region. Conversely, it was also noted that if different financial instruments or portfolios being assessed share some similar risk characteristics, then relevant forward-looking information should be applied in a comparable and consistent manner to reflect those similar characteristics.

With respect to the second issue, the ITG members noted:

- The objective of the standard is to determine ECLs by considering all reasonable and supportable information, including forward-looking information that is relevant and available without undue cost or effort. This is a challenging area. There will be a spectrum of forward-looking information available, some of which will be reasonable and supportable and some of which will have little or no supportable basis. Determining the information that is relevant and reasonable and supportable and its impact on the assessment of significant increases in credit risk and measurement of ECLs can require a high level of judgement. In addition, it can be particularly challenging and difficult to determine the economic consequences (or 'second-order effects') of uncertain future outcomes. For example, while it may be possible to assess the likelihood of a particular event occurring, it may be more difficult to determine the effect of the event on the risk of a default occurring and/or on the credit loses that would be associated with that event using reasonable and supportable information.
- The objective of the IFRS 9 requirements for measuring ECLs is to reflect probability-weighted outcomes. Accordingly, information should not be excluded from the assessment of ECLs simply because:
  - (a) the event has a low or remote likelihood of occurring; or
  - (b) the effect of that event on the credit risk or the amount of ECLs is uncertain.
- An entity should make an effort in good faith to estimate the impact of uncertain future events, including second-order effects, on the credit risk of financial instruments and the measurement of ECLs. The estimate should be based on all reasonable and supportable information that is relevant and available without undue cost and effort. Furthermore:
  - (a) Estimates of ECLs should reflect an entity's own expectations of credit losses; however, entities should be able to explain how they have arrived at their estimate and how it is based on reasonable and supportable information.

(b) Estimates of ECLs are, by their nature, approximations, which will be updated as more reasonable and supportable information becomes available over time.

(c) Information does not necessarily need to flow through a statistical model or credit-rating process in order to determine whether it is reasonable and supportable and relevant for a particular financial instrument or group of financial instruments.

- If an entity could determine that an uncertain event has an impact on the risk of a default occurring, then it should be possible to make an estimate of the impact on ECLs, despite the potentially large range of outcomes. However, in some exceptional cases, it was acknowledged that it may not be possible to estimate the impact on ECLs, despite an entity's best efforts.
- In this regard, the importance of disclosure of forward-looking information that is relevant, but that cannot be incorporated into the determination of significant increases in credit risk and/or the measurement of ECLs because of the lack of reasonable and supportable information was emphasised. Such disclosures should be consistent with the objective in IFRS 7, which is to enable users of the financial statements to understand the credit risk to which the entity is exposed.
- The need for good governance and processes in this area, because of the uncertainties and continually changing circumstances associated with forward-looking information. Furthermore, an entity should be able to explain what information it had considered and why that information had been included or excluded from the determination of ECLs.

This ITG discussion pre-dated that in December 2015 on the use of probability-weighted multiple economic scenarios (see 5.4.4 above) and some of what was noted by the ITG probably needs to be updated in the context of the later discussion. For instance, the ITG members noted that the impact of scenarios about some uncertain future events for which there is reasonable and supportable information may need to be incorporated through the use of overlays to the 'base model', on a collective basis. Applying a multiple scenario approach, an entity will not use just one base model, and if the lender needs to estimate ECLs by considering multiple economic scenarios, it would follow that many shock events will be included in that process, with the event and its various possible consequences occurring in some scenarios and not in others. There may still need to be cases when the effect of shock events is added through an additional 'overlay' to the modelled calculation of ECLs but, if so, as noted by the ITG members, care needs to be taken to avoid double counting the consequences of the event with what has already been assumed in the model.

Banks will also need to take account of guidance from their regulators (see 5.6.1 below).

The ITG members also noted that the effects of uncertain future events may need to be reflected in the assessment of whether there has been a significant increase in credit risk.

5.5 General approach: determining significant increases in credit risk

One of the major challenges in implementing the general approach in the IFRS 9 ECL model is to track and determine whether there have been significant increases in the credit risk of an entity's credit exposures since initial recognition.

The assessment of significant deterioration is key in establishing the point of switching between the requirement to measure an allowance based on 12-month ECLs and one that is based on lifetime ECLs. The standard is prescriptive that an entity cannot align the timing of significant increases in credit risk and the recognition of lifetime ECLs with the time when a financial asset is regarded as credit-impaired or to an entity's internal definition of default. *[IFRS 9.B5.5.21]*. Financial assets should normally be assessed as having increased significantly in credit risk earlier than when they become credit-impaired (see 5.3.1 above) or default occurs. *[IFRS 9.B5.5.7]*.

As this area involves significant management judgement, entities are required to provide both qualitative and quantitative disclosures under IFRS 7 to explain the inputs, assumptions and estimation used to determine significant increases in credit risk of financial instruments and any changes in those assumptions and estimates (see 5.13 below and Chapter 54 at 5.2.3). *[IFRS 7.35F(a), 35G(a)(ii), 35G(c)]*.

However, a number of operational simplifications and presumptions are available to help entities make this assessment (as described further below).

At its meeting in December 2015, the ITG members reaffirmed that unless a more specific exception applies, IFRS 9 requires an entity to assess whether there has been a significant increase in credit risk for *all* financial instruments, including those with a maturity of 12 months or less. Consistently with this requirement, IFRS 7 requires corresponding disclosures that distinguish between financial instruments for which the loss allowance is equal to 12-month or lifetime ECLs. In addition, the ITG members noted that:

- the assessment of significant increases in credit risk is distinct from the measurement of ECLs as highlighted by paragraph 5.5.9 of IFRS 9. For example, a collateralised financial asset may have suffered a significant increase in credit risk, but owing to the value of the collateral there may not be an increase in the amount of ECLs even if measured on a lifetime rather than a 12-month basis;
- assessing changes in credit risk would be consistent with normal credit risk management practices; and
- the expected life of a financial instrument may change if it has suffered a significant increase in credit risk.

Finally, the ITG noted the importance of the IFRS 7 disclosure requirements and observed that disclosing information regarding the increase in credit risk since initial recognition provides users of financial statements with useful information regarding the changes in the risk of default occurring in respect of that financial instrument (see 5.13 below and Chapter 54 at 5.2.3). Similar to measuring ECLs, an entity may use different approaches when assessing significant increases in credit risk for different financial instruments. An approach that does not include PD as an explicit input can be consistent with the impairment requirements as long as the entity is able to separate the changes in the risk of a default occurring from changes in other drivers of ECLs (e.g. collateral) and considers the following when making the assessment: *[IFRS 9.B5.5.12]*

- the change in the risk of a default occurring since initial recognition;
- the expected life of the financial instrument; and
- reasonable and supportable information that is available, without undue cost or effort, that may affect credit risk.

In addition, because of the relationship between the expected life and the risk of default occurring, the change in credit risk cannot be assessed simply by comparing the change in the absolute risk of default over time, because the risk of default usually decreases as time passes if the credit risk is unchanged. *[IFRS 9.B5.5.11]*.

Entities that do not use probability of loss as an explicit input will have to use other criteria to identify a change in the risk of default occurring. These might include deterioration in a behavioural score or other indicators of a heightened risk of default. A collective approach may also be an appropriate supplement or substitute for an assessment at the individual instrument level (see 5.5.5 below).

5.5.1 *Change in the risk of a default occurring*

In order to make the assessment of whether there has been significant credit deterioration, an entity should consider reasonable and supportable information that is available without undue cost or effort and compare: *[IFRS 9.5.5.9]*

- the risk of a default occurring on the financial instrument over its life as at the reporting date; and
- the risk of a default occurring on the financial instrument over its life as at the date of initial recognition.

For loan commitments, an entity should consider changes in the risk of a default occurring on the potential loan to which a loan commitment relates. For financial guarantee contracts, an entity should consider the changes in the risk that the specified debtor will default. *[IFRS 9.B5.5.8]*.

At each reporting date, an entity is required to assess significant increases in credit risk based on the change in the risk of a default occurring over the expected life of the financial instrument rather than the change in the amount of ECLs. *[IFRS 9.5.5.9]*. In a departure from the Basel regulatory wording and to avoid suggesting that statistical models are required (including the PD approach), the IASB changed the terminology from 'probability of a default occurring' to 'risk of a default occurring'. *[IFRS 9.BC5.157]*.

In order to make the IFRS 9 impairment model operational, the IASB considered a number of alternative methods for determining significant increases in credit risk, but these were rejected for the following reasons:

- *Absolute level of credit risk*: The IASB considered whether an entity should be required to recognise lifetime ECLs on all financial instruments at, or above, a particular credit risk at the reporting date. Although this approach is operationally simpler to apply (because an entity is not required to track changes in credit risk), such an approach would provide very different information. It would not approximate the economic effect of changes in credit loss expectations subsequent to initial recognition. In addition, it may also result in overstatement or understatement of ECLs, depending on the threshold set for recognising lifetime ECLs. *[IFRS 9.BC5.160]*. However, the IASB noted that an absolute approach could be used for portfolios of financial instruments with similar credit risk at initial recognition, by determining the maximum initial credit risk accepted and then comparing the maximum initial credit risk to the credit risk at the reporting date (see 5.5.4.E below). *[IFRS 9.BC5.161]*.

- *Change in the credit risk management objective*: The IASB also considered whether the assessment of significant deterioration should be based on whether an entity's credit risk management objective changes (e.g. monitoring of financial assets on an individual basis, or a change from collecting past due amounts to the recovery of these amounts). This approach is operationally relatively easy to apply. However, it is likely to have a similar effect to the IAS 39 incurred loss model and, hence, may result in a delayed recognition of ECLs. *[IFRS 9.BC5.162]*.
- *Credit underwriting policies*: The IASB further considered whether the change in the entity's credit underwriting limit for a particular class of financial instrument at the reporting date (i.e. an entity would not originate new loans on the same terms) should form the basis of assessing significant increase in credit risk. The IASB noted that this approach is similar to the absolute approach above. Moreover, the change in an entity's credit underwriting limits may be driven by other factors that are not related to a change in the credit risk of its borrowers (e.g. the entity may incorporate favourable terms to maintain a good business relationship or to increase lending), or are dependent on circumstances existing at the reporting date that are not relevant to the particular vintages of financial instruments. *[IFRS 9.BC5.163, BC5.164, BC5.165]*.

As already stressed, the assessment is based on the change in the lifetime risk of default, not the amount of ECLs. Hence the allowance for a fully collateralised asset may need to be based on lifetime ECLs (because there has been a significant increase in the risk of default) even though no loss is expected to arise. *[IFRS 9.5.5.9]*. In such instances, the fact that the asset is being measured using lifetime ECLs may have more significance for disclosure than for measurement (see 5.13 below).

The interaction between collateral, assessment of significant increases in credit risk and measurement of ECLs is illustrated in the following example from the standard. *[IFRS 9 IG Example 3, IE18-IE23]*.

Example 50.22: Highly collateralised financial asset

Company H owns real estate assets which are financed by a five-year loan from Bank Z with a loan-to-value (LTV) ratio of 50 per cent. The loan is secured by a first-ranking security over the real estate assets. At initial recognition of the loan, Bank Z does not consider the loan to be credit-impaired as defined in Appendix A of IFRS 9.

Subsequent to initial recognition, the revenues and operating profits of Company H have decreased because of an economic recession. Furthermore, expected increases in regulations have the potential to further negatively affect revenue and operating profit. These negative effects on Company H's operations could be significant and ongoing.

As a result of these recent events and expected adverse economic conditions, Company H's free cash flow is expected to be reduced to the point that the coverage of scheduled loan payments could become tight. Bank Z estimates that a further deterioration in cash flows may result in Company H missing a contractual payment on the loan and becoming past due.

Recent third party appraisals have indicated a decrease in the value of the real estate properties, resulting in a current LTV ratio of 70 per cent.

At the reporting date, the loan to Company H is not considered to have low credit risk in accordance with paragraph 5.5.10 of IFRS 9. Bank Z therefore needs to assess whether there has been a significant increase in credit risk since initial recognition in accordance with paragraph 5.5.3 of IFRS 9, irrespective of the value of the collateral it holds. It notes that the loan is subject to considerable credit risk at the reporting date because even a slight deterioration in cash flows could result in Company H missing a contractual payment on the loan. As a result, Bank Z determines that the credit risk (i.e. the risk of a default occurring) has increased significantly since initial recognition. Consequently, Bank Z recognises lifetime ECLs on the loan to Company H.

Although lifetime ECLs should be recognised, the measurement of the ECLs will reflect the recovery expected from the collateral (adjusting for the costs of obtaining and selling the collateral) on the property as required by paragraph B5.5.55 of IFRS 9 and may result in the ECLs on the loan being very small.

The ITG (see 5.1.5 above) discussed in April 2015 whether an entity should consider the ability to recover cash flows through a financial guarantee contract that is integral to the contract when assessing whether there has been a significant increase in the credit risk of the guaranteed debt instrument since initial recognition. IFRS 9 requires that measurement of the ECLs of the guaranteed debt instrument includes cash flows from the integral financial guarantee contract (see 5.4.7 above). *[IFRS 9.B5.5.55]*. However, some ITG members commented that IFRS 9 is clear that recoveries from integral financial guarantee contracts should be excluded from the assessment of significant increases in credit risk of the guaranteed debt instrument. *[IFRS 9.5.5.9]*. This is because the focus of the standard is about the risk of the borrower defaulting when making such an assessment, as highlighted in the examples in B5.5.17 of the standard. These examples clarify that information about a guarantee (or other credit enhancement) may be relevant to assessing changes in credit risk, but only to the extent that it affects the likelihood of the borrower defaulting on the instrument (see 5.5.2 below for the list of examples). *[IFRS 9.B5.5.17]*. Furthermore, excluding recoveries from the financial guarantee contract, when assessing significant increases in credit risk, would be consistent with the treatment of other forms of collateral.

While the value of collateral does not normally affect the assessment of significant increases in credit risk, if significant changes in the value of the collateral supporting the obligation are expected to reduce the borrower's economic incentive to make scheduled contractual payments, then this would have an effect on the risk of a default occurring. The standard provides an example where if the value of collateral declines because house prices decline, borrowers in some jurisdictions have a greater incentive to default on their mortgages. *[IFRS 9.B5.5.17(j)]*.

The other examples provided by the standard of situations where the value of a credit enhancement could have an impact on the ability or economic incentive of the borrower to repay relate to guarantees or financial support provided by a shareholder, parent entity or other affiliate and to interests issued in securitisations. These are included in the examples listed in the next section of this chapter (see 5.5.2 below), where subordinated interests are expected to be capable of absorbing ECLs:

- a significant change in the quality of the guarantee provided by a shareholder (or an individual's parent) if the shareholder (or parent) has an incentive and financial ability to prevent default by capital or cash infusion; *[IFRS 9.B5.5.17(k)]* and

- significant changes, such as reductions, in financial support from a parent entity or other affiliate or an actual or expected significant change in the quality of credit enhancement, that are expected to reduce the borrower's ability to make scheduled contractual payments. For example, such a situation could occur if a parent decides to no longer provide financial support to a subsidiary, which as a result would face bankruptcy or receivership. This could in turn result in that subsidiary prioritising payments for its operational needs (such as payroll and crucial suppliers) and assigning a lower priority to payments on its financial debt, resulting in an increase in the risk of default on those liabilities. Credit quality enhancements or support include the consideration of the financial condition of the guarantor and/or, for interests issued in securitisations, whether subordinated interests are expected to be capable of absorbing ECLs (for example, on the loans underlying the security). *[IFRS 9.B5.5.17(l)]*.

The last example, referring to the effect of subordinated interests in a securitisation deserves some comment. IFRS 9 sets out rules to determine whether an investment in a contractually linked instrument such as a tranche of a securitisation qualifies to be measured at amortised cost (see Chapter 47 at 6.5). Where these tests are met, the instrument is deemed to represent solely payments of principle and interest, in which case any failure of the instrument to pay the investor the full amount due must be treated as a default and an estimation of the amount of any losses that will be incurred must be reflected in the credit loss allowance. Paragraph B5.5.17(l) should be interpreted as saying that the investment should be measured based on lifetime ECLs if there are sufficient losses expected on the instruments underlying the securitisation such that they may not be absorbed by subordinated interests in the structure, and so there is a significantly increased risk that the investor will suffer loss.

Under the loss rate approach, introduced at 5.4.2.B above, an entity develops loss-rate statistics on the basis of the amount written off over the life of the financial assets rather than using separate PD and LGD statistics. Entities then must adjust these historical credit loss trends for current conditions and expectations about the future.

The standard is clear that although a loss rate approach may be applied, an entity needs to be able to separate the changes in the risk of a default occurring from changes in other drivers of ECLs for the purpose of assessing if there has been a significant increase in credit risk. *[IFRS 9.B5.5.12]*. Under the loss rate approach, the entity does not distinguish between a risk of a default occurring and the loss incurred following a default. This is not so much of an issue for measuring 12-month or lifetime ECLs. However, under the loss rate approach, an entity would not be able to implement the assessment of significant increases in credit risk that is based on the change in the risk of a default. Therefore, entities using the loss rate approach would need an overlay of measuring and forecasting the level of defaults, as illustrated in the extract of Example 9 from the Implementation Guidance (see Example 50.19 above). For entities that currently use only expected loss rates it may be easier to develop a PD approach than to use the method described in this example.

5.5.2 *Factors or indicators of changes in credit risk*

Similar to measuring ECLs (see 5.4 above), when assessing significant increases in credit risk, an entity should consider all reasonable and supportable information that is available without undue cost or effort (see 5.4.8 above) and that is relevant for an individual financial instrument, a portfolio, portions of a portfolio, and groups of portfolios. *[IFRS 9.B5.5.15, B5.5.16]*.

The IASB notes that it did not intend to prescribe a specific or mechanistic approach to assess changes in credit risk and that the appropriate approach will vary for different levels of sophistication of entities, the financial instrument and the availability of data. *[IFRS 9.BC5.157]*. It is important to stress that the assessment of significant increases in credit risk often involves a multifactor and holistic analysis. The importance and relevance of each specific factor will depend on the type of product, characteristics of the financial instruments and the borrower as well as the geographical region. *[IFRS 9.B5.5.16]*. The guidance in the standard is clear that in certain circumstances, qualitative and non-statistical quantitative information may be sufficient to determine that a financial instrument has met the criterion for the recognition of lifetime ECLs. That is, the information does not need to flow through a statistical model or credit ratings process in order to determine whether there has been a significant increase in the credit risk of the financial instrument. In other cases, the assessment may be based on quantitative information or a mixture of quantitative and qualitative information. *[IFRS 9.B5.5.18]*.

The standard provides a non-exhaustive list of factors or indicators which an entity should consider when determining whether the recognition of lifetime ECLs is required. This list of factors or indicators is as follows: *[IFRS 9.B5.5.17]*

- significant changes in internal price indicators of credit risk as a result of a change in credit risk since inception, including, but not limited to, the credit spread that would result if a particular financial instrument, or similar financial instrument with the same terms and the same counterparty were newly originated or issued at the reporting date;
- other changes in the rates or terms of an existing financial instrument that would be significantly different if the instrument was newly originated or issued at the reporting date (such as more stringent covenants, increased amounts of collateral or guarantees, or higher income coverage) because of changes in the credit risk of the financial instrument since initial recognition;
- significant changes in external market indicators of credit risk for a particular financial instrument or similar financial instruments with the same expected life. Changes in market indicators of credit risk include, but are not limited to: the credit spread; the credit default swap prices for the borrower; the length of time or the extent to which the fair value of a financial asset has been less than its amortised cost; and other market information related to the borrower (such as changes in the price of a borrower's debt and equity instruments). The IASB noted that market prices are an important source of information that should be considered in assessing whether credit risk has changed, although market prices themselves cannot solely determine whether

significant deterioration has occurred because market prices are also affected by non-credit risk related factors such as changes in interest rates or liquidity risks; *[IFRS 9.BC5.123]*

- an actual or expected significant change in the financial instrument's external credit rating;
- an actual or expected internal credit rating downgrade for the borrower or decrease in behavioural scoring used to assess credit risk internally. Internal credit ratings and internal behavioural scoring are more reliable when they are mapped to external ratings or supported by default studies;
- existing or forecast adverse changes in business, financial or economic conditions that are expected to cause a significant change in the borrower's ability to meet its debt obligations, such as an actual or expected increase in interest rates or an actual or expected significant increase in unemployment rates;
- an actual or expected significant change in the operating results of the borrower. Examples include actual or expected declining revenues or margins, increasing operating risks, working capital deficiencies, decreasing asset quality, increased balance sheet leverage, liquidity, management problems or changes in the scope of business or organisational structure (such as the discontinuance of a segment of the business) that result in a significant change in the borrower's ability to meet its debt obligations;
- significant increases in credit risk on other financial instruments of the same borrower;
- an actual or expected significant adverse change in the regulatory, economic, or technological environment of the borrower that results in a significant change in the borrower's ability to meet its debt obligations, such as a decline in the demand for the borrower's sales product because of a shift in technology;
- significant changes in the value of the collateral supporting the obligation or in the quality of third-party guarantees or credit enhancements, which are expected to reduce the borrower's economic incentive to make scheduled contractual payments or to otherwise have an effect on the risk of a default occurring. For example, if the value of collateral declines because house prices decline, borrowers in some jurisdictions have a greater incentive to default on their mortgages;
- a significant change in the quality of the guarantee provided by a shareholder (or an individual's parents) if the shareholder (or parents) have an incentive and financial ability to prevent default by capital or cash infusion;
- significant changes, such as reductions, in financial support from a parent entity or other affiliate or an actual or expected significant change in the quality of credit enhancement, that are expected to reduce the borrower's economic incentive to make scheduled contractual payments. For example, such a situation could occur if a parent decides to no longer provide financial support to a subsidiary, which as a result would face bankruptcy or receivership. This could in turn result in that subsidiary prioritising payments for its operational needs (such as payroll and crucial suppliers) and assigning a lower priority to

payments on its financial debt, resulting in an increase in the risk of default on those liabilities. Credit quality enhancements or support include the consideration of the financial condition of the guarantor and/or, for interests issued in securitisations, whether subordinated interests are expected to be capable of absorbing ECLs (for example, on the loans underlying the security);

- expected changes in the loan documentation (i.e. changes in contract terms) including an expected breach of contract that may lead to covenant waivers or amendments, interest payment holidays, interest rate step-ups, requiring additional collateral or guarantees, or other changes to the contractual framework of the instrument;
- significant changes in the expected performance and behaviour of the borrower, including changes in the payment status of borrowers in the group (for example, an increase in the expected number or extent of delayed contractual payments or significant increases in the expected number of credit card borrowers who are expected to approach or exceed their credit limit or who are expected to be paying the minimum monthly amount);
- changes in the entity's credit management approach in relation to the financial instrument, i.e. based on emerging indicators of changes in the credit risk of the financial instrument, the entity's credit risk management practice is expected to become more active or to be focused on managing the instrument, including the instrument becoming more closely monitored or controlled, or the entity specifically intervening with the borrower; and
- past due information, including the more than 30 days past due rebuttable presumption (see 5.5.4.B below).

This list raises the question as to whether an entity will be required to look at each of these factors or indicators as soon as the information is readily available, even though they may not be fully integrated in the entity's credit risk management systems and processes. This relates to our earlier discussion about which information is available without undue cost or effort (see 5.4.8.A above) and the Basel guidance (discussed at 5.6.1 below).

We also make the following observations:

- Many financial institutions should have readily available information about the pricing and terms of various types of loans issued to a specific customer (e.g. overdraft, credit cards and mortgage loans) in their credit risk management systems and processes. However, in practice, it would often be difficult to use such information because changes in pricing and terms on the origination of a similar financial instrument at the reporting date may not be so obviously related to a change in credit risk as other, more commercial, factors come into play (e.g. different risk appetites, change in management approach and underwriting standards). It may be challenging to link the two sets of information (i.e. pricing processes on the one hand and credit risk management on the other).
- Some of the factors or indicators are only relevant for the assessment of significant deterioration on an individual basis and not on a portfolio basis. For example, change in external market indicators of credit risk, including the credit

spread, the credit default swap prices of the borrower and the extent of decline in fair value. However, it is worth noting that external market information that is available for a quoted instrument may be useful to help assess another instrument that is not quoted but which is issued by the same debtor or one who operates in the same sector.

- It is important to stress that the approach required by the standard is more holistic and qualitative than is necessarily captured by external credit ratings, which are adjusted for discrete events and may not reflect gradual degradations in credit quality. External credit ratings should not, therefore, be used on their own but only in conjunction with other qualitative information. Furthermore, although ratings are forward-looking, it is sometimes suggested that changes in credit ratings may not be reflected in a timely matter. Therefore, entities may have to take account of expected change in ratings in assessing whether exposures are low risk (Example 50.26 below illustrates that there could be significant differences between using agencies' credit ratings or using market data such as CDS spreads). The same point can of course be made about the use of internal credit ratings, especially if they are only reassessed on an annual basis (see the discussion at the September 2015 ITG meeting later in this section).
- Also, some of the factors or indicators are very forward-looking, such as forecasts of adverse changes in business, financial or economic conditions that are expected to result in significant future financial difficulty of the borrower in repaying its debt. In practice, the analysis may have to be performed at the level of a portfolio rather than at an individual level when forward-looking information is not available at the individual level.

With IFRS 9 not being prescriptive, we observe differences in how banks intend to implement the assessment of significant increase in credit risk. These differences reflect various schools of thought along with differences in credit processes, business model, sophistication, use of advanced models for regulatory capital purposes, availability of data (e.g. historic data at origination) and consistency of definitions across businesses or multiple systems. As use of models and availability of data can vary within a bank, it is probable that a number of approaches will be adopted within a single institution.

In general, banks are considering the use of a combination of quantitative and qualitative drivers to assess significant increases in credit risk. Some of these are regarded as primary, others as secondary and some as backstops. The primary driver is usually expected to be the most forward looking indicator and is generally based on a relative measure. The most common primary drivers being considered by the larger banks are:

- changes in the lifetime risk of a default occurring, guided by scores and ratings;
- changes in the 12-month probability of default; or
- changes in ratings or credit scores for retail exposures and ratings for corporate exposures.

Forbearance and watchlists are likely to be used as secondary drivers and delinquency (usually 30 days past due) as a backstop.

The consideration of various factors or indicators when assessing significant increases in credit risk since initial recognition is illustrated in Examples 49.19 and 49.20, which are based on Examples 1 and 2 in the Implementation Guidance for the standard. *[IFRS 9 IG Example 1, IG Example 2, IE7-IE17]*.

Example 50.23: Significant increase in credit risk

Company Y has a funding structure that includes a senior secured loan facility with different tranches. The security on the loan affects the loss that would be realised if a default occurs, but does not affect the risk of a default occurring, so it is not considered when determining whether there has been a significant increase in credit risk since initial recognition as required by paragraph 5.5.3 of IFRS 9. Bank X provides a tranche of that loan facility to Company Y. At the time of origination of the loan by Bank X, although Company Y's leverage was relatively high compared with other issuers with similar credit risk, it was expected that Company Y would be able to meet the covenants for the life of the instrument. In addition, the generation of revenue and cash flow was expected to be stable in Company Y's industry over the term of the senior facility. However, there was some business risk related to the ability to grow gross margins within its existing businesses.

At initial recognition, because of the considerations outlined above, Bank X considers that despite the level of credit risk at initial recognition, the loan is not an originated credit-impaired loan because it does not meet the definition of a credit-impaired financial asset in Appendix A of IFRS 9.

Subsequent to initial recognition, macroeconomic changes have had a negative effect on total sales volume and Company Y has underperformed on its business plan for revenue generation and net cash flow generation. Although spending on inventory has increased, anticipated sales have not materialised. To increase liquidity, Company Y has drawn down more on a separate revolving credit facility, thereby increasing its leverage ratio. Consequently, Company Y is now close to breaching its covenants on the senior secured loan facility with Bank X.

Bank X makes an overall assessment of the credit risk on the loan to Company Y at the reporting date, by taking into consideration all reasonable and supportable information that is available without undue cost or effort and that is relevant for assessing the extent of the increase in credit risk since initial recognition. This may include factors such as:

(a) Bank X's expectation that the deterioration in the macroeconomic environment may continue in the near future, which is expected to have a further negative impact on Company Y's ability to generate cash flows and to de-leverage.

(b) Company Y is closer to breaching its covenants, which may result in a need to restructure the loan or reset the covenants.

(c) Bank X's assessment that the trading prices for Company Y's bonds have decreased and that the credit margin on newly originated loans have increased reflecting the increase in credit risk, and that these changes are not explained by changes in the market environment (for example, benchmark interest rates have remained unchanged). A further comparison with the pricing of Company Y's peers shows that reductions in the price of Company Y's bonds and increases in credit margin on its loans have probably been caused by company-specific factors.

(d) Bank X has reassessed its internal risk grading of the loan on the basis of the information that it has available to reflect the increase in credit risk.

Bank X determines that there has been a significant increase in credit risk since initial recognition of the loan in accordance with paragraph 5.5.3 of IFRS 9. Consequently, Bank X recognises lifetime ECLs on its senior secured loan to Company Y. Even if Bank X has not yet changed the internal risk grading of the loan it could still reach this conclusion – the absence or presence of a change in risk grading in itself is not determinative of whether credit risk has increased significantly since initial recognition.

Example 50.24: No significant increase in credit risk

Company C is the holding company of a group that operates in a cyclical production industry. Bank B provided a loan to Company C. At that time, the prospects for the industry were positive, because of expectations of further increases in global demand. However, input prices were volatile and given the point in the cycle, a potential decrease in sales was anticipated.

In addition, in the past Company C has been focused on external growth, acquiring majority stakes in companies in related sectors. As a result, the group structure is complex and has been subject to change, making it difficult for investors to analyse the expected performance of the group and to forecast the cash that will be available at the holding company level. Even though leverage is at a level that is considered acceptable by Company C's creditors at the time that Bank B originates the loan, its creditors are concerned about Company C's ability to refinance its debt because of the short remaining life until the maturity of the current financing. There is also concern about Company C's ability to continue to service interest using the dividends it receives from its operating subsidiaries.

At the time of the origination of the loan by Bank B, Company C's leverage was in line with that of other customers with similar credit risk and based on projections over the expected life of the loan, the available capacity (i.e. headroom) on its coverage ratios before triggering a default event, was high. Bank B applies its own internal rating methods to determine credit risk and allocates a specific internal rating score to its loans. Bank B's internal rating categories are based on historical, current and forward-looking information and reflect the credit risk for the tenor of the loans. On initial recognition, Bank B determines that the loan is subject to considerable credit risk, has speculative elements and that the uncertainties affecting Company C, including the group's uncertain prospects for cash generation, could lead to default. However, Bank B does not consider the loan to be originated credit-impaired.

Subsequent to initial recognition, Company C has announced that three of its five key subsidiaries had a significant reduction in sales volume because of deteriorated market conditions but sales volumes are expected to improve in line with the anticipated cycle for the industry in the following months. The sales of the other two subsidiaries were stable. Company C has also announced a corporate restructure to streamline its operating subsidiaries. This restructuring will increase the flexibility to refinance existing debt and the ability of the operating subsidiaries to pay dividends to Company C.

Despite the expected continuing deterioration in market conditions, Bank B determines, in accordance with paragraph 5.5.3 of IFRS 9, that there has not been a significant increase in the credit risk on the loan to Company C since initial recognition. This is demonstrated by factors that include:

(a) Although current sale volumes have fallen, this was as anticipated by Bank B at initial recognition. Furthermore, sales volumes are expected to improve, in the following months.

(b) Given the increased flexibility to refinance the existing debt at the operating subsidiary level and the increased availability of dividends to Company C, Bank B views the corporate restructure as being credit enhancing. This is despite some continued concern about the ability to refinance the existing debt at the holding company level.

(c) Bank B's credit risk department, which monitors Company C, has determined that the latest developments are not significant enough to justify a change in its internal credit risk rating.

As a consequence, Bank B does not recognise a loss allowance at an amount equal to lifetime ECLs on the loan. However, it updates its measurement of the 12-month ECLs for the increased risk of a default occurring in the next 12 months and for current expectations of the credit losses that would arise if a default were to occur.

Example 50.25: Assessment of a significant increase in credit risk based on a PD approach

This example is based on the same loan presented in Example 50.18 above.

On 31 December 2015, Bank A originates a 10-year bullet loan with a gross carrying amount of $1,000,000, interest being due at the end of each year. Based on statistical and qualitative information – including forward looking, Bank A has estimated a **BBB rating** for the loan.

Based on this rating, Bank A has computed a PD term structure at origination. Bank A's PD term structure is estimated with the annual PD expected for each future period. The lifetime PD is the product of each marginal PD during the considered period:

$$\text{lifetime PD}_k = 1 - \prod_{k=i}^{n} (1 - \text{marginal PD}_i)$$

Finally, based on the marginal PD computed for each future period, Bank A is able to compute the forward lifetime PD as follows:

Year	Cumulative PD at origination	Marginal 12-month PD	Remaining lifetime PD	Remaining annualised lifetime PD
2015				
2016	0.17%	0.17%	4.50%	0.46%
2017	0.49%	0.32%	4.34%	0.49%
2018	0.86%	0.37%	4.03%	0.51%
2019	1.38%	0.53%	3.67%	0.53%
2020	1.84%	0.47%	3.16%	0.53%
2021	2.37%	0.54%	2.71%	0.55%
2022	2.85%	0.49%	2.18%	0.55%
2023	3.30%	0.46%	1.70%	0.57%
2024	3.84%	0.56%	1.24%	0.62%
2025	4.50%	0.69%	0.69%	0.69%

For the first year, the remaining lifetime PD is the cumulative PD at origination. Then, after a year, it starts decreasing, considering that the remaining period is shorter. After 2 years it is 4.03% and after 3 years it is only 3.67%. At the end of the loan, the remaining lifetime PD ends up at 0%.

In common with many institutions, Bank A chooses to compare an annualised lifetime PD instead of a cumulative PD. This has the advantage that business lines and risk analysts can easily map a 12-month PD onto a rating scale. It also enables an absolute change in annualised lifetime PD, e.g. 20bp, to be set as a 'filter', to exclude small changes in lifetime PD from being assessed as significant that are considered to be 'noise'. For this purpose, Bank A calculates a 12m equivalent PD, using the residual cumulative curve. The annualised lifetime PD is calculated as follows:

$$\text{annualised lifetime PD}_k = 1 - (1 - \text{lifetime PD}_k)^{1/t}$$

when t = horizon of the lifetime PD expressed in years

2017: no significant increase in credit risk: Stage 1

On 31 December 2017 – 2 years after origination, Bank A updates the rating of its obligor. The rating is now BB+.

A new PD term structure is estimated based on this information:

Year	Cumulative lifetime PD
2018	0.67%
2019	1.53%
2020	3.70%
2021	5.58%
2022	5.89%
2023	6.51%
2024	7.45%
2025	8.70%
Remaining annualised lifetime PD	1.13%
Forecast at origination	0.51%
Increase (multiple)	**2.20**

In this example, Bank A uses a significant increase in credit risk threshold of a 2.5 multiple of PD. For simplicity we ignore any qualitative or other indicators that a bank might use to make this assessment.

Had Bank A used a cumulative lifetime PD approach, it would compare 8.70% to 4.03%, an increase of ×2.2. Comparing the remaining annualised PD estimated at origination (0.51%) with the remaining annualised PD at the reporting date (1.13%), the increase is still only ×2.2. The significant deterioration threshold set by Bank A is not met and therefore the loan remains in stage 1.

2018: significant increase in credit risk: stage 2

On 31 December 2018 – 3 years after origination, Bank A updates the rating of its obligor. Its rating is now BB–. Then Bank A updates its historical information for current economic conditions as well as reasonable and supportable forecasts of future economic conditions.

Year	Cumulative lifetime PD
2019	1.40%
2020	3.87%
2021	8.82%
2022	12.84%
2023	16.04%
2024	18.98%
2025	21.60%
Remaining annualised lifetime PD	3.42%
Forecast at origination	0.53%
Increase (multiple)	**6.41**

Had Bank A used a cumulative lifetime PD approach the comparison would be of 21.6% to 3.67%, a 6.41 fold increase. As before, Bank A compares the remaining annualised PD estimated at origination (0.53%) with the remaining annualised PD at the reporting date (3.42%), an increase of 6.45 times the original PD. This time, the threshold of significant deterioration is met and the loan is moved to stage 2.

At its meeting on 16 September 2015, the ITG (see 5.1.5 above) discussed two issues concerning how an entity should determine whether there has been a significant increase in credit risk:

- How to identify a significant increase in credit risk for a portfolio of retail loans when identical pricing and contractual terms are applied to customers across broad credit quality bands.
- The possibility of using behavioural indicators of credit risk for the purpose of the assessment of significant increases in credit risk since initial recognition.[31]

The first question was influenced by one of the operational simplifications introduced by the IASB, discussed at 5.5.4.E below, which allows an entity to assess if there has been a significant increase in credit risk by determining the maximum initial credit risk accepted for portfolios with similar credit risks on original recognition, and by reviewing which exposures now exceed this limit. The ITG discussed an example of a retail loan portfolio (Portfolio A) comprising customers who had been assigned initial credit grades between 1 and 5 (based on a 10-grade rating scale where 1 is the highest credit quality) and had been issued loans with the same contractual terms and pricing. The question was whether it would be appropriate to make the determination of significant increases in credit risk by using a single threshold approach such as that outlined for Portfolio 1 in Illustrative Example 6 of IFRS 9, on the basis that the exposures in Portfolio A could be considered to have a similar initial credit risk, or whether there were other more appropriate approaches such as, for example, defining a significant increase in credit risk as a specific number of notch increases in credit grade.

The ITG members observed that:

- The appropriateness of using a credit grading system will always depend on an entity's specific facts and circumstances. It would depend upon the range of factors taken into account in determining individual credit grades, how the credit grading system operates and how it relates to the risk of a default occurring. However, when assessing whether there has been a significant increase in credit risk, an entity should be mindful of achieving the objective of the impairment requirements, i.e. to recognise lifetime ECLs for all financial instruments for which there have been significant increases in credit risk since initial recognition.
- Consequently, the impairment model is based on an assessment of changes in credit risk since initial recognition, rather than the identification of a specific level of credit risk at the reporting date and a smaller absolute change in the risk of default occurring will be more significant for an asset that is of high quality on initial recognition than for one that is of low quality.
- In Illustrative Example 6 in IFRS 9, the assessment of significant increases in credit risk of Portfolio 1 was made using a form of absolute approach. However, it was pointed out that this approach was still consistent with the objective of identifying significant increases in credit risk since initial recognition. In particular, only loans with an initial credit grade of 3 or 4 were included in Portfolio 1 and furthermore, the entity had concluded that a movement from

Chapter 50

credit grade 3 to 4 did not represent a significant increase in credit risk. Consequently, using a single threshold of credit grade 5 as a means of identifying a significant increase in credit risk since initial recognition served to capture changes in credit risk in a manner that achieved the objective of the impairment requirements.

- In contrast, in the fact pattern discussed, Portfolio A contained loans with initial credit grades ranging between 1 and 5. Questions were raised as to whether such a broad range of credit grades could be considered to represent a similar initial credit risk and the ITG members noted that in order to conclude that the assessment could be based on whether loans had a credit rating worse than 5, the entity would need to have determined that movements between credit grades 1 and 5 did not represent a significant increase in credit risk.
- When assessing whether there has been a significant increase in credit risk, it would not be appropriate for the entity to consider only factors such as pricing and contractual terms. In this regard, while the concept of economic loss was considered in developing the IFRS 9 model, the standard requires an assessment of changes in credit risk based on a wide range of factors including internal and external indicators of credit risk, changes to contractual terms, actual and expected performance/behaviours and forecasts of future conditions
- Credit grading systems were not designed with the requirements of IFRS 9 in mind, and thus it should not be assumed that they will always be an appropriate means of identifying significant increases in credit risk. The appropriateness of using internal credit grading systems as a means of assessing changes in credit risk since initial recognition depends on whether the credit grades are reviewed with sufficient frequency, include all reasonable and supportable information and reflect the risk of default over the expected life of the financial instrument. As credit grading systems vary, care needs to be taken when referring to movements in credit grades and how this reflects an increased risk of default occurring. In addition, the assessment of whether a change in credit risk grade represents a significant increase in credit risk in accordance with IFRS 9 depends on the initial credit risk of the financial instrument being assessed. Because the relationship between credit grades and changes in the risk of default occurring differs between credit grading systems (e.g. in some cases the changes in the risk of a default occurring may increase exponentially between grades whereas in others it may not), this requires particular consideration.
- Information available at an individual financial instrument level and/or built into a credit risk grading system may not incorporate forward-looking information as required by IFRS 9. Consequently, the assessment of significant increases in credit risk may need to be supplemented by a collective assessment to capture forward-looking information. However, a collective assessment should not obscure significant increases in credit risk at an individual financial instrument level. In this regard, portfolio segmentation is important, noting that entities should ensure that sub-portfolios are not defined too widely.

The second question was whether the following behavioural indicators of credit risk could be used, on their own, as a proxy to determine if there has been a significant increase in credit risk:

- where a customer has made only the minimum monthly repayment for a specified number of months;
- where a customer has failed to make a payment on a loan with a different lender; or
- where a customer has failed to make a specified number of minimum monthly repayments.

The ITG members noted that:

- When assessing whether there has been a significant increase in credit risk, entities are required to consider a range of indicators rather than focussing on only one. Furthermore, while behavioural indicators have a role to play, the above behavioural indicators are often lagging indicators of increases in credit risk and consequently, they should be considered in conjunction with other, more forward-looking information. In this regard, an entity must consider how to source and incorporate forward-looking information into the assessment of significant increases in credit risk and may need to do this on a collective basis if forward-looking information is not available at an individual financial instrument level.
- When considering the use of behavioural indicators, an entity should:
  - (a) Focus on identifying pre-delinquency behavioural indicators of increases in credit risk, e.g. increased utilisation rates or increased cash drawings on specific products.
  - (b) Only use indicators that are relevant to the risk of default occurring.
  - (c) Establish a link between the behavioural indicators of credit risk and changes in the risk of default occurring since initial recognition.
  - (d) Be mindful that while behavioural indicators are often predictive of defaults in the short term, they are often less predictive of defaults in the longer term, and hence might be lagging. Consequently they may not, on their own, signal significant increases in credit risk in a timely manner.
  - (e) Consider whether the use of behavioural indicators is appropriate for the type of product being assessed, e.g. if a loan has only back-ended payments, behavioural indicators based on timeliness of payment will not be appropriate.
- An entity is required to consider all information available without undue cost and effort and it should not be limited by the information that is available internally. For example, an entity should consider using third-party information from sources such as credit bureaus. However, information that is available to entities will vary across jurisdictions.
- When making the assessment of significant increases in credit risk, an entity should consider the possibility of segmenting the portfolio into groups of financial instruments with shared credit characteristics in such a way that similar indicators of credit risk could be used to identify increases in credit risk for specific sub-portfolios.
- It would not be appropriate to use the above behavioural indicators for the purposes of identifying low credit risk assets in accordance with paragraph 5.5.10

of IFRS 9 (see 5.5.4.A below), on the basis that such measures would not constitute a globally accepted definition of low credit risk as required by IFRS 9.

Other behavioural indicators, beyond those mentioned above, including items such as the level of cash advances, changes in expected payment patterns (e.g. moving from full payment to something less than full payment), and higher-than-expected utilisation of the facility, were raised at the meeting. Individually, these kinds of behaviours may not be determinative of a significant increase in credit risk but, when observed together, they may prove to be more indicative. By combining these indicators, an entity has the potential to transfer assets between stage 1 and stage 2 more meaningfully.

We also note that that one of the challenges with using behavioural information is that it depends on the starting point. That is, if the obligor's risk of default initially is consistent with a super-prime rating, the kind of deteriorating behaviour noted above would likely signal a significant shift. However, if the obligor originally had a sub-prime rating, then such behaviour might not indicate a significant increase in risk. Also, while indicators that are more lagging may show a greater correlation with subsequent default, they are also likely to be less forward-looking and so make it more necessary to apply an additional collective approach.

Although a probability of default approach may seem more sophisticated and forward looking, it is still generally fed by behavioural information, even if it is combined, segmented and modelled in a more sophisticated way. If the only borrower-specific information is his behaviour, a forward looking portfolio overlay will generally be required, whether a PD or a behavioural approach is used.

5.5.3 *What is significant?*

The assessment of whether credit risk has significantly increased depends, critically, on an interpretation of the word 'significant'. Some constituents who commented on the 2013 Exposure Draft requested the IASB to quantify the term significant, however, the IASB decided not to do so, for the following reasons: *[IFRS 9.BC5.171, BC5.172]*

- specifying a fixed percentage change in the risk of default would require all entities to use the risk of default approach. As not all entities (apart from regulated financial institutions) use PDs as an explicit input, this would have increased the costs and effort for those entities that do not use such an approach; and
- defining the amount of change in the risk of a default occurring would be arbitrary and this would depend on the type of products, maturities and initial credit risk.

The standard emphasises that the determination of the significance of the change in the risk of a default occurring depends on:

- the original credit risk at initial recognition: the same absolute change in PD for a financial instrument with a lower initial credit risk will be more significant than those with a higher initial credit risk (see 5.5.4.E below and Example 50.29); *[IFRS 9.B5.5.9]* and
- the expected life or term structure: the risk of a default occurring for financial instruments with similar credit risk increases the longer the expected life of the financial instruments. Due to the relationship between the expected life and the risk of a default occurring, an entity cannot simply compare the absolute risk

of a default occurring over time. For example, if the risk of a default occurring for a financial instrument with an expected life of 10 years at initial recognition is the same after five years, then this indicates that the credit risk has increased. The standard also states that, for financial instruments that have significant payment obligations close to the maturity of the financial instrument (e.g. those where the principal is only repaid at maturity), the risk of a default occurring may not necessarily decrease as time passes. In such cases, an entity needs to consider other qualitative factors. We note, however, that while the risk of default may decrease less quickly for an instrument with payment obligations throughout its contractual life, normally, the risk of default will still decrease as maturity approaches. *[IFRS 9.B5.5.10, B5.5.11]*.

Some of these challenges are illustrated by examining the historical levels of default associated with the credit ratings of agencies, such as Standard & Poor's.

- It is apparent that the PDs increase at a geometrical, rather than an arithmetic, rate as the credit ratings decline. Hence, the absolute increase in the PD between two relatively low risk credit ratings is considerably less than between two relatively higher risk ratings.
- The relative increase in PD between each of these ratings might be considered significant, since most involve a doubling or trebling of the PD. In contrast, because credit rating is an art rather than a science, the smaller changes in credit risk associated with the plus or minus notches in the grading system are less likely to be viewed as significant.
- In addition, as the time horizon increases, the PDs also increase across all credit ratings (i.e. the PD increases with a longer maturity).

The majority of credit exposures that are assessed for significant credit deterioration will not have been rated by a credit rating agency. However, the same logic will apply when entities have developed their own PD models and are able to classify their exposure by PD levels. It is important to stress that the approach required by the standard is more holistic and qualitative than is necessarily captured by external credit ratings, which are adjusted for discrete events and may not reflect gradual degradations in credit quality. External credit ratings should not, therefore, be used on their own but only in conjunction with other qualitative information. The same point can of course be made about the use of internal credit ratings, especially if they are only reassessed on an annual basis.

The determination of what is significant will, for the larger banks, be influenced by the guidance issued by banking regulators (see 5.6.1 below). This assessment remains very much work in progress, as banks are currently testing different sets of triggers and these triggers will have to be set differently for retail and corporate businesses, and also by portfolio and country and taking into account the level of risk at origination.

Given the exponential shape of the PD curve relative to ratings, some banks are considering that a bigger downgrade, as measured by the number of grades, would be significant for a higher quality loan than for one with a lower quality. The extent to which this is appropriate will depend on how the different grades map to PDs.

Also, the calibration of a significant deterioration has to take into account the fact that PD multiples for very good ratings only represent very small movements in absolute risk, whereas the same multiple applied to bad ratings can represent a significant change in the absolute amount of PD. A number of banks have sought to remove 'noise' from the assessment of what is significant by excluding any increase in absolute risk below a certain threshold level, such as (for instance) 50 basis points per year.

Banks are also exploring various metrics to assess the effect of different approaches to assess significant increase in credit risk and for management information. Examples include the volume of stage 2 assets compared to the total portfolio and compared to 12-months of lifetime expected losses, the volume of movement (back and forth) between stages 1 and 2, the amount of assets that jump directly from stage 1 to stage 3, the proportion of assets in stage 3 which went via stage 2, and how long assets were in stage 2 before moving to stage 3.

5.5.4 Operational simplifications

When assessing significant increases in credit risk, there are a number of operational simplifications available. These are discussed below.

5.5.4.A Low credit risk operational simplification

The standard contains an important simplification that, if a financial instrument has a low credit risk, then an entity is allowed to assume at the reporting date that no significant increases in credit risk have occurred. The low credit risk concept was intended, by the IASB, to provide relief for entities from tracking changes in the credit risk of high quality financial instruments. This simplification is only optional and the low credit risk simplification can be elected on an instrument-by-instrument basis. *[IFRS 9.BC5.184]*.

This is a change from the 2013 Exposure Draft, in which a low risk exposure was deemed not to have suffered significant deterioration in credit risk. *[IFRS 9.BC5.181, BC5.182, BC5.183]*. The amendment to make the simplification optional was made in response to requests from constituents, including regulators. The Basel Committee guidance (see 5.6.1 below) considers the use of the low credit risk simplification a low-quality implementation of the ECL model and that the use of this exemption should be limited, except for holdings in securities.

For low risk instruments for which the simplification is used, the entity would recognise an allowance based on 12-month ECLs. *[IFRS 9.5.5.10]*. However, if a financial instrument is not or no longer considered to have low credit risk at the reporting date, it does not follow that the entity is required to recognise lifetime ECLs. In such instances, the entity has to assess whether there has been a significant increase in credit risk since initial recognition which requires the recognition of lifetime ECLs. *[IFRS 9.5.5.24]*.

The standard states that a financial instrument is considered to have low credit risk if: *[IFRS 9.5.5.22]*

- the financial instrument has a low risk of default;
- the borrower has a strong capacity to meet its contractual cash flow obligations in the near term; and
- adverse changes in economic and business conditions in the longer term may, but will not necessarily, reduce the ability of the borrower to fulfil its contractual cash flow obligations.

A financial instrument is not considered to have low credit risk simply because it has a low risk of loss (e.g. for a collateralised loan, if the value of the collateral is more than the amount lent (see 5.4.7 above)) or it has lower risk of default compared to the entity's other financial instruments or relative to the credit risk of the jurisdiction within which the entity operates. *[IFRS 9.B5.5.22]*.

The description of low credit risk is equivalent to investment grade quality assets, equivalent to a Standard and Poor's rating of BBB– or better, Moody's rating of Baa3 or better and Fitch's rating of BBB– or better. When applying the low credit risk simplification, financial instruments are not required to be externally rated. However, the IASB's intention was to use a globally comparable notion of low credit risk instead of a level of risk determined, for example, by an entity or jurisdiction's view of risk based on entity-specific or jurisdictional factors. *[IFRS 9.BC5.188]*. Therefore, an entity may use its internal credit ratings to assess what is low credit risk as long as this is consistent with the globally understood definition of low credit risk (i.e. investment grade) or the market's expectations of what is deemed to be low credit risk, taking into consideration the terms and conditions of the financial instruments being assessed. *[IFRS 9.B5.5.23]*.

The Consultative guidance of the Basel Committee guidance (see 5.6.1 below) states that the investment grade category used by ratings agencies is not considered homogeneous enough to be automatically considered low credit risk, and internationally active and sophisticated banks are expected to rely primarily on their own credit assessments.

In practice, entities with internal credit ratings will attempt to map their internal rating to the external credit ratings and definitions, such as Standard & Poor's, Moody's and Fitch. The description of the credit quality ratings by these major rating agencies are illustrated below.[32]

Figure 50.4 External credit ratings and definitions from the 3 major rating agencies

Standard & Poor's	*Moody's*	*Fitch*
Investment grade would usually refer to categories AAA to BBB (with BBB– being lowest investment grade considered by market participants).	Investment grade would usually refer to categories Aaa to Baa (with Baa3 being lowest investment grade considered by market participants).	Investment grade would usually refer to categories AAA to BBB (with BBB– being lowest investment grade considered by market participants).
BBB **Adequate capacity** to meet financial commitments, but more subject to **adverse economic conditions**.	**Baa** Obligations rated Baa are judged to be medium-grade and subject to moderate credit risk and as such may possess certain speculative characteristics.	**BBB: Good credit quality** Indicates that expectations of **default risk are currently low**. The capacity for payment of financial commitments is considered adequate but adverse business or economic conditions are more likely to impair this capacity.
The dividing line between investment grade and speculative grade		
BB Less vulnerable in the near-term but faces major on-going uncertainties to adverse business, financial and economic conditions.	**Ba** Obligations rated Ba are judged to be speculative and are subject to substantial credit risk.	**BB: Speculative** Indicates an elevated vulnerability to default risk, particularly in the event of adverse changes in business or economic conditions over time; however, business or financial flexibility exists which supports the servicing of financial commitments.

Examining the historical levels of default associated with the credit ratings of agencies such as Standard & Poor's, the PD of a BBB-rated loan is approximately treble that of one that is rated A. Hence, many entities would consider the increase in credit risk to be significant, if the low risk simplification is not used.

The low credit risk simplification will not be relevant if an entity originates or purchases a financial instrument with a credit risk which is already non-investment grade. Similarly, this simplification will also have limited use when the financial instrument is originated or purchased with a credit quality that is marginally better than a non-investment grade (i.e. at the bottom of the investment grade rating), because any credit deterioration into the non-investment grade rating would require the entity to assess whether the increase in credit risk has been significant.

Partly because of the Basel Committee guidance, most sophisticated banks intend to apply the low risk simplification only to securities. It is yet to be seen whether less sophisticated banks will use this operational simplification widely for their loan portfolios. Investors that hold externally rated debt instruments are more likely to rely on external rating agencies data and use the low credit risk simplification. However, some sophisticated banks are intending not to use it at all, preferring to use the same criteria as for other exposures. It is also important to emphasise that although ratings are forward-looking, it is sometimes suggested that changes in credit ratings may not be reflected in a timely matter. Therefore, entities may have to take account of expected change in ratings in assessing whether exposures are low risk.

The following example from the standard illustrates the application of the low credit risk simplification. *[IFRS 9 IG Example 4, IE24-IE28].*

Example 50.26: Public investment-grade bond

Company A is a large listed national logistics company. The only debt in the capital structure is a five-year public bond with a restriction on further borrowing as the only bond covenant. Company A reports quarterly to its shareholders. Entity B is one of many investors in the bond. Entity B considers the bond to have low credit risk at initial recognition in accordance with paragraph 5.5.10 of IFRS 9. This is because the bond has a low risk of default and Company A is considered to have a strong capacity to meet its obligations in the near term. Entity B's expectations for the longer term are that adverse changes in economic and business conditions may, but will not necessarily, reduce Company A's ability to fulfil its obligations on the bond. In addition, at initial recognition the bond had an internal credit rating that is correlated to a global external credit rating of investment grade.

At the reporting date, Entity B's main credit risk concern is the continuing pressure on the total volume of sales that has caused Company A's operating cash flows to decrease.

Because Entity B relies only on quarterly public information and does not have access to private credit risk information (because it is a bond investor), its assessment of changes in credit risk is tied to public announcements and information, including updates on credit perspectives in press releases from rating agencies.

Entity B applies the low credit risk simplification in paragraph 5.5.10 of IFRS 9. Accordingly, at the reporting date, Entity B evaluates whether the bond is considered to have low credit risk using all reasonable and supportable information that is available without undue cost or effort. In making that evaluation, Entity B reassesses the internal credit rating of the bond and concludes that the bond is no longer equivalent to an investment grade rating because:

(a) The latest quarterly report of Company A revealed a quarter-on-quarter decline in revenues of 20 per cent and in operating profit by 12 per cent.

(b) Rating agencies have reacted negatively to a profit warning by Company A and put the credit rating under review for possible downgrade from investment grade to non-investment grade. However, at the reporting date the external credit risk rating was unchanged.

(c) The bond price has also declined significantly, which has resulted in a higher yield to maturity. Entity B assesses that the bond prices have been declining as a result of increases in Company A's credit risk. This is because the market environment has not changed (for example, benchmark interest rates, liquidity, etc. are unchanged) and comparison with the bond prices of peers shows that the reductions are probably company specific (instead of being, for example, changes in benchmark interest rates that are not indicative of company-specific credit risk).

While Company A currently has the capacity to meet its commitments, the large uncertainties arising from its exposure to adverse business and economic conditions have increased the risk of a default occurring on the bond. As a result of the factors described above, Entity B determines that the bond does not have low credit risk at the reporting date. As a result, Entity B needs to determine whether the increase in credit risk since initial recognition has been significant. On the basis of its assessment, Company B determines that the credit risk has increased significantly since initial recognition and that a loss allowance at an amount equal to lifetime ECLs should be recognised in accordance with paragraph 5.5.3 of IFRS 9.

Some of the challenges in assessing whether there has been a significant increase in credit risk (including the use of the low credit risk simplification) and estimating the ECLs, are illustrated in the following example. It illustrates different ways of identifying a significant change in credit quality and different input parameters for calculating ECLs for a European government bond, which result in very different outcomes and volatility of the IFRS 9 ECL allowance. It should also be stressed that the default rates provided by external rating agencies are historical information. Entities need to understand the sources of these historical default rates and update the data for current and forward-looking information (see 5.4.8 above) when measuring ECLs or assessing credit deterioration.

Example 50.27: Use of credit ratings and/or CDS spreads to determine whether there have been significant increases in credit risk and to estimate expected credit losses

Introduction

A significant challenge in applying the IFRS 9 impairment requirements to quoted bonds is that the credit ratings assigned by agencies such as Standard & Poor's (S&P), and the historical experience of losses by rating grade, can differ significantly with the view of the market, as reflected in, for instance, credit default swap (CDS) spreads and bond spreads.

To illustrate the challenges of applying IFRS 9 to debt securities, we have examined how the ECL could be determined for a real bond issued by a European government on 16 September 2008 and due to mature in 2024. For three dates, we applied the IFRS 9 calculations to this bond, which is assumed to have been acquired at inception. In January 2009, the Standard & Poor's credit rating of the government was AA+, as at origination, but by January 2012, its rating was downgraded to A. The bond was further downgraded to BBB– in March 2014 before recovery to BBB in May 2014.

Three approaches

Shown below are three approaches:

- Approach 1: Use of S&P credit ratings both to determine whether the bond has significantly increased in credit risk and to estimate ECLs.
- Approach 2: Use of S&P credit ratings to determine whether the bond has significantly increased in credit risk and CDS spreads to estimate ECLs.
- Approach 3: Use of CDS spreads both to determine whether the bond has significantly increased in credit risk and to estimate ECLs.

Based on the historical corporate PDs from each assessed S&P credit rating (approach 1) and based on the CDS spreads (approaches 2 and 3), the loan loss percentages were calculated below. For the calculations, an often used LGD of 60% was applied. (Because the LGD represents a percentage of the present value of the gross carrying amount, this example does not illustrate the effect of the time value of money).

The percentage loss allowances were, as follows:

	Credit ratings	Historical 12-month PD based on ratings	12-month PD based on CDS spread	Lifetime PD based on CDS spread	Percentage of loss allowance		
					Approach 1	Approach 2	Approach 3
1 January 2009	AA+	0.02%	0.44%	12.81%	–	–	–
31 January 2009	AA+	0.02%	1.84%	30.48%	0.01	1.10	18.29
31 January 2012	A	0.06%	4.96%	51,48%	0.04	2.98	30.89
31 March 2014	BBB–	0.31%	0.57%	23.01%	0.18	0.34	13.81

Approach 1

According to the credit ratings, the bond was investment grade throughout this period. Hence, using the low risk simplification, the loss allowance would have been based on 12-month ECLs. Using the corporate historical default rates implied by the credit ratings and an assumption of 60% LGD to calculate the ECLs, the 12-month allowance would have increased from 0.01% on 31 January 2009 to 0.04% three years later, increasing to 0.18% by 31 March 2014. It should be stressed that the historical default rates implied by credit ratings are historical rates for corporate debt and so they would not, without adjustment, satisfy the requirements of the standard. IFRS 9 requires the calculation of ECLs, based on current conditions and forecasts of future conditions, to be based on reasonable and supportable information. This is likely to include market indicators such as CDS and bond spreads, as illustrated by Approach 2.

Approach 2

In contrast to Approach 1, using credit default swap spreads to calculate the ECLs and the same assumption of 60% LGD to calculate the ECLs, the 12-month allowance would have increased from 1.1% on 31 January 2009 to 2.98% three years later, declining to 0.34% by 31 March 2014. The default rates implied by the CDSs are significantly higher than would have been expected given the ratings of these bonds. The loss allowances are, correspondingly, very much higher and very volatile. It might be argued that CDS spreads are too responsive to short term market sentiment to calculate long term ECLs, but it may appear difficult to find other reasonable and supportable information to adjust these rates so as to dampen the effects of market volatility.

Approach 3

Credit ratings are often viewed by the market as lagging indicators. For these bonds, the ratings are difficult to reconcile with the default probabilities as assessed by the markets. It might be argued that it is not sufficient to focus only on credit ratings when assessing whether assets are low risk since, according to CDS spreads, the bond was not low risk at any time in the period covered in this example, as it showed a significant increase in 1 year PD after inception (based on CDS spreads). The 1 year PDs increased from 0.44% on issue to 1.84% by 31 January 2009. Assessing the bond as requiring a lifetime ECL at all three dates, based on CDS spreads, would have given much higher loss allowances of 18.29%, 30.89% and 13.81%.

The counter-view might be that CDS spreads are too volatile to provide a sound basis for determining significant deterioration. Perhaps the best way to make the assessment of whether a bond has increased significantly in credit risk is to use more than one source of data and to take account of the qualitative indicators as described in the standard.

Conclusion

The calculated ECL figures differ significantly depending on the approach taken as to how to determine a significant change in credit quality and the parameters used for the calculation. Those based on CDS spreads are both large and very volatile, reflecting the investor uncertainty during the period, when the possibility of default depended more on the political will of the European Union to maintain the integrity of the Eurozone than the economic forecasts for the particular country. As a result, the disparity between the effect of the use of credit grades and CDSs is probably more marked than for most other security investments. Nevertheless, the same challenges will be found with other securities, albeit on a smaller scale.

5.5.4.B *Past due status and more than 30 days past due rebuttable presumption*

The IASB is concerned that past due information is a lagging indicator. Typically, credit risk increases significantly before a financial instrument becomes past due or other lagging borrower-specific factors (for example, a modification or restructuring) are observed. Consequently, when reasonable and supportable information that is more forward-looking than past due information is available without undue cost or effort, it must be used to assess changes in credit risk and an entity cannot rely solely on past due information. *[IFRS 9.5.5.11, B5.5.2]*. However, the IASB acknowledged that many entities manage credit risk on the basis of information about past due status and have a limited ability to assess credit risk on an instrument-by-instrument basis in more detail on a timely basis. *[IFRS 9 BC5.192]*. Therefore, if more forward-looking information (either on an individual or collective basis) is not available without undue cost or effort, an entity may use past due information to assess changes in credit risks. *[IFRS 9.5.5.11]*.

This simplification includes a the rebuttable presumption that the credit risk on a financial asset has increased significantly since initial recognition when contractual payments are more than 30 days past due. *[IFRS 9.5.5.11]*. The IASB decided that this rebuttable presumption was required to ensure that the application of the simplification does not result in an entity reverting to an incurred loss model. *[IFRS 9.BC5.190]*.

The more than 30 days past due rebuttable presumption is intended to serve as a backstop even when forward-looking information is used (e.g. macroeconomic factors on a portfolio level). *[IFRS 9.B5.5.19]*. This presumption would therefore not apply if significant increases in credit risk have already occurred before contractual payments are more than 30 days past due.

Moreover, as already stressed earlier, the standard is clear that an entity cannot align the definition and criteria used to identify significant increases in credit risk (and the resulting recognition of lifetime ECLs) to when a financial asset is regarded as credit-impaired or to an entity's internal definition of default. *[IFRS 9.B5.5.21]*. An entity should normally identify significant increases in credit risk and recognise lifetime ECLs before default occurs or the financial asset becomes credit-impaired, either on an individual or collective basis (see 5.5.5 below).

An entity can rebut the presumption if it has reasonable and supportable information that is available without undue cost or effort, that demonstrates that credit risk has not increased significantly even though contractual payments are more than 30 days past due. *[IFRS 9.5.5.11]*. Such evidence may include knowledge that a missed non-payment is because of administrative oversight rather than financial difficulty of the borrower, or historical information that suggests significant increases in credit risks only occur when payments are more than 60 days past due. *[IFRS 9.B5.5.20]*.

Similar to the low credit risk simplification discussed above (see 5.5.4.A above), the Basel Committee guidance (see 5.6.1 below) has proposed that sophisticated banks should only use the 30 days past due simplification rarely for their loan portfolios.

Our observations of emerging practice amongst the more sophisticated banks is that 30 days past due rebuttable presumption is likely to be used as a backstop, as opposed to a primary driver of significant increase in credit risk. Also, most of these banks do not intend to rebut the 30 days past due presumption and those who do are more likely to do so only for credit card facilities.

Given the wording in the standard, it will be interesting to see whether any less sophisticated banks will argue that they do not have, or are unable to use, more forward-looking indicators (either at an individual or a collective level) to supplement past due status.

5.5.4.C *12-month risk as an approximation for change in lifetime risk*

In determining whether there has been a significant increase in credit risk, an entity must assess the change in the risk of default occurring over the expected life of the financial instrument. Despite this, the standard states that: '...changes in the risk of a default occurring over the next 12 months may be a reasonable approximation...unless circumstances indicate that a lifetime assessment is necessary'. *[IFRS 9.B5.5.13]*.

The IASB observed in its Basis for Conclusions that changes in the risk of a default occurring within the next 12 months generally should be a reasonable approximation of changes in the risk of a default occurring over the remaining life of a financial instrument and thus would not be inconsistent with the requirements. Also, some entities use a 12-month PD measure for prudential regulatory requirements and these entities can continue to use their existing systems and methodologies as a starting point for determining significant increases in credit risk, thus reducing the costs of implementation. *[IFRS 9.BC5.178]*.

However, for some financial instruments, or in some circumstances, the use of changes in the risk of default occurring over the next 12 months may not be appropriate to determine whether lifetime ECLs should be recognised. For a financial instrument with a maturity longer than 12 months, the standard gives the following examples: *[IFRS 9.B5.5.14]*

- the financial instrument only has significant payment obligations beyond the next 12 months;
- changes in relevant macroeconomic or other credit-related factors occur that are not adequately reflected in the risk of a default occurring in the next 12 months; or
- changes in credit-related factors only have an impact on the credit risk of the financial instrument (or have a more pronounced effect) beyond 12 months.

At its meeting on 16 September 2015, the ITG members discussed the use of changes in 12-month risk of default as a surrogate for changes in lifetime risk and commented as follows:

- An entity would be expected to complete a robust analysis up front in order to support the conclusion that changes in the 12-month risk of a default occurring was a reasonable approximation for the assessment of changes in the lifetime risk of default occurring.
- The level of initial analysis required would depend on the specific type of financial instrument being considered. Consequently in some cases, a qualitative analysis would suffice whereas in less clear-cut cases, a quantitative analysis may be necessary. Also, it may be appropriate to segregate portfolios (e.g. by maturity) in order to facilitate the analysis for groups of similar financial instruments.
- An entity would need to be satisfied on an ongoing basis that the use of changes in the 12-month risk of a default occurring continued to be a reasonable approximation for changes in the lifetime risk of a default occurring.

At the meeting, the ITG members also discussed:

- The appropriate type of review that should be undertaken on an ongoing basis. While a quantitative review would not necessarily be required, it would depend on the specific facts and circumstances. One way of approaching an ongoing review would be as follows:
  - (a) identify the key factors that would affect the appropriateness of using changes in the 12-month risk of a default occurring as an approximation of changes in the lifetime risk of default occurring;
  - (b) monitor these factors on an ongoing basis as part of a qualitative review of circumstances; and
  - (c) consider whether any changes in those factors indicated that changes in the 12-month risk of a default occurring was no longer an appropriate proxy for changes in a lifetime risk of default occurring.
- If it were determined that changes in the 12-month risk of a default occurring were no longer a reasonable approximation for the assessment of changes in the lifetime risk of a default occurring, an entity would be required to determine an appropriate approach to capture changes in the lifetime risk of a default occurring.
- The importance to emphasise that the guidance which permits an entity to use changes in the 12-month risk of a default as an approximation for the lifetime risk of default, is only relevant for the assessment of significant increases in credit risk and does *not* relate to the measurement of ECLs. When an entity is required to measure lifetime ECLs, that measurement must always reflect the lifetime risk of a default occurring.
- IFRS 9 does not prescribe how an entity should determine whether the use of changes in the 12-month risk of a default was an appropriate proxy for assessing changes in the lifetime risk of a default. However, it was noted that entities are required to disclose how they make the assessment of significant increases in credit risk, in accordance with IFRS 7.

Some of the more sophisticated banks currently intend to use the 12-month risk of default for assessing if there has been a significant increase in credit risk. Movements in a 12-month risk of default are, for most products and conditions, strongly correlated with movements in the lifetime risk. However, these banks appreciate that 12-month PDs may need to be adjusted or calibrated to reflect the longer term macroeconomic outlook. Also, there are products such as interest-only mortgages and those with an introductory period in which no repayments are required, where additional procedures may need to be implemented in order to ensure that they are transferred to stage 2 appropriately.

5.5.4.D Assessment at the counterparty level

As indicated by Example 7 in the Implementation Guidance of IFRS 9, assessment of significant deterioration in credit risk can be made at the level of the counterparty rather than the individual financial instrument. Such assessment at the counterparty level is only allowed if the outcome would not be different to the outcome if the financial instruments had been individually assessed. *[IFRS 9.BC5.168]*. In certain circumstances, assessment at the counterparty level would not be consistent with the impairment requirements. Both these situations are illustrated in the example below, based on Example 7 in the Implementation Guidance for the standard. *[IFRS 9 IG Example 7, IE43-IE47].*

Example 50.28: Counterparty assessment of credit risk

Scenario 1

In 2010 Bank A granted a loan of $10,000 with a contractual term of 15 years to Company Q when the company had an internal credit risk rating of 4 on a scale of 1 (lowest credit risk) to 10 (highest credit risk). The risk of a default occurring increases exponentially as the credit risk rating deteriorates so, for example, the difference between credit risk rating grades 1 and 2 is smaller than the difference between credit risk rating grades 2 and 3. In 2015, when Company Q had an internal credit risk rating of 6, Bank A issued another loan to Company Q for $5,000 with a contractual term of 10 years. In 2017 Company Q fails to retain its contract with a major customer and correspondingly experiences a large decline in its revenue. Bank A considers that as a result of losing the contract, Company Q will have a significantly reduced ability to meet its loan obligations and changes its internal credit risk rating to 8.

Bank A assesses credit risk on a counterparty level for credit risk management purposes and determines that the increase in Company Q's credit risk is significant. Although Bank A did not perform an individual assessment of changes in the credit risk on each loan since its initial recognition, assessing the credit risk on a counterparty level and recognising lifetime ECLs on all loans granted to Company Q, meets the objective of the impairment requirements as stated in paragraph 5.5.4 of IFRS 9. This is because, even since the most recent loan was originated, its credit risk has increased significantly. The counterparty assessment would therefore achieve the same result as assessing the change in credit risk for each loan individually.

Scenario 2

Bank A granted a loan of $150,000 with a contractual term of 20 years to Company X in 2010 when the company had an internal credit risk rating of 4. During 2014 economic conditions deteriorate and demand for Company X's products has declined significantly. As a result of the reduced cash flows from lower sales, Company X could not make full payment of its loan instalment to Bank A. Bank A re-assesses Company X's internal credit risk rating, and determines it to be 7 at the reporting date. Bank A considered the change in credit risk on the loan, including considering the change in the internal credit risk rating, and determines that there has been a significant increase in credit risk and recognises lifetime ECLs on the loan of $150,000.

Despite the recent downgrade of the internal credit risk rating, Bank A grants another loan of $50,000 to Company X in 2016 with a contractual term of 5 years, taking into consideration the higher credit risk at that date.

The fact that Company X's credit risk (assessed on a counterparty basis) has previously been assessed to have increased significantly, does not result in lifetime ECLs being recognised on the new loan. This is because the credit risk on the new loan has not increased significantly since the loan was initially recognised. If Bank A only assessed credit risk on a counterparty level, without considering whether the conclusion about changes in credit risk applies to all individual financial instruments provided to the same customer, the objective in paragraph 5.5.4 of IFRS 9 would not be met.

Most banks manage their credit exposures on a counterparty basis and would be keen to use their existing risk management processes where they can. This is particularly the case for those banks who are seeking to use processes such as the use of watch lists to make the assessment. However, this will be challenging if the standard only allows use of a counterparty basis when it can be demonstrated that it would make no difference from making the assessment at an individual instrument level. It may be necessary for these banks to add procedures to track increase in the risk of default at the instrument level in order to comply with the standard.

5.5.4.E Determining maximum initial credit risk for a portfolio

The IFRS 9 credit risk assessment that determines whether a financial instrument should attract a lifetime ECL allowance, or only a 12-month ECL allowance, is based on whether there has been a *relative* increase in credit risk. One of the challenges identified by some constituents in responding to the 2013 Exposure Draft is that many credit risk systems monitor *absolute* levels of risk, without tracking the history of individual loans (see 5.5.1 above). To help address this concern the standard contains an approach that turns a relative system into an absolute one, by segmenting the portfolio sufficiently by loan quality at origination.

As indicated by Illustrative Example 6 in the Implementation Guidance of IFRS 9 on which Example 50.29 below is based, an entity can determine the maximum initial credit risk accepted for portfolios with similar credit risks on initial recognition. *IFRS 9 IG Example 6, IE40-IE42].* Thereby, an entity may be able to establish an absolute threshold for recognising lifetime ECLs.

Example 50.29: Comparison to maximum initial credit risk

Bank A has two portfolios of automobile loans with similar terms and conditions in Region W. Bank A's policy on financing decisions for each loan is based on an internal credit rating system that considers a customer's credit history, payment behaviour on other products with Bank A and other factors, and assigns an internal credit risk rating from 1 (lowest credit risk) to 10 (highest credit risk) to each loan on origination. The risk of a default occurring increases exponentially as the credit risk rating deteriorates so, for example, the difference between credit risk rating grades 1 and 2 is smaller than the difference between credit risk rating grades 2 and 3. Loans in Portfolio 1 were only offered to existing customers with a similar internal credit risk rating and at initial recognition all loans were rated 3 or 4 on the internal rating scale. Bank A determines that the maximum initial credit risk rating at initial recognition it would accept for Portfolio 1 is an internal rating of 4. Loans in Portfolio 2 were offered to customers that responded to an advertisement for automobile loans and the internal credit risk ratings of these customers range between 4 and 7 on the internal rating scale. Bank A never originates an automobile loan with an internal credit risk rating worse than 7 (i.e. with an internal rating of 8-10).

For the purposes of assessing whether there have been significant increases in credit risk, Bank A determines that all loans in Portfolio 1 had a similar initial credit risk. It determines that given the risk of default reflected in its internal risk rating grades, a change in internal rating from 3 to 4 would not represent a significant increase in credit risk but that there has been a significant increase in credit risk on any loan in this portfolio that has an internal rating worse than 5. This means that Bank A does not have to know the initial credit rating of each loan in the portfolio to assess the change in credit risk since initial recognition. It only has to determine whether the credit risk is worse than 5 at the reporting date to determine whether lifetime ECLs should be recognised in accordance with paragraph 5.5.3 of IFRS 9.

However, determining the maximum initial credit risk accepted at initial recognition for Portfolio 2 at an internal credit risk rating of 7, would not meet the objective of the requirements as stated in paragraph 5.5.4 of IFRS 9. This is because Bank A determines that significant increases in credit risk arise not only when credit risk increases above the level at which an entity would originate new financial assets (i.e. when the internal rating is worse than 7). Although Bank A never originates an automobile loan with an internal credit rating worse than 7, the initial credit risk on loans in Portfolio 2 is not of sufficiently similar credit risk at initial recognition to apply the approach used for Portfolio 1. This means that Bank A cannot simply compare the credit risk at the reporting date with the lowest credit quality at initial recognition (for example, by comparing the internal credit risk rating of loans in Portfolio 2 with an internal credit risk rating of 7) to determine whether credit risk has increased significantly because the initial credit quality of loans in the portfolio is too diverse. For example, if a loan initially had a credit risk rating of 4 the credit risk on the loan may have increased significantly if its internal credit risk rating changes to 6.

At its September 2015 meeting, the ITG discussed identification of a significant increase of credit risk for a portfolio of retail loans with identical pricing and contractual terms (see 5.5.2 above). However, in the fact pattern, the same terms were applied to customers across a broad credit quality band. The ITG members generally agreed that it is not appropriate to assume that just because loans are priced the same that they share similar risk characteristics.

5.5.5 Collective assessment

Banks have hundreds of thousands, or even millions, of small exposures to retail customers and small businesses. Much of the information available to monitor them is based on whether payments are past due and behavioural information that is mostly historical rather than forward looking. As a result such exposures tend to be managed on an aggregated basis, combining past due and behavioural data with historical statistical experience and sometimes macroeconomic indicators, such as interest rates and unemployment levels, that tend to correlate with future defaults. Also, even when exposures are managed on an individual basis, as is the case for most commercial loans, the information used to manage them may not be sufficiently forward looking to comply with the standard.

To address these concerns, the standard introduces the idea of making a collective assessment for financial assets, to determine if there has been a significant increase in credit risk, if an entity cannot make the assessment adequately on an individual instrument level. It is, however, worth noting that the language on when this is required is not entirely consistent within the standard. Paragraph B5.5.1 states that 'it *may be* necessary to perform the assessment' on a collective basis, which is consistent with the requirement in paragraph 5.5.11, that 'an entity cannot rely on solely on past due information if reasonable and supportable forward-looking information is available without undue cost or effort'. However, paragraph B5.5.4 states that if 'an entity does not have reasonable and supportable information that is available without undue cost or effort to measure lifetime ECLs on an individual instrument basis...lifetime credit losses *shall be* recognised on a collective basis' (emphasis added for each quotation). Banking regulators will probably ensure that this 'shall be' wording will be applied, at least for more sophisticated banks (see 5.1.6 above and 5.6.1 below).

That raises a second concern: once significant deterioration has been identified for a portfolio, whether the entire portfolio would have to be measured using lifetime ECLs. This outcome would result in sudden, massive increases in provisions as soon as conditions begin to decline. Consequently the Board, in finalising the standard, also had to devise a method by which only a segment or portion of the portfolio would be changed to lifetime ECLs.

Illustrative Example 5 in the Implementation Guidance for the standard illustrates how an entity may assess whether its individual assessment should be complemented with a collective one whenever the information at individual level is not sufficiently comprehensive and up-to-date. The following examples have been adapted from that guidance.

As a benchmark, Scenario 1 (an individual assessment) illustrates a situation where a bank has sufficient information at individual exposure level to identify a significant deterioration of credit quality.

Example 50.30: Individual assessment in relation to responsiveness to changes in credit risk

The bank assesses each of its mortgage loans on a monthly basis by means of an automated behavioural scoring process based on current and historical past due statuses, levels of customer indebtedness, loan-to-value (LTV) measures, customer behaviour on other financial instruments with the bank, the loan size and the time since the origination of the loan. It is said that historical data indicates a strong correlation between the value of residential property and the default rates for mortgages.

The bank updates the LTV measures on a regular basis through an automated process that re-estimates property values using recent sales in each post code area and reasonable and supportable forward-looking information that is available without undue cost or effort. Therefore, an increased risk of a default occurring due to an expected decline in residential property value adjusts the behavioural scores and the Bank is therefore able to identify significant increases in credit risk on individual customers before a mortgage becomes past due if there has been a deterioration in the behavioural score.

The example concludes that if the bank is unable to update behavioural scores to reflect the expected declines in property prices, it would use reasonable and supportable information that is available without undue cost or effort to undertake a collective assessment to determine the loans on which there has been a significant increase in credit risk since initial recognition and recognize lifetime ECLs for those loans.

It should be noted that, in this example, the main source of forward-looking information is expected future property prices. No account would appear to be taken of other economic data such as future levels of employment or interest rates. We assume that the Board took this approach to make the example simple, but it implies that future property prices are considered to provide a sufficiently good guide to future defaults that it is not necessary to take account of other data as well.

If an entity does not have reasonable and supportable information that is available without undue cost or effort to measure lifetime ECLs on an individual instrument basis, the standard first specifies that it must assess lifetime losses on a collective basis. This exercise must consider comprehensive information that incorporates not only past due data but other relevant credit information, such as forward-looking macroeconomic information. The objective is to approximate the result of using comprehensive credit information that incorporates forward-looking information at an individual instrument level. *[IFRS 9.B5.5.4]*.

Hence, even if a financial asset is normally managed on an individual basis, it should also be assessed collectively (i.e. based on macroeconomic indicators), if the entity does not have sufficient forward-looking information at the individual level to make the determination. The way that this might work is not very different from the IAS 39 requirement to assess an asset collectively for impairment if it has already been assessed individually and found not to be impaired.

Next, the standard sets out how financial instruments may be grouped together in order to determine whether there has been a significant increase in credit risk. Any instruments assessed collectively must possess shared credit risk characteristics. It is not permitted to aggregate exposures that have different risks and, in so doing, obscure significant increases in risk that may arise on a sub-set of the portfolio. Examples of shared credit risk characteristics given in the standard include, but are not limited to: *[IFRS 9.B5.5.5]*

- instrument type;
- credit risk ratings;
- collateral type;
- date of initial recognition;
- remaining term to maturity;
- industry;
- geographical location of the borrower; and
- the value of collateral relative to the asset (the loan-to-value or LTV ratio), if this would have an impact on the risk of a default occurring.

The standard also states that the basis of aggregation of financial instruments to assess whether there have been changes in credit risk on a collective basis may have to change over time, as new information on groups of, or individual, financial instruments becomes available. *[IFRS 9.B5.5.6]*.

We make the following observations:

- As has been stressed earlier, the assessment of significant deterioration is intended to reflect the risk of default, not the risk of loss, hence collateral should normally be ignored for the assessment. The standard nonetheless explains that the value of collateral relative to the financial asset would be relevant to the collective assessment if it has an impact on the risk of a default occurring. It cites, as an example, non-recourse loans in certain jurisdictions. The question of when such an arrangement would always meet the IFRS 9 classification and measurement characteristics of the asset test is beyond the scope of this chapter. However, the standard also gives, as an example, LTV ratios, without explaining why these are likely to have an impact on the risk of a default occurring. *[IFRS 9.B5.5.5]*. LTV or a house price index may be a useful indicator of significant collective deterioration in a wider range of circumstances than just where the loans are non-recourse. First, house prices are themselves a useful barometer of the economy and so higher LTVs and lower indices correlate with declining economic conditions. Second, loans that were originally advanced at higher LTVs may reflect more aggressive lending practices, with the consequence that such loans may exhibit a higher PD if economic conditions decline. Third, a borrower in trouble with a lower LTV will likely sell his house to redeem the mortgage rather than defaulting on the mortgage (and, conversely, a borrower with a high LTV will have less incentive not to default).
- By date of original recognition, we assume that the Board did not intend that loans should be assessed in separate groups for each year of origination, but that vintages may be aggregated into groups that share similar credit risk characteristics. Loan products and lending practices, including the extent of due diligence, and key ratios, such as the LTV and loan to income, change over time, often reflecting the economic conditions at the time of origination.

The consequence is that loans from particular years are inherently more risky than others. For some banks, this might mean isolating those loans advanced just prior to the financial crisis from those originated earlier or in the subsequent, more careful lending environment. Also, there is a phenomenon termed seasoning, which describes how loans that been serviced adequately for a number of years, over a business cycle, are statistically less likely to default in future, suggesting that older loans should be assessed separately

- Although the examples in the standard refer to regions, as the geographical location of borrowers, the groupings could be much larger, such as by country, or much smaller, if there are particular issues associated with particular towns. Hence the choice of geographical groupings will depend very much on the environment in which a bank operates.
- Other ways that loans might be grouped according to shared credit risk characteristics could include by credit score, by payment history, whether previously restructured or subject to forbearance but subsequently restored to a 12-month ECL allowance, and manner of employment (as featured in Illustrative Example 5 in the Implementation Guidance for the standard under the bottom up assessment discussed in Example 50.31 below).
- The requirement that financial instruments that are assessed together must share similar credit risk characteristics means that a bank may have a substantial number of portfolios. Even a relatively small bank might have six different products (taking into account terms to maturity and types of collateral), three regions and three different vintage groups which, multiplied out, would give fifty four different assessment groups. A larger, global bank might need to monitor many more different portfolios. However, a balance will need to be struck between ensuring that portfolios are small enough to have sufficient homogeneity and yet not so small that there is too little historical data for losses to be reliably estimated.
- Also, the requirement that groupings may have to be amended over time means that there must be put in place processes to reassess whether loans continue to share similar credit risk characteristics. Yet, in practice, there will need to be a sufficient level of stability in the construction of portfolios to allow enough historical data to be gathered for reliable estimation of losses.
- Finally, paragraph B5.5.6 in IFRS 9 adds that, 'if an entity is not able to group financial instruments for which the credit risk is considered to have increased significantly since original recognition based on shared credit risk characteristics, the entity should recognise lifetime ECLs on a portion of the financial assets for which credit risk is deemed to have increased significantly'. As clarified by the IASB in its webcast on forward-looking information in July 2106, it is possible that a bank is aware of differences in sensitivities of credit risk to a change in a particular parameter but is unable to group the assets on the basis of such sensitivity. In such instances, the bank may determine that the expected forward-looking scenario would result in significant increases in credit risk for a certain proportion of its portfolio.

The main standard does not amplify how a collective assessment would be made but Illustrative Example 5 in the Implementation Guidance of IFRS 9 provides two scenarios that explore the approach. *[IFRS 9 IG Example 5, IE29-IE39].*

Example 50.31: Collective assessment in relation to responsiveness to changes in credit risk ('bottom up' approach)

Region Two of Illustrative Example 5 in the Implementation Guidance for the standard introduces the so-called bottom up method. It deals with a mining community within a region that faces unemployment risk due to a decline in coal exports and, consequently, anticipated future mine closures. Although most of the loans are not yet 30 days past due and, further, the borrowers are not yet unemployed, the bank re-segments its mortgage portfolio so as to separate loans to customers employed in the mining industry (based on information in the original mortgage application form).

For these loans (plus any others that are more than 30 days past due), Bank ABC recognises lifetime ECLs, while it continues to recognise 12-month ECLs for the other mortgage loans in the region. Any new loans to borrowers who rely on the coal industry would also attract only a 12-month allowance, until they also demonstrate a significant increase in credit risk.

The bottom up method is described as an example of how to assess credit deterioration by using information that is more forward-looking than past due status. But this example also illustrates that collectively assessed groups may need to change over time, to ensure that they share similar credit risk characteristics. Once the coal mining industry begins to decline, those loans connected with it would no longer share the same risk characteristics as other loans to borrowers in the region, and so would need to be assessed separately. We also note that this example assumes that macroeconomic factors can be linked to the ECLs of a very specific portfolio. Further, in practice, most banks may not have the data to achieve this level of segmentation.

As already described above (possible criteria for grouping of financial assets with similar credit risk characteristics), the bottom up approach could be applied to sub-portfolios differentiated by type of instrument, risk rating, type of collateral, date of initial recognition, remaining term to maturity, industry, geographical location of the borrower, or the LTV ratio. A good example of this approach might be for exposures to borrowers that are expected to suffer major economic difficulties due to war or political upheaval, or borrowers with the weakest credit scores, who are expected to be more sensitive to a change in a relevant macroeconomic factor. In addition, as underwriting standards may vary or change, the portfolio might be sub-divided so as to reflect this. Note that the coal mines closures are, as yet, only anticipated, hence this example helps show how the standard is intended to look much further forward than the consequent unemployment that would probably trigger an IAS 39 impairment provision. The need to look forward is also illustrated in the next example.

Example 50.32: Collective assessment in relation to responsiveness to changes in credit risk ('top down' approach)

For Region Three of Illustrative Example 5 in the Implementation Guidance for the standard, Bank ABC anticipates an increase in defaults following an expected rise in interest rates. We are told that, historically, an increase in interest rates has been a lead indicator of future defaults on floating rate mortgages in the region. The bank regards the portfolio of variable rate mortgage loans in that region to be homogenous and it is incapable of identifying particular sub portfolios on the basis of shared credit risk characteristics. Hence, it uses what is described as a top down method.

Based on historical data, the bank estimates that a 200 basis points rise in interest rates will cause a significant increase in credit risk on 20 per cent of the mortgages. As a result, presumably because the bank expects a 200 basis points rise in rates, it recognises lifetime ECLs on 20 per cent of the portfolio (along with those loans that are more than 30 days past due) and 12-month ECLs on the remainder of mortgages in the region.

The challenge posed by the top down method is how to calculate the percentage of loans that have significantly deteriorated. That a rise in interest rates will likely lead to a significant deterioration in credit risk for some floating rate borrowers, is not controversial. But working out whether they make up 5 per cent, 20 per cent or 35 per cent of the portfolio would appear to be more of an art than science, and no two banks are likely to arrive at the same figure.

The IASB brought some useful clarification on this example in its July 2016 webcast on forward-looking information:

- First, they clarified that one financial instrument cannot exist in stage 1 and in stage 2 at the same time. Therefore, the Board in the above example did not mean that each asset in the portfolio is to be regarded as 20% in stage 2 and 80% in stage 1. Instead, 20% of the assets are in stage 2, even if the bank does not yet know which.
- This allocation is intended to reflect that some assets in the portfolio will respond more adversely to a given change to the macroeconomic factor (e.g. unemployment rate) than others. Therefore, some assets in the portfolio may be considered to have significantly increased in credit risk while others have not. Judgment is required to determine how much of the portfolio should move to stage 2. An entity may, for example, determine that given the range of possible scenarios, 20% of the portfolio moves to stage 2 considering the different level of sensitivity of the assets in the portfolio to the different relevant credit risk drivers.
- As further explained in the next section on using multiple scenarios for the staging assessment (see 5.5.6 below), it is important to note that the 20% is not the probability of occurrence of the more adverse scenario. Rather, it reflects the proportion of the portfolio deemed to have already significantly deteriorated based on the most recent probability-weighted average PD. This is due to the heightened sensitivity of this proportion of the portfolio to certain macroeconomic factors.

A further issue with the top down approach is the question of what the lender should do if it subsequently finds that differences in risk characteristics emerge within the portfolio, such that certain assets need to be measured using lifetime ECLs using the bottom up approach. A similar question arises if individual assets subsequently need to be measured using lifetime ECLs, for instance, because they become 30 days past due. Presumably, in each case the lender will need to reallocate part of the portion of the portfolio already measured using lifetime losses based on the top down approach. For example, if 20% of the portfolio had been assessed using the top down approach and now 15% are 30 days past due, perhaps the most logical approach would be to consider the 15% to form part of the 20%, already in stage 2.

Presumably the proportion of the portfolio ECLs in stage 2 can be measured once again using 12-month ECLs if economic conditions are expected to improve. However, the standard seems to make it clear that it is not possible to rebut the 30 days past due presumption just because of a favourable economic outlook. *[IFRS 9.B5.5.19]*.

Because of these and similar difficulties, we are not currently aware of any banks who intend to use the top down approach in the manner set out in the Illustrative Example. Banks prefer to know which loans are measured using lifetime ECLs, rather than a notional percentage of the population. In practice, the methods that are being explored by banks are closer to a mixture of the bottom up and top down approaches, as described in Examples 50.31 and 50.32 above. Macroeconomic indicators are assessed, as in the top down approach, but the effect is determined by assessing the effect on particular exposures. One possible method is to determine the expected migration of loans through a bank's risk classification system, by recalibrating the probabilities of default based on forward-looking data. This could be used to forecast how many additional loans will get downgraded as well as the associated ECLs. Another is to focus on more vulnerable categories of lending, such as interest-only mortgages, secured loans with high loan-to-value ratios, or property development loans, and assess how these might respond to the economic outlook, The more information about customers that a lender possesses, the more this might look like the illustrated bottom up approach. It is likely that banks will use different approaches for different portfolios, depending on how they are managed and what data is available.

All the examples in the Illustrative Examples simplify the fact pattern to focus on just one driver of credit losses, whereas in reality there will be many, and it may not be possible to find a historical precedent for the combination of economic indicators that may now be present. Further, to delve into the past to predict the future requires a level of data that banks may lack. The example in the standard bases the percentage on historical experience, but it is more than 20 years since most developed countries last saw a 200 basis points rise in interest rates, and products and lending practices were then very different, as was the level of interest rates before they began to rise and the extent of the increase. Hence, the past may not be a reliable guide to the future. In practice, banks will need to determine the main macroeconomic variables that correlate with credit losses and focus on modelling these key drivers of loss. The banks can make use of work that has already been carried out for stress testing. Also, it should be stressed that banks will generally use one single model to estimate forward-looking PDs for both for the assessment of significant increases in credit risk and the measurement of ECLs (see 5.4.8.C above).

The example of an anticipated increase in interest rates is very topical, given that rates in many countries are expected to rise in future from the all-time low levels that have been experienced since the financial crisis. This gives rise to an observation that is relevant to any ECL model: banks and (hopefully) borrowers have presumably known that new variable loans made since the crisis would likely increase in rate as the economy improves. If the increase was anticipated at the time of origination, expectation of a rise in interest rate should not be viewed as a significant deterioration in credit risk. Yet, there is a concern that rising rates will bring difficulty for many borrowers who have over stretched themselves, implying that the inevitable rise was not fully factored into lending decisions. With any forward-looking approach it is necessary to understand what risks were already taken into account when loans are first made, to assess whether there has been a significant increase in risk.

Some kind of collective adjustment or overlay will be needed for many retail lending portfolios, given that most customer-specific information will not be forward looking. In contrast, for commercial loans, the lender will typically have access to much more information and a forward-looking approach may already have been built into loan grading systems. Nevertheless, we are aware of some banks who consider that they might need to introduce an additional overlay for commercial loans so as to be more responsive to emerging macroeconomic and other risk developments. Other banks intend to achieve this by using their existing watch list approaches, to supplement using their credit grading system to assess significant increases in credit risk, because watch list systems tend to be more reactive to changing circumstances than formal credit gradings. Any one bank is likely to employ a variety of methods, depending on its products, systems and data.

5.5.6 Multiple scenarios for 'staging' assessment

At its December 2015 meeting the Impairment Transition resource Group (ITG) discussed not only the need to consider multiple scenarios for measurement of ECLs (see 5.4.4 above) but also for the purposes of assessing whether exposures should be measured on a lifetime loss basis.

Similar to the measurement of ECLs, the ITG members noted that where there is a non-linear relationship between the different forward looking scenarios and the associated risks of default, using a single scenario would not meet the objectives of the standard. Consequently, in such cases, an entity would need to consider more than one forward looking scenario. Further, there should be consistency, to the extent relevant, between the information used to measure ECLs and that used to assess significant increases in credit risk. An example of when the information might not be relevant is the value of collateral. It may be necessary to calculate the effect of multiple scenarios to value collateral to measure ECLs, but this information may not be relevant to assessing significant changes in credit risk unless the value has an effect on the probability of default occurring.[33]

As with the measurement of ECLs, the ITG members noted that IFRS 9 does not prescribe particular methods of assessing for significant increases in credit risk. Consequently, various methods could be applied, depending on facts and circumstances and these may include both quantitative and qualitative approaches. An entity should not restrict itself by considering only quantitative approaches when considering how to incorporate multiple forward-looking scenarios. Whichever approach is taken, it should be consistent with IFRS 9, considering reasonable and supportable information that is available without undue cost and effort. Once again, this is an area of judgement and so appropriate disclosures would need to be provided to comply with the requirements of IFRS 7 (see 5.13 below and Chapter 54 at 5.2.3).

A further issue was raised at the ITG meeting, which was not referred to in the minutes but was addressed in the 25 July 2016 IASB webcast. If a number of scenarios are applied to an individual asset, in some of which there is no significant increase in credit risk and in others there is, is it possible that it could be measured partly based on 12 month losses and partly on lifetime losses? It was not the intention of the IASB that an asset should be regarded as being in more than one stage at the same time. For staging as well as for measurement, IFRS 9 applies to the unit of account which is the individual financial instrument. The financial asset cannot be considered to have partly significantly deteriorated and partly not. Hence, for instance, if the staging assessment is based on a mechanistic approach which considers the change in the lifetime probability of default, the entity should use the multiple scenario probability-weighted lifetime probability of default to assess whether there has been a significant increase in credit risk. The asset should then be measured using the weighted 12-month probability of default if it is considered to be in stage 1 or the weighted lifetime probability of default if it is considered to be in stage 2.

However, the webcast went on to note, for a collectively assessed portfolio of assets, a proportion of the portfolio only may be deemed to have significantly deteriorated while the rest of the portfolio has not, due to differences in sensitivities of credit risk to a change in a particular parameter. It is possible that an entity is aware of differences in sensitivities of credit risk to a change in a particular parameter but is unable to subdivide the portfolio on the basis of such sensitivity. In such instances, an entity may determine that the expected forward-looking scenario would result in a significant deterioration for a certain proportion of its portfolio. For instance, some assets in the portfolio may respond more adversely to a given change to the unemployment rate than others. In that case, judgement is required to determine how much of the portfolio should move to stage 2. An entity may, for example, determine that, given the range of possible scenarios, 20% of the portfolio moves to stage 2 considering the different level of sensitivity of the assets in the portfolio to the different relevant credit risk drivers.

The IASB also illustrated how multiple scenarios can be reflected in a non-PD-based approach, using the example of a scorecard system. If the entity determines that there is non-linearity in the effect of the scenarios on the credit risk of the customers, one possibility is to look at the scorecard inputs and to determine which of these inputs have a non-linear relationship with the macroeconomic parameters. The entity then adjusts the scorecard, for example, using a scaling factor to reflect the impact of non-linearity, assesses whether there has been a significant increase in credit risk and measures ECL on the basis of the adjusted scorecard.

The approach set out in this discussion is broadly the same as 'the top down' approach to collective assessments illustrated by Example 50.32 in 5.5.5 above.

It is important to note that the ITG did not state that it is always necessary to *use* multiple scenarios and probability-weighted lifetime probabilities of default to assess significant increases in credit risk.

What it did state is that:

(a) it is necessary to *consider* more than one scenario if there is non-linearity in the possible distribution of losses;

(b) qualitative approaches may be included as well as quantitative ones, so that, for instance, it might be possible to take account of non-linearities by scaling the output from score cards; and

(c) the assessment should be based on reasonable and supportable information that is available without undue cost or effort (see 5.4.8 above).

Nevertheless, the ITG did state that there should be consistency, to the extent relevant, between the forward-looking information used for measurement and for the assessment of significant increases in credit risk. There would not always be a direct mapping of the relevant information, because in some cases information might have an impact on the measurement of ECLs but not on the assessment of significant increases in credit risk (and *vice versa*). Also, various methods of assessing for significant increases in credit risk could be applied, depending on the particular facts and circumstances, and an entity should not restrict itself by considering only quantitative approaches when considering how to incorporate multiple forward-looking scenarios. However, many banks that use multiple scenarios of lifetime probabilities of default to measure assets in stage 2, intend to use them also for assessing if there has been a significant increase in credit risk. Also, as with measurement, banks will need to consider regulators' expectations (see 5.6.1 below).

In the July 2016 webcast, the IASB also stressed the importance of adequate disclosures. Because there is no one right approach and because this area involves a high level of judgment, disclosures are very important to enable users of financial statements to understand how entities' credit risk is affected by forward-looking scenarios and how they have affected the application of the ECL model. It would also be useful to disclose if relevant forward looking information has not been reflected in the assessment of significant deterioration on the basis that it is not reasonable and supportable.

As of the time of writing, many banks have not yet decided how they will respond to the ITG's guidance. It is possible that once they have considered the effects of multiple scenarios, some may conclude that the effect is not material, since it will vary with portfolio and economic location. Others may consider that they cannot access sufficient reasonable and supportable forward looking information to make the assessment using multiple scenarios.

5.6 Other matters and issues in relation to the IFRS 9 impairment requirements

This section discusses other matters and issues that are relevant to applying the IFRS 9 impairment requirements.

5.6.1 *Other guidance on accounting for expected credit losses*

The Basel Committee published the final version of its *Guidance on Credit Risk and Accounting for Expected Credit Losses* (sometimes referred to as 'G-CRAECL' but in this publication as 'the Basel guidance' or just 'the guidance') in December 2015 (see 5.1.6 above). It updates the Basel Committee's previous guidance on Sound Credit Risk Assessment and Valuation of Loans, often referred to as 'SCRAVL'. The new guidance deals with lending exposures, and not debt securities, and does not address the consequent capital requirements. The guidance was originally drafted for internationally active banks and more sophisticated banks in the business of lending. The final version does not limit its scope but allows less complex banks to apply, 'a proportionate approach' that is commensurate with the size, nature and complexity of their lending exposures. It also extends this notion to individual portfolios of more complex banks. It follows that determining what is proportionate will be a key judgement to be made, which is likely to be guided in some jurisdictions by banking regulators (see, for instance, the discussion later in this section on the consultation paper issued by the European Banking Authority). The guidance issued in June 2016 by the GPPC (see section 5.6.2 below) will also be relevant in making this determination. The final version of the guidance acknowledges that due consideration may also be given to materiality.

The main section of the Basel Committee's guidance is intended to be applicable in all jurisdictions (i.e. for banks reporting under US GAAP as well as for banks reporting under IFRS) and contains 11 supervisory principles. The guidance is supplemented by an appendix that outlines additional supervisory requirements specific to jurisdictions applying the IFRS 9 ECL model.

It is important to stress that the guidance is not intended to conflict with IFRS 9 (and, indeed, this has been confirmed by the IASB), but it goes further than IFRS 9 and, in particular, removes some of the simplifications that are available in the standard. It also insists that any approximation to what would be regarded as an 'ideal' implementation of ECL accounting should be designed and implemented so as to avoid 'bias'. The term 'avoidance of bias' is used several times in the guidance and we understand it to have its normal accounting meaning of neutrality. Hence, for instance, if a bank were ever dependent on past-due information to assess whether an exposure should be measured on a lifetime ECL basis, it is guided to 'pay particular attention to their measurement of the 12-month allowance to ensure that ECLs are appropriately captured in accordance with the measurement objective of IFRS 9.'[34]

Perhaps one of the most significant pieces of guidance provided by the Basel Committee relates to the important requirement in IFRS 9 that ECLs should be measured using 'reasonable and supportable information'. The Committee accepts that in certain circumstances, information relevant to the assessment and measurement of credit risk may not be reasonable and supportable and should therefore be excluded from the ECL assessment and measurement process. But, given that credit risk management is a core competence of banks, 'these circumstances would be exceptional in nature'.[35] This attitude pervades the guidance. It also states that management is expected 'to apply its credit judgement to consider future scenarios' and '[t]he Committee does not view the unbiased consideration of forward looking information as speculative'.[36] The guidance, therefore, establishes a high hurdle for when it is not possible for an internationally active bank to estimate the effects of forward looking information. It is possible that banking regulators would expect banks to make an estimate of the effects of events with an uncertain binary outcome that is highly significant, such as the result of a referendum as discussed by the ITG in September 2015 (see 5.4.8.C above).

A connected piece of the guidance relates to another important principle in IFRS 9, that reasonable and supportable information should be available 'without undue cost or effort'. The guidance states that banks are not expected to read this 'restrictively'. It goes on to say that, 'Since the objective of the IFRS 9 model is to deliver fundamental improvements in the measurement of credit losses ... this will potentially require costly upfront investment in new systems and processes'. Such costs 'should therefore not be considered undue'.[37]

Much of the guidance relates to systems and controls and so is outside the scope of this publication. The requirements of the main section that relate to accounting include:

1. There should be commonality in the processes, systems, tools and data used to assess credit risk and to measure ECLs for accounting and for regulatory capital purposes.[38]
2. When a bank's individual assessment of exposures does not adequately consider forward-looking information, it is appropriate to group lending exposures with shared credit risk characteristics to estimate the impact of forward-looking information, including macroeconomic factors (see 5.5.5 above).[39] The grouping of lending exposures into portfolios with shared credit risk characteristics must be re-evaluated regularly (including re-segmentation in light of relevant new information or changes in the bank's expectations). Groupings must be granular enough to assess changes in credit risk and changes in a part of the portfolio must not be masked by the performance of the portfolio as a whole.[40]
3. 'Adjustments' may be used to address events, circumstances or risk factors that are not fully considered in credit rating and modelling processes. But the Committee expects that such adjustments will be temporary. If the reason for an adjustment is not expected to be temporary then the processes should be updated to incorporate that risk driver. The guidance goes on to say that adjustments require judgement and create the potential for bias. Therefore, they should be subject to appropriate governance processes.[41]
4. The 'consideration of forward-looking information and macroeconomic factors is considered essential to the proper implementation of an ECL model. It cannot be avoided on the basis that the banks considers the costs to be excessive or unnecessary or because there is uncertainty in formulating forward looking scenarios'. However, the Committee recognises that an ECL is 'an estimate and thus may not perfectly predict actual outcomes. Accordingly, the need to incorporate such information is likely to increase the inherent degree of subjectivity in ECL estimates, compared with impairment measured using incurred loss approaches'. Also, the Basel Committee recognises that it may not always be possible to demonstrate a strong link in formal statistical terms between certain types of information and the credit risk drivers. Consequently, a bank's experienced credit judgement will be crucial in establishing the appropriate level for the individual or collective allowance.[42]
5. Although the final version of the guidance notes less about disclosures than the draft version, given the publication of the Enhanced Disclosure Task Force (EDTF) recommendations, disclosure remains one of the key principles (see 5.13 below or Chapter 54 at 9).

The guidance is supplemented by an appendix that outlines additional supervisory requirements specific to jurisdictions applying the IFRS 9 ECL model. The key requirements are outlined below:

1. A bank's definition of default adopted for accounting purposes should be guided by the definition used for regulatory purposes, which includes both a qualitative 'unlikeliness to pay' criterion and an objective 90-days-past-due criterion, described by the Committee as a 'backstop'.
2. The IFRS 9 requirement to assess whether exposures have significantly increased in credit risk 'is demanding in its requirements for data, analysis and use of experienced credit judgement'. The determination should be made 'on a timely and holistic basis', considering a wide range of current information. This should include 'all reasonable and supportable forward looking information, in addition to information about current conditions and historical data', covering 'macroeconomic conditions and the economic sector and geographical region relevant to a particular borrower or a group of borrowers'. It is critical that banks have processes in place to ensure that financial instruments, whether assessed individually or collectively, are moved from the 12-month to the lifetime ECL measurement as soon as credit risk has increased significantly. Credit losses very often begin to deteriorate a considerable period of time before an actual delinquency occurs and delinquency data are generally backward-looking. Therefore, 'the Committee believes that they will seldom on their own be appropriate in the implementation of an ECL approach by a bank.' Instead, banks need to consider the linkages between macroeconomic factors and borrower attributes, using historical information to identify the main risk drivers, and current and forecast conditions and experienced credit judgement to determine loss expectations. This will apply not only to collective assessments of portfolios but also for assessments of individual loans. The guidance gives the example of a commercial property loan, for which the bank should assess the sensitivity of the property market to the macroeconomic environment and use information such as interest rates or vacancy rates to make the assessment.[43]
3. In assessing whether there has been a significant increase in credit risk, banks should not rely solely on quantitative analysis. The guidance draws banks' attention to the list of qualitative indicators set out in paragraph B5.5.17 of the standard. It also emphasises that particular consideration should be given to a list of conditions, including an increased credit spread for a particular loan, a decision to strengthen collateral and/or covenant requirements, a downgrade by a credit rating agency or within the bank's internal credit rating system, a deterioration in future cash flows, or an expectation of forbearance or restructuring Also, the guidance stresses that the sensitivity of the risk of a default occurring to rating downgrades increases strongly as rating quality declines. Therefore, the widths of credit risk grades need to be set appropriately, so that significant increases in credit risk are not masked. Also, 'if a decision is made to intensify the monitoring of a borrower or class of borrowers, it is unlikely that such action would have been taken ... had the increase in credit risk not been perceived as significant.'[44]

4. Exposures that are transferred to stage 2 and that are subsequently renegotiated or modified, but not derecognised, should not be moved back to stage 1 until there is sufficient evidence that the credit risk over the remaining life is no longer significantly higher than on initial recognition. 'Typically, a customer would need to demonstrate consistently good payment behaviour over a period of time before the credit risk is considered to have decreased.'[45]
5. IFRS 9 includes a number of practical expedients (see 5.5.4 above). However, as banks are in the business of lending and it is unlikely that obtaining relevant information will involve undue cost or effort, the Basel Committee expects their limited use by internationally active banks. For instance:
   a. The long-term benefit of a high-quality implementation of an ECL model that takes into account all reasonable and supportable information far outweighs the associated costs.
   b. The use of the low credit risk simplification is considered a low-quality implementation of the ECL model and its use should be limited (except for holdings in debt securities, which are out of scope of the guidance). Also, the reference to an investment grade rating in the standard is only given as an example of a low credit risk exposure. An investment grade rating given by a rating agenda cannot automatically be considered low credit risk because banks are expected to rely primarily on their own credit assessments.
   c. Delinquency is a lagging indicator. Therefore, the Committee expects banks not to use the more-than-30-days-past-due rebuttable presumption as a primary indicator of a significant increase in credit risk. Banks may only use the rebuttable presumption as a backstop measure, alongside other, earlier indicators, while any rebuttal of the presumption would have to be accompanied by a thorough analysis to show that 30 days past due is not correlated with a significant increase in credit risk.[46]

In June 2016, the Canadian Office of the Superintendent of Financial Institutions (OSFI) issued local guidance in a new guideline *IFRS 9 Financial Instruments and Disclosures*. The Canadian guideline sets out OSFI's expectations on the application of IFRS 9's ECL requirements for deposit-taking institutions (DTIs) in the business of lending and emphasises the importance of a disciplined, high-quality, robust and consistent application of IFRS 9 and sets the expectation that banks should invest appropriate resources to thoroughly incorporate all available forward-looking information, including macroeconomic factors, into the measurement of ECLs. These expectations are scaled with some applying to DTIs using internal-ratings based approaches to calculate regulatory capital requirements (IRB DTIs) and others applicable to DTIs using a standardised approach (standardised DTIs). For a third category, DTIs not in the business of lending, foreign bank branches and insurance companies, the guidelines simply require the application of IFRS 9 as issued by the IASB without further regulatory guidance. The guidance applicable for IRB DTIs reproduces the Basel Committee guidance almost entirely, including the proposals to limit the use of some of the simplifications available in IFRS 9. However, for standardised DTIs that are in the business of lending, separate guidance scaled for their nature, size, complexity and risk profile has been written (attempting to define in more specific terms, it appears, a 'proportional approach' as described in the Basel Committee guidance for smaller institutions). This approach for standardised DTIs emphasises the need to still consider forward-looking information and the use of experienced credit judgement when calculating ECLs, and also sets out an expectation that they will limit the use of the 30 day past due presumption as a primary indicator of transfer to lifetime ECL measurement. In addition, both IRB and standardised DTIs will be required to pre-notify OSFI of any material changes to either their ECL methodology or the level of ECL impairment allowance. This will permit OSFI to review and provide feedback on changes in a timely manner, allowing for early supervisory engagement and reducing the risk of prudential issues arising after changes are made. Furthermore, it will help to increase consistency of allowance methodologies amongst DTIs since OSFI will be able to draw comparisons between all of them.

On 26 July 2016, the European Banking Authority ('the EBA') issued a Consultation Paper (the 'CP') providing *Draft guidelines on credit institutions' credit risk management practices and accounting for expected credit losses.* The scope of the proposed guidelines is for all credit institutions who report under IFRS on an individual, sub-consolidated or consolidated basis.

The CP is broadly the same as the Basel guidance. But since the EBA guidelines would apply to all credit institutions reporting under IFRS, however small, a key element is the application of proportionality. The CP states that, 'Credit institutions should comply with these guidelines in a manner that is appropriate to their size, internal organization and their nature, scope and complexity of activities and, more generally, all other relevant facts and circumstances of the credit institution and the group (if any) to which it belongs.'[47] The CP goes on to say that 'taking into account the proportionality principle set out in these guidelines, credit institutions which are both smaller and less complex may reasonably rely more on the use of practical expedients'. But then it states 'credit institutions should consider the need to make adjustments when using practical expedients to avoid any resulting bias...'[48]

The CP also cross refers the expected loss accounting guidelines to other EBA requirements on forbearance, probation periods and the definition of default, so as to encourage consistency in their treatment for accounting and regulatory purposes.

5.6.2 Global Public Policy Committee (GPPC) guidance

On 17 June 2016, the GPPC published *The implementation of IFRS 9 impairment by banks – Considerations for those charged with governance of systemically important banks* ('the GPPC guidance'). The GPPC is the Global Public Policy Committee of representatives of the six largest accounting networks. This publication was issued to promote high-quality implementation of the accounting for ECLs in accordance with IFRS and to help those charged with governance to identify the elements of a high-quality implementation. It was designed to complement other guidance such as that issued by the Basel Committee (see 5.6.1 above) and the EDTF (see Chapter 54 at 9.2). It does not purport to amend or interpret the requirements of IFRS 9 in any way. The first half of the GPCC guidance sets out key areas of focus for those charged with governance. This includes governance and controls, transition issues and ten questions that those charged with governance might wish to discuss. The second half of the guidance sets out a sophisticated approach to implementing each aspect of the requirements of IFRS 9, along with considerations for a simpler approach and what is not compliant. Where relevant to understanding the accounting requirements of IFRS 9, this guidance is reflected in this chapter.

The GPPC guidance regards determination of the level of sophistication of the approach to be used as one of the key areas of focus for those charged with governance. Consequently, it provides guidance on how to make this determination for particular portfolios. It sets out factors to consider at the level of the entity, such as the extent of systemic risk that the bank poses, whether it is listed or a public interest entity, the size of its balance sheet and off balance sheet credit exposures, and the level and volatility of historical credit losses. Portfolio-level factors include its size relative to that of the total balance sheet and its complexity, the sophistication of other lending-related modelling methodologies, the extent of available data, the level of historical losses and the level and volatility of losses expected in the future. The document stresses that a simpler approach is not necessarily a lower quality approach if it is applied to an appropriate portfolio.

5.6.3 Measurement dates of expected credit losses

5.6.3.A Derecognition and initial recognition for foreign currency exposures

Impairment must be assessed and measured at the reporting date. IFRS 9 also requires a derecognition gain or loss to be measured relative to the carrying amount at the date of derecognition (see Chapter 54 at 4.2.1 and 7.1.1). This necessitates an assessment and measurement of ECLs for that particular asset as at the date of derecognition, as was confirmed by the discussions at the April 2015 ITG meeting.

At that meeting, the ITG also discussed a more difficult question, whether impairment must be measured as at the date of initial recognition, for foreign currency monetary assets. The significance of this is whether subsequent gains and losses arising from foreign currency retranslation in the first accounting period should be calculated based on the initial gross amortised cost or a net amount, after deducting an impairment allowance. This would affect the allocation of subsequent gains and losses of the asset in this period to impairment or to foreign currency retranslation, so that it would be reported in different lines of the profit or loss account.

Differing views were expressed at the April 2015 ITG meeting:

- A few ITG members supported the view that while IFRS 9 does not expressly require ECLs to be measured at the date of initial recognition, the requirements of other IFRSs, e.g. IAS 21 may result in an entity measuring ECLs at the date of initial recognition. Also, Illustrative Example 14 in IFRS 9 implies the need to include ECLs on initial recognition in the measurement of foreign exchange gains and losses in respect of a foreign currency-denominated asset (see Example 50.35 at 5.8 below). However, these members questioned the frequency with which an entity needed to perform that calculation and pointed out that considerations of materiality would be a key factor in making this decision.

- Some other ITG members were of the view that an entity is required to measure a financial asset at its fair value upon initial recognition and that consequently measuring ECLs at initial recognition would be inconsistent with that requirement. *[IFRS 9.5.1.1]*. IFRS 9 includes impairment as part of the subsequent measurement of a financial asset and, consequently, only requires an entity to begin measuring ECLs at the first reporting date after initial recognition (or on derecognition if that occurs earlier). *[IFRS 9.3.2.12, 9.5.5.3, 9.5.5.5, 9.5.5.13]*. While the requirements of other IFRSs should be applied to the loss allowance at that point, the application of those requirements should not result in an entity having to measure ECLs at a date earlier than that specifically required by IFRS 9.

Also, the ITG noted that the illustrative examples are non-authoritative and illustrate only one way of applying the requirements of IFRS 9. Measuring a 12-month expected loss using point in time, forward-looking information, every time that a foreign currency exposure is first recognised would not be feasible. Given that there was no consensus on this issue, we expect that there may be diversity in practice.

A similar issue is whether impairment needs to be measured at the date that an asset is modified (see 5.7 below).

5.6.3.B Trade date and settlement date accounting

For financial assets measured at amortised cost or at fair value through other comprehensive income, IFRS 9 requires entities to use the trade date as the date of initial recognition for the purposes of applying the impairment requirements. *[IFRS 9.5.7.4]*. This means that entities that use settlement date accounting may have to recognise a loss allowance for financial assets which they have purchased but not yet recognised and, correspondingly, no loss allowance for assets that they have sold but not yet derecognised. (See Chapter 48 at 2.2 for further details on trade date accounting and settlement date accounting).

Irrespective of the accounting policy choice for trade date accounting versus settlement date accounting, the recognition of the loss allowance on the trade date ensures that entities recognise the loss allowance at the same time; otherwise entities could choose settlement date accounting to delay recognising the loss allowance until the settlement date. The effect of this is similar to accounting for fair value changes on financial assets measured at fair value through other comprehensive income and those measured at fair value through profit or loss when settlement date accounting is applied (i.e. a measurement change needs to be recognised in profit or loss and the statement of financial position even if the related assets that are being measured are only recognised slightly later).

For settlement date accounting, the recognition of a loss allowance for an asset that has not yet been recognised raises the question of how that loss allowance should be presented in the statement of financial position. The time between the trade date and the settlement date is somewhat similar to a loan commitment in that the accounting is off balance sheet, which suggests presentation of the loss allowance as a provision.

In practice, some entities tend to opt for settlement date accounting for financial assets recorded at amortised cost, because they do not need the additional systems capabilities to account for the financial assets on trade date (i.e. they do not need to account for financial assets that will be measured at amortised cost until settlement date). The change from the IAS 39 incurred loss model to the IFRS 9 ECL model means that the settlement date accounting simplification for financial assets measured at amortised cost would lose much of its benefit from an operational perspective.

5.6.4 Interaction between the initial measurement of debt instruments acquired in a business combination and the impairment model of IFRS 9

Consistent with IFRS 9 and IFRS 13, IFRS 3 – *Business Combinations* – requires financial assets acquired in a business combination to be measured by the acquirer on initial recognition at their fair value (see Chapter 48 at 3.2.4 and Chapter 9 at 5.5.5). *[IFRS 3.18, IFRS 3.36]*. IFRS 3 contains application guidance explaining that an acquirer should not recognise a separate valuation allowance (i.e. loss allowance for ECLs) in respect of loans and receivables acquired in a business combination for contractual cash flows that are deemed to be uncollectible at the acquisition date. This is because the effects of uncertainty about future cash flows are included in the fair value measure. *[IFRS 3.B41]*.

Consequently, the accounting for impairment of debt instruments measured at amortised cost or fair value through other comprehensive income under IFRS 9 does not affect the accounting for the business combination. At the acquisition date, the acquired debt instruments are measured at their acquisition-date fair value in accordance with IFRS 3. No loss allowance is recognised as part of the initial measurement of debt instruments that are acquired in a business combination.

Subsequent accounting for debt instruments acquired in a business combination after their initial recognition is in the scope of IFRS 9. The impairment requirements in IFRS 9 are part of the subsequent measurement of those debt instruments. *[IFRS 9.5.5, 9.5.2.1, 9.5.2.2]*. At the first reporting date after the business combination, following the guidance in IFRS 9, a loss allowance is recognised. *[IFRS 9.5.5.3, 9.5.5.5]*. This will result in an impairment loss that is recognised in profit or loss (rather than an adjustment to goodwill), just as would be the case if the entity were to originate those assets or acquire them as a portfolio, rather than acquire them through a business combination. *[IFRS 9.5.5.8]*.

Despite the colloquial reference to a 'day one' loss that results from the ECL impairment model in IFRS 9, it is important to understand that the recognition of a loss allowance for newly acquired (whether purchased or originated) debt instruments that are in the scope of the impairment requirements of IFRS 9 is a matter of subsequent measurement of those financial instruments. This means that the acquirer recognises the loss allowance for all debt instruments acquired in a business combination (that are subject to impairment accounting) in the reporting period that includes the business combination but not as part of that business combination, and with a corresponding impairment loss in profit or loss.

The only exception to this is the specific accounting for purchased or originated credit-impaired financial assets which applies to the extent that the portfolio includes financial assets which are credit-impaired at the acquisition date (i.e. the EIR is determined using a cash flow estimate that includes all ECLs and no allowance is made for ECLs). A financial asset is credit-impaired when one or more events that have a detrimental impact on the estimated future cash flows of that financial asset have occurred (see 5.3.1 above).

5.7 Modified financial assets

If the contractual cash flows on a financial asset are renegotiated or modified, the holder needs to assess whether the financial asset should be derecognised (see Chapter 51 at 3.4 and 6.2 for further details on modification and derecognition). While IAS 39 contains guidance on when financial liabilities that have been renegotiated or modified should be derecognised, it does not do so for financial assets. Similarly, as the derecognition literature in IAS 39 has been carried forward to IFRS 9, the IASB has still not established criteria for analysing when a modification of a financial asset constitutes a derecognition event. However, an entity may refer to the decision made by the IFRS Interpretations Committee in May 2012. The Interpretations Committee was asked to consider the accounting treatment of Greek government bonds (GGBs). The principal issue raised was whether the portion of the old GGBs to be exchanged for new bonds with different maturities and interest rates should result in derecognition of the whole asset, or only part of it, in accordance with IAS 39 or, conversely, be accounted for as a modification that would not require derecognition. The Interpretations Committee concluded that this assessment can be made, either on the basis of:

- the extinguishment of the contractual rights to the cash flows from the assets as per paragraph 17(a) of IAS 39 (now under paragraph 3.2.3 of IFRS 9); or
- by analogy to the notion of a substantial change of the terms of financial liabilities as per paragraph 40 of IAS 39 (now paragraph 3.3.2 of IFRS 9).[49]

IFRS 9 acknowledges that in some circumstances, the renegotiation or modification of the contractual cash flows of a financial asset can lead to the derecognition of the existing financial asset and subsequently, the recognition of a new financial asset. *[IFRS 9.B5.5.25]*. This means that the entity is starting afresh and the date of the modification will also be the date of initial recognition of the new financial asset. Typically, the entity will recognise a loss allowance based on 12-month ECLs at each reporting date until the requirements for the recognition of lifetime ECLs are met. However, in what the standard describes as 'some unusual circumstances' following a modification that results in derecognition of the original financial asset, there may be evidence that the new financial asset is credit-impaired on initial recognition (see 5.3.3 above), and thus, the financial asset should be recognised as an originated credit-impaired financial asset. In practice, we believe that more restructured financial assets will be treated as originated credit-impaired than the Board seems to have envisaged. *[IFRS 9.B5.5.26]*.

In other circumstances, the renegotiation or modification of the contractual cash flows of a financial asset does not lead to the derecognition of the existing financial asset as per IFRS 9. In such situations, the entity will:

- continue with its current accounting treatment for the existing asset that has been modified;
- recognise a modification gain or loss in profit or loss by recalculating the gross carrying amount of the financial asset as the present value of the renegotiated or modified contractual cash flows, discounted at the financial asset's original EIR (or the credit-adjusted EIR for purchased or originated credit-impaired financial assets). Any costs or fees incurred adjust the carrying amount of the modified financial asset and are amortised over the remaining term of the modified financial asset (see 3.2.1 above); *[IFRS 9.5.4.3, Appendix A]*
- assess whether there has been a significant increase in the credit risk of the financial instrument, by comparing the risk of a default occurring at the reporting date (based on the modified contractual terms) and the risk of a default occurring at initial recognition (based on the original, unmodified contractual terms). A financial asset that has been renegotiated or modified is not automatically considered to have lower credit risk. The assessment should consider the credit risk over the expected life of the asset based on historical and forward-looking information, including information about the circumstances that led to the modification. Evidence that the criteria for the recognition of lifetime ECLs are subsequently no longer met may include a history of up-to-date and timely payment in subsequent periods. This means a minimum period of observation will often be necessary before a financial asset may qualify to return to stage 1; *[IFRS 9.5.5.12, B5.5.27]* and
- make the appropriate quantitative and qualitative disclosures required for renegotiated or modified assets to enable users of financial statements to understand the nature and effect of such modifications (including the effect on the measurement of ECLs) and how the entity monitors its assets that have been modified (see 5.13 below and Chapter 54 at 5.2.3). *[IFRS 7.35F(f), B8B, 35J]*.

As highlighted above, IFRS 9 introduces explicit guidance on measuring financial assets that have been modified but not derecognised. Under IAS 39, there is no clear guidance on the treatment of modification gains or loss in profit or loss. For entities that have recognised the modification gain or loss over the remaining life of the financial asset by adjusting the EIR prospectively rather than an adjustment to the carrying amount, there will be a need on transition to IFRS 9 to re-assess as at the time of modification, the change in carrying value of the financial asset using the original EIR. (Note that there may be situations where there is an increase rather than a reduction in the carrying value (see BC5.241 of IFRS 9)). The difference in the carrying amounts after taking into account the subsequent amortisation will be recorded in retained earnings on transition.

Reductions in the carrying value will be partially offset by an increase in amortisation in the period between the date of modification and the date of transition, as the original EIR will be used to amortise the modified assets during this period.

The following example has been adapted from Example 11 of the Implementation Guidance in the standard to illustrate the accounting treatment of a loan that is modified. *[IFRS 9 IG Example 11, IE66-IE73].*

Example 50.33: Modification of contractual cash flows

Bank A originates a five-year loan that requires the repayment of the outstanding contractual amount in full at maturity. Its contractual par amount is €1,000 with an interest rate of 5 per cent, payable annually. The EIR is 5 per cent. At the end of the first reporting period in Year 1, Bank A recognises a loss allowance at an amount equal to 12-month ECLs because there has not been a significant increase in credit risk since initial recognition. A loss allowance balance of €20 is recognised. In Year 2, Bank A determines that the credit risk on the loan has increased significantly since initial recognition. As a result, Bank A recognises lifetime ECLs on the loan. The loss allowance balance is €150.

At the end of Year 3, following significant financial difficulty of the borrower, Bank A modifies the contractual cash flows on the loan. It forgoes interest payments and extends the contractual term of the loan by one year so that the remaining term at the date of the modification is three years. The modification does not result in the derecognition of the loan by Bank A.

As a result of that modification, Bank A recalculates the gross carrying amount of the financial asset as the present value of the modified contractual cash flows discounted at the loan's original EIR of 5 per cent. The difference between this recalculated gross carrying amount and the gross carrying amount before the modification is recognised as a modification gain or loss. Bank A recognises the modification loss (calculated as €136) against the gross carrying amount of the loan, reducing it to €864, and a modification loss of €136 in profit or loss.

Bank A also remeasures the loss allowance, taking into account the modified contractual cash flows and evaluates whether the loss allowance for the loan should continue to be measured at an amount equal to lifetime ECLs. Bank A compares the current credit risk (taking into consideration the modified cash flows) to the credit risk (on the original unmodified cash flows) at initial recognition. Bank A determines that the loan is not credit-impaired at the reporting date but that credit risk has still significantly increased compared to the credit risk at initial recognition. It continues to measure the loss allowance at an amount equal to lifetime ECLs, which are €110 at the reporting date.

At each subsequent reporting date, Bank A continues to evaluate whether there has been a significant increase in credit risk by comparing the loan's credit risk at initial recognition (based on the original, unmodified cash flows) with the credit risk at the reporting date (based on the modified cash flows).

Two reporting periods after the loan modification (Year 5), the borrower has outperformed its business plan significantly compared to the expectations at the modification date. In addition, the outlook for the business is more positive than previously envisaged. An assessment of all reasonable and supportable information that is available without undue cost or effort indicates that the overall credit risk on the loan has decreased and that the risk of a default occurring over the expected life of the loan has decreased, so Bank A adjusts the borrower's internal credit rating at the end of the reporting period.

Given the positive overall development, Bank A re-assesses the situation and concludes that the credit risk of the loan has decreased and there is no longer a significant increase in credit risk since initial recognition. As a result, Bank A once again measures the loss allowance at an amount equal to 12-month ECLs.

Year	Beginning gross carrying amount	Impairment (loss)/gain	Modification (loss)/gain	Interest revenue	Cash flows	Ending gross carrying amount	Loss allowance	Ending amortised cost amount
	A	B	C	D Gross: A × 5%	E	F = A + C + D – E	G	H = F – G
1	€1,000	(€20)		€50	€50	€1,000	€20	€980
2	€1,000	(€130)		€50	€50	€1,000	€150	€850
3	€1,000	€40	(€136)	€50	€50	€864	€110	€754
4	€864	€24		€43		€907	€86	€821
5	€907	€72		€45		€952	€14	€938
6	€952	€14		€48	€1,000	€0	€0	€0

The ITG at its meeting on 22 April 2015 (see 5.1.5 above) discussed the measurement of ECLs in respect of a modified financial asset where the modification does not result in derecognition, but the cash flows have been renegotiated to be consistent with those previously expected to be paid.[50]

The ITG noted that IFRS 9 is clear that an entity is required to calculate a new gross carrying amount and the gain or loss on modification taken to profit or loss should be based on the renegotiated or modified contractual cash flows and excludes ECLs unless it is a purchased or originated credit-impaired financial asset. *[IFRS 9.5.4.3, Appendix A]*. Consequently, an entity must calculate the gain or loss on modification as a first step before going on to consider the revised ECL allowance required on the modified financial asset. Thereafter, the entity is required to continue to apply the impairment requirements to the modified financial asset in the same way as it would for other unmodified financial instruments, taking into account the revised contractual terms. *[IFRS 9.5.5.12]*. The revised ECL cannot be assumed to be nil as, in accordance with paragraph 5.5.18 of IFRS 9, an entity is required to consider the possibility that a credit loss occurs, even if the likelihood of that credit loss occurring is very low. *[IFRS 9.5.5.18]*.

The ITG also discussed the appropriate presentation and disclosure requirements pertaining to modifications. These are discussed further in Chapter 54 at 7.1.1.

We note that if an entity has no reasonable expectations of recovering a portion of the financial asset, which is subsequently forgiven, then this amount should arguably be written off, as a partial derecognition. The gross carrying amount would be reduced directly before a modification gain or loss is calculated. *[IFRS 9.5.4.4, B5.4.9]*. This will mean that the loss will be recorded as an impairment loss, rather than as a loss on modification, and presented differently in the profit or loss account. Whether it is possible to treat forgiveness of a portion of a loan as a write off event rather than as a modification might usefully be addressed by the ITG.

5.8 Financial assets measured at fair value through other comprehensive income

Based on the accounting treatment of financial assets measured at fair value through other comprehensive income (described at 2.3 above), the ECLs do not reduce the carrying amount of the financial assets in the statement of financial position, which remains at fair value. Instead, an amount equal to the allowance that would arise if the asset was measured at amortised cost is recognised in other comprehensive income as the 'accumulated impairment amount'. *[IFRS 9.4.1.2A, 5.5.2, Appendix A]*.

The accounting treatment and journal entries for debt instruments measured at fair value through other comprehensive income are illustrated in the following example, based on Illustrative Example 13 in the Implementation Guidance for the standard. *[IFRS 9 IG Example 13, IE78-IE81]*.

Example 50.34: Debt instrument measured at fair value through other comprehensive income

An entity purchases a debt instrument with a fair value of £1,000 on 15 December 2017 and measures the debt instrument at fair value through other comprehensive income (FVOCI). The instrument has an interest rate of 5 per cent over the contractual term of 10 years, and has a 5 per cent EIR. At initial recognition the entity determines that the asset is not purchased or originated credit-impaired.

	Debit	Credit
Financial asset – FVOCI	£1,000	
Cash		£1,000

(To recognise the debt instrument measured at its fair value)

On 31 December 2017 (the reporting date), the fair value of the debt instrument has decreased to £950 as a result of changes in market interest rates. The entity determines that there has not been a significant increase in credit risk since initial recognition and that ECLs should be measured at an amount equal to 12-month ECLs, which amounts to £30. For simplicity, journal entries for the receipt of interest revenue are not provided.

	Debit	Credit
Impairment loss (profit or loss)	£30	
Other comprehensive income[(a)]	£20	
Financial asset – FVOCI		£50

(To recognise 12-month ECLs and other fair value changes on the debt instrument)

(a) The cumulative loss in other comprehensive income at the reporting date was £20. That amount consists of the total fair value change of £50 (i.e. £1,000 – £950) offset by the change in the accumulated impairment amount representing 12-month ECLs that was recognised (£30).

Disclosure would be provided about the accumulated impairment amount of £30.

On 1 January 2018, the entity decides to sell the debt instrument for £950, which is its fair value at that date.

	Debit	Credit
Cash	£950	
Financial asset – FVOCI		£950
Loss (profit or loss)	£20	
Other comprehensive income		£20

(To derecognise the fair value through other comprehensive income asset and recycle amounts accumulated in other comprehensive income to profit or loss, i.e. £20).

This means that in contrast to financial assets measured at amortised cost, there is no separate allowance but, instead, impairment gains or losses are accounted for as an adjustment of the revaluation reserve accumulated in other comprehensive income, with a corresponding charge to profit or loss (which is then reflected in retained earnings).

The above example is relatively straightforward. A more complicated one, based on a foreign currency denominated financial asset which is also the subject of an interest rate hedge, is provided below. It also illustrates the complexity that arises from the interaction between fair value (FV) hedge accounting and the new impairment model (see 5.4.6 above). It is based on Illustrative Example 14 in the Implementation Guidance for the standard but extended so as to illustrate the complexities that could arise in practice. *[IFRS 9.IE82-IE102]*.

Example 50.35: Interaction between the fair value through other comprehensive income measurement category and foreign currency denomination, fair value hedge accounting and impairment

The example assumes the following fact pattern and that, on initial recognition, ECLs are included when measuring foreign exchange gains and losses (see 5.6.2 above):

- An entity purchases a bond denominated in a foreign currency (FC) for its fair value of FC100,000 on 1 January 2017.
- The bond is held within a business model whose objective is achieved by both collecting contractual cash flows and selling financial assets and has contractual cash flows which are solely payments of principal and interest on the principal amount outstanding. Therefore, the entity classifies the bond as measured at fair value through other comprehensive income.
- The bond has five years remaining to maturity and a fixed coupon of 5 per cent over its contractual life on the contractual par amount of FC100,000.
- The entity hedges the bond for its interest rate related fair value risk. The fair value of the corresponding interest rate swap at the date of initial recognition is nil.
- On initial recognition, the bond has a 5 per cent EIR which results in a gross carrying amount that equals the fair value at initial recognition.
- The entity's functional currency is its local currency (LC).
- As at 1 January 2017, the exchange rate is FC1 to LC1.
- At initial recognition, the entity determines that the bond is not purchased credit-impaired. The entity applies a 12-month PD for its impairment calculation and assumes that payment default occurs at the end of the reporting period (i.e. after 12 months). In particular, the entity estimates the PD over the next 12 months at 2 per cent and the LGD at FC60,000, resulting in an (undiscounted) expected cash shortfall of FC1,200. The discounted expected cash shortfall is FC1,143 at 5 per cent EIR (see the example below for the detailed calculation).
- For simplicity, amounts for interest revenue are not provided. It is assumed that interest accrued is received in the period. Differences of 1 in the calculations and reconciliations are due to rounding.

The entity hedges its risk exposures using the following risk management strategy:

(a) for fixed interest rate risk (in FC) the entity decides to link its interest receipts in FC to current variable interest rates in FC. Consequently, the entity uses interest rate swaps denominated in FC under which it pays fixed interest and receives variable interest in FC; and

(b) for foreign exchange (FX) risk, the entity decides not to hedge against any variability in LC arising from changes in foreign exchange rates.

The entity designates the following hedging relationship: a fair value hedge of the bond in FC as the hedged item with changes in benchmark interest rate risk in FC as the hedged risk. The entity enters into a swap that pays fixed and receives variable interest in FC on the same day and designates the swap as the hedging instrument. The tenor of the swap matches that of the hedged item (i.e. five years). This example assumes that all qualifying criteria for hedge accounting are met (see paragraph 6.4.1 of IFRS 9). The description of the designation is solely for the purpose of understanding this example (i.e. it is not an example of the complete formal documentation required in accordance with paragraph 6.4.1 of IFRS 9).

This example assumes that no hedge ineffectiveness arises in the hedging relationship. This assumption is made in order to better focus on illustrating the accounting mechanics in a situation that entails measurement at fair value through other comprehensive income of a foreign currency financial instrument that is designated in a fair value hedge relationship, and also to focus on the recognition of impairment gains or losses on such an instrument.

Situation as per 1 January 2017

The table below illustrates the amounts recognised in the financial statements as per 1 January 2017, as well as the shadow amortised cost calculation for the bond, based on the fact pattern described above (debits are shown as positive numbers and credits as negative numbers):

	Financial Statements			**Shadow Calculation**	
	FC	**LC**		**FC**	**LC**
	Statement of financial position				
Bond (FV)	100,000	100,000	Gross carrying amount	100,000	100,000
Swap (FV)	–	–	Loss allowance	(1,143)	(1,143)
			Amortised cost	98,857	98,857
	Statement of profit or loss				
Impairment	1,143	1,143	FV hedge adjustment	–	–
FV hedge (bond)	–	–	Adjusted gross carrying amt.	100,000	100,000
FX gain/loss (bond)	–	–	Adjusted amortised cost	98,857	98,857
FV hedge (swap)	–	–			
FX gain/loss (swap)	–	–			
	Statement of OCI				
FV changes	–	–			
Impairment offset	(1,143)	(1,143)			
FV hedge recycling	–	–			

As per 1 January 2017, the entity recognises the bond and the swap at their initial fair values of LC100,000 and nil, respectively. The loss allowance of FC1,143 is recognised in profit or loss. The amount is calculated as the difference between all contractual cash flows that are due to the entity in accordance with the contract and all the cash flows that the entity expects to receive (i.e. all cash shortfalls), discounted at the original effective interest of 5 per cent, and weighted by the probability of the scenario occurring. To keep the example simple, it is assumed that default on the bond occurs one year after the date of the initial recognition, at which point the recoverable amount of the bond is received. This means that in the case of a default the entity expects cash flows of FC45,000 (which is the principal of FC100,000 plus one year of interest of FC5,000 less the LGD of FC60,000). The latter loss is discounted by the 5 per cent EIR and weighted by the 2 per cent PD to arrive at the loss allowance. The table below shows the calculation:

1 January 2017		**Year 1**	**Year 2**	**Year 3**	**Year 4**	**Year 5**
Contractual cash flows		5,000	5,000	5,000	5,000	105,000
Gross carrying amount	100,000					
EIR	5%					
Expected cash flows		45,000				
Amortised cost (NPV[1] at 5%)	42,857					
Expected cash shortfalls		40,000	(5,000)	(5,000)	(5,000)	(105,000)
NPV at 5%	(57,143)					
PD	2%					
Net present value (probability weighted) – this is the ECL	(1,143)					

1 Stands for net present value

2 Stands for present value

The table above shows how the ECL is calculated as the net present value of the cash shortfalls, i.e. the difference between contractual and expected cash flows on each relevant date. An alternative is to calculate the probability-weighted present value for the two scenarios (FC100,000 × 98% plus FC42,857 × 2% = FC98,857) and determine the difference to the gross carrying amount (FC98,857 – FC100,000 = (FC1,143)).

In accordance with paragraph 16A of IFRS 7, the loss allowance for financial assets measured at fair value through other comprehensive income is not presented separately as a reduction of the carrying amount of the financial asset. As a consequence, the offsetting entry to the impairment loss of LC1,143 is recorded in other comprehensive income in the same period.

Situation as at 31 December 2017

As of 31 December 2017 (the reporting date), the entity observes the following facts:

- The fair value of the bond has decreased from FC100,000 to FC96,370, mainly because of an increase in market interest rates.
- The fair value of the swap has increased to FC1,837.
- In addition, as at 31 December 2017, the entity determines that there has been no change to the credit risk on the bond since initial recognition. The entity still estimates the PD over the next 12 months at 2 per cent and the LGD at FC60,000, resulting in an (undiscounted) expected shortfall of FC1,200.
- As at 31 December 2017, the exchange rate is FC1 to LC1.4.

The table below illustrates the amounts recognised in the financial statements between 1 January 2017 (after the entries for the impairment loss of FC1,143 at 1 January, shown above) and 31 December 2017, as well as the shadow amortised cost calculation for the bond (debits are shown as positive numbers and credits as negative numbers):

	Financial Statements			**Shadow Calculation**	
	FC	**LC**		**FC**	**LC**
	Statement of financial position				
Bond (FV)	96,370	134,918	Gross carrying amount	100,000	140,000
Swap (FV)	1,837	2,572	Loss allowance	(1,110)	(1,555)
			Amortised cost	98,890	138,445
	Statement of profit or loss				
Impairment	(32)	(45)	FV hedge adjustment	(1,837)	(2,572)
FV hedge (bond)	1,837	2,572	Adjusted gross carrying amount	98,163	137,428
FX gain/loss (bond)		(39,543)	Adjusted amortised cost	97,053	135,874
FV hedge (swap)	(1,837)	(2,572)			
FX gain/loss (swap)	–	–			
	Statement of OCI				
FV changes	3,630	4,625			
Impairment offset	32	45			
FV hedge recycling	(1,837)	(2,572)			

At this point, the example reveals the operational complexity of the fact pattern. As highlighted in the introduction to this example, it is important to understand that the hedging relationship adjusts the gross carrying amount and the amortised cost of the bond which leads to an adjusted EIR. This follows from the definition of the EIR as 'the rate that exactly discounts the estimated future cash payments or receipts through the expected life of the financial asset or the financial liability to the gross carrying amount of a financial asset or to the amortised cost of a financial liability.' and the effect of a fair value hedge, that is, the hedging gain/loss adjusts the carrying amount of the hedged item. *[IFRS 9 Appendix A]*.

The table below outlines the calculation:

31 December 2017		Year 2	Year 3	Year 4	Year 5
Contractual cash flows		5,000	5,000	5,000	105,000
Adjusted gross carrying amount[1]	98,163				
Updated EIR[2]	5.5%				
Expected cash flows		45,000			
Adjusted amortised cost (NPV at 5.5%)	42,644				
Expected cash shortfalls		40,000	(5,000)	(5,000)	(105,000)
NPV at 5.5%	(55,519)				
PD	2%				
Net present value (probability weighted) – this is the ECL	(1,110)				

1 The adjusted gross carrying amount equals the gross carrying amount adjusted for the fair value hedge adjustment and forms the new basis of the EIR calculation

2 The updated EIR is the interest rate that exactly discounts the contractual cash flows to the adjusted gross carrying amount

Again, the table above shows how the ECL is calculated as the net present value of the cash shortfalls, i.e. the difference between contractual and expected cash flows on each relevant date. The alternative calculation based on the probability-weighted present value for the two scenarios (FC98,163 × 98% plus FC42,644 × 2% = FC97,053) and then determining the difference to the gross carrying amount (including the fair value hedge adjustment) gives the same result (FC97,053 – FC98,163 = (FC1,110)).

This calculation means that there is an impairment gain recognised in profit or loss of FC32 (or LC45, respectively). This is because, to show more clearly how the accounting works, we have maintained the same expected cash flows as a year earlier, even though interest rates have now increased by 0.5 per cent. With a higher EIR, the ECLs are discounted at a higher rate. There are three effects that influence the impairment loss: the unwinding of the discount, the adjustment of the EIR and the change in the estimate of the timing of the payment default, which has moved 12 months into the future (i.e. from 31 December 2017 to 31 December 2018). The table below provides a reconciliation of those amounts:

31 December 2017 (values in FC)		
Loss allowance at the end of 1 January 2017	(1,143)	
Previous loss allowance rolled forward to reporting date (at 5% EIR)	(1,200)	
Unwinding of discount		**(57)**
Effect of adjusting the EIR		**32**
Effect of changes in estimate		**57**
Total change in loss allowance		**32**

Because we have maintained the expected cash shortfall pattern and its probability of occurring, the change in estimate is just the effect of deferral by a year of the expected date of default, which exactly offsets the unwinding of the discount.

In accordance with paragraph 16A of IFRS 7, the loss allowance for financial assets measured at fair value through other comprehensive income is not presented separately as a reduction of the carrying amount of the financial asset. As a consequence, the offsetting entry of the impairment gain FC32 (LC45) is recorded as a debit to other comprehensive income in the same period.

The bond is a monetary asset. Consequently, the entity recognises the changes arising from movements in foreign exchange rates in profit or loss in accordance with paragraphs 23(a) and 28 of IAS 21 and recognises other changes in accordance with IFRS 9. For the purposes of applying paragraph 28 of IAS 21, the asset is treated as an asset measured at amortised cost in the foreign currency.

The change in the fair value of the bond since 1 January 2016 amounts to LC34,918 and is recognised as a fair value adjustment to the carrying amount of the bond on the entity's statement of financial position.

The gain of LC39,543 due to the changes in foreign exchange rates is recognised in profit or loss. It consists of the impact of the change in the exchange rates during 2017:

- on the original gross carrying amount of the bond, amounting to LC40,000;
- offset by the loss allowance of the bond, amounting to LC457 (i.e. the difference of FC1,143 translated at the exchange rate as at 1 January 2017 of FC1 to LC1 and FC1,143 translated at the exchange rate as at 31 December 2017 of FC1 to LC1.4).

The difference between the change in fair value (LC34,918) and the gain recognised in profit or loss that is due to the changes in foreign exchange rates (LC39,543) is recognised in OCI. That difference amounts to LC4,625.

A gain of LC2,572 (FC1,837) on the swap is recognised in profit or loss and, because it is assumed that there is no hedge ineffectiveness, this amount coincides with the loss on the hedged item (as an absolute amount). Because this is a fair value hedge of a debt instrument at fair value through other comprehensive income this loss is recycled from other comprehensive income in the same period.

Situation as at 31 December 2018

As of 31 December 2018 (the reporting date), the entity observes the following facts:

- The fair value of the bond has further decreased from FC96,370 to FC87,114.
- The fair value of the swap has increased to FC2,092.
- Based on adverse macroeconomic developments in the industry in which the bond issuer operates, the entity assumes a significant increase in credit risk since initial recognition, and recognises the lifetime ECL for the bond.
- The entity updates its impairment estimate and now estimates the lifetime PD at 20 per cent and the LGD at FC48,500, resulting in (undiscounted) expected cash shortfalls of FC9,700. (For simplicity, this example assumes that payment default will happen on maturity when the entire face value becomes due).
- As at 31 December 2018, the exchange rate is FC1 to LC1.25.

The table below illustrates the amounts recognised in the financial statements between 31 December 2017 and 31 December 2018, as well as the shadow amortised cost calculation for the bond (debits are shown as positive numbers and credits as negative numbers):

	Financial Statements			**Shadow Calculation**	
	FC	**LC**		**FC**	**LC**
	Statement of financial position				
Bond (FV)	87,114	108,893	Gross carrying amount	100,000	125,000
Swap (FV)	2,092	2,615	Loss allowance	(8,195)	(10,244)
			Amortised cost	91,805	114,756
	Statement of profit or loss				
Impairment	7,085	8,856	FV hedge adjustment	(2,092)	(2,615)
FV hedge (bond)	255	319	Adj. gross carrying amt.	97,908	122,385
FX gain/loss (bond)		14,558	Adj. amortised cost	89,713	112,141
FV hedge (swap)	(255)	(319)			
FX gain/loss (swap)		276			
	Statement of OCI				
FV changes	9,256	11,468			
Impairment offset	(7,085)	(8,856)			
FV hedge recycling	(255)	(319)			

Similar to the situation as at 31 December 2017, the fair value hedge adjustment leads to an adjusted EIR. The table below illustrates the calculation:

31 December 2018 (values in FC)		**Year 3**	**Year 4**	**Year 5**
Contractual cash flows		5,000	5,000	105,000
Adjusted gross carrying amount[1]	97,908			
Updated EIR[2]	5.8%			
Expected cash flows		5,000	5,000	56,500
Adjusted amortised cost (NPV at 5.8%)	56,931			
Expected cash shortfalls		–	–	(48,500)
NPV at 5.8%	(40,977)			
PD	20%			
Net present value (probability weighted) – this is the ECL	(8,195)			

1 The adjusted gross carrying amount equals the gross carrying amount adjusted for the fair value hedge adjustment and forms the new basis of the EIR calculation

2 The updated EIR is the interest rate that exactly discounts the contractual cash flows to the adjusted gross carrying amount

Again, the table above shows how the ECL is calculated as the net present value of the cash shortfalls, i.e. the difference between contractual and expected cash flows on each relevant date. The alternative calculation based on the probability-weighted present value for the two scenarios (FC97,908 × 80% plus FC56,931 × 20% = FC89,713) and then determining the difference to the gross carrying amount (including the fair value hedge adjustment) gives the same result (FC FC89,713 – FC97,908 = (FC8,195)).

As at 31 December 2018, there are three effects that influence the impairment loss of FC8,398 (LC10,498) recognised in profit or loss: the unwinding of the discount, the adjustment of the EIR and the increase in credit risk (change in estimate). The table below provides a reconciliation of those amounts:

31 December 2018 (values in FC)		
Loss allowance at the beginning of the period	(1,110)	
Previous loss allowance rolled forward to reporting date (at 5.5% EIR)	(1,172)	
Unwinding of discount		**(61)**
Effect of adjusting the EIR		**60**
Effect of changes in estimate		**(7,083)**
Total change in loss allowance		**(7,085)**

The offsetting entry of the impairment loss FC7,085 (LC8,856) is recorded in other comprehensive income in the same period.

The change in the fair value of the bond since 31 December 2017 amounts to a decrease of LC26,026 and is recognised as a fair value adjustment to the carrying amount of the bond on the entity's statement of financial position.

The loss of LC14,558 due to the changes in foreign exchange rates is recognised in profit or loss. It consists of the impact of the change in the exchange rates during 2018:

- on the original gross carrying amount of the bond, amounting to a loss of LC15,000;
- on the loss allowance of the bond, amounting to a gain of LC167;
- on the fair value hedge adjustment, amounting to a gain of LC276.

The difference between the change in fair value (decrease of LC26,026) and the loss recognised in profit or loss that is due to the changes in foreign exchange rates (–LC14,558) is recognised in OCI. That difference amounts to LC11,468.

A gain of LC319 (FC255) on the swap is recognised in profit or loss and, because it is assumed that there is no hedge ineffectiveness, this amount coincides with the loss on the hedged item (as an absolute amount). Because this is a fair value hedge of a debt instrument at fair value through other comprehensive income this loss is recycled from other comprehensive income in the same period.

Situation as at 1 January 2019

On 1 January 2019, the entity decides to sell the bond for FC87,114, which is its fair value at that date and also closes out the swap at its fair value. For simplicity, all amounts, including the foreign exchange rate, are assumed to be the same as at 31 December 2018.

Upon derecognition, the entity reclassifies the cumulative amount recognised in OCI of (LC3,248) ((FC2,599)) to profit or loss. This amount is equal to the difference between the fair value and the adjusted amortised cost amount of the bond at the time of its derecognition. The table below presents a reconciliation of those amounts.

Reconciliation of loss on derecognition (values in LC) to cumulative OCI

Fair value per 1 January 2019	87,114			
Adjusted amortised cost per 1 January 2019	89,713			
Loss	**(2,599)**			
	Cum. OCI	1 January 2017	31 December 2017	31 December 2018
FV changes	**12,886**	–	3,630	9,256
Impairment	**(8,195)**	(1,143)	32	(7,085)
FV hedge recycling	**(2,092)**	–	(1,837)	(255)
Total OCI to be reclassified	**2,599**			

This table presents the amount that has not yet been recycled and, therefore, must be reclassified to profit or loss on derecognition.

5.9 Trade receivables, contract assets and lease receivables

The standard provides some operational simplifications for trade receivables, contract assets and lease receivables. These are the requirement or policy choice to apply the simplified approach that does not require entities to track changes in credit risk (see 5.3.2 above) and the practical expedient to calculate ECLs on trade receivables using a provision matrix (see 5.9.1 below).

5.9.1 Trade receivables and contract assets

It is a requirement for entities to apply the simplified approach for trade receivables or contract assets that do not contain a significant financing component. However, entities have a policy choice to apply either the general approach (see 5.3.1 above) or the simplified approach separately to trade receivables and contract assets that do contain a significant financing component (see 5.3.2 above). *[IFRS 9.5.5.15(a)]*.

Also, entities are allowed to use practical expedients when measuring ECLs, as long as the approach reflects a probability-weighted outcome, the time value of money and reasonable and supportable information that is available without undue cost or effort at the reporting date about past events, current conditions and forecasts of future economic conditions. *[IFRS 9.5.5.17, B5.5.35]*.

One of the approaches suggested in the standard is the use of a provision matrix as a practical expedient for measuring ECLs on trade receivables. For instance, the provision rates might be based on days past due (e.g. 1 per cent if not past due, 2 per cent if less than 30 days past due, etc.) for groupings of various customer segments that have similar loss patterns. The grouping may be based on geographical region, product type, customer rating, the type of collateral or whether covered by trade credit insurance, and the type of customer (such as wholesale or retail). To calibrate the matrix, the entity would adjust its historical credit loss experience with forward-looking information. *[IFRS 9.B5.5.35]*.

In practice, many corporates use a provision matrix to calculate their current impairment allowances. However, in order to comply with the IFRS 9 requirements, corporates would need to consider how current and forward-looking information might affect their customers' historical default rates and, consequently, how the information would affect their current expectations and estimates of ECLs. The use of the provision matrix is illustrated in the following example. *[IFRS 9 IG Example 12, IE74-IE77]*.

Example 50.36: Provision matrix

Company M, a manufacturer, has a portfolio of trade receivables of €30 million in 2017 and operates only in one geographical region. The customer base consists of a large number of small clients and the trade receivables are categorised by common risk characteristics that are representative of the customers' abilities to pay all amounts due in accordance with the contractual terms. The trade receivables do not have a significant financing component in accordance with IFRS 15. In accordance with paragraph 5.5.15 of IFRS 9, the loss allowance for such trade receivables is always measured at an amount equal to lifetime ECLs.

To determine the ECLs for the portfolio, Company M uses a provision matrix. The provision matrix is based on its historical observed loss rates over the expected life of the trade receivables and is adjusted for forward-looking estimates. At every reporting date, the historical observed loss rates are updated and changes in the forward-looking estimates are analysed. In this case it is forecast that economic conditions will deteriorate over the next year.

On that basis, Company M estimates the following provision matrix:

	Current	1-30 days past due	31-60 days past due	61-90 days past due	More than 90 days past due
Loss rate	0.3%	1.6%	3.6%	6.6%	10.6%

The trade receivables from the large number of small customers amount to €30 million and are measured using the provision matrix.

Chapter 50

	Gross carrying amount	Lifetime ECL allowance (Gross carrying amount × lifetime ECL rate)
Current	€15,000,000	€45,000
1-30 days past due	€7,500,000	€120,000
31-60 days past due	€4,000,000	€144,000
61-90 days past due	€2,500,000	€165,000
More than 90 days past due	€1,000,000	€106,000
	€30,000,000	**€580,000**

It should be noted that this example, like many in the standard, ignores the need to consider explicitly the time value of money, presumably in this case because the effect is considered immaterial.

5.9.2 *Lease receivables*

For lease receivables, entities have a policy choice to apply either the general approach (see 5.3.1 above) or the simplified approach (see 5.3.2 above) separately to finance and operating lease receivables (see Chapter 24 and Chapter 25). *[IFRS 9.5.5.15(b)]*.

When measuring ECLs for lease receivables, an entity should:

- use the cash flows that are used in measuring the lease receivables in accordance with IAS 17 or IFRS 16 (when applied); *[IFRS 9.B5.5.34]* and
- discount the ECLs using the same discount rate used in the measurement of the lease receivables in accordance with IAS 17 or IFRS 16 (when applied). *[IFRS 9.B5.5.46, IAS 17.4, IFRS 7 Appendix A]*.

There has been some discussion on whether the unguaranteed residual value (URV) of the asset subject to a finance lease should be included in the calculation of ECLs under IFRS 9. The URV is part of the gross investment in the finance lease, together with the minimum lease payments receivable by the lessor. Changes to URV arise from fluctuations in the price that could be received for the leased asset at the end of the lease term. Paragraph 2.1(b) of IFRS 9 scopes out rights and obligations under leases to which IAS 17 applies, except for the impairment of finance lease receivables (i.e. net investments in finance leases) and operating lease receivables recognised by a lessor (see 5.2 above). Furthermore, IAS 17 does not provide guidance on impairment of lease receivables as this is subject to IFRS 9. However, IAS 17 and IFRS 16 (when applied) provide guidance on measurement of the URV, which means that such measurement is within the scope of IAS 17 or IFRS16 (when applied) rather than the impairment requirements of IFRS 9. *[IFRS 7.41, IFRS 16.77]*. As IAS 17 has not been amended by IFRS 9, in our view, the URV of the asset underlying a finance lease is excluded from the calculation of ECLs under IFRS 9. This means that the collateral that is taken into account in measuring ECLs should exclude any amounts attributed to URV and recorded on the lessor's statement of financial position.

5.10 Loan commitments and financial guarantee contracts

The description of 'loan commitment' and the definition of 'financial guarantee contract' remain unchanged from IAS 39. Loan commitments (see Chapter 43 at 3.5) are described in IFRS 9 as 'firm commitments to provide credit under pre-specified terms and conditions', while a financial guarantee contract (see Chapter 43 at 3.4) is defined as 'a contract that requires the issuer to make specified payments to reimburse the holder for a loss it incurs because a specified debtor fails to make payment when due in accordance with the original or modified terms of a debt instrument'. *[IFRS 9.BCZ2.2, Appendix A, IAS 39.9, BC15]*.

The IFRS 9 impairment requirements apply to loan commitments and financial guarantee contracts that are not measured at fair value through profit or loss under IFRS 9, with some exceptions (see 5.2 above).

The ITG (see 5.1.5 above) discussed in April 2015 whether the impairment requirements in IFRS 9 must also be applied to other commitments to extend credit such as:

- a commitment (on inception of a finance lease) to commence a finance lease at a date in the future (i.e. a commitment to transfer the right to use an asset at the lease commencement date in return for a payment or series of payments in the future); and
- a commitment by a retailer through the issue of a store account to provide a customer with credit when the customer buys goods or services from the retailer in the future.

The ITG appeared to agree with the IASB's staff analysis that the impairment requirements of IFRS 9 apply to an agreement that contains a commitment to extend credit by virtue of paragraph 2.1(g) if:

- the agreement meets the description of a loan commitment; *[IFRS 9.BCZ2.2]*
- the agreement meets the definition of a financial instrument; *[IAS 32.11]* and
- none of the specific exemptions from the requirements of IFRS 9 apply. *[IFRS 9.2.1]*.

The IASB staff paper stated that some contracts, such as irrevocable finance lease agreements, might clearly contain a firm commitment at inception to provide credit under pre-specified terms and conditions. However, other cases might not be so clear cut, depending upon the specific terms of the agreement and other facts and circumstances (e.g. if the issuer of a store account has the discretion to refuse to sell products or services to a customer with a store card and hence can avoid extending credit).[51]

In the examples discussed above, the finance lease and store account do not meet the definition of a financial instrument until the contractual right to receive cash is established, that is likely to be at the commencement of the lease term or when goods or services are sold. *[IAS 32.11, AG20]*. Only lease receivables are scoped into the IFRS 9 impairment requirements (see 5.9.2 above). *[IFRS 9.2.1(b)]*. Consequently, there is no need to make provision for ECLs in accordance with IFRS 9 until a financial lease receivable or a financial asset within the scope of IFRS 9 is recognised.

The application of the model to financial guarantees and loan commitments warrants some further specification regarding some of the key elements, such as the determination of the credit quality on initial recognition, cash shortfalls and the EIR to be used in the ECL calculations. These specifications are summarised in the table below, which also highlights the differences in recognising and measuring ECLs for financial assets measured at amortised cost or at fair value through other comprehensive income, loan commitments and financial guarantee contracts.

	Financial assets measured at amortised cost or at fair value through other comprehensive income	Loan commitments	Financial guarantee contracts
Date of initial recognition in applying the impairment requirements (see 5.6.3 above and 6.2.1 below)	Trade date. *[IFRS 9.5.7.4]*.	Date that an entity becomes a party to the irrevocable commitment. *[IFRS 9.5.5.6]*.	Date that an entity becomes a party to the irrevocable commitment. *[IFRS 9.5.5.6]*.
Period over which to estimate ECLs (see 5.4.3 above)	The expected life up to the maximum contractual period (including extension options at the discretion of the borrower) over which the entity is exposed to credit risk and not a longer period. *[IFRS 9.5.5.19]*.	The expected life up to the maximum contractual period over which an entity has a present contractual obligation to extend credit. *[IFRS 9.B5.5.38]*. However, for revolving credit facilities (see 5.11 below), this period extends beyond the contractual period over which the entity is exposed to credit risk and the ECLs would not be mitigated by credit risk management actions. *[IFRS 9.5.5.20, B5.5.39, B5.5.40]*.	The expected life up to the maximum contractual period over which an entity has a present contractual obligation to extend credit. *[IFRS 9.B5.5.38]*.
Cash shortfalls in measuring ECLs (see 5.4.1 above)	Cash shortfalls between the cash flows that are due to an entity in accordance with the contract and the cash flows that the entity expects to receive. *[IFRS 9.B5.5.28]*.	Cash shortfalls between the contractual cash flows that are due to the entity if the holder of the loan commitment draws down the loan and the cash flows that the entity expects to receive if the loan is drawn down. *[IFRS 9.B5.5.30]*.	Cash shortfalls are the expected payments to reimburse the holder for a credit loss that it incurs less any amounts that the entity (issuer) expects to receive from the holder, the debtor or any other party. *[IFRS 9.B5.5.32]*.
EIR used in discounting ECLs (see 5.4.5 above)	The EIR is determined or approximated at initial recognition of the financial instrument. *[IFRS 9.B5.5.44]*.	The EIR of the resulting asset will be applied and if this is not determinable, then the current rate representing the risk of the cash flows is used. *[IFRS 9.B5.5.47, B5.5.48]*.	The current rate representing the risk of the cash flows is used. *[IFRS 9.B5.5.48]*.
Assessment of significant increases in credit risk (see 5.5 above)	An entity considers changes in the risk of a default occurring on the financial asset. *[IFRS 9.5.5.9]*.	An entity considers changes in the risk of a default occurring on the loan to which a loan commitment relates. *[IFRS 9.B5.5.8]*.	An entity considers the changes in the risk that the specified debtor will default on the contract. *[IFRS 9.B5.5.8]*.

At its meeting in April 2015, the ITG (see 5.1.5 above) also discussed the measurement of ECLs for an issued financial guarantee contract that requires the holder to pay further premiums in the future. Some members of the ITG agreed with the staff's analysis that the issuer of a financial guarantee contract should exclude future premium receipts due from the holder when measuring ECLs in respect of the expected cash outflows payable under the guarantee.[52] When estimating the cash shortfalls, the amounts that the entity expects to receive from the holder should relate only to recoveries or reimbursements of claims for losses and would not include receipts of premiums. *[IFRS 9.B5.5.32]*. Moreover, the expected cash outflows under the guarantee depend upon the risk of default of the guaranteed asset, while the expected future premiums receipts are subject to the risk of default by the holder of the guarantee. Hence, these risks of default should be considered separately.

In addition, an ITG member noted that the terms of a financial guarantee contract may affect the period of exposure to credit risk on the guarantee, for example if the guarantee were contingent or cancellable. This should be taken into consideration when measuring the ECLs of the guarantee.

The 'higher of' test required by IFRS 9 for the subsequent measurement affects the recognition of the ECL provision for financial guarantees and off-market loan commitments (see 2.8 above). *[IFRS 9.4.2.1(c), 4.2.1(d)]*. Consequently, the timing of premium payments can result in no ECL provision being recognised.

5.11 Revolving credit facilities

The 2013 Exposure Draft specified that the maximum period over which ECLs are to be calculated should be limited to the contractual period over which the entity is exposed to credit risk.[53] This would mean that the allowance for commitments that can be withdrawn at short notice by a lender, such as overdrafts and credit card facilities, would be limited to the ECLs that would arise over the notice period, which might be only one day. However, banks will not normally exercise their right to cancel the commitment until there is already evidence of significant deterioration, which exposes them to risk over a considerably longer period. The IASB responded to the concerns of respondents by setting out further guidance and an example addressing such arrangements.

The guidance relates to financial instruments that 'include both a loan and an undrawn commitment component and for which the entity's contractual ability to demand repayment and cancel the commitment does not limit the entity's exposure to credit losses to the contractual notice period'. *[IFRS 9.5.5.20]*. Despite the use of the word 'both', the ITG agreed, in April 2015, that this guidance applies even if the facility has yet to be drawn down. It also applies if the facility has been completely drawn down, as it is the nature of revolving facilities that the drawn down component is periodically paid off before further amounts will be drawn down again in future.

The standard goes on to describe three characteristics generally associated with such instruments: *[IFRS 9.B5.5.39]*

- they usually have no fixed term or repayment structure and usually have a short contractual cancellation period;
- the contractual ability to cancel the contract is not enforced in day-to-day management, but only when the lender is aware of an increase in credit risk at the facility level; and
- they are managed on a collective basis.

At its December 2015 meeting, the ITG discussed the scope of the revolving credit facilities exception in paragraph 5.5.20 of IFRS 9. In particular, they debated whether:

- multi-purpose credit facilities, some of which have the ability to be drawn down in a number of different ways (e.g. as a revolving overdraft, a variable or fixed rate loan (with or without a fixed term) or an amortising loan such as a mortgage) would fall within the scope exception;
- the general characteristics identified in paragraph B5.5.39 of IFRS 9 should be considered to be required characteristics, or merely examples of typical characteristics; and
- the lack of a fixed term would prevent a facility from falling within the scope exception.

The ITG commented that:

- The supporting application guidance in paragraph B5.5.39 of IFRS 9 reinforces the features described in paragraph 5.5.20 of IFRS 9 by setting out general characteristics which, while not determinative, are consistent with those features.
- The Basis for Conclusions of IFRS 9 provides further context around the type of financial instruments that the Board envisaged would fall within the scope exception. In particular, the exception was intended to be limited in nature and that it was introduced in order to address specific concerns raised by respondents in relation to revolving credit facilities that were managed on a collective basis. Also, it was understood that these types of financial instruments included both a loan and an undrawn commitment component and that they were managed, and ECLs were estimated, on a facility level; i.e. the drawn and undrawn exposure were viewed as one single cash flow from the borrower. *[IFRS 9.BC5.254-BC5.261]*.
- Consequently, both the drawn and undrawn components of these facilities were understood to have similar short contractual maturities, i.e. the lender had both the ability to withdraw the undrawn commitment component and demand repayment of the drawn component at short notice.

- An immediately revocable facility which has a fixed maturity (e.g. 5 years) would be consistent with the type of facility within the scope exception because the fixed term feature does not negate the lender's contractual right to cancel the undrawn component at any time. In contrast, an immediately revocable facility that has no fixed maturity but when drawn, can take the form of a loan with a fixed maturity (i.e. once it has been drawn, the lender no longer has the right to demand immediate repayment at its discretion) would not be consistent with the type of facility envisaged to be within the scope exception. This is because the fixed term feature does negate the lender's contractual right to demand repayment of the undrawn component. However, regarding this characteristic, the ITG members also highlighted the following:
  - (a) an entity would first need to establish the unit of account to which the requirements of IFRS 9 should be applied. In this regard, they noted that even if there was only one legal contract supporting a particular multi-purpose credit facility, there might be more than one unit of account to consider; and
  - (b) if the fixed-term feature was for a shorter period, judgement would be required in order to determine whether such a fixed-term feature would prevent a particular financial instrument from falling within the scope exception (e.g. whether the borrower could consider the exposure on the drawn and undrawn components to be one single cash flow).
- IFRS 7 requires an entity to explain, among other things, the assumptions used to measure ECLs. Within the context of multi-purpose credit facilities, such disclosures are likely to be important in order to meet the disclosure objectives (see 5.13 below and Chapter 54 at 5.2.3).

While, according to the ITG, the drawn and undrawn exposures are viewed as 'one single cash flow from the borrower', the standard's Basis for Conclusions (paragraph BC5.259) is slightly clearer. It states that the loan and undrawn commitment 'are managed, and ECLs are estimated on a facility level. In other words, there is only one set of cash flows from the borrower that relates to both components'. Hence, the drawn and undrawn elements of a revolving facility within the scope of the exception would normally be viewed as only one unit of account. The ITG discussion seems to suggest that a new unit of account would be recognised if a borrower chose to draw down on a multi-purpose facility in the form of a term loan, because this is the point where this specific drawn portion ceases to share the key characteristic of a revolving facility, i.e. the entity's contractual ability to demand repayment and cancel the commitment.

According to the standard, 'for such financial instruments, and only those financial instruments, the entity shall measure ECLs over the period that the entity is exposed to credit risk and ECLs would not be mitigated by credit risk management actions, even if that period extends beyond the maximum contractual period'. *[IFRS 9.5.5.20]*. In order to calculate the period for which ECLs are assessed, 'an entity should consider factors such as historical information and experience about:

(a) the period over which the entity was exposed to credit risk on similar financial instruments;

(b) the length of time for related defaults to occur on similar financial instruments following a significant increase in credit risk; and

(c) the credit risk management actions that an entity expects to take once the credit risk on the financial instrument has increased, such as the reduction or removal of undrawn limits.' *[IFRS 9.B5.5.40]*.

This wording in the standard is not very easy to interpret or apply.

This following example illustrates the calculation of impairment for revolving credit facilities, based on Illustrative Example 10 in the Implementation Guidance for the standard. *[IFRS 9 IG Example 10, IE58-IE65]*. For the sake of clarity, the assumptions and calculations have been adapted from the IASB example as it is not explicit on the source of the parameters and how they are computed. The example has also been expanded to show the calculation of the loss allowances. However, to simplify the example, we have ignored the need to discount ECLs or whether the credit conversion factor would change if an exposure has significantly deteriorated in credit risk.

Example 50.37: Revolving credit facilities

Bank A provides credit cards with a one day cancellation right and manages the drawn and undrawn commitment on each card together, as a facility. Bank A sub-divides the credit card portfolio by segregating those amounts for which a significant increase in credit risk was identified at the individual facility level from the remainder of the portfolio. The remainder of this example only illustrates the calculation of ECLs for the sub-portfolio for which a significant increase in credit risk was not identified at the individual facility level. At the reporting date, the outstanding balance on the sub-portfolio is £6,000,000 and the undrawn facility is £4,000,000. The Bank determines the sub-portfolio's expected life as 30 months (using the guidance set out above) and that the credit risk on 25 per cent of the sub-portfolio has increased significantly since initial origination, making up £1,500,000 of the outstanding balance and £1,000,000 of the undrawn commitment (see the calculation of the exposure in the table below).

To calculate its EAD, Bank A uses an approach whereby it adds the amounts that are drawn at the reporting date and additional draw-downs that are expected in the case that a customer defaults. For those expected additional draw-downs, Bank A uses a credit conversion factor that represents the estimate of what percentage of that part of committed credit facilities that is unused at the reporting date would be drawn by a customer before he defaults. Using its credit models, the bank determines this credit conversion factor as 95 per cent. The EAD on the portion of facilities measured on a lifetime ECL basis is therefore £2,450,000, made up of the drawn balance of £1,500,000 and £950,000 of expected further draw-downs before the customers default. For the remainder of the facilities, the EAD that is measured on a 12-month ECL basis is £7,350,000, being the remaining drawn balance of £4,500,000 plus additional expected draw-downs for customers defaulting over the next 12 months of £2,850,000 (see the calculation for the EAD in the table below).

Bank A has estimated that the PD for the next 12 months is 5 per cent, and 30 per cent for the next 30 months. The estimate for the LGD on the credit cards in the sub-portfolio is 90 per cent. That results in lifetime ECLs of £661,500 and 12-month ECLs of £330,750 (see calculation for ECLs in the table below).

For the presentation in the statement of financial position, the ECLs against the drawn amount of £607,500 would be recognised as an allowance against the credit card receivables and the remainder of the ECLs that relates to the undrawn facilities of £384,750 would be recognised as a liability (see table below).

Determination made at facility level		*Drawn*	*Undrawn*	*Total*
Facility		£6,000,000	£4,000,000	£10,000,000
Exposure				
Subject to lifetime ECLs (25% of the facility has been determined to have significantly increased in credit risk)	25%	£1,500,000	£1,000,000	£2,500,000
Subject to 12-month ECLs (the remaining 75% of the facility)	75%	£4,500,000	£3,000,000	£7,500,000
Credit conversion factor (CCF) *A uniform CCF is used irrespective of deterioration, which reflects that the CCF is contingent on default which is the same reference point for a 12-month and lifetime ECL calculation*	95%			
EAD *EAD for undrawn balances is calculated as exposure × CCF*				
Subject to lifetime ECLs		£1,500,000	£950,000	£2,450,000
Subject to 12-month ECLs		£4,500,000	£2,850,000	£7,350,000
PD				
Exposures subject to lifetime ECLs	30%			
Exposures subject to 12-month ECLs	5%			
LGD	90%			
ECLs (EAD × PD × LGD)				
Exposures subject to lifetime ECLs		£405,000	£256,500	£661,500
Exposures subject to 12-month ECLs		£202,500	£128,250	£330,750
		£607,500 *presented as loss allowance against assets*	£384,750 *presented as provision*	£992,250

We make the following observations:

- Example 10 of the standard (on which our Example 50.37 above is based), does not explain how the entity has concluded that 25% of the portfolio has significantly increased in credit risk. Collective assessment is discussed at 5.5.5 above.
- Example 10 in the standard does not show how the 30-month period was calculated.
- We use the same credit conversion factor, of 95%, for calculating the EAD, irrespective of whether it is an input for 12-month or lifetime ECLs. This is based on an assumption that the extent of future draw-downs in the event that the customer defaults does not differ depending on whether at the reporting date there had been a significant increase in credit risk. In practice, for many credit cards, the exposure in the event of default reaches close to the credit limit and may even exceed it. However, as discussed further below, the standard does not permit the use of a credit conversion factor of more than 100%. For this reason, the use of a conventional credit conversion factor model for estimating the EAD may need to be adjusted to comply with the standard.

The ITG in April 2015, discussed how to determine the appropriate period when measuring ECLs for a portfolio of revolving credit card exposures in stages 1, 2 and 3 and commented that:

- An entity's ability to segment and stratify the portfolio into different sections of exposures in accordance with how those exposures are being managed will be relevant. For example, an entity may be able to identify exposures with specific attributes that are considered more likely to default and consequently would have shorter average lives than those that are expected to continue performing (see 5.5.5 above).
- While IFRS 9 requires a period in excess of the maximum contractual period to be used when measuring ECLs, the fundamental aim was still to determine the period over which the entity is exposed to credit risk and an entity must consider all three factors set out in paragraph B5.5.40. Consequently, expected defaults or potential credit risk management actions such as reduction or removal of undrawn limits could result in a shorter period of exposure than that indicated by the historical behavioural life of the facility. That is, the time horizon is not the period over which the lender expects the facility to be used, but the period over which the lender is, in practice, exposed to credit risk.

At its December 2015 meeting, the ITG continued the discussion on how an entity should determine the maximum period to consider when measuring ECLs for revolving credit facilities. This divided into two sub-questions: when does this period start and when does it end?

With respect to the starting-point, the ITG members observed that the requirements of paragraph B5.5.40 of IFRS 9 do not alter the starting-point of the maximum period to consider when measuring ECLs and consequently, the appropriate starting-point should be the reporting date.

With respect to the ending-point, ITG members focused on which credit risk management actions an entity should take into account and noted that:

- An entity should consider:
  - (a) only credit risk management actions that it expects to take rather than all credit risk management actions that it is legally and operationally able to take;
  - (b) only those credit risk management actions that serve to mitigate credit risk and consequently, actions that do not mitigate credit risk such as the reinstatement of previously curtailed credit limits should not be considered; and
  - (c) all credit risk management actions that it expects to take and that serve to either terminate or limit the credit risk exposure in some way.
- An entity's expected actions must be based on reasonable and supportable information. In this regard, consideration should be given to an entity's normal credit risk mitigation process, past practice and future intentions.
- The ending-point could be limited by the expected timing of the entity's next review process, but only if the entity's normal business practice is to take credit risk mitigation actions as part of this review process. Consequently, it may not always be appropriate to use the timing of the entity's next review process as a basis for determining the ending-point. (We make some observations on this element of the ITG discussion, below).
- In respect of assets in stage 2, the probability of assets curing and defaulting would need to be taken into account when determining the maximum period to consider when measuring ECLs.
- It was noted that a distinction should be made between credit risk management actions such as the reinstatement of a previously curtailed credit limit (that should not be taken into account) and considering how a particular stage 2 exposure that has not yet been subject to any credit risk mitigation actions will develop. For example, an entity may have determined that there has been a significant increase in credit risk since initial recognition in respect of a particular exposure but may not yet have taken any specific credit risk mitigation actions such as the curtailment or termination of the credit limit. In this case, consideration should be given to the possibility that the exposure may cure rather than default. In contrast, if an entity had taken credit risk mitigation action in respect of that exposure such as the curtailment of the credit limit, it would not be appropriate to take into consideration the possibility that the exposure may subsequently cure, resulting in a reinstatement of the previously curtailed credit limit when determining the maximum exposure period. In this regard, appropriate portfolio segmentation is crucial, in particular in relation to financial assets in stage 2.

- There is only one maximum exposure period to consider, which applies equally to both the drawn and undrawn components of a revolving credit facility, which is consistent with the way in which the facility is managed. Nevertheless, in measuring ECLs, credit risk mitigation actions may affect the drawn and undrawn components differently. For example, when an entity cancels the undrawn component, the possibility of any future drawdowns is removed, whereas when an entity demands repayment of the drawn component the recovery period associated with that drawn exposure still needs to be considered in measuring ECLs.
- Ultimately, the estimation of the maximum period to consider would require judgement and consequently the disclosure requirements of IFRS 7 (such as those explaining inputs, assumptions and estimation techniques in relation to ECLs) would be important (see 5.13 below and Chapter 54 at 5.2.3).

Perhaps the portion of the ITG's discussion that is least clear is whether it is possible to limit the period over which to measure ECLs by the expected timing of the entity's next credit review process. As an example, a bank may have a policy of carrying out a thorough review of all its credit card facilities every year and this has in the past resulted in mitigation activity. Does that mean that the entity would set the period over which to measure ECLs to only the timing of this annual review? As at the time of writing, we are aware of two very different views.

One view is that as long as the credit review is thorough as would be carried out when a card is first issued, and it does result in credit risk mitigation (i.e. some facilities are reduced or withdrawn), then the timing of the next review should be regarded as the end of the measurement period. (However, a longer period would be appropriate for any drawn down components if collection may take a little longer.)

A second view is that a periodic credit review should only ever be taken into account when assessing the period over which to measure losses *to the extent that* it is expected to result in actual limits reduction or withdrawal. Hence, for example, if normally 20% of facilities are withdrawn based on an annual review, then for 20% of the outstanding facilities the period to measure losses should be limited by the timing of this next review. For the other 80% of the facilities, three things may happen: they may someday default, the facility may someday be reduced or withdrawn, or the borrower may someday cease to use the card. For the 80% it is necessary to model each of these possibilities, which means that the period over which to measure ECLs may extend for a number of years into the future. Under this view the standard's requirement for any facilities measured using lifetime ECLs can be simply summarised as 'how much do you expect to lose'? The length of the period over which losses are measured is of secondary importance except that it is necessary to know when defaults are expected to occur, in order to determine the appropriate discounting.

Although use of the first view would be limited to those banks who do carry out a thorough periodic credit review, given the potential for diversity of practice, it would be useful for this issue to be explored further by the ITG.

It should be stressed that this issue is of relevance mostly for those facilities that are measured using lifetime credit losses. The allowance for those assets in stage 1 will be calculated based only on losses associated with default in the next twelve months, which is likely to be the period used to measure ECLs unless the entity's risk mitigation activities indicate that a shorter period should be used.

At its April 2015 meeting, the ITG also discussed the date of initial recognition when assessing significant increases in credit risk for a portfolio of revolving credit facilities. There will typically be a diverse customer base, ranging from long-standing customers who have been with the bank for many years, to new customers who have only recently opened an account. One view is that the date of initial recognition is the date the facility was issued and this should only be changed if there had been a derecognition of the original facility. The challenge would be how to determine when changes are sufficiently significant to result in a derecognition of the original facility and recognition of a new facility. Judgement would be required in making this assessment, which would depend on the specific facts and circumstances. For example:

- in some circumstances, issuing a new card may be indicative that the original facility has been derecognised (e.g. replacement of a student credit card with a new credit card upon graduation), but in other cases, this may be a purely operational process and thus would not indicate that a new facility has been issued; and
- credit reviews or revision to credit limits in themselves may not indicate that a new facility has been issued.

Against the view that it is necessary to look back to an original recognition date, others would argue that this is inappropriate for a revolving facility, since the credit decisions are periodically refreshed and those made on origination are no longer relevant. Particularly, if there is a periodic formal reassessment, as thorough as that as on original recognition, the date of this reassessment may be a more appropriate reference date. This is consistent with paragraph BC5.260 in the Basis of Conclusions, 'if an entity decides to renew or extend its commitment to extend credit, it will be a new instrument for which the entity has the opportunity to revise the terms and conditions.'

Given that it is neither practical nor seems very relevant to look back many years to assess whether there has been a significant increase in credit risk, it is likely that judgment will be used to determine more appropriate dates. However, to limit diversity in practice it would be useful for this issue to be explored further by the ITG.

At its meeting on 16 September 2015, the ITG (see 5.1.5 above) discussed how an entity should estimate future drawdowns on undrawn lines of credit when an entity has a history of allowing customers to exceed their contractually set credit limits on overdrafts and other revolving credit facilities. The ITG members noted that:

- The impairment model in IFRS 9 is based on the contractual terms of a financial instrument. Specifically:
  - (a) the definition of credit losses refers to a comparison between the contractual cash flows that are due to an entity in accordance with the contract and all the cash flows that the entity expects to receive; and
  - (b) the maximum period to consider when measuring ECLs is the maximum contractual period (including extension options) over which the entity is exposed to credit risk and not a longer period, even if that period is consistent with business practice.

- The exception for some types of revolving credit facilities set out in paragraph 5.5.20 of IFRS 9 relates to the contractual commitment period and does not address the contractual credit limit. The standard was clear in this regard and consequently, it would not be appropriate to analogise this specific exception to the contractual credit limit.
- Some members of the ITG pointed out that, in practice, the tenor and amount of revolving credit facilities are inextricably linked, because banks not only extend credit for a period in excess of their maximum contractual commitment period but also allow customers to make drawdowns in excess of the maximum contractually agreed credit limit as notified to the customer. Consequently, if amounts in excess of the maximum contractually agreed credit limits are not taken into account, there would be a potential disconnect between the accounting and credit risk management view.
- However, it was concluded that IFRS 9 limits the estimation of future drawdowns to the contractually agreed credit limit.

At its December 2015 meeting, the ITG went on further to discuss how future drawdowns should be estimated for charge cards if there is no specified credit limit in the contract when measuring of ECLs. The ITG members considered a specific fact pattern where the bank has the ability to approve each transaction at the time of sale based on the customer's perceived spending capacity using statistical models and inputs such as spending history and known income. The ITG members noted that because the bank has the right to refuse each transaction at its discretion, and on the assumption that the bank actually exercises that right in practice, then:

- the contractual credit limit should be considered to be zero and consequently future drawdowns would not be taken into account; and
- furthermore, the facility described would not fall within the scope exception because there would be no undrawn commitment component (i.e. there is no firm commitment to extend credit).

However, the ITG members noted that their discussions focussed on the very specific fact pattern presented and observed that the conclusion could differ in other situations.

5.12 Presentation of expected credit losses in the statement of financial position

IFRS 9 uses the term 'loss allowance' throughout the standard as an umbrella term for ECLs that are recognised in the statement of financial position. However, that umbrella term leaves open the question of how those ECLs should be presented in that statement. Their presentation differs by the type of the credit risk exposures that are in scope of the impairment requirements. *[IFRS 9 Appendix A]*. This section explains how presentation applies in the different situations.

Any adjustment to the loss allowance balance due to an increase or decrease of the amount of ECLs recognised in accordance with IFRS 9, is reflected in profit or loss in a separate line as an impairment gain or loss. *[IAS 1.82(ba), IFRS 9.5.5.8, Appendix A]*.

5.12.1 *Allowance for financial assets measured at amortised cost, contract assets and lease receivables*

ECLs on financial assets measured at amortised cost, lease receivables (see Chapter 24 and 25) and contract assets (see Chapter 30) are presented as an allowance, i.e. as an integral part of the measurement of those assets in the statement of financial position.

Unlike the requirement to show impairment losses as a separate line item in the statement of profit or loss, there is no similar consequential amendment to IAS 1 – *Presentation of Financial Statements* – to present the loss allowance as a separate line item in the statement of financial position. *[IAS 1.82(ba)]*.

It is clear from the standard that the definition of *amortised cost* of a financial asset is after adjusting for any loss allowance and hence, the loss allowance would reduce the *gross carrying amount* in the statement of financial position (which is why an allowance is sometimes referred to as a contra asset account). *[IFRS 9 Appendix A]*. Accordingly, financial assets measured at amortised cost, contract assets and lease receivables should be presented net of the loss allowance at their amortised cost in the statement of financial position.

This was confirmed at the ITG meeting in December 2015, when the ITG discussed whether an entity is required to present the loss allowance for financial assets measured at amortised cost (or trade receivables, contract assets or lease receivables) separately in the statement of financial position. The ITG members first noted that irrespective of how the loss allowance is presented or how it is included in the measurement of the financial instrument, IFRS 7 contains disclosure requirements pertaining to the loss allowance for all financial instruments within the scope of the IFRS 9 impairment requirements. The ITG members also noted that, in contrast to the case of financial assets measured at fair value through other comprehensive income, neither IFRS 9 nor IFRS 7 contains any specific requirements regarding the presentation of the loss allowance for financial assets measured at amortised cost (or trade receivables, contract assets or lease receivables) on the face of the statement of financial position. In accordance with the general requirements of IAS 1, the financial statements should fairly present the financial position of an entity. However, the ITG members noted that paragraph 54 of IAS 1 does not list the loss allowance as an amount that is required to be separately presented on the face of the statement of financial position.

5.12.1.A *Write-off*

IFRS 9 provides guidance on when the allowance should be used, i.e. when it should be applied against the gross carrying amount of a financial asset. This occurs when there is a write-off on a financial asset, which happens when the entity has no reasonable expectations of recovering the contractual cash flows on a financial asset in its entirety or a portion thereof. A write-off is considered a derecognition event. *[IFRS 9.5.4.4, B3.2.16(r)]*. No similar guidance is provided in IAS 39 and its derecognition guidance does not refer to write-offs.

For example, a lender plans to enforce the collateral on a loan and expects to recover no more than 30 per cent of the value of the loan from selling the collateral. If the lender has no reasonable prospects of recovering any further cash flows from the loan, it should write off the remaining 70 per cent. *[IFRS 9.B5.4.9]*. The example given in the standard demonstrates that write-offs can be for only a partial amount instead of the entire gross carrying amount.

If the amount of loss on write-off is greater than the accumulated loss allowance, the difference will be an additional impairment loss. In situations where a further impairment loss occurs, the question has arisen as to how it should be presented: simply as a loss in profit or loss with a credit directly to the gross carrying amount; or first, as an addition to the allowance that is then applied against the gross carrying amount. The difference between those alternatives is whether the additional impairment loss flows through the allowance, showing up in a reconciliation of the allowance as an addition and a use (i.e. a write-off), or whether such additional impairment amounts bypass the allowance. The IASB's original 2009 Exposure Draft (see 5.1.1 above) explicitly mandated that all write-offs could only be debited against the allowance, meaning that any direct write-offs against profit or loss without flowing through the allowance were prohibited.[54] IFRS 9 does not include any similar explicit guidance on this issue.

In addition, IFRS 7 requires an entity to disclose its policies in relation to write-offs and also, the amounts written off during the period that are still subject to enforcement activity (see 5.13 below and Chapter 54 at 5.2.3). *[IFRS 7.35F(e), 35L]*. It should be noted that there is a tension between this requirement and the criteria in IFRS 9 for write-off, since it may be difficult to argue that there is no reasonable expectation of recovering the contractual cash flows if the loan is still subject to enforcement activity.

5.12.1.B *Presentation of the gross carrying amount and expected credit loss allowance for credit-impaired assets*

For financial assets that are credit-impaired in stage 3, the application of the EIR to the amortised cost of the financial asset applies only to the calculation and presentation of interest revenue. The Basis for Conclusions confirms that this does not affect the measurement of the loss allowance. *[IFRS 9.BC5.75]*. As long as the asset was not credit-impaired on initial recognition, the EIR is based on the contractual cash flows, excluding ECLs and this does not change when the asset becomes credit-impaired. *[IFRS 9.B5.4.4, Appendix A]*. Consequently, the calculation of the gross carrying amount and the ECL allowance are not affected by the recognition of interest revenue moving from a gross to a net basis.

During its meeting in December 2015, the ITG discussed the measurement of the gross carrying amount and loss allowance for credit-impaired financial assets that are measured at amortised cost (excluding those that are purchased or originated credit-impaired). Interest revenue for credit-impaired financial assets is required to be reported in profit or loss based on the original EIR multiplied by the amortised cost (i.e. the gross carrying amount less the loss allowance). A question was raised on how the disclosed figures for the gross carrying amount and loss allowance should each be calculated. This is illustrated in the example below.[55]

Example 50.38: Measuring the gross carrying amount and loss allowance for credit-impaired financial assets that are not purchased or originated credit-impaired

The Bank has a credit-impaired financial asset with an amortised cost of $100 and an EIR of 10% per annum. On 31 December 2016, an impairment allowance was recognised of $60. During 2017, no cash is received, and on 31 December 2017, there is no change in the expected cash flows. Accordingly, the amortised cost becomes $44 (being $40 + ($40 × 10%)). Three different ways could be used to reflect the changes in the net amortised cost in the gross carrying amount and the loss allowance:

Approach	A	B	C
	$	$	$
Gross carrying amount	110	104	100
Loss allowance	(66)	(60)	(56)
Amortised cost	44	44	44

It was acknowledged by the ITG members that IAS 39 provides no specific guidance on this matter and that there is diversity in current practice.

The ITG members appeared to agree that only Approach A is IFRS 9-compliant. Thereby, for assets in stage 3, it is necessary to 'gross up' accrued interest income, to increase both the disclosed gross carrying amount and loss allowance in the notes to the financial statements. This is because IFRS 9, unlike IAS 39, defines the gross carrying amount. Approach A requires the entity to calculate:

(a) the gross carrying amount by discounting the estimated contractual cash flows (without considering ECLs) using the original EIR; and

(b) the loss allowance by discounting the expected cash shortfalls using the original EIR.

This conclusion has caused some discussion. Some have pointed out that, assuming no further loss is expected, this results in an increase in the amount of the impairment allowance over time that is not presented as an impairment loss, even though all movements in the allowance are required by paragraph 82 of IAS 1 to be reported in a separate line in the income statement. Presumably the IASB considers the requirements of IFRS 9 to be more relevant, since it is specific on how the gross carrying amount is defined and how interest should be recognised. However, it would be useful for IAS 1 to be amended so as to be consistent.

Depending on the legal form of the loan, we assume that once interest is no longer contractually due – for instance when the bank moves to take possession of collateral, there would be no need to continue to make these gross up entries.

5.12.2 Provisions for loan commitments and financial guarantee contracts

In contrast to the presentation of impairment of assets, ECLs on loan commitments and financial guarantee contracts are presented as a provision in the statement of financial position, i.e. as a liability. *[IFRS 9 Appendix A]*.

For financial institutions that offer credit facilities, commitments may often be partially drawn down, i.e. an entity may have a facility that includes both a loan (a financial asset) and an undrawn commitment (a loan commitment). If the entity cannot separately identify the ECLs attributable to the drawn amount and the undrawn commitment, IFRS 7 requires an entity to present the provision for ECLs on the loan commitment together with the allowance for the financial asset. IFRS 7 states, further, that if the combined ECLs exceed the gross carrying amount of the financial asset, then the ECLs should be recognised as a provision. *[IFRS 7.B8E]*.

5.12.3 *Accumulated impairment amount for debt instruments measured at fair value through other comprehensive income*

Rather than presenting ECLs on financial assets measured at fair value through other comprehensive income as an allowance, this amount is presented as the 'accumulated impairment amount' in other comprehensive income. This is because financial assets measured at fair value through other comprehensive income are measured at fair value in the statement of financial position and the accumulated impairment amount cannot reduce the carrying amount of these assets (see 5.8 above for further details). *[IFRS 9.4.1.2A, 5.5.2, Appendix A]*.

5.13 Disclosures

The credit risk disclosure requirements are less onerous than were proposed in the 2013 Exposure Draft. Nevertheless, they have been expanded significantly when compared to those currently in IFRS 7 and are supplemented by some detailed implementation guidance. The disclosure requirements in relation to the IFRS 9 ECL model are dealt with in more detail in Chapter 54 at 5.2.3, and this section provides only a high level summary.

The new credit risk disclosure requirements will enable users of financial statements to understand better an entity's credit risk management practices, its credit risk exposures, ECL estimates and changes in credit risks. *[IFRS 7.35B]*. In order to meet this objective, an entity will need to disclose both quantitative and qualitative information that includes the following:

- inputs, assumptions and estimation used (and any changes) to determine significant increases in credit risk of financial instruments, including the application of the low credit risk and more than 30 days past due operational simplifications (see 5.5 above); *[IFRS 7.35F(a), 35G(a)(ii), 35G(c)]*
- inputs, assumptions and techniques used (and any changes) in measuring 12-month and lifetime ECLs, including the definition of default and the incorporation of forward-looking information (see 5.4 above); *[IFRS 7.35F(b), 35G(a)(i), 35G(b), 35G(c), B8A]*
- how the financial instruments were grouped if the measurement of ECLs was performed on a collective basis (see 5.5.5 above); *[IFRS 7.35F(c)]*
- how collateral and other credit enhancements affect the estimate of ECLs, including a description of the nature and quality of collateral held and quantitative information about the collateral for financial assets that are credit-impaired (see 5.4.7 above); *[IFRS 7.35K, B8F, B8G]*

- a reconciliation of the opening and closing balance of the loss allowance and explanations of the changes. This disclosure is required to be shown separately for:
  - financial instruments that are measured using 12-month ECLs;
  - those that are measured using lifetime ECLs; financial assets that are credit-impaired on initial recognition;
  - those that are subsequently credit-impaired; and
  - trade receivables, contract assets and lease receivables measured under the simplified approach; *[IFRS 7.35H]*
- explanation of how significant changes in the gross carrying amount of financial instruments during the period contributed to changes in the loss allowance; *[IFRS 7.35I]*
- inputs, assumptions and techniques used (and any changes) to determine whether a financial asset is credit-impaired (see 5.3.1 and 5.3.3 above); *[IFRS 7.35F(d), 35G(a)(iii), 35G(c)]*
- for modified financial assets (see 5.7 above):
  - the credit risk management practices (how an entity determines that a financial asset that is modified when its loss allowance was measured based on lifetime ECLs has improved to the extent that its allowance can now be reduced to 12-month ECLs, and how an entity monitors the extent to which such a loss allowance should subsequently be brought back to lifetime ECLs);
  - the amortised cost before the modification and the net modification gain or loss recognised during the period for modified financial assets with a loss allowance measured at lifetime ECLs;
  - the gross carrying amount of those modified financial assets for which the loss allowance has changed from lifetime to 12-month ECLs during the period; and
  - quantitative information that will assist users to understand any subsequent increase in credit risk, including information about modified financial assets for which the loss allowance has reverted from 12-month ECLs to lifetime ECLs; *[IFRS 7.35F(f), B8B, 35J]*
- the entity's credit risk exposure and significant credit risk concentrations, including the gross carrying amount of financial assets and the exposure to credit risk on loan commitments and financial guarantee contracts, by credit risk rating grades or past due status. This disclosure is required to be shown separately for:
  - those instruments that are measured using 12-month ECLs;
  - those that are measured using lifetime ECLs;
  - financial assets that are credit-impaired on initial recognition;
  - those that are subsequently credit-impaired;
  - trade receivables, contract assets and lease receivables measured under the simplified approach; *[IFRS 7.35M, B8H, B8I]* and
- the write-off policy and amounts written off during the period that are still subject to enforcement activity (see 5.12.1.A above). *[IFRS 7.35F(e), 35L]*.

It is critical for entities to align their credit risk management and financial reporting systems and processes, not only to estimate the loss allowance for ECLs, but also to produce a sufficient level of detailed information to meet the disclosure requirements in IFRS 7.

In addition, the EDTF has developed common ECL disclosure practices (see Chapter 54 at 9.2).

6 EFFECTIVE DATE AND TRANSITION

This section provides a high level summary of the transition issues specific to subsequent measurement. This summary covers only the requirements that are applicable when an entity applies the final version of IFRS 9 (issued in July 2014) and had not applied the earlier versions of IFRS 9. The requirements that are applicable for the earlier versions are not covered in this edition, but are described in earlier editions of this publication.

6.1 Effective date

IFRS 9 is effective for annual periods beginning on or after 1 January 2018. Entities are permitted to apply the standard earlier, although if they do, this fact should be disclosed and all of the requirements (including the classification and measurement, impairment and hedge accounting requirements) in the standard must be applied at the same time. *[IFRS 9.7.1.1]*. However, early application may be subject to approval or endorsement by the local jurisdiction.

Previously, the IASB moved the mandatory effective date of IFRS 9 from annual periods beginning on or after 1 January 2013 to 1 January 2015. Its later decision to defer the mandatory effective date to annual periods beginning on or after 1 January 2018, was intended to allow sufficient time for entities to develop systems and processes and to gather historical data in order to make the calculations.

It is likely that systems and processes will be based on those used for credit risk management and regulatory capital calculations. However, most banks will need, at least in part, to build new systems and processes in order to comply with the standard, while there will need to be a much closer alignment of credit risk management and financial reporting functions than may currently be the case.

Many banks are seeking to run the new processes in parallel with the old during at least part of 2017. An advantage of a parallel run is that such banks would not only be able to get used to the new systems, processes and governance arrangements for calculating ECLs, but will also have a robust basis to be able to communicate the effect of transition to stakeholders, such as shareholders and regulators, in advance of the effective date.

6.2 Transition

IFRS 9 contains a general requirement that it should be applied retrospectively, including the impairment requirements. However, the standard does specify a number of exceptions and reliefs. *[IFRS 9.7.2.1, 7.2.15, 7.2.17]*. These are covered below.

6.2.1 Date of initial application

A number of the transition provisions refer to the 'date of initial application'. This is the beginning of the first reporting period in which the entity adopts IFRS 9, and not the beginning of the first restated comparative period presented. It must be the beginning of a reporting period after the issue of the standard. *[IFRS 9.7.2.2]*.

6.2.2 Restatement of comparatives

Notwithstanding the general requirement to apply the standard retrospectively, perhaps the most important transitional relief is that IFRS 9 does not require restatement of prior periods. Indeed, an entity is permitted to restate prior periods only if it is able to do so without the use of hindsight. *[IFRS 9.7.2.15]*. The IASB noted that as entities were not required to recognise or disclose ECLs for accounting purposes in the past, there was a risk that hindsight would be needed to recognise and measure the amount of ECLs in prior periods. *[IFRS 9.BC7.75(b)]*. This applies to situations where it is impracticable to calculate the period-specific effect or the cumulative effect of the change and hence, it is impossible for entities to objectively distinguish the historical information that is relevant for estimating ECLs from the information that would not have been available at that earlier date. *[IFRS 9.BC7.74, IAS 8.50-53]*.

It should be stressed that other IFRS transition requirements, such as the requirement that the business model should be assessed as at the date of initial application and that the application is not retrospective for assets derecognised prior to that date, may mean that comparative information may not, in any case, be very meaningful. To the extent financial assets were held during any prior periods but were sold before the date of initial application, their impairment will be measured under IAS 39 if comparative information is restated.

We are aware that some banks are considering providing pro forma comparative impairment information in their annual report in the year of initial application as if IFRS 9 were applied to all financial assets throughout the comparative period. Such entities will need to make it clear that these do not represent comparative numbers according to IFRS 9.

If an entity is required to provide comparative information for two prior periods (e.g. US Foreign Private Issuers as required by the US Securities Exchange Commission), we believe that the requirement in paragraph 7.2.15 of IFRS 9 does not represent an all-or-nothing option, i.e. if the entity can only restate the latest comparative period without the use of hindsight but would need to use hindsight to restate the earlier comparative period, this does not preclude a restatement only of the latest comparative period. Therefore, the entity could choose to restate the latest comparative period for which the financial information does not involve the use of hindsight, while it would not restate the earlier comparative period for which the use of hindsight would be involved. Such circumstances may arise if the entity has chosen to do a parallel run for impairment only a year before the mandatory application date of IFRS 9, in which case they would be able to restate the latest comparative period without the use of hindsight but may not be able to do so for the earlier period. The same applies to any other information about prior periods, such as historical summaries of financial data. This treatment is consistent with the requirements in IAS 8 where for retrospective application of a new accounting policy, an entity need to only go back to the beginning of the earliest period for which retrospective applicable is practicable. *[IAS 8.24, 25, 26, IFRS 9.BC7.13]*.

When prior periods are not restated, any difference between the previously reported carrying amounts and the new carrying amounts of financial instruments at the beginning of the annual reporting period that includes the date of initial application must be recognised in the opening retained earnings (or other component of equity, as appropriate) of the annual reporting period that includes the date of initial application. However, if an entity restates prior periods, the restated financial statements must reflect all of the requirements in the standard. *[IFRS 9.7.2.15]*. For impairment purposes, the cumulative impairment loss allowance is recognised in the opening retained earnings for all credit exposures.

When interim financial reports are prepared in accordance with IAS 34 – *Interim Financial Reporting*, the requirements in IFRS 9 need not be applied to interim periods prior to the date of initial application if it is impracticable (as defined in IAS 8). *[IFRS 9.7.2.16]*.

6.2.3 Own credit requirements

The 2013 version of IFRS 9 made the own credit requirements for non-derivative financial liabilities available for early application before the completed version of the standard was issued. These provisions require an entity to present in other comprehensive income the fair value gains and losses attributable to changes in the entity's own credit risk for non-derivative financial liabilities designated as measured at fair value through profit or loss (see 2.1 above). This would mean that, before the mandatory effective date of IFRS 9, entities may elect to change only their accounting policy for own credit risk while continuing to account for their financial instruments in accordance with IAS 39. If an entity elects to apply early only those provisions, it shall disclose that fact and provide on an ongoing basis the related disclosures. *[IFRS 9.7.1.2]*.

6.2.4 Hybrid financial assets measured at fair value through profit or loss

A hybrid financial asset that is measured at fair value through profit or loss in accordance with IFRS 9, may previously have been accounted for as a host financial asset and a separate embedded derivative in accordance with IAS 39. In these circumstances, at the end of each comparative reporting period, the fair value of the hybrid contract is deemed to be the sum of the fair values of the components (i.e. the non-derivative host and the embedded derivative) where the fair value of the hybrid contract had not been determined in those comparative reporting periods. *[IFRS 9.7.2.6]*.

At the date of initial application, any difference between the fair value of the entire hybrid contract at the date of initial application and the sum of the fair values of the components of the hybrid contract at the date of initial application should be recognised in the opening retained earnings (or other component of equity, as appropriate) of the reporting period that includes the date of initial application. *[IFRS 9.7.2.7]*.

6.2.5 Effective interest rate

It may be impracticable to apply retrospectively the effective interest method to a financial asset or financial liability that is measured at amortised cost in accordance with IFRS 9, e.g. if it was previously classified at fair value through profit or loss. In those circumstances, the fair value of the financial asset or financial liability at the end of each comparative period should be treated as the gross carrying amount or the amortised cost amount, respectively. Also, the fair value of the financial asset or financial liability at the date of initial application should be treated as its new gross carrying amount or amortised cost amount, respectively, at that date. *[IFRS 9.7.2.11]*.

6.2.6 Unquoted equity investments

An investment in an unquoted equity instrument (or a derivative that is linked to and must be settled by delivery of such an unquoted equity instrument) might previously have been measured at cost in accordance with IAS 39. In those circumstances the instrument should be measured at fair value at the date of initial application of IFRS 9. Any difference between the previous carrying amount and fair value should be recognised in the opening retained earnings of the reporting period that includes the date of initial application. *[IFRS 9.7.2.12-13]*. This means that that previous periods cannot be restated. The Board explains that this is because as an entity would not have previously determined the fair value of an investment in an unquoted equity instrument and it will not now have the necessary information to determine fair value retrospectively without using hindsight. *[IFRS 9.BC7.15]*.

6.2.7 Initial credit risk and significant increases in credit risk on transition

At the date of initial application, in order to determine the loss allowance that would be recognised under the IFRS 9 impairment requirements, an entity is required to determine whether there has been a significant increase in credit risk since initial recognition, by comparing: *[IFRS 9.7.2.18, B8E]*

- the credit risk at the date that a financial instrument was initially recognised (or for loan commitments and financial guarantee contracts, at the date that the entity became a party to the irrevocable commitment); and
- the credit risk at the date of initial application of IFRS 9.

On transition, the standard allows an entity to *approximate* the credit risk on initial recognition of the financial instrument (or for loan commitments and financial guarantee contracts the date that the entity became a party to the irrevocable commitment), by considering all reasonable and supportable information that is available without undue cost or effort (see 5.4.8.A above). *[IFRS 9.7.2.18, B7.2.2, B8E]*. An entity may consider internal and external information, including information used for collective assessment (see 5.5.5 above) and information about similar products or peer group experience for comparable financial instruments. *[IFRS 9.B7.2.3, B7.2.4]*. When determining whether there have been significant increases in credit risk since initial recognition, an entity is not required to undertake an exhaustive search for information. *[IFRS 9.B7.2.2]*.

In addition, when determining whether there has been a significant increase in credit risk since initial recognition, an entity may use the low credit risk operational simplification (see 5.5.4.A above) or the more than 30 days past due rebuttable presumption if significant deterioration is assessed solely based on delinquency (see 5.5.4.B above). *[IFRS 9.7.2.19]*. The IASB also noted that an entity can assess the change in the credit risk of a financial instrument on a portfolio basis if the initial credit risk is not determinable for an individual financial instrument (see 5.5.5 above). *[IFRS 9.BC7.81]*.

If an entity is unable to determine whether there have been significant increases in credit risk since initial recognition without undue cost or effort, then the entity must recognise a loss allowance based on lifetime ECLs at each reporting date until the financial instrument is derecognised. Only if at subsequent reporting dates, the entity is able to determine that the financial instrument has low credit risk at the reporting date, then it would recognise a loss allowance based only on 12-month ECLs. *[IFRS 9.B7.2.2, 7.2.20]*.

As with the approximation of EIRs (see 5.4.5 above), entities will be faced with a challenge in interpreting how much flexibility is afforded by the term 'to approximate'. Also, it is unclear to what extent entities would need to search for information that is available without undue cost or effort.

The requirement to recognise lifetime ECLs may encourage entities to look for and use information about the initial credit risk and hence, will enhance comparability and the quality of the information provided. On the other hand, some entities may be discouraged to use such information if they are able to absorb lifetime ECLs on transition. While such an approach may result in inconsistency between entities, the IASB believes that the transition requirements and reliefs are the best way to balance the provision of useful and relevant information with the associated cost of providing it. *[IFRS 9.BC7.79]*.

References

---

1 Whilst paragraph 5.7.10 of IFRS 9 could be read as saying that the modification gains or losses should not be recognised in profit or loss, we understand that it was the IASB's intention that they should be recognised in profit or loss. This is clear from reading paragraph 5.7.11 of IFRS 9 in conjunction with paragraph 5.4.3 of IFRS 9, and therefore we view this as drafting error in paragraph 5.7.10 of IFRS 9.

2 *IGC Q&A 73-1.*

3 *IGC Q&A 10-19.*

4 *IGC Q&A 76-1.*

5 Based on the example in IAS 39.B.25.

6 *IFRIC Update*, July 2008.

7 Information for Observers (May 2008 IFRIC meeting), *Application of the Effective Interest Rate Method*, IASB, May 2008, Appendix.

8 Information for Observers, 6.

9 *IFRIC Update*, July 2008.

10 Information for Observers (July 2008 IFRIC meeting), *Application of the Effective Interest Rate Method*, IASB, July 2008, 4.

11 Position Paper, *IAS 39 – Financial Instruments: Recognition and Measurement – assets and liabilities linked to an inflation index which are not measured at fair value (continuation to the paper published in February 2008)*, Israel Accounting Standards Board, August 2008.

12 *IFRIC Update*, May 2009.
13 *IFRIC Update*, July 2008.
14 G20 Declaration on Strengthening the Financial System, April 2009.
15 Report of the Financial Crisis Advisory Group, July 2009.
16 IASB Snapshot: Financial Instruments: Expected Credit Losses Exposure Draft, March 2013.
17 Based on illustration provided by the IASB in *Snapshot: Financial Instruments: Expected Credit Losses Exposure Draft*, p.9, March 2013.
18 IASB Website Announcement. IASB to establish transition resource group for impairment of financial instruments, 23 June 2014 and Transition Resource Group for Impairment of Financial Instruments – Meeting Summary, 22 April 2015.
19 IASB Transition Resource Group for Impairment of Financial Instruments, Meeting Summary, 22 April 2015.
20 IASB Transition Resource Group for Impairment of Financial Instruments, Meeting Summary, 16 September 2015.
21 IASB Transition Resource Group for Impairment of Financial Instruments, Meeting Summary, 11 December 2015.
22 Basel Committee on Banking Supervision, *International Convergence of Capital Measurement and Capital Standards, June 2006 and Basel III:A global regulatory framework for more resilient banks and banking systems*, June 2011.
23 Regulation (EU) No 575/2013 of the European Parliament and of the Council of 26 June 2013 on prudential requirements for credit institutions and investment firms and amending Regulation (EU) No 648/2012.
24 Transition Resource Group for Impairment of Financial Instruments, Agenda ref 1, *The maximum period to consider when measuring expected credit losses,* 22 April 2015.
25 IASB Transition Resource Group for Impairment of Financial Instruments, Meeting Summary, Paragraph 49, 11 December 2015.
26 IASB Transition Resource Group for Impairment of Financial Instruments, Meeting Summary, Paragraphs 50 and 51, 11 December 2015.
27 IASB Transition Resource Group for Impairment of Financial Instruments, Meeting Summary, Paragraphs 53, 11 December 2015.
28 IASB Transition Resource Group for Impairment of Financial Instruments, Meeting Summary, Paragraphs 56, 11 December 2015.
29 Q&A 2012/01 IFRS for SMEs General topics: Application of 'undue cost or effort', April 2012, para. 2.
30 Transition Resource Group for Impairment of Financial Instruments, Agenda ref 4, *Forward-looking information*, 16 September 2015.
31 Transition Resource Group for Impairment of Financial Instruments, Agenda ref 1, *Significant increases in credit risk,* 16 September 2015.
32 IASB Agenda paper 5B, Financial Instruments: Impairment, Operational simplifications – 30dpd and low credit risk, 28 October – 1 November 2013.
33 IASB Transition Resource Group for Impairment of Financial Instruments, Meeting Summary, Paragraphs 58 and 59, 11 December 2015.
34 Basel Committee on Banking Supervision, *Guidance on credit risk and accounting for expected credit losses*, Paragraph A55, December 2015.
35 Basel Committee on Banking Supervision, *Guidance on credit risk and accounting for expected credit losses*, Paragraph 22, December 2015.
36 Basel Committee on Banking Supervision, *Guidance on credit risk and accounting for expected credit losses*, Paragraph 21, December 2015.
37 Basel Committee on Banking Supervision, *Guidance on credit risk and accounting for expected credit losses*, Paragraph A47, December 2015.
38 Basel Committee on Banking Supervision, *Guidance on credit risk and accounting for expected credit losses*, Paragraph 69, December 2015.
39 Basel Committee on Banking Supervision, *Guidance on credit risk and accounting for expected credit losses*, Paragraph 57, December 2015.
40 Basel Committee on Banking Supervision, *Guidance on credit risk and accounting for expected credit losses*, Paragraphs 46 - 49, December 2015.
41 Basel Committee on Banking Supervision, *Guidance on credit risk and accounting for expected credit losses*, Paragraphs 50, 51 and 58, December 2015.
42 Basel Committee on Banking Supervision, *Guidance on credit risk and accounting for expected credit losses*, Paragraphs 64 and 65, December 2015.
43 Basel Committee on Banking Supervision, *Guidance on credit risk and accounting for expected credit losses*, Paragraphs A15 to A21, December 2015.

44 Basel Committee on Banking Supervision, *Guidance on credit risk and accounting for expected credit losses*, Paragraphs A23 to A30, December 2015.
45 Basel Committee on Banking Supervision, *Guidance on credit risk and accounting for expected credit losses*, Paragraphs A44, December 2015.
46 Basel Committee on Banking Supervision, *Guidance on credit risk and accounting for expected credit losses*, Paragraphs A45 to A55, December 2015.
47 European Banking Authority, EBA/CP/2016/10, Consultation Paper, *Draft Guidelines on credit institutions' credit risk management practices and accounting for expected credit losses*, Paragraph 17, 26 July 2016.
48 European Banking Authority, EBA/CP/2016/10, Consultation Paper, *Draft Guidelines on credit institutions' credit risk management practices and accounting for expected credit losses*, Paragraph 129, 26 July 2016.
49 *IFRIC update*, May 2012.
50 Transition Resource Group for Impairment of Financial Instruments, Agenda ref 8, *Measurement of expected credit losses in respect of a modified financial asset*, 22 April 2015.
51 Transition Resource Group for Impairment of Financial Instruments, Agenda ref 3, *Loan Commitments – Scope*, 22 April 2015.
52 Transition Resource Group for Impairment of Financial Instruments, Agenda ref 6, *Measurement of expected credit losses for an issued financial guarantee contract*, 22 April 2015.
53 *Exposure Draft – Financial Instruments: Expected Credit Losses*, March 2013, para. 17.
54 *Exposure Draft – Financial Instruments: Amortised Cost and Impairment*, November 2009, para. B23.
55 Transition Resource Group for Impairment of Financial Instruments, Agenda ref 9, *Measurement of the loss allowance for credit-impaired financial assets*, 11 December 2015.

Chapter 51 Financial instruments: Derecognition

List of examples

Chapter 51 Financial instruments: Derecognition

1 INTRODUCTION

This Chapter deals with the question of when financial instruments should be removed ('derecognised') from financial statements. At what point should an item already recognised in financial statements cease to be included? If an entity sells a quoted share in the financial markets, it may cease to be entitled to all the benefits, and exposed to all the risks, inherent in owning that share somewhat earlier than the date on which it ceases to be registered as the legal owner. However, the question of derecognition goes much further than this, as it encroaches on what is commonly referred to as 'off-balance sheet' finance.

1.1 Off-balance sheet finance

In order to understand the rationale for the requirements of IFRS for the derecognition of financial assets and financial liabilities, it is necessary to appreciate the fact that those requirements, and those in equivalent national standards, have their origins in the response by financial regulators to the growing use of off-balance sheet finance from the early 1980s onwards.

'Off-balance sheet' transactions can be difficult to define, and this poses the first problem in discussing the subject. The term implies that certain things belong on the statement of financial position and that those which escape the net are deviations from this norm. The practical effect of off-balance sheet transactions is that the financial statements do not fully present the underlying activities of the reporting entity. This is generally for one of two reasons. The items in question may be included in the statement of financial position but presented 'net' rather than 'gross' – for example, by netting off loans received against the assets they finance. Alternatively, the items might be excluded from the statement of financial position altogether on the basis that they do not represent present assets and liabilities. Examples include operating lease commitments (at least until IFRS 16 – *Leases* – is applied – see Chapter 25) and certain contingent liabilities.

The result in all cases will be that the statement of financial position may suggest less exposure to assets and liabilities than really exists, with a consequential flattering effect on certain ratios, such as the debt/equity ratio and return on assets employed. There is usually an income statement dimension to be considered as well, perhaps because assets taken off-balance sheet purport to have been sold (with a possible profit effect), and also more generally because the presentation of off-balance sheet activity influences the timing or disclosure of associated revenue items. In particular, the presence or absence of items in the statement of financial position usually affects whether the finance cost implicit in a transaction is reported as such or included within another item of income or expense.

Depending on their roles, different people react differently to the term 'off-balance sheet finance'. To some accounting standard setters, or other financial regulators, the expression carries the connotation of devious accounting, intended to mislead the reader of financial statements. Off-balance sheet transactions are those which are designed to allow an entity to avoid reflecting certain aspects of its activities in its financial statements. The term is therefore pejorative and carries the slightly self-righteous inference that those who indulge in such transactions are up to no good and need to be stopped. However, there is also room for a more honourable use of the term 'off-balance sheet finance'. Entities may wish, for sound commercial reasons, to engage in transactions which share with other parties the risks and benefits associated with certain assets and liabilities.

In theory, it should be possible to determine what items belong in the statement of financial position by reference to general principles such as those in the IASB's *Conceptual Framework for Financial Reporting* and similar concepts statements. In practice, however, such principles on their own have not proved adequate to deal with off-balance sheet finance, including routine transactions such as debt factoring and mortgage securitisation.

Accordingly, standard-setters throughout the world, including the IASB, have developed increasingly detailed rules to deal with the issue. This 'anti-avoidance' aspect of the derecognition rules helps to explain why, rather unusually, IFRS considers not only the economic position of the entity at the reporting date, but also prior transactions which gave rise to that position and the reporting entity's motives in undertaking them.

For example, an entity that enters into a forward contract to purchase a specified non-derivative asset for a fixed price will normally recognise that arrangement as a derivative. However, an entity which previously owned the specified non-derivative asset and entered into an identical forward contract at the same time as selling the asset would normally recognise the entire arrangement as a financing transaction. It would leave the (sold) asset on its statement of financial position and recognise a non-derivative liability for the purchase price specified in the forward contract.

The IASB has proposed changes to its conceptual framework, including the addition of new guidance addressing derecognition which is covered in more detail at 7 below.

2 DEVELOPMENT OF IFRS

Under IFRS, many definitions relating to financial instruments are in IAS 32 – *Financial Instruments: Presentation* – while derecognition of financial assets and financial liabilities is currently addressed in IAS 39 – *Financial Instruments: Recognition and Measurement* – or IFRS 9 – *Financial Instruments.*

The provisions of IFRS 10 – *Consolidated Financial Statements* – are also very relevant to certain aspects of the derecognition of financial assets and financial liabilities. IFRS 10 is discussed in Chapter 6, but it is also referred to at various points below.

Whilst IFRS 9 introduces major changes to the way in which financial instruments are reflected in financial statements, its requirements relating to derecognition are substantially the same as those in IAS 39. Disclosure requirements in respect of transfers of financial assets are included in IFRS 7 – *Financial Instruments: Disclosures* – and these are discussed in Chapter 54 at 6.

2.1 Definitions

The following definitions in IAS 32, IAS 39, IFRS 9 and IFRS 13 – *Fair Value Measurement* – are generally relevant to the discussion in this chapter.

A *financial instrument* is any contract that gives rise to a financial asset of one entity and a financial liability or equity instrument of another entity. *[IAS 32.11]*.

A *financial asset* is any asset that is:

(a) cash;

(b) an equity instrument of another entity;

(c) a contractual right:

  (i) to receive cash or another financial asset from another entity; or

  (ii) to exchange financial assets or financial liabilities with another entity under conditions that are potentially favourable to the entity; or

(d) a contract that will or may be settled in the entity's own equity instruments and is:

  (i) a non-derivative for which the entity is or may be obliged to receive a variable number of the entity's own equity instruments; or

  (ii) a derivative that will or may be settled other than by the exchange of a fixed amount of cash or another financial asset for a fixed number of the entity's own equity instruments. For this purpose the entity's own equity instruments do not include puttable financial instruments classified as equity ..., instruments that impose on the entity an obligation to deliver to another party a *pro rata* share of the net assets of the entity only on liquidation and are classified as equity ..., or instruments that are themselves contracts for the future receipt or delivery of the entity's own equity instruments. *[IAS 32.11]*.

A *financial liability* is any liability that is:

(a) a contractual obligation:

  (i) to deliver cash or another financial asset to another entity; or

  (ii) to exchange financial assets or financial liabilities with another entity under conditions that are potentially unfavourable to the entity; or

(b) a contract that will or may be settled in the entity's own equity instruments and is:

  (i) a non-derivative for which the entity is or may be obliged to deliver a variable number of the entity's own equity instruments; or

  (ii) a derivative that will or may be settled other than by the exchange of a fixed amount of cash or another financial asset for a fixed number of the entity's own equity instruments. For this purpose the entity's own equity instruments do not include puttable financial instruments classified as equity ..., instruments that impose on the entity an obligation to deliver to another party a *pro rata* share of the net assets of the entity only on liquidation and are classified as equity ..., or instruments that are themselves contracts for the future receipt or delivery of the entity's own equity instruments. *[IAS 32.11]*.

An *equity instrument* is any contract that evidences a residual interest in the assets of an entity after deducting all of its liabilities. *[IAS 32.11]*.

A *derivative* is a financial instrument or other contract within the scope of IAS 39 or IFRS 9 (see Chapter 44 at 2) with all three of the following characteristics:

- its value changes in response to the change in a specified interest rate, financial instrument price, commodity price, foreign exchange rate, index of prices or rates, credit rating or credit index, or other variable, provided in the case of a non-financial variable that the variable is not specific to a party to the contract (sometimes called the 'underlying');
- it requires no initial net investment or an initial net investment that is smaller than would be required for other types of contracts that would be expected to have a similar response to changes in market factors; and
- it is settled at a future date. *[IAS 39.9, IFRS 9 Appendix A]*.

Fair value is the price that would be received to sell an asset or paid to transfer a liability in an orderly transaction between market participants at the measurement date. *[IFRS 13.9, Appendix A]*.

3 DERECOGNITION – FINANCIAL ASSETS

3.1 Background

The requirements of IAS 39 and IFRS 9 for derecognition of financial assets are primarily designed to deal with the accounting challenges posed by various types of off-balance sheet finance. As a result, the real focus of many of the rules for derecognition of assets is in fact the recognition of liabilities. The starting point for most of the transactions discussed below is that the reporting entity receives cash or other consideration in return for a transfer or 'sale' of all or part of a financial asset. This raises the question of whether such consideration should be treated as sales proceeds or as a liability. IAS 39 and IFRS 9 effectively answer that question by determining whether the financial asset to which the consideration relates should be derecognised (the consideration is treated as sales proceeds and there is a gain or loss on disposal) or should continue to be recognised while the consideration is treated as a liability.

This underlying objective of the derecognition criteria helps to explain why IAS 39 and IFRS 9 consider not only the economic position of the entity at the reporting date, but also prior transactions which gave rise to that position and the reporting entity's motives in undertaking them. For example, if, at a reporting date, an entity has two identical forward contracts for the purchase of a financial asset, the accounting treatment of the contracts may vary significantly if one contract relates to the purchase of an asset previously owned by the entity and the other does not.

This is because the derecognition rules of IAS 39 and IFRS 9 are based on the premise that, if a transfer of an asset leaves the transferor's economic exposure to the transferred asset much as if the transfer had never taken place, the financial statements should represent that the transferor still holds the asset. Thus, if an entity sells (say) a listed bond subject to a forward contract to repurchase the bond from the buyer at a fixed price, IAS 39 and IFRS 9 argue that the entity is exposed to the risks and rewards of that bond as if it had never sold it, but has simply borrowed an amount equivalent to the original sales proceeds secured on the bond. IAS 39 and IFRS 9 therefore conclude that the bond should not be removed from the statement of financial position and the sale proceeds should be accounted for as a liability (in effect the obligation to repurchase the bond under the forward contract – see 4 below).

By contrast, if the entity were to enter into a second identical forward contract over another bond (i.e. one not previously owned by the entity), IAS 39 and IFRS 9 would simply require it to be accounted for as a derivative at fair value (see Chapter 44). This might seem a rather counter-intuitive outcome of a framework that purports to report economically equivalent transactions in a consistent and objective manner. However, the IASB would argue that the two transactions are not economically equivalent: they are distinguished by the fact that, on entering into the forward contract over the originally owned asset, the entity received a separate cash inflow (i.e. the 'sale' proceeds from the counterparty), whereas, on entering into the second contract, it did not. This reinforces the point that the real focus of IAS 39 and IFRS 9 is to determine the appropriate accounting treatment for that cash inflow and not that of the previously owned bond *per se*.

3.2 Decision tree

The provisions of IAS 39 and IFRS 9 concerning the derecognition of financial assets are complex, but are summarised in the flowchart below. *[IAS 39.AG36, IFRS 9.B3.2.1]*. It may be helpful to refer to this while reading the discussion that follows.

It will be seen that the process presupposes that the reporting entity has correctly consolidated all its subsidiaries in accordance with IFRS 10, including any entities identified as consolidated structured entities, often called special purpose entities (SPEs) (see Chapter 6).

Under IFRS, a vehicle (or a structured entity) that, though not meeting a traditional definition of a subsidiary based on ownership of equity, is still controlled by the entity is often referred to as a (consolidated) special purpose entity or SPE. IFRS 10 requires a reporting entity to consolidate another entity, including an SPE, when the reporting entity is exposed, or has rights, to variable returns from its involvement with the investee entity and has the ability to affect those returns through its power over the investee entity (see 3.6 below).

It is clearly highly significant from an accounting perspective that an entity to which a financial asset or liability is transferred is a subsidiary or a consolidated SPE of the transferor. A financial asset (or financial liability) transferred from an entity to its subsidiary or consolidated SPE (on whatever terms) will continue to be recognised in the entity's consolidated financial statements through the normal consolidation procedures set out in IFRS 10. Thus, the requirements discussed at 3.3 to 3.9 below are irrelevant to the treatment, in an entity's consolidated financial statements, of any transfer of a financial asset by the entity to a subsidiary or consolidated SPE. Requiring consolidation of subsidiaries and certain SPEs means that the same derecognition analysis applies whether the entity transfers the financial assets directly to a third party investor or to a subsidiary or consolidated SPE that carries out the transfer.

However, the criteria may be relevant to any onward transfer by the subsidiary or consolidated SPE, and to the transferor's separate financial statements, if prepared (see Chapter 8). Moreover, the criteria may well be relevant to determining whether the transferee is an SPE that should be consolidated. A transfer that leaves the entity, through its links with the transferee, exposed to risks and rewards similar to those arising from its former direct ownership of the transferred asset, may in itself indicate that the transferee is an SPE that should be consolidated.

Figure 51.1: Derecognition flowchart [IAS 39.AG36, IFRS 9.B3.2.1]

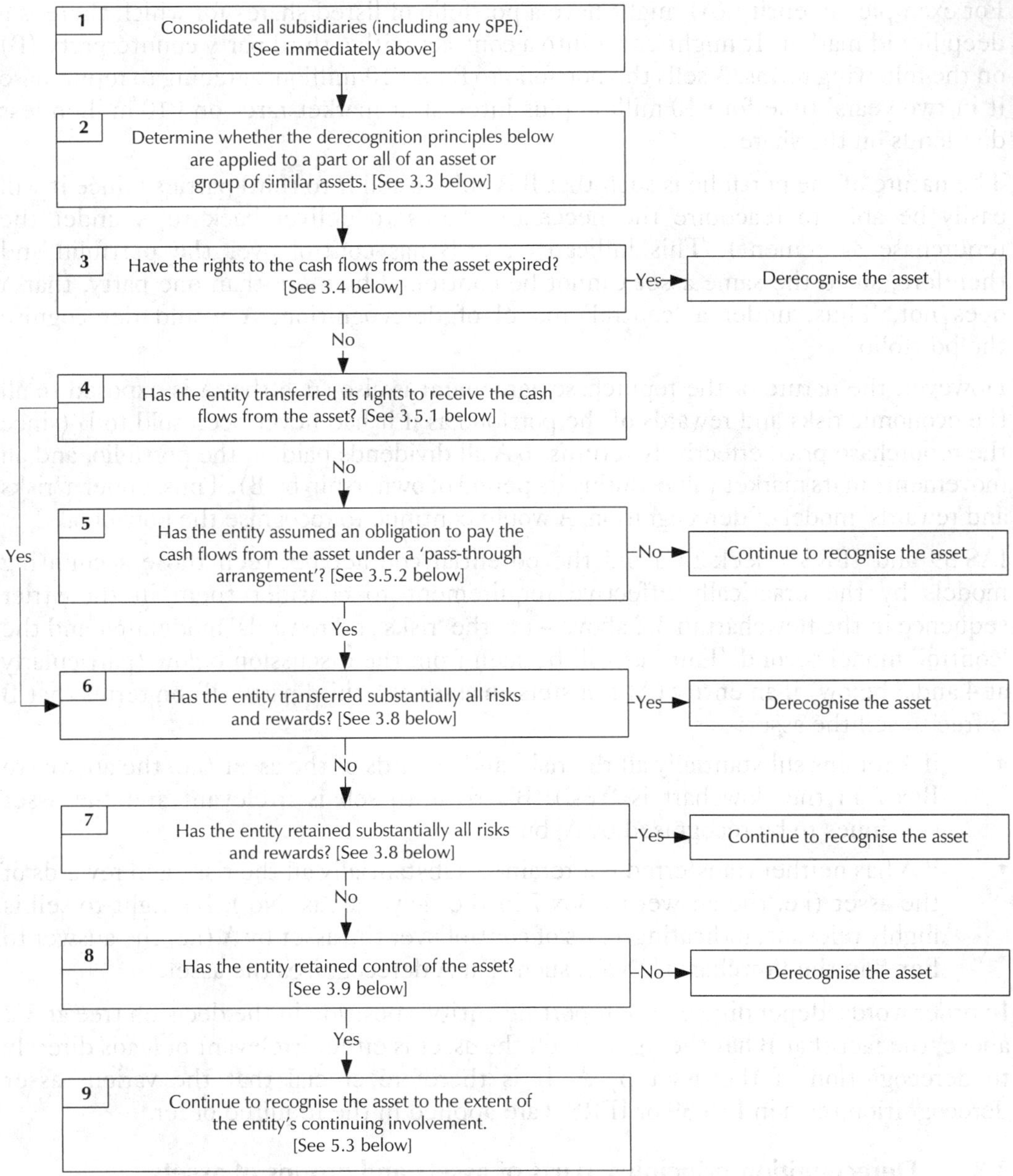

The subsequent steps towards determining whether derecognition is appropriate are discussed below. Some examples of how these criteria might be applied to some common transactions in financial assets are given in 4 below. The accounting consequences of the derecognition of a financial asset are discussed at 5 below.

3.2.1 Importance of applying tests in sequence

The derecognition rules in IAS 39 and IFRS 9 are based on several different accounting concepts, in particular a 'risks and rewards' model and a 'control' model, which may lead to opposite conclusions.

For example, an entity (A) might have a portfolio of listed shares for which there is a deep liquid market. It might enter into a contract with a third party counterparty (B) on the following terms. A sells the portfolio to B for €10 million, agreeing to repurchase it in two years' time for €10 million plus interest at market rates on €10 million less dividends on the shares.

The nature of the portfolio is such that B is able to sell it to third parties (since it will easily be able to reacquire the necessary shares to deliver back to A under the repurchase agreement). This indicates that B has control over the portfolio and therefore, since the same asset cannot be controlled by more than one party, that A does not. Thus, under a 'control' model of derecognition, A would derecognise the portfolio.

However, the nature of the repurchase agreement is also such that A is exposed to all the economic risks and rewards of the portfolio as if it had never been sold to B (since the repurchase price effectively returns to A all dividends paid on the portfolio, and all movements in its market value, during its period of ownership by B). Thus, under a 'risks and rewards' model of derecognition, A would continue to recognise the portfolio.

IAS 39 and IFRS 9 seek to avoid the potential conflict between those accounting models by the practically effective requirement to consider them in the strict sequence in the flowchart in 3.2 above – i.e. the 'risks and rewards' model first and the 'control' model second. Thus, as will be seen from the discussion below (particularly at 4 and 5 below) if an entity (A) transfers an asset to a third party (B) on terms that B is free to sell the asset:

- if A retains substantially all the risks and rewards of the asset (i.e. the answer to Box 7 in the flowchart is 'Yes'), B's right to sell is irrelevant and the asset continues to be recognised by A; but
- if A has neither transferred nor retained substantially all the risks and rewards of the asset (i.e. the answer to Box 7 in the flowchart is 'No'), B's right to sell is highly relevant, indicating a loss of control over the asset by A (i.e. the answer to Box 8 in the flowchart is 'No'), such that A derecognises the asset.

In other words, depending on the reporting entity's position in the decision tree at 3.2 above, the fact that B has the right to sell the asset is either irrelevant or leads directly to derecognition of the asset by A. It is therefore crucial that the various asset derecognition tests in IAS 39 or IFRS 9 are applied in the required order.

3.3 Derecognition principles, parts of assets and groups of assets

The discussion in this section relates to Box 2 in the flowchart at 3.2 above.

IAS 39 and IFRS 9 require an entity, before evaluating whether, and to what extent, derecognition is appropriate, to determine whether the provisions discussed at 3.4 and following below should be applied to the whole, or a part only, of a financial asset (or the whole or, a part only, of a group of similar financial assets).

It is important to remember throughout the discussion below that these are criteria for determining at what level the derecognition rules should be applied, not for determining whether the conditions in those rules have been satisfied.

The derecognition provisions must be applied to a part of a financial asset (or a part of a group of similar financial assets) if, and only if, the part being considered for derecognition meets one of the three conditions set out in (a) to (c) below.

(a) The part comprises only specifically identified cash flows from a financial asset (or a group of similar financial assets).

For example, if an entity enters into an interest rate strip whereby the counterparty obtains the right to the interest cash flows, but not the principal cash flows, from a debt instrument, the derecognition provisions are applied to the interest cash flows.

(b) The part comprises only a fully proportionate (*pro rata*) share of the cash flows from a financial asset (or a group of similar financial assets).

For example, if an entity enters into an arrangement in which the counterparty obtains the rights to 90% of all cash flows of a debt instrument, the derecognition provisions are applied to 90% of those cash flows. The test in this case is whether the reporting entity has retained a 10% proportionate share of the *total* cash flows. If there is more than one counterparty, it is not necessary for each of them to have a proportionate share of the cash flows.

(c) The part comprises only a fully proportionate (*pro rata*) share of specifically identified cash flows from a financial asset (or a group of similar financial assets).

For example, if an entity enters into an arrangement whereby the counterparty obtains the rights to a 90% share of interest cash flows from a financial asset, the derecognition provisions are applied to 90% of those interest cash flows. The test is whether the reporting entity has (in this case) retained a 10% proportionate share of the *interest* cash flows. As in (b), if there is more than one counterparty, it is not necessary for each of them to have a proportionate share of the specifically identified cash.

If none of the criteria in (a) to (c) above is met, the derecognition provisions are applied to the financial asset in its entirety (or to the group of similar financial assets in their entirety). For example, if an entity transfers the rights to the first or the last 90% of cash collections from a financial asset (or a group of financial assets), or the rights to 90% of the cash flows from a group of receivables, but provides a guarantee to compensate the buyer for any credit losses up to 8% of the principal amount of the receivables, the derecognition provisions are applied to the financial asset (or a group of similar financial assets) in its entirety. *[IAS 39.16, IFRS 9.3.2.2]*.

The various examples above illustrate that the tests in (a) to (c) are to be applied very strictly. It is essential that the entity transfers 100%, or a lower fixed proportion, of a definable cash flow. In the arrangement in the previous paragraph, the transferor provides a guarantee the effect of which is that the transferor may have to return some part of the consideration it has already received. This has the effect that the derecognition provisions must be applied to the asset in its entirety and not just to the proportion of cash flows transferred. If the guarantee had not been given, the arrangement would have satisfied condition (b) above, and the derecognition provisions would have been applied only to the 90% of cash flows transferred.

The criteria above must be applied to the whole, or a part only, of a financial asset or the whole, or a part only, of a group of similar financial assets. This raises the question of what comprises a 'group of similar financial assets' – an issue that has been discussed by the Interpretations Committee and the IASB but without them being able to reach any satisfactory conclusions (see 3.3.2 below).

3.3.1 Credit enhancement through transferor's waiver of right to future cash flows

IAS 39 and IFRS 9 give an illustrative example, the substance of which is reproduced as Example 51.15 at 5.4.4 below, of the accounting treatment of a transaction in which 90% of the cash flows of a portfolio of loans are sold. All cash collections are allocated 90:10 to the transferee and transferor respectively, but subject to any losses on the loans being fully allocated to the transferor until its 10% retained interest in the portfolio is reduced to zero, and only then allocated to the transferee. IAS 39 and IFRS 9 indicate that in this case it is appropriate to apply the derecognition criteria to the 90% sold, rather than the portfolio as whole.

At first sight, this seems inconsistent with the position in the scenario in the penultimate paragraph of 3.3 above, where application of the derecognition criteria to the 90% transferred is precluded by the transferor's having given a guarantee to the transferee. Is not the arrangement in Example 51.15 below (whereby the transferor may have to cede some of its right to receive future cash flows to the transferee) a guarantee in all but name?

Whilst IAS 39 and IFRS 9 do not expand on this explicitly, a possible explanation could be that the two transactions can be distinguished as follows:

(a) the transaction in Example 51.15 may result in the transferor losing the right to receive a future cash inflow, whereas a guarantee arrangement may give rise to an obligation to return a past cash inflow;

(b) the transaction in Example 51.15 gives the transferee a greater chance of recovering its full 90% share, but does not guarantee that it will do so. For example, if only 85% of the portfolio is recovered, the transferor is under no obligation to make up the shortfall.

It must be remembered that, at this stage, we are addressing the issue of whether or not the derecognition criteria should be applied to all or part of an asset, not whether derecognition is actually achieved.

In many cases an asset transferred subject to a guarantee by the transferor would not satisfy the derecognition criteria, since the guarantee would mean that the transferor had not transferred substantially all the risks of the asset. For derecognition to be possible, the scope of the guarantee would need to be restricted so that some significant risks are passed to the transferee. However, if the guarantee has been acquired from a third party, there are additional issues to consider that may affect the derecognition of the asset and/or the guarantee (see 3.3.2 below).

3.3.2 Derecognition of groups of financial assets

As described above, the derecognition provisions of IAS 39 and IFRS 9 apply to the whole, or a part only, of a financial asset or a group, or a part of a group, of *similar* financial assets (our emphasis). However, transfers of financial assets, such as debt factoring or securitisations (see 3.6 below), typically involve the transfer of a group of assets (and possibly liabilities) comprising:

- the non-derivative financial assets (i.e. the trade receivables or securitised assets) that are the main focus of the transaction;
- financial instruments taken out by the transferor in order to mitigate the risk of those financial assets. These arrangements may either have already been in place for some time, or they may have been entered into to facilitate the transfer; and
- non-derivative financial guarantee contracts that are transferred with the assets. These are not always recognised separately as financial assets, e.g. mortgage indemnity guarantees which compensate the lending bank if the borrower defaults and there is a deficit when the secured property is sold. Such guarantees may be transferred together with the mortgage assets to which they relate.

Financial instruments transferred with the 'main' assets typically include derivatives such as interest rate and currency swaps. The entity may have entered into such arrangements in order to swap floating rate mortgages to fixed rate, or to change the currency of cash flows receivable from financial assets to match the currency of the borrowings, e.g. sterling into euros.

Both the Interpretations Committee and the IASB have considered whether the reference to transfers of 'similar' assets in IAS 39 (and hence in IFRS 9) is intended to require:

- a single derecognition test for the whole 'package' of transferred non-derivative assets, and any associated financial instruments, as a whole; or
- individual derecognition tests for each type of instrument (e.g. debtor, interest rate swap, guarantee or credit insurance) transferred.

The IASB and Interpretations Committee did not succeed in clarifying the meaning of 'similar assets'. The Interpretations Committee came to a tentative decision but passed the matter to the IASB, together with some related derecognition issues, in particular, the types of transaction that are required to be treated as 'pass through' and the effect of conditions attached to the assets that have been transferred (discussed at 3.5 below). In November 2006 the Interpretations Committee issued a tentative decision not to provide formal guidance, based on the views publicly expressed by the IASB in the *IASB Update* for September 2006. The Interpretations Committee's decision not to proceed was withdrawn in January 2007 on the basis of comment letters received by the Interpretations Committee that demonstrated that the IASB's 'clarification' was, in fact, unworkable and further guidance was required after all. The Interpretations Committee announced this as follows:

> 'In November 2006, the IFRIC published a tentative agenda decision not to provide guidance on a number of issues relating to the derecognition of financial assets. After considering the comment letters received on the tentative agenda decision, the IFRIC concluded that additional guidance is required in this area. The IFRIC therefore decided to withdraw the tentative agenda decision [not to provide further guidance] and add a project on derecognition to its agenda. The IFRIC noted that any Interpretation in this area must have a tightly defined and limited scope, and directed the staff to carry out additional research to establish the questions that such an Interpretation should address.'[1]

The next section describes the Interpretations Committee's and IASB's attempts to establish the meaning of 'similar', which demonstrated the absence of a clear principle. There is bound to be diversity in practice in the light of the failure to provide an interpretation, so it is most important that entities establish an accounting policy that they apply consistently to the derecognition of groups of financial assets.

3.3.2.A The IASB's view and the Interpretations Committee's tentative conclusions

Although the Interpretations Committee initially tended to the view that the IASB intended a single test to be undertaken,[2] the IASB itself indicated that derivatives transferred together with non-derivative financial assets were not 'similar' to non-derivative financial assets for the purposes of paragraph 16 of IAS 39 (paragraph 3.2.2 of IFRS 9). Therefore, an entity would apply the derecognition tests in IAS 39 or IFRS 9 to non-derivative financial assets (or groups of similar non-derivative financial assets) and derivative financial assets (or groups of similar derivative financial assets) separately, even if they were transferred at the same time.[3] The IASB also indicated that, in order to qualify for derecognition, transferred derivatives that could be assets or liabilities (such as interest rate swaps) would have to meet both the financial asset and the financial liability derecognition tests[4] – see the further discussion of this issue at 6.4 below. Whilst the IASB's published decision referred only to derivatives transferred with the main non-derivative assets, observers of the relevant meeting reported that the IASB also took the view that the derecognition tests must also be applied separately to other financial assets, such as guarantees and credit insurance, transferred with the main assets.

This could have had practical effects on many securitisations as currently structured (see 3.6 below). The interpretation could have made it easier to derecognise certain items (particularly non-derivative assets) than at present. Many derivatives themselves might not meet the appropriate derecognition criteria at all and would continue to be recognised. By contrast, a transaction might achieve a transfer of substantially all the risks and rewards (see Box 6 in Figure 51.1 at 3.2 above, and 3.8 below) of a transferred asset considered separately from any associated derivatives or guarantees, but not if the asset and the associated derivatives or guarantees are considered as a whole. However, the interpretation could well have resulted in far more arrangements falling into the category of 'continuing involvement', where the entity has neither retained nor disposed of substantially all of the risks and rewards of ownership.

Suppose that an entity transfers a fixed rate loan subject to prepayment risk and a credit guarantee, but retains prepayment risk through an amortising interest rate swap, linked to the principal amount of the transferred loan, with the transferee. On the view that the loan and guarantee should be considered for derecognition as a whole, there was no real credit risk prior to the transfer because of the guarantee. The entity was exposed to prepayment risk and the risk of failure by the counterparty to the guarantee. On the assumption that the latter risk could be considered negligible, the only real risk was prepayment risk. Thus, on the view that the loan and guarantee should be considered for derecognition as a whole, they would probably not be derecognised because the entity would retain the only substantial risk (prepayment risk) to which it was exposed before the transfer – i.e. the transaction would fail the test of transferring substantially all risks and rewards in Box 6 in Figure 51.1.

Following the IASB's decision, the implication is that the derecognition criteria would be applied separately to the loan and the guarantee. Considered individually, the loan gives rise to prepayment risk and credit risk. On this analysis, the transfer would leave the entity with only one of the two substantial risks (i.e. prepayment risk, but not credit risk) that it bore previously. This could lead to the conclusion that the entity had neither transferred nor retained substantially all the risks of the loan, and that the loan would therefore be recognised only to the extent of the entity's continuing involvement (in this example, the interest rate swap) – see Box 9 in Figure 51.1 at 3.2 above, and 5.3 below.

This could well lead to more transactions being accounted for as a continuing involvement than previously. This is unfortunate since, as discussed further at 5.3 below, IAS 39 and IFRS 9 give no clear general principles to be applied in accounting for continuing involvements.

3.3.2.B What are 'similar assets'?

There are a number of different derivative and derivative-like instruments that can be transferred together with a non-derivative, including:

- hedging instruments that are always assets, e.g. interest rate caps;
- hedging instruments that are always liabilities, e.g. written options;
- hedging instruments that may be an asset or liability at any point in time, e.g. interest rate swaps;
- purchased financial guarantee contracts and credit insurance; and
- guarantees that are not financial guarantee contracts but are commonly accounted for as derivatives, e.g. mortgage indemnity guarantee contracts.

The IASB's interpretation, repeated in its Exposure Draft – *Derecognition* – referred to at 2 above, would require each of the first three to meet different derecognition treatments. Derivatives that could be financial assets or financial liabilities depending on movements in market value (e.g. interest rate and credit default swaps) would need to meet both the financial asset and financial liability derecognition requirements of IAS 39 or IFRS 9 (even though at any one time they would be either an asset or a liability). The derecognition of liabilities requires *inter alia* legal release by the counterparty (see 6 below). In many securitisations there is no cancellation, novation or discharge of swaps 'transferred' to a structured entity, in which case the transferor would not be able to derecognise the instrument. This would raise issues regarding the treatment of the retained swap, as it does not actually expose the entity to risks and rewards. This is discussed further at 3.6.5 below.

The interpretation raises the difficulty of allocating the single cash flow received from the transferee to the various financial instruments transferred. This is discussed further at 3.5.1 below.

Given the withdrawal of the Interpretations Committee 'non-interpretation', there is no underlying principle that would prevent any of the instruments described above being considered 'similar' to the main non-derivative. Therefore, an entity must establish an accounting policy that it applies consistently to all transactions involving the derecognition of assets, not only to those associated with securitisation arrangements. It must bear in mind that a narrow concept of 'similar', in which instruments are treated as separate assets, may make it easier to derecognise some of them but more likely to have to engage with the problems of continuing involvement and more difficult to achieve pass through (see 3.5.2 below). Regardless of the accounting policy followed, a derivative that involves two-way payments between parties (i.e. the payments are, or could be, from or to either of the parties) should be derecognised only when both the derecognition criteria for a financial asset and the derecognition criteria for a financial liability are met (see 6.4 below).

Once an entity has determined what is 'similar', it must consider the derecognition tests (pass through and transfer of risk and rewards) by reference to the same group of 'similar' assets (see 3.5 below).

3.3.3 Transfer of asset (or part of asset) for only part of its life

The examples given in IAS 39 and IFRS 9 implicitly appear to have in mind the transfer of a tranche of cash flows from the date of transfer for the remainder of the life of an instrument. This raises the question of the appropriate accounting treatment where (for example) an entity with a loan receivable repayable in 10 years' time enters into a transaction whereby all the interest flows for the next 5 years only (or those for years 6 to 10) are transferred to a third party. There is no reason why such a transaction could not be considered for partial derecognition.

3.3.4 'Financial asset' includes whole or part of a financial asset

In the derecognition provisions in IAS 39 and IFRS 9, as well as the discussion in sections 3 to 5 of this chapter, the term 'financial asset' is used to refer to either the whole, or a part, of a financial asset (or the whole or a part of a group of similar financial assets). *[IAS 39.16, IFRS 9.3.2.2]*. It is therefore important to remember throughout the following discussion that a reference to an asset being derecognised 'in its entirety' does not necessarily mean that 100% of the asset is derecognised.

It may mean, for example, that there has been full derecognition of, say, 80% of the asset to which the derecognition rules have applied separately (in accordance with the criteria above).

3.4 Have the contractual rights to cash flows from the asset expired?

The discussion in this section refers to Box 3 in the flowchart at 3.2 above.

The first step in determining whether derecognition of a financial asset is appropriate is to establish whether the contractual rights to the cash flows from that asset have expired. If they have, the asset is derecognised. Examples might be:

- a loan receivable is repaid;
- the holder of a perpetual debt, whose terms provide for ten annual 'interest' payments that, in effect, provide both interest and a return of capital, receives the final payment of interest; or
- a purchased option expires unexercised.

If the cash flows from the financial asset have not expired, it is derecognised when, and only when, the entity 'transfers' the asset within the specified meaning of the term in IAS 39 and IFRS 9 (see 3.5 below), and the transfer has the effect that the entity has either:

- transferred substantially all the risks and rewards of the asset (see 3.8 below); or
- neither transferred nor retained substantially all the risks and rewards of the asset (see 3.8 below), and has not retained control of the asset (see 3.9 below). *[IAS 39.17, IFRS 9.3.2.3]*.

3.4.1 Renegotiation of the terms of an asset

It is common for an entity, particularly but not necessarily when in financial difficulties, to approach its major creditors for a restructuring of its debt commitments. The restructuring may involve a modification to the terms of a loan or an exchange of one debt instrument issued by the borrower for another. In these circumstances, IAS 39 contains accounting requirements for the borrower to apply which address whether the restructured debt should be regarded as:

- the continuation of the original liability, perhaps with no gain or loss recognised as a consequence of the restructuring; or
- a new financial liability which replaces the original liability that is hence derecognised. In this case the borrower would recognise a gain or loss based on the difference between the fair value of the restructured debt and the carrying amount of the original liability (see 6.2 below).

However, IAS 39 contains no equivalent requirements for the lender.

In practice, different entities have developed their own accounting policies for such arrangements, often based broadly on the guidance for financial liabilities. Nevertheless, IAS 39 is clear that a loss should be recognised on a renegotiated or modified asset that is impaired (see Chapter 49 at 4.2.2). Therefore, it would be inappropriate to maintain the carrying amount of an impaired financial asset (as one might do for a financial liability) to avoid recognising such a loss.[5]

This could be an important accounting policy for banks and other financial institutions if they frequently renegotiate the terms of their loans and receivables and, accordingly, IFRS 7 suggests such policies should be disclosed (see Chapter 54 at 4.1). HSBC includes the following in its financial statements:

Extract 51.1: HSBC Holdings plc (2015)

Notes on the Financial Statements [extract]
1 – Basis of preparation and significant accounting policies [extract]
(k) Impairment of loans and advances and available-for-sale financial assets [extract]
Renegotiated loans [extract]

[...] A loan that is renegotiated is derecognised if the existing agreement is cancelled and a new agreement made on substantially different terms or if the terms of an existing agreement are modified such that the renegotiated loan is substantially a different financial instrument. [...]

The requirements in IFRS 9 for determining when to derecognise financial assets are unchanged from those in IAS 39, but the basis for conclusions does contain some new references to this topic. In particular, it is noted that some modifications of contractual cash flows result in the derecognition of a financial instrument and the recognition of a new instrument, but frequently they do not. *[IFRS 9.BC5.216, BC5.227].*

The Interpretations Committee has acknowledged that determining when a modification of an asset should result in its derecognition is an issue that arises in practice and considered undertaking a narrow-scope project to clarify the requirements of IFRS 9 and IAS 39. However, in May 2016 the committee concluded that the broad nature of the issue meant it could not be resolved in an efficient manner and decided not to further consider such a project.[6]

The measurement consequences for financial assets that are classified at amortised cost or debt instrument measured at fair value through other comprehensive income in accordance with IFRS 9 and which are modified but not derecognised are considered in Chapter 50 at 5.7.

3.4.2 Interpretations Committee discussions on asset restructuring in the context of Greek government debt

In February 2012, the Greek government announced the terms of a restructuring of certain of its issued bonds. One aspect involved the exchange of 31.5% of the principal amount of the bonds for twenty new bonds with different maturities and interest rates. The remaining portions of the bonds were either forgiven or exchanged for other securities issued by the European Financial Stability Facility, a special purpose entity established by Eurozone states. In addition, for each new bond, the holder received another security issued by the Greek government, payments on which are linked to Greece's gross domestic product.

Soon afterwards, the Interpretations Committee was asked to address the appropriate accounting treatment for certain aspects of the restructuring, which they did initially in May 2012. One question the Committee considered was whether the exchange of 31.5% of the principal amount of the original bonds for new bonds could be regarded as a continuation of that portion of the original asset or whether that portion should also be derecognised (it being widely accepted that the remaining portions of the bonds should be derecognised).

In addressing this question, the Committee made an assumption that it was appropriate to analyse this aspect of the restructuring in isolation even though many individual members expressed the view during their discussions that the restructuring should be analysed as a whole. (The IFRIC was clear that if the analysis considered the restructuring as a whole, the bonds should be derecognised in their entirety.)

The committee first addressed whether the exchange should be regarded as a transfer. They noted that the bonds were transferred back to the issuer rather than to a third party and, as a consequence, concluded this particular restructuring should not be regarded as a transfer (see 3.5.1 below). Instead, it should be evaluated to determine whether it amounted to an actual or in-substance expiry or extinguishment of the original cash flows.

The staff analysis was clear that a modification of terms *can* result in expiry of the asset's original rights to cash flows, although it would not always do so. This is because it is implicit within the requirements for measuring impairment losses that a modification would sometimes be regarded as a continuation of the original, albeit impaired, asset. Therefore an entity would assess the modifications made against the notion of 'expiry' of the rights to the cash flows.[7]

The staff analysis indicated that the 'hierarchy' in IAS 8 – *Accounting Policies, Changes in Accounting Estimates and Errors* – would be applied in developing an appropriate accounting policy. Whilst this requires the application of judgement, it is not an absolute discretion. Consequently, it would be appropriate to analogise, at least to some extent, to those requirements in IAS 39 applying to modifications and exchanges of financial liabilities, particularly the notion of 'substantial modification' and the fact that modifications and exchanges between an existing lender and borrower are seen as equivalent. However, applying the '10% test' to determine whether a modification is substantial would not always be appropriate because of potential inconsistencies with the requirements in IAS 39 for impaired financial assets.[8] For example, IAS 39 envisages some modifications of cash flows that are accounted for as impairment of the original financial asset (for instance, a deferral of the due dates of the original cash flows), *[IAS 39.IC.E.4.3]*, that could well produce a difference in discounted cash flows of greater than 10% (see Chapter 49 at 4.2.2).

The committee did not explicitly conclude on this part of the staff analysis, particularly the question of when it would be appropriate to regard a modification or exchange as the expiry or in-substance extinguishment of the original asset. Instead they simply noted that, in their view, derecognition of the original Greek government bonds would be the appropriate accounting treatment however this particular transaction was assessed, i.e. whether it was viewed as (a) an actual expiry of the rights of the original asset or (b) as a substantial modification that should be accounted for as an extinguishment of the original asset (because of the extensive changes in the assets' terms). An agenda decision setting out the committee's conclusions was published in September 2012.[9]

Whilst that discussion resolved most of the issues associated with the restructuring of Greek government bonds, the wider topic continues to require the application of judgement and, as a result, potentially leads to inconsistent approaches being applied by different entities. In responding to the committee's tentative agenda decision published in May 2012, some important regulators, particularly in Europe, called for the topic to be addressed more comprehensively.[10]

3.4.3 Novation of contracts to intermediary counterparties

A change in the terms of a contract may take the legal form of a 'novation'. In this context novation means that the parties to a contract agree to change that contract so that an original counterparty is replaced by a new counterparty.

For example, a derivative between a reporting entity and a bank may be novated to a central counterparty (CCP) as a result of the introduction of new laws or regulations. In these circumstances, the IASB explains that through novation to a CCP the contractual rights to cash flows from the original derivative have expired and as a consequence the novation meets the derecognition criteria for a financial asset. *[IAS 39.BC220A-220F]*.

Whilst the IASB reached the above conclusion in relation to novations of over-the-counter derivatives, it is our view that the principle is applicable to all novations of contracts underlying a financial instrument. Accordingly, when a counterparty changes as a result of a novation, the financial instrument should be derecognised and a new financial instrument should be recognised. Although such a change may not be expected to give rise to a significant gain or loss when the financial instrument derecognised and the new financial instrument recognised are both measured at fair value through profit or loss, the bid/ask spread and the effect of change in counterparty on credit risk may cause some value differences. Furthermore, a novation may result in discontinuation of hedge accounting if the original financial instrument was a derivative designated in a hedging relationship (see Chapter 52 at 4.2.3.A and Chapter 53 at 11.3 for further details).

3.4.4 Write-offs

When an entity applies IFRS 9, it is required to directly reduce the gross carrying amount of a financial asset when it has no reasonable expectations of recovery. Such a write-off is regarded as the asset being derecognised – effectively it is seen as an in-substance expiry of the associated rights. Write-offs can also relate to a portion of an asset. For example, consider an entity that plans to enforce the collateral on a financial asset and expects to recover no more than 30% of the financial asset from the collateral. If the entity has no reasonable prospects of recovering any further cash flows from the financial asset, it should write off the remaining 70%. *[IFRS 9.5.4.4, B3.2.16(r), B5.4.9]*.

3.5 Has the entity 'transferred' the asset?

An entity is regarded by IAS 39 and IFRS 9 as 'transferring' a financial asset if, and only if, it either:

(a) transfers the contractual rights to receive the cash flows of the financial asset (see 3.5.1 below); or

(b) retains the contractual rights to receive the cash flows of the financial asset, but assumes a contractual obligation to pay the cash flows on to one or more recipients in an arrangement that meets the conditions in 3.5.2 below *[IAS 39.18, IFRS 9.3.2.4]* (a so-called 'pass-through arrangement').

This might be the case where the entity is a special purpose entity or trust, and issues to investors beneficial interests in financial assets that it owns and provides servicing of those assets. *[IAS 39.AG37, IFRS 9.B3.2.2]*.

These conditions are highly significant for securitisations and similar transactions that fall within (b) because the entity retains the contractual right to receive cash.

3.5.1 *Transfers of contractual rights to receive cash flows*

The discussion in this section refers to Box 4 in the flowchart at 3.2 above.

IAS 39 and IFRS 9 do not define what they mean by the phrase 'transfers the contractual rights to receive the cash flows of the financial asset' in (a) in 3.5 above, possibly on the assumption that this is self-evident. However, this is far from the case, since the phrase raises a number of questions of interpretation.

There are two key uncertainties about the meaning of 'transferring the contractual rights' (which in turn determines whether a transaction falls within (a) or (b) in 3.5 above):

- whether it is restricted to transfers of legal title only or also encompasses transfers of equitable title or an equitable interest (see 3.5.1.A below); and
- the effect of conditions attached to the transfers (see 3.5.1.B below).

While both of these are of great significance to securitisations (see 3.6 below), they also have implications for other transactions. These issues were discussed in 2006 by both the Interpretations Committee and the IASB. However, as described at 3.3.2 above, the Interpretations Committee's tentative decision not to issue further guidance and the interpretation of the issues that had so far been published were both withdrawn in January 2007. There is no clear evidence that practice has changed as a result of the views that had been expressed by the IASB and the Interpretations Committee but, as this has demonstrated a lack of clear underlying principles, it would be no surprise to find that entities have different interpretations of the requirements.

In the context of the restructuring of Greek government bonds (see 3.4.2 above), the Interpretations Committee considered whether an exchange of debt instruments between a borrower and a lender should be regarded as a transfer. It was noted that the bonds were transferred back to the issuer rather than to a third party and, as a consequence, it was agreed that this particular restructuring should not be regarded as a transfer.[11] However, it was noted during the committee's discussion and in the comment process that applying such a conclusion more widely might not always be appropriate, e.g. in the case of a short-term sale and repurchase agreement over a bond with the bond issuer or the simple repurchase of a bond by the issuer for cash.

3.5.1.A Meaning of 'transfers the contractual rights to receive the cash flows'

In many jurisdictions, the law recognises two types of title to property: (a) legal title; and (b) 'equitable', or beneficial title. In general, legal title defines who owns an asset at law and equitable title defines who is recognised as entitled to the benefit of the asset. Transfers of legal title give the transferee the ability to bring an action against a debtor to recover the debt in its own name. In equitable transfers, however, the transferee joins the transferor in an action to sue the debtor for recovery of debt. As noted above, the issue here is whether 'transfers of contractual rights' are limited to transfers of legal title.

We have commented in previous editions of this book that the requirement to transfer 'the *contractual* rights to receive cash flows' suggests that transfer must have the effect that the transferee has a direct legal claim on those cash flows. Under this interpretation, if a corporate entity securitises the future cash flows from a portfolio of trade receivables it has arguably 'transferred' them for the purposes of IAS 39 or IFRS 9 if, and only if, the finance provider could, directly and in its own name, sue the debtor for default (see 3.6 below). In many jurisdictions, this would simply not be possible without either:

- a tri-partite agreement between the corporate entity, the finance provider and the debtor; or
- a clause in the standard terms of trade allowing such a transfer at the sole discretion of the corporate entity without the express consent of the debtor, so that transfer can be effected by a subsequent bi-partite agreement between the corporate entity and the finance provider.

The consent of the debtor is not normally obtained, or indeed practically obtainable, in many securitisations and similar transactions. In these arrangements, all cash flows that are collected are contractually payable to a new eventual recipient – i.e. the debtor continues to pay the transferor, while the transferor loses the right to retain any cash collected from the debtor without actually transferring the contract itself.

In March 2006 the Interpretations Committee began to consider whether there can be a transfer of the contractual right to receive cash flows in an equitable transfer.[12] The Interpretations Committee had already concluded, in November 2005, that retaining servicing rights (i.e. continuing to administer collections and distributions of cash as agent for the transferee) does not in itself preclude derecognition.[13] However, the Interpretations Committee then considered whether retention by the transferor of the contractual right to receive the cash from debtors for distribution on to other parties (as must inevitably happen if debtors are not notified) means that such a transaction does not meet test (a) in 3.5 above, and thus must meet test (b) (pass-through) in order to achieve derecognition. The Interpretations Committee referred this issue to the IASB, which indicated in September 2006 that:

> 'a transaction in which an entity transfers all the contractual rights to receive the cash flows (without necessarily transferring legal ownership of the financial asset), would not be treated as a pass-through. An example might be a situation in which an entity transfers all the legal rights to specifically identified cash flows of a financial asset (for example, a transfer of the interest or principal of a debt instrument). Conversely, the pass-through test would be applicable when the entity does not transfer all the

contractual rights to cash flows of the financial asset, such as disproportionate transfers.'[14] (Disproportionate transfers are discussed at 3.3 above).

The statement that such a transaction 'would not be treated as a pass-through' means (in terms of the flowchart in Figure 51.1 at 3.2 above) that the answer to Box 4 is 'Yes', such that the pass-through test in Box 5 (see 3.5.2 below) is by-passed.

The IASB's conclusion appears to concede that the reference in IAS 39 (and hence in IFRS 9) to a transfer of the 'contractual' right to cash flows was intended to include an *equitable* transfer of those rights, a conclusion that the IASB repeated in its April 2009 Exposure Draft – *Derecognition*.

The IASB commented that 'the pass-through test would be applicable when the entity does not transfer all the contractual rights to cash flows of the financial asset, such as disproportionate transfers'.

For example, if an entity transfers the rights to 90% of the cash flows from a group of receivables but provides a guarantee to compensate the buyer for any credit losses up to 8% of the principal amount of the receivables, the derecognition provisions are applied to the group of financial assets in its entirety. *[IAS 39.16(b), IFRS 9.3.2.2(b)]*. This means that the answer to Box 4 in the flowchart will be 'No' (since some, not all, of the cash flows of the entire group of assets have been transferred), thus requiring the pass-through test in Box 5 to be applied. In contrast, the pass-through test would not need to be applied where the entity transfers the contractual right to receive 100% of the cash flows even if it guarantees losses up to a certain percentage of the principal.

It is hard to see the circumstances in which the pass-through test would ever be successfully applied to a disproportionate transfer. Accordingly, this view from the IASB would, in effect, disqualify virtually all disproportionate transfers from derecognition.

The IASB's interpretation gives no answer to an even more critical question. If the derecognition rules need to be applied separately to loans and derivatives or guarantees, how does this affect:

- the definition of a 'transfer' (if all the cash flows are transferred); or
- the application of the pass-through test (if the transfer is of a disproportionate share of the cash flow)?

Before this re-examination by the IASB of the meaning of 'transfer', it was common in some jurisdictions to apply the legal title test to transfers of financial assets to a SPE in securitisation arrangements, rather than relying on an equitable transfer. After the withdrawal of the 'non-interpretation' (see 3.3.2 above), it is likely that those entities have continued to apply their previous practice. However the discussions have, yet again, highlighted the uncertainty at the heart of the derecognition rules in IAS 39 and IFRS 9 which means that there must be different treatments in practice. Until there is a conclusive interpretation, entities must establish an accounting policy that they apply consistently to all such transactions, whether they are transfers or pass-throughs.

The implications of the IASB's discussion on securitisation transactions are discussed further at 3.6.5 below.

3.5.1.B Transfers subject to conditions

An entity may transfer contractual rights to cash flows but subject to conditions. The Interpretations Committee identified the following main types of condition:

- *Conditions relating to the existence and legal status of the asset at the time of the transfer*

  These include normal warranties as to the condition of the asset at the date of transfer and other guarantees affecting the existence and accuracy of the amount of the receivable that may not be known until after the date of transfer.

- *Conditions relating to the performance of the asset after the time of transfer*

  These include guarantees covering future default, late payment or changes in credit risk, guarantees relating to changes in tax, legal or regulatory requirements, where the buyer may be able to require additional payments if it is disadvantaged or – in some cases – demand reversal of the transaction, or guarantees covering future performance by the seller that might affect the recoverable amount of the debtor.

- *Offset arrangements*

  The original debtor may have the right to offset amounts against balances owed to the transferor for which the transferor will compensate the transferee. There may also be tripartite offset arrangements where a party other than the original debtor (e.g. a subcontractor) has such offset rights.[15]

All securitisations (and indeed, most derecognitions, whether of financial or non-financial assets) include express or implied warranties regarding the condition of the asset at the date of transfer. In the case of a securitisation of credit card receivables, these might include a representation that, for example, all the debtors transferred are resident in a particular jurisdiction, or have never been in arrears for more than one month in the previous two years. In our view, such warranties should not affect whether or not the transaction achieves derecognition.

It is a different matter when it comes to guarantees of post-transfer performance. In particular, one of the issues identified by the Interpretations Committee – guarantees covering future default, late payment or changes in credit risk – links to the related debate regarding the transfer of groups of financial assets where the guarantees may have been provided by a third party (see 3.3.2 above).

In July 2006 the Interpretations Committee decided to refer this issue to the IASB, which considered it at its September 2006 meeting. The IASB broadly confirmed our view as set out above. In its view neither conditions relating to the existence and value of transferred cash flows at the date of transfer nor conditions relating to the future performance of the asset would affect whether the entity has transferred the contractual rights to receive cash flows[16] (i.e. Box 4 in Figure 51.1 at 3.2 above). In other words, a transaction with such conditions that otherwise met the criteria in Box 4 would not be subject to the pass-through test in Box 5.

However, the existence of conditions relating to the future performance of the asset might affect the conclusion related to the transfer of risks and rewards (i.e. Box 6 in Figure 51.1 at 3.2 above) as well as the extent of any continuing involvement by the transferor in the transferred asset (i.e. Box 9 in Figure 51.1 at 3.2. above).[17]

These interpretations were also withdrawn by the Interpretations Committee in January 2007 together with the views that had been expressed regarding 'similar' assets and transfers of assets (see 3.3.2 above). Although the IASB repeated them in the April 2009 Exposure Draft – *Derecognition* – an entity must take a view that is consistent with its policies on these matters and, as in these other cases, hold this view consistently when considering the derecognition of any financial asset.

An example of a two-party offset arrangement is when the original debtor (e.g. a borrower or customer) has the right to offset amounts it is owed by the transferor (e.g. balances in a deposit account or arising from a credit note issued by the transferor) against the transferred asset. If such a right is exercised after the asset is transferred the transferor would be required to compensate the transferee. This would not, in our view, normally affect whether the entity has transferred the contractual rights to receive the cash flows of the original financial asset. Payments made by the transferor to the transferee as a result of the right of offset being exercised simply transfer to the transferee the value the transferor obtained when its liability to the original debtor was settled.

3.5.2 Retention of rights to receive cash flows subject to obligation to pay over to others (pass-through arrangement)

The discussion in this section refers to Box 5 in the flowchart at 3.2 above.

It is common in certain securitisation and debt sub-participation transactions (see 3.6 below) for an entity to enter into an arrangement whereby it continues to collect cash receipts from a financial asset (or more typically a pool of financial assets), but is obliged to pass on those receipts to a third party that has provided finance in connection with the financial asset. Whilst the term 'pass-through' for these arrangements does not actually appear in IAS 39 or IFRS 9 it has become part of the language of the financial markets.

Under IAS 39 and IFRS 9, an arrangement whereby the reporting entity retains the contractual rights to receive the cash flows of a financial asset (the 'original asset'), but assumes a contractual obligation to pay the cash flows to one or more recipients (the 'eventual recipients') is regarded as a transfer of the original asset if, and only if, all of the following three conditions are met:

(a) the entity has no obligation to pay amounts to the eventual recipients unless it collects equivalent amounts from the original asset. Short-term advances by the entity with the right of full recovery of the amount lent plus accrued interest at market rates do not violate this condition (see 3.6.1 and 3.6.2 below);

(b) the entity is prohibited by the terms of the transfer contract from selling or pledging the original asset other than as security to the eventual recipients for the obligation to pay them cash flows; and

(c) the entity has an obligation to remit any cash flows it collects on behalf of the eventual recipients without material delay. In addition, the entity is not entitled to reinvest such cash flows, except in cash or cash equivalents as defined in IAS 7 – *Statement of Cash Flows* (see Chapter 38 at 3) during the short settlement period from the collection date to the date of required remittance to the eventual recipients, with any interest earned on such investments being passed to the eventual recipients. *[IAS 39.19, IFRS 9.3.2.5].*

These conditions are discussed further at 3.6.4 below.

IAS 39 and IFRS 9 note that an entity that is required to consider the impact of these conditions on a transaction is likely to be either:

- the originator of the financial asset in a securitisation transaction (see 3.6 below); or
- a group that includes a consolidated special purpose entity that has acquired the financial asset and passes on cash flows to unrelated third party investors. *[IAS 39.AG38, IFRS 9.B3.2.3]*.

3.6 Securitisations

Securitisation is a process whereby finance can be raised from external investors by enabling them to invest in parcels of specific financial assets. The first main type of assets to be securitised was domestic mortgage loans, but the technique is regularly extended to other assets, such as credit card receivables, other consumer loans, or lease receivables. Securitisations are a complex area of financial reporting beyond the scope of a general text such as this to discuss in detail. However, it may assist understanding of the IASB's thinking to consider a 'generic' example of such a transaction.

A typical securitisation transaction involving a portfolio of mortgage loans would operate as follows. The entity which has initially advanced the loans in question (the 'originator') will sell them to another entity set up for the purpose (the 'issuer'). The issuer will typically be a subsidiary or consolidated SPE of the originator (and therefore consolidated – see 3.2 above) and its equity share capital, which will be small, will often be owned by a trustee on behalf of a charitable trust. The issuer will finance its purchase of these loans by issuing loan notes on interest terms which will be related to the rate of interest receivable on the mortgages and to achieve this it may need to enter into derivative instruments such as interest rate swaps. The swap counterparty may be the originator or a third party. The originator will continue to administer the loans as before, for which it will receive a service fee from the issuer.

The structure might therefore be as shown in this diagram:

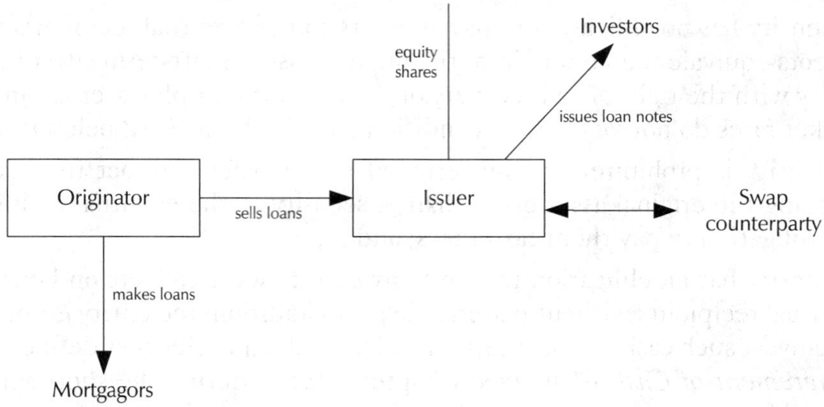

Potential investors in the mortgage-backed loan notes will want to be assured that their investment is relatively risk-free and the issue will normally be supported by obtaining a high rating from a credit rating agency. This may be achieved by using a range of credit enhancement techniques which will add to the security already inherent in the quality of the mortgage portfolio. Such techniques can include the following:

- limited recourse to the originator in the event that the income from the mortgages falls short of the interest payable to the investors under the loan notes and other expenses. This may be made available in a number of ways; for example, by the provision of subordinated loan finance from the originator to the issuer; by the deferral of part of the consideration for the sale of the mortgages; or by the provision of a guarantee (see 3.6.1 below);
- the provision of loan facilities to meet temporary shortfalls as a result of slow payments of mortgage interest (see 3.6.2 below); or
- insurance against default on the mortgages (see 3.6.3 below).

The overall effect of the arrangement is that outside investors have been brought in to finance a particular portion of the originator's activities. These investors have first call on the income from the mortgages which back their investment. The originator is left with only the residual interest in the differential between the rates paid on the notes and earned on the mortgages, net of expenses; generally, this profit element is extracted by adjustments to the service fee or through the mechanism of interest rate swaps. It has thus limited its upside interest in the mortgages, while its remaining downside risk on the whole arrangement will depend on the extent to which it has assumed obligations under the credit enhancement measures.

3.6.1 Recourse to originator

The conditions in 3.5.2 above clearly have the effect that an arrangement that does not transfer the contractual rights to receive the cash flows but provides for direct recourse to the originator does not meet the definition of a 'transfer' for the purposes of pass-through and therefore does not qualify to be considered for derecognition. Direct recourse would include an arrangement whereby part of the consideration for the financial asset transferred was deferred depending on the performance of the asset.

In our view, however, certain techniques for providing indirect recourse do not breach the conditions for transfer. These include, for example, the provision of certain types of insurance (see 3.6.3 below).

3.6.2 Short-term loan facilities

Enhancing a securitised asset with the provision of loan facilities to meet temporary shortfalls as a result of slow payments from the asset would not preclude an arrangement being regarded as a pass-through (see 3.5.2 above), but only where the loans:

- are made on a 'short-term' basis;
- are repayable irrespective of whether the slow payments are eventually received; and
- bear interest at market rates.

The purpose of these restrictions is to ensure that IAS 39 and IFRS 9 allow derecognition of assets subject to such facilities only where the facilities are providing a short-term cash flow benefit to the investor, and not when they effectively transfer slow payment risk back to the originator (as would be the case if the originator made significant interest-free loans to the investor). Clearly, therefore, the circumstances in which such funds can be advanced must be very tightly defined if pass-through is to be achieved.

3.6.3 Insurance protection

The conditions for 'transfer' are not, in our view, breached by the originator purchasing an insurance contract for the benefit of investors in the event of a shortfall in cash collections from the securitised assets, provided that the investors' only recourse is to the insurance policy. In other words, the originator cannot give a guarantee to investors to make good any shortfalls should the insurer become insolvent, nor can the originator provide any support to the insurer through a guarantee arrangement or a reinsurance contract.

The implications of the derecognition and pass-through requirements of IAS 39 (and hence of IFRS 9) for transfers of groups of financial assets including insurance contracts have been reconsidered by the Interpretations Committee and the IASB but their tentative conclusions were withdrawn. For a discussion of the issues and the alternative interpretations of 'similar' assets, see 3.3.2 above.

3.6.4 Treatment of collection proceeds

Securitisation contracts rarely require any amount received on the securitised assets to be immediately transferred to investors. This is for the obvious practical reason that it would be administratively inefficient, in the case of a securitisation of credit card receivables for example, to transfer the relevant portion of each individual, and relatively small, cash flow received from the hundreds, if not thousands, of cards in the portfolio. Instead, it is usual for transfers to be made in bulk on a periodic basis (e.g. weekly or monthly). This raises the question of what happens to the cash in the period between receipt by the issuer and onward transfer to the investors.

IAS 39 and IFRS 9 require cash flows from transferred financial assets for which derecognition is sought to be:

- passed to the eventual recipients 'without material delay'; and
- invested only in cash or cash equivalents as defined in IAS 7 entirely for the benefit of the investors (see condition (c) in 3.5.2 above).

These requirements mean that many securitisation arrangements may well fail to satisfy the pass-through test in 3.5.2 above, as explained below.

Suppose that a credit card issuer wishes to raise five year finance secured on its portfolio of credit card receivables. The assets concerned are essentially short term (being in most cases settled in full within four to eight weeks), whereas the term of the borrowings secured on them is longer. In practice, what generally happens is that, at the start of the securitisation, a 'pool' of balances is transferred to the issuer. The cash receipts from that 'pool' are used to pay interest on the borrowings, and to fund new advances on cards in the 'pool' or to purchase other balances. Such an arrangement, commonly referred to as a 'revolving' structure, appears to breach the requirement of the pass-through tests to:

- pass on cash receipts without material delay (since only the amount of cash receipts necessary to pay the interest on the borrowings is passed on, with the balance being reinvested until the principal of the borrowings falls due); and
- only invest in cash or cash equivalents as defined in IAS 7 in the period prior to passing them onto the investor. This is because the cash not required to pay interest on the borrowings is invested in further credit card receivables, which are not cash or cash equivalents as defined in IAS 7.

The Interpretations Committee confirmed in November 2005 that 'revolving' structures do not meet the requirements of the pass-through test for funds to be passed on without material delay and to be invested only in cash and cash equivalents.[18]

In practice, we have observed the pass-through tests are applied very strictly such that any arrangement that provides for even a small tranche of the interest from such short-term deposits to be retained by or for the benefit of the originator will not satisfy the criteria for transfer under IAS 39 or IFRS 9. Moreover, IAS 39 and IFRS 9 require that the reporting entity 'is not entitled' to invest the cash other than in cash or cash equivalents as described above. Thus, it appears that the criteria for transfer are not satisfied merely where the entity does not in fact invest the cash in any other way – it must be contractually prohibited from doing so. In practice, this is often achieved by having the funds paid into a trustee bank account that can be used only for the benefit of the providers of finance.

The IASB does not expand further on the term 'without material delay'. It is not, in our view, intended to require settlement to noteholders on an unrealistically frequent basis such as daily, although we would normally expect payments to be made by the next quarterly coupon payment date to meet this condition.

The strict requirements of IAS 39 and IFRS 9 in respect of cash received from assets subject to a pass-through arrangement raise the related, but broader, issue of the appropriate treatment of client money which is discussed at 3.7 below.

3.6.5 *Transfers of non-optional derivatives along with a group of financial assets*

As discussed at 3.3.2 above, interest rate swaps that are transferred along with a group of non-derivative financial assets may be derecognised only when any associated obligation is discharged, cancelled or expires (see 6 below). This, however, does not occur in most securitisations.

In a securitisation transaction involving the equitable transfer of an interest rate swap to an SPE, the swap would continue to be recognised by the transferor. The ongoing accounting consequences of this are less clear. The swap must clearly continue to be measured at fair value through profit or loss in accordance with the general requirement of IAS 39 or IFRS 9 for the measurement of derivatives not in a hedging relationship (see Chapter 44). However, this would have the effect that the reporting entity reflected gains and losses in the income statement for a derivative in which it no longer has a beneficial interest. In such a case, the entity should presumably recognise the notional back-to-back swap which it has effectively entered into with the transferee, so as to offset the income statement effect of the original swap.

3.6.6 *'Empty' subsidiaries or SPEs*

If an entity enters into a transaction whereby:

- the entity transfers an asset to a subsidiary or SPE; and
- the subsidiary or SPE transfers the asset to noteholders on terms that satisfy the pass-through derecognition criteria in IAS 39 or IFRS 9 discussed at 3.5.2 and 3.6 above,

the overall effect will be that the individual financial statements of the subsidiary or SPE will include neither the transferred asset nor the finance raised from noteholders. This may well mean that the financial statements show nothing apart from the relatively small amount of equity of the entity and any related assets. This analysis is likely to be applicable only for relatively simple transfers, and not, for example, when derivatives are transferred along with the non-derivative assets.

3.7 Client money

A number of financial institutions and other entities hold money on behalf of clients. The terms on which such money is held can vary widely. In the case of normal deposits with a bank, the bank is free to use the client's money for its own purposes, with the client being protected by the capital requirements imposed by the regulatory authorities. By contrast there are cases (e.g. in the case of certain monies held by legal advisers on behalf of their clients in some jurisdictions) where funds held on behalf of clients must be kept in a bank account completely separate from that of the depositary entity itself, with all interest earned on the account being for the benefit of clients. There are also intermediate situations where, for example:

- funds are required to be segregated in separate bank accounts but the depositary entity is allowed to retain some or all of the interest on the client accounts; or
- client funds are allowed to be commingled with those of the depositary entity, but some or all income on the funds must be passed on to clients.

This raises the question of how client monies should be accounted for in the financial statements under IFRS. In particular, whether the assets should be recognised in the first place, and if so whether, in the absence of specific guidance, the rules for the treatment of funds received under a pass-through arrangement (see 3.6.4 above) should be applied.

The types of arrangement to deal with client money are so varied that it is impossible to generalise as to the appropriate treatment. Key considerations include:

- which party is at risk from the failure of assets, such as bank accounts, in which the client money is held;
- the status of the funds in the event of the insolvency of either the reporting entity or its client;
- whether the reporting entity can use the cash for its own purposes as opposed to administering the cash on behalf of the client in its capacity as an agent; and
- which party has the benefit of income from the assets.

The analysis for the two extreme cases seems relatively straightforward. In the case of a bank deposit (or any arrangement where the entity may freely use client cash for its own benefit), the general recognition criteria of IAS 39 and IFRS 9 indicate that an asset and a liability should be recognised. Conversely, where the entity is required to hold funds held on behalf of clients in a bank account completely separate from that of the entity itself, with all interest earned on the account being for the benefit of clients, it is hard to see how such funds meet the general definition of an asset under the *Conceptual Framework for Financial Reporting*. Whilst the entity administers such funds in its capacity as an agent on behalf of the client, it can derive no economic benefits from them. The intermediate cases may be harder to deal with.

Sometimes the appropriate analysis will be that the depositary entity enjoys sufficient use of the client money that it should be recognised as an asset with a corresponding liability due to the client. This will be the case, for example, if the client money is commingled with the reporting entity's cash for a short period of time. During this period the reporting entity is exposed to the credit risk associated with the cash and is entitled to all income accruing. Hence, the reporting entity would recognise the cash as an asset and a corresponding liability. If the cash is later moved to a segregated client trust account, an analysis should be performed to determine whether or not the cash and the corresponding liability should be removed from the reporting entity's statement of financial position.

3.8 Has the entity transferred or retained substantially all the risks and rewards of ownership?

The discussion in this section refers to Boxes 6 and 7 in the flowchart at 3.2 above.

Once an entity has established that it has transferred a financial asset (see 3.5 above), IAS 39 and IFRS 9 then require it to evaluate the extent to which it retains the risks and rewards of ownership of the financial asset. *[IAS 39.20, IFRS 9.3.2.6]*.

If the entity transfers substantially all the risks and rewards of ownership of the financial asset, the entity must derecognise the financial asset and recognise separately as assets or liabilities any rights and obligations created or retained in the transfer. *[IAS 39.20(a), IFRS 9.3.2.6(a)]*. Examples of such transactions are given at 3.8.1 and 4.1. If an entity determines that, as a result of the transfer, it has transferred substantially all the risks and rewards of ownership of the transferred asset, it does not recognise the transferred asset again in a future period, unless it reacquires the transferred asset in a new transaction. *[IAS 39.AG41, IFRS 9.B3.2.6]*.

If the entity retains substantially all the risks and rewards of ownership of the financial asset, the entity continues to recognise the financial asset. *[IAS 39.20(b), IFRS 9.3.2.6(b)]*. Examples of such transactions are given at 3.8.2, 4.1 and 4.3 below.

If the entity neither transfers nor retains substantially all the risks and rewards of ownership of the financial asset (see 3.8.3 below), the entity determines whether it has retained control of the financial asset *[IAS 39.20(c), IFRS 9.3.2.6(c)]* (see 3.9 below).

IAS 39 and IFRS 9 clarify that the transfer of risks and rewards should be evaluated by comparing the entity's exposure, before and after the transfer, to the variability in the amounts and timing of the net cash flows of the transferred asset. *[IAS 39.21, IFRS 9.3.2.7]*. Often it will be obvious whether the entity has transferred or retained substantially all risks and rewards of ownership. In other cases, it will be necessary to determine this by computing and comparing the entity's exposure to the variability in the present value (discounted at an appropriate current market interest rate) of the future net cash flows before and after the transfer. All reasonably possible variability in net cash flows is considered, with greater weight being given to those outcomes that are more likely to occur. *[IAS 39.22, IFRS 9.3.2.8].*

3.8.1 Transfers resulting in transfer of substantially all risks and rewards

An entity has transferred substantially all the risks and rewards of ownership of a financial asset if its exposure to the variability in the amounts and timing of the net cash flows of the transferred asset is no longer significant in relation to the total such variability. IAS 39 and IFRS 9 give the following examples of transactions that transfer substantially all the risks and rewards of ownership:

- an unconditional sale of a financial asset;
- a sale of a financial asset together with an option to repurchase the financial asset at its fair value at the time of repurchase (since this does not expose the entity to any risk of loss or give any opportunity for profit);
- a sale of a financial asset together with a put or call option that is deeply out of the money (i.e. an option that is so far out of the money it is highly unlikely to go into the money before expiry); or
- the sale of a fully proportionate share of the cash flows from a larger financial asset in an arrangement, such as a loan sub-participation, that satisfies the criteria for a 'transfer' in 3.5.2 above. *[IAS 39.21, AG39, IFRS 9.3.2.7, B3.2.4].*

Such transactions are discussed in more detail at 4 below.

It is important to note that, in order for derecognition to be achieved, it is necessary that the entity's exposure to the variability in the amounts and timing of the net cash flows of the transferred asset is considered not in isolation, but 'in relation to the total such variability' (see above). Thus derecognition is not achieved simply because the entity's remaining exposure to the risks or rewards of an asset is small in absolute terms. It has also become clear, from the Interpretations Committee and IASB's discussions described at 3.3.2 above, that derecognition also depends on the interpretation of 'asset' and of groups of similar assets that is applied by the entity.

3.8.2 Transfers resulting in retention of substantially all risks and rewards

An entity has retained substantially all the risks and rewards of ownership of a financial asset if its exposure to the variability in the present value of the future net cash flows from the financial asset does not change significantly as a result of the transfer. IAS 39 and IFRS 9 give the following examples of transactions in which an entity has retained substantially all the risks and rewards of ownership:

- a sale and repurchase transaction where the repurchase price is a fixed price or the sale price plus a lender's return;
- a securities lending agreement;
- a sale of a financial asset together with a total return swap that transfers the market risk exposure back to the entity;
- a sale of a financial asset together with a deeply in the money put or call option (i.e. an option that is so far in the money that it is highly unlikely to go out of

the money before expiry). It will be in the holder's interest to exercise such an option, so that the asset will almost certainly revert to the transferor; and

- a sale of short-term receivables in which the entity guarantees to compensate the transferee for credit losses that are likely to occur. *[IAS 39.21, AG40, IFRS 9.3.2.7, B3.2.5]*.

Such transactions are discussed in more detail at 4.1 below.

3.8.3 Transfers resulting in neither transfer nor retention of substantially all risks and rewards

IAS 39 and IFRS 9 give the following examples of transactions in which an entity has neither transferred nor retained substantially all the risks and rewards of ownership:

- a sale of a financial asset together with a put or call option that is neither deeply in the money nor deeply out of the money. *[IAS 39.AG51(g)-(h), IFRS 9.B3.2.16(g)-(h)]*. The effect of such an option is that the transferor will have either (in the case of purchased call option) capped its exposure to a loss in value of the asset but have potentially unlimited access to increases in value or (in the case of a written put option) capped its potential access to increases in value in the asset but assumed potential exposure to a total loss in value of the asset; and
- a sale of 90% of a loan portfolio with significant transfer of prepayment risk, but retention of a 10% interest, with losses allocated first to that 10% retained interest. *[IAS 39.AG52, IFRS 9.B3.2.17]*.

Such transactions are discussed in more detail at 4 below.

3.8.4 Evaluating the extent to which risks and rewards are transferred – practical example

The following example illustrates one approach to evaluating the extent to which risks and rewards associated with a portfolio of assets have been transferred.

Example 51.1: Risks and rewards analysis – variability in the amounts and timing of net cash flows

Entity X sells a portfolio of trade receivables with a face value of £1 million and an average due date of 45 days from the issuance of the invoice to Entity Y, an unrelated third party. After the sale, X does not retain any residual beneficial interests in the receivables. However, X guarantees losses on the transferred portfolio up to a percentage of the total face value. Default losses, including late payments, as a percentage of face value ranged historically from 3% to 5%.

Assume the following two hypothetical situations:

- Fact pattern 1 – Entity X guarantees first losses on the portfolio up to 3.5% of the total face value.
- Fact pattern 2 – Entity X guarantees first losses on the portfolio up to 4% of the total face value.

The following calculations illustrate one possible approach for calculating the exposure to the variability in the amounts and timing of net cash flows.

Under this approach the reporting entity (Entity X) determines a number of reasonably possible scenarios that reflect the expected variability in the amounts and timing of net cash flows; these scenarios are then assigned a probability, with greater weighting being given to those outcomes that are more likely to occur. Next, Entity X calculates the expected future net cash flows for each scenario, discounted using an appropriate current market rate. The expected variability is then calculated using an appropriate statistical technique. The above steps are duplicated for net cash flows that the transferor, Entity X, remains exposed to after the transfer. Finally, the exposure to expected variability of net cash flows post transfer is compared to the corresponding expected variability before the transfer.

In this example, the expected variability is calculated by adding up the individual (negative or positive) deviations of the expected discounted future net cash flows for each scenario from the total expected value of the net cash flows for all possible scenarios. As the receivables are relatively short-term, the calculations below focus primarily on credit risk, including delinquency risk. For simplicity, the calculations below ignore the effect of discounting.

Fact pattern 1: Entity X guarantees first losses on the portfolio up to 3.5% of total face value.

Based on historical experience and supportable expectations Entity X has defined five scenarios of possible variability, each of which has been assigned a probability based on historical experience and current market information. These scenarios and probabilities are set out below.

Before Transfer

Face value = £1,000,000 = A

Possible credit loss B	Discounted expected cash flows C= A – [A×B]	Probability D	Probability weighted discounted cash flows E=C×D	Variability F=C–Σ(E)	Probability weighted negative variability G= F×D if F<0	Probability weighted positive variability H=F×D if F>0
	£		£	£	£	£
3.0%	970,000	3.5%	33,950	11,550	–	404.25
3.5%	965,000	20.0%	193,000	6,550	–	1,310.00
4.0%	960,000	30.0%	288,000	1,550	–	465.00
4.5%	955,000	35.0%	334,250	(3,450)	(1,207.50)	–
5.0%	950,000	11.5%	109,250	(8,450)	(971.75)	–
		100.0%	958,450		**(2,179.25)**	**2,179.25**
					K	**K**
		I	**£41,550**	**=A – Σ(E)**		

After Transfer

Face value = £1,000,000 = A

Possible credit loss B	Discounted expected cash flows C=[A×(B)], max 35,000	Probability D	Probability weighted discounted cash flows E=C×D	Variability F=C–Σ(E)	Probability weighted negative variability G=F×D if F<0	Probability weighted positive variability H=F×D if F>0
	£		£	£	£	£
3.0%	30,000	3.5%	1,050	(4,825)	(168.88)	–
3.5%	35,000	20.0%	7,000	175	–	35.00
4.0%	35,000	30.0%	10,500	175	–	52.50
4.5%	35,000	35.0%	12,250	175	–	61.25
5.0%	35,000	11.5%	4,025	175	–	20.13
		100.0%	34,825		**(168.88)**	**168.88**
			M		**L**	**L**
Percentage of variability retained by Entity X				**L÷K**	**(7.75)%**	**7.75%**

To avoid a mechanical determination and to leave room for judgement, IAS 39 does not establish any bright-lines on what constitutes 'substantially all' risks and rewards of ownership. Therefore, judgement is needed to assess what is 'substantially all' in each particular situation considering, for example, the sensitivity of the calculation to certain changes in assumptions.

Assuming that Entity X determined that 'substantially all' represents 90% of total expected variability in the amounts and timing of net cash flows, it will conclude that it has transferred substantially all risks and rewards of ownership.

This conclusion may seem counterintuitive given that Entity X has retained 83.81% of the total expected losses (M÷I=34,825÷41,550). However, IAS 39 is clear that the transfer of risks and rewards should be evaluated by comparing the transferor's exposure, before and after the transfer, to the variability in the amounts and timing of net cash flows of the transferred asset. In practice, even when factoring with limited recourse, the transferor very often retains exposure to losses in excess of those reasonably expected to arise such that substantially all the variability is retained by the transferor.

Fact pattern 2: Entity X guarantees first losses on the portfolio up to 4% of the total face value.

Face value = £1,000,000 = A

Before Transfer

Possible credit loss B	Discounted expected cash flows C= A – [A×B]	Probability D	Probability weighted discounted cash flows E=C×D	Variability F=C–Σ(E)	Probability weighted negative variability G= F×D if F<0	Probability weighted positive variability H=F×D if F>0
	£		£	£	£	£
3.0%	970,000	3.5%	33,950	11,550	–	404.25
3.5%	965,000	20.0%	193,000	6,550	–	1,310.00
4.0%	960,000	30.0%	288,000	1,550	–	465.00
4.5%	955,000	35.0%	334,250	(3,450)	(1,207.50)	–
5.0%	950,000	11.5%	109,250	(8,450)	(971.75)	–
		100.0%	958,450		**(2,179.25)**	**2,179.25**
					K	**K**
		I	**£41,550**	**A – Σ(E)**		

After Transfer

Possible credit loss B	Discounted expected cash flows C=[A×(B), max 40,000]	Probability D	Probability weighted discounted cash flows E=C×D	Variability F=C–Σ(E)	Probability weighted negative variability G=F×D if F<0	Probability weighted positive variability H=F×D if F>0
	£		£	£	£	£
3.0%	30,000	3.5%	1,050	(8,650)	(302.75)	–
3.5%	35,000	20.0%	7,000	(3,650)	(730.00)	–
4.0%	40,000	30.0%	12,000	1,350	–	405.00
4.5%	40,000	35.0%	14,000	1,350	–	472.50
5.0%	40,000	11.5%	4,600	1,350	–	155.25
		100.0%	38,650		**(1,032.75)**	**1,032.75**
			M		**L**	**L**
Percentage of variability retained by Entity X				**L÷K**	**(47.39)%**	**47.39%**

Now that Entity X stands ready to cover first losses up to 4% which is in the middle of the range of expected losses (3% to 5%), it is not a surprise that its exposure to variability has increased to 47.39%. This means that Entity X has neither transferred nor retained substantially all risks and rewards of ownership in this case. Again, the fact that the seller now covers, after the sale, 93.02% (M÷I=38,650÷41,550) of the total expected losses is not relevant to the analysis.

In this case, derecognition will depend on whether the transferee (Entity Y) has the practical ability to sell the trade receivables unilaterally and without imposing additional restrictions on the transfer. The conclusion needs to take into account many factors. For example: (i) whether the transferee has legal title to the transferred receivables (ii) whether there is a market for the transferred receivables or not; (iii) whether or not the seller has a call option or has written a put option over the transferred receivables; (iv) whether or not the guarantee of Entity X is transferable with the receivables; (v) whether the receivables are 'ring-fenced' in a SPE as a pledge for securities collateralised by the transferred assets, etc. This aspect of the analysis is covered in 3.9 below.

3.9 Has the entity retained control of the asset?

The discussion in this section relates to Boxes 8 and 9 of the flowchart at 3.2 above.

If the transferring entity has neither transferred nor retained substantially all the risks and rewards of a transferred financial asset, IAS 39 and IFRS 9 require the entity to determine whether or not it has retained control of the financial asset. If the entity has not retained control, it must derecognise the financial asset and recognise separately as assets or liabilities any rights and obligations created or retained in the transfer. If the entity has retained control, it must continue to recognise the financial asset to the extent of its continuing involvement in the financial asset (see 5.3 below). *[IAS 39.20(c), IFRS 9.3.2.6(c)]*.

IAS 39 and IFRS 9 require the question of whether the entity has retained control of the transferred asset to be determined by the transferee's ability to sell the asset. If the transferee:

- has the practical ability to sell the asset in its entirety to an unrelated third party; and
- is able to exercise that ability unilaterally and without needing to impose additional restrictions on the transfer,

the entity has not retained control (see below).

In all other cases, the entity has retained control. *[IAS 39.23, IFRS 9.3.2.9]*.

3.9.1 *Transferee's 'practical ability' to sell the asset*

IAS 39 and IFRS 9 clarify that the transferee will have the practical ability to sell a transferred asset if the asset is traded in an active market, on the basis that the transferee will have the ability to repurchase the transferred asset in the market if it needs to return the asset to the entity.

If a transferred asset is sold subject to an option that allows the entity to repurchase it, the transferee may (subject to the further considerations discussed below) have the practical ability to sell the asset if it can readily obtain the transferred asset in the market if the option is exercised. *[IAS 39.AG42, IFRS 9.B3.2.7]*.

The transferee has the practical ability to sell the transferred asset only if the transferee can sell the transferred asset in its entirety to an unrelated third party and is able to exercise that ability unilaterally and without imposing additional restrictions on the transfer. IAS 39 and IFRS 9 require that to be determined by considering what the transferee is able to do in practice, rather than solely by reference to any contractual rights or prohibitions. The standard notes that a contractual right to dispose of the transferred asset has little practical effect if there is no market for the transferred asset. *[IAS 39.AG43, IFRS 9.B3.2.8]*.

An ability to dispose of the transferred asset also has little practical effect if it cannot be exercised freely. Accordingly, the transferee's ability to dispose of the transferred asset must be a unilateral ability independent of the actions of others. In other words, the transferee must be able to dispose of the transferred asset without needing to attach conditions to the transfer (e.g. conditions about how a loan asset is serviced, or an option giving the transferee the right to repurchase the asset). *[IAS 39.AG43, IFRS 9.B3.2.8]*.

For example, the entity might sell a financial asset to a transferee but the transferee has an option to put the asset back to the entity or has a performance guarantee from the entity. IAS 39 and IFRS 9 argue that such an option or guarantee might be so valuable to the transferee that it would not, in practice, sell the transferred asset to a third party without attaching a similar option or other restrictive conditions. Instead, the transferee would hold the transferred asset so as to obtain payments under the guarantee or put option. Under these circumstances IAS 39 and IFRS 9 regard the transferor as having retained control of the transferred asset. *[IAS 39.AG44, IFRS 9.B3.2.9]*.

However, the fact that the transferee is simply unlikely to sell the transferred asset does not, of itself, mean that the transferor has retained control of the transferred asset. *[IAS 39.AG44, IFRS 9.B3.2.9]*.

4 PRACTICAL APPLICATION OF THE DERECOGNITION CRITERIA

IAS 39 and IFRS 9 give a number of practical examples of the application of the derecognition criteria, which are discussed below. In some cases, it has to be said that the guidance in IAS 39 and IFRS 9 is less than satisfactory, amounting to little more than repetition of the standard.

In order to provide a link with Figure 51.1 at 3.2 above we have used the following convention:

'Box 6, Yes'	The transaction would result in the answer 'Yes' at Box 6 in the flowchart.
'Box 7, No'	The transaction would result in the answer 'No' at Box 7 in the flowchart.

4.1 Repurchase agreements ('repos') and securities lending

4.1.1 Agreements to return the same asset

If a financial asset is:

- sold under an agreement to repurchase it at a fixed price or at the sale price plus a lender's return; or
- loaned under an agreement to return it to the transferor,

the asset is not derecognised, because the transferor retains substantially all the risks and rewards of ownership, *[IAS 39.AG51(a), IFRS 9.B3.2.16(a)]*, (Figure 51.1, Box 7, Yes). The accounting treatment of such transactions is discussed at 5.2 below.

4.1.1.A Transferee's right to pledge

If the transferee obtains the right to sell or pledge an asset that is the subject of such a transaction, the transferor reclassifies the asset on its statement of financial position as, for example, a loaned asset or repurchase receivable. *[IAS 39.AG51(a), IFRS 9.B3.2.16(a)]*.

It appears that this accounting treatment is required merely where the transferee has the 'right' to sell or pledge the asset. This contrasts with the requirements for determining whether an asset subject to a transaction in which the entity neither transfers nor retains substantially all the risks and rewards associated with the asset (Figure 51.1, Box 7, No) nevertheless qualifies for derecognition because the transferee has control (Figure 51.1, Box 8). In order for the transferee to be regarded as having control for the purposes of Box 8, any rights of the transferee to sell an asset must have economic substance – see 3.9 above.

The accounting treatment of such transactions is discussed at 5.2 below.

4.1.2 Agreements with right to return the same or substantially the same asset

If a financial asset is:

- sold under an agreement to repurchase the same or substantially the same asset at a fixed price or at the sale price plus a lender's return; or
- loaned under an agreement to return the same or substantially the same asset to the transferor,

the asset is not derecognised because the transferor retains substantially all the risks and rewards of ownership, *[IAS 39.AG51(b), IFRS 9.B3.2.16(b)]*, (Figure 51.1, Box 7, Yes). The accounting treatment of such transactions is discussed at 5.2 below.

4.1.3 Agreements with right of substitution

If a financial asset is the subject of:

- a repurchase agreement at a fixed repurchase price or a price equal to the sale price plus a lender's return; or
- a similar securities lending transaction,

that provides the transferee with a right to substitute assets that are similar and of equal fair value to the transferred asset at the repurchase date, the asset sold or lent is not derecognised because the transferor retains substantially all the risks and rewards of ownership, *[IAS 39.AG51(c), IFRS 9.B3.2.16(c)]*, (Figure 51.1, Box 7, Yes). The accounting treatment of such transactions is discussed at 5.2 below.

4.1.4 Net cash-settled forward repurchase

IAS 39 and IFRS 9 give some guidance on the treatment of net cash-settled options over transferred assets (see 4.2.5 below), which in passing refers to net cash-settled forward contracts. This guidance indicates that the key factor for determining whether derecognition is appropriate remains whether or not the entity has transferred substantially all the risks and rewards of the transferred asset. *[IAS 39.AG51(k), IFRS 9.B3.2.16(k)]*. This suggests that an asset sold subject to a fixed price net-settled forward contract to reacquire it should not be derecognised (see 4.1.1 to 4.1.3 above) until the forward contract is settled (Figure 51.1, Box 7, Yes).

The accounting treatment of such transactions is discussed at 5.2 below.

4.1.5 *Agreement to repurchase at fair value*

A transfer of a financial asset subject only to a forward repurchase agreement with a repurchase price equal to the fair value of the financial asset at the time of repurchase results in derecognition because of the transfer of substantially all the risks and rewards of ownership, *[IAS 39.AG51(j), IFRS 9.B3.2.16(j)]*, (Figure 51.1, Box 6, Yes). The accounting treatment of such transactions is discussed at 5.1 below.

4.1.6 *Right of first refusal to repurchase at fair value*

If an entity sells a financial asset and retains only a right of first refusal to repurchase the transferred asset at fair value if the transferee subsequently sells it, the entity derecognises the asset because it has transferred substantially all the risks and rewards of ownership, *[IAS 39.AG51(d), IFRS 9.B3.2.16(d)]*, (Figure 51.1, Box 6, Yes).

IAS 39 and IFRS 9 do not address the treatment of a financial asset sold with a right of first refusal to repurchase the transferred asset at a predetermined value that might well be lower or higher than fair value (e.g. an amount estimated, at the time at which the original transaction was entered into, as the future market value of the asset). One analysis might be that, since the transferee is under no obligation to put the asset up for sale, derecognition is still appropriate. Another analysis might be that, if the asset can ultimately only be realised by onward sale, the arrangement is nearer in substance to a transferor's call option (see 4.2 below).

4.1.7 *Wash sale*

A 'wash sale' is the repurchase of a financial asset shortly after it has been sold. Such a repurchase does not preclude derecognition provided that the original transaction met the derecognition requirements. However, if an agreement to sell a financial asset is entered into concurrently with an agreement to repurchase the same asset at a fixed price or the sale price plus a lender's return, then the asset is not derecognised. *[IAS 39.AG51(e), IFRS 9.B3.2.16(e)]*. Such a transaction would be equivalent to those in 4.1.1 to 4.1.4 above.

4.2 Transfers subject to put and call options

An option contract is a contract which gives one party to the contract the right, but not the obligation, to buy from, or sell to, the other party to the contract the asset that is the subject of the contract for a given price (often, but not always, a price that is fixed) at a future date (or during a longer period ending on a future date). An option giving the right to buy an asset is referred to as a 'call' option and one giving the right to sell as a 'put' option. An option is referred to as a 'bought' or 'purchased' option from the perspective of the party with the right to buy or sell (the 'holder') and as a 'written' option from the perspective of the party with the potential obligation to buy or sell. An option is referred to as 'in the money' when it would be in the holder's interest to exercise it and as 'out of the money' when it would not be in the holder's interest to exercise it.

Under IAS 39 and IFRS 9 an option is:

- 'deeply in the money' when it is so far in the money that it is highly unlikely to go out of the money before expiry; *[IAS 39.AG40(d), IFRS 9.B3.2.5(d)]* and
- 'deeply out of the money' when it is so far out of the money that it is highly unlikely to become in the money before expiry. *[IAS 39.AG39(c), IFRS 9.B3.2.4(c)]*.

IAS 39 and IFRS 9 do not elaborate on what it means by 'highly unlikely' in this context, although the Implementation Guidance clarifies that 'highly probable' (in the context of a 'highly probable forecast transaction' subject to a hedge) indicates a much greater likelihood of happening than the term 'more likely than not'. *[IAS 39.F.3.7]*.

Option contracts that are within the scope of IAS 39 or IFRS 9 (see Chapter 44 at 2) are recognised as assets or liabilities when the holder or writer becomes a party to the contract. *[IAS 39.AG35(d), IFRS 9.B3.1.2(d)]*.

4.2.1 Deeply in the money put and call options

If a transferred financial asset can be called back by the transferor, and the call option is deeply in the money, the transfer does not qualify for derecognition because the transferor has retained substantially all the risks and rewards of ownership (Figure 51.1, Box 7, Yes).

Similarly, if the financial asset can be put back by the transferee, and the put option is deeply in the money, the transfer does not qualify for derecognition because the transferor has retained substantially all the risks and rewards of ownership, *[IAS 39.AG51(f), IFRS 9.B3.2.16(f)]*, (Figure 51.1, Box 7, Yes).

The accounting treatment for such transactions would be similar to that for 'repos' as set out in Example 51.9 at 5.2 below.

If a transferred asset continues to be recognised because of a transferor's call option or transferee's put option, but the option subsequently lapses unexercised, the asset and any associated liability would then be derecognised.

4.2.2 Deeply out of the money put and call options

A financial asset that is transferred subject only to a transferee's deeply out of the money put option, or a transferor's deeply out of the money call option, is derecognised. This is because the transferor has transferred substantially all the risks and rewards of ownership, *[IAS 39.AG51(g), IFRS 9.B3.2.16(g)]*, (Figure 51.1, Box 6, Yes).

4.2.3 Options that are neither deeply out of the money nor deeply in the money

Where a financial asset is transferred subject to an option (whether a transferor's call option or a transferee's put option) that is neither deeply in the money nor deeply out of the money, the result is that the entity neither transfers nor retains substantially all the risks and rewards associated with the asset, *[IAS 39.AG51, IFRS 9.B3.2.16]*, (Figure 51.1, Box 7, No). It is therefore necessary to determine whether or not the transferor has retained control of the asset under the criteria summarised in 3.9 above.

If a transferred asset continues to be recognised because of a transferor's call option or transferee's put option, but the option subsequently lapses unexercised, the asset and any associated liability would then be derecognised.

4.2.3.A Assets readily obtainable in the market

If the transferor has a call option over a transferred financial asset that is readily obtainable in the market, IAS 39 and IFRS 9 consider that control of the asset has passed to the transferee (Figure 51.1, Box 8, No – see 3.9 above). *[IAS 39.AC51(h), IFRS 9.B3.2.16(h)]*. This would presumably also be the conclusion where the transferee has a put option over a transferred financial asset that is readily obtainable in the market, although IAS 39 and IFRS 9 do not specifically address this.

4.2.3.B Assets not readily obtainable in the market

If the transferor has a call option over a transferred financial asset that is not readily obtainable in the market, IAS 39 and IFRS 9 consider that control of the asset remains with the transferor (Figure 51.1, Box 8, Yes – see 3.9 above). Accordingly, derecognition is precluded to the extent of the amount of the asset that is subject to the call option. *[IAS 39.AG51(h), IFRS 9.B3.2.16(h)]*.

If the transferee has a put option over a transferred financial asset that is not readily obtainable in the market, IAS 39 and IFRS 9 require the transferee's likely economic behaviour to be assessed – in effect to determine whether the option gives the transferee the practical ability to sell the transferred asset (see 3.9.1 above).

If the put option is sufficiently valuable to prevent the transferee from selling the asset, the transferor is considered to retain control of the asset and should account for the asset to the extent of its continuing involvement, *[IAS 39.AG51(i), IFRS 9.B3.2.16(h)]*, (Figure 51.1, Box 9). The accounting treatment required is discussed at 5.3 below.

If the put option is not sufficiently valuable to prevent the transferee from selling the asset, the transferor is considered to have ceded control of the asset, and should derecognise it, *[IAS 39.AG51(i), IFRS 9.B3.2.16(i)]*, (Figure 51.1, Box 8, No).

The requirements above beg two questions. First the question of whether or not a put option is sufficiently valuable to prevent the transferee from selling the asset is not a matter of objective fact, but rather a function of the transferee's appetite for risk, its need for liquidity and so forth. It is not clear how the transferor can readily assess these factors.

Second, IAS 39 and IFRS 9 are not explicit as to the accounting consequences (if any) of an option that was considered at the time of the original transfer to be deeply out of the money subsequently becoming neither deeply in the money nor deeply out of the money, or even deeply in the money, (or any other of the possible permutations). This is discussed further at 4.2.9 below.

4.2.4 Option to put or call at fair value

A transfer of a financial asset subject only to a put or call option with an exercise price equal to the fair value of the financial asset at the time of repurchase results in derecognition because of the transfer of substantially all the risks and rewards of ownership, *[IAS 39.AG51(j), IFRS 9.B3.2.16(j)]*, (Figure 51.1, Box 6, Yes).

4.2.5 Net cash-settled options

Where a transfer of a financial asset is subject to a put or call option that will be settled net in cash, IAS 39 and IFRS 9 require the entity to evaluate the transfer so as to determine whether it has retained or transferred substantially all the risks and rewards of ownership. *[IAS 39.AG51(k), IFRS 9.B3.2.16(k)]*. IAS 39 and IFRS 9 comment that 'if the entity has not retained substantially all the risks and rewards of ownership of the transferred asset, it determines whether it has retained control of the transferred asset' – a repetition of the basic principles of the standard adding no clarification specific to this type of transaction.

4.2.6 Removal of accounts provision

A 'removal of accounts provision' is an unconditional repurchase (i.e. call) option that gives an entity the right to reclaim transferred assets subject to some restrictions. Provided that such an option results in the entity neither retaining nor transferring substantially all the risks and rewards of ownership, IAS 39 and IFRS 9 allow derecognition, except to the extent of the amount subject to repurchase (assuming that the transferee cannot sell the assets).

For example, if an entity transfers loan receivables with a carrying amount of €100,000 for proceeds of €100,000, subject only to the right to call back any individual loan(s) up to a maximum of €10,000, €90,000 of the loans would qualify for derecognition. *[IAS 39.AG51(l), IFRS 9.B3.2.16(l)]*.

4.2.7 Clean-up call options

A 'clean-up call' option is an option held by an entity that services transferred assets (and may be the transferor of those assets) to purchase remaining transferred assets when the cost of servicing the assets exceeds the entity's participation in their benefits. If such a clean-up call results in the entity neither retaining nor transferring substantially all the risks and rewards of ownership, and the transferee cannot sell the assets, IAS 39 and IFRS 9 preclude derecognition only to the extent of the amount of assets subject to the call option. *[IAS 39.AG51(m), IFRS 9.B3.2.16(m)]*.

4.2.8 Same (or nearly the same) price put and call options

IAS 39 and IFRS 9 do not specifically address the transfer of an asset subject to both a transferee's option to put, and a transferor's option to call, the asset at a fixed price rather than at fair value (as discussed in 4.2.4 above). Assuming that:

- both options can be exercised simultaneously; and
- both the transferor and transferee behave rationally,

it will clearly be in the interest of either the transferor or the transferee to exercise its option, so that the asset will be reacquired by the transferor. This indicates that the transferor has retained substantially all the risks and rewards of ownership.

However, if the two options were exercisable on different dates or at different prices the effects of each option would need to be considered carefully.

4.2.9 Changes in probability of exercise of options after initial transfer of asset

As noted at 4.2.3 above, IAS 39 and IFRS 9 are not explicit as to the accounting consequences (if any) of an option that was considered at the time of the original transfer to be deeply out of the money subsequently becoming neither deeply in the money nor deeply out of the money, or even deeply in the money, (or any other of the possible permutations). This is explored further in Examples 51.2 to 51.4 below.

Example 51.2: Financial asset transferred subject only to deeply out of the money call option

On 1 January 2014 an entity transferred a financial asset to a counterparty, subject only to a call option to repurchase the asset at any time up to 31 December 2018. At 1 January 2014 the option was considered deeply out of the money and the asset was accordingly derecognised (see 4.2.2 above).

At 31 December 2017 market conditions have changed considerably and the option is now deeply in the money. What is the accounting consequence of this change?

There are no accounting consequences since, as noted at 3.8 above, IAS 39 paragraph AG41 (IFRS 9 paragraph B3.2.6) specifies that an asset previously derecognised because substantially all the risks and rewards associated with the asset have been transferred (as would be the analysis for an asset transferred subject only to a deeply out of the money call – see 4.2.2 above) is not re-recognised in a future period unless it is reacquired. Instead the increase in the fair value of the option would be captured in the financial statements as a gain under the normal requirement of IAS 39 or IFRS 9 to account for derivatives at fair value with changes in value reflected in profit or loss (see Chapter 44).

However, if the market changes were not demonstrably beyond any reasonable expectation as at 1 January 2015, there might be an argument (given the definition of a deeply out of the money option as an option that is 'highly unlikely' to become in the money before expiry – see 4.2.3 above) that the fact that the option is now not merely in the money, but deeply in the money, indicates that the original assessment that that option was deeply out of the money was in fact an accounting error requiring correction under IAS 8 (see Chapter 3 at 4.6).

Example 51.3: Financial asset transferred subject only to deeply in the money call option

On 1 January 2014 an entity transferred a financial asset to a counterparty, subject only to a call option to repurchase the asset at any time up to 31 December 2018. At 1 January 2014 the option was considered deeply in the money and the asset was accordingly not derecognised (see 4.2.1 above).

At 31 December 2017 market conditions have changed considerably and the option is now deeply out of the money. What is the accounting consequence of this change?

This is the mirror image of the fact pattern in Example 51.2. However, whereas IAS 39 and IFRS 9 make it clear that an asset previously derecognised is not re-recognised, there is no comparable provision that an asset that previously did not qualify for derecognition on the origination of a particular transaction may not later be derecognised as a result of a subsequent change in the assessed likely impact of the transaction. Because the standard does not explain the consequences, it is not clear when the asset is derecognised or whether there is any basis for derecognising the asset before the expiry of the option.

In our view, however, the original assessment as to whether or not the asset should be derecognised should not be subsequently revisited, unless (in exceptional circumstances) the original assessment was an accounting error within the scope of IAS 8. Thus, in Example 51.3 above the asset would not be derecognised. However, the fall in the value of the option indicates an impairment of the asset which is likely to be required to be reflected in the financial statements under the normal requirements of IAS 39 (see Chapter 49 at 4). This would in turn appear to require a corresponding adjustment to the liability recognised for the sale proceeds, so as to avoid recognising a net loss in the income statement that has not actually been suffered.

Example 51.4: Financial asset transferred subject to call option neither deeply in the money nor deeply out of the money

On 1 January 2014 an entity transferred a financial asset (an equity share) to a counterparty, subject only to a call option to repurchase the asset at any time up to 31 December 2018. At 1 January 2014 the option was considered to be neither deeply in the money nor deeply out of the money. However, the asset was readily marketable and freely transferable by the transferor and was accordingly derecognised because the entity, while neither transferring nor retaining substantially all the risks and rewards of the asset, no longer controls it (see 4.2.3 above).

At 31 December 2017 the financial asset that was the subject of the transfer ceases to be listed and is therefore not readily marketable. Had this been the case at the time of the original transfer, the entity would have been regarded as retaining control of the asset, which would not have been derecognised (see 4.2.3.B above). What is the accounting consequence of this change?

Again, matters are not entirely clear. The rule in paragraph AG41 of IAS 39 (paragraph B3.2.6 of IFRS 9) that a previously derecognised asset should not be re-recognised (other than on reacquisition of the asset) applies, as drafted, only where derecognition results from a transfer of substantially all the risks and rewards associated with the asset. In this case, derecognition has resulted from a loss of control over, not a transfer of substantially all the risks and rewards associated with, the asset. There is therefore some ambiguity as to whether AG41 is to be read:

- *generally* as prohibiting any re-recognition of a derecognised asset; or
- *specifically* as referring only to circumstances where derecognition results from transfer of substantially all the risks and rewards (i.e. it applies only to 'Box 6, Yes' transactions, and not to 'Box 8, No' transactions).

Again, however, we take the view that the original decision to derecognise the asset should not be revisited, unless (in exceptional circumstances) the original assessment was an accounting error within the scope of IAS 8. The fact that the asset was transferred on terms that the transferee could freely dispose of it means that the transferor did indeed lose control.

4.3 Subordinated retained interests and credit guarantees

Where a financial asset is transferred, an entity may provide the transferee with credit enhancement by subordinating some or all of its interest retained in the transferred asset. Alternatively, an entity may provide the transferee with credit enhancement in the form of a credit guarantee that could be unlimited or limited to a specified amount. *[IAS 39.AG51(n), IFRS 9.B3.2.16(n)]*. Such techniques are commonly used in securitisation transactions (see 3.6 above).

IAS 39 and IFRS 9 note that, if the entity retains substantially all the risks and rewards of ownership of the transferred asset, the asset continues to be recognised in its entirety. If the entity retains some, but not substantially all, of the risks and rewards of ownership and has retained control, derecognition is precluded to the extent of the amount of cash or other assets that the entity could be required to pay. *[IAS 39.AG51(n), IFRS 9.B3.2.16(n)]*. This 'guidance' is really no more than a repetition of the basic principles of the standard, adding no real clarification specific to this type of transaction.

4.4 Transfers by way of swaps

4.4.1 *Total return swaps*

An entity may sell a financial asset to a transferee and enter into a total return swap with the transferee, whereby the transferor pays an amount equivalent to fixed or floating rate interest on the consideration for the transfer and receives an amount equivalent to the cash flows from, together with any increases or decreases in the fair value of, the underlying asset. In such a case, derecognition of all of the asset is prohibited, *[IAS 39.AG51(o), IFRS 9.B3.2.16(o)]*, since the transaction has the effect that substantially all the risks and rewards associated with the asset are retained by the transferor (Figure 51.1, Box 7, Yes).

4.4.2 *Interest rate swaps*

An entity may transfer a fixed rate financial asset and enter into an interest rate swap with the transferee to receive a fixed interest rate and pay a variable interest rate based on a notional amount equal to the principal amount of the transferred financial asset. IAS 39 and IFRS 9 state that the interest rate swap does not preclude derecognition of the transferred asset, provided that the payments on the swap are not conditional on payments being made on the transferred asset. *[IAS 39.AG51(p), IFRS 9.B3.2.16(p)]*. It is interesting that this is included as guidance as it does not follow from the principles. There are situations in which the entity retains substantially all of the risks by retaining interest rate risk.

If, however, the transferor were to transfer an asset subject to prepayment risk (e.g. a domestic mortgage), and the transferor and transferee were to enter into an amortising interest rate swap (i.e. one whose notional amount amortises so that it equals the principal amount of the transferred financial asset outstanding at any point in time), the transferor would generally retain substantial prepayment risk through the swap. In this case, the transferor would (depending on the other facts of the transaction, such as the transfer or retention of credit risk) continue to recognise the transferred asset either in its entirety (Figure 51.1, Box 7, Yes) or to the extent of the transferor's continuing involvement (Figure 51.1, Box 9). *[IAS 39.AG51(q), IFRS 9.B3.2.16(q)]*.

Conversely, if the transferor and the transferee were to enter into an amortising interest rate swap, the amortisation of the notional amount of which is not linked to the principal amount outstanding on the transferred asset, the transferor would no longer retain prepayment risk. Therefore such a swap would not preclude derecognition of the transferred asset, provided the payments on the swap were not conditional on interest payments being made on the transferred asset and the swap did not result in the entity retaining any other significant risks and rewards of ownership on the transferred asset. *[IAS 39.AG51(q), IFRS 9.B3.2.16(q)]*.

4.5 Factoring of trade receivables

IAS 39 and IFRS 9 do not specifically address one of the more common forms of 'off-balance sheet finance' – the factoring of trade receivables. The common aim of all factoring structures is to provide cash flow from trade receivables quicker than would arise from normal cash collections, which is generally achieved by a 'sale' of all, or certain selected, receivables to a financial institution. However, the conditions of such 'sales' are extremely varied (which may well explain the lack of any generic guidance in the standard), ranging from true outright sales and pass-through arrangements (resulting in full derecognition), to transactions with continuing involvement through guarantee or subordination arrangements. It will therefore be necessary for an entity to consider the terms of its particular debt-factoring arrangement(s) carefully in order to determine the appropriate application of the derecognition provisions of IAS 39 or IFRS 9. Operational matters, for example how cash receipts from a debtor are allocated to particular invoices outstanding, could also be relevant to the analysis.

Depending on circumstances, Examples 51.5 (see 5.1 below), 51.6 (see 5.1.1 below), 51.10 (see 5.4.1 below) and 51.15 (see 5.4.4 below) may also be of particular relevance.

5 ACCOUNTING TREATMENT

This part of the chapter deals with the accounting consequences of the derecognition criteria for financial assets – in other words how the principles discussed above translate into accounting entries.

In order to provide a link with Figure 51.1 at 3.2 above we have used the following convention:

'Box 6, Yes'	The transaction would result in the answer 'Yes' at Box 6 in the flowchart.
'Box 7, No'	The transaction would result in the answer 'No' at Box 7 in the flowchart.

5.1 Transfers that qualify for derecognition

It is important to remember throughout this section that references to an asset being derecognised in its entirety include situations where a part of an asset to which the derecognition criteria are applied separately is derecognised in its entirety (see 3.3 above). In this context, IAS 39 and IFRS 9 use the phrase 'in its entirety' in contrast to the accounting treatment applied to assets where there is continuing involvement (see 5.3 below) where some, but not all, of a financial asset, or part of an asset, is derecognised.

If, as a result of a transfer, a financial asset is derecognised in its entirety but the transfer results in the transferor obtaining a new financial asset or servicing asset or assuming a new financial liability, or a servicing liability (see 5.1.2 below), IAS 39 and IFRS 9 require the entity to recognise the new financial asset, servicing asset, financial liability or servicing liability at fair value. *[IAS 39.24-25, IFRS 9.3.2.10-11]*.

On derecognition of a financial asset in its entirety, IAS 39 and IFRS 9 require the difference between:

(a) the carrying amount of the asset; and

(b) the consideration received (including any new asset obtained less any new liability assumed)

to be recognised in profit or loss. *[IAS 39.26, IFRS 9.3.2.12]*. In addition, any cumulative gain or loss in respect of that asset which was previously recognised in other comprehensive income should be reclassified from equity to profit or loss if the asset is:

- classified as available-for-sale in accordance with IAS 39; *[IAS 39.26, 55(b)]* or
- a debt instrument accounted for at fair value through other comprehensive income under IFRS 9. *[IFRS 9.3.2.10]*.

Example 51.5 illustrates these requirements.

Example 51.5: Derecognition of whole of financial asset in its entirety

At 1 October 2017 an entity has an available-for-sale financial asset carried at €1,400 in respect of which a cumulative gain of €200 has been recognised in equity. At that date, the asset is unconditionally sold to a third party in exchange for cash of €2,500 and a loan note issued to the third party. The loan note bears a fixed rate interest below current market rates and is repayable at €1,150 but is considered to have a fair value of €1,100. The following accounting entries are made by the entity to record the disposal:

	€	€
Cash	2,500	
Equity ('recycling' of cumulative gain on asset)	200	
Gain on disposal		200
Asset		1,400
Loan note		1,100

Thereafter the loan note will be accreted up to its repayable amount of €1,150 over its expected life using the effective interest method (see Chapter 49 at 3).

If the asset had been of a type eligible for accounting using the amortised cost method, and had been so accounted for, and had a carrying amount of (say) €1,300 at the date of the transfer, the accounting entry would have been:

	€	€
Cash	2,500	
Profit on disposal		100
Asset		1,300
Loan note		1,100

5.1.1 Transferred asset part of larger asset

If the transferred asset is part of a larger financial asset, for example when an entity transfers interest cash flows that are part of a debt instrument (see 3.3 above), and the part transferred qualifies for derecognition in its entirety, IAS 39 and IFRS 9 require the previous carrying amount of the larger financial asset to be allocated between the part that continues to be recognised and the part that is derecognised. The allocation is based on the relative fair values of those parts on the date of the transfer. For this purpose, a retained servicing asset (see 5.1.2 below) is to be treated as a part that continues to be recognised.

IAS 39 and IFRS 9 require the difference between:

(a) the carrying amount allocated to the part derecognised; and

(b) the sum of:

  (i) the consideration received for the part derecognised (including any new asset obtained less any new liability assumed); and

  (ii) any cumulative gain or loss allocated to it previously recognised directly in equity

to be recognised in profit or loss. Any cumulative gain or loss that had been recognised in equity is allocated between the part that continues to be recognised and the part that is derecognised, based on the relative fair values of those parts. *[IAS 39.27, IFRS 9.3.2.13]*.

The requirement in (b)(ii) above for 'recycling' of any cumulative gain or loss previously recognised directly in equity applies to assets accounted for as available-for-sale in accordance with IAS 39 and the same logic would apply to debt instruments accounted for at fair value through other comprehensive income under IFRS 9.

IAS 39 and IFRS 9 note that the accounting treatment prescribed for the derecognition of a part (or parts) of a financial asset requires an entity to determine the fair value of the part(s) that continue to be recognised. Where the entity has a history of selling parts similar to the part that continues to be recognised, or other market transactions exist for such parts, IAS 39 and IFRS 9 require recent prices of actual transactions to be used to provide the best estimate of its fair value. When there are no price quotations or recent market transactions to support the fair value of the part that continues to be recognised, the best estimate of the fair value is the difference between:

- the fair value of the larger financial asset as a whole; and
- the consideration received from the transferee for the part that is derecognised. *[IAS 39.28, IFRS 9.3.2.14]*.

The requirements of IFRS 13 that deal with the determination of fair value should also be used *[IAS 39.AG46, IFRS 9.B3.2.11]* – see Chapter 14.

Example 51.6 illustrates the requirements for full derecognition of a part of an asset.

Example 51.6: Derecognition of part of financial asset in its entirety

On 1 January 2012 an entity invested €1 million in a loan with a par value of €1 million. The loan pays interest of €75,000 on 31 December annually in arrears and is to be redeemed at par on 31 December 2021. The entity accounts for the loan at amortised cost.

On 1 January 2017 it unconditionally sells the right to receive the remaining five interest payments to a bank. The derecognition provisions of IAS 39 or IFRS 9 are applied to the interest payments as an identifiable part of the asset, leading to the conclusion that they are required to be derecognised.

The consideration received for, and the fair value of, the future interest payments (based on the net present value, as at 1 January 2017, of the payments at the current market interest rate that would be available to the borrower of 5%)[19] is €324,711 (€75,000 × $[1/1.05 + 1/1.05^2 ... + 1/1.05^5]$). By the same methodology the fair value of the principal repayment can be calculated as €783,526 (€1,000,000 × $1/1.05^5$), giving a total fair value for the loan of €1,108,237.

In order to calculate the gain or loss on disposal, the total carrying value of the loan of €1,000,000 is allocated between the part disposed of and the part retained, based on the fair values of those parts. This allocates €292,998 (€1,000,000 × 324,711 ÷ 1,108,237) to the interest payments disposed of and €707,002 (€1,000,000 × 783,526 ÷ 1,108,237) to the retained right to the repayment of principal. This generates the accounting entry:

	€	€
Cash	324,711	
Loan (portion of carrying amount allocated to interest payments)		292,998
Gain on disposal		31,713

If the loan had instead been a quoted bond accounted for as available-for-sale, it would have already have been carried at €1,108,237, so that the basic disposal journal would simply be:

	€	€
Cash	324,711	
Bond (portion of carrying amount allocated to interest payments)		324,711

However, as the bond was accounted for as available-for-sale, it would also be necessary to recycle that portion of the cumulative revaluation gain of €108,237 that relates to the interest 'component' of the total carrying value from equity to the income statement. IAS 39 requires a pro-rata allocation of the cumulative gain or loss in equity based on the total fair value of the interest and principal – this would deem €31,713 (€108,237 × €324,711 ÷ 1,108,237) of the cumulative revaluation gain to relate to interest. This would give rise to the further journal, resulting in the same gain on disposal as above:

	€	€
Equity	31,713	
Gain on disposal (income statement)		31,713

5.1.2 *Servicing assets and liabilities*

It is common for an entity to transfer a financial asset (or part of a financial asset) in its entirety, but to retain the right or obligation to service the asset, i.e. to collect payments as they fall due and undertake other administrative tasks, in return for a fee.

When an entity transfers a financial asset in a transfer that qualifies for derecognition in its entirety and retains the right to service the financial asset for a fee, IAS 39 and IFRS 9 require the entity to recognise either a servicing asset or a servicing liability for that servicing contract, as follows:

- If the fee to be received is not expected to compensate the entity adequately for performing the servicing, the entity should recognise a servicing liability for the servicing obligation at its fair value.
- If the fee to be received is expected to be more than adequate compensation for the servicing, the entity should recognise a servicing asset for the servicing right. This should be recognised at an amount determined on the basis of an allocation of the carrying amount of the larger financial asset (as described in 5.1.1 above). *[IAS 39.24, IFRS 9.3.2.10].*

It is not immediately clear what is meant by this requirement. The application guidance expands on the point, as follows.

An entity may retain the right to a part of the interest payments on transferred assets as compensation for servicing those assets. The part of the interest payments that the entity would give up upon termination or transfer of the servicing contract is allocated to the servicing asset or servicing liability. The part of the interest payments that the entity would not give up is an interest-only strip receivable.

For example, if the entity would not give up any interest upon termination or transfer of the servicing contract, the entire interest spread is an interest-only strip receivable. Presumably, as the entity will still have a liability to service the portfolio, it will have to account for this if it allocates none of the interest spread to a servicing asset. For the purposes of applying the requirements for disposals of part of an asset discussed in 5.1.1 above, the fair values of the servicing asset and interest-only strip receivable are used to allocate the carrying amount of the receivable between the part of the asset that is derecognised and the part that continues to be recognised. If there is no servicing fee specified, or the fee to be received is not expected to compensate the entity adequately for performing the servicing, a liability for the servicing obligation is recognised at fair value. *[IAS 39.AG45, IFRS 9.B3.2.10]*.

Unfortunately, IAS 39 and IFRS 9 do not provide examples of what exactly is meant here, but we believe that something along the lines of Example 51.7 below was intended.

Example 51.7: Servicing assets and liabilities

An entity has a portfolio of originated domestic mortgages which are accounted for at amortised cost and have a carrying amount of £10 million. The mortgages bear interest at a fixed rate of 7.5%. The average life of the mortgages in the portfolio (taking account of prepayment risk) is 12 years and the fair value of the portfolio is £11 million, representing £4.5 million in respect of future interest payments and £6.5 million in respect of the principal amounts. The entity assesses the amount that would compensate it for servicing the assets to be £0.5 million.

The entity sells the entire portfolio to a bank (on terms such that it qualifies for derecognition under IAS 39 or IFRS 9) but continues to service the portfolio. If the entity does not retain any part of the interest payments, the selling price would be the fair value of the assets of £11 million (or very close to it). It would then assume a servicing liability of £0.5 million, giving rise to the accounting entry:

	£m	£m
Cash	11.0	
Mortgage portfolio		10.0
Servicing liability		0.5
Profit on disposal		0.5

Alternatively, it retains interest payments of 1% and the right to service the portfolio. The entity estimates that the fair value of the right to receive interest payments of 1% is £0.6 million. In this case, the bank would be expected to pay fair value of £10.4 million (or very close to it).

The standard states – see above – that, if (as is the case here) the entity would not give up any interest on termination or transfer of the contract, then the whole of the interest spread is an interest-only strip receivable. In order to calculate the amount of the portfolio to be derecognised, the carrying value of £10 million is pro-rated (as in Example 51.6 above) as to £9.45 million disposed of (£10m × 10.4/11) and the part retained of £0.55 million (£10m × 0.6/11). However, as it has allocated the full amount of the interest spread to an interest-only strip receivable, it would need to recognise a servicing liability of £0.5 million in respect of its obligations under the contract. This gives rise to the following accounting entry:

	£m	£m
Cash	10.40	
Interest-only strip receivable	0.55	
Mortgage portfolio (£9.45m disposed of plus £0.55m reclassified as interest-only strip receivable)		10.00
Servicing liability		0.50
Profit on disposal		0.45

If the entity were to retain only £0.1 million of the interest spread on termination or transfer of the servicing contract, then IAS 39 and IFRS 9 require – see above:

- the part of the interest payments that the entity would not give up, i.e. the part which is not contingent on fulfilment of the servicing obligation (£0.1 million) to be treated as an interest-only strip receivable; and
- the part of the interest payments that the entity would give up (i.e. £0.45 million – £0.55 million as above less £0.1 million in previous bullet) upon termination or transfer of the servicing contract to be allocated to the servicing asset or servicing liability.

This suggests that the following accounting entry would be made:

	£m	£m
Cash	10.40	
Interest-only strip receivable	0.10	
Mortgage portfolio (£9.45m disposed of plus £0.1m reclassified as interest-only strip receivable and £0.45m allocated to servicing liability)		10.00
Servicing liability (£0.5m gross cost less interest payments that would be lost on termination or transfer – £0.45m)		0.05
Profit on disposal		0.45

A servicing asset is a non-financial asset representing a right to receive a higher than normal amount for performing future services. Accordingly it would normally be accounted for in accordance with IAS 38 – *Intangible Assets*. Similarly, a servicing liability represents consideration received in advance for services to be performed in the future and would normally be accounted for as deferred revenue in accordance with IAS 18 – *Revenue* – or IFRS 15 – *Revenue from Contracts with Customers*.

5.2 Transfers that do not qualify for derecognition through retention of risks and rewards

If a transfer does not result in derecognition because the entity has retained substantially all the risks and rewards of ownership of the transferred asset (see 3.8 above), IAS 39 and IFRS 9 require the entity to continue to recognise the transferred asset in its entirety and recognise a financial liability for any consideration received. In subsequent periods, the entity recognises any income on the transferred asset and any expense incurred on the financial liability. *[IAS 39.29, IFRS 9.3.2.15]*. This treatment is illustrated by Examples 51.8 and 51.9 below.

It should be noted that these provisions apply only where derecognition does not occur as a result of retention by the transferor of substantially all the risks and rewards of ownership of the transferred asset (Figure 51.1, Box 7, Yes). They do not apply where derecognition does not occur as a result of continuing involvement in an asset of which substantially all the risks and rewards of ownership are neither retained nor transferred (Figure 51.1, Box 8, Yes). Such transactions are dealt with by the separate provisions discussed in 5.3 and 5.4 below.

Example 51.8: Asset not qualifying for derecognition (risks and rewards retained)

An entity holds a loan of £1,000 made on 1 January 2013, paying interest of £65 annually in arrears and redeemable at par on 31 December 2017, which it accounts for at amortised cost (see Chapter 49 at 3).

On 1 January 2017 it enters into a transaction whereby the loan is sold to a bank for its then fair value of €985, but with full recourse to the entity for any default on the loan. The guarantee provided by the entity has the effect that it retains substantially all the risks and rewards of the loan, which is therefore not derecognised (Figure 51.1, Box 7, Yes – see 3.8.2 above). *[IAS 39.AG47, IFRS 9.B3.2.12]*.

The entity therefore continues to recognise the loan, and interest on it, as if it still held the loan. It accounts for the £985 proceeds as a liability which must be accreted up using the effective interest method (see Chapter 49 at 3) so that it will be equal to the carrying amount of the asset on the date on which it is expected that the asset will be derecognised.

In this case, the asset will be derecognised at maturity on 31 December 2017, when a payment of £1,065 (the final instalment of interest of £65 and return of principal of £1,000) is due. Accordingly, the liability must be accreted from £985 to £1,065 during the year ended 31 December 2017. The following accounting entries are made by the entity:

	£	£
1 January 2017		
Cash	985	
Liability		985
Consideration received from bank		
1 January-31 December 2017		
Loan (£1,065 at 31.12.17 – £1,000 at 1.1.17)	65	
Interest on loan (income statement)		65
Interest on liability (income statement)	80	
Liability (£1,065 at 31.12.17 – £985 at 1.1.17)		80
Accretion of interest income loan and liability		
31 December 2017		
Liability	1,065	
Loan receivable		1,065
'Redemption' of loan and 'discharge' of liability		

This accounting treatment recognises an overall loss of £15 in 2017, which would be expected, as representing the difference between the carrying value of the asset at the date of transfer (£1,000) and the consideration received (£985). However, IAS 39 and IFRS 9 require the various elements of the transaction to be shown separately – it would not have been acceptable for the income statement simply to show a net loss of £15.

If the transferred asset had been accounted for at fair value through profit or loss, it would already have been carried at £985 at the date of transfer – i.e. the loss of £15 would already have been reflected in the financial statements. The accounting entries at 1 January and 31 December 2017 would be the same as above. However, the following accounting entries would then have been made during the year ended 31 December:

	£	£
1 January-31 December 2017		
Interest on liability (income statement)	80	
Liability (£1,065 at 31.12.17 – £985 at 1.1.17)		80
Loan (£1,065 at 31.12.17 – £985 at 1.1.17)	80	
Interest on loan (income statement)		65
Change in fair value of loan (income statement)		15
Recognition of interest on, and change in fair value of, loan and accretion of interest on liability		

Whilst the total amounts recorded in the income statement net to nil, they are arrived at by different methodologies – the £80 increase in the carrying value of the loan receivable is recognised as it occurs whereas the £80 interest on the liability is accrued at a constant effective rate. This means that, if the entity were to prepare financial statements at an interim date, it might well show a net gain or loss on the transaction at that date, notwithstanding that ultimately no gain or loss will be reflected.

It would presumably be possible for the entity to avoid this result by designating the liability as at fair value through profit or loss (see Chapter 46 at 2.2 and Chapter 47 at 7), such that changes in the fair value of the liability would be matched in line with those in the fair value of the asset.

Example 51.9: Asset not qualifying for derecognition ('repo' transaction)

An entity holds a government bond of £2,000 issued on 1 January 2013, paying interest of £50 semi-annually in arrears and redeemable at par on 31 December 2018, which it accounts for as a held-to-maturity investment at amortised cost (see Chapter 49 at 3).

A Gross-settled transaction

On 1 January 2017 the entity enters into a transaction whereby the bond is sold to a bank for its then fair value of £1,800, and the entity agrees to repurchase it on 1 January 2018 for £1,844. As the legal owner of the loan at 30 June 2017 and 31 December 2017, the bank will receive the £100 interest payable on the bond for the calendar year 2017. This £100, together with the £44 difference between the sale and repurchase price gives the bank £144, representing a lender's return of 8% on the £1,800 sale proceeds. Accordingly, the effect of the transaction is that the entity has retained substantially all the risks and rewards of ownership of the bond (Figure 51.1, Box 7, Yes – see 4.1 above).

The entity therefore continues to recognise the bond, and interest on it, as if it still held the bond. It accounts for the £1,800 proceeds as a liability which must be accreted up to £1,844 (the repurchase price due on 31 December 2017) over the period to 31 December 2017 using the effective interest method (see Chapter 49 at 3). The following accounting entries are made by the entity:

	£	£
1 January 2017		
Cash	1,800	
Liability		1,800
Consideration received from bank		
1 January-31 December 2017		
Interest on liability (income statement)	144	
Liability (£1,944 at 31.12.17 – £1,800 at 1.1.17)		144
Bond (£2,100 at 31.12.17 – £2,000 at 1.1.17)	100	
Interest on bond (income statement)		100
Accretion of income on bond and finance cost of liability		
1 January-31 December 2017		
Liability	100	
Bond		100
Notional receipt of interest on bond at 30 June and 31 December and notional transfer thereof to bank		
1 January 2018		
Liability	1,844	
Cash		1,844
Execution of repurchase contract		

The above is arguably the strict translation into accounting entries of the accounting analysis of IAS 39 or IFRS 9 that the entity still retains ownership of the bond throughout 2017. As a matter of practicality, however, the same overall result could have been obtained by the following 'short-cut' approach, which avoids recording the notional receipt and transfer to the bank of bond interest received on 30 June and 31 December:

	£	£
1 January 2017		
Cash	1,800	
Liability		1,800
Consideration received from bank		
1 January-31 December 2017		
Interest on liability (income statement)	144	
Interest on bond (income statement)		100
Liability (statement of financial position)		44
Accretion of income on bond and finance cost of liability		
1 January 2018		
Liability	1,844	
Cash		1,844
Execution of repurchase contract		

If (as would be likely, given the nature of the transferred asset) the bank has the right to sell or pledge the bond during the period of its legal ownership, it would be necessary to reclassify the bond as a repurchase receivable during the period of the bank's ownership (see 4.1.1.A above). In other words, the following additional accounting entries would be required.

	£	£
1 January 2017		
Repurchase receivable	2,000	
Bond		2,000
1 January 2018		
Bond	2,000	
Repurchase receivable		2,000

B Net-settled transaction

The entity might enter into the transaction above, but on terms that the repurchase contract was to be net-settled. In other words, on 1 January 2018, a payment would be made to or by the bank for the difference between £1,844 (the notional repurchase price) and the fair value of the bond at that date. Assuming that the fair value of the bond at 1 January 2018 is £1,860, the bank would be required to pay the entity £16 (£1,860 – £1,844).

In this case, matters are further complicated by the fact that the economic effect of the net-settled forward is the same as if the entity sold the bond on 1 January 2018. As this is before the maturity date of the bond, it is questionable whether the entity can any longer classify it as held-to-maturity. In such a case, IAS 39 requires it to be reclassified as available-for-sale (see Chapter 46 at 3.3). The following accounting entries would be made:

	£	£
1 January 2017		
Cash	1,800	
Liability		1,800
Consideration received from bank		
Equity	200	
Bond (£2,000 carrying amount less £1,800 fair value)		200
Restatement of bond to fair value		
Repurchase receivable	1,800	
Bond		1,800
Reclassification of bond as receivable (see 4.1.1.A above)		
1 January-31 December 2017		
Interest on liability (income statement)	144	
Interest on bond (income statement)		100
Liability (statement of financial position)		44
Repurchase receivable	60	
Equity		60
Accretion of income on bond and finance cost of liability and restatement of repurchase receivable (represented by fair value of underlying bond accounted for as available-for-sale – £1,860)		
1 January 2018		
Cash	16	
Liability	1,844	
Repurchase receivable		1,860
Loss on disposal	140	
Equity		140
Net settlement of repurchase contract and 'recycling' of cumulative losses in equity		

The loss on disposal at 1 January 2018 of £140 arises because the net-settled contract is equivalent to the entity disposing of the bond for its then fair value of £1,860, which is £140 lower than its amortised cost, at the date of reclassification from held-to-maturity to available-for-sale, of £2,000.

This illustrates the point that, where the terms of net-settled forward contract over a transferred asset are such that the original asset cannot be derecognised, the result will be that the entity's statement of financial position shows a gross position – i.e. the original asset and a liability for the consideration for the transfer. This may seem a strange accounting reflection of a contract that is required to be settled net. However, the IASB was to some extent forced into this approach as an anti-avoidance measure. It is clear from the analysis in 4.1.1 to 4.1.4 above that an asset sold subject to the obligation to repurchase the same or similar asset at a fixed price should not be derecognised. If the accounting treatment were to vary merely because the contract was net-settled, it would be possible to avoid the requirements of IAS 39 or IFRS 9 for continued recognition of assets subject to certain forward repurchase agreements simply by altering the terms of the agreement to allow net settlement.

5.3 Transfers with continuing involvement – summary

If an entity neither transfers nor retains substantially all the risks and rewards of ownership of a transferred asset, but retains control of the transferred asset (see 3.9 above), IAS 39 and IFRS 9 require the entity to continue to recognise the transferred asset to the extent of its 'continuing involvement' – i.e. the extent to which it is exposed to changes in the value of the transferred asset. *[IAS 39.30, IFRS 9.3.2.16]*. Such transactions fall within Box 9 of the flowchart at 3.2 above.

The concept of 'continuing involvement' was first introduced in the exposure draft of proposed amendments to IAS 32 and IAS 39 published in June 2002. The IASB's intention at that time was to move towards an accounting model for derecognition based entirely on continuing involvement. However, this approach (or at least the methodology for implementing it proposed in the exposure draft) received little support in the exposure period and the IASB decided to abandon it and revert largely to an accounting model for derecognition based on the transfer of risks and rewards. *[IAS 39.BC44-BC52, IFRS 9.BCZ3.4-BCZ3.12]*. However, the continuing involvement approach remains relevant for certain transactions – mainly transfers of assets which result in the sharing, rather than the substantial transfer, of the risks and rewards.

The accounting requirements in respect of assets in which the entity has continuing involvement are particularly complex, and are summarised at 5.3.1 to 5.3.5 below, with worked examples at 5.4 below. In particular, and in contrast to the treatment for transactions that do not qualify for derecognition through retention of risks and rewards (see 5.2 above), the associated liability is often calculated as a balancing figure that will not necessarily represent the proceeds received as the result of the transfer (see 5.3.3 below).

We have a general concern regarding the required accounting treatment for a continuing involvement, namely that IAS 39 and IFRS 9 provide examples of how to deal with certain specific transactions rather than clear underlying principles. It can be difficult to determine the appropriate treatment for a continuing involvement that does not correspond fairly exactly to one of the examples in IAS 39 or IFRS 9.

5.3.1 Guarantees

When the entity's continuing involvement takes the form of guaranteeing the transferred asset, the extent of the entity's continuing involvement is the lower of:

- the carrying amount of the asset; and
- the maximum amount of the consideration received that the entity could be required to repay ('the guarantee amount'). *[IAS 39.30(a), IFRS 9.3.2.16(a)]*.

An example of this treatment is given at 5.4.1 below.

It follows that if the transferor guarantees the entire amount of the transferred asset, no derecognition would be achieved, even though it may have passed other significant risks to the transferee.

5.3.2 Options

When the entity's continuing involvement takes the form of a written and/or purchased option (including a cash-settled option or similar provision) on the transferred asset, the extent of the entity's continuing involvement is the amount of the transferred asset that the entity may repurchase. However, in case of a written put option (including a cash-settled option or similar provision) on an asset measured at fair value, the extent of the entity's continuing involvement is limited to the lower of the fair value of the transferred asset and the option exercise price. *[IAS 39.30(b)-(c), IFRS 9.3.2.16(b)-(c)]*.

Examples of this treatment are given at 5.4.2 and 5.4.3 below.

5.3.3 Associated liability

When an entity continues to recognise an asset to the extent of its continuing involvement, IAS 39 and IFRS 9 require the entity to recognise an associated liability. *[IAS 39.31, IFRS 9.3.2.17]*. IAS 39 and IFRS 9 provide that 'despite the other measurement requirements in this Standard', the transferred asset and the associated liability are to be measured on a basis that reflects the rights and obligations that the entity has retained. The associated liability is measured in such a way that the net carrying amount of the transferred asset and the associated liability is equal to:

- if the transferred asset is measured at amortised cost, the amortised cost of the rights and obligations retained by the entity; or
- if the transferred asset is measured at fair value, the fair value of the rights and obligations retained by the entity when measured on a stand-alone basis. *[IAS 39.31, IFRS 9.3.2.17]*.

This has the effect that the 'liability' is often calculated as a balancing figure that will not necessarily represent the proceeds received as the result of the transfer (see Examples 51.10 to 51.13 at 5.4 below). This does not fit very comfortably with the normal rules in IAS 39 and IFRS 9 for the initial measurement of financial liabilities (see Chapter 48 at 3) – hence the comment that this treatment applies 'despite the other measurement requirements in this Standard'.

5.3.4 Subsequent measurement of assets and liabilities

IAS 39 and IFRS 9 require an entity to continue to recognise any income arising on the transferred asset to the extent of its continuing involvement and to recognise any expense incurred on the associated liability. *[IAS 39.32, IFRS 9.3.2.18]*. This is comparable to the requirements in respect of assets not derecognised through retention of substantially all risks and rewards (see 5.2 above).

When the transferred asset and associated liability are subsequently measured, IAS 39 and IFRS 9 require recognised changes in the fair value of the transferred asset and the associated liability to be accounted for consistently with each other in accordance with the general provisions of IAS 39 and IFRS 9 for measuring gains and losses (see Chapter 49 at 2 and Chapter 50 at 2) and not offset. *[IAS 39.33, IFRS 9.3.2.19]*. Moreover, if the transferred asset is measured at amortised cost, the option in IAS 39 and IFRS 9 to designate a financial liability as at fair value through profit or loss (see Chapter 46 at 2.2 and Chapter 47 at 7) is not applicable to the associated liability. *[IAS 39.35, IFRS 9.3.2.21]*.

5.3.5 Continuing involvement in part only of a larger asset

An entity may have continuing involvement in a part only of a financial asset, for example where the entity retains an option to repurchase part of a transferred asset, or retains a residual interest in part of an asset, such that the entity does not retain substantially all the risks and rewards of ownership, but does retain control.

In such a case, IAS 39 and IFRS 9 require the entity to allocate the previous carrying amount of the financial asset between the part that it continues to recognise under continuing involvement, and the part that it no longer recognises on the basis of the relative fair values of those parts on the date of the transfer. The allocation is to be made on the same basis as applies on derecognition of part only of a larger financial asset – see 5.1.1 and 5.1.2 above.

The difference between:

(a) the carrying amount allocated to the part that is no longer recognised; and

(b) the sum of:

  (i) the consideration received for the part no longer recognised; and

  (ii) any cumulative gain or loss allocated to it that had been recognised directly in equity

is recognised in profit or loss. A cumulative gain or loss that had been recognised in equity is allocated between the part that continues to be recognised and the part that is no longer recognised on the basis of the relative fair values of those parts. *[IAS 39.27, IFRS 9.3.2.13]*.

The requirement in (b)(ii) above for 'recycling' of any cumulative gain or loss previously recognised directly in equity applies to assets accounted for as available-for-sale in accordance with IAS 39 and the same logic would apply to debt instruments accounted for at fair value through other comprehensive income under IFRS 9.

This topic is discussed further at 5.4.4 below.

5.4 Transfers with continuing involvement – accounting examples

The provisions summarised at 5.3 above, even judged by the standards of IAS 39 and IFRS 9, are unusually impenetrable. However, the application guidance provides a number of clarifications and examples, the substance of which is reproduced below.

5.4.1 Transfers with guarantees

If a guarantee provided by an entity to pay for default losses on a transferred asset prevents the transferred asset from being derecognised to the extent of the continuing involvement, IAS 39 and IFRS 9 require:

(a) the transferred asset at the date of the transfer to be measured at the lower of:

  (i) the carrying amount of the asset; and

  (ii) the maximum amount of the consideration received in the transfer that the entity could be required to repay ('the guarantee amount'); and

(b) the associated liability to be initially measured at the guarantee amount plus the fair value of the guarantee (which is normally the consideration received for the guarantee).

Subsequently, the initial fair value of the guarantee is recognised in profit or loss on a time proportion basis in accordance with IAS 18 or IFRS 15 and the carrying value of the asset is reduced by any impairment losses. *[IAS 39.AG48(a), IFRS 9.B3.2.13(a)]*.

This is illustrated in Example 51.10 below (which is based on the circumstances in Example 51.15 below).

Example 51.10: Continuing involvement through guarantee

An entity has a loan portfolio carried at €10 million with a fair value of €10.5 million. It sells the rights to 100% of the cash flows to a third party for a payment of €10.55 million, which includes a payment of €50,000 in return for the entity agreeing to absorb the first €1 million of default losses on the portfolio. The loans are fixed rate loans with significant prepayment risk.

The guarantee has the effect that the entity has transferred substantially all the rewards, but not substantially all the risks, of the portfolio (Figure 51.1, Box 6, No). The prepayment risk and interest rate risk have been transferred to the transferee, so that the entity does not retain all significant risks of the loans (Figure 51.1, Box 7, No). The portfolio is not a readily marketable asset, so that the entity retains control of the asset (Figure 51.1, Box 8, Yes – see also 3.9 above), and the continuing involvement provisions of IAS 39 and IFRS 9 apply (Figure 51.1, Box 9).

The entity turns to the requirements above. The continuing involvement in the transferred asset must be measured at the lower of:

(i) the amount of the asset transferred – i.e. €10 million; and

(ii) the maximum amount of the consideration received in the transfer that the entity could be required to repay – i.e. €1 million (the amount guaranteed).

Therefore, the entity will set up an asset that represents its continuing involvement in the transferred asset of €1 million.

The entity then considers the carrying amount of the liability. This is required to be measured at the guarantee amount (i.e. €1 million) plus the fair value of the guarantee (i.e. the €50,000 guarantee payment), a total of €1.05 million. Therefore, the entity's continuing involvement in the transaction will be reflected as follows:

	€m	€m
Cash	10.55	
Loan portfolio transferred		10.00
Continuing involvement in the transferred asset	1.00	
Liability		1.05
Profit on disposal*		0.50

* Cash received (€10.55m) less guarantee payment (€50,000) = consideration for portfolio (€10.5m) less carrying amount of portfolio (€10m).

Over the remaining life of the transaction, the €50,000 of the liability that represents the consideration received for the guarantee is amortised to the income statement on a time proportion basis. This has the effect that the income earned by the entity for entering into the guarantee arrangement is reported as revenue on a time proportion basis. This is exactly the same result as would have been obtained by simply recognising the €50,000 as a liability and amortising it (as would have been required by IAS 18 or IFRS 15).

If in a subsequent period credit losses of €0.2 million are suffered, requiring a payment under the guarantee, IAS 39 and IFRS 9 require the following accounting entries to be made: *[IAS 39.AG52, IFRS 9.B3.2.17]*

	€m	€m
Profit or loss (loss under guarantee)	0.20	
Cash (paid to transferee)		0.20
Liability	0.20	
Continuing involvement in the transferred asset		0.20

5.4.2 *Transfers of assets measured at amortised cost*

If a put or call option prevents derecognition (see 3.8.3 and 4 above) of a transferred asset measured at amortised cost, IAS 39 and IFRS 9 require the associated liability to be measured at cost (i.e. the consideration received) and subsequently adjusted for the amortisation of any difference between that cost and the amortised cost of the transferred asset at the expiration date of the option, as illustrated by Example 51.11 below. *[IAS 39.AG48(b), IFRS 9.B3.2.13(b)]*.

Example 51.11: Asset measured at amortised cost

An entity has a financial asset, accounted for at amortised cost, carried at £98. It transfers the asset to a third party in return for consideration of £95. The asset is subject to a call option whereby the entity can compel the transferee to sell the asset back to the entity for £102. The amortised cost of the asset on the option exercise date will be £100. The option is considered to be neither deeply in the money nor deeply out of the money. IAS 39 and IFRS 9 therefore require the entity to continue to recognise the asset to the extent of its continuing involvement (Figure 51.1, Box 9 – see also 4.2.3 above).

The initial carrying amount of the associated liability is £95. This is then accreted to £100 (i.e. the amortised cost of the asset on exercise date – *not* the £102 exercise price) through profit or loss using the effective interest method. Because the transferred asset is measured at amortised cost, the associated liability must also be accounted for at amortised cost, and not at fair value through profit or loss (see 5.3.4 above). This will give rise to the accounting entries:

	£	£
Date of transfer		
Cash	95	
Liability		95
After date of transfer		
Interest on liability	5	
Liability (£100 – £95)		5
Asset (£100 – £98)	2	
Income on asset		2

If the option is exercised, any difference between the carrying amount of the associated liability and the exercise price is recognised in profit or loss. This last requirement has the possibly counter-intuitive effect that the question of whether the entity records a profit or loss on exercise of the option is essentially a function of the difference between the liability (representing the amortised cost of the transferred asset) and the cash paid, not of whether it has in fact (i.e. in economic terms) made a gain or loss.

Thus, if the entity were to exercise its option at £102 it would apparently record the accounting entry:

	£	£
Liability	100	
Loss	2	
Cash		102

However, the entity would not have exercised the option unless the asset had been worth at least £102 (i.e. £2 more than its carrying amount), suggesting that the more appropriate treatment would be to add the £2 to the cost of the asset.

Likewise, if instead of the entity having a call option, the transferee had a put option at £98 which it exercised, the entity would apparently record the accounting entry:

	£	£
Liability	100	
Profit		2
Cash		98

However, the transferee would not have exercised its option unless the asset had been worth less than £98 (i.e. £2 less than its carrying amount). In this case, however, the IASB's thinking may have been that the exercise of the transferee's put option suggests an impairment of the asset which is required to be recognised in the financial statements (see Chapter 49 at 4). This would not necessarily be the case (e.g. where a fixed-interest asset has a fair value below cost because of movements in interest rates but is not intrinsically impaired).

If the option were to lapse unexercised, the entity would simply derecognise the transferred asset and the associated liability, i.e.:

	£	£
Liability	100	
Asset		100

5.4.3 Transfers of assets measured at fair value

IAS 39 and IFRS 9 discuss the application of continuing involvement accounting to transferred assets measured at fair value in terms of transferred assets subject to:

- a transferor's call option (see 5.4.3.A below);
- a transferee's put option (see 5.4.3.B below); and
- a 'collar' – i.e. a transferor's call option combined with a transferee's put option (see 5.4.3.C below).

The way in which the rules are articulated in IAS 39 and IFRS 9 is somewhat confusing, but in general the effect is that the transferred asset is recognised at:

- in the case of an asset subject to a transferor call option, its fair value (on the basis that the call option gives the transferor access to any increase in the fair value of the asset); and
- in the case of an asset subject to a transferee put option, the lower of fair value and the option exercise price (on the basis that the put option denies the transferor access to any increase in the fair value of the asset above the option price).

This methodology summarised below is applied both on the date on which the option is written and subsequently.

5.4.3.A Transferor's call option

If a transferor's call option prevents derecognition (see 3.8.3 and 4 above) of a transferred asset measured at fair value, the asset continues to be measured at its fair value. The associated liability is measured:

- if the option is in or at the money, at the option exercise price less the time value of the option; or
- if the option is out of the money, at the fair value of the transferred asset less the time value of the option.

The adjustment to the measurement of the associated liability ensures that the net carrying amount of the asset and the associated liability is the fair value of the call option right, as illustrated by Example 51.12 below. *[IAS 39.AG48(c), IFRS 9.B3.2.13(c)]*.

Example 51.12: Asset measured at fair value subject to transferor's call option

An entity has a financial asset, accounted for at fair value through profit or loss, carried at €80. It transfers the asset to a third party, subject to a call option whereby the entity can compel the transferee to sell the asset back to the entity for €95. At the date of transfer, the call option has a time value of €5.

The option is considered to be neither deeply in the money nor deeply out of the money. IAS 39 and IFRS 9 therefore require the entity to continue to recognise the asset to the extent of its continuing involvement (Figure 51.1, Box 9 – see also 4.2.3 above), and to continue recording it at fair value. At the date of transfer, the call option is out of the money. IAS 39 and IFRS 9 therefore require the liability to be measured at the fair value of the transferred asset less the time value of the option, i.e. €80 – €5 = €75. This has the result that the net of the carrying value of the asset (€80) and the carrying value of the liability (€75) equals the time value of the option (€5), i.e.

	€	€
Date of transfer		
Cash	75	
Liability		75

A Transferred asset increases in value

Suppose that one year later the fair value of the asset is €100 and the time value of the option is now €3. The option is now in the money, so that the liability is measured at the option exercise price less the time value of the option, i.e. €95 – €3 = €92. This has the result that the net of the carrying value of the asset (€100) and the carrying value of the liability (€92) equals the fair value of the option (€8, representing €3 time value and €5 intrinsic value). The liability could have been more straightforwardly calculated as the fair value of the asset (€100) less the fair value of the option (€8) = €92. This gives rise to the following accounting entries:

	€	€
During year 1		
Asset (€100 – €80)	20	
Liability (€92 – €75)		17
Gain (profit or loss)		3

The €3 gain recorded in profit or loss effectively represents the increase in the fair value of the option from €5 to €8 over the period. If the entity were able to exercise the option at this point, and did so, it would record the entry:

	€	€
Liability	92	
Loss (profit or loss)	3	
Cash		95

The particular transaction results in no overall gain or loss being reflected in profit or loss (i.e. €3 gain during the year less €3 loss on exercise of option). This represents the net of the €20 gain in the fair value of the asset (€100 at the end of period less €80 at the start) and the net cash outflow of €20 (€75 in on initial transfer, €95 out on exercise of option).

B Asset decreases in value

Suppose instead that during the first year the fair value of the asset fell to €65 and the time value of the option at the end of the year was only €1. The liability would be measured at the fair value of the transferred asset less the time value of the option, i.e. €65 – €1 = €64. This would generate the accounting entries:

	€	€
During year 1		
Liability (€64 – €75)	11	
Loss (profit or loss)	4	
Asset (€65 – €80)		15

Again the overall loss shown in profit or loss represents the movement in the fair value of the option over the period from €5 to €1. Suppose that one year later there was no change in the fair value of the asset, and the option expired unexercised. The entity would then record the accounting entry:

	€	€
At end of year 2		
Liability	64	
Loss (profit or loss)	1	
Asset (statement of financial position)		65

This results in an overall loss for the transaction as a whole of €5 (€4 in year 1 and €1 in year 2), which represents the difference between the carrying value of the asset at the date of original transfer (€80) and the proceeds received (€75).

The amount of any consideration received is in principle not relevant to the measurement of the liability. If, for example, the entity originally received consideration of €72, it would still record a liability of €75 and a 'day one' loss of €3. If it received consideration of €80, it would still record a liability of €75 and a 'day one' profit of €5. The IASB no doubt presumed that such transactions are likely to be undertaken only by sophisticated market participants such that the consideration received will always be equivalent to the fair value of the asset less the fair value of the option. However, there may well be instances where this is not the case, such as in transactions between members of the same group or other related parties.

5.4.3.B Transferee's put option

If a transferee's put option prevents derecognition (see 3.8.3 and 4 above) of a transferred asset measured at fair value, IAS 39 and IFRS 9 require the asset to be measured at the lower of fair value and the option exercise price. The basis for this treatment is that the entity has no right to increases in the fair value of the transferred asset above the exercise price of the option. The associated liability is measured at the option exercise price plus the time value of the option. This ensures that the net carrying amount of the asset and the associated liability is the fair value of the put option obligation, as illustrated by Example 51.13 below. *[IAS 39.AG48(d), IFRS 9.B3.2.13(d)]*.

Example 51.13: Asset measured at fair value subject to transferee's put option

An entity has a financial asset, accounted for at fair value. On 1 January 2017 it transfers the asset, then carried at €98, to a third party, subject to a put option whereby the transferee can compel the entity to reacquire the asset for €100. The option is considered to be neither deeply in the money nor deeply out of the money. IAS 39 and IFRS 9 therefore require the entity to continue to recognise the asset to the extent of its continuing involvement (Figure 51.1, Box 9 – see also 4.2.3 above), and to continue recording it at the lower of (a) fair value and (b) €100 (the exercise price of the option). Assuming that the transferee pays €106 for the asset, representing €98 fair value of the asset plus €8 time value of the option, the entity would record the accounting entry:

	€	€
1 January 2017		
Cash	106	
Liability		106

A Transferred asset increases in value

Suppose that at 31 December 2017, the option has a time value of €5 and the fair value of the asset is €120. IAS 39 and IFRS 9 require the carrying value of the asset to be restricted to €100 (the exercise price of the option). The liability is measured at the exercise price plus the time value of the option,[20] i.e. €100 + €5 = €105. This has the result that the net of the carrying value of the asset (€100) and the carrying value of the liability (€105) equals the fair value of the option to the transferor (–€5).

This gives the accounting entry:

	€	€
31 December 2017		
Asset (€100 – €98)	2	
Liability (€105 – €106)	1	
Gain (profit or loss)		3

The gain of €3 effectively represents the decrease in the time value of the option (a *gain* from the transferor's perspective) from €8 to €5.

If the option were then to lapse unexercised, with no further change in the fair value of the asset, the entity would record the accounting entry:

	€	€
On lapse of option		
Liability	105	
Asset		100
Gain (profit or loss)		5

The total gain on the transaction of €8 (€3 in Year 1 and €5 on lapse) represents the option premium of €8 (i.e. the difference between the total consideration of €106 and the carrying value of the asset of €98) received at the outset.

B Transferred asset decreases in value

Suppose instead that at 31 December 2017, the option has a time value of €5 but the fair value of the asset is €90. IAS 39 and IFRS 9 require the carrying value of the asset to be measured at its fair value of €90. The liability is measured at the exercise price plus the time value of the option (i.e. to the transferee), i.e. €100 + €5 = €105.

This gives the accounting entry:

	€	€
31 December 2017		
Liability (€105 – €106)	1	
Loss (profit or loss)	7	
Asset (€90 – €98)		8

This has the result that the net of the carrying value of the asset (€90) and the liability (€105), i.e. €(–15) represents the fair value of the option to the transferor (i.e. intrinsic value €(–10) [€100 exercise price versus €90 value of asset] + time value €(–5)). The €7 loss represents the increase in the fair value of the option (a loss to the transferor) from €8 at the outset to €15 at 31 December 2017.

If the transferee were able to, and did, exercise its option at that point, the entity would record the accounting entry:

	€	€
On exercise of option		
Liability	105	
Cash		100
Gain (profit or loss)		5

The overall €2 loss (i.e. €5 gain above and €7 loss during Year 1) represents the net cash of €8 received from the transferee (€108 in at inception less €100 out on exercise) less the €10 fall in fair value of the transferred asset (€100 at inception less €90 at exercise).

5.4.3.C 'Collar' put and call options

Assets may be transferred in a way designed to ensure that the transferee is shielded from excessive losses on the transferred asset but has to pass significant gains on the asset back to the transferor. Such an arrangement is known as a 'collar', on the basis that it allocates a range of potential value movements in the asset to the transferee, with movements outside that range accruing to the transferor. A simple example would be the transfer of an asset subject to a purchased call option (allowing the transferor to reacquire the asset if it increases in value beyond a certain level) and a written put option (allowing the transferee to compel the transferor to reacquire the asset if it falls in value beyond a certain level).

If a collar, in the form of a purchased call and written put option, prevents derecognition (see 3.8.3 and 4 above) of a transferred asset measured at fair value,

IAS 39 and IFRS 9 require the entity to continue to measure the asset at fair value. The associated liability is measured at:

- if the call option is in or at the money, the sum of the call exercise price and the fair value of the put option less the time value of the call option; or
- if the call option is out of the money, the sum of the fair value of the asset and the fair value of the put option less the time value of the call option.

The adjustment to the associated liability ensures that the net carrying amount of the asset and the associated liability is the fair value of the options held and written by the entity, as illustrated by Example 51.14 below. *[IAS 39.AG48(e), IFRS 9.B3.2.13(e)]*.

Example 51.14: Asset measured at fair value subject to collar put and call options

An entity has a financial asset, accounted for at fair value, carried at €100. On 1 January 2017 it transfers the asset to a third party, subject to:

- a call option whereby the entity can compel the transferee to sell the asset back to the entity for €120; and
- a put option whereby the transferee can compel the entity to reacquire the asset for €80.

The options are considered to be neither deeply in the money nor deeply out of the money. IAS 39 and IFRS 9 therefore require the entity to continue to recognise the asset to the extent of its continuing involvement (Figure 51.1, Box 9 – see also 4.2.3 above), and to continue recording it at fair value.

At the date of transfer, the time value of the put and call are €1 and €5 respectively. At the date of transfer, the call option is out of the money, so that the associated liability is calculated as the sum of the fair value of the asset and the fair value of the put option less the time value of the call option, i.e. (€100+€1) – €5 = €96. The net of this and the fair value of the asset (€100) is €4 which is the net fair value of the two options (call €5 less put €1). Assuming that the transaction is undertaken at arm's length, the transferee would pay €96 for the asset and the entity would record the accounting entry:

	€	€
Cash	96	
Liability		96

A Transferred asset increases in value

Suppose that, at 31 December 2017, the fair value of the asset is €140, and the time value of the put and call are €0.5 and €2 respectively. The call option is now in the money, so that IAS 39 and IFRS 9 require the entity to recognise a liability equal to the sum of the call exercise price and fair value of the put option less the time value of the call option, i.e. (€120 + €0.5) – €2 = €118.5. The net of this and the carrying value of the asset (€140) is €21.5 which is the net fair value of the two options (call €22 [time value €2 plus intrinsic value €20] less put €0.5 = €21.5). This gives the accounting entry:

	€	€
31 December 2017		
Asset (€140 – €100)	40.0	
Gain (profit or loss)		17.5
Liability (€118.5 – €96)		22.5

The gain represents the increase in fair value of the call option of €17 (€5 at outset and €22 at 31 December 2017) plus the €0.5 decrease (a gain from the transferor's perspective) in the fair value of the put option (€1 at outset and €0.5 at 31 December 2017).

If the entity were able to, and did, exercise its call option, it would record the entry:

	€	€
Exercise of call option		
Liability	118.5	
Loss (profit or loss)	1.5	
Cash		120.0

The overall gain of €16 on the transaction (€1.5 loss above and €17.5 profit recorded in 2017) represents the increase in fair value of the asset of €40 (€100 at outset, €140 at 31 December 2017) less the net €24 paid to the transferee (€120 paid on exercise of call less €96 received on initial transfer).

B Transferred asset decreases in value

Suppose instead that, at 31 December 2017, the fair value of the asset is €78, and the time value of the put and call are €0.5 and €2 respectively. The call option is now out of the money, so that IAS 39 and IFRS 9 require the entity to recognise a liability equal to the sum of the fair value of the asset and the fair value of the put option (i.e. €2.5 – time value €0.5 plus intrinsic value €2 [€80 exercise price versus €78 fair value of asset]) less the time value of the call option, i.e. (€78 + €2.5) – €2 = €78.5.

The net of this and the carrying value of the asset (€78) is €(–0.5) which is the net fair value of the two options (call €2 less put €2.5 = €(–0.5)). This gives the accounting entry:

	€	€
31 December 2017		
Liability (€78.5 – €96)	17.5	
Loss (profit or loss)	4.5	
Asset (€78 – €100)		22.0

The loss represents the decrease in the fair value of the call option of €3 (€5 at outset and €2 at 31 December 2017) plus the €1.5 increase (a decrease from the transferor's perspective) in the fair value of the put option (€1 at outset and €2.5 at 31 December 2017).

If the transferee were able to, and did, exercise its put option, the entity would record the entry:

	€	€
Exercise of put option		
Liability	78.5	
Loss (profit or loss)	1.5	
Cash		80.0

The overall loss of €6 on the transaction (€1.5 loss above and €4.5 loss recorded in 2017) represents the decrease in fair value of the asset of €22 (€100 at outset, €78 at 31 December 2017) offset by the net €16 received from the transferee (€96 received on initial transfer less €80 paid on exercise of put).

5.4.4 Continuing involvement in part only of a financial asset

IAS 39 and IFRS 9 give the following example of the application of the continuing involvement approach to continuing involvement in part only of a financial asset. *[IAS 39.AG52, IFRS 9.B3.2.17]*.

Example 51.15: Continuing involvement in part only of a financial asset

An entity has a portfolio of prepayable loans whose coupon and effective interest rate is 10% and whose principal amount and amortised cost is €10 million. It enters into a transaction in which, in return for a payment of €9.115 million, the transferee obtains the right to €9 million of any collections of principal plus 9.5% interest.

The entity retains rights to €1 million of any collections of principal plus interest at 10%, plus the remaining 0.5% ('excess spread') on the remaining €9 million of principal. Collections from prepayments are allocated between the entity and the transferee proportionately in the ratio of 1:9, but any defaults are deducted from the entity's interest of €1 million until that interest is exhausted.

The fair value of the loans at the date of the transaction is €10.1 million and the estimated fair value of the excess spread of 0.5 per cent is €40,000.

The entity determines that it has transferred some significant risks and rewards of ownership (for example, significant prepayment risk) but has also retained some significant risks and rewards of ownership because of its subordinated retained interest (Figure 51.1, Box 7, No) and has retained control (Figure 51.1, Box 8, Yes). It therefore applies the continuing involvement approach (Figure 51.1, Box 9).

The entity analyses the transaction as:

- a retention of a fully proportionate retained interest of €1 million, plus
- the subordination of that retained interest to provide credit enhancement to the transferee for credit losses.

The entity calculates that €9.09 million (90% of €10.1 million) of the consideration received of €9.115 million represents the consideration for a fully proportionate 90% share. The remainder of the consideration (€25,000) received represents consideration received by the entity for subordinating its retained interest to provide credit enhancement to the transferee for credit losses. In addition, the excess spread of 0.5% represents consideration received for the credit enhancement. Accordingly, the total consideration received for the credit enhancement is €65,000 (€25,000 received from transferee plus €40,000 fair value of excess spread).

The entity first calculates the gain or loss on the sale of the 90% share of cash flows. Assuming that separate fair values of the 10% part transferred and the 90% part retained are not available at the date of the transfer, the entity allocates the carrying amount of the asset pro-rata to the fair values of those parts (see 5.1.1 and 5.1.2 and 5.3.5 above). The total fair value of the portfolio is considered to be €10.1 million (see above), and the fair value of the consideration for the part disposed of €9.09 million. The carrying amount of the whole portfolio is €10 million. This implies a carrying amount for the part disposed of €10m × 9.09/10.1 = €9 million, and for the part retained €1 million. The gain on the sale of the 90% is therefore €90,000 (€9.09 million – €9 million).

In addition, IAS 39 and IFRS 9 require the entity to recognise the continuing involvement that results from the subordination of its retained interest for credit losses. Accordingly, it recognises an asset of €1 million (the maximum amount of the cash flows it would forfeit under the subordination), and an associated liability of €1.065 million (the maximum amount of the cash flows it would forfeit under the subordination, i.e. €1 million, plus the consideration for the subordination of €65,000). It also recognises an asset for the fair value of the excess spread which forms part of the consideration for the subordination.

This gives rise to the accounting entry:

	€000	€000
Cash	9,115	
Asset for the subordination of the residual interest	1,000	
Excess spread received for subordination	40	
Loan portfolio		9,000
Liability for subordination		1,065
Gain on disposal		90

It is crucial to an understanding of this example that, as a result of the transaction, the original asset (the portfolio of prepayable loans) is being accounted for as two separate assets. Because the cash flows from the portfolio are split in fully proportionate (pro-rata) shares (see 3.3 above), each of these assets must be considered separately.

The first of these assets, the right to cash flows of €9 million, continues to be recognised only to the extent of the entity's continuing involvement, which in this case is via the credit enhancement. The approach is very similar to continuing involvement through guarantee (see Example 51.10 at 5.4.1 above), except that the liability for subordination includes the maximum cash flow that the entity might not receive from its retained share (i.e. €1 million) rather than, as in Example 51.10, a potential cash outflow (the guarantee amount, which is the maximum amount that the entity could be required to repay). This is aggregated with the fair value of the amount received in respect of the credit enhancement, in order to calculate the full liability for subordination. This is similar to the way in which the fair value of the guarantee is added to the guarantee amount in order to calculate the associated liability. *[IAS 39.AG48(a), IFRS 9.B3.2.13(a)]*.

The second asset is the entity's proportionate retained share of €1 million. It is, seemingly, irrelevant to the accounting analysis in IAS 39 and IFRS 9 that this has already been taken into account in calculating the entity's continuing involvement in the remaining €9 million of the portfolio.

The effect is to gross up the statement of financial position with a subordination asset and liability. As IAS 39 and IFRS 9 note, immediately following the transaction, the carrying amount of the asset is €2.04 million (i.e. €1 million part retained plus €1 million subordination asset plus €40,000 excess spread) – in respect of an asset whose fair value is only €1.01 million!

We have some reservations concerning the example above. First, we challenge whether, as a point of principle, it is appropriate to apply the derecognition criteria to part of an asset where the part that is retained provides credit enhancement for the transferee. As discussed more fully at 3.3.1 above, it is possible that IAS 39 and IFRS 9 are implicitly drawing a distinction between:

- a guarantee that could result in an outflow of the total resources of the transferor, or a return of consideration for the transfer already received (which would not allow partial derecognition); and
- a guarantee that could result in the transferor losing the right to receive a specific future cash inflow, but not being obliged to make any other payment should that specific future cash inflow not materialise.

Moreover, even in the context of the analysis presented by IAS 39 and IFRS 9, we do not understand the basis of the treatment of the excess spread. The example simply asserts that this forms part of the consideration for providing the subordination, although it is not clear that it forms any more or any less of the consideration for the subordination than the interest and principal on the 10% of the portfolio retained.

In our view, a more logical analysis would have been that:

- the entity has disposed of not 90% of the whole portfolio, but 90% of the principal balances and 9.5% interest on that 90%; and
- the consideration for the subordination is still €65,000, on the basis that if:
  - the fair value of the consideration for a fully proportionate share of 90% (i.e. including 10% interest) is €9,090,000; and
  - the fair value of the excess spread of 0.5% interest is €40,000, then

  the fair value of consideration for a fully proportionate share less the excess spread is €9,050,000 (i.e. €9,090,000 less €40,000). This in turn means that the balance of the total consideration of €9,115,000 (i.e. €65,000) relates to the subordination.

In addition, of course, Example 51.15 ignores the possibility that the excess spread is retained by the transferor because it continues to service the portfolio, although this may be an attempt to avoid overcomplicating matters even further.

A further issue is that, if the excess spread is regarded as part of the asset retained, rather than the consideration received, it would seem more appropriate to recognise it on a basis consistent with the accounting treatment of the original transferred asset (typically, amortised cost) rather than at fair value.

5.5 Miscellaneous provisions

IAS 39 and IFRS 9 contain a number of accounting provisions generally applicable to transfers of assets, as discussed below.

5.5.1 Offset

IAS 39 and IFRS 9 provide that, if a transferred asset continues to be recognised, the entity must not offset:

- the asset with the associated liability; or
- any income arising from the transferred asset with any expense incurred on the associated liability. *[IAS 39.36, IFRS 9.3.2.22]*.

Whilst IAS 39 and IFRS 9 do not say so specifically, this is clearly intended to apply both to assets that continue to be recognised in full and to those that continue to be recognised to the extent of their continuing involvement.

This requirement apparently over-rides the offset criteria in IAS 32 *[IAS 32.42]*, as illustrated, for example, by the various situations highlighted in the discussion at 4 and 5.1 to 5.4 above where a transaction required to be net-settled (which would normally be required to be accounted for as such under IAS 32) is accounted for as if it were to be gross-settled.

5.5.2 Collateral

If a transferor provides non-cash collateral (such as debt or equity instruments) to the transferee, the accounting treatment for the collateral by both the transferor and the transferee depends on:

- whether the transferee has the right to sell or repledge the collateral; and
- whether the transferor has defaulted.

If the transferee has the right by contract or custom to sell or repledge a collateral asset, the transferor should reclassify that asset in its statement of financial position (e.g. as a loaned asset, pledged equity instruments or repurchase receivable) separately from other assets.

If the transferee sells collateral pledged to it, it recognises the proceeds from the sale and a liability measured at fair value for its obligation to return the collateral.

If the transferor defaults under the terms of the contract and is no longer entitled to redeem the collateral, it derecognises the collateral, and the transferee either:

- recognises the collateral as its asset initially measured at fair value; or
- if it has already sold the collateral, derecognises its obligation to return the collateral.

In no other circumstances should the transferor derecognise, or the transferee recognise, the collateral as an asset. *[IAS 39.37, IFRS 9.3.2.23]*.

5.5.3 *Rights or obligations over transferred assets that continue to be recognised*

Where a transfer of a financial asset does not qualify for derecognition, the transferor may well have contractual rights or obligations related to the transfer, such as options or forward repurchase contracts that are derivatives of a type that would normally be required to be recognised under IAS 39 and IFRS 9.

IAS 39 and IFRS 9 prohibit separate recognition of such derivatives, if recognition of the derivative together with either the transferred asset or the liability arising from the transfer would result in recognising the same rights or obligations twice.

For example, IAS 39 and IFRS 9 note that a call option retained by the transferor may prevent a transfer of financial assets from being accounted for as a sale (see 4 above). In that case, the call option must not be separately recognised as a derivative asset. *[IAS 39.AG49, IFRS 9.B3.2.14]*.

5.6 Reassessing derecognition

IAS 39 and IFRS 9 state that if an entity determines that, as a result of the transfer, it has transferred substantially all the risks and rewards of ownership of the transferred asset, it does not recognise the transferred asset again in a future period, unless it reacquires the transferred asset in a new transaction. *[IAS 39.AG41, IFRS 9.B3.2.6]*. We have noted earlier that there is some ambiguity as to whether this rule in AG41 is to be read generally as prohibiting any re-recognition of a derecognised asset or specifically as referring only to circumstances where derecognition results from transfer of substantially all the risks and rewards (i.e. it applies only to 'Box 6, Yes' transactions, and not to 'Box 8, No' transactions). Our view, as expressed at 4.2 above, is that the broader interpretation should be applied and the requirement still applies if derecognition occurs for another reason, e.g. loss of control.

The risks and rewards of ownership retained by the entity may change as a result of market changes in such a way that, had the revised conditions existed at inception, they would have prevented derecognition of the asset. However, the original decision to derecognise the asset should not be revisited, unless (in exceptional circumstances) the original assessment was an accounting error within the scope of IAS 8.

5.6.1 *Reassessment of consolidation of subsidiaries and SPEs*

The effect of IFRS 10, combined with the derecognition provisions of IAS 39 or IFRS 9 is that a transaction (commonly, but not exclusively, in a securitisation) may result in derecognition of the financial asset concerned in the seller's own financial statements, but the 'buyer' may be a consolidated SPE, so that the asset is immediately re-recognised in the consolidated financial statements in which the seller is included. However, an entity may derecognise assets if they are transferred to an SPE that is not consolidated because, having considered all of the facts and circumstances, the entity concludes that it does not control the SPE. The assessment as to whether a particular SPE is controlled by the reporting entity is discussed in Chapter 6.

IFRS 10 requires an investor to reassess whether it controls an investee if facts and circumstances indicate that there are changes to any elements of control, including the investor's exposure, or rights, to variable returns from its involvement with the investee (see Chapter 6). *[IFRS 10.8]*.

6 DERECOGNITION – FINANCIAL LIABILITIES

The provisions of IAS 39 and IFRS 9 with respect to the derecognition of financial liabilities are generally more straightforward and less subjective than those for the derecognition of financial assets. However, they are also very different from the asset derecognition rules which focus primarily on the economic substance of the transaction. By contrast, the rules for derecognition of liabilities, like the provisions of IAS 32 for the identification of instruments as financial liabilities (see Chapter 45), focus more on legal obligations than on economic substance – or, as the IASB would doubtless argue, they are based on the view that the economic substance of whether an entity has a liability to a third party is ultimately dictated by the legal rights and obligations that exist between them.

IAS 39 and IFRS 9 contain provisions relating to:

- the extinguishment of debt (see 6.1 below);
- the substitution or modification of debt by the original lender (see 6.2 below); and
- the calculation of any profit or loss arising on the derecognition of debt (see 6.3 below).

6.1 Extinguishment of debt

IAS 39 and IFRS 9 require an entity to derecognise (i.e. remove from its statement of financial position) a financial liability (or a part of a financial liability – see 6.1.1 below) when, and only when, it is 'extinguished', that is, when the obligation specified in the contract is discharged, cancelled, or expires. *[IAS 39.39, IFRS 9.3.3.1]*. This will be achieved when the debtor either:

- discharges the liability (or part of it) by paying the creditor, normally with cash, other financial assets, goods or services; or
- is legally released from primary responsibility for the liability (or part of it) either by process of law or by the creditor. *[IAS 39.AG57, IFRS 9.B3.3.1]*. Extinguishment of liabilities by legal release is discussed further at 6.1.2 below.

If the issuer of a debt instrument repurchases the instrument, the debt is extinguished even if the issuer is a market maker in that instrument, or otherwise intends to resell or reissue it in the near term. *[IAS 39.AG58, IFRS 9.B3.3.2]*. IAS 39 and IFRS 9 focus only on whether the entity has a legal obligation to reissue the debt, not on whether there is a commercial imperative for it to do so.

6.1.1 What constitutes 'part' of a liability?

The requirements of IAS 39 and IFRS 9 for the derecognition of liabilities apply to all or 'part' of a financial liability. It is not entirely clear what is meant by 'part' of a liability in this context. The rules, and the examples, in IAS 39 and IFRS 9 seem to be drafted in the context of transactions that settle all remaining cash flows (i.e. interest and principal) of a proportion of a liability, such as the repayment of £25 million of a £100 million loan, together with any related interest payments.

However, these provisions are presumably also intended to apply in situations where an entity prepays the interest only (or a proportion of future interest payments) or the principal only (or a proportion of future principal payments) on a loan.

6.1.2 Legal release by creditor

A liability can be derecognised by a debtor if the creditor legally releases the debtor from the liability. It is clear that IAS 39 and IFRS 9 regard legal release as crucial, with the effect that very similar (if not identical) situations may lead to different results purely because of the legal form.

For example, IAS 39 and IFRS 9 provide that:

- where a debtor is legally released from a liability, derecognition is not precluded by the fact that the debtor has given a guarantee in respect of the liability; *[IAS 39.AG57(b), IFRS 9.B3.3.1(b)]* but
- if a debtor pays a third party to assume an obligation and notifies its creditor that the third party has assumed the debt obligation, the debtor derecognises the debt obligation if, and only if, the creditor legally releases the debtor from its obligations. *[IAS 39.AG60, IFRS 9.B3.3.4]*.

The effect of these requirements is shown by Example 51.16.

Example 51.16: Transfer of debt obligations with and without legal release

Scenario 1

Entity A issues bonds that have a carrying amount and fair value of $1,000,000. A pays $1,000,000 to Entity B for B to assume responsibility for paying interest and principal on the bonds to the bondholders. The bondholders are informed that B has assumed responsibility for the debt. However, A is not legally released from the obligation to pay interest and principal by the bondholders. Accordingly, if B does not make payments when due, the bondholders may seek payment from A.

Scenario 2

Entity A issues bonds that have a carrying amount and fair value of $1,000,000. A pays $1,000,000 to Entity B for B to assume responsibility for paying interest and principal on the bonds to the bondholders. The bondholders are informed that B has assumed responsibility for the debt and legally release A from any further obligation under the debt. However, A enters into a guarantee arrangement whereby, if B does not make payments when due, the bondholders may seek payment from A.

It is clear, in our view, that in either scenario above the bondholders are in the same economic and legal position – they will receive payments from B and, if B defaults, they will have recourse to A.

However, IAS 39 and IFRS 9 give rise to the, in our view, anomalous result that:

- Scenario 1 is accounted for by the continuing recognition of the debt because no legal release has been obtained; but
- Scenario 2 is accounted for by derecognition of the debt, and recognition of the guarantee, notwithstanding that the effect of the guarantee is to put A back in the same position as if it had not been released from its obligations under the original bond.

IAS 39 and IFRS 9 also clarify that, if a debtor:

- transfers its obligations under a debt to a third party and obtains legal release from its obligations by the creditor; but
- undertakes to make payments to the third party so as to enable it to meet its obligations to the creditor,

it should derecognise the original debt, but recognise a new debt obligation to the third party. *[IAS 39.AG60, IFRS 9.B3.3.4]*.

Legal release may also be achieved through the novation of a contract to an intermediary counterparty. For example, a derivative between a reporting entity and a bank may be novated to a central counterparty (CCP). In these circumstances, the IASB explains that the novation to the CCP releases the bank from the responsibility to make payments to the reporting entity. Consequently, the original derivative meets the derecognition criteria for a financial liability and a new derivative with the CCP is recognised. *[IAS 39.BC220D]*. However, for hedge accounting purposes only, it is sometimes possible in these circumstances to treat the new derivative as a continuation of the original (see Chapter 52 at 4.2.3.A and Chapter 53 at 11.3).

6.1.3 *'In-substance defeasance' arrangements*

Entities sometimes enter into so-called 'in-substance defeasance' arrangements in respect of financial liabilities. These typically involve a lump sum payment to a third party (other than the creditor) such as a trust, which then invests the funds in (typically) very low-risk assets to which the entity has no, or very limited, rights of access. These assets are then applied to discharge all the remaining interest and principal payments on the financial liabilities that are purported to have been defeased. It is sometimes argued that the risk-free nature of the assets, and the entity's lack of access to them, means that the entity is in substance in no different position than if it had actually repaid the original financial liability.

IAS 39 and IFRS 9 regard such arrangements as not giving rise to derecognition of the original liability in the absence of legal release by the creditor. *[IAS 39.AG59, IFRS 9.B3.3.3]*.

6.1.4 *Extinguishment in exchange for transfer of assets not meeting the derecognition criteria*

IAS 39 and IFRS 9 note that in some cases legal release may be achieved by transferring assets to the creditor which do not meet the criteria for derecognition (see 3 above). In such a case, the debtor will derecognise the liability from which it has been released, but recognise a new liability relating to the transferred assets that may be equal to the derecognised liability. *[IAS 39.AG61, IFRS 9.B3.3.5]*. It is not entirely clear what is envisaged here, but it may be some such scenario as the following.

Example 51.17: Extinguishment of debt in exchange for transfer of assets not meeting derecognition criteria

An entity has a bank loan of €1 million. The bank agrees to accept in full payment of the loan the transfer to it by the entity of a portfolio of corporate bonds with a market value of €1 million. The entity and the bank then enter into a put and call option over the bonds, the effect of which will be that the entity will repurchase the bonds in three years' time at a price that gives the bank a lender's return on €1 million. As discussed further at 4.2.8 above, this would have the effect that the entity is unable to derecognise the bonds.

Under the provisions of IAS 39 and IFRS 9, the entity would be able to derecognise the original bank loan, as it has been legally released from it. The provisions under discussion here have the overall result that a loan effectively continues to be recognised. Strictly, however, the analysis is that the original loan has been derecognised and a new one recognised. In effect the accounting is representing that the entity has repaid the original loan and replaced it with a new one secured on a bond portfolio.

However, as the new loan is required to be initially recognised at fair value whereas the old loan may well have been recognised at amortised cost (see Chapter 49 at 3), there may well be a gain or loss to record as the result of the different measurement bases being used – see 6.2 and 6.3 below.

6.2 Exchange or modification of debt by original lender

It is common for an entity, particularly but not necessarily when in financial difficulties, to approach its major creditors for a restructuring of its debt commitments – for example, an agreement to postpone the repayment of principal in exchange for higher interest payments in the meantime, or to roll up interest into a single 'bullet' payment of interest and principal at the end of the term. Such changes to the terms of debt can be effected in a number of ways, in particular:

- a notional repayment of the original loan followed by an immediate re-lending of all or part of the proceeds of the notional repayment as a new loan ('exchange'); or
- legal amendment of the original loan agreement ('modification').

The accounting issue raised by such transactions is essentially whether there is, in fact, anything to account for. For example, if an entity owes £100 million at floating rate interest and negotiates with its bankers to change the interest to a fixed coupon of 7%, should the accounting treatment reflect the fact that:

(a) the entity still owes £100 million to the same lender, and so is in the same position as before; or
(b) the modification of the interest profile has altered the net present value of the total obligations under the loan?

IAS 39 and IFRS 9 require an exchange between an existing borrower and lender of debt instruments with 'substantially different' terms to be accounted for as an extinguishment of the original financial liability and the recognition of a new financial liability. Similarly, a substantial modification of the terms of an existing financial liability, or a part of it, (whether or not due to the financial difficulty of the debtor) should be accounted for as an extinguishment of the original financial liability and the recognition of a new financial liability. *[IAS 39.40, IFRS 9.3.3.2]*.

The accounting consequences for an exchange or a modification that results in extinguishment and one that does not lead to extinguishment are discussed in further detail at 6.2.1 to 6.2.3 below.

IAS 39 and IFRS 9 regard the terms of exchanged or modified debt as 'substantially different' if the net present value of the cash flows under the new terms (including any fees paid net of any fees received) discounted at the original effective interest rate is at least 10% different from the discounted present value of the remaining cash flows of the original debt instrument. *[IAS 39.AG62, IFRS 9.B3.3.6]*. This comparison is commonly referred to as 'the 10% test'.

Whilst IAS 39 and IFRS 9 do not say so explicitly, it seems clear that the discounted present value of the remaining cash flows of the original debt instrument used in the

10% test must also be determined using the original effective interest rate, so that there is a 'like for like' comparison. This amount should also represent the amortised cost of the liability prior to modification.

Also, it is not clear from the standards whether the cash flows under the new terms should include only fees payable to the lender or whether they should also include other fees and costs that would be considered transaction costs, such as amounts payable to the entity's legal advisers. Read literally the standards suggest only fees should be included, but as the accounting treatment for fees and costs incurred on a modification are identical, some would argue that both should be included in the test. At the time of writing this matter was being considered by the Interpretations Committee which had tentatively concluded only fees payable to the lender should be considered when applying the 10% test.[21]

IAS 39 and IFRS 9 do not explicitly prohibit an entity from accounting for an exchange or modification of a liability where the net present value of the cash flows under the new terms is less than 10% different from the discounted present value of the remaining cash flows of the original debt instrument. Indeed, there may be situations where the modification of the debt is so fundamental that immediate derecognition is appropriate whether or not the 10% test is satisfied. The following are examples of situations where derecognition of the original instrument could be required:

- An entity has issued a 'plain vanilla' debt instrument and restructures the debt to include an embedded equity instrument.
- An entity has issued a 5% euro-denominated debt instrument and restructures the instrument to an 18% Turkish lire-denominated debt instrument.

The present value of the cash flows of the restructured debts, discounted at the original effective interest rate, may not be significantly different from the discounted present value of the remaining cash flows of the original financial liability. However, even if the 10% test is not satisfied, the introduction of the equity-linked feature or a change in currency could significantly alter the future economic risk exposure of the instrument. In these circumstances the modification of terms should, in our view, be regarded as representing a substantial change which would lead to derecognition of the original liability.

6.2.1 Costs and fees

An entity will almost always be required to pay fees to the lender and incur costs (such as legal expenses) on an exchange or modification of a financial liability.

If an exchange of debt instruments or modification of terms is accounted for as an extinguishment of the original debt, IAS 39 and IFRS 9 require any costs or fees incurred to be recognised as part of the gain or loss on the extinguishment (see 6.3 below). *[IAS 39.AG62, IFRS 9.B3.3.6]*.

Where the exchange or modification is not accounted for as an extinguishment, any costs or fees incurred adjust the carrying amount of the liability and are amortised over the remaining term of the modified liability. *[IAS 39.AG62, IFRS 9.B3.3.6]*. Neither IAS 39 nor IFRS 9 specify a particular method for amortising such costs and fees. In our view, applying the effective interest method or another approach that approximates this such as a straight-line method would be appropriate. This is illustrated in the following example.

Example 51.18: Fees and costs incurred on modification of debt not treated as extinguishment

On 1 January 2015 an entity borrowed $100 million on, at that time, arm's length market terms, so that interest of 6% was to be paid annually in arrears and the loan repaid in full on 31 December 2019. Transaction costs of $4 million were incurred. Assuming that the loan had run to term, the entity would have recorded the following amounts using the effective interest method. The loan is originally recorded at the issue proceeds of $100 million less transaction costs of $4 million, and the effective interest rate of 6.975% is derived by a computer program or trial and error. For a more detailed discussion of the effective interest method, see Chapter 49 at 3 and Chapter 50 at 3.

Year	Liability b/f $m	Interest at 6.975% $m	Cash paid $m	Liability c/f $m
1.1.2015	96.00			96.00
2015	96.00	6.70	(6.00)	96.70
2016	96.70	6.74	(6.00)	97.44
2017	97.44	6.80	(6.00)	98.24
2018	98.24	6.85	(6.00)	99.09
2019	99.09	6.91	(106.00)	–

During the latter part of 2016 the entity considers expanding its business in a way that would crystallise the lender's right to demand immediate repayment of the loan because such an action is not permitted under the detailed terms of the loan. Therefore the entity approaches the lender with a view to amending those terms to permit the planned expansion, but without changing the cash flows on the loan. On 1 January 2017, the lender agrees to amend the terms in return for which it charges the entity a fee of $450,000. The entity also incurs directly attributable legal costs of $50,000, bringing the total fees and costs incurred to $500,000.

It can be shown that the net present value of the cash flows under the new terms, including the $0.45 million of fees paid (but excluding the $0.05 million of legal costs in line with the Interpretations Committee's tentative conclusion noted at 6.2 above), discounted at the original effective interest rate is $97.89 million. This compares to the carrying amount of $97.44 million and because the remaining cash flows have not changed, the difference between the two simply represents the fees paid. This difference is just 0.46% of the original carrying amount, significantly less than 10%. The entity does not consider the changes to the detailed terms of the loan to be substantial and therefore concludes the modification should not result in the extinguishment of the liability.

Accordingly the carrying amount of the liability is adjusted by the $500,000 fees and costs incurred so that the revised carrying amount is $96.94 million ($97.44 million less $0.50 million). In order to amortise this adjustment over the remaining term of the loan, the entity could reset the effective interest rate of the loan, in this case to 7.169%, so that it is amortised in accordance with the effective interest method as follows.

Year	Liability b/f $m	Interest at 7.169% $m	Cash paid $m	Liability c/f $m
1.1.2017	96.94			96.94
2017	96.94	6.95	(6.00)	97.89
2018	97.89	7.02	(6.00)	98.91
2019	98.91	7.09	(106.00)	–

Another way would be to view the liability as comprising two components: the unadjusted carrying amount of $97.44 million, to which the effective interest method would be applied using the original effective interest rate of 6.975%; and the adjustment of $500,000 which would be amortised on some other basis, such as straight line. This would give rise to substantially the same interest expense in each period, detailed calculations showing a slight change in 2017 and 2019 to $6.96 million and $7.08 million respectively.

6.2.2 Modification gains and losses

In Example 51.18 above, the remaining cash flows on the loan remained the same after the modification, but in practice they will often change. For example, in the situation set out in Example 51.18, the lender might have agreed to charge additional interest of, say, $170,000 per year for the remaining three year term of the loan instead of the $450,000 fee at the time of the modification. Detailed calculations show an almost identical outcome when applying the 10% test to these revised facts, with the net present value of the cash flows under revised terms being $97.89 million excluding the $50,000 of costs, a difference of $0.45 million or 0.46%. Again it would be concluded that the modification does not result in derecognition of the liability.

As noted at 6.2.1 above, the standards are clear that the costs and fees incurred should be amortised over the remaining term of the liability, but how should the entity account for changes to the future contractual cash flows? Neither IAS 39 nor IFRS 9 provide a conclusive answer to this question. Guidance to the original version of IAS 39[22] made it clear that the difference between the present values under the old and new terms was to be amortised over the remaining term of the liability. This treatment applied irrespective of the extent to which the difference arose from fees or costs incurred at the time of the modification or from changes to the remaining cash flows. Given the related requirements of the original version of IAS 39 were carried forward into the current version (and now into IFRS 9) without major change, it could be argued that this approach remains appropriate.

However, other parts of IAS 39 and IFRS 9 might suggest a different treatment. In particular, both IAS 39 and IFRS 9 are clear that if an entity's estimates of the contractual cash flows on a debt instrument change, the amortised cost of the instrument should be adjusted to the net present value of the revised cash flows discounted at the original effective interest rate, with the difference recognised in profit or loss (see Chapter 49 at 3.2.1 and Chapter 50 at 3.2.1). Although this requirement is intended to apply to changes in estimated cash flows under the terms of an unmodified contract, some would argue it is appropriate to apply a similar approach when the contractual terms change. Further, IFRS 9 is clear that modifications to the contractual cash flows of a financial asset measured at amortised cost that do not result in derecognition of that asset give rise to a modification gain or loss (see Chapter 50 at 5.7).

In our view, in the absence of more definitive guidance, both approaches are acceptable. In our experience, the approach most commonly applied is that based on the guidance to the original version of IAS 39. When IFRS 9 is applied, the more explicit requirements for modifications of financial assets should lead entities to review, and possibly change, their accounting policies for modifications to financial liabilities, although that remains to be seen. Before that happens, however, the Interpretations Committee may provide more clarity. The issue has been submitted to the committee and, at the time of writing, the issue was being analysed with an expectation it would be considered at a future meeting,[23] possibly later in 2016.

Applying the second approach to the situation discussed above would result in the entity recognising a modification loss of $0.45 million, being the net present value of the additional interest payable of $170,000 per annum, discounted at the original effective interest rate of 6.975%. This might seem counter-intuitive to some when compared to the original facts in Example 51.18. The only difference between the two scenarios is that in the first the borrower makes an immediate cash payment to the lender of $0.45 million in the form of a fee, whereas in the second it makes payments to the lender over the next three years (in the form of additional interest) which have a net present value of $0.45 million. Therefore, one might ask, why would the timing of the associated expense depend on the form and timing of the cash flows? Nevertheless, this treatment is clearly required by IFRS 9 for financial assets.

6.2.3 *Illustrative examples*

Examples 51.19 and 51.20 below illustrate some more complex modifications of debt.

Example 51.19: Modification of debt not treated as extinguishment

On 1 January 2012 an entity borrowed £100 million on, at that time, arm's length market terms, so that interest of 7% was to be paid annually in arrears and the loan repaid in full on 31 December 2021. Transaction costs of £5 million were incurred. Assuming that the loan had run to term, the entity would have recorded the following amounts using the effective interest method. The loan is originally recorded at the issue proceeds of £100 million less transaction costs of £5 million, and the effective interest rate is 7.736%.

Year	Liability b/f	Interest at 7.736%	Cash paid	Liability c/f
	£m	£m	£m	£m
1.1.2012	95.00			95.00
2012	95.00	7.35	(7.00)	95.35
2013	95.35	7.38	(7.00)	95.73
2014	95.73	7.40	(7.00)	96.13
2015	96.13	7.44	(7.00)	96.57
2016	96.57	7.47	(7.00)	97.04
2017	97.04	7.51	(7.00)	97.55
2018	97.55	7.55	(7.00)	98.10
2019	98.10	7.59	(7.00)	98.69
2020	98.69	7.63	(7.00)	99.32
2021	99.32	7.68	(107.00)	–

During 2016 the entity is in financial difficulties and approaches the lender for a modification of the terms of the loan. These are agreed on 1 January 2017, as follows. No cash interest will be paid in 2017 or 2018, although a fee of £2 million must be paid to the lender immediately. From 2019 onwards interest of 9% will be paid annually in arrears and the term of the loan will be extended for two years until 31 December 2023. Legal fees and other costs incurred are not material.

The entity is required to compute the present value of the new arrangement using the original effective interest rate of 7.736%. This gives a net present value for the modified debt of £92.53 million, calculated as follows:

Year	Cash flow	£m	Discount factor	£m
1.1.2017	Fee	2.00	1	2.00
2019	Interest	9.00	$1/1.07736^3$	7.20
2020	Interest	9.00	$1/1.07736^4$	6.68
2021	Interest	9.00	$1/1.07736^5$	6.20
2022	Interest	9.00	$1/1.07736^6$	5.75
2023	Interest and principal	109.00	$1/1.07736^7$	64.70
			Total	92.53

This represents 95.4% of the current carrying value of the debt as at the end of 2016 of £97.04 million, so that the net present value of the modified loan (discounted at the effective interest rate of the original loan) is 4.6% different from that of the original loan. This is less than 10%, so that the modification is not automatically required to be treated as an extinguishment under IAS 39 or IFRS 9.

If the entity selects an accounting policy to recognise modification gains or losses over the remaining term of the liability, the current carrying value of £97.04 million must stand and a new effective interest rate is derived.

Under this approach the carrying value of the loan at the end of 2016 of £97.04 million, net of the £2 million fees, is treated as a new borrowing of £95.04 million, accounted for as follows, using a newly derived effective interest rate of 6.905%.

Year	Liability b/f	Interest at 6.905%	Cash paid	Liability c/f
	£m	£m	£m	£m
2017	95.04	6.56		101.60
2018	101.60	7.01		108.61
2019	108.61	7.50	(9.00)	107.11
2020	107.11	7.40	(9.00)	105.51
2021	105.51	7.28	(9.00)	103.79
2022	103.79	7.17	(9.00)	101.96
2023	101.96	7.04	(109.00)	–

However, the entity may have selected an accounting policy under which it recognises an immediate gain or loss when the cash flows on a loan are modified and the liability is not derecognised. The application of such an approach in this situation would result in the recognition of a gain of £6.51 million (£97.04 million current carrying value less £90.53 million recalculated net present value, excluding the fees, which as set out at 6.2.1 above adjust the carrying amount of the liability and are amortised over its remaining term). Allocating the fee based upon the effective interest method would result in an increase in the effective interest rate to 8.1213%.

The adjusted carrying amount of the liability £88.53 million (£90.53 million net present value of cash flows on the borrowing less £2 million fee) would be accreted using the effective interest method as follows:

Year	Liability b/f	Interest at 8.1213%	Cash paid	Liability c/f
	£m	£m	£m	£m
2017	88.53	7.19	–	95.72
2018	95.72	7.77	–	103.49
2019	103.49	8.41	(9.00)	102.90
2020	102.90	8.36	(9.00)	102.26
2021	102.26	8.30	(9.00)	101.56
2022	101.56	8.25	(9.00)	100.81
2023	100.81	8.19	(109.00)	–

Example 51.20: Modification of debt treated as extinguishment

Assume the same facts as in Example 51.19 above, except that on 1 January 2017 the entity comes to an arrangement with the lender to modify the terms of the loan as follows.

No cash interest will be paid in 2017 or 2018, although a fee of £2 million must be paid to the lender immediately. From 2019 onwards interest of 12.5% will be paid annually in arrears, and the term of the loan will be extended for three years until 31 December 2024. Legal fees and other costs incurred are not material.

As in Example 51.19 above, the entity is required to compute the net present value of the new arrangement using the original effective interest rate of 7.736%. This gives a net present value for the modified debt of £107.3 million calculated as follows.

Year	Cash flow	£m	Discount factor	£m
1.1.2017	Fee	2.00	1	2.00
2019	Interest	12.50	$1/1.07736^3$	10.00
2020	Interest	12.50	$1/1.07736^4$	9.28
2021	Interest	12.50	$1/1.07736^5$	8.61
2022	Interest	12.50	$1/1.07736^6$	7.99
2023	Interest	12.50	$1/1.07736^7$	7.42
2024	Interest and principal	112.50	$1/1.07736^8$	61.98
			Total	107.28

This represents 110.6% of the current carrying value of the debt as at the end of 2016 of £97.04 million, so that the net present value of the modified loan (discounted at the effective interest rate of the original loan) is 10.6% different from that of the original loan. This is greater than 10%, so that the modification is required to be treated as an extinguishment under IAS 39 and IFRS 9.

This will involve derecognising the existing liability and recognising a new liability. The issue is then at what amount the new liability should be recognised. It is not the £107.28 million above, since this includes the fee of £2 million, which is required to be treated as integral to the cash flows of the modified loan for the purposes of comparing it with the original loan, but is then required to be expensed immediately if the test identifies an extinguishment.

Moreover, as the accounting treatment is intended to represent the derecognition of an existing liability and the recognition of a new one, the modified loan must – in accordance with the initial measurement provisions of IAS 39 and IFRS 9 (see Chapter 48) – be recognised at fair value and amortised using its own effective interest rate, not that applicable to the original loan.

The difficulty is obviously in determining the fair value of the modified loan. If the loan was in the form of a quoted bond, a market value might be available. Another possible approach might be to discount the cash flows of the modified loan at the interest rate at which the entity could have issued a new loan on similar terms to the modified loan. However, where (as may well be the case) the modification is being undertaken because the entity is in serious financial difficulty, it might be that no lender would be prepared to advance new finance, so that there is no readily available 'notional' borrowing rate. Nevertheless, IAS 39 and IFRS 9 contain no exemption from making an estimate of the fair value of the modified loan.

If the view were taken that the fair value of the modified loan was £98 million, the accounting treatment for the modification would be (see also 6.3 below):

	£m	£m
Original loan	97.04	
Loss on extinguishment of debt (income statement)	2.96	
Modified loan		98.00
Cash (fee)		2.00

In this particular case, this has the result that the actual gain or loss recognised is actually somewhat smaller than the difference calculated between the net present value of the original and modified loan that led to the requirement to recognise the gain or loss in the first place. This differential will obviously be reflected in higher interest costs as the transaction matures. If the borrower was in financial difficulties, it is possible for the fair value of the modified loan to be significantly below its principal amount, which could give rise to a large profit on modification followed by very high interest charges over the remaining term.

6.2.4 *Settlement of financial liability with issue of new equity instrument*

A related area is the accounting treatment to be adopted where an entity issues non-convertible debt, but subsequently enters into an agreement with the debt-holder to discharge the liability under the debt in full or in part for an issue of equity instruments. This most often occurs when the entity is in financial difficulties. This topic is now dealt with in IFRIC 19 – *Extinguishing Financial Liabilities with Equity Instruments* – which is discussed in Chapter 45 at 7.

6.3 Gains and losses on extinguishment of debt

When a financial liability (or part of a liability) is extinguished or transferred to another party, IAS 39 and IFRS 9 require the difference between the carrying amount of the transferred financial liability (or part of a liability) and the consideration paid, including any non-cash assets transferred or liabilities assumed, to be recognised in profit or loss. *[IAS 39.41, IFRS 9.3.3.3]*.

If an entity repurchases only a part of a financial liability, it calculates the carrying value of the part disposed of (and hence the gain or loss on disposal) by allocating the previous carrying amount of the financial liability between the part that continues to be recognised and the part that is derecognised based on the relative fair values of those parts on the date of the repurchase. *[IAS 39.42, IFRS 9.3.3.4]*. In other words, the carrying amount of the liability is not simply reduced by consideration received.

This is illustrated in Example 51.21 below.

Example 51.21: Partial derecognition of debt

On 1 January 2014 an entity issues 500 million €1 10-year bonds which are traded in the capital markets. Issue costs of €15 million were incurred and the carrying value of the bonds at 31 December 2017 is €490 million. On 31 December 2017 the entity makes a market purchase of 120 million bonds at their then current market price of €0.97. The entity records the following accounting entry:

	€m	€m
Bonds (120/500 × €490m)	117.6	
Cash (120m × €0.97)		116.4
Gain on repurchase of debt		1.2

In some cases, as discussed in 6.2 above, a creditor may release a debtor from its present obligation to make payments, but the debtor assumes an obligation to pay if the party assuming primary responsibility defaults. In such a case, IAS 39 and IFRS 9 require the debtor to recognise:

(a) a new liability based on the fair value for the obligation for the guarantee; and

(b) a gain or loss based on the difference between:

  (i) any proceeds; and

  (ii) the carrying amount of the original liability (including any related unamortised costs) less the fair value of the new liability. *[IAS 39.AG63, IFRS 9.B3.3.7]*.

6.4 Derivatives that can be financial assets or financial liabilities

Historically, IAS 39 did not address the required treatment for the transfer of a non-optional derivative, such as a swap or forward contract, that by its nature can be either a financial asset or a financial liability at various times during its life. However, in finalising the amendments made to IAS 39 and IFRS 9 that addressed hedge accounting when a hedging instrument is novated to a central counterparty (see 3.4.3 above, Chapter 52 at 4.2.3.A and Chapter 53 at 11.3), the IASB noted that 'a derivative should be derecognised only when it meets both the derecognition criteria for a financial asset and the derecognition criteria for a financial liability in circumstances in which the derivative involves two-way payments between parties, i.e. the payments are or could be from and to each of the parties'. *[IAS 39.BC220B, IFRS 9.BC6.333]*. In practice, any transfer of such derivatives is likely to require the consent of the counterparty to the entity's legal release from its obligations under the contract, and the possible payment of a fee to compensate the counterparty for the difference between the creditworthiness of the entity and that of the transferee. Such procedures are much closer to those envisaged in the derecognition rules for financial liabilities than those implicit in the derecognition rules for financial assets.

On many occasions, the IASB has made it clear that a non-optional derivative that could be either an asset or liability can be derecognised only if the derecognition criteria for both assets and liabilities are satisfied (see 3.3.2 above).

6.5 Supply-chain finance

An increasingly common type of arrangement involves the provision of finance linked to the supply of goods or services. These arrangements, which can vary significantly in both form and substance, are often referred to as 'supply-chain finance', but other terms are also used including 'supplier finance', 'reverse factoring' and 'structured payable transactions'. Whilst the terms of such arrangements can vary widely, they typically contain a number of the following features:

- they involve a purchaser of goods and/or services, a group of its suppliers and a financial intermediary;
- the purchaser is often a large, creditworthy entity that uses a number of suppliers, many of which will have a higher credit risk than the purchaser;
- the arrangement is nearly always initiated by the purchaser rather than the supplier;
- the arrangements operate continuously for all future purchases until the arrangement is cancelled;
- they are often put in place in connection with the purchaser attempting to secure extended payment terms from its suppliers;
- the intermediary/service provider is often a financial institution who will normally make available IT systems to facilitate the arrangement;
- the intermediary makes available to suppliers an optional invoice discounting or factoring facility for invoices accepted or agreed by the purchaser, often on terms that enable the supplier to derecognise the receivable;
- the purchaser will commit to pay the invoice on the due date, sometimes by using a payment facility operated by the intermediary;
- interest terms will be included in the supply agreement to protect the intermediary in the event of the purchaser defaulting or missing the payment date;
- those interest terms will be similar to ones included in most supply agreements, although they are rarely enforced by suppliers;

- the credit risk the intermediary is taking on is that of the purchaser, but it may be able to charge a higher financing cost to the supplier (in the form of the discount) than it would if lending to the supplier directly; and
- it can be difficult to determine the overall financing costs of the arrangement, and who bears those costs, especially if the supply involves items for which the pricing is subjective/unobservable.

The primary accounting concern with these types of arrangement is whether the purchaser should present the resulting financial liability as debt or as a trade or similar payable. This determination could have a significant impact on the purchaser's financial position, particularly its leverage or gearing ratios. However, whilst IFRS does not address the issue directly, a number of standards could be regarded as relevant.

IAS 1 – *Presentation of Financial Statements* – addresses the presentation of the statement of financial position and can certainly be relevant to this determination. IAS 1 requires that entities include line items that present (a) trade and other payables and (b) other financial liabilities. *[IAS 1.54]*. These are considered sufficiently different in nature or function to warrant separate presentation, *[IAS 1.57]* but additional line items should be presented when relevant to an understanding of the entity's financial position, for example depending on the size, nature or function of the item. This may be achieved by disaggregating the two line items noted above. *[IAS 1.55, 57]*. In addition, it may be appropriate to amend the descriptions used and the ordering of items or aggregation of similar items according to the nature of the entity and its transactions. *[IAS 1.57]*.

These requirements provide a framework for determining the structure of an entity's statement of financial position. Liabilities that are clearly financing in nature, for example those arising from bonds, bank borrowings and other loans, are normally presented together and described as debt or another similar term. Conversely, liabilities that are more clearly in the nature of working capital are normally presented within trade and other payables, with further analysis of the component balances within the notes. In this context, IAS 7 might also be considered relevant given an entity is required to classify its cash flows according to whether they arise from operating, financing or investing activities and one would expect broad consistency between the statement of cash flows and the statement of financial position. Therefore the definitions of operating activities and financing activities (see Chapter 38 at 4) might assist an entity in determining the appropriate presentation of liabilities.

The requirements in IAS 39 and IFRS 9 dealing with derecognition of financial liabilities can be relevant in determining the appropriate presentation of liabilities arising from supply-chain financing arrangements. If the arrangement results in derecognition of the original liability (e.g. if the purchaser is legally released from its original obligation to the supplier), an entity will need to determine the appropriate classification of the new liability which may well represent an amount due to the intermediary rather than the supplier. As the intermediary is typically a financial institution, presentation as debt could be more appropriate than as a trade or other payable. Derecognition can also occur and presentation as debt can also be appropriate if the purchaser is not legally released from the original obligation but the terms of the obligation are amended in a way that is considered a substantial modification. Where those revised terms are more consistent with a financing transaction than a trade or other payable, classification of that new liability as debt will be appropriate.

However, even when the arrangement results in derecognition of the original trade payable, there is a view that if there are no significant changes to the payment terms, the new liability is not necessarily in the nature of debt and so presentation as trade or other payables might be appropriate. Conversely, even if the original liability is not derecognised, other factors may indicate that the substance and nature of the arrangements mean that the liability should no longer be presented as a trade payable. Instead the liability would be reclassified and presented as debt (in a similar way to transferred assets that are not derecognised, which IAS 39 and IFRS 9 require to be reclassified within the statement of financial position – see 4.1.1.A above). Circumstances which could result in reclassification include the payment of referral fees or commissions by the intermediary to the purchaser.

In practice, the appropriate presentation of any such arrangement is likely to involve a high degree of judgement in the light of specific facts and circumstances. Whatever the presentation adopted, we believe additional disclosures will often be necessary to explain the nature of the arrangements and the financial reporting judgements made. In fact, the need for clear disclosure of complex supplier arrangements under IFRS is something that has been emphasised by at least one European regulator[24] and the SEC has, in the past, highlighted the presentation of these arrangements under US GAAP as an area of focus. Therefore, it is quite possible this topic will become the focus of wider regulatory scrutiny in the future, and perhaps also be subject to consideration by the IFRS Interpretations Committee.

7 FUTURE DEVELOPMENTS

The IASB's *Conceptual Framework for Financial Reporting* is discussed in Chapter 2 but currently does not address derecognition in any meaningful way. However, in May 2015, the IASB issued an exposure draft proposing a revised version which would contain a new chapter addressing both recognition and derecognition of assets and liabilities. The exposure draft proposes that accounting requirements for derecognition should aim to represent faithfully both:[25]

(a) the assets and liabilities retained after the transaction or other event that led to the derecognition (including any asset or liability acquired, incurred or created as part of the transaction or other event); and

(b) the change in the entity's assets and liabilities as a result of that transaction or other event

and goes on to explain that those aims are normally achieved by:[26]

- derecognising any assets or liabilities that have been transferred, consumed, collected or fulfilled, or have expired and recognising any resulting income or expense; and
- continuing to recognise the assets or liabilities retained, if any (the retained component), which become a separate unit of account. Accordingly, no income or expenses are recognised on the retained component as a result of the derecognition of the transferred component.

The exposure draft explains that if an entity transfers a previously recognised asset (or liability) to another party that is acting as its agent the asset is still controlled by the transferor (the liability is still an obligation of the transferor) and derecognition would not faithfully represent the transferor's assets, liabilities, income and expenses.[27] Further, if an entity retains exposure to positive or negative variations in the amount of economic benefits produced by an economic resource, this may indicate that the entity retains control of that economic resource, in which case derecognition is not appropriate.[28] However, the IASB has not advocated a 'control' approach in all circumstances, nor does it advocate a 'risks and rewards' approach. Instead, it notes that the aim set out in (a) above is more consistent with a control approach and the aim set out in (b) more consistent with a risks and rewards approach.[29]

The IASB acknowledges it will sometimes be difficult to achieve both of the aims set out above. This might be the case if, for example, the transferor of an asset retains a disproportionate exposure to variations in the asset's economic benefits or if it must or may repurchase the asset. In these circumstances, derecognition may not faithfully represent the extent of changes in the entity's assets and liabilities and might in fact misrepresent the entity's financial position.[30] In some such situations derecognition might meet the aims set out above if supported by separate presentation or explanatory disclosure in the notes to the financial statements, but in others there may be a need to continue recognising the transferred component as well as the retained component, perhaps separately presented or with explanatory disclosure.[31]

The exposure draft also addresses the modification of contracts, which will include those giving rise to financial assets and financial liabilities. The proposals note that modifications normally do one or both of the following:[32]

- reduce or eliminate existing rights and obligations (for which the discussions above are relevant in deciding whether to derecognise those rights or obligations); and
- add new rights or new obligations.

For rights and obligations created by a modification that are distinct from those created by the original terms of the contract, it may be appropriate to treat the additions as new assets or liabilities.[33] However, if they are not distinct it may be appropriate to treat the new rights and obligations as part of the same unit of account as the existing rights and obligations.[34] Furthermore, some modifications both reduce or eliminate existing rights and obligations and add new rights and obligations. The combined effects of such changes would be considered in order to provide the most relevant information in the way that most faithfully represents their effect.[35]

The proposed recognition and derecognition chapter does not address whether partial derecognition (where the transferred component is derecognised and the retained component continues to be recognised) or full derecognition (where the entire asset or liability is derecognised and any retained component is recognised as a new asset or liability) should be used. This question is seen as more closely linked to how the 'unit of account' is determined and how the measurement basis for the retained component is selected, topics addressed elsewhere in the exposure draft.[36]

At the time of writing the IASB was aiming to finalise its work on the conceptual framework in 2017. Whilst it had not made any decisions about the concepts dealing with derecognition, the IASB was planning to consider them later in 2016. Even if the proposals are finalised in something like their current form, it seems unlikely the IASB would make any changes to the related requirements in IAS 39 or IFRS 9 in the short- or medium-term. However, the concepts being introduced could potentially influence the way in which entities develop their accounting policies when dealing with situations for which the requirements in the standards are not clear.

References

1 *IFRIC Update*, January 2007.
2 *IFRIC Update*, May 2006.
3 *IASB Update*, September 2006.
4 *IASB Update*, September 2006.
5 Staff Paper (May 2012 Interpretations Committee Meeting), *IAS 39 Financial Instruments: Recognition and Measurement – Derecognition of financial assets (Agenda reference 10-B)*, IASB, May 2012, paras. 8 to 10.
6 *IFRIC Update*, May 2016.
7 Staff Paper (May 2012 Interpretations Committee Meeting), *IAS 39 Financial Instruments: Recognition and Measurement – Derecognition of financial assets (Agenda reference 10-A)*, IASB, May 2012, paras. 32 to 36.
8 Staff Paper (May 2012 Interpretations Committee Meeting), *IAS 39 Financial Instruments: Recognition and Measurement – Derecognition of financial assets (Agenda reference 10-A)*, IASB, May 2012, paras. 37 to 42.
9 *IFRIC Update*, September 2012.
10 For example, *The IFRS Interpretations Committee's tentative agenda decision on IAS 39 Financial Instruments: Recognition and Measurement – Accounting for different aspects of restructuring Greek government bonds*, ESMA, July 2012 and *Final Comment Letter on the IFRS Interpretations Committee tentative rejection notice in relation to the restructuring of Greek government bonds*, EFRAG, August 2012.
11 *IFRIC Update*, September 2012.
12 *Information for Observers*, IFRIC, March 2006.
13 *IFRIC Update*, November 2005.
14 *IASB Update*, September 2006.
15 *Information for Observers*, IFRIC, March 2006.
16 *IASB Update*, September 2006.
17 *IASB Update*, September 2006.
18 *IFRIC Update*, November 2005.
19 In practice, other factors might be relevant to the valuation.
20 The fair value of an in the money option is positive for the buyer and negative for the writer.
21 *IFRIC Update*, May 2016.
22 IGC Q&A 62-1.
23 Staff Paper (July 2016 Interpretations Committee Meeting), *IFRS Interpretations Committee Work in Progress (Agenda reference 8)*, IASB, July 2016, para. 4.
24 Press Release 74/14, *FRC urges clarity in the reporting of complex supplier arrangements by retailers and other businesses*, FRC, December 2014.
25 Exposure Draft ED/2015/3, *Conceptual Framework for Financial Reporting*, IASB, May 2015, para. 5.26.
26 Exposure Draft ED/2015/3, *Conceptual Framework for Financial Reporting*, IASB, May 2015, para. 5.27.
27 Exposure Draft ED/2015/3, *Conceptual Framework for Financial Reporting*, IASB, May 2015, para. 5.28.
28 Exposure Draft ED/2015/3, *Conceptual Framework for Financial Reporting*, IASB, May 2015, para. 5.29.
29 Exposure Draft ED/2015/3, *Conceptual Framework for Financial Reporting*, IASB, May 2015, para. BC5.57.
30 Exposure Draft ED/2015/3, *Conceptual Framework for Financial Reporting*, IASB, May 2015, para. 5.30.
31 Exposure Draft ED/2015/3, *Conceptual Framework for Financial Reporting*, IASB, May 2015, paras. 5.31 and 5.32.

32 Exposure Draft ED/2015/3, *Conceptual Framework for Financial Reporting,* IASB, May 2015, para. 5.33.
33 Exposure Draft ED/2015/3, *Conceptual Framework for Financial Reporting,* IASB, May 2015, para. 5.34.
34 Exposure Draft ED/2015/3, *Conceptual Framework for Financial Reporting,* IASB, May 2015, para. 5.35.
35 Exposure Draft ED/2015/3, *Conceptual Framework for Financial Reporting,* IASB, May 2015, para. 5.36.
36 Exposure Draft ED/2015/3, *Conceptual Framework for Financial Reporting,* IASB, May 2015, para. BC5.58.

Chapter 52 Financial instruments: Hedge accounting (IAS 39)

Chapter 52

List of examples

Chapter 52 Financial instruments: Hedge accounting (IAS 39)

1 INTRODUCTION

1.1 Background

Chapter 42 provides a general background to the development of accounting for financial instruments and notes the fundamental changes that have been experienced in international financial markets. The markets for derivatives, especially, have seen remarkable and continued growth over the past two to three decades. This reflects the increasing use of such instruments by businesses, commonly to 'hedge' their financial risks. Accordingly, the accounting treatment for derivatives and hedging activities has taken on a high degree of importance. Historically, however, the accounting guidance has struggled to keep up with business practices and, at best, issues were dealt with very much on a piecemeal basis. Therefore, until the development of standards such as IAS 39 – *Financial Instruments: Recognition and Measurement*, entities were left largely to their own devices in developing accounting policies for hedges so that their financial statements reflected the objectives for entering into such transactions.

'Hedging' itself is a much wider topic than hedge accounting and is *not* the primary subject of this chapter. It is an imprecise term although standard setters frequently describe hedging in terms of designating a hedging instrument that has a value that is expected, wholly or partly, to offset changes in the value or cash flows of a 'hedged position'.[1] In this context, hedged positions normally include those arising from recognised assets and liabilities, contractual commitments and expected, but uncontracted, future transactions. Whilst this may be an appropriate description for many hedges, it does not necessarily capture the essence of all risk management activities involving financial instruments. Nevertheless, it forms the basis for the hedge accounting requirements under IFRS.

1.2 What is hedge accounting?

Hedge accounting is often seen as 'correcting' deficiencies in the accounting requirements that would otherwise apply to each leg of the hedge relationship. These deficiencies are an inevitable consequence of using a mixed-measurement model of accounting. Typically, hedge accounting involves recognising gains and losses on a hedging instrument in the same period(s) and/or in the same place in the financial statements as gains or losses on the hedged position. It may be used in a number of situations, for example to adjust (or correct) for:

- *Measurement differences*

  These might arise where the hedge is of a recognised asset or liability that is measured on a different basis to the hedging instrument. An example might be inventory that is recorded in the financial statements at cost, but whose value is hedged by a forward contract that enables inventory of the same nature to be sold at a predetermined price. In this case, both the hedging instrument and the hedged position exist and are recognised in the financial statements, but they are likely to be measured on different bases.

  Avoiding the measurement difference could in this situation theoretically be achieved in a number of ways. One alternative would be not to recognise unrealised gains or losses on the forward contract, and realised gains or losses could be deferred (e.g. separately as assets or liabilities or by including them within the carrying amount of the inventory) until the inventory is sold. On the other hand, if unrealised gains or losses on the forward contract were recognised in profit or loss, the measurement basis of the inventory could be changed to reflect changes in its fair value in profit or loss.

- *Performance reporting differences*

  Even if the measurement bases of the hedging instrument and hedged item are the same, performance reporting differences might arise if gains and losses are reported in a different place in the financial statements. An example might be where an investment in shares is classified as available-for-sale (see Chapter 46 at 5) and whose value is hedged by a put option. The investment and the put option are both measured at fair value. However, gains or losses on the investment are recognised in other comprehensive income whilst those on the put option are recognised in profit or loss, therefore resulting in a mismatch in the income statement (or statement of comprehensive income). Similarly, gains or losses on retranslating the net assets of a foreign operation are recorded in other comprehensive income whilst retranslation gains or losses on a borrowing used to hedge that net investment are, absent any form of hedge accounting, recorded in profit or loss.

  In the case of the inventory and the forward contract, hedge accounting might involve reporting gains and losses on the inventory in profit or loss, or gains and losses on the forward contract in other comprehensive income. For the foreign operation, hedge accounting normally involves reporting the retranslation gains and losses on both the borrowing and the foreign operation in other comprehensive income.

- *Recognition differences*

  These might arise where the hedge is of contractual rights or obligations that are not recognised in the financial statements. An example is a foreign currency denominated operating lease where the unrecognised contractual commitment to pay lease rentals in another currency is hedged by a series of forward currency contracts (i.e. each payment is effectively 'fixed' in functional currency terms). In this case, one solution might be to treat the lease as a 'synthetic' functional currency denominated lease. A similar outcome would be obtained if unrealised gains and losses on each forward contract remained unrecognised until the accrual of the lease payment it was hedging.

- *Existence differences*

  These might arise where the hedge is of cash flows arising from an uncontracted future transaction, i.e. a transaction that does not yet exist. An example is a foreign currency denominated sale expected next year that is hedged by a forward currency contract.

  Again, a solution to this issue might involve treating the future sale as a 'synthetic' functional currency sale or it might involve deferring the gain or loss on the forward contract until the sale is recognised in profit or loss.

1.3 Development of hedge accounting standards

The first comprehensive hedge accounting requirements issued by the IASB were contained in IAS 39. This standard was published in 1999 (see Chapter 42 at 1.2), and since then has been subject to numerous amendments.

In November 2013, as part of its project to replace IAS 39, the IASB published amendments to IFRS 9 – *Financial Instruments* – including revised requirements for hedge accounting. IFRS 9 is effective for periods beginning on or after 1 January 2018 and will replace substantially all of IAS 39, including the hedge accounting requirements. However, IFRS 9 allows entities an accounting policy choice to continue applying the hedge accounting requirements of IAS 39 instead of those in IFRS 9. *[IFRS 9.7.2.21]*. The hedge accounting requirements of IFRS 9 are discussed in Chapter 53.

IFRS 9 does not provide any particular solutions specifically tailored to so-called 'macro hedge' accounting, the term used to describe the more complex risk management practices used by entities such as banks. In May 2012 the Board decided to decouple accounting for macro hedging from IFRS 9, and a separate project was set up to develop an accounting solution for dynamic risk management. In consideration of this fact, for a fair value hedge of the interest rate exposure of a portfolio of financial assets or financial liabilities (and only for such a hedge), an entity may apply the hedge accounting requirements in IAS 39 instead of those in IFRS 9. This choice relates only to a fair value portfolio hedge as described in IAS 39 81A, 89A and AG114-AG132 of IAS 39. A decision to continue to apply this IAS 39 guidance is not part of the accounting policy choice to defer IAS 39 mention above.

In April 2014, the IASB issued the Discussion Paper – *Accounting for Dynamic Risk Management: a Portfolio Revaluation Approach to Macro Hedging.* The six-month comment period ended in October 2014. Most respondents supported the need for the project, but there was no consensus on a solution. In July 2016 the IASB decided that the project should remain in the research phase, with the aim of publishing a second discussion paper (see 6 below).

2 HEDGING INSTRUMENTS AND HEDGED ITEMS

In the terminology of IAS 39, the two main ingredients of a hedge are the hedging instrument and the hedged item. The definition of these and related terms are as follows:

- *Hedging instrument:* a designated derivative or (for a hedge of the risk of changes in foreign currency exchange rates only) a designated non-derivative financial asset or non-derivative financial liability whose fair value or cash flows are expected to offset changes in the fair value or cash flows of a designated hedged item.
- *Hedged item:* an asset, liability, firm commitment, highly probable forecast transaction or net investment in a foreign operation that (a) exposes the entity to risk of changes in fair value or future cash flows and (b) is designated as being hedged.
- *Firm commitment:* a binding agreement for the exchange of a specified quantity of resources at a specified price on a specified future date or dates.

  In addition to simple agreements to purchase a given quantity of units on a given date for a given amount of money, other arrangements may also be firm commitments, for example construction contracts under which payments are made periodically based on documented progress or achievement of milestones.
- *Forecast transaction:* an uncommitted but anticipated future transaction. *[IAS 39.9]*.

2.1 Hedging instruments

There are a number of restrictions on what type of item may be used as the hedging instrument in a 'valid' hedge, i.e. one that can qualify for hedge accounting, and these operate on many levels as set out below. One of these restrictions stems from the definition of a hedging instrument and requires an entity to have an expectation that its fair value or cash flows will offset changes in the fair value or cash flows of the hedged item attributable to the hedged risk. This requirement principally manifests itself in the provisions on hedge effectiveness, which are dealt with at 5.3 below. Hedging instruments must also involve a party that is external to the reporting group. *[IAS 39.73]*. More detail is provided on this point at 2.3 below.

2.1.1 Derivative financial instruments

The distinction between derivative and non-derivative financial instruments is covered in Chapter 44. With the exception of certain written options (see 2.1.1.A below), the circumstances in which a derivative may be designated as a hedging instrument are not restricted, provided the conditions for hedge accounting set out at 5 below are met. *[IAS 39.72]*. Those conditions mean that a derivative that is not carried at fair value, because it is linked to and must be settled by delivery of an unquoted equity instrument whose fair value cannot be reliably measured (see Chapter 49 at 2.6), cannot be designated as a hedging instrument. *[IAS 39.AG96]*.

In order to be able to qualify as a hedging instrument, the derivative must be accounted for as such under IAS 39. Therefore, an embedded derivative that is accounted for separately from its host contract (see Chapter 44 at 4) can be used as a hedging instrument. However, a contract that is considered a normal sale or purchase, and is therefore accounted for as an executory contract, cannot (see Chapter 43 at 4). *[IAS 39.F.1.2]*.

Example 52.1: Hedging with a sales commitment

Company J has the Japanese yen as its functional currency. J has issued a fixed-rate debt instrument with semi-annual interest payments that matures in two years with principal due at maturity of US$5 million. It has also entered into a fixed price sales commitment for US$5 million that matures in two years and is not accounted for as a derivative because it qualifies for the normal sales exemption.

Because the sales commitment is accounted for as a firm commitment rather than a derivative instrument it cannot be a hedging instrument in a hedge of the foreign currency risk associated with the debt instrument. However, if the foreign currency component of the sales commitment was required to be separated as an embedded derivative (essentially a forward contract to buy US dollars for yen) that component could be designated as the hedging instrument in such a hedge. *[IAS 39.F.1.2]*.

Similarly, a forecast transaction or planned future transaction cannot be the hedging instrument as it is not a recognised financial instrument, *[IAS 39.AG35(e), F.1.6]*, and is therefore not a derivative.

2.1.1.A Options and collars

It is explained in IAS 39 that an option an entity writes is not effective in reducing the profit or loss exposure of a hedged item. In other words, the potential loss on a written option could be significantly greater than the potential gain in value of a related hedged item. Therefore, a written option is prohibited from qualifying as a hedging instrument unless it is designated as an offset to a purchased option, including one that is embedded in another financial instrument. An example of this might be a written call option that is used to hedge a callable liability. In contrast, a purchased option has potential gains equal to or greater than losses and therefore has the potential to reduce profit or loss exposure from changes in fair values or cash flows. Accordingly, a purchased option can qualify as a hedging instrument. *[IAS 39.AG94]*.

It follows that a derivative such as an interest rate collar that includes a written option cannot be designated as a hedging instrument if it is a net written option. *[IAS 39.77]*. However, a derivative instrument that includes a written option may be designated as a hedging instrument if it is a net purchased option or zero cost collar. *[IAS 39.F.1.3(a)]*.

The following factors, taken together, indicate that an instrument is not a net written option:

- no net premium is received, either at inception or over the life of the instrument – the distinguishing feature of a written option is the receipt of a premium to compensate for the risk incurred;
- except for the strike prices, the critical terms and conditions of the written and purchased option components are the same, including underlying variable(s), currency denomination and maturity date; and
- the notional amount of the written option component is not greater than that of the purchased option component. *[IAS 39.F.1.3(b)]*.

The application of these requirements is illustrated in the following two examples.

Example 52.2: Foreign currency collar (or 'cylinder option')

Company E, which has sterling as its functional currency, has forecast that it is highly probable it will receive €1,000 in six months' time in respect of an expected sale to a customer in France.

E is concerned that sterling might have appreciated by the time the payment is received and wishes to protect the profit margin on the sale without paying the premium that would be required with an ordinary currency option. E also wishes to benefit from some of the upside in the event that sterling depreciates, so would prefer not to use a forward contract.

Accordingly, E enters into an instrument under which it effectively:

- purchases an option that allows it to buy sterling for €1,000 from the counterparty at €1.53:£1.00; and
- sells an option that allows the counterparty to sell sterling to E for €1,000 at €1.47:£1.00.

In the foreign currency markets, such an instrument is often called a 'cylinder option' rather than a 'collar' and it operates as follows. If, in six months' time, the spot exchange rate exceeds €1.53:£1.00, E will exercise its option to sell €1,000 at €1.53:£1.00, effectively fixing its minimum proceeds on the sale (in sterling terms) at £654. Similarly, if the rate is below €1.47:£1.00, the counterparty will exercise its option to buy €1,000 at €1.47:£1.00, effectively capping E's maximum proceeds on the sale at £680. If the rate is between €1.47:£1.00 and €1.53:£1.00, both options will lapse unexercised and E will be able to sell its €1,000 for sterling at the spot rate, generating between £654 and £680.

The premium that E would pay to acquire the purchased option equals the premium it would receive to sell the written option and therefore no premium is paid or received on inception. The critical terms and conditions, including the notional amounts, of the written and purchased option components are the same except for the strike price. Therefore, E concludes that the instrument is not a net written option and, consequently, it may be used as the hedging instrument in a hedge of the foreign currency risk associated with the future sale.

It is possible that the counterparty might, instead, have offered E a variation on the instrument described above. If the notional amount on E's purchased option component had been reduced, say to €500, the counterparty could have offered a better rate on that component, say €1.51. However, in this case, the notional amount on the written option component is twice that of the purchased option component and the instrument would be seen as a net written option. Accordingly, even if E had very good business reasons for using such an instrument to manage its foreign exchange risk, it could not qualify as a hedging instrument under IAS 39. Therefore, hedge accounting would be precluded.

Example 52.3: 'Knock-out' swap

Company Y has a significant amount of long-dated floating rate borrowings. In order to hedge the cash flow interest rate risk arising from these borrowings, Y has entered into a number of matching pay-fixed, receive-floating interest rate swaps that effectively convert the interest rates on the borrowings to fixed-rate.

Under the terms of one of these swaps, on each fifth anniversary of its inception until maturity the swap counterparty may choose to simply terminate the swap at no cost. This is often referred to as a knock-out feature. In return for agreeing to this, Y benefits by paying a lower interest rate on the fixed leg of the swap than it would on a conventional swap. In other words, Y receives a premium for taking on the risk of the counterparty cancelling the swap.

This instrument contains a net written option, i.e. the knock-out feature, and therefore cannot be used as a hedging instrument unless it is used in a hedge of an equivalent purchased option. (In practice, it is unlikely that the hedged borrowings will contain such an option feature.)

2.1.1.B Credit break clauses

It is not uncommon for certain derivatives (e.g. long-term interest rate swaps) to contain terms that allow the counterparties to settle the instrument at a so-called 'fair value' in certain circumstances. The 'fair value' is usually not a true fair value as it excludes changes in credit risk. Such terms, often called 'credit break clauses', enable the counterparties to manage their credit risk in markets where collateral or margin accounts and master netting agreements are not used. They are particularly common where a long-duration derivative is transacted between a financial and non-financial institution. For example, the terms of a twenty-year interest rate swap may allow either party to settle the instrument at fair value on the fifth, tenth and fifteenth anniversary of its inception.

These terms can be seen as options on counterparty credit risk. However, provided the two parties have equivalent rights to settle the instrument at 'fair value', the credit break clause will generally not prevent the derivative from qualifying as a hedging instrument. Particularly, in assessing whether a premium is received for agreeing to the incorporation of such terms into an instrument, care needs to be exercised. For example, marginally better underlying terms offered by one potential counterparty (as a result of market imperfections) should not be mistaken for a very small option premium.

2.1.2 Cash instruments

In contrast to the position for derivatives, there are significant restrictions over the use as hedging instruments of non-derivative financial assets and liabilities, or 'cash instruments' as the IASB sometimes refer to them. *[IAS 39.BC144]*. Essentially, a cash instrument may be designated as a hedging instrument only for a hedge of foreign currency risk. *[IAS 39.72]*.

This would allow, say, a held-to-maturity investment carried at amortised cost to be designated as a hedging instrument in a hedge of foreign currency risk, *[IAS 39.AG95]*, as well as other instruments such as loans and receivables, available for sale debt instruments and borrowings. However, an investment in an unquoted equity instrument that is not carried at fair value because its fair value cannot be reliably measured (see Chapter 49 at 2.6), cannot be designated as a hedging instrument. *[IAS 39.AG96]*.

The following two examples illustrate the types of permitted hedge relationships where the hedging instrument is a non-derivative.

Example 52.4: Hedging with a non-derivative liability

In Example 52.1 above, Company J had issued a fixed rate debt instrument with principal due at maturity in two years of US$5 million. J had also entered into a fixed price sales commitment, accounted for as an executory contract, for US$5 million that matured in two years as well.

J could not designate the debt instrument as a hedge of the exposure to *all* fair value changes of the fixed price sales commitment because the hedging instrument is a non-derivative (and it would not be a good economic hedge anyway). However, J could designate the fixed rate debt instrument as a hedge of the foreign currency exposure associated with the future receipt of US dollars on the fixed price sales commitment. *[IAS 39.F.1.2]*.

Example 52.5: Hedge of foreign currency bond

Company J has also issued US$5 million five year fixed rate debt and owns a US$5 million five year fixed rate bond, which is classified as available for sale.

J's bond has exposure to changes in both foreign currency and interest rates, as does the liability. However, the liability can only be designated as a hedge of the bond's foreign currency, not interest rate, risk because it is a non-derivative instrument.

In Example 52.5 above, hedge accounting is unnecessary because the amortised cost of the hedging instrument and the hedged item are both remeasured using closing rates with differences recognised in profit or loss as required by IAS 21 – *The Effects of Changes in Foreign Exchange Rates*. *[IAS 39.F.1.1]*.

In principle, there is no reason why a non-derivative financial instrument cannot be a hedging instrument in one hedge (of foreign currency risk) and a hedged item in another hedge (for example in a hedge of interest rate risk).

In developing the hedge accounting requirements for inclusion in IFRS 9 the IASB has decided that a non-derivative financial asset or financial liability measured at fair value through profit or loss may qualify as a hedging instrument, including for risks other than foreign currency risk, provided it is not a financial liability designated as at fair value through profit or loss with changes in its credit risk recognised in other comprehensive income (see Chapter 53 at 4.2). *[IFRS 9.6.2.2, BC6.140-141]*.

2.1.3 Combinations of instruments

Two or more derivatives, or proportions of them (see 2.1.4 below) may be viewed in combination and jointly designated as a hedging instrument. This is the case even when the risk(s) arising from some derivatives offset(s) those arising from others. However, two or more instruments (or proportions of them) may be designated as a hedging instrument only if *none of them* is a written option or a net written option. *[IAS 39.77]*. Although this restriction on individual net written options does not appear in IFRS 9 (see Chapter 53 at 4.1), there is still a requirement that any combination can only be designated as a hedged item if the combination is not a net written option.

In practice, many zero cost collars are transacted as legally separate written and purchased options. On the face of it, therefore, such transactions cannot be treated as a combined hedging instrument, even if the combination is not a net written option. However, we are not at all convinced the IASB intended such a prohibition to take effect in practice. This is especially the case if the reason the collar takes the legal form of two options is for the seller's administrative ease, which would in many cases be irrelevant to the entity purchasing the collar. In fact, if it can be demonstrated that the only substantive business purpose for entering into such an arrangement is to purchase a zero cost collar to hedge an underlying exposure, the logic in some of the implementation guidance would *require* these contracts to be treated as a single instrument for this purpose (see 2.3.3 below and Chapter 44 at 3.2). We therefore believe that a combination of two or more derivatives, having the same critical terms, but including a derivative that on its own is a written (or net written) option, can be designated as a hedging instrument if they meet the following criteria:

- for accounting purposes, those options are parts of a single financial instrument and not different financial instruments (see below); and
- the combined instrument does not meet the definition of a net written option. (see 2.1.1.A above)

Whether a combination of options constitutes a single financial instrument or separate financial instruments for accounting purposes is a matter of judgement that depends on the circumstances of the transactions from which they arise. Indicators that in substance there is only a single financial instrument that is treated as such for accounting purposes include: *[IAS 39.B.6]*

- the options are entered into at the same time and in contemplation of one another;
- the options have the same counterparty;
- the options relate to the same risk;
- there is no apparent economic need or substantive business purpose for structuring the transactions separately that could not also have been accomplished in a single transaction.

When documenting the hedging relationship it is important that the formal designation reflects the consideration that the hedging instrument is a single financial instrument.

In the case of a hedge of foreign currency risk, the standard also allows two or more non-derivatives, or proportions of them, to be viewed in combination and designated as a hedging instrument. Further, a combination of derivatives and non-derivatives, or proportions of them, may be similarly combined. *[IAS 39.77]*.

Unlike for combinations of derivatives, the standard does not clarify whether it is acceptable for these combinations to contain offsetting terms although in the absence of an indication to the contrary we believe it is.

For example, an entity with the euro as its functional currency may have issued a yen denominated floating rate borrowing and entered into a matching receive-yen floating (plus principal at maturity), pay-US dollar floating (plus principal at maturity) cross-currency interest rate swap. These instruments, which effectively synthesise a US dollar floating rate borrowing, contain offsetting terms, i.e. the whole of the borrowing and the yen leg of the swap. The entity could designate the combination of these two instruments in a hedge of the entity's foreign currency risk arising from, say, an asset with an identifiable exposure to US dollar exchange rates.

2.1.4 Portions and proportions of hedging instruments

In contrast to the position for hedged financial items (see 2.2.1 below), there are significant restrictions on what components of an individual financial instrument can be carved out and designated as a hedging instrument. It is explained that there is normally a single fair value measure for a hedging instrument in its entirety and the factors that cause changes in its fair value are co-dependent. Normally, therefore, a financial instrument (or proportion thereof – see 2.1.4.C below) can only be designated as a hedging instrument in its entirety. *[IAS 39.74]*.

Example 52.6: Combination of written and purchased options

Company Y transacts a combination of a written option and purchased option (such as an interest rate collar) as a single instrument with one counterparty. Y cannot split the derivative instrument into its written and purchased option components and designate just the purchased option component as a hedging instrument. *[IAS 39.F.1.8]*.

Similarly, the 'knock-out swap' in Example 52.3 above could not be split into a conventional interest rate swap, to be used as a hedging instrument, and the knock-out feature (a written swaption, i.e. an option for the counterparty to enter into an offsetting interest rate swap with the same terms as the conventional swap).

However, there are a number of exceptions to this general rule:

- the time value of options may be separated (see 2.1.4.A below);
- interest elements of forwards may be separated (see 2.1.4.B below);
- a proportion only of a hedging instrument may be designated in a hedging relationship (see 2.1.4.C below);
- the spot rate retranslation risk of a foreign currency cash instrument may be separated (see 2.1.4.D below); and
- a derivative may be separated into notional component parts when each part is designated as a hedge and qualifies for hedge accounting (see 2.1.4.E below).

IFRS 9 retains most of those exceptions. Further, IFRS 9 introduces the concept of costs of hedging to account for the time value of options and the interest element of forward contracts, should an entity chose to separate those elements from the hedged designation. Applying costs of hedging can further reduce volatility in profit or loss (see Chapter 53 at 4.5 and 7).

2.1.4.A Time value of options

IAS 39 permits an entity to separate the intrinsic value and time value of an option contract and designate as the hedging instrument only the change in intrinsic value of the option and exclude changes in its time value. This is permitted because, as the standard explains, the intrinsic value of the option can generally be measured separately. *[IAS 39.74]*. However, this explanation is slightly hollow as the same would apply to the type of instrument discussed in Example 52.6 above.

An entity may choose to designate the variability of future cash flow outcomes resulting from a price increase (but not a decrease) of a forecast commodity purchase. In such a situation, only cash flow losses that result from an increase in the price above the specified level are designated. However, only the intrinsic value of a purchased option, not its time value, reflects this one-sided risk in the hedged item (assuming that it has the same principal terms as the designated risk). The hedged risk of, say, a forecast transaction does not have features similar to the time value of a purchased option because that is not a component of the forecast transaction that affects profit or loss (see 5.3.10 below). *[IAS 39.AG99BA]*.

Excluding the time value may make it administratively easier to process the hedges and it can certainly improve a hedge's effectiveness from an accounting perspective. However, even though separated from the hedging relationship, the changes in the fair value of time value over the term of the hedge still affect profit or loss.

The use of this exception is not mandatory. For example, a dynamic hedging strategy that assesses both the intrinsic value and time value of an option contract can qualify for hedge accounting (see 5.1.2 below), *[IAS 39.74]*, although the time value is likely to result in some ineffectiveness.

In some cases, an entity may use an option to hedge an exposure that itself contains optionality. Section 5.3.11 below covers the challenges that arise with such a designation.

2.1.4.B *Interest elements of forwards*

IAS 39 also permits (but does not require) an entity to separate the interest element and spot price of a forward contract because the premium on the forward can generally (like the time value of an option) be measured separately. *[IAS 39.74]*.

Excluding this portion may be consistent with the entity's overall hedging strategy, such as where the interest element of forward contracts are managed with the rest of the entity's interest rate exposures rather than in conjunction with the associated spot rate exposures. Similar to the treatment of the time value of an option, if the interest element of a forward contract is excluded from the hedge relationship, changes in the fair value of that element will continue to impact profit or loss (see 5.3.3 below).

2.1.4.C *Proportions of instruments*

In addition to the above exceptions, a proportion of the entire hedging instrument, such as 50% of the notional amount, may also be designated in a hedging relationship. However, a hedging relationship may not be designated for only a portion of the time period in which the hedging instrument is outstanding. *[IAS 39.75]*.

A literal reading of the second sentence in paragraph 75 might suggest that a hedge relationship may not be designated for a shorter period of time than the period for which the hedging instrument can remain outstanding. For example, if an interest rate swap has a remaining maturity of five years, then it might be concluded this could not be a hedging instrument in a hedge relationship that would only last four years. However, we do not believe that this is the intended meaning of the guidance. We believe that there is no restriction on the period of the hedge relationship itself, but only a restriction on what can be used as the hedging instrument. For example, in the case of the interest rate swap above, the payments and receipts over the next four years (i.e. ignoring those in year five) could not be designated as the hedging instrument. Instead, the whole derivative (i.e. including payments and receipts in year five) must be designated as the hedging instrument, although the hedging relationship may itself last for only four years. However, hedge accounting can only be applied if the hedge is determined to be effective (see 5.3 below), which may be difficult where there are significant mismatches in maturity between the hedged item and the hedging instrument.

2.1.4.D *Cash instruments*

There is one further situation where a portion of an instrument may be designated as a hedging instrument (in fact, is required to be). In the case of a cash instrument used as a hedge of foreign currency risk, it is essentially only the spot rate retranslation risk of, say, a borrowing that is used as the hedging instrument and not the other components, such as its changes in fair value arising from interest rate risk. *[IAS 39.89(a), IG.F.1.1]*.

2.1.4.E Notional decomposition

We also believe it is acceptable in certain circumstances to split a derivative (or allowable portion thereof – see 2.1.4.A to 2.1.4.C above) into component parts provided all of those components are designated and qualify for hedge accounting. For example a 'functional currency leg' could be introduced into a derivative that is denominated in two currencies (such as a forward contract or cross-currency interest rate swap) and the components designated separately in more than one hedging relation. In fact, the implementation guidance effectively contains examples of just such an approach (see Examples 52.7 and 52.8 and 2.1.6 below for further details) and the IFRS Interpretations Committee has confirmed that it considers such an approach to be acceptable.[2]

2.1.4.F Restructuring of derivatives

An entity may exchange a derivative that does not qualify as a hedging instrument (say, the knock-out swap in Example 52.3 above) for two separate derivatives that, together, have the same fair value as the original instrument (say, a conventional interest rate swap and a written swaption). Such an exchange is likely to be motivated by a desire to obtain hedge accounting for one of these new instruments.

In order to determine whether the new arrangement can be treated as two separate derivatives, rather than a continuation of the original derivative, we believe it is necessary to determine whether the exchange transaction has any substance, which is clearly a matter of judgement. If the exchange has no substance then hedge accounting would still be precluded as the two 'separate' derivatives would in substance be a continuation of the original derivative (see 2.3.3 below and Chapter 44 at 3.2).

In the case of the knock-out swap, if the two new contracts had the same counterparty and, in aggregate, the same terms as the original contract this would not necessarily lead to the conclusion that the exchange lacked substance. However if, in addition, the swaption would be settled by delivery of the conventional interest rate swap in the event that it was exercised, this is a strong indicator that the exchange does lack substance.

2.1.5 Reduction of risk

The implementation guidance explains that risk exposures should be assessed on a transaction basis and, therefore, a hedging instrument need not reduce risk at an entity-wide level. For example, if an entity has a fixed rate asset and a fixed rate liability, each with the same principal terms, it may enter into a pay-fixed, receive-variable interest rate swap to hedge the fair value of the asset even though the effect of the swap is to create an interest rate exposure for the entity that previously did not exist. *[IAS 39.F.2.6]*. However, such a hedge designation would of course only make sense when the hedge is offsetting an economic risk. For example, in the situation described above, the hedge designation might only be a proxy for a hedge of a cash flow risk that does not qualify for hedge accounting.

The IASB discussed the concept of proxy hedging as part of the deliberations on the IFRS 9 hedge accounting guidance and decided that proxy hedging is permitted, provided the designation is directionally consistent with the actual risk management activities (see Chapter 53 at 5.5).

A derivative which does not reduce risk at the transaction level cannot be a hedging instrument. Consider a 'basis swap' that effectively converts one variable interest rate index (say a central bank base rate) on a liability to another (say LIBOR). A relationship of this nature would not normally qualify for hedge accounting because the hedging instrument does not reduce or eliminate risk in any meaningful way – it simply converts one risk to another similar risk. For this reason, such an economic strategy would not qualify as either a fair value or cash flow hedge relationship (see 3.1 and 3.2 below).

A basis swap or similar instrument may qualify as a hedging instrument when considered in combination with another instrument (see 2.1.3 above). For example, the basis swap described above and a pay-fixed, receive-LIBOR interest rate swap may qualify as a hedging instrument in a cash flow hedge of a borrowing that pays interest based on a central bank rate. It may also be used on its own in a hedge of offsetting asset and liability positions (see 2.1.6 below).

2.1.6 *Hedging different risks with one instrument*

A single hedging instrument may be designated as a hedge of more than one type of risk, provided that:

- the risks hedged can be identified clearly;
- the effectiveness of the hedge can be demonstrated ; and
- it is possible to ensure that there is specific designation of the hedging instrument and different risk positions. *[IAS 39.76]*.

The implementation guidance provides the following example to illustrate this point.

Example 52.7: Foreign currency forward hedging positions in two foreign currencies

Company J, which has Japanese yen as its functional currency, issues five year floating rate US dollar debt and acquires a ten year fixed rate sterling bond. The principal amounts of the asset and liability, when converted into Japanese yen, are the same. J enters into a single foreign currency forward contract to hedge its foreign currency exposure on both instruments under which it receives US dollars and pays sterling at the end of five years.

Designating a single hedging instrument as a hedge of multiple types of risk is permitted if three conditions are met:

- the hedged risks can be clearly identified.

  In this case the risks are exposures to changes in the US dollar/yen and yen/sterling exchange rates respectively;
- the effectiveness of the hedge can be demonstrated.

  For the sterling bond, effectiveness can be measured as the degree of offset between the fair value of the principal repayment in sterling and the fair value of the sterling payment on the forward exchange contract.

  For the US dollar liability, effectiveness can be measured as the degree of offset between the fair value of the principal repayment in US dollars and the US dollar receipt on the forward exchange contract.

  Even though the bond has a ten year life and the forward only protects it for the first five years, hedge accounting is permitted for only a portion of the exposure (see 2.2.1.B below); and
- it is possible to ensure that there is a specific designation of the hedging instrument and the different risk positions.

  The hedged exposures are identified as the principal amounts of the liability and the bond in their respective currency of denomination.

The hedging instrument satisfies all of these conditions and J can designate the forward as a hedging instrument in a cash flow hedge against the foreign currency exposure on the principal repayments of both instruments and qualify for hedge accounting. *[IAS 39.F.1.13]*.

In this example, the hedging instrument is effectively decomposed and viewed as two forward contracts, each with an offsetting position in yen, i.e. J's functional currency. Each of the decomposed forward contracts is then designated in an eligible hedge accounting relationship.

The implementation guidance also explains that a single hedging instrument may be designated in both a cash flow hedge and a fair value hedge, provided the above conditions are met (section 3 covers the three different types of hedge recognised by IAS 39). For example, entities may use a cross currency interest rate swap to convert a variable rate position in a foreign currency to a fixed rate position in the functional currency. Such a swap could be designated separately as a fair value hedge of the currency risk and a cash flow hedge of the interest rate risk. *[IAS 39.F.1.12]*. However it could also be designated as a single cash flow hedge of foreign exchange and interest rate risk with the interest rate and currency swap in combination as the hedging instrument.

The IASB's implementation guidance takes the concept of hedging different risks a little further, as set out in the following example.

Example 52.8: Cross-currency interest rate swap hedging two foreign currency exchange rate exposures and fair value interest rate exposure

Company J whose functional currency is Japanese yen issues five-year floating rate US dollar debt and acquires a ten-year fixed rate sterling bond and wishes to hedge the foreign currency exposure on both the bond and the debt as well as the fair value interest rate exposure on the bond. To do this it enters into a matching cross-currency interest rate swap to receive floating rate US dollars, pay fixed rate sterling and exchange the US dollars for sterling at the end of five years.

Hedge accounting is permitted for components of risk, provided effectiveness can be measured. A single hedging instrument may be designated as a hedge of more than one type of risk if the risks can be identified clearly, effectiveness can be demonstrated, and specific designation of the hedging instrument and the risk positions can be ensured.

Therefore, the swap may be designated as a hedging instrument in a fair value hedge of the sterling bond against exposure to changes in its fair value associated with the interest rate payments on the bond until year five and the change in value of the principal payment due at maturity to the extent affected by changes in the yield curve relating to the five years of the swap (see Example 52.11 at 2.2.1.B below) as well as the exchange rate between sterling and US dollars.

In summary, the swap would be measured at fair value with changes in fair value recognised in profit or loss. The carrying amount of the receivable would be adjusted for changes in its fair value caused by changes in UK interest rates for the first five-year portion of the yield curve. Both the receivable and payable are remeasured using spot exchange rates under IAS 21 and the changes to their carrying amounts recognised in profit or loss. *[IAS 39.F.2.18]*.

Taken literally, the designation set out above takes no account of the existence of the US dollar liability and thereby suggests that the exchange rate between sterling and US dollars (the hedged risk) is seen as a component of the risk associated with the sterling bond (the hedged item). Mathematically this is clearly true from the point of view of a yen functional entity – together, the sterling/US dollar rate and the US dollar/yen rate give the sterling/yen exchange rate, i.e. the true foreign currency risk arising on the sterling bond. However, without considering the US dollar liability (which does not appear to be part of the designated hedge relationship) the hedge provides no real offset against the currency risk of the sterling liability. Instead it simply converts one foreign currency risk (exposure to sterling) to another (exposure to US dollars) and this would not normally be considered an acceptable hedging relationship. The IASB obviously sees the existence of the US dollar liability as important (otherwise it would not have been introduced into the example) but the point it is trying to articulate is not perfectly clear. In all likelihood, their failure to refer to the US dollar liability in the description of the hedge designation was simply an oversight. We believe that a hedge relationship to reflect the hedge of the foreign exchange risk on the US dollar liability would also need to be designated.

By analogy with Examples 52.7 and 52.8 above, we believe it would be acceptable to use a basis swap as a hedge of relevant asset and liability positions. For example, an entity may have made a $1m loan that earns LIBOR based interest and incurred a $1m liability that pays interest based on the central bank rate. In this case it may use as a hedging instrument an interest rate swap under which it pays LIBOR based interest and receives interest based on the central bank rate on a notional amount of $1m. In this case, the basis swap could be decomposed into two interest rate swaps, both with an offsetting $1m fixed rate leg, to facilitate hedge designations for each of the LIBOR loan and central bank deposit within separate cash flow hedges.

Decomposition of a derivative hedging instrument by imputing a notional leg is an acceptable means of splitting the fair value of a derivative hedging instrument into multiple components in order to achieve hedge accounting, as long as the split does not result in the recognition of cash flows that do not exist in the contractual terms of the derivative instrument.

The guidance above discussed combinations of (a) different cash flow hedges, (b) different fair value hedges and (c) a cash flow hedge and a fair value hedge. However, there appears to be no reason why a single instrument could not, in theory, be designated in other combinations of hedges, for example a cash flow hedge and a hedge of a net investment.

When a single hedging instrument is designated as a hedge of more than one type of risk, the IFRS Interpretations Committee has confirmed that the method of effectiveness testing is not prescribed. The method of assessing effectiveness should be captured in the hedge documentation on designation. Accordingly, the effectiveness assessment may be carried out for the total hedged position, i.e. incorporating all risks identified if these risks are inextricably linked, or for the decomposed parts separately, i.e. individually each for hedge relationship that includes a decomposed part of the derivative.[3] However, if the assessment is undertaken separately we believe that the assessment needs to be passed for each hedge relationship that includes a decomposed part, otherwise the assessment fails overall. This restriction is necessary as a financial instrument can only be designated as hedging instrument in its entirety (see 2.1.4 above). *[IAS 39.74]*.

2.1.7 Own equity instruments

An entity's own equity instruments are not financial assets or liabilities of the entity and, therefore, cannot be hedging instruments. *[IAS 39.AG97]*. This prohibition would also apply to instruments that give rise to non-controlling interests in consolidated financial statements – under IFRS it is clear that non-controlling interests are part of a reporting entity's equity.

2.2 Hedged items

The basic requirement for a hedged item is for it to be one of the following:

- a recognised asset or liability;
- an unrecognised firm commitment;
- a highly probable forecast transaction; or
- a net investment in a foreign operation,

and it should expose the entity to the risk of changes in fair value or future cash flows. *[IAS 39.78]*.

Recognised assets and liabilities can include financial items and non-financial items such as inventory. They can also include firm commitments that are not routinely recognised as assets or liabilities absent the effects of hedge accounting for such items. Most internally-generated intangibles (e.g. for a bank, a core deposit intangible – see 2.2.10 below) are not recognised assets and therefore cannot be hedged items. *[IAS 39.F.2.3]*.

In general, for hedge accounting purposes, only exposures that involve a party external to the entity can be designated as hedged items. However, there are some exceptions which are covered at 2.3.4 below. *[IAS 39.80]*.

Financial assets and liabilities need not be within the scope of IAS 39 to qualify as hedged items. For example, although rights and obligations under lease agreements are for most purposes scoped out of IAS 39, finance lease payables or receivables still meet the definition of a financial instrument and could therefore be hedged items in a hedge of interest rate or foreign currency risk.

In the case of a financial asset or liability containing an embedded derivative (see Chapter 44 at 4), if the embedded derivative is accounted for separately from the host instrument, the hedged item would be the host instrument or cash flows from the host (or portion thereof – see 2.2.1 below); otherwise it would be based on the hybrid instrument (i.e. the instrument including the embedded derivative) or cash flows from the hybrid.

As well as designating all changes in the cash flows or fair value of a hedged item in a hedging relationship, an entity can also designate only changes in the cash flows or fair value of a hedged item above or below a specified price or other variable (a one-sided risk). For example, an entity can designate the variability of future cash flow outcomes resulting from a price increase of a forecast commodity purchase, without including the risk of a price decrease within the hedge relationship. Such a situation may arise if the entity wanted to retain the opportunity to benefit from lower commodities prices, but protect itself against an increase. In such a situation, only cash flow losses that result from an increase in the price above the specified level are designated. *[IAS 39.AG99BA]*.

2.2.1 *Financial items: portions and proportions*

If the hedged item is a financial asset or liability, the standard contains a general principle that it may be a hedged item with respect to the risks associated with only a portion of its cash flows or fair value, such as one or more selected contractual cash flows or portions of them or a percentage of the fair value (i.e. a proportion of the asset or liability) provided that effectiveness can be measured. *[IAS 39.81]*. The ability to designate a proportion or a percentage of an exposure as a hedged item is similar to the guidance for hedging instruments. However the ability to identify a portion of an exposure as the hedged item is very different to the restrictions imposed on hedging instruments discussed in 2.1.4 above. For example:

(a) all of the cash flows of a financial instrument may be designated for cash flow or fair value changes attributable to some (but not all) risks; or

(b) some (but not all) of the cash flows of a financial instrument may be designated for cash flow or fair value changes attributable to all or only some risks (i.e. a 'portion' of the cash flows of the financial instrument may be designated for changes attributable to all or only some risks). *[IAS 39.AG99E]*.

Only the portion of cash flows or fair value of a financial instrument that are designated as the hedged item are subject to the hedge accounting requirements. The accounting for other portions that are not designated as the hedged item remains unchanged.

The guidance also adds that to be eligible for hedge accounting, the designated risks and portions must be separately identifiable components of the financial instrument, and changes in the cash flows or fair value of the entire financial instrument arising from the designated risks and portions must be reliably measurable. *[IAS 39.AG99F]*. This is considered further below.

2.2.1.A Benchmark portions of interest rate risk

As an example of the general principle above, an identifiable and separately measurable portion of the interest rate exposure of an interest-bearing asset or liability may be designated as the hedged risk. Such a portion might be a risk-free interest rate or other benchmark interest rate component of the total interest rate exposure of a hedged financial instrument. This is always subject to the proviso that effectiveness can be measured (see 5.3 below). *[IAS 39.81]*.

For a fixed-rate financial instrument hedged for changes in fair value attributable to changes in a risk-free or other benchmark interest rate, the implementation guidance explains that the risk-free or other benchmark rate is normally regarded as both a separately identifiable component of the financial instrument and reliably measurable. *[IAS 39.AG99F(a)]*.

For example, consider an entity that issues five year debt with a fixed coupon of 5%, for which the pricing was based on a prevailing benchmark curve of 2% for five years, plus 3% credit risk spread. The entity then transacts an interest rate swap at the prevailing five year benchmark rate (i.e. pay benchmark, receive 2%). It would be possible for the entity to designate the portion of the debt's cash flow represented by the debt principal and a 2% benchmark component of the coupon as the hedged item. In general, if a portion of the cash flows of a financial asset or liability is designated as the hedged item, that designated portion must be less than its total cash flows. For example, in the case of a liability whose effective interest rate is below LIBOR, designating the following components is not permitted:

- a portion of the liability equal to the principal amount plus interest at LIBOR; and
- a negative residual portion.

This restriction gives risk to what is often referred to as the sub-LIBOR issue. In these cases, all of the cash flows of the entire financial asset or liability may be designated as the hedged item in a hedge of only one particular risk (e.g. only for changes that are attributable to changes in LIBOR). Consider a financial liability whose effective interest rate is 100 basis points (1%) below LIBOR (i.e. the cash flows represent repayment of the principal plus interest at LIBOR minus 100 basis points). It is not possible to designate cash flows representing a LIBOR component of that liability, but the entire liability can be designated as the hedged item in a hedge of changes in the fair value or cash flows attributable to changes in LIBOR. This means that the full cash flows from the liability are designated within the hedge relationship, but for changes in LIBOR.

For example, in the case of a financial liability whose effective interest rate is 100 basis points below LIBOR, an entity can designate as the hedged item the entire liability (i.e. principal plus interest at LIBOR minus100 basis points) and hedge the change in the fair value or cash flows of that entire liability that is attributable to changes in LIBOR. *[IAS 39.AG99C]*. This is likely to be an effective hedge as changes in the credit risk of the borrower are excluded from the hedged relationship. However such a hedge will not be perfectly effective. Although the variability of cash flows in the hedged item and hedging instrument may be the same, the absolute cash flows are not due to the inclusion of the negative spread in the hedged item. Accordingly, the effect of discounting those cash flows will not offset. The discount curve used to discount the hedged cash flows needs to reflect LIBOR (as the hedged risk). However, there is a choice between discounting the hedged cash flows at LIBOR or at LIBOR minus the negative credit spread (100 basis points in the example above). The negative credit spread would not need to be updated for changes in the borrower's credit risk as that risk is excluded from the hedge relationship. The second option may improve effectiveness but some ongoing ineffectiveness is likely to remain.

In the example above, if the hedged item included an embedded floor at zero, the hedge might still be effective, in particular if LIBOR has not and is not expected to go below 100 basis points. This is because the hedged item will have the same cash flow variability as a liability without a floor if LIBOR remains above 100 basis points. However, when considering changes in fair value of the hedged item due to the hedged risk, the change in value of the embedded floor should also be considered. (see 5.3.11 below). If the floor is expected to become active, there are a number of other issues to be considered, such as the disappearance of variability in the cash flows stemming from the hedged item.

The standard explains that, in order to improve the effectiveness of the hedge, a hedge ratio of other than one-to-one may be chosen. *[IAS 39.AG99C]*. This is relevant for hedged items in both cash flow hedges (e.g. a floating rate debt security which refixes to 3 month LIBOR less a 0.5% spread every 3 months) and fair value hedges (e.g. a fixed rate loan with an effective interest rate which is 1% less than the prevailing benchmark rate for that term). See Chapter 53 at 3.4.5 for further information on this topic.

The guidance goes on to explain that, if a fixed rate financial instrument is hedged some time after its origination, and interest rates have changed in the meantime, a portion equal to a benchmark rate that is actually higher than the contractual rate paid on the item *can* be designated as the hedged item in some circumstances. This is provided that the benchmark rate is less than the effective interest rate calculated on the assumption that the instrument had been purchased on the day it was first designated as the hedged item. *[IAS 39.AG99D]*. This is illustrated below.

Example 52.9: Hedge of a portion of an existing fixed rate financial asset following a rise in interest rates

Company B originates a fixed rate financial asset of €100 that has an effective interest rate of 6% at a time when LIBOR is 4%. B begins to hedge that asset some time later when LIBOR has increased to 8% and the fair value of the asset has decreased to €90.

B calculates that if it had purchased the asset on the date it first designated it as the hedged item for its then fair value of €90, the effective yield would have been 9.5%. Because LIBOR is less than this effective yield, the entity can designate a LIBOR portion of 8% that consists partly of the contractual interest cash flows and partly of the difference between the current fair value (€90) and the amount repayable on maturity (€100). *[IAS 39.AG99D]*.

The guidance illustrated in Example 52.9 above will assist entities in designating hedges in a way that significantly reduces ineffectiveness. In fact, as noted at 5.3.8 below, the ability to designate a portion of a financial instrument as the hedged item can enable many hedges to be designated in a way that minimises or even eliminates ineffectiveness in some cases.

The negative interest rate environment in some countries, mainly Switzerland and certain countries in the Eurozone, has further implications on the designation of risk components in connection with the sub-LIBOR issue. The following example illustrates this.

Example 52.10: Negative interest rates and fair value hedges

Assume the following scenarios

a) Bank A enters into a €1 million loan to a corporate at a fixed coupon of 3.5%. The coupon has been determined considering the negative EONIA rate (the benchmark) of –0.15% plus a credit spread of 3.65%.

b) Bank B acquires a government debt security in the secondary market with the same terms as the loan in scenario a). In this fact pattern the debt was issued some years ago when benchmark interest rates were much higher. The purchase price of the debt was €1.185 million which resulted in an effective interest rate of –0.18%, consisting of the negative EONIA rate (the benchmark) when the debt was acquired of –0.15% and a credit spread of –0.03%.

Both, Bank A and Bank B want to hedge the fixed rate benchmark component and enter into an interest rate swap paying fixed –0.15% and receiving EONIA. The banks wish to designate the benchmark component in a fair value hedge for changes in EONIA.

In scenario a) it seems acceptable for the bank to designate the benchmark risk component because:

- it is included in the pricing of the hedged item and therefore separately identifiable and reliably measureable;
- the benchmark can be positive or negative, therefore the cash flows representing that benchmark rate can also be positive or negative, even if they are part of overall positive cash flows (which is similar to a benchmark component of 4% hedging the benchmark risk in a coupon of 5%, except that the benchmark is negative in this case); and
- the benchmark cash flows are less than the cash flows in the hedged items (i.e. minus 0.15% which is less than 3.5%).

We would find it difficult to reach the same conclusion for scenario b) as the benchmark rate is higher than the effective interest rate (i.e. minus 0.15% which is greater than minus 0.18%). *[IAS 39.AG99D]*. This is consistent with the fact that if a debt instrument were to be issued at par bearing a coupon of –0.18%, which included credit spread of –0.03%, when the benchmark rate was –0.15% it would not be possible to identify a benchmark component for hedge accounting purposes. *[IAS 39 AG99C]*.

In both scenarios, the banks would not be permitted to designate a payment of 0.15% of the principal as an eligible component of a receipt of a 3.5% coupon, as it is difficult to argue that a payment of 0.15% of the principal is a portion of a receipt of 3.5% of that principal. However, this is not that relevant in scenario a) as it would be possible to designate a separately identifiable benchmark component in the total cash flows, as noted above. *[IAS 39.AG99E(b)]*.

Notwithstanding the above, in both cases, the banks can designate all the cash flows in the financial asset for changes in the benchmark rate, although this is likely to result in some ineffectiveness. *[IAS 39.AG99E(a)]*.

2.2.1.B Partial term hedging

The example below illustrates a different portion of interest rate risk that is eligible for designation. It is the ability to designate a hedged item for the portion of risk that represents only part of the term that a hedged item remains outstanding.

Example 52.11: Partial term hedging

Company A acquires a 10% fixed-rate government bond with a remaining term to maturity of ten years and classifies it as available-for-sale. To hedge against the fair value exposure on the bond associated with the first five years' interest payments, it acquires a five year pay-fixed receive-floating swap.

The swap may be designated as hedging the fair value exposure of the interest rate payments on the government bond until year five and the change in value of the principal payment due at maturity to the extent affected by changes in the yield curve relating to the five years of the swap. *[IAS 39.F.2.17]*.

2.2.1.C Foreign currency risk associated with publicly quoted shares

The implementation guidance explains that the foreign currency risk associated with a holding of publicly traded shares may be hedged if they give rise to a clear and identifiable exposure to changes in foreign exchange rates. It is asserted that this will be the case if:

- the shares are not traded on an exchange, or other established market, in which trades are denominated in the same currency as the functional currency of the holder; and
- dividends on the shares are not denominated in the functional currency of the holder.

Consequently, if the share trades in multiple currencies, one of which is the holder's functional currency, hedge accounting would not be permitted. *[IAS 39.F.2.19]*. However, this restriction does not stand up to close scrutiny, as illustrated in the following example.

Example 52.12: Foreign currency risk associated with equity shareholding

ABC plc, a UK company whose functional currency is sterling, acquires a small shareholding in IJK Limited. IJK is a South African company whose operations are based solely in that country and whose income, expenditure and dividends are all denominated in South African rand. IJK's shares are listed on the Johannesburg Stock Exchange where trades are denominated in rand.

The implementation guidance suggests that, potentially, ABC could hedge the foreign currency risk arising from the sterling/rand exchange rate on its IJK holding, which appears quite sensible. If, on day 1, the shares trade at R50 and the exchange rate is R10 to £1, the shares would have a sterling value of £5.00 (= R50 ÷ 10). If, on day 2, the exchange rate moves to R8 to £1, all other things being equal, the rand value of IJK should not change, but its sterling value would be £6.25 (= R50 ÷ 8), exactly mirroring the exchange rate movement.

If IJK subsequently obtained a secondary listing on the London Stock Exchange where trades were denominated in sterling, but its business fundamentals were unchanged, in the scenario outlined above ABC's foreign exchange exposure would be exactly the same. In fact, the operation of the markets should ensure that the share price in London on the equivalent of days 1 and 2 is £5.00 and £6.25 respectively. However, the guidance suggests that because of the secondary listing, ABC no longer has a clear and identifiable exposure to changes in foreign exchange rates on the IJK shares and therefore hedge accounting would not be permitted.

2.2.1.D Inflation risk

Although there has been significant debate by many interested parties over the years, the implementation guidance in IAS 39 states that inflation is not separately identifiable and reliably measurable and cannot be designated as a risk portion of a financial instrument. There is one exception: the contractually specified inflation portion of the cash flows of a recognised inflation-linked bond (assuming there is no requirement to account for an embedded derivative separately) is considered to be separately identifiable and reliably measurable as long as other cash flows of the instrument are not affected by the inflation portion. Therefore inflation risk would not be eligible as a designated risk or portion of a fixed interest rate borrowing that does not also reference inflation. *[IAS 39.AG99F(b)-(c), BC11D, BC172C]*.

However, this approach will be softened on application of IFRS 9 which introduces a rebuttable presumption (rather than prohibition) that, unless contractually specified, inflation is not separately identifiable and reliably measurable (see Chapter 53 at 3.4.4).

2.2.1.E Other portions

While IAS 39 permits hedging of some portions of risk for financial assets or liabilities, there are intended to be some restrictions, i.e. a portion cannot be simply anything. It also noted that IAS 39 requires a hedged portion to have an effect on the price of the hedged item or transaction that is separately measurable from the hedged item or transaction itself. Consequently, a portion cannot be a residual; i.e. an entity is not permitted to designate as a portion the residual fair value or cash flows of a hedged item or transaction if that residual does not have a separately measurable effect on the hedged item or transaction. It is for this reason that it is not considered possible to determine that credit risk is an eligible risk component of a debt instrument.

This position was reaffirmed by the IASB in IFRS 9. *[IAS 39.BC6.470]*. However, IFRS 9 does introduce an alternative accounting solution for entities undertaking economic credit risk hedging activity (see Chapter 53 at 10.1).

2.2.2 *Non-financial items: portions*

It is explained that changes in the price of an ingredient or component of a non-financial asset or liability generally do not have a predictable, separately measurable effect on the price of the item that is comparable to the effect of, say, a change in market interest rates on the price of a bond. Therefore, because of the difficulty of isolating and measuring the appropriate portion of cash flows or fair value changes attributable to specific risks (other than foreign currency risks) a non-financial asset or liability can be designated as a hedged item only:

- in its entirety for all risks; or
- for foreign exchange risks. *[IAS 39.82, AG100].*

A number of commentators disagree with this assertion, at least in certain situations, and some urged the IASB in revising IAS 39 to reconsider this restriction. For example, Swiss International Air Lines, in responding to the June 2002 exposure draft, wrote the following:

> 'Like any airline SWISS is short of jet fuel. The Company is exposed to the daily price fluctuations of crude oil and the prices of inter product spreads (cracks, differentials) that convert crude oil into gas oil and finally into jet fuel.
>
> There is more liquidity in crude oil for positions beyond two years. Therefore, it is part of SWISS' fuel risk management strategy to do long-term hedges with crude oil. These positions are then rolled into gas oil and jet fuel as they move closer to the settlement dates.
>
> Paragraphs 129-130 [of the Exposure Draft] state that non-financial assets and liabilities can only be hedged in their entirety or separately with respect to foreign exchange risk.
>
> Crude oil hedges therefore must be designated as hedging the risk of price movements of jet fuel in its entirety. The critical terms of the hedging instrument and the hedged item therefore do not perfectly match – frequently a certain ineffectiveness will result. Even if the hedge can be expected to be highly effective due to a high historical correlation of the price movements of crude and jet fuel, actual effectiveness might fall outside the 80-125% range in some periods and the hedge will have to be dedesignated.
>
> We believe that due to the special properties of jet fuel prices, it should be allowed to designate the price changes of a jet fuel component such as crude oil as the hedged risk.
>
> The reason given in paragraphs 129 and 130 is that risk components of non-financial instruments generally do not have a predictable, separately measurable effect on the price of the entire item. This is a generalization that does not account for the special properties of jet fuel pricing.
>
> Jet fuel is a derivative of crude oil. Crude oil is then converted into gas oil. The difference of the crude and the gas oil price is called gas oil crack. Gas oil is finally converted into jet fuel, the price difference being called jet differential.
>
> It is not difficult to isolate and measure the portion of the changes of jet fuel prices attributable to the price risk of these components. Crude, gas oil crack,

and jet differential are separately traded and market prices are available through market information systems such as Platt's as for jet fuel itself. The price of jet fuel actually is calculated from the prices of its components.

Changes in the price of the components of jet fuel do have a predictable, separately measurable effect on the price of jet fuel. This effect can be compared to the effect of a change in the market interest rates on the price of a bond.'[4]

However, in spite of protestations such as this, the IASB noted that, in many cases, changes in the cash flows or fair value of a portion of a non-financial hedged item *are* difficult to isolate and measure and therefore the restriction was retained largely unchanged. *[IAS 39.BC137, BC138]*. This was much to the disappointment of various airlines and entities with similar fuel requirements who would have preferred the standard to adopt a different approach, e.g. to establish a 'rebuttable presumption' that components could not be identified and separately hedged. In fact, it appears that this message had not been fully appreciated because it was again put to the IFRS Interpretations Committee and discussed in October 2004, where it was again reiterated that it was not possible to designate a risk component of a non-financial item other than foreign exchange risk.[5]

Interestingly, with the aim of bringing hedge accounting closer to risk management practices, the IASB has revisited risk components of non-financial items when developing the revised hedge accounting requirements for inclusion in IFRS 9. The hedge accounting requirements of IFRS 9 pick up the above jet fuel hedging example and permit risk components of non-financial items to be eligible hedged items, provided the risk component is separately identifiable and reliably measurable (see Chapter 53 at 3.4.3).

However, it is possible for an amount of highly probable forecast non-financial hedged items to be designated in a hedge relationship that is less than the full amount expected to occur. Such a designation is only possible if the forecast transaction can be identified and documented with sufficient specificity so that when the transaction occurs, it is clear whether the transaction is or is not the hedged transaction (see 5.2 below).

Furthermore, the guidance in IAS 39 does not prevent an entity hedging a specified range of absolute values of a non-financial item, i.e. a one sided risk (see 2.2 above). For example, an entity may hedge the risk that its gold inventory will fall in value by purchasing a cash-settled at-the-money put option that allows (but does not require) the entity to sell a fixed amount of gold for a price that is fixed at its market value at inception of the contract – in this case the hedged risk is the risk that the value of the gold inventory will fall below a specified price.

The IASB also considered whether the interest rate risk portion of loan servicing rights could be designated as the hedged item on the grounds that this portion can be separately identified and measured, and that changes in market interest rates have a predictable and separately measurable effect on the value of such rights. In fact the possibility of treating loan servicing rights as financial assets rather than non-financial assets, perhaps on an elective basis, was also considered. However, it was concluded that no exceptions should be permitted for this matter either. *[IAS 39.BC140-BC143]*.

It seems reasonably clear from the logic of the above restriction that an entity may also hedge a non-financial exposure for all risks *except* foreign currency risk (even if it is not clear from the standard itself), as illustrated in the following example.

Example 52.13: Hedge of foreign currency denominated commodity risk

Company P has the FC as its functional currency. It has forecast, with a high probability, the need to purchase a fixed quantity of crude oil for US Dollars in twelve months' time. To hedge part of its exposure to the price risk inherent in this purchase P enters into an exchange traded twelve-month cash-settled crude oil forward contract. The strike price of the forward is denominated in US dollars (there is no active market in FC denominated crude oil futures) and P therefore fixes the US dollar price of the oil to be purchased. P chooses not to hedge the risk associated with FC to US dollar exchange rates. This might be because of illiquidity in the foreign currency markets for FCs or, perhaps, because P has forecast US dollar inflows that provide a natural hedge of the foreign exchange risk.

P may designate the forward contract as the hedging instrument in a hedge of the exposure to the US dollar denominated price risk associated with its forecast purchase of crude oil.

In many cases it will be difficult to identify a separately measurable effect on non-financial assets, even for foreign currency risk, as illustrated in the following example from the implementation guidance.

Example 52.14: Foreign currency borrowings hedging fixed assets

A Danish shipping company, D, has a US subsidiary that has the same functional currency as the parent, the Danish krone. Accordingly in D's consolidated financial statements, ships owned by the subsidiary, which are carried at depreciated historical cost, are reported in Danish krone using historical exchange rates. To hedge the potential currency risk on the disposal of the ships in US dollars, purchases of ships are normally financed with loans denominated in US dollars.

US dollar borrowings cannot be classified as fair value hedges of a ship because ships do not contain any separately measurable foreign currency risk even if their purchase was, and sale is likely to be, denominated in US dollars.

The proceeds from the anticipated sale of the ship may, however, be designated in a cash flow hedge, provided all the hedging criteria are met. Those conditions require that the sale is highly probable, which is only likely if the sale is expected to occur in the immediate future. *[IAS 39.F.6.5]*.

Unfortunately, the statement that a ship does not contain any separately measurable foreign currency risk is not explained any further, which makes it difficult to apply this guidance in other situations. For example, it is hard to argue that a commodity such as crude oil, which is traded throughout the world in US dollars, does not contain a measurable exposure to US dollars. If another commodity is regularly traded and quoted both in US dollars and in euro (the implementation guidance suggests this might be the case for natural gas – see Chapter 44 at 5.2.1.B) it might seem sensible to treat that commodity as containing both US dollar and euro exposures. However, by analogy with the guidance on quoted shares (see 2.2.1.C above), *[IAS 39 F.2.19]*, a commodity that is traded and quoted in more than one currency would probably be deemed to create no measurable currency exposure for an entity whose functional currency is one of those currencies.

Inevitably, for many hedges of non-financial items there will be a difference between the terms of the hedging instrument and the hedged item. As well as the restriction on hedging portions of the non-financial item, there may simply be no perfectly matching hedging instruments. For example, a forward contract to purchase Colombian coffee might be used as a hedge of the forecast purchase of Brazilian coffee on otherwise similar terms. Such a hedge may, nonetheless, qualify for hedge accounting, provided all the hedging criteria are met. *[IAS 39.AG100]*.

To meet these criteria, it must be expected that the hedge will be highly effective. For this purpose, the amount of the hedging instrument may be greater or less than that of the hedged item if this improves the effectiveness of the hedging relationship (see 5.3 below for more on assessing the hedge effectiveness). For example, a regression analysis (see 5.3.6 below) could be performed to establish a statistical relationship between the hedged item (e.g. a transaction in Brazilian coffee) and the hedging instrument (e.g. a transaction in Columbian coffee). If there is a valid statistical relationship between the two variables (i.e. between the unit prices of Brazilian coffee and Columbian coffee), the slope of the regression line can be used to establish the designated hedge ratio that will maximise expected effectiveness. For example, if the slope of the regression line is 1.02, a hedge ratio based on 0.98 quantities of hedged items to 1.00 quantities of the hedging instrument maximises expected effectiveness. However, the hedging relationship may result in ineffectiveness that is recognised in profit or loss during the term of the hedging relationship. *[IAS 39.AG100]*. The continued existence of a valid statistical relationship is required to be proven as part of the ongoing hedge effectiveness assessment in order to continue with hedge accounting prospectively (see 5.3 below). This idea is a recurring theme in the standard and is referred to a number of times.

As discussed in Chapter 43 at 2.2.1, current tax receivable (payable) is a non-financial asset (liability) because it arises from statutory requirements imposed by governments rather than a contract. Therefore it is not possible to designate a portion of current tax as a hedged item except for foreign exchange risk. This is the case even where the portion arises indirectly from foreign exchange risk. For example, an entity may be taxed at, say, 30% on exchange gains or losses arising on a specified monetary item but the portion of its tax charge which is payable or receivable in respect of those foreign currency gains and losses may not be a hedged item. Consequently, gains and losses on the hedging instrument (which in some cases will offset the corresponding portion of the tax charge or credit in the right period without the need for hedge accounting) could not be offset against the tax charge in profit or loss (see Chapter 54 at 7.1.3).

2.2.3 *Groups of items as hedged items*

The standard explains that a hedged item can be a single item or a group of such items with similar risk characteristics. *[IAS 39.78]*. To aggregate and hedge similar assets or liabilities as a group, the individual items need to share the risk exposure for which they are hedged. Further, the standard requires that fair value changes attributable to the hedged risk for each individual item should be approximately proportional to the equivalent fair value change of the entire group. *[IAS 39.83]*.

For example, a group of mortgage loans may be considered a hedged item with respect to interest rate risk as long as the changes in fair value attributable to changes in the hedged risk for each loan are expected to be approximately proportional to the overall change in fair value of the entire group of loans due to the hedged risk. Factors to consider might include the interest rate applied to the individual mortgage loans in the group (fixed or floating) the actual coupon rate for fixed rate mortgages, the denominated currency and the maturity of the loans. However, the risk characteristics of the individual shares in a portfolio designed to replicate a share index will be different from each other and from the portfolio as a whole. For example the fair value of an individual share may go up whereas the fair value of the portfolio as a whole goes down. Therefore, the portfolio could not be hedged with respect to movements in the index *[IAS 39.F.2.20]* even though, in economic terms, the portfolio of shares may well be perfectly (or near perfectly) hedged. In situations like this, an entity may be able to designate the assets within the portfolio at fair value through profit or loss so that gains and losses from the hedging instrument and hedged items should offset within profit or loss (but of course designation could only take place on initial recognition and all fair value movements would be recognised, not just those with respect to the hedged risk – see Chapter 46 at 2.2).

The IFRS 9 guidance on hedge accounting for groups of items no longer requires that fair value changes attributable to the hedged risk for each individual item should be approximately proportional to the equivalent fair value change of the entire group (see Chapter 53 at 3.6.1).

IAS 39 states that, in general, hedge effectiveness is assessed by comparing the change in value or cash flow of hedging instruments and of hedged items. Therefore, an overall net position, e.g. the net of all fixed rate assets and fixed rate liabilities with similar maturities, cannot be a hedged item. *[IAS 39.84]*. Similarly, the net cash flows arising from a portfolio of floating rate assets and liabilities cannot be designated as the hedged item. *[IAS 39.F.2.21]*. Accordingly, many financial institutions apply the special portfolio hedge accounting solutions (see 6 below).

However, approximately the same effect on profit or loss can be achieved by designating a gross part of the underlying items as the hedged position. For example, a European company with firm commitments to make purchases and sales of US$100 and US$90 respectively could hedge the net exposure by acquiring a derivative and designating it as a hedging instrument associated with gross purchases of US$10. Similarly, a bank with €100 of assets and €90 of liabilities with risks and terms of a similar nature could hedge the net exposure by designating €10 of those assets as the hedged item. *[IAS 39.AG101]*.

2.2.4 Hedges of general business risk

To qualify for hedge accounting, the hedge must relate to a specific identified and designated risk, and not merely to the entity's general business risks; also, it must ultimately affect profit or loss (see the definitions of the types of hedging relationships in IAS 39 at 3 below). A hedge of the risk of obsolescence of a physical asset or the risk of expropriation of property by a government is not eligible for hedge accounting (effectiveness cannot be measured because those risks are not measurable reliably). *[IAS 39.AG110]*. Similarly, the risk that a transaction will not occur is an overall business risk that is not eligible as a hedged item. *[IAS 39.F.2.8]*.

2.2.5 Hedges of a firm commitment to acquire a business

A firm commitment to acquire a business in a business combination cannot be a hedged item, except for foreign exchange risk (see further discussion at 4.4 below), because the other risks being hedged cannot be specifically identified and measured. These other risks are also said to be general business risks. *[IAS 39.AG98]*. However, transactions of the business to be acquired (for example floating rate interest payments on its borrowings) may potentially qualify as hedged items. For this to be the case, it would need to be demonstrated that, from the perspective of the acquirer, those hedged transactions are highly probable which may not be straightforward as this requirement applies to both the business combination and the hedged transactions themselves.

2.2.6 Held-to-maturity investments

Unlike loans and receivables, a held-to-maturity investment (whether it pays fixed or floating interest rates) cannot be a hedged item with respect to interest rate risk or prepayment risk. This is because designating an investment as held-to-maturity requires an intention to hold the investment until maturity without regard to changes in the fair value or cash flows of such an instrument attributable to changes in interest rates (see Chapter 46 at 3). *[IAS 39.79, F.2.9]*.

However, a held-to-maturity investment (or related cash flows) can be a hedged item in the following circumstances:

- the investment may be a hedged item with respect to risks from changes in foreign currency exchange rates and credit risk; *[IAS 39.79]*
- the forecast purchase of such an investment may be a hedged item, say to lock in current interest rates – this is because an investment is not given an IAS 39 classification until it is actually recognised; *[IAS 39.F.2.10]* and
- the forecast reinvestment of fixed or variable interest receipts can be hedged items with respect to the risk of interest rate changes, as these hedged interest flows relate to forecast debt instruments that have not yet been classified for accounting purposes. *[IAS 39.F.2.11]*.

  It should be noted that this hedge relationship is significantly different from a hedge of the interest rate risk on the held-to-maturity investment itself. The hedge of interest flows from forecast reinvestment is most commonly used as a building block in the cash flow macro-hedging model (see 6 below).

2.2.7 Derivatives and instruments measured at fair value through profit or loss

A derivative cannot be a hedged item. The implementation guidance explains that this is because such instruments are always deemed held for trading and measured at fair value with gains and losses recognised in profit or loss unless they are designated and effective hedging instruments. *[IAS 39.F.2.1]*.

This has the effect that cash flows from a forecast derivative transaction also cannot be hedged items. For example, a company with the euro as its functional currency that expects to issue floating rate debt in three months' time may wish to enter into a forward starting euro denominated pay-fixed receive-floating interest rate swap to fix the cash flows on that debt before it is issued, and those cash flows could qualify as hedged items. However, that entity may expect to issue US dollar denominated debt and, immediately after issuance, swap it into floating rate euro debt by way of a cross currency interest rate swap. In this case, the forecast floating rate euro interest payments (i.e. the combination of the US dollar denominated debt in combination with the cross currency interest rate swap) are not valid hedged items as they partly arise from a forecast derivative contract.

Consider a further example where a commodity trading entity (which produces part of the commodities that it trades) accounts for all of its sales contracts at fair value through profit or loss (see Chapter 43 at 4). The costs of production are incurred in euros, which is also the entity's functional currency. Commodities are traded in US dollars and the entity has US dollar debt that was used to finance the production assets. In this example, the entity cannot hedge the foreign exchange risk arising from its expected gross sales in US dollars (i.e. the forecast transactions) with its US dollar debt as the expected gross sales arise from forecast derivatives.

Similarly, a 'synthetic hedged item' created by combining a derivative with a non-derivative financial instrument cannot be a hedged item. For example, if an entity issued foreign currency denominated fixed rate debt and converted it into functional currency floating rate debt using a cross-currency interest rate swap, it would not be possible to designate the synthetic functional currency floating rate debt as a hedged item, as it is made up of combination of debt and a derivative.[6]

In what is a significant change, the IASB decided to allow aggregated exposures (i.e. a combination of a derivative and a risk exposure) to qualify as a hedged item under the IFRS 9 hedge accounting requirements. This allows hedge accounting to be applied to many common risk management strategies, such as where an entity initially only hedges the price risk of a highly probable forecast purchase of a raw material denominated in a foreign currency, then later hedges the foreign exchange risk too (see Chapter 53 at 3.3).

It does not immediately appear that it would be useful to designate a recognised hedged item that is measured at fair value through profit or loss in a hedge relationship. However, for certain variable rate instruments measured at fair value through profit or loss designation as the hedged item in a cash flow hedge relationship may be desirable. Although the variable hedged item would be measured at fair value through profit or loss, an entity may still seek to hedge variability of cash flows by entering into a hedging derivative. Because of the variable nature of the hedged item, such instruments may not be significantly exposed to changes in fair value caused by movements in the hedged risk whereas the hedging derivative will be. In this instance application of cash flow hedge accounting facilitates deferral of fair value changes in the hedging derivative to the cash flow reserve, which may better reflect the risk management strategy.

The implementation guidance of IAS 39 seems to be clear that financial instruments that are held for trading cannot be designated as a hedged item as stated above. However, the position is less clear for items held at fair value through profit or loss that are not held for trading such as those to which the fair value option has been applied (see Chapter 46 at 2.2). The guidance in IFRS 9 is more explicit, and provides the following example: an entity could use a swap to change floating rate debt to fixed-rate and apply cash flow hedge accounting, even if the debt is measured at fair value through profit or loss. This is because there is a systematic way in which the cash flow hedge reserve can be reclassified, i.e. in the same way interest payments on the instrument occur. *[IFRS 9.B6.5.2]*.

However, in other cases there might be no systematic way in which the cash flow hedge reserve can be reclassified. A forecast purchase of an equity instrument that, once acquired, will be accounted for at fair value through profit or loss, is mentioned as an example of an item that cannot be the hedged item in a cash flow hedge, because any gain or loss on the hedging instrument that would be deferred could not be appropriately reclassified to profit or loss during a period in which it would achieve offset. *[IFRS 9.B6.5.2]*. We believe that the principles set out by the examples above could also be applied to non-derivative instruments to which the fair value option has been applied, that are designated as hedged items in a cash flow hedges under IAS 39 (see also Chapter 53 at 3.6.7).

2.2.8 *Forecast acquisition or issuance of foreign currency monetary items*

Changes in foreign exchange rates prior to acquisition or issuance of a monetary item denominated in a foreign currency do not impact profit or loss. Therefore an entity cannot hedge the foreign currency risk associated with the forecast acquisition or issuance of a monetary item denominated in a foreign currency, such as the expected issuance for cash of borrowings denominated in a currency other than the entity's functional currency. This is because there is a need for the hedged risk to have the potential to impact profit or loss in order to achieve hedge accounting. *[IAS 39.86(b)]*.

2.2.9 *Own equity instruments*

Transactions in an entity's own equity instruments (including distributions to holders of such instruments) are generally recognised directly in equity by the issuer (see Chapter 45) and do not affect profit or loss. Therefore, such instruments cannot be designated as a hedged item. Similarly, a forecast transaction in an entity's own equity instruments (e.g. a forecast dividend payment) cannot qualify as a hedged item. However, a declared dividend that qualifies for recognition as a financial liability, e.g. because the entity has become legally obliged to make the payment, may qualify as a hedged item. For example, a recognised liability to pay a dividend in a foreign currency would give rise to foreign exchange risk. *[IAS 39.F.2.7]*.

2.2.10 *Core deposits*

Financial institutions often receive a significant proportion of their funding from demand deposits, such as current account balances, savings accounts and other accounts that behave in a similar manner. Even though the total balance from all such customer deposits may vary, a financial institution typically determines a level of core deposits that it believes will be maintained for a particular time frame, and hence will behave for that time frame like a fixed interest rate exposure from an interest rate risk perspective.

These customer deposits or accounts usually pay a zero or low, stable interest rate which is generally insensitive to changes in market interest rates. Hence both existing and new deposits are generally considered fungible for interest rate risk management purposes as new deposits will usually be on the same terms as any withdrawn deposits that they replace. Financial institutions cannot determine which customer deposits will make up the core deposits. While these deposits can be withdrawn at little or short notice, typically they are left as a deposit for a long and generally predictable time despite the low interest paid.

Risk management of the 'deemed' fixed rate interest rate risk exposure that financial institutions attribute to core deposits will often result in the need to transact interest rate derivatives, although achieving hedge accounting for these derivatives can be difficult.[7]

In order for items to be eligible hedged items in a fair value hedge, the fair value of the hedged items must vary with the hedged risk. However, IFRS 13 – *Fair Value Measurement* – states that the fair value of a financial liability with a demand feature (e.g. a demand deposit) is not less than the amount payable on demand, discounted from the first date that the amount could be required to be paid. *[IFRS 13.47]*. Therefore the fair value of demand deposits will not vary with the hedged risk, and fair value hedge accounting is precluded.

An alternative consideration is whether it is possible to designate a core deposit intangible (representing the value of this source of funding to the financial institution) as an eligible hedged item. The term 'core deposit intangible' could be used to represent the difference between:

(a) the fair value of a portfolio of core deposits; and

(b) the aggregate of the individual fair values of the liabilities within the portfolio, normally calculated in accordance with the requirements of IAS 39.

Generally, an internally-generated core deposit intangible cannot be a hedged item because it is not a recognised asset. If a core deposit intangible is acquired together with a related portfolio of deposits, it is required to be recognised separately as an intangible asset (or as part of the related acquired portfolio of deposits) if it meets the recognition criteria in IAS 38 – *Intangible Assets* – *[IAS 39.F.2.3]* which it normally will (see Chapter 9 at 5.5.2).

Theoretically, therefore, a recognised purchased core deposit intangible asset could be designated as a hedged item. However this will only be the case if it meets the conditions for hedge accounting, including the requirement that the effectiveness of the hedge can be measured reliably. The implementation guidance explains that, because it is often difficult to measure reliably the fair value of a core deposit intangible asset other than on initial recognition, it is unlikely that this requirement will be met. *[IAS 39.F.2.3]*. In fact, this probably understates the difficulty.

For the reasons set out above, financial institutions are not able to designate core deposits with the associated hedging instruments in hedge accounting relationships, despite the economic validity of these risk management activities. Accordingly, many financial institutions apply the special portfolio or macro hedge accounting guidance (see 6 below).

2.2.11 Pension scheme assets

An entity may wish to enter into transactions to hedge the risk associated with assets held by a pension scheme or other long-term employee benefit fund. We consider that, for many reasons, plan assets are unlikely to qualify as hedged items under IAS 39. For example, a pension scheme is, in many respects, a non-financial asset or liability and, therefore, the portion of the risk associated with only the assets could not be a hedged item (see 2.2.2 above).

2.3 Internal hedges and other group accounting issues

One of the most pervasive impacts that IAS 39 can have on groups, especially those operating centralised treasury functions, is the need to reassess hedging strategies that involve intra-group transactions. To a layman this might come as something of a surprise because the standard does little more than reinforce the general principle that transactions between different entities within a group should be eliminated in the consolidated financial statements of that group. Nevertheless, a significant amount of the standard and related implementation guidance is devoted to this subject.

2.3.1 *Internal hedging instruments*

The starting point for this guidance is the principle of preparing consolidated financial statements in IFRS 10 – *Consolidated Financial Statements* – that requires 'intragroup assets and liabilities, equity, income, expenses and cash flows to be eliminated in full'. *[IFRS 10.B86, IAS 39.F.1.4]*.

Although individual entities within a consolidated group (or divisions within a single legal entity) may enter into hedging transactions with other entities within the group (or divisions within the entity), such as internal derivative contracts to transfer risk exposures between different companies (or divisions), any such intragroup (or intra-entity) transactions are eliminated on consolidation. Therefore, such hedging transactions do not qualify for hedge accounting in the consolidated financial statements of the group, *[IAS 39.73, F.1.4]*, (or in the individual or separate financial statements of an entity for hedging transactions between divisions of the entity). Effectively, this is because they do not exist in an accounting sense.

As a consequence, IAS 39 makes it very clear that for hedge accounting purposes only instruments that involve a party external to the reporting entity (i.e. external to the group or individual entity that is being reported on) can be designated as hedging instruments. *[IAS 39.73]*.

The implementation guidance explains that IAS 39 does not specify how an entity should *manage* its risk. Accordingly, where an internal contract is offset with an external party, the external contract may be regarded as the hedging instrument. In such cases, the hedging relationship (which is between the external transaction and the item that is the subject of the internal hedge) may qualify for hedge accounting. *[IAS 39.F.1.4]*. The following example illustrates this.

Example 52.15: Internal derivatives

The banking division of Bank A enters into an internal interest rate swap with A's trading division. The purpose is to hedge the interest rate risk exposure of a loan (or group of similar loans) in the banking division's loan portfolio. Under the swap, the banking division pays fixed interest payments to the trading division and receives variable interest rate payments in return.

Assuming a hedging instrument is not acquired from an external party, hedge accounting treatment for the hedging transaction undertaken by the banking and trading divisions is not allowed, because only derivatives that involve a party external to the entity can be designated as hedging instruments. Further, any gains or losses on intragroup or intra-entity transactions should be eliminated on consolidation. Therefore, transactions between different divisions within A cannot qualify for hedge accounting treatment in Bank A's financial statements. Similarly, transactions between different entities within a group cannot qualify for hedge accounting treatment in A's consolidated financial statements.

However, if, in addition to the internal swap in the above example, the trading division entered into an interest rate swap or other contract with an external party that offset the exposure hedged in the internal swap, hedge accounting would be permitted. For the purposes of IAS 39, the hedged item is the loan (or group of similar loans) in the banking division and the hedging instrument is the external interest rate swap or other contract.

The trading division may aggregate several internal swaps or portions of them that are not offsetting each other (see 2.3.2 below) and enter into a single third party derivative contract that offsets the aggregate exposure. Such external hedging transactions may qualify for hedge accounting treatment provided that the hedged items in the banking division are identified and the other conditions for hedge accounting are met. *[IAS 39.F.1.4]*.

It follows that internal hedges may qualify for hedge accounting in the individual or separate financial statements of individual entities within the group, provided they are external to the individual entity that is being reported on. *[IAS 39.73]*.

The implementation guidance contains the following summary of the application of IAS 39 to internal hedging transactions:

- IAS 39 does not preclude an entity from using internal derivative contracts for risk management purposes and it does not preclude internal derivatives from being accumulated at the treasury level or some other central location so that risk can be managed on an entity-wide basis or at some higher level than the separate legal entity or division;
- Internal derivative contracts between two separate entities within a consolidated group can qualify for hedge accounting by those entities in their individual or separate financial statements, even though the internal contracts are not offset by derivative contracts with a party external to the consolidated group;
- Internal derivative contracts between two separate divisions within the same legal entity can qualify for hedge accounting in the individual or separate financial statements of that legal entity only if those contracts are offset by derivative contracts with a party external to the legal entity;
- Internal derivative contracts between separate divisions within the same legal entity and between separate entities within the consolidated group can qualify for hedge accounting in the consolidated financial statements only if the internal contracts are offset by derivative contracts with a party external to the consolidated group;
- If the internal derivative contracts are not offset by derivative contracts with external parties, the use of hedge accounting by group entities and divisions using internal contracts must be reversed on consolidation. *[IAS 39.F.1.4]*.

The premise on which the restriction on internal hedging instruments is based is not completely true. In fact, foreign currency intragroup balances may well give rise to gains and losses in profit or loss under IAS 21 that are not fully eliminated on consolidation. Such intra-group monetary items, as well as forecast intragroup transactions, may qualify as a hedged item in the consolidated financial statements if the other conditions for hedge accounting are met (see 2.3.4 below). However, this does not change the fact that internal transactions, even those that affect consolidated profit or loss, cannot be used as hedging instruments in consolidated financial statements. This is somewhat surprising as one might consider the same arguments that led to the exception permitting intragroup monetary items and forecast intragroup transactions to be hedged items to support allowing intragroup monetary items to be hedging instruments. However, during its deliberations of the hedge accounting model under IFRS 9 the IASB decided to retain this restriction. *[IFRS 9.BC6.142-147]*.

IFRS 8 – *Operating Segments* – requires disclosure of segment information that is reported to the chief operating decision maker even if this is on a non-GAAP basis (see Chapter 34 at 3.1). Consequently, for a hedge to qualify for hedge accounting in segment reporting, it is not always necessary for the hedging instrument to involve a party external to the segment.

2.3.2 *Offsetting internal hedging instruments*

As noted at 2.3.1 above, if an internal contract used in a hedging relationship is offset with an external party, the external contract may be regarded as a hedging instrument and the hedge may qualify for hedge accounting. *[IAS 39.F.1.4]*. The implementation guidance elaborates on this further in the context of both interest rate and foreign currency risk management, particularly in the situation where the exposure from internal derivatives are offset before being laid off with a third party.

2.3.2.A *Interest rate risk*

Sometimes, central treasury functions enter into internal derivative contracts with subsidiaries and, perhaps, divisions within the consolidated group to manage interest rate risk on a centralised basis. If, before laying off the risk, the internal contracts are first netted against each other and only the net exposure is offset in the marketplace with external derivative contracts, the internal contracts cannot qualify for hedge accounting in the consolidated financial statements. *[IAS 39.F.1.5]*.

An internal contract designated at the subsidiary level, or by a division, as a hedge results in the recognition of changes in the fair value of the item being hedged in profit or loss (for a fair value hedge – see 4.1.1 below) or in the recognition of the changes in the fair value of the internal derivative in other comprehensive income (for a cash flow hedge – see 4.2.1 below). On consolidation, there is no basis for changing the measurement attribute of the item being hedged in a fair value hedge unless the exposure is offset with an external derivative. Similarly, on consolidation, there is no basis for including the gain or loss on the internal derivative in other comprehensive income for one entity and recognising it in profit or loss by the other entity unless it is offset with an external derivative. *[IAS 39.F.1.5]*.

Where two or more internal derivatives used to manage interest rate risk on assets or liabilities at the subsidiary or division level are offset at the treasury level, the effect of designating the internal derivatives as hedging instruments is that the hedged non-derivative exposures at the subsidiary or division levels would be used to offset each other on consolidation. Accordingly, since IAS 39 does not permit designating non-derivatives as hedging instruments (except for foreign currency exposures – see 2.1.2 above), the results of hedge accounting from the use of internal derivatives at the subsidiary or division level that are not laid off with external parties must be reversed on consolidation. *[IAS 39.F.1.5]*.

It should be noted, however, that if the hedges were perfectly effective at the subsidiary level, there will be no effect on profit or loss and equity of reversing the effect of hedge accounting on consolidation for internal derivatives that offset each other at the consolidation level if they are used in the same type of hedging relationship at the subsidiary or division level and, in the case of cash flow hedges, where the hedged items affect profit or loss in the same period. Just as the internal derivatives offset at the treasury level, their use as fair value hedges by two separate entities or divisions within the consolidated group will also result in the offset of the fair value amounts recognised in profit or loss. Similarly, their use as cash flow hedges by two separate entities or divisions within the consolidated group will also result in the fair value amounts being offset against each other in other comprehensive income. *[IAS 39.F.1.5]*.

However, there may be an effect on individual line items in both the consolidated income statement (or statement of comprehensive income) and the consolidated statement of financial position. For example when internal derivatives that hedge assets (or liabilities) in a fair value hedge are offset by internal derivatives that are used as a fair value hedge of other assets (or liabilities) that are recognised in a different statement of financial position or income statement (or statement of comprehensive income) line item. In addition, to the extent that one of the internal contracts is used as a cash flow hedge and the other is used in a fair value hedge, the effect on profit or loss and equity would not offset since the gain (or loss) on the internal derivative used as a fair value hedge would be recognised in profit or loss and the corresponding loss (or gain) on the internal derivative used as a cash flow hedge would be recognised in other comprehensive income. *[IAS 39.F.1.5]*. However, the reversal of the fair value hedge adjustment would also be recognised in profit or loss when reversing hedge accounting on consolidation for internal derivatives.

Notwithstanding this, under the principles set out at 2.2.3 above, it may be possible to designate the external derivative as a hedge of *some* of the underlying exposures as illustrated in the following example.

Example 52.16: Single external derivative offsets internal contracts on a net basis

Company A uses what it describes as internal derivative contracts to document the transfer of responsibility for interest rate risk exposures from individual divisions to a central treasury function. The central treasury function aggregates the internal derivative contracts and enters into a single external derivative contract that offsets the internal derivative contracts on a net basis.

On one particular day the central treasury function enters into three internal receive-fixed, pay-variable interest rate swaps that lay off the exposure to variable interest cash flows on variable rate liabilities in other divisions and one internal receive-variable, pay-fixed interest rate swap that lays off the exposure to variable interest cash flows on variable rate assets in another division. It enters into an interest rate swap with an external counterparty that exactly offsets the four internal swaps.

A hedge of an overall net position does not qualify for hedge accounting. However, designating a part of the underlying items as the hedged position on a gross basis is permitted. *[IAS 39.84, AG101]*. Therefore, even though the purpose of entering into the external derivative was to offset internal derivative contracts on a net basis, hedge accounting is permitted if the hedging relationship is defined and documented as a hedge of a part of the underlying cash inflows or cash outflows on a gross basis and assuming that the hedge accounting criteria are met. *[IAS 39.F.2.15]*.

2.3.2.B Foreign exchange risk

Although much of the discussion at 2.3.2.A above applies equally to hedges of foreign currency risk, there is one important distinction between the two situations. IAS 39 allows non-derivative financial instruments to be used as the hedging instrument in the hedge of foreign currency risk. Therefore, in this case, internal derivatives may be used as a basis for *identifying* non-derivative external transactions that could qualify as hedging instruments or hedged items, provided that the internal derivatives represent the transfer of foreign currency risk on underlying non-derivative financial assets or liabilities (see Case 3 in Example 52.17 below). However, for consolidated financial statements, it is necessary to *designate* the hedging relationship so that it involves only external transactions. *[IAS 39.F.1.6]*.

Forecast transactions and unrecognised firm commitments cannot qualify as hedging instruments under IAS 39. Accordingly, to the extent that two or more offsetting internal derivatives represent the transfer of foreign currency risk on such items, hedge accounting cannot be applied. As a result, if any cumulative net gain or loss on an internal derivative has been included in the initial carrying amount of an asset or liability (a 'basis adjustment') or recognised in other comprehensive income (see 4.2.1 and 4.2.2 below), it would have to be reversed on consolidation if it cannot be demonstrated that the offsetting internal derivative represented the transfer of a foreign currency risk on a financial asset or liability to an external hedging instrument. *[IAS 39.F.1.6]*.

The following example illustrates this principle – it also illustrates the mechanics of accounting for fair value hedges and cash flow hedges, which are discussed in more detail at 4.1 and 4.2 below. *[IAS 39.F.1.7]*.

Example 52.17: Using internal derivatives to hedge foreign currency risk

In each of the following cases, 'FC' represents a foreign currency, 'LC' represents the local currency (which is the entity's functional currency) and 'TC' the group's treasury centre.

Case 1: Offset of fair value hedges

Subsidiary A has trade receivables of FC100, due in 60 days, which it hedges using a forward contract with TC. Subsidiary B has payables of FC50, also due in 60 days, which it hedges using a forward contact with TC.

TC nets the two internal derivatives and enters into a net external forward contract to pay FC50 and receive LC in 60 days.

At the end of month 1, FC weakens against LC. A incurs a foreign exchange loss of LC10 on its receivables, offset by a gain of LC10 on its forward contract with TC. B makes a foreign exchange gain of LC5 on its payables, offset by a loss of LC5 on its forward contract with TC. TC makes a loss of LC10 on its internal forward contract with A, a gain of LC5 on its internal forward contract with B and a gain of LC5 on its external forward contract.

Accordingly, the following entries are made in the individual or separate financial statements of A, B and TC at the end of month 1 (assuming that forward foreign exchange and spot exchange rates are exactly the same, which is unlikely in reality). Entries reflecting intra-group transactions or events are shown in italics.

A's entries

	LC	LC
Foreign exchange loss	10	
Receivables		10
Internal contract (TC)	*10*	
Internal gain (TC)		*10*

B's entries

	LC	LC
Payables	5	
Foreign exchange gain		5
Internal loss (TC)	*5*	
Internal contract (TC)		*5*

TC's entries

	LC	LC
Internal loss (A)	*10*	
Internal contract (A)		*10*
Internal contract (B)	*5*	
Internal gain (B)		*5*
External forward contract	5	
Foreign exchange gain		5

Both A and B could apply hedge accounting in their individual financial statements provided all necessary conditions were met. However, because gains and losses on the internal derivatives and the offsetting losses and gains on the hedged receivables and payables are recognised immediately in profit or loss without hedge accounting, hedge accounting is unnecessary (see 3.3 for further information on hedges of foreign currency denominated monetary items).

In the consolidated financial statements, the internal derivative transactions are eliminated. In economic terms, B's payable hedges FC50 of A's receivables. The external forward in TC hedges the remaining FC50 of A's receivable. In the consolidated financial statements, hedge accounting is again unnecessary because monetary items are measured at spot foreign exchange rates under IAS 21 irrespective of whether hedge accounting is applied.

The net balances, before and after elimination of the accounting entries relating to the internal derivatives, are the same, as set out below. Accordingly, there is no need to make any further accounting entries to meet the requirements of IAS 39.

	LC	LC
Receivables	–	10
Payables	5	–
External forward contract	5	–
Gains and losses	–	–
Internal contracts	–	–

Case 2: Offset of cash flow hedges

To extend the example, A also has highly probable future revenues of FC200 on which it expects to receive cash in 90 days. B has highly probable future expenses of FC500 (advertising cost), also to be paid for in 90 days. A and B enter into separate forward contracts with TC to hedge these exposures and TC enters into an external forward contract to receive FC300 in 90 days.

As before, FC weakens at the end of month 1. A incurs a 'loss' of LC20 on its anticipated revenues because the LC value of these revenues decreases and this is offset by a gain of LC20 on its forward contract with TC. Similarly, B incurs a 'gain' of LC50 on its anticipated advertising cost because the LC value of the expense decreases and this is offset by a loss of LC50 on its transaction with TC.

TC incurs a gain of LC50 on its internal transaction with B, a loss of LC20 on its internal transaction with A and a loss of LC30 on its external forward contract.

Both A and B complete the necessary documentation, the hedges are effective and both A and B qualify for hedge accounting in their individual financial statements. A recognises the gain of LC20 on its internal derivative transaction in other comprehensive income and B does the same with its loss of LC50. TC does not claim hedge accounting, but measures both its internal and external derivative positions at fair value, which net to zero.

Accordingly, the following entries are made in the individual or separate financial statements of A, B and TC at the end of month 1. Entries reflecting intra-group transactions or events are shown in italics.

A's entries

	LC	LC
Internal contract (TC)	*20*	
Other comprehensive income		*20*

B's entries

	LC	LC
Other comprehensive income	*50*	
Internal contract (TC)		*50*

TC's entries

	LC	LC
Internal loss (A)	*20*	
Internal contract (A)		*20*
Internal contract (B)	*50*	
Internal gain (B)		*50*
Foreign exchange loss	30	
External forward contract		30

IAS 39 requires that, in the consolidated financial statements, the accounting effects of the internal derivative transactions must be eliminated.

If there were no hedge designation for the consolidated financial statements, the gains and losses recognised in other comprehensive income and profit or loss on the internal derivatives would be reversed. Consequently, a loss of LC30 would be recognised in profit or loss in respect of the external forward contract held by TC.

However, for the consolidated financial statements, TC's external forward contract on FC300 *is* designated, at the beginning of month 1, as a hedging instrument of the first FC300 of B's highly probable future expenses. Therefore, LC30 of the gain recognised in other comprehensive income by B may remain in other comprehensive income on consolidation, because it involves an external derivative. Accordingly, the net balances, before and after elimination of the accounting entries relating to the internal derivatives, are as set out below and there is no need to make any further accounting entries in order for the requirements of IAS 39 to be met.

	LC	LC
External forward contract	–	30
Other comprehensive income	30	–
Gains and losses	–	–
Internal contracts	–	–

Case 3: Offset of fair value and cash flow hedges

The example is extended further and it is assumed that the exposures and the internal derivative transactions are the same as in Cases 1 and 2. In other words, Subsidiary A has trade receivables of FC100, due in 60 days, and highly probable future revenues of FC200 on which it expects to receive cash in 90 days. Subsidiary B has payables of FC50, due in 60 days, and highly probable future expenses of FC500 to be paid for in 90 days. Each of these exposures is hedged using forward contacts with TC. However, in this case, instead of entering into two external derivatives to hedge separately the fair value and cash flow exposures, TC enters into a single net external derivative to receive FC250 in exchange for LC in 90 days.

Consequently, TC has four internal derivatives, two maturing in 60 days and two maturing in 90 days. These are offset by a net external derivative maturing in 90 days. The interest rate differential between FC and LC is minimal, and therefore the ineffectiveness resulting from the mismatch in maturities is expected to have a minimal effect on profit or loss in TC.

As in Cases 1 and 2, A and B apply hedge accounting for their cash flow hedges and TC measures its derivatives at fair value. A recognises a gain of LC20 on its internal derivative transaction in other comprehensive income and B does the same with its loss of LC50.

Accordingly, the following entries are made in the individual or separate financial statements of A, B and TC at the end of month 1. Entries reflecting intra-group transactions or events are shown in italics.

A's entries

	LC	LC
Foreign exchange loss	10	
Receivables		10
Internal contract (TC)	*10*	
Internal gain (TC)		*10*
Internal contract (TC)	*20*	
Other comprehensive income		*20*

B's entries

	LC	LC
Payables	5	
Foreign exchange gain		5
Internal loss (TC)	*5*	
Internal contract (TC)		*5*
Other comprehensive income	*50*	
Internal contract (TC)		*50*

TC's entries

	LC	LC
Internal loss (A)	*10*	
Internal contract (A)		*10*
Internal loss (A)	*20*	
Internal contract (A)		*20*
Internal contract (B)	*5*	
Internal gain (B)		*5*
Internal contract (B)	*50*	
Internal gain (B)		*50*
Foreign exchange loss	25	
External forward contract		25

The gains and losses recognised on the internal contracts in A and B can be summarised as follows:

	A LC	B LC	Total LC
Profit or loss (fair value hedges)	10	(5)	5
Other comprehensive income (cash flow hedges)	20	(50)	(30)
Total	30	(55)	(25)

In the consolidated financial statements, IAS 39 requires the accounting effects of the internal derivative transactions to be eliminated.

If there were no hedge designation for the consolidated financial statements, the gains and losses recognised in other comprehensive income and profit or loss on the internal derivatives would be reversed. Consequently, a loss of LC30 would be recognised in profit or loss in respect of the external receivable and payable held by A (loss LC10) and B (gain LC5) respectively and the external forward contract held by TC (loss LC25).

However, for the consolidated financial statements, the following designations are made at the beginning of month 1:

- the payable of FC50 in B is designated as a hedge of the first FC50 of the highly probable future revenues in A.

  Therefore, at the end of month 1, the following entries are made in the consolidated financial statements: Dr Payable LC5; Cr Other comprehensive income LC5;
- the receivable of FC100 in A is designated as a hedge of the first FC100 of the highly probable future expenses in B.

  Therefore, at the end of month 1, the following entries are made in the consolidated financial statements: Dr Other comprehensive income LC10, Cr Receivable LC10; and
- the external forward contract on FC250 in TC is designated as a hedge of the next FC250 of highly probable future expenses in B.

  Therefore, at the end of month 1, the following entries are made in the consolidated financial statements: Dr Other comprehensive income LC25; Cr External forward contract LC25.

Combining these entries produces the total net balances as follows:

	LC	LC
Receivables	–	10
Payables	5	–
External forward contract	–	25
Other comprehensive income	30	–
Gains and losses	–	–
Internal contracts	–	–

Case 4: Offset of fair value and cash flow hedges with adjustment to carrying amount of inventory

Similar transactions to those in Case 3 are assumed except that the anticipated cash outflow of FC500 in B relates to the purchase of inventory that is delivered after 60 days. It is also assumed that the entity has a policy of basis-adjusting hedged forecast non-financial items (see 4.2.2 below).

To recap, Subsidiary A has trade receivables of FC100, due in 60 days, and highly probable future revenues of FC200 on which it expects to receive cash in 90 days. Subsidiary B has payables of FC50, due in 60 days, and a highly probable future purchase of inventory for FC500, to be delivered in 60 days and paid for in 90 days. Each of these exposures is hedged using forward contracts with TC, and TC enters into a single net external derivative to receive FC250 in exchange for LC in 90 days.

At the end of month 2, there are no further changes in exchange rates or fair values. At that date, the inventory is delivered and the loss of LC50 on B's internal derivative, recognised in other comprehensive income in month 1, is removed from equity and adjusts the carrying amount of inventory in B. The gain of LC20 on A's internal derivative is recognised in other comprehensive income as before.

In the consolidated financial statements, there is now a mismatch compared with the result that would have been achieved by unwinding and redesignating the hedges. The external derivative (FC250) and the proportion of receivable (FC50) in A offset FC300 of the anticipated inventory purchase in B. Offset will occur between the FC50 payable in B and a FC50 proportion of the receivable in A. There is a natural hedge between the remaining FC200 of anticipated cash outflow in B (inventory) and the anticipated cash inflow of FC200 in A (revenue). This last relationship does not qualify for hedge accounting under IAS 39 as no valid hedging instrument exists, hence this time there is only a partial offset between gains and losses on the internal derivatives that hedge these amounts.

Accordingly, the following entries are made in the individual or separate financial statements of A, B and TC at the end of month 1. Entries reflecting intra-group transactions or events are shown in italics.

A's entries (all at the end of month 1)

	LC	LC
Foreign exchange loss	10	
Receivables		10
Internal contract (TC)	*10*	
Internal gain (TC)		*10*
Internal contract (TC)	*20*	
Other comprehensive income		*20*

B's entries (at the end of month 1)

	LC	LC
Payables	5	
Foreign exchange gain		5
Internal loss (TC)	*5*	
Internal contract (TC)		*5*
Other comprehensive income	*50*	
Internal contract (TC)		*50*

B's entries (at the end of month 2)

	LC	LC
Inventory	50	
Other comprehensive income		50

TC's entries (all at the end of month 1)

	LC	LC
Internal loss (A)	*10*	
Internal contract (A)		*10*
Internal loss (A)	*20*	
Internal contract (A)		*20*
Internal contract (B)	*5*	
Internal gain (B)		*5*
Internal contract (B)	*50*	
Internal gain (B)		*50*
Foreign exchange loss	25	
External forward contract		25

The gains and losses recognised on the internal contracts in A and B can be summarised as follows:

	A	B	Total
	LC	LC	LC
Profit or loss (fair value hedges)	10	(5)	5
Other comprehensive income (cash flow hedges)	20	–	20
Basis adjustment (inventory)	–	(50)	(50)
Total	30	(55)	(25)

Combining these amounts with the external transactions (i.e. those not marked in italics above) produces the total net balances before elimination of the internal derivatives as follows:

	LC	LC
Receivables	–	10
Payables	5	–
External forward contract	–	25
Other comprehensive income	–	20
Basis adjustment (inventory)	50	–
Gains and losses	–	–
Internal contracts	–	–

For the consolidated financial statements, the following designations are made at the beginning of month 1:

- The payable of FC50 in B is designated as a hedge of the first FC50 of the highly probable future revenues in A.

  Therefore, at the end of month 1, the following entry is made in the consolidated financial statements: Dr Payables LC5; Cr Other comprehensive income LC5.
- The receivable of FC100 in A is designated as a hedge of the first FC100 of the highly probable future inventory purchase in B.

  Therefore, at the end of month 1, the following entries are made in the consolidated financial statements: Dr Other comprehensive income LC10; Cr Receivable LC10; and at the end of month 2, Dr Inventory LC10; Cr Other comprehensive income LC10.
- The external forward contract on FC250 in TC is designated as a hedge of the next FC250 of highly probable future inventory purchase in B.

  Therefore, at the end of month 1, the following entry is made in the consolidated financial statements: Dr Other comprehensive income LC25; Cr External forward contract LC25; and at the end of month 2, Dr Inventory LC25; Cr Other comprehensive income LC25.

This leaves FC150 of the future revenue in A and FC150 of future inventory purchase in B not designated in a hedge accounting relationship in the consolidated financial statements.

The total net balances after elimination of the accounting entries relating to the internal derivatives are as follows:

	LC	LC
Receivables	–	10
Payables	5	–
External forward contract	–	25
Other comprehensive income	–	5
Basis adjustment (inventory)	35	–
Gains and losses	–	–
Internal contracts	–	–

Chapter 52

These total net balances are different from those that would be recognised if the internal derivatives were not eliminated, and it is these net balances that IAS 39 requires to be included in the consolidated financial statements. The accounting entries required to adjust the total net balances before elimination of the internal derivatives are as follows:

- to reclassify LC15 of the loss on B's internal derivative that is included in inventory to reflect that FC150 of the forecast purchase of inventory is not hedged by an external instrument (neither the external forward contract of FC250 in TC nor the external payable of FC100 in A); and
- to reclassify the gain of LC15 on A's internal derivative to reflect that the forecast revenues of FC150 to which it relates is not hedged by an external instrument.

The net effect of these two adjustments is as follows:

	LC	LC
Other comprehensive income	15	
Inventory		15

It is apparent that extending the principles set out in this relatively simple example to the more complex and higher volume situations that are likely to be encountered in practice is not going to be straightforward.

2.3.3 *Offsetting external hedging instruments*

The implementation guidance explains that where two offsetting derivatives are transacted at the same time, it is generally not permitted to designate one of them as a hedging instrument in a hedge when the derivatives are viewed as one unit. The two derivatives would not be accounted for as one unit if:

- the second derivative was not entered into in contemplation of the first; or
- there is a 'substantive business purpose' for structuring the transactions separately.

This issue is also discussed in Chapter 44 at 8. It is emphasised that judgement should be applied in determining what is a substantive business purpose. For example, a centralised treasury entity may enter into third party derivative contracts on behalf of other subsidiaries to hedge their interest rate exposures and, to track those exposures within the group, enter into internal derivative transactions with those subsidiaries. It may also enter into a derivative contract with the same counterparty during the same business day with substantially the same terms as a contract entered into as a hedging instrument on behalf of another subsidiary as part of its trading operations, or because it wishes to rebalance its overall portfolio risk. In this case, there is a valid business purpose for entering into each contract. However, a desire to achieve fair value accounting for the hedged item is deemed not to be a substantive business purpose. *[IAS 39.F.1.14]*.

The following example, based on the implementation guidance, explores this issue a little further.

Example 52.18: External derivative contracts settled net

A company uses internal derivative contracts to transfer interest rate risk exposures from individual divisions to a central treasury function. For each internal derivative contract, the central treasury function enters into a derivative contract with a single external counterparty that offsets the internal derivative contract. For example, if the central treasury function has entered into a receive-5% fixed, pay-LIBOR interest rate swap with another division that has entered into the internal contract with central treasury to hedge the exposure to variability in interest cash flows on a pay-LIBOR borrowing, central treasury would enter into a pay-5% fixed, receive-LIBOR interest rate swap on the same principal terms with the external counterparty.

Although each external derivative contract is formally documented as a separate contract, only the net of the payments on all of the external derivative contracts is settled since there is a netting agreement with the external counterparty.

Even though the external derivatives are settled on a net basis, the individual external derivative contracts, such as the pay-5% fixed, receive-LIBOR interest rate swap above, can generally be designated as hedging instruments of underlying gross exposures, such as the exposure to changes in variable interest payments on the pay-LIBOR borrowing above, assuming that all the other hedge accounting criteria are met.

External derivative contracts that are legally separate contracts and serve a valid business purpose, such as laying off risk exposures on a gross basis, qualify as hedging instruments even if those external contracts are settled on a net basis with the same external counterparty, provided the hedge accounting criteria in IAS 39 are met. *[IAS 39.F.2.16]*.

In the context of interest rate instruments, the facts in this example appear a little unlikely. This is because most master netting agreements have a practical effect only in the event of default by, or insolvency of, one of the counterparties – otherwise payments tend to be made gross. However, the above situation has become more relevant as many jurisdictions recently introduced (or plan to introduce) requirements to settle over-the-counter derivatives through a central clearing house (discussed at 4.2.3.A below).

For foreign currency instruments, a number of financial institutions provide services that are broadly analogous to the one described in Example 52.18 above. Under these arrangements a treasury function will transact, say, legally separate forward exchange contracts with the financial institution to offset each internal derivative it has entered into with a subsidiary or division. These contracts will be administered under a centralised facility with settlements being made on a net basis. Further, the financial institution will often price these contracts to reflect the reduced credit risk and administrative burden associated with the arrangements so that the cost of transacting individual contracts is significantly reduced.

Some may express surprise that the guidance explains that arrangements such as those illustrated in Example 52.18 above may qualify for hedge accounting. In substance, they are little different from the entity offsetting its internal contracts before entering into an offsetting external transaction, which as explained at 2.3.2 above, would not permit hedge accounting to be applied for each item hedged using an internal contract. However, this is nothing compared to what follows. The implementation guidance considers an extension to the arrangement set out above:

> 'Treasury observes that by entering into the external offsetting contracts and including them in the centralised portfolio, it is no longer able to evaluate the exposures on a net basis. Treasury wishes to manage the portfolio of offsetting external derivatives separately from other exposures of the entity. Therefore, it enters into an additional, single derivative to offset the risk of the portfolio.' *[IAS 39.F.2.16]*.

The guidance explains that the purpose of structuring the external derivatives like this is consistent with the entity's risk management policies and strategies and, generally, hedge accounting may still be used. Even if this final external derivative is effected with the same counterparty under the same netting arrangement, and notwithstanding the fact that all exposures with that counterparty will, as a result, net to zero, it is implied that this constitutes a substantive business purpose as described at the start of this sub-section. *[IAS 39.F.2.16]*.

In essence, the guidance appears to suggest that the use of internal derivatives for hedge accounting is allowed, provided that an agreement is reached with a third party to give the appearance of laying off the exposure even though the risk is immediately taken back again. This seems a long way from what the standard requires and, in fact, begs the question of why an entity should even go to the trouble of creating such an artificial external agreement that appears to lack any commercial substance. We have serious reservations over this part of the guidance, particularly we question whether it really would be possible to demonstrate the existence of a valid business purpose for such an arrangement.

2.3.4 *Internal hedged items*

Only assets, liabilities, firm commitments or highly probable forecast transactions that involve a party external to the entity can be designated as hedged items. It follows that hedge accounting can be applied to transactions between entities in the same group only in the individual or separate financial statements of those entities and not in the consolidated financial statements of the group. However, there are two exceptions – intragroup monetary items and forecast intragroup transactions, discussed at 2.3.4.A and 2.3.4.B below. *[IAS 39.80]*.

2.3.4.A *Intragroup monetary items*

IAS 39 allows the foreign currency risk of an intra-group monetary item (e.g. a payable or receivable between two subsidiaries) to qualify as a hedged item in the consolidated financial statements if it results in an exposure to foreign exchange rate gains or losses under IAS 21 that are not fully eliminated on consolidation. Foreign exchange gains and losses on such items are not fully eliminated on consolidation when they are transacted between two group entities that have different functional currencies (see Chapter 15 at 6.3), *[IAS 39.80]*, as illustrated in the following example.

Example 52.19: Intragroup monetary items that will affect consolidated profit or loss

Company A has two subsidiaries, Company B and Company C. A and B have the euro as their functional currencies, while C has the US dollar as its functional currency. On 31 March, C purchases goods from B for US$110, payable on 30 June.

In this case, the intragroup monetary item of US$110 may be designated as a hedged item in a hedge of foreign currency risk both by B in its separate financial statements and by A in its consolidated financial statements.

While B's foreign currency receivable is eliminated against C's foreign currency payable on consolidation, the exchange differences that arise for B cannot be eliminated since C has no corresponding exchange differences.

Thus, the intragroup monetary item results in an exposure to variability in the foreign currency amount of the intra-group monetary item that will affect profit or loss in the consolidated financial statements. Therefore, the intragroup monetary item may be designated as a hedged item in a foreign currency hedge.[8]

2.3.4.B Forecast intragroup transactions

IAS 39 also contains a second exception allowing the foreign currency risk of a highly probable forecast intragroup transaction to qualify as a hedged item in a cash flow hedge in consolidated financial statements in certain circumstances. The transaction must be denominated in a currency other than the functional currency of the entity entering into that transaction (e.g. parent, subsidiary, associate, joint venture or branch) and the foreign currency risk must affect consolidated profit or loss (otherwise it cannot qualify as a hedged item). *[IAS 39.80, AG99A]*.

Normally, royalty payments, interest payments and management charges between members of the same group will not affect consolidated profit or loss unless there is a related external transaction. However, by way of example, a forecast sale or purchase of inventory between members of the same group will affect profit or loss if there is an onward sale of the inventory to a party external to the group. Similarly, a forecast intragroup sale of plant and equipment from the group entity that manufactured it to a group entity that will use it in its operations may affect consolidated profit or loss. This could occur, for example, because the plant and equipment will be depreciated by the purchasing entity and the amount initially recognised for the plant and equipment may change if the forecast intragroup transaction is denominated in a currency other than the functional currency of the purchasing entity. *[IAS 39.AG99A]*.

Although the standard refers exclusively to forecast intragroup transactions, we believe there is no reason why these provisions should not also apply to intragroup firm commitments.

2.3.5 *Hedged item and hedging instrument held by different group entities*

The implementation guidance explains that, in a group, it is not necessary for the hedging instrument to be held by the same entity as the one that has the exposure being hedged in order to qualify for hedge accounting in the consolidated financial statements. *[IAS 39.F.2.14]*. This is illustrated in the following example.

Example 52.20: Subsidiary's foreign exchange exposure hedged by parent

Company S is based in Switzerland and prepares consolidated financial statements in Swiss francs. It has an Australian subsidiary, Company A, whose functional currency is the Australian dollar and is included in the consolidated financial statements of S. A has forecast purchases in Japanese yen that are highly probable and S enters into a forward contract to hedge the change in yen relative to the Australian dollar.

Because A did not hedge the foreign currency exchange risk associated with the forecast purchases in yen, the effects of exchange rate changes between the Australian dollar and the yen will affect A's profit or loss and, therefore, would also affect consolidated profit or loss. Therefore that hedge may qualify for hedge accounting in S's consolidated financial statements provided the other hedge accounting criteria in IAS 39 are met. *[IAS 39.F.2.14]*.

3 TYPES OF HEDGING RELATIONSHIPS

There are three types of hedging relationship defined in IAS 39: *[IAS 39.86]*

- *fair value hedge:* a hedge of the exposure to changes in the fair value of a recognised asset or liability or an unrecognised firm commitment, or an identified portion of such an asset, liability or firm commitment, that is attributable to a particular risk and could affect profit or loss;
- *cash flow hedge:* a hedge of the exposure to variability in cash flows that:
  (i) is attributable to a particular risk associated with a recognised asset or liability (such as all or some future interest payments on variable rate debt) or a highly probable forecast transaction; and
  (ii) could affect profit or loss; and
- *hedge of a net investment in a foreign operation*: as defined in IAS 21 (see Chapter 15 at 2.3).

These definitions are considered further in the remainder of this section.

3.1 Fair value hedges

An example of a fair value hedge is a hedge of the exposure to changes in the fair value of a fixed rate debt instrument (not measured at fair value through profit or loss) as a result of changes in interest rates – if interest rates increase, the fair value of the debt decreases and *vice versa.* Such a hedge could be entered into either by the issuer or by the holder, *[IAS 39.AG102]*, (provided, in the case of the holder, it was not classified as held-to-maturity – see 2.2.6 above).

On the face of it, if a fixed rate loan that is classified within loans and receivables is held until it matures (as is the case for many such loans), changes in the fair value of the loan would not affect profit or loss. However, the implementation guidance explains that such assets may be hedged items in a fair value hedge because the loan *could* be sold, in which case fair value changes *would* affect profit or loss. *[IAS 39.F.2.13]*. The same would be true of a fixed rate borrowing for which settlement before maturity is very unlikely.

A variable rate debt may be the hedged item in a fair value hedge in certain circumstances. For example, the fair value of such an instrument will change if the issuer's credit risk changes. Accordingly variable rate debt could be designated in a hedge of all changes in its fair value. There may also be changes in its fair value relating to movements in the market rate in the periods between which the variable rate is reset. For example, if a debt instrument provides for annual interest payments reset to the market rate each year, a portion of the debt instrument has an exposure to changes in fair value during the year. *[IAS 39.F.3.5]*.

The exposure to changes in the price of inventories that are carried at the lower of cost and net realisable value may also be the subject of a fair value hedge because their fair value will affect profit or loss when they are sold or written down. For example, a copper forward may be used as the hedging instrument in a hedge of the copper price associated with copper inventory. *[IAS 39.F.3.6]*.

An equity method investment cannot be a hedged item in a fair value hedge because the equity method recognises in profit or loss the investor's share of the associate's profit or loss, rather than changes in the investment's fair value. For a similar reason, an investment in a consolidated subsidiary cannot be a hedged item in a fair value hedge in the consolidated financial statements of a parent because consolidation recognises in profit or loss the subsidiary's profit or loss, rather than changes in the investment's fair value. *[IAS 39.AG99]*. However, it would in our view be possible to hedge the foreign exchange risk in the carrying value of a foreign currency denominated investment in the parent entity's separate financial statements. Further, we believe it would be possible to hedge the change in the entire fair value of the investment even if the fair value is not reflected in the financial statements. This hedge relationship would most likely be treated as a fair value hedge and would require an adjustment to be made to the carrying value of the investment.

The ongoing accounting for fair value hedges is described at 4.1 below.

3.1.1 *Hedges of firm commitments*

A hedge of a firm commitment (e.g. a hedge of the change in fuel price relating to an unrecognised contractual commitment by an electricity utility to purchase fuel at a fixed price) is considered a hedge of an exposure to a change in fair value. Accordingly, such a hedge is a fair value hedge. However, a hedge of the foreign currency risk of a firm commitment may be accounted for as a fair value hedge or a cash flow hedge (this is discussed further at 3.2.2 below). *[IAS 39.87, AG104]*.

3.1.2 *Hedges of foreign currency monetary items*

A foreign currency monetary asset or liability that is hedged using a forward exchange contract may be treated as a fair value hedge because its fair value will change as foreign exchange rates change. Alternatively, it may be treated as a cash flow hedge because changes in exchange rates will affect the amount of cash required to settle the item (as measured by reference to the entity's functional currency) (see 4.2.2 below). *[IAS 39.F3.3-F3.4]*.

3.2 Cash flow hedges

An example of a cash flow hedge is the use of an interest rate swap to change floating rate debt to fixed rate debt, i.e. a hedge of a future transaction where the future cash flows being hedged are the future interest payments. *[IAS 39.AG103]*.

As noted at 3.1 above, a hedge of the exposure to changes in the fair value of a fixed rate debt instrument as a result of changes in interest rates could be treated as a fair value hedge. This could not be a cash flow hedge because changes in interest rates will not affect the cash flows on the hedged item, only its fair value. *[IAS 39.F.3.1]*.

It was also noted at 3.1 above that a copper forward, say, may be used in a fair value hedge of copper inventory. Alternatively, the same hedging instrument may qualify as a cash flow hedge of the future sale of the inventory. *[IAS 39.F.3.6]*.

The following example from the implementation guidance explains how a company might lock in current interest rates by way of a cash flow hedge of the anticipated issuance of fixed rate debt.

Example 52.21: Hedge of anticipated issuance of fixed rate debt

Company R periodically issues new bonds to refinance maturing bonds, provide working capital, and for various other purposes. When R decides it will be issuing bonds, it sometimes hedges the risk of changes in long-term interest rates to the date the bonds are issued. If long-term interest rates go up (down), the bond will be issued either at a higher (lower) rate, with a higher (smaller) discount or with a smaller (higher) premium than was originally expected. The higher (lower) rate being paid or decrease (increase) in proceeds is normally offset by the gain (loss) on the hedge.

In August 2017 R decides it will issue £2m seven-year bonds in January 2018. Historical correlation studies suggest that a seven-year treasury bond adequately correlates to the bonds R expects to issue, assuming a hedge ratio of 0.93 future contracts to one debt unit. Therefore, it hedges the anticipated issuance of the bonds by selling ('shorting') £1.86m worth of futures on seven-year treasury bonds.

From August 2017 to January 2018 interest rates increase and the short futures positions are closed on the date the bonds are issued. This results in a £120,000 gain, which offsets the increased interest payments on the bonds and, therefore, will affect profit or loss over the life of the bonds. The hedge may qualify as a cash flow hedge of the interest rate risk on the forecast debt issuance (assuming all other conditions for hedge accounting are met). *[IAS 39.F.2.2]*.

Similarly, the forecast reinvestment of interest cash flows from a fixed rate asset can be the subject of a cash flow hedge using, say, a forward rate agreement to lock in the interest rate that will be received on that reinvestment. *[IAS 39.F.3.2]*.

The ongoing accounting for cash flow hedges is described at 4.2 below.

3.2.1 All-in-one hedges

There are situations where an instrument that is accounted for as a derivative under IAS 39 is expected to be settled gross by delivery of the underlying asset in exchange for the payment of a fixed price. The implementation guidance states that such an instrument can be designated as the hedging instrument in a cash flow hedge of the variability of the consideration to be paid or received in the future transaction that will occur on gross settlement of the derivative contract itself. It is explained that this is acceptable because there *would* be an exposure to variability in the purchase or sale price without the derivative. It is important to note that, in order to qualify for a hedge of a highly probable forecast transaction, the hedging entity must have the intention (and the ability) to gross settle the derivative. For example, consider an entity that enters into a fixed price contract to sell a commodity and that contract is accounted for as a derivative under IAS 39 (see Chapter 43 at 4). This might be because the entity has a practice of settling such contracts net in cash or of taking delivery of the underlying and selling it within a short period after delivery for the purpose of generating a profit from short-term fluctuations in price or dealer's margin. In this case, the fixed price contract may be designated as a cash flow hedge of the variability of the consideration to be received on the sale of the asset (a future transaction) even though the fixed price contract is the contract under which the asset will be sold. *[IAS 39.F.2.5]*.

Similarly, an entity may enter into a forward contract to purchase a debt instrument (which will not be classified at fair value through profit or loss) that will be settled by delivery, but the forward contract is a derivative. This will be the case if its term exceeds the regular way delivery period in the marketplace (see Chapter 48 at 2.2). In this case the forward may be designated as a cash flow hedge of the variability of the consideration to be paid to acquire the debt instrument (a future transaction), even though the derivative is the contract under which the debt instrument will be acquired. *[IAS 39.F.2.5]*. If the debt instrument was to be classified at fair value through profit or loss, the all-in-one hedge strategy could not be applied (see 2.2.7 above).

It might come as a surprise to many entities that such contracts are, in fact, derivatives as defined. *[IAS 39.9]*. Therefore, the use of an 'all-in-one hedge' strategy for such instruments could prove useful in keeping fair value gains and losses, on what might be considered little more than purchase or sale orders, from being recognised immediately in profit or loss.

However, it seems best to accept the all-in-one hedge for what it is, i.e. a pragmatic concession, rather than trying to determine how it is derived from the principles of the standard. For example, the hedged item in each of the above two paragraphs, i.e. the spot price payment on the future purchase or sale of the asset, appears to be a cash flow that will never happen because the asset will be purchased or sold for the fixed price specified in the contract. Further, the hedged item (i.e. the contracted sale or purchase) also appears to be accounted for as a derivative, which is generally prohibited (see 2.2.7 above).

3.2.2 *Hedges of firm commitments*

A hedge of the foreign currency risk of a firm commitment may be accounted for as a cash flow hedge or a fair value hedge (see 3.1.1 above). *[IAS 39.87, AG104]*. This is because foreign currency risk affects both the cash flows and the fair value of the hedged item. Accordingly, a foreign currency cash flow hedge of a forecast transaction need not be redesignated as a fair value hedge when the forecast transaction becomes a firm commitment. *[IAS 39.BC154]*.

3.2.3 *Hedges of foreign currency monetary items*

A foreign currency monetary asset or liability that is hedged using a forward exchange contract may be treated as a fair value hedge because its fair value will change as foreign exchange rates change. Alternatively, it may be treated as a cash flow hedge because changes in exchange rates will affect the amount of cash required to settle the item (as measured by reference to the entity's functional currency) (see 4.2.2 below). *[IAS 39.F3.3-F3.4]*.

3.3 Hedges of net investments in foreign operations

Many reporting entities have investments in foreign operations which may be subsidiaries, associates, joint ventures or branches. As set out in Chapter 15 at 4, IAS 21 requires an entity to determine the functional currency of each of its foreign operations as the currency of the primary economic environment of that operation. When translating the results and financial position of its foreign operation into a presentation currency, it should recognise foreign exchange differences in other comprehensive income until disposal of the foreign operation. *[IFRIC 16.1]*.

From the perspective of an investor (e.g. a parent) it is clear that an investment in a foreign operation is likely to give rise to a degree of foreign currency exchange rate risk and an entity with many foreign operations may be exposed to a number of foreign currency risks. *[IFRIC 16.4]*. Whilst equity method investments and investments in consolidated subsidiaries cannot be hedged items in a fair value hedge because changes in the investments' fair value are not recognised in profit or loss, they may be designated in a net investment hedge relationship. A hedge of a net investment in a foreign operation is said to be different because it is a hedge of the foreign currency exposure, not a fair value hedge of the change in the value of the investment. *[IAS 39.AG99]*.

Conceptually, net investment hedging is somewhat unsatisfactory, as it mixes foreign currency translation risk (largely an accounting exposure) with transactional risk (much more an economic exposure). IFRIC 16 – *Hedges of a Net Investment in a Foreign Operation* – addresses the question of what does and does not constitute a valid hedging relationship, a topic on which IAS 39 provided very little guidance.

IFRIC 16 applies to any entity that hedges the foreign currency risk arising from its net investments in foreign operations and wishes to qualify for hedge accounting in accordance with IAS 39. *[IFRIC 16.7]*. It only applies to those hedges and should not be applied by analogy to other types of hedge accounting. *[IFRIC 16.8]*. For the avoidance of doubt, IFRIC 16 explains that such a hedge can be applied only when the net assets of that foreign operation are included in the financial statements. This will be the case for consolidated financial statements, financial statements in which investments such as associates or joint ventures are accounted for using the equity method or those that include a branch or a joint operation (as defined in IFRS 11 – *Joint Arrangements*). *[IFRIC 16.2]*. For convenience, IFRIC 16 refers to such an entity as a parent entity and to the financial statements in which the net assets of foreign operations are included as consolidated financial statements and this section follows this convention.

Investments in foreign operations may be held directly by a parent entity or indirectly by its subsidiary or subsidiaries.

The requirements of IFRIC 16 are discussed in more detail at 3.3.1 to 3.3.4 below and, in the case of assessing and measuring the effectiveness of such a hedge, at 5.3.13 below.

3.3.1 Nature of the hedged risk

Perhaps the most important decision made by the IFRS Interpretations Committee was that hedge accounting may be applied only to the foreign exchange differences arising between the functional currency of the foreign operation and the parent entity's functional currency. *[IFRIC 16.10]*. Furthermore, the hedged risk may be designated as the foreign currency exposure arising between the functional currency of the foreign operation and the functional currency of any parent entity (the immediate, intermediate or ultimate parent entity) of that foreign operation. The fact that the net investment may be held through an intermediate parent does not affect the nature of the economic risk arising from the foreign currency exposure to the ultimate parent entity. *[IFRIC 16.12]*. This principle is illustrated in the following example.

Example 52.22: Nature of the hedged risk in a net investment hedge

Company P is the ultimate parent entity of a group and presents its consolidated financial statements in its functional currency of euro. It has two direct wholly owned subsidiaries, Company A whose functional currency is Japanese yen and Company B whose functional currency is sterling. B has a wholly owned subsidiary, Company C, whose functional currency is US dollars. P's net investment in A is ¥400,000 million which includes A's external borrowings of US$300 million. P's net investment in B is £500 million including the equivalent of £159 million representing B's net investment in C of US$300 million. This corporate structure is illustrated as follows:

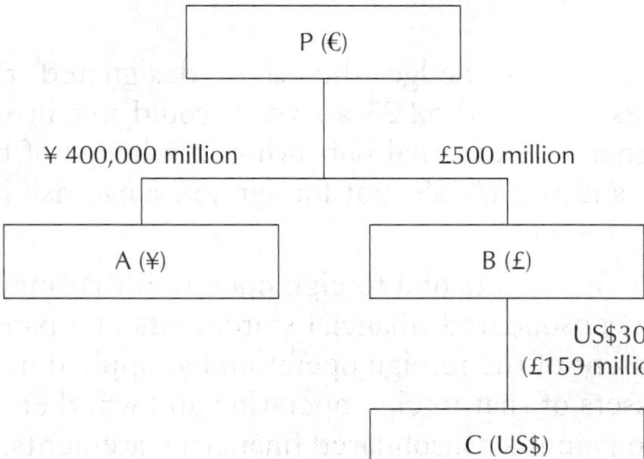

P, in its consolidated financial statements, could hedge its net investment in each of A, B and C for the foreign exchange risk between their functional currencies (Japanese yen, sterling and US dollars respectively) and euro. P could also hedge the foreign exchange risk between the functional currencies of B (sterling) and C (US dollars).

In its consolidated financial statements, B could hedge its net investment in C for the foreign exchange risk between C's functional currency (US dollars) and its own (pounds sterling). *[IFRIC 16.AG1-AG3].*

Where a non-derivative instrument is used as the hedging instrument, the designated risk should be the spot foreign exchange risk; if the hedging instruments were forward contracts, the forward or the spot foreign exchange risk could be designated as the hedged risk (see 5.3.13 below). *[IFRIC 16.AG2].*

3.3.2 *Amount of the hedged item for which a hedging relationship may be designated*

The hedged item can be an amount of net assets equal to or less than the carrying amount of the net assets of the foreign operation in the consolidated financial statements of the parent entity. *[IFRIC 16.11].*

Example 52.23: Amount of hedged item in a net investment hedge

The facts are as in Example 52.22 above. If P wished to hedge the foreign exchange risk from its net investment in C, the hedged item could be an amount of net assets equal to or less than the US$300 million carrying amount of C in P's consolidated financial statements. *[IFRIC 16.AG4].*

The carrying amount of the net investment takes account of monetary items receivable from or payable to a foreign operation for which settlement is neither planned nor likely to occur in the future. Under IAS 21 these balances are considered to be, in substance, part of the reporting entity's net investment in the foreign operation. In the case of a loan made to the foreign operation this will increase the amount that can be hedged; if a loan is made by the foreign operation, the amount that can be hedged will be reduced. *[IFRIC 16.AG14].*

In many cases the full economic value of a net investment will not be recognised in the financial statements. The most common reason will be the existence of, say, goodwill or intangible assets that are either not recognised or measured at an amount below their current value. In these situations, if an investor hedges the entire economic value of its net investment it will not be able to obtain hedge accounting for the proportion of the hedging instrument that exceeds the recognised net assets.

A single hedging instrument can hedge the same designated risk only once. Consequently, in Examples 52.22 and 52.23 above, P could not in its consolidated financial statements designate A's external borrowing in a hedge of both the €/US$ spot foreign exchange risk and the £/US$ spot foreign exchange risk in respect of its net investment in C. *[IFRIC 16.AG6]*.

The carrying amount of the net assets of a foreign operation that may be designated as the hedged item in the consolidated financial statements of a parent depends on whether any lower level parent of the foreign operation has applied hedge accounting for all or part of the net assets of that foreign operation and whether that accounting has been maintained in the parent's consolidated financial statements. *[IFRIC 16.11]*. An exposure to foreign currency risk arising from a net investment in a foreign operation may qualify for hedge accounting only once in the consolidated financial statements. Therefore, if the same net assets of a foreign operation are hedged by more than one parent entity within the group (for example, both a direct and an indirect parent entity) for the same risk, only one hedging relationship will qualify for hedge accounting in the consolidated financial statements of the ultimate parent. *[IFRIC 16.13]*. This is illustrated in the following example.

Example 52.24: Amount of hedged item in a net investment hedge (different hedged risks)

The facts are the same as in Examples 52.22 and 52.23 above except that P's net assets include £500 million and US$300 million of external borrowings. If P wished to hedge the foreign exchange risk in relation to its net investments in B and C, the designations it could make in its consolidated financial statements include the following: *[IFRIC 16.AG10]*

- US$300 million of the US dollar borrowings designated as a hedge of the net investment in C with the risk being the spot foreign exchange exposure (€/US$) between P and C and up to £341 million of the sterling borrowings designated as a hedge of the net investment in B with the risk being the spot foreign exchange exposure (€/£) between P and B; or
- US$300 million of the US dollar borrowings as a hedge of the net investment in C with the risk being the spot foreign exchange exposure (£/US$) between B and C and up to £500 million of the sterling borrowings designated as a hedge of the net investment in B with the risk being the spot foreign exchange exposure (€/£) between P and B.

The €/US$ risk from P's net investment in C is a different risk from the €/£ risk from P's net investment in B. However, in the first case described above, P would have already fully hedged the €/US$ risk from its net investment in C and if P also designated its £500 million of borrowings as a hedge of its net investment in B, £159 million of that net investment, representing the sterling equivalent of its US dollar net investment in C, would be hedged twice for £/€ risk in P's consolidated financial statements. *[IFRIC 16.AG11]*. In the second case described above, because the designation of the US$/£ risk between B and C does not include the £/€ risk, P is also able to designate up to £500 million of its net investment in B with the risk being the spot foreign exchange exposure (£/€) between P and B. *[IFRIC 16.AG12]*.

A hedging relationship designated by one parent entity in its consolidated financial statements need not be maintained by another higher level parent entity. However, if it is not maintained by the higher level parent entity, the hedge accounting applied by the lower level parent must be reversed before the higher level parent's hedge accounting is recognised. *[IFRIC 16.13]*. This is illustrated in the following example.

Example 52.25: Hedge accounting applied by intermediate parent

The facts are the same as in Examples 52.22 and 52.23 above, except that P's net assets include £500 million of external borrowings and B's net assets of £341 million include US$300 million of external borrowings which it designates as a hedge of the £/US$ risk of its net investment in C in its own consolidated financial statements.

P could maintain B's designation of that hedging instrument as a hedge of its net investment in C for the £/US$ risk and P could designate its £500 million external borrowings as a hedge of its entire net investment in B. The first hedge, designated by B, would be assessed by reference to B's functional currency (sterling) and the second hedge, designated by P, would be assessed by reference to P's functional currency (euro). In this case, only the £/US$ risk from P's net investment in C has been hedged in its consolidated financial statements by B's US dollar borrowings, not the entire €/US$ risk. Therefore, the entire €/£ risk from P's net investment in B may be hedged in P's consolidated financial statements. *[IFRIC 16.AG13]*.

Alternatively, P could reverse the hedging relationship designated by B. In this case, it could designate B's US$300 million external borrowing as a hedge of its net investment in C for the €/US$ risk and designate £341 million of its borrowings as a hedge of part of the net investment in B. In this case the effectiveness of both hedges would be computed by reference to P's functional currency (euro). Consequently, both the US$/£ and £/€ changes in value of B's US$300 million borrowing would be included in P's foreign currency translation reserve. Because P has already fully hedged the €/US$ risk from its net investment in C, it could hedge only up to £341 million for the €/GBP risk of its net investment in B. *[IFRIC 16.AG15]*.

3.3.3 Where the hedging instrument can be held

The hedging instrument(s) may be held by any entity or entities within the group, including the foreign operation being hedged, provided the designation, documentation and effectiveness requirements of IAS 39 are satisfied. The hedging strategy of the group should be clearly documented because of the possibility of different designations at different levels of the group (see 3.3.2 above). *[IFRIC 16.14, BC24A, BC24B]*.

Where the entity holding the hedging instrument has a functional currency that is not the same as the parent by which the hedged risk is defined, this could result in the recognition of ineffectiveness in profit or loss – this is discussed further at 5.3.12 below.

Clearly the reporting entity (which, in the case of consolidated financial statements, includes any subsidiary consolidated by the parent) must be a party to the hedging instrument. In Examples 52.22 and 52.23 above, therefore, B could not apply hedge accounting in its consolidated financial statements in respect of a hedge involving the US$300 million borrowing issued by A because the hedging instrument is held outside of the group headed by B. *[IFRIC 16.AG6]*.

3.3.4 Disposal of a hedged foreign operation

When a foreign operation that was hedged is disposed of, the amount reclassified from the foreign currency translation reserve to profit or loss in respect of the hedging instrument is the amount that IAS 39 requires to be identified, being the cumulative gain or loss on the hedging instrument that was determined to be an effective hedge (see 5.3.12 below). *[IFRIC 16.16]*. If the step-by-step method of consolidation is used, this amount could be different to the equivalent amount of gains or losses accumulated within equity arising on the retranslation of that entity (see Chapter 15 at 6.1.5 and at 6.6). *[IFRIC 16.17]*.

Example 52.26: Disposal of foreign operation

Based on the same facts as in Examples 52.22 and 52.23 above, the group has designated US$300 million of the US dollar borrowings of A as a hedge of the net investment in C with the risk being the spot foreign exchange exposure (€/US$) between P and C. If C were disposed of, the amounts reclassified to profit or loss in P's consolidated financial statements from its foreign currency translation reserve would be: *[IFRIC 16.17, AG8]*

- in respect of A's borrowing, the amount that IAS 39 requires to be identified, i.e. the total change in value in respect of foreign exchange risk that was recognised in other comprehensive income as the effective portion of the hedge; and
- in respect of the net investment in C, the amount determined by the entity's consolidation method. If P uses the direct method, its foreign currency translation reserve ('FCTR') in respect of C will be determined directly by the EUR/USD foreign exchange rate. If P uses the step-by-step method, its FCTR in respect of C will be determined by the FCTR recognised by B reflecting the GBP/USD foreign exchange rate, translated to P's functional currency using the EUR/GBP foreign exchange rate. P's use of the step-by-step method for consolidation in prior periods does not require it to or preclude it from determining the amount of FCTR to be reclassified when it disposes of C to be the amount that it would have recognised if it had always used the direct method, however, it is an accounting policy choice which should be followed consistently for all net investments.

4 ACCOUNTING FOR EFFECTIVE HEDGES

If there is a designated hedging relationship between a hedging instrument and a hedged item as described at 3 above and it meets the conditions set out at 5 below, the accounting for the gain or loss on the hedging instrument and the hedged item will be as set out in the remainder of this section. *[IAS 39.71]*. This is referred to as 'hedge accounting' and is said to recognise the offsetting effects on profit or loss of changes in the fair values of the hedging instrument and the hedged item. *[IAS 39.85]*.

4.1 Fair value hedges

4.1.1 Ongoing fair value hedge accounting

If a fair value hedge (see 3.1 above) meets the qualifying conditions set out at 5 below during the period, it should be accounted for as follows:

- the gain or loss from remeasuring the hedging instrument at fair value (for a derivative hedging instrument) or the foreign currency component of its carrying amount measured in accordance with IAS 21 (for a non-derivative hedging instrument) is recognised in profit or loss; and
- the carrying amount of the hedged item is adjusted for the change in its value attributable to the hedged risk and the gain or loss is recognised in profit or loss. This applies if the hedged item is an available-for-sale financial asset (and that gain or loss would otherwise be recognised in other comprehensive income) or if it is otherwise measured at cost. *[IAS 39.89]*.

It will be rare for the change in fair value of the hedging instrument (or, for non-derivative hedging instruments, foreign exchange gains or losses) to be exactly the same as the change in fair value of the hedged item attributable to the hedged risk, even for highly effective hedges. To the extent these amounts differ, a net amount will be recognised in profit or loss. The recognition of this difference is commonly referred to as the measurement of hedge ineffectiveness. Although not clearly evident from the standard, we believe the gain or loss from remeasuring the hedging instrument and the gain or loss from adjusting the hedged item should be recognised in the same line item in profit or loss to reflect the offsetting effect of hedge accounting (see Chapter 54 at 7.1.3).

The following simple example illustrates how the treatment above might apply to a hedge of fair value interest rate risk on an investment in fixed rate debt.

Example 52.27: Fair value hedge

At the beginning of Year 1 an investor purchases a fixed rate debt security for £100 and classifies it as available-for-sale. At the end of Year 1, the fair value of the asset is £110. To protect this value, the investor enters into a hedge by acquiring a derivative with a nil fair value. By the end of Year 2, the derivative has a fair value of £5 and the debt security has a corresponding decline in fair value (its fair value does not change as a result of any factors other than interest rates).

The investor would record the following accounting entries:

Year 1

Beginning of year	£	£
Debt security	100	
Cash		100

To reflect the acquisition of the security.

End of year	£	£
Debt security	10	
Other comprehensive income		10

To record the increase in the security's fair value in other comprehensive income.

Year 2

Beginning of year	£	£
Derivative	–	
Cash		–

To record the acquisition of the derivative at its fair value of nil.

End of year	£	£
Derivative	5	
Profit or loss		5

To recognise the increase in the derivative's fair value in profit or loss.

	£	£
Profit or loss	5	
Debt security		5

To recognise the decrease in the security's fair value in profit or loss.

The example is taken from the original version of the standard and was not carried forward into the December 2003 version of the standard, although it is not entirely clear why not. Even if it was considered too simplistic to be a useful practical example (it does not deal, for example, with net cash settlements on the derivative, coupon payments on the debt or the subsequent impact on the recognition of interest under the effective interest method), it does illustrate the basic mechanics of fair value hedge accounting quite well.

The standard explains that if only particular risks attributable to a hedged financial instrument are hedged, the recognised changes in the fair value of the hedged item that are unrelated to the hedged risk should be recognised as set out in Chapter 49 at 2. *[IAS 39.90]*. Therefore, for instruments measured at amortised cost, these other gains and losses would generally not be recognised; for available-for-sale assets those gains and losses would generally be recognised in other comprehensive income. Exceptions to this would include foreign currency retranslation gains or losses on monetary items and impairment losses, which would be recognised in profit or loss in any event. The following example illustrates this.

Example 52.28: Hedging foreign currency risk of publicly traded shares

Company C, whose functional currency is sterling, acquires 100,000 shares in a listed US corporation for US$1m, which it classifies as available-for-sale. It is assumed the shares gives rise to a clear and identifiable exposure to changes in the US dollar/sterling exchange rate and to protect itself from changes in this exchange rate, C enters into a forward contract to sell US$0.75m which it intends to roll over for as long as the shares are held.

A portion of an exposure may be designated as a hedged item, and so the forward contract may be designated as a hedge of part of the shareholding. It could be a fair value hedge of the foreign exchange exposure of US$0.75m associated with the shares (alternatively it could be a cash flow hedge of a forecast sale of the shares but only if the timing of the sale is identified with sufficient certainty). Any variability in the fair value of the shares in US dollars would not affect the assessment of hedge effectiveness unless their fair value fell below US$0.75m. *[IAS 39.F.2.19]*.

Gains and losses on the forward contract would be recognised in profit or loss. Gains and losses arising from remeasuring the dollar value of the hedged portion of the shares to sterling would also be recognised in profit or loss and the remainder would be recognised in other comprehensive income (as would all of the foreign currency amount were it not for the hedge relationship).

The basic hedge accounting treatment above applies equally to fair value hedges of unrecognised firm commitments. Therefore, where an unrecognised firm commitment is designated as a hedged item in a fair value hedge, the subsequent cumulative change in its fair value attributable to the hedged risk should be recognised as an asset or liability with a corresponding gain or loss recognised in profit or loss. Thereafter, the firm commitment would be a *recognised* asset or liability (albeit that its carrying amount will not represent either its cost or, necessarily, its fair value). The changes in the fair value of the hedging instrument would also be recognised in profit or loss. *[IAS 39.93]*.

It can be seen that applying fair value hedge accounting adjustments does not change the accounting for the hedging instrument. This is true whether the hedging instrument is a derivative or non-derivative instrument (in a hedge of foreign currency risk). For example, if a foreign currency cash instrument was designated as the hedging instrument in a fair value hedge (see 2.1.2 above), the foreign currency component of its carrying amount would continue to be measured in accordance with IAS 21. *[IAS 39.89(a)]*.

4.1.2 Dealing with adjustments to the hedged item

In general, adjustments to the hedged asset or liability arising from the application of hedge accounting as described at 4.1.1 above are dealt with in accordance with the normal accounting treatment for that item. For example, copper inventory might be the hedged item in a fair value hedge of the exposure to changes in the copper price. In this case, the adjusted carrying amount of the copper inventory becomes the cost basis for the purpose of applying the lower of cost and net realisable value test under IAS 2 – *Inventories* (see Chapter 22 at 3). *[IAS 39.F.3.6]*.

Where the hedged item is a financial instrument for which the effective interest method of accounting is used, the adjustment should be amortised to profit or loss. Amortisation may begin as soon as the adjustment exists and should begin no later than when the hedged item ceases to be adjusted for changes in its fair value attributable to the hedged risk. The adjustment should be based on a recalculated effective interest rate at the date amortisation begins and should be fully amortised by maturity. *[IAS 39.92]*.

When an entity enters into a firm commitment to acquire an asset or assume a liability that is a hedged item in a fair value hedge, the initial carrying amount of the asset or liability that results from the entity meeting the firm commitment is adjusted to include the cumulative change in the fair value of the firm commitment attributable to the hedged risk that was recognised in the statement of financial position. *[IAS 39.94]*.

Example 52.29: Hedge of a firm commitment to acquire equipment

Company X has the euro as its functional currency. It has chosen to treat all hedges of foreign currency risk associated with firm commitments as fair value hedges. In January 2017 it contracts with a US supplier (with the US dollar as its functional currency) to purchase an item of machinery it intends to use in its business. The machine will be delivered at the start of July 2017 and the contracted price, payable on delivery, is US$1,000.

X has no appetite to take on foreign currency exchange risk in relation to euro/US dollar exchange rates and so contracts with a bank to purchase US$1,000 at the start of July in exchange for €900 (six month forward exchange rate is US$1:€0.90). In other words, X has effectively fixed the price it will pay for the machine (in euro terms) at €900.

If the fair value of the forward contract at the end of March 2017 (X's year end) is €30 positive to X, on delivery is €50 positive to X (spot exchange rate is US$1:€0.95) and assuming the hedge is perfectly effective (this might be the case if the hedged risk is identified as the forward exchange rate rather than the spot rate – see 5.3.3 below) and meets all the requirements for hedge accounting, the journal entries to record this hedging relationship would be as follows:

January 2017

No entries are required as the firm commitment is unrecognised, the forward contract is recognised but has a zero fair value and no cash is paid or received.

March 2017

	€	€
Forward contract	30	
Profit or loss		30

To recognise the change in fair value of the forward contract in profit or loss.

	€	€
Profit or loss	30	
Firm commitment		30

To recognise the change in fair value of the (previously) unrecognised firm commitment in respect of changes in forward exchange rates in profit or loss.

July 2017

	€	€
Forward contract	20	
Profit or loss		20

To recognise the change in fair value of the forward contract in profit or loss.

	€	€
Profit or loss	20	
Firm commitment		20

To recognise the change in fair value of the (now recognised) firm commitment in respect of changes in forward exchange rates in profit or loss.

	€	€
Cash	50	
Forward contract		50

To record the settlement of the forward contract at its fair value.

	€	€
Machine	950	
Cash		950

To record the settlement of the firm commitment at the contracted price of US$1,000 at the spot rate of US$1:€0.95.

	€	€
Firm commitment	50	
Machine		50

To remove the carrying amount of the firm commitment from the statement of financial position and adjust the initial carrying amount of the machine that results from the firm commitment.

In summary, the result of these accounting entries is as follows:

	€	€
Machine	900	
Cash		900

which is somewhat reassuring given the starting presumption, i.e. that X had effectively fixed the purchase price of its machine at €900.

4.1.3 Discontinuing fair value hedge accounting

The ongoing fair value hedge accounting set out at 4.1.1 above should be discontinued prospectively if any one of the following occurs:

- the hedging instrument expires or is sold, terminated, or exercised.

  For this purpose, the replacement or a rollover of a hedging instrument into another is not an expiration or termination if that is part of the documented hedging strategy.

  Further, an expiration or termination of the hedging instrument is not considered to have occurred for this purpose if:

  - as a consequence of laws or regulations or the introduction of laws or regulations, the parties to the hedging instrument agree that one or more clearing counterparties replace their original counterparty to become the new counterparty to each of the parties. For this purpose, a clearing counterparty is a central counterparty (sometimes called a 'clearing organisation' or 'clearing agency') or an entity or entities, for example, a clearing member of a clearing organisation or a client of a clearing member of a clearing organisation, that are acting as counterparty in order to effect clearing by a central counterparty. However, when the parties to the hedging instrument replace their original counterparties with different counterparties this paragraph shall apply only if each of those parties effects clearing with the same central counterparty; and
  - other changes, if any, to the hedging instrument are limited to those that are necessary to effect such a replacement of the counterparty. Such changes are limited to those that are consistent with the terms that would be expected if the hedging instrument were originally cleared with the clearing counterparty. These changes include changes in the collateral requirements, rights to offset receivables and payables balances, and charges levied;
- the hedge no longer meets the hedge effectiveness criteria for hedge accounting; or
- the designation is revoked. *[IAS 39.91]*.

If the reason the hedge no longer meets the criteria for qualification for hedge accounting is that it does not meet the hedge effectiveness criteria, hedge accounting should be discontinued from the last date on which compliance with hedge effectiveness was demonstrated. However, if the event or change in circumstances that caused the hedging relationship to fail the effectiveness criteria can be identified, and it can be demonstrated that the hedge was effective before the event or change in circumstances occurred, the hedge accounting should be discontinued from the date of the event or change in circumstances. *[IAS 39.AG113]*.

Example 52.30: Hedge of foreign exchange risk from currency pegged to the US dollar

Company Z has the euro as its functional currency and prepares annual financial statements for the year ended 31 December. It also prepares interim financial statements for the six months ended 30 June and, in general, assesses the effectiveness of hedges at these dates.

In January 2017, Z acquires an equity instrument issued by a company whose functional currency is the FC. It is assumed the investment has a clear and identifiable exposure to changes in the FC/euro exchange rate and is classified as available-for-sale. For many years the value of the FC has been pegged to the US dollar and historical studies show that during this time the FC/US dollar exchange rate has never moved outside of a corridor representing 2.5% of the mean rate. Furthermore, there is no evidence to suggest that the peg will not continue for the foreseeable future.

Accordingly, in January 2017, Z is able to designate a US dollar denominated borrowing as a highly effective hedge of the foreign currency risk associated with part of the equity instrument.

At the end of June 2017, Z performs an effectiveness assessment and determines that the hedge has been highly effective and, therefore, changes in the value of the equity instrument attributable to changes in the FC/euro exchange rate are recognised in profit or loss rather than other comprehensive income, together with the exchange differences on the US dollar borrowing.

At the beginning of October 2017, there is an unexpected financial crisis, the peg ceases and the FC is devalued by 25% relative to the US dollar.

When Z assesses the effectiveness of the hedge in December 2017 it concludes that, because of the cessation of the peg and consequent devaluation, the hedge can no longer be regarded as highly effective and that hedge accounting should cease.

However, Z is able to determine that the failure of the hedge arose because of the cessation of the FC/US dollar peg and subsequent devaluation at the beginning of October 2017. Therefore, it is able to apply hedge accounting for the first three months of its second interim period. Thus, changes in the value of the equity instrument attributable to changes in the FC/euro exchange rate for that period will be recognised in profit or loss, but thereafter will be recognised in other comprehensive income when accounting for the available-for-sale asset at fair value.

In other cases, hedge accounting should be discontinued from the date the hedging instrument expires or is sold, terminated or exercised, or the hedge designation is revoked. For example, if the forward contract in Example 52.29 above were settled (or the hedge designation was revoked) at the end of March 2016, no further adjustments to the carrying value of the firm commitment (€30) would be made after that date.

4.2 Cash flow hedges

4.2.1 Ongoing cash flow hedge accounting

If a cash flow hedge (see 3.2 above) meets the qualifying conditions set out in 5 below, it should be accounted for as follows:

- the portion of the gain or loss on the hedging instrument that is determined to be an effective hedge should be recognised in other comprehensive income; and
- the ineffective portion should be recognised immediately in profit or loss. *[IAS 39.95, F.4.5]*.

More specifically, the accounting should be as follows:

- the separate component of equity associated with the hedged item is adjusted to the lesser of the following (in absolute amounts):
  - (i) the cumulative gain or loss on the hedging instrument from inception of the hedge; and
  - (ii) the cumulative change in fair value (present value) of the expected future cash flows on the hedged item from inception of the hedge;
- any remaining gain or loss on the hedging instrument or designated component of it (that is not an effective hedge) is recognised in profit or loss; and
- if the documented risk management strategy for a particular hedging relationship excludes from the assessment of hedge effectiveness a specific component of the gain or loss or related cash flows on the hedging instrument, that excluded component of gain or loss is recognised as set out in Chapter 49 at 2 (effectively in profit or loss for a derivative hedging instrument).

  Those excluded components can include the time value of an option, the interest element of a forward contract or a proportion of an instrument (see 2.1.4 above). *[IAS 39.96].*

The requirements set out in the first two bullets are often referred to as the 'lower of' requirements. This accounting treatment is illustrated in the following examples.

Example 52.31: Cash flow hedge of anticipated commodity sale

On 30 September 2017, Company A hedges the anticipated sale of 24 tonnes of pulp on 1 March 2018 by entering into a short forward contract. The contract requires net settlement in cash, determined as the difference between the future spot price of 24 tonnes of pulp on a specified commodity exchange and £1m. A expects to sell the pulp in a different, local market.

A determines that the forward contract is an effective hedge of the anticipated sale and that the other conditions for hedge accounting are met. It assesses hedge effectiveness by comparing the entire change in the fair value of the forward contract with the change in the fair value of the expected cash inflows. On 31 December 2017, the spot price of pulp has increased both in the local market and on the exchange, although the increase in the local market exceeds the increase on the exchange. As a result, the present value of the expected cash inflow from the sale on the local market is £1.1m and the fair value of the forward is £85,000 negative. The hedge is determined to be still highly effective.

The cumulative change in the fair value of the forward contract is £85,000, while the fair value of the cumulative change in expected future cash flows on the hedged item is £100,000. Ineffectiveness is not recognised in the financial statements because the cumulative change in the fair value of the hedged cash flows exceeds the cumulative change in the value of the hedging instrument. The whole of the fair value change in the forward contract would be recognised in other comprehensive income.

December 2017

	£'000	£'000
Other comprehensive income	85	
Forward contract		85

However, if A concluded that the hedge was no longer highly effective, it would discontinue hedge accounting prospectively as from the date the hedge ceased to be highly effective (see 4.2.3 below). *[IAS 39.F.5.3].*

Example 52.32: Cash flow hedge of a floating rate liability

Company A has a floating rate liability of £1m with five years remaining to maturity. It enters into a five year pay-fixed, receive-floating interest rate swap with the same principal terms to hedge the exposure to variable cash flow payments on the floating rate liability attributable to interest rate risk.

At inception, the swap's fair value is £nil. Subsequently, there is an increase of £49,000 which consists of a change of £50,000 resulting from an increase in market interest rates and a change of minus £1,000 resulting from an increase in the credit risk of the swap counterparty. There is no change in the fair value of the floating rate liability, but the fair value (present value) of the future cash flows needed to offset the exposure to variable interest cash flows on the liability increases by £50,000.

Even if A determines that the hedge of interest rate risk is 'highly effective' (simplistically, the offset ratio is 49,000 ÷ 50,000 or 98%, so this is quite likely), it is not fully effective if part of the change in the fair value of the derivative is due to the counterparty's credit risk (see 5.3.4 below). However, because the hedge relationship is still 'highly effective', A credits the effective portion of the swap's fair value change, £49,000, to other comprehensive income. There is no debit to profit or loss for the change in fair value of the swap attributable to the deterioration in the credit quality of the swap counterparty because the cumulative change in the present value of the future cash flows needed to offset the exposure to variable interest cash flows on the hedged item, £50,000, exceeds the cumulative change in value of the hedging instrument, £49,000. If A concluded that the hedge was no longer highly effective, it would discontinue hedge accounting prospectively as from the date the hedge ceased to be highly effective (see 4.2.3 below).

Alternatively, if the fair value of the swap increased to £51,000 of which £50,000 results from the increase in market interest rates and £1,000 from a decrease in the swap counterparty's credit risk, there would be a credit to profit or loss of £1,000 for the change in the swap's fair value attributable to the improvement in the counterparty's credit quality. This is because the cumulative change in the value of the hedging instrument, £51,000, exceeds the cumulative change in the present value of the future cash flows needed to offset the exposure to variable interest cash flows on the hedged item, £50,000. The difference of £1,000 represents the excess ineffectiveness attributable to the swap, and is recognised in profit or loss. *[IAS 39.F.5.2].*

It can be seen that the measurement of hedge ineffectiveness differs for a cash flow hedge when compared to a fair value hedge. In a cash flow hedge, if the fair value of the derivative increases by €10 and the present value of the hedged expected cash flows change by only €8, the €2 difference is recognised in profit or loss (as would be the case for a fair value hedge). However, if the present value of the hedged expected cash flows changes by €10, but the fair value of the derivative changes by only €8, this €2 of hedge ineffectiveness is *not* recognised in profit or loss (which would not be the case for a fair value hedge).

Because of this, an entity might consider deliberately under-hedging an exposure in a cash flow hedge. It might do this by targeting an offset of, say, 85% to 90%, which would keep it within the prescribed 80% to 125% range (see 5.3.1 below) but avoid the need to recognise ineffectiveness in profit or loss. However, such an approach is not permitted by IAS 39. *[IAS 39.AG107A, BC136A].*

4.2.2 Reclassification of gains and losses recognised in other comprehensive income from equity to profit or loss

If a hedged forecast transaction subsequently results in the recognition of a *financial* asset or liability, the associated gains or losses that were recognised in other comprehensive income should be reclassified from equity to profit or loss in the same period(s) during which the hedged forecast cash flows (or asset acquired or liability assumed) affect profit or loss, e.g. in the periods that interest income or interest expense is recognised. This reclassification is often referred to as 'recycling'. However, if it is expected that all or a portion of a loss recognised in other comprehensive income will not be recovered in one or more future periods, the amount that is not expected to be recovered should be reclassified from equity to profit or loss immediately. *[IAS 39.97]*.

If a hedged forecast transaction subsequently results in the recognition of a *non-financial* asset or liability (or a forecast transaction for a *non-financial* asset or liability becomes a firm commitment for which fair value hedge accounting is applied) then a choice of accounting policies is available. In these circumstances, an entity should either:

- reclassify the associated gains and losses that were recognised in other comprehensive income from equity to profit or loss in the same period(s) during which the asset acquired or liability assumed affects profit or loss, e.g. in the periods that depreciation expense or cost of sales is recognised. However, if it is expected that all or a portion of a loss recognised in other comprehensive income will not be recovered in one or more future periods, the amount that is not expected to be recovered should be reclassified from equity to profit or loss. Essentially this is the same treatment as for hedges of financial items; or
- remove the associated gains and losses that were recognised in other comprehensive income and include them in the initial cost or other carrying amount of the asset or liability, *[IAS 39.98]*, as a 'basis adjustment'.

An entity should adopt one of these as its accounting policy and apply it consistently to all relevant hedges. *[IAS 39.99]*. These treatments are illustrated in the following example.

Example 52.33: Hedge of a firm commitment to acquire equipment

Consider a variation of the situation in Example 52.29 at 4.1.2 above whereby Company X has chosen to treat all hedges of foreign currency risk associated with firm commitments as cash flow hedges, rather than as fair value hedges, as permitted by the standard (see 3.2.2 above). In the first case, X's accounting policy is to apply a basis adjustment to cash flow hedges that result in the recognition of non-financial assets or liabilities; in the second case it does not. Otherwise, the underlying facts and assumptions are the same. The accounting entries made at the end of March 2017 have not been shown separately (as they were in Example 52.29) because they are not relevant to the issue being illustrated.

Case 1: Basis adjustment

The journal entries to record this hedging relationship would be as follows:

January 2017

No entries are required as the firm commitment is unrecognised, the forward contract is recognised but has a zero fair value and no cash is paid or received.

July 2017

	€	€
Forward contract	50	
Other comprehensive income		50

To recognise the change in fair value of the forward contract and, because no ineffectiveness arises, the whole of this change is recognised in other comprehensive income.

	€	€
Cash	50	
Forward contract		50

To record the settlement of the forward contract at its fair value.

	€	€
Machine	950	
Cash		950

To record the settlement of the firm commitment at the contracted price of US$1,000 at the spot rate of US$1:€0.95.

	€	€
Other comprehensive income	50	
Machine		50

To remove the gain recognised in other comprehensive income and adjust the carrying amount of the machine that results from the hedged transaction by this amount.

In summary, the result of these accounting entries is as follows:

	€	€
Machine	900	
Cash		900

which again reflects the starting presumption, i.e. that X had effectively fixed the purchase price of its machine at €900.

Case 2: No basis adjustment

The journal entries to record this hedging relationship would be as follows:

January 2017

No entries are required as the firm commitment is unrecognised, the forward contract is recognised but has a zero fair value and no cash is paid or received.

July 2017

	€	€
Forward contract	50	
Other comprehensive income		50

To recognise the change in fair value of the forward contract and, because no ineffectiveness arises, the whole of this change is recognised in other comprehensive income.

	€	€
Cash	50	
Forward contract		50

To record the settlement of the forward contract at its fair value.

	€	€
Machine	950	
Cash		950

To record the settlement of the firm commitment at the contracted price of US$1,000 at the spot rate of US$1:€0.95.

In summary, the result of these accounting entries is as follows:

	€	€
Machine	950	
Cash		900
Other comprehensive income		50

The gain recognised in other comprehensive income would be reclassified from equity to profit or loss as the machine affects profit or loss, e.g. as it is depreciated, impaired or derecognised. If the machine has a very long useful economic life, this might involve tracking this adjustment for many years. The result might be considered less intuitive than the outcome on case 1.

The hedge accounting requirements of IFRS 9 eliminate the accounting policy choice and require a basis adjustment (see Chapter 53 at 8.1).

For all other cash flow hedges (i.e. those that do not result in the recognition of an asset or a liability), amounts that had been recognised in other comprehensive income should be reclassified from equity to profit or loss in the same period or periods during which the hedged forecast cash flows (or transaction) affects profit or loss, e.g. when a forecast sale occurs, *[IAS 39.100]*, or when variable rate interest income or expense is recognised. Although not clearly evident from the standard, we believe the reclassification from accumulated other comprehensive income to profit or loss should be recognised in the same line item in profit or loss as the hedged transaction to reflect the offsetting effect of hedge accounting (see Chapter 54 at 7.1.3).

When instruments such as conventional interest rate swaps are used as a hedging instrument in a cash flow hedge, it is common for entities to recognise net interest income or expense on the hedging instrument directly in profit or loss on an accruals basis. Other changes in fair value of the hedging instrument (i.e. the 'clean value' – excluding accrued interest) are recognised in other comprehensive income, subject to the 'lower of' requirements (see 4.2.1 above). Such an approach avoids the need to reclassify from equity to profit or loss the net interest as the hedged item impacts profit or loss. However, care must be taken to ensure the portion of the gain or loss on the hedging instrument that is recognised in other comprehensive income appropriately excludes ineffectiveness, which should be recognised in profit or loss. The hedging derivative would still be recognised in the statement of financial position at the full fair value.

If a hedge of a foreign currency forecast intragroup transaction qualifies for hedge accounting (see 2.3.4.B above), any gain or loss that is recognised in other comprehensive income should be reclassified from equity to profit or loss in the same period(s) during which the foreign currency risk of the hedged transaction affects consolidated profit or loss. *[IAS 39.AG99B]*.

It was stated at 3.2.3 above that using a forward exchange contract to hedge a foreign currency payable or receivable could be treated either as a fair value hedge, or a cash flow hedge, under IAS 39. In a fair value hedge, the gain or loss on remeasurement of the forward contract and the hedged item are recognised immediately in profit or loss. However, in a cash flow hedge, the gain or loss on remeasuring the forward contract is recognised in other comprehensive income and reclassified from equity to profit or loss when the payable or receivable affects profit or loss. Because the payable or receivable is remeasured continuously in respect of changes in foreign exchange rates, the gain or loss on the forward contract will be reclassified from equity to profit or loss as the payable or receivable is remeasured, not when the payment occurs. *[IAS 39.F.3.3-F.3.4]*. Where cash flow hedge accounting is applied, the effective portion of the gain or loss on the forward contract should be recognised in other comprehensive income and then reclassified from equity to profit or loss in the same period or periods during which the hedged item(s) impact profit or loss.

The interest element of the fair value of a forward may be excluded from the designated hedge relationship (designation of the spot exchange risk only – see 2.1.4.B above) although in this case changes in the fair value of the interest element would be recognised immediately in profit or loss, outside the hedge accounting. *[IAS 39.F.6.4]*. Designating the forward exchange rate or the spot exchange rate as the hedged risk could result in different results as illustrated in Example 52.37 at 5.3.3 below.

4.2.3 *Discontinuing cash flow hedge accounting*

Cash flow hedge accounting should be discontinued prospectively in any of the following circumstances:

(a) the hedging instrument expires or is sold, terminated, or exercised.

In this case the cumulative gain or loss that has been recognised in other comprehensive income in the period when the hedge was effective should remain in equity until the forecast transaction occurs. That is, the cumulative gain or loss on the hedging instrument that has been recognised in other comprehensive income should be reclassified from equity to profit or loss in the same period(s) during which the hedged forecast cash flows (or asset acquired or liability assumed) affect profit or loss. The standard does not entertain the possibility that, subsequently, the hedged forecast transaction might not occur. However, it would only make sense to deal with this situation in the same way as for hedges where the hedged instrument has not been terminated, i.e. as in (c) below;

The replacement or rollover of a hedging instrument into another hedging instrument is not an expiration or termination if such replacement or rollover is part of the entity's documented hedging strategy.

As a result of amendments made to IAS 39 in July 2013, for this purpose an expiration or termination of the hedging instrument is not considered to have occurred if:

- as a consequence of laws or regulations or the introduction of laws or regulations, the parties to the hedging instrument agree that one or more clearing counterparties replace their original counterparty to become the new counterparty to each of the parties. For this purpose, a clearing counterparty is a central counterparty (sometimes called a 'clearing organisation' or 'clearing agency') or an entity or entities, for example, a clearing member of a clearing organisation or a client of a clearing member of a clearing organisation, that are acting as counterparty in order to effect clearing by a central counterparty. However, when the parties to the hedging instrument replace their original counterparties with different counterparties this paragraph shall apply only if each of those parties effects clearing with the same central counterparty;
- other changes, if any, to the hedging instrument are limited to those that are necessary to effect such a replacement of the counterparty. Such changes are limited to those that are consistent with the terms that would be expected if the hedging instrument were originally cleared with the clearing counterparty. These changes include changes in the collateral requirements, rights to offset receivables and payables balances, and charges levied.

(b) the hedge no longer meets the criteria for hedge accounting.

In this case, the cumulative gain or loss that has been recognised in other comprehensive income is dealt with in same way as in (a) above;

(c) the forecast transaction is no longer expected to occur.

In this case, the cumulative gain or loss on the hedging instrument that has been recognised in other comprehensive income should be reclassified from equity to profit or loss. However, a forecast transaction that is no longer highly probable (and therefore the hedge no longer meets the criteria for hedge accounting) may still be expected to occur, in which case (b) above will apply, not (c);

(d) the designation as a hedge is revoked.

In this case, the cumulative gain or loss that has been recognised in other comprehensive income is dealt with in same way as in (a) above. However, if the transaction is no longer expected to occur, (c) applies. *[IAS 39.101]*.

As for fair value hedges, if the reason the hedge no longer meets the criteria for qualification for hedge accounting is that it does not meet the hedge effectiveness criteria, hedge accounting should normally be discontinued from the last date on which compliance with hedge effectiveness was demonstrated. However, if the event or change in circumstances that caused the hedging relationship to fail the effectiveness criteria can be identified, and it can be demonstrated that the hedge was effective before the event or change in circumstances occurred, the hedge accounting should be discontinued from the date of the event or change in circumstances. *[IAS 39.AG113]*.

4.2.3.A Impact of central clearing regulations on cash flow hedges

The collapse of some financial institutions during the financial crisis highlighted the potential impact of credit risk on the global derivatives markets. In response to this, several jurisdictions have introduced, or are in the process of introducing, legal or regulatory requirements that require over-the-counter (OTC) derivatives to be novated to a central clearing party (CCP) or incentivise financial institutions to do so. The CCP would usually require the derivatives to be collateralised, thereby reducing (potentially significantly) the counterparty credit risk. Examples of such legislation include the Dodd-Frank Wall Street Reform and Consumer Protection Act (Dodd-Frank Act) in the United States and the European Market Infrastructure Regulation (EMIR) in the European Union.

Following an urgent request, the IFRS Interpretation Committee concluded in January 2013 that an entity is required to discontinue hedge accounting where an OTC derivative that is designated as hedging instrument in a hedging relationship is novated to a CCP (unless, very unusually, the novation represented a replacement or rollover of the hedging instrument as part of a documented hedging strategy). This is because the novated derivative is derecognised and the new derivative contract, with the CCP as a counterparty, is recognised at the time of the novation. However, if the new derivative was designated in a cash flow hedge relationship accounting ineffectiveness would likely arise if the derivative had a fair value other than zero (see 5.3.5 below). Consequently, the Interpretations Committee decided to recommend that the IASB make a narrow-scope amendment to IAS 39 to permit continuation of hedge accounting in such narrow circumstances.[9] In July 2013 the IASB amended IAS 39 after the publication of an exposure draft in February 2013.

The exception applies to some, but not all, voluntary novations to a CCP. In order for hedge accounting to continue, a voluntary novation should at least be associated with laws or regulations that are relevant to central clearing of derivatives. For example, a voluntary novation could be in anticipation of regulatory changes. However, the mere possibility of laws or regulations being introduced is not, in the view of the IASB, a sufficient basis for continuation of hedge accounting. *[IAS 39.BC220O-BC220Q]*.

Further, the exception applies to so-called 'indirect clearing' arrangements where a clearing member of a CCP provides an indirect clearing service to its client or where a group entity is clearing on behalf of another entity within the same group since they are consistent with the objective of the amendments. *[IAS 39.BC220R, BC220S]*.

For this purpose, a clearing counterparty is a central counterparty (sometimes called a 'clearing organisation' or 'clearing agency') or an entity or entities, for example, a clearing member of a clearing organisation or a client of a clearing member of a clearing organisation, that are acting as counterparty in order to effect clearing by a central counterparty. However, when the parties to the hedging instrument replace their original counterparties with different counterparties this paragraph shall apply only if each of those parties effects clearing with the same central counterparty. *[IAS 39.101(a)(i)]*.

Finally, in order to qualify for the exception, any changes (if any) to the hedging instrument, as a result of a novation, should be limited to those that are necessary to effect the novation. Such changes are limited to those that are consistent with the terms that would be expected if the hedging instrument were originally cleared with the clearing counterparty. These changes include changes in the collateral requirements, rights to offset receivables and payables balances, and charges levied. *[IAS 39.101(a)(ii)]*.

The other criteria for achieving hedge accounting will still need to be met in order to continue hedge accounting, including the effectiveness assessment (see at 5.3.4.A below).

In December 2015, the London Clearing House (LCH) changed its rule book to introduce a new type of settled-to-market (STM) interest rate swap that becomes available in addition to the previously existing collateralized-to-market (CTM) swaps.

In the existing CTM model, transactions cleared through LCH are subject to daily cash variation margining. This means that the replacement value of the trade is in effect paid or received as cash each day and there is no ability to recover any of the variation margin unless the fair value of the interest rate swap changes. In addition, the variation margin is also used to settle the periodic swaps payments, and, in case of early settlement, the variation margin is used to settle the outstanding derivative position. Interest is paid on the variation margin based on a risk free overnight rate.

In the new STM model, transactions have the same economic exposure and overall cash flows as in the CTM model, except that the previous daily variation margin is now treated as a settlement of the interest rate swap's outstanding fair value. While the swap is gradually settled, it remains the same swap with the same original terms (e.g. the fixed rate, the maturity date etc.). In order to maintain the same economics, a new feature of the STM swap pricing is the Price Alignment Interest (PAI) that essentially replicates what would have been the interest on the collateral for a CTM swap into the STM swap pricing.

The introduction of the new STM swaps was primarily driven by the potentially different regulatory treatment they attract and at first sight it may appear that the accounting impact is limited since the existing CTM swap replacement values and related cash collateral are already normally offset in the statement of financial position. There are however some important accounting considerations if swaps designated in on-going hedging relationships are migrated from the CTM model to the STM model. The first question that arises is whether the change results in the de-designation of the existing hedge relationship and hence the need to re-designate a new hedging relationship with a derivative that is now likely to have a non-zero fair value (and so give rise to ineffectiveness if designated in a cash flow hedge). The second question that arises is how the PAI should be considered in the hedge effectiveness testing and measurement and whether any hypothetical derivative can be assumed to reflect these new terms (see 5.3.2 below). To date, few LCH clearing members have moved to the STM model and no consistent interpretation of the accounting requirements has yet emerged. This topic is also currently being discussed with some national regulators which may also influence the final conclusions.

4.2.4 *Acquisitions and disposals*

Where a reporting entity acquires a subsidiary that is applying cash flow hedge accounting, additional considerations arise. In applying the purchase method of accounting in its consolidated financial statements, the reporting entity does not inherit the subsidiary's existing cash flow hedge reserve, since this clearly represents cumulative pre-acquisition gains and losses.[10] This has implications for the assessment of hedge effectiveness and the measurement of ineffectiveness because, so far as the group is concerned, it has effectively started a new hedge relationship with a hedging instrument that is likely to have a non-zero fair value (see 5.1.1 and 5.3.5 below).

The standard does not address the situation when the hedge relationship ceases because there is a change in the relationship between the reporting entity and the entity that is holding the hedging instrument and/or is exposed to the hedged transaction, for example when a subsidiary is disposed of. This issue is covered in more detail in Chapter 7 at 3.2.

4.3 Accounting for hedges of a net investment in a foreign operation

Hedges of a net investment in a foreign operation (see 3.3 above), including a hedge of a monetary item that is accounted for as part of the net investment (see Chapter 15 at 6.3.1), should be accounted for in a similar way to cash flow hedges: *[IAS 39.102]*

- the portion of the gain or loss on the hedging instrument that is determined to be an effective hedge should be recognised in other comprehensive income and (as clarified by IFRIC 16) included with the foreign exchange differences arising on translation of the results and financial position of the foreign operation; *[IFRIC 16.3]* and
- the ineffective portion should be recognised in profit or loss.

The gain or loss on the hedging instrument relating to the effective portion of the hedge that has been recognised in other comprehensive income should be reclassified from equity to profit or loss on disposal or, in certain circumstances, partial disposal of the foreign operation in accordance with IAS 21 (see Chapter 15 at 6.6). *[IAS 39.102]*.

The meaning of 'in a similar way to cash flow hedges' is not immediately clear. It is readily understood that the portion of the gain or loss on the hedging derivative that is determined to be an effective hedge should be recognised in other comprehensive income (as it would for a cash flow hedge). However, the wording in the standard also seems to indicate that ineffectiveness should be measured in the same way as for cash flow hedges, i.e. no ineffectiveness is recognised in profit or loss if the gain or loss on the hedging instrument is less, in absolute terms, than the gain or loss on the hedged item, (see 4.2.1 above). This is despite the fact that there appears to be no good reason why ineffectiveness should not also be recognised in profit or loss if the gain or loss on the hedging instrument is less, in absolute terms, than the gain or loss on the hedged item. This is different to the accounting for net investment hedges under US GAAP,[11] for which it is clear that ineffectiveness should be recognised in profit or loss for under-hedges as well as over-hedges.

In its March 2016 meeting, the IFRS Interpretations Committee discussed this issue with respect to IFRS 9. The IFRS Interpretations Committee concluded that the guidance in IFRS 9 is sufficiently clear and would require an entity to apply the lower of test for net investment hedges. One of the arguments put forward was that the application of the lower of test in determining the effective portion of the gains or losses arising from the hedging instrument when accounting for net investment hedges, avoids the recycling of exchange differences arising from the hedged item that have been recognised in other comprehensive income before the disposal of the foreign operation. Such an outcome would be consistent with the requirements of IAS 21.[12]

IFRS 9 uses the same wording as IAS 39 when stating that net investment hedges should be accounted for 'in a similar way to cash flow hedges'. *[IAS 39.102, IFRS 9.6.5.13]*. However, the guidance in IFRS 9 specifically refers to paragraph 6.5.11 of IFRS 9, which deals with the accounting for cash flow hedges, whereas the equivalent guidance in IAS 39 makes reference to the qualifying criteria of a hedge relationship. Therefore, some might argue that the requirement to apply the 'lower of' test is clearer in IFRS 9 and an entity should be allowed not to apply the 'lower of test' for net investment hedges under IAS 39. However, the argument stated above arguably also applies for net investment hedges under IAS 39. Furthermore, the IFRS Interpretations Committee noted that it did not receive evidence of significant diversity among entities applying IAS 39 in determining the effective portion of the gains or losses arising from the hedging instrument by applying the 'lower of' test when accounting for net investment hedges.

Given that hedges of a net investment in a foreign operation are accounted for similar to cash flow hedges, we expect the accounting for the discontinuation of such hedges also to be similar to what is described at 4.2.3 above.

4.4 Hedges of a firm commitment to acquire a business

A firm commitment to acquire a business in a business combination cannot be a hedged item, except for foreign exchange risk (see 2.2.5 above).

Consider the situation where an entity with euro as its functional currency enters into a binding agreement to purchase a subsidiary in six months. The subsidiary's functional currency is the US dollar. The consideration is denominated in US dollars and is payable in cash. The entity decides to enter into a forward contract to buy US dollars for euros to hedge its foreign currency risk on the firm commitment. The following options exist and the entity may choose the most appropriate accounting treatment:

- Because the hedge is a *purchase* of US dollars, it is, arguably, not a fair value hedge of the acquisition, since the acquisition is itself naturally hedged for changes in the fair value in the US dollar – that is, the entity is committed to buy a group of US dollar denominated assets and liabilities for a price denominated in US dollars. Nevertheless, the entity may still designate the transaction as the hedged item in a fair value hedge relationship, *[IAS 39.87]*, although this may not make intuitive sense.
- The entity could instead designate the forward contract as a hedge of the cash flows associated with the committed purchase, which is a cash flow hedge. *[IAS 39.87]*.
- If the anticipated business combination in this example is only a highly probable forecast transaction and not a firm commitment, then the entity can only apply cash flow hedging.

If the transaction is a fair value hedge, then the carrying amount of the hedged item is adjusted for the gain or loss attributable to the hedged risk. Since separately identifiable assets acquired and liabilities assumed must be recognised on initial consolidation at fair value in the consolidated financial statements of the acquirer, it follows that the gain or loss attributable to the hedged risk must be included in the consideration paid. In other words, the impact of the hedge affects the calculation of goodwill, that is otherwise determined by the application of IFRS 3 – *Business Combinations* – see Chapter 9 at 6.[13]

During the hedging period, the effective portion of the gain or loss on a hedging instrument in a cash flow hedge is recognised in other comprehensive income. Upon initial recognition of the acquisition, gains or losses recognised in other comprehensive income may be:

- deferred in other comprehensive income until the goodwill acquired affects profit or loss; or
- included in the consideration paid for the business combination that is designated as the hedged item. *[IAS 39.98]*.

The adjusted carrying amount of goodwill, including the gain or loss from hedge accounting, will then be subject to the normal requirements to test for annual impairment (see Chapter 20 at 5).

Once the purchase price is paid and the transaction is completed, the entity is 'long' US dollars as a result of recognising the US dollar net assets of the acquired entity. Those net assets would then be eligible for net investment hedging which would require selling US dollars to create an eligible hedging instrument, for example by entering into a foreign currency forward (see 3.3 and 4.3 above).

5 QUALIFYING CONDITIONS FOR HEDGE ACCOUNTING

A hedging relationship qualifies for hedge accounting as set out at 4 above if, and only if, all of the following conditions are met:

- at the inception of the hedge there is formal designation and documentation both of the hedging relationship and the entity's risk management objective and strategy for undertaking the hedge;
- the hedge is expected to be highly effective in achieving offsetting changes in fair value or cash flows attributable to the hedged risk, consistently with the originally documented risk management strategy for that particular hedging relationship;
- a forecast transaction that is the subject of a cash flow hedge must be highly probable and must present an exposure to variations in cash flows that could ultimately affect net profit or loss;
- the effectiveness of the hedge can be reliably measured, i.e. the fair value or cash flows of the hedged item that are attributable to the hedged risk and the fair value of the hedging instrument can be reliably measured (see Chapter 14 for guidance on determining fair value and Chapter 49 at 2.6 for a discussion of when fair values may not be reliably measurable); and
- the hedge is assessed on an ongoing basis and determined actually to have been highly effective throughout the financial reporting periods for which the hedge was designated. *[IAS 39.88]*.

These conditions are considered in further detail in the remainder of this section.

5.1 Documentation and designation

The documentation supporting the hedge should include the identification of:

- the hedging instrument;
- the hedged item or transaction;
- the nature of the risk being hedged; and
- how the entity will assess the hedging instrument's effectiveness in offsetting the exposure to changes in the hedged item's fair value or cash flows attributable to the hedged risk. *[IAS 39.88(a)]*.

Designation of a hedge relationship takes effect prospectively from the date all of the criteria at 5 above are met. In particular, hedge accounting can be applied only from the date all of the necessary documentation is completed. Therefore, hedge relationships cannot be designated retrospectively. *[IAS 39.F.3.8]*.

Where an ongoing hedge relationship fails the retrospective effectiveness test (see 5.3.1 below), an entity is not precluded from redesignating the hedging instrument in a hedge of the same financial asset or liability. Therefore, hedge accounting may be obtained for a subsequent period in which the hedge is effective provided the hedge meets the requirements set out at 5 above.[14] This would require documentation as a new hedge relationship. Similarly, an instrument that has been dedesignated as a hedging instrument may be redesignated in a new hedge relationship for which the hedged item is the same or a different exposure provided all other conditions for hedge accounting are met.

Hedge designation need not take place at the time a hedging instrument is entered into. For example, a derivative contract may be designated and formally documented as a hedging instrument any time after entering into the derivative contract. Hedge accounting will apply prospectively from designation, provided all other conditions are met. *[IAS 39.F.3.9]*. However, there is often a hidden danger when designating a derivative as a hedging instrument subsequent to its inception. For non-option derivatives, such as forwards or interest rate swaps, any fair value is likely to create 'noise' in a hedge effectiveness assessment that may not be fully offset by changes in the hedged item, especially in the case of a cash flow hedge. Consequently, there is likely to be more ineffectiveness recognised and, in extremis, could cause the hedge not be regarded as highly effective (see 5.3.5 below). Only by coincidence will a derivative still have a fair value that is zero, or close to zero, which would minimise this problem.

5.1.1 Business combinations

In a business combination accounted for using the purchase method of accounting where the acquiree has designated hedging relationships, the question arises of whether the acquirer should:

- be permitted to continue to apply the hedge accounting model to hedge relationships designated previously by the acquiree, assuming it is consistent with the acquirer's strategies and policies; or
- be required to re-designate hedge relationships at the acquisition date.[15]

IFRS 3 provides guidance that in order to obtain hedge accounting in their consolidated financial statements, acquirers are required to redesignate the acquiree's hedges. *[IFRS 3.15, 16(b)]*. Further, the acquirer should not recognise in its consolidated financial statements any amounts in equity in respect of any cash flow hedges of the acquiree relating to the period prior to acquisition. Redesignating the hedge relationships at the acquisition date means that if the hedging instrument has a fair value other than zero, it is likely that ineffectiveness will be introduced in a hedge that may have been nearly 100% effective prior to the acquisition. In fact, it is possible that a hedge relationship that would continue to be effective for the acquiree had the business combination not occurred will fail to qualify for hedge accounting in the acquirer's consolidated financial statements if the hedging instrument has a significant fair value at the acquisition date, particularly for cash flow hedges. To mitigate this, the acquirer may, subsequent to the combination, choose to settle the hedging instruments and replace them with more effective ones.

5.1.2 Dynamic hedging strategies

The standard explains that a dynamic hedging strategy that assesses both the intrinsic value and time value of an option contract can qualify for hedge accounting. *[IAS 39.74]*. The implementation guidance explains that this allows the use of a delta-neutral hedging strategy as well as other dynamic hedging strategies under which the quantity of the hedging instrument is constantly adjusted in order to maintain a desired hedge ratio (e.g. to achieve a delta-neutral position, insensitive to changes in the fair value of the hedged item), to qualify for hedge accounting. For example, a portfolio insurance strategy that seeks to ensure that the fair value of the hedged item does not drop below a certain level, while allowing the fair value to increase, may qualify for hedge accounting. *[IAS 39.F.1.9]*.

For a dynamic hedging strategy to qualify for hedge accounting, the documentation must specify how the hedge will be monitored and updated and how effectiveness will be measured. In addition, the entity must be able to track properly all terminations and redesignations of the hedging instrument, in addition to demonstrating that all other criteria for hedge accounting are met. Also, the entity must demonstrate that the hedge is expected to be highly effective for a specified short period of time during which adjustment of the hedge is not expected. *[IAS 39.F.1.9]*. However, this does not mean that no ineffectiveness will arise.

This guidance is applicable when the quantity of the hedging instrument is constantly adjusted in order to maintain a desired hedge ratio for the existing hedged item(s), often referred to as a closed portfolio. Accounting for dynamic risk management of open portfolios, to which new exposures are frequently added, existing exposures mature, where frequent changes also occur to the hedged item(s), and the associated risk is managed directly was the subject of a Discussion Paper DP/2014/1 – *Accounting for Dynamic Risk management: A Portfolio Revaluation Approach to Macro Hedging* (see at 6 below).

5.2 Forecast transactions

In the case of a hedge of a forecast transaction, the documentation should identify the date on, or time period in which, the forecast transaction is expected to occur. This is because, in order to qualify for hedge accounting:

- the hedge must relate to a specific identified and designated risk;
- it must be possible to measure its effectiveness reliably; and
- the hedged forecast transaction must be highly probable.

To meet these criteria, entities are not required to predict and document the exact date a forecast transaction is expected to occur. However, the time period in which the forecast transaction is expected to occur should be identified and documented within a reasonably specific and generally narrow range of time from a most probable date, as a basis for assessing hedge effectiveness. To determine that the hedge will be highly effective, it is necessary to ensure that changes in the fair value of the expected cash flows are offset by changes in the fair value of the hedging instrument. The implementation guidance suggests in one example that this test may be met only if the timing of the cash flows occur within close proximity to each other. *[IAS 39.F.3.11]*. However, the approach adopted elsewhere in the implementation guidance (see paragraph below) focuses more on the need to pass the effectiveness assessment, which would reflect differences in timing of the hedged and hedging cash flows.

If a forecast transaction such as a commodity sale is properly designated in a cash flow hedge relationship and, subsequently, its expected timing changes to an earlier (or later) period, this does not affect the validity of the original designation. If the entity can conclude that this transaction is the same as the one designated as being hedged, then hedge accounting may be able to continue. However, this is subject to passing the effectiveness assessment, which may well be affected by the change in timing, as the assessment would be based on the up to date expectation of the timing of the hedged forecast transaction. For example, if the forecast transaction was now expected earlier than originally thought, the hedging instrument will be designated for the remaining period of its existence, which will exceed the period to the forecast sale. *[IAS 39.F.5.4]*.

Further, hedged forecast transactions must be identified and documented with sufficient specificity so that when the transaction occurs, it is clear whether the transaction is, or is not, the hedged transaction. Therefore, a forecast transaction may be identified as the sale of the first 15,000 units of a specific product during a specified three-month period, but it could not be identified as the last 15,000 units of that product sold because they cannot be identified when they occur. For the same reason, a forecast transaction cannot be specified solely as a percentage of sales or purchases during a period. *[IAS 39.F.3.10]*.

Finally, the standard requires a forecast transaction that is the subject of a cash flow hedge to be 'highly probable'. The implementation guidance explains that this term indicates a *much* greater likelihood of happening than the term 'more likely than not' (a term used throughout the IASB's work to describe, or define, 'probable'). The guidance states that probability should be supported by observable facts and attendant circumstance and should not be based solely on management intent, because intentions are not verifiable. In making this assessment, consideration should be given to the following circumstances:

- the frequency of similar past transactions;
- the financial and operational ability to carry out the transaction;
- substantial commitments of resources to a particular activity, e.g. a manufacturing facility that can be used in the short run only to process a particular type of commodity;
- the extent of loss or disruption of operations that could result if the transaction does not occur;
- the likelihood that transactions with substantially different characteristics might be used to achieve the same business purpose, e.g. there are several ways of raising cash ranging from a short-term bank loan to a public share offering; and
- the entity's business plan.

The length of time until a forecast transaction is projected to occur is also a consideration in determining probability. Other factors being equal, the more distant a forecast transaction is, the less likely it is to be considered highly probable and the stronger the evidence that would be needed to support an assertion that it is highly probable. For example, a transaction forecast to occur in five years may be less likely to occur than a transaction forecast to occur in one year. However, forecast interest payments for the next 20 years on variable-rate debt would typically be highly probable if supported by an existing contractual obligation.

In addition, other factors being equal, the greater the physical quantity or future value of a forecast transaction in proportion to transactions of the same nature, the less likely it is that the transaction would be considered highly probable and the stronger the evidence that would be required to support such an assertion. For example, less evidence would generally be needed to support forecast sales of 100,000 units in the next month than 950,000 units when recent sales have averaged 950,000 units for each of the past three months. *[IAS 39.F.3.7]*.

The implementation guidance uses the following example to elaborate on this:

Example 52.34: Hedge of foreign currency revenues

An airline operator uses sophisticated models based on past experience and economic data to project its revenues in various currencies. If it can demonstrate that forecast revenues for a period of time into the future in a particular currency are 'highly probable', it may designate the future revenue stream in a cash flow hedge.

However, it is unlikely that 100% of revenues for a future year could be reliably predicted. On the other hand, it is possible that a portion of predicted revenues, normally those expected in the short-term, will meet the 'highly probable' criterion. *[IAS 39.F.2.4]*.

It is also explained that cash flows arising after the prepayment date on an instrument that is prepayable at the issuer's option may be highly probable for a group or pool of similar assets for which prepayments can be estimated with a high degree of accuracy, e.g. mortgage loans, or if the prepayment option is significantly out of the money. In addition, the cash flows after the prepayment date may be designated as the hedged item if a comparable option exists in the hedging instrument. *[IAS 39.F.2.12]*.

The implementation guidance states that a history of having designated hedges of forecast transactions and then determining that the forecast transactions are no longer expected to occur, calls into question both the ability to accurately predict forecast transactions and the propriety of using hedge accounting in the future for similar forecast transactions. *[IAS 39.F.3.7]*. This is clearly common sense, however the standard contains no prescriptive 'tainting' provisions in this area akin to those applied to held-to-maturity investments (see Chapter 46 at 3.3). Therefore, entities are not automatically prohibited from using cash flow hedge accounting if a forecast transaction fails to occur. Instead, whenever such a situation arises the particular facts, circumstances and evidence should be assessed to determine whether doubt has, in fact, been cast on an entity's ongoing hedging strategies.

5.3 Assessing hedge effectiveness

One of the fundamental requirements of IAS 39 is that to use hedge accounting, the hedge must be an effective one. To this end, hedge effectiveness is defined as:

> 'the degree to which changes in the fair value or cash flows of the hedged item that are attributable to a hedged risk are offset by changes in the fair value or cash flows of the hedging instrument.' *[IAS 39.9]*.

There is little doubt that demonstrating the effectiveness of a hedge can be one of the most challenging aspects of IAS 39. The assessment of a hedge's effectiveness has the potential to be an extremely difficult exercise, involving the use of complex statistical techniques and valuation models of which many accountants have, at best, only limited experience. All of this is not helped by the fact that the IASB has provided very limited practical guidance on how to go about testing effectiveness and the IFRS Interpretations Committee has shied away from developing application guidance in this area.[16]

5.3.1 Basic requirements

Three of the qualifying conditions for hedge accounting involve hedge effectiveness as follows:

- the entity should expect the hedge to be highly effective in achieving offsetting changes in fair value or cash flows attributable to the hedged risk, consistently with the originally documented risk management strategy for that particular hedging relationship;
- the effectiveness of the hedge can be reliably measured, i.e. the fair value or cash flows of the hedged item that are attributable to the hedged risk and the fair value of the hedging instrument can be reliably measured; and
- the hedge should be assessed on an ongoing basis and determined actually to have been highly effective throughout the financial reporting periods for which the hedge was designated. *[IAS 39.88]*.

Qualification for hedge accounting is based on an expectation of future (prospective) effectiveness, the objective of which is to ensure there is firm evidence to support an expectation of high effectiveness, and an evaluation of actual (retrospective) effectiveness. *[IAS 39.BC136, BC136B]*. The application guidance explains that a hedge is regarded as highly effective only if both of the following conditions are met:

(a) at the inception of the hedge, and in subsequent periods, the hedge is expected to be highly effective in achieving offsetting changes in fair value or cash flows attributable to the hedged risk during the period for which the hedge is designated.

Such an expectation can be demonstrated in various ways, including a comparison of past changes in the fair value or cash flows of the hedged item that are attributable to the hedged risk with past changes in the fair value or cash flows of the hedging instrument, or by demonstrating a high statistical correlation between the fair value or cash flows of the hedged item and those of the hedging instrument. A hedge ratio of other than one to one may be chosen in order to improve the effectiveness of the hedge (see 2.2.2 above); and

(b) the actual results of the hedge are within a range of 80% to 125%.

For example, if actual results are such that the loss on the hedging instrument is €120 and the gain on the cash instrument is €100, offset can be measured by 120 ÷ 100, which is 120%, or by 100 ÷ 120, which is 83%. In this example, assuming the hedge meets the condition in (a), it would be concluded that the hedge has been highly effective. *[IAS 39.AG105]*.

Effectiveness should be assessed, at a minimum, at the time annual or interim financial reports are prepared. *[IAS 39.AG106]*. However, there is nothing to prevent effectiveness assessments being performed more frequently. In fact this might be desirable if there is a risk of the hedge ceasing to be considered highly effective (although the prospective test should ensure such a risk is actually very low). The sooner an ineffective hedge is identified, the sooner the accounting volatility that results from a failure to obtain hedge accounting can be managed. For example, following a failure, it might be possible to redesignate the hedge (perhaps with some adjustment to the hedging instrument) but hedge accounting for that new hedge relationship will be available only prospectively.

No single method for assessing hedge effectiveness is specified by IAS 39 – the method used will depend on the entity's risk management strategy adopted. For example, if the risk management strategy is to adjust the amount of the hedging instrument periodically to reflect changes in the hedged position, it needs to be demonstrated that the hedge is expected to be highly effective only for the period until the amount of the hedging instrument is next adjusted. *[IAS 39.AG107]*.

Hedge effectiveness may also be assessed on a pre-tax or after-tax basis. If effectiveness is to be assessed on an after-tax basis, this should be designated at inception as part of the formal documentation of the hedging strategy. *[IAS 39.F.4.1]*.

In some cases, an entity will adopt different methods for different types of hedges. The documentation of its hedging strategy should include its procedures for assessing effectiveness and those procedures should state whether the assessment will include all of the gain or loss on a hedging instrument or for example whether the time value of the instrument is excluded (see 2.1.4 above). *[IAS 39.AG107]*.

The appropriateness of a given method will depend on the nature of the risk being hedged and the type of hedging instrument used. The method must be reasonable and consistent with other similar hedges unless different methods are explicitly justified. An entity is required to document, at the inception of the hedge, how effectiveness will be assessed and then to apply that effectiveness test on a consistent basis for the duration of the hedge. Several mathematical techniques can be used including ratio analysis, i.e. a comparison of hedging gains and losses to the corresponding gains and losses on the hedged item at a point in time, and statistical measurement techniques such as regression analysis (see 5.3.6 below). If regression analysis is used, the entity's documented policies for assessing hedge effectiveness must specify how the results of the regression will be assessed. *[IAS 39.F.4.4]*.

Expected hedge effectiveness may be assessed on a cumulative basis if that is how the hedge is designated and that condition is reflected in the hedging documentation. Therefore, even if a hedge is not expected to be highly effective in a particular period, hedge accounting is not precluded if effectiveness is expected to remain sufficiently high over the life of the hedging relationship. *[IAS 39.F.4.2]*. Whether hedge effectiveness is to be assessed on a cumulative or period to period basis should form part of the hedge documentation.

Example 52.35: Cumulative hedge effectiveness

A company designates an interest rate swap linked to LIBOR as a hedge of a borrowing whose interest is a UK base rate plus a margin. The UK base rate changes, perhaps, once each quarter or less, in increments of 25 to 50 basis points, while LIBOR changes daily. Over a one to two year period, the hedge is expected to be highly effective. However, there will be quarters when the UK base rate does not change at all while LIBOR has changed significantly. This would not necessarily preclude hedge accounting. *[IAS 39.F.4.2]*.

The time value of money will generally need to be considered in assessing the effectiveness of a hedge. The fair value of an interest rate swap derives from its net settlements and the fixed and variable rates on a swap can be changed without affecting the net settlement if both are changed by the same amount. In other words, a pay-7% fixed, receive-LIBOR swap should have the same fair value as a pay-6% fixed, receive-LIBOR minus 1% swap with otherwise identical terms. Consequently, the fixed rate on a hedged item need not exactly match the fixed rate on a swap designated as a fair value hedge. Nor does the variable rate on an interest-bearing asset or liability need to be the same as the variable rate on a swap designated as a cash flow hedge. *[IAS 39.AG112]*.

In the case of interest rate risk, it is suggested that hedge effectiveness may be assessed by preparing a maturity schedule for financial assets and liabilities that shows the net interest rate exposure for each time period, provided that the net exposure is associated with a specific asset or liability (or a specific group of assets or liabilities or a specific portion of them) giving rise to the net exposure, and hedge effectiveness is assessed against that asset or liability. *[IAS 39.AG111]*. The macro-hedging models (see 6 below) have their origins in just such an approach.

An important point to note is that the method used in the *assessment* of hedge *effectiveness* need not be the same as that used in the *measurement* (i.e. recognition in profit or loss) of hedge *ineffectiveness*. Therefore, even if the calculations used to measure ineffectiveness would not support a retrospective hedge effectiveness test performed using the 'dollar-offset' method (see 5.3.2 below), hedge accounting would not necessarily be precluded, provided the hedge passed the originally documented retrospective hedge effectiveness test, for example regression analysis (see 5.3.6 below).[17]

5.3.2 The 'dollar-offset' method

One method that may be used to assess hedge effectiveness is a comparison of hedging gains and losses to the corresponding gains and losses on the hedged item at a point in time. *[IAS 39.F.4.4]*.

This method essentially uses the mechanics of *measuring* hedge ineffectiveness set out at 4.1.1 and 4.2.1 above as a basis for *assessing* effectiveness. In other words, it compares the monetary amounts of the change in fair value of the hedging instrument with the monetary amount of the change in fair value or cash flows of the hedged item or transactions attributable to the hedged risk over the assessment period. To the extent that dividing these monetary amounts results in a fraction between 0.80 and 1.25, the hedge will be seen as highly effective on a retrospective basis. Largely because of the terminology used under US GAAP, this has become known as the 'dollar-offset' method.

The dollar-offset method is commonly used as a basis for assessing hedge effectiveness on an ongoing basis because it uses the calculations that have to be performed for determining the hedge accounting bookkeeping entries (i.e. measurement of hedge ineffectiveness), therefore it requires limited additional effort and is relatively easily understood.

Example 52.36 below contains a very comprehensive illustration of the dollar-offset method for a cash flow hedge that is based on the implementation guidance to IAS 39. Although it is somewhat esoteric, and many accountants will find the calculations difficult to follow, it is an important example. Particularly, it establishes two relatively practical methods of measuring ineffectiveness, and assessing effectiveness, for cash flow hedges. They are normally referred to as the 'hypothetical derivative method' and the 'change in fair value method' (which is what they are called under US GAAP).

As its name suggests, the hypothetical derivative method involves establishing a notional derivative that would be the ideal hedging instrument for the hedged exposure (normally an interest rate swap or forward contract with no unusual terms and a zero fair value at inception of the hedge relationship). The fair value of the hypothetical derivative is then used as a proxy for the net present value of the hedged future cash flows against which changes in value of the actual hedging instrument are compared to assess effectiveness and measure ineffectiveness.

Example 52.36: Measuring effectiveness for a hedge of a forecast transaction in a debt instrument

A forecast investment in an interest-earning asset or forecast issue of an interest-bearing liability creates a cash flow exposure to interest rate changes because the related interest payments will be based on the market rate that exists when the forecast transaction occurs. The objective of a cash flow hedge of the exposure to interest rate changes is to offset the effects of future changes in interest rates so as to obtain a single fixed rate, usually the rate that existed at the inception of the hedge that corresponds with the term and timing of the forecast transaction. However, during the period of the hedge, it is not possible to determine what the market interest rate for the forecast transaction will be at the time the hedge is terminated or when the forecast transaction occurs.

During this period, effectiveness can be measured on the basis of changes in interest rates between the designation date and the interim effectiveness measurement date. The interest rates used to make this measurement are the interest rates that correspond with the term and occurrence of the forecast transaction that existed at the inception of the hedge and that exist at the measurement date as evidenced by the term structure of interest rates.

Generally it will not be sufficient simply to compare cash flows of the hedged item with cash flows generated by the derivative hedging instrument as they are paid or received, since such an approach ignores the entity's expectations of whether the cash flows will offset in subsequent periods and whether there will be any resulting ineffectiveness.

It is assumed that Company X expects to issue a €100,000 one-year debt instrument in three months. The instrument will pay interest quarterly with principal due at maturity. X is exposed to interest rate increases and establishes a hedge of the interest cash flows of the debt by entering into a forward starting interest rate swap. The swap has a term of one year and will start in three months to correspond with the terms of the forecast debt issue. X will pay a fixed rate and receive a variable rate, and it designates the risk being hedged as the LIBOR-based interest component in the forecast issue of the debt.

Yield curve

The yield curve provides the foundation for computing future cash flows and the fair value of such cash flows both at the inception of, and during, the hedging relationship. It is based on current market yields on applicable reference bonds that are traded in the marketplace. Market yields are converted to spot interest rates ('spot rates' or 'zero coupon rates') by eliminating the effect of coupon payments on the market yield. Spot rates are used to discount future cash flows, such as principal and interest rate payments, to arrive at their fair value. Spot rates also are used to compute forward interest rates that are used to compute the estimated variable future cash flows. The relationship between spot rates and one-period forward rates is shown by the following formula:

Spot-forward relationship

$$F = \frac{(1 + SR_t)^t}{(1 + SR_{t-1})^{t-1}} - 1$$

where F = forward rate (%)

SR = spot rate (%)

t = period in time (e.g. 1, 2, 3, 4, 5)

It is assumed that the following quarterly-period term structure of interest rates using quarterly compounding exists at the inception of the hedge.

Yield curve at inception (beginning of period 1)

Forward periods	*1*	*2*	*3*	*4*	*5*
Spot rates	3.75%	4.50%	5.50%	6.00%	6.25%
Forward rates	3.75%	5.25%	7.51%	7.50%	7.25%

The one-period forward rates are computed on the basis of spot rates for the applicable maturities. For example, the current forward rate for Period 2 calculated using the formula above is equal to $[1.0450^2 \div 1.0375] - 1 = 5.25\%$. The current one-period forward rate for Period 2 is different from the current spot rate for Period 2, since the spot rate is an interest rate from the beginning of Period 1 (spot) to the end of Period 2, while the forward rate is an interest rate from the beginning of Period 2 to the end of Period 2.

Hedged item

In this example, X expects to issue a €100,000 one-year debt instrument in three months with quarterly interest payments. X is exposed to interest rate increases and would like to eliminate the effect on cash flows of interest rate changes that may happen before the forecast transaction takes place. If that risk is eliminated, X would obtain an interest rate on its debt issue that is equal to the one-year forward coupon rate currently available in the marketplace in three months. That forward coupon rate, which is different from the forward (spot) rate, is 6.86%, computed from the term structure of interest rates shown above. It is the market rate of interest that exists at the inception of the hedge, given the terms of the forecast debt instrument. It results in the fair value of the debt being equal to par at its issue.

At the inception of the hedging relationship, the expected cash flows of the debt instrument can be calculated on the basis of the existing term structure of interest rates. For this purpose, it is assumed that interest rates do not change and that the debt would be issued at 6.86% at the beginning of Period 2. In this case, the cash flows and fair value of the debt instrument would be as follows at the beginning of Period 2.

Issue of fixed rate debt (beginning of period 2) – no rate changes (spot based on forward rates)

	Total					
Original forward periods		*1*	*2*	*3*	*4*	*5*
Remaining periods			*1*	*2*	*3*	*4*
Spot rates			5.25%	6.38%	6.75%	6.88%
Forward rates			5.25%	7.51%	7.50%	7.25%
	€		€	€	€	€
Cash flows:						
Fixed interest at 6.86%			1,716	1,716	1,716	1,716
Principal						100,000
Fair value:						
Interest*	6,592		1,694	1,663	1,632	1,603
Principal*	93,408					93,408
	100,000					

* cash flow discounted at the spot rate for the relevant period, e.g. fair value of principal is calculated as $€100{,}000 \div (1 + [0.0688 \div 4])^4 = €93{,}408$

Since it is assumed that interest rates do not change, the fair value of the interest and principal amounts equals the par amount of the forecast transaction. The fair value amounts are computed on the basis of the spot rates that exist at the inception of the hedge for the applicable periods in which the cash flows would occur had the debt been issued at the date of the forecast transaction. They reflect the effect of discounting those cash flows on the basis of the periods that will remain after the debt instrument is issued. For example, the spot rate of 6.38% is used to discount the interest cash flow that is expected to be paid in Period 3, but it is discounted for only two periods because it will occur two periods after the forecast transaction.

The forward interest rates are the same as shown previously, since it is assumed that interest rates do not change. The spot rates are different but they have not actually changed. They represent the spot rates one period forward and are based on the applicable forward rates.

Hedging instrument

The objective of the hedge is to obtain an overall interest rate on the forecast transaction and the hedging instrument that is equal to 6.86%, which is the market rate at the inception of the hedge for the period from Period 2 to Period 5. This objective is accomplished by entering into a forward starting interest rate swap that has a fixed rate of 6.86%. Based on the term structure of interest rates that exist at the inception of the hedge, the interest rate swap will have such a rate. At the inception of the hedge, the fair value of the fixed rate payments on the interest rate swap will equal the fair value of the variable rate payments, resulting in the interest rate swap having a fair value of zero. The expected cash flows of the interest rate swap and the related fair value amounts are shown as follows:

Interest rate swap

	Total					
Original forward periods		*1*	*2*	*3*	*4*	*5*
Remaining periods			*1*	*2*	*3*	*4*
	€		€	€	€	€
Cash flows:						
Fixed interest at 6.86%			1,716	1,716	1,716	1,716
Forecast variable interest*			1,313	1,877	1,876	1,813
Forecast based on forward rate			*5.25%*	*7.51%*	*7.50%*	*7.25%*
Net interest			(403)	161	160	97
Fair value						
Discount rate (spot)			*5.25%*	*6.38%*	*6.75%*	*6.88%*
Fixed interest	6,592		1,694	1,663	1,632	1,603
Forecast variable interest	6,592		1,296	1,819	1,784	1,693
Fair value of interest rate swap	0		(398)	156	152	90

* forecast variable rate cash flow based on forward rate, e.g. €1,313 = €100,000 × (0.0525 ÷ 4)

At the inception of the hedge, the fixed rate on the forward swap is equal to the fixed rate X would receive if it could issue the debt in three months under terms that exist today.

Measuring hedge effectiveness

If interest rates change during the period the hedge is outstanding, the effectiveness of the hedge can be measured in various ways.

Assume that interest rates change as follows immediately before the debt is issued at the beginning of Period 2 (this effectively uses the yield curve existing at Period 1 with a 200 basis point (2%) shift).

Yield curve assumption

Forward periods	*1*	*2*	*3*	*4*	*5*
Remaining periods		*1*	*2*	*3*	*4*
Spot rates		5.75%	6.50%	7.50%	8.00%
Forward rates		5.75%	7.25%	9.51%	9.50%

Under the new interest rate environment, the fair value of the pay-fixed at 6.86%, receive-variable interest rate swap that was designated as the hedging instrument would be as follows.

Fair value of interest rate swap

	Total					
Original forward periods		*1*	*2*	*3*	*4*	*5*
Remaining periods			*1*	*2*	*3*	*4*
	€		€	€	€	€
Cash flows:						
Fixed interest at 6.86%			1,716	1,716	1,716	1,716
Forecast variable interest			1,438	1,813	2,377	2,376
Forecast based on new forward rate			*5.75%*	*7.25%*	*9.51%*	*9.50%*
Net interest			(279)	97	661	660

	Total					
Original forward periods		*1*	*2*	*3*	*4*	*5*
Remaining periods			*1*	*2*	*3*	*4*
	€		€	€	€	€
Fair value						
New discount rate (spot)			*5.75%*	*6.50%*	*7.50%*	*8.00%*
Fixed interest	6,562		1,692	1,662	1,623	1,585
Forecast variable interest	7,615		1,417	1,755	2,248	2,195
Fair value of interest rate swap	1,053		(275)	93	625	610

In order to compute the effectiveness of the hedge, it is necessary to measure the change in the present value of the cash flows or the value of the hedged forecast transaction. There are at least two methods of accomplishing this measurement.

Method A – Compute change in fair value of debt

	Total					
Original forward periods		*1*	*2*	*3*	*4*	*5*
Remaining periods			*1*	*2*	*3*	*4*
	€		€	€	€	€
Cash flows:						
Fixed interest at 6.86%			1,716	1,716	1,716	1,716
Principal						100,000
Fair value:						
New discount rate (spot)			*5.75%*	*6.50%*	*7.50%*	*8.00%*
Interest	6,562		1,692	1,662	1,623	1,585
Principal	92,385					*92,385
Total	98,947					
Fair value at inception	100,000					
Difference	(1,053)					

* $€100,000 \div (1 + [0.08 \div 4])^4$

Under Method A, a computation is made of the fair value in the new interest rate environment of debt that carries interest that is equal to the coupon interest rate that existed at the inception of the hedging relationship (6.86%). This fair value is compared with the expected fair value as of the beginning of Period 2 that was calculated on the basis of the term structure of interest rates that existed at the inception of the hedging relationship, as illustrated above, to determine the change in the fair value. Note that the difference between the change in the fair value of the swap and the change in the expected fair value of the debt (€1,053) exactly offset in this example, since the terms of the swap and the forecast transaction match each other.

Method B – Compute change in fair value of cash flows

	Total					
Original forward periods		*1*	*2*	*3*	*4*	*5*
Remaining periods			*1*	*2*	*3*	*4*
Market rate at inception			6.86%	6.86%	6.86%	6.86%
Current forward rate			5.75%	7.25%	9.51%	9.50%
Rate difference			1.11%	(0.39%)	(2.64%)	(2.64%)
Cash flow difference (principal × rate)			€279	(€97)	(€661)	(€660)
Discount rate (spot)			*5.75%*	*6.50%*	*7.50%*	*8.00%*
Fair value of difference	(€1,053)		€275	(€93)	(€625)	(€610)

Under Method B, the present value of the change in cash flows is computed on the basis of the difference between the forward interest rates for the applicable periods at the effectiveness measurement date and the interest rate that would have been obtained if the debt had been issued at the market rate that existed at the inception of the hedge. The market rate that existed at the inception of the hedge is the one-year forward coupon rate in three months. The present value of the change in cash flows is computed on the basis of the current spot rates that exist at the effectiveness measurement date for the applicable periods in which the cash flows are expected to occur. This method also could be referred to as the 'theoretical swap' method (or 'hypothetical derivative' method) because the comparison is between the hedged fixed rate on the debt and the current variable rate, which is the same as comparing cash flows on the fixed and variable rate legs of an interest rate swap.

As before, the difference between the change in the fair value of the swap and the change in the present value of the cash flows exactly offset in this example.

Other considerations

There is an additional computation that should be performed to compute ineffectiveness before the expected date of the forecast transaction that has not been considered for the purpose of this illustration. The fair value difference has been determined in each of the illustrations as of the expected date of the forecast transaction immediately before the forecast transaction, i.e. at the beginning of Period 2. If the assessment of hedge effectiveness is performed before the forecast transaction occurs, the difference should be discounted to the current date to arrive at the actual amount of ineffectiveness. For example, if the measurement date were one month after the hedging relationship was established and the forecast transaction is now expected to occur in two months, the amount would have to be discounted for the remaining two months before the forecast transaction is expected to occur to arrive at the actual fair value. This step would not be necessary in the examples provided above because there was no ineffectiveness. Therefore, additional discounting of the amounts, which net to zero, would not have changed the result.

Under Method B, ineffectiveness is computed on the basis of the difference between the forward coupon interest rates for the applicable periods at the effectiveness measurement date and the interest rate that would have been obtained if the debt had been issued at the market rate that existed at the inception of the hedge. Computing the change in cash flows based on the difference between the forward interest rates that existed at the inception of the hedge and the forward rates that exist at the effectiveness measurement date is inappropriate if the objective of the hedge is to establish a single fixed rate for a series of forecast interest payments. This objective is met by hedging the exposures with an interest rate swap as illustrated in the above example. The fixed interest rate on the swap is a blended interest rate composed of the forward rates over the life of the swap. Unless the yield curve is flat, the comparison between the forward interest rate exposures over the life of the swap and the fixed rate on the swap will produce different cash flows whose fair values are equal only at the inception of the hedging relationship. This difference is shown in the table below.

	Total					
Original forward periods		*1*	*2*	*3*	*4*	*5*
Remaining periods			*1*	*2*	*3*	*4*
Forward rate at inception			5.25%	7.51%	7.50%	7.25%
Current forward rate			5.75%	7.25%	9.51%	9.50%
Rate difference			(0.50%)	0.26%	(2.00%)	(2.25%)
Cash flow difference (principal × rate)			(€125)	€64	(€501)	(€563)
Discount rate (spot)			*5.75%*	*6.50%*	*7.50%*	*8.00%*
Fair value of difference	€1,055		(€123)	€62	(€474)	(€520)
Fair value of interest rate swap	€1,053					
Ineffectiveness	(€2)					

If the objective of the hedge is to obtain the forward rates that existed at the inception of the hedge, the interest rate swap is ineffective because the swap has a single blended fixed coupon rate that does not offset a series of different forward interest rates. However, if the objective of the hedge is to obtain the forward coupon rate that existed at the inception of the hedge, the swap is effective, and the comparison based on differences in forward interest rates suggests ineffectiveness when none may exist. Computing ineffectiveness based on the difference between the forward interest rates that existed at the inception of the hedge and the forward rates that exist at the effectiveness measurement date would be an appropriate measurement of ineffectiveness if the hedging objective is to lock in those forward interest rates. In that case, the appropriate hedging instrument would be a series of forward contracts each of which matures on a repricing date that corresponds with the date of the forecast transactions.

It also should be noted that it would be inappropriate to compare only the variable cash flows on the interest rate swap with the interest cash flows in the debt that would be generated by the forward interest rates. That methodology has the effect of measuring ineffectiveness only on a portion of the derivative, and IAS 39 does not permit the bifurcation of a derivative for the purposes of assessing effectiveness in this situation[18] – see 2.1.4 above. It is recognised, however, that if the fixed interest rate on the interest rate swap is equal to the fixed rate that would have been obtained on the debt at inception, there will be no ineffectiveness assuming that there are no differences in terms and no change in credit risk or it is not designated in the hedging relationship. *[IAS 39.F.5.5]*.

Although the calculations are set out in longhand, the above example is still simplified. The 'hypothetical derivative' method should not be seen as a method in its own right that results in zero ineffectiveness for a hedge with matching terms. There are likely to be elements that are relevant for determining the fair value of the hedging instrument, such as credit risk, that are either not present in the hedged item or that differ between the hedged item and the hedging instrument (see also 5.3.4 below). When developing the revised hedge accounting requirements for inclusion in IFRS 9, the IASB discussed the role of hypothetical derivatives, see Chapter 53 at 5.3 and 6.4.2 for further details.

5.3.2.A Law of small numbers

The dollar-offset method of assessing effectiveness is commonly used because it requires limited additional effort over and above that required to determine the amount of ineffectiveness to be recognised in profit or loss. However, there can be significant problems in achieving high correlation, particularly when the actual movements in fair value or cash flows of the hedging instrument and hedged item are both small.

Consider a fair value hedge of a fixed interest rate bond where interest rates barely change in the period. The change in fair value of the hedging instrument for the period might be €1,000 and the corresponding change in fair value of the hedged item €2,000, being an increase from €1,000,000 to €1,002,000. This would indicate that the hedging relationship was only 50% effective and would therefore not qualify for hedge accounting. However, the changes in fair value are very small in relation to the fair value of the contract being hedged. In fact, it might be possible to demonstrate that had interest rates moved by a more noticeable amount, the change in value of the hedged item and the hedging instrument would have been, say, €50,000 and €49,000 respectively, i.e. the strategy would actually have been highly effective. This scenario is often described as 'the law of small numbers' problem. Although well documented, the standard does not address this phenomenon and certainly offers no insight as to how an entity might deal with it.

A common approach, for the purposes of *assessing* hedge effectiveness, is simply to ignore changes in fair value that are below a given fixed limit (strictly, for the purpose of *measuring* ineffectiveness, these amounts should be recognised but they will not be material). This limit should be established at the inception of the hedge and should be included in the hedge documentation. Care should be taken in setting this limit – too high and the entity could be accused of not establishing an appropriate method of assessing effectiveness; too low and the risk of failing the assessment is increased.

5.3.3 Dollar-offset: comparison of spot rate and forward rate methods

It was explained at 2.1.4.B above that the spot and interest elements of a forward contract could be treated separately for the purposes of hedge designation. The next example, based on the implementation guidance, contrasts two variations of the dollar-offset method. Case 1 can be used when the whole of a forward contract is treated as the hedging instrument and the hedged risk is identified by reference to changes attributable to the forward rate (forward rate method). Case 2 can be used when the interest component is excluded and the hedged risk is identified by reference to changes attributable to the spot rate (spot rate method).

To demonstrate these methods, the implementation guidance uses a type of hedge that is very common in practice, the hedging of foreign currency risk associated with future purchases using a forward exchange contract. The example also illustrates the difference in the accounting for such hedges depending on whether the spot and interest elements of a forward contract are treated separately for the purposes of hedge designation.

Example 52.37: Cash flow hedge of firm commitment to purchase inventory in a foreign currency

Company A has the Local Currency (LC) as its functional and presentation currency. A's accounting policy is to apply basis adjustments to non-financial assets that result from hedged forecast transactions and it chooses to treat hedges of the foreign currency risk of a firm commitment as cash flow hedges.

On 30 June 2017, A enters into a forward exchange contract to receive Foreign Currency (FC) 100,000 and deliver LC109,600 on 30 June 2018 at an initial cost and fair value of zero. On inception, it designates the forward exchange contract as a hedging instrument in a cash flow hedge of a firm commitment to purchase a certain quantity of paper for FC100,000 on 31 March 2018 and, thereafter, as a fair value hedge of the resulting payable of FC100,000, which is to be paid on 30 June 2018. It is assumed that all hedge accounting conditions in IAS 39 are met.

The relevant foreign exchange rates and associated fair values for the forward exchange contract are provided in the following table:

Date	Spot rate	Forward rate to 30 June 2018	Fair value of forward contract
30 June 2017	1.072	1.096	–
31 December 2017	1.080	1.092	(388)
31 March 2018	1.074	1.076	(1,971)
30 June 2018	1.072	–	(2,400)

The applicable yield curve in the local currency is flat at 6% per annum throughout the period. The fair value of the forward exchange contract is negative LC388 on 31 December 2017 ({[1.092 × 100,000] – 109,600} ÷ $1.06^{(6/12)}$), negative LC1,971 on 31 March 2018 ({[1.076 × 100,000] – 109,600} ÷ $1.06^{(3/12)}$), and negative LC2,400 on 30 June 2018 (1.072 × 100,000 – 109,600).

Case 1: Changes in the fair value of the forward contract are designated in the hedge

Ignoring ineffectiveness that may arise from other elements that have an impact on the fair value of the hedging instrument, the hedge is expected to be fully effective because the critical terms of the forward exchange contract and the purchase contract are otherwise the same. The assessments of hedge effectiveness are based on the forward price.

The accounting entries are as follows.

30 June 2017

	LC	LC
Forward	–	
Cash		–

To record the forward exchange contract at its initial fair value, i.e. zero.

31 December 2017

	LC	LC
Other comprehensive income	388	
Forward – liability		388

To recognise the change in the fair value of the forward contract between 30 June 2017 and 31 December 2017, i.e. 388 – 0 = LC388, in other comprehensive income. The hedge is fully effective because the loss on the forward exchange contract, LC388, exactly offsets the change in cash flows associated with the purchase contract based on the forward price {([1.092 × 100,000] – 109,600) ÷ $1.06^{(6/12)}$} – {([1.096 × 100,000] – 109,600) ÷ 1.06} = –LC388. The negative figure denotes a reduction in the net present value of cash outflows and, therefore, effectively represents a 'gain' to offset the loss on the forward in other comprehensive income.

31 March 2018

	LC	LC
Other comprehensive income	1,583	
Forward – liability		1,583

To recognise the change in the fair value of the forward contract between 1 January 2018 and 31 March 2018, i.e. 1,971 – 388 = LC1,583, in other comprehensive income. The hedge is fully effective because the loss on the forward exchange contract, LC1,583, exactly offsets the change in cash flows associated with the purchase contract based on the forward price {([1.076 × 100,000] – 109,600) ÷ $1.06^{(3/12)}$} – {([1.092 × 100,000] – 109,600) ÷ $1.06^{(6/12)}$} = –LC1,583. The negative figure denotes a reduction in the net present value of cash outflows and, therefore, effectively represents a 'gain' to offset the loss on the forward in other comprehensive income.

	LC	LC
Paper (purchase price)	107,400	
Paper (hedging loss)	1,971	
Other comprehensive income		1,971
Payable		107,400

To record the purchase of the paper at the spot rate (1.074 × 100,000 = LC 107,400) and remove the cumulative loss on the forward recognised in other comprehensive income from equity, LC1,971, and include it in the initial measurement of the purchased paper. Accordingly, the initial measurement of the purchased paper is LC 109,371 consisting of a purchase consideration of LC 107,400 and a hedging loss of LC 1,971. The payable is recorded as a foreign currency monetary item of FC100,000, equivalent to LC107,400 (100,000 × 1.074) on initial recognition.

30 June 2018

	LC	LC
Payable	107,400	
Cash		107,200
Profit or loss		200

To record the settlement of the payable at the spot rate (100,000 × 1.072 = LC107,200) and recognise the associated exchange gain of LC200 = 107,400 – 107,200 in profit or loss.

	LC	LC
Profit or loss	429	
Forward – liability		429

To recognise the loss on the forward exchange contract between 1 April 2018 and 30 June 2018, i.e. 2,400 – 1,971 = LC429) in profit or loss. The hedge is considered to be fully effective because the loss on the forward exchange contract, LC429, exactly offsets the change in the fair value of the payable based on the forward price [1.072 × 100,000] – 109,600 – {([1.076 × 100,000] – 109,600) ÷ $1.06^{(3/12)}$} = –LC429. The negative figure denotes a reduction in the net present value of the payable and, therefore represents a gain to offset the loss on the forward contract.

	LC	LC
Forward – liability	2,400	
Cash		2,400

To record the net settlement of the forward exchange contract.

Although this arrangement has been set up to be a 'perfect hedge', the loss on the forward in the last three months is significantly different from the exchange gain recognised on retranslating the hedged payable. The principal reason for this is that the change in the fair value of the forward contract includes changes in its interest element, as well as its currency element, whereas the payable is translated at the spot foreign exchange rate. *[IAS 21.23(a)]*.

Case 2: Changes in the spot element of the forward contract only are designated in the hedge

Ignoring ineffectiveness that may arise from other elements that have an impact on the fair value of the hedging instrument, the hedge is expected to be fully effective because the critical terms of the forward exchange contract and the purchase contract are the same and the change in the premium or discount on the forward contract is excluded from the assessment of effectiveness.

30 June 2017

	LC	LC
Forward	–	
Cash		–

To record the forward exchange contract at its initial fair value, i.e. zero.

31 December 2017

	LC	LC
Profit or loss (interest element of forward)	1,165	
Other comprehensive income (spot element)		777
Forward – liability		388

To recognise the change in the fair value of the forward contract between 30 June 2017 and 31 December 2017, i.e. 388 – 0 = LC388. The change in the present value of spot settlement of the forward exchange contract is a gain of LC777 = $\{([1.080 \times 100{,}000] - 107{,}200) \div 1.06^{(6/12)}\} - \{([1.072 \times 100{,}000] - 107{,}200) \div 1.06\}$), which is recognised in other comprehensive income. The change in the interest element of the forward exchange contract (the residual change in fair value) is a loss of LC1,165 = 388 + 777, which is recognised in profit or loss. The hedge is fully effective because the gain in the spot element of the forward contract, LC777, exactly offsets the change in the purchase price at spot rates $\{([1.080 \times 100{,}000] - 107{,}200) \div 1.06^{(6/12)}\} - \{([1.072 \times 100{,}000] - 107{,}200) \div 1.06\}$ = LC777. The positive figure denotes an increase in the net present value of cash outflows and, therefore, effectively represents a 'loss' to offset the gain on the forward in other comprehensive income.

31 March 2018

	LC	LC
Other comprehensive income (spot element)	580	
Profit or loss (interest element)	1,003	
Forward – liability		1,583

To recognise the change in the fair value of the forward contract between 1 January 2018 and 31 March 2018, i.e. 1,971 – 388 = LC1,583. The change in the present value of spot settlement of the forward exchange contract is a loss of LC580 = $\{([1.074 \times 100{,}000] - 107{,}200) \div 1.06^{(3/12)}\} - \{([1.080 \times 100{,}000] - 107{,}200) \div 1.06^{(6/12)}\}$, which is recognised in other comprehensive income. The change in the interest element of the forward contract (the residual change in fair value) is a loss of LC1,003 = 1,583 – 580), which is recognised in profit or loss. The hedge is fully effective because the loss in the spot element of the forward contract, LC580, exactly offsets the change in the purchase price at spot rates $\{([1.074 \times 100{,}000] - 107{,}200) \div 1.06^{(3/12)}\} - \{([1.080 \times 100{,}000] - 107{,}200) \div 1.06^{(6/12)}\}$ = –LC580. The negative figure denotes a reduction in the net present value of cash outflows and, therefore, effectively represents a 'gain' to offset the loss on the forward in other comprehensive income.

	LC	LC
Paper (purchase price)	107,400	
Other comprehensive income	197	
Paper (hedging gain)		197
Payable		107,400

To recognise the purchase of the paper at the spot rate (1.074 × 100,000 = LC 107,400) and remove the cumulative gain on the spot element of the forward contract that has been recognised in other comprehensive income (777 – 580 = LC197) and include it in the initial measurement of the purchased paper. Accordingly, the initial measurement of the purchased paper is LC107,203 consisting of a purchase consideration of LC107,400 and a hedging gain of LC197.

30 June 2018

	LC	LC
Payable	107,400	
Cash		107,200
Profit or loss		200

To record the settlement of the payable at the spot rate (100,000 × 1.072 = LC107,200) and recognise the associated exchange gain of LC200 (= – [1.072 – 1.074] × 100,000) in profit or loss.

	LC	LC
Profit or loss (spot element)	197	
Profit or loss (interest element)	232	
Forward – liability		429

To recognise the change in the fair value of the forward between 1 April 2018 and 30 June 2018, i.e. 2,400 – 1,971 = LC429). The change in the present value of spot settlement of the forward exchange contract is a loss of LC197 = {[1.072 × 100,000] – 107,200 – {([1.074 × 100,000] – 107,200) ÷ $1.06^{(3/12)}$}, which is recognised in profit or loss. The change in the interest element of the forward contract (the residual change in fair value) is a loss of LC232 = 429 – 197, which is recognised in profit or loss. The hedge is fully effective because the loss in the spot element of the forward contract, LC197, exactly offsets the gain on the payable reported using spot rates = {[1.072 × 100,000] – 107,200 – {([1.074 × 100,000] – 107,200) ÷ $1.06^{(3/12)}$} = –LC197. The negative figure denotes a reduction in the net present value of the payable and, therefore represents a gain to offset the loss on the forward contract.

	LC	LC
Forward – liability	2,400	
Cash		2,400

To record the net settlement of the forward exchange contract.

The following table provides an overview of the components of the change in fair value of the hedging instrument over the term of the hedging relationship. It illustrates that the way in which a hedging relationship is designated affects the subsequent accounting for that hedging relationship, including the assessment of hedge effectiveness and the recognition of gains and losses. *[IAS 39.F.5.6]*.

Period ending	Change in spot settlement LC	Fair value of change in spot settlement LC	Change in forward settlement LC	Fair value of change in forward settlement LC	Fair value of change in interest element LC
30 June 2017	–	–	–	–	–
31 December 2017	800	777	(400)	(388)	(1,165)
31 March 2018	(600)	(580)	(1,600)	(1,583)	(1,003)
30 June 2018	(200)	(197)	(400)	(429)	(232)
Total	–	–	(2,400)	(2,400)	(2,400)

Ignoring ineffectiveness that may arise from elements that affect the fair value of the hedging instrument only or that may be different from the hedged item to the hedging instrument, both designations result in effective hedges as a result of the way effectiveness is measured. However, there is a significant difference in profit or loss. In part (a) all gains and losses on the forward are recognised in other comprehensive income when designated as a cash flow hedge whereas in part (b) changes in the fair value of the interest element of the forward are immediately recognised in profit or loss. The example also sets out how a single hedge can initially be a cash flow hedge of the future sale and then become a fair value hedge of the associated payable, provided it is documented as such.

The example also indicates that the time value of money is relevant for the assessment of effectiveness even when the spot element is designated in a hedge relationship. However, diversity in practice exists with respect to discounting of the spot element for hedge effectiveness purposes. This is perhaps because in many circumstances the effect of discounting the revaluation of the spot element may not be material. However, some might argue that by saying that 'in assessing the effectiveness of a hedge, an entity generally considers the time value of money' IAS 39 is not entirely clear on the issue of discounting the spot element. *[IAS 39.AG112]*. This guidance could be interpreted as meaning that there are cases where an entity would not be required to consider the time value of money. Furthermore, many entities consider that the spot element should not be discounted as by definition the 'interest or forward element is excluded'. Nevertheless, IFRS 9 is more explicit and states that 'when measuring hedge ineffectiveness, an entity shall consider the time value of money.' *[IFRS 9.B6.5.4]*. Therefore, we expect that this diversity in practice might disappear under IFRS 9. See Chapter 53 at 6.4.1.

5.3.4 *The impact of the hedging instrument's credit quality*

The application guidance to IAS 39 states that a hedge of interest rate risk using a derivative would not be fully effective if part of the change in the fair value of the derivative is attributable to the counterparty's credit risk. *[IAS 39.AG109]*. The implementation guidance explains that when assessing effectiveness, both at inception and thereafter, the risk of counterparty default should be considered. For a fair value hedge, the implications of this guidance are clear. If there is a change in the derivative counterparty's creditworthiness, the hedging instrument's fair value will change but there is unlikely to be an offsetting change in fair value for the hedged item. This will affect its effectiveness as measured and should also be taken into account in the assessment of whether it continues to qualify for hedge accounting. *[IAS 39.F.4.3]*.

For a cash flow hedge, the implications of the guidance are slightly less clear. The application guidance noted above is included within a section of the standard titled 'Assessing hedge effectiveness'. This strongly suggests that it is applicable to the assessment of cash flow hedges as well as to their measurement (for which the credit risk of the counterparty is certainly something to be taken into account – see Example 52.32 above).

Some might argue that, to qualify for hedge accounting, the test is that the hedging instrument will be highly effective in achieving offsetting changes in fair value *or cash flows* attributable to the hedged risk. *[IAS 39.88(b), 88(d), AG105(a)]*. Further, in the context of a cash flow hedge, the implementation guidance explains that, if default becomes probable, the hedging relationship is unlikely to achieve offsetting cash flows and hedge accounting will be discontinued. *[IAS 39.F.4.3]*. Together, these might suggest that the assessment of a cash flow hedge's effectiveness should be affected only by significant changes in the counterparty's credit risk, i.e. where default became probable. This is the approach US GAAP adopts. Under US GAAP, if a hedged cash flow is probable of occurring, hedge accounting is permitted and changes in the risk of non-performance (e.g. credit spreads) within certain ranges, all of which still reflect the cash flow remaining probable of occurring, are not relevant to the measurement of hedge ineffectiveness because they will not *change* the amount of the ultimate cash flow or represent a source of variability. In other words, as long as the cash flows remain probable overall, changes in degrees of probability, as long as overall probability can still be asserted, are not measured under any of the three permitted methods for measuring ineffectiveness in cash flow hedges.[19] Each method contains accommodations for cash flow hedges that are intended to eliminate the generation of hedge ineffectiveness attributable to the use of different yield curves for measuring cash flows related to the hedged item and the derivative. These accommodations involve utilizing the *same* credit adjusted discount curve for both the derivative and the hedged item in all three methods. However, there is no equivalent guidance in IAS 39. Also, some would view ignoring changes in the credit risk component of a hedging instrument's fair value as inappropriately excluding a portion of the hedging instrument from the hedge relationship (see 2.1.4 above).

We note that the application guidance of IFRS 9 states in the context of the 'hypothetical derivative' method that one cannot include features in the value of the hedged item that only exist in the hedging instrument, but not in the hedged item. Arguably, both the hedged item and the hedging instrument include credit risk. However, the credit risk in the hedged item is likely to be different from the credit risk in the hedging instrument. This is true even when the specific credit risk that exists in the hedged item is not included in the hedge relationship as a benchmark interest rate has been designated as the hedged risk (see 2.2.1.A above). Consequently, at least when applying IFRS 9, credit risk also needs to be considered when assessing the effectiveness of cash flow hedges (see Chapter 53 at 5.3), although some may argue that this approach should also be applied under IAS 39. *[IFRS 9.B6.5.5]*.

In addition to changes in the counterparty's credit risk, changes in the reporting entity's own credit risk may also affect the fair value of the hedging instrument in ways that are not replicated in the hedged item (see Chapter 53 at 5.3 and Chapter 14 at 11.3). The impact will be more pronounced where the hedging derivative is longer term, has a significant negative fair value and there exist no other credit enhancements such as collateral agreements or credit break clauses. Consequently, changes in the hedging instrument's fair value arising from the reporting entity's own credit risk will need to be considered when measuring hedge effectiveness and assessing the effectiveness of fair value hedges. The extent to which they need to be considered when assessing the effectiveness of a cash flow hedge is subject to the same uncertainties as noted further above.

During the financial crisis the IASB's Expert Advisory Panel acknowledged that, in practice, this is an area that had received limited attention by many entities, possibly because such changes in value have been considered insignificant or immaterial. However the financial crisis, which started in the second half of 2007, brought the related issues into focus as the fair values of some instruments were impacted to a greater extent by credit risk than they had historically and IFRS 13 is clear that credit risk should be taken into account when measuring the fair value of derivatives (see Chapter 14 at 11.3).

Nowadays, most over-the-counter derivative contracts between financial institutions are cash collateralised. Furthermore, current initiatives in several jurisdictions, such as, the European Market Infrastructure Regulation (EMIR) in the European Union or the Dodd-Frank Act in the United States, will result in more derivative contracts being collateralised by cash. Cash collateralisation significantly reduces the credit risk for both parties involved.

5.3.4.A Discount rates for calculating the fair value of derivatives

Historically, the fair values of derivatives have been calculated using LIBOR-based swap curve as the discount factor, since it reflected the cost of funding for banks. However, the use of LIBOR as the standard discount rate ignores the fact that a number of derivative transactions are collateralised. For cash collateralised trades, a more relevant discount rate is an overnight rate rather than LIBOR.

While there has always been a difference between LIBOR and the overnight index swap (OIS) rates, the difference had historically been equal to a few basis points. However, the basis differential widened significantly during the 2008 financial crisis and is not expected to revert in the foreseeable future. Therefore, market participants generally consider an instrument's real cash flows including collateral, and OIS rate curves are generally being used to discount those derivatives that are fully cash collateralised. In other words, LIBOR (forward) rates are only used to project the future floating cash flows in collateralised derivatives but the cash flows are then discounted using OIS rates.

The use of two different yield curves (often referred to as the 'multi curve issue') has an effect on the fair value of the derivative and therefore also can have an effect on hedge accounting if the derivative is used in a hedge accounting relationship:

- For fair value hedges, it is likely that there will be ineffectiveness. This is because different curves are used for the calculation of future floating cash flows and discounting the cash flows from the derivative, while only one curve is used for discounting the hedged item's fixed cash flows.
- In the case of cash flow hedges, the situation is less clear and comes back to the discussion about the use of the 'hypothetical derivative' method set out above at 5.3.4 above. However, the situation appears to be clearer on application of IFRS 9 given the guidance on hypothetical derivatives in paragraph B6.5.5 of IFRS 9 which precludes including features in the value of the hedged item that only exist in the hedging instrument, but not in the hedged item (see Chapter 53 at 6.4.2). Accordingly under IFRS 9 it is not permissible to assume a hypothetical derivative is subject to the credit risk inherent in an OIS rate, if in fact the hedged item is subject to the credit risk inherent in a LIBOR rate. This will likely result in ineffectiveness under IFRS 9, although some may argue that this approach should be applied under IAS 39.
- A derivative that is novated to a central clearing party may as a result become cash collateralised (see 4.2.3.A above). The application guidance clarifies that the change in the fair value of the hedging instrument that results from the changes to the contract in connection with the novation (e.g. a change in the collateral arrangements) must be included in measurement of hedge ineffectiveness. This would also affect the hedge effectiveness assessment. *[IAS 39.AG113A]*.

5.3.4.B Currency basis risk in cross-currency interest rate swaps

Another phenomenon of the financial crisis is the increase in currency basis spreads. The currency basis is the charge above the risk-free rate in a foreign country to compensate for country and liquidity risk. Consequently, currency basis is sensitive to changes in the relative sovereign ratings of the two currencies involved. Historically, basis spreads had been low, but increased significantly after the financial crisis and the following sovereign crisis. Volatility in currency basis can create hedge ineffectiveness when using a cross currency interest rate swap (CCIRS) to hedge the foreign exchange and interest rate risk of a debt instrument issued in a foreign currency.

When designating the CCIRS in a fair value hedge, the gain or loss on the hedged item attributable to changes in the hedged interest rate risk is determined based on the foreign currency interest rate curve, therefore excluding currency basis. IAS 21 then requires such a monetary item in a foreign currency to be translated to the functional currency using the spot exchange rate. *[IAS 21.23]*. Contrary, the fair value of the CCIRS incorporates the currency basis spread which results in ineffectiveness.

By contrast, IFRS 9 identifies cross currency basis spread as a 'cost of hedging' for which a new accounting approach was developed. Guidance in IFRS 9 permits an appropriate portion of the change in the fair value of cross currency basis spreads to be taken to OCI rather than immediately recognised in the profit, see Chapter 53 at 7.2.2.

5.3.5 Hedging using instruments with a non-zero fair value

The application guidance to IAS 39 states that a hedge of a highly probable forecast purchase of a commodity with a forward contract is likely to be highly effective if, among other things, the fair value of the forward contract at inception is zero. *[IAS 39.AG108]*. (See 5.3.8 below). A non-optional derivative, such as a forward or swap contract, that has a non-zero fair value is unlikely to be a perfectly effective hedging instrument, especially in a cash flow hedge. This is because the derivative contains a 'financing' element (the initial fair value), gains and losses on which will not be replicated in the hedged item and therefore the hedge contains an inherent source of ineffectiveness. In extreme cases it may not be possible to determine that the hedge will be highly effective. This situation can arise when a derivative is designated or redesignated in a hedging relationship subsequent to its initial recognition or in a business combination (see 5.1.1 above).[20]

5.3.6 Regression analysis and other statistical methods

The use of regression analysis is referred to in the standard in the context of optimising the ratio of hedging instrument quantities to hedged item quantities in order to improve the effectiveness of a hedge. *[IAS 39.AG100]*. The implementation guidance also explains that statistical measurement techniques such as regression analysis may also be used for assessing hedge effectiveness. *[IAS 39.F.4.4]*. This section sets out the basic concepts underlying linear regression analysis, together with guidelines and considerations that we believe are appropriate when determining whether a hedge relationship can be considered highly effective when using this approach to test effectiveness.

5.3.6.A Basic concepts of regression

Linear regression is a method of identifying and describing the relationship between variables, for example y and x; linear refers to the assumption of a straight-line relationship between the variables. Regression analysis identifies a line of 'best fit' through a swarm of data using least squares analysis to minimise the total squared distances of the plotted points from the line. Some regression analyses will indicate a wider scatter of data points around the regression line than others; these wider scatters indicate a relationship between the variables that is less strong than a regression with a narrow scatter.

The regression is represented by the algebraic formula:

$$y = \alpha + \beta x + \varepsilon$$

In this equation, y is the dependent variable, x is the independent variable, α is the intercept, β is the slope of the regression line, and ε is the residual, or error term. In the context of hedge effectiveness, it is convenient to define y as the change in the fair value of the hedged item, and x as the change in fair value of the hedging instrument.

The following example of a regression describes the formula's terms in more detail:

Figure 52.1: The line of best fit, drawn through a series of correlated observations of changes in the x and y variables (such a line is likely to incorporate a non-zero intercept, if only due to random error)

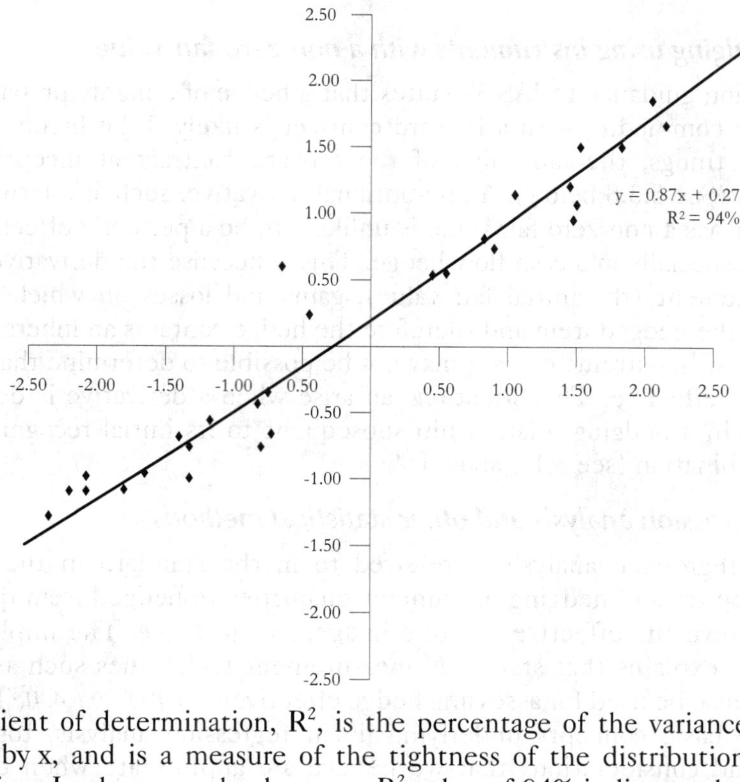

The coefficient of determination, R^2, is the percentage of the variance in y that is 'explained' by x, and is a measure of the tightness of the distribution around the regression line. In the example above, an R^2 value of 94% indicates that 94% of the variance in y can be explained by x. When assessing hedge effectiveness, the closer the line is to the actual results, the less ineffectiveness there will be. Higher R^2 values indicate a stronger relationship. The square root of this value, R, is often referred to as the coefficient of correlation. We consider that the value of R^2 should be at least 80% in order to indicate an effective hedge relationship.

The slope of the regression line is known as β or beta. In Figure 52.1 above, the slope of 0.87 indicates that, given an increase in x of 1, we would expect an increase in y of 0.87.

As noted at 2.2.2 above, IAS 39 describes a situation in which expected hedge effectiveness is maximised if the ratio between the hedging instrument and the hedged item is set at a level other than 1.00. In such circumstances it may be easier to demonstrate hedge effectiveness by multiplying the y observations by the hedge ratio so as to bring the slope closer to 1.

The intercept is the point at which the regression line crosses the y-axis – the expected value of y when x is 0. In Figure 52.1 above, the intercept is 0.27. The presence of a non-zero intercept increases the likelihood of hedge ineffectiveness, as it implies that y will change even when there is no change in x. While a small y intercept will not necessarily invalidate a hedging relationship, it is easier to demonstrate that a hedge is effective by forcing the line of regression to have a y intercept of zero, although this will reduce the value of R^2, and may also alter the slope. The chart below illustrates the impact of forcing the regression line through the origin. The effect is a reduction of the R^2 to 88% but (as described further below) an increase in the 'confidence' of the estimate.

Figure 52.2: The line of best fit, drawn through a series of correlated x and y movements so that it passes though the origin

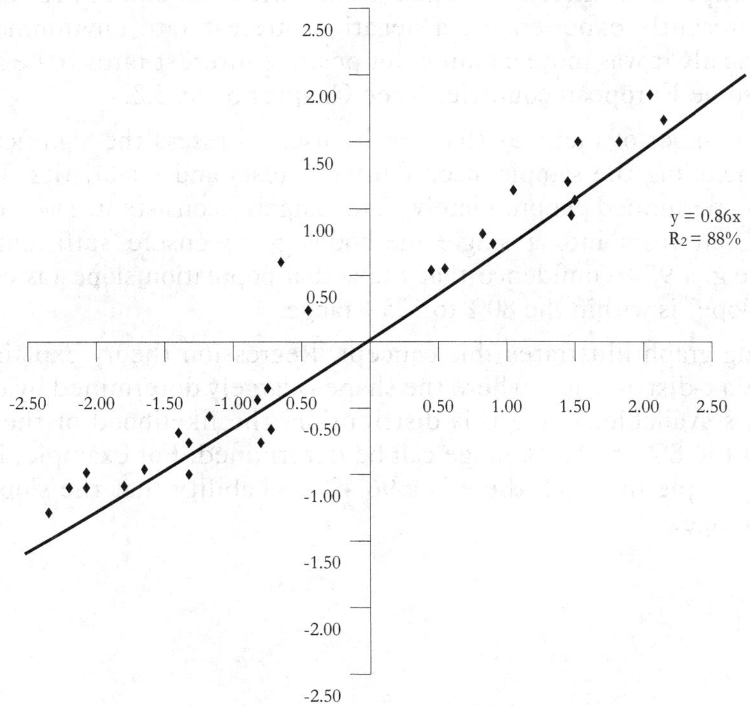

When performing regression analysis, an important notion is the concept of the sample as opposed to the population. The sample represents observations, whereas the population is the relationship between the variables that we are attempting to find. Estimates of the parameters of the population are based on the parameters of the sample. Statistical techniques can be used to express the confidence in the estimate.

For this reason, it is important to consider the statistical significance of the sample regression parameters: the degree to which the sample will provide an indication of the true (population) regression parameters. This will largely be driven by the number of data points sampled and the consistency between these points. Without some consideration of the confidence in the regression analysis, it is possible that a high R^2 could be calculated and an appropriate slope based on the sample (implying that a hedge will be highly effective), even though the sample is not a fair reflection of the population as a whole. If this were the case, it would not be appropriate to conclude that the hedge relationship will be highly effective, and there is a higher possibility of the hedge relationship failing to satisfy a retrospective test of effectiveness in future periods. In practice, when an entity enters into a new hedge relationship, it may not have the number of data points necessary to generate a reasonable population for regression analysis. In such situations, entities often generate additional data points by looking to periods prior to the inception of the hedge relationship. Effectively, the historic data points are used to help simulate how the hedge relationship would have performed under historically observed conditions, but this only makes sense provided such data is representative of those subsequent to inception. This issue is particularly relevant for relationships that include hedged items with an embedded floor within economies presently experiencing a negative interest rate environment but for which historically it was more common for positive interest rates to be applied, for example in some European countries – see Chapter 53 at 5.2.

There are a number of methods that can be used to assess the significance of the regression, including the sample size, T tests, F tests and P statistics. While these tests, when performed appropriately, are largely consistent, we recommend incorporating all tests into a single methodology to ensure sufficient statistical significance e.g. a 95% confidence that the actual population slope (as compared to the sample slope) is within the 80% to 125% range.

The following graph illustrates this concept. Regression theory explains that the slope follows a t-distribution, where the shape is largely determined by the number of data points available. Using this distribution, the likelihood of the true slope being within the 80% to 125% range can be determined. For example, Figure 52.3 illustrates a sample in which there is a 96.4% probability that the slope is within the desired range.

Figure 52.3: The probability distribution of the true slope, for the given sample, follows a t-distribution, with a 96.4% probability that the slope is within the 80% to 125% range

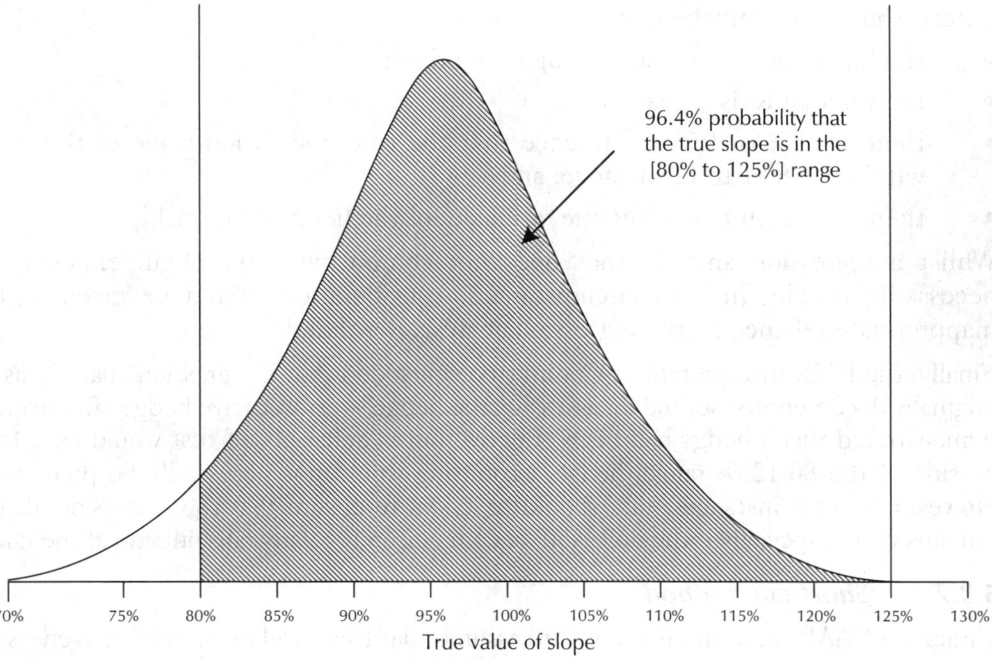

The error term ε represents the unpredicted or unexplained variation in the hedged item. In a perfectly valid regression, the error terms should be normally distributed, with constant variance, and should be independent of each other (i.e. should have no 'autocorrelation'[21]). This is an impossible expectation for real market data as financial markets almost always incorporate autocorrelation of some sort. However the imperfections most likely to invalidate regression conclusions, such as significant trends, are less likely to occur in financial price data due to the existence of arbitrage activities that take advantage of such inefficiencies.

Finally, when considering whether to use regression analysis, we believe that there must be a logical, a priori, expectation of a relationship between the relevant variables (sometimes referred to as causality). It would be inappropriate to establish a hedge relationship based solely on statistics, as there is a greater possibility of the hedge relationship being coincidental or temporary, and so breaking down in the future if it has no ongoing economic or intuitive rationale. In fact, the hedge accounting requirements under IFRS 9 explicitly require an economic relationship between the hedged item and the hedging instrument to qualify for hedge accounting (see Chapter 53 at 5.2).

5.3.6.B Summary

In order to assess a hedge relationship as highly effective (either on a prospective or retrospective basis) using regression analysis, we believe that all of the following criteria should normally be met:

- the line of best fit passes through the origin;
- the value of R^2 is at least 80%;
- there is at least 95% confidence that the true population slope of the line is within the 80% to 125% range; and
- there is an intuitive economic rationale for the hedge relationship.

Whilst a regression analysis that does not comply with these guidelines is not necessarily invalid, in such circumstances, consideration should be given so that inappropriate reliance on the regression analysis is avoided.

Finally, the IFRS Interpretations Committee concluded that if regression analysis, as the originally documented method for assessing the hedge's retrospective hedge effectiveness, demonstrated that a hedge had been effective but a 'dollar-offset' test would have fallen outside of the 80-125% range, hedge accounting would not necessarily be precluded.[22] However, in such instances, care should be taken to ensure that the regression analysis remains valid, especially if the dollar-offset comparison regularly falls outside of the range.

5.3.7 'Short-cut method'

Under US GAAP, an entity is allowed to assume that there will be no ineffectiveness in a hedge of interest rate risk using an interest rate swap as the hedging instrument, provided specified criteria are met. This is known as the 'short-cut method' for assessing hedge effectiveness. *[IAS 39.BC132]*. The original version of IAS 39 precluded such an approach and during the improvements project many commentators urged the IASB to permit the use of the short-cut method under IAS 39. *[IAS 39.BC133]*. However, one of the general principles of IAS 39 is that ineffectiveness in a hedging relationship is measured and recognised in profit or loss and the IASB did not want to make an exception to this principle. Therefore, IAS 39 was not amended to permit the short-cut method. *[IAS 39.BC134]*.

5.3.8 'Critical terms match' approach

The application guidance explains that if the principal terms of the hedging instrument and of the hedged asset, liability, firm commitment or highly probable forecast transaction are the same, the changes in fair value and cash flows attributable to the risk being hedged may be likely to offset each other fully, both when the hedge is entered into and afterwards. For example, a hedge of a highly probable forecast purchase of a commodity with a forward contract is likely to be highly effective if:

- the forward contract is for the purchase of the same quantity of the same commodity at the same time and location as the hedged forecast purchase;
- the fair value of the forward contract at inception is zero; and
- either the change in the discount or premium on the forward contract is excluded from the assessment of effectiveness and included directly in profit or loss or the change in expected cash flows on the forecast transaction is based on the forward price for the commodity (see 5.3.3 above). *[IAS 39.AG108]*.

Similarly, an interest rate swap is likely to be an effective hedge if the notional and principal amounts, term, repricing dates, dates of interest and principal receipts and payments, and basis for measuring interest rates are the same for the hedging instrument and the hedged item. *[IAS 39.AG108]*. However, an entity would of course have to consider other potential elements of ineffectiveness, such as the ones described at 5.3.4 above.

Sometimes the hedging instrument offsets only part of the hedged risk. For example, if the hedging instrument and hedged item are denominated in different currencies that do not move in tandem, the hedge would not be fully effective. *[IAS 39.AG109]*.

In deciding not to permit the short-cut method, the IASB noted that IAS 39 permits the hedging of portions of financial assets and liabilities in cases where US GAAP does not. Therefore, an entity may hedge a portion of a financial instrument (e.g. interest rate risk – see 2.2.1 above) and if the critical terms of the hedging instrument and the hedged item are the same, the entity will in many cases be able to conclude that the hedge is perfectly effective based on a qualitative assessment. *[IAS 39.BC135]*. The implementation guidance continues with this theme and explains that, to improve hedge effectiveness, an entity may designate only certain risks in an overall exposure as being hedged. For example, if an interest rate swap issued by a counterparty with a AA credit rating is used to hedge the fair value of a fixed interest rate debt instrument, designating only the exposure in the debt related to AA rated interest rate movements will reduce the impact on effectiveness of market changes in the debt counterparty credit spreads. *[IAS 39.F.4.7]*.

Therefore it can be seen, at least for hedges of financial items, that the designation of the hedge can be tailored to reduce the ineffectiveness that can feasibly occur, sometimes significantly. However, because ineffectiveness may still arise as a result of other attributes (e.g. liquidity of the hedging instrument or its credit risk – see 5.3.4 above), hedge effectiveness cannot be assumed throughout the life of the hedge even if the principal terms of the hedging instrument and hedged item are the same. *[IAS 39.F.4.7]*.

It is clear from the guidance discussed above that IAS 39 acknowledges a method of assessing *prospective* hedge effectiveness that involves comparing the critical terms of the hedging instrument and the hedged item, supplemented by a qualitative review of counterparty credit risk and other factors such as liquidity and credit risk of the hedging instrument (a 'critical terms match' approach). US GAAP also allows a 'critical terms match' approach to be used for retrospectively assessing the effectiveness of cash flow hedges,[23] but the lack of any equivalent guidance in IAS 39 has led some to say that a quantitative assessment is always necessary.

In fact, the extent of testing that is required to qualify for hedge accounting is not an accounting question, but more a regulatory issue. We have seen increasing evidence of financial reporting (and auditing) regulators setting their own benchmarks as to what they consider to be appropriate methods to use in practice, with many being reluctant to accept retrospective assessments based on the matching of critical terms and other qualitative factors. Recent years have seen new challenges to the use of seemingly simple methods for assessing hedge effectiveness, including:

- the emergence of the multi-curve issue in determining the fair value of derivatives (see 5.3.4.A above);
- a widening of basis risk spreads within cross-currency interest rate swaps (see 5.3.4.B above) and the fact that the IASB highlighted basis risk as a source of hedge ineffectiveness in the hedge accounting requirements of IFRS 9 (see Chapter 53 at 7.2.2); and
- the increased impact of credit risk on the fair value of derivatives, including an explicit requirement in IFRS 13 to take account of credit risk, including the reporting entity's own credit risk, when estimating fair values (see Chapter 14 at 11.3).

These make it increasingly difficult to justify the use of such methods and whilst they have sometimes been accepted by regulators in the past, we would advise strong caution against their continued use. In general, a quantitative method will give rise to a much lower risk of challenge than a qualitative method. The risk is heightened because, if it is determined that the selected method of assessing effectiveness is inappropriate, then hedge accounting should arguably never have been applied even if the hedge was demonstrably effective by other means such as a simple dollar-offset calculation (an approach the SEC appears to follow rigorously).[24]

5.3.9 Interest accruals and 'clean' versus 'dirty' values

Another problem that entities can face when assessing the effectiveness of hedging instruments such as interest rate swaps, is the fair value 'noise' that is generated between interest rate reset dates. The payments on an interest rate swap are typically established at the beginning of a reset period and paid at the end of that period. Between these two dates the swap is no longer a pure pay-fixed receive-variable (or *vice versa*) instrument because both the next payment and the next receipt are fixed. Accordingly, the corresponding changes in the fair value of the hedged item (e.g. fixed rate debt) will not strictly mirror that of the swap. This problem becomes more acute the less frequently variable interest rates are reset to market rates.

The IASB does not seem to see this as a potential source of ineffectiveness. For example, it is stated in IAS 39 that 'an interest rate swap is likely to be an effective hedge if the notional and principal amounts, term, repricing dates, dates of interest and principal receipts and payments, and basis for measuring interest rates are the same for the hedging instrument and the hedged item.' *[IAS 39.AG108]*. Further, given the IASB's statements (see 5.3.7 above) regarding the decision not to permit the short-cut method, which is only available for hedge relationships involving interest rate swaps, it seems safe to assume that they do not normally expect ineffectiveness from interest rate re-pricings to arise on such relationships where the hedge is 'perfect'. In fact, it is interesting to note that the one comprehensive example showing the measurement of effectiveness of an interest rate swap (see Example 52.36 at 5.3.2 above) completely avoids this issue.

Entities are therefore left with little practical guidance in dealing with the ineffectiveness that results from hedges that seem highly effective. In deliberating the accounting for macro hedging (see 6 below) the IASB staff concluded that 'hedge ineffectiveness can arise from movements in the fair value of hedging instruments owing to changes in ... floating legs within hedging derivatives'.[25]

A common approach to avoid much of this noise is to use 'clean' fair values (which effectively ignore the effects of the next net settlement or interest payment) rather than 'dirty' fair values (which includes them) for assessment of effectiveness. The mathematics of an effectiveness assessment using this approach should mean there is a much lower likelihood of the hedge failing the test. This approach is likely to prove acceptable in many situations, especially where the interval between re-pricings is frequent enough, e.g. quarterly rather than yearly, so as to minimise the changes in fair value from the fixed net settlement or next interest payment.

However, ineffectiveness should always be measured and recognised in profit or loss. This ineffectiveness is likely to be more significant when interest rates are more volatile, as experienced by a number of entities during the 'credit crunch' starting in the second half of 2007.

5.3.10 Effectiveness of options

It was explained at 2.1.4.A above that the time value of an option may be excluded from the hedge relationship and, in many cases, this may make it easier to demonstrate the effectiveness of a hedge. In such cases, if the documented hedged risk is appropriately customised there will, in many cases, be no ineffectiveness to recognise, as set out in the following example.

Example 52.38: Out of the money put option used to hedge an equity share

Company A has an investment in one hundred shares of Company Z. The share is classified as available-for-sale, therefore associated fair value gains and losses are recognised in other comprehensive income. The shares have a quoted price of £100 each and to partially protect itself against decreases in the share price, A acquires a put option, which gives it the right to sell one hundred shares in Z for £90 each.

A is permitted to designate changes in the option's intrinsic value as the hedging instrument. The changes in the intrinsic value of the option provide protection against the risk of variability in Z's share price below or equal to the strike price of the put of £90. For prices above £90, the option is out of the money and has no intrinsic value. Accordingly, gains and losses on the shares in Z for prices above £90 are not attributable to the hedged risk for the purposes of assessing hedge effectiveness and recognising gains and losses on the hedged item.

Therefore, changes in the fair value of the shares in Z are recognised in other comprehensive income if associated with variations in share price above £90. Changes in the fair value of the shares in Z associated with price declines below £90 form part of the designated fair value hedge and are recognised in profit or loss. Assuming the hedge is effective, those changes are offset by changes in the intrinsic value of the put, which are also recognised in profit or loss (see 4.1.1 above).

Changes in the time value of the put are excluded from the designated hedging relationship and recognised in profit or loss as they arise. *[IAS 39.F.1.10]*.

Under US GAAP, implementation guidance sets out a method of assessing effectiveness and measuring ineffectiveness of an entire option (i.e. including its time value) in certain cash flow hedges, which normally resulted in the measurement of no ineffectiveness.[26] This allows entities to recognise all changes in the fair value of an option (including the time value) in other comprehensive income until the hedged transaction affects profit or loss.

This guidance appears to be an exception to, rather than an interpretation of, the general principles of hedge accounting under US GAAP. Consequently, the use of this method was seen by many as incompatible with IAS 39. The topic was brought to the attention of the IFRS Interpretations Committee and in September 2007 the committee decided not to take the issue onto its agenda as the IASB's project on 'portions' would make it clear that such an approach is not allowed by IAS 39.[27]

The IASB's project resulted in amendments to IAS 39 being issued in July 2008 which added implementation guidance to the standard. The guidance reiterates that if the principal terms of a forecast transaction and an option are the same, excluding the time value of the option from the hedging instrument may result in a hedging relationship that is perfectly effective in achieving offsetting changes in cash flows attributable to the hedged one-sided risk. *[IAS 39.AG110A]*.

Conversely, if a purchased option is designated in its entirety as the hedging instrument of a one-sided risk arising from a forecast transaction, the hedging relationship will not be perfectly effective. This is because the premium paid for the option includes time value and, as discussed at 2.1.4.A above, a designated one-sided risk does not include the time value of an option. Therefore, in this situation, there will be no offset between the cash flows relating to the time value of the option premium paid and the designated hedged risk. *[IAS 39.AG110B]*.

5.3.11 Hedged items with embedded optionality

As described at 2.1.4.A above, an entity can exclude the time value of the hedging instrument from the hedging relationship when hedging with options. Although the entity would need to recognise any changes in the fair value of the time value directly in profit or loss, it most likely would achieve a higher effectiveness from an accounting perspective.

However, if the hedged item contains embedded optionality, which is matched by optionality within the hedging instrument, including the time value from both the hedged item and hedging instrument in the hedge relationship would result in a highly effective hedge. This is because offset would arise for changes in the fair value of the time value of the hedging option, from changes in the value of the embedded time value in the hedged item. The following fact patterns provide examples where offset from the time value of embedded options in hedge items could occur:

- Entity A has purchased 10 year fixed rate debt. At the end of years five and seven, the issuer has the option to prepay the debt at par. Entity A may choose to eliminate variability in the fair value of the fixed rate debt by transacting a pay fixed receive floating interest rate swap, with matching prepayment options at five and seven years.
- Entity B has floating rate debt which includes an embedded floor (e.g. interest is floored at 0%). Entity B could choose to eliminate the variability in the cash flows above the floor (and lock in current low rates), by transacting either a pay fixed swap with an embedded or standalone floor or by purchasing a cap.

In the case of Entity A above, it is relatively easy to conclude that the change in value of the embedded prepayment option should form part of the effectiveness assessment and measurement of ineffectiveness, as a fair value hedge. *[IAS 39. F.6.2]*. However, it is less clear in the case of Entity B which is a cash flow hedge.

IAS 39 provides guidance on hedge accounting for purchased options hedging a one-sided risk in a forecast transaction. The guidance explains that the hedged risk cannot include option time value because time value is not a component of the forecast transaction that affects profit or loss. Therefore, if an entity designates a purchased option in its entirety, as the hedging instrument of a one-sided risk arising from a forecast transaction, the hedging relationship will not be perfectly effective. In this situation, there will be no offset between the cash flows relating to the time value of the option premium paid and the designated hedged risk. *[IAS 39.AG99BA, AG110B]*.

This might indicate that including the change in the time value of the embedded option in the hedged item as part of the change in value of the hedged item for effectiveness purposes is not permissible under IAS 39. However, the above guidance is specifically for forecast transactions that do not include time value, whereas hedged items with embedded optionality do include time value. Therefore, it could be argued that the guidance referred to above is not relevant for hedged items that do include optionality.

IAS 39 defines a cash flow hedge as a hedge of an exposure to variability in cash flows that could impact profit or loss. *[IAS 39.86(b)]*. Arguably, a change in the value of the time value of an embedded option within the hedged item does not impact profit or loss nor does it result in cash flow variability. However, we believe that it is the hedged risk, ordinarily the underlying of the host hedged item and embedded option, for which cash flow variability and the potential to impact profit or loss must be demonstrated. In measuring ineffectiveness, the cumulative change in fair value (present value) of the expected future cash flows on the hedged item is incorporated. *[IAS 39.96(a)(i)]*. The fair value of the hedged cash flows, which include the embedded optionality, includes the time value, not just the intrinsic value.

Furthermore, the standard requires that the hedge is expected to be highly effective in achieving offsetting changes in fair value or cash flows attributable to the hedged risk. *[IAS 39.88(b)]*. Ordinarily, in order to demonstrate compliance with this requirement, it is not acceptable to only compare cash flows but to consider the time value of money by discounting the cash flows. The time value of money also does not impact profit or loss or cause variability in the cash flows in a cash flow hedge, but is considered a factor in the cumulative fair value (present value) of the future cash flow (consistent with IAS 39.96(a)(i)). This same approach should be applied to the time value of the embedded optionality with respect to the hedged risk.

5.3.12 Net investment hedges: identifying the effective portion

As set out at 3.3.1 above, IFRIC 16 explains that the hedged risk in a net investment hedge is defined by reference to the functional currency of a parent of the foreign operation that is the subject of the hedge. For the purpose of assessing effectiveness, the change in value of the hedging instrument in respect of foreign exchange risk should be computed by reference to the functional currency of this parent entity. *[IFRIC 16.15]*.

This change in value is also the amount that should be reclassified from equity to profit or loss if the hedged foreign operation is disposed of. *[IFRIC 16.16]*.

Depending on where the hedging instrument is held, in the absence of hedge accounting the total change in its value might be recognised in profit or loss, in other comprehensive income, or both. *[IFRIC 16.15]*. For example, consider the situation outlined in Example 52.22 above (see 3.3.1 above). In the absence of hedge accounting, the total US$/€ foreign exchange difference on A's US$300 million external borrowing would be recognised in P's consolidated financial statements as follows: *[IFRIC 16.AG5]*

- US$/¥ spot foreign exchange rate change, translated to euro, in profit or loss; and
- ¥/€ spot foreign exchange rate change in other comprehensive income.

The interpretation states that the assessment of effectiveness should not be affected by where the change in value of the hedging instrument would be recognised. In applying hedge accounting, the total effective portion of the change should be included in other comprehensive income. *[IFRIC 16.15]*. Nevertheless, the application guidance indicates that in certain situations there may be ineffectiveness recognised in profit or loss.

Consider the situation set out in Example 52.22 above. If A's borrowings were designated in a hedge of the €/US$ spot risk associated with P's net investment in C, the application guidance states that all of the €/US$ foreign exchange difference would, after the application of hedge accounting, be recognised in other comprehensive income and be included in the foreign currency translation reserve relating to C. The guidance says this is because the change in value of both the hedging instrument and the hedged item are computed by reference to the functional currency of P (euro) against the functional currency of C (US dollars). *[IFRIC 16.AG4, AG7]*.

However, if the borrowing was designated as a hedge of the £/US$ spot foreign exchange risk between C and B, the guidance states that the total US$/€ foreign exchange difference on A's borrowing would instead be recognised in P's consolidated financial statements as follows: *[IFRIC 16.AG5]*

- the £/US$ spot foreign exchange rate change (the effective portion of the hedging instrument) in the foreign currency translation reserve relating to C;
- £/¥ spot foreign exchange rate change, translated to euro, in profit or loss; and
- ¥/€ spot foreign exchange rate change in other comprehensive income.

Finally, it states that if P held the US$ denominated borrowings and designated them in a hedge of the spot foreign exchange exposure (£/US$) between B and C, only the £/US$ part of the change in the value of the borrowings (the effective portion of the hedging instrument) would be included in P's foreign currency translation reserve relating to C. The remainder of the change (equivalent to the £/€ change on £159 million) would be included in P's consolidated profit or loss. *[IFRIC 16.AG12]*.

The assessment of effectiveness is not affected by whether the hedging instrument is a derivative or a non-derivative instrument or by the method of consolidation. *[IFRIC 16.15, AG7]*.

5.3.13 Net investment hedges: other practical issues

There can be a number of other issues surrounding what constitutes a valid net investment hedge and the remainder of this section deals with some of the other practical aspects of such hedges on the assumption that the hedge relationship is considered valid.

5.3.13.A Non-derivative liabilities used as the hedging instrument

A foreign currency denominated non-derivative financial liability, such as a borrowing, can be used as the hedging instrument in a hedge of a net investment in a foreign operation. This can be seen as a pure 'accounting' hedge, i.e. the retranslation gain or loss on the borrowing (an accounting entry representing a part of its change in fair value that is accounted for on a continuous basis) can offset the retranslation gain or loss on the net investment (another accounting entry). In fact, if the liability is:

- denominated in the same currency as the functional currency of the hedged net investment;
- held by an entity with the same functional currency as the parent by which the hedged risk is defined;
- has an amortised cost that is lower than the net investment in the foreign operation; and
- is designated appropriately,

the hedge is likely to be perfectly effective in terms of the offsetting retranslation gains and losses on the liability and the hedged proportion of the net investment.

If a borrowing or similar liability is denominated in a different currency to the functional currency of the net investment, it may still be possible to designate it as the hedging instrument. However, it will need to be demonstrated that the two currencies are sufficiently correlated so that the hedging instrument is expected to result in offsetting gains and losses over the period that the hedge is designated. This might be the case if the two currencies are formally pegged or otherwise linked to one another or if the relevant exchange rates move in tandem because of, say, similarities in the underlying economies.

Even if such a hedge is highly effective, it is likely to result in some ineffectiveness. Under US GAAP it is suggested that the retranslation gains and losses on the actual instrument should be compared to those on a hypothetical non-derivative (e.g. a borrowing in the correct currency) with any difference recognised in profit or loss.[28] This approach should normally be acceptable under IAS 39, if applied in conjunction with the accounting requirements for net investment hedges (see 4.3 above).

5.3.13.B Derivatives used as the hedging instrument

It is harder to determine what types of derivative may be used in a hedge of a net investment. The same definition of effectiveness applies to such hedges as to others, but what are the changes in the fair value or cash flows of the hedged item that are attributable to the hedged risk that are to be offset by changes in the fair value or cash flows of the hedging instrument? In many respects it is only an accounting entry that is being hedged but, unlike in 5.3.13.A above, the hedging instrument will be accounted for at fair value. Even for the simplest derivative that fair value is likely to reflect factors other than changes in the spot exchange rate.

Under US GAAP a number of interpretations to ASC 815 have been issued setting out what types of derivative may be designated in a net investment hedge and how changes in the value of those derivatives should be accounted for. This guidance is summarised in the following table:[29]

	Method of assessing effectiveness under US GAAP*	
Type of derivative	**Spot rate method**	**Forward rate method**
Forward contract	Changes in value attributable to spot rate changes recognised in other comprehensive income Changes in value of interest element recognised in profit or loss	All changes in value (including interest element) recognised in other comprehensive income
Purchased option	Changes in intrinsic value recognised in other comprehensive income Changes in time value recognised in profit or loss	All changes in value (including time value) recognised in other comprehensive income
Cross-currency interest rate swap: both legs floating rate	Interest settlements accrued in profit or loss All other changes in value recognised in other comprehensive income	All changes in value (including interest settlements) recognised in other comprehensive income
Cross-currency interest rate swap: both legs fixed rate	Changes in value from retranslating notional at spot exchange rates recognised in other comprehensive income Interest settlements accrued in profit or loss Other changes in value (e.g. from changes in interest rates) recognised in profit or loss	All changes in value (including interest settlements) recognised in other comprehensive income
Cross-currency interest rate swap: one floating rate leg, one fixed	Hedge accounting not available	Hedge accounting not available

* one method to be applied consistently for all derivatives designated as hedges of a net investment.

This table assumes the contracts are denominated in the same currency as the functional currency of the hedged net investment and that there are no other sources of ineffectiveness. The applicability of this guidance to IAS 39 is considered below.

I Forward currency contracts

It is very common for forward currency contracts to be used as the hedging instrument in a hedge of a net investment – in fact, this is the one example that is acknowledged in the implementation guidance. Therefore, applying the US GAAP guidance under IAS 39 seems relatively uncontroversial and has effectively been endorsed in IFRIC 16. *[IFRIC 16.15, AG2]*. However, implementation guidance in IAS 39 makes it clear that where the spot rate method is used (i.e. the interest element of the forward is excluded from the hedge relationship) the premium or discount cannot be amortised to profit or loss. *[IAS 39.F.6.4]*. Inevitably, therefore, some volatility will arise in profit or loss and the longer the term of the forward, the greater is the potential volatility.

Some may wonder why entities might choose the spot rate method over the forward rate method. Prior to the development of standards such as IAS 39, the interest element of a forward contract (and similar instruments) was commonly recognised as interest on an accruals basis. Depending on the relative interest rates of the two currencies in the forward, accounting for the interest element in this way could potentially result in a credit to profit or loss, which is clearly desirable from the perspective of preparers of the financial statements. Where an entity is prepared to accept the volatility associated with this method, a similar effect on profit or loss (over time) may be achieved by using the spot rate method.

If the forward contract is denominated in a different currency to the functional currency of the net investment it is likely that, at best, some ineffectiveness will arise (unless the link between the two currencies is perfect). Under US GAAP, a comparison of the forward contract with a hypothetical derivative (a forward contract in the right currency) would be made to measure the amount of ineffectiveness[30] and this approach would normally be acceptable under IAS 39.

II Purchased options

The spot rate method involves designating the intrinsic value of a purchased option as the hedging instrument (i.e. its time value is excluded from the hedge relationship). This is clearly acceptable under IAS 39 (see 2.1.4.A and 5.3.10 above), although this will cause some volatility in profit or loss, which over time will always result in an expense being recognised in profit or loss as the time value decays.

Under the forward rate method applied under US GAAP, the whole option would be designated as the hedging instrument. However, as discussed at 5.3.10 above, designating the entire purchased option as the hedging instrument under IAS 39 is likely to result in high levels of ineffectiveness which could result in hedge failure. This is because no offset will arise for changes in the time value of the purchased option, as the time value is not a component of the hedged net investment. *[IAS 39.AG110B]*.

III Cross-currency interest rate swaps

Like forward contracts, these instruments are commonly used as hedging instruments in net investment hedges. At a conceptual level, it is easy to see that the changes in value of a cross-currency swap with two floating-rate legs are likely to offset the retranslation gains and losses of a net investment, provided the floating rate resets sufficiently frequently. It is also reasonably easy to see that a swap with one floating-rate leg and one fixed-rate leg is unlikely to provide the necessary offset because the fixed rate leg will give rise to changes in the swap's value that are unrelated to changes in exchange rates.

It is less easy to see that the change in value of a swap with two fixed-rate legs will provide a good hedge against the retranslation gains and losses (again the fixed-rate legs will give rise to changes in the swap's value that are unrelated to changes in exchange rates). However, such an instrument may be viewed as a combination of forward contracts, albeit ones that, individually, are likely to have non-zero fair values, which could be designated in a hedge of a net investment based on the forward rate method (see I above). Designating a fixed-for-fixed currency swap in a cash flow hedge based on the forward rate implies that the amount of hedged item would be equal to the sum of the undiscounted foreign currency interest and principal payments which would be higher than the notional amount of the swap. However, since the conceptual basis of a net investment hedge is not that clear, we do not think such designation by analogy to a cash flow hedge would be required.

The 'spot rate' treatment under US GAAP which permits changes in value other than the retranslation of the notional at spot exchange rates to be included in other comprehensive income, however, is generally considered to have limited technical merit. We believe that application of the US GAAP spot rate method as described for forward contracts is more appropriate.

5.3.13.C Combinations of derivative and non-derivative instruments used as the hedging instrument

It is not uncommon for entities to hedge their net investments using synthetic foreign currency debt instruments. For example, consider a parent with the euro as its functional currency that has a net investment in a Japanese subsidiary with yen as its functional currency. The parent might borrow in US dollars and enter into a pay-Japanese yen, receive-US dollar cross-currency interest rate swap. In this way the two instruments might be considered a synthetic Japanese yen borrowing, although they are required to be accounted for separately (see Chapter 44 at 8).

As noted at 2.1.3 above, a combination of derivatives and non-derivatives may be viewed in combination and jointly designated as a hedging instrument under IAS 39. *[IAS 39.77]*. However, all the hedging instruments must be clearly identified in the hedge documentation. *[IAS 39.88(a)]*.

The Japanese parent in the above fact pattern may wish to designate the spot rate only when hedging a net investment with a combination of derivatives and non-derivatives. Designation of the combination as hedging a forward rate is more problematic given the issues noted in 5.3.13.B III above and the fact that the hedging instrument includes a foreign currency monetary item for which the accounting for foreign exchange is at the spot rate. *[IAS 21.23(a)]*.

Another alternative may be to notionally decompose the cross currency swap by introducing an interest bearing functional currency denominated leg and designating one part as a hedge of the borrowing and the other as a hedge of the net investment (see 2.1.4.E above).

5.3.13.D Individual or separate financial statements

It is common for an entity with an investment in a subsidiary, associate or joint venture to be party to a financial instrument (a borrowing, say) that in the entity's consolidated financial statements is designated as the hedging instrument in a hedge of its net investment in the subsidiary, associate or joint venture. However, in the entity's individual or separate financial statements, the investment will generally be accounted for as an asset measured at cost or as a financial asset in accordance with IAS 39. *[IAS 27.10]*. In other words, it will not be accounted for by way of consolidation or the equity method.

Accordingly, from the perspective of the individual or separate financial statements, the reporting entity will not have a net investment in a foreign operation. Therefore, the borrowing could not be designated as the hedging instrument in a net investment hedge for the purposes of the separate financial statements. However, if hedge accounting is desirable, it may be possible to designate the borrowing as the hedging instrument in another type of hedge. Typically, this would be a fair value hedge of the foreign currency risk arising from the investment. This will be an independent hedge relationship, separate from the net investment hedge in the consolidated financial statements. Therefore, all of the other hedge accounting criteria (including the documentation requirements) will need to be met for this hedge too. Of course, the effects of this hedge accounting will need to be reversed when preparing the group's consolidated financial statements (otherwise those financial statements will reflect as an asset or liability certain changes in the fair value of a parent's investment in its subsidiary which would be contrary to the general principles of IFRS 10).

6 PORTFOLIO (OR MACRO) HEDGING

At a detailed level, the topic of portfolio (or macro) hedging for banks and similar financial institutions is beyond the scope of a general financial reporting publication such as this. However, no discussion of hedge accounting would be complete without an overview of the high level issues involved and an explanation of how the standard setters have tried to accommodate these entities.

The underlying philosophy of IAS 39's approach to hedge accounting is that individual hedging instruments are designated as hedging individual assets, liabilities or other risk exposures. However, banks and similar financial institutions typically manage their interest rate risk exposures dynamically on a portfolio (or macro) level. New exposures are frequently added to the portfolio and existing exposures mature. So as the net risk of the portfolio changes, risk managers will react accordingly to meet the risk management objective. Given that the focus is on the net risk position and natural offsets frequently arise as the exposures in the portfolio change, the distinction between hedged item and hedging instrument becomes less relevant. Accordingly, there is a fundamental difference between the risk management activities of the financial institution and the main hedge accounting requirements of the standard.

IAS 39 includes some specific guidance that was developed with a view to assist financial institutions in achieving hedge accounting for their portfolio interest rate risk management activities. This guidance is as follows:

- Fair value hedge of the interest rate exposure of a portfolio of financial assets or financial liabilities; *[IAS 39.78, 81A, 89A, 92, AG114-AG132, BC173-220, IE1-IE31, DO1-DO2]*
- Management of interest rate risk in financial institutions (colloquially known as the macro cash flow approach). *[IAS 39.F.6.1-F.6.3]*.

Unfortunately, even with these two approaches, it is often difficult to accommodate the risk management activities of financial institutions within the IAS 39 hedge accounting requirements. In particular, there are significant restrictions on the way the fair value of financial liabilities with a demand feature are measured (see Chapter 14 at 11.5) and this effectively prevents banks from applying fair value hedge accounting to the majority of their current and deposit accounts (see 2.2.10 above). In fact, the EC endorsed version of IAS 39 has certain parts of the hedge accounting requirements carved out in a direct response to the cited difficulties of financial institutions achieving hedge accounting under IAS 39,[31] thereby allowing the use of hedge accounting in situations that the full version of IAS 39 would not.

In view of these factors, a project was set up by the IASB to develop a new accounting approach for dynamic risk management that would be based on an entity's risk management activities. This project was originally part of the IASB's project to replace IAS 39 with IFRS 9. However, the IASB realised that developing the new accounting model would take time and probably be a different concept from hedge accounting. In May 2012, the Board therefore decided to decouple the part of the project that related to accounting for dynamic risk management from IFRS 9, allowing more time to develop an accounting model without affecting the timeline for the completion of the other elements of IFRS 9.[32]

Although mainly focused on financial institutions, the accounting model for dynamic risk management might also be beneficial for some corporate entities applying macro-type hedging strategies.

In April 2014, the IASB issued the Discussion Paper – *Accounting for Dynamic Risk Management: a Portfolio Revaluation Approach to Macro Hedging*. The six-month comment period ended in October 2014. Most respondents supported the need for the project, but there was no consensus on a solution. Given the diversity in views, in July 2015 the IASB concluded that the insights that it had received from the comment letters and feedback so far did not enable it to develop proposals for an exposure draft. Accordingly, the IASB decided that the project should remain in the research programme, with the aim of publishing a second discussion paper. The next step for the project was to focus on identifying the information needed to provide more decision useful information on dynamic risk management. In May 2016, the IASB confirmed that the project should remain on the active research section of their work plan. At that meeting it was discussed that a focus on identifying information needs has proved to be challenging. Because of this, they returned the focus of their work to recognition and measurement for Dynamic Risk Management.

References

1 For example, see IAS 39 (2000), *Financial Instruments: Recognition and Measurement*, IASC, December 1998 to October 2000, para. 10.
2 *IFRIC Update*, July 2007.
3 *IFRIC Update*, July 2007.
4 *Comments of Swiss International Air Lines Ltd. on Paragraphs 129 and 130 of the 'Exposure Draft of Proposed Amendments to IAS 39 Financial Instruments: Recognition and Measurement'*, Swiss International Air Lines Ltd, October 2002.
5 *IFRIC Update*, October 2004.
6 *IFRIC Update*, July 2009.
7 DP/2014/1 1.14 -1.15 and 3.9.1-3.9.16.
8 IGC Q&A 137-13.
9 *IFRIC Update*, January 2013.
10 Information for Observers (February 2007 IASB meeting), *Business Combinations II: Reassessments (Agenda Paper 2B)*, IASB, February 2007, para. 28 and Information for Observers (April 2007 IASB meeting), *Classification and Designation of Assets, Liabilities and Equity Instruments Acquired or Assumed in a Business Combination (Agenda Paper 2B)*, IASB, April 2007, item #5, table following para. 14.
11 ASC 815-35-35-1 through 35-26 (formerly, Statement 133 Implementation Issue H8, *Foreign Currency Hedges: Measuring the Amount of Ineffectiveness in a Net Investment Hedge*).
12 *IFRIC Update,* March 2016
13 *IFRIC Update*, January 2011.
14 *IFRIC Update*, June 2005.
15 Information for Observers (February 2007 IASB meeting), *Business Combinations II: Reassessments (Agenda Paper 2B)*, IASB, February 2007, para. 25.
16 *IFRIC Update*, September 2006.
17 *IFRIC Update*, November 2006.
18 *IFRIC Update*, March 2007.
19 ASC 815-30-35-10 through 35-32 (formerly, Statement 133 Implementation Issue G7, *Cash Flow Hedges: Measuring the Ineffectiveness of a Cash Flow Hedge under Paragraph 30(b) When the Shortcut Method is not Applied*) and ASC 815-20-35-14 through 35-18 (formerly, Statement 133 Implementation Issue G10, *Cash Flow Hedges: Need to Consider Possibility of Default by the Counterparty to the Hedging Derivative)*.
20 IAS 39.AG108, *IFRIC Update*, March 2007, Information for Observers (January 2007 IFRIC meeting), *IAS 39 Financial Instruments: Recognition and Measurement – Assessing Hedge Effectiveness of an Interest Rate Swap in a Cash Flow Hedge (Agenda Paper 14(v))*, IASB, January 2007, Information for Observers (February 2007 IASB meeting), *Business Combinations II: Reassessments (Agenda Paper 2B)*, IASB, February 2007, para. 29 and Information for Observers (April 2007 IASB meeting), *Classification and Designation of Assets, Liabilities and Equity Instruments Acquired or Assumed in a Business Combination (Agenda Paper 2B)*, IASB, April 2007, item #5, table following para. 14.
21 Autocorrelation is the correlation of a variable with itself (i.e. the risk of repeating patterns in the error term).
22 *IFRIC Update*, November 2006.
23 ASC 815-20-25-84 (formerly, SFAS 133.65).
24 Speech by SEC Staff, *Remarks Before the 2006 AICPA National Conference on Current SEC and PCAOB Developments by Timothy S. Kviz*, U.S. Securities and Exchange Commission, December 2006.
25 Staff paper 4A, paragraph 14, October 2012 IASB Meeting.
26 ASC 815-20-25-126 to 25-129, 55-209 through 55-211, 815-30-35-33 to 35-37 and 55-127 (formerly, Statement 133 Implementation Issue G20, *Cash Flow Hedges: Assessing and Measuring the Effectiveness of a Purchased Option Used in a Cash Flow Hedge*).
27 *IFRIC Update*, September 2007.
28 ASC 815-35-35-1 to 35-26 (formerly, Statement 133 Implementation Issue H8, *Foreign Currency Hedges: Measuring the Amount of Ineffectiveness in a Net Investment Hedge*).
29 ASC 815-35-35-1 to 35-26 (formerly, Statement 133 Implementation Issue H8, Question 1) and ASC 815-20-25-67 to 25-68A; 25-71 (formerly, Statement 133 Implementation Issue H9, *Foreign Currency Hedges: Hedging a Net Investment with a Compound Derivative That Incorporates Exposure to Multiple Risks*).
30 ASC 815-35-35-1 to 35-26 (formerly, Statement 133 Implementation Issue H8, Question 2).

31 IAS 39, *Financial Instruments: Recognition and Measurement*, *Regulation* No. 2086/2004, European Commission, 19 November 2004, paras. 35, AG107A, AG124(a) and AG130 and parts of paras. 81A, AG31, AG99C, AG99D, AG114(c) and (g), AG118, AG119(d), (e) and (f), AG121, AG122, AG124(d), AG126, AG127 and AG129.

32 *IASB Update*, May 2012.

Chapter 53 Financial instruments: Hedge accounting (IFRS 9)

Chapter 53

List of examples

Chapter 53 Financial instruments: Hedge accounting (IFRS 9)

1 INTRODUCTION

1.1 Background

The majority of the IASB's current work on financial instruments began in conjunction with the FASB as part of their Memorandum of Understanding,[1] when both Boards agreed to work jointly on a research project to reduce the complexity of the accounting for financial instruments. As part of this project, the Boards had a joint objective to simplify or eliminate the need for hedge accounting.[2] In March 2008 the IASB issued a discussion paper – *Reducing Complexity in Reporting Financial Instruments* – which contained many proposals, including a number related to hedge accounting.[3] Although this was not a joint IASB-FASB document, the FASB also published it so as to obtain input for its own efforts at simplifying the accounting for financial instruments.[4]

Meanwhile, the financial crisis resulted in a significant amount of political pressure being brought to bear on standard setters in general and the IASB specifically. Responding to this pressure, in April 2009 the IASB announced a detailed six-month timetable for publishing a proposal to replace IAS 39 – *Financial Instruments: Recognition and Measurement*.[5] In order to expedite the replacement of IAS 39, the IASB divided the project into three phases: classification and measurement; amortised cost and impairment of financial assets; and hedge accounting.

In December 2010, the IASB issued the Exposure Draft ('ED' or the exposure draft) *Hedge Accounting*, being the proposals for the third part of IFRS 9 – *Financial Instruments*. After redeliberating the proposals in 2011, in September 2012 the Board published a draft of *Chapter 6 – Hedge Accounting* – of IFRS 9, together with consequential changes to other parts of IFRS 9 and other IFRSs (the draft standard). The idea of the draft standard was to enable constituents to familiarise themselves with the new requirements.[6]

Although the IASB did not ask for comments, a number of constituents asked the IASB to clarify certain elements of the draft standard. As a result, the IASB redeliberated some elements of the IFRS 9 hedge accounting requirements in its January 2013 and April 2013 meetings.

This resulted in the third version of IFRS 9, issued in November 2013, which included the new hedge accounting requirements. Finally, in July 2014 the IASB issued the all-encompassing final version of IFRS 9 that includes the new impairment requirements (see Chapter 49 at 5) and some amendments to the classification and measurement requirements (see Chapter 46). This also involved some minor consequential amendments to the hedge accounting requirements in IFRS 9, mainly because of the introduction of a new category for debt instruments measured at fair value through other comprehensive income with subsequent reclassification adjustments.

The standard does not provide any particular solutions specifically tailored to so-called 'macro hedge' accounting, the term used to describe the more complex risk management practices used by entities such as banks. In May 2012 the Board decided to decouple accounting for macro hedging from IFRS 9.[7] An accounting model specifically for macro hedging is being developed in a separate project and the discussion paper – *Accounting for Dynamic Risk Management: a Portfolio Revaluation Approach to Macro Hedging* – was published in April 2014 (see 3.6.5 below).

The IASB also allowed entities an accounting policy choice to continue applying hedge accounting as set out in IAS 39 to all hedges until the project on accounting for macro hedging is completed, instead of the requirements of Chapter 6 of IFRS 9. *[IFRS 9.7.2.21]*. See 3.6.6 below.

Rather than providing a comprehensive summary of hedge accounting, this chapter focuses on the differences between hedge accounting under IAS 39 and the hedge accounting requirements in IFRS 9. Therefore, much of what is discussed in Chapter 52 also applies to this chapter.

1.2 The main changes in the IFRS 9 hedge accounting requirements

Hedge accounting under IAS 39 is often criticised as being complex and rules-based, and thus, ultimately not reflecting an entity's risk management activities. This is unhelpful for preparers and users of the financial statements alike. The IASB took this concern as the starting point of its project for a new hedge accounting model. Consequently, the objective of IFRS 9 is to reflect the effect of an entity's risk management activities in the financial statements. *[IFRS 9.6.1.1]*.

This means that the new model specifically aims to provide a better linkage between what the standard describes as the entity's risk management strategy and what is termed the entity's risk management objective, and the impact of hedging activity on the financial statements. The risk management objective determines whether or not an entity can designate a hedging relationship and whether or not it needs to discontinue an existing hedging relationship. Risk management strategy and risk management objective are covered at 2 below, the general eligibility criteria for hedge accounting are described at 5.1 below and the criteria for discontinuation of hedge accounting at 6.3 below.

In addition, IFRS 9 widens the range of eligible hedged items. This is particularly helpful for non-financial institutions as it opens up the possibility for more hedging activities to meet the criteria for hedge accounting. It includes, for example, the possibility to designate an aggregated exposure which includes a derivative as the hedged item in a second hedging relationship (see 3.3 below). It also includes the possibility to designate non-financial risk components as the hedged risk. Under IAS 39 this was only possible for financial items (see 3.4 below). The standard also introduces further guidance related to hedging of layer components (see 3.4 below) and the hedging of groups of items including net positions (see 3.5 below).

Qualifying hedging instruments are covered at 4 below. Probably the most significant change related to hedging instruments is that under IFRS 9, entities are permitted to designate, as hedging instruments, non-derivative financial assets or non-derivative financial liabilities that are accounted for at fair value through profit or loss (see 4.2 below). It is also now possible to designate standalone written options as hedging instruments within a combination of instruments, as long as the combination does not constitute a net written option (see 4.1 below).

Perhaps the most significant change compared to IAS 39 is the replacement of rules as to whether a hedge relationship is eligible with more principle-based requirements. This includes deleting some of the arbitrary rules, such as the 80%-125% effectiveness requirement. The new effectiveness requirements focus on the economic relationship between the hedged item and hedging instrument, the designated hedge ratio and the effect of credit risk on that relationship. The effectiveness test is now only prospective and will normally be qualitative. The qualifying criteria are described at 5 and the subsequent assessment of the hedge effectiveness at 6.1 below.

It should be emphasised, however, that while the standard relaxes the criteria for hedge accounting, so that many more hedge relationships will qualify for hedge accounting and far fewer will 'fail', any actual ineffectiveness must continue to be measured and recognised in profit or loss as it arises.

In order to align hedge accounting with actual risk management, the standard requires, in certain circumstances, an entity to rebalance a hedging relationship, should the expected change in fair value or cash flows associated with the quantities of the hedged item and hedging instrument no longer offset each other to the extent originally expected, due to basis risk. In such cases, an entity can (or is even required to) adjust the quantity of the hedged item or hedging instrument on a prospective basis, such that the respective changes in the fair value are expected to offset in future periods. Rebalancing is covered in more detail at 6.2 below.

Further, IFRS 9 introduces the possibility that the time value of an option, the forward element of a forward contract and any foreign currency basis spread can be excluded from the designation of a financial instrument as the hedging instrument, and need to be (for the time value of option) or can be (for the forward points or the foreign currency basis spread) accounted for as 'costs of hedging'. This means that, instead of the fair value changes of these elements affecting profit or loss like a trading instrument, these amounts get allocated to profit or loss in a similar manner to transaction costs, while fair value changes are temporarily recognised in other comprehensive income. Cost of hedging is further covered at 7 below.

Most of the basics of hedge accounting do not change as a result of IFRS 9. There are still three types of hedging relationships:

- fair value hedges;
- cash flow hedges; and
- hedges of net investments in foreign operations. *[IFRS 9.6.5.2]*.

Hedges of net investments in foreign operations must still be accounted for similarly to cash flow hedges. *[IFRS 9.6.5.13]*. There are only some consequential amendments to IFRIC 16 – *Hedges of a Net Investment in a Foreign Operation*.

While IFRS 9 does not significantly change how the different types of hedges are presented (see 8 below), it extends the range of disclosures an entity is required to provide. Consistent with the objective of the standard, the disclosures should allow the reader of the financial statements to understand the risk management strategy of the entity and how it is applied to manage risk, the amount, timing and uncertainty of future cash flows as well as the effect of hedge accounting on the financial position and performance of the entity. More information related to disclosures is provided at 9 below.

Hedge accounting remains optional and can only be applied to hedging relationships that meet the qualifying criteria (discussed at 5 below). *[IFRS 9.6.5.1]*. This means that an entity does not have to designate hedging relationships to the same extent or in exactly the same manner as it hedges for risk management purposes (see 5.5 below). However, IFRS 9 introduces a prohibition on voluntary discontinuation of hedge relationships, only mandatory discontinuation is permitted. The circumstances for mandatory discontinuation are described at 6.3 below. The standard also introduces alternatives to hedge accounting such as the fair value option for credit risk exposures and a fair value option for own use contracts. Both alternatives are described at 10 below.

2 RISK MANAGEMENT

2.1 Objective of hedge accounting

Every entity is exposed to business risks from its daily operations. Many of those risks have an impact on the cash flows or the value of assets and liabilities, and therefore, ultimately affect profit or loss. In order to manage these risk exposures, companies often enter into derivative contracts (or, less commonly, other financial instruments) to hedge them. Hedging can therefore be seen as a risk management activity in order to change an entity's risk profile.

Applying the IFRS accounting requirements to those risk management activities can result in accounting mismatches, when the gains or losses on a hedging instrument are not recognised in the same period(s) and/or in the same place in the financial statements as gains or losses on the hedged exposure. Many believe that the resulting accounting mismatches are not a good representation of those risk management activities (see Chapter 52 at 1.2). The objective of the IFRS 9 hedge accounting requirements is to 'represent, in the financial statements, the effect of an entity's risk management activities'. The aim of the objective is 'to convey the context of hedging instruments for which hedge accounting is applied in order to allow insight into their purpose and effect'. *[IFRS 9.6.1.1]*. Similar to IAS 39, this is achieved by reducing the accounting mismatch by changing either the measurement or (in the case of certain firm commitments) recognition of the hedged exposure, or the accounting for the hedging instrument, but with some important improvements.

This is a rather broad objective that focuses on an entity's risk management activities and reflects what the Board wanted to achieve with the new accounting requirements. However, this broad objective does not override any of the hedge accounting requirements, which is why the Board noted that hedge accounting is only permitted if all the new qualifying criteria are met (see 5 below). *[IFRS 9.BC6.82]*.

2.2 Risk management strategy versus risk management objective

Linking hedge accounting with an entity's risk management activities requires an understanding of what those risk management activities are. IFRS 9 distinguishes between the *risk management strategy* and the *risk management objective*. One of the qualifying criteria for hedge accounting is that the risk management objective and strategy are documented. *[IFRS 9.6.4.1(b)]*.

The *risk management strategy* is established at the highest level of an entity and identifies the risks to which the entity is exposed, and whether and how the risk management activities should address those risks. For example, a risk management strategy could identify changes in interest rates of loans as a risk and define a specific target range for the fixed to floating rate ratio for those loans. The strategy is typically maintained for a relatively long period of time. However, it may include some flexibility to react to changes in circumstances. *[IFRS 9.B6.5.24]*.

IFRS 9 refers to the risk management strategy as normally being set out in 'a general document that is cascaded down through an entity through policies containing more specific guidelines.' *[IFRS 9.B6.5.24]*. However, in our view, this does not need to be a formal written risk management strategy document in all circumstances. Small and medium-sized entities with limited risk management activities that use financial instruments may not have a formal written document outlining their overall risk management strategy that they have in place. In some instances, there might be an informal risk management strategy empowering an individual within the entity to decide on what is done for risk management purposes. In such situations entities do not have the benefit of being able to incorporate the risk management strategy in their hedge documentation by reference to a formal policy document, but instead have to include a description of their risk management strategy directly in their hedge documentation. Also, there are disclosure requirements for the risk management strategy that apply irrespective of whether an entity uses a formal written policy document as part of its risk management activities. Consequently, a more informal risk management strategy should be both reflected in the disclosures and 'compensated' by a more detailed documentation of the hedging relationships.

The risk management strategy is an important cornerstone of the hedge accounting requirements in IFRS 9. Consequently, the Board added specific disclosure requirements to IFRS 7 – *Financial Instruments: Disclosures* – that should allow users of the financial statements to understand the risk management activities of an entity and how they affect the financial statements (see 9 below). *[IFRS 7.21A(a)]*.

The *risk management objective,* on the contrary, is set at the level of an individual hedging relationship. It defines how a particular hedging instrument is designated to hedge a particular hedged item, and how that hedging instrument is used to achieve the risk management strategy. For example, this would define how a specific interest rate swap is used to 'convert' a specific fixed rate liability into a floating rate liability. Hence, a risk management strategy would usually be supported by many risk management objectives. *[IFRS 9.B6.5.24]*.

Example 53.1: Risk management strategies with related risk management objectives

The table below shows two examples of a risk management strategy with a related risk management objective.

Risk management strategy	Risk management objective
Maintain 40% of financial debt at floating interest rate	Designate an interest rate swap as a fair value hedge of a GBP 100m fixed rate liability
Hedge foreign currency risk of up to 70% of forecast sales in USD up to 12 months	Designate a foreign exchange forward contract to hedge the foreign exchange risk of the first USD 100 sales in March 2017

It is essential to understand the difference between the risk management strategy and the risk management objective. In particular, a change in a risk management objective, may affect the entity's ability to continue applying hedge accounting. Furthermore, voluntary discontinuation of a hedging relationship without a respective change in the risk management objective is not allowed. This is described at 6.3 below.

3 HEDGED ITEMS

3.1 General requirements

The general requirements of what qualifies as an eligible hedged item are unchanged compared to IAS 39. A hedged item can be:

- a recognised asset or liability;
- an unrecognised firm commitment;
- a highly probable forecast transaction; or
- a net investment in a foreign operation.

All of above can either be a single item or a group of items, provided the specific requirements for group of items are met (see 3.6 below). *[IFRS 9.6.3.1]*.

Only assets, liabilities, firm commitments and forecast transactions with an external party qualify for hedge accounting. *[IFRS 9.6.3.5]*. As an exception, a hedge of the foreign currency risk of an intragroup monetary item qualifies for hedge accounting if that foreign currency risk affects consolidated profit or loss. In addition, the foreign currency risk of a highly probable forecast intragroup transaction would also qualify as a hedged item if that transaction affects consolidated profit or loss. *[IFRS 9.6.3.6]*. These requirements are unchanged from IAS 39 (for further details see Chapter 52 at 2.3.4).

As with IAS 39, the item being hedged must still be reliably measurable. *[IFRS 9.6.3.2]*. Also unchanged from IAS 39, a forecast transaction must be highly probable. *[IFRS 9.6.3.3]*.

However, what has changed in IFRS 9, compared to IAS 39, is how hedged items are designated in a hedging relationship. In particular, the designation of risk components and nominal components, and the designation of aggregated exposures and groups of items have changed. These changes, which should ultimately lead to more risk management activities qualifying for hedge accounting, all stem from the broader goal of the hedge accounting project, to better align an entity's risk management approach with the accounting outcome.

In the remainder of this section, we focus on changes in the designation of hedged items compared to IAS 39. (For details on hedged items under IAS 39 see Chapter 52 at 2.)

3.2 Hedges of exposures affecting other comprehensive income

Only hedges of exposures that could affect profit or loss qualify for hedge accounting. The sole exception to this rule is when an entity is hedging an investment in equity instruments for which it has elected to present changes in fair value in other comprehensive income (OCI), as permitted by IFRS 9. Using that election, gains or losses on the equity investments will never be recognised in profit or loss (see Chapter 49 at 2.2). *[IFRS 9.6.5.3]*.

For such a hedge, the fair value change of the hedging instrument is recognised in OCI. *[IFRS 9.6.5.8]*. Any hedge ineffectiveness is also recognised in OCI. *[IFRS 9.6.5.3]*. On sale of the investment, gains or losses accumulated in OCI are not reclassified to profit or loss (see Chapter 50 at 5). Consequently, the same also applies for any accumulated fair value changes on the hedging instrument, including any ineffectiveness.

3.3 Aggregated exposures

3.3.1 Introduction

A well-known criticism of IAS 39 hedge accounting is that it does not always permit an entity to reflect the effect of its risk management activities in the financial statements (see 1.2 above). A scenario where this often occurs is where risk management is undertaken for a hedged position that includes a derivative, as IAS 39 precludes designation of derivatives as hedged items. It may be the case that some form of hedge accounting could be achieved for this scenario, but any such hedge designation is unlikely to fully reflect the risk management undertaken and may result in higher than expected accounting ineffectiveness (see 3.3.2 below).

IFRS 9 introduced a new hedge accounting concept known as 'an aggregated exposure'; the purpose of which was to facilitate hedge accounting that reflects the effect of risk management undertaken for a hedged position that includes a derivative. An aggregated exposure is described as a combination of an exposure that could qualify as a hedged item, and a derivative designated as a hedged item. *[IFRS 9.6.3.4]*. The new guidance does not change the unit of account for instruments making up the aggregated exposure, specifically it is not accounted for as a 'synthetic' single item. Instead, an entity should consider the combined effect of the aggregated exposure for the purpose of assessing hedge effectiveness and measuring hedge ineffectiveness.

Whilst the ability to designate an aggregated exposure as a hedged item in a hedge relationship should allow an entity to reflect better the effect of its risk management in the financial statements, the steps required to achieve this hedge accounting are quite complex. Furthermore, although some detailed examples of hedge accounting for aggregated exposures are provided in the implementation guidance in the standard, there are still some areas of uncertainty. *[IFRS 9.IE115-147]*. We outline below the general requirements for hedge accounting for aggregated exposures.

3.3.2 Background

Entities often purchase or sell items (in particular commodities) that expose them to more than one type of risk (e.g. commodity and foreign exchange risk). When hedging those risk exposures, entities do not always hedge each risk for the same time period. This is best explained with an example:

Example 53.2: Aggregated exposure – copper purchase in a foreign currency

An entity manufacturing electrical wires is expecting to purchase copper in 12 months. The functional currency of the entity is euro (EUR). The copper price is fluctuating and is denominated in US dollars (USD), which is a foreign currency for the entity. The entity is exposed to two main risks, the copper price risk and the foreign exchange risk.

The entity first decides to hedge the copper price fluctuation risk, using a copper futures contract. By doing so, the entity now has a fixed-price copper purchase denominated in a foreign currency and is therefore still exposed to foreign exchange risk. (In this example we assume there is no 'basis risk' between the copper price exposures in the expected purchase and the futures contract, such as the effect of quality and the location of delivery). (See 6.2.1 below).

Three months later, the entity decides to hedge the foreign exchange risk by entering into a foreign exchange forward contract to buy a fixed amount of USD in nine months. By doing so, the entity is hedging the aggregated exposure, which is the combination of the original exposure to variability of the copper price and the copper futures contract. The diagram below illustrates the two economic hedging relationships.

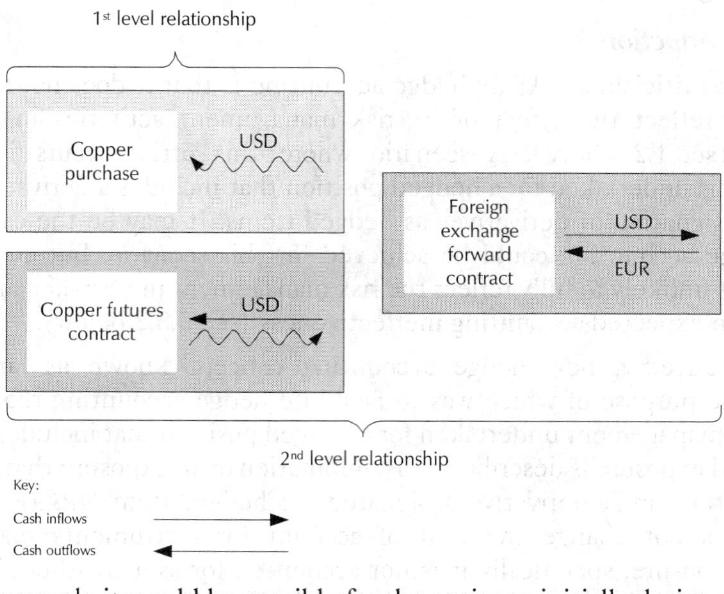

In the above example it would be possible for the entity to initially designate the copper futures contract as hedging variations in the copper purchase price in a cash flow hedge relationship, under both IFRS 9 and IAS 39. This is on the assumption that the relevant hedge accounting eligibility criteria are met. (See 5 below and Chapter 52 at 5). However, when the entity transacts the foreign exchange forward contract three months later,

IAS 39 precludes derivatives from being designated as part of a hedged item for accounting purposes (see Chapter 52 at 2.2.7) and so the entity would have two choices under IAS 39:

- discontinue the first hedging relationship (i.e. the copper price risk hedge) and re-designate a new relationship with joint designation of the copper futures contract and the foreign exchange forward contract as the hedging instrument. This is likely to lead to some 'accounting' hedge ineffectiveness as the copper futures contract will now have a non-zero fair value on designation of the new relationship (see Chapter 52 at 5.3.5); or
- maintain the copper price risk hedge and designate the foreign exchange forward contract in a second relationship as a hedge of the variable USD copper purchase price. Even if the other IAS 39 requirements could be met, this means that the volume of hedged item is constantly changing as it is the variable copper purchase price that is now hedged for foreign exchange risk, (i.e. without consideration of the effect of the copper futures). This will likely have an impact on the effectiveness of the hedging relationship, in particular if the variable USD copper price falls, as there may not be sufficient volume of USD cash flows from the designated hedged item in order to match the foreign currency forward contract.

As mentioned above, IFRS 9 expands the range of eligible hedged items by including aggregated exposures that are a combination of an exposure that could qualify as a hedged item and a derivative. *[IFRS 9.6.3.4]*.

Consequently, in the scenario described in Example 53.2 above, the entity could designate the foreign exchange forward contract in a cash flow hedge of the combination of the original exposure and the copper futures contract (i.e. the aggregated exposure) without affecting the first hedging relationship. In other words, it would no longer be necessary to discontinue and re-designate the first hedging relationship, as demonstrated in the table below:

IFRS 9 designations	**1st level hedge relationship**	**2nd level hedge relationship**
Hedge relationship	Cash flow hedge	Cash flow hedge
Hedged risk	Copper price	USD/EUR exchange rate
Hedged item	Copper purchases	Combination of copper purchases and copper futures contract
Hedging instrument	Copper futures contracts	Foreign exchange forward contract
Designation	Designated when copper futures are transacted. Hedge is not impacted by 2nd level hedge designation	Designated when foreign exchange forward contracts are transacted

It is important to keep in mind that the individual items in the aggregated exposure are accounted for separately, applying the normal requirements of hedge accounting (i.e. there is no change in the unit of account; the aggregated exposure is not treated as a 'synthetic' single item). For example, when hedging a combination of a variable rate loan and a pay fixed/receive variable interest rate swap (IRS), the loan would still be accounted for at amortised cost with the IRS accounted for at fair value through profit or loss, and presented separately in the statement of financial position. An entity would not be allowed to present the IRS and the loan (i.e. the aggregated exposure) together in one line item (i.e. as if it was one single fixed rate loan). *[IFRS 9.B6.3.4]*.

However, when assessing the effectiveness and measuring the ineffectiveness of a hedge of an aggregated exposure, the combined effect of the items in the aggregated exposure has to be taken into consideration. *[IFRS 9.B6.3.4]*. This is of particular relevance if the terms of the hedged item and the hedging instrument in the first hedging relationship do not perfectly match, e.g. if there is basis risk. Any ineffectiveness in the first level relationship would automatically also lead to some ineffectiveness in the second level relationship. However, this does not mean that the same ineffectiveness is recognised twice.

3.3.3 Accounting for aggregated exposures

The following three examples, partly derived from illustrative examples in the implementation guidance of IFRS 9, help explain the concept of a hedge of an aggregated exposure:

Example 53.3: Fixed rate loan in a foreign currency – cash flow hedge of an aggregated exposure

This fact pattern is based on Example 17 in the implementation guidance. *[IFRS 9.IE128-137]*. An entity has a fixed rate borrowing denominated in a foreign currency (FC) and is therefore exposed to foreign exchange risk and fair value risk due to changes in interest rates. The entity decides to swap the borrowing into a functional currency (LC) floating rate borrowing using a cross currency interest rate swap (CCIRS). The CCIRS is designated as the hedging instrument in a fair value hedge (first-level relationship). By doing so, the entity has eliminated both the foreign exchange risk and the fair value risk due to changes in interest rates. However, it is now exposed to variable functional currency interest payments.

Later, the entity decides to fix the amount of functional currency interest payments by entering into an interest rate swap (IRS) to pay fixed and receive floating interest in its functional currency. By doing so, the entity is hedging the aggregated exposure, which is the combination of the original exposure and the CCIRS. The IRS is designated as the hedging instrument in a cash flow hedge (second-level relationship). *[IFRS 9.IE128]*. The diagram below illustrates the two hedging relationships.

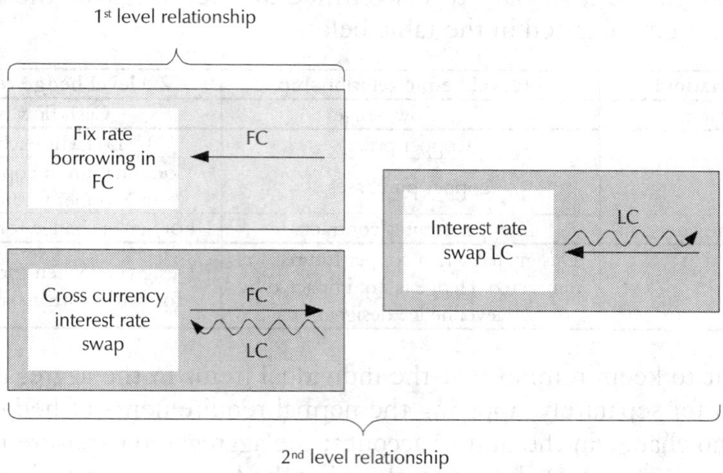

As noted above, the accounting for aggregated exposures can be complex. In this example the complexity lies in the calculation of the present value (PV) of the variability of cash flows of the aggregated exposure. This calculation is necessary in order to calculate the ineffectiveness in the second level relationship, in line with the usual hedge accounting requirements for cash flow hedges. *[IFRS 9.6.5.11(a)(ii)]*.

The implementation guidance in Example 17 demonstrates that the variability of the cash flows of the aggregated exposure can be calculated by creating a 'synthetic' aggregated exposure for calculation purposes. *[IFRS 9.IE.134(a)]*. This is similar to creating what is often referred to as a 'hypothetical derivative' for hedge relationships that do not include aggregated exposures. (See 6.4.2 below).

One leg of the synthetic aggregated exposure is based on the gross cash flows from the aggregated exposure, and the other leg is 'fixed at a blended rate' such that the present value of the whole synthetic aggregated exposure is nil on initial hedge designation. Similar to the role of the fixed leg in a hypothetical derivative, the fixed leg in the synthetic aggregated exposure is designed to reflect the level at which the hedged risk in the aggregated exposure could be locked in on initial designation of the second level relationship. The purpose of this is to capture the present value of the variability of cash flows of the aggregated exposure from that point onwards.

In this particular fact pattern, the leg in the synthetic aggregated exposure that represents the cash flows of the aggregated exposure is a combination of the future foreign currency cash outflows on the liability and the local and foreign currency cash outflows and inflows on the CCIRS. The 'blended' rate for the fixed leg of the synthetic aggregated exposure is calibrated so that the present value of the synthetic aggregated exposure in total is nil on designation of the second level relationship.

In the example in the implementation guidance, all the cash flows contributing to the leg that represents the cash flows of the aggregated exposure, are recorded and valued on a gross basis. It follows that if the cash flows from the foreign currency fixed rate liability and those from the receive fixed foreign currency leg of the CCIRS do not exactly offset, then the resultant 'net cash flow' will contribute to the synthetic aggregated exposure leg that represents the cash flows of the aggregated exposure. However, the need to consider gross cash flows could also indicate that the valuation techniques used to calculate the local currency present value for each cash flow making up the leg that reflects the aggregated exposure, must be appropriate for the instrument from which the cash flows arise. Consequently, even if the cash flows from the foreign currency liability and the foreign currency leg of the CCIRS offset completely, the local currency present value of each may not. This could be due to valuation differences such as cross currency basis spreads or the credit risk of the CCIRS. Accordingly, gross cash flows must be considered without any netting of cash flows from separate instruments. *[IFRS 9.IE134(a)]*.

The diagram below illustrates the methodology described above. The grey field identifies the output from the calculation, which is the calibrated fixed leg of the synthetic aggregated exposure that results in a zero present value for the overall synthetic aggregated exposure on initial designation of the second level relationship.

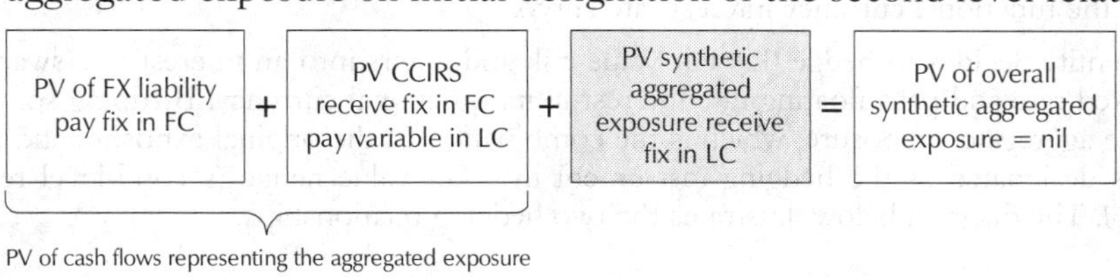

While, as stated above, the implementation guidance indicates that valuation techniques used to calculate the present value for each gross cash flow making up the leg that represents the aggregated exposure, must be appropriate for the instrument from which the cash flows arise, it is not entirely clear which valuation basis should be used when calibrating the synthetic fixed rate leg such that the overall synthetic aggregated exposure has a zero present value on designation.

In each subsequent period, the present values are updated for the changes in the cash flows representing the aggregated exposure and discount rates, while holding the previously calibrated blended fixed rate on the synthetic aggregated exposure constant, similar to a hypothetical derivative (see 6.4.2 below). The sum of the resulting present values of cash flows (which previously was calibrated to be nil as per designation) then equals the present value of the cash flow variability of the aggregated exposure, which is used for measurement of ineffectiveness. *[IFRS 9.IE134]*.

This is illustrated in the diagram below. The grey field represents the output from this calculation which is the current present value of the cash flow variability of the aggregated exposure.

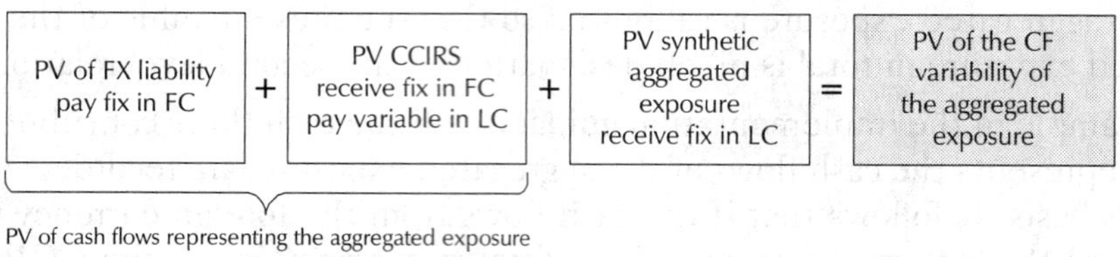

Ineffectiveness is then determined by comparing the change in calculated present value of the cash flow variability of the aggregated exposure and the fair value of the hedging instrument, (i.e. the local currency IRS). The normal ongoing cash flow hedge accounting treatment is applied to the change in fair value of the hedging instrument, as described in Chapter 52 at 4.2.1. The accounting for the first level relationship in Example 53.3 above continues unaffected by the second level relationship.

Example 53.4: Floating rate loan in a foreign currency – fair value hedge of an aggregated exposure

This fact pattern is based on Example 18 in the implementation guidance. *[IFRS 9.IE138-147]*. An entity has a floating rate borrowing denominated in a foreign currency (FC) and is therefore exposed to foreign exchange risk and cash flow risk due to changes in interest rates. The entity decides to swap the borrowing into a functional currency (LC) fixed rate borrowing using a cross currency interest rate swap (CCIRS). The CCIRS is designated as the hedging instrument in a cash flow hedge (first-level relationship). By doing so, the entity has eliminated both the foreign exchange risk and the cash flow risk due to changes in interest rates. However, it is now exposed to a fair value risk resulting from changes in the functional currency interest rate curve.

Later, the entity decides to hedge this fair value risk and enters into an interest rate swap (IRS) that receives fixed rate and pays floating rate interest in its functional currency. By doing so, the entity is hedging the aggregated exposure, which is the combination of the original exposure and the CCIRS. The IRS is designated as the hedging instrument in a fair value hedge (second-level relationship). *[IFRS 9.IE138]*. The diagram below illustrates the two hedging relationships.

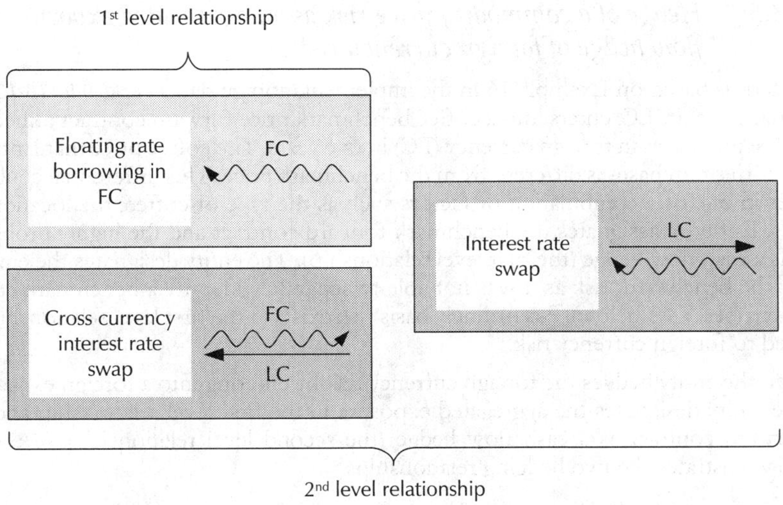

The concept of economically hedging aggregated exposures as such is straightforward. However, the accounting for such relationships includes some complexity. As for any hedge accounting relationship, there is a need to calculate the cumulative change in present value of the aggregated exposure, in order to measure ineffectiveness in the second level hedge relationship. Paragraph IE144 in the IFRS 9 implementation guidance provides some direction as to how this should be achieved as follows: similar to Example 53.3 above, this can be calculated as the change in present value of the gross cash flows from the instruments making up the aggregated exposures. However, in this example there is no requirement to create a synthetic blended fixed leg, as the aggregated exposure itself is essentially fixed.

An additional complexity in Example 53.4 above, is that it is a cash flow hedge in the first-level relationship that is then designated as the hedged item in a fair value hedge. This means that the cross-currency interest rate swap is both a hedging instrument (first level cash flow hedge relationship) and part of a hedged item (second level fair value relationship) at the same time. Accordingly, its fair value changes are initially recognised in other comprehensive income (OCI) through the first level cash flow hedge accounting, but at the same time, should also offset the fair value changes in profit or loss of the hedging interest rate swap in the second-level fair value relationship. This requires a reclassification of the amounts recognised in OCI to profit or loss (to the extent they relate to the second-level relationship) to achieve the offset in the second-level fair value hedge relationship. Consequently, applying fair value hedge accounting to a cross currency interest rate swap designated as the hedged item as part of an aggregated exposure affects where the hedging gains or losses are recognised (i.e. reclassification from the cash flow hedge reserve to profit or loss. *[IFRS 9.IE143]*.

As explained in the illustrative examples in the implementation guidance, the application of hedge accounting to an aggregated exposure gets even more complicated when basis risk is involved in one of the hedging relationships, in particular if basis risk is present in the first-level relationship. This is shown in Example 53.5 below.

Example 53.5: Hedge of a commodity price risk as an aggregated exposure in a cash flow hedge of foreign currency risk

This fact pattern is based on Example 16 in the implementation guidance. *[IFRS 9.IE116-127]*. Entity A, with functional currency LC, enters into a coffee benchmark price forward contract to hedge its highly probable coffee purchases in foreign currency (FC) in five years. The coffee price that Entity A expects to pay for its coffee purchases is different from the benchmark price. This differential could be because of differences in one or a combination of factors such as the type of coffee, the location or delivery arrangements. Entity A designates the benchmark forward contract and the highly probably forecast transaction as a cash flow hedge (the first level relationship). The entity designates the entire price risk and not only the benchmark risk as it was not able to separately identify a benchmark component in the hedged item (see 3.4.3 below). Accordingly basis risk exists in the first level relationship. The entity is still exposed to foreign currency risk.

One year later, the entity hedges the foreign currency risk by entering into a foreign exchange forward contract. The entity designates the aggregated exposure in the first level relationship and the foreign exchange forward contract as a cash flow hedge (the second level relationship). *[IFRS 9.IE117]*. The diagram below illustrates the two hedging relationships.

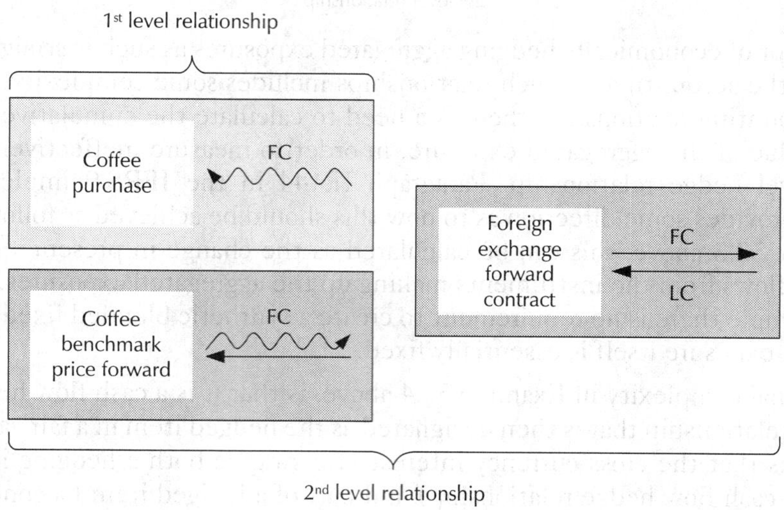

Illustrative example 16 in the implementation guidance of IFRS 9 demonstrates the accounting effort required in order to achieve hedge accounting for the aggregated exposure. First, the entity calculates the change in fair value of the hedged item and hedging instrument in the first level cash flow hedge relationship in foreign currency and translates them into local currency, using spot rates. Using these local currency equivalents, the entity calculates the ineffectiveness in the first level hedging relationship in the usual way. Second, the entity calculates the change in fair value of the aggregated exposure and the hedging instrument in the second-level cash flow hedge relationship in local currency. This results in the second level ineffectiveness.

The existence of basis risk within the first level relationship complicates the measurement of ineffectiveness described above. The aggregated exposure is a combination of the foreign currency cash flows expected from the highly probable coffee purchases and the gain or loss on the commodity hedging contract. If the first level relationship was a 'perfect hedge', the resultant foreign currency cash flow to be hedged in the second level relationship would be known. However, as commodity basis risk exists in the first level relationship, the hedged amount of foreign currency in the second level relationship will vary, as the basis spread between the price of the forecast coffee purchases and the underlying coffee price in the hedging contract varies. The hedging instrument in the second level relationship is just a foreign exchange forward contract, and so its fair value changes are insensitive to commodity basis risk. Accordingly, additional ineffectiveness may arise in the second level relationship, due to the commodity basis risk that exists in the first level relationship. *[IFRS 9.IE119(b)]*.

For example, at inception of the second level relationship, an entity might have expected a hedged aggregated cash flow of FC 990 based on the price achieved in the commodity hedging contract and the level of basis risk that then existed. However, at the date when the entity calculates the ineffectiveness, the expected aggregated cash flow might be FC 1000 due to changes in the commodity basis risk in the first level relationship. The expected aggregated hedged cash flow is calculated as follows:

Designated volume of hedged coffee purchases X prevailing forward coffee price for coffee purchases
plus
Market value of designated hedging coffee benchmark forward contracts

If the expected hedged cash flow has changed since inception of the second level relationship, an entity would need to measure effectiveness as if the current expected hedged cash flow from the aggregated exposure was always the expectation at inception (i.e. FC 1000 in the example given above). *[IFRS 9.IE122, IE123]*. Specifically, ineffectiveness to be reported in the profit or loss, is the change in fair value of the actual hedging instrument less the effective portion taken to OCI. The effective portion taken to OCI would be calculated as the lower of the following amounts: *[IFRS 9.6.5.11(a)]*

Change in fair value of the current expected hedge cash flows as if it had existed since inception.
(e.g. based on a hedged cash flow of FC 1000)
and
Change in fair value of the actual hedging instrument
(e.g. based on original assumption of hedged flow of FC 990)

The example demonstrates that to reduce the basis risk the entity may chose a hedge ratio other than 1:1 for the first level relationship (see 5.4 below). In the example the entity selects the volume of foreign exchange forward contract for the hedging instrument in the second level relationship based on the implied coffee forward price at the time the first level relationship was designated. This assumes the entity's original long term expectations of the basis spread have not changed since the coffee forward was transacted, which may not always be the case. Alternatively when identifying the optimal volume of the hedging instrument, an entity may conclude that the appropriate basis spread is the prevailing basis spread at the time of designation of the second level relationship. However, of course, the actual basis spread the entity will suffer is unknown.

Another layer of complexity would be added if the entity subsequently needed to rebalance the hedge relationship because of changes in the expected basis. The example, however, does not include this. Although the accounting for the second level relationship may be complex, the accounting for the first level hedge relationship in this example would continue to be unaffected by the existence of the second level relationship.

The definition of an aggregated exposure includes a forecast transaction of an aggregated exposure. *[IFRS 9.6.3.4]*. An example, where this might be helpful, is when pre-hedging the interest rate risk in a forecast foreign currency debt issue:

Example 53.6: Aggregated exposure – interest rate pre-hedge of forecast foreign currency debt issue

Assume it is highly probable that an entity will issue fixed rate foreign currency debt in six months' time. It is also highly probable that on issue the entity will transact a CCIRS, converting the debt to functional currency variable rate. The combination of the forecast *foreign currency* fixed rate debt issuance and the forecast transaction of the CCIRS is economically a forecast *functional currency* variable rate debt issuance.

The entity wishes to hedge itself against increases in the variable functional currency interest rate between today and the issue of the debt in six months as well as the term of the debt. Therefore, the entity enters into a forward starting pay fixed/receive variable functional currency IRS. The entity designates the IRS as a hedging instrument in a cash flow hedge of the forecast aggregated exposure.

In this example the first level relationship does not exist yet, as both the hedged item (fixed rate foreign currency debt) and the hedging instrument (CCIRS) are forecast transactions. Hedge accounting for the 'second level hedge relationship' of the forecast aggregated exposure is still permitted though.

As an aggregated exposure is a combination of an exposure and a derivative, the aggregated exposure is often a hedging relationship itself (the first-level relationship). In order for the aggregated exposure to qualify for hedge accounting, IFRS 9 only requires that the first-level relationship *could* qualify for hedge accounting and not that hedge accounting is actually applied. However, applying hedge accounting to the aggregated exposure gets even more complex when hedge accounting is not applied to the first-level relationship, and the entity is also unlikely to achieve its desired accounting result. *[IFRS 9.BC6.167]*. Therefore, in many cases we expect entities to apply hedge accounting to the first-level relationship, even if not required.

However, just because an entity enters into an additional derivative transaction that relates to an existing hedging relationship does not mean that this relationship qualifies as an aggregated exposure. This is demonstrated by the following example.

Example 53.7: Cash flow hedging of an exposure that includes a net investment in a foreign operation

Parent A with functional currency Australian dollars (AUD) has a US dollar (USD) net investment exposure. It transacts a pay floating USD receive floating AUD cross currency interest rate swap (CCIRS) and designates it in a hedge of a net investment in a foreign operation. By doing so, the group is exposed to cash flow variability due to the floating rate exposure in AUD and USD. The parent A enters into a pay floating/receive fixed AUD interest rate swap (IRS) to eliminate cash flow variability from changes in AUD interest rate risk, and wishes to designate this derivative as the hedging instrument item in a cash flow hedge for the aggregated exposure including the net investment in a foreign operation.

While there is an economic relationship between the net investment exposure and the CCIRS for foreign exchange risk, there is no economic relationship between the aggregated exposure and the IRS for interest rate risk. This is because the USD floating interest rate cash flows on the CCIRS are not offset by the USD net investment, as it does not have cash flow variability that is closely linked to interest rates. Furthermore, aggregated exposures can only be designated if they are managed as one exposure for a particular risk, which is unlikely to be the case in this fact pattern given the lack of interest risk associated with the net investment. *[IFRS 9.B6.3.3]*.

3.4 Risk components

3.4.1 General requirements

Instead of hedging the total changes in fair values or cash flows, risk managers often enter into derivatives to hedge only specific risk components. Managing a specific risk component reflects that hedging all risks is often not economical and hence not desirable, or even not possible (because of a lack of suitable hedging instruments).

However, under IAS 39, a non-financial item can only be designated as the hedged item for its foreign currency risk or all its risks in their entirety (see Chapter 52 at 2.2.2). There is no such restriction for financial items, therefore creating an inconsistency in hedge accounting for risks of financial and non-financial items. This results in many risk management activities, in particular those of non-financial services entities, not qualifying for hedge accounting under IAS 39, or else hedge ineffectiveness being artificially overstated.

In what many believe to be the single most important change from IAS 39, the hedge accounting requirements in IFRS 9 now permit an entity to designate a risk component of a non-financial item as the hedged item in a hedging relationship, provided the risk component is separately identifiable and reliably measurable. This means that only changes in the cash flows or fair value of the hedged item with respect to the designated risk are subject to the hedge accounting requirements. This is likely to enable many more common risk management strategies to qualify for hedge accounting and will result in less ineffectiveness being recognised in profit or loss. *[IFRS 9.6.3.7(b)]*. A risk component may be contractually specified or it may be implicit in the fair value or the cash flows of the item to which the component belongs. *[IFRS 9.B6.3.10]*. However, the mere fact that a physical component is part of the make-up of the whole item does not mean that the component necessarily qualifies as a risk component for hedge accounting purposes. A physical component is neither required nor by itself sufficient to meet the criteria for risk components that are eligible as a hedged item. However, depending on what the standard refers to as 'the market structure', a physical component can help meet those criteria (see 3.4.3 below). For example, just because rubber is a physical component of car tyres that does not mean that an entity can automatically designate rubber as a risk component in a hedge of forecast tyre purchases or sales, since the price of tyres may be related only indirectly to the price of rubber. Further analysis of the pricing structure of the whole car tyre would be required.

3.4.2 Contractually specified risk components

Purchase or sales agreements sometimes contain clauses that link the contract price via a specified formula to a benchmark price of a commodity. Examples of contractually specified risk components include:

- the price of natural gas contractually linked in part to a gas oil benchmark price and in part to a fuel oil benchmark price;
- the price of electricity contractually linked in part to a coal benchmark price and in part to transmission charges that include an inflation indexation;
- the price of wires contractually linked in part to a copper benchmark price and in part to a variable tolling charge reflecting energy costs; and
- the price of coffee contractually linked in part to a benchmark price of Arabica coffee and in part to transportation charges that include a diesel price indexation.

In each case, it is assumed that the pricing component would not require separation as an embedded derivative (see Chapter 43 at 4 and 5). When contractually specified, a risk component would usually be considered *separately identifiable*. [IFRS 9.BC6.174]. Further, the risk component element of a price formula would usually be referenced to observable data, such as a published price index. Therefore, the risk component would usually also be considered *reliably measurable*. However, difficulties will still arise where a negative spread exists in the hedged item. A negative spread arises when the formula for the contract price includes a spread that is subtracted from the risk component, so that the contract price is lower than the risk component. This has become termed the 'sub-LIBOR issue' (discussed at 3.4.5 below).

Example 53.8: Hedge of a contractually specified risk component – coal supply contract linked to the coal benchmark price and the Baltic Dry Index

An entity purchases coal from its coal supplier under a contract that sets out a variable price for coal linked to the coal benchmark price, represented by futures contracts for coal loaded at the Newcastle Coal Terminal in Australia, plus a logistics charge that is indexed to the Baltic Dry Index, reflecting that the delivery is at an overseas location. The contract sets out minimum purchase quantities for each month covered by its term.

The entity wishes to hedge itself against price changes related to the benchmark coal price but does not want to hedge the price variability resulting from the logistics costs represented by the indexation of the coal price to the Baltic Dry Index. Therefore, the entity enters into Newcastle coal futures contracts whereby it purchases coal for the relevant delivery months. For each relevant delivery month the entity designates the futures contracts as a hedging instrument in a cash flow hedge of the benchmark coal price risk component of the future coal purchases under its supply contract.

In this case the risk component is contractually specified by the pricing formula in the supply contract. This means it is separately identifiable, because the entity knows exactly which part of the change in the future purchase price of coal under its particular supply contract results from changes in the benchmark price for coal and what part of the price change results from changes in the Baltic Dry Index. The risk component can also be reliably measured using the price in the futures market for the relevant delivery months as inputs for calculating the present value of the cumulative change in the hedged cash flows. An entity could also decide to hedge only its exposure to variability in the coal price that is related to transportation costs. For example, the entity could enter into forward freight agreements and designate them as hedging instruments, with the hedged item being only the variability in the coal price under its supply contract that results from the indexation to the Baltic Dry Index.

3.4.3 Non-contractually specified risk components

Not all contracts define the various pricing elements and, therefore, specify risk components. In fact, we expect most risk components of financial and non-financial items not to be contractually specified. While it is certainly easier to determine that a risk component is separately identifiable and reliably measurable if it is specified in the contract, IFRS 9 is clear that there is no need for a component to be contractually specified in order to be eligible for hedge accounting. The assessment of whether a risk component qualifies for hedge accounting (i.e. whether it is separately identifiable and reliably measurable) has to be made 'within the context of the particular market structure to which the risk or risks relate and in which the hedging activity takes place'. *[IFRS 9.B6.3.9]*. We understand the relevance of the market structure to be that the risk component must have a distinguishable effect on changes in the value or the cash flows that an entity is exposed to. Depending on the situation, the market structure can reflect a 'market convention' that establishes, for example, a benchmark interest rate that has a pervasive effect on the value and cash flows for debt instruments. In other situations the market structure reflects the particular purchasing or selling market of an entity. For example, this is the case when an entity buys goods from its particular supplier based on a benchmark price plus other charges, as in the examples listed at 3.4.2 above. Even if the pricing under such a supply arrangement is not a wider 'market convention', its pricing formula represents the exposure of the particular entity to variability in cash flows from its purchases. The existence of contractually specified risk components in similar transactions can be a relevant factor in the assessment of the market structure and so help identify non-contractually specified risk components such as risk components of forecast transactions that have not been contractually specified. The following example from the application guidance of IFRS 9 illustrates the 'separately identifiable and reliably measurable' assessment. *[IFRS 9.B6.3.10(b)]*.

Example 53.9: Hedge of a non-contractually specified risk component – coffee purchases with a benchmark price risk component

An entity purchases a particular quality of coffee of a particular origin from its supplier under a contract that sets out a variable price linked to the benchmark price for coffee. The price is represented by the coffee futures price plus a fixed spread, reflecting the different quality of the coffee purchased compared to the benchmark plus a variable logistics services charge reflecting that the delivery is at a specific manufacturing site of the entity. The fixed spread is set for the current harvest period. For the deliveries that fall into the next harvest period this type of supply contract is not yet available.

The entity analyses the market structure for its coffee supplies, taking into account how the eventual deliveries of coffee that it receives are priced. The entity can enter into similar supply contracts for each harvest period once the crop relevant for its particular purchases is known and the spread can be set. In that sense, the knowledge about the pricing under the supply contracts also informs the entity's analysis of the market structure more widely, including forecast purchases which are not yet contractually specified. This allows the entity to conclude that its exposure to variability of cash flows resulting from changes in the benchmark coffee price is a risk component that is separately identifiable and reliably measurable for coffee purchases under the variable price supply contract for the current harvest period as well as for forecast purchases that fall into the next harvest period.

In this case the entity can enter into coffee futures contracts to hedge its exposure to the variability in cash flows from the benchmark coffee price and designate that risk component as the hedged item. This means that changes in the coffee price from the variable logistics services charge as well as future changes in the spread reflecting the different coffee qualities would be excluded from the hedging relationship.

The assessment of whether a risk component qualifies for hedge accounting is mainly driven by an analysis of whether there are different pricing factors that have a distinguishable effect on the item as a whole (in terms of its value or its cash flows). This evaluation would always have to be based on relevant facts and circumstances.

The standard uses the refinement of crude oil to jet fuel as an example to demonstrate how the assessment of the market structure could be made to conclude that crude oil in a particular situation is an eligible risk component of jet fuel. *[IFRS 9.B6.3.10(c)]*. Crude oil is a physical input of the most common production process for jet fuel and there is a well-established price relationship between the two.

Extending this example, crude oil is also a major input in the production process for plastic. However, the manufacturing process is complex and involves a number of steps. The process starts with crude oil being distilled into its separate 'fractions', of which only one (naphtha) is used for making plastic. Naphtha then undergoes a number of further processes before the various types of plastic are finally produced. Consequently any impact of a change in the price of crude oil on the price of plastic is likely to be significantly diluted by the costs of manufacturing and the passage of time.

Generally, the further 'downstream' in the production process an item is, the more difficult it is to find a distinguishable effect of any single pricing factor. The mere fact that a commodity is a major physical input in a production process does not automatically translate into a separately identifiable effect on the price of the item as a whole. For example, the price for pasta at food retailers in the medium to long term also responds to changes in the price for wheat, but there is no distinguishable direct effect of wheat prices changes on the retail price for pasta, which remains unchanged for longer periods even though the wheat price changes. If retail prices are periodically adjusted in a way that also directionally reflects the effect of wheat price changes, that is not sufficient to constitute a separately identifiable risk component.

Allowing non-contractually specified risk components as eligible hedged items opens up a new area for judgement. The assessment of the market structure will normally require the involvement of staff with a good understanding of the drivers of market prices (e.g. members of the sales or procurement departments responsible for the underlying transactions). Practice will evolve in this area as to what are commonly accepted non-contractual risk components and the approach taken to determine their existence. However judgement will need to continue to be applied to the particular facts and circumstances.

3.4.4 *Inflation as a risk component*

Under IAS 39, inflation cannot be designated as a hedged risk component for financial instruments, unless the inflation risk component is contractually specified (see Chapter 52 at 2.2.1.D). For non-financial instruments, inflation risk cannot be designated under IAS 39 as a risk component at all.

For financial instruments IFRS 9 introduces a rebuttable presumption that, unless contractually specified, inflation is not separately identifiable and reliably measureable. This means that there are limited cases under which it is possible to identify a non-contractually specified risk component of a financial instrument for inflation and designate that inflation component in a hedging relationship. Similar to other non-contractually specified risk components, the analysis would have to be based on the particular circumstances in the respective market, which is, in this case, the debt market. *[IFRS 9.B6.3.13]*.

The example below, derived from the application guidance of IFRS 9, explains a situation in which the presumption that inflation does not qualify as a risk component of a financial instrument can be rebutted.

Example 53.10: Inflation risk as an eligible risk component of a debt instrument

An entity wishes to hedge the inflation risk component of a debt instrument. The debt instrument is issued in a currency and country in which inflation-linked bonds are actively traded in a significant volume. The volume, liquidity and term structure of these inflation-linked bonds allow the computation of a real interest yield curve. This situation supports that inflation is a factor that is separately considered in the debt market in a way that it is a separately identifiable and reliably measureable risk component. *[IFRS 9.B6.3.14]*.

There are not many currencies with a liquid market for inflation-linked debt instruments, therefore limiting the availability of designating non-contractually specified inflation risk components of financial instruments.

IFRS 9 does not specify whether the analysis of inflation as an eligible risk component has to be made by currency or by country, or both. This is particularly relevant for countries forming a monetary union together with other countries, but having different inflation rates (e.g. within the Eurozone). We believe the relevant 'market structure' for inflation will usually be given by the currency.

While IFRS 9 defines in what circumstances inflation can be a risk component for a financial instrument, inflation can under IFRS 9 be treated as a risk component for non-financial items in the same manner as any other risk component (as described at 3.4.2 and 3.4.3 above), i.e. the rebuttable presumption described in this section applies only to financial instruments. For example, a contractually specified inflation risk component would normally qualify as a hedged item (e.g. in a sales contract, a price formula linked to the consumer price index) under IFRS 9, whereas it would not under IAS 39.

3.4.5 The 'sub-LIBOR issue'

Some financial institutions are able to raise funding at interest rates that are below a benchmark interest rate (e.g. LIBOR minus 15 basis points (bps)). In such a scenario, the entity may wish to remove the variability in future cash flows caused by movements in LIBOR benchmark interest rates. However, like IAS 39 (see Chapter 52 at 2.2.1.A), IFRS 9 does not allow the designation of a 'full' LIBOR risk component (i.e. LIBOR flat), as a component cannot be more than the total cash flows of the entire item. This is sometimes referred to as the 'sub-LIBOR issue'. *[IFRS 9.B6.3.22]*.

Part of the reason for this restriction is that a contractual interest rate is often 'floored' at zero, so that interest will never become negative. Hence, for a borrowing at, say, LIBOR minus 15bps but floored at zero, if benchmark interest rates decrease below 15bps, any further reduction in the benchmark would not cause any cash flow variability for the hedged item. Consequently, any designated component has to be less than or equal to the cash flows of the entire item. *[IFRS 9.B6.3.21, BC6.226-228]*.

In the above scenario, where the interest rate is at LIBOR minus 15bps, the entity could instead designate, as the hedged item, the variability in cash flows of the entire liability (or a proportion of it) but only for changes attributable to LIBOR. *[IFRS 9.B6.3.24]*. This would result in some ineffectiveness for financial instruments that have an interest rate floor of zero in situations in which the forward curve for a part of the remaining hedged term is below 15bps, because the hedged item will have less variability in cash flows as a result of interest rate changes than a swap without such a floor.

While the example in the standard uses LIBOR as the benchmark component, it is clear that the requirement relates not just to financial items in general, or the LIBOR benchmark component in particular, but is a general prohibition on the cash flows of hedged risk components being larger than the cash flows of the entire hedged item. This means that the sub-LIBOR issue is also applicable to non-financial items where the contract price is linked to a benchmark price minus a differential. This is best demonstrated using an example derived from the application guidance of IFRS 9.

Example 53.11: Sub-LIBOR issue – Selling crude oil at below benchmark price

An entity has a long-term sales contract to sell crude oil of a specific quality to a specified location. The contract includes a clause that sets the price per barrel at West Texas Intermediate (WTI) minus USD 10 with a minimum price of USD 30. The entity wishes to hedge the WTI benchmark price risk by entering into a WTI future. As outlined above, the entity cannot designate a 'full' WTI component, i.e. a WTI component that ignores the price differential and the minimum price.

However, the entity could designate the WTI future as a hedge of the entire cash flow variability under the sales contract that is attributable to the change in the benchmark price. When doing so, the hedged item would have the same cash flow variability as a sale of crude oil at the WTI price (or above), as long as the forward price for the remaining hedged term does not fall below USD 40. *[IFRS 9.B6.3.25]*.

Where the hedged item has the same cash flow variability as the hedging instrument there may be an expectation that the hedge relationship will meet the effectiveness criteria. However this needs to be determined prospectively and any ineffectiveness recorded in profit or loss. How ineffectiveness is calculated when the entire hedged item is designated, but only for changes in the value of a risk component, is discussed in Chapter 52 at 2.2.1.A.

In some cases the contract price may not be defined as a benchmark price minus a fixed differential but as a benchmark price plus a pricing differential that is sometimes positive and sometimes negative (the 'basis spread'). The market structure may reveal that items are priced that way and there may even be derivatives available for the basis spread (i.e. basis swaps, for example the benchmark gas oil crack spread derivative which is a derivative for the price differential between crude oil and gas oil – a refining margin *[IFRS 9.B6.3.10(c)(i)]*). Similar to Example 53.11 above, an entity could not designate the benchmark price component as the hedged item given that the cash flows of the benchmark component could be more than the total cash flows of the entire item. Unfortunately, the standard does not provide any guidance as to how an entity has to assess whether the basis spread could be negative or not. For example, it is not clear whether an entity is only required to look at the forward benchmark prices or whether it has to consider all reasonably possible scenarios. The use of 'reasonably possible scenarios' in other places in IFRS 9 might indicate that the latter is the case.

A related question is whether the entity could designate the entire cash flow variability that is attributable to changes in only the benchmark risk (as the entity alternatively does in Example 53.11 above) if that risk is a non-contractually specified risk component. This assessment is likely to be similar to whether a non-contractually specified risk component is separately identifiable and reliably measurable (as outlined at 3.4.3 above), which would be required in order to determine the variability of the entire cash flows with respect to changes in the benchmark.

However, the presence of a spread that is sometimes negative could make this assessment more difficult. An entity needs to prove that the benchmark cash flows plus or minus the spread make up the total cash flows. This might be the case, for example, if it can be proven that there are quality differences, such that the benchmark is sometimes of better quality and sometimes worse than the hedged exposure. On the other hand, if the basis spread switches between positive and negative because of individual supply and demand drivers in the benchmark price and the price of the hedged exposure, this may indicate that the benchmark is not implicit in the fair value or cash flows of the hedged exposure. To illustrate this with an example, take WTI and Brent crude oil prices. While both prices might be highly correlated, WTI could not be identified as a benchmark component in Brent because both prices have their own supply and demand drivers. Furthermore, it would not be possible to determine whether either WTI is a risk component of Brent or *vice versa*, which demonstrates that there is no risk component that can be designated in a hedge relationship. In that case, hedge accounting would only be permitted if the full cash flows were designated for all changes in the contract price, and assuming the other eligibility requirements are met.

The negative interest rate environment in some countries, mainly countries in the Eurozone and Switzerland has further implications on the designation of risk components in connection with the sub-LIBOR issue. However, this not only relates to hedge accounting under IFRS 9 but also under IAS 39 and is therefore covered in Chapter 52 at 2.2.1.A.

3.5 Components of a nominal amount

3.5.1 Definition

A component of a nominal amount is a specified part of the amount of an item. *[IFRS 9.6.3.7]*. This could be a proportion of an entire item (such as, 60% of a fixed rate loan of EUR 100 million) or a layer component (for example, the 'bottom layer' of EUR 60 million of a EUR 100 million fixed rate loan that can be prepaid at fair value. 'Bottom layer' here refers to the portion of the loan that will be prepaid last). *[IFRS 9.B6.3.16]*.

Nominal components are frequently used in risk management activities in practice. Examples include:

- Part of a monetary transaction volume, for example, the first USD 1 million cash flows from sales to customers in a given period.
- Part of a physical volume, for example, the 50 tonnes bottom layer of coal inventory in a particular location.
- A part of a physical or other transaction volume, for example, the sale of the first 15,000 units of widgets during January 2015.
- A layer from the nominal amount of the hedged item, for example, the top layer of a CHF 100 million fixed rate liability that can be prepaid at fair value. 'Top layer' refers to the portion of the liability that will be prepaid first. *[IFRS 9.B6.3.18]*.

3.5.2 Hedge accounting requirements in IAS 39

IAS 39 allows (as does IFRS 9) the designation of nominal components for a group of forecast cash flows, such as the sale of the first 15,000 units of widgets used as an example above. Such a designation accommodates the fact that there may be a level of uncertainty as to the quantity of the hedged item and that this uncertainty does not form part of the hedging relationship (see also Chapter 52 at 5.2).

However, IAS 39 does not allow the designation of layer components for fair value hedges. Consequently, an entity that wishes to hedge part of a group of items within a fair value hedge must identify specific items within the group (and designate those items only) or designate a percentage of the total as the hedged item. The premise of the IAS 39 model is to replicate, on a portfolio basis, the hedge accounting result that would arise on an individual hedged item basis.

Financial institutions often apply economic layer hedging strategies. However, as illustrated in the example below, they cannot be directly reflected in the financial statements by using hedge accounting in accordance with IAS 39.

Example 53.12: Hedging a bottom layer of a loan portfolio (IAS 39)

A bank holds a portfolio of fixed rate loans with a total nominal amount of CU 100m. The borrowers can, at any time during the tenor, prepay 20% of their (original) loan amount at par.

For risk management purposes, the loans are considered together with variable rate borrowings of CU100m. As a result, the bank is exposed to an interest margin risk resulting from the fix-to-floating rate mismatch. The bank expects CU 20m of loans to be prepaid.

As part of the risk management strategy, the bank decides to hedge the interest margin by entering into a pay fixed/receive variable interest rate swap (IRS). The objective is to hedge the amount of loans that is not prepayable using an IRS with a notional amount of CU 80m. The IRS is designated as a fair value hedge of 80% of the CU 100m loan portfolio.

After two years loans of CU 10m are prepaid, which is less than 20% and therefore does not affect the economic hedge in place. However, because of the proportionate designation, this is considered a reduction in the hedged amount for hedge accounting purposes. As a result, the entity now has an IRS of CU 80m designated as a hedge of loans of CU 72m ([CU 100m – CU 10m] × 80%), which will inevitably lead to some ineffectiveness.

3.5.3 Hedge accounting requirements in IFRS 9

In what is seen by many as an important change, IFRS 9 now allows, for fair value hedges, the designation of layer components from a defined nominal amount or a defined, but open, population. *[IFRS 9.B6.3.18]*. This designation should be consistent with an entity's risk management objective. *[IFRS 9.B6.3.16]*. IFRS 9 still includes some restrictions, in particular that a layer component that includes a prepayment option does not qualify as a hedged item in a fair value hedge if the fair value of the prepayment option is affected by changes in the hedged risk (unless the changes in fair value of the prepayment option as a result of changes in the hedged risk are included when measuring the change in fair value of the hedged item – see Example 53.13 below). *[IFRS 9.B6.3.20]*.

If an entity has an option to prepay a loan at fair value, the fair value of the option is not affected by changes in the hedged risk. Consequently, an entity would be able to designate a hedge as described in Example 53.15 below:

Example 53.13: Hedging a top layer of a loan

An entity borrows money by issuing a CU 10m five-year fixed rate loan. The entity has a prepayment option to pay back CU 5m at fair value. The entity wants to be able to make use of the prepayment option without the amount repayable on early redemption being affected by interest rate changes. Consequently, the entity would like to hedge the fair value interest rate risk of the prepayable part of the loan. To achieve this, the entity enters into a five-year receive fixed/pay variable interest rate swap (IRS) with a notional amount of CU 5m. The entity designates the IRS in a fair value hedge of the interest rate risk of the CU 5m top layer of the loan attributable to the benchmark interest rate. As a result, the top layer is adjusted for changes in the fair value attributable to changes in the hedged risk. The bottom layer, which cannot be prepaid, remains at amortised cost.

The gain or loss on the IRS will offset the change in fair value on the top layer attributable to the hedged risk. On prepayment, the fair value hedge adjustment of the top layer is part of the gain or loss from derecognition of a part of the loan as the result of the early repayment.

The situation illustrated by Example 53.13 of a hedge of a top layer of a loan would not often be found in practice, as most prepayment options in loan agreements allow, in our experience, for prepayment at the nominal amount (instead of at fair value). Moreover, if a financial asset included an option that allowed prepayment at fair value, that would affect the assessment of the characteristics of the contractual cash flows. That assessment is a part of the classification of financial assets and such a prepayment option would not be consistent with payments that are solely principal and interest (see Chapter 46 at 6.4.5). However, the ability to designate a top layer in a fair value hedge could be helpful when hedging a group of fixed rate readily transferable financial instruments, see 3.6.2 below.

If prepayment is at the nominal amount, the fair value of the prepayment option would be affected by changes in the hedged interest rate risk. Therefore, a top or bottom layer would not normally qualify for hedge accounting unless the effect of the related prepayment option is included when measuring the fair value change of the hedged item. *[IFRS 9.B6.3.20]*.

When deciding on which instruments to transact in order to manage the interest rate risk in a prepayable portfolio, an entity will usually consider the likelihood of prepayment in a bottom layer. In particular it will consider whether the risk of prepayment is sufficient to justify the added expense of transacting a hedging instrument that can also be cancelled (e.g. an interest rate swap cancellable at zero cost). As part of these considerations it is relatively common that from an economic perspective, an entity might view a bottom layer as having no prepayment risk attached at all and transact a non-cancellable hedging instrument accordingly. Despite this economic view, the IFRS 9 hedge accounting guidance requires consideration of the fair value changes of that bottom layer based on the contractual terms of the hedged item, which would include the prepayment option. Hence, for many economic hedges of bottom layers of prepayable hedged items, the changes in the fair values of the hedging instrument and the hedged item will not normally be the same. The consequence is that there is likely to be a level of ineffectiveness in the accounting hedge relationship, to be measured and recognised. 'Bottom layer' hedging strategies that avoid this source of ineffectiveness can only be applied if the hedged layer is not affected by the prepayment risk. This is best demonstrated based on the scenario already used in Example 53.12 above, but this time making use of the new IFRS 9 designation for nominal components.

Example 53.14: Hedging a bottom layer of a loan portfolio (IFRS 9)

A bank holds a portfolio of fixed rate loans with a total nominal amount of CU 100m. The borrowers can, at any time during the tenor, prepay 20% of their (original) loan amount at par.

For risk management purposes, the loans are considered together with variable rate borrowings of CU 100m. As a result, the bank is exposed to an interest margin risk resulting from the fix-to-floating rate mismatch. The bank expects CU 20m of loans to be prepaid.

As part of the risk management strategy, the bank decides to hedge a part of the interest margin by entering into a pay fixed/receive variable interest rate swap (IRS). The objective is to hedge 95% of the amount of loans that is not prepayable using an IRS with a notional amount of CU 76m (95% of CU 80m). The hedged layer does not include a prepayment option. Therefore, the IRS is designated in a fair value hedge of the interest rate risk of the CU 76m bottom layer of the CU 100m loan portfolio.

As a result, the bottom layer is adjusted for changes in the fair value attributable to changes in the hedged risk (i.e. benchmark interest rate risk). The extent to which the borrowers exercise their prepayment option does not affect the hedging relationship. Also, if the bank were to derecognise any of the loans for any other reason, the first CU 4m of non-prepayable amount of derecognised loans would not be part of the hedged item (i.e. the CU 76m bottom layer).

As already mentioned above, IFRS 9 does not preclude hedge accounting for layers including a prepayment option. However, in order to achieve hedge accounting for such a designation, changes in fair value of the prepayment option as a result of changes in the hedged risk have to be included when measuring the change in fair value of the hedged item. Example 53.15 illustrates what this means in practice:

Example 53.15: Hedging a bottom layer including prepayment risk

A bank originates a CU 10m five-year fixed rate loan with a prepayment option to pay back CU 5m at any time at par.

For risk management purposes, the loan is considered together with variable rate borrowings of CU 10m. As a result, the bank is exposed to an interest margin risk resulting from the fix-to-floating rate mismatch. The bank expects the borrower to prepay CU 2m and, therefore, wishes to hedge

CU 8m only. The bank enters into a five-year pay fixed/receive variable interest rate swap (IRS) with a notional amount of CU 8m and designates CU 5m of the IRS in a fair value hedge of the benchmark interest rate risk of the CU 5m layer of the non-prepayable loan amount. In addition, the bank enters into a swaption with a notional amount of CU 3m that is jointly designated with CU 3m of the IRS to hedge the benchmark interest rate risk of the last remaining CU 3m of the CU 5m prepayable amount of the loan (a bottom layer).

As a result, the CU 5m non-prepayable loan amount is adjusted for changes in the fair value attributable to changes in the hedged risk (the fixed rate benchmark interest rate risk of a fixed term instrument). This is also true for the CU 3m bottom layer of the prepayable amount, but in addition it must also be adjusted for the effect of the prepayment option on the changes in the fair value attributable to the interest rate risk. The CU 2m top layer remains at amortised cost.

Therefore, the first CU 2m of prepayments would have a gain or loss on derecognition determined as the difference between the amortised cost of the prepaid amount and par. For any further prepayments exceeding CU 2m, the gain or loss on derecognition would be determined as the difference between the amortised cost including the fair value hedge adjustment and par.

While IFRS 9 provides an effective solution for portfolios that feature a bottom layer that is not prepayable, as explained in Examples 53.14 and 53.15 above, it does not provide an answer for portfolios that are fully prepayable (for example, a residential fixed rate mortgage portfolio). The IASB decided to address hedging of such portfolios in its separate macro hedging project, as described at 3.6.5 below. Until that project is finalised, entities are allowed to apply the portfolio fair value hedging guidance in IAS 39 as described at 3.6.6 below and in Chapter 52 at 6).

3.6 Groups of items

Hedge accounting under IAS 39 was primarily designed from a single instrument view point. A hedging relationship would typically include a single hedging instrument (e.g. an interest rate swap) hedging a single item (e.g. a loan). However, for operational reasons entities often economically hedge several items together on a group basis. IAS 39 allows several items to be hedged together as a group, but there are restrictions such that there are relatively few types of groups that are eligible as hedged items (see Chapter 52 at 2.2.3).

Under IAS 39, a group of items is eligible as a designated hedged item for accounting purposes only if:

- the individual items within the group share the same designated risk exposure; and
- the change in the fair value attributable to the hedged risk for each individual item in the group is 'approximately proportional' to the overall change in the fair value attributable to the hedged risk of the group. *[IAS 39.83]*.

Many hedges will fail to fulfil the second criterion. For example, when hedging a portfolio of shares that replicates a market index, the individual shares would usually not move in tandem with the entire portfolio.

IAS 39 also prohibits designating hedges of groups of items that contain off setting position (i.e. net positions). *[IAS 39.84]*.

3.6.1 General requirements

In an effort to address the issues raised by these restrictions, the IASB has broadened the eligibility criteria for groups of items in IFRS 9. Under IFRS 9, hedge accounting may be applied to a group of items if:

- the group consists of items or components of items that would individually qualify for hedge accounting; and
- for risk management purposes, the items in the group are managed together on a group basis. *[IFRS 9.6.6.1]*.

Example 53.16: Hedging a portfolio of shares

An entity holds a portfolio of shares of Swiss companies that replicates the Swiss Market Index (SMI). The entity elected to account for the shares at fair value through other comprehensive income without subsequent reclassification to profit or loss, as allowed by IFRS 9. The entity decides to lock in the current value of the portfolio by entering into corresponding SMI futures contracts.

The individual shares would be eligible hedged items if hedged individually. As the objective of the portfolio is to replicate the SMI, the entity can also demonstrate that the shares are managed together on a group basis. The entity also assesses the effectiveness criteria for hedge accounting (see 5 below). Consequently, the entity designates the SMI futures contracts as the hedging instrument in a hedge of the fair value of the portfolio. As a result, the gains or losses on the SMI futures are accounted for in OCI (without subsequent reclassification to profit or loss) as well as the shares, thus eliminating the accounting mismatch.

Whether the items in the group are managed together on a group basis is a matter of fact, i.e. it depends on an entity's behaviour and cannot be achieved by mere documentation.

The IFRS 9 eligibly criteria for groups of items for hedge accounting also permit designation of net positions, however some restrictions for cash flow hedges of net positions are retained (see 3.6.3 below). *[IFRS 9 BC6.435, BC6.436]*. IFRS 9 also contains special presentation requirements when hedging net positions, which are discussed at 8.3 below.

3.6.2 Hedging a component of a group

A group designation can also consist of a component of a group of items, such as a layer component of a group. A component could also be a proportion of a group of items, such as 50% of a fixed rate bond series with a total volume of CU 100 million. Whether an entity designates a layer component or a proportionate component depends on the entity's risk management objective. *[IFRS 9.6.6.2, 6.6.3]*.

The benefits of identifying a layer component, as discussed at 3.5.3 above, are relevant when applied to a group of items. The bottom layer hedging strategy discussed in Example 53.15 above is, in fact, a designation of a component of a group.

Another example is a bond issue of CU 50million that is made up of 50,000 fixed rate bonds with a face value of CU 1,000 each. If the issuer expects that it might repurchase up to CU 10million of the issue volume before maturity, it could hedge the benchmark component of the fair value interest rate risk with a receive fixed/pay variable interest rate swap that has a notional amount of CU 10million. From an economic perspective, that hedge would allow repurchases of up to CU 10million total face value for which the gain or loss from changes in the benchmark interest rate would be compensated by the gain or loss on the swap. However, this can only be reflected in the accounting if the entity can designate a CU 10million top layer (i.e. for the first CU 10million of face value that are repurchased, the entity would include a fair value hedge gain or loss on the full face value when determining the gain or loss on derecognition of the bonds). If it was not permitted to designate a layer of a group of items, entities would in such cases either have to identify individual items within the group and designate them on a standalone basis, or prorate the fair value hedge gain or loss to the entire bond issue volume. The IASB believes this would result in arbitrary accounting results and decided to allow a layer component designation for a group of items. *[IFRS 9.BC6.438, BC6.439]*.

A layer component of a group of items only qualifies for hedge accounting if:

- the layer is separately identifiable and reliably measurable;
- the risk management objective is to hedge a layer component;
- the items in the group from which the layer is identified are exposed to the same hedged risk (so that measurement of the hedged layer is not significantly affected by which particular items from the overall group form part of the hedged layer);
- for a hedge of existing items, the items in the group can be identified and tracked; and
- any items in the group containing prepayment options meet the requirements for components of a nominal amount (see 3.5.3 above). *[IFRS 9.6.6.3]*.

3.6.3 Cash flow hedge of a net position

Many entities are exposed to foreign exchange risk arising from purchases and sales of goods or services denominated in foreign currencies. Cash inflows and outflows occurring on forecast transactions in the same foreign currency are often economically hedged on a net basis. For example, consider an entity that has forecast foreign currency sales of FC 100 and purchases of FC 80, both in 6 months. It hedges the net exposure using a single foreign exchange forward contract to sell FC 20 in 6 months.

Hedging of such a net position does not qualify for hedge accounting under IAS 39 as hedge accounting for net positions is prohibited. However, hedge accounting could still be achieved by designating the foreign exchange forward contract as hedging FC 20 of the FC 100 forecast sales. By doing so, hedge accounting would result in FC 20 of the total forecast sales of FC 100 being recorded at the hedged rate, while the remaining sales and the purchases will be measured at the then prevailing spot rate (see Chapter 52 at 2.2.3).

However this IAS 39 hedge accounting approach only truly reflects the net risk management in the financial statements if the timing of the impact on profit or loss from the hedged cash flows is aligned. This may not be the case if the timing of hedged cash flows is not aligned or if the flows are accounted for in different ways. In these circumstances the natural hedge within the net position is not reflected for accounting purposes.

Example 53.17: Accounting mismatch for a 'natural hedge' of foreign currency cash flows (IAS 39)

An entity anticipates foreign currency denominated sales of FC 100 in 12 months and also intends to purchase fixed assets of FC 80 in 12 months (both denominated in the same foreign currency). The cash inflows of the forecast sales are hedged on a net basis together with the cash outflows for the forecast purchase of the fixed assets. The forecast sales will have an immediate effect upon profit or loss when they occur, while the forecast asset purchases will only affect profit or loss as the assets are depreciated over their useful lives.

In the Exposure Draft, the IASB proposed to permit a group of items that result in a net position to be an eligible hedged item. *[IFRS 9.BC6.432]*. However, the Board also decided to limit the application for cash flow hedges to groups where the offsetting risk positions affect profit or loss in the same period. *[IFRS 9.BC6.447]*. This was considered by many constituents to conflict with the broader goal of the hedge accounting project, to reflect risk management activities in the financial statements. *[IFRS 9.BC6.449]*.

When redeliberating the proposals, the Board confirmed its earlier decision to allow net positions as eligible hedged items, but softened the limitation on cash flow hedges so that net positions that affect profit or loss in different periods can be a hedged item in a cash flow hedge. However, designation of a net position in a cash flow hedge is limited to hedges of foreign exchange risk. The instance where this limitation should be applied is defined in IFRS 9 paragraph 6.6.1(c) for hedged items as follows: 'in the case of a cash flow hedge of a group of items whose variabilities in cash flows are not expected to be approximately proportional to the overall variability in cash flows of the group so that offsetting or net risk positions arise'. This guidance could appear to reintroduce the IAS 39 'approximately proportional' requirement for cash flow hedges of groups of items under IFRS 9 (see 3.6 above). However, we do not believe that this is the case, as consistently elsewhere within IFRS 9, the key the limitation on designating cash flow hedges is whether net or offsetting positions exist within a group of hedged items. *[IFRS 9.6.6.1(c), B6.6.7, BC6.455]*.

The standard mechanics of cash flow hedge accounting cannot be applied to a hedged net position whose cash flows affect profit or loss in different periods. Applying standard cash flow hedge accounting to Example 53.17 above, the gain or loss accumulated in other comprehensive income (OCI) on the FC 20 of hedging instrument would be reclassified to profit or loss when the revenue transaction occurs. However, this will only set off the gain or loss on FC 20 of the FC 100 hedged revenue while the remaining revenue of FC 80 and the fixed asset purchase of FC 80 (i.e. the economic hedge) would still be measured at the spot rate. This would result in the bottom line profit for the period(s) not reflecting the economic hedge.

IFRS 9 changes the cash flow hedge accounting for such a net position in that the foreign exchange gain or loss on the FC 80 revenue cash flows that affect profit or loss in the earlier period must be carried forward to offset the foreign exchange gain or loss on the fixed asset purchase cash flows that will affect profit or loss in later periods. This is achieved by deferring the gain or loss on the natural hedge in OCI, with a reclassification to profit or loss once the offsetting cash flows affect profit or loss (see 8.3.1 and Example 53.18 below).

However, the transactions that make up the net position would each need to be recognised when they arise and be measured at the spot foreign currency rate ruling at that time. Hence, they are not adjusted to reflect the result of the hedge. The whole impact of hedge accounting has to be presented in a separate line item in profit or loss. *[IFRS 9.6.6.4]*.

This separate line item includes:

- The reclassification adjustment of gains or losses on the hedge of the net position.
- The gain or loss on the natural hedge, with the counter-entry being recognised in OCI.
- The later reclassification adjustment of the gain or loss on the natural hedge from OCI to profit or loss.

The rather complicated accounting described above is best illustrated using an example:

Example 53.18: Cash flow hedge of a foreign currency net position

An entity having the CAD as functional currency anticipates sales of GBP 100m in 12 months and also plans a major capital expenditure (fixed assets) of GBP 80m in 12 months. The anticipated sales and capital expenditure (i.e. the group of forecast transactions) are designated as the hedged item and the resulting net position is hedged with a forward contract to sell GBP 20m in 12 months. The fixed assets will be depreciated on a straight-line basis over eight years. For simplicity, assume the spot rate equals the forward rate.

GBP/CAD spot rate	
At inception of the hedge (beginning of year 1)	1.50
After 12 months (end of year 1)	1.60

The entity would record the following journal entries (amounts in millions):

Year 1

	CAD	CAD
Other comprehensive income	2	
Hedging derivative		2

To account for the fair value change in the hedging instrument (GBP 20 × [1.50 – 1.60]).

Cash	160	
Revenue from sales		160

To account for the sales volume of GBP 100 at the current spot rate of 1.60 (GBP 100 × 1.60).

Property, plant and equipment	128	
Cash		128

To account for the purchase of GBP 80 fixed assets at the current spot rate of 1.60 (GBP 80 × 1.60).

Hedging derivative	2	
Cash		2

To account for the settlement of the forward contract.

Net position hedging gains/losses	2	
Other comprehensive income		2

To reclassify the cash flow hedge reserve from OCI to profit or loss.

Net position hedging gains/losses	8	
Other comprehensive income		8

To defer the natural hedge gain from profit or loss to OCI (GBP 80 × [1.60 – 1.50]).

Chapter 53

The net profit for the period is CAD 150, which represents the sale of GBP 100 at the hedged rate of 1.50 (albeit presented in two different line items).

Years 2 to 9

	CAD	CAD
Depreciation	16	
Property, plant and equipment		16

To account for the straight line depreciation of the fixed assets (CAD 128 × 12.5%).

Other comprehensive income	1	
Net position hedging gains/losses		1

To reclassify part of the deferred gain from OCI to profit or loss (CAD 8 × 12.5%).

The net loss for each period is 15, which represents depreciation (at 12.5%) of a fixed asset of GBP 80 purchased at the hedged rate of 1.50.

Overview

Income statement (CAD)	Y1	Y2	Y3	Y4	Y5	Y6	Y7	Y8	Y9	Total
Revenue from sale of goods	160									160
Depreciation		(16)	(16)	(16)	(16)	(16)	(16)	(16)	(16)	(128)
Net position hedging gains/losses	(10)	1	1	1	1	1	1	1	1	(2)
Profit for the period	150	(15)	(15)	(15)	(15)	(15)	(15)	(15)	(15)	30

Statement of financial position (CAD)	Y1	Y2	Y3	Y4	Y5	Y6	Y7	Y8	Y9
Cash	30								
Property, plant and equipment	128	112	96	80	64	48	32	16	0
Hedging reserve (OCI)	(8)	(7)	(6)	(5)	(4)	(3)	(2)	(1)	0

The transactions within a net position still have to be measured at their spot rates, while the effect of the hedge is presented in a separate line item. *[IFRS 9.B6.6.15]*. In other words, as although an entity may be economically hedged from a bottom line (or net) perspective, volatility will still arise in the amounts reported for the individual hedged transactions (on a gross basis), and it is only the bottom line of profit or loss that will reflect the benefits of the hedge.

For a net position to qualify for cash flow hedge accounting the hedge documentation has to include, for each type of item within the net position, its amount and nature as well as the reporting period in which it is expected to affect profit or loss. This is expected to be a relatively detailed record of what makes up the net position and how it will impact profit or loss, including the depreciation profile, if relevant. *[IFRS 9.6.6.1, B6.6.7-B6.6.8]*.

3.6.4 *Nil net positions*

As part of its introduction of the concept of net positions as hedged items, IFRS 9 also addresses hedges of nil net positions. Sometimes entities hedge a group of items where the hedged items themselves fully offset the risk that is managed. An example would be similar to the scenario illustrated by Example 53.18 above but where the entity anticipates sales of GBP 100m in 12 months and also plans a major capital expenditure of GBP 100m in 12 months. An entity is allowed to designate such a nil net position in a hedging relationship, provided that:

- the hedge is part of a rolling net risk hedging strategy;
- hedging instruments are used to hedge the net risk when the hedged net position changes in size over the life of the rolling hedging strategy and is not a nil net position;
- the entity would normally apply hedge accounting to such net positions when the net position is not nil; and
- not applying hedge accounting to the nil net position would result in inconsistent accounting outcomes over time (because in a period in which the net position is nil, hedge accounting would not be available for what is otherwise the same type of exposure). *[IFRS 9.6.6.6]*.

3.6.5 *Macro hedging*

Financial institutions, especially retail banks, have as a core business the collection of funds by depositors that are subsequently invested as loans to customers. This typically includes instruments such as current and savings accounts, deposits and borrowings, loans and mortgages that are usually accounted for at amortised cost. The difference between interest received and interest paid on these instruments (i.e. the net interest margin) is a main source of profitability.

A bank's net interest margin is exposed to changes in interest rates, a risk most banks (economically) hedge by entering into derivatives (mainly interest rate swaps). Applying the hedge accounting requirements (as set out in IAS 39 or IFRS 9) to such hedging strategies on an individual item-by-item basis can be difficult as a result of the characteristics of the underlying financial assets and liabilities:

- Prepayment options are common features of many fixed rate loans to customers. Customers exercise these options for many reasons, such as when they move house, and so not necessarily in response to interest rate movements. Their behaviour can be predicted better on a portfolio basis rather than an item-by-item basis.
- As a result of the sheer number of financial instruments involved, banks typically apply their hedging strategies on a macro (or portfolio) basis, with the number of individual instruments in the hedged portfolio constantly churning.

Although IAS 39 can be applied to macro hedging situations, and guidance exists for portfolio fair value, *[IAS 39.81A, 89A, AG114-132]*, and cash flow hedge accounting, *[IAS 39.F6.1-6.3]*, for interest rate risk, entities do not always use hedge accounting in those situations. This is because: not all sources of interest rate risk qualify for hedge accounting, use of IAS 39 can be operationally complex and cash flow hedge solutions result in volatility of other comprehensive income. Some European banks have, instead, made use of the European Union's carve out of certain sections of the IAS 39 hedge accounting rules.

Instead of developing particular hedge accounting requirements in IFRS 9 that are specifically tailored to macro hedging strategies, the IASB is seeking to create a separate accounting model for macro hedging situations that would be based on an entity's risk management activities. The accounting for macro hedging was originally part of the IASB's project to replace IAS 39 with IFRS 9. However, the IASB realised that developing the new accounting model would take time and probably be a different concept from hedge accounting. In May 2012, the Board therefore decided to decouple the part of the project that is related to accounting for macro hedging from IFRS 9, allowing more time to develop an accounting model without affecting the timeline for the completion of the other elements of IFRS 9.[8]

Although mainly focused on financial institutions, the accounting model for macro hedging might also be beneficial for some corporate entities applying macro-type hedging strategies.

In April 2014, the IASB issued the Discussion Paper – *Accounting for Dynamic Risk Management: a Portfolio Revaluation Approach to Macro Hedging*. The six-month comment period ended in October 2014. Most respondents supported the need for the project, but there was no consensus on a solution. Given the diversity in views, in July 2015 the IASB concluded that the insights that it had received from the comment letters and feedback so far did not enable it to develop proposals for an Exposure Draft. Accordingly, the IASB decided that the project should remain in the Research Programme, with the aim of publishing a second Discussion Paper.[9] The next step for the project was to focus on identifying the information needed to provide more decision useful information on Dynamic Risk Management. In May 2016, the IASB confirmed that the project should remain on the active research section of their work plan. At that meeting it was stated that a focus on identifying information needs has proved to be challenging. Because of this, they have returned the focus of their work to recognition and measurement for Dynamic Risk Management.

3.6.6 Applying hedge accounting for macro hedging strategies under IFRS 9

Because of its pending project on an accounting model specifically tailored to macro hedging situations (see 3.6.5 above), the IASB created a scope exception from the IFRS 9 hedging accounting requirements that allows entities to use the fair value hedge accounting for portfolio hedges of interest rate risk, and only for such hedges, as defined and set out in IAS 39, until the project is finalised and becomes effective. *[IFRS 9.6.1.3]*. The specific guidance that defines what is meant by the fair value hedge accounting for portfolios of interest rate risk is set out in IAS 39.81A, 89A, AG114-AG132 (see Chapter 52 at 6).

However, IFRS 9 does not include a similar scope exception for the 'macro' cash flow hedge accounting commonly applied by financial institutions to interest rate positions for which interest rate risk is managed on a net basis. *[IAS 39.IG F.6.2, F.6.3]*. The IASB are of the view that as the macro cash flow hedge accounting model is an application of the general hedge accounting model under IAS 39, the macro cash flow hedge accounting model should remain an application of the IFRS 9 hedge accounting guidance. Accordingly the IASB did not want to make an exception for the macro cash flow hedge accounting approach and so decided to retain an earlier decision not to carry forward any IAS 39 implementation guidance on hedge accounting to IFRS 9. *[IFRS 9 BC6.91-95]*.

As a result, many financial institutions were concerned that they would not be able to continue with their existing macro cash flow hedging strategies under IFRS 9.

In its January 2013 meeting, the IASB confirmed its earlier decision and clarified that not carrying forward the implementation guidance was without prejudice (i.e. it did not mean that the IASB had rejected that guidance and so had not intended to imply that entities cannot apply macro cash flow hedge accounting under IFRS 9).[10]

This was, however, not the end of the story. Several constituents continued to lobby EFRAG and the IASB to allow entities to either apply the hedge accounting requirements in IAS 39 or IFRS 9 until the project on accounting for macro hedging is finalised.[11]

Eventually, the IASB decided to give entities the following choices until the project on accounting for macro hedging is completed:

- to apply the new hedge accounting requirements as set out in IFRS 9, in full;
- to apply the new hedge accounting requirements as set out in IFRS 9 to all hedges except fair value hedges of the interest rate exposure of a portfolio of financial assets or financial liabilities; in that case an entity must also apply the paragraphs that were added to IAS 39 when that particular type of hedge was introduced (IAS 39.81A, 89A and AG114-AG132) – i.e. an entity must apply *all* the hedge accounting requirements of IAS 39 (e.g. the 80%-125% bright line effectiveness test) *including* the paragraphs that specifically address fair value hedges of the interest rate exposure of a portfolio of financial assets or financial liabilities); the choice to apply IAS 39 in these situations is the result of the scope of the hedge accounting requirements of IFRS 9 and available on a case-by-case basis (i.e. it is not an accounting policy choice); *[IFRS 9.6.1.3]* or
- to continue applying hedge accounting as set out in IAS 39 until the project on accounting for macro hedging is completed, to all hedges; this is an accounting policy choice. *[IFRS 9.7.2.21]*. Because it is an accounting policy choice, an entity may later on change its policy and start applying the hedge accounting requirements of IFRS 9 (subject to the transition requirements of IFRS 9 for hedge accounting). However, even if an entity chooses to continue to apply the hedge accounting requirements of IAS 39, the entity still has to provide the new hedge accounting disclosures that were developed during the IFRS 9 project because those disclosure requirements have become a part of IFRS 7 for which no similar accounting policy choice to continue to apply the previous requirements was provided. *[IFRS 9.BC6.104]*. Once an entity changes its accounting policy and starts to apply the hedge accounting requirements of IFRS 9, it cannot go back to IAS 39. (See 11.1 below for more details).

3.6.7 Hedged items held at fair value through profit or loss

It does not immediately appear that it would be useful to designate a hedged item that is measured at fair value through profit or loss in a hedge relationship. However, for certain variable rate instruments measured at fair value through profit or loss, designation as the hedged item in a cash flow hedge relationship may be desirable. Although the variable hedged item would be measured at fair value through profit or loss, an entity may still seek to hedge variability of cash flows by entering into a hedging derivative. Because of the variable nature of the hedged item, such instruments may not be significantly exposed to changes in fair value caused by movements in the hedged risk whereas the hedging derivative will be. In this instance, application of cash flow hedge accounting facilitates deferral of fair value changes in the hedging derivative to the cash flow hedge reserve, which may better reflect the risk management strategy.

However, not all instruments measured at fair value through profit or loss will be eligible hedged items, as it will depend on the reason why the instrument is measured at fair value through profit or loss. Classification of an item at fair value through profit or loss could be because such an item is held for trading, managed on a fair value basis, designated as measured at fair value through profit or loss using the fair value option or because the contractual terms of the financial asset give rise on specified dates to cash flows that are not solely payments of principal and interest on the principal amount outstanding. (See Chapter 46 at 2).

For a portfolio of financial assets that is managed and whose performance is evaluated on a fair value basis, an entity is primarily focused on fair value information and uses that information to assess the assets' performance and to make decisions *[IFRS 9.B4.1.6]*. In our view if the hedging instrument is also part of the same portfolio (or business model), and the entity has by definition determined that fair value is the most appropriate measure for that portfolio, then this would be inconsistent with the idea of cash flow hedging, whereby part of the fair value movements would be recorded in other comprehensive income, separately from the remaining fair values movements that would be recorded in profit or loss. We therefore believe cash flow hedge accounting would not ordinarily be appropriate in this scenario.

However there may be some situations where the cash flow interest rate risk on an asset that is part of a portfolio managed on a fair value basis, may be managed outside of the portfolio (or business model). In such cases any instrument hedging the interest rate risk would also be held separately from the managed portfolio. In such a scenario, cash flow hedge accounting is not necessarily inconsistent with the hedged asset being held at fair value through profit or loss. Such a situation is shown in the following example:

Example 53.19: Interest rate risk managed separately from a credit risk portfolio managed on a fair value basis

Entity A has various investment portfolios for which the credit risk is managed by individual portfolio managers on a fair value basis. The individual managers are likely to manage the fair value of the portfolio using credit risk derivatives such as credit default swaps. The entity wishes to retain the management of interest rate risk centrally and therefore instructs each portfolio manager to invest in order to achieve a 3m Libor based rate of return. Accordingly the majority of assets within the portfolio will attract a floating rate and hence most of the portfolio's fair value volatility will arise from changes in credit risk. The interest rate risk is managed centrally and so any interest rate swaps used to fix some of the variability in the future cash flows from changes in interest rate risk are transacted centrally and not part of any investment portfolio. Each portfolio is managed based on its fair value, has discreet fair value financial information and each portfolio manager is assessed on the fair value performance of their portfolio. The entity concludes that the business model test should be applied at the portfolio level and as such each investment portfolio is measured at fair value through profit or loss.

It is possible that in these circumstances the decision to enter into interest rate swaps and apply cash flow hedge accounting to an asset within the investment portfolios is not inconsistent with the fact the instrument is held at fair value through profit or loss, since that designation is driven by management of the fair value of credit and not the interest rate element.

A portfolio that is held for trading is one where assets and liabilities are acquired or incurred principally for the purpose of selling or repurchasing or the purpose of short-term profit-taking. An entity achieves those objectives by either selling or repurchasing the financial instruments or to enter into an opposite trade to lock-in a gain. We believe in this case cash flow hedging will not be appropriate for the reasons set out below:

- A trading portfolio is likely to be managed on a fair value basis and so a number of the considerations above will also apply. Furthermore, it is unlikely that any of the risks within the trading portfolio will be managed separately outside of the trading portfolio.
- In a trading portfolio where an entity plans to sell an asset in the near team, the asset will not be eligible for cash flow hedging as the future cash flows will not be highly probable.
- In a trading portfolio where an entity plans to enter into an offsetting position to lock in the gain, there will be no net position remaining to economically hedge or to be managed separately outside of the portfolio.

Hence, overall we do not believe cash flow hedge accounting is appropriate for positions in a trading portfolio.

Where instruments are classified as fair value through profit or loss because they fail the contractual cash flow characteristics test (see Chapter 46 at 6), the above arguments do not apply and so it appears that such instruments may be designated as the hedged item in a cash flow hedge.

IFRS 9 provides confirmation that cash flow hedge accounting is not prohibited for all hedged items measured at fair value through profit or loss by way of the following example: an entity could use a swap to change floating rate debt to fixed-rate and apply cash flow hedge accounting, even if the debt is measured at fair value through profit or loss. This is because there is a systematic way in which the cash flow hedge reserve can be reclassified, i.e. in the same way interest payments on the instrument happen. A further example is given of a forecast purchase of an equity instrument that, once acquired, will be accounted for at fair value through profit or loss. This is mentioned as an example of an item that cannot be the hedged item in a cash flow hedge, because any gain or loss on the hedging instrument that would be deferred could not be appropriately reclassified to profit or loss during a period in which it would achieve offset. *[IFRS 9.B6.5.2]*.

As well as providing confirmation that cash flow hedge accounting is not precluded for hedged items measured at fair value through profit or loss, the guidance in IFRS 9.B6.5.2 also appears to introduce an additional requirement that there is a systematic way in which the cash flow hedge reserve can be reclassified for such a hedge.

4 HEDGING INSTRUMENTS

IAS 39 places several restrictions on the types of instruments that can qualify as hedging instruments for hedge accounting purposes. This is to reflect that hedge accounting was mainly intended to address accounting mismatches that resulted from requiring derivatives to be accounted for at fair value through profit or loss (see Chapter 52 at 2.1). IFRS 9 takes a different approach that focuses on what instruments are used for hedging and expands the list of what can be permitted as a hedging instrument. However, the requirement that the hedging instrument has to be a contract with a party external to the reporting entity remains. *[IFRS 9.6.2.3]*.

4.1 General requirements

Unchanged from IAS 39, derivatives measured at fair value through profit or loss qualify as hedging instruments. *[IFRS 9.6.2.1]*. The sole exception to this rule continues to be written options, unless the written option is designated to offset a purchased option. Purchased options include those that are embedded in another financial instrument. *[IFRS 9.B6.2.4]*. Although not specifically mentioned, we believe that embedded purchased options in non-financial instruments that are not required to be bifurcated could also be designated as being hedged by a written option.

Two or more financial instruments can be jointly designated as hedging instruments. *[IFRS 9.6.2.5]*. This was already permitted under IAS 39. Also unchanged is the requirement that a single instrument combining a written option and a purchased option, such as an interest rate collar, cannot be a hedging instrument if it is a net written option at the date of the designation. *[IFRS 9.6.2.6]*.

Contrary to IAS 39, IFRS 9 specifically permits options that are transacted as legally separate contracts to be jointly designated as hedging instruments if the combined instrument is not a net written option at the date of designation. *[IFRS 9.6.2.6]*. However, this is consistent with how we interpreted IAS 39 for certain combinations of options that have the same critical terms (see Chapter 52 at 2.1.3). However, under IFRS 9 more combinations will be permitted, for example, as there is no requirement for the options to be with the same counterparty.

Example 53.20: Hedging foreign exchange risk of a forecast transaction using a combined option instrument

An entity is exposed to foreign exchange risk resulting from a highly probably forecast transaction in a foreign currency. In order to hedge that exposure, the entity enters into a collar by combining a long call and a short put option. The premium paid on the long call option equals the premium received on the short put option (i.e. it is what is termed a 'zero cost collar').

The entity designates the combination of the two instruments in a cash flow hedge of its highly probable forecast transaction.

4.2 Non-derivative financial instruments

Under IFRS 9, entities are permitted to designate, as hedging instruments, non-derivative financial assets or non-derivative financial liabilities that are accounted for at fair value through profit or loss. *[IFRS 9.6.2.2]*. This is meant in a strict sense. Consequently:

- A liability designated as at fair value through profit or loss (for which the amount of its change in fair value that is attributable to changes in the credit risk of that liability is presented in other comprehensive income (OCI)) does not qualify as a hedging instrument. *[IFRS 9.6.2.2]*. This is because the entire fair value change is not recognised in profit or loss, which would in effect allow the entity to ignore its own credit risk when assessing and measuring hedge ineffectiveness and thus conflict with the concepts of hedge accounting.
- An equity instrument for which an entity has elected to present changes in fair value in OCI does not qualify as a hedging instrument in a hedge of foreign currency risk. *[IFRS 9.6.2.2]*. Again, this reflects that fair value changes are not recognised in profit or loss, which is incompatible with the mechanics of fair value hedges and cash flow hedges.

Example 53.21: Hedge of a forecast commodity purchase with an investment in a commodity fund or an exchange traded commodity

An entity is exposed to variability in cash flows from highly probable forecast purchases of crude oil that is indexed to Brent crude oil. The entity wants to hedge its cash flow risk from changes in the price of Brent crude oil. Instead of using derivative contracts, the entity purchases exchange traded investments that replicate the performance of Brent futures contracts such as commodity funds or exchange traded commodities (ETCs). ETCs have the legal form of debentures that are coupled to the price development of a commodity (either directly at the spot price or with a commodity futures contract). They can be traded like exchange traded funds but, because they are legally debt securities, they involve credit risk of the issuer (which is usually mitigated by collateralisation through physically deposited commodities or other suitable collateral).

These investments are financial instruments that (under IFRS 9) would be accounted for at fair value through profit or loss. Consequently, they could qualify as hedging instruments if all other qualifying criteria for hedge accounting are met. In particular, the effectiveness assessment would have to consider that the fair value change of the investments will differ from the present value of the cumulative change in the cash flows for the forecast purchases of crude oil. This is because of aspects such as 'tracking errors' (i.e. that investment does not perfectly replicate the performance of futures contracts) and that the investments are fully funded cash-instruments whereas the cash flows on the forecast transactions will only occur in the future.

The ability to designate non-derivative hedging instruments can be helpful if an entity does not have access to derivatives markets (e.g. because of local regulations that prohibit the entity from holding such instruments), or if an entity does not want to be subject to margining requirements nor enter into uncollateralised over-the-counter derivatives. Purchasing and selling financial investments in such cases can be operationally easier for entities than transacting derivatives.

For hedges other than of foreign exchange risk, when an entity designates a non-derivative financial asset or liability measured at fair value through profit or loss as a hedging instrument, it may only designate the non-derivative financial instrument in its entirety or a proportion of it. *[IFRS 9 B6.2.5]*.

4.3 Hedges of a portion of a time period

IAS 39 contains a restriction that a hedging relationship cannot be designated for only a portion of the time period during which a hedging instrument remains outstanding (see Chapter 52 at 2.1.4.C). In essence, this restriction remains; however, it is now formulated more precisely, in that a hedging instrument may not be designated for a part of its change in fair value that results from only a portion of the time period during which the hedging instrument remains outstanding. This clarifies that an entity cannot designate a 'partial-term' component of a financial instrument as the hedging instrument, but only the entire instrument for its remaining life (notwithstanding that an entity may exclude from designation the time value of an option, the forward element of a forward contract or the foreign currency basis spread, see 7.1 and 7.2 below). *[IFRS 9.6.2.4]*. This does not mean that the hedge relationship must necessarily continue for the entire remaining life of the hedging instrument – the usual hedge discontinuation requirements apply (see 6.3 below).

4.4 Hedges of foreign currency risk

For hedges of foreign currency risk, the foreign currency risk component of a non-derivative financial instrument is determined in accordance with IAS 21 – *The Effects of Changes in Foreign Exchange Rates*. *[IFRS 9.B6.2.3]*. This means that an entity could, for example, hedge the spot risk of highly probable forecast sales in 12 months' time that are denominated in a foreign currency with a 7-year financial liability in the same foreign currency. However, when measuring ineffectiveness, IFRS 9 is now explicit that the revaluation of the forecast sales for foreign currency risk would have to be on a discounted basis (i.e. a present value calculation of the spot revaluation, reflecting the time between the reporting date and the future cash flow date), whereas the hedging instrument (i.e. the IAS 21-based foreign currency component of the financial liability) would not. This would result in some ineffectiveness (see 6.4.1 below). *[IFRS 9.B6.5.4]*.

4.5 Time value of money, forward element and currency basis spread

Consistent with IAS 39, an entity can exclude from the designation as the hedging instrument the changes in fair value attributable to the time value of an option or the forward element of a forward contract (see 7.1 and 7.2 below). IFRS 9 expands this by also allowing the separation and exclusion of the foreign currency basis spread when designating a financial instrument as the hedging instrument (see 7.2.2 below).

A significant change from IAS 39 is that fluctuations over time in the fair value of the parts excluded from the hedge relationship are recorded in other comprehensive income instead of profit or loss. This is referred to as the cost of hedging treatment (see Chapter 7).

4.6 Embedded derivatives

Derivatives that are embedded in hybrid contracts, but that are not separately accounted for, cannot be designated as separate hedging instruments. *[IFRS 9 B6.2.1]*. Given that embedded derivatives in financial assets are not accounted for separately under IFRS 9, this guidance precludes designation of embedded derivatives in financial assets as separate hedging instruments. *[IFRS 9 BC6.117-122]*.

5 QUALIFYING CRITERIA

5.1 General requirements

Unchanged from IAS 39, in order to qualify for hedge accounting, a hedging relationship has to consist of eligible hedging instruments and eligible hedged items (see 3 and 4 above). Also, at inception of the hedging relationship, there still has to be a formal designation and documentation. This would include the entity's risk management strategy and the objective underlying the hedging relationship. The documentation has to include an identification of the hedging instrument, the hedged item, the nature of the risk being hedged and how the entity will assess whether the hedging relationship meets the hedge effectiveness requirements. *[IFRS 9.6.4.1]*.

However, compared to IAS 39, the entity's risk management strategy and objective are more important under IFRS 9 because of the effect on discontinuation of hedge accounting and the hedge accounting related disclosures. IFRS 9 also requires documentation of the hedge ratio and potential sources of ineffectiveness (that may have to be updated as part of a continuing hedging relationship). *[IFRS 9.B6.5.26, 6.4.1(b)]*.

Entities can still only designate one of three types of hedging relationships: a fair value hedge, a cash flow hedge or a hedge of a net investment in a foreign operation. For hedges of the foreign currency risk of a firm commitment, an entity may still designate either a fair value hedge or a cash flow hedge. *[IFRS 9.6.5.2, 6.5.4]*.

The requirements for assessing effectiveness are another change compared to IAS 39. The effectiveness assessment under IFRS 9 is only prospective, does not involve any 'bright lines' and, depending on the circumstances, may often be qualitative. The method for assessing effectiveness may need to be changed in response to changes in circumstances. In such cases, the hedge documentation is updated but without resulting in discontinuation of the hedging relationship. *[IFRS 9.B6.4.17, B6.4.19]*.

Under IFRS 9 a hedging relationship qualifies for hedge accounting if it meets *all* of the following effectiveness requirements:

- there is 'an economic relationship' between the hedged item and the hedging instrument;
- the effect of credit risk does not 'dominate the value changes' that result from that economic relationship; and
- 'the hedge ratio of the hedging relationship is the same as that resulting from the quantity of hedged item that the entity actually hedges and the quantity of the hedging instrument that the entity actually uses to hedge that quantity of hedged item. However, that designation shall not reflect an imbalance between the weightings of the hedged item and the hedging instrument that would create hedge ineffectiveness (irrespective of whether recognised or not) that could result in an accounting outcome that would be inconsistent with the purpose of hedge accounting'. *[IFRS 9.6.4.1(c)]*. The second part of this requirement is an anti-abuse clause that is explained in more detail in at 5.4 below.

These initial effectiveness requirements also form the basis for the subsequent effectiveness assessment in order to continue to achieve hedge accounting, which is discussed at 6 below.

The required steps for designating a hedging relationship can be summarised in a flow chart as follows:

Figure 53.1: How to achieve hedge accounting

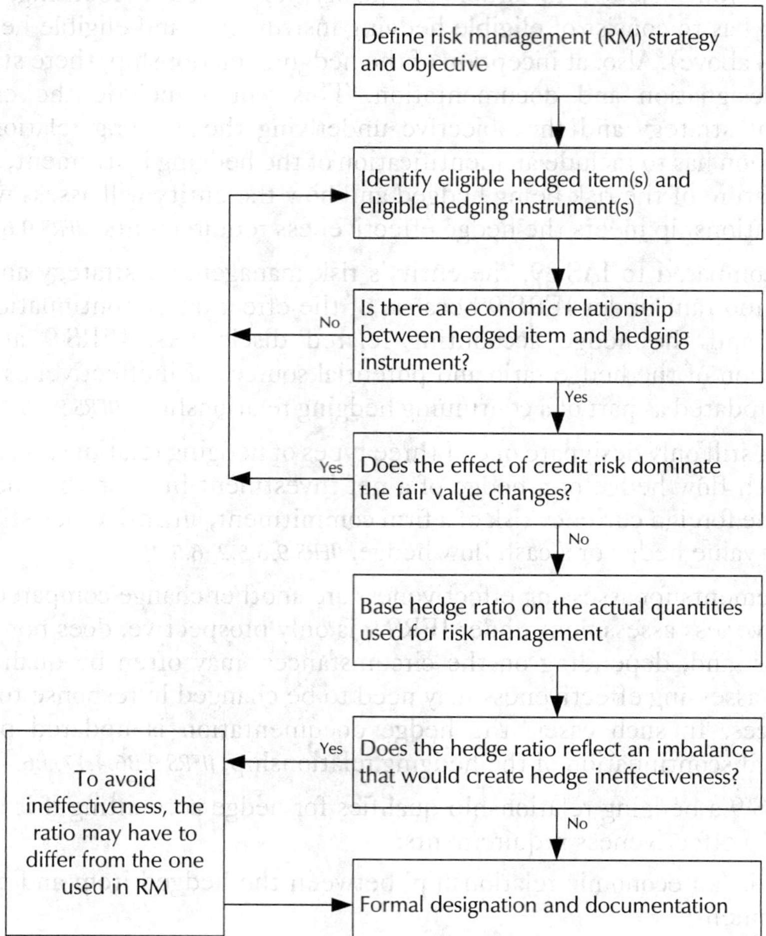

The individual steps in the new effectiveness assessment are discussed in more detail below.

5.2 Economic relationship

The first effectiveness requirement means that the hedging instrument and the hedged item must generally be expected to move in opposite directions as a result of a change in the hedged risk. The guidance does not require that the value changes of the hedging instrument and the hedged item are expected to move in the opposite direction for the hedged risk in all circumstances, but that generally there is an expectation that they will systematically move in opposite directions. The degree to which the hedged item and hedging instrument are expected to move in opposite directions is not relevant for the assessment of an economic relationship. *[IFRS 9.B6.4.4, B6.4.5, BC6.238]*.

The assessment should be based on an economic rationale rather than just by chance, as could be the case if the relationship is based only on a statistical correlation. That is, causality cannot be assumed purely from correlation or, to quote the IASB, 'the mere existence of a statistical correlation between two variables does not, by itself, support a valid conclusion that an economic relationship exists'. *[IFRS 9.B6.4.6]*. Conversely, a statistical correlation may provide corroboration of an economic rationale. For example, if it can be seen that value drivers exist such that there is an expectation that the value of the hedged item and hedging instrument would generally move in opposite directions, but that significant sources of ineffectiveness exist within a relationship that may counteract the offset, then quantitative analysis may assist in determining whether an economic relationship exists or not. However, as noted above a quantitative assessment alone is not enough to establish an economic relationship.

The requirement of an economic relationship will automatically be fulfilled for many hedging relationships, as the underlying of the hedging instrument often matches, or is closely aligned with, the hedged risk. *[IFRS 9.B6.4.14]*. Even when there are differences between the hedged item and the hedging instrument, the economic relationship will often be capable of being demonstrated using a qualitative assessment. However, when the critical terms of the hedging instrument and hedged item are not closely aligned, IFRS 9 suggests that 'it might only be possible for an entity to conclude [that there is an economic relationship] on the basis of a quantitative assessment.' *[IFRS 9.B6.4.16, BC6.269]*. However, the standard does not provide any guidance on the point at which quantitative assessment might be required or how it would be made. This is an area where practice will develop, but we expect the need for a quantitative assessment over and above what is already undertaken for risk management purposes, to be relatively infrequent. The standard also mentions hedging relationships where a derivative with a non-zero fair value is designated as the hedging instruments as an example of a situation where a quantitative assessment might be required to establish an economic relationship. *[IFRS 9.B6.4.15]*. However, as noted above, the standard does not provide guidance on how large the non-zero fair value would have to be in order that an economic relationship would not be considered to exist or when a quantitative assessment is required.

The assessment, whether qualitative or quantitative, would need to consider, amongst other possible sources of mismatch between the designated hedged item and the hedging instrument:

- maturity;
- volume or nominal amount;
- cash flow dates;
- interest rate basis, or quality and location basis differences;
- day count methods; and
- the extent that the hedging instrument is already 'in the money', or 'out of the money' when designated.

The assessment should also include an analysis of the possible behaviour of the hedging relationship during its term to ascertain whether it can be expected to meet the risk management objective. *[IFRS 9.B6.4.6]*. The assessment must be forward looking at all times, without solely relying on actual retrospective offset. This does not mean that retrospective offset is never relevant, but it should only be relied upon if there is a reasonable expectation that it is representative of the future.

IFRS 9 does not specify a method for assessing whether an economic relationship exists. An entity should use a method capturing all the relevant characteristics of the hedging relationship including the sources of ineffectiveness. *[IFRS 9.B6.4.13]*. Which methods, including statistical methods such as regression or sensitivity analysis, as well as the thresholds attached to them, is an area where we expect that best practice will emerge over time. No 'bright lines' are mandated by the guidance, nor is there a requirement for an entity to determine their own bright lines. Instead, judgement is required in determining whether an economic relationship exists or not. However, it follows from the objective of the hedge accounting requirements to represent the effect of an entity's risk management activities, that the main source of information to perform the assessment would be an entity's risk management activities. *[IFRS 9.6.1.1, B6.4.18]*. In practice, an entity will have normally assessed the economic relationship for risk management purposes and, in most cases, assuming sound risk management, we would expect that this assessment to be appropriate for accounting purposes as well. However, in some cases, existing risk management techniques might not adequately consider all sources of ineffectiveness, such that additional quantitative analysis may be required, although this is likely to be rare. The chosen quantitative technique should depend on the complexity of the relationship, availability of data, the time value of money and the level of uncertainty of offset in the hedge relationship. If there are changes in circumstances that affect hedge effectiveness, an entity may have to change the method for assessing whether an economic relationship exists. *[IFRS 9.B6.4.17]*.

The standard also mentions that a quantitative method, (e.g. regression analysis), might help demonstrate a suitable hedge ratio (see 5.4 below). *[IFRS 9.B6.4.16]*.

The following example illustrates an approach that uses a qualitative assessment.

Example 53.22: Economic relationship between HKD and USD

An entity has foreign currency exposures in both Hong Kong dollars (HKD) and US dollars (USD). The entity aggregates its exposures in the two currencies and only uses USD linked hedges to hedge those currency exposures.

Because the HKD is pegged to the USD in a way that allows fluctuations only within a very narrow band (between HKD 7.75 – HKD 7.85 per USD) the entity concludes that an economic relationship exists between its USD linked hedges (with the USD as the underlying) and its HKD denominated foreign currency exposures.

The entity monitors the currency peg for changes and treats the movements of the HKD within the narrow band as a source of some ineffectiveness for all hedges in which the hedged item relates to amounts denominated in HKD.

When using a statistical method such as regression analysis, either to corroborate an economic relationship or to determine a suitable hedging ratio, an entity is required to consider its expectations of future developments. A prominent recent example is negative interest rates in some European countries. Many variable debt instruments such as mortgages include an explicit or implicit floor while the interest rates swaps used to hedge the variability of cash flows of those exposures usually do not. Although the interest cash flows of the hedged item and the variable leg of the hedging instrument may well have been highly correlated in the past, in an environment where interest rates are expected to be negative in the foreseeable future, this may no longer be expected because of the floor in the hedged item. This means that an entity needs to incorporate changes in expectations and re-calibrate its regression analysis accordingly (see Chapter 52 at 5.3.6.A).

5.3 Credit risk and the effectiveness assessment

IFRS 9 requires that, to achieve hedge accounting, the impact of credit risk should not be of a magnitude such that it dominates the value changes, even if there is an economic relationship between the hedged item and hedging instrument. Credit risk can arise on both the hedging instrument and the hedged item in the form of counterparty credit risk or the entity's own credit risk.

Judgement has to be used in determining when the impact of credit risk is 'dominating' the value changes. But clearly, to 'dominate' would mean that there would have to be a very significant effect on the fair value of the hedged item or the hedging instrument. The standard provides guidance that small effects should be ignored even when, in a particular period, they affect the fair values more than changes in the hedged risk. *[IFRS 9.B6.4.7]*. An example of credit risk dominating a hedging relationship would be when an entity hedges an exposure to commodity price risk with an uncollateralised derivative and the credit standing of the counterparty to that derivative deteriorates severely, such that the effect of the changes in the counterparty's credit standing might outweigh the effect of changes in the commodity price on the fair value of the hedging instrument. *[IFRS 9.B6.4.8]*.

5.3.1 Credit risk on the hedging instrument

IFRS 13 – *Fair Value Measurement* – is clear that the effect of credit risk, both the counterparty's credit risk and the entity's own credit risk, has to be reflected in the measurement of fair value (see Chapter 14 at 11.3.2). The effect of counterparty and own credit risk on the measurement of the hedging instrument would obviously result in some hedge ineffectiveness. The expected effect of that ineffectiveness should not be of a magnitude that it frustrates the offsetting impact of a change in the values of the hedging instrument and the hedged item that results from the economic relationship (as explained at 5.2 above).

We expect the assessment of the effect of credit risk to be a qualitative assessment in most cases. For example, entities typically have counterparty risk limits defined as part of their risk management policy. The credit standing of the counterparties is monitored on a regular basis. However, a quantitative assessment of the impact of credit risk on the value changes of the hedging relationship might be required in some instances, if the customer's credit standing deteriorates.

Nowadays, most over-the-counter derivative contracts between financial institutions are cash collateralised. Furthermore, current initiatives in several jurisdictions, such as, the European Market Infrastructure Regulation (EMIR) in the European Union or the Dodd-Frank Act in the United States, will result in more derivative contracts being collateralised by cash. Cash collateralisation significantly reduces the credit risk for both parties involved, meaning that credit risk is unlikely to dominate the change in fair value of such hedging instruments.

5.3.2 Credit risk on the hedged item

The analysis of the hedged item is somewhat different, as credit risk does not apply to all types of hedged items. For example, while loan assets typically have counterparty credit risk and financial liabilities bear the issuing entity's own credit risk, inventory and forecast transactions do not pose credit risk.

Credit risk is defined as 'risk that one party to a financial instrument will cause a financial loss for the other party by failing to discharge an obligation'. *[IFRS 7 Appendix A]*. Credit risk cannot dominate the value change in a hedge of a forecast transaction as the transaction is, by definition, only anticipated but not committed. *[IFRS 9 Appendix A]*. For the same reason, inventory also does not involve credit risk. Consequently, credit risk can only apply if the entity enters into a contract (e.g. if the hedged item is a firm commitment or a financial instrument). This should be contrasted with the assessment of whether a forecast transaction is highly probable. Even though such a transaction does not involve credit risk, depending on the possible counterparties for the anticipated transaction, the credit risk that affects them can indirectly affect the assessment of whether the forecast transaction is highly probable. For example, assume an entity sells a product to only one particular customer abroad for which the sales are denominated in a foreign currency and the entity does not have alternative customers to sell the product to in that currency (or other sales in that currency). In that case, the credit risk of that particular customer would indirectly affect the likelihood of the entity's forecast sales in that currency occurring. Conversely, if the entity has a wider customer base for sales of its product that are denominated in the foreign currency then the potential loss of a particular customer would not significantly (or even not at all) affect the likelihood of the entity's forecast sales in that currency occurring.

For regulatory and accounting purposes, banks usually have systems in place to determine the credit risk on their loan portfolios. Therefore, banks should be able to identify loans for which credit risk is so high that it would require an assessment of whether credit risk is dominating the value changes in the hedging relationship. The introduction of the new impairment model of IFRS 9 (see Chapter 49 at 5) has raised the question of whether there is a linkage between:

- the impairment model concept of a significant increase in credit risk (i.e. the move from 'stage one' to 'stage two') and the subsequent transfer of a credit-impaired financial assets to 'stage three'; and
- the concept of when the effect of credit risk dominates the value changes of the hedged item that represent the hedged risk.

There is no direct link between the stages of the impairment model and credit risk eligibility criterion of the hedge accounting model. However in practice, an entity may consider the indicators cited in the definition of a credit-impaired financial asset (see Chapter 49 at 5.3.3). This is because those indicators characterise situations with a magnitude of credit risk that normally suggests that its effect would dominate the value changes of the hedged item that represent the hedged risk. This suggests that normally the hedge effectiveness criteria would cease to be met no later than when a financial asset is classified as credit-impaired (i.e. in stage three). How much earlier the hedge effectiveness criteria might be failed is a matter of judgement, which may need to be supported by quantitative assessment in some situations. But also, in the context of stage three of the impairment model, it should be remembered that the effect of credit risk on the fair value of an item involves not only the probability of default but also the loss given default, whereas the indicators cited in the definition of a credit-impaired financial asset relate only to the probability of default. That difference is relevant when assessing whether credit risk is dominant in the case of items that are highly collateralised.

In practice, we expect that entities with a sound risk management would be unlikely to struggle with the assessment of when the effect of credit risk dominates the value changes of the hedged item that represent the hedged risk. This is because such entities would have developed suitable criteria for when risk exposures can no longer be hedged because credit risk creates too much uncertainty as to whether that exposure will eventually crystallise as per the terms in the contract from which it arises. Entities normally evaluate this for risk management purposes because they want to avoid being 'over-hedged' as a result of the offset from the hedged item for the gains or losses on the hedging instrument being eroded by credit risk. In other words, this is predominantly an economic question rather than an accounting consideration (similar to the discussion at 5.3.1 above regarding the credit risk of hedging instruments and entities' criteria for selecting counterparties for those instruments).

Theoretically there is also interaction between the hedge accounting model and the impairment model regarding the effect that a fair value hedge has on the measurement of the expected credit loss for an item whose carrying amount is adjusted for fair value hedge gains and losses. Because the fair value hedge adjustment is a part of the carrying value of the financial asset that is hedged, the measurement of the loss allowance should presumably take that adjustment into account. This could be achieved by adjusting the effective interest rate used to measure the expected credit loss allowance, although IFRS 9 does not seem to prescribe this treatment. A similar requirement was illustrated by the implementation guidance of IAS 39. *[IAS 39.IG E.4.4]*. If the effective interest rate used for discounting the expected credit loss is adjusted for the effect of fair value hedging, the main difference compared to IAS 39 in terms of operational complexity is, of course, that under IFRS 9 every debt instrument recorded at amortised cost or at fair value through other comprehensive income has an associated loss allowance. This would mean, for every fair value hedge in relation to such financial assets, the measurement of the loss allowance requires taking into account the effect of the fair value hedge accounting. This is discussed further in Chapter 49 at 5.4.6.

The assessment of the effect of credit risk on value changes for hedge effectiveness purposes, which often may be made on a qualitative basis, should not be confused with the requirement to measure and recognise the impact of credit risk on the hedging instrument and, where appropriate, the designated hedged item, which will normally give rise to hedge ineffectiveness recognised in profit or loss (see Chapter 52 at 5.3.4).

The systems used to assess the credit risk of loans would also usually permit banks to determine the appropriate economic hedge when hedging the interest rate risk of such loans, as illustrated by Example 53.23 below:

Example 53.23: Designating interest rate hedges of loan assets when credit risk is expected

Assume a bank wishes to hedge the interest rate risk of a portfolio of loans that have similar credit risk characteristics. Economically, the bank should hedge only the cash flows it expects to collect. When expecting to collect 95% of all cash flows in a loan portfolio, the bank should designate the first 95% of cash flows only. A designation of more than 95% would result in an economic over-hedge and would also increase the risk of credit risk dominating the value changes of the hedging relationship.

As a significant change compared to IAS 39, the designation of such a nominal component (often referred to as a bottom layer) is now possible under IFRS 9 (as discussed at 3.5.3 above). This type of designation would require that all items included in the layer are exposed to the same hedged risk so that the measurement of the hedged layer is not significantly affected by items that make up the 95% layer from the overall 100% of the portfolio. *[IFRS 9.6.6.3(c)]*. Therefore, the entity has to designate the same kind of benchmark interest rate risk component of each loan to make up the bottom layer. If there is a deterioration in the credit risk of a particular loan that results in credit risk dominating the economic relationship with the benchmark interest rate, such that its benchmark interest rate risk component will no longer qualify to be designated as a hedged item, it would not be considered to be part of the bottom layer unless and until those loans for which credit risk dominates the economic relationship would exceed 5% of the portfolio.

The example should not be taken to imply that for an individual loan with an expected loss of, say, 5% an entity may not hedge the interest rate risk using an interest rate swap that has a notional amount equal to the loan's face value. However, if the loan deteriorated in its credit quality to an extent where the credit risk-related changes in fair value start to dominate the interest rate risk-related changes, the hedging relationship would have to be discontinued.

5.4 Setting the hedge ratio

The hedge ratio is the ratio between the amount of hedged item and the amount of hedging instrument. For many hedging relationships, the hedge ratio would be 1:1 as the underlying of the hedging instrument perfectly matches the designated hedged risk.

Some hedging relationships may include basis risk such that the fair value changes of the hedged item and the hedging instrument do not have a simple 1:1 relationship. In such cases, risk managers will generally set the hedge ratio so as to be other than 1:1, in order to improve the effectiveness of the hedge. Consequently, the third effectiveness requirement is that the hedge ratio used for accounting should ordinarily be the same as that used for risk management purposes. *[IFRS 9.6.4.1(c)(iii)]*.

Example 53.24: Setting the hedge ratio

An entity purchases a raw material whose price is at a discount to the commodity benchmark price, reflecting that the raw material is not yet processed to the same extent as the benchmark commodity, as well as quality differences. The entity runs a rolling 12-month regression analysis at each month end to ascertain that the price of the commodity in the futures market and the price of the raw material remain highly correlated. The slopes of the regression analyses (commodity benchmark price to raw material price) over recent months varied between 1.237 and 1.276.

The entity considers that the pattern of its regression analyses is consistent with its longer term view that the raw material trades at an approximately 20% discount to the commodity benchmark price and does not indicate a change in trend but fluctuations around that discount. Therefore, the entity uses a notional amount of 1 tonne of a forward contract for the benchmark commodity to hedge highly probable forecast purchases of 1.25 tonnes of the raw material. Note that this is not exactly the same as the particular slope of the most recent monthly regression, which is not required because the standard requires only that the entity uses the hedge ratio that it actually uses for risk management purposes, and not that it is required to minimise ineffectiveness. The example also illustrates what the standard acknowledges: there is no 'right' answer, as different entities would run different regression analyses (e.g. in terms of frequency and data inputs used, which means there is no one hedge ratio that could be required). The fluctuation of the actual discount around the particular hedge ratio chosen for designating the hedging relationship will give rise to some ineffectiveness.

However, the standard requires the hedge ratio for accounting purposes to be different from the hedge ratio used for risk management if the latter hedge ratio reflects an imbalance that would create hedge ineffectiveness 'that could result in an accounting outcome that would be inconsistent with the purpose of hedge accounting.' *[IFRS 9.6.4.1(c)(iii), B6.4.10]*. This complex language was introduced because the Board is specifically concerned with deliberate 'under-hedging', either to minimise recognition of ineffectiveness in cash flow hedges or the creation of additional fair value adjustments to the hedged item in fair value hedges. *[IFRS 9.B6.4.11(a)]*.

Example 53.25: Deliberate under-hedging in a cash flow hedge to avoid recognition of ineffectiveness

Consistent with the equivalent requirements of IAS 39 (see Chapter 52 at 4.2.1), IFRS 9 requires the cash flow hedge reserve to be adjusted for the lower of (a) the cumulative gain or loss on the hedging instrument or (b) the cumulative change in fair value of the hedged item. *[IFRS 9.6.5.11(a)]*. If (a) exceeds (b), the difference is recognised in profit or loss as ineffectiveness. On the other hand, no ineffectiveness is recognised if (b) exceeds (a). An entity has highly probable forecast purchases of a raw material used in its manufacturing process. The average volume of raw material purchases is expected to be Russian Rouble (RUB) 200m per month. The entity wishes to hedge the commodity price risk on those forecast purchases. The only derivative available does not have an underlying risk exactly matching the one from the actual raw material hedged. The slope of a linear regression analysis is 0.93, indicating the ideal hedge ratio.

To seek to avoid recognition of accounting ineffectiveness, the entity ensures (b) will exceed (a), applying the accounting requirement discussed above. It enters into derivatives with a notional amount of only RUB 150m per month and designates the RUB 150m of forward contracts as hedging instruments in cash flow hedges of highly probable forecast purchases of RUB 200m (thereby setting the hedge ratio at 0.75:1).

In this scenario, the hedge ratio would be considered unbalanced and only entered into to avoid recognition of accounting ineffectiveness. For hedge accounting purposes, the hedge ratio would have to be based on the expected sensitivity between the hedged item and the hedging instrument (in this example possibly around the 0.93:1 based on the linear regression analysis, which would give a hedged volume of RUB 161m). As a result, if the relative change in the fair value of the hedging instrument is greater than that on the hedged item because the relationship between the underlyings changes, some ineffectiveness will have to be recognised.

Example 53.26: Deliberate under-hedging in a fair value hedge to create fair value accounting

An entity acquires a CU 50million portfolio of debt instruments. The debt instruments fail the 'cash flow characteristics test' of IFRS 9 (i.e. the contractual cash flows do not solely represent payments of principal and interest on the principal amount outstanding) and are therefore accounted for at fair value through profit or loss (see Chapter 46 at 6). *[IFRS 9.4.1.2(b), 4.1.2A(b)]*.

The treasurer dislikes the profit or loss volatility resulting from the fair value accounting. He realises that one of the entity's fixed rate bank borrowings has a similar term structure and that fair value changes on the liability would more or less offset the fair value changes on the asset portfolio. However, at the time of entering into the bank borrowing, the entity did not apply the fair value option to this liability (see Chapter 46 at 3).

The treasurer enters into a CU 1m receive fixed/pay variable interest rate swap (IRS) and designates the IRS in a fair value hedge of CU 50m of fixed rate liability (thereby setting the hedge ratio at 0.02:1). As a result, the entire CU 50m of liability would be adjusted for changes in the hedged interest rate risk.

In this scenario, the hedge ratio is unbalanced as the real purpose of the hedging relationship is to achieve fair value accounting (related to changes in interest rate risk) for CU 49m of the liability. The hedge ratio used for hedge accounting purposes would have to be different (likely close to 1:1).

The above examples are of course extreme scenarios and instances of unbalanced hedge designations are likely to be rare; IFRS 9 does not require an entity to designate a 'perfect hedge'. For instance, if the hedging instrument is only available in multiples of 25 metric tonnes as the standard contract size, an imbalance due to using, say, 400 metric tonnes nominal value of hedging instrument to hedge 409 metric tonnes of forecast purchases, would not be regarded as resulting in an outcome 'that would be inconsistent with the purpose of hedge accounting' and so would meet the qualifying criteria. *[IFRS 9.B6.4.11(b)]*.

The subsequent prospective effectiveness assessment requires consideration as to whether the accounting hedge ratio is still appropriate, or indeed whether a change is required. This 'rebalancing' of a live hedge relationship is a new concept introduced within IFRS 9 (see 6.2 below for further details).

5.5 Designating 'proxy hedges'

The objective of the standard is 'to represent, in the financial statements, the effect of an entity's risk management activities'. *[IFRS 9.6.1.1]*. However, this does not mean that an entity can only designate hedging relationships that exactly mirror its risk management activities. The Basis for Conclusions notes that, in some circumstances, the designation for hedge accounting purposes is inevitably not the same as an entity's risk management view of its hedging, but that the designation reflects risk management in that it relates to the same type of risk that is being managed and the instruments used for this purpose. The IASB refer to this situation as 'proxy hedging' (i.e. designations that do not exactly represent the actual risk management). In redeliberating the September 2012 draft standard, the Board decided that proxy hedging is permitted, provided the designation is directionally consistent with the actual risk management activities.[12] *[IFRS 9.BC6.97-BC6.101]*. The examples below are common proxy hedging designations:

Example 53.27: Common proxy hedging designations

Net position cash flow hedging

An entity holds Australian Dollar (AUD) 2m of variable rate loan assets and AUD 10m of variable rate borrowings. The treasurer is hedging the cash flow risk exposure on the net position of AUD 8m, by entering into a pay fixed/receive variable interest rate swap (IRS) with a nominal amount of AUD 8m. Rather than designate the net AUD 8m as the hedged item, the entity designates the IRS in a hedge of variable rate interest payments on a portion of AUD 8m of its AUD 10m borrowing.

Macro hedging strategies

Permitting proxy hedging is of particular relevance for banks wishing to apply macro cash flow hedging strategies (see Chapter 52 at 6). Typically, banks manage the interest margin risk resulting from fixed-floating mismatches of financial assets and financial liabilities held at amortised cost on their banking books. Assume the assets are floating rate and the liabilities are fixed rate. The fixed-floating mismatches are offset by entering into receive fixed/pay variable interest rate swaps. There is no hedge accounting model that perfectly accommodates such hedges of the interest margin. Consequently, banks are forced to use either fair value hedge accounting for the liabilities or cash flow hedge accounting for the assets, although the actual risk management activity is neither to hedge fair values nor cash flows, but to hedge the interest margin. Both cash flow hedge accounting and fair value hedge accounting would be directionally consistent with the risk management activity and so acceptable as proxy hedging designations.

IFRS 9 limits the designation of net positions in cash flow hedges to hedges of foreign exchange risk (see 3.6.3 above). *[IFRS 9.6.6.1(c)]*. However, in practice, entities often hedge other types of risk on a net cash flow basis. Such entities could still designate the net position as a gross designation. *[IFRS 9 BC6.100(a)]*.

6 SUBSEQUENT ASSESSMENT OF EFFECTIVENESS, REBALANCING AND DISCONTINUATION

6.1 Assessment of effectiveness

Under IFRS 9 there is no retrospective effectiveness assessment, and the IAS 39 quantitative assessment using the 80%-125% 'bright lines' has been removed. It is important, however, to stress that, unchanged from IAS 39, an entity still has to measure and recognise any ineffectiveness that has actually occurred, as described in Chapter 52 at 4.1.1 and 4.2.1. Also, the elimination of a retrospective effectiveness assessment does not mean that hedge accounting continues irrespective of how effective the hedge turns out to be. A prospective effectiveness assessment is still required on an ongoing basis, in a similar manner as at the inception of the hedging relationship (see 5.1 above) and, as a minimum, at each reporting date. *[IFRS 9.B6.4.12]*.

Figure 53.2: Effectiveness assessment and rebalancing

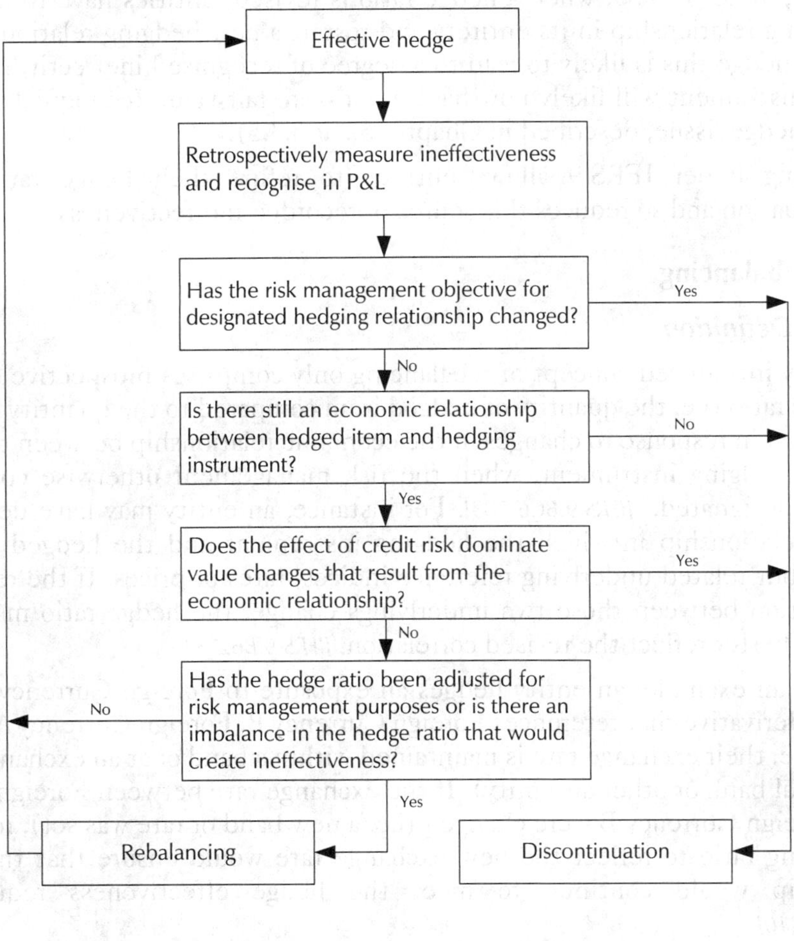

Chapter 53

Each accounting period an entity first has to assess whether the risk management objective for the hedging relationship has changed. A change in risk management objective is a matter of fact that triggers discontinuation. Discontinuation of hedging relationships is discussed at 6.3 below.

An entity would also have to discontinue hedge accounting if it turns out that there is no longer an economic relationship. This makes sense as whether there is an economic relationship is a matter of fact that cannot be altered by adjusting the hedge ratio. The same is true for the impact of credit risk; if credit risk is now dominating the hedging relationship, then the entity has to discontinue hedge accounting. *[IFRS 9.6.5.6]*.

But the hedge ratio may need to be adjusted if it turns out that the hedged item and hedging instrument do not move in relation to each other as expected. The entity has to assess whether it expects this to continue to be the case going forward. If so, the entity is required to 'rebalance' the hedge ratio to reflect the change in the relationship between the underlyings. Rebalancing refers to the adjustments made to the designated quantities of the hedged item or hedging instrument of an already existing hedging relationship for the purpose of maintaining the a hedge ratio that complies with the hedge effectiveness requirements. *[IFRS 9.B6.5.7]*.

Currently, under IAS 39, when a hedge ratio is revised, entities have to discontinue the hedging relationship in its entirety and restart a new hedging relationship. For a cash flow hedge this is likely to lead to a degree of recognised ineffectiveness, as the hedging instrument will likely now have a non-zero fair value (colloquially known as the 'late hedge' issue, described in Chapter 52 at 5.3.5).

Rebalancing under IFRS 9 allows entities to refine their hedge ratio without discontinuation and so reduces this source of recorded ineffectiveness.

6.2 Rebalancing

6.2.1 Definition

The newly introduced concept of rebalancing only comprises prospective changes to the hedge ratio (i.e. the quantity of hedged item compared to the quantity of hedging instrument) in response to changes in the economic relationship between the hedged item and hedging instrument, when the risk management otherwise continues as originally designated. *[IFRS 9.BC6.303]*. For instance, an entity may have designated a hedging relationship in which the hedging instrument and the hedged item have different but related underlying reference indices, rates or prices. If the relationship or correlation between those two underlyings change, the hedge ratio may need to change to better reflect the revised correlation. *[IFRS 9.B6.5.9]*.

By way of an example; an entity hedges an exposure to Foreign Currency A using a currency derivative that references Foreign Currency B. Foreign Currency A and B are pegged (i.e. their exchange rate is maintained within a band or at an exchange rate set by a central bank or other authority). If the exchange rate between Foreign Currency A and Foreign Currency B were changed (i.e. a new band or rate was set), rebalancing the hedging ratio to reflect the new exchange rate would ensure that the hedging relationship would continue to meet the hedge effectiveness requirements. *[IFRS 9.B6.5.10]*.

Any other changes made to the quantities of the hedged item or hedging instrument, for instance, a reduction in the quantity of the hedged item because some cash flows are no longer highly probable, would not be rebalancing. Such other changes to the designated quantities would need to be treated as a partial discontinuation if the entity reduces the extent to which it hedges, and a new designation of a hedging relationship if the entity increases it. *[IFRS 9.B6.5.7]*.

Changes that risk managers may make to improve hedge effectiveness but that do not alter the quantities of the hedged item or the hedging instrument are not rebalancing either. An example of such a change is the transaction of derivatives related to a risk that was not considered in the original hedge relationship.

Therefore, rebalancing is only relevant if there is basis risk between the hedged item and the hedging instrument. Basis risk, in the context of hedge accounting, refers to any difference in price sensitivity of the underlyings of the hedging instrument and the hedged item. The existence of basis risk in a hedge relationship usually results in a degree of hedge ineffectiveness. For example, hedging a cotton purchase in India with NYMEX cotton futures contracts is likely to result in some ineffectiveness, as the hedged item and the hedging instrument do not share exactly the same underlying price. Rebalancing only affects the expected relative sensitivity between the hedged item and the hedging instrument going forward, as ineffectiveness from past changes in the sensitivity will have already been recognised in profit or loss.

The following example provides some indications as to how to distinguish rebalancing from other changes to a hedge relationship:

Example 53.28: Rebalancing

Fact pattern 1

An entity is exposed to price changes in commodity A which is not widely traded as a derivative. The entity has proven that there is an economic relationship between commodity A and B and commodity B is widely traded as a derivative. In that case, the entity may use commodity B derivatives to hedge the price risk in commodity A. An initial hedge ratio of 1:1.1 is based on the expected relationship between the prices of commodity A and commodity B. The relationship subsequently changes such that a ratio of 1:1.15 is expected to be more effective.

The entity can account for the changes in the hedging relationship as rebalancing because the difference between the prices is caused by basis risk.

Fact pattern 2

An entity swaps a base rate floating rate loan into a fixed interest rate using a pay LIBOR receive fixed swap. At inception, the entity is able to prove that there is an economic relationship between the base rate and LIBOR and designates the swap and the loan in a cash flow hedge, although it expects some level of ineffectiveness. Similar to fact pattern 1, the entity may use rebalancing to account for changes in the basis spread between the base rate and LIBOR.

However, the entity subsequently transacts a LIBOR versus base rate swap in order to eliminate the basis risk. The accounting consequences would depend on the reason for doing so and here we consider two scenarios:

a) The entity can no longer prove that there is an economic relationship between the base rate and LIBOR.

b) The entity can still prove that there is an economic relationship between the base rate and LIBOR, but no longer wishes to suffer the resultant ineffectiveness arising from the basis risk.

In scenario a), the hedging relationship no longer meets the eligibility criteria and needs to be discontinued, as there is no longer an economic relationship between the hedged item and the hedging instrument. The entity cannot use rebalancing to avoid discontinuation because the hedge no longer meets the qualifying criteria.

In scenario b), the entity tries to avoid ineffectiveness by contracting another hedging instrument. Arguably, the entity could continue with the original designation and account for the LIBOR versus base rate swap as a derivative measured at fair value through profit or loss. However, given that the entity seeks to avoid ineffectiveness, it might want to apply hedge accounting to the base rate swap as well. If the entity wants to include the LIBOR versus base rate swap in the original hedging relationship, it would represent a change in the documented risk management objective which requires discontinuation of the existing and re-designation of a new hedging relationship. Alternatively, the entity may be able to designate the base rate swap as hedging the aggregated exposure of the based rate floating rate loan and pay LIBOR interest rate swap (see 3.3 above).

Fact pattern 3

An entity with US dollars as its functional currency designated a fix rate loan denominated in EUR and a USD dollars /Euro forward exchange contract in a cash flow hedge. Subsequently, the borrower suffers significant financial difficulties and the entity only expects to receive 90% of the contractual cash flows on the loan.

The entity cannot apply rebalancing because the changes in the cash flows of the hedged item are not caused by basis risk but by credit risk. Instead, the entity is required to assess whether credit risk dominates the fair value changes of the hedged item in which case the hedging relationship needs to be discontinued (see 5.3 above). The entity might, however, still adjust the amount of the hedging instrument and treat this as a partial dedesignation (see 6.3 below).

Fact pattern 4

An airline with a functional currency of Swiss francs enters into a firm commitment to purchase ten new wide-bodied airplanes in two years' time. The contract to purchase those airplanes is denominated in US dollars and the airline enters into a forward exchange contract to hedge the foreign currency exposure. There is no embedded foreign currency derivative to bifurcate, as sales of wide-bodied aircrafts appear to be routinely denominated in US dollars around the world (see Chapter 44 at 5.2.1.B). The airline designates the firm commitment and the derivative in a fair value hedge. Six months into the contract, the aircraft manufacturer informs the airline that it has suffered significant delays in production and that the aircrafts will not be delivered in two years as originally planned but in three years. Payment is due when the airplanes are delivered.

The delay in payment may result in some ineffectiveness as the forward exchange and discounting rates for two years and three years are likely to be different. However, the airline could not avoid this ineffectiveness by rebalancing, because the ineffectiveness is caused by the timing difference and not basis risk that was present in the original designation.

6.2.2 *Requirement to rebalance*

Whether an entity is required to rebalance a hedging relationship is first and foremost a matter of fact, which is, whether the hedge ratio has changed for risk management purposes. An entity has to rebalance a hedging relationship if that relationship has an unchanged risk management objective but no longer meets the hedge effectiveness requirements regarding the hedge ratio. This will, in effect, be the case if the hedge ratio is no longer the one that is actually used for risk management (see 5.4 above). *[IFRS 9.6.5.5]*.

However, consistent with initial designation, the hedge ratio used for hedge accounting purposes may have to differ from the hedge ratio used for risk management if the latter would result in ineffectiveness that could result in an accounting outcome that would be inconsistent with the purpose of hedge accounting. *[IFRS 9.B6.5.14]*.

IFRS 9 clarifies that 'not every change in the extent of offset between the hedging instrument and the hedged item constitutes a change in the relationship' that requires rebalancing. For example, hedge ineffectiveness arising from a fluctuation around an otherwise valid hedge ratio cannot be reduced by adjusting the hedge ratio. *[IFRS 9.B6.5.11, B6.5.12]*. A trend in the amount of ineffectiveness on the other hand might suggest that retaining the hedge ratio would result in increased ineffectiveness going forward. This guidance in IFRS 9 further clarifies that an accounting outcome that would be inconsistent with the purpose of hedge accounting as the result of failing to adjust the hedge ratio for risk management purposes, would not meet the qualifying criteria for hedge accounting. This simply means that the qualifying criteria treat inappropriate hedge ratios in the same way, irrespective of whether they were achieved by acting (inappropriate designation) or failure to act (by not adjusting a designation that has become inappropriate). *[IFRS 9.B6.5.13]*.

Accordingly, in order to continue to apply hedge accounting, an entity must rebalance the hedge ratio if required for accounting purposes as part of the prospective effectiveness assessment. IFRS 9 acknowledges that such an assessment is usually inherent in effective risk management monitoring, and so in many cases existing risk management process may be sufficient to determine whether accounting rebalancing is required or not. *[IFRS 9 BC6.301]*.

IFRS 9 does not specify the nature of the assessment to determine if rebalancing is required. Therefore, the nature of the assessment requires judgment based on the facts and circumstances of the hedge relationship. For example, a hedge involving two underlyings with correlation that has been historically volatile would likely require more robust analysis than two underlyings that have shown consistent correlation over many years. As another example, a relationship that has been under-hedging for four consecutive quarters would likely require more robust analysis than a relationship constantly moving to and from an over- and under-hedge position.

Regardless of the chosen assessment methodology, it is clear that rebalancing is not a mathematical optimization exercise. Accordingly hedges are not required to be perfectly effective, but judgement will be required to determine if rebalancing is necessary or not. *[IFRS 9 BC6.310]*. Therefore at each reporting date entities should document the work performed to determine whether rebalancing was necessary or not, and any judgements made.

6.2.3 *Mechanics of rebalancing*

Rebalancing can be achieved by:

- increasing the volume of the hedged item;
- increasing the volume of the hedging instrument;
- decreasing the volume of the hedged item; or
- decreasing the volume of the hedging instrument. *[IFRS 9.B6.5.16]*.

Decreasing the volume of the hedging instrument or hedged item does not mean that the respective transactions or items no longer exist or are no longer expected to occur. As demonstrated in Example 53.29 below, rebalancing only changes what is designated in the particular hedging relationship.

Example 53.29: Rebalancing the hedge ratio by decreasing the volume of the hedging instrument

1 January

An entity expects to purchase 1m barrels of West Texas Intermediate (WTI) crude oil in 12 months. The entity designates a futures contract of 1.05m barrels of Brent crude oil in a cash flow hedge to hedge the highly probable forecast purchase of 1m barrels of WTI crude oil (hedge ratio of 1.05:1).

30 June

At 30 June, the cumulative change in the value of the hedged item is CU 200, while the cumulative change in the fair value of the hedging instrument is CU 229.

The entity would account for the hedging relationship as follows:

	CU	CU
Hedging gain/loss – other comprehensive income	200	
Hedge ineffectiveness	29	
Derivatives – hedging instruments		229

The treasurer of the entity is very sensitive to ineffectiveness and therefore considers rebalancing the hedging relationship.

The analysis of the treasurer shows that the sensitivity of Brent crude oil to WTI crude oil prices was not as expected. Going forward, the treasurer expects a different relationship between the two benchmark prices and decides to reset the hedge ratio to 0.98:1.

Rebalancing on 30 June

The treasurer can either designate more WTI exposure or de-designate part of the hedging instrument. The entity decides to do the latter, that is, discontinue hedge accounting for 0.07m barrels of Brent crude oil derivatives.

Of the total of 1.05m barrels of Brent derivative, 0.07m are no longer part of the hedging relationship. Therefore, the entity needs to reclassify 7/105 (or 6.7%) of the hedging instrument in the statement of financial position to a held for trading derivative, measured at fair value through profit or loss. The hedge documentation is updated accordingly.

The entity accounts for the rebalancing as follows:

	CU	CU
Derivatives – hedging instruments	15	
Derivatives – trading		15

To reflect that a part of the derivative is no longer part of a hedging relationship.

In Example 53.29 above, the entity no longer needs to hold this portion of the derivative any longer for hedging purposes and could, therefore, close it out. If the entity chooses to keep that portion of the derivative it will of course continue to result in volatility in the profit or loss, although it would no longer be presented as hedge ineffectiveness. As mentioned, the entity could have also rebalanced by designating more WTI exposure (assuming that the higher level of exposure is highly probable of occurring). In that case, there would not be any immediate accounting entries; the entity would simply designate more WTI exposure. However, the ongoing accounting can be more complex, which is discussed in more detail below. The same would be true when rebalancing by increasing the volume of hedging instrument, in which case the entity would simply designate more of the same hedging instruments within the hedge relationship. This could be achieved either by entering into additional hedging instruments via a market transaction, or designating existing derivatives that are not currently designated within a hedge relationship. *[IFRS 9.B6.5.16-20]*.

Example 53.30: Rebalancing the hedge ratio by decreasing the volume of hedged item

1 April

An entity has highly probable forecast purchases of diesel over the next 12 months. The entity expects to get monthly deliveries of 10,000 metric tonnes at the local market price. The entity designates a futures contract referenced to the Platts Diesel D2 price with a nominal amount of 9,500 metric tonnes in a cash flow hedge, to hedge 10,000 metric tonnes of highly probable diesel purchases in September (giving a hedge ratio of 1:0.95).

30 June

At 30 June, the cumulative change in the value of hedged item is CU 820, while the cumulative change in the fair value of hedging instrument is CU 650.

The entity would account for the hedging relationship as follows:

	CU	CU
Hedging reserve – other comprehensive income	650	
Derivatives – hedging instruments		650

To account for the fair value change of the hedging instrument.

Despite the hedge only being 79% effective, no hedging ineffectiveness is recorded as a result of the 'lower of test' in the standard. *[IFRS 9.6.5.11(a)]*. As per that paragraph, the amount accumulated in other comprehensive income has to be the lower of:

i) the cumulative gain or loss on the hedging instrument; and

ii) the cumulative change in fair value of the hedged item, with any remaining gain or loss on the hedging instrument being recorded in profit or loss.

Based on an analysis, the entity now believes that the appropriate hedge ratio going forward is 1:1.05. Consequently, the entity can either increase the volume of hedging instrument or decrease the volume of hedged item. Based on a cost-benefit analysis the entity decides to reduce the volume of hedged item by 953 metric tonnes.

Rebalancing on 30 June

Rebalancing a hedge ratio by decreasing the volume of hedged item is considered a partial discontinuation of the hedging relationship. *[IFRS 9.B6.5.27]*. The entity is discontinuing 952 (10,000 – (9,500/1.05) = 952) metric tonnes of diesel purchases while 9,048 metric tonnes of forecast purchases remain in the hedging relationship. The hedge documentation is updated accordingly. No accounting entry is required (however, the entity would have to retain the information that 952 metric tonnes of diesel were the hedged item for some part of the total life of the hedging relationship and which amount in the cash flow hedge reserve relates to this quantity of diesel).

Even though the standard allows adjusting either the quantity of hedging instrument or the quantity of the hedged item, when rebalancing, entities should consider that adjusting the hedged item will be operationally more complex than adjusting the hedging instrument because of the need to track the history of different quantities that were designated during the term of the hedging relationship. For example, if a quantity of 10 tonnes of a hedged item were added to increase the quantity of hedged item and later deducted to decrease it, those 10 tonnes would have been part of the hedged item for only a part of the life of the hedging relationship. However, any cash flow hedge adjustment would still, in part, relate to that quantity, even though it is not currently part of a cash flow hedge. Therefore ongoing tracking of the 10 tonnes is

Chapter 53

required to ensure appropriate recycling of the amounts previously taken to the cash flow hedge reserve. This can get more complex in situations in which the hedging relationship needs frequent rebalancing, if not all hedged transactions occur at the same time, or in conjunction with the cost formulas used for the measurement of the cost of inventory (for example a first in first out formula) (see Chapter 22 at 3.2). In addition, risk management would normally adjust the quantity of the designated hedging instruments when rebalancing, since the hedged exposure is normally the 'given' and drives what hedges are needed.

When rebalancing a hedging relationship, an entity must update its analysis of the sources of ineffectiveness in the hedge documentation. *[IFRS 9 B6.5.21]*.

6.3 Discontinuation

The accounting for discontinuation of a hedge relationship is unchanged from IAS 39 (see Chapter 52 at 4.1.3 and 4.2.3). As already discussed above, an entity would have to discontinue hedge accounting if the qualification criteria are no longer met. *[IFRS 9.6.5.6]*. As also mentioned at 6.1 above, this includes if the risk management objective for the hedging relationship has changed. However, these are the only circumstances when discontinuation occurs as voluntary discontinuation is no longer permitted under IFRS 9.

In an important change to IAS 39, IFRS 9 introduces partial discontinuation of hedge accounting, which means that hedge accounting continues for the remaining part of the hedging relationship. *[IFRS 9.6.5.6]*.

The table below summarises the main scenarios resulting in either full or partial discontinuation:

Scenario	Discontinuation
The risk management objective has changed	Full or partial
There is no longer an economic relationship between the hedged item and the hedging instrument	Full
The effect of credit risk dominates the value changes of the hedging relationship	Full
As part of rebalancing, the volume of the hedged item or the hedging instrument is reduced	Partial
The hedging instrument expires	Full
The hedging instrument is (in full or in part) sold, terminated or exercised	Full or partial
The hedged item (or part of it) no longer exists or is no longer highly probable	Full or partial

The application guidance in IFRS 9 contains three examples elaborating what constitutes a change in risk management objective. *[IFRS 9.B6.5.24]*. We believe that a change in risk management objective has to be a matter of fact that can be observed in the entity's actual risk management. The examples below, the first of which is derived from the application guidance to IFRS 9, demonstrate how this could be assessed in practice.

Example 53.31: Partial discontinuation as a result of a change in risk management objective

ABC Ltd is currently fully financed with variable rate borrowings (the tables in this example show nominal amounts in millions of Euro (EUR)):

Non-current financial liabilities as of 1 January 20x1	Variable rate	Fixed rate
Variable rate borrowings	100	
Fixed rate borrowings		0
Total	100	0
	100%	0%

Risk management strategy

To maintain between 20% and 40% of long term debt at a fixed rate.

Risk management activity

Consequently, the treasurer of ABC enters into a pay fixed/receive variable interest rate swap (IRS) and designates the IRS in a hedging relationship.

Risk management objective

Use a pay fixed/receive floating interest rate swap with a notional amount of EUR 30m in a cash flow hedge to hedge the interest payments on EUR 30m of the variable rate borrowings in order to maintain 30% of the long term borrowings at fixed rate.

Non-current financial liabilities as of 1 January 20x1	Variable rate	Fixed rate
Variable rate borrowings	100	
Fixed rate borrowings		0
Pay fixed/receive variable interest rate swap	(30)	30
Total	70	30
	70%	30%

On 31 March 20x2, the entity needs further funding and takes advantage of lower interest rates by issuing a EUR 50m fixed rate bond. At the same time, the entity decides to set its fixed rate exposure at 40% of total borrowings, still being within the risk management strategy.

Non-current financial liabilities as of 31 March 20x2	Variable rate	Fixed rate
Variable rate borrowings	100	
Fixed rate borrowings		50
Pay fixed/receive variable interest rate swap	(30)	30
Total	70	80
	47%	53%

It is evident that ABC is no longer within the target range of its risk management strategy. In order to execute the risk management strategy, ABC no longer needs part of its interest rate swap. In other words, the risk management objective for the hedging relationship has changed. Consequently, ABC discontinues EUR 20m of the hedging relationship (a partial discontinuation) and would most likely close out the risk from EUR 20m of the IRS.

Going forward, ABC's debt financing and risk profile will be as follows: *[IFRS 9.B6.5.24]*

Non-current financial liabilities as of 31 March 20x2	Variable rate	Fixed rate
Variable rate borrowings	100	
Fixed rate borrowings		50
Pay fixed/receive floating interest rate swap	(10)	10
Total	90	60
	60%	40%

Chapter 53

The above example only illustrates the outcome of one particular course of action. The entity could also have adjusted its interest rate exposure in a different way in order to remain in the target range for its fixed rate funding, for instance by swapping EUR 20m of the new fixed rate bond into variable rate funding. In that case, instead of discontinuing a part of the already existing cash flow hedge, the entity could have designated a new fair value hedge. The example in the application guidance of the standard is obviously a simplified one. In practice, entities tend to have staggered maturities for different parts of their financing. In such situations it would often be obvious from the maturity of the new interest rate swaps if they are a fair value hedge of the debt or a reduction of the already existing cash flow hedge volume. For example, if the new EUR 50m fixed rate bond is for a longer period than the existing debt and the new interest rate swap is for the same longer period, it would suggest that it is a fair value hedge of the new fixed rate bond instead of a reduction of the cash flow hedge for the already existing debt. Conversely, a reduction of the cash flow hedge volume would be consistent with entering into a new interest rate swap that has the same remaining maturity as the existing interest rate swap and offsets its fair value changes on a part of the notional amount.

Example 53.32: Partial discontinuation of an interest margin hedge

XYZ Bank is holding a combination of fixed and variable rate assets and liabilities on its banking book. For risk management purposes, the bank allocates all the assets and liabilities to time bands based on their contractual maturity. As of 1 January 20x1 the bank holds the following instruments in the 5-year time bucket (the tables in this example show nominal amounts in millions of Euro (EUR)):

Summary of instruments with a 5-year maturity	**Assets: fixed rate**	**Liabilities: fixed rate**	**Assets: variable rate**	**Liabilities: variable rate**
Bonds held			20	
Mortgages	30		10	
Retail loans	30		10	
Client term deposits				(60)
Bonds issued		(30)		(10)
Total	60	(30)	40	(70)
Fixed-variable interest mismatch		30		(30)

The fixed-variable mismatch results in interest margin risk due to changes in interest rates.

Risk management strategy

To eliminate the interest margin risk resulting from fixed-variable interest mismatches.

Risk management activity

In order to achieve the risk management strategy, XYZ Bank enters into a pay fixed/receive variable interest rate swap (IRS) with a notional amount of EUR 30m. For accounting purposes, the bank could either designate the IRS in a cash flow hedge of EUR 30m of specific variable rate liabilities or in a fair value hedge of EUR 30m of specific fixed rate assets. Under the local regulatory requirements, fair value hedges are more favourable for the bank's regulatory capital.

Risk management objective

Using a EUR 30m pay fixed/receive variable IRS in a fair value hedge of EUR 30m of fixed rate retail loans to hedge a fixed-variable interest mismatch on fixed and variable rate assets and liabilities in the 5-year time bucket of XYZ Bank's banking book.

At the beginning of year 20x3, XYZ Bank attracts EUR 10m of client term deposits as a result of a successful marketing campaign. The new term deposits all have a fixed interest rate for a maturity of three years, therefore, matching the (remaining) maturity of the instruments in the above time bucket. The XYZ Bank uses the proceeds from the new term deposits to buy back EUR 10m of variable rate bonds that it has issued. The new situation in the (now) 3-year time bucket is:

Summary of instruments with a 3-year maturity	**Assets: fixed rate**	**Liabilities: fixed rate**	**Assets: variable rate**	**Liabilities: variable rate**
Bonds held			20	
Mortgages	30		10	
Retail loans	30		10	
Client term deposits		(10)		(60)
Bonds issued		(30)		(0)
Total	60	(40)	40	(60)
Fixed-variable interest mismatch	20		(20)	
Pay fixed/receive variable interest rate swap	(30)		30	

As a result of the change in funding, the risk management objective of the hedging relationship has changed. XYZ Bank is over-hedged and needs to discontinue EUR10m of its hedging relationship.

A logical consequence of linking the discontinuation to the risk management objective is that voluntary discontinuations are no longer permitted just for accounting purposes. This change, gave rise to concern among some constituents who argued that, given hedge accounting is optional, voluntary discontinuation should be retained. *[IFRS 9.BC6.324]*.

In our view, entities have often voluntarily discontinued hedge accounting to adjust, for instance, the hedge ratio for a change in the expected relationship between the hedged item and the hedging instrument. Other reasons were because the entity wanted to hedge a secondary risk (i.e. an entity first hedged the commodity price risk in a commodity purchase contract in foreign currency but later decided to hedge the foreign currency risk as well), because the chosen effectiveness method no longer was appropriate, or because some of the hedged cash flows were no longer expected to occur.

This is addressed in IFRS 9 by introducing a new effectiveness assessment, rebalancing, the ability to achieve hedge accounting for aggregated exposures and partial discontinuation. Hence, voluntary discontinuation is no longer needed in such situations.

In its redeliberations, the IASB noted that hedge accounting is an exception to the general accounting principles in IFRS, in order to (better) present in the financial statements a particular risk management objective of a risk management activity. If that risk management objective is unchanged and the qualifying criteria for hedge accounting are still met, a voluntary discontinuation would be inconsistent with the original (valid) reason for applying hedge accounting. The Board believes that hedge accounting, including its discontinuation, should have a meaning and should not be a mere accounting exercise. *[IFRS 9.BC6.327]*. Based on this, the IASB decided not to allow voluntary discontinuation for hedges with unchanged risk management objectives. *[IFRS 9.BC6.331]*.

It is important to note that the risk management objective of an individual hedging relationship can change although the risk management strategy of the entity remains unchanged. *[IFRS 9.BC6.331]*. In fact, in most cases where an entity might wish to voluntarily dedesignate a hedging relationship, this is usually driven by a change in the risk management objective, in which case the entity would actually be required to amend its hedge accounting under IFRS 9. The standard only prohibits voluntary dedesignations when they are only made for accounting purposes.

6.4 Measuring ineffectiveness

IFRS 9 only adds two paragraphs in the application guidance on how to measure ineffectiveness, dealing with the time value of money and hypothetical derivatives. Although intended as a clarification, these two paragraphs might have wider implications for some practices currently used by entities. Except for the matters mentioned in this section, the guidance on measurement of ineffectiveness are the same as under IAS 39 and are covered in Chapter 52 at 4.1.1 and 4.2.1.

6.4.1 *The effect of the time value of money*

Entities have to consider the time value of money when measuring hedge ineffectiveness. This means that an entity has to determine the value of the hedged item on a present value basis (thereby including the effect of the time value of money). *[IFRS 9.B6.5.4].*

The guidance in IFRS 9 does not clarify more than what was (theoretically) already clear under IAS 39 (see Chapter 52 at 5.3.1). In valuation practice, the effect of the time value of money is also included when measuring the fair value of financial instruments. Consequently, it is more than logical to apply the same principle to the hedged item as well.

Example 53.33: Impact of time value of money when measuring ineffectiveness

A manufacturing company in India, having the Indian Rupee as its functional currency, is expecting forecast sales in USD. The company assesses sales of USD 1m per month for the next twelve months to be highly probable and wishes to hedge the related foreign currency exposure. The company also holds a borrowing of USD 20m with a bullet repayment in fourteen months' time. Instead of entering into foreign currency forward contracts, the company designates the US dollar borrowing as a hedging instrument in hedges of the spot risk of the monthly highly probable US dollar sales.

When measuring hedge ineffectiveness, the revaluation of the forecast sales for foreign currency risk would have to be made on a discounted basis (i.e. a present value calculation reflecting the time between the reporting date and the future cash flow date), whereas the revaluation of the hedging instrument would not (as this follows the requirements of IAS 21).

On application of either IFRS 9 or IAS 39 it is possible to designate a spot element of a hedged item if it can be determined to be an eligible risk component (see 3.4 above and Chapter 52 at 2.2.1 and 2.2.2). Whilst a spot designation is relatively common place for both foreign exchange and commodity risk, the need to consider the time value of money for effectiveness purposes for spot designations has been a matter of some debate. The Guidance in Implementing IAS 39 contains an example in which an entity designated changes in the spot element only (see Chapter 52 at 5.3.3). The example indicates that the time value of money is relevant for the assessment of effectiveness even when the spot element is designated in a hedge relationship but, similar to all the other implementation guidance in IAS 39, this example has not been carried forward to IFRS 9. *[IAS 39.IG.F.5.6].*

However, the requirement to calculate ineffectiveness on a present value basis intuitively makes sense in cases where the cash flows of the hedged item and hedging instrument are not aligned. It would seem inappropriate to have no ineffectiveness under a spot designation, for example in the situation described at 4.4 above, where a 7-year financial liability denominated in a foreign currency is used as the hedging instrument for a 12 month forecast sale in that foreign currency.

Currently under IAS 39 there is diversity in practice with respect to the discounting of the spot element for hedge effectiveness measurement purposes. This is perhaps because in many circumstances the effect of discounting the revaluation of the spot element is unlikely to be material. It has been suggested by some that use of a spot designation would override the general principle of IFRS 9 that measurement of ineffectiveness needs to be made on a discounted basis. They argue that the spot element is a specific component, for which any discounting effect is only relevant to the residual forward element which is not part of the hedged risk when the spot element is designated. However, given that the requirement to measure effectiveness on a present value basis appears to be clearer in IFRS 9, combined with the lack of explicit guidance permitting spot designations to be treated differently in this regard, it appears difficult to override the requirements of paragraph B6.5.4.

6.4.2 Hypothetical derivatives for measuring ineffectiveness

Although not specifically addressed in IAS 39, a method commonly used in practice to measure (and assess) ineffectiveness of cash flow hedges is the use of a so-called 'hypothetical derivative'. Although IFRS 9 brings more clarity in this regard, the basic method has not changed compared to IAS 39. The method involves establishing a notional derivative that has terms that match the critical terms of the hedged exposure (normally an interest rate swap or forward contract with no unusual terms and a zero fair value at inception of the hedging relationship). The fair value of the hypothetical derivative is then used to measure the change in the value of the hedged item against which changes in value of the actual hedging instrument are compared, to assess effectiveness and measure ineffectiveness (see Chapter 52 at 5.3.2).

IFRS 9 confirms that use of a hypothetical derivative is one possible way of determining the change in the value of the hedged item when measuring ineffectiveness. However, IFRS 9 also clarifies that a hypothetical derivative has to be a replication of the hedged item and that any different method for determining the change in the value of the hedged item would have to give the same outcome. Consequently, an entity cannot include features in the hypothetical derivative that only exist in the hedging instrument, but not in the hedged item. *[IFRS 9.B6.5.5]*.

What appears to be a logical requirement may have wider implications for cash flow hedges than many would have expected. IFRS 9 is clear that the hypothetical derivative is supposed to represent the hedged item and not the 'perfect hedge'. In other words, an entity cannot simply assume no ineffectiveness for a cash flow hedge because the principal terms of the hedging instrument exactly match the principal terms of a hedged item, if there are differences in other features of the hedging instrument and the hedged item.

For example, IFRS 13 requires an entity to reflect both the counterparty's credit risk and the entity's own credit risk when determining the fair value of a derivative. The counterparty credit risk of a derivative designated in a hedging relationship is likely to be different from the counterparty credit risk identified in the hedged item. This difference in credit risk would result in some ineffectiveness (see 5.3 above and Chapter 52 at 5.3.2 and 5.3.4). Paragraph B6.5.5 of IFRS 9 is clear that, when using a hypothetical derivative for measuring ineffectiveness in a cash flow hedge, the counterparty credit risk on the hedging instrument could not be deemed to equally be a feature also present in the hedged item. *[IFRS 9.B6.5.5]*. For example, if the hedged item is a highly probable forecast transaction it may not involve any credit risk at all, so that there is no offset for any credit risk affecting the fair value of the hedging instrument. This would give rise to some ineffectiveness recorded in profit or loss.

If the credit risk of the hedged item is excluded from the hedge relationship then, unless any change in the credit risk of the hedged item either dominates the value changes in the hedge relationship or results in forecast hedged cash flows no longer being highly probable, any change in the credit risk should not affect the hedge relationship and its associated effectiveness. However, as noted above, changes in the credit risk of the hedging instrument may well cause ineffectiveness, as the credit risk of the hedging instrument cannot be excluded from the hedge relationship.

Example 53.34: Impact on ineffectiveness of changes in credit risk in the hedged item when the hedged risk is a benchmark component

Entity A has issued floating rate debt, paying a benchmark floating rate plus a credit spread of 1%. Entity A also transacts a pay fixed, receive benchmark interest rate swap in order to eliminate variability in cash flows from changes in the benchmark rate. The entity designates this as a hedge of the benchmark component of the issued debt and excludes credit risk on the debt from the hedge relationship. Accordingly, if subsequently Entity A's credit rating changes such that the current credit spread is now 0.95%, this will have no impact on the change in value of the hedged item for the purposes of measuring ineffectiveness, as credit risk in the hedged item has been excluded from the hedge relationship. Conversely, if there is a change in the credit risk with respect to the interest rate swap (either that of the counterparty or the entity itself), resulting in a change in the fair value of the interest rate swap, this would affect the measurement of hedge ineffectiveness. The credit risk associated with the interest rate swap includes both counterparty and own credit risk (see Chapter 52 at 5.3.4).

As a consequence of the guidance in B6.5.5 a (maybe unexpected) source of ineffectiveness is the discount rate used for measuring the fair value of cash collateralised interest rate swaps (IRS). Historically, the fair values of interest rate swaps have been calculated using LIBOR-based discount rates. As per its definition, LIBOR is the average rate at which the reference banks can fund *unsecured* cash in the interbank market for a given currency and maturity.[13] However, the use of LIBOR as the standard discount rate ignores the fact that many derivative transactions are now collateralised and have therefore a lower credit risk than LIBOR would suggest. For cash-collateralised trades, a more relevant discount rate is an overnight rate rather than LIBOR. Overnight index swaps (OIS) are interest rate swaps where the floating leg is linked to a benchmark interest rate for overnight unsecured lending. OIS rates much better reflect the credit risk of cash collateralised IRS.

When measuring the fair value of cash-collateralised LIBOR indexed interest rate swap, an entity would have to use a LIBOR-based forward curve to determine the future floating cash flows, but these are then discounted using an OIS swap curve. This would result in a different fair value compared to a non-collateralised IRS for which both the forward rates and the discount rates are derived from the LIBOR swap curve. The significance of this is that when, for example, a collateralised LIBOR-base IRS is used as the designated hedging instrument in a fair value hedge of a fixed rate bond for changes in LIBOR, this will likely lead to recorded hedge ineffectiveness. This is because the calculation of the change in fair value of the bond for hedge accounting purposes will be based on a discount rate that includes the credit risk associated with the hedged risk (i.e. LIBOR), whereas the hedging IRS will be discounted at an OIS rate.

The resulting ineffectiveness is sometimes referred to as the 'multi curve issue' (see also Chapter 52 at 5.3.4.A). For cash flow hedges, the situation is less clear under IAS 39. For example, a collateralised IRS is used to hedge the variability of cash flows of a variable rate bond due to changes in LIBOR. Consequentially, the IRS is designated as the hedging instrument in a cash flow hedge of the variable rate bond. The question arises which credit risk should be considered when the 'hypothetical derivative' is set up. However, by saying that 'the hypothetical derivative replicates the hedged item' IFRS 9 can be read to suggest that the 'hypothetical derivative' should be valued using a discount rate that represents the credit risk associated with the hedged risk. If so, the appropriate discount rate would be LIBOR. *[IFRS 9.B6.5.5]*. This is an area where we expect practice will emerge. Historically, the difference between LIBOR and OIS rates has been only a few basis points. However, the basis differential widened significantly during the financial crisis and is not expected to revert in the foreseeable future.

For cash-collateralised derivatives, both parties to the contract would have equal collateral requirements, significantly reducing the credit risk of both parties to the contract. This would improve the economic effectiveness of a hedging relationship while at the same time, may also result in more accounting ineffectiveness.

Another example of when the features of the hedging instrument and the hedging item could differ is when an entity hedges a debt instrument denominated in a foreign currency in a cash flow hedge (irrespective of whether it is fixed-rate or variable-rate debt). When using a hypothetical derivative to calculate ineffectiveness, the hypothetical derivative cannot simply impute a charge for exchanging different currencies (i.e. the foreign currency basis spread) even though actual derivatives (for example, cross-currency interest rate swaps) under which different currencies are exchanged might include such a charge. *[IFRS 9.B6.5.5]*. Although cross-currency interest rate swaps are used to highlight the fact that foreign currency basis spreads should not be replicated in hypothetical derivatives, this issue is also likely to arise in other foreign exchange contacts settled in the future. To address this, the IASB introduced the possibility to account for the foreign currency basis spread as a cost of hedging (see 7.2.2 below).

7 ACCOUNTING FOR THE COSTS OF HEDGING

Currently under IAS 39, entities can designate the intrinsic value of an option or the spot element of a forward contract (see Chapter 52 at 2.1.4.A and 2.1.4.B). When doing so, the changes in fair value of the time value of the option or the forward points are accounted for in profit or loss, therefore resulting in volatility. This was criticised by many constituents as they see the time value or forward points as an unavoidable cost of hedging that should be accounted for accordingly. In response to these concerns, the IFRS 9 hedging model contains a new accounting requirement when only the intrinsic value or the spot element is designated in the hedge relationship. All the fluctuation in the fair value of the time value or forward points over time is recorded in other comprehensive income instead of affecting profit or loss immediately. Although the cost of hedging will ultimately be recognised in profit or loss, this will be in a manner consistent with the risk management activity. This new treatment also applies to foreign currency basis spreads.

7.1 Time value of options

7.1.1 *General requirements*

The fair value of an option consists of its intrinsic value and its time value. Unchanged from IAS 39, an entity can either designate an option as a hedging instrument in its entirety, or it can separate the intrinsic value and the time value and designate only the intrinsic value. *[IFRS 9.6.2.4(a)]*.

Under IAS 39, if the option is designated in its entirety as a hedge of a non-option item, changes in the portion of the fair value attributable to the option time value result in ineffectiveness. This is because only changes in the intrinsic value of the option will provide offset to the fair value changes attributable to the hedged risk (the situation is different if the hedged item also includes optionality, see 4.1 above, or if a delta-neutral hedging strategy is applied, see Chapter 52 at 5.1.2). Depending on the level of ineffectiveness, an entity might even not pass the prospective effectiveness assessment or be forced to discontinue hedge accounting as a result of changes in the time value.

Alternatively, when designating the intrinsic value of the option only, the time value has to be accounted for at fair value through profit or loss, thus, also resulting in potentially significant profit or loss volatility, albeit without the risk of failing the effectiveness assessment. In either case, the change in the time value will be recognised in profit or loss (see also Chapter 52 at 2.1.4.A).

From a risk management perspective, entities typically consider the premium paid on an option (which, on inception, is often only time value) as a cost of hedging rather than a trading position. Economically, the time value could be considered as a premium for protection against risk (i.e. an 'insurance premium'). *[IFRS 9.BC6.387]*. IFRS 9 does not change how an option is designated in a hedging relationship (i.e. whether in its entirety or the intrinsic value only). However, the IASB has acknowledged these concerns and introduced a new accounting treatment for changes in the fair value of the time value if only the intrinsic value is designated in the hedging relationship. It is worth noting that this treatment is not an accounting policy choice, as the treatment must be applied for all hedge relationships for which only the intrinsic value of the hedging instrument is designated within the hedge relationship.

Changes in the fair value of the time value of options to the extent that they relate to the hedged item, are first recognised in other comprehensive income (OCI). The subsequent treatment depends on the nature of the hedged transaction. The standard differentiates between transaction related hedged items and time-period related hedged items: *[IFRS 9.6.5.15, B6.5.29]*

- Transaction related hedged item: the time value of an option used to hedge such an item has the character of part of the cost of the transaction. An example would be a hedge of a forecast commodity purchase.

  The amount that is accumulated in OCI is removed similarly to amounts accumulated in the cash flow hedge reserve (see 8.1 below), i.e. if the hedged transaction subsequently results in the recognition of a non-financial item, the amount becomes a 'basis adjustment', otherwise the amount is reclassified to profit or loss in the same period or periods during which the hedged cash flows affect profit or loss.

- Time-period related hedged item: the time value of an option used to hedge such an item has the character of the cost of protection against a risk over a particular period of time. An example would be a hedge of commodity inventory over a six month period.

  The amount that will be accumulated in OCI is amortised on a systematic and rational basis to profit or loss as a reclassification adjustment. The amortisation period is the period during which the hedge adjustment for the option's intrinsic value could affect profit or loss (or other comprehensive income if the option is designated as a hedge of an equity instrument accounted for at fair value through other comprehensive income).

The distinction between transaction related hedged items and time-period related hedged items reflects that the accounting for the time value of the option should follow general IFRS principles for how to account for payments that are akin to insurance premiums (the 'insurance premium view' mentioned above). So, in making the distinction, an entity needs to consider how the accounting for the hedged item will eventually affect profit or loss.

If the hedged item later results in a transaction for which the transactions costs are accounted for as part of a one-off event (like a purchase or a sale of an item), the option's time value relates to a transaction related hedged item. Examples are hedges of forecast purchases of inventory or property, plant and equipment, and forecast sales, as well as purchases or sales resulting from firm commitments.

If the hedged item later results in protection against risk for a particular period that does not involve a transaction for which the transactions costs are accounted for as part of a one-off event, the option's time value relates to a time-period related hedged item. Examples are hedges of interest expense or income in particular periods, already existing inventory hedged for fair value changes or a hedge of a net investment in a foreign operation. In the case of a forward starting interest rate option, the time value would be amortised over the interest periods that the option covers (i.e. the amortisation period would exclude the initial part of the option's life). *[IFRS 9.B6.5.30]*.

It is important to note that because this accounting for 'costs of hedging' only applies if the time value of the option is excluded from the designation of the hedging relationship, the amounts deferred in accumulated other comprehensive income are not part of the cash flow hedge reserve but instead a different component of equity. The cash flow hedge reserve only includes amounts that are gains or losses on hedging instruments that are determined to be an effective hedge (i.e. amounts that are included in the designation of a hedging relationship).

By default, the time value will be zero at expiry of an option contract. For a transaction related hedged item, recognising the fair value changes of the time value in OCI means that on expiry, the time value that existed at designation will have accumulated in OCI. Once the hedged transaction happens, the accounting for the accumulated time value follows the accounting for any changes in fair value of the intrinsic value of the option. The latter will also accumulate in OCI, but as part of the cash flow hedge reserve. *[IFRS 9.6.5.15]*.

If hedge accounting is discontinued for a time-period related hedge relationship for which the cost of hedging treatment has been applied to the time value of the hedging option, the net amount (i.e. including cumulative amortisation) that has been accumulated in OCI must be immediately reclassified to profit or loss. This appears to be the case whether or not the hedged item is still expected to occur. *[IFRS 9.6.5.15(c), BC6.399]*. In contracts there is no equivalent guidance for discontinuation of transaction related hedges when the transaction is still expected to take place, and so there does not seem to be a need to reclassify the net amount accumulated in OCI immediately to profit or loss in that scenario, although this is an area of uncertainty given the standard as drafted.

Example 53.35: Hedging the purchase of equipment (transaction related)

In the first quarter of a year, a manufacturing entity plans to purchase a new machine for its manufacturing process. Delivery of the machine is expected in the third quarter and the purchase price will be Swedish Krona (SEK) 5m. The entity has the Norwegian Krone (NOK) as its functional currency and, therefore, is exposed to foreign currency risk on this forecast transaction. The entity buys a call option to purchase SEK 5m, as it wishes to hedge the downside risk only. The terms of the option match the terms of the forecast transaction. The entity designates only the intrinsic value of the call option in a cash flow hedge of the highly probable forecast purchase of the machine.

At inception, the time value of the option amounts to NOK 30,000. The time value of the option amounts to NOK 16,000 at the end of the first quarter, NOK 7,000 at the end of the second quarter and zero at maturity.

Applying the IFRS 9 accounting requirements to the time value of the option results in the following movement within other comprehensive income (OCI), specifically the reserve within equity for accumulating amounts in relation to the time value of options associated with transaction related hedged items:

(All amounts in NOK thousands)	**Q1**	**Q2**	**Q3**
Reserve at beginning of quarter	–	(14)	(23)
Change in time value of option	(14)	(9)	(7)
Basis adjustment to machine			30
Reserve at end of quarter	(14)	(23)	–
Effect on OCI for the period	(14)	(9)	23

For time-period related hedged items, the standard does not prescribe what 'on a systematic and rational basis' means in the context of amortising the time value from OCI to profit or loss. We believe a straight-line amortisation to be appropriate in most cases.

Example 53.36: Hedging interest rate risk of a bond (time period related) (1)

An entity issues a seven-year floating rate bond and wishes to protect itself against increases in the interest expense for the first two years. Therefore, the entity purchases an interest rate cap with a maturity of two years. Only the intrinsic value of the cap is designated as a hedging instrument in a cash flow hedge.

The time value on designation is CU 20, which is amortised to profit or loss on a straight-line basis over the protection period (i.e. the first two years). The time value of the option amounts to CU 13 at the end of the first year and zero at maturity.

Applying the IFRS 9 accounting requirements to the time value of the option results in the following movement within other comprehensive income (OCI), specifically the reserve within equity for accumulating amounts in relation to the time value of options associated with time-period related hedged items:

	Year 1	Year 2
Reserve at beginning of year	–	3
Change in time value of option	(7)	(13)
Amortisation of time value at inception	10	10
Reserve at end of year	3	–
Effect on OCI for the year	3	(3)
Effect on profit or loss for the year	(10)	(10)

The accounting for the time value of options would also apply to combinations of options, for example, when hedging a highly probable forecast transaction with a zero-cost collar. When designating the intrinsic value only, the volatility resulting from changes in the time values of the two options would be recognised in other comprehensive income. However, the amortisation (in the case of time-period related hedged items) or the transaction costs deferred at the end of the life of the hedging relationship (for transaction related hedged items) would be nil when using a zero-cost collar, as the cumulative change in time value over the period would be nil. *[IFRS 9.B6.5.31]*.

7.1.2 Aligned time value

Examples 53.35 and 53.36 above both assume that the critical terms of the option match the hedged item. However, in practice, this is not always the case. The accounting treatment described above applies only to the extent the time value relates to the hedged item. An additional assessment has to be made if the critical terms of the option do not match the hedged item. For that purpose, the actual time value has to be compared with that of a hypothetical option that perfectly matches the critical terms of the hedged item (in IFRS 9 referred to as the 'aligned time value'). *[IFRS 9.B6.5.32]*.

When the terms of the option are not aligned with the hedged item, the accounting for the time value in situations in which the aligned time value exceeds the actual time value is different to situations in which the actual time value exceeds the aligned time value. *[IFRS 9.B6.5.33]*.

If, at inception, the actual time value exceeds the aligned time value:

- the aligned time value at inception is treated in line with the general requirements outlined in 7.1 above, depending on whether it is a time period or transaction related hedged item;
- the change in the fair value of the aligned time value is recognised in OCI; and
- the remaining difference in change in fair value between the actual time value and the aligned time value is recognised in profit or loss.

If, at inception, the aligned time value exceeds the actual time value:

- the actual time value at inception is treated in line with the general requirements outlined in 7.1 above, depending on whether it is a time period or transaction related hedged item;
- the lower of the cumulative change in the fair value of the actual time value and the aligned time value is recognised in OCI; and
- the remaining difference in change in fair value between the actual time value and the aligned time value, if any, is recognised in profit or loss. *[IFRS 9.B6.5.33]*.

For the hedging strategy introduced in Example 53.36 above, this would change the accounting as follows:

Example 53.37: Hedging interest rate risk of a bond (time period related) (2)

Scenario 1: Actual time value exceeds aligned time value

The actual time value at inception is CU 20. The aligned time value at inception is CU 15.

	Year 1	Year 2
Change in actual time value of option	(7)	(13)
Change in aligned time value of option	(6)	(9)
Reserve in equity at beginning of year	–	1.5
Change in time value of option (based on aligned time value)	(6)	(9)
Amortisation of time value at inception (based on aligned time value)	7.5	7.5
Reserve in equity at end of year	1.5	–
Effect on OCI for the year	1.5	(1.5)
Remaining change in (actual) time value recognised in profit or loss (difference between the change in aligned time value and the actual time value of the option)	(1)	(4)
Effect on profit or loss for the year	(8.5)	(11.5)

The above accounting treats the difference between the actual and the aligned time value, consistent with its default classification, as a derivative at fair value through profit or loss.

Scenario 2: Actual time value is lower than aligned time value

The actual time value at inception is CU 20. The aligned time value at inception is CU 24.

	Year 1	Year 2
Change in actual time value of option	(7)	(13)
Change in aligned time value of option	(14)	(10)
Reserve in equity at beginning of year	–	2
Change in time value of option (based on the lower of the cumulative change in aligned time value and actual time value)	(7)	(13)
Amortisation of time value at inception (based on actual time value)	10	10
Reserve in equity at end of year	3	–
Effect on OCI for the year	3	(3)
Remaining change in (actual) time value recognised in profit or loss (zero, because the aligned time value of the option exceeds the actual time value of the option at inception)	–	–
Effect on profit or loss for the year	(10)	(10)

The above 'lower of test' for the accounting of the time value ensures that the entity does not recognise more expense in profit or loss than the entity actually incurred (based on the time value at inception). However, for this scenario, on maturity of the option the cumulative change in fair value of the actual time value will be lower than the cumulative change in fair value of the aligned time value, as the actual time value was lower at inception of the hedge relationship.

IFRS 9 does not define the 'aligned time value' in much detail but it is clear that it is part of the concept of 'costs of hedging'. Therefore, regular pricing features, such as dealer margins, are part of the aligned time value of an option, reflecting that they are part of the fair value of the financial instrument whose intrinsic value is designated as the hedging instrument. This is different from using a hypothetical derivative, which has the purpose of measuring the hedged item. For that purpose, features that are only in the hedging instrument but not the hedged item cannot be taken into account, whereas the same rationale does not apply for the purpose of accounting for the costs of hedging. This becomes clearer from the example of the foreign currency basis spread (see 7.2.2 below); it cannot be included as part of a hypothetical derivative to measure the hedged item but it is a cost of hedging.

7.2 Forward element of forward contracts and foreign currency basis spread of financial instruments

7.2.1 General requirements

Under IAS 39, entities using foreign currency forward contracts in hedging relationships can designate the instrument in its entirety or designate the spot element. Designating the spot element results in the forward points (often also called the 'forward element') being accounted for at fair value through profit or loss (see Chapter 52 at 2.1.4.B).

When designating the entire instrument, IAS 39 allows the hedged item alternatively to be measured at the forward rate instead of the spot rate. For example, when hedging a highly probable forecast transaction, the hedged item, once transacted, would be measured at the forward rate at designation. This is often referred to as the 'forward rate method' (see Chapter 52 at 5.3.3). However, IAS 21 requires monetary financial assets and liabilities denominated in a foreign currency to be measured at the spot rate. As a result, the forward rate method does not provide a similar solution for hedges of such monetary items under IFRS 9 because of how IAS 21 works. *[IFRS 9.BC6.422]*.

IFRS 9 introduces an optional treatment similar to the accounting for time value of options when only the spot element is designated. This is, however, not an accounting policy choice, but an election for each designation. *[IFRS 9.BC6.417]*.

Some assistance is provided in the implementation guidance of IAS 39 as to how the spot and forward elements of a simple forward contract can be identified (see also Example 52.37). *[IAS 39 F.5.6]*.

When designating the spot element, the change in fair value of the forward element is recognised in other comprehensive income (OCI) and accumulated in a separate component of equity. The accounting for the forward element that exists at inception also follows the distinction between transaction related hedged items and time-period related hedged items that is made when accounting for the time value of an option (see at 7.1.1 above). This means, in the case of a transaction related hedged item, that the change in the fair value of the forward element is deferred in OCI and included, like transaction costs, in the measurement of the hedged item (or it is reclassified to profit or loss when a hedged sale occurs). In case of a time-period related hedged item, the forward element that exists at inception is amortised from the separate component of equity to profit or loss on a rational basis. *[IFRS 9.6.5.16, B6.5.34]*.

As a result of the above accounting, fluctuations in the fair value of the forward element over time will affect other comprehensive income, and the amount accumulated in OCI will be recognised in profit or loss when the hedged item affects profit or loss (in case of a transaction related hedged item), or be amortised to profit or loss (in case of a time-period related hedged item). The following example is designed to demonstrate the accounting for the forward element of a hedging derivative, as a cost of hedging. The fact pattern is intentionally simplified in order to isolate the cost of hedging accounting.

Example 53.38: Funding swaps – designating the spot risk only

A bank, having the Singapore Dollar (SGD) as its functional currency, borrows money by entering into a two-year zero coupon loan denominated in Japanese Yen (JPY). The bank transfers the JPY funds into its functional currency and lends the money as a SGD denominated two-year zero coupon loan. To hedge the SGD/JPY exchange risk, the bank enters into a foreign exchange forward contract to buy JPY against SGD in two years' time and designates it as a hedge of the JPY foreign exchange risk. The fair value of the forward element at inception is SGD 20,000 and it is SGD 13,000 at the end of the first year and zero at maturity.

From an economic standpoint, the bank has now hedged the foreign exchange risk and locked in the interest margin for the entire two-year period.

In economic theory, the forward points represent the difference in interest rates between the two currencies involved. Hence, the forward element that exists at inception is seen as one element of the interest margin (however, see also 7.2.2 below).

Applying the IFRS 9 accounting for cost of hedging to the forward element of the forward contract results in the following movement within other comprehensive income (OCI):

(All amounts in SGD thousands)	Year 1	Year 2
Reserve in equity at beginning of year	–	3
Change in fair value of forward element	(7)	(13)
Amortisation of forward element at inception	10	10
Reserve in equity at end of year	3	–
Effect on OCI for the year	3	(3)
Effect on profit or loss for the year	(10)	(10)

The bank would present the amortisation of the forward element in the income statement within the interest margin, together with the interest income from the loan and the interest expense from the borrowing, showing the economically fixed interest margin in SGD of the transaction.

The forward element cost of hedging treatment is not solely applicable for simple foreign exchange forward contract, but applies equally to forward contracts with respect to other risks, such as commodity or interest rate. *[IFRS 9 BC6.416]*. We would also expect the treatment to apply to a fixed-for-fixed currency swap as that is no more than a series of forward contracts.

Just like for the accounting for the time value of an option, the accounting for the forward element as a cost of hedging applies only to the extent of the so-called 'aligned' forward element (i.e. only to the extent that the forward element relates to the hedged item – see 7.1.2 above).

7.2.2 Foreign currency basis spreads

IFRS 9 also introduces a new accounting treatment for currency basis spreads. The currency basis spread, a phenomenon that became very significant during the financial crisis, is a charge embedded in financial instruments that compensates for aspects such as country and liquidity risk as well as demand and supply factors. This charge only applies to transactions involving the exchange of foreign currencies at a future point in time (as, for example, in currency forward contracts or cross currency interest rate swaps (CCIRS)).

Historically, the difference between the spot and forward prices of currency forward contracts and CCIRS represented the differential between the interest rates of the two currencies involved. However, basis spreads increased significantly during the financial crisis and during the subsequent sovereign debt crisis, and have become a significant and volatile component of the pricing of longer term forward contracts and CCIRS.

The standard cites currency basis spread as an example of an element that is only present in the hedging instrument, but not in a hedged item that is a single currency instrument. Consequently, this would result in some ineffectiveness even when using a hypothetical derivative for measuring ineffectiveness (see 6.4.2 above). *[IFRS 9.B6.5.5]*.

When using a foreign currency forward contract or a CCIRS in a hedge, the currency basis spread is an unavoidable 'cost' of the hedging instrument. In its redeliberations after the publication of the draft standard, the Board decided that currency basis spreads are a 'cost of hedging'. The cost of a hedging activity should be recognised in profit or loss at the same time as the hedged transaction. Consequently, the Board decided to expand the requirements regarding the accounting for costs of hedging to also include currency basis spreads in a way similar to the forward element of forward contracts.[14] This means that, when designating a hedging instrument, an entity may exclude the currency basis spread and account for it separately in the same way as the accounting for the forward element of the forward rate, as described in 7.2.1 above. *[IFRS 9.6.5.16]*. Consistent with the approach to designation of the forward element as a cost of hedging, designation of cross currency basis as a cost of hedging is not an accounting policy choice, but an election for each designation. However, if an entity designates the entire hedging instrument, fair value changes due to changes in the currency basis spread would result in some ineffectiveness.

It may be the case for some hedging instruments that contain both a forward element and cross currency basis that it is more operationally efficient to calculate the combined cost of hedging, rather than the forward element and cross currency basis individually. The standard does not explicitly permit a combined treatment, but for many scenarios the aggregate of the individual cost of hedging accounting will equate to the cost of hedging accounting calculated on a combined basis.

Similarly, it may also be the case that for some forward foreign exchange contracts designated as the hedging instrument for changes in the forward foreign exchange element under IAS 39 (see Chapter 52 at 5.3.3), it may be more operationally efficient to designate it as a hedge of the spot element and apply the cost of hedging treatment to the forward element and cross currency basis under IFRS 9. See 11.3.2 below for the transition guidance on this issue.

8 PRESENTATION

8.1 Cash flow hedges

The general mechanics of how ongoing cash flow hedges are presented does not change compared with IAS 39. Entities would continue to accumulate in what the standard now calls the 'cash flow hedge reserve' (i.e. in other comprehensive income in equity), the lower of the cumulative gain or loss on the hedging instrument and the cumulative change in fair value of the hedged item. *[IFRS 9.6.5.11(a)]*. This is often referred to as the 'lower-of-test' and basically ensures that, in line with the IASB's *Conceptual Framework*, an entity is not recognising an asset or liability that does not exist.

IFRS 9 is less flexible than IAS 39 as to how the amount accumulated in the hedging reserve is subsequently accounted for. IAS 39 provides an accounting policy choice to entities that hedge a forecast transaction resulting in the recognition of a non-financial item, to account for the amount accumulated in equity either as a basis adjustment or as a reclassification adjustment (see Chapter 52 at 4.2.2). This accounting policy choice is not available under IFRS 9 – see below for the required treatment.

IFRS 9 requires that those amounts accumulated in the cash flow hedging reserve shall be reclassified from the cash flow hedge reserve as a reclassification adjustment in the same period or periods during which the hedged future cash flow affects profit or loss.

The guidance provides as an example of the period over such a reclassification should occur as the 'periods that interest income or interest expense is recognised'. *[IFRS 9.6.5.11(d)(ii)]*. This clarifies that entities cannot simply account for the net interest payment on an interest rate swap straight into profit or loss but would have to present this as a reclassification adjustment between OCI and profit or loss. There is a requirement to disclose reclassification adjustments in the statement of comprehensive income. *[IAS 1.92]*.

Apart from the above, IFRS 9 did not introduce further changes and the amount accumulated in the hedging reserve is subsequently accounted for depending on the nature of the underlying hedged transaction:

- If the hedged transaction subsequently results in the recognition of a non-financial item, the amount accumulated in equity is removed from the separate component of equity and included in the initial cost or other carrying amount of the hedged asset or liability. This accounting entry, sometimes referred to as 'basis adjustment', does not affect OCI of the period.
- The above accounting treatment would equally apply to situations where the hedged forecast transaction of a non-financial asset or non-financial liability subsequently becomes a firm commitment for which fair value hedge accounting is applied.
- For any other cash flow hedges, the amount accumulated in equity is reclassified to profit or loss as a reclassification adjustment in the same period or periods during which the hedged cash flows affect profit or loss. This accounting entry *does* affect OCI of the period. *[IFRS 9.6.5.11(d)]*.

If cash flow hedge accounting is discontinued, the amount that has been accumulated in OCI shall:

- remain in accumulated OCI if the hedged future cash flows are still expected to occur; or
- be immediately reclassified to profit or loss as a reclassification adjustment if the hedged future cash flows are no longer expected to occur. *[IFRS 9.6.5.12]*.

After discontinuation, once the previously still expected hedged cash flow occurs, any amount remaining in accumulated OCI shall be accounted for depending on the nature of the underlying transaction (as described above). *[IFRS 9.6.5.12]*. In a change from IAS 39, partial discontinuations are permitted under IFRS 9 (see 6.3 above for more details). The guidance on the treatment of the cash flow hedge reserve on discontinuation should also be applied to partial discontinuations,

8.2 Fair value hedges

IFRS 9 does not change how fair value hedges are presented. Entities would continue to recognise the gain or loss on the hedging instrument in profit or loss and adjust the carrying amount of the hedged item for the hedging gain or loss with the adjustment being recognised in profit or loss.

For hedged items that are debt instruments measured at fair value through OCI in accordance with paragraph 4.1.2A of IFRS 9, the gain or loss on the hedged item results in reclassification of that amount from accumulated OCI to profit or loss. This means fair value hedge accounting changes the timing of reclassification from the revaluation reserve of the debt instrument whereas the measurement of the debt instrument at fair value remains unaffected.

For hedged items that are equity instruments for which an entity has elected to present fair value changes in OCI without subsequent reclassification to profit or loss, the accounting for a fair value hedge is different because it does not affect profit or loss but instead only OCI (see 3.2 above). *[IFRS 9.6.5.8]*.

8.3 Hedges of groups of items

8.3.1 Cash flow hedges

When designating a group of items in a cash flow hedge, the presentation of the related hedging gains or losses in the statement of profit or loss depends on the nature of the group position. *[IFRS 9.B6.6.13-B6.6.15]*.

Nature of position	Line items affected in profit or loss	Presentation in the income statement
Gross position	One line item	The amount reclassified from equity to profit or loss has to be presented in the same line item as the underlying hedged transaction.
	Multiple line items	The amount reclassified from equity to profit or loss has to be allocated to the line items affected by the hedged items on a systematic and rational basis and shall not result in a gross up of the net gains or losses on the hedging instrument.
Net position	Multiple line items	The amount reclassified from equity to profit or loss has to be presented in a separate line item.

Note that the designation of a net position cash flow hedge is only permitted when hedging foreign currency risk (see 3.6.3 above).

The above requirement for net position cash flow hedges might not seem very attractive, as the presentation of the hedged transactions would not reflect the effect of the hedge. However, the Board was concerned that grossing-up the hedging gain or loss would result in non-existing gains or losses being recognised in the statement of profit or loss, which would be in conflict with general accounting principles. *[IFRS 9.BC6.457]*. The Board also considered that such a presentation makes it transparent that an entity is hedging on a net basis and would clearly present the effect of those hedges of net positions on the face of the statement of profit or loss. *[IFRS 9.BC6.461]*. However because of this presentation, in practice some entities may choose to continue to designate a proportion of a gross position consistent with the IAS 39 approach, rather than a net designation. Such a 'proxy designation' would be permitted provided the designation is directionally consistent with the actual risk management activities *[IFRS 9.BC6.98, 100(a)]*. (See 5.5 above).

8.3.2 Fair value hedges

For fair value hedges of groups of items with offsetting risk positions (i.e. hedges of a net position), entities would have to present the hedging gains or losses in a separate line item in the income statement in order to avoid grossing up the hedging gain or loss on a single instrument into multiple line items. *[IFRS 9.6.6.4, B6.6.16]*.

However, the treatment in the statement of financial position is different, in that the individual items in the group are separately adjusted for the change in fair value due to changes in the hedged risk. *[IFRS 9.6.6.5]*.

9 DISCLOSURES

For a comprehensive overview of the financial instruments related disclosure requirements of IFRS 7 see Chapter 53. This section on disclosures only addresses some of the hedge accounting related disclosures and aims primarily at illustrating them. Nevertheless, the new IFRS 7 disclosures must be applied even if an entity makes the accounting policy choice to continue to apply IAS 39 hedge accounting, as discussed in 11.1 below.

9.1 Background and general requirements

The disclosure requirements for entities applying hedge accounting are set out in IFRS 7. Those disclosure requirements were amended as a consequence of the new hedge accounting requirements.

Many constituents, users in particular, have asked for improved disclosures that link more clearly an entity's risk management activities and how it applies hedge accounting. *[IFRS 7.BC35C]*. Linking the two requires an understanding of an entity's risk management strategy, which is why the IASB has introduced a requirement for a much more detailed qualitative description of the risk management strategy of the entity. *[IFRS 7.BC35P]*. These disclosures of risk management strategies will, however, only be required where hedge accounting is applied. *[IFRS 7.21A]*.

The objective of the new hedge accounting disclosures is that entities shall disclose information about:

- the risk management strategy and how it is applied to manage risks;
- how the risk management activities may affect the amount, timing and uncertainty of future cash flows; and
- the effect that hedge accounting has had on the statement of financial position, the statement of comprehensive income and the statement of changes in equity. *[IFRS 7.21A]*.

In applying this objective an entity has to consider the necessary level of detail, the balance between different disclosure requirements, the appropriate level of disaggregation and whether additional explanations are necessary to meet the objective. *[IFRS 7.21D]*.

The hedge accounting disclosures should be presented in a single note or a separate section of the financial statements. An entity may include information by cross-referencing to information presented elsewhere, such as a risk report, provided that information is available to users of the financial statements on the same terms as the financial statements and at the same time. *[IFRS 7.21B]*.

The IASB made it clear that it would require entities to give clear disclosures about their risk management activities. *[IFRS 7.BC35D]*. These should be specific to the entity rather than generic or 'boiler plate'.

9.2 Risk management strategy

The risk management strategy has to be described, by type of risk, and this description has to include how each risk arises and how, and to what extent, the risk is managed. This description must also include whether the entity hedges only a part of the risk exposure, such as a nominal component or selected contractual cash flows. *[IFRS 7.22A]*. To satisfy this requirement, an entity must disclose:

- the hedging instruments and how they are used to hedge the risk exposure;
- why the entity believes there is an economic relationship between the hedged item and the hedging instrument;
- how the hedge ratio is determined; and
- the expected sources of ineffectiveness. *[IFRS 7.22B]*.

When only a risk component of an exposure is hedged, an entity must also disclose how it determined the component and how the component relates to the item in its entirety. *[IFRS 7.22C]*. In our view this would include a description of whether the risk component is contractually specified, and if not, how the entity determined that the non-contractually specified risk component is separately identifiable and reliably measurable.

Example 53.39: Illustrative disclosure of risk management strategy for commodity price risk

Coffee price risk

Fluctuations in the coffee price are the main source of market risk for the Alpha Beta Coffee Group (the Group). The Group purchases Arabica coffee from various suppliers in South America. For this purpose, the Group enters into long-term contracts (for between one and three years) with its suppliers, in which the future coffee price is indexed to the USD Arabica benchmark coffee price, adjusted for transport cost that are indexed to diesel prices plus a quality coefficient that is reset annually for a crop period. In order to secure the volume of coffee needed, supply contracts are always entered into (or renewed) at least one year prior to harvest.

The Group forecasts the monthly volume of expected coffee purchases for a period of 18 months and manages the coffee price risk exposure on a 12-month rolling basis. For this purpose, the Group enters into futures contracts on the Arabica benchmark price and designates the futures contracts in cash flow hedges of the USD Arabica benchmark price risk component of its future coffee purchases. Some of those purchases are committed minimum volumes under the contracts and some purchases are highly probable forecast transactions (i.e. quantities in excess of the minimum purchases volumes and sometime for periods for which no contract has yet been entered into). The underlying risk of the coffee futures contracts is identical to the hedged risk component (i.e. the USD Arabica benchmark price). Therefore, the Group has established a hedge ratio of 1:1 for all its hedging relationships. The USD Arabica benchmark price risk component is contractually specified in its purchase contracts, therefore, the Group considers the risk component to be separately identifiable and reliably measurable based on the price of coffee futures.

The Group does not hedge its exposure to the variability in the purchase price of coffee that results from the annual reset of the quality coefficient, because hedging that risk would require highly bespoke financial instruments that in the Group's view are not economical.

The Group's exposure to the variability in the purchase price of coffee that results from the diesel price indexation of the transport costs is integrated into its general risk management of logistics costs that aggregates exposures resulting from various logistics processes of the Group (see Section XYZ below).

The Group determined the USD Arabica benchmark coffee price risk component that it designates as the hedged item on the basis of the pricing formula in the Group's coffee supply contracts (see the above description). That benchmark component is the largest pricing element. The quality coefficient depends on the particular crop in the region from which the Group sources its coffee, depending mainly on weather conditions that affect size and quality of the crop. Sometimes pest and plant diseases can have similar effects. Over the last 10 crop periods the quality coefficient ranged between US cents 2-27 per pound (lb). For the effect of the diesel price indexation, refer to the section 'Logistics costs management' in the Risk Management Report that is included in this Annual Report.

More information about how the Group manages its risk, including the extent to which the Group hedges, the hedging instruments used and sources of ineffectiveness, is provided in the Risk Management Report (see section 'Commodity Price Risk Management').

The risk management strategy disclosures are an important cornerstone of the new hedge accounting model, as they provide the link between an entity's risk management activities and how they affect the financial statements. The notes should also disclose the key judgements the entity has used in applying the new hedge accounting model (including those used to determine whether an economic relationship exists between the hedged item and the hedging instrument, how the hedge ratio was set and how risk components were identified, just to mention a few).

Disclosures have to be made by type of risk, rather than the type of hedging relationship (e.g. cash flow hedge or fair value hedge). *[IFRS 7.21C]*. This should enable users to follow the various disclosures by type of risk, resulting in a much better understanding of the hedging activities and their impact on the financial statements.

9.3 The amount, timing and uncertainty of future cash flows

Further to the risk management strategy, entities have to disclose the 'terms and conditions of hedging instruments and how they affect the amount, timing and uncertainty of future cash flows'. *[IFRS 7.23A]*. More precisely, an entity has to disclose, by category of risk:

- a profile of the timing of the nominal amount of the hedging instrument; and
- if applicable, the average price or rate of the hedging instrument. This could be a strike price or a forward rate. *[IFRS 7.23B]*.

In the Exposure Draft, the IASB proposed also to require the disclosure of the total volume of risk the entity managed, irrespective of whether the entity actually hedges the full exposure. *[IFRS 7.BC35U]*. Many constituents disagreed with this proposal as they believed this to result in disclosure of commercially sensitive information. *[IFRS 7.BC35W]*. The Board acknowledged this concern and decided not to carry this requirement forward to the final standard. *[IFRS 7.BC35X]*.

Entities also have to disclose a description of the sources of hedge ineffectiveness that are expected to affect the hedging relationship during its term. *[IFRS 7.23D]*. This would include an update of new sources of ineffectiveness that emerge in a hedging relationship over the term. *[IFRS 7.23E]*.

Finally, if an entity has previously designated forecast transactions as hedged items in a cash flow hedging relationship and these are no longer expected to occur, this fact and a description of the forecast transaction have to be disclosed. *[IFRS 7.23F]*.

Example 53.40: Illustrative disclosure of timing, nominal amount and average price of coffee futures contracts

As of 31 December 20x0, Alpha Beta Coffee Group is holding the following coffee futures contracts to hedge the exposure on its coffee purchases over the next twelve months:

	Jan	Feb	Mar	Apr	May	...	Dec	Total
Notional amount of coffee futures contracts (in lb thousands) by month of their maturity	1,275	1,425	1,350	1,312.5	1,350	...	1,200	**16,275**
Average hedged rate (in US cents per lb)	122	125	128	133	135	...	139	**133**

Disclosure of the profile of nominal amounts of hedging instruments and their average prices, as required by paragraph 23B of IFRS 7, would not be very meaningful when an entity applies a dynamic hedging process in which both the amount of hedged item and hedging instrument change frequently. *[IFRS 7.23B, BC35Z]*. Consequently, an entity using a dynamic hedging process is exempt from providing these disclosures. Instead, such an entity must disclose:

- a description of what the ultimate risk management strategy is in relation to those dynamic hedging relationships;
- a description of how it reflects this risk management strategy by using hedge accounting and designating those particular hedging relationships; and
- an indication of how frequently the hedging relationships are discontinued and restarted as part of the entity's process in relation to those hedging relationships. *[IFRS 7.23C]*.

If, at the reporting date, the volume of hedging relationships (which is part of the disclosures discussed at 9.4 below) to which the above exemption applies is not representative of the normal volumes hedged during the period, an entity has to disclose this fact and the reason it believes the volumes are not representative. *[IFRS 7.24D]*.

9.4 The effects of hedge accounting on the financial position and performance

IFRS 7 sets out a specific requirement to disclose the effect hedge accounting has on the entity's financial position and the performance. All disclosures are required to be provided in a tabular format and by type of risk. *[IFRS 7.24A-24C]*.

Instead of reproducing the specific requirements of IFRS 7 (see Chapter 54 at 4.3.2) we provide examples below of how those disclosures might look.

Example 53.41: Illustrative disclosure of the effects of hedge accounting on the financial position and performance

The impact of hedging instruments designated in hedging relationships as of 31 December 20x0 on the statement of financial position of Alpha Beta Coffee Group (the Group) is as follows:

Cash flow hedges	Notional amount	Carrying amount	Line item in the statement of financial position	Change in fair value used for measuring ineffectiveness for the period
Coffee price risk				
Arabica coffee futures	16,275lbs (thousands)	(4.5)	Short-term derivative financial liabilities	(1.0)
Interest rate risk				
Pay fixed/receive variable interest rate swap	EUR 50m	4.0	Long-term derivative financial assets	1.0

Fair value hedges	Notional amount	Carrying amount	Line item in the statement of financial position	Change in fair value used for measuring ineffectiveness for the period
Interest rate risk				
Receive fixed/pay variable interest rate swap	EUR 200m	(10.0)	Long-term derivative financial liabilities	(2.0)

The impact of hedged items designated in hedging relationships as of 31 December 20x0 on the statement of financial position of the Group is as follows:

Cash flow hedges	Change in value used for measuring ineffectiveness	Cash flow hedge reserve
Coffee price risk		
Coffee purchases	1.0	4.5
Interest rate risk		
Forecast interest payments	(0.9)	(3.9)

Fair value hedges	Carrying amount	Thereof accumulated fair value adjustments	Line item in the statement of financial position	Change in fair value used for measuring ineffectiveness for the period
Interest rate risk				
Fixed rate borrowings	211.0	11.0	Long-term borrowings	2.1

The above hedging relationships affected profit or loss and other comprehensive income as follows:

Cash flow hedges	Hedging gain or loss recognised in OCI	Ineffectiveness recognised in profit or loss	Line item in the statement of profit or loss	Amount reclassified from OCI to profit or loss	Line item in the statement of profit or loss
Coffee price risk					
Hedges of forecast coffee purchases	(1.0)				
Interest rate risk					
Forecast interest payments	0.9	0.1	Other financial income	0.5	Interest expense

Fair value hedges	Ineffectiveness recognised in profit or loss	Line item in the statement of profit or loss
Interest rate risk		
Hedge of fixed rate borrowings	(0.1)	Other financial expenses

Note that the cash flow hedges of the coffee price risk result in an adjustment to the purchase price of the coffee purchases (a basis adjustment), which means that the amounts that are removed from the cash flow hedge reserve are not reclassification adjustments and hence do not affect OCI or profit or loss (see 8.1 above).

IFRS 7 further requires a reconciliation of the components of equity that arise in connection with hedge accounting (such as the hedging reserve) and an analysis of OCI. That information needs to be disaggregated by risk category, which can be given in the notes to the financial statements. *[IFRS 7.24E, 24F]*.

10 ALTERNATIVES TO HEDGE ACCOUNTING

10.1 Credit risk exposures

Many financial institutions hedge the credit risk arising from loans or loan commitments using credit default swaps (CDS). This would often result in an accounting mismatch, as loans and loan commitments are typically not accounted for at fair value through profit or loss. The most natural approach to hedge accounting would be to designate the credit risk as a risk component in a hedging relationship. However, the IASB noted that due to the difficulty in isolating the credit risk as a separate risk it does not meet the eligibility criteria for risk components. As a result, the accounting mismatch creates profit or loss volatility. *[IFRS 9.BC6.470]*. The Exposure Draft leading up to IFRS 9 did not propose any changes in this area, however, the IASB asked its constituents to comment on three alternative approaches, none of which were that credit risk could be deemed an eligible risk component for hedge accounting. The feedback from constituents showed that accounting for credit risk hedging strategies is a major concern for many financial institutions. *[IFRS 9.BC6.491]*.

In its redeliberations the Board reconfirmed its view that credit risk does not qualify as a separate risk component. *[IFRS 9.BC6.504]*. However, the IASB decided that an entity undertaking economic credit risk hedging may, at any time, elect to account for all or a proportion of a debt instrument (such as a loan or a bond), a loan commitment or a financial guarantee contract, to the extent that any of these instruments is managed for changes in its credit risk, at fair value through profit or loss. This was one of the alternative approaches set out in the Exposure Draft. This election can only be made if the asset referenced by the credit derivative has the same issuer and subordination as the hedged exposure (i.e. both the issuer's name and seniority of the exposure match). The accounting for the credit derivative would not change, i.e. it would continue to be accounted at fair value through profit or loss. *[IFRS 9.6.7.1]*.

If the election is made, the difference at that time between the carrying value (if any) and the fair value of the financial instrument designated as at fair value through profit or loss is immediately recognised in profit or loss; in case of a debt instrument accounted for as at fair value through other comprehensive income the carrying amount (i.e. fair value) does not change but instead the gain or loss that has been accumulated in the revaluation reserve has to be reclassified to profit or loss. *[IFRS 9.6.7.2]*. This gain or loss would not only reflect any change in credit risk, but also any change in other risks such as interest rate risk. Also different to a fair value hedge, once elected, the financial instruments hedged for credit risk are measured at their full fair value instead of just being adjusted for changes in the risk actually hedged. As a result, by economically hedging the credit risk exposure and applying the fair value option consistent with the guidance in paragraph 6.7.1, the entity also has to revalue the financial instrument for the general effect of interest rate risk, which may result in profit or loss volatility.

An entity has to discontinue the specific accounting for credit risk hedges in line with its actual risk management. This would be the case when the credit risk either no longer exists or if the credit risk is no longer managed using credit derivatives (irrespective of whether the credit derivative still exists or is sold, terminated or settled). *[IFRS 9.6.7.3]*.

On discontinuation, the accounting for the financial instrument reverts to the same measurement category that had applied before the designation as at fair value through profit or loss. However, the fair value of the financial instrument on the date of discontinuing the accounting at fair value through profit or loss becomes the new carrying amount on that date. *[IFRS 9.6.7.4]*. For example, the fair value of a loan at the time of discontinuation becomes its new deemed amortised cost which is the basis to determine its new effective interest rate. This applies also to a debt instrument that reverts to accounting at fair value through other comprehensive income because it is required to affect profit or loss in the same way as a financial instrument at amortised cost. *[IFRS 9.5.7.11]*. This means the revaluation reserve only includes the gains and losses that arise after the date on which the accounting at fair value through profit or loss ceased.

For a loan commitment or a financial guarantee contract the fair value at the date on which the accounting at fair value through profit or loss ceased is amortised over the remaining life of the instrument in accordance with the principles of IFRS 15 – *Revenue from Contracts with Customers* – unless the impairment requirements of IFRS 9 would require a higher amount than the remaining unamortised balance (see Chapter 50 at 2.8).

In contrast to the fair value option under IFRS 9, the possibility to elect to measure at fair value through profit or loss those financial instruments whose credit risk is managed using credit derivatives, has the following advantages:

- the election can be made after initial recognition of the financial instrument;
- the election is available for a proportion of the instrument (instead of only the whole instrument); and
- the fair value through profit or loss accounting can be discontinued.

Consequently, even though it is not an equivalent to fair value hedge accounting, this accounting does address several, but not all, concerns of entities that use CDSs for hedging credit exposures.

10.2 Own use contracts

Contracts accounted for in accordance with IFRS 9 include those contracts to buy or sell non-financial items that can be settled net in cash, as if they were financial instruments (i.e. they are in substance similar to financial derivatives). Many commodity purchase and sale contracts meet the criteria for net settlement in cash because the commodities are readily convertible to cash. However, such contracts are excluded from the scope of IFRS 9 if they were entered into and continue to be held for the purpose of the receipt or delivery of a non-financial item in accordance with the entity's expected purchase, sale or usage requirements. *[IFRS 9.2.4]*. This is commonly referred to as the 'own use' scope exception. Own use contracts are further discussed in Chapter 43 at 4 (the scope exception was carried over to IFRS 9).

Own use contracts are accounted for as normal sales or purchase contracts (i.e. executory contracts), with the idea that any fair value change of the contract is not relevant given the contract is used for the entity's own use. However, some entities in certain industries enter into contracts for own use and similar financial derivatives for risk management purposes and manage all these contracts together. In such a situation, own use accounting leads to an accounting mismatch as the fair value change of the derivative positions used for risk management purposes cannot be offset against fair value changes of the own use contracts.

To eliminate the accounting mismatch, an entity could apply hedge accounting by designating an own use contract as the hedged item in a fair value hedging relationship. However, hedge accounting in these circumstances is administratively burdensome. Furthermore, entities enter into large volumes of commodity contracts and, within the large volume of contracts, some positions may offset each other. An entity would therefore typically hedge on a net basis.

Example 53.42: Processing and brokerage of soybeans and sunflowers

An entity is in the business of procuring, transporting, storing, processing and merchandising soybeans and sunflower seeds. The inputs and the outputs are agricultural commodities which are traded in liquid markets. The entity has both a broker business and a processing business, which are operationally distinct. However, the entity analyses and monitors its net commodity risk position, comprising inventories, physically settled forward purchase and sales contracts and exchange traded futures and options. The target is to keep the net fair value risk position close to nil.

Under IAS 39, the physically settled forward contracts from the processing business have to be accounted for as own use contracts, whereas all other contracts are accounted for at fair value through profit or loss. The resulting accounting mismatch does not reflect how the entity is managing the overall fair value risk of those contracts.

As part of its project to replace IAS 39, the IASB introduced a fair value option for own use contracts. At inception of a contract, an entity may make an irrevocable designation to measure an own use contract at fair value through profit or loss (the 'fair value option'). However, such designation is only allowed if it eliminates or significantly reduces an accounting mismatch. *[IFRS 9.2.5]*.

Some entities, especially in the power and utilities sector, enter into long-term own use contracts, sometimes for as long as 15 years. The business model of those entities would often be to manage those contracts together with other contracts on a fair value basis. However, there are often no derivatives available with such long maturities, while fair values for longer dated contracts may be difficult to determine. Hence, a fair value based management approach might only be used for the time horizon in which derivatives are available. The fair value option is, however, only available on inception of the own use contract. Consequently the fair value option will mainly be useful for entities that apply a fair value based risk management strategy for entire contracts, which is more likely to be the case for shorter-term own use contracts.

11 EFFECTIVE DATE AND TRANSITION

11.1 Effective date

The version of IFRS 9 issued in July 2014 has a mandatory effective date of annual periods beginning on or after 1 January 2018. Early application is permitted. *[IFRS 9.7.1.1]*. Early application can only start from the beginning of a reporting period, which is the date of initial application and must be after the date IFRS 9 was issued, i.e. after 24 July 2014. *[IFRS 9.7.2.2]*. Although not explicit in the standard, we believe that reporting period can be an annual reporting period or an interim reporting period.

This version of IFRS 9 supersedes the three earlier versions of IFRS 9 (issued in 2009, 2010 and 2013). However, the IASB provided a 'grace period' that allowed an entity to adopt those earlier versions of IFRS 9 but only if it did so by choosing a date of initial application before 1 February 2015. *[IFRS 9.7.3.2]*.

Taken together, this means an entity that has early applied one of the earlier versions of IFRS 9 (when that option was still available) can continue to apply that version until the version issued in July 2014 becomes mandatorily effective in 2018. Furthermore, an entity that wants to apply the new hedge accounting requirements of IFRS 9 but does not want to early apply the new impairment model would have to apply the version of IFRS 9 issued in November 2013, which would require choosing a date of initial application that was the beginning of an annual or interim reporting period beginning before 1 February 2015. Such an entity would have to apply the new impairment model (as well as the changes to classification and measurement that are included in IFRS 9 issued in July 2014) only from 2018.

As stated at 3.6.6 above, an entity has the accounting policy choice to continue applying hedge accounting as set out in IAS 39 to all hedges until the project on accounting for macro hedging is completed, instead of the requirements of Chapter 6 of IFRS 9. *[IFRS 9.7.2.21]*. We believe that an entity can chose to adopt the IFRS 9 hedge accounting requirements subsequent to the initial adoption of IFRS 9, as there is nothing in the transition guidance that indicates that an entity must continue to apply the accounting policy choice until the macro hedging project is finished. *[IFRS 9 BC6.104]*. However, it is not possible to switch back to the hedge accounting provisions of IAS 39 once Chapter 6 of IFRS 9 has been applied. Furthermore, for first time adopters of IFRS, the transition guidance in IFRS 9 is not relevant, and hence the accounting policy choice to apply the hedge accounting requirements of IAS 39 is not available.

The accounting policy choice to continue to apply the hedge accounting requirements of IAS 39, effectively defers all of the Chapter 6 of IFRS 9, (although not the IFRS 7 disclosure requirements on hedge accounting introduced by IFRS 9). As the guidance on designating credit exposures at fair value through profit or loss is included within Chapter 6 of IFRS 9, we believe it cannot be applied if an entity chooses to remain on IAS 39 for hedge accounting. See 10.1 above for more details on designating credit exposures at fair value through profit or loss.

Furthermore, if an entity has an equity instrument classified at fair value through other comprehensive income as permitted by paragraph 5.7.5, and has chosen to continue to

Chapter 53

apply the IAS 39 hedge accounting requirements; we believe that such an equity instrument is not an eligible hedged item as it will not impact profit or loss. *[IAS 39.86]*. This is because the specific guidance in paragraph 6.5.8 of IFRS 9 which permits designation of an equity instrument for which an entity has elected to present changes in fair value in other comprehensive income in a fair value hedges is not applicable if the entity remains on IAS 39 hedge accounting.

11.2 Prospective application in general

A hedging relationship can only be designated on a prospective basis, in order to avoid the use of hindsight. The same concern about using hindsight would also apply if the new hedge accounting requirements were to be applied retrospectively. Consequently, the IASB decided that hedge accounting in accordance with IFRS 9 has to be applied prospectively, with some limited exceptions. *[IFRS 9.7.2.22]*. Because the date of initial application can only be the beginning of a reporting period, an entity can only start applying the new hedge accounting requirements of IFRS 9 prospectively from the beginning of a reporting period, and only if all qualifying criteria – including the hedge accounting documentation that conforms to IFRS 9 – are met on that date. *[IFRS 9.7.2.23, 7.2.2]*.

Many preparers will already be applying hedge accounting under IAS 39 before transitioning to IFRS 9. For such entities, the standard clarifies that hedging relationships under IAS 39 which also qualify for hedge accounting under IFRS 9, are treated as continuing hedging relationships. *[IFRS 9.7.2.24]*. Hedge accounting under IAS 39 ceases in the very same second as hedge accounting under IFRS 9 starts, therefore resulting in no accounting entries on transition. However, entities might have to rebalance their hedges on transition to fulfil the new effectiveness requirements under IFRS 9 in which case any resulting gain or loss must be recognised in profit or loss. *[IFRS 9.7.2.25]*.

Entities that are already applying IAS 39 hedge accounting will need to ensure the existing IAS 39 hedge documentation is updated to meet the requirements of IFRS 9 on the date of initial application. As a minimum this would include the following:

- reconsideration of the documented risk management strategy and objective;
- the approach and rationale for concluding the eligibility criteria are met, specifically an explanation of the economic relationship, the effect of credit risk, and the hedge ratio;
- identification of all major sources of ineffectiveness;
- justification for designation of any risk components;
- deletion of retrospective effectiveness assessment; and
- the approach to cost of hedging (if applicable).

11.3 Limited retrospective application

The exceptions from prospective application of the new standard are for the new accounting treatment for the time value of options, when only the intrinsic value is designated; and, at the option of the entity, for the forward element of forward contracts, when only the spot element is designated, and the foreign currency basis spread of financial instruments (see 7 above).

The transition requirements for hedge accounting in IFRS 9 also replicate the retrospective application for the amendments that were made to IAS 39 by *Novation of Derivatives and Continuation of Hedge Accounting*. *[IFRS 9.7.2.26(c), IAS 39.108D]*. (See Chapter 52 at 4.2.3.A.)

11.3.1 Accounting for the time value of options

Entities have to apply the new accounting treatment for the time value of options retrospectively, if in accordance with IAS 39, only the hedging option's intrinsic value was designated as part of the hedge relationship. However, retrospective treatment is only applied to hedging relationships that existed at the beginning of the earliest comparative period and hedging relationships designated thereafter. *[IFRS 9.7.2.26(a)]*. This means that, for example, foreign entities registered and reporting with the United States Securities and Exchange Commission and required to present two comparative years of income statements, would have a longer period to cover for the retrospective application of the new requirements.

Applying the new accounting requirement retrospectively might have a much wider impact than anticipated. Depending on the type of hedging relationship, many line items in the primary statements and many disclosures in the notes might be affected.

Example 53.43: Retrospective application of accounting for time value of option

An entity applies the IFRS hedge accounting requirements as of 1 January 2017 and 1 January 2016 is the beginning of its earliest comparative period presented.

As of 1 January 2016, the entity had a hedging relationship in place in which the intrinsic value of an option was designated as the hedging instrument of a highly probable forecast purchase of a machine as of 31 March 2016. When preparing the 2017 financial statements, the entity would have to:

- determine the time value of that option as of 1 January 2016 and restate accumulated other comprehensive income (OCI) against retained earnings as of that date;
- determine the time value of that option as of 31 March 2016 and restate accumulated OCI against retained earnings as of that date;
- restate the initial carrying amount of the machine as of 31 March 2016 (the basis adjustment of amount accumulated in OCI);
- determine the new depreciation amount for 2016 and restate the carrying amount of the machine as of 31 December 2016 against retained earnings as of that date;
- reflect the restatement in the statement of profit or loss and other comprehensive income, the statement of changes in equity and the statement of financial position; and
- reflect the restatement in the notes disclosures.

11.3.2 Accounting for the forward element of forward contracts and foreign currency basis spread

Different to the accounting for the time value of options, entities will have a choice of whether to apply retrospectively the new accounting for the forward element of forward contracts or not, for hedge relationships where, in accordance with IAS 39, only changes in the spot element of a hedging forward contract were designated within the hedge relationship. However, the choice applies on an all or nothing basis (i.e. if an entity elects to apply the accounting retrospectively, it has to be applied to all hedging relationships that qualify for the election). The retrospective application would also only apply to those hedging relationships that existed at the beginning of the earliest comparative period or that were designated thereafter. *[IFRS 9.7.2.26(b)]*. Consequently, assets and liabilities cannot be adjusted to reflect hedges that had already finished at the start of the comparative period. Furthermore, this retrospective application does not appear to apply if under IAS 39 a forward designation was made, yet on application of IFRS 9 a spot designation is deemed preferable.

A similar retrospective transition requirement applies for the accounting for foreign currency basis spreads (see at 7.2.2 above). However, in contrast to the transition requirements for the forward element of forward contracts, the decision to apply retrospectively the cost of hedging guidance on foreign currency basis spreads can be made on a hedge by hedge basis, without a requirement that cross currency basis had been excluded from the designation under IAS 39. This is owing to the differences in circumstances: IAS 39 did not have an exception for excluding a foreign currency basis spread from the designation of a financial instrument as a hedging instrument. *[IFRS 9.7.2.26(b), BC7.49]*.

11.3.3 Re-designation of hedge relationships for non-financial risk components

IFRS 9 permits the designation of eligible risk components in non-financial hedged items (see 3.4 above). Such a designation was not possible under IAS 39. This means, even if entities were economically hedging a risk component, they were obliged to designate the change in the entire hedged item as the hedged risk in order to achieve hedge accounting. Such a designation was likely to result in the recognition of ineffectiveness in profit or loss and in some cases failure of the effectiveness requirements.

On transition to IFRS 9, entities may wish to amend hedge accounting relationships such that the hedged risk is an eligible risk component for non-financial hedged items. The question is whether that change in the documented hedged risk must result in the discontinuation of the original hedge relationship and the start of a new hedge relationship, or whether it can be treated as an amendment to the original designation such that the original hedge relationship continues. This question is particularly relevant for cash flow hedges, as on re-designation the non-zero fair value of the hedging instrument can result in subsequent ineffectiveness recorded in profit or loss.

We believe that such a change in the documented hedged risk should be treated as a discontinuation of the original hedge relationship and the re-designation of a new hedge relationship because it can be seen as either a change in the hedged item or a change in the documented risk management objective which both require discontinuation of a hedging relationship. *[IFRS 9.B6.5.26(a)]*.

The IASB was very nervous of permitting any retrospective application of the IFRS 9 hedge accounting requirements, as such an application could involve the use of hindsight, for example as to whether it is beneficial or not to change the hedged risk to be an eligible risk component. The specific scenarios where retrospective application is permitted are those that either do not involve the use of hindsight as IFRS 9 application relied on particular choices that had already been made under

IAS 39 (e.g. the designation of the intrinsic value of an option or the spot element of a forward) or where retrospective application was already permitted in IAS 39 (novation of a derivative through a central counterparty). *[IFRS 9.BC7.44-51]*. Due to the absence of a specific respective transition relief, it follows that such a hedge relationship cannot continue. A dual-designation at the inception of the hedge is not possible either because of the same arguments.

The logical follow-on question is whether an entity can continue with the original designation although it does not exactly represent the entity's risk management objective. We note that although the objective of hedge accounting under IFRS 9 is to represent an entity's risk management activities, *[IFRS 9.6.1.1]*, it does not require that it is an exact match. The Basis for Conclusions notes that, in some circumstances, the designation for hedge accounting purposes is inevitably not the same as an entity's risk management view of its hedging, but that the designation reflects risk management in that it relates to the same type of risk that is being managed and the instruments used for this purpose. The IASB refer to this situation as 'proxy hedging', which is an eligible way of designating the hedged item under IFRS 9 as long as that still reflects risk management. One example of proxy hedging mentioned is those instances where the risk management objective is to hedge a risk component but the accounting hedge designation is for the full price risk. Where there is a choice of accounting hedge designation, there is no requirement for an entity to select the designation that most closely matches the risk management view of hedging as long as the chosen approach still reflects risk management. *[IFRS 9.BC6.97,98,100(b)]*. Consequently, we believe that it is permitted, on transition, to continue with an accounting designation of the full price risk even if the management objective was always to hedge a component of risk.

Both questions above have been debated by the IFRS Interpretations Committee in September 2015 and January 2016. The final agenda decision reached by the IFRS Interpretations Committee is consistent with the analysis presented above.[15]

11.3.4 Designation of own use contracts at fair value through profit or loss

On introduction of this fair value option for own use contracts, the IASB considered the need for specific transition requirements. As a result, the IASB allowed that on transition to IFRS 9, entities can apply the fair value option on an 'all-or-nothing' basis for similar types of (already existing) own use contracts. *[IFRS 9.7.2.14A]*.

References

1 *A Roadmap for Convergence between IFRSs and US GAAP* – 2006-2008, issued in February 2006, updated in 2008 and reaffirmed in November 2009.

2 *IASB Update*, October 2005 and April 2006 and Project Update, *Financial Instruments*, IASB, 18 January 2006.

3 Discussion Paper, *Reducing Complexity in Reporting Financial Instruments*, IASB, March 2008.

4 Invitation to Comment, *Reducing Complexity in Reporting Financial Instruments* (including IASB Discussion Paper, *Reducing Complexity in Reporting Financial Instruments)*, FASB, March 2008.

5 Press Release, *IASB sets out timetable for IAS 39 replacement and its conclusions on FASB FSPs*, IASB, April 2009.

6 Press Release, *Draft of forthcoming IFRS on general hedge accounting*, September 2012.

7 *IASB Update*, May 2012.

8 *IASB Update*, May 2012.

9 *IASB Update*, July 2015.

10 *IASB Update*, January 2013.

11 For example: *Request to allow hedge accounting to comply with either IAS 39 or IFRS 9 while the macro hedging project is developed*, letter from EFRAG to the IASB, 22 March 2013.

12 *IASB Update*, January 2013.

13 www.bbalibor.com/explained/definitions (24 July 2013).

14 *IASB Update*, January 2013.

15 *IFRIC Update*, January 2016.

Chapter 54 Financial instruments: Presentation and disclosure

List of examples

Chapter 54 Financial instruments: Presentation and disclosure

1 INTRODUCTION

Disclosure of financial instruments is largely dealt with in IFRS 7 – *Financial Instruments: Disclosures* – and presentation in IAS 32 – *Financial Instruments: Presentation.* The development of these standards is outlined below.

1.1 IAS 32

The original version of IAS 32 – *Financial Instruments: Disclosure and Presentation* – was published in March 1995 and, as its title suggested, contained requirements about the disclosures entities should make about financial instruments. These requirements were superseded by IFRS 7 (see 1.2 below) which also changed the name of the standard.

One of the topics IAS 32 continues to address is when entities should offset financial assets and financial liabilities, the associated requirements for which are discussed at 7.4.1 below. It also addresses the classification of financial instruments as equity, financial liabilities or financial assets, a topic covered in Chapter 45. IAS 32 has been amended a number of times since publication, including in December 2011 when the IASB addressed certain practical problems it had identified in its offsetting requirements.

1.2 IFRS 7

IFRS 7 emerged from a project principally focused on revising IAS 30 – *Disclosures in the Financial Statements of Banks and Similar Financial Institutions* – a standard which, at the time, set out additional disclosure requirements for banks and similar entities. It was published in August 2005 and superseded IAS 30.

The objective of IFRS 7 is to require entities to provide disclosures in their financial statements that enable users to evaluate: *[IFRS 7.1]*

- the significance of financial instruments for the entity's financial position and performance; and
- the nature and extent of risks arising from financial instruments to which the entity is exposed during the period and at the reporting date, and how the entity manages those risks.

These objectives manifest themselves in two disclosure principles (see 4 and 5 below) which are designed to complement those for recognising, measuring and presenting financial assets and financial liabilities in IAS 32, IAS 39 – *Financial Instruments: Recognition and Measurement* – or, when applied, IFRS 9 – *Financial Instruments* (see Chapters 42 to 53). *[IFRS 7.2]*.

IFRS 7 has been subject to significant amendment since its original publication, in particular to address concerns raised during the financial crisis. These amendments aimed to improve the disclosures entities provide in a number of areas including liquidity risk, transfers of financial assets, offsetting and fair values (most of the disclosures for which are now included in IFRS 13 – *Fair Value Measurement* – see Chapter 14).

In July 2014, the IASB published the final version of IFRS 9, its replacement for IAS 39. The new standard changes the framework for classifying and measuring financial assets and financial liabilities; introduces an expected loss approach for determining impairment losses on financial assets and amends the requirements for applying hedge accounting. It also makes a number of consequential amendments to IFRS 7, introducing extensive new disclosures in respect of impairment (see 5.2.3 below) and hedge accounting (see 4.3.2 below) as well as making other changes which are noted throughout this chapter. The final version of IFRS 9 and its consequential amendments to IFRS 7 are effective for periods beginning on or after 1 January 2018.

2 SCOPE OF IFRS 7

2.1 Entities required to comply with IFRS 7

Although IFRS 7 evolved from a project to update IAS 30 (which applied only to banks and similar financial institutions) it applies to all entities preparing their financial statements in accordance with IFRS that have financial instruments. *[IFRS 7.BC6]*. The IASB considered exempting certain entities, including insurers, subsidiaries and those that are small or medium-sized (SMEs), but decided that IFRS 7 should apply to all entities applying IFRS. *[IFRS 7.BC9, BC10, BC11]*. Entities applying the IFRS for SMEs are required to provide only reduced disclosures about financial instruments.

2.2 Financial instruments within the scope of IFRS 7

Sections 3 and 4 of Chapter 43 contain a detailed explanation of the scope of IFRS 7. It is important to recognise that the scope of IFRS 7 is generally somewhat wider than that of IAS 39 and IFRS 9. Therefore IFRS 7 can apply to instruments that are not subject to the recognition and measurement provisions of IAS 39 or IFRS 9, for example lease liabilities and certain loan commitments. *[IFRS 7.4]*. Conversely, some financial instruments within the scope of IAS 39 or IFRS 9, particularly those held in disposal groups or as part of discontinued operations, are not subject to all of the requirements in IFRS 7.

2.3 Interim reports

IAS 34 – *Interim Financial Reporting* – sets out the minimum content of an interim financial report. When an event or transaction is significant to an understanding of the changes in an entity's financial position or performance since the last annual financial period, IAS 34 requires the report to provide an explanation of, and update to, the information included in the last annual financial statements. *[IAS 34.15]*. The standard emphasises that relatively insignificant updates need not be provided. *[IAS 34.15A]*. The following disclosures which relate to financial instruments are required if significant: *[IAS 34.15B]*

- losses recognised from the impairment of financial assets;
- changes in the business or economic circumstances that affect the fair value of the entity's financial assets and financial liabilities, whether recognised at fair value or amortised cost;
- any loan default or breach of a loan agreement that has not been remedied on or before the end of the reporting period;
- transfers between levels of the fair value hierarchy used in the measurement of the fair value of financial instruments; and
- changes in the classification of financial assets as a result of a change in the purpose or use of those assets.

In considering the extent of disclosures necessary to meet the requirements above, IAS 34 refers to the guidance included in other IFRSs, *[IAS 34.15C]*, which would include IFRS 7, but does not ordinarily require compliance with all the requirements in those standards.

IAS 34 also specifies additional disclosures to be given (normally on a financial year-to-date basis) about the fair value of financial instruments, including those discussed at 4.5 below and a number required by IFRS 13. *[IAS 34.16A(j)]*. This requirement is not subject to the qualifications noted above and so, as discussed in further detail in Chapter 39 at 4.5, these disclosures should always be given unless the information is not material.

The disclosures about offsetting of financial assets and financial liabilities (see 7.4.2 below) need not be provided in condensed interim financial statements unless required by the more general requirements of IAS 34, a position clarified by the IASB in September 2014.

3 STRUCTURING THE DISCLOSURES

The main text of IFRS 7 is supplemented by application guidance, which is an integral part of the standard,[1] and by implementation guidance, which accompanies, but is not part of, the standard.[2] The implementation guidance suggests possible ways of applying some of the requirements of the standard but, it is emphasised, does not create additional requirements. *[IFRS 7.IG1]*.

Although the implementation guidance discusses each disclosure requirement in IFRS 7 separately, disclosures would normally be presented as an integrated package and individual disclosures might satisfy more than one requirement. For example, information about concentrations of risk might also convey information about exposure to credit or other risk. *[IFRS 7.IG2]*. This chapter follows a similar approach whereby each topic is considered individually in the context of the requirements of the standard as well as related application and implementation guidance.

3.1 Level of detail

Entities need to decide, in the light of their circumstances, how much detail to provide to satisfy the requirements of IFRS 7, how much emphasis to place on different aspects of the requirements and how information is aggregated to display the overall picture without combining information with different characteristics. It is necessary to strike a balance between overburdening financial statements with excessive detail that may not assist users of financial statements and obscuring important information as a result of too much aggregation. For example, important information should not be obscured by including it among a large amount of insignificant detail. Similarly, information should not be aggregated so that it obscures important differences between individual transactions or associated risks. *[IFRS 7.B3]*.

This means that not all of the information suggested, say, in the implementation guidance is necessarily required. *[IFRS 7.IG5]*. On the other hand, there is a reminder that IAS 1 – *Presentation of Financial Statements* – requires additional disclosures when compliance with the specific requirements in IFRSs is insufficient to enable users to understand the impact of particular transactions, other events and conditions on the entity's financial position and financial performance (see Chapter 3 at 4.1.1.A). *[IFRS 7.IG6]*.

3.2 Materiality

The implementation guidance to the original version of IFRS 7 drew attention to the definition of materiality in IAS 1 (see Chapter 3 at 4.1.5.A): *[IFRS 7(2010).IG3]*

> 'Omissions or misstatements of items are material if they could, individually or collectively, influence the economic decisions that users make on the basis of the financial statements. Materiality depends on the size and nature of the omission or misstatement judged in the surrounding circumstances. The size or nature of the item, or a combination of both, could be the determining factor.' *[IAS 1.7]*.

It then noted that a specific disclosure requirement need not be satisfied if the information is not material, *[IFRS 7(2010).IG3]*, and drew attention to the following explanation in IAS 1: *[IFRS 7(2010).IG4]*

> 'Assessing whether an omission or misstatement could influence economic decisions of users, and so be material, requires consideration of the characteristics of those users. The *Framework for the Preparation and Presentation of Financial Statements* states that "users are assumed to have a reasonable knowledge of business and economic activities and accounting and a willingness to study the information with reasonable diligence."[3] Therefore, the assessment needs to take into account how users with such attributes could reasonably be expected to be influenced in making economic decisions.' *[IAS 1.7]*.

The inclusion of such guidance could have been seen as curious given that it is no more or less applicable to IFRS 7 than any other standard. What it amounted to was a degree of reassurance that entities with few financial instruments and few risks (for example a manufacturer whose only financial instruments are accounts receivable and accounts payable) will give few disclosures, something that was borne out in other references within the standard and accompanying material. *[IFRS 7.IN4, BC10]*.

However, in May 2010, the IASB removed all references to materiality from IFRS 7 because they thought that some of these references could imply that other disclosures in IFRS 7 are required even if those disclosures are not material, which was not the intention. *[IFRS 7.BC47A]*. Accordingly the above guidance continues to be relevant even though it has been removed from the standard.

3.3 Classes of financial instrument

Certain disclosures required by IFRS 7 should be provided by class of financial instrument (see 4.2.4, 4.4.7, 4.5.1, 4.5.2, 5.2.2, 5.2.3 and 6 below). For these, entities should group financial instruments into classes that are appropriate to the nature of the information disclosed and take into account the characteristics of those instruments. *[IFRS 7.6]*. It is clear from this requirement that the classes used need not be the same for each disclosure provided, e.g. one set of classes may be used to present information about credit risk (see 5.2.2 or 5.2.3 below) and another for information about day 1 profits (see 4.5.2 below).

It is emphasised that these classes should be determined by the entity and are, thus, distinct from the categories of financial instruments specified in IAS 39 or IFRS 9 which determine how financial instruments are measured and where changes in fair value are recognised. *[IFRS 7.B1]*. However, in determining classes of financial instrument an entity should, as a minimum, distinguish instruments measured at amortised cost from those measured at fair value and treat as a separate class or classes those financial instruments outside the scope of IFRS 7. *[IFRS 7.B2]*.

For disclosures given by class of instrument, sufficient information should be provided to permit the information to be reconciled to the line items presented in the statement of financial position. *[IFRS 7.6]*.

4 SIGNIFICANCE OF FINANCIAL INSTRUMENTS FOR AN ENTITY'S FINANCIAL POSITION AND PERFORMANCE

The IASB decided that the disclosure requirements in this area should result from the following disclosure principle:

> 'An entity shall disclose information that enables users of its financial statements to evaluate the significance of financial instruments for its financial position and performance.'

Further, they concluded that this principle could not be satisfied unless other specified disclosures (which are dealt with at 4.1 to 4.5 below) are also provided. *[IFRS 7.7, BC13]*.

Chapter 54

4.1 Accounting policies

The main body of IFRS 7 contains a reminder of IAS 1's requirement for an entity to disclose its significant accounting policies, comprising the measurement basis (or bases) used in preparing the financial statements and the other accounting policies used that are relevant to an understanding of the financial statements. *[IFRS 7.21]*.

For financial assets or financial liabilities designated at fair value through profit or loss in accordance with IAS 39 (see Chapter 46 at 2.2), such disclosure may include: *[IFRS 7.B5(a)]*

- the nature of the financial assets or financial liabilities designated at fair value through profit or loss;
- the criteria for so designating such financial assets or financial liabilities on initial recognition; and
- how the conditions in IAS 39 for such designation have been satisfied.

  For instruments designated to eliminate or significantly reduce a measurement or recognition inconsistency, this should include a narrative description of the circumstances underlying the inconsistency that would otherwise arise.

  For groups of instruments that are managed and the performance evaluated on a fair value basis, this should include a narrative description of how designation at fair value through profit or loss is consistent with the entity's documented risk management or investment strategy.

For financial assets and financial liabilities designated as measured at fair value through profit or loss in accordance with IFRS 9 (see Chapter 47 at 7), such disclosure may include: *[IFRS 7.B5(a), B5(aa)]*

- the nature of the financial assets or financial liabilities designated as measured at fair value through profit or loss;
- the criteria for designating financial liabilities on initial recognition; and
- how the conditions or criteria in IFRS 9 for such designation have been satisfied.

Other policies that might be appropriate include: *[IFRS 7.B5(b), (c), (e), (f), (g)]*

- the criteria for designating financial assets as available for sale in accordance with IAS 39;
- whether regular way purchases and sales of financial assets are accounted for at trade date or at settlement date (see Chapter 48 at 2.2); and
- how net gains or net losses on each category of financial instrument are determined (see 4.2.1 below), for example whether the net gains or net losses on items measured at fair value through profit or loss include interest or dividend income.

  In our view, interest income and interest expense (including, for example, that arising on short positions) should be treated consistently, i.e. both included or both excluded from the net gains and losses disclosed;

- the criteria an entity applying IAS 39 uses to determine that there is objective evidence that an impairment loss has occurred; and
- for entities applying IAS 39, when the terms of financial assets that would otherwise be past due (see 5.2.2.C below) or impaired have been renegotiated, the accounting policy for financial assets that are the subject of renegotiated terms.

  In contrast to its specific requirements for the derecognition of financial liabilities, IAS 39 does not explicitly address whether or in what circumstances a financial asset whose terms are subject to renegotiation should be derecognised by the holder or whether it should be regarded as a continuation of the existing asset (see Chapter 51 at 3.4.1 and 3.4.2). Therefore, this could be an important accounting policy for banks and other financial institutions if they frequently renegotiate the terms of their loans and receivables.

  Such an accounting policy may also be relevant to entities applying IFRS 9, although when adopted, IFRS 7 is amended to specify additional disclosures about financial instruments that have been renegotiated and not derecognised (see 5.2.3 below).

For entities applying IAS 39, when an allowance account (such as a bad debt provision) is used to reduce the carrying amount of financial assets impaired by credit losses, the accounting policies may need to indicate: *[IFRS 7.B5(d)]*

- the criteria for determining when the carrying amount of impaired financial assets is reduced directly (or, in the case of a reversal of a write-down, increased directly) and when the allowance account is used; and
- the criteria for writing off amounts charged to the allowance account against the carrying amount of impaired financial assets (as set out at 4.4.7 below, a reconciliation of changes in the allowance account should be given).

When IFRS 9 is adopted, the guidance immediately above is deleted and replaced by extensive new disclosure requirements about impairments which are covered primarily at 5.2.3 below.

The application guidance also contains a reminder that IAS 1 requires entities to disclose the judgements, apart from those involving estimations, that management has made in the process of applying the entity's accounting policies and that have the most significant effect on the amounts recognised in the financial statements (see Chapter 3 at 5.1.1.B). *[IFRS 7.B5]*.

4.2 Income, expenses, gains and losses

Under IFRS 7, entities are required to disclose various items of income, expense, gains and losses. The disclosures below may be provided either on the face of the financial statements or in the notes. *[IFRS 7.20]*.

4.2.1 Gains and losses by measurement category

The IASB concluded that disclosure of net gains or net losses arising on the following categories of instrument is necessary to understand the financial performance of an entity's financial instruments given the different measurement bases in IAS 39: *[IFRS 7.20(a), BC33]*

- financial assets or financial liabilities at fair value through profit or loss, showing separately those on financial instruments designated as such upon initial recognition, and those on financial instruments classified as held for trading.

  The implementation guidance to IAS 39 explains that IFRS 7 neither requires nor prohibits the further analysis of gains and losses according to internal classifications used in an entity's business. For example, the change in fair value of those derivatives that IAS 39 classifies as held for trading but the entity classifies as part of risk management activities outside of the trading portfolio may be disclosed separately. *[IAS 39.G.1]*.

  In our view, these amounts should not be shown net of funding costs if the associated financial liabilities are not classified at fair value through profit or loss;
- available-for-sale financial assets, showing separately the amount of gain or loss recognised directly in other comprehensive income during the period and the amount reclassified from equity to profit or loss for the period;
- held-to-maturity investments;
- loans and receivables; and
- financial liabilities measured at amortised cost.

These disclosures are designed to complement the statement of financial position disclosure requirement described at 4.4.1 below. *[IFRS 7.BC33]*.

Some entities include interest and dividend income in gains and losses on financial assets and financial liabilities held for trading and others do not. To assist users in comparing income arising from financial instruments across different entities, entities are required to disclose how the income statement amounts are determined. For example, an entity should disclose whether net gains and losses on financial assets or financial liabilities held for trading include interest and dividend income (see 4.1 above). *[IFRS 7.BC34]*.

On application of IFRS 9, the disclosure requirements above are amended to align them with that standard. Consequently, disclosure should be given of net gains or net losses arising on the following categories of instrument: *[IFRS 7.20]*

- financial assets or financial liabilities measured at fair value through profit or loss, showing separately those on financial assets or liabilities:
  - designated as such upon initial recognition (or subsequently when the credit risk of a financial asset is managed using a credit derivative); and
  - mandatorily measured at fair value in accordance with IFRS 9, e.g. liabilities held for trading.

  For financial liabilities designated at fair value through profit or loss, the amount of gain or loss recognised in other comprehensive income, i.e. relating to changes in fair value attributable to changes in credit risk (see Chapter 50 at 2.1), should be shown separately;

- financial assets measured at amortised cost.

  IFRS 7 requires disclosure of an analysis of the gain or loss arising from derecognition of such assets showing separately gains and losses. The reasons for derecognition should also be given. *[IFRS 7.20A]*. These gains and losses should also be shown separately on the face of the income statement or statement of comprehensive income (see 7.1.1 below); *[IAS 1.82(aa)]*
- financial liabilities measured at amortised cost;
- investments in equity instruments designated at fair value through other comprehensive income; and
- debt instruments measured at fair value through other comprehensive income, showing separately:
  - the amount of gain or loss recognised in other comprehensive income during the period; and
  - the amount reclassified upon derecognition from accumulated other comprehensive income to profit or loss for the period.

4.2.2 Interest income and expense

For financial assets or financial liabilities that are not measured at fair value through profit or loss, total interest income and total interest expense (calculated using the effective interest method) should be disclosed. Interest income on impaired financial assets (accrued as described in Chapter 49 at 4.5) should be disclosed by entities applying IAS 39. Where IFRS 9 is applied, interest revenue for financial assets measured at amortised cost should be shown separately from interest revenue on debt instruments measured at fair value through other comprehensive income. *[IFRS 7.20(b), (d)]*.

Financial instruments containing discretionary participation features fall within the scope of IFRS 4 – *Insurance Contracts* – rather than IAS 39 or IFRS 9 (see Chapter 43 at 3.3.2 and Chapter 55 at 6). However, IFRS 7 does apply to such instruments and IFRS 4 acknowledges that the interest expense disclosed need not be calculated using the effective interest method. *[IFRS 4.35(d)]*.

Similarly, lease liabilities and finance lease receivables are within the scope of IFRS 7 (see Chapter 43 at 3.2) but are not accounted for using the effective interest method. However, there is no equivalent acknowledgement in IAS 17 – *Leases*, IFRS 16 – *Leases*, IAS 39, or IFRS 9 that the disclosure of interest income and interest expense should be made on the basis of the finance cost and finance revenue recognised under the relevant standard for leases. Nevertheless, this seems little more than an oversight and we consider it appropriate to include in the disclosure the amounts actually recognised rather than amounts calculated in accordance with the effective interest method.

4.2.3 Fee income and expense

Entities should disclose fee income and expense (excluding amounts included in the effective interest rate calculation) arising from: *[IFRS 7.20(c)]*

- financial assets or financial liabilities that are not measured at fair value through profit or loss; and
- trust and other fiduciary activities that result in the holding or investing of assets on behalf of individuals, trusts, retirement benefit plans, and other institutions.

This information is said to indicate the level of such activities and help users to estimate possible future income of the entity. *[IFRS 7.BC35]*.

4.2.4 Impairment losses

For entities applying IAS 39, the amount of any impairment loss should be disclosed for each class of financial asset. *[IFRS 7.20(e)]*. Significant additional disclosures are required for entities applying IFRS 9 which are covered at 5.2.3 below.

4.3 Hedge accounting

4.3.1 Hedge accounting disclosures for entities applying IAS 39

When hedge accounting is applied (see Chapter 52), entities applying IAS 39 are required to disclose the following, separately for each type of hedge (i.e. fair value hedges, cash flow hedges, and hedges of net investments in foreign operations): *[IFRS 7.22]*

- a description of each type of hedge;
- a description of the financial instruments designated as hedging instruments and their fair values at the reporting date; and
- the nature of the risks being hedged.

A single hedging instrument may be simultaneously designated in a cash flow hedge and a fair value hedge. The situations in which this might occur are considered further in Chapter 52 at 2.1.6. Such an instrument would need to be included separately in the disclosures above both for cash flow hedges and fair value hedges. *[IAS 39.F.1.12]*.

For cash flow hedges, entities are also required to disclose: *[IFRS 7.23]*

- the periods when the cash flows are expected to occur and when they are expected to affect profit or loss;
- a description of any forecast transaction for which hedge accounting has previously been used, but which is no longer expected to occur;
- the amount that was recognised in other comprehensive income during the period;
- the amount that was reclassified from equity to profit or loss for the period, showing the amount included in each line item in the income statement; and
- the amount that was removed from equity during the period and included in the initial cost or other carrying amount of a non-financial asset or non-financial liability whose acquisition or incurrence was a hedged highly probable forecast transaction.

Finally, the following information is also required: *[IFRS 7.24]*

- for fair value hedges, gains or losses:
  - on the hedging instrument; and
  - on the hedged item attributable to the hedged risk;
- the ineffectiveness recognised in profit or loss that arises from cash flow hedges; and
- the ineffectiveness recognised in profit or loss that arises from hedges of net investments in foreign operations.

The financial statements of Deutsche Telekom include the following disclosure about hedges.

Extract 54.1: Deutsche Telekom AG (2014)

Notes to the consolidated financial statements [extract]

37. Financial instruments and risk management [extract]

Hedge accounting

Fair value hedges.

To hedge the fair value risk of fixed-interest liabilities, Deutsche Telekom primarily used interest rate swaps and forward interest rate swaps (pay variable, receive fixed) denominated in EUR, GBP, NOK and USD. Fixed-income bonds/MTNs denominated in EUR, GBP, NOK and USD were designated as hedged items. The changes in the fair values of the hedged items resulting from changes in the Euribor, GBP Libor, NOK OIBOR or USD Libor swap rate are offset against the changes in the value of the interest rate swaps. In addition, a cross-currency swap totalling AUD 125 million has been designated as fair value hedge, which converts a fixed-interest MTN into a variable interest-bearing security. The aim of this hedging is to transform the fixed-income bonds into variable-interest debt, thus hedging the fair value of the financial liabilities. Credit risks are not part of the hedging.

The effectiveness of the hedging relationship is tested prospectively and retrospectively at each reporting date using statistical methods in the form of a regression analysis. All hedging relationships were sufficiently effective as of the reporting date.

In the reporting period, new fair value hedges with a total nominal volume of EUR 3.5 billion were designated for reducing the fair value risk.

As the list of the fair values of derivatives shows (see TABLE 171, PAGE 257), Deutsche Telekom had interest rate derivatives with a net fair value of EUR 0.2 billion (December 31, 2013: EUR – 0.2 billion) designated as fair value hedges at December 31, 2014. The remeasurement of the hedged items results in losses of EUR 0.4 billion being recorded in other financial income/expense in the 2014 financial year (2013: gains of EUR 0.4 billion); the changes in the fair values of the hedging transactions result in gains of EUR 0.4 billion (2013: losses of EUR 0.4 billion) being recorded in other financial income/expense.

Cash flow hedges – interest rate risks.

Deutsche Telekom entered into payer interest rate swaps and forward payer interest rate swaps (pay fixed, receive variable) to hedge the cash flow risk of variable-interest debt. The interest payments to be made in the hedging period are the hedged items and are recognized in profit or loss in the same period. The changes in the cash flows of the hedged items resulting from changes in the Euribor and Libor rates are offset against the changes in the cash flows of the interest rate swaps. The aim of this hedging is to transform the variable-interest bonds into fixed-income debt, thus hedging the cash flows of the financial liabilities. The terms of the hedging relationships will end in the years 2015 through 2018. Credit risks are not part of the hedging.

The effectiveness of the hedging relationship is tested prospectively and retrospectively using statistical methods in the form of a regression analysis.

Ineffectiveness of EUR 19 million (income) was recognized in profit or loss under other financial income/expense in the reporting year (2013: expense of EUR 21 million).

All designated hedging relationships were sufficiently effective as of the reporting date.

As the list of fair values of derivatives shows (see TABLE 171), Deutsche Telekom had interest rate derivatives with a fair value of EUR –0.3 billion (December 31, 2013: EUR –0.3 billion) amounting to a nominal total of EUR 3.1 billion (December 31, 2013: EUR 5.0 billion) designated as hedging instruments for the hedging of interest rate risks as part of cash flow hedges at December 31, 2014.

The recognition directly in equity of the change in the fair value of the hedging instruments resulted in losses (before taxes) of EUR 97 million (2013: gains of EUR 36 million) in shareholders' equity in the 2014 financial year. Losses amounting to EUR 77 million (2013: losses of EUR 124 million) recognized directly in equity were reclassified to other financial income/expense in the income statement in the 2014 financial year.

Cash flow hedges – currency risks.

Deutsche Telekom entered into currency derivative and cross-currency swap agreements to hedge cash flows not denominated in a functional currency. The payments in foreign currency to be made in the hedging period are the hedged items and are recognized in profit or loss in the same period. The terms of the hedging relationships will end in the years 2015 through 2033. The effectiveness of the hedging relationship is tested prospectively and retrospectively using statistical methods in the form of a regression analysis. All designated hedging relationships were sufficiently effective as of the reporting date.

No new cash flow hedges of this kind were designated in the reporting period.

In the 2014 financial year, gains (before taxes) totaling EUR 362 million (2013: losses of EUR 199 million) resulting from the change in the fair values of currency derivatives were taken directly to equity (hedging reserve). These changes constitute the effective portion of the hedging relationship. In the 2014 financial year, gains totalling EUR 338 million recognized directly in equity were reclassified to other financial income/expense and gains totalling EUR 6 million on were reclassified to profit/loss from operations (2013: losses of EUR 70 million were reclassified to other financial income/expense and gains of EUR 16 million to profit/loss from operations). There was no material ineffectiveness of these hedges recorded as of the reporting date.

As the list of the fair values of derivatives shows (see TABLE 171), Deutsche Telekom had currency forwards of a net fair value of EUR –5 million (December 31, 2013: EUR +21 million), that are the result of foreign currency purchases totalling EUR 0.2 billion and foreign currency sales totalling EUR 0.4 billion (December 31, 2013: foreign currency purchases of EUR 0.3 billion and foreign currency sales of EUR 0.8 billion), as well as cross-currency swaps of a net fair value of EUR 0.1 billion (December 31, 2013: EUR –0.3 billion) and a total volume of EUR 4.8 billion (December 31, 2013: EUR 4.8 billion) designated as hedging instruments for cash flow hedges as of December 31, 2014.

Hedging of a net investment.

The hedge of the net investment in T-Mobile US against fluctuations in the U.S. dollar spot rate designated in 2012 did not generate any effects in 2014. The level of gains/losses recognized directly in equity (total other comprehensive income) remained unchanged at EUR –0.4 billion (before taxes).

Derivatives.

TABLE 171 shows the fair values of the various derivatives carried. A distinction is made depending on whether these are part of an effective hedging relationship as set out in IAS 39 (fair value hedge, cash flow hedge, net investment hedge) or not. Other derivatives can also be embedded, i.e. a component of a composite instrument that contains a non-derivative host contract.

T 171 millions of €	Net carrying amounts Dec. 31, 2014	Net carrying amounts Dec. 31, 2013
Assets		
Interest rate swaps		
Held for trading	53	54
In connection with fair value hedges	222	62
In connection with cash flow hedges	–	–
Currency forwards/currency swaps		
Held for trading	67	26
In connection with cash flow hedges	4	24
Cross-currency swaps		
Held for trading	531	358
In connection with fair value hedges	–	–
In connection with cash flow hedges	282	89
Other derivatives in connection with cash flow hedges	–	–
Other derivatives without a hedging relationship	1	–
Embedded derivatives	183	158
Liabilities and shareholders' equity		
Interest rate swaps		
Held for trading	235	226
In connection with fair value hedges	–	264
In connection with cash flow hedges	252	336
Currency forwards/currency swaps		
Held for trading	229	39
In connection with cash flow hedges	9	3
In connection with net investment hedges	–	–
Cross-currency swaps		
Held for trading	185	316
In connection with fair value hedges	8	12
In connection with cash flow hedges	162	387
Other derivatives in connection with cash flow hedges	–	–
Other derivatives without a hedging relationship	15	–
Embedded derivatives	–	–

4.3.2 Hedge accounting disclosures for entities applying IFRS 9

For entities applying IFRS 9, the disclosure requirements in respect of hedge accounting are expanded significantly when compared to IAS 39. Those requirements are also supplemented by some detailed implementation guidance. The hedge accounting requirements of IFRS 9 are dealt with in Chapter 53 which includes some discussion of the disclosure requirements set out below.

When an entity applies IFRS 9 it may choose to continue applying certain, or all, of the hedge accounting requirements of IAS 39 rather than those in IFRS 9 (see Chapter 52 at 1.3 and Chapter 53 at 3.6.6). In these circumstances the disclosure requirements introduced by IFRS 9 and covered in this section should be followed, rather than those set out at 4.3.1 above, even for those hedges that continue to be accounted for in accordance with IAS 39. *[IFRS 9.BC6.104]*.

The requirements set out at 4.3.2.A to 4.3.2.D below apply for those risk exposures that an entity hedges and for which it elects to apply hedge accounting. The objective of these disclosures is to provide information about: *[IFRS 7.21A]*

- the entity's risk management strategy and how it is applied to manage risk (see 4.3.2.A below);
- how the entity's hedging activities may affect the amount, timing and uncertainty of its future cash flows (see 4.3.2.B below); and
- the effect that hedge accounting has had on the entity's statement of financial position, statement of comprehensive income and statement of changes in equity (see 4.3.2.C and 4.3.2.D below).

In order to meet these objectives, an entity will need to determine how much detail to disclose, how much emphasis to place on different aspects of the disclosure requirements, the appropriate level of aggregation or disaggregation and whether additional explanations are needed to evaluate the quantitative information disclosed. The level of aggregation or disaggregation should be consistent with that used for meeting the disclosure requirements of related information elsewhere in IFRS 7 and in IFRS 13 (see Chapter 14 at 20.1.2). *[IFRS 7.21D]*.

Some of the disclosure requirements at 4.3.2.A to 4.3.2.C are required to be given by 'risk category'. This is not a defined term, but each risk category should be determined on the basis of the risk exposures an entity decides to hedge and for which hedge accounting is applied. These categories should be determined consistently for all hedge accounting disclosures. *[IFRS 7.21C]*.

These disclosures should be presented in a single note or separate section of the financial statements. To avoid duplication, IFRS 7 allows this information to be incorporated by cross-reference from the financial statements to some other statement that is available to users of the financial statements on the same terms and at the same time, such as a management commentary or risk report. Without the information incorporated by cross-reference, the financial statements are incomplete. *[IFRS 7.21B]*.

4.3.2.A The risk management strategy

An entity should explain its risk management strategy for each risk category of risk exposures that it decides to hedge and for which hedge accounting is applied. This explanation should enable users of financial statements to evaluate, for example: *[IFRS 7.22A]*

- how each risk arises;
- how each risk is managed.

  This includes whether the entity hedges an item in its entirety for all risks or hedges a risk component (or components) of an item and why; and
- the extent of risk exposures that are managed.

To meet these requirements, the information should include, but is not limited to, a description of: *[IFRS 7.22B]*

- the hedging instruments that are used (and how they are used) to hedge risk exposures;
- how the economic relationship between the hedged item and the hedging instrument is determined for the purpose of assessing hedge effectiveness;
- how the hedge ratio is established; and
- the sources of hedge ineffectiveness.

When a specific risk component is designated as a hedged item, qualitative or quantitative information should be provided about: *[IFRS 7.22C]*

- how the risk component that is designated as the hedged item was determined, including a description of the nature of the relationship between the risk component and the item as a whole; and
- how the risk component relates to the item in its entirety. For example, the designated risk component may historically have covered on average 80% of the changes in fair value of the item as a whole.

4.3.2.B *The amount, timing and uncertainty of future cash flows*

For most hedge relationships, quantitative information should be disclosed by risk category that allows the evaluation of the terms and conditions of the hedging instruments and how they affect the amount, timing and uncertainty of future cash flows. *[IFRS 7.23A]*. This should include a breakdown disclosing the profile of the timing of the hedging instrument's nominal amount and, if applicable, its average price or rate (e.g. strike or forward prices). *[IFRS 7.23B]*. However, different information should be given where a dynamic hedging process is used.

A dynamic process may be used in which both the exposure and the hedging instruments used to manage that exposure remain the same for only short periods of time because both the hedging instrument and the hedged item frequently change and the hedging relationship is frequently reset (or discontinued and restarted). This might occur, for example, when hedging the interest rate risk of an open portfolio of debt instruments. In these situations, the following should be disclosed: *[IFRS 7.23C]*

- information about what the ultimate risk management strategy is in relation to those hedging relationships;
- a description of how the risk management strategy is reflected by using hedge accounting and designating those particular hedging relationships; and
- an indication of how frequently the hedging relationships are discontinued and restarted as part of the process in relation to those hedging relationships.

When the volume of hedging relationships in a dynamic process is unrepresentative of normal volumes during the period (i.e. the volume at the reporting date does not reflect the volumes during the period) that fact should be disclosed along with the reason volumes are believed to be unrepresentative. *[IFRS 7.24D]*.

For all hedges, a description of the sources of hedge ineffectiveness that are expected to affect the hedging relationship during its term should be disclosed by risk category. *[IFRS 7.23D]*. If other sources of hedge ineffectiveness emerge in a hedging relationship, those sources should be disclosed by risk category along with an explanation of the resulting hedge ineffectiveness. *[IFRS 7.23E]*.

For cash flow hedges, a description of any forecast transaction for which hedge accounting had been used in the previous period, but which is no longer expected to occur, should be disclosed. *[IFRS 7.23F]*.

4.3.2.C The effects of hedge accounting on financial position and performance

The following amounts related to designated hedging instruments should be disclosed:

- the carrying amount of the hedging instruments, presenting financial assets separately from financial liabilities;
- the line item in the statement of financial position that includes the hedging instrument;
- the change in fair value of the hedging instrument used as the basis for recognising hedge ineffectiveness for the period; and
- the nominal amounts (including quantities such as tonnes or cubic metres) of the hedging instruments.

This information should be given in a tabular format, separately by risk category and for fair value hedges, cash flow hedges and hedges of a net investment in a foreign operation, *[IFRS 7.24A]*, and the implementation guidance suggests it might be given in the following format. *[IFRS 7.IG13C]*.

Example 54.1: Amounts related to hedged instruments

	Nominal amount of the hedging instrument	Carrying amount of the hedging instrument		Line item in the statement of financial position where the hedging instrument is located	Changes in fair value used for calculating hedge ineffective-ness for 20X1
		Assets	Liabilities		
Cash flow hedges					
Commodity price risk					
– Forward sales contracts	xx	xx	xx	Line item XX	xx
Fair value hedges					
Interest rate risk					
– Interest rate swaps	xx	xx	xx	Line item XX	xx
Foreign exchange risk					
– Foreign currency loan	xx	xx	xx	Line item XX	xx

The following amounts related to hedged items should be disclosed:

- for fair value hedges:
  - the carrying amount of the hedged item recognised in the statement of financial position, presenting assets separately from liabilities;
  - the accumulated amount of adjustments to the hedged item included in its carrying amount, again presenting assets separately from liabilities;

- the line item in the statement of financial position that includes the hedged item;
- the change in value of the hedged item used as the basis for recognising hedge ineffectiveness for the period; and
- the accumulated amount of adjustments to hedged financial instruments measured at amortised cost that have ceased to be adjusted for hedging gains and losses and which remain in the statement of financial position;

- for cash flow hedges and hedges of a net investment in a foreign operation:
  - the change in value of the hedged item used as the basis for recognising hedge ineffectiveness for the period;
  - the balances in the cash flow hedge reserve and the foreign currency translation reserve for continuing hedges; and
  - the balances remaining in the cash flow hedge reserve and the foreign currency translation reserve from any hedging relationships for which hedge accounting is no longer applied.

This information should be given in a tabular format, separately by risk category, *[IFRS 7.24B]*, and the implementation guidance suggests it might be given in the following format. *[IFRS 7.IG13D]*.

Example 54.2: Amounts related to hedged items

	Carrying amount of the hedged item		**Accumulated amount of fair value hedge adjustments on the hedged item included in the carrying amount of the hedged item**		**Line item in the statement of financial position in which the hedged item is included**	**Change in value used for calculating hedge ineffective-ness for 20X1**	**Cash flow hedge reserve**
	Assets	**Liabilities**	**Assets**	**Liabilities**			
Cash flow hedges							
Commodity price risk							
– Forecast sales	n/a	n/a	n/a	n/a	n/a	xx	xx
– Discontinued hedges (forecast sales)	n/a	n/a	n/a	n/a	n/a	n/a	xx
Fair value hedges							
Interest rate risk							
– Loan payable	–	xx	–	xx	Line item XX	xx	n/a
– Discontinued hedges (Loan payable)	–	xx	–	xx	Line item XX	n/a	n/a
Foreign exchange risk							
– Firm commitment	xx	xx	xx	xx	Line item XX	xx	n/a

The following amounts affecting the statement of comprehensive income should be disclosed:

- for fair value hedges:
  - hedge ineffectiveness, i.e. the difference between the hedging gains or losses of the hedging instrument and the hedged item, recognised in profit or loss (or other comprehensive income for hedges of an equity instrument for which changes in fair value are presented in other comprehensive income); and
  - the line item in the statement of comprehensive income that includes the recognised hedge ineffectiveness;
- for cash flow hedges and hedges of a net investment in a foreign operation:
  - hedging gains or losses that were recognised in other comprehensive income in the reporting period;
  - hedge ineffectiveness recognised in profit or loss;
  - the line item in the statement of comprehensive income that includes the recognised hedge ineffectiveness;
  - the amount reclassified from the cash flow hedge reserve or the foreign currency translation reserve into profit or loss as a reclassification adjustment, differentiating in the case of cash flow hedges between:
    - amounts for which hedge accounting had previously been used, but for which the hedged future cash flows are no longer expected to occur; and
    - amounts that have been transferred because the hedged item has affected profit or loss;
  - the line item in the statement of comprehensive income that includes the reclassification adjustment; and
  - for hedges of net positions, the hedging gains or losses recognised in a separate line item in the statement of comprehensive income.

This information should be given in a tabular format, separately by risk category, *[IFRS 7.24C]*, and the implementation guidance suggests it might be given in the following format. *[IFRS 7.IG13E]*.

Example 54.3: Amounts affecting the statement of comprehensive income.

Cash flow hedges (a)	Separate line item recognised in profit or loss as a result of a hedge of a net position(b)	Change in the value of the hedging instrument recognised in other comprehensive income	Hedge ineffective-ness recognised in profit or loss	Line item in profit or loss (that includes hedge ineffectiveness)	Amount reclassified from the cash flow hedge reserve to profit or loss	Line item affected in profit or loss because of the reclassification
Commodity price risk						
Commodity X	n/a	xx	xx	Line item XX	xx	Line item XX
– Discontinued hedge	n/a	n/a	n/a	n/a	xx	Line item XX

(a) The information disclosed in the statement of changes in equity (cash flow hedge reserve) should have the same level of detail as these disclosures.
(b) This disclosure only applies to cash flow hedges of foreign currency risk.

Fair value Hedges	Ineffectiveness recognised in profit or loss	Line item(s) in profit or loss (that include(s) hedge ineffectiveness)
Interest rate risk	xx	Line item XX
Foreign exchange risk	xx	Line item XX

IAS 1 requires the presentation of a reconciliation of each component of equity and an analysis of other comprehensive income (see 7.2 and 7.3 below). The level of information given in the reconciliation and analysis should: *[IFRS 7.24E]*

- differentiate between hedging gains or losses recognised in other comprehensive income and amounts reclassified to profit or loss, separately for:
  - cash flow hedges for which the hedged future cash flows are no longer expected to occur;
  - those hedges for which the hedged item has affected profit or loss; and
  - amounts related to hedged forecast transactions that subsequently result in the recognition of a non-financial asset or liability, or a hedged forecast transaction for a non-financial asset or liability becomes a firm commitment for which fair value hedge accounting is applied, that are included directly in the initial cost or other carrying amount of the asset or the liability;
- differentiate between amounts associated with the time value of options that hedge transaction related hedged items and those that hedge time-period related hedged items where the time value of the option is recognised initially in other comprehensive income; and
- differentiate between amounts associated with forward elements of forward contracts and the foreign currency basis spreads of financial instruments that hedge transaction related hedged items and those that hedge time-period related hedged items where those amounts are recognised initially in other comprehensive income.

The information in the bullets above should be disclosed separately by risk category, although this disaggregation may be provided in the notes to the financial statements. *[IFRS 7.24F]*.

Further examples of how these disclosures might be provided are set out in Chapter 53 at 9.

4.3.2.D Option to designate a credit exposure as measured at fair value through profit or loss

If a financial instrument, or a proportion of it, has been designated as measured at fair value through profit or loss because a credit derivative is used to manage the credit risk of that financial instrument, the following should be disclosed: *[IFRS 7.24G]*

- a reconciliation of each of the nominal amount and the fair value of the credit derivative at the beginning and end of the period;
- the gain or loss recognised in profit or loss on initial designation; and
- on discontinuation of measuring a financial instrument, or a proportion of it, at fair value through profit or loss, the fair value of that financial instrument that becomes the new carrying amount and the related nominal or principal amount.

  Except for providing comparative information in accordance with IAS 1, this information need not be given in subsequent periods.

4.4 Statement of financial position

4.4.1 Categories of financial assets and financial liabilities

For entities applying IAS 39, the carrying amounts of each of the following categories of financial instrument should be disclosed, either on the face of the statement of financial position or in the notes: *[IFRS 7.8]*

- financial assets at fair value through profit or loss, showing separately:
  - those designated as such upon initial recognition; and
  - those classified as held for trading;
- held-to-maturity investments;
- loans and receivables;
- available-for-sale financial assets;
- financial liabilities at fair value through profit or loss, showing separately:
  - those designated as such upon initial recognition; and
  - those classified as held for trading; and
- financial liabilities measured at amortised cost.

The IASB concluded that such disclosure would assist users in understanding the extent to which accounting policies affect the amounts at which financial assets and financial liabilities are recognised. *[IFRS 7.BC14]*.

Although accounted for identically, the carrying amounts of financial instruments that are classified as held for trading and those designated at fair value through profit or loss are shown separately because designation is at the discretion of the entity. *[IFRS 7.BC15]*.

On application of IFRS 9, the disclosure requirements above are amended to align them with that standard. Consequently, disclosure should be made using the following categories: *[IFRS 7.8]*

- financial assets measured at fair value through profit or loss, showing separately:
  - those designated as such upon initial recognition; and
  - those mandatorily measured at fair value in accordance with IFRS 9;
- financial liabilities at fair value through profit or loss, showing separately:
  - those designated as such upon initial recognition; and
  - those that meet the definition of held for trading in IFRS 9;
- financial assets measured at amortised cost;
- financial liabilities measured at amortised cost; and
- financial assets measured at fair value through other comprehensive income, showing separately:
  - debt instruments held within a business model to both collect contractual cash flows from, and to sell, the assets; and
  - investments in equity instruments designated to be measured as such upon initial recognition.

A derivative that is designated as a hedging instrument in an effective hedge relationship does not fall within any of the above categories and, strictly, should not be included in these disclosures. Disclosure requirements for hedges are set out at 4.3 above.

4.4.2 *Financial liabilities designated at fair value through profit or loss*

4.4.2.A *Entities applying IAS 39*

Where a (non-derivative) financial liability has been designated at fair value through profit or loss, i.e. it is not classified as trading, the amount of change during the period and cumulatively (i.e. since initial recognition) in its fair value that is attributable to changes in credit risk should be disclosed. *[IFRS 7.10(a)]*.

Unless an alternative method more faithfully represents this amount, it should be determined as the amount of change in the fair value of the liability that is not attributable to changes in market conditions that give rise to market risk. Changes in market conditions that give rise to market risk include changes in a benchmark interest rate, commodity price, foreign exchange rate or index of prices or rates. For contracts that include a unit-linking feature, changes in market conditions include changes in the performance of an internal or external investment fund. *[IFRS 7.10(a)]*. If the only relevant changes in market conditions for a financial liability are changes in an observed (benchmark) interest rate, the amount to be disclosed can be estimated as follows:

(a) first, the liability's internal rate of return at the start of the period is computed using the observed market price and contractual cash flows at that time and from this is deducted the observed (benchmark) interest rate at the start of the period, to arrive at an instrument specific component of the internal rate of return;

(b) next, the present value of the cash flows associated with the liability is calculated using the liability's contractual cash flows at the end of the period and a discount rate equal to the sum of the observed (benchmark) interest rate at the end of the period and the instrument-specific component of the internal rate of return at the start of the period as determined in (a); and

(c) the difference between the observed market price of the liability at the end of the period and the amount determined in (b) is the change in fair value that is not attributable to changes in the observed (benchmark) interest rate and this is the amount to be disclosed.

This assumes that changes in fair value other than those arising from changes in the instrument's credit risk or from changes in interest rates are not significant. If the instrument contained an embedded derivative, the change in fair value of the embedded derivative would be excluded in determining the amount to be disclosed. *[IFRS 7.B4]*.

The default method will produce an amount which includes any changes in the liquidity spread charged by market participants because such changes are not considered to be 'attributable to changes in market conditions that give rise to market risk'. This seems appropriate when the effect of a liquidity spread cannot be isolated from that of the credit spread.

This method is illustrated in the following example. *[IFRS 7.IG7]*.

Example 54.4: Estimating the change in fair value of an instrument attributable to its credit risk

On 1 January 2017, Company J issues a 10-year bond with a par value of €150,000 and an annual fixed coupon rate of 8%, which is consistent with market rates for bonds with similar characteristics. J uses LIBOR as its observable (benchmark) interest rate. At the date of inception of the bond, LIBOR is 5%. At the end of the first year:

- LIBOR has decreased to 4.75%; and
- the fair value of the bond is €153,811, consistent with an interest rate of 7.6% [the remaining cash flows on the bond, i.e. €12,000 per year for nine years and €150,000 at the end of nine years, discounted at 7.6% equals €153,811].

J assumes a flat yield curve, that all changes in interest rates result from a parallel shift in the yield curve, and that the changes in LIBOR are the only relevant changes in market conditions.

The amount of change in the fair value of the bond that is not attributable to changes in market conditions that give rise to market risk is estimated as follows:

Step (a)

The bond's internal rate of return at the start of the period is 8%. Because the observed (benchmark) interest rate (LIBOR) is 5%, the instrument-specific component of the internal rate of return is 3%.

Step (b)

The contractual cash flows of the instrument at the end of the period are:

- interest: €12,000 [€150,000 × 8%] per year for each of years 2018 to 2026; and
- principal: €150,000 in 2026

The discount rate to be used to calculate the present value of the bond is thus 7.75%, which is the 4.75% end of period LIBOR rate, plus the 3% instrument-specific component calculated as at the start of the period which gives a notional present value of €152,367 [€12,000 × (1 – 1.0775^{-9}) ÷ 0.0775) + €150,000 × 1.0775^{-9}], on the assumption that there has been no change in the instrument-specific component.

Step (c)

The market price of the liability at the end of the period (which will reflect the real instrument-specific component at the end of the period) is €153,811, therefore J should disclose €1,444 [€153,811 – €152,367] as the increase in fair value of the bond that is not attributable to changes in market conditions that give rise to market risk. *[IFRS 7.IG8, IG9, IG10, IG11].*

If another method more faithfully represents the amount of change in the fair value of the liability that is attributable to changes in credit risk, that method should be used. *[IFRS 7.10(a)(ii)].*

Whatever the chosen method(s), it (they) should be disclosed. Further, if the disclosure is not considered to represent faithfully the change in the fair value of the financial liability attributable to changes in credit risk, the reasons for reaching this conclusion and the factors believed to be relevant should also be disclosed. *[IFRS 7.11].* This second requirement is somewhat curious and, where provided, could be regarded as undermining the entity's compliance with the requirements above.

In addition, the IASB concluded that the difference between the carrying amount of such a liability and the amount the entity would be contractually required to pay at maturity to the holder of the obligation should also be disclosed. *[IFRS 7.10(b)].* The fair value may differ significantly from the settlement amount, particularly for liabilities with a long duration when the entity has experienced a significant deterioration in creditworthiness subsequent to issuance and the IASB concluded that knowledge of this difference would be useful. Also, the settlement amount is important to some financial statement users, particularly creditors. *[IFRS 7.BC22].*

4.4.2.B Entities applying IFRS 9

For entities applying IFRS 9, very similar disclosure requirements to those set out at 4.4.2.A above apply, although they are supplemented by a number of additional requirements. Further, entities should follow the requirements of IFRS 9 for determining changes in the fair value of a financial liability attributable to credit risk (see Chapter 50 at 2.1.1) rather than those in IFRS 7, although they are very similar. *[IFRS 7.10, 10A, 11].*

Where changes in the fair value of a financial liability attributable to credit risk are recognised in other comprehensive income (see Chapter 50 at 2.1), any transfers of the cumulative gain or loss within equity should be disclosed, including the reason for such transfers. *[IFRS 7.10(c)]*. Also, if a financial liability is derecognised during the period, the amount (if any) presented in other comprehensive income that was realised at derecognition should be disclosed. *[IFRS 7.10(d)]*.

When disclosing the method used to calculate the change in fair value attributable to changes in credit risk, a detailed description of that method should be given, including an explanation of why the method is appropriate. *[IFRS 7.11(a)]*.

Entities should also provide a detailed description of the methodology or methodologies used to determine whether presenting changes in the fair value of a liability attributable to credit risk in other comprehensive income would create or enlarge an accounting mismatch in profit or loss (see Chapter 50 at 2.1.2). Where an entity is required to present such changes in profit or loss, this disclosure should include a detailed description of the economic relationship between the financial liability and other financial instrument(s) measured at fair value through profit or loss that are expected to offset those changes. *[IFRS 7.11(c)]*.

4.4.3 Financial assets designated as measured at fair value through profit or loss

Additional disclosure requirements apply to loans and receivables (or groups of such assets) that are designated at fair value through profit or loss in accordance with IAS 39. Where IFRS 9 has been applied, the disclosure requirements apply to debt instruments that would otherwise be measured at fair value through other comprehensive income or at amortised cost.

These requirements are: *[IFRS 7.9]*

- the maximum exposure to credit risk (see 5.2.2.A or 5.2.3.D below) at the reporting date of the loan or receivable (or group of loans or receivables);
- the amount by which any related credit derivatives or similar instruments mitigate that maximum exposure to credit risk;
- the amount of change during the period and cumulatively (i.e. since initial recognition) in the fair value of the loan or receivable (or group of loans or receivables) that is attributable to changes in credit risk (see below); and
- the amount of change in the fair value of any related credit derivative or similar instrument that has occurred during the period and cumulatively since the loan or receivable was designated.

Calculating the change in fair value attributable to changes in credit risk is approached in the same way as for financial liabilities (see 4.4.2 above). It may be determined either as the amount of change in fair value that is not attributable to changes in market conditions that give rise to market risk or by using an alternative method that more faithfully represents the amount of change in its fair value that is attributable to changes in credit risk. *[IFRS 7.9]*. The chosen method(s) should be disclosed and if the disclosure is not considered to represent faithfully the change in the fair value of the financial asset attributable to changes in credit risk, the reasons for reaching this conclusion and the factors believed to be relevant should be disclosed. *[IFRS 7.11]*.

Although this is not addressed explicitly within the standard, we believe that the disclosure requirements above apply to hybrid financial assets that would, absent the designation, be accounted for as a loan or receivable and a separate embedded derivative in accordance with IAS 39, not just those financial assets that meet the definition of loans and receivables in their entirety.

On application of IFRS 9, very similar disclosure requirements to those set out above apply for a financial asset (or group of financial assets) designated as measured at fair value through profit or loss that would otherwise be measured at amortised cost. *[IFRS 7.9]*. When disclosing the method used to calculate the change in fair value attributable to changes in credit risk, an entity applying IFRS 9 should also provide a detailed description of that method, including an explanation of why the method is appropriate. *[IFRS 7.11(a)]*.

4.4.4 Investments in equity instruments designated at fair value through other comprehensive income (IFRS 9)

Where IFRS 9 is applied and investments in equity instruments have been designated to be measured at fair value through other comprehensive income (see Chapter 47 at 2 and 8), the following should be disclosed: *[IFRS 7.11A]*

- which investments in equity instruments have been designated to be measured at fair value through other comprehensive income;
- the reasons for using this presentation alternative;
- the fair value of each such investment at the end of the reporting period;
- dividends recognised during the period, showing separately those related to investments derecognised during the reporting period and those related to investments held at the end of the reporting period; and
- any transfers of the cumulative gain or loss within equity during the period, including the reason for such transfers.

Where such investments are derecognised during the reporting period, the following should also be disclosed: *[IFRS 7.11B]*

- the reasons for disposing of the investments;
- the fair value of the investments at the date of derecognition; and
- the cumulative gain or loss on disposal.

4.4.5 Reclassification

The circumstances in which financial instruments should or may be reclassified from one category to another are discussed in Chapter 46 at 6 for those entities applying IAS 39 and, where IFRS 9 is applied, in Chapter 47 at 9.

4.4.5.A Reclassifications in accordance with the October 2008 'reclassification' amendments to IAS 39

If an entity has reclassified a financial asset out of the fair value through profit or loss category (see Chapter 46 at 6.1.1) or out of the available-for-sale category (see Chapter 46 at 6.2) in accordance with the October 2008 amendments to IAS 39, it should disclose: *[IFRS 7.12A]*

(a) the amount reclassified into and out of each category;

(b) for each reporting period until derecognition, the carrying amounts and fair values of all financial assets that have been reclassified in the current and previous reporting periods;

(c) if a financial asset was reclassified as a result of 'rare circumstances' (see Chapter 46 at 6.1.1.B), the rare situation and the facts and circumstances indicating that the situation was rare;

(d) for the reporting period when the financial asset was reclassified, the fair value gain or loss on the financial asset recognised in profit or loss or other comprehensive income in that reporting period and in the previous reporting period;

(e) for each reporting period following the reclassification (including the reporting period in which the financial asset was reclassified) until derecognition of the financial asset, the fair value gain or loss that would have been recognised in profit or loss or other comprehensive income if the financial asset had not been reclassified, and the gain, loss, income and expense recognised in profit or loss; and

(f) the effective interest rate and estimated amounts of cash flows the entity expects to recover, as at the date of reclassification of the financial asset.

The IASB regarded such information as useful because the reclassification of a financial asset can have a significant effect on the financial statements. *[IFRS 7.BC23A]*. A survey by CESR of one hundred European financial companies' financial statements clearly demonstrates this to have been true. It found that €550 billion of assets had been reclassified in 2008 and the amount reported in profit or loss and other comprehensive income was an aggregate €28 billion higher as a result. Unfortunately, CESR also found some significant deficiencies in the compliance by these companies with the requirements above, particularly (d) and (f).[4]

4.4.5.B Other reclassifications under IAS 39

Under IAS 39, financial assets should be reclassified from held-to-maturity investments to available-for-sale assets and *vice versa* in certain circumstances, for example as a result of a change in intention or ability to hold a debt instrument to maturity (see Chapter 46 at 6.3). Where this occurs, the amount reclassified into and out of each category should be disclosed, together with the reason for that reclassification. *[IFRS 7.12]*.

This disclosure should also be provided for those unquoted equity instruments and related derivative assets that cease to be measured at cost or at fair value because a reliable measure of fair value becomes available or ceases to be available (see Chapter 49 at 2.1, 2.4 and 2.6). *[IFRS 7.12]*. Strictly, this requirement does not appear to apply to similar derivative liabilities whose measurement basis changes from cost to fair value or *vice versa*, although it would seem sensible to make equivalent disclosures.

4.4.5.C Reclassifications of financial assets in accordance with IFRS 9

Where IFRS 9 is applied, there are circumstances in which a financial asset will be reclassified in response to a change in an entity's business model (see Chapter 47 at 9). If, in the current or previous reporting periods, any such reclassifications have occurred, the following should be disclosed: *[IFRS 7.12B]*

- the date of reclassification;
- a detailed explanation of the change in business model and a qualitative description of its effect on the entity's financial statements; and
- the amount reclassified into and out of each category.

For assets previously measured at fair value through profit or loss that are reclassified so that they are measured at amortised cost or at fair value through other comprehensive income, the following information should be disclosed in each reporting period following reclassification until derecognition: *[IFRS 7.12C]*

- the effective interest rate determined on the date of reclassification; and
- the interest income or expense recognised.

Where financial assets previously measured at fair value through other comprehensive income have been reclassified since the last annual reporting date so that they are measured at amortised cost, the following should be disclosed: *[IFRS 7.12D]*

- the fair value of the financial assets at the end of the reporting period; and
- the fair value gain or loss that would have been recognised in profit or loss during the reporting period if the financial assets had not been reclassified.

4.4.6 Collateral

Where an entity has pledged financial assets as collateral for liabilities or contingent liabilities it should disclose the carrying amount of those assets and the terms and conditions relating to its pledge. This also applies to transfers of non-cash collateral where the transferee has the right, by contract or custom, to sell or repledge the collateral (see Chapter 51 at 5.5.2). *[IFRS 7.14]*.

When an entity holds collateral (of financial or non-financial assets) and is permitted to sell or repledge the collateral in the absence of default by the owner of the collateral, it should disclose: *[IFRS 7.15]*

- the fair value of the collateral held;
- the fair value of any such collateral sold or repledged, and whether the entity has an obligation to return it; and
- the terms and conditions associated with its use of the collateral.

Although some respondents to the exposure draft that preceded IFRS 7 (ED 7) argued for an exemption from this disclosure in cases where it is impracticable to obtain the fair value of the collateral held, the IASB concluded that it is reasonable to expect an entity to know the fair value of collateral that it holds and can sell even where there is no default. *[IFRS 7.BC25]*. Entities have continued to question the usefulness of this requirement and requested that it be removed, but the IASB has shown no inclination do so.[5]

4.4.7 Allowance account for credit losses

For entities applying IAS 39, IFRS 7 requires disclosures to be made when impairments of financial assets are recorded in a separate account (for example, an allowance account used to record individual impairments or a similar account used to record a collective impairment of assets) rather than directly reducing the carrying amount of the asset. In such cases an entity should disclose a reconciliation of changes in that account during the period for each class of financial assets. *[IFRS 7.16]*. The components of the reconciliation are not specified, thereby allowing entities flexibility in determining the most appropriate format for their needs. *[IFRS 7.BC26]*.

Equivalent information is not required for entities that do not use an allowance account. However, the IASB believes that IAS 39's requirement to consider impairment on a group or collective basis (see Chapter 49 at 4) necessitates the use of an allowance or similar account for virtually all entities. The disclosures required by IFRS 7 in respect of accounting policies (see 4.1 above) also include information about the use of direct adjustments to carrying amounts of financial assets. *[IFRS 7.BC27]*.

This requirement applies to all entities, not just financial institutions, and the following extracts from the financial statements of Deutsche Telekom and the Nationwide Building Society show how this requirement has been dealt with in practice.

Extract 54.2: Deutsche Telekom AG (2014)

Notes to the consolidated statement of financial position [extract]

2 Trade and other receivables [extract]

The allowances on trade receivables developed as follows:

millions of €	**2014**	2013
Allowances as of January 1	**1,344**	1,316
Currency translation adjustments	**15**	(15)
Additions (allowances recognized as expense)	**641**	642
Use	**(410)**	(479)
Reversal	**(222)**	(120)
Allowances as of December 31	**1,368**	1,344

Extract 54.3: Nationwide Building Society (2015)

Notes to the Accounts [extract]

10 Impairment provisions on loans and advances to customers [extract]

The following provisions have been deducted from the appropriate asset values in the balance sheet:

2015 Group	**Prime residential**	**Specialist residential**	**Consumer banking**	**Commercial lending**	**Other lending**	**Total**
	£m	**£m**	**£m**	**£m**	**£m**	**£m**
At 5 April 2014	**18**	**84**	**173**	**1,001**	**12**	**1,288**
Charge for the year	**13**	**45**	**89**	**52**	**34**	**233**
Amounts written off during the year	**(10)**	**(41)**	**(56)**	**(276)**	**(6)**	**(389)**
Amounts recovered during the year	**1**	**1**	**15**	**15**	**–**	**32**
Disposals	**–**	**–**	**–**	**(428)**	**(36)**	**(464)**
Unwind of discount	**–**	**(1)**	**(5)**	**(42)**	**–**	**(48)**
At 4 April 2015	**22**	**88**	**216**	**322**	**4**	**652**

2014 Group	**Prime residential**	**Specialist residential**	**Consumer banking**	**Commercial lending**	**Other lending**	**Total**
	£m	**£m**	**£m**	**£m**	**£m**	**£m**
At 5 April 2013	32	133	87	958	14	1,224
Charge for the year	–	–	60	309	11	380
Amounts written off during the year	(15)	(52)	(3)	(215)	(9)	(294)
Amounts recovered during the year	1	4	33	10	–	48
Disposals	–	–	–	–	(4)	(4)
Unwind of discount	–	(1)	(4)	(61)	–	(66)
At 4 April 2014	18	84	173	1,001	12	1,288

The Group impairment provision of £652 million at 4 April 2015 (2014: £1,288 million) comprises individual provisions of £341 million (2014: £959 million) and collective provisions of £311 million (2014: £329 million).

The charge for the year for prime and specialist residential loans primarily results from refinements to credit risk provision assumptions, which reflect a segmental review of actual loss experience and take account of the impacts of the prolonged low interest rate environment.

The increase in impairment provisions on consumer banking is driven by a change in the accounting treatment for charged off accounts in 2014. Previously these accounts had been written off in full with subsequent recoveries taken to profit when received. Balances on charged off accounts are now held on the balance sheet, together with relevant provisions, where at least partial recovery is still expected.

The £464 million for disposals relates to divestment activity undertaken during the year in relation to non-core commercial real estate lending and out of policy treasury assets.

When IFRS 9 is applied, the requirement above is withdrawn and replaced by a requirement to disclose in the notes the loss allowance in respect of debt instruments measured at fair value through other comprehensive income. *[IFRS 7.16A]*. In addition, more extensive disclosures about credit risk and loss allowances on financial assets measured at amortised cost are required as set out at 5.2.3 below.

4.4.8 Compound financial instruments with multiple embedded derivatives

Where an instrument has been issued that contains both a liability and an equity component and the instrument has multiple embedded derivatives whose values are interdependent, such as a callable convertible debt instrument (see Chapter 45 at 6.4.2), the existence of these features should be disclosed. *[IFRS 7.17]*. Accordingly, the impact on the amounts reported as liabilities and equity will be highlighted, something the IASB sees as important given the acknowledged arbitrary nature of the allocation under IAS 32 of the joint value attributable to this interdependence. *[IFRS 7.BC31]*.

4.4.9 Defaults and breaches of loans payable

Loans payable are defined as 'financial liabilities other than short-term trade payables on normal credit terms.' *[IFRS 7 Appendix A]*. It is considered that disclosures about defaults and breaches of loans payable and other loan agreements provide relevant information about the entity's creditworthiness and its prospects of obtaining future loans. *[IFRS 7.BC32]*.

Accordingly, for any loans payable recognised at the reporting date, an entity is required to disclose: *[IFRS 7.18]*

- details of any defaults during the period of principal, interest, sinking fund, or redemption terms;
- the carrying amount of the loans payable in default at the reporting date; and
- whether the default was remedied, or the terms of the loans payable were renegotiated, before the financial statements were authorised for issue.

If, during the period, there were breaches of loan agreement terms other than those described above, the same information should be disclosed if those breaches permitted the lender to demand accelerated repayment (unless the breaches were remedied, or the terms of the loan were renegotiated, on or before the reporting date). *[IFRS 7.19]*.

It is noted that any defaults or breaches may affect the classification of the liability as current or non-current in accordance with IAS 1 (see Chapter 3 at 3.1.4). *[IFRS 7.IG12]*.

4.4.10 Interests in other entities accounted for in accordance with IAS 39 or IFRS 9

IAS 28 – *Investments in Associates and Joint Ventures* – allows an interest in an associate or a joint venture held by a venture capital or similar organisation to be measured at fair value through profit or loss in accordance with IAS 39 or IFRS 9 (see Chapter 11 at 5.3). In these circumstances, IFRS 12 – *Disclosure of Interests in Other Entities* – contains additional disclosure requirements, over and above those in IFRS 7, which are dealt with in Chapter 13 at 2.2.3.D and 5.

4.5 Fair values

4.5.1 General disclosure requirements

The IASB sees the disclosure of information about the fair value of financial assets and liabilities as being an important requirement. It is explained in the following terms:

> 'Many entities use fair value information internally in determining their overall financial position and in making decisions about individual financial instruments. It is also relevant to many decisions made by users of financial statements because, in many circumstances, it reflects the judgement of the financial markets about the present value of expected future cash flows relating to an instrument. Fair value information permits comparisons of financial instruments having substantially the same economic characteristics, regardless of why they are held and when and by whom they were issued or acquired. Fair values provide a neutral basis for assessing management's stewardship by indicating the effects of its decisions to buy, sell or hold financial assets and to incur, maintain or discharge financial liabilities.'

Therefore, when financial assets or liabilities are not measured on a fair value basis, information on fair values should be given by way of supplementary disclosures to assist users in comparing entities on a consistent basis. *[IFRS 7.BC36]*.

More specifically, except as set out below, the fair value of each class of financial assets and liabilities should be disclosed in a way that permits comparison with the corresponding carrying amounts. *[IFRS 7.25]*. In providing this disclosure, instruments should be offset only to the extent that their related carrying amounts are also offset in the statement of financial position. *[IFRS 7.26]*. IFRS 13 contains guidance on determining fair values and includes more extensive disclosure requirements about the fair values disclosed. These are discussed in Chapter 14 at 20.

Pragmatically, disclosure of fair values is not required for instruments whose carrying amount reasonably approximates their fair value, for example short-term trade receivables and payables. *[IFRS 7.29(a)]*.

Fair values need not be given for investments in unquoted equity instruments, or derivatives linked to such instruments, that are measured at cost because their fair value cannot be measured reliably (see Chapter 49 at 2.6). When IFRS 9 is applied, this concession ceases to apply. *[IFRS 7.29(b)]*.

As set out in Chapter 43 at 3.3.2 some instruments (normally life insurance policies) contain a discretionary participation feature. If the fair value of that feature cannot be reliably measured, disclosures of fair value are not required. *[IFRS 7.29(c)]*.

When IFRS 16 is applied, disclosure need not be given of the fair value of lease liabilities. *[IFRS 7.29(d)]*. IFRS 16 is effective for periods commencing on or after 1 January 2019 (see 8.4 below).

However, additional disclosures should be given about instruments for which the fair value cannot be reliably measured. This is to assist users of the financial statements in making their own judgements about the extent of possible differences between the carrying amount of such contracts and their fair value. In particular, the following should be disclosed: *[IFRS 7.30]*

- the fact that fair value has not been disclosed because it cannot be reliably measured;
- a description of the instruments, their carrying amount, and an explanation of why fair value cannot be measured reliably;
- information about the market for the instruments;
- information about whether and how the entity intends to dispose of the instruments; and
- for instruments whose fair value previously could not be reliably measured that are derecognised:
  - that fact;
  - their carrying amount at the time of derecognition; and
  - the amount of gain or loss recognised.

For all other financial instruments, the IASB believes it is reasonable to expect that fair value can be determined with sufficient reliability within constraints of timeliness and cost. It therefore concluded that there should be no exception from the requirement to disclose fair value information for these instruments. *[IFRS 7.BC37]*.

4.5.2 Day 1 profits

In certain situations there will be a difference between the transaction price for a financial asset or financial liability and the fair value that would be determined at that date in accordance with IFRS 13 (commonly known as a day 1 profit). *[IFRS 7.28]*. As set out in Chapter 48 at 3.2, an entity should not recognise a day 1 profit on initial recognition of the financial instrument if the fair value is neither evidenced by a quoted price in an active market for an identical asset or liability (known as a Level 1 input) nor based on a valuation technique that uses only data from observable markets. Instead, the difference will be recognised in profit or loss in subsequent periods in accordance with IAS 39 or IFRS 9 and the entity's accounting policy. *[IFRS 7.IG14]*.

Where such a difference exists, IFRS 7 requires disclosure, by class of financial instrument of: *[IFRS 7.28]*

- the accounting policy for recognising that difference in profit or loss to reflect a change in factors (including time) that market participants would take into account when setting a price for the financial instrument;
- the aggregate difference yet to be recognised in profit or loss at the beginning and end of the period and a reconciliation of changes in the amount of this difference; and
- why it was concluded that the transaction price was not the best evidence of fair value, including a description of the evidence that supports the fair value.

In other words, disclosure is required of the profits an entity might think it has made but which it is prohibited from recognising, at least for the time being. This disclosure is illustrated in the following example based on the implementation guidance. It is rather curious in that it illustrates a day 1 loss, not profit.

Example 54.5: Disclosure of deferred day 1 profits

On 1 January 2016 Company R purchases financial assets that are not traded in an active market for €15 million which represents their fair value at initial recognition. After initial recognition, R applies a valuation technique to measure the fair value of the financial assets. This valuation technique uses inputs other than data from observable markets. At initial recognition, the same valuation technique would have resulted in an amount of €14 million, which differs from fair value by €1 million. R has only one class of such financial assets with existing differences of €5 million at 1 January 2016. The disclosure in R's 2017 financial statements would include the following: *[IFRS 7.IG14]*

Accounting policies

R uses the following valuation technique to measure the fair value of financial instruments that are not traded in an active market: [insert description of technique, not included in this example] Differences may arise between the fair value at initial recognition (which, in accordance with IFRS 13 and IAS 39 or IFRS 9, is normally the transaction price) and the amount determined at initial recognition using the valuation technique. Any such differences are [description of R's accounting policy].

In the notes to the financial statements

As discussed in note X, [insert name of valuation technique] is used to measure the fair value of the following financial instruments that are not traded in an active market. However, in accordance with IFRS 13 and IAS 39 or IFRS 9, the fair value of an instrument at inception is normally the transaction price. If the transaction price differs from the amount determined at inception using the valuation technique, that difference is [description of R's accounting policy].

The differences yet to be recognised in profit or loss are as follows:

	2017 €m	2016 €m
Balance at beginning of year	5.3	5.0
New transactions	–	1.0
Recognised in profit or loss during the year	(0.7)	(0.8)
Other increases	(0.1)	(0.1)
Balance at end of year	4.5	5.3

UBS discloses the following information about recognition of day 1 profits.

Extract 54.4: UBS AG (2014)

Notes to the UBS AG consolidated financial statements [extract]

24 Fair value measurement [extract]

d) Valuation adjustments [extract]

Day-1 reserves [extract]

For new transactions where the valuation technique used to measure fair value requires significant inputs that are not based on observable market data, the financial instrument is initially recognized at the transaction price. The transaction price may differ from the fair value obtained using a valuation technique, and any such difference is deferred and not recognized in the income statement. These day-1 profit or loss reserves are reflected, where appropriate, as valuation adjustments.

The table below provides the changes in deferred day-1 profit or loss reserves during the respective period. Amounts deferred are released and gains or losses are recorded in *Net trading income* when pricing of equivalent products or the underlying parameters become observable or when the transaction is closed out.

Deferred day-1 profit or loss	**For the year ended**		
CHF million	31.12.14	31.12.13	31.12.12
Balance at the beginning of the year	486	474	433
Profit/(loss) deferred on new transactions	344	694	424
(Profit)/loss recognized in the income statement	(384)	(653)	(367)
Foreign currency translation	35	(29)	(16)
Balance at the end of the year	480	486	474

4.6 Business combinations

IFRS 3 – *Business Combinations* – requires an acquirer to disclose additional information about financial instruments arising from business combinations that occur during the reporting period. These requirements are discussed below.

4.6.1 Acquired receivables

Some constituents were concerned that prohibiting the use of an allowance account when accounting for acquired receivables at fair value (see Chapter 48 at 3.2.4) could make it impossible to determine the contractual cash flows due on those assets and the amount of those cash flows not expected to be collected. They asked for additional disclosure to help in assessing considerations of credit quality used in estimating those fair values, including expectations about receivables that will be uncollectible.

[IFRS 3.BC258]. Consequently, the IASB decided to require the following disclosures to be made about such assets acquired in a business combination:

- fair value of the receivables;
- gross contractual amounts receivable; and
- the best estimate at the acquisition date of the contractual cash flows not expected to be collected.

This information should be provided by major class of receivable, such as loans, direct finance leases and any other class of receivables. *[IFRS 3.B64(h)]*.

Although these requirements will produce some of the information users need to evaluate the credit quality of receivables acquired, the IASB acknowledged that it may not provide all such information. However, this is seen as an interim measure and the IASB will monitor a related FASB project with a view to improving the disclosure requirements in the future, *[IFRS 3.BC260]*, although it is not clear when such a project might be completed.

4.6.2 *Contingent consideration and indemnification assets*

The following information about contingent consideration arrangements and indemnification assets (see Chapter 43 at 3.7.1 and 3.12 respectively) should be given: *[IFRS 3.B64(g)]*

- the amount recognised as at the acquisition date;
- a description of the arrangement and the basis for determining the amount of the payment; and
- an estimate of the range of outcomes (undiscounted) or, if a range cannot be estimated, that fact and the reasons why a range cannot be estimated.

  If the maximum amount of the payment is unlimited, that fact should be disclosed.

These are requirements of IFRS 3 and apply irrespective of whether such items meet the definition of a financial instrument (which they normally will).

5 NATURE AND EXTENT OF RISKS ARISING FROM FINANCIAL INSTRUMENTS

IFRS 7 establishes a second key principle, namely:

> 'An entity shall disclose information that enables users of its financial statements to evaluate the nature and extent of risks arising from financial instruments to which the entity is exposed at the reporting date.' *[IFRS 7.31]*.

Again this is supported by related disclosure requirements which focus on qualitative and quantitative aspects of the risks arising from financial instruments and how those risks have been managed. *[IFRS 7.32]*.

Providing qualitative disclosures in the context of quantitative disclosures enables users to link related disclosures and hence form an overall picture of the nature and extent of risks arising from financial instruments. The interaction between qualitative and quantitative disclosures contributes to disclosure of information in a way that better enables users to evaluate an entity's exposure to risks. *[IFRS 7.32A]*.

These risks typically include, but are not limited to, credit risk, liquidity risk and market risk, which are defined as follows: *[IFRS 7 Appendix A]*

(a) *Credit risk*, the risk that one party to a financial instrument will cause a financial loss for the other party by failing to discharge an obligation;

(b) *Liquidity risk*, the risk that an entity will encounter difficulty in meeting obligations associated with financial liabilities that are settled by delivering cash or another financial asset.

(c) *Market risk*, the risk that the fair value or future cash flows of a financial instrument will fluctuate because of changes in market prices. It comprises three separate types of risk:

  (i) *Currency risk*, the risk that the fair value or future cash flows of a financial instrument will fluctuate because of changes in foreign exchange rates.

  Currency risk (or foreign exchange risk) arises on financial instruments that are denominated in a foreign currency, i.e. in a currency other than the functional currency in which they are measured. For the purpose of IFRS 7, currency risk does not arise from financial instruments that are non-monetary items or from financial instruments denominated in an entity's functional currency. *[IFRS 7.B23]*. Therefore if a parent with the euro as its functional and presentation currency owns a subsidiary with the pound sterling as its functional currency, monetary items held by the subsidiary that are denominated in sterling do not give rise to any currency risk in the consolidated financial statements of the parent.

  (ii) *Interest rate risk*, the risk that the fair value or future cash flows of a financial instrument will fluctuate because of changes in market interest rates.

  It is explained that interest rate risk arises on interest-bearing financial instruments recognised in the statement of financial position (e.g. debt instruments acquired or issued) and on some financial instruments not recognised in the statement of financial position (e.g. some loan commitments). *[IFRS 7.B22]*.

  (iii) *Other price risk*, the risk that the fair value or future cash flows of a financial instrument will fluctuate because of changes in market prices (other than those arising from interest rate risk or currency risk), whether those changes are caused by factors specific to the individual financial instrument or its issuer, or factors affecting all similar financial instruments traded in the market.

  Other price risk arises on financial instruments because of changes in, for example, commodity prices, equity prices, prepayment risk (i.e. the risk that one party to a financial asset will incur a financial loss because the other party repays earlier or later than expected), and residual value risk (e.g. a lessor of motor cars that writes residual value guarantees is exposed to residual value risk). *[IFRS 7.B25, IG32]*.

  Two examples of financial instruments that give rise to equity price risk are a holding of equities in another entity, and an investment in a trust, which in turn holds investments in equity instruments. Other examples include forward contracts and options to buy or sell specified quantities of an equity instrument and swaps that are indexed to equity prices. The fair values of such financial instruments are affected by changes in the market price of the underlying equity instruments. *[IFRS 7.B26]*.

The specified disclosures can be provided either in the financial statements or may be incorporated by cross-reference from the financial statements to some other statement that is available to users of the financial statements on the same terms and at the same time, such as a management commentary or risk report (preparation of which might be required by a regulatory authority). Without the information incorporated by cross-reference, the financial statements are incomplete. *[IFRS 7.B6, BC46]*.

Consistent with the approach outlined at 3 above, it is emphasised that the extent of these disclosures will depend on the extent of an entity's exposure to risks arising from financial instruments. *[IFRS 7.BC41]*. Therefore, entities with many financial instruments and related risks should provide more disclosure and those with few financial instruments and related risks may provide less extensive disclosure. *[IFRS 7.BC40(b)]*.

The IASB recognised that entities view and manage risk in different ways and that some entities undertake limited management of risks. Therefore, disclosures based on how risk is managed are unlikely to be comparable between entities and, for some entities, would convey little or no information about the risks assumed. Accordingly, whilst at a high level the disclosures are approached from the perspective of information provided to management (see 5.2 below), certain minimum disclosures about risk exposures are specified to provide a common and relatively easy to implement benchmark across different entities. Obviously, those entities with more developed risk management systems would provide more detailed information. *[IFRS 7.BC42]*.

It is explained in the basis for conclusions that the implementation guidance, which illustrates how an entity might apply IFRS 7, is consistent with the disclosure requirements for banks developed by the Basel Committee (known as Pillar 3), so that banks can prepare, and users receive, a single co-ordinated set of disclosures about financial risk. *[IFRS 7.BC41]*. The standard was originally written before the financial crisis and there have been a number of subsequent initiatives to improve the reporting of risk by financial institutions, both from a regulatory and a financial reporting perspective, for example as set out at 9 below.

In developing the standard, the IASB considered various arguments that risk disclosures should not be included within the financial statements (even by cross-reference). For example, concerns were expressed that the information would be difficult and costly to audit and that it did not meet the criteria of comparability, faithful representation and completeness because it is subjective, forward-looking and based on management's judgement. It was also suggested that the subjectivity involved in the sensitivity analyses could undermine the credibility of the fair values recognised in the financial statements. However, the IASB was not persuaded and these arguments were rejected. *[IFRS 7.BC43, BC44, BC45, BC46]*.

5.1 Qualitative disclosures

For each type of risk arising from financial instruments, an entity is required to disclose: *[IFRS 7.33(a), (b)]*

(a) the exposures to risk and how they arise; and

(b) its objectives, policies and processes for managing the risk and the methods used to measure the risk.

Any changes in either (a) or (b) above compared to the previous period, together with the reasons for the change, should be disclosed. These changes may result from changes in exposure to risk or the way those exposures are managed. *[IFRS 7.33(c), IG17]*.

The type of information that might be disclosed to meet these requirements includes, but is not limited to, a narrative description of: *[IFRS 7.IG15]*

- the entity's exposures to risk and how they arose, which might include details of exposures, both gross and net of risk transfer and other risk-mitigating transactions;
- the entity's policies and processes for accepting, measuring, monitoring and controlling risk, which might include:
  - the structure and organisation of the entity's risk management function(s), including a discussion of independence and accountability;
  - the scope and nature of the entity's risk reporting or measurement systems;
  - the entity's policies for hedging or mitigating risk, including its policies and procedures for taking collateral; and
  - the entity's processes for monitoring the continuing effectiveness of such hedges or mitigating devices; and
- the entity's policies and procedures for avoiding excessive concentrations of risk.

It is noted that information about the nature and extent of risks arising from financial instruments is more useful if it highlights any relationship between financial instruments that can affect the amount, timing or uncertainty of an entity's future cash flows. The extent to which a risk exposure is altered by such relationships might be apparent from other required disclosures, but in some cases further disclosures might be useful. *[IFRS 7.IG16]*.

The following extract from the financial statements of Origin Energy shows the type of disclosure that can be seen in practice.

Extract 54.5: Origin Energy Limited (2014)

Notes to the Financial Statements [extract]

24. Financial Instruments [extract]

(A) Financial risk management

Financial risk factors

The consolidated entity's activities expose it to a variety of financial risks: market risk (including foreign exchange risk and price risk), credit risk, liquidity risk and interest rate risk.. The consolidated entity's overall risk management program focuses on the unpredictability of financial and commodity markets and seeks to manage potential adverse effects of these on the consolidated entity's financial performance. The consolidated entity uses a range of derivative financial instruments to hedge these exposures.

Risk management is carried out under policies approved by the Board of Directors. Financial risks are identified, evaluated and hedged in close co-operation with the consolidated entity's operating units. The consolidated entity has written policies covering specific areas, such as foreign exchange risk, interest rate risk, electricity price risk, oil price risk, credit risk, use of derivative financial instruments and non-derivative financial instruments, and the investment of excess liquidity.

(i) Market risk

Foreign exchange risk

The consolidated entity operates internationally and is exposed to foreign exchange risk arising from various currency exposures, primarily with respect to the New Zealand dollar, US dollar and Euro. Foreign exchange risk arises from future commercial transactions (including interest payments and principal debt repayments on long-term borrowings, the sale of oil, the sale and purchase of LPG and the purchase of capital equipment), the recognition of assets and liabilities (including foreign receivables and borrowings) and net investments in foreign operations.

To manage the foreign exchange risk arising from future commercial transactions, the consolidated entity uses forward foreign exchange contracts. To manage the foreign exchange risk arising from the future principal and interest payments required on foreign currency denominated long-term borrowings, the consolidated entity uses cross currency interest rate swaps (both fixed to fixed and fixed to floating) which convert the foreign currency denominated future principal and interest payments into the functional currency for the relevant entity for the full term of the underlying borrowings. In certain circumstances borrowings are left in the foreign currencies, or hedged from one foreign currency to another to match payments of interest and principal against expected future business cash flows in that foreign currency.

External derivative contracts are designated at the consolidated entity level as hedges of foreign exchange risk on specific assets, liabilities or future transactions on a gross basis.

The consolidated entity has certain investments in foreign operations whose net assets are exposed to foreign currency translation risk. Currency exposure arising from the net assets of the consolidated entity's foreign operations is managed primarily through borrowings denominated in the relevant foreign currencies.

Price risk

The consolidated entity is exposed to price risk from the purchase and sale of electricity, oil, gas, environmental scheme certificates and related commodities. To manage its price risks, the consolidated entity utilises a range of financial and derivative instruments including fixed priced swaps, options, futures and fixed price forward purchase contracts.

The consolidated entity's risk management policy for commodity price risk is to hedge forecast future transactions. The consolidated entity has a risk management policy framework that manages the exposure arising from its commodity-based activities. The policy permits the active hedging of price and volume exposure arising from the retailing, generation and portfolio management activities, within prescribed risk capacity limits. The policy prescribes the maximum risk exposures permissible over prescribed periods for each commodity within the portfolio, under defined worse case scenarios. The full portfolio is subject to ongoing testing against these limits at prescribed intervals, and reported monthly.

(ii) Credit risk

The consolidated entity manages its exposure to credit risk via credit risk management policies which allocate credit limits based on the overall financial and competitive strength of the counterparty. Publicly available credit information from recognised providers is utilised for this purpose where available. Credit policies cover exposures generated from the sale of products and the use of derivative instruments. Derivative counterparties are limited to high-credit-quality financial institutions and other organisations in the relevant industry. The consolidated entity has Board approved policies that limit the amount of credit exposure to each financial institution and derivate counterparty. The consolidated entity also utilises International Swaps and Derivative Association (ISDA) agreements with all derivative counterparties in order to limit exposure to credit risk through the netting of amounts receivable from and amounts payable to individual counterparties.

The carrying amounts of financial assets recognised in the statement of financial position, and disclosed in more detail in notes 6, 7 and 19 best represents the consolidated entity's maximum exposure to credit risk at the reporting date. In respect of those financial assets and the credit risk embodied within them, the consolidated entity holds no significant collateral as security and there are no other significant credit enhancements in respect of these assets. The credit quality of all financial assets that are neither past due nor impaired is constantly monitored in order to identify any potential adverse changes in the credit quality. There are no significant financial assets that have had renegotiated terms that would otherwise, without that renegotiation, have been past due or impaired.

The consolidated entity has provided certain funding to Australia Pacific LNG by way of subscription up to an amount of $3.75 billion for mandatorily redeemable cumulative preference shares (MRCPS) issued by Australia Pacific LNG. Each holder of the ordinary shares of Australia Pacific LNG also holds MRCPS in an equivalent proportion to its share in the ordinary equity of the joint venture entity. The MRCPS attract a market-based fixed dividend, reflective of the assessed credit risk of Australia Pacific LNG, have a mandatory redemption date of 31 December 2022 and accordingly are recorded in "other non-current financial assets". The carrying value of the loan at 30 June 2014, as disclosed in note 7, reflects the consolidated entity's view that the shares will be fully redeemed for their full issue price prior to 31 December 2022 from the cash flows generated from Australia Pacific LNG's export operations. There are no conditions existing at the reporting date which indicate that Australia Pacific LNG will be unable to repay the full carrying value. Accordingly, the loan is valued at amortised cost, and reflects the cash provided to Australia Pacific LNG.

(iii) Liquidity risk

Prudent liquidity risk management implies maintaining sufficient cash and marketable securities, the availability of funding through an adequate amount of committed credit facilities and the ability to close out market positions. Due to the dynamic nature of the underlying businesses, the consolidated entity aims to maintain flexibility in funding by keeping committed credit lines available. Certain of the consolidated entity's interest-bearing liability obligations are subject to change in control provisions under the agreements with third-party lenders. As at 30 June 2014 those provisions were not triggered.

(iv) Interest rate risk (cash flow and fair value)

The consolidated entity's income and operating cash flows are substantially independent of changes in market interest rates. The consolidated entity's interest rate risk arises from long-term borrowings. Borrowings issued at variable rates expose the consolidated entity to cash flow interest rate risk. Borrowings issued at fixed rates expose the consolidated entity to fair value interest rate risk. The consolidated entity's risk management policy is to manage interest rate exposures using Profit at Risk and Value at Risk methodologies using 95 per cent statistical confidence levels. Exposure limits are set to ensure that the consolidated entity is not exposed to excess risk from interest rate volatility. The consolidated entity manages its cash flow interest rate risk by using floating-to-fixed interest rate swaps. Such interest rate swaps have the economic effect of converting borrowings from floating rates to fixed rates.

5.2 Quantitative disclosures

5.2.1 General matters

For each type of risk arising from financial instruments (see 5 above), entities are required to disclose summary quantitative data about their exposure to that risk at the reporting date. It should be based on the information provided internally to key management personnel of the entity as defined in IAS 24 – *Related Party Disclosures* (see Chapter 37 at 2.2.1.D), for example the board of directors or chief executive officer. *[IFRS 7.34(a)]*.

This 'management view' approach was adopted by the IASB because it was considered to: *[IFRS 7.BC47]*

- provide a useful insight into how the entity views and manages risk;
- result in information that has more predictive value than information based on assumptions and methods that management does not use, for instance, in considering the entity's ability to react to adverse situations;
- be more effective in adapting to changes in risk measurement and management techniques and developments in the external environment;
- have practical advantages for preparers of financial statements, because it allows them to use the data they use in managing risk; and
- be consistent with the approach used in segment reporting (see Chapter 34).

When several methods are used to manage a risk exposure, the information disclosed should use the method(s) that provide the most relevant and reliable information. It is noted, in this context, that IAS 8 – *Accounting Policies, Changes in Accounting Estimates and Errors* – discusses relevance and reliability (see Chapter 3 at 4.3). *[IFRS 7.B7]*.

Where the quantitative data disclosed as at the reporting date are unrepresentative of an entity's exposure to risk during the period, further information that is representative should be provided. *[IFRS 7.35]*. For example, if an entity typically has a large exposure to a particular currency, but at year-end unwinds the position, the entity might disclose a graph that shows the exposure at various times during the period, or it might disclose the highest, lowest and average exposures. *[IFRS 7.IG20]*.

In developing IFRS 7, the IASB considered whether quantitative information about average risk exposures during the period should be given in all cases. However, they considered that such information is more informative only if the risk exposure at the reporting date is not representative of the exposure during the period. They also considered it would be onerous to prepare. Consequently, they decided that IFRS 7 would only require disclosure by exception, i.e. when the position at the reporting date was unrepresentative of the exposure during the reporting period. *[IFRS 7.BC48]*.

5.2.2 Credit risk (entities applying IAS 39)

Many of the credit risk disclosures are to be given by class and it is noted that financial instruments in the same class should reflect shared economic characteristics with respect to the risk being disclosed, credit risk in this case (see 3.3 above). Therefore, a lender might determine that residential mortgages, unsecured consumer loans, and commercial loans each have different economic characteristics. *[IFRS 7.IG21]*.

5.2.2.A Maximum exposure to credit risk

For each class of financial instrument, entities should disclose the amount that best represents its maximum exposure to credit risk at the reporting date without taking account of any collateral held or other credit enhancements (e.g. netting agreements that do not qualify for offset in accordance with IAS 32). This disclosure is not required for financial instruments whose carrying amount best represents this amount. *[IFRS 7.36(a)]*.

For a financial asset, the maximum exposure to credit risk is typically the gross carrying amount, net of any amounts offset in accordance with IAS 32 (see 7.4.1 below) and any impairment losses recognised in accordance with IAS 39 (see Chapter 49 at 4). *[IFRS 7.B9]*. This disclosure is required even if there are no identified problems in, say, a loan portfolio. *[IFRS 7.BC49]*.

Activities that give rise to credit risk and the associated maximum exposure to credit risk include, but are not limited to: *[IFRS 7.B10]*

- granting loans to customers and placing deposits with other entities. In these cases, the maximum exposure to credit risk is the carrying amount of the related financial assets;
- entering into derivative contracts, e.g. foreign exchange contracts, interest rate swaps and purchased credit derivatives. When a resulting asset is measured at fair value, the maximum exposure to credit risk at the reporting date will equal the carrying amount;

  It is recognised that this disclosure does not always reflect potential *future* exposure to credit risk (because fair value could increase), but the disclosure requirement is for the exposure *at the reporting date*; *[IFRS 7.BC50]*
- granting financial guarantees. In this case, the maximum exposure to credit risk is the maximum amount the entity could have to pay if the guarantee is called on, which may be significantly greater than the amount recognised as a liability; and
- making a loan commitment that is irrevocable over the life of the facility or is revocable only in response to a material adverse change. If the issuer cannot settle the loan commitment net in cash or another financial instrument, the maximum credit exposure is the full amount of the commitment. This is because it is uncertain whether the amount of any undrawn portion may be drawn upon in the future. This may be significantly greater than the amount recognised as a liability.

The following extracts from the financial statements of Deutsche Telekom and HSBC illustrate how these disclosures may be provided in practice – clearly credit risk is much more significant to an entity such as HSBC.

Extract 54.6: Deutsche Telekom AG (2014)

Notes to the consolidated financial statements [extract]

37. Financial instruments and Risk management. [extract]

Credit risks. Deutsche Telekom is exposed to a credit risk from its operating activities and certain financing activities. As a rule, transactions with regard to financing activities are only concluded with counterparties that have at least a credit rating of BBB+/Baa1, in connection with an operational credit management system. At the level of operations, the outstanding debts are continuously monitored in each area, i.e. locally. Credit risks are taken into account through individual and collective allowances.

The solvency of the business with corporate customers, especially international carriers, is monitored separately. In terms of the overall risk exposure from the credit risk, however, the receivables from these counterparties are not so extensive as to justify extraordinary concentrations of risk.

Offsetting is applied in particular to receivables and liabilities and Deutsche Telekom AG and Telekom Deutschland GmbH for the routing of international calls via the fixed network and for roaming fees in the mobile network.

In line with the contractual provisions, in the event of insolvency all derivatives with a positive or negative fair value that exist with the respective counterparty are offset against each other, leaving a net receivable or liability. The net amounts are normally recalculated every bank working day and offset against each other. When the netting of the positive and negative fair values of all derivatives was positive from Deutsche Telekom's perspective, the counterparty provided Deutsche Telekom with cash pursuant to the collateral contracts mentioned in Note 1 "Cash and cash equivalents.". The credit risk was thus further reduced.

When the netting of the positive and negative fair values of all derivatives was negative from Deutsche Telekom's perspective, Deutsche Telekom provided cash collateral to counterparties pursuant to collateral agreements. The net amounts are normally recalculated every bank working day and offset against each other. The cash collateral paid (please also refer to Note 8 "Other financial assets", PAGE 214) is offset by corresponding negative net derivative positions of EUR 467 million at the reporting date, which is why it was not exposed to any credit risks in this amount as of the reporting date. The collateral paid is reported under originated loans and receivables within other financial assets. On account of its close connection to the corresponding derivatives, the collateral paid constitutes a separate class of financial assets. Likewise, the collateral received, which is reported as other interest-bearing liabilities under financial liabilities, constitutes a separate class of financial liabilities on account of its close connection to the corresponding derivatives.

In accordance with the terms of bonds issued by a Deutsche Telekom subsidiary, this subsidiary has the right to terminate the bonds prematurely under specific conditions. The rights of termination constitute embedded derivatives and are accounted for separately as derivative financial assets. The conversion rights maintained in Mandatory Convertible Preferred Stock issued by a subsidiary of Deutsche Telekom constitute an embedded derivative and are recognized separately as a derivative. Since these rights of termination and conversion rights are not exposed to a credit risk, they constitute a separate class of financial instruments.

No other significant agreements reducing the maximum exposure to the credit risks of financial assets existed. The maximum exposure to credit risk of the other financial assets thus corresponds to their carrying amounts.

In addition, Deutsche Telekom is exposed to a credit risk through the granting of financial guarantees. Guarantees amounting to a nominal total of EUR 50 million had been pledged as of the reporting date (December 31, 2013: EUR 70 million), which also represent the maximum exposure to credit risk.

There were no indications as of the reporting date that Deutsche Telekom will incur a loss from a financial guarantee.

Extract 54.7: HSBC Holdings plc (2014)

Report of the Directors: Risk [extract]

Maximum exposure to credit risk *(Audited)* [extract]

The table presents our maximum exposure to credit risk from balance sheet and off-balance sheet financial instruments before taking account of any collateral held or other credit enhancements (unless such enhancements meet accounting offsetting requirements). For financial assets recognised on the balance sheet, the maximum exposure to credit risk equals their carrying amount; for financial guarantees and similar contracts granted, it is the maximum amount that we would have to pay if the guarantees were called upon. For loan commitments and other credit-related commitments, it is generally the full amount of the committed facilities.

The offset in the table relates to amounts where there is a legally enforceable right of offset in the event of counterparty default and where, as a result, there is a net exposure for credit risk purposes. However, as there is no intention to settle these balances on a net basis under normal circumstances, they do not qualify for net presentation for accounting purposes.

In the case of derivatives the offset column also includes collateral received in cash and other financial assets.

While not disclosed as an offset in the 'Maximum exposure to credit risk' table, other arrangements are in place which reduce our maximum exposure to credit risk. These include a charge over collateral over borrowers' specific assets such as residential properties. Other credit risk mitigants include short positions in securities and financial assets held as part of linked insurance/investment contracts where the risk is predominantly borne by the policyholder. In addition, we hold collateral in the form of financial instruments that are not recognised on the balance sheet.

Maximum exposure to credit risk (Audited)

	2014		
	Maximum exposure	**Offset**	**Net**
	US$m	US$m	US$m
Cash and balances at central banks	129,957	–	129,957
Items in the course of collection from other banks	4,927	–	4,927
Hong Kong Government certificates of indebtedness	27,674	–	27,674
Trading assets	228,944	–	228,944
-Treasury and other eligible bills	16,170	–	16,170
-debt securities	141,532	–	141,532
-loan and advances to banks	27,581	–	27,581
-loans and advances to customers	43,661	–	43,661
Financial assets designated at fair value	9,031	–	9,031
-Treasury and other eligible bills	56	–	56
-debt securities	8,891	–	8,891
-loan and advances to banks	84	–	84
-loans and advances to customers	–	–	–
Derivatives	345,008	(313,300)	31,708
Loans and advances to customers held at amortised cost	974,660	(67,094)	907,556
-personal	388,954	(4,412)	384,542
-corporate and commercial	535,184	(59,197)	475,987
-financial (non-bank financial institutions)	50,522	(3,485)	47,037
Loans and advances to banks held at amortised cost	112,149	(258)	111,891
Reverse repurchase agreements – non trading	161,713	(5,750)	155,963
Financial investments	404,773	–	404,773
-Treasury and other similar bills	81,517	–	81,517
-debt securities	323,256	–	323,256
Other assets	35,264	–	35,264
-assets held for sale	1,375	–	1,375
-endorsements and acceptances	10,775	–	10,775
-other	23,114	–	23,114
Financial guarantees and similar contracts	47,078	–	47,078
Loan and other credit-related commitments	651,380	–	651,380
At 31 December	3,132,558	(386,402)	2,746,156

Entities should provide by class of financial instrument a description of collateral held as security and of other credit enhancements, and their financial effect (e.g. a quantification of the extent to which collateral and other credit enhancements mitigate credit risk) in respect of the amount that best represents the maximum exposure to credit risk (whether disclosed separately or represented by the carrying amount of a financial instrument). *[IFRS 7.36(b)]*.

The requirement may be met by disclosing: *[IFRS 7.IG22]*

- the policies and processes for valuing and managing collateral and other credit enhancements obtained;
- a description of the main types of collateral and other credit enhancements (examples of the latter being guarantees and credit derivatives, as well as netting agreements that do not qualify for offset in accordance with IAS 32);
- the main types of counterparties to collateral and other credit enhancements and their creditworthiness; and
- information about risk concentrations within the collateral or other credit enhancements.

It is not entirely clear how detailed this additional information is intended to be. For example, whilst the standard suggests it should, or at least could, involve disclosure of quantitative information, the implementation guidance implies more discursive disclosures might suffice in some cases. In practice, entities will need to make a judgment based on their own specific circumstances and in the light of emerging practice.

5.2.2.B *Credit quality of financial assets*

Entities should also provide information about the credit quality of financial assets that are neither past due (see 5.2.2.C below) nor impaired. *[IFRS 7.36(c)]*. The IASB believes this gives a greater insight into the credit risk of assets and helps users assess whether such assets are more or less likely to become impaired in the future. Because this information will vary between entities, no particular method for giving this information is specified. Rather, each entity should devise a method that is appropriate to its circumstances. *[IFRS 7.BC54]*. This might include: *[IFRS 7.IG23]*

- an analysis of credit exposures using an external or internal credit grading system;
  When external ratings are considered when managing and monitoring credit quality, information might be disclosed about: *[IFRS 7.IG24]*
  - the amounts of credit exposures for each external credit grade;
  - the rating agencies used;
  - the amount of an entity's rated and unrated credit exposures; and
  - the relationship between internal and external ratings.

  When internal credit ratings are considered when managing and monitoring credit quality, information might be disclosed about: *[IFRS 7.IG25]*
  - the internal credit ratings process;
  - the amounts of credit exposures for each internal credit grade; and
  - the relationship between internal and external ratings.
- the nature of the counterparty;
- historical information about counterparty default rates; and
- any other information used to assess credit quality.

It should be noted that the above disclosures do not need to include the fair value of all collateral held (except where the lender is entitled to sell or repledge in the absence of default – see 4.4.6 above). The IASB recognised that such information would often be onerous to collect and may sometimes be misleading (for example if information about over- and under-collateralised assets is aggregated). Of more relevance will be the extent of under-collateralised loans. *[IFRS 7.BC51, BC52].*

The following extracts from the financial statements of Volkswagen, Essentra, Aviva and the Coventry Building Society illustrate a variety of ways in which these disclosures have been dealt with in practice. Volkswagen discloses an analysis of receivables by internal credit ratings; Essentra analyses current trade receivables between new and established customers; Aviva shows an analysis of investments by external credit ratings; and Coventry Building Society provides various information about its loan assets including the extent of collateral.

Extract 54.8: Volkswagen Aktiengesellschaft (2014)

Notes to the Consolidated Financial Statements [extract]

34 Financial risk management and financial instruments [extract]

2. Credit and Default Risk [extract]

CREDIT RATING OF THE GROSS CARRYING AMOUNTS OF FINANCIAL ASSETS THAT ARE NEITHER PAST DUE NOR IMPAIRED

€ million	**Risk class 1**	**Risk class 2**	**Dec. 31, 2014**	Risk class 1	Risk class 2	Dec. 31, 2013
Measured at amortized cost						
Financial services receivables	**86,099**	**13,696**	**99,795**	71,592	14,996	86,588
Trade receivables	**8,546**	**137**	**8,682**	8,218	1	8,219
Other receivables	**10,765**	**35**	**10,800**	9,402	40	9,442
Measured at fair value	**13,593**	**–**	**13,593**	12,009	–	12,009
	119,003	**13,868**	**132,871**	101,221	15,037	116,258

The Volkswagen Group performs a credit assessment of borrowers in all loan and lease agreements, using scoring systems for the high-volume business and rating systems for corporate customers and receivables from dealer financing. Receivables rated as good are contained in risk class 1. Receivables from customers whose credit rating is not good but have not yet defaulted are contained in risk class 2.

Extract 54.9: Essentra plc (2014)

Notes [extract]

1. Financial risk management [extract]

i) Credit risk [extract]

Trade and other receivables

Essentra's exposure to credit risk is driven by the profile of its customers. This is influenced by the demographics of the customer base, including the industry and country in which customers operate. Trade and other receivables are generally due from customers who are unlikely to seek credit ratings as part of their normal course of business.

Essentra monitors significant customers' credit limits and there is an allowance for impairment that represents the estimate of potential losses in respect of trade and other receivables. The components of this allowance are a specific allowance for individual losses and a collective allowance for losses that have been incurred but not yet identified. The collective allowance takes account of historical experience and the profile of customers.

As at 31 December 2014, gross trade receivables were £151.8m (2013: £130.7m) of which £25.1m (2013: £19.4m) were past due but not impaired. The ageing analysis of trade receivables past due but not impaired is as follows:

	2014 £m	2013 £m
Up to 3 months	**25.1**	19.4

As at 31 December 2014, trade receivables of £6.3m (2013: £5.7m) were provided for as they were considered to be impaired. The ageing of the impaired receivables provided for is as follows:

	2014 £m	2013 £m
Up to 3 months	**1.6**	2.1
Over 3 months	**4.7**	3.6
	6.3	5.7

The movement in the provision for impaired receivables is as follows:

	2014 £m	2013 £m
Beginning of year	**5.7**	4.9
Impaired receivables acquired	**0.5**	1.5
Impairment loss recognised	**2.8**	0.6
Release in the year	**(1.6)**	(0.4)
Utilisation	**(1.1)**	(0.9)
End of year	**6.3**	5.7

Derivative assets

Credit risk with respect to derivatives is controlled by limiting transactions to major banking counterparties where internationally agreed standard form documentation exists. The credit ratings of these counterparties are monitored.

Cash and cash equivalents

Credit risk relating to cash and cash equivalents is monitored daily, on a counterparty by counterparty basis. The credit limits imposed specify the maximum amount of cash which can be invested in, or with, any single counterparty. These limits are determined by geographic presence, expertise and credit rating. Essentra monitors the credit ratings of counterparties.

The following credit risk table provides information regarding the credit risk exposure of Essentra by classifying derivative assets and cash and cash equivalents according to credit ratings of the counterparties. AAA is the highest possible rating and all of the assets are neither impaired nor past due.

2014	AAA £m	AA £m	A £m	BBB £m	BB £m	Not rated £m	Total £m
Derivative assets	–	0.1	0.3	3.5	–	–	3.9
Cash and cash equivalents	–	2.6	13.9	27.5	1.0	1.0	46.0
	–	**2.7**	**14.2**	**31.0**	**1.0**	**1.0**	**49.9**

2013	AAA £m	AA £m	A £m	BBB £m	BB £m	Not rated £m	Total £m
Derivative assets	–	–	0.2	–	–	–	0.2
Cash and cash equivalents	–	9.5	29.0	3.6	0.6	1.4	44.1
	–	**9.5**	**29.2**	**3.6**	**0.6**	**1.4**	**44.3**

Essentra's maximum credit risk exposure is £209.4m (2013: £180.3m) and no collateral is held against this amount (2013: £nil).

Extract 54.10: Aviva plc (2014)

Notes to the consolidated financial statements [extracts]

58 Risk management [extract]

(b) Credit risk [extracts]

Financial exposures by credit ratings [extracts]

Financial assets are graded according to current external credit ratings issued. AAA is the highest possible rating. Investment grade financial assets are classified within the range of AAA to BBB ratings. Financial assets which fall outside this range are classified as sub-investment grade. The following table provides information regarding the aggregated credit risk exposure of the Group for financial assets with external credit ratings, excluding assets 'held for sale'. 'Not rated' assets capture assets not rated by external ratings agencies.

As at 31 December 2014	AAA	AA	A	BBB	Speculative grade	Not rated	Carrying value including held for sale	Less: Amounts classified as held for sale	Carrying value £m
Debt securities	13.6%	35.6%	21.3%	21.9%	2.1%	5.5%	131,661	–	131,661
Reinsurance assets	0.3%	71.3%	21.9%	0.1%	0.0%	6.4%	7,958	–	7,958
Other investments	0.0%	0.1%	1.3%	0.0%	0.2%	98.4%	35,358	–	35,358
Loans	1.3%	9.0%	2.1%	0.2%	0.0%	87.4%	25,260	–	25,260
Total							200,237	–	200,237

As at 31 December 2013	AAA	AA	A	BBB	Speculative grade	Not rated	Carrying value including held for sale	Less: Amounts classified as held for sale	Carrying value £m
Debt securities	13.0%	33.1%	20.8%	24.9%	2.8%	5.4%	126,805	(2,420)	124,385
Reinsurance assets	0.3%	53.6%	37.1%	1.1%	0.1%	7.8%	7,257	(37)	7,220
Other investments	0.0%	0.2%	0.7%	1.0%	0.1%	98.0%	32,517	(201)	32,316
Loans	3.8%	12.1%	1.2%	0.0%	0.3%	82.6%	23,879	–	23,879
Total							190,458	(2,658)	187,800

Extract 54.11: Coventry Building Society (2014)

Risk Management Report [extracts]

Retail credit risk [extracts]

Retail credit risk profile

The nature of the Society's lending has remained focused on low risk residential mortgage business, including buy to let. Limited non-traditional lending in the form of near-prime mortgages and self-certification was discontinued in 2008 and 2009 respectively and these portfolios are reducing over time. Commercial loans in the Stroud & Swindon portfolio were added to the Society's assets upon merger of the two Societies in 2010. These balances also continue to reduce over time, with no new lending activity being undertaken in this portfolio. There has been no new unsecured lending since 2009.

Loans and advances to customers, gross of impairment provisions, are shown below:

Loans and advances to customers (Audited)	**2014 £m**	**2014 %**	2013 £m	2013 %
Residential mortgages: owner-occupier	**16,835.2**	**62.4**	15,161.1	62.8
Residential mortgages: buy to let	**9,657.4**	**35.8**	8,419.8	34.9
Total traditional residential mortgages	**26,492.6**	**98.2**	23,580.9	97.7
Residential near-prime mortgages	**105.2**	**0.4**	116.0	0.5
Residential self-certification mortgages	**331.6**	**1.2**	382.6	1.6
Commercial mortgages	**6.3**	**–**	8.3	–
Total non-traditional mortgages	**443.1**	**1.6**	506.9	2.1
Unsecured personal loans	**50.0**	**0.2**	56.7	0.2
Total gross balance	**26,985.7**	**100.0**	24,144.5	100.0

Geographical concentration (Audited)

The residential mortgage portfolio is well diversified and reflects the national coverage of the Society's distribution channels. The geographical split of residential mortgages by balance, gross of impairment provisions is shown below:

Region	**2014 %**	2013 %
East of England	**12.6**	12.4
London	**14.8**	14.2
Midlands	**15.1**	16.0
North East	**9.0**	9.1
North West	**8.6**	8.6
Scotland & Northern Ireland	**4.6**	4.6
South Central	**12.9**	12.6
South East	**10.8**	10.6
South West & Wales	**11.6**	11.9
Total	**100.0**	100.0

Loan to value

The Society's low risk approach to lending is reflected in the loan to value profile of the residential mortgage book. The estimated value of the residential mortgage portfolio is updated on a quarterly basis using the Nationwide regional House Price Index.

The residential mortgage book as at 31 December 2014 is analysed below, together with an analysis of gross new lending in the year. The following tables are by value unless stated otherwise:

Total mortgage book profile (by number of accounts) (Audited)	**2014 %**	2013 %
Indexed loan to value:		
<50%	**48.1**	45.0
50% to 65%	**25.9**	26.6
65% to 75%	**13.0**	13.7
75% to 85%	**8.8**	9.1
85% to 95%	**3.7**	4.1
> 95%	**0.5**	1.5
Total	**100.0**	100.0
Average indexed loan to value of stock (simple average)	**48.6**	50.0
Average indexed loan to value of stock (balance weighted)	**55.6**	57.7

Chapter 54

New business profile (Gross lending) (Audited)	**2014**	2013
	%	%
Owner-occupier purchase	**38.8**	36.7
Owner-occupier remortgages	**23.8**	24.0
Buy to let	**37.4**	39.3
Total	**100.0**	100.0
Average loan to value (simple average)	**64.6**	63.6
Average loan to value (balance weighted)	**66.6**	66.5

Identifying impaired loans (Audited)

Loans are categorised by arrears status in line with industry practice and are identified as being either not past due and not impaired (if up to date at the balance sheet date), past due up to three months but not impaired, or impaired if more than three months in arrears or in possession.

In terms of impaired mortgages, the Society's performance is compared with figures published by the Council of Mortgage Lenders (CML). From these figures it can be seen that the performance of the Society has remained strong, with arrears reducing over the year, and favourable to the industry.

The Society's number of accounts in arrears as a percentage of loans and advances to customers compared with the CML data is shown below:

	2014		2013	
	Society	**CML**	Society	CML
(Audited)	**%**	**%**	%	%
Greater than three months	**0.68**	**1.33**	0.90	1.68
Greater than six months	**0.26**	**0.70**	0.41	0.91
Greater than one year	**0.08**	**0.28**	0.12	0.37
In possession	**0.02**	**0.06**	0.03	0.08

An analysis of past due and impaired loans by loan to value is shown below:

As at 31 December 2014 (Audited)	Not impaired		Impaired				
Indexed loan to value:	Not past due	Past due up to three months	Past due over three to six months	Past due over six months or in litigation	In possession	Impairment provision	Total
	£m	£m	£m	£m	£m	£m	£m
<50%	9,697.5	97.3	24.3	10.9	0.1	(3.7)	9,826.4
50% to 65%	8,324.8	92.7	28.3	16.6	0.2	(4.3)	8,458.3
65% to 75%	4,228.2	62.4	19.9	15.5	0.4	(2.7)	4,323.7
75% to 85%	2,871.0	50.7	14.9	13.3	0.2	(3.0)	2,947.1
85% to 95%	1,140.5	28.5	15.1	11.7	0.9	(2.8)	1,193.9
>95%	131.6	15.2	8.4	8.7	5.9	(5.2)	164.6
Unsecured	45.6	3.5	0.6	0.3	–	(4.4)	45.6
Total	26,439.2	350.3	111.5	77.0	7.7	(26.1)	26,959.6

The Society held properties valued at £6.4 million (2013: £9.1 million) pending their sale against balances of £5.8 million (net of provisions) (2013: £8.2 million). Shortfalls between expected sale proceeds (less anticipated costs) and the balance outstanding are fully provided.

The table below provides further information regarding the impaired status of mortgages and loans. Balances are shown gross of impairment provisions.

As at 31 December 2014 (Audited)	Not impaired		Impaired				
	Not past due £m	Past due up to three months £m	Past due over three to six months £m	Past due over six months or in litigation £m	In possession £m	Impairment provision £m	Total £m
Residential mortgages							
Owner-occupier	16,484.3	223.1	73.6	51.6	2.6	(9.0)	16,826.2
Buy to let	9,562.9	69.9	13.1	9.4	2.1	(9.5)	9,647.9
Non-traditional mortgages							
Residential near-prime	57.9	22.7	14.1	9.2	1.3	(1.1)	104.1
Residential self-certified	283.1	30.3	10.1	6.4	1.7	(1.3)	330.3
Commercial lending	5.5	0.8	–	–	–	(0.8)	5.5
Unsecured	45.5	3.5	0.6	0.4	–	(4.4)	45.6
Total	26,439.2	350.3	111.5	77.0	7.7	(26.1)	26,959.6

5.2.2.C *Financial assets that are either past due or impaired*

A financial asset is defined as 'past due' when a counterparty has failed to make a payment when contractually due. *[IFRS 7 Appendix A]*. For example, consider an entity that enters into a lending agreement that requires interest to be paid every month. On the first day of the next month, if interest has not been paid, the loan is past due. Past due does not mean that the counterparty will never pay, but it can trigger various actions such as renegotiation, enforcement of covenants, or legal proceedings. *[IFRS 7.IG26]*.

This definition may seem rigid when compared to internal management reporting, which may not classify an asset as overdue provided payment is made within a commercially accepted interval, e.g. 30 days after the contractual due date. However, the IASB is not inclined to change the definition and notes that entities are encouraged to disclose their methods used to measure credit risk which would allow them to explain any differences between internal reporting and the ageing analysis required by IFRS 7.[6]

When the terms and conditions of financial assets that have been classified as past due are renegotiated (a practice often referred to as forbearance), the terms and conditions of the new contractual arrangement should be applied to determine whether the financial asset remains past due. *[IFRS 7.IG27]*. Accounting for and disclosure of banks' forbearance practices has become a common area of scrutiny by financial reporting regulators in the wake of the financial crisis.

To provide information about financial assets with the greatest credit risk, entities are required to disclose the following for each class of financial asset (including trade receivables): *[IFRS 7.37, BC55]*

- an analysis of the age of financial assets that are past due as at the reporting date but not impaired (essentially to identify those financial assets that are more likely to become impaired and help users to estimate the level of future impairment losses *[IFRS 7.BC55(a)]*).

  Judgement should be used to determine an appropriate number of time bands. For example, the following time bands might be considered appropriate: *[IFRS 7.IG28]*

  - not more than three months;
  - more than three months and not more than six months;
  - more than six months and not more than one year; and
  - more than one year.

  In most cases it will be appropriate to analyse the assets by reference to the period of time the asset has been past due rather than, say, by reference to the amount of time since the financial asset was initially recognised. For example, if a borrower had missed only the most recent interest payment due 20 days before the lender's reporting date, the fact that the payment is 20 days past due seems far more relevant to assessing its credit risk than the date the asset was originated which could have been many years earlier.

  There is no exemption from this disclosure requirement for financial assets classified as at fair value through profit or loss or as available for sale. Consequently, an ageing analysis of such financial assets should be provided, even though their carrying amounts reflect their credit status;[7] and

- an analysis of financial assets that are individually determined to be impaired as at the reporting date, including the factors the entity considered in determining that they are impaired.

  This analysis might include: *[IFRS 7.IG29]*

  - the carrying amount, before deducting any impairment loss;
  - the amount of any related impairment loss; and
  - the nature and fair value of collateral available and other credit enhancements obtained.

  It might also include an analysis of such assets by factors other than age, such as the nature of the counterparty or a geographical analysis of the impaired assets. *[IFRS 7.BC55(b)]*.

Extracts 54.9 and 54.11 above (Essentra and Coventry Building Society) contain examples of how this disclosure requirement has been dealt with in practice.

5.2.2.D *Collateral and other credit enhancements obtained*

When an entity obtains financial or non-financial assets during the period by taking possession of collateral it holds as security, or calling on other credit enhancements such as guarantees, and these assets meet the recognition criteria in other standards, it should disclose for such assets held at the reporting date: *[IFRS 7.38]*

- the nature and carrying amount of the assets; and
- when the assets are not readily convertible into cash, its policies for disposing of such assets or for using them in its operations.

This disclosure is intended to provide information about the frequency of such activities and the entity's ability to obtain and realise the value of the collateral. *[IFRS 7.BC56]*.

5.2.3 Credit risk (entities applying IFRS 9)

For entities applying IFRS 9, the disclosure requirements in respect of impairment are expanded significantly when compared to IAS 39. Those requirements are also supplemented by some detailed implementation guidance. The requirements of IFRS 9 relating to the measurement of impairments are dealt with in Chapter 50 at 5.

5.2.3.A Scope and objectives

The objective of these disclosures is to enable users to understand the effect of credit risk on the amount, timing and uncertainty of future cash flows. To achieve this objective, the disclosures should provide: *[IFRS 7.35B]*

- information about the entity's credit risk management practices and how they relate to the recognition and measurement of expected credit losses, including the methods, assumptions and information used to measure those losses (see 5.2.3.B below);
- quantitative and qualitative information that allows users of financial statements to evaluate the amounts in the financial statements arising from expected credit losses, including changes in the amount of those losses and the reasons for those changes (see 5.2.3.C below); and
- information about the entity's credit risk exposure, i.e. the credit risk inherent in its financial assets and commitments to extend credit, including significant credit risk concentrations (see 5.2.3.D below).

An entity will need to determine how much detail to disclose, how much emphasis to place on different aspects of the disclosure requirements, the appropriate level of aggregation or disaggregation and whether additional explanations are necessary to evaluate the quantitative information disclosed. *[IFRS 7.35D]*. If the disclosures provided are insufficient to meet the objectives above, additional information that is necessary to meet those objectives should be disclosed. *[IFRS 7.35E]*.

To avoid duplication, IFRS 7 allows this information to be incorporated by cross-reference from the financial statements to some other statement that is available to users of the financial statements on the same terms and at the same time, such as a management commentary or risk report. Without the information incorporated by cross-reference, the financial statements are incomplete. *[IFRS 7.35C]*.

A number of the disclosures about credit risk are required to be given by class (see 3.3 above). In determining these classes, financial instruments in the same class should reflect shared economic characteristics with respect to credit risk. A lender, for example, might determine that residential mortgages, unsecured consumer loans and commercial loans each have different economic characteristics. *[IFRS 7.IG21]*.

Unless otherwise stated, the disclosure requirements set out at 5.2.3.B to 5.2.3.D below are applicable only to financial instruments to which the impairment requirements in IFRS 9 are applied. *[IFRS 7.35A]*.

5.2.3.B Credit risk management practices

An entity should explain its credit risk management practices and how they relate to the recognition and measurement of expected credit losses. To meet this objective it should disclose information that enables users to understand and evaluate: *[IFRS 7.35F]*

- how it has determined whether the credit risk of financial instruments has increased significantly since initial recognition, including if and how:
  - financial instruments are considered to have low credit risk, including the classes of financial instruments to which it applies; and
  - the presumption that there have been significant increases in credit risk since initial recognition when financial assets are more than 30 days past due has been rebutted;
- its definitions of default, including the reasons for selecting those definitions. This may include: *[IFRS 7.B8A]*
  - the qualitative and quantitative factors considered in defining default;
  - whether different definitions have been applied to different types of financial instruments; and
  - assumptions about the cure rate, i.e. the number of financial assets that return to a performing status, after a default has occurred on the financial asset;
- how the instruments were grouped if expected credit losses were measured on a collective basis;
- how it has determined that financial assets are credit-impaired; and
- its write-off policy, including the indicators that there is no reasonable expectation of recovery and information about the policy for financial assets that are written-off but are still subject to enforcement activity.

  An asset (or portion thereof) should be written off only if there is no reasonable expectation of recovery. *[IFRS 9.5.4.4]*. Consequently, it is not entirely clear in which circumstances such an asset might still be subject to enforcement activity; and
- how the requirements for the modification of contractual cash flows of financial instruments have been applied, including how the entity:
  - determines whether the credit risk on a financial asset that has been modified while the loss allowance was measured at an amount equal to lifetime expected credit losses has improved to the extent that the loss allowance reverts to being measured at an amount equal to 12-month expected credit losses; and
  - monitors the extent to which the loss allowance on financial assets meeting the criteria in the previous bullet is subsequently remeasured at an amount equal to lifetime expected credit losses.

Quantitative information that will assist users in understanding the subsequent increase in credit risk of modified financial assets may include information about modified financial assets meeting the criteria above for which the loss allowance has reverted to being measured at an amount equal to lifetime expected credit losses, i.e. a deterioration rate. *[IFRS 7.B8B]*.

An entity should also explain the inputs, assumptions and estimation techniques used to apply the impairment requirements of IFRS 9. For this purpose it should disclose: *[IFRS 7.35G]*

- the basis of inputs and assumptions and the estimation techniques used to:
  - measure 12-month and lifetime expected credit losses;
  - determine whether the credit risk of financial instruments has increased significantly since initial recognition; and
  - determine whether a financial asset is credit-impaired.

  This may include information obtained from internal historical information or rating reports and assumptions about the expected life of financial instruments and the timing of the sale of collateral; *[IFRS 7.B8C]*
- how forward-looking information has been incorporated into the determination of expected credit losses, including the use of macroeconomic information; and
- changes in estimation techniques or significant assumptions made during the reporting period and the reasons for those changes.

5.2.3.C *Quantitative and qualitative information about amounts arising from expected credit losses*

An entity should explain the changes in the loss allowance and reasons for those changes by presenting a reconciliation of the opening balance to the closing balance. This should be given in a table for each relevant class of financial instruments, showing separately the changes during the period for: *[IFRS 7.35H]*

- the loss allowance measured at an amount equal to 12-month expected credit losses;
- the loss allowance measured at an amount equal to lifetime expected credit losses for:
  - financial instruments for which credit risk has increased significantly since initial recognition but that are not credit-impaired financial assets;
  - financial assets that are credit-impaired at the reporting date (but were not credit-impaired when purchased or originated); and
  - trade receivables, contract assets or lease receivables for which the loss allowance is measured using a simplified approach based on lifetime expected credit losses; and
- financial assets that were credit-impaired when purchased or originated.

  The total amount of undiscounted expected credit losses on initial recognition of any such assets during the reporting period should also be disclosed.

In addition, it may be necessary to provide a narrative explanation of the changes in the loss allowance during the period. This narrative explanation may include an analysis of the reasons for changes in the loss allowance during the period, including: *[IFRS 7.B8D]*

- the portfolio composition;
- the volume of financial instruments purchased or originated; and
- the severity of the expected credit losses.

For loan commitments and financial guarantee contracts the loss allowance is recognised as a provision. Information about changes in the loss allowance for financial assets should be shown separately from those for loan commitments and financial guarantee contracts. However, if a financial instrument includes both a loan (i.e. financial asset) and an undrawn loan commitment (i.e. loan commitment) component and the expected credit losses on the loan commitment component cannot be separately identified from those on the financial asset component, the expected credit losses on the loan commitment should be recognised together with the loss allowance for the financial asset. To the extent that the combined expected credit losses exceed the gross carrying amount of the financial asset, the expected credit losses should be recognised as a provision. *[IFRS 7.B8E]*.

An explanation should also be provided of how significant changes in the gross carrying amount of financial instruments during the period contributed to changes in the loss allowance. This information should be provided separately for financial instruments that represent the loss allowance as listed in paragraph 35H of IFRS 7 (see above). Examples of changes in the gross carrying amount of financial instruments that contribute to changes in the loss allowance may include: *[IFRS 7.35I]*

- changes because of financial instruments originated or acquired during the reporting period;
- the modification of contractual cash flows on financial assets that do not result in a derecognition of those financial assets;
- changes because of financial instruments that were derecognised, including those that were written-off during the reporting period; and
- changes arising from the measurement of the loss allowance moving from 12-month expected credit losses to lifetime losses (or *vice versa*).

The information disclosed should provide an understanding of the nature and effect of modifications of contractual cash flows on financial assets that have not resulted in derecognition as well as the effect of such modifications on the measurement of expected credit losses. The following information should therefore be given: *[IFRS 7.35J]*

- the amortised cost before the modification and the net modification gain or loss recognised for financial assets for which the contractual cash flows have been modified during the reporting period while they had a loss allowance based on lifetime expected credit losses; and
- the gross carrying amount at the end of the reporting period of financial assets that have been modified since initial recognition at a time when the loss allowance was based on lifetime expected credit losses and for which the loss allowance has changed during the reporting period to an amount equal to 12-month expected credit losses.

These requirements apply to all modifications whether they are as a result of credit related or other commercial reasons. However, if an entity has the ability to separately identify different types of modifications and considers that the separate disclosure of these items is relevant to achieving the overall objective of the disclosures in this section, the entity could provide this additional detail as part of the disclosure.[8]

The following example illustrates how this information might be presented. *[IFRS 7.IG20B]*.

Example 54.6: Information about changes in the loss allowance

Mortgage loans – loss allowance	**12-month expected credit losses**	**Lifetime expected credit losses (collectively assessed)**	**Lifetime expected credit losses (individually assessed)**	**Credit-impaired financial assets (lifetime expected credit losses)**
CU'000				
Loss allowance as at 1 January	X	X	X	X
Changes due to financial instruments recognised as at 1 January:				
– Transfer to lifetime expected credit losses	(X)	X	X	–
– Transfer to credit-impaired financial assets	(X)	–	(X)	X
– Transfer to 12-month expected credit losses	X	(X)	(X)	–
– Financial assets that have been derecognised during the period	(X)	(X)	(X)	(X)
New financial assets originated or purchased	X	–	–	–
Write-offs	–	–	(X)	(X)
Changes in models/risk parameters	X	X	X	X
Foreign exchange and other movements	X	X	X	X
Loss allowance as at 31 December	X	X	X	X

Significant changes in the gross carrying amount of mortgage loans that contributed to changes in the loss allowance were:

- The acquisition of the ABC prime mortgage portfolio increased the residential mortgage book by x per cent, with a corresponding increase in the loss allowance measured on a 12-month basis.
- The write off of the CUXX DEF portfolio following the collapse of the local market reduced the loss allowance for financial assets with objective evidence of impairment by CUX.
- The expected increase in unemployment in Region X caused a net increase in financial assets whose loss allowance is equal to lifetime expected credit losses and caused a net increase of CUX in the lifetime expected credit losses allowance.

The significant changes in the gross carrying amount of mortgage loans are further explained below:

Mortgage loans – gross carrying amount	**12-month expected credit losses**	**Lifetime expected credit losses (collectively assessed)**	**Lifetime expected credit losses (individually assessed)**	**Credit impaired financial assets (lifetime expected credit losses)**
CU'000				
Gross carrying amount as at 1 January	X	X	X	X
Individual financial assets transferred to lifetime expected credit losses	(X)	–	X	–
Individual financial assets transferred to credit-impaired financial assets	(X)	–	(X)	X
Individual financial assets transferred from credit-impaired financial assets	X	–	X	(X)
Financial assets assessed on collective basis	(X)	X	–	–
New financial assets originated or purchased	X	–	–	–
Write-offs	–	–	(X)	(X)
Financial assets that have been derecognised	(X)	(X)	(X)	(X)
Changes due to modifications that did not result in derecognition	(X)	–	(X)	(X)
Other changes	X	X	X	X
Gross carrying amount as at 31 December	X	X	X	X

Where the loss allowance for trade receivables or lease receivables is measured using a simplified approach based on lifetime expected credit losses, the information about modifications need be given only if those financial assets are modified while more than 30 days past due. *[IFRS 7.35A(a)]*.

To provide an understanding of the effect of collateral and other credit enhancements on the amounts arising from expected credit losses, the following should be disclosed by class of financial instrument: *[IFRS 7.35K]*

- the amount that best represents the maximum exposure to credit risk at the end of the reporting period without taking account of any collateral held or other credit enhancements (e.g. netting agreements that do not qualify for offset in accordance with IAS 32);
- a narrative description of collateral held as security and other credit enhancements, including:
  - a description of the nature and quality of the collateral held;
  - an explanation of any significant changes in the quality of that collateral or credit enhancements as a result of deterioration or changes in the entity's collateral policies during the reporting period; and
  - information about financial instruments for which a loss allowance has not been recognised because of the collateral.

  This might include information about: *[IFRS 7.B8G]*

  - the main types of collateral held as security and other credit enhancements, examples of the latter being guarantees, credit derivatives and netting agreements that do not qualify for offset in accordance with IAS 32;

- the volume of collateral held and other credit enhancements and its significance in terms of the loss allowance;
- the policies and processes for valuing and managing collateral and other credit enhancements;
- the main types of counterparties to collateral and other credit enhancements and their creditworthiness; and
- information about risk concentrations within the collateral and other credit enhancements; and

- quantitative information about the collateral held as security and other credit enhancements, e.g. quantification of the extent to which collateral and other credit enhancements mitigate credit risk, on financial assets that are credit-impaired at the reporting date.

Disclosure of information about the fair value of collateral and other credit enhancements is not required, nor is a quantification of the exact value of the collateral included in the calculation of expected credit losses (i.e. the loss given default). *[IFRS 7.B8F]*. Further, these requirements do not apply to lease receivables. *[IFRS 7.35A(b)]*.

For a financial asset, the maximum exposure to credit risk is typically the gross carrying amount, net of any amounts offset in accordance with IAS 32 and any impairment losses recognised in accordance with IFRS 9. *[IFRS 7.B9]*. Activities that give rise to credit risk and the associated maximum exposure to credit risk include, but are not limited to: *[IFRS 7.B10]*

- granting loans to customers and placing deposits with other entities. In these cases, the maximum exposure to credit risk is the carrying amount of the related financial assets;
- entering into derivative contracts, e.g. foreign exchange contracts, interest rate swaps and purchased credit derivatives. When the resulting asset is measured at fair value, the maximum exposure to credit risk at the reporting date will equal the carrying amount;
- granting financial guarantees. In this case, the maximum exposure to credit risk is the maximum amount the entity could have to pay if the guarantee is called on, which may be significantly greater than the amount recognised as a liability; and
- making a loan commitment that is irrevocable over the life of the facility or is revocable only in response to a material adverse change. If the issuer cannot settle the loan commitment net in cash or another financial instrument, the maximum credit exposure is the full amount of the commitment. This is because it is uncertain whether the amount of any undrawn portion may be drawn upon in the future. This may be significantly greater than the amount recognised as a liability.

The contractual amount outstanding on financial assets that were written off during the reporting period and which are still subject to enforcement activity should be disclosed. *[IFRS 7.35L]*.

5.2.3.D Credit risk exposure

Users should be able to assess an entity's credit risk exposure and understand its significant credit risk concentrations. Therefore, an entity should disclose, by 'credit risk rating grades' (see below), the gross carrying amount of financial assets and the exposure to credit risk on loan commitments and financial guarantee contracts. This information should be provided separately for financial instruments: *[IFRS 7.35M]*

- for which the loss allowance is measured at an amount equal to 12-month expected credit losses;
- for which the loss allowance is measured at an amount equal to lifetime expected credit losses and that are:
  - financial instruments for which credit risk has increased significantly since initial recognition but are not credit-impaired financial assets;
  - financial assets that are credit-impaired at the reporting date (but were not credit-impaired when purchased or originated); and
  - trade receivables, contract assets or lease receivables for which the loss allowances are measured using a simplified approach based on lifetime expected credit losses. Information for these assets may be based on a provision matrix; *[IFRS 7.35N]* and
- that are financial assets that were credit-impaired when purchased or originated.

The following examples illustrate how this information might be presented. *[IFRS 7.IG20C, 20D].*

Example 54.7: Information about credit risk exposures and significant credit risk concentrations

Consumer loan credit risk exposure by internal rating grades

20XX	**Consumer–credit card**		**Consumer–automotive**	
CU'000	**Gross carrying amount**		**Gross carrying amount**	
	Lifetime	**12-month**	**Lifetime**	**12-month**
Internal Grade 1-2	X	X	X	X
Internal Grade 3-4	X	X	X	X
Internal Grade 5-6	X	X	X	X
Internal Grade 7	X	X	X	X
Total	X	X	X	X

Corporate loan credit risk profile by external rating grades

20XX	**Corporate–equipment**		**Corporate–construction**	
CU'000	**Gross carrying amount**		**Gross carrying amount**	
	Lifetime	**12-month**	**Lifetime**	**12-month**
AAA-AA	X	X	X	X
A	X	X	X	X
BBB-BB	X	X	X	X
B	X	X	X	X
CCC-CC	X	X	X	X
C	X	X	X	X
D	X	X	X	X
Total	X	X	X	X

Corporate loan risk profile by probability of default

20XX	**Corporate–unsecured**		**Corporate–secured**	
CU'000	**Gross carrying amount**		**Gross carrying amount**	
	Lifetime	**12-month**	**Lifetime**	**12-month**
0.00-0.10	X	X	X	X
0.11-0.40	X	X	X	X
0.41-1.00	X	X	X	X
1.01-3.00	X	X	X	X
3.01-6.00	X	X	X	X
6.01-11.00	X	X	X	X
11.01-17.00	X	X	X	X
17.01-25.00	X	X	X	X
25.01-50.00	X	X	X	X
50.00+	X	X	X	X
Total	X	X	X	X

Example 54.8: Information about credit risk exposures using a provision matrix

The reporting entity manufactures cars and provides financing to both dealers and end customers. It discloses its dealer financing and customer financing as separate classes of financial instruments and applies the simplified approach to its trade receivables so that the loss allowance is always measured at an amount equal to lifetime expected credit losses. The following table illustrates the use of a provision matrix as a risk profile disclosure under the simplified approach:

20XX CU'000	**Trade receivables days past due**				
Dealer financing	**Current**	**More than 30 days**	**More than 60 days**	**More than 90 days**	**Total**
Expected credit loss rate	0.10%	2%	5%	13%	
Estimated total gross carrying amount at default	CU20,777	CU1,416	CU673	CU235	CU23,101
Lifetime expected credit losses – dealer financing	CU21	CU28	CU34	CU31	CU114
Customer financing					
Expected credit loss rate	0.20%	3%	8%	15%	
Estimated total gross carrying amount at default	CU19,222	CU2,010	CU301	CU154	CU21,687
Lifetime expected credit losses – customer financing	CU38	CU60	CU24	CU23	CU145

Credit risk rating grades are defined as ratings of credit risk based on the risk of a default occurring on the financial instrument. *[IFRS 7.A]*. The number of credit risk rating grades used to disclose the information above should be consistent with the number that the entity reports to key management personnel for credit risk management purposes. If past due information is the only borrower-specific information available and past due information is used to assess whether credit risk has increased significantly since initial recognition, an analysis by past due status should be provided for that class of financial assets. *[IFRS 7.B8I]*.

When expected credit losses are measured on a collective basis, it may not be possible to allocate the gross carrying amount of individual financial assets or the exposure to credit risk on loan commitments and financial guarantee contracts to the credit risk rating grades for which lifetime expected credit losses are recognised. In that case, the disclosure requirement above should be applied to those financial instruments that can be directly allocated to a credit risk rating grade and separate disclosure should be given of the gross carrying amount of financial instruments for which lifetime expected credit losses have been measured on a collective basis. *[IFRS 7.B8J]*.

A concentration of credit risk exists when a number of counterparties are located in a geographical region or are engaged in similar activities and have similar economic characteristics that would cause their ability to meet contractual obligations to be similarly affected by changes in economic or other conditions. Information should be provided to enable users to understand whether there are groups or portfolios of financial instruments with particular features that could affect a large portion of that group of financial instruments, such as concentration to particular risks. This could include, for example, loan-to-value groupings, geographical, industry or issuer-type concentrations. *[IFRS 7.B8H]*.

For financial instruments within the scope of IFRS 7 to which the impairment requirements in IFRS 9 are *not* applied, disclosure should be given by class of instrument of the amount that best represents the entity's maximum exposure to credit risk at the reporting date (see 5.2.2.A above). The amount disclosed should not take account of any collateral held or other credit enhancements (e.g. netting agreements that do not qualify for offset in accordance with IAS 32). This disclosure is not required for financial instruments whose carrying amount best represents this amount. *[IFRS 7.36(a)]*.

Entities should also provide, by class of financial instrument to which the impairment requirements in IFRS 9 are not applied, a description of collateral held as security and of other credit enhancements, and their financial effect (e.g. a quantification of the extent to which collateral and other credit enhancements mitigate credit risk) in respect of the amount that best represents the maximum exposure to credit risk. This applies irrespective of whether the maximum exposure to credit risk is disclosed separately or is represented by the carrying amount of a financial instrument. *[IFRS 7.36(b)]*. The requirement may be met by disclosing: *[IFRS 7.IG22]*

- the policies and processes for valuing and managing collateral and other credit enhancements obtained;

- a description of the main types of collateral and other credit enhancements (examples of the latter being guarantees and credit derivatives, as well as netting agreements that do not qualify for offset in accordance with IAS 32);
- the main types of counterparties to collateral and other credit enhancements and their creditworthiness; and
- information about risk concentrations within the collateral or other credit enhancements.

It is not entirely clear how detailed this additional information is intended to be. For example, whilst the standard suggests it should, or at least could, involve disclosure of quantitative information, the implementation guidance implies more discursive disclosures might suffice in some cases. In practice, entities will need to make a judgment based on their own specific circumstances and in the light of emerging practice.

5.2.3.E Collateral and other credit enhancements obtained

When an entity obtains financial or non-financial assets during the period by taking possession of collateral it holds as security, or calling on other credit enhancements such as guarantees, and these assets meet the recognition criteria in other standards, it should disclose for such assets held at the reporting date: *[IFRS 7.38]*

- the nature and carrying amount of the assets; and
- when the assets are not readily convertible into cash, its policies for disposing of such assets or for using them in its operations.

This disclosure is intended to provide information about the frequency of such activities and the entity's ability to obtain and realise the value of the collateral. *[IFRS 7.BC56]*.

5.2.4 *Liquidity risk*

5.2.4.A Information provided to key management

As set out at 5.2.1 above, an entity should disclose summary quantitative data about its exposure to risk on the basis of the information provided internally to key management personnel and IFRS 7 emphasises that this requirement applies to liquidity risk too. *[IFRS 7.B10A, BC58A(b)]*.

Entities should provide an explanation of how the data disclosed are determined. If the outflows of cash (or other financial assets) included in the data could occur significantly earlier than indicated, that fact should be stated and quantitative information should be provided to enable users of the financial statements to evaluate the extent of this risk, unless that information is included in the contractual maturity analyses (see 5.2.4.B below). Similar information should be given if the outflows of cash (or other financial assets) could be for significantly different amounts than those indicated in the data. This might be required, for example, if a derivative is included in the data on a net settlement basis, but the counterparty has the option of requiring gross settlement. *[IFRS 7.B10A]*.

5.2.4.B Maturity analyses

To illustrate liquidity risk, the principal minimum numerical disclosures required are: *[IFRS 7.39(a), (b)]*

- a maturity analysis for non-derivative financial liabilities (including issued financial guarantee contracts) that shows their remaining contractual maturities; and
- a maturity analysis for derivative financial liabilities which includes the remaining contractual maturities for those derivative financial liabilities for which contractual maturities are essential for an understanding of the timing of the cash flows.

  The contractual maturities of the following would be essential for an understanding of the timing of the cash flows: *[IFRS 7.B11B]*

  - an interest rate swap with a remaining maturity of five years in a cash flow hedge of a variable rate financial asset or liability; and
  - all loan commitments.

  Derivatives entered into for trading purposes that are typically settled before their contractual maturity (e.g. in response to fair value movements) are an example of the type of instrument that might not need to be included in the maturity analysis.[9]

These requirements are discussed further in the remainder of this sub-section.

Although these minimum disclosures address only financial liabilities, other aspects of IFRS 7 mean that most financial institutions will be required to disclose a maturity analysis of financial assets too (see 5.2.4.C below).

I Time bands

The time bands to be used in the maturity analyses are not specified. Rather, entities should use their judgement to determine what is appropriate. For example, an entity might determine that the following are appropriate: *[IFRS 7.B11]*

- not later than one month;
- later than one month and not later than three months;
- later than three months and not later than one year; and
- later than one year and not later than five years.

In practice it is rare for entities outside of the financial services sector to present more than one time band covering amounts payable within one year. However, it is quite common for more than one time band to be given covering amounts payable later than one year and within five years as Unilever and Nestlé have done (Extracts 54.13 and 54.14 respectively at VII below). For banks and similar institutions an 'on demand' category could also be relevant.

When applied, IFRS 16 requires lessees to disclose a maturity analysis of lease liabilities applying paragraphs 39(a) and B11 of IFRS 7 separately from the maturity analyses of other financial liabilities. *[IFRS 16.58]*. It also adds guidance to IFRS 7 illustrating a number of different approaches, each of which takes into account the maturity of the financial liabilities being presented. Two of these examples simply show lease liabilities as a separate line within a table. A third example illustrates an entity with all financial liabilities due within three years except lease liabilities which extend for 25 years. For this entity, two tables are presented, one including all financial liabilities using the following time bands:

- less than 1 month;
- 1-6 months;
- 6 months – 1 year;
- 1-2 years;
- 2-3 years; and
- more than 3 years;

and a second analysing only the lease liabilities but using the following time bands:

- less than 1 year;
- 1-5 years;
- 5-10 years;
- 10-15 years;
- 15-20 years; and
- 20-25 years. *[IFRS 7.IG31A]*.

IFRS 16 is effective for periods commencing on or after 1 January 2019 (see 8.4 below).

When a counterparty has a choice of when an amount is paid, the liability should be included on the basis of the earliest date on which the entity can be required to pay. For example, financial liabilities such as demand deposits that an entity can be required to repay on demand should be included in the earliest time band. *[IFRS 7.B11C(a)]*. This means that the disclosure shows a worst case scenario, even if there is only a remote possibility that the entity could be required to pay its liabilities earlier than expected, *[IFRS 7.BC57]*, (although the disclosures at 5.2.4.C below may be relevant in these circumstances, i.e. those which are based on the information used by management to manage liquidity risk).

No guidance is given on how to deal with instruments where the issuer has a choice of when an amount is paid. For example, borrowings containing embedded issuer call or issuer prepayment options might be included in the analysis for non-derivative financial liabilities based on the earliest, latest or expected contractual payment dates. Where an entity has a material amount of such instruments it would be appropriate to explain the basis of the analyses presented.

When an entity is committed to make amounts available in instalments, each instalment should be allocated to the earliest period in which the entity can be required to pay. For example, an undrawn loan commitment would be included in the time band containing the earliest date it could be drawn down. *[IFRS 7.B11C(b)]*.

For issued financial guarantee contracts, amounts included in the maturity analysis should be allocated to the earliest period in which the guarantee could be called. *[IFRS 7.B11C(c)]*.

Chapter 54

II Cash flows: general requirements

The amounts that should be disclosed in the maturity analyses are the contractual undiscounted cash flows, for example:

- gross finance lease obligations (before deducting finance charges);
- prices specified in forward agreements to purchase financial assets for cash;
- net amounts for pay-floating/receive-fixed interest rate swaps for which net cash flows are exchanged;
- contractual amounts to be exchanged in a derivative financial instrument (e.g. a currency swap) for which gross cash flows are exchanged; and
- gross loan commitments.

These undiscounted cash flows will differ from the amount included in the statement of financial position because the latter amount is based on discounted cash flows. *[IFRS 7.B11D]*.

When the amount payable is not fixed, the amount disclosed should be determined by reference to the conditions existing at the reporting date. For example, if the amount payable varies with changes in an index, the amount disclosed may be based on the level of the index at the reporting date. *[IFRS 7.B11D]*. The standard does not explain whether the amount should be based on the spot or forward price of the index and, in practice, both approaches are used. Where a material difference between the two approaches could arise it would be appropriate to explain the basis on which the information is prepared as Berendsen plc does.

Extract 54.12: Berendsen plc (2014)

Notes to the consolidated financial statements [extract]

17. Financial risk management [extract]

17.1 Financial risk factors [extract]

c) Liquidity risk [extract]

The table below analyses the group's financial liabilities, excluding break clauses, which will be settled on a net basis into relative maturity groupings based on the remaining period at the balance sheet to the contract maturity date. The amounts disclosed in the table are contractual undiscounted cash flows using spot interest and foreign exchange rates at 31 December 2014. Balances due within 12 months equal their carrying balances as the impact of the discount is not significant.

The definition of liquidity risk includes only financial liabilities that will result in the outflow of cash or another financial asset (see 5 above) which means that financial liabilities that will be settled in the entity's own equity instruments and liabilities within the scope of IFRS 7 that are settled with non-financial assets will not be included in the maturity analysis. *[IFRS 7.BC58A(a)]*.

III Cash flows: borrowings

It follows from the requirements at II above that the cash flows included in the analysis of non-derivative financial liabilities in respect of interest-bearing borrowings should reflect coupon as well as principal payments (although the standard does not say this explicitly). Quite how perpetual debt obligations should be dealt with in this analysis remains to be seen because the amount the standard requires in the latest maturity category is infinity!

A number of companies show coupon payments separately from payments of principal, for example Unilever (Extract 54.13 at VII below). However, separate disclosure is not required and coupon payments are commonly aggregated with principal payments as Nestlé and Volkswagen have (Extracts 54.14 and 54.15 respectively).

The following example illustrates the cash flows that should be included in the maturity analysis for non-derivative financial liabilities for a simple floating rate borrowing.

Example 54.9: Maturity analysis: floating rate borrowing

On 1 January 2017, Company P borrowed €100 million from a bank on the following terms: coupons are payable on the entire principal on 30 June and 31 December each year at the annual rate of LIBOR plus 1% as determined on the previous 1 January and 1 July; the principal is repayable on 31 December 2020.

At the end of 2017, P's reporting period, LIBOR is 5% and there is no difference between spot and forward interest rates (i.e. the yield curve is flat). Accordingly, P would include the following cash flows in its maturity analysis:

	€ million
30 June 2018	3
31 December 2018	3
30 June 2019	3
31 December 2019	3
30 June 2020	3
31 December 2020	103
Total	118

IV *Cash flows: derivatives*

In the case of derivatives that are settled by a gross exchange of cash flows, it is not entirely clear whether entities should disclose the related cash inflow as well as the cash outflow, although such information might be considered useful. Further, because the analysis is of financial liabilities, it seems clear that, strictly, cash outflows from a derivative *asset* that is settled by a gross exchange of cash should not be included. However, the contractual cash flows on these instruments would appear to be no less relevant than on those that have a negative fair value and should be disclosed where relevant.

A number of approaches to these issues were seen in practice as illustrated in Extracts 54.13 to 54.16 at VII below. Unilever and Nestlé both included cash inflows as well as outflows whereas Volkswagen showed only the cash outflows; Unilever included only derivative liabilities whereas Nestlé and Volkswagen included gross-settled derivative assets too. The size of the figures disclosed by entities with gross-settled derivatives can be staggering – Volkswagen, for example, disclosed gross cash outflows of nearly €30 billion from its derivatives.

The IASB staff has been clear that disclosure of only the outflow on derivatives that were in a liability position was explicitly required. However, IFRS 7 now emphasises the need to provide a maturity analysis of assets where such information is necessary to enable users of financial statements to evaluate the nature and extent of the entity's liquidity risk (see 5.2.4.C below). This change is likely to bring derivative assets within the scope of the maturity analyses[10] and, by analogy, related gross cash inflows. Similar issues can arise on commodity contracts that are accounted for under IAS 39 or IFRS 9 which will often be settled by exchanging the commodity for cash. An additional complication with these is that one leg of the contract may not involve a cash flow.

Further issues can arise in the case of a derivative liability settled by exchanging net cash flows in a number of future periods. For example, the relevant index for a long-term interest rate swap might predict that in some periods the entity could have cash inflows. Although this issue was identified by the IASB staff,[11] it has not been addressed and it remains unclear whether and how these inflows should be included within the analyses.

V Cash flows: embedded derivatives

The application guidance to IFRS 7 explains that where an embedded derivative is separated from a hybrid (combined) financial instrument (see Chapter 44 at 4), the entire instrument should be dealt with in the maturity analysis for non-derivative instruments. *[IFRS 7.B11A]*.

No guidance is given for dealing with embedded derivatives separated from non-financial contracts. However, applying a similar approach to those separated from financial instruments would result in them being excluded from the maturity analyses altogether. This is because the hypothecated cash flows of the embedded derivative would be treated as cash flows of the non-financial contract and such contracts are not within the scope of IFRS 7. This is consistent with the IASB staff analysis when developing the above requirement: they planned to exclude from the maturity analysis all separated embedded derivatives except those for which the hybrid contract was a financial liability because including them was unhelpful in understanding the liquidity information provided.[12]

VI Cash flows: financial guarantee contracts and written options

For issued financial guarantee contracts, IFRS 7 requires the maximum amount of the guarantee to be included in the maturity analysis, *[IFRS 7.B11C(c)]*, but credit default swaps and written options are not directly addressed. However, the IASB staff have noted that the question of what to include in the maturity analysis is the same for such instruments and, in our view, the maximum amount that could be payable should be included in the analysis.[13]

VII Examples of disclosures in practice

The following extracts from the financial statements of Unilever, Nestlé, Volkswagen and Royal Bank of Scotland show a variety of ways that companies applied the requirements of IFRS 7 in practice.

Extract 54.13: Unilever PLC and Unilever N.V. (2014)

Notes to the Consolidated Financial Statements [extract]

16A. Management of liquidity risk [extract]

The following table shows Unilever's contractually agreed undiscounted cash flows, including expected interest payments, which are payable under financial liabilities at the balance sheet date:

Undiscounted cash flows	**€ million** Due within 1 year	**€ million** Due between 1 and 2 years	**€ million** Due between 2 and 3 years	**€ million** Due between 3 and 4 years	**€ million** Due between 4 and 5 years	**€ million** Due after 5 years	**€ million** Total	**€ million** Net carrying amount as shown in balance sheet
2014								
Non-derivative financial liabilities:								
Preference shares	(4)	(4)	(4)	(4)	(4)	(72)	(92)	(68)
Bank loans and overdrafts	(601)	(257)	(272)	–	–	–	(1,130)	(1,114)
Bonds and other loans	(4,758)	(647)	(1,289)	(511)	(1,418)	(4,513)	(13,136)	(10,573)
Finance lease creditors	(25)	(48)	(23)	(19)	(18)	(172)	(305)	(199)
Other financial liabilities	(230)	–	–	–	–	(188)	(418)	(418)
Trade payables excluding social security and sundry taxes	(12,051)	(378)	–	–	–	–	(12,429)	(12,429)
Issued financial guarantees	(11)	–	–	–	–	–	(11)	–
	(17,680)	(1,334)	(1,588)	(534)	(1,440)	(4,945)	(27,521)	(24,801)
Derivative financial liabilities:								
Interest rate derivatives:								
Derivatives contracts – receipts	289	229	230	17	–	–	765	
Derivative contracts – payments	(429)	(255)	(277)	(19)	–	–	(980)	
Foreign exchange derivatives:								
Derivatives contracts – receipts	9,957	2	–	347	–	–	10,306	
Derivative contracts – payments	(10,284)	(2)	–	(304)	–	–	(10,590)	
Commodity derivatives:								
Derivatives contracts – receipts	405	–	–	–	–	–	405	
Derivative contracts – payments	(421)	–	–	–	–	–	(421)	
	(483)	(26)	(47)	41	–	–	(515)	(514)
Total	(18,163)	(1,360)	(1,635)	(493)	(1,440)	(4,945)	(28,036)	(25,315)

Extract 54.14: Nestlé S.A. (2014)

Notes [extract]

13. Financial instruments [extract]

13.2b Liquidity risk [extract]

Contractual maturities of financial liabilities and derivatives (including interest) [extract]

In millions of CHF

	In the first year	In the second year	In the third to the fifth year	After the fifth year	Contractual amount	Carrying amount
Financial assets						**27,833**
Trade and other payables	**(17,437)**	**(357)**	**(60)**	**(1,474)**	**(19,328)**	**(19,279)**
Commercial paper (a)	(5,573)	–	–	–	(5,573)	(5,569)
Bonds (a)	(672)	(1,419)	(6,403)	(5,042)	(13,536)	(12,257)
Other financial debt	(2,963)	(203)	(326)	(115)	(3,607)	(3,380)
Total financial debt	**(9,208)**	**(1,622)**	**(6,729)**	**(5,157)**	**(22,716)**	**(21,206)**
Financial liabilities	**(26,645)**	**(1,979)**	**(6,789)**	**(6,631)**	**(42,044)**	**(40,485)**
Non-currency derivative assets	39	5	3	(6)	41	41
Non-currency derivative liabilities	(215)	(29)	(42)	(7)	(293)	(289)
Gross amount receivable from currency derivatives	11,589	458	2,204	495	14,746	14,553
Gross amount payable from currency derivatives	(11,370)	(489)	(2,435)	(550)	(14,844)	(14,662)
Net derivatives	**43**	**(55)**	**(270)**	**(68)**	**(350)**	**(357)**
Net financial position						**(13,009)**
Of which derivatives under cash flow hedges (b)	(105)	(29)	(42)	(7)	(183)	(180)

(a) Commercial paper of CHF 3571 million and bonds of CHF 76 million have maturities of less than three months.

(b) The periods when the cash flow hedges affect the income statement do not differ significantly from the maturities disclosed above.

Extract 54.15: Volkswagen Aktiengesellschaft (2014)

Notes to the Consolidated Financial Statements [extract]

34. Financial risk management and financial instruments [extract]

3. LIQUIDITY RISK [extract]

The solvency and liquidity of the Volkswagen Group are ensured at all times by rolling liquidity planning, a liquidity reserve in the form of cash, confirmed credit lines and globally available debt issuance programs.

Local cash funds in certain countries (e.g. Brazil, Argentina, Ukraine, Malaysia, India and Taiwan) are only available to the Group for cross-border transactions subject to exchange controls. There are no significant restrictions over and above these.

The following overview shows the contractual undiscounted cash flows from financial instruments.

MATURITY ANALYSIS OF UNDISCOUNTED CASH FLOWS FROM FINANCIAL INSTRUMENTS

€ million	Remaining contractual maturities			
	under one year	within one to five years	over five years	2014
Put options and compensation rights granted to noncontrolling interest shareholders	3,185	–	–	3,185
Financial liabilities	67,634	63,926	12,011	142,941
Trade payables	19,526	4	–	19,530
Other financial liabilities	4,652	1,470	94	6,216
Derivatives	61,623	51,265	207	113,094
	156,619	116,034	12,312	284,965

When calculating cash outflows related to put options and compensation rights, it was assumed that shares would be tendered at the earliest possible repayment date.

Derivatives comprise both cash flows from derivative financial instruments with negative fair values and cash flows from derivatives with positive fair values for which gross settlement has been agreed. The cash outflows from derivatives for which gross settlement has been agreed are matched in part by cash inflows. These cash inflows are not reported in the maturity analysis. If these cash inflows were also recognized, the cash outflows presented would be substantially lower.

The cash outflows from irrevocable credit commitments are presented in note 38, classified by contractual maturities.

The maximum potential liability under financial guarantees amounted to €674 million as of December 31, 2014. Financial guarantees are assumed to be due immediately in all cases. They relate primarily to guarantees.

Chapter 54

Extract 54.16: The Royal Bank of Scotland Group plc (2014)

Notes on the consolidated accounts [extract]

12. Financial instruments – maturity analysis [extracts]

Assets and liabilities by contractual cash flow maturity [extract]

The tables below show the contractual undiscounted cash flows receivable and payable, up to a period of 20 years, including future receipts and payments of interest of financial assets and liabilities by contractual maturity.

Financial liabilities are included at the earliest date on which the counterparty can require repayment, regardless of whether or not such early repayment results in a penalty. If the repayment of a financial instrument is triggered by, or is subject to, specific criteria such as market price hurdles being reached, the asset is included in the time band that contains the latest date on which it can be repaid, regardless of early repayment.

The liability is included in the time band that contains the earliest possible date on which the conditions could be fulfilled, without considering the probability of the conditions being met.

For example, if a structured note is automatically prepaid when an equity index exceeds a certain level, the cash outflow will be included in the less than three months period, whatever the level of the index at the year end. The settlement date of debt securities in issue, issued by certain securitisation vehicles consolidated by RBS, depends on when cash flows are received from the securitised assets. Where these assets are prepayable, the timing of the cash outflow relating to securities assumes that each asset will be prepaid at the earliest possible date. As the repayments of assets and liabilities are linked, the repayment of assets in securitisations is shown on the earliest date that the asset can be prepaid, as this is the basis used for liabilities.

The principal amounts of financial assets and liabilities that are repayable after 20 years or where the counterparty has no right to repayment of the principal are excluded from the table, as are interest payments after 20 years.

Held-for-trading assets of £498.2 billion (2013 - £452.1 billion; 2012 - £666.5 billion) and liabilities of £477.1 billion (2013 - £423.3 billion; 2012 - £628.2 billion) have been excluded from the following tables in view of their short term nature.

2014	0-3 months £m	3-12 months £m	1-3 years £m	3-5 years £m	5-10 years £m	10-20 years £m
Liabilities by contractual maturity						
Deposits by banks	8,287	754	793	8	575	140
Debt securities in issue	2,591	7,585	12,952	8,536	8,897	1,926
Subordinated liabilities	1,243	2,731	3,045	4,365	13,394	3,698
Settlement balances and other liabilities	6,295	5	4	–	–	–
Total maturing liabilities	18,416	11,075	16,794	12,909	22,866	5,764
Customer accounts	328,158	7,884	3,170	1,082	114	23
Derivatives held for hedging	140	348	789	543	949	1,010
	346,714	19,307	20,753	14,534	23,929	6,797
Maturity gap	82,122	(4,772)	(11,561)	(8,179)	(16,748)	(3,162)
Cumulative maturity gap	82,122	77,350	65,789	57,610	40,862	37,700
Guarantees and commitments – notional amounts						
Guarantees	16,721	–	–	–	–	–
Commitments	212,777	–	–	–	–	–
	229,498	–	–	–	–	–

5.2.4.C Management of associated liquidity risk

In addition to the maturity analyses for financial liabilities, the entity should provide a description of how it manages the liquidity risk inherent in those analyses. *[IFRS 7.39(c)]*. These disclosures are, in effect, intended to 'reconcile' the maturity analyses which are prepared on a worst case scenario notion (see 5.2.4.B above) with how an entity actually manages liquidity risk (see 5.2.4.A above).[14]

It is emphasised that a maturity analysis of financial assets held for managing liquidity risk (e.g. financial assets that are readily saleable or expected to generate cash inflows to meet cash outflows on financial liabilities) is required if that information is necessary to enable users of financial statements to evaluate the nature and extent of the entity's liquidity risk. *[IFRS 7.B11E, BC58D]*. IFRS 7 does not specify the basis on which such an analysis should be provided and in practice they are often prepared on the basis of expected rather than contractual maturities as this is considered more relevant information.

Other factors that might be considered when making this disclosure include, but are not limited to, whether the entity: *[IFRS 7.B11F]*

- has committed borrowing facilities (e.g. commercial paper facilities) or other lines of credit (e.g. stand-by credit facilities) that it can access to meet liquidity needs;

- holds deposits at central banks to meet liquidity needs;
- has very diverse funding sources;
- has significant concentrations of liquidity risk in either its assets or its funding sources;
- has internal control processes and contingency plans for managing liquidity risk;
- has instruments that include accelerated repayment terms (e.g. on the downgrade of the entity's credit rating);
- has instruments that could require the posting of collateral (e.g. margin calls for derivatives);
- has instruments that allow the entity to choose whether it settles its financial liabilities by delivering cash (or another financial asset) or by delivering its own shares; or
- has instruments that are subject to master netting agreements.

5.2.4.D *Puttable financial instruments classified as equity*

Certain puttable financial instruments that meet the definition of financial liabilities are classified as equity instruments (see Chapter 45 at 4.6). In spite of this classification, the IASB recognises that these instruments give rise to liquidity risk and consequently requires the following disclosures about them: *[IAS 1.136A]*

- summary quantitative data about the amount classified as equity;
- the entity's objectives, policies and processes for managing its obligation to repurchase or redeem the instruments when required to do so by the instrument holders, including any changes from the previous period;
- the expected cash outflow on redemption or repurchase of that class of financial instruments; and
- information about how the expected cash outflow on redemption or repurchase was determined.

5.2.5 *Market risk*

IFRS 7 requires entities to provide disclosure of their sensitivity to market risk in one of two ways which are set out at 5.2.5.A and 5.2.5.B below. The sensitivity analyses should cover the whole of an entity's business, but different types of sensitivity analysis may be provided for different classes of financial instruments. *[IFRS 7.B21]*. This is considered by the IASB to be simpler and more suitable than the disclosure of terms and conditions of financial instruments previously required by IAS 32 and for which there is no direct equivalent within IFRS 7. *[IFRS 7.BC59]*.

No sensitivity analysis is required for financial instruments that an entity classifies as equity instruments. Such instruments are not remeasured so that neither profit or loss nor equity will be affected by the equity price risk of those instruments. *[IFRS 7.B28]*.

5.2.5.A 'Basic' sensitivity analysis

Except where the disclosures set out at 5.2.5.B below are provided, entities should disclose: *[IFRS 7.40]*

- a sensitivity analysis for each type of market risk to which the entity is exposed at the reporting date, showing how profit or loss and equity would have been affected by changes in the relevant risk variable that were reasonably possible at that date.

  The sensitivity of profit or loss (which arises, for example, from instruments measured at fair value through profit or loss and, where IFRS 9 is not applied, impairments of available-for-sale financial assets) should be disclosed separately from the sensitivity of equity (which arises, for example, from instruments classified as available for sale or, where IFRS 9 is applied, from investments in equity instruments whose changes in fair value are presented in other comprehensive income). *[IFRS 7.B27]*.

  The term 'profit or loss' is used in IAS 1 to mean profit after tax. Therefore, it might well be argued that the amounts disclosed should take account of any related tax effects, a view corroborated by the illustrative disclosures in the implementation guidance to IFRS 7 (see Example 54.10 below). However, as noted below, the application guidance suggests this requirement should (and the implementation guidance might suggest it could) be met by disclosing the impact on interest expense, a pre-tax measure of profit. Given this conflicting guidance, it is difficult to say that a pre-tax approach fails to comply with the standard and, in practice, both approaches are seen.

  Where a post-tax figure is disclosed, it will not always be straightforward to determine the related tax effects, especially for a multinational group, and it may be appropriate to use the guidance in Chapter 31 at 10 which deals with the allocation of income tax between profit or loss, other comprehensive income and equity.

  This requirement focuses exclusively on accounting sensitivity, and does not include market risk sensitivities that do not directly impact profit and loss or equity, e.g. interest rate risk arising on fixed rate financial assets held at amortised cost. In December 2008, the IASB considered encouraging entities to discuss the effect of changes in the relevant risk variable on economic value not manifest in profit and loss or equity, but decided not to;[15]
- the methods and assumptions used in preparing the sensitivity analysis; and
- changes from the previous period in the methods and assumptions used, and the reasons for such changes.

The standard contains a reminder of the general guidance at 3.1 above and explains that an entity should decide how it aggregates information to display the overall picture without combining information with different characteristics about exposures to risks from significantly different economic environments. For example, an entity that trades financial instruments might disclose this information separately for financial instruments held for trading and those not held for trading. Similarly, an entity would not aggregate its exposure to market risks from areas of hyperinflation with its exposure to the same market risks from areas of very low inflation. However, an entity that has exposure to only one type of market risk in only one economic environment, would not show disaggregated information. *[IFRS 7.B17]*.

Risk variables that are relevant to disclosing market risk include, but are not limited to: *[IFRS 7.IG32]*

- the yield curve of market interest rates.

  It may be necessary to consider both parallel and non-parallel shifts in the yield curve;
- foreign exchange rates.

  The standard requires a sensitivity analysis to be disclosed for each currency to which an entity has significant exposure; *[IFRS 7.B24]*
- prices of equity instruments; and
- market prices of commodities.

When disclosing how profit or loss and equity would have been affected by changes in the relevant risk variable, there is no requirement to determine what the profit or loss for the period would have been if the relevant risk variables had been different during the reporting period. The requirement is subtly different because the effect that is disclosed assumes that a reasonably possible change in the relevant risk variable had occurred *at the reporting date* and had been applied to the risk exposures in existence *at that date*. For example, if an entity has a floating rate liability at the reporting date, the entity would disclose the effect on profit or loss (i.e. interest expense) for the current year if interest rates had varied by reasonably possible amounts. Further, this disclosure is not required for each change within a range of reasonably possible changes, only at the limits of the reasonably possible range. *[IFRS 7.B18]*.

The following example illustrates how the amounts to be included in these disclosures in respect of a number of different instruments might be determined – for simplicity, tax effects are ignored.

Example 54.10: Illustration of how sensitivity disclosures can be determined

Company X, which has the euro as its functional currency, is party to the following instruments at 31 December 2017, X's reporting date:

- a €100m floating rate borrowing;
- a forward contract to sell US$10m in July 2018 that is designated in an effective hedge of a highly probable forecast sale that is denominated in US dollars;
- a short-term loan of £10m made to a related party;
- an interest rate swap that is not designated as a hedge;
- investments in fixed rate debt securities that are classified as held-to-maturity (IAS 39) or financial assets measured at amortised cost (IFRS 9);
- investments in similar securities that are classified as available-for-sale (IAS 39) or debt instruments measured at fair value through other comprehensive income (IFRS 9); and
- investments in a portfolio of US equities with a fair value of US$50m.

Floating rate borrowing

Changes in interest rates will result in this instrument impacting on X's profit or loss. If X concludes that a reasonably possible change in interest rates is 50 basis points (0.5%), €0.5m [€100m × 0.5%] would be included in the amount disclosed as the impact on profit or loss of this reasonably possible change.

Chapter 54

Forward contract

Changes in exchange rates will have an impact on the fair value (and carrying value) of this instrument, but this would be recognised in other comprehensive income, not profit or loss (assuming ineffectiveness is insignificant). If a reasonably possibly change in exchange rates would change the value of the contract by €0.3m, this would be included in the amount disclosed as the impact on equity of this reasonably possible change.

Foreign currency loan

Changes in spot exchange rates will have an impact on the carrying amount of this asset with changes recognised in profit or loss as a result of the application of IAS 21 – *The Effects of Changes in Foreign Exchange Rates*. If a reasonably possible change in the exchange rate would alter the carrying value of the contract by €1.0m, this would be included in the amount disclosed as the impact on profit or loss of this reasonably possible change.

If the loan were made to a subsidiary of X that had sterling as its functional currency, the loan itself would eliminate on consolidation but the impact of retranslating it into euros in X's own financial statements would remain in consolidated profit or loss. Therefore, in these circumstances, the loan would still be included in the sensitivity analysis for X's consolidated financial statements.

Interest rate swap

Changes in interest rates will have an impact on the fair value (and carrying value) of this instrument and such changes would be recognised in profit or loss. If a reasonably possible change of 50 basis points in interest rates would change the value of the contract by €0.4m, this would be included in the amount disclosed as the impact on profit or loss of this reasonably possible change.

Fixed rate debt securities

Changes in interest rates will have an impact on the fair value of all these instruments. However, because those classified as held-to-maturity (IAS 39) or financial assets measured at amortised cost (IFRS 9) are not measured at fair value, the carrying amount only of those that are classified as available-for-sale (IAS 39) or debt instruments measured at fair value through other comprehensive income (IFRS 9) will change as interest rates move and such change will normally be recognised in other comprehensive income. Therefore, if a reasonably possible 50 basis point change in interest rates would change the fair value of each group of instruments by €0.5m, only the amount in respect of the available-for-sale securities (IAS 39) or debt instruments measured at fair value through other comprehensive income (IFRS 9) would be included in the sensitivity disclosure as an impact on equity. Of course there would be nothing to preclude disclosure, as additional information (if considered relevant), of the sensitivity of the fair value of held-to-maturity investments to changes in interest rates.

US equity securities

The impact of a reasonably possible change in the market prices of these securities should be included in the amount disclosed as X's sensitivity to equity price risk. Changes in exchange rates might be considered to impact the fair value of these investments. However, as noted at (c)(i) at 5 above, financial instruments that are non-monetary items do not give rise to foreign currency risk for the purposes of IFRS 7 – essentially the foreign currency risk is seen as part of the market price risk associated with such instruments. Therefore, X should take no account of these investments when disclosing its sensitivity to changes in the euro/US dollar exchange rate. Nevertheless, this information may be provided as additional disclosure where it is considered relevant.

Relevant risk variables for the purpose of this disclosure might include: *[IFRS 7.IG33]*

- prevailing market interest rates, for interest-sensitive financial instruments such as a variable-rate loan; or
- currency rates and interest rates, for foreign currency financial instruments such as foreign currency bonds.

For interest rate risk, the sensitivity analysis might show separately the effect of a change in market interest rates on:

- interest income and expense;
- other line items of profit or loss (such as trading gains and losses); and
- when applicable, equity.

An entity might disclose a sensitivity analysis for interest rate risk for each currency in which the entity has material exposures to interest rate risk. *[IFRS 7.IG34]*.

In determining what a reasonably possible change in the relevant risk variable is, the economic environment(s) in which the entity operates and the time frame over which it is making the assessment should be considered. A reasonably possible change should not include remote or 'worst case' scenarios or 'stress tests'. Moreover, if the rate of change in the underlying risk variable is stable, the chosen reasonably possible change in the risk variable need not be altered.

For example, assume that interest rates are 5 percent and an entity determines that a fluctuation in interest rates of ±50 basis points is reasonably possible. It would disclose the effect on profit or loss and equity if interest rates were to change to 4.5 percent or 5.5 percent. In the next period, interest rates have increased to 5.5 percent. The entity continues to believe that interest rates may fluctuate by ±50 basis points (i.e. that the rate of change in interest rates is stable). The entity would disclose the effect on profit or loss and equity if interest rates were to change to 5 percent or 6 percent. The entity would not be required to revise its assessment that interest rates might reasonably fluctuate by ±50 basis points, unless there is evidence that interest rates have become significantly more volatile. *[IFRS 7.B19]*.

However, when market conditions change significantly, for example as occurred in many markets in the second half of 2008, an entity's assessment of what constitutes a reasonably possible change should be reassessed.[16]

The time frame over which a reasonably possible change should be assessed is defined by the period until these disclosures will next be presented. This will normally coincide with the next annual reporting period, *[IFRS 7.B19]*, although in some jurisdictions such information may be included in interim reports.

Because the factors affecting market risk will vary according to the specific circumstances of each entity, the appropriate range to be considered in providing a sensitivity analysis of market risk will also vary for each entity and for each type of market risk. *[IFRS 7.IG35]*.

Where an entity has exposure to other price risk, it might disclose the effect of a decrease in a specified stock market index, commodity price, or other risk variable. For example, if residual value guarantees that are financial instruments are given, the disclosure could include an increase or decrease in the value of the assets to which the guarantee applies. *[IFRS 7.B25]*.

The following example from the implementation guidance illustrates the type of disclosure that might be provided for an entity still applying IAS 39.

Example 54.11: Illustrative disclosure of sensitivity analyses

Interest rate risk

At 31 December 2017, if interest rates at that date had been 10 basis points lower with all other variables held constant, post-tax profit for the year would have been €1.7 million (2016: €2.4 million) higher, arising mainly as a result of lower interest expense on variable borrowings, and other comprehensive income would have been €2.8 million (2016: €3.2 million) higher, arising mainly as a result of an increase in the fair value of fixed rate financial assets classified as available-for-sale.

If interest rates had been 10 basis points higher, with all other variables held constant, post-tax profit would have been €1.5 million (2016: €2.1 million) lower, arising mainly as a result of higher interest expense on variable borrowings, and other comprehensive income would have been €3.0 million (2016: €3.4 million) lower, arising mainly as a result of a decrease in the fair value of fixed rate financial assets classified as available-for-sale.

Profit is more sensitive to interest rate decreases than increases because of borrowings with capped interest rates. The sensitivity is lower in 2017 than in 2016 because of a reduction in outstanding borrowings that has occurred as the entity's debt has matured (see note X).

Foreign currency exchange rate risk

At 31 December 2017, if the euro had weakened 10 percent against the US dollar with all other variables held constant, post-tax profit for the year would have been €2.8 million (2016: €6.4 million) lower, and other comprehensive income would have been €1.2 million (2016: €1.1 million) higher.

Conversely, if the euro had strengthened 10 percent against the US dollar with all other variables held constant, post-tax profit would have been €2.8 million (2016: €6.4 million) higher, and other comprehensive income would have been €1.2 million (2016: €1.1 million) lower.

The lower foreign currency exchange rate sensitivity in profit in 2017 compared with 2016 is attributable to a reduction in foreign currency denominated debt. Equity is more sensitive in 2017 than in 2016 because of the increased use of hedges of foreign currency purchases, offset by the reduction in foreign currency debt. *[IFRS 7.IG36].*

Similar disclosures could be given by an entity that has adopted IFRS 9, although it would not hold assets classified as available for sale.

The following extracts from the financial statements of Hunting illustrates how one company has addressed this disclosure requirement in respect of certain of its interest rate and foreign currency exposures. Extract 54.18 (BP) at 5.2.5.B below contains another example, this time for its exposure to embedded derivatives.

Extract 54.17: Hunting plc (2014)

Notes to the Financial Statements [extract]

31. Financial Instruments: Sensitivity Analysis [extract]

The following sensitivity analysis is intended to illustrate the sensitivity to changes in market variables on the Group's and Company's financial instruments and show the impact on profit or loss and shareholders' equity. Financial instruments affected by market risk include cash and cash equivalents, borrowings, deposits and derivative financial instruments. The sensitivity analysis relates to the position as at 31 December 2014.

The analysis excludes the impact of movements in market variables on the carrying value of pension and other post-retirement obligations, provisions and on the non-financial assets and liabilities of foreign operations.

The following assumptions have been made in calculating the sensitivity analysis:

- Foreign exchange rate and interest rate sensitivities have an asymmetric impact on the Group's results, that is, an increase in rates does not result in the same amount of movement as a decrease in rates.
- For floating rate assets and liabilities, the amount of asset or liability outstanding at the balance sheet date is assumed to be outstanding for the whole year.
- Fixed rate financial instruments that are carried at amortised cost are not subject to interest rate risk for the purpose of this analysis.
- The carrying values of financial assets and liabilities carried at amortised cost do not change as interest rates change.

Positive figures represent an increase in profit or equity.

(i) Interest Rate Sensitivity

The sensitivity rate of 0.25% (2013 – 0.25%) for US interest rates represents management's assessment of a reasonably possible change, based on historical volatility and a review of analysts' research and banks' expectations of future interest rates.

Group

The post-tax impact on the income statement, with all other variables held constant, at 31 December, for an increase of 0.25% (2013 – 0.25%) in US interest rates, is to reduce profits by $0.2m (2013 – $0.5m). If US interest rates were to decrease by 0.25% (2013 – 0.25%), then the post-tax impact on the income statement would be to increase profits by $0.2m (2013 – $0.5m). The movements arise on US dollar denominated borrowings. There is no impact on other comprehensive income ("OCI") for a change in interest rates.

(ii) Foreign Exchange Rate Sensitivity

The sensitivity rate of 10% (2013 – 10%) for Sterling and Canadian dollar exchange rates represents management's assessment of a reasonably possible change, based on historical volatility and a review of analysts' research and banks' expectations of future foreign exchange rates.

The table below shows the post-tax impact for the year of a reasonable change in foreign exchange rates, with all other variables held constant, at 31 December.

	2014		2013	
	Income statement	**OCI**	Income statement	OCI
	$m	**$m**	$m	$m
Sterling exchange rates +10% (2013: +10%)	**(0.5)**	**1.6**	(12.6)	18.6
Sterling exchange rates –10% (2013: –10%)	**0.9**	**(2.0)**	2.1	(22.4)
Canadian dollar exchange rates +10% (2013: +10%)	**(0.8)**	**(5.1)**	(0.1)	(1.8)
Canadian dollar exchange rates –10% (2013: –10%)	**0.9**	**5.5**	0.1	2.2

The movements in the income statement arise from cash, bank overdrafts, intra-group balances and accrued expenses where the functional currency of the entity is different from the currency that the monetary items are denominated in.

The movements in OCI in 2014 arise from net Sterling and Canadian dollar borrowings designated in a hedge of net investments in foreign subsidiaries and from US and Canadian dollar denominated loans that have been recognised as part of the Group's net investment in foreign subsidiaries. The movements in OCI in 2013 arise from Sterling and Canadian dollar denominated loans that have been recognised as part of the Group's net investment in foreign subsidiaries.

5.2.5.B Value-at-risk and similar analyses

Where an entity prepares a sensitivity analysis, such as value-at-risk, that reflects interdependencies between risk variables (e.g. interest rates and exchange rates) and uses it to manage financial risks, it may disclose that analysis in place of the information specified at 5.2.5.A above. *[IFRS 7.41]*. If this disclosure is given, the effects on profit or loss and equity at 5.2.5.A above need not be given. *[IFRS 7.BC61]*.

In these cases the following should also be disclosed: *[IFRS 7.41]*

- an explanation of the method used in preparing such a sensitivity analysis, and of the main parameters and assumptions underlying the data provided; and
- an explanation of the objective of the method used and of limitations that may result in the information not fully reflecting the fair value of the assets and liabilities involved.

This applies even if such a methodology measures only the potential for loss and does not measure the potential for gain. Such an entity might comply with the disclosure requirements above by detailing the type of value-at-risk model used (e.g. whether the model relies on Monte Carlo simulations), an explanation about how the model works and the main assumptions (e.g. the holding period and confidence level). Entities might also disclose the historical observation period and weightings applied to observations within that period, an explanation of how options are dealt with in the calculations, and which volatilities and correlations (or, alternatively, Monte Carlo probability distribution simulations) are used. *[IFRS 7.B20]*.

The basic sensitivity analysis considered at 5.2.5.A above incorporates only the effects of financial instruments and other contracts within the scope of IFRS 7. In contrast, value-at-risk and similar analyses can incorporate the effects of items outside the scope of IFRS 7, for example trading inventories, own use contracts and insurance contracts. This is because the standard requires entities to disclose the analysis actually used in the management of the business which will often include such items.

It has been suggested that disclosure of potential losses due to stress conditions would be of greater use than the disclosure requirements for value-at-risk and similar methodologies that do not contemplate extraordinary market movements. However, in December 2008, the IASB noted this would be inconsistent with the 'basic' sensitivity analysis (see 5.2.5.A above) and decided not to add such a requirement to IFRS 7.[17]

BP provides the following market risk disclosures which includes the value-at-risk limit it uses to manage that risk.

Extract 54.18: BP p.l.c. (2014)

Notes on financial statements [extract]

27 Financial instruments and financial risk factors [extract]

(a) Market risk [extract]

Market risk is the risk or uncertainty arising from possible market price movements and their impact on the future performance of a business. The primary commodity price risks that the group is exposed to include oil, natural gas and power prices that could adversely affect the value of the group's financial assets, liabilities or expected future cash flows. The group enters into derivatives in a well-established entrepreneurial trading operation. In addition, the group has developed a control framework aimed at managing the volatility inherent in certain of its natural business exposures. In accordance with the control framework the group enters into various transactions using derivatives for risk management purposes.

The major components of market risk are commodity price risk, foreign currency exchange risk and interest rate risk, each of which is discussed below.

> **(i) Commodity price risk**
>
> The group's integrated supply and trading function uses conventional financial and commodity instruments and physical cargoes and pipeline positions available in the related commodity markets. Oil and natural gas swaps, options and futures are used to mitigate price risk. Power trading is undertaken using a combination of over-the-counter forward contracts and other derivative contracts, including options and futures. This activity is on both a standalone basis and in conjunction with gas derivatives in relation to gas-generated power margin. In addition, NGLs are traded around certain US inventory locations using over-the-counter forward contracts in conjunction with over-the-counter swaps, options and physical inventories.
>
> The group measures market risk exposure arising from its trading positions in liquid periods using value-at-risk techniques. These techniques make a statistical assessment of the market risk arising from possible future changes in market prices over a one-day holding period. The value-at-risk measure is supplemented by stress testing. Trading activity occurring in liquid periods is subject to value-at-risk limits for each trading activity and for this trading activity in total. The board has delegated a limit of $100 million value at risk in support of this trading activity. Alternative measures are used to monitor exposures which are outside liquid periods and which cannot be actively risk managed.

5.2.5.C *Other market risk disclosures*

When the sensitivity analyses discussed at 5.2.5.A and 5.2.5.B above are unrepresentative of a risk inherent in a financial instrument, that fact should be disclosed together with the reason for believing the sensitivity analyses are unrepresentative. *[IFRS 7.42]*.

This can occur when the year-end exposure does not reflect the exposure during the year *[IFRS 7.42]* or a financial instrument contains terms and conditions whose effects are not apparent from the sensitivity analysis, e.g. options that remain out of (or in) the money for the chosen change in the risk variable. *[IFRS 7.IG37(a)]*. Additional disclosures in this second case might include:

- the terms and conditions of the financial instrument (e.g. the options);
- the effect on profit or loss if the term or condition were met (i.e. if the options were exercised); and
- a description of how the risk is hedged.

For example, an entity may acquire a zero-cost interest rate collar that includes an out-of-the-money leveraged written option (e.g. the entity pays ten times the amount of the difference between a specified interest rate floor and the current market interest rate if that current rate is below the floor). The entity may regard the collar as an inexpensive economic hedge against a reasonably possible increase in interest rates. However, an unexpectedly large decrease in interest rates might trigger payments under the written option that, because of the leverage, might be significantly larger than the benefit of lower interest rates. Neither the fair value of the collar nor a sensitivity analysis based on reasonably possible changes in market variables would indicate this exposure. In this case, the entity might provide the additional information described above. *[IFRS 7.IG38]*.

Where financial assets are illiquid, e.g. when there is a low volume of transactions in similar assets and it is difficult to find a counterparty, additional disclosures might be required, *[IFRS 7.IG37(b)]*, for example the reasons for the lack of liquidity and how the risk is hedged. *[IFRS 7.IG39]*.

A large holding of a financial asset that, if sold in its entirety, would be sold at a discount or premium to the quoted market price for a smaller holding could also require additional disclosure. *[IFRS 7.IG37(c)]*. This might include: *[IFRS 7.IG40]*

- the nature of the security (e.g. entity name);
- the extent of holding (e.g. 15 percent of the issued shares);
- the effect on profit or loss; and
- how the entity hedges the risk.

5.2.6 Concentrations of risk

Concentrations of risk should be disclosed if not otherwise apparent from the disclosures made to comply with the requirements set out at 5.2.1 to 5.2.5 above. *[IFRS 7.34(c)]*. This should include:

- a description of how management determines concentrations;
- a description of the shared characteristic that identifies each concentration (for example, counterparty, geographical area, currency or market).

  For example, the shared characteristic may refer to geographical distribution of counterparties by groups of countries, individual countries or regions within countries; *[IFRS 7.IG19]* and
- the amount of the risk exposure associated with all financial instruments sharing that characteristic.

Concentrations of risk arise from financial instruments that have similar characteristics and are affected similarly by changes in economic or other conditions. It is emphasised that the identification of concentrations of risk requires judgement taking into account the circumstances of the entity. *[IFRS 7.B8]*. For example, they may arise from:

- Industry sectors.

  If an entity's counterparties are concentrated in one or more industry sectors (such as retail or wholesale), it would disclose separately exposure to risks arising from each concentration of counterparties;
- Credit rating or other measure of credit quality.

  If an entity's counterparties are concentrated in one or more credit qualities (such as secured loans or unsecured loans) or in one or more credit ratings (such as investment grade or speculative grade), it would disclose separately exposure to risks arising from each concentration of counterparties;
- Geographical distribution.

  If an entity's counterparties are concentrated in one or more geographical markets (such as Asia or Europe), it would disclose separately exposure to risks arising from each concentration of counterparties; and
- A limited number of individual counterparties or groups of closely related counterparties.

Similar principles apply to identifying concentrations of other risks, including liquidity risk and market risk. For example, concentrations of liquidity risk may arise from the repayment terms of financial liabilities, sources of borrowing facilities or reliance on a particular market in which to realise liquid assets. Concentrations of foreign exchange risk may arise if an entity has a significant net open position in a single foreign currency, or aggregate net open positions in several currencies that tend to move together. *[IFRS 7.IG18]*.

5.2.7 Operational risk

In developing IFRS 7, the IASB considered whether disclosure of information about operational risk should be required by the standard. However, the definition and measurement of operational risk were considered to be in their infancy and were not necessarily related to financial instruments. Also, such disclosures were believed to be more appropriately located outside the financial statements. Consequently, this issue was deferred for consideration in the management commentary project (see Chapter 3 at 2.3). *[IFRS 7.BC65]*.

5.2.8 Capital disclosures

The IASB considers that the level of an entity's capital and how it is managed are important factors for users of financial statements to consider in assessing the risk profile of an entity and its ability to withstand unexpected adverse events. It might also affect an entity's ability to pay dividends. Consequently, ED 7 contained proposed disclosures about capital. *[IAS 1.BC86]*.

However, some commentators questioned the relevance of the capital disclosures in a standard dealing with disclosures relating to financial instruments and the IASB noted that an entity's capital does not relate solely to financial instruments and, thus, they have more general relevance. Accordingly, whilst these disclosures were retained, they were included in IAS 1, rather than IFRS 7. *[IAS 1.BC88]*. Those disclosures required by IAS 1 are dealt with in Chapter 3 at 5.4.

6 TRANSFERS OF FINANCIAL ASSETS

The objective of these requirements, which were introduced into IFRS 7 in October 2010, is that entities should disclose information that enables users of its financial statements: *[IFRS 7.42B]*

(a) to understand the relationship between transferred financial assets that are not derecognised in their entirety and the associated liabilities; and

(b) to evaluate the nature of, and risks associated with, the entity's continuing involvement in derecognised financial assets.

The standard specifies detailed disclosure requirements to support objectives (a) and (b) which are discussed below at 6.2 and 6.3 below respectively. However, an entity should disclose any additional information, over and above that specified by IFRS 7, that it considers necessary to meet these objectives. *[IFRS 7.42H]*.

Rather unusually, the standard specifies that these disclosures should be presented in a single note to the financial statements. *[IFRS 7.42A]*. Presumably this is to prevent entities 'hiding' these disclosures by having the detailed information scattered across a number of notes.

These requirements supplement the other requirements of IFRS 7 and apply when an entity transfers financial assets. They apply for all transferred financial assets that are not derecognised, and for any continuing involvement in a transferred asset, that exist at the reporting date, irrespective of when the related transfer occurred. *[IFRS 7.42A]*.

6.1 The meaning of 'transfer'

For the purposes of applying the disclosure requirements in this section, an entity transfers all or a part of a financial asset (the transferred financial asset) if, and only if, it either: *[IFRS 7.42A]*

(a) transfers the contractual rights to receive the cash flows of that financial asset; or

(b) retains the contractual rights to receive the cash flows of that financial asset, but assumes a contractual obligation to pay the cash flows to one or more recipients in an arrangement.

The transactions encompassed by (a) should be the same ones that would be regarded as transfers under the derecognition requirements of IAS 39 or IFRS 9 (see Chapter 51 at 3.5.1).

However, the transactions falling within (b) represent a larger group than those which would be regarded as 'pass-through arrangements' for the purposes of those requirements (see Chapter 51 at 3.5.2).

6.2 Transferred financial assets that are not derecognised in their entirety

Financial assets may have been transferred in such a way that part or all of the financial assets do not qualify for derecognition. This might occur if:

- the contractual rights to the cash flows have been transferred but substantially all risks and rewards are retained, e.g. a sale and repurchase agreement, so that the assets are not derecognised;
- the rights to the cash flows have been transferred, the risks and rewards partially transferred and control of the assets has been retained so that the assets continue to be recognised to the extent of the entity's continuing involvement; or
- an obligation has been assumed to pay the cash flows from the asset to other parties but in a way that does not meet the 'pass-through' requirements (see Chapter 51 at 3.5.2).

  Where securitisations and similar arrangements do not meet the pass-through requirements, careful analysis will be required to determine whether they are within the scope of these disclosures. If such a transaction is not considered to be within the scope of these requirements, the disclosures about collateral discussed at 4.4.6 above are likely to be applicable.

The following disclosures should be given for each class of transferred financial assets that are not derecognised in their entirety: *[IFRS 7.42D]*

(a) the nature of the transferred assets;

(b) the nature of the risks and rewards of ownership to which the reporting entity is exposed;

(c) a description of the nature of the relationship between the transferred assets and the associated liabilities, including restrictions arising from the transfer on the reporting entity's use of the transferred assets;

(d) when the counterparty (counterparties) to the associated liabilities has (have) recourse only to the transferred assets, a schedule that sets out the fair value of the transferred assets, the fair value of the associated liabilities and the net position, i.e. the difference between the fair value of the transferred assets and the associated liabilities;

(e) when the reporting entity continues to recognise all of the transferred assets, the carrying amounts of the transferred assets and the associated liabilities; and

(f) when the reporting entity continues to recognise the assets to the extent of its continuing involvement, the total carrying amount of the original assets before the transfer, the carrying amount of the assets that the entity continues to recognise, and the carrying amount of the associated liabilities.

These disclosures should be given at each reporting date at which the entity continues to recognise the transferred financial assets, regardless of when the transfers occurred. *[IFRS 7.B32]*.

The above requirements clearly apply to transfers of entire financial assets where the transferred assets continue to be recognised in their entirety. They also apply to transfers of entire assets where the transferred assets are recognised to the extent of the transferor's continuing involvement.

However, the derecognition criteria in IAS 39 and IFRS 9 are sometimes applied to specified parts of a financial asset (or group of similar financial assets). For example, an entity might transfer a proportion of an entire financial asset, such as 50% of all cash flows on a bond. Similarly, it may transfer specified cash flows from a financial asset, such as all the coupon payments or only the principal payment on a bond, commonly known as an interest strip and principal strip respectively. Further, if the derecognition criteria are met, it is possible for the specified parts of the financial asset to be derecognised whilst the remainder of the asset remains on the statement of financial position (see Chapter 51, particularly at 3.3). This begs the question of whether the disclosure requirements in this section should be applied to such transfers.

Whilst the financial asset has not been derecognised in its entirety, it will normally be the case that the asset has not been transferred in its entirety either. Therefore, it might seem more appropriate for the disclosure requirements to follow the way in which the derecognition requirements of IAS 39 or IFRS 9 have been applied, i.e. they should focus on the specified part of the asset that has been transferred. Nevertheless, in the absence of specific guidance, we believe the alternative view could be supported too so that the disclosures would address the entire asset.

In our view these disclosure requirements do not apply where an entity provides non-cash financial assets as collateral to a third party and the transferee's right to control the asset (normally evidenced by its ability to resell or repledge those assets) is conditional on default of the transferor. Instead the disclosures about collateral set out at 4.4.6 above would apply.

The following example illustrates how an entity that has not adopted IFRS 9 might meet the quantitative disclosure requirements in (d) and (e) above. *[IFRS 7.IG40C]*.

Example 54.12: Quantitative disclosures for transferred assets not fully derecognised

	Financial assets at fair value through profit or loss		**Loans and receivables**		**Available-for-sale financial assets**
	CU million		CU million		CU million
	Trading securities	Derivatives	Mortgages	Consumer loans	Equity investments
Carrying amount of assets	X	X	X	X	X
Carrying amount of associated liabilities	(X)	(X)	(X)	(X)	(X)
For those liabilities that have recourse only to the transferred assets:					
Fair value of assets	X	X	X	X	X
Fair value of associated liabilities	(X)	(X)	(X)	(X)	(X)
Net position	X	X	X	X	X

Very similar disclosures could be given by an entity that has adopted IFRS 9, although the asset classifications would be different. *[IFRS 7.IG40B]*.

6.3 Transferred financial assets that are derecognised in their entirety

An entity may have transferred financial assets in such a way that they are derecognised in their entirety but the entity has 'continuing involvement' in those assets. Where this is the case, the additional disclosures set out at 6.3.2 below should be given. In this context, the term continuing involvement has a different meaning to that used in the derecognition requirements of IAS 39 or IFRS 9 (see Chapter 51 at 3.2 and 5.3) which is discussed at 6.3.1 below.

In practice the application of these requirements is likely to be limited given that few transfers with any form of continuing involvement (as that term is used here) will qualify for full derecognition. One example is a transfer of a readily obtainable financial asset subject to a call option that is neither deeply in the money nor deeply out of the money (see Chapter 51 at 4.2.3.A).

An entity may have derecognised financial assets under its previous GAAP, or an early version of IAS 39, in a transaction that would not have qualified for derecognition under IAS 39. Further, IFRS 1 – *First-time Adoption of International Financial Reporting Standards* – or the transitional provisions of IAS 39 mean these financial assets may remain derecognised. In our view it is not clear whether the disclosures covered in this section should be given for any remaining continuing involvement in such assets and an entity should establish an accounting policy and apply that policy consistently to all similar transactions.

6.3.1 Meaning of continuing involvement

In this context, continuing involvement arises if, as part of the transfer, the entity retains any of the contractual rights or obligations inherent in the transferred financial asset or obtains any new contractual rights or obligations relating to it. *[IFRS 7.42C]*.

For example, a financial asset transferred subject only to either (a) a deeply out of the money put option granted to the transferee or (b) a deeply out of the money call option retained by the transferor would be derecognised. This is because substantially all the risks and rewards of ownership have been transferred. *[IAS 39.AG51(g), IFRS 9.B3.2.16(g)]*. However, the put or call option would constitute continuing involvement in the asset.

Similarly, a readily obtainable asset transferred subject to a call option that is neither deeply in the money nor deeply out of the money would also be derecognised. This is because the entity has neither transferred nor retained substantially all of the risks and rewards of ownership and has not retained control. *[IAS 39.AG51(h), IFRS 9.B3.2.16(h)]*. However, the call option would constitute continuing involvement in the asset.

The following do not constitute continuing involvement for these purposes: *[IFRS 7.42C]*

(a) normal representations and warranties relating to fraudulent transfer and concepts of reasonableness, good faith and fair dealings that could invalidate a transfer as a result of legal action;

(b) forward, option and other contracts to reacquire the transferred financial asset for which the contract price (or exercise price) is the fair value of the transferred financial asset; or

(c) an arrangement whereby an entity retains the contractual rights to receive the cash flows of a financial asset but assumes a contractual obligation to pay the cash flows to one or more entities in a 'pass-through arrangement' (see Chapter 51 at 3.5.2).

An entity does not have a continuing involvement in a transferred financial asset if, as part of the transfer, it neither retains any of the contractual rights or obligations inherent in the transferred financial asset nor acquires any new contractual rights or obligations relating to the transferred financial asset. Also, an entity does not have continuing involvement in a transferred financial asset if it has neither an interest in the future performance of the transferred financial asset nor a responsibility under any circumstances to make payments in respect of the transferred financial asset in the future. The term 'payment' in this context does not include cash flows of the transferred financial asset that an entity collects and is required to remit to the transferee. *[IFRS 7.B30]*.

When an entity transfers a financial asset, it may retain the right to service that financial asset for a fee, e.g. by entering into a servicing contract. Such a contract should be assessed in accordance with the guidance above to determine whether it gives rise to continuing involvement for the purposes of these disclosures. For example, a servicer will have continuing involvement in the transferred financial asset if the servicing fee is dependent on the amount or timing of the cash flows collected from the transferred financial asset. Similarly, the right to a fixed fee that would not be paid in full as a result of non-performance of the transferred financial asset would also represent continuing involvement.

This is because the servicer has an interest in the future performance of the transferred financial asset. Any such assessment is independent of whether the fee to be received is expected to compensate the entity adequately for performing the servicing. *[IFRS 7.B31]*.

As originally published IFRS 7 was unclear whether servicing rights or obligations related to derecognised financial assets represented continuing involvement for the purpose of these disclosure requirements. However, in September 2014 the IASB added the above guidance to clarify its intention. This guidance is effective for periods commencing on or after 1 January 2016 and earlier application was permitted, although an entity should have disclosed that it had done so. The guidance need not be applied for any period presented that begins before the annual period for which an entity first applies that guidance. *[IFRS 7.44AA]*. In other words, comparative periods need not be restated.

An entity might transfer a fixed rate financial asset and at the same time enter into an interest rate swap with the transferee that has the same notional amount as the transferred asset. If payments on the swap are not conditional on payments being made on the transferred financial asset and the notional of the swap is not linked to the notional amount of the loan this would not, in our view, represent continuing involvement.

The assessment of continuing involvement in a transferred financial asset should be made at the level of the reporting entity. For example, a subsidiary may transfer to an unrelated third party a financial asset in which the parent of the subsidiary has continuing involvement. In the subsidiary's stand-alone financial statements the parent's involvement should not be included in the assessment of whether the reporting entity (the subsidiary) has continuing involvement in the transferred asset. However, in the parent's consolidated financial statements, its continuing involvement (or that of another member of the group) in a financial asset transferred by its subsidiary would be included in determining whether the group has continuing involvement in the transferred asset. *[IFRS 7.B29]*.

Continuing involvement in a transferred financial asset may result from contractual provisions in the transfer agreement or in a separate agreement with the transferee or a third party entered into in connection with the transfer. *[IFRS 7.B31]*. In our view it would not encompass arrangements entered into some time after the financial asset was transferred that were not contemplated at the time of the transfer.

6.3.2 *Disclosure requirements*

When an entity derecognises transferred financial assets in their entirety but has continuing involvement in those assets, it should disclose, as a minimum, the following for each type of continuing involvement at each reporting date: *[IFRS 7.42E]*

(a) the carrying amount of the assets and liabilities that are recognised in the entity's statement of financial position and represent the entity's continuing involvement in the derecognised financial assets, and the line items in which the carrying amount of those assets and liabilities are recognised;

(b) the fair value of the assets and liabilities that represent the entity's continuing involvement in the derecognised financial assets;

(c) the amount that best represents the entity's maximum exposure to loss from its continuing involvement in the derecognised financial assets, and information showing how the maximum exposure to loss is determined;

(d) the undiscounted cash outflows that would or may be required to repurchase derecognised financial assets (e.g. the strike price in an option agreement) or other amounts payable to the transferee in respect of the transferred assets.

If the cash outflow is variable then the amount disclosed should be based on the conditions that exist at each reporting date;

(e) a maturity analysis of the undiscounted cash outflows that would or may be required to repurchase the derecognised financial assets or other amounts payable to the transferee in respect of the transferred assets, showing the remaining contractual maturities of the entity's continuing involvement.

This analysis should distinguish between cash flows that are required to be paid (e.g. forward contracts), cash flows the entity may be required to pay (e.g. written put options) and cash flows the entity might choose to pay (e.g. purchased call options). *[IFRS 7.B34]*.

Entities should use judgement to determine an appropriate number of time bands in preparing the maturity analysis. For example, it might be determined that the following maturity time bands are appropriate: *[IFRS 7.B35]*

(i) not later than one month;

(ii) later than one month and not later than three months;

(iii) later than three months and not later than six months;

(iv) later than six months and not later than one year;

(v) later than one year and not later than three years;

(vi) later than three years and not later than five years; and

(vii) more than five years.

If there is a range of possible maturities, the cash flows should be included on the basis of the earliest date on which the entity can be required or is permitted to pay; *[IFRS 7.B36]* and

(f) qualitative information that explains and supports the quantitative disclosures set out in (a) to (e) above.

This should include a description of the derecognised financial assets and the nature and purpose of the continuing involvement retained after transferring those assets. It should also include a description of the risks to which an entity is exposed, including: *[IFRS 7.B37]*

(i) a description of how the entity manages the risk inherent in its continuing involvement in the derecognised financial assets;

(ii) whether the entity is required to bear losses before other parties, and the ranking and amounts of losses borne by parties whose interests rank lower than the entity's interest in the asset (i.e. its continuing involvement in the asset); and

(iii) a description of any triggers associated with obligations to provide financial support or to repurchase a transferred financial asset.

The types of continuing involvement into which these disclosures and those referred to below are analysed should be representative of the entity's exposure to risks. For example, the analysis may be given by type of financial instrument (e.g. guarantees or call options) or by type of transfer (e.g. factoring of receivables, securitisations and securities lending). *[IFRS 7.B33]*.

If an entity has more than one type of continuing involvement in respect of a particular derecognised financial asset the information above may be aggregated and reported under one type of continuing involvement. *[IFRS 7.42F]*.

The following example illustrates how an entity that has not adopted IFRS 9 might meet the quantitative disclosure requirements in (a) to (e) above. *[IFRS 7.IG40C]*.

Example 54.13: Quantitative disclosures for transferred assets fully derecognised

	Cash outflows to repurchase transferred (derecognised) assets CU million	Carrying amount of continuing involvement in statement of financial position CU million			Fair value of continuing involvement CU million		Maximum exposure to loss CU million
Type of continuing involvement		**Held for trading**	**Available-for-sale financial assets**	**Financial liabilities at fair value through profit or loss**	**Assets**	**Liabilities**	
Written put options	(X)			(X)		(X)	X
Purchased call options	(X)	X			X		X
Securities lending	(X)		X	(X)	X	(X)	X
		X	X	(X)	X	(X)	X

Undiscounted cash flows to repurchase transferred assets

	Maturity of continuing involvement CU million							
Type of continuing involvement	Total	less than 1 month	1-3 months	3-6 months	6 months-1 year	1-3 years	3-5 years	more than 5 years
Written put options	X		X	X	X	X		
Purchased call options	X			X	X	X		X
Securities lending	X	X	X					

Very similar disclosures could be given by an entity that has adopted IFRS 9, although the asset classifications would be different. *[IFRS 7.IG40B]*.

In addition to the information above, the following should be disclosed for each type of continuing involvement: *[IFRS 7.42G]*

(a) the gain or loss recognised at the date of transfer of the assets.

Disclosure should also be given if a gain or loss on derecognition arose because the fair values of the components of the previously recognised asset (i.e. the interest in the asset derecognised and the interest retained by the entity) were different from the fair value of the previously recognised asset as a whole. In that situation, disclosure should be made of whether the fair value measurements included significant inputs that were not based on observable market data; *[IFRS 7.B38]*

(b) income and expenses recognised, both in the reporting period and cumulatively, from the entity's continuing involvement in the derecognised financial assets (e.g. fair value changes in derivative instruments); and

(c) if the total amount of proceeds from transfer activity (that qualifies for derecognition) in a reporting period is not evenly distributed throughout the reporting period (e.g. if a substantial proportion of the total amount of transfer activity takes place in the closing days of a reporting period):

  (i) when the greatest transfer activity took place within that reporting period (e.g. the last five days before the end of the reporting period);

  (ii) the amount (e.g. related gains or losses) recognised from transfer activity in that part of the reporting period; and

  (iii) the total amount of proceeds from transfer activity in that part of the reporting period.

This information should be provided for each period for which a statement of comprehensive income is presented. *[IFRS 7.42G]*.

7 PRESENTATION ON THE FACE OF THE FINANCIAL STATEMENTS AND RELATED DISCLOSURES

Although it requires certain minimum disclosures, IFRS 7 provides little guidance as to where financial instruments and related gains and losses should be presented on the face of the financial statements nor how such items should be disaggregated. Further, the disclosures required need not always reflect how items are presented on the face of the statements. Therefore, for the time being at least, management must use its judgement in deciding how best to present much of the information relating to financial instruments, taking account of the minimum requirements of IFRS 7 and other related standards such as IAS 1.

7.1 Gains and losses recognised in profit or loss

7.1.1 Presentation on the face of the statement of comprehensive income (or income statement)

The effects of an entity's various activities, transactions and other events (including those relating to financial instruments) differ in frequency, potential for gain or loss and predictability. Accordingly, IAS 1 explains, disclosing the components of financial performance assists in providing an understanding of the financial performance achieved and in making projections of future results. *[IAS 1.86]*.

IAS 1 prescribes requirements for line items to be included on the face of the statement of comprehensive income (or income statement). Where IFRS 9 is applied, these requirements include:

- gains and losses arising from the derecognition of financial assets measured at amortised cost. *[IAS 1.82(aa)]*. In order to determine the amount of this gain or loss, the carrying amount of the financial asset should, in principle, be updated to the date of derecognition. It should, therefore, include a revised estimate of expected credit losses determined as at the date of derecognition. However, considerations of materiality would also need to be taken into account;[18]
- impairment losses (including reversals of impairment losses or impairment gains) determined in accordance with IFRS 9. *[IAS 1.82(ba)]*. This will include losses in respect of loan commitments and financial guarantee contracts as well as financial assets.

  Some might argue this line item should also include modification gains or losses, particularly if the reason for the modification was credit-related. However, a summary of the April 2015 meeting of the Transition Resource Group for Impairment of Financial Instruments, published on the IASB's website, suggests this would not be appropriate. Instead, it says that if disclosing gains and losses from impairments and modifications on a net basis would provide relevant information (for example, if the reason for the modification was credit-related), this could be dealt with through additional disclosure in the notes.

  The summary also says that modification gains and losses should be presented separately if considered appropriate.[19] Consequently, another way in which a net figure could be presented on the face of the income statement involves presenting modification gains and losses (or at least those arising from credit-related events) in a separate line item that is adjacent to the one showing impairment losses and gains, together with a subtotal that includes these two amounts;
- where a financial asset previously measured at amortised cost is reclassified so that it is measured at fair value through profit or loss, any gain or loss arising from a difference between the previous carrying amount and its fair value at the reclassification date; *[IAS 1.82(ca)]* and
- where a financial asset previously classified at fair value through other comprehensive income is reclassified as measured at fair value through profit or loss, any cumulative gain or loss previously recognised in other comprehensive income that is reclassified to profit or loss. *[IAS 1.82(cb)]*.

Otherwise, only one caption, 'finance costs', clearly relates to financial instruments. *[IAS 1.82(b)]*. The implementation guidance to IFRS 7 explains that this caption includes total interest expense (see 4.2.2 above) but may also include amounts associated with non-financial liabilities, for example the unwinding of the discount on long-term provisions (see Chapter 28 at 4.3.5). *[IFRS 7.IG13]*.

The Interpretations Committee concluded that it is not permissible to present a line item 'net finance costs' (or a similar term) on the face of the statement without showing the finance costs and finance revenue composing it. However, the presentation of finance revenue followed immediately by finance costs and a subtotal, e.g. 'net finance costs', is allowed.[20]

The demand for safe investments can sometimes result in a negative yield on very high quality financial assets (e.g. certain government bonds or reserve bank deposits). The IFRS Interpretations Committee has considered this phenomenon and in January 2015 noted that interest resulting from a negative effective interest rate on a financial asset does not meet the definition of interest revenue in IAS 18 – *Revenue* – because it reflects a gross outflow, not a gross inflow, of economic benefits. Consequently, such expenses should not be presented as interest revenue, but in an appropriate expense classification.[21] This might be a separate line item titled, for example, 'financial expenses on liquid short term assets' or 'other financial expenses' or using another appropriate description. Alternatively, it could be appropriate to include within another expense line, for example, 'other expenses'. Similarly, we believe negative interest on financial liabilities, which will represent a form of income, should not be offset against positive interest expense.

Additional line items, headings and subtotals should be presented on the face of the statement of comprehensive income (or income statement) when such presentation is relevant to an understanding of the elements of an entity's financial performance. Factors that should be considered include materiality and the nature and function of the components of income and expenses. For example, a financial institution may amend the descriptions to provide information that is relevant to the operations of a financial institution. *[IAS 1.85, 86]*. This may also be relevant where an entity recognises negative interest on financial assets or financial liabilities.[22]

Any additional subtotals presented should: *[IAS 1.85A]*

- comprise line items made up of amounts recognised and measured in accordance with IFRS;
- be presented and labelled in a manner that makes the line items that constitute the subtotal clear and understandable;
- be consistent from period to period, as required by IAS 1 (see Chapter 3 at 4.1.4); and
- not be displayed with more prominence than the subtotals and totals required in IFRS for the statement(s) presenting profit or loss and other comprehensive income.

The following items should also be disclosed on the face of the statement of comprehensive income (or income statement) as allocations of profit or loss for the period: *[IAS 1.81B(a)]*

- profit or loss attributable to non-controlling interests; and
- profit or loss attributable to owners of the parent.

7.1.2 Further analysis of gains and losses recognised in profit or loss

As noted at 4.2.2 above, entities are required to disclose total interest income and total interest expense, calculated using the effective interest method, for financial assets and financial liabilities that are not at fair value through profit or loss. Whilst leases are included within the scope of IFRS 7, strictly they are not accounted for using the effective interest method (although for many leases the method prescribed in IAS 17 or IFRS 16 results in a very similar treatment). Accordingly, where material, it appears that finance income (charges) arising on leases should be shown separately from the interest income (expense) shown above. Until IFRS 15 – *Revenue from Contracts with Customers* – is applied, IAS 18 also requires separate disclosure of interest income arising on assets that do not arise from leases. *[IAS 18.6(a), 35(b)(iii)]*. In fact, it will often be appropriate to include such items within the same caption on the face of the statement of comprehensive income (or income statement) and include a sub-analysis in the notes.

Dividends classified as an expense (for example those payable to holders of redeemable preference shares) may be presented either with interest on other liabilities or as a separate item. Such items are subject to the requirements of IAS 1. In some circumstances, because of the differences between interest and dividends with respect to matters such as tax deductibility, it is desirable to disclose them separately in the statement of comprehensive income (or income statement). *[IAS 32.40]*.

The following gains and losses reported in profit or loss should also be disclosed:

- the amount of revenue arising from dividends. *[IAS 18.35(b)(iv)]*. Where IFRS 9 is applied and equity investments are designated at fair value through other comprehensive income, dividends recognised should be disclosed, showing separately the amounts arising on investments derecognised during the reporting period and those related to investments held at the end of the reporting period; *[IFRS 7.11A(d)]*
- changes in fair value that relate to instruments at fair value through profit or loss (see 4.2.1 above).

  Little guidance is given on disaggregating gains and losses from instruments classified as at fair value through profit or loss. For example, the components of the change in fair value of a debt instrument can include:

  - interest accruals;
  - foreign currency retranslation;
  - movements arising from changes in the issuer's credit risk; and
  - changes in market interest rates.

  An entity is neither required to disaggregate, nor prohibited from disaggregating, these components on the face of the statement of comprehensive income (or income statement) provided the minimum disclosure requirements are met (e.g. see 4.2 above). Accordingly, in our view the interest accrual component, say, may be included separately within an interest receivable caption or it may be included within the same caption as other components of the gain or loss such as dealing profit. As noted at 4.1 above, whatever the entity's approach, it should be explained in its accounting policies; and
- the amount of exchange differences recognised in profit or loss under IAS 21 except for those arising on financial instruments measured at fair value through profit or loss. *[IAS 21.52(a)]*.

When IFRS 9 is applied, dividends recognised during the period arising on equity investments designated at fair value through other comprehensive income should be disclosed. Those dividends arising on investments derecognised during the reporting period and those arising on investments held at the end of the reporting period should be shown separately. *[IFRS 7.11A(d)]*.

In IAS 1 it is explained that when items of income and expense are material, their nature and amount are required to be disclosed separately. *[IAS 1.97]*. Circumstances that can give rise to separate disclosure include the disposal of investments *[IAS 1.98]* (e.g. available-for-sale assets) and the early settlement of liabilities. However, gains and losses should not be reported as extraordinary items, either on the face of the statement of comprehensive income (or income statement) or in the notes. *[IAS 1.87]*.

7.1.3 Offsetting and hedges

IAS 1 explains that income and expenses should not be offset unless required or permitted by another standard. This is because offsetting detracts from the ability of users to understand fully the transactions, other events and conditions that have occurred and to assess the entity's future cash flows (except where it reflects the substance of the transaction or other event). *[IAS 1.32, 33]*. It goes on to explain that gains and losses on the disposal of non-current investments (such as many available-for-sale assets) are reported by deducting the carrying amount of the asset and related selling expenses from the proceeds on disposal rather than showing gross proceeds as revenue *[IAS 1.34]* – in the case of available-for-sale assets the profit or loss on disposal will also include any gains and losses that are reclassified from equity. It also explains that gains and losses arising from groups of similar transactions should be reported on a net basis, for example gains and losses arising on financial instruments held for trading or foreign exchange differences. The individual transactions should, however, be reported separately if they are material. *[IAS 1.35]*.

Whilst IAS 32 prescribes when financial assets and liabilities should be offset in the statement of financial position (see 7.4.1 below) it contains no guidance on when related income and expenses should be offset. IAS 39 states that hedge accounting 'recognises the offsetting effects on profit or loss of changes in the fair values of the hedging instrument and the hedged item.' *[IAS 39.85]*. This is a little short of an explicit requirement or permission to show income or expenses net of related hedging gains and losses. However, it is entirely consistent with the objective of hedge accounting to include within a caption in profit or loss related hedging gains and losses even if that results in a degree of offset. Further support for this position was found within IAS 30, which explained that income and expense items 'shall not be offset except for those relating to hedges and to assets and liabilities that have been offset...',[23] although we believe it would also be acceptable to present gains and losses on hedging instruments in a separate line item.

Chapter 54

Example 54.14: Presenting the effects of a hedge of a forecast sale

Company K has the euro as its functional currency. On 1 January 2017 it forecasts the sale of certain goods in dollars in six months and, to hedge that exposure, enters into a forward foreign exchange contract maturing on 1 July 2017. The hedge is designated as a cash flow hedge and meets the conditions for hedge accounting throughout the term of the hedge.

On 1 July 2017 the forecast sale occurs and is recorded using the prevailing spot rate resulting in, say, €1,000 being recognised in revenue. The forward contract is settled on this date at which point a related loss of, say, €100 has been recognised in other comprehensive income.

The mechanics of cash flow hedge accounting require the €100 loss to be reclassified from equity to profit or loss on 1 July 2017. Using the analysis above, K presents the €100 loss as a deduction from revenue resulting in the hedged sale being recognised at a net amount of €900.

Although the €100 loss reclassified from equity is being offset in profit or loss it will, however, be disclosed in the statement of comprehensive income or statement of changes in equity (see 7.2 below) or notes thereto.

IFRS 9 is more prescriptive than IAS 39 about the presentation of gains or losses on hedging instruments, specifying the following:

- if a group of hedged items in a cash flow hedge contains no offsetting risk positions and will affect different line items in profit or loss, the gains or losses on the hedging instrument should be apportioned to the line items affected by the hedged items when reclassified to profit or loss.

  This might be the case, for example, if a group of foreign currency expense transactions are hedged for foreign currency risk and those expenses will affect, say, both distribution costs and administrative expenses.

  The basis of apportionment between line items should be systematic and rational and not result in the grossing up of net gains or losses arising from a single hedging instrument; *[IFRS 9.B6.6.13, B6.6.14]*
- if a group of hedged items contains offsetting risk positions, i.e. a net position is hedged and the hedged risk affects different line items in profit or loss, the gains or losses on the hedging instrument should be presented in a line separate from those affected by the hedged items. Consequently, the line item relating to the hedged item will remain unaffected by the hedge accounting. *[IFRS 9.6.6.4, B6.6.13]*.

  This would apply, for example, to a cash flow hedge of a group of foreign currency denominated sales and expenses. The hedging gains or losses would be presented in a line item that is separate from both revenue and the relevant expense line item(s). *[IFRS 9.B6.6.15]*.

  Another example would be a fair value hedge of a net position involving a fixed-rate asset and a fixed-rate liability. Hedge accounting would normally involve recognising the net interest accrual on the interest rate swap in profit or loss. In this case the net interest accrual should be presented in a line item separate from gross interest revenue and gross interest expense.

  This is to avoid the grossing up of net gains or losses on a single instrument into offsetting gross amounts and recognising them in different line items. *[IFRS 9.B6.6.16]*.

These requirements imply that gains and losses from hedging instruments in other hedging relationships would be presented in the same line item that is affected by the hedged item (at least to the extent the hedge is effective) rather than being shown separately, although this is not explicitly stated in IFRS 9.

7.1.4 *Embedded derivatives*

IAS 39 and IFRS 9 explicitly state that they do not address whether embedded derivatives should be presented separately in the statement of financial position. However, both standards are silent about the presentation in profit or loss. *[IAS 39.11, IFRS 9.4.3.4]*. In practice, it will depend on the nature both of the hybrid and the host whether related gains and losses are included in the same or separate captions within profit or loss.

For example, an investment in a credit linked note that is accounted for as a debt instrument host and an embedded credit derivative might give rise to interest income and credit losses respectively that would normally be reported in separate captions within profit or loss. Alternatively, changes in the fair value of an embedded prepayment option in a host debt instrument that is accounted for separately may be included in the same caption within profit or loss as interest on the debt instrument if the value of the option varies largely as a result of change in interest rates.

7.1.5 *Entities whose share capital is not equity*

Gains and losses related to changes in the carrying amount of a financial liability are recognised as income or expense in profit or loss even when they relate to an instrument that includes a right to the residual interest in the assets of the entity in exchange for cash or another financial asset, such as shares in mutual funds and co-operatives (see Chapter 45 at 4.6). Any gain or loss arising from the remeasurement of such an instrument (including the impact of dividends paid, where appropriate) should be presented separately on the face of the statement of comprehensive income (or income statement) when it is relevant in explaining the entity's performance. *[IAS 32.41]*.

The following example illustrates a format for a statement of comprehensive income (or income statement) that may be used by entities such as mutual funds that do not have equity as defined in IAS 32, although other formats may be acceptable.

Example 54.15: Statement of comprehensive income (or income statement) format for a mutual fund

Statement of comprehensive income (income statement) for the year ended 31 December 2017 *[IAS 32.IE32]*

	2017 €	2016 €
Revenue	2,956	1,718
Expenses (classified by nature or function)	(644)	(614)
Profit from operating activities	2,312	1,104
Finance costs		
– other finance costs	(47)	(47)
– distributions to members	(50)	(50)
Change in net assets attributable to unit holders	2,215	1,007

Although it may not be immediately clear, the final line item in this format is an expense. Therefore the entity's 'profit or loss' (as that term is used in IAS 1) for 2017 is €2,312 – €47 – €50 – €2,215 = €nil.

The next example illustrates a format for a statement of comprehensive income (or income statement) that may be used by entities whose share capital is not equity as defined in IAS 32 because the entity has an obligation to repay the share capital on demand, for example co-operatives, but which do have some equity (such as other reserves). Again, other formats may be acceptable.

Example 54.16: Statement of comprehensive income (income statement) format for a co-operative

Statement of comprehensive income (income statement) for the year ended 31 December 2017 *[IAS 32.IE33]*

	2017	2016
	€	€
Revenue	472	498
Expenses (classified by nature or function)	(367)	(396)
Profit from operating activities	105	102
Finance costs		
– other finance costs	(4)	(4)
– distributions to members	(50)	(50)
Change in net assets attributable to members	51	48

In this example, the line item 'Finance costs – distributions to members' is an expense and the final line item is equivalent to 'profit or loss'.

Corresponding statement of financial position formats for both of these examples are shown at 7.4.6 below.

7.2 Gains and losses recognised in other comprehensive income

IAS 1 requires income and expense not recognised within profit or loss to be included in a statement of comprehensive income. *[IAS 1.82A]*.

Material items of income and expense and gains and losses that result from financial assets and financial liabilities which are included in other comprehensive income are required to be disclosed separately and should include at least the following:

- changes in fair value of available-for-sale financial assets, *[IAS 39.C.1]*, including: *[IFRS 7.20(a)(ii)]*
  - the amount of any gain or loss recognised in other comprehensive income during the period; and
  - the amount that was reclassified from equity to profit or loss for the period; and
- for cash flow hedges: *[IFRS 7.23(c), (d), (e)]*
  - the amount of gains or losses on designated hedging instruments recognised in other comprehensive income for the period;
  - the amount reclassified from equity to profit or loss during the period; and
  - the amount removed from equity during the period and included in the initial measurement of the acquisition cost of hedged non-financial assets or liabilities.

The implementation guidance to IAS 39 states that disclosure should be provided of changes in the fair value of hedging instruments that are recognised in other comprehensive income. *[IAS 39.C.1]*. This will include, in aggregate, gains and losses on hedging instruments in both cash flow hedges and hedges of net investments. However, this may often be dealt with by presenting for hedges of net investments similar information to that noted above for cash flow hedges.

When IFRS 9 is applied, the available-for-sale financial assets category is eliminated, although gains and losses on other categories of instrument are recognised in other comprehensive income which should be disclosed as follows:

- the amount of gain or loss attributable to changes in a liability's credit risk for those financial liabilities designated as at fair value through profit or loss; *[IFRS 7.20(a)(i)]*
- the revaluation gain or loss arising on equity investments designated at fair value through other comprehensive income; *[IFRS 7.20(a)(vii)]* and
- revaluation gains or losses arising on debt instruments measured at fair value through other comprehensive income, showing separately: *[IFRS 7.20(a)(viii)]*
  - the amount of gain or loss recognised in other comprehensive income during the period; and
  - the amount reclassified upon derecognition from accumulated other comprehensive income to profit or loss for the period.

In finalising IFRS 9, the IASB reconsidered the journal entry that arises when an entity removes a gain or loss on a cash flow hedge that was recognised in other comprehensive income in order to include it in the initial cost or other carrying amount of a non-financial asset or liability. It decided this should not be regarded as a reclassification adjustment and hence should not affect, or be included within, other comprehensive income. *[IFRS 9.BC6.380]*.

The following items should also be disclosed on the face of the statement of comprehensive income as allocations of total comprehensive income for the period: *[IAS 1.81B(b)]*

- total comprehensive income attributable to non-controlling interests; and
- total comprehensive income attributable to owners of the parent.

7.3 Statement of changes in equity

The following information should be included in the statement of changes in equity: *[IAS 1.106]*

- total comprehensive income for the period, showing separately the total amounts attributable to owners of the parent and to non-controlling interests; and
- for each component of equity, a reconciliation between the carrying amount at the beginning and the end of the period, separately disclosing changes resulting from:
  - profit or loss;
  - other comprehensive income; and
  - transactions with owners acting in their capacity as owners, showing separately:
    - contributions by and distributions to owners; and
    - changes in ownership interests in subsidiaries that do not result in a loss of control.

An analysis of other comprehensive income by item should be presented for each component of equity, either in the statement or in the notes. *[IAS 1.106A]*.

Where hedge accounting is applied in accordance with IFRS 9, IFRS 7 specifies additional information that should be presented within the reconciliation and analysis noted above or the notes thereto. This is covered in more detail at 4.3.2.C above.

In finalising IFRS 9, the IASB also reconsidered the nature of the journal entry that arises when an entity removes a gain or loss on a cash flow hedge that was recognised in other comprehensive income in order to include it in the initial cost or other carrying amount of a non-financial asset or liability. It decided it should not be regarded as a reclassification adjustment and hence should not affect, or be included within, other comprehensive income. *[IFRS 9.BC6.380]*. Such an entry should be presented within the statement of changes of equity (because it affects an entity's net assets and hence its equity), albeit separately from other comprehensive income.

The amount of dividends recognised as distributions to owners during the period should be disclosed on the face of the statement of changes in equity or in the notes. *[IAS 1.107]*.

In addition, IAS 32 notes that IAS 1 requires the amount of transaction costs accounted for as a deduction from equity in the period to be disclosed separately. *[IAS 32.39]*.

If an entity reacquires its own equity instruments from related parties disclosure should be provided in accordance with IAS 24 (see Chapter 37). *[IAS 32.34]*.

If an entity such as a mutual fund or a co-operative has no issued equity instruments, it may still need to present a statement of changes in equity. For example, such an entity may have gains or losses arising on available-for-sale assets that are recognised in equity; also co-operatives, for example, may have a balance on equity.

7.4 Statement of financial position

7.4.1 Offsetting financial assets and financial liabilities

It is common for reporting entities to enter into offsetting arrangements with their counterparties. Offsetting arrangements allow market participants to manage counterparty credit risks, and manage liquidity risk. In particular, netting arrangements generally reduce the credit risk exposures of market participants to counterparties relative to their gross exposures. Such mechanisms also permit the management of existing market risk exposures by taking on offsetting contracts with the same counterparty rather than assuming additional counterparty risk by entering into an offsetting position with a new counterparty. Furthermore, for a regulated financial institution, position netting may also have regulatory capital implications.

IAS 1 sets out a general principle that assets and liabilities should not be offset except where such offset is permitted or required by an accounting standard or interpretation (see Chapter 3 at 4.1.5.B). *[IAS 1.32]*. This general prohibition on offset is due to the fact that net presentation of assets and liabilities generally does not provide a complete depiction of the assets and liabilities of an entity. In particular, offsetting obscures the existence of some assets and liabilities in the statement of financial position and it impacts key financial ratios such as gearing, and measures such as total assets or liabilities.

IAS 32 provides some exceptions to this general rule in the case of financial assets and liabilities. IAS 32 *requires* a financial asset and a financial liability to be offset and the net amount reported in the statement of financial position when, and only when, an entity:

(a) currently has a legally enforceable right to set off the recognised amounts; and

(b) intends either to settle on a net basis, or to realise the asset and settle the liability simultaneously.

These two conditions are often called the *IAS 32 Offsetting Criteria.* There is, however, one exception to the offsetting requirement. This exception arise when a transferred financial asset does not qualify for derecognition. In such a circumstance, the transferred asset and the associated liability must not be offset, *[IAS 32.42]*, even if they otherwise satisfy the offsetting criteria (see Chapter 51 at 5.5.1).

IAS 32 argues that offset is appropriate in the circumstances set out in (a) and (b) above, because the entity has, in effect, a right to, or an obligation for, only a single net future cash flow and, hence, a single net financial asset or financial liability. In other circumstances, financial assets and financial liabilities are presented separately from each other, consistently with their characteristics as resources or obligations of the entity. *[IAS 32.43]*. Furthermore, the amount resulting from offsetting must also reflect the reporting entity's expected future cash flows from settling two or more separate financial instruments. *[IAS 32.BC94]*.

Offset is not equivalent to derecognition, since offsetting does not result in the financial asset or the financial liability being removed from the statement of financial position, but in net presentation of a net financial asset or a net financial liability. Moreover, no gain or loss can ever arise on offset, but may arise on derecognition. *[IAS 32.44]*.

IAS 32 acknowledges that an enforceable right to set off a financial asset and a financial liability affects the rights and obligations associated with that asset and liability and may affect an entity's exposure to credit and liquidity risk. However, such a right is not, in itself, a sufficient basis for offsetting. The entity may still realise the asset and liability separately and, in the absence of an intention to exercise the right or to settle simultaneously, the amount and timing of an entity's future cash flows are not affected. Similarly, an intention by one or both parties to settle on a net basis without the legal right to do so is not sufficient to justify offsetting because the rights and obligations associated with the individual financial asset and financial liability remain unaltered. *[IAS 32.46, AG38E]*.

IAS 32 elaborates further on the detail of the offsetting criteria as set out in the following subsections.

7.4.1.A Criterion (a): Enforceable legal right of set-off

IAS 32 describes a right of set-off as a debtor's legal right, by contract or otherwise (for example, it may arise as a result of a provision in law or a regulation), to settle or otherwise eliminate all or a portion of an amount due to a creditor by applying against that amount an amount due from the creditor. The enforceability of the right of set-off is thus essentially a legal matter, so that the specific conditions supporting the right may vary from one legal jurisdiction to another. *[IAS 32.45]*. Care must therefore be taken to establish which laws apply to the relationships between the parties.

In unusual circumstances, a debtor (A) may have a legal right to apply an amount due from a third party (B) against an amount due to a creditor (C), provided that there is an agreement among A, B and C that clearly establishes A's right to set off amounts due from B against those due to C. *[IAS 32.45]*. For example, a foreign branch of a US bank makes a loan to a foreign subsidiary of a US parent with the parent required to deposit an amount equal to the loan in the US bank for the same term. The terms of the transactions may give the bank a legal right to set off the amount due to the parent against the amount owed by the foreign subsidiary. Another example is bank accounts maintained for a group of companies where each member of the group agrees that its credit balance may be the subject of set-off in respect of debit balances of other members of the group. In our experience, not all jurisdictions recognise this type of contractual multilateral set-off arrangement, particularly in bankruptcy scenarios.

A right of set-off may currently be available or it may be contingent on a future event (e.g. the right may be triggered or exercisable only on the occurrence of some future event, such as the default, insolvency or bankruptcy of one of the counterparties). Even if the right of set-off is not contingent on a future event, it may only be legally enforceable in the normal course of business, or in the event of default, or in the event of insolvency or bankruptcy, of one or all of the counterparties. *[IAS 32.AG38A]*.

The revised application guidance makes it clear that, in order for an entity to currently have a legally enforceable right of set-off, the right: *[IAS 32.AG38B]*

- must not be contingent on a future event; and
- must be legally enforceable in all of the following circumstances:
  - the normal course of business;
  - the event of default; and
  - the event of insolvency or bankruptcy of the entity and all of the counterparties.

The nature and extent of the right of set-off, including any conditions attached to its exercise and whether it would remain in the event of default or insolvency or bankruptcy, may vary from one legal jurisdiction to another. Consequently, it cannot be assumed that the right of set-off is automatically available outside of the normal course of business. For example, the bankruptcy or insolvency laws of a jurisdiction may prohibit, or restrict, the right of set-off in the event of bankruptcy or insolvency in some circumstances. *[IAS 32.AG38C]*. Therefore, contractual provisions, the laws governing the contract, or the default, insolvency or bankruptcy laws applicable to the parties need to be considered to ascertain whether the right of set-off is enforceable in the circumstances set out above. *[IAS 32.AG38D]*. In assessing whether an agreement meets these conditions, entities will need to make a legal determination, which may involve obtaining legal advice.

The basis for conclusions suggests that to meet the criteria for offsetting, these rights must exist for all counterparties. Thus, if one party, including the reporting entity, will not or cannot perform under the contract, the other counterparties will be able to enforce that right to set-off against the party that has defaulted or become insolvent or bankrupt. *[IAS 32.BC80]*. However, the revised application guidance above appears to focus only on whether the rights of the reporting entity are legally enforceable. It is also clear that the above reference to 'all of the counterparties' pertains to the legal enforceability in the circumstances listed (i.e. the normal course of business, the events of default, insolvency or bankruptcy), and not who holds the set-off right.

In our view, normally the standard and its application guidance would prevail over the basis for conclusions and we consider that the IASB's most likely intention, consistent with the wording in the body and application guidance of the standard, was to require only the reporting entity to have a legal right to set off in the circumstances noted above – including, in the event of the reporting entity's own default, insolvency or bankruptcy.

The requirement that a reporting entity must be able to legally enforce a right of set-off in the event of its own bankruptcy means that the counterparty (or counterparties) to a netting agreement must not have the ability to force gross settlement in the event of the reporting entity's default, insolvency or bankruptcy. It also means that the reporting entity may need to obtain legal advice as to whether its legal right to net settle will survive the bankruptcy laws of the jurisdiction in which it is located.

Many contracts give only the non-defaulting party the right to enforce the netting provisions in case of default, insolvency or bankruptcy of any of the parties to the agreement. Unless the insolvency laws in the relevant jurisdiction would force net settlement, such contracts would fail the IAS 32 criteria because the reporting entity cannot enforce such rights of set-off in the event of its own bankruptcy, regardless of the fact that in practice it is highly unlikely that the non-defaulting party would insist on gross settlement. In practice, most of these contracts would not achieve offsetting under IAS 32 anyway, because the legal right of set-off available under such contracts is usually not enforceable in the normal course of business. Generally speaking, these contracts are structured this way because entities do not intend to settle net other than in situations of default. In other circumstances, entities need to determine if the right to enforce net settlement would survive their own bankruptcy.

A right of set-off that can be exercised only upon the occurrence of a future event is often referred to as a 'conditional' right of set-off. For example, an entity may have a right of set-off that is exercisable on changes to particular legislation or change in control of the counterparties. Conditional rights of set-off such as these do not meet the offsetting criteria and, hence, the financial asset and financial liability subject to such rights of set-off would not qualify to be offset.

As the description of a right of set-off itself envisages an amount being due to each party either now or in the future, the passage of time and uncertainties relating to amounts to be paid do not preclude an entity from currently having a legally enforceable right of set-off. The fact that payments subject to a right of set-off will only arise at a future date is not in itself a condition or form of contingency that prevents offsetting. *[IAS 32.BC83]*.

However, if the right of set-off is not exercisable during a period when amounts are due and payable, then the entity does not meet the offsetting criterion as it has no right to set off those payments. Similarly, a right of set-off that could disappear or that would no longer be enforceable after a future event that could take place in the normal course of business or in the event of default, or in the event of insolvency or bankruptcy, such as a ratings downgrade, would not meet the currently (legally enforceable) criterion. *[IAS 32.BC84]*.

Some contracts include representation clauses under which the right to set-off is automatically invalidated if any undertakings or representations in the contract turns out to be incorrect in a material respect. In our view, such clauses would generally not render the right of set-off a conditional right of set-off.

In certain circumstances, an entity may, in order to exercise its right of set-off, need to unilaterally take a procedural action within its control. For example, an entity may be required to notify the counterparty, in the form of a letter in advance, in order to effect net settlement under the terms of the contract. In some cases, an entity may need to apply to a court to effect set-off when a counterparty becomes bankrupt (as a matter of process), although that right is assured and is upheld in the event of default of a counterparty in that jurisdiction. In our view, the mere fact that such actions are needed before an entity can exercise the right of set-off would not make the exercisability of that right contingent on a future event. However, in the latter example, the probability of favourable or unfavourable judgement from the court would have to be assessed separately as part of the 'legal enforceability' requirement to conclude whether the right of set-off meets the offsetting criteria in IAS 32.

Unlike US GAAP, IAS 32 does not specify a particular level of assurance required to meet the 'legally enforceable' criterion. Instead, it leaves such determination to judgement and consideration of the relevant facts and circumstances. In practice, entities are expected, in their day to day business, to obtain reasonable assurance on enforceability of contractual rights as part of prudent risk management regardless of the accounting requirements.

7.4.1.B Master netting agreements

It is common practice for an entity that undertakes a number of financial instrument transactions with a single counterparty to enter into a 'master netting arrangement' with that counterparty. These arrangements are typically used by financial institutions to restrict their exposure to loss in the event of bankruptcy or other events that result in a counterparty being unable to meet its obligations. Such an agreement commonly creates a conditional right of set-off that becomes enforceable, and affects the realisation or settlement of individual financial assets and financial liabilities, only following a specified event of default or in other circumstances not expected to arise in the normal course of business. Entities who enter into such master netting agreements other than not meeting the legal right of set-off requirement also typically do not intend to settle net in the normal course of business.

Where an entity has entered into such an agreement, the agreement does not provide the basis for the offset of assets and liabilities unless both of the offsetting criteria are satisfied. *[IAS 32.50, AG38]*. For enforceable master netting arrangements that create a conditional right of set off, this will typically be the case only if the default (or other event specified in the contract) has actually occurred. When financial assets and financial liabilities subject to a master netting arrangement are not offset, the effect of the arrangement falls within the scope of the disclosure requirements of IFRS 7(see 7.4.2 below).

7.4.1.C Criterion (b): Intention to settle net or realise the gross amount simultaneously ('the net settlement criterion')

An entity's intention to settle net or settle simultaneously may be demonstrated through its past experience of executing set-off or simultaneous settlement in similar situations, its usual operating practices or by reference to its documented risk policies. Thus, incidental net or simultaneous settlement of a financial asset or financial liability does not meet the criterion above.

The requirement for an intention to settle net or to settle simultaneously is, however, considered only from the reporting entity's perspective.

IAS 32 notes that an entity's intentions with respect to settlement of particular assets and liabilities may be influenced by its normal business practices, the requirements of the financial markets and other circumstances that may limit the ability to settle net or simultaneously. *[IAS 32.47]*. In practice, even though a reporting entity has the right to settle net, it may settle gross either because of lack of appropriate arrangements or systems to effect net settlement or to facilitate operations. In such circumstances, the entity presents such assets and liabilities on a net basis in the statement of financial position only when the entity intends to settle the asset and the liability simultaneously.

Simultaneous settlement of two financial instruments may occur through, for example, the operation of a clearing house in an organised financial market or a face-to-face exchange. *[IAS 32.48]*. The procedures of the clearing house or exchange may provide that the amount to be paid or received for different products be settled gross. However, such payments may be made simultaneously. Hence, even though the parties may make payment or receive payment separately for different product types, settlement occur at the same moment and there is exposure only to the net amount.

The standard states that the reference to 'simultaneous' settlement in the conditions for offset above is to be interpreted literally, as applying only to the realisation of a financial asset and settlement of a financial liability at the same moment. *[IAS 32.48]*. For example, the settlement of a financial asset and a financial liability at the same nominal time but in different time zones is not considered to be simultaneous.

Nevertheless, it became apparent to the IASB that there was diversity in practice related to the interpretation of 'simultaneous' settlement in IAS 32. In practice, due to processing constraints, settlement of gross amounts rarely occurs at exactly the same moment, even when using a clearing house or settlement system. Rather, actual settlement takes place over a period of time (e.g. clearing repos and reverse repos in batches during the day). Arguably, therefore, 'simultaneous' is not operational and ignores settlement systems that are established to achieve what is economically equivalent to net settlement. Consequently, IAS 32 has often been interpreted to mean that settlement through a clearing house does meet the simultaneous settlement criterion, even if not occurring at the same moment. The IASB agreed that some, but not all, settlement systems should be seen as equivalent to net settlement and, in order to reduce diversity of accounting treatment, introduced guidance into IAS 32 in December 2011 to clarify how criterion (b) should be assessed in these circumstances. *[IAS 32.BC94-BC100]*.

The amendments explain that if an entity can settle amounts in a manner such that the outcome is, in effect, equivalent to net settlement, the entity will meet the net settlement criterion. This will occur if, and only if, the gross settlement mechanism has features that (i) eliminate or result in insignificant credit and liquidity risk, and that (ii) will process receivables and payables in a single settlement process or cycle. For example, a gross settlement system that has all of the following characteristics would meet the net settlement criterion: *[IAS 32.AG38F]*

- financial assets and financial liabilities eligible for set-off are submitted at the same point in time for processing;
- once the financial assets and financial liabilities are submitted for processing, the parties are committed to fulfil the settlement obligation;
- there is no potential for the cash flows arising from the assets and liabilities to change once they have been submitted for processing (unless the processing fails – see next item below);
- assets and liabilities that are collateralised with securities will be settled on a securities transfer or similar system (e.g. delivery versus payment), so that if the transfer of securities fails, the processing of the related receivable or payable for which the securities are collateral will also fail (and *vice versa*);
- any transactions that fail, as outlined in the previous item above, will be re-entered for processing until they are settled;
- settlement is carried out through the same settlement institution (e.g. a settlement bank, a central bank or a central securities depository); and
- an intraday credit facility is in place that will provide sufficient overdraft amounts to enable the processing of payments at the settlement date for each of the parties, and it is virtually certain that the intraday credit facility will be honoured if called upon.

The IASB deliberately chose the language above so that it was clear that settlement systems established by clearing houses or other central counterparties should not automatically be assumed to meet the net settlement criterion. Conversely, irrespective of the names used in a particular jurisdiction, other settlement systems may meet the net settlement criterion if that system eliminates or results in insignificant credit and liquidity risk and processes receivables and payables in the same settlement process or cycle. *[IAS 32.BC101]*.

7.4.1.D Situations where offset is not normally appropriate

An entity may enter into a number of different financial instruments designed to replicate, as a group, the features of a single financial instrument (such a replication is sometimes referred to as creating a 'synthetic instrument'). For example, if an entity issues floating rate debt and then enters into a 'pay fixed/receive floating' interest rate swap, the combined economic effect is that the entity has issued fixed rate debt.

IAS 32 argues that each of the individual financial instruments that together constitute a 'synthetic instrument':

- represents a contractual right or obligation with its own terms and conditions;
- may be transferred or settled separately; and
- is exposed to risks that may differ from those to which the other financial instruments in the 'synthetic instrument' are exposed.

Accordingly, when one financial instrument in a 'synthetic instrument' is an asset and another is a liability, they are not offset and presented on an entity's statement of financial position on a net basis unless they meet the offsetting criteria. *[IAS 32.49(a), AG39]*.

Other circumstances where the offsetting criteria are generally not met, and therefore offsetting is usually inappropriate, include: *[IAS 32.49(b), (c), (d), (e)]*

(a) financial assets and financial liabilities which arise from financial instruments having the same primary risk exposure (e.g. assets and liabilities within a portfolio of forward contracts or other derivative instruments) but involving different counterparties;

(b) financial or other assets that are pledged as collateral for non-recourse financial liabilities (see 7.4.1.F below);

(c) financial assets which are set aside in trust by a debtor for the purpose of discharging an obligation without those assets having been accepted by the creditor in settlement of the obligation (e.g. a sinking fund arrangement); or

(d) obligations incurred as a result of events giving rise to losses that are expected to be recovered from a third party by virtue of a claim made under an insurance policy.

Derivative assets and liabilities that are not transacted through central clearing systems are very unlikely to qualify for offsetting. For example, it is rare that they will be settled net in the normal course of business and even where associated offsetting agreements exist they are usually conditional on the default of one of the counterparties.

7.4.1.E Cash pooling arrangements

Groups often use what are commonly known as cash pooling arrangements. Typically these will involve a number of subsidiaries within a group each having a legally separate bank account with the same bank that may have positive or negative (overdrawn) balances. In many respects these accounts will be managed on an aggregated basis, for example interest will normally be determined on a notional basis using the net balance of all accounts; similarly any overdraft limit will normally apply to the net balance.

These arrangements may or may not give the group a legally enforceable right to set off the balances in these accounts. Clearly if there is no such right the balances should not be offset in the group financial statements. However, where such a right exists and meets criterion (a), the entity should assess whether there is an intention to settle the balances net or simultaneously, i.e. to what extent criterion (b) is met.

The Interpretations Committee considered criterion (b) for a particular cash pooling arrangement where:

- the group instigated regular physical transfers of balances into a single netting account;
- such transfers were not required under the terms of the cash-pooling arrangement and were not performed at the reporting date; and
- at the reporting date, the group expected that its subsidiaries would use their bank accounts before the next net settlement date by placing further cash on deposit or by withdrawing cash to settle other obligations.

The committee observed that the group expects cash movements to take place on individual bank accounts before the next net settlement date because the group expects its subsidiaries to use those bank accounts in their normal course of business. Consequently, to the extent the group did not expect to settle its subsidiaries' period-end account balances on a net basis, it would not be appropriate for the group to assert it had the intention to settle the entire period-end balances on a net basis at the reporting date. Therefore, presenting these balances net would not appropriately reflect the amounts and timings of the expected future cash flows, taking into account the entity's normal business practices.

In other cash-pooling arrangements, a group's expectations regarding how subsidiaries will use their bank accounts before the next net settlement date may be different. Consequently, in those circumstances, the group would be required to apply judgement in determining whether there was an intention to settle on a net basis at the reporting date. The committee also noted that many different cash pooling arrangements exist in practice and the determination of what constitutes an intention to settle on a net basis would depend on the individual facts and circumstances of each case. The related disclosure requirements (see 7.4.2 below) should also be considered.[24]

7.4.1.F Offsetting collateral amounts

Many central counterparty clearing houses require cash collateral in the form of variation margin to cover the fluctuations in the market value of 'over-the-counter' and exchange-traded derivatives. Historically IAS 32 has not addressed the offsetting of collateral although entities sometimes did offset the market values of the derivatives against the cash collateral, on the basis that all payments on the derivatives will be made net using the cash collateral already provided. In effect, the collateral is represented as an advance payment for settlement of the cash flows arising on the derivatives.

In the basis for conclusions to the 2011 amendment, the IASB clarified that the offsetting criteria do not give special consideration to items referred to as 'collateral'. Accordingly, a recognised financial instrument designated as collateral should be set off against the related financial asset or financial liability if, and only if, it meets the offsetting criteria in IAS 32. This might be the case, for instance, if variation margin is used to settle cash flows on derivative contracts. However, the IASB also noted that if an entity can be required to return or receive back collateral, the entity would not currently have a legally enforceable right of set-off in all relevant circumstances and therefore offsetting would not be appropriate. *[IAS 32.BC103]*.

In practice, to set off collateral against related financial assets and liabilities, a reporting entity would also need to assess, among other factors: (i) whether the amounts paid or received can be construed as partial settlement of the amounts due under the derivative contracts (see below); (ii) whether the right of offset is legally enforceable in the event of default, insolvency or bankruptcy of either party as well as in the normal course of business; (iii) whether the right to offset the collateral and the open position is conditional on a future event; (iv) whether the collateral will form part of the actual net settlement of the underlying contracts; and (v) whether there is a single process for both the settlement of the underlying contracts and the transfer of the collateral.

The analysis of whether payments or receipts described as margin payments are in fact partial settlements of an open position, and hence result in partial derecognition of the derivative, requires the application of significant judgement, including an assessment of the legal relationship between the clearing member and the clearing house. When the strike price of a derivative contract is effectively reset each day following a margin payment based on the contract's change in fair value, this might indicate it is appropriate to regard the margin payment as a partial settlement of the derivative. This situation sometimes occurs with exchange traded futures for which gains and losses on the open position are realised over time as opposed to being accumulated until the final settlement date.

7.4.1.C Unit of account

IAS 32 does not specify the 'unit of account' to which the offsetting requirements should be applied. For example, they could be applied to individual financial instruments, such as entire derivative assets or liabilities, or they could be applied to identifiable cash flows arising on those financial instruments. In practice, both approaches are seen with the former being more commonly applied by financial institutions and the latter by energy producers and traders. This diversity became apparent to the IASB during its project that amended IAS 32 in December 2011. Nevertheless, whilst the IASB considered imposing an approach based on individual cash flows (which, on a conceptual level, it favoured), it concluded that the different interpretations applied today do not result in inappropriate application of the offsetting criteria. The Board also concluded that the benefits of amending IAS 32 would not outweigh the costs for preparers. *[IAS 32.BC105-BC111]*. Accordingly, IAS 32 was not amended, thereby allowing this diversity to continue. Reporting entities should establish an accounting policy and apply that policy consistently.

7.4.2 Offsetting financial assets and financial liabilities: disclosure

This section discusses the requirements of IFRS 7 introduced by the IASB in December 2011. These requirements are similar to requirements introduced into US GAAP by the FASB at around the same time and are intended to assist users in identifying major differences between the effects of the IFRS and US GAAP offsetting requirements (without requiring a full reconciliation). *[IAS 32.BC77]*.

7.4.2.A Objective

The objective of these requirements is to disclose information to enable users of financial statements to evaluate the effect or potential effect of netting arrangements, including rights of set-off associated with recognised financial assets and liabilities, on the reporting entity's financial position. *[IFRS 7.13B]*.

To meet this objective, the minimum quantitative disclosure requirements considered at 7.4.2.C below may need to be supplemented with additional (qualitative) disclosures. Whether such disclosures are necessary will depend on the terms of an entity's enforceable master netting arrangements and related agreements, including the nature of the rights of set-off, and their effect or potential effect on the entity's financial position. *[IFRS 7.B53]*.

7.4.2.B Scope

The disclosure requirements considered at 7.4.2.C below are applicable not only to all recognised financial instruments that are set off in accordance with IAS 32 (see 7.4.1 above), but also to recognised financial instruments that are subject to an *enforceable* master netting arrangement or 'similar agreement' that covers similar financial instruments and transactions, irrespective of whether they are set off in accordance with IAS 32. *[IFRS 7.13A, B40]*.

In this context, enforceability has two elements: first, enforceability as a matter of law under the governing laws of the contract; and second, consistency with the bankruptcy laws of the jurisdictions where the reporting entity and counterparty are located. The latter is critical since, regardless of the jurisdiction selected to govern the contract, local insolvency laws in an insolvent counterparty's jurisdiction can override contractual terms in the event of insolvency. Determining whether an agreement is enforceable for the purposes of these disclosures may require judgement based on a legal analysis that is sometimes, but not necessarily, based on legal advice.

These 'similar agreements' include, but are not limited to, derivative clearing agreements, global master repurchase agreements, global master securities lending agreements, and any related rights to financial collateral. The 'similar financial instruments and transactions' include, but are not restricted to, derivatives, sale and repurchase agreements, reverse repurchase agreements, securities borrowing and securities lending agreements. However, loans and customer deposits with the same financial institution would not be within the scope of these disclosure requirements, unless they are set off in the statement of financial position; nor would financial instruments that are subject *only* to a collateral agreement. *[IFRS 7.B41]*.

The scope of equivalent disclosures in US GAAP is restricted to derivatives, repurchase and reverse repurchase agreements and securities lending and borrowing arrangements. In November 2012, the IASB considered this and effectively confirmed that the scope of IFRS 7 is broader than US GAAP. As a result, trade or other receivables and payables, such as balances with brokers, that are subject to an umbrella netting arrangement (normally where an entity's customer is also a supplier, and *vice versa*), are likely to fall within the scope of these disclosure requirements. Extract 54.19 (BP) illustrates one company providing these disclosures about receivables and payables in addition to derivatives.

7.4.2.C Disclosure requirements

To meet the objective at 7.4.2.A above, the standard requires entities to disclose, at the end of the reporting period, in a tabular format unless another format is more appropriate, the following information separately for recognised financial assets and for recognised financial liabilities: *[IFRS 7.13C]*

- the gross amounts of those recognised financial assets and recognised financial liabilities within the scope of the disclosures (see 7.4.2.B above) [Amount (a)].

  This excludes any amounts recognised as a result of collateral agreements that do not meet the offsetting criteria in IAS 32. Instead these will be disclosed in Amount (d) (see below); *[IFRS 7.B43]*
- the amounts that are set off in accordance with the criteria in IAS 32 when determining the net amounts presented in the statement of financial position [Amount (b)].

  These amounts will be disclosed in both the financial asset and financial liability disclosures. However, the amounts disclosed (in, for example, a table) should be limited to the amounts subject to set-off. For example, an entity may have a recognised derivative asset and a recognised derivative liability that meet the offsetting criteria. If the gross amount of the asset is larger than the gross amount of the liability, the financial asset disclosure table will include the entire amount of the derivative asset in Amount (a) and the entire amount of the derivative liability in Amount (b). However, while the financial liability disclosure table will include the entire amount of the derivative liability in Amount (a), it will only include the amount of the derivative asset that is equal to the amount of the derivative liability in Amount (b); *[IFRS 7.B44]*
- the net amounts presented in the statement of financial position [Amount (c) = Amount (a) – Amount (b)].

  For instruments that are within the scope of these disclosure requirements but which do not meet the offsetting criteria in IAS 32, the amounts included in Amount (c) would equal the amounts included in Amount (a). *[IFRS 7.B45]*.

  Amount (c) should be reconciled to the individual line item amounts presented in the statement of financial position. For example, if an entity determines that the aggregation or disaggregation of individual line item amounts provides more relevant information, it should reconcile the aggregated or disaggregated amounts included in Amount (c) back to the individual line item amounts presented in the statement of financial position; *[IFRS 7.B46]*
- the amounts subject to an enforceable master netting arrangement or similar agreement that are not included in the amounts subject to set-off above [Amount (d)], including:
  - amounts related to recognised financial instruments that do not meet some or all of the offsetting criteria in IAS 32 [Amount (d)(i)].

    This might include, for example, current rights of set-off where there is no intention to settle the open positions subject to these rights net or simultaneously, or conditional rights of set-off that are enforceable and exercisable only in the event of the default, insolvency or bankruptcy of any of the counterparties; *[IFRS 7.B47]* and
  - amounts related to *financial* collateral (including cash collateral) [Amount (d)(ii)].

    The fair value of those financial instruments that have been pledged or received as collateral should be disclosed. To ensure that the disclosures reflect the maximum net exposure to credit risk, the amendments require the amounts disclosed for financial collateral not offset to include *actual* collateral received, whether recognised or not as well as actual collateral pledged. The amounts disclosed should not relate to any payables or receivables recognised to return or receive back such collateral. *[IFRS 7.B48]*. The amounts disclosed for collateral would exclude non-financial collateral, for instance, land and buildings.

References to Amounts (a), (b), et seq. can be traced through to Example 54.17 at 7.4.2.D below.

The total amount included in Amount (d) for any instrument is limited to the amount included in Amount (c) for that instrument. *[IFRS 7.13D]*. In other words, an entity takes into account the effects of over-collateralisation by financial instrument, so that, for example, an over-collateralisation on one asset does not make an under-collateralisation on another. To do so, it first deducts the amounts included in Amount (d)(i) from the amount included in Amount (c). It then limits the amounts included in Amount (d)(ii) to the remaining amount in Amount (c) for the related financial instrument. However, if rights to collateral are available to cover multiple contracts with the same counterparty, for example through a cross collateralisation agreement, such rights can be taken into account in arriving at Amount (d)(ii). *[IFRS 7.B49]*.

Entities should provide a description of the rights of set-off associated with the entity's financial instruments included in Amount (d), including the nature and type of those rights. For example, conditional rights would need to be described. For instruments subject to rights of set-off that are not contingent on a future event but that do not meet the remaining criteria in IAS 32, the description should include the reasons why the criteria are not met. For any financial collateral received or pledged, it would be appropriate to disclose the terms of the collateral (such as why the collateral is restricted); *[IFRS 7.13E, B50]* and

- the net amount after deducting Amount (d) from Amount (c) [Amount (e)].

The financial instruments disclosed in accordance with the requirements above may be subject to different measurement requirements, for example a payable related to a repurchase agreement may be measured at amortised cost, while a derivative will be measured at fair value. Instruments should be included at their recognised amounts and any resulting measurement differences should be described in the related disclosures. *[IFRS 7.B42]*.

The disclosures may be grouped by type of financial instrument or transaction (e.g. derivatives, repurchase and reverse repurchase agreements or securities borrowing and securities lending agreements). *[IFRS 7.B51]*.

Alternatively, disclosure of Amounts (a) to (c) may be grouped by type of financial instrument with disclosure of Amounts (c) to (e) by counterparty. Amounts that are individually significant in terms of total counterparty amounts should be separately disclosed with the remaining individually insignificant counterparty amounts aggregated into one line item. Names of the counterparties need not be given, although designation of counterparties (Counterparty P, Counterparty Q, Counterparty R, etc.) should remain consistent from year to year for the periods presented to maintain comparability. Qualitative disclosures should be considered so that further information can be given about the types of counterparties. *[IFRS 7.B52]*.

If the above quantitative and qualitative disclosures are included in more than one note to the financial statements, the amendments require the information in the individual notes to be cross-referenced to each other. This is intended to increase the transparency of the disclosures and enhance the value of information. *[IFRS 7.13F]*.

7.4.2.D Offsetting disclosures – illustrative examples

The amendment that introduced the disclosures related to offsetting financial instruments provides the following example illustrating ways in which an entity might provide the required quantitative disclosures described above. However, these illustrations do not address all possible ways of applying the disclosure requirements. *[IFRS 7.IG40D]*.

Example 54.17: Illustration of offsetting disclosures

Background

An entity has entered into transactions subject to an enforceable master netting arrangement or similar agreement with the following counterparties. The entity has the following recognised financial assets and financial liabilities resulting from those transactions that meet the scope of the disclosure requirements.

Counterparty A:

The entity has a derivative asset (fair value of CU100 million) and a derivative liability (fair value of CU80 million) with Counterparty A that meet the IAS 32 offsetting criteria. Consequently, the gross derivative liability is set off against the gross derivative asset, resulting in the presentation of a net derivative asset of CU20 million in the entity's statement of financial position. Cash collateral has also been received from Counterparty A for a portion of the net derivative asset (CU10 million). The cash collateral of CU10 million does not meet the IAS 32 offsetting criteria, but it can be set off against the net amount of the derivative asset and derivative liability in the case of default and insolvency or bankruptcy, in accordance with an associated collateral arrangement.

Counterparty B:

The entity has a derivative asset (fair value of CU100 million) and a derivative liability (fair value of CU80 million) with Counterparty B that do not meet the IAS 32 offsetting criteria, but which the entity has the right to set off in the case of default and insolvency or bankruptcy. Consequently, the gross amount of the derivative asset (CU100 million) and the gross amount of the derivative liability (CU80 million) are presented separately in the entity's statement of financial position.

Cash collateral has also been received from Counterparty B for the net amount of the derivative asset and derivative liability (CU20 million). The cash collateral of CU20 million does not meet the IAS 32 offsetting criteria, but it can be set off against the net amount of the derivative asset and derivative liability in the case of default and insolvency or bankruptcy, in accordance with an associated collateral arrangement.

Counterparty C:

The entity has entered into a sale and repurchase agreement with Counterparty C that is accounted for as a collateralised borrowing. The carrying amount of the financial assets (bonds) used as collateral and posted by the entity for the transaction is CU79 million and their fair value is CU85 million. The carrying amount of the collateralised borrowing (repo payable) is CU80 million.

The entity has also entered into a reverse sale and repurchase agreement with Counterparty C that is accounted for as a collateralised lending. The fair value of the financial assets (bonds) received as collateral (and not recognised in the entity's statement of financial position) is CU105 million. The carrying amount of the collateralised lending (reverse repo receivable) is CU90 million.

The transactions are subject to a global master repurchase agreement with a right of set-off only in default and insolvency or bankruptcy and therefore do not meet the IAS 32 offsetting criteria. Consequently, the related repo payable and repo receivable are presented separately in the entity's statement of financial position.

Illustration of the disclosures by type of financial instrument

Financial assets subject to offsetting, enforceable master netting arrangements and similar agreements

CU million

As at 31 December 20XX	(a)	(b)	(c)=(a)–(b)	(d) Related amounts not set off in the statement of financial position		(e)=(c)–(d)
	Gross amounts of recognised financial assets	Gross amounts of recognised financial liabilities set off in the statement of financial position	Net amounts of financial assets presented in the statement of financial position	(d)(i), (d)(ii) Financial instruments	(d)(ii) Cash collateral received	Net amount
Description						
Derivatives	200	(80)	120	(80)	(30)	10
Reverse repurchase, securities borrowing and similar agreements	90	–	90	(90)	–	–
Other financial instruments	–	–	–	–	–	–
Total	290	(80)	210	(170)	(30)	10

Financial liabilities subject to offsetting, enforceable master netting arrangements and similar agreements

CU million

As at 31 December 20XX	(a)	(b)	(c)=(a)–(b)	(d) Related amounts not set off in the statement of financial position		(e)=(c)–(d)
	Gross amounts of recognised financial liabilities	Gross amounts of recognised financial assets set off in the statement of financial position	Net amounts of financial liabilities presented in the statement of financial position	(d)(i), (d)(ii) Financial instruments	(d)(ii) Cash collateral pledged	Net amount
Description						
Derivatives	160	(80)	80	(80)	–	–
Repurchase, securities lending and similar agreements	80	–	80	(80)	–	–
Other financial instruments	–	–	–	–	–	–
Total	240	(80)	160	(160)	–	–

Illustration of amounts offset disclosed by type of financial instrument and amounts not offset by counterparty

Financial assets subject to offsetting, enforceable master netting arrangements and similar agreements

CU million

As at 31 December 20XX	(a) Gross amounts of recognised financial assets	(b) Gross amounts of recognised financial liabilities set off in the statement of financial position	(c)=(a)–(b) Net amounts of financial assets presented in the statement of financial position
Description			
Derivatives	200	(80)	120
Reverse repurchase, securities borrowing and similar agreements	90	–	90
Other financial instruments	–	–	–
Total	290	(80)	210

Net financial assets subject to enforceable master netting arrangements and similar agreements, by counterparty

CU million

As at 31 December 20XX	(c)	(d)		(e)=(c)–(d)
		Related amounts not set off in the statement of financial position		
	Net amounts of financial assets presented in the statement of financial position	(d)(i), (d)(ii) Financial instruments	(d)(ii) Cash collateral received	Net amount
Counterparty A	20	–	(10)	10
Counterparty B	100	(80)	(20)	–
Counterparty C	90	(90)	–	–
Other	–	–	–	–
Total	210	(170)	(30)	10

Financial liabilities subject to offsetting, enforceable master netting arrangements and similar agreements

CU million

As at 31 December 20XX	(a)	(b)	(c)=(a)–(b)
	Gross amounts of recognised financial liabilities	Gross amounts of recognised financial assets set off in the statement of financial position	Net amounts of financial liabilities presented in the statement of financial position
Description			
Derivatives	160	(80)	80
Repurchase, securities lending and similar agreements	80	–	80
Other financial instruments	–	–	–
Total	240	(80)	160

Net financial liabilities subject to enforceable master netting arrangements and similar agreements, by counterparty

CU million

As at 31 December 20XX	(c)	(d)		(e)=(c)–(d)
		Related amounts not set off in the statement of financial position		
	Net amounts of financial liabilities presented in the statement of financial position	(d)(i), (d)(ii) Financial instruments	(d)(ii) Cash collateral pledged	Net amount
Counterparty A	–	–	–	–
Counterparty B	80	(80)	–	–
Counterparty C	80	(80)	–	–
Other	–	–	–	–
Total	160	(160)	–	–

BP provides the following disclosures about the extent of its offsetting.

Extract 54.19: BP p.l.c. (2014)

Notes on financial statements[extract]
27. Financial instruments and financial risk factors [extract]
(b) Credit risk [extract]

Financial instruments subject to offsetting, enforceable master netting arrangements and similar agreements

The following table shows the gross amounts of recognized financial assets and liabilities (i.e. before offsetting) and the amounts offset in the balance sheet.

Amounts which cannot be offset under IFRS, but which could be settled net under the terms of master netting agreements if certain conditions arise, and collateral received or pledged, are also shown in the table to show the total net exposure of the group.

$ million

At 31 December 2014	Gross amounts of recognized financial assets (liabilities)	Amounts set off	Net amounts presented on the balance sheet	Related amounts not set off in the balance sheet: Master netting arrangements	Cash collateral (received) pledged	Net amount
Derivative assets	11,515	(2,383)	9,132	(1,164)	(458)	7,510
Derivative liabilities	(8,971)	2,383	(6,588)	1,164	–	(5,424)
Trade receivables	10,502	(6,080)	4,422	(485)	(145)	3,792
Trade payables	(9,062)	6,080	(2,982)	485	–	(2,497)

Chapter 54

7.4.3 Assets and liabilities

IAS 1 does not prescribe the order or format in which items are to be presented on the face of the statement of financial position, but states that the following items relating to financial instruments, are sufficiently different in nature or function to warrant separate presentation: *[IAS 1.54, 57]*

- trade and other receivables;
- cash and cash equivalents;
- other financial assets;
- trade and other payables;
- provisions; and
- other financial liabilities.

However, additional line items, headings and subtotals should be presented on the face of the statement of financial position when the size, nature or function of an item or aggregation of similar items is such that separate presentation is relevant to an understanding of the entity's financial position. Additional line items may also be presented by disaggregating the line items noted above. *[IAS 1.55, 57(a)]*.

Any additional subtotals presented should: *[IAS 1.55A]*

- comprise line items made up of amounts recognised and measured in accordance with IFRS;
- be presented and labelled in a manner that makes the line items that constitute the subtotal clear and understandable;
- be consistent from period to period, as required by IAS 1 (see Chapter 3 at 4.1.4); and
- not be displayed with more prominence than the subtotals and totals required in IFRS for the statement of financial position.

The judgement on whether additional items are presented separately should be based on an assessment of: *[IAS 1.58]*

- the nature and liquidity of assets;
- the function of assets within the entity; and
- the amounts, nature and timing of liabilities.

The descriptions used and the ordering of items or aggregation of similar items may be amended according to the nature of the entity and its transactions, to provide information that is relevant to an understanding of the entity's financial position. For example, a financial institution may amend the descriptions to provide information that is relevant to the operations of a financial institution. *[IAS 1.57(b)]*.

Although, for measurement purposes, IAS 39 classifies financial assets into four categories (see Chapter 46), other descriptors for these categories or other categorisations may be used when presenting information on the face of the financial statements. *[IAS 39.45]*. Whilst not explicitly stated in IFRS 9, entities should also be able to use categorisations that are different from the measurement categories in that standard (see Chapter 47) when it is applied.

However, the use of different measurement bases for different classes of assets suggests that their nature or function differs and, therefore, that they should be presented as separate line items. *[IAS 1.59]*. For example, loans and receivables measured at amortised cost would normally be presented separately from available-for-sale assets measured at fair value, particularly by a financial institution.

As noted at 7.1.4 above, IAS 39 and IFRS 9 explicitly state that they do not address whether embedded derivatives should be presented separately in the statement of financial position. *[IAS 39.11, IFRS 9.4.3.4]*. Although the guidance in the previous paragraph suggests that embedded derivatives will often be presented separately on the face of the statement of financial position, this will not always be the case, e.g. for the 'puttable instruments' shown in Example 54.18 below, which is based on IAS 32.

Further sub-classifications of the line items presented should be disclosed, either on the face of the statement of financial position or in the notes, classified in a manner appropriate to the entity's operations. *[IAS 1.77]*. The detail provided in sub-classifications will depend on the size, nature and function of the amounts involved and will vary for each item. For example, receivables should be disaggregated into amounts receivable from trade customers, receivables from related parties and other amounts. Assets included within receivables that are not financial instruments, such as many prepayments, should also be shown separately. *[IAS 1.78(b)]*.

The presentation in the statement of financial position of liabilities arising from supply-chain financing arrangements is an area where particular judgement is necessary. This issue is discussed in more detail in Chapter 51 at 6.5.

7.4.4 The distinction between current and non-current assets and liabilities

For entities presenting a statement of financial position that distinguishes between current and non-current assets and liabilities, the requirements of IAS 1 for determining whether items are classified as current or non-current are dealt with in Chapter 3 at 3.1.1 to 3.1.4. This section deals with five interpretive issues that have arisen in applying those requirements to financial instruments.

7.4.4.A Derivatives

IAS 1 requires assets and liabilities held 'primarily for the purpose of trading' to be classified as current. *[IAS 1.66, 69]*. Where a derivative is not designated as a hedging instrument in an effective hedge, it is classified by IAS 39 or IFRS 9 as held for trading irrespective of the purpose for which it is held (see Chapter 46 at 2.1 and Chapter 47 at 4). *[IAS 39.9, IFRS 9.A]*. This does not mean that any derivative not designated as a hedging instrument in an effective hedge must always be classified as current because the IAS 39 or IFRS 9 classification is for measurement purposes only. Whilst a derivative held primarily for trading purposes should be presented as current regardless of its maturity date, other derivatives should be classified as current or non-current on the basis of their settlement date. Accordingly, derivatives that have maturities of less than 12 months from the end of the reporting period, or derivatives that have maturities of more than 12 months from the end of the reporting period but are expected to be settled within 12 months should be presented as a current asset or liability. Conversely, derivatives that have a maturity of more than twelve months and are expected to be held for more than twelve months after the reporting period should be presented as non-current assets or liabilities. *[IAS 1.BC38B, BC38C]*.

Although the Interpretations Committee and the IASB have considered how to split into current and non-current components the carrying amount of derivatives with staggered payment dates, both have decided not to address this issue. Consequently, entities will need to apply judgement in determining an appropriate split. For example, the current component of a five-year interest rate swap with interest payments exchanged quarterly could be determined as the present value of the net interest cash flows of the swap for the forthcoming twelve months after the reporting date.[25]

7.4.4.B Convertible loans

Where an entity issues convertible bonds that are accounted for as an equity component (i.e. the holders' rights to convert the bonds into a fixed number of the issuer's equity instruments) and a liability component (i.e. the entity's obligation to deliver cash to holders at the maturity date), the issue arises whether the liability component should be classified as current or non-current if the conversion option may be exercised at any time before maturity. IAS 1 now explains that any terms of a liability which could, at the option of the counterparty, result in its settlement by the issue of equity instruments do not affect its classification. *[IAS 1.69(d)]*. In other words, provided the entity could not be required to settle the liability component directly within one year, it would be classified as non-current even if the holder could exercise the conversion (thereby requiring the liability component to be derecognised) within one year.

7.4.4.C Long-term loans with repayment on demand terms

IAS 1 requires liabilities for which the entity does not have an unconditional right to defer settlement for at least twelve months after the reporting date to be classified as current. *[IAS 1.69(d)]*. Some long-term loan agreements, particularly in Hong Kong, contain clauses allowing the lender an absolute right to demand repayment at any time before maturity. Historically, borrowers often approached these clauses in the same way as more conventional covenants because the risk of exercise was considered very low (except in situations that might adversely affect the borrower's ability to repay). Consequently, the clause would result in classification of a loan as current only if such adverse matters relating to the borrower existed at the end of the reporting period.[26]

However, in 2010, the Interpretations Committee addressed this situation, noting that the requirements of IAS 1 are clear, i.e. such terms should always result in the loan being classified as current.[27]

7.4.4.D Debt with refinancing or roll over agreements

IAS 1 states that if an entity expects, and has the discretion, to refinance or roll over an obligation for at least twelve months after the reporting period under an existing loan facility, the obligation should be classified as non-current even if it would otherwise be due within a shorter period. *[IAS 1.73]*. The Interpretations Committee has been considering the circumstances in which the guidance in paragraph 73 should apply for some time.

One particular area of concern has been the classification of liabilities arising from a short-term commercial paper programme that is backed by a long-term loan facility. In these arrangements the commercial paper is typically issued for a term of 90 or 180 days; the issuer will normally attempt to issue new instruments to replace those maturing; and a bank (often the sponsor or manager of the scheme) will have provided the entity with a longer-term loan facility that may be drawn down if any issue of commercial paper is under-subscribed. In this situation, *prima facie* the entity has in place an agreement (the loan facility) that can be used to refinance the short-term liability (from the commercial paper) on a long-term basis and might consider classifying the liability arising from commercial paper as non-current.

However, in January 2011 after analysing outreach requests, the IFRS Interpretations Committee noted that there is no charted diversity in practice where an agreement is reached to refinance an existing borrowing with a different lender – here paragraph 73 is not considered applicable, whatever the terms of the new facility, and the existing borrowing would be classified as current. Therefore the commercial paper liabilities should be classified as current.[28] In February 2015 the IASB proposed an amendment to IAS 1 that would remove the reference in paragraph 73 to 'refinance' and bring the wording of the standard into line with the committee's view on how it should be (and is being) applied. At the time of writing, the IASB was expecting to finalise these amendments during 2017.

7.4.4.E Loan covenants

If an entity does not have an unconditional right to defer settlement of the liability for at least twelve months after the reporting period the liability should be reported as current. *[IAS 1.69(a)]*. Further, when an entity breaches a provision of a long-term loan arrangement (commonly called a covenant) on or before the end of the reporting period with the effect that the liability becomes payable on demand, the liability should be classified as current because, at the end of the reporting period, it does not have an unconditional right to defer settlement for at least twelve months after that date. *[IAS 1.73]*. The application of these requirements, including in some commonly occurring situations, and proposals issued by the IASB in February 2015 to clarify these requirements are discussed in more detail in Chapter 3 at 3.1.4 and 6.3 respectively. At the time of writing, the IASB was expecting to finalise these proposals during 2017.

7.4.5 Equity

IAS 1 explains that the face of the statement of financial position should include line items that present the following amounts within equity: *[IAS 1.54(q), (r)]*

- non-controlling interests, presented within equity; and
- issued capital and reserves attributable to owners of the parent.

As for assets and liabilities, additional line items, headings and subtotals should be presented on the face of the statement of financial position when such presentation is relevant to an understanding of the entity's financial position and additional line items may also be presented by disaggregating the line items noted above. *[IAS 1.55]*. Further sub-classifications of the line items presented should be disclosed, either on the face of the statement of financial position or in the notes, classified in a manner appropriate to the entity's operations. *[IAS 1.77]*. The detail provided in the sub-classifications will depend on the size, nature and function of the amounts involved and will vary for each item. For example, equity capital and reserves should be disaggregated into various classes, such as paid-in capital, share premium and reserves. *[IAS 1.78(e)]*. A description of the nature and purpose of each reserve within equity should also be provided. *[IAS 1.79(b)]*.

For each class of share capital, the following information should be disclosed, either on the face of the statement of financial position or in the notes: *[IAS 1.79(a)]*

- the number of shares authorised;
- the number of shares issued and fully paid, and issued but not fully paid;
- par value per share, or that the shares have no par value;
- a reconciliation of the number of shares outstanding at the beginning and at the end of the period;
- the rights, preferences and restrictions attaching to that class including restrictions on the distribution of dividends and the repayment of capital;
- shares in the entity held by the entity or by its subsidiaries (treasury shares *[IAS 32.34]*) or associates; and
- shares reserved for issue under options and contracts for the sale of shares, including the terms and amounts.

An entity without share capital, such as a partnership or trust, should disclose equivalent information, showing changes during the period in each category of equity interest, and the rights, preferences and restrictions attaching to each category of equity interest, *[IAS 1.80]*, (assuming of course it has actually issued instruments that meet the definition of equity).

Where puttable financial instruments and obligations arising on liquidation (see Chapter 45 at 4.6) are reclassified between financial liabilities and equity, entities are required to disclose the amount reclassified into and out of each category and the timing and reason for that reclassification. *[IAS 1.80A]*. This requirement was introduced by the amendments to IAS 32 and IAS 1 dealing with the classification of puttable financial instruments and obligations arising on liquidation.

7.4.6 Entities whose share capital is not equity

Continuing Examples 54.15 and 54.16 at 7.1.5 above, the following examples illustrate corresponding statement of financial position formats that may be used by entities such as mutual funds that do not have equity as defined in IAS 32, or entities such as co-operatives whose share capital is not equity as defined in IAS 32 because the entity has an obligation to repay the share capital on demand.

Example 54.18: Statement of financial position format for a mutual fund

Statement of financial position at 31 December 2017 *[IAS 32.IE32]*

	2017		2016	
	€	€	€	€
ASSETS				
Non-current assets (classified in accordance with IAS 1)	91,374		78,484	
Total non-current assets		91,374		78,484
Current assets (classified in accordance with IAS 1)	1,422		1,769	
Total current assets		1,422		1,769
Total assets		92,796		80,253

LIABILITIES				
Current liabilities (classified in accordance with IAS 1)	647		66	
Total current liabilities		(647)		(66)
Non-current liabilities excluding net assets attributable to unit holders (classified in accordance with IAS 1)	280		136	
		(280)		(136)
Net assets attributable to unit holders		91,869		80,051

As for the equivalent income statement format, it may not be immediately clear what the final line item in this format represents. It is, in fact, a liability and therefore the entity's 'equity' (as that term is used in IAS 1) at the end of 2017 is €92,796 – €647 – €280 – €91,869 = €nil.

Example 54.19: Statement of financial position format for a co-operative

Statement of financial position at 31 December 2017 *[IAS 32.IE33]*	2017		2016	
	€	€	€	€
ASSETS				
Non-current assets (classified in accordance with IAS 1)	908		830	
Total non-current assets		908		830
Current assets (classified in accordance with IAS 1)	383		350	
Total current assets		383		350
Total assets		1,291		1,180
LIABILITIES				
Current liabilities (classified in accordance with IAS 1)	372		338	
Share capital repayable on demand	202		161	
Total current liabilities		(574)		(499)
Total assets less current liabilities		717		681
Non-current liabilities (classified in accordance with IAS 1)	187		196	
		187		196
RESERVES*				
Reserves, e.g. revaluation reserve, retained earnings	530		485	
		530		485
		717		681
MEMORANDUM NOTE				
TOTAL MEMBERS' INTERESTS				
Share capital repayable on demand		202		161
Reserves		530		485
		732		646

*In this example, the entity has no obligation to deliver a share of its reserves to its members.

Chapter 54

The line item 'Share capital repayable on demand' is part of the entity's liabilities and the items within 'Reserves' represent its equity.

Although not required by IAS 1, an entity adopting this type of format for its statement of financial position may choose to present an analysis of movements in (or reconciliation of) total members' interests (often defined as equity plus share capital repayable on demand, perhaps adjusted for other balances with members) if this is considered to provide useful information; this would not remove the need to present a statement of changes in equity.

7.5 Statement of cash flows

The implementation guidance to IAS 39 and IFRS 9 acknowledges that the terminology in IAS 7 – *Statement of Cash Flows* – was not updated to reflect the publication of these standards, but does explain that the classification of cash flows arising from hedging instruments within the statement of cash flows should be consistent with the classification of these instruments as hedging instruments. In other words, such cash flows should be classified as operating, investing or financing activities, on the basis of the classification of the cash flows arising from the hedged item. *[IAS 39.G.2, IFRS 9.G.2]*.

8 EFFECTIVE DATES AND TRANSITIONAL PROVISIONS

This section contains information that is relevant for annual periods beginning on or after 1 January 2016. For earlier periods, equivalent requirements are dealt with in *International GAAP 2016* and other predecessors to this publication.

8.1 Adoption of IFRS 9: effective date and transitional provisions

This section is prepared for entities applying the version of IFRS 9 published in July 2014 in its entirety. IFRS 9 and the consequential amendments to IFRS 7 and IAS 1, which are noted throughout this chapter, are effective for periods beginning on or after 1 January 2018. Entities are permitted to apply the standard earlier, however if they do, this fact should be disclosed. *[IFRS 9.7.1.1]*. Comparative periods need not be restated when IFRS 9 is first applied. *[IFRS 9.7.2.15]*.

8.2 Adoption of IFRS 9: disclosure requirements

When IFRS 9 is first applied, the following information should be disclosed, in a table unless another format is more appropriate, for each class of financial assets and financial liabilities at the date of initial application: *[IFRS 7.42I]*

- the original measurement category and carrying amount determined in accordance with IAS 39;
- the new measurement category and carrying amount determined in accordance with IFRS 9; and
- the amount of any financial assets and financial liabilities that were previously designated as measured at fair value through profit or loss but are no longer so designated, distinguishing between those that are required to be reclassified and those which an entity elects to reclassify.

In addition, qualitative information should be disclosed to provide an understanding of: *[IFRS 7.42J]*

- how the classification requirements in IFRS 9 were applied to those financial assets whose classification has changed as a result of applying IFRS 9; and
- the reasons for any designation or de-designation of financial assets or financial liabilities as measured at fair value through profit or loss.

The following additional disclosures should also be provided on the application of IFRS 9: *[IFRS 7.44S, IFRS 9.7.2.13]*

- at the date of initial application of IFRS 9, changes in the classifications of financial assets and financial liabilities, showing separately: *[IFRS 7.42L]*
  - changes in the carrying amounts on the basis of their measurement categories in accordance with IAS 39 (i.e. not resulting from a change in measurement attribute on transition to IFRS 9); and
  - the changes in the carrying amounts arising from a change in measurement attribute on transition to IFRS 9; and
- in the reporting period in which IFRS 9 is initially applied, for financial assets and financial liabilities that have been reclassified so that they are measured at amortised cost and, in the case of financial assets, that have been reclassified out of fair value through profit or loss so that they are measured at fair value through other comprehensive income, as a result of the transition to IFRS 9: *[IFRS 7.42M]*
  - the fair value of the financial assets or financial liabilities at the end of the reporting period; and
  - the fair value gain or loss that would have been recognised in profit or loss or other comprehensive income during the reporting period if the financial assets or financial liabilities had not been reclassified;
- for financial assets and financial liabilities that have been reclassified out of fair value through profit or loss as a result of the transition to IFRS 9: *[IFRS 7.42N]*
  - the effective interest rate determined on the date of initial application; and
  - the interest income or expense recognised.

  If an entity treats the fair value of a financial asset or a financial liability as its amortised cost at the date of initial application (see Chapter 47 at 10.2.7.B), these disclosures should be made for each reporting period following reclassification until derecognition. *[IFRS 7.42N]*.

These disclosures, together with other information in the financial statements, must permit reconciliation as at the date of initial application between: *[IFRS 7.42O]*

- the measurement categories presented in accordance with IAS 39 and IFRS 9; and
- the class of financial instrument.

Information should be disclosed that permits the reconciliation as at the date of initial application of the ending impairment allowances in accordance with IAS 39 and the provisions in accordance with IAS 37 – *Provisions, Contingent Liabilities and Contingent Assets* – to the opening loss allowances determined in accordance with IFRS 9. For financial assets, this disclosure should be provided by the related financial assets'

Chapter 54

measurement categories in accordance with IAS 39 and IFRS 9 and show separately the effect of the changes in the measurement category on the loss allowance at that date. *[IFRS 7.42P]*.

In the reporting period that includes the date of initial application of IFRS 9, an entity is not required to disclose the line item amounts that would have been reported in accordance with the classification and measurement requirements (including the requirements related to amortised cost measurement of financial assets and impairment) of IFRS 9 for prior periods or IAS 39 for the current period: *[IFRS 7.42Q]*

If, at the date of initial application of IFRS 9, it is impracticable (as defined in IAS 8) to assess:

- a modified time value of money element based on the facts and circumstances that existed at the initial recognition of a financial asset; or
- whether the fair value of a prepayment feature was insignificant based on the facts and circumstances that existed at the initial recognition of a financial asset,

the contractual cash flow characteristics of that asset should be based on the facts and circumstances that existed at that time without taking into account the requirements related to the modification of the time value of money or the exception for prepayment features as appropriate. The carrying amount of the financial assets whose contractual cash flow characteristics have been assessed in this way should be disclosed, separately for each of the two situations above, at each reporting date until those financial assets are derecognised. *[IFRS 7.42R, 42S]*.

These disclosures should be provided irrespective of whether comparatives are restated.

8.3 Other amendments to IFRS 7

The application guidance added to IFRS 7 clarifying the meaning of 'continuing involvement' for the purposes of disclosures about transfers of financial assets (see 6.3.1 above) is effective for periods commencing on or after 1 January 2016. Earlier application was permitted, although an entity should have disclosed that it had done so. The guidance need not be applied for any period presented that begins before the annual period for which an entity first applies that guidance. *IFRS 7.44AA]*. In other words, comparative periods need not be restated.

The amendments clarifying that disclosures about offsetting are not normally required in interim reports (see 2.3 above) has the same effective date and the same requirement to disclose if this was applied in earlier periods. *[IFRS 7.44AA]*.

8.4 IFRS 16

IFRS 16, which amends some of the disclosure requirements for financial instruments arising from leases (see particularly 4.5.1 and 5.2.4.B I above), is effective for periods commencing on or after 1 January 2019. Earlier application is permitted for entities that apply IFRS 15 at or before the date of initial application of IFRS 16, although an entity should disclose that it has done so. *[IFRS 16.C1]*. There are many transitional provisions and these are covered in detail in Chapter 25 at 10.2 to 10.5.

9 FUTURE DEVELOPMENTS

9.1 General developments

Disclosure requirements are considered important by the IASB and those in respect of financial instruments have been expanded significantly as a result of changes made following the financial crisis. However, it seems unlikely that further major changes will be forthcoming in the near term.

The IASB's disclosure initiative (see Chapter 3 at 6.1) may influence the way entities present their disclosures about financial instruments. Initiatives by other bodies, such as reports and surveys of the Enhanced Disclosure Task Force of the Financial Stability Board (see 9.2 below) and the Basel Committee on Banking Supervision, may also influence the disclosures provided, particularly by financial institutions. In addition, we may see a gradual evolution of disclosure requirements in the light of practical experience.

In the longer term, any new accounting requirements arising from the IASB's project addressing macro hedge accounting (see Chapter 53 at 3.6.5) will likely be accompanied by extensive new disclosure requirements.

9.2 Enhanced Disclosure Task Force

The Enhanced Disclosure Task Force ('EDTF') is a private sector group comprising representatives from financial institutions, investors and analysts, credit rating agencies and external auditors. It was formed by the Financial Stability Forum in May 2012 and its objectives include the development of principles for enhanced disclosures about market conditions and risks, including ways to enhance the comparability of those disclosures and identifying those disclosures seen as leading practice.

In October 2012 the EDTF issued its first report. Seven fundamental principles for achieving enhanced risk disclosures were identified, namely that disclosures should:

- be clear, balanced and understandable;
- be comprehensive and include all of the bank's key activities and risks;
- present relevant information;
- reflect how the bank manages its risks;
- be consistent over time;
- be comparable among banks; and
- be provided on a timely basis.

The report also identified a number of detailed recommendations for enhancing risk disclosures, grouped under the following subjects (as well as addressing more general matters):

- risk governance and risk management strategies/business model;
- capital adequacy and risk-weighted assets;
- liquidity;
- funding;
- market risk;
- credit risk; and
- other risks.

These were accompanied by illustrative examples as well as observations on and extracts from recent reports issued by banks. The EDTF has issued further reports charting the progress of a number of banks in applying the principles and recommendations set out in the first report.

The latest of these reports, published in December 2015, noted that a user group of investors and analysts found that significant opportunity remains for banks to improve credit risk disclosures. This is before the transition to the new standards requiring an expected credit loss impairment approach for which high quality disclosure will be particularly important since it will differ from the calculation of expected losses for regulatory capital purposes and because model-based provisioning is inherently complex. Consequently, at the same time, the EDTF published guidance for banks in this area. This aims to enhance their disclosures, help the market understand the upcoming change in provisioning based on expected credit losses (whether under IFRS or US GAAP) and promote consistency and comparability of disclosures across internationally-active banks.

The guidance builds on the existing fundamental principles and recommendations noted above and addresses the following key areas of focus:

- concepts, interpretations and policies developed to implement the new expected credit loss approaches, including the significant credit deterioration assessment required by IFRS 9;
- the specific methodologies and estimation techniques developed;
- the impact of moving from an incurred to an expected credit loss approach;
- understanding the dynamics of changes in impairment allowances and their sensitivity to significant assumptions, including those as a result of the application of macro-economic assumptions;
- any changes made to the governance over financial reporting, and how they link with existing governance over other areas including credit risk management and regulatory reporting; and
- understanding the differences between the expected credit losses applied in the financial statements and those used in determining regulatory capital.

The guidance suggests that a gradual and phased approach during the transition period would be most useful to users, in order to give them clearer insights into the likely impacts of the new standards as implementation progresses and to allow them to make increasingly useful comparisons between banks. It also suggests that the initial focus should have been on qualitative disclosures and that proposed quantitative disclosures should be added as soon as they can be practicably determined and are reliable but, for IFRS reporters, at the latest in 2017 annual reports. At the time of writing, banks had started to explain the impacts of adopting IFRS 9 in more detail in their annual reports, although most of these disclosures were qualitative in nature.

References

1 IFRS 7, Appendix B, Application guidance, para. after main heading.

2 IFRS 7, Guidance on implementing, para. after main heading.

3 In September 2010 the IASB replaced the *Framework* with the *Conceptual Framework for Financial Reporting*, Chapter 3 of which contains guidance on materiality. However, the guidance on materiality in IAS 1 has not been updated to reflect this.

4 CESR Statement, *Application of and disclosures related to the reclassification of financial instruments*, CESR, July 2009.

5 Information for Observers (December 2008 IASB Meeting), *IFRS 7 Financial Instruments: Disclosures – Minor Amendments (Agenda paper 14)*, IASB, December 2008, paras. 93 to 98 and *IASB Update*, December 2008.

6 Information for Observers (December 2008 IASB Meeting), *IFRS 7 Financial Instruments: Disclosures – Minor Amendments (Agenda paper 14)*, IASB, December 2008, paras. 30 to 40 and *IASB Update*, December 2008.

7 Information for Observers (December 2008 IASB Meeting), *IFRS 7 Financial Instruments: Disclosures – Minor Amendments (Agenda paper 14)*, IASB, December 2008, para. 32.

8 Transition Resource Group for Impairment of Financial Instruments, *Meeting Summary – 22 April 2015*, IASB, April 2015, para. 57(b).

9 Information for Observers (January 2009 IASB Meeting), *Proposed amendments on liquidity risk disclosures (Agenda paper 14B)*, IASB, January 2009, para. 32.

10 Information for Observers (September 2008 IASB Meeting), *IFRS 7 Financial Instruments: Disclosures, Liquidity risk (Agenda paper 2A)*, IASB, September 2008, para. 34(b) and Information for Observers (January 2009 IASB Meeting), *Proposed amendments on liquidity risk disclosures (Agenda paper 14B)*, IASB, January 2009, para. 35(a).

11 Information for Observers (September 2008 IASB Meeting), *IFRS 7 Financial Instruments: Disclosures, Liquidity risk (Agenda paper 2A)*, IASB, September 2008, para. 34(c).

12 Information for Observers (September 2008 IASB Meeting), *IFRS 7 Financial Instruments: Disclosures, Liquidity risk (Agenda paper 2A)*, IASB, September 2008, paras. 40 and 41.

13 Information for Observers (September 2008 IASB Meeting), *IFRS 7 Financial Instruments: Disclosures, Liquidity risk (Agenda paper 2A)*, IASB, September 2008, paras. 34(d).

14 Information for Observers (September 2008 IASB Meeting), *IFRS 7 Financial Instruments: Disclosures, Liquidity risk (Agenda paper 2A)*, IASB, September 2008, para. 25.

15 Information for Observers (December 2008 IASB Meeting), *IFRS 7 Financial Instruments: Disclosures – Minor Amendments (Agenda paper 14)*, IASB, December 2008, paras. 71 to 79 and IASB Update, December 2008.

16 Information for Observers (December 2008 IASB Meeting), *IFRS 7 Financial Instruments: Disclosures – Minor Amendments (Agenda paper 14)*, IASB, December 2008, para. 86.

17 Information for Observers (December 2008 IASB Meeting), *IFRS 7 Financial Instruments: Disclosures – Minor Amendments (Agenda paper 14)*, IASB, December 2008, paras. 80 to 88 and IASB Update, December 2008.

18 Transition Resource Group for Impairment of Financial Instruments, *Meeting Summary – 22 April 2015*, IASB, April 2015, paras. 24 and 25.

19 Transition Resource Group for Impairment of Financial Instruments, *Meeting Summary – 22 April 2015*, IASB, April 2015, para. 57(a).

20 *IFRIC Update*, October 2004 and November 2006.

21 *IFRIC Update*, January 2015.

22 *IFRIC Update*, January 2015.

23 IAS 30, *Disclosures in the Financial Statements of Banks and Similar Financial Institutions*, IASB, August 1990 to December 2003, para. 13.

24 *IFRIC Update*, March 2016.

25 Information for Observers (March 2007 IFRIC meeting), *Current or non-current presentation of derivatives that are not designated as hedging instruments in effective hedges*, IASB, March 2007, paras. 14 and 17 and Information for Observers (11 March 2008 IASB meeting), *ED Annual improvements process – Comment analysis: IAS 1 Current/non-current classification of derivatives (Q6)*, IASB, March 2008, para. 12.

26 Staff Paper (September 2010 IFRS Interpretations Committee Meeting), *Current/non-current classification of callable term loan*, IASB, September 2010.

27 *IFRIC Update*, September 2010.

28 *IFRIC Update*, January 2011 and Staff Paper (January 2011 IFRS Interpretations Committee Meeting), *IAS 1 Presentation of Financial Statements – current/non-current classification of debt (rollover agreements) – outreach results*, IASB, January 2011.

Chapter 55 Insurance contracts

List of examples

Chapter 55 Insurance contracts

1 INTRODUCTION

1.1 The history of the IASB's insurance project

The IASB and its predecessor, the IASC, have been attempting to develop a comprehensive standard on insurance contracts since 1997 when a Steering Committee was established to carry out the initial project work. *[IFRS 4.BC3]*. It was decided to develop a standard on insurance contracts because:

(a) there was no standard on insurance contracts, and insurance contracts were excluded from the scope of existing standards that would otherwise have been relevant; and

(b) accounting practices for insurance contracts are diverse, and also often differ from practices in other sectors. *[IFRS 4.BC2]*.

Historically, the IASB and its predecessor have avoided dealing with specific accounting issues relating to insurance contracts by excluding them from the scope of their accounting standards. Currently, insurance contracts are excluded from the scope of the following standards:

- IAS 18 – *Revenue*;
- IAS 32 – *Financial Instruments: Presentation*;
- IAS 36 – *Impairment of Assets*;
- IAS 37 – *Provisions, Contingent Liabilities and Contingent Assets*;
- IAS 38 – *Intangible Assets*;
- IAS 39 – *Financial Instruments: Recognition and Measurement*;
- IFRS 7 – *Financial Instruments: Disclosures*;
- IFRS 9 – *Financial Instruments*; and
- IFRS 15 – *Revenue from Contracts with Customers*.

An alternative to developing a standard on insurance contracts would have been for the IASB to remove the insurance contract scope exemptions from these standards. Revenue would then have to be measured in accordance with IAS 18 (or IFRS 15) and most insurance contract liabilities would have to be recognised in accordance with either IAS 39 (or IFRS 9) or IAS 37 depending on their nature. However, the IASB and its predecessor were persuaded that an insurance contract is sufficiently unique to warrant its own accounting standard and have so far spent fourteen years attempting to decide what accounting that standard should require.

The Steering Committee established in 1997 published an Issues Paper – *Insurance* – in December 1999 which attracted 138 comment letters. Following a review of the comment letters, the committee developed a report to the IASB that was published in 2001 as a *Draft Statement of Principles – Insurance Contracts* (DSOP). The DSOP was never approved. *[IFRS 4.BC3]*.

The IASB began discussing the DSOP in November 2001. However, at its May 2002 meeting the IASB concluded that it would not be realistic to expect the implementation of a full recognition and measurement standard for insurance contracts by 2005 (in time for the adoption of IFRS in the EU).[1]

Consequently, the insurance project was split into two phases: Phase I, which became IFRS 4 – *Insurance Contracts* – and Phase II, which encompasses the IASB's subsequent work to develop a full recognition and measurement standard for insurance contracts.

A Discussion Paper (DP) – *Preliminary Views on Insurance Contracts* – was issued in May 2007, an Exposure Draft (2010 ED), *ED 2010/8 – Insurance Contracts* – was published in July 2010 and a revised Exposure Draft (revised ED), ED/2013/7 – *Insurance Contracts* – was published in June 2013. The revised ED and its subsequent deliberations are discussed at 12 below.

At the time of writing, the new insurance accounting standard (the Phase II standard, also referred to as IFRS 17 – *Insurance Contacts*) is expected to be issued by the IASB in 2017 with an effective date not before 2021.

Amendments made to IFRS 4 (designed to address concerns about the different effective dates of IFRS 9) and the forthcoming new insurance contract standard are discussed at 1.3 and 11 below.

1.2 The development of IFRS 4

IFRS 4 was the result of Phase I of the IASB's insurance contract project. It was finalised in a relatively short period by the IASB once it became clear that a standard was required in time for the EU adoption of IFRS in 2005. An exposure draft, ED 5 – *Insurance Contracts* – was issued in July 2003 with a comment period expiring on 31 October 2003. The IASB was extremely responsive to comment letters with most of the major concerns of the insurance industry being addressed in the final standard when it was issued in March 2004. IFRS 4 was first applicable for accounting periods beginning on or after 1 January 2005 with earlier adoption encouraged. *[IFRS 4.41]*.

One significant concern that the IASB was unable to address was the mismatching of financial assets and insurance liabilities. Under IAS 39, many financial investments are held at fair value and, if those assets are classified as available-for-sale, unrealised fair value movements are recognised in other comprehensive income. By contrast all movements in insurance liabilities are normally recognised in profit or loss and most non-life insurance liabilities under most existing local GAAP models are undiscounted. A number of respondents to ED 5 suggested the creation of an investment category called 'investments held to back insurance contracts' (or words similar to that). Investments in this category would be held at amortised cost. However, the IASB concluded that changing the measurement requirements for financial assets in IAS 39, even temporarily, would diminish the relevance and reliability of an insurer's financial statements. In the view of the IASB this mismatch is caused by imperfections in the insurance liability measurement model rather than deficiencies in the financial investments measurement model and hence the suggestion went no further. *[IFRS 4.BC166-174]*.

Although IFRS 4 has now been in force for twelve years the standard was intended originally to be a temporary one that would last no more than a few years. As discussed at 12 below, the Phase II standard is unlikely to be issued until 2017 and the effective date is unlikely to be before 2021.

1.3 Mitigating the impact on insurers of applying IFRS 9 before the new insurance accounting standard

The delay in issuing the Phase II standard has meant that the effective date of this new standard is expected to be three years after the effective date of IFRS 9. Consequently, the IASB was asked to address concerns that additional accounting mismatches and profit or loss volatility could result if IFRS 9 was applied before the Phase II standard. The IASB agreed that these concerns should be addressed and, in September 2016, issued *Applying IFRS 9 Financial Instruments with IFRS 4 Insurance Contracts* that amends IFRS 4 in order to address these concerns. These amendments are discussed at 11 below. An entity may apply these amendments for annual periods beginning on or after 1 January 2018.

Chapter 55

1.4 Existing accounting practices for insurance contracts

Existing local accounting practices for insurance contracts are diverse. Typically such practices, including the definition of what constitutes an insurance contract, are driven by regulatory requirements. There may also be separate GAAP and regulatory rules for insurers. For example, in the European Union, there are separate financial statement presentation requirements for insurance entities which differ from those for non-insurance entities.

Many jurisdictions have also evolved different accounting rules for non-life (property/casualty) or short-term insurance and life or long-term insurance. However, the boundaries between what is considered non-life and life insurance can vary between jurisdictions and even within jurisdictions.

1.4.1 Non-life insurance

Non-life or short-term insurance transactions under local GAAP are typically accounted for on a deferral and matching basis. This means that premiums are normally recognised as revenue over the contract period, usually on a time apportionment basis. Claims are usually recognised on an incurred basis with no provision for claims that have not occurred at the reporting date. Within this basic model differences exist across local GAAPs on various points of detail which include:

- whether or not claims liabilities are discounted;
- the basis for measuring claims liabilities (e.g. best estimate or a required confidence level);
- whether and what acquisition costs are deferred;
- whether a liability adequacy test (see 7.2.2 below) is performed on the unearned revenue or premium balance and the methodology and level of aggregation applied in such a test; and
- whether reinsurance follows the same model as direct insurance and whether immediate gains on retroactive reinsurance contracts are permitted or not (see 7.2.6 below).

1.4.2 Life insurance

Most local GAAP life insurance accounting models recognise premiums when receivable and insurance contract liabilities are typically measured under some form of discounted cash flow approach that calculates the cash flows expected over the lifetime of the contract. In many jurisdictions the key inputs to the calculation (e.g. discount rates, mortality rates) are set by regulators. Key assumptions may be current or 'locked-in' at the contract inception. Differences across jurisdictions also include:

- whether or not certain investment-type products are subject to 'deposit accounting' (i.e. only fees are recognised as revenue rather than all cash inflows from policyholders);
- if, and how (contracts with) discretionary participation features are accounted for (discussed at 6 below);
- whether and what acquisition costs are deferred;
- how to account for options and guarantees embedded within contracts; and
- the use of contingency reserves or provisions for adverse deviation.

1.4.3 Embedded value

The embedded value (EV) of a life insurance business is an estimate of its economic worth excluding any value which may be attributed to future new business. The EV is the sum of the value placed on the entity's equity and the value of the in-force business. Typically, an embedded value calculation would involve discounting the value of the stream of after tax profits. For insurance liabilities the income stream would normally be calculated by using the income stream from the backing invested assets as a proxy.

EV is used as an alternative (non-GAAP) performance measure by some life insurers to illustrate the performance and value of their business because local accounting is rarely seen as providing this information. This is because local accounting is often driven by what management consider are 'unrealistic' regulatory rules and assumptions. *[IFRS 4.BC140]*.

There is no standardised global measure of embedded value and embedded value practices are diverse. For example, in Europe, the CFO Forum, an organisation comprising the Chief Financial Officers of Europe's leading life and property and casualty insurers, has published both *European Embedded Values (EEV)* and *Market Consistent Embedded Value Principles (MCEV)*. Either of these embedded value models can be applied by Forum members.[2]

The potential use of embedded value under IFRS 4 is discussed at 8.2.4 below.

2 THE OBJECTIVES AND SCOPE OF IFRS 4

2.1 The objectives of IFRS 4

The stated objectives of IFRS 4 are:

(a) to make limited improvements to accounting by insurers for insurance contracts; and

(b) to require disclosures that identify and explain the amounts in an insurer's financial statements arising from insurance contracts and help users of those financial statements understand the amount, timing and uncertainty of future cash flows from insurance contracts. *[IFRS 4.1]*.

It is not IFRS 4's stated objective to determine, in a comprehensive way, how insurance contracts are recognised, measured and presented. This will be addressed by the Phase II standard. Instead, issuers of insurance contracts are permitted, with certain limitations, to continue to apply their existing, normally local, GAAP. This is discussed further at 7 below.

2.2 The scope of IFRS 4

2.2.1 Definitions

The following definitions are relevant to the application of IFRS 4. *[IFRS 4 Appendix A]*.

An *insurer* is the party that has an obligation under an insurance contract to compensate a policyholder if an insured event occurs.

An *insurance contract* is a contract under which one party (the insurer) accepts significant insurance risk from another party (the policyholder) by agreeing to compensate the policyholder if a specified uncertain future event (the insured event) adversely affects the policyholder.

A *reinsurer* is the party that has an obligation under a reinsurance contract to compensate a cedant if an insured event occurs.

A *reinsurance contract* is an insurance contract issued by one insurer (the reinsurer) to compensate another insurer (the cedant) for losses on one or more contracts issued by the cedant.

An *insured event* is an uncertain future event that is covered by an insurance contract and creates insurance risk.

An *insurance asset* is an insurer's net contractual rights under an insurance contract.

A *reinsurance asset* is a cedant's net contractual rights under a reinsurance contract.

An *insurance liability* is an insurer's net contractual obligations under an insurance contract.

A *cedant* is the policyholder under a reinsurance contract.

A *policyholder* is a party that has a right to compensation under an insurance contract if an insured event occurs.

Fair value is the price that would be received to sell an asset or paid to transfer a liability in an orderly transaction between market participants at the measurement date. This definition of fair value is the same as in IFRS 13 – *Fair Value Measurement*.

Guaranteed benefits are payments or other benefits to which a particular policyholder or investor has an unconditional right that is not subject to the contractual discretion of the issuer.

A *discretionary participation feature* (DPF) is a contractual right to receive, as a supplement to guaranteed benefits, additional benefits:

(a) that are likely to be a significant portion of the total contractual benefits;

(b) whose amount or timing is contractually at the discretion of the issuer; and

(c) that are contractually based on:

  (i) the performance of a specified pool of contracts or a specified type of contract;

  (ii) realised and/or unrealised investment returns on a specified pool of assets held by the issuer; or

  (iii) the profit or loss of the company, fund or other entity that issues the contract.

A *financial guarantee contract* is a contract that requires the issuer to make specified payments to reimburse the holder for a loss it incurs because a specified debtor fails to make payment when due in accordance with the original or modified terms of a debt instrument.

2.2.2 *Transactions within the scope of IFRS 4*

Unless specifically excluded from its scope (see 2.2.3 below) IFRS 4 must be applied to:

(a) insurance contracts (including reinsurance contracts) issued by an entity and reinsurance contracts that it holds; and

(b) financial instruments that an entity issues with a discretionary participation feature (see 6.2 below). *[IFRS 4.2]*.

It can be seen from this that IFRS 4 applies to insurance contracts and not just to entities that specialise in issuing insurance contracts. Consistent with other IFRSs it is a transaction-based standard. Consequently, non-insurance entities will be within its scope if they issue contracts that meet the definition of an insurance contract.

IFRS 4 describes any entity that issues an insurance contract as an insurer whether or not the entity is regarded as an insurer for legal or supervisory purposes. *[IFRS 4.5]*.

Often an insurance contract will meet the definition of a financial instrument but IAS 39 (and IFRS 9) contains a scope exemption for both insurance contracts and for contracts that would otherwise be within its scope but are within the scope of IFRS 4 because they contain a discretionary participation feature (see 6 below). *[IAS 39.2(e), IFRS 9.2.1(e)]*.

Although the recognition and measurement of financial instruments (or investment contracts) with a discretionary participation feature is governed by IFRS 4, for disclosure purposes they are within the scope of IFRS 7. *[IFRS 4.2(b)]*.

Contracts that fail to meet the definition of an insurance contract are within the scope of IAS 39 or IFRS 9 if they meet the definition of a financial instrument (unless they contain a DPF). This will be the case even if such contracts are regulated as insurance contracts under local legislation. These contracts are commonly referred to as 'investment contracts'.

Consequently, under IFRS, many insurers have different measurement and disclosure requirements applying to contracts that, under local GAAP or local regulatory rules, might, or might not, have been subject to the same measurement or disclosure requirements. The following table illustrates the standards applying to such contracts.

Type of contract	*Recognition and Measurement*	*Disclosure*
Insurance contract issued (both with and without a DPF)	IFRS 4	IFRS 4
Reinsurance contract held and issued	IFRS 4	IFRS 4
Investment contract with a DPF	IFRS 4	IFRS 7/IFRS 13
Investment contract without a DPF	IAS 39/IFRS 9	IFRS 7/IFRS 13

Many local GAAPs and local regulatory regimes prescribe different accounting requirements for life (long term) and non-life (short-term) insurance contracts (see 1.3 above). However, IFRS 4 does not distinguish between different types of insurance contracts.

IFRS 4 confirms that a reinsurance contract is a type of insurance contract and that all references to insurance contracts apply equally to reinsurance contracts. *[IFRS 4.6]*.

Because all rights and obligations arising from insurance contracts and investment contracts with a DPF are also scoped out of IAS 39 (and IFRS 9), IFRS 4 applies to all the assets and liabilities arising from insurance contracts. *[IAS 39.2(e), IFRS 9.2.1(e)]*. These include:

- insurance and reinsurance receivables owed by the policyholder direct to the insurer;
- insurance receivables owed by an intermediary to an insurer on behalf of the policyholder where the intermediary is acting in a fiduciary capacity;
- insurance claims agreed with the policyholder and payable;
- insurance contract policy liabilities;
- claims handling cost provisions;
- the present value of acquired in-force business (discussed at 9.1 below);
- deferred or unearned premium reserves;
- reinsurance assets (i.e. expected reinsurance recoveries in respect of claims incurred);
- deferred acquisition costs; and
- discretionary participation features (DPF).

However, payables and receivables arising out of investment contracts fall within the scope of IAS 39 (or IFRS 9) and the capitalisation and deferral of costs arising from such contracts currently fall within the scope of IAS 18, IAS 38 and IAS 39 (or IFRS 9).

Receivables due from intermediaries to insurers that have a financing character and balances due from intermediaries not acting in a fiduciary capacity, for example loans to intermediaries repayable from commissions earned, would also seem to be outside the scope of IFRS 4 as they do not arise from insurance contracts.

2.2.3 Transactions not within the scope of IFRS 4

IFRS 4 does not address other aspects of accounting by insurers, such as accounting for financial assets held by insurers and financial liabilities issued by insurers (which are within the scope of IAS 32, IAS 39, IFRS 7 and IFRS 9), except: *[IFRS 4.3]*.

- insurers that meet specified criteria are permitted to apply a temporary exemption from IFRS 9 for annual periods beginning on or after 1 January 2018 (see 11.1 below);
- insurers are permitted to apply what the IASB describes as the 'overlay approach' to designated financial assets for annual periods beginning on or after 1 January 2018 (see 11.2 below); and
- insurers are permitted to reclassify in specified circumstances some or all of their financial assets so that the assets are measured at fair value through profit or loss (see 8.4 below).

IFRS 4 also describes transactions to which IFRS 4 is not applied. These primarily relate to transactions covered by other standards that could potentially meet the definition of an insurance contract. It was not the intention of the IASB in issuing IFRS 4 to reopen issues addressed by other standards unless the specific features of insurance contracts justified a different treatment. *[IFRS 4.BC10(c)]*. These transactions are discussed below.

2.2.3.A Product warranties

Product warranties issued directly by a manufacturer, dealer or retailer are outside the scope of IFRS 4. These are accounted for under IAS 18 and IAS 37. *[IFRS 4.4(a)]*.

Without this exception many product warranties would have been covered by IFRS 4 as they would normally meet the definition of an insurance contract. The IASB has excluded them from the scope of IFRS 4 because they are closely related to the underlying sale of goods and because IAS 37 addresses product warranties while IAS 18 (or IFRS 15 – *Revenue from Contracts with Customers*) deals with the revenue received for such warranties. *[IFRS 4.BC71]*.

However, a product warranty is within the scope of IFRS 4 if an entity issues it on behalf of another party i.e. the contract is issued indirectly. *[IFRS 4.BC69]*.

Other types of warranty are not specifically excluded from the scope of IFRS 4. For example, a warranty given by a vendor to the purchaser of a business, such as in respect of contingent liabilities related to unagreed tax computations of the acquired entity, is an example of a transaction that may also fall within the scope of this standard. However, since IFRS 4 does not prescribe a specific accounting treatment, issuers of such warranties are likely to be able to apply their existing accounting policies.

2.2.3.B *Assets and liabilities arising from employment benefit plans*

Employers' assets and liabilities under employee benefit plans and retirement benefit obligations reported by defined benefit retirement plans are excluded from the scope of IFRS 4. These are accounted for under IAS 19 – *Employee Benefits*, IFRS 2 – *Share-based Payment* – and IAS 26 – *Accounting and Reporting by Retirement Benefit Plans*. *[IFRS 4.4(b)]*.

Many defined benefit pension plans and similar post-employment benefits meet the definition of an insurance contract because the payments to pensioners are contingent on uncertain future events such as the continuing survival of current or retired employees. Without this exception they would have been within the scope of IFRS 4.

2.2.3.C *Contingent rights and obligations related to non-financial items*

Contractual rights or contractual obligations that are contingent on the future use of, or right to use, a non-financial item (for example, some licence fees, royalties, contingent or variable lease payments and similar items) are excluded from the scope of IFRS 4, as well as a lessee's residual value guarantee embedded in a finance lease which is accounted for under IAS 17 – *Leases* (or in any lease accounted for under IFRS 16 – *Leases*). *[IFRS 4.4(c)]*.

2.2.3.D *Financial guarantee contracts*

Financial guarantee contracts are excluded from the scope of IFRS 4 unless the issuer has previously asserted explicitly that it regards such contracts as insurance contracts and has used accounting applicable to insurance contracts, in which case the issuer may elect to apply either IAS 32, IAS 39 (or IFRS 9) and IFRS 7 or IFRS 4 to them. The issuer may make that election contract by contract, but the election for each contract is irrevocable. *[IFRS 4.4(d)]*.

Where an insurer elects to use IFRS 4 to account for its financial guarantee contracts, its accounting policy defaults to its previous GAAP for such contracts (subject to any limitations discussed at 7.2 below) unless subsequently modified as permitted by IFRS 4 (see 8 below).

IFRS 4 does not elaborate on the phrase 'previously asserted explicitly'. However, the application guidance to IAS 39 and IFRS 9 states that assertions that an issuer regards contracts as insurance contracts are typically found throughout the issuer's communications with customers and regulators, contracts, business documentation and financial statements. Furthermore, insurance contracts are often subject to accounting requirements that are distinct from the requirements for other types of transaction, such as contracts issued by banks or commercial companies. In such cases, an issuer's financial statements typically include a statement that the issuer has used those accounting requirements. *[IAS 39.AG4A, IFRS 9.B2.6]*. Therefore, it is likely that insurers that have previously issued financial guarantee contracts and accounted for them under an insurance accounting and regulatory framework will meet these criteria. It is unlikely that an entity not subject to an insurance accounting and regulatory framework, or new insurers (start-up companies) and existing insurers that had not previously issued financial guarantee contracts would meet this criteria because they would not have previously made the necessary assertions.

Accounting for financial guarantee contracts by issuers that have not elected to use IFRS 4 is discussed in Chapter 43 at 3.4.2.

The approach to financial guarantee contracts in the revised ED is the same as IFRS 4. Therefore, entities would either account for financial guarantee contracts in accordance with the new insurance contract standard or in accordance with IFRS 9.

2.2.3.E *Contingent consideration payable or receivable in a business combination*

Contingent consideration payable or receivable in a business combination is outside the scope of IFRS 4. *[IFRS 4.4(e)]*. Contingent consideration in a business combination is required to be recognised at fair value at the acquisition date with subsequent remeasurements of non equity consideration included in profit or loss. *[IFRS 3.58]*.

2.2.3.F *Direct insurance contracts in which the entity is the policyholder*

Accounting by policyholders of direct insurance contracts (i.e. those that are not reinsurance contracts) is excluded from the scope of IFRS 4 because the IASB did not regard this as a high priority for Phase I. *[IFRS 4.4(f), BC73]*. However, holders of reinsurance contracts (cedants) are required to apply IFRS 4. *[IFRS 4.4(f)]*. The IASB originally intended to address accounting by policyholders of direct insurance contracts in the Phase II standard but changed its mind and excluded them from the revised ED on the grounds that there are 'no pressing reasons to address this topic'.[3]

A policyholder's rights and obligations under an insurance contract are also excluded from the scope of IAS 32, IAS 39 (or IFRS 9) and IFRS 7. However, the IAS 8 – *Accounting Policies, Changes in Accounting Estimates and Errors* – hierarchy does apply to policyholders when determining an accounting policy for direct insurance contracts. IAS 37 addresses accounting for reimbursements from insurers for expenditure required to settle a provision and IAS 16 – *Property, Plant and Equipment* – addresses some aspects of compensation from third parties for property, plant and equipment that is impaired, lost or given up. *[IFRS 4.BC73]*.

The principal outlined in IAS 37 is that reimbursements and contingent assets can only be recognised if an inflow of economic benefits is virtually certain. *[IAS 37.33, 56]*. IAS 16 requires that compensation from third parties for property, plant and equipment impaired, lost or given up is included in profit or loss when it 'becomes receivable'. *[IAS 16.66(c)]*. These are likely to be more onerous recognition tests than any applied under IFRS 4 for cedants with reinsurance assets which will be based on local insurance GAAP.

2.2.4 *The product classification process*

Because of the need to determine which transactions should be within the scope of IFRS 4, and which transactions are not within its scope, one of the main procedures required of insurers as part of their first-time adoption of IFRS 4 is to conduct a product classification review.

Many large groups developed a product classification process to determine the appropriate classification on a consistent basis. In order to ensure consistency, the product classification process is typically set out in the group accounting manual.

The assessment of the appropriate classification for a contract will include an assessment of whether the contract contains significant insurance risk (discussed at 3 below), and whether the contract contains embedded derivatives (discussed at 4 below), deposit components (discussed at 5 below) or discretionary participation features (discussed at 6 below).

The diagram below illustrates a product classification decision tree.

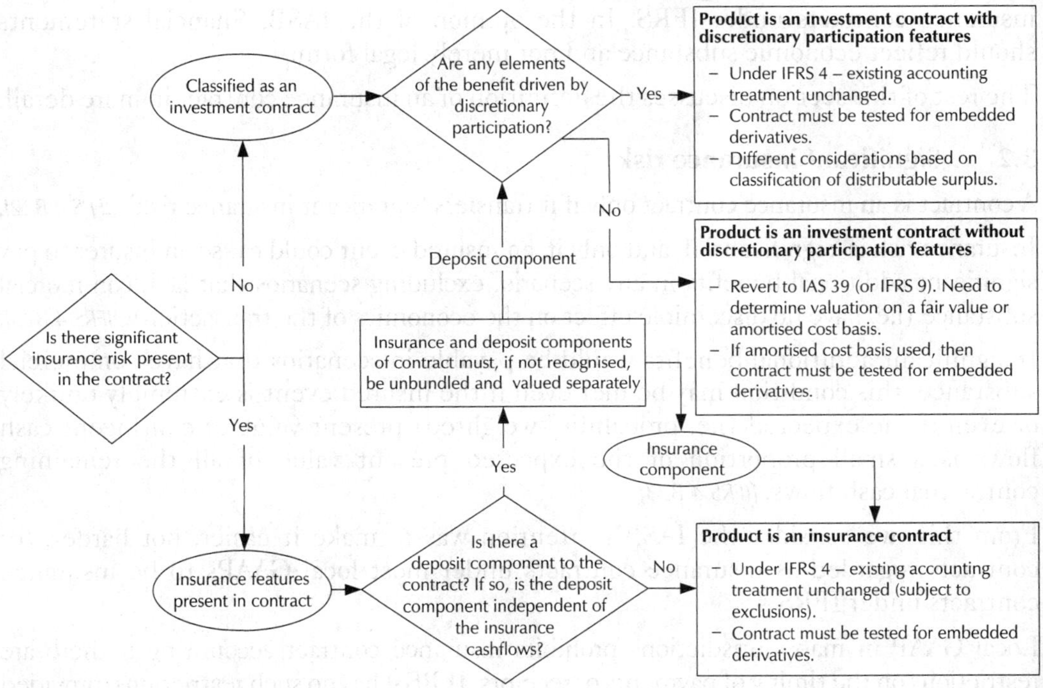

3 THE DEFINITION OF AN INSURANCE CONTRACT

3.1 The definition

The definition of an insurance contract in IFRS 4 is:

'A contract under which one party (the insurer) accepts significant insurance risk from another party (the policyholder) by agreeing to compensate the policyholder if a specified uncertain future event (the insured event) adversely affects the policyholder'. *[IFRS 4 Appendix A].*

This definition determines which contracts are within the scope of IFRS 4 rather than other standards.

The IASB rejected using existing national definitions because they believed it unsatisfactory to base the definition used in IFRS on definitions that may vary from country to country and may not be the most relevant for deciding which IFRS ought to apply to a particular type of contract. *[IFRS 4.BC12].*

In response to concerns that the definition in IFRS 4 could ultimately lead to changes in definitions used for other purposes, such as insurance law, insurance supervision or tax, the IASB made it clear that any definition within IFRS is solely for financial reporting and is not intended to change or pre-empt definitions used for other purposes. *[IFRS 4.BC13]*.

This means that contracts which have the legal form of insurance contracts in their country of issue are not necessarily insurance contracts under IFRS. Conversely, contracts which may not legally be insurance contracts in their country of issue can be insurance contracts under IFRS. In the opinion of the IASB, financial statements should reflect economic substance and not merely legal form.

The rest of this section discusses the definition of an insurance contract in more detail.

3.2 Significant insurance risk

A contract is an insurance contract only if it transfers 'significant insurance risk'. *[IFRS 4.B22]*.

Insurance risk is 'significant' if, and only if, an insured event could cause an insurer to pay significant additional benefits in any scenario, excluding scenarios that lack commercial substance (i.e. have no discernible effect on the economics of the transaction). *[IFRS 4.B23]*.

If significant additional benefits would be payable in scenarios that have commercial substance, this condition may be met even if the insured event is extremely unlikely or even if the expected (i.e. probability-weighted) present value of contingent cash flows is a small proportion of the expected present value of all the remaining contractual cash flows. *[IFRS 4.B23]*.

From this, we consider the IASB's intention was to make it easier, not harder, for contracts regarded as insurance contracts under most local GAAPs to be insurance contracts under IFRS 4.

Local GAAP in many jurisdictions prohibits insurance contract accounting if there are restrictions on the timing of payments or receipts. IFRS 4 has no such restrictions, provided there is significant insurance risk, although clearly the existence of restrictions on the timing of payments may mean that the policy does not transfer significant insurance risk.

3.2.1 The meaning of 'significant'

No quantitative guidance supports the determination of 'significant' in IFRS 4. This was a deliberate decision because the IASB considered that if quantitative guidance was provided it would create an arbitrary dividing line that would result in different accounting treatments for similar transactions that fall marginally on different sides of that line and would therefore create opportunities for accounting arbitrage. *[IFRS 4.BC33]*.

The IASB also rejected defining the significance of insurance risk by reference to the definition of materiality within IFRS because, in their opinion, a single contract, or even a single book of similar contracts, could rarely generate a loss that would be material to the financial statements as a whole. *[IFRS 4.BC34]*. The IASB also rejected the notion of defining significance of insurance risk by expressing the expected (probability weighted) average of the present values of the adverse outcomes as a proportion of the expected present value of all outcomes, or as a proportion of the premium. This idea would have required the constant monitoring of contracts over their life to see whether they continued to transfer insurance risk. As discussed at 3.3 below, an assessment of whether significant insurance risk has been transferred is normally only required at the inception of a contract. *[IFRS 4.BC35]*.

The IASB believes that 'significant' means that the insured benefits certainly must be greater than 101% of the benefits payable if the insured event did not occur and it expressed this in the implementation guidance as illustrated below. It is, however, unclear how much greater than 101% the insured benefits must be to meet the definition of 'significant'.

Example 55.1: Significant insurance risk

Entity A issues a unit-linked contract that pays benefits linked to the fair value of a pool of assets. The benefit is 100% of the unit value on surrender or maturity and 101% of the unit value on death.

In this situation the implementation guidance states that if the insurance component (the additional death benefit of 1%) is not unbundled then the whole contract is an investment contract. The insurance component in this arrangement is insignificant in relation to the whole contract and so would not meet the definition of an insurance contract in IFRS 4. *[IFRS 4.IG2 E1.3]*.

Some jurisdictions have their own guidance as to what constitutes significant insurance risk. However, as with IFRS 4, other jurisdictions offer no quantitative guidance. Some US GAAP practitioners apply a guideline that a reasonable possibility of a significant loss is a 10% probability of a 10% loss although this guideline does not appear in US GAAP itself. *[IFRS 4.BC32]*. It is not disputed in the basis for conclusions that a 10% chance of a 10% loss results in a transfer of significant insurance risk and, indeed, the words 'extremely unlikely' and 'a small proportion' (see 3.2 above) suggests to us that the IASB envisages that significant insurance risk can exist at a different threshold than a 10% probability of a 10% loss.

This lack of a quantitative definition means that insurers must apply their own judgement as to what constitutes significant insurance risk. Although the IASB did not want to create an 'arbitrary dividing line', the practical impact of this lack of guidance is that insurers have to apply their own criteria to what constitutes significant insurance risk and there probably is inconsistency in practice as to what these dividing lines are, at least at the margins.

There is no requirement under IFRS 4 for insurers to disclose any thresholds used in determining whether a contract has transferred significant insurance risk. However, IAS 1 – *Presentation of Financial Statements* – requires an entity to disclose the judgements that management has made in the process of applying the entity's accounting policies that have the most significant effect on the amounts recognised in the financial statements (see Chapter 3 at 5.1.1.B). Liverpool Victoria made the following disclosures about significant insurance risk in its 2013 financial statements.

Extract 55.1: Liverpool Victoria Friendly Society Limited (2013)

Notes to the financial statements [extract]
Note 1.3 **Accounting policies** [extract]
b. **Contract classification** [extract]

Insurance contracts are those contracts that transfer significant insurance risk. Such contracts may also transfer financial risk. As a general guideline, the Group defines as significant insurance risk the possibility of having to pay benefits on the occurrence of an insured event that are at least 10% more than the benefits payable if the insured event did not occur.

The revised ED contains application guidance which states that a contract does not transfer significant insurance risk if there is no scenario that has commercial substance in which the present value of the net cash flows paid by the issuer can exceed the present value of the premiums. However, if a reinsurance contract does not expose the issuer to the possibility of a significant loss, that contract would be deemed to transfer significant insurance risk if it transfers to the reinsurer substantially all of the insurance risk relating to the reinsured portions of the underlying insurance contracts. This would be a change from IFRS 4.[4] In subsequent discussions, the IASB has tentatively decided to clarify the guidance in the revised ED that significant insurance risk only occurs when there is a possibility that an issuer will incur a loss on a present value basis.[5]

3.2.2 *The level at which significant insurance risk is assessed*

Significant insurance risk must be assessed by individual contract, rather than by blocks of contracts or by reference to materiality to the financial statements. Thus, insurance risk may be significant even if there is a minimal probability of material losses for a whole book of contracts. *[IFRS 4.B25]*.

The IASB's reasons for defining significant insurance risk in relation to a single contract were that:

(a) although contracts are often managed and measured on a portfolio basis, the contractual rights and obligations arise from individual contracts; and

(b) an assessment contract by contract is likely to increase the proportion of contracts that qualify as insurance contracts. The IASB intended to make it easier, not harder, for a contract previously regarded as an insurance contract under local GAAP to meet the IFRS 4 definition. *[IFRS 4.BC34]*.

However, where a relatively homogeneous book of small contracts is known to consist of contracts that all transfer insurance risk, the standard does not require that an insurer examine each contract within that book to identify a few non-derivative contracts that transfer insignificant insurance risk. *[IFRS 4.B25]*.

Multiple, mutually linked contracts entered into with a single counterparty (or contracts that are otherwise interdependent) should be considered a single contract for the purposes of assessing whether significant insurance risk is transferred. *[IFRS 4.B25fn7]*. This requirement is intended to prevent entities entering into contracts that individually transfer significant insurance risk but collectively do not and accounting for part(s) of what is effectively a single arrangement as (an) insurance contract(s).

If an insurance contract is unbundled (see 5 below) into a deposit component and an insurance component, the significance of insurance risk transferred is assessed by reference only to the insurance component. The significance of insurance risk transferred by an embedded derivative is assessed by reference only to the embedded derivative (see 4 below). *[IFRS 4.B28]*.

3.2.2.A *Self insurance*

An insurer can accept significant insurance risk from a policyholder only if it issues an insurance contract to an entity separate from itself. Therefore, 'self insurance', such as a self-insured deductible where the insured cannot claim for losses below the excess limit of an insurance policy, is not insurance because there is no insurance contract. Accounting for self insurance and related provisions is covered by IAS 37 which requires that a provision is recognised only if there is a present obligation as a result of a past event, if it is probable that an outflow of resources will occur and a reliable estimate can be determined. *[IAS 37.14]*.

3.2.2.B Insurance mutuals

A mutual insurer accepts risk from each policyholder and pools that risk. Although policyholders bear the pooled risk collectively in their capacity as owners, the mutual has still accepted the risk that is the essence of an insurance contract and therefore IFRS 4 applies to those contracts. *[IFRS 4.B17]*.

3.2.2.C Intragroup insurance contracts

Where there are insurance contracts between entities in the same group these would be eliminated in the consolidated financial statements as required by IFRS 10 – *Consolidated Financial Statements*. If any intragroup insurance contract is reinsured with a third party that is not part of the group this third party reinsurance contract should be accounted for as a direct insurance contract in the consolidated financial statements of a non-insurer because the intragroup contract will be eliminated on consolidation. This residual direct insurance contract (i.e. the policy with the third party) is outside the scope of IFRS 4 from the viewpoint of the consolidated financial statements of a non-insurer because policyholder accounting is excluded from IFRS 4 as discussed at 2.2.3.F above.

3.2.3 Significant additional benefits

The 'significant additional benefits' described at 3.2 above refer to amounts that exceed those that would be payable if no insured event occurred. These additional amounts include claims handling and claims assessment costs, but exclude:

(a) the loss of the ability to charge the policyholder for future services, for example where the ability to collect fees from a policyholder for performing future investment management services ceases if the policyholder of an investment-linked life insurance contract dies. This economic loss does not reflect insurance risk and the future investment management fees are not relevant in assessing how much insurance risk is transferred by a contract;

(b) the waiver on death of charges that would be made on cancellation or surrender of the contract. Because the contract brought these charges into existence, the waiver of them does not compensate the policyholder for a pre-existing risk. Hence, they are not relevant in determining how much insurance risk is transferred by a contract;

(c) a payment conditional on an event that does not cause a significant loss to the holder of the contract, for example where the issuer must pay one million currency units if an asset suffers physical damage causing an insignificant economic loss of one currency unit to the holder. The holder in this case has transferred to the insurer the insignificant insurance risk of losing one currency unit. However, at the same time the contract creates non-insurance risk that the issuer will need to pay 999,999 additional currency units if the specified event occurs;

(d) possible reinsurance recoveries. The insurer will account for these separately; *[IFRS 4.B24]* and

(e) the original policy premium (but not additional premiums payable in the event of claims experience – see Example 55.26 below).

The definition of insurance risk refers to risk that the insurer accepts from the policyholder. Consequently, insurance risk must be a pre-existing risk transferred from the policyholder to the insurer. A new risk, such as the inability to charge the policyholder for future services, is not insurance risk. *[IFRS 4.B12]*. The following example illustrates this.

Example 55.2: Loan contract with prepayment fee

A loan contract contains a prepayment fee that is waived if the prepayment results from the borrower's death.

This is not an insurance contract since before entering into the contract the borrower faced no risk corresponding to the prepayment fee. Hence, although the loan contract exposes the lender to mortality risk, it does not transfer a pre-existing risk from the borrower. Thus, the risk associated with the possible waiver on death of the prepayment fee is not insurance risk. *[IFRS 4.IG2 E1.23]*.

It follows from this that if a contract pays a death benefit exceeding the amount payable on survival (excluding waivers under (b) above), the contract is an insurance contract unless the additional death benefit is insignificant (judged by reference to the contract rather than to an entire book of contracts). Similarly, an annuity contract that pays out regular sums for the rest of a policyholder's life is an insurance contract, unless the aggregate life-contingent payments are insignificant. In this case, the insurer could suffer a significant loss on an individual contract if the annuitant survives longer than expected. *[IFRS 4.B26]*.

Additional benefits could include a requirement to pay benefits earlier than expected if the insured event occurs earlier provided the payment is not adjusted for the time value of money. An example could be whole life insurance cover that provides a fixed death benefit whenever a policyholder dies. Whilst it is certain that the policyholder will die, the timing of death is uncertain and the insurer will suffer a loss on individual contracts when policyholders die early, even if there is no overall expected loss on the whole book of contracts. *[IFRS 4.B27]*.

3.3 Changes in the level of insurance risk

It is implicit within IFRS 4 that an assessment of whether a contract transfers significant insurance risk should be made at the inception of a contract. *[IFRS 4.B29]*. Further, a contract that qualifies as an insurance contract at inception remains an insurance contract until all rights and obligations are extinguished or expire. *[IFRS 4.B30]*. This applies even if circumstances have changed such that insurance contingent rights and obligations have expired. The IASB considered that requiring insurers to set up systems to continually assess whether contracts continue to transfer significant insurance risk imposed a cost that far outweighed the benefit that would be gained from going through the exercise. *[IFRS 4.BC38]*.

Conversely, contracts that do not transfer insurance risk at inception may become insurance contracts if they transfer insurance risk at a later time, as explained in the following example. This is because IFRS 4 imposes no limitations on when contracts can be assessed for significant insurance risk. The reclassification of contracts as insurance contracts occurs based on changing facts and circumstances, although there is no guidance on accounting for the reclassification.

Example 55.3: Deferred annuity with policyholder election

Entity A issues a deferred annuity contract whereby the policyholder will receive, or can elect to receive, a life-contingent annuity at rates prevailing when the annuity begins.

This is not an insurance contract at inception if the insurer can reprice the mortality risk without constraints. However, it will become an insurance contract when the annuity rate is fixed (unless the contingent amount is insignificant in all scenarios that have commercial substance). *[IFRS 4.IG2 E1.7].*

In practice, in the accumulation phase of an annuity, there are other guaranteed benefits such as premium refunds that might still make this an insurance contract prior to the date when the annuity rate is fixed.

Some respondents to ED 5 suggested that a contract should not be regarded as an insurance contract if the insurance-contingent rights and obligations expire after a very short time. The IASB considered that the requirement to ignore scenarios that lack commercial substance in assessing significant insurance risk and the fact that there is no significant transfer of pre-existing risk in some contracts that waive surrender penalties on death is sufficient to cover this issue. *[IFRS 4.BC39].*

IFRS 3 – *Business Combinations* – confirms that there should be no reassessment of the classification of contracts previously classified as insurance contracts under IFRS 4 which are acquired as a part of a business combination. *[IFRS 3.17(b)].*

3.4 Uncertain future events

Uncertainty (or risk) is the essence of an insurance contract. Accordingly, IFRS 4 requires at least one of the following to be uncertain at the inception of an insurance contract:

(a) whether an insured event will occur;

(b) when it will occur; or

(c) how much the insurer will need to pay if it occurs. *[IFRS 4.B2].*

An insured event will be one of the following:

- the discovery of a loss during the term of the contract, even if the loss arises from an event that occurred before the inception of the contract;
- a loss that occurs during the term of the contract, even if the resulting loss is discovered after the end of the contract term; *[IFRS 4.B3]* or
- the discovery of the ultimate cost of a claim which has already occurred but whose financial effect is uncertain. *[IFRS 4.B4].*

This last type of insured event arises from 'retroactive' contracts, i.e. those providing insurance against events which have occurred prior to the policy inception date. An example is a reinsurance contract that covers a direct policyholder against adverse development of claims already reported by policyholders. In this case the insured event is the discovery of the ultimate cost of those claims.

Local GAAP in some jurisdictions, including the US, prohibits the recognition of gains on inception of retroactive reinsurance contracts. IFRS 4 contains no such prohibition. Therefore, such gains would be recognised if that was required by an insurer's existing accounting policies. However, as discussed at 10.1.3 below, the amount of any such gains recognised should be disclosed.

3.5 Payments in kind

Insurance contracts that require or permit payments to be made in kind are treated the same way as contracts where payment is made directly to the policyholder. For example, some insurers replace an article directly rather than compensating the policyholder. Others use their own employees, such as medical staff, to provide services covered by the contract. *[IFRS 4.B5]*.

3.5.1 Service contracts

Some fixed-fee service contracts in which the level of service depends on an uncertain event may meet the definition of an insurance contract. However, in some jurisdictions these are not regulated as insurance contracts. For example, a service provider could enter into a maintenance contract in which it agrees to repair specified equipment after a malfunction. The fixed service fee is based on the expected number of malfunctions but it is uncertain whether a particular machine will break down. Similarly, a contract for car breakdown services in which the provider agrees, for a fixed annual fee, to provide roadside assistance or tow the car to a nearby garage could meet the definition of an insurance contract even if the provider does not agree to carry out repairs or replace parts. *[IFRS 4.B6]*.

In respect of the type of service contracts described above, their inclusion within IFRS 4 seems an unintended consequence of the definition of an insurance contract. However, the IASB stresses that applying IFRS 4 to these contracts should be no more burdensome than applying other IFRSs since:

(a) there are unlikely to be material liabilities for malfunctions and breakdowns that have already occurred;

(b) if the service provider applied accounting policies consistent with IAS 18, this would be acceptable either as an existing accounting policy or, possibly, an improvement of existing policies (see 8 below);

(c) whilst the service provider would be required to apply the liability adequacy test discussed at 7.2.2 below if the cost of meeting its contractual obligation to provide services exceeded the revenue received in advance, it would have been required to apply IAS 37 to determine whether its contracts were onerous if IFRS 4 did not apply; and

(d) the disclosure requirements in IFRS 4 are unlikely to add significantly to the disclosures required by other IFRSs. *[IFRS 4.B7]*.

The revised ED proposes to exclude from the scope of the standard fixed-fee service contracts that have, as their primary purpose, the provision of services and meet all of the following conditions:

- the entity does not reflect an assessment of the risk that is associated with an individual customer in setting the price of the contract with that customer;
- the contracts compensate customers by providing a service, rather than cash payment; and
- the insurance risk that is transferred by the contract arises primarily from the customer's use of services.

These contracts will be accounted for under the new revenue recognition standard.[6]

However, in subsequent discussions the IASB tentatively decided that entities should be permitted an accounting policy choice whether to apply IFRS 15 to the fixed fee service contracts that meet the criteria above or whether to account for these contracts under the new insurance accounting standard.[7]

3.6 The distinction between insurance risk and financial risk

The definition of an insurance contract refers to 'insurance risk' which is defined as 'risk, other than financial risk, transferred from the holder of a contract to the issuer'. *[IFRS 4 Appendix A]*.

A contract that exposes the reporting entity to financial risk without significant insurance risk is not an insurance contract. *[IFRS 4.B8]*. 'Financial risk' is defined as 'the risk of a possible future change in one or more of a specified interest rate, financial instrument price, foreign exchange rate, index of prices or rates, credit rating or credit index or other variable, provided in the case of a non-financial variable that variable is not specific to a party to the contract'. *[IFRS 4 Appendix A]*.

An example of a non-financial variable that is not specific to a party to the contract is an index of earthquake losses in a particular region or an index of temperature in a particular city. An example of a non-financial variable that is specific to a party to the contract is the occurrence or non-occurrence of a fire that damages or destroys an asset of that party.

The risk of changes in the fair value of a non-financial asset is not a financial risk if the fair value reflects not only changes in the market prices for such assets (a financial variable) but also the condition of a specific non-financial asset held by a party to the contract (a non-financial variable). For example if a guarantee of the residual value of a specific car exposes the guarantor to the risk of changes in that car's condition, that risk is insurance risk. *[IFRS 4.B9]*.

Chapter 55

Example 55.4: Residual value insurance

Entity A issues a contract to Entity B that provides a guarantee of the fair value at the future date of an aircraft (a non-financial asset) held by B. A is not the lessee of the aircraft (residual value guarantees given by a lessee under a lease within the scope of IAS 17 or IFRS 16).

This is an insurance contract (unless changes in the condition of the asset have an insignificant effect on its value). The risk of changes in the fair value of the aircraft is not a financial risk because the fair value reflects not only changes in market prices for similar aircraft but also the condition of the specific asset held.

However, if the contract compensated B only for changes in market prices and not for changes in the condition of B's asset, the contract would be a derivative and within the scope of IAS 39 or IFRS 9. *[IFRS 4.IG2 E1.15]*.

Contracts that expose the issuer to both financial risk and significant insurance risk can be insurance contracts. *[IFRS 4.B10]*.

Example 55.5: Contract with insurance and financial risk

Entity A issues a catastrophe bond to Entity B under which principal, interest payments or both are reduced significantly if a specified triggering event occurs and the triggering event includes a condition that B has suffered a loss.

The contract is an insurance contract because the triggering event includes a condition that B has suffered a loss, and contains an insurance component (with the issuer as policyholder and the holder as the insurer) and a deposit component. A discussion of the separation of these two components is set out at 5 below. *[IFRS 4.IG2 E1.20]*.

Contracts where an insured event triggers the payment of an amount linked to a price index are insurance contracts provided the payment that is contingent on the insured event is significant.

An example would be a life contingent annuity linked to a cost of living index. Such a contract transfers insurance risk because payment is triggered by an uncertain future event, the survival of the annuitant. The link to the price index is an embedded derivative but it also transfers insurance risk. If the insurance risk transferred is significant the embedded derivative meets the definition of an insurance contract (see 4 below for a discussion of derivatives embedded within insurance contracts). *[IFRS 4.B11]*.

3.7 Adverse effect on the policyholder

For a contract to be an insurance contract the insured event must have an adverse effect on the policyholder. In other words, there must be an insurable interest.

Without the notion of insurable interest the definition of an insurance contract would have encompassed gambling. The IASB believed that without this notion the definition of an insurance contract might have captured any prepaid contract to provide services whose cost is uncertain and that would have extended the scope of the term 'insurance contract' too far beyond its traditional meaning. *[IFRS 4.BC26-28]*. In the IASB's opinion the retention of insurable interest gives a principle-based distinction, particularly between insurance contracts and other contracts that happen to be used for hedging and they preferred to base the distinction on a type of contract rather than the way an entity manages a contract or group of contracts. *[IFRS 4.BC29]*.

The adverse effect on the policyholder is not limited to an amount equal to the financial impact of the adverse event. So, the definition includes 'new for old' coverage that replaces a damaged or lost asset with a new asset. Similarly, the definition does not limit payment under a term life insurance contract to the financial loss suffered by a deceased's dependents nor does it preclude the payment of predetermined amounts to quantify the loss caused by a death or accident. *[IFRS 4.B13]*.

A contract that requires a payment if a specified uncertain event occurs which does not require an adverse effect on the policyholder as a precondition for payment is not an insurance contract. Such contracts are not insurance contracts even if the holder uses the contract to mitigate an underlying risk exposure. Conversely, the definition of an insurance contract refers to an uncertain event for which an adverse effect on the policyholder is a contractual precondition for payment. This contractual precondition does not require the insurer to investigate whether the uncertain event actually caused an adverse effect, but permits the insurer to deny payment if it is not satisfied that the event caused an adverse effect. *[IFRS 4.B14]*.

The following example illustrates the concept of insurable interest.

Example 55.6: Reinsurance contract with 'original loss warranty' clause

Entity A agrees to provide reinsurance cover to airline insurer B for $5m against losses suffered. The claims are subject to an original loss warranty of $50m meaning that only losses suffered by B up to $5m from events exceeding a cost of $50m in total can be recovered under the contract. This is an insurance contract as B can only recover its own losses arising from those events.

If the contract allowed B to claim up to $5m every time there was an event with a cost exceeding $50m regardless of whether B had suffered a loss from that event then this would not be an insurance contract because there would be no insurable interest in this arrangement.

3.7.1 *Lapse, persistency and expense risk*

Lapse or persistency risk (the risk that the policyholder will cancel the contract earlier or later than the issuer had expected in pricing the contract) is not insurance risk because, although this can have an adverse effect on the issuer, the cancellation is not contingent on an uncertain future event that adversely affects the policyholder. *[IFRS 4.B15]*.

Similarly, expense risk (the risk of unexpected increases in the administrative costs incurred by the issuer associated with the serving of a contract, rather than the costs associated with insured events) is not insurance risk because an unexpected increase in expenses does not adversely affect the policyholder. *[IFRS 4.B15]*.

Therefore, a contract that exposes the issuer to lapse risk, persistency risk or expense risk is not an insurance contract unless it also exposes the issuer to significant insurance risk.

3.7.2 *Insurance of non-insurance risks*

If the issuer of a contract which does not contain significant insurance risk mitigates the risk of that contract by using a second contract to transfer part of that first contract's risk to another party, this second contract exposes that other party to insurance risk because the policyholder of the second contract (the issuer of the first contract) is subject to an uncertain event that adversely affects it and thus it meets the definition of an insurance contract. *[IFRS 4.B16]*. This is illustrated by the following example.

Example 55.7: Insurance of non-insurance risks

Entity A agrees to compensate Entity B for losses on a series of contracts issued by B that do not transfer significant insurance risk. These could be investment contracts or, for example, a contract to provide services.

The contract is an insurance contract if it transfers significant insurance risk from B to A, even if some or all of the underlying individual contracts do not transfer significant insurance risk to B. The contract is a reinsurance contract if any of the contracts issued by B are insurance contracts. Otherwise, the contract is a direct insurance contract. *[IFRS 4.IG2 E1.29]*.

3.8 Accounting differences between insurance and non insurance contracts

Making a distinction between insurance and non-insurance contracts is important because the accounting treatment will usually differ.

Insurance contracts under IFRS 4 will normally be accounted for under local GAAP (see 7 below). Typically, local GAAP (see 1.3 above) will recognise funds received or due from a policyholder as premiums (revenue) and amounts due to a policyholder as claims (an expense). However, if a contract does not transfer significant insurance risk and is therefore not an insurance contract under IFRS 4 it will probably be accounted for as an investment contract under IAS 39 (or IFRS 9). Under IAS 39 (or IFRS 9) the receipt of funds relating to financial assets or financial liabilities will result in the creation of a liability for the value of the remittance rather than a credit to profit or loss. This accounting treatment is sometimes called 'deposit accounting'. *[IFRS 4.B20]*.

A financial liability within the scope of IAS 39 (or IFRS 9) is measured at either amortised cost or fair value or possibly a mixture (e.g. if the instrument contains an embedded derivative). However, under IFRS 4, an insurance liability is measured under the entity's previous local GAAP accounting policies, unless these have been subsequently changed as discussed at 8 below. These may well result in the measurement of a liability that is different from that obtained by applying IAS 39 (or IFRS 9).

Additionally, the capitalisation of any acquisition costs related to the issuance of a contract is also likely to be different for insurance and investment contracts. IAS 18 (and IFRS 15) permits only incremental costs associated with obtaining an investment management contract to be capitalised. IAS 39 (or IFRS 9) requires transaction costs directly attributable to a financial asset or financial liability not at fair value through profit or loss to be included in its initial measurement. Transaction costs relating to financial assets and financial liabilities held at fair value through profit or loss are required to be expensed immediately. IFRS 4 does not provide any guidance as to what acquisition costs can be capitalised so reference to existing local accounting policies should apply (see 7.2.6.B below). In most cases, these will differ from the requirements outlined in IAS 18 (or IFRS 15) and IAS 39 (or IFRS 9).

If non-insurance contracts (see 3.9.2 below) do not create financial assets or financial liabilities then IAS 18 or IFRS 15 applies to the recognition of associated revenue. The principle outlined in IAS 18 is to recognise revenue associated with a transaction involving the rendering of services by reference to the stage of completion of the transaction if the revenue can be estimated reliably. The principle outlined in IFRS 15 is to recognise revenue associated with a transaction involving the rendering of services when (or as) an entity satisfies a performance obligation by transferring the promised service to a customer in an amount that reflects the consideration to which the entity expects to be entitled. *[IFRS 4.B21]*. This could differ from revenue recognition for insurance contracts measured under local GAAP.

3.9 Examples of insurance and non-insurance contracts

The section contains examples given in IFRS 4 of insurance and non-insurance contracts.

3.9.1 Examples of insurance contracts

The following are examples of contracts that are insurance contracts, if the transfer of insurance risk is significant:

(a) insurance against theft or damage to property;

(b) insurance against product liability, professional liability, civil liability or legal expenses;

(c) life insurance and prepaid funeral plans (although death is certain, it is uncertain when death will occur or, for some types of life insurance, whether death will occur within the period covered by the insurance);

(d) life-contingent annuities and pensions (contracts that provide compensation for the uncertain future event – the survival of the annuitant or pensioner – to assist the annuitant or pensioner in maintaining a given standard of living, which would otherwise be adversely affected by his or her survival);

(e) disability and medical cover;

(f) surety bonds, fidelity bonds, performance bonds and bid bonds (i.e. contracts that provide compensation if another party fails to perform a contractual obligation, for example an obligation to construct a building);

(g) credit insurance that provides for specified payments to be made to reimburse the holder for a loss it incurs because a specified debtor fails to make payment when due under the original or modified terms of a debt instrument. These contracts could have various legal forms, such as that of a guarantee, some types of letter of credit, a credit derivative default contract or an insurance contract. Although these contracts meet the definition of an insurance contract they also meet the definition of a financial guarantee contract and are within the scope of IAS 39 (or IFRS 9) and IFRS 7 and not IFRS 4 unless the issuer has previously asserted explicitly that it regards such contracts as insurance contracts and has used accounting applicable to such contracts (see 2.2.3.D above);

(h) product warranties issued by another party for goods sold by a manufacturer, dealer or retailer are within the scope of IFRS 4. However, as discussed at 2.2.3.A above, product warranties issued directly by a manufacturer, dealer or retailer are outside the scope of IFRS 4;

(i) title insurance (insurance against the discovery of defects in title to land that were not apparent when the contract was written). In this case, the insured event is the discovery of a defect in the title, not the title itself;

(j) travel assistance (compensation in cash or in kind to policyholders for losses suffered while they are travelling);

(k) catastrophe bonds that provide for reduced payments of principal, interest or both if a specified event adversely affects the issuer of the bond (unless the specified event does not create significant insurance risk, for example if the event is a change in an interest rate or a foreign exchange rate);

(l) insurance swaps and other contracts that require a payment based on changes in climatic, geological and other physical variables that are specific to a party to the contract; and

(m) reinsurance contracts. *[IFRS 4.B18]*.

These examples are not intended to be an exhaustive list.

The following illustrative examples provide further guidance on situations where there is significant insurance risk:

Example 55.8: Deferred annuity with guaranteed rates

Entity A issues a contract to a policyholder who will receive, or can elect to receive, a life-contingent annuity at rates guaranteed at inception.

This is an insurance contract unless the transfer of insurance risk is not significant. The contract transfers mortality risk to the insurer at inception, because the insurer might have to pay significant additional benefits for an individual contract if the annuitant elects to take the life-contingent annuity and survives longer than expected. *[IFRS 4.IG2 E1.6]*.

This example contrasts with Example 55.3 above where the rates were not set at the inception of the policy and therefore that was not an insurance contract at inception.

Example 55.9: Guarantee fund established by contract

A guarantee fund is established by contract. The contract requires all participants to pay contributions to the fund so that it can meet obligations incurred by participants (and, perhaps, others). Participants would typically be from a single industry, e.g. insurance, banking or travel.

The contract that establishes the guarantee fund is an insurance contract. *[IFRS 4.IG2 E1.13]*.

This example contrasts with Example 55.15 below where a guarantee fund has been established by law and not by contract.

Example 55.10: Insurance contract issued to employees related to a defined contribution pension plan

An insurance contract is issued by an insurer to its employees as a result of a defined contribution pension plan. The contractual benefits for employee service in the current and prior periods are not contingent on future service. The insurer also issues similar contracts on the same terms to third parties.

This is an insurance contract. However, if the insurer pays part or all of its employee's premiums, the payment by an insurer is an employee benefit within the scope of IAS 19 and is not accounted for under IFRS 4 because the insurer is the employer and would be paying its own insurance premiums. *[IFRS 4.IG2 E1.22]*.

Defined benefit pension liabilities are outside the scope of IFRS 4 as discussed at 2.2.3.B above.

Example 55.11: No market value adjustment for maturity benefits

A contract permits the issuer to deduct a market value adjustment (MVA), a charge which varies depending on a market index, from surrender values or death benefits to reflect current market prices for the underlying assets. It does not permit an MVA for maturity benefits.

The policyholder obtains an additional survival benefit because no MVA is applied at maturity. That benefit is a pure endowment because the insured person receives a payment on survival to a specified date but beneficiaries receive nothing if the insured person dies before then. If the risk transferred by that benefit is significant, the contract is an insurance contract. *[IFRS 4.IG2 E1.25]*.

Example 55.12: No market value adjustment for death benefits

A contract permits the issuer to deduct a market value adjustment (MVA) from surrender values or maturity payments to reflect current market prices for the underlying assets. It does not permit an MVA for death benefits.

The policyholder obtains an additional death benefit because no MVA is applied on death. If the risk transferred by that benefit is significant, the contract is an insurance contract. *[IFRS 4.IG2 E1.26].*

3.9.2 Examples of transactions that are not insurance contracts

The following are examples of transactions that are not insurance contracts:

(a) investment contracts that have the legal form of an insurance contract but do not expose the insurer to significant insurance risk, for example life insurance contracts in which the insurer bears no significant mortality risk;

(b) contracts that have the legal form of insurance, but pass all significant risk back to the policyholder through non-cancellable and enforceable mechanisms that adjust future payments by the policyholder as a direct result of insured losses, for example some financial reinsurance contracts or some group contracts;

(c) self insurance, in other words retaining a risk that could have been covered by insurance. There is no insurance contract because there is no agreement with another party (see 3.2.2.A above);

(d) contracts (such as gambling contracts) that require a payment if an unspecified uncertain future event occurs, but do not require, as a contractual precondition for payment, that the event adversely affects the policyholder. However, this does not preclude the specification of a predetermined payout to quantify the loss caused by a specified event such as a death or an accident (see 3.7 above);

(e) derivatives that expose one party to financial risk but not insurance risk, because they require that party to make payment based solely on changes in one or more of a specified interest rate, financial instrument price, commodity price, foreign exchange rate, index of prices or rates, credit rating or credit index or other variable, provide in the case of a non-financial variable that the variable is not specific to a party to the contract;

(f) a credit-related guarantee (or letter of credit, credit derivative default contract or credit insurance contract) that requires payments even if the holder has not incurred a loss on the failure of a debtor to make payments when due;

(g) contracts that require a payment based on a climatic, geological or other physical variable that is not specific to a party to the contract. These are commonly described as weather derivatives and are accounted for under IAS 39 (or IFRS 9); and

(h) catastrophe bonds that provide for reduced payments of principal, interest or both, based on a climatic, geological or other physical variable that is not specific to a party to the contract. *[IFRS 4.B19].*

The following examples illustrate further situations where IFRS 4 is not applicable.

Example 55.13: Investment contract linked to asset pool

Entity A issues an investment contract in which payments are contractually linked (with no discretion) to returns on a pool of assets held by the issuer.

This contract is within the scope of IAS 39 (or IFRS 9) because the payments are based on asset returns and there is no significant insurance risk. *[IFRS 4.IG2 E1.10].*

Example 55.14: Credit-related guarantee

Entity A issues a credit-related guarantee that does not, as a precondition for payment, require that the holder is exposed to, and has incurred a loss on, the failure of the debtor to make payments on the guaranteed asset when due.

This is a derivative within the scope of IAS 39 (or IFRS 9) because there is no insurable interest. *[IFRS 4.IG2 E1.12].*

Example 55.15: Guarantee fund established by law

Guarantee funds established by law exist in many jurisdictions. Typically they require insurers to contribute funds into a pool in order to pay policyholder claims in the event of insurer insolvencies. They may be funded by periodic (usually annual) levies or by levies only when an insolvency arises. The basis of the funding requirement varies although typically most are based on an insurer's premium income.

The commitment of participants to contribute to the fund is not established by contract so there is no insurance contract. Obligations to guarantee funds are within the scope of IAS 37. *[IFRS 4.IG2 E1.14].*

Example 55.16: Right to recover future premiums

Entity A issues an insurance contract which gives it an enforceable and non-cancellable contractual right to recover all claims paid out of future premiums, with appropriate compensation for the time value of money.

Insurance risk is insignificant because all claims can be recovered from future premiums and consequently the insurer cannot suffer a significant loss. Therefore the contract is a financial instrument within the scope of IAS 39 (or IFRS 9). *[IFRS 4.IG2 E1.18].*

Example 55.17: Catastrophe bond linked to index

Entity A issues a catastrophe bond in which principal, interest payments or both are reduced if a specified triggering event occurs and that triggering event does not include a condition that the issuer of the bond suffered a loss.

This is a financial instrument with an embedded derivative. Both the holder and the issuer should measure the embedded derivative at fair value through profit or loss under IAS 39 (or IFRS 9). *[IFRS 4.IG2 E1.19].*

Example 55.18: Insurance policy issued to defined benefit pension plan

Entity A issues an insurance contract to either (a) a defined benefit pension plan, covering the employees of A, and/or (b) the employees of another entity consolidated within the same group financial statements as A.

This contract will generally be eliminated on consolidation from the group financial statements which will include:

(a) the full amount of the pension obligation under IAS 19 with no deduction for the plan's right under the contract;

(b) no liability to policyholders under the contract; and

(c) the assets backing the contract. *[IFRS 4.IG2 E1.21].*

In January 2008, the Interpretations Committee considered a request for guidance on the accounting for investment or insurance policies that are issued by an entity to a pension plan covering its own employees (or the employees of an entity that is consolidated into the same group as the entity issuing the policy). The Interpretations Committee noted the definitions of plan assets, assets held by a long-term employee benefit plan and a qualifying insurance policy as defined by IAS 19 and considered that, if a policy was issued by a group company to the employee benefit fund then the treatment would depend on whether the policy was a 'non-transferable financial instrument issued by the reporting entity'. Since the policy was issued by a related party, the Interpretations Committee concluded that it could not meet the definition of a qualifying insurance policy as defined by IAS 19. Because of the narrow scope of this issue the Interpretations Committee declined to either issue an Interpretation or to add the issue to its agenda.[8]

Example 55.19: Market value adjustment without death or maturity benefits

A contract permits the issuer to deduct an MVA from surrender payments to reflect current market prices for the underlying assets. The contract does not permit a MVA for death and maturity benefits. The amount payable on death or maturity is the amount originally invested plus interest.

The policyholder obtains an additional benefit because no MVA is applied on death or maturity. However, that benefit does not transfer insurance risk from the policyholder because it is certain that the policyholder will live or die and the amount payable on death or maturity is adjusted for the time value of money. Therefore, the contract is an investment contract because there is no significant insurance risk. This contract combines the two features discussed in Examples 55.11 and 55.12 at 3.9.1 above. When considered separately, these two features transfer insurance risk. However, when combined, they do not transfer insurance risk. Therefore, it is not appropriate to separate this contract into two insurance components.

If the amount payable on death were not adjusted in full for the time value of money, or were adjusted in some other way, the contract might transfer insurance risk. *[IFRS 4.IG2 E1.27].*

4 EMBEDDED DERIVATIVES

Insurance contracts may contain policyholder options or other clauses that meet the definition of an embedded derivative under IAS 39 (or IFRS 9). A derivative is a financial instrument within the scope of IAS 39 (or IFRS 9) with all three of the following characteristics:

- its value changes in response to a change in a specified interest rate, financial instrument price, commodity price, foreign exchange rate, index of prices or rates, credit rating or credit index, or other variable, provided in the case of a non-financial variable that the variable is not specific to the underlying of the contract;
- it requires no initial net investment or an initial net investment that would be smaller than would be required for other types of contracts that would be expected to have a similar response to changes in market factors; and
- it is settled at a future date. *[IAS 39.9, IFRS 9 Appendix A].*

An embedded derivative is a component of a hybrid (combined) instrument that also includes a non-derivative host contract. An embedded derivative causes some or all of the cash flows that would otherwise be required by the contract to be modified according to a specified interest rate, financial instrument price, commodity price, foreign exchange rate, index of prices or rates, credit rating or credit index, or other variable provided that in the case of a non-financial variable that the variable is not specific to the party to the contract. *[IAS 39.10, IFRS 9.4.3.1]*.

The following are examples of embedded derivatives that may be found in insurance contracts:

- benefits, such as death benefits, linked to equity prices or an equity index;
- options to take life-contingent annuities at guaranteed rates;
- guarantees of minimum interest rates in determining surrender or maturity values;
- guarantees of minimum annuity payments where the annuity payments are linked to investment returns or asset prices;
- a put option for the policyholder to surrender a contract. These can be specified in a schedule, based on the fair value of a pool of interest-bearing securities or based on an equity or commodity price index;
- an option to receive a persistency bonus (an enhancement to policyholder benefits for policies that remain in-force for a certain period);
- an industry loss warranty where the loss trigger is an industry loss as opposed to an entity specific loss;
- a catastrophe trigger where a trigger is defined as a financial variable such as a drop in a designated stock market;
- an inflation index affecting policy deductibles;
- contracts where the currency of claims settlement differs from the currency of loss; and
- contracts with fixed foreign currency rates.

IAS 39 requires that an embedded derivative is separated from its host contract and measured at fair value with changes in fair value included in profit or loss if:

- its economic characteristics and risks are not closely related to the economic characteristics and risks of the host contract;
- it meets the definition of a derivative; and
- the combined instrument is not measured at fair value through profit or loss. *[IAS 39.11]*.

IFRS 9 has identical requirements, although they do not apply to contracts that are financial assets. *[IFRS 9.4.3.3]*.

The IASB considered and rejected arguments that insurers should be exempt from the requirement to separate embedded derivatives contained in a host insurance contract under IAS 39 (or IFRS 9) because, in the IASB's opinion, fair value is the only relevant measure for derivatives. *[IFRS 4.BC190]*.

However, the IASB decided to exclude derivatives embedded in an insurance contract from the IAS 39 (or IFRS 9) measurement requirements if the embedded derivative is itself an insurance contract. *[IFRS 4.7]*.

The IASB determined that it would be contradictory to require the measurement at fair value of an embedded derivative that met the definition of an insurance contract when such accounting is not required for a stand-alone insurance contract. Similarly, the IASB concluded that an embedded derivative is closely related to the host insurance contract if the embedded derivative and the host insurance contract are so interdependent that an entity cannot measure the embedded derivative separately. Without this conclusion IAS 39 (or IFRS 9) would have required an insurer to measure the entire insurance contract at fair value. *[IFRS 4.BC193]*.

This means that derivatives embedded within insurance contracts do not have to be separated and accounted for under IAS 39 (or IFRS 9) if the policyholder benefits from the embedded derivative only when the insured event occurs.

IFRS 4 also states that an insurer need not (but may) separate, and measure at fair value, a policyholder's option to surrender an insurance contract for a fixed amount (or for an amount based on a fixed amount and an interest rate) even if the exercise price differs from the carrying amount of the host insurance liability. This appears to overrule the requirement in IAS 39 (or IFRS 9) that a call, put or prepayment option embedded in a host insurance contract must be separated from the host insurance contract unless the option's exercise price is approximately equal on each exercise date to the carrying amount of the host insurance contract. *[IAS 39.AG30(g), IFRS 9.B4.3.5(e)]*. Because surrender values of insurance contracts often do not equal their amortised cost, without this concession in IFRS 4 fair value measurement of the surrender option would be required. *[IFRS 4.8]*. This relief also applies to investment contracts with a discretionary participation feature. *[IFRS 4.9]*.

The diagram below illustrates an embedded derivative decision tree.

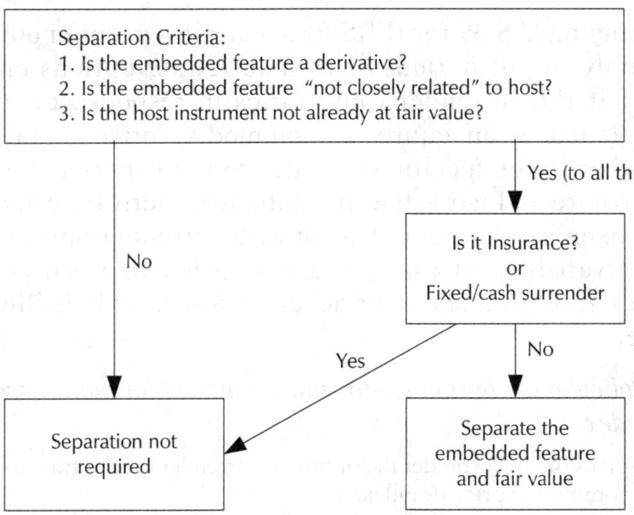

The example below illustrates an embedded derivative in an insurance contract that is not required to be separated and accounted for under IAS 39 (or IFRS 9).

Example 55.20: Death or annuitisation benefit linked to equity prices or index

A contract has a death benefit linked to equity prices or an equity index and is payable only on death or when annuity payments begin and not on surrender or maturity.

The equity-index feature meets the definition of an insurance contract (unless the life-contingent payments are insignificant) because the policyholder benefits from it only when the insured event occurs. The embedded derivative is not required to be separated for accounting purposes. *[IFRS 4.IG4 E2.1]*.

The following two examples illustrate the application of the concession that IFRS 4 gives from the requirements in IAS 39 (or IFRS 9) to separate and measure at fair value surrender options for which the exercise price is not amortised cost as discussed above.

Example 55.21: Life contingent annuity option

An insurance contract gives the policyholder the option to take a life-contingent annuity at a guaranteed rate i.e. a combined guarantee of interest rates and mortality changes.

The embedded option is an insurance contract (unless the life-contingent payments are insignificant) because the option is derived from mortality changes. Fair value measurement is not required but not prohibited even though the guaranteed rate may differ from the carrying amount of the insurance liability. *[IFRS 4.IG4 E2.3]*.

Example 55.22: Policyholder option to surrender contract for cash surrender value

An insurance contract gives the policyholder the option to surrender the contract for a cash surrender value specified in a schedule i.e. not indexed and does not accumulate interest.

Fair value measurement is not required (but not prohibited) because the surrender option is for a fixed amount even though that fixed amount may differ from the carrying amount of the insurance liability. The surrender value may be viewed as a deposit component, but IFRS 4 does not require an insurer to unbundle a contract if it recognises all its obligations arising under the deposit component (see 5 below).

If this was an investment contract measured at amortised cost then fair value measurement of the option would be required if the surrender value was not approximately equal to the amortised cost at each exercise date. *[IFRS 4.IG4 E2.12]*.

The relief from applying IAS 39 (or IFRS 9) to certain surrender options discussed above does not apply to put options or cash surrender options embedded in an insurance contract if the surrender value varies in response to the change in a financial variable (such as an equity or commodity price or index) or a non-financial variable that is not specific to a party to the contract. Furthermore, the requirement to separate and fair value the embedded derivative also applies if the holder's ability to exercise the put option or cash surrender option is triggered by a change in such a variable, for example a put option that can be exercised if a stock market index reaches a specified level. *[IFRS 4.8]*. This is illustrated by the following example.

Example 55.23: Policyholder option to surrender contract for value based on a market index

An insurance contract gives the policyholder the option to surrender the contract for a surrender value based on an equity or commodity price or index.

The option is not closely related to the host insurance contract because the surrender value is derived from an index and is not specific to a party to the contract. Therefore, measurement of the option at its fair value is required. *[IFRS 4.IG4 E2.14]*.

Embedded derivatives in insurance contracts are also required to be separated where they do not relate to insurance risk and are not otherwise closely related to the host contract. An example of this is illustrated below.

Example 55.24: Persistency bonus

An insurance contract gives policyholders a persistency bonus paid at maturity in cash (or as a period-certain maturity).

The embedded derivative (the option to receive the persistency bonus) is not an insurance contract because, as discussed at 3.7 above, insurance risk does not include lapse or persistency risk. Therefore, measurement of the option at its fair value is required. *[IFRS 4.IG4 E2.17]*.

If the persistency bonus was paid at maturity as an enhanced life-contingent annuity then the embedded derivative would be an insurance contract and separate accounting would not be required. *[IFRS 4.IG4 E2.18]*.

Non-guaranteed participating dividends contained in an insurance contract are discretionary participation features rather than embedded derivatives and are discussed at 6 below.

Although the relief given by IFRS 4 from the requirements of IAS 39 (or IFRS 9) to separately account for embedded derivatives is therefore significant, some derivatives embedded in insurance contracts may still be required to be separated from the host instrument and accounted for at fair value under IAS 39 (or IFRS 9) as illustrated in Examples 55.23 and 55.24 above. In some circumstances this can be a challenging and time consuming task.

The revised ED contains similar requirements to IFRS 4. It proposes that an entity should separate an embedded derivative from the host contract and account for the embedded derivative under IAS 39 (or IFRS 9) if, and only if:

- the economic characteristics and risks of the embedded derivative are not closely related to the economic characteristics and risks of the host contract; and
- a separate financial instrument with the same terms as the embedded derivative would meet the definition of a derivative and would be within the scope of IAS 39 or IFRS 9 (for example, the derivative itself is not an insurance contract).[9]

Chapter 55

4.1 Unit-linked features

A unit-linked feature (i.e. a contractual term that requires payments denominated in units of an internal or external investment fund) embedded in a host insurance contract (or financial instrument) is considered to be closely related to the host contract if the unit-denominated payments are measured at current unit values that reflect the fair values of the assets of the fund. *[IAS 39.AG33(g), IFRS 9.B4.3.8(g)]*.

IAS 39 (or IFRS 9) also considers that unit-linked investment liabilities should be normally regarded as puttable instruments that can be put back to the issuer at any time for cash equal to a proportionate share of the net asset value of an entity, i.e. they are not closely related. Nevertheless, the effect of separating an embedded derivative and accounting for each component is to measure the combined instrument at the redemption amount that is payable at the reporting date if the unit holders had exercised their right to put the instrument back to the issuer. *[IAS 39.AG32, IFRS 9.B4.3.7]*. This seems somewhat to contradict the fact that the unit-linked feature is regarded as closely related (which means no separation of the feature is required) but the accounting treatment is substantially the same.

5 UNBUNDLING OF DEPOSIT COMPONENTS

The definition of an insurance contract distinguishes insurance contracts within the scope of IFRS 4 from investments and deposits within the scope of IAS 39 (or IFRS 9). However, most insurance contracts contain both an insurance component and a 'deposit component'. *[IFRS 4.10]*. Indeed, virtually all insurance contracts have an implicit or explicit deposit component, because the policyholder is generally required to pay premiums before the period of the risk and therefore the time value of money is likely to be one factor that insurers consider in pricing contracts. *[IFRS 4.BC40]*.

A deposit component is 'a contractual component that is not accounted for as a derivative under IAS 39 (or IFRS 9) and would be within the scope of IAS 39 (or IFRS 9) if it were a separate instrument'. *[IFRS 4 Appendix A]*.

IFRS 4 requires an insurer to 'unbundle' those insurance and deposit components in certain circumstances, *[IFRS 4.10]*, i.e. to account for the components of a contract as if they were separate contracts. *[IFRS 4 Appendix A]*. In other circumstances unbundling is either allowed (but not required) or is prohibited.

Unbundling has the following accounting consequences:

(a) the insurance component is measured as an insurance contract under IFRS 4;

(b) the deposit component is measured under IAS 39 (or IFRS 9) at either amortised cost or fair value which may not be consistent with the measurement basis used for the insurance component;

(c) premiums for the deposit component are not recognised as revenue, but rather as changes in the deposit liability. Premiums for the insurance component are typically recognised as revenue (see 3.8 above); and

(d) a portion of the transaction costs incurred at inception is allocated to the deposit component if this allocation has a material effect. *[IFRS 4.12, BC41]*.

The IASB's main reason for making unbundling mandatory only in limited circumstances was to give relief to insurers from having to make costly systems changes. These changes might be needed to identify and separate the various deposit components that might exist in certain contracts (e.g. surrender values in traditional life insurance contracts) which may then need to be reversed in Phase II (see 11 below). However, the IASB generally regards unbundling as appropriate for all large customised contracts, such as some financial reinsurance contracts, because a failure to unbundle them might lead to the complete omission of material contractual rights and obligations from the statement of financial position. *[IFRS 4.BC44-46]*.

The revised ED proposes to require separation of any investment component of an insurance contract and account for it in accordance with IAS 39 or IFRS 9 if that investment component is distinct. An investment component is distinct if a contract with equivalent terms is sold, or could be sold, separately in the same market or same jurisdiction either by entities that issue insurance contracts or by other entities. However, if the investment component and insurance component are highly interrelated the entire contract would be accounted for as an insurance contract. This would be the case if:

- the entity is unable to measure the one without considering the other, e.g. the value of one component varies according to the value of the other; or
- the policyholder is unable to benefit from one component unless the other is also present, e.g. if the lapse or maturity of one component in a contract causes the lapse or maturity of the other.[10]

5.1 The unbundling requirements

Unbundling is required only if both the following conditions are met:

(a) the insurer can measure the deposit component (including any embedded surrender options) separately (i.e. without considering the insurance component); and

(b) the insurer's accounting policies do not otherwise require it to recognise all obligations and rights arising from the deposit component. *[IFRS 4.10(a)]*.

Unbundling is permitted, but not required, if the insurer can measure the deposit component separately as in (a) but its accounting policies require it to recognise all obligations and rights arising from the deposit component. This is regardless of the basis used to measure those rights and obligations. *[IFRS 4.10(b)]*.

Unbundling is prohibited when an insurer cannot measure the deposit component separately. *[IFRS 4.10(c)]*.

Example 55.25: Unbundling

A cedant receives compensation for losses from a reinsurer but the contract obliges the cedant to repay the compensation in future years. That obligation arises from a deposit component.

If the cedant's accounting policies would otherwise permit it to recognise the compensation as income without recognising the resulting obligation, unbundling is required. *[IFRS 4.11]*.

5.2 Unbundling illustration

The implementation guidance accompanying IFRS 4 provides an illustration of the unbundling of the deposit component of a reinsurance contract which is reproduced in full below.

Example 55.26: Unbundling a deposit component of a reinsurance contract

Background

A reinsurance contract has the following features:

(a) the cedant pays premiums of CU10 every year for five years;

(b) an 'experience account' is established equal to 90% of the cumulative premiums (including the additional premiums discussed in (c) below) less 90% of the cumulative claims;

(c) if the balance in the experience account is negative (i.e. cumulative claims exceed cumulative premiums), the cedant pays an additional premium equal to the experience account balance divided by the number of years left to run on the contract;

(d) at the end of the contract, if the experience account balance is positive (i.e. cumulative premiums exceed cumulative claims), it is refunded to the cedant; if the balance is negative, the cedant pays the balance to the reinsurer as an additional premium;

(e) neither party can cancel the contract before maturity; and

(f) the maximum loss that the reinsurer is required to pay in any period is CU200.

The contract is an insurance contract because it transfers significant risk to the reinsurer. For example, in case 2 discussed below, the reinsurer is required to pay additional benefits with a present value, in year 1, of CU35, which is clearly significant in relation to the contract.

The following discussion addresses the accounting by the reinsurer. Similar principles apply to the accounting by the cedant.

Application of requirements: case 1 – no claims

If there are no claims, the cedant will receive CU45 in year 5 (90% of the cumulative premiums of CU50). In substance, the cedant has made a loan, which the reinsurer will repay in one instalment of CU45 in year 5.

If the reinsurer's accounting policies require it to recognise its contractual liability to repay the loan to the cedant, unbundling is permitted but not required. However, if the reinsurer's accounting policies would not require it to recognise the liability to repay the loan, the reinsurer is required to unbundle the contract.

If the reinsurer is required, or elects, to unbundle the contract, it does so as follows. Each payment by the cedant has two components: a loan advance (deposit component) and a payment for insurance cover (insurance component). Applying IAS 39 or IFRS 9 to the deposit component, the reinsurer is required to measure it initially at fair value. Fair value could be determined by discounting the future cash flows from the deposit component. Assume that an appropriate discount rate is 10% and that the insurance cover is equal in each year, so that the payment for insurance cover is the same in each year. Each payment of CU10 by the cedant is then made up of a loan advance of CU6.7 and an insurance premium of CU3.3.

The reinsurer accounts for the insurance component in the same way it accounts for a separate insurance contract with an annual premium of CU3.3.

The movements in the loan are shown below.

Year	Opening balance	Interest at 10%	Advance (repayment)	Closing balance
	CU	CU	CU	CU
0	0.00	0.00	6.70	6.70
1	6.70	0.67	6.70	14.07
2	14.07	1.41	6.70	22.18
3	22.18	2.21	6.70	31.09
4	31.09	3.11	6.70	40.90
5	40.90	4.10	(45.00)	0.00
Total		11.50	(11.50)	

Application of requirements: case 2 – claim of CU150 in year 1

Consider now what happens if the reinsurer pays a claim of CU150 in year 1. The changes in the experience account, and the resulting additional premiums, are as follows:

Year	Premium	Additional premium	Total premium	Cumulative premium	Claims	Cumulative claims	Cumulative premiums less claims	Experience account
	CU	CU	CU	CU	CU	CU	CU	CU
0	10	0	10	10	0	0	10	9
1	10	0	10	20	(150)	(150)	(130)	(117)
2	10	39	49	69	0	(150)	(81)	(73)
3	10	36	46	115	0	(150)	(35)	(31)
4	10	31	41	156	0	(150)	6	6
Total		106	156		(150)			

Incremental cash flows because of the claim in year 1

The claim in year 1 leads to the following incremental cash flows, compared with case 1:

Year	Additional premium	Claims	Refund in case 2	Refund in case 1	Net incremental cash flow	Present value at 10%
	CU	CU	CU	CU	CU	CU
0	0	0			0	0
1	0	(150)			(150)	(150)
2	39	0			39	35
3	36	0			36	30
4	31	0			31	23
5	0	0	(6)	(45)	39	27
Total	106	(150)	(6)	(45)	(5)	(35)

The incremental cash flows have a present value, in year 1, of CU35 (assuming a discount rate of 10% is appropriate). Applying paragraphs 10-12 of IFRS 4, the cedant unbundles the contract and applies IAS 39 or IFRS 9 to this deposit component (unless the cedant already recognises its contractual obligation to repay the deposit component to the reinsurer). If this were not done, the cedant might recognise the CU150 received in year 1 as income and the incremental payments in years 2-5 as expenses. However, in substance, the reinsurer has paid a claim of CU35 and made a loan of CU115 (CU150 less CU35) that will be repaid in instalments.

The following table shows the changes in the loan balance. The table assumes that the original loan shown in case 1 and the new loan shown in case 2 meet the criteria for offsetting in IAS 32. Amounts shown in the table are rounded.

Year	Opening balance	Interest at 10%	Payments per original schedule	Additional payments in case 2	Closing balance
	CU	CU	CU	CU	CU
0	–	–	6	–	6
1	6	1	7	(115)	(101)
2	(101)	(10)	7	39	(65)
3	(65)	(7)	7	36	(29)
4	(29)	(3)	6	31	5
5	5	1	(45)	39	0
Total		(18)	(12)	30	

Although the example refers to 'in year' the calculations indicate that most of the cash flows occur at the end of each year. The present value table showing the incremental cash flows resulting from the claim 'in year 1' appear to show the present values at the end of year 1. *[IFRS 4.IG5 E3]*.

5.3 Practical difficulties

In unbundling a contract the principal difficulty is identifying the initial fair value of any deposit component. In the IASB's illustration at 5.2 above a discount rate is provided but in practice contracts will not have a stated discount rate. The issuer and the cedant will therefore have to determine an appropriate discount rate in order to calculate the fair value of the deposit component. The IASB illustration is also unclear as to whether the discount rate is a risk adjusted rate. Fair value measurement would require an adjustment for credit risk.

However, the potential burden on insurers is reduced by the fact that the IASB has limited the requirement to unbundle to only those contracts where the rights and obligations arising from the deposit component are not recognised under insurance accounting. As noted above the IASB is principally concerned with ensuring that large reinsurance contracts with a significant financing element have all of their obligations properly recorded, although the requirements apply equally to direct insurance contracts. *[IFRS 4.IG5]*.

Some examples of clauses within insurance contracts that might indicate the need for unbundling are:

- 'funds withheld' clauses where part or all of the premium is never paid to the reinsurer or claims are never received;
- 'no claims bonus', 'profit commission' or 'claims experience' clauses which guarantee that the cedant will receive a refund of some of the premium;
- 'experience accounts' used to measure the profitability of the contract. These are often segregated from other funds and contain interest adjustments that may accrue to the benefit of the policyholder;
- 'finite' clauses that limit maximum losses or create a 'corridor' of losses not reinsured under a contract;
- contracts that link the eventual premium to the level of claims;
- commutation clauses whose terms guarantee that either party will receive a refund of amounts paid under the contract; and
- contracts of unusual size where the economic benefits to either party are not obviously apparent.

The unbundling requirements in IFRS 4 do not specifically address the issue of contracts artificially separated through the use of side letters, the separate components of which should be considered together. The IASB believes that it is a wider issue for a future project on linkage (accounting for separate transactions that are connected in some way). However, IFRS 4 does state that linked contracts entered into with a single counterparty (or contracts that are otherwise interdependent) form a single contract, for the purposes of assessing whether significant insurance risk is transferred, although the standard is silent on linked transactions with different counterparties (see 3.2.2 above). *[IFRS 4.BC54]*.

6 DISCRETIONARY PARTICIPATION FEATURES

A discretionary participation feature (DPF) is a contractual right to receive, as a supplement to guaranteed benefits, additional benefits:

(a) that are likely to be a significant portion of the total contractual benefits;

(b) whose amount or timing is contractually at the discretion of the issuer; and

(c) that are contractually based on:

   (i) the performance of a specified pool of contracts or a specified type of contract;

   (ii) realised and/or unrealised investment returns on a specified pool of assets held by the issuer; or

   (iii) the profit or loss of the company, fund or other entity that issues the contract. *[IFRS 4 Appendix A]*.

Guaranteed benefits are payments or other benefits to which the policyholder or investor has an unconditional right that is not subject to the contractual discretion of the issuer. Guaranteed benefits are always accounted for as liabilities.

Insurance companies in many countries have issued contracts with discretionary participation features. For example, in Germany, insurance companies must return to the policyholders at least 90% of the investment profits on certain contracts, but may give more. In France, Italy, the Netherlands and Spain, realised investment gains are distributed to the policyholder, but the insurance company has discretion over the timing of realising the gains. In the United Kingdom, bonuses are added to the policyholder account at the discretion of the insurer. These are normally based on the investment return generated by the underlying assets but sometimes include allowance for profits made on other contracts. The following are two examples of contracts with a DPF.

Example 55.27: Unitised with-profits policy

Premiums paid by the policyholder are used to purchase units in a 'with-profits' fund at the current unit price. The insurer guarantees that each unit added to the fund will have a minimum value which is the bid price of the unit. This is the guaranteed amount. In addition, the insurer may add two types of bonus to the with-profits units. These are a regular bonus, which may be added daily as a permanent increase to the guaranteed amount, and a final bonus that may be added on top of those guaranteed amounts when the with-profits units are cashed in. Levels of regular and final bonuses are adjusted twice per year. Both regular and final bonuses are discretionary amounts and are generally set based on expected future returns generated by the funds.

Example 55.28: DPF policy with minimum interest rates

An insurance contract provides that the insurer must annually credit each policyholder's 'account' with a minimum interest rate (3%). This is the guaranteed amount. The insurer then has discretion with regard to whether and what amount of the remaining undistributed realised investment returns from the assets backing the participating policies are distributed to policyholders in addition to the minimum. The contract states that the insurer's shareholders are only entitled to share up to 10% in the underlying investment results associated with the participating policies. As that entitlement is up to 10%, the insurer can decide to credit the policyholders with more than the minimum sharing rate of 90%. Once any additional interest above the minimum interest rate of 3% is credited to the policyholder it becomes a guaranteed liability.

DPF can appear in both insurance contracts and investment contracts. However, to qualify as a DPF, the discretionary benefits must be likely to be a 'significant' portion of the total contractual benefits. The standard does not quantify what is meant by 'significant' but it could be interpreted in the same sense as in the definition of an insurance contract (see 3.2.1 above).

The definition of a DPF does not capture an unconstrained contractual discretion to set a 'crediting rate' that is used to credit interest or other returns to policyholders (as found in contracts described in some countries as 'universal life' contracts). For example, some contracts may not meet the criterion of (c) above if the discretion to set crediting rates is not contractually bound to the performance of a specified pool of assets or the profit or loss of the entity or fund that issues the contract. The IASB, however, acknowledges that some view these features as similar to a DPF because crediting rates are constrained by market forces and it proposed to revisit the treatment of these features in Phase II. *[IFRS 4.BC162]*. However, the revised ED does not specifically revisit the treatment of these features. That is because the definition of DPF has been changed (see below).

With contracts that have discretionary features, the issuer has discretion over the amount and/or timing of distributions to policyholders although that discretion may be subject to some contractual constraints (including related legal and regulatory constraints) and competitive constraints. Distributions are typically made to policyholders whose contracts are still in force when the distribution is made. Thus, in many cases, a change in the timing of a distribution, apart from the change in the value over time, means that a different generation of policyholders might benefit. *[IFRS 4.BC154]*.

Although the issuer has contractual discretion over distributions it is usually likely that current or future policyholders will ultimately receive some, if not most, of the accumulated surplus available at the reporting date. In Example 55.28 above policyholders are contractually entitled to a minimum of 90% of any discretionary distribution. Management can decide on any (total) amount. The main accounting question is whether that part of the discretionary surplus is a liability or a component of equity. *[IFRS 4.BC155]*.

The problem caused by discretionary features is that it is difficult to argue they meet the definition of a liability under IFRS. However, they can be integral to the economics of a contract and would clearly have to be considered in determining its fair value.

The definition of a liability in the IASB's *Conceptual Framework for Financial Reporting* ('*Framework*') requires there to be a present obligation. An obligation is a duty or responsibility to act or perform in a certain way. *[Framework 4.15]*. This can be contractual or constructive. However, a financial liability under IAS 32 must be a 'contractual obligation' *[IAS 32.11]* and discretionary obligations normally would not meet this requirement because of their discretionary nature.

IAS 37 requires provisions to be established once an 'obligating event' has occurred. Obligating events can be constructive but constructive obligations do require an entity to have indicated its responsibilities to other parties by an established pattern of past practice, published policies, or a sufficiently specific current statement, such that the entity has created a valid expectation on the part of those other parties that it will discharge those responsibilities. *[IAS 37.10]*. Say, for example, that an entity has previously paid discretionary bonuses to policyholders in the past five years of 5%, 15%, 0%, 10% and 5%. What 'valid expectation' has it created at the reporting date to policyholders in the absence of any public statement of management intent or, say, a published policy that discretionary bonuses will be linked to a particular profit figure?

If a DPF does not meet the definition of a liability then, under IAS 32, it would default to being equity, which is the residual interest in an entity's assets after deduction of its liabilities. This appears counter-intuitive and would result in discretionary distributions to policyholders being recorded as equity transactions outside of profit or loss or other comprehensive income. Taking this approach, a contract with a DPF would be bifurcated between liability and equity components like a bond convertible into equity shares.

The IASB's response to this difficult conceptual issue is to ignore it altogether in IFRS 4 and permit entities to have a choice as to whether to present contracts with a DPF within liabilities or equity. The difficult decisions have been deferred until Phase II. The IASB considers that the factor making it difficult to determine the appropriate accounting for these features is 'constrained discretion', being the combination of discretion and constraints on that discretion. If participation features lack discretion they are embedded derivatives and are within the scope of IAS 39. *[IFRS 4.BC161]*.

There may be timing differences between accumulated profits under IFRS and distributable surplus (i.e. the accumulated amount that is contractually eligible for distribution to holders of a DPF), for example, because distributable surplus excludes unrealised investment gains that are recognised under IAS 39 or IFRS 9. IFRS 4 does not address the classification of such timing differences. *[IFRS 4.BC160]*.

In November 2005, the Interpretations Committee rejected a request for further interpretative guidance on the definition of a DPF. The Interpretations Committee had been informed of concerns that a narrow interpretation of a DPF would fail to ensure clear and comprehensive disclosure about contracts that included these features. In response, the Interpretations Committee noted that disclosure was particularly important in this area, drawing attention to the related implementation guidance, discussed at 10 below, but declined to add the topic to its agenda because it involved some of the most difficult questions that the IASB will need to resolve in Phase II.[11]

In January 2010, the Interpretations Committee also rejected a request to provide guidance on whether features contained in ownership units issued by certain Real Estate Investment Trusts (REITs) met the definition of a DPF. In some of the trusts, the contractual terms of the ownership units require the REIT to distribute 90% of the Total Distributable Income (TDI) to investors. The remaining 10% may be distributed at the discretion of management. The request was to provide guidance on whether the discretion to distribute the remaining 10% of TDI met the definition of a DPF. If so, IFRS 4 would permit the ownership units to be classified as a liability in its entirety rather than a compound instrument with financial liability and equity components under IAS 32. The Interpretations Committee noted that the definition of a DPF in IFRS 4 requires, among other things, that the instrument provides the holder with guaranteed benefits and that the DPF benefits are in addition to these guaranteed benefits. Furthermore, it noted that such guaranteed benefits were typically found in insurance contracts. In other words, the Interpretations Committee was very sceptical about this presentation. However, it considered that providing guidance on this issue would be in the nature of application rather than interpretive guidance and therefore declined to add the issue to its agenda.[12]

The lack of interpretative guidance as to what constitutes a DPF has led to diversity in practice as to what is recognised as a DPF liability. For example, IFRS 4 is silent as to whether that part of an undistributed surplus on a participating contract which does not belong to policyholders should be treated as a liability or equity. This is illustrated by the following example.

Example 55.29: DPF recognition

A minimum of 90% of an investment surplus on a participating contract may be distributed to policyholders although any distribution is entirely at the discretion of the insurer. However, IFRS 4 is silent as to whether the 10% of the surplus which does not belong to policyholders is part of the DPF if it has not been distributed and consequentially there is diversity in practice among insurers as to whether the undistributed DPF liability includes the amount attributable to shareholders. Some insurers recognise the 90% as a liability and the 10% as a component of equity whereas others recognise the entire 100% as a liability until it is distributed.

The revised ED states that an investment contract with a DPF is within the scope of the proposed insurance contract standard provided that the reporting entity also issues insurance contracts, which is a change from IFRS 4. All insurance contracts, both with and without a DPF, are within the scope of the revised ED. Compared with the definition of a DPF in IFRS 4, the definition of an investment contract with a DPF in the revised ED requires that the additional returns must be contractually based on the returns from a specified pool of *insurance* contracts or a specified type of *insurance* contract rather just a contract or contracts *per se*.[13]

In subsequent discussions on accounting for participating contracts, the IASB has tentatively decided to create a class of participating contracts described as 'contracts with direct participation features' which will be eligible for a measurement model described as the 'variable fee' approach (discussed at 12.4 below). These are contracts for which:

- the contractual terms specify that the policyholder participates in a defined share of a clearly identified pool of underlying items;
- the entity expects to pay to the policyholder an amount equal to a substantial share of the returns from the underlying items; and
- a substantial proportion of the cash flows that the entity expects to pay to the policyholder should be expected to vary with the cash flows from the underlying items.[14]

By default, participating contracts not eligible for the 'variable fee' approach will be accounted for under the general model for insurance contracts.

6.1 Discretionary participation features in insurance contracts

Whilst IFRS 4 permits previous accounting practices for insurance contracts (see 7 below), the IASB considered there was a need to specify special accounting requirements for DPF features within these contracts. This might seem odd but the IASB's main concerns were:

- to prevent insurers classifying contracts with a DPF as an intermediate category that is neither liability nor equity as may have been permitted under some existing local accounting practices, such an intermediate category being incompatible with the *Framework*; *[IFRS 4.BC157]* and
- to ensure consistency with the treatment of DPF in investment contracts. *[IFRS 4.BC158]*.

IFRS 4 requires any guaranteed element (i.e. the obligation to pay guaranteed benefits included in a contract that contains a DPF) within an insurance contract to be recognised as a liability. However, insurers have an option as to whether to present a DPF either as a liability or as a component of equity. The following requirements apply:

(a) where the guaranteed element is not recognised separately from the DPF the whole contract must be classified as a liability;

(b) where the DPF is recognised separately from the guaranteed element the DPF can be classified as either a liability or as equity. IFRS 4 does not specify how an insurer determines whether the DPF is a liability or equity. The insurer may split the DPF into liability and equity components but must use a consistent accounting policy for such a split; and

(c) a DPF cannot be classified as an intermediate category that is neither liability nor equity. *[IFRS 4.34(a)-(b)]*.

An insurer may recognise all premiums received as revenue without separating any portion that relates to the equity component. *[IFRS 4.34(c)]*. The use of the word 'may' means that an insurer can classify some of the DPF as equity but continue to record all of the contract premiums as income. Conceptually, the IASB has admitted that if part or all of the DPF is classified as a component of equity, then the related portion of the premium should not be included in profit or loss. However, it concluded that requiring each incoming premium on a contract with a DPF to be split between liability and equity would requires systems changes beyond the scope of Phase I. Therefore, it decided that an issuer could recognise the entire premium as revenue without separating the portion that relates to the equity component. *[IFRS 4.BC164]*. This conclusion is inconsistent with those discussed at 4 and 5 above where IFRS 4 requires the separation of embedded derivatives and deposit elements of contracts in certain circumstances regardless of the 'systems changes' that may be required as a result.

Subsequent changes in the measurement of the guaranteed element and in the portion of the DPF classified as a liability must be recognised in profit or loss. If part or all of the DPF is classified in equity, that portion of profit or loss may be attributable to that feature (in the same way that a portion may be attributable to a non-controlling interest). The insurer must recognise the portion of profit or loss attributable to any equity component of a DPF as an allocation of profit or loss, not as expense or income. *[IFRS 4.34(c)]*.

IFRS 4 also requires an insurer to:

(a) apply IAS 39 (or IFRS 9) to a derivative embedded within an insurance contract containing a DPF if it is within the scope of IAS 39 (or IFRS 9) (see 4 above); and

(b) continue its existing accounting policies for such contracts, unless it changes those accounting policies in a way that complies with IFRS 4 (subject to the constraints noted above and those discussed at 8 below). *[IFRS 4.34(d)-(e)]*.

Chapter 55

AMP provide the following detail as to how DPF contracts have been allocated in their income statement and statement of financial position.

Extract 55.2: AMP Limited (2008)

Notes to the financial statements [extract]

Note 1 Summary of significant accounting policies [extract]

Allocation of operating profit and unvested policyholder benefits

The operating profit arising from discretionary participating contracts is allocated between shareholders and participating policyholders by applying the MoS principles in accordance with the Life Insurance Act 1995 (Life Act).

Once profit is allocated to participating policyholders it can only be distributed to these policyholders. Any distribution of this profit to shareholders is only allowed for overseas business with specific approval of the regulators.

Profit allocated to participating policyholders is recognised in the Income statement as an increase in policy liabilities. Both the element of this profit that has not yet been allocated to specific policyholders (i.e. unvested) and that which has been allocated to specific policyholders by way of bonus distributions (i.e. vested) are included within life insurance contract liabilities.

Bonus distributions to participating policyholders are merely a change in the nature of the liability from unvested to vested and, as such, do not alter the amount of profit attributable to shareholders.

The principles of allocation of the profit arising from discretionary participating business determined under the Life Act and MoS are as follows:

(i) Investment income (net of tax and investment expenses) on retained earnings in respect of discretionary participating business is allocated between policyholders and shareholders in proportion to the balances of policyholders' and shareholders' retained earnings, being 80:20.

(ii) Other MoS profits arising from discretionary participating business (excluding the additional tax attributable to shareholders in respect of Australian superannuation business) are allocated 80% to policyholders and 20% to shareholders, with the following exceptions:

– The profit arising from New Zealand corporate superannuation business is apportioned such that shareholders are allocated 15% of the profit allocated to policyholders.

– The profit arising in respect of Preservation Superannuation Account business is allocated 92.5% to policyholders and 7.5% to shareholders.

(iii) Additional tax on taxable income to shareholders in respect of Australian superannuation business is allocated to shareholders only.

(iv) All profits arising from non-participating business, including net investment returns on shareholder capital and retained earnings in life statutory funds (excluding retained earnings dealt with in (i) above) are allocated to shareholders.

6.2 Discretionary participation features in financial instruments

As discussed at 2.2.2 above, a financial instrument containing a DPF is also within the scope of IFRS 4, not IAS 39 (or IFRS 9), and issuers of these contracts are permitted to continue applying their existing accounting policies to them rather than apply the rules in IAS 39 or IFRS 9.

The requirements discussed at 6.1 above apply equally to financial instruments that contain a DPF. However, in addition:

(a) if the issuer classifies the entire DPF as a liability, it must apply the liability adequacy test discussed at 7.2.2 below to the whole contract, i.e. to both the guaranteed element and the DPF. The issuer need not determine separately the amount that would result from applying IAS 39 (or IFRS 9) to the guaranteed element;

(b) if the issuer classifies part or all of the DPF of that instrument as a separate component of equity, the liability recognised for the whole contract should not be less than the amount that would result from applying IAS 39 (or IFRS 9) to the guaranteed element. That amount should include the intrinsic value of an option to surrender the contract, but need not include its time value if IFRS 4 exempts that option from fair value measurement (see 4 above). The issuer need not disclose the amount that would result from applying IAS 39 (or IFRS 9) to the guaranteed element, nor need it present the guaranteed amount separately. Furthermore, it need not determine the guaranteed amount if the total liability recognised for whole contract is clearly higher; and

(c) the issuer may continue to recognise all premiums (including the premiums from the guaranteed element) as revenue and recognise as an expense the resulting increase in the carrying amount of the liability even though these contracts are financial instruments.

The IASB has admitted that, conceptually, the premium for the guaranteed element of these investment contracts is not revenue but believes that the treatment of the discretionary element could depend on matters that will not be resolved until Phase II. It has also decided to avoid requiring entities to make systems changes in order to split the premium between the guaranteed and discretionary elements which might later become redundant. Therefore, entities can continue to present premiums or deposits received from investment contracts with a DPF as revenue, with an expense representing the corresponding change in the liability. *[IFRS 4.BC163]*.

AXA's accounting policy for revenue recognition gives an example of an accounting policy that includes premiums from investment contracts with a DPF as revenue.

Extract 55.3: AXA Group (2008)

Notes to the Consolidated Financial Statements of AXA Group [extract]

1.18. Revenue Recognition [extract]

1.18.1. Gross written premiums

Gross written premiums correspond to the amount of premiums written by insurance and reinsurance companies on business incepted in the year with respect to both insurance contracts and investment contracts with discretionary participating features, net of cancellations and gross of reinsurance ceded. For reinsurance, premiums are recorded on the basis of declarations made by the ceding company, and may include estimates of gross written premiums.

The disclosure requirements of IFRS 7 and IFRS 13 apply to financial instruments containing a DPF even though they are accounted for under IFRS 4. *[IFRS 4.2(b)]*. However, disclosure of the fair value of a contract containing a DPF (as described in IFRS 4) is not required if the fair value of that DPF cannot be measured reliably. *[IFRS 7.29(c)]*. Further, IFRS 4 allows the disclosed amount of interest expense for such contracts to be calculated on a basis other than the effective interest method. *[IFRS 4.35(d)]*. All of the other disclosure requirements of IFRS 7 and IFRS 13 apply to investment contracts with a DPF without modification, for example the contractual maturity analysis showing undiscounted cash flows and the fair value hierarchy categorisation if the contracts are measured at fair value.

As discussed at 6 above, an investment contract with a DPF is within the scope of the revised ED provided that the reporting entity also issues insurance contracts, which is a change from IFRS 4. In addition, the definition of an investment contract with a DPF is modified such that the additional returns must be contractually based on the returns from a specified pool of *insurance* contracts or a specified type of *insurance* contract rather just a contract or contracts.

6.3 Practical issues

6.3.1 Negative DPF

Cumulative unallocated realised and unrealised returns on investments backing insurance and investment contracts with a DPF may become negative and result in an unallocated amount that is negative (a cumulative unallocated loss).

Negative DPF is not addressed in IFRS 4 and does not appear to have been contemplated by the IASB at the time the standard was issued.

Assuming an insurer normally classifies contracts with a DPF as a liability, where such amounts become negative we believe that the insurer is prohibited from recognising an asset or debiting the contract liability related to the cumulative unallocated losses (realised or unrealised) on the investments backing contracts that include DPF features except to the extent that:

- the insurer is contractually entitled to pass those losses to the contract holders; or
- the insurer's previous local GAAP accounting for insurance or investment contracts with a DPF permitted the recognition of such an asset or the debiting of the contract liability when the unallocated investment results of the investments backing a DPF contract were negative.

An insurer is permitted to continue existing GAAP accounting for insurance contracts and investment contracts with a DPF as discussed at 7 below. If an existing GAAP accounting policy specifically allows the recognition of an asset or the reduction of contract liabilities related to cumulative unallocated DPF losses then in our view continuation of that policy is permitted because IFRS 4 specifically excludes accounting policies for insurance contracts from paragraphs 10-12 of IAS 8. If the existing GAAP accounting policy does not permit the recognition of an asset or the reduction of contract liabilities in such circumstances then the introduction of such a policy would need to satisfy the relevance and reliability criteria discussed at 8.1 below to be permissible.

Examples of situations in which an insurer is contractually entitled to (partially) recover losses can include contracts with a fixed surrender charge or a market value adjustment feature.

6.3.2 Contracts with switching features

Some contracts may contain options for the counterparty to switch between terms that would, *prima facie*, result in classification as an investment contract without DPF features (accounted for under IAS 39 (or IFRS 9)) and terms that would result in a classification as an investment contract with DPF features (accounted for under IFRS 4).

We believe that the fact that this switch option makes these contracts investment contracts with a DPF means that the issuer should continuously be able to demonstrate that the DPF feature still exists and also be able to demonstrate actual switching to a DPF in order to classify these contracts as investment contracts with a DPF under IFRS 4.

7 SELECTION OF ACCOUNTING POLICIES

IFRS 4 provides very little guidance on accounting policies that should be used by an entity that issues insurance contracts or investment contracts with a DPF (hereafter for convenience, at 7 and 8 below, referred to as 'insurance contracts').

Instead of providing detailed guidance, the standard:

(a) creates an exemption from applying the hierarchy in IAS 8 (the 'hierarchy exemption') that specifies the criteria an entity should use in developing an accounting policy if no IFRS applies specifically to an item (see 7.1 below);

(b) limits the impact of the hierarchy exemption by imposing five specific requirements relating to catastrophe provisions, liability adequacy, derecognition, offsetting and impairment of reinsurance assets (see 7.2 below); and

(c) permits some existing practices to continue but prohibits their introduction (see 8.2.1 below).

The importance of the hierarchy exemption is that without it certain existing accounting practices would be unlikely to be acceptable under IFRS as they would conflict with the *Framework* or other standards such as IAS 37, IAS 39 (or IFRS 9), IAS 18 or IFRS 15. For example, the deferral of acquisition costs that are not incremental or directly attributable to the issue of an insurance contract are unlikely to meet the *Framework's* definition of an asset. Similarly, a basis of liability measurement, such as the gross premium valuation, which includes explicit estimates of future periods' cash inflows in respect of policies which are cancellable at the policyholder's discretion would be unlikely to be acceptable.

The IASB considered that, without the hierarchy exemption, establishing acceptable accounting policies for insurance contracts could have been costly and that some insurers might have made major changes to their policies on adoption of IFRS followed by further significant changes in Phase II. *[IFRS 4.BC77]*.

The practical result of the hierarchy exemption is that an insurer is permitted to continue applying the accounting policies that it was using when it first applied IFRS 4, subject to the exceptions noted at 7.2 below. *[IFRS 4.BC83]*.

Usually, but not exclusively, these existing accounting policies will be the insurer's previous GAAP, but IFRS 4 does not specifically require an insurer to follow its local accounting pronouncements. This is mainly because of the problems in defining local GAAP. Additionally, some insurers, such as non-US insurers with a US listing, apply US GAAP to their insurance contracts rather than the GAAP of their own country which would have given rise to further definitional problems. *[IFRS 4.BC81]*. The IASB also wanted to give insurers the opportunity to improve their accounting policies even if there was no change to their local GAAP. *[IFRS 4.BC82]*.

The practical result of this is a continuation of the diversity in accounting practices whose elimination was one of the primary objectives of the IASC's project on insurance contracts originally initiated in 1997.

To illustrate this point, below are extracts from the financial statements of Prudential and Münchener Rück (Munich Re), both of which apply IFRS. Prudential is a UK insurance group and applies UK GAAP to its insurance contracts whereas Munich Re is a German insurance group that applies US GAAP to its insurance contracts.

Extract 55.4: Prudential plc (2008)

Note on the Group financial statements [extract]

A3 Critical accounting policies, estimates and judgements[extract]

Insurance contract accounting

With the exception of certain contracts described in note D1, the Group's life assurance contracts are classified as insurance contracts and investment contracts with discretionary participating features. As permitted by IFRS 4, assets and liabilities of these contracts (see below) are accounted for under previously applied GAAP. Accordingly, except as described below, the modified statutory basis (MSB) of reporting as set out in the revised Statement of Recommended Practice (SORP) issued by the Association of British Insurers (ABI) in November 2003 has been applied.

Extract 55.5: Münchener Rückversicherungs – Gesellschaft Aktiengesellschaft (2008)

Note to the consolidated financial statements [extract]

Application of International Financial Reporting Standards [extract]

In accordance with the rules of IFRS 4, underwriting items are recognised and measured on the basis of US GAAP (United States Generally Accepted Accounting Principles). We have also observed the German accounting standards (DRSs) adopted by the German Standardisation Council (DSR) provided they do not contradict the applicable IFRSs.

7.1 The hierarchy exemption

Paragraphs 10-12 of IAS 8 provide guidance on the development and application of accounting policies in the absence of a standard or interpretation that specifically applies to a transaction. In particular, it explains the applicability and relative weighting to be given to other IFRS sources, the use of guidance issued by other standard-setting bodies and other accounting literature and accepted industry practices.

An insurer is not required to apply paragraphs 10-12 of IAS 8 for:

(a) insurance contracts that it issues (including related acquisition costs and related intangible assets); and

(b) reinsurance contracts that it holds. *[IFRS 4.13]*.

What this means is that an insurer need not consider:

- whether its existing accounting policies are consistent with the *Framework*;
- whether those accounting policies regarding insurance contracts are consistent with other standards and interpretations dealing with similar and related issues; or
- whether they result in information that is 'relevant' or 'reliable'.

This exemption was controversial within the IASB and resulted in five members of the IASB dissenting from the issue of the standard. It was also opposed by some respondents to ED 5 on the grounds that it would permit too much diversity in practice and allow fundamental departures from the *Framework* that could prevent an insurer's financial statements from presenting information that is understandable, relevant, reliable and comparable. The IASB admitted that the exemption is 'unusual' but believed that it was necessary to minimise disruption in 2005 for both users and preparers. *[IFRS 4.BC79]*.

7.2 Limits on the hierarchy exemption

In order to prevent insurers continuing with accounting policies that the IASB considered would either not be permitted in Phase II or which conflict too greatly with other standards, such as IAS 39 (or IFRS 9) or IAS 37, IFRS 4 imposes several limits on the hierarchy exception. These are in respect of:

- catastrophe and equalisation provisions;
- liability adequacy testing;
- derecognition of insurance liabilities;
- offsetting of reinsurance contracts against relating direct insurance contracts; and
- impairment of reinsurance assets. *[IFRS 4.14]*.

These are discussed below.

7.2.1 Catastrophe and equalisation provisions

Catastrophe provisions are provisions that are generally built up over the years out of premiums received, perhaps following a prescribed regulatory formula, until an amount, possibly specified by the regulations, is reached. These provisions are usually intended to be released on the occurrence of a future catastrophic loss that is covered by current and future contracts. Equalisation provisions are usually intended to cover random fluctuations of claim expenses around the expected value of claims for some types of insurance contract (such as hail, credit guarantee and fidelity insurance) perhaps using a formula based on experience over a number of years. *[IFRS 4.BC87]*. Consequently, these provisions tend to act as income smoothing mechanisms that reduce profits in reporting periods in which insurance claims are low and reduce losses in reporting periods in which insurance claims are high. As catastrophe and/or equalisation provisions are normally not available for distribution to shareholders, the solvency position of an insurer can be improved.

The recognition of a liability (such as catastrophe and equalisation provisions) for possible future claims, if these claims arise from insurance contracts that are not in existence at the end of the reporting period, is prohibited. *[IFRS 4.14(a)]*.

The IASB considers there is no credible basis for arguing that equalisation or catastrophe provisions are recognisable liabilities under IFRS. Such provisions are not liabilities as defined in the *Framework* because the insurer has no present obligation for losses that will occur after the end of the contract period. Without the hierarchy exemption the recognition of these provisions as liabilities would have been allowed and therefore this requirement preserves that prohibition. Further, there is no realistic prospect that the IASB will permit them in Phase II. *[IFRS 4.BC89-90]*.

The IASB views the objective of financial statements as not to enhance solvency but to provide information that is useful to a wide range of users for economic decisions. *[IFRS 4.BC89(d)]*. Present imperfections in the measurement of insurance liabilities do not, in the IASB's opinion, justify the recognition of items that do not meet the definition of a liability. *[IFRS 4.BC92(a)]*.

Although the recognition of catastrophe and equalisation provisions in respect of claims arising from insurance contracts that are not in force at the end of the reporting period are prohibited, such provisions are permitted to the extent that they were permitted under previous accounting policies and they are attributable to policies in force at the end of the reporting period.

Although IFRS 4 prohibits the recognition of these provisions as a liability, it does not prohibit their segregation as a component of equity. Consequently, insurers are free to designate a proportion of their equity as an equalisation or catastrophe provision. *[IFRS 4.BC93]*.

Aviva Insurance Limited discloses that its equalisation provisions are included within retained earnings in equity.

Extract 55.6: Aviva Insurance Limited (2013)

Accounting policies [extract]

(AA) Equalisation provision

Equalisation provisions are established in accordance with UK company law. These provisions are in addition to the provisions required to meet the anticipated ultimate cost of settlement of outstanding claims at the balance sheet date. Under IFRS, the provisions are not reported in the balance sheet as no liability exists but are included within the non-distributable element of retained earnings, net of attributable tax relief.

When a catastrophe or equalisation provision has a tax base but is not recognised in the IFRS financial statements, then a taxable temporary difference will arise that should be accounted for under IAS 12 – *Income Taxes*.

7.2.2 Liability adequacy testing

Many existing insurance accounting models have mechanisms to ensure that insurance liabilities are not understated, and that related amounts recognised as assets, such as deferred acquisition costs, are not overstated. However, because there is no guarantee that such tests are in place in every jurisdiction and are effective, the IASB was concerned that the credibility of IFRS could suffer if an insurer claims to comply with IFRS but fails to recognise material and reasonably foreseeable losses arising from existing contractual obligations.

Therefore, a requirement for the application of a 'liability adequacy test' (an assessment of whether the carrying amount of an insurance liability needs to be increased, or the carrying amount of related deferred acquisition costs or related intangible assets decreased, based on a review of future cash flows) was introduced into IFRS 4. This assessment of liability adequacy is required at each reporting date. *[IFRS 4.BC94]*.

If the assessment shows that the carrying amount of the recognised insurance liabilities (less related deferred acquisition costs and related intangible assets such as those acquired in a business combination or portfolio transfer discussed at 9 below) is inadequate in the light of the estimated future cash flows, the entire deficiency must be recognised immediately in profit or loss. *[IFRS 4.15]*.

The purpose of this requirement is to prevent material liabilities being unrecorded.

7.2.2.A *Using a liability adequacy test under existing accounting policies*

As many existing insurance accounting models have some form of liability adequacy test, the IASB was keen to ensure that insurers using such models, as far as possible, did not have to make systems changes. Therefore, if an insurer applies a liability adequacy test that meets specified minimum requirements, IFRS 4 imposes no further requirements. The minimum requirements are the following:

(a) the test considers current estimates of all contractual cash flows, and of related cash flows such as claims handling costs, as well as cash flows resulting from embedded options and guarantees; and

(b) if the test shows that the liability is inadequate, the entire deficiency is recognised in profit or loss. *[IFRS 4.16]*.

If the insurer's liability adequacy test meets these requirements then the test should be applied at the level of aggregation specified in that test. *[IFRS 4.18]*.

The standard does not specify:

- what criteria in the liability adequacy test determine when existing contracts end and future contracts start;
- at what level of aggregation the test should be performed;
- whether or how the cash flows are discounted to reflect the time value of money or adjusted for risk and uncertainty;
- whether the test considers both the time value and intrinsic value of embedded options and guarantees; or
- whether additional losses recognised because of the test are recognised by reducing the carrying amount of deferred acquisition costs or by increasing the carrying amount of the related insurance liabilities. *[IFRS 4.BC101]*.

Additionally, the standard does not state whether this existing liability adequacy test can be performed net of expected related reinsurance recoveries. However, the liability adequacy test discussed at 7.2.2.B below explicitly excludes reinsurance.

The standard provides only minimum guidelines on what a liability adequacy test comprises. This avoids insurers having to make systems changes that may have to be reversed in Phase II but allows the continuation of a diversity of practice among insurers, for example in the use (or not) of discounting. However, some existing practices may not meet these minimum requirements, for example if they use cash flows locked-in at inception rather than current estimates.

An example of the details of a liability adequacy test can be found in the financial statements of Allianz.

> *Extract 55.7: Allianz SE (2008)*
>
> **Notes to the consolidated financial statements** [extract]
>
> **Note 2 Summary of significant accounting policies** [extract]
>
> ***Reserves for insurance and investment contracts and financial liabilities for unit-linked contracts*** [extract]
>
> Liability adequacy tests are performed for each insurance portfolio on the basis of estimates of future claims, costs, premiums earned and proportionate investment income. For short duration contracts, a premium deficiency is recognised if the sum of expected claim costs and claim adjustment expenses, expected dividends to policyholders, unamortized acquisition costs, and maintenance expenses exceeds related unearned premiums while considering anticipated investment income. For long duration contracts, if actual experience regarding investment yields, mortality, morbidity, terminations or expense indicate that existing contract liabilities, along with the present value of future gross premiums, will not be sufficient to cover the present value of future benefits and to recover deferred policy acquisition costs, then a premium deficiency is recognised.

7.2.2.B Using the liability adequacy test specified in IFRS 4

If an insurer's accounting policies do not require a liability adequacy test that meets the minimum criteria discussed, it should:

(a) determine the carrying amount of the relevant insurance liabilities less the carrying amount of:

   (i) any related deferred acquisition costs; and

   (ii) any related intangible assets. However, related reinsurance assets are not considered because an insurer assesses impairment for them separately (see 7.2.5 below).

(b) determine whether the amount described in (a) is less than the carrying amount that would be required if the relevant insurance liabilities were within the scope of IAS 37. If it is less, the entire difference should be recognised in profit or loss and the carrying amount of the related deferred acquisition costs or related intangible assets should be reduced or the carrying amount of the relevant insurance liabilities should be increased. *[IFRS 4.17]*.

This test should be performed at the level of a portfolio of contracts that are subject to broadly similar risks and managed together as a single portfolio. *[IFRS 4.18]*.

Investment margins should be reflected in the calculation if, and only if, the carrying amounts of the liabilities and any related deferred acquisition costs and intangible assets also reflect those margins. *[IFRS 4.19]*.

IAS 37 was used as a basis for this liability adequacy test as it was an existing measurement basis that minimised the need for exceptions to existing IFRS principles. *[IFRS 4.BC95, 104]*.

IAS 37 requires an amount to be recognised as a provision that is the best estimate of the expenditure required to settle the present obligation. This is the amount that an entity would rationally pay to settle the obligation at the reporting date or transfer it to a third party at that time. *[IAS 37.36-47]*. Although IAS 37 refers to 'expenditure' there appears to be no specific prohibition from considering future premiums. This might be appropriate if it can be argued that the expenditures are a function of the future premiums.

The end result is that the IAS 37 requirements are potentially more prescriptive and onerous than those applying if an insurer has an existing liability adequacy test which meets the minimum IFRS 4 criteria discussed above.

7.2.2.C Investment contracts with a discretionary participation feature

As discussed at 6.2 above the accounting requirements for investment contracts with a DPF depend on whether the entity has classified the DPF as a liability or as equity. Where the DPF is classified entirely as a liability then the liability adequacy test is applied to the whole contract, i.e. both the guaranteed element and the DPF. Where the DPF is classified in part or in total as a separate component of equity then IFRS 4 states that the amount recognised as a liability for the whole contract should be not less than the amount that would result from applying IAS 39 (or IFRS 9) to the guaranteed element. IFRS 4 does not specify whether the IAS 39 (or IFRS 9) measurement basis should be amortised cost or fair value. It is also not clear if this requirement relates to the gross liability or to the net carrying amount, i.e. less any related deferred acquisition costs or related intangible assets. *[IFRS 4.35(b)]*.

7.2.2.D Interaction between the liability adequacy test and shadow accounting

IFRS 4 does not address the interaction between the liability adequacy test and shadow accounting (discussed at 8.3 below). The liability adequacy test requires all deficiencies to be recognised in profit or loss whereas shadow accounting permits certain unrealised losses to be recognised in other comprehensive income.

We believe that a company can apply shadow accounting to offset an increase in insurance liabilities to the extent that the increase is caused directly by market interest rate movements that lead to changes in the value of investments that are recognised directly in other comprehensive income. Although IFRS 4 does not specify the priority of shadow accounting over the LAT, because the LAT is to be applied as a final test to the amount recognised under the insurer's accounting policies, it follows that shadow accounting has to be applied first. This is illustrated in the example below.

Example 55.30: Shadow loss recognition

An insurer has classified certain investments backing insurance liabilities as available-for-sale financial assets. It has issued a guaranteed single premium product backed by an investment in a government bond with the same effective interest rate, duration and currency.

The opening position in the statement of financial position, perfectly matched in currency, interest rates and duration is as follows:

	CU		CU
Bond @ 6% effective rate, initial value	100	Equity	10
Other assets	10	Contract @ 6% guarantee	100
Total assets	110	Total liabilities and equity	110

Chapter 55

The position in the statement of financial position, one year after issuance, after a significant decline in market interest rates is as follows:

	CU		CU
Bond @ market value	116	Equity	20
Other assets	10	Contract @ 6% guarantee	106
Total assets	126	Total liabilities and equity	126

Given the market interest rate movement, the 'matched' situation no longer shows in the statement of financial position as the investment is valued at CU 116 and the liability at CU 106. The current market return on the assets funding the insurance contract at the time of performing the liability adequacy test (LAT) is no longer 6%. It is now 5.2% (CU 6 ÷ CU 116).

The increase in shareholders' equity could be used for, or considered available for, dividend payments. Part of the cash value of the investment is no longer allocated to the insurance liability, but to shareholders' equity. This is not correct because the entire investment, regardless of its carrying amount, is needed to provide the annual investment return (CU 6) to fund the growth of the liability (CU 6).

The bond's unrealised gain results in a decline in its market interest yield to below 6%. Therefore the liability needs to increase (in other words a higher amount of the investment needs to be allocated to it) to the level where the nominal CU 6 is earned.

IFRS 4 states that any increase in the liability needs to be charged to profit or loss. However, in this case the increase is caused by a market interest movement that has produced an unrealised gain on an investment. This unrealised gain has been credited to other comprehensive income rather than profit or loss. If the liability increase is charged to profit or loss there will be a mismatch between this and the related unrealised gain in other comprehensive income.

To the extent that the increase in the liability is related to other causes, the insurer should recognise a loss in the income statement.

This example assumes that the effect of the change in market interest rates on the fair value of investments is recorded in other comprehensive income and was exactly the same as the opposite change in the fair value of the liability. In reality these two effects may not match exactly, so there could be a difference between the change in the fair value of the available-for-sale (AFS) assets and the change required in the carrying amount of the liability before the LAT is performed. The impact of shadow accounting needs to be limited to the change in value that was directly recorded in other comprehensive income arising from changes in the fair value carrying amount of the AFS assets.

7.2.3 Insurance liability derecognition

An insurance liability, or a part of such a liability, can be removed from the statement of financial position (derecognised) when, and only when, it is extinguished i.e. when the obligation specified in the contract is discharged, cancelled or expires. *[IFRS 4.14(c)]*.

This requirement is identical to that contained in IAS 39 (or IFRS 9) for the derecognition of financial liabilities. *[IAS 39.39, IFRS 9.3.3.1]*. The IASB said it could identify no reasons for the derecognition requirements for insurance liabilities to differ from those for financial liabilities. *[IFRS 4.BC105]*.

Accordingly, insurance liabilities should not normally be derecognised as a result of entering into a reinsurance contract because this does not usually discharge the insurer's liability to the policyholder. This applies even if the insurer has delegated all claims settlement authority to the reinsurer or if a claim has been fully reinsured.

Derecognition should be distinguished from remeasurement. The carrying amounts of many insurance liabilities are estimates and an insurer should re-estimate its claims liabilities, and hence change their carrying amounts, if that is required by its accounting policies. However, in certain situations the distinction between the two concepts can be blurred, for example where there is a dispute or other uncertainty over the contractual terms of an insurance policy.

IFRS 4 contains no guidance on when or whether a modification of an insurance contract might cause derecognition of that contract. The revised ED contains detailed guidance on when a modification of an insurance contract results in derecognition of that contract and recognition of a new contract. The revised ED states that if an insurance contract does not meet the criteria for derecognition due to modification, it is derecognised when, and only when, it is extinguished (i.e. when the obligation specified in the insurance contract is discharged, cancelled or expired).[15]

7.2.4 Offsetting of insurance and related reinsurance contracts

IFRS 4 prohibits offsetting of:

(a) reinsurance assets against the related insurance liabilities; and

(b) income or expense from reinsurance contracts against the expense or income from the related insurance contracts. *[IFRS 4.14(d)]*.

This prohibition broadly aligns the offsetting criteria for insurance assets and liabilities with those required for financial assets and financial liabilities under IAS 32, which requires that financial assets and financial liabilities can only be offset where an entity:

(a) has a legally enforceable right to set-off the recognised amounts; and

(b) intends to settle on a net basis, or to realise both the asset and settle the liability simultaneously. *[IAS 32.42]*.

Because a cedant normally has no legal right to offset amounts due from a reinsurer against amounts due to the related underlying policyholder the IASB considers a gross presentation gives a clearer picture of the cedant's rights and obligations. *[IFRS 4.BC106]*.

As a result, balances due from reinsurers should be shown as assets in the statement of financial position, whereas the related insurance liabilities should be shown as liabilities. Because of the relationship between the two, some insurers provide linked disclosures in the notes to their IFRS financial statements as discussed at 10.1.2.A below.

The IFRS 4 requirements, however, appear to be less flexible than those in IAS 32 in that they provide no circumstances in which offsetting can be acceptable. So, for example, 'pass through' contracts that provide for reinsurers to pay claims direct to the underlying policyholder would still have to be shown gross in the statement of financial position. IAS 32 also does not address offsetting in the income statement.

The revised ED requires separate presentation of portfolios of insurance and reinsurance contracts and also separate presentation of portfolios of insurance and reinsurance contracts that are assets from those that are liabilities. This means that balances on individual contracts within a portfolio that are assets are presented on a net basis together with balances on individual contracts that are liabilities.[16] In the statement of profit or loss and other comprehensive income, the revised ED requires that an entity should not offset income or expense from reinsurance contracts against the expense or income from insurance contracts and that income or expense from the underlying items is not offset against expense or income from the insurance contract.[17]

7.2.5 Impairment of reinsurance assets

If the IASB had required that the impairment model in IAS 36 be applied to reinsurance assets (as proposed in ED 5) many cedants would have been compelled to change their accounting model for reinsurance contracts in a way that was inconsistent with the accounting for the underlying direct insurance liability. This would have required the cedant to address matters such as discounting and risk, together with the attendant systems implications. Consequently, the IASB concluded that the impairment test should focus on credit risk (arising from the risk of default by the reinsurer and also from disputes over coverage) and not address matters arising from the measurement of the underlying direct insurance liability. It decided the most appropriate way to achieve this was to introduce an incurred loss model based on that contained in IAS 39. *[IFRS 4.BC107-108]*.

Consequently, a reinsurance asset should be impaired if, and only if:

(a) there is objective evidence, as a result of an event that occurred after initial recognition of the asset, that the cedant may not receive all amounts due to it under the terms of the contract; and

(b) that event has a reliably measureable impact on the amounts that the cedant will receive from the reinsurer. *[IFRS 4.20]*.

Where a reinsurance asset is impaired, its carrying amount should be reduced accordingly and the impairment loss recognised in profit or loss.

IAS 39 provides various indicators of impairment for financial assets, such as the significant financial difficulty of the obligor and a breach of contract, such as a default in interest or principal payments. IFRS 4 does not provide any specific indicators of impairment relating to reinsurance assets. In the absence of such indicators, it would seem appropriate for insurers to refer to those in IAS 39 as a guide to determining whether reinsurance assets are impaired.

Zurich Financial Services discloses details of impairment indicators considered in determining whether reinsurance assets are impaired.

Extract 55.8: Zurich Financial Services Group (2008)

Notes to the consolidated financial statements [extract]

Note 3 Summary of significant accounting policies [extract]

b) Insurance contracts and investment contracts with discretionary participating features [extract]

Reinsurance [extract]

Reinsurance assets are assessed for impairment on a regular basis for any events that may trigger impairment. Triggering events may include legal disputes with third parties, changes in capital and surplus levels, change in credit ratings of a counterparty and historic experience regarding collectability from specific reinsurers.

The use of this impairment model means that provisions cannot be recognised in respect of credit losses expected to arise from future events.

IAS 39 permits a portfolio approach to determining impairment provisions for financial assets carried at amortised cost. More specifically, IAS 39 permits a collective evaluation of impairment for assets that are grouped on the basis of similar credit risk characteristics that are indicative of the debtors' ability to pay all amounts due according to the contractual terms (for example on the basis of a credit risk evaluation or grading process that considers asset type, industry, geographical location, collateral type, past-due status and other relevant factors). *[IAS 39.AG87]*.

It is questionable whether an insurer's reinsurance assets would normally exhibit sufficiently similar credit risk characteristics to permit such an approach to determining impairment. That said, IAS 39 is clear that impairment losses recognised on a group basis represent an interim step pending the identification of impairment losses on individual assets in the group of financial assets that are collectively assessed for impairment. As soon as information is available that specifically identifies losses on individually impaired assets in a group, those assets are removed from the group. *[IAS 39.AG88]*.

IFRS 9 does not contain any consequential amendments to IFRS 4 in respect of impairment of reinsurance assets. Therefore, if the new insurance accounting standard is not yet adopted when IFRS 9 is applied, insurers will continue to use an incurred loss impairment model for reinsurance assets notwithstanding the fact that an expected loss model will be used for financial assets within the scope of IFRS 9.

The revised ED proposes that a cedant should consider the risk of non-performance by the reinsurer, including the effects of collateral and losses from disputes within the fulfilment cash flows, on an expected present value basis.[18]

7.2.6 Accounting policy matters not addressed by IFRS 4

7.2.6.A Derecognition of insurance and reinsurance assets

IFRS 4 does not address the derecognition of insurance or reinsurance assets. The IASB could identify no reason why the derecognition criteria for insurance assets should differ from those for financial assets accounted for under IAS 39 (or IFRS 9), but declined to address the issue 'because derecognition of financial assets is a controversial topic'. *[IFRS 4.BC105]*. Consequently, derecognition of insurance assets should be dealt with under existing accounting practices which may differ from the requirements of IAS 39 (or IFRS 9).

AEGON discloses the following policy concerning the derecognition of reinsurance assets.

Extract 55.9: AEGON N.V. (2008)

Notes to the consolidated financial statements [extract]

Note 2.12 Reinsurance assets [extract]

Reinsurance assets are measured consistently with the amounts associated with the underlying insurance contracts and in accordance with the terms of each reinsurance contract. They are subject to impairment testing and are derecognized when the contractual rights are extinguished or expire or when the contract is transferred to another party.

The revised ED states that where an entity buys reinsurance, it should derecognise the underlying insurance contract or contracts if, and only if, the underlying insurance contract or contracts are extinguished.[19]

7.2.6.B Impairment of insurance assets

IFRS 4 is silent on the impairment model to be used for receivables arising under insurance contracts that are not reinsurance assets (discussed at 7.2.5 above). An example of these would be premium receivables due from policyholders. Insurers should therefore apply their existing accounting policies for determining impairment provisions for these assets, although an impairment model similar to that required by IAS 39 for financial assets would also appear to be appropriate. IFRS 9 changes the impairment model from an incurred loss model to an expected loss model (see Chapter 50).

The revised ED is also silent on impairment of insurance assets although, under the proposed model, premiums (including premium adjustments and instalment premiums) from policyholders and any additional cash flows that result from those premiums are included within the fulfilment cash flows.[20]

7.2.6.C Gains and losses on buying reinsurance

Some local accounting requirements often define reinsurance contracts more strictly than direct insurance contracts to avoid income statement distortion caused by contracts that have the legal form of reinsurance but do not transfer significant insurance risk. Such contracts are sometimes described as financial reinsurance. One such source of distortion is caused because many local GAAPs do not require the discounting of non-life insurance claims liabilities. If the insurer buys reinsurance, the premium paid to the reinsurer reflects the present value of the underlying liability and is, therefore, potentially less than the existing carrying amount of the liability. This could result in a gain on the initial recognition of the reinsurance contract (a 'day 1' gain) where a reinsurance asset is recognised at an amount equivalent to the undiscounted liability and this is less than the premium payable for the reinsurance contract. This day 1 gain arises largely because of the inability to discount the underlying liability. Initial recognition of gains could also arise if the underlying insurance liability is measured with excessive prudence. *[IFRS 4.BC110]*.

IFRS 4 defines a reinsurance contract using the same terms as an insurance contract. The IASB decided not to use the definition of a reinsurance contract to address the problems described above because it found no conceptual reason to define a reinsurance contract any differently to a direct insurance contract. It considered making a distinction for situations where significant distortions in reported profit were most likely to occur, such as retroactive contracts, but eventually considered that developing such a distinction would be time-consuming and difficult, and there would have been no guarantee of success. *[IFRS 4.BC111, 113]*.

Consequently, IFRS 4 does not restrict the recognition of gains on entering into reinsurance contracts but instead requires specific disclosure of the gains and losses that arise (see 10.1.3 below).

Insurers are therefore permitted to continue applying their existing accounting policies to gains and losses on the purchase of reinsurance contracts (which may or may not prohibit gains on initial recognition) and are also permitted to change those accounting policies according to the criteria discussed at 8 below.

The revised ED proposes that day 1 gains or losses on the purchase of reinsurance contracts held are normally treated as a contractual service margin and not recognised immediately in profit or loss. However, day 1 losses are recognised in profit or loss as an expense if the reinsurance coverage relates to events that occurred before the purchase of the reinsurance contract.[21] In subsequent discussions, the IASB tentatively decided that, after inception, an entity should recognise in profit or loss any changes in estimates of fulfilment cash flows for a reinsurance contract that an entity holds when those changes arise as a result of changes in estimates of fulfilment cash flows for an underlying direct insurance contract that are recognised immediately in profit or loss.[22]

7.2.6.D Acquisition costs

IFRS 4 is silent on how to account for the costs of acquiring insurance contracts. 'Acquisition costs' are not defined within the standard, although the Basis for Conclusions states that they are 'the costs that an insurer incurs to sell, underwrite and initiate a new insurance contract', *[IFRS 4.BC116]*, a description that would appear to exclude costs associated with amending an existing contract.

IFRS 4 neither prohibits nor requires the deferral of acquisition costs, nor does it prescribe what acquisition costs should be deferred, the period and method of their amortisation, or whether an insurer should present deferred acquisition costs as an asset or as a reduction in insurance liabilities. *[IFRS 4.BC116].*

The IASB decided that the treatment of acquisition costs was an integral part of existing insurance models that could not easily be amended without a more fundamental review of these models in Phase II. *[IFRS 4.BC116].*

Insurers are therefore permitted to continue applying their existing accounting policies for deferring the costs of acquiring insurance contracts.

Zurich Financial Services and Generali provide examples of the diversity in practice regarding which acquisition costs are capitalised. Zurich apply US GAAP to their insurance contracts and only capitalise expenses that are directly related to and vary with the acquisition. Generali apply Italian GAAP to their insurance contracts and also capitalise indirect expenses.

Extract 55.10: Zurich Financial Services Group (2008)

Notes to the consolidated financial statements [extract]

Note 4 Critical accounting estimates and judgements [extract]

f) Deferred policy acquisition costs [extract]

Deferred policy acquisition costs generally consist of commissions, underwriting expenses and policy issuance costs. The amount of acquisition costs to be deferred is dependent on judgements as to which issuance costs are directly related to and vary with the acquisition. The related asset is amortized over the premium earning pattern for non-life and certain life products. For most life products, amortization is based on the estimated future profitability of the contract throughout its life. The estimation of profitability considers both historical and future experience as regards assumptions, such as lapse rates or investment income.

> *Extract 55.11: Assicurazioni Generali S.p.A. (2008)*
> **Notes to the consolidated financial statements** [extract]
> **Part D Summary of significant accounting policies** [extract]
> **6.2 – Deferred acquisition costs**
> In accordance with IFRS 4, deferred acquisition costs are accounted for in line with local GAAP. This item includes acquisition commissions and other expenses directly or indirectly attributable to the acquisition or renewal contracts and deferrable over the term of the contracts.

Both IAS 18 and IFRS 15 permit only incremental costs that are associated with obtaining an investment management contract to be recognised as an asset. An incremental cost is one that would not have been incurred if the entity had not secured the investment management contract. *[IAS 18.IE14(b)(iii), IFRS 15.91-93]*. These criteria may be different from those applied to acquisition costs for insurance contracts under local GAAP.

The revised ED proposes that directly attributable acquisition costs that can be allocated on a rational and consistent basis to the individual portfolios of insurance contracts are included in the estimates of cash flows used to determine the fulfilment cash flows which form part of the initial measurement of an insurance contract. No distinction is made between the costs of successful acquisition efforts and unsuccessful efforts.[23]

7.2.6.E Salvage and subrogation

Some insurance contracts permit the insurer to sell (usually damaged) property acquired in settling the claim (salvage). The insurer may also have the right to pursue third parties for payment of some or all costs (subrogation). IFRS 4 contains no guidance on whether potential salvage and subrogation recoveries should be presented as separate assets or netted against the related insurance liability. This will be considered in Phase II. *[IFRS 4.BC120]*.

Royal & SunAlliance is an example of an entity which discloses that its insurance liabilities are stated net of anticipated salvage and subrogation.

> *Extract 55.12: Royal & SunAlliance Insurance Group plc (2008)*
> **Significant accounting policies** [extract]
> **Insurance liabilities** [extract]
> The provisions for claims outstanding, whether reported or not, comprise the estimated cost of claims incurred but not settled at the balance sheet date. It includes related expenses and a deduction for the expected value of salvage and other recoveries.

The revised ED proposes that potential recoveries (such as salvage and subrogation) on past and future claims should be included as part of the contractual cash flows to the extent that they do not qualify for recognition as separate assets.[24]

7.2.6.F Policy loans

Some insurance contracts permit the policyholder to obtain a loan from the insurer with the insurance contract acting as collateral for the loan. IFRS 4 is silent on whether an insurer should treat such loans as a prepayment of the insurance liability or as a separate financial asset. This is because the IASB does not regard the issue as a priority. *[IFRS 4.BC122]*.

Consequently, insurers can either present these loans either as separate assets or as a reduction of the related insurance liability depending on their local GAAP requirements.

The revised ED does not explicitly address policy loans but implies that these are part of the contractual cash flows and included within the overall insurance contract asset or liability.

7.2.6.G Investments held in a fiduciary capacity

Insurers often make investments on behalf of policyholders as well as on behalf of shareholders. In some cases, this can result in the insurer holding an interest in an entity which, either on its own, or when combined with the interest of the policyholder, gives the insurer control of that entity (as defined by IFRS 10).

8 CHANGES IN ACCOUNTING POLICIES

IFRS 4 imposes a number of constraints that apply whenever an insurer wishes to change its accounting policies for insurance contracts. These requirements apply both to changes made by an insurer that already applies IFRS and to changes made by an insurer adopting IFRS for the first time. *[IFRS 4.21]*.

They reflect the IASB's concern that insurers might change their existing policies to ones that are less relevant or reliable contrary to the requirements of IAS 8. One option would have been for the IASB to prohibit any changes in accounting policies to prevent lack of comparability (especially within a country) and management discretion to make arbitrary changes. However, it decided to permit changes in accounting policies for insurance contracts provided they can be justified, as is required for any change in accounting policy under IFRS. *[IFRS 4.BC123, 125]*.

The general and specific requirements relating to changes in accounting policies are discussed below.

8.1 Criteria for accounting policy changes

An insurer may change its accounting policies for insurance contracts if, and only if, the change makes the financial statements more relevant to the economic decision-making needs of users and no less reliable, or more reliable and no less relevant to those needs. Relevance and reliability should be judged by the criteria in IAS 8. *[IFRS 4.22]*.

Relevance relates to the economic decision-making needs of users and reliability, in reference to the financial statements, relates to faithful representation, the economic substance of transactions and not merely their legal form, freedom from bias, prudence and completion in all material respects. *[IAS 8.10]*. In making judgements regarding relevance and reliability management should refer to the requirements in IFRSs dealing with similar and related issues and the definitions, recognition criteria and measurement concepts in the IASB *Framework*. Management may also consider the most recent pronouncements of other standard-setting bodies that use a similar conceptual framework to develop accounting standards, other accounting literature and accepted industry practices to the extent that they do not conflict with IFRS. *[IAS 8.11-12]*.

The Board also considers that as its conclusions for Phase II develop they will give insurers further context for judgements about whether a change in accounting policy will make the financial statements more relevant and reliable. *[IFRS 4.BC123]*. More specifically, the change should bring the insurer's financial statements closer to meeting the criteria in IAS 8, but need not achieve full compliance with those criteria. *[IFRS 4.23]*.

IAS 8 requires changes in accounting policies for which there are no specific transitional provisions to be applied retrospectively. As IFRS 4 does not contain any transitional provisions for changes in accounting policies for insurance contracts, any such changes will have to be retrospective, unless impracticable. *[IAS 8.19]*.

Aviva's financial statements illustrate an example of a change in an accounting policy used for insurance contracts.

Extract 55.13: Aviva plc (2008)

Notes to the consolidated financial statements [extract]

Note 2 **Presentation changes** [extract]

(b) (i) **Restatement for the change in accounting policy for latent reserves** [extract]

As part of the Company's aim to continuously improve the relevance and reliability of its financial reporting, Aviva undertook a review of the Group's general insurance reserving in 2008.

As part of this review, the Group concluded that estimating our latent claim provisions on an undiscounted basis, and discounting back to current values, represented an improvement to the existing estimation technique. This approach is in line with best practice for long-term liabilities and moves the measurement of latent claims onto a more economic basis, consistent with our internal model for economic capital and the measurement model being proposed for both IFRS Phase II and Solvency II. This approach also improves consistency with the reporting of other long-tail classes of business which are already discounted, namely certain London Market latent claims and our Dutch Permanent health and Injury Business.

The discount rate that has been applied is based on the relevant swap curve in the relevant currency at the reporting date, having due regard to the duration of the expected settlement of the claims. The discount rate is set at the start of the accounting period with any change in rates between the start and end of the accounting period being reflected below operating profit as an economic assumption change. The range of discount rates used is shown in note 38c and depends on the duration of the claim and the reporting date. We estimate that latent claims will be payable for around the next 35 to 40 years with an average duration of 15 years.

The application of discounting to our latent claims represents a change in accounting policy and has been applied retrospectively. The cumulative impact of discounting in our opening reserves as at 1 January 2007 is to reduce insurance liabilities by £214 million and reinsurance assets by £61 million, and to increase retained earnings by £153 million. These have been treated as prior year adjustments in these financial statements.

8.2 Specific issues

In addition to the more general criteria considered at 8.1 above, certain changes of accounting policy are specifically addressed in IFRS 4. The need for the IASB to establish requirements in respect of these issues perhaps indicates that the criteria above are not as clear-cut on certain matters as the IASB would like.

The following are discussed below:

- continuation of existing practices;
- current market interest rates;
- prudence; and
- future investment margins. *[IFRS 4.23]*.

Shadow accounting is discussed separately at 8.3 below.

8.2.1 Continuation of existing practices

An insurer may continue the following practices but the introduction of any of them after IFRS has been adopted is not permitted because the IASB believes that they do not satisfy the criteria discussed at 8.1 above. *[IFRS 4.25]*.

8.2.1.A Measuring insurance liabilities on an undiscounted basis

Under many bodies of local GAAP, non-life insurance liabilities are not discounted to reflect the time value of money. In the IASB's view, discounting of insurance liabilities results in financial statements that are more relevant and reliable. Hence, a change from a policy of discounting to not discounting liabilities is not permitted. *[IFRS 4.25(a)]*. The IASB decided against requiring insurance liabilities to be discounted in IFRS 4 because it had not addressed the issue of the discount rate(s) to be used and the basis for any risk adjustments which is being addressed in Phase II. *[IFRS 4.BC126]*.

8.2.1.B Measuring contractual rights to future investment management fees in excess of their fair value

It is not uncommon to find insurance contracts that give the insurer an entitlement to receive a periodic investment management fee. Some local GAAP accounting policies permit the insurer, in determining the value of its contractual rights and obligations under the insurance contract, to discount the estimated cash flows related to those fees at a discount rate that reflects the risks associated with the cash flows. This approach is found in some embedded value methodologies. *[IFRS 4.BC128]*.

In the IASB's opinion, however, this approach can lead to results that are not consistent with fair value measurement. The IASB considers that if the insurer's contractual asset management fee is in line with the fee charged by other insurers and asset managers for comparable asset management services, the fair value of the contractual right to that fee would be approximately equal to what it would cost insurers and asset managers to acquire similar contractual rights. This approach is considered by the IASB to be consistent with how to account for servicing rights and obligations in IAS 39 (or IFRS 9). Therefore, IFRS 4 does not permit an insurer to introduce an accounting policy that measures those contractual rights at more than their fair value as implied by fees charged by others for comparable services. *[IFRS 4.BC129]*.

The reasoning behind this requirement is that the fair value at inception of such contractual rights will equal the origination costs paid, unless future investment management fees and related costs are out of line with market comparables. *[IFRS 4.25(b)]*.

8.2.1.C Introducing non-uniform accounting policies for the insurance contracts of subsidiaries

IFRS 10 requires consolidated financial statements to be prepared using uniform accounting policies for like transactions. *[IFRS 10.19]*. However, under current local requirements, some insurers consolidate subsidiaries without using the parent company's accounting policies for the measurement of the subsidiaries' insurance liabilities (and related deferred acquisition costs and intangible assets) which continue to be measured under the relevant local GAAP applying in each jurisdiction. *[IFRS 4.BC131]*.

The use of non-uniform accounting policies in consolidated financial statements reduces the relevance and reliability of financial statements and is not permitted by IFRS 10. However, prohibiting this practice in IFRS 4 would have forced some insurers to change their accounting policies for the insurance liabilities for some of their subsidiaries, requiring systems changes now that might not be subsequently required following Phase II. Therefore, the IASB decided that an insurer could continue to use non-uniform accounting policies to account for insurance contracts. If those accounting policies are not uniform, an insurer may change them if the change does not make the accounting policies more diverse and also satisfies the criteria set out at 8.1 above. *[IFRS 4.25(c), BC132]*.

There is one exception to this requirement which is discussed at 8.2.2 below.

Old Mutual is an example of a company that applies non-uniform accounting policies to the measurement of its insurance contract liabilities.

Extract 55.14: Old Mutual plc (2008)

Accounting policies [extract]

(d) Insurance and investment contracts [extract]

(v) Insurance contract provisions [extract]

Insurance contract provisions for African businesses have been computed using a gross premium valuation method. Provisions in respect of African business have been made in accordance with the Financial Soundness Valuation basis as set out in the guidelines issued by the Actuarial Society of South Africa in Professional Guidance Note (PGN) 104 (2001). Under this guideline provisions are valued using realistic expectations of future experience, with margins for prudence and deferral of profit emergence.

Provisions for investment contracts with a discretionary participating feature are also computed using the gross premium valuation method in accordance with the Financial Soundness Valuation basis. Surplus allocated to policyholders but not yet distributed (i.e. bonus smoothing reserve) related to these contracts is included as a provision.

For the US business, the insurance contract provisions are calculated using the net premium method, based on assumptions as to investment yields, mortality, withdrawals and policyholder dividends. For the term life products, the assumptions are set at the time the contracts are issued, whereas the assumptions are updated annually, based on the experience for the annuity products.

Universal life and deferred annuity reserves are computed on the retrospective deposit method, which produces reserves equal to the cash value of the contracts.

Reserves on immediate annuities and guaranteed payments are computed on the prospective deposit method, which produces reserves equal to the present value of future benefit payments.

For other territories, the valuation bases adopted are in accordance with local actuarial practices and methodologies.

8.2.2 Current market interest rates

An insurer is permitted, but not required, to change its accounting policies so that it remeasures designated insurance liabilities (including related deferred acquisition costs and related intangible assets) to reflect current market interest rates. Any changes in these rates would need to be recognised in profit or loss. At that time, it may also introduce accounting policies that require other current estimates and assumptions for the designated liabilities. An insurer may change its accounting policies for designated liabilities without applying those policies consistently to all similar liabilities as IAS 8 would otherwise require. If an insurer designates liabilities for this election, it should apply current market interest rates (and, if applicable, the other current estimates and assumptions) consistently in all periods to all those liabilities until they are extinguished. *[IFRS 4.24]*.

The purpose of this concession is to allow insurers to move, in whole or in part, towards the use of fair value-based measures for insurance contracts.

AXA is an example of an insurance group which has used this option for some of its insurance contracts.

Extract 55.15: AXA Group (2008)

Notes to the consolidated financial statements [extract]

1.13.2 Insurance contracts and investment contracts with discretionary participating features [extract]

Some guaranteed benefits such as Guaranteed Minimum Death or Income Benefits (GMDB or GMIB), or certain guarantees on return proposed by reinsurance treaties, are covered by a risk management program using derivative instruments. In order to minimize the accounting mismatch between liabilities and hedging derivatives, AXA has chosen to use the option allowed under IFRS 4.24 to re-measure its provisions: this revaluation is carried out at each accounts closing based on guarantee level projections and takes into account interest rates and other market assumptions. The liabilities revaluation impact in the current period is recognized through income, symmetrically with the impact of the change in value of hedging derivatives. This change in accounting principles was adopted on first time application of IFRS on January 1, 2004 for contracts portfolios covered by the risk management program at that date. Any additional contracts portfolios covered by the risk management program after that date are valued on the same terms as those applied on the date the program was first applied.

Our view is that, where an entity has elected to account for some, but not all, of its insurance products using current market interest rates, or other current estimates and assumptions, it cannot selectively disregard an input variable, such as a change in interest rates, to determine the value of those liabilities. The input variable must be used every time those insurance contracts are valued.

8.2.3 Prudence

In the IASB's opinion, insurers sometimes measure insurance liabilities on what is intended to be a highly prudent basis that lacks the neutrality required by the IASB's *Framework*. This may be particularly true for insurers who are required under local GAAP to measure their liabilities on a regulatory basis. However, IFRS 4 does not define how much prudence is 'sufficient' and therefore does not require the elimination of 'excessive prudence'. *[IFRS 4.BC133]*. As a result, insurers are not required under IFRS 4 to change their accounting policies to eliminate excessive prudence. However, if an insurer already measures its insurance contracts with sufficient prudence, it should not introduce additional prudence. *[IFRS 4.26]*.

The liability adequacy test requirements discussed at 7.2.2 above address the converse issue of understated insurance liabilities.

8.2.4 Future investment margins

An insurer need not change its accounting policies for insurance contracts to eliminate the recognition of future investment margins (which may occur under some forms of embedded value accounting). However, IFRS 4 imposes a rebuttable presumption that an insurer's financial statements will become less relevant and reliable if it introduces an accounting policy that reflects future investment margins in the measurement of insurance contracts, unless those margins directly affect the contractual payments.

Two examples of accounting policies that reflect those margins are:

(a) using a discount rate that reflects the estimated return on the insurer's assets; and

(b) projecting the returns on those assets at an estimated rate of return, discounting those projected returns at a different rate and including the rate in the measurement of the liability. *[IFRS 4.27]*.

Such accounting policies are used in some embedded value methodologies. For example, the CFO Forum European Embedded Value (EEV) Principles state that the value of future cash flows from in-force covered business should be the present value of future shareholder cash flows projected to emerge from the assets backing the liabilities of the in-force covered business reduced by the value of financial options and guarantees.[25] The EEV methodology is considered to be an indirect method of measuring the insurance liability because the measurement of the liability is derived from the related asset. In contrast, direct methods measure the liability by discounting future cash flows arising from the book of insurance contracts only. If the same assumptions are made in both direct and indirect methods, they can produce the same results. *[IFRS 4.BC138]*.

The IASB appears to have been concerned that insurers might take advantage of the lack of specific accounting guidance for insurance contracts in IFRS 4 as an opportunity to change their accounting policies to an embedded value basis on the grounds that this was more relevant and no less reliable, or more reliable and no less relevant than their existing accounting policies (possibly prepared on an 'excessively prudent' regulatory basis). The use of embedded value measures by insurers is discussed at 1.3.3 above.

The IASB's view is that the cash flows arising from an asset are irrelevant for the measurement of a liability unless those cash flows affect (a) the cash flows arising from the liability or (b) the credit characteristics of the liability. Therefore, the IASB considers that the following two embedded value approaches involve practices that are incompatible with IFRS, namely:

- applying an asset discount rate to insurance liabilities; and
- measuring contractual rights to investment management fees at an amount that exceeds their fair value (see 8.2.1.B above).

However, the IASB concluded that it could not eliminate these practices, where they were existing accounting policies, until Phase II gives guidance on the appropriate discount rates and the basis for risk adjustments and therefore the use of asset-based discount rates for the measurement of insurance liabilities is not prohibited. *[IFRS 4.BC142]*.

In addition, where embedded values are generally determined on a single best estimate basis, the IASB considers that they do not reflect a full range of possible outcomes and do not generally adequately address liabilities arising from embedded guarantees and options. Further, the IASB believes that existing embedded value approaches are largely unregulated and there is diversity in their application. *[IFRS 4.BC141]*.

It is possible for insurers to introduce accounting policies that use an embedded value approach even if that involves the use of asset-based discount rates for liabilities if they can overcome the rebuttable presumption described above. This will be if, and only if, the other components of a change in accounting policies increase the relevance and reliability of its financial statements sufficiently to outweigh the decrease in relevance and reliability caused by the inclusion of future investment margins. For example, suppose an insurer's existing accounting policies for insurance contracts involves excessively prudent assumptions set at inception and a discount rate prescribed by a regulator without direct reference to market conditions, and the assumptions ignore some embedded options and guarantees. The insurer might make its financial statements more relevant and no less reliable by switching to a basis of accounting that is widely used and involves:

(a) current estimates and assumptions;

(b) a reasonable (but not excessively prudent) adjustment to reflect risk and uncertainty;

(c) measurements that reflect both the intrinsic value and time value of embedded options and guarantees; and

(d) a current market discount rate, even if that discount rate reflects the estimated return on the insurer's assets. *[IFRS 4.28]*.

In some measurement approaches, the discount rate is used to determine the present value of a future profit margin. That profit margin is then attributed to different periods using a formula. In those approaches, the discount rate affects the measurement of the liability only indirectly. In these circumstances, the IASB has concluded that the use of a less appropriate discount rate has a limited or no effect on the measurement of the liability at inception. However, in other approaches, the IASB considers that the discount rate determines the measurement of the liability directly. In the latter case, because the introduction of an asset-based discount rate has a more significant effect, the IASB believes that it is highly unlikely that an insurer could overcome the rebuttable presumption described above. *[IFRS 4.29]*.

The IASB believes that in most applications of embedded value the discount rate determines the measurement of the liability directly and therefore it is highly unlikely that an insurer could overcome the rebuttable presumption described above if it wanted to change its accounting policies for insurance contracts to an embedded value basis. *[IFRS 4.BC144]*.

8.3 Shadow accounting

IFRS 4 grants relief to insurers allowing them to mitigate an accounting mismatch occurring when unrealised gains or losses on assets backing insurance contracts affect the measurement of the insurance contracts. This relief, known as 'shadow accounting', ensures that all gains and losses on investments affect the measurement of the insurance assets and liabilities in the same way, regardless of whether they are realised or unrealised and regardless of whether the unrealised investment gains and losses are recognised in profit or loss or in other comprehensive income using a revaluation reserve. In particular, the relief permits certain gains or losses arising from remeasuring insurance contracts to be recognised in other comprehensive income whereas IFRS 4 otherwise requires all gains and losses arising from insurance contracts to be recognised in profit or loss. Normally, this change in accounting policy would be adopted upon transition to IFRS. Application of shadow accounting is always voluntary and in practice it is also applied selectively.

In many local GAAP accounting models, gains or losses on an insurer's assets have a direct effect on the measurement of some or all of its insurance liabilities, related deferred acquisition costs and related intangible assets. *[IFRS 4.30]*. In some of these models, prior to the introduction of IFRS, the insurer's assets were measured at cost or amortised cost and unrealised fair value movements were not recognised. Under IFRS, most of an insurer's assets are likely to be held at either fair value through profit or loss or available-for-sale with unrealised fair value gains recognised in profit or loss or other comprehensive income respectively. If the unrealised gains on the insurance liabilities (or deferred acquisition costs and intangible assets) which the assets back were not also recognised there would be an accounting mismatch.

The IASB believe that, in principle, gains or losses on an asset should not influence the measurement of an insurance liability unless the gains or losses on the asset alter the amounts payable to policyholders. Nevertheless, this was a feature of some existing measurement models for insurance liabilities and the IASB decided that it was not feasible to eliminate this practice. The IASB also acknowledged that shadow accounting might mitigate volatility caused by differences between the measurement basis for assets and the measurement basis for insurance liabilities. However, that is a by-product of shadow accounting and not its primary purpose. *[IFRS 4.BC183]*.

IFRS 4 permits, but does not require, a change in accounting policies so that a recognised but unrealised gain or loss on an asset affects the related insurance liabilities in the same way that a realised gain or loss does. In other words, a measurement adjustment to an insurance liability (or deferred acquisition cost or intangible asset) arising from the remeasurement of an asset would be recognised in other comprehensive income if, and only if, the unrealised gains or losses on the asset are also recognised in other comprehensive income. *[IFRS 4.30]*.

Recognition of movements in insurance liabilities (or deferred acquisition costs or intangible assets) in other comprehensive income only applies when unrealised gains on assets are recognised in other comprehensive income such as for available-for-sale investments accounted for under IAS 39, debt securities classified at fair value through other comprehensive income under IFRS 9 or property, plant and equipment accounted for using the revaluation model under IAS 16. *[IFRS 4.IG10]*.

Shadow accounting is not applicable for liabilities arising from investment contracts accounted for under IAS 39 (or IFRS 9). However, shadow accounting may be applicable for a DPF within an investment contract if the measurement of that feature depends on asset values or asset returns. *[IFRS 4.IG8].*

Further, shadow accounting may not be used if the measurement of an insurance liability is not driven by realised gains and losses on assets held, for example if the insurance liabilities are measured using a discount rate that reflects a current market rate but that measurement does not depend directly on the carrying amount of any assets held. *[IFRS 4.IG9].*

The implementation guidance to IFRS 4 includes an illustrative example to show how shadow accounting through other comprehensive income might be applied. This example is reproduced in full below.

Example 55.31: Shadow accounting

Background

Under some national requirements for some insurance contracts, deferred acquisition costs (DAC) are amortised over the life of the contract as a constant proportion of estimated gross profits (EGP). EGP includes investment returns, including realised (but not unrealised) gains and losses. Interest is applied to both DAC and EGP, to preserve present value relationships. For simplicity, this example ignores interest and ignores re-estimation of EGP.

At the inception of a contract, insurer A has DAC of CU20 relating to that contract and the present value, at inception, of EGP is CU100. In other words, DAC is 20 per cent of EGP at inception. Thus, for each CU1 of realised gross profits, insurer A amortises DAC by CU0.20. For example, if insurer A sells assets and recognises a gain of CU10, insurer A amortises DAC by CU2 (20 per cent of CU10).

Before adopting IFRSs for the first time in 2013, insurer A measured financial assets on a cost basis. (Therefore, EGP under those national requirements considers only realised gains and losses.) However, under IFRSs, it does not apply IFRS 9 and classifies its financial assets as available for sale. Thus, insurer A measures the assets at fair value and recognises changes in their fair value directly in other comprehensive income. In 2013, insurer A recognises unrealised gains of CU10 on the assets backing the contract.

In 2014, insurer A sells the assets for an amount equal to their fair value at the end of 2013 and, to comply with IAS 39, transfers the now-realised gain of CU10 from other comprehensive income to profit or loss.

Application of paragraph 30 of IFRS 4

Paragraph 30 of IFRS 4 permits, but does not require, insurer A to adopt shadow accounting. If insurer A adopts shadow accounting, it amortises DAC in 2013 by an additional CU2 (20 per cent of CU10) as a result of the change in the fair value of the assets. Because insurer A recognised the change in the assets' fair value in other comprehensive income, it recognises the additional amortisation of CU2 directly in other comprehensive income.

When insurer A sells the assets in 2014, it makes no further adjustment to DAC, but transfers DAC amortisation of CU2 relating to the now-realised gain from other comprehensive income to profit or loss.

In summary, shadow accounting treats an unrealised gain in the same way as a realised gain, except that the unrealised gain and resulting DAC amortisation are (a) recognised in other comprehensive income rather than in profit or loss and (b) transferred to profit or loss when the gain on the asset becomes realised.

If insurer A does not adopt shadow accounting, unrealised gains on assets do not affect the amortisation of DAC (i.e. the CU2 of DAC amortisation would have been recognised in profit or loss in 2013). *[IFRS 4.IG10, IE4].*

Old Mutual is an example of an entity that applies shadow accounting.

> *Extract 55.16: Old Mutual plc (2008)*
>
> **Accounting policies** [extract]
>
> **(d) Insurance and investment contracts** [extract]
>
> ***(v) Insurance contract provisions*** [extract]
>
> The group applies shadow accounting in relation to certain insurance contract provisions in the South Africa long-term business, and DAC and PVIF assets in the United States long-term business, in respect of owner occupied properties or available-for-sale financial assets, in order for recognised unrealised gains or losses on those assets to affect the measurement of the insurance contract provisions, DAC or PVIF assets in the same way that the recognised gains or losses do.
>
> In respect of the South Africa long-term business, shadow accounting is applied to insurance contract provisions where the underlying measurement of the policyholder liability depends directly on the value of owner-occupied property and the unrealised gains and losses on such property, which are recognised in equity. The shadow accounting adjustment to insurance contract provisions is recognised in equity to the extent that the unrealised gains or losses on owner-occupied property backing insurance contract provisions are also directly recognised in equity.
>
> In respect of the United States long-term business, shadow accounting adjustments are made to the amortisation of DAC and PVIF assets in respect of unrealised gains and losses on available-for-sale financial assets to the extent that those unrealised gains and losses would impact the calculation of DAC or PVIF amortisation were they recognised in income. The shadow DAC and PVIF amortisation charge is recognised in equity in line with the unrealised gains and losses on the relevant financial assets until such time as those assets are sold or otherwise disposed of, at which point the accumulated amortisation recognised in equity is recycled to the income statement in the same way as the unrealised gains or losses on those financial assets.

IFRS 4 does not specifically address the interaction between shadow accounting and the liability adequacy test. We believe that shadow accounting is applied before the liability adequacy test and the implications of this are discussed at 7.2.2.D above.

Shadow accounting, as described in IFRS 4, is not permitted in the revised ED or in the subsequent deliberations of the revised ED. However, the new Phase II standard does contain proposals that can produce a similar effect to shadow accounting. For example, the IASB has tentatively decided that an entity should have an accounting policy choice at an insurance portfolio level whether to present the effect of changes in discount rates in profit or loss or in other comprehensive income.[26]

8.4 Redesignation of financial assets

IAS 39 generally prohibits the reclassification of a financial asset into the 'fair value through profit or loss' category while it is held or issued. *[IAS 39.50]*. IFRS 9 allows such reclassifications only when an entity changes its business model for financial assets. *[IFRS 9.4.4.1]*. However, when an insurer changes its accounting policies for insurance liabilities, it is permitted, but not required, to reclassify some or all of its financial assets at fair value through profit or loss. This reclassification is permitted if an insurer changes its accounting policies when it first applies IFRS 4 and also if it makes a subsequent policy change permitted by IFRS 4. This reclassification is a change in accounting policy and the requirements of IAS 8 apply, i.e. it must be performed retrospectively unless impracticable. *[IFRS 4.45]*.

The IASB decided to grant this exemption from IAS 39 (or IFRS 9) in order to allow an insurer to avoid an accounting mismatch when it improves its accounting policies for insurance contracts and to remove unnecessary barriers for insurers wishing to move to a measurement basis that reflects fair values. *[IFRS 4.BC145]*.

This concession cannot be used to reclassify financial assets out of the fair value through profit or loss category. These remain subject to the normal IAS 39 (or IFRS 9) requirements.

The revised ED proposes that insurers would be permitted, but not required, upon adopting the new standard, to redesignate a financial asset as measured at fair value through profit or loss if doing so would eliminate or significantly reduce an inconsistency in measurement or recognition. In addition, insurers would be required to revoke previous designations of financial assets at fair value through profit or loss if the initial application of the new standard eliminates the accounting mismatch that led to the previous designation. Insurers that had adopted IFRS 9 previously would also be able to designate an investment in an equity instrument as at fair value through other comprehensive income or revoke a previous such designation.[27] In subsequent discussions, the IASB tentatively decided to confirm the transition relief proposals in the revised ED and to consider providing further relief to permit or require an entity to reassess the business model for financial assets at the date of initial application of the new insurance contracts standard.[28]

8.5 Practical issues

8.5.1 Changes to local GAAP

As most entities are applying some form of local GAAP for their insurance contracts under IFRS 4, a common issue is whether an entity is obliged to change its accounting policy when local GAAP changes or whether the decision to change accounting policy for IFRS purposes is one that remains solely with the insurer.

We believe that the decision to change an accounting policy established on the initial adoption of IFRS is at the discretion of the entity. Accordingly, any change in local GAAP for insurance contracts that was used as the basis for the initial adoption of IFRS does not oblige the insurer to change its accounting policies.

Although an entity is not required to change its policies when local GAAP changes, it can make voluntary changes provided the revised accounting policy makes the financial statements more relevant and no less reliable or more reliable and no less relevant, as discussed at 8.1 above.

When a local accounting standard is changed, it is likely that the change is made for a reason. Therefore, there would normally be a rebuttable presumption that any change in local GAAP is an improvement to the existing standard and so is more relevant and no less reliable or more reliable and no less relevant to users than the previous standard would have been.

The fact that an entity can decide whether or not to apply changes in local GAAP will inevitably, over time, lead to further diversity in practice and potentially encourage 'cherry picking' of accounting policies. This emphasises the need for a comprehensive recognition and measurement standard sooner rather than later.

Chapter 55

The financial statements of AXA provide an example of a change in accounting policy caused by a change to local GAAP.

Extract 55.17: AXA Group (2007)

Notes to the consolidated financial statements of AXA Group [extract]

Note 1.12.2 Insurance contracts and investment contracts with discretionary participating features [extract]

Following the adoption of UK Financial Reporting standard FRS27, reserves relating to with-profit contracts and the FFA were subject to a change in accounting policies in 2006, that was applied retrospectively, consistently with what other UK insurance companies applied. Reserves were adjusted on a "realistic" basis, and related deferred acquisition costs and unearned revenues reserves were cancelled. These adjustments had no impact on net income or shareholders' equity. The presentational impact of applying this standard is detailed in note 14. This change in accounting principles only applied to the Group's UK with-profit contracts.

An entity should not state that it uses a particular local GAAP for insurance contracts if it no longer complies with that GAAP due to it not implementing a local GAAP accounting policy change.

9 INSURANCE CONTRACTS ACQUIRED IN BUSINESS COMBINATIONS AND PORTFOLIO TRANSFERS

9.1 Expanded presentation of insurance contracts

IFRS 3 requires most assets and liabilities, including insurance liabilities assumed and insurance assets acquired, in a business combination to be measured at fair value. *[IFRS 4.31]*. The IASB saw no compelling reason to exempt insurers from these requirements. *[IFRS 4.BC153]*.

However, an insurer is permitted, but not required, to use an expanded presentation that splits the fair value of acquired insurance contracts into two components:

(a) a liability measured in accordance with the acquirer's accounting policies for insurance contracts that it issues; and

(b) an intangible asset, representing the difference between (i) the fair value of the contractual insurance rights acquired and insurance obligations assumed and (ii) the amount described in (a). The subsequent measurement of this asset should be consistent with the measurement of the related insurance liabilities. *[IFRS 4.31(a), (b)]*.

We note that technically this IFRS 4 intangible has no intrinsic value that can be actuarially calculated. It is no more than the balancing number between the purchase price allocated to the insurance liability and the amount recorded for the insurance liability by the purchaser under the purchaser's existing GAAP. The more prudent (higher) the basis of liability measurement, the higher the value of the intangible.

This alternative presentation had often been used in practice under many local GAAPs. Life insurers have variously described this intangible asset as the 'present value of in-force business' (PVIF), 'present value of future profits' (PVFP or PVP) or 'value of business acquired' (VOBA). Similar principles apply in non-life insurance, for example, if claims liabilities are not discounted. *[IFRS 4.BC147]*.

The IASB decided to let these existing practices continue because:

- they wished to avoid insurers making systems changes for Phase I that might need to be reversed in Phase II. In the IASB's opinion the disclosures about the intangible asset provide transparency for users;
- IFRS 4 gives no guidance on how to determine fair values (although IFRS 13 does not exclude insurance contracts from its scope – see 9.1.1.B below); and
- it might be difficult for insurers to integrate a fair value measurement at the date of a business combination into subsequent insurance contract accounting without requiring systems changes that could become obsolete in Phase II. *[IFRS 4.BC148]*.

An insurer acquiring a portfolio of insurance contracts (separate from a business combination) may also use the expanded presentation described above. *[IFRS 4.32]*.

An illustration of how a business combination might be accounted for using the expanded presentation is given below.

Example 55.32: Business combination under IFRS 4

Insurance entity A purchases an insurance business owned by Entity B for £10 million. Under A's existing accounting policies for insurance contracts the carrying value of the insurance contract liabilities held by B is £8 million. Entity A estimates the fair value of the insurance contract liabilities to be £6 million. The fair value of other net assets acquired, including intangible assets, after recognising any additional deferred tax, is £13 million. The tax rate is 25%.

This gives rise to the following journal entry to record the acquisition of B in A's consolidated financial statements:

	£m	£m
Cash		10.0
Present value of in-force (PVIF) business intangible (£8m less £6m)	2.0	
Carrying value of insurance liabilities (A's existing accounting policies)		8.0
Goodwill	3.5	
Other net assets acquired	13.0	
Deferred taxation on PVIF		0.5

The intangible asset described at (b) above is excluded from the scope of both IAS 36 and IAS 38; instead IFRS 4 requires its subsequent measurement to be consistent with the measurement of the related insurance liabilities. *[IFRS 4.33]*. As a result, it is generally amortised over the estimated life of the contracts. Some insurers use an interest method of amortisation, which the IASB considers is appropriate for an asset that essentially comprises the present value of a set of contractual cash flows. However, the IASB considers it doubtful whether IAS 38 would have permitted such a method, hence the scope exclusion from IAS 38. This intangible asset is included within the scope of the liability adequacy test discussed at 7.2.2 above which acts as a quasi-impairment test on its carrying amount and hence is also excluded from the scope of IAS 36. *[IFRS 4.BC149]*.

Generali is one entity that uses the expanded presentation discussed above and its accounting policy for acquired insurance contracts is reproduced below.

Extract 55.18: Assicurazioni Generali S.p.A. (2008)

Notes to the consolidated financial statements [extract]

Part D **Summary of significant accounting policies** [extract]

Note 1.2.1 **Insurance contracts acquired in a business combination or portfolio transfer** [extract]

In case of acquisition of non-life insurance contracts in a business combination or portfolio transfer, the group recognises an intangible asset, i.e. the value of the acquired contractual relationships (Value of Business Acquired).

The VOBA is the present value of the pre-tax future profit arising from the contracts in force at the purchase date, taking into account the probability of renewals of the one year contracts. The related deferred taxes are accounted for as liabilities in the consolidated balance sheet.

The VOBA is amortized over the effective life of the contracts acquired, by using an amortization pattern reflecting the expected future profit recognition. Assumptions used in the development of the VOBA amortization pattern are consistent with the ones applied in its initial measurement. The amortization pattern is reviewed on a yearly basis to assess its reliability and to verify the consistency with the assumptions used in the valuation of the corresponding insurance provisions.

The difference between the fair value of the insurance contracts acquired in a business combination or a portfolio transfer, and the insurance liabilities measured in accordance with the acquirer's accounting policies for the insurance contracts that it issues is recognised as intangible asset and amortized over the period in which the acquirer recognises the corresponding profits.

The Generali Group applies this accounting treatment to the insurance liabilities assumed in the acquisition of insurance portfolios. Therefore, the assumed insurance liabilities are recognized in the balance sheet according to the acquirer's accounting policies for the insurance contracts that it issues. The intangible assets are not in the scope of IAS 38 and IAS 36.

The future VOBA recoverable amount is tested on yearly basis.

Investment contracts within the scope of IAS 39 (or IFRS 9) are required to be measured at fair value when acquired in a business combination.

As discussed at 3.3 above, there should be no reassessment of the classification of contracts previously classified as insurance contracts under IFRS 4 which are acquired as a part of a business combination.

The revised ED proposes that an entity treats the consideration paid or received in a portfolio transfer (excluding any amounts received or paid for any other assets and liabilities acquired in the same transaction) as a pre-coverage cash flow. In accordance with the general requirements of the revised ED, the entity would measure the insurance contracts as the sum of the fulfilment cash flows and the contractual service margin, if any.[29] In subsequent discussions, the IASB tentatively decided to clarify that contracts acquired through a portfolio transfer or a business combination should be accounted for as if they had been issued by the entity at the date of the portfolio transfer or business combination.[30]

9.1.1 Practical issues

9.1.1.A The difference between a business combination and a portfolio transfer

When an entity acquires a portfolio of insurance contracts the main accounting consideration is to determine whether that acquisition meets the definition of a business. IFRS 3 defines a business as 'an integrated set of activities and assets that is capable of being conducted and managed for the purpose of providing a return in the form of dividends, lower costs or other economic benefits directly to investors, or other owners, members or participants'. *[IFRS 3 Appendix A]*. The application guidance to IFRS 3 notes that a business consists of inputs and processes applied to those inputs that have the ability to create outputs. Although businesses usually have outputs they do not need to be present for an integrated set of assets and activities to be a business. *[IFRS 3.B7]*. Where it is considered that a business is acquired, goodwill may need to be recognised as may deferred tax liabilities in respect of any acquired intangibles. For an isolated portfolio transfer, neither goodwill nor deferred tax should be recognised.

The determination of whether a portfolio of contracts or a business has been acquired will be a matter of judgement based on the facts and circumstances. Acquisitions of contracts that also include the acquisition of underwriting systems and/or the related organised workforce are more likely to meet the definition of a business than merely the acquisition of individual or multiple contracts.

Rights to issue or renew contracts in the future (as opposed to existing insurance contracts) are separate intangible assets and the accounting for the acquisition of such rights is discussed at 9.2 below.

9.1.1.B Fair value of an insurer's liabilities

IFRS 4 does not prescribe a method for determining the fair value of insurance liabilities. However, the definition of fair value in IFRS 4 is the same as that in IFRS 13 and insurance contracts are not excluded from the scope of IFRS 13. Therefore, any calculation of fair value must be consistent with IFRS 13's valuation principles.

Deferred acquisition costs (DAC) are generally considered to have no value in a business combination and are usually subsumed into the PVIF intangible. The fair value of any unearned premium reserve will include any unearned profit element as well as the present value of the claims obligation in respect of the unexpired policy period at the acquisition date which is likely to be different from the value under existing accounting policies.

9.1.1.C Deferred taxation

IAS 12 requires deferred tax to be recognised in respect of temporary differences arising in business combinations, for example if the tax base of the asset or liability remains at cost when the carrying amount is fair value. IFRS 4 contains no exemption from these requirements. Therefore, deferred tax will often arise on temporary differences created by the recognition of insurance liabilities at their fair value or on the related intangible asset. The deferred tax adjusts the amount of goodwill recognised as illustrated in Example 55.32 at 9.1 above. *[IAS 12.19]*.

9.1.1.D Negative intangible assets

There are situations where the presentation described at 9.1 above may result in the creation of a negative intangible asset, at least in theory. This could arise, for example, where the acquirer's existing accounting policies are such that the contractual liabilities acquired are measured at an amount less than their fair value although this is likely to raise questions about whether the carrying value of the liabilities are adequate (see 7.2.2 above). IFRS 4 is silent on the subject of negative intangible assets but there appears to be no prohibition on their recognition.

9.2 Customer lists and relationships not connected to contractual insurance rights and obligations

The requirements discussed at 9.1 above apply only to contractual insurance rights and obligations that existed at the date of a business combination or portfolio transfer.

Therefore, they do not apply to customer lists and customer relationships reflecting the expectation of future contracts that are not part of the contractual insurance rights and contractual insurance obligations existing at the date of the transaction. *[IFRS 4.33]*. IAS 36 and IAS 38 apply to such transactions as they apply to other intangible assets.

The following example deals with customer relationships acquired together with a portfolio of one-year motor insurance contracts.

Example 55.33: Purchase of portfolio of one-year motor insurance contracts

Background

Parent A obtained control of insurer B in a business combination on 31 December 2014. B has a portfolio of one-year motor insurance contracts that are cancellable by policyholders.

Analysis

Because B establishes its relationships with policyholders through insurance contracts, the customer relationship with the policyholders meets the contractual-legal criterion for recognition as an intangible asset. IAS 36 and IAS 38 apply to the customer relationship intangible asset. *[IFRS 3.IE30(d)]*.

10 DISCLOSURE

One of the two main objectives of IFRS 4 is to require entities issuing insurance contracts to disclose information about those contracts that identifies and explains the amounts in an insurer's financial statements arising from these contracts and helps users of those financial statements understand the amount, timing and uncertainty of future cash flows from those insurance contracts. *[IFRS 4.IN1]*.

For many insurers, the disclosure requirements of the standard had a significant impact when IFRS 4 was applied for the first time because they significantly exceeded what were required under most local GAAP financial reporting frameworks.

In drafting the disclosure requirements, the main objective of the IASB appears to have been to impose similar requirements for insurance contracts as for financial assets and financial liabilities under IFRS 7.

The requirements in the standard itself are relatively high-level and contain little specific detail. For example, reconciliations of changes in insurance liabilities, reinsurance assets and, if any, related deferred acquisition costs are required but no details about the line items those reconciliations should contain are specified. By comparison, however, other standards such as IAS 16, provide details of items required to be included in similar reconciliations for other amounts in the statement of financial position.

The lack of specific disclosure requirements is probably attributable to the diversity of accounting practices permitted under IFRS 4. We suspect the IASB probably felt unable to give anything other than generic guidance within the standard to avoid the risk that local GAAP requirements may not fit in with more specific guidance.

However, the disclosure requirements outlined in the standard are supplemented by sixty nine paragraphs of related implementation guidance which explains how insurers may or might apply the standard. According to this guidance, an insurer should decide in the light of its circumstances how much emphasis to place on different aspects of the requirements and how information should be aggregated to display the overall picture without combining information that has materially different characteristics. Insurers should strike a balance so that important information is not obscured either by the inclusion of a large amount of insignificant detail or by the aggregation of items that have materially different characteristics. To satisfy the requirements of the standard an insurer would not typically need to disclose all the information suggested in the guidance. *[IFRS 4.IG12]*.

The implementation guidance does not, however, create additional disclosure requirements. *[IFRS 4.IG12]*. On the other hand, there is a reminder that IAS 1 requires additional disclosures when compliance with the specific requirements in IFRSs is insufficient to enable users to understand the impact of particular transactions, other events and conditions on the entity's financial position and financial performance. *[IFRS 4.IG13]*. The guidance also draws attention to the definition and explanation of materiality in IAS 1. *[IFRS 4.IG15-16]*.

The disclosure requirements are sub-divided into two main sections:

(a) information that identifies and explains the amounts in the financial statements arising from insurance contracts; and

(b) information that enables users of its financial statements to evaluate the nature and extent of risks arising from insurance contracts.

Each of these is discussed in detail below. They are accompanied by examples illustrating how some of disclosure requirements have been applied in practice.

As discussed at 2.2.2 above, disclosures for investment contracts with a DPF are within the scope of IFRS 7 and IFRS 13, not IFRS 4.

10.1 Explanation of recognised amounts

The first disclosure principle established by the standard is that an insurer should identify and explain the amounts in its financial statements arising from insurance contracts. *[IFRS 4.36]*.

To comply with this principle an insurer should disclose:

(a) its accounting policies for insurance contracts and related assets, liabilities, income and expense;

(b) the recognised assets, liabilities, income and expense (and cash flows if its statement of cash flows is presented using the direct method) arising from insurance contracts. Furthermore, if the insurer is a cedant it should disclose:

  (i) gains or losses recognised in profit or loss on buying reinsurance; and

  (ii) if gains and losses on buying reinsurance are deferred and amortised, the amortisation for the period and the amounts remaining unamortised at the beginning and the end of the period;

(c) the process used to determine the assumptions that have the greatest effect on the measurement of the recognised amounts described in (b). When practicable, quantified disclosure of these assumptions should be given;

(d) the effect of changes in assumptions used to measure insurance assets and insurance liabilities, showing separately the effect of each change that has a material effect on the financial statements; and

(e) reconciliations of changes in insurance liabilities, reinsurance assets and, if any, related deferred acquisitions costs. *[IFRS 4.37]*.

Each of these is discussed below.

10.1.1 Disclosure of accounting policies

As noted at 10.1 above, IFRS 4 requires an insurer's accounting policies for insurance contracts and related liabilities, income and expense to be disclosed. *[IFRS 4.37(a)]*. The implementation guidance suggests that an insurer might need to address the treatment of some or all of the following:

(a) premiums (including the treatment of unearned premiums, renewals and lapses, premiums collected by agents and brokers but not passed on and premium taxes or other levies on premiums);

(b) fees or other charges made to policyholders;

(c) acquisition costs (including a description of their nature);

(d) claims incurred (both reported and unreported), claims handling costs (including a description of their nature) and liability adequacy tests (including a description of the cash flows included in the test, whether and how the cash flows are discounted and the treatment of embedded options and guarantees in those tests – see 7.2.2 above). Disclosure of whether insurance liabilities are discounted might be given together with an explanation of the methodology used;

(e) the objective of methods used to adjust insurance liabilities for risk and uncertainty (for example, in terms of a level of assurance or level of sufficiency), the nature of those models, and the source of information used in those models;

(f) embedded options and guarantees including a description of whether:
   (i) the measurement of insurance liabilities reflects the intrinsic value and time value of these items; and
   (ii) their measurement is consistent with observed current market prices;

(g) discretionary participation features (including an explanation of how the insurer classifies those features between liabilities and components of equity) and other features that permit policyholders to share in investment performance;

(h) salvage, subrogation or other recoveries from third parties;

(i) reinsurance held;

(j) underwriting pools, coinsurance and guarantee fund arrangements;

(k) insurance contracts acquired in business combinations and portfolio transfers, and the treatment of related intangible assets; and

(l) the judgements, apart from those involving estimations, management has made in the process of applying the accounting policies that have the most significant effect on the amounts recognised in the financial statements as required by IAS 1. The classification of a DPF is an example of an accounting policy that might have a significant effect. *[IFRS 4.IG17]*.

Because an insurer's accounting policies will normally be based on its previous local GAAP, the policies for such items will vary from entity to entity.

Set out below are the accounting policies for premiums and claims for Aviva. These are based on UK GAAP which has different requirements for recognition of premiums from life and general (non-life) insurance business.

Extract 55.19: Aviva plc (2008)

Accounting policies [extract]

(G) Premiums earned

Premiums on long-term insurance contracts and participating investment contracts as recognised as income when receivable, except for investment-linked premiums which are accounted for when the corresponding liabilities are recognised. For single premium business, this is the date from which the policy is effective. For regular premium contracts, receivables are taken at the date when payments are due. Premiums are shown before deduction of commission and before any sale-based taxes or duties. Where policies lapse due to non-receipt of premiums, then all related premium income accrued but not received from the date they are deemed to have lapsed is offset against premiums.

General insurance and health premiums written reflect direct business incepted during the year, and exclude any sales-based taxes or duties. Unearned premiums are those proportions of the premiums written in a year that relate to periods of risk after the balance sheet date. Unearned premiums are calculated on either a daily or monthly pro rata basis. Premiums collected by intermediaries, but not yet received, are assessed based on estimates from underwriting or past experience, and are included in premiums written.

Deposits collected under investment contracts without a discretionary participation feature (non-participating contracts) are not accounted for through the income statement, except for fee income (covered in policy H) and the investment income attributable to those contracts, but are accounted for directly through the balance sheet as an adjustment to the investment contract liability.

(K) Insurance and participating investment contract liabilities [extract]

Claims

Long-term business claims reflect the cost of all claims arising during the year, including claims handling costs, as well as policyholder bonuses accrued in anticipation of bonus declarations.

General insurance and health claims include all losses occurring during the year, whether reported or not, related handling costs, a reduction for the value of salvage and other recoveries, and any adjustments to claims outstanding from previous years.

Claims handling costs include internal and external costs incurred in connection with the negotiation and settlement of claims. Internal costs include all direct expenses of the claims department and any part of the general administrative costs directly attributable to the claims function.

Long-term business provision

Under current IFRS requirements, insurance and participating investment contract liabilities are measured under accounting policies consistent with those adopted previously under existing accounting practices, with the exception of liabilities remeasured to reflect current market interest rates and those relating to UK with-profit and non-profit contracts, to be consistent with the value of the backing assets. For liabilities relating to UK with-profit-contracts, the Group has adopted FRS 27, *Life Assurance*, which adds to the requirements of IFRS but does not vary them in any way. Further details are given in policy A above.

In the United States, shadow adjustments are made to the liabilities or related deferred acquisition costs and are recognised directly in equity. This means that the measurement of these items is adjusted for unrealised gains or losses on the backing assets such as AFS financial investments (see policy S), that are recognised directly in equity, in the same way as if those gains or losses had been realised.

The long-term business provisions are calculated separately for each life operation, based either on local regulatory requirements or existing local GAAP at the later of the date of transition to IFRS or the date of acquisition of the entity, and actuarial principles consistent with those applied in the UK. Each calculation represents a determination within a range of possible outcomes, where the assumptions used in the calculations depend on circumstances prevailing in each life operation. The principal assumptions are disclosed in note 38(b). For liabilities of the UK with-profit fund, FRS 27 requires liabilities to be calculated as the realistic basis liabilities as set out by the UK Financial Services Authority, adjusted to remove the shareholders' share of future bonuses. For UK non-profit insurance contracts, the Group applies the realistic regulatory basis as set out in the FSA Policy Statement 06/14, *Prudential Changes for Insurers,* where applicable.

General insurance and health provisions [extract]

(i) Outstanding claims provisions [extract]

General insurance and health outstanding claims provisions are based on the estimated ultimate cost of all claims incurred but not settled at the balance sheet date, whether reported or not, together with related claims handling costs. Significant delays are experienced in the notification and settlements of certain types of general insurance claims, particularly in respect of liability business, including environmental and potential exposures, the ultimate cost of which cannot be known with certainty at the balance sheet date. Provisions for certain claims are discounted, using rates having regard to the returns generated by the assets supporting the liabilities. Any estimate represents a determination within a range of possible outcomes. Further details of estimation techniques are given in note 38(c).

Provisions for latent claims are discounted, using rates based on the relevant swap curve, in the relevant currency at the reporting date, having due regard to the duration of the expected settlement date of the claims. The discount rate is set at the start of the accounting period with any change in rates between the start and end of the accounting period being reflected below operating profit as an economic assumption change. The range of discount rates used is described in note 38c. This is a change in accounting policy, the effects of which are given in note 2(b)(i).

(ii) Provision for unearned premiums

The proportion of written premiums, gross of commission payable to intermediaries, attributable to subsequent periods is deferred as a provision for unearned premiums. The change in this provision is taken to the income statement in order that revenue is recognised over the period of risk.

The following example from Allianz illustrates an accounting policy for reinsurance contracts based on US GAAP.

Extract 55.20: Allianz SE (2008)

Notes to the consolidated financial statements [extract]

2. Summary of significant accounting policies [extract]

Reinsurance contracts

The Allianz Group's consolidated financial statements reflect the effects of ceded and assumed reinsurance contracts. Assumed reinsurance refers to the acceptance of certain insurance risks by Allianz that other companies have underwritten. Ceded reinsurance refers to the transfer of insurance risk, along with the respective premiums, to one or more reinsurers who will share in the risks. When the reinsurance contracts do not transfer significant insurance risk according to SFAS 113, deposit accounting is applied as required under SOP 98-7.

Assumed reinsurance premiums, commissions and claim settlements, as well as the reinsurance element of technical provisions are accounted for in accordance with the conditions of the reinsurance contracts and with consideration of the original contracts for which the reinsurance was concluded.

Premiums ceded for reinsurance and reinsurance recoveries on benefits and claims incurred are deducted from premiums earned and insurance and investment contract benefits. Assets and liabilities related to reinsurance are reported on a gross basis. Amounts ceded to reinsurers from reserves for insurance and investment contracts are estimated in a manner consistent with the claim liability associated with the reinsured risks. Revenues and expenses related to reinsurance agreements are recognised in a manner consistent with the underlying risk of the business reinsured.

To the extent that the assuming reinsurers are unable to meet their obligations, the Group remains liable to its policyholders for the portion reinsured. Consequently, allowances are made for receivables on reinsurance contracts which are deemed uncollectible.

An example of an accounting policy showing a split of contracts with a DPF between liability and equity (AMP) is shown at 6.1 above.

An example of an accounting policy for a liability adequacy test (Allianz) is shown at 7.2.2 above.

Examples of accounting policies for deferred acquisition costs (Zurich Financial Services and Generali) are shown at 7.2.6.B above.

An example of an accounting policy for salvage and subrogation (Royal & SunAlliance) is shown at 7.2.6.C above.

If the financial statements disclose supplementary information, for example embedded value information, that is not prepared on the basis used for other measurements in the financial statements, it would be appropriate to explain the basis of preparation. Disclosures about embedded value methodology might include information similar to that described above, as well as disclosure of whether, and how, embedded values are affected by estimated returns from assets and by locked-in capital and how those effects are estimated. *[IFRS 4.IG18]*.

10.1.2 Recognised assets, liabilities, income and expense

As noted at 10.1 above, IFRS 4 requires disclosure of the recognised assets, liabilities, income and expense (and cash flows if using the direct method) arising from insurance contracts. *[IFRS 4.37(b)]*.

10.1.2.A Assets and liabilities

IAS 1 requires minimum disclosures on the face of the statement of financial position. *[IAS 1.54]*. In order to satisfy these requirements, an insurer may need to present separately on the face of its statement of financial position the following amounts arising from insurance contracts:

(a) liabilities under insurance contracts and reinsurance contracts issued;

(b) assets under insurance contracts and reinsurance contracts issued; and

(c) assets under reinsurance contracts ceded which, as discussed at 7.2.4 above, should not be offset against the related insurance liabilities. *[IFRS 4.IG20]*.

Neither IAS 1 nor IFRS 4 prescribe the descriptions and ordering of the line items presented on the face of the statement of financial position. An insurer could amend the descriptions and ordering to suit the nature of its transactions. *[IFRS 4.IG21]*.

IAS 1 requires the presentation of current and non-current assets and liabilities as separate classifications on the face of the statement of financial position except where a presentation based on liquidity provides information that is reliable and more relevant. *[IAS 1.60]*. In practice, a current/non-current classification is not normally considered relevant for insurers, and they usually present their IFRS statements of financial position in broad order of liquidity.

IAS 1 permits disclosure, either on the face of the statement of financial position or in the notes, of sub-classifications of the line items presented, classified in a manner appropriate to the entity's operations. The appropriate sub-classifications of insurance liabilities will depend on the circumstances, but might include items such as:

(a) unearned premiums;

(b) claims reported by policyholders;

(c) claims incurred but not reported (IBNR);

(d) provisions arising from liability adequacy tests;

(e) provisions for future non-participating benefits;

(f) liabilities or components of equity relating to discretionary participating features. If these are classified as a component of equity IAS 1 requires disclosure of the nature and purpose of each reserve within equity;

(g) receivables and payables related to insurance contracts (amounts currently due to and from agents, brokers and policyholders); and

(h) non-insurance assets acquired by exercising rights to recoveries. *[IFRS 4.IG22]*.

Similar sub-classifications may also be appropriate for reinsurance assets, depending on their materiality and other relevant circumstances. For assets under insurance contracts and reinsurance contracts issued an insurer might need to distinguish:

(a) deferred acquisition costs; and

(b) intangible assets relating to insurance contracts acquired in business combinations or portfolio transfers. *[IFRS 4.IG23]*.

If non-uniform accounting policies for the insurance liabilities of subsidiaries are adopted, it might be necessary to disaggregate the disclosures about the amounts reported to give meaningful information about amounts determined using different accounting policies. *[IFRS 4.IC30]*.

Munich Re's gross technical provisions on the face of the statement of financial position are illustrated below, together with some further detail shown in selected notes.

Extract 55.21: Münchener Rückversicherungs – Gesellschaft Aktiengesellschaft (2008)

Consolidated balance sheet as at 31 December 2008 [extract]
Equity and liabilities [extract]

	Notes			Prev. year	Change	balance sheet
		€m	€m	€m	€m	%
C. Gross technical provisions						
I. Unearned premiums	(19)	6,421		5,719	702	12.3
II. Provision for future policy benefits	(20)	98,738		94,933	3,805	4.0
III. Provision for outstanding claims	(21)	45,031		44,560	471	1.1
IV. Other technical provisions	(22)	9,292		10,536	–1,244	–11.8
Thereof: Provision for deferred premium refunds relating to disposal groups	(16)	–		–172	172	100.0
			159,482	155,748	3,734	2.4
D. Gross technical provisions for life insurance policies where the investment risk is borne by the policyholders	(23)		**2,940**	2,308	632	27.4

Note 20 Provision for future policy benefits [extract]

Gross provision for future policy benefits according to types of insurance cover

€m	31.12.2008	Prev. year
Life	77,638	74,882
Reinsurance	9,338	9,993
Primary insurance	68,300	64,889
Term life insurance	2,529	2,297
Other life insurance	40,772	40,544
Annuity insurance	23,956	21,026
Disability insurance	1,037	918
Contracts with combination of more than one risk	6	4
Health	20,503	19,037
Reinsurance	5	5
Primary insurance	20,498	19,032
Property-casualty	597	1,014
Reinsurance	299	748
Primary insurance	298	266
Total	**98,738**	**94,933**

Chapter 55

The provision for future policy benefits in life reinsurance largely involves contracts where the mortality or morbidity risk predominates. In reinsurance, annuity contracts have a significantly lower weight than in primary insurance.

In reinsurance, measurement is carried out partly individually for each risk and partly collectively for reinsured portfolios, using biometric actuarial assumptions based on the tables of the national actuarial associations. These are adjusted for the respective reinsured portfolio, in line with the probabilities observed for the occurrence of an insured event. A discount rate is chosen that is based on a conservative capital-market scenario.

In primary insurance, measurement is generally carried out individually for each risk. For German life and health primary insurance, to which approx. 87% of the provisions for future policy benefits are apportionable, biometric actuarial assumptions based on the tables of the German Association of Actuaries are used. We also largely use the tables of the national actuarial associations for the rest of the primary insurance business. The actuarial interest rate employed for discounting is limited by the respective maximum actuarial interest rate prescribed by the supervisory authorities.

Essentially the same actuarial assumptions have been used as in the previous year for measuring the provisions for future policy benefits for business in force.

Further information on the underwriting risks and discount rates can be found under (36) Risks from insurance contracts in the life and health segment and (37) Risks from insurance contracts in the property-casualty segment.

Note 21 Provision for outstanding claims [extract]
Gross provisions by type

	Reinsurance		*Primary insurance*		*Total*	
€m	31.12.2008	Prev. year	31.12.2008	Prev. year	31.12.2008	Prev. year
Life and health segment						
Disability claims provisions	1,470	1,537	897	860	2,367	2,397
Provision for other benefit cases	1,941	1,977	1,438	1,327	3,379	3,304
Property-casualty segment (claims reserve)						
Case reserve	17,668	17,602	3,908	3,801	21,576	21,403
IBNR reserve	16,455	16,342	1,254	1,114	17,709	17,456
Total	**37,534**	**37,458**	**7,497**	**7,102**	**45,031**	**44,560**

In the life and health segment, the provision for outstanding claims consists of a provision for disability cases and a provision for other benefit cases. The disability claims provision involves periodic payments and is usually due long term. It is calculated as the present value of the expected future payments. Discount rates are disclosed in Note (36) Risks from insurance contracts in the life and health segment. The biometric actuarial assumptions are selected using appropriate actuarial principles. The provision for other benefit cases is largely measured at face value and is usually due short term. This provision includes an IBNR reserve, whose amounts are estimated using actuarial methods.

In the property-casualty segment, the claims reserve consists of the case reserve and the IBNR reserve. The case reserve reflects the amount which is expected to be needed to settle claims which are known and reported at the balance sheet date. The major part of this provision is measured at face value. A smaller part refers to provisions for annuities in personal accident, liability and workers' compensation insurance. These are calculated as the present value of the expected future payments. The respective discount rates are disclosed in Note (37) Risks from insurance contracts in the property-casualty segment. The biometric actuarial assumptions are selected using appropriate actuarial principles. The IBNR reserve is calculated using actuarial methods on the basis of historical claims development data and taking into account foreseeable future trends.

CNP Assurances provided the following analysis of its insurance contract liabilities.

Extract 55.22: CNP Assurances (2008)

Notes to the financial statements [extract]

Note 10 Insurance and financial liabilities [extract]

Note 10.1 Analysis of insurance and financial liabilities [extract]

The following tables show the subclassifications of insurance liabilities that require separate disclosure under IFRS.

10.1.1 Analysis of insurance and financial liabilities at 31 December 2008 [extract]

In € millions	**31/12/2008**		
	Before reinsurance	**Net of reinsurance**	**Reinsurance**
Non-life technical reserves	**5,227.0**	**4,551.5**	**675.6**
Unearned premium reserves	184.4	168.1	16.3
Outstanding claims reserves	750.4	677.4	73.0
Bonuses and rebates (including claims equalisation reserve on group business maintained in liabilities)	56.5	53.6	3.0
Other technical reserves	4,235.7	3,652.4	583.3
Liability adequacy test reserves	0.0	0.0	0.0
Life technical reserves	**81,069.3**	**75,650.3**	**5,419.1**
Unearned premium reserves	79,590.2	74,215.6	5,374.6
Outstanding claims reserves	1,160.7	1,120.4	40.3
Policyholder surplus reserves	208.6	204.4	4.2
Other mathematical reserves	109.8	109.8	0.0
Liability adequacy test reserves	0.0	0.0	0.0
Financial instruments with DPF	**148,776.8**	**148,776.5**	**0.3**
Unearned premium reserves	145,111.0	145,110.7	0.3
Outstanding claims reserves	1,727.1	1,727.1	0.0
Policyholder surplus reserves	1,938.5	1,938.5	0.0
Other mathematical reserves	0.1	0.1	0.0
Liability adequacy test reserves	0.0	0.0	0.0
Financial instruments without DPF	**6,439.8**	**6,229.5**	**210.4**
Derivative instruments embedded in financial instruments with or without DPF	**0.0**	**0.0**	**0.0**
Deferred participation reserve	**356.7**	**356.7**	**0.0**
Total insurance and financial liabilities	**243,092.2**	**236,786.8**	**6,305.3**

IFRS 7 requires an entity to disclose the carrying amount of financial assets pledged as collateral for liabilities, the carrying amount of financial assets pledged as collateral for contingent liabilities, and any terms and conditions relating to assets pledged as collateral. *[IFRS 7.14-15]*. In complying with this requirement, it might be necessary to disclose segregation requirements that are intended to protect policyholders by restricting the use of some of the insurer's assets. *[IFRS 4.IG23A]*.

Prudential makes the following disclosures in respect of the segregation of various of its assets and liabilities.

Extract 55.23: Prudential plc (2008)

Notes on the group financial statements [extract]

D5: Capital position statement for life assurance business[extract]

d Transferability of available capital

For PAC and all other UK long-term insurers, long-term business assets and liabilities must, by law, be maintained in funds separate from those for the assets and liabilities attributable to non-life insurance business or to shareholders. Only the 'established surplus' – the excess of assets over liabilities in the long-term fund determined through a formal valuation – may be transferred so as to be available for other purposes. Distributions from the with-profits sub-fund to shareholders reflect the shareholders' one-ninth share of the cost of declared policyholders' bonuses.

Accordingly, the excess of assets over liabilities of the PAC long-term fund is retained within that company. The retention of the capital enables it to support with-profits and other business of the fund by, for example, providing the benefits associated with smoothing and guarantees. It also provides investment flexibility for the fund's assets by meeting the regulatory capital requirements that demonstrate solvency and by absorbing the costs of significant events or fundamental changes in its long-term business without affecting the bonus and investment policies.

For other UK long-term business subsidiaries, the amounts retained within the companies are at levels which provide an appropriate level of capital strength in excess of the regulatory minimum.

For Jackson, capital retention is maintained at a level consistent with an appropriate rating by Standard & Poor's. Currently Jackson is rated AA. Jackson can pay dividends on its capital stock only out of earned surplus unless prior regulatory approval is obtained. Furthermore, dividends which exceed the greater of 10 per cent of Jackson's statutory surplus or statutory net gain from operations for the prior year require prior regulatory approval.

For Asian subsidiaries, the amounts retained within the companies are at levels that provide an appropriate level of capital strength in excess of the local regulatory minimum. For ring-fenced with-profits funds, the excess of assets over liabilities is retained with distribution tied to the shareholders' share of bonuses through declaration of actuarially determined surplus. The Singapore and Malaysian businesses may, in general, remit dividends to the UK, provided the statutory insurance fund meets the capital adequacy standard required under local statutory regulations.

Available capital of the non-insurance business units is transferable to the life assurance businesses after taking account of an appropriate level of operating capital, based on local regulatory solvency targets, over and above basis liabilities. The economic capital model described in section D1 (concentration of risks) takes into account restrictions on mobility of capital across the Group with capital transfers to and from business units triggered at a solvency level consistent with these targets. The model takes into account restrictions on the availability to the Group of the estate of the various with-profits funds throughout the Group.

10.1.2.B Income and expense

IAS 1 lists minimum line items that an entity should present on the face of its income statement. It also requires the presentation of additional line items when this is necessary to present fairly the entity's financial performance. To satisfy these requirements, disclosure of the following amounts on the face of the income statement might be required:

(a) revenue from insurance contracts issued (without any deduction for reinsurance held);

(b) income from contracts with reinsurers;

(c) expense for policyholder claims and benefits (without any reduction for reinsurance held); and

(d) expenses arising from reinsurance held. *[IFRS 4.IG24]*.

The extracts below show two alternative methods of presenting revenue and expense on the face of the income statement. Royal & SunAlliance presents sub-totals of net premiums (premiums net of reinsurance premiums) and net claims (claims net of reinsurance claims) on the face of its income statement. AEGON presents reinsurance premiums within expenses and reinsurance claims within income on the face of its income statement.

Extract 55.24: Royal & SunAlliance Insurance Group plc (2008)

Consolidated income statement [extract]

For the year ended 31 December 2008

	Notes	**2008 £m**	2007 £m
Continuing operations			
Income			
Gross written premiums		**7,273**	6,596
Less: reinsurance premiums		**(811)**	(759)
Net written premiums		**6,462**	5,837
Change in the gross provision for unearned premiums		**(112)**	(235)
Less: change in provision for unearned premiums, reinsurers' share		**8**	5
Change in provision for unearned premiums		**(104)**	(230)
Net earned premiums		**6,358**	5,607
Net investment return	2	**681**	709
Other operating income	4	**104**	113
Total income		**7,143**	6,429
Expenses			
Gross claims incurred		**(4,205)**	(4,044)
Less: claims recoveries from reinsurers		**63**	387
Net claims and benefits	3	**(4,142)**	(3,657)
Underwriting and policy acquisition costs		**(1,925)**	(1,776)
Unwind of discount		**(92)**	(81)
Other operating expenses	4	**(117)**	(119)
Total expenses		**(6,276)**	(5,633)

Chapter 55

Extract 55.25: AEGON N.V. (2008)

Consolidated Income Statement of AEGON Group For The Year Ended December 31 [extract]

Amount in EUR million (except per share data)	Note	2008	2007	2006
Income				
Premium income	31	22,409	26,900	24,570
Investment income	32	9,965	10,457	10,376
Fee and commission income	33	1,703	1,900	1,665
Other revenues	34	5	14	4
Total revenues		34,082	39,271	36,615
Income from reinsurance ceded	35	1,633	1,546	1,468
Results from financial transactions	36	(28,195)	4,545	9,397
Other income	37	6	214	11
TOTAL INCOME		7,526	45,576	47,491
Charges				
Premiums to reinsurers	31	1,571	1,606	1,671
Policyholder claims and benefits	38	(808)	34,135	35,267
Profit sharing and rebates	39	98	83	133
Commissions and expenses	40	6,109	5,939	6,085
Impairment charges/(reversals)	41	1,113	117	33
Interest charges and related fees	42	526	474	362
Other charges	43	2	181	1
TOTAL CHARGES		8,611	42,535	43,552

IAS 18 requires an entity to disclose the amount of each significant category of revenue recognised during the period, and specifically requires disclosure of revenue arising from the rendering of services. *[IAS 18.35(b)]*. Although revenue from insurance contracts is outside the scope of IAS 18, similar disclosures may be appropriate for insurance contracts. IFRS 4 does not prescribe a particular method for recognising revenue and recording expenses so a variety of models are used, the most common ones being:

- recognising premiums earned during the period as revenue and recognising claims arising during the period (including estimates of claims incurred but not reported) as an expense;
- recognising premiums received as revenue and at the same time recognising an expense representing the resulting increase in the insurance liability; and
- initially recognising premiums received as deposit receipts. Revenue will include charges for items such as mortality, and expenses will include the policyholder claims and benefits related to those charges. *[IFRS 4.IG25]*.

IAS 1 requires additional disclosures of various items of income and expense. To meet this requirement the following additional items might need to be disclosed, either on the face of the income statement or in the notes:

(a) acquisition costs (distinguishing those recognised as an expense immediately from the amortisation of deferred acquisition costs);

(b) the effects of changes in estimates and assumptions (see 10.1.5 below);

(c) losses recognised as a result of applying liability adequacy tests;

(d) for insurance liabilities measured on a discounted basis:

  (i) accretion of interest to reflect the passage of time; and

  (ii) the effect of changes in discount rates; and

(e) distributions or allocations to holders of contracts that contain a DPF. The portion of profit or loss that relates to any equity component of those contracts is an allocation of profit or loss, not expense or income (see 6.1 above). *[IFRS 4.IG26]*.

These items should not be offset against income or expense arising from reinsurance held. *[IFRS 4.IG28]*.

Some insurers present a detailed analysis of the sources of their earnings from insurance activities, either in the income statement, or in the notes. Such an analysis may provide useful information about both the income and expense of the current period and risk exposures faced during the period. *[IFRS 4.IG27]*.

To the extent that gains or losses from insurance contracts are recognised in other comprehensive income, e.g. as a result of applying shadow accounting (see 8.3 above), similar considerations to those discussed above will apply.

If non-uniform accounting policies for the insurance liabilities of subsidiaries are adopted, it might be necessary to disaggregate the disclosures about the amounts reported to give meaningful information about amounts determined using different accounting policies. *[IFRS 4.IG30]*.

10.1.2.C Cash flows

If an insurer presents its cash flow statement using the direct method, IFRS 4 also requires it to disclose the cash flows that arise from insurance contracts although it does not require disclosure of the component cash flows associated with its insurance activity. *[IFRS 4.IG19]*.

10.1.3 Gains or losses on buying reinsurance

Gains or losses on buying reinsurance may, using some measurement models, arise from imperfect measurements of the underlying direct insurance liability. Furthermore, some measurement models require a cedant to defer some of those gains and losses and amortise them over the period of the related risk exposures, or some other period. *[IFRS 4.IG29]*.

Therefore, a cedant is required to provide specific disclosure about gains or losses on buying reinsurance as discussed at 7.2.6 and 10.1 above. In addition, if gains and losses on buying reinsurance are deferred and amortised, disclosure is required of the amortisation for the period and the amounts remaining unamortised at the beginning and end of the period. *[IFRS 4.37(b)(i)-(ii)]*.

Zurich Financial Services is one insurer that defers and amortises gains on buying reinsurance for 'retroactive' reinsurance contracts in accordance with its existing accounting policies, which are derived from US GAAP.

Extract 55.26: Zurich Financial Services Group (2008)

Consolidated financial statements [extract]

3. Summary of significant accounting policies [extract]

b) Insurance contracts and investment contracts with discretionary participating features (DPF) [extract]

Reinsurance [extract]

Premiums paid under the retroactive contracts are included in reinsurance recoverables in the balance sheet. If the amount of gross claims provisions reinsured is higher than the premium paid, reinsurance receivables are increased by the difference, and the gain is deferred and amortized over the period in which the underlying claims are paid.

10.1.4 Process used to determine significant assumptions

As noted at 10.1 above, IFRS 4 requires disclosure of the process used to determine the assumptions that have the greatest effect on the measurement of the recognised amounts. Where practicable, quantified disclosure of these assumptions should also be given. *[IFRS 4.37(c)].*

Some respondents to ED 5 expressed concern that information about assumptions and changes in assumptions (see 10.1.5 below) might be costly to prepare and of limited usefulness. They argued that there are many possible assumptions that could be disclosed and excessive aggregation would result in meaningless information, whereas excessive disaggregation could be costly, lead to information overload, and reveal commercially sensitive information. In response to these concerns, the IASB determined that disclosure about assumptions should focus on the process used to derive them. *[IFRS 4.BC212].* Further, the standard refers only to those assumptions 'that have the greatest effect on the measurement of' the recognised amounts.

IFRS 4 does not prescribe specific assumptions that should be disclosed, because different assumptions will be more significant for different types of contracts. *[IFRS 4.IG33].*

For some disclosures, such as discount rates or assumptions about future trends or general inflation, it may be relatively easy to disclose the assumptions used (aggregated at a reasonable but not excessive level, when necessary). For other assumptions, such as mortality rates derived from tables, it may not be practicable to disclose quantified assumptions because there are too many, in which case it is more important to describe the process used to generate the assumptions. *[IFRS 4.IG31].*

The description of the process used to describe assumptions might include a summary of the most significant of the following:

(a) the objective of the assumptions, for example, whether the assumptions are intended to be neutral estimates of the most likely or expected outcome ('best estimates') or to provide a given level of assurance or level of sufficiency. If they are intended to provide a quantitative or qualitative level of assurance that level could be disclosed;

(b) the source of data used as inputs for the assumptions that have the greatest effect, for example, whether the inputs are internal, external or a mixture of the two. For data derived from detailed studies that are not carried out annually, the criteria used to determine when the studies are updated and the date of the latest update could be disclosed;

(c) the extent to which the assumptions are consistent with observable market prices or other published information;

(d) a description of how past experience, current conditions and other relevant benchmarks are taken into account in developing estimates and assumptions. If a relationship would normally be expected between past experience and future results, the reasons for using assumptions that differ from past experience and an indication of the extent of the difference could be explained;

(e) a description of how assumptions about future trends, such as changes in mortality, healthcare costs or litigation awards were developed;

(f) an explanation of how correlations between different assumptions are identified;

(g) the policy in making allocations or distributions for contracts with discretionary participation features. In addition, the related assumptions that are reflected in the financial statements, the nature and extent of any significant uncertainty about the relative interests of policyholders and shareholders in the unallocated surplus associated with those contracts, and the effect on the financial statements of any changes during the period in that policy or those assumptions could be disclosed; and

(h) the nature and extent of uncertainties affecting specific assumptions. In addition, to comply with IAS 1, an insurer may need to disclose the assumptions it makes about the future, and other major sources of estimation uncertainty, that have a significant risk of resulting in a material adjustment to the carrying amounts of insurance assets and liabilities within the next financial year. *[IFRS 4.IG32]*.

Ping An disclose the following assumptions in relation to their insurance liabilities together with further detail about those assumptions.

Extract 55.27: Ping An Insurance (Group) Company of China Ltd (2008)

Notes to financial statements [extract]

4. Critical accounting estimates and judgements in applying accounting policies [extract]

(2) Estimates and assumptions [extract]

Life insurance contract liabilities

The liability for life insurance contracts (including investment contracts with DPF) is either based on current assumptions or on assumptions established at inception of the contract, reflecting the best estimate at the time increased with a margin for risk and adverse deviation. All contracts are subject to a liability adequacy test, which reflect management's best current estimate of future cash flows.

Certain acquisition costs related to the sale of new policies are recorded in deferred policy acquisition costs and are amortized to the income statement over time. If the assumptions relating to future profitability of these policies are not realized, the amortization of these costs could be accelerated and may require additional write-offs to the income statement.

The main assumptions used relate to mortality, morbidity, investment returns, expenses, lapses and surrender rates. The Group base mortality and morbidity tables on standard industry tables which reflect historical experiences, adjusted when appropriate to reflect the Group's unique risk exposure, product characteristics, target markets and own claims severity and frequency experiences.

Estimates are also made as to future investment income arising from the assets backing life insurance contracts. These estimates are based on current market returns as well as expectations about future economic and financial developments.

Assumptions on future expense are based on current expense levels, adjusted for expected expense inflation adjustments if appropriate.

Lapse and surrender rates depend on product features, policy duration and external circumstance, such as sale trends. Credible own experience is used in establishing these assumptions.

Property and casualty and short term life insurance contract liabilities

For property and casualty and short term life insurance contracts, estimates have to be made both for the expected ultimate cost of claims reported at the balance sheet date and for the expected ultimate cost of claims incurred but not yet reported at the balance sheet date ("IBNR"). It may take a significant period of time before the ultimate claims cost can be established with certainty and for some type of policies, IBNR claims form the majority of the balance sheet liability. The ultimate cost of outstanding claims is estimated by using a range of standard actuarial claims projection techniques, such as the Chain Ladder and Bornheutter-Ferguson methods.

The main assumption underlying these techniques is that a company's past claims development experience can be used to project future claims development and hence ultimate claims costs. As such, these methods extrapolate the development of paid and incurred losses, average costs per claim and claim numbers based on the observed development of earlier years and expected loss ratios. Historical claims development is mainly analyzed by accident year, but can also be further analyzed by geographical areas, as well as by significant business lines and claim types. Large claims are usually separately addressed, either by being reserved at the face value of loss adjustor estimates or separately projected in order to reflect their future development. In most cases, no explicit assumptions are made regarding future rates of claims inflation or loss ratios. Instead, the assumptions used are those implicit in the historic claims development data on which the projections are based. Additional qualitative judgment is used to assess the extent to which past trends may not apply in future (for example to reflect one-off occurrences, changes in external or maker factors such as public attitudes to claiming, economic conditions, levels of claims inflation, judicial decisions and legislation, as well as internal factors such as portfolio mix, policy conditions and claims handling procedures), so as to arrive at the estimated ultimate cost of claims that present the likely outcome from the range of possible outcomes, taking account of all the uncertainties involved.

41. Risk and capital management [extract]

1(a) Long term life insurance contracts and investment contracts with DPF [extract]

Assumptions

Material judgment is required in determining the liabilities and in the choice of assumptions relating to both long term life insurance contracts and investment contracts. Such assumptions are determined as appropriate and prudent estimates at the date of valuation.

The key assumptions to which the estimation of liabilities is particularly sensitive are as follows:

Mortality, morbidity and lapse rates

Mortality and morbidity rates, varying by age of the insured, and lapse rates, varying by contract type, are based upon expected experience at the date of contract issue plus, where applicable, a margin for adverse deviation. The mortality, morbidity and lapse assumptions are based on experience studies of the Group's actual experience.

For long term life insurance policies, increased mortality rates will lead to a larger number of claims and claims will occur sooner than anticipated, which will increase the expenditure and reduce profits for the shareholders.

For annuity contracts, a high mortality will decrease payments, thereby reducing expenditure and increase profits.

The impact of an increase in lapse rates at early duration of the policy would tend to reduce profits for the shareholders but lapse rates at later policy durations is broadly neutral in effect.

Investment return

Future investment return for non-investment-linked life insurance contracts has been changed to be 4.25% in 2009 and to increase by 0.25% every year to 5.5% by 2014 and thereafter. These rates have been derived by consideration of the current market condition and the Group's current and expected future asset allocation. They are the best estimate rates used in gross premium reserve valuation and liability adequacy test on a portfolio basis.

An increase in investment return assumption may lead to a decrease in policyholders' liabilities.

Expenses

Maintenance expenses assumptions reflect the projected costs of maintaining and servicing in force policies. The assumption for policy administration expenses is determined based on expected unit costs. Unit costs have been based on an analysis of actual experience.

Others

Other assumptions include taxation, future bonus rates, etc.

The assumptions used to estimate the liabilities of the Group's long term life insurance contracts and investment contracts with DPF require judgement and are subject to uncertainty.

Chapter 55

Some life insurers give details of the mortality tables used for measuring their insurance contract liabilities. AMP provide an example of the type of disclosures made.

Extract 55.28: AMP Limited (2008)

Notes to the financial statements [extract]

19. Life insurance contracts [extract]

(a) Assumptions and methodology applied in the valuation of life insurance contract liabilities [extract]

(ix) Mortality and morbidity [extract]

Standard mortality tables, based on national or industry wide data, are used (e.g. IA95-97 and IM(F)80 in Australia and New Zealand). These are then adjusted by factors that take account of AMP Life's own experience, primarily over the past three years. For annuity business, adjustment is also made for mortality improvements prior to and after the valuation date.

Rates of mortality assumed at 31 December 2008 are 1% to 6% lower than those assumed at 31 December 2007 in Australia and New Zealand. Rates of annuitant mortality in are unchanged.

Typical mortality assumptions, in aggregate, are as follows:

	Conventional – % of IA95-97		Term – % of IA95-97	
Risk products	Male	Female	Male	Female
Australia	80%	80%	63%	63%
New Zealand	78%	78%	63%	63%

Annuities	Male – % of IM80	Female – % of IF80
Australia	72%	61%

For disability income business, the claim assumptions are currently based on CIDA85, which is derived from North American experience. It is adjusted for AMP Life's experience, with the adjustment dependent on age, sex, waiting period, occupation, smoking status and claim duration. Incidence rates and termination rates are both unchanged as at 31 December 2008 compared to those at 31 December 2007.

For trauma cover, standard tables are not available and so assumptions are mostly based on Australian population statistics, with adjustment for smoking status as well as AMP Life's recent claim experience. Assumptions at 31 December 2008 are unchanged from those used at 31 December 2007.

The Actuarial tables used were:

IA95-97 – A mortality table developed by the Institute of Actuaries of Australia based on Australian insured lives experience from 1995-1997.

IM80* / IF80* – IM80 and IF80 are mortality tables developed by the Institute of Actuaries and the Faculty of Actuaries based on United Kingdom annuitant lives experience from 1979-1982. The tables refer to male and female lives, respectively, and incorporate factors that allow for mortality improvements since the date of the investigation. *IM80 and IF80 are these published tables amended for some specific AMP experience.

CIDA85 – A disability table developed by the Society of Actuaries based on North American disability income experience from 1973-1979.

Prudential provides the following disclosures about allocations and distributions in respect of contracts with a DPF.

Extract 55.29: Prudential plc (2008)

Notes on the financial statements [extract]
D: Life assurance business [extract]
D2: UK insurance operations [extract]

i With-profits products and PAC with-profits sub-fund

Within the balance sheet of UK insurance operations at 31 December 2008, as shown in note D2(a), there are policyholder liabilities and unallocated surplus of £72.1 billion (2007: £90.5 billion) that relate to the WPSF. These amounts include the liabilities and capital of Prudential Annuities Limited, a wholly owned subsidiary of the fund. The WPSF mainly contains with-profits business but it also contains some non-profit business (unit-linked, term assurances and annuities). The WPSF's profits are apportioned 90 per cent to its policyholders and 10 per cent to shareholders as surplus for distribution is determined via the annual actuarial valuation.

> With-profits products provide returns to policyholders through bonuses that are 'smoothed'. There are two types of bonuses: 'annual' and 'final'. Annual bonuses are declared once a year, and once credited, are guaranteed in accordance with the terms of the particular product. Unlike annual bonuses, final bonuses are guaranteed only until the next bonus declaration.
>
> When determining policy payouts, including final bonuses, Prudential considers policyholders' reasonable expectations, the need to smooth claim values and payments from year to year and competitive considerations, together with 'asset shares' for specimen policies. Asset shares broadly reflect the value of premiums paid plus the investment return on the assets notionally attributed to the policy, less the other items to be charged such as expenses and the cost of the life insurance cover.
>
> For many years, UK with-profits product providers, such as Prudential, have been required by law and regulation to consider the reasonable expectations of policyholders in setting bonus levels. This concept is established by statute but is not defined. However, it is defined within the regulatory framework, which also more recently contains an explicit requirement to treat customers fairly.
>
> The WPSF held a provision of £42 million at 31 December 2008 (2007: £45 million) to honour guarantees on a small amount of guaranteed annuity products. SAIF's exposure to guaranteed annuities is described below.
>
> Beyond the generic guarantees described above, there are very few explicit options or guarantees such as minimum investment returns, surrender values or annuities at retirement and any granted have generally been at very low levels.

10.1.5 The effects of changes in assumptions

As noted at 10.1 above, IFRS 4 requires disclosure of the effects of changes in assumptions used to measure insurance assets and insurance liabilities, showing separately the effect of each change that has a material impact on the financial statements. *[IFRS 4.37(d)]*. This requirement is consistent with IAS 8, which requires disclosure of the nature and amount of a change in an accounting estimate that has an effect in the current period or is expected to have an effect in future periods. *[IFRS 4.IG34]*.

Assumptions are often interdependent. When this is the case, any analysis of changes by assumption may depend on the order in which the analysis is performed and may be arbitrary to some extent. Not surprisingly, IFRS 4 does not specify a rigid format or content for this analysis. This allows insurers to analyse the changes in a way that meets the objective of the disclosure requirement and is appropriate for their particular circumstances. If practicable, the impact of changes in different assumptions might be disclosed separately, particularly if changes in those assumptions have an adverse effect and others have a beneficial effect. The impact of interdependencies between assumptions and the resulting limitations of any analysis of the effect of changes in assumption might also be described. *[IFRS 4.IG35]*.

The effects of changes in assumptions both before and after reinsurance held might be disclosed, especially if a significant change in the nature or extent of an entity's reinsurance programme is expected or if an analysis before reinsurance is relevant for an analysis of the credit risk arising from reinsurance held. *[IFRS 4.IG36]*.

Old Mutual make the following disclosures in respect of the impact of changes in assumptions.

Extract 55.30: Old Mutual plc (2008)

Notes to the consolidated financial statements [extract]

23 Long term and general business policyholder liabilities [extract]

(v) Assumptions [extract]

Various assumption changes have been made which have resulted in a net increase in the value of insurance contract provisions of £11 million (2007: £22 million) on the Published basis. The reserve for investment guarantees which have been calculated on a market-consistent basis was increased by £27 million (including a discretionary margin), as a result of the reduction in swap yields and increases in volatilities. Lower economic assumptions also led to an increase in underlying policyholder liabilities of £8 million. The basis for terminations and alterations was strengthened leading to an increase in liabilities of £35 million. Lower expense and mortality assumptions reduced liabilities by £39 million and £13 million respectively. Methodology changes and error corrections reduced liabilities by £6 million.

Aviva disclose the impact of changes in assumptions for their insurance business in a tabular format.

Extract 55.31: Aviva plc (2008)

Consolidated financial statements [extract]

42 – Effects of changes in assumptions and estimates during the year [extract]

This disclosure only allows for the impact on liabilities and related assets, such as reinsurance, deferred acquisition costs and AVIF, and does not allow for offsetting movements in the value of backing financial assets.

	Effect on profit 2008 £m	Effect on profit 2007 £m
Assumptions		
Long term insurance business		
Interest rates	**(521)**	850
Expenses	**24**	(13)
Persistency rates	**2**	(2)
Mortality for assurance contracts	**44**	16
Mortality for annuity contracts	**26**	11
Tax and other assumptions	**93**	60
Investment contracts		
Interest rates	**(75)**	12
Expenses	**(27)**	5
Persistency	**2**	–
Tax and other assumptions	**36**	7
General insurance and health business		
Change in loss ratio assumptions	**(1)**	–
Change in discount rate assumptions	**(94)**	3
Change in expense ratio assumptions	**–**	(4)
Total	**(491)**	945

> The impact of interest rates for long-term business relates primarily to the UK, Ireland and the Netherlands, driven by the market level of risk-free rates. Lower valuation interest rates in 2008 had the effect of increasing liabilities for traditional business and hence a negative impact on profit. This follows an increase in market interest rates in 2007 which had the reverse effect. The overall impact on profit also depends on movements in the value of assets baking the liabilities, which is not included in this disclosure.
>
> Favourable impacts for expense and mortality assumption changes for insurance contracts relate mainly to the UK. Other assumption changes include further implementation of FSA Policy Statement PS06/14 for non-profit business and expense inflation adjustments in the UK, and reserve releases in Asia, partly offset by compensation for unit-linked policies in the Netherlands.

10.1.6 Reconciliations of changes in insurance assets and liabilities

As noted at 10.1 above, IFRS 4 requires reconciliations of changes in insurance liabilities, reinsurance assets and, if any, related deferred acquisition costs, although it does not prescribe the line items that should appear in the reconciliations. *[IFRS 4.37(e)]*.

The changes need not be disaggregated into broad classes, but they might be if different forms of analysis are more relevant for different types of liability. For insurance liabilities the changes might include:

(a) the carrying amount at the beginning and end of the period;

(b) additional insurance liabilities arising during the period;

(c) cash paid;

(d) income and expense included in profit or loss;

(e) liabilities acquired from, or transferred to, other insurers; and

(f) net exchange differences arising on the translation of the financial statements into a different presentation currency, and on the translation of a foreign operation into the presentation currency of the reporting entity. *[IFRS 4.IG37]*.

This reconciliation is also required for each period for which comparative information is presented. *[IFRS 4.IG38]*.

The reconciliations given by CNP Assurances for life insurance, non-life insurance and investment contracts with a DPF are shown below. In the tables the amounts are shown before and after the impact of reinsurance.

Extract 55.32: CNP Assurances (2008)

Notes to the financial statements [extract]

10. Insurance and financial liabilities [extract]

10.2 Change in technical reserves [extract]

This note presents changes in technical reserves by category, such as those arising from changes in the assumptions applied to measure insurance liabilities. Each change with a material impact on the consolidated financial statements is shown separately. Movements are presented before and after reinsurance.

10.2.1.1 Changes in mathematical reserves – life insurance – 2008 [extract]

In € millions		**2008**	
	Before reinsurance	**Net of reinsurance**	**Reinsurance**
Mathematical reserves at the beginning of the period	**216,835.0**	**211,703.6**	**5,131.4**
Premiums	24,530.7	24,049.3	481.4
Extinguished liabilities (benefit payments)	(17,456.2)	(17,238.7)	(217.5)
Locked-in gains	7,213.5	7,109.3	104.2
Change in value of unit-linked portfolios	(5,591.2)	(5,591.2)	0.0
Changes in scope (acquisitions/divestments)	(20.2)	(20.0)	(0.2)
Asset loading	(1,016.7)	(1,016.7)	0.0
Surpluses/deficits	0.0	0.0	0.0
Currency effect	(435.0)	(435.0)	0.0
Changes in assumptions	0.2	0.2	0.0
Consolidation of Marfin Insurance Holdings Ltd	467.1	467.1	0.0
Other	174.0	298.4	(124.4)
Mathematical reserves at the end of the period	**224,701.2**	**219,326.3**	**5,374.9**

10.2.2.1 Changes in mathematical reserves – non-life insurance – 2008 [extract]

In € millions		**2008**	
	Before reinsurance	**Net of reinsurance**	**Reinsurance**
Outstanding claims reserves at the beginning of the period	**678.5**	**608.7**	**69.8**
Claims expense for the period	1,416.1	1,275.3	140.8
Prior period surpluses/deficits	(3.3)	(1.0)	(2.3)
Total claims expenses	**1,412.8**	**1,274.3**	**138.5**
Current period claims settled during the period	(1,322.5)	(1,172.6)	(149.9)
Prior period claims settled during the period	(37.4)	(34.9)	(2.5)
Total paid claims	**(1,359.9)**	**(1,207.5)**	**(152.4)**
Changes in scope of consolidation and changes of method	0.0	0.0	0.0
Translation adjustment	(22.9)	(22.9)	0.0
Changes in scope of consolidation: Marfin Insurance Holding	42.0	24.9	17.1
Outstanding claims reserves at the end of the period	**750.4**	**677.4**	**73.0**

10.2.3 Changes in mathematical reserves – financial instruments with DPF [extract]

In € millions	**2008**		
	Before reinsurance	**Net of reinsurance**	**Reinsurance**
Mathematical reserves at the beginning of the period	**7,881.2**	**7,553.8**	**327.4**
Premiums	795.0	768.8	26.2
Extinguished liabilities (benefit payments)	(961.8)	(935.0)	(26.8)
Locked-in gains	43.9	43.9	0.0
Change in value of unit-linked portfolios	(1,203.5)	(1,087.1)	(116.4)
Changes in scope (acquisitions/divestments)	(13.1)	(13.1)	0.0
Currency effect	(111.8)	(111.8)	0.0
Changes in scope of consolidation	0.0	0.0	0.0
Other	10.0	10.0	0.0
Mathematical reserves at the end of the period	**6,439.9**	**6,229.5**	**210.4**

A reconciliation of deferred acquisition costs might include:

(a) the carrying amount at the beginning and end of the period;

(b) the amounts incurred during the period;

(c) the amortisation for the period;

(d) impairment losses recognised during the period; and

(e) other changes categorised by cause and type. *[IFRS 4.IG39]*.

ING's reconciliation of deferred acquisition costs is illustrated below.

Extract 55.33: ING Groep N.V. (2008)

Notes to the consolidated financial statements [extract]

10. Deferred acquisition costs

Changes in deferred acquisition costs

	Investment contracts		Life insurance		Non-Life insurance		Total	
	2008	2007	**2008**	2007	**2008**	2007	**2008**	2007
Opening balance	**101**	83	**10,183**	9,645	**408**	435	**10,692**	10,163
Capitalised	**50**	31	**2,495**	2,766	**126**	257	**32,671**	3,054
Amortisation and unlocking	**–12**	–12	**–1,884**	–1,294	**–130**	–274	**–2,026**	–1,580
Effect of unrealised revaluations in equity			**1,523**	43			**1,523**	43
Changes in the composition of the group	**–34**		**–1,289**		**–104**	–5	**–1,427**	–5
Exchange rate differences	**–16**	–1	**461**	–938	**–35**	10	**410**	–929
Disposal of portfolios				–39		–15		–54
Closing balance	**89**	101	**11,489**	10,183	**265**	408	**11,843**	10,692

For flexible life insurance contracts the growth rate assumption used to calculate the amortisation of the deferred acquisition costs for 2008 is 6.4% gross and 5.6% net of investment management fees (2007: 6.6% gross and 5.6% net of investment management fees).

In 2008, Changes in the composition of the group related for EUR 1,164 million to the sale of ING Life Taiwan.

Chapter 55

An insurer may have intangible assets related to insurance contracts acquired in a business combination or portfolio transfer. IFRS 4 does not require any disclosures for intangible assets in addition to those required by IAS 38 (see 9.2 above). *[IFRS 4.IG40]*.

10.2 Nature and extent of risks arising from insurance contracts

The second key disclosure principle established by IFRS 4 is that information should be disclosed to enable the users of the financial statements to evaluate the nature and extent of risks arising from insurance contracts. *[IFRS 4.38]*.

To comply with this principle, an insurer needs to disclose:

(a) its objectives, policies and processes for managing risks arising from insurance contracts and the methods used to manage those risks;

(b) information about insurance risk (both before and after risk mitigation by reinsurance), including information about:

  (i) sensitivity to insurance risk;

  (ii) concentrations of insurance risk, including a description of how management determines concentrations and a description of the shared characteristic that identifies each concentration (e.g. type of insured event, geographical area or currency); and

  (iii) actual claims compared with previous estimates (i.e. claims development). This disclosure has to go back to the period when the earliest material claim arose for which there is still uncertainty about the amount and timing of the claims payments, but need not go back more than ten years. Information about claims for which uncertainty about the amount and timing of claims payments is typically resolved within one year need not be disclosed;

(c) information about credit risk, liquidity risk and market risk that would be required by IFRS 7 if insurance contracts were within the scope of that standard. However:

  (i) an insurer need not provide the maturity analyses required by IFRS 7 if it discloses information about the estimated timing of the net cash outflows resulting from recognised insurance liabilities instead. This may take the form of an analysis, by estimated timing, of the amounts recognised in the statement of financial position rather than gross undiscounted cash flows; and

  (ii) if an alternative method to manage sensitivity to market conditions, such as an embedded value analysis is used, an insurer may use that sensitivity analysis to meet the requirements of IFRS 7. However, disclosures are still required explaining the methods used in preparing that alternative analysis, its main parameters and assumptions, and an explanation of the objectives of the method and of its limitations; and

(d) information about exposures to market risk arising from embedded derivatives contained in a host insurance contract if the insurer is not required to, and does not, measure the embedded derivatives at fair value. *[IFRS 4.39]*.

These disclosures are based on two foundations:

(a) there should be a balance between quantitative and qualitative disclosures, enabling users to understand the nature of risk exposures and their potential impact; and

(b) disclosures should be consistent with how management perceives its activities and risks, and the objectives, policies and processes that management uses to manage those risks so that they:

  (i) generate information that has more predictive value than information based on assumptions and methods that management does not use, for example, in considering the insurer's ability to react to adverse situations; and

  (ii) are more effective in adapting to the continuing change in risk measurement and management techniques and developments in the external environment over time. *[IFRS 4.IG41]*.

In developing disclosures to satisfy the requirements, it might be useful to group insurance contracts into broad classes appropriate for the nature of the information to be disclosed, taking into account matters such as the risks covered, the characteristics of the contracts and the measurement basis applied. These broad classes may correspond to classes established for legal or regulatory purposes, but IFRS 4 does not require this. *[IFRS 4.IG42]*.

Under IFRS 8 – *Operating Segments* – the identification of operating segments reflects the way in which management allocates resources and assesses performance. It might be useful to adopt a similar approach to identify broad classes of insurance contracts for disclosure purposes, although it might be appropriate to disaggregate disclosures down to the next level. For example, if life insurance is identified as an operating segment for IFRS 8, it might be appropriate to report separate information about, say, life insurance, annuities in the accumulation phase and annuities in the payout phase. *[IFRS 4.IG43]*.

In identifying broad classes for separate disclosure, it is useful to consider how best to indicate the level of uncertainty associated with the risks underwritten, so as to inform users whether outcomes are likely to be within a wider or a narrower range. For example, an insurer might disclose information about exposures where there are significant amounts of provisions for claims incurred but not reported (IBNR) or where outcomes and risks are unusually difficult to assess, e.g. for asbestos-related claims. *[IFRS 4.IG45]*.

It may also be useful to disclose sufficient information about the broad classes identified to permit a reconciliation to relevant line items on the statement of financial position. *[IFRS 4.IG46]*.

Information about the nature and extent of risks arising from insurance contracts will be more useful if it highlights any relationship between classes of insurance contracts (and between insurance contracts and other items, such as financial instruments) that can affect those risks. If the effect of any relationship would not be apparent from disclosures required by IFRS 4, additional disclosure might be useful. *[IFRS 4.IG47]*.

A more detailed analysis of risk disclosures made by insurers is discussed below.

10.2.1 Objectives, policies and processes for managing insurance contract risks

As noted at 10.2 above, IFRS 4 requires an insurer to disclose its objectives, policies and processes for managing risks arising from insurance contracts and the methods used to manage those risks. *[IFRS 4.39(a)]*.

Such disclosure provides an additional perspective that complements information about contracts outstanding at a particular time and might include information about:

(a) the structure and organisation of the entity's risk management function(s), including a discussion of independence and accountability;

(b) the scope and nature of its risk reporting or measurement systems, such as internal risk measurement models, sensitivity analyses, scenario analysis, and stress testing, and how these are integrated into the entity's operating activities. Useful disclosure might include a summary description of the approach used, associated assumptions and parameters (including confidence intervals, computation frequencies and historical observation periods) and strengths and limitations of the approach;

(c) the processes for accepting, measuring, monitoring and controlling insurance risks and the entity's underwriting strategy to ensure that there are appropriate risk classification and premium levels;

(d) the extent to which insurance risks are assessed and managed on an entity-wide basis;

(e) the methods employed to limit or transfer insurance risk exposures and avoid undue concentrations of risk, such as retention limits, inclusion of options in contracts, and reinsurance;

(f) asset and liability management (ALM) techniques; and

(g) the processes for managing, monitoring and controlling commitments received (or given) to accept (or contribute) additional debt or equity capital when specified events occur.

It might be useful to provide disclosures both for individual types of risks insured and overall. They might include a combination of narrative descriptions and specific quantified data, as appropriate to the nature of the contracts and their relative significance to the insurer. *[IFRS 4.IG48]*.

The following extract from AMP provides an example of disclosures concerning the management of life insurance risks.

Extract 55.34: AMP Limited (2008)

Notes to the consolidated financial statements [extract]

19. Life insurance contracts [extract]

(h) Life insurance risk

The life insurance activities of AMP Life involve a number of non-financial risks concerned with the pricing, acceptance and management of the mortality, morbidity and longevity risks accepted from policyholders, often in conjunction with the provision of wealth management products. Financial risks involved in AMP Life are covered in Note 20.

The design of products carrying insurance risk is managed to ensure that policy wording and promotional materials are clear, unambiguous and do not leave AMP Life open to claims from causes that were not anticipated. Product prices are set through a process of financial analysis, including review of previous AMP Life and industry experience and specific product design features. The variability inherent in insurance risk is managed by having a large portfolio of individual risks, underwriting and the use of reinsurance.

Underwriting is managed through a dedicated underwriting department, with formal underwriting limits and appropriate training and development of underwriting staff. Individual policies carrying insurance risk are underwritten on their merits and are generally not issued without having been examined and underwritten individually. Individual policies which are transferred from a group scheme are generally issued without underwriting. Group risk insurance policies meeting certain criteria are underwritten on the merits of the employee group as a whole.

Claims are managed through a dedicated claims management team, with formal claims acceptance limits and appropriate training and development of staff to ensure payment of all genuine claims. Claims experience is assessed regularly and appropriate actuarial reserves are established to reflect up-to-date experience and any anticipated future events. This includes reserves for claims incurred but not yet reported.

AMP Life reinsures (cedes) to specialist reinsurance companies a proportion of its portfolio or certain types of insurance risk. This serves primarily to:
– reduce the net liability on large individual risks
– obtain greater diversification of insurance risks
– provide protection against large losses.

The specialist reinsurance companies are regulated by APRA or industry regulators in other jurisdictions and have strong credit ratings from A+ to AAA.

This extract from Beazley Group illustrates the disclosure of non-life insurance and reinsurance risk policies and processes.

Extract 55.35: Beazley Group plc (2008)

Notes to the financial statements [extract]
2 Risk management [extract]
2.1 Insurance risk [extract]

The group's insurance business assumes the risk of loss from persons or organisations that are directly exposed to an underlying loss. Insurance risk arises from this risk transfer due to inherent uncertainties about the occurrence, amount and timing of insurance liabilities. The four key components of insurance risk are underwriting, reinsurance, claims management, reserving and ultimate reserves. Each element is considered below.

a) Underwriting risk [extract]

Underwriting risk comprises four elements that apply to all insurance products offered by the group:

• Cycle risk – the risk that business is written without full knowledge as to the (in)adequacy of rates, terms and conditions;

• Event risk – the risk that individual risk losses or catastrophes lead to claims that are higher than anticipated in plans and pricing;

• Pricing risk – the risk that the level of expected loss is understated in the pricing process; and

• Expense risk – the risk that the allowance for expenses and inflation in pricing is inadequate.

The group's underwriting strategy is to seek a diverse and balanced portfolio of risks in order to limit the variability of outcomes. This is achieved by accepting a spread of business over time, segmented between different products, geography and size.

The annual business plans for each underwriting team reflect the group's underwriting strategy, and set out the classes of business, the territories in which business is to be written and the industry sectors to which the group is prepared to expose itself. These plans are approved by the board and monitored by the monthly underwriting committee.

Our underwriters calculate premiums for risks written based on a range of criteria tailored specifically to each individual risk. These factors include but are not limited to the financial exposure, loss history, risk characteristics, limits, deductibles, terms and conditions and acquisition expenses.

The group also recognises that insurance events are, by their nature, random, and the actual number and size of events during any one year may vary from those estimated using established statistical techniques.

To address this, the group sets out the exposure that it is prepared to accept in certain territories to a range of events such as natural catastrophes and specific scenarios which may result in large industry losses. This is monitored through regular calculation of realistic disaster scenarios (RDS). The aggregate position is monitored at the time of underwriting a risk, and reports are regularly produced to highlight the key aggregations to which the group is exposed.

The group uses a number of modelling tools to monitor aggregation and to simulate catastrophe losses in order to measure the effectiveness of its reinsurance programmes. Stress and scenario tests are also run using these models. The range of scenarios considered include natural catastrophes, marine, liability, political, terrorism and war events.

One of the largest types of event exposure relates to natural catastrophe events such as flood damage, windstorm or earthquake. Where possible the group measures geographic accumulations and uses its knowledge of the business, historical loss behaviour and commercial catastrophe modelling software to assess the probable maximum loss (PML). Upon application of the reinsurance coverage purchased, the key gross and net exposures are calculated on the basis of extreme events at a range of return periods.

The group's high-level catastrophe risk appetite is set by the board and the business plans of each team are determined within these parameters. The board may adjust these limits over time as conditions change. Currently, the group operates to catastrophe risk appetite for a probabilistic 1 in 250 year US event of $340m net of reinsurance.

To manage underwriting exposures, the group has developed limits of authority and business plans which are binding upon all staff authorized to underwrite and are specific to underwriters, classes of business and industry. In 2008, the normal maximum gross PML line that any one underwriter could commit the managed syndicates to was $100m. In most cases, maximum lines for classes of business were much lower than this.

These authority limits are enforced through a comprehensive sign-off process for underwriting transactions including dual sign-off for all line underwriters and peer review for all risks exceeding individual underwriters' authority limits. Exception reports are also run regularly to monitor compliance.

All underwriters also have a right to refuse renewal or change the terms and conditions of insurance contracts upon renewal. Rate monitoring details, including limits, deductibles, exposures, terms and conditions and risk characteristics are also captured and the results are combined to monitor the rating environment for each class of business.

b) Reinsurance risk [extract]

Reinsurance risk to the group arises where reinsurance contracts put in place to reduce gross insurance risk do not perform as anticipated, result in coverage disputes or prove inadequate in terms of the vertical or horizontal limits purchased. Failure of a reinsurer to pay a valid claim is considered a credit risk which is detailed separately below.

The group's reinsurance programmes complement the underwriting team business plans and seek to protect group capital from an adverse volume or volatility of claims on both a per risk and per event basis. In some cases the group deems it more economic to hold capital than purchase reinsurance. These decisions are regularly reviewed as an integral part of the business planning and performance monitoring process.

The reinsurance security committee (RSC) examines and approves all reinsurers to ensure that they possess suitable security. The group's ceded reinsurance team ensures that these guidelines are followed, undertakes the administration of reinsurance contracts, monitors and instigates our responses to any erosion of the reinsurance programmes.

10.2.2 Insurance risk – general matters

As noted at 10.2 above, IFRS 4 requires disclosure about insurance risk (both before and after risk mitigation by reinsurance). *[IFRS 4.39(c)]*.

These disclosures are intended to be consistent with the spirit of the disclosures required by financial instruments. The usefulness of particular disclosures about insurance risk depends on individual circumstances. Therefore, the requirements have been written in general terms to allow practice in this area to evolve. *[IFRS 4.BC217]*.

Disclosures made to satisfy this requirement might build on the following foundations:

(a) information about insurance risk might be consistent with (though less detailed than) the information provided internally to the entity's key management personnel as defined in IAS 24 – *Related Party Disclosures* – so that users can assess the entity's financial position, performance and cash flows 'through the eyes of management';

(b) information about risk exposures might report exposures both gross and net of reinsurance (or other risk mitigating elements, such as catastrophe bonds issued or policyholder participation features). This is especially relevant if a significant change in the nature or extent of an entity's reinsurance programme is expected or if an analysis before reinsurance is relevant for an analysis of the credit risk arising from reinsurance held;

(c) in reporting quantitative information about insurance risk, disclosure of the strengths and limitations of those methods, the assumptions made, and the effect of reinsurance, policyholder participation and other mitigating elements might be useful;

(d) risk might be classified according to more than one dimension. For example, life insurers might classify contracts by both the level of mortality risk and the level of investment risk. It may sometimes be useful to display this information in a matrix format;

(e) if risk exposures at the reporting date are unrepresentative of exposures during the period, it might be useful to disclose that fact; and

(f) the following disclosures required by IFRS 4 might also be relevant:

  (i) the sensitivity of profit or loss and equity to changes in variables that have a material effect on them (see 10.2.3 below);

  (ii) concentrations of insurance risk (see 10.2.4 below); and

  (iii) the development of prior year insurance liabilities (see 10.2.5 below). *[IFRS 4.IG51]*.

Disclosures about insurance risk might also include:

(a) information about the nature of the risk covered, with a brief summary description of the class (such as annuities, pensions, other life insurance, motor, property and liability);

(b) information about the general nature of participation features whereby policyholders share in the performance (and related risks) of individual contracts or pools of contracts or entities. This might include the general nature of any formula for the participation and the extent of any discretion held by the insurer; and

(c) information about the terms of any obligation or contingent obligation for the insurer to contribute to government or other guarantee funds established by law which are within the scope of IAS 37 as illustrated by Example 55.16 at 3.8.2 above. *[IFRS 4.IG51A]*.

Legal & General provide the following narrative disclosures about the type of life insurance contracts that it issues.

Extract 55.36: Legal & General Group plc (2008)

Notes to the financial statements [extract]

50. Risk management and control [extract]

Long term insurance risks [extract]

Protection business (individual and group)

The Group offers protection products which provide mortality or morbidity benefits. They may include health, disability, critical illness and accident benefits; these additional benefits are commonly provided as supplements to main life policies but can also be sold separately. The benefit amounts would usually be specified in the policy terms. Some sickness benefits cover the policyholder's mortgage repayments and are linked to the prevailing mortgage interest rates. In addition to these benefits, some contracts may guarantee premium rates, provide guaranteed insurability benefits and offer policyholders conversion options.

Life savings business

A range of contracts are offered in a variety of different forms to meet customers' long term savings objectives. Policyholders may choose to include a number of protection benefits within their savings contracts. Typically, any guarantees under the contract would only apply on maturity or earlier death. On certain older contracts there may be provisions guaranteeing surrender benefits. Savings contracts may or may not guarantee policyholders an investment return. Where the return is guaranteed, the Group may be exposed to interest rate risk with respect to the backing assets.

Pensions (individual and corporate)

These are long term savings contracts through which policyholders accumulate pension benefits. Some older contracts contain a basic guaranteed benefit expressed as an amount of pension payable or a guaranteed annuity option, which exposes the Group to interest rate and longevity risk. These guarantees become more costly during periods when interest rates are low or when annuitant mortality improves faster than expected. The ultimate cost will also depend on the take-up rate of any option and the final form of annuity selected by the policyholder.

Other options provided by these contracts include an open market option on maturity, early retirement and late retirement. The Group would generally have discretion over the terms on which these options are offered.

Annuities

Deferred and immediate annuity contracts are offered. Immediate annuities provide a regular income stream to the policyholder, purchased with a lump sum investment, where the income stream starts immediately after the purchase. The income stream from a deferred annuity is delayed until a specified future date. Bulk annuities are also offered, where the Group manages the assets and accepts the liabilities of a company pension scheme or a life fund.

Non-participating deferred annuities written by the Group do not contain guaranteed cash options.

Annuity products provide guaranteed income for a specified time, usually the life of the policyholder, in exchange for a lump sum capital payment. No surrender value is available under any of these products. The primary risks to the Group from annuity products are therefore mortality improvements and investment performance.

There is a block of immediate and deferred annuities within the UK non profit business with benefits linked to changes in the RPI, but with contractual maximum or minimum increases. In particular, most of these annuities have a provision that the annuity will not reduce if RPI falls. The total of such annuities in payment at 31 December 2008 was £226m (2007: £162m). Thus, 1% negative inflation, which was reversed in the following year, would result in a guarantee cost of approximately £2m (2007: £2m). Negative inflation sustained over a longer period would give rise to significantly greater guarantee costs. Some of these guarantee costs have been partially matched through the purchase of negative inflation hedges and limited price indexation bonds.

The following extract from the financial statements of Amlin illustrates a tabular presentation of insurance risk showing information about premiums and line sizes by class of business.

Extract 55.37: Amlin plc (2008)

Notes to the accounts [extract]

3. Risk disclosures [extract]

3.1 Underwriting risk [extract]

C. Marine risks [extract]

Marine classes

	2008 Gross premium	Current maximum line size	2008 Average line size
	£m	£m	£m
Hull	17	10	1.4
Cargo	32	17	3.5
Energy	39	20	3.3
War and terrorism	25	17	8.7
Specie	9	24	6.3
Bloodstock	21	4	0.6
Yacht (hull and liability)	30	4	1.0
Liability	21	57	4.3

Notes:

1) Limits are set in US dollars converted at a rate of exchange of £1 = US$1.5 and therefore currency rate of exchange changes may increase or reduce the sterling limits.

2) Maximum line size is after business written and ceded by specific proportional treaties to Amlin Bermuda Ltd.

3) Premium are stated net of acquisition costs.

The hull and cargo account is worldwide, covering property damage to ships and loss, or damage to a large variety of cargo or goods in transit. The hull account can include machinery breakdown and the account written is generally targeted towards lower value tonnage, smaller "brownwater" vessels and fishing boats. These accounts can be impacted by attritional claims of a small size as well as a single individual large claim. The cargo account in particular could also be involved in a major natural catastrophe loss. In an economic recession, it is expected that premium income will fall from these areas as trade reduces and hull values are impacted by reduced freight rates. It is also possible that claims frequency increases due to increased economic pressures affecting fraud and theft claims.

The energy portfolio is mainly offshore rig and construction policies which may be impacted by large individual claims from construction fault or property damage such as fire or explosion but is also exposed to severe catastrophe losses in the North Sea and Gulf of Mexico. The account includes control of well to limit loss of oil and avoid pollution and also some business interruption cover which indemnifies companies for loss of production.

War business includes aviation, marine and on land terrorism coverage and is exposed to single incidents or a series of losses arising from concerted action. A small amount of political risk, confiscation and contract frustration is written.

Specie business consists of the insurance against damage or theft to fine art, the contents of vaults and other high value goods including jewellers' block and cash in transit. The fine art may be shown at exhibitions which have very high aggregate values at risk. The class is therefore exposed to the potential for a frequency of small claims and also large individual losses. Some specie is written in catastrophe zones e.g. California.

The bloodstock account protects for death, illness or injury to horses mainly in the UK but business from the USA, Australia and South Africa is also written. This covers racing and eventing horses or breeding studs. The average value insured is below £1 million but there is the potential for an aggregate loss such as a stable fire which could cause multiple claims.

Chapter 55

> Yacht business covers property damage and third party injury for small leisure boats and craft. The bulk of the account is smaller value yachts in the UK and Europe, although there are a number of binders written by coverholders elsewhere, such as Scandinavia, Canada and Australia. There is an expectation of a large number of small claims, as average values are low in comparison to other claims written in the Group. Third party liability yacht claims arise from injury or damage caused by one of our policyholders to third parties. There is also the potential for a large catastrophe loss such as a UK windstorm where there are large aggregate sums insured in coastal regions such as southern England.
>
> The marine liability portfolio is written to protect ship-owners, harbours, charterers and energy companies against damage or injury to third parties. This includes the potential for pollution damage and clean up claims. The account could suffer a large catastrophe incident from a collision causing death of crew and passengers or an oil or chemical spill which could require large clean up costs.

10.2.3 Insurance risk – sensitivity information

As noted at 10.2 above, IFRS 4 requires disclosures about sensitivity to insurance risk. *[IFRS 4.39(c)(i)]*.

To comply with this requirement, disclosure is required of either:

(a) a sensitivity analysis that shows how profit or loss and equity would have been affected had changes in the relevant risk variable that were reasonably possible at the end of the reporting period occurred; the methods and assumptions used in preparing that sensitivity analysis; and any changes from the previous period in the methods and assumptions used. However, if an insurer uses an alternative method to manage sensitivity to market conditions, such as an embedded value analysis, it may meet this requirement by disclosing that alternative sensitivity analysis. Where this is done, the methods used in preparing that alternative analysis, its main parameters and assumptions, and its objectives and limitations should be explained; or

(b) qualitative information about sensitivity, and information about those terms and conditions of insurance contracts that have a material effect on the amount, timing and uncertainty of future cash flows. *[IFRS 4.39A]*.

Quantitative disclosures may be provided for some insurance risks and qualitative information about sensitivity and information about terms and conditions for other insurance risks. *[IFRS 4.IG52A]*.

Although sensitivity tests can provide useful information, such tests have limitations. Disclosure of the strengths and limitations of the sensitivity analyses performed might be useful. *[IFRS 4.IG52]*.

Insurers should avoid giving a misleading sensitivity analysis if there are significant non-linearities in sensitivities to variables that have a material effect. For example, if a change of 1% in a variable has a negligible effect, but a change of 1.1% has a material effect, it might be misleading to disclose the effect of a 1% change without further explanation. *[IFRS 4.IG53]*.

Further, if a quantitative sensitivity analysis is disclosed and that sensitivity analysis does not reflect significant correlations between key variables, the effect of those correlations may need to be explained. *[IFRS 4.IG53A]*.

If qualitative information about sensitivity is provided, disclosure of information about those terms and conditions of insurance contracts that have a material effect on the amount, timing and uncertainty of cash flows should be made. This might be achieved by disclosing the information discussed at 10.2.2 above and 10.2.6 below. An entity should decide in the light of its circumstances how best to aggregate information to display an overall picture without combining information with different characteristics. Qualitative information might need to be more disaggregated if it is not supplemented with quantitative information. *[IFRS 4.IG54A]*.

QBE provide the following quantitative information about non-life insurance sensitivities in their financial statements:

Extract 55.38: QBE Insurance Group (2008)

Notes to the financial statements [extract]

3. Critical accounting estimates and judgements [extract]

(A) Ultimate liability arising from claims under insurance contracts [extract]

(vii) Impact of changes in key variables on the outstanding claims provision [extract]

The impact of changes in key outstanding claims variables is summarised in the table below. Each change has been calculated in isolation from the other changes and each change shows the after tax impact on profit and equity assuming that there is no change to:

- Any of the other variables – This is considered unlikely as, for example, an increase in interest rates is normally accompanied by an increase in the rate of inflation. As can be seen from the table below, the impact of a change in discount rates is largely offset by the impact of a change in the rate of inflation. The impact on financial assets of a change in interest rates is shown in note 5(A)(ii).
- The probability of adequacy – It is likely that if, for example, the central estimate was to increase by 5%, at least part of the increase would result in a decrease in the probability of adequacy, which is currently estimated to be 86.1%. Likewise, if the coefficient of variation were to increase by 1%, it is likely that the probability of adequacy would reduce from its current level and that the change would therefore impact the amount of risk margins held rather than net profit after income tax or equity.

		FINANCIAL IMPACT (1)			
	MOVEMENT IN VARIABLE %	PROFIT (LOSS) 2008 $M	EQUITY 2008 $M	PROFIT (LOSS) 2007 $M	EQUITY 2007 $M
Central estimate	+5	**(524)**	**(524)**	(430)	(430)
	–5	**524**	**524**	430	430
Inflation rate	+1	**(283)**	**(283)**	(248)	(248)
	–1	**268**	**268**	236	236
Discount rate	+1	**265**	**265**	251	251
	–1	**(284)**	**(284)**	(270)	(270)
Coefficient of variation	+1	**(115)**	**(115)**	(148)	(148)
	–1	**113**	**113**	137	137
Weighted average term to settlement	+10	**68**	**68**	123	123
	–10	**(68)**	**(68)**	(125)	(125)

(1) Determined at the consolidated entity level net of reinsurance and taxation at the prima facie rate of 30%.

The consolidated entity has adopted government bond rates appropriate to the mean term and currency of the outstanding claims provision. This has resulted in a probability of adequacy of 86.1%. If the consolidated entity had applied swap rates appropriate to the mean term and currency of the outstanding claims provision, the probability of adequacy would have been 89.4%.

The following extract from Legal & General's financial statements shows sensitivity analysis on a European Embedded Value basis for life insurance liabilities.

Extract 55.39: Legal & General Group plc (2008)

Notes to the financial statements [extract]

50. Risk management and control [extract]

Sensitivity analysis [extract]

Table 6 below shows the effect of alternative assumptions on the long term embedded value, prepared in accordance with the guidance issued by the CFO Forum in October 2005. These sensitivities correspond to those contained within the Supplementary Financial Statements on page 172 of the Annual Report and Accounts.

Table 6 – Effect on embedded value [extract]

As at 31 December 2008	As published £m	1% lower risk discount rate £m	1% higher risk discount rate £m	1% lower interest rate £m	1% higher interest rate £m	1% higher equity/ property yields £m
UK	6,146	384	(336)	(73)	5	110
International	1,463	126	(109)	17	(23)	3
	7,609	**510**	**(445)**	**(56)**	**(18)**	**113**

As at 31 December 2008	As published £m	10% lower equity/ property values £m	10% lower maint- enance expenses £m	10% lower lapse rates £m	5% lower mortality (UK annuities) £m	5% lower mortality (other business) £m
UK	6,146	(248)	68	66	(111)	40
International	1,463	(6)	12	59	n/a	95
	7,609	**(254)**	**80**	**125**	**(111)**	**135**

Opposite sensitivities are broadly symmetrical.

The Group uses embedded value (EV) financial information to manage and monitor performance, and to manage interdependences between different aspects of financial risks, for example for market risk. This provides information about the value which is being created on the Group's long term insurance contracts.

EV information is calculated for the Group's life and pensions business (covered business). All other businesses are accounted for on the IFRS basis adopted in the primary financial statements.

The EV methodology requires assets of an insurance company, as reported in the primary financial statements, to be attributed between those supporting the covered business and the remainder. The method accounts for assets in the covered business on an EV basis and the remainder of the Group's assets on the IFRS basis adopted in the primary financial statements. Sensitivities have been presented for covered business only. In this context the non covered business is considered not to be material. Whilst EV sensitivities do not directly reflect the short term movements under IFRS, they more closely reflect the long term economic out turn.

Cash flow projections are determined using realistic assumptions for each component of cash flow and for each policy group. Future economic and investment return assumptions are based on conditions at the end of the financial year. Future investment returns are projected by one of two methods. The first method is based on an assumed investment return attributed to assets at their market value. The second, which is used in the US, where the investments of that subsidiary are substantially all fixed interest, projects the cash flows from the current portfolio of assets and assumes an investment return on reinvestment of surplus cash flows. The assumed discount and inflation rates are consistent with the investment return assumptions. The main assumptions are provided on page 161 in the Supplementary Financial Statements.

10.2.4 Insurance risk – concentrations of risk

As noted at 10.2 above, IFRS 4 requires disclosure of concentrations of insurance risk, including a description of how management determines concentrations and a description of the shared characteristic that identifies each type of concentration (e.g. type of insured event, geographical area, or currency). *[IFRS 4.39(c)(ii)]*.

Such concentrations could arise from, for example:

(a) a single insurance contract, or a small number of related contracts, for example when an insurance contract covers low-frequency, high-severity risks such as earthquakes;

(b) single incidents that expose an insurer to risk under several different types of insurance contract. For example, a major terrorist incident could create exposure under life insurance contracts, property insurance contracts, business interruption and civil liability;

(c) exposure to unexpected changes in trends, for example unexpected changes in human mortality or in policyholder behaviour;

(d) exposure to possible major changes in financial market conditions that could cause options held by policyholders to come into the money. For example, when interest rates decline significantly, interest rate and annuity guarantees may result in significant losses;

(e) significant litigation or legislative risks that could cause a large single loss, or have a pervasive effect on many contracts;

(f) correlations and interdependencies between different risks;

(g) significant non-linearities, such as stop-loss or excess of loss features, especially if a key variable is close to a level that triggers a material change in future cash flows; and

(h) geographical and sectoral concentrations. *[IFRS 4.IG55]*.

Disclosure of concentrations of insurance risk might include a description of the shared characteristic that identifies each concentration and an indication of the possible exposure, both before and after reinsurance held, associated with all insurance liabilities sharing that characteristic. *[IFRS 4.IG56]*.

Disclosure about the historical performance of low-frequency, high-severity risks might be one way to help users assess cash flow uncertainty associated with those risks. For example, an insurance contract may cover an earthquake that is expected to happen, on average, once every 50 years. If the earthquake occurs during the current reporting period the insurer will report a large loss. If the earthquake does not occur during the current reporting period the insurer will report a profit. Without adequate disclosure of long-term historical performance, it could be misleading to report 49 years of large profits, followed by one large loss, because users may misinterpret the insurer's long-term ability to generate cash flows over the complete cycle of 50 years. Therefore, describing the extent of the exposure to risks of this kind and the estimated frequency of losses might be useful. If circumstances have not changed significantly, disclosure of the insurer's experience with this exposure may be one way to convey information about estimated frequencies. *[IFRS 4.IG57]*. However, there is no specific requirement to disclose a probable maximum loss (PML) in the event of a catastrophe because there is no widely agreed definition of PML. *[IFRS 4.BC222]*.

ING discloses its concentration to various industries and geographical areas in a tabular format.

Extract 55.40: ING Groep N.V. (2008)

Notes to the consolidated annual accounts [extract]

Risk management [extract]

Risk concentration: ING insurance portfolio, by economic sector (1)

	Insurance Americas		Insurance Europe		Insurance Asia/Pacific		Total ING Insurance	
	2008	2007	**2008**	2007	**2008**	2007	**2008**	2007
Non-Bank Financial Institutions	**53.3%**	52.3%	**26.4%**	19.6%	**18.7%**	16.8%	**39.1%**	34.7%
Central governments	**3.2%**	1.7%	**33.7%**	35.8%	**22.7%**	38.1%	**16.6%**	20.1%
Commercial banks	**6.2%**	11.0%	**12.8%**	8.1%	**23.7%**	16.2%	**10.8%**	10.8%
Private Individuals	**3.5%**	3.5%	**10.5%**	13.9%	**11.8%**	7.8%	**7.1%**	7.9%
Real estate	**8.7%**	7.9%	**1.7%**	1.6%	**2.0%**	1.6%	**5.4%**	4.6%
Utilities	**4.0%**	4.0%	**1.7%**	1.4%	**4.0%**	2.9%	**3.2%**	2.9%
Natural Resources	**3.5%**	3.5%	**0.6%**	1.1%	**1.6%**	1.4%	**2.2%**	2.3%
Other	**17.6%**	16.1%	**12.6%**	18.5%	**15.5%**	14.6%	**15.6%**	16.7%
	100.0%	100.0%	**100.0%**	100.0%	**100.0%**	100.0%	**100.0%**	100.0%

(1) Based on credit risk measurement contained in lending, pre-settlement, money market and investment activities. The ratings reflect probabilities of default and does not take collateral into consideration.

Overall risk concentrations remained stable in 2008 for ING Insurance with a small shift towards Commercial Banks as a result of increased equity derivatives trading business at Insurance Europe. Private Individuals in Europe decreased, due to the sale of EUR 4.5 billion in residential mortgages to Retail Banking (Nationale Nederlanden Hypotheek Bedrijf). Food, Beverages and Personal Care accounted for 2.5% in 2007, but fell below the 2.0% threshold in 2008. All other industries not shown in the table above have less than 2.0% concentrations.

Largest economic exposures: ING Insurance portfolio by country (1,2)

	Insurance Americas		Insurance Europe		Insurance Asia/Pacific		Total ING Insurance	
amounts in billions of euros	**2008**	2007	**2008**	2007	**2008**	2007	**2008**	2007
United States	**58.6**	56.2	**2.0**	1.7	**1.1**	2.3	**61.7**	60.2
Netherlands	**0.8**	0.7	**14.6**	22.0	**0.2**	0.3	**15.6**	23.0
France	**0.3**	0.4	**6.8**	5.9	**0.1**	0.5	**7.2**	6.8
Italy	**0.3**	0.3	**5.9**	6.4	**0.2**	0.2	**6.4**	6.9
South Korea	**0.1**	0.1			**6.2**	6.6	**6.3**	6.7
United Kingdom	**1.8**	1.9	**3.5**	0.4	**0.4**	0.4	**5.7**	5.4
Germany	**0.3**	0.3	**5.3**	0.1	**0.1**	0.3	**5.7**	6.7
Canada	**5.5**	6.0	**0.1**				**5.6**	6.1

(1) Only covers total exposures in excess of EUR 5 billion, including intercompany exposure with ING Bank.

(2) Country is based on the country of residence of the obligor.

The portfolio in the Netherlands decreased principally due to the sale of residential mortgages to retail Banking (Nationale Nederlanden Hypotheek Bedrijf). There were no other significant shifts in the portfolio concentration.

Brit Insurance discloses the potential impact of modelled realistic disaster scenarios (estimated losses incurred from a hypothetical catastrophe).

Extract 55.41: Brit Insurance Holdings plc (2008)

Notes to the financial statements [extract]

4. Risk management policies [extract]

iv) Aggregate exposure management [extract]

As a further guide to the level of catastrophe exposure written by the Group, the table below shows hypothetical claims as at 1 January 2009 for various RDSs.

Event	Modelled industry claims US$m	Brit insurance gross claims £m	Brit Insurance net claims £m	Comments
Florida hurricane – Tampa bay	125,000	299	171	Category 4 storm on the SS Scale, landfalling in Tampa. Brit Insurance estimates include demand surge, flood associated with the hurricane, and non-property exposures.
Florida hurricane – Miami	125,000	257	129	Category 5 storm on the SS Scale, landfalling in Miami. Brit Insurance claim estimates include demand surge, flood associate with the hurricane, and non-property exposures.
US north east coast hurricane	78,000	263	151	Category 4 storm on the SS Scale, landfalling in Suffolk County, New York State. Brit Insurance claim estimates include demand surge, flood associated with the hurricane, and non-property exposures.
California earthquake – Los Angeles	78,000	290	115	Magnitude 7.2 earthquake on the MMI scale, on the Elsinore fault in Los Angeles. Brit Insurance claim estimates include demand surge, fire following the earthquake, and non-property exposures.
California earthquake – San Francisco	78,000	300	120	Magnitude 7.4 earthquake on the MMI scale, on the San Andreas Fault in San Francisco. Brit Insurance claim estimates include demand surge, fire following the earthquake, and non-property exposures.

Europe windstorm	31,000	244	99	A winter storm with peak gusts in excess of 112mph resulting in a broad swath of damage across southern England, France, Belgium, Netherlands, Luxembourg, Germany and Denmark. Brit Insurance claim estimates include demand surge and UK coastal flood.
Japan earthquake	51,000	196	101	Based on a repeat of the Great Kanto event in 1923, a magnitude 7.9 earthquake in the Tokyo Metropolitan Area.

10.2.5 Insurance risk – claims development information

As noted at 10.2 above, IFRS 4 requires disclosure of actual claims compared with previous estimates (i.e. claims development). The disclosure about claims development should go back to the period when the earliest material claim arose for which there is still uncertainty about the amount and the timing of the claims payments, but need not go back more than ten years. Disclosure need not be provided for claims for which uncertainty about claims payments is typically resolved within one year. *[IFRS 4.39(c)(iii)]*.

These requirements apply to all insurers, not only to property and casualty insurers. However, the IASB consider that because insurers need not disclose the information for claims for which uncertainty about the amount and timing of payments is typically resolved within a year, it is unlikely that many life insurers will need to give the disclosure. *[IFRS 4.IG60, BC220]*. Additionally, the implementation guidance to IFRS 4 states that claims development disclosure should not normally be needed for annuity contracts because each periodic payment is regarded as a separate claim about which there is no uncertainty. *[IFRS 4.IG60]*.

It might also be informative to reconcile the claims development information to amounts reported in the statement of financial position and disclose unusual claims expenses or developments separately, allowing users to identify the underlying trends in performance. *[IFRS 4.IG59]*.

The implementation guidance to IFRS 4 provides an illustrative example of one possible format for presenting claims development which is reproduced in full below. From this it is clear that the IASB is expecting entities to present some form of claims development table. This example presents discounted claims development information by underwriting year. *[IFRS 4.IG61 IE5]*. Other formats are permitted, including for example, presenting information by accident year or reporting period rather than underwriting year. *[IFRS 4.IG61]*.

Example 55.34: Disclosure of claims development

This example illustrates a possible format for a claims development table for a general insurer. The top half of the table shows how the insurer's estimates of total claims for each underwriting year develop over time. For example, at the end of 2010, the insurer estimated that it would pay claims of CU680 for insured events relating to insurance contracts underwritten in 2010. By the end of 2011, the insurer had revised the estimate of cumulative claims (both those paid and those still to be paid) to CU673.

The lower half of the table reconciles the cumulative claims to the amount appearing in the statement of financial position. First, the cumulative payments are deducted to give the cumulative unpaid claims for each year on an undiscounted basis. Second, if the claims liabilities are discounted, the effect of discounting is deducted to give the carrying amount in the statement of financial position.

Underwriting year	2010 CU	2011 CU	2012 CU	2013 CU	2014 CU	Total CU
Estimate of cumulative claims:						
At end of underwriting year	680	790	823	920	968	
One year later	673	785	840	903		
Two years later	692	776	845			
Three years later	697	771				
Four years later	702					
Estimate of cumulative claims	702	771	845	903	968	
Cumulative payments	(702)	(689)	(570)	(350)	(217)	
	–	82	275	553	751	1,661
Effect of discounting	–	(14)	(68)	(175)	(285)	(542)
Present value recognised in the statement of financial position	–	68	207	378	466	1,119

The example appears to be gross of reinsurance but IFRS 4 is silent on whether development information should be given on both a gross basis and a net basis. If the effect of reinsurance is significant it would seem appropriate to provide such information both gross and net of reinsurance.

The illustrative example also provides only five years of data although the standard itself requires ten (subject to the transitional relief upon first-time adoption). Given the long tail nature of many non-life insurance claims liabilities it is likely that many non-life insurers will still have claims outstanding at the reporting date that are more than ten years old and which will need to be included in a reconciliation of the development table to the statement of financial position.

IFRS 4 is also silent on the presentation of:

- exchange differences associated with insurance liabilities arising on retranslation;
- claims liabilities acquired in a business combination or portfolio transfer; and
- claims liabilities disposed of in a business combination or portfolio transfer.

As IFRS 4 is silent on these matters, a variety of treatments would appear to be permissible provided they are adequately explained to the users of the financial statements and consistently applied in each reporting period. For example, exchange rates could be fixed at the date the claims are incurred, the original reporting period dates or amounts could be retranslated at each reporting date. Claims liabilities acquired in a business combination or portfolio transfer could be reallocated to the prior reporting periods in which they were originally incurred by the acquiree or all liabilities could be allocated to the reporting period in which the acquisition/portfolio transfer occurred.

Aviva's loss (claims) development tables are shown below. These are presented on an accident year basis. Aviva discloses both gross and net insurance liabilities in this format.

Extract 55.42: Aviva plc (2007)

Notes to the consolidated financial statements [extract]

38 Insurance liabilities [extract]

(d) Loss development tables

(i) Description of tables

The tables that follow present the development of claim payments and the estimated ultimate cost of claims for the accident years 2001 to 2007. The upper half of the tables shows the cumulative amounts paid during successive years related to each accident year. For example, with respect to the accident year 2002, by the end of 2007 £5,618 million had actually been paid in settlement of claims. In addition, as reflected in the lower section of the table, the original estimated ultimate cost of claims of £6,250 million was re-estimated to be £6,122 million at 31 December 2007. This decrease from the original estimate is due to the combination of a number of factors. The original estimates will be increased or decreased, as more information becomes known about the individual claims and overall claim frequency and severity.

In 2005, the year of adoption of IFRS, only five years were required to be disclosed. This is being increased in each succeeding additional year, until ten years of information is included.

The Group aims to maintain strong reserves in respect of its non-life and health business in order to protect against adverse future claims experience and development. As claims develop and the ultimate cost of claims become more certain, the absence of adverse claims experience will then result in a release from earlier accident years as shown in the loss development tables. However, in order to maintain reserve adequacy, the Group transfers releases to current accident year (2007) reserves where the development of claims is less mature and there is much greater uncertainty attaching to the ultimate cost of claims. The release from prior accident year reserves during 2007 is also due to an improvement in the estimated ultimate cost of claims.

(ii) Gross figures

Before the effect of reinsurance, the loss development table is:

Accident year	All prior years £m	2001 £m	2002 £m	2003 £m	2004 £m	2005 £m	2006 £m	2007 £m	**Total £m**
Gross cumulative claim payments									
At end of accident year		(3,029)	(2,952)	(2,819)	(2,971)	(3,345)	(3,653)	(4,393)	
One year later		(4,766)	(4,486)	(4,190)	(4,561)	(5,011)	(5,525)		
Two years later		(5,303)	(4,921)	(4,613)	(4,981)	(5,449)			
Three years later		(5,701)	(5,233)	(4,972)	(5,263)				
Four years later		(5,966)	(5,466)	(5,258)					
Five years later		(6,121)	(5,618)						
Six years later		(6,223)							

Estimate of gross ultimate claims									
At end of accident year		6,590	6,250	6,385	6,891	7,106	7,533	8,530	
One year later		6,770	6,372	6,172	6,557	6,938	7,318		
Two years later		6,775	6,287	6,124	6,371	6,813			
Three years later		6,798	6,257	6,036	6,178				
Four years later		6,754	6,205	5,932					
Five years later		6,679	6,122						
Six years later		6,630							
Estimate of gross ultimate claims		6,630	6,122	5,932	6,178	6,813	7,318	8,530	
Cumulative payments		(6,223)	(5,618)	(5,258)	(5,263)	(5,449)	(5,525)	(4,393)	
	3,201	407	504	674	915	1,364	1,793	4,137	**12,995**
Effect of discounting	(266)	(4)	(4)	(4)	(2)	(3)	(5)	(9)	**(297)**
Present value	2,935	403	500	670	913	1,361	1,788	4,128	**12,698**
Cumulative effect of foreign exchange movements	–	19	24	37	46	36	99	–	**261**
Effect of acquisitions	12	3	2	63	17	23	29	34	**183**
Present value recognised in the balance sheet	2,947	425	526	770	976	1,420	1,916	4,162	**13,142**

(iii) Net of reinsurance

After the effect of reinsurance, the loss development table is:

Accident year	All prior years £m	2001 £m	2002 £m	2003 £m	2004 £m	2005 £m	2006 £m	2007 £m	**Total £m**
Net cumulative claim payments									
At end of accident year		(2,970)	(2,913)	(2,819)	(2,870)	(3,281)	(3,612)	(4,317)	
One year later		(4,624)	(4,369)	(4,158)	(4,378)	(4,925)	(5,442)		
Two years later		(5,088)	(4,779)	(4,565)	(4,712)	(5,344)			
Three years later		(5,436)	(5,064)	(4,924)	(4,986)				
Four years later		(5,648)	(5,297)	(5,180)					
Five years later		(5,763)	(5,424)						
Six years later		(5,841)							
Estimate of net ultimate claims									
At end of accident year		6,186	6,037	6,218	6,602	6,982	7,430	8,363	
One year later		6,333	6,038	6,093	6,266	6,818	7,197		
Two years later		6,321	5,997	6,037	6,082	6,688			
Three years later		6,329	5,973	5,942	5,882				
Four years later		6,286	5,912	5,851					
Five years later		6,219	5,855						
Six years later		6,173							
Estimate of net ultimate claims		6,173	5,855	5,851	5,882	6,688	7,197	8,363	
Cumulative payments		(5,841)	(5,424)	(5,180)	(4,986)	(5,344)	(5,442)	(4,317)	
	1,634	332	431	671	896	1,344	1,755	4,046	**11,109**
Effect of discounting	(39)	(3)	(4)	(4)	(2)	(3)	(5)	(9)	**(69)**
Present value	1,595	329	427	667	894	1,341	1,750	4,037	**11,040**
Cumulative effect of foreign exchange movements	–	13	21	34	45	34	97	–	**244**
Effect of acquisitions	8	2	2	43	16	22	28	19	**140**
Present value recognised in the balance sheet	1,603	344	450	744	955	1,397	1,875	4,056	**11,424**

> In the loss development tables shown above, the cumulative claim payments and estimates of cumulative claims for each accident year are translated into sterling at the exchange rates that applied at the end of that accident year. The impact of using varying exchange rates is shown at the bottom of each table. Disposals are dealt with by treating all outstanding and IBNR claims of the disposed entity as "paid" at the date of disposal.
> The loss development tables above include information on asbestos and environmental pollution claims provisions from business written before 2001. The claim provisions, net of reinsurance, in respect of this business at 31 December 2007 were £323 million (*2006: £312 million*). The movement in the year reflects strengthening of provisions by £20 million (*2006: £9 million*), foreign exchange rate movements and timing differences between claim payments and reinsurance recoveries.

10.2.6 Credit risk, liquidity risk and market risk disclosures

As noted at 10.2 above, IFRS 4 also requires disclosure of information about credit risk, liquidity risk and market risk that would be required by IFRS 7 if insurance contracts were within the scope of that standard. *[IFRS 4.39(d)]*.

Such disclosure should include:

- summary quantitative data about exposure to those risks based on information provided internally to key management personnel; and
- to the extent not already covered by the disclosures discussed above, the information required by IFRS 7.

IFRS 7 allows disclosures about credit risk, liquidity risk and market risk to be either provided in the financial statements or incorporated by cross-reference to some other statement, such as a management commentary or risk report, that is available to users of the financial statements on the same terms as the financial statements and at the same time. This approach is also permitted for the equivalent disclosures about insurance contracts. *[IFRS 4.IG62]*.

To be informative, the disclosure about credit risk, liquidity risk and market risk might include:

(a) information about the extent to which features such as policyholder participation features might mitigate or compound those risks;

(b) a summary of significant guarantees, and of the levels at which guarantees of market prices or interest rates are likely to alter cash flows; and

(c) the basis for determining investment returns credited to policyholders, such as whether the returns are fixed, based contractually on the return of specified assets or partly or wholly subject to the insurer's discretion. *[IFRS 4.IG64]*.

10.2.6.A Credit risk disclosures

Credit risk is defined in IFRS 7 as 'the risk that one party to a financial instrument will fail to discharge an obligation and cause the other party to incur a financial loss'.

For a reinsurance contract, credit risk includes the risk that the insurer incurs a financial loss because a reinsurer defaults on its obligations under a reinsurance contract. Furthermore, disputes with reinsurers could lead to impairments of the cedant's reinsurance assets. The risk of such disputes may have an effect similar to credit risk. Thus, similar disclosure might be relevant. Balances due from agents or brokers may also be subject to credit risk. *[IFRS 4.IG64A]*.

The specific disclosure requirements about credit risk in IFRS 7 are:

(a) an amount representing the maximum exposure to credit risk at the reporting date without taking account of any collateral held or other credit enhancements;

(b) in respect of the amount above, a description of the collateral held as security and other credit enhancements;

(c) information about the credit quality of financial assets that are neither past due nor impaired;

(d) the carrying amount of financial assets that would otherwise be past due or impaired whose terms have been renegotiated;

(e) for financial assets:

  (i) an analysis of the age of those that are past due at the reporting date but not impaired;

  (ii) an analysis of those that are individually determined to be impaired as at the reporting date, including the factors considered in determining that they are impaired; and

  (iii) for the amounts disclosed above a description of collateral held as security and other credit enhancements and, unless impracticable, an estimate of the fair value of this collateral or credit enhancement.

(f) when financial or non financial assets held as security are taken possession of during the reporting period and such assets meet the recognition criteria in other IFRSs disclosure is required of:

  (i) the nature and carrying amount of the assets obtained; and

  (ii) when the assets are not readily convertible into cash, the entity's policies for disposing of such assets or for using them in its operations.

The disclosures in (a) to (e) above are to be given by class of financial instrument. *[IFRS 7.36-38]*.

IFRS 7 also contains a requirement to disclose a reconciliation of an entity's allowance account for credit losses. However, this requirement does not apply to insurance contracts as the relevant paragraph in IFRS 7 is not specified in IFRS 4 as one of those that should be applied to insurance contracts. Nevertheless, this requirement does apply to financial assets held by insurers that are within the scope of IAS 39 (or IFRS 9), such as mortgages and other loans and receivables due from intermediaries which have a financing character or are due from those not acting in a fiduciary capacity.

Zurich Financial Services provides the following disclosures about the credit risk for reinsurance assets and insurance receivables.

Extract 55.43: Zurich Financial Services Group (2008)

Consolidated financial statements [extract]
Risk review [extract]
Credit risk relating to reinsurance assets [extract]

As part of our overall risk management strategy, the Group cedes insurance risk through proportional, non-proportional and specific risk reinsurance treaties. While these cessions mitigate insurance risk, the recoverables from reinsurers and receivables arising from ceded reinsurance expose the Group to credit risk.

Our Corporate Reinsurance Security Committee manages the credit quality of our cessions and reinsurance assets. The Group typically cedes new business to authorized reinsurers with a minimum rating of BBB. The premiums ceded to reinsurers that are below investment grade or not rated are to a large extent collateralized.

Reinsurance assets include reinsurance recoverables of USD 18,595 million and USD 26,970 million as of December 31, 2008 and 2007, respectively, which are the reinsurer's share of reserves for insurance contracts, and receivables arising from ceded reinsurance of USD 1,166 million and USD 1,372 million as of December 31, 2008 and 2007, respectively. Expected reserves for uncollectable amounts of reinsurance assets amount to USD 206 million and USD 239 million as of December 31, 2008 and 2007, respectively.

Reinsurance assets in the table below are shown before taking into account the fair value of credit default swaps, bought by the Group to mitigate credit risks of the reinsurance exposure, and other collateral such as cash or letters of credit from banks rated at least 'A', which can be converted into cash and deposits received under ceded reinsurance contracts. The decrease of reinsurance assets in 2008 compared with 2007 is mainly attributable to the sale of a pension annuity portfolio to the reinsurer, subsequent to the approval from the UK High Court, effective on June 30, 2008.

The weighted average credit quality of the reinsurance assets (including receivables, but after deduction of collateral) was 'A' as of December 31, 2008 and 2007, respectively. For credit risk assessment purposes collateral has been taken into account at nominal value as an approximation for fair value. For collateral we apply minimum requirements, such as a minimum rating for the issuers of letters of credit and guarantees, and for pledged assets a minimum coverage ratio of 100 per cent.

Table 10 – Reinsurance premiums ceded and reinsurance assets by rating of reinsurer

for the years ended December 31	**2008**				2007			
	Premiums ceded		**Reinsurance assets**		Premiums ceded		Reinsurance assets	
	USD millions	**% of total**	**USD millions**	**% of total**	USD millions	% of total	USD millions	% of total
Rating								
AAA	189	3%	417	2%	234	2%	542	2%
AA	1,495	24%	9,106	47%	9,203	70%	18,149	65%
A	2,465	40%	6,368	33%	1,796	14%	5,956	21%
BBB	706	11%	1,291	7%	670	5%	1,320	5%
BB	172	3%	280	1%	215	2%	461	2%
B	70	1%	96	–	15	–	162	1%
Unrated	1,129	18%	1,996	10%	1,064	8%	1,513	5%
Total	**6,226**	**100%**	**19,554**	**100%**	**13,197**	**100%**	**28,103**	**100%**

> **Credit risk relating to receivables**
>
> The Group's credit risk exposure to receivables from third party agents, brokers and other intermediaries arises where they collect premiums from customers to be paid to the Group or pay claims to customers on behalf of the Group. Receivables from ceded reinsurance form part of the reinsurance assets and are managed accordingly. The Group has policies and standards to manage and monitor credit risk from intermediaries with a focus in day-to-day monitoring of the largest positions. As part of these standards the Group requires that intermediaries maintain segregated cash accounts for policyholder money. Additionally, the Group requires intermediaries to satisfy minimum requirements in terms of their capitalization, reputation and experience as well as providing short-dated business credit terms. Past due but not impaired receivables should be regarded as unsecured, but some of these receivable positions may be offset by collateral.

10.2.6.B Liquidity risk disclosures

Liquidity risk is defined in IFRS 7 as 'the risk that an entity will encounter difficulty in meeting obligations associated with financial liabilities that are settled by delivering cash or another financial asset'.

The specific disclosure requirements in IFRS 7 relating to liquidity risk are:

(a) a maturity analysis for non-derivative financial liabilities (including issued financial guarantee contracts) that shows the remaining contractual maturities;

(b) a maturity analysis for derivative financial liabilities. The maturity analysis should include the remaining contractual maturities for those derivative financial liabilities for which contractual maturities are essential for an understanding of the timing of cash flows; and

(c) a description of how the liquidity risk inherent in (a) and (b) is managed. *[IFRS 7.39]*.

IFRS 7 also requires disclosure of a maturity analysis of financial assets an entity holds for managing liquidity risk (e.g. financial assets that are readily saleable or expected to generate cash inflows to meet cash outflows on financial liabilities) if that information is necessary to enable users of its financial statements to evaluate the nature and extent of liquidity risk. *[IFRS 7.B11E]*. As most insurers hold financial assets in order to manage liquidity risk (i.e. to pay claims) they are likely to have to provide such an analysis and, indeed, some insurers have historically provided such an analysis.

For financial liabilities within the scope of IFRS 7 the maturity analysis should present undiscounted contractual amounts. *[IFRS 7.B11D]*. However, an insurer need not present the maturity analyses of insurance liabilities using undiscounted contractual cash flows if it discloses information about the estimated timing of the net cash outflows resulting from recognised insurance liabilities instead. This may take the form of an analysis, by estimated timing, of the amounts recognised in the statement of financial position. *[IFRS 4.39(d)(i)]*. The guidance in respect of the maturity analysis for financial assets is silent as to whether such analysis should be on a contractual undiscounted basis or on the basis of the amounts recognised in the statement of financial position.

The reason for this concession is to avoid insurers having to disclose detailed cash flow estimates for insurance liabilities that are not required for measurement purposes. Because various accounting practices for insurance contracts are permitted, an insurer may not need to make detailed estimates of cash flows to determine the amounts recognised in the statement of financial position. *[IFRS 4.IG65B]*.

However, this concession is not available for investment contracts whether or not they contain a DPF. These contracts are within the scope of IFRS 7 not IFRS 4. Consequently, a maturity analysis of contractual undiscounted amounts is required for these liabilities.

An insurer might need to disclose a summary narrative description of how the flows in the maturity analysis (or analysis by estimated timing) could change if policyholders exercised lapse or surrender options in different ways. If lapse behaviour is likely to be sensitive to interest rates, that fact might be disclosed as well as whether the disclosures about market risk (see 10.2.6.C below) reflect that interdependence. *[IFRS 4.IG65C]*.

Prudential's liability maturity analysis for its UK insurance operations is shown below. The disclosure is on a discounted basis and includes investment contracts although, as stated in a footnote to the table, an undiscounted maturity profile of those investment contracts is disclosed elsewhere in the financial statements.

Extract 55.44: Prudential plc (2008)

Notes on the group financial statements [extract]

D2. UK insurance operations [extract]

K. Duration of liabilities

With the exception of most unitised with-profit bonds and other whole of life contracts the majority of the contracts of the UK insurance operations have a contract term. However, in effect, the maturity term of contracts reflects the earlier of death, maturity, or lapsation. In addition, with-profit contract liabilities as noted in D2(g) above include projected future bonuses based on current investment values. The actual amounts payable will vary with future investment performance of SAIF and the WPSF.

The tables below show the carrying value of the policyholder liabilities. Separately, the Group uses cash flow projections of expected benefit payments as part of the determination of the value of in-force business when preparing EEV basis results. The tables below also show the maturity profile of the cash flows used for 2008 and 2007 for that purpose for insurance contracts, as defined by IFRS, i.e. those containing significant insurance risk, and investment contracts, which do not.

	2008 £m								
	With-profits business			Annuity business (insurance contracts)			Other		
	Insurance contracts	Investment contracts	Total	PAL	PRIL	Total	Insurance contracts	Investment contracts	Total
Policyholder liabilities	39,010	23,367	62,377	11,477	12,513	23,990	9,756	11,584	21,340
	2008%								
Expected maturity:									
0 to 5 years	47	26	38	30	29	29	31	32	32
5 to 10 years	26	23	25	24	23	23	23	22	23
10 to 15 years	13	19	15	18	17	18	18	18	18
15 to 20 years	7	15	10	12	13	13	12	12	12
20 to 25 years	4	11	7	8	8	8	8	7	7
Over 25 years	3	6	5	8	10	9	8	9	8

Notes
i The cash flow projections of expected benefit payments used in the maturity profile table above are from value of in-force business and exclude the value of future new business, including vesting of internal pension contracts.
ii Benefit payments do not reflect the pattern of bonuses and shareholder transfers in respect of the with profits business.
iii Investment contracts under Other comprise certain unit-linked and similar contracts accounted for under IAS 39 and IAS 18.
iv For business with no maturity term included within the contracts, for example with-profits investment bonds such as Prudence Bond, an assumption is made as to likely duration based on prior experience.
v The maturity tables shown above have been prepared on a discounted basis. Details of undiscounted cash flow for investment contracts are shown in note G2.

10.2.6.C Market risk disclosures

Market risk is defined in IFRS 7 as 'the risk that the fair value or future cash flows of a financial instrument will fluctuate because of changes in market prices'. Market risk comprises three types of risk: currency risk, interest rate risk and other price risk.

The specific disclosure requirements in respect of market risk are:

(a) a sensitivity analysis for each type of market risk to which there is exposure at the reporting date, showing how profit or loss and equity would have been affected by changes in the relevant risk variable that were reasonably possible at that date;

(b) the methods and assumptions used in preparing that sensitivity analysis; and

(c) changes from the previous reporting period in the methods and assumptions used, and the reasons for such changes. *[IFRS 7.40]*.

These disclosures are required for insurance contracts. However, if an insurer uses an alternative method to manage sensitivity to market conditions, such as an embedded value analysis, it may use that sensitivity analysis to meet the requirements of IFRS 4. *[IFRS 4.39(d)(ii)]*. In addition, it should also disclose:

(a) an explanation of the method used in preparing such a sensitivity analysis, and of the main parameters and assumptions underlying the data provided; and

(b) an explanation of the objective of the method used and of limitations that may result in the information not fully reflecting the fair value of the assets and liabilities involved. *[IFRS 7.41]*.

Because two approaches are permitted, an insurer might use different approaches for different classes of business. *[IFRS 4.IG65G]*.

Where the sensitivity analysis disclosed is not representative of the risk inherent in the instrument (for example because the year-end exposure does not reflect the exposure during the year), that fact should be disclosed together with the reasons the sensitivity analyses are unrepresentative. *[IFRS 7.42]*.

If no reasonably possible change in a relevant risk variable would affect either profit or loss or equity, that fact should be disclosed. A reasonably possible change in the relevant risk variable might not affect profit or loss in the following examples:

- if a non-life insurance liability is not discounted, changes in market interest rates would not affect profit or loss; and
- some entities may use valuation factors that blend together the effect of various market and non-market assumptions that do not change unless there is an assessment that the recognised insurance liability is not adequate. In some cases a reasonably possible change in the relevant risk variable would not affect the adequacy of the recognised insurance liability. *[IFRS 4.IG65D]*.

In some accounting models, a regulator may specify discount rates or other assumptions about market risk variables that are used in measuring insurance liabilities and the regulator may not amend those assumptions to reflect current market conditions at all times. In such cases, compliance with the requirements might be achieved by disclosing:

(a) the effect on profit or loss or equity of a reasonably possible change in the assumption set by the regulator; and

(b) the fact that the assumption set by the regulator would not necessarily change at the same time, by the same amount, or in the same direction, as changes in market prices, or market rates, would imply. *[IFRS 4.IG65E]*.

An insurer might be able to take action to reduce the effect of changes in market conditions. For example, it may have discretion to change surrender values or maturity benefits, or to vary the amount or timing of policyholder benefits arising from discretionary participation features. There is no requirement for entities to consider the potential effect of future management actions that may offset the effect of the disclosed changes in any relevant risk variable. However, disclosure is required of the methods and assumptions used to prepare any sensitivity analysis. To comply with this requirement, disclosure of the extent of available management actions and their effect on the sensitivity analysis might be required. *[IFRS 4.IG65F]*.

Because some insurers manage sensitivity to market conditions using alternative methods as discussed above, different sensitivity approaches may be used for different classes of insurance contracts. *[IFRS 4.IG65G]*.

Some insurers combine their market risk disclosures with their other sensitivity disclosures. Extract 55.39 (Legal & General) at 10.2.3 above is an illustration of this.

Many life insurance contract liabilities are backed by matching assets. In these circumstances giving isolated disclosures about the variability of, say, interest rates on the valuation of the liabilities without linking this to the impact on the assets could be misleading to users of the financial statements. In these circumstances it may be useful to provide information as to the linkage of market risk sensitivities.

10.2.7 Exposures to market risk from embedded derivatives

As noted at 10.2 above, disclosure is required if there are exposures to market risk arising from embedded derivatives contained in a host insurance contract if the insurer is not required to, and does not, measure the embedded derivatives at fair value. *[IFRS 4.39(e)]*.

Fair value measurement is not required for derivatives embedded in an insurance contract if the embedded derivative is itself an insurance contract (see 4 above). Examples of these include guaranteed annuity options and guaranteed minimum death benefits as illustrated below. *[IFRS 4.IG66]*.

Example 55.35: Contract containing a guaranteed annuity option

An insurer issues a contract under which the policyholder pays a fixed monthly premium for thirty years. At maturity, the policyholder can elect to take either (a) a lump sum equal to the accumulated investment value or (b) a lifetime annuity at a rate guaranteed at inception (i.e. when the contract started). This is an example of a contract containing a guaranteed annuity option.

For policyholders electing to receive the annuity, the insurer could suffer a significant loss if interest rates decline substantially or if the policyholder lives much longer than the average. The insurer is exposed to both market risk and significant insurance risk (mortality risk) and the transfer of insurance risk occurs at inception of the contract because the insurer fixed the price for mortality risk at that date. Therefore, the contract is an insurance contract from inception. Moreover, the embedded guaranteed annuity option itself meets the definition of an insurance contract, and so separation is not required. *[IFRS 4.IG67]*.

Example 55.36: Contract containing minimum guaranteed death benefits

An insurer issues a contract under which the policyholder pays a monthly premium for 30 years. Most of the premiums are invested in a mutual fund. The rest is used to buy life cover and to cover expenses. On maturity or surrender, the insurer pays the value of the mutual fund units at that date. On death before final maturity, the insurer pays the greater of (a) the current unit value and (b) a fixed amount. This is an example of a contract containing minimum guaranteed death benefits. It is an insurance contract because the insurer is exposed to significant insurance risk as the fixed amount payable on death before maturity could be greater than the unit value.

It could be viewed as a hybrid contract comprising (a) a mutual fund investment and (b) an embedded life insurance contract that pays a death benefit equal to the fixed amount less the current unit value (but zero if the current unit value is more than the fixed amount). *[IFRS 4.IG68]*.

Both of the examples of embedded derivatives above meet the definition of an insurance contract where the insurance risk is deemed significant. However, in both cases, market risk or interest rate risk may be much more significant than the mortality risk. So, if interest rates or equity markets fall substantially, these guarantees would have significant value. Given the long-term nature of the guarantees and the size of the exposures, an insurer might face extremely large losses in certain scenarios. Therefore, particular emphasis on disclosures about such exposures might be required. *[IFRS 4.IG69]*.

To be informative, disclosures about such exposures may include:

- the sensitivity analysis discussed at 10.2.6.C above;
- information about the levels where these exposures start to have a material effect on the insurer's cash flows; and
- the fair value of the embedded derivative, although this is not a required disclosure. *[IFRS 4.IG70]*.

An extract of Aviva's disclosures in respect of financial guarantees and options is shown below.

Extract 55.45: Aviva plc (2008)

Notes to the consolidated financial statements [extract]

Note 40 Financial guarantees and options [extract]

(iii) Ireland

Guaranteed annuity options

Products with similar GAO's to those offered in the UK have been issued in Ireland. The current net of reinsurance provision for such options is £180 million (2007: £160 million). This has been calculated on a deterministic basis, making conservative assumptions for the factors which influence the cost of the guarantee, principally annuitant mortality option take-up and long-term interest rates.

These GAOs are "in the money" at current interest rates but the exposure to interest rates under these contracts has been hedged through the use of reinsurance, using derivatives (swaptions). The swaptions effectively guarantee that an interest rate of 5% will be available at the vesting date of these benefits so there is reduced exposure to a further decrease in interest rates.

"No MVR" guarantees

Certain unitised with-profit policies containing "no MVR" guarantees, similar to those in the UK, have been sold in Ireland.

These guarantees are currently "in-the-money" by £16 million (2007: "out-of-the-money" by £53 million). This has been calculated on a deterministic basis as the excess of the current policy surrender value over the discounted value (excluding terminal bonus) of the guarantees. The value of these guarantees is sensitive to the performance of investments held in the with-profit fund. Amounts payable under these guarantees are determined by the bonuses declared on these policies. It is estimated that the guarantees would be "in-the-money" by £16 million (2007: "out-of-the-money" by£46 million) if yields were to increase by 1% per annum and by £16 million (2007: "out-of-the-money" by £29 million) if equity markets were to decline by 10% from year end 2008 levels. There is no sensitivity to either interest rates or equity markets since there is no longer any exposure to equity in those funds and a matching strategy has been implemented for bonds.

Return of premium guarantee

Until 2005, Hibernian Life wrote two tranches of linked bonds with a return of premium guarantee, or a price floor guarantee, after five or six years. The provision for these over and above unit and sterling reserves, at the end of 2008 is £18 million (2007: £0.1 million).

It is estimated that the provision would increase by £4 million (2007: £1 million) if equity markets were to decline by 10% from year end 2008 levels. However, the provision increase would be broadly off-set by an increase in the value of the hedging assets that were set up on sale of these policies. We would not expect any significant impact on this provision as a result of interest rate movements. It is estimated that the provision would increase by £2 million if property values were to decline by 10% from year end 2008 levels. This would be offset by an increase in the value of the hedging assets by £1 million, the difference reflecting the fact that only the second tranche was hedged for property exposure.

10.2.8 Other disclosure matters

10.2.8.A IAS 1 capital disclosures

Most insurance entities are exposed to externally imposed capital requirements and therefore the IAS 1 disclosures in respect of these requirements are likely to be applicable.

Where an entity is subject to externally imposed capital requirements, disclosures are required of the nature of these requirements and how these requirements are incorporated into the management of capital. Disclosure of whether these requirements have been complied with in the reporting period is also required and, where they have not been complied with, the consequences of such non-compliance. *[IAS 1.135]*.

Many insurance entities operate in several jurisdictions. Where an aggregate disclosure of capital requirements and how capital is managed would not provide useful information or distorts a financial statement user's understanding of an entity's capital resources separate information should be disclosed for each capital requirement to which an entity is subject. *[IAS 1.136]*.

Although there is no explicit requirement to disclose the amounts of the regulatory capital requirements, some insurers do so to assist users of the financial statements. Ping An is an example of an entity that discloses its externally imposed regulatory capital requirements.

Extract 55.46: Ping An Insurance (Group) Company of China Ltd (2008)

Notes to the financial statements [extract]

41. Risk and capital management [extract]

(6) Capital management [extract]

The Group's capital requirements are primarily dependent on the scale and the type of business that it underwrites, as well as the industry and geographic location in which it operates. The primary objectives of the Group's capital management are to ensure that the Group complies with externally imposed capital requirements and that the Group maintains healthy capital ratios in order to support its business and to maximize shareholders' value.

The Group manages its capital requirements by assessing shortfalls, if any, between the reported and the required capital levels on a regular basis. Adjustments to current capital levels are made in light of changes in economic conditions and risk characteristics of the Group's activities. In order to maintain or adjust the capital structure, the Group may adjust the amount of dividends paid, return capital to ordinary shareholders or issue capital securities.

The Group fully complied with the externally imposed capital requirements as at 31 December 2008 and no changes were made to its capital base, objectives, policies and processes from the previous year.

The table below summarizes the minimum regulatory capital for major insurance subsidiaries of the Group and the regulatory capital held against each of them.

	December 31, 2008			December 31, 2007		
(in RMB million)	**Regulatory capital held**	**Minimum regulatory capital**	**Solvency margin ratio**	Regulatory capital held	Minimum regulatory capital	Solvency margin ratio
The Group	**88,270**	**28,663**	**308.0%**	121,104	24,883	486.7%
Ping An life	**33,752**	**18,371**	**183.7%**	45,218	15,704	287.9%
Ping An Property & casualty	**5,047**	**3,293**	**153.3%**	4,895	2,695	181.6%

As discussed at 7.2.1 above, equalisation and catastrophe provisions are not liabilities but are a component of equity. Therefore, they are subject to the disclosure requirements in IAS 1 for equity. IAS 1 requires disclosure of a description of the nature and purpose of each reserve within equity. *[IFRS 4.IG58]*.

10.2.8.B *Financial guarantee contracts*

A financial guarantee contract reimburses a loss incurred by the holder because a specified debtor fails to make payment when due. The holder of such a contract is exposed to credit risk and is required by IFRS 7 to make disclosures about that credit risk. However, from the perspective of the issuer, the risk assumed by the issuer is insurance risk rather than credit risk. *[IFRS 4.IG64B]*.

As discussed at 2.2.3.D above, the issuer of a financial guarantee contract should provide disclosures complying with IFRS 7 if it applies IAS 39 (or IFRS 9) in recognising and measuring the contract. However, if the issuer elects, when permitted, to apply IFRS 4 in recognising and measuring the contract, it provides disclosures complying with IFRS 4. The main implications are as follows:

(a) IFRS 4 requires disclosure about actual claims compared with previous estimates (claims development), but does not require disclosure of the fair value of the contract; and

(b) IFRS 7 requires disclosure of the fair value of the contract, but does not require disclosure of claims development. *[IFRS 4.IG65A]*.

10.2.8.C Fair value disclosures

Insurance contracts are not excluded from the scope of IFRS 13 and therefore any insurance contracts measured at fair value are also subject to the disclosures required by IFRS 13. However, insurance contracts are excluded from the scope of IFRS 7.

Disclosure of the fair value of investment contracts with a DPF is not required by IFRS 7 if the fair value of that feature cannot be measured reliably. *[IFRS 7.29(c)]*. However, IFRS 7 does require additional information about fair value in these circumstances including disclosure that fair value information has not been provided because fair value cannot be reliably measured, an explanation of why fair value cannot be reliably measured, information about the market for the instruments, information about whether and how the entity intends to dispose of the financial instruments and any gain or loss recognised on derecognition. *[IFRS 7.30]*.

For insurance contracts and investment contract liabilities with and without a DPF which are measured at fair value, disclosures required by IFRS 13 include the level in the fair value hierarchy in which the liabilities are categorised. *[IFRS 13.93]*. Very few insurance or investment contract liabilities are likely to have quoted prices (unadjusted) in active markets and are therefore likely to be Level 2 or Level 3 measurements under IFRS 13.

For investment contract liabilities without a DPF measured at amortised cost, disclosure of the fair value of those contracts is required as well as the assumptions applied in determining those fair values and the level of the fair value hierarchy in which those fair value measurements are categorised. *[IFRS 13.97]*.

When unit-linked investment liabilities are matched by associated financial assets some have argued that there is no fair value adjustment for credit risk as the liability is simply the value of the asset. However, there will be at least some risk, however small, of non-payment with regard to the liability. Therefore, it would be appropriate to provide some form of qualitative disclosure that credit risk was taken into account in assessing the fair value of the liability or why it was thought to be immaterial and/or relevant only in extreme situations.

10.2.8.D Key performance indicators

IFRS 4 does not require disclosure of key performance indicators. However, such disclosures might be a useful way for an insurer to explain its financial performance during the period and to give an insight into the risks arising from insurance contracts. *[IFRS 4.IG71]*.

11 APPLYING IFRS 9 – FINANCIAL INSTRUMENTS – WITH IFRS 4 – INSURANCE CONTRACTS

It has become clear that the effective date of IFRS 4 Phase II will be three years after the effective date of IFRS 9. Consequently, the IASB was asked to address concerns expressed by various parties that additional accounting mismatches and profit or loss volatility could result if IFRS 9 was applied before the forthcoming insurance contracts standard. The IASB agreed that these concerns should be addressed. *[IFRS 4.BC229]*.

Consequently, in September 2016, the IASB issued *Applying IFRS 9 Financial Instruments with IFRS 4 Insurance Contracts* that addresses these concerns by amending IFRS 4 to introduce:

- an optional temporary exemption from IFRS 9 for insurers whose activities are predominantly connected with insurance. The temporary exemption is available until an insurer's first accounting period beginning on or after 1 January 2021 (see 11.1 below); and
- an optional overlay approach that permits insurers to reclassify between profit or loss and other comprehensive income an amount equal to the difference between the amount reported in profit or loss for designated financial assets applying IFRS 9 and the amount that would have been reported in profit or loss for those assets if the insurer had applied IAS 39 (see 11.2 below).

As both the temporary exemption and the overlay approach are optional an insurer can still apply IFRS 9 as issued by the IASB and not use either of the permitted alternatives.

In this context, an insurer includes an entity that issues financial instruments that contain a discretionary participation feature. *[IFRS 4.5]*. Therefore, both the temporary exemption and the overlay approach are also available to an issuer of a financial instrument that contains a discretionary participation feature. *[IFRS 4.35A]*.

An entity should apply these amendments for annual periods beginning on or after 1 January 2018. *[IFRS 4.46]*. The overlay approach may be applied only when an entity first applies IFRS 9 and therefore an insurer which early applies IFRS 9 may also adopt the overlay approach at the same time. *[IFRS 4.35C, 48]*. An entity that has previously applied any version of IFRS 9, other than only the requirements for the presentation in OCI of gains and losses arising from changes in own credit risk on financial liabilities designated at fair value through profit or loss (see Chapter 50 at 2.1), is not permitted to use either the temporary exemption or the overlay approach. *[IFRS 4.20B, 35C(b)]*.

IAS 8 requires an entity to disclose information when it has not applied a new IFRS that has been issued but is not yet effective. *[IAS 8.30]*. Accordingly, the IASB believes that insurers are required to provide information about the expected date of these amendments before they are effective including whether the insurer expects to apply the temporary exemption from IFRS 9. *[IFRS 4.BC273]*.

The diagram below summarises the various implementation routes an entity may choose from, based on three potential scenarios for the effective date of the new insurance contract standard.

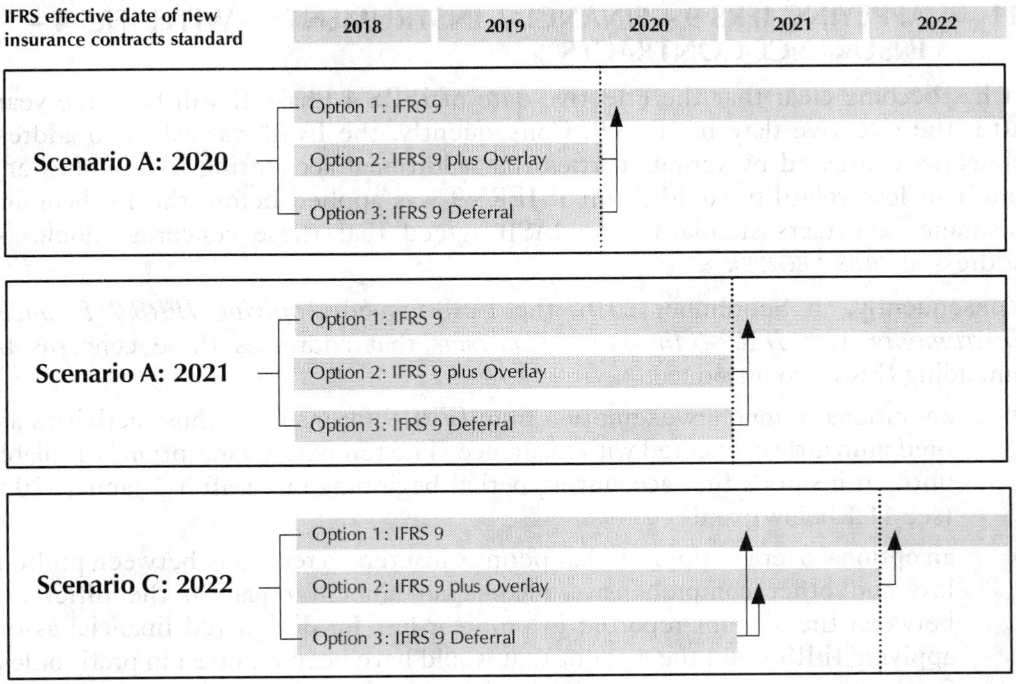

11.1 The temporary exemption from IFRS 9

For an insurer that meets the eligibility criteria, the temporary exemption permits, but does not require, the insurer to apply IAS 39 rather than IFRS 9 for annual reporting periods beginning before 1 January 2021. Therefore, an insurer that applies the temporary exemption does not adopt IFRS 9. *[IFRS 4.20A]*. As a result, an insurer applies either IAS 39 (if it applies the temporary exemption from IFRS 9) or IFRS 9 (if the temporary exemption is not applied) to all its financial assets and financial liabilities.

An insurer that applies the temporary exemption from IFRS 9 should: *[IFRS 4.20A]*

- use the requirements in IFRS 9 that are necessary to provide the disclosures discussed at 11.1.5 below; and
- apply all other applicable IFRSs to its financial instruments except as described below.

Eligibility for the temporary exemption is assessed at the reporting entity level. That is, an entity as a whole is assessed by considering all of its activities. *[IFRS 4.BC252]*. So, for example, a conglomerate financial institution assesses its eligibility to apply the temporary exemption in its consolidated financial statements by reference to the entire group. This indicates that a separate eligibility assessment is required for the separate financial statements of the parent company of the group. Subsidiaries within the conglomerate that issue their own separate, individual or consolidated financial statements must also assess the eligibility criteria at the relevant reporting entity level. Consequently, it is unlikely that all reporting entities consolidated within group financial statements will meet the criteria for the temporary exemption even if the criteria is met in the consolidated financial statements. This means that conglomerates that elect to use the temporary exemption, where permitted, are likely to have some subsidiaries required to apply IFRS 9 in the subsidiaries' own financial statements.

The following examples illustrate how eligibility would be determined at the reporting entity level. Example 55.37 illustrates the situation when the predominant activity of the group is an insurance business and Example 55.38 illustrates the situation when the predominant activity of the group is not an insurance business.

Example 55.37: Determination of eligibility for the temporary exemption at reporting entity level when the group is eligible for the temporary exemption

The activities of the HoldCo group as a whole, HoldCo itself and Subsidiary A are predominantly connected with insurance (see 11.1.1 below). The activities of Subsidiary B are not predominantly connected with insurance.

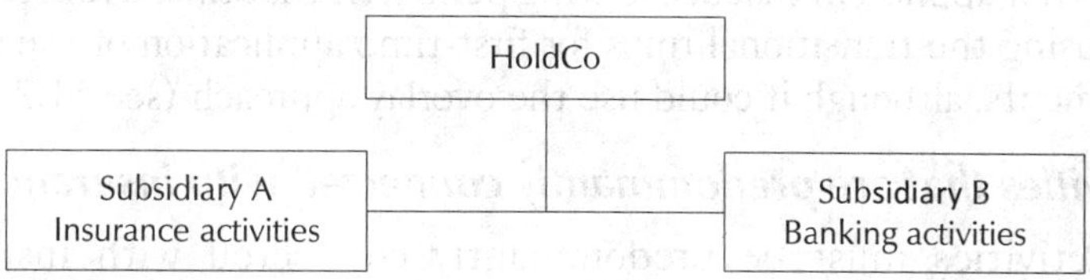

The temporary exemption would be available for HoldCo's consolidated financial statements, HoldCo's separate financial statements and Subsidiary A's individual financial statements. However, the temporary exemption is not available for Subsidiary B's individual financial statements. In those financial statements IFRS 9 must be applied although the overlay approach may be available (see 11.2 below) for designated financial assets.

Example 55.38: Determination of eligibility for the temporary exemption at reporting entity level when the group is not eligible for the temporary exemption

The activities of the HoldCo group as a whole, HoldCo itself and Subsidiary B are not predominantly connected with insurance (see 11.1.1 below). The activities of Subsidiary A are predominantly connected with insurance.

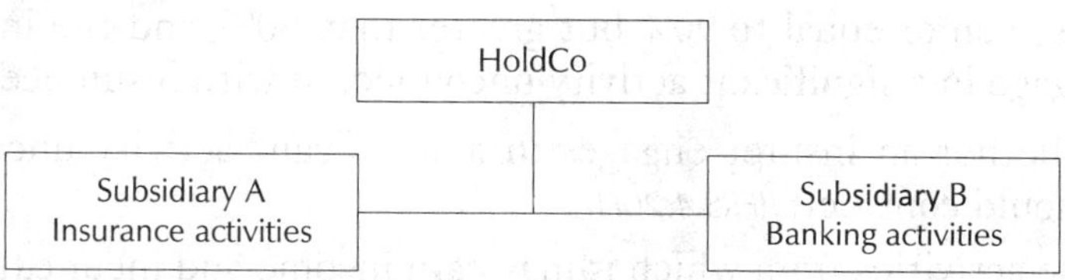

HoldCo and Subsidiary B are not eligible to apply the temporary exemption and must apply IFRS 9, in HoldCo's case, in both its consolidated and separate financial statements. However, they may be eligible to apply the overlay approach (see 11.2 below) to designated financial assets. Subsidiary A is eligible to apply the temporary exemption.

An insurer may apply the temporary exemption from IFRS 9 if, and only if: *[IFRS 4.20B]*

- it has not previously applied any version of IFRS 9, other than only the requirements for the presentation in OCI of gains and losses attributable to changes in the entity's own credit risk on financial liabilities designated at fair value through profit or loss; and
- its activities are predominantly connected with insurance (see 11.1.1 below) at its annual reporting date that immediately precedes 1 April 2016, or at a subsequent reporting date when reassessed (see 11.1.2 below).

An insurer applying the temporary exemption from IFRS 9 is permitted to elect to apply only the requirements of IFRS 9 for the presentation in OCI of gains and losses attributable to changes in an entity's own credit risk on financial liabilities designated as at fair value through profit or loss. If an insurer elects to apply those requirements, it should apply the relevant transition provisions in IFRS 9, disclose the fact that it has applied those requirements and provide on an ongoing basis the related disclosures set out in IFRS 7 and discussed in Chapter 54 at 4.4.2. *[IFRS 4.20C]*.

As IFRS 4 is worded, the ability to use the temporary exemption from IFRS 9 would cease automatically in an entity's first accounting period beginning on or after 1 January 2021. This cessation would occur even if the new insurance contract accounting standard has not been issued or is not applied in that accounting period. At that time a reporting entity must apply IFRS 9 (using the transitional rules for first-time application of the standard) to its financial instruments, although it could use the overlay approach (see 11.2 below).

11.1.1 Activities that are predominantly connected with insurance

An insurer's activities must be predominantly connected with insurance for the temporary exemption from IFRS 9 to be used. An insurer's activities are predominantly connected with insurance if, and only if: *[IFRS 4.20D]*

- the carrying amount of its liabilities arising from contracts within the scope of IFRS 4, which includes any deposit components or embedded derivatives unbundled from insurance contracts (see 4 and 5 above), is significant compared to the total carrying amount of all its liabilities; and
- the percentage of the total carrying amount of its liabilities connected with insurance relative to the total carrying amount of all its liabilities is:
  - greater than 90%; or
  - less than or equal to 90% but greater than 80%, and the insurer does not engage in a significant activity unconnected with insurance.

In assessing whether an insurer engages in a significant activity unconnected with insurance, it should consider: *[IFRS 4.20F]*

- only those activities from which it may earn income and incur expenses; and
- quantitative or qualitative factors (or both), including publicly available information such as industry classification that users of financial statements apply to the insurer.

For this purpose, liabilities connected with insurance comprise: *[IFRS 4.20E]*

- liabilities arising from contracts with the scope of IFRS 4, which includes any deposit components or embedded derivatives that are unbundled from insurance contracts (see 4 and 5 above);
- non-derivative investment contract liabilities measured at fair value through profit or loss (FVPL) applying IAS 39, including those liabilities designated at fair value through profit or loss to which the insurer has elected to apply the requirements in IFRS 9 for the presentation of gains and losses (see 11.1 above); and
- liabilities that arise because the insurer issues, or fulfils obligations arising from, the contracts noted in the preceding two bullet points. Examples of such liabilities include derivatives used to mitigate risks arising from those contracts and from the assets backing those contracts, relevant tax liabilities such as the deferred tax liabilities for taxable temporary differences on liabilities arising from those contracts, and debt instruments that are included in the insurer's regulatory capital.

Although not specifically mentioned in the standard, the Basis for Conclusions states that other connected liabilities include liabilities for salaries and other employment benefits for the employees of the insurance activities. *[IFRS 4.BC255(b)]*. Employee benefit liabilities would include, for example, defined benefit pension liabilities.

The Basis for Conclusions observes that, although non-derivative investment contract liabilities measured at FVPL applying IAS 39 (including those designated at fair value through profit or loss to which the insurer has applied the requirements in IFRS 9 for the presentation in OCI of gains and losses arising from changes in the entity's own credit risk) do not meet the definition of an insurance contract, those investment contracts are sold alongside similar products with significant insurance risk and are regulated as insurance contracts in many jurisdictions. Accordingly, the IASB concluded that insurers with significant investment contracts measured at FVPL should not be precluded from applying the temporary exemption. However, the IASB noted that insurers generally measure at amortised cost most non-derivative financial liabilities that are associated with non-insurance activities and therefore decided that such financial liabilities (i.e. non-derivative financial liabilities associated with non-insurance liabilities measured at amortised cost) cannot be treated as connected with insurance. *[IFRS 4.BC255(a)]*. In our view, this would not preclude non-derivative financial liabilities measured at amortised cost being included within the numerator provided such liabilities are connected with insurance activities.

The 90% threshold for predominance was set to avoid ambiguity and undue effort in determining eligibility for the temporary exemption from IFRS 9. Nevertheless, the IASB acknowledged that an assessment based solely on this 90% threshold has shortcomings. Accordingly, the IASB decided that when an insurer narrowly fails to meet the threshold, the insurer is still able to qualify for the temporary exemption as long as more than 80% of its liabilities are connected with insurance and it does not engage in a significant activity unconnected with insurance. *[IFRS 4.BC256]*.

When a reporting entity's liabilities connected with insurance are greater than 80% but less than 90% of all of its liabilities and the insurer wishes to apply the temporary exemption, additional disclosures are required (see 11.1.5 below). A reporting entity is not permitted to apply the temporary exemption if its liabilities connected with insurance are less than 80% of all of its liabilities at initial assessment (see 11.1.2 below).

The diagram below illustrates the assessment of the temporary exemption.

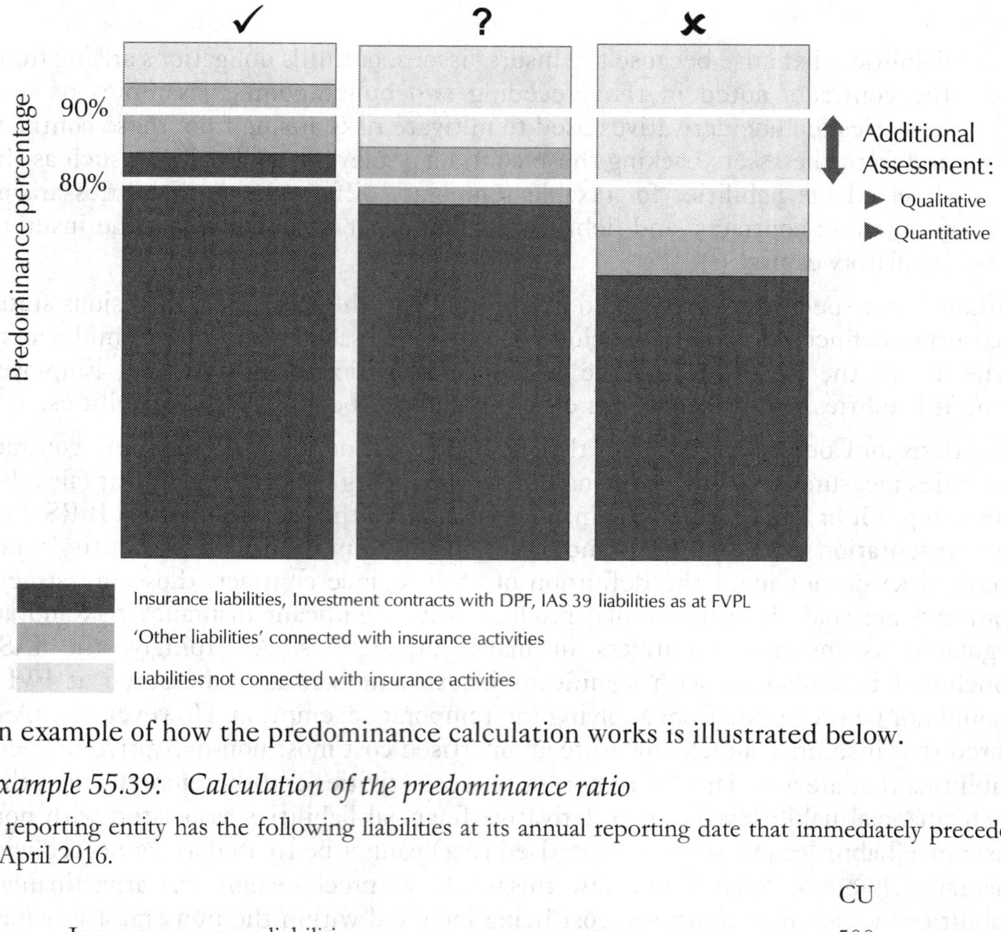

An example of how the predominance calculation works is illustrated below.

Example 55.39: Calculation of the predominance ratio

A reporting entity has the following liabilities at its annual reporting date that immediately precedes 1 April 2016.

	CU
Insurance contract liabilities	500
Investment contract liabilities at FVPL	200
Debt issued for regulatory capital	100
Derivatives used for hedges of insurance liabilities	60
Employee benefit liabilities of insurance employees	50
Banking liabilities at amortised cost	90
Total liabilities	1,000

Predominance ratio = 91% (i.e. 500+200+100+60+50/1,000).
Therefore, the reporting entity's liabilities are predominantly connected with insurance activities.

11.1.2 Initial assessment and reassessment of the temporary exemption

An insurer is required to assess whether it qualifies for the temporary exemption from IFRS 9 at its annual reporting date that immediately precedes 1 April 2016. After that date: *[IFRS 4.20G]*

- an entity that previously qualified for the temporary exemption from IFRS 9 should reassess whether its activities are predominantly connected with insurance at a subsequent annual reporting date if, and only if, there was a change in the entity's activities (as described below) during the annual period that ended on that date; and
- an entity that previously did not qualify for the temporary exemption from IFRS 9 is permitted to reassess whether its activities are predominantly connected with insurance at a subsequent annual reporting date before 31 December 2018 if, and only if, there was a change in the entity's activities, as described below, during the annual period that ended on that date.

The initial assessment date is prior to the issuance of the amendments to IFRS 4 that introduced the temporary exemption from IFRS 9. The Basis for Conclusions explains that this date was selected in response to feedback from respondents who told the IASB that entities would need to perform the assessment earlier than the application date of IFRS 9 because they would need adequate time to implement IFRS 9 if they did not qualify for the temporary exemption. *[IFRS 4.BC264]*.

A reassessment of the predominance criteria is triggered by a change in activities not a change in the predominance ratio. Therefore, an entity whose predominance ratio, say, fell below 80% at the end of a subsequent reporting period (or rose above 80% in a subsequent reporting period) would not reassess its ability to use the temporary exemption unless this was accompanied by a change in its activities. The IASB considered that a change merely in the level of an entity's insurance liabilities relative to its total liabilities over time would not trigger a reassessment because such a change, in the absence of other events, would be unlikely to indicate a change in the entity's activities. *[IFRS 4.BC265]*.

The Basis for Conclusions clarifies that an entity's financial statements reflect the effect of a change in its activities only after the change has been completed. Therefore, an entity performs the reassessment using the carrying amounts of its liabilities at the annual reporting date immediately following the completion of the change in its activities. For example, an entity would reassess whether its activities are predominantly connected with insurance at the annual reporting date immediately following the completion of an acquisition. *[IFRS 4.BC266]*.

A change in an entity's activities that would result in a reassessment is a change that: *[IFRS 4.20H]*

- is determined by the entity's senior management as a result of internal or external changes;
- is significant to the entity's operations; and
- is demonstrable to external parties.

Accordingly, such a change occurs only when the entity begins or ceases to perform an activity that is significant to its operations or significantly changes the magnitude of one of its activities; for example, when the entity has acquired, disposed of or terminated a business line.

The IASB expects a change in an entity's activities that would result in reassessment to occur very infrequently. The following are examples of changes that would not result in a reassessment: *[IFRS 4.20I]*

- a change in the entity's funding structure that in itself does not affect the activities from which the entity earns income and incurs expenses; and
- the entity's plan to sell a business line, even if the assets and liabilities are classified as held for sale applying IFRS 5 – *Non-current Assets Held for Sale and Discontinued Operations.* A plan to sell a business activity could change the entity's activities and give rise to a reassessment in the future but has yet to affect the liabilities recognised on its balance sheet. This means that a disposal must have completed for it to trigger a reassessment.

If an entity no longer qualifies for the temporary exemption from IFRS 9 as a result of reassessment, then the entity is permitted to continue to apply IAS 39 only until the end of the annual period that began immediately after that reassessment. Nevertheless, the entity must apply IFRS 9 for annual periods beginning on or after 1 January 2021. This is illustrated in the following example. *[IFRS 4.20J]*.

Example 55.40: Discontinuation of the temporary exemption

A reporting entity has a 31 December reporting date and qualifies for the temporary exemption in its annual reporting period ending 31 December 2015 (i.e. its reporting period immediately preceding 1 April 2016). Following a reassessment, after a change in its activities, the reporting entity determines that it no longer qualifies for the temporary exemption from IFRS 9 at the end of its annual reporting period ending 31 December 2018. As a result, it is permitted to continue using the temporary exemption from IFRS 9 only until 31 December 2019. After 31 December 2019, it can either apply IFRS 9 or apply IFRS 9 with the overlay approach.

When an entity, having previously qualified for the temporary exemption, concludes that its activities are no longer predominantly connected with insurance, additional disclosures are required – see 11.1.5.A below.

An insurer that previously elected to apply the temporary exemption from IFRS 9 may always, at the beginning of any subsequent annual period, irrevocably elect to apply IFRS 9 rather than IAS 39. *[IFRS 4.20K]*. The transitional requirements of IFRS 9 would apply in those circumstances. An insurer ceasing to use the temporary exemption may also elect to use to overlay approach in the first reporting period in which it applies IFRS 9.

11.1.3 First-time adopters

A first-time adopter, as defined in IFRS 1 – *First-time Adoption of International Financial Reporting Standards*, may apply the temporary exemption if, and only if, it meets the criteria described at 11.1 above. A first-time adopter is required to assess and reassess predominance on the same reporting dates as an existing user of IFRS. This means that a first-time adopter initially performs the predominance calculation (see 11.1.1 above) using the carrying amounts determined applying IFRSs as at its annual reporting date that immediately precedes 1 April 2016. This reporting period is used even if the entity first applies IFRS 1 with a later date of transition to IFRSs (e.g. the period ended 31 December with a 1 January 2017 date of transition). A first-time adopter that qualifies for the temporary exemption at its annual reporting date that immediately precedes 1 April 2016 must reassess eligibility if there is a change in its activities (see 11.1.2 above). A first-time adopter that does not qualify for the temporary exemption on initial assessment is permitted to reassess whether its activities are predominantly connected with insurance at a subsequent annual reporting date before 31 December 2018 if, and only if, there is a change in its activities. *[IFRS 4.20L]*. The Basis for Conclusions states that the IASB was prepared to allow first-time adopters to use the temporary exemption if, and only if, those first-time adopters met the same criteria as existing users of IFRS (i.e. the initial assessment of eligibility for the temporary exemption was performed for the same reporting period). *[IFRS 4.BC282]*.

Other requirements in IFRS 1, for example the elections available to a subsidiary that becomes a first-time adopter later than its parent or to an entity that becomes a first-time adopter later than its subsidiary (discussed in Chapter 5 at 5.9), do not override the conditions for using the temporary exemption. Therefore, nothing overrides the requirement that a first-time adopter must meet the predominance criteria at an annual reporting date that immediately precedes 1 April 2016, or, in certain circumstances, at a later date, to apply the temporary exemption from IFRS 9. *[IFRS 4.20M]*.

When making the disclosure required by entities using the temporary exemption (see 11.1.5 below), a first-time adopter should use the requirements and exemptions in IFRS 1 that are relevant to making the assessments required for those disclosures. *[IFRS 4.20N]*.

11.1.4 Relief for investors in associates and joint ventures

IAS 28 – *Investments in Associates and Joint Ventures* – requires an entity to use uniform accounting policies when applying the equity method to account for interests in associates and joint ventures. Nevertheless, for accounting periods beginning before 1 January 2021, an entity is permitted, but not required, to retain the relevant accounting policies applied by the associate or joint venture as follows: *[IFRS 4.20O]*

- the entity applies IFRS 9 but the associate or joint venture uses the temporary exemption from IFRS 9; or
- the entity applies the temporary exemption from IFRS 9 but the associate or joint venture applies IFRS 9.

These reliefs are intended to reduce the costs of applying the equity method when an entity does not qualify for the temporary exemption from IFRS 9, and thus applies IFRS 9, but one or more of its associates and joint ventures is eligible and chooses to continue to apply IAS 39 (or *vice versa*). *[IFRS 4.BC279]*. The effect is that the underlying financial assets and liabilities held by individual associates and joint ventures, which contribute to the equity accounted result, can be valued on a different basis to those of the reporting entity. This election may be applied separately to each associate or joint venture. *[IFRS 4.20Q]*.

When an entity uses the equity method to account for its investment in an associate or joint venture: *[IFRS 4.20P]*

- if IFRS 9 was previously applied in the financial statements used to apply the equity method to that associate or joint venture (after reflecting any adjustments made by the entity), then IFRS 9 should continue to be applied; and
- if the temporary exemption from IFRS 9 was previously applied in the financial statements used to apply the equity method to that associate or joint venture (after reflecting any adjustments made by the entity), then IFRS 9 may be subsequently applied. This election may be applied separately for each associate or joint venture. *[IFRS 4.20Q]*.

This relief is not limited to consolidated financial statements and could also be applied under the temporary exemption in separate or individual financial statements when associates and joint ventures are accounted for using the equity method.

When an entity uses fair value through profit or loss to measure an investment in associate or joint venture, as permitted by paragraph 18 of IAS 28, this election does not apply (as the election applies only to associates and joint ventures accounted for using the equity method).

11.1.5 Disclosures required for entities using the temporary exemption

Insurers that apply the temporary exemption should disclose information to enable users of their financial statements to: *[IFRS 4.39B]*

- understand how the insurer qualified for the temporary exemption; and
- compare insurers applying the temporary exemption with entities applying IFRS 9.

The standard contains detailed disclosure requirements for each of these principles which are described at 11.1.5.A and 11.1.5.B below. An insurer that uses the temporary exemption from IFRS 9 should use the transitional provisions in IFRS 9 that are relevant to making the assessments required for these disclosures. The date of initial application for that purpose should be deemed to be the beginning of the first annual period beginning on or after 1 January 2018. *[IFRS 4.47]*.

11.1.5.A Disclosures required to understand how an insurer qualified for the temporary exemption

In order to comply with the overall disclosure objective an insurer should disclose: *[IFRS 4.39C]*

- the fact that it is applying the temporary exemption from IFRS 9; and
- how it concluded on the relevant date (see 11.1.2 above) that it qualifies for the temporary exemption from IFRS 9, including:
  - if the carrying amount of its liabilities arising from contracts within the scope of IFRS 4 was less than or equal to 90% of the total carrying amount of all its liabilities, the nature and carrying amount of the liabilities connected with insurance that are not liabilities arising from contracts within the scope of IFRS 4 (e.g. non-derivative investment contract liabilities measured at fair value through profit or loss applying IAS 39,

liabilities that arise because the insurer issues or fulfils obligations arising from contracts within the scope of IFRS 4 and non-derivative investment contract liabilities measured at fair value through profit or loss) – see 11.1.1 above;

- if the percentage of the total carrying amount of its liabilities connected with insurance relative to the total carrying amount of all its liabilities was less than or equal to 90% but greater than 80%, how the insurer determined that it did not engage in a significant activity unconnected with insurance, including what information it considered; and
- if the insurer qualified for the temporary exemption from IFRS 9 on the basis of a reassessment (see 11.1.2 above):
  - the reason for the reassessment;
  - the date on which the relevant change in its activities occurred; and
  - a detailed explanation of the change in its activities and a qualitative description of the effect of that change on the insurer's financial statements.

If an entity, having previously qualified for the temporary exemption, concludes that its activities are no longer predominantly connected with insurance, it should disclose the following information in each reporting period before it begins to apply IFRS 9: *[IFRS 4.39D]*

- the fact that it no longer qualifies for the temporary exemption from IFRS 9;
- the date on which the relevant change in its activities occurred; and
- a detailed explanation of the change in the its activities and a qualitative description of the effect of that change on the entity's financial statements.

11.1.5.B Disclosures required in order to compare insurers applying the temporary exemption with entities applying IFRS 9

To comply with this disclosure principle, an insurer should disclose the fair value at the end of the reporting period and the amount of change in fair value during that period for the following two groups of financial assets separately: *[IFRS 4.39E]*

- financial assets with contractual terms that give rise on specified dates to cash flows that are solely payments of principal and interest on the principal amount outstanding, excluding any financial asset that meets the definition of held for trading under IFRS 9 or that is managed and whose performance is evaluated on a fair value basis: that is, any financial asset (see Chapter 47 at 2.1):
  - that is measured at amortised cost under IFRS 9;
  - that is a debt instrument that is measured at fair value through OCI under IFRS 9; or
  - that meets the criteria in IFRS 9 to be measured at amortised cost or the criteria in IFRS 9 for a debt instrument to be measured fair value through OCI but is measured at fair value through profit or loss in order to avoid an accounting mismatch; and

- all financial assets other than those specified above; that is, any financial asset:
  - with contractual terms that do not give rise on specified dates to cash flows that are solely payments of principal and interest on the principal amount outstanding (which includes equity instruments measured at fair value through OCI under IFRS 9);
  - that meets the definition of held for trading under IFRS 9; or
  - that is managed or whose performance is evaluated on a fair value basis.

When disclosing the fair value at the end of the reporting period and the change in fair value of the two groups, the insurer: *[IFRS 4.39F]*

- may use the carrying amount of a financial asset measured at amortised cost as its fair value if that is a reasonable approximation (e.g. for short-term receivables); and
- should consider the level of detail necessary to enable users of the financial statements to understand the characteristics of the financial assets.

This disclosure requirement means that insurers applying the temporary exemption need to allocate their financial assets into the two groups above, an exercise that will be of similar complexity to that required on adoption of IFRS 9.

There is no explicit requirement to distinguish between the different measurement models used under IFRS 9 for financial assets in each group (e.g. to distinguish between those assets measured at amortised cost and those at fair value through OCI or fair value through profit or loss) although there is a requirement to consider the detail necessary to enable users of the financial statements to understand the characteristics of the financial assets. In addition, there is no requirement to sub-analyse the change in fair value of the financial assets within each group (e.g. between realised and unrealised gains or losses). As IFRS 7 and IFRS 13 already require disclosure of the fair value of financial assets measured at amortised cost (see Chapter 14 at 20.4) information about fair values at each reporting date should generally be available although not analysed by the two groupings required.

As well as disclosing fair values and changes in fair values, an insurer should also disclose information about credit risk exposure, including significant credit risk concentration, inherent in the first group of financial assets. At a minimum, an insurer should disclose the following information for those financial assets at the end of the reporting period: *[IFRS 4.39G]*

- the carrying amounts applying IAS 39 (before adjusting for any impairment allowances in the case of financial assets measured at amortised cost) by credit risk rating grades as defined in IFRS 7; and
- the fair value and carrying amount applying IAS 39 (before adjusting for any impairment allowances in the case of financial assets measured at amortised cost) for those financial assets that do not have low credit risk at the end of the reporting period. IFRS 9 sets out guidance assessing whether the credit risk on a financial instrument is considered low (see Chapter 50 at 5.5.2).

As with the requirement to disclose fair values and changes in fair values, there is no explicit requirement to distinguish between the different measurement models used under IFRS 9 for financial assets in each group (e.g. to distinguish between those assets measured at amortised cost, those at fair value through OCI or those at fair value through profit or loss). Details of impairment losses for those financial assets under IFRS 9 are also not required. In addition, there is no requirement for credit risk information for the second group of financial assets in addition to the disclosures required already by IFRS 7.

An insurer should also disclose information about where a user of financial statements can obtain any publicly available IFRS 9 information that relates to an entity within the group that is not already provided in the group's consolidated financial statements for the relevant reporting period. Such information could be obtained from publicly available individual or separate financial statement of an entity within the group that has applied IFRS 9. *[IFRS 4.39H]*.

When an entity elects to apply the exemption from using uniform accounting policies for associates and joint ventures, discussed at 11.1.4 above, it should disclose that fact. *[IFRS 4.39I]*.

In addition, if an entity applied the temporary exemption from IFRS 9 when accounting for its investment in an associate or joint venture using the equity method it should disclose the following in addition to the information required by IFRS 12 – *Disclosure of Interests in Other Entities*: *[IFRS 4.39J]*

- the information required above (e.g. fair value analysis and credit risk disclosures) for each associate or joint venture that is material to the entity. The amounts disclosed should be those included in the IFRS financial statements of the associate or joint venture after reflecting any adjustments made by the entity when using the equity method rather than the entity's share of those amounts (see Chapter 13 at 5.1.1); and
- the quantitative information required above (e.g. fair value analysis and credit risk disclosures) in aggregate for individually immaterial associates or joint ventures. The aggregate amounts:
  - disclosed should be the entity's share of those amounts; and
  - for associates should be disclosed separately from the aggregate amounts disclosed for joint ventures.

If applicable, this requires disclosure of financial assets which are not shown separately on the reporting entity's balance sheet (as only the net equity investment in an associate or joint venture is disclosed). Therefore, this will require the reporting entity to have access to the underlying records of the associate(s) and joint venture(s). As worded, these disclosure requirements apply only for an associate or joint venture where the reporting entity applies IFRS 9 but elects to apply the temporary exemption in equity accounting for its associate or joint venture. They do not apply for any associate and joint venture when the reporting entity applies the temporary exemption but elects to apply IFRS 9 when equity accounting for an associate or joint venture. As discussed at 11.1.4 above, this election can be made separately for each associate or joint venture.

11.2 The overlay approach

An insurer is permitted, but not required, to apply the overlay approach to designated financial assets. *[IFRS 4.35B]*. The overlay approach is intended to address the additional accounting mismatches and volatility in profit or loss that may arise if an insurer applies IFRS 9 before the forthcoming insurance contracts standard. *[IFRS 4.BC240]*.

The overlay approach is elective on an instrument-by-instrument basis. Insurers may therefore choose whether to apply the overlay approach and to what extent. There is no 'predominance test' (see 11.1.1 above) and therefore the overlay approach can be applied to designated financial instruments by any reporting entity, such as a financial conglomerate, that has activities which are not predominantly connected with insurance. The IASB acknowledged that the availability of choice reduces comparability among insurers but decided not to require insurers to apply the overlay approach to all eligible financial assets because there is no loss of information when an insurer applies the overlay approach to only some financial assets. *[IFRS 4.BC241]*.

An insurer may elect to apply the overlay approach only when it first applies IFRS 9, including when it first applies IFRS 9 after previously applying: *[IFRS 4.35C]*

- the temporary exemption discussed at 11.1 above; or
- only the requirements in IFRS 9 for the presentation in OCI of gains and losses attributable to changes in the entity's own credit risk on financial liabilities designated at fair value through profit or loss.

An insurer that applies the overlay approach when applying IFRS 9 should: *[IFRS 4.35B]*

- reclassify between profit or loss and other comprehensive income an amount that results in the profit or loss at the end of the reporting period for the designated financial assets being the same as if the entity had applied IAS 39 to the designated financial assets. Accordingly, the amount reclassified is equal to the difference between:
  - the amount reported in profit or loss for the designated financial assets applying IFRS 9; and
  - the amount that would have been reported in profit or loss for the designated financial assets if the insurer had applied IAS 39.
- apply all other applicable IFRSs to its financial instruments, except for the application of the overlay approach.

An insurer should present the amount reclassified between profit and loss and other comprehensive income applying the overlay approach: *[IFRS 4.35D]*

- in profit or loss as a separate line item; and
- in other comprehensive income as a separate component of other comprehensive income.

The use of the overlay approach will result in financial instruments in the statement of financial position being recognised and measured in accordance with IFRS 9 but profit or loss and other comprehensive income will reflect a mixed measurement model (i.e. gains and losses from some financial assets will reflect the requirements of IAS 39 whilst gains and losses on other financial assets and all financial liabilities will reflect the requirements of IFRS 9). The IASB has acknowledged that different entities could use different approaches to designating financial assets (see 11.2.1 below) but notes that all financial assets will be accounted for in the statement of financial position under IFRS 9 and considers that the proposed presentation and disclosure requirements (see 11.2.4 below) will make the effect of the overlay approach transparent.

Unlike the temporary exemption from IFRS 9 (see 11.1 above), there is no expiry date for the overlay approach so an insurer is able to continue to use this approach until the new insurance contract accounting standard supersedes IFRS 4. The overlay approach is available only for designated financial assets. Financial liabilities cannot be designated for the overlay approach.

When an entity elects to apply the overlay approach it should: *[IFRS 4.49]*

- apply that approach retrospectively to designated financial assets on transition to IFRS 9. Accordingly, for example, an entity should recognise as an adjustment to the opening balance of accumulated other comprehensive income an amount equal to the difference between the fair value of designated financial assets determined applying IFRS 9 and their carrying amount determined applying IAS 39; and
- restate comparative amounts to reflect the overlay approach if, and only if, the entity restated comparative information applying IFRS 9.

If an insurer applies the overlay approach, shadow accounting (see 8.3 above) may be applicable. *[IFRS 4.35L]*.

The reclassification between profit or loss and other comprehensive income may have consequential effects for including other amounts in other comprehensive income, such as income taxes. The relevant IFRS (e.g. IAS 12) should be applied to determine any such consequential effects. *[IFRS 4.35M]*.

11.2.1 Designation and de-designation of eligible financial assets

Eligible financial assets can be designated for the overlay approach on an instrument-by-instrument basis. *[IFRS 4.35C]*.

A financial asset is eligible for the overlay approach if, and only if, the following criteria are met: *[IFRS 4.35E]*

- it is measured at fair value through profit or loss applying IFRS 9 but would not have been measured at fair value through profit or loss in its entirety applying IAS 39; and
- it is not held in respect of an activity that is unconnected with contracts within the scope of IFRS 4. Examples of financial assets that would not be eligible for the overlay approach are those assets held in respect of banking activities or financial assets held in funds relating to investment contracts that are outside the scope of IFRS 4.

The first criterion above limits the application of the overlay approach to those financial assets for which application of IFRS 9 may result in additional volatility in profit or loss. The Basis for Conclusions states that an example of such a financial asset is one that is measured at fair value through profit or loss applying IFRS 9 but that would have been bifurcated into a derivative and a host applying IAS 39. *[IFRS 4.BC240(b)(i)]*.

The second criterion above is expressed in the negative (i.e. an asset is eligible if it is not held in respect of an activity that is unconnected with contracts within the scope of IFRS 4). Logically, this means that a financial asset is eligible for the overlay approach if it is held in respect of a business activity that is connected with contracts within the scope of IFRS 4. In the majority of situations this is likely to be obvious (e.g. the assets are held to back insurance liabilities). In other situations, application depends on the specific facts and circumstances. Although not mentioned in the text of the standard, the Basis for Conclusions clarifies that financial assets held for insurance regulatory requirements (or for internal capital requirements for the insurance business) are eligible for the overlay approach on the grounds that the forthcoming insurance contracts standard may affect them. *[IFRS 4.BC240(b)(ii)]*.

An insurer may designate an eligible financial asset for the overlay approach when it elects to apply the overlay approach (see 11.2 above). Subsequently, it may designate an eligible financial asset for the overlay approach when, and only when: *[IFRS 4.35F]*

- that asset is initially recognised; or
- that asset newly meets the criteria above having previously not met that criteria.

For the purpose of applying the overlay approach to a newly designated financial asset: *[IFRS 4.35H]*

- its fair value at the date of designation should be its new amortised cost carrying amount; and
- the effective interest rate should be determined based on its fair value at the date of designation (i.e. the new amortised cost carrying amount).

An entity should continue to apply the overlay approach to a designated financial asset until that financial asset is derecognised. However, an entity: *[IFRS 4.35I]*

- should de-designate a financial asset if the financial asset no longer meets the second criterion specified above. For example a financial asset will no longer meet that criterion when an entity transfers that asset so that it is held in respect of its banking activities or when an entity ceases to be an insurer. When an entity de-designates a financial asset in this way it should reclassify from other comprehensive income to profit or loss as a reclassification adjustment any balance relating to that financial asset; *[IFRS 4.35J]* and
- may, at the beginning of any annual period, stop applying the overlay approach to all designated financial assets. An entity that elects to stop applying the overlay approach should apply IAS 8 to account for the change in accounting policy (i.e. account for the change retrospectively unless impracticable).

An entity that stops using the overlay approach because it elects to do so or because it is no longer an insurer should not subsequently apply the overlay approach. However, an insurer that has elected to apply the overlay approach but has no eligible financial assets may subsequently apply the overlay approach when it has eligible financial assets. *[IFRS 4.35K]*.

11.2.2 First-time adopters

First-time adopters are permitted to apply the overlay approach. A first-time adopter that elects to apply the overlay approach should restate comparative information to reflect the overlay approach if, and only if, it restates comparative information to comply with IFRS 9. IFRS 1 allows a first-time adopter not to apply IFRS 9 to its comparative period if its first IFRS reporting period begins before 1 January 2019 (see Chapter 5 at 5.24). *[IFRS 4.35N]*.

11.2.3 Disclosures required for entities applying the overlay approach

Insurers that apply the overlay approach should disclose information to enable users of the financial statements to understand: *[IFRS 4.39K]*

- how the amount reclassified from profit or loss to other comprehensive income in the reporting period is calculated; and
- the effect of that reclassification on the financial statements.

To comply with these principles an insurer should disclose: *[IFRS 4.39L]*

- the fact that it is applying the overlay approach;
- the carrying amount at the end of the reporting period of financial assets to which the entity applies the overlay approach by class of financial assets ('class' is explained in Chapter 54 at 3.3);
- the basis for designating financial assets for the overlay approach, including an explanation of any designated financial assets are held outside the legal entity that issues contracts within the scope of IFRS 4;
- an explanation of the total amount reclassified between profit or loss and other comprehensive income in the reporting period in a way that enables users of the financial statements to understand how that amount is derived, including:
  - the amount reported in profit or loss for the designated financial assets applying IFRS 9; and
  - the amount that would have been reported in profit or loss for the designated financial assets if the insurer had applied IAS 39;
- the effect of the reclassification and consequential effects (e.g. income taxes) on each affected line item in profit or loss; and
- if during the reporting period the insurer has changed the designation of financial assets:
  - the amount reclassified between profit or loss and other comprehensive in the reporting period relating to newly designated financial assets applying the overlay approach;
  - the amount that would have been reclassified between profit or loss and other comprehensive income in the reporting period if the financial assets had not been de-designated; and
  - the amount reclassified in the reporting period to profit or loss from accumulated other comprehensive income for financial assets that have been de-designated.

If an entity applies the overlay approach when accounting for its investment in an associate or joint venture using the equity method it should disclose the following, in addition to information required by IFRS 12: *[IFRS 4.39M]*

- the information set out above for each associate or joint venture that is material to the entity. The amounts disclosed should be those included in the IFRS financial statements of the associate or joint venture after reflecting any adjustments made by the entity when using the equity method rather than the reporting entity's share of those amounts (see Chapter 13 at 5.1.1); and

- the quantitative information set out above and the effect of the reclassification on profit and loss and other comprehensive income in aggregate for all individually immaterial associates or joint ventures. The aggregate amounts:
  - disclosed should be the entity's share of those amounts; and
  - for associates should be disclosed separately from the aggregate amounts disclosed for joint ventures.

Designation of financial assets is always voluntary on an instrument-by-instrument basis under the overlay approach. Therefore, an entity could always avoid the need for these disclosures for associates and joint ventures by not designating an investee's financial assets for the overlay approach.

12 FUTURE DEVELOPMENTS IN INSURANCE CONTRACT ACCOUNTING

12.1 The Phase II discussion paper

In May 2007 the IASB published a Discussion Paper (DP) – *Preliminary Views on Insurance Contracts*. The DP contained the IASB's preliminary views on various recognition and measurement issues to be considered in accounting for insurance contracts and set out the issues that were still under consideration.

The key proposal of the DP was that insurance contract liabilities would be measured at the amount that an insurer would expect to pay at the reporting date to transfer its remaining contractual rights and obligations immediately to another party. The IASB referred to this measurement model as 'current exit value'.

Nearly all of the respondents to the discussion paper had significant concerns about particular aspects of the building blocks proposed in the DP. As a result, at its June 2009 meeting, the IASB rejected the 'current exit value' model proposed by the DP.[31]

12.2 The Phase II Exposure Draft

In July 2010, the IASB published an Exposure Draft (2010 ED), ED 2010/8 – *Insurance Contracts*.

The 2010 ED proposed that an insurer should measure insurance liabilities using a model based on the 'present value of fulfilment cash flows' plus a residual margin when required to eliminate day 1 gains. The residual margin is set up at inception and recognised over the policy coverage period. It is not re-estimated. For most short-duration contracts a modified version of the measurement approach will apply. In the modified version, the fulfilment cash flows approach will be used only for events that have already occurred (incurred claims liability). During the contract period, the insurer would measure the contract using an allocation of the total premium for that period, on a basis similar to the unearned premium approach used in much existing practice.

The 2010 ED proposed that the modified method be mandatory for those contracts whose coverage period is approximately one year or less that do not contain significant embedded options or derivatives. Consequently, entities that write both short-term and long-term contracts would have two different measurements and two different sets of disclosure requirements.

The 'present value of fulfilment cash flows' approach uses the following building blocks:

- a current estimate of future cash flows;
- a discount rate that adjusts those cash flows for the time value of money; and
- an explicit risk adjustment.

An entity should incorporate, in an unbiased way, all available information about the amount, timing and uncertainty of all cash flows that will arise as the contract is fulfilled. Cash flows should also be remeasured at the end of each reporting period and any movements reported in profit or loss.

The discount rate should adjust the cash flows for the time value of money in a way that captures the characteristics of the liability. It is implied that the discount rate is based on the risk-free rate adjusted for the characteristics unique to the liability such as illiquidity. Own credit risk is specifically excluded. If the cash flows depend wholly, or in part, on the performance of specific assets then the measurement of the contract should reflect that fact.

The risk adjustment is intended to capture the effects of uncertainty associated with the cash flows arising from the contract. It should be the maximum amount that the insurer would rationally pay to be relieved of the risk that the ultimate fulfilment cash flows may exceed those expected. The risk adjustment should be determined for each separate portfolio of insurance contracts without any credit for diversification of risk between those portfolios.

A high-level summary of other matters addressed by the 2010 ED is as follows:

- financial investments with a DPF are included within the scope of the proposed standard only if they invest in the same pool of assets as insurance contracts;
- fixed-fee service contracts are excluded from the scope of the proposed standard;
- financial guarantee contracts are included within the scope of the proposed standard and not IAS 39 (or IFRS 9);
- an entity must recognise an insurance obligation at the earlier of when it is bound by the contract or first exposed to risk. Accordingly, an insurer may have to recognise a contract prior to the start of the coverage period;
- a contract boundary is defined as the point at which an insurer either: (a) is no longer required to provide coverage, or (b) has the right and practical ability to reassess the risk of a particular policyholder and, as a result, can set a price that fully reflects that risk;
- entities are required to unbundle components of contracts that are not closely related to the insurance coverage;
- reinsurance contracts are measured initially at the present value of the fulfilment cash flows including the risk of non-performance by the reinsurer. If the present

value of the fulfilment cash flows for the reinsurance contract is greater than zero a gain is recognised in profit or loss. However, if the present value of the fulfilment cash flows is less than zero then the cedant should record the difference as a residual margin within the reinsurance asset;

- acquisition costs can be included in the present value of fulfilment cash flows only to the extent that they are incremental at an individual contract level. These increase the present value of the fulfilment cash flows thereby decreasing the residual margin. Non incremental costs are expensed as incurred;
- all expected cash flows resulting from participating features should be included in the measurement of insurance contracts in the same way as any other contractual cash flow;
- insurance contracts acquired via business combinations must be measured at the higher of the fair value of the portfolio and the present value of the fulfilment cash flows. If the fair value is higher, the difference is recognised as a residual margin. If the fair value is lower, the difference is additional goodwill;
- insurance contracts acquired via portfolio transfers are initially measured at the higher of either the consideration received or the present value of the fulfilment cash flows. If the consideration is higher, then the difference is recognised as a residual margin. If the present value of fulfilment cash flows is higher, then a loss should be recognised immediately.

The 2010 ED proposed a presentation model that focused on margins and other key performance information. The presentation model required those contracts not using the simplified short-term model to treat all premiums as deposits and all claims and benefits as repayments to the policyholder. As a result, volume measures such as premiums and claims were not permitted to be shown on the face of the income statement. Instead, minimum disclosures included changes to the risk adjustment in the period, the release of the residual margin, changes in estimates and the interest on insurance liabilities. This was a major change from most existing models where premiums and claims are shown on the face of the income statement.

For those contracts accounted for using the alternative short-term model an insurer was permitted to present premium revenue and claims incurred on the face of the income statement.

12.3 The revised Phase II Exposure Draft

In June 2013, the IASB published a revised Exposure Draft (revised ED), ED 2013/7 – *Insurance Contracts*. The revised ED took into account the re-deliberations by the IASB since the July 2010 ED.

The measurement principles for insurance contracts that are set out in the revised ED are similar to those of the 2010 ED, i.e. a current value measurement model comprising of the expected present value of future cash flows, a risk adjustment and a contractual service margin (referred to as a residual margin in the 2010 ED). One of the main criticisms of the 2010 ED was that the proposed model, especially for long duration contracts, would, in effect force insurers to measure both assets and liabilities on a current value basis with the effects of remeasurement reported through profit or loss. Many comment letters on the 2010 ED expressed significant concern about the earnings volatility that would ensue because changes in market conditions would usually have a different impact on financial assets and insurance liabilities. In the respondents' view, such fluctuations would highlight short-term market fluctuations rather than reflect the expected long-term performance of an insurer. Another key concern was the presentation model in the statement of comprehensive income, in particular the removal of volume information such as premiums and claims caused by the IASB's decision to focus on summarised margin information. The comment letters in response to the 2010 ED also raised many other issues such as which cash flows and acquisition expenses to include, unbundling, the application of the simplified model and the treatment of reinsurance contracts.

Consequently, the IASB took on the challenges raised in the comment letters as part of its re-deliberations and made changes to many areas of the proposals. Although the IASB decided that re-exposure of the draft standard was necessary, it wanted to avoid re-opening areas that in its view had already been deliberated sufficiently during past discussions. As a result, the IASB invited comment only on five areas where it believed significant changes had been made compared with the 2010 ED:

- adjusting the contractual service margin for differences between current and previous estimates of future cash flows related to future coverage and other future services provided the contractual service margin is sufficient to absorb any unfavourable changes (the 2010 ED proposed that the margin was not adjusted subsequently);
- measuring fulfilment cash flows for certain types of contracts with participating features that vary directly with returns on underlying items by reference to the carrying amount of the underlying items with changes to the liabilities presented in profit or loss or other comprehensive income on the same basis as changes in the value of the underlying items (the 2010 ED did not contain such specific measurement and presentation guidance for these contracts);
- presentation of insurance contract revenue and expenses in profit or loss (the 2010 ED proposed that entities would use a summarised margin approach);
- recognising in other comprehensive income the impact of measuring the current value of the insurance contract using the current discount rate compared with the discount rate at contract inception (the 2010 ED proposed that all effects of changes in discount rates should always be presented in profit or loss); and
- proposing that, on transition, an entity should apply the standard retrospectively in accordance with IAS 8 unless impracticable in which case simplified transition requirements would be applied (the 2010 ED proposed that an entity should recognise no contractual service margin for contracts in force at the beginning of the earliest period presented).

Although the IASB only invited comment on these five areas, a number of other important changes were made compared with the 2010 ED which include the following:

- in determining which cash flows are included within the model, the 2010 ED made reference to cash flows that are incremental at the portfolio level. The revised ED includes all cash flows that relate directly to the fulfilment of a portfolio of contracts, including an allocation of fixed and variable overheads that are directly attributable to fulfilling that portfolio;
- in determining which cash flows are included in the model, the 2010 ED used acquisition costs that are incremental at the individual contract level. The revised ED uses acquisition costs which are directly attributable at the portfolio level that can be allocated on a rational and consistent basis, for both successful and unsuccessful efforts;
- the revised ED clarifies that two approaches can be used to establish discount rates: a 'top-down' approach and a 'bottom-up' approach. Guidance is also included that requires an insurer to estimate the inputs necessary to determine the relevant rates to the extent observable information is not available;
- the revised ED eliminates the guidance included in the 2010 ED that permitted only three methods for estimating the risk adjustment. Instead, the application guidance now focuses on setting out the characteristics that the risk adjustment should meet;
- the revised ED states that the contractual service margin should be recognised systematically in profit or loss over the coverage period in a way that best reflects the transfer of services under the contract. The 2010 ED proposed that the margin would be recognised in profit or loss in a way that best reflects the exposure from providing insurance coverage;
- the simplified model (referred to as the modified approach in the 2010 ED) is optional (rather than mandatory as in the 2010 ED) for those contracts which would produce measurements that are a reasonable approximation to those that would be produced using the building block approach or the coverage period of the contract at initial recognition arising from all premiums within the contract boundary is one year or less;
- the revised ED proposes that a cedant records any difference between the future cash inflows plus the risk adjustment and the future cash outflows of an acquired insurance contract as a contractual service margin. This means that, in contrast to the model for underlying direct contracts, the contractual service margin can be both positive and negative. However, if a reinsurance contract reimburses a cedant for liabilities incurred as a result of past events a negative contractual service margin is recognised in profit or loss immediately;
- ceded premiums are presented net of ceding commissions;
- cash flows that affect either the amount of ceded premiums or ceding commissions that are contingent on claims or benefits experience should be recognised as claims or benefit cash flows rather than premiums;

- the revised ED retains the 2010 ED definition of an insurance contract but adds that a reinsurance contract is deemed to transfer significant insurance risk if substantially all of the insurance risk is assumed by the reinsurer;
- there are additional criteria for scope exclusions regarding fixed-fee service contracts but the existing scoping for financial guarantee contracts from IFRS 4 has now been retained so that those contracts previously regarded as insurance contracts by the issuer would be accounted for under the new standard rather than IAS 39 (or IFRS 9);
- the revised ED clarifies that the standard would apply to financial instruments with discretionary participation features by an entity that also issues insurance contracts but eliminates the additional requirement from the 2010 ED that such contracts participate in the same pool of assets as insurance contracts;
- the definition of a portfolio is changed compared with the 2010 ED by adding a requirement that a portfolio of insurance contracts is priced similarly commensurate to the risk taken;
- the term 'unbundling' is no longer used; instead the revised ED refers to 'separating components from an insurance contract'. The revised ED requires an insurer to separate from an insurance contract (i) embedded derivatives if they meet certain specified criteria; (ii) distinct investment components; and (iii) performance obligations to provide goods and services;
- the revised ED requires an insurer to exclude from the statement of comprehensive income insurance contract revenue and incurred claims in respect of investment components that have not been separated;
- the revised ED clarifies that an insurance contract should be recognised at the earliest of: the beginning of the coverage period; the date when payments from the policyholder become due; or when there is evidence that a portfolio of insurance contracts is onerous. The 2010 ED proposed that an insurer should recognise an insurance contract when it becomes party to an insurance contract;
- the revised ED introduces guidance on how to treat modifications to insurance contracts;
- the revised ED clarifies that the date of recognition for contracts acquired in a portfolio transfer or business combination is the date of the transfer or the business combination; and
- the revised ED requires extensive disclosures in respect of reconciliations from the opening to the closing balance of the aggregate carrying amounts of insurance contract liabilities and insurance contract assets.

The revised ED did not propose an effective date but instead stated that the effective date will be around three years after the issuance of the final standard.

12.4 Subsequent decisions made by the IASB during deliberations of the revised ED

Comments on the revised ED were due by 25 October 2013. In its subsequent deliberations to 22 July 2016, the IASB has made the following major tentative decisions which will result in changes from the proposals in the revised ED:

- an entity will be able to make an accounting policy choice at a portfolio level whether to present the effects of changes in discount rates in profit or loss or in other comprehensive income (the revised ED proposed that the effects of all changes in discount rates would be presented in other comprehensive income);
- subsequent changes in cash flow estimates of reinsurance contracts held should be recognised in profit or loss by the cedant when changes in the expected reinsured losses of the underlying direct contracts are recognised in profit or loss. This would occur when, for example, the underlying contracts have become onerous and the contractual service margin on those contracts has been reduced to zero;
- a loss for onerous contracts should be recognised only when the contractual service margin is negative for a group of contracts and that the group should comprise contracts that at inception (i) have cash flows that the entity expects will respond in similar ways to key drivers in terms of amount and timing and (ii) have similar profitability (i.e. similar contractual margin as a percentage of the premium). The IASB explicitly confirmed that this means that contracts with dissimilar profitability, even as a consequence of regulation, may not be grouped for determining onerous contracts and for the allocation of the contractual service margin;
- the IASB confirmed the principle in the 2013 ED that an entity should recognise the remaining contractual service margin in profit or loss over the coverage period in the systematic way that best reflects the remaining transfer of the services that are provided under an insurance contract. For non-participating contracts, the coverage period that best represents the transfer of service represented by the contractual service margin is insurance coverage that (i) is provided on the basis of the passage of time and (ii) reflects the expected number of contracts in force. The IASB also tentatively decided that the contractual service margin should be measured using the group used for deciding which contracts are onerous (see above);
- the contractual service margin should not only be adjusted for subsequent changes in estimates of future cash flows but also for subsequent changes to the risk adjustment. The IASB also decided not to permit or require in the general model the remeasurement of the contractual service margin using current discount rates;
- for contracts acquired through a portfolio transfer or in a business combination such contracts should be accounted for as if they had been issued by the entity as at the date of the portfolio transfer or business combination;
- significant insurance risk occurs only when there is a possibility that an issuer will incur a loss on a present value basis;

- reconciliations should be required of opening and closing balances of the components of the insurance contract asset or liability, of premiums received in the period to insurance premium revenue, inputs used in determining the insurance contract revenue recognised in the period and the effect of insurance contracts that are initially recognised in the period on the amounts that are recognised in the statement of financial position;
- for all insurance contracts, an entity should present changes in estimates of the amount of cash flows that result from changes in market variables consistently with the way that the effects of the changes in discount rates are presented. For example, if the changes in discount rates are presented in other comprehensive income, those cash flow effects should also be presented in other comprehensive income;
- the standard will specify the objective for disaggregating changes in the carrying amount of insurance contracts arising from changes in market variables between profit or loss and other comprehensive income, but it will not specify detailed mechanics for the determination of the insurance investment expense (i.e. the expense for interest accretion on the insurance liability) using a cost measurement basis (i.e. an effective yield approach); and
- on transition, several simplifications have to be applied if the full retrospective approach would be impracticable according to IAS 8.

The IASB spent some time deliberating an alternative approach to the measurement and presentation exception ('mirroring approach') proposed in the revised ED for participating contracts which was generally criticised by respondents. As a result of the deliberations, the IASB tentatively decided that the mirroring approach should not be permitted or required. Instead, for participating contracts, the IASB has tentatively decided that:

- for insurance contracts with direct participation features, it would modify the general measurement model so that changes in the estimate of the fee that the entity expects to earn from the contract are adjusted in the contractual service margin (the 'variable fee' approach). The fee that the entity expects to earn from the contract is equal to the entity's expected share of the returns on underlying items, less any expected cash flows that do not vary directly with the underlying item for participating contracts (e.g. guarantee minimum benefits and expenses). The IASB tentatively decided that contracts with direct participation features should be defined as contracts for which:
  - the contractual terms specify that the policyholder participates in a share of a clearly identified pool of underlying items;
  - the entity expects to pay to the policyholder a substantial share of the returns from the underlying items; and
  - a substantial proportion of the cash flows that the entity expects to pay to the policyholder should be expected to vary with thee cash flows from the underlying items.
- for all insurance contracts with participation features, an entity should recognise the contractual service margin in profit or loss on the basis of the passage of time (and reflecting the expected number of contracts in force);

- for contracts (i) that meet the scope of the variable fee approach and (ii) for which the entity holds the underlying items, the insurance investment expense item is determined consistently with the accounting returns reflected in profit or loss for those underlying assets (this is referred to as 'the current period book yield approach');
- when an entity is required to change between the effective yield approach and the current period book yield approach (and *vice versa*) the standard will specify the mechanics of how this is to be implemented;
- the option to fully recognise the impact of changes in market variables in profit or loss as an accounting policy choice will be extended to contracts with participating features;
- a simplified approach for determining the insurance investment expense for contracts in which changes in market variables affects the amount of cash flows will be permitted when retrospective application of the new standard is impracticable;
- when an entity uses the variable fee approach to measure insurance contracts and uses a derivative measured at fair value through profit or loss to mitigate the financial risk from a guarantee embedded in the insurance contract, the entity would be permitted to recognise in profit or loss the changes in the value of the guarantee determined using fulfilment cash flows provided certain conditions are met including documentation of the entity's risk management objectives and strategy for using the derivative in this way.[32]

The IASB has now completed its technical decisions, confirmed that it is satisfied that all necessary due process steps have been taken and instructed staff to commence the drafting process.

12.5 The road ahead

Currently, the IASB expects to issue the new standard in 2017. Considering the IASB's stated intent to set an effective date no earlier than three years after issuance of the final standard, if the standard is issued in 2017, it is unlikely to have an effective date before accounting periods commencing in 2021.

References

1 *IASB Update*, May 2002.
2 www.cfoforum.nl
3 ED/2013/7, Insurance Contracts, IASB, June 2013, para. BCA154.
4 ED/2013/7, para. B19.
5 *Effect of board redeliberations on the 2013 Exposure Draft Insurance Contracts*, IASB, June 2016, p.57.
6 ED/2013/7, para. 7(e).
7 *Effect of board redeliberations on the 2013 Exposure Draft Insurance Contracts*, IASB, June 2016, p.6.
8 *IFRIC Update*, January 2008, p.3.
9 ED/2013/7, para. 10(a).
10 ED/2013/7, paras. 10(b) and B31-32.
11 *IFRIC Update*, November 2005, p.6.
12 *IFRIC Update*, January 2010, p.2.
13 ED/2013/7, paras. 3(c), Appendix A.

14 *Effect of board redeliberations on the 2013 Exposure Draft Insurance Contracts*, IASB, June 2016, p.18.
15 ED/2013/7, paras. 49-50.
16 ED/2013/7, paras. 54-55.
17 ED/2013/7, paras. 63 and 67.
18 ED/2013/7, para. 41(b)(iii).
19 ED/2013/7, para. 51.
20 ED/2013/7, para. B66(a).
21 ED/2013/7, para. 41(c).
22 *Effect of board redeliberations on the 2013 Exposure Draft Insurance Contracts*, IASB, June 2016, p.26.
23 ED/2013/7, para. B66(c).
24 ED/2013/7, para. B66(j).
25 *European Embedded Value Principles*, CFO Forum, May 2004, p.3.
26 *Effect of board redeliberations on the 2013 Exposure Draft Insurance Contracts*, IASB, June 2016, p.33.
27 ED/2013/7, paras. C11-C12.
28 *Effect of board redeliberations on the 2013 Exposure Draft Insurance Contracts*, IASB, June 2016, pp.94-95.
29 ED/2013/7, paras. 44-46.
30 *Effect of board redeliberations on the 2013 Exposure Draft Insurance Contracts*, IASB, June 2016, p.27.
31 *IASB Update*, June 2009.
32 *Effect of board redeliberations on the 2013 Exposure Draft Insurance Contracts*, IASB, June 2016.

Index of extracts from financial statements

Index of standards

Framework

IFRS 1

IFRS 2

IFRS 3 (2007)

IFRS 3

IFRS 4

IFRS 6

IFRS 7 (2010)

IFRS 7

IFRS 8

IFRS 9 (2012)

IFRS 9 (2014)

IFRS 9

IFRS 10

IFRS 11

IFRS 12

IFRS 13

IFRS 14

IFRS 15

IFRS 16

IAS 1

IAS 7

IAS 10

IAS 11

IAS 12

IAS 16

IAS 17

IAS 18 (2008)

IAS 18

IAS 19

IAS 20

IAS 21

IAS 23

IAS 24

IAS 27 (2012)

IAS 27

IAS 28

IAS 29

IAS 33

IAS 34

IAS 36

IAS 37

IAS 38

IAS 39 (2012)

IAS 39

IAS 40

IAS 41 (2008)

IAS 41 (2012)

IAS 41

IFRIC 1

IFRIC 13

IFRIC 14

IFRIC 15

IFRIC 16

IFRIC 17

IFRIC 18

IFRIC 19

IFRIC 2

IFRIC 21

SIC 7

SIC 10

SIC 12

SIC 15

SIC 25

SIC 27

SIC 29

SIC 31

SIC 32

MC

Index

Notes

Notes

International GAAP® 2017

Gener… e
under … ds

Martin Be… nkhurst
Mike Bon…
Linzi Carr… oddubnaya
Victor Ch… tt
Wei Li Ch… on
Angela C… -Tan
Mike Davi… a
Pieter De… o
Julie Dem… ila
Tim Dent… ng
Dennis De… n
Dennis Es…

EY
Building a bet… working world

This edition first published in 2017 by John Wiley & Sons Ltd.

The United Kingdom firm of Ernst & Young LLP is a member of Ernst & Young Global Limited.
International GAAP® is a registered trademark of Ernst & Young LLP.
http://www.internationalgaap.com

Registered office
John Wiley & Sons Ltd, The Atrium, Southern Gate, Chichester, West Sussex, PO19 8SQ, United Kingdom

For details of our global editorial offices, for customer services and for information about how to apply for permission to reuse the copyright material in this book please see our website at www.wiley.com

ISBN 978-1-119-34448-3 (paperback)
[EY personnel only ISBN 978-1-119-34453-7]

ISBN 978-1-119-34449-0 (ebk)
ISBN 978-1-119-34452-0 (ebk)

A catalogue record for this book is available from the British Library.

Printed and bound by CPI Group (UK) Ltd, Croydon, CR0 4YY

This book is printed on acid-free paper responsibly manufactured from sustainable forestry.

About this book

International GAAP® 2017 has been fully revised and updated in order to:

- Include a new chapter on the new leases standard IFRS 16 (*Leases*). This is a joint standard issued by the IASB and FASB which is likely to affect all entities in all industries, and will result in more assets and liabilities being recognised on the Statement of Financial Position.
- Explore the implementation issues arising as entities plan for the future adoption of IFRS 9 (*Financial Instruments*) and IFRS 15 (*Revenue from Contracts with Customers*), including those referred to the IFRS Transition Resource Group for Impairment of Financial Instruments and the Joint Transition Resource Group for Revenue Recognition.
- Address amended standards and new interpretations issued since the preparation of the 2016 edition.
- Explain the many other initiatives that are currently being discussed by the IASB and by the IFRS Interpretations Committee and the potential consequential changes to accounting requirements. In particular, projects on insurance contracts and the conceptual framework for financial reporting may all result in significant changes to current accounting practice.
- Provide insight on the many issues relating to the practical application of IFRS, based on the extensive experience of the book's authors in dealing with recent day-to-day issues.

The book is published in three volumes. The 54 chapters – listed on pages ix to xi – are split between the three volumes as follows:

- Volume 1 - Chapters 1 to 23,
- Volume 2 - Chapters 24 to 41,
- Volume 3 - Chapters 42 to 55.

Each chapter includes a detailed list of contents and list of illustrative examples.

Each of the three volumes contains the following indexes covering all three volumes:

- an index of extracts from financial statements,
- an index of references to standards and interpretations,
- a general index.

Preface

The IASB reported earlier this year that 122 of the 147 jurisdictions they have researched require the use of IFRS for all or most listed companies and financial institutions, and a further 13 jurisdictions permit the use of IFRS. Several large economies like China, India and Japan do not require IFRS for all or most of their listed companies, but they have made considerable progress to move towards or to converge with IFRS. While it is unlikely that the United States will adopt IFRS in the near term, there are more than 500 foreign IFRS reporters with a significant market capitalisation listed on US markets and many US investors are familiar with IFRS-based financial statements. Global financial reporting is now in a position where there are essentially only two global-scale systems of financial reporting – IFRS and US GAAP.

In 2016, the IASB completed its project on lease accounting and made considerable efforts to provide implementation and adoption support regarding the new revenue recognition and financial instruments standards.

The publication of IFRS 16 – *Leases*, which is effective from 1 January 2019 onwards, marks the completion of the IASB's long-running project on lease accounting. The main objective of the new standard – to bring most lease obligations that are currently not recognised, on to the balance sheet – is converged with the FASB's objective. However, certain requirements for the recognition, measurement, presentation and disclosure of leases by lessees and lessors differ. IFRS 16 is more complex than its predecessor, IAS 17 – *Leases*, and is giving rise to implementation questions that the IASB will need to address in a timely manner.

IFRS 9 – *Financial Instruments* – and IFRS 15 – *Revenue from Contracts with Customers*, which are effective from 1 January 2018, introduce important improvements and fill major gaps in the existing literature. The joint IASB/FASB transition resource group for revenue recognition (TRG) and the IASB's transition resource group for impairment of financial instruments have provided valuable forums for identifying interpretation questions that inevitably arise when entities implement complex accounting standards. In April 2016, the IASB published amendments that improve the guidance in IFRS 15 and address some issues that the TRG discussed. These amendments and the many interpretations and emerging practices regarding the new standards have been included in this edition of *International GAAP* and will help companies that are implementing these standards.

In the past year, the IASB has worked on its projects on insurance contracts and the conceptual framework. The work on insurance contracts, the IASB's longest running project, is crucial because as Hans Hoogervorst noted in comments to the European

Parliament: '[i]nsurance is an extremely important business with substantial systemic risks. These risks are currently amplified by the current environment of persistently low interest rates. … There is no real global standard and there is a wide variety of practices around the world. Some of these standards provide information that is clearly wrong.' In February 2016, the Board concluded that it had completed all the necessary due process steps and instructed the staff to commence the drafting process. A final standard is now expected to be published in the first half of 2017. In order to address the complex interaction between IFRS 9 and the insurance contracts project, the IASB published, in September 2016, amendments to IFRS 4 – *Insurance Contracts*. These amendments provide certain reliefs to insurers that are intended to mitigate the impact of applying IFRS 9 until the new insurance contracts standard becomes effective.

The IASB is redeliberating its revised conceptual framework based on the comments received in response to the exposure draft *Conceptual Framework for Financial Reporting*. Some of the most challenging areas being discussed are measurement, the distinction between debt and equity, and the role of profit and loss versus other comprehensive income. While it is hard to make progress on such major conceptual issues, these are nevertheless the areas that will be most important to constituents. The IASB expects to publish the revised conceptual framework in the first half of 2017.

The IASB has recently been considering its priorities for the period from 2016 to 2020, based on the feedback it received in response to its request for views *2015 Agenda Consultation*. The IASB's new work programme can be broken down into the following main categories, each of which contains a number of projects:

- *Standard-setting and relating projects* – conceptual framework, disclosure initiative: materiality practice statement, insurance contracts, and rate-regulated activities;
- *Implementation and other activities* – implementation and adoption support activities, post-implementation reviews, and a public consultation on small and medium-sized entities;
- *Active research agenda* – principles of disclosure, primary financial statements, financial instruments with characteristics of equity, goodwill and impairment, dynamic risk management, and business combinations under common control; and
- *Research pipeline* – equity method of accounting, extractive activities, pollutant pricing mechanisms, provisions, contingent liabilities and contingent assets (review of IAS 37), variable and contingent consideration, and feasibility studies (on small and medium-sized entities, post-employment benefits that depend on asset returns, and high inflation).

We believe that these are important areas of accounting where the IASB will be able to make meaningful improvements in financial reporting. In particular, the IASB is addressing the needs of users and preparers of financial statements by focussing on better communication (by way of better disclosures and presentation), implementation and adoption support, and post-implementation reviews of existing standards.

We think that it is important for the IASB to consider carefully the scope of a new project before starting the development of a new standard. This is to avoid scope-creep and projects taking longer than necessary to complete. In addition, the decision to undertake a major project should not automatically lead to the decision not to address urgent practical issues affecting the same area of accounting. In our view, such a situation might warrant two projects: one to solve the existing practical issue; and one to address the more fundamental and conceptual issues.

The IFRS Foundation Trustees identified, in the 2015 review of the organisation, the consistency of application and implementation of IFRS as one of the IFRS Foundation's primary strategic goals. They correctly see this in a holistic manner as requiring: clear drafting of standards; guidance that is consistent with a principle-based approach to standard setting; a responsive approach towards requests for interpretations; close co-operation with enforcers and educational efforts.

We believe the IASB should take its time in the final drafting stages of a standard, i.e. between the final redeliberations and the issuance of the standard, thereby ensuring that the drafting of the standard is clear and unambiguous. Drafting accounting standards for a worldwide audience involves a particular level of complexity because constituents interpret the wording in the context of their own experience and background. In addition, the operability of a standard enhances its quality to a large degree and we believe that the benefits of spending more time on this during the drafting phase outweigh the costs of doing so.

The consistent application of IFRS remains essential to its credibility. We believe that *International GAAP*, now in its twelfth edition, plays an important role in ensuring consistent application. Our team of authors and reviewers hails from all parts of the world, and includes not only our global technical experts but also senior client-facing staff. This gives us an in-depth knowledge of practice in many different countries and industry sectors, enabling us to go beyond mere recitation of the requirements of standards to explaining their application in many varied situations.

We are deeply indebted to many of our colleagues within the global organisation of EY for their selfless assistance and support in the publication of this book. It has been a truly international effort, with valuable contributions from EY people around the globe.

Our thanks go particularly to those who reviewed, edited and assisted in the preparation of drafts, most notably: John Alton, Mark Barton, Silke Blaschke, Jason Bond, Brian Byrne, Larissa Clark, Tony Clifford, Muriel Courel, Tai Danmola, Jackson Day, Alison Dobbie, Chantelle Duffy, Charles Feeney, Lisa Filomia-Atkas, Josh Forgione, Peter Gittens, Lindsay Gotsman, Laure Guégan, Paul Hebditch, Jennifer Hillenmeyer, Deborah Jones, Guy Jones, Akashi Kohno, Steinar Kvifte, Vincent de La Bachelerie, Martin Lee, Twan van Limpt, Meredith Lloyd, Michiel van der Lof, James Luke, Mark Mahar, Robert McCracken, Joseph McGrath, Ellie Morris, John O'Grady, Eric Ohlund, Gerard van Santen, Cyra Sharma, Rachel Simons, Alison Spivey, Paul Sutcliffe, Leo van der Tas, Evangelia Tsakiroglou, Hans van der Veen, Emma VanEmon, Jana Wahrisch, Arne Weber, Chris White and Luci Wright.

Our thanks also go to everyone who directly or indirectly contributed to the book's creation, including the following members of the Financial Reporting Group in the UK: Denise Brand, Rob Carrington, Larissa Connor, Anna Costigan, Diego Fernandez, Prahalad Halgeri, Parbin Khatun, Maria Kingston, Andrea Maylor, Bunmi Oluitan, Anna Pickup and Claire Taylor.

We also thank Jeremy Gugenheim for his assistance with the production technology throughout the period of writing.

London,
October 2016

Martin Beyersdorff
Mike Bonham
Linzi Carr
Victor Chan
Wei Li Chan
Angela Covic
Mike Davies
Pieter Dekker
Julie Dempers
Tim Denton
Dennis Deysel
Dennis Esterhuizen
Jane Hurworth
Praveen Jindal
Ted Jones
Bernd Kremp
Dean Lockhart
Thomas Luescher
Sharon MacIntyre
Takahiro Makino
Amanda Marrion
Steve Martin
Emily Moll
Richard Moore
Margaret Pankhurst
Tina Patel
Alexandra Poddubnaya
Michael Pratt
Tim Rogerson
Serene Seah-Tan
Anna Sirocka
Charlene Teo
Michael Varila
Tracey Waring
Jane Watson

Lists of chapters

Volume 1

The lists of chapters in volumes 2 and 3 follow overleaf.

Volume 2

The list of chapters in volume 3 follows overleaf.

Volume 3

Abbreviations

The following abbreviations are used in this book:

Professional and regulatory bodies:

AASB	Australian Accounting Standards Board
AcSB	Accounting Standards Board of Canada
AICPA	American Institute of Certified Public Accountants
AOSSG	Asian-Oceanian Standard-Setters Group
APB	Accounting Principles Board (of the AICPA, predecessor of the FASB)
ARC	Accounting Regulatory Committee of representatives of EU Member States
ASAF	Accounting Standards Advisory Forum
ASB	Accounting Standards Board in the UK
ASBJ	Accounting Standards Board of Japan
ASU	Accounting Standards Update
CASC	China Accounting Standards Committee
CESR	Committee of European Securities Regulators, an independent committee whose members comprised senior representatives from EU securities regulators (replaced by ESMA)
CICA	Canadian Institute of Chartered Accountants
EC	European Commission
ECB	European Central Bank
ECOFIN	The Economic and Financial Affairs Council
EDTF	Enhanced Disclosure Task Force of the (FSB)
EFRAG	European Financial Reporting Advisory Group
EITF	Emerging Issues Task Force in the US
EPRA	European Public Real Estate Association
ESMA	European Securities and Markets Authority (see CESR)
EU	European Union
FAF	Financial Accounting Foundation
FASB	Financial Accounting Standards Board in the US

FCAG	Financial Crisis Advisory Group
FEE	Federation of European Accountants
FSB	Financial Stability Board (successor to the FSF)
FSF	Financial Stability Forum
G4+1	The (now disbanded) group of four plus 1, actually with six members, that comprised an informal 'think tank' of staff from the standard setters from Australia, Canada, New Zealand, UK, and USA, plus the IASC
G7	The Group of Seven Finance Ministers (successor to G8)
G8	The Group of Eight Finance Ministers
G20	The Group of Twenty Finance Ministers and Central Bank Governors
GPPC	Global Public Policy Committee of the six largest accounting networks
HKICPA	Hong Kong Institute of Certified Public Accountants
ICAI	Institute of Chartered Accountants of India
IASB	International Accounting Standards Board
IASC	International Accounting Standards Committee. The former Board of the IASC was the predecessor of the IASB
IASCF	International Accounting Standards Committee Foundation (predecessor of the IFRS Foundation)
ICAEW	Institute of Chartered Accountants in England and Wales
ICAS	Institute of Chartered Accountants of Scotland
IFAC	International Federation of Accountants
IFASS	International Forum of Accounting Standard Setters
IFRIC	The IFRS Interpretations Committee (formerly the International Financial Reporting Interpretations Committee) of the IASB
IGC	Implementation Guidance Committee on IAS 39 (now disbanded)
IOSCO	International Organisation of Securities Commissions
IPSASB	International Public Sector Accounting Standards Board
IPTF	International Practices Task Force (a task force of the SEC Regulations Committee)
ISDA	International Swaps and Derivatives Association
IVSC	International Valuation Standards Council
KASB	Korea Accounting Standards Board
RICS	Royal Institution of Chartered Surveyors
SAC	Standards Advisory Council, predecessor of the IFRS Advisory Council which provides advice to the IASB on a wide range of issues
SEC	Securities and Exchange Commission (the US securities regulator)
SIC	Standing Interpretations Committee of the IASC (replaced by IFRIC)

TEG	Technical Expert Group, an advisor to the European Commission
TRG	Joint Transition Resource Group for Revenue Recognition

Accounting related terms:

ADS	American Depositary Shares
AFS	Available-for-sale investment
ARB	Accounting Research Bulletins (issued by the AICPA)
ARS	Accounting Research Studies (issued by the APB)
ASC	Accounting Standards Codification®. The single source of authoritative US GAAP recognised by the FASB, to be applied to non-governmental entities for interim and accounting periods ending after 15 September 2009
ASU	Accounting Standards Update
CCIRS	Cross Currency Interest Rate Swap
CDO	Collateralised Debt Obligation
CGU	Cash-generating Unit
CU	Currency Unit
DD&A	Depreciation, Depletion and Amortisation
DPF	Discretionary Participation Feature
E&E	Exploration and Evaluation
EBIT	Earnings Before Interest and Taxes
EBITDA	Earnings Before Interest, Taxes, Depreciation and Amortisation
EIR	Effective Interest Rate
EPS	Earnings per Share
FAS	Financial Accounting Standards (issued by the FASB). Superseded by Accounting Standards Codification® (ASC)
FC	Foreign currency
FICE	Financial Instruments with the Characteristics of Equity
FIFO	First-In, First-Out basis of valuation
FRS	Financial Reporting Standard (issued by the ASB)
FTA	First-time Adoption
FVLCD	Fair value less costs of disposal
FVLCS	Fair value less costs to sell (following the issue of IFRS 13, generally replaced by FVLCD)
GAAP	Generally accepted accounting practice (as it applies under IFRS), or generally accepted accounting principles (as it applies to the US)
HTM	Held-to-maturity investment

IAS	International Accounting Standard (issued by the former board of the IASC)
IBNR	Incurred but not reported claims
IFRS	International Financial Reporting Standard (issued by the IASB)
IGC Q&A	Implementation guidance to the original version of IAS 39 (issued by the IGC)
IPO	Initial Public Offering
IPR&D	In-process Research and Development
IPSAS	International Public Sector Accounting Standard
IRR	Internal Rate of Return
IRS	Interest Rate Swap
JA	Joint Arrangement
JCA	Jointly Controlled Asset
JCE	Jointly Controlled Entity
JCO	Jointly Controlled Operation
JO	Joint Operation
JV	Joint Venture
LAT	Liability Adequacy Test
LC	Local Currency
LIBOR	London Inter Bank Offered Rate
LIFO	Last-In, First-Out basis of valuation
NCI	Non-controlling Interest
NBV	Net Book Value
NPV	Net Present Value
NRV	Net Realisable Value
OCI	Other Comprehensive Income
PP&E	Property, Plant and Equipment
R&D	Research and Development
SCA	Service Concession Arrangement
SE	Structured Entity
SFAC	Statement of Financial Accounting Concepts (issued by the FASB as part of its conceptual framework project)
SFAS	Statement of Financial Accounting Standards (issued by the FASB). Superseded by Accounting Standards Codification® (ASC)
SME	Small or medium-sized entity
SPE	Special Purpose Entity
SV	Separate Vehicle

TSR	Total Shareholder Return
VIU	Value In Use
WACC	Weighted Average Cost of Capital

References to IFRSs, IASs, Interpretations and supporting documentation:

AG	Application Guidance
AV	Alternative View
B, BCZ	Basis for Conclusions on IASs
BC	Basis for Conclusions on IFRSs and IASs
DI	Draft Interpretation
DO	Dissenting Opinion
DP	Discussion Paper
ED	Exposure Draft
IE	Illustrative Examples on IFRSs and IASs
IG	Implementation Guidance
IN	Introduction to IFRSs and IASs
PIR	Post-implementation Review

Authoritative literature

The content of this book takes into account all accounting standards and other relevant rules issued up to September 2016. Consequently, it covers the IASB's *Conceptual Framework for Financial Reporting* and authoritative literature listed below.

References in the main text of each chapter to the pronouncements below are generally to the versions of those pronouncements as approved and expected to be included in the Blue Book edition of the Bound Volume 2017 International Financial Reporting Standards – IFRS – Consolidated without early application – Official pronouncements applicable on 1 January 2017, to be published by the IASB.

References to those pronouncements below which have an effective date after 1 January 2017 (such as IFRS 9 – *Financial Instruments*) are to the versions of those pronouncements as denoted by the ISBN references noted below. These are expected to be included in the Red Book edition of the Bound Volume 2017 International Financial Reporting Standards – IFRS – Official pronouncements issued at 1 January 2017, to be published by the IASB.

References in the main text to pronouncements that applied only to periods beginning before 1 January 2017 are generally denoted by the last version of the Blue Book edition of the Bound Volume in which they were included. For example, IFRS 3 (2007) refers to IFRS 3 – *Business Combinations*, which was included in the Blue Book edition of the Bound Volume 2007 International Financial Reporting Standards – IFRS – Consolidated without early application – Official pronouncements applicable on 1 January 2007.

US GAAP accounting standards are organised within a comprehensive FASB Accounting Standards Codification®, which is now the single source of authoritative US GAAP recognised by the FASB to be applied to non-governmental entities and has been applied in this publication.

† The standards and interpretations marked with a dagger have been withdrawn or superseded.

IASB Framework

The Conceptual Framework for Financial Reporting

International Financial Reporting Standards (2017 Bound Volume)

IFRS 1	First-time Adoption of International Financial Reporting Standards
IFRS 2	Share-based Payment
IFRS 3	Business Combinations
IFRS 4	Insurance Contracts
IFRS 5	Non-current Assets Held for Sale and Discontinued Operations

IFRS 6	Exploration for and Evaluation of Mineral Resources
IFRS 7	Financial Instruments: Disclosures
IFRS 8	Operating Segments
IFRS 10	Consolidated Financial Statements
IFRS 11	Joint Arrangements
IFRS 12	Disclosure of Interests in Other Entities
IFRS 13	Fair Value Measurement
IFRS 14	Regulatory Deferral Accounts

International Financial Reporting Standards (mandatory after 1 January 2017)

IFRS 9	Financial Instruments	ISBN 978-1-909704-47-3
IFRS 15	Revenue from Contracts with Customers	ISBN 978-1-909704-33-6
IFRS 16	Leases	ISBN 978-1-911040-03-3

International Accounting Standards (2017 Bound Volume)

IAS 1	Presentation of Financial Statements
IAS 2	Inventories
IAS 7	Statement of Cash Flows
IAS 8	Accounting Policies, Changes in Accounting Estimates and Errors
IAS 10	Events after the Reporting Period
IAS 11	Construction Contracts
IAS 12	Income Taxes
IAS 16	Property, Plant and Equipment
IAS 17	Leases
IAS 18	Revenue
IAS 19	Employee Benefits
IAS 20	Accounting for Government Grants and Disclosure of Government Assistance
IAS 21	The Effects of Changes in Foreign Exchange Rates
IAS 23	Borrowing Costs
IAS 24	Related Party Disclosures
IAS 26	Accounting and Reporting by Retirement Benefit Plans
IAS 27	Separate Financial Statements
IAS 28	Investments in Associates and Joint Ventures
IAS 29	Financial Reporting in Hyperinflationary Economies
IAS 32	Financial Instruments: Presentation
IAS 33	Earnings per Share
IAS 34	Interim Financial Reporting
IAS 36	Impairment of Assets
IAS 37	Provisions, Contingent Liabilities and Contingent Assets
IAS 38	Intangible Assets
IAS 39	Financial Instruments: Recognition and Measurement
IAS 40	Investment Property
IAS 41	Agriculture

IFRS Interpretations Committee Interpretations

IFRIC 1	Changes in Existing Decommissioning, Restoration and Similar Liabilities
IFRIC 2	Members' Shares in Co-operative Entities and Similar Instruments
† IFRIC 3	Emission Rights
IFRIC 4	Determining whether an Arrangement contains a Lease
IFRIC 5	Rights to Interests arising from Decommissioning, Restoration and Environmental Rehabilitation Funds
IFRIC 6	Liabilities arising from Participating in a Specific Market – Waste Electrical and Electronic Equipment
IFRIC 7	Applying the Restatement Approach under IAS 29 Financial Reporting in Hyperinflationary Economies
IFRIC 9	Reassessment of Embedded Derivatives
IFRIC 10	Interim Financial Reporting and Impairment
IFRIC 12	Service Concession Arrangements
IFRIC 13	Customer Loyalty Programmes
IFRIC 14	IAS 19 – The Limit on a Defined Benefit Asset, Minimum Funding Requirements and their Interaction
IFRIC 15	Agreements for the Construction of Real Estate
IFRIC 16	Hedges of a Net Investment in a Foreign Operation
IFRIC 17	Distributions of Non-cash Assets to Owners
IFRIC 18	Transfer of Assets from Customers
IFRIC 19	Extinguishing Financial Liabilities with Equity Instruments
IFRIC 20	Stripping Costs in the Production Phase of a Surface Mine
IFRIC 21	Levies

Standing Interpretations Committee Interpretations

SIC-7	Introduction of the Euro
SIC-10	Government Assistance – No Specific Relation to Operating Activities
SIC-15	Operating Leases – Incentives
SIC-25	Income Taxes – Changes in the Tax Status of an Entity or its Shareholders
SIC-27	Evaluating the Substance of Transactions Involving the Legal Form of a Lease
SIC-29	Service Concession Arrangements: Disclosures
SIC-31	Revenue – Barter Transactions Involving Advertising Services
SIC-32	Intangible Assets – Web Site Costs

IASB Exposure Drafts

ED/2013/7	Insurance Contracts
ED/2014/4	Measuring Quoted Investments in Subsidiaries, Joint Ventures and Associates at Fair Value (Proposed amendments to IFRS 10, IFRS 12, IAS 27, IAS 28 and IAS 36 and Illustrative Examples for IFRS 13)
ED/2015/1	Classification of Liabilities (Proposed amendments to IAS 1)
ED/2015/3	Conceptual Framework for Financial Reporting
ED/2015/4	Updating References to the Conceptual Framework (Proposed amendments to IFRS 2, IFRS 3, IFRS 4, IFRS 6, IAS 1, IAS 8, IAS 34, SIC-27 and SIC-32)

ED/2015/5	Remeasurement on a Plan Amendment, Curtailment or Settlement/Availability of a Refund from a Defined Benefit Plan (Proposed amendments to IAS 19 and IFRIC 14)
ED/2015/7	Effective Date of Amendments to IFRS 10 and IAS 28
ED/2015/9	Transfers of Investment Property (Proposed amendments to IAS 40)
ED/2016/1	Definition of a Business and Accounting for Previously Held Interests (Proposed amendments to IFRS 3 and IFRS 11)

IFRS Interpretations Committee Exposure Drafts

DI/2012/2	Put Options Written on Non-controlling Interests	ISBN 978-1-907877-61-2
DI/2015/1	Uncertainty over Income Tax Treatments	ISBN 978-1-909704-99-2
DI/2015/2	Foreign Currency Transactions and Advance Consideration	ISBN 978-1-909704-98-5

IASB Discussion Papers

DP/2014/1	Accounting for Dynamic Risk Management: a Portfolio Revaluation Approach to Macro Hedging	ISBN 978-1-909704-39-8
DP/2014/2	Reporting the Financial Effects of Rate Regulation	ISBN 978-1-909704-58-9

Other IASB publications

IFRS for SMEs	International Financial Reporting Standard (IFRS) for Small and Medium-sized Entities (SMEs)	ISBN 978-1-911040-07-1

Chapter 24 Leases (IAS 17)

List of Examples

Chapter 24 Leases (IAS 17)

1 INTRODUCTION

Although a lease is an agreement that gives a lessee the right to use an asset for an agreed period of time in return for a payment or series of payments, companies are required in certain circumstances to capitalise assets in their statements of financial position, together with the corresponding obligations, irrespective of the fact that legal title to those assets is vested in another party.

The term 'lease' also applies to arrangements that do not take the legal form of leases. They may combine rights to use assets and the provision of services or outputs, for agreed periods of time in return for a payment or series of payments, e.g. outsourcing arrangements that include the provision of assets and services. Entities have to consider the substance of these arrangements to see if they are, or contain, leases. If so, then the elements identified as a lease will be subject to the requirements of IAS 17 – *Leases*. The objective of IAS 17 is to prescribe, for lessees and lessors, the appropriate accounting policies and disclosure to apply in relation to leases. *[IAS 17.1]*.

IAS 17 has been in place for many years, having been originally issued in September 1982. So has its equivalent standard in the US, SFAS 13 – *Accounting for Leases* (1976) – (now ASC 840). For several years, the IASB and the Financial Accounting Standards Board (FASB) worked on a joint project to develop a new approach to lease accounting. In January 2016, the IASB issued IFRS 16 – *Leases* – which will replace IAS 17, and in February 2016, the FASB issued its new lease accounting standard, ASU 2016-02 *Leases* (ASC 842). Whilst the IASB and FASB reached the same conclusions on many areas of lease accounting, there are some areas for which they did not reach the same conclusions. Therefore differences do exist between the new IASB and FASB standards. IFRS 16 will be effective for annual periods beginning on or after 1 January 2019, and is discussed in Chapter 25.

2 WHAT IS A LEASE?

IAS 17 defines a lease as 'an agreement whereby the lessor conveys to the lessee in return for a payment or series of payments the right to use an asset for an agreed period of time.' *[IAS 17.4]*. The standard applies to agreements that transfer the right to use assets even though substantial services by the lessor may be called for in connection with the operation or maintenance of such assets. It does not apply to agreements that are contracts for services that do not transfer the right to use assets from one contracting party to the other. The definition of a lease includes contracts for the hire of an asset that contain a provision giving the hirer an option to acquire title to the asset when agreed conditions have been complied with, sometimes known as hire purchase contacts. *[IAS 17.6]*.

There are types of arrangements that do not take the legal form of leases. They take many forms, and may combine rights to use assets and the provision of services or outputs, for agreed periods of time in return for a payment or series of payments. These issues are dealt with in IFRIC 4 – *Determining whether an Arrangement contains a Lease* – which is considered further in 2.1 below. Some of the arrangements under service concession arrangements give rise to further accounting issues that have been separately addressed by the Interpretations Committee; service concessions have been excluded from the scope of lease accounting and are discussed in Chapter 27.

The SIC had previously considered whether all transactions in the legal form of a lease should be considered under IAS 17. The results of these deliberations, SIC-27 – *Evaluating the Substance of Transactions Involving the Legal Form of a Lease*, are covered in 2.2 below.

2.1 Determining whether an arrangement contains a lease

IFRIC 4 notes that there are arrangements that do not take the legal form of a lease but that nevertheless convey rights to use items for agreed periods of time in return for a payment or series of payments. *[IFRIC 4.1]*. IFRIC 4 has the objective only of dealing with the practical issues that arise when applying IAS 17 to arrangements that are not (or do not contain) leases in form: how to identify an arrangement that is in substance a lease, when to make the assessment and how to measure the lease element. *[IFRIC 4.5]*. The Interpretation does not provide any guidance for determining lease classification under IAS 17, *[IFRIC 4.2]*, in other words, it could be a finance lease or an operating lease under IAS 17, nor does it expect the guidance to extend the scope of that standard.

If an arrangement turns out to contain a lease or licence of a type excluded from the scope of IAS 17 (see 3.1.1 below), the Interpretation does not apply. Service concession arrangements to which IFRIC 12 – *Service Concession Arrangements* – applies are also out of scope (see Chapter 27). *[IFRIC 4.4]*. However, in some service concession arrangements, the operator of a service concession arrangement may be required to make contractual payments to the grantor that are linked to a right to use a tangible asset that is separate from the infrastructure. The Interpretations Committee observed that, in such cases, the operator should assess whether the arrangement contains a lease of that tangible asset. If the arrangement contains a lease, that portion of the arrangement would be in scope of IAS 17.[1]

IFRIC 12 considers the accounting implications of arrangements such as the following, in all of which an entity (the supplier) conveys a right to use an asset to another entity (the purchaser), together with related services or outputs:

- outsourcing arrangements, including outsourcing of the data processing functions of an entity;
- arrangements in the telecommunications industry, where suppliers of network capacity enter into contracts to provide purchasers with rights to capacity; and
- take-or-pay and similar contracts, in which purchasers must make specified payments regardless of whether they take delivery of the contracted products or services (e.g. where purchasers are committed to acquiring substantially all of the output of a supplier's power generator). *[IFRIC 4.1]*.

The Interpretations Committee concluded that an arrangement of one of these types could be within the scope of IAS 17 if it met the definition of a lease, i.e. if it conveyed to the lessee the right to use an asset for an agreed period of time in return for a payment or series of payments. *[IFRIC 4.BC2]*. IAS 17 applies to the lease element of the arrangement notwithstanding the related services or outputs because IAS 17 applies to 'agreements that transfer the right to use assets even though substantial services by the lessor may be called for in connection with the operation or maintenance of such assets.' *[IAS 17.3]*. This is regardless of the fact that the arrangement is not described as a lease and is likely to grant rights that are significantly different from those in a formal lease agreement.

2.1.1 Identification of an asset

The first condition that must be met to determine whether an arrangement is, or contains a lease is that fulfilment of the arrangement depends on a specific asset or assets. *[IFRIC 4.6]*.

IAS 17 applies only to an arrangement in which there is a 'right to use an asset', so an arrangement will not contain a lease unless it depends on a specific asset or assets.

A specific asset that is explicitly identified by the arrangement will not be the subject of a lease if the arrangement is not dependent on the asset. If the seller is required under the arrangement to deliver a specified quantity of goods or services and has the right or ability to provide those goods using other assets not specified in the agreement, the arrangement will not contain a lease. *[IFRIC 4.7]*.

However, an arrangement may still contain a lease if a specific asset is not explicitly identified but it would not be economically feasible or practical for the supplier to provide the use of alternative items. For example, the supplier may only own one suitable asset. *[IFRIC 4.8]*.

Some arrangements may allow the supplier to replace the specified asset with a similar asset if the original asset is unavailable, e.g. because it is unexpectedly inoperable. The Interpretations Committee takes the view that as such a requirement is in effect a warranty obligation it does not preclude lease treatment. *[IFRIC 4.7]*.

To take a relatively simple example, an arrangement in which an entity (the purchaser) outsources its product delivery department to another organisation (the supplier) will not contain a lease if the supplier is obliged to make available a certain number of delivery vehicles of a certain standard specification and the supplier is a delivery organisation with many suitable vehicles available. However, if the supplier has to supply and maintain a specified number of specialist vehicles in the purchaser's branding, then this arrangement is more likely to contain a lease. The latter arrangement may be commercially more akin to outsourcing the purchaser's acquisitions of delivery vehicles rather than its delivery functions. Similar issues would have to be taken into account if data processing functions are outsourced as these may require substantial investment by the supplier in computer hardware dedicated to the use of a single customer.

Where arrangements are likely to contain leases (delivery vehicles in the purchaser's branding, dedicated hardware), the purchaser cannot be unaware that there are specific assets underlying the service. There would have been negotiations between supplier and purchaser that would probably be reflected in the contract documentation. By contrast, if the purchaser does not know what assets are used to provide the service (beyond the fact that they are trucks and computers, of course), and in the circumstances it is reasonable not to know, it is plausible that there is no underlying lease in the arrangement. This remains true even if the supplier has dedicated specific assets to the service being provided and expects their cost to be recouped during the course of the contractual relationship.

2.1.2 Parts of assets and the unit of account

IFRIC 4 notes that some arrangements transfer the right to use an asset that is a component of a larger asset but the issue of whether and when such rights should be accounted for as leases is not dealt with in the Interpretation. The Interpretation states merely that 'arrangements in which the underlying asset would represent a unit of account' in either IAS 16 – *Property, Plant and Equipment* – or IAS 38 – *Intangible Assets* – are within the scope of the Interpretation. *[IFRIC 4.3]*. 'Unit of account' presumably means an asset whose cost, replacement, impairment and depreciation are separately accounted for under one of these standards (see Chapters 17 and 18). However, the opposite is not necessarily the case. It does not mean that a component of one of these assets cannot be the underlying asset. Generally, in the case of physical assets a portion of a larger asset that is not physically distinct is not considered to be a specified asset. Many intangible assets are capable of being subdivided with the part subject to the lease itself meeting the definition of an intangible asset, as discussed further at 3.1.2 below.

There are many arrangements in practice that demonstrate the issue of the unit of account. For example, a plant may contain more than one production unit or line that might be regarded as a single 'component' (because each makes the same product) or alternatively each of its units or lines might be regarded as separate 'components'. Depending on other aspects of the arrangement, a particular production line may be the asset that is the subject of a lease, if the supplier cannot transfer production to a different line to supply the goods.

Similar examples from the telecommunications industry include fibre optical cable, satellite and wireless tower arrangements. Fibre agreements vary from those that allow use of the whole or portions of a cable, to those that specify the wavelength or spectrum within a fibre. Many arrangements are essentially for transmission capacity within the vendor's fibre cable or network. As a result, arrangements have to be examined carefully to determine if they do specify an asset.

2.1.3 *The arrangement conveys a right to use the item*

In order to contain a lease, the arrangement must convey a right to use the asset. *[IFRIC 4.6]*. An arrangement does not convey the right to use an asset unless the purchaser has the right to control the use of the underlying item, which depends on any one of the following conditions being met: *[IFRIC 4.9]*

(a) the purchaser has the ability or right to operate the asset or direct others to operate the asset in a manner it determines while obtaining or controlling more than an insignificant amount of the output or other utility of the asset;

(b) the purchaser has the ability or right to control physical access to the underlying asset while obtaining or controlling more than an insignificant amount of the output or other utility of the asset; or

(c) facts and circumstances indicate:

 (i) it is remote that one or more parties other than the purchaser will take more than an insignificant amount of the output or other utility that will be produced or generated by the asset during the term of the arrangement; and

 (ii) the price that the purchaser will pay for the output is neither contractually fixed per unit of output; nor equal to the current market price per unit of output as of the time of delivery of the output.

Therefore, control of the asset may be obtained in circumstances in which an entity obtains 'more than an insignificant amount of the output' but *only* if it has the ability or right to operate (or direct others to operate) the asset in a manner that it determines or if it has the ability or right to control physical access to the asset ((a) and (b) above).

When the arrangement involves a single purchaser taking substantially all of the output from a specific asset other than at market price per unit of output and the price varies other than in response to market price changes, the variability ('off-market' nature) is regarded by IFRIC 4 as indicating that payment is being made for the right to use the asset rather than for the actual use of or output from the asset. In these circumstances the arrangement would also convey the right to use the asset, even though the purchaser would have neither the ability nor right to operate the asset, or direct others to operate the asset in a manner it determines, nor have the ability or right to control physical access to the underlying asset.

The effects of this are demonstrated by the following examples.

Example 24.1 contains two scenarios that illustrate arrangements that contain a lease. Scenario (a) is based on an illustrative example in IFRIC 4. *[IFRIC 4.IE1-2]*.

Example 24.1: Arrangements that contain a lease

(a) Take-or-pay contract that depends on a specific asset (a gas supply facility)

A production company (the purchaser) enters into an arrangement with a third party (the supplier) to supply a minimum quantity of gas needed in its production process for a specified period of time. The supplier designs and builds a facility near to the purchaser's plant to produce the gas and maintains ownership and control over all significant aspects of operating the facility. The agreement provides for the following:

- The facility is explicitly identified in the arrangement, and the supplier has the contractual right to supply gas from other sources, although supplying gas from other sources is not economically feasible or practicable.
- The supplier has the right to provide gas to other customers and to remove and replace the facility's equipment and modify or expand the facility to enable the supplier to do so. However, at inception of the arrangement, the facility is designed to meet only the purchaser's needs and the supplier has no plans to modify or expand the facility.
- The supplier is responsible for repairs, maintenance and capital expenditures.
- The supplier must stand ready to deliver a minimum quantity of gas each month.
- On a monthly basis, the purchaser will pay a fixed capacity charge and a variable charge based on actual production taken. The purchaser must pay the fixed capacity charge irrespective of whether it takes any of the facility's production. The variable charge includes the facility's actual energy costs, which comprise approximately 90 per cent of the facility's total variable costs. The supplier is subject to increased costs resulting from the facility's inefficient operations.
- If the facility does not produce the stated minimum quantity, the supplier must return all or a portion of the fixed capacity charge.

The arrangement contains a lease within the scope of IAS 17. An asset (the facility) is explicitly identified in the arrangement and fulfilment of the arrangement is dependent on the facility. While the supplier has the right to supply gas from other sources, its ability to do so is not substantive. The purchaser has obtained the right to use the facility because, on the facts presented – in particular, that the facility is designed to meet only the purchaser's needs and the supplier has no plans to expand or modify the facility – it is remote that one or more parties other than the purchaser will take more than an insignificant amount of the facility's output and the price the purchaser will pay is neither contractually fixed per unit of output nor equal to the current market price per unit of output as of the time of delivery of the output.

(b) Take-or-pay contract that depends on a specific asset (indefeasible right of use)

Entity A (supplier), a telecom company, owns a large fibre network and enters into an agreement with Entity B (purchaser), another telecom company. The agreement specifies that fibre strands four, five and six will be used to carry the traffic of Entity B's customers for a 10-year period in exchange for a fixed up-front capacity payment. Entity B will handle all transmissions by connecting its switching equipment to the ends of the fibre strands. Entity A cannot substitute other fibre strands to fulfil the agreement. Entity A retains physical control over the PP&E and the ability to operate the PP&E. However, Entity B will obtain substantially all of the output and utility of the specified fibres during the term of the arrangement (i.e. no other customers will be able to use the specified fibres). The price of the agreement is fixed, regardless of how much Entity B uses the fibre.

The arrangement contains a lease within the scope of IAS 17. The agreement involves the use of explicitly identified PP&E (i.e. fibre strands four, five and six). Entity B does not have the ability or right to direct the operation of or control physical access to the PP&E. However, the contract conveys the right to use specified PP&E because Entity B will take substantially all of the PP&E's output (i.e. the likelihood is remote that one or more parties other than Entity B will take more than a minor amount of the output), and the price it will pay is neither fixed per unit of output nor equal to the market price per unit.

Having concluded that the arrangement contains a lease, it is then necessary to classify it as an operating or a finance lease. Identifying the relevant lease payments is discussed in 2.1.6 below.

The three scenarios in the next example illustrate arrangements that do not contain a lease. Scenarios (a) and (b) describe circumstances in which an arrangement does not contain a lease because no specific asset has been identified. The significance of the control concept is shown in scenario (c) based on the second illustrative example in IFRIC 4. *[IFRIC 4.IE3-4]*.

Example 24.2: Arrangements that do not contain leases

(a) Take-or-pay contract that does not depend on a specific asset (gas supply)

A purchaser enters into a take-or-pay contract to buy industrial gases from a supplier. The supplier is a large company operating similar plants at various locations. The amount of gas that the purchaser is committed to buy is roughly equivalent to the total output of one of the plants. Because a good distribution network is available, the supplier is able to provide gas from various locations to fulfil its supply obligation.

In this example, the arrangement does not depend on a specific asset. This is because it is economically feasible and practical for the supplier to fulfil the arrangement by providing use of more than one plant. A specific asset has therefore not been identified either explicitly or implicitly.

Payments under the contract may be unavoidable because it is a take-or-pay arrangement and the purchaser may in fact take all of the output of a single plant but the arrangement does not convey a right to use the asset. The purchaser does not have the right to control the use of the underlying asset. It does not have the ability or right to operate the asset in a manner it determines (or to direct others to do so on its behalf), and it does not control physical access. The arrangement does not contain a lease.

(b) Take-or-pay contract that does not depend on a specific asset (indefeasible right of use)

Taking the same facts as used in scenario (b) in Example 24.1 above, except that the agreement does not specify which fibre strands will carry the traffic of Entity B's customers. Entity A has the right and ability (i.e. Entity A has multiple fibre strands available to transmit the data and it is feasible and practicable to use those other assets) to use any of its fibre strands to carry Entity B's customers' traffic.

Although the agreement involves the use of PP&E, fulfilment of the agreement does not depend on specified PP&E. Therefore, the arrangement does not contain a lease.

(c) The right to control the use of an underlying asset is not conveyed

A manufacturing company (the purchaser) enters into an arrangement with a third party (the supplier) to supply a specific component part of its manufactured product for a specified period of time. The supplier designs and constructs a plant next to the purchaser's factory to produce the component part. The designed capacity of the plant exceeds the purchaser's current needs, and the supplier maintains ownership and control over all significant aspects of operating the plant.

The supplier's plant is explicitly identified in the arrangement, but the supplier has the right to fulfil the arrangement by shipping the component parts from another plant owned by the supplier. However, to do so for any extended period of time would be uneconomical. The supplier must stand ready to deliver a minimum quantity. The purchaser is required to pay a fixed price per unit for the actual quantity taken. Even if the purchaser's needs are such that they do not need the stated minimum quantity, they still pay only for the actual quantity taken.

The supplier has the right to sell the component parts to other customers and has a history of doing so by selling in the replacement parts market, so it is expected that parties other than the purchaser will take more than an insignificant amount of the component parts produced at the supplier's plant.

The supplier is responsible for repairs, maintenance, and capital expenditures of the plant.

This arrangement does not contain a lease. An asset (the plant) is explicitly identified in the arrangement and fulfilment of the arrangement is dependent on the facility. While the supplier has the right to supply component parts from other sources, the supplier would not have the ability to do so because it would be uneconomical. However, the purchaser has not obtained the right to use the plant because it does not control it, for the following reasons:

(a) the purchaser does not have the ability or right to operate or direct others to operate the plant or control physical access to the plant;

(b) the likelihood that parties other than the purchaser will take more than an insignificant amount of the component parts produced at the plant is more than remote, based on the facts presented; and

(c) the price paid by the purchaser is fixed per unit of output taken but see the following section where this is discussed further.

2.1.4 Fixed or current market prices and control of the asset

The third control condition states that an arrangement will not contain a lease, notwithstanding that a purchaser takes all but an insignificant amount of the output or other utility if the price is contractually fixed per unit of output. We consider that by this the Interpretation means absolutely fixed, with no variance per unit based on underlying costs or volumes, whether discounts or stepped pricing.

In the manufacturing industry 'lifetime' agreements with step pricing between the supplier and the purchaser are not uncommon. The parties to the agreement agree in advance on progressive unit price reductions on achievement of specified production volume levels, reflecting the supplier's increasing efficiencies and economies of scale. These types of contracts should be closely analysed, especially to see whether one of the other two conditions, the 'right to operate the asset' or the 'right to control the physical access to the asset', is met before concluding that the arrangement contains a lease.

'Current market price per unit of output' means that the cost is solely a market price for the output of the asset without any other pricing factors. A 'market price per KWH plus x per cent change in the price of natural gas' would not be the current market price per unit of the output of the asset. Price increases based on a general index such as a retail and price indices are unlikely to result in a current market price for the output in question.

Example 24.3: Fixed prices per unit

Purchaser P and supplier S enter into a parts supply agreement for the lifetime of the finished product concerned. S uses tooling equipment that is specific to the needs of P. The tooling is explicitly identified in the agreement and S could not use an alternative asset. The estimated capacity of the tooling equipment is 500,000 units which corresponds to the total production of the finished product units over its life cycle. P takes substantially all of the output produced by S using the specific tooling.

Purchaser P and supplier S agree on the following unit price reductions in the parts supply agreement to reflect S's increasing efficiencies and economies of scale:

- from 0 to 100,000 units, price per unit €150;
- from 100,001 to 200,000, price per unit €140;
- from 200,001 to 300,000, price per unit €135;
- from 300,001 to 400,000, price per unit €132;
- above 400,000, price per unit €130.

The fulfilment of the arrangement depends on the use of a specific asset, the tooling. P has obtained the right to use the tooling because, on the facts presented, the likelihood is remote that one or more parties other than the P will take more than an insignificant amount of the tooling's output. As the estimated capacity of the tooling equipment corresponds to the total production of the finished product units produced by P, P takes substantially all of the output produced using that tooling.

Stepped pricing does not mean a price 'fixed per unit of output' and, particularly as the stepped pricing is agreed in advance, it is not equal to the current market price per unit as of the time of delivery of the output. The arrangement contains a lease within the scope of IAS 17. The purchaser will have to determine whether it is a finance or operating lease.

2.1.5 When to assess the arrangements

IFRIC 4 states that assessing whether an arrangement contains a lease should be made at the inception of the arrangement, which is the earlier of the date of the arrangement and the date of commitment by the parties to the principal terms of the arrangement, on the basis of all the facts and circumstances. A reassessment of whether the arrangement contains a lease should be made only if: *[IFRIC 4.10]*

(a) there is a change in the terms of the contract, except for a renewal or extension of the arrangement;

(b) a renewal option is exercised or an extension is agreed to, unless the term of the renewal or extension had been taken into account in the original assessment of the lease term in accordance with IAS 17; *[IAS 17.4]*

(c) there is a change in whether or not the arrangement depends on specified item; or

(d) there is a substantial physical change to the specified assets.

Changes to estimates, for example of the amount of output that would be taken by the purchaser, would not trigger a reassessment. *[IFRIC 4.11]*.

If the arrangement is reassessed and found to contain a lease, or not to contain a lease, lease accounting will be applied or discontinued as from the time that the arrangement is reassessed. The same applies if a renewal option is exercised when this was not previously anticipated, as described in (b) above. *[IFRIC 4.11]*. The exercise of renewal options is discussed at 3.2.3 below.

2.1.6 Separation of leases from other payments within the arrangement

If an arrangement contains a lease within the scope of IAS 17 (see 3.1 below), both parties to the arrangement are to apply IAS 17 to the lease element of the arrangement. Other elements of the arrangement must be accounted for in accordance with the appropriate standards. *[IFRIC 4.12]*.

It must be stressed that this means that the lease element of the arrangement may be classified as either an operating or finance lease. Therefore, having identified the lease payments, the entity may still classify the arrangement as an operating lease if it does not transfer substantially all the risks and rewards incidental to ownership of an asset (see 3.2 below). *[IAS 17.4, 8]*.

In order to apply IAS 17, the payments and other consideration under the arrangement must be separated at inception or on reassessment between those for the lease of the asset (that will meet the definition of minimum lease payments, see 3.4.3 below) and those for other services and outputs. IFRIC 4 requires this to be done on the basis of their relative fair values. *[IFRIC 4.13]*. This may require the purchaser to use estimation techniques – this appears to be somewhat of an understatement as, unless the price to be paid for both elements is clear and they have both been negotiated at market value, it will always be necessary to use some form of estimation.

The Interpretation suggests that it may be possible to estimate either the lease payments (by comparison with similar leases that do not contain other elements) or the other elements (using comparable arrangements) and then deduct the estimated amount from the total under the arrangement. *[IFRIC 4.14]*. This is not a straightforward exercise and the Interpretation does not go into any further detail as to how it would be carried out. There may be no market-based evidence of fair value of the underlying assets because of their specialised nature or because they are rarely sold, in which case it will be necessary to use valuation techniques.

Discounted cash flow projections based on estimated future cash flows that will be generated by specialised assets may be difficult to obtain, although it should be possible to make some form of estimate, if need be with the assistance of valuation experts. The service elements within these agreements are by no means standardised and it may not be easy to identify comparable arrangements. The exercise will be complicated by the fact that the fair value of a bundle of services is not necessarily the same as the aggregation of their individual fair values and making such an assumption could lead to an overstatement of the service element and consequent understatement of the fair value of the lease element or *vice versa.*

The discount rates should reflect current market assessments of the uncertainty and timing of the cash flows, i.e. the risk inherent in the separate elements of the transaction. There are usually very different risk profiles for the provision of services and for leasing assets. If, as suggested by the Interpretation, the entity estimates one of the elements under the arrangement and derives the other by deduction, i.e. it uses a residual method, it will always be necessary to carry out a 'sense check' on the derived payments.

IFRIC 4 suggests that only in rare cases will a purchaser conclude that it is impracticable to separate the payments reliably. In the case of a finance lease, the entity should recognise an asset at an amount equal to the fair value of the underlying asset that it has identified as the subject of the lease, as described in 2.1.1 above. A liability should be set up at the same amount as the asset. The entity would impute a finance charge based on the purchaser's incremental borrowing rate of interest (see 3.4.5 below) and, from this, compute the reduction in the liability as payments are made. *[IFRIC 4.15]*. Presumably the Interpretations Committee considers that the entity's incremental borrowing rate would have to be used because, if it were possible to determine the interest rate implicit in the lease, the arrangement would not be one in which it was impracticable to separate the payments reliably.

What this means is that an entity may be required to account for an asset held under a finance lease when it is, in fact, unable to identify the lease payments. This will not often happen in practice as obtaining control is likely to result in an entity being able to identify the underlying payment streams.

If the lease is assessed as an operating lease, applying the Interpretation might affect the recognition of costs and revenue over the term of the arrangement. IAS 17 requires lessors and lessees to recognise operating lease payments on a straight-line basis over the lease term unless another systematic basis is more representative (see 5.1.2 below) and this may not be in line with the payments for the lease element so some adjustments might be required. *[IFRIC 4.BC39]*.

See below for disclosure implications if the arrangement is deemed to contain an operating lease and the purchaser concludes that it is impracticable to separate the payments reliably.

2.1.7 *Disclosure requirements*

IAS 17 requires a general description of the lessee's material leasing arrangements. *[IAS 17.31(e)]*. This will require disclosure of the details of major transactions that have fallen within IFRIC 4.

As long as the entity is able to distinguish the lease payments from other elements of the lease, the disclosed information will relate only to the lease element of the arrangement. There appears to be no intention to require entities to disclose the service (executory) element of arrangements.

If the arrangements are assessed as containing finance leases, these arrangements are deemed to be within the scope of IAS 17 and therefore within its disclosure requirements (see 9 below).

However, if it were considered to be an operating lease, the Interpretation may result in additional disclosures, because IAS 17 specifies that the lessor and lessee should disclose the future minimum lease payments. Although the arrangements discussed in the Interpretation typically represent significant future commitments, purchasers are not required to disclose them in the financial statements unless they fall within the scope of IAS 17. The Interpretations Committee argues that bringing such arrangements within the scope of IAS 17 will provide users of financial statements with relevant information that is useful for assessing the purchaser's solvency, liquidity and adaptability. *[IFRIC 4.BC39]*.

If the arrangement is one of those in which it is impracticable to separate the payments reliably, the Interpretation requires disclosure of all payments under the arrangement separately from other minimum lease payments, together with a statement that the disclosed payments also include payments for non-lease elements in the arrangement. *[IFRIC 4.15]*.

2.2 Transactions that involve the legal form of a lease but are not, in substance, leases

While there are some arrangements that contain leases that are not formally lease contracts, the reverse is also true: there are some formal lease contracts that do not, in substance, contain leases. These issues are addressed by SIC-27.

Essentially, SIC-27 deals with the issue of how to evaluate the substance of transactions, or a series of linked transactions, in the legal form of a lease. The main purpose of the Interpretation is to reinforce the principle of substance over form, and to ensure that, where appropriate, a series of linked transactions should be accounted for as one transaction. If the transaction does not meet the definition of a lease under IAS 17, SIC-27 deals with the extent to which the arrangement gives rise to other assets and liabilities of the reporting entity, the reporting of any other obligations and the recognition of fee income. *[SIC-27.2]*.

An entity may enter into a transaction or a series of structured transactions (an arrangement) with an unrelated party or parties (an investor) that involves the legal form of a lease. Although the details may vary considerably, a typical example involves an entity leasing or selling assets to an investor and leasing the same assets back. The lease and leaseback transactions are often entered into so that the investor may achieve a tax advantage. *[SIC-27.1]*. In recent years these arrangements have become less common as taxation authorities in various jurisdictions have restricted the tax benefits. The following example illustrates an arrangement that does not, in substance, involve a lease under IAS 17. *[SIC-27.A2(a)]*.

Example 24.4: Substance of an arrangement

Entity A leases a specialised asset that it requires to conduct its business to an Investor and leases the same asset back for a shorter period of time under a sublease. At the end of the sublease period, Entity A has the right to buy back the rights of the Investor under a purchase option. If Entity A does not exercise its purchase option, the Investor has options available to it under each of which it receives a minimum return on its investment in the headlease – the Investor may put the underlying asset back to Entity A, or require it to provide a return on the Investor's investment in the headlease.

The arrangement achieves a tax advantage for the Investor who pays a fee to Entity A and prepays the lease payment obligations under the headlease. The agreement requires the amount prepaid to be invested in risk-free assets and, as a requirement of finalising the execution of the legally binding arrangement, placed into a separate investment account held by a Trustee outside of the control of the entity.

Over the term of the sublease, the sublease payment obligations are satisfied with funds of an equal amount withdrawn from the separate investment account. Entity A guarantees the sublease payment obligations, and will be required to satisfy the guarantee should the separate investment account have insufficient funds. Entity A, but not the Investor, has the right to terminate the sublease early under certain circumstances (e.g. a change in local or international tax law causes the Investor to lose part or all of the tax benefits, or Entity A decides to dispose of (e.g. replace, sell or deplete) the underlying asset) and on payment of a termination value to the Investor. If Entity A chooses early termination, then it would pay the termination value from funds withdrawn from the separate investment account, and if the amount remaining in the separate investment account is insufficient, the difference would be paid by Entity A.

A series of transactions that involve the legal form of a lease should be accounted for as one transaction when the overall economic effect cannot be understood without reference to the series of transactions as a whole. All aspects and implications of an arrangement should be evaluated to determine the substance of the arrangement, with greater weight given to those aspects and implications that will have an economic effect in practice. The accounting should reflect the substance of the arrangement. *[SIC-27.3, 4]*.

2.2.1 The arrangement

First, the series of transactions must be part of a single 'arrangement'; a series of transactions may be closely interrelated, negotiated as a single transaction, and take place concurrently or in a continuous sequence. *[SIC-27.3]*.

Second, there must be indicators that individually demonstrate that an arrangement may not, in substance, involve a lease under IAS 17. SIC-27 states that in circumstances such as those in Example 24.4 above, these indicators are as follows:

(a) the entity retains all the risks and rewards of ownership and there is no significant change in its rights to use the asset;

(b) the primary reason for the arrangement is to achieve a particular tax result, and not to convey the right to use an asset; and

(c) the options on which the arrangement depends are included on terms that make their exercise almost certain (e.g. a put option that is exercisable at a price sufficiently higher than the expected fair value when it becomes exercisable). *[SIC-27.5]*.

In other words, the entity retains more rights than it would in a straightforward sale and finance leaseback. In Example 24.4 above, for instance, it retains all of the residual interests in the asset. The investor has no interest at all in the underlying asset while a lessor under a finance lease will often retain title and some residual value in the asset. The investor has only entered into the transaction to obtain a tax benefit.

2.2.2 *Accounting for assets and liabilities arising under the arrangement*

The balances arising under the arrangement (in Example 24.4 these comprise the separate investment account and the lease payment obligations under the sublease) must be assessed to see whether they represent assets and liabilities of the entity. SIC-27 refers to definitions of assets and liabilities and guidance in the *Conceptual Framework for Financial Reporting ('Framework')*. *[Framework 4.4-19]*. It argues that:

(a) the investment account is not an asset of the entity because it cannot control it;

(b) there is only a remote risk that the entity will have to pay out under the guarantee or reimburse the entire amount of any fee received; and

(c) once the arrangement has been set up and the initial payments have been made, no further cash flows will be made by the entity.

The entity cannot use the cash in the investment account for its own benefit, nor can it prevent it from being used to make lease payments to the investor. The lease payments will be satisfied solely from funds withdrawn from the separate investment account established with the initial cash flows. In the example, the terms of the arrangement require that a prepaid amount is invested in risk-free assets that are expected to generate sufficient cash flows to satisfy the lease payment obligations. *[SIC-27.6]*. This also demonstrates, among other things, that the entity is not, in substance, entering into a financing arrangement, as it has no need for the funds.

Care must be taken to ensure that the assets in which the prepayment is invested are in fact 'risk-free' and this will have to be monitored throughout the arrangement. The financial crisis in 2008 revealed that many so-called 'AAA' or 'risk-free' assets, including sovereign debt, were not risk-free, leaving entities exposed to shortfalls in the cash held in the investment account for which they may have been required to make provision.

Other obligations of the entity, including any guarantees provided and obligations incurred on early termination, should be accounted for under IFRS 4 – *Insurance Contracts*, IAS 37 – *Provisions, Contingent Liabilities and Contingent Assets* – or IAS 39 – *Financial Instruments: Recognition and Measurement* (or IFRS 9 – *Financial Instruments* – if the entity applies that standard), depending on the terms of the arrangement. *[SIC-27.7]*. Therefore, if Entity A were to elect to terminate the arrangement, it would have to provide for its exposure in excess of the available funds in the investment account. In addition, if the arrangement is within a special purpose entity or trust, the entity will need to consider the effect of IFRS 10 – *Consolidated Financial Statements.* The interaction of IFRS 10 and IAS 17 in connection with special purpose entities leaves room for interpretation, but the Interpretations Committee decided in May 2015 not to clarify the matter (see Chapter 6 at 4.1.3).

2.2.3 Fee income

SIC-27 addresses the recognition of fee income. There are many factors that could affect the economic substance and nature of the fee, and it may not be appropriate to recognise it in its entirety at the inception of the agreement if the entity has significant future performance obligations, retained risks or a significant risk of repayment. Factors to be taken into account include:

(a) obligations that are conditions of earning the fee so that entering into the agreement is not the most significant act required by the arrangement;

(b) limitations are put on the use of the underlying asset that lead to significant changes in the entity's rights to use the asset, e.g. the entity's right to deplete or sell it or pledge it as collateral;

(c) the possibility of reimbursing any amount of the fee and possibly paying some additional amount is not remote. This occurs when, for example:

    (i) the underlying asset is essential for the entity's business, in which case there is a possibility that the entity may be prepared to pay to terminate the arrangement early and be required to repay all or part of the fee; or

    (ii) the possibility that there are insufficient assets in the investment account to meet the lease payment obligations is not remote, and therefore it is possible that the entity may be required to pay some additional amount. This may occur if the entity is required, or has some or total discretion, to invest in assets carrying more than an insignificant amount of risk (e.g. currency, interest rate or credit risk). *[SIC-27.8]*.

An entity must take great care before it considers any investment as carrying an insignificant amount of risk.

2.2.4 Presentation and disclosure requirements.

The fee must be presented in the income statement based on its economic substance and nature. *[SIC-27.9]*. The entity must disclose the following in each period that an arrangement exists:

An entity has to make the disclosures that are necessary to understand the arrangement and the accounting treatment adopted, including the following:

(a) a description of the arrangement including:
   (i) the underlying asset and any restrictions on its use;
   (ii) the life and other significant terms of the arrangement;
   (iii) the transactions that are linked together, including any options; and
(b) the accounting treatment of any fee received, the amount that has been recognised as income in the period, and the line item of the income statement in which it is included.

These disclosures should be provided individually for each arrangement or in aggregate for each class of arrangement. A class is a grouping of arrangements with underlying assets of a similar nature. *[SIC-27.10, 11]*.

3 SCOPE AND DEFINITIONS OF IAS 17

3.1 Scope of IAS 17

The standard applies in accounting for all leases other than:

- lease agreements to explore for or use minerals, oil, natural gas and similar non-regenerative resources (see Chapter 41); and
- licensing agreements for such items as motion picture films, video recordings, plays, manuscripts, patents and copyrights.

The standard should not be applied to the measurement by:

- lessees of investment property held under finance leases;
- lessors of investment property leased out under operating leases, as in these cases IAS 40 – *Investment Property* – applies (see Chapter 19);
- lessees of biological assets held under finance leases; or
- lessors of biological assets leased out under operating leases, as in these cases IAS 41 – *Agriculture* – applies (see Chapter 40). *[IAS 17.2]*.

3.1.1 Leases and licensing agreements

IAS 17 does not define a licensing agreement so the distinction between 'leases' and 'licensing agreements' is not clear.

Whether or not the arrangement is within scope of IAS 17 does not depend on the type of asset or as discussed in 2.2 above on how the contract is labelled, but rather on the nature of that arrangement.

IAS 17 does not apply to agreements that do not transfer the right to use assets from one contracting party to the other. A conventional licence over an intangible asset such as a film or video commonly gives a non-exclusive right of 'access' to show or view the video simultaneously with many others but not a 'right of use' of the original film or video itself because the licensee does not control that asset. This puts many licence agreements outside the scope of IAS 17. However, if the right to use the intangible asset is provided in the license agreement, the arrangement may be a lease; see the discussion in 2.1 above regarding IFRIC 4 and the right to use the asset.

The assets subject to licensing agreements excluded from the scope of IAS 17 (such as motion picture films, video recordings, plays, manuscripts, patents and copyrights) are specific intangible assets but arrangements involving, for example, motion picture films are not out of scope simply because of the nature of that asset but rather because the nature of arrangements over such assets typically grants a non-exclusive right of access to those assets rather than a right of use.

It follows, therefore, that an arrangement that has been labelled a 'licence' *will* be within scope of IAS 17 if it transfers a right of use of the asset that is the subject of the arrangement to the licensee. This 'licence' will include features in addition to those in a conventional licence described above.

3.1.2 Arrangements over intangible assets

IAS 17 applies to leases over intangible assets.

IAS 38 excludes from its scope 'intangible assets that are within the scope of another Standard.' *[IAS 38.2]*. It emphasises that 'if another Standard prescribes the accounting for a specific type of intangible asset, an entity applies that Standard instead of this Standard. For example, this Standard does not apply to... leases that are within the scope of IAS 17 *Leases*.' *[IAS 38.3]*. This is because rights themselves arising under a number of accounting standards could be seen as intangible assets, e.g. deferred tax assets as well as assets arising under lease agreements. Therefore, IAS 38 excludes intangible assets that fall within the scope of another standard from its scope, thereby avoiding any potential ambiguity about the applicable standard. *[IAS 38.3]*. It does not mean that the underlying items that are the subject of the lease arrangement are not intangible assets, but that recognition and measurement are within scope of IAS 17. IAS 38's clarification of the applicable standard applies to all rights arising under lease agreements, whether over tangible or intangible assets. Subsequent accounting for the asset, e.g. amortisation, is in accordance with IAS 38. *[IAS 38.6]*. See 4.1.4 below.

However, there are additional issues for applying IAS 17 to rights to an intangible asset. First, the 'right' must meet the definition of an intangible asset in IAS 38. Second, because many of these rights are either acquired for an up-front sum or for a series of periodic payments and by definition the period covered by the payments equals the life of the right, there is divergence in practice in how to account for them, i.e. whether they are leases (and if so, whether finance or operating leases) or whether they are acquisitions of assets on deferred payment terms.

Many intangible assets are capable of being subdivided with some part of the whole meeting the definition of an intangible asset (see Chapter 17 at 2.1). If the rights are exclusive, the lease part will meet the definition of an intangible asset because it is embodied in legal rights that allow the acquirer to control the benefits arising from the asset. For example, an entity might sell to another entity rights to distribute its product in a particular geographical market. If the right is not on an exclusive basis then it may not be within the scope of IAS 38, e.g. it may be a licensing agreement as discussed above. Other arrangements may be for services and not for a right of use of an intangible asset.

Note that it is irrelevant to the analysis whether the original right was recognised prior to the arrangement in the financial statements of the lessor.

Rights that meet the definition of an intangible asset usually have a finite life, e.g. a radio station may acquire a licence that gives it a right to broadcast over specified frequencies for a period of seven years. Yet the underlying asset on which the right depends exists both before and after the 'right' has been purchased and may have an indefinite life, as is the case with the broadcast spectrum. Many intangible rights can be purchased for an upfront sum, which will be accounted for as the acquisition of an intangible asset that is capitalised at cost. As an alternative to up-front purchase, an entity may pay in a series of instalments over a period of time. Does it become an operating lease because it is only a short period out of the life of the underlying asset? Usually the answer is no: these rights will not be accounted for as operating leases by comparison to the total life of the underlying asset as the arrangement is over the *right* in question. If the arrangement is considered to be a lease, then it will be accounted for in accordance with IAS 17, and classified by reference to the right rather than the underlying asset.

If, rather than as a lease, the arrangement is seen as the acquisition of an asset on deferred payment terms, the effective interest rate method is mandated. The effective interest rate is the rate that exactly discounts estimated future cash payments or receipts through the expected life of the financial instrument or, when appropriate, a shorter period, to the carrying amount of the financial asset or financial liability. This will take account of estimated future cash payments or receipts through the expected life of the financial instrument, to the extent required by IAS 39 or IFRS 9, which may include some of the 'contingent' payments that are excluded from the measurement of finance leases (see 3.5 below).

Therefore, there are arguments as to whether there are assets and liabilities to be recognised and, even if recognition is accepted, measurement depends on the view that is taken of the applicable standard.

3.2 Lease classification

3.2.1 Finance and operating leases

A finance lease is a 'lease that transfers substantially all the risks and rewards incidental to ownership of an asset', and an operating lease is 'a lease other than a finance lease', *[IAS 17.4]*, i.e. a lease that does not transfer substantially all the risks and rewards incidental to ownership.

The individual circumstances of a lessor and lessee may differ in respect of a single lease contract. As a result, it is perfectly possible that the application of the definitions to the different circumstances of the lessor and lessee may result in the same lease being classified differently by them. For example, a lease may be classified as an operating lease by the lessee and as a finance lease receivable by the lessor if it includes a residual value guarantee provided by a third party. *[IAS 17.9]*. These are discussed further at 3.4.6 below.

3.2.2 Determining the substance of transactions

The classification of leases adopted in the standard is based on the extent to which the risks and rewards incidental to ownership of a leased asset lie with the lessor or the lessee. 'Risks include the possibilities of losses from idle capacity or technological obsolescence and of variations in return due to changing economic conditions. Rewards may be represented by the expectation of profitable operation over the asset's economic life and of gain from appreciation in value or realisation of a residual value.' *[IAS 17.7]*.

Some national standards include the rebuttable presumption that the transfer of substantially all of the risks and rewards occurs if, at the inception of the lease, the present value of the minimum lease payments amounts to substantially all (normally 90% or more) of the fair value of the leased asset. IAS 17 provides no numerical guidelines to be applied in classifying a lease as either finance or operating. It seems that it was a conscious decision of the (then) IASC Board not to refer to a percentage such as 90% in the standard, as it wanted to avoid the possibility of lease classification being reduced to a single pass or fail test.

Instead, the standard takes a more principles-based substance over form approach. It makes the statement that the classification of a lease depends on the substance of the transaction rather than the form of the contract, and lists a number of examples of situations that individually or in combination would normally lead to a lease being classified as a finance lease: *[IAS 17.10]*

(a) the lease transfers ownership of the asset to the lessee by the end of the lease term;

(b) the lessee has the option to purchase the asset at a price which is expected to be sufficiently lower than the fair value at the date the option becomes exercisable such that, at the inception of the lease, it is reasonably certain that the option will be exercised (frequently called a 'bargain purchase' option);

(c) the lease term is for the major part of the economic life of the asset even if title is not transferred;

(d) at the inception of the lease the present value of the minimum lease payments amounts to at least substantially all of the fair value of the leased asset; and

(e) the leased assets are of a specialised nature such that only the lessee can use them without major modifications being made.

All of these are indicators that the lessor will only look to the lessee to obtain a return from the leasing transaction, so it can be presumed that the lessee will, in fact, pay for the asset.

Although the first criterion refers to title being transferred, it is clear from the standard that title does not have to be transferred to the lessee for a lease to be classified as a finance lease. *[IAS 17.4]*. The point is that the lease will almost certainly be classified as a finance lease if title does transfer.

The lease term must be measured by reference to economic life, which is the period for which the leased asset is expected to be usable by one or more users. The economic life will usually be shorter than the physical life if the asset is subject to technological obsolescence. A computer may be capable of use for six or seven years but would rarely be used beyond three years. It is less well appreciated that buildings suffer from technological obsolescence which means that an office building which may remain structurally sound for sixty years may have an economic life of half of that. This is because it becomes increasingly hard to adapt buildings to rapidly-changing IT or energy efficiency requirements. The residual value of these assets at the end of the economic life is minimal.

The economic life would therefore include additional lease terms with the same or different lessees. It is not the same as the useful life which is specific to the lessee and is the estimated remaining period, from the commencement of the lease term but without the limitation of the lease term, over which the entity expects to consume the economic benefits embodied in the asset (see 4.1.4 below).

'Fair value' is defined as the amount for which an asset could be exchanged or a liability settled, between knowledgeable, willing parties in an arm's length transaction (see 3.4.2 below). *[IAS 17.4]*. IFRS 13 – *Fair Value Measurement* – does not apply because the IASB states that IAS 17 uses 'fair value' in a way that differs in some respects from the definition in IFRS 13. *[IFRS 13.6, IAS 17.6A]*.

Options such as those referred to under (b) above are common in lease agreements. The bargain purchase option is designed so that the lessee will exercise it and to give the lessor its expected lender's return (comprising interest on its investment perhaps together with a relatively small fee) but no more, over the life of the agreement.

Criteria (c) and (d) above also include the unquantified expressions 'major part of' and 'substantially all', which means that judgement must be used in determining their effect on the risks and rewards of ownership. By contrast, in US GAAP the equivalent to (c) above in ASC 840 does quantify when a lease will be a capital lease, the equivalent of a finance lease. In ASC 840, if the lease term is equal to 75% or more of the estimated economic life of the leased asset, the lease will normally be a capital lease (there is an exception if the beginning of the lease term falls within the last 25% of the total estimated economic life of the leased property, including earlier years of use, where this criterion is not used for purposes of classifying the lease, plus additional criteria specific to lessors).[2] However in practice, if the lease is for the major part of the economic life of the asset then it is unlikely that the lessor will rely on any party other than the lessee to obtain its return from the lease. This would still not be conclusive evidence that the lease should be classified as a finance lease. There could be other terms that indicate that the significant risks and rewards of ownership rest with the lessor, e.g. lease payments might be reset periodically to market rates or there might be significant technological, obsolescence or damage risks borne by the lessor.

Similarly, whilst (d) above refers to the present value of the minimum lease payments being at least 'substantially all of the fair value of the asset', it does so without putting a percentage to it. We have already speculated as to why this may be; nevertheless, we see no harm in practice in applying the '90% test' described above as a rule of thumb benchmark as part of the overall process in reaching a judgement as to the classification of a lease. Clearly, though, it cannot be applied as a hard and fast rule.

For an example of the 90% test, see Example 24.9 at 3.4.9 below. In that example, the present value of the minimum lease payments is calculated to be 92.74% of the asset's fair value; as this exceeds 90%, this would normally indicate that the lease is a finance lease. Nevertheless, the other criteria discussed above would need to be considered as well.

Consequently, we stress that the 90% test is not an explicit requirement of the standard and should not be applied as a rule or in isolation, but it may be a useful tool to use in practice in attempting to determine the economic substance of a lease arrangement.

The standard then goes on to list the following indicators of situations that, individually or in combination, could also lead to a lease being classified as a finance lease: *[IAS 17.11]*

(a) if the lessee can cancel the lease, the lessor's losses associated with the cancellation are borne by the lessee;

(b) gains or losses from the fluctuation in the fair value of the residual fall to the lessee (for example, in the form of a rent rebate equalling most of the sale proceeds at the end of the lease); and

(c) the lessee has the ability to continue the lease for a secondary period at a rent which is substantially lower than market rent.

IAS 17 notes that these examples are only indications and are not always conclusive. A right to purchase the residual asset for its fair value or an expectation to pay substantially all of the fair value of the asset if contingent rents are taken into account will not necessarily give the lessee substantially all of the risks and rewards of ownership. *[IAS 17.12]*.

In our view, other considerations that could be made in determining the economic substance of the lease arrangement include the following:

- are the lease rentals based on a market rate for use of the asset (which would indicate an operating lease) or a financing rate for use of the funds, which would be indicative of a finance lease? and
- is the existence of put and call options a feature of the lease? If so, are they exercisable at a predetermined price or formula (indicating a finance lease) or are they exercisable at the market price at the time the option is exercised (indicating an operating lease)?

Note that these two considerations mean that an arrangement for the whole of an asset's useful life may be an operating lease, as may an agreement in which the lessee has a right to obtain title to the asset at market value.

3.2.2.A Residual value guarantees by the lessee

One of the indicators listed in IAS 17 that may lead to a lease being classified as a finance lease is where gains or losses from the fluctuation in the fair value of the residual accrue to the lessee *[IAS 17.11]*. However, this does not mean that a lease where the residual value is guaranteed by the lessee will necessarily be classified as a finance lease. The lease itself may be structured so that the most likely outcome of events relating to the residual value indicates that no significant risk will attach to the lessee.

Example 24.5: A lease structured such that the most likely outcome is that the lessee has no significant residual risk

Brief details of a motor vehicle lease are:

Fair value	–	€10,000
Rentals	–	20 monthly payments of €300, followed by a final rental of €2,000

At the end of the lease, the lessee sells the vehicle as an agent for the lessor and if sold for:

(i) more than €3,000, the sales proceeds are paid to the lessor and 99% of the excess is repaid to the lessee; or

(ii) less than €3,000, the sales proceeds are paid to the lessor and lessee pays the deficit to the lessor up to a maximum of 40 eurocents per kilometre above 25,000 kilometres p.a. on average that the leased vehicle has done.

The net present value of the minimum lease payments excluding the guarantee amounts to €7,365.

This lease involves a guarantee by the lessee of the residual value of the leased vehicle of €3,000, as a result of (ii) above. However, the guarantee will only be called on if both:

(a) the vehicle's actual residual value is less than €3,000; and

(b) the vehicle has travelled more than 25,000 kilometres per year on average over the lease term.

Further, the lessee is only liable to pay a certain level of the residual; namely, €100 for each 2,500 kilometres above 25,000 kilometres that the vehicle has done (if the lessee chooses to drive such amount).

Classification depends on the substance of the arrangement, as described above. In assessing the risks and rewards of ownership, the entity will take account of the residual guarantee, which may be zero if the lessee chooses not to drive the vehicle over 25,000 kilometres.

The risks and rewards of ownership are determined in a lease classification by the substance of the arrangement, including the substance of any residual guarantee arrangements.

Therefore the guarantee would be considered in evaluating the substance of the arrangement on a qualitative basis, to the extent that experience or expectations of the sales price and/or mileage that vehicles have driven (and the inter-relationship between these) indicate that a residual payment by the lessee will be made.

If a lease is determined to be a finance lease, IAS 17 requires initial recognition of the asset at fair value or at the NPV of the minimum lease payments. The residual value guarantee could then affect the asset's residual value as explained in Example 24.16 at 4.3.1.A below.

3.2.2.B Rental rebates

IAS 17 suggests that an indicator that the lease is a finance lease is that 'the gains or losses from the fluctuation in the fair value of the residual accrue to the lessee (for example, in the form of a rent rebate equalling most of the sales proceeds at the end of the lease)'. *[IAS 17.11]*. This is because a lessee that obtains most of the sales proceeds has received most of the risks and rewards of the residual value in the asset. This would indicate that the lessor has already been compensated for the transaction and hence that it is a finance lease.

Other leases require the asset to be sold at the end of the lease but the lessor receives the first tranche of proceeds and only those proceeds above a certain level are remitted to the lessee. These arrangements may have a different significance as the lessor may be taking the proceeds to meet its unguaranteed residual value. Lessors are prepared to take risks on residual values of such assets if there is an established and reliable market in which to sell them. This could mean that the gains or losses from the fluctuation in the fair value of the residual do not fall predominantly to the lessee and, in the absence of other factors, could indicate that it is an operating lease.

Example 24.6: Rental rebates

The lease arrangements are as in Example 24.5, except that at end of the lease, the lessee sells the vehicle as an agent for the lessor, and if it is sold for:

(i) up to €3,000, all of the proceeds are received by the lessor; or

(ii) more than €3,000, 99% of the excess is repaid to the lessee.

The lessee does not have to make good any deficit, should one arise.

In this example, it appears that the lessor is using the sale proceeds to meet its unguaranteed residual value but it is also taking the first loss provision. Only thereafter does the lessee gain or lose from the fluctuations in the fair value. The lessee's minimum lease payments have a net present value of €7,365, it has not guaranteed the residual value at all and is not exposed to any risk of any fall in value, although it may benefit from increases in the fair value in excess of €3,000. On balance this indicates that the arrangement is an operating lease.

3.2.3 Changes to lease terms and provisions

Lease classification is made at the inception of the lease, which is the earlier of the date of the lease agreement or of a commitment by the parties to the principal provisions of the lease. *[IAS 17.4]*. Lease classification is only changed 'if at any time the lessee and the lessor agree to change the provisions of the lease, other than by renewing the lease, in a manner that would have resulted in a different classification of the lease under the criteria in paragraphs 7-12 if the changed terms had been in effect at the inception of the lease...' (see 3.2.2 above). The revised agreement is regarded as a new agreement over its term. *[IAS 17.13]*. Changes in estimates (for example, changes in estimates of the economic life or of the residual value of the leased item) or changes in circumstances (for example, default by the lessee) do not result in the lease being reclassified for accounting purposes. *[IAS 17.13]*.

The distinction between changes to the provisions of the lease and changes in estimate is that the former, unlike the latter, are always the result of agreements between the lessee and lessor.

This section does not address the measurement of these changes, as measurement is addressed in section 6 below.

IAS 17 does not discuss or illustrate these requirements.

(a) Changes to the provisions or terms of an existing lease ('modifications')

Changes to the provisions or terms of an existing lease (referred to here as a 'modification') are changes to the contractual terms and conditions that are not part of the original lease. Modifications that affect a lease's classification are those that affect the risks and rewards incidental to ownership of the asset by changing the terms and cash flows of the existing lease. Examples of modifications that could affect classification include those that change the duration of the lease and the number, amount and timing of lease payments or inserting into the agreement an option to acquire the asset that was not previously part of the lease terms. Some changes to lease terms will not affect the cash flows at all, e.g. those that change terms such as the names of the contracting parties.

The revised agreement resulting from the modification is considered as if it were a new agreement which should be accounted for appropriately, as a finance or operating lease, prospectively over the remaining term of the lease.

IAS 17 does not give any specific guidance on how to assess whether modified lease terms give rise to a new classification so the general classification rules described in 3.2.2 above must be applied. Nor does it explain how to measure modifications of leases if changes affect the value of the assets and liabilities for both lessor and lessee. These issues are discussed at 6 below. Sections 6.1.1 and 6.1.2 below discuss how to assess whether the classification has changed, based on the revised cash flows, and how to account for the reclassification. Example 24.23 at 6.1.1 below describes circumstances in which a lease term is extended mid-term, changing the cash flows over the remainder of the original lease term as well as requiring the lessee to make payments during the extended term.

If lease terms are modified but the classification does not change, the entity will still have to account for the modified cash flows. How to account for the changes if a finance lease remains a finance lease is discussed at 6.1.3 below. Accounting for changes to the terms of operating leases, where those changes do not result in reclassification, is considered at 6.1.5 below.

(b) The lessee and lessor renew the lease

If the lessee and lessor renew the lease, this could mean one of the following:

- The lessee exercises an option to extend the lease when the option was not included in the original lease term (i.e. exercise of the renewal option was not reasonably certain at lease inception). Changes in circumstances or intentions such as exercising an option that was excluded from the initial lease term do not give rise to a new classification of the original lease.
- The lessee enters into a new lease with the lessor at the end of the lease term. For example, in the absence of a contractual right, an entity may have a right to 'renew' a lease of business premises for a further term after expiry of the initial lease term at the market rent. This is not a change to the terms of the original lease. In some jurisdictions the ability to renew at market rates is a statutory right to ensure that businesses are not forced to relocate. This is similar in effect to an option to extend at market value so under a risks and rewards model the renewal period would not pass the significant risks and rewards to the lessee.

  Orange SA discloses that it holds commercial leases that it may choose to renew on expiry of the term.

Extract 24.1: Orange (2014)

Financial report [extract]
Consolidated financial statements [extract]
14.1 Operational activities commitments [extract]
Operating leases [extract]

The property lease commitments in France represent 65% of the total of the property lease commitments.

The Group may choose whether or not to renew these commercial leases upon expiration or replace them by other leases with renegotiated terms and conditions.

- The lessee and lessor could revoke the original lease and enter into a new one in its place, which would also be considered a renewal. It is necessary to ensure that the new lease terms are at fair value at the time the new lease is entered into so it does not reflect, for example, underpayments or overpayments made by the lessee under the terms of the original lease.

- The lessee and lessor could agree to extend the existing lease without changing any other term, e.g. with the consent of the lessor, continuing to use the asset for a period of time after the original expiry at the original rental. This is similar to the requirements in IFRIC 4, discussed at 2.1.5 above, under which an entity does not have to reassess an arrangement to see if it contains a lease if a change in the contractual terms only renews or extends the arrangement. *[IFRIC 4.10]*. This has to be distinguished from a negotiation between the lessee and lessor that changes the terms of the original lease before its expiry, although this would probably also include other changes such as a different rental and. in which case, the accounting would fall under (a) above.

A new or extended lease will be classified according to its own terms.

Example 24.7 below illustrates various scenarios and their effects or otherwise on classification.

Example 24.7: Lease classification

Consider the following scenarios:

(a) Entity A leases a motor vehicle from Entity B for a non-cancellable three-year period. At the inception of the lease, the lease was assessed as an operating lease. The lease did not contain any explicit option in the lease contract to extend the term of the lease. A short period of time before the end of the lease term, Entity A negotiates with Entity B to extend the lease for a further two years. This extension is granted by the leasing company at fair value.

The lease modification results in a new forward starting lease, not a change in the provisions of the original lease, which will be accounted for on its own terms. This does not affect the classification of the original lease. Although the lease inception of the new lease would be the date on which negotiations were completed, the new lease would not be accounted for until its commencement, which will be after the termination of the original lease.

(b) Entity C leases a machine tool from Entity D for 5 years, expecting to purchase a new asset after the lease expires. After 3 years, Entity C concludes that it is more economically viable for it to lease the asset from Entity D for a total of 8 years. The lessor agrees to revised lease terms and the lease is extended by 3 years, giving a total term of 8 years. At the same time the lease payments for years 4 and 5 are revised so that Entity C will pay a new rental for each of the years 4 to 8.

This is a lease modification as it has resulted in a change to the terms of the original lease. The entity will have to assess whether the revised lease is an operating or finance lease.

(c) Entity E leases an asset from Entity F for 10 years. The lease includes a purchase option under which Entity E may purchase the asset from Entity F at the end of the lease. The exercise price is fair value. Entity E is required to give notice of its intention to purchase no later than the end of the eighth year of the lease (since this arrangement allows Entity F time to market the leased asset for sale). On inception, Entity E classifies the lease as an operating lease, believing it was not reasonably certain that it would exercise the option. Near the end of the eighth year of the lease, Entity E serves notice that it will purchase the asset, thereby creating a binding purchase commitment.

Entity E exercises an option that was not considered reasonably certain at inception; this is a change in estimate and does not affect lease classification. Many entities would consider the arrangement to be executory at the time that the notice is given even though there is a legal obligation to make the option payment (see Chapter 28 at 2.2.1.A) and therefore would account for the purchase option only when it is exercised.

3.3 Leases of land – finance or operating leases?

The standard requires an entity to assess the classification of leases over land as finance or operating leases in accordance with the general rules in paragraphs 7-13 that are described above. Many leases include elements for both land and buildings and both parts must be considered separately as discussed in 3.3.2 below.

The standard includes a reminder that 'in determining whether the land element is an operating or a finance lease, an important consideration is that land normally has an indefinite economic life'. *[IAS 17.15A]*. A lease term for the major part of the economic life of the asset can indicate that a lease is a finance lease, even if title is not transferred, *[IAS 17.10]*, and by repeating this in paragraph 15A, which was introduced in an amendment that came into force on 1 January 2010, the IASB is stressing that this particular feature of finance leases is not likely to be met. Prior to amendment in 2009, IAS 17 required initial classification of land leases to be based on whether or not title had passed. Where title to the land had not passed and it had an indefinite economic life, the land was normally classified as an operating lease, while the buildings element was an operating lease or finance lease according to the classification in the standard.[3]

The Board expected the amendment to affect lease classification of land, noting that it will be an improvement in accounting for leases and the significance of this issue in countries in which property rights are obtained under long-term leases. *[IAS 17.BC8E]*. In these jurisdictions these interests are frequently purchased for single lease premiums in a manner comparable to the purchase of a freehold, although there may also be a small annual rent payable (e.g. a 'ground rent' in the UK). The Basis for Conclusions suggests that the lessee in leases of this type 'will typically be in a position economically similar to an entity that purchased the land and buildings. The present value of the residual value of the property in a lease with a term of several decades would be negligible. The Board concluded that accounting for the land element as a finance lease in such circumstances would be consistent with the economic position of the lessee.' *[IAS 17.BC8C]*. Therefore, the fact that land has an indefinite life will be assessed alongside other features that distinguish finance leases from operating leases. As well as considering whether the minimum lease payments amount to substantially all of the fair value, it is necessary to consider whether the lease includes other features that indicate that the significant risks and rewards of ownership rest with the lessor rather than the lessee. These include significant contingent rentals, rentals that are reset to market rates and fair value purchase options, all of which could indicate that the lease is an operating lease.

Some have questioned whether a purchase of a right to use land could ever be classified as a fixed asset, i.e. as plant, property and equipment (PP&E) under IAS 16 or an intangible asset under IAS 38, especially in circumstances in which the right can be extended indefinitely, as happens in some jurisdictions. The Interpretations Committee noted that a lease could be indefinite with extensions or renewals so the fact that the right to use could have an indefinite period does not prevent it from qualifying as a lease in accordance with IAS 17. In the particular country, entities can purchase a right to exploit or build on land that can be extended indefinitely, subject to government rights to take back possession at the end of the term or otherwise with compensation. The Committee concluded that the particular arrangement should be classified as a lease. However, because the circumstances were specific to a jurisdiction, the Committee decided not to take the matter onto its agenda.[4]

An advantage of classifying certain land leases as finance leases is that they can then be presented in the financial statements as property, plant and equipment. Under the previous standard, unless title to the land transfers to the lessee, premiums paid for a leasehold interest in land always represented pre-paid lease payments to be amortised over the lease term in accordance with the pattern of benefits provided.[5] This treatment is now reserved for prepaid land rentals that are not classified as finance leases. An example would be a lease premium that comprises ten year's prepaid rentals, which is most unlikely to be classified as a finance lease.

A company that reclassified land leases as finance leases as a result of the change to IAS 17 is Wm Morrison Supermarkets PLC. The amounts reclassified as finance leases were large, amounting to £271 million in 2011.

Extract 24.2: Wm Morrison Supermarkets PLC (2011)

Consolidated financial statements under International Financial Reporting Standards [extract]

Group accounting policies [extract]

Long-leasehold land

The amendment to IAS 17 Leases is effective for annual periods beginning on or after 1 January 2010. During the period, the Group has reassessed the classification of unexpired land leases between operating and finance leases. Leases newly classified as finance leases have been accounted for retrospectively in accordance with IAS 8 Accounting policies, changes in accounting estimates and errors, and the required disclosures have been made.

The adoption of the amendment to IAS 17 Leases has resulted in a) derecognising long-lease land premiums previously classified within non-current asset lease prepayments, and the current element classified within debtors; and b) recognising a corresponding increase in the closing net book value of leasehold land and buildings to reflect the carrying value of the leased assets.

3.3.1 Measurement and presentation of operating leases over land

Prepayments that are classified as operating leases over land and buildings are disclosed as current or non-current assets, as appropriate, in the entity's statement of financial position. If certain costs arise at the inception of the lease that are necessary to consummate the agreement and enable a lessee to exercise its rights under the lease agreement, these costs are incurred as a direct result of the lease. Therefore, it is appropriate to consider these as lease-related costs that should be subject to the same accounting treatment as prepaid lease payments. Initial direct costs of leases are discussed at 3.4.8 below.

The following is an example of presentation of pre-paid operating leases in the statement of financial position, together with the supporting note.

Extract 24.3: VTech Holdings Limited (2014)

Consolidated Financial Statements [extract]

Consolidated Balance Sheet [extract]

As at 31 March 2014

	Note	**31 March 2014 US$ million**	31 March 2013 (Restated) US$ million	1 April 2012 (Restated) US$ million
Non-current assets				
Tangible assets	7	**85.9**	88.4	91.0
Leasehold land payments	8	**5.1**	5.2	5.1
Investments		**0.1**	0.1	0.2
Deferred tax assets	9(b)	**2.5**	4.6	7.0
		93.6	98.3	103.3

Notes to the Financial Statements [extract]

Principal Accounting Policies [extract]

J Leases [extract]

Leasehold land payments are up-front payments to acquire long-term leasehold interests in land. These payments are stated at cost and are amortised on a straight-line basis over the respective period of the leases.

8 Leasehold Land Payments

	Note	**2014 US$ million**	2013 US$ million
Net book value at 1 April		**5.2**	5.1
Amortisation	2	**(0.1)**	(0.1)
Effect of changes in exchange rates		**–**	0.2
Net book value at 31 March (*note (i)*)		**5.1**	5.2
Leasehold land payments in respect of:			
Owner-occupied properties		**5.1**	5.2

Note:

(i) Included in leasehold land payments is the amount of US$3.0 million (2013: US$3.0 million) paid for the acquisition of certain sites in the PRC.

3.3.2 *Separating land and buildings*

A characteristic of property leases in some jurisdictions (such as the UK) is that it is not possible to lease a building without leasing the land on which it stands – under UK property law all such leases are leases of land and everything attached to it. There is no separate fair value for the land and buildings elements as they cannot be disposed of separately and the IASB noted that in substance such leases may differ little from buying a property. *[IAS 17.BC5]*. Notwithstanding this, the standard states explicitly that the land and buildings elements of leases are considered separately for the purposes of lease classification. *[IAS 17.15A]*. Each part must be classified as an operating or finance lease in the same way as leases of other assets.[6] This does not apply to leases of investment properties where there is no requirement to separate the land and buildings elements; see 3.3.3 below.

Entities may need to make the allocation between the land and buildings elements even if both are clearly finance leases as there could be a difference in amortisation methods, although this would be very unusual. *[IAS 17.BC8F]*. Much more common is a difference in useful economic life, where an entity takes out a lease for land and buildings where the term is longer than the useful life of any building on the land, e.g. a lease of 75 years over land on which there is a building that has a remaining useful life of 30 years.

If either or both parts of the lease comprise a finance lease, the minimum lease payments need to be allocated between the land and buildings elements in proportion to the respective fair values of the leasehold interest in the land and buildings elements at the inception of the lease. The minimum lease payments must, of course, include any up-front payments, such as the payment for a lease premium. *[IAS 17.16]*.

The allocation of the minimum lease payments should be weighted to reflect the fair value of the land and buildings components to the extent they are the subject of the lease. This means that the amount that is being allocated is the lessee's leasehold interest in the land and buildings and the compensation received by the lessor, not the relative fair values of the land and buildings. The amount for which the land could be purchased at the inception of the lease is not the same as the value of that interest to the lessee. As land has an indefinite life, the value to the lessor may not be significantly affected by the grant of the lease. *[IAS 17.BC9-11]*.

The standard addresses the fact that it may not be possible to determine the fair values of the elements at inception and allows the following:

- if it is difficult or impossible to allocate the payments between the two elements, then the entire lease may be classified as a finance lease unless it is obvious that both the land and buildings elements are operating leases; and *[IAS 17.16]*
- if the land element is immaterial, the lease may be treated as a single unit and classified as a finance or operating lease. The economic life of the entire leased asset will be the economic life of the buildings. *[IAS 17.17]*.

Some examples of the ways in which these exemptions may operate in practice are as follows:

Example 24.8: Leases of land and buildings

Consider the following scenarios:

- Company A leases a building (and the underlying land) for 10 years. The remaining economic life of the building when the lease is entered into is 30 years. The lease is for considerably less than the economic life of the building so it is clear that both the land and buildings elements are operating leases and no separation is necessary.
- Company B enters into a 30-year lease of a new building and the underlying land. It is on a retail park and almost all of the value is ascribed to the building as land values are low. Although the building has a fabric life of 60 years, its economic life is estimated to be 30 years, after which it is expected to be technologically obsolete. The lease is for a major part of the economic life of the buildings and the present value of the minimum lease payments amounts to substantially all of the fair value of the building. It is not legally possible to lease the building without leasing the underlying land. In any event, the lessor retains the residual value in the land and the lessee's interest in the land alone will be insignificant because of the low land values. The entire lease is accounted for as a finance lease with an economic life of 30 years.

- Company C takes out a 25 year non-cancellable lease of premises in the centre of a major town where land values are high. There are upward-only rent reviews every 5 years. It is a modern building that may have a remaining economic life of 35 years (or perhaps more, as the building has a fabric life of 60 years) and the land is clearly valuable to the lessor, who will want a reasonable return from it over the lease term. In this case the interest in the building may or may not be a finance lease and the lessee's leasehold interest in the land is not insignificant. Company C will have to undertake a valuation exercise to determine the allocation of minimum lease payments between the land and building elements of the lease in order to determine whether or not it has finance or operating leases over the land and buildings.

In some circumstances it may be unclear whether the lessee has a finance or operating lease over land and buildings. In such cases it will probably be necessary to obtain the help of a valuation expert.

There are four elements that need to be taken into account in the apportionment: the value within the lease of the buildings and the land, and the residual value of both buildings and land. In the UK, The Royal Institution of Chartered Surveyors issued guidance that analyses the apportionments based on these elements for lease classification under IFRSs, which could be of more general interest.[7] The principal steps are as follows:

(a) assess the freehold value of the land and buildings;

(b) apportion the freehold value between the value within the lease and the residual (reversionary) value;

(c) apportion the freehold value between land and buildings by calculating the value of one or other interest (usually, in practice, the building element) and deducting this from the value obtained in (b) to obtain the other;

(d) apportion the value of the buildings element calculated at (c) between the residual and the value within the lease;

(e) the value within the lease (b) can now be allocated between the buildings element (calculated at (d)) and the land element ((b) less (d)); and

(f) apportion minimum lease payment between land and buildings in the ratio in (e) above.

This methodology makes it possible to calculate the implicit interest rate separately for the building as all elements needed for the calculation are known (fair value of the building, value of its residual and an appropriate proportion of the rentals paid).[8]

3.3.3 Leases and investment properties

IAS 17 requires leases to be separated into land and building components, subject to this being possible or the land element being immaterial. If the interest is an investment property carried at fair value in accordance with IAS 40 (the interest may be a finance or operating lease under IAS 17, see Chapter 19 at 2.1), there is no requirement to separate the land and buildings elements of the lease. *[IAS 17.18]*.

If the lessee has classified a property interest held under an operating lease as if it were held under a finance lease, as permitted by IAS 40 (see Chapter 19 at 2.1), it must apply the fair value model and it must continue to do so even if subsequent changes in circumstances mean that the property interest is no longer an investment property to the lessee. IAS 17 gives two examples:

(a) the lessee occupies the property, in which case it is transferred to owner-occupied property at fair value at the date of change of use; or

(b) the lessee grants a sublease over substantially all of its property interest to an unrelated third party. It will treat the sublease as a finance lease to the third party even though the interest may well be accounted for as an operating lease by that party. *[IAS 17.19]*.

In some arrangements, a developer may acquire a headlease over land and sell its rights under that same headlease. In these circumstances the developer may apply an IAS 40 analysis and treat the transaction as a purchase and sale of the same investment property. However, this does depend on the disposal in substance of the same asset as the one that has been acquired.

Further discussion about investment properties and leases is included in Chapter 19.

3.4 Defined terms

3.4.1 Inception and commencement of the lease

The standard distinguishes between the inception of the lease (when leases are classified) and the commencement of the lease term (when recognition takes place). The *inception* of the lease is the earlier of the date of the lease agreement and the date of commitment of the parties to the principal terms of the lease. This is the date on which a lease is classified as a finance or operating lease and, for finance leases, the date at which the amounts to be recognised at commencement are determined. *[IAS 17.4]*. The *commencement* of the lease term is the date on which the lessee is entitled to exercise its right to use the leased asset and is the date of initial recognition of the assets, liabilities, income and expenses of the lease in the financial statements. *[IAS 17.4]*. This means that the entity makes an initial calculation of the assets and liabilities under a finance lease at inception of the lease but does not recognise these in the financial statements until the commencement date, if this is later. These amounts may in some circumstances be revised.

It is not uncommon for these two dates to be different, especially if the asset is under construction. Lease payments may be adjusted for changes in the lessor's costs during the period between inception and commencement. The lease may allow for changes in respect of costs of construction, acquisition costs, changes in the lessor's financing costs and any other factor, such as changes in general price levels, during the construction period. Changes to the lease payments as a result of such events are deemed to take place at inception of the lease, i.e. are taken into account in establishing, at inception, whether it is a finance or operating lease. *[IAS 17.5]*. In other words, if the final cost of the asset, and hence its fair value, is not known until after the date of inception, hindsight is used to establish that fair value.

The fair value may be known at inception but payment delayed until commencement, which may happen with large but routinely constructed assets such as aircraft or railway locomotives. The lease liability will increase between the date of inception and the date of commencement, taking account of payments made and the interest rate implicit in the lease (see 3.4.5 below). Although IAS 17 does not address this, the lessee will add the increase in the liability until the commencement date to the asset. It is not a finance cost on the liability (no liability is recognised prior to commencement) and nor need it be an expense. It is not appropriate to recognise at commencement the liability that was calculated at inception as that would change the interest rate implicit in the lease.

The standard also considers what will happen if the lease terms are changed so radically (but without entering into a new lease agreement) that it would have been classified in a different way, e.g. it would have been a finance lease instead of an operating lease. Such changes could happen at any stage during the lease (see 3.2.3 above) but if they happen in the period between inception and commencement, the lease will be classified at inception in accordance with the revised terms as if they had existed as at that date. Accounting for modifications is discussed at 6 below.

3.4.2 Fair value

Fair value is defined as the amount for which an asset could be exchanged or a liability settled, between knowledgeable, willing parties in an arm's length transaction. *[IAS 17.4]*. In practice, the transaction price, i.e. the purchase price of the asset that is the subject of the lease, will be its fair value, unless there is evidence to the contrary. IFRS 13 does not apply because IAS 17 uses 'fair value' in a way that differs in some respects from the definition in the IFRS. *[IFRS 13.6, IAS 17.6A]*. As a result lessees and lessors are also exempt from IFRS 13's disclosure requirements.

3.4.3 Minimum lease payments

The minimum lease payments are the payments over the lease term that the lessee is or can be required to make, excluding contingent rent, costs for services and taxes to be paid by and reimbursed to the lessor, together with:

(a) for a lessee, any amounts guaranteed by the lessee or by a party related to the lessee;

(b) for a lessor, any residual guaranteed to the lessor by:

  (i) the lessee or by a party related to the lessee; or

  (ii) a third party unrelated to the lessor who is financially capable of discharging the obligations under the guarantee.

The lessee may have an option to purchase the asset at a price that is expected to be sufficiently lower than the fair value at the date the option becomes exercisable so that, at the inception of the lease, it is reasonably certain to be exercised. In this case the minimum lease payments comprise the minimum payments payable over the lease term to the expected date of exercise of this purchase option and the payment required to exercise it. *[IAS 17.4]*.

3.4.4 Lease term and non-cancellable period

The lease term is the non-cancellable period for which the lessee has contracted to lease the asset, together with any further terms for which the lessee has the option to continue to lease the asset, with or without further payment, if it is reasonably certain at the inception of the lease that the lessee will exercise the option. *[IAS 17.4]*. A non-cancellable lease is either a lease that has no cancellation terms or one that has terms that effectively force the lessee to continue to use the asset for the period of the agreement. Therefore, a lease is considered to be non-cancellable if it can be cancelled only:

(a) on the occurrence of a remote contingency;

(b) with the permission of the lessor;

(c) if the lessee enters into a new lease with the same lessor for the same or an equivalent asset; or

(d) if the lessee is required to pay additional amounts that make it reasonably certain at inception that the lessee will continue the lease. *[IAS 17.4]*.

An example of (d) is a requirement that the lessee pays a termination payment equivalent to the present value of the remaining lease payments.

3.4.5 Interest rate implicit in the lease and incremental borrowing rate

The interest rate implicit in the lease ('IIR') is the discount rate that, at the inception of the lease, causes the aggregate present value of:

(a) the minimum lease payments; and

(b) the unguaranteed residual value,

to be equal to the sum of the fair value of the leased asset and any initial direct costs of the lessor. Example 24.9 at 3.4.9 below illustrates the calculation of the implicit interest rate.

If it is not practicable to determine this then the lessee may use its incremental borrowing rate of interest, which it is the rate of interest the lessee would have to pay on a similar lease or, if that is not determinable, the rate that, at the inception of the lease, the lessee would have to pay to borrow over a similar term, and with a similar security, the funds necessary to purchase the asset. *[IAS 17.4]*.

3.4.6 Residual value

The guaranteed residual value is:

(a) for a lessee, the part of the residual value that is guaranteed by itself or by one of its related parties. The amount of the guarantee is the maximum amount that could, in any event, become payable; and

(b) for a lessor, it is the part of the residual value that is guaranteed by the lessee or by a third party unrelated to the lessor who is financially capable of discharging the obligations under the guarantee.

The lessor's unguaranteed residual value is any part of the residual value of the leased asset, the realisation of which is not assured or is guaranteed solely by a party related to it. *[IAS 17.4]*.

If the net present value of the residual value of an asset is significant and is not guaranteed by the lessee or a party related to it, then the lease is likely to be classified as an operating lease by the lessee. The lessee will not bear the risks of recovering the significant residual value; consequently it is unlikely that 'substantially all' of the risks and rewards of ownership will have passed to the lessee. However, as can be seen from Example 24.5 at 3.2.2.A above, the provision of a residual value guarantee by a lessee does not necessarily mean that the lease will not be classified as an operating lease by the lessee.

There are frequently problems of interpretation regarding the significance of residual values in lease classification. Lessees may find it difficult to obtain information in order to calculate the unguaranteed residual values. If lessees guarantee all or part of the residual value of the asset, this has to be taken into account in the lease classification.

3.4.6.A Residual value guarantors

A lessee and lessor may legitimately classify the same lease differently if the lessor has received a residual value guarantee provided by a third party. *[IAS 17.9]*. Residual value guarantors undertake to acquire the assets from the lessor at an agreed amount at the end of the lease term because they can dispose of the assets on a ready and reliable market. As a result, such a lease is an operating lease for the lessee and a finance lease for the lessor. Residual value guarantors may be prepared to take the residual risk with many types of assets as long as there is a second-hand market. This is particularly common with vehicle leases where there is an efficient second-hand market, including price guides, many car dealers and car auctions.

3.4.7 Contingent rents and embedded derivatives

Contingent rents, which are excluded from minimum lease payments, are defined in the standard as that portion of the lease payments that are not fixed in amount, but are based on a factor other than just the passage of time (for example, percentage of sales, amount of usage, price indices, market rates of interest). *[IAS 17.4]*.

Contingent rents are embedded derivatives, as defined by IAS 39 (or IFRS 9, should the entity apply that IFRS), and in principle within the scope of that standard. An embedded derivative is a component of a hybrid or combined instrument that also includes a non-derivative host contract; it has the effect that some of the cash flows of the combined instrument vary in a similar way to a stand-alone derivative. In other words, it causes some or all of the cash flows that otherwise would be required by the contract to be modified according to a specified underlying. *[IAS 39.10]*. Embedded derivatives have to be separated from the host contract and recognised separately in the financial statements of the entity unless they are closely related to the economic characteristics and risks of the host contract. *[IAS 39.11]*.

IAS 39 specifically identifies the examples of contingent rents referred to in IAS 17 as being 'closely related' to the lease contract and hence not separately accounted for. *[IAS 39.11, AG33(f)]*. This means that lessees continue to expense such contingent payments as they arise.

However, other types of contingent rent could be embedded derivatives, e.g. an index that relates to inflation in another economic environment. *[IAS 39.AG33(f)]*.

A contingent rent may be subject to a cap or floor, e.g. a rental payment increases annually in line with an inflation index but there is a maximum or minimum increase, or both.

IAS 39 allows embedded floors or caps on the interest rate on a debt contract to be closely related to the host contract as long as the cap is at or above and the floor similarly at or below current market rates of interest and they are not leveraged in relation to the host contract. *[IAS 39.11, AG33(b)]*. Therefore caps and floors on closely related derivatives in leases that meet these criteria and are not otherwise leveraged are themselves considered to be closely related and not accounted for separately.

In the case of more complex lease terms, reference should be made to IAS 39 paragraphs 10 to 13 (see Chapter 44 at 5).

A lease is classified as a finance lease if it transfers substantially all the risks and rewards incidental to ownership. *[IAS 17.8]*. Contingent payments will be taken into account in assessing whether substantially all of the risks and rewards of ownership have been transferred e.g. property rentals that are periodically reset to market rates would tend to indicate that risks and rewards rest with the lessor – see the discussion at 3.2.2 above. This still leaves open to debate whether a particular 'contingency' is in fact contingent or is so certain that it ought to be reflected in the minimum lease payments for the purposes of classifying the lease. IAS 17 contains no explicit guidance in this respect, and in practice, this will be based on an assessment of the individual circumstances. However, unlike IAS 17, IFRS 16 explicitly addresses in-substance fixed lease payments, being those payments that may, in form, contain variability but that, in substance, are fixed. *[IFRS 16.B42]*. The IASB understands that the approach to in-substance fixed lease payments required by IFRS 16 is similar to the way in which entities apply IAS 17, even though IAS 17 does not contain explicit requirements in this respect. *[IFRS 16.BC164]*. As such, the guidance on in-substance fixed lease payments provided by IFRS 16 may be helpful to those entities still applying IAS 17. The identification of in-substance fixed lease payments under IFRS 16 is discussed at Chapter 25 at 4.5.1.

Lessees under finance leases need to disclose the minimum lease payments payable under finance leases and contingent rents recognised as an expense in the period (see 9.2 below). *[IAS 17.31(b), 31(c)]*.

3.4.7.A Contingent rents and operating leases

IAS 17 specifies that lessees expense contingent rents relating to finance leases in the period in which they are incurred. *[IAS 17.25]*. However, the standard is not explicit in the treatment of contingent elements of operating lease rentals.

In its May 2006 meeting, the Interpretations Committee considered whether an estimate of contingent rents should be included in the total operating lease payments or lease income to be recognised on a straight-line basis over the lease term. It concluded in July 2006 that current practice was to exclude such amounts and did not, therefore, add the matter to its agenda for further consideration. Accordingly, lease payments or receipts under operating leases may exclude contingent amounts.

Views are divided on whether minimum lease payments determined at the inception of the lease are revised on the occurrence of the contingency, e.g. whether minimum lease payments change when there are rent revisions that are stipulated in the original lease agreement, either for straight-line recognition or disclosure purposes.

Contingent property rents are common. They usually fall into one of two categories: rents that vary in accordance with an index (e.g. a cost or retail price index) or those that vary with turnover or a similar contingency. In the case of contingencies based on an index, it is our view that disclosure should reflect all contingencies that have occurred in future minimum lease disclosures. This is on the basis that the contingency has occurred and IAS 17 specifies disclosure of future minimum lease payments. If the initial payment before any indexation changes was 100 per year and at the end of year 1, the index was 102.5, the minimum lease payments for disclosure purposes would be 102.5 for each remaining year of the lease term.

Lease disclosures relating to minimum lease payments and contingent rents are discussed at 9 below.

3.4.8 *Initial direct costs*

Initial direct costs are incremental costs that are directly attributable to negotiating and arranging a lease, except for such costs incurred by manufacturer or dealer lessors. *[IAS 17.4]*.

If the lessee incurs costs that are directly attributable to activities it has performed to obtain a finance lease, these are added to the amount recognised as an asset. *[IAS 17.24]*. IAS 17 is silent on the treatment of initial direct costs of operating leases but there seems to be no restriction, in principle, to an entity selecting a policy of recognising initial direct costs as assets and amortising them, as appropriate, over the lease term. Initial direct costs of lessors include amounts such as commissions, legal fees and internal costs that are incremental and directly attributable to negotiating and arranging a lease. Internal costs must exclude general overheads such as those incurred by a sales or marketing team. *[IAS 17.38]*. The Interpretations Committee confirmed in March 2014 that incremental costs are those that would not have been incurred if the entity had not negotiated and arranged a lease. This means that the fixed salary costs of permanent staff involved in negotiating and arranging new leases (and loans) do not qualify as 'incremental costs'. Lessors must add internal direct costs to the carrying value of leased assets under both finance and operating leases – see 4.2 and 5.2 below – unless they are manufacturer and dealer lessors, in which case they must be expensed – see 4.4 below.

3.4.9 *Calculation of the implicit interest rate and present value of minimum lease payments*

An entity will frequently have to calculate the net present value of the minimum lease payments in order to classify a lease as a finance or operating lease as well as in accounting for finance leases. Once it has the necessary information it can calculate the implicit interest rate and present value of minimum lease payments, as in the following example:

Example 24.9: Calculation of the implicit interest rate and present value of minimum lease payments

Details of a non-cancellable lease are as follows:

(i) Fair value = €10,000

(ii) Five annual rentals payable in advance of €2,100

(iii) Lessor's unguaranteed estimated residual value at end of five years = €1,000

The implicit interest rate in the lease is that which gives a present value of €10,000 for the five rentals plus the total estimated residual value at the end of year 5. This rate can be calculated as 6.62%, as follows:

Year	Capital sum at start of period	Rental paid	Capital sum during period	Finance charge (6.62% per annum)	Capital sum at end of period
	€	€	€	€	€
1	10,000	2,100	7,900	523	8,423
2	8,423	2,100	6,323	419	6,742
3	6,742	2,100	4,642	307	4,949
4	4,949	2,100	2,849	189	3,038
5	3,038	2,100	938	62	1,000
		10,500		1,500	

In other words, 6.62% is the implicit interest rate that, at the inception of the lease, causes the aggregate present value of the minimum lease payments (€10,500) and the unguaranteed residual value (€1,000) to be equal to the fair value of the leased asset. Lessor's initial direct costs have been excluded for simplicity.

This implicit interest rate is then used to calculate the present value of the minimum lease payments, i.e. €10,500 discounted at 6.62%. This can be calculated at €9,274, which is 92.74% of the asset's fair value, indicating that the present value of the minimum lease payments is substantially all of the fair value of the leased asset and a finance lease classification is therefore indicated.

It would be appropriate for the lessee to record the asset at €9,274 as the present value of the minimum lease payments is lower than the fair value and this would take account of the lessor's residual interest in the asset.

The lessor will know all of the information in the above example, as it will have been used in the pricing decision for the lease. However, the lessee may not know either the fair value or the unguaranteed residual value and, therefore, not know the implicit interest rate. In such circumstances the lessee will substitute a rate from a similar lease or its incremental borrowing rate. The lessee is also unlikely to know the lessor's initial direct costs even if the other information is known, but this is unlikely to have more than a marginal effect on the implicit interest rate.

3.5 Leases as financial instruments

In accordance with the accounting model in IAS 17, a finance lease is essentially regarded as an entitlement to receive, and an obligation to make, a stream of payments that are substantially the same as blended payments of principal and interest under a loan agreement. Consequently, the lessor accounts for its investment in the amount receivable under the lease contract rather than the leased asset itself. An operating lease, on the other hand, is regarded primarily as an uncompleted contract committing the lessor to provide the use of an asset in future periods in exchange for consideration similar to a fee for a service. The lessor continues to account for the leased asset itself rather than any amount receivable in the future under the contract.

Accordingly, a finance lease is regarded by IAS 32 – *Financial Instruments: Presentation* – as a financial instrument and an operating lease is not, except as regards individual payments currently due and payable. *[IAS 32.AG9]*.

In general the lease rights and obligations that come about as a result of IAS 17's recognition and measurement rules are not included within the scope of IAS 39 (or IFRS 9, should an entity apply that standard, as it incorporates IAS 39's scope).

Finance lease assets and liabilities are not necessarily stated at the same amount as they would be if they were measured under IAS 39. The most obvious differences are those between the implicit interest rate and the effective interest rate. The IIR (as described in 3.4.5 above) is the discount rate that, at the inception of the lease, causes the aggregate present value of the minimum lease payments (receivable during the non-cancellable lease term and any option periods that it is reasonably certain at inception the lessee will exercise) and the unguaranteed residual value to be equal to the sum of the fair value of the leased asset and any initial direct costs of the lessor. *[IAS 17.4]*. The effective interest rate, by contrast, is the rate that exactly discounts estimated future cash payments or receipts through the expected life of the financial instrument (see Chapter 49 at 3). *[IAS 39.9]*. The latter may include payments that would be considered contingent rentals, and hence excluded, from the calculation of the IIR and may take account of cash flows over a different period.

However, the following aspects of accounting for leases are within IAS 39's scope:

(a) finance lease payables recognised by a lessee are subject to the derecognition provisions (see 4.3.1 below);

(b) lease receivables recognised by a lessor, which are subject to the derecognition and impairment provisions of IAS 39 (see 4.3.2 below); and

(c) derivatives that are embedded in leases are subject to IAS 39's embedded derivatives provisions (see 3.4.7 above). *[IAS 39.2(b)]*.

IAS 39 (or IFRS 9) has little impact on traditional, straightforward leases. However, its requirements will have to be considered in many more complex situations and in relation to sub-leases and back-to-back leases, as described in 8 below.

4 ACCOUNTING FOR FINANCE LEASES

Lessees recognise finance leases as assets and liabilities in their statements of financial position at the commencement of the lease term at amounts equal to the fair value of the leased item or, if lower, at the present value of the minimum lease payments, each determined at the inception of the lease. In calculating the present value of the minimum lease payments the discount factor is the interest rate implicit in the lease, if this is practicable to determine; if not, the lessee's incremental borrowing rate should be used. Any initial direct costs of the lessee are added to the recognised asset. *[IAS 17.20, 21]*. 'Fair value', 'minimum lease payments' and 'initial direct costs' are defined in 3.4.2, 3.4.3 and 3.4.8 above.

The fair value and the present value of the lease payments are both determined as at the inception of the lease. At commencement, the asset and liability for the future lease payments are recognised in the statement of financial position at the same amount (except for any initial direct costs added to the recognised asset). *[IAS 17.22]*. Both asset and liability must be recognised separately, with an appropriate distinction between current and non-current liabilities being made. *[IAS 17.23]*. The terms and calculations of initial recognition by lessees are discussed further in 4.1 below.

Lease payments made by the lessee are apportioned between the finance charge and the reduction of the outstanding liability. The finance charge should be allocated to periods during the lease term so as to produce a constant periodic rate of interest on the remaining balance of the liability for each period. [IAS 17.25]. This is covered in 4.1.2 below.

Lessors recognise assets held under a finance lease as receivables in their statement of financial position and present them as a receivable at an amount equal to the net investment in the lease. [IAS 17.36]. Lessors who are not manufacturers or dealers include costs that they have incurred in connection with arranging and negotiating a lease as part of the initial measurement of the finance lease receivable. Initial recognition by lessors, which is in many respects a mirror image of lessee recognition, is discussed at 4.2 below. The recognition of finance income and other issues in connection with subsequent measurement of the lessor's assets arising from finance leases is dealt with in 4.2.1 to 4.2.4 below. The consequences of terminating a finance lease are described in 4.3.

Manufacturer or dealer lessors have specific issues with regard to recognition of selling profit and finance income. These are dealt with at 4.4 below.

4.1 Accounting by lessees

4.1.1 Initial recognition

At commencement of the lease, the asset and liability for the future lease payments are recorded in the statement of financial position at the same amount, which is an amount equal to the fair value of the leased asset or the present value of the minimum lease payments, if lower, with initial direct costs of the lessee being added to the asset. [IAS 17.22]. An example of the calculation is given in Example 24.9 at 3.4.9 above.

4.1.2 Allocation of finance costs

The standard requires that lease payments should be apportioned between the finance charge and the reduction of the outstanding liability. The finance charge should be allocated to periods during the lease term so as to produce a constant periodic rate of interest on the remaining balance of the liability for each period. [IAS 17.25].

Example 24.10: Allocation of finance costs

In Example 24.9 above, the present value of the lessee's minimum lease payments (payable at the beginning of each period) was calculated at €9,274 by using the implicit interest rate of 6.62%. The total finance charges of €1,226 (total rentals paid of €10,500 less their present value of €9,274) are allocated over the lease term as follows:

Year	Liability at start of period	Rental paid	Liability during period	Finance charge (6.62% per annum)	Liability at end of period
	€	€	€	€	€
1	9,274	2,100	7,174	475	7,649
2	7,649	2,100	5,549	368	5,917
3	5,917	2,100	3,817	253	4,070
4	4,070	2,100	1,970	130	2,100
5	2,100	2,100	–	–	–
		10,500		1,226	

The standard notes that, in practice, when allocating the finance charge to periods during the lease term some form of approximation may be used to simplify the calculation. *[IAS 17.26]*. However, it provides no guidance as to the methodology that should be applied in allocating finance charges to accounting periods.

Two methods that are used as approximations are the 'sum of the digits' ('rule of 78') or simply taking the finance costs on a straight-line basis over the lease term. The 'sum of digits' method is based on allocating the finance charge based on the cumulative number of payments still outstanding as illustrated in the example below. These are progressively easier to apply but also give progressively less accurate answers. There is, therefore, a trade-off to be made between the costs versus the benefits of achieving complete accuracy, but in making this trade-off, the question of materiality is important. If differences between allocated finance charges under each method are immaterial, the simplest method may be used for convenience. The converse also applies and, of course, a number of individually immaterial differences may in aggregate be material.

The following example illustrates the implicit interest rate and sum of the digits methods of allocating finance charges to accounting periods.

Example 24.11: Sum-of-digits allocation as compared to implicit interest rate

Continuing the lease example from Example 24.9 above, the sum of the digits method calculation is as follows:

Year	Number of rentals not yet due	×	total finance charge / sum of number of rentals	=	Finance charge per annum
					€
1	4	×	€1,226 ÷ 10	=	490
2	3	×	€1,226 ÷ 10	=	368
3	2	×	€1,226 ÷ 10	=	245
4	1	×	€1,226 ÷ 10	=	123
5	–	×	€1,226 ÷ 10	=	–
	10				1,226

We can now compare the finance charges in each of the five years under the implicit interest rate (IIR) as calculated in Example 24.9 and sum of the digits methods:

	Annual finance charge		Annual finance charge as % of total rentals	
	IIR	Sum of the digits	IIR	Sum of the digits
Year	€	€	%	%
1	475	490	39	40
2	368	368	30	30
3	253	245	20	20
4	130	123	11	10
5	–	–	–	–
	1,226	1,226	100	100

As can be seen above, in situations where the lease term is not very long (typically not more than seven years) and interest rates are not very high, the sum of the digits method gives an allocation of finance charges that is close enough to that under the implicit interest rate method to allow the simpler approach to be used.

4.1.3 Recording the liability

The carrying amount of the liability will always be calculated in the same way, by adding the finance charge (however calculated) to the outstanding balance and deducting cash paid. The finance charge depends on the method used to apportion the finance costs. If the IIR method is used, the liability in each of the years, as apportioned between the current and non-current liability, is as follows:

Example 24.12: Lessee's liabilities and interest expense

The entity entering into the lease in Example 24.9 will record the following liabilities and interest expense in its statement of financial position:

Year	Liability at end of period	Current liability at end of period	Non-current liability at end of period	Interest expense (at 6.62%) for the period
	€	€	€	€
1	7,649	2,100	5,549	475
2	5,917	2,100	3,817	368
3	4,070	2,100	1,970	253
4	2,100	2,100	–	130
5	–	–	–	–
				1,226

4.1.4 Accounting for the leased asset

At commencement of the lease, the asset and liability for the future lease payments are recorded in the statement of financial position at the same amount, with initial direct costs of the lessee being added to the asset. *[IAS 17.22]*. These are costs that are directly attributable to the lease and are added to the carrying value, *[IAS 17.24]*, in an analogous way to the treatment of the acquisition costs of property, plant and equipment.

Accounting for the leased asset follows the general rules for accounting for property, plant and equipment or intangible assets. A finance lease gives rise to a depreciation expense for depreciable assets as well as a finance expense for each accounting period. The depreciation policy for depreciable leased assets should be consistent with that for depreciable assets that are owned, and the depreciation recognised should be calculated in accordance with IAS 16 (see Chapter 18) and IAS 38 (see Chapter 17). *[IAS 17.27]*. The useful life is the estimated remaining period, from the commencement of the lease term but without the limitation of the lease term, over which the entity expects to consume the economic benefits embodied in the asset. This is different from the economic life which takes account of the period of time for which the asset is economically usable by one or more users and would therefore include additional lease terms with the same or different lessees. *[IAS 17.4]*. If there is reasonable certainty that the lessee will obtain ownership by the end of the lease term, the period of expected use is the useful life of the asset, otherwise the asset is depreciated over the shorter of its useful life or the lease term. *[IAS 17.28]*. IAS 17 does not address the situation in which an entity expects to extend a lease but it is not reasonably certain at inception that it will do so. In our view, the entity is not precluded from depreciating assets either over the lease term or over the shorter of the asset's useful life and the period for which the entity expects to extend the lease. See also Chapter 18 at 5.4.

Because the interest expense and depreciation must be calculated separately and are unlikely to be the same it is not appropriate simply to treat the lease payments as an expense for the period. *[IAS 17.29]*. This is demonstrated in the following example.

Example 24.13: Lessee's depreciation and interest expense

The entity that has entered into the lease agreement described in Example 24.9 will depreciate the asset (whose initial carrying value, disregarding initial direct costs, is €9,274) on a straight-line basis over five years in accordance with its depreciation policy for owned assets, i.e. an amount of €1,855 per annum. The balances for asset and liability in the financial statements in each of the years 1-5 will be as follows:

Year	Carrying value of asset at end of period	Total liability at end of period	Total charged to income statement*	Lease payments
	€	€	€	€
1	7,419	7,649	2,330	2,100
2	5,564	5,917	2,222	2,100
3	3,709	4,070	2,108	2,100
4	1,855	2,100	1,985	2,100
5	–	–	1,855	2,100
			10,500	10,500

* The total charge combines the annual depreciation of €1,855 and the interest calculated according to the IIR method in Example 24.10, which is in aggregate the initial carrying value of the asset of €9,274 and the total finance charge of €1,226, i.e. the total rent paid of €10,500. Note that this example assumes that the asset is being depreciated to a residual value of zero over the lease term, which is shorter than its useful life, so IAS 16's requirement to reconsider the residual value and useful life at least at each financial year end is unlikely to have an effect. *[IAS 16.51]*.

An entity applies IAS 36 – *Impairment of Assets* – to determine whether the leased asset has become impaired in value (see Chapter 20). *[IAS 17.30]*.

Leased assets may also be revalued using the revaluation model but the entire class of assets (both owned and those held under finance leases) must be revalued. *[IAS 16.36]*. See Chapter 18 at 6.5.

Whilst it is not explicit in IAS 16, in our view, to obtain the fair value of an asset held under a finance lease for financial reporting purposes, the assessed value must be adjusted to take account of any recognised finance lease liability. The mechanism for achieving this, which is mainly an issue for investment properties, is set out in detail in Chapter 19 at 6.7.

4.2 Accounting by lessors

Under a finance lease, a lessor retains legal title to an asset but passes substantially all the risks and rewards of ownership to the lessee in return for a stream of rentals. In substance, therefore, the lessor provides finance and expects a return thereon.

The standard requires lessors to recognise assets held under a finance lease in their statement of financial position as a receivable at an amount equal to the net investment in the lease. *[IAS 17.36]*. The lease payments received from the lessee are treated as repayments of principal and finance income. *[IAS 17.37]*. Initial direct costs may include commissions, legal fees and internal costs that are incremental and directly attributable to negotiating and arranging the lease. Incremental costs are those that would not have been incurred if the entity had not negotiated and arranged a lease (see 3.4.8 above). They do not include general overheads such as the costs of the sales and marketing departments, including the employees' fixed salaries. They are included in the measurement of the net investment in the lease at inception and reflected in the calculation of the implicit interest rate, except for manufacturers and dealers (see 4.4 below). *[IAS 17.38]*.

The recognition of finance income should be based on a pattern reflecting a constant periodic rate of return on the lessor's net investment outstanding in respect of the finance lease. *[IAS 17.39]*.

4.2.1 The lessor's net investment in the lease

The lessor's gross investment in the lease is the aggregate of the minimum lease payments receivable by the lessor under a finance lease and any guaranteed and unguaranteed residual value to which the lessor is entitled. The net investment in the lease is the gross investment discounted at the interest rate implicit in the lease, *[IAS 17.4]*, i.e. at any point in time it comprises the gross investment after deducting gross earnings allocated to future periods.

The lessor's gross investment is, therefore, the same as the aggregate figures used to calculate the implicit interest rate and the net investment is the present value of those same figures – see 3.4.9 and Example 24.9 above.

Therefore, at inception, the lessor's net investment in the lease is the cost of the asset as increased by its initial direct costs. The difference between the net and gross investments is the gross finance income to be allocated over the lease term. Example 24.14 below illustrates this point.

4.2.2 Allocation of finance income

The lessor recognises finance income based on a pattern reflecting a constant periodic rate of return on the lessor's net investment outstanding in respect of the finance lease. *[IAS 17.39]*. Lease payments, excluding costs for services, are applied against the gross investment in the lease to reduce both the principal and the unearned finance income. *[IAS 17.40]*. The standard does not refer to the use of approximations by lessors and, accordingly, the alternative methods described in 4.1.2 above should not be used unless the differences are clearly immaterial.

Example 24.9 at 3.4.9 above can be examined from the lessor's perspective:

Example 24.14: The lessor's gross and net investment in the lease

The lease has the same facts as described in Example 24.9, i.e. the asset has a fair value of €10,000, the lessee is making five annual rentals payable in advance of €2,100 and the total unguaranteed estimated residual value at the end of five years is estimated to be €1,000. The lessor's direct costs have been excluded for simplicity.

The lessor's gross investment in the lease is the total rents receivable of €10,500 and the unguaranteed residual value of €1,000. The gross earnings are therefore €1,500. The initial carrying value of the receivable is its fair value of €10,000, which is also the present value of the gross investment discounted at the interest rate implicit in the lease of 6.62%.

Year	Receivable at start of period €	Rental received €	Finance income (6.62% per annum) €	Gross investment at end of period €	Gross earnings allocated to future periods €	Receivable at end of period €
1	10,000	2,100	523	9,400	977	8,423
2	8,423	2,100	419	7,300	558	6,742
3	6,742	2,100	307	5,200	251	4,949
4	4,949	2,100	189	3,100	62	3,038
5	3,038	2,100	62	1,000	–	1,000
		10,500	1,500			

The gross investment in the lease at any point in time comprises the aggregate of the rentals receivable in future periods and the unguaranteed residual value, e.g. at the end of year 2, the gross investment of €7,300 is three years' rental of €2,100 plus the unguaranteed residual of €1,000. The net investment, which is the amount at which the debtor will be recorded in the statement of financial position, is €7,300 less the earnings allocated to future periods of €558 = €6,742.

4.2.3 *Residual values*

Residual values have to be taken into account in assessing whether a lease is a finance or operating lease as well as affecting the calculation of the IIR and finance income.

- Unguaranteed residual values have to be estimated in order to calculate the IIR and finance income receivable under a finance lease. Any impairment in the residual must be taken into account; this is illustrated in 4.2.3.A below.
- Residual values can be guaranteed by the lessee or by a third party. The effects of third party guarantees on risks and rewards are described in 3.4.6.A above.
- The terms of a lease guarantee can affect the assessment of the risks and rewards in the arrangement as in the example in 3.2.2.A above.
- A common form of lease requires the asset to be sold at the end of the lease term. The disposition of the proceeds has to be taken into account in assessing who bears residual risk, as described in 3.2.2.B above.

4.2.3.A Unguaranteed residual values

Income recognition by lessors can be extremely sensitive to the amount recognised as the asset's residual value. This is because the amount of the residual directly affects the computation of the amount of finance income earned over the lease term – this is illustrated in Example 24.15 below. The standard gives no guidance regarding the estimation of unguaranteed residual values but it does require them to be reviewed regularly. If there has been a reduction in the estimated value, the income allocation over the lease term is revised and any reduction in respect of amounts accrued is recognised immediately. *[IAS 17.41]*.

Example 24.15: Reduction in residual value

Taking the same facts as used in Example 24.14 above, the lessor concludes at the end of year 2 that the residual value of the asset is only €500 and revises the income allocation over the lease term accordingly. It continues to apply the same implicit interest rate, 6.62%, as before.

Year	Receivable at start of period €	Rental received €	Finance income (6.62% per annum) €	Gross investment at end of period* €	Gross earnings allocated to future periods €	Receivable at end of period €
2	8,423	2,100	419	6,800	471	6,329
3	6,329	2,100	280	4,700	191	4,509
4	4,509	2,100	160	2,600	31	2,569
5	2,569	2,100	31	500	–	500

* The gross investment in the lease now takes account of the revised unguaranteed residual of €500, rather than the original €1,000.

The lessor will have to write off €413, being the difference between the carrying amount of the receivable as previously calculated in Example 24.14 and the revised balance above (€6,742 – €6,329). This is the present value as at the end of year 2 of €500 and represents the part of the unguaranteed residual written off.

Impairment of lease receivables is within the scope of IAS 39, *[IAS 39.2(b)]*, and this methodology is required by IAS 39 paragraph 63, *[IAS 39.63]*, described in 4.3.2.A below.

4.2.4 Disposals by lessors of assets held under finance leases – measurement

If a lessor is to dispose of an asset under a finance lease that is classified as held for sale, or is included in a disposal group that is so classified, it is to apply the requirements of IFRS 5 – *Non-current Assets Held for Sale and Discontinued Operations* – to the disposal. *[IAS 17.41A]*. The 'asset under a finance lease' is the receivable from the lessee, which is not a financial asset under IAS 39; see 3.5 above for an analysis of the extent to which assets and liabilities under leases are within scope of that standard. This means that measurement as well as classification of the asset under the finance lease is within scope of IFRS 5, unlike financial assets within scope of IAS 39 that are subject only to its classification rules. Once classified as held for sale, it must be measured at the lower of carrying amount and fair value less costs to sell. Any residual interest in the leased asset once the lease has ended and the asset is returned to the lessor would be accounted for under IAS 16 or IAS 38, and is clearly within scope of IFRS 5. The requirements of IFRS 5 are dealt with in Chapter 4.

4.3 Termination of finance leases

The expectations of lessors and lessees regarding the timing of termination of a lease may affect the classification of a lease as either operating or finance. This is because it will affect the expected lease term, level of payments under the lease and expected residual value of the lease assets.

Termination during the primary lease term will generally not be anticipated at the lease inception because the lessee can be assumed to be using the asset for at least that period. In addition, early termination will be unlikely because most leases are non-cancellable. A termination payment is usually required which will give the lessor an amount equivalent to most or all of the rental receipts which would have been received if no termination had taken place, which means that it is reasonably certain at inception that the lease will continue to expiry.

However, there are consequences if the lease is terminated. The issues for finance lessees and lessors are discussed in the following sections.

4.3.1 Termination of finance leases by lessees

Finance lease payables recognised by a lessee are subject to the derecognition provisions of IAS 39 (or IFRS 9, should the entity apply that standard). *[IAS 39.2(b)]*.

IAS 39 requires an entity to derecognise (i.e. remove from its statement of financial position) a financial liability (or a part of a financial liability) when, and only when, it is 'extinguished', that is, when the obligation specified in the contract is discharged, cancelled, or expires. *[IAS 39.39]*. This will be achieved when the debtor either:

- discharges the liability (or part of it) by paying the creditor, normally with cash, other financial assets, goods or services; or
- is legally released from primary responsibility for the liability (or part of it) either by process of law or by the creditor. *[IAS 39.AG57]*.

The difference between the carrying amount of a financial liability (or part of a financial liability) extinguished or transferred to another party and the consideration paid, including any non-cash assets transferred or liabilities assumed, is recognised in profit or loss.

In order to identify the part of a liability derecognised, an entity allocates the previous carrying amount of the financial liability between the part that continues to be recognised and the part that is derecognised based on the relative fair values of those parts on the date of the repurchase. *[IAS 39.41-42]*. Derecognition of part of a lease liability will most likely come about in the context of a lease renegotiation, discussed at 6 below.

The derecognition of financial liabilities under IAS 39 (or IFRS 9) is dealt with in Chapter 51.

4.3.1.A Early termination by lessees

Except as part of a renegotiation or business combination or similar larger arrangement, early termination of a finance lease results in derecognition of the capitalised asset by the lessee, with any remaining balance of the capitalised asset being written off as a loss on disposal. Any payment made by the lessee will reduce the lease obligation that is being carried in the statement of financial position. If either a part of this obligation is not eliminated or the termination payment exceeds the previously existing obligation, then the remainder or excess will be included as a gain or loss respectively on derecognition of a financial liability.

A similar accounting treatment is required where the lease terminates at the expected date and there is a residual at least partly guaranteed by the lessee. For the lessee, a payment made under such a guarantee will reduce the obligation to the lessor as the guaranteed residual would obviously be included in the lessee's finance lease obligation.

If any part of the guaranteed residual is not called on, then the lessee would treat this as a profit on derecognition of a financial liability.

The effect on the derecognition of the capitalised asset will depend on the extent to which the lessee expected to make the residual payment as this will have affected the level to which the capitalised asset has been depreciated. For example, if the total guaranteed residual was not expected to become payable by the lessee, then the depreciation charge may have been calculated to give a net book value at the end of the lease term equal to the residual element not expected to become payable. If this estimate was correct then the remaining obligation will equal the net book value of the relevant asset, so that the gain on derecognition of the liability will be equal to the loss on derecognition of the asset.

Example 24.16: Early termination of finance leases by lessees

In Example 24.5 above there is effectively a guarantee of a residual of €3,000 dependent on the mileage driven by the leased vehicle. Assuming the lease is capitalised as a finance lease, if the lessee considered, at the lease inception, that the guarantee will not be called on, the vehicle will be depreciated to an estimated residual value of €3,000 over the lease term. In the event that this estimate is found to be correct, the loss on disposal of the asset at its written down value will be equal and opposite to the gain on derecognition of the lease obligation of €3,000. However, if, for example, €1,000 of the guarantee was called on, then the net book value of €3,000 (which assumes that the lessee had not previously adjusted the residual value of the leased asset for depreciation purposes, nor impaired the leased asset) and the unused guarantee of €2,000 will both be derecognised. As a result, a loss of €1,000 will be recorded on disposal of the vehicle.

4.3.2 Termination and impairment of finance leases by lessors

Although lease receivables are not financial instruments within scope of IAS 39 (or IFRS 9, if applied), the carrying amounts recognised by a lessor are subject to the derecognition and impairment provisions of those standards. Generally, a financial asset is derecognised when the contractual rights to the cash flows from that asset have expired. *[IAS 39.17]*. This will apply to most leases at the end of the term when the lessor has no more right to cash flows from the lessee.

If the cash flows from the financial asset have not expired, it is derecognised when, and only when, the entity 'transfers' the asset within the specified meaning of the term in IAS 39, and the transfer has the effect that the entity has either:

(a) transferred substantially all the risks and rewards of the asset; or

(b) neither transferred nor retained substantially all the risks and rewards of the asset and has not retained control of the asset. *[IAS 39.20]*. If the rights to the cash are retained then there are other tests that must be met. *[IAS 39.19]*.

These requirements are relevant to common lease situations such as sub-leases and back-to-back leases, dealt with in 8 below. Derecognition of financial assets is a complex area discussed in Chapter 51 at 3.

4.3.2.A Impairment of lease receivables

If a lease receivable is impaired, for example, because the lessee is in default of lease payments, the amount of the impairment is measured as the difference between the carrying value of the receivable and the present value of the estimated future cash flows, discounted at the implicit interest rate used on initial recognition. Therefore, if the lessor makes an arrangement with the lessee and reschedules and/or reduces amounts due under the lease, the loss is by reference to the new carrying amount of the receivable, calculated by discounting the estimated future cash flows at the original implicit interest rate. *[IAS 39.63]*. This methodology has been used in Example 24.15 at 4.2.3.A above.

4.3.2.B Early termination of finance leases for lessors

Any termination payment received by a lessor on an early termination will reduce the lessor's net investment in the lease shown as a receivable. The recognition of a gain or loss on early termination will depend upon the amount of termination payment received, and the value of the leased asset returned to the lessor on termination of the lease. If the sum of the termination payment and value of asset returned is greater than the carrying amount of the net investment, the lessor will account for a gain on derecognition of the lease; conversely, if the sum of the termination payment and the value of the leased asset returned is smaller than the net investment, a loss will be shown. If the leased asset is retained by the lessee on early termination of the lease, the gain or loss recognised by the lessor will depend upon whether the termination payments is greater or smaller than the net investment in the lease.

Losses on termination in the ordinary course of business are less likely to arise because a finance lease usually has termination terms so that the lessor is compensated fully for early termination and the lessor has legal title to the asset. The lessor can continue to include the asset in current assets as a receivable to the extent that sales proceeds or new finance lease receivables are expected to arise. If the asset is then re-leased under an operating lease, the asset may be transferred to property, plant and equipment (PP&E) and depreciated over its remaining useful life. There is no guidance about the amount at which the asset is recognised in PP&E. Although the net investment (i.e. the lease receivable recognised by the lessor) is not a financial instrument within scope of IAS 39, *[IAS 39.2(b)]*, in general we expect that entities would use the carrying amount of the net investment as the cost of the reacquired item of PP&E. However, in the absence of authoritative guidance we would expect there to be divergence in practice. If the asset is designated as held for sale then the requirements of IFRS 5 will apply (see Chapter 4). The aspects of lease assets and liabilities that are within scope of IAS 39 are described at 3.5 above.

4.4 Manufacturer or dealer lessors

Manufacturers or dealers often offer customers the choice of either buying or leasing an asset. While there is no selling profit on entering into an operating lease because it is not the equivalent of a sale, *[IAS 17.55]*, a finance lease of an asset by a manufacturer or dealer lessor gives rise to two types of income:

(a) the profit or loss equivalent to the profit or loss resulting from an outright sale of the asset being leased, at normal selling prices, reflecting any applicable volume or trade discounts; and

(b) the finance income over the lease term. *[IAS 17.43]*.

If the customer is offered the choice of paying the cash price for the asset immediately or paying for it on deferred credit terms then, as long as the credit terms are the manufacturer or dealer's normal terms, the cash price (after taking account of applicable or volume discounts) can be used to determine the selling profit. *[IAS 17.42]*. However, in many cases such an approach should not be followed as the manufacturer or dealer's marketing considerations often influence the terms of the lease. For example, a car dealer may offer 0% finance deals instead of reducing the normal selling price of his cars. It would be inappropriate in this instance for the dealer to record a profit on the sale of the car and no finance income under the lease.

The standard, therefore, requires sales revenue to be based on the fair value of the asset (i.e. the cash price) or, if lower, the present value of the minimum lease payments computed at a market rate of interest. As a result, if artificially low rates of interest are quoted, selling profit is restricted to that which would apply if a commercial rate of interest were charged. *[IAS 17.44-45]*. The cost of sales is reduced to the extent that the lessor retains an unguaranteed residual interest in the asset. *[IAS 17.44]*.

Initial direct costs should be recognised as an expense in the income statement at the inception of the lease. This is not the same as the treatment when a lessor arranges a finance lease where the costs are added to the finance lease receivable; the standard argues that this is because the costs are related mainly to earning the selling profit. *[IAS 17.46]*. If the manufacturer or dealer is in the position of incurring an overall loss because the total rentals receivable under the finance lease are less than the cost to it of the asset then, this loss should be taken to profit or loss at the inception of the lease. IAS 17 assumes that the manufacturer or dealer will have a normal implicit interest rate based on its other leasing activity. However, in other situations where the manufacturer or dealer does not conduct other leasing business, an estimate will have to be made of the implicit rate for the leasing activity.

Example 24.17: Manufacturer or dealer lessors

A company manufactures specialised machinery. The company offers customers the choice of either buying or leasing the machinery. A customer chooses to lease the machinery. Details of the arrangement are as follows:

(i) The lease commences on 1 January 20X1 and lasts for three years.

(ii) The lessee makes three annual rentals payable in arrears of €57,500.

(iii) The leased machinery is returned to the lessor at the end of the lease.

(iv) Fair value of the machinery is €150,000, which is equivalent to the selling price of the machinery.

(v) The machinery cost €100,000 to manufacture. The lessor incurred costs of €2,500 to negotiate and arrange the lease.

(vi) The expected useful life of the machinery is 3 years. The machinery has an expected residual value of €10,000 at the end of year three. The estimated residual value does not change over the term of the lease.

(vii) The interest rate implicit in the lease is 10.19%.

The lessor classifies the lease as a finance lease.

The cost to the lessor of providing the machinery for lease consists of the book cost of the machinery (€100,000), plus the initial direct costs associated with entering into the lease (€2,500), less the future income expected from disposing of the machinery at the end of the lease (the present value of the unguaranteed residual value of €10,000, being €7,475). This gives a cost of sale of €95,025.

The lessor records the following entries at the commencement of the lease:

	Debit €	Credit €
Lease receivable	150,000	
Cost of sales	95,025	
Inventory		100,000
Revenue		142,525
Creditors / cash (initial direct costs)		2,500

The sales profit recognised by the lessor at the commencement of the lease is therefore €47,500 (€142,525 – €95,025). This is equal to the fair value of the machinery of €150,000, less the book value of the machinery (€100,000) and the initial direct costs of entering into the lease (€2,500). Revenue is equal to the lease receivable (€150,000), less the present value of the unguaranteed residual value (€7,475).

Lease payments received from the lessee will then be allocated over the lease term as follows:

Year	Lease receivable at the start of the year (€) (a)	Lease payments (€) (b)	Interest income (10.19% per annum) (€) (c)	Decrease in lease receivable (€) (d)=(b)–(c)	Lease receivable at the end of the year (€) (e)=(a)–(d)
1	150,000	57,500	15,280	42,220	107,780
2	107,780	57,500	10,979	46,521	61,260
3	61,260	57,500	6,240	51,260	10,000

The lessor will record the following entries:

		Debit €	Credit €
Year 1	Cash	57,500	
	Lease receivable		42,220
	Interest income		15,280
Year 2	Cash	57,500	
	Lease receivable		46,521
	Interest income		10,979
Year 3	Cash	57,500	
	Lease receivable		51,260
	Interest income		6,240

At the end of the three year lease term, the leased machinery will be returned to the lessor, who will record the following entries:

	Debit €	Credit €
Inventory	10,000	
Lease receivable		10,000

5 ACCOUNTING FOR OPERATING LEASES

5.1 Operating leases in the financial statements of lessees

IAS 17 requires lease payments under an operating lease, excluding costs for services such as insurance and maintenance, to be recognised as an expense on a straight-line basis over the lease term unless another systematic basis is representative of the time pattern of the user's benefit, even if the payments are not on that basis. *[IAS 17.33, 34]*. Generally, the only other acceptable bases are where rentals are based on a unit of use or unit of production.

IAS 17 requires a straight-line recognition of the lease expenses even when amounts are not payable on this basis. This does not require the entity to anticipate contingent rental increases, such as those that will result from a periodic re-pricing to market rates or those that are based on some other index (see 3.4.7 above). However, lease payments may vary over time for other reasons that will have to be taken into account in calculating the annual charge. Described in more detail below are some examples: leases that are inclusive of services, leases with increments intended to substitute for inflation and security deposits made with lessors that attract low or no interest. Lease incentives are another feature that may affect the cash flows under a lease; they are dealt with in more detail in 5.1.4 (for lessees) and 5.2.2 (for lessors) below. Operating leases often contain clauses which specify that the lessee should incur periodic charges for maintenance, make good dilapidations or other damage occurring during the rental period or return the asset to the configuration that existed as at inception of the lease. The accounting for these obligations is addressed in Chapter 28 at 6.9.

5.1.1 Leases that include payments for services

There is a wide range of services that can be subsumed into a single 'lease' payment. For a vehicle, the payment may include maintenance and servicing. Property leases could include cleaning, security, reception services, gardening, utilities and local and property taxes. Single payments for operating facilities may include lease payments for the plant and the costs of operating them, as discussed in the context of IFRIC 4; see Example 24.1 at 2.1.3 above. IAS 17 says in the definition of minimum lease payments that the costs of services should be excluded to arrive at the lease payments. *[IAS 17.4]*. This is straightforward enough if the payments are made by the lessor and quantified in the payments made by the lessee. It will be somewhat less so if, for example, the lessor makes all maintenance payments but does not specify the amounts; instead, payments are increased periodically to take account of changes in such costs. In such a case the lessee will have to estimate the amount paid for services and deduct them from the total. The remaining payments, which relate solely to the right to use the asset, will then be spread on a straight-line basis over the non-cancellable term of the lease.

5.1.2 Straight-line recognition over the lease term

Operating lease payments must be recognised on a straight-line basis over the lease term, unless another systematic basis is more representative of the time pattern of the user's benefit. *[IAS 17.33]*. There are some lease payments that increase annually by fixed increments intended to compensate for expected annual inflation over the lease period.

In considering the issue, the Interpretations Committee noted that IAS 17 does not incorporate adjustments to operating lease payments to reflect the time value of money. Except in those cases where another basis is more appropriate, it requires all operating leases to be taken on a straight-line basis. They concluded that to allow recognition of these increases on an annual basis would be inconsistent with the treatment of other operating leases.[9]

Some leases allow for an annual increase in line with an index but with a fixed minimum increment. As discussed in 3.4.7 above, contingent rents are excluded from the lease payments but the fixed minimum increment will have to be spread so as to take the payments on a straight-line basis over the lease term.

Example 24.18: Operating lease expenses with fixed annual increment

Entity A leases a property at an initial rent of €1,000,000 per annum. The lease has a non-cancellable term of 30 years and rent increases annually in line with the Retail Prices Index (RPI) of the country in which the property is situated but with a minimum increase of 2.5% (the estimated long-term rate of inflation in the country in question) and a maximum of 5% per annum.

The annual increase of 2.5% must be taken into account in calculating the operating lease payment charged to profit or loss. On a straight-line basis this will be €1,463,000 per annum. Therefore, by the end of year 15 (at which point the amounts payable under the lease will exceed the straight-lined amount) the entity will have paid rentals of €15 million, charged €22 million to income and will be recording an accrual of €7 million.

If the increase in the RPI exceeds 2.5% these additional amounts will be charged to income as contingent rents.

5.1.3 Notional or actual interest paid to lessors

Lessees are sometimes required to place security deposits with lessors that are refunded at termination to the extent that they have not been utilised by the lessor. Lessees often receive either no or a reduced rate of interest on such deposits. In accordance with IAS 39, the lessee initially measures the deposit at fair value and subsequently at amortised cost (assuming that the deposit is classified as a loan and receivable *[IAS 39.46]*) using the effective interest method; accordingly interest income is recognised through profit and loss over the useful life of the deposit. *[IAS 39.9]*. At inception of an operating lease, the difference between the nominal value of the deposit and its fair value should be considered additional rent payable to the lessor. This will be expensed on a straight-line basis over the lease term.

Example 24.19: Operating lease expenses reflecting interest payments to the lessor

A lessee makes an interest-free security deposit of €1,000 on entering into a five year lease. It assesses an appropriate rate of interest for the deposit to be 4% and accordingly the fair value of the deposit at inception is €822. On making the deposit, it will record it as follows:

Year		€	€
1	Security deposit	822	
	Advance rentals	178	
	Cash		1,000

During the five years of the lease, it will record interest income and additional rental expense as follows:

Year	Interest income	Rental expense	Difference
1	33	(36)	(3)
2	34	(35)	(1)
3	36	(36)	–
4	37	(36)	1
5	38	(35)	3
	178	(178)	

5.1.4 Lease incentives – accounting by lessees

Incentives that may be given by a lessor to a lessee to enter into a new or renewed operating lease agreement include an up-front cash payment to the lessee or the reimbursement or assumption by the lessor of costs of the lessee, such as relocation costs, leasehold improvements and costs associated with a pre-existing lease commitment of the lessee. Alternatively, the lessor may grant the lessee rent-free or reduced rent initial lease periods. *[SIC-15.1]*.

The consensus reached by the SIC in Interpretation SIC-15 – *Operating Leases – Incentives* – was that all incentives for the agreement of a new or renewed operating lease should be recognised as an integral part of the net consideration agreed for the use of the leased asset, irrespective of the incentive's nature or form or the timing of payments. *[SIC-15.3]*. The lessee should recognise the aggregate benefit of incentives as a reduction of rental expense over the lease term, on a straight-line basis unless another systematic basis is representative of the time pattern of the lessee's benefit from the use of the leased asset. *[SIC-15.5]*. Finally, SIC-15 requires costs incurred by the lessee, including costs in connection with a pre-existing lease (for example, costs for termination, relocation or leasehold improvements), to be accounted for by the lessee in accordance with the IAS applicable to those costs, including costs which are effectively reimbursed through an incentive arrangement. *[SIC-15.6]*.

The following two examples, based on those in the Illustrative Examples to SIC-15, illustrate how to apply the Interpretation:

Example 24.20: Accounting for lease incentives under SIC-15

Example 1

An entity agrees to enter into a new lease arrangement with a new lessor. As an incentive for entering into the new lease, the lessor agrees to pay the lessee's relocation costs. The lessee's moving costs are €1,000. The new lease has a term of 10 years, at a fixed rate of €2,000 per year.

The lessee recognises relocation costs of €1,000 as an expense in Year 1. Both the lessor and lessee would recognise the net rental consideration of €19,000 (€2,000 for each of the 10 years in the lease term, less the €1,000 incentive) over the 10 year lease term using a single amortisation method in accordance with SIC-15. *[SIC-15.4, 5]*.

Example 2

An entity agrees to enter into a new lease arrangement with a new lessor. The lessor agrees to a rent-free period for the first three years. The new lease has a term of 20 years, at a fixed rate of $5,000 per annum for years 4 through 20.

Net consideration of $85,000 consists of $5,000 for each of 17 years in the lease term. Both the lessor and lessee would recognise the net consideration of $85,000 over the 20-year lease term using a single amortisation method. *[SIC-15.4, 5]*.

One point about SIC-15 that has attracted considerable debate is its requirement to spread incentives over the lease term. The validity of this has been questioned if rentals are re-priced to market rates at periodic intervals. It is argued that in these circumstances the rent-free period is being given solely to compensate for an above-market rental in the primary period.

The Interpretations Committee rejected this view in August 2005. It did not accept that the lease expense of a lessee after an operating lease is re-priced to market ought to be comparable with the lease expense of an entity entering into a new lease at that same time at market rates. Nor did it believe that the re-pricing itself would be reflective of a change in the time patterns of the lessee's benefit from the use of the leased asset. In other words, incentives are seen in the context of the total cash flows under the lease and, except where the benefit of the lease is not directly related to the time during which the entity has the right to use the asset, IAS 17 requires these to be taken on a straight-line basis.

There is a similar argument when lessees assert that they should not be obliged to spread rentals over a void period as they are not actually benefiting from the property during this time – it is a fit-out period or a start-up so activities are yet to increase to anticipated levels. However, the argument against this is no different to the above: the lessee's period of benefit from the use of the asset is the lease term, so the rentals should be spread over the lease term, including the void period. This was reinforced by the Interpretations Committee in September 2008, when it noted that IAS 16 and IAS 38 require an entity to recognise the use of productive assets using the method that best reflects 'the pattern in which the asset's future economic benefits are expected to be consumed by the entity', *[IAS 16.60, IAS 38.97]*, but IAS 17 refers to the time pattern of the user's benefit. *[IAS 17.33]*. Therefore, any alternative to the straight-line recognition of lease expense under an operating lease must reflect the time pattern of the use of the leased property rather than the amount of use or other factor related to economic benefits. The Interpretations Committee has not shown any indication that it is prepared to accept economic arguments for other than straight-line treatment.

5.1.5 Onerous contracts

IAS 37 prohibits the recognition of provisions for future operating losses, *[IAS 37.63]*, but the standard specifically addresses the issue of onerous contracts. It requires that if an entity has a contract that is onerous, the present obligation under the contract should be recognised and measured as a provision. *[IAS 37.66]*.

The standard defines an onerous contract as 'a contract in which the unavoidable costs of meeting the obligations under it exceed the economic benefits expected to be received under it'. *[IAS 37.10]*. This is taken to mean that the contract itself is onerous to the point of being directly loss-making, not simply uneconomic by reference to current prices. A common example of an onerous contract seen in practice relates to operating leases for the rent of property, and the standard includes the following example: *[IAS 37 IE Example 8]*

Example 24.21: An onerous contract

An entity operates profitably from a factory that it has leased under an operating lease. During December 20X0 the entity relocates its operations to a new factory. The lease on the old factory continues for the next four years, it cannot be cancelled and the factory cannot be re-let to another user.

Present obligation as a result of a past obligating event	The obligating event is the signing of the lease contract, which gives rise to a legal obligation.
Transfer of economic benefits in settlement	When the lease becomes onerous, a transfer of economic benefits is probable. Until then, the entity accounts for the lease by applying IAS 17.
Conclusion	A provision is recognised for the best estimate of the unavoidable lease payments. *[IAS 37.5(c), 14, 66]*.

Care must be taken to ensure that the lease itself is onerous. If an entity has a number of retail outlets and one of these is loss-making, this is not sufficient to make the lease onerous. However, if the entity vacates the premises and could reasonably sub-let them only at an amount less than the rent it is paying, then the lease becomes onerous and the entity should provide for its best estimate of the unavoidable lease payments. The unavoidable costs of the lease will be the remaining lease commitment reduced by the estimated sub-lease rentals that the entity could reasonably obtain, regardless of whether or not the entity intends to enter into a sublease. One company which has provided for onerous leases is Wm Morrison Supermarkets, as indicated by the following extract.

Extract 24.4: Wm Morrison Supermarkets PLC (2014)

Notes to the Group financial statements [extract]

5.5 Provisions [extract]

Part of onerous leases relate to sublet and vacant properties, with commitments ranging from one to 58 years. The provision is revised regularly in response to market conditions. During the year, £118m has been charged to onerous lease provisions in respect of the impairment detailed in note 1.4. The utilisation of onerous lease provisions this year mostly relates to the assignment of Kiddicare leases.

Accounting for onerous contracts is discussed in more detail in Chapter 28 at 6.2.

5.2 Operating leases in the financial statements of lessors

5.2.1 Accounting for assets subject to operating leases

Lessors should present assets subject to operating leases in their statement of financial position according to the nature of the asset, i.e. usually as PP&E or as an intangible asset. Lease income from operating leases should be recognised in income on a straight-line basis over the lease term, unless another systematic basis is more representative of the time pattern in which, the standard states, 'use benefit derived from the leased asset is diminished'. *[IAS 17.49, 50]*. Generally, the only other basis that is encountered is based on unit-of-production or service.

Lease income excludes receipts for services provided such as insurance and maintenance. IAS 18 – *Revenue* – provides guidance on how to recognise service revenue – see Chapter 29 at 3.8. Costs, including depreciation, incurred in earning the lease income are recognised as an expense. *[IAS 17.51]*. Initial direct costs incurred specifically to earn revenues from an operating lease are added to the carrying amount of the leased asset and allocated to income over the lease term in proportion to the recognition of lease income. *[IAS 17.52]*. This means that the costs will be depreciated on a straight-line basis if this is the method of recognising the lease income, regardless of the depreciation basis of the asset.

The depreciation policy for depreciable leased assets is to be consistent with the entity's policy for similar assets that are not subject to leasing arrangements and calculated in accordance with IAS 16 or IAS 38, as appropriate. *[IAS 17.53]*. If the lessor does not use similar assets in its business then the depreciation policy must be set solely by reference to IAS 16 and IAS 38. This also means that the lessor is obliged in accordance with IAS 16 to consider the residual value and economic life of the assets at least at each financial year-end. *[IAS 16.51]*. There are similar requirements in the case of intangible assets, although IAS 38 notes that they rarely have a residual value. *[IAS 38.100]*. These matters are discussed in Chapters 17 and 18. These assets are also tested for impairment in a manner consistent with other tangible and intangible fixed assets; IAS 17 refers to IAS 36 (discussed in Chapter 20) in providing guidance on the need to assess the possibility of an impairment of assets. *[IAS 17.54]*.

5.2.2 *Lease incentives – accounting by lessors*

In negotiating a new or renewed operating lease, a lessor may provide incentives for the lessee to enter into the arrangement. In the case of a property lease, the tenant may be given a rent-free period but other types of incentive include up-front cash payments to the lessee or the reimbursement or assumption by the lessor of lessee costs such as relocation costs, leasehold improvements and costs associated with a pre-existing lease commitment of the lessee. SIC-15 states that the lessor should recognise the aggregate cost of incentives as a reduction of rental income over the lease term, on a straight-line basis unless another systematic basis is representative of the time pattern over which the benefit of the leased asset is diminished. *[SIC-15.4]*. The SIC rejected the argument that lease incentives for lessors are part of the initial direct costs of negotiating or arranging the contract; instead concluding that they are in substance, related to the amount of consideration received by the lessor for the use of the asset. This view was confirmed in the IASB's 2003 revision of IAS 17, which requires initial direct costs to be capitalised as part of the carrying value of the asset – see 3.4.8 above. Lessor accounting is, therefore, the mirror image of lessee accounting for the incentives, as described in 5.1.4 above.

5.3 Payments made in connection with the termination of operating leases

Payments for terminating operating leases or payments between a lessee and a third party regarding a lease are common but not all are directly addressed by either IAS 17 or SIC-15. In addition, neither statement addresses payments made between a lessee and a third party in connection with a lease. The following example addresses a variety of payments that might arise in connection with terminating an operating lease over a property:

Example 24.22: Payments made in connection with terminating an operating lease

	Treatment in the financial statements of		
Transaction	*Lessor*	*Old tenant*	*New tenant*
Lessor pays			
Old tenant – lessor intends to renovate the building.	Expense immediately, or Capitalise as part of the carrying amount of the leased asset if the payment meets the definition of construction costs in IAS 16 (note 1)	Recognise income immediately (note 1)	
Old tenant – new lease with higher quality tenant	Expense immediately (note 1)	Recognise income immediately (note 1)	
New tenant – an incentive to occupy	Prepayment amortised over the lease term on a straight-line basis under SIC-15 (see 5.2.2 above)		Deferred lease incentive amortised over the lease term on a straight-line basis under SIC-15 (see 5.1.4 above).
Building alterations specific to the tenant with no further value to the lessor after completion of the lease period.	Prepayment amortised over the lease term on a straight-line basis under SIC-15 (see 5.2.2 above)		Leasehold improvements capitalised and depreciated. Deferred lease incentive amortised over the lease term on a straight-line basis under SIC-15 (see 5.1.4 above).

Transaction	*Lessor*	*Old tenant*	*New tenant*
Old tenant pays			
Lessor, to vacate the leased premises early	Recognised as income immediately to the extent not already recognised (note 2)	Recognised as expense immediately to the extent not already recognised (note 2)	
New tenant to take over the lease		Recognise as an expense immediately (note 3)	Recognise as income immediately, unless compensation for above market rentals, in which case amortise over expected lease term (note 3)
New tenant pays			
Lessor to secure the right to obtain a lease agreement	Recognise as deferred revenue under IAS 17 and amortise over the lease term on a straight-line basis (see 5.2.1 above)		Recognise as a prepayment under IAS 17 and amortise over the lease term on a straight-line basis (see 5.1.2 above).
Old tenant to buy out the lease agreement		Recognise as a gain immediately (note 4)	Recognised as an intangible asset with a finite economic life (note 4)

Note 1 A payment by a lessor to a lessee to terminate the lease is not dealt with under IAS 17 or SIC-15. If the lessor's payment meets the definition of a cost of an item of PP&E, which might be the case if the lessor intends to renovate, it must be capitalised. *[IAS 16.7]*. If not, the payment will be expensed, as it does not meet the definition of an intangible asset in IAS 38. *[IAS 38.8]*. A payment by a lessor to a lessee to terminate the lease in order to re-let it to another tenant does not meet the definition of initial direct costs for arranging a new lease. *[IAS 17.4]*. This is because the cost is incurred in relation to the lease with the old tenant, and is not directly related to the new lease, even if the new lease has been entered into. As the lessee has no further performance obligation the receipt should be income.

Note 2 A payment made by the lessee to the lessor to get out of a lease agreement does not meet the appropriate definitions of an asset in IAS 16 or IAS 38 and does not fall within IAS 17 as there is no longer a lease – the payments are not for the use of the asset. Therefore it should be expensed. Similarly, from the lessor's perspective, income should be recorded. However, if the payment to the lessor to vacate the premises was already stipulated in the original lease contract and the payment was assessed as probable during the life of the contract, both the lessee and lessor would have accrued this over the lease term in accordance with the principles of IAS 17.

Note 3 A payment made by an existing tenant to a new tenant to take over the lease would also not meet the definition of an asset under IAS 16 or IAS 38 (see notes above) and falls outside IAS 17 as the lease no longer exists. The old tenant must expense the cost. The new tenant will recognise the payment as income except to the extent that it is compensation for an above-market rental (similar in nature to an incentive to enter into a lease), in which case the receipt is deferred and amortised over the lease term (see 5.1.4 above).

Note 4 The new tenant has made a payment to an old tenant, and while it is in connection with the lease arrangements, it is not directly related to the actual lease as it was made to a party outside the lease contract. Therefore it cannot be accounted for under IAS 17. The old tenant will treat the receipt as a gain immediately. Any remaining balances of the lease will be removed and a net gain (or loss) recorded. The payment by the lessee will generally meet the definition of an intangible asset in IAS 38 and therefore will be amortised over the useful life, usually the term of the lease. However, if other conditions and circumstances in the arrangement mean that this definition is not met, the payment will be expensed in the period in which it is incurred.

5.3.1 *Compensation for loss of profits*

Compensation amounts paid by lessors to lessees are sometimes described as 'compensation for loss of profits' or some similar term. This is a method of calculating the amount to be paid and the receipt is not a substitute for the revenue or profits that the lessee would otherwise have earned. The description will not affect the treatment described above.

6 MODIFYING THE TERMS OF LEASES

Lessees may renegotiate lease terms for a variety of reasons. They may wish to extend the term over which they have a right to use the asset or to alter the number of assets that they have a right to use. They may consider that the lease is too expensive by comparison with current market terms. The renegotiations may deal with several such issues simultaneously.

Lessors may also renegotiate leases, for example one lessor may sell the lease to another that offers to provide a cheaper lease service to the lessee, usually because the new lessor's transactions have different tax consequences. Lease contracts may allow for changes in payments if specified contingencies occur, for example a change in taxation or interest rates.

6.1 IAS 17 and accounting for renegotiations

The standard has little to say on the consequences of such renegotiations. It states:

> 'If at any time the lessee and the lessor agree to change the provisions of the lease, other than by renewing the lease, in a manner that would have resulted in a different classification of the lease ... if the changed terms had been in effect at the inception of the lease, the revised agreement is regarded as a new agreement over its term.' *[IAS 17.13]*.

As described at 3.2.3 above, the consequences of a different classification are clear. A revised agreement that is reclassified (e.g. an operating lease is reassessed as a finance lease or *vice versa*) is accounted for prospectively in accordance with the revised terms. However, IAS 17 leaves many questions of application unanswered. It provides no practical guidance on what to take into account to determine whether there would have been a different classification. It does not explain how to account for the consequences of modifications, and whether or not they would lead to a different classification. These matters are described below.

Other changes to lease terms that do not lead to reclassification but that nevertheless need to be accounted for, for example variations due to changes in rates of taxation or interest rates, are discussed in 6.1.4 below.

Changes in estimates, for example changes in estimates of the economic life or of the residual value of the leased item, or changes in circumstances, for example default by the lessee, do not result in a different classification. *[IAS 17.13]*. Changes in estimates also include the renewal of a lease or the execution of a purchase option, if these were not considered reasonably certain at the inception of the lease (see 3.2.3 above).

6.1.1 Determining whether there is a different classification

This section addresses various approaches to determining whether lease classification has changed as a result of changes to its terms. It does not address accounting for the reclassified lease, which is considered at 6.1.2 below, if there is a revised classification.

For a modification to result in a change in classification, it must be one that affects the risks and rewards incidental to ownership of the asset by changing the terms and cash flows of the existing lease, for example a renegotiation that changes the duration and/or the payments due under the lease.

One of the indicators used in practice to determine whether a modified lease results in a different classification from the original lease is an assessment of the net present value of the minimum lease payments and whether or not these amount to substantially all of the fair value of the leased asset. An entity might use this test to help assess whether the revised lease is a finance or operating lease, in conjunction with a reassessment of the other factors described at 3.2.2 above. The entity might use one of the following methods to calculate the net present value:

(a) recalculate as per the original date of inception of the lease the net present value based on the revised lease term and cash flows (and revised residual value, if relevant), which will result in a different implicit interest rate to that used in the original calculation;

(b) take into consideration the changes in the agreement but calculate the present value of the asset and liability using the interest rate implicit in the original lease. This approach is consistent with the remeasurement of the carrying value of financial instruments applying the effective interest rate method, as required by IAS 39; *[IAS 39.AG8]* or

(c) consider the revised agreement to be a new lease and assess the classification based on the terms of the new agreement and the fair value and useful life of the asset at the date of the revision. The inference of this method, unlike (a) and (b) above, is that the entity already considers that there is likely to be a new classification to the lease, based on an assessment of other factors, e.g. as a result of the revised terms, the lease term is now the whole of the economic life of the asset or a bargain purchase option has been introduced.

A lessee under an operating lease will be able to apply method (c) but methods (a) and (b) will not be available to it unless it has sufficient information to be able to calculate the IIR at the inception of the original lease, which includes the fair value of the asset at inception. Lessees that are party to more complex leases or sale and leaseback arrangements are more likely to have the necessary information available to them.

It must be stressed that all features of any arrangement must be considered in order to assess whether or not the modified lease transfers substantially all of the risks and rewards of ownership.

Each of these three approaches is likely to lead to a different net present value for the minimum lease payments.

They are compared in the following example.

Example 24.23: Modifying the terms of leases

Details of a non-cancellable lease taken out on the first day of the year are as follows:

(i) Fair value = €25,000

(ii) Estimated useful life of asset = 8 years

(iii) Five annual rentals payable in advance of €4,200

(iv) At the end of year 5, the asset must be sold and all proceeds up to €8,292 taken by the lessor. If any amount in excess of €8,292 is received, 99% of the excess is repaid to the lessee.

The lease does not contain any renewal options.

The lessee assesses this as an operating lease because the terms suggest that substantially all of the risks and rewards of ownership have not been transferred to it – the lease term is only 62.5% of the useful life of the asset and there is clearly significant residual value.

At the end of year 2, the parties renegotiate the lease, with the changes coming into effect on the first day of year 3. The lease term is to be extended for a further two years, making the term seven years in total. Payments for the four years 3-6 have been reduced to €4,000 and €1,850 is payable for year 7. At the time of the renegotiation the estimated fair value of the asset is €17,500 and its residual value at the end of year 7 is €1,850.

The implicit interest rate in the original lease can be calculated because the maximum amount receivable by the lessor on the sale of the asset at the end of the lease term is the residual value (on the assumption that the lessor disregards any potential upside in its contingent 1%); the IIR is 5.92%, as follows:

Year	Capital sum at start of period	Rental paid	Capital sum during period	Finance charge (IIR 5.92% per annum)	Capital sum at end of period
	€	€	€	€	€
1	25,000	4,200	20,800	1,231	22,031
2	22,031	4,200	17,831	1,056	18,887
3	18,887	4,200	14,687	869	15,556
4	15,556	4,200	11,356	672	12,028
5	12,028	4,200	7,828	464	8,292
		21,000		4,292	

This supports the lessee's assessment that this is an operating lease as the present value of the minimum lease payments (the rentals to be paid over the term discounted at the IIR of 5.92%) is €18,780, which is 75% of the fair value of the asset at the commencement of the lease.

If the revised terms had been in existence at inception then the implicit interest rate and NPV calculation would have been as follows. This corresponds to (a) above.

Year	Capital sum at start of period €	Rental paid €	Capital sum during period €	Finance charge (IIR 4.10% per annum) €	Capital sum at end of period €
1	25,000	4,200	20,800	853	21,653
2	21,653	4,200	17,453	715	18,168
3	18,168	4,000	14,168	581	14,749
4	14,749	4,000	10,749	441	11,190
5	11,190	4,000	7,190	294	7,484
6	7,484	4,000	3,484	143	3,627
7	3,627	1,850	1,777	73	1,850
		26,250		3,100	

The NPV of the lessee's minimum lease payments (per the rentals paid above) discounted at the IIR of 4.1% is €23,603 which is 94% of the fair value of the asset at the commencement of the lease. The lease would be classified as a finance lease.

Method (b) results in the following calculation:

Year	Capital sum at start of period €	Rental paid €	Capital sum during period €	Finance charge (IIR 5.92% per annum) €	Capital sum at end of period €
1	25,000	4,200	20,800	1,231	22,031
2	22,031	4,200	17,831	1,056	**18,887**
3	**17,566**	4,000	13,566	803	14,369
4	14,369	4,000	10,369	613	10,982
5	10,982	4,000	6,982	414	7,396
6	7,396	4,000	3,396	201	3,597
7	3,597	1,850	1,747	103	1,850
		26,250		4,421	

The present value of the total rentals paid over the revised lease term at the original discount rate of 5.92% is €22,585, which is 90.3% of the fair value of the asset at commencement of the lease. In addition, the residual value of €1,850 would have had a present value of only €1,237; it is a feature of the methodology that the present value of the lease payments and the present value of the residual do not add up to the fair value of the asset at inception. In order to make the computation, an adjustment is made to the capital amount as at the date that the lease is renegotiated. The outstanding amount is recomputed from €18,887 (the balance at the end of year 2 calculated using the original assumptions) to €17,566, the amount that corresponds to the new assumptions. Note that it is not relevant that the method results in a change to the 'capital sum' of only 7% ((18,887 – 17,566) ÷ 18,887). The assessment is based on the net present value of the minimum lease payments over the lease term and other features of the revised agreement.

If method (c) is applied, the modified lease is considered as if it were a new five year lease. The IIR calculated prospectively over the remaining term is now 6.13%:

Year	Capital sum at start of period	Rental paid	Capital sum during period	Finance charge (IIR 6.13% per annum)	Capital sum at end of period
	€	€	€	€	€
3	17,500	4,000	13,500	827	14,327
4	14,327	4,000	10,327	633	10,960
5	10,960	4,000	6,960	426	7,386
6	7,386	4,000	3,386	207	3,593
7	3,593	1,850	1,743	107	1,850
		17,850		2,200	

The present value of the remaining rental payments to be made discounted at the IIR of 6.13% is €16,126, which is 92.15% of the fair value of the asset (€17,500) at the date of entering into the new lease.

In this example, all three methods result in a present value of the minimum lease payments that exceeds 90% but this would not, of course, always be the case.

6.1.2 Accounting for reclassified leases

IAS 17 states that the revised agreement is treated as a new agreement over its term.

If the original lease was a finance lease and the revised lease is an operating lease, then the balances relating to the finance lease must be derecognised. For the lessee, this involves derecognising both the asset (which will have been depreciated up to the point of derecognition over the shorter of the useful life or the lease term) and the finance lease liability. Finance lease derecognition is discussed further at 4.3 above.

If the original lease was an operating lease and the revised lease is a finance lease, then any balances resulting from recognising the lease cost on a straight-line basis will be expensed and the balances relating to the finance lease must be recognised for the first time unless payments made under the original operating lease affect the terms of the new finance lease. For example, an entity might have made an up-front prepayment under the terms of the original lease of which part relates to the period after the renegotiation. This is taken into account in the revised terms and become a prepayment over the relevant period under the new finance lease.

Although the standard says that 'the revised agreement is regarded as a new agreement over its term', *[IAS 17.13]*, this refers to classification; there is no consensus regarding the measurement of assets and liabilities as at this point.

- The revised lease may be accounted for as a new lease as from the date on which the terms were changed, based on an implicit interest rate modified to reflect the revised lease term and revised cash flows (method (a) in 6.1.1 above) or the revised lease term, cash flows, and the fair value of the assets as at the date of revision (method (c) in 6.1.1 above). In the facts as in Example 24.23 above, the assets and liabilities under the finance lease would be recognised initially as;

- €16,655, being the present value of the revised remaining lease payments applying method (a) from 6.1.1 above; or
- €16,126, being the present value of the revised remaining lease payments applying method (c) from 6.1.1 above.

- The new lease can be recognised using method (b) above, by taking into consideration the changes in the agreement but calculating the present value of the asset and liability by using the interest rate implicit in the original lease. This uses an accepted methodology and is consistent with the fact that there has, in fact, only been a change to the original terms and not a completely new lease; it also has the advantage that the revised fair value of the assets does not have to be known.

  In the facts as in Example 24.23 above, this means that the asset and liability would be recorded at €16,178.

If the original lease agreement and the revised lease agreement are both finance leases, then the modification will have accounting consequences that are discussed in the following section.

6.1.3 Accounting for modifications to finance leases

If the rights under a finance lease have changed without a change in the classification, these changes to lease term and cash flows must be accounted for. Once again, the accounting consequences are not dealt with by IAS 17.

The two most obvious methods of calculating the impact of the changes are as follows:

(a) Account for the revised agreement as if it were a new lease, even though the classification has not changed. The calculation will be based on the fair value and useful life of the asset at the date of the revision.

(b) Use the original IIR to discount the revised minimum lease payments and (for a lessee) adjust any change in lease liability to the carrying amount of the asset. Lessors will adjust the carrying value of the asset, taking gains or losses to income. As noted before, this approach is consistent with the requirements of IAS 39 when the effective interest rate method is applied and the cash flows change. *[IAS 39.AG8]*.

These are described in 6.1.1 and Example 24.23 above (method (b) and method (c)). For lessees, both of these methods will affect the carrying value of the asset and hence its future amortisation.

Another method that might be considered is to reflect changes prospectively over the remaining term of the lease; this is only likely to be appropriate if the cash flows are modified but all other rights remain unchanged. Some of the circumstances in which such changes can arise are considered at 6.1.4 below.

Example 24.24: Accounting for lease modifications

The details of a lease are as in Example 24.23 above, except that the lease has an original duration of six years with an annual rent of €4,200, rather than five years. The present value of the minimum lease payments based on the total rental paid discounted using the IIR of 5.92% is €21,931, which is 87.72% of the fair value of the leased asset, calculated as follows:

Year	Capital sum at start of period €	Rental paid €	Capital sum during period €	Finance charge (IIR 5.92% per annum) €	Capital sum at end of period €
1	21,931	4,200	17,731	1,050	18,780
2	18,780	4,200	14,580	863	15,443
3	15,443	4,200	11,243	666	11,909
4	11,909	4,200	7,709	456	8,165
5	8,165	4,200	3,965	235	4,200
6	4,200	4,200	-	-	-
		25,200		3,270	

The directors of the entity assess this as a finance lease, taking account of all of the circumstances surrounding the agreement. The entity capitalise the asset at €21,931 at commencement of the lease and recognise an equivalent liability.

At the end of year 2, the lease term is extended for a further year, making the term seven years in total. Payments for the four years 3-6 are reduced to €4,000 and €1,850 is payable for year 7.

The asset (which has a useful life to the lessee of six years) has been depreciated on a straight-line basis for two years and its carrying amount is €14,620, while the lessee's lease liability (as calculated above) is €15,443:

(a) If the modification is treated as a new lease, it will be accounted for as follows, using the revised fair value of €16,126 and IIR of 6.13% calculated at Example 24.23(c) above:

Year	Capital sum at start of period €	Rental paid €	Capital sum during period €	Finance charge (IIR 6.13% per annum) €	Capital sum at end of period €
3	16,126	4,000	12,126	743	12,868
4	12,868	4,000	8,868	543	9,412
5	9,412	4,000	5,412	331	5,743
6	5,743	4,000	1,743	107	1,850
7	1,850	1,850	–	–	–
		17,850		1,724	

Therefore, the entity will derecognise both the leased asset of €14,620 and liability of €15,443, recognising a net gain of €823. The new asset of €16,126 will be depreciated prospectively over the remaining life of 5 years.

(b) If the modification is accounted for by restating the liability using the original IIR of 5.92%, the liability will be €16,178 calculated as follows:

Year	Capital sum at start of period €	Rental paid €	Capital sum during period €	Finance charge (IIR 5.92% per annum) €	Capital sum at end of period €
3	16,178	4,000	12,178	721	12,899
4	12,899	4,000	8,899	526	9,425
5	9,425	4,000	5,425	322	5,747
6	5,747	4,000	1,747	103	1,850
7	1,850	1,850	–	–	–
		17,850		1,672	

The entity will increase the lease liability by €735 (from €15,443 to €16,178) but it will increase the asset's carrying amount by the same amount from €14,620 to €15,355 which will be depreciated prospectively over the asset's remaining life of 5 years.

6.1.4 *Tax and interest variation clauses*

The relationship between leasing and taxation is frequently complex. It depends on whether tax deductions or taxable income are based on amounts receivable or payable in accordance with the lease or on the amounts that are taken to the income statement. It further depends on the availability of tax deductions for the cost of leased assets and who is able to claim these deductions. Some lessors draw up leases that are based on a post-tax return that takes account of these factors. These leases include tax variation clauses that enable lessors to change the amounts receivable from the lessee so that their post-tax return remains constant. The rental could be adjusted in a number of different ways, e.g. a new fixed payment, an up-front sum or an adjustment on a rental-by-rental basis.

The variations are unlikely of themselves to change the lease classification because their potential impact will have been taken into account in making that original assessment. Nor are they likely to lead to an impairment of a lessor's finance lease asset as the profitability of the lease (on a post-tax basis) is unaffected.

IAS 17 does not refer to variation clauses so the question is whether the change is a variety of contingent rent, defined by the standard as that portion of the lease payments that is not fixed in amount but is based on a factor that varies other than with the passage of time, such as percentage of sales, amount of usage, price indices or market rates of interest, *[IAS 17.4]*, or another type of event. Contingent rent is recognised when it is incurred. This means that a reduction in rentals because of a reduction in rates of taxation would be a negative contingent rent.

Leases may also contain interest variation clauses which adjust the rental by reference to movements in bank base rates or similar. As market rates of interest are specific examples of contingent rent in the standard, they must be accounted for as such. These movements could be positive or negative over the lease term.

6.1.5 *Accounting for changes to the terms of operating leases*

Lessees may seek to renegotiate terms with lessors, e.g. in circumstances in which the lessee has financial difficulties or where there is evidence that the lease terms are at higher than market rates or to extend the lease term while, at the same time, changing the payments made under the lease agreement. If the revised lease is still classified as an operating lease, the revised terms should be taken into account prospectively from the date of the agreement.

The lessee now has a contractual obligation to continue the lease and the effect on any existing straight-line prepayment or accrual should be taken into account. Both previously recognised amounts and aggregate future minimum lease payments should be recognised on a straight-line basis prospectively over the remaining revised lease term, whether or not the original lease contract contained a renewal option.

Accounting for the original lease until its expiry and then treating the modification (e.g. the extended term) as if it were a new lease may be an attractive option as it avoids any change if there are straight-line prepayments or accruals; these will reduce to zero at the end of the original lease term. However, it is inconsistent with the fact that there has been a contractual change to the existing lease.

Because tenants in financial difficulties may negotiate changes to their lease terms, any asset that is being spread forward may need to be assessed for impairment.

7 SALE AND LEASEBACK TRANSACTIONS

These transactions involve the original owner of an asset selling it to a provider of finance and immediately leasing it back. The lease payment and the sale price are usually interdependent because they are negotiated as a package. These parties will be termed the seller/lessee (the original owner) and buyer/lessor (the finance provider) respectively. Sometimes, instead of selling the asset outright, the original owner will lease the asset to the other party under a finance lease and then lease it back. Such a transaction is known as a 'lease and leaseback' and has similar effects so for these purposes is included within the term 'sale and leaseback'.

Sale and leaseback transactions are a fairly common feature in sectors where entities own many properties, such as the retail and hotel industries. Many parties are involved as buyer/lessors, not only finance houses and banks but also pension funds and property groups. From a commercial point of view, the important point of difference lies between an entity that decides that it is cheaper to rent than to own – and is willing to pass on the property risk to the landlord – and an entity which decides to use the property as a means of raising finance – and will therefore retain the property risk. However from the accounting point of view, a major consideration is whether a profit can be reported on such transactions.

The buyer/lessor will treat the lease in the same way as it would any other lease that was not part of a sale and leaseback transaction. The accounting treatment of the transaction by the seller/lessee depends on the type of lease involved, i.e. whether the leaseback is under a finance or an operating lease. *[IAS 17.58]*.

7.1 Sale and finance leaseback

In order to assess whether the leaseback is under a finance lease, the seller/lessee will apply the qualitative tests in IAS 17 that are described at 3.2.2 above. If a sale and leaseback transaction results in a finance lease, any excess of sales proceeds over the carrying amount should not be recognised immediately as income by a seller/lessee. Instead, the excess is deferred and amortised over the lease term. *[IAS 17.59]*. It is inappropriate to show a profit on disposal of an asset which has, in substance, been reacquired by the entity under a finance lease. The lessor is providing finance to the lessee with the asset as security. *[IAS 17.60]*. The asset will be restated to its fair value (or the present value of the minimum lease payments, if lower) in exactly the same way as any other asset acquired under a finance lease.

Example 24.25: Sale and finance leaseback – accounting for the excess sale proceeds

An asset that has a carrying value of €700 and a remaining useful life of 7 years is sold for €1,200 and leased back on a finance lease. This is accounted for as a disposal of the original asset and the acquisition of an asset under a finance lease for €1,200. The excess of sales proceeds of €500 over the original carrying value should be deferred and amortised (i.e. credited to profit or loss) over the lease term.

The net impact on income of the charge for depreciation based on the carrying value of the asset held under the finance lease of €171 (€1200 over 7 years) and the amortisation of the deferred income of €71 (€500 over 7 years) is the same as the annual depreciation of €100 based on the original carrying amount.

In 2007 the Interpretations Committee considered the related area of sale and repurchase options, concluding that IAS 17 itself contains 'the more specific guidance with respect to sale and leaseback transactions'.[10]

However, some consider that there is an alternative treatment which they believe is more consistent with the substance of the arrangement and with the approach in SIC-27 described at 2.2 above, which deals with transactions that have the form but not the substance of leases. It follows the standard's description of the transaction as 'a means whereby the lessor provides finance to the lessee, with the asset as security'. *[IAS 17.60]*. The previous carrying value is left unchanged, with the sales proceeds being shown as a liability. This is consistent with IAS 18 which states that a transaction is not a sale and revenue is not recognised if the entity retains significant risks of ownership. *[IAS 18.16]*. By definition the entity will have retained the significant risks and rewards, because it now holds the asset under a finance lease.

Both methods of accounting for sale and leaseback transactions are seen in practice. Therefore, an entity should select a treatment as a matter of accounting policy and apply it consistently.

If the sales value is less than the carrying amount then the apparent 'loss' need not be taken to income unless there has been an impairment under IAS 36. *[IAS 17.64]*. There may be an obvious reason why the sales proceeds are less than the carrying value; for example, the fair value of a second-hand vehicle or item of plant and machinery is frequently lower than its book value, especially soon after the asset has been acquired by the entity. This fall in fair value after sale has no effect on the asset's value-in-use. This means that, in the absence of impairment, a deficit (sales proceeds lower than carrying value) will be deferred in the same manner as a profit and spread over the lease term.

7.2 Operating leaseback

If a sale and leaseback transaction results in an operating lease, and it is clear that the transaction is established at fair value, any profit or loss should be recognised immediately. If the sale price is below fair value, any profit or loss should be recognised immediately unless the loss is compensated by future lease payments at below market price, in which case it should be deferred and amortised in proportion to the lease payments over the period for which the asset is expected to be used. If the sale price is above fair value, the excess over fair value should be deferred and amortised over the period for which the asset is expected to be used. *[IAS 17.61-63]*.

The rationale behind these treatments is that if the sales value is not based on fair values then it is likely that the normal market rents will have been adjusted to compensate. For example, a sale at above fair value followed by above-market rentals is similar to a loan of the excess proceeds by the lessor that is being repaid out of the rentals. Accordingly, the transaction should be recorded as if it had been based on fair value.

However, this will not always be the case. Where the sales value is less than fair value there may be legitimate reasons for this to be so, for example where the seller has had to raise cash quickly. In such situations, as the rentals under the lease have not been reduced to compensate, the profit or loss should be based on the sales value.

The standard includes an Appendix, which comprises the following table of the standard's requirements concerning sale and leaseback transactions, and is aimed at providing guidance in interpreting the various permutations of facts and circumstances that are set out in the requirements.

Sale price established at fair value (paragraph 61)	*Carrying amount equal to fair value*	*Carrying amount less than fair value*	*Carrying amount above fair value*
Profit	no profit	recognise profit immediately	not applicable
Loss	no loss	not applicable	recognise loss immediately
Sale price below fair value (paragraph 61)			
Profit	no profit	recognise profit immediately	no profit (note 1)
Loss *not* compensated by future lease payments at below market price	recognise loss immediately	recognise loss immediately	(note 1)
Loss compensated by future lease payments at below market price	defer and amortise loss	defer and amortise loss	(note 1)
Sale price above fair value (paragraph 61)	*Carrying amount equal to fair value*	*Carrying amount less than fair value*	*Carrying amount above fair value*
Profit	defer and amortise profit(note 3)	defer and amortise profit (note 3)	defer and amortise profit (note 2)
Loss	no loss	no loss	(note 1)

Note 1 These parts of the table represent circumstances that would have been dealt with under paragraph 63 of the Standard. Paragraph 63 requires the carrying amount of an asset to be written down to fair value where it is subject to a sale and leaseback.

Note 2 The profit would be the difference between fair value and sale price as the carrying amount would have been written down to fair value in accordance with paragraph 63.

Note 3 Any excess profit (the excess of sale price over fair value) is deferred and amortised over the period for which the asset is expected to be used. Any excess of fair value over carrying amount is recognised immediately.

IAS 17's disclosure requirements for lessees and lessors apply equally to sale and leaseback transactions. The requirement of the standard for lessees to give a general description of their significant leasing arrangements will lead to the disclosure of unique or unusual provisions of the agreement or terms of the sale and leaseback transactions. *[IAS 17.35(d), 65]*. Furthermore, sale and leaseback transactions may meet the separate disclosure criteria set out in IAS 1 – *Presentation of Financial Statements* (see Chapter 3). *[IAS 17.66]*.

Sale and leaseback arrangements may also include features such as repurchase options. These are not addressed by IAS 17 and are discussed below.

7.3 Sale and leaseback arrangements including repurchase agreements and options

IAS 17 does not deal explicitly with the function of options in the context of sale and leaseback arrangements, where circumstances could be complex and there may be a variety of options that may affect the overall assessment of the lease.

The Interpretations Committee considered whether these arrangements would have to meet the derecognition criteria in IAS 18 in order to recognise the sale of the asset. If this were the case then it would be unlikely that the seller/lessee would ever achieve derecognition. Arguably the seller/lessee would retain effective control through continuing managerial involvement to the degree usually associated with ownership. It might also retain the significant risks and rewards of ownership, e.g. through fixed price repurchase terms that allowed it to retain the rewards but not the risks of ownership. *[IAS 18.14]*.

The Interpretations Committee concluded that there was no such requirement as IAS 17 itself contained 'the more specific guidance with respect to sale and leaseback transactions'. However, these transactions may be outside the scope IAS 17 because they do not 'convey a right to use an asset' as defined by SIC-27 and IFRIC 4, whose requirements are described at 2.1 above. If the purchaser/lessor does not have a right of use, the transaction is outside the scope of IAS 17 and the sale and leaseback accounting in IAS 17 should not be applied.

The Interpretations Committee considered that 'significantly divergent interpretations do not exist in practice on this issue and that it would not expect such divergent interpretations to emerge'. Consequently, the Interpretations Committee decided not to take the issue onto its agenda.[11]

The Interpretations Committee considers, therefore, that entities should use IFRIC 4 and SIC-27 to analyse whether or not the arrangement contains a lease and then apply IAS 18 to determine whether or not there is revenue relating to the transaction. SIC-27 is helpful in the analysis; it includes the following indicators that an arrangement is not in substance a lease:

(a) the entity retains all the risks and rewards of ownership and there is no significant change in its rights to use the asset; and

(b) the options on which the arrangement depends are included on terms that make their exercise almost certain (e.g. a put option that is exercisable at a price sufficiently higher than the expected fair value when it becomes exercisable). *[SIC-27.5]*.

In practice entities may well have obtained the same answer by moving straight to IAS 18 and applying a 'risks and rewards' analysis, rather than considering whether the arrangement contains a lease, which could explain the lack of divergence in practice.

7.3.1 Sale and leaseback arrangements with put and call options

If a lease arrangement includes an option that can only be exercised by the seller/lessee at the then fair value of the asset in question, the risks and rewards inherent in the residual value of the asset have passed to the buyer/lessor. The option amounts to a right of first refusal to the seller/lessee.

Where there is both a put and a call option on equivalent terms at a determinable amount other than the fair value, it is clear that the asset will revert to the seller/lessee. It is in the interests of one or other of the parties to exercise the option so as to secure a profit or avoid a loss. Therefore the likelihood of the asset remaining the property of the buyer/lessor rather than reverting to the seller would be remote. In such a case, this is a bargain purchase option (see 3.2.2 above) and the seller/lessee has entered into a finance leaseback.

However, the position is less clear where there is only a put option or only a call option, rather than a combination of the two. Where there is only a put option by the buyer/lessor, the effect will be (in the absence of other factors) that the seller/lessee has disposed of the rewards of ownership to the buyer/lessor but retained the risks. This is because the buyer/lessor will only exercise his option to put the asset back to the seller/lessee if its value at the time is less than the repurchase price payable under the option. This means that if the asset continues to rise in value the buyer/lessor will keep it and reap the benefits of that enhanced value; conversely if the value of the asset falls, the option will be exercised and the downside on the asset will be borne by the seller/lessee.

This analysis does not of itself answer the question of whether the deal should be treated as an operating or financing leaseback. The overall commercial effect will still have to be evaluated, taking account of all the terms of the arrangement and by considering the motivations of both of the parties in agreeing to the various terms of the deal; in particular it will need to be considered why they have each agreed to have this one-sided option.

Where there is only a call option exercisable by the seller/lessee, the position will be reversed. In this case, the seller/lessee has disposed of the risks, but retained the rewards to be attained if the value of the asset exceeds the repurchase price specified in the option. Once again, though, the overall commercial effect of the arrangement has to be evaluated in deciding how to account for the deal. Emphasis has to be given to what is likely to happen in practice, and it is instructive to look at the arrangement from the point of view of both parties to see what their expectations are and what has induced them to accept the deal on the terms that have been agreed. It may be obvious from the overall terms of the arrangement that the call option will be exercised, in which case the deal will again be a financing arrangement and should be accounted for as such. For example, the exercise price of the call option may be set at a significant discount to expected market value, the seller/lessee may need the asset to use on an ongoing basis in its business, or the asset may provide in effect the only source of the seller/lessee's future income. Equally, the financial effects of *not* exercising the option, such as continued exposure to escalating costs, may make it obvious that the option will have to be exercised (so-called 'economic compulsion').

The following is an example of a sale and leaseback deal where the seller has a call option to repurchase the asset but has no commitment to do so:

Example 24.26: Sale and leaseback transaction involving escalating rentals and call options

Company S sells a property to Company B for £100,000,000 and leases it back on the following terms:

Rental for years 1 to 5	£1,475,000 per annum
Rental for years 6 to 10	£2,900,000 per annum
Rental for years 11 to 15	£5,500,000 per annum
Rental for years 16 to 20	£10,800,000 per annum
Rental for years 21 to 25	£19,100,000 per annum
Rental for years 26 to 30	£30,025,000 per annum
Rental for years 31 to 35	£45,150,000 per annum
Rental thereafter	open market rent

Rentals are payable annually in advance.

Company S has a call option to buy back the property at the following dates and prices:

At the end of year 5	£125,000,000
At the end of year 10	£150,000,000
At the end of year 15	£168,000,000
At the end of year 20	£160,000,000
At the end of year 25	£100,000,000

Company B has no right to put the property back to Company S.

An analysis of the economics of this deal suggests that whilst Company S has no legal obligation to repurchase the property, there is no genuine commercial possibility that the option will not be exercised. This is because the rentals and option prices are structured in such a way as to give the buyer of the property a lender's return whilst, at the same time, there is no commercial logic for the seller not to exercise the option at year 25, if not earlier. Exercising the option at the end of year 25 will mean that Company S will regain ownership of the property and will have had the use of the £100,000,000 at an effective rate of approximately 6% per annum; failure to exercise the option will mean additional lease obligations of £375,875,000 over the ten years from years 25 to 35, followed by the obligation to pay market rents thereafter.

8 SUB-LEASES AND BACK-TO-BACK LEASES

8.1 Introduction

Sometimes there are more parties to a lease arrangement than simply one lessor and one lessee. This section relates to situations involving an original lessor, an intermediate party and an ultimate lessee. The intermediate party is unrelated to both lessor and lessee and may be acting either as both a lessee and lessor of the asset concerned or, alternatively, as an agent of the lessor in the transaction.

Both sub-leases and back-to-back leases involve the intermediate party acting as both lessor and lessee of the asset. The difference between the two arrangements is that, for a back-to-back lease, the terms of the two lease agreements match to a greater extent than would be the case for a sub-lease arrangement. This difference is really only one of degree. The important decision to be made concerns whether the intermediate party is acting as both lessee and lessor in two related but independent transactions or whether the nature of the interest is such that it need not recognise the rights and obligations under the leases in its financial statements.

8.1.1 The original lessor and the ultimate lessee

The accounting treatment adopted by these parties will not be affected by the existence of sub-leases or back-to-back leases. The original lessor has an agreement with the intermediate party, which is not affected by any further leasing of the assets by the intermediate party unless the original lease agreement is thereby replaced.

Similarly, the ultimate lessee has a lease agreement with the intermediate party. The lessee will have use of the asset under that agreement and must make a decision, in the usual way, as to whether the lease is of a finance or operating type under the requirements of IAS 17.

8.1.2 The intermediate party

It is common for entities whose business is the leasing of assets to third parties to finance these assets themselves through leasing arrangements. There are also arrangements in which a party on-leases assets as an intermediary between a lessor and a lessee while taking a variable degree of risk in the transaction. The appropriate accounting treatment by the intermediate party depends on the substance of the series of transactions. Either the intermediate party will act as lessee to the original lessor and lessor to the ultimate lessee or, if in substance it has transferred the risks and rewards of ownership, it may be able to derecognise the assets and liabilities under its two lease arrangements and recognise only its own commission or fee income.

In order to analyse the issues that may arise, the various combinations of leases between lessor/intermediate and intermediate/lessee are summarised in the following table:

	Lessor	Intermediate party		Lessee
	Lease to Intermediate	*Lease from Lessor*	*Lease to Lessee*	*Lease from Intermediate*
(1)	Operating lease	Operating lease	Operating lease	Operating lease
(2)	Finance lease	Finance lease	Operating lease	Operating lease
(3)	Finance lease	Finance lease	Finance lease	Finance lease

Only in unusual circumstances could there be an operating lease from the lessor to the intermediate and a finance lease from the intermediate to the lessee. The intermediate would have to acquire an additional interest in the asset from a party other than the lessor in order to be in a position to transfer substantially all of the risks and rewards incidental to ownership of that asset to the lessee.

There are no significant accounting difficulties for the intermediate party regarding (1), an operating lease from the lessor to the intermediate and from the intermediate to the lessee. The intermediate may be liable to the lessor if the lessee defaults, in which case it would have to make an appropriate provision, but otherwise both contracts are executory and will be accounted for in the usual way.

In situation (2), the intermediate will record at commencement of the lease term an asset acquired under a finance lease and an obligation to the lessor of an equal and opposite amount. As it has granted an operating lease to the lessee, its risks and rewards incidental to ownership of the asset exceed those assumed by the lessee under the lease. It is appropriate for the intermediate party to record a fixed asset, which it will have to depreciate as set out in 4.1.4 above.

However, under scenario (3), the intermediate is the lessee under a finance lease with the lessor and lessor under a finance lease with the lessee. Its statement of financial position, *prima facie*, records a finance lease receivable from the lessee and a finance lease obligation to the lessor. Both of these are treated as if they are financial instruments for derecognition purposes (see 3.5 above for the circumstances in which lease assets and liabilities are within scope of IAS 39).

The intermediate may be in a position to derecognise its financial asset and liability if it transfers to the lessor the contractual right to receive the cash flows of the lessee and thereby extinguishes its liability under the lease. *[IAS 39.18]*. However, it is more likely that it retains the contractual right to receive the cash flow under the lease and takes on a contractual obligation to pay the cash flows to the lessor. In accordance with the derecognition rules in IAS 39 it can derecognise its asset and liability if, and only if, it meets certain criteria, which are summarised below and described in detail in Chapter 51.

In the context of leases, the most important of these conditions is that the intermediate has no obligation to pay amounts to the lessor unless in collects equivalent amounts from the lessee. *[IAS 39.19]*. If the ultimate lessee defaults on its lease obligations (for whatever reason), the original lessor must have no recourse against the intermediate party for the outstanding payments under the lease if derecognition is to be appropriate. Another important factor is what happens if the original lessor defaults, for example through insolvency. The analysis will also have to take account of the following conditions for derecognition of a financial asset in IAS 39 (or IFRS 9 if the entity applies that standard):

(a) the entity (i.e. the intermediate party) is prohibited by the terms of the transfer contract from selling or pledging the original asset; and

(b) the entity has an obligation to remit any cash flows it collects without material delay. Investment in cash or cash equivalents is permitted, but interest earned must be passed to the eventual recipients. *[IAS 39.19]*.

If all of these factors indicate that the intermediate party has derecognised its interest in the two leases, i.e. commercially it is acting merely as a broker or agent for the original lessor, it should not include any asset or obligation relating to the leased asset in its statement of financial position. The income received by such an intermediary should be taken to profit or loss on a systematic and rational basis – the discussion of the recognition of fee income in SIC-27, as discussed in 2.2 above, may be helpful. If, on the other hand, the intermediate party is taken to be acting as both lessee and lessor in two independent although related transactions, the assets and obligations under finance leases should be recognised in the normal way.

It should not be inferred from the above discussion that all situations encountered can be relatively easily analysed. In practice this is unlikely to be the case, as the risks and rewards will probably be spread between the parties involved. This is especially likely where more than the three parties discussed above are involved. Therefore, even if the arrangements meet the definition of a 'transfer' under IAS 39, the intermediate may have retained some of the risks and rewards of ownership or control of the asset and it may be necessary to recognise other assets and liabilities in this respect. The complex area concerning derecognition of financial assets is dealt with in Chapter 51 at Section 3.

9 DISCLOSURES REQUIRED BY IAS 17

This section deals only with the disclosure requirements of IAS 17 and those of other accounting standards to which it specifically refers. Disclosures required by SIC-27 are dealt with in 2.2.4 above.

9.1 Disclosures relating to financial assets and liabilities

Because finance lease assets and obligations and individual payments currently due and payable under operating leases are financial assets and liabilities, lessees and lessors must make the disclosures required by IFRS 7 – *Financial Instruments: Disclosures.* This principally applies to the general requirements regarding classification and disclosure of financial assets and liabilities in the statement of financial position and disclosure of interest income and expense, together with other gains and losses arising from financial instruments, whether reflected in profit or loss or other comprehensive income. IFRS 7's disclosure requirements are covered in Chapter 54.

9.2 Disclosure by lessees

9.2.1 Disclosure of finance leases

As well as meeting the IFRS 7 disclosure requirements, IAS 17 requires lessees to make the following disclosures for finance leases: *[IAS 17.31]*

(a) for each class of asset, the net carrying amount at the reporting date. Assets that are recognised under a finance lease will generally be considered to be the same class of assets with a similar nature that are owned, so there is no need to provide separate reconciliations of movements in owned assets from assets under finance leases;

(b) a reconciliation between the total of future minimum lease payments at the reporting date, and their present value. The minimum lease payments will include adjustments that have been made following a rent review. In addition, an entity shall disclose the total of future minimum lease payments at the reporting date, and their present value, for each of the following periods:

 (i) not later than one year;

 (ii) later than one year and not later than five years;

 (iii) later than five years.

(c) contingent rents recognised as an expense in the period. See 3.4.7 above for a discussion about the meaning for disclosure purposes of future minimum lease payments and contingent rents;

(d) the total of future minimum sublease payments expected to be received under non-cancellable subleases at the reporting date;

(e) a general description of the lessee's material leasing arrangements including, but not limited to, the following:
   (i) the basis on which contingent rent payable is determined;
   (ii) the existence and terms of renewal or purchase options and escalation clauses; and
   (iii) restrictions imposed by lease arrangements, such as those concerning dividends, additional debt, and further leasing.

The following is an example of disclosures made in practice:

Extract 24.5: Deutsche Telekom AG (2014)

Notes to the Consolidated Financial Statements [extract]
34 **Leases** [extract]
Deutsche Telekom as lessee [extract]

Finance leases. When a lease transfers substantially all risks and rewards to Deutsche Telekom as lessee, Deutsche Telekom initially recognizes the leased assets in the statement of financial position at the lower of fair value or present value of the future minimum lease payments. Most of the leased assets carried in the statement of financial position as part of finance leases relate to long-term rental and lease agreements for office buildings and cell towers or mobile communications facilities. The average lease term is 18 years. The agreements include extension and purchase options. Table 156 shows the net carrying amounts of leased assets capitalized in connection with a finance lease as of the reporting date:

T156

millions of €	Dec. 31, 2014	Of which: sale and leaseback transactions	Dec. 31, 2013	Of which: sale and leaseback transactions
Land and buildings	599	347	680	394
Technical equipment and machinery	455	0	362	0
Other	8	0	8	0
Net carrying amounts of leased assets capitalized	**1,062**	**347**	**1,050**	**394**

At the inception of the lease term, Deutsche Telekom recognizes a lease liability equal to the carrying amount of the leased asset. In subsequent periods, the liability decreases by the amount of lease payments made to the lessors using the effective interest method. The interest component of the lease payments is recognized in the income statement.

Table 157 provides a breakdown of these amounts:

T157
millions of €

	Minimum lease payments		Interest component		Present values	
	Total	Of which: sale and leaseback	Total	Of which: sale and leaseback	Total	Of which: sale and leaseback
Dec. 31, 2014						
Maturity						
Within 1 year	278	108	98	49	180	59
In 1 to 3 years	509	206	178	82	331	124
In 3 to 5 years	372	183	133	60	239	123
After 5 years	1,028	393	317	165	711	228
	2,187	**890**	**726**	**356**	**1,461**	**534**
Dec. 31, 2013						
Maturity						
Within 1 year	260	109	98	52	162	57
In 1 to 3 years	475	209	183	90	292	119
In 3 to 5 years	398	198	140	70	258	128
After 5 years	1,079	472	345	189	734	283
	2,212	**988**	**766**	**401**	**1,446**	**587**

In addition, the leased asset is accounted for as property, plant and equipment, an intangible asset or other asset of the reporting entity and the requirements for disclosure in accordance with IAS 16 (Chapter 18), IAS 36 (Chapter 20), IAS 38 (Chapter 17), IAS 40 (Chapter 19) and IAS 41 (Chapter 40) are applicable, as appropriate. *[IAS 17.32]*.

9.2.2 *Disclosure of operating leases*

In addition to meeting the requirements of IFRS 7, lessees must make the following disclosures for operating leases: *[IAS 17.35]*

(a) the total of future minimum lease payments under non-cancellable operating leases for each of the following periods:
  - (i) not later than one year;
  - (ii) later than one year and not later than five years;
  - (iii) later than five years.

(b) the total of future minimum sublease payments expected to be received under non-cancellable subleases at the reporting date;

(c) lease and sublease payments recognised as an expense in the period, with separate amounts for minimum lease payments, contingent rents, and sublease payments. See 3.4.7.A above for a discussion about the meaning for disclosure purposes of future minimum lease payments and contingent rents;

(d) a general description of the lessee's significant leasing arrangements including, but not limited to, the following:

(i) the basis on which contingent rent payable is determined;

(ii) the existence and terms of renewal or purchase options and escalation clauses; and

(iii) restrictions imposed by lease arrangements, such as those concerning dividends, additional debt and further leasing.

An example of the disclosures made by a lessee in respect of their obligations under operating leases is as follows.

Extract 24.6: Deutsche Telekom AG (2014)

Notes to the Consolidated Financial Statements [extract]

34 Leases [extract]

Deutsche Telekom as lessee [extract]

Operating leases. Beneficial ownership of a lease is attributed to the lessor if this is the party to which all the substantial risks and rewards incidental to ownership of the asset are transferred. The lessor recognizes the leased asset in its statement of financial position. Deutsche Telekom recognizes the lease payments made during the term of the operating lease in profit or loss. Deutsche Telekom's obligations arising from operating leases are mainly related to long-term rental or lease agreements for cell towers, network infrastructure, and real estate.

Some leases include extension options and provide for stepped rents. Most of these leases relate to cell towers in the United States.

The operating lease expenses recognized in profit or loss amounted to EUR 3.3 billion in the 2014 financial year (2013: EUR 3.2 billion; 2012: EUR 2.8 billion). Table 158 provides a breakdown of future obligations arising from operating leases:

T158
millions of €

	Dec. 31, 2014	Dec. 31, 2013
Maturity		
Within 1 year	2,918	2,684
In 1 to 3 years	4,856	4,490
In 3 to 5 years	3,971	3,770
After 5 years	7,164	6,496
	18,909	**17,440**

9.3 Disclosure by lessors

9.3.1 *Disclosure of finance leases*

In addition to meeting the requirements in IFRS 7 (see 9.1 above), lessors must disclose the following for finance leases:

(a) a reconciliation between the gross investment in the lease at the reporting date, and the present value of minimum lease payments receivable at the reporting date. In addition, an entity shall disclose the gross investment in the lease and the present value of minimum lease payments receivable at the reporting date, for each of the following periods:

  (i) not later than one year;

  (ii) later than one year and not later than five years;

  (iii) later than five years;

(b) unearned finance income;

(c) the unguaranteed residual values accruing to the benefit of the lessor;

(d) the accumulated allowance for uncollectible minimum lease payments receivable;

(e) contingent rents recognised as income in the period; and

(f) a general description of the lessor's material leasing arrangements. *[IAS 17.47]*.

IAS 17 also recommends but does not require disclosure of the gross investment less unearned income in new business added during the period, after deducting the relevant amounts for cancelled leases as a useful indicator of growth. *[IAS 17.48]*.

Deutsche Telekom discloses its activities as a finance lessor as follows:

Extract 24.7: Deutsche Telekom AG (2014)

Notes to the Consolidated Financial Statements [extract]

34 Leases [extract]

Deutsche Telekom as lessor [extract]

Finance Leases. Deutsche Telekom is a lessor in connection with finance leases. Essentially, these relate to the leasing of routers and other hardware, which Deutsche Telekom provides to its customers for data and telephone network solutions. Deutsche Telekom recognizes a receivable in the amount of the net investment in the lease. The lease payments made by the lessees are split into an interest component and a principal component using the effective interest method. The lease receivable is reduced by the principal received. The interest component of the payments is recognized as finance income in the income statement. Table 159 shows how the amount of the net investment in a finance lease is determined:

T159
millions of €

	Dec. 31, 2014	Dec. 31, 2013
Minimum lease payments	242	208
Unguaranteed residual value	2	10
Gross investment	244	218
Unearned finance income	(17)	(15)
Net investment (present value of the minimum lease payments)	**227**	**203**

Table 160 presents the gross investment amounts and the present value of payable minimum lease payments:

T160
millions of €

	Dec. 31, 2014		Dec. 31, 2013	
	Gross investment	Present value of minimum lease payments	Gross investment	Present value of minimum lease payments
Maturity				
Within 1 year	98	90	104	79
In 1 to 3 years	113	103	92	91
In 3 to 5 years	31	33	12	23
After 5 years	2	1	10	10
	244	**227**	**218**	**203**

9.3.2 *Disclosure of operating leases*

Lessors must, in addition to meeting the requirements of IFRS 7 (Chapter 54), disclose the following for operating leases:

(a) the future minimum lease payments under non-cancellable operating leases in the aggregate and for each of the following periods:
 (i) not later than one year;
 (ii) later than one year and not later than five years;
 (iii) later than five years;

(b) total contingent rents recognised as income in the period; and

(c) a general description of the lessor's leasing arrangements. *[IAS 17.56].*

Depending on facts and circumstances, additional disclosures can be necessary that would improve users' understanding of the lessor's operating leases (e.g. disclosures required by IAS 37 on contingent liabilities arising from lease transactions).

Deutsche Telekom's lessor interests in operating leases are disclosed as follows.

Extract 24.8: Deutsche Telekom AG (2014)

Notes to the Consolidated Financial Statements [extract]
34 Leases [extract]
Deutsche Telekom as lessor [extract]

Operating leases. If Deutsche Telekom is a lessor in connection with operating leases, it continues to recognize the leased assets in its statement of financial position. The lease payments received are recognized in profit or loss. The leases mainly relate to the rental of cell towers and building space and have an average term of 15 years. Table 161 presents the future minimum lease payments arising from non-cancelable operating leases:

T161
millions of €

	Dec. 31, 2014	Dec. 31, 2013
Maturity		
Within 1 year	314	275
In 1 to 3 years	380	382
In 3 to 5 years	289	302
After 5 years	507	603
	1,490	**1,562**

In addition, the leased asset is accounted for as a fixed asset of the reporting entity and the requirements for disclosure in accordance with IAS 16 (Chapter 18), IAS 36 (Chapter 20), IAS 38 (Chapter 17), IAS 40 (Chapter 19) and IAS 41 (Chapter 40) are applicable, as appropriate. *[IAS 17.57].*

References

1 *IFRIC Update*, July 2016.
2 ASC 840-10-25-1.
3 IAS 17 (2008) para. 15.
4 *IFRIC Update*, September 2012.
5 IAS 17(2008) para 14.
6 Prior to amendment in 2009, IAS 17 required initial classification of land leases to be based on whether or not title passed. Where title to the land did not pass and it had an indefinite economic life, the land was normally classified as an operating lease while the buildings element was an operating lease or finance lease according to the classification in the standard. IAS 17 (2008) para. 15.
7 RICS Valuation – Professional Standards UK January 2014 (revised April 2015), p.130.
8 RICS Valuation – Professional Standards UK January 2014 (revised April 2015), p.130.
9 *IFRIC Update*, November 2005.
10 *IFRIC Update*, March 2007.
11 *IFRIC Update*, March 2007.

Chapter 25 Leases (IFRS 16)

List of examples

Chapter 25 Leases (IFRS 16)

1 INTRODUCTION

The IASB issued IFRS 16 – *Leases* – in January 2016, which requires lessees to recognise assets and liabilities for most leases. The IASB issued the standard after joint deliberations with the US FASB, which issued a similar standard. However, there are significant differences between the IASB and FASB standards (e.g. lessees classify leases as finance or operating leases under the FASB standard). These differences will result in certain transactions being accounted for differently under IFRS and US GAAP.

The current lease accounting requirements in IAS 17 – *Leases*, have been criticised for failing to meet the needs of users of the financial statements, particularly because IAS 17 does not require lessees to recognise assets and liabilities arising from operating leases. IFRS 16 addresses those criticisms by requiring lessees to recognise most leases on their statements of financial position and providing enhanced disclosures. The IASB believes this will result in a more faithful representation of lessees' assets and liabilities and greater transparency about lessees' financial obligations and leasing activities.

Under IFRS 16, leases are accounted for based on a 'right-of-use model'. The model reflects that, at the commencement date, a lessee has a financial obligation to make lease payments to the lessor for its right to use the underlying asset during the lease term. The lessor conveys that right to use the underlying asset at lease commencement, which is the time when it makes the underlying asset available for use by the lessee.

Entities will need to focus on whether an arrangement contains a lease or a service agreement because there are significant differences in the accounting. Although IFRS 16 changes how the definition of a lease is applied, we believe that the assessment of whether a contract contains a lease will be straightforward in most arrangements. However, judgement may be required in applying the definition of a lease to certain arrangements, particularly those that include significant services.

For lessees, the income statement presentation and expense recognition pattern will be similar to finance leases under IAS 17 (i.e. separate interest and depreciation expense with higher periodic expense in the earlier periods of a lease).

Lessor accounting is substantially unchanged from current accounting. Lessors will classify all leases using the same classification principle as in IAS 17 and distinguish between operating and finance leases.

IFRS 16 is effective for annual periods beginning on or after 1 January 2019. Early application is permitted, provided the new revenue standard, IFRS 15 – *Revenue from Contracts with Customers* – has been applied, or is applied at the same date as IFRS 16.

IFRS 16's transition provisions permit lessees to use either a full retrospective or a modified retrospective approach for leases existing at the date of initial application of the standard (i.e. the beginning of the annual reporting period in which an entity first applies the standard), with options to use certain transition reliefs.

2 OBJECTIVE AND SCOPE OF IFRS 16

2.1 Objective of IFRS 16

IFRS 16 sets out the principles for the recognition, measurement, presentation and disclosure of leases. The objective is to ensure that lessees and lessors provide relevant information in a manner that faithfully represents those transactions. This information gives a basis for users of financial statements to assess the effect that leases have on the financial position, financial performance and cash flows of an entity. *[IFRS 16.1]*.

IFRS 16 requires an entity to consider the terms and conditions of contracts and all relevant facts and circumstances, and to apply the standard consistently to contracts with similar characteristics and in similar circumstances. *[IFRS 16.2]*.

2.2 Scope of IFRS 16

IFRS 16 applies to all leases, including leases of right-of-use assets in a sublease, except for:

(a) Leases to explore for or use minerals, oil, natural gas and similar non-regenerative resources;

(b) Leases of biological assets within the scope of IAS 41 – *Agriculture* – held by a lessee;

(c) Service concession arrangements within the scope of IFRIC 12 – *Service Concession Arrangements*;

(d) Licences of intellectual property granted by a lessor within the scope of IFRS 15 – *Revenue from Contracts with Customers*; and

(e) Rights held by a lessee under licensing agreements within the scope of IAS 38 – *Intangible Assets* – for such items as motion picture films, video recordings, plays, manuscripts, patents and copyrights. *[IFRS 16.3]*.

A lessee may, but is not required to, apply IFRS 16 to leases of intangible assets other than those described in (e) above. *[IFRS 16.4]*.

2.3 Recognition exemptions

A lessee can elect not to apply the recognition requirements to:

(a) Short term leases; and

(b) Leases for which the underlying asset is of low value. *[IFRS 16.5]*.

These recognition exemptions are discussed in further detail at 5.1.1 and 5.1.2 below.

3 WHAT IS A LEASE?

IFRS 16 defines a lease as 'a contract, or part of a contract, that conveys the right to use an asset (the underlying asset) for a period of time in exchange for consideration'. *[IFRS 16.Appendix A]*. The determination of whether an arrangement contains a lease is performed at the inception of the contract.

The assessment of whether a contract is or contains a lease will be straightforward in most arrangements. However, judgement may be required in applying the definition of a lease to certain arrangements. For example, in contracts that include significant services, we believe that determining whether the contracts conveys the right to direct the use of an identified asset may be challenging. We discuss this further at 3.1 below.

3.1 Determining whether an arrangement contains a lease

At inception of a contract, an entity assesses whether the contract is, or contains, a lease. A contract is, or contains, a lease if the contract conveys the right to control the use of an identified asset for a period of time in exchange for consideration. *[IFRS 16.9]*. See 3.1.2 below for additional discussion on identified assets.

A period of time may be described in terms of the amount of use of an identified asset (for example, the number of production units that an item of equipment will be used to produce). *[IFRS 16.10]*.

To assess whether a contract conveys the right to control the use of an identified asset for a period of time, an entity assesses whether, throughout the period of use, the customer has both of the following:

(a) the right to obtain substantially all of the economic benefits from use of the identified asset (see 3.1.4 below); and

(b) the right to direct the use of the identified asset (see 3.1.5 below). *[IFRS 16.B9]*.

If the customer has the right to control the use of an identified asset for only a portion of the term of the contract, the contract contains a lease for that portion of the term. *[IFRS 16.B10]*.

An entity assesses whether a contract contains a lease for each potential separate lease component. *[IFRS 16.B12]*. See 3.2 below.

3.1.1 Joint arrangements

Entities often enter into joint arrangements with other entities for certain activities. For example, the exploration of oil and gas fields, or the development of pharmaceutical products.

A contract to receive goods or services may be entered into by the joint arrangement, or on behalf of the joint arrangement, as defined in IFRS 11 – *Joint Arrangements*. In this case the joint arrangement is considered to be the customer in the contract. In assessing whether such a contract contains a lease, the entity assesses whether the joint arrangement has the right to control the use of an identified asset throughout the period of use. *[IFRS 16.B11]*.

When two or more parties form a joint arrangement, as defined in IFRS 11, the parties can decide to lease assets to be used in the joint arrangement's operations. The joint arrangement may be a joint venture or a joint operation. The contract might be signed by the joint arrangement itself if the joint arrangement has its own legal identity, or it might be signed by one or more of the parties to the joint arrangement on behalf of the joint arrangement. In these cases, the IASB decided to clarify that an entity should consider the joint arrangement to be the customer when assessing whether the contract contains a lease, i.e. the parties to the joint arrangement should not each be considered to be a customer. Accordingly, if the parties to the joint arrangement collectively have the right to control the use of an identified asset throughout the period of use through their joint control of the arrangement, the contract contains a lease. In that scenario, it would be inappropriate to conclude that a contract does not contain a lease on the grounds that each of the parties to the joint arrangement either obtains only a portion of the economic benefits from use of the underlying asset or does not unilaterally direct the use of the underlying asset. *[IFRS 16.BC126]*.

3.1.2 Identified asset

An arrangement only contains a lease if there is an identified asset. This concept is generally consistent with the 'specified asset' concept in IFRIC 4 – *Determining whether an Arrangement contains a Lease*.

An asset is typically identified by being explicitly specified in a contract. However, an asset can also be identified by being implicitly specified at the time that the asset is made available for use by the customer. *[IFRS 16.B13]*.

Example 25.1: Implicitly specified asset

Customer X enters into a five year contract with Supplier Y for the use of rolling stock specifically designed for Customer X. The rolling stock is designed to transport materials used in Customer X's production process and is not suitable for use by other customers. The rolling stock is not explicitly specified in the contract, but Supplier Y owns only one rolling stock that is suitable for Customer X's use. If the rolling stock does not operate properly, the contract requires Supplier Y to repair or replace the rolling stock. Assume that Supplier Y does not have a substantive substitution right (see 3.1.3 below).

Analysis: The rolling stock is an identified asset. While the rolling stock is not explicitly specified in the contract (e.g. by serial number), it is implicitly specified because Supplier Y must use it to fulfil the contract.

Example 25.2: Identified asset – implicitly specified at the time the asset is made available for use by the customer

Customer X enters into a five year contract with Supplier Y for the use of a car. The specification of the car is contained in the contract (brand, type, colour, options, etc.). At inception of the contract the car is not yet built.

Analysis: The car is an identified asset. Although the car cannot be identified at inception of the contract, it is apparent that it will be identifiable at commencement of the lease. The car is identified by being implicitly specified at the time it is made available for use by the customer (i.e. at the commencement date).

A capacity portion of an asset is an identified asset if it is physically distinct (for example, a floor of a building). A capacity or other portion of an asset that is not physically distinct (for example, a capacity portion of a fibre optic cable) is not an identified asset, unless it represents substantially all of the capacity of the asset and thereby provides the customer with the right to obtain substantially all of the economic benefits from use of the asset. *[IFRS 16.B20]*.

Some contracts involve a dedicated cable that is part of the larger network infrastructure (e.g. unbundled network element arrangements for the 'last mile' to a customer location, 'special access' arrangements for a dedicated connection between two locations). Under IAS 17, an entity may not treat the dedicated cable as a specified asset. IFRS 16 does not specify or provide examples that clarify whether these arrangements are identified assets. However, the FASB's new standard includes an additional example that is similar to a dedicated cable (i.e. a segment of a pipeline that connects a single customer to a larger pipeline). That example clarifies that such segments of a larger pipeline are identified assets. As the IASB has stated that it and the FASB have reached the same conclusions on the definition of a lease, we believe that, under IFRS 16, the last mile of a network that connects a single customer to a larger network may be an identified asset. Entities will need to be sensitive to this matter in both these and similar arrangements.

Example 25.3: Identified asset – physically distinct portion of a larger asset

Customer X enters into a 12-year contract with Supplier Y for the right to use three fibres within a fibre optic cable between New York and London. The contract identifies three of the cable's 20 fibres for use by Customer X. The three fibres are dedicated solely to Customer X's data for the duration of the contract term. Assume that Supplier Y does not have a substantive substitution right (see 3.1.3 below).

Analysis: The three fibres are identified assets because they are physically distinct and explicitly specified in the contract.

Example 25.4: Identified asset – capacity portion of an asset

Scenario A:

Customer X enters into a five-year contract with Supplier Y for the right to transport oil from Country A to Country B through Supplier Y's pipeline. The contract provides that Customer X will have the right to use 95% of the pipeline's capacity throughout the term of the arrangement.

Analysis: The capacity portion of the pipeline is an identified asset. While 95% of the pipeline's capacity is not physically distinct from the remaining capacity of the pipeline, it represents substantially all of the capacity of the entire pipeline and thereby provides Customer X with the right to obtain substantially all of the economic benefits from use of the pipeline.

Scenario B:

Assume the same facts as in Scenario A, except that Customer X has the right to use 60% of the pipeline's capacity throughout the term of the arrangement.

Analysis: The capacity portion of the pipeline is not an identified asset because 60% of the pipeline's capacity is less than substantially all of the capacity of the pipeline. Customer X does not have the right to obtain substantially all of the economic benefits from use of the pipeline.

3.1.3 Substantive substitution rights

Even if an asset is specified, a customer does not have the right to use an identified asset if, at inception of the contract, a supplier has the substantive right to substitute the asset throughout the period of use (i.e. the total period of time that an asset is used to fulfil a contract with a customer, including the sum of any non-consecutive periods of time). A substitution right is substantive when both of the following conditions are met:

- the supplier has the practical ability to substitute alternative assets throughout the period of use (e.g. the customer cannot prevent the supplier from substituting an asset and alternative assets are readily available to the supplier or could be sourced by the supplier within a reasonable period of time); and
- the supplier would benefit economically from the exercise of its right to substitute the asset (i.e. the economic benefits associated with substituting the asset are expected to exceed the costs associated with substituting the asset). *[IFRS 16.B14]*.

The IASB indicated in the Basis for Conclusions to IFRS 16 that the conditions above are intended to differentiate between substitution rights that result in a supplier controlling the use of an asset, rather than the customer, and rights that do not change the substance or character of the contract. *[IFRS 16.BC113]*.

If the supplier has a right or an obligation to substitute the asset only on or after either a particular date or the occurrence of a specified event, the supplier's substitution right is not substantive because the supplier does not have the practical ability to substitute alternative assets throughout the period of use. *[IFRS 16.B15]*.

An entity's evaluation of whether a supplier's substitution right is substantive is based on facts and circumstances at inception of the contract. At inception of the contract, an entity should not consider future events that are not likely to occur. IFRS 16 provides the following examples of circumstances that, at inception of the contract, are not likely to occur and, thus, are excluded from the evaluation of whether a supplier's substitution right is substantive throughout the period of use:

- an agreement by a future customer to pay an above market rate for use of the asset;
- the introduction of new technology that is not substantially developed at inception of the contract;
- a substantial difference between the customer's use of the asset, or the performance of the asset, and the use or performance considered likely at inception of the contract; and
- a substantial difference between the market price of the asset during the period of use, and the market price considered likely at inception of the contract. *[IFRS 16.B16]*.

The requirement that a substitution right must benefit the supplier economically in order to be substantive is a new concept. In many cases, it will be clear that the supplier will not benefit from the exercise of a substitution right because of the costs associated with substituting an asset. *[IFRS 16.BC113]*. If an asset is located at the customer's premises or elsewhere, the costs associated with substitution are generally higher than when located at the supplier's premises, and therefore, are more likely to exceed the benefits associated with substituting the asset. *[IFRS 16.B17]*. However, simply because a supplier concludes that the cost of substitution is not significant does not automatically mean that it would economically benefit from the right of substitution.

IFRS 16 further clarifies that a customer should presume that a supplier's substitution right is not substantive when the customer cannot readily determine whether the supplier has a substantive substitution right. *[IFRS 16.B19]*. This requirement is intended to clarify that a customer is not expected to exert undue effort to provide evidence that a substitution right is not substantive. We believe that the Board did not include a similar provision for suppliers, because they should have sufficient information to make a determination of whether a substitution right is substantive.

Contract terms that allow or require a supplier to substitute alternative assets only when the underlying asset is not operating properly (e.g. a normal warranty provision) or when a technical upgrade becomes available do not create a substantive substitution right. *[IFRS 16.B18]*.

Example 25.5: Substitution rights

Scenario A:

Assume that an electronic data storage provider (supplier) provides services, through a centralised data centre, that involve the use of a specified server (Server No. 9). The supplier maintains many identical servers in a single, accessible location and determines, at inception of the contract, that it is permitted to and can easily substitute another server without the customer's consent throughout the period of use. Further, the supplier would benefit economically from substituting an alternative asset, because doing this would allow the supplier to optimise the performance of its network at only a nominal cost. In addition, the supplier has made clear that it has negotiated this right of substitution as an important right in the arrangement, and the substitution right affected the pricing of the arrangement.

Analysis: The customer does not have the right to use an identified asset because, at the inception of the contract, the supplier has the practical ability to substitute the server and would benefit economically from such a substitution. However, if the customer could not readily determine whether the supplier had a substantive substitution right (e.g. there is insufficient transparency into the supplier's operations), the customer would presume the substitution right is not substantive and conclude that there is an identified asset.

Scenario B:

Assume the same facts as in Scenario A except that Server No. 9 is customised, and the supplier does not have the practical ability to substitute the customised asset throughout the period of use. Additionally, it is unclear whether the supplier would benefit economically from sourcing a similar alternative asset.

Analysis: Because the supplier does not have the practical ability to substitute the asset and there is no evidence of economic benefit to the supplier from substituting the asset, the substitution right is non-substantive, and Server No. 9 would be an identified asset. In this case, neither of the conditions of a substitution right is met. As a reminder, both conditions must be met for the supplier to have a substantive substitution right.

3.1.4 Right to obtain substantially all of the economic benefits from use of the identified asset

To control the use of an identified asset, a customer is required to have the right to obtain substantially all of the economic benefits from use of the asset throughout the period of use (for example, by having exclusive use of the asset throughout that period). A customer can obtain economic benefits from use of an asset directly or indirectly in many ways, such as by using, holding or sub-leasing the asset. The economic benefits from use of an asset include its primary output and by-products (including potential cash flows derived from these items), and other economic benefits from using the asset that could be realised from a commercial transaction with a third party. *[IFRS 16.B21]*.

The term 'substantially all' is not defined in IFRS 16. However, entities might consider the term similarly to how it is used in IAS 17 in the context of lease classification. Economic benefits arising from construction or ownership of the identified asset (e.g. tax benefits related to excess tax depreciation and investment tax credits) are not considered economic benefits derived from the use of the asset. Therefore, they are not considered when assessing whether a customer has the right to obtain substantially all of the economic benefits.

When assessing the right to obtain substantially all of the economic benefits from use of an asset, an entity considers the economic benefits that result from use of the asset within the defined scope of a customer's right to use the asset. For example:

(a) if a contract limits the use of a motor vehicle to only one particular territory during the period of use, an entity considers only the economic benefits from use of the motor vehicle within that territory, and not beyond; or

(b) if a contract specifies that a customer can drive a motor vehicle only up to a particular number of miles during the period of use, an entity considers only the economic benefits from use of the motor vehicle for the permitted mileage, and not beyond. *[IFRS 16.B22]*.

If a contract requires a customer to pay the supplier or another party a portion of the cash flows derived from use of an asset as consideration, those cash flows paid as consideration are considered to be part of the economic benefits that the customer obtains from use of the asset. For example, if the customer is required to pay the supplier a percentage of sales from use of retail space as consideration for that use, that requirement does not prevent the customer from having the right to obtain substantially all of the economic benefits from use of the retail space. This is because the cash flows arising from those sales are considered to be economic benefits that the customer obtains from use of the retail space, a portion of which it then pays to the supplier as consideration for the right to use that space. *[IFRS 16.B23]*.

3.1.5 Right to direct the use of the identified asset

A customer has the right to direct the use of an identified asset throughout the period of use when either:

- the customer has the right to direct how and for what purpose the asset is used throughout the period of use; or
- the relevant decisions about how and for what purpose an asset is used are predetermined; and
  - the customer either has the right to operate the asset, or to direct others to operate the asset in a manner that it determines, throughout the period of use, without the supplier having the right to change those operating instructions; or
  - the customer designed the asset, or specific aspects of the asset, in a way that predetermines how and for what purpose the asset will be used throughout the period of use. *[IFRS 16.B24]*.

Requiring a customer to have the right to direct the use of an identified asset is a change from IFRIC 4. A contract may have met IFRIC 4's control criterion if, for example, the customer obtained substantially all of the output of an underlying asset and met certain price-per-unit-of-output criteria even though the customer did not have the right to direct the use of the identified asset as contemplated by IFRS 16. Under IFRS 16, such arrangements would no longer be considered leases.

3.1.5.A How and for what purpose the asset is used

A customer has the right to direct how and for what purpose the asset is used if, within the scope of its right of use defined in the contract, it can change how and for what purpose the asset is used throughout the period of use. In making this assessment, an entity considers the decision-making rights that are most relevant to changing how and for what purpose the asset is used throughout the period of use. Decision-making rights are relevant when they affect the economic benefits to be derived from use. The decision-making rights that are most relevant are likely to be different for different contracts, depending on the nature of the asset and the terms and conditions of the contract. *[IFRS 16.B25]*.

How and for what purpose an asset is used is a single concept (i.e. 'how' an asset is used is not assessed separately from 'for what purpose' an asset is used).

The IASB have indicated that decisions about how and for what purpose an asset is used can be viewed as similar to the decisions made by a board of directors. Decisions made by a board of directors about the operating and financing activities of an entity are generally the most relevant decisions rather than the actions of individuals implementing those decisions. *[IFRS 16.BC120]*.

Examples of decision-making rights that, depending on the circumstances, grant the right to change how and for what purpose the asset is used, within the defined scope of the customer's right of use, include:

(a) rights to change the type of output that is produced by the asset (for example, to decide whether to use a shipping container to transport goods or for storage, or to decide upon the mix of products sold from retail space);

(b) rights to change when the output is produced (for example, to decide when an item of machinery or a power plant will be used);

(c) rights to change where the output is produced (for example, to decide upon the destination of a truck or a ship, or to decide where an item of equipment is used); and

(d) rights to change whether the output is produced, and the quantity of that output (for example, to decide whether to produce energy from a power plant and how much energy to produce from that power plant). *[IFRS 16.B26]*.

Examples of decision-making rights that do not grant the right to change how and for what purpose the asset is used include rights that are limited to operating or maintaining the asset. Such rights can be held by the customer or the supplier. Although rights such as those to operate or maintain an asset are often essential to the efficient use of an asset, they are not rights to direct how and for what purpose the asset is used and are often dependent on the decisions about how and for what purpose the asset is used. However, rights to operate an asset may grant the customer the right to direct the use of the asset if the relevant decisions about how and for what purpose the asset is used are predetermined. *[IFRS 16.B27]*.

The customer does not need the right to operate the underlying asset to have the right to direct its use. That is, the customer may direct the use of an asset that is operated by the supplier's personnel. However, as discussed at 3.1.5.B below, the right to operate an asset will often provide the customer the right to direct the use of the asset if the relevant decisions about how and for what purpose the asset is used are predetermined.

3.1.5.B Relevant decisions about how and for what purpose the asset is used are predetermined

In some cases, it will not be clear whether the customer has the right to direct the use of the identified asset. This could be the case when the most relevant decisions about how and for what purpose an asset is used are predetermined by contractual restrictions on the use of the asset (e.g. the decisions about the use of the asset are agreed to by the customer and the supplier in negotiating the contract, and those decisions cannot be changed). This could also be the case when the most relevant decisions about how and for what purpose an asset is used are, in effect, predetermined by the design of the asset. The IASB indicated that it would expect decisions about how and for what purpose an asset is used to be predetermined in few cases. *[IFRS 16.BC121]*. In such cases, a customer has the right to direct the use of an identified asset throughout the period of use when the customer either:

- has the right to operate the asset, or direct others to operate the asset in a manner it determines, throughout the period of use without the supplier having the right to change those operating instructions; or
- designed the asset (or specific aspects of the asset) in a way that predetermines how and for what purpose the asset will be used throughout the period of use. *[IFRS 16.B24]*.

Significant judgement may be required to assess whether a customer designed the asset (or specific aspects of the asset) in a way that predetermines how and for what purpose the asset will be used throughout the period of use.

3.1.5.C Specifying the output of an asset before the period of use

The relevant decisions about how and for what purpose the asset is used can be predetermined in a number of ways. For example, the relevant decisions can be predetermined by the design of the asset or by contractual restrictions on the use of the asset. *[IFRS 16.B28]*.

In assessing whether a customer has the right to direct the use of an asset, an entity considers only rights to make decisions about the use of the asset during the period of use, unless the customer designed the asset (or specific aspects of the asset) as described in paragraph B24(b)(ii). See 3.1.5 above. Consequently, unless the conditions in paragraph B24(b)(ii) exist, an entity does not consider decisions that are predetermined before the period of use. For example, if a customer is able only to specify the output of an asset before the period of use, the customer does not have the right to direct the use of that asset. The ability to specify the output in a contract before the period of use, without any other decision-making rights relating to the use of the asset, gives a customer the same rights as any customer that purchases goods or services. *[IFRS 16.B29]*.

3.1.5.D Protective rights

A contract may include terms and conditions designed to protect the supplier's interest in the asset or other assets, to protect its personnel, or to ensure the supplier's compliance with laws or regulations. These are examples of protective rights. For example, a contract may (i) specify the maximum amount of use of an asset or limit where or when the customer can use the asset, (ii) require a customer to follow particular operating practices, or (iii) require a customer to inform the supplier of changes in how an asset will be used. Protective rights typically define the scope of the customer's right of use but do not, in isolation, prevent the customer from having the right to direct the use of an asset. *[IFRS 16.B30]*.

Example 25.6: Right to direct the use of an asset

Customer X enters into a contract with Supplier Y to use a vehicle for a three year period. The vehicle is identified in the contract. Supplier Y cannot substitute another vehicle unless the specified vehicle is not operational (e.g. it breaks down).

Under the contract:

- Customer X operates the vehicle (i.e. drives the vehicle) or directs others to operate the vehicle (e.g. hires a driver);
- Customer X decides how to use the vehicle (within contractual limitations, discussed below). For example, throughout the period of use, Customer X decides where the vehicle goes as well as when or whether it is used and what it is used for. Customer X can also change these decisions throughout the period of use; and
- Supplier Y prohibits certain uses of the vehicle (e.g. moving it overseas) and modifications to the vehicle to protect its interest in the asset.

Analysis: Customer X has the right to direct the use of the identified vehicle throughout the period of use. Customer X has the right to direct the use of the vehicle because it has the right to change how the vehicle is used, when or whether the vehicle is used, where the vehicle goes and what the vehicle is used for.

Supplier Y's limits on certain uses for the vehicle and modifications to it are considered protective rights that define the scope of Customer X's use of the asset but do not affect the assessment of whether Customer X directs the use of the asset.

3.1.6 Flowchart of the decision making process

IFRS 16 contains a flowchart that depicts the decision making process for determining whether an arrangement contains a lease. *[IFRS 16.B31]*. This has been provided below.

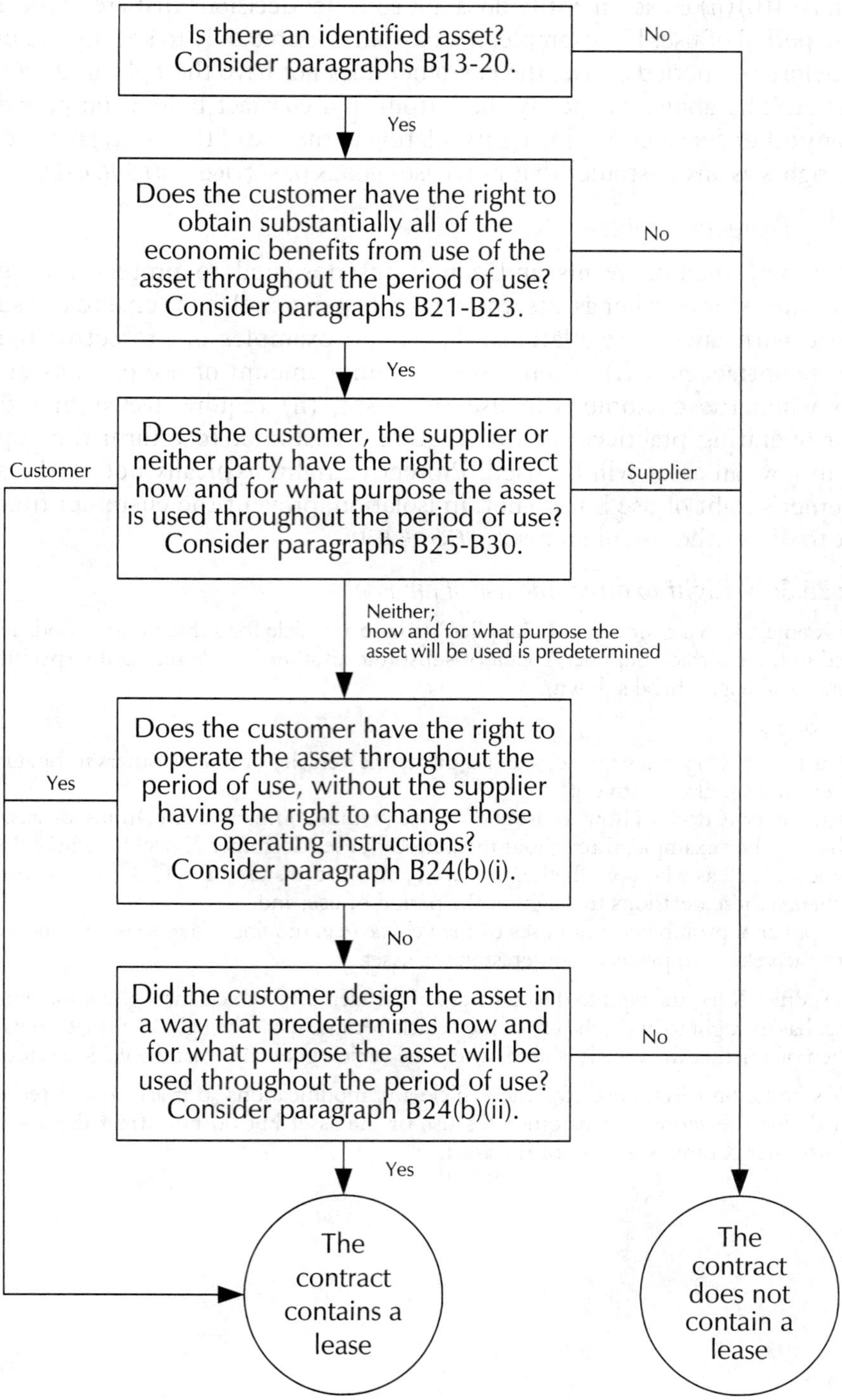

3.1.7 *Reassessment of the contract*

An entity reassesses whether a contract is, or contains, a lease only if the terms and conditions of the contract are changed. *[IFRS 16.11]*. A change in the terms and conditions of a contract does not include the exercise of an option (e.g. a renewal option) or failure to exercise an option that is included in the contract.

3.2 Identifying and separating lease and non-lease components of a contract

3.2.1 *Identifying and separating lease components of a contract*

An entity accounts for each lease component within a contract as a lease separately from non-lease components of the contract, unless the entity (lessees only) applies the practical expedient in paragraph 15 of IFRS 16. *[IFRS 16.12]*. See 3.2.2.B below.

The right to use an underlying asset is a separate lease component if both:

(a) the lessee can benefit from use of the underlying asset either on its own or together with other resources that are readily available to the lessee. Readily available resources are goods or services that are sold or leased separately (by the lessor or other suppliers) or resources that the lessee has already obtained (from the lessor or from other transactions or events); and

(b) the underlying asset is neither highly dependent on, nor highly interrelated with, the other underlying assets in the contract. For example, the fact that a lessee could decide not to lease the underlying asset without significantly affecting its rights to use other underlying assets in the contract might indicate that the underlying asset is not highly dependent on, or highly interrelated with, those other underlying assets. *[IFRS 16.B32]*.

If one or both of these criteria are not met, the right to use multiple assets is considered a single lease component.

A contract may include an amount payable by the lessee for activities and costs that do not transfer a good or service to the lessee. For example, a lessor may include in the total amount payable a charge for administrative tasks, or other costs it incurs associated with the lease, that do not transfer a good or service to the lessee. Such amounts payable do not give rise to a separate component of the contract, but are considered to be part of the total consideration that is allocated to the separately identified components of the contract. *[IFRS 16.B33]*.

Example 25.7: Identifying and separating lease components

Scenario A

Assume that a lessee enters into a lease of a warehouse and the surrounding car park that is used for deliveries and truck parking. The lessee is a local trucking company that intends to use the warehouse as the hub for its shipping operations.

Analysis: From the perspective of the lessee, the contract contains one lease component. The lessee would be unable to benefit from the use of the warehouse without also using the car park. Therefore, the warehouse space is dependent upon the car park.

Scenario B

Assume the same facts as in Scenario A, except that the contract also conveys the right to use an additional plot of land that is adjacent to the car park. This plot of land could be developed by the lessee for other uses (e.g. to construct a truck maintenance facility).

Analysis: From the perspective of the lessee, the contract contains two lease components: a lease of the warehouse (together with the car park) and a lease of the adjacent plot of land. Because the adjacent land could be developed for other uses independent of the warehouse and car park, the lessee can benefit from the adjacent plot of land on its own or together with other readily available resources. The lessee can also benefit from the use of the warehouse and car park on its own or together with other readily available resources.

For contracts that involve the right to use land and buildings, IFRS 16 requires a lessor to classify (see 6.1 below) and account for the right to use land as a separate lease component, unless the accounting effect of doing so is immaterial to the lease. *[IFRS 16.B57]*. For example, separation of the land may not be necessary when the amount that would be recognised for the land lease component is immaterial to the lease. If the lease payments cannot be allocated reliably between the land and the buildings, the entire lease is classified as a finance lease, unless it is clear that both elements are operating leases (i.e. the entire lease is classified as an operating lease). *[IFRS 16.B56]*. An entity that leases an entire building (i.e. 100% of the building) is inherently leasing the land underneath the building and would potentially account for the land and building as separate lease components. However, this would not necessarily be the case when an entity only leases part of the building.

3.2.2 *Identifying and separating lease from non-lease components of a contract*

Many contracts contain a lease coupled with an agreement to purchase or sell other goods or services (non-lease components). The non-lease components are identified and accounted for separately from the lease component in accordance with other standards, unless the lessee applies the practical expedient as discussed at 3.2.2.B below. *[IFRS 16.16]*. For example, the non-lease components may be accounted for as executory arrangements by lessees (customers) or as contracts subject to IFRS 15 by lessors (suppliers).

Some contracts contain items that do not relate to the transfer of goods or services by the lessor to the lessee (e.g. fees or other administrative costs a lessor charges a lessee). These items are not considered separate lease or non-lease components, and lessees and lessors do not allocate consideration in the contract to these items. See 3.2.3.B below. However, if the lessor provides services (e.g. maintenance, supply of utilities) or operates the underlying asset (e.g. vessel charter, aircraft wet lease), the contract would generally contain non-lease components.

Identifying non-lease components of contracts may change practice for some lessees. Under IAS 17, entities may not focus on identifying lease and non-lease components because the accounting treatment (e.g. accounting for an operating lease and a service contract is often the same.

3.2.2.A Lessee reimbursements

Under IFRS 16, payments for maintenance activities, including common area maintenance (e.g. cleaning the common areas of a building, removing snow from a car park for employees and customers) and other goods or services transferred to the tenant (e.g. providing utilities or rubbish removal) are considered non-lease components because they provide the lessee with a service.

In some leases, a lessee may also reimburse (or make certain payments on behalf of) the lessor that relate to the leased asset for activities and costs that do not transfer a good or service to the lessee (e.g. payments made for real estate taxes that would be owed by the lessor regardless of whether it leased the building and regardless of who the lessee is, payments made for insurance that protects the lessor's investment in the asset and the landlord will receive the proceeds from any claim). Under IFRS 16, such costs are not separate components of the contract because they do not represent payments for goods or services and are considered to be part of the total consideration that is allocated to the separately identified components of the contract (i.e. the lease and non-lease components). Entities also need to evaluate whether such payments are fixed (or in-substance fixed) lease payments or variable lease payments. See 4.5 below.

Example 25.8: Activities that are not components of a lease contract

A lessee enters into a three-year lease of equipment, with fixed annual payments of CU 12,000. The contract itemises the fixed annual payments as follows: CU 9,000 for rent, CU 2,500 for maintenance and CU 500 of administrative tasks.

Analysis: The contract contains two components – one lease component (lease of equipment) and a non-lease component (maintenance). The amount paid for administrative tasks does not transfer a good or service to the lessee. Therefore, the total consideration in the contract of CU 36,000 will be allocated to the lease component (equipment) and the non-lease component (maintenance).

3.2.2.B Practical expedient – lessees

As a practical expedient, a lessee may elect, by class of underlying asset, not to separate non-lease components from lease components, and instead account for each lease component and any associated non-lease components as a single lease component. A lessee cannot apply this practical expedient to embedded derivatives that meet the criteria in paragraph 4.3.3 of IFRS 9 – *Financial Instruments*. *[IFRS 16.15]*. See Chapter 44 at 4.

IFRS 16 provides this expedient to alleviate concerns that the costs and administrative burden of allocating consideration to separate lease and non-lease components may not be justified by the benefit of more precisely reflecting the right-of-use asset and the lease liability. Furthermore, the IASB expects the practical expedient to most often be used when the non-lease components of a contract are not significant when compared with the lease components of a contract. *[IFRS 16.BC135]*. The practical expedient does not allow lessees to account for multiple lease components of a contract as a single lease component.

Lessees that make the policy election to account for each separate lease component of a contract and any associated non-lease components as a single lease component allocate all of the contract consideration to the lease component. Therefore, the initial and subsequent measurement of the lease liability and right-of-use asset is higher than if the policy election was not applied.

3.2.3 Determining and allocating the consideration in the contract – lessees

3.2.3.A Determining the consideration in the contract

IFRS 16 does not define 'consideration' in a contract, nor is 'consideration' defined in the IFRS Glossary. However, we believe that the consideration in a contract for a lessee would include all the lease payments described at 4.5 below, as well as certain other consideration in the contract regardless of whether it is labelled as lease payments or payments for non-lease components of a contract, including other fixed payments (e.g. monthly service charges) or in-substance fixed payments, variable payments that depend on an index or a rate, initially measured using the index or rate at the commencement date, less any incentives paid or payable to the lessee, other than those included in lease payments.

3.2.3.B Allocating the consideration in the contract – lessees

For a contract that contains a lease component and one or more additional lease or non-lease components, a lessee allocates the consideration in the contract to each lease component on the basis of the relative stand-alone price of the lease component and the aggregate stand-alone price of the non-lease components. *[IFRS 16.13]*.

The relative stand-alone price of lease and non-lease components is determined on the basis of the price the lessor, or a similar supplier, would charge an entity for that component, or a similar component, separately. If an observable stand-alone price is not readily available, the lessee estimates the stand-alone price, maximising the use of observable information. *[IFRS 16.14]*. A contractually stated price may be the stand-alone price for a good or service but it is not presumed to be for accounting purposes.

Example 25.9: Allocating contract consideration to lease and non-lease components – lessees

A lessee enters into a lease of equipment. The contract stipulates the lessor will perform maintenance of the leased equipment and receive consideration for that maintenance service. The contract includes the following fixed prices for the lease and non-lease component:

Lease	CU80,000
Maintenance	CU10,000
Total	CU90,000

The stand-alone prices cannot be readily observed, so the lessee makes estimates, maximising the use of observable information, of the lease and non-lease components, as follows:

Lease	CU85,000
Maintenance	CU15,000
Total	CU100,000

Analysis: The stand-alone price for the lease component represents 85% of total estimated stand-alone prices. The lessee allocates the consideration in the contract (CU90,000), as follows:

Lease	CU76,500	(1)
Maintenance	CU13,500	(2)
Total	CU90,000	

(1) 85% × CU90,000
(2) 15% × CU90,000

3.2.4 Determining and allocating the consideration in the contract – lessors

3.2.4.A Determining the consideration in the contract

As discussed at 3.2.3.A above, IFRS 16 does not define 'consideration' in a lease contract, nor is 'consideration' defined in the IFRS Glossary. However, we believe that the consideration in a lease contract for a lessor would include the following:

- lease payments as described at 4.5 below;
- the following other payments not labelled in the contract as lease payments:
  - any other fixed payments (e.g. monthly service charges, non-lease components such as maintenance) or in-substance fixed payments made during the lease term, less any incentives paid or payable to the lessee;
  - any other variable payments that depend on an index or a rate made during the lease term and initially measured using the index or rate at the commencement date; and
  - any other variable payment amounts that would be included in the transaction price in accordance with the requirements on variable consideration in IFRS 15 that specifically relate to either of the following:
    - the lessor's efforts to transfer one or more goods or services that are not leases; or
    - an outcome from transferring one or more goods or services that are not leases.

Variable consideration is defined broadly in IFRS 15 and can take many forms. Consideration can vary because of discounts, rebates, refunds, credits, price concessions, incentives, performance bonuses, penalties or other similar items. It is important for lessors to appropriately identify the different types of variable consideration included in the contract because estimating variable consideration requires lessors to apply a constraint to each type of variable consideration. See Chapter 30 at 5.2.3 for further discussion on variable consideration under IFRS 15.

3.2.4.B Allocating the consideration in the contract – lessors

For a contract that contains a lease component and one or more additional lease or non-lease components, a lessor allocates the consideration in the contract applying paragraphs 73 to 90 of IFRS 15. *[IFRS 16.17]*.

Paragraphs 73 to 86 of IFRS 15 require the lessor to allocate the consideration in the contract between the lease and non-lease components on a relative stand-alone selling price basis. In addition, lessors are required to apply paragraphs 87-90 of IFRS 15 to allocate any subsequent changes in the consideration of the contract between the lease and non-lease components. The stand-alone selling price is the price at which an entity would sell a promised good or service separately to a customer. When stand-alone selling prices are not directly observable, the lessor must estimate the stand-alone selling price. Paragraph 79 of IFRS 15 provides suitable methods for estimating the stand-alone selling price. See Chapter 30 at 6.1 for further discussion on estimating stand-alone selling prices under IFRS 15.

The following example from the IFRS 16 illustrative examples illustrates the allocation of consideration in a contract to lease and non-lease components by a lessee. *[IFRS 16.IE4].*

Example 25.10: Lessee allocation of consideration to lease and non-lease components of a contract (IFRS 16 Example 12)

Lessor leases a bulldozer, a truck and a long-reach excavator to Lessee to be used in Lessee's mining operations for four years. Lessor also agrees to maintain each item of equipment throughout the lease term. The total consideration in the contract is CU600,000[(a)], payable in annual instalments of CU150,000, and a variable amount that depends on the hours of work performed in maintaining the long-reach excavator. The variable payment is capped at 2 per cent of the replacement cost of the long-reach excavator. The consideration includes the cost of maintenance services for each item of equipment.

Lessee accounts for the non-lease components (maintenance services) separately from each lease of equipment applying paragraph 12 of IFRS 16. Lessee does not elect the practical expedient in paragraph 15 of IFRS 16. Lessee considers the requirements in paragraph B32 of IFRS 16 and concludes that the lease of the bulldozer, the lease of the truck and the lease of the long-reach excavator are each separate lease components. This is because:

(a) Lessee can benefit from use of each of the three items of equipment on its own or together with other readily available resources (for example, Lessee could readily lease or purchase an alternative truck or excavator to use in its operations); and

(b) although Lessee is leasing all three items of equipment for one purpose (i.e. to engage in mining operations), the machines are neither highly dependent on, nor highly interrelated with, each other.

Lessee's ability to derive benefit from the lease of each item of equipment is not significantly affected by its decision to lease, or not lease, the other equipment from Lessor. Consequently, Lessee concludes that there are three lease components and three non-lease components (maintenance services) in the contract. Lessee applies the guidance in paragraphs 13–14 of IFRS 16 to allocate the consideration in the contract to the three lease components and the non-lease components.

Several suppliers provide maintenance services for a similar bulldozer and a similar truck. Accordingly, there are observable standalone prices for the maintenance services for those two items of leased equipment. Lessee is able to establish observable stand-alone prices for the maintenance of the bulldozer and the truck of CU32,000 and CU16,000, respectively, assuming similar payment terms to those in the contract with Lessor. The long-reach excavator is highly specialised and, accordingly, other suppliers do not lease or provide maintenance services for similar excavators. Nonetheless, Lessor provides four-year maintenance service contracts to customers that purchase similar long-reach excavators from Lessor. The observable consideration for those four-year maintenance service contracts is a fixed amount of CU56,000, payable over four years, and a variable amount that depends on the hours of work performed in maintaining the long-reach excavator.

That variable payment is capped at 2 per cent of the replacement cost of the long-reach excavator. Consequently, Lessee estimates the stand-alone price of the maintenance services for the long-reach excavator to be CU56,000 plus any variable amounts. Lessee is able to establish observable stand-alone prices for the leases of the bulldozer, the truck and the long-reach excavator of CU170,000, CU102,000 and CU224,000, respectively.

Lessee allocates the fixed consideration in the contract (CU600,000) to the lease and non-lease components as follows:

CU	Bulldozer	Truck	Long-reach excavator	Total
Lease	170,000	102,000	224,000	496,000
Non-lease				104,000
Total fixed consideration				600,000

Lessee allocates all of the variable consideration to the maintenance of the long-reach excavator, and, thus, to the non-lease components of the contract. Lessee then accounts for each lease component applying the guidance in IFRS 16, treating the allocated consideration as the lease payments for each lease component.

(a) In these Illustrative Examples, currency amounts are denominated in 'currency units' (CU).

3.3 Contract combinations

An entity combines two or more contracts entered into at or near the same time with the same counterparty (or related parties of the counterparty), and accounts for the contracts as a single contract if one or more of the following criteria are met:

(a) the contracts are negotiated as a package with an overall commercial objective that cannot be understood without considering the contracts together;

(b) the amount of consideration to be paid in one contract depends on the price or performance of the other contract; or

(c) the rights to use underlying assets conveyed in the contracts (or some rights to use underlying assets conveyed in each of the contracts) form a single lease component. *[IFRS 16.B2]*.

The IASB developed these criteria to address concerns that separately accounting for multiple contracts may not result in a faithful representation of the combined transaction. *[IFRS 16.BC130-132]*.

4 KEY CONCEPTS

4.1 Inception of a contract

IFRS 16 requires customers and suppliers to determine whether a contract is a lease at inception of the contract. The inception date is the earlier of the date of a lease agreement and the date of commitment by the parties to the principal terms and conditions of the lease. *[IFRS 16.Appendix A]*.

The underlying asset is the asset that is subject to a lease, for which the right to use that asset has been provided by a lessor to a lessee. *[IFRS 16.Appendix A]*.

4.2 Commencement date of the lease

The commencement date is the date on which the lessor makes an underlying asset available for use by a lessee. *[IFRS 16.Appendix A]*. In some cases, the commencement date of the lease may be before the date stipulated in the lease agreement (e.g. the date on which rents become due and payable). This often occurs when the leased space is modified by the lessee prior to commencing operations in the leased space (e.g. during the period a lessee uses the leased space to construct its own leasehold improvements). If a lessee takes possession of, or is given control over, the use of the underlying asset before it begins operations or making lease payments under the terms of the lease, the lease term has commenced even if the lessee is not required to pay rent or the lease arrangement states the lease commencement date is a later date. The timing of when lease payments begin under the contract does not affect the commencement date of the lease. For example, a lessee (except for a lessee applying the short-term lease or low-value asset exemption discussed at 5.1.1 and 5.1.2 below) initially recognises a lease liability and related right-of-use asset on the commencement date and a lessor (for finance leases) initially recognises its net investment in the lease on the commencement date.

4.3 Lessee involvement with the underlying asset before the commencement date

An entity may negotiate a lease before the underlying asset is available for use by the lessee. For some leases, the underlying asset may need to be constructed or redesigned for use by the lessee. Depending on the terms and conditions of the contract, a lessee may be required to make payments relating to the construction or design of the asset. *[IFRS 16.B43]*.

If a lessee incurs costs relating to the construction or design of an underlying asset, the lessee accounts for those costs applying other IFRS, such as IAS 16 – *Property, Plant and Equipment*. Costs relating to the construction or design of an underlying asset do not include payments made by the lessee for the right to use the underlying asset. Payments for the right to use an underlying asset are payments for a lease, regardless of the timing of those payments. *[IFRS 16.B44]*.

A lessee may obtain legal title to an underlying asset before that legal title is transferred to the lessor and the asset is leased to the lessee. Obtaining legal title does not in itself determine how to account for the transaction. *[IFRS 16.B45]*.

If the lessee controls (or obtains control of) the underlying asset before that asset is transferred to the lessor, the transaction is a sale and leaseback transaction that is accounted for as described at 8 below. *[IFRS 16.B46]*.

However, if the lessee does not obtain control of the underlying asset before the asset is transferred to the lessor, the transaction is not a sale and leaseback transaction. For example, this may be the case if a manufacturer, a lessor and a lessee negotiate a transaction for the purchase of an asset from the manufacturer by the lessor, which is in turn leased to the lessee. The lessee may obtain legal title to the underlying asset before legal title transfers to the lessor. In this case, if the lessee obtains legal title to the underlying asset but does not obtain control of the asset before it is transferred to the lessor, the transaction is not accounted for as a sale and leaseback transaction, but as a lease. *[IFRS 16.B47]*.

4.4 Lease term and purchase options

An entity determines the lease term as the non-cancellable period of the lease, together with both:

- Periods covered by an option to extend the lease if the lessee is reasonably certain to exercise that option; and
- Periods covered by an option to terminate the lease if the lessee is reasonably certain not to exercise that option. *[IFRS 16.18]*.

The phrase 'reasonably certain' was also used in IAS 17 and is generally interpreted as a high threshold. Therefore, the IASB does not anticipate a change in practice.

Purchase options are assessed in the same way as options to extend or terminate the lease. The IASB indicated that an option to purchase an underlying asset is economically similar to an option to extend the lease term for the remaining economic life of the underlying asset. *[IFRS 16.BC173]*.

The lease term begins at the commencement date and includes any rent-free periods provided to the lessee by the lessor. *[IFRS 16.B36]*.

In assessing whether a lessee is reasonably certain to exercise an option to extend a lease, or not to exercise an option to terminate a lease, an entity considers all relevant facts and circumstances that create an economic incentive for the lessee to exercise the option to extend the lease, or not to exercise the option to terminate the lease. *[IFRS 16.19]*.

At the commencement date, an entity assesses whether the lessee is reasonably certain to exercise an option to extend the lease or to purchase the underlying asset, or not to exercise an option to terminate the lease. The entity considers all relevant facts and circumstances that create an economic incentive for the lessee to exercise, or not to exercise, the option, including any expected changes in facts and circumstances from the commencement date until the exercise date of the option. Examples of factors to consider include, but are not limited to:

(a) contractual terms and conditions for the optional periods compared with market rates, such as:
  (i) the amount of payments for the lease in any optional period;
  (ii) the amount of any variable payments for the lease or other contingent payments, such as payments resulting from termination penalties and residual value guarantees; and
  (iii) the terms and conditions of any options that are exercisable after initial optional periods (for example, a purchase option that is exercisable at the end of an extension period at a rate that is currently below market rates).

(b) significant leasehold improvements undertaken (or expected to be undertaken) over the term of the contract that are expected to have significant economic benefit for the lessee when the option to extend or terminate the lease, or to purchase the underlying asset, becomes exercisable;

(c) costs relating to the termination of the lease, such as negotiation costs, relocation costs, costs of identifying another underlying asset suitable for the lessee's needs, costs of integrating a new asset into the lessee's operations, or termination penalties and similar costs, including costs associated with returning the underlying asset in a contractually specified condition or to a contractually specified location;

(d) the importance of that underlying asset to the lessee's operations, considering, for example, whether the underlying asset is a specialised asset, the location of the underlying asset and the availability of suitable alternatives; and

(e) conditionality associated with exercising the option (i.e. when the option can be exercised only if one or more conditions are met), and the likelihood that those conditions will exist. *[IFRS 16.B37]*.

The longer the period from commencement of the lease to the exercise date of an option, the more difficult it will be, in certain cases, to determine whether the exercise of the option is reasonably certain. The difficulty arises from several factors. For example, a lessee's estimates of its future needs for the leased asset become less precise the further into the future the forecast goes. Also, the future fair value of certain assets such as those involving technology is more difficult to predict than the future fair value of a relatively stable asset, such as a fully leased commercial office building located in a prime area.

The further into the future that the option date is, the lower the option price must be in relation to the estimated future fair value to conclude that the lessee is reasonably certain to exercise the option. The difference between the option price and the estimated future fair value of an asset that is subject to significant changes in value also should be greater than would be the case for an asset with a relatively stable value.

An artificially short lease term (e.g. a lease of a corporate headquarters, distribution facility, manufacturing plant or other key property with a four-year lease term), may effectively create a significant economic incentive for the lessee to exercise a purchase or renewal option. This may be evidenced by the significance of the underlying asset to the lessee's continuing operations and whether, absent the option, the lessee would have entered into such a lease.

Similarly, the significance of the underlying asset to the lessee's operations may affect a lessee's decisions about whether it is reasonably certain to exercise a purchase or renewal option. For example, a company that leases a specialised facility (e.g. manufacturing plant, distribution facility, corporate headquarters) and does not exercise a purchase or renewal option would face a significant economic penalty if an alternative facility is not readily available. This would potentially have an adverse effect on the company while it searched for a replacement asset.

An option to extend or terminate a lease may be combined with one or more other contractual features (for example, a residual value guarantee) such that the lessee guarantees the lessor a minimum or fixed cash return that is substantially the same regardless of whether the option is exercised. In such cases, and notwithstanding the guidance on in-substance fixed payments (see 4.5.1 below), an entity assumes that the lessee is reasonably certain to exercise the option to extend the lease, or not to exercise the option to terminate the lease. *[IFRS 16.B38]*.

The shorter the non-cancellable period of a lease, the more likely a lessee is to exercise an option to extend the lease or not to exercise an option to terminate the lease. This is because the costs associated with obtaining a replacement asset are likely to be proportionately higher the shorter the non-cancellable period. *[IFRS 16.B39]*.

A lessee's past practice regarding the period over which it has typically used particular types of assets (whether leased or owned), and its economic reasons for doing so, may provide information that is helpful in assessing whether the lessee is reasonably certain to exercise, or not to exercise, an option. For example, if a lessee has typically used particular types of assets for a particular period of time or if the lessee has a practice of frequently exercising options on leases of particular types of underlying assets, the lessee considers the economic reasons for that past practice in assessing whether it is reasonably certain to exercise an option on leases of those assets. *[IFRS 16.B40]*.

Example 25.11: Determining the lease term

Scenario A

Assume that Entity P enters into a lease for equipment that includes a non-cancellable term of four years and a two-year fixed-priced renewal option with future lease payments that are intended to approximate market rates at lease inception. There are no termination penalties or other factors indicating that Entity P is reasonably certain to exercise the renewal option.

Analysis: At the lease commencement date, the lease term is four years.

Scenario B

Assume that Entity Q enters into a lease for a building that includes a non-cancellable term of four years and a two-year, market-priced renewal option. Before it takes possession of the building, Entity Q pays for leasehold improvements. The leasehold improvements are expected to have significant value at the end of four years, and that value can only be realised through continued occupancy of the leased property.

Analysis: At lease commencement, Entity Q determines that it is reasonably certain to exercise the renewal option because it would suffer a significant economic penalty if it abandoned the leasehold improvements at the end of the initial non-cancellable period. At lease commencement, Entity Q concludes that the lease term is six years.

Chapter 25

4.4.1 Cancellable leases

In determining the lease term and assessing the length of the non-cancellable period of a lease, an entity applies the definition of a contract and determine the period for which the contract is enforceable. A lease is no longer enforceable when the lessee and the lessor each has the right to terminate the lease without permission from the other party with no more than an insignificant penalty. *[IFRS 16.B34]*.

Any non-cancellable periods (by the lessee and lessor) in contracts that meet the definition of a lease are considered part of the lease term. If only a lessee has the right to terminate a lease, that right is considered to be an option to terminate the lease available to the lessee that an entity considers when determining the lease term. If only a lessor has the right to terminate a lease, the non-cancellable period of the lease includes the period covered by the option to terminate the lease. *[IFRS 16.B35]*.

Example 25.12: Cancellable leases

A lease contract has an initial non-cancellable period of one year and an extension for an additional year if both the lessee and the lessor agree. There is no penalty if the lessee and the lessor do not agree. The initial one-year non-cancellable period meets the definition of a contract because it creates enforceable rights and obligations. However, the one-year extension period does not meet the definition of a contract because both the lessee and the lessor could unilaterally elect to not extend the arrangement without penalty.

4.4.2 Reassessment of lease term and purchase options – lessees

After lease commencement, IFRS 16 requires lessees to monitor leases for significant changes that could trigger a change in the lease term. A lessee reassesses whether it is reasonably certain to exercise an extension option, or not to exercise a termination option, upon the occurrence of either a significant event or a significant change in circumstances that:

(a) is within the control of the lessee; and

(b) affects whether the lessee is reasonably certain to exercise an option not previously included in its determination of the lease term, or not to exercise an option previously included in its determination of the lease term. *[IFRS 16.20]*.

Examples of significant events or changes in circumstances that would trigger a reassessment include:

(a) significant leasehold improvements not anticipated at the commencement date that are expected to have significant economic benefit for the lessee when the option to extend or terminate the lease, or to purchase the underlying asset, becomes exercisable;

(b) a significant modification to, or customisation of, the underlying asset that was not anticipated at the commencement date;

(c) the inception of a sublease of the underlying asset for a period beyond the end of the previously determined lease term; and

(d) a business decision of the lessee that is directly relevant to exercising, or not exercising, an option (for example, a decision to extend the lease of a complementary asset, to dispose of an alternative asset or to dispose of a business unit within which the right-of-use asset is employed). *[IFRS 16.B41]*.

An entity revises the lease term if there is a change in the non-cancellable period of a lease. For example, the non-cancellable period of a lease will change if:

(a) the lessee exercises an option not previously included in the entity's determination of the lease term;

(b) the lessee does not exercise an option previously included in the entity's determination of the lease term;

(c) an event occurs that contractually obliges the lessee to exercise an option not previously included in the entity's determination of the lease term; or

(d) an event occurs that contractually prohibits the lessee from exercising an option previously included in the entity's determination of the lease term. *[IFRS 16.21]*.

As a lessee is required to reassess the lease term upon the occurrence of either a significant event or a significant change in circumstances that is within the control of the lessee, the revision of the lease term often happens before the actual exercise of the option in these circumstances. Additionally, if the reassessment of lease term or the exercise of a purchase option results in a change, lessees would remeasure the lease liability, using revised inputs (e.g. discount rate) at the reassessment date, and would adjust the right-of-use asset. However, if the right-of-use asset is reduced to zero, a lessee would recognise any remaining amount in profit or loss. See 4.5.9 below.

4.4.3 *Reassessment of lease term and purchase options – lessors*

IFRS 16 requires a lessor to revise the lease term to account for a lessee's exercise of an option to extend or terminate the lease or purchase the underlying asset.

4.5 Lease payments

Lease payments are payments made by a lessee to a lessor relating to the right to use an underlying asset during the lease term, comprising the following:

(a) fixed payments (including in-substance fixed payments), less any lease incentives;

(b) variable lease payments that depend on an index or a rate;

(c) the exercise price of a purchase option if the lessee is reasonably certain to exercise that option; and

(d) payments of penalties for terminating the lease, if the lease term reflects the lessee exercising an option to terminate the lease.

For the lessee, lease payments also include amounts expected to be payable by the lessee under residual value guarantees. Lease payments do not include payments allocated to non-lease components of a contract, unless the lessee elects to combine non-lease components with a lease component and to account for them as a single lease component.

For the lessor, lease payments also include any residual value guarantees provided to the lessor by the lessee, a party related to the lessee or a third party unrelated to the lessor that is financially capable of discharging the obligations under the guarantee. Lease payments do not include payments allocated to non-lease components. *[IFRS 16.Appendix A]*.

4.5.1 *In-substance fixed lease payments*

Lease payments include any in-substance fixed lease payments. In-substance fixed lease payments are payments that may, in form, contain variability but that, in substance, are unavoidable. In-substance fixed lease payments exist, for example, if:

(a) payments are structured as variable lease payments, but there is no genuine variability in those payments. Those payments contain variable clauses that do not have real economic substance. Examples of those types of payments include:

  (i) payments that must be made only if an asset is proven to be capable of operating during the lease, or only if an event occurs that has no genuine possibility of not occurring; or

  (ii) payments that are initially structured as variable lease payments linked to the use of the underlying asset but for which the variability will be resolved at some point after the commencement date so that the payments become fixed for the remainder of the lease term. Those payments become in-substance fixed payments when the variability is resolved;

(b) there is more than one set of payments that a lessee could make, but only one of those sets of payments is realistic. In this case, an entity considers the realistic set of payments to be lease payments; or

(c) there is more than one realistic set of payments that a lessee could make, but it must make at least one of those sets of payments. In this case, an entity considers the set of payments that aggregates to the lowest amount (on a discounted basis) to be lease payments. *[IFRS 16.B42]*.

4.5.2 *Lease incentives*

Lease incentives are defined as 'payments made by a lessor to a lessee associated with a lease, or the reimbursement or assumption by a lessor of costs of a lessee'. *[IFRS 16.Appendix A]*.

A lease agreement with a lessor might include incentives for the lessee to sign the lease, such as an up-front cash payment to the lessee, payment of costs for the lessee (such as moving expenses) or the assumption by the lessor of the lessee's pre-existing lease with a third party.

For lessees, lease incentives that are paid or payable to the lessee are deducted from lease payments and reduce the initial measurement of a lessee's right-of-use asset. Lease incentives that are payable to the lessee at lease commencement reduce a lessee's lease liability.

For lessors, lease incentives that are paid or payable to the lessee are also deducted from lease payments and affect the lease classification test. For finance leases, lease incentives that are payable to the lessee reduce the expected lease receivables at the commencement date and thereby the initial measurement of the lessor's net investment in the lease. For operating leases, lessors should defer the cost of any lease incentives paid or payable to the lessee and recognise that cost as a reduction to lease income over the lease term.

4.5.3 *Variable lease payments that depend on an index or rate*

Variable lease payments that depend on an index or a rate include, for example, payments linked to a consumer price index, payments linked to a benchmark interest rate (such as LIBOR) or payments that vary to reflect changes in market rental rates. *[IFRS 16.28]*. The payments are included in the lease payments and are measured using the prevailing index or rate at the measurement date (e.g. lease commencement date for initial measurement). The IASB indicated in the Basis for Conclusions that, despite the measurement uncertainty associated with changes to index- or rate-based payments, the payments meet the definition of an asset (lessor) and a liability (lessee) because they are unavoidable. *[IFRS 16.BC165]*. Lessees subsequently remeasure the lease liability if there is a change in the cash flows (i.e. when the adjustment to the lease payments takes effect) for future payments resulting from a change in index or rate used to determine lease payments.

Example 25.13: Variable lease payment that depends on an index or rate

Assume that Entity A enters into a 10-year lease of property. The lease payment for the first year is CU1,000. The lease payments are linked to the consumer price index (CPI), i.e. not a floating interest rate. The CPI at the beginning of the first year is 100. Lease payments are updated at the end of every second year. At the end of year one, the CPI is 105. At the end of year two, the CPI is 108.

Analysis: At the lease commencement date, the lease payments are CU1,000 per year for 10 years. Entity A does not take into consideration the potential future changes in the index. At the end of year one the payments have not changed, so the liability is not updated. At the end of year two, when the lease payments change, Entity A updates the remaining eight lease payments to CU1,080 per year (CU1,000 / 100 × 108) and does not change its discount rate to remeasure the lease liability (and right-of-use asset).

4.5.4 *The exercise price of a purchase option*

If the lessee is reasonably certain to exercise a purchase option, the exercise price is included as a lease payment. That is, entities consider the exercise price of asset purchase options included in lease contracts consistently with the evaluation of lease renewal and termination options. See 4.4 above.

4.5.5 *Payments for penalties for terminating a lease*

If it is reasonably certain that the lessee will not terminate a lease, the lease term is determined assuming that the termination option would not be exercised, and any termination penalty is excluded from the lease payments. Otherwise, the lease termination penalty is included as a lease payment. The determination of whether to include lease termination penalties as lease payments is similar to the evaluation of lease renewal options.

4.5.6 *Amounts expected to be payable under residual value guarantees – lessees only*

IFRS 16 requires lessees to include amounts expected to be payable to the lessor under residual value guarantees as lease payments.

A lessee may provide a guarantee to the lessor that the value of the underlying asset it returns to the lessor at the end of the lease will be at least a specified amount. Such guarantees are enforceable obligations that the lessee has assumed by entering into the lease. Uncertainty related to a lessee's guarantee of a lessor's residual value affects the measurement of the obligation rather than the existence of an obligation.

A lessee is required to remeasure the lease liability if there is a change in the amounts expected to be payable under a residual value guarantee.

Example 25.14: Residual value guarantee included in lease payments

Entity R (lessee) enters into a lease and guarantees that the lessor will realise CU15,000 from selling the asset to another party at the end of the lease. At lease commencement, based on Entity R's estimate of the residual value of the underlying asset, Entity R determines that it expects that it will owe CU6,000 at the end of the lease.

Analysis: Because it is expected that it will owe the lessor CU6,000 under the residual value guarantee, Entity R includes that amount as a lease payment.

IFRS 16 does not state how frequently reassessment should occur for expected changes under residual value guarantees. However, we would expect entities to apply judgement to determine the frequency of reassessment based on the relevant facts and circumstances.

4.5.7 *Amounts expected to be payable under residual value guarantees – lessors only*

IFRS 16 requires lessors to include in the lease payments, any residual value guarantees provided to the lessor by the lessee, a party related to the lessee, or a third party unrelated to the lessor that is financially capable of discharging the obligations under the guarantee. This amount included in lease payments is different to that for a lessee which only includes the amount expected to be payable. See 4.5 above.

4.5.8 Amounts not included in lease payments

Variable lease payments that do not depend on an index or rate and are not in-substance fixed (see 4.5.1 above), such as those based on performance (e.g. a percentage of sales) or usage of the underlying asset (e.g. the number of hours flown, the number of units produced), are not included as lease payments. Instead they are recognised in profit or loss (unless they are included in the carrying amount of another asset in accordance with other IFRS) in the period in which the event that triggers the payment occurs. *[IFRS 16.38]*.

Lease payments do not include payments allocated to the non-lease components of a contract. However, lease payments include amounts that would otherwise be allocable to the non-lease components of a contract when the lessee makes an accounting policy election to account for the lease and non-lease components as a single lease component.

4.5.9 Reassessment of the lease liability

IFRS 16 contains specific requirements about how to remeasure the lease liability to reflect changes to the lease payments (see 5.4 below). A lessee recognises the amount of the remeasurement of the lease liability as an adjustment to the right-of-use asset. However, if the carrying amount of the right-of-use asset is reduced to zero and there is a further reduction in the measurement of the lease liability, a lessee recognises any remaining amount of the remeasurement in profit or loss. *[IFRS 16.39]*.

4.5.10 Remeasurement by lessors

Lessors remeasure the lease payments upon a modification (i.e. a change in the scope of a lease, or the consideration for a lease that was not part of its original terms and conditions) that is not accounted for as a separate contract. See 6.4 below.

4.6 Discount rates

Discount rates are used to determine the present value of the lease payments which are used to determine lease classification (see 6.1 below) and to measure a lessor's net investment in the lease and a lessee's lease liability.

The discount rate for lessors is the interest rate implicit in the lease, which is defined as the rate that causes the present value of (a) the lease payments and (b) the unguaranteed residual value to equal the sum of (i) the fair value of the underlying asset and (ii) any initial direct costs of the lessor. *[IFRS 16.Appendix A]*.

Initial direct costs, other than those incurred by manufacturer or dealer lessors, are included in the initial measurement of the net investment in the lease and reduce the amount of income recognised over the lease term.

For lessees, lease payments are discounted using the interest rate implicit in the lease if that rate can be readily determined. If that rate cannot be readily determined, the lessee uses the incremental borrowing rate. *[IFRS 16.26]*.

The incremental borrowing rate is the rate of interest that a lessee would have to pay to borrow over a similar term, and with a similar security, the funds necessary to obtain an asset of a similar value to the right-of-use asset in a similar economic environment. *[IFRS 16.Appendix A]*.

In determining the incremental borrowing rate, the lessee considers borrowings with a similar term and security to the right-of-use asset, not the underlying asset. Observable rates, such as a property yield can be used as a starting point to determine the incremental borrowing rate but adjustments need to be considered for the specific right-of-use asset.

The interest rate implicit in the lease is not necessarily the rate stated in the contract and reflects, among other things, the lessor's initial direct costs and estimates of residual value. Therefore, lessees may find it difficult to determine the interest rate implicit in the lease, in which case they will need to determine the incremental borrowing rate.

4.7 Initial direct costs

Initial direct costs are incremental costs of obtaining a lease that would not have been incurred if the lease had not been obtained, except for such costs incurred by a manufacturer or dealer lessor in connection with a finance lease. *[IFRS 16.Appendix A]*.

Initial direct costs, other than those incurred by manufacturer or dealer lessors, are included in the initial measurement of the net investment in the lease and reduce the amount of income recognised over the lease term. The interest rate implicit in the lease is defined in such a way that the initial direct costs are included automatically in the net investment in the lease and there is no need to add them separately. *[IFRS 16.69]*.

IFRS 16 requires lessees to include their initial direct costs in their initial measurement of the right-of-use asset. As noted above, initial direct costs are incremental costs that would not have been incurred if the lease had not been obtained (e.g. commissions, certain payments made to an existing lessee to incentivise that lessee to terminate its lease). Lessees and lessors apply the same definition of initial direct costs. The requirements under IFRS 16 for initial direct costs are consistent with the concept of incremental costs in IFRS 15. Under IAS 17, initial direct costs are incremental costs that are directly attributable to negotiating and arranging a lease, except for such costs incurred by manufacturer or dealer lessors. The revised definition under IFRS 16 could result in some changes in practice for lessors. Lessor's initial direct costs will now also exclude costs incurred regardless of whether the lease is obtained (e.g. certain legal advice).

4.8 Economic life

The economic life is either the period over which an asset is expected to be economically usable by one or more users or the number of production or similar units expected to be obtained from an asset by one or more users. *[IFRS 16.Appendix A]*.

4.9 Fair value

The fair value for the purposes of applying the lessor accounting requirements in IFRS 16 is the amount for which an asset could be exchanged, or a liability settled, between knowledgeable, willing parties in an arm's length transaction. *[IFRS 16.Appendix A]*.

The fair value definition for lessors has been carried forward from IAS 17.

5 LESSEE ACCOUNTING

5.1 Initial recognition

At the commencement date, a lessee recognises a right-of-use asset and a lease liability. [IFRS 16.22]. This applies to all leases unless the lessee elects the short-term lease and/or low-value asset recognition exemptions, discussed below. If an entity applies the exemptions it must disclose that fact. [IFRS 16.60].

5.1.1 Short-term leases

A short-term lease is a lease that, at the commencement date, has a lease term of 12 months or less. A lease that contains a purchase option is not a short-term lease. [IFRS 16.Appendix A].

The short-term lease exemption can be made by class of underlying asset to which the right of use relates. A class of underlying asset is a grouping of underlying assets of a similar nature and use in an entity's operations. [IFRS 16.8].

A lessee that makes this accounting policy election does not recognise a lease liability or right-of-use asset on its balance sheet. Instead, the lessee recognises the lease payments associated with those leases as an expense on either a straight-line basis over the lease term or another systematic basis. The lessee is required to apply another systematic basis if that basis is more representative of the pattern of the lessee's benefit. [IFRS 16.6].

When determining whether a lease qualifies as a short-term lease, a lessee evaluates the lease term in the same manner as all other leases. That is, the lease term includes the non-cancellable term of the lease, periods covered by an option to extend the lease if the lessee is reasonably certain to exercise that option and periods covered by an option to terminate the lease if the lessee is reasonably certain not to exercise that option. In addition, to qualify as a short-term lease, the lease cannot include an option to purchase the underlying asset.

A lease that qualifies as a short-term lease at the commencement is a new lease if there is a lease modification or a change in a lessee's assessment of the lease term (e.g. the lessee exercises an option not previously included in the determination of the lease term). [IFRS 16.7]. The new lease is evaluated to determine whether it qualifies for the short-term exemption, similar to any other new lease.

The short-term lease accounting policy election is intended to reduce the cost and complexity of applying IFRS 16. However, a lessee that makes the election must make certain quantitative and qualitative disclosures about short-term leases (see 5.8.2 below).

Once a lessee establishes a policy for a class of underlying assets, all future short-term leases for that class are required to be accounted for in accordance with the lessee's policy. A lessee evaluates any potential change in its accounting policy in accordance with IAS 8 – Accounting Policies, Changes in Accounting Estimates and Errors.

Example 25.15: Short-term lease

Scenario A

A lessee enters into a lease with a nine-month non-cancellable term with an option to extend the lease for four months. At the lease commencement date, the lessee concludes that it is reasonably certain to exercise the extension option because the monthly lease payments during the extension period are significantly below market rates.

Analysis: The lease term is greater than 12 months i.e. 13 months. Therefore, the lessee may not account for the lease as a short-term lease.

Scenario B

Assume the same facts as Scenario A except, at the lease commencement date, the lessee concludes that it is not reasonably certain to exercise the extension option because the monthly lease payments during the optional extension period are at what the lessee expects to be market rates and there are no other factors that would make exercise of the renewal option reasonably certain.

Analysis: The lease term is 12 months or less, i.e. nine months. Therefore, the lessee may (subject to its accounting policy, by class of underlying asset) account for the lease under the short-term lease exemption, i.e. it recognises lease payments as an expense on a either a straight-line basis over the lease term or another systematic basis and does not recognise a lease liability or right-of-use asset on its balance sheet, similar to an operating lease under IAS 17.

5.1.2 Leases of low-value assets

Lessees can also make a similar election for leases of low-value assets, which can be made on a lease-by-lease basis. *[IFRS 16.8]*. A lessee that makes this accounting policy election does not recognise a lease liability or right-of-use asset on its statement of financial position. Instead, the lessee recognises the lease payments associated with those leases as an expense on either a straight-line basis over the lease term or another systematic basis. The lessee is required to apply another systematic basis if that basis is more representative of the pattern of the lessee's benefit. *[IFRS 16.6]*.

A lessee assesses the value of an underlying asset based on the value of the asset when it is new, regardless of the age of the asset being leased. *[IFRS 16.B3]*. The assessment of whether an underlying asset is of low value is performed on an absolute basis. Leases of low-value assets qualify for the exemption regardless of whether those leases are material to the lessee. The assessment is not affected by the size, nature or circumstances of the lessee. Accordingly, different lessees are expected to reach the same conclusion about whether a particular underlying asset is of low-value. *[IFRS 16.B4]*. At the time of reaching its decisions about the exemption, the IASB had in mind leases of underlying assets with a value, when new, of US$5,000 or less. Examples of low-value assets include desktop and laptop computers, small items of office furniture, telephones and other low-value equipment. *[IFRS 16.B8]*.

An underlying asset can only be of low-value if both:

- the lessee can benefit from use of the assets on their own, or together with, other resources that are readily available to the lessee; and
- the underlying asset is not dependent on, or highly interrelated with, other assets. *[IFRS 16.B5]*.

For example, an entity may lease a truck for use in its business and the lease includes the use of the tyres attached to the truck. To use the tyres for their intended purpose, they can only be used with the truck and therefore are dependent on, or highly interrelated with the truck. Therefore the tyres would not qualify for the low-value asset exemption.

A lease of an underlying asset does not qualify as a lease of a low-value asset if the nature of the asset is such that, when new, the asset is typically not of low value. For example, leases of cars would not qualify as leases of low-value assets because a new car would typically not be of low value. *[IFRS 16.B6]*.

An intermediate lessor who subleases, or expects to sublease an asset, cannot account for the head lease as a lease of a low-value asset. *[IFRS 16.B7]*.

5.2 Initial measurement

5.2.1 Right-of-use assets

At commencement date, a lessee measures the right-of-use asset at cost. *[IFRS 16.23]*.

The cost of a right-of-use asset comprises:

- the amount of the initial measurement of the lease liability;
- any lease payments made at or before the commencement date, less any lease incentives received;
- any initial direct costs incurred by the lessee; and
- an estimate of costs to be incurred by the lessee in dismantling and removing the underlying asset, restoring the site on which it is located or restoring the underlying asset to the condition required by the terms and conditions of the lease, unless those costs are to produce inventories. The lessee incurs the obligation for those costs either at the commencement date or as a consequence of having used the underlying asset during a particular period. *[IFRS 16.24]*.

A lessee recognises dismantling, removal and restoration costs above as part of the cost of the right-of-use asset when it incurs an obligation for those costs. A lessee applies IAS 2 – *Inventories* – to costs that are incurred during a particular period as a consequence of having used the right-of-use asset to produce inventories during that period. The obligations for such costs are recognised and measured applying IAS 37 – *Provisions, Contingent Liabilities and Contingent Assets*. *[IFRS 16.25]*.

5.2.2 Lease liabilities

At the commencement date, a lessee measures the lease liability at the present value of the lease payments that are not paid at that date. The lease payments are discounted using the interest rate implicit in the lease, if that rate can be readily determined. If that rate cannot be readily determined, the lessee uses the lessee's incremental borrowing rate. *[IFRS 16.26]*.

At the commencement date, the lease payments included in the measurement of the lease liability comprise the following payments for the right to use the underlying asset during the lease term that are not paid at the commencement date:

- fixed payments (including in-substance fixed payments), less any lease incentives receivable;
- variable lease payments that depend on an index or a rate, initially measured using the index or rate as at the commencement date;
- amounts expected to be payable by the lessee under residual value guarantees;
- the exercise price of a purchase option if the lessee is reasonably certain to exercise that option; and
- payments of penalties for terminating the lease, if the lease term reflects the lessee exercising an option to terminate the lease. *[IFRS 16.27]*.

5.3 Subsequent measurement

5.3.1 Right-of-use assets

After the commencement date, a lessee measures the right-of-use asset applying a cost model, unless it applies either of the measurement models described in 5.3.1.B below. *[IFRS 16.29]*.

5.3.1.A Cost model

To apply the cost model, the lessee measures the right-of-use asset at cost:

- less any accumulated depreciation and accumulated impairment losses; and
- adjusted for the remeasurement of the lease liability described in 5.4 below. *[IFRS 16.30]*.

A lessee applies the depreciation requirements in IAS 16 in depreciating the right-of-use asset, subject to the following requirements. *[IFRS 16.31]*.

If the lease transfers ownership of the underlying asset to the lessee by the end of the lease term or if the cost of the right-of-use asset reflects that the lessee will exercise a purchase option, the lessee depreciates the right-of-use asset from the commencement date to the end of the useful life of the underlying asset. Otherwise, the lessee depreciates the right-of-use asset from the commencement date to the earlier of the end of the useful life of the right-of-use asset or the end of the lease term. *[IFRS 16.32]*.

Depreciation of the right-of-use asset is recognised in a manner consistent with existing standards for property, plant and equipment. IAS 16 is not prescriptive about the methods of depreciation, mentioning straight line, diminishing balance and units of production as possibilities. The overriding requirement of IAS 16 is that the depreciation charge reflects the pattern of consumption of the benefits the asset brings over its useful life, and is applied consistently from period to period.

A lessee applies IAS 36 – *Impairment of Assets* – to determine whether the right-of-use asset is impaired and to account for any impairment loss identified. *[IFRS 16.33]*.

5.3.1.B Other measurement models

If a lessee applies the fair value model in IAS 40 – *Investment Property* – to its investment property, the lessee also applies that fair value model to right-of-use assets that meet the definition of investment property in IAS 40. *[IFRS 16.34]*.

If right-of-use assets relate to a class of property, plant and equipment to which the lessee applies the revaluation model in IAS 16, a lessee may elect to apply that revaluation model to all of the right-of-use assets that relate to that class of property, plant and equipment. *[IFRS 16.35]*.

5.3.2 Lease liabilities

After the commencement date, a lessee measures the lease liability by:

(a) increasing the carrying amount to reflect interest on the lease liability;

(b) reducing the carrying amount to reflect the lease payments made; and

(c) remeasuring the carrying amount to reflect any reassessment or lease modifications specified, or to reflect revised in-substance fixed lease payments. *[IFRS 16.36]*.

Interest on the lease liability in each period during the lease term is the amount that produces a constant periodic rate of interest on the remaining balance of the lease liability. The periodic rate of interest is the discount rate described at commencement, unless a reassessment requiring a change in the discount rate has been triggered. *[IFRS 16.37]*.

5.3.3 Expense recognition

After the commencement date, the lessee recognises depreciation and impairment of the right-of-use asset in profit or loss (unless the lessee applies the fair value model described in at 5.3.1.B above).

A lessee also recognises in profit or loss, unless the costs are included in the carrying amount of another asset applying other IFRS, both:

(a) interest on the lease liability; and

(b) variable lease payments not included in the measurement of the lease liability in the period in which the event or condition that triggers those payments occurs. *[IFRS 16.38]*.

When a lessee depreciates the right-of-use asset on a straight-line basis, the total periodic expense (i.e. the sum of interest and depreciation expense) is generally higher in the early periods and lower in the later periods. Because a constant interest rate is applied to the lease liability, the interest expense decreases as cash payments are made during the lease term and the lease liability decreases. Therefore, more interest expense is incurred in the early periods and less in the later periods. This trend in the interest expense, combined with straight-line depreciation of the right-of-use asset, results in a front-loaded expense recognition pattern. This expense pattern is consistent with the subsequent measurement of finance leases under IAS 17.

If a lessee determines that a right-of-use asset is impaired, it recognises an impairment loss and measures the right-of-use asset at its carrying amount immediately after the impairment. A lessee subsequently depreciates, generally on a straight-line basis, the right-of-use asset from the date of the impairment to the earlier of the end of the useful life of the right-of-use asset or the end of the lease term. However, the depreciation period is the remaining useful life of the underlying asset if the lessee is reasonably certain to exercise an option to purchase the underlying asset or if the lease transfers ownership of the underlying asset to the lessee by the end of the lease term. See 5.6.1 below for additional discussion of impairment of right-of-use assets.

Example 25.16: Lessee accounting

Entity H (lessee) enters into a three-year lease of equipment. Entity H agrees to make the following annual payments at the end of each year: CU10,000 in year one, CU12,000 in year two and CU14,000 in year three. For simplicity, there are no other elements to the lease payments (e.g. purchase options, lease incentives from the lessor or initial direct costs). The initial measurement of the right-of-use asset and lease liability is CU33,000 (present value of lease payments using a discount rate of approximately 4.235%). Entity H uses its incremental borrowing rate because the rate implicit in the lease cannot be readily determined. Entity H depreciates the right-of-use asset on a straight-line basis over the lease term.

Analysis: At lease commencement, Entity H would recognise the lease-related asset and liability:

Right-of-use asset	CU33,000	
Lease liability		CU33,000
To initially recognise the lease-related asset and liability		

The following journal entries would be recorded in the first year:

Interest expense	CU1,398	
Lease liability		CU1,398
To record interest expense and accrete the lease liability using the interest method (CU33,000 × 4.235%)		
Depreciation expense	CU11,000	
Right-of-use asset		CU11,000
To record depreciation expense on the right-of-use asset (CU33,000 ÷ 3 years)		
Lease liability	CU10,000	
Cash		CU10,000

A summary of the lease contract's accounting (assuming no changes due to reassessment) is as follows:

	Initial	**Year 1**	**Year 2**	**Year 3**
	CU	CU	CU	CU
Cash lease payments		10,000	12,000	14,000
Lease expense recognised				
Interest expense		1,398	1,033	569
Depreciation expense		11,000	11,000	11,000
Total periodic expense		12,398	12,033	11,569
Statement of financial position				
Right-of-use asset	33,000	22,000	11,000	–
Lease liability	(33,000)	(24,398)	(13,431)	–

5.4 Remeasurement of lease liabilities and right-of-use assets

After the commencement date, a lessee remeasures the lease liability to reflect changes to the lease payments. A lessee recognises the amount of the remeasurement of the lease liability as an adjustment to the right-of-use asset. However, if the carrying amount of the right-of-use asset is reduced to zero and there is a further reduction in the measurement of the lease liability, a lessee recognises any remaining amount of the remeasurement in profit or loss. *[IFRS 16.39]*.

A lessee remeasures the lease liability by discounting the revised lease payments using a revised discount rate, if:

(a) there is a change in the lease term. A lessee determines the revised lease payments on the basis of the revised lease term; or

(b) there is a change in the assessment of an option to purchase the underlying asset, assessed considering the events and circumstances in the context of a purchase option. A lessee determines the revised lease payments to reflect the change in amounts payable under the purchase option. *[IFRS 16.40]*.

The lessee determines the revised discount rate as the interest rate implicit in the lease for the remainder of the lease term, if that rate can be readily determined, or the lessee's incremental borrowing rate at the date of reassessment, if the interest rate implicit in the lease cannot be readily determined. *[IFRS 16.41]*.

A lessee remeasures the lease liability by discounting the revised lease payments, if:

(a) there is a change in the amounts expected to be payable under a residual value guarantee. A lessee determines the revised lease payments to reflect the change in amounts expected to be payable under the residual value guarantee.

(b) there is a change in future lease payments resulting from a change in an index or a rate used to determine those payments, including for example a change to reflect changes in market rental rates following a market rent review. The lessee remeasures the lease liability to reflect those revised lease payments only when there is a change in the cash flows (i.e. when the adjustment to the lease payments takes effect). A lessee determines the revised lease payments for the remainder of the lease term based on the revised contractual payments. *[IFRS 16.42]*.

In applying paragraph 42 above, a lessee uses an unchanged discount rate, unless the change in lease payments results from a change in floating interest rates. In that case, the lessee uses a revised discount rate that reflects changes in the interest rate. *[IFRS 16.43]*.

5.5 Lease modifications

A lease modification is a change in the scope of a lease, or the consideration for a lease, that was not part of the original terms and conditions of the lease (for example, adding or terminating the right to use one or more underlying assets, or extending or shortening the contractual lease term). *[IFRS 16.Appendix A]*.

If a lease is modified, the modified contract is evaluated to determine whether it is or contains a lease (see 3.1 above). If a lease continues to exist, the lease modification can result in:

- a separate lease (see 5.5.1 below); or
- a change in the accounting for the existing lease (i.e. not a separate lease) (see 5.5.2 below).

The exercise of an existing purchase or renewal option or a change in the assessment of whether such options are reasonably certain to be exercised are not lease modifications but can result in the remeasurement of lease liabilities and right-of-use assets (see 5.4 above).

5.5.1 Determining whether a lease modification results in a separate lease

A lessee accounts for a lease modification as a separate lease when both of the following conditions are met:

- the modification increases the scope of the lease by adding the right to use one or more underlying assets; and
- the consideration for the lease increases commensurate with the stand-alone price for the increase in scope and any adjustments to that stand-alone price reflect the circumstances of the particular contract. *[IFRS 16.44]*.

If both of these conditions are met, the lease modification results in two separate leases, the unmodified original lease and a separate new lease. Lessees account for the separate contract that contains a lease in the same manner as other new leases. If either of the conditions are not met, the modified lease is not accounted for as a separate lease (see 5.5.2 below).

5.5.2 Lessee accounting for a modification that does not result in a separate lease

For a lease modification that is not accounted for as a separate lease, at the effective date of the lease modification the lessee:

(a) allocates the consideration in the modified contract;

(b) determines the lease term of the modified lease; and

(c) remeasures the lease liability by discounting the revised lease payments using a revised discount rate. The revised discount rate is determined as the interest rate implicit in the lease for the remainder of the lease term, if that rate can be readily determined, or the lessee's incremental borrowing rate at the effective date of the modification, if the interest rate implicit in the lease cannot be readily determined. *[IFRS 16.45]*.

For a lease modification that is not accounted for as a separate lease, the lessee accounts for the remeasurement of the lease liability by:

(a) decreasing the carrying amount of the right-of-use asset to reflect the partial or full termination of the lease for lease modifications that decrease the scope of the lease. The lessee recognises in profit or loss any gain or loss relating to the partial or full termination of the lease; or

(b) making a corresponding adjustment to the right-of-use asset for all other lease modifications. *[IFRS 16.46]*.

IFRS 16 contains a number of illustrative examples on modifications, which are reproduced below. *[IFRS 16.IE7]*.

Example 25.17: Lease modifications (IFRS 16 Examples 15 to 19)

IFRS 16 Example 15 – Modification that is a separate lease

Lessee enters into a 10-year lease for 2,000 square metres of office space.

At the beginning of Year 6, Lessee and Lessor agree to amend the original lease for the remaining five years to include an additional 3,000 square metres of office space in the same building. The additional space is made available for use by Lessee at the end of the second quarter of Year 6. The increase in total consideration for the lease is commensurate with the current market rate for the new 3,000 square metres of office space, adjusted for the discount that Lessee receives reflecting that Lessor does not incur costs that it would otherwise have incurred if leasing the same space to a new tenant (for example, marketing costs).

Lessee accounts for the modification as a separate lease, separate from the original 10-year lease. This is because the modification grants Lessee an additional right to use an underlying asset, and the increase in consideration for the lease is commensurate with the stand-alone price of the additional right-of-use adjusted to reflect the circumstances of the contract. In this example, the additional underlying asset is the new 3,000 square metres of office space. Accordingly, at the commencement date of the new lease (at the end of the second quarter of Year 6), Lessee recognises a right-of-use asset and a lease liability relating to the lease of the additional 3,000 square metres of office space. Lessee does not make any adjustments to the accounting for the original lease of 2,000 square metres of office space as a result of this modification.

IFRS 16 Example 16 – Modification that increases the scope of the lease by extending the contractual lease term

Lessee enters into a 10-year lease for 5,000 square metres of office space. The annual lease payments are CU100,000 payable at the end of each year. The interest rate implicit in the lease cannot be readily determined. Lessee's incremental borrowing rate at the commencement date is 6 per cent per annum. At the beginning of Year 7, Lessee and Lessor agree to amend the original lease by extending the contractual lease term by four years. The annual lease payments are unchanged (i.e. CU100,000 payable at the end of each year from Year 7 to Year 14). Lessee's incremental borrowing rate at the beginning of Year 7 is 7 per cent per annum.

At the effective date of the modification (at the beginning of Year 7), Lessee remeasures the lease liability based on: (a) an eight-year remaining lease term, (b) annual payments of CU100,000 and (c) Lessee's incremental borrowing rate of 7 per cent per annum. The modified lease liability equals CU597,130. The lease liability immediately before the modification (including the recognition of the interest expense until the end of Year 6) is CU346,511. Lessee recognises the difference between the carrying amount of the modified lease liability and the carrying amount of the lease liability immediately before the modification (CU250,619) as an adjustment to the right-of-use asset.

IFRS 16 Example 17 – Modification that decreases the scope of the lease

Lessee enters into a 10-year lease for 5,000 square metres of office space. The annual lease payments are CU50,000 payable at the end of each year. The interest rate implicit in the lease cannot be readily determined. Lessee's incremental borrowing rate at the commencement date is 6 per cent per annum. At the beginning of Year 6, Lessee and Lessor agree to amend the original lease to reduce the space to only 2,500 square metres of the original space starting from the end of the first quarter of Year 6. The annual fixed lease payments (from Year 6 to Year 10) are CU30,000. Lessee's incremental borrowing rate at the beginning of Year 6 is 5 per cent per annum.

At the effective date of the modification (at the beginning of Year 6), Lessee remeasures the lease liability based on: (a) a five-year remaining lease term, (b) annual payments of CU30,000 and (c) Lessee's incremental borrowing rate of 5 per cent per annum. This equals CU129,884.

Lessee determines the proportionate decrease in the carrying amount of the right-of-use asset on the basis of the remaining right-of-use asset (i.e. 2,500 square metres corresponding to 50 per cent of the original right-of-use asset).

50 per cent of the pre-modification right-of-use asset (CU184,002) is CU92,001. Fifty per cent of the pre-modification lease liability (CU210,618) is CU105,309. Consequently, Lessee reduces the carrying amount of the right-of-use asset by CU92,001 and the carrying amount of the lease liability by CU105,309. Lessee recognises the difference between the decrease in the lease liability and the decrease in the right-of-use asset (CU105,309 – CU92,001 = CU13,308) as a gain in profit or loss at the effective date of the modification (at the beginning of Year 6).

Lessee recognises the difference between the remaining lease liability of CU105,309 and the modified lease liability of CU129,884 (which equals CU24,575) as an adjustment to the right-of-use asset reflecting the change in the consideration paid for the lease and the revised discount rate.

IFRS 16 Example 18 – Modification that both increases and decreases the scope of the lease

Lessee enters into a 10-year lease for 2,000 square metres of office space. The annual lease payments are CU100,000 payable at the end of each year. The interest rate implicit in the lease cannot be readily determined. Lessee's incremental borrowing rate at the commencement date is 6 per cent per annum. At the beginning of Year 6, Lessee and Lessor agree to amend the original lease to (a) include an additional 1,500 square metres of space in the same building starting from the beginning of Year 6 and (b) reduce the lease term from 10 years to eight years. The annual fixed payment for the 3,500 square metres is CU150,000 payable at the end of each year (from Year 6 to Year 8). Lessee's incremental borrowing rate at the beginning of Year 6 is 7 per cent per annum.

The consideration for the increase in scope of 1,500 square metres of space is not commensurate with the stand-alone price for that increase adjusted to reflect the circumstances of the contract. Consequently, Lessee does not account for the increase in scope that adds the right to use an additional 1,500 square metres of space as a separate lease.

The pre-modification right-of-use asset and the pre-modification lease liability in relation to the lease are as follows.

	Lease liability				Right-of-use asset		
	Beginning balance	6% interest expense	Lease payment	Ending balance	Beginning balance	Depreciation charge	Ending balance
Year	CU	CU	CU	CU	CU	CU	CU
1	**736,009**	44,160	(100,000)	**680,169**	**736,009**	(73,601)	**662,408**
2	**680,169**	40,810	(100,000)	**620,979**	**662,408**	(73,601)	**588,807**
3	**620,979**	37,259	(100,000)	**558,238**	**588,807**	(73,601)	**515,206**
4	**558,238**	33,494	(100,000)	**491,732**	**515,206**	(73,601)	**441,605**
5	**491,732**	29,504	(100,000)	**421,236**	**441,605**	(73,601)	**368,004**
6	**421,236**				**368,004**		

At the effective date of the modification (at the beginning of Year 6), Lessee remeasures the lease liability on the basis of: (a) a three-year remaining lease term, (b) annual payments of CU150,000 and (c) Lessee's incremental borrowing rate of 7 per cent per annum. The modified liability equals CU393,647, of which (a) CU131,216 relates to the increase of CU50,000 in the annual lease payments from Year 6 to Year 8 and (b) CU262,431 relates to the remaining three annual lease payments of CU100,000 from Year 6 to Year 8.

Decrease in the lease term

At the effective date of the modification (at the beginning of Year 6), the pre-modification right-of-use asset is CU368,004. Lessee determines the proportionate decrease in the carrying amount of the right-of-use asset based on the remaining right-of-use asset balance for the original 2,000 square metres of office space (i.e. a remaining three-year lease term rather than the original five-year lease term). The remaining right-of-use asset for the original 2,000 square metres of office space is CU220,802 (i.e. CU368,004 ÷ 5 × 3 years).

At the effective date of the modification (at the beginning of Year 6), the pre-modification lease liability is CU421,236. The remaining lease liability for the original 2,000 square metres of office space is CU267,301 (i.e. present value of three annual lease payments of CU100,000, discounted at the original discount rate of 6 per cent per annum).

Consequently, Lessee reduces the carrying amount of the right-of-use asset by CU147,202 (CU368,004 – CU220,802), and the carrying amount of the lease liability by CU153,935 (CU421,236 – CU267,301). Lessee recognises the difference between the decrease in the lease liability and the decrease in the right-of-use asset (CU153,935 – CU147,202 = CU6,733) as a gain in profit or loss at the effective date of the modification (at the beginning of Year 6).

Lease liability	CU153,935	
Right-of-use asset		CU147,202
Gain		CU6,733

At the effective date of the modification (at the beginning of Year 6), Lessee recognises the effect of the remeasurement of the remaining lease liability reflecting the revised discount rate of 7 per cent per annum, which is CU4,870 (CU267,301 – CU262,431), as an adjustment to the right-of-use asset.

Lease liability	CU4,870	
Right-of-use asset		CU4,870

Increase in the leased space

At the commencement date of the lease for the additional 1,500 square metres of space (at the beginning of Year 6), Lessee recognises the increase in the lease liability related to the increase in scope of CU131,216 (i.e. present value of three annual lease payments of CU50,000, discounted at the revised interest rate of 7 per cent per annum) as an adjustment to the right-of-use asset.

Right-of-use asset	CU131,216	
Lease liability		CU131,216

The modified right-of-use asset and the modified lease liability in relation to the modified lease are as follows.

	Lease liability				Right-of-use asset		
	Beginning balance	**7% interest expense**	**Lease payment**	**Ending balance**	**Beginning balance**	**Depreciation charge**	**Ending balance**
Year	**CU**	**CU**	**CU**	**CU**	**CU**	**CU**	**CU**
6	**393,647**	27,556	(150,000)	**271,203**	**347,148**	(115,716)	**231,432**
7	**271,203**	18,984	(150,000)	**140,187**	**231,432**	(115,716)	**115,716**
8	**140,187**	9,813	(150,000)	**–**	**115,716**	(115,716)	**–**

IFRS 16 Example 19 – Modification that is a change in consideration only

Lessee enters into a 10-year lease for 5,000 square metres of office space. At the beginning of Year 6, Lessee and Lessor agree to amend the original lease for the remaining five years to reduce the lease payments from CU100,000 per year to CU95,000 per year. The interest rate implicit in the lease cannot be readily determined. Lessee's incremental borrowing rate at the commencement date is 6 per cent per annum. Lessee's incremental borrowing rate at the beginning of Year 6 is 7 per cent per annum. The annual lease payments are payable at the end of each year.

At the effective date of the modification (at the beginning of Year 6), Lessee remeasures the lease liability based on: (a) a five-year remaining lease term, (b) annual payments of CU95,000, and (c) Lessee's incremental borrowing rate of 7 per cent per annum. Lessee recognises the difference between the carrying amount of the modified liability (CU389,519) and the lease liability immediately before the modification (CU421,236) of CU31,717 as an adjustment to the right-of-use asset.

5.6 Other lessee matters

5.6.1 *Impairment of right-of-use assets*

A lessee applies IAS 36 to determine whether the right-of-use asset is impaired and to account for any impairment loss identified. *[IFRS 16.33].*

IAS 36 requires an impairment indicator analysis at each reporting period. If any indicators are present, the entity is required to estimate the recoverable amount of the asset (or the cash-generating unit of which the asset is a part – the CGU). The entity has to recognise an impairment loss if the recoverable amount of the CGU is less than the carrying amount of the CGU. After an impairment loss is recognised, the adjusted carrying amount of the right-of-use asset would be its new basis for depreciation.

Subsequent reversal of a previously recognised impairment loss needs to be assessed if there is any indication that an impairment loss recognised in prior periods may no longer exist or may have decreased. In recognising any reversal, the increased carrying amount of the asset must not exceed the carrying amount that would have been determined after depreciation, had there been no impairment.

Lessees currently apply the same impairment analysis to assets held under finance leases. This analysis would be new for leases currently accounted for as operating leases and could significantly affect the timing of expense recognition.

5.6.2 *Leases denominated in a foreign currency*

Lessees apply IAS 21 – *The Effects of Changes in Foreign Exchange Rates* – to leases denominated in a foreign currency. As they do for other monetary liabilities, lessees remeasure the foreign currency-denominated lease liability using the exchange rate at each reporting date. Any changes to the lease liability due to exchange rate changes are recognised in profit or loss. Because the right-of-use asset is a non-monetary asset measured at historical cost, it is not affected by changes in the exchange rate.

The IASB acknowledged in the Basis for Conclusions that this approach could result in volatility in profit or loss from the recognition of foreign currency exchange gains or losses, but it will be clear to users of financial statements that the gains or losses result solely from changes in exchange rates. *[IFRS 16.BC199].*

5.6.3 *Portfolio approach*

IFRS 16 specifies the accounting for an individual lease. However, as a practical expedient, an entity may apply it to a portfolio of leases with similar characteristics if the entity reasonably expects that the effects on the financial statements of applying IFRS 16 to the portfolio would not differ materially from applying it to the individual leases within that portfolio. If accounting for a portfolio, an entity uses estimates and assumptions that reflect the size and composition of the portfolio. *[IFRS 16.B1].*

The IASB decided to include the portfolio approach to be consistent with IFRS 15. A decision to use the portfolio approach would be similar to a decision some entities make today to expense, rather than capitalise, certain assets when the accounting difference is, and would continue to be, immaterial to the financial statements.

5.6.4 Income tax accounting

IFRS 16 could affect lessees' accounting for income taxes. For lessees, IFRS 16 requires recognition of lease-related assets and liabilities that are not on the balance sheet under today's accounting (i.e. amounts related to leases that are operating leases under IAS 17) and could change the measurement of other lease-related assets and liabilities. These changes affect certain aspects of accounting for income taxes such as the following:

- recognition and measurement of deferred tax assets and liabilities; and
- assessment of the recoverability of deferred tax assets.

Deferred tax assets and liabilities are further discussed in Chapter 31 at 7 and 8.

5.7 Presentation

A lessee presents either in the statement of financial position, or discloses in the notes:

(a) right-of-use assets separately from other assets. If a lessee does not present right-of-use assets separately in the statement of financial position, the lessee:
   (i) includes right-of-use assets within the same line item as that within which the corresponding underlying assets would be presented if they were owned; and
   (ii) discloses which line items in the statement of financial position include those right-of-use assets;

(b) lease liabilities separately from other liabilities. If the lessee does not present lease liabilities separately in the statement of financial position, the lessee discloses which line items in the statement of financial position include those liabilities. *[IFRS 16.47]*.

The requirement above does not apply to right-of-use assets that meet the definition of investment property, which is presented in the statement of financial position as investment property. *[IFRS 16.48]*.

Right-of-use assets and lease liabilities are subject to the same considerations as other assets and liabilities in classifying them as current and non-current in the statement of financial position.

In the statement of profit or loss and other comprehensive income, a lessee presents interest expense on the lease liability separately from the depreciation charge for the right-of-use asset. Interest expense on the lease liability is a component of finance costs, which paragraph 82(b) of IAS 1 – *Presentation of Financial Statements* – requires to be presented separately in the statement of profit or loss and other comprehensive income. *[IFRS 16.49]*.

In the statement of cash flows, a lessee classifies:

(a) cash payments for the principal portion of the lease liability within financing activities;

(b) cash payments for the interest portion of the lease liability applying the requirements in IAS 7 – *Statement of Cash Flows* – for interest paid; and

(c) short-term lease payments, payments for leases of low-value assets and variable lease payments not included in the measurement of the lease liability within operating activities. *[IFRS 16.50]*.

The following table summarises the presentation requirements for lessees.

Financial statement	Lessee presentation
Statement of financial position	Right-of-use assets presented either: • separately from other assets (e.g. owned assets); or • together with other assets as if they were owned, with disclosures of the balance sheet line items that include right-of-use assets and their amounts. Right-of-use assets that meet the definition of investment property are presented as investment property Lease liabilities presented either: • separately from other liabilities; or • together with other liabilities with disclosure of the balance sheet line items that include lease liabilities and their amounts.
Statement of profit or loss	Lease-related depreciation and lease-related interest expense are presented separately (i.e. lease-related depreciation and lease-related interest expense cannot be combined). Interest expense on the lease liability is a component of finance costs.
Statement of cash flows	Cash payments for the principal portion of the lease liability are presented within financing activities. Cash payments for the interest portion of the lease liability are presented based on an accounting policy election in accordance with IAS 7. Lease payments for short-term leases and leases of low-value assets not recognised on the balance sheet and variable lease payments not included in the lease liability are presented within operating activities. Non-cash activity (e.g. the initial recognition of the lease at commencement) is disclosed as a supplemental non-cash item.

5.8 Disclosure

5.8.1 Disclosure objective

The objective of the disclosures is for lessees to disclose information in the notes that, together with the information provided in the statement of financial position, statement of profit or loss and statement of cash flows, gives a basis for users of financial statements to assess the effect that leases have on the financial position, financial performance and cash flows of the lessee. *[IFRS 16.51]*.

A lessee discloses information about its leases for which it is a lessee in a single note or separate section in its financial statements. However, a lessee need not duplicate information that is already presented elsewhere in the financial statements, provided that the information is incorporated by cross-reference in the single note or separate section about leases. *[IFRS 16.52]*.

5.8.2 Disclosures of assets, liabilities, expenses and cash flows

IFRS 16 includes the following disclosure requirements for lessees, for the reporting period:

(a) depreciation charge for right-of-use assets by class of underlying asset;

(b) interest expense on lease liabilities;

(c) the expense relating to short-term leases. This expense need not include the expense relating to leases with a lease term of one month or less;

(d) the expense relating to leases of low-value assets. This expense does not include the expense relating to short-term leases of low-value assets included in paragraph (c) above;

(e) the expense relating to variable lease payments not included in the measurement of lease liabilities;

(f) income from subleasing right-of-use assets;

(g) total cash outflow for leases;

(h) additions to right-of-use assets;

(i) gains or losses arising from sale and leaseback transactions; and

(j) the carrying amount of right-of-use assets at the end of the reporting period by class of underlying asset. *[IFRS 16.53]*.

A lessee provides the disclosures specified in paragraph 53, as shown above, in a tabular format, unless another format is more appropriate. The amounts disclosed include costs that a lessee has included in the carrying amount of another asset during the reporting period. *[IFRS 16.54]*.

A lessee discloses the amount of its lease commitments for short-term leases if the portfolio of short-term leases to which it is committed at the end of the reporting period is dissimilar to the portfolio of short-term leases to which the short-term lease expense disclosed applying paragraph 53(c) above relates. *[IFRS 16.55]*.

If right-of-use assets meet the definition of investment property, a lessee applies the disclosure requirements in IAS 40. In that case, a lessee is not required to provide the disclosures in paragraph 53(a), (f), (h) or (j) above, for those right-of-use assets. *[IFRS 16.56]*.

If a lessee measures right-of-use assets at revalued amounts applying IAS 16, the lessee discloses the information required by paragraph 77 of IAS 16 for those right-of-use assets. *[IFRS 16.57]*. Those disclosures include the effective date of the revaluation, whether an independent valuer was involved, the carrying amount of the class of asset that would have been recognised under the cost model and the revaluation surplus. These disclosures are discussed further in Chapter 18 at 8.2.

A lessee also discloses a maturity analysis of lease liabilities applying paragraphs 39 and B11 of IFRS 7 – *Financial Instruments: Disclosures* – separately from the maturity analyses of other financial liabilities. *[IFRS 16.58]*. The IASB indicated in the Basis for Conclusions to IFRS 16 that because the lessee accounting model is based on the premise that a lease liability is a financial liability, it is appropriate for lessees to apply the same maturity analysis disclosure requirements to lease liabilities as to those applied to other financial liabilities. *[IFRS 16.BC222]*

IFRS 16 requires disclosure of the total cash outflow for leases. It does not explicitly state that leases of low-value assets and short-term leases are excluded. Therefore, we believe the cash outflows related to those leases should be included in the disclosure.

5.8.3 Additional disclosures

In addition to the disclosures described above, a lessee discloses additional qualitative and quantitative information about its leasing activities necessary to meet the disclosure objective in paragraph 51. This additional information may include, but is not limited to, information that helps users of financial statements to assess:

(a) the nature of the lessee's leasing activities;

(b) future cash outflows to which the lessee is potentially exposed that are not reflected in the measurement of lease liabilities. This includes exposure arising from:

  (i) variable lease payments;

  (ii) extension options and termination options;

  (iii) residual value guarantees; and

  (iv) leases not yet commenced to which the lessee is committed.

(c) restrictions or covenants imposed by leases; and

(d) sale and leaseback transactions. *[IFRS 16.59]*.

6 LESSOR ACCOUNTING

IFRS 16 substantially carries forward the lessor accounting model in IAS 17. The significant differences between the lessor accounting requirements in IFRS 16 and those in IAS 17 are primarily a consequence of decisions reached about the lessee accounting model in IFRS 16. The IASB also changed elements of the lessor accounting model, including changes to the accounting for subleases, initial direct costs and lessor disclosures.

Lessor accounting under IAS 17 is discussed further in Chapter 24.

6.1 Lease classification

A lessor classifies each of its leases as either an operating lease or a finance lease. *[IFRS 16.61]*. The classification of leases under IFRS 16 is the same as under IAS 17. A lease is classified as a finance lease if it transfers substantially all the risks and rewards incidental to ownership of an underlying asset. A lease is classified as an operating lease if it does not transfer substantially all the risks and rewards of ownership of an underlying asset. *[IFRS 16.62]*.

6.1.1 Criteria for lease classification

The classification of leases is based on the extent to which the lease transfers the risks and rewards incidental to ownership of an underlying asset. Risks include the possibilities of losses from idle capacity or technological obsolescence and of variations in return because of changing economic conditions. Rewards may be represented by the expectation of profitable operation over the underlying asset's economic life and of gain from appreciation in value or realisation of a residual value. *[IFRS 16.B53]*.

Whether a lease is a finance lease or an operating lease depends on the substance of the transaction rather than the form of the contract. Examples of situations that individually or in combination would normally lead to a lease being classified as a finance lease are:

(a) the lease transfers ownership of the underlying asset to the lessee by the end of the lease term;

(b) the lessee has the option to purchase the underlying asset at a price that is expected to be sufficiently lower than the fair value at the date the option becomes exercisable for it to be reasonably certain, at the inception date, that the option will be exercised;

(c) the lease term is for the major part of the economic life of the underlying asset even if title is not transferred;

(d) at the inception date, the present value of the lease payments amounts to at least substantially all of the fair value of the underlying asset; and

(e) the underlying asset is of such a specialised nature that only the lessee can use it without major modifications. *[IFRS 16.63]*.

Indicators of situations that individually or in combination could also lead to a lease being classified as a finance lease are:

(a) if the lessee can cancel the lease, the lessor's losses associated with the cancellation are borne by the lessee;

(b) gains or losses from the fluctuation in the fair value of the residual accrue to the lessee (for example, in the form of a rent rebate equalling most of the sales proceeds at the end of the lease); and

(c) the lessee has the ability to continue the lease for a secondary period at a rent that is substantially lower than market rent. *[IFRS 16.64]*.

The examples and indicators above are not always conclusive. If it is clear from other features that the lease does not transfer substantially all the risks and rewards incidental to ownership of an underlying asset, the lease is classified as an operating lease. For example, this may be the case if ownership of the underlying asset transfers at the end of the lease for a variable payment equal to its then fair value, or if there are variable lease payments, as a result of which the lessor does not transfer substantially all such risks and rewards. *[IFRS 16.65]*.

In our view, other considerations that could be made in determining the economic substance of the lease arrangement include the following:

- Are the lease rentals based on a market rate for use of the asset (which would indicate an operating lease) or a financing rate for use of the funds, which would be indicative of a finance lease?
- Is the existence of put and call options a feature of the lease? If so, are they exercisable at a predetermined price or formula (indicating a finance lease) or are they exercisable at the market price at the time the option is exercised (indicating an operating lease)?

A lease contract may include terms and conditions to adjust the lease payments for particular changes that occur between the inception date and the commencement date (such as a change in the lessor's cost of the underlying asset or a change in the lessor's cost of financing the lease). In that case, for the purposes of classifying the lease, the effect of any such changes is deemed to have taken place at the inception date. *[IFRS 16.B54]*.

6.1.2 *Lease classification test for land and buildings*

When a lease includes both land and buildings elements, a lessor assesses the classification of each element as a finance lease or an operating lease separately. In determining whether the land element is an operating lease or a finance lease, an important consideration is that land normally has an indefinite economic life. *[IFRS 16.B55]*.

Whenever necessary in order to classify and account for a lease of land and buildings, a lessor allocates lease payments (including any lump-sum upfront payments) between the land and the buildings elements in proportion to the relative fair values of the leasehold interests in the land element and buildings element of the lease at the inception date. If the lease payments cannot be allocated reliably between these two elements, the entire lease is classified as a finance lease, unless it is clear that both elements are operating leases, in which case the entire lease is classified as an operating lease. *[IFRS 16.B56]*.

For a lease of land and buildings in which the amount for the land element is immaterial to the lease, a lessor may treat the land and buildings as a single unit for the purpose of lease classification and classify it as a finance lease or an operating lease. In such a case, a lessor regards the economic life of the buildings as the economic life of the entire underlying asset. *[IFRS 16.B57]*.

6.1.3 *Residual value guarantees included in the lease classification test*

In evaluating IFRS 16's lease classification criteria, lessors are required to include in the 'substantially all' test any (i.e. the maximum obligation) residual value guarantees provided by both lessees and any other third party unrelated to the lessor.

6.1.4 *Reassessment of lease classification*

Lease classification is made at the inception date and is reassessed only if there is a lease modification. Changes in estimates (for example, changes in estimates of the economic life or of the residual value of the underlying asset), or changes in circumstances (for example, default by the lessee), do not give rise to a new classification of a lease for accounting purposes. *[IFRS 16.66]*.

Lessors reassess lease classification as at the effective date of the modification using the modified conditions at that date. If a lease modification results in a separate new lease, that new lease would be classified in the same manner as any new lease. See 6.1.1 above.

6.2 Finance leases

At commencement date, a lessor recognises assets held under a finance lease in its statement of financial position and present them as a receivable at an amount equal to the net investment in the lease. *[IFRS 16.67]*.

The net investment in the lease is defined as 'the gross investment in the lease discounted at the interest rate implicit in the lease'. *[IFRS 16.Appendix A]*. The gross investment in the lease is 'the sum of (a) the lease payments receivable by a lessor under a finance lease and (b) any unguaranteed residual value accruing to the lessor.' *[IFRS 16.Appendix A]*.

6.2.1 *Initial measurement*

At lease commencement, a lessor accounts for a finance lease, as follows:

- derecognises the carrying amount of the underlying asset;
- recognises the net investment in the lease; and
- recognises, in profit or loss, any selling profit or selling loss.

The lessor uses the interest rate implicit in the lease to measure the net investment in the lease. In the case of a sublease, if the interest rate implicit in the sublease cannot be readily determined, an intermediate lessor may use the discount rate used for the head lease (adjusted for any initial direct costs associated with the sublease) to measure the net investment in the sublease. *[IFRS 16.68]*.

Initial direct costs, other than those incurred by manufacturer or dealer lessors, are included in the initial measurement of the net investment in the lease and reduce the amount of income recognised over the lease term. The interest rate implicit in the lease is defined in such a way that the initial direct costs are included automatically in the net investment in the lease; there is no need to add them separately. *[IFRS 16.69]*.

At the commencement date, the lease payments included in the measurement of the net investment in the lease comprise the following payments for the right to use the underlying asset during the lease term that are not received at the commencement date:

(a) fixed payments (including in-substance fixed payments), less any lease incentives payable;

(b) variable lease payments that depend on an index or a rate, initially measured using the index or rate as at the commencement date;

(c) any residual value guarantees provided to the lessor by the lessee, a party related to the lessee or a third party unrelated to the lessor that is financially capable of discharging the obligations under the guarantee;

(d) the exercise price of a purchase option if the lessee is reasonably certain to exercise that option; and

(e) payments of penalties for terminating the lease, if the lease term reflects the lessee exercising an option to terminate the lease. *[IFRS 16.70]*.

6.2.2 *Manufacturer or dealer lessors*

At the commencement date, a manufacturer or dealer lessor recognises the following for each of its finance leases:

(a) revenue being the fair value of the underlying asset, or, if lower, the present value of the lease payments accruing to the lessor, discounted using a market rate of interest;

(b) the cost of sale being the cost, or carrying amount if different, of the underlying asset less the present value of the unguaranteed residual value; and

(c) selling profit or loss (being the difference between revenue and the cost of sale) in accordance with its policy for outright sales to which IFRS 15 applies. A manufacturer or dealer lessor recognises selling profit or loss on a finance lease at the commencement date, regardless of whether the lessor transfers the underlying asset as described in IFRS 15. *[IFRS 16.71]*.

Manufacturers or dealers often offer to customers the choice of either buying or leasing an asset. A finance lease of an asset by a manufacturer or dealer lessor gives rise to profit or loss equivalent to that resulting from an outright sale of the underlying asset, at normal selling prices, reflecting any applicable volume or trade discounts. *[IFRS 16.72]*.

Manufacturer or dealer lessors sometimes quote artificially low rates of interest in order to attract customers. The use of such a rate would result in a lessor recognising an excessive portion of the total income from the transaction at the commencement date. If artificially low rates of interest are quoted, a manufacturer or dealer lessor restricts selling profit to that which would apply if a market rate of interest were charged. *[IFRS 16.73]*.

A manufacturer or dealer lessor recognises as an expense costs incurred in connection with obtaining a finance lease at the commencement date because they are mainly related to earning the manufacturer or dealer's selling profit. Costs incurred by manufacturer or dealer lessors in connection with obtaining a finance lease are excluded from the definition of initial direct costs and, thus, are excluded from the net investment in the lease. *[IFRS 16.74]*.

6.2.3 *Subsequent measurement*

After commencement a lessor recognises finance income over the lease term, based on a pattern reflecting a constant periodic rate of return on the lessor's net investment in the lease. *[IFRS 16.75]*. A lessor aims to allocate finance income over the lease term on a systematic and rational basis. A lessor applies the lease payments relating to the period against the gross investment in the lease to reduce both the principal and the unearned finance income. *[IFRS 16.76]*. Thus, the lessor reduces the net investment in the lease for lease payments received (net of interest income calculated above).

The lessor also recognises income from variable payments that are not included in the net investment in the lease (e.g. performance or usage based variable payments) separately in the period in which the income is earned.

A lessor applies the derecognition and impairment requirements in IFRS 9 to the net investment in the lease. The lessor reviews regularly estimated unguaranteed residual values used in computing the gross investment in the lease. If there has been a reduction in the estimated unguaranteed residual value, the lessor revises the income allocation over the lease term and recognise immediately any reduction in respect of amounts accrued. *[IFRS 16.77]*.

A lessor that classifies an asset under a finance lease as held for sale (or includes it in a disposal group that is classified as held for sale) applies IFRS 5 – *Non-current Assets Held for Sale and Discontinued Operations.* [IFRS 16.78].

Example 25.18: Lessor accounting for a finance lease

Assume Lessor enters into a 10-year lease of equipment with Lessee. The equipment is not specialised in nature and is expected to have alternative use to Lessor at the end of the 10-year lease term. Under the lease:

- Lessor receives annual lease payments of CU15,000, payable at the end of the year.
- Lessor expects the residual value of the equipment to be CU50,000 at the end of the 10-year lease term.
- Lessee provides a residual value guarantee that protects Lessor from the first CU30,000 of loss for a sale at a price below the estimated residual value at the end of the lease term (i.e. CU50,000).
- The equipment has an estimated remaining economic life of 15 years, a carrying amount of CU100,000 and a fair value of CU111,000.
- The lease does not transfer ownership of the underlying asset to Lessee at the end of the lease term or contain an option to purchase the underlying asset.
- The interest rate implicit in the lease is 10.078%.

Lessor classifies the lease as a finance lease because the sum of the present value of lease payments amounts to substantially all of the fair value of the underlying asset.

At lease commencement, Lessor accounts for the finance lease, as follows:

To record the net investment in the finance lease and derecognise the underlying asset:

Net investment in the lease	CU111,000	(a)		
Cost of goods sold	CU92,344	(b)		
Revenue			CU103,344	(d)
Property held for lease			CU100,000	(e)

(a) The net investment in the lease consists of (1) the present value of the 10 annual payments of CU15,000 plus the guaranteed residual value of CU30,000, both discounted at the interest rate implicit in the lease, which equals CU103,344 (i.e. the lease payment) and (2) the present value of unguaranteed residual asset of CU20,000, which equals CU7,656. Note that the net investment in the lease is subject to the same considerations as other assets in classification as current or non-current assets in a classified balance sheet (see 6.6 below).

(b) Cost of goods sold is the carrying amount of the equipment of CU100,000 less the present value of the unguaranteed residual asset of CU7,656

(c) Revenue equals the lease receivable

(d) The carrying amount of the underlying asset

At lease commencement, Lessor recognises selling profit of CU11,000 which is calculated as the lease payment of CU103,344 less the carrying amount of the asset (CU100,000), net of any unguaranteed residual asset (CU7,656), which equals CU92,344.

Year 1 journal entries for a finance lease:

Cash	CU15,000	(e)		
Net investment in the lease			CU3,813	(f)
Interest income			CU11,187	(g)

(a) Receipt of annual lease payments at the end of the year.

(b) Reduction of the net investment in the lease for lease payments received of (CU15,000), net of interest income of CU11,187.

(c) Interest income is the amount that produces a constant periodic discount rate on the remaining balance of the net investment in the lease. See computation below.

The following table summarises the interest income from this lease and the related amortisations of the net investment over the lease term:

Year	Annual rental payment	Annual interest income(a)	Net investment at end of year
	CU	CU	CU
Initial net investment	–	–	111,000
1	15,000	11,187	107,187
2	15,000	10,803	102,990
3	15,000	10,380	98,370
4	15,000	9,914	93,284
5	15,000	9,401	87,685
6	15,000	8,837	81,522
7	15,000	8,216	74,738
8	15,000	7,532	67,270
9	15,000	6,780	59,050
10	15,000	5,950	50,000(b)

(a) Interest income equals 10.078% of the net investment in the lease at the beginning of each year. For example, Year 1 annual interest income is calculated as (CU111,000 initial net investment × 10.078%).

(b) The estimated residual value of the equipment at the end of the lease term.

6.2.4 *Remeasurement of the net investment in the lease*

After lease commencement, the net investment in a lease is not remeasured unless:

- the lease is modified (i.e. a change in the scope of the lease, or the consideration for the lease, that was not part of the original terms and conditions of the lease) and the modified lease is not accounted for as a separate contract (see 6.4 below); or
- the lease term is revised when there is a change in the non-cancellable period of the lease (see 4.4 above).

6.3 Operating leases

Under IFRS 16, lessors account for operating leases in a manner similar to the requirements under IAS 17. That is, they continue to recognise the underlying asset and do not recognise a net investment in the lease on the balance sheet or initial profit (if any) on the income statement. The underlying asset continues to be accounted for in accordance with applicable accounting standards (e.g. IAS 16).

Lessors recognise lease payments as income on either a straight-line basis or another systematic basis if that basis is more representative of the pattern in which benefit derived from the use of the underlying asset is diminished. *[IFRS 16.81]*. After lease commencement, lessors recognise variable lease payments that do not depend on an index or rate (e.g. performance- or usage-based payments) as they are earned.

A lessor recognises costs, including depreciation, incurred in earning the lease income as an expense. *[IFRS 16.82]*. A lessor adds initial direct costs incurred in obtaining an operating lease to the carrying amount of the underlying asset and recognises those costs as an expense over the lease term on the same basis as the lease income. *[IFRS 16.83]*.

The depreciation policy for depreciable underlying assets subject to operating leases must be consistent with the lessor's normal depreciation policy for similar assets. A lessor calculates depreciation in accordance with IAS 16 and IAS 38. *[IFRS 16.84]*. A lessor applies IAS 36 to determine whether an underlying asset subject to an operating lease is impaired and to account for any impairment loss identified. *[IFRS 16.85]*.

A manufacturer or dealer lessor does not recognise any selling profit on entering into an operating lease because it is not the equivalent of a sale. *[IFRS 16.86]*.

6.4 Lease modifications

A lease modification is a change in the scope of a lease, or the consideration for a lease, that was not part of the original terms and conditions of the lease (for example, adding or terminating the right to use one or more underlying assets, or extending or shortening the contractual lease term). *[IFRS 16.Appendix A]*.

If a lease is modified, the modified contract is evaluated to determine whether it is or contains a lease (see 3.1 above). If a lease continues to exist, the lease modification can result in:

- a separate lease (see 6.4.1 below); or
- a change in the accounting for the existing lease (i.e. not a separate lease) (see 6.4.2 below).

6.4.1 *Determining whether a modification to a finance lease results in a separate lease*

A lessor accounts for a modification to a finance lease as a separate lease if both:

(a) the modification increases the scope of the lease by adding the right to use one or more underlying assets; and

(b) the consideration for the lease increases by an amount commensurate with the stand-alone price for the increase in scope and any appropriate adjustments to that stand-alone price to reflect the circumstances of the particular contract. *[IFRS 16.79]*.

If both of the conditions above are met, the lease modification results in two separate leases, the unmodified original finance lease and a separate lease. Lessors account for the separate lease in the same manner as other new leases. If either of the conditions is not met, the lease modification does not result in a separate lease.

6.4.2 *Lessor accounting for a modification to a finance lease that does not result in a separate lease*

For a modification to a finance lease that is not accounted for as a separate lease, a lessor accounts for the modification as follows:

(a) if the lease would have been classified as an operating lease had the modification been in effect at the inception date, the lessor:

  (i) accounts for the lease modification as a new lease from the effective date of the modification; and

  (ii) measures the carrying amount of the underlying asset as the net investment in the lease immediately before the effective date of the lease modification;

(b) otherwise, the lessor applies the requirements of IFRS 9. *[IFRS 16.80]*.

6.4.3 *Modification to an operating lease*

A lessor accounts for a modification to an operating lease as a new lease from the effective date of the modification, considering any prepaid or accrued lease payments relating to the original lease as part of the lease payments for the new lease. *[IFRS 16.87]*.

6.5 Other lessor matters

6.5.1 *Portfolio approach*

IFRS 16 specifies the accounting for an individual lease. However, as a practical expedient, an entity may apply it to a portfolio of leases with similar characteristics if the entity reasonably expects that the effects on the financial statements of applying IFRS 16 to the portfolio would not differ materially from applying it to the individual leases within that portfolio. If accounting for a portfolio, an entity uses estimates and assumptions that reflect the size and composition of the portfolio. *[IFRS 16.B1]*.

The IASB decided to include the portfolio approach to be consistent with IFRS 15. A decision to use the portfolio approach would be similar to a decision some entities make today to expense, rather than capitalise, certain assets when the accounting difference is, and would continue to be, immaterial to the financial statements.

6.6 Presentation

Similar to IAS 17, IFRS 16 requires lessors to recognise assets held under a finance lease in the statements of financial position and present them as a receivable at an amount equal to the net investment in the lease. *[IFRS 16.67]*. In addition, lessors are required under IFRS 16 to present underlying assets subject to operating leases according to the nature of that asset in the statement of financial position. *[IFRS 16.88]*.

The net investment in the lease is subject to the same considerations as other assets in classification as current or non-current assets in the statement of financial position.

6.7 Disclosure

6.7.1 *Disclosure objective*

The objective of the disclosures for lessors is to disclose information in the notes that, together with the information provided in the statement of financial position, statement of profit or loss and statement of cash flows, gives a basis for users of financial statements to assess the effect that leases have on the financial position, financial performance and cash flows of the lessor. *[IFRS 16.89]*.

6.7.2 *Disclosures for all lessors*

A lessor discloses the following amounts for the reporting period:

(a) for finance leases:

- (i) selling profit or loss;
- (ii) finance income on the net investment in the lease; and
- (iii) income relating to variable lease payments not included in the measurement of the net investment in the lease;

(b) for operating leases, lease income, separately disclosing income relating to variable lease payments that do not depend on an index or a rate. *[IFRS 16.90]*.

The disclosures specified above are provided in a tabular format, unless another format is more appropriate. *[IFRS 16.91]*.

A lessor discloses additional qualitative and quantitative information about its leasing activities necessary to meet the disclosure objective in paragraph 89 (see 6.7.1 above). This additional information includes, but is not limited to, information that helps users of financial statements to assess:

(a) the nature of the lessor's leasing activities; and

(b) how the lessor manages the risk associated with any rights it retains in underlying assets. In particular, a lessor discloses its risk management strategy for the rights it retains in underlying assets, including any means by which the lessor reduces that risk. Such means may include, for example, buy-back agreements, residual value guarantees or variable lease payments for use in excess of specified limits. *[IFRS 16.92]*.

6.7.3 *Disclosures for finance leases*

A lessor provides a qualitative and quantitative explanation of the significant changes in the carrying amount of the net investment in finance leases. *[IFRS 16.93]*.

A lessor discloses a maturity analysis of the lease payments receivable, showing the undiscounted lease payments to be received on an annual basis for a minimum of each of the first five years and a total of the amounts for the remaining years. A lessor reconciles the undiscounted lease payments to the net investment in the lease. The reconciliation must identify the unearned finance income relating to the lease payments receivable and any discounted unguaranteed residual value. *[IFRS 16.94]*.

6.7.4 *Disclosures for operating leases*

For items of property, plant and equipment subject to an operating lease, a lessor applies the disclosure requirements of IAS 16. In doing so, the lessor disaggregates each class of property, plant and equipment into assets subject to operating leases and assets not subject to operating leases. Therefore, a lessor provides the disclosures required by IAS 16 for assets subject to an operating lease (by class of underlying asset) separately from owned assets held and used by the lessor. *[IFRS 16.95]*.

A lessor applies the disclosure requirements in IAS 36, IAS 38, IAS 40 and IAS 41 for assets subject to operating leases. *[IFRS 16.96]*.

A lessor discloses a maturity analysis of lease payments, showing the undiscounted lease payments to be received on an annual basis for a minimum of each of the first five years and a total of the amounts for the remaining years. *[IFRS 16.97]*.

7 SUBLEASES

7.1 Definition

A sublease is a transaction for which an underlying asset is re-leased by a lessee ('intermediate lessor') to a third party, and the lease ('head lease') between the head lessor and lessee remains in effect. *[IFRS 16.Appendix A]*.

Lessees often enter into arrangements to sublease a leased asset to a third party while the original lease contract is in effect. In these arrangements, one party acts as both the lessee and lessor of the same underlying asset. The original lease is often referred to as a head lease, the original lessee is often referred to as an intermediate lessor or sub-lessor and the ultimate lessee is often referred to as the sublessee.

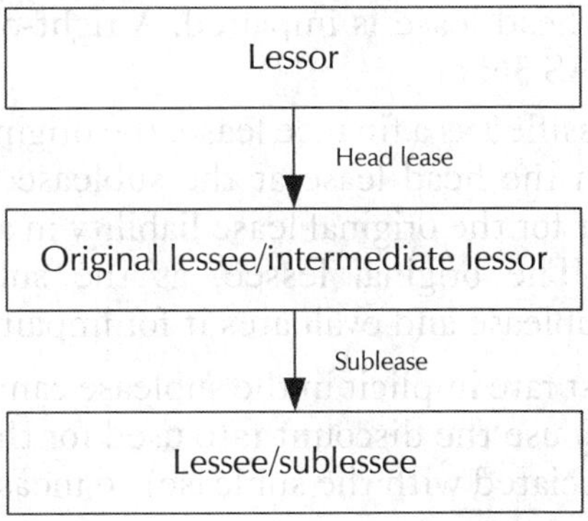

In some cases, the sublease is a separate lease agreement. In other cases, a third party assumes the original lease, but the original lessee remains the primary obligor under the original lease.

7.2 Intermediate lessor accounting

If an underlying asset is re-leased by a lessee to a third party and the original lessee retains the primary obligation under the original lease, the transaction is a sublease. That is, the original lessee generally continues to account for the original lease (the head lease) as a lessee and accounts for the sublease as the lessor (intermediate lessor).

The intermediate lessor classifies the sublease as a finance lease or an operating lease as follows:

(a) if the head lease is a short-term lease and the entity, as a lessee, has applied the short-term recognition exemption, the sublease is classified as an operating lease; or

(b) otherwise, the sublease is classified by reference to the right-of-use asset arising from the head lease, rather than by reference to the underlying asset (for example, the item of property, plant, or equipment that is the subject of the lease). *[IFRS 16.B58]*.

Example 25.19: Classification of a sublease

Entity F (original lessee/intermediate lessor) leases a building for five years. The building has an economic life of 30 years. Entity F subleases the building for four years. The sublease is classified with reference to the right-of-use asset in the head lease (and not the underlying building). For example when assessing the useful life criterion, the sublease term of four years is compared with five year right-of-use asset in the head lease and not with 30-year economic life of the building, which may result in the sublease being classified as a finance lease.

The intermediate lessor accounts for the sublease as follows:

- if the sublease is classified as an operating lease, the original lessee continues to account for the lease liability and right-of-use asset on the head lease like any other lease. If the total remaining lease cost on the head lease exceeds the anticipated sublease income, this may indicate that the right-of-use asset associated with the head lease is impaired. A right-of-use asset is assessed for impairment under IAS 36; or
- if the sublease is classified as a finance lease, the original lessee derecognises the right-of-use asset on the head lease at the sublease commencement date and continues to account for the original lease liability in accordance with the lessee accounting model. The original lessee, as the sublessor, recognises a net investment in the sublease and evaluates it for impairment.

In a sublease, if the interest rate implicit in the sublease cannot be readily determined, an intermediate lessor may use the discount rate used for the head lease (adjusted for any initial direct costs associated with the sublease) to measure the net investment in the sublease. *[IFRS 16.68]*.

When contracts are entered into at or near the same time, an intermediate lessor is required to consider the criteria for combining contracts (e.g. when the contracts are negotiated as a package with a single commercial objective, or when the consideration to be paid in one contract depends on the price or performance of the other contract). If the contracts are required to be combined, the intermediate lessor accounts for the head lease and sublease as a single combined transaction.

If a lessee subleases, or expects to sublease an asset, the head lease does not qualify as a lease of a low-value asset. *[IFRS 16.B7]*.

Example 25.20: Subleases (IFRS 16 Illustrative Examples 20 and 21)

IFRS 16 Example 20 – Sublease classified as a finance lease [IFRS 16.IE8]

Head lease – An intermediate lessor enters into a five-year lease for 5,000 square metres of office space (the head lease) with Entity A (the head lessor).

Sublease – At the beginning of Year 3, the intermediate lessor subleases the 5,000 square metres of office space for the remaining three years of the head lease to a sublessee.

The intermediate lessor classifies the sublease by reference to the right-of-use asset arising from the head lease. The intermediate lessor classifies the sublease as a finance lease, having considered the requirements in paragraphs 61–66 of IFRS 16.

When the intermediate lessor enters into the sublease, the intermediate lessor:

(a) derecognises the right-of-use asset relating to the head lease that it transfers to the sublessee and recognises the net investment in the sublease;

(b) recognises any difference between the right-of-use asset and the net investment in the sublease in profit or loss; and

(c) retains the lease liability relating to the head lease in its statement of financial position, which represents the lease payments owed to the head lessor.

During the term of the sublease, the intermediate lessor recognises both finance income on the sublease and interest expense on the head lease.

IFRS 16 Example 21 – Sublease classified as an operating lease

Head lease – An intermediate lessor enters into a five-year lease for 5,000 square metres of office space (the head lease) with Entity A (the head lessor).

Sublease – At commencement of the head lease, the intermediate lessor subleases the 5,000 square metres of office space for two years to a sublessee.

The intermediate lessor classifies the sublease by reference to the right-of-use asset arising from the head lease. The intermediate lessor classifies the sublease as an operating lease, having considered the requirements in paragraphs 61–66 of IFRS 16.

When the intermediate lessor enters into the sublease, the intermediate lessor retains the lease liability and the right-of-use asset relating to the head lease in its statement of financial position.

During the term of the sublease, the intermediate lessor:

(a) recognises a depreciation charge for the right-of-use asset and interest on the lease liability; and

(b) recognises lease income from the sublease.

7.3 Sublessee accounting

A sublessee accounts for its lease in the same manner as any other lease under IFRS 16. See 5 above.

7.4 Presentation

Intermediate lessors are not permitted to offset lease liabilities and lease assets that arise from a head lease and a sublease, respectively, unless those liabilities and assets meet the requirements in IAS 1 for offsetting. *[IFRS 16.BC235]*. Intermediate lessors apply the principal-agent provisions requirements in IFRS 15 to determine whether sublease revenue needs to be presented on a gross or net basis (i.e. reduced for head lease expenses). Intermediate lessors generally present sublease revenue on a gross basis. See Chapter 30 at 4.4.

7.5 Disclosure

Intermediate lessors, like all lessors, are required to disclose qualitative and quantitative information which gives a basis for users of financial statements to assess the effect that leases have on the financial position, financial performance and cash flows of the lessor.

8 SALE AND LEASEBACK TRANSACTIONS

A sale and leaseback transaction involves the transfer of an asset by an entity (the seller-lessee) to another entity (the buyer-lessor) and the leaseback of the same asset by the seller-lessee. Because IFRS 16 requires lessees to recognise most leases on the balance sheet (i.e. all leases except for leases of low-value assets and short-term leases depending on the lessee's accounting policy election), sale and leaseback transactions no longer provide lessees with a source of off-balance sheet financing.

If an entity (the seller-lessee) transfers an asset to another entity (the buyer-lessor) and leases that asset back from the buyer-lessor, both the seller-lessee and the buyer-lessor assess whether the transfer of the asset is a sale and account for it as described below. *[IFRS 16.98]*.

8.1 Determining whether the transfer of an asset is a sale

An entity applies the requirements for determining when a performance obligation is satisfied in IFRS 15 to determine whether the transfer of an asset is accounted for as a sale of that asset. *[IFRS 16.99]*. If control of an underlying asset passes to the buyer-lessor, the transaction is accounted for as a sale or purchase of the asset and a lease. If not, both the seller-lessee and the buyer-lessor account for the transaction as a financing transaction. See Chapter 30 at 7.3 for the requirements of IFRS 15.

Paragraph 38 of IFRS 15 includes the following indicators of the transfer of the control:

- the entity has a present right to payment for the asset – if a customer is presently obliged to pay for an asset, then that may indicate that the customer has obtained the ability to direct the use of, and obtain substantially all of the remaining benefits from, the asset in exchange;
- the customer has legal title to the asset – legal title may indicate which party to a contract has the ability to direct the use of, and obtain substantially all of the remaining benefits from, an asset or to restrict the access of other entities to those benefits. Therefore, the transfer of legal title of an asset may indicate that the customer has obtained control of the asset. If an entity retains legal title solely as protection against the customer's failure to pay, those rights of the entity would not preclude the customer from obtaining control of an asset;
- the entity has transferred physical possession of the asset – the customer's physical possession of an asset may indicate that the customer has the ability to direct the use of, and obtain substantially all of the remaining benefits from, the asset or to restrict the access of other entities to those benefits. However, physical possession may not coincide with control of an asset. For example, in some repurchase agreements and in some consignment arrangements, a customer or consignee may have physical possession of an asset that the entity controls. Conversely, in some bill-and-hold arrangements, the entity may have physical possession of an asset that the customer controls;
- the customer has the significant risks and rewards of ownership of the asset – the transfer of the significant risks and rewards of ownership of an asset to the customer may indicate that the customer has obtained the ability to direct the use of, and obtain substantially all of the remaining benefits from, the asset. However, when evaluating the risks and rewards of ownership of a promised asset, an entity is required to exclude any risks that give rise to a separate performance obligation in addition to the performance obligation to transfer the asset. For example, an entity may have transferred control of an asset to a customer but not yet satisfied an additional performance obligation to provide maintenance services related to the transferred asset; and
- the customer has accepted the asset – the customer's acceptance of an asset may indicate that it has obtained the ability to direct the use of, and obtain substantially all of the remaining benefits from, the asset. *[IFRS 15.38]*.

None of these indicators individually determine whether the buyer-lessor has obtained control of the underlying asset. Both the seller-lessee and the buyer-lessor must consider all relevant facts and circumstances to determine whether control has transferred.

Furthermore, not all of the indicators must be present to determine that the buyer-lessor has gained control. Rather, the indicators are factors that are often present when a customer has obtained control of an asset and the list is meant to help entities apply the principle of control. See Chapter 30 at 7.3.

The IASB noted that the existence of a leaseback, in isolation, does not preclude a sale. This is because a lease is different from the sale or purchase of an underlying asset, as a lease does not transfer control of the underlying asset. Instead, it transfers the right to control the use of the underlying asset for the period of the lease. However, if the seller-lessee has a substantive repurchase option for the underlying asset (i.e. a right to repurchase the asset), no sale has occurred because the buyer-lessor has not obtained control of the asset. *[IFRS 16.BC262]*.

These requirements are a significant change from current practice for seller-lessees as they must apply the requirements of IFRS 15 to determine whether a sale has occurred.

IFRS 16 does not address whether a lessee's renewal options (e.g. fixed price, fair value at the date of exercise) permitting the seller-lessee to extend the lease for substantially all of the remaining economic life of the underlying asset precludes sale accounting. We believe that a lessee that has an option to extend a lease for substantially all of the remaining economic life of the underlying asset is, economically, in a similar position to a lessee that has an option to purchase the underlying asset. Therefore, when the renewal price is not fair value at the time the renewal option is exercised, the renewal option would prohibit sale accounting under IFRS 15 and IFRS 16.

8.2 Transactions in which the transfer of an asset is a sale

8.2.1 Accounting for the sale

If the transfer of an asset by the seller-lessee satisfies the requirements of IFRS 15 to be accounted for as a sale of the asset:

(a) the seller-lessee measures the right-of-use asset arising from the leaseback at the proportion of the previous carrying amount of the asset that relates to the right of use retained by the seller-lessee. Accordingly, the seller-lessee recognises only the amount of any gain or loss that relates to the rights transferred to the buyer-lessor; and

(b) the buyer-lessor accounts for the purchase of the asset applying applicable Standards, and for the lease applying the lessor accounting requirements in this Standard. *[IFRS 16.100]*.

Although not explicitly stated in IFRS 16, we believe that if the sale and leaseback transaction is expected to result in a loss to the seller-lessee, that loss will not be deferred.

8.2.2 Accounting for the leaseback

When a sale occurs, both the seller-lessee and the buyer-lessor account for the leaseback in the same manner as any other lease, with adjustments for off-market terms. Specifically, a seller-lessee recognises a lease liability and right-of-use asset for the leaseback (subject to the optional exemptions for short-term leases and leases of low-value assets).

8.2.3 Adjustment for off-market terms

The sale transaction and the ensuing lease are generally interdependent and negotiated as a package. Consequently, some transactions could be structured with a negotiated sales price that is above or below the asset's fair value and with lease payments for the ensuing lease that are above or below the market rates. These off-market terms could distort the gain or loss on the sale and the recognition of lease expense and lease income for the lease. To ensure that the gain or loss on the sale and the lease-related assets and liabilities associated with such transactions are neither understated nor overstated, IFRS 16 requires adjustments for any off-market terms of sale and leaseback transactions, on the more readily determinable basis of the difference between the fair value of the consideration for the sale and the fair value of the asset and the difference between the present value of the contractual payments for the lease and the present value of payments for the lease at market rates.

If the fair value of the consideration for the sale of an asset does not equal the fair value of the asset, or if the payments for the lease are not at market rates, an entity makes the following adjustments to measure the sale proceeds at fair value:

(a) any below-market terms are accounted for as a prepayment of lease payments; and

(b) any above-market terms are accounted for as additional financing provided by the buyer-lessor to the seller-lessee. *[IFRS 16.101]*.

The entity measures any potential adjustment required above on the basis of the more readily determinable of:

(a) the difference between the fair value of the consideration for the sale and the fair value of the asset; and

(b) the difference between the present value of the contractual payments for the lease and the present value of payments for the lease at market rates. *[IFRS 16.102]*.

Example 25.21: Sale and leaseback transaction (IFRS 16 Illustrative Example 24) *[IFRS 16.IE11]*

An entity (Seller-lessee) sells a building to another entity (Buyer-lessor) for cash of CU2,000,000. Immediately before the transaction, the building is carried at a cost of CU1,000,000. At the same time, Seller-lessee enters into a contract with Buyer-lessor for the right to use the building for 18 years, with annual payments of CU120,000 payable at the end of each year. The terms and conditions of the transaction are such that the transfer of the building by Seller-lessee satisfies the requirements for determining when a performance obligation is satisfied in IFRS 15.

Accordingly, Seller-lessee and Buyer-lessor account for the transaction as a sale and leaseback. This example ignores any initial direct costs.

The fair value of the building at the date of sale is CU1,800,000. Because the consideration for the sale of the building is not at fair value Seller-lessee and Buyer-lessor make adjustments to measure the sale proceeds at fair value. The amount of the excess sale price of CU200,000 (CU2,000,000 – CU1,800,000) is recognised as additional financing provided by Buyer-lessor to Seller-lessee.

The interest rate implicit in the lease is 4.5 per cent per annum, which is readily determinable by Seller-lessee. The present value of the annual payments (18 payments of CU120,000, discounted at 4.5 per cent per annum) amounts to CU1,459,200, of which CU200,000 relates to the additional financing and CU1,259,200 relates to the lease – corresponding to 18 annual payments of CU16,447 and CU103,553, respectively.

Buyer-lessor classifies the lease of the building as an operating lease.

Seller-lessee

At the commencement date, Seller-lessee measures the right-of-use asset arising from the leaseback of the building at the proportion of the previous carrying amount of the building that relates to the right-of-use retained by Seller-lessee, which is CU699,555. This is calculated as: $1,000,000 (the carrying amount of the building) ÷ CU1,800,000 (the fair value of the building) × CU1,259,200 (the discounted lease payments for the 18-year right-of-use asset).

Seller-lessee recognises only the amount of the gain that relates to the rights transferred to Buyer-lessor of CU240,355 calculated as follows. The gain on sale of building amounts to CU800,000 (CU1,800,000 – CU1,000,000), of which:

(a) CU559,645 (CU800,000 ÷ CU1,800,000 × CU1,259,200) relates to the right to use the building retained by Seller-lessee; and

(b) CU240,355 (CU800,000 ÷ CU1,800,000 × (CU1,800,000 – CU1,259,200)) relates to the rights transferred to Buyer-lessor.

At the commencement date, Seller-lessee accounts for the transaction as follows.

Cash	CU2,000,000	
Right-of-use asset	CU699,555	
Building		CU1,000,000
Financial liability		CU1,459,200
Gain on rights transferred		CU240,355

Buyer-lessor

At the commencement date, Buyer-lessor accounts for the transaction as follows.

Building	CU1,800,000	
Financial asset	CU200,000*	
Cash		CU2,000,000

* 18 payments of CU16,447, discounted at 4.5 per cent per annum

After the commencement date, Buyer-lessor accounts for the lease by treating CU103,553 of the annual payments of CU120,000 as lease payments. The remaining CU16,447 of annual payments received from Seller-lessee are accounted for as (a) payments received to settle the financial asset of CU200,000 and (b) interest revenue.

8.3 Transactions in which the transfer of an asset is not a sale

If the transfer of an asset by the seller-lessee does not satisfy the requirements of IFRS 15 to be accounted for as a sale of the asset:

(a) the seller-lessee continues to recognise the transferred asset and recognises a financial liability equal to the transfer proceeds. It accounts for the financial liability applying IFRS 9; and

(b) the buyer-lessor does not recognise the transferred asset and recognises a financial asset equal to the transfer proceeds. It accounts for the financial asset applying IFRS 9. *[IFRS 16.103]*.

8.4 Disclosures

A seller-lessee may need to provide additional information relating to sale and leaseback transactions to satisfy the disclosure objective. This could include information that helps users of financial statements to assess, for example:

(a) the lessee's reasons for sale and leaseback transactions and the prevalence of those transactions;

(b) key terms and conditions of individual sale and leaseback transactions;

(c) payments not included in the measurement of lease liabilities; and

(d) the cash flow effect of sale and leaseback transactions in the reporting period. *[IFRS 16.B52]*.

A seller-lessee is also required to disclose any gains and losses arising from sale and leaseback transactions separately from gains and losses on disposals of other assets. *[IFRS 16.53(i)]*.

9 BUSINESS COMBINATIONS

9.1 Acquiree in a business combination is a lessee

Consequential amendments to IFRS 3 – *Business Combinations* – specify the initial measurement requirements for leases that are acquired in a business combination.

Paragraph 28A will be added to IFRS 3 to clarify that the acquirer recognises right-of-use assets and lease liabilities for leases identified in accordance with IFRS 16 in which the acquiree is the lessee. The acquirer is not required to recognise right-of-use assets and lease liabilities for:

- leases for which the lease term ends within 12 months of the acquisition date; or
- leases for which the underlying asset is of low-value.

Paragraph 28B will be added to IFRS 3 to clarify that the acquirer measures the lease liability at the present value of the remaining lease payments as if the acquired lease were a new lease at the acquisition date. The acquirer measures the right-of-use asset at the same amount as the lease liability, adjusted to reflect favourable or unfavourable terms of the lease when compared with market terms. Because the off-market nature of the lease is captured in the right-of-use asset, the acquirer does not separately recognise an intangible asset or liability for favourable or unfavourable lease terms relative to market. The acquirer is not required to recognise assets and liabilities relating to off-market terms for short-term leases and leases of low-value assets, as the IASB expect that the effect of off-market terms will rarely be material for these contracts. *[IFRS 16.BC298]*.

The subsequent measurement requirements for an acquired lease liability and right-of-use asset are the same as the requirements for any other existing lease arrangement.

9.2 Acquiree in a business combination is a lessor

IFRS 16 requires an acquirer to classify acquired lessor leases as either finance or operating leases using the contractual terms and conditions at the inception of the lease, or, if the terms of the contract have been modified in a manner that would change its classification, at the date of that modification. Therefore, the classification is not changed as a result of a business combination unless a lease is modified.

10 EFFECTIVE DATE AND TRANSITION

10.1 Effective date

An entity applies IFRS 16 for annual periods beginning on or after 1 January 2019. Earlier application is permitted for entities that apply IFRS 15 at or before the date of initial application of IFRS 16. If an entity applies IFRS 16 earlier, it must disclose that fact. *[IFRS 16.C1]*.

The application date for IFRS 15 is for annual periods beginning on or after 1 January 2018. The IASB has aligned several concepts in IFRS 16 with those in IFRS 15 and so some entities, particularly lessors, may consider applying IFRS 16 one year earlier in order to have one transition date for both standards.

10.2 Transition

The transition provisions of IFRS 16 are applied at the initial date of application. For this purpose, the date of initial application is the beginning of the annual reporting period in which an entity first applies IFRS 16. *[IFRS 16.C2]*.

As a practical expedient, an entity is not required to reassess whether a contract is, or contains a lease at the date of initial application. Instead, an entity is permitted:

- to apply IFRS 16 to contracts that were previously identified as leases applying IAS 17 and IFRIC 4; or
- not to apply IFRS 16 to contracts that were not previously identified as containing a lease applying IAS 17 and IFRIC 4. *[IFRS 16.C3]*.

If an entity chooses to apply the practical expedient, it discloses that fact and applies the practical expedient to all of its contracts. As a result, entities apply the requirements in paragraphs 9 to 11 (identifying a lease) only to contracts entered into after the date of initial application. *[IFRS 16.C4]*.

As the accounting for operating leases under IAS 17 is similar to the accounting for service contracts, entities may not always have focussed on determining whether an arrangement is a lease or a service contract. Some entities may need to revisit assessments made under IAS 17 and IFRIC 4 because, under IFRS 16, most leases are recognised on lessees' balance sheets and the effects of treating an arrangement as a service instead of a lease may be material. IFRS 16's practical expedient that allows an entity not to reassess whether a contract contains a lease, only applies to arrangements that were appropriately assessed under IAS 17 and IFRIC 4.

10.3 Lessee transition

A lessee applies IFRS 16 to its leases either:

- retrospectively to each prior reporting period presented applying IAS 8 (see 10.3.1 below); or
- retrospectively with the cumulative effect of initially applying IFRS 16 recognised at the date of initial application (see 10.3.2 below). *[IFRS 16.C5]*.

A lessee applies its elected transition approach consistently to all leases in which it is a lessee. *[IFRS 16.C6]*.

10.3.1 Full retrospective approach

Under the full retrospective approach, an entity applies IFRS 16 as if it had been applied since the inception of all lease contracts that are presented in the financial statements. If the standard is applied at 1 January 2019, this means that, in the 31 December 2019 financial statements, the comparative period to 31 December 2018 (assuming that this is the only comparative period presented) must be restated. A restated opening balance sheet at 1 January 2018 will also need to be disclosed as required by IAS 1.

10.3.2 Modified retrospective approach

When applying the modified retrospective approach, a lessee does not restate comparative figures. Instead, a lessee recognises the cumulative effect of initially applying IFRS 16 as an adjustment to the opening balance of retained earnings (or other component of equity, as appropriate) at the date of initial application. *[IFRS 16.C7]*.

10.3.2.A Leases previously classified as operating leases

A lessee:

- recognises a lease liability at the date of initial application for leases previously classified as an operating lease applying IAS 17. The lessee measures that lease liability at the present value of the remaining lease payments, discounted using the lessee's incremental borrowing rate at the date of initial application;
- recognises a right-of-use asset at the date of initial application for leases previously classified as an operating lease applying IAS 17. The lessee chooses, on a lease-by-lease basis, to measure that right-of-use asset at either:
  - its carrying amount as if IFRS 16 had been applied since the commencement date, but discounted using the lessee's incremental borrowing rate at the date of initial application; or
  - an amount equal to the lease liability, adjusted by the amount of any prepaid or accrued lease payments relating to that lease recognised in the statement of financial position immediately before the date of initial application; and
- applies IAS 36 to right-of-use assets at the date of initial application, unless the lessee applies the practical expedient below. *[IFRS 16.C8]*.

For leases previously classified as operating leases, applying IAS 17, a lessee:

- is not required to make any adjustments on transition for leases for which the underlying asset is of low value. The lessee accounts for those leases applying IFRS 16 from the date of initial application;
- is not required to make any adjustments on transition for leases previously accounted for as investment property using the fair value model in IAS 40. The lessee accounts for those leases applying IAS 40 and IFRS 16 from the date of initial application; and
- measures the right-of-use asset at fair value at the date of initial application for leases previously accounted for as operating leases under IAS 17 and that will be accounted for as investment property using the fair value model in IAS 40 from the date of initial application. The lessee accounts for those leases applying IAS 40 and IFRS 16 from the date of initial application. *[IFRS 16.C9]*.

A lessee may use one or more of the following practical expedients when applying the modified retrospective approach to leases previously classified as operating leases applying IAS 17. A lessee is permitted to apply these practical expedients on a lease-by-lease basis:

- a lessee may apply a single discount rate to a portfolio of leases with reasonably similar characteristics (such as leases with a similar remaining lease term for a similar class of underlying asset in a similar economic environment);
- a lessee may rely on its assessment of whether leases are onerous applying IAS 37 immediately before the date of initial application as an alternative to performing an impairment review. If a lessee chooses this practical expedient, the lessee adjusts the right-of-use asset at the date of initial application by the amount of any provision for onerous leases recognised in the statement of financial position immediately before the date of initial application;
- a lessee may elect not to recognise a lease liability and a right-of-use asset for leases for which the lease term ends within 12 months of the date of initial application. In this case, a lessee:
  - accounts for those leases in the same way as short-term leases; and
  - includes the cost associated with those leases within the disclosure of short-term lease expense in the annual reporting period that includes the date of initial application;
- a lessee may exclude initial direct costs from the measurement of the right-of-use asset at the date of initial application; and
- a lessee may use hindsight, such as in determining the lease term if the contract contains options to extend or terminate the lease. *[IFRS 16.C10]*.

10.3.2.B Leases previously classified as finance leases

For a lessee that applies the modified retrospective approach to leases that were classified as finance leases applying IAS 17, the carrying amount of the right-of-use asset and the lease liability at the date of initial application are the carrying amounts of the lease asset and lease liability immediately before that date measured applying

IAS 17. For those leases, a lessee accounts for the right-of-use asset and the lease liability applying IFRS 16 from the date of initial application. *[IFRS 16.C11]*.

10.4 Lessor transition

With the exception of subleases (see 10.4.1. below), a lessor is not required to make any adjustments on transition for leases in which it is a lessor and accounts for those leases applying IFRS 16 from the date of initial application. *[IFRS 16.C14]*.

10.4.1 Subleases

An intermediate lessor (an entity that is both a lessee and a lessor of the same underlying asset):

- reassesses subleases that were classified as operating leases applying IAS 17 and are ongoing at the date of initial application, to determine whether each sublease should be classified as an operating lease or a finance lease. The intermediate lessor performs this assessment at the date initial application on the basis of the remaining contractual terms and conditions of the head lease and sublease at that date; and
- for subleases that were classified as operating leases applying IAS 17 but finance leases applying IFRS 16, account for the sublease as a new finance lease entered into at the date of initial application. *[IFRS 16.C15]*.

10.5 Other considerations

10.5.1 Sale and leaseback transactions

An entity does not reassess sale and leaseback transactions entered into before the date of initial application to determine whether the transfer of the underlying asset satisfies the requirements in IFRS 15 to be accounted for as a sale. *[IFRS 16.C16]*.

If a sale and leaseback transaction was accounted for as a sale and a finance lease applying IAS 17, the seller-lessee:

- accounts for the leaseback in the same way as it accounts for any other finance lease that exists at the date of initial application; and
- continues to amortise any gain on sale over the lease term. *[IFRS 16.C17]*.

If a sale and leaseback transaction was accounted for as a sale and operating lease applying IAS 17, the seller-lessee:

- accounts for the leaseback in the same way as it accounts for any other operating lease that exists at the date of initial application; and
- adjusts the leaseback right-of-use asset for any deferred gains or losses that relate to off-market terms recognised in the statement of financial position immediately before the date of initial application. *[IFRS 16.C18]*.

10.5.2 Amounts previously recognised in a business combination

If a lessee previously recognised an asset or liability applying IFRS 3 relating to favourable or unfavourable terms of an operating lease acquired as part of a business combination, the lessee derecognises that asset or liability and adjusts the carrying amount of the right-of-use asset by a corresponding amount at the date of initial application. *[IFRS 16.C19]*.

10.6 Disclosure

If an entity applies IFRS 16 in full retrospectively, it is required to apply certain disclosures under IAS 8 regarding the effect of the initial application (see Chapter 3 at 4.4).

If an entity applies the modified retrospective approach above, the lessee discloses information about initial application required by paragraph 28 of IAS 8, except for the information specified in paragraph 28(f) of IAS 8, which relates to the amount of the adjustments. Instead of the information specified in paragraph 28(f) of IAS 8, the lessee discloses:

- the weighted average lessee's incremental borrowing rate applied to lease liabilities recognised in the statement of financial position at the date of initial application; and
- an explanation of any difference between:
  - operating lease commitments disclosed applying IAS 17 at the end of the annual reporting period immediately preceding the date of initial application, discounted using the incremental borrowing rate at the date of initial application; and
  - lease liabilities recognised in the statement of financial position at the date of initial application.

If a lessee uses one or more of the specified practical expedients in paragraph C10 (see 10.3.2.A above), it discloses that fact. *[IFRS 16.C13].*

Chapter 26 Government grants

List of examples

Chapter 26 Government grants

1 INTRODUCTION

IAS 20 – *Accounting for Government Grants and Disclosure of Government Assistance* – applied for the first time in 1984. *[IAS 20.41]*. With the exception of an amendment in 2008 requiring entities to quantify the benefit of a government loan at a below-market rate of interest, *[IAS 20.43]*, the standard has survived for all that time without any substantive amendment. The standard pre-dates the IASB's *Conceptual Framework* and, as the IASB itself has noted, it is inconsistent with it,[1] resulting in the recognition in the statement of financial position of deferred credits that do not meet the *Framework's* definitions of liabilities and allowing alternatives to initial measurement at fair value that could result in an asset being understated by reference to the *Framework*.

IAS 20 defines government grants in terms of assistance given to an entity in return for meeting certain conditions relating to the operating activities of the entity. *[IAS 20.3]*. SIC-10 – *Government Assistance – No Specific Relation to Operating Activities* – was issued in 1998 to clarify that IAS 20 applies even if the only condition is a requirement to operate in certain regions or industry sectors (see 2.2.1 below).

Government grants related to biological assets are excluded from the scope of IAS 20 and are dealt with in IAS 41 – *Agriculture* (see section 5 below and Chapter 40 at 3.3). *[IAS 20.2(d)]*.

A project to revise IAS 20 was deferred in 2006 and, at the time of writing, the lack of any reference to it in the IASB's Work Plan indicates that resumption of this project is not a priority.[2]

1.1 Overview of IAS 20

Government grants are transfers of resources to an entity in return for past or future compliance with certain conditions relating to the entity's operating activities. *[IAS 20.3]*. Such assistance has been available to businesses for many years, although the exact nature of such support will vary from country to country and over time as governments and their priorities change. The purpose of government grants, which may be called subsidies, subventions or premiums, *[IAS 20.6]*, and other forms of government assistance is often to encourage a private sector entity to take a course of action that it would not normally have taken if the assistance had not been provided. *[IAS 20.4]*. As the standard notes, the receipt of government assistance by an entity may be significant for the preparation of the financial statements for two reasons:

- if resources have been transferred, an appropriate method of accounting for the transfer must be found; and
- it is desirable to give an indication of the extent to which an entity has benefited from such assistance during the reporting period, because this facilitates comparison of its financial statements with those of prior periods and with those of other entities. *[IAS 20.5]*.

The main accounting issue that arises from government grants is how to deal with the benefit that the grant represents. IAS 20 adopts an income approach, whereby grants are recognised in profit or loss in the same period as the costs that the grants are intended to compensate. *[IAS 20.12]*. Accordingly, grants relating to specific expenses are recognised in profit or loss in the same period as those expenses, and grants relating to depreciable assets are recognised in profit or loss in the same periods as the related depreciation expense. *[IAS 20.17]*. This approach is applied regardless of whether the benefit is received in the form of cash; by a transfer of a non-monetary asset; or as a reduction of a liability to the government. *[IAS 20.9, 23]*.

The standard recognises that an entity may receive other forms of government assistance, such as free technical or marketing advice and the provision of guarantees, which cannot reasonably have a value placed upon them. Rather than prescribe how these should be accounted for, it requires disclosure about such assistance. *[IAS 20.35, 36]*.

1.2 Terms used in this chapter

The following terms are used in this chapter with the meanings specified:

Term	Definition
Government	Government, government agencies and similar bodies whether local, national or international. *[IAS 20.3]*
Government assistance	Action by government designed to provide an economic benefit specific to an entity or a range of entities qualifying under certain criteria. Government assistance does not include benefits provided only indirectly through action affecting general trading conditions, such as the provision of infrastructure in development areas or the imposition of trading constraints on competitors. *[IAS 20.3]*
Government grants	Assistance by government in the form of transfers of resources to an entity in return for past or future compliance with certain conditions relating to the operating activities of the entity. This excludes those forms of government assistance which cannot reasonably have a value placed upon them and transactions with government which cannot be distinguished from the normal trading transactions of the entity. *[IAS 20.3]* Government grants are sometimes called by other names such as subsidies, subventions, or premiums. *[IAS 20.6]*

Grants related to assets	Government grants whose primary condition is that an entity qualifying for them should purchase, construct or otherwise acquire long-term assets. Subsidiary conditions may also be attached restricting the type or location of the assets or the periods during which they are required to be held. *[IAS 20.3]*
Grants related to income	Government grants other than those related to assets. *[IAS 20.3]*
Forgivable loans	Loans which the lender undertakes to waive repayment under certain prescribed conditions. *[IAS 20.3]*
Fair value	The price that would be received to sell an asset or paid to transfer a liability in an orderly transaction between market participants at the measurement date. *[IAS 20.3, IFRS 13 Appendix A]*
Non-monetary government grant	A government grant that takes the form of a transfer of a non-monetary asset, such as land or other resources, for the use of the entity. *[IAS 20.23]*
Biological asset	A living animal or plant. *[IAS 41.5]*
Bearer plant	A bearer plant is a living plant that: *[IAS 41.5]* (a) is used in the production or supply of agricultural produce; (b) is expected to bear produce for more than one period; and (c) has a remote likelihood of being sold as agricultural produce, except for incidental scrap sales.
Costs to sell	The incremental costs directly attributable to the disposal of an asset, excluding finance costs and income taxes. *[IAS 41.5]*

Chapter 26

2 SCOPE OF IAS 20

IAS 20 applies in accounting for, and in the disclosure of, government grants and in the disclosure of other forms of government assistance. *[IAS 20.1]*. The distinction between government grants and other forms of government assistance is important because the standard's accounting requirements only apply to the former.

The standard regards the term 'government' to include government agencies and similar bodies whether local, national or international. *[IAS 20.3]*.

2.1 Government assistance

Government assistance is defined as action by government designed to provide an economic benefit to an entity or range of entities qualifying under certain criteria (see 3.7 below). *[IAS 20.3]*. Government assistance takes many forms 'varying both in the nature of the assistance given and in the conditions which are usually attached to it'. *[IAS 20.4]*.

However, such assistance does not include benefits provided indirectly through action affecting general trading conditions, such as the provision of infrastructure (e.g. transport, communications networks or utilities) in development areas or that are available for the benefit of an entire local community or the imposition of trading constraints on competitors. *[IAS 20.3, 38]*.

2.2 Government grants

Government grants are a specific form of government assistance. Under IAS 20, *government grants* represent assistance by government in the form of transfers of resources to an entity in return for past or future compliance with certain conditions relating to the operating activities of the entity. *[IAS 20.3]*. The standard identifies the following types of government grants:

- *grants related to assets* are government grants whose primary condition is that an entity qualifying for them should purchase, construct or otherwise acquire long-term assets. Subsidiary conditions may also be attached restricting the type or location of the assets or the periods during which they are to be acquired or held; and
- *grants related to income* are government grants other than those related to assets. *[IAS 20.3]*.

Government grants exclude:

(a) assistance to which no value can reasonably be assigned, e.g. free technical or marketing advice and the provision of guarantees; and

(b) transactions with government that cannot be distinguished from the normal trading transactions of the entity, e.g. where the entity is being favoured by a government's procurement policy. *[IAS 20.3, 35]*.

Such excluded items are to be treated as falling within the standard's disclosure requirements for government assistance (see 2.1 above and 3.7 below).

Loans at below market interest rates are also deemed to be a form of government assistance and the standard requires entities to measure and record the benefit of the below-market rate of interest in accordance with IAS 39 – *Financial Instruments: Recognition and Measurement* – or IFRS 9 – *Financial Instruments* – as appropriate. *[IAS 20.10A]*. The accounting consequences are discussed at 3.4 below.

In public-to-private service concession arrangements a government may give certain assets to the operator of the service concession. If the entire arrangement is to be accounted for under IFRIC 12 – *Service Concession Arrangements* – the assets are not a government grant. *[IFRIC 12.27]*. Service concessions are discussed in Chapter 27.

While grants of emission rights and renewable energy certificates typically meet the definition of government grants under IAS 20, the rights and certificates themselves are intangible assets. Accounting for emission rights and renewable energy certificates is discussed in Chapter 17 at 11.2 and 11.3.

2.2.1 Grants with no specific relation to operating activities (SIC-10)

SIC-10 addresses the situation in some countries where government assistance is provided to entities, but without there being any conditions specifically relating to their operating activities, other than to operate in certain regions or industry sectors. It determined that such forms of government assistance are to be treated as government grants. *[SIC-10.3]*. This ruling was made to avoid any suggestion that such forms of assistance were not governed by IAS 20 and could be credited directly to equity.

2.3 Scope exclusions

IAS 20 does not deal with:

(a) accounting for government grants if the entity prepares financial information that reflect the effects of changing prices, whether as financial statements or in supplementary information of a similar nature;

(b) government assistance in the form of benefits that are available in determining taxable profit or loss or are determined or limited on the basis of income tax liability, e.g. income tax holidays, investment tax credits, accelerated depreciation allowances and reduced income tax rates;

(c) government participation in the ownership of the entity; and

(d) government grants covered by IAS 41. *[IAS 20.2]*.

The accounting treatment of government assistance either provided by way of a reduction in taxable profit or loss; or determined or limited according to an entity's income tax liability is discussed in the context of investment tax credits at 2.3.1 below and in Chapter 31 at 4.3.

The reason for exclusion (d) above is that the presentation permitted by IAS 20 of deducting government grants from the carrying amount of the asset (see 4.1 below) was considered inconsistent with a fair value model, which can be used in the measurement of biological assets. *[IAS 41.B66]*. The IASB decided to deal with government grants related to agricultural activity in IAS 41 rather than initiate a wider review of IAS 20. *[IAS 41.B67]*. The requirements of IAS 41 in relation to government grants are set out at 5 below and in Chapter 40 at 3.3.

There are no similar exclusions for government grants in IAS 40 – *Investment Property* – which includes a similar fair value model (see Chapter 19), nor was IAS 20 revised to deal with the matter. This is probably because government grants in the investment property sector are relatively rare compared to the agricultural sector. However, governments do on occasion provide grants and subsidised loans to finance the acquisition of social housing that meets the definition of investment property. The discount on these subsidised loans is now considered to be a government grant, as described at 3.4 below.

2.3.1 Investment tax credits

IAS 20 excludes from its scope government assistance either provided by way of a reduction in taxable profit or determined or limited according to an entity's income tax liability, citing investment tax credits as an example. *[IAS 20.2(b)]*. Investment tax credits are excluded altogether from the scope of IAS 12 – *Income Taxes* – although any temporary differences that arise from them are in the scope of the standard. *[IAS 12.4]*. Accordingly, if government assistance is described as an investment tax credit, but it is neither determined or limited by the entity's income tax liability nor provided in the form of an income tax deduction, the requirements of IAS 20 apply.

This raises the question as to how an entity should account for those forms of government incentives for specific kinds of investment that are delivered through the tax system. Sometimes, a tax credit is given as a deduction from the entity's income tax liability, and sometimes as a deductible expense in computing the liability. Entitlement to assistance can be determined in a variety of ways. Some investment tax credits may relate to direct investment in property, plant and equipment. Other entities may receive investment tax credits relating to research and development activities. Some credits may be realisable only through a reduction in current or future income taxes payable, while others may be settled directly in cash if the entity does not have sufficient income taxes payable to offset the credit within a certain period. Access to the credit may be limited according to the total of all taxes paid (i.e. including taxes such as payroll and sales taxes remitted to government in addition to income taxes). There may be other conditions associated with receiving the investment tax credit, for example with respect to the conduct and continuing activities of the entity, and the credit may become repayable if ongoing conditions are not met.

The fact that both IAS 20 and IAS 12 exclude from their scope those investment tax credits that are realisable only through a reduction in current or future income taxes payable does not prohibit an entity from applying either standard in accounting for such credits. Indeed, either IAS 20 or IAS 12 will generally provide an appropriate accounting framework, by analogy under the 'GAAP hierarchy' in IAS 8 – *Accounting Policies, Changes in Accounting Estimates and Errors* (see Chapter 3).

Which standard provides the better accounting model in a particular case is a matter of judgement. In our view, such a judgement would be informed by reference to the specific terms of the arrangement including the following factors:

Feature of credit	**Indicator of IAS 20 treatment**	**Indicator of IAS 12 treatment**
Method of realisation	Directly settled in cash where there are insufficient taxable profits to allow credit to be fully offset, or available for set off against payroll taxes, VAT or amounts owed to government other than income taxes payable.	Only available as a reduction in income taxes payable (i.e. benefit is forfeit if there are insufficient income taxes payable). However, the longer the period allowed for carrying forward unused credits, the less relevant this indicator becomes.
Number of conditions not related to tax position (e.g. minimum employment, ongoing use of purchased assets)	Many	None or few
Restrictions as to nature of expenditure required to receive the grant	Highly specific	Broad criteria encompassing many different types of qualifying expenditure
Tax status of grant income	Taxable	Not taxable

In group accounts, in which entities from a number of different jurisdictions may be consolidated, it is desirable that each particular investment tax credit should be consistently accounted for under either IAS 20 or IAS 12. However, the fact that judgment is required in making this determination may mean that predominant practice in a particular jurisdiction for a specific type of tax credit has evolved differently from predominant practice in another jurisdiction for a substantially similar credit. We believe that, in determining whether IAS 20 or IAS 12 should be applied, an entity should consider the following factors in the order listed below:

- the predominant local treatment for a specific credit in the relevant tax jurisdiction;
- if there is no predominant local treatment, the group-wide accounting policy for such a credit;
- in the absence of a predominant local treatment or a group-wide accounting policy, the indicators listed in the table above should provide guidance.

This may occasionally mean that an entity operating in a number of territories adopts different accounting treatments for apparently similar arrangements in different countries, but it at least ensures a measure of comparability between different entities operating in the same tax jurisdiction.

The treatment of investment tax credits accounted under IAS 12 is discussed in Chapter 31 at 4.3.

3 RECOGNITION AND MEASUREMENT

3.1 General requirements of IAS 20

IAS 20 requires that government grants should be recognised only when there is reasonable assurance that:

(a) the entity will comply with the conditions attaching to them; and

(b) the grants will be received. *[IAS 20.7]*.

The standard does not define 'reasonable assurance', which raises the question of whether or not it means the same as 'probable' (or 'more likely than not' *[IAS 37.15]*). When developing IAS 41 the Board believed that recognition of government grants when there is 'reasonable assurance' was different from the alternative approaches it considered for biological assets, being recognition when 'it is probable that the entity will meet the conditions attaching to the government grant' and 'the entity meets the conditions attaching to the government grant'. *[IAS 41.B70]*. The Board also noted that 'it would inevitably be a subjective decision as to when there is reasonable assurance that the conditions are met and that this subjectivity could lead to inconsistent income recognition.' *[IAS 41.B69]*. Nevertheless, we would not expect an entity to recognise government grants before it was at least probable that the entity would comply with the conditions attached to them (even though these conditions may relate to future performance and other future events) and that the grants would be received. The standard notes that receiving a grant does not of itself provide conclusive evidence that the conditions attaching to the grant have been or will be fulfilled. *[IAS 20.8]*.

After an entity has recognised a government grant, any related contingent liability or contingent asset should be accounted for under IAS 37 – *Provisions, Contingent Liabilities and Contingent Assets*. *[IAS 20.11]*.

Accounting for government grants is not affected by the manner in which they are received, i.e. grants received in cash, as a non-monetary amount, or forgiveness of a government loan, are all accounted for in the same manner. *[IAS 20.9]*.

3.2 Non-monetary grants

A government grant in the form of a transfer of a non-monetary asset, such as land or other resources, which is intended for use by the entity, is usually recognised at the fair value of that asset. *[IAS 20.23]*. Fair value is defined in IFRS 13 – *Fair Value Measurement* – and applies when another IFRS requires or permits fair value measurement, including IAS 20. *[IFRS 13.5, IAS 20.45]*. Fair value is the price that would be received to sell an asset or paid to transfer a liability in an orderly transaction between market participants at the measurement date. *[IAS 20.3, IFRS 13.9]*. The requirements of IFRS 13 are discussed in Chapter 14.

An alternative of recognising such assets, and the related grant, at a nominal amount is permitted. *[IAS 20.23]*. This alternative is available even if the fair value of the asset differs materially from the nominal amount. Under IAS 8 an entity should select an accounting policy and apply it consistently to all non-monetary government grants. *[IAS 8.13]*.

3.3 Forgivable loans

A forgivable loan from government, the repayment of which will be waived under certain prescribed conditions, *[IAS 20.3]*, is to be treated as a government grant when there is reasonable assurance that the entity will meet the terms for forgiveness of the loan. *[IAS 20.10]*.

Example 26.1: Government grant by way of forgivable loan

An entity participates in a government-sponsored research and development programme under which it is entitled to receive a government grant of up to 50% of the costs incurred for a particular project. The government grant is interest-bearing and fully repayable based on a percentage ('royalty') of the sales revenue of any products developed. Although the repayment period is not limited, no repayment is required if there are no sales of the products.

The entity should account for this type of government grant as follows:

- initially recognise the government grant as a liability;
- apply the principles underlying the effective interest rate method in subsequent periods, which would involve estimating the amount and timing of future cash flows;
- review at each reporting date whether there is reasonable assurance that the entity will meet the terms for forgiveness of the loan, i.e. the entity assesses that the product will not achieve sales. If this is the case then derecognise part or all of the liability initially recorded with a corresponding profit in the income statement; and
- if the entity subsequently revises its estimates of future sales upwards, it recognises a liability for any amounts previously included in profit and recognises a corresponding loss in the income statement.

However, an arrangement only meets the definition of a forgivable loan if its terms provide for circumstances where repayment would be waived (i.e. forgiven), without any other form of settlement. In Example 26.1 above, the entity either repays some or all of the loan if the project generates any sales or, in the event that no sales are made, its liability is waived in full, with no further recourse to the government. In May 2016, the Interpretations Committee concluded on a request to clarify whether cash received to help an entity finance a research and development project would be treated as a forgivable loan in the following specific circumstances:[3]

- the loan was repayable only if the entity decided to exploit and commercialise the results of the research phase of the project;
- otherwise, the loan was not repayable in cash but instead the entity was required to transfer to the government the rights to the research.

The Interpretations Committee noted that, in this arrangement, the cash received did not meet the definition of a forgivable loan under IAS 20, because the government did not undertake to waive repayment of the loan but instead required settlement in cash or by the transfer of rights to the research. In other words, the entity could only avoid repayment by settling a non-financial obligation (to hand over the rights to the research). This requirement confirms the status of the cash receipt as a financial liability under IAS 32 – *Financial Instruments: Presentation*. *[IAS 32.20(a)]*. The Committee also noted that the financial liability should be measured under IAS 39 or IFRS 9 as appropriate. Any difference between the cash receipt and the fair value of the liability would need to be accounted for under IAS 20 as discussed at 3.4 below. The Interpretations Committee decided not to add this issue to its agenda on the basis that existing standards provide an adequate basis of accounting.[4]

3.4 Loans at lower than market rates of interest

IAS 20 requires government loans that have a below-market rate of interest to be recognised and measured in accordance with IAS 39 or IFRS 9 as appropriate, i.e. at their fair value. *[IAS 20.10A, IAS 39.43, IFRS 9.5.1.1]*. The loans could be interest-free. The difference between the initial carrying value of the loan (its fair value) and the proceeds received is treated as a government grant.

Example 26.2: Interest-free loan from a government agency

Company A secures an interest-free loan of €1,000 from a local government agency to ensure that the company invests in new equipment at its manufacturing facility. The loan is repayable over five years and carries no interest. Company A can draw down the loan on demonstrating that it has incurred qualifying expenditure on property, plant and equipment.

On initial recognition, the market rate of interest for a similar five year loan with payment of interest at maturity is 10% per year. The initial fair value of the loan is the present value of the future payment of €1,000, discounted using the market rate of interest for a similar loan of 10% for five years. This equates to €621.

The fair value of the government incentive to Company A to invest in its factory is €379, the difference between the total consideration received of €1,000 and the loan's initial fair value of €621. This difference is treated as a government grant.

Subsequently, interest will be imputed to the loan using the effective interest method, taking account of any transaction costs (see Chapter 48 at 3.2.1). The grant will not necessarily be released on a basis that is consistent with the interest expense. The standard stresses that the entity has to consider the conditions and obligations that have been, or must be, met when 'identifying the costs for which the benefit of the loan is intended to compensate'. *[IAS 20.10A]*. This process of matching the benefit to costs is discussed at 3.5 below.

As well as routine subsidised lending to meet specific objectives, loans made as part of government rescue plans are generally within scope of IAS 20 if they are at a lower than market rate of interest. In 2009 PSA Peugeot Citroën received assistance from the European Investment Bank as described in Extract 26.1 below.

Extract 26.1: PSA Peugeot Citroën (2009)

Half-Year Financial Report 2009 [extract]

17.2. REFINANCING TRANSACTIONS [extract]

– ***EIB loan***

In April 2009, Peugeot Citroën Automobiles S.A. obtained a €400 million 4-year bullet loan from the European Investment Bank (EIB). Interest on the loan is based on the 3-month Euribor plus 179 bps. At June 30, 2009 the government bonds (OATs) given by Peugeot S.A. as collateral for all EIB loans to Group companies had a market value of €160 million. In addition, 4,695,000 Faurecia shares held by Peugeot S.A. were pledged to the EIB as security for the loans. The interest rate risk on the new EIB loan has not been specifically hedged.

This new loan is at a reduced rate of interest. The difference between the market rate of interest for an equivalent loan at the inception date and the rate granted by the EIB has been recognised as a government grant in accordance with IAS 20. The grant was originally valued at €38 million and was recorded as a deduction from the capitalized development costs financed by the loan. It is being amortised on a straight-line basis over the life of the underlying projects. The loan is measured at amortised cost, in the amount of €362 million at June 30, 2009. The effective interest rate is estimated at 5.90%.

This will also affect the manner in which arrangements that are similar in substance to loans are accounted for.

Governments sometimes allow entities to retain sums that they collect on behalf of the government (e.g. value added taxes) to be retained until a future event, as in the following example:

Example 26.3: Entity allowed to retain amounts owed to government

The local government of an underdeveloped region is trying to stimulate investment by allowing local companies to retain the value added tax (VAT) on their sales. An entity participating in this scheme is entitled to retain an amount up to 40% of its investment in fixed assets. The retained VAT must be paid to the local government after 5 years.

In this example, the fact that amounts retained by the entity are required to be repaid after 5 years makes this arrangement similar in nature to an interest free loan. Accordingly, the entity would determine a value for the government assistance by comparing the amounts retained to the fair value of a 5 year loan at market rates of interest, as illustrated in Example 26.2 above. In determining an appropriate basis for recognising the benefit of the grant in profit or loss, the entity has to consider the conditions and obligations that have been, or must be, met when 'identifying the costs for which the benefit of the loan is intended to compensate'. *[IAS 20.10A]*. In the example above, because the grant is intended to stimulate investment in fixed assets, an acceptable approach would be deferral in line with depreciation of the relevant asset while recognition immediately in profit or loss upon occurrence of sales would generally not be appropriate. The judgement involved in matching the benefit to costs is discussed at 3.5 below.

3.5 Recognition in the income statement

Grants should be recognised in the income statement on a systematic basis that matches them with the related costs that they are intended to compensate. *[IAS 20.12]*. They should not be credited directly to shareholders' funds. Income recognition on a receipts basis, which is not in accordance with the accruals accounting assumption, is only acceptable if there is no basis for allocating a grant to periods other than the one in which it is received. *[IAS 20.16]*.

IAS 20 rejects a 'capital approach', under which a grant is recognised outside profit or loss (typically credited directly to equity), *[IAS 20.13]*, in favour of the 'income approach', under which grants are taken to income over one or more periods, because:

(a) government grants are receipts from a source other than shareholders. As such, they should not be credited directly to equity but should be recognised as income in appropriate periods;

(b) government grants are rarely gratuitous. An entity earns them through compliance with their conditions and meeting the envisaged obligations. They should therefore be recognised as income and matched with the associated costs which the grant is intended to compensate; and

(c) as income and other taxes are expenses, it is logical to deal also with government grants, which are an extension of fiscal policies, in the income statement. *[IAS 20.15]*.

IAS 20 envisages that in most cases, the periods over which an entity recognises the costs or expenses related to the government grant are readily ascertainable and thus grants in recognition of specific expenses are recognised as income in the same period as the relevant expense. *[IAS 20.17]*.

Grants related to depreciable assets are usually recognised as income over the periods, and in the proportions, in which depreciation on those assets is charged. *[IAS 20.17]*. Grants related to non-depreciable assets may also require the fulfilment of certain obligations, in which case they would be recognised as income over the periods in which the costs of meeting the obligations are incurred. For example, a grant of land may be conditional upon the erection of a building on the site and it may be appropriate to recognise it as income over the life of the building. *[IAS 20.18]*.

IAS 20 acknowledges that grants may be received as part of a package of financial or fiscal aids to which a number of conditions are attached. In such cases, the standard indicates that care is needed in identifying the conditions giving rise to the costs and expenses which determine the periods over which the grant will be earned. It may also be appropriate to allocate part of the grant on one basis and part on another. *[IAS 20.19]*.

Where a grant relates to expenses or losses already incurred, or for the purpose of giving immediate financial support to the entity with no future related costs, the grant should be recognised in income when it becomes receivable. If such a grant is recognised as income of the period in which it becomes receivable, the entity should disclose its effects to ensure that these are clearly understood. *[IAS 20.20-22]*.

Many of the problems in accounting for government grants relate to that of interpreting the requirement to match the grant with the related costs, particularly because of the international context in which IAS 20 is written. It does not address specific questions that relate to particular types of grant that are available in individual countries.

3.5.1 Achieving the most appropriate matching

Most problems of accounting for grants relate to implementing the requirement to match the grant against the costs that it is intended to compensate. *[IAS 20.12]*. This apparently simple principle can be difficult to apply in practice, because the essential purpose of the grant may be far from clear and, therefore, what costs are being subsidised. Moreover, grants are sometimes given for a particular kind of expenditure that forms an element of a larger project, making the allocation a highly subjective matter. For example, in trying to determine an appropriate accounting policy for government assistance that is in the form of a training grant, an entity might consider recognition in income in any of the following ways:

(a) matching against direct training costs;

(b) taking over a period of time against the salary costs of the employees being trained, for example over the estimated duration of the project;

(c) taking over the estimated period for which the company or the employees are expected to benefit from the training;

(d) matching against total project costs together with other project grants receivable;

(e) taking to income systematically over the life of the project, for example the total grant receivable may be allocated to revenue on a straight-line basis;

(f) allocating against project costs or income over the period over which the grant is paid (instead of over the project life); or

(g) taking to income when received in cash.

Determining a reasonable approach is very much dependent on the specific facts and circumstances, including those relating to the context in which the grant was offered; the conditions attached to it; and the consequences of failing to meet those conditions. There may be a number of acceptable approaches to achieve this; our observations on these alternative methods are as follows:

Under method (a), the grant could be recognised as income considerably in advance of its receipt, since often the major part of the direct training costs will be incurred at the beginning of a project and payment is usually made retrospectively. As the total grant receivable may be subject to adjustment, this may lead to a mismatch of costs and revenues. Therefore, as well as matching with the related expenditure, the policy should also reflect the conditions giving rise to the entity's entitlement to receive the grant.

Methods (b) to (e) all rely on different interpretations of the expenditure to which the grant is expected to contribute, and could all represent an appropriate form of matching. In these circumstances, an entity should also take account of any conditions attached to the grant that give rise to withdrawal of support or a requirement to refund amounts already received.

Method (f) might have less to commend it, because a policy linked to the period over which the grant is paid might not properly reflect the period over which the related costs to be compensated are incurred. *[IAS 20.12]*. However, the period of payment of the grant could in some circumstances give an indication (in the absence of better evidence) of the duration of the project for which the expenditure is to be subsidised. For example, where payment of grant is secured by submitting a summary of project expenditure incurred to date, and there are no provisions for refund, such an approach could be appropriate.

Similarly, method (g) is unlikely to be the most appropriate method *per se*, because it is not obviously linked to the recognition of the related expenditure. However, in some situations it may approximate to one of the other methods, or may, in the absence of any conclusive indication as to the expenditure intended to be subsidised by the grant, be the only practicable method that can be adopted.

In some jurisdictions grants are taxed as income on receipt; consequently, this is often the argument advanced for taking grants to income when received in cash. However, it is clear that the treatment of an item for tax purposes does not necessarily determine its treatment for accounting purposes, and immediate recognition in the income statement may result in an unacceptable departure from the principle that government grants should be matched with the costs that they are intended to compensate. *[IAS 20.16]*. Consequently, the recognition of a grant in the income statement in a different period from that in which it is taxed, gives rise to a temporary difference that should be accounted for in accordance with IAS 12 (see Chapter 31). The example below illustrates that the interpretation of the matching requirement in the standard is not always straightforward.

Example 26.4: Grant associated with investment property

The government provides a grant to an entity that owns an investment property that is let for social housing. The grant is intended to compensate the entity for the lower rent it will receive when the property is let as social housing at below market rates. That means that future rental income will be lower over the period of the lease which, at the same time, reduces the fair value of the investment property.

If the entity accounts for the investment property under the IAS 40 cost model then it could be argued that the government grant should be recognised over the term of the lease to offset the lower rental income.

Alternatively, if the entity applied the IAS 40 fair value model then the cost being compensated is the reduction in fair value of the investment property. In that case it is more appropriate to recognise the benefit of the government grant immediately.

If, instead of a grant, the government subsidises a loan used by the entity to acquire the property, then the loan will be brought in at its fair value. The difference between the face value and fair value will be a government grant and the arguments above will apply to its treatment.

If the government imposes conditions, e.g. that the building must be used for social housing for ten years, this does not necessarily mean that the grant should be taken to income over that period. Rather, it should apply a process similar to that in Example 26.1 above. The entity assesses whether there is reasonable assurance that it will meet the terms of the grant and, to that extent, treat an appropriate amount as a grant as above. This should be reviewed at each reporting date and adjustments made if it appears that the conditions will not be met (see 3.6 below).

In the face of the problems described above of attributing a grant to related costs, it is difficult to offer definitive guidance; entities will have to make their own judgements as to how the matching principle is to be applied in light of the specific facts and circumstances of the case. The only overriding considerations are that the method should be systematically and consistently applied, and that the policy adopted in respect of both capital and revenue grants, if material, should be adequately disclosed.

3.5.2 The period to be benefited by the grant

IAS 20 cautions that care is needed in identifying the conditions giving rise to the costs and expenses, which determine the periods over which the grant will be earned. *[IAS 20.19]*. The qualifying conditions that have to be satisfied are not necessarily conclusive evidence of the period to be benefited by the grant. For example, certain grants may become repayable if assets cease to be used for a qualifying purpose within a certain period; notwithstanding this condition, the grant should be recognised over the whole life of the asset, not over the qualifying period.

3.5.3 Separating grants into elements

The grant received may be part of a package, the elements of which have different costs and conditions. In such cases, it is common that the elements for which the grant is given are not specifically identified or quantified. It will often be appropriate to treat these different elements on different bases rather than accounting for the entire grant in one way. For example, a grant may be given on the basis that an entity makes approved capital expenditure in a particular area and employs a specified number of local people for an agreed period of time. The amount of grant may be based on the approved capital expenditure but this does not mean that the grant is necessarily treated wholly as a capital grant. It will be necessary to examine the full circumstances of the grant in order to determine its purpose.

In general, the most straightforward way of recognising a grant is by linking it to long-term assets where this is a possible interpretation, particularly where the receipt of the grant depends on the cost of acquisition of long-term assets. However, this approach can only be taken if there is no clear indication to the contrary.

Allocation of a grant between the elements will always be a matter of judgement and entities may place more stress on some features than on others. We believe that the most important consideration where there are significant questions over how the grant is to be recognised, and where the effect is material, is that the financial statements should explicitly state what treatment has been chosen and disclose the financial effect of adopting that treatment.

3.6 Repayment of government grants

A government grant that becomes repayable after recognition should be accounted for as a revision of an accounting estimate. Repayment of a grant related to income should be charged against the related unamortised deferred credit and any excess should be recognised as an expense immediately. *[IAS 20.32]*.

Repayment of a grant related to an asset should be recognised by increasing the carrying amount of the related asset or reducing the related unamortised deferred credit. The cumulative additional depreciation that would have been recognised to date as an expense in the absence of the grant should be charged immediately to profit or loss. *[IAS 20.32]*.

IAS 20 emphasises that the circumstances giving rise to the repayment of a grant related to an asset may require that consideration be given to the possible impairment of the asset. *[IAS 20.33]*.

3.7 Government assistance

As indicated above, IAS 20 excludes from the definition of government grants 'certain forms of government assistance which cannot reasonably have a value placed upon them and transactions with government which cannot be distinguished from the normal trading transactions of the entity'. *[IAS 20.34]*. In many cases the 'existence of the benefit might be unquestioned but any attempt to segregate the trading activities from government assistance could well be arbitrary'. *[IAS 20.35]*. The standard therefore requires disclosure of significant government assistance (see 6.1 below).

The following example describes two different forms of government assistance –

Example 26.5: Government assistance

(a) Assistance in the form of priority bidding status

A government specifies that entities below a certain size are to be given priority in bidding for a particular type of government contract by mandating a minimum number of such entities to obtain bidding status. Although the entities will benefit from the quota, the value cannot be identified and the effects of the assistance cannot be segregated from the trading activities of the entities.

(b) Assistance in the form of credit facilities at market rates

Three governments that between themselves own just over 50% of the shares in an airline participate in granting it a revolving credit facility at a market rate of interest. This is not a government grant as it is on terms that a private market participant might have accepted but it is government assistance as the benefit cannot be distinguished from normal trading activities of the airline.

Under IAS 20, 'government assistance does not include the provision of infrastructure by improvement to the general transport and communication network and the supply of improved facilities such as irrigation or water reticulation that is available on an ongoing indeterminate basis for the benefit of an entire local community.' *[IAS 20.38]*.

4 PRESENTATION OF GRANTS

4.1 Presentation of grants related to assets

Grants that are related to assets (i.e. those whose primary condition is that an entity qualifying for them should purchase, construct or otherwise acquire long-term assets) should be presented in the statement of financial position either: *[IAS 20.24]*

(a) by setting up the grant as deferred income, which is recognised as income on a systematic and rational basis over the useful life of the asset; *[IAS 20.26]* or

(b) by deducting the grant in arriving at the carrying amount of the asset, in which case the grant is recognised in income as a reduction of depreciation. *[IAS 20.27]*.

IAS 20 regards both these methods of presenting grants in financial statements as acceptable alternatives. *[IAS 20.25]*.

A company that adopted the former treatment is Greencore Group, as shown below:

Extract 26.2: Greencore Group plc (2015)

NOTES TO THE GROUP FINANCIAL STATEMENTS [extract]

1. GROUP STATEMENT OF ACCOUNTING POLICIES [extract]

GOVERNMENT GRANTS

Government grants for the acquisition of assets are recognised at their fair value when there is reasonable assurance that the grant will be received and any conditions attached to them have been fulfilled. The grant is held on the Balance Sheet as a deferred credit and released to the Income Statement over the periods necessary to match the related depreciation charges, or other expenses of the asset, as they are incurred.

An example of a company adopting a policy of deducting grants related to assets from the cost of the assets is shown below:

Extract 26.3: Akzo Nobel N.V. (2015)

Notes to the Consolidated financial statements [extract]

Note 1: Summary of significant accounting policies [extract]

Government grants

Government grants related to costs are deducted from the relevant cost to be compensated in the same period. Government grants to compensate for the cost of an asset are deducted from the cost of the related asset. Emission rights granted by the government are recorded at cost. A provision is recorded if the actual emission is higher than the emission rights granted.

4.1.1 Cash flows

The purchase of assets and the receipt of related grants can cause major movements in the cash flow of an entity. Therefore, if payments are made gross rather than net, such movements should be disclosed as separate items in the cash flow statement whether or not the grant is deducted from the related asset for the purpose of presentation in the statement of financial position. *[IAS 20.28]*.

4.1.2 Impairment testing of assets that qualified for government grants

When an asset is tested for impairment under IAS 36 – *Impairment of Assets* – the value of any government grants received in relation to those assets is taken into account regardless of whether the entity elected to deduct the grants in arriving at the carrying amount of the related assets or decided to set up the grant as deferred income.

Where grants had been deducted from the initial carrying amount of the related assets, no further adjustment is required before commencing the impairment test. However, when grants relating to assets are classified as deferred income, the unamortised balance carried in the statement of financial position should be deducted from the carrying amount of the assets or cash generating unit being tested.

If the impairment test requires the carrying value of the asset or related CGU to be reduced (because it exceeds the recoverable amount determined under IAS 36), the amount of the impairment is deducted from the carrying amount of the asset.

However, no adjustment should be made to the balance presented as deferred income, which would continue to be recognised as income over the useful life of the asset. The requirements of IAS 36 are discussed in Chapter 20.

4.2 Presentation of grants related to income

Grants related to income should be presented either as:

(a) a credit in the income statement, either separately or under a general heading such as 'other income'; or

(b) a deduction in reporting the related expense. *[IAS 20.29]*.

The standard points out that supporters of method (a) consider it inappropriate to present income and expense items on a net basis and that 'separation of the grant from the expense facilitates comparison with other expenses not affected by a grant'. *[IAS 20.30]*. Furthermore, method (a) is consistent with the general prohibition of offsetting in IAS 1 – *Presentation of Financial Statements*. *[IAS 1.32-33]*. However, supporters of method (b) would argue that 'the expenses might well not have been incurred by the entity if the grant had not been available and presentation of the expense without offsetting the grant may therefore be misleading'. *[IAS 20.30]*. The standard regards both methods as acceptable for the presentation of grants related to income. *[IAS 20.31]*. When offsetting is permitted by another standard, the general prohibition in IAS 1 does not apply. *[IAS 1.32]*. In any case, IAS 20 considers that disclosure of the grant may be necessary for a proper understanding of the financial statements. Furthermore, disclosure of the effect of grants on any item of income or expense, which should be disclosed separately, is usually appropriate. *[IAS 20.31]*.

As illustrated below, Anheuser-Busch InBev has adopted a policy of presenting grants within other operating income, although not separately on the face of the income statement, rather than as a deduction from the related expense.

Extract 26.4: Anheuser-Busch InBev NV/SA (2015)

Notes to the Consolidated Financial Statements [extract]

3. Summary of Significant Accounting Policies [extract]

(X) Income recognition [extract]

Government grants

A government grant is recognized in the balance sheet initially as deferred income when there is reasonable assurance that it will be received and that the company will comply with the conditions attached to it. Grants that compensate the company for expenses incurred are recognized as other operating income on a systematic basis in the same periods in which the expenses are incurred. Grants that compensate the company for the acquisition of an asset are presented by deducting them from the acquisition cost of the related asset in accordance with IAS 20 *Accounting for Government Grants and Disclosure of Government Assistance.*

Akzo Nobel N.V. is an example of a company presenting the grant as a deduction from the related expense in the income statement, as illustrated in Extract 26.3 above.

5 GOVERNMENT GRANTS RELATED TO BIOLOGICAL ASSETS IN THE SCOPE OF IAS 41

A different accounting treatment to that prescribed in IAS 20 is required if a government grant relates to a biological asset measured at its fair value less costs to sell, in accordance with IAS 41; or a government grant requires an entity not to engage in specified agricultural activity. *[IAS 41.38]*. In this context, the term 'biological asset' excludes bearer plants as defined in IAS 41 (see 1.2 above). *[IAS 41.5]*. Government grants involving biological assets should only be accounted for under IAS 20 if the biological asset is 'measured at its cost less any accumulated depreciation and any accumulated impairment losses' (see Chapter 40). *[IAS 41.37-38]*. For government grants relating to biological assets measured at fair value less costs to sell, the requirements of IAS 41 apply as follows.

An unconditional government grant related to a biological asset measured at its fair value less costs to sell is recognised in profit or loss when, and only when, the grant becomes receivable. *[IAS 41.34]*. An entity is therefore not permitted under IAS 41 to deduct a government grant from the carrying amount of the related asset. The IASB determined that any adjustment to the carrying value of the asset would be inconsistent with a fair value model and would give rise to no difference in the treatment of unconditional and conditional government grants, with both effectively recognised in income immediately. *[IAS 41.B66]*.

A conditional government grant related to a biological asset measured at its fair value less costs to sell is recognised only when the conditions attaching to the grant are met. *[IAS 41.35]*. IAS 41 permits an entity to recognise a government grant as income only to the extent that it (i) has met the terms and conditions of the grant and (ii) has no obligation to return the grant. This would generally be later than the point of recognition in IAS 20, where reasonable assurance that these criteria will be met is sufficient. *[IAS 20.7]*. The following example, which is taken from IAS 41, illustrates how an entity should apply these requirements. *[IAS 41.36]*.

Example 26.6: Grant relating to biological assets carried at fair value

Entity A receives a government grant under terms that require it to farm in a particular location for five years. The entire government grant has to be returned if it farms for less than five years. In this case the government grant is not recognised as income until the five years have passed.

Entity B receives a government grant on a similar basis, except it allows part of the government grant to be retained based on the passage of time. Entity B recognises the government grant as income on a time proportion basis.

6 DISCLOSURES

IAS 20 requires that entities should disclose the following information regarding government grants:

(a) the accounting policy, including the method of presentation adopted in the financial statements;

(b) a description of the nature and extent of the grants recognised and an indication of other forms of government assistance from which the entity has directly benefited; and

(c) unfulfilled conditions or contingencies attaching to government assistance that has been recognised. *[IAS 20.39]*.

The extract below illustrates how companies typically disclose government grants under IFRS. It should be noted that disclosures concerning the nature and conditions of government grants are sometimes relatively minimal, possibly because the amounts involved are immaterial.

Extract 26.5: Eskom Holdings SOC Limited (2016)

Notes to the financial statements [extract]

2. **Summary of significant accounting policies** [extract]

2.16 **Payments received in advance** [extract]

Payments received in advance consist mainly of capital contributions received from customers for the construction of assets and government grants received for electrification and energy efficiency initiatives. [...] Government grants for energy efficiency initiatives are recognised in profit or loss within other expenses when the related expenses are incurred. Government grants for electrification are recognised in deferred income when the related asset has been connected to the electricity network (refer to note 2.17).

2.17 **Deferred income** [extract]

Grants

Government grants received relating to the creation of electrification assets are included in liabilities as deferred income and are credited to profit or loss within depreciation and amortisation expense on a straight-line basis over the expected useful lives of the related assets.

		2016 Government grant Rm
27.	**Payments received in advance and deferred income** [extract]	
27.2	**Deferred income** [extract]	
	Group and company	
	Balance at beginning of the year	12 146
	Transfers from payments received in advance	2 372
	Income recognised	(753)
	Balance at end of the year	13 765
	Maturity analysis	13 765
	Non-current	12 967
	Current	798

		2016 Rm	Group 2015 Rm
38.	**Depreciation and amortisation expense** [extract]		
	Depreciation of property, plant and equipment	16,591	13 827
	Amortisation of intangible assets	693	939
	Deferred income recognised (government grant)	(753)	(651)
		16 531	14 115

Eskom Holdings also provided information relating to the parent company and for other items of deferred income that is not reproduced above for reasons of space. Additional examples of accounting policies for government grants can be found in Extracts 26.2, 26.3 and 26.4 above.

6.1 Government assistance

In addition to the disclosures noted above, for those forms of government assistance that are excluded from the definition of government grants, the significance of such benefits may be such that the disclosure of the nature, extent and duration of the assistance is necessary to prevent the financial statements from being misleading. *[IAS 20.36]*.

References

1 Work plan for IFRSs, All projects since 2006 in alphabetical order, Government grants (Deferred).

2 *IASB Work Plan* as at 20 July 2016, IASB.

3 *IFRIC Update*, May 2016.

4 *IFRIC Update*, May 2016.

Chapter 27 Service concession arrangements

Chapter 27

List of examples

Chapter 27 Service concession arrangements

1 INTRODUCTION

Service concession arrangements (SCAs) have been developed as a mechanism for governments to procure public services using private capital and management expertise. The rights and obligations of the public sector body procuring the services and the private sector entity providing the services are set out in a contract, the terms of which can be complex depending upon the nature of the SCA. The most common forms of arrangement are as follows:

- 'Build-operate-transfer' service concession arrangement – where a private sector entity takes responsibility for funding and building infrastructure assets such as roads, bridges, railways, hospitals, prisons, power stations and schools, in consideration for a long-term contract from the public sector body giving the entity the right to charge for services to the public using that infrastructure;
- 'Rehabilitate-operate-transfer' SCA – where the private sector entity restores or improves an existing facility or public service up to an agreed standard and continues to maintain and operate the related infrastructure for a contracted period. This type of arrangement includes a range of projects from the refurbishment of social housing and street lighting to major civil engineering projects to restore a city's underground rail system; and
- 'Operate-only' SCA – where a private sector entity becomes responsible for the operational management and maintenance of an existing infrastructure asset that is used to provide services to the public. This last variant, together with the development of similar arrangements between private sector bodies, has at times obscured the boundary between service concessions and outsourcing arrangements (see 2.3 below).

The accounting challenge is to reflect the substance of these arrangements fairly in the financial statements of both of the contracting parties, because the various transactions between the parties to a service concession arrangement range across a number of accounting standards and interpretations, including:

- accounting for the rights of the parties over the infrastructure assets (IAS 16 – *Property, Plant and Equipment*, IAS 17 – *Leases*, IFRIC Interpretation 4 – *Determining whether an Arrangement contains a Lease*);
- construction or refurbishment of the infrastructure assets (IAS 11 – *Construction Contracts*, IAS 18 – *Revenue*);
- accounting for the various performance obligations under the contract during the operations period of the concession (IAS 18 – *Revenue*, IAS 37 – *Provisions, Contingent Liabilities and Contingent Assets*); and
- recognition and measurement of the amounts payable or receivable under the arrangement (IAS 20 – *Accounting for Government Grants and Disclosure of Government Assistance*, IAS 23 – *Borrowing Costs*, IAS 32 – *Financial Instruments: Presentation*, IAS 37 – *Provisions, Contingent Liabilities and Contingent Assets*, IAS 38 – *Intangible Assets* – and IAS 39 – *Financial Instruments: Recognition and Measurement*).

IFRS 9 – *Financial Instruments* – will also be relevant to entities choosing to apply it instead of IAS 39,[1] as will IFRS 15 – *Revenue from Contracts with Customers* – to entities choosing to early adopt that Standard instead of applying IAS 11 and IAS 18,[2] and IFRS 16 – *Leases* – for entities choosing to early adopt that Standard instead of applying IAS 17 and IFRIC 4 – *Determining whether an Arrangement contains a Lease*.[3]

This makes it difficult to develop a coherent accounting model that deals with all of the features of service concessions simultaneously, and from the position of both the private sector (i.e. the 'operator') and public sector (i.e. the 'grantor'). Moreover, prior to the issue of IFRIC Interpretation 12 – *Service Concession Arrangements*, entrenched national positions had developed and differing accounting treatments had been widely adopted in various jurisdictions, with or without a basis in specific local accounting standards. Also, some jurisdictions accepted more than one accounting treatment for broadly similar arrangements, some of which are influenced by a taxation basis that has been agreed with the jurisdictional taxation authorities. All this resulted in considerable diversity in the accounting by IFRS reporters of seemingly similar arrangements.

In 2001, SIC-29 – *Service Concession Arrangements: Disclosures* – was issued. This did not attempt to address the accounting issues but considered the information that should be disclosed in the notes to the financial statements of an 'operator' and 'grantor' under a service concession arrangement. *[SIC-29.4]*. Its requirements are described further at 6 below.

IFRIC 12 – *Service Concession Arrangements* – addresses the accounting issues and was approved by the IASB in November 2006. The fact that the Interpretation took more than three years to develop indicates the complexity of the issues and the difficulty that the Committee encountered in fitting a solution into the existing accounting framework.

1.1 The Interpretations Committee's approach to accounting for service concessions

The Interpretations Committee limits its guidance to accounting by the operator of the service concession. *[IFRIC 12.4, 9]*. It views the primary accounting determination for the operator as being whether control over the infrastructure assets has been ceded to the operator or whether any new or existing assets under the concession arrangement are controlled by the grantor.

The Interpretations Committee suggests that arrangements where control does not rest with the grantor, and the asset is either derecognised by the grantor or is an asset constructed for the concession that the grantor never controls, can be dealt with adequately by other accounting standards or interpretations. *[IFRIC 12.BC13]*. The interrelationship with other accounting standards is discussed further at 2 below.

Infrastructure assets controlled by the grantor are the subject of IFRIC 12. This applies whether the assets are constructed or acquired by the operator for the concession, that become those of the grantor because it controls them, or existing assets that remain under the grantor's control and to which the operator is granted access. *[IFRIC 12.7]*.

'Control' is therefore a central concept in IFRIC 12. Control is not determined by attributing risks and benefits to identify the 'owner' of the infrastructure. Instead, IFRIC 12 regards control in terms of the operator's ability (or lack thereof) to decide how to use the asset during the concession term and how it will be deployed thereafter. Its definition and consequences are discussed further at 3 below.

Thus any infrastructure that remains under the control of the grantor will be accounted for using IFRIC 12. In doing so, the Interpretations Committee establishes a number of principles for accounting by the operator of a concession falling within its scope:

- the infrastructure is not recognised as property, plant and equipment by the operator; *[IFRIC 12.11]*
- the operator recognises revenue from construction services when assets are built or upgraded during the concession term; *[IFRIC 12.14]*
- a financial asset or an intangible asset is recognised as consideration for these construction services, depending upon the way in which the operator is paid for services under the contract; *[IFRIC 12.15]* and
- revenues and costs for the provision of operating services are recognised over the term of the concession arrangement in accordance with IAS 18 or IFRS 15, as appropriate. *[IFRIC 12.20]*.

The requirement to recognise an asset as consideration for construction services gives rise to two service concession models – the 'financial asset' model or the 'intangible asset' model. These are considered further at 4 below. The recognition of revenue and costs in the operations phase is discussed at 5 below.

1.2 Terms used in this chapter

The following terms are used in this chapter with the meanings specified:

Term	Definition
Grantor	A public sector body (including a governmental body, or a private sector entity to which responsibility for a public service has been devolved) that grants the service arrangement. *[IFRIC 12.3]*
Operator	A private sector entity that is contractually obliged to provide services to the public on behalf of the public sector entity. The operator is responsible for at least some of the management of the infrastructure and related services and does not merely act as an agent on behalf of the grantor. *[IFRIC 12.3]*
Service arrangement/ Service concession arrangement	A contract that obliges the operator to provide the services related to the infrastructure to the public on behalf of the grantor. The contract sets the initial prices to be levied by the operator and regulates price revisions over the period of the service arrangement. *[IFRIC 12.3]*
Infrastructure	Assets used in the provision of services to the public. Examples include roads, bridges, tunnels, prisons, hospitals, airports, water distribution facilities, energy supply and telecommunications networks. *[IFRIC 12.1]*. Infrastructure can be constructed or acquired by the operator for the purpose of the service arrangement; or can be existing assets to which the grantor gives the operator access for the purpose of the service arrangement. *[IFRIC 12.7]*
Control criteria	(a) the grantor controls or regulates what services the operator must provide with the infrastructure, to whom it must provide them, and at what price; and (b) the grantor controls any significant residual interest in the infrastructure at the end of the term of the arrangement, through ownership, beneficial entitlement or otherwise. *[IFRIC 12.5]*
Government	Refers to government, government agencies and similar bodies whether local, national or international. *[IAS 20.3]*

2 SCOPE OF IFRIC 12

The scope of IFRIC 12 is specific and relatively narrow. The Interpretations Committee decided to address only public-to-private service concession arrangements in which:

(a) the grantor controls or regulates the services that the operator must provide using the infrastructure, to whom it must provide them, and at what price; and

(b) the grantor controls any significant residual interest in the property at the end of the concession term through ownership, beneficial entitlement or otherwise. (Infrastructure used in a service concession for its entire useful life is deemed to meet this second condition because there is no significant residual interest). *[IFRIC 12.5, 6]*.

The Committee also decided to restrict its guidance to the accounting by operators in public-to-private service concession arrangements. *[IFRIC 12.4]*. Accordingly, the Interpretation does not specify the accounting by grantors. *[IFRIC 12.9]*.

The Committee acknowledged that these restrictions would exclude many arrangements that are found in practice for private sector participation in the provision of public services. However, it concluded that the above conditions were likely to be met in most of the public-to-private service concession arrangements for which guidance had been sought and that other standards apply when these conditions are not a feature of the arrangement. *[IFRIC 12.BC11-13]*. The standards that might apply for arrangements outside the scope of IFRIC 12 are set out at 2.2 below. Arrangements within scope will be those that meet the following criteria:

1. the arrangement is a public-to-private service concession (see 2.1 below); *[IFRIC 12.4]*
2. the grantor controls or regulates the services (see 3.1 below); *[IFRIC 12.5(a)]*
3. the grantor controls any significant residual interest (see 3.2 below). *[IFRIC 12.5(b)]*.

The diagram below illustrates how these criteria would be applied for a service arrangement.

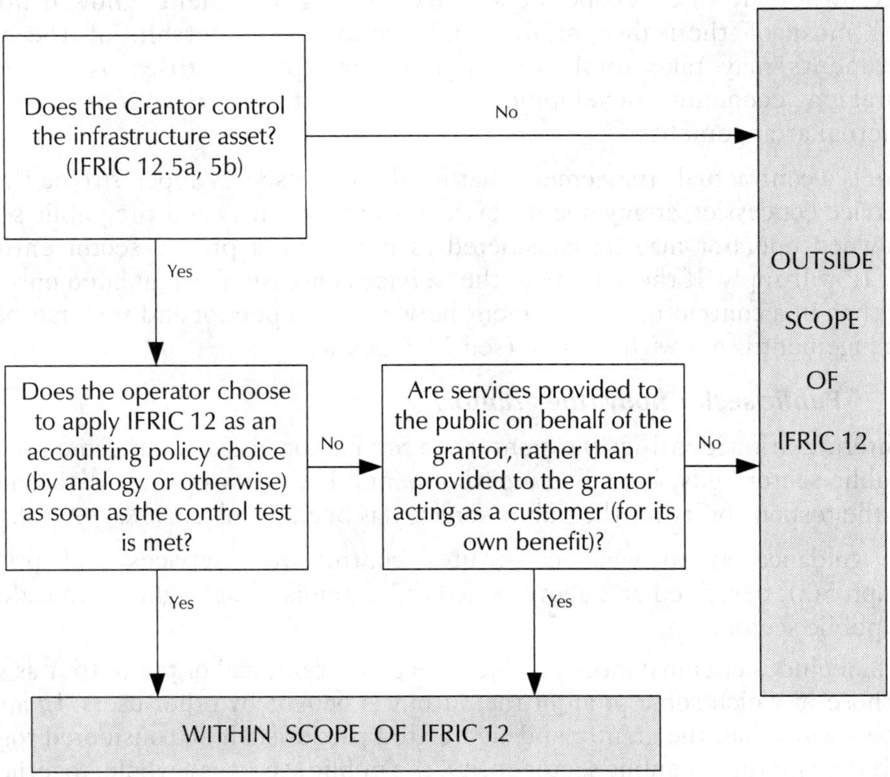

2.1 Public-to-private service concession arrangements within scope

The Committee has applied a narrow definition to the scope of IFRIC 12, restricting it to guidance on public-to-private service concession arrangements. *[IFRIC 12.4]*. A broader definition based solely on the control criteria could have applied to many existing outsourcing and similar arrangements.

Therefore, to be within the mandatory scope, an arrangement has to involve a private sector entity (the operator), a public sector body (the grantor), and a service concession. These elements are discussed below.

2.1.1 Private sector entity (the operator)

Whilst an arrangement within the scope of IFRIC 12 typically involves a private sector operator, *[IFRIC 12.2]*, the Interpretation can still apply if the operator is ultimately controlled by the state, provided that it can be demonstrated that it is acting independently and not as an agent for the grantor. *[IFRIC 12.3(b)]*.

Generally, a private sector entity would be expected to be one that was entirely independent of the state. However, there may be circumstances in which an entity is partially or wholly state-owned but allowed autonomy to conduct its own affairs. Entities such as these are common, not only in jurisdictions where there is state ownership of all economic activity. Some governments allow utilities to control most of their own affairs while retaining ownership of the utility. Governments may take total or partial ownership of entities as a means of encouraging economic development but allow the entity control over its contractual arrangements.

If there is a contractual arrangement that in all other respects appears to be the same as a service concession arrangement between a private entity and the public sector, a state-owned operator may be considered as if it were a private sector entity and IFRIC 12 will apply. If the activity of the 'service concession' is regulated only by law rather than in a contractual arrangement between the operator and the grantor, then the arrangement is not within scope (see 2.1.6 below).

2.1.2 Public sector body (the grantor)

The Interpretation identifies the grantor of a service concession arrangement in terms of a public sector body, including a governmental body or a private sector entity to which the responsibility for the public service has been devolved. *[IFRIC 12.3(a)]*.

In its guidance as to what constitutes control over services and prices in paragraph 5(a), described at 2 above, IFRIC 12 extends what might be considered to mean 'public sector':

> '... includes circumstances in which the grantor buys all of the output as well as those in which some or all of the output is bought by other users. In applying this condition, the grantor and any related parties shall be considered together. If the grantor is a public sector entity, the public sector as a whole, together with any regulators acting in the public interest, shall be regarded as related to the grantor for the purposes of this Interpretation.' *[IFRIC 12.AG2]*.

This means that the entire public may be considered as part of the 'public sector' if the grantor purchases all of the output and provides services for free, e.g. health services provided by privately operated hospitals but free at the point of delivery to the patient.

Not every related party of the grantor (as defined in paragraph 9 of IAS 24 – *Related Party Disclosures* – see Chapter 37) need be taken into account in determining whether the grantor controls the service concession. Some services may be provided simultaneously to more than one public sector body but they will only be taken into account together if they operate in concert to control the 'output'. For instance, an entity may provide similar information technology services to several government departments and local government bodies but each contract is negotiated separately; the departments and bodies are not necessarily 'related parties'.

Regulators must be taken into account although they may not be related parties of the grantor as defined by IAS 24, as they may be required to be independent to act in the public interest. If the activities of the operator are regulated, but there is no contractual arrangement between the operator and the grantor, then the arrangement is not within scope (see 2.1.5 below).

Control over services is discussed further at 3.1 below.

2.1.3 Service concession arrangement ('SCA')

IFRIC 12 does not describe the features of a service concession agreement in the scope paragraphs; instead they are included in 'background' information where they help explain what is, and what is not, a public-to-private service arrangement. The main characteristic of a service concession is the public service nature of the obligation undertaken by the operator. The services related to the infrastructure are to be provided to the public as a matter of policy, irrespective of the identity of the party that operates the services. The service concession arrangement contractually obliges the operator to provide the services to the public on behalf of the public sector entity. IFRIC 12 states that 'other common features' are:

'(a) the party that grants the service arrangement (the grantor) is a public sector entity, including a governmental body, or a private sector entity to which the responsibility for the service has been devolved.

(b) the operator is responsible for at least some of the management of the infrastructure and related services and does not merely act as an agent on behalf of the grantor.

(c) the contract sets the initial prices to be levied by the operator and regulates price revisions over the period of the service arrangement.

(d) the operator is obliged to hand over the infrastructure to the grantor in a specified condition at the end of the period of the arrangement, for little or no incremental consideration, irrespective of which party initially financed it.' *[IFRIC 12.3]*.

The meaning of the public service obligation remains a matter of judgement. SCAs fall into two broad categories where the public service obligation can be identified:

1. SCAs that provide services directly to the public (e.g. transport, water supply, sewage, landfills).
2. SCAs where the services 'related to the infrastructure' continue to be provided by the grantor, e.g. the services provided by hospitals, prisons or schools, all of which would usually be considered to be examples of service concession arrangements. However, in these cases the infrastructure that is the subject of the contractual arrangement is used to provide services directly to the public, or to a significant part of it.

In other cases, it is far less clear that there is a public service obligation. Some arrangements are controlled by government bodies that may only comprise a few municipal authorities within that jurisdiction. Some European city authorities, for example, control car parking but in the vast majority of cities car parking *per se* is not considered a public service. In these cases the entity simply has to provide services to the grantor through an asset it has constructed and the arrangement may well be the same as those it has with local supermarkets and cinemas. An arrangement to provide parking services with the city authority may meet the control criteria in paragraph 5 of IFRIC 12, described at 3 below but so, too, may a contract to provide parking services with a cinema.

The services may be those that need to be provided to the public as a matter of policy (e.g. the provision of electricity) but the contractual arrangement itself may be unrelated to any public service obligation. There are no services in addition to the provision of power (a combination of assets and services is often thought as typical of SCAs) and the grantor pays for the fixed and variable costs of the power produced, as do many private purchasers of power. Similarly, a public sector water utility might engage a private contractor to build, maintain and operate a water treatment facility but there are no services in addition to the provision of a functioning facility within the water network.

These outsourcing-type arrangements are examples of the problematic boundary between IFRIC 12 and IFRIC 4. The Interpretations Committee has attempted to deal with this, not wholly successfully, by introducing an amendment to IFRIC 4 specifically to exclude arrangements falling within the scope of IFRIC 12 from its scope. *[IFRIC 4.4]*. This is discussed at 2.3 below.

2.1.4 Infrastructure assets within the scope of IFRIC 12

Infrastructure assets within scope are those constructed or acquired for the purpose of the concession or existing infrastructure to which the operator is given access by the grantor for these purposes (see 3.3 below). *[IFRIC 12.7]*. Accounting is based on who controls the right to use the infrastructure. Crucially, control may be separated from ownership. Therefore, if the grantor controls the infrastructure assets, they should be accounted for according to one of the service concession models (see 4 below).

2.1.5 Operator does not 'merely act as an agent'

A feature of SCAs is that the operator is responsible for at least some of the management of the infrastructure and related services and does not merely act as an agent on behalf of the grantor. *[IFRIC 12.3(b)]*.

For example, an operator constructs and maintains for 25 years a building that will be used for administrative purposes by the Defence Ministry in a particular country. The building does not have any parts dedicated to services provided directly to the public although the service that is provided within the building (national security) may be considered a public service as a matter of policy. At the end of the concession term, the building reverts to the Ministry for a nominal sum. In the interests of national security, all details of the services to be provided are predetermined. In this type of arrangement there may be virtually no scope for the operator to make any management decisions, making it unlikely that the arrangement will be within scope of IFRIC 12.

This will always be a question of degree and is unlikely to be the crucial feature in making a decision but it may help distinguish SCAs within scope of IFRIC 12 from some of the 'outsourcing' type arrangements discussed at 2.3 below.

2.1.6 A contract with the grantor

An arrangement can only be an SCA if there is a contract with the grantor 'that sets out performance standards, mechanisms for adjusting prices, and arrangements for arbitrating disputes'. *[IFRIC 12.2]*.

If the operator of an asset obtains a licence to provide services but has no contractual obligation to the grantor (including parties 'related' to the grantor in the sense in which the term is used in IFRIC 12, see 3.1 below) then the arrangement will not be within scope. There are many activities that require a formal licence; in some jurisdictions these include licences to operate pharmacies, provide childcare or carry out certain waste disposal activities, any of which could be considered public service obligations in some countries. Obtaining the licence does not bring the activity into scope of IFRIC 12 unless there is a separate contractual arrangement that governs the provision of the service.

Information Note 2 to IFRIC 12, reproduced at 2.2 below, indicates that there are certain contractual arrangements between grantor and operator that are not within scope of the Interpretation. These include arrangements in which there is a service and/or maintenance contract, i.e. to perform specific tasks such as processing licence applications, where IAS 18 or IFRS 15, as appropriate, is the relevant standard. Another example is where the operator leases assets from the grantor, in which case IAS 17 or IFRS 16 would provide relevant guidance, unless, for example, the lease payments are made as part of a wider service concession, in which case the costs may have to be taken into account as part of the costs of an infrastructure asset (see 3.3 below).

However, the contractual arrangement does not need to be for construction services in respect of any infrastructure. The arrangement may be within scope of IFRIC 12 in respect of post-construction services alone. Accounting for the post-construction period is described at 5 below.

2.2 Arrangements that are not in the scope of IFRIC 12

The Committee acknowledged that in practice there are arrangements for private sector participation in the provision of public services that will not fall in the scope of IFRIC 12. However, it was satisfied that the Interpretation would apply to most of the public-to-private service concession arrangements for which guidance had been sought. Nevertheless, the Committee did consider a range of typical arrangements and decided that it could provide references to the standards that apply to those that fall outside the scope of IFRIC 12 without giving any guidance as to their application. *[IFRIC 12.BC13]*.

These references are presented in Information Note 2 to IFRIC 12 (on which the following table is based) and which shows a range of arrangements between the public and private sectors. The Interpretations Committee's view is that IFRIC 12 is interpreting IFRSs for the transactions in the middle of this range, where the application of standards was previously unclear. These are described in the table below as 'Rehabilitate-operate-transfer' and 'Build-operate-transfer' arrangements. The table also demonstrates how other standards, namely IAS 17, IAS 18 and IAS 16, apply to arrangements that do not contain the features of a public-to-private service concession as defined in the Interpretation.

Category	*Lessee*	*Service Provider*			*Owner*	
Typical arrangement types	Lease, e.g. Operator leases assets from grantor	Service and/or maintenance contract (specific tasks e.g. debt collection)	Rehabilitate-operate-transfer	Build-operate-transfer	Build-own-operate	100% Divestment, Privatisation, Corporation
Asset Ownership	Grantor				Operator	
Capital Investment	Grantor		Operator			
Demand Risk	Shared	Grantor	Operator and/or Grantor		Operator	
Typical Duration	8-20 years	1-5 years	25-30 years			Indefinite (or may be limited by licence)
Residual Interest	Grantor				Operator	
Examples of IFRSs that may apply	IAS 17	IAS 18	IFRIC 12		IAS 16	

For entities applying IFRS 15, the reference to IAS 18 in the above table is replaced with that Standard.[4] For entities applying IFRS 16, the reference to IAS 17 in the above table is replaced with that Standard.[5]

2.3 IFRIC 4 and IFRIC 12: outsourcing arrangements and SCAs

Some features of a service concession arrangement may make it difficult to distinguish from a lease. The concept of an operator's right of 'access to operate the infrastructure', *[IFRIC 12.11]*, can appear to be very similar to an arrangement that 'conveys the right to use the asset'. *[IFRIC 4.6(b), 9]*. It can therefore be unclear whether the private sector entity is a lessee or the operator of a service concession arrangement.

The guidance presented in Information Note 2 to IFRIC 12 (and reproduced at 2.2 above) identifies some differences between a leasing arrangement and a service concession, but is not always conclusive. Whilst a service concession will usually require capital investment by the operator and perhaps have a longer duration than a typical lease, under both arrangements ownership of the asset and control over the residual interest rests with the grantor. A key distinction is the degree of control that the operator/lessee has over the use to which the asset is put.

A 'right of use' conveys the right to control the use of the underlying asset. One of the conditions noted in IFRIC 4 that confirms a right of use (and therefore a lease) is that the lessee has the ability or right to operate the asset or direct others to operate the asset in a manner it determines while obtaining or controlling more than an insignificant amount of the output or other utility of the asset. *[IFRIC 4.9]*.

This feature is absent from an arrangement that meets the control criteria (discussed at 3 below) and other features of a service concession, in particular:

- in a service concession, the grantor controls or regulates what services the operator must provide with the infrastructure, to whom, and at what price; *[IFRIC 12.5]*
- a service concession contractually obliges the operator to provide services to the public on behalf of the public sector grantor; *[IFRIC 12.3]* or
- the operator in a service concession arrangement is granted access to the infrastructure; but the use to which that asset is applied is governed by the contract with the grantor. The contractual service agreement does not convey to the operator the right to control the use of the infrastructure. *[IFRIC 12.11]*.

The Interpretations Committee recognised the risk of confusion and amended IFRIC 4 to exclude arrangements falling within the scope of IFRIC 12 from its scope. *[IFRIC 4.4]*. Under IFRIC 12, whilst the operator has rights over the infrastructure, the grantor retains control over both the asset itself and how it is used. Therefore the Interpretations Committee concluded that the infrastructure should not be recognised by the operator as property, plant and equipment. *[IFRIC 12.11, BC21, BC22]*.

2.3.1 The private sector entity acting as lessor or provider of outsourcing services

While it is evident that IFRIC 4 does not apply to the treatment by the private sector entity of infrastructure assets in public-to-private service concession arrangements that are clearly within scope of IFRIC 12, *[IFRIC 4.4]*, the analysis at 2.3 above does not help if there is doubt as to whether the arrangement ought to fall within scope of IFRIC 12 in the first place. Service concessions are not the only contractual arrangements between the public sector and private sector. There are numerous examples of arrangements in which the grantor controls both the services in and the residual interest in the infrastructure asset but that would be seen as containing leases under IAS 17 by applying an IFRIC 4 analysis (see Chapter 24 at 2.1). Public sector bodies lease buildings or other property, plant and equipment from private sector entities for their own use. The private sector body might also be engaged to construct the buildings or other property before it is occupied by the public sector body. The public sector also engages independent subcontractors to outsource the operation of its internal services and functions. Sometimes the leasing of assets and the provision of outsourcing services to government are embodied in the same contract. In any event, the private sector entity would have to identify the distinct performance obligations and account for each separately. *[IAS 18.13, IFRS 15.22]*.

Examples of outsourcing arrangements include contracts for the provision of building maintenance services, accounting and information technology functions and operating employee cafeteria. *[SIC-29.1]*. It is arguable whether outsourcing-type arrangements were intended to be within scope of IFRIC 12. The Interpretations Committee noted in September 2005 that it would not expect an information technology outsourcing arrangement for a government department to be dealt with under IFRIC 12.[6] The Interpretations Committee presumably concluded that, as an outsourcing arrangement, this more properly fell within IFRIC 4. In our view a distinguishing feature is the purpose to which the leased assets or services is applied. In a service concession arrangement, the private sector operator is contracted to provide services to the public on behalf of the public sector entity. *[IFRIC 12.3]*. By contrast, in a leasing or outsourcing arrangement, the infrastructure is used by the grantor, in order that it can ultimately provide public services but it is not used itself to provide the service.

This could make a significant difference to the manner in which the arrangement is accounted for. IFRIC 12's control model and IAS 17's risks and rewards tests could result in different assets being recognised in the financial statements of operator (or lessor) and grantor (or public sector lessee). An arrangement could be accounted for under the financial asset model under IFRIC 12, so the asset would be accounted for as a receivable by the operator, yet considered an operating lease under IAS 17, in which case the private sector entity, as a lessor, would consider the asset to be PP&E. The private sector entity may have arrangements on the same terms with other private sector entities and with the public sector. It would appear strange that similar arrangements should be treated differently merely because the customer is a public sector body. One example is power supply. In many parts of the world, governments have chosen to expand power generation capacity in their countries by entering into contracts with operators. Some of these arrangements have the same features as power supply contracts to private sector purchasers to which IFRIC 4 applies. Commonly, the contract allows for a fixed charge that is payable irrespective of deliveries, which may or may not cover all of the capital expenditure, a variable charge related to the variable costs of generating power and a penalty regime under which part of the fixed cost is refundable. These are the features that are described in Chapter 24, Example 24.1, as 'An arrangement that contains a lease'. Providing power is usually considered to be a public service yet the public service element may be irrelevant to the structure of the contract. For example, the private sector entity may have no relationship with the public, instead selling its output to the government. The use to which the power is put need not affect the arrangement; for example, the power could be used solely by Government department buildings, by a government-owned industry, for naval dockyards or it could be put directly into the national electricity distribution network.

In such a case there may be no services in addition to those necessary to maintain the power supply, unlike the much more extensive services that are provided as part of what are usually considered typical SCAs such as hospitals or prisons. By contrast, other 'typical' SCAs such as toll roads and bridges have few associated services but are clearly used directly by the public. This means that the provision of significant ancillary or associated services is not sufficient by itself to distinguish SCAs from other contractual arrangements with the public sector. Whether the operator (or lessor) is directly involved in the provision of services *to the public* is an indicator of a service concession rather than a lease.

However, to require a public service to be identified in an arrangement that could equally be a service concession or a lease is not a conclusive test either. The Interpretations Committee was unable to come up with a robust definition of public service obligation. The description of the features of SCAs (discussed at 2.1.3 above), is included in a 'background' section preceding the body of the Interpretation itself. In the period since IFRIC 12 was issued, it has still not proved possible to come up with a workable definition of public service obligation. To some extent this is because the public policy component of its meaning comes from a political or ideological determination of what activities should be provided by the state. This means that there will always be a certain amount of confusion over whether an arrangement that meets the control criteria but that does not appear to contain any obvious public service obligation ought, as a matter of course, to be accounted for under IFRIC 12.

In the end, it is always likely to be a matter of judgement and there will be different views in practice. IFRIC 12 was developed because there are transactions that are so complex that it is very difficult to fit them into an existing accounting model and it is important not to lose sight of this. It appears that it was not the intention of the Interpretations Committee to change the manner in which outsourcing arrangements were accounted for solely because the contracting party is a government body but, equally, if the control criteria in paragraph 5 of IFRIC 12 apply to these arrangements many companies choose to apply IFRIC 12.

2.3.2 *Entities applying IFRS 16*

IFRS 16 was issued by the IASB in January 2016 and is effective for annual reporting periods beginning on or after 1 January 2019. Earlier application is permitted for entities that also apply IFRS 15 at or before the date of initial application of IFRS 16. *[IFRS 16.C1]*.

Like IFRIC 4, the scope of IFRS 16 excludes service concession arrangements falling within scope of IFRIC 12. *[IFRS 16.3(c)]*. However, similar issues can arise in determining the 'boundary' between IFRIC 12 and IFRS 16 as those discussed at 2.3 and at 2.3.1 above. For questions as to whether a private sector entity is the operator in a service concession arrangement or a lessee, the concept of a 'right of access' under IFRIC 12 remains an appropriate distinguishing feature. IFRS 16 defines an arrangement as containing a lease if the contract conveys the right to control the use of an identified asset for a period of time in exchange for consideration. *[IFRS 16.9]*. A right to control the use of an identified asset is then described in terms of the right to direct the use of the asset. *[IFRS 16.B9]*. As discussed at 2.3 above, a conclusion that the grantor controls or regulates what services the operator must provide with the infrastructure, to whom, and at what price, *[IFRIC 12.5]*, is not compatible with the assertion that the private sector entity has a leasehold interest in the same assets under IFRS 16.

Another question is whether a private sector entity is acting as a lessor or as a provider of outsourcing services, rather than as the operator of a service concession. The answer is no clearer under IFRS 16 than under the previous leasing standard, as discussed at 2.3.1 above. The scope exclusion will not help if there is doubt as to whether an arrangement ought to fall in scope of IFRIC 12 in the first place. Because the 'operating lease' remains a feature of IFRS 16 for lessor accounting, the assessment of whether an arrangement is in scope of IFRIC 12 or IFRS 16 could give rise to the private sector entity recognising PP&E in its financial statements. This would be the case if the arrangement were accounted for under IFRS 16 and the private sector entity was considered to be the lessor in an operating lease. However, given the nature of concession arrangements, in practice it would be more likely that, where IFRS 16 is applied, the private sector entity would be treated as lessor in a finance lease and would recognise a finance lease receivable for the contractual lease payments. *[IFRS 16.67, 81]*. For an arrangement accounted for under IFRIC 12, the private sector entity (operator) would recognise either a financial asset or an intangible asset, depending upon the nature of consideration receivable for construction or upgrade services provided. *[IFRIC 12.16-17]*. As noted at 2.3.2 above, the use to which the asset is put and the involvement of the public as consumer of services are features of the arrangement relevant to making an appropriate judgement.

IFRS 16 is discussed in Chapter 25.

2.4 Private-to-private arrangements

While the Interpretations Committee expects IFRIC 12 to be applied to arrangements that share the features of the public service obligation (see 2.1.3 above), its application to private-to-private arrangements is neither required nor prohibited. The Basis for Conclusions notes that application by analogy could be appropriate under the hierarchy in IAS 8 – *Accounting Policies, Changes in Accounting Estimates and Errors* – if the arrangement met the control criteria quoted above. *[IFRIC 12.BC14]*. Accordingly, the application of IFRIC 12 to other arrangements would be regarded as an accounting policy choice, rather than a treatment that could be determined on a case by case basis.

2.5 Accounting by grantors

The Interpretation applies only to accounting by the operator, not the grantor. *[IFRIC 12.4, 9]*. Grantor accounting was determined not to be a priority for the Committee, who noted that grantors are government bodies that do not necessarily apply IFRS. *[IFRIC 12.BC15]*. In 2011, the International Public Sector Accounting Standards Board (IPSASB) approved a new standard, IPSAS 32 – *Service Concession Arrangements: Grantor*– that addresses the grantor's accounting in such arrangements. Its approach is consistent with that used for the operator's accounting in IFRIC 12, in that an infrastructure asset is recognised by the grantor, together with an obligation comprising either a financial liability to the operator or, where an unconditional to pay cash to the operator is not a feature of the arrangement, a deferred revenue balance.[7] This chapter does not address accounting by grantors.

3 THE CONTROL MODEL

A contractual arrangement that is within the scope of IFRIC 12 includes the following features, commonly referred to as the 'control criteria':

(a) the grantor controls or regulates the services that the operator must provide using the infrastructure, to whom it must provide them, and at what price; and

(b) the grantor controls any significant residual interest in the infrastructure at the end of the concession term through ownership, beneficial entitlement or otherwise. *[IFRIC 12.5]*.

The Interpretations Committee considers that, taken together, these conditions identify when the infrastructure is controlled by the grantor for the whole of its economic life, in which case an operator is only managing the infrastructure on the grantor's behalf. *[IFRIC 12.AG6]*. Crucially, it has concluded from this that an infrastructure asset controlled by the grantor cannot be the property, plant and equipment of the operator. *[IFRIC 12.11, BC21, BC22]*. Control should be distinguished from management. If the grantor retains both the degree of control described in (a) above and any significant residual interest in the infrastructure, the operator is only managing the infrastructure on the grantors behalf – even though, in many cases, it may have wide managerial discretion. *[IFRIC 12.AG5]*.

3.1 Regulation of services

Although there has to be a contract between grantor and operator for the arrangement to be a service concession, the control or regulation of services does not have to be governed by contract as it could include control via an industry regulator. Control also extends to circumstances in which the grantor buys all of the output as well as those in which it is bought by other users.

The grantor and relevant related parties (see 2.1.2 above) must be considered together. If the grantor is a public sector entity, the public sector as a whole, together with any independent regulators acting in the public interest, are to be regarded as related to the grantor. *[IFRIC 12.AG2]*. 'Price' can mean the amount at which the grantor buys the service or the amount that the operator charges members of the public or a combination of both.

This means that many regulated public utilities (water, sewage, electricity supply etc.) will fall within (a) above. Other arrangements that fall within (a) include public health facilities that are free to users and subsidised transport facilities (rail, some toll roads and bridges) that are partly paid by public sector grant and partly by passenger fares. Of course, all of these will only be within scope of IFRIC 12 if there is also a contract between grantor and operator for the arrangement and any significant residual interest is also 'controlled' by the grantor under (b).

The Interpretations Committee stresses that the grantor does not need to have complete control of the price. It is sufficient for the price to be regulated, which could be by way of a capping mechanism (regulated utilities are usually free to charge *lower* prices). Other 'caps' may not be so apparent. A contract may give the operator freedom to set its prices but any excess is clawed back by the grantor, e.g. through setting a maximum return on an agreed investment in the infrastructure. In such a case, the operator's return is capped and the price element of the control test is substantively met. *[IFRIC 12.AG3]*.

Care should be taken to look to the substance of the agreements, so a cap that only applies in remote circumstances will be ignored.

Some arrangements only allow the grantor to control prices for part of the life of the infrastructure, particularly if it is a lease-type arrangement. For example, an operator may construct clinical facilities that are used by a government health care provider (the grantor) for a five year contract term. At the end of the term, the health care provider may extend the contract by renegotiation. If it does not do so, the operator can run the facilities for private health care. Although the prices are controlled for the first five years, this arrangement is unlikely to meet the control condition in (a) above.

Alternatively, the contract might allow regulation of the prices of some but not all of the services provided with the infrastructure. Judgement is required in determining whether arrangements involving partially regulated assets fall within the scope of IFRIC 12 (see 3.4 below).

3.2 Control of the residual interest

In order for an arrangement to be within scope of IFRIC 12, the grantor must control not only the services provided with the infrastructure but also any significant residual interest in the property at the end of the concession term through ownership, beneficial entitlement or otherwise. *[IFRIC 12.5(b)]*. The grantor's control over any significant residual interest should restrict the operator's ability to sell or pledge the infrastructure. The grantor must also have a right of use of the infrastructure throughout the concession term. *[IFRIC 12.AG4]*. As discussed below, control over the residual interest does not require the infrastructure to be returned to the grantor. It is sufficient that the grantor controls how access to the infrastructure is awarded after the concession term.

Many infrastructure assets are partially replaced during the course of the concession and the impact of this on condition (b) has been considered. If the operator has to replace part of an item of infrastructure during the life of the concession, e.g. the top layer of a road or the roof of a building, the item of infrastructure is to be considered as a whole, so that condition (b) will be met for the whole of the infrastructure, including the part that is replaced, if the grantor has the residual interest in the final replacement of that part. *[IFRIC 12.AG6]*.

IFRIC 12 pays little attention to the residual interest. Its application guidance states that 'the residual interest in the infrastructure is the estimated current value of the infrastructure as if it were already of the age and in the condition expected at the end of the period of the arrangement'. *[IFRIC 12.AG4]*. This echoes the definition of 'residual value' in IAS 16, but excludes any deduction for the estimated costs of disposal. *[IAS 16.6]*. See Chapter 18 at 5.2. However, the Interpretation does not expand on what is regarded as 'significant'. Some infrastructure assets such as toll roads and bridges generate cash flows directly and it may be possible to use estimated future cash flows to calculate the significance of the residual value, whether or not the grantor will charge tolls after reversion of the asset. It may not be possible to base the assessment of 'significance' on the cash flows received by the operator on handing back the asset to the grantor as these may be nominal amounts; indeed, the grantor may pay nothing. In such a case, the remaining useful life of the asset when it reverts may give a good indication, e.g. if a hospital is handed back to the public sector with a remaining useful life of twenty years, this residual interest is likely to be significant.

There are a number of features that indicate whether the grantor controls the residual interest. There are usually several contractual alternatives: the operator is granted a second concession term, a new operator is allowed to acquire the assets or the grantor acquires the assets and brings the arrangement 'in house'. The grantor still controls the residual as it will determine which of these alternatives applies and the option exercise price (if it or a new operator acquires the infrastructure) is irrelevant.

In some arrangements the grantor only has an option to reacquire the asset at the end of the concession term. The operator cannot control the infrastructure until the grantor decides what to do with the option. An option at fair value at the date of exercise may by itself be enough to give the grantor control over the residual under IFRIC 12 if it is sufficient to restrict the operator's ability to sell or pledge the infrastructure. This is a clear difference between a 'risks and rewards' and a 'control' model as under the former, the operator would be seen as keeping the risks and rewards of ownership if another party had the right to acquire the asset at fair value.

Example 27.1: Residual arrangements

A gas transmission system is being operated under a concession arrangement with the State Gas Authority. At the end of the term, the grantor will either acquire the infrastructure assets at their net book value, determined on the basis of the contract, or it may decide to grant a new SCA on the basis of a competitive tender, which will exclude the current operator. If the grantor elects to do the latter, the operator will be entitled to the lower of the following two amounts:

(a) the net book value of the infrastructure, determined on the basis of the contract; and

(b) the proceeds of a new competitive bidding process to acquire a new contract.

Although the operator cannot enter the competitive tender, it also has the right to enter into a new concession term but, in order to do so, it must match the best tender offer made. It has to pay to the grantor the excess of the best offer (b) above the amount in (a); should the tender offer be lower than (a), it will receive an equivalent refund.

In this arrangement, the grantor will control the residual. It can choose to take over the activities of the concession itself or it can allow potential operators, including the incumbent, to bid for a second term. The price that might be received by the operator, or paid by the grantor, is not relevant.

What if the arrangement is for the whole life of the infrastructure? Assets in service concession arrangements may revert to the grantor at the end of the concession term but they may not have much, if any, remaining useful life. Many modern buildings, for example, only have a useful life of thirty years or so and this is a common concession term. Consequently, infrastructure used in a service concession arrangement for its entire useful life ('whole of life infrastructure') is included within the scope of IFRIC 12. *[IFRIC 12.6]*.

The Interpretations Committee noted that one reason for including the 'significant residual interest' requirement was to differentiate between privatised, but still regulated, industries and service concession arrangements, thereby seeming to confirm that it had not intended regulated industries to be in scope.[8] The Interpretations Committee considers that privatised regulated industries should generally be out of scope, because they are divestitures or privatisations where it is more appropriate to treat the infrastructure as the property, plant and equipment of the operator. This is indicated in the table included as Information Note 2 to IFRIC 12 (reproduced at 2.2 above). It is usually the case in a privatisation that the infrastructure only reverts to the grantor in the event of a major breach of the conditions of the regulatory framework as otherwise the right of the operator to provide the regulated services may roll over indefinitely into a new term. In other cases it may require legislative change to bring the assets back into the control of the public sector. This means that the grantor does not control the residual interest in the property as required by IFRIC 12.

GDF SUEZ discloses that some of its concessions are not considered to be within scope of IFRIC 12 as the grantor has no rights over the infrastructure at the end of the contract. These assets (for gas distribution) are likely to have a life in excess of the contract term.

Extract 27.1: GDF SUEZ SA (2014)

Notes to the consolidated financial statements [extract]

NOTE 1 Accounting standards and methods [extract]

1.4. Accounting methods [extract]

1.4.7 Concession arrangements [extract]

For a concession arrangement to fall within the scope of IFRIC 12, usage of the infrastructure must be controlled by the concession grantor. This requirement is met when the following two conditions are met:

- the grantor controls or regulates what services the operator must provide with the infrastructure, to whom it must provide them, and at what price; and
- the grantor controls the infrastructure, i.e. retains the right to take back the infrastructure at the end of the concession.

Concessions outside the scope of IFRIC 12

Concession infrastructures that do not meet the requirements of IFRIC 12 are presented as property, plant and equipment.

This is the case of the distribution of gas in France. The related assets are recognized in accordance with IAS 16, since GrDF operates its network under long-term concession arrangements, most of which are mandatorily renewed upon expiration pursuant to French law no. 46-628 of April 8, 1946.

3.3 Assets within scope

There are two groups of assets within scope of IFRIC 12:

(a) the infrastructure that the operator constructs or acquires from a third party for the purpose of the concession; and

(b) existing infrastructure to which the grantor gives the operator access for the purpose of the concession. *[IFRIC 12.7]*.

Generally, 'infrastructure' is interpreted broadly and it is accepted that 'the infrastructure' used to provide services can include moveable assets. Although IFRIC 12 uses the word 'infrastructure' and includes examples traditionally regarded as such, including roads, bridges, hospitals and airports, *[IFRIC 12.1]*, the Interpretation is based on the definition of an asset under IFRS. An asset is 'a resource controlled by the entity as a result of past events and from which future economic benefits are expected to flow to the entity', *[CF 4.4]*, and is therefore considered to apply to all assets, including items such as buses or rolling stock that are made available by the grantor to the operator of the public service.

It is usually relatively straightforward to apply (a) above, infrastructure that the operator constructs or acquires from a third party for the purpose of the concession. The accounting for service concession arrangements in which infrastructure is leased from a party other than the grantor is discussed at 3.3.3 below.

However, there are some issues of interpretation relating to infrastructure to which the grantor has given access to the operator for the purpose of the SCA. Infrastructure under (b) above could include other arrangements in the form of leases from the grantor over assets. As part of a SCA, in addition to receiving payments for the construction and/or operation of the infrastructure, an operator may make lease payments to a grantor, e.g. it may lease the land on which a facility is to be built. These issues are discussed at 3.3.1 below.

A third group of assets comprises property, plant and equipment previously held by the operator and then used in connection with the provision of services under the SCA. The Interpretations Committee's view is that accounting for these types of assets is already covered by existing accounting standards, principally IAS 16, and therefore it does not specify how the operator should account for its previously existing assets that now form part of the infrastructure. *[IFRIC 12.8]*. The treatment of existing assets is discussed further at 3.3.2 below.

3.3.1 Periodic payments to the grantor for the right to use assets

Assets within the scope of IFRIC 12 include infrastructure that the operator constructs or acquires from a third party for the purpose of the service arrangement and existing infrastructure to which the grantor gives the operator access for the purpose of the service arrangement. *[IFRIC 12.7]*. IFRIC 12 contains no explicit guidance regarding periodic payments made to the grantor in connection with the right to use assets. The issue is whether these costs should be treated as lease costs in accordance with IAS 17, treated as executory in nature with costs expensed as incurred or otherwise recognised as a liability. If they are considered to be within scope of IFRIC 12, what are the accounting consequences? Are they part of the overall consideration paid by the grantor or recognised as an asset and, if an asset, did they form part of the 'concession asset' at the start of the concession, with an obligation to make the related payments?

This has been discussed by the Interpretations Committee on a number of occasions. The Committee decided in March 2016 that the treatment of variable payments for asset purchases, including payments that vary in relation to future activity by the purchaser, was too broad an issue for it to address, and consequently decided not to add the issue to its agenda.[9]

For fixed payments made by the operator to the grantor, the Committee observed in July 2016 that IFRIC 12 would apply, unless:

(a) they are payments for the right to a good or service that is separate from the service concession arrangement, which should be accounted for under other applicable IFRSs; or

(b) they are payments for the right to use an asset that is separate from the infrastructure within the scope of IFRIC 12, in which case the operator should assess whether the arrangement contains a lease. If the arrangement contains a lease, the operator should account for those payments by applying IAS 17, or IFRS 16 if that standard is applied.[10]

Payments that are part of the overall concession agreement but do not fall within these two exceptions will be accounted for as part of the SCA. In this case the accounting treatment will depend on whether the SCA falls within the financial asset model, the intangible asset model or is a hybrid. If the financial asset model applies, payments would be treated as reductions to the overall consideration received and therefore be offset against the financial asset receivable under the SCA. In contrast, under the intangible asset model the payments to the grantor should be recognised as a liability that increases the cost of the concession right asset. This is discussed further at 4.7 below.

3.3.2 *Previously held assets used for the concession*

IFRIC 12 does not apply to infrastructure held and recognised as property, plant and equipment by the operator before entering into the SCA. If such assets of the operator become part of the infrastructure in the SCA, then it implies that control over those assets has transferred to the grantor. Accordingly, the operator must apply the derecognition requirements of IAS 16 to determine whether it should derecognise those previously held assets. *[IFRIC 12.8]*. The Interpretations Committee's view is that accounting for assets is already covered by existing accounting standards, principally IAS 16, and therefore it is not necessary to specify how the operator should account for its previously existing assets that now form part of the infrastructure. *[IFRIC 12.BC16]*.

The implication is that losing control of a previously held asset by contractually giving control of its use to the grantor may be a deemed disposal of the asset under IAS 16. The existing asset would be derecognised and any consideration received on the disposal recognised at its fair value. *[IAS 16.72]*. This means that the total consideration received under the contract would be allocated between an amount receivable for construction and upgrade services and an amount to reflect the transfer of the asset to the control of the grantor. What was previously recorded by the operator as property, plant and equipment would be replaced by an element of either an intangible asset or a financial asset, depending on the accounting model determined to be appropriate to the particular SCA (see 4.1.1 below). Gains and losses must be calculated as the difference between any net disposal proceeds and the carrying value of the item of property, plant and equipment, *[IAS 16.71]*, and recognised in profit or loss. Derecognition of assets within scope of IAS 16 in general is discussed in Chapter 18 at 7.

The operator may use some of its existing assets for the purpose of the concession without transferring control to the grantor. These are out of scope.

Therefore, an entity may already control assets, which might include assets regarded as infrastructure that it has constructed and used for its operations before it enters into a concession arrangement. Unless the contract transfers the residual interest in these pre-existing assets to the grantor (and thereby both of the control criteria laid out at 3 above are met), these assets are out of scope of IFRIC 12. If an infrastructure asset is itself out of scope, the SCA might include, for example, extensions to that asset, upgrades to it and a contractual period of using the infrastructure asset to provide services. In this case, the total consideration payable under the concession will be allocated between the extension, upgrade and operating services within scope of IFRIC 12. Accordingly, construction revenue would be recognised at the time of the extension or upgrade work, with an additional financial asset or intangible asset recognised as appropriate.

3.3.3 Accounting for service concession arrangements for which the infrastructure is leased from a party other than the grantor

As noted at 3 above, assets within the scope of IFRIC 12 include infrastructure that the operator constructs or acquires from a third party for the purpose of the service arrangement and existing infrastructure to which the grantor gives the operator access for the purpose of the service arrangement. *[IFRIC 12.7]*. In some cases, an operator may enter into an arrangement with the grantor to provide a public service using infrastructure that is leased. For example, an operator may lease trains in order to provide rail transportation services to the public. The accounting for arrangements in which infrastructure is leased from the grantor are addressed at 3.3.1 above. Where the lessor and grantor are controlled by the same governmental body and are related parties (see 2.2.1 above), lease payments made by the operator to the lessor are, in substance, payments made to a grantor in a service concession arrangement[11] which are covered at 3.3.1 above. For arrangements in which infrastructure is leased from a third party, the first question that arises is whether such arrangements are in scope of IFRIC 12. If so, how should the operator account for any assets and liabilities arising from the arrangement with the lessor?

The Interpretations Committee has discussed these questions in respect of an arrangement where infrastructure is leased from a third party lessor, unrelated to the grantor, and the operator is not required to provide any construction or upgrade services with respect to the infrastructure. In the fact pattern discussed, the operator is contractually required to pay the lessor for the lease of the infrastructure, and has an unconditional contractual right to receive cash from the grantor to reimburse those payments. In July 2016, the Interpretations Committee observed that:

(a) Assessing whether an arrangement is in scope of IFRIC 12 requires consideration of all facts and circumstances, in particular whether the control conditions in paragraph 5 of IFRIC 12 are met (see 3 above), and whether the infrastructure falls within one the groups of assets set out in paragraph 7 of IFRIC 12 as in scope of IFRIC 12 (see 3.3 above). However, an operator is not required to provide construction or upgrade services with respect to the infrastructure for the arrangement to be in scope of IFRIC 12.

(b) If the arrangement is in scope of IFRIC 12, then it is the grantor, not the operator, that controls the right to use the infrastructure. Accordingly, the operator should assess whether it has the obligation to make payments to the lessor for the lease, or whether the grantor has this obligation.

 (i) If the grantor has the obligation to make payments to the lessor, the operator is collecting cash from the grantor that it remits to the lessor on behalf of the grantor.

 (ii) If the operator has the obligation to make payments to the lessor as part of the service concession arrangement, the operator should recognise a liability for this obligation when it is committed to the service concession arrangement and the infrastructure is made available by the lessor. At the time the operator recognises the liability, it should also recognise a financial asset because the operator has a contractual right to receive cash from the grantor to reimburse those payments. The operator should offset the liability to make payments to the lessor against the corresponding receivable from the grantor only when the criteria for offsetting a financial asset and financial liability in IAS 32 are met.[12] The offsetting criteria in IAS 32 are discussed at Chapter 54 at 7.4.

3.4 Partially regulated assets

IFRIC 12 notes that it is not uncommon for the use of infrastructure to be partly regulated and partly unregulated and gives examples while noting that these activities take a variety of forms:

'(a) any infrastructure that is physically separable and capable of being operated independently and meets the definition of a cash generating unit as defined in IAS 36 shall be analysed separately if it is used wholly for unregulated purposes. For example this might apply to a private wing of a hospital, where the remainder of the hospital is used by the grantor to treat public patients.

(b) where purely ancillary activities (such as a hospital shop) are unregulated, the control tests shall be applied as if those services did not exist, because in cases in which the grantor controls the services described in paragraph 5, the existence of ancillary activities does not detract from the grantor's control of the relevant infrastructure.' *[IFRIC 12.AG7]*.

In both of these cases, the operator may have a lease from the grantor that gives it a right to use the unregulated asset in question; if so, this is to be accounted for in accordance with IAS 17, or IFRS 16 if that Standard is applied. *[IFRIC 12.AG8]*. This would be likely to involve using the principles in IFRIC 4 (or IFRS 16 if applied) to distinguish the lease payments from other parts of the service concession arrangement (see Chapter 24 at 2.1 for entities applying IAS 17, or Chapter 25 at 3.2 for entities applying IFRS 16).

The Interpretation gives no further guidance on how an entity might interpret the term 'purely ancillary' in evaluating whether an unregulated activity is ignored for the purposes of determining if the control criteria are met or considered to detract from the grantor's control of the asset. The hospital shop is clearly insignificant by virtue of its size relative to the whole hospital, the proportion of cash flows attributable to it and the fact that the existence of a shop has no direct impact on the function of the infrastructure in the provision of regulated services. However, it is not clear at what point a secondary activity would become or cease to be 'purely ancillary' which will be a matter of judgement.

In addition, there are many concession agreements that include unregulated services that are neither purely ancillary nor delivered by using a physically separable portion of the total infrastructure, a situation not addressed by AG 7. For example, a grantor may control prices charged to children, pensioners and the unemployed who use a sports facility but the amounts charged to other adults are not controlled. The same swimming pool is being used by all, regardless of the amount that they pay. Alternatively, price regulation could apply only to services provided at certain times of the day rather than to different classes of user. In such cases it will be a matter of judgement whether enough of the service is unregulated in order to demonstrate that the grantor is not considered to control the asset, which would lead to the arrangement as a whole falling out of the scope of IFRIC 12. This assessment will be made at the beginning of the contract and will not be revisited unless errors were made in the original assessment.

However, if it transpires that there are significantly fewer unregulated users than anticipated then it is likely that the contract will be renegotiated. This is because of the public service obligation, which means that the grantor will want the service to continue to be provided to the public albeit under new terms. The new contract may be within scope of IFRIC 12. If a toll bridge has had fewer users than anticipated, the grantor might subsidise the tolls under a new arrangement.

4 ACCOUNTING BY THE CONCESSION OPERATOR: THE FINANCIAL ASSET AND INTANGIBLE ASSET MODELS

Arrangements within the scope of IFRIC 12 will be those that meet the following criteria:

1. the arrangement is a public-to-private service concession (see 2.1 above); *[IFRIC 12.4]*
2. the grantor controls or regulates the services (see 3.1 above); *[IFRIC 12.5(a)]*
3. the grantor controls any significant residual interest (see 3.2 above); *[IFRIC 12.5(b)]*
4. infrastructure is constructed or acquired (or the grantor provides access to that infrastructure) for the purpose of the service concession (see 3.3 above); *[IFRIC 12.7]* and
5. the operator has either a contractual right to receive cash from or at the direction of the grantor; or a contractual right to charge users of the service. *[IFRIC 12.16, 17]*.

The last element also determines which of IFRIC 12's accounting models, financial asset or intangible asset, should be applied.

The Interpretations Committee's accounting framework for public-to-private arrangements is summarised in the following diagram from Information Note 1 in IFRIC 12. The diagram starts with the presumption that the arrangement has already been determined to be a service concession (see 2 above):

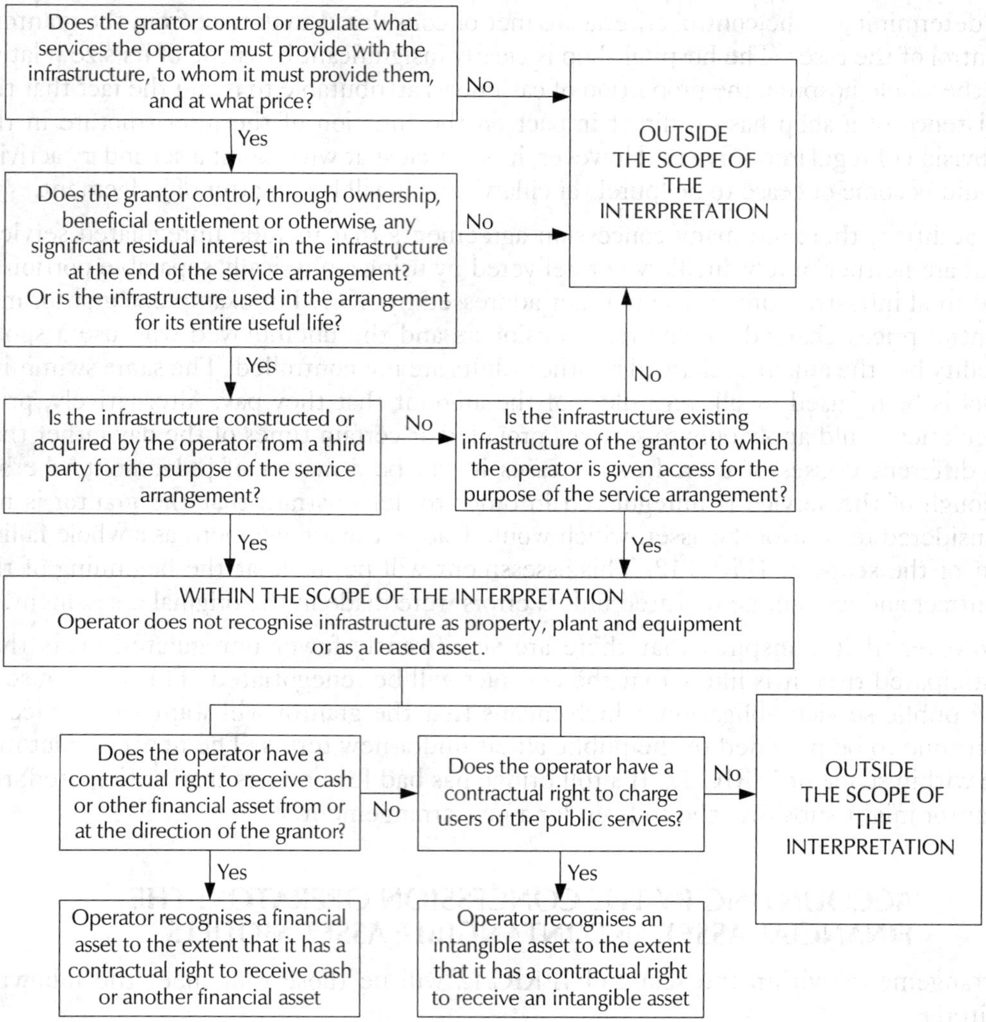

The two accounting models in IFRIC 12 apply several decisions of principle:

- the control model applies as described at 3 above, which means that the operator will not recognise infrastructure assets as its property, plant and equipment; *[IFRIC 12.11]* and
- the operator is providing 'construction services' and not, for example, constructing an item of property, plant and equipment for sale. Construction services are to be accounted for separately from 'operation services' in the operations phase of the contract. *[IFRIC 12.13, BC31]*.

There is a third important point of principle: the 'amounts due from customers' asset that arises from the application of the stage of completion method of revenue recognition required by IAS 11 or IFRS 15, as appropriate, (whose principles are used during the period of construction of the asset) is a financial asset as defined in IAS 32 (see 4.2 below).

4.1 Consideration for services provided and the choice between the two models

Most service concession agreements are for both construction (or upgrade) services and operations services. Operators almost always negotiate a single contract with the grantor and, although the Interpretation does not refer to this, this will usually include a single payment mechanism throughout the concession term, sometimes called a 'unitary payment'. The operator is unlikely to be remunerated separately for its different activities. The payment mechanism often falls into one or other of the following models:

Example 27.2: Payment mechanisms for service concessions

(a) a hospital where the payment is based on the availability of the whole hospital

The unitary payment is based on the full provision of an overall accommodation requirement which is divided into different units, such as hospital wards, consulting rooms, operating theatres, common parts and reception. Availability is defined in terms of being usable and accessible and, includes some associated core services such as heating, power and (in the case of operating theatres) appropriate cleanliness. There is a payment deduction for failure to provide an available unit according to a contractual scale. There are no separate payment streams for any of the non-core services but substandard performance can result in payment deductions.

$P = (F \times I) - (D + E)$
P = unitary payment per day
F = price per day for overall accommodation requirement
I = Indexation increase based on the retail prices index
D = deductions for unavailability
E = performance deductions

The payments for both schemes are not immediately separable between amounts attributable to the construction or other services.

b) a prison where payment is made based on the number of occupied places

The unitary payment is based on the number of occupied places. Occupied means not only that a prisoner is allocated a physical space but the associated core services and minimum requirements must be met in relation to services such as heating, mail delivery and food. No payment is made for unoccupied places. There are no separate payment streams for any of the non-core services (i.e. not associated with the definition of an occupied place) but deductions from the unitary payment can be made for substandard performance of these services.

The unitary payment is based on the following formula:

$P = (F \times I) - Z$
P = unitary payment per place
F = Fixed amount per occupied place per day
I = Indexation increase based on the retail prices index
Z = Performance deductions

IFRIC 12 clarifies the basis on which revenue is recognised in accordance with IAS 11 and IAS 18. It argues that if the operator provides separate services as part of its overall contractual arrangement it will allocate the consideration receivable by reference to their relative fair values. *[IFRIC 12.13]*. The exercise to separate the consideration receivable for the separate services (e.g. construction, upgrade or operating services) provided by the operator is expanded at 4.1.1 below. For entities applying IFRS 15,

Chapter 27

the recognition of revenue for separate services is determined in accordance with that Standard[13] (see Chapter 30). The nature of the consideration determines the accounting model, *[IFRIC 12.13]*, as described at 4.1.2 below.

Payments often start only when the infrastructure asset has been completed and accepted as suitable for purpose by the grantor. Operators usually seek payment during the construction phase but whether or not they receive any is inevitably a result of negotiation between the parties. Payments that are received are normally for services provided and not directly to meet construction costs; any amounts received will be allocated to the relevant service activity as described below.

4.1.1 Allocating the consideration

The Interpretation Committee argues that it is a requirement of IAS 18, to separate the construction services that will be accounted for under IAS 11 from the remainder of the contract. Thereafter the separate services within this contract, e.g. 'upgrade services' or 'operations services', may also be disaggregated on the basis of their 'distinct skills, requirements and risks'. *[IFRIC 12.BC31]*. IFRIC 12 argues that the operator might report different profit margins for its construction services within IAS 11 and the other services that are within IAS 18. The inference is that these different margins may also help allocate the total consideration. *[IFRIC 12.BC31]*. One must be very cautious here as IAS 11 does not permit an entity to determine what it considers to be an appropriate profit margin for the contract and use this as the basis of recognising revenue and attributable contract costs (unless, of course, it is a cost plus contract, see Chapter 23 at 3.3.1). The profit margin must be a consequence of the different fair values of the separate elements of the contract rather than driving the allocation of the consideration.

An operator may also be contractually required to make payments to the grantor. These may take the form of payments for the right of access to infrastructure or other assets, for the construction of assets or additional fees for the right to operate the concession. If the SCA falls within the financial asset model, the payments made may reduce the consideration received from the grantor. This is considered further at 4.7 below.

Although there is a single contract and a single payment mechanism, it is often straightforward in practice to identify the underlying cash flows that relate to different activities. This may be on the basis of the original contract negotiations or because the contract contains terms allowing for subsequent price adjustments by 'market testing' or benchmarking. However, the cash flows may not reflect the fair value of the underlying services so care will have to be taken. There will always be practical problems when it comes to apportioning the total contract consideration between the elements of the contract and the allocation will be a matter of judgement. For entities applying IFRS 15, the allocation of revenue for the provision of separate services is determined in accordance with that Standard[14] (see Chapter 30).

4.1.2 Determining the accounting model

IFRIC 12 states that the operator may receive a financial asset or an intangible asset as consideration for its construction services and the asset that it receives determines the subsequent treatment. *[IFRIC 12.15]*. The nature of the consideration given by the grantor to the operator shall be determined by reference to the contract terms and, when it exists, relevant contract law. *[IFRIC 12.19]*.

The Interpretations Committee decided that the boundary between the financial and the intangible asset models should be based on the operator's unconditional contractual right to receive cash from, or at the direction of, the grantor. *[IFRIC 12.16]*. The grantor does not need to pay the cash to the operator directly. Fees or tolls received from users are viewed as essentially no more than collections on behalf of the grantor if they are part of an overall arrangement under which the grantor bears ultimate responsibility. If the grantor pays but the amounts are wholly based on usage of the infrastructure and there is no minimum guaranteed payment, the entity has no unconditional contractual right to receive cash, as the amounts receivable are contingent on the extent to which the public uses the service. In this case the intangible asset model will apply.

The operator will recognise a financial asset to the extent that it has a contractual right to receive cash or other financial assets from the grantor for the construction services, where the grantor has little, if any, discretion to avoid payment. This is usually because the agreement is legally enforceable. *[IFRIC 12.16]*. The operator will recognise an intangible asset to the extent that it receives a licence to charge users of the public service. *[IFRIC 12.17]*.

Sometimes it is necessary to 'bifurcate' the operator's right to cash flows for construction services into a financial asset and an intangible asset and account separately for each component of the operator's consideration. This, the Interpretations Committee argues, is because the operator is paid for its services partly by a financial asset and partly by an intangible asset. *[IFRIC 12.18]*.

The analysis between the different models can be seen in the following table:

	Arrangement	*Applicable model*
1	Grantor pays – fixed payments	Financial asset
2	Grantor pays – payments vary with demand	Intangible asset
3	Grantor retains demand risk – users pay but grantor guarantees amounts	Financial asset or bifurcated (part financial, part intangible)
4	Grantor retains demand risk – operator collects revenues from users until it achieves specified return	Intangible asset
5	Users pay – no grantor guarantees	Intangible asset

Of the two arrangements in Example 27.2 above, the hospital is an example of (1) above: the payments are contractually fixed if all obligations and services are provided. The prison, as described in Example 27.2 above, would fall within (2) and be accounted for as an intangible asset. However, the prison operator might be paid on a different basis, e.g. it might be paid for 1,000 'available places' and receive this as long as heating and food were capable of being provided. In this case it would be no different to the hospital and be a financial asset. There are, of course, many potential variations and a combination of fixed and variable demand could lead to bifurcation.

Common examples of arrangements that fall within (3) above are transport concessions where the operator collects revenue from users but is entitled to an agreed return on capital invested in the infrastructure. The fees or tolls are considered to be collections on behalf of the grantor. There will be a financial asset to the extent of the guaranteed return. There may be an intangible asset as well if the operator retains a right to collect tolls in excess of the guaranteed amount.

However, arrangements of the type in (4) above remain to be treated as intangible assets even if the overall risk to the operator of not obtaining a specified result is very low. An arrangement that effectively caps revenue collected from users once an agreed level of return is reached, it is argued, is not a contractual right to cash but a right to collect revenues from users and it is not relevant that the risk is low or that the operator will, in effect, get a fixed return. *[IFRIC 12.BC52]*.

The following are examples of arrangements that will be accounted for using the intangible asset model:

(a) A municipality grants the operator a contract to treat all of its waste collections for which it will be paid per unit processed. The arrangement does not provide for any guaranteed volume of waste to be treated by the operator (so it does not contain a take-or-pay arrangement) or any form of guarantee by the grantor. Historically, however, the annual volume of waste has never been less than 40,000 tons and the average annual volume over the last 20 years has been 75,000 tons.

(b) An operator enters into a toll bridge concession. The operator is permitted to collect revenues from users or the grantor until it achieves a 6% return on its agreed infrastructure spend, at which point the arrangement comes to an end.

In commercial terms, the toll bridge concession may be virtually identical to a transaction that falls within (3) above, e.g. where the users pay tolls but the grantor guarantees a minimum 6% return. The crucial difference is the grantor's guarantee. The arrangement with the guarantee, which will contain a financial asset, is likely to leave more of the rewards of ownership with the operator than the intangible arrangement in (b) as the operator will be entitled to benefits in excess of the 6% return. This demonstrates that the distinction between the financial asset and intangible asset models is linked less to the transfer of commercial risk, but more by the existence (or not) of an unconditional contractual right to cash flows.

There are jurisdictions where public-to-private contract laws or the concession arrangements themselves allow an operator to ask the grantor for a revision of the tariffs for the public service when the operator's actual return is below initial expectations. Although this feature in the concession arrangement is included to reduce the operator's risk, it only gives the operator a right to re-negotiate and the outcome of that is not certain. As a result, the operator does not have an unconditional right to receive cash and, therefore, the existence of these features would not allow the operator to apply the financial asset model.

Many payment mechanisms include deductions for substandard performance of services. These do not affect the analysis of the contract as a financial asset or intangible asset and are discussed further below.

4.2 The financial asset model

Under the financial asset model, which applies if the entity has an unconditional contractual right to receive cash or another financial asset, *[IFRIC 12.16]*, the service element that relates to the construction of the infrastructure asset ('construction services') is accounted for in accordance with IAS 11 or IFRS 15, as appropriate. *[IFRIC 12.14]*. For the avoidance of doubt, an asset is not recognised for the discounted present value of *all* amounts payable by the grantor under the service concession arrangement. The entity recognises an asset for construction services performed up to the reporting date; subsequently it may recognise an asset on the same basis for upgrade services; the carrying value of the asset does not include future services yet to be performed or maintenance services that are accounted for as expenses. The consideration received by the operator for other services is addressed at 5 below.

The Interpretations Committee has argued that the 'amounts due from customers', i.e. those amounts recognised as revenue under IAS 11 from the point of initial recognition of the service concession, net of cash received, are deemed to be financial assets under IAS 32 because they represent contractual rights to receive cash or another financial asset from another entity. *[IAS 32.11]*. This analysis is not affected by the fact that this contractual right may be contingent on performance standards, as in the example of a unitary charge for a hospital in Example 27.2 above. The Interpretations Committee points out that this is no different from other circumstances and other financial assets where the payment depends on the subsequent performance of the asset. *[IFRIC 12.BC44]*.

Should the entity apply IFRS 9, the financial asset would be recognised at amortised cost, at fair value through other comprehensive income, or at fair value through profit or loss. *[IFRIC 12.24]*. This is discussed further at 5.4.3 below. Until it applies that standard, the financial asset will fall into one of the following three categories under IAS 39:

- a loan or receivable;
- an available-for-sale financial asset; or
- at fair value through profit or loss, if so designated on initial recognition.

In the first two cases, interest income will be recognised, calculated using the effective interest method. *[IFRIC 12.25]*.

The financial asset will not be classified as held-to-maturity. *[IFRIC 12.BC61]*.

It is argued that under IAS 39, amounts may only be classified as loans and receivables if the holder will receive 'substantially all of its initial investment, other than through credit deterioration'. *[IAS 39.9]*. In this regard, the potential for variation that exists in any service concession arrangement does not comprise an embedded derivative because it is specific to the parties in the contract. *[IFRIC 12.BC62]*. When the amount to be received by the operator could vary with the quality of services it provided or according to performance or efficiency targets, the arrangement does not contain an embedded derivative. These are non-financial measures and the remainder of the arrangement may still meet the definition of a loan and receivable. Non-compliance with this contractual requirement is a breach of contract and the resulting adjustment of future payments would be considered a penalty which causes forfeiture of some or the entire financial asset but it does not need to be considered part of the original financial asset.

This approach is consistent with general practice for accounting for receivables arising from the sale of goods and services with performance conditions under IASs 11 and 18. The Basis for Conclusions notes that the operator's position is the same as that of any other entity in which payment for goods or services is contingent on subsequent performance of the goods or service sold. *[IFRIC 12.BC44]*. Following this argument, the financial asset is recognised as consideration for delivering construction services and is no different from any other such receivable.

In practice many entities classify IFRIC 12 financial assets as loans and receivables.

Extract 27.2: VINCI SA (2014)

Notes to the consolidated financial statements [extract]

A. Accounting policies and measurement methods [extract]

3 Measurement rules and methods [extract]

3.5 Concession contracts [extract]

In return for its activities, the operator receives remuneration from [...]

- **The grantor: the financial asset model applies.** The operator has an unconditional contractual right to receive payments from the concession grantor, irrespective of the amount of use made of the infrastructure.

  Under this model, the operator recognises a financial asset, attracting interest, in its balance sheet, in consideration for the services it provides (design, construction, etc.). Such financial assets are recognised in the balance sheet under "Loans and receivables", in an amount corresponding to the fair value of the infrastructure on first recognition and subsequently at amortised cost. The receivable is settled by means of the grantor's payments received. The income calculated on the basis of the effective interest rate is recognised under operating income.

3.19 Other non-current financial assets [extract]

Loans and receivables at amortised cost [extract]

This category mainly comprises receivables connected with shareholdings, current account advances to companies accounted for under the equity method or unconsolidated entities, guarantee deposits, collateralised loans and receivables and other loans and financial receivables. It also includes the financial receivables relating to concession contracts and public-private partnerships whenever the concession operator has an unconditional right to receive remuneration (generally in the form of "scheduled payments") from the grantor.

When first recognised, these loans and receivables are recognised at their fair value less the directly attributable transaction costs. At each balance sheet date, these assets are measured at their amortised cost using the effective interest method.

If the contract is not classified as a loan and receivable it will most likely be classified as available-for-sale and be accounted for at fair value with changes in value taken to other comprehensive income. These definitions are further described in Chapter 46.

Whichever of these classifications apply, the financial asset will be measured on initial recognition at its fair value, and interest will be calculated on the balance using the effective interest rate method. *[IAS 39.43]*. Revenue will be recognised in accordance with IAS 11 when the contract work is performed using the percentage of completion method, *[IAS 11.26]*, or under IFRS 15, as appropriate. This means that the financial asset will be recognised from the beginning of contract activity.

How to measure this could represent a conundrum: it is necessary to recognise interest (using the effective interest rate method) on the financial asset simultaneously with recognising revenue using the percentage of completion method. Part of what would otherwise have been recognised as construction revenue is now finance income. The Illustrative Example 1 in IFRIC 12, on which Example 27.3 below is based, demonstrates how to avoid this problem by deeming the fair value of the consideration for construction services to be based on construction costs plus a margin. Potential issues with the use of a profit margin have previously been discussed at 4.1.1 above.

Borrowing costs cannot be capitalised under the financial asset model. *[IFRIC 12.22]*.

Example 27.3: The Financial Asset Model – recording the construction asset

Table 1 Concession terms

The terms of the arrangement require an operator to construct a road – completing construction within two years – and maintain and operate the road to a specified standard for eight years (i.e. years 3-10). The terms of the concession also require the operator to resurface the road at the end of year 8. At the end of year 10, the arrangement will end. The operator estimates that the costs it will incur to fulfil its obligations will be:

	Year	€
Construction services (per year)	1-2	500
Operation services (per year)	3-10	10
Road resurfacing	8	100

The terms of the concession require the grantor to pay the operator €200 per year in years 3-10 for making the road available to the public.

For the purpose of this illustration, it is assumed that all cash flows take place at the end of the year.

Table 2 Contract revenue

The operator recognises contract revenue and costs in accordance with IAS 11. The costs of each activity – construction, operation, maintenance and resurfacing – are recognised as expenses by reference to the stage of completion of that activity. Contract revenue – the fair value of the amount due from the grantor for the activity undertaken – is recognised at the same time.

The total consideration (€200 in each of years 3-8) reflects the fair values for each of the services, which are:

	Fair value		
Construction	**Forecast cost**	+	**5%**
Operation and maintenance	" "	+	**20%**
Road resurfacing	" "	+	**10%**
Lending rate to grantor	**6.18% per year**		

In year 1, for example, construction costs of €500, construction revenue of €525 (cost plus 5 per cent), and hence construction profit of €25 are recognised in the income statement.

Financial asset

The amount due from the grantor meets the definition of a receivable in IAS 39. The receivable is measured initially at fair value. It is subsequently measured at amortised cost, i.e. the amount initially recognised plus the cumulative interest on that amount calculated using the effective interest method minus repayments.

Table 3 Measurement of receivable

	€
Amount due for construction in year 1	525
Receivable at end of year 1*	525
Effective interest in year 2 on receivable at the end of year 1 (6.18% × €525)	32
Amount due for construction in year 2	525
Receivable at end of year 2	1,082
Effective interest in year 3 on receivable at the end of year 2 (6.18% × €1,082)	67
Amount due for operation in year 3 (€10 × (1 + 20%))	12
Cash receipts in year 3	(200)
Receivable at end of year 3	961

* No effective interest arises in year 1 because the cash flows are assumed to take place at the end of the year.

Chapter 27

4.3 The intangible asset model

If the financial asset model does not apply (i.e. there is no unconditional contractual right to cash or other financial assets), the operator's consideration for its construction services will be an intangible asset. *[IFRIC 12.15]*. As with the financial asset model, the operator cannot have an item of property, plant and equipment because the physical infrastructure is controlled by the grantor (see 3 above). *[IFRIC 12.11]*. Therefore, the Interpretations Committee has concluded that the right of an operator to charge users of the public service, for example the right to collect tolls from a road or a bridge, meets the definition of an intangible asset, that should be accounted for in accordance with IAS 38. It is, in effect, a licence 'bought' in exchange for construction services. *[IFRIC 12.17]*.

The Interpretations Committee has concluded that an intangible asset will be recorded during the construction phase as activity progresses, representing the operator's right to receive the licence. On this assumption, the entity will account for the construction of the infrastructure asset as follows:

(i) Revenue will be measured at the fair value of the intangible asset received. *[IFRIC 12.15]*.

(ii) It will record this contract revenue in accordance with IAS 11 as it provides 'construction services' by constructing the asset. *[IFRIC 12.14]*.

For entities applying IFRS 15, the references above to 'fair value' and IAS 11 are replaced with references to IFRS 15[15] (see Chapter 30).

The intangible asset under the concession (the licence received in return for construction services) meets the definition of a qualifying asset because it will not be ready for use until the infrastructure is constructed. Therefore borrowing costs must be capitalised during the period of construction. *[IFRIC 12.22]*. This contrasts with the treatment of borrowing costs under the financial asset model, where capitalisation is forbidden but financial income (the accretion of interest on the financial asset) is recognised.

Furthermore, it is argued that an inevitable consequence of applying the intangible asset model is that there must be an exchange transaction in which the operator receives the intangible right in exchange for its construction services. As this is an exchange of dissimilar assets, revenue must be recognised in accordance with IAS 18, which requires the recognition of revenue and a profit (or loss) based on the fair value of the assets received, unless the fair value of the assets given up can be measured more reliably. *[IFRIC 12.BC32-BC35]*. This means that the operator must establish the fair value of either the intangible asset it receives or the fair value of the construction services it has provided. The following example, based on Illustrative Example 2 in IFRIC 12, indicates how the Interpretations Committee expects this to apply in practice. The estimate of fair value is based on the cost of the construction services plus a margin – a similar methodology to that applied for the financial asset model above.

Example 27.4: The Intangible Asset Model – recording the construction asset

Arrangement terms

The terms of a service arrangement require an operator to construct a road – completing construction within two years – and maintain and operate the road to a specified standard for eight years (i.e. years 3-10). The terms of the arrangement also require the operator to resurface the road when the original surface has deteriorated below a specified condition. The operator estimates that it will have to undertake the resurfacing at the end of the year 8. At the end of year 10, the service arrangement will end. The operator estimates that the costs it will incur to fulfil its obligations will be:

Table 1 Contract costs

	Year	€
Construction services (per year)	1-2	500
Operation services (per year)	3-10	10
Road resurfacing	8	100

The terms of the arrangement allow the operator to collect tolls from drivers using the road. The operator forecasts that vehicle numbers will remain constant over the duration of the contract and that it will receive tolls of €200 in each of years 3-10.

For the purpose of this illustration, it is assumed that all cash flows take place at the end of the year.

Intangible asset

The operator provides construction services to the grantor in exchange for an intangible asset, i.e. a right to collect tolls from road users in years 3-10. In accordance with IAS 38, the operator recognises the intangible asset at cost, i.e. the fair value of consideration received or receivable.

During the construction phase of the arrangement the operator's asset (representing its accumulating right to be paid for providing construction services) is classified as an intangible asset (licence to charge users of the infrastructure). The operator estimates the fair value of its consideration received to be equal to the forecast construction costs plus 5 per cent margin. The operator also capitalises borrowing costs during the construction phase as required by IAS 23, at an estimated rate of 6.7 per cent:

Table 2 Initial measurement of intangible asset

	€
Construction services in year 1 (€500 × (1 + 5%))	525
Capitalisation of borrowing costs	34
Construction services in year 2 (€500 × (1 + 5%))	525
Intangible asset at end of year 2	1,084

The intangible asset is amortised over the period in which it is expected to be available for use by the operator, i.e. years 3-10. In this case, the directors determine that it is appropriate to amortise using a straight-line method. The annual amortisation charge is therefore €1,084 divided by 8 years, i.e. €135 per year.

Construction costs and revenue

The operator recognises the revenue and costs in accordance with IAS 11 i.e. by reference to the stage of completion of the construction. It measures contract revenue at the fair value of the consideration received or receivable. Thus in each of years 1 and 2 it recognises in its income statement construction costs of €500, construction revenue of €525 (cost plus 5 per cent) and, hence, construction profit of €25.

Toll revenue

The road users pay for the public services at the same time as they receive them, i.e. when they use the road. The operator therefore recognises toll revenue when it collects the tolls.

4.3.1 *Amortisation of the intangible asset*

The intangible asset will subsequently be accounted for in accordance with IAS 38, *[IFRIC 12.26]*, and the amount at which it is measured initially, i.e. after the exchange transaction, is its cost. *[IAS 38.45]*. It will be amortised on a systematic basis over its useful life, using a method that reflects 'the pattern in which the asset's future economic benefits are expected to be consumed by the entity'. *[IAS 38.97]*. This means that the methods permitted by IAS 38 are available (straight line, diminishing balance or unit-of-production). *[IAS 38.98]*. The requirements of IAS 38 are discussed in detail in Chapter 17. Interest methods of amortisation are forbidden. *[IFRIC 12.BC65]*.

The Interpretations Committee expressly considered unit-of-production methods to be appropriate in some circumstances; in March 2006, it was noted in the *IFRIC Update* that the Basis of Conclusions had been redrafted to avoid the impression that these methods were not allowed.[16] There were still concerns as a unit-of-production method could result in lower amortisation in the early years of the asset's operation so IAS 38 itself was amended to remove a statement discouraging methods that might have such a result.[17] This clarifies that there is no prohibition when the method is the most appropriate, whatever the resulting profile of amortisation.

Unit-of-production methods are typically considered in the context of toll roads and bridges. Obviously the method might apply if there is a right to charge a specified number of users. Questions still remained as to whether it might also be used if the basis was the estimated number of users, e.g. the number of vehicles that might use a particular road during the concession term.

The remaining issue regarding amortisation methods has been whether they could be based on revenue generated by the asset; this depends on the meaning of 'consumption of economic benefits' in the context of intangible assets with finite lives. In May 2014, the IASB issued amendments to IAS 38 to introduce a rebuttable presumption that a method of amortisation based on the revenue expected to be generated from an activity that includes the use of an intangible asset is not appropriate. This is because this method typically reflects factors that are not directly linked to the consumption of the economic benefits embodied in the asset. *[IAS 38.98A]*. See Chapter 17 at 9.2.1. Similar amendments have been made to IAS 16 except that there is no rebuttable presumption regarding depreciation based on revenue, *[IAS 16.62A]*, see Chapter 18 at 5.6.

Example 27.5 below demonstrates the potentially distorting effects for a SCA of basing amortisation on revenue.

The amendment applies for annual reporting periods beginning on or after 1 January 2016, with earlier application permitted. The amendment requires prospective application. *[IAS 38.130J]*.

However, the Board did acknowledge certain 'limited circumstances' that would give rise to an exception to this presumption. Revenue generated can be used to amortise an intangible asset when: *[IAS 38.98A]*

- the rights embodied in that intangible asset are expressed as a measure of revenue; or
- when it can be demonstrated that revenue and the consumption of economic benefits are 'highly correlated'.

The Board did not define what is meant by 'highly correlated', but it describes situations where the asset is 'expressed as a measure of revenue'. A 'highly correlated' outcome would only be achieved where a revenue-based method of amortisation is expected to give the same answer as one of the other methods permitted by IAS 38. For example, if revenue is earned evenly over the expected life of the asset, the pattern of amortisation would be similar to a straight-line basis. In situations where unit prices are fixed and all production is sold, the pattern of amortisation would replicate the use of the units-of-production method. However, when unit prices are not fixed, revenue would not provide the same answer and its use would therefore be inappropriate. The following example illustrates how a revenue-based method of amortisation diverges from the units-of-production method when the price per unit is not fixed.

Example 27.5: Output-based versus revenue-based amortisation when prices change

Entity Z enters into a twenty-five year SCA over a toll bridge. It recognises an intangible asset of £20 million and expects the bridge to be used at its full capacity of 500,000 vehicles per year. Tolls will commence at £10 per vehicle and, under the terms of the SCA, it is allowed to raise prices by 10% every five years. On this basis, the profile of amortisation on a units-of-production method (UoP) and on a revenue-based method would be as follows:

	Units	Charge UoP basis £	Revenue £	Charge Revenue basis £
Years 1-5	500,000	4,000,000	5,000,000	3,276,000
Years 6-10	500,000	4,000,000	5,500,000	3,604,000
Years 11-15	500,000	4,000,000	6,050,000	3,964,000
Years 16-20	500,000	4,000,000	6,655,000	4,360,000
Years 21-25	500,000	4,000,000	7,320,500	4,796,000
Total	2,500,000	20,000,000	30,525,500	20,000,000

Despite an expected constant level of consumption of the asset in the example above, the revenue-based method results in amortisation being delayed until the later periods of the asset's use. This distortion is caused by the increase in price rather than any factor related to the use of the intangible asset.

The Board permits revenue-based amortisation to be used when revenue is 'the predominant limiting factor that is inherent in the intangible asset'. *[IAS 38.98B]*. In other words, revenue determines the useful life of the asset, rather than, for example, a number of years or the number of units produced.

The IASB provided two examples of this circumstance in which revenue earned can be regarded as a measure of consumption of an intangible asset: *[IAS 38.98C]*

(a) a contract may allow the extraction of gold from a mine until total cumulative revenue from the sale of gold reaches $2 billion; or

(b) the right to operate a toll road could be based on a fixed total amount of revenue generated, based on cumulative tolls that have been charged.

An example of (b) is a SCA arrangement, described at 4.1.2 above, in which an operator enters into a toll bridge concession under which it is permitted to collect revenues from users or the grantor until it achieves a 6% return on its agreed infrastructure spend, at which point the arrangement comes to an end. As explained at 4.1.2, this will be accounted for as an intangible asset because the operator bears demand risk and may never achieve the revenue target. In this case the operator could calculate amortisation based on cumulative revenue as a percentage of total revenue.

The Amendment may require entities to change their current amortisation approach to an acceptable method, such as the diminishing balance method, which would recognise increased amortisation in the early part of the asset's useful life.

The choice of amortisation method is a matter of judgement. In the following extract from its accounting policies, GDF SUEZ indicates that it amortises its intangible assets on a straight line basis over the concession term to reflect the pattern of consumption.

Extract 27.3: GDF SUEZ SA (2014)

Notes to the consolidated financial statements [extract]

NOTE 1 Accounting standards and methods [extract]

1.4 Accounting methods [extract]

1.4.4 Intangible assets [extract]

1.4.4.2 Other intangible assets [extract]

Other internally-generated or acquired intangible assets

Other intangible assets include mainly:

- amounts paid or payable as consideration for rights relating to concession contracts or public service contracts;
- customer portfolios acquired on business combinations;
- capacity rights, in particular regarding power stations; the Group helped finance the construction of certain nuclear power stations operated by third parties and in consideration received the right to purchase a share of the production over the life of the assets. Said capacity rights are amortized over the useful life of the related assets, not exceeding 40 years;
- concession assets;
- the GDF Gaz de France brand and gas supply contracts acquired as part of the business combination with Gaz de France in 2008.

Intangible assets are amortized on the basis of the expected pattern of consumption of the estimated future economic benefits embodied in the asset. Amortization is calculated mainly on a straight-line basis over the following useful lives:

	Useful life	
Main amortization periods (years)	**Minimum**	**Maximum**
Concession rights	10	30
Customer portfolio	10	40
Other intangible assets	1	40

Some intangible assets (brand, etc.) with an indefinite useful life are not amortized but an impairment test has to be performed annually.

4.3.2 Impairment during the construction phase

The operator will recognise an intangible right during the construction phase of the arrangement, which is before the asset has been brought into use. There may be other circumstances in which the operator will continue to recognise an intangible asset prior to the service being provided to users. IAS 36 – *Impairment of Assets* – requires any intangible asset that has not yet been brought into use to be tested for impairment annually, irrespective of whether there are any indications of impairment. *[IAS 36.10]*. See Chapter 20 at 2.2.

4.4 Revenue recognition implications of the two models

There are major differences in the way in which revenue is measured under the two models. Under the financial asset model, total revenue over the concession term will be the same as the total cash inflows under the contract. By contrast, the fair value of the intangible asset is recognised as revenue under the intangible asset model, so total revenue measured using this model will be higher by this amount. The consequences of the two models can be demonstrated by the following simple example:

Example 27.6: Revenue under the financial asset and intangible models

An operator builds a road at a cost of 100. The construction profit is 10 and total cash inflows over the life of the concession are 200.

Under the financial asset model, the operator will recognise construction revenue of 110 and a receivable of 110. Of the future cash inflows of 200, 110 will be treated as repaying the receivable, with the remaining 90 being recognised as revenue over the life of the concession. Total revenue will be 200.

Under the intangible asset model, the operator will recognise construction revenue of 110, an intangible of 110, and a construction profit of 10. Over the life of the concession, the intangible asset of 110 would be amortised against revenues (which in this case would be from users) of 200. The net position is the same as in the financial asset case, but total revenues will be 310 rather than 200.

It is fair to say that this proved highly controversial. In fact, the September 2004 *IFRIC Update* stated that 'the majority of the Interpretations Committee strongly disliked this outcome'.[18] However, the Interpretations Committee maintained that this is the appropriate application of accounting standards to the arrangements and is consistent with the treatment generally accorded to barter transactions, *[IFRIC 12.BC35]*, although, of course, there are no other sectors where barter transactions are fundamental to the arrangement. The possible implications for many other transactions with governmental grantors where licences are granted have not been considered.

4.5 'Bifurcation' – single arrangements that contain both financial and intangible assets

The Interpretations Committee concluded that it may be necessary in certain circumstances to divide the operator's right to cash flows into a financial asset and an intangible asset. *[IFRIC 12.18]*. The *IFRIC Update* (March 2006) reported that 'With this change, the proposed amendment would better reflect the economic reality of concession arrangements: to the extent that the operator is remunerated for its construction services by obtaining a contractual right to receive cash from, or at the direction of, the grantor, the operator would recognise a financial asset and, to the extent that the operator receives only a licence to charge users, it would recognise an intangible asset.'

The Basis for Conclusions to IFRIC 12 explains more of the reasoning and potential impact. In some arrangements both parties to the contract share the risk (demand risk) that the cash flows generated by the project will not be sufficient to recover the operator's capital investment. A common mechanism for achieving this is where the grantor pays partly by a financial asset (i.e. the grantor will pay cash for the services provided) but gives the operator the right to charge for services (i.e. the operator has an intangible asset). The operator's infrastructure asset is to be split into a financial asset component for any guaranteed amount of cash and an intangible asset for the remainder. *[IFRIC 12.18, BC53]*.

These are common in transport concessions, e.g. a rail system paid for partly by grantor subsidy and partly by the payment of fares. This gives rise to difficult matters of judgement. It may not be clear how much of the arrangement is a financial asset and, therefore, where to draw the boundary between the two assets. There may be minor amounts within a contract that fall within another model and entities may conclude that these are *de minimis*.

4.6 Accounting for residual interests

Unless the infrastructure is used in a service concession arrangement for the whole of its useful life (within scope of IFRIC 12 – see 3.2 above), there will be a residual interest at the end of the contract that will be controlled by the grantor. The way in which the grantor controls the residual interest will affect the way in which the operator accounts for it. If the operator has an unconditional contractual right to cash (or another financial asset) for the residual interest in the infrastructure, this right will be a financial asset. It will be recognised as part of the consideration for the construction services. *[IFRIC 12.16]*. This is unaffected by the basis on which the consideration is calculated.

There are many different arrangements over residual interests in the infrastructure at the end of the concession term but broadly they depend on whether the grantor has a right or an option to acquire the residual interest and on the rights or options of the operator:

(a) The grantor may control the residual via an obligation to purchase the infrastructure from the operator but this could be at fair value, net book value, a notional amount or zero.

(b) It may only have an option to acquire the assets, on similar bases to (a), but it also has a right to put in place other arrangements, e.g. granting the operator a new term or selecting a new party to take on the assets. Payment might be made by the grantor or by the new operator but always at the direction of the grantor.

(c) The grantor has an option to acquire the assets but if this is not exercised then the operator may retain them.

The implications of grantor options and control of the residual interest have been discussed at 3.2 above.

If the terminal arrangements fall within (a) above the operator will have an unconditional contractual right to cash. It will recognise a financial asset, initially at fair value, which will then be accounted for according to the relevant classification under IAS 39 or IFRS 9, as appropriate (see 4.2 above). If the financial asset is classified as a loan and receivable or as available for sale then interest will be calculated using the effective interest rate method. At the end of the contract the residual interest will be stated at the operator's best estimate of the amount receivable.

Where the grantor has a right to put in place other arrangements, as in (b) above, the operator would only have an unconditional right to cash (i.e. a financial asset) after the grantor terminates the operator's involvement in the concession (by letting the contract lapse or by selecting a new party to take on the assets) if such termination will result in a payment to the operator. To the extent that the grantor can avoid any obligation to pay cash by allowing the concession term to continue, the operator has an intangible asset. The existence of such extension rights would have to be taken into account when determining the term of the concession arrangement.

If the arrangement is of the type described in (c), then the operator's residual interest is not a financial asset. Nor does it have a residual interest in the underlying property, plant and equipment because this is an arrangement within scope of IFRIC 12 and the entity cannot recognise the underlying assets, in whole or in part. *[IFRIC 12.11]*. The only option is to recognise an intangible right to receive cash or the residual interest in the assets. By contrast to the residual financial asset, it is most unlikely that the operator would be able to restate the value of this right over the term to its best estimate of the amount receivable at the end of the contract. IAS 38 only allows intangible assets to be revalued in very restricted circumstances; see Chapter 17 at 8.2.

The operator will have to account for its residual interests as described above based on the contractual rights, whatever model is being applied to its construction services. This is similar to the explicit requirements for upgrade services described at 5.1 below: IFRIC 12 recognises that upgrade services have to be recognised as construction revenue on the basis of their individual contract terms regardless of the model applied. *[IFRIC 12.14]*. The result is that an entity that has recognised an intangible asset for the major part of its construction services might have to recognise a financial asset for the residual interests – or *vice versa* if its construction services have been accounted for as a financial asset. This treatment is a variation of the bifurcation described at 4.5 above except that the financial asset relates only to the residual interest in the infrastructure rather than to a portion of the consideration receivable for the infrastructure as a whole. The residual rights will be taken into account in calculating the revenue receivable under the contract, which are described at 4.2 and 4.3 above.

As the termination arrangements can be complex, care will have to be taken to ensure that the effects are fully analysed.

Example 27.7: Contractual rights to cash in termination arrangements

The facts of the SCA are as in Example 27.1 above. At the end of the term, the grantor will either pay for the infrastructure assets at their net book value, determined on the basis of the contract, or it may decide to grant a new SCA on the basis of a competitive tender, which will exclude the current operator. If the grantor elects to do the latter, the operator will be entitled to the lower of the following two amounts:

(a) the net book value of the infrastructure, determined on the basis of the contract; and

(b) the proceeds of a new competitive bidding process to acquire a new contract.

Although the operator cannot enter the competitive tender, it also has the right to enter into a new concession term but in order to do so, it must match the best tender offer made. It has to pay to the grantor the excess of the best offer (b) above the amount in (a); should the tender offer be lower than (a), it will receive an equivalent refund.

In this arrangement, the operator has a contractual right to cash that should be recognised as a financial asset. It has a right to receive the lower of (a) and (b). It may *choose* to use its right to cash to settle part or all of the price of a new concession agreement but this does not affect the fact that it has a right to cash. This example also illustrates that calculating the fair value of the contractual right to cash may be complex as it has to take account of a number of different estimates, including the net book value of the infrastructure at the end of the contract, as well as the options available to the parties to the contract.

4.7 Accounting for contractual payments to be made by an operator to a grantor

Many arrangements require an entity to make payments to the grantor during the course of the SCA. These payments take two main forms:

(a) payments related to the use of tangible assets, including:
  - (i) payments to the grantor or third parties for making assets available (such as trains and buses) in order to provide the services required by the concession contract;
  - (ii) payments to a third party for the construction and making available of assets (such as rolling stock) that pass to the grantor at the end of the concession term; and
  - (iii) payments to the grantor for making available land on which the infrastructure assets are constructed or situated; or

(b) fees payable to the grantor for the right to operate the concession, which can be described as concession fees, development fees or access charges.

It is possible that some of these payments could be for the right to use assets controlled by the operator itself or the concession payment could relate to a distinct good or service that is separate from the concession arrangement. In July 2016, the Interpretations Committee observed:

(a) if payments made by an operator to a grantor are for a right to a good or service that is separate from the service concession arrangement, the operator should account for those payments by applying the applicable IFRS Standards; and

(b) if payments are for the right to use an asset that is separate from the infrastructure within the scope of IFRIC 12, the operator should assess whether the arrangement contains a lease. If the arrangement contains a lease, the operator should account for those payments by applying IAS 17, or IFRS 16 if that Standard has been applied.[19]

The Interpretations Committee observed that if payments made by an operator to a grantor are not for the right to a separate good or service or a right to use an asset that is a lease, the accounting for those payments should depend on whether the SCA falls within the financial asset model, the intangible asset model or is a hybrid. This means that the payments will be reflected in the carrying value of the appropriate concession asset:

- if the SCA is accounted for under the financial asset model, then the concession payment is an adjustment to the overall consideration receivable, illustrated at 4.7.2 below;
- if the intangible asset model applies, then the concession payment is part of the cost of acquiring the intangible asset recognised for the right to charge users of the service, illustrated at 4.7.3 below; and
- if the operator has both a right to charge users of the public service and a contractual right to receive cash from the grantor, then the entity should assess the extent to which the concession payment represents an adjustment to the overall consideration receivable or whether it is consideration for the intangible asset element.[20] This is determined by comparing the amount of the contractual right to receive cash from the grantor with the fair value of the operator's services.

The recommended treatment under the financial asset model is predicated on the fact that the operator has a contractual right to receive cash from the grantor and that payments between the parties are all part of this single relationship, however described. In this regard, payments to the grantor will include amounts paid to a related private sector entity to which responsibility for the service has been devolved. *[IFRIC 12.3]*.

Under the Interpretations Committee's approach for the intangible asset model, payments to the grantor that are not for a right to a good or service that is separate from the SCA, and are not an embedded lease, represent consideration for the concession, i.e. part of the cost of the intangible asset recognised. It is clearly a requirement of IAS 38 that an intangible asset be recognised when it meets the definition and other recognition criteria (see Chapter 17 at 2 and 3) and it must be recognised at its present value if payment is deferred. *[IAS 38.32]*.

Therefore, fixed fees payable over the life of a concession generate an intangible asset and give rise to a financial liability on inception, as the fixed fee will only be avoided by the operator if it withdraws from the concession, which in most circumstances is contractually and economically unfeasible.

4.7.1 Accounting for variable payments in a service concession

Some contracted payments, particularly concession fees, vary with a measure of usage of the concession asset or with another feature of the arrangement. Whilst the Interpretations Committee was able to reach a consensus on the treatment of concession fees that do not depend on future activity, as noted at 4.7 above, it has found the issue of variable payments more challenging.

In July 2013, the Committee tentatively agreed that, in cases where the variable payments do not depend on the purchaser's future activity, the fair value of those variable payments should be recognised as a liability and included as appropriate in the measurement of the related asset. The Committee was unable to reach a consensus on the treatment of payments that vary in relation to future activity and on the question of whether subsequent changes to the estimate of contingent consideration should be capitalised or expensed.[21] In March 2016, the Committee determined that the issue of variable payments for asset purchases is too broad for it to address within the confines of existing IFRS standards, and consequently decided not to add the issue to its agenda.[22] The Committee's deliberations on the treatment of variable payments for the separate acquisition of PP&E and intangible assets are also discussed in Chapter 17 at 4.5 and Chapter 18 at 4.1.9. At present, the usual treatment for an operator in a service concession is to treat contingent payments that vary in relation to future activity as executory and expense them as incurred.

4.7.2 Accounting for contractual payments under the financial asset model

If the financial asset model applies then the Interpretations Committee agreed that unless the contractual payments relate to the right to use assets controlled by the operator itself or relate to a distinct good or service that is distinct from the service concession arrangement, the contractual payment is accounted for as a reduction in the overall consideration received, i.e. it is an adjustment to the fair value of the consideration given by the grantor[23] (see 4.7 above). Another way of expressing this is that payments from the grantor reduce the financial asset while payments to the grantor increase that asset; both will also affect the amount of interest accrued on the outstanding balance. This applies whether the payment is for the right of access to an asset or described as a concession fee. This will not affect the revenue recognised under the contract which depends on the cost of providing the services. This is demonstrated in the following example.

Example 27.8: Contractual payments made to a grantor under the financial asset model

Entity A enters into a 10 year concession agreement requiring it to construct a school and be responsible for operations services (including maintenance, utilities, cleaning and catering). After a 2 year construction period, the entity will receive €300 per year during years 3-10, to operate the asset, after which the concession will cease. The entity must pay €30 per year for the use of the land on which the school is built.

The entity's estimated contract costs and contractual payments are as follows:

	Year	Annual charge €	Total €
Construction services	1-2	500	1,000
Operation services	3-10	100	800
Land use charge	1-10	30	300
Total cash paid	1-10		2,100

The operating cash flows under the contract are as follows:

Year	1 €	2 €	3 €	4 €	5 €	6 €	7 €	8 €	9 €	10 €
Concession consideration	–	–	300	300	300	300	300	300	300	300
Construction costs	(500)	(500)	(100)	(100)	(100)	(100)	(100)	(100)	(100)	(100)
Land use charge	(30)	(30)	(30)	(30)	(30)	(30)	(30)	(30)	(30)	(30)
Net cash flow	(530)	(530)	170	170	170	170	170	170	170	170

The entity estimates that the fair value of its services and total revenue from those services is as follows:

	Fair value			Total €
Construction	Forecast cost	+	5%	1,050
Operation and maintenance	" "	+	15%	920
Total revenue				1,970
Lending rate to grantor	5% per year			

Under the financial asset model, the land use charge is treated as an adjustment to the carrying value of the financial asset and is not treated as an expense. Accordingly, the gross concession profit is calculated as follows:

Year	1	2	3	4	5	6	7	8	9	10
	€	€	€	€	€	€	€	€	€	€
Concession revenue*	525	525	115	115	115	115	115	115	115	115
Construction costs	(500)	(500)	(100)	(100)	(100)	(100)	(100)	(100)	(100)	(100)
Finance income	13	25	23	20	16	13	10	7	3	–
Concession profit**	38	50	38	35	31	28	25	22	18	15

* Concession revenue comprises revenue from construction and operation and maintenance services
** Concession profit totals €300, which represents the total consideration received for services (€2,400) less the total costs including the land use charge of €2,100. In the income statement this is analysed as:

	€
Concession revenue	1,970
Construction costs	(1,800)
Finance income	130
Total	300

The financial asset is computed as follows, applying an effective interest rate of 5%.

Year	1	2	3	4	5	6	7	8	9	10
	€	€	€	€	€	€	€	€	€	€
Opening balance	0	568	1148	1016	881	742	600	455	307	155
Additions	525	525	115	115	115	115	115	115	115	115
Net cash	30	30	(270)	(270)	(270)	(270)	(270)	(270)	(270)	(270)
Finance income*	13	25	23	20	16	13	10	7	3	–
Closing balance	568	1,148	1,016	881	742	600	455	307	155	–

* Finance income is calculated on the average debtor balance outstanding.

In the above example, the land use charge is treated as an adjustment to the carrying value of the financial asset and is not treated as an expense. The effect of paying the land use charge is incorporated into the effective finance cost recognised in the income statement. This is why the total profit is €300, representing the total consideration received for services (€2,400) less the total costs including the land use charge of €2,100. If the land use charge were accounted for separately as an expense, this would not affect contract revenue, which is based on the fair value of the services provided. Instead, the additional cost of €300 would be offset by increasing the amount of finance income over the concession term from €130 to €430 (€130 + €300). It can be demonstrated that this would increase the effective interest rate on the finance debtor from 5% to 15% because only cash inflows from the grantor would be taken into account in the financial asset calculation and not the cash outflows relating to the land use charge. This is clearly an inappropriately high lending rate for this concession arrangement. Of course, in an actual concession agreement the effects of the treatment of such charges is likely to be much less marked but the principle remains the same.

4.7.3 Accounting for contractual payments under the intangible asset model

Under the intangible asset model, concession payments would be treated in accordance with IAS 38 as part of the consideration for the intangible asset.

While lease-type costs and land use charges can be part of any concession arrangement, concession fees (however called) are much more commonly a feature of arrangements which follow the intangible asset model. This is unsurprising as they are in substance payments made by the operator for the right to charge users of the concession infrastructure.

The Interpretations Committee have noted that unless the contractual payments relate to the right to use assets controlled by the operator itself or relate to a distinct good or service that is distinct from the service concession arrangement, the concession payment represents consideration for the concession right (i.e. part of the cost of the intangible asset recognised)[24] (see 4.7 above). However, the effects on reported revenues were not addressed directly. In the following illustration, the concession fee is regarded as a distinct cost in addition to the fair value of the construction services. Alternatively, the concession fee could be regarded as a cost of the IAS 11 construction contract, for example if the concession payments were for access to the land on which the infrastructure was to be constructed or for an asset used in the delivery of the construction services. In that case, the estimate of the fair value of the construction services would include an appropriate margin on top of the concession fee (see 4.3 above).

Example 27.9: Contractual payments made to a grantor under the intangible asset model

Entity B enters into a 10 year concession agreement to construct a toll road and be responsible for operations services. After a 2 year construction period, the entity expects to receive tolls of €300 per year, which it expects to remain at the same level for the duration of the concession. The entity must pay a concession fee of €50 per year in years 5-10.

The entity concludes that the obligation for the concession fee is incurred in year 1 and estimates that its present value is €209. The contract costs and contractual payments are as follows:

	Year	Annual charge €	Total €
Construction services	1-2	500	1,000
Operation services	3-10	100	800
Concession fee	5-10	50	300
Total cash paid	1-10		2,100

The entity assesses the fair value of its intangible asset to be the cost of construction services plus a margin of 5%. To this it adds an amount to reflect the present value of the obligation to pay the concession fee. This means that it will record construction revenue and additions to its intangible asset in years 1 and 2 as follows.

Year	1 €	2 €
Construction services	500	500
Revenue (uplift costs by 5%)	525	525
Concession fee (present value of obligation)	209	–
Intangible asset additions	734	525

This means that the entity recognises concession revenue for construction services totalling €1,050 (525+525) and an intangible asset of €1,259 (734+525). It concludes that, as usage is expected to be the same throughout the term, the intangible asset should be amortised in equal annual instalments commencing in year 3. The concession gross profit (revenue – contract costs – unwinding discount on the concession fee – amortisation of the intangible asset) is calculated as follows:

Year	**1**	**2**	**3**	**4**	**5**	**6**	**7**	**8**	**9**	**10**
	€	**€**	**€**	**€**	**€**	**€**	**€**	**€**	**€**	**€**
Concession revenue	525	525	300	300	300	300	300	300	300	300
Construction costs	(500)	(500)	(100)	(100)	(100)	(100)	(100)	(100)	(100)	(100)
Unwinding discount	(10)	(11)	(12)	(12)	(12)	(11)	(9)	(7)	(5)	(2)
Amortisation*	–	–	(157)	(157)	(158)	(158)	(158)	(157)	(157)	(157)
Concession profit**	15	14	31	31	30	31	33	36	38	41

* The amortisation is adjusted for rounding

** Concession profit totals €300, which represents the total consideration received from users for services (€2,400) less the total costs including the concession fee of €2,100. In the income statement this is analysed as:

	€
Concession revenue (525+525+2,400)	3,450
Contract costs	(1,800)
Unwinding discount	(91)
Amortisation	(1,259)
Total	300

5 REVENUE AND EXPENDITURE DURING THE OPERATIONS PHASE OF THE CONCESSION AGREEMENT

So far, we have described the recognition and measurement of the infrastructure asset in the accounts of the operator under the two models. A significant issue in practice is that service concession arrangements are composite transactions. They usually have a long duration (twenty-five to thirty years is not uncommon) during which time the operator has a variety of obligations. These may be in connection with the infrastructure asset itself and include:

- enhancement of the infrastructure or construction of new infrastructure;
- infrastructure components that must be replaced in their entirety;
- infrastructure subject to major cyclical repairs; and
- regular repairs and maintenance.

In addition, many service concession arrangements involve the provision of services. In the case of a hospital, for example, this could include utilities (such as water and electricity) and a wide range of 'soft' services such as cleaning, laundry, meals, portering, security and grounds maintenance, amongst others. All of these might be paid for as a single unitary charge that would probably be adjusted according to performance as in Example 27.2 above. The accounting models for service concessions must be able to deal with all of these issues.

5.1 Additional construction and upgrade services

The concession may include obligations to construct new infrastructure (construction services) or to enhance either new or existing infrastructure to a condition better than at the start of the concession (upgrade services). IFRIC 12 does not deal in detail with the treatment to be adopted other than to say that revenue and costs relating to construction or upgrade services are recognised in accordance with IAS 11 or IFRS 15, as appropriate. *[IFRIC 12.14]*. This means that all construction or upgrade services are accounted for in accordance with the appropriate model, regardless of when they take place. Contractual obligations to maintain or restore infrastructure may also include an upgrade element. *[IFRIC 12.21]*.

Upgrade or construction services are separate revenue-generating activities. This means that the contract has to require the particular service to be carried out at a specified time. This is not the same as a general requirement to maintain the asset in a specified condition.

It would be unusual for a toll road concession, for example, to require resurfacing to take place according to a predetermined schedule as road surfaces degrade with usage (based on both the number of vehicles and weight per axle) as well as weather conditions. However, the contract might require a new bridge or access road after a specified period of time and either of these could be separate upgrade services.

Upgrade services must be recognised in accordance with IAS 11, using the percentage of completion method and recognising revenue during the construction period, as described at 4.2 and 4.3 above and in Chapter 23 at 3.3.2. Accounting for construction contracts under IFRS 15 is discussed in Chapter 30.

If the financial asset model applies to the upgrade, the entity has to determine the fair value of consideration received for the upgrade services. This may be part of the allocation at inception of the contract, as shown in Example 27.3 above where part of the contract revenue is attributed to road resurfacing, or the contract may specify a separate payment when the upgrade is performed. In the latter case the entity would account for the upgrade service as a separate financial asset once it started to provide the services (e.g. started to build the bridge) which means recognising revenue during construction. If the infrastructure is being accounted for as a financial asset, the entity cannot simply add upgrade-related maintenance costs as incurred to the carrying value of an existing financial asset.

Similar issues for intangible assets are discussed in further detail below. Are the construction services part of the original asset or should they be accounted for as a new asset? If it is a new asset, when should it be recognised?

5.1.1 *Subsequent construction services that are part of the initial infrastructure asset*

In some circumstances, the 'enhancement' spend is a component of the original intangible asset and should be recognised as part of the exchange transaction to secure the right to charge users described at 4.3 above. An example of this is the common requirement in concession contracts that the operator replace certain items at the operator's cost, whether or not the items concerned have become unserviceable. For example, a water supply operator may be contractually required to replace all lead pipes for environmental and health reasons; similarly, a gas supply operator may be required to replace all cast-iron pipes for safety reasons.

Assuming that the intangible asset model is the relevant one, the first issue is whether these expenditures should be regarded as operating costs (obligations to maintain or to restore the infrastructure) and treated as described at 5.2 below or as an additional cost of the intangible asset. They do not directly increase the future economic benefits of any particular infrastructure asset when the costs are incurred and might therefore be treated as the cost of maintaining the original benefits and expensed. However, unlike most subsequent expenditure on intangible assets, which is not recognised as an asset because it cannot be distinguished from expenditure to develop the business as a whole, *[IAS 38.20]*, it is possible in the case of SCAs to attribute the expenditure directly to the cost of securing a particular intangible asset (the right to operate the concession). The requirement of the operator to incur subsequent expenditure for building, upgrading or maintaining a physical infrastructure asset is embodied in the contract entered into to secure that intangible right. IAS 16 explicitly allows such expenditure to be capitalised as part of an item of property, plant and equipment, *[IAS 16.10]*, so it would seem that capitalisation is an appropriate treatment.

These features indicate that these expenditures should be included in the measure of the consideration given for the intangible asset and therefore recognised as part of its carrying value on initial recognition. This would require the recognition of a liability for the present value of the best estimate of the amount required to replace the underlying asset, such as the pipes. Note that the revenue earned in the construction phase is based on the fair value of the building or upgrade work performed on initial recognition, in accordance with IAS 11 or IFRS 15, as appropriate. In other words, the fair value of the 'construction services' may remain unchanged although the entity has accrued additional costs in relation to the other obligations it has assumed in return for securing the right to operate the infrastructure asset and to earn related revenues.

The Interpretations Committee did not address the accounting treatment of subsequent variations in the amount of the liability for the operator's unfulfilled obligations that is recognised as part of the cost of the intangible asset (the licence) e.g. when the estimated amount of the expenditures to be incurred is revised. The situation may be regarded as analogous to the situation addressed by IFRIC Interpretation 1 – *Changes in Existing Decommissioning, Restoration and Similar Liabilities* – where the obligation is recognised as a liability in accordance with IAS 37 and as part of the cost of an asset. *[IFRIC 1.1]*. Therefore, the principles set out in IFRIC 1 should be applied, i.e. a change in the measurement of the liability should be added to, or deducted from the cost of the intangible asset, subject to impairment testing and to the extent that the amount deducted from the cost of the asset does not exceed the carrying amount of the intangible asset. *[IFRIC 1.5]*. The periodic unwinding of the discount must be recognised in income. *[IFRIC 1.8]*. IFRIC 1 is discussed in Chapter 28 at 6.3.1.

5.1.2 Subsequent construction services that comprise a new infrastructure asset

An operator may be contractually entitled to add to or upgrade the infrastructure and from this generate additional revenues. The operator may have a right to extend a distribution network and, under its right to charge for the services, it will obtain revenues from newly connected users. There is an example of such a right in Extract 27.4 below, in which Telenor ASA discloses that it has a right 'to arrange, expand, operate and provide the cellular telephone services in various areas in Thailand'.

Extract 27.4: Telenor ASA (2014)

Notes to the Consolidated Financial Statements / Telenor Group [extract]

/17/ Intangible assets [extract]

dtac operates under a concession right to operate and deliver mobile services in Thailand granted by CAT Telecom Public Company Limited (CAT). CAT allows dtac to arrange, expand, operate and provide the cellular telephone services in various areas in Thailand. The concession originally covered a 15-year period but the agreement was amended on 23 July 1993 and 22 November 1996 with the concession period being extended to 22 and 27 years, respectively. Accordingly, the concession period under the amended agreement expires in 2018.

Revenues generated by the new infrastructure will be determined under the terms of the *original* licence granted to the operator. However, in this case there is no pre-existing obligation to incur the cost of the extension work, meaning that it will only be recognised when the expenditure is made. Accordingly, that new cost is not an additional component of the cost of the original intangible asset but will be a new intangible asset in its own right, giving rise to new construction revenues and recognised using the same principles as the original as described at 4.3 above.

5.2 Accounting for the operations phase

Both the financial and intangible asset models apply the same accounting in the operations phase of the SCA. According to the September 2006 *IFRIC Update*, 'the nature of the asset recognised by the operator as consideration for providing construction services (a financial asset or an intangible asset) does not determine the accounting for the operation phase of the arrangement'.[25]

Revenue and costs for the operation services will be recognised in accordance with IAS 18 or IFRS 15, as appropriate. *[IFRIC 12.20]*. This means that most operating and maintenance costs are likely to be executory and will be accounted for as incurred. Contractual obligations, including obligations to maintain, replace or restore infrastructure, are to be recognised and measured in accordance with IAS 37, i.e. once there is a present obligation as a result of a past event, and measured at the best estimate of the expenditure required to settle the present obligation at the reporting date, as shown in Example 27.10 below. These include obligations to restore infrastructure to a specified condition before it is returned to the grantor at the end of the concession. *[IFRIC 12.21]*. These do not include any upgrade element which is treated as an additional construction service (see 5.1 above).

Distinguishing between executory maintenance expenditure and contractual obligations is not always straightforward. A concession arrangement may provide for a specified total amount of expenditure to be incurred by the operator throughout the contract. Sometimes, the contract provides for mechanisms whereby at the end of the contract, any shortfall in the agreed amount is paid in cash to the grantor by the operator. Particularly in the case of older contracts, it is common for the maintenance and repair obligation to be expressed in very general terms such as keeping the infrastructure in 'good working condition' or 'state of the art' working condition. The obligation may include the requirement that the asset be handed over with a certain number of years' useful life remaining.

Local regulations or laws also change over time. Some operators are obliged to report annually to the grantor on the level of maintenance and renewal expenditure incurred during the year and on a cumulative basis from inception of the contract. Sometimes, the operator must report on expected expenditures over some future period of time (e.g. over the next 12 months or two years) as well. In these situations, more often than not the grantor compares the cumulative expenditure at any point in time with either the operator's prior estimates of expenditures or with the level of expenditure that had been anticipated at the outset of the arrangement and was factored into the level of usage charges. In such circumstances, judgement is required in deciding whether expenditure on renewals is an obligation requiring recognition or an executory contract.

Example 27.10: Executory and contractual obligations to maintain and restore the infrastructure

The operator under a water supply service concession is required as part of the overall contractual arrangement to replace four water pumps as soon as their performance drops below certain quality levels. The operator expects this to be the case after 15 years of service. The expected cost of replacing the pumps is CU 1,000. The operator's best estimate is that the service potential of the pumps is consumed evenly over time and provision for the costs is made on this basis from inception of the service concession arrangement until the date of expected replacement. The provision is measured at the net present value of the amounts expected to be paid, using the operator's discount rate of 5%. The amount provided in the first year can be calculated as CU 33.67. Assuming no changes to estimates, in 15 years CU 1,000 would have been provided and would be utilised in replacing the pumps. The provision would be adjusted on a cumulative basis to take account of changes in estimates to the cost of replacement pumps, the manner in which they are wearing out or changes to the operator's discount rate.

The Interpretations Committee has also provided an example in Illustrative Example 2, the intangible asset model, of how operational expenditure might be accounted for in accordance with IAS 37. Although this illustration is in the context of an intangible asset, IAS 37 can apply to maintenance and other obligations whatever model applies. Major maintenance, in this case the requirement to resurface the road, will be recognised as the best estimate of the expenditure required to settle the present obligation at the reporting date and it is suggested that this might 'arise as a consequence of use of the road', therefore increasing in measurable annual increments. *[IFRIC 12.IE19]*. The basis for accounting for such obligations is discussed further in Chapter 28.

Example 27.11: The Intangible Asset Model – recording the operations phase

The terms of the arrangement are the same as in Example 27.4 above. The contract costs and initial measurement of the intangible asset are set out in Table 1 and Table 2 in that example.

Resurfacing obligations

The operator's resurfacing obligation arises as a consequence of use of the road during the operating phase. It is recognised and measured in accordance with IAS 37, i.e. at the best estimate of the expenditure required to settle the present obligation at the reporting date.

For the purpose of this illustration, it is assumed that the terms of the operator's contractual obligation are such that the best estimate of the expenditure required to settle the obligation at any date is proportional to the number of vehicles that have used the road by that date and increases by €17 (discounted to a current value) each year. The operator discounts the provision to its present value in accordance with IAS 37. The income statement charge each period is:

Table 3 Resurfacing obligation

Year	3	4	5	6	7	8	Total
	€	€	€	€	€	€	€
Obligation arising in year (€17 discounted at 6%)	12	13	14	15	16	17	87
Increase in earlier years' provision arising from passage of time	–	1	1	2	4	5	13
Total expense recognised in income statement	12	14	15	17	20	22	100

Overview of cash flows, income statement and statement of financial position

For the purpose of this illustration, it is assumed that the operator finances the arrangement wholly with debt and retained profits. It pays interest at 6.7% a year on outstanding debt. If the cash flows and fair values remain the same as those forecast, the operator's cash flows, income statement and statement of financial position over the duration of the arrangement will be:

Table 4 Cash flows

Year	1	2	3	4	5	6	7	8	9	10	Total
	€	€	€	€	€	€	€	€	€	€	€
Receipts	–	–	200	200	200	200	200	200	200	200	1,600
Contract costs	(500)	(500)	(10)	(10)	(10)	(10)	(10)	(110)	(10)	(10)	(1,180)
Borrowing costs†	–	(34)	(69)	(61)	(53)	(43)	(33)	(23)	(19)	(7)	(342)
Net inflow/ (outflow)	(500)	(534)	121	129	137	147	157	67	171	183	78

† Debt at start of year (table 6) × 6.7%

Table 5 Income statement

Year	**1**	**2**	**3**	**4**	**5**	**6**	**7**	**8**	**9**	**10**	**Total**
	€	**€**	**€**	**€**	**€**	**€**	**€**	**€**	**€**	**€**	**€**
Revenue	525	525	200	200	200	200	200	200	200	200	2,650
Amortisation	–	–	(135)	(135)	(136)	(136)	(136)	(136)	(135)	(135)	(1,084)
Resurfacing expense	–	–	(12)	(14)	(15)	(17)	(20)	(22)	–	–	(100)
Other operating costs†	(500)	(500)	(10)	(10)	(10)	(10)	(10)	(10)	(10)	(10)	(1,080)
Borrowing costs* (table 4)	–	–	(69)	(61)	(53)	(43)	(33)	(23)	(19)	(7)	(308)
Net profits	25	25	(26)	(20)	(14)	(6)	1	9	36	48	78

* Borrowing costs are capitalised during the construction phase

† Table 1

Table 6 Statement of financial position

End of Year	**1**	**2**	**3**	**4**	**5**	**6**	**7**	**8**	**9**	**10**
	€	**€**	**€**	**€**	**€**	**€**	**€**	**€**	**€**	**€**
Intangible asset	525	1,084	949	814	678	542	406	270	135	–
Cash/ (debt)*	(500)	(1,034)	(913)	(784)	(647)	(500)	(343)	(276)	(105)	78
Resurfacing obligation	–	–	(12)	(26)	(41)	(58)	(78)	–	–	–
Net assets	25	50	24	4	(10)	(16)	(15)	(6)	30	78

* Debt at start of year plus net cash flow in year (table 4)

To make this illustration as clear as possible, it has been assumed that the arrangement period is only ten years and that the operator's annual receipts are constant over the period. In practice, arrangement periods may be much longer and annual revenue may increase with time. In such circumstances, the changes in net profit from year to year could be greater.

5.3 Items provided to the operator by the grantor

Following the basic principles underlying the accounting treatment under both models, infrastructure items to which the operator is given access by the grantor for the purpose of the service concession are not recognised as its property, plant and equipment. *[IFRIC 12.27]*. This is because they remain under the control of the grantor.

There is a different treatment for assets that are given to the operator as part of the consideration for the concession that can be kept or dealt with as the operator wishes. These assets are not to be treated as government grants as defined in IAS 20. Instead, an operator applying IAS 18 and IAS 11 is required to recognise the assets, initially measured at fair value, together with a liability in respect of any unfulfilled obligations assumed in exchange for the assets. *[IFRIC 12.27]*. An entity that has adopted IFRS 15 should account for these assets as part of the transaction price and in accordance with that Standard[26] (see Chapter 30).

Chapter 27

What this means is that an operator that has been given a licence or similar arrangement over a piece of land on which a hospital is to be built does not recognise the land as an asset. If, on the other hand, the operator has been given a piece of surplus land on which it can build private housing for sale, it will recognise an asset. The consideration, which is the fair value of that land, will be aggregated with the remainder of the consideration for the transaction and accounted for according to the model being used.

5.4 Additional considerations for entities applying IFRS 15

IFRS 15 applies for annual reporting periods beginning on or after 1 January 2018, with early application permitted. *[IFRS 15.C1]*.

As discussed at 4.1.1 above, IFRIC 12 currently requires an operator to separate the revenue and costs relating to construction or upgrade services, to which IAS 11 applies, *[IFRIC 12.14]*, from the operation services under the remainder of the contract, which is accounted for under IAS 18. *[IFRIC 12.20]*. When IFRS 15 is applied, consequential amendments to IFRIC 12 refer to IFRS 15 in relation to both the accounting for construction and upgrade services and to the way the operator should account for operation services.[27]

However, IFRS 15 does not distinguish between a construction contract and any other contract for the provision of goods and services to a customer, in the way that IAS 11 and IAS 18 clearly did. Accordingly, entities applying IFRS 15 will have to refer to the general requirements of that standard in accounting for revenues under a service concession arrangement.

As discussed in Chapter 30 at 1.1, the principles in IFRS 15 will be applied using the following five steps:

1. Identify the contract(s) with a customer.
2. Identify the performance obligations in the contract.
3. Determine the transaction price.
4. Allocate the transaction price to the performance obligations in the contract.
5. Recognise revenue when (or as) the entity satisfies a performance obligation.

An entity will need to exercise judgement when considering the terms of the contract(s) and all of the facts and circumstances, including implied contract terms. At the time of writing, the following initial issues have been identified.

5.4.1 Determining the separate performance obligations to account for

IFRIC 12 distinguishes the principal performance obligations in a service concession arrangement between construction and upgrade services and operating services (where the operator operates and maintains the infrastructure used to provide a public service). *[IFRIC 12.12]*.

At contract inception, an entity applying IFRS 15 is required to assess the goods or services promised in a contract to identify performance obligations. A performance obligation is either: *[IFRS 15.22]*

(a) a good or service (or a bundle of goods or services) that is distinct; or

(b) a series of distinct goods or services that are substantially the same and that have the same pattern of transfer to the customer.

Under IFRS 15, a good or service is distinct if both of the following criteria are met: *[IFRS 15.27]*

(a) the customer can benefit from the good or service either on its own or together with other resources that are readily available to the customer (i.e. the good or service is capable of being distinct); and

(b) the entity's promise to transfer the good or service to the customer is separately identifiable from other promises in the contract (i.e. the good or service is distinct within the context of the contract).

The process for identifying distinct performance obligations is discussed in Chapter 30 at 4. In the context of a service concession arrangement, it may be determined under IFRS 15 that there are more elements to the contract than simply the delivery of construction services, upgrade services and operation services. The identification of more (and distinct) performance obligations may change the timing of revenue recognition under IFRS 15 because, as noted above, revenue is recognised as each performance obligation is satisfied.

An interesting question relates to the status of the contractual obligation of an operator to maintain the infrastructure. As discussed at 5.2 above, maintenance of the infrastructure is regarded more as a cost of operating the concession rather than as a performance obligation that would give rise to revenue. Indeed, the requirement in IFRIC 12 to recognise and measure contractual obligations to maintain or restore infrastructure in accordance with IAS 37, *[IFRIC 12.21]*, is unchanged on applying IFRS 15. This paragraph suggests that only any upgrade element would give rise to revenue. *[IFRIC 12.21]*. However, IFRS 15 includes in a list of possible goods and services 'performing a contractually agreed-upon task (or tasks) for a customer.' *[IFRS 15.26(d)]*. This could reasonably be interpreted to include maintenance services. Nevertheless, even if regarded as a separate performance obligation, it may still not give rise to a change in the revenue recognised under IFRS 15, on the basis that it is not distinct. This is discussed further in Chapter 30 at 4.2.

5.4.2 Recognising construction revenue over time or at a point in time

Under IFRS 15, an entity only recognises revenue when it satisfies an identified performance obligation by transferring a promised good or service to a customer. A good or service is generally considered to be transferred when the customer obtains control. *[IFRS 15.31]*. The standard indicates that an entity must determine, at contract inception, whether it will transfer control of a promised good or service over time. If an entity does not satisfy a performance obligation over time, the performance obligation is satisfied at a point in time. *[IFRS 15.32]*. These concepts are explored further in Chapter 30 at 7.

In a service concession arrangement, this evaluation is relevant to the determination of whether revenues from construction or upgrade services continue to be recognised, as they were under IAS 11, on a percentage of completion basis, or at the point of completing the construction element. As discussed in Chapter 30 at 7.1, one criterion for recognising revenue over time is that an entity's performance creates or enhances an asset that the customer controls. *[IFRS 15.35]*.

It would appear reasonable in the context of a service arrangement under IFRIC 12, where the grantor controls the asset, including any significant residual interest therein, *[IFRIC 12.5]*, that this criterion will be met.

As discussed further in Chapter 30, entities are seeking to address these and other implementation issues in the period leading up to first time application of IFRS 15 in 2018.

5.4.3 Additional considerations for entities applying IFRS 9 and IFRS 15

IFRIC 12 currently states that an operator may receive a financial asset or an intangible asset as consideration for its construction services. *[IFRIC 12.15]*. If the operator receives a financial asset, the financial asset is recognised from the beginning of contract activity, *[IFRIC 12.IE7]*, as discussed in 4.2 above, and measured in accordance IAS 39, or IFRS 9 if that Standard has been applied.

IFRS 15 amends IFRIC 12 to change the date of initial recognition of the financial asset. The amendment requires a contract asset to be recognised during the construction activity and requires the significant financing component in the arrangement to be accounted for in accordance with IFRS 15 until construction or upgrade is complete. Under IFRS 15 a significant financing component would be recorded if the consideration was paid more than a year after construction is complete, with is typically the case in service concession agreements. Only once construction is complete are the amounts due from the grantor accounted for in accordance with IFRS 9.[28] On initial recognition, IFRS 9 requires a financial asset to be measured at its fair value (plus or minus transaction costs). *[IFRS 9.5.1.1, 3]*. As a result, the financial asset would initially be recognised at fair value, once construction is complete. The fair value of the financial asset is impacted by changes in market interest rates. Where construction or upgrade activity takes a significant time (as is common in many infrastructure projects), it is possible that market interest rates will have moved over the construction phase of the arrangement, such that there is a difference between the initial measurement of the financial asset in accordance with IFRS 9 and the amount of construction revenue and accrued interest recognised as a contract asset in accordance with IFRS 15 during the construction period. In addition, whilst fair value under IFRS 9 is based on market interest rates, accrued interest recognised as part of the contract asset under IFRS 15 is determined using the rate 'that would be reflected in a separate financing transaction between the entity and its customer at contract inception', *[IFRS 15.64]*, i.e. a rate specific to the contract. This may also lead to differences between the amount recognised as a contract asset under IFRS 15 and the initial measurement of the financial asset under IFRS 9. IFRS 15 requires any difference between the initial measurement of the financial asset in accordance with IFRS 9 and the corresponding amount of revenue recognised under IFRS 15 to be presented as an expense. *[IFRS 15.108]*.

6 DISCLOSURE REQUIREMENTS: SIC-29

IFRIC 12 has no specific disclosure requirements although the disclosure requirements of the various applicable standards (such as IFRS 7 – *Financial Instruments: Disclosures* *[IFRIC 12.23]* – and IAS 38) will have to be made as appropriate. SIC-29, which pre-dates IFRIC 12 by several years, includes additional disclosure requirements. *[IFRIC 12.10]*. It is important to note that the scope of SIC-29 is not defined in terms of IFRIC 12 and is potentially broader in scope than IFRIC 12. It applies to a type of transaction that is described although not really defined and which does not depend on the control criteria described at 3 above. It also applies to both sides of the transaction, whereas IFRIC 12 applies only to the operator under the concession agreement.

SIC-29 describes service concessions as arrangements in which an entity (the operator) provides services on behalf of another entity (the grantor, which may be a public or private sector entity, including a governmental body) that give the public access to major economic and social facilities. The examples of service concession arrangements given by SIC-29 include water treatment and supply facilities, motorways, car parks, tunnels, bridges, airports and telecommunication networks. *[SIC-29.1]*.

SIC-29 states that the common characteristic of all service concession arrangements is that the operator both receives a right and incurs an obligation to provide public services. *[SIC-29.3]*. It excludes from its scope an entity outsourcing the operation of its internal services (e.g. employee cafeteria, building maintenance, and accounting or information technology functions). *[SIC-29.1]*. This means that some of the arrangements that do not include the construction of a major capital asset, as discussed above, may not be caught by the requirements of the SIC, although there is no hard-and-fast dividing line between service concessions and outsourcing arrangements. For example, a contract between a government department and an operator to maintain the existing computer system, including replacement of hardware and software as appropriate, may be outside the scope of SIC-29.

SIC-29 summarises the rights and obligations as follows:

For the period of the concession, the operator has received from the grantor:

(a) the right to provide services that give the public access to major economic and social facilities; and

(b) in some cases, the right to use specified tangible assets, intangible assets, and/or financial assets;

in exchange for the operator:

(a) committing to provide the services according to certain terms and conditions during the concession period; and

(b) when applicable, committing to return at the end of the concession period the rights received at the beginning of the concession period and/or acquired during the concession period. *[SIC-29.2]*.

Chapter 27

The disclosure requirements in respect of such projects are set out below:

SIC-29 requires disclosure in addition to that required by other standards that may cover part of the transaction, such as IAS 16 (see Chapter 18), IAS 17 (see Chapter 24) (or IFRS 16 if that Standard is applied (see Chapter 25)) and IAS 38 (see Chapter 17). *[SIC-29.5]*. All aspects of a service concession arrangement should be considered in determining the appropriate disclosures in the notes to the financial statements. *[SIC-29.6]*.

An operator and a grantor should disclose the following in each period:

(a) a description of the arrangement;

(b) significant terms of the arrangement that may affect the amount, timing and certainty of future cash flows (e.g. the period of the concession, re-pricing dates and the basis upon which re-pricing or re-negotiation is determined);

(c) the nature and extent (e.g. quantity, time period or amount as appropriate) of:

- (i) rights to use specified assets;
- (ii) obligations to provide or rights to expect provision of services;
- (iii) obligations to acquire or build items of property, plant and equipment;
- (iv) obligations to deliver or rights to receive specified assets at the end of the concession period;
- (v) renewal and termination options; and
- (vi) other rights and obligations (e.g. major overhauls);

(d) changes in the arrangement occurring during the period; and

(e) how the service arrangement has been classified.

These disclosures should be provided individually for each service concession arrangement or in aggregate for each class of service concession arrangements. A class is a grouping of service concession arrangements involving services of a similar nature (e.g. toll collections, telecommunications and water treatment services). *[SIC-29.6-7]*.

IFRIC 12 added a requirement to disclose 'the amount of revenue and profits or losses recognised in the period on exchanging construction services for a financial asset and an intangible asset'. *[SIC-29.6A]*.

Vinci has made aggregate disclosures for the principal terms of its arrangements. The following extract is part only of the extensive disclosures that separately address concession arrangements under the intangible asset model, financial asset model and bifurcated model.

Extract 27.5: VINCI SA (2014)

Notes to the consolidated financial statements [extract]

F. **Notes on the main features of concession and public-private partnership (PPP) contracts** [extract]

24. **Controlled subsidiaries' concession and PPP contracts** [extract]

24.1 **Main features of concession and PPP contracts** [extract]

The main features of contracts for concession and PPP contracts operated by controlled subsidiaries are as follows:

	Control and regulation of prices by concession grantor	Remuneration paid by	Grant or guarantee from concession grantor	Residual value	Concession end date	IFRIC 12 accounting model
VINCI Autoroutes						
ASF Group						
ASF 2,714 km of toll motorways (France)	Pricing law as defined in the concession contract. Price increases subject to agreement by grantor	Users	Nil	Infrastructure returned to grantor for no consideration at end of the contract unless purchased before term by the grantor on the basis of the economic value	2033	Intangible asset
Escota 459 km of toll motorways (France)	Pricing law as defined in the concession contract. Price increases subject to agreement by grantor	Users	Nil	Infrastructure returned to grantor for no consideration at end of the contract unless purchased before term by the grantor on the basis of the economic value	2027	Intangible asset

Other concessions [extract]

	Control and regulation of prices by concession grantor	Remuneration paid by	Grant or guarantee from concession grantor	Residual value	Concession end date or average duration	IFRIC 12 accounting model
MMArena Stade du Mans (France)	Pricing schedule approved by grantor	Ticket + resident club receipts + miscellaneous revenue	Investment grant and operating grant (currently suspended).	Infrastructure returned to grantor for no consideration at end of concession	2043	Bifurcated: intangible asset and financial asset
Caraïbus – bus rapid transport system (Martinique)	Annual fee paid by grantor (with no traffic level risk)	Grantor	Nil	Infrastructure returned to grantor for no consideration at end of concession	2035	Financial asset

24.2 Commitments made under concession contracts – intangible asset model [extract]
Contractual investment, renewal or financing obligations

(in € millions)	31/12/2014	31/12/2013
ASF group	1,681	2,072
Cofiroute	584	772
Société Concessionnaire Aéroports du Grand Ouest	370	374
VINCI Park (*)	–	85
Other	54	79
Total	**2,689**	**3,383**

(*) *Deconsolidated on 4 June 2014.*

Chapter 27

Contractual capital investment obligations for motorway companies (ASF group, Cofiroute) relate mainly to investment undertakings made by motorway concession companies as part of multi-year master plans. The above amounts do not include obligations relating to maintenance expenditure on infrastructure under concession.
The investments by motorway concession companies (ASF, Escota, Cofiroute, Arcour) are financed by issuing bonds on the markets, taking out new loans from the European Investment Bank (EIB) or drawing on their available credit facilities.

Collateral security connected with the financing of concessions
Some concession operating companies have given collateral security to guarantee the financing of their investments in concession infrastructure. These break down as follows:

(in € millions)	**Start date**	**End date**	**Amount**
Arcour	2008	2045	600
Other concession operating companies			23

This finance is without recourse against VINCI SA.

Vinci also disclosed the revenue and profit earned from its concession arrangements. The following extract discloses revenue from concessions as a component of revenue by business line.

Extract 27.6: VINCI SA (2014)

Notes to the consolidated financial statements [extract]
C. Information by operating segment [extract]
1. Revenue [extract]
1.1 Breakdown of revenue by business line

(in € millions)	**2014**	**2013**	**Change**
Concessions	**5,823**	**5,616**	**3.7%**
VINCI Autoroutes	4,755	4,596	3.5%
VINCI Airports	717	315	127.4%
VINCI Park(*)	259	607	(57.3%)
Other concessions	92	98	(6.2%)
Contracting	**32,916**	**34,636**	**(5.0%)**
VINCI Energies	9,309	9,248	0.7%
Eurovia	8,188	8,613	(4.9%)
VINCI Construction	15,419	16,775	(8.1%)
VINCI Immobilier	**587**	**816**	**(28.1%)**
Intragroup eliminations	**(623)**	**(731)**	**(14.8%)**
Revenue(**)	**38,703**	**40,338**	**(4.1%)**
Concession subsidiaries' revenue derived from works carried out by non-Group companies	*340*	*403*	*(15.6%)*
Total revenue	*39,043*	*40,740*	*(4.2%)*

(*) *Fully consolidated until 4 July 2014.*
(**) *Excluding concession subsidiaries' revenue derived from works carried out by non-Group companies.*

References

1 IFRS 9 – *Financial Instruments*, IASB, July 2014, applies for annual reporting periods beginning on or after 1 January 2018, with early application permitted. IFRS 9, para. 7.1.1.

2 IFRS 15 – *Revenue from Contracts with Customers*, IASB, May 2014, applies for annual reporting periods beginning on or after 1 January 2018, with early application permitted. IFRS 15, para. C1.

3 IFRS 16 – *Leases*, IASB, January 2016, applies for annual reporting periods beginning on or after 1 January 2019, with early adoption permitted for entities that also apply IFRS 15. IFRS 16, para. C1.

4 IFRS 15, Appendix D, Amendments to other Standards, IASB, May 2014.

5 IFRS 16, Appendix D, Amendments to other Standards, IASB, January 2016.

6 *IFRIC Update*, September 2005.

7 IPSAS 32, *Service Concession Arrangements: Grantor,* International Public Sector Accounting Standards Board, October 2011.

8 *IFRIC Update*, September 2005.

9 *IFRIC Update*, March 2016.

10 *IFRIC Update*, July 2016.

11 *IFRIC Staff paper*, March 2016, IFRIC 12 – *Service Concession Arrangements* – Service concession arrangements with leased infrastructure, p.11.

12 *IFRIC Update*, May 2016, Interpretations Committee's tentative agenda decisions.

13 IFRS 15 Appendix D, Amendments to other Standards, IFRIC 12.13, IASB, May 2014.

14 IFRS 15 Appendix D, Amendments to other Standards, IFRIC 12.13, IASB, May 2014.

15 IFRS 15 Appendix D, Amendments to other Standards, IFRIC 12.14, 15, IASB, May 2014.

16 *IFRIC Update*, March 2006.

17 IAS 38 (2007), *Intangible Assets*, IASB, 2007 Bound Volume, para. 98 stated that 'there is rarely, if ever, persuasive evidence to support an amortisation method for intangible assets with finite useful lives that results in a lower amount of accumulated amortisation than under the straight-line method.' This was removed by *Improvements to IFRSs*, May 2008.

18 *IFRIC Update*, September 2004.

19 *IFRIC Update*, July 2016.

20 *IFRIC Update*, July 2016.

21 *IASB Update*, July 2013.

22 *IFRIC Update*, March 2016.

23 *IFRIC Update*, July 2016.

24 *IFRIC Update*, July 2016.

25 *IFRIC Update*, September 2006.

26 IFRS 15 Appendix D, Amendments to other Standards, IFRIC 12.27, IASB, May 2014.

27 IFRS 15 Appendix D, Amendments to other Standards, IFRIC 12.14 and IFRIC 12.20, IASB, May 2014.

28 IFRIC 12(2014).IE7.

Chapter 28 Provisions, contingent liabilities and contingent assets

List of examples

Chapter 28 Provisions, contingent liabilities and contingent assets

1 INTRODUCTION

1.1 Background

IAS 37 – *Provisions, Contingent Liabilities and Contingent Assets* – applies to all provisions, contingent liabilities and contingent assets, except those relating to executory contracts that are not onerous and those provisions covered by another Standard. *[IAS 37.1]*.

For some time the IASB has considered amending IAS 37 and an exposure draft was issued in June 2005. Subsequent deliberation, including round-table meetings held with constituents to discuss their views, resulted in the Board revising its proposals and issuing a second exposure draft in January 2010. In the months that followed, other documents were issued, including:

- a working draft of a proposed new IFRS, combining the original proposals with the exposure draft on measurement and incorporating other amendments identified by the Board during its deliberations;[1] and
- an IASB Staff Paper on discussing the recognition of liabilities arising from lawsuits.[2]

However, IAS 37 was not revised and work on the liabilities project was suspended pending the outcome of the Board's 2011 consultation on its future agenda. The IASB indicated that it expected to issue a further exposure draft of the revised standard following the conclusion of that consultation.[3] Instead, in May 2012, the IASB declared its unanimous support to give priority to initiating a research programme to include, among other topics, non-financial liabilities.[4] As part of the research programme, the IASB is assessing how and when IAS 37 could be revised or replaced, taking into account the feedback received on the earlier Exposure Drafts and the likely revisions to the *Conceptual Framework* (see Chapter 2). The IASB began discussions on the Provisions, Contingent Liabilities and Contingent Assets research project during 2015. Discussions have continued during 2016. However, it is likely that the IASB will wait until it is close to finalising revisions to the Conceptual Framework before publishing any preliminary views on possible amendments to IAS 37.[5]

1.2 Interpretations related to the application of IAS 37

The Interpretations Committee has issued a number of pronouncements relating to the application of IAS 37 (although one of them was subsequently withdrawn).

1.2.1 *IFRIC 1*

IFRIC 1 – *Changes in Existing Decommissioning, Restoration and Similar Liabilities* – provides guidance on how to account for the effect of changes in the measurement of existing provisions for obligations to dismantle, remove or restore items of property, plant and equipment. This is discussed at 6.3 below.

1.2.2 *IFRIC 3*

Another issue considered by the Interpretations Committee was how to account for a 'cap and trade' emission rights scheme. In December 2004, the Interpretations Committee issued IFRIC 3 – *Emission Rights* – but this was later withdrawn in June 2005. This interpretation, *inter alia*, required that as emissions are made, a liability was to be recognised for the obligation to deliver allowances equal to the emissions that had been made by the entity. Such a liability was a provision within the scope of IAS 37, and was to be measured at the present market value of the number of allowances required to cover emissions made up to the end of the reporting period. Accounting for liabilities associated with emissions trading schemes is discussed at 6.5 below.

1.2.3 *IFRIC 5*

IFRIC 5 – *Rights to Interests arising from Decommissioning, Restoration and Environmental Rehabilitation Funds* – deals with the accounting by an entity when it participates in a 'decommissioning fund', the purpose of which is to segregate assets to fund some or all of the costs of its decommissioning or environmental liabilities for which it has to make a provision under IAS 37. This is discussed at 6.3.3 below.

1.2.4 *IFRIC 6*

IFRIC 6 – *Liabilities arising from Participating in a Specific Market – Waste Electrical and Electronic Equipment* – provides guidance on the accounting for liabilities for waste management costs. This clarifies when certain producers of electrical goods will need to recognise a liability for the cost of waste management relating to the decommissioning of waste electrical and electronic equipment (historical waste) supplied to private households. This is discussed at 6.7 below.

1.2.5 *IFRIC 21*

IFRIC 21 – *Levies* – addresses the recognition of a liability to pay a levy imposed by government if that liability is within the scope of IAS 37. It also addresses the accounting for a liability to pay a levy whose timing and amount is certain (see 6.8 below).

The number of other Interpretations that refer to IAS 37 demonstrates just how pervasive the consideration of non-financial liabilities is in developing accounting practice. For example, IAS 37 is also referred to in IFRIC 12 – *Service Concession*

Arrangements (see Chapter 27); IFRIC 13 – *Customer Loyalty Programmes* (see Chapter 29); IFRIC 14 – *IAS 19 – The Limit on a Defined Benefit Asset, Minimum Funding Requirements and their Interaction* (see Chapter 33); and IFRIC 15 – *Agreements for the Construction of Real Estate* (see Chapter 23).

1.3 Terms used in this chapter

The following terms are used in this chapter with the meanings specified:

Term	Definition
Provision	A liability of uncertain timing or amount. *[IAS 37.10]*.
Liability	A present obligation of the entity arising from past events, the settlement of which is expected to result in an outflow from the entity of resources embodying economic benefits. *[IAS 37.10]*.
Obligating event	An event that creates a legal or constructive obligation that results in an entity having no realistic alternative to settling that obligation. *[IAS 37.10]*.
Legal obligation	An obligation that derives from a contract (through its explicit or implicit terms); legislation; or other operation of law. *[IAS 37.10]*.
Constructive obligation	An obligation that derives from an entity's actions where: (a) by an established pattern of past practice, published policies or a sufficiently specific current statement, the entity has indicated to other parties that it will accept certain responsibilities; and (b) as a result, the entity has created a valid expectation on the part of those other parties that it will discharge those responsibilities. *[IAS 37.10]*.
Contingent liability	(a) a possible obligation that arises from past events and whose existence will be confirmed only by the occurrence or non-occurrence of one or more uncertain future events not wholly within the control of the entity; or (b) a present obligation that arises from past events but is not recognised because: (i) it is not probable that an outflow of resources embodying economic benefits will be required to settle the obligation; or (ii) the amount of the obligation cannot be measured with sufficient reliability. *[IAS 37.10]*.
Contingent asset	A possible asset that arises from past events and whose existence will be confirmed only by the occurrence or non-occurrence of one or more uncertain future events not wholly within the control of the entity. *[IAS 37.10]*.
Onerous contract	A contract in which the unavoidable costs of meeting the obligations under the contract exceed the economic benefits expected to be received under it. *[IAS 37.10]*.

Term	Definition
Restructuring	A programme that is planned and controlled by management, and materially changes either: (a) the scope of a business undertaken by an entity; or (b) the manner in which that business is conducted. *[IAS 37.10]*.
Executory contract	A contract under which neither party has performed any of its obligations or both parties have partially performed their obligations to an equal extent. *[IAS 37.3]*
Levy	An outflow of resources embodying economic benefits that is imposed by governments on entities in accordance with legislation (i.e. laws and or regulations), other than: (a) those outflows of resources that are within the scope of other Standards (such as income taxes that are within the scope of IAS 12); and (b) fines or other penalties that are imposed for breaches of the legislation. *[IFRIC 21.4]*.
Government	Refers to government, government agencies and similar bodies whether local, national or international. *[IFRIC 21.4]*.

2 OBJECTIVE AND SCOPE OF IAS 37

2.1 Objective

The objective of IAS 37 'is to ensure that appropriate recognition criteria and measurement bases are applied to provisions, contingent liabilities and contingent assets and that sufficient information is disclosed in the notes to enable users to understand their nature, timing and amount'. *[IAS 37 Objective]*.

2.2 Scope of IAS 37

The standard is required to be applied by all entities in accounting for provisions, contingent liabilities and contingent assets, except those arising from executory contracts (unless the contract is onerous) and those covered by another standard. *[IAS 37.1]*.

The following table lists the specific types of transaction or circumstances referred to in the standard that might give rise to a provision, contingent liability or contingent asset. In some cases, the transaction is identified in IAS 37 only to prohibit recognition of any liability, such as for future operating losses and repairs and maintenance of owned assets (see 5 below). This chapter does not address those items identified below as falling outside the scope of the standard.

Types of transaction or circumstances referred to	*In scope*	*Out of scope*	*Another standard*
Restructuring costs	•		
Environmental penalties or clean-up costs	•		
Decommissioning costs	•		
Product warranties / refunds	•		
Legal claims	•		
Reimbursement rights	•		
Future operating costs (training, relocation, etc.)	•		
Future operating losses	•		
Onerous contracts (including onerous construction contracts under IFRS 15)	•		
Repairs and maintenance costs	•		
Provisions for depreciation, impairment or doubtful debts		•	IAS 16 / IAS 38 / IAS 36 / IAS 39 / IFRS 9
Executory contracts (unless onerous)		•	
Construction contracts		•	IAS 11
Income taxes		•	IAS 12
Leases (unless onerous)		•	IAS 17 / IFRS 16
Employee benefits		•	IAS 19
Insurance contracts issued by insurers to policyholders		•	IFRS 4
Contingent liabilities acquired in a business combination		•	IFRS 3
Contingent consideration of an acquirer in a business combination		•	IFRS 3
Financial instruments and financial guarantees within the scope of IAS 39 and IFRS 9		•	IAS 39 / IFRS 9
Trade payables or accruals		•	

2.2.1 Items outside the scope of IAS 37

2.2.1.A Executory contracts, except where the contract is onerous

The standard uses the term executory contracts to mean 'contracts under which neither party has performed any of its obligations, or both parties have partially performed their obligations to an equal extent'. *[IAS 37.3]*. This means that contracts such as supplier purchase contracts and capital commitments, which would otherwise fall within the scope of the standard, are exempt.

This exemption prevents the statement of financial position from being grossed up for all manner of commitments that an entity has entered into, and in respect of which it is debatable whether (or at what point) such contracts give rise to items that meet the definition of a liability or an asset. In particular, the need for this exemption arises because the liability framework on which this standard is based includes the concept of a constructive obligation (see 3.1.1 below) which, when applied to executory contracts would otherwise give rise to an inordinate number of contingent promises requiring recognition or disclosure.

An executory contract will still require recognition as a provision if the contract becomes onerous. *[IAS 37.3]*. Onerous contracts are dealt with at 6.2 below.

2.2.1.B Items covered by another standard

Where another standard deals with a specific type of provision, contingent liability or contingent asset, it should be applied instead of IAS 37. Examples given in the standard are:

- construction contracts (for entities not adopting IFRS 15 – *Revenue from Contracts with Customers* – construction contracts are dealt with in IAS 11 – *Construction Contracts* – see Chapter 23. For entities adopting IFRS 15 see 2.2.1.C below);
- income taxes (dealt with in IAS 12 – *Income Taxes* – see Chapter 31);
- leases (for entities not adopting IFRS 16 – *Leases* – leases are dealt with in IAS 17 – *Leases* – see Chapter 24. However, IAS 37 states that if operating leases become onerous, there are no specific requirements within IAS 17 to address the issue and thus IAS 37 applies to such leases. For entities adopting IFRS 16, see 2.2.1.D below);
- employee benefits (dealt with in IAS 19 – *Employee Benefits* – see Chapter 33);
- insurance contracts (dealt with in IFRS 4 – *Insurance Contracts* – see Chapter 55). However, IAS 37 requires an insurer to apply the standard to provisions, contingent liabilities and contingent assets, other than those arising from its contractual obligations and rights under insurance contracts within the scope of IFRS 4; and
- contingent consideration of an acquirer in a business combination (dealt with in IFRS 3 – *Business Combinations* – see Chapter 9). *[IAS 37.5]*.

Contingent consideration of an acquirer in a business combination is excluded from the scope of IAS 37 as a result of changes to IFRS 3 effective for business combinations with an acquisition date on or after 1 July 2014. See Chapter 9 at 7.1.

As noted above, the scope of IAS 37 excludes income taxes that fall in the scope of IAS 12. The Interpretations Committee confirmed in July 2014 that the recognition of tax-related contingent liabilities and contingent assets should also be assessed using the guidance in IAS 12 rather than IAS 37.[6] However, the Committee also confirmed that the guidance in IAS 37 remains relevant to the disclosure of tax-related contingent liabilities and contingent assets. *[IAS 12.88]*. Tax-related contingent liabilities and assets are discussed further in Chapter 31 at 9.6.

Whilst IAS 37 contains no reference to it, IFRS 3 – *Business Combinations* – states that the requirements in IAS 37 do not apply in determining which contingent liabilities to recognise as of the acquisition date (see 4.9 below and Chapter 9 at 5.6.1). *[IFRS 3.23]*.

In addition, the standard does not apply to financial instruments (including guarantees) that are within the scope of IAS 39 – *Financial Instruments: Recognition and Measurement* – and IFRS 9 – *Financial Instruments*. *[IAS 37.2]*. This means that guarantees of third party borrowings (including those of subsidiaries, associates and joint arrangements) are not covered by IAS 37. However, the guarantee contract may meet the definition of an insurance contract in IFRS 4 – *Insurance Contracts* – and the issuer may have previously asserted that it regards such contracts as insurance contracts. In such cases, the accounting policy applied by the issuer may result in the issuer providing for probable payments under the guarantee. *[IAS 37 IE, Example 9]*. (See Chapter 43).

IAS 37 also notes that some amounts treated as provisions may relate to the recognition of revenue, for example where an entity gives guarantees in exchange for a fee, and states that the standard does not address the recognition of revenue. This is dealt with by IAS 18 – *Revenue* (see Chapter 29), and IAS 37 does not change the requirements of that standard. *[IAS 37.6]*.

The standard applies to provisions for restructurings, including discontinued operations. However, it emphasises that when a restructuring meets the definition of a discontinued operation under IFRS 5 – *Non-current Assets Held for Sale and Discontinued Operations*, additional disclosures may be required under that standard (see Chapter 4 at 3). *[IAS 37.9]*.

The standard defines a provision as 'a liability of uncertain timing or amount'. *[IAS 37.10]*. Thus it only deals with provisions that are shown as liabilities in a statement of financial position. The term 'provision' is also used widely in the context of items such as depreciation, impairment of assets and doubtful debts. Such 'provisions' are not addressed in IAS 37, since these are adjustments to the carrying amounts of assets. *[IAS 37.7]*.

2.2.1.C Entities adopting IFRS 15

In July 2015, the IASB decided to defer the mandatory effective date of IFRS 15 by one year, to annual reporting periods beginning on or after 1 January 2018. Earlier application is permitted provided that this is disclosed. *[IFRS 15.C1]*. The requirements of IFRS 15 are discussed in Chapter 30.

However, when entities apply IFRS 15 the scope of IAS 37 is amended, not only to refer to IFRS 15 instead of IAS 11, but also to state that, 'as IFRS 15 contains no specific requirements to address contracts with customers that are, or have become, onerous, this Standard applies to such cases'.[7] Onerous contracts are discussed at 6.2 below.

Furthermore, whilst an entity would apply IFRS 15 to separately purchased warranties, if a customer does not have the option to purchase a warranty separately, an entity would consider IAS 37 (see 6.10 below), unless the promised warranty, or a part of the promised warranty, provides the customer with a service in addition to the assurance that the product complies with agreed-upon specifications. *[IFRS 15.B30]*.

IFRS 15 adds that IAS 37 applies to other obligations under a contract with a customer that do not give rise to a performance obligation. For example, a law that requires an entity to pay compensation if its products cause harm or damage does not give rise to a performance obligation and IAS 37 would apply. Similarly, an entity would account for customer indemnities arising from claims of patent, copyright, trademark or other infringement in relation to its products in accordance with IAS 37. *[IFRS 15.B33]*.

2.2.1.D Entities adopting IFRS 16

IFRS 16 is effective for annual reporting periods beginning on or after 1 January 2019. Earlier application is permitted for entities that apply IFRS 15 at or before the date of initial application of IFRS 16. *[IFRS 16.C1]*. The requirements of IFRS 16 are discussed in Chapter 25.

When entities apply IFRS 16, the scope of IAS 37 is amended to apply to any lease that becomes onerous before the commencement date of the lease, as defined in IFRS 16. IAS 37 also applies to onerous short-term leases and onerous leases for which the underlying asset is of a low value that are accounted for under paragraph 6 of IFRS 16.[8]

2.2.2 *Provisions compared to other liabilities*

IAS 37 states that the feature distinguishing provisions from other liabilities, such as trade payables and accruals, is the existence of 'uncertainty about the timing or amount of the future expenditure required in settlement'. *[IAS 37.11]*. The standard compares provisions to:

(a) trade payables – liabilities to pay for goods or services that have been received or supplied and have been invoiced or formally agreed with the supplier; and

(b) accruals – liabilities to pay for goods or services that have been received or supplied but have not been paid, invoiced or formally agreed with the supplier, including amounts due to employees (for example, amounts relating to accrued vacation pay). Although it is sometimes necessary to estimate the amount or timing of accruals, the uncertainty is generally much less than for provisions.

IAS 37 also notes that accruals are often reported as part of trade and other payables whereas provisions are reported separately. *[IAS 37.11]*.

For trade payables and their associated accruals, there is little uncertainty regarding either the amount of the obligation (which would be determined by the contracted price for the goods and services being provided) or of the timing of settlement (which would normally occur within an agreed period following transfer of the goods and services in question and the issue of an invoice). In practice, however, contracts can be more complex and give rise to a wide range of possible outcomes in terms of the amount or timing of payment. In these circumstances, the difference between provisions and other liabilities is less obvious and judgement may be required to determine where the requirement to make an estimate of an obligation indicates a level of uncertainty about timing or amount that is more indicative of a provision. Such judgements, if significant to the amounts recognised in the financial statements, would merit disclosure (see Chapter 3 at 5.1.1.B). *[IAS 1.122]*.

One reason why this distinction matters is that provisions are subject to narrative disclosure requirements regarding the nature of the obligation and the uncertainties over timing and amount; and to quantitative disclosures of movements arising from their use, remeasurement or release that do not apply to other payables (see 7.1 below). In fact, although questions of recognition and measurement are important, transparency of disclosure is also a very significant matter in relation to accounting for provisions and ensuring that their effect is properly understood by users of the financial statements.

2.2.3 Distinction between provisions and contingent liabilities

There is an area of overlap between provisions and contingent liabilities. Although contingent liabilities are clearly not as likely to give rise to outflows, similar judgements are made in assessing the nature of the uncertainties, the need for disclosures and ultimately the recognition of a liability in the financial statements. The standard notes that in a general sense, all provisions are contingent because they are uncertain in timing or amount. However, in IAS 37 the term 'contingent' is used for liabilities and assets that are not recognised because their existence will be confirmed only by the occurrence of one or more uncertain future events not wholly within the entity's control. In addition, the term 'contingent liability' is used for liabilities that do not meet the recognition criteria for provisions. *[IAS 37.12]*.

Accordingly, the standard distinguishes between:

(a) provisions – which are recognised as liabilities (assuming that a reliable estimate can be made) because they are present obligations and it is probable that an outflow of resources embodying economic benefits will be required to settle the obligations; and

(b) contingent liabilities – which are not recognised as liabilities because they are either:

  (i) possible obligations, as it has yet to be confirmed whether the entity has a present obligation that could lead to an outflow of resources embodying economic benefits; or

  (ii) present obligations that do not meet the recognition criteria in the standard because either it is not probable that an outflow of resources embodying economic benefits will be required to settle the obligation, or a sufficiently reliable estimate of the amount of the obligation cannot be made. *[IAS 37.13]*.

3 RECOGNITION

3.1 Determining when a provision should be recognised

IAS 37 requires that a provision should be recognised when:

(a) an entity has a present obligation (legal or constructive) as a result of a past event;

(b) it is probable that an outflow of resources embodying economic benefits will be required to settle the obligation; and

(c) a reliable estimate can be made of the amount of the obligation.

No provision should be recognised unless all of these conditions are met. *[IAS 37.14]*.

Each of these three conditions is discussed separately below.

3.1.1 *'An entity has a present obligation (legal or constructive) as a result of a past event'*

The standard defines both legal and constructive obligations. The definition of a legal obligation is fairly straightforward and uncontroversial; it refers to an obligation that derives from a contract (through its explicit or implicit terms), legislation or other operation of law. *[IAS 37.10]*.

The definition of a constructive obligation, on the other hand, may give rise to more problems of interpretation. A constructive obligation is defined as an obligation that derives from an entity's actions where:

(a) by an established pattern of past practice, published policies or a sufficiently specific current statement, the entity has indicated to other parties that it will accept certain responsibilities; and

(b) as a result, the entity has created a valid expectation on the part of those other parties that it will discharge those responsibilities. *[IAS 37.10]*.

The following examples in IAS 37 illustrate how a constructive obligation is created.

Example 28.1: Recognising a provision because of a constructive obligation

Scenario 1: Environmental policy – contaminated land

An entity in the oil industry operates in a country with no environmental legislation. However, it has a widely published environmental policy in which it undertakes to clean up all contamination that it causes and it has a record of honouring this published policy. During the period the entity causes contamination to some land in this country.

In these circumstances, the contamination of the land gives rise to a constructive obligation because the entity (through its published policy and record of honouring it) has created a valid expectation on the part of those affected by it that the entity will clean up the site. *[IAS 37 IE Example 2B]*.

Scenario 2: Refunds policy – product returns

A retail store has a generally known policy of refunding purchases by dissatisfied customers, even though it is under no legal obligation to do so.

In these circumstances, the sale of its products gives rise to a constructive obligation because the entity (through its reputation for providing refunds) has created a valid expectation on the part of customers that a refund will be given if they are dissatisfied with their purchase. *[IAS 37 IE Example 4]*.

These examples demonstrate that the essence of a constructive obligation is the creation of a valid expectation that the entity is irrevocably committed to accepting and discharging its responsibilities.

The standard states that in almost all cases it will be clear whether a past event has given rise to a present obligation. However, it acknowledges that there will be some rare cases, such as a lawsuit against an entity, where this will not be so because the occurrence of certain events or the consequences of those events are disputed. *[IAS 37.16]*. When it is not clear whether there is a present obligation, a 'more likely than not' evaluation (taking into account all available evidence) is deemed to be sufficient to require recognition of a provision at the end of the reporting period. *[IAS 37.15]*.

The evidence to be considered includes, for example, the opinion of experts together with any additional evidence provided by events after the reporting period. If on the basis of such evidence it is concluded that a present obligation is more likely than not to exist at the end of the reporting period, a provision will be required (assuming that the other recognition criteria are met). *[IAS 37.16]*. This is an apparent relaxation of the standard's first criterion for the recognition of a provision as set out at 3.1 above, which requires there to be a definite obligation, not just a probable one. It also confuses slightly the question of the existence of an obligation with the probability criterion, which strictly speaking relates to whether it is more likely than not that there will be an outflow of resources (see 3.1.2 below). However, this interpretation is confirmed in IAS 10 – *Events after the Reporting Period*, which includes 'the settlement after the reporting period of a court case that confirms that the entity had a present obligation at the end of the reporting period' as an example of an adjusting event. *[IAS 10.9]*.

The second half of this condition uses the phrase 'as a result of a past event'. This is based on the concept of an obligating event, which the standard defines as 'an event that creates a legal or constructive obligation and that results in an entity having no realistic alternative to settling that obligation'. *[IAS 37.10]*. The standard says that this will be the case only:

(a) where the settlement of the obligation can be enforced by law; or

(b) in the case of a constructive obligation, where the event (which may be an action of the entity) creates valid expectations in other parties that the entity will discharge the obligation. *[IAS 37.17]*.

This concept of obligating event is used in the standard when discussing specific examples of recognition, which we consider further at 6 below. However, it is worth mentioning here that this concept, like that of a constructive obligation, is open to interpretation and requires the exercise of judgement, as the obligating event is not always easy to identify.

The standard emphasises that the financial statements deal with the financial position of an entity at the end of its reporting period, not its possible position in the future. Accordingly, no provision should be recognised for costs that need to be incurred to operate in the future. The only liabilities to be recognised are those that exist at the end of the reporting period. *[IAS 37.18]*. It is not always easy to distinguish between the current state at the reporting date and the entity's future possible position, especially where IAS 37 requires an assessment to be made based on the probability of obligations and expectations as to their outcome. However, when considering these questions it is important to ensure that provisions are not recognised for liabilities that arise from events after the reporting period (see Chapter 36 at 2).

Example 28.2: No provision without a past obligating event

The government introduces a number of changes to the income tax system. As a result of these changes, an entity in the financial services sector will need to retrain a large proportion of its administrative and sales staff in order to ensure continued compliance with financial services regulation. At the end of the reporting period, no training has taken place.

In these circumstances, no event has taken place at the reporting date to create an obligation. Only once the training has taken place will there be a present obligation as a result of a past event. *[IAS 37 IE Example 7]*.

IAS 37 prohibits certain provisions that might otherwise qualify to be recognised by stating that it 'is only those obligations arising from past events existing independently of an entity's future actions (i.e. the future conduct of its business) that are recognised as provisions'. In contrast to situations where the entity's past conduct has created an obligation to incur expenditure (such as to rectify environmental damage already caused), a commercial or legal requirement to incur expenditure in order to operate in a particular way in the future, will not of itself justify the recognition of a provision. It argues that because the entity can avoid the expenditure by its future actions, for example by changing its method of operation, there is no present obligation for the future expenditure. *[IAS 37.19]*.

Example 28.3: Obligations must exist independently of an entity's future actions

Under legislation passed in 2016, an entity is required to fix smoke filters in its factories by 30 June 2018. The entity has not fitted the smoke filters.

At 31 December 2017, the end of the reporting period, no event has taken place to create an obligation. Only once the smoke filters are fitted or the legislation takes effect, will there be a present obligation as a result of a past event, either for the cost of fitting smoke filters or for fines under the legislation.

At 31 December 2018, there is still no obligating event to justify provision for the cost of fitting the smoke filters required under the legislation because the filters have not been fitted. However, an obligation may exist as at the reporting date to pay fines or penalties under the legislation because the entity is operating its factory in a non-compliant way. However, a provision would only be recognised for the best estimate of any fines and penalties if, as at 31 December 2018, it is determined to be more likely than not that such fines and penalties will be imposed. *[IAS 37 IE Example 6]*.

The standard expects strict application of the requirement that, to qualify for recognition, an obligation must exist independently of an entity's future actions. Even if a failure to incur certain costs would result in a legal requirement to discontinue an entity's operations, no provision can be recognised. As discussed at 5.2 below, IAS 37 considers the example of an airline required by law to overhaul its aircraft once every three years. It concludes that no provision is recognised because the entity can avoid the requirement to perform the overhaul, for example by replacing the aircraft before the three year period has expired. *[IAS 37 IE Example 11B]*.

SSE plc describes its interpretation of the group's obligations under UK legislation to install energy efficiency improvement measures in domestic households in a manner consistent with Example 28.3 above.

Extract 28.1: SSE plc (2015)

Notes on the financial statements [extract]

3. Critical accounting judgements and key sources of estimation uncertainty [extract]

3.2 Other key accounting judgements

(iv) Energy Company Obligation (ECO) costs

The Energy Company Obligation ('ECO') legislation, in force since 1 January 2013, requires qualifying energy suppliers to meet defined targets by providing measures to improve the energy efficiency of and level of carbon emissions from UK domestic households. The targets for the Group's Energy Supply business are set based on historic customer information with delivery of the measures being required by 31 March 2017. The Group believes it is not technically obligated to provide those measures until the end of the delivery period. As a consequence and applying applicable accounting standards, the costs of ECO are recorded when measures are delivered or other qualifying expenditure has been incurred.

Significantly, however, such considerations do not apply in the case of obligations to dismantle or remove an asset at the end of its useful life, where an obligation is recognised despite the entity's ability to dispose of the asset before its useful life has expired. Such costs are required to be included by IAS 16 – *Property, Plant and Equipment* – as part of the measure of an asset's initial cost. *[IAS 16.16]*. Decommissioning provisions are discussed at 6.3 below. A further distinction can be drawn where the requirement to maintain the asset is a contractual obligation, such as when the asset in question is held under an operating lease (see 6.9 below). Accordingly, the determination of whether an obligation exists independently of an entity's future actions can be a matter of judgement that depends on the particular facts and circumstances of the case.

There is no requirement for an entity to know to whom an obligation is owed. The obligation may be to the public at large. It follows that the obligation could be to one party, but the amount ultimately payable will be to another party. For example, in the case of a constructive obligation for an environmental clean-up, the obligation is to the public, but the liability will be settled by making payment to the contractors engaged to carry out the clean-up. However, the principle is that there must be another party for the obligation to exist. It follows from this that a management or board decision will not give rise to a constructive obligation unless it is communicated in sufficient detail to those affected by it before the end of the reporting period. *[IAS 37.20]*. The most significant application of this requirement relates to restructuring provisions, which is discussed further at 6.1 below.

The standard discusses the possibility that an event that does not give rise to an obligation immediately may do so at a later date, because of changes in the law or an act by the entity (such as a sufficiently specific public statement) which gives rise to a constructive obligation. *[IAS 37.21]*. Changes in the law will be relatively straightforward to identify. The only issue that arises will be to determine exactly when that change in the law should be recognised. IAS 37 states that an obligation arises only when the legislation is virtually certain to be enacted as drafted and suggests that in many cases, this will not be until it is enacted. *[IAS 37.22]*.

The more subjective area is the possibility that an act by the entity will give rise to a constructive obligation. The example given is of an entity publicly accepting responsibility for rectification of previous environmental damage in a way that creates a constructive obligation. *[IAS 37.21]*. This seems to introduce a certain amount of flexibility to management when reporting results. By bringing forward or delaying a public announcement of a commitment that management had always intended to honour, it can affect the reporting period in which a provision is recognised. Nevertheless, the existence of a public announcement provides a more transparent basis for recognising a provision than, for example, a decision made behind the closed doors of a boardroom.

3.1.2 *'It is probable that an outflow of resources embodying economic benefits will be required to settle the obligation'*

This requirement has been included as a result of the standard's attempt to incorporate contingent liabilities within the definition of provisions. This is discussed at 3.2 below.

The meaning of *probable* in these circumstances is that the outflow of resources is more likely than not to occur; that is, it has a probability of occurring that is greater than 50%. *[IAS 37.23]*. The standard also makes it clear that where there are a number of similar obligations, the probability that an outflow will occur is based on the class of obligations as a whole. This is because in the case of certain obligations such as warranties, the possibility of an outflow for an individual item may be small (likely to be much less than 50%) whereas the possibility of at least some outflow of resources for the population as a whole will be much greater (almost certainly greater than 50%). *[IAS 37.24]*. With regard to the measurement of a provision arising from a number of similar obligations, the standard refers to the calculation of an 'expected value', whereby the obligation is estimated by weighting all the possible outcomes by their associated probabilities. *[IAS 37.40]*. Where the obligation being measured relates to a single item, the standard suggests that the best estimate of the liability may be the individual most likely outcome. *[IAS 37.40]*. For the purposes of recognition, a determination that it is more likely than not that *any* outflow of resources will be required is sufficient. The measurement of provisions is discussed at 4 below.

3.1.3 *'A reliable estimate can be made of the amount of the obligation'*

The standard takes the view that a sufficiently reliable estimate can almost always be made for a provision where an entity can determine a range of possible outcomes. Hence, the standard contends that it will only be in extremely rare cases that a range of possible outcomes cannot be determined and therefore no sufficiently reliable estimate of the obligation can be made. *[IAS 37.25]*. In these extremely rare circumstances, no liability is recognised. Instead, the liability should be disclosed as a contingent liability (see disclosure requirements at 7.2 below). *[IAS 37.26]*. Whether such a situation is as rare as the standard asserts is open to question, especially for entities trying to determine estimates relating to potential obligations that arise from litigation and other legal claims (see 6.11 below).

3.2 Contingencies

IAS 37 says that contingent liabilities and contingent assets should not be recognised, but only disclosed. *[IAS 37.27-28, 31, 34]*.

Contingent liabilities that are recognised separately as part of allocating the cost of a business combination are covered by the requirements of IFRS 3. *[IFRS 3.23]*. Such liabilities continue to be measured after the business combination at the higher of:

(a) the amount that would be recognised in accordance with IAS 37, and

(b) the amount initially recognised less, if appropriate, cumulative amortisation recognised in accordance with IAS 18. *[IFRS 3.56]*. For entities applying IFRS 15, the amount initially recognised less, if appropriate, the cumulative amount of income recognised in accordance with the principles of that Standard.[9]

The requirements in respect of contingent liabilities identified in a business combination are discussed in Chapter 9 at 5.6.1.

3.2.1 Contingent liabilities

A contingent liability is defined in the standard as:

(a) a possible obligation that arises from past events and whose existence will be confirmed only by the occurrence or non-occurrence of one or more uncertain future events not wholly within the control of the entity; or

(b) a present obligation that arises from past events but is not recognised because:

  (i) it is not probable that an outflow of resources embodying economic benefits will be required to settle the obligation; or

  (ii) the amount of the obligation cannot be measured with sufficient reliability. *[IAS 37.10]*.

At first glance, this definition is not easy to understand because a natural meaning of 'contingent' would include any event whose outcome depends on future circumstances. The meaning is perhaps clearer when considering the definition of a liability and the criteria for recognising a provision in the standard. A possible obligation whose existence is yet to be confirmed does not meet the definition of a liability; and a present obligation in respect of which an outflow of resources is not probable, or which cannot be measured reliably does not qualify for recognition. *[IAS 37.14]*. On that basis a contingent liability under IAS 37 means one of the following:

(a) an obligation that is estimated to be less than 50+% likely to exist (i.e. it does not meet the definition of a liability). Where it is more likely than not that a present obligation exists at the end of the reporting period, a provision is recognised. *[IAS 37.16(a)]*. Where it is more likely than not that no present obligation exists, a contingent liability is disclosed (unless the possibility is remote); *[IAS 37.16(b)]*

(b) a present obligation that has a less than 50+% chance of requiring an outflow of economic benefits (i.e. it meets the definition of a liability but does not meet the recognition criteria). Where it is not probable that there will be an outflow of resources, an entity discloses a contingent liability (unless the possibility is remote); *[IAS 37.23]* or

(c) a present obligation for which a sufficiently reliable estimate cannot be made (i.e. it meets the definition of a liability but does not meet the recognition criteria). In these rare circumstances, a liability cannot be recognised and it is disclosed as a contingent liability. *[IAS 37.26]*.

The term 'possible' is not defined, but literally it could mean any probability greater than 0% and less than 100%. However, the standard effectively divides this range into four components, namely 'remote', 'possible but not probable', 'probable' and 'virtually certain'. The standard requires a provision to be recognised if 'it is more likely than not that a present obligation exists at the end of the reporting period'. *[IAS 37.16(a)]*. Therefore, IAS 37 distinguishes between a 'probable' obligation (which is more likely than not to exist and, therefore requires recognition as a provision) and a 'possible' obligation (for which either the existence of a present obligation is yet to be confirmed or where the probability of an outflow of resources is 50% or less). *[IAS 37.13]*. Appendix A to IAS 37, in summarising the main requirements of the standard, uses the phrase 'a possible obligation ... that may, but probably will not, require an outflow of resources'. Accordingly, the definition restricts contingent liabilities to those where either the existence of the liability or the transfer of economic benefits arising is less than 50+% probable (or where the obligation cannot be measured at all, but as noted at 3.1.3 above, this would be relatively rare).

The standard requires that contingent liabilities are assessed continually to determine whether circumstances have changed, in particular whether an outflow of resources embodying economic benefits has become probable. Where this becomes the case, then provision should be made in the period in which the change in probability occurs (except in the rare circumstances where no reliable estimate can be made). *[IAS 37.30]*. Other changes in circumstances might require disclosure of a previously remote obligation on the grounds that an outflow of resources has become possible (but not probable).

Example 28.4: When the likelihood of an outflow of benefits becomes probable

After a wedding in 2017, ten people died, possibly as a result of food poisoning from products sold by the entity. Legal proceedings are started seeking damages from the entity. The entity disputes any liability and, up to the date on which its financial statements for the year ended 31 December 2017 are authorised for issue, its lawyers have advised that is probable that the entity will not be found liable. However, when the entity prepares its financial statements for the year ended 31 December 2018, its lawyers advise that, owing to developments in the case, it is probable that the entity will be found liable.

At 31 December 2017, no provision is recognised and the matter is disclosed as a contingent liability unless the probability of any outflow is regarded as remote. On the basis of the evidence available when the financial statements were approved, there is no obligation as a result of a past event.

At 31 December 2018, a provision is recognised for the best estimate of the amount required to settle the obligation. The fact that an outflow of economic benefits is now believed to be probable means that there is a present obligation. *[IAS 37 IE Example 10]*.

3.2.2 Contingent assets

A contingent asset is defined in a more intuitive way. It is 'a possible asset that arises from past events and whose existence will be confirmed only by the occurrence or non-occurrence of one or more uncertain future events not wholly within the control of the entity'. *[IAS 37.10]*. In this case, the word 'possible' is *not* confined to a level of probability of 50% or less, which may further increase the confusion over the different meaning of the term in the definition of contingent liabilities.

Contingent assets usually arise from unplanned or other unexpected events that give rise to the possibility of an inflow of economic benefits to the entity. An example is a claim that an entity is pursuing through legal process, where the outcome is uncertain. *[IAS 37.32]*.

The standard states that a contingent asset should not be recognised, as this could give rise to recognition of income that may never be realised. However, when the realisation of income is virtually certain, then the related asset is no longer regarded as contingent and recognition is appropriate. *[IAS 37.33]*.

Virtual certainty is not defined in the standard, but it is certainly a much higher hurdle than 'probable' and indeed more challenging than the term 'highly probable', defined in IAS 39 as indicating a much greater likelihood of happening than the term 'more likely than not', *[IAS 39.F.3.7]*, and in IFRS 5 as 'significantly more likely than probable'. *[IFRS 5 Appendix A]*. We think it reasonable that virtual certainty is interpreted as being as close to 100% as to make any remaining uncertainty insignificant. What this means in practice requires each case to be decided on its merits and any judgement should be made in the knowledge that, in any event, it is rarely possible to accurately assess the probability of the outcome of a particular event.

The standard requires disclosure of the contingent asset when the inflow of economic benefits is probable. *[IAS 37.34]*. For the purposes of the standard 'probable' means that the event is more likely than not to occur; that is, it has a probability greater than 50%. *[IAS 37.23]*. The disclosure requirements are detailed at 7.3 below.

As with contingent liabilities, any contingent assets should be assessed continually to ensure that developments are appropriately reflected in the financial statements. If it has become virtually certain that an inflow of economic benefits will arise, the asset and the related income should be recognised in the period in which the change occurs. If a previously unlikely inflow becomes probable, then the contingent asset should be disclosed. *[IAS 37.35]*.

The requirement to recognise the effect of changing circumstances in the period in which the change occurs extends to the analysis of information available after the end of the reporting period and before the date of approval of the financial statements. In our view, such information would not give rise to an adjusting event after the reporting period. In contrast to contingent liabilities (in respect of which IAS 10 includes as a specific example of an adjusting event 'the settlement after the reporting period of a court case that confirms that the entity had a present obligation at the end of the reporting period' *[IAS 10.9]*), no adjustment should be made to reflect the subsequent settlement of a legal claim in favour of the entity. In this instance, the period in which the change occurs is subsequent to the reporting period. There is also no suggestion that the example in IAS 10 is referring to anything but liabilities. An asset could only be recognised if, at the end of the reporting period, the entity could show that it was virtually certain that its claim would succeed.

3.2.2.A Obligations contingent on the successful recovery of a contingent asset

Entities may sometimes be required to pay contingent fees to a third party dependent upon the successful recovery of a contingent asset. For example, the payment of fees to a legal advisor in a contract agreed on a 'no win, no fee' basis will depend upon the successful outcome of a legal claim. In such cases, we believe that the obligation for the success fee arises from an executory contract that should be evaluated separately from the legal claim. The liability for the success fee would therefore only be recognised by the entity upon winning the claim.

IAS 37 uses the term executory contracts to mean 'contracts under which neither party has performed any of its obligations, or both parties have partially performed their obligations to an equal extent'. *[IAS 37.3]*. When a contract for services is wholly contingent on recovering a contingent asset, no service requiring payment is deemed to be provided until or unless the matter is resolved successfully. Unless the contract also required payment to be made in the event of failure, the amount of work put in by the lawyer to prepare a case and argue for recovery of the contingent asset is irrelevant to the existence of a liability to pay fees.

If the entity has deemed it appropriate to recognise an asset in respect of the claim, it would be appropriate to take account of any such fees in the measurement of that asset (in determining the net amount recoverable); but no accrual should be made for the legal fees themselves unless a successful outcome is confirmed.

This analysis is specific to a no win-no fee arrangement related to a contingent asset and may not be appropriate in other circumstances.

3.2.3 How probability determines whether to recognise or disclose

The following matrix summarises the treatment of contingencies under IAS 37:

Likelihood of outcome	*Accounting treatment: contingent liability*	*Accounting treatment: contingent asset*
Virtually certain	Recognise	Recognise
Probable	Recognise	Disclose
Possible but not probable	Disclose	No disclosure permitted
Remote	No disclosure required	No disclosure permitted

The standard does not put a numerical measure of probability on either 'virtually certain' or 'remote'. In our view, the use of such measures would downgrade a process requiring the exercise of judgement into a mechanical exercise. It is difficult to imagine circumstances when an entity could reliably determine an obligation to be, for example, 92%, 95% or 99% likely, let alone be able to compare those probabilities objectively. Accordingly, we think it reasonable to regard 'virtually certain' as describing a likelihood that is as close to 100% as to make any remaining uncertainty insignificant; to see 'remote' as meaning a likelihood of an outflow of resources that is not significant; and for significance to be a matter for judgement and determined according to the merits of each case.

3.3 Recognising an asset when recognising a provision

In most cases, the recognition of a provision results in an immediate expense in profit or loss. Nevertheless, in some cases it may be appropriate to recognise an asset. These issues are not discussed in IAS 37, which neither prohibits nor requires capitalisation of the costs recognised when a provision is made. It states that other standards specify whether expenditures are treated as assets or expenses. *[IAS 37.8]*.

Whilst the main body of IAS 37 is silent on the matter, the standard contains the following example which concludes that an asset should be recognised when a decommissioning provision is established.

Example 28.5: When the recognition of a provision gives rise to an asset

An entity operates an offshore oilfield where its licensing agreement requires it to remove the oil rig at the end of production and restore the seabed. 90% of the eventual costs relate to the removal of the oil rig and restoration of damage caused by building it, with 10% expected to arise through the extraction of oil. At the end of the reporting period, the rig has been constructed but no oil has been extracted.

A provision is recognised in respect of the probable costs relating to the removal of the rig and restoring damage caused by building it. This is because the construction of the rig, combined with the requirement under the licence to remove the rig and restore the seabed, creates an obligating event as at the end of the reporting period. These costs are included as part of the cost of the oil rig.

However, there is no obligation to rectify any damage that will be caused by the future extraction of oil. *[IAS 37 IE Example 3]*.

This conclusion is supported by IAS 16, which requires the cost of an item of property, plant and equipment to include the initial estimate of the costs of dismantling and removing an asset and restoring the site on which it is located, the obligation for which an entity incurs either when the item is acquired or as a consequence of having used the item during a particular period for purposes other than to produce inventories during that period. *[IAS 16.16(c), 18]*. The treatment of decommissioning costs is discussed further at 6.3 below.

4 MEASUREMENT

4.1 Best estimate of provision

IAS 37 requires the amount to be recognised as a provision to be the best estimate of the expenditure required to settle the present obligation at the end of the reporting period. *[IAS 37.36]*. This measure is determined before tax, as the tax consequences of the provision, and changes to it, are dealt with under IAS 12. *[IAS 37.41]*.

The standard equates this 'best estimate' with 'the amount that an entity would rationally pay to settle the obligation at the end of the reporting period or to transfer it to a third party at that time'. *[IAS 37.37]*. It is interesting that a hypothetical transaction of this kind should be proposed as the conceptual basis of the measurement required, rather than putting the main emphasis upon the actual expenditure that is expected to be incurred in the future.

The standard does acknowledge that it would often be impossible or prohibitively expensive to settle or transfer the obligation at the end of the reporting period. However, it goes on to state that 'the estimate of the amount that an entity would rationally pay to settle or transfer the obligation gives the best estimate of the expenditure required to settle the present obligation at the end of the reporting period'. *[IAS 37.37]*.

The estimates of outcome and financial effect are determined by the judgement of the entity's management, supplemented by experience of similar transactions and, in some cases, reports from independent experts. The evidence considered will include any additional evidence provided by events after the reporting period. *[IAS 37.38]*.

The standard suggests that there are various ways of dealing with the uncertainties surrounding the amount to be recognised as a provision. It mentions three, an expected value (or probability-weighted) method; the mid-point of the range of possible outcomes; and an estimate of the individual most likely outcome. An expected value approach would be appropriate when a large population of items is being measured, such as warranty costs. This is a statistical computation which weights the cost of all the various possible outcomes according to their probabilities, as illustrated in the following example taken from IAS 37. *[IAS 37.39]*.

Example 28.6: Calculation of expected value

An entity sells goods with a warranty under which customers are covered for the cost of repairs of any manufacturing defects that become apparent within the first six months after purchase. If minor defects were detected in all products sold, repair costs of £1 million would result. If major defects were detected in all products sold, repair costs of £4 million would result. The entity's past experience and future expectations indicate that, for the coming year, 75 per cent of the goods sold will have no defects, 20 per cent of the goods sold will have minor defects and 5 per cent of the goods sold will have major defects. In accordance with paragraph 24 of IAS 37 (see 3.1.2 above) an entity assesses the probability of a transfer for the warranty obligations as a whole.

The expected value of the cost of repairs is:

(75% of nil) + (20% of £1m) + (5% of £4m) = £400,000.

In a situation where there is a continuous range of possible outcomes and each point in that range is as likely as any other, IAS 37 requires that the mid-point of the range is used. *[IAS 37.39]*. This is not a particularly helpful way of setting out the requirement, as it does not make it clear what the principle is meant to be. The mid-point in this case represents the median as well as the expected value. The latter may have been what was intended, but the median could be equally well justified on the basis that it is 50% probable that at least this amount will be payable, while anything in excess of that constitutes a possible but not a probable liability, that should be disclosed rather than accrued. Interestingly, US GAAP has a different approach to this issue in relation to contingencies. FASB ASC Topic 450 – *Contingencies* – states that where a contingent loss could fall within a range of amounts then, if there is a best estimate within the range, it should be accrued, with the remainder noted as a contingent liability. However, if there is no best estimate then the *lowest* figure within the range should be accrued, with the remainder up to the maximum potential loss noted as a contingent liability.[10]

Where the obligation being measured relates to a single item, the standard suggests that the best estimate of the liability may be the individual most likely outcome. However, even in such a case, it notes that consideration should be given to other possible outcomes and where these are predominantly higher or mainly lower than the most likely outcome, the resultant 'best estimate' will be a higher or lower amount than the individual most likely outcome. To illustrate this, the standard gives an example of an entity that has to rectify a fault in a major plant that it has constructed for a customer. The most likely outcome is that the repair will succeed at the first attempt. However, a provision should be made for a larger amount if there is a significant chance that further attempts will be necessary. *[IAS 37.40]*.

4.2 Dealing with risk and uncertainty in measuring a provision

It is clear from the definition of a provision as a liability of uncertain timing or amount that entities will have to deal with risk and uncertainty in estimating an appropriate measure of the obligation at the end of the reporting period. It is therefore interesting to consider how the measurement rules detailed in IAS 37 help entities achieve a faithful representation of the obligation in these circumstances. A faithful representation requires estimates that are neutral, that is, without bias. *[Framework.QC12, QC14]*. The *Conceptual Framework* warns against the use of conservatism or prudence in estimates because this is 'likely to lead to a bias'. It adds that the exercise of prudence can be counterproductive, in that the overstatement of liabilities in one period frequently leads to overstated financial performance in later periods, 'a result that cannot be described as prudent or neutral'. *[Framework.BC3.28]*.

The standard does not refer to neutrality as such; however, it does discuss the concept of risk and the need for exercising caution and care in making judgements under conditions of uncertainty. It states that 'the risks and uncertainties that inevitably surround many events and circumstances shall be taken into account in reaching the best estimate of a provision'. *[IAS 37.42]*. It refers to risk as being variability of outcome and suggests that a risk adjustment may increase the amount at which a liability is measured. *[IAS 37.43]*. Whilst the standard provides an example of a case in which the best estimate of an obligation might have to be larger than the individual most likely outcome, *[IAS 37.40]*, it gives no indication of how this increment should be determined. It warns that caution is needed in making judgements under conditions of uncertainty, so that expenses or liabilities are not understated. However, it says that uncertainty does not justify the creation of excessive provisions or a deliberate overstatement of liabilities. Accordingly, care is needed to avoid duplicating adjustments for risk and uncertainty, for example by estimating the costs of a particularly adverse outcome and then overestimating its probability. *[IAS 37.43]*. Any uncertainties surrounding the amount of the expenditure are to be disclosed (see 7.1 below). *[IAS 37.44]*.

The overall result of all this is somewhat confusing. Whilst a best estimate based solely on the expected value approach or the mid-point of a range addresses the uncertainties relating to there being a variety of possible outcomes, it does not fully reflect risk, because the actual outcome could still be higher or lower than the estimate. Therefore, the discussion on risk suggests that an additional adjustment should be made. However, apart from indicating that the result may be to increase the recognised liability and pointing out the need to avoid duplicating the effect of risk in estimates of cash flows and probability, *[IAS 37.43]*, it is not clear quite how this might be achieved. This leaves a certain amount of scope for variation in the estimation of provisions and is further complicated when the concept of risk is combined with considerations relating to the time value of money (see 4.3.2 below).

4.3 Discounting the estimated cash flows to a present value

The standard requires that where the effect of the time value of money is material, the amount of a provision should be the present value of the expenditures expected to be required to settle the obligation. *[IAS 37.45]*. The discount rate (or rates) to be used in arriving at the present value should be 'a pre-tax rate (or rates) that reflect(s) current market assessments of the time value of money and the risks specific to the liability. The discount rate(s) shall not reflect risks for which the future cash flow estimates have been adjusted.' *[IAS 37.47]*. However, it is worth noting that no discounting is required for provisions where the cash flows will not be sufficiently far into the future for discounting to have a material impact. *[IAS 37.46]*.

The main types of provision where the impact of discounting will be significant are those relating to decommissioning and other environmental restoration liabilities. IFRIC 1 addresses some of the issues relating to the use of discounting (in the context of provisions for obligations to dismantle, remove or restore items of property, plant and equipment, referred to as 'decommissioning, restoration and similar liabilities') which are discussed at 6.3.1 below.

4.3.1 Real versus nominal rate

IAS 37 does not indicate whether the discount rate should be a real discount rate or a nominal discount rate (although a real discount rate is referred to in Example 2 in Appendix D which illustrates the narrative disclosure for decommissioning costs). The discount rate to be used depends on whether:

(a) the future cash flows are expressed in current prices, in which case a real discount rate (which excludes the effects of general inflation) should be used; or

(b) the future cash flows are expressed in expected future prices, in which case a nominal discount rate (which includes a return to cover expected inflation) should be used.

Either alternative is acceptable, and these methods may produce the same figure for the initial present value of the provision. However, the effect of the unwinding of the discount will be different in each case (see 4.3.5 below). In Extract 28.9 at 6.4 below, BP p.l.c. discloses how its provision for the costs of environmental remediation is estimated using current prices and discounted using a real rate.

4.3.2 Adjusting for risk and using a government bond rate

IAS 37 also requires that risk is taken into account in the calculation of a provision, but gives little guidance as to how this should be done. Where discounting is concerned, it merely says that the discount rate should not reflect risks for which the future cash flow estimates have been adjusted. *[IAS 37.47]*. One may use a discount rate that reflects the risk associated with the liability (a risk-adjusted rate). The following example, taken from the UK Accounting Standards Board's (ASB) Working Paper – *Discounting in Financial Reporting*,[11] shows how an entity might calculate such a risk adjusted rate.

Example 28.7: Calculation of a risk-adjusted rate[12]

A company has a provision for which the expected value of the cash outflow in three years' time is £150, and the risk-free rate (i.e. the nominal rate unadjusted for risk) is 5%. However, the possible outcomes from which the expected value has been determined lie within a range between £100 and £200. The company is risk averse and would settle instead for a certain payment of, say, £160 in three years' time rather than be exposed to the risk of the actual outcome being as high as £200. The effect of risk in calculating the present value can be expressed as either:

(a) discounting the risk-adjusted cash flow of £160 at the risk-free (unadjusted) rate of 5%, giving a present value of £138; or

(b) discounting the expected cash flow (which is unadjusted for risk) of £150 at a risk-adjusted rate that will give the present value of £138, i.e. a rate of 2.8%.

As can be seen from this example, the risk-adjusted discount rate is a *lower* rate than the unadjusted (risk-free) discount rate. This may seem counter-intuitive initially, because the experience of most borrowers is that banks and other lenders will charge a higher rate of interest on loans that are assessed to be higher risk to the lender. However, in the case of a provision a risk premium is being suffered to eliminate the possibility of the actual cost being higher (thereby capping a liability), whereas in the case of a loan receivable a premium is required to compensate the lender for taking on the risk of not recovering its full value (setting a floor for the value of the lender's financial asset). In both cases the actual cash flows incurred by the paying entity are higher to reflect a premium for risk. In other words, the discount rate for an asset is increased to reflect the risk of recovering less and the discount rate for a liability is reduced to reflect the risk of paying more.

A problem with changing the discount rate to account for risk is that this adjusted rate is a theoretical rate, as it is unlikely that there would be a market assessment of the risks specific to the liability alone. *[IAS 37.47]*. However the lower discount rate in the above example is consistent with the premise that a risk-adjusted liability should be higher than a liability without accounting for the risk that the actual settlement amount is different to the estimate. *[IAS 37.43]*. It is also difficult to see how a risk-adjusted rate could be obtained in practice. In the above example, it was obtained only by reverse-engineering; it was already known that the net present value of a risk-adjusted liability was £138, so the risk-adjusted rate was just the discount rate applied to unadjusted cash flow of £150 to give that result.

IAS 37 offers an alternative approach – instead of using a risk-adjusted discount rate, the estimated future cash flows themselves can be adjusted for risk. *[IAS 37.47]*. This does of course present the problem of how to adjust the cash flows for risk (see 4.2 above). However, this may be easier than attempting to risk-adjust the discount rate.

For the purposes of discounting post-employment benefit obligations, IAS 19 requires the discount rate to be determined by reference to market yields at the end of the reporting period on high quality corporate bonds (although in countries where there is no deep market in such bonds, the market yields on government bonds should be used). *[IAS 19.83]*. Although IAS 19 indicates that this discount rate reflects the time value of money (but not the actuarial or investment risk), *[IAS 19.84]*, we do not believe it is appropriate to use the yield on a high quality corporate bond for determining a risk-free rate to be used in discounting provisions under IAS 37. Accordingly, in our view, where an entity is using a risk-free discount rate for the purposes of calculating a provision under IAS 37, that rate should be based on a government bond rate with a similar currency and remaining term as the provision. It follows that because a risk-adjusted rate is always lower than the risk-free rate, an entity cannot justify the discounting of a provision at a rate that is higher than a government bond rate with a similar currency and term to the provision.

Whichever method of reflecting risk is adopted, IAS 37 emphasises that care must be taken that the effect of risk is not double-counted by inclusion in both the cash flows and the discount rate. *[IAS 37.47]*.

In recent years, government bond rates have been more volatile as markets have changed rates to reflect (among other factors) heightened perceptions of sovereign debt risk. In some cases, government bond yields may be negative. The question has therefore arisen whether government bond rates, at least in certain jurisdictions, should continue to be regarded as the default measure of a risk-free discount rate. Whilst the current volatility in rates has highlighted the fact that no debt (even government debt) is totally risk free, the challenge is to find a more reliable measure as an alternative. Any adjustment to the government bond rate to 'remove' the estimate of sovereign debt risk is conceptually flawed, as it not possible to isolate one component of risk from all the other variables that influence the setting of an interest rate. Another approach might be to apply some form of average bond rate over a period of 3, 6 or 12 months to mitigate the volatility inherent in applying the spot rate at the period end. However, this is clearly inappropriate given the requirements in IAS 37 to determine the best estimate of an obligation by reference to the expenditure required to settle it *'at the end of the reporting period'*, *[IAS 37.36]*, and to determine the discount rate on the basis of *'current market assessments'* of the time value of money. *[IAS 37.47]*.

With 'risk' being a measure of potential variability in returns, it remains the case that in most countries a government bond will be subject to the lowest level of variability in that jurisdiction. As such, in most countries it remains the most suitable of all the observable measures of the time value of money in a particular country. Where government bond rates are negative or, more likely, result in a negative discount rate once adjusted for risk, we believe that it is not appropriate to apply a floor of zero to the discount rate as this would result in an understatement of the liability. As discussed above, and at 4.3.1, IAS 37 offers various approaches to determining an appropriate discount rate. It may sometimes be the case that one or more of the allowed approaches result in a negative discount rate whereas the application of an alternative permitted approach would not. In order to avoid some of the presentational difficulties associated with a negative discount rate, entities faced with a negative real discount rate before risk adjustment may wish to consider the alternative approach of discounting expected future cash flows expressed in future prices, at a nominal discount rate (see 4.3.1 above), if the nominal rate is not negative. Similarly, entities that are faced with a negative risk-adjusted discount rate only because of risk adjustment (i.e. where risk free rates themselves are not negative) may wish to adopt the alternative approach of adjusting the estimated future cash flows to reflect the risks associated with the liability, rather than risk-adjusting the discount rate.

A difficulty that can arise in certain countries is finding a government bond with a similar term to the provision, for example when measuring a decommissioning provision expected to be settled in 30 years in a country where there are no government bonds with a term exceeding 10 years. In such cases, the government bond rate might be adjusted and the techniques adopted by actuaries for measuring retirement obligations with long maturities, that involve extrapolating current market rates along a yield curve, *[IAS 19.86]*, might be considered. The difficulties of finding an appropriate discount rate in the context of retirement benefit obligations are discussed in Chapter 33 at 7.6.

4.3.3 Own credit risk is not taken into account

In considering the risk factors that might give rise to a difference between the actual cash flows required to settle a liability and their previously estimated amounts, an entity would not take into account its own credit risk; that is, the risk that the entity could be unable to settle the amount finally determined to be payable. This is because IAS 37 requires the discount rate to reflect 'the risks specific to the liability'. *[IAS 37.47]*. In March 2011, the Interpretations Committee decided not to take to its agenda a request for interpretation of the phrase 'the risks specific to the liability' and whether this means that an entity's own credit risk should be excluded from any adjustments made to the discount rate used to measure liabilities. In doing so, the Interpretations Committee acknowledged that IAS 37 is not explicit on the question of own credit risk; but understood that the predominant practice was to exclude it for the reason that credit risk is generally viewed as a risk of the entity rather than a risk specific to the liability.[13]

4.3.4 Pre-tax discount rate

Since IAS 37 requires provisions to be measured before tax, it follows that cash flows should be discounted at a pre-tax discount rate. *[IAS 37.47]*. No further explanation of this is given in the standard.

This is probably because, in reality, the use of a pre-tax discount rate will be most common. Supposing, for example, that the risk-free rate of return is being used, then the discount rate used will be a government bond rate. This rate will be obtained gross. Thus, the idea of trying to determine a pre-tax rate (for example by obtaining a required post-tax rate of return and adjusting it for the tax consequences of different cash flows) will seldom be relevant.

The calculation is illustrated in the following example.

Example 28.8: Use of discounting and tax effect

It is estimated that the settlement of an environmental provision will give rise to a gross cash outflow of £500,000 in three years' time. The gross interest rate on a government bond maturing in three years' time is 6%. The tax rate is 30%.

The net present value of the provision is £419,810 (£500,000 × 1 ÷ $(1.06)^3$). Hence, a provision of £419,810 should be booked in the statement of financial position. A corresponding deferred tax asset of £125,943 (30% of £419,810) would be set up if it met the criteria for recognition in IAS 12 (See Chapter 31 at 7.4).

4.3.5 Unwinding of the discount

IAS 37 indicates that where discounting is used, the carrying amount of a provision increases in each period to reflect the passage of time, and that this increase is recognised as a borrowing cost. *[IAS 37.60]*. This is the only guidance that the standard gives on the unwinding of the discount. IFRIC 1 in relation to provisions for decommissioning, restoration and similar liabilities requires that the periodic unwinding of the discount is recognised in profit or loss as a finance cost as it occurs. The Interpretations Committee concluded that the unwinding of the discount is not a borrowing cost for the purposes of IAS 23 – *Borrowing Costs* – and thus cannot be capitalised under that standard. *[IFRIC 1.8]*. It noted that IAS 23 addresses funds borrowed specifically for the purpose of obtaining a particular asset and agreed that a decommissioning liability does not fall within this description since it does not reflect funds borrowed. Accordingly, the Interpretations Committee concluded that the unwinding of the discount is not a borrowing cost as defined in IAS 23. *[IFRIC 1.BC26]*.

However, there is no discussion of the impact that the original selection of discount rate can have on its unwinding, that is, the selection of real versus nominal rates, and risk-free versus risk-adjusted rates. The IASB appears to have overlooked the fact that these different discount rates will unwind differently. This is best illustrated by way of an example.

Example 28.9: Effect on future profits of choosing a real or nominal discount rate

A provision is required to be set up for an expected cash outflow of €100,000 (estimated at current prices), payable in three years' time. The appropriate nominal discount rate is 7.5%, and inflation is estimated at 5%. If the provision is discounted using the nominal rate, the expected cash outflow has to reflect future prices. Accordingly, if prices increase at the rate of inflation, the cash outflow will be €115,762 (€100,000 × 1.05^3). The net present value of €115,762, discounted at 7.5%, is €93,184 (€115,762 × 1 ÷ $(1.075)^3$). If all assumptions remain valid throughout the three-year period, the movement in the provision would be as follows:

	Undiscounted cash flows	*Provision*
	€	€
Year 0	115,762	93,184
Unwinding of discount (€93,184 × 0.075)		6,989
Revision to estimate		–
Year 1	115,762	100,173
Unwinding of discount (€100,173 × 0.075)		7,513
Revision to estimate		–
Year 2	115,762	107,686
Unwinding of discount (€107,686 × 0.075)		8,076
Revision to estimate		–
Year 3	115,762	115,762

If the provision is calculated based on the expected cash outflow of €100,000 (estimated at current prices), then it needs to be discounted using a real discount rate. This may be thought to be 2.5%, being the difference between the nominal rate of 7.5% and the inflation rate of 5%. However, it is more accurately calculated using the Fisher relation or formula[14] as 2.381%, being (1.075 ÷ 1.05) – 1. Accordingly, the net present value of €100,000, discounted at 2.381%, is €93,184 (€100,000 × 1 ÷ $(1.02381)^3$), the same as the calculation using future prices discounted at the nominal rate.

If all assumptions remain valid throughout the three-year period, the movement in the provision comprises both the unwinding of the discount and the increase in the level of current prices used to determine the estimate of cost, as follows:

	Undiscounted cash flows	*Provision*
	€	€
Year 0	100,000	93,184
Unwinding of discount (€93,184 × 0.02381)		2,219
Revision to estimate (€100,000 × 0.05)	5,000	4,770
Year 1	105,000	100,173
Unwinding of discount (€100,173 × 0.02381)		2,385
Revision to estimate (€105,000 × 0.05)	5,250	5,128
Year 2	110,250	107,686
Unwinding of discount (€107,686 × 0.02381)		2,564
Revision to estimate (€110,250 × 0.05)	5,512	5,512
Year 3	115,762	115,762

Although the total expense in each year is the same under either method, what will be different is the allocation of the change in provision between operating costs (assuming the original provision was treated as an operating expense) and finance charges. It can be seen from the second table in the above example that using the real discount rate will give rise to a much lower finance charge each year. However, this does not lead to a lower provision in the statement of financial position at the end of each year. Provisions have to be revised annually to reflect the current best estimate of the obligation. *[IAS 37.59]*. Thus, the provision in the above example at the end of each year needs to be adjusted to reflect current prices at that time (and any other adjustments that arise from changes in the estimate of the provision), as well as being adjusted for the unwinding of the discount. For example, the revised provision at the end of Year 1 is €100,173, being €105,000 discounted for two years at 2.381%. After allowing for the unwinding of the discount, this required an additional provision of €4,770.

A more significant difference will arise where the recognition of the original provision is included as part of the cost of property, plant or equipment, rather than as an expense, such as when a decommissioning provision is recognised. In that case, using a real discount rate will result initially in a lower charge to the income statement, since under IFRIC 1 any revision to the estimate of the provision is not taken to the income statement but is treated as an adjustment to the carrying value of the related asset, which is then depreciated prospectively over the remaining life of the asset (see 6.3.1 below).

A similar issue arises with the option of using the risk-free or the risk-adjusted discount rate. However, this is a more complex problem, because it is not clear what to do with the risk-adjustment built into the provision. This is illustrated in the following example.

Example 28.10: Effect on future profits of choosing a risk-free or risk-adjusted rate

A company is required to make a provision for which the estimated value of the cash outflow in three years' time is £150, when the risk-free rate (i.e. the rate unadjusted for risk) is 5%. However, the possible outcomes from which the expected value has been determined lie within a range between £100 and £200. The reporting entity is risk averse and would settle instead for a certain payment of, say, £160 in three years' time rather than be exposed to the risk of the actual outcome being as high as £200. The measurement options to account for risk can be expressed as either:

(a) discounting the risk-adjusted cash flow of £160 at the risk-free (unadjusted) rate of 5%, giving a present value of £138; or

(b) discounting the expected cash flow (which is unadjusted for risk) of £150 at a risk-adjusted rate that will give the present value of £138, i.e. a rate of 2.8%.

Assuming that there are no changes in estimate required to be made to the provision during the three-year period, alternative (a) will unwind to give an overall finance charge of £22 and a final provision of £160. Alternative (b) will unwind to give an overall finance charge of £12 and a final provision of £150.

In this example, the unwinding of different discount rates gives rise to different provisions. The difference of £10 (£22 – £12) relates to the risk adjustment that has been made to the provision. As the actual date of settlement comes closer, the estimates of the range of possible outcomes (and accordingly the expected value of the outflow) and the premium the entity would accept for certainty will converge. As such, the effect of any initial difference related to the decision to apply a risk-free or risk-adjusted rate will be lost in the other estimation adjustments that would be made over time.

In circumstances where a provision has been discounted using a negative discount rate (see 4.3.2 above), entities will need to give some consideration to how the unwinding of the discount should be presented in the statement of comprehensive income. The presentation of income and expense resulting from negative interest has been discussed by the Interpretations Committee in the context of financial instruments. Whilst that topic was not taken on to the Interpretations Committee's agenda, the Committee noted in their agenda decision that the expense arising on a financial asset because of a negative interest rate should not be presented as interest revenue, but in an appropriate expense classification.[15] Whilst negative interest rates on financial liabilities were not explicitly addressed in the agenda decision, the Interpretations Committee noted during discussions that an inflow of economic benefits arising from a liability cannot be characterised as revenue under IAS 18.[16] In our view, similar considerations are appropriate to the presentation of the unwinding of the discount on a provision that has been discounted using a negative nominal discount rate.

4.3.6 *The effect of changes in interest rates on the discount rate applied*

The standard requires the discount rate to reflect current market assessments of the time value of money. *[IAS 37.47]*. This means that where interest rates change, the provision should be recalculated on the basis of revised interest rates (see Example 28.11 below).

Any revision in the interest rate will give rise to an adjustment to the carrying value of the provision in addition to the unwinding of the previously estimated discount. The standard requires these movements to be disclosed in the notes to the financial statements (see 7.1 below). *[IAS 37.84(e)]*. However, the standard does not explicitly say how the effect of changes in interest rates should be classified in the income statement. We believe that this element should be treated separately from the effect of the passage of time, with only the charge for unwinding of the discount being classified as a finance cost. Any adjustment to the provision as a result of revising the discount rate is a change in accounting estimate, as defined in IAS 8 – *Accounting Policies, Changes in Accounting Estimates and Errors* (see Chapter 3 at 4.5).

Accordingly, it should be reflected in the line item of the income statement to which the expense establishing the provision was originally taken and not as a component of the finance cost. Indeed, this is the approach required by IFRIC 1 in relation to provisions for decommissioning, restoration and similar liabilities in relation to assets measured using the cost model (see 6.3.1 below). However, in that case the original provision gives rise to an asset rather than an expense, so any subsequent adjustment is not included in profit or loss, *[IAS 8.36]*, but added to or deducted from the cost of the asset to which it relates. *[IFRIC 1.5]*. The adjusted depreciable amount of the asset is then depreciated prospectively over its remaining useful life. *[IFRIC 1.7]*. Nevertheless, the effect is distinguished from the unwinding of the discount.

In addition, the standard gives no specific guidance on how or when this adjustment should be made. For example, it is unclear whether the new discount rate should be applied during the year or just at the year-end, and whether the rate should be applied to the new estimate of the provision or the old estimate. IFRIC 1 implies that the finance cost is adjusted prospectively from the date on which the liability is remeasured. Example 1 to IFRIC 1 states that if the change in the liability had resulted from a change in discount rate, instead of a change in the estimated cash flows, the change would still have been reflected in the carrying value of the related asset, but next year's finance cost would have reflected the new discount rate. *[IFRIC 1.IE5]*. This conclusion is consistent with the requirement in IAS 37 for the value of a provision to reflect the best estimate of the expenditure required to settle the obligation as at the end of the reporting period, *[IAS 37.36]*, as illustrated in the following example.

Example 28.11: Accounting for the effect of changes in the discount rate

A provision is required to be set up for an expected cash outflow of €100,000 (estimated at current prices), payable in three years' time. The appropriate nominal discount rate is 7.5%, and inflation is estimated at 5%. At future prices the cash outflow will be €115,762 (€100,000 × 1.05^3). The net present value of €115,762, discounted at 7.5%, is €93,184 (€115,762 × 1 ÷ 1.075^3).

At the end of Year 2, all assumptions remain valid, except it is determined that a current market assessment of the time value of money and the risks specific to the liability would require a decrease in the discount rate to 6.5%. Accordingly, at the end of Year 2, the revised net present value of €115,762, discounted at 6.5%, is €108,697 (€115,762 ÷ 1.065).

The movement in the provision would be reflected as follows:

	Undiscounted cash flows	*Provision*
	€	€
Year 0	115,762	93,184
Unwinding of discount (€93,184 × 0.075)		6,989
Revision to estimate		–
Year 1	115,762	100,173
Unwinding of discount (€100,173 × 0.075)		7,513
	115,762	107,686
Revision to estimate (€108,697 – €107,686)		1,011
Year 2	115,762	108,697
Unwinding of discount (€108,697 × 0.065)		7,065
Revision to estimate		–
Year 3	115,762	115,762

Chapter 28

In Year 2, the finance charge is based on the previous estimate of the discount rate and the revision to the estimate of the provision would be charged to the same line item in the income statement that was used to establish the provision of €93,184 at the start of Year 1.

Where market rates of interest are more volatile, entities may decide to reassess the applicable discount rate for a provision during an annual reporting period. Equally, it would be appropriate to revise this assessment as at the end of any interim reporting period during the financial year to the extent that the impact is material.

4.4 Anticipating future events that may affect the estimate of cash flows

The standard states that 'future events that may affect the amount required to settle an obligation shall be reflected in the amount of a provision where there is sufficient objective evidence that they will occur'. *[IAS 37.48]*. The types of future events that the standard has in mind are advances in technology and changes in legislation.

The requirement for objective evidence means that it is not appropriate to reduce the best estimate of future cash flows simply by assuming that a completely new technology will be developed before the liability is required to be settled. There will need to be sufficient objective evidence that such future developments are likely. For example, an entity may believe that the cost of cleaning up a site at the end of its life will be reduced by future changes in technology. The amount recognised has to reflect a reasonable expectation of technically qualified, objective observers, taking account of all available evidence as to the technology that will be available at the time of the clean-up. Thus it is appropriate to include, for example, expected cost reductions associated with increased experience in applying existing technology or the expected cost of applying existing technology to a larger or more complex clean-up operation than has previously been carried out. *[IAS 37.49]*.

Similarly, if new legislation is to be anticipated, there will need to be evidence both of what the legislation will demand and whether it is virtually certain to be enacted and implemented. In many cases sufficient objective evidence will not exist until the new legislation is enacted. *[IAS 37.50]*.

These requirements are most likely to impact provisions for liabilities that will be settled some distance in the future, such as decommissioning costs (see 6.3 below).

4.5 Reimbursements, insurance and other recoveries from third parties

In some circumstances an entity is able to look to a third party to reimburse part of the costs required to settle a provision or to pay the amounts directly to a third party. Examples are insurance contracts, indemnity clauses and suppliers' warranties. *[IAS 37.55]*. A reimbursement asset is recognised only when it is virtually certain to be received if the entity settles the obligation. The asset cannot be greater than the amount of the provision. No 'netting off' is allowed in the statement of financial position, with any asset classified separately from any provision. *[IAS 37.53]*. However, the expense relating to a provision can be shown in the income statement net of reimbursement. *[IAS 37.54]*. This means that if an entity has insurance cover in relation to a specific potential obligation, this is treated as a reimbursement right under IAS 37. It is not appropriate to record no provision (where the recognition criteria in the standard are met) on the basis that the entity's net exposure is expected to be zero.

The main area of concern with these requirements is whether the 'virtually certain' criterion that needs to be applied to the corresponding asset might mean that some reimbursements will not be capable of recognition at all. For items such as insurance contracts, this may not be an issue, as entities will probably be able to confirm the existence of cover for the obligation in question and accordingly be able to demonstrate that a recovery on an insurance contract is virtually certain if the entity is required to settle the obligation. Of course, it may be more difficult in complex situations for an entity to confirm it has cover against any loss. For other types of reimbursement, it may be more difficult to establish that recovery is virtually certain.

Except when an obligation is determined to be joint and several (see 4.6 below), any form of net presentation in the statement of financial position is prohibited. This is because the entity would remain liable for the whole cost if the third party failed to pay for any reason, for example as a result of the third party's insolvency. In such situations, the provision should be made gross and any reimbursement should be treated as a separate asset (but only when it is virtually certain that the reimbursement will be received if the entity settles the obligation). *[IAS 37.56]*.

If the entity has no liability in the event that the third party cannot pay, then these costs are excluded from the estimate of the provision altogether because, by its very nature, there is no liability. *[IAS 37.57]*.

Extract 28.2 at 4.6 below illustrates how Syngenta classifies amounts recoverable from third parties as separate assets.

In contrast, where an entity is assessing an onerous contract, such as a vacant leasehold property, it is common for entities to apply what looks like a net approach. However, because an onerous contract provision relates to the excess of the unavoidable costs over the expected economic benefits, *[IAS 37.68]*, there is no corresponding asset to be recognised. For example, the amount of the provision for an onerous lease is determined net of the cash flows that may be expected to arise from sub-letting the property. This is discussed further at 6.2 below.

4.6 Joint and several liability

It is interesting to contrast the approach of IAS 37 to reimbursements with the case where an entity is jointly and severally liable for an obligation. Joint and several liability arises when a number of entities are liable for a single obligation (for example, to damages), both individually and collectively. The holder of the obligation in these circumstances can collect the entire amount from any single member of the group or from any and all of the members in various amounts until the liability is settled in full. Even when the members have an agreement between themselves as to how the total obligation should be divided, each member remains liable to make good any deficiency on the part of the others. This situation is different from proportionate liability, where individual members of a group might be required to bear a percentage of the total liability, but without any obligation to make good any shortfall by another member. Joint and several liability can be established in a contract, by a court judgement or under legislation.

An entity that is jointly and severally liable recognises only its own share of the obligation, based on the amount it is probable that the entity will pay. The remainder that is expected to be met by other parties is treated only as a contingent liability. *[IAS 37.29, 58]*.

The fact that the other third parties in this situation have a direct (albeit shared) obligation for the past event itself, rather than only a contractual relationship with the entity, is enough of a difference in circumstances to allow a form of net determination of the amount to recognise. Arguably, the economic position is no different, because the entity is exposed to further loss in the event that the third parties are unable or unwilling to pay. However, IAS 37 does not treat joint and several liability in the same way as reimbursement, which would have required a liability to be set up for the whole amount with a corresponding asset recognised for the amount expected to be met by other parties.

The extract below illustrates how Syngenta describes its policy for the recognition of amounts recoverable from third parties and measurement where liability is joint and several.

Extract 28.2: Syngenta AG (2013)

Notes to the Syngenta Group Consolidated Financial Statements [extract]
30. Other new IFRSs and accounting policies [extract]
Provisions

A provision is recognized in the balance sheet when Syngenta has a legal or constructive obligation to a third party or parties as a result of a past event, the amount of which can be reliably estimated and it is probable that an outflow of economic benefits will be required to settle the obligation. The amount recognized as a provision is the best estimate of the expenditure required to settle the obligation at the balance sheet date. If the effect of discounting is material, provisions are discounted to the expected present value of their future cash flows using a pre-tax rate that reflects current market assessments of the time value of money and the risks specific to the liability. Where some or all of the expenditures required to settle a provision are expected to be reimbursed by another party, the expected reimbursement is recognized as a separate asset only when virtually certain.

Where Syngenta has a joint and several liability for a matter with one or more other parties, no provision is recognized by Syngenta for those parts of the obligation expected to be settled by another party. Syngenta self-insures or uses a combination of insurance and self-insurance for certain risks. Provisions for these risks are estimated in part by considering historical claims experience and other actuarial assumptions and, where necessary, counterparty risk.

4.7 Provisions are not reduced for gains on disposal of related assets

IAS 37 states that gains from the expected disposal of assets should not be taken into account in measuring a provision, even if the expected disposal is closely linked to the event giving rise to the provision. Such gains should be recognised at the time specified by the Standard dealing with the assets concerned. *[IAS 37.51-52]*. This is likely to be of particular relevance in relation to restructuring provisions (see 6.1.4 below). However, it may also apply in other situations. Extract 28.6 at 6.3 below illustrates an example of a company excluding gains from the expected disposal of assets in determining its provision for decommissioning costs.

4.8 Changes and uses of provisions

After recognition, a provision will be re-estimated, used and released over the period up to the eventual determination of a settlement amount for the obligation. IAS 37 requires that provisions should be reviewed at the end of each reporting period and adjusted to reflect the current best estimate. If it is no longer probable that an outflow of resources embodying economic benefits will be required to settle the obligation, the provision should be reversed. *[IAS 37.59]*. Where discounting is applied, the carrying amount of a provision increases in each period to reflect the passage of time. This increase is recognised as a borrowing cost. *[IAS 37.60]*. As discussed at 4.3.5 above, the periodic unwinding of the discount is recognised as a finance cost in the income statement, and it is not a borrowing cost capable of being capitalised under IAS 23. *[IFRIC 1.8]*.

The standard does not allow provisions to be redesignated or otherwise used for expenditures for which the provision was not originally recognised. *[IAS 37.61]*. In such circumstances, a new provision is created and the amount no longer needed is reversed, as to do otherwise would conceal the impact of two different events. *[IAS 37.62]*. This means that the questionable practice of charging costs against a provision that was set up for a different purpose is specifically prohibited.

4.9 Changes in contingent liabilities recognised in a business combination

In a business combination, the usual requirements of IAS 37 do not apply and the acquirer recognises a liability at the acquisition date for those contingent liabilities of the acquiree that represent a present obligation arising as a result of a past event and in respect of which the fair value can be measured reliably. *[IFRS 3.23]*. After initial recognition, and until the liability is settled, cancelled or expires, the acquirer measures the contingent liability recognised in a business combination at the higher of: *[IFRS 3.56]*

(a) the amount that would be recognised in accordance with IAS 37; and

(b) the amount initially recognised less, if appropriate, cumulative amortisation recognised in accordance with IAS 18. *[IFRS 3.56]*. For entities applying IFRS 15, the amount initially recognised less, if appropriate, the cumulative amount of income recognised in accordance with the principles of that Standard.[17]

This requirement does not apply to contracts accounted for in accordance with IAS 39 and IFRS 9. See Chapter 9 at 5.6.1.B.

This requirement prevents the immediate release to post acquisition profit of any contingency recognised in a business combination.

5 CASES IN WHICH NO PROVISION SHOULD BE RECOGNISED

IAS 37 sets out three particular cases in which the recognition of a provision is prohibited. They are: future operating losses, repairs and maintenance of owned assets and staff training costs. The Interpretations Committee has also considered repeated requests relating to obligations arising on entities operating in a rate-regulated environment. The Interpretations Committee concluded that there is no justification for the recognition of a special regulatory liability, although the issue of

IFRS 14 – *Regulatory Deferral Accounts* – in January 2014 provides some relief for first-time adopters of IFRS who have recognised regulatory deferral account balances under their previous GAAP (see 5.4 below). The common theme in these cases is that the potential obligation does not exist independently of an entity's future actions. In other words, the entity is able to change the future conduct of its business in a way that avoids the future expenditure. Only those obligations that exist independently of an entity's future actions are recognised as provisions. *[IAS 37.19]*. This principle is also relevant to determining the timing of recognition of a provision, whereby no liability is recognised until the obligation cannot otherwise be avoided by the entity. Examples include those arising from participation in a particular market under IFRIC 6 (see 6.7 below) and an obligation for levies imposed by government under IFRIC 21 (see 6.8 below).

5.1 Future operating losses

IAS 37 explicitly states that 'provisions shall not be recognised for future operating losses'. *[IAS 37.63]*. This is because such losses do not meet the definition of a liability and the general recognition criteria of the standard. *[IAS 37.64]*. In particular there is no present obligation as a result of a past event. Such costs should be left to be recognised as they occur in the future in the same way as future profits.

However, it would be wrong to assume that this requirement has effectively prevented the effect of future operating losses from being anticipated, because they are sometimes recognised as a result of requirements in another standard, either in the measurement of an asset of the entity or to prevent inappropriate recognition of revenue. For example:

- under IAS 2 – *Inventories* – inventories are written down to the extent that they will not be recovered from future revenues, rather than leaving the non-recovery to show up as future operating losses (see Chapter 22 at 3.4);
- under IAS 11 provision is made for losses expected on construction contracts (see Chapter 23 at 3.3.6); and
- under IAS 36 – *Impairment of Assets* – impairment is assessed on the basis of the present value of future operating cash flows, meaning that the effect of not only future operating losses but also sub-standard operating profits will be recognised (see Chapter 20). IAS 37 specifically makes reference to the fact that an expectation of future operating losses may be an indication that certain assets are impaired. *[IAS 37.65]*.

This is therefore a rather more complex issue than IAS 37 acknowledges. Indeed, IAS 37 itself has to navigate closely the dividing line between the general prohibition of the recognition of future losses and the recognition of contractual or constructive obligations that are expected to give rise to losses in future periods.

5.2 Repairs and maintenance of owned assets

Repairs and maintenance provisions in respect of owned assets are generally prohibited under IAS 37. Under the standard, the following principles apply:

(a) provisions are recognised only for obligations existing independently of the entity's future actions (i.e. the future conduct of its business) and in cases where an entity can avoid future expenditure by its future actions, for example by changing its method of operation, it has no present obligation; *[IAS 37.19]*

(b) financial statements deal with an entity's position at the end of the reporting period and not its possible position in the future. Therefore, no provision is recognised for costs that need to be incurred to operate in the future; *[IAS 37.18]* and

(c) for an event to be an obligating event, the entity can have no realistic alternative to settling the obligation created by the event. *[IAS 37.17]*.

These principles are applied strictly in the case of an obligation to incur repairs and maintenance costs in the future, even when this expenditure is substantial, distinct from what may be regarded as routine maintenance and essential to the continuing operations of the entity, such as a major refit or refurbishment of the asset. This is illustrated by two examples in an appendix to the standard.

Example 28.12: Prohibition on maintenance provisions relating to owned assets

Scenario 1: Re-lining costs of a furnace

An entity operates a furnace, the lining of which needs to be replaced every five years for technical reasons. At the end of the reporting period, the lining has been in use for three years. In these circumstances, a provision for the cost of replacing the lining is not recognised because, at the end of the reporting period, no obligation to replace the lining exists independently of the entity's future actions. Even the intention to incur the expenditure depends upon the entity deciding to continue operating the furnace or to replace the lining. Instead of a provision being recognised, the initial cost of the lining is treated as a significant part of the furnace asset and depreciated over a period of five years. *[IAS 16.43]*. The re-lining costs are then capitalised when incurred and depreciated over the next five years. *[IAS 37 IE Example 11A]*.

Scenario 2: Overhaul costs of an aircraft

An airline is required by law to overhaul its aircraft once every three years. Even with the legal requirement to perform the overhaul, there is no obligating event until the three year period has elapsed. As with Scenario 1, no obligation exists independently of the entity's future actions. The entity could avoid the cost of the overhaul by selling the aircraft before the three year period has elapsed. Instead of a provision being recognised, the overhaul cost is identified as a separate part of the aircraft asset under IAS 16 and is depreciated over three years. *[IAS 37 IE Example 11B]*.

Entities might try to argue that a repairs and maintenance provision should be recognised on the basis that there is a clear intention to incur the expenditure at the appointed time and that this means it is more likely than not, as at the end of the reporting period, that an outflow of resources will occur. However, the application of the three principles noted above, particularly that an entity should not provide for future operating costs, make an entity's intentions irrelevant. In the example above, recognition was not allowed because the entity could do all manner of things to avoid the obligation, including selling the asset, however unlikely that might be in the context of the entity's business or in terms of the relative cost of replacement as compared to repair. The existence of a legal requirement, probably resulting in the aircraft being grounded, was still not enough. This detachment from intention or even commercial reality, regarded by some as extreme, is most recently exhibited in the Interpretations Committee's approach to the recognition of levies imposed by government under IFRIC 21 (see 6.8 below).

It is interesting, however, that a similar argument had not been used in respect of the recognition of decommissioning costs, where presumably an entity could also avoid such obligations by selling, for example, its oil and gas assets.

The effect of the prohibition on setting up provisions for repairs obviously has an impact on presentation in the statement of financial position. It may not always, however, have as much impact on the statement of comprehensive income. This is because it is stated in the examples that depreciation would be adjusted to take account of the repairs. For example, in the case of the furnace lining, the lining should be depreciated over five years in advance of its expected repair. Similarly, in the case of the aircraft overhaul, the example in the standard states that an amount equivalent to the expected maintenance costs is depreciated over three years. The result of this is that the depreciation charge recognised in profit or loss over the life of the component of the asset requiring regular repair may be equivalent to that which would previously have arisen from the combination of depreciation and a provision for repair. This is the way IAS 16 requires entities to account for significant parts of an item of property, plant and equipment which have different useful lives (see Chapter 18 at 5.1). *[IAS 16.44]*.

5.3 Staff training costs

In the normal course of business it is unlikely that provisions for staff training costs would be permissible, because it would normally contravene the general prohibition in the standard on the recognition of provisions for future operating costs. *[IAS 37.18]*. In the context of a restructuring, IAS 37 identifies staff retraining as an ineligible cost because it relates to the future conduct of the business. *[IAS 37.81]*. Example 28.2 at 3.1.1 above reproduces an example in the standard where the government introduces changes to the income tax system, such that an entity in the financial services sector needs to retrain a large proportion of its administrative and sales workforce in order to ensure continued compliance with financial services regulation. The standard argues that there is no present obligation until the actual training has taken place and so no provision should be recognised. We also note that in many cases the need to incur training costs is not only future operating expenditure but also fails the 'existing independently of an entity's future actions' criterion, *[IAS 37.19]*, in that the cost could be avoided by the entity, for example, if it withdrew from that market or hired new staff who were already appropriately qualified.

This example again illustrates how important it is to properly understand the nature of any potential 'constructive obligation' or 'obligating event' and to determine separately its financial effect in relation to past transactions and events on the one hand and in relation to the future operation of the business on the other. Otherwise, it can be easy to mistakenly argue that a provision is required, such as for training costs to ensure that staff comply with new legal requirements, on the basis that the entity has a constructive obligation to ensure staff are appropriately skilled to adequately meet the needs of its customers. However, the obligation, constructive or not, declared or not, relates to the entity's future conduct, is a future cost of operation and is therefore ineligible for recognition under the standard until the training takes place.

5.4 Rate-regulated activities

In many countries, the provision of utilities (e.g. water, natural gas or electricity) to consumers is regulated by the national government. Regulations differ between countries but often regulators operate a cost-plus system under which a utility provider is allowed to make a fixed return on investment. Under certain national GAAPs, an entity may account for the effects of regulation by recognising a 'regulatory asset' that reflects the increase in future prices approved by the regulator or a 'regulatory liability' that reflects a requirement from the regulator to reduce tariffs or improve services so as to return the benefit of earlier excess profits to customers. This issue has for a long time been a matter of significant interest as entities in those countries adopt IFRS, because the recognition of these regulatory assets and liabilities is prohibited under IFRS. Just as the ability to charge higher prices for goods services to be rendered in the future does not meet the definition of an intangible asset in IAS 38 – *Intangible Assets* (see Chapter 17 at 11.1), the requirement to charge a lower price for the delivery of goods and services in the future does not meet the definition of a past obligating event, or a liability, in IAS 37.

A liability is defined in IAS 37 as 'a present obligation of the entity arising from past events, the settlement of which is expected to result in an outflow from the entity of resources embodying economic benefits'. *[IAS 37.10]*. The return to customers of amounts mandated by a regulator depends on future events including:

- future rendering of services;
- future volumes of output (generally consisting of utilities such as water or electricity) consumed by users; and
- the continuation of regulation.

Similar considerations apply to actions that a regulator may require entities to complete in the future, such as an obligation to invest in equipment to improve efficiency. Other than decommissioning obligations (see 6.3 below), such items do not meet the definition of a liability because there needs to be a present obligation at the end of the reporting period before a liability can be recognised. Such a regulatory obligation that fails to qualify for recognition under IAS 37 is illustrated in Extract 28.1 at 3.1.1 above.

Whilst the requirements of IAS 37 and the *Conceptual Framework* are clear in this respect, their perceived inflexibility in this regard has been identified as a significant barrier that prevents the entities affected by it from adopting IFRS as a whole.[18] In an effort to establish a way for certain liabilities and assets to achieve recognition under very limited circumstances, the IASB issued an exposure draft in July 2009 on rate-regulated activities. However, the IASB discontinued the project in September 2011, on the basis that the complexities of the issue could not be resolved quickly and cited resource constraints. However, it identified the following options which were then presented in its 2011 agenda consultation document:[19]

- a disclosure only standard;
- an interim standard to 'grandfather' previous GAAP accounting practices with some limited improvements;
- a medium-term project focused on the effects of rate-regulation; or
- addressing it as part of a comprehensive project on intangible assets.

In response to the feedback received, the IASB embarked on a two-tier approach. In September 2012 the IASB added to its agenda a comprehensive research project on rate-regulated activities and in December 2012 the IASB decided to develop an interim Standard on the accounting for regulatory deferral accounts that would apply for first-time adopters of IFRS until the completion of the comprehensive project.[20] The interim Standard, IFRS 14 was issued in January 2014 and is effective for annual periods beginning on or after 1 January 2016, with early application permitted *[IFRS 14.C1]*. The Standard can be applied in only very limited circumstances.

A first-time adopter is permitted (but not required) to apply IFRS 14 in its first IFRS financial statements if, and only if, it conducts rate-regulated activities (as defined in the Standard) and recognised amounts that qualify as regulatory deferral account balances in its financial statements prepared under its previous GAAP. *[IFRS 14.5]*. An entity shall not change its accounting policies in order to start to recognise regulatory deferral account balances. *[IFRS 14.13]*.

Entities can apply IFRS 14 after first-time adoption if, and only if, they had elected to apply the Standard in their first IFRS financial statements and had recognised regulatory deferral account balances in those financial statements. *[IFRS 14.6]*. Therefore, the scope for applying this standard does not extend to existing IFRS reporters; nor to first-time adopters whose previous GAAP did not allow for the recognition of regulatory assets and liabilities; nor even to first-time adopters whose previous GAAP allowed such recognition but the entity chose not to do so.

The requirements of first-time adoption of IFRS are discussed further in Chapter 5.

As regards its comprehensive research project, in September 2014 the IASB issued the discussion paper *Reporting the Financial Effects of Rate Regulation*. The discussion paper focused on developing an overall definition of rate regulation ('defined rate regulation') and was intended to obtain feedback on:

(a) the common features of rate regulation that create a combination of rights and obligations that are distinguishable from those activities that are not rate-regulated and would support the recognition of an asset or liability in the statement of financial position;

(b) whether the description of the defined rate regulation encompassed those features of regulation that have the most significant effect on the amount, timing and certainty or revenue, profit and cash flows of rate-regulated entities, for which specific accounting requirements should be developed; and

(c) what information about the financial effects of rate regulation is most relevant to users of financial statements in making investment and lending decisions.

The discussion paper did not include specific accounting proposals. Instead, it explored several possible approaches that the IASB might consider when deciding how best to report the financial effects of defined rate regulation and sought feedback on the advantages and disadvantages of those possible approaches. Based on the feedback received on the discussion paper, the IASB decided to develop a second discussion paper to help stakeholders consider a thorough analysis of the issues and possible solutions before the Board decides what changes to make to existing IFRS requirements, including IFRS 14.[21]

6 SPECIFIC EXAMPLES OF PROVISIONS AND CONTINGENCIES

IAS 37 expands on its general recognition and measurement requirements by including more specific requirements for particular situations, i.e. future restructuring costs and onerous contracts. This section discusses those situations, looks at other examples, including those addressed in an appendix to the Standard and other areas where the Interpretations Committee has considered how the principles of IAS 37 should be applied.

6.1 Restructuring provisions

IAS 37 allows entities to recognise restructuring provisions, but it has specific rules on the nature of obligations and the types of cost that are eligible for inclusion in such provisions, as discussed below. These rules ensure that entities recognise only obligations that exist independently of their future actions, *[IAS 37.19]*, and that provisions are not made for future operating costs and losses. *[IAS 37.63]*.

6.1.1 *Definition*

IAS 37 defines a restructuring as 'a programme that is planned and controlled by management, and materially changes either:

(a) the scope of a business undertaken by an entity; or

(b) the manner in which that business is conducted'. *[IAS 37.10]*.

This is said to include:

(a) the sale or termination of a line of business;

(b) the closure of business locations in a country or region or the relocation of business activities from one country or region to another;

(c) changes in management structure, for example, eliminating a layer of management; and

(d) fundamental reorganisations that have a material effect on the nature and focus of the entity's operations. *[IAS 37.70]*.

This definition is very wide and whilst it may be relatively straightforward to establish whether an operation has been sold, closed or relocated, the determination of whether an organisational change is fundamental, material or just part of a process of continuous improvement is a subjective judgement. Whilst organisational change is a perennial feature in most business sectors, entities could be tempted to classify all kinds of operating costs as restructuring costs and thereby invite the user of the financial statements to perceive them in a different light from the 'normal' costs of operating in a dynamic business environment. Even though the requirements in IAS 37 prevent such costs being recognised too early, the standard still leaves the question of classification open to judgement. As such there can be a tension between the permitted recognition of expected restructuring costs, subject to meeting the criteria set out at 6.1.2 below, and the general prohibition in IAS 37 against provision for future operating losses, which is discussed above at 5.1.

IAS 37 emphasises that when a restructuring meets the definition of a discontinued operation under IFRS 5, additional disclosures may be required under that standard (see Chapter 4 at 3). *[IAS 37.9]*.

6.1.2 Recognition of a restructuring provision

IAS 37 requires that restructuring costs are recognised only when the general recognition criteria in the standard are met, i.e. there is a present obligation (legal or constructive) as a result of a past event, in respect of which a reliable estimate can be made of the probable cost. *[IAS 37.71]*. The standard's specific requirements for the recognition of a provision for restructuring costs seek to define the circumstances that give rise to a constructive obligation and thereby restrict the recognition of a provision to cases when an entity:

(a) has a detailed formal plan for the restructuring identifying at least:
   - (i) the business or part of a business concerned;
   - (ii) the principal locations affected;
   - (iii) the location, function, and approximate number of employees who will be compensated for terminating their services;
   - (iv) the expenditures that will be undertaken; and
   - (v) when the plan will be implemented; and

(b) has raised a valid expectation in those affected that it will carry out the restructuring by starting to implement that plan or announcing its main features to those affected by it. *[IAS 37.72]*.

The standard gives examples of the entity's actions that may provide evidence that the entity has started to implement a plan, quoting the dismantling of plant or selling of assets, or the public announcement of the main features of the plan. However, it also emphasises that the public announcement of a detailed plan to restructure will not automatically create an obligation; the important principle is that the announcement is made in such a way and in sufficient detail to give rise to valid expectations in other parties such as customers, suppliers and employees that the restructuring will be carried out. *[IAS 37.73]*.

The standard also suggests that for an announced plan to give rise to a constructive obligation, its implementation needs to be planned to begin as soon as possible and to be completed in a timeframe that makes significant changes to the plan unlikely. Any extended period before commencement of implementation, or if the restructuring will take an unreasonably long time, will mean that recognition of a provision is premature, because the entity is still likely to have a chance of changing the plan. *[IAS 37.74]*.

In summary, these conditions require the plan to be detailed and specific, to have gone beyond the directors' powers of recall and to be put into operation without delay or significant alteration.

The criteria set out above for the recognition of provisions mean that a board decision, if it is the only relevant event arising before the end of the reporting period, is not sufficient. This message is reinforced specifically in the standard, the argument being made that a constructive obligation is not created by a management decision. There will only be a constructive obligation where the entity has, before the end of the reporting period:

(a) started to implement the restructuring plan; or

(b) announced the main features of the restructuring plan to those affected by it in a sufficiently specific manner to raise a valid expectation in them that the entity will carry out the restructuring. *[IAS 37.75]*.

If the restructuring is not started or announced in detail until after the end of the reporting period, no provision is recognised. Instead, the entity discloses a non-adjusting event after the reporting period. *[IAS 37.75, IAS 10.22(e)]*.

The following examples in IAS 37 illustrate how a constructive obligation for a restructuring may or may not be created.

Example 28.13: The effect of timing of the creation of a constructive obligation on the recognition of a restructuring provision

Scenario 1: Closure of a division – no implementation before end of the reporting period

On 12 December 2017, the board of Entity A decided to close down a division. No announcement was made before the end of the reporting period (31 December 2017) and no other steps were taken to implement the decision before that date.

In these circumstances, no provision is recognised because management's actions are insufficient to create a constructive obligation before the end of the reporting period. *[IAS 37 IE Example 5A]*.

Scenario 2: Closure of a division – communication/implementation before end of the reporting period

In another case, the board of Entity B decides on 12 December 2017 to close down one of its manufacturing divisions. On 20 December 2017 a detailed plan for closure was agreed by the board; letters were sent to customers warning them to seek an alternative source of supply and redundancy notices were sent to the staff of the division.

The communication of management's decision to customers and employees on 20 December 2017 creates a valid expectation that the division will be closed, thereby giving rise to a constructive obligation from that date. Accordingly, a provision is recognised at 31 December 2017 for the best estimate of the costs of closing the division. *[IAS 37 IE Example 5B]*.

The standard acknowledges that there will be circumstances where a board decision could trigger recognition, but not on its own. Only if earlier events, such as negotiations with employee representatives for termination payments or with purchasers for the sale of an operation, have been concluded subject only to board approval would the decision of the board create an obligation. In such circumstances, it is reasoned that when board approval has been obtained and communicated to the other parties, the entity is committed to restructure, assuming all other conditions are met. *[IAS 37.76]*.

There is also discussion in the standard of the situation that may arise in some countries where, for example, employee representatives may sit on the board, so that a board decision effectively communicates the decision to them, which may result in a constructive obligation to restructure. *[IAS 37.77]*.

In practice it can be very difficult to determine whether it is appropriate to recognise a provision for the future costs of a restructuring programme. The determination of whether an organisational change is fundamental, material or just part of a process of continuous improvement is a subjective judgement. Once it has been established that the activities in question constitute a restructuring rather than an ongoing operating cost, it can be difficult to determine whether management's actions before the reporting date have been sufficient to have 'raised a valid expectation in those affected'. *[IAS 37.72]*. Even if a trigger point is easily identifiable, such as the date of an appropriately detailed public announcement, it might not necessarily commit management to the *whole* restructuring, but only to specific items of expenditure such as redundancy costs. When the announcement is less clear, referring for example to consultations, negotiations or voluntary arrangements, particularly with employees, judgement is required. Furthermore, taken on its own, the 'valid expectation' test is at least as open to manipulation as one based on the timing of a board decision. Entities anxious to accelerate or postpone recognition of a liability could do so by advancing or deferring an event that signals such a commitment, such as a public announcement, without any change to the substance of their position.

In these situations it is important to consider all the related facts and circumstances and not to 'home in' on a single recognition criterion. The objective of the analysis is to determine whether there is a past obligating event at the reporting date. The guidance in the standard about restructuring, referring as it does to constructive obligations and valid expectations is ultimately aimed at properly applying the principle in IAS 37 that only those obligations arising from past events and existing independently of an entity's future actions are recognised as provisions. *[IAS 37.19]*. In essence, a restructuring provision qualifies for recognition if, as at the reporting date, it relates to a detailed plan of action from which management cannot realistically withdraw.

6.1.3 Recognition of obligations arising from the sale of an operation

IAS 37 has some further specific rules governing when to recognise an obligation arising on the sale of an operation, stating that no obligation arises for the sale of an operation until the entity is committed to the sale, i.e. there is a binding sale agreement. *[IAS 37.78]*. Thus a provision cannot be made for a loss on sale unless there is a binding sale agreement by the end of the reporting period. The standard says that this applies even when an entity has taken a decision to sell an operation and announced that decision publicly, it cannot be committed to the sale until a purchaser has been identified and there is a binding sale agreement. Until there is such an agreement, the entity will be able to change its mind and indeed will have to take another course of action if a purchaser cannot be found on acceptable terms. *[IAS 37.79]*.

Even in cases where it is part of a larger restructuring that qualifies for recognition under IAS 37, an obligation arising from the sale is not recognised until there is a binding sale agreement. Instead, the assets of the operation must be reviewed for impairment under IAS 36. This may therefore mean that an expense is recorded in the income statement; it is just that the expense gives rise to a reduction of the carrying amount of assets rather than the recognition of a liability. The standard also recognises that where a sale is only part of a restructuring, the entity could be committed to the other parts of restructuring before a binding sale agreement is in place. *[IAS 37.79]*. Hence, the costs of the restructuring will be recognised over different reporting periods.

6.1.4 Costs that can (and cannot) be included in a restructuring provision

Having met the specific tests in the standard for the recognition of a restructuring provision at the end of the reporting period, IAS 37 imposes further criteria to restrict the types of cost that can be provided for. Presumably these additional restrictions are intended to ensure that the entity does not contravene the general prohibition in IAS 37 against provision for future operating losses. *[IAS 37.63]*.

A restructuring provision should include only the direct expenditures arising from the restructuring, which are those that are both:

(a) necessarily entailed by the restructuring; and

(b) not associated with the ongoing activities of the entity. *[IAS 37.80]*.

The standard gives specific examples of costs that may not be included within the provision, because they relate to the future conduct of the business. Such costs include:

(a) retraining or relocating continuing staff;

(b) marketing; or

(c) investment in new systems and distribution networks. *[IAS 37.81]*.

Because these costs relate to the future conduct of the business, they are recognised on the same basis as if they arose independently of a restructuring. *[IAS 37.81]*. In most cases, this means that the costs are recognised as the related services are provided.

Example 28.14: Distinguishing restructuring costs from ongoing expenses

On 15 November 2017, management announced its intention to close down its operation in the North of the country and relocate to a new site in the South, primarily to be closer to its key customers. Before the end of the reporting period (31 December 2017), the principal elements of the plan were agreed with employee representatives, a lease signed for a building at the new location, and a notice to vacate the existing facility given to the landlord; all on the basis that production would start at the new location on 31 March 2018 and the existing site would be vacated on 30 April 2018. Production would cease at the existing site on 28 February 2018 to allow plant and equipment to be relocated. Inventory levels would be increased up to that date so that customers could be supplied with goods sent from the Northern facility until 31 March.

Whilst the majority of the 600 existing staff was expected to take redundancy on 28 February 2018, 50 had agreed to accept the entity's offer of relocation, including an incentive of €3,000 each towards relocation costs. Of those employees taking redundancy, 20 had agreed to continue to work for the entity until 30 June 2018, to dismantle plant and equipment at the Northern site; install it at the new facility in the South; and train new staff on its operation. A bonus of €4,500 per employee would be payable if they remained until 30 June. A further 60 had agreed to stay with the entity until 31 March 2018, to ensure

Chapter 28

that inventory was sent out to customers before the new site was operational, of which 10 would remain until 30 April 2018 to complete the decommissioning of the Northern facility. These employees would also receive a bonus for staying until the promised date.

The announcement of management's decision on 15 November 2017 and the fact that the key elements of the plan were understood by employees, customers and the landlord of the Northern site before the end of the reporting period give rise to a constructive obligation that requires a provision to be recognised at 31 December 2017 for the best estimate of the costs of the reorganisation.

However, only those direct costs of the restructuring not associated with ongoing activities can be included in the provision. For example, as follows:

Type of expense	*Direct cost of restructuring*	*Associated with ongoing activities*
Redundancy payments to 550 staff	•	
Payroll costs to 28 February 2018 (all 600 staff)		•
Relocation incentive of €3,000 per employee (50 staff)		•
Payroll costs – to 31 March 2018 (60 staff dispatching goods)		•
Payroll costs – March to June 2018 (20 staff relocating plant) Note 1		•
Payroll costs – April 2018 (10 staff decommissioning site)	•	
Costs of dismantling plant and equipment Note 1	•	•
Cost of transporting PP&E and inventory to the new site		•
Costs of recruiting and training staff for the Southern site		•
Rent of Northern site to 31 March 2018 Note 2		•
Rent of Northern site for April 2018	•	
Cost of terminating lease of Northern site	•	
Rent of new site to 31 March 2018 (pre-production)		•
Cost of invoices, forms and stationery showing new address		•

Note 1: Costs relating to dismantling plant and equipment that is no longer intended for use in the business could be regarded as a direct cost of restructuring. However, costs relating to the dismantling and installation of equipment at the new site and training staff to operate it are costs associated with ongoing operations and, therefore, ineligible for inclusion in the restructuring provision.

Note 2: This assumes that the lease of the Northern site has not become an onerous lease as at 31 December 2017.

This example shows that individual classes of expenditure should be disaggregated into components that distinguish those elements associated with ongoing activities. Even if expenditure would not have been incurred without the restructuring activity, its association with ongoing activities means that it is ineligible for inclusion in a provision. IAS 37 requires the cost to be *both* necessarily entailed by the restructuring *and* not associated with the ongoing activities of the entity. *[IAS 37.80]*.

For that reason, whilst the cost of making employees redundant is an eligible restructuring cost, any incremental amounts paid to retain staff to ensure a smooth transition of operations from one location to another are not eligible because they are incurred to facilitate ongoing activities. IAS 19 requires these to be treated as short-term employee benefits to the extent that they are expected to be settled within 12 months after the end of the reporting period.[22] Similarly, whilst the costs of dismantling plant and equipment intended to be scrapped is an eligible restructuring cost, the costs of dismantling plant and equipment intended to be relocated and installed at the new site is ineligible, because it is associated with ongoing activities.

A further rule in IAS 37 is that the provision should not include identifiable future operating losses up to the date of the restructuring, unless they relate to an onerous contract. *[IAS 37.82]*. This means that even if the operation being reorganised is loss-making, its ongoing costs are not provided for. This is consistent with the general prohibition against the recognition of provisions for future operating losses. *[IAS 37.63]*.

The general requirement in the standard that gains from the expected disposal of assets cannot be taken into account in the measurement of provisions, *[IAS 37.51]*, is also relevant to the measurement of restructuring provisions, even if the sale of the asset is envisaged as part of the restructuring. *[IAS 37.83]*. Whilst the expected disposal proceeds from asset sales might have been a significant element of the economic case for a restructuring, the income from disposal is not anticipated just because it is part of a restructuring plan.

6.2 Onerous contracts

Although future operating losses in general cannot be provided for, IAS 37 requires that 'if an entity has a contract that is onerous, the present obligation under the contract shall be recognised and measured as a provision'. *[IAS 37.66]*.

The standard notes that many contracts (for example, some routine purchase orders) can be cancelled without paying compensation to the other party, and therefore there is no obligation. However, other contracts establish both rights and obligations for each of the contracting parties. Where events make such a contract onerous, the contract falls within the scope of the standard and a liability exists which is recognised. Executory contracts that are not onerous fall outside the scope of the standard. *[IAS 37.67]*.

IAS 37 defines an onerous contract as 'a contract in which the unavoidable costs of meeting the obligations under the contract exceed the economic benefits expected to be received under it'. *[IAS 37.10]*. This requires that the contract is onerous to the point of being directly loss-making, not simply uneconomic by reference to current prices.

IAS 37 considers that 'the unavoidable costs under a contract reflect the least net cost of exiting from the contract, which is the lower of the cost of fulfilling it and any compensation or penalties arising from failure to fulfil it'. *[IAS 37.68]*. This evaluation does not require an intention by the entity to fulfil or to exit the contract. It does not even require there to be specific terms in the contract that apply in the event of its termination or breach. Its purpose is to recognise only the unavoidable costs to the entity, which in the absence of specific clauses in the contract relating to termination or breach could include an estimation of the cost of ceasing to honour the contract and having the other party go to court for compensation for the resultant breach.

There is a subtle yet important distinction between making a provision in respect of the unavoidable costs under a contract (reflecting the least net cost of what the entity has to do) compared to making an estimate of the cost of what the entity *intends* to do. The first is an obligation, which merits the recognition as a provision, whereas the second is a choice of the entity, which fails the recognition criteria because it does not exist independently of the entity's future actions, *[IAS 37.19]*, and is therefore akin to a future operating loss.

Example 28.15: Onerous supply contract

Entity P negotiated a contract in 2014 for the supply of components when availability in the market was scarce. It agreed to purchase 100,000 units per annum for 5 years commencing 1 January 2015 at a price of $20 per unit. Since then, new suppliers have entered the market and the typical price of a component is now $5 per unit. Whilst its activities are still profitable (Entity P makes a margin of $6 per unit of finished product sold) changes to the entity's own business means that it will not use all of the components it is contracted to purchase. As at 31 December 2017, Entity P expects to use 150,000 units in future and has 55,000 units in inventory. The contract requires 200,000 units to be purchased before the agreement expires in 2019. If the entity terminates the contract before 2019, compensation of $1 million per year is payable to the supplier. Each finished product contains one unit of the component.

Therefore, the entity expects to achieve a margin of $900,000 (150,000 × $6) on the units it will produce and sell; but will make a loss of $15 ($20 – $5) per unit on each of the 105,000 components (55,000 + 200,000 – 150,000) it is left with at the end of 2018 and now expects to sell in the components market.

In considering the extent to which the contract is onerous, Entity P in the example above should not concentrate solely on the net cost of the excess units of $1,575,000 (105,000 × $15) that it is contracted to purchase but which are expected to be left unsold. Instead, the entity should consider all of the related benefits of the contract, which includes the profits earned as a result of having a secure source of supply of components. Therefore the supply contract is onerous (directly loss making) only to the extent of the costs not covered by related revenues, justifying a provision of $675,000 ($1,575,000 – $900,000).

In the extract below, Centrica discloses the nature of its key onerous contract provisions, along with some detail on how each of the provisions is calculated.

Extract 28.3: Centrica plc (2015)

Notes to the Financial Statements [extract]

3 CRITICAL ACCOUNTING JUDGEMENTS AND KEY SOURCES OF ESTIMATION UNCERTAINTY [extract]

(b) Key sources of estimation uncertainty [extract]

Provisions for onerous contracts

The Group has entered into a number of commodity procurement and capacity contracts related to specific assets in the ordinary course of its business. Where the unavoidable costs of meeting the obligations under these contracts exceed the associated expected future net benefits, an onerous contract provision is recognised. The calculation of these provisions will involve the use of estimates. The key onerous provisions are as follows:

Rijnmond power station operating lease

The onerous provision is calculated by taking the unavoidable costs that will be incurred under the contract and deducting any estimated revenues.

Spalding power station onerous contract provision

During 2015, a new onerous contract provision has been calculated by taking the unavoidable costs that will be incurred under the contract, excluding those that are treated as minimum lease payments and included within the Group's finance lease liability, less any estimated revenue.

European gas transportation capacity contracts

The onerous provision is calculated using capacity costs incurred under the contracts, less any predicted income. The provision calculation assumes that contracts for capacity in continental Europe are onerous but those that enable gas to be transported directly back into the UK may be necessary to achieve security of supply in the future. Therefore no provision has been recognised relating to these latter contracts.

Direct Energy wind farm power purchase agreements

The onerous nature of the power purchase agreements is measured using estimates relating to wind forecasts, forward curves for energy prices, balancing costs and renewable energy certificates.

6.2.1 Recognition of provisions for vacant leasehold property

The most common example of an onerous contract in practice relates to leasehold property. From time to time entities may hold vacant leasehold property which they have substantially ceased to use for the purpose of their business and where sub-letting is either unlikely, or would be at a significantly reduced rental from that being paid by the entity. In these circumstances, the obligating event is the signing of the lease contract (a legal obligation) and when the lease becomes onerous, an outflow of resources embodying economic benefits is probable. Accordingly, a provision is recognised for the best estimate of the unavoidable lease payments. *[IAS 37 IE Example 8]*.

Entities have to make systematic provision when such properties become vacant, and on a discounted basis where the effect is sufficiently material. Indeed, it is not just when the properties become vacant that provision would be required, but that provision should be made at the time the expected economic benefits of using the property fall short of the unavoidable costs under the lease. This may occur prior to an entity physically vacating a property. The recognition of onerous lease provisions for occupied leasehold property when the entity has no current intention of vacating the property is addressed at 6.2.2 below. For vacant, or soon to be vacated, leasehold property consideration will need to be given to the point in time at which the lease becomes onerous and whether this may occur prior to the property being physically vacated. Although the Interpretations Committee had a preliminary discussion in December 2003 about the timing of recognition and the measurement of a provision for an onerous lease, including its application to other types of executory contracts such as a take or pay contract, it agreed that the issue should not be taken onto its agenda at that time.[23] In our view, it may be appropriate to recognise an onerous lease provision prior to physically vacating a property if an entity has made a commitment to vacate from which it cannot realistically withdraw or if the unavoidable costs of meeting the obligations under the lease exceed the economic benefits expected to be received under that lease (see 6.2.2 below).

Nevertheless, where a provision is to be recognised a number of difficulties remain. The first is how the provision should be calculated. It is unlikely that the provision will simply be the net present value of the future rental obligation, because if a substantial period of the lease remains, the entity will probably be able either to agree a negotiated sum with the landlord to terminate the lease early, or to sub-lease the building at some point in the future. Hence, the entity will have to make a best estimate of its future cash flows taking all these factors into account.

Another issue that arises from this is whether the provision in the statement of financial position should be shown net of any cash flows that may arise from sub-leasing the property, or whether the provision must be shown gross, with a corresponding asset set up for expected cash flows from sub-leasing only if they meet the recognition criteria of being 'virtually certain' to be received. Whilst the expense relating to a provision can be shown in the income statement net of reimbursement, *[IAS 37.54]*, the strict offset criteria in the standard (see 4.5 above) would suggest the latter to be required, as the entity would normally retain liability for the full lease payments if the sub-lessee defaulted. However, the standard makes no explicit reference to this issue. It is common for entities to apply a net approach for such onerous contracts under IAS 37. Indeed, it could be argued that because an onerous contract provision relates to the excess of the unavoidable costs over the expected economic benefits, *[IAS 37.68]*, there is no corresponding asset to be recognised. In its 2005 exposure draft of proposed amendments to IAS 37, the IASB confirmed that if an onerous contract is an operating lease, the unavoidable cost of the contract is the remaining lease commitment reduced by the estimated rentals that the entity could reasonably obtain, regardless of whether or not the entity intends to enter into a sublease.[24]

In the past, some entities may have maintained that no provision is required for vacant properties, because if the property leases are looked at on a portfolio basis, the overall economic benefits from properties exceed the overall costs. However, this argument is not sustainable under IAS 37, as the definition of an onerous contract refers specifically to costs and economic benefits *under the contract*. *[IAS 37.10]*.

It is more difficult to apply the definition of onerous contracts to the lease on a head office which is not generating revenue specifically. If the definition were applied too literally, one might end up concluding that all head office leases should be provided against because no specific economic benefits are expected under them. It would be more sensible to conclude that the entity as a whole obtains economic benefits from its head office, which is consistent with the way in which corporate assets are allocated to other cash generating units for the purposes of impairment testing (see Chapter 20 at 4.3.2). *[IAS 36.101]*. However, this does not alter the fact that if circumstances change and the head office becomes vacant, or the unavoidable costs of meeting the obligations under the head office lease come to exceed the economic benefits expected to be received (see 6.2.2 below), a provision should then be made in respect of the lease.

IAS 37 requires that any impairment loss that has occurred in respect of assets dedicated to an onerous contract is recognised before establishing a provision for the onerous contract. *[IAS 37.69]*. For example, any leasehold improvements that have been capitalised should be written off before provision is made for excess future rental costs.

One company which has provided for onerous leases under IAS 37 is Jardine Matheson as indicated by the following extract.

Extract 28.4: Jardine Matheson Holdings Limited (2015)

Notes to the Financial Statements [extract]

32 Provisions

	Motor vehicle warranties US$m	Closure cost provisions US$m	Obligations under onerous leases US$m	Reinstatement and restoration costs US$m	Statutory employee entitlements US$m	Others US$m	Total US$m
2015							
At 1st January	35	5	12	46	101	16	**215**
Exchange differences	(3)	–	(3)	(4)	(9)	(1)	**(20)**
Additional provisions	11	7	7	4	10	10	**49**
Unused amounts reversed	(1)	(2)	–	–	–	–	**(3)**
Utilized	(3)	(2)	–	(1)	(1)	(5)	**(12)**
At 31st December	**39**	**8**	**16**	**45**	**101**	**20**	**229**
Non-current	–	1	13	40	74	17	**145**
Current	39	7	3	5	27	3	**84**
	39	**8**	**16**	**45**	**101**	**20**	**229**
2014							
At 1st January	32	9	10	46	96	12	205
Exchange differences	(2)	–	(1)	(2)	(2)	–	(7)
Additional provisions	9	2	3	4	9	7	34
Unused amounts reversed	–	(2)	–	(1)	–	(1)	(4)
Utilized	(4)	(4)	–	(1)	(2)	(2)	(13)
At 31st December	35	5	12	46	101	16	215
Non-current	–	1	10	41	75	11	138
Current	35	4	2	5	26	5	77
	35	5	12	46	101	16	215

Motor vehicle warranties are estimated liabilities that fall due under the warranty terms offered on sale of new and used vehicles beyond that which is reimbursed by the manufacturers.

Closure cost provisions are established when legal or constructive obligations arise on closure or disposal of businesses.

Provisions are made for obligations under onerous operating leases when the properties are not used by the Group and the net costs of exiting from the leases exceed the economic benefits expected to be received.

Other provisions principally comprise provisions in respect of indemnities on disposal of businesses and legal claims.

6.2.2 Recognition of provisions for occupied leasehold property

The discussion above deals with situations where the leasehold property becomes vacant. However, it does not address the case where an entity is occupying leasehold property, which it has no current intention to vacate, and the lease becomes onerous. As noted above, IAS 37 defines an onerous contract as 'a contract in which the unavoidable costs of meeting the obligations under the contract exceed the economic benefits expected to be received under it'. *[IAS 37.10]*. In practice, it will often be where business performance declines that an entity will assess whether a lease over an occupied property has become onerous. The definition of an onerous contract requires that the contract is onerous to the point of being directly loss-making, not simply uneconomic by reference to current prices. Thus, if the entity still expects to operate profitably from the leased property, despite rental payments that come to exceed market rates, or a decline in business performance, no provision should be made. If the business operated out of the leased property has become loss-making, and the entity does not expect to be able to improve its operating results to recover the rental payments, then a provision may be necessary. However, before a separate provision for an onerous contract is established, IAS 37 requires that an entity should first recognise any impairment loss that has occurred on assets dedicated to the contract. *[IAS 37.69]*. Where the business operated out of a leased property has become loss-making, an onerous lease provision cannot be recognised to the extent that the lessee could reasonably expect to recover its own remaining lease commitment by subletting the property (see 6.2.1 above).

Home Retail Group plc includes in its property provisions an amount for those stores where the projected future trading income is insufficient to cover the lower of exit cost or cost of continuing to trade the store.

Extract 28.5: Home Retail Group plc (2015)

Notes to the financial statements [extract]
24. PROVISIONS [extract]

Property provisions comprise obligations in respect of onerous leases together with other costs or income associated with store closures. In respect of onerous leases, provision is made for onerous lease contracts on stores that have closed, or where a decision to close has been announced, and for those stores where the projected future trading income is insufficient to cover the lower of exit cost or cost of continuing to trade the store. Where the cost of continuing to trade the store is lower, the provision is based on the present value of expected future cash flows relating to rents, rates and other property costs to the end of the lease terms net of expected trading or sublet income. The majority of this provision is expected to be utilised over the period to 2020.

6.2.3 When an entity ceases to occupy part of a leased property

A further complication arises in the case of a leased property when only part of the building under lease is vacated. In our view, the existence of a single lease contract does not prevent the entity from regarding each floor as a separate unit of account if this appropriately reflects the facts and circumstances. Accordingly, it could be appropriate to regard physically separable parts of a building in isolation when determining whether the lease (or in this case part of it) is onerous. This would appear reasonable in the case of an office block with a number of floors, where it is customary for individual floors to be sub-let to other occupants.

Nevertheless, a distinction needs to be made between physically separable areas of a property that have been vacated (i.e. taken out of use by the lessee) and areas of a property that are being used inefficiently. Inefficient use does not justify the recognition of a liability, due to the prohibition in IAS 37 against provisions for future operating losses. *[IAS 37.63]*. As noted above, an entity should consider whether it is appropriate to regard each floor as a separate unit of account and therefore to recognise a provision for the rental costs related to a single floor of an office block that has been vacated. However, it is not appropriate to recognise a provision in respect of a lease or a separate unit of account within a lease (i.e. a floor) that is still partly-occupied, albeit at less than its full capacity unless the unavoidable costs of meeting the obligations under that lease, or separate unit of account within the lease, exceed the economic benefits expected to be received under the lease (see 6.2.2 above).

6.3 Decommissioning provisions

Decommissioning costs arise when an entity is required to dismantle or remove an asset at the end of its useful life and to restore the site on which it has been located, for example, when an oil rig or nuclear power station reaches the end of its economic life.

Rather than allowing an entity to build up a provision for the required costs over the life of the facility, IAS 37 requires that the liability is recognised as soon as the obligation arises. This is because the construction of the asset (and the environmental damage caused by it) creates the past obligating event requiring restoration in the future. *[IAS 37 IE Example 3]*.

The accounting for decommissioning costs is dealt with in IAS 37 by way of an example relating to an oil rig in an offshore oilfield (see Example 28.5 at 3.3 above). A provision is recognised at the time of constructing the oil rig in relation to the eventual costs that relate to its removal and the restoration of damage caused by building it. Additional provisions are recognised over the life of the oil field to reflect the need to reverse damage caused during the extraction of oil. *[IAS 37 IE Example 3]*. The total decommissioning cost is estimated, discounted to its present value and it is this amount which forms the initial provision. This 'initial estimate of the costs of dismantling and removing the item and restoring the site' is added to the corresponding asset's cost. *[IAS 16.16]*. Thereafter, the asset is depreciated over its useful life, while the discounted provision is progressively unwound, with the unwinding charge shown as a finance cost, as discussed at 4.3.5 above.

The effect of discounting on the statement of comprehensive income is to split the cost of the eventual decommissioning into two components: an expense based on the present value of the expected future cash outflows; and a finance element representing the unwinding of the discount. The overall effect is to produce a rising pattern of cost over the life of the facility, often with much of the total cost of the decommissioning classified as a finance cost.

AngloGold Ashanti's accounting policies and provisions note in respect of decommissioning obligations and restoration obligations are shown in the following extract.

Extract 28.6: AngloGold Ashanti Limited (2015)

GROUP – NOTES TO THE FINANCIAL STATEMENTS [extract]

For the year ended 31 December

1 ACCOUNTING POLICIES [extract]

1.3 SUMMARY OF ACCOUNTING POLICIES [extract]

Environmental expenditure

The group has long-term remediation obligations comprising decommissioning and restoration liabilities relating to its past operations which are based on the group's environmental management plans, in compliance with current environmental and regulatory requirements. Provisions for non-recurring remediation costs are made when there is a present obligation, it is probable that expenditure on remediation work will be required and the cost can be estimated within a reasonable range of possible outcomes. The costs are based on currently available facts, technology expected to be available at the time of the clean-up, laws and regulations presently or virtually certain to be enacted and prior experience in remediation of contaminated sites.

Contributions for the South African operations are made to Environmental Rehabilitation Trust Funds, created in accordance with local statutory requirements where applicable, to fund the estimated cost of rehabilitation during and at the end of the life of a mine. The amounts contributed to the trust funds are accounted for as non-current assets in the company. Interest earned on monies paid to rehabilitation trust funds is accrued on a time proportion basis and is recorded as interest income. For group purposes, the trusts are consolidated.

Decommissioning costs

The provision for decommissioning represents the cost that will arise from rectifying damage caused before production commences. Accordingly, a provision and a decommissioning asset is recognised and included within mine infrastructure.

Decommissioning costs are provided at the present value of the expenditures expected to settle the obligation, using estimated cash flows based on current prices. The unwinding of the decommissioning obligation is included in the income statement. Estimated future costs of decommissioning obligations are reviewed regularly and adjusted as appropriate for new circumstances or changes in law or technology. Changes in estimates are capitalised or reversed against the relevant asset. Estimates are discounted at a pre-tax rate that reflects current market assessments of the time value of money.

Gains or losses from the expected disposal of assets are not taken into account when determining the provision.

Restoration costs

The provision for restoration represents the cost of restoring site damage after the start of production. Changes in the provision are recorded in the income statement as a cost of production.

Restoration costs are estimated at the present value of the expenditures expected to settle the obligation, using estimated cash flows based on current prices and adjusted for risks specific to the liability. The estimates are discounted at a pre-tax rate that reflects current market assessments of the time value of money.

	US Dollars	
	2015	2014
28 Environmental rehabilitation and other provisions [extract]		
Environmental rehabilitation obligations [extract]		
Provision for decommissioning		
Balance at beginning of year	**296**	256
Change in estimates[(1)]	**5**	41
Transfer of liability to asset held for sale	**–**	–
Unwinding of decommissioning obligation	**11**	12
Transfer of decommissioning obligation to a third party	**–**	–
Disposals	**(11)**	–
Utilised during the year	**(3)**	(3)
Translation	**(26)**	(10)
Balance at end of year	**272**	296

Provision for restoration		
Balance at beginning of year	**555**	472
Charge to income statement	**6**	36
Change in estimates[(1)]	**(40)**	51
Transfer of liability to asset held for sale	**–**	–
Unwinding of restoration obligation	**10**	13
Transfer of restoration liability to a third party	**–**	–
Disposals	**(110)**	–
Utilised during the year	**(2)**	(13)
Translation	**(8)**	(4)
Balance at end of year	**411**	555

(1) The change in estimates is attributable to changes in discount rates due to changes in global economic assumptions and changes in mine plans resulting in a change in cash flows and changes in design of tailings storage facilities and in methodology following requests from the environmental regulatory authorities. These provisions are expected to unwind beyond the end of the life of mine.

6.3.1 *Changes in estimated decommissioning costs (IFRIC 1)*

IAS 37 requires provisions to be revised annually to reflect the current best estimate of the provision. *[IAS 37.59]*. However, the standard gives no guidance on accounting for changes in the decommissioning provision. Similarly, IAS 16 is unclear about the extent to which an item's carrying amount should be affected by changes in the estimated amount of dismantling and site restoration costs that occur *after* the estimate made upon initial measurement. This was addressed by the IASB with the publication of IFRIC 1 in May 2004. *[IFRIC 1.1]*.

IFRIC 1 applies to any decommissioning, restoration or similar liability that has been both included as part of the cost of an asset measured in accordance with IAS 16 and recognised as a liability in accordance with IAS 37. *[IFRIC 1.2]*. It addresses how the effect of the following events that change the measurement of an existing decommissioning, restoration or similar liability should be accounted for:

(a) a change in the estimated outflow of resources embodying economic benefits (e.g. cash flows) required to settle the obligation;

(b) a change in the current market-based discount rate (this includes changes in the time value of money and the risks specific to the liability); and

(c) an increase that reflects the passage of time (also referred to as the unwinding of the discount). *[IFRIC 1.3]*.

IFRIC 1 requires that (c) above, the periodic unwinding of the discount, is recognised in profit or loss as a finance cost as it occurs. *[IFRIC 1.8]*. The Interpretations Committee concluded that the unwinding of the discount is not a borrowing cost as defined in IAS 23, and thus cannot be capitalised under that standard. *[IFRIC 1.BC26-27]*.

For a change caused by (a) or (b) above, however, the adjustment is taken to the income statement only in specific circumstances. Any revision to the provision (other than to reflect the passage of time) is first recognised in the carrying value of the related asset or in other comprehensive income, depending on whether the asset is measured at cost or using the revaluation model. *[IFRIC 1.4-7]*.

Chapter 28

If the related asset is measured using the cost model, the change in the liability should be added to or deducted from the cost of the asset to which it relates. Where the change gives rise to an addition to cost, the entity should consider the need to test the new carrying value for impairment. This is particularly relevant for assets approaching the end of their useful life, as their remaining economic benefits are often small compared to the potential changes in the related decommissioning liability. Reductions over and above the remaining carrying value of the asset are recognised immediately in profit or loss. *[IFRIC 1.5]*. The adjusted depreciable amount of the asset is then depreciated prospectively over its remaining useful life. *[IFRIC 1.7]*. IFRIC 1 includes the following illustrative example.

Example 28.16: Changes in decommissioning costs – related asset measured at cost

An entity has a nuclear power plant and a related decommissioning liability. The nuclear power plant started operating on 1 January 2008. The plant has a useful life of 40 years. Its initial cost was $120,000,000; this included an amount for decommissioning costs of $10,000,000, which represented $70,400,000 in estimated cash flows payable in 40 years discounted at a risk-adjusted rate of 5%. The entity's financial year ends on 31 December.

On 31 December 2017, the plant is 10 years old. Accumulated depreciation is $30,000,000. Because of the unwinding of discount over the 10 years, the decommissioning liability has grown from $10,000,000 to $16,300,000.

On 31 December 2017, the discount rate has not changed. However, the entity estimates that, as a result of technological advances, the net present value of the expected cash flows has decreased by $8,000,000. Accordingly, the entity reduces the decommissioning liability from $16,300,000 to $8,300,000 and reduces the carrying amount of the asset by the same amount.

Following this adjustment, the carrying amount of the asset is $82,000,000 ($120,000,000 – $8,000,000 – $30,000,000), which will be depreciated over the remaining 30 years of the asset's life to give a depreciation expense for 2016 of $2,733,333 ($82,000,000 ÷ 30). The next year's finance cost for the unwinding of the discount will be $415,000 ($8,300,000 × 5%). *[IFRIC 1.IE1-4]*.

In illustrating the requirements of the Interpretation, the example in IFRIC 1 reduces the carrying value of the whole asset (comprising its construction cost and decommissioning cost) by the reduction in the present value of the decommissioning provision. The solution set out in the example does not treat the decommissioning element as a separate component of the asset. Had this been the case, the component would have had accumulated depreciation as at 31 December 2017 of $2,500,000 ($10,000,000 × 10/40), giving a carrying amount of $7,500,000 at that date and a gain of $500,000 when reduced by the decrease in the provision of $8,000,000. Accordingly, we believe that the example in IFRIC 1 indicates that it would not be appropriate to recognise any gain until the carrying value of the whole asset is extinguished.

If the related asset is measured using the revaluation model, changes in the liability alter the revaluation surplus or deficit previously recognised for that asset. Decreases in the provision are recognised in other comprehensive income and increase the value of the revaluation surplus in respect of the asset, except that:

(a) a decrease in the provision should be recognised in profit or loss to the extent that it reverses a previous revaluation deficit on that asset that was recognised in profit or loss; and

(b) if a decrease in the provision exceeds the carrying amount of the asset that would have been recognised under the cost model, the excess should be recognised in profit or loss. *[IFRIC 1.6]*.

Increases in the provision are recognised in profit or loss, except that they should be recognised in other comprehensive income, and reduce the revaluation surplus, to the extent of any credit balance existing in the revaluation surplus in respect of that asset. Changes in the provision might also indicate the need for the asset (and therefore all assets in the same class) to be revalued. *[IFRIC 1.6]*.

The illustrative examples in IFRIC 1 address this alternative.

Example 28.17: Changes in decommissioning costs – related asset carried at revaluation amount

Assume that the entity in Example 28.16 above instead adopts the revaluation model in IAS 16, and its policy is to eliminate accumulated depreciation at the revaluation date against the gross carrying amount of the asset.

The entity first revalues the asset as at 31 December 2010 when the nuclear power plant is 3 years old. The valuation of $115,000,000 comprises a gross valuation of $126,600,000 and an allowance of $11,600,000 for decommissioning costs, which represents no change to the original estimate, after the unwinding of three years' discount. The amounts included in the statement of financial position at 31 December 2010 and the related revaluation reserve movements are therefore:

	Net book value	*Valuation*	*Revaluation reserve*
	$'000	$'000	$'000
Cost or valuation	120,000	126,600	6,600
Accumulated depreciation (3/40)	(9,000)	–	9,000
Carrying amount of asset	111,000	126,600	15,600
Original provision	10,000		
Unwinding of discount (3 years @ 5%)	1,600		
	11,600	11,600	
Carrying amount less provision	99,400	115,000	15,600

The depreciation expense for 2011 is therefore $3,420,000 ($126,600,000 ÷ 37) and the discount expense for 2011 is $580,000 (5% of $11,600,000). On 31 December 2011, the decommissioning liability (before any adjustment) is $12,180,000 and the discount rate has not changed. However, on that date, the entity estimates that, as a result of technological advances, the present value of the decommissioning liability has decreased by $5,000,000. Accordingly, the entity adjusts the decommissioning liability to $7,180,000. To determine the extent to which any of the change to the provision is recognised in profit or loss, the entity has to keep a record of revaluations previously recognised in profit or loss; the carrying amount of the asset that would have been recognised under the cost model; and the previous revaluation surplus relating to that asset. *[IFRIC 1.6]*. In this example, the whole of the adjustment is taken to revaluation surplus, because it does not exceed the carrying amount that would have been recognised for the asset under the cost model of $103,000 (see below). *[IFRIC 1.IE6-10]*.

In addition, the entity decides that a full valuation of the asset is needed at 31 December 2011, in order to ensure that the carrying amount does not differ materially from fair value. Suppose that the asset is now valued at $107,000,000, which is net of an allowance of $7,180,000 for the reduced decommissioning obligation. The valuation of the asset for financial reporting purposes, before deducting this allowance, is therefore $114,180,000. The effect on the revaluation reserve of the revision to the estimate of the decommissioning provision and the new valuation can be illustrated in the table below. *[IFRIC 1.IE11-12]*.

	Cost model	*Revaluation*	*Revaluation reserve*
	$'000	$'000	$'000
Carrying amount as at 31 December 2010	111,000	126,600	15,600
Depreciation charge for 2011	(3,000)	(3,420)	
Carrying amount as at 31 December 2011	108,000	123,180	
Revision to estimate of provision	(5,000)		
Revaluation adjustment in 2011		(9,000)	(9,000)
	103,000	114,180	
Provision as at 31 December 2010	11,600	11,600	
Unwinding of discount @ 5%	580	580	
Revision to estimate	(5,000)	(5,000)	5,000
Provision as at 31 December 2011	7,180	7,180	
Carrying amount less provision	95,820	107,000	11,600

As indicated at 4.3.6 above, IAS 37 is unclear whether a new discount rate should be applied during the year or just at the year-end, and whether the rate should be applied to the new estimate of the provision or the old estimate. Although IFRIC 1 requires that changes in the provision resulting from a change in the discount rate is added to, or deducted from, the cost of the related asset in the current period, it does not deal specifically with these points. However, Example 1 in the illustrative examples to IFRIC 1 indicates that a change in discount rate would be accounted for in the same way as other changes affecting the estimate of a provision for decommissioning, restoration and similar liabilities. That is, it is reflected as a change in the liability at the time the revised estimate is made and the new estimate is discounted at the revised discount rate from that point on. *[IFRIC 1.IE5]*.

When accounting for revalued assets to which decommissioning liabilities attach, the illustrative example in IFRIC 1 states that it is important to understand the basis of the valuation obtained. For example:

(a) if an asset is valued on a discounted cash flow basis, some valuers may value the asset without deducting any allowance for decommissioning costs (a 'gross' valuation), whereas others may value the asset after deducting an allowance for decommissioning costs (a 'net' valuation), because an entity acquiring the asset will generally also assume the decommissioning obligation. For financial reporting purposes, the decommissioning obligation is recognised as a separate liability, and is not deducted from the asset. Accordingly, if the asset is valued on a net basis, it is necessary to adjust the valuation obtained by adding back the allowance for the liability, so that the liability is not counted twice. This is the case in Example 28.17 above;

(b) if an asset is valued on a depreciated replacement cost basis, the valuation obtained may not include an amount for the decommissioning component of the asset. If it does not, an appropriate amount will need to be added to the valuation to reflect the depreciated replacement cost of that component. *[IFRIC 1.IE7]*.

6.3.2 *Changes in legislation after construction of the asset*

The scope of IFRIC 1 is set out in terms of any existing decommissioning, restoration or similar liability that is both recognised as part of the cost of the asset under IAS 16; and recognised as a liability in accordance with IAS 37. *[IFRIC 1.2]*. The Interpretation does not address the treatment of obligations arising after the asset has been constructed, for example as a result of changes in legislation. *[IFRIC 1.BC23]*. Nevertheless, in our opinion the cost of the related asset should be measured in accordance with the principles set out in IFRIC 1 regardless of whether the obligation exists at the time of constructing the asset or arises later in its life.

As discussed at 3.3 in Chapter 18, IAS 16 makes no distinction in principle between the initial costs of acquiring an asset and any subsequent expenditure upon it. In both cases any and all expenditure has to meet the recognition rules, and be expensed in profit or loss if it does not. IAS 16 states that the cost of an item of property, plant and equipment includes 'the initial estimate of the costs of dismantling and removing the item and restoring the site on which it is located, the obligation for which an entity incurs either when the item is acquired or as a consequence of having used the item during a particular period for purposes other than to produce inventories during that period.' *[IAS 16.16(c)]*. For example, the introduction of new legislation to require the clean-up of sites that cease to be used as gasoline filling stations would give rise to the recognition of a decommissioning provision and, to the extent that the clean-up obligation arose as a result of the construction of the filling stations, an increase in the carrying value of the properties.

IAS 16 requires an entity to apply IAS 2 to the costs of obligations for dismantling, removing and restoring the site on which an item is located that are incurred during a particular period as a consequence of having used the item to produce inventories during that period. *[IAS 16.18]*. For example, the cost of restoring the site of a quarry would be reflected as part of the cost of the aggregate extracted from it, and not added to the carrying value of the site. Accordingly, if an entity previously had no obligation to restore the site and new legislation was introduced after 25% of the site had been excavated and 80% of that output had been sold, then 80% of the new estimate of the restoration cost would be expensed; 20% added to the cost of inventory; and none added to the carrying value of the site.

When changes in legislation give rise to a new decommissioning, restoration or similar liability that is added to the carrying amount of the related asset, it would be appropriate to perform an impairment review in accordance with IAS 36 (see Chapter 20).

6.3.3 *Funds established to meet an obligation (IFRIC 5)*

Some entities may participate in a decommissioning, restoration or environmental rehabilitation fund, the purpose of which is to segregate assets to fund some or all of the costs of decommissioning for which the entity has to make a provision under IAS 37. IFRIC 5 was issued in December 2004 to address this issue, referring to decommissioning to mean not only the dismantling of plant and equipment but also the costs of undertaking environmental rehabilitation, such as rectifying pollution of water or restoring mined land. *[IFRIC 5.1]*.

Contributions to these funds may be voluntary or required by regulation or law, and the funds may have one of the following common structures:

- funds that are established by a single contributor to fund its own decommissioning obligations, whether for a particular site, or for a number of geographically dispersed sites;
- funds that are established with multiple contributors to fund their individual or joint decommissioning obligations, where contributors are entitled to reimbursement for decommissioning expenses to the extent of their fund contributions plus any actual earnings on those contributions less their share of the costs of administering the fund. Contributors may have an obligation to make potential additional contributions, for example, in the event of the bankruptcy of another contributor;
- funds that are established with multiple contributors to fund their individual or joint decommissioning obligations when the required level of contributions is based on the current activity of a contributor, but the benefit obtained by that contributor is based on its past activity. In such cases there is a potential mismatch in the amount of contributions made by a contributor (based on current activity) and the value realisable from the fund (based on past activity). *[IFRIC 5.2]*.

Such funds generally have the following features:

- the fund is separately administered by independent trustees;
- entities (contributors) make contributions to the fund, which are invested in a range of assets that may include both debt and equity investments, and are available to help pay the contributors' decommissioning costs. The trustees determine how contributions are invested, within the constraints set by the fund's governing documents and any applicable legislation or other regulations;
- the contributors retain the obligation to pay decommissioning costs. However, contributors are able to obtain reimbursement of decommissioning costs from the fund up to the lower of the decommissioning costs incurred and the entity's share of assets of the fund; and
- the contributors may have restricted or no access to any surplus of assets of the fund over those used to meet eligible decommissioning costs. *[IFRIC 5.3]*.

IFRIC 5 applies to accounting in the financial statements of a contributor for interests arising from decommissioning funds that have both the following features:

- the assets are administered separately (either by being held in a separate legal entity or as segregated assets within another entity); and
- a contributor's right to access the assets is restricted. *[IFRIC 5.4]*.

A residual interest in a fund that extends beyond a right to reimbursement, such as a contractual right to distributions once all the decommissioning has been completed or on winding up the fund, may be an equity instrument within the scope of IAS 39 or IFRS 9, as appropriate, and is not within the scope of IFRIC 5. *[IFRIC 5.5]*.

The issues addressed by IFRIC 5 are:

(a) How should a contributor account for its interest in a fund?

(b) When a contributor has an obligation to make additional contributions, for example, in the event of the bankruptcy of another contributor, how should that obligation be accounted for? *[IFRIC 5.6]*.

6.3.3.A *Accounting for an interest in a fund*

IFRIC 5 requires the contributor to recognise its obligations to pay decommissioning costs as a liability and recognise its interest in the fund separately, unless the contributor is not liable to pay decommissioning costs even if the fund fails to pay. *[IFRIC 5.7]*.

The contributor determines whether it has control, joint control or significant influence over the fund by reference to IFRS 10 – *Consolidated Financial Statements*, IFRS 11 – *Joint Arrangements* – and IAS 28 – *Investments in Associates and Joint Ventures*. If the contributor determines that it has such control, joint control or significant influence, it should account for its interest in the fund in accordance with those standards (see Chapters 6, 12 and 11 respectively). *[IFRIC 5.8]*.

Otherwise, the contributor should recognise the right to receive reimbursement from the fund as a reimbursement in accordance with IAS 37 (see 4.5 above). This reimbursement should be measured at the lower of:

- the amount of the decommissioning obligation recognised; and
- the contributor's share of the fair value of the net assets of the fund attributable to contributors. *[IFRIC 5.9]*.

This 'asset cap' means that the asset recognised in respect of the reimbursement rights can never exceed the recognised liability. Accordingly, rights to receive reimbursement to meet decommissioning liabilities that have yet to be recognised as a provision are not recognised. *[IFRIC 5.BC14]*. Although many respondents expressed concern about this asset cap and argued that rights to benefit in excess of this amount give rise to an additional asset, separate from the reimbursement asset, the Interpretations Committee, despite having sympathy with the concerns, concluded that to recognise such an asset would be inconsistent with the requirement in IAS 37 that 'the amount recognised for the reimbursement should not exceed the amount of the provision'. *[IFRIC 5.BC19-20]*.

Changes in the carrying value of the right to receive reimbursement other than contributions to and payments from the fund should be recognised in profit or loss in the period in which these changes occur. *[IFRIC 5.9]*.

The effect of this requirement is that the amount recognised in the statement of comprehensive income relating to the reimbursement bears no relation to the expense recognised in respect of the provision, particularly for decommissioning liabilities where most changes in the measurement of the provision are not taken to the profit or loss immediately, but are recognised prospectively over the remaining useful life of the related asset (see 6.3.1 above).

One company that has been affected by the 'asset cap' is Fortum as shown below. In this extract, the company observes that because IFRS does not allow the asset to exceed the amount of the provision, *[IFRIC 5.BC19-20]*, it recognises a

Chapter 28

reimbursement asset in its statement of financial position that is lower than its actual share of the fund.

Extract 28.7: Fortum Oyj (2015)

Financial statements [extract]

30 Nuclear related assets and liabilities [extract]

Accounting policies [extract]

Fortum owns Loviisa nuclear power plant in Finland. In Fortum's consolidated balance sheet, Share in the State Nuclear Waste Management Fund and the Nuclear provisions relate to Loviisa nuclear power plant. Fortum's nuclear related provisions and the related part of the State Nuclear Waste Management Fund are both presented separately in the balance sheet. Fortum's share in the State Nuclear Waste Management Fund is accounted for according to IFRIC 5, Rights to interests arising from decommissioning, restoration and environmental rehabilitation funds which states that the fund assets are measured at the lower of fair value or the value of the related liabilities since Fortum does not have control or joint control over the State Nuclear Waste Management Fund. The Nuclear Waste Management Fund is managed by governmental authorities. The related provisions are the provision for decommissioning and the provision for disposal of spent fuel.

[...]

Fortum's actual share of the State Nuclear Waste Management Fund, related to Loviisa nuclear power plant, is higher than the carrying value of the Fund in the balance sheet. The legal nuclear liability should, according to the Finnish Nuclear Energy Act, be fully covered by payments and guarantees to the State Nuclear Waste Management Fund. The legal liability is not discounted while the provisions are, and since the future cash flow is spread over 100 years, the difference between the legal liability and the provisions are material.

30.1 Nuclear related assets and liabilities for 100% owned nuclear power plant, Loviisa [extract]

EUR million	**2015**	**2014**
Carrying values in the balance sheet		
BS Nuclear provisions	810	774
BS Fortum's share of the State Nuclear Waste Management Fund	810	774
Legal liability and actual share of the State Nuclear Waste Management Fund		
Liability for nuclear waste management according to the Nuclear Energy Act	1,094	1,084
Funding obligation target	1,094	1,074
Fortum's share of the State Nuclear Waste Management Fund	1,083	1,039
Share of the fund not recognised in the balance sheet	273	265

Legal liability for Loviisa nuclear power plant

The legal liability on 31 December 2015, decided by the Ministry of Employment and Economy in December 2015, was EUR 1,094 million.

The legal liability is based on a cost estimate, which is done every year, and a technical plan, which is made every third year. The current technical plan was updated in 2013. Following the update of the technical plan in 2013, the liability increased due to updated cost estimates relating to interim and final storage of spent fuel. The legal liability is determined by assuming that the decommissioning would start at the beginning of the year following the assessment year.

Fortum's share in the State Nuclear Waste Management Fund

According to Nuclear Energy Act, Fortum is obligated to contribute funds in full to the State Nuclear Waste Management Fund to cover the legal liability. Fortum contributes funds to the Finnish State Nuclear Waste Management Fund based on the yearly funding obligation target decided by the governmental authorities in December in connection with the decision of size of the legal liability. The current funding obligation target decided in December 2015 is EUR 1,094 million.

Nuclear provisions EUR million	**2015**	**2014**
BS 1 January	**774**	**744**
Additional provisions	10	11
Used during the year	–18	–24
Unwinding of discount	44	43
BS 31 December	**810**	**774**
Fortum's share in the State Nuclear Waste Management Fund	810	774

Nuclear provision and fund accounted according to IFRS [extract]

Nuclear provisions include the provision for decommissioning and the provision for disposal of spent fuel. The carrying value of the nuclear provisions, calculated according to IAS 37, increased by EUR 36 million compared to 31 December 2014, totaling EUR 810 million on 31 December 2015. The provisions are based on the same cash flows for future costs as the legal liability, but based on the estimated future timing of the expenditures. The main reason for the difference between the carrying value of the provision and the legal liability is the fact that the legal liability is not discounted to net present value.

The carrying value of the Fund in the balance sheet cannot exceed the carrying value of the nuclear provisions according to IFRIC Interpretation 5. The Fund is from an IFRS perspective overfunded with EUR 273 million, since Fortum's share of the Fund on 31 December 2015 was EUR 1,083 million and the carrying value in the balance sheet was EUR 810 million.

Fortum's share of the Finnish Nuclear Waste Management Fund in Fortum's balance sheet can in maximum be equal to the amount of the provisions according to IFRS. As long as the Fund is overfunded from an IFRS perspective, the effects to operating profit from this adjustment will be positive if the provisions increase more than the Fund and negative if actual value of the fund increases more than the provisions.

6.3.3.B *Accounting for obligations to make additional contributions*

IFRIC 5 requires that when a contributor has an obligation to make potential additional contributions, for example, in the event of the bankruptcy of another contributor or if the value of the investments held by the fund decreases to an extent that they are insufficient to fulfil the fund's reimbursement obligations, this obligation is a contingent liability that is within the scope of IAS 37. The contributor shall recognise a liability only if it is probable that additional contributions will be made. *[IFRIC 5.10]*.

6.3.3.C *Gross presentation of interest in the fund and the decommissioning liability*

IFRIC 5 requires the contributor to a fund to recognise its obligations to pay decommissioning costs as a liability and recognise its interest in the fund separately, unless the contributor is not liable to pay decommissioning costs even if the fund fails to pay. *[IFRIC 5.7]*. Accordingly, in most cases it would not be appropriate to offset the decommissioning liability and the interest in the fund.

The Interpretations Committee reached this conclusion because IAS 37 requires an entity that remains liable for expenditure to recognise a provision even where reimbursement is available and to recognise a separate reimbursement asset only when the entity is virtually certain that it will be received when the obligation is settled. *[IFRIC 5.BC7]*. The Interpretations Committee also noted that the conditions in IAS 32 – *Financial Instruments: Presentation* – for offsetting a financial asset and a financial liability would rarely be met because of the absence of a legal right of set off and the likelihood that settlement will not be net or simultaneous. *[IAS 32.42]*. Arguments that the existence of a fund allows derecognition of the liability by analogy to IAS 39; or a net presentation similar to a pension fund, were also rejected. *[IFRIC 5.BC8]*.

6.3.3.D *Disclosure of interests arising from decommissioning, restoration and environmental rehabilitation funds*

IFRIC 5 requires the following disclosures:

- A contributor should disclose the nature of its interest in a fund and any restrictions on access to the assets in the fund *[IFRIC 5.11]*;
- When a contributor has an obligation to make potential additional contributions that is not recognised as a liability (see 6.3.3.B above), it should provide the contingent liability disclosures required by IAS 37 (see 7.2 below); *[IFRIC 5.12]* and
- When a contributor accounts for its right to receive reimbursement from the fund as a reimbursement right under IAS 37 in accordance with paragraph 9 of IFRIC 5 (see 6.3.3.A above), it should disclose the amount of the expected reimbursement and the amount of any asset that has been recognised for that expected reimbursement. *[IFRIC 5.13]*.

6.4 Environmental provisions – general guidance in IAS 37

The standard illustrates its recognition requirements in two examples relating to environmental provisions. The first deals with the situation where it is virtually certain that legislation will be enacted which will require the clean-up of land already contaminated. In these circumstances, the virtual certainty of new legislation being enacted means that the entity has a present legal obligation as a result of the past event (contamination of the land), requiring a provision to be recognised. *[IAS 37 IE Example 2A]*. However, in its discussion about what constitutes an obligating event, the standard notes that 'differences in circumstances surrounding enactment make it impossible to specify a single event that would make the enactment of a law virtually certain. In many cases, it will be impossible to be virtually certain of the enactment of a law until it is enacted.' *[IAS 37.22]*. The second example deals with a similar situation, except that the entity is not expected to be legally required to clean it up. Nevertheless, the entity has a widely publicised environmental policy undertaking to clean up all contamination that it causes, and has a record of honouring this policy. In these circumstances a provision is still required because the entity has created a valid expectation that it will clean up the land, meaning that the entity has a present constructive obligation as a result of past contamination. *[IAS 37 IE Example 2B]*. It is therefore clear that where an entity causes environmental damage and has a present legal or constructive obligation to make it good; it is probable that an outflow of resources will be required to settle the obligation; and a reliable estimate can be made of the amount, a provision will be required. *[IAS 37.14]*.

One company making provision for environmental costs is Syngenta, which describes some of the practical difficulties and uncertainties relating to its measurement in the extract below.

Extract 28.8: Syngenta AG (2015)

Notes to the Syngenta Group Consolidated Financial Statements [extract]

29. New IFRSs and accounting policies [extract]

Other accounting policies [extract]

Environmental provisions [extract]

Provisions for remediation costs are made when there is a present obligation, it is probable that expenditures for remediation work will be required within ten years (or a longer period if specified by a legal obligation) and the cost can be estimated within a reasonable range of possible outcomes. The costs are based on currently available facts: technology expected to be available at the time of the clean up; laws and regulations presently or virtually certain to be enacted; and prior experience in remediation of contaminated sites.

Environmental liabilities are recorded at the estimated amount at which the liability could be settled at the balance sheet date, and are discounted if the impact is material [...]

19. Provisions [extract]

Movements in provisions for the year ended December 31, 2015 are as follows: [extract]

($m)	January 1	Charged to income	Release of provisions credited to income	Payments	Actuarial (gains)/ losses	Transfers offset in defined benefit assets	Currency translation effects/ other	December 31
Environmental provisions	237	3	(1)	(28)	–	–	(2)	209

25. Commitments and contingencies [extract]

Contingencies [extract]

Environmental Matters

It is reasonably possible that Syngenta may be required to make expenditures in excess of the established provisions that are reported in Note 19 to remediate environmental liabilities at some currently or formerly owned, leased and third party sites throughout the world. Further, in cases where it is not possible to estimate reliably the remediation costs that may be incurred in the future for environmental damage that has occurred at sites currently in operation and having no present obligation for environmental damage remediation, no provisions have been made. This is because it is neither possible to determine a time limit beyond which the sites will no longer be operated, nor what remediation costs may be required upon their eventual closure.

In the USA, Syngenta and/or its indemnitors or indemnitees, have been named under federal legislation (the Comprehensive Environmental Response, Compensation and Liability Act of 1980, as amended) as a potentially responsible party ("PRP") in respect of several sites. Syngenta expects to be indemnified against a proportion of the liabilities associated with a number of these sites by the sellers of the businesses associated with such sites and, where appropriate, actively participates in or monitors the clean-up activities at the sites in respect of which it is a PRP.

Chapter 28

If the expenditure relating to an environmental obligation is not expected to be incurred for some time, a significant effect of the standard is its requirement that provisions should be discounted, which can have a material impact. BP sets out its policy in the following extract.

Extract 28.9: BP p.l.c. (2015)

Notes on financial statements [extract]

1. Significant accounting policies, judgements, estimates and assumptions [extract]

Environmental expenditures and liabilities

Environmental expenditures that are required in order for the group to obtain future economic benefits from its assets are capitalized as part of those assets. Expenditures that relate to an existing condition caused by past operations that do not contribute to future earnings are expensed.

Liabilities for environmental costs are recognized when a clean-up is probable and the associated costs can be reliably estimated. Generally, the timing of recognition of these provisions coincides with the commitment to a formal plan of action or, if earlier, on divestment or on closure of inactive sites.

The amount recognized is the best estimate of the expenditure required to settle the obligation. Provisions for environmental liabilities have been estimated using existing technology, at current prices and discounted using a real discount rate. The weighted average period over which these costs are generally expected to be incurred is estimated to be approximately five years.

22. Provisions [extract]

	$ million Environmental
At 1 January 2015	2,847
Exchange adjustments	(18)
New or increased provisions	5,697
Write-back of unused provisions	(75)
Unwinding of discount	106
Change in discount rate[a]	(149)
Utilization	(392)
Reclassified to other payables	(459)
Deletions	–
At 31 December 2015	7,557
Of which – current	587
– non-current	6,970
Of which – Gulf of Mexico Oil Spill[b]	5,919

[a] Provisions for the agreements to settle all federal and state claims in relation to the Gulf of Mexico oil spill are discounted using a discount rate equal to a current interest rate that the group could obtain for a borrowing on similar terms.

[b] Further information on the financial impacts of the Gulf of Mexico oil spill is provided in Note 2.

2. Significant event – Gulf of Mexico oil spill [extract]

Environmental

The environmental provision at 31 December 2015 includes amounts payable for natural resource damage costs under the proposed Consent Decree. These amounts are payable in instalments over 16 years commencing one year after the court approves the Consent Decree; [...]

6.5 Liabilities associated with emissions trading schemes

A number of countries around the world either have, or are developing, schemes to encourage reduced emissions of pollutants, in particular of greenhouse gases.

These schemes comprise tradable emissions allowances or permits, an example of which is a 'cap and trade' model whereby participants are allocated emission rights or allowances equal to a cap (i.e. a maximum level of allowable emissions) and are permitted to trade those allowances. A cap and trade emission rights scheme typically has the following features:[25]

- an entity participating in the scheme (participant) is set a target to reduce its emissions to a specified level (the cap). The participant is issued allowances equal in number to its cap by a government or government agency. Allowances may be issued free of charge, or participants may pay the government for them;
- the scheme operates for defined compliance periods;
- participants are free to buy and sell allowances;
- if at the end of the compliance period a participant's actual emissions exceeded its emission rights, the participant will incur a penalty;
- in some schemes emission rights may be carried forward to future periods; and
- the scheme may provide for brokers – who are not themselves participants – to buy and sell emission rights.

In response to diversity in the accounting for cap and trade emission rights schemes, the Interpretations Committee added this matter to its agenda. Accordingly, in December 2004 the IASB issued IFRIC 3 to address the accounting for emission allowances that arise from cap and trade emission rights schemes.

IFRIC 3 took the view that a cap and trade scheme did not give rise to a net asset or liability, but that it gave rise to various items that were to be accounted for separately:[26]

(a) *an asset for allowances held* – Allowances, whether allocated by government or purchased, were to be regarded as intangible assets and accounted for under IAS 38. Allowances issued for less than fair value were to be measured initially at their fair value;[27]

(b) *a government grant* – When allowances are issued for less than fair value, the difference between the amount paid and fair value was a government grant that should be accounted for under IAS 20 – *Accounting for Government Grants and Disclosure of Government Assistance*. Initially the grant was to be recognised as deferred income in the statement of financial position and subsequently recognised as income on a systematic basis over the compliance period for which the allowances were issued, regardless of whether the allowances were held or sold;[28]

(c) *a liability for the obligation to deliver allowances equal to emissions that have been made* – As emissions are made, a liability was to be recognised as a provision that falls within the scope of IAS 37. The liability was to be measured at the best estimate of the expenditure required to settle the present obligation at the end of the reporting period. This would usually be the present market price of the number of allowances required to cover emissions made up to the end of the reporting period.[29]

However, the interpretation met with significant resistance because application of IFRIC 3 would result in a number of accounting mismatches:[30]

- a measurement mismatch between the assets and liabilities recognised in accordance with IFRIC 3;
- a mismatch in the location in which the gains and losses on those assets are reported; and
- a possible timing mismatch because allowances would be recognised when they are obtained – typically at the start of the year – whereas the emission liability would be recognised during the year as it is incurred.

Consequently, the IASB decided in June 2005 to withdraw IFRIC 3 despite the fact that it considered it to be 'an appropriate interpretation of existing IFRSs'.[31] The IASB activated its project on emission trading schemes in December 2007 but work was suspended in November 2010. In May 2012, IASB members gave their unanimous support to giving priority to restarting research on emission trading schemes.[32] In February 2015, the project was renamed from 'Emission trading schemes' to 'Pollutant pricing mechanisms'. This change was to reflect a decision by the Board in January 2015 to broaden the scope of the project to consider a variety of schemes that use emission allowances and other financial tools to manage the emission of pollutants. The Board also decided in January 2015 that they would take a 'fresh start' approach to the project rather than starting from the tentative decisions made in the previous project.[33] IASB discussions are ongoing and the next step is likely to be a discussion paper.[34]

In the meantime, entities can either:

(a) apply IFRIC 3, which despite having been withdrawn, is considered to be an appropriate interpretation of existing IFRS; or

(b) develop its own accounting policy for cap and trade schemes based on the hierarchy of authoritative guidance in IAS 8.

A more fulsome discussion of the issues and methods applied in practice is covered in Chapter 17 at 11.2.

6.6 Green certificates compared to emissions trading schemes

Some countries have launched schemes to promote the production of power from renewable sources based on green certificates – also known as renewable energy certificates (RECs), green tags, or tradable renewable certificates.

In a green certificates system, a producer of electricity from renewable sources is granted certificates by the government based on the power output (kWh) of green electricity produced. These certificates may be used in the current and future compliance periods as defined by the particular scheme. The certificates can be sold separately. Generally the cost to produce green electricity is higher than the cost of producing an equivalent amount of electricity generated from non-renewable sources, although this is not always the case. Distributors of electricity sell green electricity at the same price as other electricity.

In a typical green certificates scheme, distributors of electricity to consumers (businesses, households etc.) are required to remit a number of green certificates based on the kWh of electricity sold on an annual basis. Distributors must therefore purchase green certificates in the market (such certificates having been sold by producers). If a distribution company does not have the number of required certificates, it is required to pay a penalty to the environmental agency. Once the penalty is paid, the entity is discharged of its obligations to remit certificates.

It is this requirement to remit certificates that creates a market in and gives value to green certificates (the value depends on many variables but primarily on the required number of certificates that have to be delivered relative to the amount of power that is produced from renewable sources, and the level of penalty payable if the required number of certificates are not remitted).

There are similarities between green certificates and emission rights. However, green certificates are granted to generators of cleaner energy as an incentive for 'good' production achieved, irrespective of whether or not there is a subsequent sale of that cleaner energy to an end consumer. For a distributor of energy, a green certificate gives a similar 'right to pollute' as an emission right except that a distributor of energy under a green certificate regime must acquire the certificates from the market (i.e. they are not granted to the distributor by the government). As with emission rights, the topic of green certificates cuts across a number of different areas of accounting, not just provisions. A more fulsome discussion of the issues and methods applied in practice is covered in Chapter 17 at 11.3.

6.7 EU Directive on 'Waste Electrical and Electronic Equipment' (IFRIC 6)

This Directive regulates the collection, treatment, recovery and environmentally sound disposal of waste electrical or electronic equipment (WE&EE).[35] It applies to entities involved in the manufacture and resale of electrical or electronic equipment, including entities (both European and Non-European) that import such equipment into the EU. As member states in the EU began to implement this directive into their national laws, it gave rise to questions about when the liability for the decommissioning of WE&EE should be recognised. The Directive distinguishes between 'new' and 'historical' waste and between waste from private households and waste from sources other than private households. New waste relates to products sold after 13 August 2005. All household equipment sold before that date is deemed to give rise to historical waste for the purposes of the Directive. *[IFRIC 6.3]*.

The Directive states that the cost of waste management for historical household equipment should be borne by producers of that type of equipment that are in the market during a period to be specified in the applicable legislation of each Member State (the measurement period). The Directive states that each Member State shall establish a mechanism to have producers contribute to costs proportionately 'e.g. in proportion to their respective share of the market by type of equipment.' *[IFRIC 6.4]*.

The Interpretations Committee was asked to determine in the context of the decommissioning of WE&EE what constitutes the obligating event in accordance with paragraph 14(a) of IAS 37 (discussed at 3.1.1 above) for the recognition of a provision for waste management costs:

- the manufacture or sale of the historical household equipment?
- participation in the market during the measurement period?
- the incurrence of costs in the performance of waste management activities? *[IFRIC 6.8]*.

IFRIC 6 was issued in September 2005 and provides guidance on the recognition, in the financial statements of producers, of liabilities for waste management under the EU Directive on WE&EE in respect of sales of historical household equipment. *[IFRIC 6.6]*. The interpretation addresses neither new waste nor historical waste from sources other than private households. The Interpretations Committee considers that the liability for such waste management is adequately covered in IAS 37. However, if, in national legislation, new waste from private households is treated in a similar manner to historical waste from private households, the principles of IFRIC 6 are to apply by reference to the hierarchy set out in IAS 8 (see Chapter 3 at 4.3). The IAS 8 hierarchy is also stated to be relevant for other regulations that impose obligations in a way that is similar to the cost attribution model specified in the EU Directive. *[IFRIC 6.7]*.

IFRIC 6 regards participation in the market during the measurement period as the obligating event in accordance with paragraph 14(a) of IAS 37. Consequently, a liability for waste management costs for historical household equipment does not arise as the products are manufactured or sold. Because the obligation for historical household equipment is linked to participation in the market during the measurement period, rather than to production or sale of the items to be disposed of, there is no obligation unless and until a market share exists during the measurement period. It is also noted that the timing of the obligating event may also be independent of the particular period in which the activities to perform the waste management are undertaken and the related costs incurred. *[IFRIC 6.9]*.

The following example, which is based on one within the accompanying Basis for Conclusions on IFRIC 6, illustrates its requirements.

Example 28.18: Illustration of IFRIC 6 requirements

An entity selling electrical equipment in 2015 has a market share of 4 per cent for that calendar year. It subsequently discontinues operations and is thus no longer in the market when the waste management costs for its products are allocated to those entities with market share in 2017. With a market share of 0 per cent in 2017, the entity's obligation is zero. However, if another entity enters the market for electronic products in 2017 and achieves a market share of 3 per cent in that period, then that entity's obligation for the costs of waste management from earlier periods will be 3 per cent of the total costs of waste management allocated to 2017, even though the entity was not in the market in those earlier periods and has not produced any of the products for which waste management costs are allocated to 2017. *[IFRIC 6.BC5]*.

The Interpretations Committee concluded that the effect of the cost attribution model specified in the Directive is that the making of sales during the measurement period is the 'past event' that requires recognition of a provision under IAS 37 over the measurement period. Aggregate sales for the period determine the entity's obligation for a proportion of the costs of waste management allocated to that period. The measurement period is independent of the period when the cost allocation is notified to market participants. *[IFRIC 6.BC6]*.

Some constituents asked the Interpretations Committee to consider the effect of the following possible national legislation: the waste management costs for which a producer is responsible because of its participation in the market during a specified period (for example 2017) are not based on the market share of the producer during that period but on the producer's participation in the market during a previous period (for example 2016). The Interpretations Committee noted that this affects only the measurement of the liability and that the obligating event is still participation in the market during 2017. *[IFRIC 6.BC7]*.

IFRIC 6 notes that terms used in the interpretation such as 'market share' and 'measurement period' may be defined very differently in the applicable legislation of individual Member States. For example, the length of the measurement period might be a year or only one month. Similarly, the measurement of market share and the formulae for computing the obligation may differ in the various national legislations. However, all of these examples affect only the measurement of the liability, which is not within the scope of the interpretation. *[IFRIC 6.5]*.

6.8 Levies imposed by governments

When governments or other public authorities impose levies on entities in relation to their activities, as opposed to income taxes and fines or other penalties, it is not always clear when the liability to pay a levy arises and a provision should be recognised. In May 2013, the Interpretations Committee issued IFRIC 21 to address this question. *[IFRIC 21.2, 7]*. The Interpretation does not address the accounting for the costs arising out of an obligation to pay a levy, for example to determine whether an asset or expense should be recorded. Other standards should be applied in this regard. *[IFRIC 21.3]*.

The Interpretation became mandatory for accounting periods beginning on or after 1 January 2014, although it permitted earlier application. *[IFRIC 21.A1]*. It requires that, for levies within its scope, an entity should recognise a liability only when the activity that triggers payment, as identified by the relevant legislation, occurs. *[IFRIC 21.8]*.

6.8.1 Scope of IFRIC 21

A levy is defined as an outflow of resources embodying economic benefits that is imposed by governments on entities in accordance with legislation, other than:

(a) those outflows of resources that are within the scope of other Standards (such as income taxes that are within the scope of IAS 12); and

(b) fines or other penalties that are imposed for breaches of the legislation. *[IFRIC 21.4]*.

In addition to income taxes (see Chapter 31) and fines, the Interpretation does not apply to contractual arrangements with government in which the entity acquires an asset (see Chapters 17 and 18) or receives services; and it is not required to be applied to liabilities that arise from emission trading schemes (see 6.5 above). *[IFRIC 21.5, 6]*. Although IFRIC 21 does not apply to income taxes in scope of IAS 12, the Interpretations Committee concluded in 2006 that any taxes not within the scope of other standards (such as IAS 12) are within the scope of IAS 37. Therefore such taxes may be within the scope of IFRIC 21. *[IFRIC 21.BC4]*.

IFRIC 21 was developed to address concerns over the timing of recognition for government-imposed levies in which the obligation to pay depended upon participation in a particular market on a specified date. However, the definition of levy in IFRIC 21 has resulted in the scope of the interpretation being broader than entities might have expected. The term 'levy' may not be widely used across jurisdictions, and may be referred to as a charge, duty or a tax, for example. However, it is not the terminology, but the nature of the payment, that should be considered when determining if it is in the scope of IFRIC 21.

Entities should consider all payments imposed by governments pursuant to legislation to determine whether they are in scope of IFRIC 21. The interpretation provides a broad definition of government, including municipal, provincial, state, federal or international governments or government agencies or organisations controlled or administered by government. *[IFRIC 21.4]*.

IFRIC 21 clarifies that both levies that give rise to a liability under IAS 37, and levies whose timing or amounts are certain are within scope of the interpretation *[IFRIC 21.2]*. Therefore, the scope of IFRIC 21 is broader than IAS 37. For example, a non-refundable fixed fee imposed by government payable at a specific date may be a levy within the scope of IFRIC 21.

In some cases, payments may pass through one or more non-governmental bodies or entities before being received by the government. In our view, IFRIC 21 does not distinguish between recipients of the payment; they key factor is whether the payment is required by law. Therefore, as long as the payments are required by law, they are generally considered to be imposed by the government *[IFRIC 21.4]*.

Some of the legislation relating to payments imposed by governments can be complex, so entities should carefully analyse the facts and circumstances to determine whether a payment falls within the scope of IFRIC 21. However, where entities are making payments for any of the following items, it may be necessary to assess for any potential IFRIC 21 impacts:

- taxes other than income taxes, e.g. property tax, land tax and capital-based tax;
- certain fees, concessions, contributions or royalty fees imposed on industries which are regulated by government, e.g. telecommunications, mining, airline, banking, insurance, dairy produce and energy and natural resources; and
- transaction taxes based on activity in a specified market, e.g. banking and insurance.

6.8.2 *Recognition and measurement of levy liabilities*

For levies within the scope of the Interpretation, the *activity* that creates the obligation under the relevant legislation to pay the levy is the obligating event for recognition purposes. *[IFRIC 21.8]*. In many cases this activity is related to the entity's participation in a relevant market at a specific date or dates. The Interpretation states that neither a constructive nor a present obligation arises as a result of being economically compelled to continue operating; or from any implication of continuing operations in the future arising from the use of the going concern assumption in the preparation of financial statements. *[IFRIC 21.9, 10]*.

When a levy is payable progressively, for example as the entity generates revenues, the entity recognises a liability over a period of time on that basis. This is because the obligating event is the activity that generates revenues. *[IFRIC 21.11]*. If an obligation to pay a levy is triggered in full as soon as a minimum threshold is reached, such as when the entity commences generating sales or achieves a certain level of revenue, the liability is recognised in full on the first day that the entity reaches that threshold. *[IFRIC 21.12]*. If an entity pays over amounts to government before it is determined that an obligation to pay that levy exists, it recognises an asset. *[IFRIC 21.14]*.

Example 28.19: A levy is triggered in full as soon as the entity generates revenues

An entity with a calendar year end generates revenues in a specific market in 2017. The amount of the levy is determined by reference to revenues generated by the entity in the market in 2016 although the levy is only payable when revenues are generated in 2017. The entity generated revenues in the market in 2016 and starts to generate revenues in the market in 2017 on 3 January 2017.

In this example, the liability is recognised in full on 3 January 2017 because the obligating event, as identified by the legislation, is the first generation of revenues in 2017. The generation of revenues in 2016 is necessary, but not sufficient, to create a present obligation to pay a levy. Before 3 January 2017, the entity has no obligation. In other words, the activity that triggers the payment of the levy as identified by the legislation is the first generation of revenues at a point in time in 2017. The generation of revenues in 2016 is not the activity that triggers the payment of the levy. The amount of revenues generated in 2016 only affects the measurement of the liability. *[IFRIC 21.13, IE1 Example 2]*.

The table below summarises the illustrative examples that accompany IFRIC 21, which provide guidelines on how to account for the timing of the recognition for the various types of levies: [IFRIC 21.IE1]

Illustrative examples	*Obligating event*	*Recognition of liability*
Levy triggered progressively as revenue is generated in a specified period.	Generation of revenue in the specified period.	Recognise progressively. A liability must be recognised progressively because, at any point in time during the specified period, the entity has a present obligation to pay a levy on revenues generated to date.
Levy triggered in full as soon as revenue is generated in one period, based on revenues from a previous period.	First generation of revenue in subsequent period.	Full recognition at that point in time. Where an entity generates revenue in one period, which serves as the basis for measuring the amount of the levy, the entity does not become liable for the levy, and therefore cannot recognise a liability, until it first starts generating revenue in the subsequent period.
Levy triggered in full if the entity operates as a bank at the end of the annual reporting period.	Operating as a bank at the end of the reporting period.	Full recognition at the end of the annual reporting period. Before the end of the annual reporting period, the entity has no present obligation to pay a levy, even if it is economically compelled to continue operating as a bank in the future. The liability is recognised only at the end of the annual reporting period.
Levy triggered if revenues are above a minimum specified threshold (e.g. when a certain level of revenue has been achieved)	Reaching the specified minimum threshold.	Recognise an amount consistent with the obligation at that point of time. A liability is recognised only at the point that the specified minimum threshold is reached. For example, a levy is triggered when an entity generates revenues above specified thresholds: 0% for the first \$50 million and 2% above \$50 million. In this example, no liability is accrued until the entity's revenues reach the revenue threshold of \$50 million.

As set out in the table above, when a levy is triggered progressively, for example, as the entity generates revenues, the entity recognises a liability over the period of time on that basis. Some examples of progressive-type levies are set out below.

Example 28.20: Recognising a liability for levies that are triggered progressively

Scenario 1: Minimums

The legislation prescribes that no levy is triggered until revenues reach a certain threshold. There is a 0% tax rate on revenues until they reach $50 million, with a payment of 2% of revenues in excess of that amount.

For an entity that earns $49 million as at 30 June 2017, $51million as at 31 July 2017 and $100 million as at 31 December 2017, the following liabilities should be recognised:

30 June 2017 – No provision is recognised;

31 July 2017 – $20,000 provision is recognised (2% × $1 million); and

31 December 2017 – $1 million provision is recognised (2% × $50 million).

Scenario 2: Progressive tax rates

The legislation prescribes that the tax rate is escalating. There is a 2% tax rate on the first $50 million in revenues and 3% for revenues in excess of $50 million.

For an entity that earns $49 million as at 30 June 2017, $51million as at 31 July 2017 and $100 million as at 31 December 2017, the following liabilities should be recognised:

30 June 2017 – $980,000 provision is recognised (2% × $49 million);

31 July 2017 – $1,030,000 provision is recognised ((2% × $50 million) + (3% × $1 million)); and

31 December 2017 – $2.5 million provision is recognised ((2% × $50 million) + (3% × $50 million)).

Scenario 3: Specified formula

The legislation prescribes that the levy is calculated based on a specified formula that does not match the actual activity for the period. A calendar year-end entity has to pay a monthly levy based on 0.1% of a 12-month rolling average of gross profit.

Under the legislation, the 12-month period which the rolling average of the gross profit would be based on relates to the preceding 12 months, for example:

Date	Preceding 12 months	12 month rolling average ($)	Liability to be recognised ($)
30 June 2017	1 July 2016 – 30 June 2017	50 million	50,000
31 July 2017	1 August 2016 – 31 July 2017	60 million	60,000
31 December 2017	1 January 2017 – 31 December 2017	40 million	40,000

When the legislation provides that a levy is triggered by an entity operating in a market only at the end of its annual reporting period, no liability is recognised until the last day of the annual reporting period. No amount is recognised before that date in anticipation of the entity still operating in the market. Accordingly, a provision would not be permitted to be recognised in interim financial statements if the obligating event occurs only at the end of the annual reporting period. *[IFRIC 21.IE1 Example 3]*. The accounting treatment in interim reports is discussed in Chapter 39 at 9.7.5.

6.8.3 *Recognition of an asset or expense when a levy is recorded*

IFRIC 21 only provides guidance on when to recognise a liability, which is the credit side of the journal entry. The interpretation specifically states that it does not address whether the debit side of the journal entry is an asset or an expense *[IFRIC 21.3]*, except in the case of prepaid levies. *[IFRIC 21.14]*.

Prepayments may be fairly common in arrangements in which the legislation requires entities to pay levies in advance and where the obligating events for these levies are progressive. For example, property taxes that are paid in advance at a specified date (e.g. 1 January) for an obligating event that relates to future periods (e.g. 1 January to 31 December). In such instances, the entity would recognise the prepaid levy as an asset. *[IFRIC 21.14]*. In this scenario, the prepaid levy would then be amortised over the period.

Aside from prepaid levies, there are also instances when the assessment of expensing the liability or recognising a corresponding asset requires the application of other standards, such as IAS 2, IAS 11, IAS 16 or IAS 38. Given that levies are imposed by government and arise from non-exchange transactions, there would not typically be a clear linkage to future economic benefits. Consequentially, if the incurrence of the liability does not give rise to an identifiable future economic benefit to the entity, the recognition of an asset would be inappropriate as the definition of an asset would not be met. In such cases, the debit side would therefore be to an expense account.

In the case where asset recognition is appropriate under other IFRS standards, levies are generally not expected to give rise to a stand-alone asset in its own right, given that payments for the acquisition of goods or services are scoped out of IFRIC 21. *[IFRIC 21.5]*. However, a levy may form part of the acquisition costs of some other asset, provided it meets the asset recognition criteria in other IFRS standards. For example, an entity may be required to pay an import duty to the government under legislation for any large cargo trucks purchased from overseas. The entity uses the large cargo trucks as part of their operations to transport their goods to customers locally and therefore capitalises the trucks as part of property, plant and equipment under IAS 16. The import duty that is payable under the legislation may give rise to an IFRIC 21 levy, which would also be capitalised as part of the cost of the asset. *[IAS 16.16(a)]*.

6.9 Dilapidation and other provisions relating to leased assets

As discussed at 5.2 above, it is not appropriate to recognise provisions that relate to repairs and maintenance of owned assets (including assets held under finance leases). However, the position can be different in the case of obligations relating to assets held under operating leases. Nevertheless, the same principles under IAS 37 apply:

(a) provisions are recognised only for obligations existing independently of the entity's future actions (i.e. the future conduct of its business) and in cases where an entity can avoid future expenditure by its future actions, for example by changing its method of operation, it has no present obligation; *[IAS 37.19]*

(b) financial statements deal with an entity's position at the end of the reporting period and not its possible position in the future. Therefore, no provision is recognised for costs that need to be incurred to operate in the future; *[IAS 37.18]* and

(c) for an event to be an obligating event, the entity must have no realistic alternative to settling the obligation created by the event. *[IAS 37.17]*.

Operating leases often contain clauses which specify that the lessee should incur periodic charges for maintenance, make good dilapidations or other damage occurring during the rental period or return the asset to the configuration that existed as at inception of the lease. These contractual provisions may restrict the entity's ability to change its future conduct to avoid the expenditure. For example, the entity might not be able to transfer the asset in its existing condition. Alternatively, the entity could return the asset to avoid the risk of incurring costs relating to any future damage, but would have to make a payment in relation of dilapidations incurred to date. So the contractual obligations in a lease could create an environment in which a present obligation could exist as at the reporting date from which the entity cannot realistically withdraw.

Under principle (b) above, any provision should reflect only the conditions as at the reporting date. This means that a provision for specific damage done to the leased asset would merit recognition, as the event giving rise to the obligation under the lease has certainly occurred. For example, if an entity has erected partitioning or internal walls in a leasehold property and under the lease these have to be removed at the end of the term, then provision should be made for this cost (on a discounted basis, if material) at the time of putting up the partitioning or the walls. In this case, an equivalent asset would be recognised and depreciated over the term of the lease. This is similar to a decommissioning provision discussed at 6.3 above. Another example would be where an airline company leases aircraft under an operating lease, and upon delivery of the aircraft has made changes to the interior fittings and layout, but under the leasing arrangements has to return the asset to the configuration that existed as at inception of the lease.

What is less clear is whether a more general provision can be built up over time for maintenance charges and dilapidation costs in relation to a leased asset. It might be argued that in this case, the event giving rise to the obligation under the lease is simply the passage of time, and so a provision can be built up over time. However, in our view the phrase 'the event giving rise to the obligation under the lease' indicates that a more specific event has to occur; there has to be specific evidence of dilapidation etc. before any provision can be made. That is, it cannot be assumed that the condition of a leased asset has deteriorated simply because time has passed. However, in practice, it will often be the case that dilapidations do occur over time, in which case a dilapidations provision should be recognised as those dilapidations occur over the lease term. Example 28.12 at 5.2 above dealt with an owned aircraft that by law needs overhauling every three years, but no provision could be recognised for such costs. Instead, IAS 37 suggests that an amount equivalent to the expected maintenance costs is treated as a separate part of the asset and depreciated over three years. Airworthiness requirements for the airline industry are the same irrespective of whether the aircraft is owned or leased. So, if an airline company leases the aircraft under an operating lease, should a provision be made for the overhaul costs? The answer will depend on the terms of the lease.

If the lease requires the lessee to maintain the airworthiness of the aircraft and to return the aircraft at the end of the lease in the same condition as it was taken at inception of the lease, i.e. the aircraft has to be overhauled prior to its return, then the lessee should make provision. In this case the overhaul of the aircraft is a contractual obligation under the lease. The specific event that gives rise to the obligation is each flown hour or cycle completed by the aircraft as these determine the timing and nature of the overhaul that must be carried out. Provision should therefore be made for the costs of overhaul as the obligation towards the lessor arises (typically based upon the specific requirements of each aircraft type such as each flown hour or cycle), with a corresponding expense recognised in the statement of comprehensive income. For certain aircraft types and aircraft leases it is likely that the provision for the costs will be built up and then released, as the expenditure is incurred, a number of times during the term of the operating lease.

However, if the lease does not require the overhaul to be undertaken prior to the return of the aircraft (or require the lessee to make a contribution towards the next overhaul), then no provision should be made as the lessee does not have a contractual obligation to incur these costs that is independent of its own future actions.

The fact that a provision for repairs can be made at all in these circumstances might appear inconsistent with the case where the asset is owned by the entity. In that case, as discussed at 5.2 above, no provision for repairs could be made. There is, however, a difference between the two situations. Where the entity owns the asset, it has the choice of selling it rather than repairing it, and so the obligation is not independent of the entity's future actions. However, in the case of an entity leasing the asset, it can have a contractual obligation to repair any damage from which it cannot walk away.

6.10 Warranty provisions

Warranty provisions are specifically addressed in one of the examples appended to IAS 37. However, as noted at 2.2.1.C above, an entity that adopts the new revenue recognition Standard, IFRS 15, would apply that Standard to separately purchased warranties and to those warranties determined to provide the customer with a service in addition to the assurance that the product complies with agreed-upon specifications. Only if a customer does not have the option to purchase a warranty separately and the warranty is determined only to provide assurance that the product complies with agreed-upon specifications would an entity that has adopted IFRS 15 consider IAS 37. *[IFRS 15.B30]*. The requirements for warranties falling within the scope of IFRS 15 are considered further in Chapter 30.

The following example illustrates how warranty costs are addressed if IAS 37 applies.

Example 28.21: Recognition of a provision for warranty costs

A manufacturer gives warranties at the time of sale to purchasers of its product. Under the terms of the contract for sale, the manufacturer undertakes to make good, by repair or replacement, manufacturing defects that become apparent within three years from the date of sale. On past experience, it is probable (i.e. more likely than not) that there will be some claims under the warranties.

In these circumstances the obligating event is the sale of the product with a warranty, which gives rise to a legal obligation. Because it is more likely than not that there will be an outflow of resources for some claims under the warranties as a whole, a provision is recognised for the best estimate of the costs of making good under the warranty for those products sold before the end of the reporting period. *[IAS 37 IE Example 1]*.

The assessment of the probability of an outflow of resources is made across the population as a whole, and not using each potential claim as the unit of account. *[IAS 37.24]*. On past experience, it is probable that there will be some claims under the warranties, so a provision is recognised.

The assessment over the class of obligations as a whole makes it more likely that a provision will be recognised, because the probability criterion is considered in terms of whether at least one item in the population will give rise to a payment. Recognition then becomes a matter of reliable measurement and entities calculate an expected value of the estimated warranty costs. IAS 37 discusses this method of 'expected value' and illustrates how it is calculated in an example of a warranty provision. *[IAS 37.39]*. See Example 28.6 at 4.1 above.

An example of a company that makes a warranty provision is Philips Group as shown below:

Extract 28.10: Koninklijke Philips N.V. (2015)

12.9 **Notes** [extract]

1 **Significant accounting policies** [extract]

Provisions [extract]

Product warranty – A provision for warranties is recognized when the underlying products or services are sold. The provision is based on historical warranty data and a weighing of possible outcomes against their associated probabilities.

19 **Provisions**

Product warranty [extract]

The provision for product warranty reflects the estimated costs of replacement and free-of-charge services that will be incurred by the Company with respect to products sold. The Company expects the provision to be utilized mainly within the next year.

6.11 Litigation and other legal claims

IAS 37 includes an example of a court case in its appendix to illustrate how its principles distinguish between a contingent liability and a provision in such situations. See Example 28.4 at 3.2.1 above. However, the assessment of the particular case in the example is clear-cut. In most situations, assessing the need to provide for legal claims is one of the most difficult tasks in the field of provisioning. This is due mainly to the inherent uncertainty in the judicial process itself, which may be very long and drawn out. Furthermore, this is an area where either provision or disclosure might risk prejudicing the outcome of the case, because they give an insight into the entity's own view on the strength of its defence that can assist the claimant.

In principle, whether a provision should be made will depend on whether the three conditions for recognising a provision are met, i.e.

(a) there is a present obligation as a result of a past event;

(b) it is probable that an outflow of resources embodying economic benefits will be required to settle the obligation; and

(c) a reliable estimate can be made of the amount of the obligation. *[IAS 37.14]*.

In situations such as these, a past event is deemed to give rise to a present obligation if, taking account of all available evidence (including, for example, the opinion of experts), it is more likely than not that a present obligation exists at the end of the reporting period. *[IAS 37.15]*. The evidence to be considered includes any additional evidence occurring after the end of the reporting period. Accordingly, if on the basis of the evidence it is concluded that a present obligation is more likely than not to exist, a provision will be required, assuming the other conditions are met. *[IAS 37.16]*.

Condition (b) will be met if the transfer of economic benefits is more likely than not to occur, that is, it has a probability greater than 50%. In making this assessment, it is likely that account should be taken of any expert advice.

As far as condition (c) is concerned, the standard takes the view that a reasonable estimate can generally be made and it is only in extremely rare cases that this will not be the case. *[IAS 37.25]*.

Clearly, whether an entity should make provision for the costs of settling a case or to meet any award given by a court will depend on a reasoned assessment of the particular circumstances, based on appropriate legal advice.

6.12 Refunds policy

Example 28.1 at 3.1.1 above reflects an example given in the appendix of IAS 37 of a retail store that has a policy of refunding goods returned by dissatisfied customers. There is no legal obligation to do so, but the company's policy of making refunds is generally known. The example argues that the conduct of the store has created a valid expectation on the part of its customers that it will refund purchases. The obligating event is the original sale of the item, and the probability of some economic outflow is greater than 50%, as there will nearly always be some customers demanding refunds. Hence, a provision should be made, *[IAS 37 IE Example 4]*, presumably calculated on the 'expected value' basis.

This example is straightforward when the store has a very specific and highly publicised policy on refunds. However, some stores' policies on refunds might not be so clear cut. A store may offer refunds under certain conditions, but not widely publicise its policy. In these circumstances, there might be doubt as to whether the store has created a valid expectation on the part of its customers that it will honour all requests for a refund.

As with warranty costs (discussed at 6.10 above), the accounting treatment of refunds impinges into the area of revenue recognition. Currently, where products are sold with a right of return, IAS 18 requires the seller to recognise a liability for the expected returns, *[IAS 18.17]*, (see Chapter 29). Under IFRS 15, an entity recognises the amount of expected returns as a refund liability, representing its obligation to return the customer's consideration. *[IFRS 15.55]*. Even though this appears to be similar to current practice, there are other notable differences between the accounting for sales with a right of return under IFRS 15 as compared to IAS 18, which impacts the amount and timing of revenue recognition. This is discussed further in Chapter 30.

6.13 Self insurance

Another situation where entities sometimes make provisions is self insurance which arises when an entity decides not to take out external insurance in respect of a certain category of risk because it would be uneconomic to do so. The same position may arise when a group insures its risks with a captive insurance subsidiary, the effects of which have to be eliminated on consolidation. In fact, the term 'self insurance' is potentially misleading, since it really means that the entity is not insured at all and will settle claims from third parties from its own resources in the event that it is found to be liable. Accordingly, the recognition criteria in IAS 37 should be applied, with a provision being justified only if there is a present obligation as a result of a past event; if it is probable that an outflow of resources will occur; and a reliable estimate can be determined. *[IAS 37.14]*.

Therefore, losses are recognised based on their actual incidence and any provisions that appear in the statement of financial position should reflect only the amounts expected to be paid in respect of those incidents that have occurred by the end of the reporting period.

In certain circumstances, a provision will often be needed not simply for known incidents, but also for those which insurance companies call IBNR – Incurred But Not Reported – representing an estimate of claims that have occurred at the end of the reporting period but which have not yet been notified to the reporting entity. We believe that it is appropriate that provision for such expected claims is made to the extent that such items can be measured reliably.

6.14 Obligations to make donations to non-profit organisations

When an entity promises to make donations to a non-profit organisation it can be difficult to determine whether a past obligating event exists that requires a provision to be recognised or whether it is appropriate instead to account for the gift as payments are made.

Example 28.22: Accounting for donations to non-profit organisations

An entity decides to enter into an arrangement to 'donate' €1m in cash to a university. A number of different options are available for the arrangement and the entity's management want to determine whether the terms of these options make any difference to the timing, measurement or presentation of the €1m expenditure, as follows:

Option 1:
The entity enters into an unenforceable contract to contribute €1m for general purposes. The benefits to the entity are deemed only to relate to its reputation as a 'good corporate citizen'; the entity does not receive any consideration or significant benefit from the university in return for the donation.

Option 2:
As per Option 1 except the entity publishes a press release in relation to the donation and announcing that payment is to be made in equal instalments of €200,000 over 5 years.

Option 3:
As per Option 2, except that the contract is legally enforceable in the event that the entity does not pay all the instalments under the contract.

Option 4:
As per Option 2, except that the entity is only required to make the donation if the university raises €4m from other sources.

Option 5:
As per Option 2, except that the contract is legally enforceable and the funds will be used for research and development activities specified by the entity. The entity will retain proprietary rights over the results of the research.

The following principles are relevant in determining when a promise to make a donation should be recognised as an obligation:

- to the extent that there is an enforceable contract, the donor should recognise an expense and a liability upon entry into that contract;
- where the agreement is not enforceable, the donor recognises an expense and a liability when a constructive obligation arises. The timing of recognition depends on whether the donation is conditional, whether it is probable that those conditions are substantially met and whether a past event has occurred; and
- if the donor expects to receive benefits commensurate with the value of the donation, the arrangement should be treated as an exchange transaction. Such transactions are in some cases executory contracts and may also give rise to the recognition of an asset rather than an expense.

In cases where the 'donation' is made under an enforceable contract, a present obligation is created when the entity enters into that contract. When payment is required in cash, the signing of an enforceable contract gives rise to a financial liability, *[IAS 32.11]*, which is measured initially at fair value. *[IAS 39.43, IFRS 9.5.1.1]*.

Where there is no legal obligation to make the payments, a liability is recognised when a constructive obligation arises. It is a matter of judgement whether and when a constructive obligation exists. In many unenforceable contracts, a signed contract would not, in itself, be sufficient to create a constructive obligation. Hence, in the absence of other facts and circumstances that would create a constructive obligation, the donor would recognise the expenditure when the cash or other assets are transferred.

By contrast, an exchange transaction is a reciprocal transfer in which each party receives and sacrifices approximately equal value. Assets and liabilities are not recognised until each party performs their obligations under the arrangement.

Applying these principles to the options listed in Example 28.22 above:

- In Option 1, the contract is unenforceable, there is no announcement or conditions preceding payment and there is no exchange of benefits. Accordingly, an expense would be recognised only when the entity transfers cash to the university.
- For Option 2, it may be appropriate for the entity to conclude that the entity's announcement of the donation to be paid by instalments indicates that there is a constructive obligation because the entity has a created a valid expectation that it will make all of the payments promised. Alternatively, it could determine that once the first instalment is paid, the entity has created a valid expectation that it will make the remaining payments. This is a matter of judgement. In this case the entity would recognise an expense and a liability, measured at the net present value of the 5 instalments of €200,000, at the point when it is determined that a constructive obligation exists.
- Option 3 involves an enforceable contract with no exchange of benefits. Therefore a liability and an expense is recognised on signing the enforceable contract, measured at the present value of the 5 instalments of €200,000.

- Under Option 4, the contract is unenforceable and the donation is subject to a condition. In these circumstances, whether there is a constructive obligation to make the donation is a matter of judgement. Management might conclude that no constructive obligation exists until it is probable that the condition is met (which might not be until the additional funds have been collected). Only then would a liability and expense be recognised, measured at the net present value of the €1m promised.
- Option 5 involves an enforceable contract which may give rise to a liability when the contract is signed. However, there is an exchange of benefits relating to the research and development activities performed on behalf of the entity. Whether these benefits have a value of at least the present value of the 5 instalments of €200,000 is a matter of judgement. If it is determined that this is an exchange transaction that is not onerous, the entity could regard the signing of the contract as executory and could apply the criteria in IAS 38 to determine whether an asset or expense would be recognised for the related research and development costs as incurred (see Chapter 17 at 6.2).

Where the arrangement gives rise to an exchange transaction rather than a donation, the expenditure incurred by the donor is recorded in accordance with the relevant IFRS.

7 DISCLOSURE REQUIREMENTS

A significant distinction between the accounting treatment of provisions and other liabilities, such as trade payables and accruals, is the level of disclosure required.

7.1 Provisions

For each class of provision an entity should provide a reconciliation of the carrying amount of the provision at the beginning and end of the period showing:

(a) additional provisions made in the period, including increases to existing provisions;

(b) amounts used, i.e. incurred and charged against the provision, during the period;

(c) unused amounts reversed during the period; and

(d) the increase during the period in the discounted amount arising from the passage of time and the effect of any change in the discount rate.

Comparative information is not required. *[IAS 37.84]*.

It is not clear whether disclosure (d) allows a single amount to be provided for the sum of the unwinding of the discount and any change in the provision resulting from a reassessment of the discount rate to be used or it requires these amounts to be given separately. However, given our view (discussed at 4.3.6 above) that only the charge for unwinding of the discount should be classified as a finance cost, with any further charge or credit that arises if discount rates have changed being recorded in the same line item that was used to establish the provision, it would make sense to disclose these items separately. This treatment is demonstrated by BP p.l.c. in Extract 28.9 at 6.4 above. It is also interesting that there is no specific requirement in the standard to disclose the discount rate used, especially where the effect of using a different discount rate could be material, such as in the measurement of a decommissioning provision. However, entities should remember that IAS 1 – *Presentation of Financial Statements* – requires disclosure of information about major sources of estimation uncertainty that have a significant risk of resulting in a material adjustment to the carrying amounts of assets and liabilities within the next financial year. *[IAS 1.125]*.

One of the important disclosures which is reinforced here is the requirement to disclose the release of provisions found to be unnecessary. This disclosure, along with the requirement in the standard that provisions should be used only for the purpose for which the provision was originally recognised, *[IAS 37.61]*, is designed to prevent entities from concealing expenditure by charging it against a provision that was set up for another purpose.

In addition, for each class of provision an entity should disclose the following:

(a) a brief description of the nature of the obligation and the expected timing of any resulting outflows of economic benefits;

(b) an indication of the uncertainties about the amount or timing of those outflows. Where necessary to provide adequate information, an entity should disclose the major assumptions made concerning future events, as addressed in paragraph 48 of the standard (discussed at 4.4 above). This refers to future developments in technology and legislation and is of particular relevance to environmental liabilities; and

(c) the amount of any expected reimbursement, stating the amount of any asset that has been recognised for that expected reimbursement. *[IAS 37.85]*.

Section D of the implementation guidance to the standard provides examples of suitable disclosures in relation to warranties and decommissioning costs.

Most of the above disclosures are illustrated in the extract below, which includes the disclosure of provisions determined in accordance with IAS 37 and employee provisions which would be determined in accordance with IAS 19.

Extract 28.11: Roche Holding Ltd (2015)

Notes to the Roche Group Consolidated Financial Statements [extract]

19. Provisions and contingent liabilities [extract]

Provisions: movements in recognised liabilities in millions of CHF

	Legal provisions	Environ-mental provisions	Restruct-uring provisions	Employee provisions	Other provisions	Total
Year ended 31 December 2014						
At 1 January 2014	634	624	601	342	1,044	3,245
Additional provisions created	74	14	439	115	599	1,241
Unused amounts reversed	(22)	–	(139)	(13)	(200)	(374)
Utilised	(81)	(59)	(314)	(83)	(336)	(873)
Discount unwind	–	19	–	2	9	30
Business combinations						
– Acquired companies	10	–	–	–	70	80
– Deferred consideration	–	–	–	–	(7)	(7)
– Contingent consideration	–	–	–	–	640	640
Currency translation effects	62	29	19	22	129	261

At 31 December 2014	**677**	**627**	**606**	**385**	**1,948**	**4,243**
Current	668	184	386	108	1,119	2,465
Non-current	9	443	220	277	829	1,778
At 31 December 2014	**677**	**627**	**606**	**385**	**1,948**	**4,243**
Year ended 31 December 2015						
At 1 January 2015	677	627	606	385	1,948	4,243
Additional provisions created	60	130	429	130	571	1,320
Unused amounts reversed	(15)	(1)	(63)	(8)	(255)	(342)
Utilised	(17)	(153)	(319)	(107)	(239)	(835)
Discount unwind	–	12	–	1	40	53
Business combinations						
– Acquired companies	–	–	–	–	–	–
– Deferred consideration	–	–	–	–	(55)	(55)
– Contingent consideration	–	–	–	–	448	448
Other movements	–	–	–	(72)	–	(72)
Currency translation effects	(5)	(30)	(32)	(16)	(41)	(124)
At 31 December 2015	**700**	**585**	**621**	**313**	**2,417**	**4,636**
Current	670	195	284	118	1,165	2,432
Non-current	30	390	337	195	1,252	2,204
At 31 December 2015	**700**	**585**	**621**	**313**	**2,417**	**4,636**
Expected outflow of resources						
Within one year	670	195	284	118	1,165	2,432
Between one and two years	28	87	204	42	401	762
Between two and three years	1	160	54	37	394	646
More than three years	1	143	79	116	457	796
At 31 December 2015	**700**	**585**	**621**	**313**	**2,417**	**4,636**

Legal provisions

Legal provisions consist of a number of separate legal matters, including claims arising from trade, in various Group companies. By their nature the amounts and timings of any outflows are difficult to predict.

In 2015 legal expenses totalled CHF 41 million (2014: CHF 203 million) which reflect the recent developments in various legal matters. Details of the major legal cases outstanding are disclosed below.

Environmental provisions

Provisions for environmental matters include various separate environmental issues in a number of countries. By their nature the amounts and timings of any outflows are difficult to predict. Significant provisions are discounted by between 2% and 4% where the time value of money is material. The significant provisions relate to the US site in Nutley, New Jersey, the estimated remediation costs for a landfill site near Grenzach, Germany, that was used by manufacturing operations that were closed some years ago and the estimated remediation costs for the manufacturing site at Clarecastle. Ireland (see Note 6).

Restructuring provisions

These arise from planned programmes that materially change the scope of business undertaken by the Group or the manner in which business is conducted. Such provisions include only the costs necessarily entailed by the restructuring which are not associated with the recurring activities of the Group. The timings of these cash outflows are reasonably certain. These provisions are not discounted as the time value of money is not material in these matters.

In the Pharmaceuticals Division the significant provisions relate to the strategic realignment of the manufacturing network including exiting from four manufacturing sites (see Note 6), the research and development strategic realignment and field force reduction in the Europe and Asia-Pacific regions.

Employee provisions

These mostly relate to certain employee benefit obligations, such as sabbatical leave and long-service benefits. The timings of these cash outflows can be reasonably estimated based on past experience.

Other provisions

The timing of cash outflows are by their nature uncertain and other provisions relate to the items shown in the table below.

Other provisions in millions of CHF

	2015	2014	2013
Sales returns	616	706	652
Contingent consideration	1,492	815	122
Other items	309	427	270
Total other provisions	**2,417**	**1,948**	**1,044**

The standard states that in determining which provisions may be aggregated to form a class, it is necessary to consider whether the nature of the items is sufficiently similar for a single statement about them to fulfil the requirements of (a) and (b) above. An example is given of warranties: it is suggested that, while it may be appropriate to treat warranties of different products as a single class of provision, it would not be appropriate to aggregate normal warranties with amounts that are subject to legal proceedings. *[IAS 37.87]*. For entities disclosing restructuring costs, this requirement could result in material components of the costs, such as redundancies, termination of leases, etc. being disclosed separately. However, materiality will be an important consideration in judging how much analysis is required.

As indicated at 6.1.1 above, IAS 37 emphasises that when a restructuring meets the definition of a discontinued operation under IFRS 5, additional disclosures may be required under that standard (see Chapter 4 at 3). *[IAS 37.9]*.

7.2 Contingent liabilities

Unless the possibility of any outflow in settlement is remote, IAS 37 requires the disclosure for each class of contingent liability at the end of the reporting period to include a brief description of the nature of the contingent liability, and where practicable:

(a) an estimate of its financial effect, measured in accordance with paragraphs 36-52 of IAS 37 (discussed at 4 above);

(b) an indication of the uncertainties relating to the amount or timing of any outflow; and

(c) the possibility of any reimbursement. *[IAS 37.86]*.

Where any of the information above is not disclosed because it is not practicable to do so, that fact should be stated. *[IAS 37.91]*.

The guidance given in the standard on determining which provisions may be aggregated to form a class referred to at 7.1 above also applies to contingent liabilities.

A further point noted in the standard is that where a provision and a contingent liability arise from the same circumstances, an entity should ensure that the link between the provision and the contingent liability is clear. *[IAS 37.88]*. This situation may occur, for instance, when an entity stratifies a population of known and potential claimants between different classes of obligation, and accounts for each class separately. For example, an entity's actions may have resulted in environmental damage. The entity identifies the geographical area over which that damage is likely to have occurred and recognises a provision based on its 'best estimate' of value of claims it expects to be submitted from residents in that geographical area. In addition, there is a chance (albeit possible rather than probable) that the pollution is found to have had an effect beyond the geographical area established by the entity. As noted at 3.2.1 above, the latter, 'possible but not probable' obligation meets the definition of a contingent liability for which disclosure is required.

Another example of when a provision and a contingent liability may arise from the same circumstance would be where an entity is jointly and severally liable for an obligation. As noted at 4.6 above, in these circumstances the part of the obligation that is expected to be met by other parties is treated as a contingent liability.

It is not absolutely clear what is meant by 'financial effect' in (a) above. Is it the *potential* amount of the loss or is it the *expected* amount of the loss? The cross-reference to the measurement principles in paragraphs 36-52 might imply the latter, but in any event, disclosure of the potential amount is likely to be relevant in explaining the uncertainties in (b) above.

7.3 Contingent assets

IAS 37 requires disclosure of contingent assets where an inflow of economic benefits is probable. The disclosures required are:

(a) a brief description of the nature of the contingent assets at the end of the reporting period; and

(b) where practicable, an estimate of their financial effect, measured using the principles set out for provisions in paragraphs 36-52 of IAS 37. *[IAS 37.89]*.

Where any of the information above is not disclosed because it is not practicable to do so, that fact should be stated. *[IAS 37.91]*. The standard goes on to emphasise that the disclosure must avoid giving misleading indications of the likelihood of income arising. *[IAS 37.90]*.

One problem that arises with IAS 37 is that it requires the disclosure of an estimate of the potential financial effect for contingent assets to be measured in accordance with the measurement principles in the standard. Unfortunately, the measurement principles in the standard are all set out in terms of the settlement of obligations, and these principles cannot readily be applied to the measurement of contingent assets. Hence, judgement will have to be used as to how rigorously these principles should be applied.

7.4 Reduced disclosure when information is seriously prejudicial

IAS 37 contains an exemption from disclosure of information in the following circumstances. It says that, 'in extremely rare cases, disclosure of some or all of the information required by [the disclosure requirements at 7.1 to 7.3 above] can be expected to prejudice seriously the position of the entity in a dispute with other parties on the subject matter of the provision, contingent liability or contingent asset'. *[IAS 37.92]*.

In such circumstances, the information need not be disclosed. However, disclosure will still need to be made of the general nature of the dispute, together with the fact that, and the reason why, the required information has not been disclosed. *[IAS 37.92]*.

The following example, from the implementation guidance to the Standard, provides an example of the disclosures required where some of the information required by the standard is not given because it is expected to prejudice seriously the position of the entity.

Example 28.23: Reduced disclosure when information is seriously prejudicial

An entity is involved in a dispute with a competitor, who is alleging that the entity has infringed patents and is seeking damages of $100 million. The entity recognises a provision for its best estimate of the obligation, but discloses none of the information required by paragraphs 84 and 85 of IAS 37. The following information is disclosed:

Litigation is in process against the company relating to a dispute with a competitor who alleges that the company has infringed patents and is seeking damages of $100 million. The information usually required by IAS 37 Provisions, Contingent Liabilities and Contingent Assets is not disclosed on the grounds that it can be expected to prejudice seriously the outcome of the litigation. The directors are of the opinion that the claim can be successfully resisted by the company. *[IAS 37 IE Example Disclosures: Example 3]*.

In the following extract, Daimler applied this exemption in relation to antitrust investigations by the European Commission into the activities of European vehicle manufacturers.

Extract 28.12: Daimler AG (2015)

Notes to the Consolidated Financial Statements [extract]

29. Legal proceedings [extract]

In mid-January 2011, the European Commission carried out anti-trust investigations of European commercial vehicle manufacturers, including Daimler AG. If antitrust infringements are discovered, the European Commission can impose considerable fines depending on the gravity of the infringement. In November 2014, the European Commission served Daimler with its statement of objections which, from the European Commission's perspective, further explains and legally evaluates the relevant facts. Resulting from knowledge gained from access to essential documents of the European Commission's file, Daimler AG, in December 2014, decided to increase provisions by €600 million. Daimler is taking the Commission's investigation very seriously. The Company is cooperating with the authorities but will at the same time – while stating the Company's legal view – safeguard its rights in the further proceedings and is also reviewing all of its procedural options. In accordance with IAS 37.92, the Group does not provide further information on this antitrust investigation and the associated risk for the Group, especially with regard to the measures taken in this context, in order not to impair the outcome of the proceedings.

As it can be seen in the above examples, an entity applying the 'seriously prejudicial' exemption is still required to describe the general nature of the dispute, resulting in a level of disclosure that many entities might find uncomfortable in the circumstances.

References

1 Working Draft, International Financial Reporting Standard [X] – *Liabilities*, IASB, 19 February 2010.
2 IASB Staff Paper, *Liabilities – IFRS to replace IAS 37 – Recognising liabilities from lawsuits*, IASB, 7 April 2010.
3 Request for Views *Agenda Consultation 2011*, IASB, July 2011, Appendix C.
4 *IASB Update*, May 2012, p.9.
5 *IASB Staff Paper– Research project – IAS 37 Provisions, Contingent Liabilities and Contingent Assets – Agenda Consultation Feedback, April 2016.*
6 *IFRIC Update*, July 2014, p.7.
7 IAS 37.5(g) (2014).
8 IAS 37.5(c)(2016).
9 IFRS 3.56(2014).
10 FASB ASC Topic 450, Contingencies, para. 450-20-30-1.
11 *Discounting in Financial Reporting*, ASB, April 1997.
12 *Discounting in Financial Reporting*, ASB, April 1997, para. 2.10.
13 *IFRIC Update*, March 2011, p.4.
14 Fisher, Irving PhD. *The Rate of Interest*, New York: MacMillan, 1907.
15 *IFRIC Update*, January 2015.
16 *IFRIC Staff Paper – Negative interest rates: implication for presentation in the statement of comprehensive income*, January 2015, p.6.
17 IFRS 3.56(2014).
18 Exposure Draft ED/2013/5: *Regulatory Deferral Accounts*, IASB, April 2013, para. BC15.
19 Request for Views *Agenda Consultation 2011*, IASB, July 2011, Appendix C.
20 ED/2013/5, para. BC10.
21 *IASB Staff Paper – Rate-regulated activities – Project update and responses to the Agenda Consultation,* April 2016.
22 IAS 19, *Employee Benefits*, Example illustrating paragraphs 159-170.
23 *IFRIC Update*, December 2003, pp.4-5.
24 *Exposure Draft of Proposed Amendments to IAS 37 Provisions, Contingent Liabilities and Contingent Assets* (IAS 37 ED) *and IAS 19 Employee Benefits* (IAS 19 ED), IASB, June 2005, para. 58.
25 IFRIC 3, *Emission Rights*, IASB, December 2004, para. 6.
26 IFRIC 3.5.
27 IFRIC 3.6.
28 IFRIC 3.7.
29 IFRIC 3.8.
30 *IASB Update*, June 2005, p.1.
31 *IASB Update*, June 2005, p.1.
32 *IASB Update*, May 2012, p.8.
33 *IASB Update*, January 2015, p.10.
34 IASB Work plan – as at 23 June 2016.
35 Directive 2002/96/EC of the European Parliament and of the Council of 27 January 2003 on waste electrical and electronic equipment and Directive 2003/108/EC of the European Parliament and of the Council of 8 December 2003 amending Directive 2002/96/EC on waste electrical and electronic equipment.

Chapter 29 Revenue recognition (IAS 18)

List of examples

Chapter 29 Revenue recognition (IAS 18)

1 INTRODUCTION

IAS 18 – *Revenue* – was issued in its original form in 1982 and received its last major revision in 1993. *[IAS 18.2]*. IAS 18 does not address many of the complex transactions undertaken by modern business, such as those involving multiple deliverables. To address this, the International Accounting Standards Board (IASB) and Financial Accounting Standards Board (FASB) undertook a joint project to develop new revenue recognition requirements, which culminated in the IASB issuing a new revenue standard in May 2014, IFRS 15 – *Revenue from Contracts with Customers.* The new standard (as amended in April 2016), is discussed in Chapter 30.

Until the new standard comes into effect in 2018, or an entity early adopts IFRS 15, the traditional historical cost approach to revenue recognition remains in place for most practical purposes and entities and their auditors will have to continue to apply IAS 18, IAS 11 – *Construction Contracts* (see Chapter 23) and their related Interpretations.

This chapter discusses IAS 18, drawing on both IASB and FASB pronouncements. For entities reporting under IFRS, IAS 18 is the main source of authoritative literature on revenue recognition, but several other standards also address revenue recognition issues. These include IAS 11, IAS 17 – *Leases* (i.e. rental income), IFRS 4 – *Insurance Contracts*, SIC-31 – *Revenue – Barter Transactions Involving Advertising Services*, IFRIC 13 – *Customer Loyalty Programmes*, IFRIC 15 – *Agreements for the Construction of Real Estate* – and IFRIC 18 – *Transfers of Assets from Customers.* In most cases, these revenue recognition requirements were developed in order to deal with specific issues on a piecemeal basis.

US GAAP, in particular, has a substantial body of literature on revenue recognition that can, on occasion, prove useful when there is no IFRS guidance available (see 4 below). Historically, this was particularly relevant for IFRS reporting entities registered with the US Securities Exchange Commission (US SEC), e.g. foreign private issuers, who wished to avoid, as far as possible, having IFRS to US GAAP differences. This is now less significant as reconciliation to US GAAP is no longer required since the US SEC accepts from foreign private issuers, in their filings with the US SEC, financial statements prepared in accordance with IFRS as issued by the IASB. However, such differences are sometimes unavoidable and it is not always the case that a revenue recognition policy under US GAAP is acceptable under IFRS.

2 THE TIMING OF REVENUE RECOGNITION

Under the historical cost system, revenues are the inflows of assets to an entity as a result of the transfer of products and services by the entity to its customers during a period of time. They are recorded at the cash amount received or expected to be received (or, in the case of non-monetary exchanges, at their cash equivalent) as the result of these exchange transactions. However, because of the system of periodic financial reporting, it is necessary to determine the point (or points) in time when revenue should be measured and reported. This has traditionally been governed by what is known as the 'realisation principle', which acknowledges that, for revenue to be recognised, it is not sufficient merely for a sale to have been made; there has to be a certain degree of performance by the vendor as well. While there are many different (and sometime inconsistent) rules for different circumstances, the rules underlying revenue recognition have been developed from two broad approaches to the recognition of revenue: the critical event and the accretion approaches, each of which is appropriate under particular circumstances. These are discussed below.

2.1 The critical event approach

The fundamental approach to revenue recognition under IFRS has been built on the foundation of critical event theory.

The critical event approach is based on the belief that revenue is earned at the point in the operating cycle when the most critical decision is made or the most critical act is performed.[1] In theory, the critical event could occur at various stages during the operating cycle – for example, at the completion of production, at the time of sale, at the time of delivery or at the time of cash collection.

Revenue recognition is subject to a number of measurement uncertainties, which could occur at any of these points. As these uncertainties fall away at various stages throughout the operating cycle, it is necessary to identify a point in the cycle at which the remaining uncertainties can be estimated with sufficient accuracy to enable revenue to be recognised. As discussed later in this chapter, the decision is often not straightforward; further complications arise in the case of transactions that involve multiple elements and/or significant post-delivery obligations.

2.1.1 The recognition of revenue at the completion of production

An entity may enter into a firm contract for the production and delivery of a product, for which the sales price will have been determined and the selling costs will have already been incurred. Consequently, provided that both the delivery expenses and the bad debt risk can reasonably be assessed, it may be appropriate in some circumstances to report revenue on the completion of production, unless it is a transaction for which the percentage of completion method is mandated by IAS 11 or IAS 18. The completed contract method of recognising revenue on construction contracts is not common and is not permitted under IFRS (construction contracts are discussed in Chapter 23).

It has also become accepted practice in a limited number of industries to recognise revenue at the completion of production, even though a sales contract may not have been entered into. This practice has been adopted, for example, in the case of some agricultural, minerals and mineral products. IAS 2 – *Inventories* – allows commodity broker-traders to carry inventory at net realisable value if it is a 'well-established' practice, as long as changes in net realisable value are recognised in profit or loss in the period of the change. *[IAS 2.3(a)]*. IAS 2 specifies that the treatment might be appropriate if, for example, the minerals have been extracted, the sale is assured under a forward contract or a government guarantee, there is an active market and there is a negligible risk of failure to sell. *[IAS 2.4]*. Note that this is different to recognising biological products at fair value throughout the period of growth, which is an example of the accretion approach described at 2.2 below that is mandated by IAS 41 – *Agriculture* (see Chapter 40 for discussion on IAS 41).

2.1.2 The recognition of revenue at the time of sale

The point of sale is probably the most widely used basis of recognising revenue from transactions involving the sale of goods. The sale is usually the critical point in the earning process when most of the significant uncertainties are eliminated. The only uncertainties that are likely to remain are: the possible return of the goods (where the customer has the right to do so, thereby cancelling the sale); the failure to collect the sales price (in the case of a credit sale); and any future liabilities in terms of any express or implied customer warranties. Under normal circumstances, these uncertainties will be both minimal and estimable to a reasonable degree of accuracy, based, *inter alia*, on past experience.

However, what if the sale takes place before production or the delivery only takes place at some significantly distant time in the future; should revenues still be recognised at the time of sale? In practice, the time of sale is generally taken to be the point of delivery; among other reasons, this reflects the law in a large number of jurisdictions, under which title passes to the buyer upon delivery, whether or not payment has been made.

See 3.7 below for a discussion of the principles laid down in IAS 18 for determining when to recognise revenue from a transaction involving the sale of goods.

2.1.3 The recognition of revenue subsequent to delivery

The uncertainties that exist after delivery may be of such significance that recognition should be delayed beyond the normal recognition point.

If the principal uncertainty concerns collectability, it might be appropriate to defer recognition of the whole sale (and not just the profit) until collection is probable under IAS 18. *[IAS 18.14(d)]*.

The entity may sell its product, but give the customer the right to return the goods, e.g. in the case of an online business where the customer is given an approval period of 14 days. Revenue may be recognised at the time of delivery if future returns can be predicted reasonably accurately. Otherwise, it should be recognised on: receipt of payment for the goods; on customer acceptance of the goods and express or implied acknowledgement of the liability for payment; or after the 14 days have elapsed – whichever is considered to be the most appropriate under the circumstances. Note that entities may have a statutory right to cancel most sales of goods bought online or by mail order without reason; for example in the EU, customers typically have 7 days from the date of receipt.

In fact, this is an area where practice has been somewhat inconsistent. A transaction with a right of return is usually accounted for as a sale, whereas revenue from a transaction with a 14-day acceptance period is usually deferred – despite the fact that the transactions may be virtually identical in terms of the legal rights and obligations of the parties.

This area of uncertainty is dealt with in US GAAP under Accounting Standards Codification (ASC) 605-15 – *Revenue Recognition – Products* – which states that if an entity sells its product, but gives the buyer the right to return the product, revenue from the sales transaction is recognised at time of sale only if *all* of the following conditions are met:[2]

(a) the seller's price to the buyer is substantially fixed or determinable at the date of sale;

(b) the buyer has paid the seller, or the buyer is obligated to pay the seller and the obligation is not contingent on resale of the product;

(c) the buyer's obligation to the seller would not be changed in the event of theft or physical destruction or damage of the product;

(d) the buyer acquiring the product for resale has economic substance apart from that provided by the seller (i.e. the buyer does not merely exist 'on paper' with little or no physical facilities, having been established by the seller primarily for the purpose of recognising revenue);

(e) the seller does not have significant obligations for future performance to directly bring about resale of the product by the buyer; and

(f) the amount of future returns can be reasonably estimated.

Revenue that was not recognised at the time of sale because these conditions were not met should be recognised either when the return privilege has 'substantially expired' or when all the above conditions are met, whichever occurs first.[3]

The ability to make a reasonable estimate of future returns depends on many factors and will vary from one case to the next. US GAAP lists the following factors as being those that might impair a seller's ability to make such an estimate:[4]

(a) the susceptibility of the product to significant external factors, such as technological obsolescence or changes in demand;

(b) relatively long periods in which a particular product may be returned;

(c) absence of historical experience with similar types of sales of similar products, or inability to apply such experience because of changing circumstances; for example, changes in the selling entity's marketing policies or its relationships with its customers; and

(d) absence of a large volume of relatively homogeneous transactions.

The right of return is, therefore, viewed as a significant uncertainty that would preclude recognition under circumstances when the level of returns cannot be estimated. This means, for example, that a 14-day return period would not of itself require deferral of a sale, provided that the 14-day period is normal and routine and the uncertainty related to the returns is not significant.

2.2 The accretion approach

The accretion approach involves the recognition of revenue during the process of production, rather than at the end of a contract or when production is complete. There are four broad areas of entity activity where the application of the accretion approach might be appropriate.

(a) The use by others of entity resources

The traditional accrual basis of accounting recognises revenue as entity resources are used by others; this approach is followed, for example, in the case of rental or interest income. Uncertainty of collection should always be considered, in which case it might be appropriate to delay recognition until cash is received or ultimate collection is probable.

(b) Long-term contracts

The second accepted application of the accretion approach may be found in the accounting practice for long-term construction contracts. For example, under IAS 11, the amount of revenue to be recognised on construction contracts is determined according to the 'percentage-of-completion method', whereby contract revenue is matched with the contract costs incurred in reaching the stage of completion. This results in the reporting of revenue, expenses and profit that can be attributed to the proportion of work completed at each balance sheet date. *[IAS 11.25]*. Normally, the main uncertainties in the application of this approach are the estimation of the total costs and the degree of completion attained at the balance sheet date, particularly in the early stages of the contract. However, the selling price is sometimes uncertain as well, owing to contract modifications that give rise to revenue from 'extras'. Accounting for construction contracts is dealt with in Chapter 23.

(c) The rendering of services

This is probably the most widespread example of the application of the accretion approach. For example, IAS 18 requires that when the outcome of a transaction involving the rendering of services can be estimated reliably, revenue is recognised 'by reference to the stage of completion of the transaction at the end of the reporting period', *[IAS 18.20]*, (in other words, using the percentage-of-completion method). This is discussed further at 3.8 below.

(d) Natural growth and 'biological transformation'

Where an entity's activity involves production through natural growth or ageing, the accretion approach suggests that revenue should be recognised at identifiable stages during this process. For example, in the case of livestock, there could be market prices available at the various stages of growth; revenue could, therefore, be recognised throughout the production process by making comparative stock valuations and reporting the accretions at the end of each reporting period.

This is addressed in IAS 41. The standard requires application of fair value accounting for assets within its scope throughout their period of growth. The change in fair value less costs to sell of biological assets during a period is reported in profit or loss for the period. *[IAS 41.26]*. However, IAS 41 contains no guidance on revenue recognition. In fact, the term 'revenue' is not mentioned in the entire standard and in the illustration of the statement of comprehensive income set out in Example 1 of the Illustrative Examples to IAS 41, there is no revenue line. *[IAS 41.IE1]*. When it was issued, IAS 41 amended IAS 18 to exclude from the scope of IAS 18 changes in fair value and initial recognition at fair value of agricultural assets and produce before harvest (see 3.1 below). Fair value gains and revenue from the sale of biological assets and agricultural produce should not be aggregated as this may result in double counting.

IAS 41 is addressed in Chapter 40, including a discussion of the treatment of fair value movements in the statement of comprehensive income.

3 THE REQUIREMENTS OF IAS 18

3.1 Scope

Income is defined in the IASB's *Conceptual Framework for Financial Reporting ('Framework')* as 'increases in economic benefits during the accounting period in the form of inflows or enhancements of assets or decreases of liabilities that result in increases in equity, other than those relating to contributions from equity participants'. *[Framework 4.25(a)]*. IAS 18 embraces, in its objective, the definition of income from the *Framework,* adding that 'revenue is income that arises in the course of ordinary activities of an entity and is referred to by a variety of different names including sales, fees, interest, dividends and royalties'. *[IAS 18 Objective]*. However, having established the link between the *Framework's* definition of income and IAS 18's definition of revenue, IAS 18 reverts to the transactions-based critical event approach for the recognition of revenues derived from the sale of goods.

The standard explains that its objective is to prescribe the accounting treatment of revenue arising from the following types of transactions and events:

(a) the sale of goods;

(b) the rendering of services; and

(c) the use by others of entity assets yielding interest, royalties and dividends. *[IAS 18.1]*.

The term 'goods' includes goods produced by the entity for the purpose of sale and goods purchased for resale, such as merchandise purchased by a retailer or land and other property held for resale. *[IAS 18.3]*.

The rendering of services typically involves the performance by the entity of a contractually agreed task over an agreed period of time. The services may be rendered within a single period or over more than one period. However, some contracts for the rendering of services are directly related to construction contracts, for example, those for the services of project managers and architects. Consequently, revenue arising from these contracts is not specified by IAS 18, but is dealt with in accordance with the requirements for construction contracts in IAS 11 (see Chapter 23). *[IAS 18.4]*.

The use by others of an entity's assets gives rise to revenue in the form of:

(a) interest – charges for the use of cash or cash equivalents or amounts due to the entity;

(b) royalties – charges for the use of long-term assets of the entity, for example, patents, trademarks, copyrights and computer software; and

(c) dividends – distributions of profits to holders of equity investments in proportion to their holdings of a particular class of capital. *[IAS 18.5]*.

There are a number of matters that the standard expressly states that it does not deal with, because they are all dealt with in other standards. These are:

(a) lease agreements (see IAS 17). However, IAS 17 itself does not apply to licensing agreements for such items as motion picture films, video recordings, plays, manuscripts, patents and copyrights, *[IAS 17.2]*, (see Chapter 24);

(b) dividends arising from investments that are accounted for under the equity method (see Chapters 11 and 12, which address associates and joint arrangements, respectively);

(c) insurance contracts within the scope of IFRS 4 (see Chapter 55);

(d) the changes in the fair value of financial assets and financial liabilities or their disposal (for IAS 39 – *Financial Instruments: Recognition and Measurement* – see Chapters 49 and 51; or if IFRS 9 – *Financial Instruments* – is applied, see Chapters 50 and 51);

(e) the changes in the value of other current assets;

(f) revenue arising from the initial recognition and from changes in the fair value of biological assets related to agricultural activity (see Chapter 40);

(g) the initial recognition of agricultural produce (see Chapter 40); and

(h) the extraction of mineral ores (see Chapter 41). *[IAS 18.6]*.

3.2 The distinction between income, revenue and gains

The *Framework* explains that its definition of income encompasses both 'revenue' and 'gains'. Revenue arises in the course of the ordinary activities of an entity. As discussed at 3.1 above, it can include sales, fees, interest, dividends, royalties and rent. Gains represent other items that meet the definition of income and may, or may not, arise in the course of the ordinary activities of an entity. Gains include, for example, those arising on the disposal of non-current assets. The definition of income also includes unrealised gains; for example, those arising on the revaluation of marketable securities and those resulting from increases in the carrying amount of long-term assets. *[Framework 4.31]*.

The rules on offset in IAS 1 – *Presentation of Financial Statements* – distinguish between revenue and gains. That standard states that an entity undertakes, in the course of its ordinary activities, other transactions that do not generate revenue but are incidental to the main revenue-generating activities. When this presentation reflects the substance of the transaction or other event, the results of such transactions are presented by netting any income with related expenses arising on the same transaction. For example, gains and losses on the disposal of non-current assets, including investments and operating assets, are reported by deducting from the proceeds on disposal the carrying amount of the asset and related selling expenses. *[IAS 1.34]*. IAS 16 – *Property, Plant and Equipment* – has a general rule that 'gains shall not be classified as revenue'. *[IAS 16.68]*. The only exception to this rule is where an entity routinely sells property, plant and equipment (PP&E) that it has held for rental to others, which is discussed further at 5.11.1 below.

IAS 18 explains that revenue includes only the gross inflows of economic benefits received and receivable by the entity on its own account. In practice, the distinction between gross and net revenues is not always straightforward, but there is guidance regarding revenue and agency relationships, which is discussed at 3.3 below.

Amounts collected on behalf of third parties, such as sales taxes, goods and services taxes and value added taxes, are not economic benefits that flow to the entity and do not result in increases in equity. *[IAS 18.8]*. Therefore, they are excluded from revenue. See 5.8 below for a discussion of some of the factors that need to be considered in determining whether gross or net revenue presentation is appropriate in relation to excise taxes and goods and services taxes.

3.3 Revenue and agency relationships

In an agency relationship, the gross inflows of economic benefits often include amounts collected on behalf of the principal and amounts which do not result in increases in equity for the entity. The amounts collected on behalf of the principal are not revenue; instead, revenue is the amount of commission. *[IAS 18.8]*.

The Illustrative Examples to IAS 18 include guidance to help determine whether an entity is acting as a principal or as an agent. *[IAS 18.IE21]*. An entity is acting as a principal when it has exposure to the significant risks and rewards associated with the sale of goods or rendering of services. There are four criteria that, individually or in combination, indicate that an entity is acting as principal: *[IAS 18.IE21]*

- the entity has the primary responsibility for providing the goods or services to the customer or for fulfilling the order, for example by being responsible for the acceptability of the products or services ordered or purchased by the customer;
- the entity has inventory risk before or after the customer order, during shipping or on return;
- the entity has latitude in establishing prices, either directly or indirectly, for example by providing additional goods or services; and
- the entity bears the customer's credit risk on the receivable due from the customer.

Conversely, an entity is acting as agent when it does not have exposure to the significant risks and rewards associated with the sale of goods or rendering of services and this may be evidenced by the entity earning a predetermined amount, perhaps a fixed fee per transaction or a stated percentage of customer billings. *[IAS 18.IE21]*.

This above guidance is closely related to the more detailed US GAAP guidance in ASC 605-45 – *Revenue Recognition – Principal Agent Considerations* – which had been widely used as guidance on agency and gross versus net accounting. However, unlike the guidance in US GAAP, the Illustrative Examples to IAS 18 do not place more or less weight on any one of the indicators.

An entity may make sales to parties that are acting as agents. In order to recognise revenue on the sale of goods the seller must have transferred the significant risks and rewards of ownership to the buyer and must not retain either continuing managerial involvement to the degree usually associated with ownership or effective control over the goods sold. *[IAS 18.14(a), 14(b)]*. This may not be the case if the buyer is an agent of the seller. For example, revenue from sales to intermediate parties, such as distributors, dealers or others for resale is generally recognised when the risks and rewards of ownership have passed. When the buyer is acting, in substance, as an agent, the sale is treated as a consignment sale, i.e. no revenue is recognised until the goods are sold to a third party. *[IAS 18.IE6, IE2(c)]*.

3.4 Income and distributable profits

IFRS, generally, and IAS 18, specifically, do not address the issue of the distribution of profit. Whether or not revenue and gains recognised in accordance with IFRS are distributable to shareholders of an entity will depend entirely on the national laws and regulations with which the entity needs to comply. Thus, income reported in accordance with IFRS does not necessarily imply that such income would either be realised or distributable under a reporting entity's applicable national legislation.

3.5 Measurement of revenue

Revenue should be measured at the fair value of the consideration received or receivable. *[IAS 18.9]*. IAS 18 states that the amount of revenue arising on a transaction is usually determined by agreement between the entity and the buyer or user of the asset. This means that it is measured at the fair value of the consideration received or receivable taking into account the amount of any trade discounts and volume rebates allowed by the entity. *[IAS 18.10]*. Fair value is defined in IFRS 13 – *Fair Value Measurement* – as 'the price that would be received to sell an asset or paid to transfer a liability in an orderly transaction between market participants at the measurement date'. *[IAS 18.7, IFRS 13.9]*.

Usually, this will present little difficulty, as the consideration will normally be in the form of cash or cash equivalents and the amount of revenue will be the amount of cash or cash equivalents received or receivable. However, if the inflow is deferred, the fair value of the consideration will then be less than the nominal amount of cash received or receivable. IFRS 13 requires an entity to use market participant assumptions in measuring fair value and to prioritise observable inputs over those that are unobservable (see Chapter 14). Therefore, when an arrangement, or a separately identifiable component of an arrangement, effectively constitutes a financing arrangement, the fair value of the consideration would reflect market participants' assumptions about the time value of money and the risk associated with the financing arrangement. IFRS 13 requires an entity to prioritise the use of observable inputs over unobservable inputs, but does not restrict or prioritise the types of techniques an entity can use to measure fair value. However, IAS 18 requires that the fair value of the consideration be determined by discounting all future receipts using an imputed rate of interest. The imputed rate of interest is the more clearly determinable of either: *[IAS 18.11]*

(a) the prevailing rate for a similar instrument of an issuer with a similar credit rating; or

(b) a rate of interest that discounts the nominal amount of the instrument to the current cash sales price of the goods or services.

The difference between the fair value and the nominal amount of the consideration is recognised as interest revenue using the effective interest method as set out in IAS 39 (or IFRS 9, if applied). *[IAS 18.11, 30(a)]*. The application of the effective interest rate method is discussed in Chapter 49 (Chapter 50 if IFRS 9 is applied).

A further issue arises if an entity offers prompt settlement discounts to its customers. An example of a prompt settlement discount is a reduction of 5% of the selling price for paying an invoice within 7 days, instead of the usual 60 days. In such cases, in order to comply with IAS 18's requirement that revenue should be measured at the fair value of the consideration received or receivable, *[IAS 18.9]*, a prompt settlement discount should be estimated at the time of sale and deducted from revenue.

3.6 Identifying the transaction

IAS 18 states that the recognition criteria are usually applied separately to each transaction. However, in certain circumstances, it is necessary to apply the recognition criteria to the separately identifiable components of a single transaction in order to reflect the substance of the transaction. *[IAS 18.13]*. This means that transactions have to be analysed in accordance with their economic substance in order to determine whether separately identifiable components should be combined or separated for revenue recognition purposes. For example, when the selling price of a product includes an identifiable amount for subsequent servicing, that amount attributable to the servicing is deferred and recognised as revenue over the period during which the service is performed. *[IAS 18.IE11]*.

Conversely, the recognition criteria are applied to two or more transactions together when they are linked in such a way that the commercial effect cannot be understood without reference to the series of transactions as a whole – as is the case, for example, where an entity sells goods and, at the same time, enters into a separate agreement to repurchase the goods at a later date, thus negating the substantive effect of the transaction; in such a case, the two transactions are dealt with together. *[IAS 18.13]*. The following extracts from the revenue recognition policies of Sandvik and Renault illustrate this point:

Extract 29.1: Sandvik AB (publ) (2014)

SIGNIFICANT ACCOUNTING POLICIES
– ASSESSMENTS AND ASSUMPTIONS FOR ACCOUNTING PURPOSES [extract]
REVENUE [extract]
REVENUE FROM SALES AND SERVICES [extract]

Revenue from the sale of goods is recognized in profit or loss for the year when the significant risks and rewards of ownership have transferred to the buyer, that is, normally in connection with delivery. If the product requires installation at the buyer, and installation is a significant part of the contract, revenue is recognized when the installation is completed. Buy-back commitments may entail that sales revenue cannot be recognized if the agreement with the customer in reality implies that the customer has only rented the product for a certain period of time.

Extract 29.2: Renault SA (2014)

4.2.6 NOTES TO THE CONSOLIDATED FINANCIAL STATEMENT
4.2.6.2 ACCOUNTING POLICIES AND SCOPE OF CONSOLIDATION [extract]
Note 2 ACCOUNTING POLICIES [extract]
G – Revenues and margin [extract]

Sales of goods and services and margin recognition [extract]
SALES AND MARGIN RECOGNITION

Sales of automotive goods are recognized when the goods are made available to the distribution network in the case of non-Group dealers, or upon delivery to the end-user in the case of direct sales. The margin on sales is recognized immediately for normal sales by the Automotive segment, including sales with associated financing contracts that can be considered as finance leases (long-term or with a purchase option). However, no sale is recognized when an automotive item (vehicle or electric car battery) is covered by an operating lease from a Group finance company or the Group has made a buy-back commitment with a high probability of application, if the term of the contract covers an insufficient portion of the item's useful life.

In such cases, the transactions are recorded as operating leases and included in sales of services. The difference between the price paid by the customer and the buy-back price is treated as rental income, and spread over the period the automotive item is at the customer's disposal. The production cost for the new automotive item concerned is recorded in inventories for contracts of less than one year, or included in property, plant and equipment under fixed assets leased to customers when the contracts exceed one year. The sale of the automotive item as second-hand at the end of the lease gives rise to recognition of sales revenue and the related margin. The forecast resale value takes account of recent known developments on the second-hand automotive market but also future anticipated developments over the period in which the automotive goods will be sold, which may be influenced by factors both external (economic situation, taxation) and internal (changes in the range or the manufacturer's pricing strategy). As soon as a loss is expected on the resale, a provision (if the automotive item is in inventories) or additional depreciation (if the automotive item is included in property, plant and equipment) is recognized to cover the loss. When the overall position of the lease contract (rental income and income on resale) shows a loss, an additional provision is also recorded immediately to cover the future loss.

IAS 18 does not establish criteria for separating or combining revenue transactions. However, IAS 11 includes a requirement similar to that of IAS 18 in that it requires entities to apply the standard to separately identifiable components of a single construction contract, or to a group of contracts together, in order to reflect the substance of a contract or a group of contracts. *[IAS 11.7]*. The practical issues in connection with combining and segmenting contracts are considered further in Chapter 23 at 2.

In the absence of any equivalent practical guidance in IAS 18, the criteria set out in IAS 11 may be helpful in determining whether revenue transactions should be combined or separated. However, the underlying principle in IAS 18, which focuses on whether combination or separation is necessary to reflect the substance and understand the commercial effect, should remain the primary consideration in making this assessment. *[IAS 18.13]*.

IAS 18 does not provide any additional guidance on identifying the separate components to which revenue should be allocated, nor does it prescribe an allocation method. In the specific case of servicing fees included in the price of a product, it notes that part of the revenue should be deferred to meet the expected costs of the service, together with a 'reasonable profit' on those services. *[IAS 18.IE11]*. There is no further explanation of what constitutes a 'reasonable profit'. IFRIC 13 mentions two allocation methodologies – allocation based on relative fair value and allocation using the residual method. IFRIC 13 does not prescribe a hierarchy. Therefore, an entity must use its judgement to select the most appropriate methodology, taking into consideration all relevant facts and circumstances. An entity should ensure that the resulting allocation is consistent with IAS 18's objective to measure revenue at the fair value of the consideration.

The method of allocation selected should be consistently applied to similar transactions. That is, the entity will draw on its experience of transactions with similar customers. In addition, the selected method of allocation should be adequately disclosed in the accounting policies and notes to the financial statements.

In the case of certain arrangements with multiple deliverables, it may also be helpful (but not required), under the hierarchy in IAS 8 – *Accounting Policies, Changes in Accounting Estimates and Errors, [IAS 8.12]*, to refer to the US GAAP guidance codified in ASC 605-25 – *Revenue Recognition – Multiple-Element Arrangements*, which deals with the issue of separating elements of revenue. See 5.7.1 below for a discussion of how this US GAAP guidance has been applied to recognising revenue on bundled offers in the telecommunications sector.

3.7 The sale of goods

IAS 18 provides the following five criteria that must be satisfied in order to recognise revenue from the sale of goods:

(a) the entity has transferred to the buyer the significant risks and rewards of ownership of the goods;

(b) the entity retains neither continuing managerial involvement to the degree usually associated with ownership nor effective control over the goods sold;

(c) the amount of revenue can be measured reliably;

(d) it is probable that the economic benefits associated with the transaction will flow to the entity; and

(e) the costs incurred or to be incurred in respect of the transaction can be measured reliably. *[IAS 18.14]*.

If the costs incurred cannot be measured reliably, the standard requires that 'any consideration already received for the sale of the goods is recognised as a liability'. *[IAS 18.19]*.

IAS 18 views the passing of risks and rewards as the most crucial of the five criteria, giving the following four examples of situations in which an entity may retain the significant risks and rewards of ownership:

(a) when the entity retains an obligation for unsatisfactory performance not covered by normal warranty provisions;

(b) when the receipt of the revenue from a particular sale is contingent on the derivation of revenue by the buyer from its sale of the goods;

(c) when the goods are shipped subject to installation and the installation is a significant part of the contract which has not yet been completed by the entity; and

(d) when the buyer has the right to rescind the purchase for a reason specified in the sales contract and the entity is uncertain about the probability of return. *[IAS 18.16]*.

It is clear that the standard still advocates an earnings process-driven critical event approach to revenue recognition. It is, therefore, necessary to establish at which point in the earnings process both the significant risks and rewards of ownership are transferred from the seller to the buyer and any significant uncertainties (which would otherwise defer recognition) are removed. For example, the responsibilities of each party during the period between sale and delivery should be established, possibly from past practice and by examination of the customer agreements. If the goods only need to be collected by the buyer, and the seller has performed all his associated responsibilities, then the sale may be recognised immediately. However, if the substance of the sale is merely that an order has been placed, and the goods have still to be acquired or manufactured by the seller, then the sale should not be recognised. The following extract from the accounting policies of Atlas Copco illustrates the deferral of revenue recognition until installation is completed in those cases where installation is a significant part of the contract:

Extract 29.3: Atlas Copco AB (2014)

FINANCIAL STATEMENTS AND NOTES [extract]

1. Significant accounting principles, accounting estimates and judgments [extract]

Significant accounting principles [extract]

Goods sold

Revenue from goods sold is recognized when the significant risks and rewards of ownership have been transferred to the buyer, i.e. when the Group retains neither continuing right to dispose of the goods nor hold effective control of the goods sold, recovery of the consideration is probable and the amount of the revenue and associated costs can be measured reliably. When the product requires installation and this constitutes a significant part of the contract, revenue is recognized when the installation is completed. Revenue is not recorded for buy-back commitments if the substance of the agreement is that the risks and rewards of ownership have not been transferred to the buyer. No revenue is recognized if there is significant uncertainty regarding the possible return of goods.

The terms of trade, and the associated legal implications, may also be relevant in determining the timing of revenue recognition. The standard assumes that 'in most cases, the transfer of risks and rewards of ownership coincides with the transfer of legal title or the passing of possession to the buyer', but acknowledges that this may not always be the case. The standard recognises that transactions occur where the transfer of risks and rewards of ownership occurs at a different time from the transfer of legal title or the passing of possession. *[IAS 18.15]*. Transfer of legal title is, therefore, not a condition for revenue recognition under IAS 18. IAS 18 recognises that, under certain circumstances, goods are sold subject to reservation of title in order to protect the collectability of the amount due. In such circumstances, provided that the seller has transferred the significant risks and rewards of ownership, the transaction can be treated as a sale and revenue can be recognised. *[IAS 18.17]*.

This point is reinforced in the introductory paragraph to the Illustrative Examples to IAS 18, which notes that laws in different countries may mean that the recognition criteria in the standard are met at different times. In particular, the law may determine the point in time at which an entity transfers the significant risks and rewards of ownership. Therefore, the illustrative examples need to be read in the context of the laws relating to the sale of goods in the country in which the transaction takes place. *[IAS 18.IE]*.

The following extracts from the financial statements of Smith & Nephew and Roche illustrate both the measurement principles of IAS 18 and the application of the critical event approach in determining the timing of revenue recognition:

Extract 29.4: Smith & Nephew plc (2014)

Notes to the Group accounts [extract]

2.1 Revenue by business segment and geography [extract]

ACCOUNTING POLICY

Revenue comprises sales of products and services to third parties at amounts invoiced net of trade discounts and rebates, excluding taxes on revenue. Revenue from the sale of products is recognised upon transfer to the customer of the significant risks and rewards of ownership. This is generally when goods are delivered to customers. Sales of inventory located at customer premises and available for customers' immediate use are recognised when notification is received that the product has been implanted or used. Appropriate provisions for returns, trade discounts and rebates are deducted from revenue. Rebates comprise retrospective volume discounts granted to certain customers on attainment of certain levels of purchases from the Group. These are accrued over the course of the arrangement based on estimates of the level of business expected and adjusted at the end of the arrangement to reflect actual volumes.

Extract 29.5: Roche Holding Ltd (2014)

Notes to the Roche Group Consolidated Financial Statements [extract]

32. Significant accounting policies [extract]

Revenues

Sales represent amounts received and receivable for goods supplied to customers after deducting trade discounts, cash discounts and volume rebates, and exclude value added taxes and other taxes directly linked to sales. Revenues from the sale of products are recognised upon transfer to the customer of significant risks and rewards. Trade discounts, cash discounts and volume rebates are recorded on an accrual basis consistent with the recognition of the related sales. Estimates of expected sales returns, charge-backs and other rebates, including Medicaid in the US and similar rebates in other countries, are also deducted from sales and recorded as accrued liabilities or provisions or as a deduction from accounts receivable. Such estimates are based on analyses of existing contractual or legislatively mandated obligations, historical trends and the Group's experience. If the circumstances are such that the level of sales returns, and hence revenues, cannot be reliably measured, then sales are only recognised when the right of return expires, which is generally upon prescription of the products to patients. Other revenues are recorded as earned or as the services are performed. Single transactions are split into separately identifiable components to reflect the substance of the transaction, where necessary. Conversely, two or more transactions may be considered together for revenue recognition purposes, where the commercial effect cannot be understood without reference to the series of transactions as a whole.

3.8 The rendering of services

IAS 18 requires that when the outcome of a transaction involving the rendering of services can be estimated reliably, revenue is recognised 'by reference to the stage of completion of the transaction at the end of the reporting period' (in other words, using the percentage-of-completion method). *[IAS 18.20]*. The requirements of IAS 11 are 'generally applicable to the recognition of revenue and the associated expenses for a transaction involving the rendering of services'. *[IAS 18.21]*.

According to IAS 18, the outcome of a transaction can be estimated reliably when all the following conditions are satisfied:

(a) the amount of revenue can be measured reliably;

(b) it is probable that the economic benefits associated with the transaction will flow to the entity;

(c) the stage of completion of the transaction at the end of the reporting period can be measured reliably; and

(d) the costs incurred for the transaction and the costs to complete the transaction can be measured reliably. *[IAS 18.20]*.

When the outcome cannot be estimated reliably, revenue is recognised only to the extent of the expenses recognised that are recoverable. *[IAS 18.26]*. During the early stages of a transaction, it is often the case that the outcome of the transaction cannot be estimated reliably. Nevertheless, it may be probable that the enterprise will recover the transaction costs incurred. Therefore, revenue is recognised only to the extent of costs incurred that are expected to be recoverable. As the outcome of the transaction cannot be estimated reliably, no profit is recognised. *[IAS 18.27]*. For an example of this see the BT Group revenue recognition policy in Extract 29.7 below.

When the outcome of a transaction cannot be estimated reliably and it is not probable that the costs incurred will be recovered, revenue is not recognised and the costs incurred are recognised as an expense. When the uncertainties that prevented the outcome of the contract being estimated reliably no longer exist, revenue is recognised by reference to the stage of completion of the transaction at the balance sheet date. *[IAS 18.28]*.

IAS 18 provides several illustrative examples of transactions involving the rendering of services. It is clear from these examples that the performance of the service is the critical event for revenue recognition. *[IAS 18.IE10-IE19]*.

The standard claims that an entity is generally able to make reliable estimates after it has agreed to the following with the other parties to the transaction:

(a) each party's enforceable rights regarding the service to be provided and received by the parties;

(b) the consideration to be exchanged; and

(c) the manner and terms of settlement. *[IAS 18.23]*.

The standard notes that it is usually necessary for the entity to have effective systems for internal financial budgeting and reporting. The entity reviews and, when necessary, revises the estimates of revenue as the service is performed. The need for such revisions does not necessarily indicate that the outcome of the transaction cannot be estimated reliably. *[IAS 18.23]*.

When it comes to determining the stage of completion of a transaction, IAS 18 suggests three methods that may be used:

(a) surveys of work performed;

(b) services performed to date as a percentage of total services to be performed; or

(c) the proportion that costs incurred to date bear to the estimated total costs of the transaction. Only costs that reflect services performed to date are included in costs incurred to date. Only costs that reflect services performed (or to be performed) are included in the estimated total costs of the transaction. *[IAS 18.24]*.

For practical purposes, when services are performed by an indeterminate number of acts over a specified period, the standard states that revenue should be recognised on a straight-line basis over the specified period, unless there is evidence that some other method better represents the stage of completion. However, when a specific act is much more significant than any other acts, the standard requires that the recognition of revenue be postponed until the significant act is executed. *[IAS 18.25]*.

In practice, this can be seen by considering outsourcing arrangements. These are contracts that require services to be provided on an ongoing basis, often for a number of years, rather than the provision of a single service or a number of services that constitute a single project. These arrangements are common across a wide range of services including processing, provision of telecommunications services, general professional advice, help desk support, accounting advice, maintenance or cleaning, The 'service' to which IAS 18's method applies is the individual act, whether it be the individual process, answering the telephone help line or cleaning the office each night. Clearly in most cases, it would not be feasible to identify the costs and revenue for each of these acts, so revenue is recognised on a straight line basis over the contract term and costs are expensed as incurred.

The entities that provide outsourcing services frequently provide single services as well. The following revenue recognition policy for Cap Gemini illustrates both the treatment of revenue for outsourcing contracts and for its long-term contracts.

Extract 29.6: Cap Gemini S.A. (2014)

NOTES TO THE CONSOLIDATED FINANCIAL STATEMENTS FOR THE YEAR ENDED DECEMBER 31, 2014 [extract]

NOTE 5 REVENUES [extract]

The method for recognizing revenues and costs depends on the nature of the services rendered:

a. Time and materials contracts

Revenues and cost of services are recognized as services are rendered.

b. Long-term fixed-price contracts

Revenues, including systems development and integration contracts, are recognized using the "percentage-of-completion" method. Costs are recognized as they are incurred.

c. Outsourcing contracts [extract]

Revenues from outsourcing agreements are recognized over the term of the contract as the services are rendered. When the services are made up of different components which are not separately identifiable, the related revenues are recognized on a straight-line basis over the term of the contract.

The related costs are recognized as they are incurred. However, a portion of costs incurred in the initial phase of outsourcing contracts (transition and/or transformation costs) may be deferred when they are specific to a given contract, relate to future activity on the contract and/or will generate future economic benefits, and are recoverable. These costs are allocated to work-in-progress and any reimbursement by the client is recorded as a deduction from the costs incurred.

When the projected cost of the contract exceeds contract revenues, a loss to completion is recognized in the amount of the difference.

BT Group provides an illustration of an accounting policy whereby revenue from long-term contractual arrangements involving the design and build of software solutions is recognised using the percentage-of-completion method:

Extract 29.7: BT Group plc (2015)

Notes to the consolidated financial statements [extract]

3. Significant accounting policies [extract]

Revenue [extract]

Long-term contractual arrangements

Revenue from long-term contractual arrangements including fixed price contracts to design and build software solutions, is recognised based on the percentage of completion method. The stage of completion is estimated using an appropriate measure according to the nature of the contract such as the proportion of costs incurred relative to the estimated total contract costs, or other measures of completion such as the achievement of contract milestones and customer acceptance. In the case of time and materials contracts, revenue is recognised as the service is rendered.

Costs related to delivering services under long-term contractual arrangements are expensed as incurred except for an element of costs incurred in the initial contract set up, transition or transformation phase, which is deferred and recorded within non-current assets. These costs are then recognised in the income statement on a straight line basis over the remaining contract term, unless the pattern of service delivery indicates a different profile is appropriate. These costs are directly attributable to specific contracts, relate to future activity, will generate future economic benefits and are assessed for recoverability on a regular basis.

The percentage of completion method relies on estimates of total expected contract revenues and costs, as well as reliable measurement of the progress made towards completion. Unless the financial outcome of a contract can be estimated with reasonable certainty, no attributable profit is recognised. In such circumstances, revenue is recognised equal to the costs incurred to date, to the extent that such revenue is expected to be recoverable, or costs are accrued to bring the margin to nil. Recognised revenue and profits are subject to revisions during the contract if the assumptions regarding the overall contract outcome are changed. The cumulative impact of a revision in estimates is recorded in the period in which such revisions become likely and can be estimated. Where the actual and estimated costs to completion exceed the estimated revenue for a contract, the full contract life loss is recognised immediately.

3.9 Exchanges of goods and services

Under IAS 18, when goods or services are exchanged or swapped for goods or services that are of a similar nature and value, the exchange is not regarded as a transaction that generates revenue. The standard notes exchanges of commodities like oil or milk, where suppliers exchange or swap inventories in various locations to fulfil demand on a timely basis in a particular location as examples of this. There are similar reasons behind exchanges of capacity in the telecommunications sector.

If the goods or services exchanged are dissimilar, then revenue will be recognised on the transaction. The revenue is measured at the fair value of the goods or services received, adjusted by the amount of any cash or cash equivalents transferred. When the fair value of the goods or services received cannot be measured reliably, the revenue is measured at the fair value of the goods or services given up, adjusted by the amount of any cash or cash equivalents transferred. *[IAS 18.12]*.

IFRIC 18, which addresses accounting for transfers of assets from customers, provides guidance in situations where an entity receives an item of PP&E from a customer (or cash for the acquisition or construction of such items) that must then be used by the entity either to connect the customer to a network or to provide the customer ongoing access to a supply of goods or services. *[IFRIC 18.4-6]*. These arrangements are relatively common in the utilities industry. IFRIC 18 is discussed at 5.14 below.

There are specific requirements for exchanges of fixed assets within scope of IAS 16 or IAS 38 – *Intangible Assets*.

3.10 Exchanges of property plant and equipment and intangible assets

Accounting for exchanges of PP&E is dealt with in IAS 16 (see Chapter 18), which takes a different approach to IAS 18's treatment of exchanges of goods and services. IAS 38 deals with exchanges of intangible assets and includes the same requirements as IAS 16 with respect to intangible assets (see Chapter 17). *[IAS 38.45-47]*.

IAS 16 stipulates that gains arising from the derecognition of PP&E may not be classified as revenue, *[IAS 16.68]*, and it is clear that this applies equally to derecognition by way of an exchange, sale and abandonment; this means that an exchange of PP&E does not result in the recognition of revenue. The sole exception is the sale of certain ex-rental assets, discussed at 5.11.1 below. *[IAS 16.68A]*. Exchanges of assets are discussed in Chapter 18 at 4.4.

IFRS 5 – *Non-current Assets Held for Sale and Discontinued Operations* – provides additional requirements for assets held for disposal; these requirements include measurement rules that affect the measurement of the amount of the gain on disposal to be recognised. These are discussed in Chapter 4 at 2.2.

3.11 Barter transactions involving advertising services

The issue arises where an entity (the seller) enters into a barter transaction to provide advertising services in exchange for receiving advertising services from its customer. Advertisements may be displayed on websites, broadcast on television or radio, published in magazines or journals, or presented in another medium. In some cases, no cash or other consideration is exchanged between the entities although in other cases equal or approximately equal amounts of cash or other consideration may pass between them.

IAS 18 specifically addresses the recognition of revenue from advertising commissions, discussed at 5.5 below. It is clear that, under IAS 18, a seller that provides advertising services in the course of its ordinary activities recognises revenue from a barter transaction involving advertising when, amongst other criteria, the services exchanged are dissimilar and the amount of revenue can be measured reliably. *[IAS 18.12, 20(a)]*. However, an exchange of similar advertising services is not a transaction that generates revenue under IAS 18.

SIC-31 states that revenue cannot be measured reliably at the fair value of advertising services received. A seller can only measure revenue reliably at the fair value of the advertising services it provides by reference to non-barter transactions that:

(a) involve advertising similar to the advertising in the barter transaction;

(b) occur frequently;

(c) represent a predominant number of transactions and amount when compared to all transactions to provide advertising that is similar to the advertising in the barter transaction;

(d) involve cash and/or another form of consideration (e.g. marketable securities, non-monetary assets, and other services) that has a reliably measurable fair value; and

(e) do not involve the same counterparty as in the barter transaction. *[SIC-31.5].*

The conditions represent a relatively high hurdle for entities to overcome and it would seem that, in most instances, they would find it difficult to be able to recognise any revenue. For example, payments of equal or substantially equal amounts between the entities that provide and receive advertising services do not provide reliable evidence of fair value. An exchange of advertising services that also includes only partial cash payment provides reliable evidence of the fair value of the transaction to the extent of the cash component (except when partial cash payments of equal or substantially equal amounts are swapped), but does not provide reliable evidence of the fair value of the entire transaction.

Barter transactions involving services occur mainly in the media industry. German television corporation, ProSiebenSat.1 Media discloses the following accounting policy for barter transactions involving advertising:

Extract 29.8: ProSiebenSat.1 Media AG (2014)

CONSOLIDATED FINANCIAL STATEMENTS [extract]

Notes [extract]

2 Accounting policies [extract]

Recognition of income and expenses [extract]

At ProSiebenSat.1 Group, barter transactions are primarily concluded as tradeoff transactions relating to the sale of advertising time. Revenues from such barter transactions are considered revenue-generating transactions only when dissimilar goods or services are exchanged, and the amount of the proceeds and costs, as well as the economic benefit, can be clearly measured. If advertising time is exchanged for goods or products, the revenues are measured according to the fair value of the goods or products received, provided this can be determined reliably. If advertising time is exchanged for advertising time, the revenues are determined according to the fair value of the advertising time provided. Revenues from barter transactions are considered realized when ProSiebenSat.1 Group performs the service, e.g. when the agreed advertising is broadcast.

In our view, SIC-31 was issued as a specific anti-abuse rule that does not have wider implications and should not be applied to other situations by analogy.

3.12 Interest, royalties and dividends

When it is probable that the economic benefits associated with the transaction will flow to the entity and that the amount of revenue can be measured reliably, IAS 18 requires that the revenue arising from the use by others of entity assets yielding interest, royalties and dividends should be recognised as follows:

(a) *interest:* using the effective interest method as set out in IAS 39, paragraphs 9 and AG5-AG8 and discussed in Chapter 49 at 3 (or if IFRS 9 is applied, Chapter 50 at 3);

(b) *royalties:* on an accrual basis in accordance with the substance of the relevant agreement; and

(c) *dividends:* when the shareholder's right to receive payment is established. *[IAS 18.29-30]*.

When unpaid interest has accrued before the acquisition of an interest-bearing investment, the subsequent receipt of interest is allocated between pre-acquisition and post-acquisition periods; only the post-acquisition portion is recognised as revenue. *[IAS 18.32]*.

There is no distinction between pre- and post-acquisition dividends. IAS 27 – *Separate Financial Statements* – states that an entity is to recognise dividends from subsidiaries, joint ventures or associates in its separate financial statements when its right to receive the dividend is established. *[IAS 27.12]*. Entities determine as a separate exercise whether or not the investment has been impaired as a result of the dividend. IAS 36 – *Impairment of Assets* – includes specific triggers for impairment reviews on receipt of dividends. *[IAS 36.12(h)]*. The treatment of the dividends received is discussed in Chapter 8 at 2.4.

Stock dividends, whereby new shares are issued to investors in lieu of a cash dividend, are popular in certain jurisdictions. Where the investor has the option to receive cash or the equivalent value in new shares this arrangement is in substance a cash dividend with an immediate reinvestment in shares. If the investment is either an associate or a joint venture held at cost under IAS 27, or an investment classified as available for sale under IAS 39 (or IFRS 9, if applied), the stock dividend will be recorded as revenue in the normal manner when the right to receive payment is established. The debit entry will be recognised as an addition to the investment. However, if the stock dividend is compulsory with no cash alternative, or where the cash alternative is priced at such an unfavourable rate that an investor would be unlikely to take that option, the arrangement cannot be considered to be, in substance, a cash dividend with immediate reinvestment. The transaction will not result in economic benefits to the investor and, therefore, revenue will not be recognised.

Royalties accrue in accordance with the terms of the relevant agreement and are usually recognised on that basis unless, having regard to the substance of the agreement, it is more appropriate to recognise revenue on some other systematic and rational basis. *[IAS 18.33]*.

Anglo American Platinum provides a straightforward example of accounting policies for dividends, interest and royalties:

Extract 29.9: Anglo American Platinum Limited (2014)

PRINCIPAL ACCOUNTING POLICIES

for the year ended 31 December 2014 [extract]

EXISTING ACCOUNTING POLICIES [extract]

11. Revenue recognition

- Revenue from the sale of metals and intermediary products is recognised when the risk and rewards of ownership are transferred to the buyer. Gross sales revenue represents the invoiced amounts excluding value-added tax.
- Dividends are recognised when the right to receive payment is established.
- Interest is recognised on a time proportion basis, which takes into account the effective yield on the asset over the period it is expected to be held.
- Royalties are recognised when the right to receive payment is established.

3.13 Uncollectible revenue

Revenue is recognised only when it is probable that the economic benefits associated with the transaction will flow to the entity. *[IAS 18.14(d)]*. Because it is recognised at fair value, the revenue may be lower than the contracted amount, to take account of expected non-recoveries. In some cases, part or all of the revenue may not be recognised until the consideration is received or until an uncertainty is removed as, until then, its receipt is not probable. However, if the collectability of an amount already included in revenue becomes uncertain, the uncollectible amount (or the amount in respect of which recovery has ceased to be probable) is recognised as an expense, rather than as an adjustment of the amount of revenue originally recognised. *[IAS 18.18, 22, 34]*. In other words, bad and doubtful debts are recognised as expenses, not as reductions of revenue.

3.14 Disclosure

IAS 18's disclosure requirements relate to both revenue recognition policies and amounts included in the financial statements under the different categories of revenue. They are set down in the standard as follows:

(a) the accounting policies adopted for the recognition of revenue including the methods adopted to determine the stage of completion of transactions involving the rendering of services;

(b) the amount of each significant category of revenue recognised during the period including revenue arising from:

  (i) the sale of goods;
  (ii) the rendering of services;
  (iii) interest;
  (iv) royalties;
  (v) dividends; and

(c) the amount of revenue arising from exchanges of goods or services included in each significant category of revenue. *[IAS 18.35]*.

The disclosures required under (b) and (c) above may be provided in the notes to the financial statements, rather than on the face of the statement of comprehensive income or separate income statement (if presented).

3.15 Revenue in the statement of profit or loss and other comprehensive income

IAS 1 contains minimum requirements for the contents of the statement of comprehensive income. It states that an entity is to present all items of income and expense recognised in a period either in a single 'statement of profit or loss and other comprehensive income', or in two separate statements:

- a statement displaying components of profit or loss (statement of profit or loss); and
- a second statement beginning with profit or loss and displaying components of other comprehensive income (the statement of comprehensive income).

There are minimum requirements for what must be disclosed on the face of the statement of comprehensive income or separate statement of profit or loss (if presented). The formats and their requirements are described in Chapter 3.

IAS 1 requires that revenue be presented separately in the statement of comprehensive income and the separate statement of profit or loss (if presented). In addition, IAS 1 requires that additional line items, headings and subtotals are to be presented in the statement of comprehensive income and the separate statement of profit or loss (if presented) when such presentation is relevant to an understanding of the entity's financial performance. Additional line items are included, and the descriptions used and the ordering of items are amended, when this is necessary to explain the elements of financial performance. Factors to be considered include materiality and the nature and function of the components of income and expenses. *[IAS 1.85-86]*.

These requirements provide an entity with a substantial amount of flexibility with regard to the presentation of its statement of comprehensive income and separate statement of profit or loss (if presented). However, they also raise a number of practical questions about the presentation of revenue, such as:

- whether the amount for 'finance costs' can be shown net of interest and other finance income; and
- the classification in profit or loss of gains on disposal of PP&E.

3.15.1 Interest and other finance income

IAS 18 requires interest income to be disclosed as one of the categories of revenue. *[IAS 18.35(b)]*. It used to be a fairly widespread practice under a number of national GAAPs for entities to show finance costs net of interest and other finance income. However, IAS 1 states that income and expenses should not be offset unless required or permitted by a standard or an interpretation. *[IAS 1.32]*. 'Finance costs' are listed as one of the line items that must be included on the face of the statement of comprehensive income or separate statement of profit or loss (if presented). *[IAS 1.82(b)]*. Taken together, these paragraphs preclude an entity presenting 'net finance costs' on the face of the statement of comprehensive income or separate statement of profit or loss (if presented) without showing separately the finance costs and finance revenue included in the net amount, e.g. by presenting gross interest income and gross interest expense and then striking a sub-total that shows net interest. The IASB has removed a reference in IFRS 7 – *Financial Instruments: Disclosures* – paragraph IG13 to 'total interest income' as a component of finance costs. This amendment confirmed the IASB's intention that finance income and finance expense be separately disclosed on the face of profit or loss.

IAS 1 permits some gains and losses arising from a group of similar transactions to be reported on a net basis, for example, foreign exchange gains and losses or gains and losses arising on financial instruments held for trading. Such gains and losses are, however, reported separately if they are material. *[IAS 1.35]*.

Although there is no standard or interpretation that permits interest income to be offset against interest expense, we believe that net presentation is appropriate in the case of trading activities; in our view, the interest income on financial instruments (e.g. bonds) that are held as trading assets (e.g. by a financial institution) could be included within net trading income.

In January 2015,[5] the Interpretations Committee discussed the economic situation of negative effective interest rates in respect of the presentation of income and expense in the statement of comprehensive income. The Interpretations Committee decided not to add the issue to its agenda noting that interest resulting from a negative effective interest rate on a financial asset does not meet the definition of interest revenue under IAS 18 because it does not reflect a gross inflow of economic benefits. It was further noted that the expense arising on a financial asset because of the negative effective interest rate would not be presented as interest revenue and, instead, would be classified as an expense.

UBS shows interest income and expense gross in the income statement, but provides note disclosure on a net basis by business activity.

Extract 29.10: UBS AG (2014)

Financial information [extract]

UBS AG consolidated financial statements [extract]

Audited | Income statement [extract]

		For the year ended			% change from
CHF million, except per share data	Note	**31.12.14**	31.12.13	31.12.12	31.12.13
Interest income	3	**13,194**	13,137	15,968	0
Interest expense	3	**(6,639)**	(7,351)	(9,990)	(10)
Net interest income	3	**6,555**	5,786	5,978	13
Credit loss (expense)/recovery	12	**(78)**	(50)	(118)	56
Net interest income after credit loss expense		**6,477**	5,736	5,860	13
Net fee and commission income	4	**17,076**	16,287	15,396	5
Net trading income	3	**3,841**	5,130	3,526	(25)
Other income	5	**632**	580	641	9
Total operating income		**28,026**	27,732	25,423	1

Income statement notes [extract]
Note 3 Net interest and trading income [extract]

	For the year ended			% change from
CHF million	**31.12.14**	31.12.13	31.12.12	31.12.13
Net interest and trading income				
Net interest income	**6,555**	5,786	5,978	13
Net trading income	**3,841**	5,130	3,526	(25)
Total net interest and trading income	**10,396**	10,915	9,504	(5)
Wealth Management	**2,845**	2,868	2,728	(1)
Wealth Management Americas	**1,352**	1,323	1,265	2
Retail & Corporate	**2,536**	2,485	2,467	2
Global Asset Management	**0**	9	9	(100)
Investment Bank	**4,554**	5,015	3,574	(9)
of which: Corporate Client Solutions[1]	***1,047***	*1,142*	*706*	*(8)*
of which: Investor Client Services[1]	***3,507***	*3,873*	*2,868*	*(9)*
Corporate Center	**(892)**	(784)	(540)	14
of which: Core Functions	***(29)***	*(1,045)*	*(1,992)*	*(97)*
of which: own credit on financial liabilities designated at fair value[2]	***292***	*(283)*	*(2,202)*	
of which: Non-core and Legacy Portfolio	***(864)***	*261*	*1,452*	
Total net interest and trading income	**10,396**	10,915	9,504	(5)
Net interest income				
Interest income				
Interest earned on loans and advances[3]	**8,722**	8,686	9,323	0
Interest earned on securities borrowed and reverse repurchase agreements	**752**	852	1,413	(12)
Interest and dividend income from trading portfolio	**3,196**	2,913	4,482	10
Interest income on financial assets designated at fair value	**208**	364	369	(43)
Interest and dividend income from financial investments available-for-sale	**315**	322	381	(2)
Total	**13,194**	13,137	15,968	0
Interest expense				
Interest on amounts due to banks and customers	**708**	893	1,433	(21)
Interest on securities lent and repurchase agreements	**827**	829	1,208	0
Interest expense from trading portfolio[4]	**1,804**	1,846	2,442	(2)
Interest on financial liabilities designated at fair value	**919**	1,197	1,744	(23)
Interest on debt issued	**2,382**	2,586	3,163	(8)
Total	**6,639**	7,351	9,990	(10)
Net interest income	**6,555**	5,786	5,978	13

1 In 2014, comparative period figures were corrected. As a result, net interest and trading income for Investment Bank Corporate Client Solutions increased by CHF 107 million and CHF 131 million for 2013 and 2012, respectively, with an equal and offsetting decrease for Investment Bank Investor Client Services. **2** Refer to Note 24 for more information on own credit. **3** Includes interest income on impaired loans and advances of CHF 15 million for 2014, CHF 15 million for 2013 and CHF 16 million for 2012. **4** Includes expense related to dividend payment obligations on trading liabilities.

3.15.2 Gains on disposal of property, plant and equipment and intangible assets

As discussed at 3.2 above, the IASB's *Framework* explains that income includes both 'revenue' and 'gains'. Gains include, for example, those arising on the disposal of non-current assets. IAS 16 and IAS 38 also make it clear that 'gains shall not be classified as revenue'. *[IAS 16.68, IAS 38.113]*.

Therefore, gains arising on the disposal of PP&E do not form part of revenue (aside from entities that routinely sell PP&E that it has held for rental to others as discussed at 5.11.1 below). However, in our view, it is acceptable to show such gains net of any losses on disposal as part of income, while net losses on disposal should be shown within expenses.

4 REVENUE RECOGNITION UNDER US GAAP

4.1 Applicability of US literature

Although IAS 18 provides general principles of revenue recognition, there is a lack of specific guidance in relation to matters, such as multiple-element revenue arrangements and industry-specific issues, e.g. those relating to the software industry. The underlying approach to revenue recognition under US GAAP is closely aligned with that of IAS 18, in that it is based on the earnings process and realisation principle. As such, US GAAP's requirements for revenue recognition may, in many instances, be compatible with IAS 18. While the US literature does not override the specific requirements of IFRS, some entities might choose to avail themselves of the hierarchy set out in IAS 8 in order to look to US GAAP in formulating appropriate accounting policies with respect to specific transactions. *[IAS 8.12]*. However, while US GAAP might provide useful guidance in certain instances, the IAS 8 hierarchy does not require entities to refer either to US GAAP or, indeed, any other national GAAP. It is crucial to bear in mind that not all industry practices under US GAAP are permissible under IFRS. For example, utility entities should not adopt a revenue recognition policy that gives rise to regulatory assets and regulatory liabilities (although the IASB is considering the treatment of rate-regulated activities – see 5.13 below). Care always needs to be taken to ensure that the adoption of the more detailed US GAAP requirements results in IFRS compliance. It may be the case that the application of the principles in IAS 18 could result in different accounting from that which would be achieved if the detailed rules in US GAAP were applied.

4.2 The general approach to revenue recognition under US GAAP

The accounting literature of US GAAP on revenue recognition includes both broad conceptual discussions and certain industry-specific guidance. If a transaction is within the scope of specific authoritative literature that provides revenue recognition guidance, that literature should be applied. In the absence of authoritative literature addressing a specific arrangement or a specific industry, preparers consider the existing authoritative accounting standards as well as the broad revenue recognition criteria specified in the FASB's conceptual framework that contain basic guidelines for revenue recognition.[6]

Statement of Financial Accounting Concepts (C) No. 5 – *Recognition and Measurement in Financial Statements of Business Enterprises* – deals with recognition issues primarily from the angle of providing reliability of measurement. However, the broad principle for revenue recognition provided in Concepts Statement 5 is that revenues are not recognised until they are both realised or realisable and earned.[7] Concepts Statement 5 states that 'an entity's revenue-earning activities involve delivering or producing goods, rendering services, or other activities that constitute its ongoing major or central operations, and revenues are considered to have been earned when the entity has substantially accomplished what it must do to be entitled to the benefits represented by the revenues'.[8] It states that 'the two conditions (being realized or realizable and being earned) are usually met by the time product or merchandise is delivered or services are rendered to customers, and revenues from manufacturing and selling activities and gains and losses from sales of other assets are commonly recognized at time of sale (usually meaning delivery)'.[9] In addition, it states 'if services are rendered or rights to use assets extend continuously over time (for example, interest or rent), reliable measures based on contractual prices established in advance are commonly available, and revenues may be recognized as earned as time passes'.[10]

The US SEC staff believes that revenue generally is realised or realisable and earned when all of the following criteria are met:[11]

- persuasive evidence of an arrangement exists;
- delivery has occurred or services have been rendered;
- the seller's price to the buyer is fixed or determinable; and
- collectability is reasonably assured.

Generally, a sales price is not fixed or determinable when a customer has the unilateral right to terminate or cancel the contract and receive a cash refund. A sales price or fee that is variable until the occurrence of future events (other than short-term rights of return that are not considered to be cancellation privileges and fall under the guidance provided within ASC 605-15) generally is not fixed or determinable until the future event occurs. The revenue from such transactions should not be recognised in earnings until the sales price or fee becomes fixed or determinable.[12]

IAS 18 states that revenue can be recognised at the time of sale if only an insignificant risk of ownership is retained, the seller can estimate returns and it provides for them. *[IAS 18.17]*. This means that a retailer who offers refunds if the customer is not satisfied can generally recognise revenue for those sales, provided the retailer has separately provided for the estimated returns.

4.3 US GAAP requirements for multiple-element transactions

One area of US GAAP guidance that is often referred to by IFRS reporters is that relating to transactions that comprise multiple components. The guidance under IFRS is limited. IAS 18 points out that it may be necessary to apply its requirements to separately identifiable components of a single transaction in order to reflect the

Chapter 29

substance of a transaction. *[IAS 18.13]*. It does not prescribe a method of allocation, which means that allocations based on relative fair value or on a residual method could be acceptable, depending on the relevant facts and circumstances. In an example illustrating the need to defer an amount relating to subsequent servicing when this servicing fee is included in the price of a product, the entity is required to defer sufficient revenue to cover the expected costs of the service together with a 'reasonable profit' on these services (see 3.6 above). *[IAS 18.IE11]*.

The key issues relate to how the components within these multiple-element transactions should be broken down (i.e. the determination of the unit of account) and when allocated revenue on each element should be recognised.

The primary US GAAP guidance is included within ASC 605-25, although this does not apply to software arrangements which are included within industry-specific guidance and briefly explained at 5.6 below.

ASC 605-25 requires that, in multiple-element arrangements, the delivered item or items be considered a separate unit of account if both of the following criteria are met:[13]

- the delivered item or items have stand-alone value; and
- if the arrangement includes a general right of return for the delivered item, the delivery or performance of the undelivered item is probable and is substantially in the control of the seller.

Unlike IAS 18, ASC 605-25 provides specific guidance, requiring that the consideration is allocated to components based on their relative selling prices. These selling prices are calculated based upon vendor-specific objective evidence (VSOE), where available, or third party evidence where not available. If neither VSOE nor third-party evidence of selling price exists for a component, the entity should use its best estimate of the selling price for that component, i.e. the price at which the entity would transact if the component were sold by the entity regularly on a stand-alone basis.[14] These detailed requirements are not included within IFRS. Rather, IFRS reporters have always had to comply with the general principles of IAS 18. But, as discussed at 4.1 above, entities may find it useful to refer to the more detailed US GAAP guidance.

5 PRACTICAL ISSUES

IAS 18 could be said to be one of the more principles-based standards in the IFRS literature. However, the broader the principles, the more that judgement is required to apply them in practice, with the inevitable result that consistency is not always achieved. Nevertheless, consistency has tended to be achieved over time within specific industries on the basis of principles-based consensuses between the preparer, regulator and auditor communities.

The following table summarises some of the broad approaches to revenue reporting that would appear to have achieved general acceptance through existing reporting practice. The table indicates the circumstances under which it might be appropriate to apply each of the approaches.

It is essential that each situation is considered on its individual merits, with particular attention being paid to the risks and uncertainties that remain at each stage of the earnings process and the extent to which the amount of revenue can be measured reliably. Revenue recognition will also be affected by the laws in a jurisdiction and by the applicable terms of trade.

The timing of recognition	*Criteria*	*Examples of practical application*
During production (accretion)	Revenues accrue over time, and no significant uncertainty exists as to measurability or collectability. A contract of sale has been entered into and future costs can be estimated with reasonable accuracy.	Most services. The accrual of interest and dividend income. Accounting for construction contracts using the percentage-of-completion method.
At the completion of production	There is a ready market for the commodity that can rapidly absorb the quantity held by the entity; the commodity comprises interchangeable units; the market price should be determinable and stable; there should be insignificant marketing costs involved.	Certain precious metals and commodities.
At the time of sale (but before delivery)	Goods must have already been acquired or manufactured; goods must be capable of immediate delivery to the customer; selling price has been established; all material related expenses (including delivery) have been ascertained; no significant uncertainties remain (e.g. ultimate cash collection, returns).	Certain sales of goods (e.g. 'bill and hold' sales).
On delivery	Criteria for recognition before delivery were not satisfied and no significant uncertainties remain.	Most sales of goods and some services.
Subsequent to delivery	Significant uncertainty regarding collectability existed at the time of delivery; at the time of sale it was not possible to value the consideration with sufficient accuracy.	Certain sales of goods and services (e.g. where the right of return exists). Goods shipped subject to conditions (e.g. installation and inspection/ performance).
On an apportionment basis (the revenue allocation approach)	Where revenue represents the supply of initial and subsequent goods/services.	Franchise fees. Sale of goods with after sales service.

Chapter 29

As limited application guidance is given in IFRS about the timing of revenue recognition, we have devoted the remainder of this Chapter to the examination of specific areas of revenue recognition in practice that might be open to inconsistent, controversial or varied accounting practices. Some of this comprises a discussion of the issues addressed in the Illustrative Examples to IAS 18, which expands on the principles in the standard. The IFRIC Interpretations that have a particular impact on revenue recognition (IFRIC 13, IFRIC 15 and IFRIC 18) are also discussed below. Many of the issues discussed below relate to specific industries that pose particular revenue recognition challenges.

5.1 Sale of goods

The Illustrative Examples to IAS 18 identifies a number of different arrangements that may affect the point at which the risks and rewards of ownership pass to the buyer. The terms of trade agreed with a customer, as well as the law governing the sale of goods in any particular jurisdiction, must be taken into account.

5.1.1 'Bill and hold' sales

The term 'bill and hold' sale is used to describe a transaction in which delivery is delayed at the buyer's request, but the buyer takes title and accepts billing.

Under the Illustrative Examples to IAS 18, revenue is recognised when the buyer takes title, provided:

(a) it is probable that delivery will be made;

(b) the item is on hand, identified and ready for delivery to the buyer at the time the sale is recognised;

(c) the buyer specifically acknowledges the deferred delivery instructions; and

(d) the usual payment terms apply.

Revenue is not recognised when there is simply an intention to acquire or manufacture the goods in time for delivery. *[IAS 18.IE1]*.

5.1.2 Goods shipped subject to conditions

The Illustrative Examples to IAS 18 identify four scenarios in which goods are shipped subject to various conditions: *[IAS 18.IE2]*

(a) *installation and inspection*

Revenue is normally recognised when the buyer accepts delivery and installation and inspection are complete. Revenue is recognised immediately upon the buyer's acceptance of delivery when:

(i) the installation process is simple in nature, e.g. the installation of a factory-tested television receiver that only requires unpacking and connection of power and antennae; or

(ii) the inspection is performed only for purposes of final determination of contract prices, for example, shipments of iron ore, sugar or soya beans.

(b) *on approval when the buyer has negotiated a limited right of return*

If there is uncertainty about the possibility of return, revenue is recognised when the shipment has been formally accepted by the buyer or the goods have been delivered and the time period for rejection has elapsed. See the discussion at 2.1.3 above.

(c) *consignment sales under which the recipient (buyer) undertakes to sell the goods on behalf of the shipper (seller)*

Revenue is recognised by the shipper when the goods are sold by the recipient to a third party.

(d) *cash on delivery sales*

Revenue is recognised when delivery is made and cash is received by the seller or its agent.

The extract from the financial statements of Sandvik AB in Extract 29.1 at 3.6 above, illustrates a revenue recognition policy that reflects some of these requirements.

5.1.3 Layaway sales

The term 'layaway sales' applies to transactions where the goods are delivered only when the buyer makes the final payment in a series of instalments. This is fairly common in the retail sector, e.g. clothing and household goods. Revenue from such a sale is recognised when the goods are delivered. However, when experience indicates that most of such sales are completed, revenue may be recognised when a significant deposit is received, provided the goods are on hand, identified and ready for delivery to the buyer. *[IAS 18.IE3]*.

5.1.4 Payments in advance

In certain sectors (e.g. furniture and kitchen retail) payment or partial payment is received from the customer when they place their order for the goods. This is often well in advance of delivery for goods that are not presently held in inventory (if, for example, the goods are still to be manufactured or will be delivered directly to the customer by a third party). In such cases, revenue is recognised when the goods are delivered to the buyer. *[IAS 18.IE4]*.

In other sectors – for example, utilities – entities receive advance payments from customers for services to be provided in the future. In some cases, these advance payments are long term in nature. The issue that arises is whether or not interest should be accrued on these advances and, if so, how revenue should be measured in these circumstances.

IAS 18 requires entities to measure revenue 'at the fair value of the consideration received or receivable'. *[IAS 18.9]*. The standard refers to the situations in which an entity either provides interest-free credit to the buyer or accepts a note receivable bearing a below-market interest rate from the buyer as consideration for the sale of goods. If the arrangement effectively constitutes a financing transaction, IAS 18 requires that the entity determine the fair value of the consideration by discounting all future receipts using an imputed rate of interest. *[IAS 18.11]*. Although IAS 18 does not address the reverse situation of the receipt of interest-free advances from customers, a similar rationale may be applied to justify the accruing of interest, i.e. there is a financing element to the transaction and this must be taken account of if revenue is to be measured at the fair value of the consideration at the time the good or service is provided.

In drafting IFRIC 18, the Interpretations Committee considered the concept of accruing interest on advance payments received from customers, but the majority of respondents commenting on the draft disagreed that this was necessary. The Interpretations Committee subsequently agreed with this majority view and noted that 'paragraph 11 of IAS 18 requires taking the time value of money into account only when payments are deferred'. *[IFRIC 18.BC22]*.

Given this lack of clarity, we believe an entity has a policy choice to either accrue or not accrue interest on advance payments received from customers. If interest is accrued, it will be calculated based upon the incremental borrowing rate of the entity and revenue will ultimately be recognised based upon the nominal value of the advance payments received from customers plus this accrued interest. Whichever accounting policy is adopted, it should be applied consistently.

In July 2015, the Interpretations Committee considered a question received regarding whether a purchaser should accrete interest on long-term prepayments by recognising interest income. The Interpretations Committee decided not to add this to its agenda (see Chapter 22 for further discussion). However, in doing so, it noted that 'when a financing component is identified in a long-term supply contract, that financing component should be accounted for separately'. Furthermore, although the question was considered in the context of IAS 2 (from the position of the purchaser), the Interpretations Committee noted that IFRS 15 includes a requirement that the financing component of a transaction be recognised separately for both prepayment and deferral of payment (see Chapter 30).[15] Furthermore, IFRS 15 indicates that a significant financing component may exist regardless of whether promise of financing is explicitly stated in the contract or is implied by the payment terms. *[IFRS 15.60]*.

A separate issue has also been discussed by the Interpretations Committee. An entity might pay or receive consideration in a foreign currency in advance of delivering goods or services in circumstances where the resulting liability is considered a non-monetary item. In late October 2015, the Interpretations Committee published a draft interpretation – *Foreign Currency Transactions and Advance Consideration* – to address an issue on whether the date of transaction, when applying IAS 21 – *The Effects of Changes in Foreign Exchange Rates* – is the date on which the consideration paid or received in advance is recognised or a subsequent date (or dates) when the goods or services are actually delivered. It proposes that, in general, the appropriate application of IAS 21 is to use the exchange rate at the date the advanced receipt is recognised, normally the payment date. At the time of writing, the Interpretations Committee's deliberations were complete. The interpretation was expected to be finalised by the end of 2016, with an anticipated effective date of 1 January 2018 (see Chapter 15 at 5.1.1).

5.1.5 Sale and repurchase agreements

Sale and repurchase agreements take many forms: the seller concurrently agrees to repurchase the same goods at a later date; the seller has a call option to repurchase; or the buyer has a put option to require the repurchase, by the seller, of the goods.

In a sale and repurchase agreement for an asset other than a financial asset, the terms of the agreement need to be analysed to ascertain whether, in substance, the seller has transferred the risks and rewards of ownership to the buyer and hence revenue is recognised. When the seller has retained the risks and rewards of ownership, even though legal title has been transferred, the transaction is a financing arrangement (e.g. a lease arrangement) and does not give rise to revenue. Sale and leaseback arrangements, repurchase agreements and options are discussed in Chapter 24 at 7. For a sale and repurchase agreement on a financial asset, IAS 39 (or IFRS 9) applies (see Chapter 51). *[IAS 18.IE5]*.

5.1.6 Instalment sales

The term 'instalment sales' refers to sales where the goods are delivered to the customer, but payment is made by a number of instalments that include financing charges. In such cases, revenue attributable to the sale price, exclusive of interest, is recognised at the date of sale. The sale price is the present value of the consideration, determined by discounting the instalments receivable at the imputed rate of interest. The interest element is recognised as revenue as it is earned, using the effective interest method set out in IAS 39. *[IAS 18.IE8]*. The application of the effective interest rate method is discussed in Chapter 49 at 3 (Chapter 50 at 3 if IFRS 9 is applied).

5.2 Receipt of initial fees

The practice that has developed in certain industries of charging an initial fee at the inception of a service, followed by subsequent service fees, can present revenue allocation problems. This is because it is not always altogether clear what the initial fee represents; it is necessary to determine what proportion, if any, of the initial fee has been earned on receipt and how much relates to the provision of future services. In some cases, large initial fees are paid for the provision of a service, while continuing fees are relatively small in relation to future services to be provided. If it is probable that the continuing fees will not cover the cost of the continuing services to be provided plus a reasonable profit, then a portion of the initial fee should be deferred over the period of the service contract, such that a reasonable profit is earned throughout the service period. *[IAS 18.IE18(b)]*. Accounting for initial fees has proved problematic and the Interpretations Committee has addressed the issue inconclusively – see 5.2.4 below.

5.2.1 Franchise fees

Franchise agreements between franchisors and franchisees can vary widely, both in complexity and in the extent to which various rights, duties and obligations are explicitly addressed. There is no standard form of franchise agreement that would dictate standard accounting practice for the recognition of all franchise fee revenue. Only a full understanding of the franchise agreement will reveal the substance of a particular arrangement so that the most appropriate accounting treatment can be determined. Nevertheless, the following are the more common areas that are likely to be addressed in any franchise agreement and be relevant to franchise fee revenue reporting:

(a) *rights transferred by the franchisor:* the agreement gives the franchisee the right to use the trade name, processes, know-how of the franchisor for a specified period of time or in perpetuity.

(b) *the amount and terms of payment of initial fees:* payment of initial fees (where applicable) may be fully or partially due in cash, and may be payable immediately, over a specified period or on the fulfilment of certain obligations by the franchisor.

(c) *amount and terms of payment of continuing franchise fees:* the franchisee will normally be required to pay a continuing fee to the franchisor – usually on the basis of a percentage of gross revenues.

(d) *services to be provided by the franchisor initially and on a continuing basis:* the franchisor will usually agree to provide a variety of services and advice to the franchisee, such as:
  - site selection;
  - the procurement of fixed assets and equipment – these may be either purchased by the franchisee, leased from the franchisor or leased from a third party (possibly with the franchisor guaranteeing the lease payments);
  - advertising;
  - training of franchisee's personnel;
  - inspecting, testing and other quality control programmes; and
  - bookkeeping services.

(e) *acquisition of equipment, stock and supplies*: the franchisee may be required to purchase these items either from the franchisor or from designated suppliers. Some franchisors manufacture products for sale to their franchisees, whilst others act as wholesalers.

The Illustrative Examples to IAS 18 includes a broad discussion of the receipt of franchise fees, stating that they are recognised as revenue on a basis that reflects the purpose for which the fees were charged. *[IAS 18.IE18]*. The standard states that the following methods of franchise fee recognition are appropriate:

- *Supplies of equipment and other tangible assets*: the amount (based on the fair value of the assets sold) is recognised as revenue when the items are delivered or title passes.
- *Supplies of initial and subsequent services*: fees for the provision of continuing services, whether part of the initial fee or a separate fee, are recognised as revenue as the services are rendered. When the separate fee does not cover the cost of continuing services together with a reasonable profit, part of the initial fee (sufficient to cover the costs of continuing services and to provide a reasonable profit on those services) is deferred and recognised as revenue as the services are rendered.

The franchise agreement may provide for the franchisor to supply equipment, inventories, or other tangible assets, at a price lower than that charged to others or a price that does not provide a reasonable profit on those sales. In these circumstances, part of the initial fee, sufficient to cover estimated costs in excess of that price and to provide a reasonable profit on those sales, is deferred and recognised over the period the goods are likely to be sold to the franchisee. The balance of an initial fee is recognised as revenue when performance of all the initial services and other obligations required of the franchisor (such as assistance with site selection, staff training, financing and advertising) has been substantially accomplished.

The initial services and other obligations under an area franchise agreement may depend on the number of individual outlets established in the area. In this case, the fees attributable to the initial services are recognised as revenue in proportion to the number of outlets for which the initial services have been substantially completed.

If the initial fee is collectible over an extended period and there is a significant uncertainty that it will be collected in full, the fee is recognised as cash instalments are received.

- *Continuing Franchise Fees*: fees charged for the use of continuing rights granted by the agreement, or for other services provided during the period of the agreement, are recognised as revenue as the services are provided or the rights used.
- *Agency Transactions*: transactions may take place between the franchisor and the franchisee that, in substance, involve the franchisor acting as agent for the franchisee. For example, the franchisor may order supplies and arrange for their delivery to the franchisee at no profit. Such transactions do not give rise to revenue. *[IAS 18.IE18]*.

In summary, it is necessary to break down the initial fee into its various components, (e.g. the fee for franchise rights, fee for initial services to be performed by the franchisor, fair value of tangible assets sold, etc.). The individual components may be recognised at different stages. The portion that relates to the franchise rights may be recognised in full immediately, unless part of it has to be deferred because the continuing fee does not cover the cost of continuing services to be provided by the franchisor plus a reasonable profit. In this case a portion of the initial fee should be deferred and recognised as services are provided. The fee for initial services should only be recognised when the services have been 'substantially performed' (it is unlikely that substantial performance will have been completed before the franchisee opens for business). The portion of the fee which relates to tangible assets may be recognised when title passes. If the collection period for the initial fees is extended and there is doubt as to the ultimate collectability, recognition of revenue should be deferred.

5.2.2 *Advance royalty or licence receipts*

The general guidance relating to licence fees and royalties states that 'fees and royalties paid for the use of an entity's assets (such as trademarks, patents, software, music copyright, record masters and motion picture films) are normally recognised in accordance with the substance of the agreement. As a practical matter, this may be on a straight line basis over the life of the agreement, for example, when a licensee has the right to use certain technology for a specified period of time'. *[IAS 18.IE20]*.

Therefore, under normal circumstances, the accounting treatment of advance royalty or licence receipts is straightforward. Under the accruals concept, the advance should be treated as deferred income when received and released to the profit and loss account when earned under the terms of the royalty/licence agreement. Bayer Aktiengesellschaft provides an example of such an approach:

Extract 29.11: Bayer Aktiengesellschaft (2014)

Notes to the Consolidated Financial Statements of the Bayer Group [extract]

4. Basic principles, methods and critical accounting estimates [extract]

NET SALES AND OTHER OPERATING INCOME [extract]

Some of the Bayer Group's revenues are generated on the basis of licensing agreements under which third parties have been granted rights to products and technologies. Payments received, or expected to be received, that relate to the sale or outlicensing of technologies or technological expertise are recognized in profit or loss as of the effective date of the respective agreement if all rights relating to the technologies and all obligations resulting from them have been relinquished under the contract terms. However, if rights to the technologies continue to exist or obligations resulting from them have yet to be fulfilled, the payments received are deferred accordingly. Upfront payments and similar non-refundable payments received under these agreements are recorded as other liabilities and recognized in profit or loss over the estimated performance period stipulated in the agreement.

Entities in the media sector often enter into arrangements in which one party receives upfront sums of a similar nature. For example, a music company may receive fees from another party for content that will be accessed via the internet (e.g. digital downloading or streaming of music). If so, the same considerations apply and revenue will be recognised when earned under the terms of the royalty or licence agreement. Often the terms of such arrangements call for the music company to make its current product (past recordings) available and may also require that future products be made available to the other party in exchange for an upfront payment (often called a 'minimum guarantee') that is recouped against future amounts owed the music company by the other party. This revenue will generally be recognised over the term of the arrangement. However, in cases where there is no expectation or obligation to provide future content (arrangement is for past recordings only) revenue would generally be recognised by the music company once its product has been made available to the other party. In the latter instance, the arrangement would likely be viewed as an in-substance sale, as discussed below.

Advance royalty or licence receipts have to be distinguished from assignments of rights that are, in substance, sales. The Illustrative Examples to IAS 18 explain in-substance sales as follows:

'An assignment of rights for a fixed fee or non-refundable guarantee under a non-cancellable contract which permits the licensee to exploit those rights freely and the licensor has no remaining obligations to perform is, in substance, a sale. An example is a licensing agreement for the use of software when the licensor has no obligations subsequent to delivery. Another example is the granting of rights to exhibit a motion picture film in markets where the licensor has no control over the distributor and expects to receive no further revenues from the box office receipts. In such cases, revenue is recognised at the time of sale.' *[IAS 18.IE20]*.

Software revenue recognition and the granting of rights to exhibit motion pictures are discussed at 5.6 and 5.10 below respectively, but in-substance sales are not restricted to these sectors. The extract from Bayer Aktiengesellschaft in Extract 29.11 above indicates that some arrangements in the pharmaceutical sector can be accounted for as in-substance sales.

Licence fees or royalties may be receivable only on the occurrence of a future event, in which case revenue will be recognised only when it is probable that the fee or royalty will be received. This is normally when the event has occurred. *[IAS 18.IE20]*.

This means that advance receipts may comprise a number of components that may require revenue to be recognised on different bases.

5.2.3 Financial service fees

IAS 18 includes a series of illustrative examples that relate to financial service fees, pointing out that the recognition of revenue for financial service fees depends on the purposes for which the fees are assessed and the basis of accounting for any associated financial instrument. *[IAS 18.IE14]*. The description of fees for financial services may not be indicative of the nature and substance of the services provided. Therefore, it is necessary to distinguish between fees that are an integral part of the effective interest rate of a financial instrument, fees that are earned as services are provided, and fees that are earned on the execution of a significant act. The definition of the effective interest rate in IAS 39 refers to IAS 18 and is discussed in Chapter 49 at 3 (IFRS 9 defines the effective interest rate without reference to IAS 18 or IFRS 15, see Chapter 50 at 3 if IFRS 9 is applied) and the Illustrative Examples to IAS 18 make this distinction as shown below. *[IAS 18.IE14]*.

5.2.3.A Fees that are an integral part of the effective interest rate of a financial instrument

Such fees are generally treated as an adjustment to the effective interest rate. However, when the financial instrument is measured at fair value with the change in fair value recognised in profit or loss the fees are recognised as revenue when the instrument is initially recognised. *[IAS 18.IE14(a)]*.

- *Origination fees received by the entity relating to the creation or acquisition of a financial asset other than one that under IAS 39 (or IFRS 9, if applied) is classified as a financial asset 'at fair value through profit or loss':* such fees may include compensation for activities, such as evaluating the borrower's financial condition, evaluating and recording guarantees, collateral and other security arrangements, negotiating the terms of the instrument, preparing and processing documents and closing the transaction. These fees are an integral part of generating an involvement with the resulting financial instrument and, together with the related transaction costs (as defined in IAS 39), are deferred and recognised as an adjustment to the effective interest rate.

Deutsche Bank discloses a policy that reflects this requirement:

> *Extract 29.12: Deutsche Bank Aktiengesellschaft (2014)*
>
> **Notes to the Consolidated Financial Statements** [extract]
>
> **01 – Significant Accounting Policies and Critical Accounting Estimates** [extract]
>
> **Interest, Commissions and Fees** [extract]
>
> **Commission and Fee Income** [extract] – The recognition of fee revenue (including commissions) is determined by the purpose of the fees and the basis of accounting for any associated financial instruments. If there is an associated financial instrument, fees that are an integral part of the effective interest rate of that financial instrument are included within the effective yield calculation. However, if the financial instrument is carried at fair value through profit or loss, any associated fees are recognized in profit or loss when the instrument is initially recognized, provided there are no significant unobservable inputs used in determining its fair value. Fees earned from services that are provided over a specified service period are recognized over that service period. Fees earned for the completion of a specific service or significant event are recognized when the service has been completed or the event has occurred.
>
> Loan commitment fees related to commitments that are not accounted for at fair value through profit or loss are recognized in commissions and fee income over the life of the commitment if it is unlikely that the Group will enter into a specific lending arrangement. If it is probable that the Group will enter into a specific lending arrangement, the loan commitment fee is deferred until the origination of a loan and recognized as an adjustment to the loan's effective interest rate.

- *Commitment fees received by the entity to originate a loan when the loan commitment is outside the scope of IAS 39 (IFRS 9, if applied):* if it is probable that the entity will enter into a specific lending arrangement and the loan commitment is not within the scope of IAS 39 (or IFRS 9, if applied), the commitment fee received is regarded as compensation for an ongoing involvement with the acquisition of a financial instrument. Together with the related transaction costs (as defined in IAS 39), the commitment fee is deferred and recognised as an adjustment to the effective interest rate. If the commitment expires without the entity making the loan, the fee is recognised as revenue on expiry. Loan commitments that are within the scope of IAS 39 (or IFRS 9, if applied) are accounted for as derivatives and measured at fair value.
- *Origination fees received on issuing financial liabilities measured at amortised cost:* these fees are an integral part of generating an involvement with a financial liability. When a financial liability is not classified as 'at fair value through profit or loss', the origination fees received are included, with the related transaction costs (as defined in IAS 39) incurred, in the initial carrying amount of the financial liability and recognised as an adjustment to the effective yield. An entity distinguishes fees and costs that are an integral part of the effective interest rate for the financial liability from origination fees and transaction costs relating to the right to provide services, such as investment management services.

5.2.3.B *Fees earned as services are provided*

The following are examples of situations where revenue is recognised over the period of the related service: *[IAS 18.IE14(b)]*

- *Fees charged for servicing a loan:* these fees are recognised as revenue as the services are provided.
- *Commitment fees to originate a loan when the loan commitment is outside the scope of IAS 39 (or IFRS 9, if applied):* if it is unlikely that a specific lending arrangement will be entered into and the loan commitment is outside the scope of IAS 39 (or IFRS 9, if applied), the commitment fee is recognised as revenue on a time-proportionate basis over the commitment period. Loan commitments that are within the scope of IAS 39 (or IFRS 9, if applied) are accounted for as derivatives and measured at fair value.
- *Investment management fees:* fees charged for managing investments are recognised as revenue as the services are provided. Incremental costs that are directly attributable to securing an investment management contract are recognised as an asset if they can be identified separately and measured reliably and if it is probable that they will be recovered. As in IAS 39, an incremental cost is one that would not have been incurred if the entity had not secured the investment management contract. The asset represents the entity's contractual right to benefit from providing investment management services and is amortised as the entity recognises the related revenue. If the entity has a portfolio of investment management contracts, it may assess their recoverability on a portfolio basis. Some financial services contracts involve both the origination of one or more financial instruments and the provision of investment management services. An example is a long-term monthly saving contract linked to the management of a pool of equity securities. The provider of the contract distinguishes the transaction costs relating to the origination of the financial instrument from the costs of securing the right to provide investment management services.

5.2.3.C *Fees that are earned on the execution of a significant act*

The fees are recognised as revenue when the significant act has been completed, as in the examples below. *[IAS 18.IE14(c)]*.

- *Commission on the allotment of shares to a client:* the commission is recognised as revenue when the shares have been allotted.
- *Placement fees for arranging a loan between a borrower and an investor:* the fee is recognised as revenue when the loan has been arranged.
- *Loan syndication fees:* a syndication fee received by an entity that arranges a loan and retains no part of the loan package for itself (or retains a part at the same effective interest rate for comparable risk as other participants) is compensation for the service of syndication. Such a fee is recognised as revenue when the syndication has been completed.

The following extracts from the financial statements of HSBC Holdings plc and Barclays PLC illustrate the approach followed in practice:

> *Extract 29.13: HSBC Holdings plc (2014)*
>
> **Notes on the Financial Statements** [extract]
>
> **1 Basis of preparation and significant accounting policies** [extract]
>
> **(m) Operating income** [extract]
>
> **Non-interest income and expense** [extract]
>
> **Fee income** is earned from a diverse range of services provided by HSBC to its customers. Fee income is accounted for as follows:
>
> – income earned on the execution of a significant act is recognised as revenue when the act is completed (for example, fees arising from negotiating or participating in the negotiation of a transaction for a third-party, such as the arrangement for the acquisition of shares or other securities);
>
> – income earned from the provision of services is recognised as revenue as the services are provided (for example, asset management, portfolio and other management advisory and service fees); and
>
> – income which forms an integral part of the effective interest rate of a financial instrument is recognised as an adjustment to the effective interest rate (for example, certain loan commitment fees) and recorded in 'Interest income'.

By contrast to the detail disclosed by HSBC Holdings plc, Barclays PLC provides summarised information about its accounting policies and refers directly to IAS 18:

> *Extract 29.14: Barclays PLC (2014)*
>
> **Notes to the financial statements** [extract]
>
> **4 Net fee and commission income** [extract]
>
> **Accounting for net fee and commission income**
>
> The Group applies IAS 18 *Revenue.* Fees and commissions charged for services provided or received by the Group are recognised as the services are provided, for example on completion of the underlying transaction.

5.2.4 *Initial and ongoing fees received by a fund manager*

Fund managers' activities generate a number of different fees and commissions, including the payment and receipt of initial fees followed by further payments and receipts (so-called 'trail' or 'trailing' commissions) and performance fees depending on the value of investments under management. Various parties have argued that the initial fee should be recognised as revenue when receivable, or alternatively that it should be spread over the estimated life of the investment.

These fees are typically paid by an investor who makes an investment in a fund, and they are non-refundable regardless of how long the investor chooses to remain invested. An investor may pay a non-refundable fee (e.g. 5% of the initial investment) on investing in a fund and ongoing fees (e.g. 1% of the fund assets per annum) for continuing fund management. Units in the fund may be sold by an adviser from an in-house sales department of the same group as the fund manager or by a separate financial adviser. If they are sold by a separate financial adviser, that adviser will retain the upfront fee (5% in our example). There are considerable difficulties in determining the appropriate accounting and they demonstrate a tension between different accounting standards that can lead to different accounting treatments.

The Interpretations Committee has considered on a number of occasions the appropriate accounting for initial fees and trail commissions and failed to come to any conclusion, most recently in July 2008.[16] The Interpretations Committee focused on the accounting treatment by the party that receives the fee, usually the financial adviser to the investor.

Some members of the Interpretations Committee viewed the fact that the upfront fee is the same, regardless of whether it is retained by a separate financial adviser (which is independent of the group that includes the fund manager and, therefore, has no further involvement with the transaction) or by an adviser from an in-house sales department of the same group as the fund manager, as evidence that upfront services were delivered and that the fair value of those services can be measured reliably. Other members noted that the receipt of a non-refundable initial fee does not, in itself, give evidence that an upfront service has been provided or that the fair value of the consideration paid in respect of any upfront services is equal to the initial fee received.[17]

Trailing commissions raise additional problems. They are paid periodically in arrears and the amounts payable vary with values (e.g. a percentage of funds under management). In July 2008, the Interpretations Committee again did not conclude whether there were future services, but revenue recognition remains an issue even if it is assumed that there are no services provided during the arrangement. Some argue that IAS 18 should be used; revenue ought to be taken when the conditions are met as two of the basic criteria for revenue recognition cannot be demonstrated at inception (i.e. that the amount of revenue can be measured reliably and that is probable that the economic benefits associated with the transaction will flow to the entity). *[IAS 18.14]*. Paragraph 20 of the Illustrative Examples notes, in the context of licence fees or royalty whose receipt is contingent on the occurrence of a future event, that revenue is recognised only when it is probable that the fee will be received, which is normally when the event has occurred. *[IAS 18IE.20]*. Others argue that the initial fee and trailing commissions together comprise the revenue earned by the financial advisor. The fair value can be estimated and ought to be recognised at inception, using IAS 39 (or IFRS 9, if applied) as the relevant accounting standard.

Similar arrangements can be found in many industries, not all of which are financial services. For example, 'revenue share' arrangements in telecommunications share many features: an upfront commission is paid to the distributor, who receives further sums if the customer remains on the same network tariff. The corresponding treatment of the cost to the operator is also debated: whether it is an upfront liability as defined by IAS 32 – *Financial Instruments: Presentation* – and expensed as incurred and measured using IAS 39 (or IFRS 9, if applied) principles, or whether it is recognised when incurred under IAS 37 – *Provisions, Contingent Liabilities and Contingent Assets.* It is a widespread and complex problem and the arrangements create issues for the entity making the payment as well as the recipient. The Interpretations Committee decided not to add this issue to its agenda.[18] While industry practice varies, some asset management groups take the view that some front-end fees are earned over the period in which it is expected that services will be provided and other fees earned as conditions are met.

> *Extract 29.15: Henderson Group plc (2015)*
>
> **2. Accounting policies** [extract]
>
> **2.1 Significant accounting policies** [extract]
>
> **Income recognition** [extract]
>
> Gross fee income
>
> Fee income includes management fees and performance fees (including earned carried interest), net of rebates. Management fees are recognised in the accounting period in which the associated investment management service is provided. Performance fees are recognised when the prescribed performance hurdles are achieved and it is probable that a fee will crystallise as a result.

In this extract, the company discloses its policy for performance fees. This is another area where practice varies, particularly in interim financial statements.

5.2.5 *Insurance agency commissions*

The critical event for the recognition of insurance agency commissions is the commencement of the policy. Hence, the Illustrative Examples to IAS 18 states that insurance agency commissions received or receivable that does not require the agent to render further service are recognised as revenue by the agent on the effective commencement or renewal dates of the related policies. However, when it is probable that the agent will be required to render further services during the life of the policy, the commission, or part thereof, is deferred and recognised as revenue over the period during which the policy is in force. *[IAS 18.IE13].*

Some insurance agency commissions have similar features to the investment fund initial fee and 'trail commissions' noted in the preceding section, so there is a similar degree of uncertainty regarding the recognition and measurement of revenue.

5.2.6 *Credit card fees*

It is common practice in some countries for credit card entities to levy a charge, payable in advance, on its cardholders. Although such charges may be seen as commitment fees for the credit facilities offered by the card, they clearly cover the many other services available to cardholders as well. Accordingly, we would suggest that the fees that are periodically charged to cardholders should be deferred and recognised on a straight-line basis over the period the fee entitles the cardholder to use the card.[19]

5.2.7 *Admission, entrance and membership fees*

The issue of entrance and membership fees is dealt with briefly in IAS 18's Illustrative Examples, which note that revenue recognition depends on the nature of the services provided. If the fee permits only membership, and all other services or products are paid for separately, or if there is a separate annual subscription, the fee is recognised as revenue when no significant uncertainty as to its collectability exists. If the fee entitles the member to services or publications to be provided during the membership period, or to purchase goods or services at prices lower than those charged to non-members, it is recognised on a basis that reflects the timing, nature and value of the benefits provided. *[IAS 18.IE17]*.

Admission fees to 'artistic performances' and other special events are recognised when the event takes place. Fees may be allocated pro-rata to the services provided if there is a subscription to a number of events. *[IAS 18.IE15]*.

5.3 Subscriptions to publications

Publication subscriptions are generally paid in advance and are non-refundable. As the publications will still have to be produced and delivered to the subscriber, the subscription revenue cannot be regarded as having been earned until production and delivery takes place. This is the approach adopted by IAS 18, which requires that revenue is recognised on a straight-line basis over the period in which the items are despatched when the items involved are of similar value in each time period. When the items vary in value from period to period, revenue is recognised on the basis of the sales value of the item despatched in relation to the total estimated sales value of all items covered by the subscription. *[IAS 18.IE7]*.

Reed Elsevier discloses its policy for recognising revenue from subscriptions as follows:

Extract 29.16: Reed Elsevier PLC and Reed Elsevier NV (2014)

FINANCIAL STATEMENTS AND OTHER INFORMATION [extract]

Accounting policies [extract]

Revenue

Revenue represents the invoiced value of sales less anticipated returns on transactions completed by performance, excluding customer sales taxes.

Revenues are recognised for the various categories as follows: subscriptions – on periodic despatch of subscribed product or rateably over the period of the subscription where performance is not measurable by despatch; transactional – on despatch or occurrence of the transaction; and advertising – on publication or over the period of online display.

Where sales consist of two or more independent components whose value can be reliably measured, revenue is recognised on each component as it is completed by performance, based on attribution of relative value.

5.4 Installation fees

Installation fees are recognised as revenue by reference to the stage of completion of the installation, unless they are incidental to the sale of a product in which case they are recognised when the goods are sold. *[IAS 18.IE10]*. However, in certain circumstances where the installation fees are linked to a contract for future services (for example, in the telecommunications industry: see 5.7 below) it may be more appropriate to defer such fees over either the contract period or the average expected life of the customer relationship, depending on the circumstances.

5.5 Advertising revenue

IAS 18's Illustrative Examples adopt the performance of the service as the critical event for the recognition of revenue derived from the rendering of advertising services. Consequently, media commissions are recognised when the related advertisement or commercial appears before the public. Production commissions are recognised by reference to the stage of completion of the project. *[IAS 18.IE12]*. The special case of barter transactions involving advertising services is addressed at 3.11 above.

German television corporation ProSiebenSat.1 Media's revenues are derived mainly from the sale of advertising time on television as disclosed in its accounting policy:

Extract 29.17: ProSiebenSat.1 Media AG (2014)

CONSOLIDATED FINANCIAL STATEMENTS [extract]

Notes [extract]

2 Accounting policies [extract]

Recognition of income and expenses [extract]

ProSiebenSat.1 Group's **revenues** are mainly advertising revenues derived from the sale of advertising time on television. Advertising revenues are presented net of volume discounts, agency commissions, cash discounts and value-added tax.

Revenues are realized at the time when the service is provided, or when risk is transferred to the customer. Accordingly revenues are recognized once the service has been provided, the principal risks and rewards of ownership have been transferred to the buyer, the amount of the proceeds can be measured reliably, an economic benefit from the sale is sufficiently probable and the costs associated with the sale can be measured reliably.

Specifically, television advertising revenues are considered realized when the associated advertising spots are broadcast. If advertising services are agreed in return for the acquisition of company stakes ("media for equity"), the obligation for broadcasting the agreed advertising spots is initially recognized as a credit entry (deferred revenues) to reflect the equity stake capitalized and realized as revenues when the agreed advertising spots are broadcast.

Revenues from pay TV activities are considered realized when the service is provided. Revenues from the sale of merchandising licenses are realized at the agreed guarantee amount as of the inception of the license for the customer. Revenues from the sale of programming assets and ancillary programming rights are considered realized when the license term for the purchaser of the programming asset has begun and broadcast-ready materials have been delivered to the purchaser. In addition, ProSiebenSat.1 Group receives a share in the technical activation fees that end customers pay to the respective providers for programs in HD quality. Revenues from the Group's HD business are realized when the TV signal is made available to the relevant platform partner.

5.6 Software revenue recognition

The accounting issues in the software services industry relate to when to recognise revenue from contracts to develop software, software licensing fees, customer support services and data services. However, these issues have not been specifically addressed in the IFRS literature. IAS 18 provides only one sentence of guidance: fees from the development of customised software are recognised as revenue by reference to the stage of completion of the development, including completion of services provided for post delivery service support. *[IAS 18.IE19]*. Because of the nature of the products and services involved, applying the general revenue recognition principles to software transactions can sometimes be difficult. As a result, software entities have used a variety of methods to recognise revenue, often producing significantly different financial results from similar transactions.

The problem of software revenue recognition was recognised in the US by the FASB and US SEC where industry-specific guidance was issued and is codified in ASC 985-605 – *Revenue Recognition – Software*. Whilst this US GAAP guidance is not mandatory for entities reporting under IFRS, because of the absence of detailed

IFRS requirements, many entities benefit by using the hierarchy in IAS 8 to develop their accounting policy looking to the US requirements. Set out below is a broad overview of the US GAAP software accounting guidance, but the detailed requirements are beyond the scope of this publication.

5.6.1 The basic principles of ASC 985-605

Software arrangements range from those that simply provide a licence for a single software product, to those that require significant production, modification or customisation of the software. Arrangements may also include multiple products or services. The codified guidance in ASC 985-605 states that if the arrangement does not require significant production, modification or customisation of existing software (i.e. contract accounting does not apply – see below), revenue should be recognised when all of the following criteria are met:[20]

- persuasive evidence of an arrangement exists;
- delivery has occurred (and no future elements to be delivered are essential to the functionality of the delivered element);
- the vendor's fee is fixed or determinable (the 'determinable' criterion relates to the issue as to whether the fee is subject to factors such as acceptance, refund, extended payment terms); and
- collectability is probable (i.e. whether the customer has the ability to pay and will pay).

With respect to 'persuasive evidence of an arrangement', ASC 985-605 requires that if a vendor has a customary practice of obtaining written contracts, revenues should not be recognised until the contract is signed by both parties.[21] Therefore, in the absence of a signed contract, revenue should not be recognised even if the software has been delivered and payment received.

ASC 985-605 states that the fee should be allocated to the various elements based on VSOE of fair value, regardless of any separate prices stated within the contract for each element.[22] It requires deferral of all revenue from multiple-element arrangements that are not accounted for using long-term contract accounting if there is insufficient VSOE to allocate revenue to the various elements of the arrangement.

The licence fee under an arrangement with multiple elements should be allocated to the elements according to VSOE. A portion of the licence fee should be allocated to elements that are deliverable on a when-and-if-available basis, whereby a vendor agrees to deliver software only when or if it becomes available while the agreement is in effect. However, absent such features and if all other criteria are met, this means that revenue may be recognised on entering into the arrangement in respect of a licence that allows the customer to use the software for a finite period.

If there is VSOE for the fair values of the undelivered elements in an arrangement, but not for one or more of the delivered elements in the arrangement, that fee can be recognised using the 'residual method'.[23] This means deducting the values for which there is VSOE from the total revenue and treating the remaining balance as the share of revenue for the element for which there is no VSOE. These requirements under US GAAP only apply to sales of computer software which are within the scope of ASC 985-605. The US

Chapter 29

GAAP requirements in respect of other arrangements were always different to these and were significantly amended in 2008; the revised requirements in ASC 605-25 are described at 4.3 above.

5.6.2 Accounting for software arrangements with multiple elements

Software arrangements may provide licences for many products or services, such as additional software products, upgrades/enhancements, rights to exchange or return software, post-contract customer support (PCS) or other services including elements deliverable only on a 'when-and-if-available' basis. These are referred to in US GAAP as 'multiple elements'.

We have noted at 3.6 above that in certain circumstances it is necessary to apply the recognition criteria to the separately identifiable components of a single transaction in order to reflect the substance of the transaction. *[IAS 18.13]*. However, IAS 18 does not establish more detailed criteria for identifying components and little guidance on the allocation of revenue to those elements. As such, an entity must use its judgement to select the most appropriate methodology, taking into consideration all relevant facts and circumstances.

Two of the most important rules in ASC 985-605 address discounts and the effects on revenue recognition of VSOE. If there is a discount, ASC 985-605 requires a proportionate amount to be applied to each element included in the arrangement based on relative fair values, without regard to the discount. No portion of the discount should be allocated to any upgrade rights and the residual method attributes the discount entirely to the delivered elements.[24]

If there is insufficient VSOE, ASC 985-605 provides that all revenue from the arrangement should be deferred until the earlier of the date on which such sufficient VSOE is obtained or all elements of the arrangement have been delivered.[25]

VSOE is a complex area and there are many detailed rules and requirements that expand the basic points made above and deal with areas, such as upgrades, PCS, extended payment terms, rights of return and services. It is not necessary under IFRS to demonstrate VSOE in order to allocate revenue on the basis of the fair value of individual components.

5.6.3 Accounting for arrangements which require significant production, modification or customisation of software

Where entities are running well-established computer installations with systems and configurations that they do not wish to change, off-the-shelf software packages are generally not suitable for their purposes. For this reason, some software entities will enter into a customer contract whereby they agree to customise a generalised software product to meet the customer's specific requirements. A simple form of customisation is to modify the system's output reports so that they integrate with the customer's existing management reporting system. However, customisation will often entail more involved obligations, e.g. having to translate the software so that it is able to run on the customer's specific hardware configuration, data conversion, system integration, installation and testing.

The question that arises, therefore, is the basis on which a software entity recognises revenue when it enters into a contract that involves significant obligations. It is our view that the principles provided in IAS 11 should be applied in this situation. This is supported by IAS 18, which states that the requirements of IAS 11 are generally applicable to the recognition of revenue and the associated expenses for a transaction involving the rendering of services. *[IAS 18.21]*. Accounting under IAS 11 is described in Chapter 23.

Consequently, where an entity is able to make reliable estimates as to the extent of progress towards completion of a contract, the related revenues and the related costs, and where the outcome of the contract can be assessed with reasonable certainty, the percentage-of-completion method should be applied.

One company that follows this approach is BT Group for their software solutions as illustrated in Extract 29.7 at 3.8 above.

Under ASC 985-605, if an arrangement to deliver software or a software system, either alone or together with other products or services, requires significant production, modification or customisation of software, the entire arrangement should be accounted for in accordance with ASC 605-35 – *Revenue – Construction-Type and Production-Type Contracts.*[26] This will not necessarily have any relevance when applying IFRS as the entity will need to determine the most appropriate accounting policy, which may be the principles in IAS 11.

5.7 Revenue recognition issues in the telecommunications sector

There are significant revenue recognition complexities that affect the telecommunications sector and about which IFRS is effectively silent. The complexities differ depending upon the type of telecommunications services being considered. Recognition issues may differ between fixed line (principally voice and data) services and wireless (principally mobile voice and data) services. In addition, customers may purchase elements of both as part of a bundled package.

A number of general factors underlie the accounting issues. For example: local regulatory laws may dictate the way business is done by the operators; there may be restrictions on the discounting of handsets; handsets may be branded in some countries but not in others; both branded and unbranded handsets may co-exist in the same country; and there may be varying degrees of price protection.

Connection and upfront fees are an issue for both fixed line and mobile operators.

5.7.1 Recording revenue for multiple service elements ('bundled offers')

IAS 18 notes that in some instances revenue is recognised for the separately identifiable components of a single transaction and refers specifically to situations where the selling price of a product includes an identifiable amount for subsequent servicing, in which case that amount is deferred and recognised as revenue over the period during which the service is performed. *[IAS 18.13]*. This is directly relevant to some aspects of multiple deliverable arrangements offerings, where customers are offered a 'bundle' of assets and services.

When a consumer enters into a mobile phone contract with a provider, the contract may be a package that includes a handset and various combinations of 'talktime', text messages and data allowances (internet access). The bundle may also include fixed line products, such as voice, video and broadband services.

Consumers may pay for their bundle of assets and services in a number of different ways: a payment for the handset (which may be discounted); connection charges related to activation of the handset; monthly fixed or usage-based payments; and prepayments by credit card or voucher. None of these payments may relate directly to the cost of the services being provided by the operator. Operators may also offer loyalty programmes that entail the provision of future services at substantially reduced prices.

As discussed at 3.6 above, as there is limited guidance within IFRS on the subject of multiple deliverable arrangements beyond the brief references in paragraph 13 of IAS 18 referred to above, many entities use the hierarchy in IAS 8 to consider any relevant US GAAP guidance. However, it needs to be made clear that, while US GAAP might provide useful guidance in this area, the IAS 8 hierarchy does not require entities to refer to it.

5.7.1.A Accounting for handsets and monthly service arrangements

Many of the mobile operators that provide handsets to customers who subscribe to service contracts do so at heavily discounted prices or even free of charge. Most telecommunications operators have an accounting policy under which handsets and airtime are separately identifiable components, but they apply a form of 'residual method' to the amount of revenue taken for the sale of the handset, recognising no more than the amount contractually receivable for it which may, *inter alia*, be equivalent to the so-called 'cash cap' under US GAAP, now in ASC 605-25-30-5. This states, '[t]he amount allocable to a delivered unit or units is limited to the amount that is not contingent upon the delivery of additional items or meeting other specified performance conditions (the non-contingent amount)'. An example of this is Orange's policy with respect to bundled offers:

Extract 29.18: Orange (2014)

Notes to the consolidated financial statements [extract]

Note 18 Accounting policies [extract]

18.3 Revenue [extract]

Revenue [extract]

Revenues from the Group's activities are recognized and presented as follows, in accordance with IAS 18:

Separable components of bundled offers [extract]

Numerous service offers on the Group's main markets include two components: an equipment component (e.g. a mobile handset) and a service component (e.g. a talk plan).

For the sale of multiple products or services, the Group analyzes all deliverables in the arrangement to determine whether they represent separate units of account. A delivered item (sold product or rendered service) is considered a separate unit of account if (i) it has value to the customer on a standalone basis and (ii) there is objective and reliable evidence of the fair value of the undelivered item(s). The total fixed or determinable amount of the arrangement is allocated to the separate units of account based on its relative fair value. However, when an amount allocated to a delivered item is contingent upon the delivery of additional items or meeting specified performance conditions, the amount allocated to that delivered item is limited to the non-contingent amount.

Hence, for bundled offers including a handset sold at a discounted price and a telecommunications service, revenue recognized for the handset sale is limited to the amount of the arrangement that is not contingent upon the rendering of telecommunication services, i.e. the amount paid by the customer for the handset: this amount is usually the amount paid at the delivery, or the discounted amounts paid over a one or two-year period with respect to the offers paid by instalments which have been more recently placed on the market.

In March 2006, the Interpretations Committee was asked whether:

- the contracts should be treated as comprising two separately identifiable components, i.e. the sale of a telephone and the rendering of telecommunication services, as discussed in paragraph 13 of IAS 18 (under which revenue would be attributed to each component); or
- the telephones should be treated as a cost of acquiring the new customer, with no revenue being attributed to them.

The Interpretations Committee did not take this issue on to its agenda; instead, it published the following 'rejection notice' in the March 2006 issue of IFRIC Update:

'The IFRIC acknowledged that the question is of widespread relevance, both across the telecommunications industry and, more generally, in other sectors. IAS 18 does not give guidance on what it means by "separately identifiable components" and practices diverge.

'However, the IFRIC noted that the terms of subscriber contracts vary widely. Any guidance on accounting for discounted handsets would need to be principles-based to accommodate the diverse range of contract terms that arise in practice. The IASB is at present developing principles for identifying separable components within revenue contracts. In these circumstances, the IFRIC does not believe it could reach a consensus on a timely basis. The IFRIC, therefore, decided not to take the topic onto its agenda.'[27] The new standard, IFRS 15, is discussed further in Chapter 30.

The Interpretations Committee did not publish its views on how (or whether) revenue should be attributed to each component if the transaction is treated as falling under paragraph 13 of IAS 18. However, although IAS 18 requires revenue to be measured at its fair value, it does not prescribe a method of allocation. Usually, an allocation of revenue based on relative fair values would be considered an appropriate basis, but this is not an explicit requirement and there are other bases allowed in IAS 18 and in IFRS more generally. However, as discussed at 3.6 above an entity must use its judgement to select the most appropriate methodology, taking into consideration all relevant facts and circumstances. The entity should ensure that the resulting allocation is consistent with IAS 18's objective to measure revenue at the fair value of the consideration.

5.7.1.B 'Free' services

'Free' services are often included in the monthly service arrangement for contract subscribers as an additional incentive to encourage subscribers to sign up for a fixed contract period, typically one or two years.

'Free' services can either be provided upfront as inclusive services for a fixed monthly fee, or as an incentive after a specific threshold has been exceeded, intended to encourage subscribers to spend more than their specified amount.

As a result, one of the challenges for mobile operators is the accounting treatment for the 'free' service period. In our opinion, the total amount that is contractually required to be paid by the customer is recognised as revenue rateably over the entire service period, including the period in which the 'free' services are provided.

The following example illustrates the accounting for free minutes granted at subscription date by a mobile operator to a subscriber:

Example 29.1: Accounting for free minutes

An operator enters into a service contract with a customer for a period of 12 months. Under the contract specifications, the customer is offered for the first 2 months 60 free minutes talk time per month and for the remaining 10 months of the contract the customer will pay a fixed fee of €30 per month for 60 minutes of communication per month. The operator considers the recoverability of the amounts due under the contract from the customer to be probable.

In our view, since the free minutes offer is linked to the non-cancellable contract, the fee receivable for the non-cancellable contract is spread over the entire contract term.

Consequently, the fixed fee of €300 (€30 × 10 months) to be received from the subscriber would be recognised on a straight line basis over the 12 month contract period, being the stage of completion of the contract. The operator, therefore, would recognise €25 each month over the twelve month period (€30 × 10/12 = €25).

Orange's accounting policy is as follows.

Extract 29.19: Orange (2014)

Notes to the consolidated financial statements [extract]

Note 18 Accounting policies [extract]

18.3 Revenue [extract]

Revenue [extract]

Promotional offers and loyalty programs [extract]

Revenue is stated net of discounts. With respect to certain commercial offers where customers are offered a free service over a certain period in exchange for signing up for a fixed period (time-based incentives), the total revenue generated under the contract may be spread over the fixed non-cancellable period.

5.7.1.C Connection and upfront fees

Connection fees can be a feature of both the wireless (mobile) and the fixed line activities.

When the mobile telecoms industry was in its infancy, upfront costs such as connection fees, contract handling fees, registration fees, fees for changing plans etc., were commonly charged by operators. Such charges have been phased out over the years and are no longer a common feature in a number of markets.

Nevertheless, there are still occasions in which a telecommunications operator charges its subscribers a one-time non-refundable fee for connection to its network. The contract for telecommunications services between the operator and the subscriber has either a finite or an indefinite life and includes the provision of the network connection and ongoing telecommunications services. The direct and incremental costs incurred by the operator in providing the connection service are primarily the technician's salary and related benefits; this technician provides both connection and physical installation services at the same time.

In such cases, the connection service and the telecommunications services have to be analysed in accordance with their economic substance in order to determine whether they should be combined or separated for revenue recognition purposes. When the connection transaction is bundled with the service arrangement in such a way that the commercial effect cannot be understood without reference to the two transactions as a whole, the connection fee revenue should be recognised over the expected term of the customer relationship under the arrangement which generated the connection. In our view, the expected term of the customer relationship may not necessarily be the contract period, but may be the estimated average life of the customer relationship, provided that this can be estimated reliably.

Vodafone Group is an example of a company that defers customer connection fees over the period in which services are expected to be provided to the customer, another way of describing the expected life of the customer relationship.

Extract 29.20: Vodafone Group Plc (2014)

Notes to the consolidated financial statements [extract]

2. Segmental analysis [extract]

Accounting policies [extract]

Revenue [extract]

Customer connection revenue is recognised together with the related equipment revenue to the extent that the aggregate equipment and connection revenue does not exceed the fair value of the equipment delivered to the customer. Any customer connection revenue not recognised together with related equipment revenue is deferred and recognised over the period in which services are expected to be provided to the customer.

Charging fees remains relatively common for connection to a fixed telephone line. Although connection fees are commonly recognised over the contract period, upfront recognition of the non-refundable fee may be possible if there is a clearly demonstrable separate service and it is provided at the inception of the contract.

The requirements provided within IFRIC 18, which is explained at 5.14 below, may be of some help in identifying what services have been provided in return for the upfront fee, but the interpretation is not normally directly relevant because the upfront fee is not used to construct PP&E required for connection as envisaged under paragraph 6 of IFRIC 18. Nevertheless, it is a common practice amongst fixed line operators to defer activation revenue, as illustrated by the two relevant policies of Telkom SA SOC, which are similar to Vodafone Group's policy on customer connection fees included above:

Extract 29.21: Telkom SA SOC Limited (2015)

NOTES TO THE CONSOLIDATED ANNUAL FINANCIAL STATEMENTS [extract]

2. SIGNIFICANT ACCOUNTING POLICIES [extract]

2.3 Summary of significant accounting policies [extract]

Retail voice [extract]

The group provides telephone and data communication services under post-paid and pre-paid payment arrangements. Revenue includes fees for installation and activation, which are deferred over the expected customer relationship period. Costs incurred on first-time installations that form an integral part of the network are capitalised and depreciated over the expected average customer relationship period. All other installation and activation costs are expensed as incurred.

Deferred revenue and expenses

Activation revenue and costs are deferred and recognised systematically over the expected duration of the customer relationship because it is considered to be part of the customers' ongoing rights to telecommunication services and the operator's continuing involvement. Any excess of the costs over revenues is expensed immediately.

5.7.2 'Gross versus net' issues

The difficulty of deciding whether to record revenue gross or net is pervasive in the telecommunications sector. The problem occurs because of the difficulty in deciding whether the parties involved in any particular agreement are acting as principal or agent. IAS 18 states that 'in an agency relationship, the gross inflows of economic benefits include amounts collected on behalf of the principal and which do not result in increases in equity for the entity. The amounts collected on behalf of the principal are not revenue. Instead, revenue is the amount of commission'. *[IAS 18.8]*.

There is guidance in IAS 18's Illustrative Examples to help determine whether an entity is acting as a principal or as an agent. *[IAS 18.IE21]*. This guidance is discussed at 3.3 above. Despite this guidance, it can still be very challenging to make this determination in many telecoms scenarios. A frequent arrangement is where there is data content provided by third parties that is subject to a separate provider agreement.

Content, such as music, navigation and other downloads such as 'apps' can either be included in the monthly price plan or purchased separately on an *ad hoc* basis. Operators can either develop the content in-house or use third party providers to offer a range of items to their subscribers, with charges based either on duration (news, traffic updates, etc.) or on quantity (number of ringtones, games, etc.).

The issue is whether the operator should report the content revenue based on the gross amount billed to the subscriber because it has earned revenue from the sale of the services or the net amount retained (i.e. the amount billed to the subscriber less the amount paid to a supplier) because it has only earned a commission or fee. That is, whether the substance of the transaction with the supplier one of buying and on-selling goods or selling goods on consignment (i.e. an agency relationship). The two most important considerations of those listed in IAS 18's Illustrative Examples paragraph 21, for most of these arrangements, are:

- whether the operator has the primary responsibility for providing the services to the customer or for fulfilling the order, for example by being responsible for the acceptability of the services ordered or purchased by the customer; and
- whether it has discretion in establishing prices, either directly or indirectly, for example by providing additional goods or services.

Inventory risk is unlikely to be relevant for a service provision and credit risk may be only a weak indicator as the amounts are individually small and may be paid to access the download.

Therefore, if the content is an own-brand product or service then the revenue receivable from subscribers should be recorded as revenue by the operator, and the amounts payable to the third party content providers should be recorded as costs.

By contrast, if the content is a non-branded product/service that is merely using the mobile operator's network as a medium to access its subscriber base, then the amounts receivable from subscribers should not be recorded as revenue. The operator's revenue will comprise only the commissions receivable from the content providers for the use of the operator's network.

Orange discloses whether it is an agent or principal based on who has responsibility for content and setting the price to subscribers, as follows:

> *Extract 29.22: Orange (2014)*
>
> **Notes to the consolidated financial statements** [extract]
>
> **Note 18 Accounting policies** [extract]
>
> **18.3 Revenue** [extract]
>
> **Revenue** [extract]
>
> **Service revenue** [extract]
>
> The gross or net accounting for revenue sharing arrangements and supply of content depends on the analysis of the facts and circumstances surrounding each transaction. Thus, revenue is recognized on a net basis when the provider is responsible for supplying the content provided to the end-customer and for setting the price. This principle is applied notably for revenue-sharing arrangements (Audiotel, premium rate number, special numbers, etc.) and for revenues from the sale or supply of content (audio, video, games, etc.) through the Group's various communications systems (mobile, PC, TV, fixed line, etc.).

5.7.3 Accounting for roll-over minutes

Where an operator offers a subscriber a finite number of call minutes for a fixed amount per period with the option of rolling over any unused minutes, the question arises as to how the operator should account for the unused minutes that the subscriber holds. The operator is not obliged to reimburse the subscriber for unused minutes, but is obliged (normally subject to a ceiling) to provide the accumulated unused call minutes to the subscriber until the end of the contract, after which they expire.

In such cases, revenue is recognised at the time the minutes are used. Any minutes unused at the end of each month should be recognised as deferred revenue.

However, in some instances, the operator has relevant and reliable evidence that shows that a portion of those unused minutes will not be used before the expiration of the validity period. In that case, the operator could consider an alternative revenue recognition policy that would take account of the probability of unused minutes at the end of the validity period in the computation of the revenue per minute used by the subscriber. This would result in allocating a higher amount of revenue per minute used.

When the validity period expires, any remaining balance of unused minutes would be recognised as revenue immediately, since the obligation of the operator to provide the contractual call minutes is extinguished.

5.7.4 Accounting for the sale of pre-paid calling cards

Prepaid cards are normally sold by an operator either through its own sales outlet or through distributors. The communication credit sold with the cards has an expiry date that varies from one operator to another, although, in certain limited jurisdictions, there is no expiry date. For example, prepaid cards may be sold with an initial credit of €10 covering 60 minutes of communication and the credit has a validity period of 90 days from the date of activation. If not used within this period, the credit is lost.

When the cards are sold through distributors, the distributor is usually obliged to sell the cards to the customers at the face value of the card. On sale of the card, the distributor pays the operator the face value less a commission. The distributor has a right to return unsold cards to the operator. Once the distributor has sold the cards, it has no further obligation to the operator.

In our view, when an operator sells calling cards directly, revenue is recognised at the time the minutes are used. Any minutes unused at the end of each month should be recognised as deferred revenue. However, if the operator has relevant and reliable evidence that shows that a portion of those unused minutes will not be used before the expiration of the validity period then it could consider an alternative revenue recognition policy. This would take account of the probability of unused minutes at the end of the validity period in the computation of the revenue per minute recognised as the minutes are used by the customer.

When an operator sells calling cards through a distributor, the revenue is required to be recognised based on the substance of the arrangement with the distributor.

It is usually the case that the distributor is in substance acting as an agent for the operator. The revenue associated with the sale of the calling card is recognised when the subscriber uses the minutes. The difference between the card's usage value, which is charged to the subscriber, and the amount paid to the operator is the distributor's commission.

In our view, unless the distributor is also an operator or the calling card could be used on any operator's network (which is rare), it would be difficult to conclude that the distributor is the principal in the arrangement with the subscriber, because the distributor would not have the capacity to act as the principal under the terms of the service provided by the calling card to the subscriber (see 3.3 and 5.7.2 above).

5.8 Excise taxes and goods and services taxes: recognition of gross versus net revenues

Many jurisdictions around the world raise taxes that are based on components of sales or production. These include excise taxes and goods and services or value added taxes. In some cases, these taxes are, in effect, collected by the entity from customers on behalf of the taxing authority. In other cases, the taxpayer's role is more in the nature of principal than agent. The regulations (e.g. excise taxes in the tobacco and drinks industries) differ significantly from one country to another. The practical accounting issue that arises concerns the interpretation of paragraph 8 of IAS 18: should excise taxes and goods and services taxes be deducted from revenue (net presentation) or included in the cost of sales and, therefore, revenue (gross presentation)? *[IAS 18.8]*.

Clearly, the appropriate accounting treatment will depend on the particular circumstances. In determining whether gross or net presentation is appropriate, the entity needs to consider whether it is acting in a manner similar to that of an agent or principal.

We believe that there are two main indicators that should be considered when determining whether the entity is acting as principal or agent. An additional two indicators relating to the nature of the tax itself should also be considered to determine whether a net or gross presentation is applicable. No one indicator is considered to be conclusive on its own. These indicators are:

Acting as Principal or Agent:

A. whether the entity is exposed to financial risk in relation to the tax (e.g. non-recovery of the tax from the customers); and

B. whether the entity has an obligation to change prices in line with changes in the rate or amount of the tax.

Nature of Taxes:

C. basis of calculation – whether the tax is levied on sales proceeds or on units of production; and

D. point of payment – whether the entity becomes liable to pay the tax at the point of sale or at the time of production.

Whether an entity is acting as principal or agent is a matter of judgement that depends on the relevant facts and circumstances of the particular tax in the country concerned. The factors that should be taken into account in determining gross or net treatment are summarised in the following table:

Indicator	**Circumstances indicating:**	
	<u>net</u> revenue recognition	**<u>gross</u> revenue recognition**
A Whether the entity is exposed to financial risk in relation to the tax (e.g. non-recovery of the tax from the customers): (i) who benefits from any short term fluctuations? (ii) who bears the inventory risk? (iii) who bears the credit risk?	• The tax is refundable in the event that stock becomes damaged or obsolete, or receivables are not collectible.	• The entity will not be refunded for the tax paid if the stock is not sold or the receivables are not collected.
B Whether the entity has an obligation to change prices in line with changes in the rate or amount of the tax.	• The tax is included in the selling price and the selling price can never fall below taxes paid. • The entity will change or is required (by law) to change the price of the product to reflect the tax increases but is unable to increase the price above tax increases. • The entity will reduce or is required (by law) to reduce the price of the product to reflect tax decreases.	• The entity has the discretion to determine the final selling price of the products. It bears the tax and makes the decision whether to pass the tax (entire/a portion of it) to the consumer.

Indicator	Circumstances indicating:	
	net revenue recognition	**gross revenue recognition**
C Basis of calculation – Whether the tax is levied on sales proceeds or on units of production.	• The tax is computed based on the sales price or units sold rather than producing activities.	• The tax is computed based on the number of units produced rather than sold. This suggests that it is a type of production tax.
D Point of payment – Whether the entity becomes liable to pay the tax at the point of sale or at the time of production. (This is likely to be a weak indicator that should not be considered without additional factors.)	• The tax is payable to the government only when the sale has occurred or the entity is required to make payment to the government at a date relatively close to the point of sale. The closer the payment is to the point of sale the more likely it is that the tax is similar to a sales tax.	• The tax is payable to the government when the unit is produced or the entity is required to make payment to the government at a date relatively close to the point of production. The closer the payment is to the point of production the more likely it is that the tax is a production tax.

It is important that entities disclose the policies that they have adopted in accounting for duty. BP is an example of a company that provides disclosure in this area:

Extract 29.23: BP p.l.c. (2014)

Notes on financial statements [extract]

1. Significant accounting policies, judgements, estimates and assumptions [extract]

Customs duties and sales taxes

Customs duties and sales taxes which are passed on to customers are excluded from revenues and expenses. Assets and liabilities are recognized net of the amount of customs duties or sales tax except:

- Where the customs duty or sales taxes incurred on a purchase of goods and services is not recoverable from the taxation authority, in which case the customs duty or sales tax is recognized as part of the cost of acquisition of the asset.
- Receivables and payables are stated with the amount of customs duty or sales tax included.

The net amount of sales tax recoverable from, or payable to, the taxation authority is included within receivables or payables in the balance sheet.

5.9 Sales incentives

IAS 18 states that 'the amount of revenue arising on a transaction is usually determined by agreement between the entity and the buyer or user of the asset. It is measured at the fair value of the consideration received or receivable taking into account the amount of any trade discounts and volume rebates allowed by the entity'. *[IAS 18.10]*. Consequently, where an entity provides sales incentives to a customer when entering into a contract these are usually treated as rebates and will be included in the measurement of (i.e. deducted from) revenue when the goods are delivered or services provided.

Where the incentive is in the form of cash, revenue will be recognised at a reduced amount taking into account the rebate factor from the cash incentive. Depending on when the incentive is paid, this may create a liability (i.e. a rebate to be paid at a subsequent date).

Any cash consideration, including but not limited to, consideration characterised as a sales incentive given by a seller to a buyer is presumed to be a reduction of the selling prices of the supplier's goods or services. That presumption is overcome, only if the supplier receives, or will receive, an identifiable benefit (goods or services) in exchange for the consideration. 'Identifiable' means separate from the buyer's purchase of the seller's goods or services such that the seller could have entered into a separate transaction with a party other than the buyer in order to receive that benefit. However, in most of these types of arrangements (i.e. a cash incentive is offered to the buyer) the seller is not receiving any identifiable benefit from the seller. The timing of the corresponding reduction of revenue should reflect the pattern in which goods or services are sold to the buyer.

Non-cash incentives take a variety of forms. Where the seller provides 'free postage' this would impose an additional cost on the entity, but would not impact revenue. Where the seller provides free delivery and undertakes this service itself, this would either be a separate component of a multiple element transaction to which some of the transaction price should be allocated, or more commonly, where risks and rewards of the good are not transferred to the customer until delivery, the total transaction price will not be recognised until that point.

Non-cash incentives may comprise products or services from third parties. If these are provided as part of a sales transaction they will represent separate components of a multiple element transaction to which revenue must be attributed. The seller will need to determine whether they are acting as agent or principal for that element of the transaction. If the seller is acting as agent and has no further obligations in respect of that component then it will immediately recognise the margin on that element as its own revenue. If acting as principal it will recognise the full transaction price as revenue but it will need to defer any element that relates to the provision of the good or service by the third party if that party still needs to provide that good or service (for example where the incentive is in the form of a voucher that is redeemable by the third party at a later date).

Some of these non-cash incentives that are issued as part of a sales transaction will fall under the scope of IFRIC 13 (see 5.15 below). However even where it may be argued that they do not strictly fall under that Interpretation, the main principle of IFRIC 13 (whereby fair value is attributed to the incentive and deferred from revenue until the related obligation is fulfilled) will still be applicable.

If the sales incentive is in the form of a voucher that is issued independently of a sales transaction (e.g. one that entitles the customer to money off if they choose to make a purchase) there will be no impact on revenue. The entity will need to assess whether this results in an onerous contract that would need to be provided for under IAS 37.

Prompt settlement discounts (for example, customers are offered a reduction of 5% of the selling price for paying an invoice within 7 days instead of the usual 60 days) should be estimated at the time of sale and deducted from revenues.

Sanofi is an example of a company that provides various forms of sales incentives to its customers:

Extract 29.24: Sanofi(2014)

NOTES TO THE CONSOLIDATED FINANCIAL STATEMENTS

YEAR ENDED DECEMBER 31, 2014 [extract]

B/ Summary of significant accounting policies [extract]

B.14. REVENUE RECOGNITION

Revenue arising from the sale of goods is presented in the income statement under ***Net sales***. Net sales comprise revenue from sales of pharmaceutical products, active ingredients, vaccines and animal health products, net of sales returns, of customer incentives and discounts, and of certain sales-based payments paid or payable to the healthcare authorities.

Revenue is recognized when all of the following conditions have been met: the risks and rewards of ownership have been transferred to the customer; the Group no longer has effective control over the goods sold; the amount of revenue and costs associated with the transaction can be measured reliably; and it is probable that the economic benefits associated with the transaction will flow to the Group, in accordance with IAS 18 (Revenue). In particular, the contracts between SanofiPasteur and government agencies specify conditions for the supply and acceptance of batches of vaccine; revenue is recognized when those conditions are met.

The Group offers various types of price reductions on its products. In particular, products sold in the United States are covered by various governmental programs (such as Medicare and Medicaid) under which products are sold at a discount. Rebates are granted to healthcare authorities, and under contractual arrangements with certain customers. Some wholesalers are entitled to chargeback incentives based on the selling price to the end customer, under specific contractual arrangements. Cash discounts may also be granted for prompt payment.

Returns, discounts, incentives and rebates, as described above, are recognized in the period in which the underlying sales are recognized as a reduction of sales revenue.

These amounts are calculated as follows:

- Provisions for chargeback incentives are estimated on the basis of the relevant subsidiary's standard sales terms and conditions, and in certain cases on the basis of specific contractual arrangements with the customer. They represent management's best estimate of the ultimate amount of chargeback incentives that will eventually be claimed by the customer.
- Provisions for rebates based on attainment of sales targets are estimated and accrued as each of the underlying sales transactions is recognized.
- Provisions for price reductions under Government and State programs, largely in the United States, are estimated on the basis of the specific terms of the relevant regulations or agreements, and accrued as each of the underlying sales transactions is recognized.
- Provisions for sales returns are calculated on the basis of management's best estimate of the amount of product that will ultimately be returned by customers. In countries where product returns are possible, Sanofi operates a returns policy that allows the customer to return products within a certain period either side of the expiry date (usually 6 months before and 12 months after the expiry date). The provision is estimated on the basis of past experience of sales returns.

> The Group also takes account of factors such as levels of inventory in its various distribution channels, product expiry dates, information about potential discontinuation of products, the entry of competing generics into the market, and the launch of over-the-counter medicines.
>
> In each case, the provisions are subject to continuous review and adjustment as appropriate based on the most recent information available to management.
>
> The Group believes that it has the ability to measure each of the above provisions reliably, using the following factors in developing its estimates:
>
> - the nature and patient profile of the underlying product;
> - the applicable regulations and/or the specific terms and conditions of contracts with governmental authorities, wholesalers and other customers;
> - historical data relating to similar contracts, in the case of qualitative and quantitative rebates and chargeback incentives;
> - past experience and sales growth trends for the same or similar products;
> - actual inventory levels in distribution channels, monitored by the Group using internal sales data and externally provided data;
> - the shelf life of the Group's products; and
> - market trends including competition, pricing and demand.
>
> Non-product revenues, mainly comprising royalty income from license arrangements that constitute ongoing operations of the Group (see Note C.), are presented in ***Other revenues.***

5.10 Film exhibition and television broadcast rights

Revenue received from the licensing of films for exhibition at cinemas and on television should be recognised in accordance with the general recognition principles discussed in this chapter.

Contracts for the television broadcast rights of films normally allow for multiple showings within a specific period; these contracts usually expire either on the date of the last authorised telecast, or on a specified date, whichever occurs first. Rights for the exhibition of films at cinemas are generally sold either on the basis of a percentage of the box office receipts or for a flat fee.

IAS 18 states that an assignment of rights for a fixed fee or non-refundable guarantee under a non-cancellable contract which permits the licensee to exploit those rights freely and the licensor has no remaining obligations to perform is, in substance, a sale. When a licensor grants rights to exhibit a motion picture film in markets where it has no control over the distributor and expects to receive no further revenues from the box office receipts, revenue is recognised at the time of sale. *[IAS 18.IE20]*.

Therefore, it is our view that the revenue from the sale of broadcast, film or exhibition rights may be recognised in full upon commencement of the licence period provided the following conditions are met:

(a) a contract has been entered into;

(b) the film is complete and available for delivery;

(c) there are no outstanding performance obligations, other than having to make a copy of the film and deliver it to the licensee; and

(d) collectability is reasonably assured.

This applies even if the rights allow for multiple showings within a specific period for a non-refundable flat fee and the contract expires either on the date of the last authorised telecast, or on a specified date, whichever occurs first. The sale can be recognised even though the rights have not yet been used by the purchaser. We do not believe it appropriate to recognise revenue prior to the date of commencement of the licence period since it is only from this date that the licensee is able to freely exploit the rights of the licence and hence has the rewards of ownership. *[IAS 18.14(a)]*.

When the licensor is obliged to perform any significant acts or provide any significant services subsequent to delivery of the film to the licensee – for example to promote the film – it would be appropriate to recognise revenue as the acts or services are performed (or, as a practical matter, on a straight-line basis over the period of the licence).

Rights for the exhibition of a film at cinemas may be granted on the basis of a percentage of the box office receipts, in which case revenue should be recognised as the entitlement to revenue arises based on box office receipts.

If the fees only become payable when the box office receipts have exceeded a minimum level, IAS 18 suggests that revenue should not be recognised until the minimum level has been achieved. It states that revenue that is contingent on the occurrence of a future event is recognised only when it is probable that the fee or royalty will be received, in this case normally when the event has occurred. *[IAS 18.IE20]*.

In this instance, the requirement in IAS 18 supports deferral until the contingency has occurred. This differs from the arguments based on IAS 32, described in 5.2.4 above in the context of initial and ongoing fees, in which the full amount can be recognised at inception and the contingency affects measurement.

5.11 The disposal of property, plant and equipment

IAS 16 requires that the gain or loss arising from the derecognition of an item of PP&E be included in profit or loss when the item is derecognised, unless IAS 17 requires otherwise on a sale and leaseback. IAS 16 prohibits recognition of any such gain as revenue, *[IAS 16.68]*, except in the case of entities that are in the business of renting and selling the same asset.

An item is disposed of when the criteria in IAS 18 for recognising revenue from the sale of goods are met (see 3.7 above). IAS 17 applies to disposal by a sale and leaseback. *[IAS 16.69]*. IAS 18's criteria are essentially built around the transfer of significant risks and rewards of ownership. *[IAS 18.14-16]*. Although, IAS 18 states that in most cases the transfer of the risks and rewards of ownership coincide with the transfer of legal title, it acknowledges that legal title sometimes passes at a different time. *[IAS 18.15]*.

There are two significant points in the earning process that could, depending on the circumstances of the sale, be considered to be the critical event for recognition. The first point is on exchange of contracts, at which time the vendor and purchaser are both bound by a legally enforceable contract of sale. The second possible point of recognition is on completion of the contract, when legal title and beneficial ownership pass.

It is possible that the earnings process is sufficiently complete to permit recognition to take place on exchange of contracts. This is because the selling price would have been established, all material related expenses would have been ascertained and, usually, no significant uncertainties would remain. If, however, on exchange of contracts there are doubts that the sale will ultimately be completed, recognition should take place on the receipt of the sales proceeds at legal completion.

The issue arises most commonly with regard to the sale of real estate, but is not restricted to it. The two approaches had previously been supported by the Illustrative Examples to IAS 18, which stated that, in the case of real estate sales, revenue is normally recognised when legal title passes to the buyer; however, at the same time, it acknowledged that recognition might take place before legal title passes, provided that the seller has no further substantial acts to complete under the contract. *[IAS 18(2008).IE9]*. This paragraph was deleted with the introduction of IFRIC 15 (discussed at 5.12 below).

The evidence is that some entities delay profit recognition until legal completion, while others recognise profit before completion when the significant risks and returns have been transferred to the buyer. In our view, both approaches are acceptable and not affected by the amendment to IAS 18. Care must be taken before recognising profits before completion and it may be that in many cases, legal completion is the more appropriate point at which to recognise revenue. Whichever policy is adopted, it is important to ensure that all of the general conditions in IAS 18 have been met (see 3.7 above).

The two approaches are illustrated in the following extracts:

Extract 29.25: Barratt Developments PLC (2014)

Accounting Policies [extract]

Revenue

Revenue is recognised at legal completion in respect of the total proceeds of building and development. An appropriate proportion of revenue from construction contracts is recognised by reference to the stage of completion of contract activity. Revenue is measured at the fair value of consideration received or receivable and represents the amounts receivable for the property, net of discounts and VAT. The sale proceeds of part-exchange properties are not included in revenue.

Interest income is accrued on a time basis, by reference to the principal outstanding and at the effective interest rate applicable.

Extract 29.26: Intu Properties plc (2014)

Notes to the accounts [extract]

2 Accounting policies – Group and Company [extract]

Revenue recognition [extract]

– trading property income

Revenue on the sale of trading property is recognised when the significant risks and rewards of ownership have been transferred to the buyer. This will normally take place on exchange of contracts.

The gain or loss on derecognition of an item of PP&E is the difference between the net disposal proceeds, if any, and the carrying amount of the item. *[IAS 16.71]*. This means that any revaluation surplus relating to the asset disposed of is transferred within equity to retained earnings when the asset is derecognised and not reflected in profit or loss.

The consideration receivable on disposal of an item of PP&E is recognised initially at its fair value. If payment for the item is deferred, the consideration received is recognised initially at the cash price equivalent. In accordance with IAS 18, the difference between the nominal amount of the consideration and the cash price equivalent is recognised as interest revenue reflecting the effective yield on the receivable (see 3.5 above). *[IAS 16.72]*.

IFRS 5 provides additional requirements for assets held for disposal. These requirements include measurement rules, which affect the measurement of the amount of the gain on disposal to be recognised. These are discussed in Chapter 4 at 2.2.

5.11.1 Sale of assets held for rental

Until 2008, IAS 16 prohibited classification as revenue of any gains arising from the derecognition of items of property, plant and equipment. *[IAS 16.68]*. However, some entities are in the business of renting and subsequently selling the same asset. The IASB has agreed that the presentation of gross selling revenue, rather than a net gain or loss on the sale of the assets, would better reflect the ordinary activities of such entities. *[IAS 16.BC35C]*.

Therefore IAS 16 was amended to require that where an entity, in the course of its ordinary activities, routinely sells items of PP&E that it has held for rental to others to transfer the assets to inventories at their carrying amount when they cease to be rented and become held for sale. The proceeds from the sale of such assets are recognised as revenue in accordance with IAS 18. IFRS 5 does not apply when assets that are held for sale in the ordinary course of business are transferred to inventories. *[IAS 16.68A]*.

IAS 7 – *Statement of Cash Flows* – requires presentation within operating activities of cash payments to manufacture or acquire such assets and cash receipts from rents and sales of such assets. *[IAS 7.14]*. The requirements of IAS 7 are discussed further in Chapter 38.

5.12 IFRIC 15 and pre-completion contracts

When and how to recognise revenue is a complex issue in the case of real estate developments where there are agreements for sale to the ultimate buyer prior to the completion of construction. Such 'forward sale' contracts are common in areas such as multiple-unit real estate developments (for example, residential apartment blocks) and commercial property developments where agreements for sale are reached before construction is complete. In these situations, the developers start marketing the development before construction is complete (perhaps even before construction has started, i.e. 'off plan') and buyers enter into agreements to acquire either the entire building or a specific unit within the building development on completion of the construction. The contracts may require the buyer to pay a deposit and progress payments, which are refundable only if the developer fails to complete and deliver the unit. The balance of the purchase price may be payable only when the buyer gains possession, which often coincides with the point at which legal title is transferred to the buyer. However, within this broad framework, the details of the legal rights and obligations might differ quite widely and legal title may transfer at different times, depending on national laws and practices.

5.12.1 Applicable standard: IAS 18 or IAS 11

The first issue to be resolved is to determine which standard, IAS 18 or IAS 11, is the relevant standard to apply. IFRIC 15 was issued in July 2008 and applies to the accounting for revenue and associated expenses by entities that undertake the construction of real estate directly or through sub-contractors. *[IFRIC 15.4]*. In substance, IFRIC 15 argues that pre-completion sales contracts typically do not meet the IAS 11 definition of, and are distinguishable from, construction contracts. They are, instead, generally sales of goods for which IAS 18 is the applicable standard. This means that revenue is recognised only when the IAS 18 conditions are met. Such contracts may span more than one accounting period, but this does not, by itself, justify the use of the percentage of completion method.

As well as guidance as to the applicable standard, IFRIC 15 addresses when revenue from the construction of real estate should be recognised. *[IFRIC 15.6]*.

The Interpretations Committee has focused on IAS 11's definition of a construction contract as 'a contract specifically negotiated for the construction of an asset or a combination of assets...'. *[IAS 11.3]*. An agreement for the construction of real estate meets the definition of a construction contract when the buyer is able to specify the major structural elements of the design of the real estate before construction begins and/or specify major structural changes once construction is in progress (whether or not it exercises that ability). *[IFRIC 15.11]*. By contrast, the buyer may only have limited ability to influence the design of the real estate, for example to select a design from a range of options specified by the entity, or to specify only minor variations to the basic design. In practice, many agreements only give the buyer the right of choice over a few options, such as types of flooring or kitchen fittings. In this case, the agreement is for the sale of goods and is within the scope of IAS 18, rather than IAS 11. *[IFRIC 15.12]*.

The analysis assumes that there is revenue to be recognised, i.e. it assumes that the entity retains neither continuing managerial involvement to the degree usually associated with ownership nor effective control over the constructed real estate to an extent that would preclude recognition of some or all of the consideration as revenue. *[IFRIC 15.7]*. Examples are agreements in which the entity guarantees occupancy of the property for a specified period or guarantees a return on the buyer's investment for a specified period. In such circumstances, recognition of revenue may be delayed or precluded altogether. *[IFRIC 15.IE9-IE10]*.

A feature of many of these agreements is that an entity may contract to deliver goods or services in addition to the construction of real estate. *[IFRIC 15.5]*. For example, the agreement may include the sale of land or provision of property management services and it may need to be split into its separate components. *[IAS 18.13]*. The fair

Chapter 29

value of the total consideration received or receivable for the agreement is allocated to each component. The entity will apply IFRIC 15 to the component for the construction of real estate in order to determine the appropriate accounting, *[IFRIC 15.8]*, as illustrated in the following flowchart, which is based on the Information note to IFRIC 15:

Analysis of a single agreement for the construction of real estate

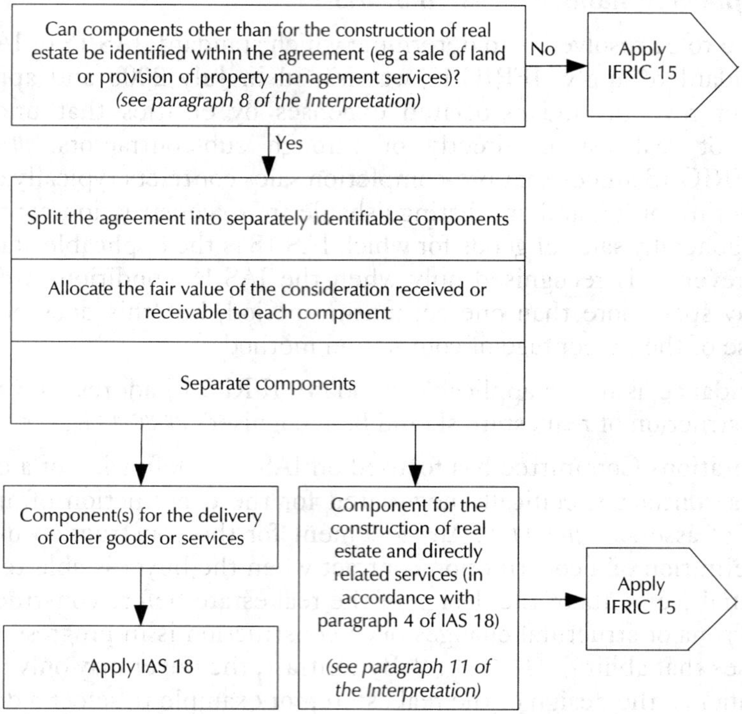

Analysis of the agreement, or the component for the construction of real estate within it, will determine whether it is a construction contract, a contract for services or a contract for the sale of goods:

(a) *the agreement is a construction contract*: if its outcome can be estimated reliably, the entity should recognise revenue by reference to the stage of completion of the contract activity in accordance with IAS 11 (see Chapter 23); *[IFRIC 15.13]*

(b) *the agreement is for the rendering of services*: the entity does not have to acquire and supply construction materials so the agreement may be for services and IAS 18 requires revenue to be recognised by reference to the stage of completion using IAS 11 principles; *[IFRIC 15.15]* (see 3.8 above); or

(c) *the agreement is an agreement for the sale of goods*: if the entity has to provide services and construction materials as part of its contractual obligation to deliver the real estate to the buyer, it is an agreement for the sale of goods to which IAS 18 applies. *[IFRIC 15.16]*. There are two alternatives depending on the transfer of control:

(i) the entity may transfer to the buyer control and the significant risks and rewards of ownership of the work-in-progress in its current state as construction progresses, i.e. in a process of continuous transfer, and the percentage of completion method will apply; *[IFRIC 15.17]* or

(ii) the entity may transfer to the buyer control and the significant risks and rewards of ownership of the real estate in its entirety at a single point in time (whether this be at completion, on or after delivery). In this case, the entity can recognise revenue only when all the criteria in paragraph 14 of IAS 18 are satisfied. *[IFRIC 15.18]*.

This means that, in addition to transferring significant risks and rewards of ownership, the entity retains neither continuing managerial involvement to the degree usually associated with ownership nor effective control over the goods sold. In addition, the amount of revenue can be measured reliably, it is probable that the economic benefits associated with the transaction will flow to the entity and the costs incurred or to be incurred in respect of the transaction can be measured reliably. See 3.7 above.

If the entity has to carry out any further work on the real estate itself that has already been delivered to the buyer, it should recognise a liability measured in accordance with IAS 37 and an expense for this work. Additional separately identifiable goods or services would already have been identified as a separate component and revenue allocated accordingly (see the flowchart above). *[IFRIC 15.19]*.

Although arrangements that meet the conditions for the 'continuous transfer' of work in progress envisaged in (c)(i) above are not construction contracts, it is appropriate to recognise revenue as the criteria are met. IFRIC 15 states that the requirements of IAS 11 are generally applicable to the recognition of revenue and the associated expenses for such a transaction, *[IFRIC 15.17]*, i.e. they will give the best approximations in this type of arrangement.

If a builder/developer 'pre-sells' a development to an institutional investor, this contractual arrangement is usually, in substance, a financing arrangement and the purchaser will not have the right to assume the work in progress. Revenue recognition will normally be deferred until a single point of time (as in (c)(ii) above), such as on completion.[28]

Chapter 29

5.12.2 Continuous transfer

Continuous transfer ((c)(i) in 5.12.1 above) is a concept developed in IFRIC 15; it allows an entity to apply percentage of completion accounting to transactions that would not otherwise qualify for this method, whether under IAS 11 as a construction contract or under IAS 18 as a contract for services. Without continuous transfer, these entities might have had to recognise revenue at a single point in time, e.g. at completion or on delivery.

Some of the features of 'continuous transfer' are described in the Illustrative Examples to IFRIC 15. They include circumstances in which the buyer has a right to take over the work in progress during construction (albeit with a penalty) and to engage a different entity to complete it. During this process the builder will have access to the land and the work in progress in order to perform its contractual obligations. This access does not necessarily imply that the builder retains continuing managerial involvement to the degree usually associated with ownership to an extent that would preclude recognition of some or all of the consideration as revenue. The builder may have control over the activities related to the performance of its contractual obligation, but not over the real estate itself. *[IFRIC 15.IE11]*.

The following example is based on the Illustrative Example 2. *[IFRIC 15.IE6-IE8]*.

Example 29.2: Applying IFRIC 15 to residential real estate

An entity is developing residential real estate and starts marketing individual units (apartments) while construction is still in progress. Buyers enter into a binding sale agreement that gives them the right to acquire a specified unit when it is ready for occupation. They pay a deposit that is refundable only if the entity fails to deliver the completed unit in accordance with the contracted terms. Buyers are also required to make progress payments between the time of the initial agreement and contractual completion. The balance of the purchase price is paid only on contractual completion, when buyers obtain possession of their unit. Buyers are able to specify only minor variations to the basic design but they cannot specify or alter major structural elements of the design of their unit.

(a) In Country A, no rights to the underlying real estate asset transfer to the buyer other than through the agreement. Consequently, the construction takes place regardless of whether sale agreements exist. The terms of the agreement and other facts and circumstances indicate that the agreement is not a construction contract. It is a forward contract that gives the buyer an asset in the form of a right to acquire, use and sell the completed real estate at a later date and an obligation to pay the purchase price in accordance with its terms. Although the buyer might be able to transfer its interest in the forward contract to another party, the entity retains control and the significant risks and rewards of ownership of the work in progress in its current state until the completed real estate is transferred. Therefore, revenue should be recognised at completion as it is only at this point that all of IAS 18's criteria are met.

(b) In Country B, the law requires the entity to transfer immediately to the buyer ownership of the real estate in its current state of completion and that any additional construction becomes the responsibility and property of the buyer as construction progresses. In this case it is possible that the entity transfers to the buyer control and the significant risks and rewards of ownership of the work in progress in its current state as construction progresses. For example, if the agreement is terminated before construction is complete, the buyer retains the work in progress and the entity has the right to be paid for the work performed. This might indicate that control is transferred along with ownership. If it does, the entity recognises revenue using the percentage of completion method taking into account the stage of completion of the whole building and the agreements signed with individual buyers.

The Interpretations Committee considered that continuous transfer would not be common. Certain specific agreements were considered in developing IFRIC 15 that may be examples of continuous transfer. These are agreements defined by law in certain jurisdictions, such as France and Belgium (Vente en l'Etat Futur d'Achèvement – otherwise known as 'VEFA' agreements) under which the seller of real estate immediately transfers the rights of ownership of the floor area and existing work to the buyer, and additional construction work becomes the property of the buyer as it is performed.[29] These terms are reflected in the Illustrative Examples.

Since IFRIC 15, was issued, the Interpretations Committee has discussed continuous transfer on three occasions. Identifying those arrangements to which continuous transfer applies is highly contentious and arrangements that might be eligible are apparently more common than the Committee had hoped.

In addition, there are different opinions about how to account for protective rights given to buyers of residential properties when they are obliged to make progress payments during the period of construction. These protective rights may be enforced by relevant public authorities; usually they protect the buyer if the developer defaults, e.g. the public authorities may have the right to appoint another developer.[30] It is not clear whether continuous transfer of control means that the buyer receives control over the part-completed work in progress or the seller loses control and the buyer gains protective rights.

In May 2014, the IASB and FASB finalised their joint revenue project. Under IFRS, this culminated in the issuance of IFRS 15. That standard requires an entity to meet one of three criteria in order to determine that control has transferred to a customer over time (see Chapter 30). Although this may appear to be a similar concept to continuous transfer, the criteria that have to be met are different.

Early in 2012, the future of IFRIC 15 was considered by the IASB at the request of the Interpretations Committee. Although the IASB considered a range of options, including withdrawing or revising IFRIC 15 (either in line with the revenue proposals or to include indicators and guidance in interpreting IAS 18), the Board's advice to the Committee was to retain IFRIC 15, as drafted.[31]

5.12.3 Separation into components

The following, based on Illustrative Example 1 that accompanies IFRIC 15, *[IFRIC 15.IE1-IE4]*, helps identify the different elements within these arrangements.

Example 29.3: Applying IFRIC 15 to commercial real estate

An entity buys a plot of land for the construction of commercial real estate. It designs an office block and applies for building permission. The entity markets the office block to potential tenants and signs conditional lease agreements.

(a) It then markets the office block itself to potential buyers and signs with one of them a conditional agreement for the sale of land and the construction of the office block. The buyer cannot put the land or the incomplete office block back to the entity. When the entity receives the building permission and all agreements become unconditional, it constructs the office block.

The agreement should be separated into a component for the sale of land and a component for the construction of the office block. The component for the sale of land is a sale of goods within the scope of IAS 18.

Because all the major structural decisions were made by the entity and were included in the designs submitted to the planning authorities before the buyer signed the conditional agreement, it is assumed that there will be no major change in the designs after the construction has begun. Consequently, the construction of the office block is not a construction contract and is within the scope of IAS 18. Construction takes place on land the buyer owns before construction begins and the buyer cannot put the incomplete office block back to the entity. This indicates that the entity transfers to the buyer control and the significant risks and rewards of ownership of the work in progress in its current state as construction progresses. Therefore, the entity recognises revenue from the construction of the office block by reference to the stage of completion using the percentage of completion method.

(b) Alternatively, assume that the construction of the office block started before the entity signed the agreement with the buyer. In that event, the agreement should be separated into three components: a component for the sale of land, a component for the partially constructed office block and a component for the construction of the office block. The entity should apply the recognition criteria separately to each component. Assuming that the other facts remain unchanged, the entity recognises revenue from the component for the construction of the office block by reference to the stage of completion using the percentage of completion method.

In this example, the sale of land is a separately identifiable component, but this will not always be the case. IFRIC 15 notes that in some jurisdictions, a condominium is legally defined as the absolute ownership of a unit based on a legal description of the airspace the unit actually occupies, plus an undivided interest in the ownership of the common elements (that includes the land and actual building itself, all the driveways, parking, lifts, outside hallways, recreation and landscaped areas) that are owned jointly with the other condominium unit owners. The undivided interest in the ownership of the common elements does not give the buyer control over the significant risks and rewards of the land. The right to the unit and the interest in the common elements are not separable. *[IFRIC 15.IE5]*.

5.12.4 Disclosure

IAS 18 has fewer disclosure requirements than IAS 11 and therefore the Interpretations Committee have inserted a number of specific disclosures in IFRIC 15 that are required when these agreements are deemed to be 'continuous transfer' arrangements that are accounted for under IAS 18: *[IFRIC 15.20-21]*

(a) When an entity recognises revenue using the percentage of completion method for agreements that meet all the criteria in paragraph 14 of IAS 18 continuously as construction progresses it should disclose:
   (i) how it determines which agreements meet all the criteria in paragraph 14 of IAS 18 continuously as construction progresses;
   (ii) the amount of revenue arising from such agreements in the period; and
   (iii) the methods used to determine the stage of completion of agreements in progress.

(b) For the agreements described in the paragraph above that are in progress at the reporting date, the entity should also disclose:
   (i) the aggregate amount of costs incurred and recognised profits (less recognised losses) to date; and
   (ii) the amount of advances received.

IFRIC 15 replaces the requirements for real estate sales that were previously included in IAS 18's Illustrative Examples. The reference to revenue generally being recognised on the passing of legal title, *[IAS 18(2008).IE9]*, has been deleted, but of course the general criteria of IAS 18 applicable to the sale of goods (see 3.7 above) will still be applicable.

5.13 Regulatory assets and liabilities

In many countries, the provision of utilities (e.g. water, natural gas or electricity) to consumers is regulated by a government agency. Regulations differ between countries, but regulators may operate a cost-plus system under which a utility is allowed to make a fixed return on investment. Consequently, the future price that a utility is allowed to charge its customers may be influenced by past cost levels and investment levels.

Under some national GAAPs (including US GAAP) accounting practices have been developed that allow an entity to account for the effects of regulation by recognising a 'regulatory liability' or 'regulatory asset' that reflects the decrease in future prices required by the regulator to compensate for an excessive return on investment, and *vice versa* where an increase would be permitted.

In September 2012, the Board decided to restart its rate-regulated activities project and issued a discussion paper in September 2014.[32] As an interim measure, the IASB issued an IFRS 14 – *Regulatory Deferral Accounts* – to help entities who currently recognise rate-regulated assets and liabilities under their national GAAP adopt IFRS. That standard permits a first-time adopter of IFRS to continue to use its previous accounting policies for rate-regulated assets and liabilities, with specific disclosure requirements (see Chapter 5).

Until any new standard is issued and becomes effective, regulatory assets and liabilities are not eligible for recognition under IFRS, unless the entity is a first-time adopter that can apply IFRS 14. For further details see Chapter 17 at 11.1.

5.14 Transfers of assets from customers and IFRIC 18

It is quite common for utilities, in particular, to receive contributions of assets from customers so that they can be connected to networks or receive services from them. IFRIC 18 provides guidance in these situations.

IFRIC 18 applies to all agreements under which an entity receives from a customer, or another party, an item of PP&E (or cash to acquire or construct such an asset) that the entity must then use either to connect the customer to a network or to provide the customer ongoing access to a supply of goods or services or both. *[IFRIC 18.3-6]*. IFRIC 18 does not apply if this transfer is a government grant within the scope of IAS 20 – *Accounting for Government Grants and Disclosure of Government Assistance* – or the asset is used in a service concession within the scope of IFRIC 12 – *Service Concession Arrangements*, *[IFRIC 18.7]*, see Chapters 26 and 27, respectively.

A typical arrangement is one in which a builder or individual householder must pay for power cables, pipes or other connections for water, electricity or other supplies. However, IFRIC 18 will also apply to many outsourcing arrangements where the existing assets are contributed to the service provider or the customer must pay for assets or both. For example, in an arrangement under which an entity outsources its telephony, it is very common for it to transfer its existing assets to the service provider and for this to be reflected in the contract price.

The following flowchart illustrates the analysis and accounting to be applied under IFRIC 18:

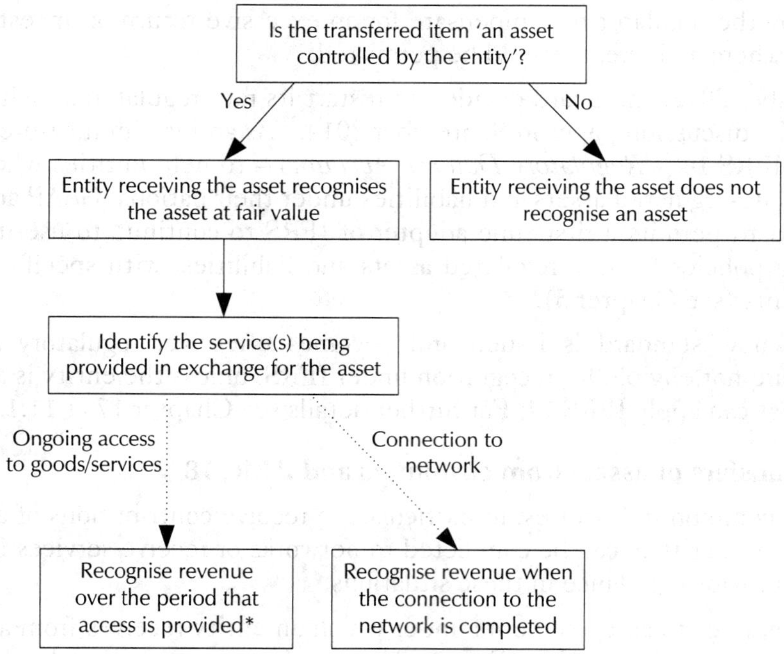

* If the agreement is silent, this is no longer than the life of the related asset.

The first step is to assess whether the item of PP&E received meets the definition of an asset. *[IFRIC 18.9]*. Paragraph 4.4(a) of the *Framework* defines an asset as 'a resource controlled by the entity as a result of past events and from which future economic benefits are expected to flow to the entity'. *[Framework 4.4(a)]*.

Something can only be an asset of the reporting entity if that entity controls it. The water pipes installed to connect the new house may be controlled by the householder from the house to the boundary of the property and the utility will control everything from the boundary. Note that a third party that has no direct connection to the ongoing service may have constructed and contributed the asset (e.g. the builder). This does not prevent the arrangement being within scope. In an outsourcing arrangement, the service provider may operate the equipment, but may or may not have rights over its maintenance and replacement which will indicate who controls the asset.

Control is not determined solely by the transfer of legal ownership, and will require a careful assessment of the facts and circumstances. Factors that would indicate that the transferred asset is controlled by the receiving entity are that entity's ability to:

- exchange the asset for other assets to deliver the same service;
- employ the asset to produce other goods or services or settle a liability;
- charge a price for others to use it; and
- determine how the transferred asset is operated and maintained and when it is replaced.

As well as establishing whether the entity controls the asset it also needs to determine whether the asset will be a source of future economic benefits.

IFRIC 18 is particularly relevant to utility entities. Utilities regulated under a 'cost of service' mechanism noted a conflict between how the regulator accounts for items contributed or funded by customers and the requirements of IFRIC 18. The aim of a 'cost of service' model is to establish rates that earn the entity a specified rate of return (or a return within a certain range) and rates are often set using formulas involving an entity's asset base. Most regulators exclude assets or portions of assets that are contributed or funded by customer contributions from the entity's asset base.

This raises the issue of whether an asset's exclusion from the rate-base calculation for establishing tariffs is an indicator that the asset definition has not been met. Arguments supporting this view are that these assets are not associated with any 'future economic benefits that will flow to the entity'. In our view, the regulator's decision to exclude items of PP&E from the rate setting process is not an indicator that the asset definition has not been met. While contributed assets may not increase the overall level of returns permitted by the regulator, the utility does have the benefit of having an additional customer as a result of the connection. As these customers consume the ongoing service of the utility, they contribute directly to the revenues of the utility. Also, in some markets, only a portion of the utility's business is regulated and these additional customers may potentially contribute to revenues in unregulated portions of the utility's business. An entity's ability to sell the asset is also an indication that future economic benefits exists. Finally, contributed assets are usually only one of the many differences between the regulated asset and the asset in financial statements prepared under IFRS. For example, regulators may permit capitalisation of expenditure that would be considered repairs or maintenance under IAS 16 and accounted for as an expense.

Any asset transferred to the reporting entity will be measured initially at its fair value, which will become its cost for accounting purposes. *[IAS 18.12, IFRIC 18.11]*. It will be necessary to identify the separate services that are to be provided in exchange for the item of PP&E. *[IFRIC 18.14]*. This is because revenue needs to be recognised as it is an exchange transaction involving dissimilar goods and services, *[IFRIC 18.13]*, (see 3.9 above). The nature of the services provided will determine the manner in which revenue is recognised.

The service may simply be connection of the customer to the network. This may be a separately identifiable service if connection represents stand-alone value to the customer. *[IFRIC 18.15]*. Although IFRIC 18 does not provide a definition of stand-

Chapter 29

alone value, stand-alone selling price is defined by IFRS 15 as 'the price at which the entity would sell a good or service separately to the customer'[33] (see Chapter 30). US GAAP currently has a broader definition of stand-alone value – 'if they are sold separately by any vendor or the customer could resell the delivered item on a stand-alone basis'.[34]

Other factors that could be considered in determining if the connection has stand-alone value are:

- does the customer have a choice of service provider? If there is no choice in providers, this may indicate that connection does not have stand-alone value; and
- if the customer is able to choose the service provider, does the connection allow a future purchaser of the property to avoid connection charges with the new provider (i.e. a connection enhances the value of a property)? A connection that increases a property's value relative to a property that is not connected to the network indicates that the connection has stand-alone value.

Another feature that indicates that the connection is a separately identifiable service is if the fair value of the connection service can be measured reliably. *[IFRIC 18.15]*. This may not always be straightforward, particularly when the connection is not sold separately.

It may be possible to identify the services that the entity is providing in exchange for the contributed asset by looking at how the ongoing goods and services are priced. If the customer who made the contribution would pay the same amount for the ongoing goods and services as others who have not done so, this suggests that connection is the only service provided in exchange for the contributed asset. *[IFRIC 18.17]*. By contrast, a lower price than is available to other customers suggests that the future goods and services are, at least to some extent, provided in return for the contributed asset. *[IFRIC 18.16]*. The existence of any rate regulation, so common in the utilities industry, may make it harder to interpret this indicator. Prices established in a free market may approximate a measure of the fair value of the ongoing service. Accordingly, if that price is the same for all customers irrespective of whether they contributed to the cost of the utility's assets, there is no ongoing benefit to those customers that made a contribution. However, where the price charged to customers is regulated, it does not follow that that price is a true measure of the fair value of the ongoing service obligation. In these circumstances, use of ongoing prices as an indicator can be inconclusive.

IFRIC 18 does not attribute a weighting or a priority to any of these features, and as a result, utility entities may find indicators that point to different conclusions. For example, many utilities have a legal obligation to provide ongoing services at set rates to all customers, indicating that the asset has been contributed in exchange for the connection, but the connection service may not have stand-alone value to the customer, which implies the opposite. In our opinion, no individual indicator is definitive and, as such, entities must consider all of them, along with other relevant facts and circumstances and exercise its own judgment in reaching its conclusion.

Once the services that have been provided in return for the asset have been identified, the fair value of the total consideration received or receivable under the agreement (i.e. including the fair value of the contributed asset) is allocated to each service. *[IFRIC 18.19]*. This enables the entity to determine the period over which the revenue is recognised. If there are no ongoing goods and services provided in exchange, revenue is recognised as soon as the connection is complete. The revenue for ongoing access will be recognised in accordance with the terms of the agreement if it has a specified term; otherwise the revenue will be recognised over a period not exceeding the useful life of the contributed item of PP&E. *[IFRIC 18.20]*. The following example based on Illustrative Example 3 in IFRIC 18 illustrates issues concerning revenue recognition (rather than asset recognition). *[IFRIC 18.IE6-IE9]*.

Example 29.4: Recognising revenue when assets are transferred for services

An entity enters into an agreement with a customer involving the outsourcing of information technology (IT) functions. As part of the agreement, the customer transfers ownership of its existing IT equipment to the entity. Initially, the entity must use the equipment to provide the service required by the outsourcing agreement. The entity is responsible for maintaining the equipment and for replacing it when it decides to do so. The useful life of the equipment is estimated to be three years. The outsourcing agreement requires service to be provided for ten years for a fixed price that is lower than the price the entity would have charged if the IT equipment had not been transferred.

These facts indicate that the IT equipment is an asset of the entity, which will recognise the equipment and measure its cost on initial recognition at its fair value, together with a liability to provide the service. Because the price charged for the service is lower than the price the entity would charge without the transfer of the IT equipment, this service is a separately identifiable service included in the agreement. The facts also indicate that it is the only service to be provided in exchange for the transfer of the IT equipment. Therefore, the entity should recognise revenue arising from the exchange transaction when the service is performed, i.e. over the ten-year term of the outsourcing agreement.

Alternatively, assume that after the first three years, the price the entity charges under the outsourcing agreement increases to reflect the fact that it will then be replacing the equipment the customer transferred. In this case, the reduced price for the services provided under the outsourcing agreement reflects the useful life of the transferred equipment. For this reason, the entity should recognise revenue from the exchange transaction over the first three years of the agreement.

IFRIC 12 and IFRIC 13 may be used for guidance on allocating the fair value, which are based on the fair values of the separate components. *[IFRIC 18.BC19]*. IFRIC 12 is discussed in Chapter 27 and IFRIC 13 at 5.15 below.

The analysis and accounting to be applied when the entity receives cash that it must use to construct or acquire the assets is similar to the above. The entity needs to assess whether the agreement is within scope of IFRIC 18 and, if so, it will need to assess whether an asset is required to be recognised. The PP&E acquired or constructed will be recognised in accordance with IAS 16 and revenue, at the amount of cash received, will be recognised accordingly to each separately identifiable service provided. *[IFRIC 18.21]*.

5.15 Customer loyalty programmes and IFRIC 13

Customer loyalty programmes are now an integral element of a wide range of businesses – from airlines to retailers and from consumer credit to mobile telecommunications. Customer loyalty programmes are used by entities to provide incentives to their customers to buy their products or use their services. Customer loyalty is recognised through the grant of award credits, such as 'points' or 'air miles'; customers can then redeem the award credits for free or discounted goods or services.

The programmes operate in a variety of ways. Customers may be required to accumulate a specified minimum number or value of award credits before they are able to redeem them. Award credits may be linked to individual purchases or groups of purchases, or to continued custom over a specified period of time. An entity may operate the customer loyalty programme itself or participate in a programme operated by a third party. The awards offered may include goods and services supplied by the entity itself and/or rights to claim goods or services from another vendor. *[IFRIC 13.2]*.

In addressing the issue, the Interpretations Committee rejected two approaches. It did not accept that an obligation for expenses is recognised as an expense at the time of the initial sale, measured by reference to the amount required to settle it, in accordance with IAS 37. Nor did it consider the accounting should depend on the nature of the customer loyalty programme (e.g. as a marketing expense or revenue), depending on significance. Instead it has concluded that some of the consideration received from the customer should be allocated to the award credits and deferred as a liability until the entity fulfils its obligations to deliver awards to customers. The liability is measured by reference to the value of the award credits to the customer (not their cost to the entity) and recognised as a deferral of revenue (not an expense). In support of this approach, it is argued that:

(a) award credits are an element of the market exchange of economic benefits between the entity and the customer. They represent rights granted to a customer, for which the customer is implicitly paying. They can be distinguished from marketing expenses because they are granted to the customer as part of a sales transaction; and

(b) award credits are separately identifiable from the other goods or services sold as part of the initial sale.

In the Interpretations Committee's view, paragraph 13 of IAS 18 applies if a single transaction requires two or more separate goods or services to be delivered at different times; it ensures that revenue for each item is recognised only when that item is delivered. In contrast, paragraph 19 of IAS 18 applies only if the entity has to incur further costs directly related to items already delivered – for example, to meet warranty claims. In the Interpretation Committee's view, loyalty awards are not costs that directly relate to the goods and services already delivered – rather, they are separate goods or services delivered at a later date. *[IFRIC 13.BC9(a)]*.

Although the issue of customer loyalty programmes was discussed by the US Emerging Issues Task Force, no conclusion was reached. As a result, under US GAAP, there is no specific authoritative accounting guidance on accounting for the issue of award credits, and in practice entities commonly recognise an expense on original sale or when the obligation is fulfilled. In the airline sector – where such arrangements are pervasive – the majority of airlines have historically used the first approach.

5.15.1 The scope of IFRIC 13

IFRIC 13 applies to customer loyalty award credits that an entity grants to its customers as part of a sales transaction (i.e. a sale of goods, rendering of services or use by a customer of entity assets) as a result of which, subject to meeting any further qualifying conditions, those customers can redeem the credits for free or discounted goods and services. *[IFRIC 13.3]*. In other words, it applies to schemes whereby the award credits offered to customers derive from a past transaction. This means that it does not apply to the distribution of 'money off' vouchers or other schemes that do not involve an initial sales transaction.

IFRIC 13 does not specifically address the situation where an operator of a loyalty programme (e.g. an airline) sells award credits to another entity (e.g. a credit card company) and that other entity grants the purchased award credits to its own customers who are also members of the loyalty programme. This type of transaction is a direct sale of the award credits to a third party and therefore is within the scope of IAS 18, as opposed to IFRIC 13. As the cardholders/members can redeem the awards directly with the programme operator, the programme operator still has an obligation that should be recognised through the deferral of some or all of the sales proceeds. Furthermore, the award credits granted to programme members directly by the programme operator versus those granted by third parties will, in both cases, have the same rights attaching to them and are indistinguishable from one another in the members' accounts.

Where a programme operator sells its award credits to a third party, it is likely that the sale will involve a number of components. For example, an airline selling its air miles to a credit card company is likely to be selling both a travel component (for redemption by the third party's customers) and a marketing component for allowing the third party access to its loyalty programme and customer base. In determining how much revenue should be recognised on the sale of the air miles to the third party, the airline determines how much of the consideration should be attributed to these components, since it is likely that the consideration related to marketing component may not require revenue deferral. This is discussed in more detail in 5.15.3 below.

Chapter 29

5.15.2 The requirements of IFRIC 13

Under IFRIC 13, an entity must account for award credits as a separately identifiable component of the sales transaction(s) in which they are granted (the 'initial sale'). The fair value of the consideration received or receivable in respect of the initial sale must be allocated between the award credits and the other components of the sale. *[IFRIC 13.5]*.

IAS 18 does not prescribe an allocation method for multiple-element transactions. Its overall objective is to determine the amount the customer is paying for each component, which can be estimated by drawing on the entity's experience of transactions with similar customers. Hence, IFRIC 13 requires the consideration allocated to award credits to be measured by reference to their fair value.

IFRIC 13 does not specify whether the amount allocated to the award credits should be:

(a) equal to their fair value (irrespective of the fair values of the other elements); or

(b) a proportion of the total consideration based on the fair value of the award credits relative to the fair values of the other elements of the sale.

The Interpretations Committee noted that IAS 18 does not specify which of these methods should be applied, or in what circumstances and decided that the Interpretation should not be more prescriptive than IAS 18. The selection of one or other method is, therefore, left to management's judgement.

The measurement of fair value is discussed in more detail in 5.15.3 below.

Since not all award credits will ultimately be redeemed, IFRIC 13 specifies the basis on which revenue should be recognised, depending on whether the awards are supplied by the entity itself or by a third party. If the entity supplies the awards itself, it should recognise the consideration allocated to award credits as revenue when award credits are redeemed and it fulfils its obligations to supply awards. The amount of revenue recognised should be based on the number of award credits that have been redeemed in exchange for awards, relative to the total number expected to be redeemed. *[IFRIC 13.7]*.

The practical application of this approach is illustrated in Example 1 of the Illustrative Examples appended to IFRIC 13, as follows: *[IFRIC 13.IE1-IE5]*

Example 29.5: Awards supplied by the entity

A grocery retailer operates a customer loyalty programme. It grants programme members loyalty points when they spend a specified amount on groceries. Programme members can redeem the points for further groceries. The points have no expiry date. In one period, the entity grants 100 points. Management expects 80 of these points to be redeemed. Management estimates the fair value of each loyalty point to be $1, and defers revenue of $100.

Year 1

At the end of the first year, 40 of the points have been redeemed in exchange for groceries, i.e. half of those expected to be redeemed. The entity recognises revenue of (40 points ÷ 80 points) × $100 = $50.

Year 2

In the second year, management revises its expectations. It now expects 90 points to be redeemed altogether.

During the second year, 41 points are redeemed, bringing the total number redeemed to 40 + 41 = 81 points. The cumulative revenue that the entity recognises is (81 points ÷ 90 points) × $100 = $90. The entity has already recognised revenue of $50 in the first year, so it recognises $40 in the second year.

Year 3

In the third year, a further nine points are redeemed, taking the total number of points redeemed to 81 + 9 = 90. Management continues to expect that only 90 points will ever be redeemed, i.e. that no more points will be redeemed after the third year. So the cumulative revenue to date is (90 points ÷ 90 points) × $100 = $100. The entity has already recognised $90 of revenue ($50 in the first year and $40 in the second year), so it recognises the remaining $10 in the third year. All of the revenue initially deferred has now been recognised.

When the fair value of the award credit is calculated by reference to the value of the awards for which they could be redeemed, the value of the awards for which they could be redeemed must be adjusted to reflect expected forfeitures, as well as the discounts or incentives that would otherwise be offered to customers who have not earned award credits from an initial sale. *[IFRIC 13.AG2]*. Therefore, each loyalty point issued could be redeemed for groceries valued at $1.25, but the fair value of the award credits is calculated at $100, being the 100 points issued multiplied by 80% (given the 20% forfeiture rate) of $1.25.

If a third party supplies the awards, the entity must assess whether it is collecting the consideration allocated to the award credits on its own account (i.e. as the principal in the transaction) or on behalf of the third party (i.e. as an agent for the third party).

(a) If the entity is collecting the consideration on behalf of the third party, it must:

  (i) measure its revenue as the net amount retained on its own account, i.e. the difference between the consideration allocated to the award credits and the amount payable to the third party for supplying the awards; and

  (ii) recognise this net amount as revenue when the third party becomes obliged to supply the awards and entitled to receive consideration for doing so. These events may occur as soon as the award credits are granted. Alternatively, if the customer can choose to claim awards from either the entity or a third party, these events may occur only when the customer chooses to claim awards from the third party.

(b) If the entity is collecting the consideration on its own account, it must measure its revenue as the gross consideration allocated to the award credits and recognise the revenue when it fulfils its obligations in respect of the awards. *[IFRIC 13.8]*.

The practical application of this approach is illustrated in Example 2 of the illustrative examples appended to IFRIC 13, as follows: *[IFRIC 13.IE6-IE10]*

Example 29.6: Awards supplied by a third party

A retailer of electrical goods participates in a customer loyalty programme operated by an airline. It grants programme members one air mile with each $1 they spend on electrical goods. Programme members can redeem the air miles for air travel with the airline, subject to availability. The retailer pays the airline $0.009 for each air mile.

In one period, the retailer sells electrical goods for consideration totalling $1 million and grants 1 million air miles.

Allocation of consideration to air miles

The retailer estimates that the fair value of an air mile is $0.01. It allocates to the air miles 1 million × $0.01 = $10,000 of the consideration it has received from the sales of its electrical goods.

Revenue recognition

Having granted the air miles, the retailer has fulfilled its obligations to the customer. The airline is obliged to supply the awards and entitled to receive consideration for doing so. Therefore the retailer recognises revenue from the air miles when it sells the electrical goods.

Revenue measurement

If the retailer has collected the consideration allocated to the air miles on its own account, it measures its revenue as the gross $10,000 allocated to them. It separately recognises the $9,000 paid or payable to the airline as an expense. If the retailer has collected the consideration on behalf of the airline, i.e. as an agent for the airline, it measures its revenue as the net amount it retains on its own account. This amount of revenue is the difference between the $10,000 consideration allocated to the air miles and the $9,000 passed on to the airline.

Normally, the deferred consideration will exceed the unavoidable costs of meeting the obligation to supply the awards. However, if at any time the unavoidable costs of meeting the obligations to supply the awards are expected to exceed the consideration received and receivable for them (i.e. the consideration allocated to the award credits at the time of the initial sale that has not yet been recognised as revenue plus any further consideration receivable when the customer redeems the award credits), the entity has onerous contracts. A liability must be recognised for the excess in accordance with IAS 37 (see Chapter 28). The need to recognise such a liability could arise if the expected costs of supplying awards increase, for example if the entity revises its expectations about the number of award credits that will be redeemed. *[IFRIC 13.9]*.

5.15.3 Measuring the fair value of award credits

IAS 18 requires revenue to be measured at the fair value of the consideration received or receivable. *[IAS 18.9]*. Hence, the amount of revenue attributed to award credits should be the fair value of the consideration received for them (measured in accordance with IFRS 13, see Chapter 14).

IFRIC 13 requires also that the consideration allocated to the award credits must be measured by reference to their fair value. The brief Application Guidance set out in the Appendix to IFRIC 13 notes that this amount is often not directly observable and in such circumstances, it must be estimated. *[IFRIC 13.AG1]*.

This can lead to some confusion as, for example, airlines also sell air miles/award credits to third parties to use in their marketing programs. However, airlines would not consider the amount for which the credits are sold separately to be the same as the fair value of air miles issued as part of the sale of a ticket. The reason is that, when airlines sell air miles to third parties, they are selling both a travel component (for redemption by the third party's customers) and a marketing component for allowing the third party access to their loyalty program and customer base. In such cases, these sales would themselves be required to be accounted for under IAS 18 with an estimation required for the two components.

It is expected that in the majority of cases the fair value will need to be estimated. IFRIC 13 sets out in the application guidance that an entity may estimate the fair value of award credits by reference to the fair value of the awards for which they could be redeemed. It goes further and notes that if customers can choose from a range of different awards, the fair value of the award credits will reflect the fair values of the range of available awards, weighted in proportion to the frequency with which each award is expected to be selected. *[IFRIC 13.AG2]*.

This means, for example, that airlines may be required to estimate the fair value of an air mile by reference to a weighted average ticket value using an equivalent restricted fare as a proxy for tickets representing the profile of actual redemptions. These would depend on which routes, classes of travel and the time of flights for which the miles are redeemed. Therefore, an airline would be expected to determine the fair value of the air miles on a basis that is 'weighted in proportion to the frequency with which each award is expected to be selected'. Entities will be required in a number of cases to maintain comprehensive redemption data covering all variables subject to estimation, and that this is likely to place an onerous burden on many entities that grant loyalty awards.

However, the Application Guidance goes on to state that, in some circumstances, other estimation techniques may be available. *[IFRIC 13.AG3]*. For example, if a third party will supply the awards and the entity pays the third party for each award credit it grants, it could estimate the fair value of the award credits by reference to the amount it pays the third party, adding a reasonable profit margin. The Application Guidance then ends merely by stating that '[j]udgement is required to select and apply the valuation technique that satisfies the requirements of paragraph 6 of the consensus and is most appropriate in the circumstances'. *[IFRIC 13.AG3]*. Clearly, this provides preparers with substantial flexibility in choosing the estimation techniques that they apply in practice, provided they are consistent with the requirements of IFRS 13. At the same time, though, it needs to be recognised that in most cases the amount of revenue that is attributable to the award credits is not directly observable because the award credits are granted as part of a larger sale.

5.16 Revenue recognition from gambling

Many gambling activities are derivative financial instruments if they are legally enforceable, which means they meet the definition of a financial liability. *[IAS 32.11]*. These activities are accounted for in accordance with IAS 39 (or IFRS 9, if applied) (see Chapter 44). However, some gambling contracts or activities are not in scope of IAS 39 (or IFRS 9, if applied), in which case IAS 18 applies and the operator has to assess whether it acts as a principal or an agent.

If the operator is acting as a principal, revenue is recognised gross at the amount collected from players, with prizes awarded to winners classified as an expense.

Presenting revenue on a gross basis may present practical challenges if the entity's systems records information on a net basis. An entity could be, for example, recording net amounts collected from slot machines at the end of each day. Even if the cash flows received are net, an entity that is deemed to be the principal presents revenue on gross basis.

The general criteria in IAS 18 for determining whether an entity is an agent or principal are described in 3.3 above. The most applicable of these indicators to gambling is likely to be the ability of the operator to establish prices, but the general characteristics of an agent are also highly relevant. An agent does not have exposure to the significant risks and rewards associated with the rendering of services and the amount the entity earns may be predetermined, being either a fixed fee per transaction or a stated percentage of the amount billed to the customer. *[IAS 18.IE21]*.

When assessing whether the entity is a principal or agent, the following indicators should be considered. These indicators have not been ranked and they are not intended to be exhaustive. This assessment is based on the weight of evidence available. In making this assessment, it is generally helpful to consider the responsibilities of the operator under the contract.

Indicators that the operator is acting as principal	*Indicators that the operator is acting as an agent*
(a) The operator has latitude in establishing the prices for players to participate in the game.	The operator does not set the price to enter the game.
(b) The operator participates in the game.	The operator facilitates the game for the benefit of the players.
(c) The amount the operator earns is not predetermined, for example, it is not limited to a fixed percentage or fixed amount of the wagers.	The amount the operator earns is predetermined, for example, it may be limited to a predefined percentage or the entity may only be entitled to a fixed amount of the wagers.
(d) The operator is not required to pay out a prescribed amount of the wagers.	The operator is required, for example, by law or regulation, to pay a prescribed amount (e.g. a fixed percentage) of the wagers.

(a) In some gambling activities, the operator might set the price or the minimum stake for a player to participate. An example could include the sale of bingo cards for a fixed price. This might indicate the operator is the principal. However, in other gambling activity, the price might be set by the players, perhaps by mutual agreement, for example, in a game of poker, or be predetermined as part of the game rules. The price might also be set by a regulator, with the operator entitled to a fixed percentage of total amounts wagered, for example, the price to purchase a lottery ticket. This might indicate the operator is not the principal.

(b) In games, such as poker, the players play against each other and the operator facilitates the game, for example, by providing the venue, the chips, cards and dealer. This might indicate the operator is acting as an agent. In other games, the operator might be a participant (i.e. the players place wagers against the operator). Examples of this include roulette, blackjack and slot machines. In such situations, the operator might be the principal.

(c) Sports betting is commonly performed through a bookmaker or through various online outlets. The bookmaker can accept wagers for different outcomes. If the bookmaker has the option to accept or reject the wagers, it may indicate the operator is the principal.

If the amount to which the operator is entitled is predetermined or capped, it may indicate the operator is an agent. In games such as poker, for example, where players play against each other, the house takes a commission, which might be a fixed percentage of the pot (i.e. combined amount wagered by the players), up to a predetermined maximum amount.

The operator's ability to determine the spread may indicate the operator is the principal. For example, in sports betting the role of the bookmaker is generally to act as a market maker for the wagers, many of which have a binary outcome (e.g. a team either wins or loses) and/or have fixed odds. The bookmaker usually accepts wagers for either outcome and maintains a spread, which ensures a profit for the bookmaker regardless of the outcome of the wager.

(d) A requirement to pay a fixed percentage of all amounts wagered to the winners, either in cash or in kind, may indicate the operator is acting as an agent. However, if that requirement is contained in laws or regulations, the operator may need to look to other indicators to determine whether it is a principal or acting as an agent.

References

1 John H. Myers, '*The Critical Event and Recognition of Net Profit*', Accounting Review 34, October 1959, pp.528-532.
2 FASB Accounting Standards Codification (ASC) 605-15-25-1.
3 ASC 605-15-25-1.
4 ASC 605-15-25-3.
5 *IFRIC Update*, January 2015.
6 ASC 605-10-S99.
7 Statement of Financial Accounting Concepts (Concepts Statement) No. 5, para. 83.
8 Concepts Statement No. 5, para. 83(b).
9 Concepts Statement No. 5, para. 84(a).
10 Concepts Statement No. 5, para. 84(d).
11 ASC 605-10-S99.
12 ASC 605-10-S99.
13 ASC 605-25-25-5.
14 ASC 605-25-30-2.
15 *IFRIC Update*, November 2015.
16 *IFRIC Update*, July 2008.
17 *IFRIC Update*, January 2007.
18 *IFRIC Update*, September 2008.
19 This is also the view taken under US GAAP; see ASC 310-20-35-5.
20 ASC 985-605-25-3.
21 ASC 985-605-25-16.
22 ASC 985-605-25-6.
23 ASC 985-605-25-10.
24 ASC 985-605-25-8.
25 ASC 985-605-25-9.
26 ASC 985-605-25-2.
27 *IFRIC Update*, March 2006, p.7.
28 *IFRIC Update*, May 2008.
29 Agenda Paper 2B to the May 2008 IFRIC meeting, para. 12.
30 *IFRIC Update*, May 2011 and November 2012.
31 *IASB Update*, February 2012.
32 Discussion Paper DP/2014/2, *Reporting the Financial Effects of Rate Regulation.*
33 IFRS 15, Appendix A.
34 ASC 605-25-25-5.

Chapter 30 Revenue from contracts with customers (IFRS 15)

Chapter 30

List of examples

Chapter 30 Revenue from contracts with customers (IFRS 15)

1 OBJECTIVE, EFFECTIVE DATE AND TRANSITION

In May 2014, the International Accounting Standards Board (IASB) and the US Financial Accounting Standards Board (FASB) (collectively, the Boards) respectively issued largely converged new revenue standards: IFRS 15 – *Revenue from Contracts with Customers* – and Accounting Standards Codification (ASC) 606 – *Revenue from Contracts with Customers* – (created by Accounting Standards Update (ASU) 2014-09) (together with IFRS 15, the standards). These new revenue standards will supersede virtually all revenue recognition requirements in IFRS and US GAAP, respectively. Throughout this chapter, when we refer to the FASB's standard, we mean ASC 606 (including the recent amendments), unless otherwise noted.

The standards provide accounting requirements for all revenue arising from contracts with customers. They affect all entities that enter into contracts to provide goods or services to their customers, unless the contracts are in the scope of other IFRSs or US GAAP requirements, such as the leasing standards. The standards also specify the accounting for costs an entity incurs to obtain and fulfil a contract to provide goods and services to customers (see 9.3 below) and provide a model for the measurement and recognition of gains and losses on the sale of certain non-financial assets, such as property, plant or equipment.

As a result, the standards will likely affect an entity's financial statements, business processes and internal controls over financial reporting. While some entities will be able to implement the standard with limited effort, others may find implementation a significant undertaking. Successful implementation will require an assessment of and a plan for managing the change. Unless early adopting, IFRS preparers and US GAAP public entities, as defined[1], will need to apply the standards beginning in 2018 (see 1.2 below).

Following issuance of the standards, the Boards created the Joint Transition Resource Group for Revenue Recognition (TRG) to help them determine whether more application guidance is needed on their new revenue standards. TRG members include financial statement preparers, auditors and users from a variety of industries, countries, as well as public and private entities. Members of the TRG met six times in 2014 and 2015. In January 2016, the IASB announced that it did not plan to schedule further meetings of the IFRS constituents of the TRG, but said it will monitor any discussions of the US GAAP group, which met in April 2016 and is scheduled to meet again in November 2016.

While the TRG members' views are non-authoritative, entities should consider them as they implement the new standards. In a recent public statement, the European Securities and Markets Authority (ESMA) encouraged issuers to consider the TRG discussions when implementing IFRS 15. Furthermore, the Chief Accountant of the US Securities and Exchange Commission (SEC) has previously made public statements that he expects SEC registrants to use the TRG discussions and meeting minutes to inform their implementation of the standards and has said that his office strongly encourages registrants, including foreign private issuers, that want to use accounting that differs from TRG discussions to discuss their accounting with the SEC staff.[2]

We have incorporated our summaries of topics on which TRG members generally agreed at joint meetings in 2014, 2015 and at the April 2016 meeting of the FASB TRG throughout this chapter. Unless otherwise specified, these summaries represent the discussions of the joint TRG. The TRG members representing IFRS constituents did not participate in the April 2016 meeting. However, certain members of the IASB and its staff observed the meeting. At its May 2016 meeting, the IASB received an oral update of the April 2016 FASB TRG meeting. Where possible, we indicate if members of the IASB or its staff commented on the FASB TRG discussions.

Recently, the Boards amended their respective standards to address several implementation issues raised by constituents, many of which had been discussed by the TRG. The Boards did not agree on the nature and breadth of all of the changes to their revenue standards. However, the Boards expect the amendments to result in similar outcomes in many circumstances (see 1.1.2 below).

This chapter summarises the IASB's standard and highlights significant differences from the FASB's standard. It addresses the amendments the IASB has issued, along with topics on which the members of the TRG reached general agreement. It also discusses our views on certain topics.

The views we express in this chapter may evolve as implementation continues and additional issues are identified. The conclusions we describe in our illustrations are also subject to change as views evolve. Conclusions in seemingly similar situations may differ from those reached in the illustrations due to differences in the underlying facts and circumstances.

1.1 Overview of the standard

The new revenue standards the Boards issued in May 2014 were largely converged. IFRS 15 and the FASB's standard will supersede virtually all revenue recognition requirements in IFRS and US GAAP, respectively. Noting several concerns with existing requirements for revenue recognition under both IFRS and US GAAP, the Boards' goal in the joint deliberations was to develop new revenue standards that would:

- remove inconsistencies and weaknesses in the current revenue recognition literature;
- provide a more robust framework for addressing revenue recognition issues;
- improve comparability of revenue recognition practices across industries, entities within those industries, jurisdictions and capital markets;
- reduce the complexity of applying revenue recognition requirements by reducing the volume of the relevant standards and interpretations; and
- provide more useful information to users through expanded disclosure requirements. *[IFRS 15.IN5]*.

The standards provide accounting requirements for all revenue arising from contracts with customers. They affect all entities that enter into contracts to provide goods or services to their customers, unless the contracts are in the scope of other IFRSs or US GAAP requirements, such as the leasing standards. The standards also specify the accounting for costs an entity incurs to obtain and fulfil a contract to provide goods and services to customers (see 9.3 below) and provide a model for the measurement and recognition of gains and losses on the sale of certain non-financial assets, such as property, plant or equipment. When effective, IFRS 15 will replace all of the current revenue standards and interpretations in IFRS, including IAS 11 – *Construction Contracts*, IAS 18 – *Revenue*, IFRIC 13 – *Customer Loyalty Programmes*, IFRIC 15 – *Agreements for the Construction of Real Estate*, IFRIC 18 – *Transfers of Assets from Customers* – and SIC-31 – *Revenue – Barter Transactions Involving Advertising Services*. *[IFRS 15.IN3, C10]*.

When they were issued in 2014, the standards were converged, except for a handful of differences.[3] Since then, the Boards have issued some converged amendments to their standards, but they have also issued different amendments to the same topics (see 1.1.2 below for a discussion of the changes to the standards since issuance). The FASB has also issued several amendments that the IASB has not issued. For the sake of completeness, we highlight these differences throughout this chapter. However, the primary purpose of this chapter is to highlight the IASB's standard, including all amendments to date, and focuses on the effects for IFRS preparers. As such, we generally refer to the singular 'standard' in this chapter.

1.1.1 Core principle of the standard

The standard describes the principles an entity must apply to measure and recognise revenue and the related cash flows. *[IFRS 15.1]*. The core principle is that an entity will recognise revenue at an amount that reflects the consideration to which the entity expects to be entitled in exchange for transferring goods or services to a customer. *[IFRS 15.2]*.

The principles in IFRS 15 are applied using the following five steps:

1. Identify the contract(s) with a customer.
2. Identify the performance obligations in the contract.
3. Determine the transaction price.
4. Allocate the transaction price to the performance obligations in the contract.
5. Recognise revenue when (or as) the entity satisfies a performance obligation.

Entities will need to exercise judgement when considering the terms of the contract(s) and all of the facts and circumstances, including implied contract terms. Entities will also have to apply the requirements of the standard consistently to contracts with similar characteristics and in similar circumstances. *[IFRS 15.3]*. To assist entities, IFRS 15 includes detailed application guidance. The IASB also included more than 60 illustrative examples.

1.1.2 Changes to the standard since issuance

Since the issuance of the standards, the Boards have finalised various amendments to their respective standards, as summarised below. Throughout the chapter, we highlight these amendments and discuss the amended requirements. The Boards did not agree on the nature and breadth of all of the changes to their respective revenue standards. However, the Boards have said they expect the amendments to result in similar outcomes in many circumstances.

In September 2015, the IASB deferred the effective date of IFRS 15 by one year to give entities more time to implement it (see 1.2 below).[4] In addition, in April 2016, the IASB issued *Clarifications to IFRS 15* Revenue from Contracts with Customers (the IASB's amendments) to address several implementation issues (many of which were discussed by the TRG) on key aspects of the standard.

The IASB's amendments:

- clarify when a promised good or service is separately identifiable from other promises in a contract (i.e. distinct within the context of the contract), which is part of an entity's assessment of whether a promised good or service is a performance obligation (see 4.2 below);
- clarify how to apply the principal versus agent application guidance to determine whether the nature of an entity's promise is to provide a promised good or service itself (i.e. the entity is a principal) or to arrange for goods or services to be provided by another party (i.e. the entity is an agent) (see 4.4 below);
- clarify for a licence of intellectual property when an entity's activities significantly affect the intellectual property to which the customer has rights, which is a factor in determining whether the entity recognises revenue over time or at a point in time (see 8 below);
- clarify the scope of the exception for sales-based and usage-based royalties related to licences of intellectual property (the royalty constraint) when there are other promised goods or services in the contract (see 8.5 below); and
- add two practical expedients to the transition requirements of IFRS 15 for: (a) completed contracts under the full retrospective transition method; and (b) contract modifications at transition (see 1.3 below).

The FASB also deferred the effective date of its standard by one year for US GAAP public and non-public entities, as defined, which keeps the standards' effective dates converged under IFRS and US GAAP.

Like the IASB, the FASB also finalised amendments to its revenue standard to address principal versus agent considerations, identifying performance obligations, licences of intellectual property and certain practical expedients on transition.[5] The FASB's amendments for principal versus agent considerations and clarifying when a promised good or service is separately identifiable when identifying performance obligations are converged with those of the IASB as discussed above. However, the FASB's other amendments were not the same as those of the IASB. The FASB has also issued amendments relating to immaterial goods and services in a contract, accounting for shipping and handling, collectability, non-cash consideration and the presentation of sales and other similar taxes, which the IASB has not issued. We highlight these differences throughout this chapter.

In May 2016, the FASB proposed nine technical corrections and improvements related to its revenue standard.[6] Comments were due by 2 July 2016. To finalise these changes, the FASB will need to issue final amendments. The IASB is not expected to propose similar amendments. We highlight certain of these proposed differences throughout this chapter.

1.2 Effective date

IFRS 15 is now effective for annual reporting periods beginning on or after 1 January 2018 (as a result of the IASB issuing an amendment in September 2015 to defer the standard's effective date by one year, see 1.1.2 above). Early adoption is permitted, provided that fact is disclosed. *[IFRS 15.C1]*.

In April 2016, the IASB issued amendments to IFRS 15. The amendments are also effective for annual reporting periods beginning on or after 1 January 2018. Early adoption is permitted, provided that fact is disclosed. *[IFRS 15.C1B]*.

Figure 30.1 below illustrates the effective date of IFRS 15 for entities with differing year-ends and assumes that entities report results twice a year (annual and half-year).

Figure 30.1: Illustrative effective dates for IFRS 15

Year-end	Mandatory adoption	Early adoption
31 December	1 January 2018 adoption date. Present for the first time in 30 June 2018 interim financial statements or 31 December 2018 annual financial statements.	Possible adoption dates include, but are not limited to: • 1 January 2014 adoption date. Present for the first time in 30 June 2014 interim financial statements or 31 December 2014 annual financial statements. • 1 January 2015 adoption date. Present for the first time in 30 June 2015 interim financial statements or 31 December 2015 annual financial statements. • 1 January 2016 adoption date. Present for the first time in 30 June 2016 interim financial statements or 31 December 2016 annual financial statements.

		• 1 January 2017 adoption date. Present for the first time in 30 June 2017 interim financial statements or 31 December 2017 annual financial statements.
30 June	1 July 2018 adoption date. Present for the first time in 31 December 2018 interim financial statements or 30 June 2019 annual financial statements.	Possible adoption dates include, but are not limited to: • 1 July 2014 adoption date. Present for the first time in 31 December 2014 interim financial statements or 30 June 2015 annual financial statements. • 1 July 2015 adoption date. Present for the first time in 31 December 2015 interim financial statements or 30 June 2016 annual financial statements. • 1 July 2016 adoption date. Present for the first time in 31 December 2016 interim financial statements or 30 June 2017 annual financial statements. • 1 July 2017 adoption date. Present for the first time in 31 December 2017 interim financial statements or 30 June 2018 annual financial statements.

The FASB also deferred the effective date of its standard by one year. As a result, the FASB's standard is effective for public entities, as defined,[7] for fiscal years beginning after 15 December 2017 and interim periods therein. Non-public entities (i.e. an entity that does not meet the definition of a public entity in the FASB's standard) are required to adopt the standard for fiscal years beginning after 15 December 2018 and interim periods within fiscal years beginning after 15 December 2019. That is, non-public entities are not required to apply the standard in interim periods in the year of adoption.

US GAAP public and non-public entities will be permitted to adopt the standard as early as the original public entity effective date (i.e. annual reporting periods beginning after 15 December 2016 and interim periods therein). Early adoption prior to that date is not permitted.

1.3 Transition methods

IFRS 15 requires retrospective application. The Board decided to allow either 'full retrospective' adoption in which the standard is applied to all of the periods presented or a 'modified retrospective' adoption (see 1.3.1 and 1.3.2 below, respectively).

In April 2016, the IASB amended IFRS 15 to permit an entity: (a) under the full retrospective method, not to restate contracts that are completed contracts at the beginning of the earliest period presented; (b) under the modified retrospective method, to either apply IFRS 15 to only contracts that are not completed contracts at the date of initial application; or to all contracts including completed contracts at the date of initial application; (c) under either transition method, to use hindsight when evaluating contract modifications for transition purposes.

The IASB also clarified in the Basis for Conclusions that any remaining accounting for a completed contract, including revenue still to be recognised, after the date of initial application will be in accordance with its accounting policies based on current IFRS, i.e. IAS 11, IAS 18 and related Interpretations. *[IFRS 15.BC445E]*.

IFRS 15 defines the following terms: *[IFRS 15.C2]*

- *The date of initial application* – the start of the reporting period in which an entity first applies IFRS 15. For example, for an entity whose annual reporting period ends on 30 June, the mandatory date of initial application will be 1 July 2018, regardless of the transition method selected.
- *Completed contract* – a contract in which the entity has fully transferred all of the identified goods and services before the date of initial application. Depending on the manner an entity elects to transition to IFRS 15, an entity may not need to apply IFRS 15 to contracts if they have completed performance before the date of initial application, even if they have not yet received the consideration and that consideration is still subject to variability.

  The IASB noted in the Basis for Conclusions that 'transferred all of the goods or services' is not meant to imply that an entity would apply the 'transfer of control' notion in IFRS 15 to goods or services that have been identified in accordance with current IFRS. Rather it is performance in accordance with current requirements (i.e. IAS 11, IAS 18 and related Interpretations). *[IFRS 15.BC441]*. 'Consequently, in many situations the term "transferred" would mean "delivered" within the context of contracts for the sale of goods and "performed" within the context of contracts for rendering services and construction contracts. In some situations, the entity would use judgement when determining whether it has transferred goods or services to the customer.' *[IFRS 15.BC445D]*.

  Consider the following examples:

  - Contract is completed – a retailer sells products to a customer on 31 December 2017, with immediate delivery. The customer has a poor credit history. Therefore, the retailer requires the customer to pay half of the consideration upfront and half within 60 days. In accordance with IAS 18, the retailer recognises half of the consideration at the time of the sale. However, the retailer concludes it is not probable that it will be able to collect the remainder and defers recognition of this amount. Because the goods are delivered prior to the date of initial application of the new standard (e.g. 1 January 2018), the contract is considered completed under the new standard.

Chapter 30

- Contract is not completed – an entity enters into a contract to provide a service and loyalty points to a customer on 31 January 2017. In accordance with IFRIC 13, the entity defers a portion of the total contract consideration for the loyalty points and defers recognition until the points are exercised on 15 January 2018. The entity completes the required service within six months and recognises revenue related to the service over that period in accordance with IAS 18. As at the date of initial application of the new standard (e.g. 1 January 2018), the entity has not yet performed in relation to the loyalty points. As a result, the contract is not considered completed under the new standard.

The definition of a 'completed contract' is not converged between IFRS and US GAAP. A completed contract under ASC 606 is defined as one for which all (or substantially all) of the revenue was recognised in accordance existing US GAAP requirements that applied at the date of initial application.[8]

The different definitions could lead to entities having a different population of contracts to transition to the new revenue standards under IFRS and US GAAP, respectively. However, the Board noted in the Basis for Conclusions that an entity could avoid the consequences of these different definitions by choosing to apply IFRS 15 retrospectively to all contracts, including completed contracts. *[IFRS 15.BC445I]*.

1.3.1 Full retrospective adoption

Entities electing the full retrospective adoption will apply the provisions of IFRS 15 to each period presented in the financial statements in accordance with IAS 8 – *Accounting Policies, Changes in Accounting Estimates and Errors*, subject to the practical expedients created to provide relief. The requirements of IAS 8 are discussed in Chapter 3.

Under the full retrospective method, entities will have to apply IFRS 15 as if it had been applied since the inception of all its contracts with customers that are presented in the financial statements. That is, an entity electing the full retrospective method will have to transition all of its contracts with customers to IFRS 15 (subject to the practical expedients described below), not just those that are not considered completed contracts as at the beginning of the earliest period presented. This means that for contracts that were considered completed (as defined) before the beginning of the earliest period, an entity will still need to evaluate the contract under IFRS 15 in order to determine whether there was an effect on revenue recognised in any of the year's presented in the period of initial application (unless an entity elects to use one of the practical expedients described below).

During deliberations on the original standard, the IASB seemed to prefer the full retrospective method, under which all contracts with customers are recognised and measured consistently in all periods presented within the financial statements, regardless of when the contracts were entered into. This method also provides users of the financial statements with useful trend information across all periods presented.

However, to ease the potential burden of applying it on a fully retrospective basis, the IASB provided relief. An entity may use one or more of the following practical expedients when applying this standard retrospectively:

'(a) for completed contracts, an entity need not restate contracts that:
  (i) begin and end within the same annual reporting period; or
  (ii) are completed contracts at the beginning of the earliest period presented.

(b) for completed contracts that have variable consideration, an entity may use the transaction price at the date the contract was completed rather than estimating variable consideration amounts in the comparative reporting periods.

(c) for contracts that were modified before the beginning of the earliest period presented, an entity need not retrospectively restate the contract for those contract modifications in accordance with paragraphs 20-21. Instead, an entity shall reflect the aggregate effect of all of the modifications that occur before the beginning of the earliest period presented when:
  (i) identifying the satisfied and unsatisfied performance obligations;
  (ii) determining the transaction price; and
  (iii) allocating the transaction price to the satisfied and unsatisfied performance obligations.

(d) for all reporting periods presented before the date of initial application, an entity need not disclose the amount of the transaction price allocated to the remaining performance obligations and an explanation of when the entity expects to recognise that amount as revenue (see paragraph 120).' *[IFRS 15.C5]*.

While the practical expedients will provide some relief, an entity will still need to use judgement and make estimates. For example, an entity will need to use judgement in estimating stand-alone selling prices when there has been a wide range of selling prices and when allocating the transaction price to satisfied and unsatisfied performance obligations if there have been several performance obligations or contract modifications over an extended period. Furthermore, if an entity applies the practical expedient for contract modifications, it will still be required to apply the standard's contract modification requirements (see 3.4 below) to modifications made after the beginning of the earliest period presented under IFRS 15.

The FASB's standard includes a similar practical expedient for contract modifications at transition for entities that elect to apply the full retrospective method. Entities would also apply the FASB's practical expedient to all contract modifications that occur before the beginning of the earliest period presented under the new standard in the financial statements. However, this could be a different date for IFRS preparers and US GAAP preparers depending on the number of comparative periods included within an entity's financial statements (e.g. US GAAP preparers often include two comparative periods in their financial statements).

Unlike IFRS 15, the FASB's standard does not allow an entity that uses the full retrospective method to apply ASC 606 only to contracts that are not completed (as defined) as at the beginning of the earliest period presented.

Entities may elect to apply none, some or all of these expedients. However, if an entity elects to use any of them, it must apply that expedient consistently to all contracts within all periods presented. It would not be appropriate to apply the selected expedient to some, but not all, of the periods presented. Entities that choose to use some, or all, of the relief will be required to provide additional qualitative disclosures (i.e. the types of relief the entity has applied and the likely effect of that application). *[IFRS 15.C6]*.

An entity that elects to apply the standard retrospectively is also required to provide the disclosures required in IAS 8, including:

'(a) the title of the IFRS;

(b) when applicable, that the change in accounting policy is made in accordance with its transitional provisions;

(c) the nature of the change in accounting policy;

(d) when applicable, a description of the transitional provisions;

(e) when applicable, the transitional provisions that might have an effect on future periods;

(f) for the current period and each prior period presented, to the extent practicable, the amount of the adjustment.

  (i) for each financial statement line item affected; and

  (ii) if IAS 33 – *Earnings per Share* – applies to the entity, for basic and diluted earnings per share;

(g) the amount of the adjustment relating to periods before those presented, to the extent practicable; and

(h) if retrospective application is impracticable for a particular prior period, or for periods before those presented, the circumstances that led to the existence of that condition and a description of how and from when the change in accounting policy has been applied.

Financial statements for subsequent periods need not repeat these disclosures.' *[IAS 8.28]*.

An entity must make the above disclosures in the period in which a new standard is applied for the first time. Financial statements in subsequent periods need not repeat the required disclosures. The IASB provided some additional relief from disclosures for an entity that elects to apply IFRS 15 on a fully retrospective basis. Although permitted to do so, an entity need not present the quantitative information required by (f) above for periods other than the annual period immediately preceding the first annual period for which IFRS 15 is applied (the 'immediately preceding period'). *[IFRS 15.C4]*.

1.3.2 Modified retrospective adoption

Entities that elect the modified retrospective method will apply the standard retrospectively to only the most current period presented in the financial statements (i.e. the initial period of application). To do so, the entity will have to recognise the cumulative effect of initially applying IFRS 15 as an adjustment to the opening balance of retained earnings (or other appropriate components of equity) at the date of initial application. *[IFRS 15.C7]*.

Under this method, IFRS 15 will be applied either to all contracts at the date of initial application (e.g. 1 January 2018, see 1.2 above) or only to contracts that are not completed at this date. *[IFRS 15.C7]*. Depending on how an entity elects to apply the modified retrospective method, it will have to evaluate either all contracts or only those that are not completed before the date of initial application as if the entity had applied the new standard to them since inception. An entity will be required to disclose how it has applied the modified retrospective method (i.e. either to all contracts or only to contracts that are not completed at the date of initial application).

An entity may choose to apply the modified retrospective method to all contracts as at the date of initial application (rather than only to contracts that are not completed) in order to apply the same accounting to similar contracts after the date of adoption. Consider the example discussed at 1.3 above, a sale by a retailer on 31 December 2017, the contract in that example is considered a completed contract as at the date of initial application (e.g. 1 January 2018). If the retailer adopts the standard only for contracts that are not completed, it would not restate revenue for this contract and would continue to account for the remaining revenue to be recognised under current IFRS (i.e. IAS 18) after adoption of IFRS 15. However, any similar sales on or after 1 January 2018 would be subject to the requirements of IFRS 15. Accordingly, if the retailer prefers to account for similar transactions under the same accounting model, it could choose to adopt the standard for all contracts, rather than only to those that are not completed under the new standard.

Entities that use the modified retrospective method will need to make this election at the entity-wide level. That is, they will need to carefully consider whether to apply the standard to all contracts or only to contracts that are not completed as at the date of initial application, considering the totality of all of the entity's revenue streams and the potential disparity in accounting treatment for the same or similar types of transactions after they adopt the standard.

Under the modified retrospective method, an entity will: *[IFRS 15.C7-C8]*

- present comparative periods in accordance with prior revenue standards (e.g. IAS 11, IAS 18, etc.);
- apply IFRS 15 to new and existing contracts (either all existing contracts or only contracts that are not completed contracts) from the effective date onwards; and
- recognise a cumulative catch-up adjustment to the opening balance of retained earnings at the effective date either for all contracts or only for existing contracts that still require performance by the entity in the year of adoption, disclose the amount by which each financial statement line item was affected as a result of applying IFRS 15 and an explanation of significant changes.

An entity that chooses the modified retrospective method can use only one of the five practical expedients available to entities that apply the full retrospective method, relating to contract modifications. However, under the modified retrospective method, entities can choose whether to apply the expedient to all contract modifications that occur before either: (a) the beginning of the earliest period presented (e.g. before 1 January 2017 if an entity with a December year-end presents only one comparative period); or (b) the date of initial application (e.g. 1 January 2018). Under the expedient, an entity can reflect the aggregate effect of all modifications that occur before either of these dates under IFRS 15 when identifying the satisfied and unsatisfied performance obligations, determining the transaction price and allocating the transaction price to the satisfied and unsatisfied performance obligations for the modified contract at transition. *[IFRS 15.C7A]*.

An entity that uses this expedient will have to identify all contract modifications from the inception of the contract until either: (a) the beginning of the earliest period presented under IFRS 15; or (b) the date of initial application. It will then have to determine how each modification affected the identification of performance obligations as at the modification date. However, the entity would not need to determine or allocate the transaction price as at the date of each modification. Instead, at the beginning of the earliest period presented under the standard or the date of initial application of the standard, the entity would determine the transaction price for all satisfied and unsatisfied performance obligations identified in the contract from contract inception. The entity would then perform a single allocation of the transaction price to those performance obligations, based on their relative stand-alone selling prices.

If an entity electing the modified retrospective method uses the practical expedient for contract modifications, it will be required to provide additional qualitative disclosures (i.e. the type of relief the entity applied and the likely effects of that application). *[IFRS 15.C7A]*.

While this practical expedient will provide some relief, an entity will still need to use judgement and make estimates. For example, an entity will need to use judgement in estimating stand-alone selling prices when there has been a wide range of selling prices and when allocating the transaction price to satisfied and unsatisfied performance obligations if there have been several performance obligations or contract modifications over an extended period. Furthermore, it will still be required to apply the standard's contract modification requirements (see 3.4 below) to modifications made after the beginning of the earliest period presented under IFRS 15.

The FASB's standard includes a similar practical expedient for contract modifications at transition. However, ASC 606 only permits an entity to apply the practical expedient under the modified retrospective method to contract modifications that occur before the beginning of the earliest period presented under the new standard in the financial statements (e.g. 1 January 2018).

The following example illustrates the potential effects of the modified retrospective method:

Example 30.1: Cumulative effect of adoption under the modified retrospective method

A software vendor with a 31 December year-end adopts IFRS 15 on 1 January 2018. The vendor adopts the standard using the modified retrospective method and elects to apply IFRS 15 only to contracts that are not completed.

The vendor frequently enters into contracts to provide a software licence, professional services and post-delivery service support. It previously accounted for its contracts in accordance with IAS 18, particularly paragraph IE19 of IAS 18. As a result, it recognised fees from the development of its software by reference to the stage of completion of the development, which included the completion of post-delivery service support services. In effect, the software vendor treated the development of software and post-delivery service support as a single deliverable.

IFRS 15 provides more detailed requirements for determining whether promised goods and services are performance obligations (discussed further at 4.2 below) than IAS 18 provided regarding the number of deliverables to identify.

As a result, the vendor's analysis of contracts in progress as at 1 January 2018 may result in the identification of different performance obligations from those it previously used for revenue recognition. As part of this assessment, the entity would need to allocate the estimated transaction price, based on the relative stand-alone selling price method (see 6.2 below), to the newly identified performance obligations.

The vendor would compare the revenue recognised for each contract, from contract inception through to 31 December 2017, to the amount that would have been recognised if the entity had applied IFRS 15 since contract inception. The difference between those two amounts would be accounted for as a cumulative catch-up adjustment and recognised as at 1 January 2018 in opening retained earnings. From 1 January 2018 onwards, revenue recognised would be based on IFRS 15.

An entity that elects to apply the modified retrospective method will be required to make certain disclosures in the year of initial application. Specifically, the entity must disclose the amount by which each financial statement line item is affected as a result of applying IFRS 15. Furthermore, an entity must disclose an explanation of the reasons for any significant changes between the reported results under IFRS 15 and under IAS 11, IAS 18 and related Interpretations.

Depending on an entity's prior accounting policies, applying the modified retrospective method may be more difficult than an entity would anticipate. Situations that may make application under this method more complex include the following:

- the performance obligations identified under IFRS 15 are different from the elements/deliverables identified under current requirements;
- the relative stand-alone selling price allocation required by IFRS 15 results in different amounts of the consideration being allocated to performance obligations than had been allocated in the past; or
- the contract contains variable consideration and the amount of variable consideration that can be included in the allocable consideration differs from the amount under current requirements.

In addition, the modified retrospective method effectively requires an entity to keep two sets of accounting records in the year of adoption in order to comply with the requirement to disclose all line items in the financial statements as if they were prepared under current IFRS.

1.3.3 Other transition considerations

Regardless of the transition method they choose, many entities will have to apply the standard to contracts entered into in prior periods. The population of contracts will be larger under the full retrospective method. However, under the modified retrospective method, entities will, at a minimum, have to apply IFRS 15 to all contracts that are not completed as at the date of initial application, regardless of when those contracts commenced. Questions on the mechanics of retrospective application are likely to arise.

The Board has provided some relief from a full retrospective method, in the form of several practical expedients, and provided the option of a modified retrospective method, which provides one practical expedient. However, there are still a number of application issues that may make applying IFRS 15 difficult and/or time-consuming, for example:

- In the case of full retrospective adoption, entities will likely be required to perform an allocation of the transaction price because of changes to the identified deliverables, the transaction price or both. If an entity previously performed a relative fair value allocation, this step may be straightforward. Regardless, an entity will be required to determine the stand-alone selling price of each performance obligation as at inception of the contract. Depending on the age of the contract, this information may not be readily available and the prices may differ significantly from current stand-alone selling prices. While the standard is clear as to when it is acceptable to use hindsight in respect of variable consideration to determine the transaction price (see 5.2 below for a discussion on variable consideration), it is silent on whether the use of hindsight is acceptable for other aspects of the model (e.g. for the purpose of allocating the transaction price) or whether it would be acceptable to use current pricing information if that were the only information available.
- Estimating variable consideration for all contracts for prior periods will likely require significant judgement. The standard is clear that hindsight cannot be used for contracts that are not completed when applying the full retrospective method. The standard is silent on whether the use of hindsight is acceptable for entities applying the modified retrospective method. However, the Board's discussion in the Basis for Conclusions implies that it originally intended to provide no practical expedients for the modified retrospective method. *[IFRS 15.BC439-BC443]*. Furthermore, since entities applying the modified retrospective method may only be adjusting contracts that are not completed, it seems likely that the use of hindsight is not acceptable. As a result, entities must make this estimate based only on information that was available at contract inception. Contemporaneous documentation clarifying what information was available to management, and when it was available, will likely be needed to support these estimates. In addition to estimating variable consideration using the expected value or a most likely amount method, entities will have to make conclusions about whether such variable consideration is subject to the constraint (see 5.2.3 below for further discussion).
- The modified retrospective method does not require entities to restate the amounts reported in prior periods. However, at the date of initial application, entities electing this method will still have to calculate, either for all contracts or only for contracts that are not completed (depending on how the entity elects to apply this transition method), the revenues they would have recognised as if they had applied IFRS 15 since contract inception. This is needed in order to determine the cumulative effect of adopting the new standard. It is likely to be most challenging for contracts in which the identified elements/deliverables or allocable consideration change when the new requirements are applied.

Finally, entities will need to consider a number of other issues as they prepare to adopt IFRS 15. For example, entities with significant deferred revenue balances under current IFRS may experience 'lost revenue' if those amounts were deferred at the adoption date of IFRS 15 and will, ultimately, be reflected in the restated prior periods or as part of the cumulative adjustment upon adoption, but are never reported as revenue in a current period within the financial statements.

1.3.4 Disclosures prior to adoption of IFRS 15

When an entity has not applied a new standard that has been issued but is not yet effective, IAS 8 requires an entity to disclose that fact and known or reasonably estimable information relevant to assessing the possible impact that application of a standard will have on the financial statements in the period of initial application. *[IAS 8.30]*. In producing this disclosure, an entity is required to consider disclosing all of the following: *[IAS 8.31]*

- the title of the new standard;
- the nature of the impending change or changes in accounting policy;
- the date by which application of the standard is required;
- the date as at which it plans to apply the standard initially; and
- a discussion of the impact that initial application of the standard is expected to have on the entity's financial statements or, if that impact is not known or reasonably estimable, a statement to that effect.

In July 2016, ESMA made a public statement regarding the implementation of IFRS 15.[9] The statement highlighted the need for consistent and high-quality implementation and for transparency on the impact of IFRS 15 to assist users of financial statements. In relation to the requirements in IAS 8, outlined above, ESMA commented that:

- An entity's IAS 8 disclosures should evolve as more information about the effects of the new standard becomes available and an entity should gradually be able to provide more entity-specific quantitative and qualitative information.
- For most issuers, the effect of IFRS 15 should be known or reasonably estimable by the time they prepare their 2017 interim financial statement. Therefore, in ESMA's view, in most cases, it would not be appropriate to provide disclosures about the magnitude and impact of IFRS 15 only in the 2017 annual financial statements.
- If the impact is expected to be significant, 'ESMA expects issuers to:
  - (a) provide information about the accounting policy choices that are to be taken upon first application of IFRS 15 (such as the accounting policy to apply a full retrospective approach, the cumulative catch-up transition method or the use of practical expedients);
  - (b) disaggregate the expected impact depending on its nature (i.e. whether the impact will modify the amount of revenue to be recognised, the timing or both) and by revenue streams; and
  - (c) explain the nature of the impacts so that users of financial statements understand the changes to current practices and their key drivers when compared with the existing principles on recognition and measurement in IAS 11, IAS 18 and related interpretations.'[10]

The public statement also provides, by way of illustration, the types of information ESMA expects to be disclosed for each interim and annual reporting for 2016 and 2017 when an entity expects the standard to have a significant impact.

Some entities may not know, or be able to make, a reasonable estimate of the impact IFRS 15 will have on its financial statements and will make a statement to that effect.

Like ESMA, other regulators may expect an entity's disclosures to become more robust as time passes as more information about the effects of the new standard becomes available.

1.4 Definitions

The following table summarises the terms that are defined in IFRS 15. *[IFRS 15 Appendix A]*.

Figure 30.2: IFRS 15 Definitions

Term	Definition
Contract	An agreement between two or more parties that creates enforceable rights and obligations.
Contract asset	An entity's right to consideration in exchange for goods or services that the entity has transferred to a customer when that right is conditioned on something other than the passage of time (for example, the entity's future performance).
Contract liability	An entity's obligation to transfer goods or services to a customer for which the entity has received consideration (or the amount is due) from the customer.
Customer	A party that has contracted with an entity to obtain goods or services that are an output of the entity's ordinary activities in exchange for consideration.
Income	Increases in economic benefits during the accounting period in the form of inflows or enhancements of assets or decreases of liabilities that result in an increase in equity, other than those relating to contributions from equity participants.
Performance obligation	A promise in a contract with a customer to transfer to the customer either: (a) a good or service (or a bundle of goods or services) that is distinct; or (b) a series of distinct goods or services that are substantially the same and that have the same pattern of transfer to the customer.
Revenue	Income arising in the course of an entity's ordinary activities.
Stand-alone selling price (of a good or service)	The price at which an entity would sell a promised good or service separately to a customer.
Transaction price (for a contract with a customer)	The amount of consideration to which an entity expects to be entitled in exchange for transferring promised goods or services to a customer, excluding amounts collected on behalf of third parties.

2 SCOPE

IFRS 15 applies to all entities and all contracts with customers to provide goods or services in the ordinary course of business, except for the following contracts, which are specifically excluded: *[IFRS 15.5]*

- lease contracts within the scope of IAS 17– *Leases* (or IFRS 16 – *Leases*);
- insurance contracts within the scope of IFRS 4 – *Insurance Contracts*;
- financial instruments and other contractual rights or obligations within the scope of IFRS 9 – *Financial Instruments* – or IAS 39 – *Financial Instruments: Recognition and Measurement*, IFRS 10 – *Consolidated Financial Statements*, IFRS 11 – *Joint Arrangements*, IAS 27 – *Separate Financial Statements* – and IAS 28 – *Investments in Associates and Joint Ventures*; and
- non-monetary exchanges between entities in the same line of business to facilitate sales to customers or potential customers.

In addition, arrangements must meet the criteria set out in paragraph 9 of IFRS 15, which are discussed at 3.1 below, in order to be accounted for as a revenue contract under the standard.

For certain arrangements, entities will have to evaluate their relationship with the counterparty to the contract in order to determine whether a vendor-customer relationship exists. Some collaboration arrangements, for example, are more akin to a partnership, while others have a vendor-customer relationship. Only transactions that are determined to be with a customer are within the scope of IFRS 15. See 2.3 below for a discussion on collaborative arrangements.

2.1 Other scope considerations

Certain arrangements executed by entities include repurchase provisions, either as a component of a sales contract or as a separate contract that relates to the same or similar goods in the original agreement. The form of the repurchase agreement and whether the customer obtains control of the asset will determine whether the agreement is within the scope of the standard. See 7.4 below for a discussion on repurchase agreements.

Entities may enter into transactions that are partially within the scope of IFRS 15 and partially within the scope of other standards. In these situations, the standard requires an entity to apply any separation and/or measurement requirements in the other standard first, before applying the requirements in IFRS 15. See 2.4 below for further discussion.

The standard also specifies the accounting requirements for certain costs, such as the incremental costs of obtaining a contract and the costs of fulfilling a contract. However, the standard is clear that these requirements only apply if there are no other applicable requirements in IFRS for those costs. See 9.3 below for further discussion on the requirements relating to contract costs in the standard.

In addition, as part of the consequential amendments associated with IFRS 15, the existing requirements for the recognition of a gain or loss on the disposal of a non-financial asset (e.g. assets within the scope of IAS 16 – *Property, Plant and Equipment* – or IAS 38 – *Intangible Assets*) will be amended. The recognition and measurement requirements in IFRS 15 will apply when recognising and measuring any gains or losses on disposal of such non-financial assets, when that disposal is not in the ordinary course of business. An entity will be required to look to the control model in IFRS 15 to determine when to derecognise the non-financial asset (i.e. when control is transferred). The entity will estimate consideration to measure the gain or loss following the requirements in IFRS 15 for determining the transaction price. Any subsequent changes to the estimated consideration will also be accounted for following the requirements of IFRS 15. The measurement of any gain or loss resulting from the consequential amendments may differ from the gain or loss measured by following the current requirements in IAS 18.

2.2 Definition of a customer

The standard defines a customer 'as a party that has contracted with an entity to obtain goods or services that are an output of the entity's ordinary activities in exchange for consideration'. *[IFRS 15 Appendix A]*. IFRS 15 does not define the term 'ordinary activities' because it is already widely used in IFRS. In many transactions, a customer is easily identifiable. However, in transactions involving multiple parties, it may be less clear which counterparties are customers of the entity. For some arrangements, multiple parties could all be considered customers of the entity. However, for other arrangements, only some of the parties involved are considered customers.

Example 30.2 below shows how a party considered to be the customer may differ, depending on the specific facts and circumstances. The identification of the performance obligations in a contract (discussed further at 4 below) can have a significant effect on the determination of which party is the entity's customer. Also see the discussion of the identification of an entity's customer when applying the application guidance on consideration paid or payable to a customer at 5.7 below.

Example 30.2: Identification of a customer

An entity provides internet-based advertising services to companies. As part of those services, the entity purchases banner-space on various websites from a selection of publishers. For certain contracts, the entity provides a sophisticated service of matching the ad placement with the pre-identified criteria of the advertising party (i.e. the customer). In addition, the entity pre-purchases the banner-space from the publishers before it finds advertisers for that space. Assume that the entity appropriately concludes it is acting as the principal in these contracts (see 4.4 below for further discussion on this topic). Accordingly, the entity identifies that its customer in this transaction is the advertiser to whom it is providing services.

In other contracts, the entity simply matches advertisers with the publishers in its portfolio, but the entity does not provide any sophisticated ad-targeting services or purchase the advertising space from the publishers before it finds advertisers for that space. Assume that the entity appropriately concludes it is acting as the agent in these contracts. Accordingly, the entity identifies that its customer is the publisher to whom it is providing services.

2.3 Collaborative arrangements

In certain transactions, a counterparty may not always be a 'customer' of the entity. Instead, the counterparty may be a collaborator or partner that shares in the risks and benefits of developing a product to be marketed. *[IFRS 15.6]*. This is common in the pharmaceutical, bio-technology, oil and gas, and health care industries. However, depending on the facts and circumstances, these arrangements may also contain a vendor-customer relationship component. Such contracts could still be within the scope of IFRS 15, at least partially, if the collaborator or partner meets the definition of a customer for some, or all, aspects of the arrangement.

The IASB decided not to provide additional application guidance for determining whether certain revenue-generating collaborative arrangements would be within the scope of IFRS 15. In the Basis for Conclusions, the IASB explained that it would not be possible to provide application guidance that applies to all collaborative arrangements. *[IFRS 15.BC54]*. Therefore, the parties to such arrangements need to consider all of the facts and circumstances to determine whether a vendor-customer relationship exists that is subject to the standard.

However, the IASB did determine that, in some circumstances, it may be appropriate for an entity to apply the principles in IFRS 15 to collaborations or partnerships (e.g. when there are no applicable or more relevant requirements that could be applied). *[IFRS 15.BC56]*.

Under current IFRS, identifying the customer can be difficult, especially when multiple parties are involved in the transaction. This evaluation may require significant judgement and the new standard does not provide additional factors to consider.

Furthermore, transactions among partners in collaboration arrangements are not within the scope of IFRS 15. Therefore, entities will need to use judgement to determine whether transactions are between partners acting in their capacity as collaborators or reflect a vendor-customer relationship.

2.4 Interaction with other standards

The standard provides requirements for arrangements partially within the scope of IFRS 15 and partially within the scope of other standards. IFRS 15 states that if the other standards specify how to separate and/or initially measure one or more parts of the contract, then an entity shall first apply the separation and/or measurement requirements in those standards. An entity shall exclude from the transaction price (as discussed at 5 below) the amount of the part (or parts) of the contract that are initially measured in accordance with other standards and shall apply the allocation requirements in IFRS 15 (as discussed at 6 below) to allocate the amount of the transaction price that remains (if any) to each performance obligation within the scope of IFRS 15. If the other standards do not specify how to separate and/or initially measure one or more parts of the contract, then the entity shall apply IFRS 15 to separate and/or initially measure the part (or parts) of the contract. *[IFRS 15.7]*.

Only after applying other applicable standards will an entity apply IFRS 15 to the remaining components of an arrangement. Some examples of where separation and/or allocation are addressed in other IFRS include the following:

- IAS 39 requires that a financial instrument be recognised at fair value at initial recognition. For contracts that include the issuance of a financial instrument and revenue components, the fair value of the financial instrument is first measured and the remainder of the estimated contract consideration is allocated among the other components in the contract in accordance with IFRS 15.
- IFRIC 4 – *Determining whether an Arrangement contains a Lease* – requires the allocation of an arrangement's consideration between a lease and other components within a contractual arrangement using a relative fair value approach. *[IFRIC 4.13]*. Note that, in March 2016, the IASB issued a new leases standard, IFRS 16. The new leases standard is effective annual periods beginning after 1 January 2019 (i.e. one year after IFRS 15). Early adoption is permitted for all entities, provided IFRS 15 has been applied or is applied at the same date as IFRS 16.

As stated above, if a component of the arrangement is covered by another standard or interpretation, but that standard or interpretation does not specify how to separate and/or initially measure that component, the entity will apply IFRS 15 to separate and/or measure each component. For example, specific requirements do not exist for the separation and measurement of the different parts of an arrangement when an entity sells a business and also enters into a long-term supply agreement with the other party. See 6.6 below for further discussion on the effect on the allocation of arrangement consideration when an arrangement includes both revenue and non-revenue components.

Entities entering into transactions that fall within the scope of multiple standards need to separate those transactions into components, so that each component can be accounted for under the relevant standards. IFRS 15 does not change this requirement. However, under current IFRS, revenue transactions must often be separated into components that are accounted for under different revenue standards and/or interpretations (e.g. a transaction involving the sale of goods and a customer loyalty programme that falls within the scope of both IAS 18 and IFRIC 15, respectively). This will no longer be relevant as there is a single revenue recognition model under IFRS 15.

IAS 18 currently specifies the accounting treatment for the recognition and measurement of interest and dividends. Interest and dividend income are excluded from the scope of IFRS 15. Instead, the relevant recognition and measurement requirements have been moved to IFRS 9 or IAS 39.

2.4.1 Implementation questions on scope

2.4.1.A Islamic financing transactions

Islamic financial institutions (IFIs) enter into Sharia-compliant instruments and transactions that do not result in IFIs earning interest on loans. Instead, these transactions involve purchases and sales of real assets (e.g. vehicles) on which IFIs can earn a premium to compensate them for deferred payment terms. Typically, an IFI makes a cash purchase of the underlying asset, takes legal possession, even if only for a short time, and immediately sells the asset on deferred payment terms. The financial instruments created by these transactions are within the scope of the financial instruments standards.[11]

At the January 2015 TRG meeting, the IASB TRG members discussed whether (before applying the financial instruments standards) deferred-payment transactions that are part of Sharia-compliant instruments and transactions are within the scope of IFRS 15. The IASB TRG members generally agreed that Sharia-compliant instruments and transactions may be outside the scope of the standard. However, the analysis would depend on the specific facts and circumstances. This may require significant judgement as contracts often differ within and between jurisdictions. The FASB TRG members did not discuss this issue.[12]

2.4.1.B Certain fee-generating activities of financial institutions

The TRG considered an issue raised by US GAAP stakeholders whether certain fee-generating activities of financial institutions are in the scope of the new revenue standard (i.e. servicing and sub-servicing financial assets, providing financial guarantees and providing deposit-related services).[13]

The FASB TRG members generally agreed that the standard provides a framework for determining whether certain contracts are in the scope of the FASB's standard, ASC 606, or other standards. As discussed above, the standard's scope includes all contracts with customers to provide goods or services in the ordinary course of business, except for contracts with customers that are within the scope of certain other ASC topics that are listed as scope exclusions. If another standard specifies the accounting for the consideration (e.g. a fee) received in the arrangement, the consideration is outside the scope of ASC 606. If other standards do not specify the accounting for the consideration and there is a separate good or service provided, the consideration is in (or at least partially in) the scope of ASC 606. The FASB staff applied this framework in the TRG agenda paper to arrangements to service financial assets, provide financial guarantees and provide deposit-related services.

The FASB TRG members generally agreed that income from servicing financial assets (e.g. loans) is not within the scope of ASC 606. An asset servicer performs various services, such as communication with the borrower and payment collection, in exchange for a fee. The FASB TRG members generally agreed that an entity should look to ASC 860 – *Transfers and Servicing* – to determine the appropriate accounting for these fees. This is because ASC 606 contains a scope exception for contracts that fall under ASC 860, which provides requirements on the recognition of the fees (despite not providing explicit requirements on revenue accounting).

The FASB TRG members generally agreed that fees from providing financial guarantees are not within the scope of ASC 606. A financial institution may receive a fee for providing a guarantee of a loan. These types of financial guarantees are generally within the scope of ASC 460 – *Guarantees* – or ASC 815 – *Derivatives and Hedging*. FASB TRG members generally agreed that an entity should look to ASC 460 or ASC 815 to determine the appropriate accounting for these fees. This is because ASC 606 contains a scope exception for contracts that fall within those topics, which provide principles an entity can follow to determine the appropriate accounting to reflect the financial guarantor's release from risk (and credit to earnings).

The FASB TRG members also generally agreed that fees from deposit-related services are within the scope of ASC 606. In contrast to the decisions for servicing income and financial guarantees, the guidance in ASC 405 – *Liabilities* – that financial institutions apply to determine the appropriate liability accounting for customer deposits, does not provide a model for recognising fees related to customer deposits (e.g. ATM fees, account maintenance or dormancy fees). Accordingly, the FASB TRG members generally agreed that deposit fees and charges are within the scope of ASC 606, even though ASC 405 is listed as a scope exception in ASC 606, because of the lack of guidance on the accounting for these fees in ASC 405.

It should be noted that, while this was not specifically discussed by the IASB TRG, IFRS preparers may find the FASB TRG's discussions helpful in assessing whether certain contracts are within the scope of IFRS 15 or other standards.

2.4.1.C Credit card arrangements

A bank that issues credit cards can have various income streams (e.g. annual fees) from a cardholder under various credit card arrangements. Some of these fees may entitle cardholders to ancillary services (e.g. concierge services, airport lounge access). The card issuer may also provide rewards to cardholders based on their purchases. At the July 2015 TRG meeting, the TRG members discussed a question raised by US GAAP stakeholders regarding whether such fees and programmes are within the scope of the revenue standard, particularly when a good or service is provided to a cardholder.[14]

While this question has only been raised by US GAAP stakeholders, IASB TRG members generally agreed that an IFRS preparer would first need to determine whether the credit card fees are within the scope of IFRS 9 or IAS 39. IFRS 9 and IAS 39 require that any fees that are an integral part of the effective interest rate for a financial instrument be treated as an adjustment to the effective interest rate. Conversely, any fees that are not an integral part of the effective interest rate of the financial instrument will generally be accounted for under IFRS 15.

The FASB TRG members generally agreed that credit card fees that are accounted for under ASC 310 – *Receivables* – are not in the scope of ASC 606. This includes annual fees that may entitle cardholders to ancillary services. The FASB TRG members noted that this conclusion is consistent with current US GAAP requirements for credit card fees. However, the observer from the US SEC noted that the nature of the arrangement must truly be that of a credit card lending arrangement in order to be in the scope of ASC 310. As such, entities will need to continue to evaluate their arrangements as new programmes develop. Credit card fees could, therefore, be treated differently under IFRS and US GAAP.

2.4.1.D Credit card-holder rewards programmes

The FASB TRG members also discussed whether cardholder rewards programmes are within the scope of ASC 606. The FASB TRG members generally agreed that if all consideration (i.e. credit card fees discussed in 2.4.1.C above) related to the rewards programme is determined to be within the scope of ASC 310, the rewards programme would not be in the scope of ASC 606. However, this determination would have to be made based on the facts and circumstances due to the wide variety of credit card reward programmes offered. The IASB TRG members did not discuss this issue because the question was only raised in relation to existing US GAAP.[15]

2.4.1.E Contributions

Currently, not-for-profit entities that report under US GAAP follow ASC 958-605 – *Not-for-Profit Entities – Revenue Recognition* – to account for contributions (i.e. unconditional promises of cash or other assets in voluntary non-reciprocal transfers). Contributions are not explicitly excluded from the scope of the FASB's standard. However, ASC 958-605 will not be wholly superseded by ASC 606.

In March 2015, the FASB TRG members discussed a question raised by US GAAP stakeholders and generally agreed that contributions are not within the scope of ASC 606 because they are non-reciprocal transfers. That is, contributions are generally not given in exchange for goods or services that are an output of the entity's ordinary activities. The IASB TRG members did not discuss this issue because the question was only raised in relation to existing US GAAP.[16]

2.4.1.F Fixed-odds wagering contracts

US GAAP stakeholders had questioned whether fixed-odds wagering contracts are within the scope of the new revenue standard. The IASB TRG members did not discuss this issue because the question was only raised in relation to existing US GAAP. Under IFRS, consistent with a July 2007 IFRS Interpretations Committee agenda decision, wagers that meet the definition of a derivative are within the scope of IFRS 9 or IAS 39. Those that do not meet the definition of a derivative would be within the scope of IFRS 15.

The FASB TRG members generally agreed that it was not clear whether fixed-odds wagering contracts should be in the scope of the FASB's new revenue standard or ASC 815. ASC 606 scopes in all contracts with customers unless the contracts are within the scope of other requirements, such as ASC 815. The FASB TRG members agreed that it was possible that fixed–odds wagering contracts would meet the definition of a derivative under ASC 815 and, therefore, be scoped out of ASC 606. If the FASB believes that these contracts should be considered as revenue arrangements and should be accounted for under ASC 606, once the industry-specific standard is superseded, FASB TRG members recommended that a clarification be codified within US GAAP.[17]

In May 2016, the FASB proposed a technical correction to create a scope exception to exclude fixed-odds wagering contracts from the derivatives guidance and clarify that these contracts are in the scope of ASC 606. Comments were due by 2 July 2016. To finalise this change, the FASB will need to issue a final amendment. The IASB is not expected to propose a similar change.

3 IDENTIFY THE CONTRACT WITH THE CUSTOMER

To apply the model in IFRS 15, an entity must first identify the contract, or contracts, to provide goods and services to customers. A contract must create enforceable rights and obligations to fall within the scope of the model in the standard. Such contracts may be written, oral or implied by an entity's customary business practices. For example, if an entity has an established practice of starting performance based on oral agreements with its customers, it may determine that such oral agreements meet the definition of a contract. *[IFRS 15.10]*.

As a result, an entity may need to account for a contract as soon as performance begins, rather than delay revenue recognition until the arrangement is documented in a signed contract, as is often the case under current practice. Certain arrangements may require a written contract to comply with laws or regulations in a particular jurisdiction. These requirements must be considered when determining whether a contract exists.

In the Basis for Conclusions, the Board acknowledged that entities will need to look at the relevant legal framework to determine whether the contract is enforceable because factors that determine enforceability may differ among jurisdictions. *[IFRS 15.BC32]*. The Board also clarified that, while the contract must be legally enforceable to be within the scope of the model in the standard, all of the promises do not have to be enforceable to be considered performance obligations (see 4.1 below). That is, a performance obligation can be based on the customer's valid expectations (e.g. due to the entity's business practice of providing an additional good or service that is not specified in the contract). In addition, the standard clarifies that some contracts may have no fixed duration and can be terminated or modified by either party at any time. Other contracts may automatically renew on a specified periodic basis. Entities are required to apply IFRS 15 to the contractual period in which the parties have present enforceable rights and obligations. *[IFRS 15.11]*. Contract enforceability and termination clauses are discussed at 3.2 below.

Example 30.3: Oral contract

IT Support Co. provides online technology support for customers remotely via the internet. For a fixed fee, IT Support Co. will scan a customer's personal computer (PC) for viruses, optimise the PC's performance and solve any connectivity problems. When a customer calls to obtain the scan services, IT Support Co. describes the services it can provide and states the price for those services. When the customer agrees to the terms stated by the representative, payment is made over the telephone. IT Support Co. then gives the customer the information it needs to obtain the scan services (e.g. an access code for the website). It provides the services when the customer connects to the internet and logs onto the entity's website (which may be that day or a future date).

In this example, IT Support Co. and its customer are entering into an oral agreement, which is legally enforceable in this jurisdiction, for IT Support Co. to repair the customer's PC and for the customer to provide consideration by transmitting a valid credit card number and authorisation over the telephone. The required criteria for a contract with a customer (discussed further at 3.1 below) are all met. As such, this agreement will be within the scope of the model in the standard at the time of the telephone conversation, even if the entity has not yet performed the scanning services.

3.1 Attributes of a contract

To help entities determine whether (and when) their arrangements with customers are contracts within the scope of the model in the standard, the Board identified certain attributes that must be present. The Board noted in the Basis for Conclusions that the criteria are similar to those in previous revenue recognition requirements and in other existing standards and are important in an entity's assessment of whether the arrangement contains enforceable rights and obligations. *[IFRS 15.BC33]*.

IFRS 15 requires an entity to account for a contract with a customer that is within the scope of the model in the standard only when all of the following criteria are met: *[IFRS 15.9]*

(a) the parties to the contract have approved the contract (in writing, orally or in accordance with other customary business practices) and are committed to perform their respective obligations;

(b) the entity can identify each party's rights regarding the goods or services to be transferred;

(c) the entity can identify the payment terms for the goods or services to be transferred;

(d) the contract has commercial substance (i.e. the risk, timing or amount of the entity's future cash flows is expected to change as a result of the contract); and

(e) it is probable that the entity will collect the consideration to which it will be entitled in exchange for the goods or services that will be transferred to the customer. In evaluating whether collectability of an amount of consideration is probable, an entity shall consider only the customer's ability and intention to pay that amount of consideration when it is due. The amount of consideration to which the entity will be entitled may be less than the price stated in the contract if the consideration is variable because the entity may offer the customer a price concession.

These criteria are assessed at the inception of the arrangement. If the criteria are met at that time, an entity does not reassess these criteria unless there is an indication of a significant change in facts and circumstances. *[IFRS 15.13]*. For example, as noted in paragraph 13 of IFRS 15, if the customer's ability to pay significantly deteriorates, an entity would have to reassess whether it is probable that the entity will collect the consideration to which it is entitled in exchange for transferring the remaining goods and services under the contract. The updated assessment is prospective in nature and would not change the conclusions associated with goods and services already transferred. That is, an entity would not reverse any receivables, revenue or contract assets already recognised under the contract. *[IFRS 15.BC34]*.

If the criteria are not met, the arrangement is not considered a revenue contract under the standard and the requirements discussed at 3.5 below must be applied.

3.1.1 Parties have approved the contract and are committed to perform their respective obligations

Before applying the model in IFRS 15, the parties must have approved the contract. As indicated in the Basis for Conclusions, the Board included this criterion because a contract might not be legally enforceable without the approval of both parties. *[IFRS 15.BC35]*. Furthermore, the Board decided that the form of the contract (i.e. oral, written or implied) is not determinative, in assessing whether the parties have approved the contract. Instead, an entity must consider all relevant facts and circumstances when assessing whether the parties intend to be bound by the terms and conditions of the contract. In some cases, the parties to an oral or implied contract may have the intent to fulfil their respective obligations. However, in other cases, a written contract may be required before an entity can conclude that the parties have approved the arrangement. *[IFRS 15.10]*.

In addition to approving the contract, the entity must also be able to conclude that both parties are committed to perform their respective obligations. That is, the entity must be committed to providing the promised goods or services. In addition, the customer must be committed to purchasing those promised goods and services. In the Basis for Conclusions, the Board clarified that an entity and a customer do not always have to be committed to fulfilling all of their respective rights and obligations for a contract to meet this requirement. *[IFRS 15.BC36]*. The Board cited, as an example, a supply agreement between two parties that includes stated minimums. The customer does not always buy the required minimum quantity and the entity does not always enforce its right to require the customer to purchase the minimum quantity. In this situation, the Board stated that it may still be possible for the entity to determine that there is sufficient evidence to demonstrate that the parties are substantially committed to the contract. This criterion does not address a customer's intent and ability to pay the consideration (i.e. collectability). Collectability is a separate criterion and is discussed at 3.1.5 below.

Termination clauses are also an important consideration when determining whether both parties are committed to perform under a contract and, consequently, whether a contract exists. See 3.2 below for further discussion of termination clauses and how they affect contract duration.

Current IFRS does not provide specific application guidance on oral contracts. However, entities are required to consider the underlying substance and economic reality of an arrangement and not merely its legal form. *The Conceptual Framework for Financial Reporting* states that representing a legal form that differs from the economic substance of the underlying economic phenomenon may not result in a faithful representation. *[Framework BC3.26]*.

Despite the focus on substance over form in IFRS, treating oral or implied agreements as contracts may be a significant change in practice for some entities. It may lead to earlier accounting for oral agreements, i.e. not waiting until such agreements are formally documented.

3.1.2 Each party's rights regarding the goods or services to be transferred can be identified

This criterion is relatively straightforward. If the goods and services to be provided in the arrangement cannot be identified, it is not possible to conclude that an entity has a contract within the scope of the model in IFRS 15. The Board indicated that if the promised goods and services cannot be identified, the entity cannot assess whether those goods and services have been transferred because the entity would be unable to assess each party's rights with respect to those goods and services. *[IFRS 15.BC37]*.

3.1.3 Payment terms can be identified

Identifying the payment terms does not require that the transaction price be fixed or stated in the contract with the customer. As long as there is an enforceable right to payment (i.e. enforceability as a matter of law) and the contract contains sufficient information to enable the entity to estimate the transaction price (see further discussion at 5 below), the contract would qualify for accounting under the standard (assuming the remaining criteria set out in paragraph 9 of IFRS 15 have been met – see 3.1 above).

3.1.4 Commercial substance

The Board included a criterion that requires arrangements to have commercial substance (i.e. the risk, timing or amount of the entity's future cash flows is expected to change as a result of the contract) to prevent entities from artificially inflating revenue. *[IFRS 15.BC40]*. The model in IFRS 15 does not apply if an arrangement does not have commercial substance. Historically, some entities in high-growth industries allegedly engaged in transactions in which goods and services were transferred back and forth between the same entities in an attempt to show higher transaction volume and gross revenue (sometimes known as 'round-tripping'). This is also a risk in arrangements that involve non-cash consideration.

Determining whether a contract has commercial substance for the purposes of IFRS 15 may require significant judgement. In all situations, the entity must be able to demonstrate a substantive business purpose for the nature and structure of its transactions.

In a change from the existing requirements in SIC-31, IFRS 15 does not contain requirements specific to advertising barter transactions. We anticipate entities will need to carefully consider the commercial substance criterion when evaluating these types of transactions.

3.1.5 Collectability

Under IFRS 15, collectability refers to the customer's ability and intent to pay the amount of consideration to which the entity expects to be entitled in exchange for the goods and services that will be transferred to the customer. An entity should assess a customer's ability to pay based on the customer's financial capacity and its intention to pay considering all relevant facts and circumstances, including past experiences with that customer or customer class. *[IFRS 15.BC45]*.

In the Basis for Conclusions, the Board noted that the purpose of the criteria in paragraph 9 of IFRS 15 is to require an entity to assess whether a contract is valid and represents a genuine transaction. The collectability criterion (i.e. determining whether the customer has the ability and the intention to pay the promised consideration) is a key part of that assessment. In addition, the Board noted that, in general, entities only enter into contracts in which it is probable that the entity will collect the amount to which it will be entitled. *[IFRS 15.BC43]*. That is, in most instances, an entity would not enter into a contract with a customer if there was significant credit risk associated with that customer without also having adequate economic protection to ensure that it would collect the consideration. The IASB expects that only a small number of arrangements may fail to meet the collectability criterion. *[IFRS 15.BC46E]*.

The standard requires an entity to evaluate at contract inception (and when significant facts and circumstances change) whether it is probable that it will collect the consideration to which it will be entitled in exchange for the goods or services that will be transferred to a customer. This is consistent with current IFRS, where revenue recognition is permitted only when it is probable that the economic benefits associated with the transaction will flow to the entity (assuming other basic revenue recognition criteria have been met).

For purposes of this analysis, the meaning of the term 'probable' is consistent with the existing definition in IFRS, i.e. 'more likely than not'. *[IFRS 5 Appendix A]*. If it is not probable that the entity will collect amounts to which it is entitled, the model in IFRS 15 is not applied to the contract until the concerns about collectability have been resolved. However, other requirements in IFRS 15 apply to such arrangements (see 3.5 below for further discussion).

Paragraph 9(e) of IFRS 15 specifies that an entity should only assess only the consideration to which it will be entitled in exchange for the goods or services that will be transferred to the customer (rather than the total amount promised for all goods or services in the contract). In the Basis for Conclusions, the Board noted that, if the customer were to fail to perform as promised and the entity were able to stop transferring additional goods or services to the customer in response, the entity would not consider the likelihood of payment for those goods or services that would not be transferred in its assessment of collectability. *[IFRS 15.BC46]*.

In the Basis for Conclusions, the Board also noted that the assessment of collectability criteria requires an entity to consider how the entity's contractual rights to the consideration relate to its performance obligations. That assessment considers the business practices available to the entity to manage its exposure to credit risk throughout the contract (e.g. through advance payments or the right to stop transferring additional goods or services). *[IFRS 15.BC46C]*.

The amount of consideration that is assessed for collectability is the amount to which the entity will be entitled, which under the standard is the transaction price for the goods or services that will be transferred to the customer, rather than the stated contract price for those items. Entities will need to first determine the transaction price before assessing the collectability of that amount. The contract price and transaction price most often will differ because of variable consideration (e.g. rebates, discounts or explicit or implicit price concessions) that reduces the amount of consideration stated in the contract. For example, the transaction price for the items expected to be transferred may be less than the stated contract price for those items if an entity concludes that it has offered, or is willing to accept, a price concession on products sold to a customer as a means to assist the customer in selling those items through to end-consumers. As discussed at 5.2.1.A below, an entity will deduct from the contract price any variable consideration that would reduce the amount of consideration to which an entity expects to be entitled (e.g. the estimated price concession) at contract inception in order to derive the transaction price for those items.

The standard provides the following example of how an entity would assess the collectability criterion. *[IFRS 15.IE3-IE6]*.

Example 30.4: Collectability of the consideration

An entity, a real estate developer, enters into a contract with a customer for the sale of a building for CU1 million. The customer intends to open a restaurant in the building. The building is located in an area where new restaurants face high levels of competition and the customer has little experience in the restaurant industry.

The customer pays a non-refundable deposit of CU50,000 at inception of the contract and enters into a long-term financing agreement with the entity for the remaining 95 per cent of the promised consideration. The financing arrangement is provided on a non-recourse basis, which means that if the customer defaults, the entity can repossess the building, but cannot seek further compensation from the customer, even if the collateral does not cover the full value of the amount owed. The entity's cost of the building is CU600,000. The customer obtains control of the building at contract inception.

In assessing whether the contract meets the criteria in paragraph 9 of IFRS 15, the entity concludes that the criterion in paragraph 9(e) of IFRS 15 is not met because it is not probable that the entity will collect the consideration to which it is entitled in exchange for the transfer of the building. In reaching this conclusion, the entity observes that the customer's ability and intention to pay may be in doubt because of the following factors:

- the customer intends to repay the loan (which has a significant balance) primarily from income derived from its restaurant business (which is a business facing significant risks because of high competition in the industry and the customer's limited experience);
- the customer lacks other income or assets that could be used to repay the loan; and
- the customer's liability under the loan is limited because the loan is non-recourse.

Because the criteria in paragraph 9 of IFRS 15 are not met, the entity applies paragraphs 15-16 of IFRS 15 to determine the accounting for the non-refundable deposit of CU50,000. The entity observes that none of the events described in paragraph 15 have occurred – that is, the entity has not received substantially all of the consideration and it has not terminated the contract. Consequently, in accordance with paragraph 16, the entity accounts for the non-refundable CU50,000 payment as a deposit liability. The entity continues to account for the initial deposit, as well as any future payments of principal and interest, as a deposit liability, until such time that the entity concludes that the criteria in paragraph 9 are met (i.e. the entity is able to conclude that it is probable that the entity will collect the consideration) or one of the events in paragraph 15 has occurred. The entity continues to assess the contract in accordance with paragraph 14 to determine whether the criteria in paragraph 9 are subsequently met or whether the events in paragraph 15 of IFRS 15 have occurred.

While this requirement is similar to the current requirements in IAS 18, applying the concept to a portion of the contractual amount, instead of the total, may be a significant change. Before revenue can be recognised under IAS 18, it must be probable that the economic benefits associated with the transaction will flow to the entity. *[IAS 18.14(b), 18, 20(b)]*. In practice, entities likely consider the entire contractually agreed consideration under IAS 18. If so, the requirements in IFRS 15 could result in the earlier recognition of revenue for a contract in which a portion of the contract price (but not the entire amount) is considered to be at risk.

Significant judgement will be required to determine when an expected partial payment indicates that there is an implied price concession in the contract, there is an impairment loss or the arrangement lacks sufficient substance to be considered a contract under the standard. See 5.2.1.A below for further discussion on implicit price concessions.

ASC 606 also uses the term 'probable' for the collectability assessment. However, 'probable' under US GAAP is a higher threshold than under IFRS.[18]

In May 2016, the FASB amended its standard to clarify the intention of the collectability assessment. The IASB decided not to make any clarifications or amendments to IFRS 15. As part of its April 2016 amendments, the IASB added a discussion to the Basis for Conclusions on IFRS 15 that it does not expect the FASB's amendments to result in differences in outcomes under IFRS and US GAAP in relation to the evaluation of the collectability criterion. *[IFRS 15.BC46E]*.

3.1.5.A Assessing collectability for a portfolio of contracts

At the January 2015 TRG meeting, the TRG members considered how an entity would assess collectability if it has a portfolio of contracts. The TRG members generally agreed that if an entity has determined it is probable that a customer will pay amounts owed under a contract, but the entity has historical experience that it will not collect consideration from some of the customers within a portfolio of contracts (see 3.3.1 below), it would be appropriate for the entity to record revenue for the contract in full and separately evaluate the corresponding contract asset or receivable for impairment.[19] That is, the entity would not conclude the arrangement contains an implicit price concession and would not reduce revenue for the uncollectable amounts. See 5.2.1.A below for a discussion of evaluating whether an entity has offered an implicit price concession.

Consider the following example included in the TRG agenda paper: an entity has a large volume of similar customer contracts for which it invoices its customers in arrears, on a monthly basis. Before accepting a customer, the entity performs procedures designed to determine if it is probable that the customer will pay the amounts owed. It does not accept customers if it is not probable that the customer will pay the amounts owed. Because these procedures are only designed to determine whether collection is probable (and, thus, not a certainty), the entity anticipates that it will have some customers that will not pay all of the amounts owed. While the entity collects the entire amount due from the vast majority of its customers, on average, the entity's historical evidence (which is representative of its expectations for the future) indicates that the entity will only collect 98% of the amounts invoiced. In this case, the entity would recognise revenue for the full amount due and recognise a bad debt expense for 2% of the amount due (i.e. the amount the entity does not expect to collect).[20]

In this example, the entity concludes that collectability is probable for each customer based on procedures it performed prior to accepting each customer and on its historical experience with this customer class, while also accepting that there is some credit risk inherent with this customer class. Furthermore, the entity concludes that any amounts not collected do not represent implied price concessions. Instead, they are due to general credit risk that was present in a limited number of customer contracts. Some TRG members cautioned that the analysis to determine whether to recognise a bad debt expense for a contract in the same period in which revenue is recognised (instead of reducing revenue for an anticipated price concession) will require judgement.

3.1.5.B Determining when to reassess collectability

As discussed at 3.1 above, IFRS 15 requires an entity to reassess whether it is probable that it will collect the consideration to which it will be entitled when significant facts and circumstances change. Example 4 in IFRS 15 illustrates a situation in which a customer's financial condition declines and its current access to credit and available cash on hand is limited. In this case, the entity does not reassess the collectability criterion. However, in a subsequent year, the customer's financial condition further declines after losing access to credit and its major customers. Example 4 in IFRS 15 illustrates that this subsequent change in the customer's financial condition is so significant that a reassessment of the criteria for identifying a contract is required, resulting in the collectability criterion not being met. As noted in the TRG agenda paper, this example illustrates that it was not the Board's intent to require an entity to reassess collectability when changes occur that are relatively minor in nature (i.e. those that do not call into question the validity of the contract). The TRG members generally agreed that entities will need to exercise judgement to determine whether changes in the facts and circumstances are significant enough to indicate that a contract no longer exists under the standard.[21]

3.2 Contract enforceability and termination clauses

An entity will have to first determine the term of the contract to apply certain aspects of the revenue model (e.g. identifying performance obligations, determining the transaction price). The contract term to be evaluated is the period in which parties to the contract have present enforceable rights and obligations, as described in the standard.

The standard states that entities are required to apply IFRS 15 to the contractual period in which the parties have present enforceable rights and obligations. *[IFRS 15.11]*. For the purpose of applying IFRS 15, a contract does not exist if each party has the unilateral enforceable right to terminate a wholly unperformed contract without compensating each other or other parties. The standard defines a wholly unperformed contract as one for which 'both of the following criteria are met: (a) the entity has not yet transferred any promised goods or services to the customer; and (b) the entity has not yet received, and is not yet entitled to receive, any consideration in exchange for promised goods or services.' *[IFRS 15.12]*.

The period in which enforceable rights and obligations exist may be affected by termination provisions in the contract. For example, an entity may apply the standard to only a portion of a contract with a stated term when the contract allows either party to terminate it at any time without penalty. Significant judgement will be required to determine the effect of termination provisions on the contract term. The contract term to which the standard is applied may affect the number of performance obligations identified and the determination of the transaction price. It may also affect the amounts disclosed in some of the required disclosures.

If each party has the unilateral right to terminate a 'wholly unperformed' contract (as defined in paragraph 12 of IFRS 15) without compensating the counterparty, IFRS 15 states that, for purposes of the standard, a contract does not exist and its accounting and disclosure requirements would not apply. This is because the contracts would not affect an entity's financial position or performance until either party performs. Any arrangement in which the vendor has not provided any of the contracted goods or services and has not received or is not entitled to receive any of the contracted consideration is considered to be a 'wholly unperformed' contract.

The requirements for 'wholly unperformed' contracts do not apply if the parties to the contract have to compensate the other party if they exercise their right to terminate the contract and that termination payment is considered substantive. Significant judgement will be required to determine whether a termination payment is substantive and all facts and circumstances related to the contract should be considered.

Evaluating termination provisions will be a change from current IFRS. Under IAS 18, entities apply the revenue requirements for the stated term of the contract and generally account for terminations when they occur. Under IFRS 15, entities may be required to account for contracts with stated terms as month-to-month (or possibly a shorter duration) contracts if the parties can terminate the contract without penalty.

3.2.1 *Implementation questions on contract enforceability and termination clauses*

3.2.1.A *Evaluating termination clauses and termination payments in determining the contract term*

Entities will need to carefully evaluate termination clauses and any related termination payments to determine how they affect contract duration (i.e. the period in which there are enforceable rights and obligations). TRG members generally agreed that enforceable rights and obligations exist throughout the term in which each party has the unilateral enforceable right to terminate the contract by compensating the other party. For example, if a contract includes a substantive termination payment, the duration of the contract would equal the term throughout which a termination penalty would be due (which could be the stated contractual term or a shorter duration if the termination penalty did not extend to the end of the contract). However, the TRG members observed that the determination of whether a termination penalty is substantive, and what constitutes enforceable rights and obligations under a contract, will require judgement and consideration of the facts and circumstances.

The TRG members also agreed that when a contract with a stated contractual term can be terminated by either party at any time for no consideration, the contract term ends when control of the goods or services that have already been provided transfers to the customer (e.g. a month-to-month service contract), regardless of its stated contractual term. Entities will need to consider whether a contract includes a notification or cancellation period (e.g. the contract can be terminated with 90 days' notice) that would cause the contract term to extend beyond the date when control of the goods or services that have already been provided were transferred to the customer. In these cases, the contract term would be shorter than the stated contractual term, but would extend beyond the date when control of the goods or services that have already been provided were transferred to the customer.[22]

3.2.1.B *Evaluating the contract term when only the customer has the right to cancel the contract without cause*

Enforceable rights and obligations exist throughout the term in which each party has the unilateral enforceable right to terminate the contract by compensating the other party. The TRG members did not view a customer-only right to terminate sufficient to warrant a different conclusion than one in which both parties have the right to terminate, as discussed in 3.2.1.A above.

The TRG members generally agreed that a substantive termination penalty payable by a customer to the entity is evidence of enforceable rights and obligations of both parties throughout the period covered by the termination penalty. For example, consider a four-year service contract in which the customer has the right to cancel without cause at the end of each year, but for which the customer would incur a termination penalty that decreases each year and is determined to be substantive. The TRG members generally agreed that the arrangement would be treated as a four-year contract.

The TRG members also discussed situations in which a contractual penalty would result in including optional goods or services in the accounting for the original contract (see 4.6.1.D below).

The TRG members observed that the determination of whether a termination penalty is substantive, and what constitutes enforceable rights and obligations under a contract, will require judgement and consideration of the facts and circumstances.

If enforceable rights and obligations do not exist throughout the entire term stated in the contract the TRG members generally agreed that customer cancellation rights would be treated as customer options. Examples include, when there are no (or non-substantive) contractual penalties that compensate the entity upon cancellation and when the customer has the unilateral right to terminate the contract for reasons other than cause or contingent events outside the customer's control. In the Basis for Conclusions, the Board noted that a cancellation option or termination right can be similar to a renewal option. *[IFRS 15.BC391]*. An entity would need to determine whether a cancellation option indicates that the customer has a material right that would need to be accounted for as a performance obligation (e.g. there is a discount for goods or services provided during the cancellable period that provides the customer with a material right) (see 4.6 below).[23]

3.2.1.C *Evaluating the contract term when an entity has a past practice of not enforcing termination payments*

A TRG agenda paper for the October 2014 TRG meeting noted that the evaluation of the termination payment in determining the duration of a contract depends on whether the law (which may vary by jurisdiction) would consider past practice as limiting the parties' enforceable rights and obligations. An entity's past practice of allowing customers to terminate the contract early without enforcing collection of the termination payment only affects the contract term in cases in which the parties' legally enforceable rights and obligations are limited because of the lack of enforcement by the entity. If that past practice does not change the parties' legally enforceable rights and obligations, the contract term should equal the term throughout which a substantive termination penalty would be due (which could be the stated contractual term or a shorter duration if the termination penalty did not extend to the end of the contract).[24]

3.2.1.D *Accounting for a partial termination of a contract*

We believe an entity should account for the partial termination of a contract (e.g. a change in the contract term from three years to two years prior to the beginning of year two) as a contract modification (see 3.4 below) because it results in a change in the scope of the contract. IFRS 15 states that 'a contract modification exists when the parties to a contract approve a modification that either creates new or changes existing enforceable rights and obligations of the parties to the contract'. *[IFRS 15.18]*. A partial termination of a contract results in a change to the enforceable rights and obligations in the existing contract. This conclusion is consistent with TRG agenda paper no. 48, which states, 'a substantive termination penalty is evidence of enforceable rights and obligations throughout the contract term. The termination penalty is ignored until the contract is terminated at which point it will be accounted for as a modification'.[25] Consider the following example:

An entity enters into a contract with a customer to provide monthly maintenance services for three years at a fixed price of CU500 per month (i.e. total consideration of CU18,000). The contract includes a termination clause that allows the customer to cancel the third year of the contract by paying a termination penalty of CU1,000 (which is considered substantive for the purpose of this example). The penalty would effectively result in an adjusted price per month for two years of CU542 (i.e. total consideration of CU13,000). At the end of the first year, the customer decides to cancel the third year of the contract and pays the CU1,000 termination penalty specified in the contract.

In this example, the modification would not be accounted for as a separate contract because it does not result in the addition of distinct goods or services (see 3.4.2 below). Since the remaining services are distinct, the entity would apply the requirements in paragraph 21(a) of IFRS 15 and account for the modification prospectively. The remaining consideration of CU7,000 (CU6,000 per year under the original contract for the second year, plus the CU1,000 payment upon modification) would be recognised over the remaining revised contract period of one year. That is, the entity would recognise the CU1,000 termination penalty over the remaining performance period.

3.3 Combining contracts

In most cases, entities will apply the model to individual contracts with a customer. However, the standard requires entities to combine contracts entered into at, or near, the same time with the same customer (or related parties of the customer) if they meet one or more of the following criteria: *[IFRS 15.17]*

(a) the contracts are negotiated as a package with a single commercial objective;

(b) the amount of consideration to be paid in one contract depends on the price or performance of the other contract; or

(c) the goods or services promised in the contracts (or some goods or services promised in each of the contracts) are a single performance obligation.

In the Basis for Conclusions, the Board explained that it included the requirements on combining contracts in the standard because, in some cases, the amount and timing of revenue may differ depending on whether an entity accounts for contracts as a single contract or separately. *[IFRS 15.BC71]*.

Entities will need to apply judgement to determine whether contracts are entered into at or near the same time because the standard does not provide a bright line for making this assessment. In the Basis for Conclusions, the Board noted that the longer the period between entering into different contracts, the more likely it is that the economic circumstances affecting the negotiations of those contracts will have changed. *[IFRS 15.BC75]*.

Negotiating multiple contracts at the same time is not sufficient evidence to demonstrate that the contracts represent a single arrangement for accounting purposes. In the Basis for Conclusions, the Board noted that there are pricing interdependencies between two or more contracts when either of the first two criteria (i.e. the contracts are negotiated with a single commercial objective or the price in one contract depends on the price or performance of the other contract) are met, so the amount of consideration allocated to the performance obligations in each contract may not faithfully depict the value of the goods or services transferred to the customer if those contracts were not combined. The Board also explained that it decided to include the third criterion (i.e. the goods or services in the contracts are a single performance obligation) to avoid any structuring opportunities that would effectively allow entities to bypass the requirements for identifying performance obligations. *[IFRS 15.BC73]*.

IFRS 15 provides more requirements on when to combine contracts than IAS 18. IAS 18 indicates that the recognition criteria should be applied to two or more transactions on a combined basis 'when they are linked in such a way that the commercial effect cannot be understood without reference to the series of transactions as a whole'. *[IAS 18.13]*.

The IFRS 15 contract combination requirements are similar to those in IAS 11, but there are some notable differences. IAS 11 allows an entity to combine contracts with several customers, provided the relevant criteria for combination are met. In contrast, the contract combination requirements in IFRS 15 only apply to contracts with the same customer or related parties of the customer. Unlike IFRS 15, IAS 11 does not require that contracts be entered into at or near the same time.

IAS 11 also requires that all criteria be met before contracts can be combined, while IFRS 15 requires that one or more of its criteria to be met. The criteria for combination in the two standards are similar. The main difference is the criterion in paragraph 17(c) of IFRS 15, which considers a performance obligation across different contracts. In contrast, IAS 11 considers concurrent or sequential performance. *[IAS 11.9(c)]*.

Overall, the criteria are generally consistent with the underlying principles in the existing revenue standards on combining contracts. However, since IFRS 15 explicitly requires an entity to combine contracts if one or more of the criteria in paragraph 17 of IFRS 15 are met, some entities that do not currently combine contracts may need to do so.

3.3.1 Portfolio approach practical expedient

Under the standard, the five-step model is applied to individual contracts with customers. However, the IASB recognised that there may be situations in which it may be more practical for an entity to combine contracts for revenue recognition purposes rather than attempt to account for each contract separately. Specifically, the standard includes a practical expedient that allows an entity to apply IFRS 15 to a portfolio of contracts (or performance obligations) with similar characteristics if the entity reasonably expects that application of this practical expedient will not differ materially from applying IFRS 15 to the individual contracts (or performance obligations) within the portfolio. Furthermore, an entity is required to use estimates and assumptions that reflect the size and composition of the portfolio. *[IFRS 15.4]*.

As noted above, in order to use the portfolio approach, an entity must reasonably expect that the accounting result will not be materially different from the result of applying the standard to the individual contracts. However, in the Basis for Conclusions, the Board noted that it does not intend for an entity to quantitatively evaluate every possible outcome when concluding that the portfolio approach is not materially different. Instead, they indicated that an entity should be able to take a reasonable approach to determine the portfolios that would be representative of its types of customers and that an entity should use judgement in selecting the size and composition of those portfolios. *[IFRS 15.BC69]*.

Application of the portfolio approach will likely vary based on the facts and circumstances of each entity. Management will need to determine whether to apply the portfolio approach to some or all of the entity's business lines. In addition, an entity may choose to apply the portfolio approach to only certain aspects of the new model (e.g. determining the transaction price in Step 3).

See 3.1.5.A above for a discussion on how an entity would assess collectability for a portfolio of contracts.

3.4 Contract modifications

Parties to an arrangement frequently agree to modify the scope or price (or both) of their contract. If that happens, an entity must determine whether the modification it is accounted for as a new contract or as part of the existing contract. Generally, it is clear when a contract modification has taken place, but in some circumstances that determination is more difficult. To assist entities when making this determination, the standard states 'a contract modification is a change in the scope or price (or both) of a contract that is approved by the parties to the contract. In some industries and jurisdictions, a contract modification may be described as a change order, a variation or an amendment. A contract modification exists when the parties to a contract approve a modification that either creates new or changes existing enforceable rights and obligations of the parties to the contract. A contract modification could be approved in writing, by oral agreement or implied by customary business practices. If the parties to the contract have not approved a contract modification, an entity shall continue to apply this Standard to the existing contract until the contract modification is approved.' *[IFRS 15.18]*.

The standard goes on to state 'a contract modification may exist even though the parties to the contract have a dispute about the scope or price (or both) of the modification or the parties have approved a change in the scope of the contract but have not yet determined the corresponding change in price. In determining whether the rights and obligations that are created or changed by a modification are enforceable, an entity shall consider all relevant facts and circumstances including the terms of the contract and other evidence.' *[IFRS 15.19]*. If the parties to a contract have approved a change in the scope of the contract but have not yet determined the corresponding change in price, an entity shall estimate the change to the transaction price arising from the modification in accordance with the requirements for estimating and constraining estimates of variable consideration. *[IFRS 15.19]*.

These requirements illustrate that the Board intended the requirements to apply more broadly than only to finalised modifications. That is, IFRS 15 indicates that an entity may have to account for a contract modification prior to the parties reaching final agreement on changes in scope or pricing (or both). Instead of focusing on the finalisation of a modification, IFRS 15 focuses on the enforceability of the changes to the rights and obligations in the contract. Once an entity determines the revised rights and obligations are enforceable, it accounts for the contract modification.

The standard provides the following example to illustrate this point. *[IFRS 15.IE42-IE43]*.

Example 30.5: Unapproved change in scope and price

An entity enters into a contract with a customer to construct a building on customer-owned land. The contract states that the customer will provide the entity with access to the land within 30 days of contract inception. However, the entity was not provided access until 120 days after contract inception because of storm damage to the site that occurred after contract inception. The contract specifically identifies any delay (including *force majeure*) in the entity's access to customer-owned land as an event that entitles the entity to compensation that is equal to actual costs incurred as a direct result of the delay. The entity is able to demonstrate that the specific direct costs were incurred as a result of the delay in accordance with the terms of the contract and prepares a claim. The customer initially disagreed with the entity's claim.

The entity assesses the legal basis of the claim and determines, on the basis of the underlying contractual terms, that it has enforceable rights. Consequently, it accounts for the claim as a contract modification in accordance with paragraphs 18-21 of IFRS 15. The modification does not result in any additional goods and services being provided to the customer. In addition, all of the remaining goods and services after the modification are not distinct and form part of a single performance obligation. Consequently, the entity accounts for the modification in accordance with paragraph 21(b) of IFRS 15 by updating the transaction price and the measure of progress towards complete satisfaction of the performance obligation. The entity considers the constraint on estimates of variable consideration in paragraphs 56-58 of IFRS 15 when estimating the transaction price.

Once an entity has determined that a contract has been modified, the entity determines the appropriate accounting treatment for the modification. Certain modifications are treated as separate stand-alone contracts (discussed at 3.4.1 below), while others are combined with the original contract (discussed at 3.4.2 below) and accounted for in that manner. In addition, some modifications are accounted for on a prospective basis and others on a cumulative catch-up basis. The Board developed different approaches to account for different types of modifications with an overall objective of faithfully depicting an entity's rights and obligations in each modified contract. *[IFRS 15.BC76]*.

The following figure illustrates these requirements.

Figure 30.3: Contract modifications

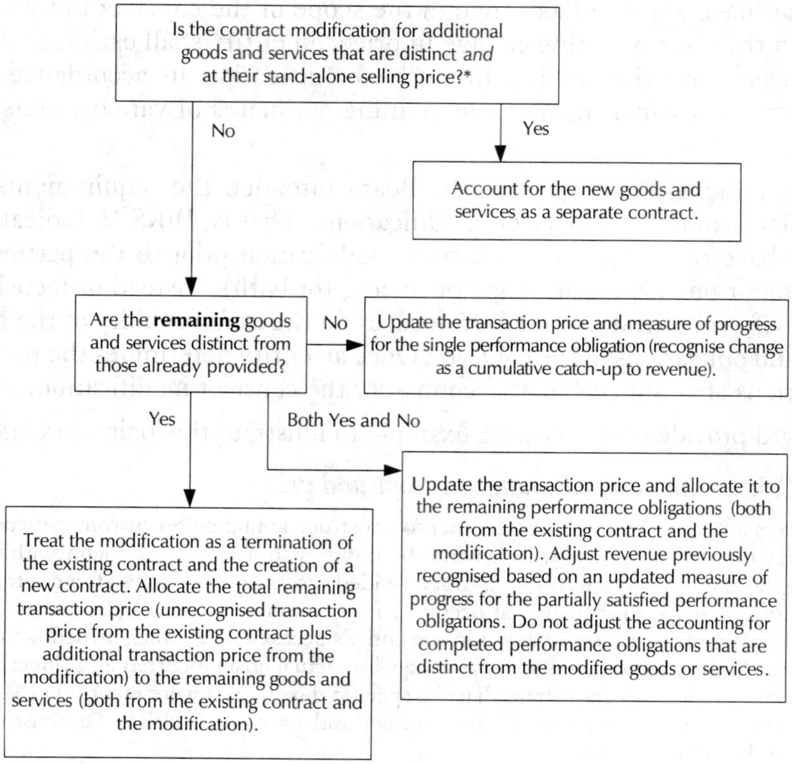

* In accordance with paragraph20 of IFRS 15, an entity may make appropriate adjustments to the stand-alone selling price to reflect the circumstances of the contract and still meet the criteria to account for the modification as a separate contract

When assessing how to account for a contract modification, an entity must consider whether any additional goods or services are distinct, often giving careful consideration to whether those goods or services are distinct within the context of the modified contract (see 4.2.1 below for further discussion on evaluating whether goods or services are distinct). That is, although a contract modification may add a new good or service that would be distinct in a stand-alone transaction, that new good or service may not be distinct when considered in the context of the contract, as modified. For example, in a building renovation project, a customer may request a contract modification to add a new room. The construction firm may commonly sell the construction of an added room on a stand-alone basis, which would indicate that the service is capable of being distinct. However, when that service is added to an existing contract and the entity has already determined that the entire project is a single performance obligation, the added goods and services would normally be combined with the existing bundle of goods and services.

In contrast to the construction example (for which the addition of otherwise distinct goods or services are combined with the existing single performance obligation and accounted for in that manner), a contract modification that adds distinct goods or services to a single performance obligation that is a series of distinct goods or services (see 4.2.2 below) is accounted for either as a separate contract or as the termination of the old contract and the creation of a new contract (i.e. prospectively). In the Basis for Conclusions, the Board explained that it clarified the accounting for modifications that affect a single performance obligation that is made up of a series of distinct goods or services (e.g. repetitive service contracts) to address some stakeholders' concerns that an entity otherwise would have been required to account for these modifications on a cumulative catch-up basis. *[IFRS 15.BC79]*.

The requirement to determine whether to treat a change in contractual terms as a separate contract or a modification to an existing contract is similar to the requirements in IAS 11 for construction contracts. *[IAS 11.13]*. In contrast, IAS 18 does not provide detailed application guidance on how to determine whether a change in contractual terms is treated as a separate contract or a modification to an existing contract. Despite there being some similarities to current IFRS, the requirements in IFRS 15 for contract modifications are much more detailed. Therefore, the requirements in IFRS 15 could result in a change in practice for some entities. Entities should evaluate whether their current processes and controls for contract modifications will need to be updated for the new requirements.

3.4.1 Contract modification represents a separate contract

Certain contract modifications are treated as separate, new contracts. *[IFRS 15.20]*. For these modifications, the accounting for the original contract is not affected by the modification and the revenue recognised to date on the original contract is not adjusted. Furthermore, any performance obligations remaining under the original contract continue to be accounted for under the original contract. The accounting for this modification approach reflects the fact that there is no economic difference between a separate contract for additional goods and services and a modified contract for those same items, provided the two criteria required for this modification approach are met.

The first criterion that must be met for a modification to be treated as a separate contract is that the additional promised goods or services in the modification must be distinct from the promised goods or services in the original contract. This assessment is done in accordance with IFRS 15's general requirements for determining whether promised goods or services are distinct (see 4.2.1 below). Only modifications that add distinct goods or services to the arrangement can be treated as separate contracts. Arrangements that reduce the amount of promised goods or services or change the scope of the original promised goods and services cannot, by their very nature, be considered separate contracts. Instead, they would be considered modifications of the original contract (see 3.4.2 below). *[IFRS 15.20(a)]*.

The second criterion is that the amount of consideration expected for the added promised goods or services must reflect the stand-alone selling prices of those promised goods or services. However, when determining the stand-alone selling price entities have some flexibility to adjust the stand-alone selling price, depending on the facts and circumstances. For example, a vendor may give an existing customer a discount on additional goods because the vendor would not incur selling-related costs that it would typically incur for new customers. In this example, the entity (vendor) may determine that the additional transaction consideration meets the criterion, even though the discounted price is less than the stand-alone selling price of that good or service for a new customer. In another example, an entity may conclude that, with the additional purchases, the customer qualifies for a volume-based discount (see 4.6.1.E and 4.6.1.F below on volume discounts). *[IFRS 15.20(b)]*.

The following example illustrates a contract modification that represents a separate contract. *[IFRS 15.IE19-IE21]*.

Example 30.6: Modification of a contract for goods

An entity promises to sell 120 products to a customer for CU12,000 (CU100 per product). The products are transferred to the customer over a six-month period. The entity transfers control of each product at a point in time. After the entity has transferred control of 60 products to the customer, the contract is modified to require the delivery of an additional 30 products (a total of 150 identical products) to the customer. The additional 30 products were not included in the initial contract.

Case A – Additional products for a price that reflects the stand-alone selling price

When the contract is modified, the price of the contract modification for the additional 30 products is an additional CU2,850 or CU95 per product. The pricing for the additional products reflects the stand-alone selling price of the products at the time of the contract modification and the additional products are distinct (in accordance with paragraph 27 of IFRS 15) from the original products.

In accordance with paragraph 20 of IFRS 15, the contract modification for the additional 30 products is, in effect, a new and separate contract for future products that does not affect the accounting for the existing contract. The entity recognises revenue of CU100 per product for the 120 products in the original contract and CU95 per product for the 30 products in the new contract.

3.4.2 Contract modification is not a separate contract

In instances in which the criteria discussed at 3.4.1 above are not met (i.e. distinct goods or services are not added or the distinct goods or services are not priced at their stand-alone selling price), contract modifications are accounted for as changes to the original contract and not as separate contracts. This includes contract modifications that modify or remove previously agreed-upon goods and services or reduce the price of the contract. An entity would account for the effects of these modifications differently, depending on which of the following three scenarios ((A)-(C) below) described in paragraph 21 of IFRS 15 most closely aligns with the facts and circumstances of the modification. *[IFRS 15.21]*.

(A) If the remaining goods and services after the contract modification are distinct from the goods or services transferred on, or before, the contract modification, the entity accounts for the modification as if it were a termination of the old contract and the creation of a new contract.

The amount of consideration to be allocated to the remaining performance obligations (or to the remaining distinct goods or services in a single performance obligation identified in accordance with paragraph 22(b) of IFRS 15, see 4.2.2 below) is the sum of:

(i) the consideration promised by the customer (including amounts already received from the customer) that was included in the estimate of the transaction price and that had not been recognised as revenue; and

(ii) the consideration promised as part of the contract modification.

For these modifications, the revenue recognised to date on the original contract (i.e. the amount associated with the completed performance obligations) is not adjusted. Instead, the remaining portion of the original contract and the modification are accounted for, together, on a prospective basis by allocating the remaining consideration (i.e. the unrecognised transaction price from the existing contract plus the additional transaction price from the modification) to the remaining performance obligations, including those added in the modification. This scenario is illustrated as follows. *[IFRS 15.IE19, IE22-IE24]*.

Example 30.7: Modification of a contract for goods

An entity promises to sell 120 products to a customer for CU12,000 (CU100 per product). The products are transferred to the customer over a six-month period. The entity transfers control of each product at a point in time. After the entity has transferred control of 60 products to the customer, the contract is modified to require the delivery of an additional 30 products (a total of 150 identical products) to the customer. The additional 30 products were not included in the initial contract.

Case B – Additional products for a price that does not reflect the stand-alone selling price

During the process of negotiating the purchase of an additional 30 products, the parties initially agree on a price of CU80 per product. However, the customer discovers that the initial 60 products transferred to the customer contained minor defects that were unique to those delivered products. The entity promises a partial credit of CU15 per product to compensate the customer for the poor quality of those products. The entity and the customer agree to incorporate the credit of CU900 (CU15 credit × 60 products) into the price that the entity charges for the additional 30 products. Consequently, the contract modification specifies that the price of the additional 30 products is CU1,500 or CU50 per product. That price comprises the agreed-upon price for the additional 30 products of CU2,400, or CU80 per product, less the credit of CU900.

At the time of modification, the entity recognises the CU900 as a reduction of the transaction price and, therefore, as a reduction of revenue for the initial 60 products transferred. In accounting for the sale of the additional 30 products, the entity determines that the negotiated price of CU80 per product does not reflect the stand-alone selling price of the additional products. Consequently, the contract modification does not meet the conditions in paragraph 20 of IFRS 15 to be accounted for as a separate contract. Because the remaining products to be delivered are distinct from those already transferred, the entity applies the requirements in paragraph 21(a) of IFRS 15 and accounts for the modification as a termination of the original contract and the creation of a new contract.

Consequently, the amount recognised as revenue for each of the remaining products is a blended price of CU93.33 {[(CU100 × 60 products not yet transferred under the original contract) + (CU80 × 30 products to be transferred under the contract modification)] ÷ 90 remaining products}.

In Example 30.7 above, the entity attributed a portion of the discount provided on the additional products to the previously delivered products because they contained minor defects. That portion of the discount was recognised as a reduction of the transaction price (and, therefore, revenue) on the date of the modification.

In similar situations, an entity needs to have sufficient evidence to indicate that a portion of the discount on the additional products specifically relates to the previously delivered products to make a similar conclusion. In many circumstances, this evidence may not exist so the discount will only be attributed to the additional products and recognised when control of those products transfers to the customer.

(B) The remaining goods and services to be provided after the contract modification may not be distinct from those goods and services already provided and, therefore, form part of a single performance obligation that is partially satisfied at the date of modification.

If this is the case, the entity accounts for the contract modification as if it were part of the original contract. The entity adjusts revenue previously recognised (either up or down) to reflect the effect that the contract modification has on the transaction price and updates the measure of progress (i.e. the revenue adjustment is made on a cumulative catch-up basis). This scenario is illustrated as follows. *[IFRS 15.IE37-IE41]*.

Example 30.8: Modification resulting in a cumulative catch-up adjustment to revenue

An entity, a construction company, enters into a contract to construct a commercial building for a customer on customer-owned land for promised consideration of CU1 million and a bonus of CU200,000 if the building is completed within 24 months. The entity accounts for the promised bundle of goods and services as a single performance obligation satisfied over time in accordance with paragraph 35(b) of IFRS 15 (discussed at 7.1.2 below) because the customer controls the building during construction. At the inception of the contract, the entity expects the following:

	CU
Transaction price	1,000,000
Expected costs	700,000
Expected profit (30%)	300,000

At contract inception, the entity excludes the CU200,000 bonus from the transaction price because it cannot conclude that it is highly probable that a significant reversal in the amount of cumulative revenue recognised will not occur. Completion of the building is highly susceptible to factors outside the entity's influence, including weather and regulatory approvals. In addition, the entity has limited experience with similar types of contracts.

The entity determines that the input measure, on the basis of costs incurred, provides an appropriate measure of progress towards complete satisfaction of the performance obligation. By the end of the first year, the entity has satisfied 60 per cent of its performance obligation on the basis of costs incurred to date (CU420,000) relative to total expected costs (CU700,000). The entity reassesses the variable consideration and concludes that the amount is still constrained in accordance with paragraphs 56-58 of IFRS 15. Consequently, the cumulative revenue and costs recognised for the first year are as follows:

	CU
Revenue	600,000
Costs	420,000
Gross profit	180,000

In the first quarter of the second year, the parties to the contract agree to modify the contract by changing the floor plan of the building. As a result, the fixed consideration and expected costs increase by CU150,000 and CU120,000, respectively. Total potential consideration after the modification is CU1,350,000 (CU1,150,000 fixed consideration + CU200,000 completion bonus). In addition, the allowable time for achieving the CU200,000 bonus is extended by 6 months to 30 months from the original contract inception date. At the date of the modification, on the basis of its experience and the remaining work to be performed, which is primarily inside the building and not subject to weather conditions, the entity concludes that it is highly probable that including the bonus in the transaction price will not result in a significant reversal in the amount of cumulative revenue recognised in accordance with paragraph 56 of IFRS 15 and includes the CU200,000 in the transaction price.

In assessing the contract modification, the entity evaluates paragraph 27(b) of IFRS 15 and concludes (on the basis of the factors in paragraph 29 of IFRS 15) that the remaining goods and services to be provided using the modified contract are not distinct from the goods and services transferred on or before the date of contract modification; that is, the contract remains a single performance obligation.

Consequently, the entity accounts for the contract modification as if it were part of the original contract (in accordance with paragraph 21(b) of IFRS 15). The entity updates its measure of progress and estimates that it has satisfied 51.2 per cent of its performance obligation (CU420,000 actual costs incurred ÷ CU820,000 total expected costs). The entity recognises additional revenue of CU91,200 [(51.2 per cent complete × CU1,350,000 modified transaction price) – CU600,000 revenue recognised to date] at the date of the modification as a cumulative catch-up adjustment.

(C) Finally, a change in a contract may also be treated as a combination of the two: a modification of the existing contract and the creation of a new contract.

In this case, an entity would not adjust the accounting treatment for completed performance obligations that are distinct from the modified goods or services. However, the entity would adjust revenue previously recognised (either up or down) to reflect the effect of the contract modification on the estimated transaction price allocated to performance obligations that are not distinct from the modified portion of the contract and would update the measure of progress.

See 10.1.1.E below for a discussion on how an entity would account for a contract asset that exists when a contract is modified if the modification is treated as the termination of an existing contract and the creation of a new contract.

3.4.3 *Implementation questions on contract modifications*

3.4.3.A *Reassessing the contract criteria if a contract is modified*

When an arrangement that has already been determined to meet the standard's contract criteria is modified, would an entity need to reassess whether that arrangement still meets the criteria to be considered a contract within the scope of the model in the standard? There is no specific requirement in the standard to reconsider whether a contract meets the definition of a contract when it is modified. However, if a contract is modified, we believe that may indicate that 'a significant change in facts and circumstances' has occurred (see 3.1 above) and that the entity should reassess the criteria in paragraph 9 of IFRS 15 for the modified contract. Any reassessment is prospective in nature and would not change the conclusions associated with goods and services already transferred. That is, an entity would not reverse any receivables, revenue or contract assets already recognised under the contract because of the reassessment of the contract criteria in paragraph 9 of IFRS 15. However, due to the contract modification accounting (see 3.4.2 above), the entity may need to adjust contract assets or cumulative revenue recognised in the period of the contract modification.

See 4.6.1.G below for a discussion on how an entity would account for the exercise of a material right. See 8.1.5.A below for a discussion on how entities would account for modifications to licences of intellectual property.

3.5 Arrangements that do not meet the definition of a contract under the standard

If an arrangement does not meet the criteria to be considered a contract under the standard, the standard specifies how to account for it. The standard states that when a contract with a customer does not meet the criteria in paragraph 9 of IFRS 15 (i.e. the criteria discussed at 3.1 above) and an entity receives consideration from the customer, the entity shall recognise the consideration received as revenue only when either of the following events has occurred:

(a) the entity has no remaining obligations to transfer goods or services to the customer and all, or substantially all, of the consideration promised by the customer has been received by the entity and is non-refundable; or

(b) the contract has been terminated and the consideration received from the customer is non-refundable. *[IFRS 15.15]*.

The standard goes on to specify that an entity shall recognise the consideration received from a customer as a liability until one of the events described above occurs or until the contract meets the criteria to be accounted for within the revenue model. *[IFRS 15.16]*.

Entities are required to continue to assess the criteria in paragraph 9 of IFRS 15 throughout the term of the arrangement to determine whether they are subsequently met. Once the criteria are met, the model in the standard applies, rather than the requirements discussed below. *[IFRS 15.14]*.

If an arrangement does not meet the criteria in paragraph 9 of IFRS 15 (and continues not to meet them), an entity only recognises non-refundable consideration received as revenue when one of the events outlined above has occurred (i.e. full performance and substantially all consideration received or the contract has been terminated) or the arrangement subsequently meets the criteria in paragraph 9 of IFRS 15.

Until one of these events happens, any consideration received from the customer is initially accounted for as a liability (not revenue) and the liability is measured at the amount of consideration received from the customer.

In the Basis for Conclusions, the Board indicated that it intended this accounting to be 'similar to the "deposit method" that was previously included in US GAAP and applied when there was no consummation of a sale.' *[IFRS 15.BC48]*

As noted in the Basis for Conclusions, the Board decided to include the requirements in paragraphs 14-16 of IFRS 15 (discussed earlier in this section) to prevent entities from seeking alternative guidance or improperly analogising to the model in IFRS 15 in circumstances in which an executed contract does not meet the criteria in paragraph 9 of IFRS 15. *[IFRS 15.BC47]*.

In May 2016, the FASB amended its standard to add an additional event for when an entity can recognise revenue in relation to consideration received from a customer when the arrangement does not meet the criteria to be accounted for as a revenue contract under the standard. Under this amendment, an entity would recognise revenue in the amount of the non-refundable consideration received when the entity has transferred control of the goods or services and has stopped transferring (and has no obligation to transfer) additional goods or services.

The IASB considered this issue, but decided not to propose any clarifications or amendments to IFRS 15. However, as part of its April 2016 amendments, the IASB added discussion to the Basis for Conclusions on IFRS 15 that explains that contracts often specify that an entity has a right to terminate the contract in the event of non-payment. Furthermore, such clauses would not generally affect the entity's legal rights to recover any amounts due. Therefore, the IASB concluded that the requirements in

IFRS 15 would allow an entity to conclude that a contract is terminated when it stops providing goods or services to the customer. *[IFRS 15.BC46H]*.

3.5.1 *Implementation questions on arrangements that do not meet the definition of a contract under the standard*

3.5.1.A *Determining when a contract is terminated for the purpose of applying paragraph 15(b) of IFRS 15*

Determining whether a contract is terminated may require significant judgement. In the Basis for Conclusions on IFRS 15, 'the IASB noted that contracts often specify that an entity has the right to terminate the contract in the event of non-payment by the customer and that this would not generally affect the entity's rights to recover any amounts owed by the customer. The IASB also noted that an entity's decision to stop pursuing collection would not typically affect the entity's rights and the customer's obligations under the contract with respect to the consideration owed by the customer. On this basis, ... the existing requirements in IFRS 15 are sufficient for an entity to conclude... that a contract is terminated when it stops providing goods or services to the customer.' *[IFRS 15.BC46H]*.

4 IDENTIFY THE PERFORMANCE OBLIGATIONS IN THE CONTRACT

To apply the standard, an entity must identify the promised goods and services within the contract and determine which of those goods and services are separate performance obligations. As noted in the Basis for Conclusions, the Board developed the notion of a 'performance obligation' to assist entities with appropriately identifying the unit of account for the purposes of applying the standard. *[IFRS 15.BC85]*. Because the standard requires entities to allocate the transaction price to performance obligations, identifying the correct unit of account is fundamental to recognising revenue on a basis that faithfully depicts the entity's performance in transferring the promised goods or services to the customer.

With respect to identifying the performance obligations in a contract, the standard states that, at contract inception, an entity is required to assess the goods or services promised in a contract to identify performance obligations. A performance obligation is either: *[IFRS 15.22]*

(a) a good or service (or a bundle of goods or services) that is distinct; or

(b) a series of distinct goods or services that are substantially the same and that have the same pattern of transfer to the customer.

The standard goes on to clarify that a series of distinct goods or services has the same pattern of transfer to the customer if both of the following criteria are met: *[IFRS 15.23]*

- each distinct good or service in the series that the entity promises to transfer to the customer would meet the criteria to be a performance obligation satisfied over time (see 7.1 below); and
- the same method would be used to measure the entity's progress towards complete satisfaction of the performance obligation to transfer each distinct good or service in the series to the customer.

4.1 Identifying the promised goods and services in the contract

As a first step in identifying the performance obligation(s) in the contract, the standard requires an entity to identify, at contract inception, the promised goods and services in the contract. However, unlike current IFRS, which does not define elements/deliverables, the new standard provides guidance on the types of items that may be goods or services promised in the contract.

'A contract with a customer generally explicitly states the goods or services that an entity promises to transfer to a customer. However, the performance obligations identified in a contract with a customer may not be limited to the goods or services that are explicitly stated in that contract. This is because a contract with a customer may also include promises that are implied by an entity's customary business practices, published policies or specific statements if, at the time of entering into the contract, those promises create a valid expectation of the customer that the entity will transfer a good or service to the customer.' *[IFRS 15.24]*.

'Performance obligations do not include activities that an entity must undertake to fulfil a contract unless those activities transfer a good or service to a customer. For example, a services provider may need to perform various administrative tasks to set up a contract. The performance of those tasks does not transfer a service to the customer as the tasks are performed. Therefore, those setup activities are not a performance obligation.' *[IFRS 15.25]*.

Identifying which promised goods or services are distinct is very important. The standard includes the following examples of promised goods or services: *[IFRS 15.26]*

- sale of goods produced by an entity (e.g. inventory of a manufacturer);
- resale of goods purchased by an entity (e.g. merchandise of a retailer);
- resale of rights to goods or services purchased by an entity (e.g. a ticket resold by an entity acting as a principal – see 4.4 below);
- performing a contractually agreed-upon task (or tasks) for a customer;
- providing a service of standing ready to provide goods or services (e.g. unspecified updates to software that are provided on a when-and-if-available basis – see 4.1.2.B below) or of making goods or services available for a customer to use as and when the customer decides;
- providing a service of arranging for another party to transfer goods or services to a customer (e.g. acting as an agent of another party – see 4.4 below);
- granting rights to goods or services to be provided in the future that a customer can resell or provide to its customer (e.g. an entity selling a product to a retailer promises to transfer an additional good or service to an individual who purchases the product from the retailer);
- constructing, manufacturing or developing an asset on behalf of a customer;
- granting licences (see 8 below); and
- granting options to purchase additional goods or services when those options provide a customer with a material right (see 4.6 below).

In addition, the standard makes clear that certain activities are not promised goods or services, such as activities that an entity must perform to satisfy its obligation to deliver the promised goods and services (e.g. internal administrative activities). After identifying the promised goods or services in the contract, an entity will then determine which of these promised goods or services (or bundle of goods and services) represent separate performance obligations.

In order for an entity to identify the promised goods and services in a contract, IFRS 15 indicates that an entity would consider whether there is a valid expectation on the part of the customer that the entity will provide a good or service. If the customer has a valid expectation that it will receive certain goods or services, it would likely view those promises as part of the negotiated exchange. This expectation will most commonly be created from an entity's explicit promises in a contract to transfer a good(s) or service(s) to the customer.

However, in other cases, promises to provide goods or services might be implied by the entity's customary business practices or standard industry norms (i.e. outside of the written contract). As discussed at 3 above, the Board clarified that, while the contract must be legally enforceable to be within the scope of the revenue model, not all of the promises (explicit or implicit) have to be enforceable to be considered when determining the entity's performance obligations. *[IFRS 15.BC32, BC87]*. That is, a performance obligation can be based on a customer's valid expectations (e.g. due to the entity's business practice of providing an additional good or service that is not specified in the contract).

In addition, some items commonly considered to be marketing incentives will have to be evaluated under IFRS 15 to determine whether they represent promised goods and services in the contract. Such items may include 'free' handsets provided by telecommunication entities, 'free' maintenance provided by automotive manufacturers and customer loyalty points awarded by supermarkets, airlines, and hotels. *[IFRS 15.BC88]*. Although an entity may not consider those goods or services to be the 'main' items that the customer contracts to receive, the Board concluded that they are goods or services for which the customer pays and to which the entity would allocate consideration for the purpose of recognising revenue. *[IFRS 15.BC89]*.

Paragraph 26 of IFRS 15 provides examples of promised goods or services that may be included in a contract with a customer. Several of them would be considered deliverables under current IFRS, including a good produced by an entity or a contractually agreed-upon task (or service) performed for a customer. However, the IASB also included other examples that may not be considered deliverables in practice currently. For example, paragraph 26(e) of IFRS 15 describes a stand-ready obligation as a promised service that consists of standing ready to provide goods or services or making goods or services available for a customer to use as and when it decides to use it. *[IFRS 15.26(e)]*. That is, a stand-ready obligation is the promise that the customer will have access to a good or service, rather than a promise to transfer the underlying good or service itself. Stand-ready obligations are common in the software industry (e.g. unspecified updates to software on a when-and-if-available basis) and may be present in other industries. See 4.1.2.B and 4.1.2.C below for further discussion on stand-ready obligations.

Paragraph 26(g) of IFRS 15 notes that a promise to a customer may include granting rights to goods or services to be provided in the future that the customer can resell or provide to its own customers. *[IFRS 15.26(g)]*. Such a right may represent promises to the customer if it existed at the time that the parties agreed to the contract. As noted in the Basis for Conclusions, the Board thought it was important to clarify that a performance obligation may exist for a promise to provide a good or service in the future (e.g. when an entity makes a promise to provide goods or services to its customer's customer). *[IFRS 15.BC92]*. These types of promises exist in distribution networks in various industries and are common in the automotive industry.

The standard includes the following example to illustrate how an entity would identify the promised goods and services in a contract (including both explicit and implicit promises). *[IFRS 15.IE59-IE65A]*. The example also evaluates whether the identified promises are performance obligations, which we discuss at 4.2.

Example 30.9: Explicit and implicit promises in a contract

An entity, a manufacturer, sells a product to a distributor (i.e. its customer) who will then resell it to an end customer.

Case A – Explicit promise of service

In the contract with the distributor, the entity promises to provide maintenance services for no additional consideration (i.e. 'free') to any party (i.e. the end customer) that purchases the product from the distributor. The entity outsources the performance of the maintenance services to the distributor and pays the distributor an agreed-upon amount for providing those services on the entity's behalf. If the end customer does not use the maintenance services, the entity is not obliged to pay the distributor.

The contract with the customer includes two promised goods or services – (a) the product and (b) the maintenance services. The promise of maintenance services is a promise to transfer goods or services in the future and is part of the negotiated exchange between the entity and the distributor. The entity assesses whether each good or service is distinct in accordance with paragraph 27 of IFRS 15. The entity determines that both the product and the maintenance services meet the criterion in paragraph 27(a) of IFRS 15. The entity regularly sells the product on a stand-alone basis, which indicates that the customer can benefit from the product on its own. The customer can benefit from the maintenance services together with a resource the customer already has obtained from the entity (i.e. the product).

The entity further determines that its promises to transfer the product and to provide the maintenance services are separately identifiable (in accordance with paragraph 27(b) of IFRS 15) on the basis of the principle and the factors in paragraph 29 of IFRS 15. The product and the maintenance services are not inputs to a combined item in the contract. The entity is not providing a significant integration service because the presence of the product and the services together in this contract do not result in any additional or combined functionality. In addition, neither the product nor the services modify or customise the other. Lastly, the product and the maintenance services are not highly interdependent or highly interrelated because the entity would be able to fulfil each of the promises in the contract independently of its efforts to fulfil the other (i.e. the entity would be able to transfer the product even if the customer declined maintenance services and would be able to provide maintenance services in relation to products sold previously through other distributors). The entity also observes, in applying the principle in paragraph 29 of IFRS 15, that the entity's promise to provide maintenance is not necessary for the product to continue to provide significant benefit to the customer. Consequently, the entity allocates a portion of the transaction price to each of the two performance obligations (i.e. the product and the maintenance services) in the contract.

Case B – Implicit promise of service

The entity has historically provided maintenance services for no additional consideration (i.e. 'free') to end customers that purchase the entity's product from the distributor. The entity does not explicitly promise maintenance services during negotiations with the distributor and the final contract between the entity and the distributor does not specify terms or conditions for those services.

However, on the basis of its customary business practice, the entity determines at contract inception that it has made an implicit promise to provide maintenance services as part of the negotiated exchange with the distributor. That is, the entity's past practices of providing these services create valid expectations of the entity's customers (i.e. the distributor and end customers) in accordance with paragraph 24 of IFRS 15. Consequently, the entity assesses whether the promise of maintenance services as a performance obligation. For the same reasons as in Case A, the entity determines that the product and maintenance services are separate performance obligations.

Case C – Services are not a promised service

In the contract with the distributor, the entity does not promise to provide any maintenance services. In addition, the entity typically does not provide maintenance services and, therefore, the entity's customary business practices, published policies and specific statements at the time of entering into the contract have not created an implicit promise to provide goods or services to its customers. The entity transfers control of the product to the distributor and, therefore, the contract is completed. However, before the sale to the end customer, the entity makes an offer to provide maintenance services to any party that purchases the product from the distributor for no additional promised consideration.

The promise of maintenance is not included in the contract between the entity and the distributor at contract inception. That is, in accordance with paragraph 24 of IFRS 15, the entity does not explicitly or implicitly promise to provide maintenance services to the distributor or the end customers. Consequently, the entity does not identify the promise to provide maintenance services as a performance obligation. Instead, the obligation to provide maintenance services is accounted for in accordance with IAS 37 – *Provisions, Contingent Liabilities and Contingent Assets.*

Although the maintenance services are not a promised service in the current contract, in future contracts with customers the entity would assess whether it has created a business practice resulting in an implied promise to provide maintenance services.

Current IFRS does not specifically address contracts with multiple deliverables, focusing instead on identifying the transaction. This includes identifying separate elements so as to reflect the substance of the transaction. *[IAS 18.13]*. As a result, many IFRS preparers have looked to US GAAP for guidance in this area. Current US GAAP requires entities to identify the 'deliverables' within an arrangement, but does not define that term. In contrast, IFRS 15 indicates the types of items that may be goods or services promised in the contract. In addition, the standard makes clear that certain activities are not promised goods or services, such as activities that an entity must perform to satisfy its obligation to deliver the promised goods and services (e.g. internal administrative activities).

Some 'free' goods or services that may be treated as marketing incentives currently will have to be evaluated under the standard to determine whether they represent promised goods and services in a contract.

The FASB's standard allows entities to elect to account for shipping and handling activities performed after the control of a good has been transferred to the customer as a fulfilment cost (i.e. an expense). Without such an accounting policy choice, a US GAAP entity that has shipping arrangements after the customer has obtained control may determine that the act of shipping is a performance obligation under the standard. If that were the case, the entity would be required to allocate a portion of the transaction price to the shipping service and recognise it when (or as) the shipping occurs.

The IASB has not permitted a similar policy choice in IFRS 15. In the Basis for Conclusions, the IASB noted that paragraph 22 of IFRS 15 requires an entity to assess the goods or services promised in a contract with a customer in order to identify performance obligations. Such a policy choice would override that requirement. Furthermore, a policy choice is applicable to all entities and it is possible that entities with significant shipping operations may make different policy choices. Therefore, it could also reduce comparability between entities, including those within the same industry. *[IFRS 15.BC116U]*. Since the FASB's standard includes a policy choice that IFRS 15 does not, it is possible that diversity between IFRS and US GAAP entities may arise in practice.

Another difference is that FASB uses different language in relation to implied contractual terms and whether those implied terms represent a promised good or service to a customer. IFRS 15 states that promised goods or services are not limited to explicit promises in a contract, but could be created by a 'valid expectation of the customer'. ASC 606 refers to a 'reasonable expectation of the customer'. The FASB used this language in order to avoid confusion with the term 'valid expectation' because ASC 606 states that promises to provide goods or services do not need to be legally enforceable (although the overall arrangement needs to be enforceable). The use of the term 'valid' in IFRS 15 is consistent with the requirements for constructive obligations in IAS 37 – *Provisions, Contingent Liabilities and Contingent Assets.* While the terms used in IFRS 15 and ASC 606 are different, we do not expect this to result in a difference in practice.

4.1.1 Identifying promised goods or services that are not identified as deliverables under current revenue requirements

Following the issuance of IFRS 15, stakeholders questioned whether they will have to identify promised goods or services under the new standard that they do not identify as deliverables today. The question had been raised, in part, because the Board said in the Basis for Conclusions that it intentionally 'decided not to exempt an entity from accounting for performance obligations that the entity might regard as being perfunctory or inconsequential. Instead, an entity should assess whether those performance obligations are immaterial to its financial statements'. *[IFRS 15.BC90]*.

In January 2015, the TRG members discussed this issue and generally agreed that the standard is not intended to require the identification of promised goods or services that are not accounted for as deliverables today. At the same time, entities may not disregard items that they deem to be perfunctory or inconsequential and will need to consider whether 'free' goods and services represent promises to a customer. For example, telecommunications entities may have to allocate consideration to the 'free' handsets that they provide. Likewise, automobile manufacturers may have to allocate consideration to 'free' maintenance that may be considered a marketing incentive under current practice. However, entities would consider materiality in determining whether items are promised goods or services.[26]

The Board subsequently considered the TRG members' discussion and agreed that it does not expect entities to identify significantly more performance obligations than the deliverables that are identified under current IFRS.

The FASB's standard allows entities to disregard promises that are deemed to be immaterial in the context of a contract. That is, ASC 606 permits entities to disregard items that are immaterial at the contract level and does not require that the items be aggregated and assessed for materiality at the entity level. However, ASC 606 also emphasises that entities will still need to evaluate whether customer options for additional goods or services are materials rights to be accounted for in accordance with the related requirements (see 4.6 below).

IFRS 15 does not include explicit language to indicate an entity can disregard promised goods and services that are immaterial in the context of the contract. However, in the Basis for Conclusions, the IASB noted that it did not intend for entities to identify every possible promised good or services in a contract and that entities should consider materiality and the overall objective of IFRS 15 when assessing promised goods or services and identifying performance obligations.

The IASB also noted that revenue standards under current IFRS do not contain similar language to the current guidance issued by the staff of the US SEC on inconsequential or perfunctory performance obligations under current US GAAP. *[IFRS 15.BC116A-BC116E]*. The TRG's discussion highlighted that the concerns raised about identifying performance obligations that are not identified as deliverables today primarily relate to potential changes in practice under US GAAP when comparing this existing US SEC guidance to ASC 606.

4.1.2 Implementation questions on identifying promised goods or services

4.1.2.A Assessing whether pre-production activities are a promised good or service

The TRG members generally agreed that the determination of whether pre-production activities are a promised good or service or fulfilment activities will require judgement and consideration of the facts and circumstances. Entities often need to perform pre-production activities before delivering any units under a production contract. For example, some long-term supply arrangements require an entity to perform up-front engineering and design services to create new, or adapt existing, technology to the needs of a customer.

The TRG members generally agreed that if an entity is having difficulty determining whether a pre-production activity is a promised good or service in a contract, the entity should consider whether control of that good or service transfers to the customer. For example, if an entity is performing engineering and development services as part of developing a new product for a customer and the customer will own the resulting intellectual property (e.g. patents), the entity would likely conclude that it is transferring control of the intellectual property and that the engineering and development activities are a promised good or service in the contract.

The TRG members noted that assessing whether control transfers in such arrangements may be challenging. In some arrangements, legal title of the good or service created from the pre-production activity is transferred to the customer. However, the TRG members generally agreed that an entity would have to consider all indicators of control transfer under IFRS 15 and that the transfer of legal title is not a presumptive indicator.

If a pre-production activity is determined to be a promised good or service, an entity will allocate a portion of the transaction price to that good or service (as a single performance obligation or as part of a combined performance obligation that includes the pre-production activities along with other goods and services). If the pre-production activities are included in a performance obligation satisfied over time, they would be considered when measuring progress toward satisfaction of that performance obligation (see 7.2 below).[27]

4.1.2.B The nature of the promise in a typical stand-ready obligation

Stakeholders raised questions about the nature of the promise in a 'typical' stand-ready obligation.

At the January 2015 TRG meeting, the TRG members discussed numerous examples of stand-ready obligations and generally agreed that the nature of the promise in a stand-ready obligation is the promise that the customer will have access to the good or service, not the delivery of the underlying good or service.[28] The standard describes a stand-ready obligation as a promised service that consists of standing ready to provide goods or services or making goods or services available for a customer to use as and when it decides to do so. Stand-ready obligations are common in the software industry (e.g. unspecified updates to software on a when-and-if-available basis) and may be present in other industries.

The TRG agenda paper included the following types of promises to a customer that could be considered stand-ready obligations, depending on the facts and circumstances:[29]

- obligations for which the delivery of the good, service or intellectual property is within the control of the entity, but is still being developed (e.g. a software vendor's promise to transfer unspecified software upgrades at its discretion);
- obligations for which the delivery of the underlying good or service is outside the control of the entity and the customer (e.g. an entity's promise to remove snow from an airport runway in exchange for a fixed fee for the year);
- obligations for which the delivery of the underlying good or service is within the control of the customer (e.g. an entity's promise to provide periodic maintenance on a when-and-if needed basis on a customer's equipment after a pre-established amount of usage by the customer); and
- obligations to make a good or service available to a customer continuously (e.g. a gym membership that provides unlimited access to a customer for a specified period of time).

An entity will need to carefully evaluate the facts and circumstances of its contracts to appropriately identify whether the nature of a promise to a customer is the delivery of the underlying good(s) or service(s) or the service of standing ready to provide goods or services. Entities will also have to consider other promises in a contract that includes a stand-ready obligation to appropriately identify the performance obligations in the contract. The TRG members generally agreed that all contracts with a stand-ready element do not necessarily include a single performance obligation (see 4.1.2.C below).[30]

At the TRG meeting, a FASB staff member also indicated that the staff does not believe that the FASB intended to change current practice under US GAAP for determining when software or technology transactions include specified upgrade rights (i.e. a separate performance obligation) or unspecified upgrade rights (i.e. a stand-ready obligation).[31] For details of TRG members' discussion on measuring progress toward satisfaction for a stand-ready obligation that is satisfied over time see 7.2.4.A below.

4.1.2.C *Considering whether contracts with a stand-ready element include a single performance obligation that is satisfied over time*

At the November 2015 TRG meeting, the TRG members considered whether all contracts with a stand-ready element include a single performance obligation that is satisfied over time.

The TRG members generally agreed that the stand-ready element in a contract does not always represent a single performance obligation satisfied over time. This conclusion is consistent with the discussion in 4.1.2.B above that, when identifying the nature of a promise to a customer, an entity may determine that a stand-ready element exists, but it is not the promised good or service for revenue recognition purposes. Instead, the underlying goods or services are the goods or services promised to the customer and accounted for by the entity.

As an example, an entity may be required to stand ready to produce a part for a customer under a master supply arrangement. The customer is not obligated to purchase any parts (i.e. there is no minimum guaranteed volume). However, it is highly likely the customer will purchase parts because the part is required to manufacture the customer's product and it is not practical for the customer to buy parts from multiple suppliers. The TRG members generally agreed that the nature of the promise in this example is the delivery of the parts, rather than a service of standing ready. When the customer submits a purchase order under the master supply arrangement, it is contracting for a specific number of distinct goods and the purchase order creates new performance obligations for the entity. However, if the entity determined that the nature of the promise is a service of standing ready, the contract would be accounted for as a single performance obligation satisfied over time. In that situation, the entity may be required to estimate the number of purchases to be made throughout the contract term (i.e. make an estimate of variable consideration and apply the constraint on variable consideration) and continually update the transaction price and its allocation among the transferred goods and services.

The TRG agenda paper also noted that, in this example, the entity is not obligated to transfer any parts until the customer submits a purchase order (i.e. the customer makes a separate purchasing decision). This contrasts with a stand-ready obligation, which requires the entity to make a promised service available to the customer and does not require the customer to make any additional purchasing decisions.[32]

See 4.6.1.C below for further discussion on determining whether a contract involving variable quantities of goods or services should be accounted for as variable consideration (i.e. if the nature of the promise is to transfer one overall service to the customer, such as a stand-ready obligation) or a contract containing customer options (i.e. if the nature of the promise is to transfer the underlying distinct goods or services).

4.2 Determining when promises are performance obligations

After identifying the promised goods and services within a contract, an entity determines which of those goods and services will be treated as separate performance obligations. That is, the entity identifies the individual units of account. Promised goods or services represent separate performance obligations if the goods or services are distinct (by themselves, or as part of a bundle of goods and services) or if the goods and services are part of a series of distinct goods and services that are substantially the same and have the same pattern of transfer to the customer (see 4.2.2 below).

If a promised good or service is not distinct, an entity is required to combine that good or service with other promised goods or services until it identifies a bundle of goods or services that, together, is distinct. *[IFRS 15.30]*.

An entity will be required to account for all the goods or services promised in a contract as a single performance obligation if the entire bundle of promised goods and services is the only performance obligation identified. See 4.3 below for further discussion.

A single performance obligation may include a licence of intellectual property and other promised goods or services. IFRS 15 identifies two examples of licences of intellectual property that are not distinct from other promised goods or services in a contract: (1) a licence that is a component of a tangible good and that is integral to the functionality of the tangible good and (2) a licence that the customer can benefit from only in conjunction with a related service (e.g. an online hosting service that enables a customer to access the content provided by the licence of intellectual property). *[IFRS 15.B54]*. See 8.1.2 below for further discussion on these two examples.

The standard also specifies that the following items are performance obligations:

- Customer options for additional goods or services that provide material rights to customers (see 4.6 below). *[IFRS 15.B39-B43]*.
- Service-type warranties (see 9.1 below). *[IFRS 15.B28-B33]*.

Entities will not apply the general model to determine whether these goods or services are performance obligations because the Board deemed them to be performance obligations if they are identified as promises in a contract.

4.2.1 Determination of 'distinct'

IFRS 15 outlines a two-step process for determining whether a promised good or service (or a bundle of goods and services) is distinct:

- Consideration at the level of the individual good or service (i.e. the good or service is capable of being distinct).
- Consideration of whether the good or service is separable from other promises in the contract (i.e. the good or service is distinct within the context of the contract).

Both of these criteria must be met to conclude that the good or service is distinct. If these criteria are met, the individual good or service must be accounted for as a separate unit of account (i.e. a performance obligation).

The Board concluded that both steps are important in determining whether a promised good or service should be accounted for separately. The first criterion (i.e. capable of being distinct) establishes the minimum characteristics for a good or service to be accounted for separately. However, even if the individual goods or services promised in a contract may be capable of being distinct, it may not be appropriate to account for each of them separately because doing so would not result in a faithful depiction of the entity's performance in that contract or appropriately represent the nature of an entity's promise to the customer. *[IFRS 15.BC102]*.

Therefore, an entity would also need to consider the interrelationship of those goods or services to apply the second criterion (i.e. distinct within the context of the contract) and determine the performance obligations within a contract.

The standard specifies that a promised good or service is distinct if it meets both of the following criteria:

(a) the customer can benefit from the good or service either on its own or together with other resources that are readily available to the customer (i.e. the good or service is capable of being distinct); and

(b) the entity's promise to transfer the good or service to the customer is separately identifiable from other promises in the contract (i.e. the promise to transfer the good or service is distinct within the context of the contract). *[IFRS 15.27]*.

4.2.1.A Capable of being distinct

The first criterion requires that a promised good or service must be capable of being distinct by providing a benefit to the customer either on its own or together with other resources that are readily available to the customer.

The standard states that a customer can benefit from a good or service if the good or service could be used, consumed, sold for an amount greater than scrap value or otherwise held in a way that generates economic benefits. A customer may be able to benefit from some goods or services on their own or in conjunction with other readily available resources. A readily available resource is a good or service that is sold separately (by the entity or another entity) or a resource that the customer has already obtained from the entity (including goods or services that the entity will have already transferred to the customer under the contract) or from other transactions or events. The fact that an entity regularly sells a good or service separately indicates that a customer can benefit from that good or service on its own or with readily available resources. *[IFRS 15.28]*.

Determining whether a good or service is capable of being distinct will be straightforward in many situations. For example, if an entity regularly sells a good or service separately, this fact would demonstrate that the good or service provides benefit to a customer on its own or with other readily available resources.

The evaluation may require more judgement in other situations, particularly when the good or service can only provide benefit to the customer with readily available resources provided by other entities. These are resources that meet either of the following conditions:

- they are sold separately by the entity (or another entity); or
- the customer has already obtained them from the entity (including goods or services that the entity will have already transferred to the customer under the contract) or from other transactions or events.

As noted in the Basis for Conclusions, the assessment of whether the customer can benefit from the goods or services (either on its own or with other readily available resources) is based on the characteristics of the goods or services themselves instead of how the customer might use the goods or services. *[IFRS 15.BC100]*. Consistent with this notion, an entity disregards any contractual limitations that may prevent the customer from obtaining those readily available resources from a party other than the entity when making this assessment (as illustrated below in Example 30.15 at 4.2.3 below).

In the Basis for Conclusions, the Board explained that 'the attributes of being distinct are comparable to the previous revenue recognition requirements for identifying separate deliverables in a multiple-element arrangements, which specified that a delivered item must have "value to the customer on a stand-alone basis" for an entity to account for that item separately.' However, the Board did not use similar terminology in IFRS 15 so as to avoid implying that an entity must assess a customer's intended use for a promised good or service when it is identifying performance obligations. It observed that it would be difficult, if not impossible, for an entity to know a customer's intent. *[IFRS 15.BC101]*.

4.2.1.B Distinct within the context of the contract

In April 2016, the IASB amended IFRS 15 to clarify when a promised good or service is 'separately identifiable' from other promises in a contract (i.e. distinct within the context of the contract). The amendments: (1) reframed the principle for determining whether promised goods or services are separately identifiable to emphasise that the evaluation hinges on whether the multiple promised goods or services work together to deliver a combined output(s); (2) aligned the standard's three indicators for determining whether a promised good or service is separately identifiable with this principle; and (3) added new examples and amended others to help entities apply these concepts.

Once an entity has determined whether a promised good or service is capable of being distinct based on the individual characteristics of the promise, the entity considers the second criterion of whether the good or service is separately identifiable from other promises in the contract (i.e. whether the promise to transfer the good or service is distinct within the context of the contract). The standard states that, when assessing whether an entity's promises to transfer goods or services to the customer are separately identifiable from other promises in the contract, the objective is 'to determine whether the nature of the promise, within the context of the contract, is to transfer each of those goods or services individually or, instead, to transfer a combined item or items to which the promised goods or services are inputs. Factors that indicate that two or more promises to transfer goods or services to a customer are not separately identifiable include, but are not limited to, the following:

(a) the entity provides a significant service of integrating the goods or services with other goods or services promised in the contract into a bundle of goods or services that represent the combined output or outputs for which the customer has contracted. In other words, the entity is using the goods or services as an input to produce or deliver the combined output or outputs specified by the customer. A combined output or outputs might include more than one phase, element or unit.

(b) one or more of the goods or services do significantly modifies or customises, or are significantly modified or customised by, one or more of the other goods or services promised in the contract.

(c) the goods or services are highly dependent or highly interrelated. In other words, each of the goods or services is significantly affected by one or more of the other goods or services in the contract. For example, in some cases, two or more goods or services are significantly affected by each other because the entity would not be able to fulfil its promise by transferring each of the goods or services independently.' *[IFRS 15.29]*.

(a) Separately identifiable principle

To determine whether promised goods or services are separately identifiable (i.e. whether a promise to transfer a good or service is distinct within the context of the contract), an entity will need to evaluate whether its promise is to transfer each good or service individually or a combined item (or items) that comprises the individual goods or services promised in the contract. Therefore, an entity would evaluate whether the promised goods or services in the contract are outputs or they are inputs to a combined item (or items). In the Basis for Conclusions, the Board noted that, in many cases, a combined item (or items) would be more than (or substantially different from) the sum of the underlying promised goods and services. *[IFRS 15.BC116J]*.

The evaluation of whether an entity's promise is separately identifiable considers the relationship between the various goods or services in the context of the process to fulfil the contract. Therefore, an entity considers the level of integration, interrelation or interdependence among the promises to transfer goods or services. In the Basis for Conclusion, the Board observed that, rather than considering whether one item, by its nature, depends on the other (i.e. whether two items have a functional relationship), an entity evaluates whether there is a transformative relationship between the two or more items in the process of fulfilling the contract. *[IFRS 15.BC116K]*.

The Board also emphasised that the separately identifiable principle is applied within the context of the bundle of promised goods or services in the contract. It is not within the context of each individual promised good or service. That is, the separately identifiable principle is intended to identify when an entity's performance in transferring a bundle of goods or services in a contract is fulfilling a single promise to a customer. Therefore, to apply the 'separately identifiable' principle, an entity evaluates whether two or more promised goods or services significantly affect each other in the contract (and are, therefore, highly interdependent or highly interrelated). *[IFRS 15.BC116L]*.

As an example of this evaluation, the IASB discussed in the Basis for Conclusions a typical construction contract that involves transferring to the customer many goods and services that are capable of being distinct (e.g. various building materials, labour, project management services). In this example, the IASB concluded that identifying all of the individual goods and services as separate performance obligations would be impractical and would not faithfully represent the nature of the entity's promise to the customer. That is, the entity would recognise revenue when the materials and other inputs to the construction process are provided rather than when it performs (and uses those inputs) in the construction of the item the customer has contracted to receive (e.g. a building, a house). As such, when determining whether a promised good or service is distinct, an entity will not only determine whether the good or service is capable of being distinct but also whether the promise to transfer the good or service is distinct within the context of the contract. *[IFRS 15.BC102]*.

Paragraph 29 of IFRS 15 includes three factors (discussed individually below) that are intended to help entities identify when the promises in a bundle of promised goods or services are not separately identifiable and, therefore, should be combined into a single performance obligation. *[IFRS 15.29]*. In the Basis for Conclusions, the IASB noted that these three factors are not an exhaustive list and that not all of the factors need to exist in order to conclude that the entity's promises to transfer goods or services are not separately identifiable. The three factors also are not intended to be criteria that are evaluated independently of the separately identifiable principle. Given the wide variety of arrangements that are within the scope of IFRS 15, the Board expects that there will be some instances in which the factors will be less relevant to the evaluation of the separately identifiable principle. *[IFRS 15.BC116N]*. Entities may need to apply significant judgement to evaluate whether a promised good or service is separately identifiable. The evaluation will require a thorough understanding of the facts and circumstances present in each contract.

(i) Significant integration service

The first factor (included in paragraph 29(a) of IFRS 15) is the presence of a significant integration service. *[IFRS 15.29(a)]*. The IASB determined that, when an entity provides a significant service of integrating a good or service with other goods or services in a contract, the bundle of integrated goods or services represents a combined output or outputs. In other words, when an entity provides a significant integration service, the risk of transferring individual goods or services is inseparable from the bundle of integrated goods or services because a substantial part of an entity's promise to the customer is to make sure the individual goods or services are incorporated into the combined output or outputs. *[IFRS 15.BC107]*.

This factor applies even if there is more than one output. Furthermore, as described in the standard, a combined output or outputs may include more than one phase, element or unit.

In the Basis for Conclusions, the IASB noted that this factor may be relevant in many construction contracts in which a contractor provides an integration (or contract management) service to manage and coordinate the various construction tasks and to assume the risks associated with the integration of those tasks. An integration service provided by the contractor often includes coordinating the activities performed by any subcontractors and making sure the quality of the work performed is in compliance with contract specifications and that the individual goods or services are appropriately integrated into the combined item that the customer has contracted to receive. *[IFRS 15.BC107]*. The Board also observed that this factor could apply to other industries as well. *[IFRS 15.BC108]*.

(ii) Significant modification or customisation

The second factor in paragraph 29(b) of IFRS 15 is the presence of significant modification or customisation. *[IFRS 15.29(b)]*. In the Basis for Conclusions, the IASB explained that in some industries, the notion of inseparable risks is more clearly illustrated by assessing whether one good or service significantly modifies or customises another. This is because if a good or service modifies or customises another good or service in a contract, each good or service is being assembled together (as an input) to produce a combined output. *[IFRS 15.BC109]*.

For example, assume that an entity promises to provide a customer with software that it will significantly customise to make the software function with the customer's existing infrastructure. Based on its facts and circumstances, the entity determines that it is providing the customer with a fully integrated system and that the customisation service requires it to significantly modify the software in such a way that the risks of providing it and the customisation service are inseparable (i.e. the software and customisation service are not separately identifiable).

(iii) Highly interdependent or highly interrelated

The third factor in paragraph 29(c) of IFRS 15 is whether the promised goods or services are highly interdependent or highly interrelated. *[IFRS 15.29(c)]*. Promised goods or services are highly interdependent or highly interrelated if each of the promised goods or services is significantly affected by one or more of the other goods or services in the contract. As discussed above, the Board clarified that an entity would evaluate whether there is a two-way dependency or transformative relationship between the promised goods or services to determine whether the promises are highly interdependent or highly interrelated.

(b) Examples

The IASB included a number of examples in the standard that illustrate the application of the requirements for identifying performance obligations. The examples include analysis of how an entity may determine whether the promises to transfer goods or services are distinct within the context of the contract. See 4.2.3 below for full extracts of several of these examples.

IAS 18 indicates that an entity may need to apply its recognition criteria to separately identifiable elements in order to reflect the substance of the transaction. However, it does not provide additional application guidance for determining those separate elements. As such, the requirements in IFRS 15 may change practice.

Many IFRS preparers have developed their current accounting policies by reference to current US GAAP. Whether the new standard results in a change in practice may depend on which current US GAAP requirements they have considered when developing their policies.

The first step of the two-step process to determine whether goods or services are distinct is similar to the principles for determining separate units of accounting under today's US GAAP requirements in ASC 605-25 – *Revenue Recognition – Multiple-Element Arrangements*. However, the second step of considering the goods or services within the context of the contract is a new requirement. Therefore, entities will need to carefully evaluate this second step to determine whether their historical units of account for revenue recognition may need to change. This evaluation may require an entity to use significant judgement.

Entities that have looked to other current US GAAP requirements to develop their accounting policies, such as ASC 985-605 – *Software – Revenue Recognition*, may also reach different conclusions under IFRS 15.

It is important to note that the assessment of whether a good or service is distinct must consider the specific contract with a customer. That is, an entity cannot assume that a particular good or service is distinct (or not distinct) in all instances. The manner in which promised goods and services are bundled within a contract can affect the conclusion of whether a good or service is distinct. We anticipate that entities may treat the same goods and services differently, depending on how those goods and services are bundled within a contract.

4.2.2 Series of distinct goods and services that are substantially the same and have the same pattern of transfer

As discussed above, paragraph 22(b) of IFRS 15 defines, as a second type of performance obligation, a promise to transfer to the customer a series of distinct goods or services that are substantially the same and that have the same pattern of transfer, if both of the following criteria from paragraph 23 of IFRS 15 are met: *[IFRS 15.22(b), 23]*

- each distinct good or service in the series that the entity promises to transfer represents a performance obligation that would be satisfied over time in accordance with paragraph 35 of IFRS 15 (see 4.2.2.A and 7.1 below), if it were accounted for separately; and
- the entity would measure its progress toward satisfaction of the performance obligation using the same measure of progress for each distinct good or service in the series (see 7.2 below).

If a series of distinct goods or services meets the criteria in paragraph 22(b) of IFRS 15 and paragraph 23 of IFRS 15 (the series requirement), an entity is required to treat that series as a single performance obligation (i.e. it is not optional). The Board incorporated this requirement to simplify the model and promote consistent identification of performance obligations in cases when an entity provides the same good or service over a period of time. *[IFRS 15.BC113]*. Without the series requirement, the Board noted that applying the revenue model might present operational challenges because an entity would have to identify multiple distinct goods or services, allocate the transaction price to each distinct good or service on a stand-alone selling price basis and then recognise revenue when those performance obligations are satisfied. The IASB determined that this would not be cost effective. Instead, an entity will identify a single performance obligation and allocate the transaction price to that performance obligation. It will then recognise revenue by applying a single measure of progress to that performance obligation. *[IFRS 15.BC114]*.

For distinct goods or services to be accounted for as a series, they must be substantially the same. In the Basis for Conclusions, the Board provided three examples of repetitive services (i.e. cleaning, transaction processing and delivering electricity) that meet the series requirement. *[IFRS 15.BC114]*. In addition, the TRG members generally agreed that when determining whether distinct goods or services are substantially the same, entities will need to first determine the nature of their promise. This is because a series could consist of either specified quantities of the underlying good or service delivered (e.g. each unit of a good) or distinct time increments (e.g. an hourly service), depending on the nature of the promise. That is, if the nature of the promise is to deliver a specified quantity of service (e.g. monthly payroll services over a defined contract period), the evaluation considers whether each service is distinct and substantially the same. In contrast, if the nature of the entity's promise is to stand ready or provide a single service for a period of time (i.e. because there is an unspecified quantity to be delivered), the evaluation considers whether each time increment (e.g. hour, day), rather than the underlying activities, is distinct and substantially the same.[33]

It is important to highlight that even if the underlying activities an entity performs to satisfy a promise vary significantly throughout the day and from day to day, that fact, by itself, does not mean the distinct goods or services are not substantially the same. Consider an example where the nature of the promise is to provide a daily hotel management service. The service is comprised of activities that may vary each day (e.g. cleaning services, reservation services, property maintenance). However, the entity determines that the daily hotel management services are substantially the same because the nature of the entity's promise is the same each day and the entity is providing the same overall management service each day. See 4.2.2.C below for further discussion on determining the nature of an entity's promise and evaluating the 'substantially the same' criterion.

A TRG agenda paper discussed at the July 2015 TRG meeting explained that, when considering the nature of the entity's promise and the applicability of the series requirement (including whether a good or service is distinct), it may be helpful to consider which over-time criterion in paragraph 35 of IFRS 15 was met (i.e. why the entity concluded that the performance obligation is satisfied over time).[34] As discussed further at 7.1 below, a performance obligation is satisfied over time if one of three criteria are met. For example, if a performance obligation is satisfied over time because the customer simultaneously receives and consumes the benefits provided as the entity performs (i.e. the first over-time criterion in paragraph 35(a) of IFRS 15), that may indicate that each increment of service is capable of being distinct. If that is the case, the entity would need to evaluate whether each increment of service is separately identifiable (and substantially the same). If a performance obligation is satisfied over time based on one of the other two criteria in paragraph 35 of IFRS 15 (i.e. (1) the entity's performance creates or enhances an asset that the customer controls as the asset is created or enhanced; or (2) the entity's performance does not create an asset with an alternative use to the entity and the entity has an enforceable right to payment for performance completed to date), the nature of that promise might be to deliver a single specified good or service (e.g. a contract to construct a single piece of equipment), which would not be considered a series because the individual goods or services within that performance obligation are not distinct.

An entity's determination of whether a performance obligation is a single performance obligation comprising a series of distinct goods or services or a single performance obligation comprising goods or services that are not distinct from one another will affect the accounting in the following areas: (1) allocation of variable consideration (see 6 below); (2) contract modifications (see 3.4 above); and (3) changes in transaction price (see 6.5 below). As the IASB discussed in the Basis for Conclusions and the TRG members discussed at their March 2015 meeting, an entity considers the underlying distinct goods or services in the contract, rather than the single performance obligation identified under the series requirement, when applying the requirements for these three areas of the model.[35] *[IFRS 15.BC115]*.

The following example, included in a TRG agenda paper, illustrates how the allocation of variable consideration may differ for a single performance obligation identified under the series requirement and a single performance obligation comprising non-distinct goods and/or services. Consider a five-year service contract that includes payment terms of a fixed annual fee plus a performance bonus upon completion of a milestone at the end of year two. If the entire service period is determined to be a single performance obligation comprising a series of distinct services, the entity may be able to conclude that the variable consideration (i.e. the bonus amount) should be allocated directly to its efforts to perform the distinct services up to the date that the milestone is achieved (e.g. the underlying distinct services in years one and two). This would result in the entity recognising the entire bonus amount, if earned, at the end of year two. See 4.2.2.C below for several examples of services for which it would be reasonably to conclude that they meet the series requirement.[36]

In contrast, if the entity determines that the entire service period is a single performance obligation that is comprised of non-distinct services, the bonus would be included in the transaction price (subject to the constraint on variable consideration – see 5.2.3 below) and recognised based on the measure of progress determined for the entire service period. For example, assume the bonus becomes part of the transaction price at the end of year two (when it is probable to be earned and not subject to a revenue reversal). In that case, a portion of the bonus would be recognised at that the end of year two based on performance completed to date and a portion would be recognised as the remainder of the performance obligation is satisfied. As a result, the bonus amount would be recognised as revenue through to the end of the five-year service period.

The series requirement is a new concept. We believe that entities may need to apply significant judgement when determining whether a promised good or service in a contract with a customer meets the criteria to be accounted for as a series of distinct goods or services. As illustrated in 4.2.2.C below, promised goods or services that meet the series criteria are not limited to a particular industry and can encompass a wide array of promised goods and services.

Entities should consider whether they need to add or make changes to their business processes or internal controls as a result of this new requirement.

4.2.2.A *The series requirement: concurrent versus consecutive transfer of goods or services*

In March 2015, the TRG members discussed whether the goods or services must be consecutively transferred to be considered under the series requirement. The TRG members generally agreed that a series of distinct goods or services need not be consecutively transferred. That is, the series requirement must be applied even when there is a gap or an overlap in an entity's transfer of goods or services, provided that the other criteria are met.[37] The IASB TRG members also noted that entities may need to carefully consider whether the series requirement applies, depending on the length of the gap between an entity's transfer of goods or services.

Stakeholders had asked this question because the Basis for Conclusions uses the term 'consecutively' when it discusses the series requirement. *[IFRS 15.BC113, BC116]*. However, the TRG agenda paper concluded that the Board's discussion was not meant to imply that the series requirement only applies to circumstances in which the entity provides the same good or service consecutively over a period of time.

The TRG agenda paper included an example of a contract under which an entity provides a manufacturing service producing 24,000 units of a product over a two-year period. The conclusion in the TRG agenda paper was that the criteria for the series requirement in paragraph 23 of IFRS 15 were met because the units produced under the service arrangement were substantially the same and were distinct services that would be satisfied over time (see 7.1 below). This is because the units are manufactured to meet the customer's specifications (i.e. the entity's performance does not create an asset with alternative use to the entity). Furthermore, if the contract were to be cancelled, the entity would have an enforceable right to payment (cost plus a reasonable profit margin).[38]

The conclusion in the TRG agenda paper was not influenced by whether the entity would perform the service evenly over the two-year period (e.g. produce 1,000 units per month). That is, the entity could produce 2,000 units in some months and none in others, but this would not be a determining factor in concluding whether the contract met the criteria to be accounted for as a series.

4.2.2.B *The series requirement versus treating the distinct goods or services as separate performance obligations*

At the March 2015 TRG meeting, the TRG members were asked whether, in order to apply the series requirement, the accounting result needs to be the same as if the underlying distinct goods and services were accounted for as separate performance obligations.

The TRG members generally agreed that the accounting result does not need to be the same. Furthermore, an entity is not required to prove that the result would be the same as if the goods and services were accounted for as separate performance obligations.[39]

4.2.2.C *Assessing whether a performance obligation consists of distinct goods or services that are 'substantially the same'*

At the July 2015 TRG meeting, the TRG members were asked to consider how an entity would assess whether a performance obligation consists of distinct goods or services that are 'substantially the same' in order to apply the series requirement.[40]

As discussed above, the TRG members generally agreed that the TRG paper, which primarily focused on the application of the series requirement to service contracts, will help entities understand how to determine whether a performance obligation consists of distinct goods or services that are 'substantially the same' under IFRS 15.

The TRG agenda paper noted that, when making the evaluation of whether goods or services are distinct and substantially the same, an entity first needs to determine the nature of the entity's promise in providing services to the customer. That is, if the nature of the promise is to deliver a specified quantity of service (e.g. monthly payroll services over a defined contract period), the evaluation should consider whether each service is distinct and substantially the same. In contrast, if the nature of the entity's promise is to stand ready or provide a single service for a period of time (i.e. because there is an unspecified quantity to be delivered), the evaluation would consider whether each time increment (e.g. hour, day), rather than the underlying activities, is distinct and substantially the same. The TRG agenda paper noted that the Board intended that a series could consist of either specified quantities of the underlying good or service delivered (e.g. each unit of a good) or distinct time increments (e.g. an hourly service), depending on the nature of the promise.

As discussed at 4.2.2 above, it is important to highlight that the underlying activities an entity performs to satisfy a performance obligation could vary significantly throughout a day and from day to day. However, the TRG agenda paper noted that this not determinative in the assessment of whether a performance obligation consists of goods or services that are distinct and substantially the same. Consider an example where the nature of the promise is to provide a daily hotel management service. The hotel management service comprises various activities that may vary each day (e.g. cleaning services, reservation services, property maintenance). However, the entity determines that the daily hotel management services are substantially the same because the nature of the entity's promise is the same each day and the entity is providing the same overall management service each day.

The TRG agenda paper included several examples of promised goods and services that may meet the series requirement and the analysis that supports that conclusion. The evaluation of the nature of the promise for each example is consistent with Example 13 of IFRS 15, *[IFRS 15.IE67-IE68]*, on monthly payroll processing. Below we have summarised some of the examples and analysis in the TRG agenda paper.

Example 30.10: IT outsourcing[41]

A vendor and customer execute a 10-year information technology (IT) outsourcing arrangement in which the vendor continuously delivers the outsourced activities over the contract term (e.g. it provides server capacity, manages the customer's software portfolio, runs an IT help desk). The total monthly invoice is calculated based on different units consumed for the respective activities. The vendor concludes that the customer simultaneously receives and consumes the benefits provided by its services as it performs (meeting the over-time criterion in paragraph 35(a) of IFRS 15).

The vendor first considers the nature of its promise to the customer. Because the vendor has promised to provide an unspecified quantity of activities, rather than a defined number of services, the TRG agenda paper noted that the vendor could reasonably conclude that the nature of the promise is an obligation to stand ready to provide the integrated outsourcing service each day. If the nature of the promise is the overall IT outsourcing service, each day of service could be considered distinct because the customer can benefit from each day of service on its own and each day is separately identifiable. The TRG agenda paper also noted that the vendor could reasonably conclude that each day of service is substantially the same. That is, even if the individual activities that comprise the performance obligation vary from day to day, the nature of the overall promise is the same from day to day. Accordingly, it would be reasonable for an entity to conclude that this contract meets the series requirement.

Example 30.11: Transaction processing[42]

A vendor enters into a 10-year contract with a customer to provide continuous access to its system and to process all transactions on behalf of the customer. The customer is obligated to use the vendor's system, but the ultimate quantity of transactions is unknown. The vendor concludes that the customer simultaneously receives and consumes the benefits as it performs.

If the vendor concludes that the nature of its promise is to provide continuous access to its system, rather than process a particular quantity of transactions, it might conclude that there is a single performance obligation to stand ready to process as many transactions as the customer requires. If that is the case, the TRG agenda paper noted that it would be reasonable to conclude that there are multiple distinct time increments of the service. Each day of access to the service provided to the customer could be considered substantially the same since the customer is deriving a consistent benefit from the access each day, even if a different number of transactions are processed each day.

If the vendor concludes that the nature of the promise is the processing of each transaction, the TRG agenda paper noted that each transaction processed could be considered substantially the same even if there are multiple types of transactions that generate different payments. Furthermore, the TRG agenda paper noted that each transaction processed could be a distinct service because the customer could benefit from each transaction on its own and each transaction could be separately identifiable. Accordingly, it would be reasonable for an entity to conclude that this contract meets the series requirement.

Example 30.12: Hotel management[43]

A hotel manager (HM) enters into a 20-year contract to manage properties on behalf of a customer. HM receives monthly consideration of 1% of the monthly rental revenue, as well as reimbursement of labour costs incurred to perform the service and an annual incentive payment. HM concludes that the customer simultaneously receives and consumes the benefits of its services as it performs.

HM considers the nature of its promise to the customer. If the nature of its promise is the overall management service (because the underlying activities are not distinct from each other), the TRG agenda paper noted that each day of service could be considered distinct because the customer can benefit from each day of service on its own and each day of service is separately identifiable.

Assuming the nature of the promise is the overall management service, the TRG agenda paper noted that the service performed each day could be considered distinct and substantially the same. This is because, even if the individual activities that comprise the performance obligation vary significantly throughout the day and from day to day, the nature of the overall promise to provide the management service is the same from day to day. Accordingly, it would be reasonable for an entity to conclude that this contract meets the series requirement.

4.2.3 Examples of identifying performance obligations

The standard includes several examples that illustrate the application of the requirements for identifying performance obligations. The examples explain the judgements made to determine whether the promises to transfer goods or services are capable of being distinct and distinct within the context of the contract. We have extracted these examples below.

The following example illustrates contracts with promised goods and services that, while capable of being distinct, are not distinct within the context of the contract because of a significant integration service that combines the inputs (the underlying goods and services) into a combined output. *[IFRS 15.IE45-IE48C]*.

Example 30.13: Goods and services are not distinct

Case A – Significant integration service

An entity, a contractor, enters into a contract to build a hospital for a customer. The entity is responsible for the overall management of the project and identifies various promised goods and services, including engineering, site clearance, foundation, procurement, construction of the structure, piping and wiring, installation of equipment and finishing.

The promised goods and services are capable of being distinct in accordance with paragraph 27(a) of IFRS 15. That is, the customer can benefit from the goods and services either on their own or together with other readily available resources. This is evidenced by the fact that the entity, or competitors of the entity, regularly sells many of these goods and services separately to other customers. In addition, the customer could generate economic benefit from the individual goods and services by using, consuming, selling or holding those goods or services.

However, the promises to transfer the goods and services are not separately identifiable in accordance with paragraph 27(b) of IFRS 15 (on the basis of the factors in paragraph 29 of IFRS 15). This is evidenced by the fact that the entity provides a significant service of integrating the goods and services (the inputs) into the hospital (the combined output) for which the customer has contracted.

Because both criteria in paragraph 27 of IFRS 15 are not met, the goods and services are not distinct. The entity accounts for all of the goods and services in the contract as a single performance obligation.

Case B – Significant integration service

An entity enters into a contract with a customer that will result in the delivery of multiple units of a highly complex, specialised device. The terms of the contract require the entity to establish a manufacturing process in order to produce the contracted units. The specifications are unique to the customer, based on a custom design that is owned by the customer and that were developed under the terms of a separate contract that is not part of the current negotiated exchange. The entity is responsible for the overall management of the contract, which requires the performance and integration of various activities including procurement of materials, identifying and managing subcontractors, and performing manufacturing, assembly and testing.

The entity assesses the promises in the contract and determines that each of the promised devices is capable of being distinct in accordance with paragraph 27(a) of IFRS 15 because the customer can benefit from each device on its own. This is because each unit can function independently of the other units.

The entity observes that the nature of its promise is to establish and provide a service of producing the full complement of devices for which the customer has contracted in accordance with the customer's specifications. The entity considers that it is responsible for overall management of the contract and for providing a significant service of integrating various goods and services (the inputs) into its overall service and the resulting devices (the combined output) and, therefore, the devices and the various promised goods and services inherent in producing those devices are not separately identifiable in accordance with paragraph 27(b) and paragraph 29 of IFRS 15. In this case, the manufacturing process provided by the entity is specific to its contract with the customer. In addition, the nature of the entity's performance and, in particular, the significant integration service of the various activities means that a change in one of the entity's activities to produce the devices has a significant effect on the other activities required to produce the highly complex, specialised devices such that the entity's activities are highly interdependent and highly interrelated. Because the criterion in paragraph 27(b) of IFRS 15 is not met, the goods and services that will be provided by the entity are not separately identifiable and, therefore, are not distinct. The entity accounts for all of the goods and services promised in the contract as a single performance obligation.

The determination of whether a 'significant integration service' exists within a contract, as illustrated in Case A and Case B above, will require significant judgement and will be heavily dependent on the unique facts and circumstances for each individual contract with a customer.

The following example illustrates how the significance of installation services can affect an entity's conclusion about the number of identified performance obligations for similar fact patterns. *[IFRS 15.IE49-IE58]*. In Case A, each of the promised goods and services are determined to be distinct. In Case B, two of the promised goods and services are combined into a single performance obligation because one promise (the installation) significantly customises another promise (the software).

Example 30.14: Determining whether goods or services are distinct

Case A – Distinct goods or services

An entity, a software developer, enters into a contract with a customer to transfer a software licence, perform an installation service and provide unspecified software updates and technical support (online and telephone) for a two-year period. The entity sells the licence, installation service and technical support separately. The installation service includes changing the web screen for each type of user (for example, marketing, inventory management and information technology). The installation service is routinely performed by other entities and does not significantly modify the software. The software remains functional without the updates and the technical support.

The entity assesses the goods and services promised to the customer to determine which goods and services are distinct in accordance with paragraph 27 of IFRS 15. The entity observes that the software is delivered before the other goods and services and remains functional without the updates and the technical support. The customer can benefit from the updates together with the software licence transferred at the start of the contract. Thus, the entity concludes that the customer can benefit from each of the goods and services either on their own or together with the other goods and services that are readily available and the criterion in paragraph 27(a) of IFRS 15 is met.

The entity also considers the principle and the factors in paragraph 29 of IFRS 15 and determines that the promise to transfer each good and service to the customer is separately identifiable from each of the other promises (thus the criterion in paragraph 27(b) of IFRS 15 is met). In reaching this determination, the entity considers that, although it integrates the software into the customer's system, the installation services do not significantly affect the customer's ability to use and benefit from the software licence because the installation services are routine and can be obtained from alternative providers. The software updates do not significantly affect the customer's ability to use and benefit from the software licence during the licence period. The entity further observes that none of the promised goods or services significantly modify or customise one another, nor is the entity providing a significant service of integrating the software and the services into a combined output. Lastly, the entity concludes that the software and the services do not significantly affect each other and, therefore, are not highly interdependent or highly interrelated, because the entity would be able to fulfil its promise to transfer the initial software licence independently from its promise to subsequently provide the installation service, software updates or technical support.

On the basis of this assessment, the entity identifies four performance obligations in the contract for the following goods or services:

(a) the software licence;

(b) an installation service;

(c) software updates; and

(d) technical support.

The entity applies paragraphs 31-38 of IFRS 15 to determine whether each of the performance obligations for the installation service, software updates and technical support are satisfied at a point in time or over time. The entity also assesses the nature of the entity's promise to transfer the software licence in accordance with paragraph B58 of IFRS 15 (see Example 54 in paragraphs IE276-IE277).

Case B – Significant customisation

The promised goods and services are the same as in Case A, except that the contract specifies that, as part of the installation service, the software is to be substantially customised to add significant new functionality to enable the software to interface with other customised software applications used by the customer. The customised installation service can be provided by other entities.

The entity assesses the goods and services promised to the customer to determine which goods and services are distinct in accordance with paragraph 27 of IFRS 15. The entity first assesses whether the criterion in paragraph 27(a) has been met. For the same reasons as in Case A, the entity determines that the software licence, installation, software updates and technical support each meet that criterion. The entity next assesses whether the criterion in paragraph 27(b) has been met by evaluating the principle and the factors in paragraph 29 of IFRS 15. The entity observes that the terms of the contract result in a promise to provide a significant service of integrating the licensed software into the existing software system by performing a customised installation service as specified in the contract. In other words, the entity is using the licence and the customised installation service as inputs to produce the combined output (i.e. a functional and integrated software system) specified in the contract (see paragraph 29(a) of IFRS 15).The software is significantly modified and customised by the service (see paragraph 29(b) of IFRS 15). Consequently, the entity determines that the promise to transfer the licence is not separately identifiable from the customised installation service and, therefore, the criterion in paragraph 27(b) of IFRS 15 is not met. Thus, the software licence and the customised installation service are not distinct.

On the basis of the same analysis as in Case A, the entity concludes that the software updates and technical support are distinct from the other promises in the contract.

On the basis of this assessment, the entity identifies three performance obligations in the contract for the following goods or services:

(a) software customisation (which comprises the licence for the software and the customised installation service;

(b) software updates; and

(c) technical support.

The entity applies paragraphs 31-38 of IFRS 15 to determine whether each performance obligation is satisfied at a point in time or over time.

The following examples illustrate contracts that include multiple promised goods or services, all of which are determined to be distinct. The example highlights the importance of considering both the separately identifiable principle and the underlying factors in paragraph 29 of IFRS 15. *[IFRS 15.IE58A-IE58K]*.

Case C illustrates a contract that includes the sale of equipment and installation services. The equipment can be operated without any customisation or modification. The installation is not complex and can be performed by other vendors. The entity determines that the two promises in the contract are distinct.

Case D illustrates that certain types of contractual restrictions, including those that require a customer to only use the entity's services, should not affect the evaluation of whether a promised good or service is distinct.

Case E illustrates a contract that includes the sale of equipment and specialised consumables to be used with the equipment. Even though the consumables can only be produced by the entity, they are sold separately. The entity determines that the two promises in the contract are distinct and the example walks through the analysis for determining whether the promises are capable of being distinct and distinct in the context of the contract.

Example 30.15: Determining whether goods or services are distinct

Case C – Promises are separately identifiable (installation)

An entity contracts with a customer to sell a piece of equipment and installation services. The equipment is operational without any customisation or modification. The installation required is not complex and is capable of being performed by several alternative service providers.

The entity identifies two promised goods and services in the contract: (a) equipment and (b) installation. The entity assesses the criteria in paragraph 27 of IFRS 15 to determine whether each promised good or service is distinct. The entity determines that the equipment and the installation each meet the criterion in paragraph 27(a) of IFRS 15. The customer can benefit from the equipment on its own, by using it or reselling it for an amount greater than scrap value, or together with other readily available resources (for example, installation services available from alternative providers). The customer also can benefit from the installation services together with other resources that the customer will already have obtained from the entity (i.e. the equipment).

The entity further determines that its promises to transfer the equipment and to provide the installation services are each separately identifiable (in accordance with paragraph 27(b) of IFRS 15). The entity considers the principle and the factors in paragraph 29 of IFRS 15 in determining that the equipment and the installation services are not inputs to a combined item in this contract. In this case, each of the factors in paragraph 29 of IFRS 15 contributes to, but is not individually determinative of, the conclusion that the equipment and the installation services are separately identifiable as follows:

(a) The entity is not providing a significant integration service. That is, the entity has promised to deliver the equipment and then install it; the entity would be able to fulfil its promise to transfer the equipment separately from its promise to subsequently install it. The entity has not promised to combine the equipment and the installation services in a way that would transform them into a combined output.

(b) The entity's installation services will not significantly customise or significantly modify the equipment.

(c) Although the customer can benefit from the installation services only after it has obtained control of the equipment, the installation services do not significantly affect the equipment because the entity would be able to fulfil its promise to transfer the equipment independently of its promise to provide the installation services. Because the equipment and the installation services do not each significantly affect the other, they are not highly interdependent or highly interrelated.

On the basis of this assessment, the entity identifies two performance obligations in the contract for the following goods or services:

(i) the equipment; and

(ii) installation services.

The entity applies paragraphs 31–38 of IFRS 15 to determine whether each performance obligation is satisfied at a point in time or over time.

Case D – Promises are separately identifiable (contractual restrictions)

Assume the same facts as in Case C, except that the customer is contractually required to use the entity's installation services.

The contractual requirement to use the entity's installation services does not change the evaluation of whether the promised goods and services are distinct in this case. This is because the contractual requirement to use the entity's installation services does not change the characteristics of the goods or services themselves, nor does it change the entity's promises to the customer. Although the customer is required to use the entity's installation services, the equipment and the installation services are capable of being distinct (i.e. they each meet the criterion in paragraph 27(a) of IFRS 15) and the entity's promises to provide the equipment and to provide the installation services are each separately identifiable, i.e. they each meet the criterion in paragraph 27(b) of IFRS 15. The entity's analysis in this regard is consistent with that in Case C.

Case E – Promises are separately identifiable (consumables)

An entity enters into a contract with a customer to provide a piece of off-the-shelf equipment (i.e. the equipment is operational without any significant customisation or modification) and to provide specialised consumables for use in the equipment at predetermined intervals over the next three years. The consumables are produced only by the entity, but are sold separately by the entity.

The entity determines that the customer can benefit from the equipment together with the readily available consumables. The consumables are readily available in accordance with paragraph 28 of IFRS 15, because they are regularly sold separately by the entity (i.e. through refill orders to customers that previously purchased the equipment). The customer can benefit from the consumables that will be delivered under the contract together with the delivered equipment that is transferred to the customer initially under the contract. Therefore, the equipment and the consumables are each capable of being distinct in accordance with paragraph 27(a) of IFRS 15.

The entity determines that its promises to transfer the equipment and to provide consumables over a three-year period are each separately identifiable in accordance with paragraph 27(b) of IFRS 15. In determining that the equipment and the consumables are not inputs to a combined item in this contract, the entity considers that it is not providing a significant integration service that transforms the equipment and consumables into a combined output. In addition, neither the equipment nor the consumables are significantly customised or modified by the other. Lastly, the entity concludes that the equipment and the consumables are not highly interdependent or highly interrelated because they do not significantly affect each other. Although the customer can benefit from the consumables in this contract only after it has obtained control of the equipment (i.e. the consumables would have no use without the equipment) and the consumables are required for the equipment to function, the equipment and the consumables do not each significantly affect the other. This is because the entity would be able to fulfil each of its promises in the contract independently of the other. That is, the entity would be able to fulfil its promise to transfer the equipment even if the customer did not purchase any consumables and would be able to fulfil its promise to provide the consumables, even if the customer acquired the equipment separately.

On the basis of this assessment, the entity identifies two performance obligations in the contract for the following goods or services:

(a) the equipment; and

(b) the consumables.

The entity applies paragraphs 31–38 of IFRS 15 to determine whether each performance obligation is satisfied at a point in time or over time.

4.3 Promised goods and services that are not distinct

If a promised good or service does not meet the criteria to be considered distinct, an entity is required to combine that good or service with other promised goods or services until the entity identifies a bundle of goods or services that, together, is distinct. This could result in an entity combining a good or service that is not considered distinct with another good or service that, on its own, would have met the criteria to be considered distinct (see 4.2.1 above). *[IFRS 15.30]*.

The standard provides two examples of contracts with promised goods and services that, while capable of being distinct, are not distinct in the context of the contract because of a significant integration service that combines the inputs (the underlying goods and services) into a combined output – see Example 30.13 at 4.2.3 above.

4.4 Principal versus agent considerations

When more than one party is involved in providing goods or services to a customer, the standard requires an entity to determine whether it is a principal or an agent in these transactions by evaluating the nature of its promise to the customer. An entity is a principal (and, therefore, records revenue on a gross basis) if it controls a promised good or service before transferring that good or service to the customer. *[IFRS 15.B35]*. An entity is an agent (and, therefore, records as revenue the net amount that it retains for its agency services) if its role is to arrange for another entity to provide the goods or services. *[IFRS 15.B36]*.

In April 2016, the IASB issued amendments that clarified how an entity identifies the unit of account (i.e. the specified good or service) for the principal versus agent evaluation and how the control principle applies to certain types of arrangements, such as service transactions. The amendments also reframed the indicators to focus on evidence that an entity is acting as a principal rather than as an agent, revised existing examples and added new ones.

In the Basis for Conclusions, the Board explained that in order for an entity to conclude that it is providing the good or service to the customer, it must first control that good or service. That is, the entity cannot provide the good or service to a customer if the entity does not first control it. If an entity controls the good or service, the entity is a principal in the transaction. If an entity does not control the good or service before it is transferred to the customer, the entity is an agent in the transaction. *[IFRS 15.B36, BC385D]*.

In the Basis for Conclusions, the Board noted that an entity that itself manufactures a good or performs a service is always a principal if it transfers control of that good or service to another party. There is no need for such an entity to evaluate the principal versus agent application guidance because it transfers control of or provides its own good or service directly to its customer without the involvement of another party. For example, if an entity transfers control of a good to an intermediary that is a principal in providing that good to an end-customer, the entity records revenue as a principal in the sale of the good to its customer (the intermediary). *[IFRS 15.BC385E]*.

Consistent with current practice, entities will need to carefully evaluate whether a gross or net presentation is appropriate. IFRS 15 includes application guidance on determining whether an entity is a principal or agent in an arrangement that is similar to current IFRS. However, the standard includes the notion of considering whether an entity has control of the goods or services as part of the evaluation, which adds an overarching principle for entities to evaluate in addition to the indicators. This may affect the assessment of whether an entity is a principal or agent in an arrangement.

The standard states that when other parties are involved in providing the specified goods or services to an entity's customer, the entity must determine whether its performance obligation is to provide the specified good or service itself (i.e. the entity is a principal) or to arrange for another party to provide the specified good or service (i.e. the entity is an agent). An entity makes this determination for each specified good or service promised to the customer. The standard also notes that, if a contract includes more than one specified good or service, an entity could be a principal for some and an agent for others. *[IFRS 15.B34]*.

In order to determine the nature of its promise (as a principal or an agent), the entity must (a) identify the specified goods or services to be provided to the customer; and (b) assess whether it controls each specified good or service before that good or service is transferred to the customer. *[IFRS 15.B34A]*. As noted above, an entity is a principal if it controls a promised good or service before transferring that good or service to the customer. However, an entity may not necessarily control a specified good if it only momentarily obtains legal title to that good before legal title is transferred to a customer. Furthermore, the standard notes that a principal may satisfy its performance obligation to provide the specified good or service itself or it may engage another party to satisfy some, or all, of the performance obligation on its behalf. *[IFRS 15.B35]*.

4.4.1 *Identifying the specified good or service*

In accordance with paragraph B34A of IFRS 15, an entity must first identify the specified good or service (or unit of account for the principal versus agent evaluation) to be provided to the customer in the contract in order to determine the nature of its promise (i.e. whether it is to provide the specified goods or services or to arrange for those goods or services to be provided by another party). A specified good or service is defined as 'a distinct good or service (or a distinct bundle of goods or services) to be provided to the customer'. *[IFRS 15.B34]*. While this definition is similar to that of a performance obligation (see 4.2 above), the IASB noted in the Basis for Conclusions that it created this new term because using 'performance obligation' would have been confusing in agency relationships. *[IFRS 15.BC385B]*. That is, because an agent's performance obligation is to arrange for goods or services to be provided by another party, providing the specified goods or services to the end-customer is not the agent's performance obligation.

A specified good or service may be a distinct good or service or a distinct bundle of goods and services. In the Basis for Conclusions, the Board noted that if individual goods or services are not distinct from one another, they may be inputs to a combined item and each good or service may represent only a part of a single promise to the customer. For example, in a contract in which goods or services provided by another party are inputs to a combined item (or items), the entity would assess whether it controls the combined item (or items) before that item (or items) is transferred to the customer. *[IFRS 15.BC385Q]*. That is, in determining whether it is a principal or an agent, an entity should evaluate that single promise to the customer, rather than the individual inputs that make up that promise.

Appropriately identifying the good or service to be provided is a critical step in determining whether an entity is a principal or an agent in a transaction. In many situations, especially those involving tangible goods, identifying the specified good or service will be relatively straightforward. For example, if an entity is reselling laptop computers, the specified good that will be transferred to the customer is a laptop computer.

However, the assessment may require significant judgement in other situations, such as those involving intangible goods or services. In accordance with paragraph B34A(a) of IFRS 15, the specified good or service may be the underlying good or service a customer ultimately wants to obtain (e.g. a flight, a meal) or a right to obtain that good or service (e.g. in the form of a ticket or voucher). *[IFRS 15.B34A(a)]*. In the Basis for Conclusions, the Board noted that when the specified good or service is a right to a good or service that will be provided by another party, the entity would determine whether its performance obligation is a promise to provide that right (and it is, therefore, a principal) or whether it is arranging for the other party to provide that right (and it is, therefore, an agent). The fact that the entity will not provide the underlying goods or services itself is not determinative. *[IFRS 15.BC385O]*.

The Board acknowledged that it may be difficult in some cases to determine whether the specified good or service is the underlying good or service, or a right to obtain that good or service. Therefore, it provided examples in the standard. Example 30.17 at 4.4.4 below involves an airline ticket reseller. In this example, the entity pre-purchases airline tickets that it will later sell to customers. While the customer ultimately wants airline travel, the conclusion in Example 30.17 is that the specified good or service is the right to fly on a specified flight (in the form of a ticket) and not the underlying flight itself. The entity itself does not fly the plane and it cannot change the service (e.g. change the flight time or destination). However, the entity obtained the ticket prior to identifying a specific customer to purchase the ticket. As a result, the entity holds an asset (in the form of a ticket) that represents a right to fly. The entity could, therefore, transfer that right to a customer (as depicted in the example) or decide to use the right itself.

Example 30.16 at 4.4.4 below involves an office maintenance service provider. In this example, the entity concludes that the specified good or service is the underlying office maintenance service (rather than a right to that service). While the entity obtained the contract with the customer prior to engaging a third party to perform the requested services, the right to the subcontractor's services never transfers to the customer. Instead, the entity retains the right to direct the service provider. That is, the entity can direct the right to use the subcontractor's services as it chooses (e.g. to fulfil the customer contract, to fulfil another customer contract, to service its own facilities). Furthermore, the customer in Example 30.16 is indifferent as to who carries out the office maintenance services. This is not the case in Example 30.17, in which the customer wants the ticket reseller to sell one of its tickets on a specific flight.

If a contract with a customer includes more than one specified good or service, IFRS 15 clarifies that an entity may be a principal for some specified goods or services and an agent for others. *[IFRS 15.B34]*. Example 30.19 at 4.4.4 below provides an illustration of this.

As discussed above, appropriately identifying the specified good or service to be provided to the customer is a critical step in identifying whether the nature of an entity's promise is to act as a principal or an agent. Entities may need to apply significant judgement to determine whether the specified good or service is the underlying good or service or a right to obtain that good or service.

4.4.2 Control of the specified good or service

In accordance with paragraph B34A of IFRS 15, the second step in determining the nature of the entity's promise (i.e. whether it is to provide the specified goods or services or to arrange for those goods or services to be provided by another party) is for the entity to determine whether the entity controls the specified good or service before it is transferred to the customer. An entity cannot provide the specified good or service to a customer (and, therefore, be a principal) unless it controls that good or service prior to its transfer. That is, as the Board noted in the Basis for Conclusions, control is the determining factor when assessing whether an entity is a principal or an agent. *[IFRS 15.BC385S]*.

In assessing whether an entity controls the specified good or service prior to transfer to the customer, paragraph B34A(b) of IFRS 15 requires the entity to consider the definition of control that is included in Step 5 of the model, in accordance with paragraph 33 of IFRS 15 (discussed further at 7 below). *[IFRS 15.B34A(b)]*.

If, after evaluating the requirement in paragraph 33 of IFRS 15, an entity concludes that it controls the specified good or service before it is transferred to the customer, the entity is a principal in the transaction. If the entity does not control that good or service before transfer to the customer, it is an agent.

Stakeholder feedback indicated that the control principle was easier to apply to tangible goods than to intangible goods and services because intangible goods and services generally exist only at the moment they are delivered. To address this concern, the standard includes application guidance on how the control principle applies to certain types of arrangements (including service transactions) by explaining what a principal controls before the specified good or service is transferred to the customer. Specifically, the standard states that '[w]hen another party is involved in providing goods or services to a customer, an entity that is a principal obtains control of any one of the following:

(a) a good or another asset from the other party that it then transfers to the customer.

(b) a right to a service to be performed by the other party, which gives the entity the ability to direct that party to provide the service to the customer on the entity's behalf.

(c) a good or service from the other party that it then combines with other goods or services in providing the specified good or service to the customer. For example, if an entity provides a significant service of integrating goods or services (see paragraph 29(a)) provided by another party into the specified good or service for which the customer has contracted, the entity controls the specified good or service before that good or service is transferred to the customer. This is because the entity first obtains control of the inputs to the specified good or service (which includes goods or services from other parties) and directs their use to create the combined output that is the specified good or service.' *[IFRS 15.B35A]*.

In the Basis for Conclusions, the Board observed that an entity can control a service to be provided by another party when it controls the right to the specified service that will be provided to the customer. *[IFRS 15.BC385U]*. Generally, the entity will then either transfer the right (in the form of an asset, such as a ticket) to its customer, in accordance with paragraph B35A(a) of IFRS 15 (as in Example 30.17 at 4.4.4 below involving the airline ticket reseller that is discussed at 4.4.1 above), or use its right to direct the other party to provide the specified service to the customer on the entity's behalf, in accordance with paragraph B35A(b) of IFRS 15 (as in Example 30.16 at 4.4.4 below involving the office maintenance services that is discussed at 4.4.1 above).

The condition described in paragraph B35A(a) of IFRS 15 would include contracts in which an entity transfers to the customer a right to a future service to be provided by another party. If the specified good or service is a right to a good or service to be provided by another party, the entity evaluates whether it controls the right to the good or service before that right is transferred to the customer (rather than whether it controls the underlying goods or services). In the Basis for Conclusions, the Board noted that, in assessing such rights, it is often relevant to assess whether the right is created only when it is obtained by the customer or whether the right exists before the customer obtains it. If the right does not exist before the customer obtains it, an entity would not be able to control right before it is transferred to the customer. *[IFRS 15.BC385O]*.

The standard includes two examples to illustrate this point. In Example 30.17 (discussed at 4.4.1 above and included at 4.4.4 below) involving an airline ticket reseller, the specified good or service is determined to be the right to fly on a specified flight (in the form of a ticket). One of the determining factors for the principal-agent evaluation in this example is that the entity pre-purchases the airline tickets before a specific customer is identified. Accordingly, the right existed prior to a customer obtaining it. The example concludes that the entity controls the right before it is transferred to the customer (and is, therefore, a principal).

In Example 30.18 (included at 4.4.4 below), an entity sells vouchers that entitle customers to future meals at specified restaurants selected by the customer. The specified good or service is determined to be the right to a meal (in the form of a voucher). One of the determining factors for the principal-agent evaluation is that the entity does not control the voucher (the right to a meal) at any time. It does not pre-purchase or commit itself to purchase the vouchers from the restaurants before they are sold to a customer. Instead, the entity waits to purchase the voucher until a customer requests a voucher for a particular restaurant. In addition, vouchers are created only at the time that they are transferred to a customer and do not exist before that transfer. Accordingly, the right does not exist before the customer obtains it. Therefore, the entity does not at any time have the ability to direct the use of the vouchers or obtain substantially all of the remaining benefits from the vouchers before they are transferred to customers. The example concludes that the entity does not control the right before it is transferred to the customer (and is, therefore, an agent).

In the Basis for Conclusions, the IASB acknowledged that determining whether an entity is a principal or an agent may be more difficult when evaluating whether a contract falls under paragraph B35A(b) of IFRS 15. That is, it may be difficult to determine whether an entity has the ability to direct another party to provide the service on its behalf (and is, therefore, a principal) or is only arranging for the other party to provide the service (and is, therefore, an agent). As depicted in Example 30.16 (as discussed at 4.4.1 above and included at 4.4.4 below), an entity could control the right to the specified service and be a principal by entering into a contract with the subcontractor in which the entity defines the scope of service to be performed by the subcontractor on its behalf. This situation is equivalent to the entity fulfilling the contract using its own resources. Furthermore, the entity would remain responsible for the satisfactory provision of the specified service in accordance with the contract with the customer. In contrast, when the specified service is provided by another party and the entity does not have the ability to direct those services, the entity would typically be an agent because the entity would be facilitating, rather than controlling the rights to, the service. *[IFRS 15.BC385V]*.

In accordance with paragraph B35A(c) of IFRS 15, if an entity provides a significant service of integrating two or more goods or services into a combined item that is the specified good or service the customer contracted to receive, the entity controls that specified good or service before it is transferred to the customer. This is because the entity first obtains control of the inputs to the specified good or service (which can include goods or services from other parties) and directs their use to create the combined item that is the specified good or service. The inputs would be a fulfilment cost to the entity. However, as noted by the Board in the Basis for Conclusions, if a third party provides the significant integration service, the entity's customer for its good or services (which would be inputs to the specified good or service) is likely to be the third party. *[IFRS 15.BC385R]*.

4.4.2.A Principal indicators

After considering the application guidance discussed above, it still may not be clear whether an entity controls the specified good or service. Therefore, the standard provides three indicators of when an entity controls the specified good or service (and is, therefore, a principal):

'Indicators that an entity controls the specified good or service before it is transferred to the customer (and is therefore a principal (see paragraph B35)) include, but are not limited to, the following:

(a) the entity is primarily responsible for fulfilling the promise to provide the specified good or service. This typically includes responsibility for the acceptability of the specified good or service (for example, primary responsibility for the good or service meeting customer specifications). If the entity is primarily responsible for fulfilling the promise to provide the specified good or service, this may indicate that the other party involved in providing the specified good or service is acting on the entity's behalf.

(b) the entity has inventory risk before the specified good or service has been transferred to a customer or after transfer of control to the customer (for example, if the customer has a right of return). For example, if the entity obtains, or commits itself to obtain, the specified good or service before obtaining a contract with a customer, that may indicate that the entity has the ability to direct the use of, and obtain substantially all of the remaining benefits from, the good or service before it is transferred to the customer.

(c) the entity has discretion in establishing the price for the specified good or service. Establishing the price that the customer pays for the specified good or service may indicate that the entity has the ability to direct the use of that good or service and obtain substantially all of the remaining benefits. However, an agent can have discretion in establishing prices in some cases. For example, an agent may have some flexibility in setting prices in order to generate additional revenue from its service of arranging for goods or services to be provided by other parties to customers.' *[IFRS 15.B37]*.

The above indicators are meant to support an entity's assessment of control, not to replace it. Each indicator explains how it supports the assessment of control. As emphasised in the Basis for Conclusions, the indicators do not override the assessment of control, should not be viewed in isolation and do not constitute a separate or additional evaluation. Furthermore, they should not be considered a checklist of criteria to be met or factors to be considered in all scenarios. Considering one or more of the indicators will often be helpful and, depending on the facts and circumstances, individual indicators will be more or less relevant or persuasive to the assessment of control. *[IFRS 15.B37A, BC385H]*.

The first indicator that an entity is a principal, in paragraph B37(a) of IFRS 15, is that the entity is primarily responsible for both fulfilling the promise to provide the specified good or service to the customer and for the acceptability of the specified good or service. We believe that one of the reasons that this indicator supports the assessment of control of the specified good or service is because an entity will generally control a specified good or service that it is responsible for transferring control to a customer.

The terms of the contract and representations (written or otherwise) made by an entity during marketing will generally provide evidence of which party is responsible for fulfilling the promise to provide the specified good or service and for the acceptability of that good or service.

It is possible that one entity may not be solely responsible for both providing the specified good or service and for the acceptability of that same good or service. For example, a reseller may sell goods or services that are provided to the customer by a supplier. However, if the customer is dissatisfied with the goods or services it receives, the reseller may be solely responsible for providing a remedy to the customer. The reseller may promote such a role during the marketing process or may agree to such a role as claims arise in order to maintain its relationship with its customer. In this situation, both the reseller and the supplier possess characteristics of this indicator. Therefore, other indicators will likely need to be considered to determine which entity is the principal. However, if the reseller is responsible for providing a remedy to a dissatisfied customer, but can then pursue a claim against the supplier to recoup any remedies it provides, that may indicate that the reseller is not ultimately responsible for the acceptability of the specified good or service.

The second indicator that an entity is a principal, in paragraph B37(b) of IFRS 15, is that the entity has inventory risk (before the specified good or service is transferred to the customer or upon customer return). Inventory risk is the risk normally taken by an entity that acquires inventory in the hope of reselling it at a profit. Inventory risk exists if a reseller obtains (or commits to obtain) the specified good or service before it is ordered by a customer. Inventory risk also exists if a customer has a right of return and the reseller will take back the specified good service if the customer exercises that right.

This indicator supports the assessment of control of the specified good or service because when an entity obtains (or commits to obtain) the specified good or service before it has contracted with a customer, it likely has the ability to direct the use of and obtain substantially all of the remaining benefits from the good or service. For example, inventory risk can exist in a customer arrangement involving the provision of services if an entity is obligated to compensate the individual service provider(s) for work performed, regardless of whether the customer accepts that work. However, this indicator will often not apply to intangible goods and services.

Factors may exist that mitigate a reseller's inventory risk. For example, a reseller's inventory risk may be significantly reduced or eliminated if it has the right to return to the supplier goods it cannot sell or goods that are returned by customers. Another example is if a reseller receives inventory price protection from the supplier. In these cases, the inventory risk indicator may be less relevant or persuasive to the assessment of control.

The third principal indicator, in paragraph B37(c) of IFRS 15, is that the entity has discretion in establishing the price of the specified good or service. Reasonable latitude, within economic constraints, to establish the price with a customer for the product or service may indicate that the entity has the ability to direct the use of that good or service and obtain substantially all of the remaining benefits (i.e. the entity controls the specified good or service). However, because an agent may also have discretion in establishing the price of the specified good or service, the facts and circumstances of the transaction will need to be carefully evaluated.

The three indicators in paragraph B37 of IFRS 15 are similar to some of those included in current IFRS. However, the indicators in IFRS 15 are based on the concepts of identifying performance obligations and the transfer of control of goods and services. In addition, the new standard does not carry forward some other indicators from IAS 18 (e.g. those relating to exposure to credit risk and the form of the consideration as a commission).

Accordingly, in the Basis for Conclusions, the IASB acknowledged that entities could reach different conclusions under the new standard than they did under IAS 18. *[IFRS 15.BC385I]*. Entities will likely need to reconsider their principal versus agent conclusions under the new standard.

4.4.3 Recognising revenue as principal or agent

The determination of whether the entity is acting as a principal or an agent affects the amount of revenue the entity recognises. When the entity is the principal in the arrangement, the revenue recognised is the gross amount to which the entity expects to be entitled. *[IFRS 15.B35B]*. When the entity is the agent, the revenue recognised is the net amount that the entity is entitled to retain in return for its services as the agent. The entity's fee or commission may be the net amount of consideration that the entity retains after paying the other party the consideration received in exchange for the goods or services to be provided by that party. *[IFRS 15.B36]*.

After an entity determines whether it is the principal or the agent and the amount of gross or net revenue that would be recognised, the entity recognises revenue when or as it satisfies its performance obligation. An entity satisfies its performance obligation by transferring control of the specified good or service underlying the performance obligation, either at a point in time or over time (as discussed at 7 below). That is, a principal would recognise revenue when (or as) it transfers the specified good or service to the customer. An agent would recognise revenue when its performance obligation to arrange for the specified good or service is complete.

In the Basis for Conclusions, the Board noted that, in some contracts in which the entity is the agent, control of specified goods or services promised by the agent may transfer before the customer receives related goods or services from the principal. For example, an entity might satisfy its promise to provide customers with loyalty points when those points are transferred to the customer if:

- the entity's promise is to provide loyalty points to customers when the customer purchases goods or services from the entity;
- the points entitle the customers to future discounted purchases with another party (i.e. the points represent a material right to a future discount); or
- the entity determines that it is an agent (i.e. its promise is to arrange for the customers to be provided with points) and the entity does not control those points (i.e. the specified good or service) before they are transferred to the customer.

In contrast, if the points entitle the customers to future goods or services to be provided by the entity, the entity may conclude it is not an agent. This is because the entity's promise is to provide those future goods or services and, therefore, the entity controls both the points and the future goods or services before they are transferred to the customer. In these cases, the entity's performance obligation may only be satisfied when the future goods or services are provided.

In other cases, the points may entitle customers to choose between future goods or services provided by either the entity or another party. In this situation, the nature of the entity's performance obligation may not be known until the customer makes its choice. That is, until the customer has chosen the goods or services to be provided (and, therefore, whether the entity or the third party will provide those goods or services), the entity is obliged to stand ready to deliver goods or services. Therefore, the entity may not satisfy its performance obligation until it either delivers the goods or services or is no longer obliged to stand ready. If the customer subsequently chooses to receive the goods or services from another party, the entity would need to consider whether it was acting as an agent and would, therefore, only recognise revenue for a fee or commission that it received for arranging the ultimate transaction between the customer and the third party. *[IFRS 15.BC383-BC385]*.

The above discussion illustrates that control of specified goods or services promised by an agent may transfer before the customer receives related goods or services from the principal. An entity will need to assess each loyalty programme in accordance with the principles of the principal versus agent application guidance to determine if revenue would be reported on a gross or net basis.

Although an entity may be able to transfer its obligation to provide its customer specified goods or services, the standard says that such a transfer may not always satisfy the performance obligation. Specifically, it states that '[i]f another entity assumes the entity's performance obligations and contractual rights in the contract so that the entity is no longer obliged to satisfy the performance obligation to transfer the specified good or service to the customer (i.e. the entity is no longer acting as the principal), the entity shall not recognise revenue for that performance obligation. Instead, the entity shall evaluate whether to recognise revenue for satisfying a performance obligation to obtain a contract for the other party (i.e. whether the entity is acting as an agent).' *[IFRS 15.B38]*.

4.4.4 Examples of principal verses agent assessments

The standard includes six examples to illustrate the principal versus agent application guidance discussed above. We have extracted four of them below.

The standard includes the following example of when the specified good or service (see 4.4.1 above) is the underlying service, rather than the right to obtain that service. The entity in this example is determined to be a principal. *[IFRS 15.IE238A-IE238C]*.

Example 30.16: Promise to provide goods or services (entity is a principal)

An entity enters into a contract with a customer to provide office maintenance services. The entity and the customer define and agree on the scope of the services and negotiate the price. The entity is responsible for ensuring that the services are performed in accordance with the terms and conditions in the contract. The entity invoices the customer for the agreed-upon price on a monthly basis with 10-day payment terms.

The entity regularly engages third-party service providers to provide office maintenance services to its customers. When the entity obtains a contract from a customer, the entity enters into a contract with one of those service providers, directing the service provider to perform office maintenance services for the customer. The payment terms in the contracts with the service providers are generally aligned with the payment terms in the entity's contracts with customers. However, the entity is obliged to pay the service provider even if the customer fails to pay.

To determine whether the entity is a principal or an agent, the entity identifies the specified good or service to be provided to the customer and assesses whether it controls that good or service before the good or service is transferred to the customer.

The entity observes that the specified services to be provided to the customer are the office maintenance services for which the customer contracted, and that no other goods or services are promised to the customer. While the entity obtains a right to office maintenance services from the service provider after entering into the contract with the customer, that right is not transferred to the customer. That is, the entity retains the ability to direct the use of, and obtain substantially all the remaining benefits from, that right. For example, the entity can decide whether to direct the service provider to provide the office maintenance services for that customer, or for another customer, or at its own facilities. The customer does not have a right to direct the service provider to perform services that the entity has not agreed to provide. Therefore, the right to office maintenance services obtained by the entity from the service provider is not the specified good or service in its contract with the customer.

The entity concludes that it controls the specified services before they are provided to the customer. The entity obtains control of a right to office maintenance services after entering into the contract with the customer but before those services are provided to the customer. The terms of the entity's contract with the service provider give the entity the ability to direct the service provider to provide the specified services on the entity's behalf (see paragraph B35A(b)). In addition, the entity concludes that the following indicators in paragraph B37 of IFRS 15 provide further evidence that the entity controls the office maintenance services before they are provided to the customer:

(a) the entity is primarily responsible for fulfilling the promise to provide office maintenance services. Although the entity has hired a service provider to perform the services promised to the customer, it is the entity itself that is responsible for ensuring that the services are performed and are acceptable to the customer (i.e. the entity is responsible for fulfilment of the promise in the contract, regardless of whether the entity performs the services itself or engages a third-party service provider to perform the services).

(b) the entity has discretion in setting the price for the services to the customer.

The entity observes that it does not commit itself to obtain the services from the service provider before obtaining the contract with the customer. Thus, the entity has mitigated inventory risk with respect to the office maintenance services. Nonetheless, the entity concludes that it controls the office maintenance services before they are provided to the customer on the basis of the evidence in paragraph IE238E.

Thus, the entity is a principal in the transaction and recognises revenue in the amount of consideration to which it is entitled from the customer in exchange for the office maintenance services.

The standard also includes the following example of when the specified good or service is the right to obtain a service and not the underlying service itself. The entity in this example is determined to be a principal. *[IFRS 15.IE239-IE243].*

Example 30.17: Promise to provide goods or services (entity is a principal)

An entity negotiates with major airlines to purchase tickets at reduced rates compared with the price of tickets sold directly by the airlines to the public. The entity agrees to buy a specific number of tickets and must pay for those tickets regardless of whether it is able to resell them. The reduced rate paid by the entity for each ticket purchased is negotiated and agreed in advance.

The entity determines the prices at which the airline tickets will be sold to its customers. The entity sells the tickets and collects the consideration from customers when the tickets are purchased.

The entity also assists the customers in resolving complaints with the service provided by the airlines. However, each airline is responsible for fulfilling obligations associated with the ticket, including remedies to a customer for dissatisfaction with the service.

To determine whether the entity's performance obligation is to provide the specified goods or services itself (i.e. the entity is a principal) or to arrange for those goods or services to be provided by another party (i.e. the entity is an agent), the entity identifies the specified good or service to be provided to the customer and assesses whether it controls that good or service before the good or service is transferred to the customer.

The entity concludes that, with each ticket that it commits itself to purchase from the airline, it obtains control of a right to fly on a specified flight (in the form of a ticket) that the entity then transfers to one of its customers (see paragraph B35A(a)). Consequently, the entity determines that the specified good or service to be provided to its customer is that right (to a seat on a specific flight) that the entity controls. The entity observes that no other goods or services are promised to the customer.

The entity controls the right to each flight before it transfers that specified right to one of its customers because the entity has the ability to direct the use of that right by deciding whether to use the ticket to fulfil a contract with a customer and, if so, which contract it will fulfil. The entity also has the ability to obtain the remaining benefits from that right by either reselling the ticket and obtaining all of the proceeds from the sale or, alternatively, using the ticket itself.

The indicators in paragraphs B37(b)–(c) of IFRS 15 also provide relevant evidence that the entity controls each specified right (ticket) before it is transferred to the customer. The entity has inventory risk with respect to the ticket because the entity committed itself to obtain the ticket from the airline before obtaining a contract with a customer to purchase the ticket. This is because the entity is obliged to pay the airline for that right regardless of whether it is able to obtain a customer to resell the ticket to or whether it can obtain a favourable price for the ticket. The entity also establishes the price that the customer will pay for the specified ticket.

Thus, the entity concludes that it is a principal in the transactions with customers. The entity recognises revenue in the gross amount of consideration to which it is entitled in exchange for the tickets transferred to the customers.

In the following example, the entity also determines that the specified good or service is the right to obtain a service and not the underlying service itself. However, the entity in this example is determined to be an agent. *[IFRS 15.IE244-IE248]*.

Example 30.18: Arranging for the provision of goods or services (entity is an agent)

An entity sells vouchers that entitle customers to future meals at specified restaurants. The sales price of the voucher provides the customer with a significant discount when compared with the normal selling prices of the meals (for example, a customer pays CU100 for a voucher that entitles the customer to a meal at a restaurant that would otherwise cost CU200). The entity does not purchase or commit itself to purchase vouchers in advance of the sale of a voucher to a customer; instead, it purchases vouchers only as they are requested by the customers. The entity sells the vouchers through its website and the vouchers are non-refundable.

The entity and the restaurants jointly determine the prices at which the vouchers will be sold to customers. Under the terms of its contracts with the restaurants, the entity is entitled to 30 per cent of the voucher price when it sells the voucher.

The entity also assists the customers in resolving complaints about the meals and has a buyer satisfaction programme. However, the restaurant is responsible for fulfilling obligations associated with the voucher, including remedies to a customer for dissatisfaction with the service.

To determine whether the entity is a principal or an agent, the entity identifies the specified good or service to be provided to the customer and assess whether it controls the specified good or service before that good or service is transferred to the customer.

A customer obtains a voucher for the restaurant that it selects. The entity does not engage the restaurants to provide meals to customers on the entity's behalf as described in the indicator in paragraph B37(a) of IFRS 15. Therefore, the entity observes that the specified good or service to be provided to the customer is the right to a meal (in the form of a voucher) at a specified restaurant or restaurants, which the customer purchases and then can use itself or transfer to another person. The entity also observes that no other goods or services (other than the vouchers) are promised to the customers.

The entity concludes that it does not control the voucher (right to a meal) at any time. In reaching this conclusion, the entity principally considers the following:

(a) the vouchers are created only at the time that they are transferred to the customers and, thus, do not exist before that transfer. Therefore, the entity does not at any time have the ability to direct the use of the vouchers, or obtain substantially all of the remaining benefits from the vouchers, before they are transferred to customers.

(b) the entity neither purchases, nor commits itself to purchase, vouchers before they are sold to customers. The entity also has no responsibility to accept any returned vouchers. Therefore, the entity does not have inventory risk with respect to the vouchers as described in the indicator in paragraph B37(b) of IFRS 15.

Thus, the entity concludes that it is an agent with respect to the vouchers. The entity recognises revenue in the net amount of consideration to which the entity will be entitled in exchange for arranging for the restaurants to provide vouchers to customers for the restaurants' meals, which is the 30 per cent commission it is entitled to upon the sale of each voucher.

Paragraph B34 of IFRS 15 clarifies that an entity may be a principal for some specified goods or services in a contract and an agent for others. The standard includes the following example of a contract in which an entity is both a principal and an agent. *[IFRS 15.IE248A-IE248F]*.

Example 30.19: Entity is a principal and an agent in the same contract

An entity sells services to assist its customers in more effectively targeting potential recruits for open job positions. The entity performs several services itself, such as interviewing candidates and performing background checks. As part of the contract with a customer, the customer agrees to obtain a licence to access a third party's database of information on potential recruits. The entity arranges for this licence with the third party, but the customer contracts directly with the database provider for the licence. The entity collects payment on behalf of the third-party database provider as part of the entity's overall invoicing to the customer. The database provider sets the price charged to the customer for the licence, and is responsible for providing technical support and credits to which the customer may be entitled for service down time or other technical issues.

To determine whether the entity is a principal or an agent, the entity identifies the specified goods or services to be provided to the customer, and assesses whether it controls those goods or services before they are transferred to the customer.

For the purpose of this example, it is assumed that the entity concludes that its recruitment services and the database access licence are each distinct on the basis of its assessment of the requirements in paragraphs 27-30 of IFRS 15. Accordingly, there are two specified goods or services to be provided to the customer – access to the third party's database and recruitment services.

The entity concludes that it does not control the access to the database before it is provided to the customer. The entity does not at any time have the ability to direct the use of the licence because the customer contracts for the licence directly with the database provider. The entity does not control access to the provider's database – it cannot, for example, grant access to the database to a party other than the customer, or prevent the database provider from providing access to the customer.

As part of reaching that conclusion, the entity also considers the indicators in paragraph B37 of IFRS 15. The entity concludes that these indicators provide further evidence that it does not control access to the database before that access is provided to the customer:

(a) the entity is not responsible for fulfilling the promise to provide the database access service. The customer contracts for the licence directly with the third-party database provider and the database provider is responsible for the acceptability of the database access (for example, by providing technical support or service credits).

(b) the entity does not have inventory risk because it does not purchase, or commit itself to purchase, the database access before the customer contracts for database access directly with the database provider.

(c) the entity does not have discretion in setting the price for the database access with the customer because the database provider sets that price.

Thus, the entity concludes that it is an agent in relation to the third party's database service. In contrast, the entity concludes that it is the principal in relation to the recruitment services because the entity performs those services itself and no other party is involved in providing those services to the customer.

4.4.5 *Implementation questions on principal versus agent considerations*

4.4.5.A Presentation of amounts billed to customers (e.g. shipping and handling, reimbursement of out-of-pocket expenses and taxes)

In July 2014, the TRG members were asked to consider how an entity would determine the presentation of amounts billed to customers (e.g. shipping and handling, reimbursement of out-of-pocket expenses and taxes) under the standard (i.e. as revenue or as a reduction of costs).[44]

The TRG members generally agreed that the standard is clear that any amounts not collected on behalf of third parties would be included in the transaction price (i.e. revenue). As discussed at 5 below, paragraph 47 of IFRS 15 says that 'the transaction price is the amount of consideration to which an entity expects to be entitled in exchange for transferring promised goods or services to a customer, excluding amounts collected on behalf of third parties (for example, some sales taxes)'. Therefore, if the amounts were incurred by the entity in fulfilling its performance obligations, the amounts will be included in the transaction price and recorded as revenue.

Several TRG members noted that this would require entities to evaluate taxes collected in all jurisdictions in which they operate to determine whether a tax is levied on the entity or the customer. TRG members generally agreed that an entity would apply the principal versus agent application guidance when it is not clear whether the amounts are collected on behalf of third parties. This could result in amounts billed to a customer being recorded as an offset to costs incurred (i.e. on a net basis), even when the amounts are not collected on behalf of third parties.

The FASB's standard allows an entity to make an accounting policy choice to present revenue net of certain types of taxes collected from a customer (including sales, use, value-added and some excise taxes). The FASB included this policy choice to address a concern expressed by stakeholders in the US as to the operability of the requirements under US GAAP. IFRS 15 does not provide a similar accounting policy choice in IFRS 15 for the following reasons: it would reduce comparability; the requirements in IFRS 15 are consistent with those in current IFRS; *[IAS 18.8]*; and it would create an exception to the five-step model. *[IFRS 15.BC188D]*. Since entities do not have a similar accounting policy choice under IFRS, differences could arise between IFRS and US GAAP.

Another difference relates to determining the transaction price when an entity is the principal, but is unable to determine the ultimate price charged to the customer. In the Basis for Conclusions to its May 2016 amendments, the FASB stated that, if uncertainty related to the transaction price is not ultimately expected to be resolved, it would not meet the definition of variable consideration and, therefore, should not be included in the transaction price.[45] Stakeholders had raised a question about how an entity that is a principal would estimate the amount of revenue to recognise if it were not aware of the amounts being charged to end-customers by an intermediary that is an agent. The IASB did not specifically consider how the transaction price requirements would be applied in these situations (i.e. when an entity that is a principal does not know and expects not to know the price charged to its customer by an agent), but concluded in the Basis for Conclusions that an entity that is a principal would generally be able to apply judgement and determine the consideration to which it is entitled using all information available to it. *[IFRS 15.BC385Z]*. Accordingly, we believe that it is possible that IFRS and US GAAP entities will reach different conclusions on estimating the gross transaction price in these situations.

4.5 Consignment arrangements

The standard provides specific application guidance for a promise to deliver goods on a consignment basis to other parties. See 7.5 below.

4.6 Customer options for additional goods or services

Many sales contracts give customers the option to acquire additional goods or services. These additional goods and services may be priced at a discount or may even be free of charge. Options to acquire additional goods or services at a discount can come in many forms, including sales incentives, volume-tiered pricing structures, customer award credits (e.g. frequent flyer points) or contract renewal options (e.g. waiver of certain fees, reduced future rates). *[IFRS 15.B39]*.

The standard specifies that when an entity grants a customer the option to acquire additional goods or services, that option is only a separate performance obligation if it provides a material right to the customer that the customer would not receive without entering into the contract (e.g. a discount that exceeds the range of discounts typically given for those goods or services to that class of customer in that geographical area or market). If the option provides a material right to the customer, the customer has, in effect, paid in advance for future goods or services. As such, the entity recognises revenue when those future goods or services are transferred or when the option expires. *[IFRS 15.B40]*. In the Basis for Conclusions, the IASB indicated that the purpose of this requirement is to identify and account for options that customers are paying for (often implicitly) as part of the current transaction. *[IFRS 15.BC386]*.

The Board did not provide any bright lines as to what constitutes a 'material' right. However, the standard requires that if the discounted price the customer would receive by exercising the option reflects the stand-alone selling price that a customer without an existing relationship with the entity would pay, the option does not provide a material right. The entity is deemed to have made a marketing offer. The standard states that this is the case even if the option can only be exercised because the customer entered into the earlier transaction. An entity that has made a marketing offer accounts for it in accordance with IFRS 15 only when the customer exercises the option to purchase the additional goods or services. *[IFRS 15.B41]*.

Current IFRS does not provide application guidance on how to distinguish between an option and a marketing offer (i.e. as an expense). Nor does it address how to account for options that provide a material right. As a result, some entities may have effectively accounted for such options as marketing offers. IFRS 15's requirements on the amount of the transaction price to be allocated to the option will likely differ significantly from current practice due to the lack of guidance in current IFRS (see 6.1.5 below).

Significant judgement may be required to determine whether a customer option represents a material right. This determination is important because it will affect the accounting and disclosures for the contract at inception and throughout the life of the contract.

The standard includes the following example to illustrate the determination of whether an option represents a material right (see 6.1.5 below for a discussion of the measurement of options that are separate performance obligations). *[IFRS 15.IE250-IE253]*.

Example 30.20: Option that provides the customer with a material right (discount voucher)

An entity enters into a contract for the sale of Product A for CU100. As part of the contract, the entity gives the customer a 40 per cent discount voucher for any future purchases up to CU100 in the next 30 days. The entity intends to offer a 10 per cent discount on all sales during the next 30 days as part of a seasonal promotion. The 10 per cent discount cannot be used in addition to the 40 per cent discount voucher.

Because all customers will receive a 10 per cent discount on purchases during the next 30 days, the only discount that provides the customer with a material right is the discount that is incremental to that 10 per cent (i.e. the additional 30 per cent discount). The entity accounts for the promise to provide the incremental discount as a performance obligation in the contract for the sale of Product A.

To estimate the stand-alone selling price of the discount voucher in accordance with paragraph B42 of IFRS 15, the entity estimates an 80 per cent likelihood that a customer will redeem the voucher and that a customer will, on average, purchase CU50 of additional products. Consequently, the entity's estimated stand-alone selling price of the discount voucher is CU12 (CU50 average purchase price of additional products × 30 per cent incremental discount × 80 per cent likelihood of exercising the option). The stand-alone selling prices of Product A and the discount voucher and the resulting allocation of the CU100 transaction price are as follows:

Performance obligations	Stand-alone selling price	
	CU	
Product A	100	
Discount voucher	12	
Total	112	
	Allocated transaction price	
Product A	89	(CU100 ÷ CU112 × CU100)
Discount voucher	11	(CU12 ÷ CU112 × CU100)
Total	100	

The entity allocates CU89 to Product A and recognises revenue for Product A when control transfers. The entity allocates CU11 to the discount voucher and recognises revenue for the voucher when the customer redeems it for goods or services or when it expires.

4.6.1 Implementation questions on customer options for additional goods or services

4.6.1.A Which transactions to consider when assessing customer options for additional goods or services

At their October 2014 meeting, the TRG members discussed whether entities should consider only the current transaction or also past and future transactions with the same customer when determining whether an option for additional goods and services provides the customer with a material right.

The TRG members generally agreed that entities should consider all relevant transactions with a customer (i.e. current, past and future transactions), including those that provide accumulating incentives, such as loyalty programmes, when determining whether an option represents a material right. That is, the evaluation is not solely performed in relation to the current transaction.[46]

4.6.1.B Nature of evaluation of customer options: quantitative versus qualitative

In October 2014, the TRG members considered whether the material right evaluation is solely a quantitative evaluation or whether it should also consider qualitative factors.

The TRG members generally agreed that the evaluation should consider both quantitative and qualitative factors (e.g. what a new customer would pay for the same service, the availability and pricing of competitors' service alternatives, whether the average customer life indicates that the fee provides an incentive for customers to remain beyond the stated contract term, whether the right accumulates). This is because a customer's perspective on what constitutes a 'material right' may consider qualitative factors. This is consistent with the notion that when identifying promised goods or services in Step 2, an entity considers reasonable expectations of the customer that the entity will transfer a good or service to it.[47]

4.6.1.C Distinguishing between a customer option and variable consideration

In November 2015, the TRG members were asked to consider how an entity would distinguish between a contract that contains an option to purchase additional goods and services and a contract that includes variable consideration (see 5.2 below) based on a variable quantity (e.g. a usage-based fee).[48]

The TRG members generally agreed that this determination requires judgement and consideration of the facts and circumstances. They also generally agreed that the TRG agenda paper on this question provides a framework that will help entities to make this determination.

This determination is important because it will affect the accounting for the contract at inception and throughout the life of the contract, as well as disclosures. If an entity concludes that a customer option for additional goods or services provides a material right, the option itself is deemed to be a performance obligation in the contract, but the underlying goods or services are not accounted for until the option is exercised (as discussed at 4.6.1.D below). As a result, the entity will be required to allocate a portion of the transaction price to the material right at contract inception and to recognise that revenue when or as the option is exercised or the option expires. If an entity, instead, concludes that an option for additional goods or services is not a material right, there is no accounting for the option and no accounting for the underlying optional goods or services until those subsequent purchases occur.

However, if the contract includes variable consideration (rather than a customer option), an entity will have to estimate at contract inception the variable consideration expected over the life of the contract and update that estimate each reporting period (subject to the constraint on variable consideration) (see 5.2 below). There are also more disclosures required for variable consideration (e.g. the requirement to disclose the remaining transaction price for unsatisfied performance obligations) (see 10.4.1 below) than for options that are not determined to be material rights.

The TRG agenda paper explained that the first step (in determining whether a contract involving variable quantities of goods or services should be accounted for as a contract containing customer options or variable consideration) is for the entity to determine the nature of its promise in providing goods or services to the customer and the rights and obligations of each party.

In a contract in which the variable quantity of goods or services results in variable consideration, the nature of the entity's promise is to transfer to the customer an overall service. In providing this overall service, an entity may perform individual tasks or activities. At contract inception, the entity is presently obligated by the terms and conditions of the contract to transfer all promised goods or services provided under the contract and the customer is obligated to pay for those promised goods or services. The customer's subsequent actions to utilise the service affect the measurement of revenue (in the form of variable consideration).

For example, consider a contract between a transaction processor and a customer in which the processor will process all of the customer's transactions in exchange for a fee paid for each transaction processed. The ultimate quantity of transactions that will be processed is not known. The nature of the entity's promise is to provide the customer with continuous access to the processing platform so that submitted transactions are processed. By entering into the contract, the customer has made a purchasing decision that obligates the entity to provide continuous access to the transaction processing platform. The consideration paid by the customer results from events (i.e. additional transactions being submitted for processing to the processor) that occur after (or as) the entity transfers the payment processing service. The customer's actions do not obligate the processor to provide additional distinct goods or services because the processor is already obligated (starting at contract inception) to process all transactions submitted to it.

Another example described in the TRG agenda paper of contracts that may include variable consideration was related to certain information technology outsourcing contracts. Under this type of contract (similar to the transaction processing contract discussed above), the vendor provides continuous delivery of a service over the contract term and the amount of service provided is variable.

In contrast, with a customer option the nature of the entity's promise is to provide the quantity of goods or services specified in the contract. The entity is not obligated to provide additional distinct goods or services until the customer exercises the option. The customer has a contractual right that allows it to choose the amount of additional distinct goods or services to purchase, but the customer has to make a separate purchasing decision to obtain those additional distinct goods or services. Prior to the customer's exercise of that right, the entity is not obligated to provide (nor does it have a right to consideration for transferring) those goods or services.

The TRG agenda paper included the following example of a contract that includes a customer option (rather than variable consideration): Entity B enters into a contract to provide 100 widgets to Customer Y in return for consideration of CU10 per widget. Each widget is a distinct good transferred at a point in time. The contract also gives Customer Y the right to purchase additional widgets at the stand-alone selling price of CU10 per widget. Therefore, the quantity that may be purchased by Customer Y is variable.

The conclusion in the TRG agenda paper was that, while the quantity of widgets that may be purchased is variable, the transaction price for the existing contract is fixed at CU1,000 [100 widgets × CU10/widget]. That is, the transaction price only includes the consideration for the 100 widgets specified in the contract and the customer's decision to purchase additional widgets is an option. While Entity B may be required to deliver additional widgets in the future, Entity B is not legally obligated to provide the additional widgets until Customer Y exercises the option. In this example, the option is accounted for as a separate contract because there is no material right, since the pricing of the option is at the stand-alone selling price of the widgets.

The TRG agenda paper also included the following example of a contract in which the variable quantity of goods or services includes a customer option.

Example 30.21: Customer option[49]

A supplier enters into a five-year master supply arrangement in which the supplier is obligated to produce and sell parts to a customer at the customer's request. That is, the supplier is not obligated to transfer any parts until the customer submits a purchase order. In addition, the customer is not obligated to purchase any parts; however, it is highly likely it will do so because the part is required to manufacture the customer's product and it is not practical to obtain parts from multiple suppliers. Each part is determined to a distinct good that transfers to the customer at a point in time.

The conclusion in the TRG agenda paper was that the nature of the promise in this example is the delivery of parts (and not a service of standing ready to produce and sell parts). That is, the contract provides the customer with a right to choose the quantity of additional distinct goods (i.e. it provides a customer option), rather than a right to use the services for which control to the customer has (or is currently being) transferred (such as in the transaction processor example above). Similarly, the supplier is not obligated to transfer any parts until the customer submits the purchase order (another important factor in distinguishing a customer option from variable consideration). In contrast, in the other fact patterns the vendor is obligated to make the promised services available to the customer without any additional decisions made by the customer.

The TRG agenda paper contrasted this example with other contracts that may include a stand-ready obligation (e.g. a customer's use of a health club). When the customer submits a purchase order under the master supply arrangement, it is contracting for a specific number of distinct goods, which creates new performance obligations for the supplier. In contrast, a customer using services in a health club is using services that the health club is already obligated to provide under the present contract. That is, there are no new obligations arising from the customer's usage.

The TRG agenda paper also included the following example of a contract in which the variable quantity of goods or services results in variable consideration.

Example 30.22: Variable consideration[50]

Entity A enters into a contract to provide equipment to Customer X. The equipment is a single performance obligation transferred at a point in time. Entity A charges Customer X based on its usage of the equipment at a fixed rate per unit of consumption. The contract has no minimum payment guarantees. Customer X is not contractually obligated to use the equipment. However, Entity A is contractually obligated to transfer the equipment to Customer X.

The conclusion in the TRG agenda paper was that the usage of the equipment by Customer X is a variable quantity that affects the amount of consideration owed to Entity A. It does not affect

Entity A's performance obligation, which is to transfer the piece of equipment. That is, Entity A has performed by transferring the distinct good. Customer X's actions, which result in payment to Entity A, occur after the equipment has been transferred and do not require Entity A to provide additional goods or services.

4.6.1.D *When, if ever, to consider the goods or services underlying a customer option as a separate performance obligation when there are no contractual penalties*

At their November 2015 meeting, TRG members generally agreed that, even if an entity believes that it is virtually certain that a customer will exercise its option for additional goods and services, it would not identify the additional goods and services underlying the option as promised goods or services (or performance obligations) if there are no contractual penalties. Only the option would be assessed to determine whether it represents a material right to be accounted for as a performance obligation. As a result, consideration that would be received in return for optional goods or services is not included in the transaction price at contract inception.[51]

The TRG agenda paper included the following example of a contract in which it is virtually certain that a customer will exercise its option for additional goods or services:

Example 30.23: Customer option with no contractual penalties[52]

An entity sells equipment and consumables, both of which are determined to be distinct goods that are recognised at a point in time. The stand-alone selling price of the equipment and each consumable is CU10,000 and CU100, respectively. The equipment costs CU8,000 and each consumable costs CU60. The entity sells the equipment for CU6,000 (i.e. at a 40% discount on its stand-alone selling price) with a customer option to purchase each consumable for CU100 (i.e. equal to its stand-alone selling price). There are no contractual minimums, but the entity estimates the customer will purchase 200 parts over the next two years. This is an exclusive contract in which the customer cannot purchase the consumables from any other vendors during the contract term.

TRG members generally agreed that the consumables underlying each option would not be considered part of the contract. Furthermore, the option does not represent a material right because it is priced at the stand-alone selling price for the consumable. This is the case even though the customer is compelled to exercise its option for the consumables because the equipment cannot function without the consumables and the contract includes an exclusivity clause that requires the customer to acquire the consumables only from the entity. Accordingly, the transaction price is CU6,000 and it is entirely attributable to the equipment. This would result in a loss for the entity of CU2,000 when it transfers control of the equipment to the customer.

If contractual penalties exist (e.g. termination fees, monetary penalties assessed for not meeting contractual minimums), the entity will need to further analyse the goods or services underlying customer options to determine which optional goods or services would be accounted for in the present contract. If there are substantive contractual penalties, it may be appropriate to include some or all of the goods or services underlying customer options as part of the contract at inception. This is because the penalty effectively creates a minimum purchase obligation for the goods or services that would be purchased if the penalty were enforced.

Example 30.24: Customer option with contractual penalties[53]

Consider the same facts as in Example 30.23 above, except that the customer will incur a penalty if it does not purchase at least 200 consumables. That is, the customer will be required to repay some or all of the CU4,000 discount provided on the equipment. Per the contract terms, the penalty decreases as each consumable is purchased at a rate of CU20 per consumable.

The conclusion in the TRG agenda paper was that the penalty is substantive and it effectively creates a minimum purchase obligation. As a result, the entity would conclude that the minimum number of consumables required to avoid the penalty would be evidence of enforceable rights and obligations. The entity would then calculate the transaction price as CU26,000 [(200 consumables × CU100/consumable) + CU6,000 (the selling price of the equipment)]. Furthermore, the conclusion in the TRG agenda paper was that, if the customer failed to purchase 200 consumables, the entity would account for the resulting penalty as a contract modification.

4.6.1.E Volume rebates and/or discounts on goods or services: customer options versus variable consideration

Should volume rebates and/or discounts on goods or services be accounted for as variable consideration or as customer options to acquire additional goods or services at a discount? It will depend on whether rebate or discount programme is applied retrospectively or prospectively.

Generally, if a volume rebate or discount is applied prospectively, we believe the rebate or discount would be accounted for as a customer option (not variable consideration). This is because the consideration for the goods or services in the present contract is not contingent upon or affected by any future purchases. Rather, the discounts available from the rebate programme affect the price of future purchases. Entities will need to evaluate whether the volume rebate or discount provides the customer with an option to purchase goods or services in the future at a discount that represents a material right (and is, therefore, accounted for as a performance obligation) (see 4.6.1.D below).

However, we believe a volume rebate or discount that is applied retrospectively will be accounted for as variable consideration (see 5.2 below). This is because the final price of each good or service sold depends upon the customer's total purchases that are subject to the rebate programme. That is, the consideration is contingent upon the occurrence or non-occurrence of future events. This view is consistent with Example 24 in the standard (which is included as Example 30.26 at 5.2.1 below).

Entities should keep in mind that they will need to evaluate whether contract terms, other than those specific to the rebate or discount programme, create variable consideration that would need to be separately evaluated (e.g. if the goods subject to the rebate programme are also sold with a right of return).

4.6.1.F Considering whether prospective volume discounts determined to be customer options are material rights

At the April 2016 FASB TRG meeting, the FASB TRG members were asked to consider how an entity should consider whether prospective volume discounts determined to be customer options are material rights.[54]

The FASB TRG members generally agreed that in making this evaluation, an entity would first evaluate whether the option exists independently of the existing contract. That is, would the entity offer the same pricing to a similar high-volume customer independent of a prior contract with the entity? If yes, it indicates that the volume discount is not a material right, as it is not incremental to the discount typically offered to a similar high-volume customer. If the entity typically charges a higher price to a similar customer, it may indicate that the volume discount is a material right as the discount is incremental.

The TRG agenda paper included the following example: Entity enters into a long-term master supply arrangement with Customer A to provide an unspecified volume of non-customised parts. The price of the parts in subsequent years is dependent upon Customer A's purchases in the current year. That is, Entity charges Customer A CU1.00 per part in year one and if Customer A purchases more than 100,000 parts, the year two price will be CU0.90.

When making the determination of whether the contract between Entity and Customer A includes a material right, Entity first evaluates whether the option provided to Customer A exists independently of the existing contract. To do this, Entity would compare the discount offered to Customer A with the discount typically offered to a similar high-volume customer that receives a discount independent of a prior contract with Entity. Such a similar customer could be Customer B who places a single order with Entity for 105,000 parts. Comparing the price offered to Customer A in year two with offers to other customers that also receive pricing that is contingent on prior purchases would not help Entity determine whether Customer A would have been offered the year two price had it not entered into the original contract.

The evaluation of when volume rebates result in a material right will likely require significant judgement.

4.6.1.G Accounting for the exercise of a material right

At the March 2015 TRG meeting, the TRG members were asked to consider how an entity would account for the exercise of an option for additional goods and services that provides the customer with a material right (a material right).[55]

The TRG members generally agreed that it would be reasonable for an entity to account for the exercise of a material right as either a contract modification or as a continuation of the existing contract (i.e. a change in the transaction price). TRG members also generally agreed that it would not be appropriate to account for the exercise of a material right as variable consideration.

Although the TRG members generally agreed that the standard could be interpreted to allow either approach, many TRG members favoured treating the exercise of a material right as a continuation of the existing contract because the customer decided to purchase additional goods or services that were contemplated in the original contract (and not as part of a separate, subsequent negotiation). Under this approach, if a customer exercises a material right, an entity would update the transaction price of the contract to include any consideration to which the entity expects to be entitled as a result of the exercise, in accordance with the requirements for changes in the transaction price included in paragraphs 87-90 of IFRS 15 (see 6.5 below).

Under these requirements, changes in the total transaction price are generally allocated to the separate performance obligations on the same basis as the initial allocation. However, paragraph 89 of IFRS 15 requires an entity to allocate a change in the transaction price entirely to one or more, but not all, performance obligations if the criteria in paragraph 85 of IFRS 15 are met. These criteria (discussed further at 6.3 below) are that the additional consideration specifically relates to the entity's efforts to satisfy the performance obligation(s) and that allocating the additional consideration entirely to one or more, but not all, performance obligation(s) is consistent with the standard's allocation objective (see 6 below). The additional consideration received for the exercise of the option would likely meet the criteria to be allocated directly to the performance obligation(s) underlying the material right. Revenue would be recognised when (or as) the performance obligation(s) is satisfied.

The TRG agenda paper included the following example.

Example 30.25: Exercise of a material right under the requirements for changes in the transaction price[56]

Entity enters into a contract with Customer to provide two years of Service A for CU100 and includes an option for Customer to purchase two years of Service B for CU300. The stand-alone selling prices of Services A and B are CU100 and CU400, respectively. Entity concludes that the option represents a material right and its estimate of the stand-alone selling price of the option is CU33. Entity allocates the CU100 transaction price to each performance obligation as follows:

	Transaction price	Stand-alone selling price	%	Allocation
Service A		CU100	75%	CU75
Option		CU33	25%	CU25
Total	CU100	CU133	100%	CU100

Upon executing the contract, Customer pays CU100 and Entity begins transferring Service A to Customer. The consideration of CU75 that is allocated to Service A is recognised over the two-year service period. The consideration of CU25 that is allocated to the option is deferred until Service B is transferred to the customer or the option expires. Six months after executing the contract, Customer exercises the option to purchase two years of Service B for CU300. Under this approach, the consideration of CU300 related to Service B is added to the amount previously allocated to the option to purchase Service B (i.e. CU300 + 25 = CU325). This is recognised as revenue over the two-year period in which Service B is transferred. Entity is able to allocate the additional consideration received for the exercise of the option to Service B because it specifically relates to Entity's efforts to satisfy the performance obligation and the allocation in this manner is consistent with the standard's allocation objective.

The TRG members who favoured the contract modification approach generally did so because the exercise of a material right also meets the definition of a contract modification in the standard (i.e. a change in the scope and/or price of a contract). Under this approach, an entity would follow the contract modification requirements in paragraphs 18-21 of IFRS 15 (see 3.4 above).

Since more than one approach would be acceptable, the TRG members generally agreed that an entity will need to consider which approach is most appropriate, based on the facts and circumstances, and consistently apply that approach to similar contracts.[57]

4.6.1.H Customer options that provide a material right: Evaluating whether there is a significant financing component

At their March 2015 TRG meeting, the TRG members discussed whether an entity is required to evaluate a customer option that provides a material right to determine if it includes a significant financing component and, if so, how entities would perform this evaluation.

The TRG members generally agreed that an entity will have to evaluate whether a material right includes a significant financing component (see 5.5 below) in the same way as it would evaluate any other performance obligation. This evaluation will require judgement and consideration of the facts and circumstances.[58]

On this question, the TRG agenda paper discussed a factor that may be determinative in this evaluation. Paragraph 62(a) of IFRS 15 indicates that if a customer provides advance payment for a good or service, but the customer can choose when the good or service is transferred, no significant financing component exists. *[IFRS 15.62(a)]*. As a result, if the customer can choose when to exercise the option, it is unlikely that there will be a significant financing component.[59]

4.7 Sale of products with a right of return

An entity may provide its customers with a right to return a transferred product. A right of return may be contractual, an implicit right that exists due to the entity's customary business practice or a combination of both (e.g. an entity has a stated return period, but generally accepts returns over a longer period). A customer exercising its right to return a product may receive a full or partial refund, a credit that can be applied to amounts owed, a different product in exchange or any combination of these items. *[IFRS 15.B20]*.

Offering a right of return in a sales agreement obliges the selling entity to stand ready to accept any returned product. Paragraph B22 of IFRS 15 states that such an obligation does not represent a performance obligation. *[IFRS 15.B22]*. Instead, the Board concluded that an entity makes an uncertain number of sales when it provides goods with a return right. That is, until the right of return expires, the entity is not certain how many sales will fail. Therefore, the Board concluded that an entity does not recognise revenue for sales that are expected to fail as a result of the customer exercising its right to return the goods. *[IFRS 15.BC364]*. Instead, the potential for customer returns needs to be considered when an entity estimates the transaction price because potential returns are a component of variable consideration. This concept is discussed further at 5.4.1 below.

Paragraph B26 of IFRS 15 clarifies that exchanges by customers of one product for another of the same type, quality, condition and price (e.g. one colour or size for another) are not considered returns for the purposes of applying the standard. *[IFRS 15.B26]*. Furthermore, contracts in which a customer may return a defective product in exchange for a functioning product need to be evaluated in accordance with the requirements on warranties included in IFRS 15. *[IFRS 15.B27]*. See further discussion on warranties at 9.1 below.

Under current IFRS, revenue is recognised at the time of sale for a transaction that provides a customer with a right of return, provided the seller can reliably estimate future returns. In addition, the seller is required to recognise a liability for the expected returns. *[IAS 18.17]*. The new standard's requirements are, therefore, not significantly different from current IFRS.

We do not expect the net impact of these arrangements to change materially. However, there may be some differences as IAS 18 does not specify the presentation of a refund liability or the corresponding debit. IFRS 15 requires that a return asset be recognised in relation to the inventory that may be returned. In addition, the refund liability is required to be presented separately from the corresponding asset (i.e. on a gross basis, rather than a net basis, see 5.2.2, 5.3 and 5.4.1 below).

5 DETERMINE THE TRANSACTION PRICE

When (or as) an entity satisfies a performance obligation, an entity recognises revenue at the amount of the transaction price (which excludes constrained estimates of variable consideration – see 5.2.3 below) that is allocated to that performance obligation. *[IFRS 15.46]*. The standard states that 'an entity shall consider the terms of the contract and its customary business practices to determine the transaction price. The transaction price is the amount of consideration to which an entity expects to be entitled in exchange for transferring promised goods or services to a customer, excluding amounts collected on behalf of third parties (for example, some sales taxes). The consideration promised in a contract with a customer may include fixed amounts, variable amounts, or both.' *[IFRS 15.47]*.

The nature, timing and amount of consideration promised by a customer affect the estimate of the transaction price. When determining the transaction price, an entity shall consider the effects of all of the following: *[IFRS 15.48]*

(a) variable consideration;

(b) constraining estimates of variable consideration;

(c) the existence of a significant financing component in the contract;

(d) non-cash consideration; and

(e) consideration payable to a customer.

For the purpose of determining the transaction price, an entity shall assume that the goods or services will be transferred to the customer as promised in accordance with the existing contract and that the contract will not be cancelled, renewed or modified. *[IFRS 15.49]*.

The transaction price is based on the amount to which the entity expects to be 'entitled'. This amount is meant to reflect the amount to which the entity has rights under the present contract (see 3.2 above on contract enforceability and termination clauses). That is, the transaction price does not include estimates of consideration resulting from future change orders for additional goods and services. The amount to which the entity expects to be entitled also excludes amounts collected on behalf of another party, such as sales taxes. As noted in the Basis for Conclusions, the Board decided that the transaction price would not include the effects of the customer's credit risk, unless the contract includes a significant financing component (see 5.5 below). *[IFRS 15.BC185]*.

Determining the transaction price is an important step in applying IFRS 15 because this amount is allocated to the identified performance obligations and is recognised as revenue when (or as) those performance obligations are satisfied. In many cases, the transaction price is readily determinable because the entity receives payment when it transfers promised goods or services and the price is fixed (e.g. a restaurant's sale of food with a no refund policy). Determining the transaction price is more challenging when it is variable, when payment is received at a time that differs from when the entity provides the promised goods or services or when payment is in a form other than cash. Consideration paid or payable by the entity to the customer may also affect the determination of the transaction price.

5.1 Presentation of sales (and other similar) taxes

The standard includes a general principle that an entity will determine the transaction price exclusive of amounts collected on behalf of third parties (e.g. some sales taxes). Following the issuance of the standard, some stakeholders informed the Board's staff that there could be multiple interpretations regarding whether certain items that are billed to customers need to be presented as revenue or as a reduction of costs. Examples of such amounts include shipping and handling fees, reimbursements of out-of-pocket expenses and taxes or other assessments collected and remitted to government authorities.

At the July 2014 TRG meeting, the TRG members generally agreed that the standard is clear that any amounts that are not collected on behalf of third parties would be included in the transaction price (i.e. revenue). That is, if the amounts were incurred by the entity in fulfilling its performance obligations, the amounts will be included in the transaction price and recorded as revenue.

Several TRG members noted that this would require entities to evaluate taxes collected in all jurisdictions in which they operate to determine whether a tax is levied on the entity or the customer. In addition, the TRG members indicated that an entity would apply the principal versus agent application guidance (see 4.4 above) when it is not clear whether the amounts are collected on behalf of third parties. This could result in amounts billed to a customer being recorded net of costs incurred (i.e. on a net basis).[60]

In May 2016, the FASB issued amendments to its standard to allow an entity to make an accounting policy election to present revenue net of certain types of taxes (including sales, use, value-added and some excise taxes) with a requirement for preparers to disclose the policy. As a result, entities that make this election would not need to evaluate taxes that they collect (e.g. sales, use, value-added, some excise taxes) in all jurisdictions in which they operate in order to determine whether a tax is levied on the entity or the customer. This type of evaluation would otherwise be necessary to meet the standard's requirement to exclude from the transaction price any 'amounts collected on behalf of third parties (for example, some sales taxes)'. *[IFRS 15.47]*.

The IASB decided not to make similar amendments, noting that the topic was not an interpretative question and the requirements of IFRS 15 are consistent with current IFRS requirements. *[IFRS 15.BC188D]*. Since this accounting policy is only being available under US GAAP, differences may arise between entities applying IFRS 15 and those applying ASC 606.

5.2 Variable consideration

The transaction price reflects an entity's expectations about the consideration to which it will be entitled to receive from the customer. 'If the consideration promised

Chapter 30

in a contract includes a variable amount, an entity shall estimate the amount of consideration to which the entity will be entitled in exchange for transferring the promised goods or services to a customer.'

'An amount of consideration can vary because of discounts, rebates, refunds, credits, price concessions, incentives, performance bonuses, penalties or other similar items. The promised consideration can also vary if an entity's entitlement to the consideration is contingent on the occurrence or non-occurrence of a future event. For example, an amount of consideration would be variable if either a product was sold with a right of return or a fixed amount is promised as a performance bonus on achievement of a specified milestone.' *[IFRS 15.50-51]*.

In some cases, the variability relating to the promised consideration may be explicitly stated in the contract. In addition to the terms of the contract, the standard states that the promised consideration is variable if either of the following circumstances exists:

- the customer has 'a valid expectation arising from an entity's customary business practices, published policies or specific statements that the entity will accept an amount of consideration that is less than the price stated in the contract. That is, it is expected that the entity will offer a price concession. Depending on the jurisdiction, industry or customer this offer may be referred to as a discount, rebate, refund or credit.'
- other facts and circumstances that indicate 'the entity's intention, when entering into the contract with the customer, is to offer a price concession to the customer.' *[IFRS 15.52]*.

These concepts are discussed in more detail below.

5.2.1 Forms of variable consideration

As indicated in paragraph 51 of IFRS 15, 'variable consideration' is defined broadly and can take many forms, including discounts, rebates, refunds, credits, price concessions, incentives, performance bonuses and penalties. *[IFRS 15.51]*. Variable consideration can result from explicit terms in a contract to which the parties to the contract agreed or can be implied by an entity's past business practices or intentions under the contract. It is important for entities to appropriately identify the different instances of variable consideration included in a contract because the second step of estimating variable consideration requires entities to apply a constraint (as discussed further at 5.2.3 below) to all variable consideration.

Many types of variable consideration identified in IFRS 15 are also considered variable consideration under current IFRS. An example of this is where a portion of the transaction price depends on an entity meeting specified performance conditions and there is uncertainty about the outcome. This portion of the transaction price would be considered variable (or contingent) consideration under both current IFRS and IFRS 15.

The Board noted in the Basis for Conclusions that consideration can be variable even when the stated price in the contract is fixed. This is because the entity may be entitled to consideration only upon the occurrence or non-occurrence of a future event. *[IFRS 15.BC191]*. For example, IFRS 15's definition of variable consideration includes amounts resulting from variability due to customer refunds or returns. As a result, a contract to provide a customer with 100 widgets at a fixed price per widget would be considered to include a variable component if the customer has the ability to return the widgets (see 5.4.1 below).

In many transactions, entities have variable consideration as a result of rebates and/or discounts on the price of products or services they provide to customers once the customers meet specific volume thresholds. The standard contains the following example relating to volume discounts. *[IFRS 15.IE124-IE128]*.

Example 30.26: Volume discount incentive

An entity enters into a contract with a customer on 1 January 20X8 to sell Product A for CU100 per unit. If the customer purchases more than 1,000 units of Product A in a calendar year, the contract specifies that the price per unit is retrospectively reduced to CU90 per unit. Consequently, the consideration in the contract is variable.

For the first quarter ended 31 March 20X8, the entity sells 75 units of Product A to the customer. The entity estimates that the customer's purchases will not exceed the 1,000-unit threshold required for the volume discount in the calendar year.

The entity considers the requirements in paragraphs 56–58 of IFRS 15 on constraining estimates of variable consideration, including the factors in paragraph 57 of IFRS 15. The entity determines that it has significant experience with this product and with the purchasing pattern of the entity. Thus, the entity concludes that it is highly probable that a significant reversal in the cumulative amount of revenue recognised (i.e. CU100 per unit) will not occur when the uncertainty is resolved (i.e. when the total amount of purchases is known). Consequently, the entity recognises revenue of CU7,500 (75 units × CU100 per unit) for the quarter ended 31 March 20X8.

In May 20X8, the entity's customer acquires another company and in the second quarter ended 30 June 20X8 the entity sells an additional 500 units of Product A to the customer. In the light of the new fact, the entity estimates that the customer's purchases will exceed the 1,000-unit threshold for the calendar year and therefore it will be required to retrospectively reduce the price per unit to CU90.

Consequently, the entity recognises revenue of CU44,250 for the quarter ended 30 June 20X8. That amount is calculated from CU45,000 for the sale of 500 units (500 units × CU90 per unit) less the change in transaction price of CU750 (75 units × CU10 price reduction) for the reduction of revenue relating to units sold for the quarter ended 31 March 20X8 (see paragraphs 87 and 88 of IFRS 15).

See 4.6.1.E above for discussion on whether volume rebates and/or discounts on goods or services should be accounted for as variable consideration or as customer options to acquire additional goods or services at a discount. See 4.6.1.C above for a discussion on distinguishing between a contract that contains an option to purchase additional goods and services and a contract that includes variable consideration based on a variable quantity (e.g. a usage-based fee).

5.2.1.A Implicit price concessions

For some contracts, the stated price has easily identifiable variable components. However, for other contracts, the consideration may be variable because the facts and circumstances indicate that the entity may accept a lower price than the amount stated in the contract (i.e. it expects to provide an implicit price concession). This could be as a result of the customer's valid expectation that the entity will reduce its price because of the entity's customary business practices, published policies or specific statements made by the entity.

An implicit price concession could also result from other facts and circumstances indicating that the entity intended to offer a price concession to the customer when it entered into the contract. For example, an entity may accept a lower price than the amount stated in the contract to develop or enhance a customer relationship or because the incremental cost of providing the service to the customer is not significant and the total consideration it expects to collect provides a sufficient margin.

The standard provides the following example of when an implicit price concession exists and the transaction price, therefore, is not the amount stated in the contract. *[IFRS 15.IE7-IE9]*.

Example 30.27: Consideration is not the stated price – implicit price concession

An entity sells 1,000 units of a prescription drug to a customer for promised consideration of CU1 million. This is the entity's first sale to a customer in a new region, which is experiencing significant economic difficulty. Thus, the entity expects that it will not be able to collect from the customer the full amount of the promised consideration. Despite the possibility of not collecting the full amount, the entity expects the region's economy to recover over the next two to three years and determines that a relationship with the customer could help it to forge relationships with other potential customers in the region.

When assessing whether the criterion in paragraph 9(e) of IFRS 15 is met, the entity also considers paragraphs 47 and 52(b) of IFRS 15. Based on the assessment of the facts and circumstances, the entity determines that it expects to provide a price concession and accept a lower amount of consideration from the customer. Accordingly, the entity concludes that the transaction price is not CU1 million and, therefore, the promised consideration is variable. The entity estimates the variable consideration and determines that it expects to be entitled to CU400,000.

The entity considers the customer's ability and intention to pay the consideration and concludes that even though the region is experiencing economic difficulty, it is probable that it will collect CU400,000 from the customer. Consequently, the entity concludes that the criterion in paragraph 9(e) of IFRS 15 is met based on an estimate of variable consideration of CU400,000. In addition, on the basis of an evaluation of the contract terms and other facts and circumstances, the entity concludes that the other criteria in paragraph 9 of IFRS 15 are also met. Consequently, the entity accounts for the contract with the customer in accordance with the requirements in IFRS 15.

Variable consideration may also result from extended payment terms in a contract and any resulting uncertainty about whether the entity will be willing to accept a lower amount when it is paid in the future. That is, an entity will have to evaluate whether the extended payment terms represent an implied price concession because the entity does not intend to, or will not be able to, collect all amounts due in future periods.

However, in the Basis for Conclusions, the IASB acknowledged that in some cases, it may be difficult to determine whether the entity has implicitly offered a price concession or whether the entity has chosen to accept the risk of the customer defaulting on the contractually agreed consideration (i.e. impairment losses). *[IFRS 15.BC194]*. The Board did not develop detailed application guidance to assist in distinguishing between price concessions (recognised as variable consideration, within revenue) and impairment losses (recognised as a bad debt expense, outside of revenue). Therefore, entities will need to consider all relevant facts and circumstances when analysing situations in which an entity is willing to accept a lower price than the amount stated in the contract.

Appropriately distinguishing between price concessions (i.e. reductions of revenue) and customer credit risk (i.e. bad debt) for collectability concerns that were known at contract inception is important because it will affect whether a valid contract exists (see 3.1.5 above) and the subsequent accounting for the transaction. If an entity determines at contract inception that a contract includes a price concession (i.e. variable consideration), any change in the estimate of the amount the entity expects to collect, absent an identifiable credit event, will be accounted for as a change in the transaction price. That is, a decrease in the amount the entity expects to collect would be recorded as a reduction in revenue and not as a bad debt expense, unless there is an event that affects a customer's ability to pay some or all of the transaction price (e.g. a known decline in a customer's operations, a bankruptcy filing). As illustrated in Example 30.27 above, entities may estimate a transaction price that is significantly lower than the stated invoice or contractual amount, but still consider the difference between those amounts to be variable consideration (e.g. a price concession), rather than a collectability issue related to bad debt. Under current IFRS, such amounts are likely expensed as bad debts, rather than being reflected as a reduction of revenue.

5.2.1.B *Liquidated damages, penalties or compensation from other similar clauses: variable consideration versus warranty provisions*

Should liquidated damages, penalties or compensation from other similar clauses be accounted for as variable consideration or warranty provisions under the standard? Most liquidated damages, penalties and similar payments should be accounted for as variable consideration. However, in limited situations, we believe that amounts that are based on the actual performance of a delivered good or service may be considered similar to warranty payments (e.g. in situations in which an entity pays the customer's direct costs to remedy a defect).

Some contracts provide for liquidated damages, penalties or other damages if an entity fails to deliver future goods or services or if the goods or services fail to meet certain specifications. Paragraph 51 of IFRS 15 includes 'penalties' as an example of variable consideration and describes how promised consideration in a contract can be variable if the right to receive the consideration is contingent on the occurrence or non-occurrence of a future event (e.g. the contract specifies that a vendor pays a penalty if it fails to perform according to the agreed upon terms). *[IFRS 15.51]*.

Penalties and other clauses that are considered similar to warranty provisions would be accounted for as:

(a) consideration paid or payable to a customer (which may be variable consideration, see 5.7 below); or

(b) an assurance-type or service-type warranty (see 9.1 below on warranties).

Cash fines or penalties paid to a customer would generally be accounted for under the requirements on consideration payable to a customer. However, we believe there may be situations in which it is appropriate to account for cash payments as an assurance-type warranty (e.g. an entity's direct reimbursement to the customer for costs paid by the customer to a third party for the repair of a product).

5.2.1.C *Identifying variable consideration: undefined quantities with fixed per unit contractual prices*

At the July 2015 TRG meeting, the TRG members were asked whether the consideration is variable in a contract that includes a promise to provide an undefined quantity of outputs or to perform an undefined quantity of tasks, but has a contractual rate per unit that is fixed. The TRG members generally agreed that if a contract includes an unknown quantity of tasks throughout the contract period, for which the entity has enforceable rights and obligations (i.e. the unknown quantity of tasks is not an option to purchase additional goods and services, as described at 4.6.1.C above) and the consideration received is contingent upon the quantity completed, the total transaction price would be variable. This is because the contract has a range of possible transaction prices and the ultimate consideration will depend on the occurrence or non-occurrence of a future event (e.g. customer usage), even though the rate per unit is fixed.

The TRG agenda paper on this topic noted that an entity would need to consider contractual minimums (or other clauses) that would make some or all of the consideration fixed.[61]

5.2.1.D *If a contract is denominated in a currency other than that of the entity's functional currency, should changes in the contract price due to exchange rate fluctuations be accounted for as variable consideration?*

We believe that changes to the contract price due to exchange rate fluctuations do not result in variable consideration. These price fluctuations are a consequence of entering into a contract that is denominated in a foreign currency, rather than a result of a contract term like a discount or rebate or one that depends on the occurrence or non-occurrence of a future event, as described in paragraph 51 of IFRS 15. *[IFRS 15.51]*.

The variability resulting from changes in foreign exchange rates relates to the form of the consideration (i.e. it is in a currency other than the entity's functional currency). As such, we believe that it should not be considered variable consideration when determining the transaction price. This variability may, instead, need to be accounted for in accordance with IFRS 9 or IAS 39 if it is a separable embedded derivative. Otherwise, an entity would account for this variability in accordance with IAS 21 – *The Effects of Changes in Foreign Exchange Rates*.

In late October 2015, the Interpretations Committee published a draft interpretation – *Foreign Currency Transactions and Advance Consideration* – to address an issue on whether the date of transaction (when applying IAS 21) is the date on which the consideration paid or received in advance is recognised or a subsequent date (or dates) when the goods or services are actually delivered. It proposed that, in general, the appropriate application of IAS 21 is to use the exchange rate at the date the advanced receipt is recognised, normally the payment date. At the time of writing, the Interpretations Committee's deliberations were complete and the interpretation was expected to be finalised by the end of 2016, with an anticipated effective date of 1 January 2018 (see Chapter 15 at 5.1.1).

5.2.2 Estimating variable consideration

An entity is required to estimate an amount of variable consideration by using either of the following methods, depending on which method the entity expects to better predict the amount of consideration to which it will be entitled:

- *The expected value* – 'the expected value is the sum of probability-weighted amounts in a range of possible consideration amounts. An expected value may be an appropriate estimate of the amount of variable consideration if an entity has a large number of contracts with similar characteristics.'
- *The most likely amount* – 'the most likely amount is the single most likely amount in a range of possible consideration amounts (i.e. the single most likely outcome of the contract). The most likely amount may be an appropriate estimate of the amount of variable consideration if the contract has only two possible outcomes' (e.g. an entity either achieves a performance bonus or does not). *[IFRS 15.53]*.

An entity applies one method consistently throughout the contract when estimating the effect of an uncertainty on an amount of variable consideration to which the entity will be entitled. In addition, an entity is required to consider all the information (historical, current and forecast) that is reasonably available to the entity and identify a reasonable number of possible consideration amounts. The standard states that the information an entity uses to estimate the amount of variable consideration would typically be similar to the information that the entity's management uses during the bid-and-proposal process and in establishing prices for promised goods or services. *[IFRS 15.54]*.

An entity is required to choose between the expected value method and the most likely amount method based on which method better predicts the amount of consideration to which it will be entitled. That is, the method selected is not meant to be a 'free choice'. Rather, an entity selects the method that is best suited, based on the specific facts and circumstances of the contract. *[IFRS 15.53]*.

An entity applies the selected method consistently to each type of variable consideration throughout the contract term and updates the estimated variable consideration at the end of each reporting period. Once it selects a method, an entity is required to apply that method consistently for similar types of variable consideration in similar types of contracts. In the Basis for Conclusions, the Board noted that a contract may contain different types of variable consideration. *[IFRS 15.BC202]*. As such, it may be appropriate for an entity to use different methods (i.e. expected value or most likely amount) for estimating different types of variable consideration within a single contract.

Entities will determine the expected value of variable consideration using the sum of probability-weighted amounts in a range of possible amounts under the contract. To do this, an entity identifies the possible outcomes of a contract and the probabilities of those outcomes. The Board indicated in the Basis for Conclusions that the expected value method may better predict expected consideration when an entity has a large number of contracts with similar characteristics. *[IFRS 15.BC200]*. This method may also better predict consideration when an entity has a single contract with a large number of possible outcomes. The IASB clarified that an entity preparing an expected value calculation is not required to consider all possible outcomes, even if the entity has extensive data and can identify many possible outcomes. Instead, the IASB noted in the Basis for Conclusions that, in many cases, a limited number of discrete outcomes and probabilities can provide a reasonable estimate of the expected value. *[IFRS 15.BC201]*.

Entities will determine the most likely amount of variable consideration using the single most likely amount in a range of possible consideration amounts. The Board indicated in the Basis for Conclusions that the most likely amount method may be the better predictor when the entity expects to be entitled to one of two possible amounts. *[IFRS 15.BC200]*. For example, a contract in which an entity is entitled to receive all or none of a specified performance bonus, but not a portion of that bonus.

The standard requires that when applying either of these methods, an entity considers all information (historical, current and forecast) that is reasonably available to the entity. Some stakeholders questioned whether an entity would be applying the portfolio approach practical expedient in paragraph 4 of IFRS 15 (see 3.3.1 above) when considering evidence from other, similar contracts to develop an estimate of variable consideration using an expected value method. The TRG members discussed this question and generally agreed that an entity would not be applying the portfolio approach practical expedient if it used a portfolio of data from its historical experience with similar customers and/or contracts. The TRG members noted that an entity could choose to apply the portfolio approach practical expedient, but would not be required to do so.[62] Use of this practical expedient requires an entity to assert that it does not expect the use of the expedient to differ materially from applying the standard to an individual contract. The TRG agenda paper noted that using a portfolio of data is not equivalent to using the portfolio approach practical expedient, so entities that use the expected value method to estimate variable consideration would not be required to assert that the outcome from the portfolio is not expected to materially differ from an assessment of individual contracts.

Many entities will see significant changes in how they account for variable consideration on adoption of IFRS 15. This will be an even more significant change for entities that currently do not attempt to estimate variable consideration and simply recognise such amounts when received or known with a high degree of certainty (e.g. upon receipt of a report from a customer detailing the amount of revenue due to the entity).

As an example, the standard may change practice for many entities that sell their products through distributors or resellers. Before revenue can be recognised, paragraph 14 of IAS 18 requires that the amount of revenue can be measured reliably and that it be probable that the economic benefits associated with the transaction will flow to the entity. *[IAS 18.14]*. As a result, when the sales price charged to the distributor or reseller is not finalised until the product is sold to the end-customer, entities may wait until the product is sold to the end-customer to recognise revenue.

Under IFRS 15, waiting until the end-sale has occurred will no longer be acceptable if the only uncertainty is the variability in the pricing. This is because IFRS 15 requires an entity to estimate the variable consideration (i.e. the end-sales price) based on the information available, taking into consideration the effect of the constraint on variable consideration. However, in some cases, the outcomes under IFRS 15 and current IFRS may be similar if a significant portion of the estimated revenue is constrained.

5.2.3 Constraining estimates of variable consideration

Before it can include any amount of variable consideration in the transaction price, an entity must consider whether the amount of variable consideration is constrained. The Board explained in the Basis for Conclusions that it created this constraint on variable consideration to address concerns raised by many constituents that the standard could otherwise require recognition of revenue before there was sufficient certainty that the amounts recognised would faithfully depict the consideration to which an entity expects to be entitled in exchange for the goods or services transferred to a customer. *[IFRS 15.BC203]*.

The IASB explained in the Basis for Conclusions that it did not intend to eliminate the use of estimates from the revenue recognition standard. Instead, it wanted to make sure the estimates are robust and result in useful information. *[IFRS 15.BC204]*. Following this objective, the Board concluded that it was appropriate to include estimates of variable consideration in revenue only when an entity has a 'high degree of confidence' that revenue will not be reversed in a subsequent reporting period. Therefore, the constraint is aimed at preventing the over-recognition of revenue (i.e. the standard focuses on potential significant reversals of revenue). The standard requires an entity to include in the transaction price some or all of an amount of variable consideration estimated only to the extent that it is highly probable that a significant reversal in the amount of cumulative revenue recognised will not occur when the uncertainty associated with the variable consideration is subsequently resolved. *[IFRS 15.56]*.

In making this assessment, an entity is required to consider both the likelihood and the magnitude of the revenue reversal. The standard includes factors that could increase the likelihood or the magnitude of a revenue reversal. These include, but are not limited to, any of the following: *[IFRS 15.57]*

'(a) the amount of consideration is highly susceptible to factors outside the entity's influence. Those factors may include volatility in a market, the judgement or actions of third parties, weather conditions and a high risk of obsolescence of the promised good or service.

(b) the uncertainty about the amount of consideration is not expected to be resolved for a long period of time.

(c) the entity's experience (or other evidence) with similar types of contracts is limited, or that experience (or other evidence) has limited predictive value.

(d) the entity has a practice of either offering a broad range of price concessions or changing the payment terms and conditions of similar contracts in similar circumstances.

(e) the contract has a large number and broad range of possible consideration amounts.'

The standard does have an exception 'for consideration in the form of a sales or usage-based royalty that is promised in exchange for a licence of intellectual property.' *[IFRS 15.58]*.

To include variable consideration in the estimated transaction price, the entity has to conclude that it is 'highly probable' that a significant revenue reversal will not occur in future periods. For the purpose of this analysis, the meaning of the term 'highly probable' is consistent with the existing definition in IFRS 5 – *Non-current Assets Held for Sale and Discontinued Operations*, i.e. 'significantly more likely than probable'. *[IFRS 5 Appendix A]*. For US GAAP preparers, ASC 606 uses the term 'probable' as the confidence threshold for applying the constraint, rather than 'highly probable', which is defined as 'the future event or events are likely to occur'.[63] However, the meaning of 'probable' under US GAAP is intended to be the same as 'highly probable' under IFRS. *[IFRS 15.BC211]*.

Furthermore, the IASB noted that an entity's analysis to determine whether its estimate of variable consideration should be constrained will largely be qualitative. *[IFRS 15.BC212]*. That is, an entity will need to use judgement to evaluate whether it has met the objective of the constraint (i.e. it is highly probable that a significant revenue reversal will not occur in future periods) considering the factors provided in the standard that increase the probability of a significant revenue reversal.

An entity will need to consider both the likelihood and magnitude of a revenue reversal to apply the constraint.

- *Likelihood* – assessing the likelihood of a future reversal of revenue will require significant judgement. Entities will want to ensure they adequately document the basis for their conclusions. The presence of any one of the indicators cited in the extract above does not necessarily mean that a reversal will occur if the variable consideration is included in the transaction price. The standard includes 'factors', rather than 'criteria', to signal that the list of items to consider is not a checklist for which all items need to be met. In addition, the factors provided are not meant to be an all-inclusive list and entities may consider additional factors that are relevant to their facts and circumstances.
- *Magnitude* – when assessing the probability of a significant revenue reversal, an entity is also required to assess the magnitude of that reversal. The constraint is based on the probability of a reversal of an amount that is 'significant' relative to the cumulative revenue recognised for the contract. When assessing the significance of the potential revenue reversal, the cumulative revenue recognised at the date of the potential reversal includes both fixed and variable consideration and includes revenue recognised from the entire contract, not just the transaction price allocated to a single performance obligation.

There are some types of variable consideration that are frequently included in contracts that have significant uncertainties. It is likely to be more difficult for an entity to assert it is highly probable that these types of estimated amounts will not be subsequently reversed. Examples of the types of variable consideration include the following:

- payments contingent on regulatory approval (e.g. regulatory approval of a new drug);
- long-term commodity supply arrangements that settle based on market prices at the future delivery date; and
- contingency fees based on litigation or regulatory outcomes (e.g. fees based on the positive outcome of litigation or the settlement of claims with government agencies).

When an entity determines that it cannot meet the highly probable threshold if it includes all of the variable consideration in the transaction price, the amount of variable consideration that must be included in the transaction price is limited to the amount that would not result in a significant revenue reversal. That is, an entity is required to include in the transaction price the portion of variable consideration that will not result in a significant revenue reversal when the uncertainty associated with the variable consideration is subsequently resolved.

The standard includes an example in which the application of the constraint limits the amount of variable consideration included in the transaction price and one in which it does not. *[IFRS 15.IE116-IE123]*.

Example 30.28: Price concessions

An entity enters into a contract with a customer, a distributor, on 1 December 20X7. The entity transfers 1,000 products at contract inception for a price stated in the contract of CU100 per product (total consideration is CU100,000). Payment from the customer is due when the customer sells the products to the end customers. The entity's customer generally sells the products within 90 days of obtaining them. Control of the products transfers to the customer on 1 December 20X7.

On the basis of its past practices and to maintain its relationship with the customer, the entity anticipates granting a price concession to its customer because this will enable the customer to discount the product and thereby move the product through the distribution chain. Consequently, the consideration in the contract is variable.

Case A – Estimate of variable consideration is not constrained

The entity has significant experience selling this and similar products. The observable data indicate that historically the entity grants a price concession of approximately 20 per cent of the sales price for these products. Current market information suggests that a 20 per cent reduction in price will be sufficient to move the products through the distribution chain. The entity has not granted a price concession significantly greater than 20 per cent in many years.

To estimate the variable consideration to which the entity will be entitled, the entity decides to use the expected value method (see paragraph 53(a) of IFRS 15) because it is the method that the entity expects to better predict the amount of consideration to which it will be entitled. Using the expected value method, the entity estimates the transaction price to be CU80,000 (CU80 × 1,000 products).

The entity also considers the requirements in paragraphs 56–58 of IFRS 15 on constraining estimates of variable consideration to determine whether the estimated amount of variable consideration of CU80,000 can be included in the transaction price. The entity considers the factors in paragraph 57 of IFRS 15 and determines that it has significant previous experience with this product and current market information that supports its estimate. In addition, despite some uncertainty resulting from factors outside its influence, based on its current market estimates, the entity expects the price to be resolved within a short time frame. Thus, the entity concludes that it is highly probable that a significant reversal in the cumulative amount of revenue recognised (i.e. CU80,000) will not occur when the uncertainty is resolved (i.e. when the total amount of price concessions is determined). Consequently, the entity recognises CU80,000 as revenue when the products are transferred on 1 December 20X7.

Case B – Estimate of variable consideration is constrained

The entity has experience selling similar products. However, the entity's products have a high risk of obsolescence and the entity is experiencing high volatility in the pricing of its products. The observable data indicate that historically the entity grants a broad range of price concessions ranging from 20–60 per cent of the sales price for similar products. Current market information also suggests that a 15–50 per cent reduction in price may be necessary to move the products through the distribution chain.

To estimate the variable consideration to which the entity will be entitled, the entity decides to use the expected value method (see paragraph 53(a) of IFRS 15) because it is the method that the entity expects to better predict the amount of consideration to which it will be entitled. Using the expected value method, the entity estimates that a discount of 40 per cent will be provided and, therefore, the estimate of the variable consideration is CU60,000 (CU60 × 1,000 products).

The entity also considers the requirements in paragraphs 56–58 of IFRS 15 on constraining estimates of variable consideration to determine whether some or all of the estimated amount of variable consideration of CU60,000 can be included in the transaction price. The entity considers the factors in paragraph 57 of IFRS 15 and observes that the amount of consideration is highly susceptible to factors outside the entity's influence (i.e. risk of obsolescence) and it is likely that the entity may be required to provide a broad range of price concessions to move the products through the distribution chain. Consequently, the entity cannot include its estimate of CU60,000 (i.e. a discount of 40 per cent) in the transaction price because it cannot conclude that it is highly probable that a significant reversal in the amount of cumulative revenue recognised will not occur. Although the entity's historical price concessions have ranged from 20–60 per cent, market information currently suggests that a price concession of 15–50 per cent will be necessary. The entity's actual results have been consistent with then-current market information in previous, similar transactions. Consequently, the entity concludes that it is highly probable that a significant reversal in the cumulative amount of revenue recognised will not occur if the entity includes CU50,000 in the transaction price (CU100 sales price and a 50 per cent price concession) and therefore, recognises revenue at that amount. Therefore, the entity recognises revenue of CU50,000 when the products are transferred and reassesses the estimates of the transaction price at each reporting date until the uncertainty is resolved in accordance with paragraph 59 of IFRS 15.

In some situations, it will be appropriate for an entity to include in the transaction price an estimate of variable consideration that is not a possible outcome of an individual contract. The TRG discussed this topic using the following example from the TRG agenda paper.

Example 30.29: Estimating variable consideration using the expected value method[64]

Entity A develops websites for customers. The contracts include similar terms and conditions and contain a fixed fee, plus variable consideration for a performance bonus related to the timing of Entity A completing the website. Based on Entity A's historical experience, the bonus amounts and associated probabilities for achieving each bonus are as follows:

Bonus amount	Probability of outcome
–	15%
CU50	40%
CU100	45%

Analysis

Entity A determines that using the expected value method would better predict the amount of consideration to which it will be entitled than using the most likely amount method because it has a large number of contracts that have characteristics that are similar to the new contract.

Under the expected value method, Entity A estimates variable consideration of CU65,000 [(0 × 15%) + (50,000 × 40%) + (100,000 × 45%)]. Entity A must then consider the effect of applying the constraint on variable consideration. To do this, Entity A considers the factors that could increase the likelihood of a revenue reversal in paragraph 57 of IFRS 15 and concludes that it has relevant historical experience with similar types of contracts and that the amount of consideration is not highly susceptible to factors outside of its influence.

In determining whether the entity would include CU50,000 or CU65,000 in the transaction price, TRG members generally agreed that when an entity has concluded that the expected value approach is the appropriate method to estimate variable consideration, the constraint is also applied based on the expected value method. That is, the entity is not required to switch from an expected value method to a most likely amount for purposes of applying the constraint. As a result, if an entity applies the expected value method for a particular contract, the estimated transaction price may not be a possible outcome in an individual contract. Therefore, the entity could conclude that, in this example, CU65,000 is the appropriate estimate of variable consideration to include in the transaction price. It is important to note that in this example, the entity had concluded that none of the factors in paragraph 57 of IFRS 15 or any other factors indicate a likelihood of a significant revenue reversal.

When an entity uses the expected value method and determines that the estimated amount of variable consideration is not a possible outcome in the individual contract, the entity must still consider the constraint on variable consideration. Depending on the facts and circumstances of each contract, an entity may need to constrain its estimate of variable consideration, even though it has used an expected value method, if the factors in paragraph 57 of IFRS 15 indicate a likelihood of a significant revenue reversal. However, using the expected value method and considering probability-weighted amounts sometimes achieves the objective of the constraint on variable consideration. When an entity estimates the transaction price using the expected value method, the entity reduces the probability of a revenue reversal because the estimate does not include all of the potential consideration due to the probability weighting of the outcomes. In some cases, the entity may not need to constrain the estimate of variable consideration if the factors in paragraph 57 of IFRS 15 do not indicate a likelihood of a significant revenue reversal.

The standard provides the following example of a situation in which a qualitative analysis of the factors in paragraph 57 of IFRS 15 indicates that it is not highly probable that a significant reversal would not occur if an entity includes a performance-based incentive fee in the transaction price of an investment management contract. *[IFRS 15.IE129-IE133]*.

Example 30.30: Management fees subject to the constraint

On 1 January 20X8, an entity enters into a contract with a client to provide asset management services for five years. The entity receives a two per cent quarterly management fee based on the client's assets under management at the end of each quarter. In addition, the entity receives a performance-based incentive fee of 20 per cent of the fund's return in excess of the return of an observable market index over the five-year period. Consequently, both the management fee and the performance fee in the contract are variable consideration.

The entity accounts for the services as a single performance obligation in accordance with paragraph 22(b) of IFRS 15, because it is providing a series of distinct services that are substantially the same and have the same pattern of transfer (the services transfer to the customer over time and use the same method to measure progress – that is, a time-based measure of progress).

At contract inception, the entity considers the requirements in paragraphs 50–54 of IFRS 15 on estimating variable consideration and the requirements in paragraphs 56–58 of IFRS 15 on constraining estimates of variable consideration, including the factors in paragraph 57 of IFRS 15. The entity observes that the promised consideration is dependent on the market and thus is highly susceptible to factors outside the entity's influence. In addition, the incentive fee has a large number and a broad range of possible consideration amounts. The entity also observes that although it has experience with similar contracts, that experience is of little predictive value in determining the future performance of the market. Therefore, at contract inception, the entity cannot conclude that it is highly probable that a significant reversal in the cumulative amount of revenue recognised would not occur if the entity included its estimate of the management fee or the incentive fee in the transaction price.

At each reporting date, the entity updates its estimate of the transaction price. Consequently, at the end of each quarter, the entity concludes that it can include in the transaction price the actual amount of the quarterly management fee because the uncertainty is resolved. However, the entity concludes that it cannot include its estimate of the incentive fee in the transaction price at those dates. This is because there has not been a change in its assessment from contract inception – the variability of the fee based on the market index indicates that the entity cannot conclude that it is highly probable that a significant reversal in the cumulative amount of revenue recognised would not occur if the entity included its estimate of the incentive fee in the transaction price. At 31 March 20X8, the client's assets under management are CU100 million. Therefore, the resulting quarterly management fee and the transaction price is CU2 million.

At the end of each quarter, the entity allocates the quarterly management fee to the distinct services provided during the quarter in accordance with paragraphs 84(b) and 85 of IFRS 15. This is because the fee relates specifically to the entity's efforts to transfer the services for that quarter, which are distinct from the services provided in other quarters, and the resulting allocation will be consistent with the allocation objective in paragraph 73 of IFRS 15. Consequently, the entity recognises CU2 million as revenue for the quarter ended 31 March 20X8.

See 6 below for a discussion of allocating the transaction price.

We anticipate that questions will arise involving the application of the constraint on variable consideration to specific fact patterns, including the determination of when it is highly probable that a significant revenue reversal would not occur. The constraint is a new way of evaluating variable consideration and it applies to all types of variable consideration in all transactions. However, there are specific requirements for sales-based or usage-based royalties associated with a licence of intellectual property that constrain the recognition of those royalties, which may result in a similar outcome to fully constraining the estimate of those royalties.

For a number of entities, the treatment of variable consideration under the new standard could represent a significant change from current practice.

Under current IFRS, preparers often defer measurement of variable consideration until revenue is reliably measurable, which could be when the uncertainty is removed or when payment is received.

Furthermore, current IFRS permits recognition of contingent consideration, but only if it is probable that the economic benefits associated with the transaction will flow to the entity and the amount of revenue can be reliably measured. *[IAS 18.14, 18, IAS 11.11]*. Some entities, therefore, defer recognition until the contingency is resolved.

Some entities have looked to US GAAP to develop their accounting policies in this area. Currently, US GAAP has various requirements and thresholds for recognising variable consideration. As a result, the accounting treatment varies depending on which US GAAP standard is applied to a transaction. For example, the revenue recognition requirements in ASC 605-25 limit the recognition of contingent consideration when the amounts depend on the future performance of the entity and SAB Topic 13 requires that the transaction price be fixed or determinable in order to recognise revenue.[65]

In contrast, the constraint on variable consideration in the new standard is an entirely new way of evaluating variable consideration and is applicable to all types of variable consideration in all transactions. As a result, depending on the requirements entities were previously applying, some entities may recognise revenue sooner under the new standard, while others may recognise revenue later.

5.2.3.A *Applying the constraint on variable consideration: contract level versus performance obligation level*

At the January 2015 TRG meeting, the TRG members were asked whether an entity was required to apply the constraint on variable consideration at the contract level or at the performance obligation level.

The TRG members generally agreed that the constraint would be applied at the contract level and not at the performance obligation level. That is, the significance assessment of the potential revenue reversal would consider the total transaction price of the contract (and not the portion of transaction price allocated to a performance obligation).[66]

Stakeholders raised this question because the standard refers to 'cumulative revenue recognised' without specifying the level at which this assessment would be performed (i.e. at the contract level or performance obligation level). Furthermore, the Basis for Conclusions could be read to indicate that the assessment should occur in relation to the cumulative revenue recognised for a performance obligation. *[IFRS 15.BC217]*.

5.2.3.B *Do the variable consideration requirements (including application of the constraint) apply to all types of variable consideration?*

The requirements for variable consideration apply to all types of variable consideration. However, there are specific requirements for sales-based or usage-based royalties associated with a licence of intellectual property that constrain the recognition of those royalties, which may result in a similar outcome to fully constraining the estimate of those royalties. Such royalties are not recognised as revenue until the later of when:

(1) the subsequent sales or usage occurs; or

(2) the performance obligation, to which some or all of the sales-based or usage-based royalty has been allocated, has been satisfied (or partially satisfied), as discussed further at 8.5 below.

5.2.3.C *Would an entity be required to follow a two-step approach to estimate variable consideration?*

The Board noted in the Basis for Conclusions that an entity is not required to strictly follow a two-step process (i.e. first estimate the variable consideration and then apply the constraint to that estimate) if its internal processes incorporate the principles of both steps in a single step. *[IFRS 15.BC215]*. For example, if an entity already has a single process to estimate expected returns when calculating revenue from the sale of goods in a manner consistent with the objectives of applying the constraint, the entity would not need to estimate the transaction price and then separately apply the constraint.

A TRG agenda paper also noted that applying the expected value method, which requires an entity to consider probability-weighted amounts, may sometimes achieve the objective of the constraint on variable consideration.[67] That is, in developing its estimate of the transaction price in accordance with the expected value method, an entity reduces the probability of a revenue reversal and may not need to further constrain its estimate of variable consideration. However, to meet the objective of the constraint, the entity's estimated transaction price would need to incorporate its expectations of the possible consideration amounts (e.g. products not expected to be returned) at a level at which it is highly probable that including the estimate of variable consideration in the transaction price would not result in a significant revenue reversal (e.g. such that it is highly probable that additional returns above the estimated amount would not result in a significant reversal).

5.2.4 Reassessment of variable consideration

The standard specifies that at the end of each reporting period, an entity must 'update the estimated transaction price (including updating its assessment of whether an estimate of variable consideration is constrained) to represent faithfully the circumstances present at the end of the reporting period and the changes in circumstances during the reporting period.' The entity accounts for changes in the transaction price in accordance with paragraphs 87–90 of IFRS 15. *[IFRS 15.59]*.

When a contract includes variable consideration, an entity will need to update its estimate of the transaction price throughout the term of the contract to depict conditions that exist at the end of each reporting period. This will involve updating the estimate of the variable consideration (including any amounts that are constrained) to reflect an entity's revised expectations about the amount of consideration to which it expects to be entitled, considering uncertainties that are resolved or new information that is gained about remaining uncertainties. See 6.5 below for a discussion of allocating changes in the transaction price after contract inception.

5.3 Refund liabilities

An entity may receive consideration that it will need to refund to the customer in the future because the consideration is not an amount to which the entity ultimately will be entitled under the contract. If an entity expects to refund some or all of that consideration, the amounts received (or receivable) will need to be recorded as refund liabilities.

A refund liability is measured 'at the amount of consideration received (or receivable) for which the entity does not expect to be entitled (i.e. amounts not included in the transaction price).' The refund liability (and corresponding change in the transaction price) is updated at the end of each reporting period for changes in circumstances. The standard also notes that, if a refund liability relates to a sale with a right of return, an entity applies the specific application guidance for sales with a right of return. *[IFRS 15.55]*.

While the most common form of refund liabilities may be related to sales with a right of return, the refund liability requirements also apply when an entity expects that it will need to refund consideration received due to poor customer satisfaction with a service provided (i.e. there was no good delivered or returned) and/or if an entity expects to have to provide retrospective price reductions to a customer (e.g. if a customer reaches a certain threshold of purchases, the unit price will be retrospectively adjusted). For a discussion of the accounting for sales with a right of return, see 5.4.1 below. We address the question of whether a refund liability is a contract liability (and, therefore, subject to the presentation and disclosure requirements of a contract liability) at 10.1.1.D below.

5.4 Accounting for specific types of variable consideration

5.4.1 Rights of return

The standard notes that, in some contracts, an entity may transfer control of a product to a customer, but grant the customer the right to return. In return, the customer may receive a full or partial refund of any consideration paid; a credit that can be applied against amounts owed, or that will be owed, to the entity; another product in exchange; or any combination thereof. *[IFRS 15.B20]*. As discussed at 4.7 above, the standard states that a right of return does not represent a separate performance obligation. *[IFRS 15.B22]*. Instead, a right of return affects the transaction price and the amount of revenue an entity can recognise for satisfied performance obligations. In other words, rights of return create variability in the transaction price.

Under IFRS 15, rights of return do not include exchanges by customers of one product for another of the same type, quality, condition and price (e.g. one colour or size for another). *[IFRS 15.B26]*. Nor do rights of return include situations where a customer may return a defective product in exchange for a functioning product; these are, instead, evaluated in accordance with the warranties application guidance on warranties (see 9.1 below). *[IFRS 15.B27]*.

'To account for the transfer of products with a right of return (and for some services that are provided subject to a refund), an entity shall recognise all of the following:

(a) revenue for the transferred products in the amount of consideration to which the entity expects to be entitled (therefore, revenue would not be recognised for the products expected to be returned);

(b) a refund liability; and

(c) an asset (and corresponding adjustment to cost of sales) for its right to recover products from customers on settling the refund liability.' *[IFRS 15.B21]*.

Under the standard, an entity will estimate the transaction price and apply the constraint to the estimated transaction price to determine the amount of consideration to which the entity expects to be entitled. In doing so, it will consider the products expected to be returned in order to determine the amount to which the entity expects to be entitled (excluding consideration for the products expected to be returned). The entity will recognise revenue based on the amount to which it expects to be entitled through to the end of the return period (considering expected product returns). An entity will not recognise the portion of the revenue subject to the constraint until the amount is no longer constrained, which could be at the end of the return period. The entity will recognise the amount received or receivable that is expected to be returned as a refund liability, representing its obligation to return the customer's consideration (see 5.3 above). Subsequently, at the end of each reporting period, the entity updates its assessment of amounts for which it expects to be entitled and make a corresponding change to the transaction price (and, therefore, to the amount of revenue recognised). *[IFRS 15.B23]*.

As part of updating its estimate, an entity must update its assessment of expected returns and the related refund liabilities. *[IFRS 15.B24]*. This remeasurement is performed at the end of each reporting period and reflects any changes in assumptions about expected returns. Any adjustments made to the estimate will result in a corresponding adjustment to amounts recognised as revenue for the satisfied performance obligations (e.g. if the entity expects the number of returns to be lower than originally estimated, it would have to increase the amount of revenue recognised and decrease the refund liability). *[IFRS 15.B23, B24]*.

Finally, when customers exercise their rights of return, the entity may receive the returned product in a saleable or repairable condition. Under the standard, at the time of the initial sale (i.e. when recognition of revenue is deferred due to the anticipated return), the entity recognises a return asset (and adjusts the cost of goods sold) for its right to recover the goods returned by the customer. *[IFRS 15.B21]*. The entity initially measures this asset at the former carrying amount of the inventory, less any expected costs to recover the goods, including any potential decreases in the value of the returned goods. Along with remeasuring the refund liability at the end of each reporting period, the entity updates the measurement of the asset recorded for any revisions to its expected level of returns, as well as any additional decreases in the value of the returned products. *[IFRS 15.B25]*.

IFRS 15 requires the carrying value of the return asset to be presented separately from inventory and to be subject to impairment testing on its own, separately from inventory on hand. The standard also requires the refund liability to be presented separately from the corresponding asset (on a gross basis, rather than a net basis). *[IFRS 15.B25]*.

The standard provides the following example of rights of return. *[IFRS 15.IE110-IE115]*.

Example 30.31: Right of return

An entity enters into 100 contracts with customers. Each contract includes the sale of one product for CU100 (100 total products × CU100 = CU10,000 total consideration). Cash is received when control of a product transfers. The entity's customary business practice is to allow a customer to return any unused product within 30 days and receive a full refund. The entity's cost of each product is CU60.

The entity applies the requirements in IFRS 15 to the portfolio of 100 contracts because it reasonably expects that, in accordance with paragraph 4, the effects on the financial statements from applying these requirements to the portfolio would not differ materially from applying the requirements to the individual contracts within the portfolio.

Because the contract allows a customer to return the products, the consideration received from the customer is variable. To estimate the variable consideration to which the entity will be entitled, the entity decides to use the expected value method (see paragraph 53(a) of IFRS 15) because it is the method that the entity expects to better predict the amount of consideration to which it will be entitled. Using the expected value method, the entity estimates that 97 products will not be returned.

The entity also considers the requirements in paragraphs 56-58 of IFRS 15 on constraining estimates of variable consideration to determine whether the estimated amount of variable consideration of CU9,700 (CU100 × 97 products not expected to be returned) can be included in the transaction price. The entity considers the factors in paragraph 57 of IFRS 15 and determines that although the returns are outside the entity's influence, it has significant experience in estimating returns for this product and customer class. In addition, the uncertainty will be resolved within a short time frame (i.e. the 30-day return period). Thus, the entity concludes that it is highly probable that a significant reversal in the cumulative amount of revenue recognised (i.e. CU9,700) will not occur as the uncertainty is resolved (i.e. over the return period).

The entity estimates that the costs of recovering the products will be immaterial and expects that the returned products can be resold at a profit.

Upon transfer of control of the 100 products, the entity does not recognise revenue for the three products that it expects to be returned. Consequently, in accordance with paragraphs 55 and B21 of IFRS 15, the entity recognises the following:

- revenue of CU9,700 (CU100 × 97 products not expected to be returned);
- a refund liability of CU300 (CU100 refund × 3 products expected to be returned); and
- an asset of CU180 (CU60 × 3 products for its right to recover products from customers on settling the refund liability).

While IFRS 15's accounting treatment for rights of return may not significantly change current practice, there are some notable differences. Under IFRS 15, an entity will estimate the transaction price and apply the constraint to the estimated transaction price. In doing so, it will consider the products expected to be returned in order to determine the amount to which the entity expects to be entitled (excluding the products expected to be returned). *[IFRS 15.B23]*.

Consistent with paragraph 17 of IAS 18, an entity will recognise the amount of expected returns as a refund liability, representing its obligation to return the customer's consideration. *[IFRS 15.B21, IAS 18.17]*. If the entity estimates returns and applies the constraint, the portion of the revenue that is subject to the constraint will not be recognised until the amounts are no longer constrained, which could be at the end of the return period.

The classification in the statement of financial position for amounts related to the right of return asset may be a change from current practice. Under current IFRS, an entity typically recognises a liability and corresponding expense, but may not recognise a return asset for the inventory that may be returned, as is required by IFRS 15. In addition, IFRS 15 is clear that the carrying value of the return asset (i.e. the product expected to be returned) is subject to impairment testing on its own, separately from inventory on hand. IFRS 15 also requires the refund liability to be presented separately from the corresponding asset (on a gross basis, rather than a net basis).

The topic of product sales with rights of return is one that has not received as much attention as other topics for a variety of reasons. However, the changes in this area (primarily treating the right of return as a type of variable consideration to which the variable consideration requirements apply, including the constraint) may affect manufacturers and retailers that, otherwise, would not be significantly affected by IFRS 15. Entities will need to assess whether their current methods for estimating returns are appropriate, given the need to consider the constraint.

See 7.4.2.A for a discussion on whether a conditional call option held by an entity to remove and replace expired products (e.g. out-of-date perishable goods, expired medicine) prevents a customer from obtaining control of the products or is akin to a right of return.

5.4.1.A Is an entity applying the portfolio approach practical expedient when accounting for rights of return?

An entity can, but would not be required to, apply the portfolio approach practical expedient to estimate variable consideration for expected returns using the expected value method. Similar to the discussion at 5.2.2 above on estimating variable consideration, the July 2015 TRG agenda paper noted that an entity can consider evidence from other, similar contracts to develop an estimate of variable consideration using the expected value method without applying the portfolio approach practical expedient. In order to estimate variable consideration in a contract, an entity frequently will make judgements considering its historical experience with other, similar contracts. Considering historical experience does not necessarily mean the entity is applying the portfolio approach practical expedient.[68]

This question arises, in part, because Example 22 in IFRS 15 (see Example 30.31 at 5.4.1 above) states that the entity is using the portfolio approach practical expedient in paragraph 4 of IFRS 15 to calculate its estimate of returns. Use of this practical expedient requires an entity to assert that it does not expect the use of the expedient to differ materially from applying the standard to an individual contract.

We expect that entities will often use the expected value method to estimate variable consideration related to returns because doing so would likely better predict the amount of consideration to which the entities will be entitled. This is despite the fact that there are two potential outcomes for each contract from the variability of product returns: the product either will be returned or will not be returned. That is, the revenue for each contract ultimately either will be 100% or will be 0% of the total contract value (assuming returns create the only variability in the contract). However, entities may conclude that the expected value is the appropriate method for estimating variable consideration because they have a large number of contracts with similar characteristics. The TRG agenda paper noted that using a portfolio of data is not equivalent to using the portfolio approach practical expedient, so entities that use the expected value method to estimate variable consideration for returns would not be required to assert that the outcome from the portfolio is not expected to materially differ from an assessment of individual contracts.

5.4.1.B *Accounting for restocking fees for goods that are expected to be returned*

Entities sometimes charge customers a 'restocking fee' when a product is returned. This fee may be levied by entities to compensate them for the costs of repackaging, shipping and/or reselling the item at a lower price to another customer. Stakeholders had raised questions about how to account for restocking fees and related costs.[69]

At the July 2015 TRG meeting, the TRG members generally agreed that restocking fees for goods that are expected to be returned would be included in the estimate of the transaction price at contract inception and recorded as revenue when (or as) control of the good transfers.

For example, assume that an entity enters into a contract with a customer to sell 10 widgets for CU100 each. The customer has the right to return the widgets, but if it does so, it will be charged a 10% restocking fee (or CU10 per returned widget). The entity estimates that 10% of all widgets that are sold will be returned. Upon transfer of control of the 10 widgets, the entity will recognise revenue of CU910 [(9 widgets not expected to be returned × CU100 selling price) + (1 widget expected to be returned × CU10 restocking fee)]. A refund liability of CU90 will also be recorded [1 widget expected to be returned × (CU100 selling price – CU10 restocking fee)].

5.4.1.C Accounting for restocking costs for goods that are expected to be returned

At the July 2015 TRG meeting, the TRG members generally agreed that restocking costs (e.g. shipping and repackaging costs) would be recorded as a reduction of the amount of the return asset when (or as) control of the good transfers. This accounting treatment will be consistent with the new revenue standard's requirement that the returned asset be initially measured at the former carrying amount of the inventory, less any expected costs to recover the goods (e.g. restocking costs).[70]

5.4.2 Sales-based and usage-based royalties on licences of intellectual property

The standard provides explicit application guidance for recognising consideration from sales and usage-based royalties provided in exchange for licences of intellectual property. The standard states that an entity recognises sales and usage-based royalties as revenue only at the later of when:

(1) the subsequent sales or usage occurs; or

(2) the performance obligation, to which some or all of the sales-based or usage-based royalty has been allocated, has been satisfied (or partially satisfied). *[IFRS 15.B63]*.

In many cases, this application guidance will result in the same pattern of revenue recognition as fully constraining the estimate of variable consideration associated with the future royalty stream. See 8.5 below for further discussion about the sales-based and usage-based royalty exception on licences of intellectual property.

5.5 Significant financing component

For some transactions, the receipt of the consideration does not match the timing of the transfer of goods or services to the customer (e.g. the consideration is prepaid or is paid after the services are provided). When the customer pays in arrears, the entity is effectively providing financing to the customer. Conversely, when the customer pays in advance, the entity has effectively received financing from the customer.

IFRS 15 states that 'in determining the transaction price, an entity shall adjust the promised amount of consideration for the effects of the time value of money if the timing of payments agreed to by the parties to the contract (either explicitly or implicitly) provides the customer or the entity with a significant benefit of financing the transfer of goods or services to the customer. In those circumstances, the contract contains a significant financing component. A significant financing component may exist regardless of whether the promise of financing is explicitly stated in the contract or implied by the payment terms agreed to by the parties to the contract.' *[IFRS 15.60]*.

The standard goes on to clarify that 'the objective when adjusting the promised amount of consideration for a significant financing component is for an entity to recognise revenue at an amount that reflects the price that a customer would have paid for the promised goods or services if the customer had paid cash for those goods or services when (or as) they transfer to the customer (i.e. the cash selling price). An entity shall consider all relevant facts and circumstances in assessing whether a contract contains a financing component and whether that financing component is significant to the contract, including both of the following:

(a) the difference, if any, between the amount of promised consideration and the cash selling price of the promised goods or services; and

(b) the combined effect of both of the following:

 (i) the expected length of time between when the entity transfers the promised goods or services to the customer and when the customer pays for those goods or services; and

 (ii) the prevailing interest rates in the relevant market.' *[IFRS 15.61]*

Notwithstanding this assessment, a contract with a customer would not have a significant financing component if any of the following factors exist: *[IFRS 15.62]*

- the customer paid for the goods or services in advance and the timing of the transfer of those goods or services is at the discretion of the customer;
- a substantial amount of the consideration promised by the customer is variable and the amount or timing of that consideration varies on the basis of the occurrence or non-occurrence of a future event that is not substantially within the control of the customer or the entity (e.g. if the consideration is a sales-based royalty); or
- the difference between the promised consideration and the cash selling price of the good or service (as described in (a) above) arises for reasons other than the provision of finance to either the customer or the entity, and the difference between those amounts is proportional to the reason for the difference. For example, the payment terms might provide the entity or the customer with protection from the other party failing to adequately complete some or all of its obligations under the contract.

This assessment may be difficult in some circumstances, so the Board provided a practical expedient. An entity 'need not adjust the promised amount of consideration for the effects of a significant financing component if the entity expects, at contract inception, that the period between when the entity transfers a promised good or service to a customer and when the customer pays for that good or service will be one year or less.' *[IFRS 15.63]*.

When an entity concludes that a financing component is significant to a contract, it determines the transaction price by discounting the amount of promised consideration. The entity uses the same discount rate that it would use if it were to enter into a separate financing transaction with the customer at contract inception. The discount rate has to reflect the credit characteristics of the borrower in the contract, as well as any collateral or security provided by the customer or the entity, including assets transferred in the contract. The standard notes that an entity 'may be able to determine that rate by identifying the rate that discounts the nominal amount of the promised consideration to the price that the customer would pay in cash for the goods or services when (or as) they transfer to the customer.'

The entity does not update the discount rate for changes in circumstances or interest rates after contract inception. *[IFRS 15.64]*.

The Board explained in the Basis for Conclusions that, conceptually, a contract that includes a financing component is comprised of two transactions – one for the sale of goods and/or services and one for the financing. *[IFRS 15.BC229]*. Accordingly, the Board decided to only require entities to adjust the amount of promised consideration for the effects of financing if the timing of payments specified in the contract provides the customer or the entity with a significant benefit of financing. The IASB's objective in requiring entities to adjust the promised amount of consideration for the effects of a significant financing component is for entities to recognise as revenue the 'cash selling price' of the underlying goods or services at the time of transfer. *[IFRS 15.BC230]*.

However, an entity is not required to adjust the promised amount of consideration for the effects of a significant financing component if the entity expects, at contract inception, that the period between when the entity transfers a promised good or service to a customer and when the customer pays for that good or service will be one year or less. The Board added this practical expedient to the standard because it simplifies the application of this aspect of IFRS 15 and because the effect of accounting for a significant financing component (or of not doing so) should be limited in financing arrangements with a duration of less than 12 months. *[IFRS 15.BC236]*. If an entity uses this practical expedient, it would apply the expedient consistently to similar contracts in similar circumstances. *[IFRS 15.BC235]*.

Entities may need to apply judgement to determine whether the practical expedient applies to some contracts. For example, the standard does not specify whether entities should assess the period between payment and performance at the contract level or at the performance obligation level. In addition, the TRG discussed how an entity should consider whether the practical expedient applies to contracts with a single payment stream for multiple performance obligations. See 5.5.2.D below.

Absent the use of the practical expedient, to determine whether a significant financing component exists, an entity will need to consider all relevant facts and circumstances, including:

(1) the difference between the cash selling price and the amount of promised consideration for the promised goods or services; and

(2) the combined effect of the expected length of time between the transfer of the goods or services and the receipt of consideration and the prevailing market interest rates. The Board acknowledged that a difference in the timing between the transfer of and payment for goods and services is not determinative, but the combined effect of timing and the prevailing interest rates may provide a strong indication that an entity is providing or receiving a significant benefit of financing. *[IFRS 15.BC232]*.

Even if conditions in a contract would otherwise indicate that a significant financing component exists, the standard includes several situations that the Board has determined do not provide the customer or the entity with a significant benefit of financing. These situations, as described in paragraph 62 of IFRS 15, include the following:

- The customer has paid for the goods or services in advance and the timing of the transfer of those goods or services is at the discretion of the customer. In these situations (e.g. prepaid phone cards, customer loyalty programmes), the Board noted in the Basis for Conclusions that the payment terms are not related to a financing arrangement between the parties and the costs of requiring an entity to account for a significant financing component would outweigh the benefits because an entity would need to continually estimate when the goods or services will transfer to the customer. *[IFRS 15.BC233]*.
- A substantial amount of the consideration promised by the customer is variable and is based on factors outside the control of the customer or entity. In these situations, the Board noted in the Basis for Conclusions that the primary purpose of the timing or terms of payment may be to allow for the resolution of uncertainties that relate to the consideration, rather than to provide the customer or the entity with the significant benefit of financing. In addition, the terms or timing of payment in these situations may be to provide the parties with assurance of the value of the goods or services (e.g. an arrangement for which consideration is in the form of a sales-based royalty). *[IFRS 15.BC233]*.
- The difference between the promised consideration and the cash selling price of the good or service arises for reasons other than the provision of financing to either the customer or the entity (e.g. a payment is made in advance or in arrears in accordance with the typical payment terms of the industry or jurisdiction). In certain situations, the Board determined the purpose of the payment terms may be to provide the customer with assurance that the entity will complete its obligations under the contract, rather than to provide financing to the customer or the entity. Examples include a customer withholding a portion of the consideration until the contract is complete (illustrated in Example 30.33 at 5.5.1 below) or a milestone is reached, or an entity requiring a customer to pay a portion of the consideration upfront in order to secure a future supply of goods or services. See 5.5.2.A below for further discussion.

As explained in the Basis for Conclusions, the Board decided not to provide an overall exemption from accounting for the effects of a significant financing component arising from advance payments. This is because ignoring the effects of advance payments may skew the amount and timing of revenue recognised if the advance payment is significant and the purpose of the payment is to provide the entity with financing. *[IFRS 15.BC238]*. For example, an entity may require a customer to make advance payments in order to avoid obtaining the financing from a third party. If the entity obtained third-party financing, it would likely charge the customer additional amounts in order to cover the finance costs incurred. The Board decided that an entity's revenue should be consistent regardless of whether it receives the significant financing benefit from a customer or from a third party because, in either scenario, the entity's performance is the same.

In order to conclude that an advance payment does not represent a significant financing component, we believe that an entity will need to support why the advance payment does not provide a significant financing benefit and describe its substantive business purpose.[71] As a result, it is important that entities analyse all of the relevant facts and circumstances. Example 30.35 at 5.5.1 below illustrates an entity's determination that a customer's advance payment represents a significant financing component. Example 30.36 at 5.5.1 below illustrates an entity's determination that a customer's advance payment does not represent a significant financing component.

The assessment of significance is made at the individual contract level. As noted in the Basis for Conclusions, the Board decided that it would be an undue burden to require an entity to account for a financing component if the effects of the financing component are not significant to the individual contract, but the combined effects of the financing components for a portfolio of similar contracts would be material to the entity as a whole. *[IFRS 15.BC234]*.

When an entity concludes that a financing component is significant to a contract, in accordance with paragraph 64 of IFRS 15, it determines the transaction price by applying an interest rate to the amount of promised consideration. The entity uses the same interest rate that it would use if it were to enter into a separate financing transaction with the customer. The interest rate needs to reflect the credit characteristics of the borrower in the contract, which could be the entity or the customer, depending on who receives the financing. Using the risk-free rate or a rate explicitly stated in the contract that does not correspond with a separate financing rate would not be acceptable. *[IFRS 15.BC239]*. While not explicitly stated in the standard, we believe an entity would consider the expected term of the financing when determining the interest rate in light of current market conditions at contract inception. In addition, paragraph 64 of IFRS 15 is clear that an entity does not update the interest rate for changes in circumstances or market interest rates after contract inception.

The standard requires that the interest rate be a rate similar to that the entity would have used in a separate financing transaction with the customer. Because most entities are not in the business of entering into free-standing financing arrangements with their customers, they may find it difficult to identify an appropriate rate. However, most entities perform some level of credit analysis before financing purchases for a customer, so they will likely have some information about the customer's credit risk. For entities that have different pricing for products depending on the time of payment (e.g. cash discounts), the standard indicates that the appropriate interest rate, in some cases, could be determined by identifying the rate that discounts the nominal amount of the promised consideration to the cash sales price of the good or service.

Entities will likely have to exercise significant judgement to determine whether a significant financing component exists when there is more than one year between the transfer of goods or services and the receipt of contract consideration. Entities should consider sufficiently documenting their analyses to support their conclusions.

5.5.1 Examples of significant financing components

The standard includes the following examples to illustrate these concepts. Example 30.32 illustrates a contract that contains a significant financing component because the cash selling price differs from the promised amount of consideration and there are no other factors present that would indicate that this difference arises for reasons other than financing. In this example, the contract also contains an implicit interest rate that is determined to be commensurate with the rate that would be reflected in a separate financing transaction between the entity and its customer at contract inception, as follows. *[IFRS 15.IE135-IE140]*.

Example 30.32: Significant financing component and right of return

An entity sells a product to a customer for CU121 that is payable 24 months after delivery. The customer obtains control of the product at contract inception. The contract permits the customer to return the product within 90 days. The product is new and the entity has no relevant historical evidence of product returns or other available market evidence.

The cash selling price of the product is CU100, which represents the amount that the customer would pay upon delivery for the same product sold under otherwise identical terms and conditions as at contract inception. The entity's cost of the product is CU80.

The entity does not recognise revenue when control of the product transfers to the customer. This is because the existence of the right of return and the lack of relevant historical evidence means that the entity cannot conclude that it is highly probable that a significant reversal in the amount of cumulative revenue recognised will not occur in accordance with paragraphs 56-58 of IFRS 15. Consequently, revenue is recognised after three months when the right of return lapses.

The contract includes a significant financing component, in accordance with paragraphs 60-62 of IFRS 15. This is evident from the difference between the amount of promised consideration of CU121 and the cash selling price of CU100 at the date that the goods are transferred to the customer.

The contract includes an implicit interest rate of 10 per cent (i.e. the interest rate that over 24 months discounts the promised consideration of CU121 to the cash selling price of CU100). The entity evaluates the rate and concludes that it is commensurate with the rate that would be reflected in a separate financing transaction between the entity and its customer at contract inception. The following journal entries illustrate how the entity accounts for this contract in accordance with paragraphs B20-B27 of IFRS 15.

- When the product is transferred to the customer, in accordance with paragraph B21 of IFRS 15:

Asset for right to recover product to be returned	CU80(a)	
Inventory		CU80

(a) This example does not consider expected costs to recover the asset.

- During the three-month right of return period, no interest is recognised in accordance with paragraph 65 of IFRS 15 because no contract asset or receivable has been recognised.
- When the right of return lapses (the product is not returned):

Receivable	CU100(a)	
Revenue		CU100
Cost of sales	CU80	
Asset for product to be returned		CU80

(a) The receivable recognised would be measured in accordance with IFRS 9. This example assumes there is no material difference between the fair value of the receivable at contract inception and the fair value of the receivable when it is recognised at the time the right of return lapses. In addition, this example does not consider the impairment accounting for the receivable.

Until the entity receives the cash payment from the customer, interest revenue would be recognised in accordance with IFRS 9. In determining the effective interest rate in accordance with IFRS 9, the entity would consider the remaining contractual term.

In Example 30.33, the difference between the promised consideration and the cash selling price of the good or service arises for reasons other than the provision of financing. In this example, the customer withholds a portion of each payment until the contract is complete in order to protect itself from the entity failing to complete its obligations under the contract, as follows. *[IFRS 15.IE141-IE142]*.

Example 30.33: Withheld payments on a long-term contract

An entity enters into a contract for the construction of a building that includes scheduled milestone payments for the performance by the entity throughout the contract term of three years. The performance obligation will be satisfied over time and the milestone payments are scheduled to coincide with the entity's expected performance. The contract provides that a specified percentage of each milestone payment is to be withheld (i.e. retained) by the customer throughout the arrangement and paid to the entity only when the building is complete.

The entity concludes that the contract does not include a significant financing component. The milestone payments coincide with the entity's performance and the contract requires amounts to be retained for reasons other than the provision of finance in accordance with paragraph 62(c) of IFRS 15. The withholding of a specified percentage of each milestone payment is intended to protect the customer from the contractor failing to adequately complete its obligations under the contract.

Example 30.34 illustrates two situations. *[IFRS 15.IE143-IE147]*. In Case A, a contractual discount rate reflects the rate in a separate financing transaction. In Case B, it does not.

Example 30.34: Determining the discount rate

An entity enters into a contract with a customer to sell equipment. Control of the equipment transfers to the customer when the contract is signed. The price stated in the contract is CU1 million plus a five per cent contractual rate of interest, payable in 60 monthly instalments of CU18,871.

Case A – Contractual discount rate reflects the rate in a separate financing transaction

In evaluating the discount rate in the contract that contains a significant financing component, the entity observes that the five per cent contractual rate of interest reflects the rate that would be used in a separate financing transaction between the entity and its customer at contract inception (i.e. the contractual rate of interest of five per cent reflects the credit characteristics of the customer).

The market terms of the financing mean that the cash selling price of the equipment is CU1 million. This amount is recognised as revenue and as a loan receivable when control of the equipment transfers to the customer. The entity accounts for the receivable in accordance with IFRS 9.

Case B – Contractual discount rate does not reflect the rate in a separate financing transaction

In evaluating the discount rate in the contract that contains a significant financing component, the entity observes that the five per cent contractual rate of interest is significantly lower than the 12 per cent interest rate that would be used in a separate financing transaction between the entity and its customer at contract inception (i.e. the contractual rate of interest of five per cent does not reflect the credit characteristics of the customer). This suggests that the cash selling price is less than CU1 million.

In accordance with paragraph 64 of IFRS 15, the entity determines the transaction price by adjusting the promised amount of consideration to reflect the contractual payments using the 12 per cent interest rate that reflects the credit characteristics of the customer. Consequently, the entity determines that the transaction price is CU848,357 (60 monthly payments of CU18,871 discounted at 12 per cent). The entity recognises revenue and a loan receivable for that amount. The entity accounts for the loan receivable in accordance with IFRS 9.

Example 30.35 illustrates a contract with an advance payment from the customer that the entity concludes represents a significant benefit of financing. It also illustrates a situation in which the implicit interest rate does not reflect the interest rate that would be used in a separate financing transaction between the entity and its customer at contract inception, as follows. *[IFRS 15.IE148-IE151]*.

Example 30.35: Advance payment and assessment of discount rate

An entity enters into a contract with a customer to sell an asset. Control of the asset will transfer to the customer in two years (i.e. the performance obligation will be satisfied at a point in time). The contract includes two alternative payment options: payment of CU5,000 in two years when the customer obtains control of the asset or payment of CU4,000 when the contract is signed. The customer elects to pay CU4,000 when the contract is signed.

The entity concludes that the contract contains a significant financing component because of the length of time between when the customer pays for the asset and when the entity transfers the asset to the customer, as well as the prevailing interest rates in the market.

The interest rate implicit in the transaction is 11.8 per cent, which is the interest rate necessary to make the two alternative payment options economically equivalent. However, the entity determines that, in accordance with paragraph 64 of IFRS 15, the rate to be used in adjusting the promised consideration is six per cent, which is the entity's incremental borrowing rate.

The following journal entries illustrate how the entity would account for the significant financing component:

- recognise a contract liability for the CU4,000 payment received at contract inception:

Cash	CU4,000	
Contract liability		CU4,000

- during the two years from contract inception until the transfer of the asset, the entity adjusts the promised amount of consideration (in accordance with paragraph 65 of IFRS 15) and accretes the contract liability by recognising interest on CU4,000 at six per cent for two years:

Interest expense	CU494[(a)]	
Contract liability		CU494

(a) CU494 = CU4,000 contract liability × (6 per cent interest per year for two years).

- recognise revenue for the transfer of the asset:

Contract liability	CU4,494	
Revenue		CU4,494

In Example 30.36, involving a contract with an advance payment from the customer, the entity determines that a significant financing component does not exist because the difference between the amount of promised consideration and the cash selling price of the good or service arises for reasons other than the provision of financing, as follows. *[IFRS 15.IE152-IE154]*.

Example 30.36: Advance payment

An entity, a technology product manufacturer, enters into a contract with a customer to provide global telephone technology support and repair coverage for three years along with its technology product. The customer purchases this support service at the time of buying the product. Consideration for the service is an additional CU300. Customers electing to buy this service must pay for it upfront (i.e. a monthly payment option is not available).

To determine whether there is a significant financing component in the contract, the entity considers the nature of the service being offered and the purpose of the payment terms. The entity charges a single upfront amount, not with the primary purpose of obtaining financing from the customer but, instead, to maximise profitability, taking into consideration the risks associated with providing the service. Specifically, if customers could pay monthly, they would be less likely to renew and the population of customers that continue to use the support service in the later years may become smaller and less diverse over time (i.e. customers that choose to renew historically are those that make greater use of the service, thereby increasing the entity's costs). In addition, customers tend to use services more if they pay monthly rather than making an upfront payment. Finally, the entity would incur higher administration costs such as the costs related to administering renewals and collection of monthly payments.

In assessing the requirements in paragraph 62(c) of IFRS 15, the entity determines that the payment terms were structured primarily for reasons other than the provision of finance to the entity. The entity charges a single upfront amount for the services because other payment terms (such as a monthly payment plan) would affect the nature of the risks assumed by the entity to provide the service and may make it uneconomical to provide the service. As a result of its analysis, the entity concludes that there is not a significant financing component.

5.5.2 Implementation questions on identifying and accounting for significant financing components

See 4.6.1.H above for discussion on whether an entity is required to evaluate if a customer option that provides a material right includes a significant financing component.

5.5.2.A Payment terms reflect reasons other than the provision of finance

According to IFRS 15, a significant financing component does not exist if the difference between the promised consideration and the cash selling price of the good or service arises for reasons other than the provision of finance. *[IFRS 15.62(c)]*. At the March 2015 TRG meeting, the TRG members discussed whether this factor should be broadly or narrowly applied.

The TRG members generally agreed that there will likely be significant judgement involved in determining whether either party is providing financing or the payment terms are for another reason. The TRG members also generally agreed that the Board did not seem to intend to create a presumption that a significant financing component exists if the cash selling price differs from the promised consideration.

The TRG agenda paper noted that, although paragraph 61 of IFRS 15 states that the measurement objective for a significant financing component is to recognise revenue for the goods and services at an amount that reflects the cash selling price, this measurement objective is only followed when an entity has already determined that a significant financing component exists. The fact that there is a difference in the promised consideration and the cash selling price is not a principle for determining whether a significant financing component actually exists. It is only one factor to consider.[72]

Many of the TRG members noted that it will require significant judgement in some circumstances to determine whether a transaction includes a significant financing component.[73]

5.5.2.B Existence of a financing component when the promised consideration is equal to the cash selling price

Under IFRS 15, an entity must consider the difference, if any, between the amount of promised consideration and the cash selling price of a promised good or service when determining whether a significant financing component exists in a contract. *[IFRS 15.61(a)]*. At the March 2015 TRG meeting, the TRG members were asked to consider whether a financing component exists if the promised consideration is equal to the cash selling price.

The TRG members generally agreed that even if the list price, cash selling price and promised consideration of a good or service are all equal, an entity should not automatically assume that a significant financing component does not exist. This would be a factor to consider, but it would not be determinative.[74]

As discussed at 5.5.2.A above, while paragraph 61 of IFRS 15 states that the measurement objective for a significant financing component is to recognise revenue for the goods and services at an amount that reflects the cash selling price, this measurement objective is only followed when an entity has already determined that a significant financing component exists. The fact that there is no difference between the promised consideration and the cash selling price is not determinative in the evaluation of whether a significant financing component actually exists. It is a factor to consider, but it is not the only factor and is not determinative. As discussed above, an entity needs to consider all facts and circumstances in this evaluation.

The TRG agenda paper noted that the list price may not always equal the cash selling price (i.e. the price that a customer would have paid for the promised goods or services if the customer had paid cash for those goods or services when (or as) they transfer to the customer, as defined in paragraph 61 of IFRS 15). For example, if a customer offers to pay cash upfront when the entity is offering 'free' financing to customers, the customer that offers the upfront payment may be able to pay less than the list price. Determining a 'cash selling price' may require judgement and the fact that an entity provides 'interest-free financing' does not necessarily mean that the cash selling price is the same as the price another customer would pay over time. Entities would have to consider the cash selling price in comparison to the promised consideration in making the evaluation based on the overall facts and circumstances of the arrangement.

This notion is consistent with paragraph 77 of IFRS 15 on allocating the transaction price to performance obligations based on stand-alone selling prices (see 6.1 below), which indicates that a contractually stated price or a list price for a good or service may be (but is not presumed to be) the stand-alone selling price of that good or service. The TRG agenda paper noted that it may be possible for a financing component to exist, but that it may not be significant. As discussed at 5.5 above, entities will need to apply judgement in determining whether the financing component is significant.[75]

5.5.2.C Accounting for financing components that are not significant

At the March 2015 TRG meeting, the TRG members generally agreed that the standard does not preclude an entity from deciding to account for a financing component that is not significant. For example, an entity may have a portfolio of contracts in which there is a mix of significant and insignificant financing components. An entity could choose to account for all of the financing components as if they were significant in order to avoid having to apply different accounting methods to each.

An entity electing to apply the requirements for significant financing components to an insignificant financing component would need to be consistent in its application to all similar contracts with similar circumstances.[76]

5.5.2.D Determining whether the significant financing component practical expedient applies to contracts with a single payment stream for multiple performance obligations

The standard includes a practical expedient that allows an entity not to assess a contract for a significant financing component if the period between the customer's payment and the entity's transfer of the goods or services is one year or less. *[IFRS 15.63]*.

The TRG members were asked, at the March 2015 TRG meeting, how entities should consider whether the practical expedient applies to contracts with a single payment stream for multiple performance obligations.

The TRG members generally agreed that entities will either apply an approach of allocating any consideration received:

(1) to the earliest good or service delivered; or

(2) proportionately between the goods and services depending on the facts and circumstances.

The TRG agenda paper on this topic provided an example of a telecommunications entity that enters into a two-year contract to provide a device at contract inception and related data services over 24 months in exchange for 24 equal monthly instalments.[77] Under approach (1) above, an entity would be allowed to apply the practical expedient because the period between transfer of the good or service and customer payment would be less than one year for both the device and the related services. This is because, in the example provided, the device would be 'paid off' after five months. Under approach (2) above, an entity would not be able to apply the practical expedient because the device would be deemed to be paid off over the full 24 months (i.e. greater than one year).

Approach (2) above may be appropriate in circumstances similar to the example in the TRG agenda paper, when the cash payment is not directly tied to a particular good or service in a contract. However, approach (1) may be appropriate when the cash payment is directly tied to the earliest good or service delivered in a contract. However, the TRG members noted it may be difficult to tie a cash payment directly to a good or service because cash is fungible. Accordingly, judgement will be required based on the facts and circumstances.[78]

5.5.2.E *Calculating the adjustment to revenue for significant financing components*

At the March 2015 TRG meeting, the TRG members discussed how an entity would calculate the adjustment to revenue for contracts that include a significant financing component.

The TRG members generally agreed that the standard does not contain requirements for how to calculate the adjustment to the transaction price due to a significant financing component. A financing component will be recognised as interest expense (when the customer pays in advance) or interest income (when the customer pays in arrears). Entities need to consider requirements outside IFRS 15 to determine the appropriate accounting treatment (i.e. IFRS 9 or IAS 39).[79]

5.5.2.F *Allocating a significant financing component when there are multiple performance obligations in a contract*

At the March 2015 TRG meeting, the TRG members discussed how an entity would allocate a significant financing component when there are multiple performance obligations in a contract.

The standard is clear that, when determining the transaction price in Step 3 of the model, the effect of financing is excluded from the transaction price prior to the allocation of the transaction price to performance obligations (which occurs in Step 4). However, stakeholders had questioned whether an adjustment for a significant financing component could ever be attributed to only one or some of the performance obligations in the contract, rather than to all of the performance obligations in the contract. This is because the standard only includes examples in which there is a single performance obligation.

The TRG members generally agreed that it may be reasonable for an entity to attribute a significant financing component to one or more, but not all, of the performance obligations in the contract. In doing so, the entity may analogise to the exceptions for allocating variable consideration and/or discounts to one or more (but not all) performance obligations, if specified criteria are met (see 6.3 and 6.4 below, respectively).[80] However, attribution of a financing component to one (or some) of the performance obligations will require the use of judgement, especially because cash is fungible.

5.5.3 Financial statement presentation of financing component

As discussed at 5.5 above, when a significant financing component exists in a contract, the transaction price is adjusted so that the amount recognised as revenue is the 'cash selling price' of the underlying goods or services at the time of transfer. Essentially, a contract with a customer that has a significant financing component would be separated into a revenue component (for the notional cash sales price) and a loan component (for the effect of the deferred or advance payment terms). *[IFRS 15.BC244]*. Consequently, the accounting for accounts receivable arising from a contract that has a significant financing component should be comparable to the accounting for a loan with the same features. *[IFRS 15.BC244]*.

The amount allocated to the significant financing component would have to be presented separately from revenue recognised from contracts with customers. The financing component is recognised as interest expense (when the customer pays in advance) or interest income (when the customer pays in arrears). The interest income or expense is recognised over the financing period using the effective interest method described in IFRS 9 or IAS 39. The standard notes that interest is only recognised to the extent that a contract asset, contract liability or receivable is recognised in accordance with IFRS 15. *[IFRS 15.65]*. The IASB noted in the Basis for Conclusions that an entity may present interest income as revenue only when interest income represents income from an entity's ordinary activities. *[IFRS 15.BC247]*.

Impairment losses on receivables, with or without a significant financing component, are presented in line with the requirements of IAS 1 – *Presentation of Financial Statements* – and disclosed in accordance with IFRS 7 – *Financial Instruments: Disclosures*. However, IFRS 15 makes it clear that such amounts are 'disclosed separately from impairment losses from other contracts.' *[IFRS 15.113(b)]*.

5.6 Non-cash consideration

Customer consideration may be in the form of goods, services or other non-cash consideration (e.g. property, plant and equipment, a financial instrument). When an entity (i.e. the seller or vendor) receives, or expects to receive, non-cash consideration, the fair value of the non-cash consideration is included in the transaction price. *[IFRS 15.66]*.

An entity will likely apply the requirements of IFRS 13 – *Fair Value Measurement* – or IFRS 2 – *Share-based Payment* – when measuring the fair value of any non-cash consideration. If an entity cannot reasonably estimate the fair value of non-cash consideration, it measures the non-cash consideration indirectly by reference to the stand-alone selling price of the promised goods or services. *[IFRS 15.67]*.

For contracts with both non-cash consideration and cash consideration, an entity will need to measure the fair value of the non-cash consideration and it will look to other requirements within IFRS 15 to account for the cash consideration. For example, for a contract in which an entity receives non-cash consideration and a sales-based royalty, the entity would measure the fair value of the non-cash consideration and refer to the requirements within the standard for the sales-based royalties.

The fair value of non-cash consideration may change both because of the form of consideration (e.g. a change in the price of a share an entity is entitled to receive from a customer) and for reasons other than the form of consideration (e.g. a change in the exercise price of a share option because of the entity's performance). Under IFRS 15, if an entity's entitlement to non-cash consideration promised by a customer is variable for reasons other than the form of consideration (i.e. there is uncertainty as to whether the entity will receive the non-cash consideration if a future event occurs or does not occur), the entity considers the constraint on variable consideration. *[IFRS 15.68]*.

In some transactions, a customer contributes goods or services, such as equipment or labour, to facilitate the fulfilment of the contract. If the entity obtains control of the contributed goods or services, it would consider them non-cash consideration and account for that consideration as described above. *[IFRS 15.69]*.

The Board also noted that any assets recognised as a result of non-cash consideration are accounted for in accordance with other relevant standards (e.g. IAS 16).

The standard provides the following example of a transaction for which non-cash consideration is received in exchange for services provided. *[IFRS 15.IE156-IE158]*.

Example 30.37: Entitlement to non-cash consideration

An entity enters into a contract with a customer to provide a weekly service for one year. The contract is signed on 1 January 20X1 and work begins immediately. The entity concludes that the service is a single performance obligation in accordance with paragraph 22(b) of IFRS 15. This is because the entity is providing a series of distinct services that are substantially the same and have the same pattern of transfer (the services transfer to the customer over time and use the same method to measure progress – that is, a time-based measure of progress).

In exchange for the service, the customer promises 100 shares of its common stock per week of service (a total of 5,200 shares for the contract). The terms in the contract require that the shares must be paid upon the successful completion of each week of service.

The entity measures its progress towards complete satisfaction of the performance obligation as each week of service is complete. To determine the transaction price (and the amount of revenue to be recognised), the entity measures the fair value of 100 shares that are received upon completion of each weekly service. The entity does not reflect any subsequent changes in the fair value of the shares received (or receivable) in revenue.

The concept of accounting for non-cash consideration at fair value is consistent with current IFRS. IAS 18 requires non-cash consideration to be measured at the fair value of the goods or services received. 'When this amount cannot be measured reliably, non-cash consideration is measured at the fair value of the goods or services given up.' *[IAS 18.12]*. IFRIC 18 also requires any revenue recognised as a result of a transfer of an assets from a customer to be measured at fair value, *[IFRIC 18.13]* consistent with the requirement in IAS 18. Therefore, we do not expect IFRS 15 to result in a significant change to current practice in respect of the measurement of non-cash consideration.

SIC-31 specifies that a seller can reliably measure revenue at the fair value of the advertising services it provides in a barter transaction, by reference to non-barter transactions that meet specified criteria. IFRS 15 does not contain similar requirements. Therefore, significant judgement and consideration of the specific facts and circumstances are likely to be needed when accounting for advertising barter transactions.

5.6.1 Non-cash consideration implementation considerations

Stakeholders raised questions about the date that should be used when measuring the fair value of non-cash consideration for inclusion within the transaction price. In addition, constituents noted that the variability of non-cash consideration could arise both from its form (e.g. shares) and for other reasons (e.g. performance factors that affect the amount of consideration to which the entity will be entitled). Consequently, they questioned how the constraint on variable consideration would be applied in such circumstances.

At the January 2015 TRG meeting, the TRG members discussed these questions and agreed that, while the standard requires non-cash consideration (e.g. shares, advertising provided as consideration from a customer) to be measured at fair value, it is unclear when that fair value must be measured (i.e. the measurement date). The TRG members discussed three measurement date options: contract inception; when it is received; or when the related performance obligation is satisfied. Each view received support from some TRG members. Since IFRS 15 does not specify the measurement date, an entity will need to use its judgement to determine the most appropriate measurement date when measuring the fair value of non-cash consideration. However, in accordance with paragraph 126 of IFRS 15, information about the methods, inputs and assumptions used to measure non-cash consideration will need to be disclosed. *[IFRS 15.BC254E]*.

IFRS 15 requires that the constraint on variable consideration be applied to non-cash consideration only if the variability is due to factors other than the form of consideration (i.e. variability arising for reasons other than changes in the price of the non-cash consideration). The constraint will not apply if the non-cash consideration varies because of its form (e.g. listed shares for which the share price changes). However, the standard does not address how the constraint would be applied when the non-cash consideration is variable due to both its form and other reasons. While some of the TRG members said the standard could be interpreted to require an entity to split the consideration based on the source of the variability, other TRG members highlighted that this approach would be overly complex and would not provide useful information.

The FASB issued amendments to its standard in May 2016 to specify that the fair value of non-cash consideration be measured at contract inception when determining the transaction price. Any subsequent changes in the fair value of the non-cash consideration due to its form (e.g. changes in share price) are not included in the transaction price and would be recognised, if required, as a gain or loss in accordance with other accounting standards, but would not be recognised as revenue from contracts with customers. However, in the Basis for Conclusions, the IASB observed that this issue has important interactions with other standards (including IFRS 2 and IAS 21) and there was a concern about the risk of unintended consequences. Therefore the Board decided that, if needed, these issues would be considered more comprehensively in a separate project. *[IFRS 15.BC254C]*. Since the IASB did not make amendments to IFRS 15 that are similar to those made by the FASB, it acknowledged in the Basis for Conclusions, that the use of a measurement date other than contract inception would not be precluded under IFRS. Consequently, it is possible that diversity between IFRS and US GAAP entities may arise in practice. Unlike US GAAP, existing IFRS does not contain specific requirements regarding the measurement date for non-cash consideration related to revenue transactions. As such, the IASB does not expect IFRS 15 to create more diversity than currently exists in relation to this issue. *[IFRS 15.BC254E]*.

The FASB also specified that when the variability of non-cash consideration is due to both the form of the consideration and other reasons, the constraint on variable consideration would apply only to the variability for reasons other than its form. While the IASB did not issue a similar amendment, the Board noted in the Basis for Conclusions that it decided to constrain variability in the estimate of the fair value of the non-cash consideration if that variability relates to changes in the fair value for reasons other than the form of the consideration. It also noted the view of some TRG members that, in practice, it might be difficult to distinguish between variability in the fair value due to the form of the consideration and other reasons, in which case applying the variable consideration constraint to the whole estimate of the non-cash consideration might be more practical. *[IFRS 15.BC252]*. However, for reasons similar to those on the measurement date for non-cash consideration, the IASB decided not to issue a similar amendment to that of the FASB. Consequently, the IASB acknowledged that differences may arise between an entity reporting under IFRS and an entity reporting under US GAAP. *[IFRS 15.BC254H]*.

5.7 Consideration paid or payable to a customer

Many entities make payments to their customers. In some cases, the consideration paid or payable represents purchases by the entity of goods or services offered by the customer that satisfy a business need of the entity. In other cases, the consideration paid or payable represents incentives given by the entity to entice the customer to purchase, or continue purchasing, its goods or services.

The standard states that consideration payable to a customer includes 'cash amounts that an entity pays, or expects to pay, to the customer (or to other parties that purchase the entity's goods or services from the customer). Consideration payable to a customer also includes credit or other items (e.g. a coupon or voucher) that can be applied against amounts owed to the entity (or to other parties that purchase the entity's goods or services from the customer).' *[IFRS 15.70]*.

To determine the appropriate accounting treatment, an entity must first determine whether the consideration paid or payable to a customer is: a payment for a distinct good or service; a reduction of the transaction price; or a combination of both. For a payment by the entity to a customer to be treated as something other than a reduction of the transaction price, the good or service provided by the customer must be distinct (as discussed at 4.2.1 above). The standard also states that, if the consideration payable to a customer includes a variable amount, an entity must estimate the transaction price in accordance with the requirements for estimating (and constraining) variable consideration (see 5.2 above). *[IFRS 15.70]*.

If consideration payable to a customer is a payment for a distinct good or service from the customer, an entity is required to account for the purchase of the good or service in the same way that it accounts for other purchases from suppliers. If the amount of consideration payable to the customer exceeds the fair value of the distinct good or service that the entity receives from the customer, the entity is required to account for the excess as a reduction of the transaction price. If the entity cannot reasonably estimate the fair value of the good or service received from the customer, it is required to account for all of the consideration payable to the customer as a reduction of the transaction price. *[IFRS 15.71]*.

If consideration payable to a customer is accounted for as a reduction of the transaction price, it is recognised as a reduction of revenue when (or as) the later of when:

(a) the entity recognises revenue for the transfer of the related goods or services to the customer; and

(b) the entity pays or promises to pay the consideration (even if the payment is conditional on a future event), which might be implied by the entity's customary business practices. *[IFRS 15.72]*.

The standard indicates that an entity accounts for the consideration payable to a customer, regardless of whether the purchaser receiving the consideration is a direct or indirect customer of the entity. This includes consideration to any purchasers of the entity's products at any point along the distribution chain. This would include entities that make payments to the customers of resellers or distributors that purchase directly from the entity (e.g. manufacturers of breakfast cereals may offer coupons to end-consumers, even though their direct customers are the grocery stores that sell to end-consumers). The requirements in IFRS 15 apply to entities that derive revenue from sales of services, as well as entities that derive revenue from sales of goods.

5.7.1 Determining who is an entity's customer when applying the requirements for consideration payable to a customer

When applying the requirements for consideration payable to a customer, it is important to determine who is an entity's customer. This was considered by the TRG members at both the March 2015 and July 2015 TRG meetings.

The TRG members generally agreed that the requirements for consideration payable to a customer apply to all payments made to entities/customers in the distribution chain of that contract. However, they agreed that there could also be situations in which the requirements would apply to payments made to any customer of an entity's customer outside the distribution chain if both parties are considered the entity's customers. For example, in an arrangement with a principal, an agent and an end-customer, an agent may conclude its only customer is the principal or it may conclude that it has two customers – the principal and the end-customer. Regardless of this assessment, an agent's payment to a principal's end-customer that was contractually required based on an agreement between the entity (agent) and the principal would represent consideration payable to a customer. Absent similar contract provisions that clearly indicate when an amount is consideration payable, the TRG members agreed that agents will need to evaluate their facts and circumstances to determine whether payments made to an end-customer would be considered a reduction of revenue or a marketing expense.[81]

5.7.2 Classification of different types of consideration paid or payable to a customer

To determine the appropriate accounting treatment, an entity must first determine whether the consideration paid or payable to a customer is a payment for a distinct good or service, a reduction of the transaction price or a combination of both.

For a payment by the entity to a customer to be treated as something other than a reduction of the transaction price, the good or service provided by the customer must be distinct (as discussed at 4.2.1 above). However, if the payment to the customer is in excess of the fair value of the distinct good or service received, the entity must account for such excess as a reduction of the transaction price.

5.7.3 Forms of consideration paid or payable to a customer

Consideration paid or payable to customers commonly takes the form of discounts and coupons, among others. Furthermore, the promise to pay the consideration may be implied by the entity's customary business practice.

Consideration paid or payable to a customer can take many different forms. Therefore, entities will have to carefully evaluate each transaction to determine the appropriate treatment of such amounts. Some common examples of consideration paid to a customer are given below.

- *Slotting fees* – Manufacturers of consumer products commonly pay retailers fees to have their goods displayed prominently on store shelves. Those shelves can be physical (i.e. in a building where the store is located) or virtual (i.e. they represent space in an internet reseller's online catalogue). Generally, such fees do not provide a distinct good or service to the manufacturer and are treated as a reduction of the transaction price.
- *Co-operative advertising arrangements* – In some arrangements, a vendor agrees to reimburse a reseller for a portion of costs incurred by the reseller to advertise the vendor's products. The determination of whether the payment from the vendor is in exchange for a distinct good or service at fair value will depend on a careful analysis of the facts and circumstances of the contract.
- *Price protection* – A vendor may agree to reimburse a retailer up to a specified amount for shortfalls in the sales price received by the retailer for the vendor's products over a specified period of time. Normally such fees do not provide a distinct good or service to the manufacturer and are treated as a reduction of the transaction price.

- *Coupons and rebates* – An indirect customer of a vendor may receive a refund of a portion of the purchase price of the product or service acquired by returning a form to the retailer or the vendor. Generally, such fees do not provide a distinct good or service to the manufacturer and are treated as a reduction of the transaction price.
- *'Pay-to-play' arrangements* – In some arrangements, a vendor pays an upfront fee to the customer in order to obtain a new contract. In most cases, these payments are not associated with any distinct good or service to be received from the customer and are treated as a reduction of the transaction price.
- *Purchase of goods or services* – Entities often enter into supplier-vendor arrangements with their customers in which the customers provide them with a distinct good or service. For example, a software entity may buy its office supplies from one of its software customers. In such situations, the entity has to carefully determine whether the payment made to the customer is solely for the goods and services received, or whether part of the payment is actually a reduction of the transaction price for the goods and services the entity is transferring to the customer.

IFRS 15's accounting for consideration payable to a customer is similar to current practice under IFRS. However, the requirement to determine whether a good or service is 'distinct' in order to treat the consideration payable to a customer as anything other than a reduction of revenue is new. While many of the illustrative examples to IAS 18 imply that the vendor would have to receive an 'identifiable benefit' from the customer that is sufficiently separable from the customer's purchases of the vendor's products, it is not explicitly discussed in current IFRS. As such, some entities may need to reassess their current treatment of consideration paid or payable to a customer.

5.7.3.A Payments to a customer that are within the scope of the requirements for consideration payable to a customer

At both the March 2015 and July 2015 TRG meetings, the TRG members discussed which payments made to a customer would be within the scope of the requirements for consideration payable to a customer.

The TRG members generally agreed that an entity may not need to separately analyse each payment to a customer if it is apparent that the payment is for a distinct good or service acquired in the normal course of business at market prices. However, if the business purpose of a payment to a customer is unclear or the goods or services are acquired in a manner that is inconsistent with market terms that other entities would receive when purchasing the customer's good or services, the payment needs to be evaluated under these requirements.[82] In the Basis for Conclusions, the IASB noted that the amount of consideration received from a customer for goods or services and the amount of any consideration paid to that customer for goods or services may be linked even if they are separate events. *[IFRS 15.BC257]*.

5.7.4 Timing of recognition of consideration paid or payable to a customer

If the consideration paid or payable to a customer is a discount or refund for goods or services provided to a customer, this reduction of the transaction price (and, ultimately, revenue) is recognised at the later of when the entity transfers the promised goods or services to the customer, or the entity promises to pay the consideration. *[IFRS 15.72]*. For example, if goods subject to a discount through a coupon are already delivered to the retailers, the discount would be recognised when the coupons are issued. However, if a coupon is issued that can be used on a new line of products that have not yet been sold to retailers, the discount would be recognised upon sale of the products to a retailer.

However, to determine the appropriate timing of recognition of consideration payable to a customer, entities will also need to consider the requirements for variable consideration. That is, the standard's definition of variable consideration is broad and includes amounts such as coupons or other forms of credits that can be applied to the amounts owed to an entity by the customer (see 5.2.1 above). IFRS 15 requires that all potential variable consideration be considered and reflected in the transaction price at contract inception and reassessed as the entity performs. In other words, if an entity has a history of providing this type of consideration to its customers, the requirements on estimating variable consideration would require that such amounts be considered at contract inception, even if the entity has not yet provided or explicitly promised this consideration to the customer.

The TRG discussed the potential inconsistency that arises between the requirements on consideration payable to a customer and variable consideration, as the requirements specific to consideration payable to a customer indicate that such amounts are not recognised as a reduction of revenue until the *later* of when:

- the related sales are recognised, or
- the entity promises to provide such consideration.[83]

A literal read of these requirements seems to suggest that an entity need not anticipate offering these types of programmes, even if it has a history of doing so, and would only recognise the effect of these programmes at the later of when the entity transfers the promised goods or services or makes a promise to pay the customer. The TRG members generally agreed that if an entity has a history of providing this type of consideration to customers, the requirements on estimating variable consideration would require the entity to consider such amounts at contract inception when the transaction price is estimated, even if the entity has not yet provided or promised to provide this consideration to the customer.[84] If the consideration paid or payable to a customer includes variable consideration in the form of a discount or refund for goods or services provided, an entity would use either the expected value method or most likely amount method to estimate the amount to which the entity expects to be entitled and apply the constraint to the estimate (see 5.2.3 above for further discussion) to determine the effect of the discount or refund on the transaction price.

The standard includes the following example of consideration paid to a customer. *[IFRS 15.IE160-IE162]*.

Chapter 30

Example 30.38: Consideration payable to a customer

An entity that manufactures consumer goods enters into a one-year contract to sell goods to a customer that is a large global chain of retail stores. The customer commits to buy at least CU15 million of products during the year. The contract also requires the entity to make a non-refundable payment of CU1.5 million to the customer at the inception of the contract. The CU1.5 million payment will compensate the customer for the changes it needs to make to its shelving to accommodate the entity's products.

The entity considers the requirements in paragraphs 70–72 of IFRS 15 and concludes that the payment to the customer is not in exchange for a distinct good or service that transfers to the entity. This is because the entity does not obtain control of any rights to the customer's shelves. Consequently, the entity determines that, in accordance with paragraph 70 of IFRS 15, the CU1.5 million payment is a reduction of the transaction price.

The entity applies the requirements in paragraph 72 of IFRS 15 and concludes that the consideration payable is accounted for as a reduction in the transaction price when the entity recognises revenue for the transfer of the goods. Consequently, as the entity transfers goods to the customer, the entity reduces the transaction price for each good by 10 per cent (CU1.5 million ÷ CU15 million). Therefore, in the first month in which the entity transfers goods to the customer, the entity recognises revenue of CU1.8 million (CU2.0 million invoiced amount less CU0.2 million of consideration payable to the customer).

The general agreement by TRG members that entities will need to consider the requirements on variable consideration to determine the appropriate timing of recognition of consideration payable to a customer may result in a change in practice for some entities. Significant judgement may be needed to determine the appropriate timing of recognition.

5.8 Non-refundable upfront fees

In certain circumstances, entities may receive payments from customers before they provide the contracted service or deliver a good. Upfront fees generally relate to the initiation, activation or set-up of a good to be used or a service to be provided in the future. Upfront fees may also be paid to grant access to or to provide a right to use a facility, product or service. In many cases, the upfront amounts paid by the customer are non-refundable. Examples include fees paid for membership to a health club or buying club and activation fees for phone, cable or internet services. *[IFRS 15.B48]*.

Entities must evaluate whether a non-refundable upfront fee relates to the transfer of a promised good or service. If it does, the entity is required to determine whether to account for the promised good or service as a separate performance obligation (see 4 above). *[IFRS 15.B49, B50]*.

The standard notes that, even though a non-refundable upfront fee relates to an activity that the entity is required to undertake at or near contract inception in order to fulfil the contract, in many cases that activity will not result in the transfer of a promised good or service to the customer. Instead, in many situations, an upfront fee represents an advance payment for future goods or services. In addition, the existence of a non-refundable upfront fee may indicate that the contract includes a renewal option for future goods and services at a reduced price (if the customer renews the agreement without the payment of an additional upfront fee). In such circumstances, an entity would need to assess whether the option is a material right (i.e. another performance obligation in the contract) (see 4.6 above). *[IFRS 15.B49]*. If the entity concludes that the non-refundable upfront fee does not provide a material right, the fee would be part of the consideration allocable to the goods or services in the contract and would be recognised when (or as) the good or service to which the consideration was allocated is transferred to the customer. If an entity concludes that the non-refundable upfront fee provides a material right, the amount of the fee allocated to the material right would be recognised over the period of benefit of the fee, which may be the estimated customer life.

In some cases, an entity may charge a non-refundable fee in part as compensation for costs incurred in setting up a contract (or other administrative tasks). If those set-up activities do not satisfy a performance obligation, the entity is required to disregard those activities (and related costs) when measuring progress (see 7.2 below). This is because the costs of set-up activities do not depict the transfer of services to the customer. In addition, the entity is required to assess whether costs incurred in setting up a contract are costs incurred to fulfil a contract that meet the requirements for capitalisation in IFRS 15 (see 9.3.2 below). *[IFRS 15.B51]*.

The following illustration depicts the allocation of a non-refundable upfront fee determined to be a material right.

Example 30.39: Non-refundable upfront fees

A customer signs a one-year contract with a health club and is required to pay both a non-refundable initiation fee of CU150 and an annual membership fee in monthly instalments of CU40. At the end of each year, the customer can renew the contract for an additional year without paying an additional initiation fee. The customer is then required to pay an annual membership fee in monthly instalments of CU40 for each renewal period. The club's activity of registering the customer does not transfer any service to the customer and, therefore, is not a performance obligation. By not requiring the customer to pay the upfront membership fee again upon renewal, the club is effectively providing a discounted renewal rate to the customer.

The club determines that the renewal option is a material right because it provides a renewal option at a lower price than the range of prices typically charged for new customers. Therefore, it is a separate performance obligation. Based on its experience, the club determines that its customers, on average, renew their annual memberships twice before terminating their relationship with the club. As a result, the club determines that the option provides the customer with the right to two annual renewals at a discounted price. In this scenario, the club would allocate the total transaction consideration of CU630 (CU150 upfront membership fee + CU480 (CU40 × 12 months)) to the identified performance obligations (monthly services for the one-year contract and renewal option) based on the relative stand-alone selling price method. The amount allocated to the renewal option would be recognised as each of the two renewal periods is either exercised or forfeited.

Alternatively, the club could value the option by 'looking through' to the optional goods and services using the practical alternative provided in paragraph B42 of IFRS 15 (see 6.1.5 below). In that case, the club would determine that the total hypothetical transaction price (for purposes of allocating the transaction price to the option) is the sum of the upfront fee plus three years of service fees (i.e. CU150 + CU1,440) and would allocate that amount to all of the services expected to be delivered or 36 months of membership (or CU44.17 per month). Therefore, the total consideration in the contract of CU630 would be allocated to the 12 months of service (CU530 (CU44.17 × 12 months)) with the remaining amount being allocated to the renewal option (CU100 (CU630 – 530)). The amount allocated to the renewal option (CU100) would be recognised as revenue over each renewal period. One acceptable approach would be to reduce the initial CU100 deferred revenue balance for the material right by CU4.17 each month (CU100/24 months remaining), assuming that the estimated renewal period of two years remains unchanged.

See 4.6 above and 6.1.5 below for a more detailed discussion of the treatment of options (including the practical alternative allowed under paragraph B42 of IFRS 15) and 6.1 and 6.2 below for a discussion of estimating stand-alone selling prices and allocating consideration using the relative stand-alone selling price method.

5.8.1 Implementation questions on non-refundable upfront fees

5.8.1.A Recognition period for a non-refundable upfront fee that does not relate to the transfer of a good or service

At the March 2015 TRG meeting, the TRG members were asked over what period an entity should recognise a non-refundable upfront fee (e.g. fees paid for membership to a club, activation fees for phone, cable or internet services) that does not relate to the transfer of a good or service.

The TRG members generally agreed that the period over which a non-refundable upfront fee will be recognised depends on whether the fee provides the customer with a material right with respect to future contract renewals.[85] For example, assume that an entity charges a one-time activation fee of CU50 to provide CU100 of services to a customer on a month-to-month basis. If the entity concludes that the activation fee provides a material right, the fee would be recognised over the service period during which the customer is expected to benefit from not having to pay an activation fee upon renewal of service. That period may be the estimated customer life in some situations. If the entity concludes that the activation fee does not provide a material right, the fee would be recognised over the contract term (i.e. one month).

5.9 Changes in the transaction price

Changes in the transaction price can occur for various reasons, including 'the resolution of uncertain events or other changes in circumstances that change the amount of consideration to which an entity expects to be entitled in exchange for the promised goods or services'. *[IFRS 15.87]*. See 6.5 below for additional requirements on accounting for a change in transaction price.

6 ALLOCATE THE TRANSACTION PRICE TO THE PERFORMANCE OBLIGATIONS

The standard's allocation objective is to allocate the transaction price to each performance obligation (or distinct good or service) in an amount that depicts the amount of consideration to which the entity expects to be entitled in exchange for transferring the promised goods or services to the customer. *[IFRS 15.73]*. As noted above, the allocation is generally done in proportion to the stand-alone selling prices (i.e. on a relative stand-alone selling price basis). *[IFRS 15.74]*.

Once the separate performance obligations are identified and the transaction price has been determined, the standard generally requires an entity to allocate the transaction price to the performance obligations in proportion to their stand-alone selling prices (i.e. on a relative stand-alone selling price basis). The Board noted in the Basis for Conclusions that, in most cases, an allocation based on stand-alone selling prices will faithfully depict the different margins that may apply to promised goods or services. *[IFRS 15.BC266]*.

When allocating on a relative stand-alone selling price basis, any discount within the contract is generally allocated proportionately to all of the performance obligations in the contract. However, as discussed further below, there are some exceptions. For example, an entity could allocate variable consideration to a single performance obligation in some situations. IFRS 15 also contemplates the allocation of any discount in a contract only to certain performance obligations, if specified criteria are met. *[IFRS 15.74]*. An entity would not apply the allocation requirements if the contract has only one performance obligation (except for a single performance obligation that is made up of a series of distinct goods and services and includes variable consideration). *[IFRS 15.75]*.

6.1 Determining stand-alone selling prices

To allocate the transaction price on a relative stand-alone selling price basis, an entity must first determine the stand-alone selling price of the distinct good or service underlying each performance obligation. *[IFRS 15.76]*. Under the standard, this is the price at which an entity would sell a good or service on a stand-alone (or separate) basis at contract inception. *[IFRS 15.77]*.

IFRS 15 indicates the observable price of a good or service sold separately provides the best evidence of stand-alone selling price. *[IFRS 15.77]*. However, in many situations, stand-alone selling prices will not be readily observable. In those cases, the entity must estimate the stand-alone selling price. *[IFRS 15.78]*.

When estimating a stand-alone selling price, an entity is required to consider all information (including market conditions, entity-specific factors and information about the customer or class of customer) that is reasonably available to the entity. In doing so, an entity maximises the use of observable inputs and applies estimation methods consistently in similar circumstances. *[IFRS 15.78]*.

Stand-alone selling prices are determined at contract inception and are not updated to reflect changes between contract inception and when performance is complete. *[IFRS 15.88]*. For example, assume an entity determines the stand-alone selling price for a promised good and, before it can finish manufacturing and deliver that good, the underlying cost of the materials doubles. In such a situation, the entity would not revise its stand-alone selling price used for this contract. However, for future contracts involving the same good, the entity would need to determine whether the change in circumstances (i.e. the significant increase in the cost to produce the good) warrants a revision of the stand-alone selling price. If so, the entity would use that revised price for allocations in future contracts (see 6.1.3 below).

Furthermore, if the contract is modified and that modification is treated as a termination of the existing contract and the creation of a new contract (see 3.4.2 above), the entity would update its estimate of the stand-alone selling price at the time of the modification. If the contract is modified and the modification is treated as a separate contract (see 3.4.1 above), the accounting for the original contact would not be affected (and the stand-alone selling prices of the underlying goods and services would not be updated), but the stand-alone selling prices of the distinct goods or services of the new, separate contract would have to be determined at the time of the modification.

The new requirements for the allocation of the transaction price to performance obligations could result in a change in practice for many entities.

IAS 18 does not prescribe an allocation method for arrangements involving multiple goods or services. IFRIC 13 mentions two allocation methodologies: allocation based on relative fair value; and allocation using the residual method. However, IFRIC 13 does not prescribe a hierarchy. Therefore, currently an entity must use its judgement to select the most appropriate methodology, taking into consideration all relevant facts and circumstances and ensuring the resulting allocation is consistent with IAS 18's objective to measure revenue at the fair value of the consideration.

Given the limited guidance in current IFRS on arrangements involving multiple goods or services, some entities have looked to US GAAP to develop their accounting policies. The requirement to estimate a stand-alone selling price if a directly observable selling price is not available will not be a new concept for entities that have developed their accounting policies by reference to the multiple-element arrangements requirements in ASC 605-25. The requirements in IFRS 15 for estimating a stand-alone selling price are generally consistent with ASC 605-25, except that they do not require an entity to consider a hierarchy of evidence to make this estimate.

Some entities have looked to the provisions of ASC 605-25 by developing estimates of selling prices for elements within an arrangement that may exhibit 'highly variable' pricing, as described at 6.1.2 below. IFRS 15 may allow those entities to revert to a residual approach.

The requirement to estimate a stand-alone selling price may be a significant change for entities reporting under IFRS that have looked to other US GAAP requirements to develop their accounting policies for revenue recognition, such as the software revenue recognition requirements in ASC 985-605. Those requirements have a different threshold for determining the stand-alone selling price, requiring observable evidence and not management estimates. Some of these entities may find it difficult to determine a stand-alone selling price, particularly for goods or services that are never sold separately (e.g. specified upgrade rights for software). In certain circumstances, an entity may be able to estimate the stand-alone selling price of a performance obligation using a 'residual approach' (see 6.1.2 below).

We anticipate that personnel responsible for an entity's revenue recognition policies will need to consult with personnel beyond those in the accounting or finance departments. Specifically, they would need to consult with personnel that are involved in the entity's pricing decisions in order to determine estimated stand-alone selling prices, especially when there are limited or no observable inputs. This may be a change for some entities.

6.1.1 Factors to consider when estimating the stand-alone selling price

To estimate the stand-alone selling price (if not readily observable), an entity may consider the stated prices in the contract, but the standard says an entity cannot presume that a contractually stated price or a list price for a good or service is the stand-alone selling price. *[IFRS 15.77]*. The standard states that an 'entity shall consider all information (including market conditions, entity-specific factors and information about the customer or class of customer) that is reasonably available to the entity' to estimate a stand-alone selling price. *[IFRS 15.78]*. An entity will also need to maximise the use of observable inputs in its estimate. This is a very broad requirement for which an entity will need to consider a variety of data sources.

The following list, which is not all-inclusive, provides examples of market conditions to consider:

- potential limits on the selling price of the product;
- competitor pricing for a similar or identical product;
- market awareness and perception of the product;
- current market trends that will likely affect the pricing;
- the entity's market share and position (e.g. the entity's ability to dictate pricing);
- effects of the geographic area on pricing;
- effects of customisation on pricing; and
- expected life of the product, including whether significant technological advances are expected in the market in the near future.

Examples of entity-specific factors include:

- profit objectives and internal cost structure;
- pricing practices and pricing objectives (including desired gross profit margin);
- effects of customisation on pricing;
- pricing practices used to establish pricing of bundled products;
- effects of a proposed transaction on pricing (e.g. the size of the deal, the characteristics of the targeted customer); and
- expected life of the product, including whether significant entity-specific technological advances are expected in the near future.

To document its estimated stand-alone selling price, an entity should consider describing the information that it has considered (e.g. the factors listed above), especially if there is limited observable data or none at all.

6.1.2 Possible estimation approaches

Paragraph 79 of IFRS 15 discusses three estimation approaches: (1) the adjusted market assessment approach; (2) the expected cost plus a margin approach; and (3) a residual approach. *[IFRS 15.79]*. All of these are discussed further below. When applying IFRS 15, an entity may need to use a different estimation approach for each of the distinct goods or services underlying the performance obligations in a contract. In addition, an entity may need to use a combination of approaches to estimate the stand-alone selling prices of goods or services promised in a contract if two of more of those goods and services have highly variable or uncertain stand-alone selling prices. This may be applicable when an entity is using the residual approach to allocate consideration because there are two or more goods or services with highly variable or uncertain stand-alone selling prices, but at least one of the goods or services in the contract has an observable stand-alone selling price. *[IFRS 15.80]*. For example, the Board noted in the Basis for Conclusions (and discussed further below) that an entity in such

Chapter 30

a situation might apply the residual approach to estimate the aggregate of the stand-alone selling prices for all the promised goods or services with highly variable or uncertain stand-alone selling prices, and then use another approach to estimate the stand-alone selling prices of each of those promised goods or services. *[IFRS 15.BC272]*.

Furthermore, these are not the only estimation approaches permitted. IFRS 15 allows any reasonable estimation approach: as long as it is consistent with the notion of a stand-alone selling price; maximises the use of observable inputs and is applied on a consistent basis for similar goods and services and customers. *[IFRS 15.80]*.

In some cases, an entity may have sufficient observable data to determine the stand-alone selling price. For example, an entity may have sufficient stand-alone sales of a particular good or service that provide persuasive evidence of the stand-alone selling price of a particular good or service. In such situations, no estimation would be necessary. *[IFRS 15.77]*.

In many instances, an entity may not have sufficient stand-alone sales data to determine the stand-alone selling price based solely on those sales. In those instances, it must maximise the use of whatever observable inputs it has available in order to make its estimate. That is, an entity would not disregard any observable inputs when estimating the stand-alone selling price of a good or service. *[IFRS 15.78]*. An entity should consider all factors contemplated in negotiating the contract with the customer and the entity's normal pricing practices factoring in the most objective and reliable information that is available. While some entities may have robust practices in place regarding the pricing of goods and services, some may need to improve their processes to develop estimates of stand-alone selling prices.

The standard includes the following estimation approaches. *[IFRS 15.79]*.

- *Adjusted market assessment approach* – this approach focuses on the amount that the entity believes the market in which it sells goods or services is willing to pay for a good or service. For example, an entity might refer to competitors' prices for similar goods and services and adjust those prices, as necessary, to reflect the entity's costs and margins. When using the adjusted market assessment approach, an entity considers market conditions, such as those listed at 6.1.1 above. Applying this approach will likely be easiest when an entity has sold the good or service for a period of time (such that it has data about customer demand), or a competitor offers similar goods or services that the entity can use as a basis for its analysis. Applying this approach may be difficult when an entity is selling an entirely new good or service because it may be difficult to anticipate market demand. In these situations, entities may want to use the market assessment approach, with adjustments as necessary, to reflect the entity's costs and margins, in combination with other approaches to maximise the use of observable inputs (e.g. using competitors' pricing, adjusted based on the market assessment approach in combination with an entity's planned internal pricing strategies if the performance obligation has never been sold separately).
- *Expected cost plus margin approach* – this approach focuses more on internal factors (e.g. the entity's cost basis), but has an external component as well. That is, the margin included in this approach must reflect the margin the market

would be willing to pay, not just the entity's desired margin. The margin may have to be adjusted for differences in products, geographies, customers and other factors. The expected cost plus margin approach may be useful in many situations, especially when the performance obligation has a determinable direct fulfilment cost (e.g. a tangible product or an hourly service). However, this approach may be less helpful when there are no clearly identifiable direct fulfilment costs or the amount of those costs is unknown (e.g. a new software licence or specified upgrade rights).

- *Residual approach* – this approach allows an entity to estimate the stand-alone selling price of a promised good or service as the difference between the total transaction price and the observable (i.e. not estimated) stand-alone selling prices of other promised goods or services in the contract, provided one of two criteria are met. Because the standard indicates that this approach can only be used for contracts with multiple promised goods or services when the selling price of one or more goods or services is unknown (either because the historical selling price is highly variable or because the goods or services have not yet been sold), we anticipate that the use of this approach will likely be limited. However, allowing entities to use a residual technique will provide relief to entities that rarely, or never, sell goods or services on a stand-alone basis, such as entities that sell intellectual property only with physical goods or services.

  Assume, for example, that an entity frequently sells software, professional services and maintenance, bundled together, at prices that vary widely. The entity also sells the professional services and maintenance individually at relatively stable prices. The Board indicated that it may be appropriate to estimate the stand-alone selling price for the software as the difference between the total transaction price and the observable selling prices of the professional services and maintenance. See Example 30.44, at 6.4 below Cases B and C, for examples of when the residual approach may or may not be appropriate.

  As mentioned above, the Board clarified in the Basis for Conclusions that an entity could also use the residual approach if there are two or more goods or services in the contract with highly variable or uncertain stand-alone selling prices, provided that at least one of the other promised goods or services in the contract has an observable stand-alone selling price. The Board observed that, in such an instance, an entity may need to use a combination of techniques to estimate the stand-alone selling prices. *[IFRS 15.BC272]*. For example, an entity may apply the residual approach to estimate the aggregate of the stand-alone selling prices for all of the promised goods or services with highly variable or uncertain stand-alone selling prices, but then use another approach (e.g. adjusted market assessment, expected cost plus margin) to estimate the stand-alone selling prices of each of those promised goods or services with highly variable or uncertain stand-alone selling prices.

The standard includes the following example in which two estimation approaches are used to estimate stand-alone selling prices of two different goods in a contract. *[IFRS 15.IE164-IE166]*.

Example 30.40: Allocation methodology

An entity enters into a contract with a customer to sell Products A, B and C in exchange for CU100. The entity will satisfy the performance obligations for each of the products at different points in time. The entity regularly sells Product A separately and therefore the stand-alone selling price is directly observable. The stand-alone selling prices of Products B and C are not directly observable.

Because the stand-alone selling prices for Products B and C are not directly observable, the entity must estimate them. To estimate the stand-alone selling prices, the entity uses the adjusted market assessment approach for Product B and the expected cost plus a margin approach for Product C. In making those estimates, the entity maximises the use of observable inputs (in accordance with paragraph 78 of IFRS 15). The entity estimates the stand-alone selling prices as follows:

Product	**Stand-alone selling price**	**Method**
	CU	
Product A	50	Directly observable (see paragraph 77 of IFRS 15)
Product B	25	Adjusted market assessment approach (see paragraph 79(a) of IFRS 15)
Product C	75	Expected cost plus a margin approach (see paragraph 79(b) of IFRS 15)
Total	150	

The customer receives a discount for purchasing the bundle of goods because the sum of the stand-alone selling prices (CU150) exceeds the promised consideration (CU100). The entity considers whether it has observable evidence about the performance obligation to which the entire discount belongs (in accordance with paragraph 82 of IFRS 15) and concludes that it does not. Consequently, in accordance with paragraphs 76 and 81 of IFRS 15, the discount is allocated proportionately across Products A, B and C. The discount, and therefore the transaction price, is allocated as follows:

Product	**Allocated transaction price**	
	CU	
Product A	33	(CU50 ÷ CU150 × CU100)
Product B	17	(CU25 ÷ CU150 × CU100)
Product C	50	(CU75 ÷ CU150 × CU100)
Total	100	

Given the flexibility provided by the standard, it is both appropriate and necessary for entities to tailor the approach(es) used to estimate the stand-alone selling prices to their specific facts and circumstances. Regardless of whether the entity uses a single approach or a combination of approaches to estimate the stand-alone selling price, the entity would evaluate whether the resulting allocation of the transaction price is consistent with the overall allocation objective in paragraph 73 of IFRS 15 and the requirements for estimating stand-alone selling prices above. *[IFRS 15.80]*.

In accordance with IFRS 15, an entity must make a reasonable estimate of the stand-alone selling price for the distinct good or service underlying each performance obligation if an observable selling price is not readily available. In developing this requirement, the Board believed that, even in instances in which limited information is available, entities should have sufficient information to develop a reasonable estimate.

Estimating stand-alone selling prices may require a change in practice. IAS 18 does not prescribe an allocation method for arrangements involving multiple goods or services. As a result, entities have used a variety of approaches, which may not be based on current selling prices.

In addition, entities that have developed their accounting policies by reference to the US GAAP requirements in ASC 605-25 should note that there will no longer be a hierarchy such as is in that standard, which requires them to first consider vendor-specific objective evidence (VSOE), then third-party evidence and, finally, best estimate of selling price. In addition, entities that have looked to current requirements in ASC 985-605 to develop their accounting policies will no longer need to establish VSOE based on a significant majority of their transactions.

As a result, we expect that many entities will need to establish approaches to estimate their stand-alone selling prices. However, as these estimates may have limited underlying observable data, it will be important for entities to have robust documentation to demonstrate the reasonableness of the calculations they make in estimating stand-alone selling prices. It is not clear how much an entity's estimate of stand-alone selling price will change as a result of applying the new requirements.

6.1.3 *Updating estimated stand-alone selling prices*

IFRS 15 does not specifically address how frequently estimated stand-alone selling prices must be updated. Instead, it indicates that an entity must make this estimate for each distinct good or service underlying each performance obligation in a contract with a customer, which suggests constantly updating prices.

In practice, we anticipate that entities will be able to consider their own facts and circumstances in order to determine how frequently they will need to update their estimates. If, for example, the information used to estimate the stand-alone selling price for similar transactions has not changed, an entity may determine that it is reasonable to use the previously determined stand-alone selling price. However, in order for the changes in circumstances to be reflected in the estimate in a timely manner, we anticipate that an entity would formally update the estimate on a regular basis (e.g. monthly, quarterly, semi-annually).

The frequency of updates should be based on the facts and circumstances of the distinct good or service underlying each performance obligation for which the estimate is made. An entity uses current information each time it develops or updates its estimate. While the estimates may be updated, the approach used to estimate a stand-alone selling price does not change (i.e. an entity must use a consistent approach), unless facts and circumstances change. *[IFRS 15.78]*.

6.1.4 *Additional considerations for determining the stand-alone selling price*

While this is not explicitly stated in IFRS 15, we anticipate that a single good or service could have more than one stand-alone selling price. That is, the entity may be willing to sell goods or services at different prices to different customers. Furthermore, an entity may use different prices in different geographies or in markets where it uses different methods to distribute its products (e.g. it may use a distributor or reseller, rather than selling directly to the end-customer) or for other reasons (e.g. different cost structures or strategies in different markets). Accordingly, an entity may need to stratify its analysis to determine its stand-alone selling price for each class of customer, geography and/or market, as applicable.

6.1.4.A When estimating the stand-alone selling price, does an entity have to consider its historical pricing for the sale of the good or service involved?

We believe that an entity should consider its historical pricing in all circumstances, but it may not be determinative. Historical pricing is likely to be an important input as it may reflect both market conditions and entity-specific factors and can provide supporting evidence about the reasonableness of management's estimate. For example, if management determines, based on its pricing policies and competition in the market, that the stand-alone selling price of its good or service is X, historical transactions within a reasonable range of X would provide supporting evidence for management's estimate. However, if historical pricing was only 50% of X, this may indicate that historical pricing is no longer relevant due to changes in the market, for example, or that management's estimate is flawed.

Depending on the facts and circumstances, an entity may conclude that other factors such as internal pricing policies are more relevant to its determination of a stand-alone selling price. When historical pricing has been established using the entity's normal pricing policies and procedures, it is more likely that this information will be relevant in the estimation.

If the entity has sold the product separately or has information on competitors' pricing for a similar product, the entity would likely find historical data relevant to its estimate of stand-alone selling prices, among other factors. In addition, we believe it may be appropriate for entities to stratify stand-alone selling prices based on: the type or size of customer; the amount of product or services purchased; the distribution channel; the geographic location; or other factors.

6.1.4.B When using an expected cost plus margin approach to estimate a stand-alone selling price, how would an entity determine an appropriate margin?

When an entity elects to use the expected cost plus margin approach, it is important for the entity to use an appropriate margin. Determining an appropriate margin will likely require the use of significant judgement and will involve the consideration of many market conditions and entity-specific factors, discussed at 6.1.1 above. For example, it would not be appropriate to determine that the entity's estimate of stand-alone selling price is equivalent to cost plus a 30% margin if a review of market conditions demonstrates that customers are only willing to pay the equivalent of cost plus a 12% margin for a comparable product. Similarly, it would be inappropriate to determine that cost plus a specified margin represents the stand-alone selling price if competitors are selling a comparable product at twice the determined estimate. Furthermore, it is likely the determined margin will have to be adjusted for differences in products, geographic locations, customers and other factors.

6.1.5 Measurement of options that are separate performance obligations

An entity that determines that an option is a separate performance obligation (because the option provides the customer with a material right, as discussed further at 4.6 above) needs to determine the stand-alone selling price of the option. *[IFRS 15.B42]*.

If the option's stand-alone selling price is not directly observable, the entity estimates it. The estimate takes into consideration the discount the customer would receive in a stand-alone transaction and the likelihood that the customer would exercise the option. *[IFRS 15.B42]*. Generally, option pricing models consider both the intrinsic value of the option (i.e. the value of the option if it were exercised today) and its time value (e.g. the option may be more or less valuable based on the amount of time until its expiration date and/or the volatility of the price of the underlying good or service). An entity is only required to measure the intrinsic value of the option under paragraph B42 of IFRS 15 when estimating the stand-alone selling price of the option. In the Basis for Conclusions, the Board noted that the benefits of valuing the time value component of an option would not justify the cost of doing so. *[IFRS 15.BC390]*. Example 30.20 at 4.6 above illustrates the measurement of an option determined to be a material right under paragraph B42 of IFRS 15.

Paragraph B43 of IFRS 15 provides an alternative to estimating the stand-alone selling price of an option. This practical alternative applies when the goods or services are both: (1) similar to the original goods and services in the contract (i.e. the entity continues to provide what it was already providing); *[IFRS 15.BC394]*; and (2) provided in accordance with the terms of the original contract. The standard indicates that this alternative will generally apply to options for contract renewals (i.e. the renewal option approach). *[IFRS 15.B43]*.

Under this alternative, a portion of the transaction price is allocated to the option (i.e. the material right that is a performance obligation) by reference to the total goods or services expected to be provided to the customer (including expected renewals) and the corresponding expected consideration. That is, the total amount of consideration expected to be received from the customer (including consideration from expected renewals) is allocated to the total goods or services expected to be provided to the customer, including the expected contract renewals. The amount allocated to the goods or services that the entity is required to transfer to the customer under the contract (i.e. excluding the optional goods or services that will be transferred if the customer exercises the renewal option(s)) is then subtracted from the total amount of consideration received (or that will be received) for transferring those goods or services. The difference is the amount that is allocated to the option at contract inception. An entity using this alternative would need to apply the constraint on variable consideration (as discussed at 5.2.3 above) to the estimated consideration for the optional goods or services prior to performing the allocation (see Example 30.41, Scenario B, below). *[IFRS 15.B43]*.

It is important to note that the calculation of total expected consideration (i.e. the hypothetical transaction price), including consideration related to expected renewals, is only performed for the purpose of allocating a portion of the hypothetical transaction price to the option at contract inception. It does not change the enforceable rights or obligations in the contract, nor does it affect the actual transaction price for the goods or services that the entity is presently obligated to transfer to the customer (which would not include expected renewals). Accordingly, the entity would not include any remaining hypothetical transaction price in its disclosure of remaining performance obligations (see 10.4.1 below). In this respect, the renewal option approach is consistent with the conclusion in 4.6.1.D above that, even if an entity may think that it is almost certain that a customer will exercise an option to buy additional goods and services, an entity does not include the additional goods and services underlying the option as promised goods or services (or performance obligations), unless there are substantive contractual penalties.

Subsequent to contract inception, if the actual number of contract renewals is different from an entity's initial expectations, the entity would update the hypothetical transaction price and allocation accordingly. However, as discussed at 6.1 above, the estimate of the stand-alone selling prices at contract inception would not be updated.

The following example illustrates the two possible approaches for measuring options included in a contract.

Example 30.41: Measuring an option

A machinery maintenance contract provider offers a promotion to new customers who pay full price for the first year of maintenance coverage that would grant them an option to renew their services for up to two years at a discount. The entity regularly sells maintenance coverage for CU750 per year. With the promotion, the customer would be able to renew the one-year maintenance contract at the end of each year for CU600. The entity concludes that the ability to renew is a material right because the customer would receive a discount that exceeds any discount available to other customers. The entity also determines that no directly observable stand-alone selling price exists for the option to renew at a discount.

Scenario A – Estimate the stand-alone selling price of the option directly (paragraph B42 of IFRS 15)

Since the entity has no directly observable evidence of the stand-alone selling price for the renewal option, it estimates the stand-alone selling price of an option for a CU150 discount on the renewal of service in years two and three. When developing its estimate, the entity would consider factors such as the likelihood that the option will be exercised and the price of comparable discounted offers. For example, the entity may consider the selling price of an offer for a discounted price of similar services found on a 'deal of the day' website.

The option will then be included in the relative stand-alone selling price allocation. In this example, there will be two performance obligations: one-year of maintenance services; and an option for discounted renewals. The consideration of CU750 is allocated between these two performance obligations based on their relative stand-alone selling prices.

Example 30.20 at 4.6 above illustrates the estimation of the stand-alone selling price of an option determined to be a material right under paragraph B42 of IFRS 15.

Scenario B – Practical alternative to estimating the stand-alone selling price of the option using the renewal option approach (paragraph B43 of IFRS 15)

If the entity chooses to use the renewal option approach, it would allocate the transaction price to the option for maintenance services by reference to the maintenance services expected to be provided (including expected renewals) and the corresponding expected consideration. Since there is a discount offered on renewal of the maintenance service, this calculation will result in less revenue being allocated to the first year of the maintenance service when compared to the amount of consideration received. The difference between the consideration received (or that will be received) for the first year of maintenance service and the revenue allocated to the first year of maintenance service will represent the amount allocated to the option using the renewal option approach.

Assume the entity obtained 100 new customers under the promotion. Based on its experience, the entity anticipates approximately 50% attrition annually, after giving consideration to the anticipated effect of the CU150 discount will have on attrition. The entity considers the constraint on variable consideration and concludes that it is not highly probable that a significant revenue reversal will not occur. Therefore, the entity concludes that, for this portfolio of contracts, it will ultimately sell 175 contracts, each contract providing one-year of maintenance services (100 customers in the first year, 50 customers in the second year and 25 customers in the third year).

The total consideration the entity expects to receive is CU120,000 [(100 × CU750) + (50 × CU600) + (25 × CU600)] (i.e. the hypothetical transaction price). Assuming the stand-alone selling price for each maintenance contract period is the same, the entity allocates CU685.71 (CU120,000/175) to each maintenance contract sold.

During the first year, the entity will recognise revenue of CU68,571 (100 one-year maintenance service contracts sold × the allocated price of CU685.71 per maintenance service contract). Consequently, at contract inception, the entity would allocate CU6,429 to the option to renew (CU75,000 cash received – CU68,571 revenue to be recognised in the first year).

If the actual renewals in years two and three differ from expectations, the entity would have to update the hypothetical transaction price and allocation accordingly. However, as discussed at 6.1 above, the estimate of the stand-alone selling prices at contract inception would not be updated.

For example, assume that the entity experiences less attrition than expected (e.g. 40% attrition annually, instead of 50%). Therefore, the entity estimates that it will ultimately sell 196 one-year maintenance services (100 + 60 renewals after year one + 36 renewals after year two). Accordingly, the total consideration that the entity expects to receive is CU132,600 [(100 × CU750) + (60 × CU600) + (36 × CU600)] (i.e. the updated hypothetical transaction price). The entity would not update its estimates of the stand-alone selling prices (which were assumed to be the same for each maintenance period). As such, the entity allocates CU676.53 (CU132,600/196) to each maintenance period. This would require the entity to reduce the amount of revenue it recognises in year one by CU918 (CU68,571 – (100 × CU676.53)) because the amount allocated to the option would have been higher at contract inception.

The requirement to identify and allocate contract consideration to an option (that has been determined to be a performance obligation) on a relative stand-alone selling price basis will likely be a significant change in practice for many IFRS preparers.

For entities that developed their accounting policy for allocation of revenue in an arrangement involving multiple goods or services by reference to US GAAP, the requirements are generally consistent with the current requirements in ASC 605-25. However, ASC 605-25 requires the entity to estimate the selling price of the option (unless other objective evidence of the selling price exists) and does not provide an alternative method (i.e. no renewal option approach) for measuring the option.

6.1.5.A *Could the form of an option (e.g. a gift card versus a coupon) affect how an option's stand-alone selling price is estimated?*

We believe that the form of an option should not affect how the stand-alone selling price is estimated. Consider, for example, a retailer that gives customers who spend more than CU100 during a specified period a CU15 discount on a future purchase in the form of a coupon or a gift card that expires two weeks from the sale date. If the retailer determines that this type of offer represents a material right (see 4.6 above), it will need to allocate a portion of the transaction price to the option on a relative stand-alone selling price basis.

As discussed at 6.1 above, the standard requires that an entity first look to any directly observable stand-alone selling price. This will require the retailer to consider the nature of the underlying transaction. In this example, while a customer can purchase a CU15 gift card for its face value, that transaction is not the same in substance as a transaction in which the customer is given a CU15 gift card or coupon in connection with purchasing another good or service. As such, the retailer could conclude that there is no directly observable stand-alone selling price for a 'free' gift card or coupon obtained in connection with the purchase of another good or service. It would then need to estimate the stand-alone selling price in accordance with paragraph B42 of IFRS 15.

The estimated stand-alone selling price of an option given in the form of a gift card or a coupon would be the same because both estimates would reflect the likelihood that the option will be exercised (i.e. breakage, as discussed at 7.10 below).

6.2 Applying the relative stand-alone selling price method

Once an entity has determined the stand-alone selling price for the separate goods and services in a contract, the entity allocates the transaction price to those performance obligations. *[IFRS 15.76]*. The standard requires an entity to use the relative stand-alone selling price method to allocate the transaction price, except in the two specific circumstances (variable consideration and discounts), which are described at 6.3 and 6.4 below.

Under the relative stand-alone selling price method, the transaction price is allocated to each performance obligation based on the proportion of the stand-alone selling price of each performance obligation to the sum of the stand-alone selling prices of all of the performance obligations in the contract, as described in Example 30.42 below. *[IFRS 15.76]*.

We have provided the following example of a relative stand-alone selling price allocation:

Example 30.42: Relative stand-alone selling price allocation

Manufacturing Co. entered into a contract with a customer to sell a machine for CU100,000. The total contract price included installation of the machine and a two-year extended warranty. Assume that Manufacturing Co. determined there were three performance obligations and the stand-alone selling prices of those performance obligations were as follows: machine – CU75,000, installation services – CU14,000 and extended warranty – CU20,000.

The aggregate of the stand-alone selling prices (CU109,000) exceeds the total transaction price of CU100,000, indicating there is a discount inherent in the contract. That discount must be allocated to each of the individual performance obligations based on the relative stand-alone selling price of each performance obligation. Therefore, the amount of the CU100,000 transaction price is allocated to each performance obligation as follows:

Machine – CU68,807 (CU100,000 × (CU75,000 / CU109,000))

Installation – CU12,844 (CU100,000 × (CU14,000 / CU109,000))

Warranty – CU18,349 (CU100,000 × (CU20,000 / CU109,000))

The entity would recognise as revenue the amount allocated to each performance obligation when (or as) each performance obligation is satisfied.

The method of allocation in IFRS 15 is not significantly different from the mechanics of applying the methods that are mentioned in IFRIC 13 to allocate consideration, such as a relative fair value approach. However, the methodology may be complicated when an entity applies one or both of the exceptions provided in IFRS 15 (described at 6.3 and 6.4 below). In addition, the new standard will likely require a change in practice for entities that do not apply a relative allocation approach under current IFRS (e.g. entities that currently apply the residual approach).

6.3 Allocating variable consideration

The relative stand-alone selling price method is the default method for allocating the transaction price. However, the Board noted in the Basis for Conclusion on IFRS 15 that this method may not always result in a faithful depiction of the amount of consideration to which an entity expects to be entitled from the customer. *[IFRS 15.BC280]*. Therefore, the standard provides two exceptions to the relative selling price method of allocating the transaction price.

The first relates to the allocation of variable consideration (see 6.4 below for the second exception). This exception requires variable consideration to be allocated entirely to a specific part of a contract such as one or more (but not all) performance obligations in the contract, (e.g. a bonus may be contingent on an entity transferring a promised good or service within a specified period of time) or one or more (but not all) distinct goods or services promised in a series of distinct goods or services that form part of a single performance obligation (see 4.2.2 above). For example, the consideration promised for the second year of a two-year cleaning contract will increase on the basis of movements in a specified index. This exception will be applied to a single performance obligation, a combination of performance obligations or distinct goods or services that make up part of a performance obligation depending on the facts and circumstances of each contract. *[IFRS 15.84]*.

Two criteria must be met to apply this exception, as follows:

(a) the terms of a variable payment relate specifically to the entity's efforts to satisfy the performance obligation or transfer the distinct good or service (or to a specific outcome from satisfying the performance obligation or transferring the distinct good or service); and

(b) allocating the variable amount of consideration entirely to the performance obligation or the distinct good or service is consistent with the allocation objective (see 6 above) when considering all of the performance obligations and payment terms in the contract. *[IFRS 15.85]*.

The general allocation requirements (see 6.1 above) must then be applied to allocate the remaining amount of the transaction price that does not meet the above criteria. *[IFRS 15.86]*.

While the language in above criteria (from paragraph 85 of IFRS 15) implies that this exception is limited to allocating variable consideration to a single performance obligation or a single distinct good or service within a series, paragraph 84 of IFRS 15 indicates that the variable consideration can be allocated to 'one or more, but not all' performance obligations or distinct goods or services within a series. We understand it was not the Board's intent to limit this exception to a single performance obligation or a single distinct good or service within a series, even though the standard uses a singular construction for the remainder of the discussion and does not repeat 'one or more, but not all'.

The Board noted in the Basis for Conclusions that this exception is necessary because allocating contingent amounts to all performance obligations in a contract may not reflect the economics of a transaction in all cases. *[IFRS 15.BC278]*. Allocating variable consideration entirely to a distinct good or service may be appropriate when the result is that the amount allocated to that particular good or service is reasonable relative to all other performance obligations and payment terms in the contract. Subsequent changes in variable consideration must be allocated in a consistent manner.

Entities may need to exercise significant judgement to determine whether they meet the requirements to allocate variable consideration to specific performance obligations or distinct goods or services within a series. Firstly, entities will need to determine whether they meet the first criterion in paragraph 85 of IFRS 15, which requires the terms of a variable payment to specifically relate to an entity's efforts to satisfy a performance obligation or transfer a distinct good or service that is part of a series. In performing this assessment, entities will need to consider the nature of the promise identified and whether the variable payment relates to that promise. For example, an entity may conclude that the nature of the promise to provide hotel management services (including management of the hotel employees, accounting services, training, procurement) is a series of distinct services (i.e. daily hotel management). For providing this service, the entity receives a variable fee (e.g. based on a percentage of occupancy rates and reimbursement of accounting services). An entity will likely determine it meets the first criterion because the uncertainty related to the consideration is resolved on a daily basis as the entity satisfies its obligation to perform daily hotel management services. This is because the variable payments specifically relate to transferring the distinct service that is part of a series of distinct goods or services (i.e. the daily management service). The fact that the payments do not directly correlate with each of the underlying activities performed each day does not affect this assessment. See 4 above for further discussion on identifying the nature of the goods and services promised in a contract, including whether they meet the series requirement.

Secondly, entities will need to determine whether they meet the second criterion in paragraph 85 of IFRS 15; to confirm that allocating the consideration in this manner is consistent with the overall allocation objective of the standard in paragraph 73 of IFRS 15. That is, an entity should allocate to each performance obligation (or distinct good or service in a series) the portion of the transaction price that reflects the amount of consideration the entity expects to be entitled in exchange for transferring those goods or services to the customer.

The TRG discussed four different types of contracts that may be accounted for as a series of distinct goods or services (see 4.2.2 above) and for which an entity may reasonably conclude that the allocation objective has been met (and the variable consideration could be allocated to each distinct period of service, such as day, month or year) which are detailed below.[86]

- IT outsourcing contract in which the events that trigger the variable consideration are the same throughout the contract, but the per unit price declines over the life of the contract – the allocation objective could be met if the pricing is based on market terms (e.g. if the contract contains a benchmarking clause) or the changes in price are substantive and linked to changes in an entity's cost to fulfil the obligation or value provided to the customer.
- Transaction processing contract with unknown quantity of transactions, but fixed contractual rate per transaction – the allocation objective could be met if the fees are priced consistently throughout the contract and the rates charged are consistent with the entity's standard pricing practices with similar customers.
- Hotel management contract in which monthly consideration is based on a percentage of monthly rental revenue, reimbursement of labour costs and an annual incentive payment – the allocation objective could be met for each payment stream as follows. The base monthly fees could meet the allocation objective if the consistent measure throughout the contract period (e.g. 1% of monthly rental revenue) reflects the value to the customer. The cost reimbursements could meet the allocation objective if they are commensurate with an entity's efforts to fulfil the promise each day. The annual incentive fee could also meet the allocation objective if it reflects the value delivered to the customer for the annual period and is reasonable compared with incentive fees that could be earned in other periods.
- Franchise agreement in which franchisor will receive a sales-based royalty of 5% in addition to a fixed fee – the allocation objective could be met if the consistent formula throughout the licence term reasonably reflects the value to the customer of its access to the franchisor's intellectual property (e.g. reflected by the sales that have been generated by the customer).

It is important to note that allocating variable consideration to one or more, but not all, performance obligations or distinct goods or services in a series is a requirement, not a policy choice. If the above criteria are met, the entity must allocate the variable consideration to the related performance obligation(s). *[IFRS 15.85]*.

The standard provides the following example to illustrate when an entity may or may not be able to allocate variable consideration to a specific part of a contract. Note that the example focuses on licences of intellectual property, which are discussed at 8 below. *[IFRS 15.IE178-IE187]*.

Example 30.43: Allocation of variable consideration

An entity enters into a contract with a customer for two intellectual property licences (Licences X and Y), which the entity determines to represent two performance obligations each satisfied at a point in time. The stand-alone selling prices of Licences X and Y are CU800 and CU1,000, respectively.

Case A – Variable consideration allocated entirely to one performance obligation

The price stated in the contract for Licence X is a fixed amount of CU800 and for Licence Y the consideration is three per cent of the customer's future sales of products that use Licence Y. For purposes of allocation, the entity estimates its sales-based royalties (i.e. the variable consideration) to be CU1,000, in accordance with paragraph 53 of IFRS 15.

To allocate the transaction price, the entity considers the criteria in paragraph 85 of IFRS 15 and concludes that the variable consideration (i.e. the sales-based royalties) should be allocated entirely to Licence Y. The entity concludes that the criteria in paragraph 85 of IFRS 15 are met for the following reasons:

(a) the variable payment relates specifically to an outcome from the performance obligation to transfer Licence Y (i.e. the customer's subsequent sales of products that use Licence Y); and

(b) allocating the expected royalty amounts of CU1,000 entirely to Licence Y is consistent with the allocation objective in paragraph 73 of IFRS 15. This is because the entity's estimate of the amount of sales-based royalties (CU1,000) approximates the stand-alone selling price of Licence Y and the fixed amount of CU800 approximates the stand-alone selling price of Licence X. The entity allocates CU800 to Licence X in accordance with paragraph 86 of IFRS 15. This is because, based on an assessment of the facts and circumstances relating to both licences, allocating to Licence Y some of the fixed consideration in addition to all of the variable consideration would not meet the allocation objective in paragraph 73 of IFRS 15.

The entity transfers Licence Y at inception of the contract and transfers Licence X one month later. Upon the transfer of Licence Y, the entity does not recognise revenue because the consideration allocated to Licence Y is in the form of a sales-based royalty. Therefore, in accordance with paragraph B63 of IFRS 15, the entity recognises revenue for the sales-based royalty when those subsequent sales occur.

When Licence X is transferred, the entity recognises as revenue the CU800 allocated to Licence X.

Case B – Variable consideration allocated on the basis of stand-alone selling prices

The price stated in the contract for Licence X is a fixed amount of CU300 and for Licence Y the consideration is five per cent of the customer's future sales of products that use Licence Y. The entity's estimate of the sales-based royalties (i.e. the variable consideration) is CU1,500 in accordance with paragraph 53 of IFRS 15.

To allocate the transaction price, the entity applies the criteria in paragraph 85 of IFRS 15 to determine whether to allocate the variable consideration (i.e. the sales-based royalties) entirely to Licence Y. In applying the criteria, the entity concludes that even though the variable payments relate specifically to an outcome from the performance obligation to transfer Licence Y (i.e. the customer's subsequent sales of products that use Licence Y), allocating the variable consideration entirely to Licence Y would be inconsistent with the principle for allocating the transaction price. Allocating CU300 to Licence X and CU1,500 to Licence Y does not reflect a reasonable allocation of the transaction price on the basis of the stand-alone selling prices of Licences X and Y of CU800 and CU1,000, respectively. Consequently, the entity applies the general allocation requirements in paragraphs 76-80 of IFRS 15.

The entity allocates the transaction price of CU300 to Licences X and Y on the basis of relative stand-alone selling prices of CU800 and CU1,000, respectively. The entity also allocates the consideration related to the sales-based royalty on a relative stand-alone selling price basis. However, in accordance with paragraph B63 of IFRS 15, when an entity licenses intellectual property in which the consideration is in the form of a sales-based royalty, the entity cannot recognise revenue until the later of the following events: the subsequent sales occur; or the performance obligation is satisfied (or partially satisfied).

Licence Y is transferred to the customer at the inception of the contract and Licence X is transferred three months later. When Licence Y is transferred, the entity recognises as revenue the CU167 (CU1,000 ÷ CU1,800 × CU300) allocated to Licence Y. When Licence X is transferred, the entity recognises as revenue the CU133 (CU800 ÷ CU1,800 × CU300) allocated to Licence X.

In the first month, the royalty due from the customer's first month of sales is CU200. Consequently, in accordance with paragraph B63 of IFRS 15, the entity recognises as revenue the CU111 (CU1,000 ÷ CU1,800 × CU200) allocated to Licence Y (which has been transferred to the customer and is therefore a satisfied performance obligation). The entity recognises a contract liability for the CU89 (CU800 ÷ CU1,800 × CU200) allocated to Licence X. This is because although the subsequent sale by the entity's customer has occurred, the performance obligation to which the royalty has been allocated has not been satisfied.

6.3.1 Implementation questions on the variable consideration allocation exception

6.3.1.A *In order to meet the criteria to allocate variable consideration entirely to a specific part of a contract, must the allocation be made on a relative stand-alone selling price basis?*

The TRG members generally agreed that a relative stand-alone selling price allocation is not required to meet the allocation objective when it relates to the allocation of variable consideration to a specific part of a contract (e.g. a distinct good or service in a series). The Basis for Conclusions notes that stand-alone selling price is the default method for meeting the allocation objective, but other methods could be used in certain instances (e.g. in allocating variable consideration). *[IFRS 15.BC279-BC280]*.

Stakeholders had questioned whether the variable consideration exception would have limited application to a series of distinct goods or services (see 4.2.2 above). That is, they wanted to know whether the standard would require that each distinct service that is substantially the same be allocated the same amount (absolute value) of variable consideration.[87] While the standard does not state what other allocation methods could be used beyond the relative stand-alone selling price basis, the TRG members generally agreed that an entity would apply reasonable judgement to determine whether the allocation results in a reasonable outcome (and, therefore, meets the allocation objective in the standard), as discussed above at 6.3 above.

6.4 Allocating a discount

The second exception to the relative stand-alone selling price allocation (see 6.3 above for the first exception) relates to discounts inherent in contracts. When an entity sells a bundle of goods and services, the selling price of the bundle is often less than the sum of the stand-alone selling prices of the individual elements. Under the relative stand-alone selling price allocation method, this discount would be allocated proportionately to all of the separate performance obligations. *[IFRS 15.81]*.

However, the standard states that if an entity determines that a discount in a contract is not related to all of the promised goods or services in the contract, the entity allocates the contract's entire discount only to the goods or services to which it relates. An entity is likely to be able to use this exception when the price of certain goods or services is largely independent of other goods or services in the contract. In these situations, an entity would be able to effectively 'carve out' an individual performance obligation, or some of the performance obligations in the contract, and allocate the contract's entire discount to that performance obligation or group of performance obligations, provided the criteria below are met. However, an entity could not use this exception to allocate only a portion of the discount to one or more, but not all, performance obligations in the contract.

The standard requires an entity to allocate a discount entirely to one or more, but not all, performance obligations in the contract if all of the following criteria are met: *[IFRS 15.82]*

(a) the entity regularly sells each distinct good or service (or each bundle of distinct goods or services) on a stand-alone basis;

(b) the entity also regularly sells on a stand-alone basis a bundle (or bundles) of some of those distinct goods or services at a discount to the stand-alone selling prices of the goods or services in each bundle; and

(c) the discount attributable to each bundle of goods or services described in (b) is substantially the same as the discount in the contract and an analysis of the goods or services in each bundle provides observable evidence of the performance obligation (or performance obligations) to which the entire discount in the contract belongs.

The IASB noted in the Basis for Conclusions that it believes the requirements in paragraph 82 of IFRS 15 will generally apply to contracts that include at least three performance obligations. While the standard contemplates that an entity may allocate the entire discount to as few as one performance obligation, the Board further clarified that it believes such a situation would be rare. *[IFRS 15.BC283]*. Instead, the Board believes it is more likely that an entity will be able to demonstrate that a discount relates to two or more performance obligations. This is because an entity will likely have observable information that the stand-alone selling price of a group of promised goods or services is lower than the price of those items when sold separately. It would likely be more difficult for an entity to have sufficient evidence to demonstrate that a discount is associated with a single performance obligation. When an entity applies a discount to one or more performance obligations in accordance with the above criteria, the standard states that the discount is allocated first before using the residual approach to estimate the stand-alone selling price of a good or service (see 6.1.2 above). *[IFRS 15.83]*.

The standard includes the following example to illustrate this exception and when the use of the residual approach for estimating stand-alone selling prices may or may not be appropriate. *[IFRS 15.IE167-IE177]*.

Example 30.44: Allocating a discount

An entity regularly sells Products A, B and C individually, thereby establishing the following stand-alone selling prices:

Product	**Stand-alone selling price**
	CU
Product A	40
Product B	55
Product C	45
Total	140

In addition, the entity regularly sells Products B and C together for CU60.

Case A – Allocating a discount to one or more performance obligations

The entity enters into a contract with a customer to sell Products A, B and C in exchange for CU100. The entity will satisfy the performance obligations for each of the products at different points in time.

The contract includes a discount of CU40 on the overall transaction, which would be allocated proportionately to all three performance obligations when allocating the transaction price using the relative stand-alone selling price method (in accordance with paragraph 81 of IFRS 15). However, because the entity regularly sells Products B and C together for CU60 and Product A for CU40, it has evidence that the entire discount should be allocated to the promises to transfer Products B and C in accordance with paragraph 82 of IFRS 15.

If the entity transfers control of Products B and C at the same point in time, then the entity could, as a practical matter, account for the transfer of those products as a single performance obligation. That is, the entity could allocate CU60 of the transaction price to the single performance obligation and recognise revenue of CU60 when Products B and C simultaneously transfer to the customer.

If the contract requires the entity to transfer control of Products B and C at different points in time, then the allocated amount of CU60 is individually allocated to the promises to transfer Product B (stand-alone selling price of CU55) and Product C (stand-alone selling price of CU45) as follows:

Product	Allocated transaction price	
	CU	
Product B	33	(CU55 ÷ CU100 total stand-alone selling price × CU60)
Product C	27	(CU45 ÷ CU100 total stand-alone selling price × CU60)
Total	60	

Case B – Residual approach is appropriate

The entity enters into a contract with a customer to sell Products A, B and C as described in Case A. The contract also includes a promise to transfer Product D. Total consideration in the contract is CU130. The stand-alone selling price for Product D is highly variable (see paragraph 79(c) of IFRS 15) because the entity sells Product D to different customers for a broad range of amounts (CU15-CU45). Consequently, the entity decides to estimate the stand-alone selling price of Product D using the residual approach.

Before estimating the stand-alone selling price of Product D using the residual approach, the entity determines whether any discount should be allocated to the other performance obligations in the contract in accordance with paragraphs 82 and 83 of IFRS 15.

As in Case A, because the entity regularly sells Products B and C together for CU60 and Product A for CU40, it has observable evidence that CU100 should be allocated to those three products and a CU40 discount should be allocated to the promises to transfer Products B and C in accordance with paragraph 82 of IFRS 15. Using the residual approach, the entity estimates the stand-alone selling price of Product D to be CU30 as follows:

Product	Stand-alone selling price	Method
	CU	
Product A	40	Directly observable (see paragraph 77 of IFRS 15)
Products B and C	60	Directly observable with discount (see Paragraph 82 of IFRS 15)
Product D	30	Residual approach (see paragraph 79(c) of IFRS 15)
Total	130	

The entity observes that the resulting CU30 allocated to Product D is within the range of its observable selling prices (CU15-CU45). Therefore, the resulting allocation (see above table) is consistent with the allocation objective in paragraph 73 of IFRS 15 and the requirements in paragraph 78 of IFRS 15.

Case C – Residual approach is inappropriate

The same facts as in Case B apply to Case C except the transaction price is CU105 instead of CU130. Consequently, the application of the residual approach would result in a stand-alone selling price of CU5 for Product D (CU105 transaction price less CU100 allocated to Products A, B and C). The entity concludes that CU5 would not faithfully depict the amount of consideration to which the entity expects to be entitled in exchange for satisfying its performance obligation to transfer Product D, because CU5 does not approximate the stand-alone selling price of Product D, which ranges from CU15-CU45. Consequently, the entity reviews its observable data, including sales and margin reports, to estimate the stand-alone selling price of Product D using another suitable method. The entity allocates the transaction price of CU105 to Products A, B, C and D using the relative stand-alone selling prices of those products in accordance with paragraphs 73-80 of IFRS 15.

The ability to allocate a discount to some, but not all, performance obligations within a contract is a significant change from current practice. This exception gives entities the ability to better reflect the economics of the transaction in certain circumstances. However, the criteria that must be met to demonstrate that a discount is associated with only some of the performance obligations in the contract will likely limit the number of transactions that will be eligible for this exception.

6.4.1 Implementation questions on the discount allocation exception

6.4.1.A Interaction between the two allocation exceptions: variable discounts

A discount that is variable in amount and/or contingent on the occurrence or non-occurrence of future events will also meet the definition of variable consideration (see 5.2 above). As a result, some stakeholders had questioned which exception would apply – allocating a discount or allocating variable consideration.

At the March 2015 TRG meeting, the TRG members generally agreed that an entity will first determine whether a variable discount meets the variable consideration exception (see 6.3 above). *[IFRS 15.86]*. If it does not, the entity will then consider whether it meets the discount exception (see 6.4 above).

In reaching that conclusion, the TRG agenda paper noted that paragraph 86 of IFRS 15 establishes a hierarchy for allocating variable consideration that requires an entity to identify variable consideration and then determine whether it should allocate variable consideration to one or some, but not all, performance obligations (or distinct goods or services that comprise a single performance obligation) based on the exception for allocating variable consideration. The entity would consider the requirements for allocating a discount only if the discount is not variable consideration (i.e. the amount of the discount is fixed and not contingent on future events) or the entity does not meet the criteria to allocate variable consideration to a specific part of the contract.[88]

6.5 Changes in transaction price after contract inception

After contract inception, 'the transaction price can change for various reasons, including the resolution of uncertain events or other changes in circumstances that change the amount of consideration to which an entity expects to be entitled in exchange for the promised goods or services.' *[IFRS 15.87]*.

Changes in the total transaction price are generally allocated to the performance obligations on the same basis as the initial allocation, whether they are allocated based on the relative stand-alone selling price (i.e. using the same proportionate share of the total) or to individual performance obligations under the variable consideration exception discussed at 6.3 above. Amounts allocated to a satisfied performance obligation should be recognised as revenue, or a reduction in revenue, in the period that the transaction price changes. As discussed at 6.1 above, stand-alone selling prices are not updated after contract inception, unless the contract has been modified. *[IFRS 15.88-89]*.

If the change in the transaction price is due to a contract modification, the contract modification requirements in paragraphs 18-21 of IFRS 15 must be followed (see 3.4 above for a discussion on contract modifications). *[IFRS 15.90]*.

However, when contracts include variable consideration, it is possible that changes in the transaction price that arise after a modification may (or may not) be related to performance obligations that existed before the modification. For changes in the transaction price arising after a contract modification that is not treated as a separate contract, an entity must apply one of the two approaches: *[IFRS 15.90]*

- if the change in transaction price is attributable to an amount of variable consideration promised before the modification and the modification was considered a termination of the existing contract and the creation of a new contract, the entity allocates the change in transaction price to the performance obligations that existed before the modification; or
- in all other cases, the change in the transaction price is allocated to the performance obligations in the modified contract (i.e. the performance obligations that were unsatisfied and partially unsatisfied immediately after the modification).

6.6 Allocation of transaction price to components outside the scope of IFRS 15

Revenue arrangements frequently contain multiple elements, including some components that are not within the scope of IFRS 15. As discussed further at 2.4 above, the standard indicates that in such situations, an entity must first apply the other standards if those standards address separation and/or measurement. *[IFRS 15.7]*.

For example, some standards require certain components, such as derivatives, to be accounted for at fair value. As a result, when a revenue contract includes that type of component, the fair value of that component must be separated from the total transaction price. The remaining transaction price is then allocated to the remaining performance obligations. The following example illustrates this concept.

Example 30.45: Arrangements with components outside the scope of the standard

Company A sells widgets to Company B. The transaction is denominated in Japanese yen. Both companies are located in Europe and the euro is their functional currency. Since Japanese yen is not the functional currency of either company, and the product is not routinely or commonly denominated in yen, Company A identifies an embedded foreign currency derivative.

Company A sells the widgets to Company B for total consideration of ¥5,650,000, which is equivalent to €50,000 at contract inception. The stand-alone selling price of the widgets and the fair value of the embedded derivative are €48,000 and €4,000, respectively.

Analysis

Company A determines that the embedded foreign currency derivative would be separable and needs to be accounted for in accordance with IAS 39.

In accordance with paragraph 7 of IFRS 15, because IAS 39 provides measurement requirements (i.e. requires that embedded derivatives in its scope be initially recognised at fair value), Company A excludes from the IFRS 15 transaction price the fair value of the embedded derivative.

Company A allocates the remaining transaction price to the widgets. The allocation of the total transaction price is as follows:

	Selling price and fair value	% Allocated discount	Allocated discount	Arrangement consideration allocation
Widgets	€48,000	100%	€2,000	€46,000
Embedded foreign currency derivative	€4,000	0%	–	€4,000
	€52,000		€2,000	€50,000

For components that must be recognised at fair value on inception, any subsequent remeasurement would be pursuant to other IFRSs (e.g. IFRS 9 or IAS 39). That is, subsequent adjustments to the fair value of those components have no effect on the amount of the transaction price previously allocated to any performance obligations included within the contract or on revenue recognised.

7 SATISFACTION OF PERFORMANCE OBLIGATIONS

Under IFRS 15, an entity only recognises revenue when it satisfies an identified performance obligation by transferring a promised good or service to a customer. A good or service is considered to be transferred when the customer obtains control. *[IFRS 15.31]*.

Recognising revenue upon a transfer of control is a different approach from the 'risks and rewards' model that currently exists in IFRS. IFRS 15 states that 'control of an asset refers to the ability to direct the use of and obtain substantially all of the remaining benefits from the asset'. Control also means the ability to prevent others from directing the use of, and receiving the benefit from, a good or service. *[IFRS 15.33]*. The Board noted that both goods and services are assets that a customer acquires (even if many services are not recognised as an asset because those services are simultaneously received and consumed by the customer). *[IFRS 15.BC118]*. The IASB explained the key terms in the definition of control in the Basis for Conclusions, which are as follows. *[IFRS 15.BC120]*

- *Ability* – a customer must have the present right to direct the use of, and obtain substantially all of the remaining benefits from, an asset for an entity to recognise revenue. For example, in a contract that requires a manufacturer to produce an asset for a customer, it might be clear that the customer will ultimately have the right to direct the use of, and obtain substantially all of the remaining benefits from, the asset. However, the entity should not recognise revenue until the customer has actually obtained that right (which, depending on the contract, may occur during production or afterwards).
- *Direct the use of* – a customer's ability to direct the use of an asset refers to the customer's right to deploy or to allow another entity to deploy that asset in its activities or to restrict another entity from deploying that asset.
- *Obtain the benefits from* – the customer must have the ability to obtain substantially all of the remaining benefits from an asset for the customer to obtain control of it. Conceptually, the benefits from a good or service are

potential cash flows (either an increase in cash inflows or a decrease in cash outflows). A customer can obtain the benefits directly or indirectly in many ways, such as: using the asset to produce goods or services (including public services); using the asset to enhance the value of other assets; using the asset to settle a liability or reduce an expense; selling or exchanging the asset; pledging the asset to secure a loan; or holding the asset. *[IFRS 15.33]*.

Under IFRS 15, the transfer of control to the customer represents the transfer of the rights with regard to the good or service. The customer's ability to receive the benefit from the good or service is represented by its right to substantially all of the cash inflows, or the reduction of the cash outflows, generated by the goods or services. *[IFRS 15.33]*. Upon transfer of control, the customer has sole possession of the right to use the good or service for the remainder of its economic life or to consume the good or service in its own operations.

The IASB explained in the Basis for Conclusions that control should be assessed primarily from the customer's perspective. While a seller often surrenders control at the same time the customer obtains control, the Board required the assessment of control to be from the customer's perspective to minimise the risk of an entity recognising revenue from activities that do not coincide with the transfer of goods or services to the customer. *[IFRS 15.BC121]*.

The standard indicates that an entity must determine, at contract inception, whether it will transfer control of a promised good or service over time. If an entity does not satisfy a performance obligation over time, the performance obligation is satisfied at a point in time. *[IFRS 15.32]*. These concepts are explored further in the following sections.

7.1 Performance obligations satisfied over time

Frequently, entities transfer the promised goods and services to the customer over time. While the determination of whether goods or services are transferred over time is straightforward in some contracts (e.g. many service contracts), it is more difficult in other contracts.

To help entities determine whether control transfers over time (rather than at a point in time), the standard states that an entity transfers control of a good or service over time (and, therefore, satisfies a performance obligation and recognises revenue over time) if one of the following criteria is met: *[IFRS 15.35]*

(a) the customer simultaneously receives and consumes the benefits provided by the entity's performance as the entity performs (see 7.1.1 below);

(b) the entity's performance creates or enhances an asset (e.g. work in progress) that the customer controls as the asset is created or enhanced (see 7.1.2 below); or

(c) the entity's performance does not create an asset with an alternative use to the entity and the entity has an enforceable right to payment for performance completed to date (see 7.1.3 below).

Examples of each of the criteria above are included in the following sections. If an entity is unable to demonstrate that control transfers over time, the presumption is that control transfers at a point in time (see 7.3 below). *[IFRS 15.32]*.

For each performance obligation identified in the contract, an entity is required to consider at contract inception whether it satisfies the performance obligation over time (i.e. whether it meets one of the three criteria for over time recognition) or at a point in time. This evaluation will require many entities to perform new analyses or to perform analyses that differ from what they do under current IFRS. For example, entities that enter in to contracts to construct real estate for a customer will no longer need to determine if the contract either meets the definition of a construction contract (in order to apply IAS 11) or is for the provision of services (under IAS 18) so as to recognise revenue over time. Instead, under IFRS 15, an entity needs to determine whether its performance obligations are satisfied over time by evaluating the three criteria for over time recognition. If an entity does not satisfy a performance obligation over time, the performance obligation is satisfied at a point in time.

7.1.1 Customer simultaneously receives and consumes benefits as the entity performs

As the Board explained in the Basis for Conclusions, in many service contracts the entity's performance creates an asset, momentarily, because that asset is simultaneously received and consumed by the customer. In these cases, the customer obtains control of the entity's output as the entity performs. Therefore, the performance obligation is satisfied over time. *[IFRS 15.BC125]*.

There may be service contracts in which it is unclear whether the customer simultaneously receives and consumes the benefit of the entity's performance over time. IFRS 15 states that, for some types of performance obligations, the assessment of whether a customer receives the benefits of an entity's performance as the entity performs and simultaneously consumes those benefits as they are received will be straightforward. Examples given by the standard include routine or recurring services (e.g. a cleaning service) in which the receipt and simultaneous consumption by the customer of the benefits of the entity's performance can be readily identified. *[IFRS 15.B3]*.

For other types of performance obligations, an entity may not be able to readily identify whether a customer simultaneously receives and consumes the benefits from the entity's performance as the entity performs. In those circumstances, IFRS 15 states that 'a performance obligation is satisfied over time if an entity determines that another entity would not need to substantially re-perform the work that the entity has completed to date if that other entity were to fulfil the remaining performance obligation to the customer'. *[IFRS 15.B4]*.

In determining whether another entity would not need to substantially re-perform the work the entity has completed to date, the standard requires an entity to make both of the following assumptions: *[IFRS 15.B4]*

- disregard potential contractual restrictions or practical limitations that otherwise would prevent the entity from transferring the remaining performance obligation to another entity; and
- presume that another entity fulfilling the remainder of the performance obligation would not have the benefit of any asset that is presently controlled by the entity (and that would remain controlled by the entity if the performance obligation were to transfer to another entity).

The IASB added this application guidance because the notion of 'benefit' can be subjective. As discussed in the Basis for Conclusions, the Board provided an example of a freight logistics contract. Assume that the entity has agreed to transport goods from Vancouver to New York City. Some stakeholders had suggested that the customer receives no benefit from the entity's performance until the goods are delivered to, in this case, New York City. However, the Board said that the customer benefits as the entity performs. This is because, if the goods were only delivered part of the way (e.g. to Chicago), another entity would not need to substantially re-perform the entity's performance to date. The Board observed that in these cases, the assessment of whether another entity would need to substantially re-perform the entity's performance to date is an objective way to assess whether the customer receives benefit from the entity's performance as it occurs. *[IFRS 15.BC126]*.

In assessing whether a customer simultaneously receives and consumes the benefits provided by an entity's performance, all relevant facts and circumstances need to be considered. This includes considering the inherent characteristics of the good or service, the contract terms and information about how the good or service is transferred or delivered. However, as noted in paragraph B4(a) of IFRS 15 (the first bullet above), an entity disregards any contractual or practical restrictions when it assesses this criterion. In the Basis for Conclusions, the IASB explained that the assessment of whether control of the goods or services has transferred to the customer is performed by making a hypothetical assessment of what another entity would need to do if it were to take over the remaining performance. Therefore, actual practical or contractual restrictions would have no bearing on the assessment of whether the entity had already transferred control of the goods or services provided to date. *[IFRS 15.BC127]*.

The standard provides the following example that illustrates a customer simultaneously receiving and consuming the benefits as the entity performs in relation to a series of distinct payroll processing services. *[IFRS 15.IE67-IE68]*.

Example 30.46: Customer simultaneously receives and consumes the benefits

An entity enters into a contract to provide monthly payroll processing services to a customer for one year.

The promised payroll processing services are accounted for as a single performance obligation in accordance with paragraph 22(b) of IFRS 15. The performance obligation is satisfied over time in accordance with paragraph 35(a) of IFRS 15 because the customer simultaneously receives and consumes the benefits of the entity's performance in processing each payroll transaction as and when each transaction is processed. The fact that another entity would not need to re-perform payroll processing services for the service that the entity has provided to date also demonstrates that the customer simultaneously receives and consumes the benefits of the entity's performance as the entity performs. (The entity disregards any practical limitations on transferring the remaining performance obligation, including setup activities that would need to be undertaken by another entity.) The entity recognises revenue over time by measuring its progress towards complete satisfaction of that performance obligation in accordance with paragraphs 39-45 and B14-B19 of IFRS 15.

The IASB clarified, in the Basis for Conclusions, that an entity does not evaluate this criterion (to determine whether a performance obligation is satisfied over time) if the entity's performance creates an asset that the customer does not consume immediately as the asset is received. Instead, an entity assesses that performance obligation using the criteria discussed at 7.1.2 and 7.1.3 below.

For some service contracts, the entity's performance will not satisfy its obligation over time because the customer does not consume the benefit of the entity's performance until the entity's performance is complete. The standard provides an example (Example 14 of IFRS 15, included as Example 30.48 at 7.1.3.B below) of an entity providing consulting services that will take the form of a professional opinion upon the completion of the services. In this situation, an entity cannot conclude that the services are transferred over time based on this criterion. Instead, the entity must consider the remaining two criteria in paragraph 35 of IFRS 15 (see 7.1.2 and 7.1.3 and Example 30.48 below).

7.1.1.A Evaluating whether a customer simultaneously receives and consumes the benefits of a commodity as the entity performs

In July 2015, the TRG members discussed the factors that an entity should consider when evaluating whether a customer simultaneously receives and consumes the benefits of a commodity (e.g. electricity, natural gas, heating oil) as the entity performs.[89]

The TRG members generally agreed that an entity would consider all known facts and circumstances when evaluating whether a customer simultaneously receives and consumes the benefits of a commodity. These may include the inherent characteristics of the commodity (e.g. whether the commodity can be stored), contract terms (e.g. a continuous supply contract to meet immediate demands) and information about infrastructure or other delivery mechanisms.

As such, revenue related to the sale of a commodity may or may not be recognised over time, depending on whether the facts and circumstances of the contract indicate that the customer will simultaneously receive and consume the benefits. This evaluation will likely require the use of significant judgement.

Whether a commodity meets this criterion and is transferred over time is important in determining whether the sale of a commodity will meet the criteria to apply the series requirement (see 4.2.2 above). This, in turn, affects how an entity will allocate variable consideration and apply the requirements for contract modifications and changes in the transaction price.

7.1.2 Customer controls asset as it is created or enhanced

The second criterion to determine whether control of a good or service is transferred over time requires entities to evaluate whether the customer controls the asset as it is being created or enhanced. An entity applies the requirements for control in paragraphs 31-34 and 38 of IFRS 15. *[IFRS 15.B5]*.

For the purpose of this determination, the definition of 'control' is the same as previously discussed (i.e. the ability to direct the use of and obtain substantially all of the remaining benefits from the asset). The IASB explained in the Basis for Conclusions that this criterion addresses situations in which the customer controls any work in progress arising from the entity's performance. *[IFRS 15.BC129]*. For example, some construction contracts may also contain clauses indicating that the customer owns any work in progress as the contracted item is being built.

Furthermore, the asset being created or enhanced can be either tangible or intangible. *[IFRS 15.B5]*.

The Board observed in the Basis for Conclusions that the second over-time criterion (related to the customer's control of the asset as it is being created or enhanced) is consistent with the rationale for the percentage-of-completion revenue recognition approach for construction contracts under current US GAAP. *[IFRS 15.BC130]*. Both approaches acknowledge that, in effect, the entity has agreed to sell its rights to the asset (i.e. work in progress) as the entity performs (i.e. a continuous sale).

7.1.3 Asset with no alternative use and right to payment

In some cases, it may be unclear whether the asset that an entity creates or enhances is controlled by the customer when considering the first two criteria (discussed at 7.1.1 and 7.1.2 above) for evaluating whether control transfers over time. Therefore, the Board added a third criterion, which requires revenue to be recognised over time if both of the following two requirements are met: *[IFRS 15.35(c)]*

- the entity's performance does not create an asset with alternative use to the entity (see 7.1.3.A below); and
- the entity has an enforceable right to payment for performance completed to date (see 7.1.3.B below).

7.1.3.A Alternative use

The IASB explained in the Basis for Conclusions that it had developed the notion of 'alternative use' to prevent over time revenue recognition when the entity's performance does not transfer control of the goods or services to the customer over time. When the entity's performance creates an asset with an alternative use to the entity (e.g. standard inventory items), the entity can readily direct the asset to another customer. In those cases, the entity (not the customer) controls the asset as it is created because the customer does not have the ability to direct the use of the asset or restrict the entity from directing that asset to another customer. The standard states that an asset created by an entity's performance 'does not have an alternative use to an entity if the entity is either restricted contractually from readily directing the asset for another use during the creation or enhancement of that asset or limited practically from readily directing the asset in its completed state for another use'. The assessment of whether an asset has an alternative use to the entity is made at contract inception. *[IFRS 15.36]*.

In assessing whether an asset has an alternative use, an entity is required to consider the effects of contractual restrictions and practical limitations on its ability to readily direct that asset for another use (e.g. selling it to a different customer). The standard clarifies that the possibility of the contract with the customer being terminated is not a relevant consideration in this assessment. *[IFRS 15.B6]*.

In making the assessment of whether a good or service has an alternative use, an entity must consider any substantive contractual restrictions. A contractual restriction is substantive if an entity expects the customer to enforce its rights to the promised asset if the entity sought to direct the asset for another use. *[IFRS 15.B7]*. Contractual restrictions that are not substantive, such as protective rights for the customer, are not considered. The Board explained in the Basis for Conclusions that a protective right typically gives an entity the practical ability to physically substitute or redirect the asset without the customer's knowledge or objection to the change. For example, a contract may specify that an entity cannot transfer a good to another customer because the customer has legal title to the good. Such a contractual term would not be substantive if the entity could physically substitute that good for another and could redirect the original good to another customer for little cost. In that case, the contractual restriction would merely be a protective right and would not indicate that control of the asset has transferred to the customer. *[IFRS 15.BC138]*. As an example, the standard notes that contractual restrictions are not substantive if an asset is largely interchangeable with other assets that the entity could transfer to another customer without breaching the contract and without incurring significant costs that otherwise would not have been incurred in relation to that contract. *[IFRS 15.B7]*.

An entity will also need to consider any practical limitations on directing the asset for another use. A significant economic loss could arise because the entity either would incur significant costs to rework the asset or would only be able to sell the asset at a significant loss. For example, an entity may be practically limited from redirecting assets that either have design specifications that are unique to a customer or are located in remote areas. *[IFRS 15.B8]*. In making this determination, the Board clarified that an entity considers the characteristics of the asset that ultimately will be transferred to the customer and assesses whether the asset in its completed state could be redirected without a significant cost of rework. The Board provided an example of manufacturing contracts in which the basic design of the asset is the same across all contracts, but substantial customisation is made to the asset. As a result, redirecting the finished asset would require significant rework and the asset would not have an alternative use because the entity would incur significant economic losses to direct the asset for another use. *[IFRS 15.BC138]*.

Considering the level of customisation of an asset may help entities assess whether an asset has an alternative use. The IASB noted in the Basis for Conclusions that, when an entity is creating an asset that is highly customised for a particular customer, it is less likely that the entity could use that asset for any other purpose. *[IFRS 15.BC135]*. That is, the entity would likely need to incur significant rework costs to redirect the asset to another customer or sell the asset at a significantly reduced price. As a result, the asset would not have an alternative use to the entity and the customer could be regarded as receiving the benefit of the entity's performance as the entity performs (i.e. having control of the asset), provided that the entity also has an enforceable right to payment (discussed at 7.1.3.B below). However, the Board clarified that although the level of customisation is a factor to consider, but it should not be a determinative factor. For example, in some real estate contracts, the asset may be standardised (i.e. not highly customised), but it still may not have an alternative use to the entity because of substantive contractual restrictions that preclude the entity from readily directing the asset to another customer. *[IFRS 15.BC137]*.

The standard provides the following example to illustrate an evaluation of practical limitations on directing an asset for another use. *[IFRS 15.IE73-IE76]*.

Example 30.47: Asset has no alternative use to the entity

An entity enters into a contract with a customer, a government agency, to build a specialised satellite. The entity builds satellites for various customers, such as governments and commercial entities. The design and construction of each satellite differ substantially, on the basis of each customer's needs and the type of technology that is incorporated into the satellite.

At contract inception, the entity assesses whether its performance obligation to build the satellite is a performance obligation satisfied over time in accordance with paragraph 35 of IFRS 15.

As part of that assessment, the entity considers whether the satellite in its completed state will have an alternative use to the entity. Although the contract does not preclude the entity from directing the completed satellite to another customer, the entity would incur significant costs to rework the design and function of the satellite to direct that asset to another customer. Consequently, the asset has no alternative use to the entity (see paragraphs 35(c), 36 and B6–B8 of IFRS 15) because the customer-specific design of the satellite limits the entity's practical ability to readily direct the satellite to another customer.

For the entity's performance obligation to be satisfied over time when building the satellite, paragraph 35(c) of IFRS 15 also requires the entity to have an enforceable right to payment for performance completed to date. This condition is not illustrated in this example.

Requiring an entity to assess contractual restrictions when evaluating this criterion may seem to contradict the requirements in paragraph B4 of IFRS 15 to ignore contractual and practical restrictions when evaluating whether another entity would need to substantially reperform the work the entity has completed to date (see 7.1.1 above). The Board explained that this difference is appropriate because each criterion provides a different method for assessing when control transfers and the criteria were designed to apply to different situations. *[IFRS 15.BC139]*.

After contract inception, an entity does not update its assessment of whether an asset has an alternative use for any subsequent changes in facts and circumstances, unless the parties approve a contract modification that substantively changes the performance obligation. *[IFRS 15.36]*. The IASB also decided that an entity's lack of an alternative use for an asset does not, by itself, mean that the customer effectively controls the asset. The entity would also need to determine that it has an enforceable right to payment for performance to date, as discussed below. *[IFRS 15.BC141]*.

Chapter 30

7.1.3.B *Enforceable right to payment for performance completed to date*

To evaluate whether it has an enforceable right to payment for performance completed to date, the entity is required to consider the terms of the contract and any laws or regulations that relate to it. *[IFRS 15.37, B12]*. The standard states that the right to payment for performance completed to date need not be for a fixed amount. However, at any time during the contract term, an entity must be entitled to an amount that at least compensates the entity for performance completed to date, even if the contract is terminated by the customer (or another party) for reasons other than the entity's failure to perform as promised. *[IFRS 15.37, B9]*. The IASB concluded that a customer's obligation to pay for the entity's performance is an indicator that the customer has obtained benefit from the entity's performance. *[IFRS 15.BC142]*.

The standard clarifies that an amount that would compensate an entity for performance completed to date would be an amount that approximates the selling price of the goods or services transferred to date (e.g. recovery of the costs incurred by an entity in satisfying the performance obligation plus a reasonable profit margin), rather than compensation for only the entity's potential loss of profit if the contract were to be terminated. *[IFRS 15.B9]*.

Compensation for a reasonable profit margin need not equal the profit margin expected if the contract was fulfilled as promised, but the standard states that an entity should be entitled to compensation for either of the following amounts: *[IFRS 15.B9]*

- a proportion of the expected profit margin in the contract that reasonably reflects the extent of the entity's performance under the contract before termination by the customer (or another party); or
- a reasonable return on the entity's cost of capital for similar contracts (or the entity's typical operating margin for similar contracts) if the contract-specific margin is higher than the return the entity usually generates from similar contracts.

The standard is clear that an entity's right to payment for performance completed to date need not be a present unconditional right to payment. In many cases, an entity will have an unconditional right to payment only at an agreed-upon milestone or upon complete satisfaction of the performance obligation. Therefore, when assessing whether it has a right to payment for performance completed to date, an entity is required to consider whether it would have an enforceable right to demand or retain payment for performance completed to date if the contract were to be terminated before completion (for reasons other than the entity's failure to perform as promised). *[IFRS 15.B10]*.

In some contracts, a customer may have a right to terminate the contract only at specified times during the life of the contract or the customer might not have any right to terminate the contract. The standard states that, if a customer acts to terminate a contract without having the right to terminate the contract at that time (including when a customer fails to perform its obligations as promised), the contract (or other laws) might entitle the entity to continue to transfer the promised goods or services in the contract to the customer and require the customer to pay the promised consideration. In those circumstances, an entity has a right to payment for performance completed to date because the entity has a right to continue to perform its obligations in accordance with the contract and to require the customer to perform its obligations (which include paying the promised consideration). *[IFRS 15.B11]*.

The IASB described in the Basis for Conclusions how the factors of 'no alternative use' and the 'right to payment' relate to the assessment of control. Since an entity is constructing an asset with no alternative use to the entity, the entity is effectively creating an asset at the direction of the customer. That asset would have little or no value to the entity if the customer were to terminate the contract. As a result, the entity will seek economic protection from the risk of customer termination by requiring the customer to pay for the entity's performance to date in the event of customer termination. The customer's obligation to pay for the entity's performance to date (or, the inability to avoid paying for that performance) suggests that the customer has obtained the benefits from the entity's performance. *[IFRS 15.BC142]*.

The enforceable right to payment criterion has two components that an entity must assess:

- the amount that the customer would be required to pay; and
- what it means to have the enforceable right to payment.

The Board provided additional application guidance on how to evaluate each of these components.

Firstly, the Board explained in the Basis for Conclusions that the focus of the analysis should be on the amount to which the entity would be entitled upon termination. *[IFRS 15.BC144]*. This amount is not the amount the entity would settle for in a negotiation and it does not need to reflect the full contract margin that the entity would earn if the contract were completed. The Board clarified in paragraph B9 of IFRS 15 that a 'reasonable profit margin' would either be a proportion of the entity's expected profit margin that reasonably reflects the entity's performance to date or a reasonable return on the entity's cost of capital. In addition, in paragraph B13 of IFRS 15, the standard clarifies that including a payment schedule in a contract does not, in and of itself, indicate that the entity has the right to payment for performance completed to date. This is because, in some cases, the contract may specify that the consideration received from the customer is refundable for reasons other than the entity failing to perform as promised in the contract. The entity must examine information that may contradict the payment schedule and may represent the entity's actual right to payment for performance completed to date. As highlighted in the Example 30.49 below, payments from a customer must approximate the selling price of the goods or services transferred to date to be considered a right to payment for performance to date. A fixed payment schedule may not meet this requirement. *[IFRS 15.B13]*.

Secondly, the IASB added application guidance in paragraph B12 of IFRS 15 to help an entity determine whether the right to payment is enforceable. Entities are required to consider any laws, legislation or legal precedent that could supplement or override the contractual terms. *[IFRS 15.B12]*. This may require entities to consult with legal counsel to establish their enforceable right to payment for performance completed to date. Paragraph B12 of IFRS 15 states that the assessment includes consideration of:

'(a) legislation, administrative practice or legal precedent confers upon the entity a right to payment for performance to date even though that right is not specified in the contract with the customer;

(b) relevant legal precedent indicates that similar rights to payment for performance completed to date in similar contracts have no binding legal effect; or

(c) an entity's customary business practices of choosing not to enforce a right to payment has resulted in the right being rendered unenforceable in that legal environment. However, notwithstanding that an entity may choose to waive its right to payment in similar contracts, an entity would continue to have a right to payment to date if, in the contract with the customer, its right to payment for performance to date remains enforceable.' *[IFRS 15.B12]*.

Furthermore, the standard indicates that an entity may have an enforceable right to payment even when the customer terminates the contract without having the right to terminate. This would be the case if the contract (or other law) entitles the entity to continue to transfer the goods or services promised in the contract and require the customer to pay the consideration promised for those goods or services (often referred to as 'specific performance'). *[IFRS 15.BC145]*. The standard also states that even when an entity chooses to waive its right to payment in other similar contracts, an entity would continue to have a right to payment for the contract if, in the contract, its right to payment for performance to date remains enforceable.

The standard provides the following example to illustrate the concepts described at 7.1.3 above. It depicts an entity providing consulting services that will take the form of a professional opinion upon the completion of the services, as follows. In this example, the entity's performance obligation meets the no alternative use and right to payment criterion in paragraph 35(c) of IFRS 15, as follows. *[IFRS 15.IE69-IE72]*.

Example 30.48: Assessing alternative use and right to payment

An entity enters into a contract with a customer to provide a consulting service that results in the entity providing a professional opinion to the customer. The professional opinion relates to facts and circumstances that are specific to the customer. If the customer were to terminate the consulting contract for reasons other than the entity's failure to perform as promised, the contract requires the customer to compensate the entity for its costs incurred plus a 15 per cent margin. The 15 per cent margin approximates the profit margin that the entity earns from similar contracts.

The entity considers the criterion in paragraph 35(a) of IFRS 15 and the requirements in paragraphs B3 and B4 of IFRS 15 to determine whether the customer simultaneously receives and consumes the benefits of the entity's performance. If the entity were to be unable to satisfy its obligation and the customer hired another consulting firm to provide the opinion, the other consulting firm would need to substantially re-perform the work that the entity had completed to date, because the other consulting firm would not have the benefit of any work in progress performed by the entity. The nature of the professional opinion is such that the customer will receive the benefits of the entity's performance only when the customer receives the professional opinion. Consequently, the entity concludes that the criterion in paragraph 35(a) of IFRS 15 is not met.

However, the entity's performance obligation meets the criterion in paragraph 35(c) of IFRS 15 and is a performance obligation satisfied over time because of both of the following factors:

(a) in accordance with paragraphs 36 and B6-B8 of IFRS 15, the development of the professional opinion does not create an asset with alternative use to the entity because the professional opinion relates to facts and circumstances that are specific to the customer. Therefore, there is a practical limitation on the entity's ability to readily direct the asset to another customer.

(b) in accordance with paragraphs 37 and B9-B13 of IFRS 15, the entity has an enforceable right to payment for its performance completed to date for its costs plus a reasonable margin, which approximates the profit margin in other contracts.

Consequently, the entity recognises revenue over time by measuring the progress towards complete satisfaction of the performance obligation in accordance with paragraphs 39-45 and B14-B19 of IFRS 15.

Example 30.49 illustrates a contract in which the fixed payment schedule is not expected to correspond, at all times throughout the contract, to the amount that would be necessary to compensate the entity for performance completed to date.

Accordingly, the entity concludes that it does not have an enforceable right to payment for performance completed to date as follows. *[IFRS 15.IE77-IE80]*.

Example 30.49: Enforceable right to payment for performance completed to date

An entity enters into a contract with a customer to build an item of equipment. The payment schedule in the contract specifies that the customer must make an advance payment at contract inception of 10 per cent of the contract price, regular payments throughout the construction period (amounting to 50 per cent of the contract price) and a final payment of 40 per cent of the contract price after construction is completed and the equipment has passed the prescribed performance tests. The payments are non-refundable unless the entity fails to perform as promised. If the customer terminates the contract, the entity is entitled only to retain any progress payments received from the customer. The entity has no further rights to compensation from the customer.

At contract inception, the entity assesses whether its performance obligation to build the equipment is a performance obligation satisfied over time in accordance with paragraph 35 of IFRS 15.

As part of that assessment, the entity considers whether it has an enforceable right to payment for performance completed to date in accordance with paragraphs 35(c), 37 and B9–B13 of IFRS 15 if the customer were to terminate the contract for reasons other than the entity's failure to perform as promised. Even though the payments made by the customer are non-refundable, the cumulative amount of those payments is not expected, at all times throughout the contract, to at least correspond to the amount that would be necessary to compensate the entity for performance completed to date. This is because at various times during construction the cumulative amount of consideration paid by the customer might be less than the selling price of the partially completed item of equipment at that time. Consequently, the entity does not have a right to payment for performance completed to date.

Because the entity does not have a right to payment for performance completed to date, the entity's performance obligation is not satisfied over time in accordance with paragraph 35(c) of IFRS 15. Accordingly, the entity does not need to assess whether the equipment would have an alternative use to the entity. The entity also concludes that it does not meet the criteria in paragraph 35(a) or (b) of IFRS 15 and thus, the entity accounts for the construction of the equipment as a performance obligation satisfied at a point in time in accordance with paragraph 38 of IFRS 15.

Example 30.50 contrasts similar situations and illustrates when revenue would be recognised over time (see 7.1 above) versus at a point in time (see 7.3 below). Specifically, this example illustrates the evaluation of the 'no alternative use' and 'right to payment for performance to date' concepts, as follows. *[IFRS 15.IE81-IE90]*.

Example 30.50: Assessing whether a performance obligation is satisfied at a point in time or over time

An entity is developing a multi-unit residential complex. A customer enters into a binding sales contract with the entity for a specified unit that is under construction. Each unit has a similar floor plan and is of a similar size, but other attributes of the units are different (for example, the location of the unit within the complex).

Case A – Entity does not have an enforceable right to payment for performance completed to date

The customer pays a deposit upon entering into the contract and the deposit is refundable only if the entity fails to complete construction of the unit in accordance with the contract. The remainder of the contract price is payable on completion of the contract when the customer obtains physical possession of the unit. If the customer defaults on the contract before completion of the unit, the entity only has the right to retain the deposit.

At contract inception, the entity applies paragraph 35(c) of IFRS 15 to determine whether its promise to construct and transfer the unit to the customer is a performance obligation satisfied over time. The entity determines that it does not have an enforceable right to payment for performance completed to date because, until construction of the unit is complete, the entity only has a right to the deposit paid by the customer. Because the entity does not have a right to payment for work completed to date, the entity's performance obligation is not a performance obligation satisfied over time in accordance with paragraph 35(c) of IFRS 15. Instead, the entity accounts for the sale of the unit as a performance obligation satisfied at a point in time in accordance with paragraph 38 of IFRS 15.

Case B – Entity has an enforceable right to payment for performance completed to date

The customer pays a non-refundable deposit upon entering into the contract and will make progress payments during construction of the unit. The contract has substantive terms that preclude the entity from being able to direct the unit to another customer. In addition, the customer does not have the right to terminate the contract unless the entity fails to perform as promised. If the customer defaults on its obligations by failing to make the promised progress payments as and when they are due, the entity would have a right to all of the consideration promised in the contract if it completes the construction of the unit. The courts have previously upheld similar rights that entitle developers to require the customer to perform, subject to the entity meeting its obligations under the contract.

At contract inception, the entity applies paragraph 35(c) of IFRS 15 to determine whether its promise to construct and transfer the unit to the customer is a performance obligation satisfied over time. The entity determines that the asset (unit) created by the entity's performance does not have an alternative use to the entity because the contract precludes the entity from transferring the specified unit to another customer. The entity does not consider the possibility of a contract termination in assessing whether the entity is able to direct the asset to another customer.

The entity also has a right to payment for performance completed to date in accordance with paragraphs 37 and B9-B13 of IFRS 15. This is because if the customer were to default on its obligations, the entity would have an enforceable right to all of the consideration promised under the contract if it continues to perform as promised.

Therefore, the terms of the contract and the practices in the legal jurisdiction indicate that there is a right to payment for performance completed to date. Consequently, the criteria in paragraph 35(c) of IFRS 15 are met and the entity has a performance obligation that it satisfies over time. To recognise revenue for that performance obligation satisfied over time, the entity measures its progress towards complete satisfaction of its performance obligation in accordance with paragraphs 39-45 and B14-B19 of IFRS 15.

In the construction of a multi-unit residential complex, the entity may have many contracts with individual customers for the construction of individual units within the complex. The entity would account for each contract separately. However, depending on the nature of the construction, the entity's performance in undertaking the initial construction works (i.e. the foundation and the basic structure), as well as the construction of common areas, may need to be reflected when measuring its progress towards complete satisfaction of its performance obligations in each contract.

Case C – Entity has an enforceable right to payment for performance completed to date

The same facts as in Case B apply to Case C, except that in the event of a default by the customer, either the entity can require the customer to perform as required under the contract or the entity can cancel the contract in exchange for the asset under construction and an entitlement to a penalty of a proportion of the contract price.

Notwithstanding that the entity could cancel the contract (in which case the customer's obligation to the entity would be limited to transferring control of the partially completed asset to the entity and paying the penalty prescribed), the entity has a right to payment for performance completed to date because the entity could also choose to enforce its rights to full payment under the contract. The fact that the entity may choose to cancel the contract in the event the customer defaults on its obligations would not affect that assessment (see paragraph B11 of IFRS 15), provided that the entity's rights to require the customer to continue to perform as required under the contract (i.e. pay the promised consideration) are enforceable.

7.1.3.C *Enforceable right to payment: does an entity need a present unconditional right to payment?*

In order to have an enforceable right to payment for performance completed to date, does an entity need to have a present unconditional right to payment? In the Basis for Conclusions, the IASB clarified that the contractual payment terms in a contract may not always align with an entity's enforceable rights to payment for performance completed to date. As a result, an entity does not need to have a present unconditional right to payment. Instead, it must have an enforceable right to demand and/or retain payment for performance completed to date upon customer termination without cause. To illustrate this point, the Board included an example of a consulting contract that requires an entity to provide a report at the end of the project. In return, the entity earns a fixed amount, which is due and payable to the entity when it delivers the report. Assume that the entity is performing under the contract and that the contract (or the law) requires the customer to compensate the entity for its performance completed to date. In that situation, the entity would have an enforceable right to payment for performance completed to date, even though an unconditional right to the fixed amount only exists at the time the report is provided to the customer. This is because the entity has a right to demand and retain payment for performance completed to date. *[IFRS 15.BC145]*.

7.1.3.D *Enforceable right to payment: non-refundable upfront payments that represent the full transaction price*

If the entity receives a non-refundable upfront payment that represents the full transaction price, an entity has a right to payment for performance completed to date. The Board explained in the Basis for Conclusions that such a payment would represent an entity's right to payment for performance completed to date provided that the entity's right to retain and not refund the payment is enforceable upon termination by the customer. This is because a full upfront payment would at least compensate an entity for the work completed to date throughout the contract. *[IFRS 15.BC146]*.

7.2 Measuring progress over time

When an entity has determined that a performance obligation is satisfied over time, the standard requires the entity to select a single revenue recognition method for the relevant performance obligation. The objective is to faithfully depict an entity's performance in transferring control of goods or services promised to a customer (i.e. the satisfaction of an entity's performance obligation). *[IFRS 15.39]*.

The standard requires the entity to select a single revenue recognition method to measure progress. The selected method must be applied consistently to similar performance obligations and in similar circumstances. At the end of each reporting period, an entity remeasures its progress towards complete satisfaction of a performance obligation satisfied over time. *[IFRS 15.40]*. Regardless of which method an entity selects, it excludes from its measure of progress any goods or services for which control has not transferred. *[IFRS 15.42]*.

As circumstances change over time, an entity updates its measure of progress to reflect any changes in the outcome of the performance obligation. Such changes to an entity's measure of progress are accounted for as a change in accounting estimate in accordance with IAS 8. *[IFRS 15.43]*.

While the standard requires an entity to update its estimates related to the measure of progress selected, it does not permit a change in method. A performance obligation is accounted for using the method the entity selects (i.e. either the specific input or output method it has chosen) from inception until the performance obligation has been fully satisfied. It would not be appropriate for an entity to start recognising revenue based on an input measure and later switch to an output measure (or to switch from one input method to a different input method). Furthermore, the standard requires that the selected method be applied to similar contracts in similar circumstances. It also requires that a single method of measuring progress be used for each performance obligation. *[IFRS 15.40]*. The Board noted that applying more than one method to measure performance would effectively override the guidance on identifying performance obligations. *[IFRS 15.BC161]*.

If an entity does not have a reasonable basis to measure its progress, revenue cannot be recognised until progress can be reasonably measured. *[IFRS 15.44]*. An entity may be able to determine that a loss will not be incurred, but may not be able to reasonably estimate the amount of profit. Until an entity is able to reasonably measure the outcome, the standard requires the entity to recognise revenue, but only up to the amount of the costs incurred. *[IFRS 15.45]*. However, the IASB explained that an entity would need to stop using this method once it is able to reasonably measure its progress towards satisfaction of the performance obligation. *[IFRS 15.BC180]*. Finally, stakeholders had asked whether an entity's inability to measure progress would mean that costs incurred would also be deferred. The Board clarified that costs cannot be deferred in these situations, unless they meet the criteria for capitalisation under paragraph 95 of IFRS 15 (see 9.3.2 below). *[IFRS 15.BC179]*.

The standard provides two methods for recognising revenue on contracts involving the transfer of goods and services over time: input methods and output methods. *[IFRS 15.41, B14]*. The standard contains the following application guidance on these methods.

- *Output methods*

  Output methods recognise revenue on the basis of direct measurements of the value to the customer of the goods or services transferred to date relative to the remaining goods or services promised under the contract. Output methods include methods such as surveys of performance completed to date, appraisals of results achieved, milestones reached, time elapsed and units produced or units delivered. *[IFRS 15.B15]*.

  When an entity evaluates whether to apply an output method to measure its progress, the standard requires that an entity consider whether the output selected would faithfully depict the entity's performance towards complete satisfaction of the performance obligation. This would not be the case if the output selected would fail to measure some of the goods or services for which control has transferred to the customer. For example, output methods based on units produced or units delivered would not faithfully depict an entity's performance in satisfying a performance obligation if, at the end of the reporting period, the entity's performance has produced work in progress or finished goods controlled by the customer that are not included in the measurement of the output. *[IFRS 15.B15]*.

As a practical expedient, if an entity has a right to consideration from a customer in an amount that corresponds directly with the value to the customer of the entity's performance completed to date (e.g. a service contract in which an entity bills a fixed amount for each hour of service provided), the entity may recognise revenue in the amount to which the entity has a right to invoice ('right to invoice' practical expedient, see 7.2.4.E and 10.4.1.D below for further discussion). *[IFRS 15.B16]*.

The disadvantages of output methods are that the outputs used to measure progress may not be directly observable and the information required to apply them may not be available to an entity without undue cost. Therefore, an input method may be necessary. *[IFRS 15.B17]*.

- *Input methods*

  Input methods recognise revenue on the basis of the entity's efforts or inputs to the satisfaction of a performance obligation (e.g. resources consumed, labour hours expended, costs incurred, time elapsed or machine hours used) relative to the total expected inputs to the satisfaction of that performance obligation. If the entity's efforts or inputs are expended evenly throughout the performance period, it may be appropriate for the entity to recognise revenue on a straight-line basis. *[IFRS 15.B18]*.

In determining the best method for measuring progress that faithfully depicts an entity's performance, an entity needs to consider both the nature of the promised goods or services and the nature of the entity's performance. *[IFRS 15.41]*. In other words, an entity's selection of a method to measure its performance needs to be consistent with the nature of its promise to the customer and what the entity has agreed to transfer to the customer. To illustrate this concept, the Basis for Conclusions cites, as an example, a contract for health club services. *[IFRS 15.BC160]*. Regardless of when, or how frequently, the customer uses the health club, the entity's obligation to stand ready for the contractual period does not change. Furthermore, the customer is required to pay the fee regardless of whether the customer uses the health club. As a result, the entity would need to select a measure of progress based on its service of standing ready to make the health club available.

Chapter 30

7.2.1 Output methods

While there is no preferable measure of progress, the IASB stated in the Basis for Conclusions that, conceptually, an output measure is the most faithful depiction of an entity's performance. This is because it directly measures the value of the goods and services transferred to the customer. *[IFRS 15.BC160]*. However, the Board discussed two output methods that may not always be appropriate: units of delivery and units of production. *[IFRS 15.BC165]*.

Units-of-delivery or units-of-production methods may not result in the best depiction of an entity's performance over time if there is material work-in-progress at the end of the reporting period. In these cases, the IASB observed that using a units-of-delivery or units-of-production method would distort the entity's performance because it would not recognise revenue for the customer-controlled assets that are created before delivery or before construction is complete. This is because, when an entity determines control transfers to the customer over time, it has concluded that the customer controls any resulting asset as it is created. Therefore, the entity must recognise revenue related to those goods or services for which control has transferred. The IASB also stated, in the Basis for Conclusions, that a units-of-delivery or units-of-production method may not be appropriate if the contract provides both design and production services because each item produced 'may not transfer an equal amount of value to the customer'. *[IFRS 15.BC166]*. That is, the items produced earlier will likely have a higher value than those that are produced later. It is important to note that 'value to the customer' in paragraph B15 of IFRS 15 refers to an objective method of measuring the entity's performance in the contract. This is not intended to be assessed by reference to the market prices, stand-alone selling prices or the value a customer perceives to be embodied in the goods or services. *[IFRS 15.BC163]*. The TRG agenda paper noted that this concept of value is different from the concept of value an entity uses to determine whether it can use the 'right to invoice' practical expedient, as discussed below. When an entity determines whether items individually transfer an equal amount of value to the customer (i.e. when applying paragraph B15 of IFRS 15), the evaluation related to how much, or what proportion, of the goods or services (i.e. quantities) have been delivered (but not the price). For example, for the purposes of applying paragraph B15 of IFRS 15, an entity might consider the amount of goods or services transferred to date in proportion to the total expected goods or services to be transferred when measuring progress. However, if this measure of progress results in material work-in-progress at the end of the reporting period, it would not be appropriate, as discussed above.[90] See the discussion at 7.2.1.A below regarding the evaluation of 'value to the customer' in the context of evaluating the 'right to invoice' practical expedient in paragraph B16 of IFRS 15.

7.2.1.A Practical expedient for measuring progress towards satisfaction of a performance obligation

The Board provided a practical expedient in paragraph B16 of IFRS 15 for an entity that is using an output method to measure progress towards completion of a performance obligation that is satisfied over time. The practical expedient only applies if an entity can demonstrate that the invoiced amount corresponds directly with the value to the customer of the entity's performance completed to date. *[IFRS 15.B16]*. In that situation, the practical expedient allows an entity to recognise revenue in the amount for which it has the right to invoice (i.e. the 'right to invoice' practical expedient). An entity may be able to use this practical expedient for a service contract in which an entity bills a fixed amount for each hour of service provided.

A TRG agenda paper noted that paragraph B16 of IFRS 15 is intended as an expedient to some aspects of Step 3, Step 4 and Step 5 in the standard. Because this practical expedient allows an entity to recognise revenue on the basis of invoicing, revenue is recognised by multiplying the price (assigned to the goods or services delivered) by the measure of progress (i.e. the quantities or units transferred). Therefore, an entity effectively bypasses the steps in the model for determining the transaction price, allocating that transaction price to the performance obligations and determining when to recognise revenue. However, it does not permit an entity to bypass the requirements for identifying the performance obligations in the contract and evaluating whether the performance obligation are satisfied over time, which is a requirement to use this expedient.[91]

To apply the practical expedient, an entity must also be able to assert that the right to consideration from a customer corresponds directly with the value to the customer of the entity's performance to date. When determining whether the amount that has been invoiced to the customer corresponds directly with the value to the customer of an entity's performance completed to date, the entity could evaluate the amount that has been invoiced in comparison to market prices, stand-alone selling prices or another reasonable measure of value to the customer. See 7.2.4.E below for the TRG discussion on evaluating value to the customer in contracts with changing rates.

Furthermore, the TRG members also noted in their discussion of the TRG agenda paper that an entity would have to evaluate all significant upfront payments or retrospective adjustments (e.g. accumulating rebates) in order to determine whether the amount the entity has a right to invoice for each good or service corresponds directly to the value to the customer of the entity's performance completed to date. That is, if an upfront payment or retrospective adjustment shifts payment for value to the customer to the front or back-end of a contract, it may be difficult for an entity to conclude that the amount invoiced corresponds directly with the value provided to the customer for goods or services.[92]

The TRG agenda paper also stated that the presence of an agreed-upon customer payment schedule does not mean that the amount an entity has the right to invoice corresponds directly with the value to the customer of the entity's performance completed to date. In addition, the TRG agenda paper stated that the existence of specified contract minimums (or volume discounts) would not always preclude the application of the practical expedient, provided that these clauses are deemed non-substantive (e.g. the entity expects to receive amounts in excess of the specified minimums).[93]

7.2.2 Input methods

Input methods recognise revenue based on an entity's efforts or inputs towards satisfying a performance obligation relative to the total expected efforts or inputs to satisfy the performance obligation. Examples of input methods mentioned in the standard include costs incurred, time elapsed, resources consumed or labour hours expended. An entity is required to select a single measure of progress for each performance obligation that depicts the entity's performance in transferring control of the goods or services promised to a customer. If an entity's efforts or inputs are used evenly throughout the entity's performance period, a time-based measure that results in a straight line recognition of revenue may be appropriate. However, there may be a disconnect between an entity's inputs (e.g. cost of non-distinct goods included in a single performance obligation satisfied over time) and the depiction of an entity's performance to date. The standard includes specific application guidance on adjustments to the measure of progress that may be necessary in those situations. See 7.2.2.A below for additional discussion.

Regardless of which method an entity selects, it excludes from its measure of progress any goods or services for which control has not transferred to the customer.

7.2.2.A Adjustments to the measure of progress based on an input method

If an entity applies an input method that uses costs incurred to measure its progress towards completion (e.g. cost to cost), the cost incurred may not always be proportionate to the entity's progress in satisfying the performance obligation. To address this shortcoming of input methods, the standard notes that a shortcoming of input methods is that there may not be a direct relationship between an entity's inputs and the transfer of control of goods or services to a customer. Therefore, an entity is required to exclude the effects of any inputs that do not depict the entity's performance (in transferring control of goods or services to the customer) from an input method. For instance, when using a cost-based input method, the standard suggests an adjustment to the measure of progress may be required in the following circumstances: *[IFRS 15.B19]*

(a) When a cost incurred does not contribute to an entity's progress in satisfying the performance obligation.

As an example, the standard states that an entity would not recognise revenue on the basis of costs incurred that are attributable to significant inefficiencies in the entity's performance that were not reflected in the price of the contract (e.g. the costs of unexpected amounts of wasted materials, labour or other resources that were incurred to satisfy the performance obligation).

(b) When a cost incurred is not proportionate to the entity's progress in satisfying the performance obligation.

In those circumstances, the standard states that the best depiction of the entity's performance may be to adjust the input method to recognise revenue only to the extent of that cost incurred. For example, a faithful depiction of an entity's performance might be to recognise revenue at an amount equal to the cost of a good used to satisfy a performance obligation if the entity expects at contract inception that all of the following conditions would be met:

(i) the good is not distinct;

(ii) the customer is expected to obtain control of the good significantly before receiving services related to the good;

(iii) the cost of the transferred good is significant relative to the total expected costs to completely satisfy the performance obligation; and

(iv) the entity procures the good from a third party and is not significantly involved in designing and manufacturing the good (but the entity is acting as a principal, see 4.4 above).

In a combined performance obligation comprised of non-distinct goods and services, the customer may obtain control of the goods before the entity provides the services related to those goods. This could be the case when goods are delivered to a customer site, but the entity has not yet integrated the goods into the overall project (e.g. the materials are 'uninstalled'). The Board concluded that, if an entity were using a percentage-of-completion method based on costs incurred to measure its progress (i.e. cost-to-cost), the measure of progress may be inappropriately affected by the delivery of these goods and that a pure application of such a measure of progress would result in overstated revenue. *[IFRS 15.BC171]*.

The standard indicates that, in such circumstances, (e.g. when control of the individual goods has transferred to the customer, but the integration service has not yet occurred), the best depiction of the entity's performance may be to recognise revenue at an amount equal to the cost of the goods used to satisfy the performance obligation (i.e. a zero margin). This is because the costs incurred are not proportionate to an entity's progress in satisfying the performance obligation. The standard specifies, in paragraph B19 of IFRS 15, that it may be more appropriate to only recognise revenue to the extent of costs incurred in these situations. It is also important to note that determining when control of the individual goods (that are part of a performance obligation) have transferred to the customer will require judgement. *[IFRS 15.B19]*.

The Board noted that the adjustment to the cost-to-cost measure of progress for uninstalled materials is generally intended to apply to a subset of construction-type goods that have a significant cost relative to the contract and for which the entity is effectively providing a simple procurement service to the customer. *[IFRS 15.BC172]*. By applying the adjustment to recognise revenue at an amount equal to the cost of uninstalled materials, an entity is recognising a margin similar to the one the entity would have recognised if the customer had supplied the materials. The IASB clarified that the outcome of recognising no margin for uninstalled materials is necessary to adjust the cost-to-cost calculation to faithfully depict an entity's performance. *[IFRS 15.BC174]*.

In addition, situations may arise in which not all of the costs incurred contribute to the entity's progress in completing the performance obligation. Paragraph B19(a) of IFRS 15 requires that, under an input method, an entity excludes these types of costs (e.g. costs related to significant inefficiencies, wasted materials, required rework) from the measure of progress, unless such costs were reflected in the price of the contract. *[IFRS 15.B19(a)]*.

The requirements for uninstalled materials may be a significant change from current practice for some entities. IAS 11 contains a requirement that when the stage of completion is determined by reference to the contract costs incurred to date, only those contract costs that reflect work performed are included. *[IAS 11.31]*. Hence, costs related to future activities, such as costs of materials (that do not have a high specificity to the contact) delivered to a contract site or set aside for use in a contract, but not yet installed, would not form part of the assessment of costs incurred to date. When installed, these would be included in the costs incurred to date. Under IFRS 15, any margin related to the uninstalled materials would be shifted to the other goods and services and recognised as the costs for those goods and services are incurred.

IFRS 15 does not dictate which approach an entity should use in these situations. However, it is clear that an entity cannot use an input method based on costs incurred to measure progress when costs are disproportionate to the entity's progress throughout the life of the contract. Not using a percentage-of-completion method (in which costs incurred are used to measure the stage of completion) in these situations may represent a significant change for some entities.

The standard includes the following example, illustrating how uninstalled materials are considered in measuring progress towards complete satisfaction of a performance obligation. *[IFRS 15.IE95-IE100]*.

Example 30.51: Uninstalled materials

In November 20X2, an entity contracts with a customer to refurbish a 3-storey building and install new elevators for total consideration of CU5 million. The promised refurbishment service, including the installation of elevators, is a single performance obligation satisfied over time. Total expected costs are CU4 million, including CU1.5 million for the elevators. The entity determines that it acts as a principal in accordance with paragraphs B34-B38 of IFRS 15, because it obtains control of the elevators before they are transferred to the customer.

A summary of the transaction price and expected costs is as follows:

	CU
Transaction price	5,000,000
Expected costs	
Elevators	1,500,000
Other costs	2,500,000
Total expected costs	4,000,000

The entity uses an input method based on costs incurred to measure its progress towards complete satisfaction of the performance obligation. The entity assesses whether the costs incurred to procure the elevators are proportionate to the entity's progress in satisfying the performance obligation, in accordance with paragraph B19 of IFRS 15. The customer obtains control of the elevators when they are delivered to the site in December 20X2, although the elevators will not be installed until June 20X3. The costs to procure the elevators (CU1.5 million) are significant relative to the total expected costs to completely satisfy the performance obligation (CU4 million). The entity is not involved in designing or manufacturing the elevators.

The entity concludes that including the costs to procure the elevators in the measure of progress would overstate the extent of the entity's performance. Consequently, in accordance with paragraph B19 of IFRS 15, the entity adjusts its measure of progress to exclude the costs to procure the elevators from the measure of costs incurred and from the transaction price. The entity recognises revenue for the transfer of the elevators in an amount equal to the costs to procure the elevators (i.e. at a zero margin).

As of 31 December 20X2 the entity observes that:

(a) other costs incurred (excluding elevators) are CU500,000; and

(b) performance is 20 per cent complete (i.e. CU500,000 ÷ CU2,500,000).

Consequently, at 31 December 20X2, the entity recognises the following:

	CU	
Revenue	2,200,000	(a)
Cost of goods sold	2,000,000	(b)
Profit	200,000	

(a) Revenue recognised is calculated as (20 per cent × CU3,500,000) + CU1,500,000. (CU3,500,000 is CU5,000,000 transaction price – CU1,500,000 costs of elevators).

(b) Cost of goods sold is CU500,000 of costs incurred + CU1,500,000 costs of elevators.

7.2.3 *Examples of measures of progress*

The following example illustrates some possible considerations when determining an appropriate measure of progress.

Example 30.52: Choosing the measure of progress

A ship-building entity enters into a contract to build 15 vessels for a customer over a three-year period. The contract includes both design and production services. The entity has not built a vessel of this type in the past. In addition, the entity expects that the first vessels may take longer to produce than the last vessels because, as the entity gains experience building the vessels, it expects to be able to construct the vessels more efficiently.

Assume that the entity has determined that the design and production services represent a single performance obligation. In this situation, it is likely that the entity would not choose a 'units-of-delivery' method as a measure of progress because that method would not accurately capture the level of performance. That is, such a method would not reflect the entity's efforts during the design phase of the contract because no revenue would be recognised until a vessel was shipped. In such situations, an entity would likely determine that an input method is more appropriate, such as a percentage-of-completion method based on costs incurred.

The standard also includes the following example on selecting an appropriate measure of progress towards satisfaction of a performance obligation. *[IFRS 15.IE92-IE94]*.

Example 30.53: Measuring progress when making goods or services available

An entity, an owner and manager of health clubs, enters into a contract with a customer for one year of access to any of its health clubs. The customer has unlimited use of the health clubs and promises to pay CU100 per month.

The entity determines that its promise to the customer is to provide a service of making the health clubs available for the customer to use as and when the customer wishes. This is because the extent to which the customer uses the health clubs does not affect the amount of the remaining goods and services to which the customer is entitled. The entity concludes that the customer simultaneously receives and consumes the benefits of the entity's performance as it performs by making the health clubs available. Consequently, the entity's performance obligation is satisfied over time in accordance with paragraph 35(a) of IFRS 15.

The entity also determines that the customer benefits from the entity's service of making the health clubs available evenly throughout the year. (That is, the customer benefits from having the health clubs available, regardless of whether the customer uses it or not.) Consequently, the entity concludes that the best measure of progress towards complete satisfaction of the performance obligation over time is a time-based measure and it recognises revenue on a straight-line basis throughout the year at CU100 per month.

7.2.4 *Implementation questions on measuring progress over time*

7.2.4.A *Measuring progress toward satisfaction of a stand-ready obligation that is satisfied over time*

At the January 2015 TRG meeting, the TRG members discussed questions raised regarding how an entity would measure progress for a stand-ready obligation that is a performance obligation satisfied over time.

The TRG members generally agreed that an entity should not default to a straight-line revenue attribution model. However, they also generally agreed that if an entity expects the customer to receive and consume the benefits of its promise throughout the contract period, a time-based measure of progress (e.g. straight-line) would be appropriate. The TRG agenda paper noted that this will generally be the case for unspecified upgrade rights, help-desk support contracts and cable or satellite television contracts. The TRG members generally agreed that rateable recognition may not be appropriate if the benefits are not spread evenly over the contract period (e.g. an annual snow removal contract that provides most benefits in winter).[94]

7.2.4.B Selecting a measure of progress when there is more than one promised good or service within a performance obligation

In July 2015, the TRG members were asked to consider whether an entity can use more than one measure of progress in order to depict an entity's performance in transferring a performance obligation comprised of two or more goods and/or services that is satisfied over time. Note that, under Step 2 of the new model, a single performance obligation may contain multiple non-distinct goods or services and/or distinct goods or services that were required to be combined with non-distinct goods or services in order to identify a distinct bundle. This bundled performance obligation is referred to as a 'combined performance obligation' for the purpose of this discussion.

The TRG members agreed that when an entity has determined that a combined performance obligation is satisfied over time, the entity has to select a single measure of progress that faithfully depicts the entity's performance in transferring the goods or services. For example, using different measures of progress for different non-distinct goods or services in the combined performance obligation would be inappropriate because doing so ignores the unit of account that has been identified under the standard (i.e. the single combined performance obligation). Furthermore, it would also be inappropriate because the entity would recognise revenue in a way that overrides the separation and allocation requirements in the standard. *[IFRS 15.BC161]*.

While the TRG members did not specifically discuss this point, the TRG agenda paper noted that a single method of measuring progress should not be broadly interpreted to mean an entity may apply multiple measures of progress as long as all measures used are either output or input measures.[95] The TRG members also acknowledged that there is currently diversity in practice and selecting a single measure of progress may represent a change for entities that currently use a multiple attribution model when deliverables cannot be separated into units of account.

7.2.4.C Determining the appropriate single measure of progress for a combined performance obligation that is satisfied over time

At the July 2015 TRG meeting, the TRG members discussed how an entity would determine the appropriate single measure of progress for a combined performance obligation that is satisfied over time.

The TRG members acknowledged that it may be difficult to appropriately determine a single measure of progress when the entity will transfer goods or services that make up the combined performance obligation over different points of time and/or the entity would otherwise use a different measure of progress (e.g. a time-based method versus a labour-based input method) if each promise was a separate performance obligation. Such a determination will require significant judgement, but the TRG members generally agreed that the measure of progress selected is not meant to be a 'free choice'. Entities need to consider the nature of the overall promise for the combined performance obligation in determining the measure of progress to use. For example, entities should not default to a 'final deliverable' methodology such that all revenue would be recognised over the performance period of the last promised good or service. Rather, an entity is required to select the single measure of progress that most faithfully depicts the entity's performance in satisfying its combined performance obligation.[96]

Some of the TRG members observed that an entity would need to consider the reasons why goods or services were bundled into a combined performance obligation in order to determine the appropriate pattern of revenue recognition. For example, if a good or service was combined with other goods or services because it was not capable of being distinct, that may indicate that it does not provide value or use to the customer on its own. As such, the entity would not contemplate the transfer of that good or service when determining the pattern of revenue recognition for the combined performance obligation.

The TRG members also generally agreed that, if an appropriately selected single measure of progress does not faithfully depict the economics of the arrangement, the entity should challenge whether the performance obligation was correctly combined (i.e. there may be more than one performance obligation).

7.2.4.D Can control of a good or service underlying a performance obligation satisfied over time be transferred at discrete points in time?

The FASB TRG members generally agreed that, if a performance obligation meets the criteria for revenue to be recognised over time (rather than at a point in time), control of the underlying good or service is not transferred at discrete points in time. Because control transfers as an entity performs, an entity's performance (as reflected using an appropriate measure of progress) should not result in the creation of a material asset in the entity's accounts (e.g. work in progress).

Stakeholders had queried whether control of a good or service underlying a performance obligation that is satisfied over time can be transferred at discrete points in time because the standard highlights several output methods, including 'milestones reached', as potentially acceptable methods for measuring progress towards satisfaction of an over-time performance obligation. The FASB TRG members generally agreed that an entity could use an output method only if that measure of progress correlates to the entity's performance to date.[97]

At the May 2016 IASB meeting, the IASB staff indicated support for the conclusions reached in the TRG agenda paper on this issue, noting that it provides some clarity about when to use milestones reached as a measure of progress. Furthermore, the members of the IASB who observed the FASB TRG meeting indicated that the FASB TRG discussion on the topic was helpful.

7.2.4.E Use of the 'right to invoice' practical expedient for a contract that includes rates that change over the contractual term

At the July 2015 TRG meeting, the TRG members were asked to consider whether the 'right to invoice' practical expedient could apply to a contract that includes rates that change over the contractual term.

The TRG members generally agreed that determining whether an entity can apply the 'right to invoice' practical expedient will require judgement. They also generally agreed that it is possible for entities to meet the requirements for the practical expedient in contracts with changing rates, provided that the changes in rates correspond directly to changes in value to the customer. That is, a contract does not need to have a fixed price per unit for the duration of a contract in order to qualify for the practical expedient. Examples of contracts that might qualify include an IT outsourcing arrangement with rates that decrease over the contract term as the level of effort to the customer decreases or a multi-year electricity contract that contemplates the forward market price of electricity. However, the SEC observer also noted that entities will need to have strong evidence that variable prices are representative of value to the customer in order to recognise variable amounts of revenue for similar goods or services.[98]

See 10.4.1.D below for a discussion on whether an entity can still use the practical expedient (under which an entity can decide not to disclose the amount of transaction price allocated to remaining performance obligation) if it determines that it has not met the criteria to use the 'right to invoice' practical expedient (e.g. because there is a substantive contractual minimum payment or a volume discount).

7.2.4.F Recognising revenue when fulfilment costs are incurred prior to the contract establishment date for a specifically anticipated contract

An entity cannot begin to recognise revenue on a contract until it meets all five criteria to be considered a contract under IFRS 15 (as discussed at 3.1 above), regardless of whether it has received any consideration or has begun performing under the terms of the arrangement.

At the March 2015 TRG meeting, the TRG members were asked to consider how an entity would recognise revenue for at the date a contract exists if an entity begins activities on a specifically anticipated contract either:

- before it agrees to the contract with the customer; or
- before the arrangement meets the criteria to be considered a contract under the standard.[99]

The TRG members generally agreed that if the goods or services that ultimately will be transferred meet the criteria to be recognised over time, revenue would be recognised on a cumulative catch-up basis at the 'contract establishment date', reflecting the performance obligation(s) that are partially or fully satisfied at that time. The TRG agenda paper noted that the cumulative catch-up method is considered to be consistent with the overall principle of the standard that revenue is recognised when (or as) an entity transfers control of goods or services to a customer.[100]

See 9.3.2.B below for the TRG members' discussion regarding contract fulfilment costs incurred prior to the contract establishment date.

7.3 Control transferred at a point in time

For performance obligations in which control is not transferred over time, control is transferred as at a point in time. *[IFRS 15.38]*. In many situations, the determination of when that point in time occurs is relatively straightforward. However, in other circumstances, this determination is more complex.

To help entities determine the point in time when a customer obtains control of a particular good or service, the standard requires an entity to consider the general requirements for control in paragraphs 31-34 of IFRS 15 (see 7 above). In addition, an entity is required to consider indicators of the transfer of control, which include, but are not limited to, the following. *[IFRS 15.38]*.

(a) *The entity has a present right to payment for the asset* – if a customer is presently obliged to pay for an asset, then that may indicate that the customer has obtained the ability to direct the use of, and obtain substantially all of the remaining benefits from, the asset in exchange.

(b) *The customer has legal title to the asset* – legal title may indicate which party to a contract has the ability to direct the use of, and obtain substantially all of the remaining benefits from, an asset or to restrict the access of other entities to those benefits. Therefore, the transfer of legal title of an asset may indicate that the customer has obtained control of the asset. If an entity retains legal title solely as protection against the customer's failure to pay, those rights of the entity would not preclude the customer from obtaining control of an asset.

(c) *The entity has transferred physical possession of the asset* – the customer's physical possession of an asset may indicate that the customer has the ability to direct the use of, and obtain substantially all of the remaining benefits from, the asset or to restrict the access of other entities to those benefits. However, physical possession may not coincide with control of an asset. For example, in some repurchase agreements (see 7.4 below) and in some consignment arrangements, a customer or consignee may have physical possession of an asset that the entity controls (see 4.5 above and 7.5 below). Conversely, in some bill-and-hold arrangements (see 7.6 below), the entity may have physical possession of an asset that the customer controls.

(d) *The customer has the significant risks and rewards of ownership of the asset* – the transfer of the significant risks and rewards of ownership of an asset to the customer may indicate that the customer has obtained the ability to direct the use of, and obtain substantially all of the remaining benefits from, the asset. However, when evaluating the risks and rewards of ownership of a promised asset, an entity is required to exclude any risks that give rise to a separate performance obligation in addition to the performance obligation to transfer the asset. For example, an entity may have transferred control of an asset to a customer but not yet satisfied an additional performance obligation to provide maintenance services related to the transferred asset.

(e) *The customer has accepted the asset* – the customer's acceptance of an asset may indicate that it has obtained the ability to direct the use of, and obtain substantially all of the remaining benefits from, the asset (see 7.3.1 below).

None of the indicators above are meant to individually determine whether the customer has gained control of the good or service. For example, while shipping terms may provide information about when legal title to a good transfers to the customer, they are not determinative when evaluating the point in time at which the customer obtains control of the promised asset. An entity must consider all relevant facts and circumstances to determine whether control has transferred. The IASB also made it clear that the indicators are not meant to be a checklist. Furthermore, not all of them must be present for an entity to determine that the customer has gained control. Rather, the indicators are factors that are often present when a customer has obtained control of an asset and the list is meant to help entities apply the principle of control. *[IFRS 15.BC155]*.

- *Present right to payment for the asset*

  As noted in the Basis for Conclusions, the IASB considered, but rejected specifying a right to payment as an overarching criterion for determining when revenue would be recognised. Therefore, while the date at which the entity has a right to payment for the asset may be an indicator of the date the customer obtained control of the asset, it does not always indicate that the customer has obtained control of the asset. *[IFRS 15.BC148]*. For example, in some contracts, a customer is required to make a non-refundable upfront payment, but receives no goods or services in return at that time.

- *Legal title and physical possession*

  The term 'title' is often associated with a legal definition denoting the ownership of an asset or legally recognised rights that preclude others' claim to the asset. Accordingly, the transfer of title often indicates that control of an asset has been transferred. Determination of which party has title to an asset does not always depend on which party has physical possession of the asset, but without contractual terms to the contrary, title generally passes to the customer at the time of the physical transfer. For example, in a retail store transaction, there is often no clear documentation of the transfer of title. However, it is generally understood that the title to a product is transferred at the time it is purchased by the customer.

  While the retail store transaction is relatively straightforward, determining when title has transferred may be more complicated in other arrangements. Transactions that involve the shipment of products may have varying shipping terms and may involve third-party shipping agents. In such cases, a clear understanding of the seller's practices and the contractual terms is required in order to make an assessment of when title transfers. As indicated in paragraph 38(b) of IFRS 15, legal title and/or physical possession may be an indicator of which party to a contract has the ability to direct the use of, and obtain substantially all of the remaining benefits from, an asset or to restrict the access of other entities to those benefits.

- *Risks and rewards of ownership*

  Although the Board included the risks and rewards of ownership as one factor to consider when evaluating whether control of an asset has transferred, it emphasised, in the Basis for Conclusions, that this factor does not change the principle of determining the transfer of goods or services on the basis of control. *[IFRS 15.BC154]*. The concept of the risks and rewards of ownership is based on how the seller and the customer share both the potential gain (the reward) and the potential loss (risk) associated with owning an asset. Rewards of ownership include the following:

- rights to all appreciation in value of the asset;
- unrestricted usage of the asset;
- ability to modify the asset;
- ability to transfer or sell the asset; and
- ability to grant a security interest in the asset.

Conversely, the risks of ownership include the following:

- absorbing all of the declines in market value;
- incurring losses due to theft or damage of the asset; and
- incurring losses due to changes in the business environment (e.g. obsolescence, excess inventory, effect of retail pricing environment).

However, as noted in paragraph 38(d) of IFRS 15, an entity does not consider risks that give rise to a separate performance obligation when evaluating whether the entity has the risks of ownership of an asset. For example, an entity does not consider warranty services that represent a separate performance obligation when evaluating whether it retains the risks of ownership of the asset sold to the customer.

7.3.1 Customer acceptance

When determining whether the customer has obtained control of the goods or services, an entity must consider any customer acceptance clauses that require the customer to approve the goods or services before it is obligated to pay for them. If a customer does not accept the goods or services, the entity may not be entitled to consideration, may be required to take remedial action or may be required to take back the delivered good.

The standard states that a customer's acceptance of an asset may indicate that the customer has obtained control of the asset. Customer acceptance clauses allow a customer to cancel a contract or require an entity to take remedial action if a good or service does not meet agreed-upon specifications. As such, an entity needs to consider such clauses when evaluating when a customer obtains control of a good or service. *[IFRS 15.B83]*.

If an entity can objectively determine that control of a good or service has been transferred to the customer in accordance with the agreed-upon specifications in the contract, customer acceptance is a formality that would not affect the entity's determination of when the customer has obtained control of the good or service. The standard gives the example of a clause that is based on meeting specified size and weight characteristics. In that situation, an entity would be able to determine whether those criteria have been met before receiving confirmation of the customer's acceptance. The entity's experience with contracts for similar goods or services may provide evidence that a good or service provided to the customer is in accordance with the agreed-upon specifications in the contract. If revenue is recognised before customer acceptance, the entity still needs to consider whether there are any remaining performance obligations (e.g. installation of equipment) and evaluate whether to account for them separately. *[IFRS 15.B84]*.

Conversely, if an entity cannot objectively determine that the good or service provided to the customer is in accordance with the agreed-upon specifications in the contract, it would not be able to conclude that the customer has obtained control until the entity receives the customer's acceptance. In that circumstance, the entity cannot determine that the customer has the ability to direct the use of, and obtain substantially all of the remaining benefits from, the good or service. *[IFRS 15.B85]*.

If an entity delivers products to a customer for trial or evaluation purposes and the customer is not committed to pay any consideration until the trial period lapses, the standard clarifies that control of the product is not transferred to the customer until either the customer accepts the product or the trial period lapses. *[IFRS 15.B86]*.

Some acceptance provisions may be straightforward, giving a customer the ability to accept or reject the goods or services based on objective criteria specified in the contract (e.g. the goods function at a specified speed). Other acceptance clauses may be subjective or may appear in parts of the contract that do not typically address acceptance matters, such as warranty provisions or indemnification clauses. Professional judgement may be required to determine the effect on revenue recognition of the latter types of acceptance clauses.

Acceptance criteria that an entity cannot objectively evaluate against the agreed-upon specifications in the contract will preclude an entity from concluding that a customer has obtained control of a good or service until formal customer sign-off is obtained or the acceptance provisions lapse. However, the entity would consider its experience with other contracts for similar goods or services because that experience may provide evidence that the entity is able to objectively determine that a good or service provided to the customer is in accordance with the agreed-upon specifications in the contract. We believe one or more of the following would represent circumstances in which the entity may not be able to objectively evaluate the acceptance criteria.

- The acceptance provisions are unusual or 'non-standard'. Indicators of 'non-standard' acceptance terms are:
  - the duration of the acceptance period is longer than in contracts for similar goods or services;
  - the majority of the vendor's contracts lack similar acceptance terms; and
  - the arrangement contains explicit customer-specified requirements that must be met prior to acceptance.
- The arrangement contains a contractual requirement for explicit notification of acceptance, in contrast to deemed acceptance. Explicit notification requirements may indicate that the criteria with which the customer is assessing compliance are not objective. Contracts may include provisions used to limit the time period within which the customer can reject delivered products. Such clauses may require the customer to provide, in writing, the reasons for the rejection of the products by the end of a specified period. When such clauses exist, acceptance can be deemed to have occurred at the end of the specified time period if notification of rejection has not been received from the customer, as long as the customer has not indicated it will reject the products.

In determining whether compliance with the criteria for acceptance can be objectively assessed (and acceptance is only a formality), the following should be considered:

- whether the acceptance terms are standard in arrangements entered into by the vendor;
- whether the acceptance is based on the delivered product performing to standard, published, specifications and whether the vendor can demonstrate that it has an established history of objectively determining that the product functions in accordance with those specifications; and
- whether the vendor is required to perform additional services for customer acceptance to occur.

As discussed above, customer acceptance should not be deemed a formality if the acceptance terms are unusual or non-standard. If an arrangement contains acceptance provisions that are based on customer-specified criteria, it may be difficult for the entity to objectively assess compliance with the criteria and the entity may not be able to recognise revenue prior to obtaining evidence of customer acceptance. However, determining that the acceptance criteria have been met (and, therefore, acceptance is merely a formality) may be appropriate if the entity can demonstrate that its product meets all of the customer's acceptance specifications by replicating, before shipment, those conditions under which the customer intends to use the product. However, if it is reasonable to expect that the product's performance (once it has been installed and is operating at the customer's facility) will be different from the performance when it was tested prior to shipment, this acceptance provision will not have been met. The entity, therefore, would not be able to conclude that the customer has obtained control until customer acceptance occurs. Factors indicating that specifications cannot be tested effectively prior to shipment include:

- the customer has unique equipment, software or environmental conditions that can reasonably be expected to make performance in that customer's environment different from testing performed by the vendor. If the arrangement includes customer acceptance criteria or specifications that cannot be effectively tested before delivery or installation at the customer's site, revenue recognition would be deferred until it can be demonstrated that the criteria are met;
- the products that are the subject of the arrangement are highly complex; and
- the vendor has a limited history of testing products prior to delivery to customers or a limited history of having customers reject products that it has previously tested.

Determining when a customer obtains control of an asset in an arrangement with customer-specified acceptance criteria requires the use of professional judgement and depends on the weight of the evidence in the particular circumstances. The conclusion could change based on a single variable, such as the complexity of the equipment, the nature of the interface with the customer's environment, the extent of the seller's experience with this type of transaction or a particular clause in the agreement. An entity may need to discuss the situation with knowledgeable project managers or engineers in making such an assessment.

In addition, each contract containing customer-specified acceptance criteria may require a separate compliance assessment of whether the acceptance provisions have been met prior to confirmation of the customer's acceptance. That is, since different customers may specify different acceptance criteria, a vendor may not be able to make one compliance assessment that applies to all contracts because of the variations in contractual terms and customer environments.

Even if an arrangement includes a standard acceptance clause, if the clause relates to a new product or one that has only been sold on a limited basis previously, a vendor may be required to initially defer revenue recognition for the product until it establishes a history of successfully obtaining acceptance.

7.4 Repurchase agreements

Some agreements include repurchase provisions, either as part of a sales contract or as a separate contract that relates to the goods in the original agreement or similar goods. These provisions affect how an entity applies the requirements on control to affected transactions. That is, when evaluating whether a customer obtains control of an asset, an entity shall consider any agreement to repurchase the asset. *[IFRS 15.34]*.

The standard clarifies the types of arrangements that qualify as repurchase agreements. It defines a repurchase agreement as 'a contract in which an entity sells an asset and also promises or has the option (either in the same contract or in another contract) to repurchase the asset. The repurchased asset may be the asset that was originally sold to the customer, an asset that is substantially the same as that asset, or another asset of which the asset that was originally sold is a component'. *[IFRS 15.B64]*.

The standard states that repurchase agreements generally come in three forms: *[IFRS 15.B65]*

- an entity's obligation to repurchase the asset (a forward);
- an entity's right to repurchase the asset (a call option); and
- an entity's obligation to repurchase the asset at the customer's request (a put option).

In order for an obligation or right to purchase an asset to be accounted for as a repurchase agreement under IFRS 15, it needs to exist at contract inception, either as a part of the same contract or in another contract. The IASB clarified that an entity's subsequent decision to repurchase an asset (after transferring control of that asset to a customer) without reference to any pre-existing contractual right, would not be accounted for as a repurchase agreement under the standard. That is, the customer is not obligated to resell that good to the entity as a result of the initial contract. Therefore, any subsequent decision to repurchase the asset does not affect the customer's ability to control the asset upon initial transfer. However, in cases in which an entity decides to repurchase a good after transferring control of the good to a customer, the Board observed that the entity should carefully consider whether the customer obtained control in the initial transaction. Furthermore, it may need to consider the application guidance on principal versus agent considerations (see 4.4 above). *[IFRS 15.BC423]*.

7.4.1 Forward or call option held by the entity

When an entity has the obligation or right to repurchase an asset (i.e. a forward or a call option), the standard indicates that the customer has not obtained control of the asset. That is, the customer is limited in its ability to direct the use of, and obtain substantially all of the remaining benefits from, the asset even though the customer may have physical possession of the asset.

Consequently, the standard requires that an entity account for a transaction including a forward or a call option based on the relationship between the repurchase price and the original selling price. The standard indicates that if the entity has the right or obligation to repurchase the asset at a price less than the original sales price (taking into consideration the effects of the time value of money), the entity would account for the transaction as a lease in accordance with IAS 17 (or IFRS 16, when adopted), unless the contract is part of a sale and leaseback transaction. If the entity has the right or obligation to repurchase the asset at a price equal to or greater than the original sales price (considering the effects of the time value of money) or if the contract is part of a sale and leaseback transaction, the entity would account for the contract as a financing arrangement in accordance with paragraph B68 of IFRS 15. *[IFRS 15.B66-B67]*.

The following figure depicts this application guidance for transactions that are not sale and leaseback transaction.

Figure 30.4: Forward or call options

Repurchase price	<	Original selling price	=	Lease
Repurchase price	≥	Original selling price	=	Financing

Under the standard, any transaction in which a seller has an option to repurchase the product must be treated as a lease or a financing arrangement (i.e. not a sale). This is because the customer does not have control of the product and is constrained in its ability to direct the use of and obtain substantially all of the remaining benefits from the good. Entities cannot consider the likelihood that a call option will be exercised in determining the accounting for the repurchase provision. However, the Board noted in the Basis for Conclusions that non-substantive call options are ignored and would not affect when a customer obtains control of an asset. *[IFRS 15.BC427]*.

If a transaction is considered a financing arrangement under the IFRS 15, in accordance with paragraph B68 of IFRS 15, the selling entity would continue to recognise the asset. In addition, it would record a financial liability for the consideration received from the customer. The difference between the consideration received from the customer and the consideration subsequently paid to the customer (upon repurchasing the asset) represents the interest and holding costs (as applicable) that are recognised over the term of the financing arrangement. If the option lapses unexercised, the entity derecognises the liability and recognises revenue at that time. *[IFRS 15.B68-B69]*.

Also note that, when effective, IFRS 16 will consequentially amend paragraph B66(a) of IFRS 15 to specify that, if the contract is part of a sale and leaseback transaction, the entity continues to recognise the asset. Furthermore, the entity recognises a financial liability for any consideration received from the customer to which IFRS 9 would apply.

Consistent with the requirements in IAS 18 and SIC-27 – *Evaluating the Substance of Transactions involving the Legal Form of a Lease*, the new standard requires an entity to consider a repurchase agreement together with the original sales agreement when they are linked in such a way that the substance of the arrangement cannot be understood without reference to the series of transactions as a whole. *[IAS 18.13, SIC-27]*. Therefore, for most entities, the requirement to consider the two transactions together would not change.

The requirement in the new standard to distinguish between repurchase agreements that are, in substance, leases or financing arrangements is broadly consistent with current IFRS. IAS 18 indicates that 'the terms of the agreement need to be analysed to ascertain whether, in substance, the seller has transferred the risks and rewards of ownership to the buyer'. *[IAS 18.IE5]*.

However, IAS 18 does not specify how to treat repurchase agreements that represent financing arrangements, except to state that such arrangements do not give rise to revenue. The requirements in IFRS 15 may, therefore, result in a significant change in practice for some entities.

Entities may find the requirements challenging to apply in practice as the standard treats all forwards and call options the same way and does not consider the likelihood that they will be exercised. In addition, since the standard provides lease requirements, it will be important for entities to understand the interaction between the lease and revenue standards.

The standard provides the following example of a call option. *[IFRS 15.IE315-IE318]*.

Example 30.54: Repurchase agreements

An entity enters into a contract with a customer for the sale of a tangible asset on 1 January 20X7 for CU1 million.

Case A – Call option: financing

The contract includes a call option that gives the entity the right to repurchase the asset for CU1.1 million on or before 31 December 20X7.

Control of the asset does not transfer to the customer on 31 December 20X7 because the entity has a right to repurchase the asset and therefore the customer is limited in its ability to direct the use of, and obtain substantially all of the remaining benefits from, the asset. Consequently, in accordance with paragraph B66(b) of IFRS 15, the entity accounts for the transaction as a financing arrangement, because the exercise price is more than the original selling price. In accordance with paragraph B68 of IFRS 15, the entity does not derecognise the asset and instead recognises the cash received as a financial liability. The entity also recognises interest expense for the difference between the exercise price (CU1.1 million) and the cash received (CU1 million), which increases the liability.

On 31 December 20X7, the option lapses unexercised; therefore, the entity derecognises the liability and recognises revenue of CU1.1 million.

7.4.2 Put option held by the customer

IFRS 15 indicates that if the customer has the ability to require an entity to repurchase an asset (i.e. a put option) at a price lower than its original selling price, the entity considers, at contract inception, whether the customer has a significant economic incentive to exercise that right. *[IFRS 15.B70]*. That is, this determination influences whether the customer truly has control over the asset received.

The determination of whether an entity has a significant economic incentive to exercise its right will determine whether the arrangement is treated as a lease or a sale with the right of return (discussed at 5.4.1 above). However, the new standard does not provide any guidance on determining whether 'a significant economic incentive' exists and judgement may be required to make this determination. An entity must consider all relevant facts and circumstances to determine whether a customer has a significant economic incentive to exercise its right, including the relationship between the repurchase price to the expected market value (taking into consideration the effects of the time value of money) of the asset at the date of repurchase and the amount of time until the right expires. The standard notes that if the repurchase price is expected to significantly exceed the market value of the asset the customer may have a significant economic incentive to exercise the put option. *[IFRS 15.B70-B71, B75]*.

- If a customer has a significant economic incentive to exercise its right, the customer is expected to ultimately return the asset. The entity accounts for the agreement as a lease because the customer is effectively paying the entity for the right to use the asset for a period of time. *[IFRS 15.B70]*. However, one exception to this would be if the contract is part of a sale and leaseback, in which case the contract would be accounted for as a financing arrangement (financing arrangements are discussed at 7.4.1 above). *[IFRS 15.B73]*. Note that, when effective, IFRS 16 will consequentially amend paragraph B70 of IFRS 15 to specify that, if the contract is part of a sale and leaseback transaction, the entity continues to recognise the asset. Furthermore, the entity recognises a financial liability for any consideration received from the customer to which IFRS 9 would apply.
- If a customer does not have a significant economic incentive to exercise its right, the entity accounts for the agreement in a manner similar to a sale of a product with a right of return. *[IFRS 15.B72]*. The repurchase price of an asset that is equal to or greater than the original selling price, but less than or equal to the expected market value of the asset, must also be accounted for as a sale of a product with a right of return, if the customer does not have a significant economic incentive to exercise its right. *[IFRS 15.B74]*. See 5.4.1 above for a discussion on sales with a right of return.

If the customer has the ability to require an entity to repurchase the asset at a price equal to, or more than, the original selling price and the repurchase price is more than the expected market value of the asset, the contract is in effect a financing arrangement.

If the option lapses unexercised, an entity shall derecognise the liability and recognise revenue. *[IFRS 15.B76]*.

The following figure depicts this application guidance.

Figure 30.5: Put options held by the customer

Repurchase price	<	Original selling price	→	Significant economic incentive to exercise?	No →	Sale with a right of return
					Yes →	Lease

Repurchase price	≥	Original selling price	and	Repurchase price	>	Expected market value of asset	=	Financing

Repurchase price	≥	Original selling price	and	Repurchase price	≤	Expected market value of asset	and	No significant economic incentive to exercise	=	Sale with a right of return

The new standard provides application guidance in respect of written put options where there is currently limited guidance under IFRS. However, the new standard does not provide any guidance on determining whether 'a significant economic incentive' exists and judgement may be required to make this determination.

The standard provides the following example of a put option. *[IFRS 15.IE315, IE319-IE321].*

Example 30.55: Repurchase agreements

An entity enters into a contract with a customer for the sale of a tangible asset on 1 January 20X7 for CU1 million.

Case B – Put option: lease

Instead of having a call option, the contract includes a put option that obliges the entity to repurchase the asset at the customer's request for CU900,000 on or before 31 December 20X7. The market value is expected to be CU750,000 on 31 December 20X7.

At the inception of the contract, the entity assesses whether the customer has a significant economic incentive to exercise the put option, to determine the accounting for the transfer of the asset (see paragraphs B70-B76 of IFRS 15). The entity concludes that the customer has a significant economic incentive to exercise the put option because the repurchase price significantly exceeds the expected market value of the asset at the date of repurchase. The entity determines there are no other relevant factors to consider when assessing whether the customer has a significant economic incentive to exercise the put option. Consequently, the entity concludes that control of the asset does not transfer to the customer, because the customer is limited in its ability to direct the use of, and obtain substantially all of the remaining benefits from, the asset.

In accordance with paragraphs B70-B71 of IFRS 15, the entity accounts for the transaction as a lease in accordance with IAS 17.

7.4.2.A *When an entity has a conditional call option to remove and replace expired products (e.g. out-of-date perishable goods, expired medicine), does the customer obtain control of the products (or is it akin to a right of return)?*

The standard does not differentiate between conditional call or forward options held by the entity and unconditional ones. Furthermore, it states that a customer does not obtain control of the asset when the entity has a right to repurchase the asset. The presence of call or forward options indicates that control is not transferred because the customer is limited in its ability to direct the use of and obtain substantially all of the remaining benefits from the asset.

However, in the case of perishable products, an entity's conditional right to remove and replace expired goods does not necessarily constrain the customer's ability to direct the use of and obtain substantially all of the remaining benefits from the products. That is, the entity is not able to remove and replace the products until they expire. Furthermore, the customer has control of the products over their entire useful life. Consequently, we believe it may be reasonable for an entity to conclude that control of the initial product does transfer to the customer in this situation and that an entity could consider this right to be a form of a right of return (see 5.4.1 above).

7.4.3 Sales with residual value guarantees

An entity that sells equipment may use a sales incentive programme under which it guarantees that the customer will receive a minimum resale amount when it disposes of the equipment (i.e. a residual value guarantee). If the customer holds a put option and has significant economic incentive to exercise, the customer is effectively restricted in its ability to consume, modify or sell the asset. In contrast, when the entity guarantees that the customer will receive a minimum amount of sales proceeds, the customer is not constrained in its ability to direct the use of, and obtain substantially all of the benefits from, the asset. Accordingly, the Board decided that it was not necessary to expand the application guidance on repurchase agreements to consider guaranteed amounts of resale. *[IFRS 15.BC427]*.

Therefore, it will be important for an entity to review all its contracts and make sure that the residual value guarantee is not accomplished through a repurchase provision, such as a put within the contract (e.g. the customer has the right to require the entity to repurchase equipment two years after the date of purchase at 85% of the original purchase price). If a put option is present, the entity would have to use the application guidance in the standard to determine whether the existence of the put option precludes the customer from obtaining control of the acquired item. In such circumstances, the entity would determine whether the customer has a significant economic incentive to exercise the put. If the entity concludes that there is no significant economic incentive, the transaction would be accounted for as a sale with a right of return, as discussed at 7.4.2 above. Alternatively, if the entity concludes there is a significant economic incentive for the customer to exercise its right, the transaction would be accounted for as a lease.

However, assume the transaction includes a residual value guarantee in which no put option is present. If the entity guarantees that it will compensate the customer (or 'make whole') on a qualifying future sale if the customer receives less than 85% of the initial sale price, the application guidance on repurchase agreements in IFRS 15 would not apply. That is because the entity is not repurchasing the asset.

In such situations, judgement will be needed to determine the appropriate accounting treatment, which will depend on the specific facts and circumstances. In some cases, an entity may need to consider the requirements of other IFRSs to appropriately account for the residual value guarantee. In other situations, IFRS 15 may apply to the entire transaction. If IFRS 15 applies, an entity would need to assess whether the guarantee affects control of the asset transferring, which will depend on the promise to the customer. In some cases, it may not affect the transfer of control. In the Basis for Conclusions, the Board noted that 'when the entity guarantees that the customer will receive a minimum amount of sales proceeds, the customer is not constrained in its ability to direct the use of, and obtain substantially all of the benefits from, the asset.' *[IFRS 15.BC431]*. However, while a residual value guarantee may not affect the transfer of control, an entity would need to consider whether it affects the transaction price (see 5 above). While the economics of a repurchase agreement and a residual value guarantee may be similar, the accounting could be quite different.

7.5 Consignment arrangements

Entities frequently deliver inventory on a consignment basis to other parties (e.g. distributor, dealer). By shipping on a consignment basis, consignors are able to better market products by moving them closer to the end-customer. However, they do so without selling the goods to the intermediary (consignee). *[IFRS 15.B77]*. The Board included indicators that an arrangement is a consignment arrangement include, but are not limited to, the following: *[IFRS 15.B78]*

'(a) the product is controlled by the entity until a specified event occurs, such as the sale of the product to a customer of the dealer or until a specified period expires;

(b) the entity is able to require the return of the product or transfer the product to a third party (such as another dealer); and

(c) the dealer does not have an unconditional obligation to pay for the product (although it might be required to pay a deposit).'

Entities entering into a consignment arrangement will need to determine the nature of the performance obligation (i.e. whether the obligation is to transfer the product to the consignee or to transfer the product to the end-customer). This determination would be based on whether control of the product passes to the consignee upon delivery. Typically, a consignor will not relinquish control of the consigned product until the product is sold to the end-customer or, in some cases, when a specified period expires. Consignees commonly do not have any obligation to pay for the product, other than to pay the consignor the agreed-upon portion of the sale price once the consignee sells the product to a third party. As a result, for consignment arrangements, revenue generally would not be recognised when the products are delivered to the consignee because control has not transferred (i.e. the performance obligation to deliver goods to the end-customer has not yet been satisfied). *[IFRS 15.B77]*.

7.6 Bill-and-hold arrangements

In some sales transactions, the selling entity fulfils its obligations and bills the customer for the work performed, but does not ship the goods until a later date. These transactions, often called bill-and-hold transactions, are usually designed this way at the request of the purchaser for a number of reasons, including a lack of storage capacity or its inability to use the goods until a later date. For example, a customer may request an entity to enter into such a contract because of the customer's lack of available space for the product or because of delays in the customer's production schedules. *[IFRS 15.B79]*.

The criteria for determining whether a bill-and-hold transaction qualifies for revenue recognition under the new standard are similar to current IFRS. *[IAS 18.IE1]*. However, consideration of a separate custodial performance obligation (as discussed in the following application guidance) may be new to IFRS preparers, as this is not addressed in IAS 18.

An entity determines when it has satisfied its performance obligation to transfer a product by evaluating when a customer obtains control of that product. For some contracts, control transfers either when the product is delivered to the customer's site or when the product is shipped, depending on the terms of the contract (including delivery and shipping terms). However, for some contracts, a customer may obtain control of a product even though that product remains in an entity's physical possession. In that case, the customer has the ability to direct the use of, and obtain substantially all of the remaining benefits from, the product even though it has decided not to exercise its right to take physical possession of that product. Consequently, the entity does not control the product. Instead, the entity provides custodial services to the customer over the customer's asset. *[IFRS 15.B80]*.

In addition to applying the general requirements for assessing whether control has transferred, for a customer to have obtained control of a product in a bill-and-hold arrangement, all of the following criteria must be met: *[IFRS 15.B81]*

(a) the reason for the bill-and-hold arrangement must be substantive (e.g. the customer has requested the arrangement);

(b) the product must be identified separately as belonging to the customer;

(c) the product currently must be ready for physical transfer to the customer; and

(d) the entity cannot have the ability to use the product or to direct it to another customer.

If an entity recognises revenue for the sale of a product on a bill-and-hold basis, the standard requires that it consider whether it has remaining performance obligations (e.g. for custodial services) to which it is required to allocate a portion of the transaction price. *[IFRS 15.B82]*.

The standard provides the following illustrative example to illustrate the application guidance on bill-and-hold arrangements. *[IFRS 15.IE323-IE327]*.

Example 30.56: Bill-and-hold arrangement

An entity enters into a contract with a customer on 1 January 20X8 for the sale of a machine and spare parts. The manufacturing lead time for the machine and spare parts is two years.

Upon completion of manufacturing, the entity demonstrates that the machine and spare parts meet the agreed-upon specifications in the contract. The promises to transfer the machine and spare parts are distinct and result in two performance obligations that each will be satisfied at a point in time. On 31 December 20X9, the customer pays for the machine and spare parts, but only takes physical possession of the machine. Although the customer inspects and accepts the spare parts, the customer requests that the spare parts be stored at the entity's warehouse because of its close proximity to the customer's factory. The customer has legal title to the spare parts and the parts can be identified as belonging to the customer. Furthermore, the entity stores the spare parts in a separate section of its warehouse and the parts are ready for immediate shipment at the customer's request. The entity expects to hold the spare parts for two to four years and the entity does not have the ability to use the spare parts or direct them to another customer.

The entity identifies the promise to provide custodial services as a performance obligation because it is a service provided to the customer and it is distinct from the machine and spare parts. Consequently, the entity accounts for three performance obligations in the contract (the promises to provide the machine, the spare parts and the custodial services). The transaction price is allocated to the three performance obligations and revenue is recognised when (or as) control transfers to the customer.

Control of the machine transfers to the customer on 31 December 20X9 when the customer takes physical possession. The entity assesses the indicators in paragraph 38 of IFRS 15 to determine the point in time at which control of the spare parts transfers to the customer, noting that the entity has received payment, the customer has legal title to the spare parts and the customer has inspected and accepted the spare parts. In addition, the entity concludes that all of the criteria in paragraph B81 of IFRS 15 are met, which is necessary for the entity to recognise revenue in a bill-and-hold arrangement. The entity recognises revenue for the spare parts on 31 December 20X9 when control transfers to the customer.

The performance obligation to provide custodial services is satisfied over time as the services are provided. The entity considers whether the payment terms include a significant financing component in accordance with paragraphs 60-65 of IFRS 15.

7.7 Recognising revenue for licences of intellectual property

IFRS 15 provides application guidance on the recognition of revenue for licences of intellectual property that is different from the general requirements for other promised goods or services. We discuss licensing in detail in Section 8 below.

7.8 Recognising revenue when a right of return exists

As discussed at 4.7 above, a right of return does not represent a separate performance obligation. Instead, the existence of a right of return affects the transaction price and the entity must determine whether the customer will return the transferred product.

Under IFRS 15, as discussed at 5 above, an entity will estimate the transaction price and apply the constraint to the estimated transaction price. In doing so, it will consider the products expected to be returned in order to determine the amount to which the entity expects to be entitled (excluding consideration for the products expected to be returned). The entity will recognise revenue based on the amounts to which the entity expects to be entitled through to the end of the return period (considering expected product returns). An entity will not recognise the portion of the revenue that is subject to the constraint until the amount is no longer constrained, which could be at the end of the return period or earlier if the entity's expectations about the products expected to be returned changes prior to the end of the return period. The entity will recognise the amount received or receivable that is expected to be returned as a refund liability, representing its obligation to return the customer's consideration. An entity will also update its estimates at the end of each reporting period. See 4.7 and 5.4.1 above for further discussion on this topic.

7.9 Recognising revenue for customer options for additional goods and services

As discussed in 4.6 above, when an entity grants a customer the option to acquire additional goods or services, that option is a separate performance obligation if it provides a material right to the customer that the customer would not receive without entering into the contract (e.g. a discount that exceeds the range of discounts typically given for those goods or services to that class of customer in that geographical area or market). If the option provides a material right to the customer, the customer has, in effect, paid the entity in advance for future goods or services. IFRS 15 requires the entity to allocate a portion of the transaction price to the material right at contract inception (see 6.1.5 above). The revenue allocated to the material right will be recognised when (or as) the option is exercised (and the underlying future goods or services are transferred) or when the option expires.

In contrast, if a customer option is not deemed to be a material right and is instead a marketing offer, the entity does not account for the option and waits to account for the underlying goods or services until those subsequent purchases occur.

See 4.6.1.G above for discussion on how an entity account would for the exercise of a material right.

7.10 Breakage and prepayments for future goods or services

In certain industries, an entity will collect non-refundable payments from its customers for goods or services that the customer has a right to receive in the future. However, a customer may ultimately leave that right unexercised (often referred to as 'breakage'). *[IFRS 15.B45]*. Retailers, for example, frequently sell gift cards that are not completely redeemed and airlines sometimes sell tickets to passengers who allow the tickets to expire unused.

When an entity receives consideration that is attributable to a customer's unexercised rights, the entity recognises a contract liability equal to the amount prepaid by the customer for the performance obligation to transfer, or to stand ready to transfer, goods or services in the future. Revenue would normally be recognised when the entity satisfies its performance obligation. *[IFRS 15.B44]*.

However, since entities will frequently not be required by customers to fully satisfy their performance obligations, the Board concluded that when an entity expects to be entitled to a breakage amount, the expected breakage would be recognised as revenue in proportion to the pattern of rights exercised by the customer. If an entity does not expect to be entitled to a breakage amount, it would not recognise any breakage amounts as revenue until the likelihood of the customer exercising its right becomes remote. *[IFRS 15.B46, BC398]*. An exception to this process is when the entity is required to remit the payment to another party (e.g. the government). Such an amount is recognised as a liability. *[IFRS 15.B47]*.

When estimating any breakage amount, an entity has to consider the constraint on variable consideration, as discussed at 5.2.3 above. *[IFRS 15.B46]*. That is, if it is highly probable that a significant revenue reversal would occur for any estimated breakage amounts, an entity would not recognise those amounts until the breakage amounts are no longer constrained.

As discussed above, the application guidance on breakage requires that an entity recognise a liability for the full amount of the prepayment. It would then recognise breakage on that liability proportionate to the pattern of rights exercised by the customer. If the prepayment element (e.g. the sale of a gift card, loyalty points) is part of a multiple-element arrangement, an entity will need to allocate the transaction price between the identified performance obligations. As a result, the deferred revenue associated with this element would be less than the 'prepaid' amount received for the unsatisfied performance obligations.

The following example depicts the sale of goods with loyalty points. In this example, the amount allocated to the points (i.e. the 'prepaid' element) is less than the stand-alone selling price of those points because of the allocation of the transaction price among the two performance obligations. *[IFRS 15.IE267-IE270]*.

Example 30.57: Customer loyalty programme

An entity has a customer loyalty programme that rewards a customer with one customer loyalty point for every CU10 of purchases. Each point is redeemable for a CU1 discount on any future purchases of the entity's products. During a reporting period, customers purchase products for CU100,000 and earn 10,000 points that are redeemable for future purchases. The consideration is fixed and the stand-alone selling price of the purchased products is CU100,000. The entity expects 9,500 points to be redeemed. The entity estimates a stand-alone selling price of CU0.95 per point (totalling CU9,500) on the basis of the likelihood of redemption in accordance with paragraph B42 of IFRS 15.

The points provide a material right to customers that they would not receive without entering into a contract. Consequently, the entity concludes that the promise to provide points to the customer is a performance obligation. The entity allocates the transaction price (CU100,000) to the product and the points on a relative stand-alone selling price basis as follows:

	CU	
Product	91,324	[CU100,000 × (CU100,000 stand-alone selling price ÷ CU109,500)]
Points	8,676	[CU100,000 × (CU9,500 stand-alone selling price ÷ CU109,500)]

At the end of the first reporting period, 4,500 points have been redeemed and the entity continues to expect 9,500 points to be redeemed in total. The entity recognises revenue for the loyalty points of CU4,110 [(4,500 points ÷ 9,500 points) × CU8,676] and recognises a contract liability of CU4,566 (CU8,676 – CU4,110) for the unredeemed points at the end of the first reporting period.

At the end of the second reporting period, 8,500 points have been redeemed cumulatively. The entity updates its estimate of the points that will be redeemed and now expects that 9,700 points will be redeemed. The entity recognises revenue for the loyalty points of CU3,493 {[(8,500 total points redeemed ÷ 9,700 total points expected to be redeemed) × CU8,676 initial allocation] – CU4,110 recognised in the first reporting period}. The contract liability balance is CU1,073 (CU8,676 initial allocation – CU7,603 of cumulative revenue recognised).

7.10.1 Implementation questions on breakage

7.10.1.A Are customers' unexercised rights (i.e. breakage) a form of variable consideration?

Although the breakage application guidance in paragraph B46 of IFRS 15 specifically refers to the constraint on variable consideration, we do not believe breakage is a form of variable consideration (see 5.2 above). This is because it does not affect the transaction price. Breakage is a recognition concept (Step 5) that could affect the timing of revenue recognition. It is not a measurement concept (Step 3). For example, the transaction price for a sale of a CU20 gift card is fixed at CU20 regardless of the expected breakage amount. The expected breakage, however, could affect the timing of revenue recognition because an entity is required under paragraph B46 of IFRS 15 to 'recognise the expected breakage amount as revenue in proportion to the pattern of rights exercised by the customer' if it expects to be entitled to a breakage amount. *[IFRS 15.B46]*.

8 LICENCES OF INTELLECTUAL PROPERTY

IFRS 15 provides application guidance specific to the recognition of revenue for licences of intellectual property, which differs from the recognition model for other promised goods and services.

Given that licences include a wide array of features and economic characteristics, the Board decided that an entity will need to evaluate the nature of its promise to grant a licence of intellectual property in order to determine whether the promise is satisfied (and revenue is recognised) over time or at a point in time. A licence will either provide: *[IFRS 15.B56]*

- a right to access the entity's intellectual property throughout the licence period, which results in revenue that is recognised over time; or
- a right to use the entity's intellectual property as it exists at the point in time in which the licence is granted, which results in revenue that is recognised at a point in time.

The standard states that licences of intellectual property establish a customer's rights to the intellectual property of an entity and may include licences for any of the following: software and technology, media and entertainment (e.g. motion pictures and music), franchises, patents, trademarks and copyrights. *[IFRS 15.B52]*.

The application guidance provided on licences of intellectual property is only applicable to licences that are distinct. When the licence is the only promised item (either explicitly or implicitly) in the contract, the application guidance is clearly applicable to that licence. The assessment as to whether the contract includes a distinct licence of intellectual property may be straightforward for many contracts. However, if there are multiple promises in a contract, entities may have to more carefully evaluate the nature of the rights conveyed.

Licences of intellectual property are frequently included in multiple-element arrangements with promises for additional goods and services that may be explicit or implicit. In these situations, an entity first applies the requirements of Step 2 of the model to determine whether the licence of intellectual property is distinct, as discussed at 4 above and 8.1 below.

For most licences that are not distinct, an entity would follow the general requirements in Step 5 of the model to account for the recognition of revenue for the performance obligation that includes the licence (i.e. the requirements in paragraphs 31-36 of IFRS 15 to determine whether the performance obligation transfers over time or at a point in time, as discussed at 7.1 and 7.3 above). Furthermore, the IASB noted in the Basis for Conclusions that there may be some situations in which, even though the licence is not distinct from the good or service transferred with the licence, the licence is the primary or dominant component (i.e. the predominant item) of the combined performance obligation. *[IFRS 15.BC407]*. In such situations, the IASB indicated that the application guidance for licences will still be applied. The Board provided no application guidance or bright lines for determining when a licence is the primary or dominant component. However, the IASB referred to an example in the Basis for Conclusions to illustrate this concept further. *[IFRS 15.BC414X]*. See 8.2.1 below for a further discussion. The determination of whether a licence is the predominant component may be obvious in some cases, but not in others. Therefore, entities may need to exercise significant judgement and consider both qualitative and quantitative factors.

8.1 Identifying performance obligations in a licensing arrangement

Contracts for licences of intellectual property frequently include explicit or implicit promises for additional goods and services (e.g. equipment, when-and-if available upgrades, maintenance and installation). Consistent with Step 2 of the general model (see 4 above), entities will need to apply the requirements on identifying performance obligations in paragraphs 22-30 of IFRS 15, when a contract with a customer includes a licence of intellectual property and other promised goods or services, in order to appropriately determine whether the licence of intellectual property and the other promises are distinct (i.e. are separate performance obligations).

In respect of identifying performance obligations in a licensing arrangement, the standard states that '[i]n addition to a promise to grant a licence to a customer, an entity may also promise to transfer other goods or services to the customer. Those promises may be explicitly stated in the contract or implied by an entity's customary business practices, published policies or specific statements (see paragraph 24). As with other types of contracts, when a contract with a customer includes a promise to grant a licence in addition to other promised goods or services, an entity applies paragraphs 22–30 to identify each of the performance obligations in the contract.' *[IFRS 15.B53]*.

As discussed at 4.2 above, the standard outlines a two-step process for determining whether a promised good or service (including a licence of intellectual property) is distinct and, therefore, is a performance obligation as follows:

(1) consideration of the individual good or service (i.e. whether the good or service is capable of being distinct); and

(2) consideration of whether the good or service is separately identifiable from other promises in the contract (i.e. whether the promise to transfer the good or service is distinct in the context of the contract).

To conclude that a good or service is distinct, an entity will need to determine that the good or service is both capable of being distinct and distinct in the context of the contract. These requirements will need to be similarly applied to determine whether a promise to grant a licence of intellectual property is distinct from other promised goods or services in the contract. Therefore, entities are required to assess whether the customer can benefit from a licence of intellectual property on its own or together with readily available resources (i.e. whether it is capable of being distinct) and whether the entity's promise to transfer a licence of intellectual property is separately identifiable from other promises in the contract (i.e. whether it is distinct in the context of the contract).The assessment of whether a licence of intellectual property is distinct will need to be based on the facts and circumstances of each contract.

8.1.1 Licences of intellectual property that are distinct

Licences are frequently capable of being distinct (i.e. the first criteria of a distinct good or service) as a customer can often obtain at least some benefit from the licence of intellectual property on its own or with other readily available resources. Consider Example 30.14, Case A, at 4.2.3 above, which includes a contract for a software licence that is transferred along with installation services, technical support and unspecified software updates. The installation service is routinely performed by other entities and does not significantly modify the software. The software licence is delivered before the other goods and services and remains functional without the updates and technical support. The entity concludes that the customer can benefit from each of the goods and services either on their own or together with other goods or services that are readily available. That is, each good or service, including the software licence, is capable of being distinct under paragraph 27 of IFRS 15.

If an entity determines that a licence of intellectual property and other promised goods or services are capable of being distinct, the second step in the evaluation is to determine whether they are distinct in the context of the contract. As part of this evaluation, an entity considers the indicators for whether the goods or services are not separately identifiable, including whether:

(1) the entity provides a significant service of integrating the licence and other goods or services into a combined output or outputs;

(2) the licence and other goods or services significantly modify or customise each other; or

(3) the licence and other goods or services are highly interdependent or highly interrelated, such that the entity would not be able to fulfil its promise to transfer the licence independently of fulfilling its promise to transfer the other goods or services to the customer.

Continuing with Example 30.14, Case A, discussed above, the entity considers the separately identifiable principle and factors in paragraph 29 of IFRS 15 and determines that the promise to transfer each good and service, including the software licence, is separately identifiable. In reaching this determination, the entity considers that the installation services are routine and can be obtained from other providers. In addition, the entity considers that, although it integrates the software into the customer's system, the software updates do not significantly affect the customer's ability to use and benefit from the software licence during the licence period. Therefore, neither the installation services nor the software updates significantly affect the customer's ability to use and benefit from the software licence. The entity further observes that none of the promised goods or services significantly modify or customise one another and the entity is not providing a significant service of integrating the software and services into one combined output. Lastly, the software and the services are not deemed to be highly interdependent or highly interrelated because the entity would be able to fulfil its promise to transfer the initial software licence independent from its promise to subsequently provide the installation service, software updates and the technical support.

The following example from the standard also illustrates a contract for which a licence of intellectual property is determined to be distinct from other promised goods or services. *[IFRS 15.IE281, IE285-IE288]*.

Example 30.58: Identifying a distinct licence

An entity, a pharmaceutical company, licenses to a customer its patent rights to an approved drug compound for 10 years and also promises to manufacture the drug for the customer. The drug is a mature product; therefore the entity will not undertake any activities to support the drug, which is consistent with its customary business practices.

Case B – Licence is distinct

In this case, the manufacturing process used to produce the drug is not unique or specialised and several other entities can also manufacture the drug for the customer.

The entity assesses the goods and services promised to the customer to determine which goods and services are distinct, and it concludes that the criteria in paragraph 27 of IFRS 15 are met for each of the licence and the manufacturing service. The entity concludes that the criterion in paragraph 27(a) of IFRS 15 is met because the customer can benefit from the licence together with readily available resources other than the entity's manufacturing service (because there are other entities that can provide the manufacturing service), and can benefit from the manufacturing service together with the licence transferred to the customer at the start of the contract.

The entity also concludes that its promises to grant the licence and to provide the manufacturing service are separately identifiable (i.e. the criterion in paragraph 27(b) of IFRS 15 is met). The entity concludes that the licence and the manufacturing service are not inputs to a combined item in this contract on the basis of the principle and the factors in paragraph 29 of IFRS 15. In reaching this conclusion, the entity considers that the customer could separately purchase the licence without significantly affecting its ability to benefit from the licence. Neither the licence, nor the manufacturing service, is significantly modified or customised by the other and the entity is not providing a significant service of integrating those items into a combined output. The entity further considers that the licence and the manufacturing service are not highly interdependent or highly interrelated because the entity would be able to fulfil its promise to transfer the licence independently of fulfilling its promise to subsequently manufacture the drug for the customer. Similarly, the entity would be able to manufacture the drug for the customer even if the customer had previously obtained the licence and initially utilised a different manufacturer. Thus, although the manufacturing service necessarily depends on the licence in this contract (i.e. the entity would not provide the manufacturing service without the customer having obtained the licence), the licence and the manufacturing service do not significantly affect each other. Consequently, the entity concludes that its promises to grant the licence and to provide the manufacturing service are distinct and that there are two performance obligations:

(a) licence of patent rights; and

(b) manufacturing service.

The entity assesses, in accordance with paragraph B58 of IFRS 15, the nature of the entity's promise to grant the licence. The drug is a mature product (i.e. it has been approved, is currently being manufactured and has been sold commercially for the last several years). For these types of mature products, the entity's customary business practices are not to undertake any activities to support the drug. The drug compound has significant stand-alone functionality (i.e. its ability to produce a drug that treats a disease or condition). Consequently, the customer obtains a substantial portion of the benefits of the drug compound from that functionality, rather than from the entity's ongoing activities. The entity concludes that the criteria in paragraph B58 of IFRS 15 are not met because the contract does not require, and the customer does not reasonably expect, the entity to undertake activities that significantly affect the intellectual property to which the customer has rights. In its assessment of the criteria in paragraph B58 of IFRS 15, the entity does not take into consideration the separate performance obligation of promising to provide a manufacturing service. Consequently, the nature of the entity's promise in transferring the licence is to provide a right to use the entity's intellectual property in the form and the functionality with which it exists at the point in time that it is granted to the customer. Consequently, the entity accounts for the licence as a performance obligation satisfied at a point in time.

The entity applies paragraphs 31-38 of IFRS 15 to determine whether the manufacturing service is a performance obligation satisfied at a point in time or over time.

8.1.2 Licences of intellectual property that are not distinct

The licences of intellectual property included in the examples above were determined to be distinct, as they met the two criteria of paragraph 27 of IFRS 15. In other situations, a licence of intellectual property may not be distinct from other promised goods or services in a contract, either because it is not capable of being distinct and/or it is not separately identifiable.

Paragraph B54 of IFRS 15 requires that a licence that is not distinct from other promised goods or services in a contract be combined into a single performance obligation. It also identifies two examples of licences of intellectual property that are not distinct from other goods or services, as follows: *[IFRS 15.B54]*

'(a) a licence that forms a component of a tangible good and that is integral to the functionality of the good; and

(b) a licence that the customer can benefit from only in conjunction with a related service (such as an online service provided by the entity that enables, by granting a licence, the customer to access content).'

In both examples, a customer only benefits from the combined output of the licence of intellectual property and the related good or service. Therefore, the licence is not distinct and would be combined with those other promised goods or services in the contract.

The standard includes other examples of licences of intellectual property that are not distinct, which are combined with other promised goods or services because the customer can only benefit from the licence in conjunction with a related service (as described in paragraph B54(b) of IFRS 15). For example, Example 55 in IFRS 15 and Example 56, Case A, in IFRS 15 (included as Example 30.59 at 8.2.1 below) illustrate contracts that include licences of intellectual property that are not distinct from other goods or services promised to the customer.

When an entity is required to bundle a licence of intellectual property with other promised goods and services in a contract, it will often need to consider the licensing application guidance to help determine the nature of its promise to the customer when the licence is the predominant item in the combined performance obligation. See 8.2.1 below for further discussion on applying the licensing application guidance to such performance obligations.

8.1.3 *Contractual restrictions*

Some licences contain substantive contractual restrictions on how the customer may employ a licence. Paragraph B62(a) of IFRS 15 explicitly states an entity must disregard restrictions of time, geography or use when determining whether the promise to transfer a licence is satisfied over time or at a point in time; such restrictions define the attributes of the promised licence, rather than define whether the entity satisfies its performance obligation at a point in time or over time. *[IFRS 15.B62(a)]*.

While stakeholders acknowledged that paragraph B62 of IFRS 15 is clear that restrictions of time, geographical region or use do not affect the licensor's determination about whether the promise to transfer a licence is satisfied over time or at a point in time, some stakeholders thought that the standard was unclear about whether particular types of contractual restrictions would affect the identification of the promised goods or services in the contract. For example, an arrangement might grant a customer a licence to a well-known television programme or movie for a period of time (e.g. three years), but the customer might be restricted in how often it can show that licensed content to only once per year during each of those three years. In this instance, stakeholders thought that it may be unclear whether contractual restrictions affect the entity's identification of its promises in the contract (i.e. do the airing restrictions affect whether the entity has granted one licence or three licences?). *[IFRS 15.BC414O]*.

In considering this issue further, the IASB explained that contracts that include a promise to grant a licence to a customer require an assessment of the promises in the contract using the criteria for identifying performance obligations, as is the case with other contracts. *[IFRS 15.BC405-BC406]*. This assessment is done before applying the criteria to determine the nature of an entity's promise in granting a licence. *[IFRS 15.BC414P]*.

In the Basis for Conclusions, the IASB further explained that they considered Example 59 in IFRS 15 (see Example 30.62 at 8.3.2 below) in the context of this issue. The entity concludes that its only performance obligation is to grant the customer a right to use the music recording. When, where and how the right can be used is defined by the attributes of time (i.e. two years), geographical scope (i.e. Country A) and permitted use (i.e. in commercials). If, instead, the entity had granted the customer rights to use the recording for two different time periods in two geographical locations, for example, years X1–X3 in Country A and years X2–X4 in Country B, the entity would need to use the criteria for identifying performance obligations in paragraphs 27-30 of IFRS 15 to determine whether the contract included one licence that covers both countries or separate licences for each country. *[IFRS 15.BC414Q]*.

Consequently, the entity considers all of the contractual terms to determine whether the promised rights result in the transfer to the customer of one or more licences. In making this determination, judgement is needed to distinguish between contractual provisions that create promises to transfer rights to use the entity's intellectual property from contractual provisions that establish when, where and how those rights may be used. Therefore, in the Board's view, the clarifications made to the requirements on identifying performance obligations in paragraphs 22-30 of IFRS 15 provide sufficient guidance to entities. *[IFRS 15.BC414P]*.

We believe a critical part of the evaluation of contractual restrictions is whether the lifting of a restriction at a future date requires an entity to *grant additional rights* to the customer at that future date in order to fulfil its promises under the contract. The presence of a requirement to grant additional rights to the customer indicates that there may be multiple performance obligations that need to be accounted for under Step 2 of the model.

Entities may need to use significant judgement to distinguish between a single promised licence with multiple attributes and a licence that contains multiple promises to the customer that may be separate performance obligations.

ASC 606 requires that entities distinguish between contractual provisions that define the attributes of a single promised licence (e.g. restrictions of time, geography or use) and contractual provisions that require them to transfer additional goods or services to customers (e.g. additional rights to use or access intellectual property). Contractual provisions that are attributes of a promised licence define the scope of a customer's rights to intellectual property and do not affect whether a performance obligation is satisfied at a point in time or over time. Nor do they affect the number of performance obligations in the contract.

The IASB decided not to clarify the requirements for identifying performance obligations in a contract containing one or more licences since it had clarified the general requirements for identifying performance obligations. *[IFRS 15.BC414P]*.

As a result, ASC 606 includes guidance on contractual restrictions that differs from the requirements in IFRS 15. However, the IASB noted in the Basis for Conclusions that, consistent with the ASC 606, an entity would need to apply the requirements in Step 2 of the general model on identifying performance obligations when distinguishing between contractual provisions that create promises to transfer additional rights from those that are merely attributes of a licence that establish when, where and how the right may be used. *[IFRS 15.BC414P]*. Under both IFRS 15 and ASC 606, an entity may need to apply significant judgement to distinguish between a single promised licence with multiple attributes and a licence that contains multiple promises to the customer that may be separate performance obligations.

8.1.4 Guarantees to defend or maintain a patent

IFRS 15 states that a guarantee provided by an entity that it has a valid patent to intellectual property and that it will defend or maintain a patent does not represent a performance obligation in a licensing contract. This is because 'the act of defending a patent protects the value of the entity's intellectual property assets and provides assurance to the customer that the licence transferred meets the specifications of the licence promised in the contract'. Furthermore, this type of guarantee does not affect the licensor's determination as to whether the licence provides a right to access intellectual property (satisfied over time) or a right to use intellectual property (satisfied at a point in time). *[IFRS 15.B62(b)]*.

8.1.5 Implementation questions on identifying performance obligations in a licensing arrangement

8.1.5.A How should entities account for modifications to licences of intellectual property?

A licence provides a customer with a right to use or a right to access the intellectual property of an entity. The terms of each licence of intellectual property are defined by the contract, which establishes the customer's rights (e.g. period of time, area of use). We believe that when a contract for a licence of intellectual property is modified, the additional and/or modified licence of intellectual property is distinct from the original licence because the new and/or modified rights will always differ from those conveyed by the original licence.

The standard contains requirements on accounting for contract modification (see 3.4 above) and requires that a modification in which the additional promised goods or services are distinct be accounted for on a prospective basis, as follows:

- the modification will be accounted for as a separate contract if the additional consideration from the modification reflects the new licence's stand-alone selling price in accordance with paragraph 20 of IFRS 15; and
- if the additional consideration does not reflect the stand-alone selling price of the new licence, the modification would be accounted for in accordance with paragraph 21 of IFRS 15.

For a modification accounted for as a termination of the original contract and creation of a new contract in accordance with paragraph 21(a) of IFRS 15, any revenue recognised to date under the original contract is not adjusted. At the date of the modification, the remaining unrecognised transaction price from the original contract (if any) and the additional transaction price from the new contract are allocated to the remaining performance obligation(s) in the new contract. Any revenue allocated to a performance obligation created at the modification date for the renewal or extension of a licence would be recognised when (or as) that performance obligation is satisfied, which may not be until the beginning of the renewal or extension period (see 8.4 below).

8.2 Determining the nature of the entity's promise in granting a licence

In April 2016, the IASB issued amendments that clarified when an entity's activities significantly affect the intellectual property to which the customer has rights, which is a factor in determining whether the entity recognises revenue over time or at a point in time for a licence of intellectual property.

Entities will need to evaluate the nature of a promise to grant a licence of intellectual property in order to determine whether the promise is satisfied (and revenue is recognised) over time or at a point in time. In order to help entities in determining whether a licence provides a customer with a right to access or a right to use the intellectual property (which is important when determining the period of performance and, therefore, the timing of revenue recognition – see 8.3 below), the Board provided application guidance that clarifies that an entity's promise is to provide a right to access the entity's intellectual property if all of the following criteria are met: *[IFRS 15.B58]*

(a) the contract requires, or the customer reasonably expects, that the entity will undertake activities that significantly affect the intellectual property to which the customer has rights;

(b) the rights granted by the licence directly expose the customer to any positive or negative effects of the entity's activities identified in (a); and

(c) those activities do not result in the transfer of a good or a service to the customer as those activities occur.

The standard lists an entity's customary business practices, published policies or specific statements as factors that may indicate that a customer could reasonably expect that an entity will undertake activities that significantly affect the intellectual property. Although not determinative, the existence of a shared economic interest (that is related to the intellectual property to which the customer has rights) between the entity and the customer (e.g. a sales-based royalty) may also provide such an indication. *[IFRS 15.B59]*.

In providing this application guidance, the Board decided to focus on the characteristics of a licence that provides a right to access the entity's intellectual property. If the licensed intellectual property does not have those characteristics, it provides a right to use the entity's intellectual property, by default. This analysis is focused on situations in which the underlying intellectual property is subject to change over the licence period.

The key determinants of whether the nature of an entity's promise is a right to access the entity's intellectual property are whether: (1) the entity is required to undertake activities that affect the licensed intellectual property (or the customer has a reasonable expectation that the entity will do so); and (2) the customer is exposed to positive or negative effects resulting from those changes.

It is important to note that when an entity is making this assessment, it excludes the effect of any other performance obligations in the contract. For example, if an entity enters into a contract to license software and provide access to any future upgrades to that software during the licence period, the entity first determines whether the licence and the promise to provide future updates are separate performance obligations. If they are separate, when the entity considers whether it has a contractual (explicit or implicit) obligation to undertake activities to change the software during the licence period, it would exclude any changes and activities associated with the performance obligation to provide future upgrades.

While the activities considered in this assessment do not include those that are a performance obligation, these activities can be part of an entity's ongoing ordinary activities and customary business practices (i.e. they do not have to be activities the entity is undertaking specifically as a result of the contract with the customer). In addition, the IASB noted, in the Basis for Conclusions, that the existence of a shared economic interest between the parties (e.g. sales-based or usage-based royalties) may be an indicator that the customer has a reasonable expectation that the entity will undertake such activities. *[IFRS 15.BC413]*.

After an entity has identified the activities for this assessment, it must determine if those activities significantly affect the intellectual property to which the customer has rights. The standard clarifies that such activities significantly affect the intellectual property if they: *[IFRS 15.B59A]*

- significantly change the form (e.g. design or content) or functionality (e.g. the ability to perform a function or task) of the intellectual property; or
- affect the ability of the customer to obtain benefit from the intellectual property (e.g. the benefit from a brand is often derived from, or dependent upon, the entity's ongoing activities that support or maintain the value of the intellectual property).

If the intellectual property has significant stand-alone functionality, the standard clarifies that the customer will derive a substantial portion of the benefit of that intellectual property from that functionality. As such, 'the ability of the customer to obtain benefit from that intellectual property would not be significantly affected by the entity's activities unless those activities significantly change its form or functionality.' Therefore, if the intellectual property has significant stand-alone functionality, revenue will be recognised at a point in time. Examples of types of intellectual property that may have significant stand-alone functionality that are mentioned in the standard include software, biological compounds or drug formulas, and completed media content. *[IFRS 15.B59A]*.

The IASB has not defined the term 'significant stand-alone functionality', but has made clarifications to the examples in the standard to illustrate when the intellectual property to which the customer has rights may have significant stand-alone functionality. In some cases, it will be clear when intellectual property has significant stand-alone functionality. If there is no significant stand-alone functionality, the benefit to the customer might be substantially derived from the value of the intellectual property and the entity's activities to support or maintain that value. The IASB noted, however, that an entity may need to apply judgement to determine whether the intellectual property to which the customer has rights has significant stand-alone functionality. *[IFRS 15.BC414I]*.

It is important for entities that provide licences of intellectual property to their customers to appropriately identify the performance obligations as part of Step 2 of the model because those conclusions may directly affect their evaluation of whether the entity's activities significantly change the form or functionality of the intellectual property or affect the ability of the customer to obtain benefit from the intellectual property.

The FASB's standard requires entities to classify intellectual property in one of two categories as detailed below.

- *Functional*: This intellectual property has significant stand-alone functionality (e.g. many types of software, completed media content such as films, television shows and music). Revenue for these licences will be recognised at the point in time when the intellectual property is made available for the customer's use and benefit if the functionality is not expected to change substantially as a result of the licensor's ongoing activities that do not transfer another good or service to the customer. If the functionality of the intellectual property is expected to substantively change because of the activities of the licensor that do not transfer promised goods or services and the customer is contractually or practically required to use the latest version of the intellectual property, revenue for the licence will be recognised over time. The FASB noted in the Basis for Conclusions of licensing amendments that it expects entities will meet the criteria to recognise licences of functional intellectual property over time infrequently, if at all.

- *Symbolic*: This intellectual property does not have significant stand-alone functionality (e.g. brands, team and trade names, character images). The utility of symbolic intellectual property is derived from the licensor's ongoing or past activities (e.g. activities that support the value of character images licensed from an animated film). Revenue from these licences will be recognised over time as the performance obligation is satisfied (e.g. over the licence period).

IFRS 15 does not require entities to classify licenses of intellectual property as either functional or symbolic. The IASB decided to clarify the approach to determining the nature of an entity's promise in providing a licence (as discussed above), rather than change that approach. *[IFRS 15.BC414K]*.

The IASB and FASB agreed that their approaches will generally result in consistent answers, but the Boards acknowledged that different outcomes may arise due to the different approaches when entities license brand names that no longer have any related ongoing activities (e.g. the licence to the brand name of a defunct sports team, such as the Brooklyn Dodgers). Under the FASB's approach, a licence of a brand name would be classified as symbolic intellectual property and revenue would be recognised over time, regardless of whether there are any related ongoing activities. Under the IASB's approach, revenue would be recognised at a point in time if there are no ongoing activities that significantly affect the intellectual property.

8.2.1 Applying the licensing application guidance to a single performance obligation that includes a licence of intellectual property

IFRS 15 does not explicitly state that an entity will need to consider the nature of its promise in granting a licence when applying the general revenue recognition model to performance obligations that are comprised of both a licence (that is not distinct) and other goods or services. However, the Board clarified in the Basis for Conclusions that to the extent that an entity is required to combine a licence with other promised goods and services in a single performance obligation and the licence is the primary or dominant component (i.e. the predominant item) of that performance obligation, the entity will need to consider the licensing application guidance to help determine the nature of its promise to the customer. *[IFRS 15.BC407]*.

If the licence is a predominant item of a single performance obligation, entities will need to consider the licensing application guidance when:

- determining whether the performance obligation is satisfied over time or at a point in time; and
- selecting an appropriate method for measuring progress of that performance obligation if it is satisfied over time.

Considering the nature of an entity's promise in granting a licence that is part of a single combined performance obligation is not a separate step or evaluation in the revenue model. Rather, it is part of the overall requirements in Step 5 of the model to determine whether that single performance obligation is satisfied over time or at a point in time and the appropriate measure of progress toward the satisfaction, if it is satisfied over time.

The Board did not provide application guidance or bright lines for determining when a licence is the primary or dominant (i.e. the predominant) component. However, the IASB explained in the Basis for Conclusions that, in some instances, not considering the nature of the entity's promise in granting a licence that is combined with other promised goods or services in a single performance obligation would result in accounting that does not best reflect the entity's performance. For example, consider a situation where an entity grants a 10-year licence that is not distinct from a one-year service arrangement. The IASB noted that a distinct licence that provides access to an entity's intellectual property over a 10-year period could not be considered completely satisfied before the end of the access period. The IASB observed in that example that it is, therefore, inappropriate to conclude that a single performance obligation that includes that licence is satisfied over the one-year period of the service arrangement. *[IFRS 15.BC414X]*.

The standard includes examples that illustrate how an entity applies the licensing application guidance to help determine the nature of a performance obligation that includes a licence of intellectual property and other promised goods or services.

In Example 30.59 below an entity licences the patent rights for an approved drug compound to its customer and also promises to manufacture the drug for the customer. The entity considers that no other entity can perform the manufacturing service because of the highly specialised nature of the manufacturing process. Therefore, the licence cannot be purchased separately from the manufacturing service and the customer cannot benefit from the licence on its own or with other readily available resources (i.e. the licence and the manufacturing service are not capable of being distinct). Accordingly, the entity's promises to grant the licence and to manufacture the drug are accounted for as a single performance obligation, as follows. *[IFRS 15.IE281-IE284]*.

Example 30.59: Identifying a distinct licence

An entity, a pharmaceutical company, licenses to a customer its patent rights to an approved drug compound for 10 years and also promises to manufacture the drug for the customer. The drug is a mature product; therefore the entity will not undertake any activities to support the drug, which is consistent with its customary business practices.

Case A – Licence is not distinct

In this case, no other entity can manufacture this drug because of the highly specialised nature of the manufacturing process. As a result, the licence cannot be purchased separately from the manufacturing services.

The entity assesses the goods and services promised to the customer to determine which goods and services are distinct in accordance with paragraph 27 of IFRS 15. The entity determines that the customer cannot benefit from the licence without the manufacturing service; therefore, the criterion in paragraph 27(a) of IFRS 15 is not met. Consequently, the licence and the manufacturing service are not distinct and the entity accounts for the licence and the manufacturing service as a single performance obligation.

The entity applies paragraphs 31–38 of IFRS 15 to determine whether the performance obligation (i.e. the bundle of the licence and the manufacturing services) is a performance obligation satisfied at a point in time or over time.

Example 30.59 above illustrates the importance of applying the licensing application guidance when determining the nature of an entity's promise in granting a licence that is combined into a single performance obligation with other promised goods or services. That is because the conclusion of whether a non-distinct licence provides the customer with a right to use intellectual property or a right to access intellectual property may have a significant effect on the timing of revenue recognition for the single combined performance obligation. In Example 30.59, the entity needs to determine the nature of its promise in granting the licence within the single performance obligation (comprising the licence and the manufacturing service) to appropriately apply the general principle of recognising revenue when (or as) it satisfies its performance obligation to the customer. If the licence in this example provided a right to use the entity's intellectual property that on its own would be recognised at the point in time in which control of the licence is transferred to the customer, the combined performance obligation would likely only be fully satisfied at the end of the fifth year, when the manufacturing service is complete. In contrast, if the licence provided a right to access the entity's intellectual property, the combined performance obligation would not be fully satisfied until the end of the 10-year licence period, which would likely extend the period of revenue recognition beyond the date when the manufacturing service is complete.

ASC 606 explicitly states that an entity considers the nature of its promise in granting a licence when applying the general revenue recognition model to a single performance obligation that includes a licence and other goods or services (i.e. when applying the general requirements, consistent with those in paragraphs 31-45 of IFRS 15, to assess whether the performance obligations are satisfied at a point in time or over time). Consequently, when the licence is not the predominant item in a single performance obligation, this may result in a US GAAP preparer considering the nature of its promise in granting a licence in a greater number of circumstances than an IFRS preparer. *[IFRS 15.BC414Y]*. The determination of whether a licence is the predominant component may be obvious in some cases, but not in others. Therefore, entities may need to exercise significant judgement and consider both qualitative and quantitative factors.

8.3 Transfer of control of licensed intellectual property

When determining whether a licence of intellectual property transfers to a customer (and revenue is recognised) over time or at a point in time, the standard states that an entity provides a customer with either:

- a right to access the entity's intellectual property throughout the licence period for which revenue is recognised over the licence period; or
- a right to use the entity's intellectual property as it exists at the point in time the licence is granted, for which revenue is recognised at the point in time, the customer can first use and benefit from the licensed intellectual property.

On the timing of revenue recognition for right-to-access and right-to-use licences, the standard states that, if the criteria in paragraph B58 of IFRS 15 are met, 'an entity shall account for the promise to grant a licence as a performance obligation satisfied over time because the customer will simultaneously receive and consume the benefit from the entity's performance of providing access to its intellectual property as the performance occurs (see paragraph 35(a)). An entity shall apply paragraphs 39–45 to select an appropriate method to measure its progress towards complete satisfaction of that performance obligation to provide access.' *[IFRS 15.B60]*.

If, instead, the criteria in paragraph B58 of IFRS 15 are not met, the standard explains that 'the nature of an entity's promise is to provide a right to use the entity's intellectual property as that intellectual property exists (in terms of form and functionality) at the point in time at which the licence is granted to the customer.' As a result, the customer will be able to direct the use of, and obtain substantially all of the remaining benefits from, the licence at the point in time at which the licence transfers. Therefore, an entity is required to account for the promise to provide a right to use the entity's intellectual property as a performance obligation satisfied at a point in time. *[IFRS 15.B61]*.

An entity applies paragraph 38 of IFRS 15 to determine the point in time at which the licence transfers to the customer. However, 'revenue cannot be recognised for a licence that provides a right to use the entity's intellectual property before the beginning of the period during which the customer is able to use and benefit from the licence. For example, if a software licence period begins before an entity provides (or otherwise makes available) to the customer a code that enables the customer to immediately use the software, the entity would not recognise revenue before that code has been provided (or otherwise made available).' *[IFRS 15.B61]*.

8.3.1 Right to access

The Board concluded that a licence that provides an entity with the right to access intellectual property is satisfied over time 'because the customer simultaneously receives and consumes the benefit from the entity's performance as the performance occurs', including the related activities undertaken by entity. *[IFRS 15.B60, BC414]*. This conclusion is based on the determination that when a licence is subject to change (and the customer is exposed to the positive or negative effects of that change), the customer is not able to fully gain control over the licence of intellectual property at any given point in time, but rather gains control over the licence period. Entities will need to apply the general requirements in paragraphs 39-45 of IFRS 15 to determine the appropriate method to measure progress (see 7.2 above).

The standard includes the following example of a right-to-access licence. *[IFRS 15.IE297-IE302]*.

Example 30.60: Access to intellectual property

An entity, a creator of comic strips, licenses the use of the images and names of its comic strip characters in three of its comic strips to a customer for a four-year term. There are main characters involved in each of the comic strips. However, newly created characters appear regularly and the images of the characters evolve over time. The customer, an operator of cruise ships, can use the entity's characters in various ways, such as in shows or parades, within reasonable guidelines. The contract requires the customer to use the latest images of the characters.

In exchange for granting the licence, the entity receives a fixed payment of CU1 million in each year of the four-year term.

In accordance with paragraph 27 of IFRS 15, the entity assesses the goods and services promised to the customer to determine which goods and services are distinct. The entity concludes that it has no other performance obligations other than the promise to grant a licence. That is, the additional activities associated with the licence do not directly transfer a good or service to the customer because they are part of the entity's promise to grant a licence.

The entity assesses the nature of the entity's promise to transfer the licence in accordance with paragraph B58 of IFRS 15. In assessing the criteria the entity considers the following:

(a) the customer reasonably expects (arising from the entity's customary business practices) that the entity will undertake activities that will significantly affect the intellectual property to which the customer has rights (i.e. the characters). This is because the entity's activities (i.e. development of the characters) change the form of the intellectual property to which the customer has rights. In addition, the ability of the customer to obtain benefit from the intellectual property to which the customer has rights is substantially derived from, or dependent upon, the entity's ongoing activities (i.e. the publishing of the comic strip).

(b) the rights granted by the licence directly expose the customer to any positive or negative effects of the entity's activities because the contract requires the customer to use the latest characters.

(c) even though the customer may benefit from those activities through the rights granted by the licence, they do not transfer a good or service to the customer as those activities occur.

Consequently, the entity concludes that the criteria in paragraph B58 of IFRS 15 are met and that the nature of the entity's promise to transfer the licence is to provide the customer with access to the entity's intellectual property as it exists throughout the licence period. Consequently, the entity accounts for the promised licence as a performance obligation satisfied over time (i.e. the criterion in paragraph 35(a) of IFRS 15 is met).

The entity applies paragraphs 39-45 of IFRS 15 to identify the method that best depicts its performance in the licence. Because the contract provides the customer with unlimited use of the licensed characters for a fixed term, the entity determines that a time-based method would be the most appropriate measure of progress towards complete satisfaction of the performance obligation.

Step 2 of the model requires an entity to identify the performance obligations in a contract. This includes identifying whether multiple distinct goods or services should be accounted for as a single performance obligation under the series requirement (see 4.2.2 above). Many licences that provide a right to access intellectual property may include a series of distinct goods or services that are substantially the same and have the same pattern of transfer to the customer (e.g. a series of distinct periods of access to intellectual property, such as monthly access or quarterly access). If a licence meets the criteria to be accounted for as a series of distinct goods or services, an entity will need to consider whether any variable consideration in the contract (e.g. royalties, milestone payments) would need to be allocated to the distinct periods of access, if certain criteria are met. See 6.3 above for a discussion of the variable consideration allocation exception and 8.5 below for a discussion of the accounting for sales-based or usage-based royalties.

8.3.2 Right to use

In contrast, when the licence represents a right to use the intellectual property as it exists at a specific point in time, the customer gains control over that intellectual property at the beginning of the period for which it has the right to use the intellectual property. *[IFRS 15.B61]*. This timing may differ from when the licence was granted. For example, an entity may provide a customer with the right to use intellectual property, but indicate that right to use does not start until 30 days after the agreement is finalised. For the purpose of determining when control transfers for the right-to-use licence, the Board was clear that the assessment is from the customer's perspective (i.e. when the customer can use the licensed intellectual property), rather than the entity's perspective (i.e. when the entity transfers the licence).

The standard includes the following example of a right-to-use licence. *[IFRS 15.IE303-IE306]*.

Example 30.61: Right to use intellectual property

An entity, a music record label, licenses to a customer a 1975 recording of a classical symphony by a noted orchestra. The customer, a consumer products company, has the right to use the recorded symphony in all commercials, including television, radio and online advertisements for two years in Country A. In exchange for providing the licence, the entity receives fixed consideration of CU10,000 per month. The contract does not include any other goods or services to be provided by the entity. The contract is non-cancellable.

The entity assesses the goods and services promised to the customer to determine which goods and services are distinct in accordance with paragraph 27 of IFRS 15. The entity concludes that its only performance obligation is to grant the licence. The entity determines that the term of the licence (two years), its geographical scope (the customer's right to use the recording only in Country A), and the defined permitted use for the recording (in commercials) are all attributes of the promised licence in the contract.

In accordance with paragraph B58 of IFRS 15, the entity assesses the nature of the entity's promise to grant the licence. The entity does not have any contractual or implied obligations to change the licensed recording. The licensed recording has significant stand-alone functionality (i.e. the ability to be played) and, therefore, the ability of the customer to obtain the benefits of the recording is not substantially derived from the entity's ongoing activities. The entity therefore determines that the contract does not require, and the customer does not reasonably expect, the entity to undertake activities that significantly affect the licensed recording (i.e. the criterion in paragraph B58(a) is not met). Consequently, the entity concludes that the nature of its promise in transferring the licence is to provide the customer with a right to use the entity's intellectual property as it exists at the point in time that it is granted. Therefore, the promise to grant the licence is a performance obligation satisfied at a point in time. The entity recognises all of the revenue at the point in time when the customer can direct the use of, and obtain substantially all of the remaining benefits from, the licensed intellectual property.

Because of the length of time between the entity's performance (at the beginning of the period) and the customer's monthly payments over two years (which are non-cancellable), the entity considers the requirements in paragraphs 60-65 of IFRS 15 to determine whether a significant financing component exists.

8.3.3 Use and benefit requirement

IFRS 15 states that revenue from a right-to-use licence cannot be recognised before the beginning of the period during which 'the customer is able to use and benefit from the licence'. *[IFRS 15.B61]*. The IASB explained in the Basis for Conclusions that if the customer cannot use and benefit from the licensed intellectual property then, by definition, it does not control the licence. *[IFRS 15.BC414]*. See 8.4 below for discussion on licence renewals.

Consider an example where an entity provides a customer with a right to use its software, but the customer requires a code before the software will function, which the entity will not provide until 30 days after the agreement is finalised. In this example, the entity is likely to conclude that control of the licence does not transfer until 30 days after the agreement is finalised because that is when the customer has the right to use and can benefit from the software.

8.4 Licence renewals

As discussed at 8.3.3 above, IFRS 15 states that revenue cannot be recognised for a licence that provides a right to use the entity's intellectual property before the beginning of the period during which the customer is able to use and benefit from the licence. *[IFRS 15.B61]*. Some stakeholders questioned whether paragraph B61 of IFRS 15 applies to the renewal of an existing licence or whether the entity could recognise revenue for the renewal when the parties agree to the renewal. Therefore, the TRG discussed the application of paragraph B61 of IFRS 15 within the context of renewals or extensions of existing licences. *[IFRS 15.BC414S]*. The discussion at the TRG indicated that this is an area in which judgement is needed and, therefore, this topic was further discussed by the IASB.[101]

The IASB decided that a clarification about the application of the contract modification requirements specifically for renewals of licensing arrangements was not necessary. The Board noted that, although some diversity may arise, IFRS 15 provides a more extensive framework for applying judgement than IAS 18. In addition, in making its decision, the Board also considered the wider implications of amending IFRS 15 before its effective date.

Therefore, when an entity and a customer enter into a contract to renew (or extend the period of) an existing licence, the entity needs to evaluate whether the renewal or extension should be treated as a new licence or as a modification of the existing contract. A modification would be accounted for in accordance with the contract modifications requirements in paragraphs 18-21 of IFRS 15. *[IFRS 15.BC414T]*.

Under ASC 606, revenue related to the renewal of a licence of intellectual property may not be recognised earlier than the beginning of the renewal period. This will be the case even if the entity provides a copy of the intellectual property in advance or the customer has a copy of the intellectual property from another transaction. The FASB also provided an additional example to illustrate this point.

IFRS 15 does not include similar requirements. Therefore, the IASB noted in the Basis for Conclusions that it is possible that IFRS entities will recognise revenue for contract renewals or extensions earlier than US GAAP entities. *[IFRS 15.BC414U]*.

8.5 Sales-based or usage-based royalties on licences of intellectual property

In April 2016, the IASB issued amendments that clarify the scope of the exception for sales-based or usage-based royalties related to licences of intellectual property (the royalty exception) when there are other promised goods or services in the contract. Under the amendments, the royalty exception must be applied to the overall royalty stream when the sole or predominant item to which the royalty relates is a licence of intellectual property.

It also clarified that the sales-based or usage-based royalty in these types of contracts will be either entirely in the scope of royalty constraint application guidance or entirely in the scope of the general variable consideration constraint guidance, but not both.

The standard provides application guidance on the recognition of revenue for sales-based or usage-based royalties on licences of intellectual property, which differs from the requirements that apply to other revenue from licences. IFRS 15 requires that sales or usage-based royalties received in exchange for licences of intellectual property are recognised at the later of when: [IFRS 15.B63]

(1) the subsequent sale or usage occurs; and

(2) the performance obligation to which some or all of the sales-based or usage-based royalty has been allocated is satisfied (or partially satisfied).

That is, an entity recognises the royalties as revenue for such arrangements when (or as) the customer's subsequent sales or usage occurs, unless that pattern of recognition accelerates revenue recognition ahead of the entity's satisfaction of the performance obligation to which the royalty solely or partially relates, based on an appropriate measure of progress (see 7.2 above). [IFRS 15.BC421I].

The Board explained in the Basis for Conclusions that for a licence of intellectual property for which the consideration is based on the customer's subsequent sales or usage, an entity does not recognise any revenue for the variable amounts until the uncertainty is resolved (i.e. when a customer's subsequent sales or usage occurs). [IFRS 15.BC219].

The IASB also explained in the Basis for Conclusions that the application guidance in paragraphs B63-B63B of IFRS 15 addresses the *recognition* of sales-based or usage-based royalties received in exchange for a licence of intellectual property, rather than when such amounts are included in the transaction price of the contract. [IFRS 15.BC421I]. As a result, this exception is a recognition constraint and the constraint on variable consideration (see 5.2.3 above) does not apply.

The Board explained that it added the royalty exception because both users and preparers of financial statements indicated that it would not be useful for entities to recognise a minimum amount of revenue for sales-based or usage-based royalties received in exchange for licences of intellectual property (following the requirements in the general model on estimating the transaction price), because that approach would inevitably require the entity to report significant adjustments to the amount of revenue recognised throughout the life of the contract as a result of changes in circumstances that are not related to the entity's performance. The Board observed that this would not result in relevant information, especially for contracts in which the sales-based or usage-based royalties are paid over a long period of time. [IFRS 15.BC415].

Paragraph B63A of IFRS 15 requires that the royalty exception be applied to the overall royalty stream when the sole or predominant item to which the royalty relates is a licence of intellectual property (including when no single licence is the predominant item to which the royalty relates, but the royalty predominantly relates to two or more licences in the contract). [IFRS 15.B63A, BC421G]. That is, this application guidance is applicable to all licences of intellectual property, regardless of whether they have been determined to be distinct. The standard does not provide a bright line for determining the 'predominant' item in a contract that includes a licence of intellectual property. The Board acknowledged in the Basis for Conclusions that significant judgement may be required to determine when a licence is the predominant item to which a royalty relates. However, the judgement for determining whether a licence is the predominant item is likely to be less than the judgement needed to apply the general requirements for variable consideration to such contracts. [IFRS 15.BC421E].

It is important to note that this application guidance applies only to licences of intellectual property for which some or all of the consideration is in the form of a sales-based or usage-based royalty. Therefore, entities cannot analogise to this application guidance for other types of transactions. For example, if consideration in a contract is in the form of a sales-based or usage-based royalty, but there is no licence of intellectual property, this application guidance would not apply. In such cases, an entity would follow the requirements in the general model on estimating variable consideration and applying the constraint on variable consideration (see 5.2 above). In some cases, it may not be obvious as to whether the arrangement is an in-substance sale of intellectual property (i.e. a promise that is in the form of a licence, but, in substance, has the characteristics of a sale) or a licence of intellectual property. In such instances, entities would have to exercise judgement to determine whether the control over the underlying intellectual property has been transferred from the entity to the customer and therefore, has been sold.

The standard provides the following example of a contract that includes two performance obligations, including a licence that provides a right to use the entity's intellectual property and consideration in the form of sales-based royalties. In the example, the licence is determined to be the predominant item to which the royalty relates. *[IFRS 15.IE307-IE308]*.

Example 30.62: Sales-based royalty for a licence of intellectual property

An entity, a movie distribution company, licenses Movie XYZ to a customer. The customer, an operator of cinemas, has the right to show the movie in its cinemas for six weeks. Additionally, the entity has agreed to: (a) provide memorabilia from the filming to the customer for display at the customer's cinemas before the beginning of the six-week screening period; and (b) sponsor radio advertisements for Movie XYZ on popular radio stations in the customer's geographical area throughout the six-week screening period. In exchange for providing the licence and the additional promotional goods and services, the entity will receive a portion of the operator's ticket sales for Movie XYZ (i.e. variable consideration in the form of a sales-based royalty).

The entity concludes that the licence to show Movie XYZ is the predominant item to which the sales-based royalty relates because the entity has a reasonable expectation that the customer would ascribe significantly more value to the licence than to the related promotional goods or services. The entity recognises revenue from the sales-based royalty, the only consideration to which the entity is entitled under the contract, wholly in accordance with paragraph B63. If the licence, the memorabilia and the advertising activities are separate performance obligations, the entity would allocate the sales-based royalty to each performance obligation.

As illustrated in Example 30.62 above, Paragraph B63B of IFRS 15 requires that, when the royalty exception is applied, the royalty stream must be accounted for either entirely under the royalty exception or entirely under the general variable consideration constraint requirements (see 5.2.3 above). *[IFRS 15.B63B]*. That is, an entity would not split a single royalty and apply the royalty exception to a portion of the sales-based royalty and the general constraint requirements for variable consideration to the remainder. The Board indicated in the Basis for Conclusions that it would be more complex to account for part of a royalty under the royalty exception and another part under the general requirements for variable consideration and that doing so would not provide any additional useful information to users of financial statements. This is because splitting a royalty would result in an entity recognising an amount at contract inception that would reflect neither the amount to which the entity expects to be entitled, based on its performance, nor the amount to which the entity has become legally entitled during the period. *[IFRS 15.BC421J]*.

Regardless of whether an entity applies the royalty exception or the general requirements for variable consideration, it is still required to allocate sales-based or usage-based royalties to separate performance obligations in a contract (as noted in Example 30.62 above). The following example from the standard also illustrates the allocation of the transaction price (including sales-based or usage-based royalties) to the performance obligations in the contract. *[IFRS 15.IE178-IE187]*.

Example 30.63: Allocation of variable consideration

An entity enters into a contract with a customer for two intellectual property licences (Licences X and Y), which the entity determines to represent two performance obligations each satisfied at a point in time. The stand-alone selling prices of Licences X and Y are CU800 and CU1,000, respectively.

Case A – Variable consideration allocated entirely to one performance obligation

The price stated in the contract for Licence X is a fixed amount of CU800 and for Licence Y the consideration is three per cent of the customer's future sales of products that use Licence Y. For purposes of allocation, the entity estimates its sales-based royalties (i.e. the variable consideration) to be CU1,000, in accordance with paragraph 53 of IFRS 15.

To allocate the transaction price, the entity considers the criteria in paragraph 85 of IFRS 15 and concludes that the variable consideration (i.e. the sales-based royalties) should be allocated entirely to Licence Y. The entity concludes that the criteria in paragraph 85 of IFRS 15 are met for the following reasons:

(a) the variable payment relates specifically to an outcome from the performance obligation to transfer Licence Y (i.e. the customer's subsequent sales of products that use Licence Y).

(b) allocating the expected royalty amounts of CU1,000 entirely to Licence Y is consistent with the allocation objective in paragraph 73 of IFRS 15. This is because the entity's estimate of the amount of sales-based royalties (CU1,000) approximates the stand-alone selling price of Licence Y and the fixed amount of CU800 approximates the stand-alone selling price of Licence X. The entity allocates CU800 to Licence X in accordance with paragraph 86 of IFRS 15. This is because, based on an assessment of the facts and circumstances relating to both licences, allocating to Licence Y some of the fixed consideration in addition to all of the variable consideration would not meet the allocation objective in paragraph 73 of IFRS 15.

The entity transfers Licence Y at inception of the contract and transfers Licence X one month later. Upon the transfer of Licence Y, the entity does not recognise revenue because the consideration allocated to Licence Y is in the form of a sales-based royalty. Therefore, in accordance with paragraph B63 of IFRS 15, the entity recognises revenue for the sales-based royalty when those subsequent sales occur.

When Licence X is transferred, the entity recognises as revenue the CU800 allocated to Licence X.

Case B – Variable consideration allocated on the basis of stand-alone selling prices

The price stated in the contract for Licence X is a fixed amount of CU300 and for Licence Y the consideration is five per cent of the customer's future sales of products that use Licence Y. The entity's estimate of the sales-based royalties (i.e. the variable consideration) is CU1,500 in accordance with paragraph 53 of IFRS 15.

To allocate the transaction price, the entity applies the criteria in paragraph 85 of IFRS 15 to determine whether to allocate the variable consideration (i.e. the sales-based royalties) entirely to Licence Y. In applying the criteria, the entity concludes that even though the variable payments relate specifically to an outcome from the performance obligation to transfer Licence Y (i.e. the customer's subsequent sales of products that use Licence Y), allocating the variable consideration entirely to Licence Y would be inconsistent with the principle for allocating the transaction price. Allocating CU300 to Licence X and CU1,500 to Licence Y does not reflect a reasonable allocation of the transaction price on the basis of the stand-alone selling prices of Licences X and Y of CU800 and CU1,000, respectively. Consequently, the entity applies the general allocation requirements in paragraphs 76-80 of IFRS 15.

The entity allocates the transaction price of CU300 to Licences X and Y on the basis of relative stand-alone selling prices of CU800 and CU1,000, respectively. The entity also allocates the consideration related to the sales-based royalty on a relative stand-alone selling price basis. However, in accordance with paragraph B63 of IFRS 15, when an entity licenses intellectual property in which the consideration is in the form of a sales-based royalty, the entity cannot recognise revenue until the later of the following events: the subsequent sales occur or the performance obligation is satisfied (or partially satisfied).

Licence Y is transferred to the customer at the inception of the contract and Licence X is transferred three months later. When Licence Y is transferred, the entity recognises as revenue the CU167 (CU1,000 ÷ CU1,800 × CU300) allocated to Licence Y. When Licence X is transferred, the entity recognises as revenue the CU133 (CU800 ÷ CU1,800 × CU300) allocated to Licence X.

In the first month, the royalty due from the customer's first month of sales is CU200. Consequently, in accordance with paragraph B63 of IFRS 15, the entity recognises as revenue the CU111 (CU1,000 ÷ CU1,800 × CU200) allocated to Licence Y (which has been transferred to the customer and is therefore a satisfied performance obligation). The entity recognises a contract liability for the CU89 (CU800 ÷ CU1,800 × CU200) allocated to Licence X. This is because although the subsequent sale by the entity's customer has occurred, the performance obligation to which the royalty has been allocated has not been satisfied.

8.5.1 Recognition of royalties for a licence that provides a right to access intellectual property

The IASB explained in the Basis for Conclusions that the royalty exception is intended to align the recognition of sales or usage-based royalties with the standard's key principle that revenue should be recognised when (or as) an entity satisfies a performance obligation. As discussed above, IFRS 15 requires that royalties received in exchange for licences of intellectual property are recognised at the later of when: (1) the subsequent sales or usage occurs; and (2) the performance obligation to which the sales-based or usage-based royalties relates has been satisfied (or partially satisfied). That is, an entity recognises the royalties as revenue for such arrangements when (or as) the customer's subsequent sales or usage occurs, unless that pattern of recognition accelerates revenue recognition ahead of the entity's satisfaction of the performance obligation to which the royalty solely or partially relates, based on an appropriate measure of progress (see 7.2 above). *[IFRS 15.BC421I]*.

Consider the following example, which was provided by the FASB, that illustrates when revenue recognition may be inappropriately accelerated ahead of an entity's performance, if revenue was recognised under paragraph B63(a) of IFRS 15 for a right-to-access licence.

Example 30.64: Licensing contract with a declining royalty rate[102]

A contract provides a customer with the right to access an entity's intellectual property and the entity receives royalties of 8% on total sales up to CU1 million, 4% on the next CU3 million in sales and 2% on all sales above CU4 million. The declining royalty rate does not reflect changing value to the customer.

In this example, the FASB noted that recognising royalties as they are due (i.e. according to the contractual formula) would not be aligned with the principle of recognising revenue only when (or as) an entity satisfies a performance obligation because the right to access the intellectual property is provided evenly over the licence term while the declining royalty rate does not reflect the value to the customer. However, the FASB stated that the existence of a declining royalty rate in a contract does not always mean that recognising revenue for sales-based or usage-based royalties as the customer's underlying sales or usage occur is inappropriate. In fact, it would be appropriate if the declining royalty rate reflects the changing value to the customer.

The above example notwithstanding, for many contracts with licences that provide a right to access an entity's intellectual property, applying the royalty exception will result in an entity recognising revenue from sales-based or usage-based royalties when (or as) the customer's underlying sales or usage occurs in accordance with paragraph B63(a) of IFRS 15. An output-based measure of progress that is the same as, or similar to, the application of the practical expedient in paragraph B16 of IFRS 15 (i.e. when the right to consideration corresponds directly with the value to the customer of the entity's performance to date) may be appropriate because the entity's right to consideration (i.e. the sales-based or usage-based royalties earned) will often correspond directly with the value to the customer of the entity's performance completed to date. The practical expedient in paragraph B16 of IFRS 15 is discussed further at 7.2.1.A above.

In addition, an output-based measure could also be appropriate for a licence that provides a right to access intellectual property in which the consideration is in the form of a fixed fee and royalties. The following example from the standard illustrates this. *[IFRS 15.IE309-IE313]*.

Example 30.65: Access to intellectual property

An entity, a well-known sports team, licenses the use of its name and logo to a customer. The customer, an apparel designer, has the right to use the sports team's name and logo on items including t-shirts, caps, mugs and towels for one year. In exchange for providing the licence, the entity will receive fixed consideration of CU2 million and a royalty of five per cent of the sales price of any items using the team name or logo. The customer expects that the entity will continue to play games and provide a competitive team.

The entity assesses the goods and services promised to the customer to determine which goods and services are distinct in accordance with paragraph 27 of IFRS 15. The entity concludes that its only performance obligation is to transfer the licence. The additional activities associated with the licence (i.e. continuing to play games and provide a competitive team) do not directly transfer a good or service to the customer because they are part of the entity's promise to grant the licence.

The entity assesses the nature of the entity's promise to transfer the licence in accordance with paragraph B58 of IFRS 15. In assessing the criteria the entity considers the following:

(a) the entity concludes that the customer would reasonably expect that the entity will undertake activities that will significantly affect the intellectual property (i.e. the team name and logo) to which the customer has rights. This is on the basis of the entity's customary business practice to undertake activities that support and maintain the value of the name and logo such as continuing to play and providing a competitive team. The entity determines that the ability of the customer to obtain benefit from the name and logo is substantially derived from, or dependent upon, the expected activities of the entity. In addition, the entity observes that because some of its consideration is dependent on the success of the customer (through the sales-based royalty), the entity has a shared economic interest with the customer, which indicates that the customer will expect the entity to undertake those activities to maximise earnings.

(b) the entity observes that the rights granted by the licence (i.e. the use of the team's name and logo) directly expose the customer to any positive or negative effects of the entity's activities.

(c) the entity also observes that even though the customer may benefit from the activities through the rights granted by the licence, they do not transfer a good or service to the customer as those activities occur.

The entity concludes that the criteria in paragraph B58 of IFRS 15 are met and the nature of the entity's promise to grant the licence is to provide the customer with access to the entity's intellectual property as it exists throughout the licence period. Consequently, the entity accounts for the promised licence as a performance obligation satisfied over time (i.e. the criterion in paragraph 35(a) of IFRS 15 is met).

The entity then applies paragraphs 39–45 of IFRS 15 to determine a measure of progress that will depict the entity's performance. For the consideration that is in the form of a sales-based royalty, paragraph B63 of IFRS 15 applies because the sales-based royalty relates solely to the licence, which is the only performance obligation in the contract. The entity concludes that recognition of the CU2 million fixed consideration as revenue rateably over time plus recognition of the royalty as revenue as and when the customer's sales of items using the team name or logo occur reasonably depicts the entity's progress towards complete satisfaction of the licence performance obligation.

In Example 30.65 above, the fixed consideration of CU2 million is an explicit term in the contract with the customer. In some contracts, fixed consideration may be implied, such as when a guaranteed minimum amount of royalties is part of the transaction price.

In addition, as discussed in 8.3.1 above, many licences that provide a right to access intellectual property may constitute a series of distinct goods or services that are substantially the same and have the same pattern of transfer to the customer (e.g. a series of distinct periods of access to intellectual property, such as monthly access or quarterly access). In cases where the criteria for a performance obligation to be accounted for as a series of distinct goods or services have been met, an entity will need to consider whether any variable consideration in the contract (e.g. sales-based or usage-based royalties) should be allocated directly to the distinct periods of access, if the criteria for certain allocation exceptions are met. The allocation of sales-based or usage-based royalties in this manner will generally result in the recognition of royalties as revenue when (or as) the customer's underlying sales or usage occurs.

An entity may need to apply significant judgement to determine the appropriate pattern of revenue recognition for royalties received on a licence that provides a right to access intellectual property.

8.5.2 Implementation questions on the sales-based or usage-based royalty exception

8.5.2.A *Can the recognition constraint for sales-based or usage-based royalties be applied to royalties that are paid in consideration for sales of intellectual property (rather than just licences of intellectual property)?*

As noted in the Basis for Conclusions, the Board discussed but decided not to expand the scope of the royalty exception to include sales of intellectual property. The Board also stated that the royalty exception is intended to apply only to limited circumstances (i.e. those circumstances involving licences of intellectual property) and, therefore, entities cannot apply it by analogy to other types of transactions. *[IFRS 15.BC421, BC421F]*.

8.5.2.B *If a contract for a licence of intellectual property includes payments with fixed amounts (e.g. milestone payments) that are determined by reference to sales-based or usage-based thresholds, would the royalty exception need to be applied?*

We generally believe the royalty exception would apply to fixed amounts of variable consideration (i.e. fixed amounts of consideration that are contingent on the occurrence of a future event), such as milestone payments, provided the amounts are determined by reference to sales-based or usage-based thresholds. This is the case even if those payments are not referred to as 'royalties' under the terms of the contract. However, entities will need to apply judgement and carefully evaluate the facts and circumstances of their contracts for licences of intellectual property to determine whether these types of payments should be accounted for using the royalty exception. Consider the following example.

Example 30.66: Application of the royalty exception to a milestone payment

A vendor enters into a contract to grant a customer a right to use the vendor's licence. The contract contains payment terms that include a CU10 million milestone payment that is payable to the vendor once the customer has achieved sales of CU100 million.

The vendor determines that the milestone payment is based on the customer's subsequent sales and represents variable consideration because it is contingent on the customer's sales reaching CU100 million. The vendor accounts for the CU10 million milestone payment in accordance with the royalty recognition constraint and only recognises revenue for the milestone payment once the customer's sales reach CU100 million.

8.5.2.C Can an entity recognise revenue for sales-based or usage-based royalties for licences of intellectual property on a lag if actual sales or usage data is not available at the end of a reporting period?

The standard requires that sales-based or usage-based royalties promised in exchange for licences of intellectual property be recognised as revenue at the later of when: (1) the subsequent sales or usage occurs and (2) the performance obligation to which the sales-based or usage-based royalties relates has been satisfied (or partially satisfied). Therefore, after the conditions in the royalty exception application guidance have been met (i.e. the underlying sales or usage has occurred and the performance obligation to which the royalties relate has been satisfied, or partially satisfied), we believe that licensors without actual sales or usage data from the licensee will need to make an estimate of royalties earned in the current reporting period in accordance with the general model in Step 3. This would include consideration of the general constraint on variable consideration. This may result in a change in practice for entities that have previously recognised revenue from royalties on a lag (i.e. in a reporting period subsequent to when the underlying sales or usage occurs).

9 OTHER MEASUREMENT AND RECOGNITION TOPICS

9.1 Warranties

Warranties are commonly included in arrangements to sell goods or services. They can be explicitly stated in the contract, required by law or implied based on the entity's customary business practices.. *[IFRS 15.B28]*

The price of a warranty may be included in the overall purchase price or listed separately as an optional product. While the standard notes that the nature of a warranty can vary significantly across industries and contracts, it identifies two types of warranties: *[IFRS 15.B28]*

- warranties that promise the customer that the delivered product is as specified in the contract (called 'assurance-type warranties'); and
- warranties that provide a service to the customer in addition to assurance that the delivered product is as specified in the contract (called 'service-type warranties').

9.1.1 Determining whether a warranty is an assurance-type or service-type warranty

If the customer has the option to purchase the warranty separately or if the warranty provides a service to the customer, beyond fixing defects that existed at the time of sale paragraph B29 of IFRS 15 states that the entity is providing a service-type warranty. *[IFRS 15.B29]*. Otherwise, it is an assurance-type warranty, which provides the customer with assurance that the product complies with agreed-upon specifications. *[IFRS 15.B30]*. In some cases, it may be difficult to determine whether a warranty provides a customer with a service in addition to the assurance that the delivered product is as specified in the contract. In assessing whether a warranty provides a customer with a service (in addition to the assurance that the product complies with agreed-upon specifications), an entity is required to consider factors such as: *[IFRS 15.B31]*

- whether the warranty is required by law – if the entity is required by law to provide a warranty, the existence of that law indicates that the promised warranty is not a performance obligation because such requirements typically exist to protect customers from the risk of purchasing defective products;
- the length of the warranty coverage period – the longer the coverage period, the more likely it is that the promised warranty is a performance obligation because it is more likely to provide a service in addition to the assurance that the product complies with agreed-upon specifications; and
- the nature of the tasks that the entity promises to perform – if it is necessary for an entity to perform specified tasks to provide the assurance that a product complies with agreed-upon specifications (e.g. a return shipping service for a defective product), then those tasks likely do not give rise to a performance obligation.

The standard specifies that the following do not give rise to performance obligations:

- 'a law that requires an entity to pay compensation if its products cause harm or damage' – the standard gives the example of a manufacturer that sells products in a jurisdiction that, by law, holds the manufacturer liable for any damages arising if a consumer has used a product for its intended purpose; and
- 'an entity's promise to indemnify a customer for liabilities and damages arising from claims of patent, copyright, trademark or other infringement by the entity's products'. *[IFRS 15.B33]*.

Entities may need to exercise significant judgement when determining whether a warranty is an assurance-type or service-type warranty. An entity's evaluation may be affected by several factors including common warranty practices within its industry and the entity's business practices related to warranties. For example, consider an automotive manufacturer that provides a five-year warranty on a luxury vehicle and a three-year warranty on a standard vehicle. The manufacturer may conclude that the longer warranty period is not an additional service because it believes the materials used to construct the luxury vehicle are of a higher quality and that latent defects would take longer to appear. In contrast, the manufacturer may also consider the length of the warranty period and the nature of the services provided under the warranty and conclude that the five-year warranty period, or some portion of it, is an additional service that needs to be accounted for as a service-type warranty. The standard excludes assurance-type warranties, which are accounted for in accordance with IAS 37. *[IFRS 15.B33]*.

See 5.2.1.B above for a discussion on whether liquidated damages, penalties or compensation from other similar clauses should be accounted for as variable consideration or warranty provisions under the standard.

9.1.1.A *Evaluating whether a product warranty is a service-type warranty (i.e. a performance obligation) when it is not separately priced*

At the March 2015 TRG meeting, the TRG members generally agreed that the evaluation of whether a warranty provides a service (in addition to the assurance that the product complies with agreed specifications) will require judgement and depend on the facts and circumstances. There is no bright line in the standard on what constitutes a service-type warranty, beyond it being separately priced.

However, the standard includes three factors that would need to be considered in each evaluation: whether the warranty is required by law; the length of the warranty coverage; and the nature of the tasks that the entity promises to perform, as stated in paragraph B31 of IFRS 15.

Consider the following example from the TRG agenda paper: A luggage company provides a life-time warranty to repair broken or damaged baggage free of charge. The luggage company evaluates the three factors and determines that they indicate the warranty is a performance obligation (in addition to the assurance that the product complies with agreed-upon specifications) because: (1) there is no law that requires the luggage company to make a promise for the lifetime of the product; (2) the length of the warranty is for the life of the baggage; and (3) the tasks include both repairs to baggage that does not meet the promised specifications and repairs for broken or damaged baggage.

Furthermore, the TRG agenda paper emphasised that entities cannot assume that their current accounting will remain unchanged under IFRS 15. Entities will need to evaluate each type of warranty offered to determine the appropriate accounting treatment.[103]

9.1.1.B *Should repairs provided outside the warranty period be accounted for as a service-type warranty?*

We believe entities will need to carefully consider the factors in paragraph B31 of IFRS 15 (e.g. the nature of the services provided, the length of the implied warranty period) to determine whether services provided outside the warranty period represent a service-type warranty. Sometimes, entities provide these services as part of their customary business practices, in addition to providing assurance-type warranties for specified periods of time. For example, an equipment manufacturer may give its customers a standard product warranty that provides assurance that the product complies with agreed-upon specifications for one year from the date of purchase. However, the entity may also provide an implied warranty by frequently repairing products for free after the one-year standard warranty period has ended. See 4.1 above for a discussion of implied performance obligations.

If the entity determines that the repairs made during the implied warranty period generally involve defects that existed when the product was sold and the repairs occur shortly after the assurance warranty period, the entity may conclude that the repairs are covered by an assurance-type warranty. That is, the term of the assurance-type warranty may be longer than that stated in the contract. However, all facts need to be considered to reach a conclusion.

9.1.1.C Customer's return of a defective item in exchange for compensation: right of return versus assurance-type warranty

Should an entity account for a customer's return of a defective item in exchange for compensation (i.e. not for a replacement item) as a right of return or an assurance-type warranty? We believe that an entity should account for the right to return a defective item in return for cash (instead of a replacement item) under the right of return application guidance in paragraphs B20-B27 of IFRS 15, rather than as an assurance-type warranty. The Basis for Conclusions states that '... the boards decided that an entity should recognise an assurance-type warranty as a separate liability to replace or repair a defective product'. *[IFRS 15.BC376]*. This description of an assurance-type warranty does not include defective products that are returned for a refund. It only contemplates defective products that are replaced or repaired. See 5.4.1 above for a discussion of rights of return.

However, there may be limited circumstances in which the cash paid to a customer for a defective item would need to be accounted for in accordance with the warranty application guidance, instead of as a right of return. For example, an entity may pay cash to a customer as reimbursement for third-party costs incurred to repair a defective item. In this case, the cash payment to the customer was incurred to fulfil the entity's warranty obligation. This assessment will require judgement and depend on the facts and circumstances.

9.1.2 Service-type warranties

The Board determined that a service-type warranty represents a distinct service and is a separate performance obligation. *[IFRS 15.BC371]*. Therefore, using the estimated stand-alone selling price of the warranty, an entity allocates a portion of the transaction price to the service-type warranty (see 6 above). The entity then recognises the allocated revenue over the period in which the service-type warranty service is provided. *[IFRS 15.B29, B32]*. This is because the customer will likely receive and consume the benefits of the warranty as the entity performs (i.e. the warranty performance obligation is likely satisfied over time in accordance with paragraph 35(a) of IFRS 15, see 7.1.1 above).

Judgement may be required to determine the appropriate pattern of revenue recognition associated with service-type warranties. For example, an entity may determine that it provides the warranty service continuously over the warranty period (i.e. the performance obligation is an obligation to 'stand ready to perform' during the stated warranty period). An entity that makes this determination will likely recognise revenue rateably over the warranty period. An entity may also conclude that a different pattern of recognition is appropriate based on data it has collected about when it provides such services. For example, an entity may recognise little or no revenue in the first year of a three-year service-type warranty if its historical data indicates that it only provides warranty services in the second and third years of the warranty period.

Considerations for determining the appropriate pattern of revenue recognition are described at 7.2 above, including those for stand-ready obligations. If payment for the service-type warranty is received upfront, an entity should also evaluate whether a significant financing component exists (see 5.5 above).

Changes in the estimate of the costs to satisfy service-type warranty performance obligations do not result in a revision to the original relative stand-alone selling price allocation (or the resulting allocated amount of the transaction price that will be recognised as revenue for the service-type warranty performance obligation). For example, an entity may discover two months after a product is shipped that the cost of a part acquired from a third-party manufacturer has tripled and that, as a result, it will cost the entity significantly more to replace that part if a warranty claim is made. This change will not affect the amount of transaction price that the entity allocates to the service-type warranty. This is because the estimate of stand-alone selling prices is performed at contract inception and is not updated to reflect changes between contract inception and when performance is complete. Therefore, the cost an entity will incur to satisfy the entity's obligation under a service-type warranty does not affect the revenue recognition. However, for future contracts involving the same warranty, the entity would need to determine whether to revise the stand-alone selling price because of the increase in the costs to satisfy the warranty and, if so, use that revised price for future allocations (see 6.1.3 above).

9.1.3 Assurance-type warranties

The Board concluded that assurance-type warranties do not provide an additional good or service to the customer (i.e. they are not separate performance obligations). By providing this type of warranty, the selling entity has effectively provided a guarantee of quality. In accordance with paragraph B30 of IFRS 15, these types of warranties are accounted for as warranty obligations and the estimated cost of satisfying them is accrued in accordance with the requirements in IAS 37. *[IFRS 15.B30, BC376]*. Once recorded, the warranty liability is assessed on an ongoing basis in accordance with IAS 37.

9.1.4 Contracts that contain both assurance and service-type warranties

Some contracts may include both an assurance-type warranty and a service-type warranty, as illustrated below. However, if an entity provides both an assurance-type and service-type warranty within a contract and the entity cannot reasonably account for them separately, the warranties are accounted for as a single performance obligation (i.e. revenue would be allocated to the combined warranty and recognised over the period the warranty services are provided). *[IFRS 15.B32]*.

When an assurance-type warranty and a service-type warranty can be accounted for separately, an entity is required to accrue for the expected costs associated with the assurance-type warranty and defer the revenue for the service-type warranty, as illustrated in Example 30.67.

Example 30.67: Service-type and assurance-type warranties

An entity manufactures and sells computers that include an assurance-type warranty for the first 90 days. The entity offers an optional 'extended coverage' plan under which it will repair or replace any defective part for three years from the expiration of the assurance-type warranty. Since the optional 'extended coverage' plan is sold separately, the entity determines that the three years of extended coverage represent a separate performance obligation (i.e. a service-type warranty).

The total transaction price for the sale of a computer and the extended warranty is CU3,600. The entity determines that the stand-alone selling prices of the computer and the extended warranty are CU3,200 and CU400, respectively. The inventory value of the computer is CU1,440. Furthermore, the entity estimates that, based on its experience, it will incur CU200 in costs to repair defects that arise within the 90-day coverage period for the assurance-type warranty. As a result, the entity will record the following entries:

Dr. Cash/Trade receivables	CU3,600	
Dr. Warranty expense	CU200	
Cr. Accrued warranty costs (assurance-type warranty)		CU200
Cr. Contract liability (service-type warranty)		CU400
Cr. Revenue		CU3,200
To record revenue and contract liabilities related to warranties.		
Dr. Cost of goods sold	CU1,440	
Cr. Inventory		CU1,440
To derecognise inventory and recognise cost of goods sold.		

The entity derecognises the accrued warranty liability associated with the assurance-type warranty as actual warranty costs are incurred during the first 90 days after the customer receives the computer. The entity recognises the contract liability associated with the service-type warranty as revenue during the contract warranty period and recognises the costs associated with providing the service-type warranty as they are incurred. The entity would need to be able to determine whether the repair costs incurred are applied against the warranty reserve already established for claims that occur during the first 90 days or recognised as an expense as incurred.

Accounting for both assurance-type warranties and service-type warranties in the same transaction may be complex. Entities may need to develop processes to match individual warranty claims with the specific warranty plans so that claims can be analysed for the appropriate accounting treatment. This individual assessment of warranty claims is necessary because the assurance-type warranty costs will have been accrued previously, while the service-type warranty costs are expenses that need to be recognised in the period in which they are incurred, as illustrated in Example 30.68.

Example 30.68: Service-type and assurance-type warranty costs

Assume the same facts as in Example 30.67, but assume the entity has sold 500 computers during the year. In January of the following year, CU10,000 of warranty claims are submitted by customers. The entity analyses each claim and identifies the specific computer sale to which the claims relate. The entity needs to do this in order to determine eligibility under the warranty plans and the appropriate accounting treatment under the warranty plans.

The entity determines that a portion of the claims, costing CU2,500 for repair and replacement parts, are covered by the assurance-type warranty plan. As shown above in Example 30.67, the expected cost of each assurance-type warranty was accrued at the time of the sale. The entity records the following entry to derecognise a portion of the warranty liability:

Dr. Accrued warranty costs (assurance-type warranty)	CU2,500	
Cr. Cash		CU2,500
To derecognise the assurance-type warranty liability as the costs are incurred.		

The entity also determines that a portion of the claims, costing CU7,000 for repair and replacement parts, are eligible under the 'extended coverage' plan (i.e. the service-type warranty). The entity records the following entry to recognise the costs associated with the service-type warranty:

Dr. Warranty expense	CU7,000	
Cr. Cash		CU7,000

To record the costs of the service-type warranty as the costs are incurred.

The entity also determines that CU500 of the claims are not eligible under either warranty plan. This is because the claims relate to incidents that occurred after the 90-day coverage period for the assurance-type warranty and the customers in those transactions did not purchase the extended warranty coverage. The entity rejects these customer claims.

The requirements for assurance-type warranties, as discussed at 9.1.3 above, are essentially the same as current practice under IFRS. The requirements for service-type warranties may differ from current practice, particularly in relation to the amount of transaction price that is allocated to the warranty performance obligation, as is discussed at 9.1.2 above. Currently, entities that provide separate extended warranties often defer an amount equal to the stated price of the warranty and record that amount as revenue evenly over the warranty period. IFRS 15 requires an entity to defer an allocated amount, based on a relative stand-alone selling price allocation, which, in most cases, will increase judgement and complexity.

9.2 Onerous contracts

The Board decided to retain existing requirements for onerous contracts. Under IFRS, the requirements in IAS 37 for onerous contracts apply to all contracts in the scope of IFRS 15. The new standard states that entities that are required to recognise a liability for expected losses on contracts under IAS 37 will continue to be required to do so. IAS 37 requires that, if an entity has a contract that is onerous, the present obligation under the contract must be recognised and measured as a provision. However, before a separate provision for an onerous contract is established, an entity recognises any impairment loss that has occurred on assets dedicated to that contract in accordance with IAS 36 – *Impairment of Assets*. *[IAS 37.66, 69]*.

IAS 37 clarifies that many contracts (e.g. some routine purchase orders) can be cancelled without paying compensation to the other party, and therefore there is no obligation. Other contracts establish both rights and obligations for each of the contracting parties. Where events make such a contract onerous, the contract falls within the scope of IAS 37 and a liability exists which is recognised. In addition, executory contracts that are not onerous fall outside its scope. IAS 37 goes on to define an onerous contract as 'a contract in which the unavoidable costs of meeting the obligations under the contract exceed the economic benefits expected to be received under it. The unavoidable costs under a contract reflect the least net cost of exiting from the contract, which is the lower of the cost of fulfilling it and any compensation or penalties arising from failure to fulfil it'. *[IAS 37.67-68]*. See Chapter 28 for further discussion.

Under current US GAAP, while requirements exist for some industries or for certain types of transactions, there is no general authoritative standard for when to recognise losses on onerous contracts and, if a loss is to be recognised, how to measure the loss. Accordingly, there is diversity in practice when such contracts are not within the scope of specific authoritative literature. The FASB retained existing requirements for situations in which an entity is expected to incur a loss on a contract (with certain consequential amendments to reflect the terminology of, and cross-references to, ASC 606, where appropriate). As the FASB's requirements on onerous contracts are not the same as IAS 37, the accounting treatment in this area is not converged.

In May 2016, the FASB proposed clarifying that the provision for losses under ASC 605-35, *Revenue Recognition – Construction-Type and Production-Type Contracts*, be determined at least at the contract level. However, the proposed amendments would allow an entity to determine the provision for losses at the performance obligation level as an accounting policy election. Comments were due by 2 July 2016. To finalise this change, the FASB will need to issue a final amendment. The IASB is not expected to propose a similar amendment to IFRS 15.

9.3 Contract costs

IFRS 15 specifies the accounting treatment for costs an entity incurs to obtain and fulfil a contract to provide goods and services to customers. An entity only applies those requirements costs incurred that relate to a contract with a customer that is within the scope of IFRS 15 (see 2 above). *[IFRS 15.8]*.

9.3.1 Costs to obtain a contract

Under IFRS 15, the incremental costs of obtaining a contract are recognised as an asset if the entity expects to recover them. *[IFRS 15.91-93]*.

To qualify for capitalisation, contract acquisition costs must be incremental and the entity must expect to recover them. Incremental costs are those that an entity would not have incurred if the contract had not been obtained. *[IFRS 15.92]*. For example, salaries and benefits of sales employees that are incurred (i.e. paid to the employee) regardless of whether a contract was obtained are not incremental costs. An entity can expect to recover contract acquisition costs through direct recovery (i.e. reimbursement under the contract) or indirect recovery (i.e. through the margin inherent in the contract).

However before applying the cost requirements, entities will need to consider the scoping provisions of the requirements. Specifically, an entity will need to first consider whether the requirements on consideration payable to a customer under IFRS 15 (see 5.7 above for a discussion on accounting for consideration paid or payable to a customer) apply to the costs.

The standard cites sales commissions as a type of an incremental cost that may require capitalisation under the standard. For example, commissions that are related to sales from contracts signed during the period may represent incremental costs that would require capitalisation. The standard does not explicitly address considerations for different types of commission programmes. Therefore, entities will have to exercise judgement to determine whether sales commissions are incremental costs and, if so, the point in time when the costs would be capitalised. For example, variable commissions, commissions paid for contract renewals or modifications, commissions paid to supervisors and commissions not directly linked to any single contract (e.g. commissions based on reaching a specified level of sales overall) may require additional analysis.

The TRG members discussed the underlying principle for capitalising costs under the standard and generally agreed that IFRS 15 did not amend the current requirements for liabilities (e.g. IAS 37). Therefore, entities would first refer to the applicable liability standards to determine when they are required to accrue for certain costs. Entities would then use the requirements in IFRS 15 to determine whether the related costs need to be capitalised. The TRG members acknowledged that certain aspects of the cost requirements will require entities to apply significant judgement in analysing the facts and circumstances and determining the appropriate accounting treatment.[104]

In addition, the TRG agenda paper observed that incremental costs of obtaining a contract are not limited to initial incremental costs. Commissions recognised subsequent to contract inception (e.g. commissions paid on modifications, commissions subject to contingent events or clawback) because they did not meet the recognition criteria for liabilities at contract inception would still be considered for capitalisation as costs to obtain the contract when the liability is recognised. This would include contract renewals because, as the TRG agenda paper noted, a renewal is a contract and there is nothing in the requirements for costs to obtain a contract that suggests a different treatment for contracts that are renewals of existing contracts. That is, the only difference between the two costs would be the timing of recognition based on when a liability has been incurred.[105]

The following example illustrates how these principles may be applied to a fact pattern with sales commissions paid to a supervisor and sales commissions paid for renewals:

Example 30.69: Sales commissions

Entity X has a commission plan whereby each salesperson is paid CU1,000 for each new contract entered into with a customer as a result of the salesperson's efforts. In addition, the salesperson is paid CU200 every time that customer renews its contract with the company. The Vice President (VP) of sales also receives a CU50 commission every time an initial contract or renewal is signed, which is not contingent on other performance metrics. The margin inherent in each new contract is sufficient to recover the commissions for each new contract and renewal.

Entity X would record a liability of CU1,050 (the commission for the salesperson and the VP of sales) at contract inception, since at this point in time it is probable that an outflow of resources embodying economic benefits will be required to settle the obligation and a reliable estimate of the amount can be made. *[IAS 37.14]*. The entity would separately evaluate the commissions paid to the salesperson and to the VP of sales to determine whether it would have incurred those commissions if it had not obtained the contract and whether it will recover them. If Entity X determines these criteria are met for both commissions, it would capitalise CU1,050 when the liability is recognised.

Entity X would, likewise, record a liability of CU250 when each renewal is signed because that is the point in time when the renewal commissions would meet the recognition criteria in IAS 37. The entity would evaluate whether the commissions are incremental (i.e. they would not have been incurred if the renewal contract had not been obtained) and are recoverable. Even if the renewal was anticipated at contract inception, the estimated commission would not be accrued or capitalised at that time because a liability would not have been incurred for the renewal at contract inception.

Unlike many commissions, some incentive payments, such as bonuses and other compensation that are based on other quantitative or qualitative metrics that are not related to contracts obtained (e.g. profitability, earnings per share (EPS), performance evaluations) will be unlikely to meet the criteria for capitalisation because they are not incremental costs of obtaining a contract. However, a legal contingency cost may be an incremental cost of obtaining a contract when a lawyer agrees to receive payment only upon the successful completion of a negotiation. Determining which costs must be capitalised under the standard may require judgement.

The standard provides the following example regarding incremental costs of obtaining a contract. *[IFRS 15.IE189-IE191]*.

Example 30.70: Incremental costs of obtaining a contract

An entity, a provider of consulting services, wins a competitive bid to provide consulting services to a new customer. The entity incurred the following costs to obtain the contract:

	CU
External legal fees for due diligence	15,000
Travel costs to deliver proposal	25,000
Commissions to sales employees	10,000
Total costs incurred	50,000

In accordance with paragraph 91 of IFRS 15, the entity recognises an asset for the CU10,000 incremental costs of obtaining the contract arising from the commissions to sales employees because the entity expects to recover those costs through future fees for the consulting services. The entity also pays discretionary annual bonuses to sales supervisors based on annual sales targets, overall profitability of the entity and individual performance evaluations. In accordance with paragraph 91 of IFRS 15, the entity does not recognise an asset for the bonuses paid to sales supervisors because the bonuses are not incremental to obtaining a contract. The amounts are discretionary and are based on other factors, including the profitability of the entity and the individuals' performance. The bonuses are not directly attributable to identifiable contracts.

The entity observes that the external legal fees and travel costs would have been incurred regardless of whether the contract was obtained. Therefore, in accordance with paragraph 93 of IFRS 15, those costs are recognised as expenses when incurred, unless they are within the scope of another Standard, in which case, the relevant provisions of that Standard apply.

As a practical expedient, the standard permits an entity to immediately expense contract acquisition costs when the asset that would have resulted from capitalising such costs would have been amortised within one year or less. *[IFRS 15.94]*. While this is not explicitly stated, we believe entities would need to apply this approach consistently to all short-term contract acquisition costs.

IFRS 15 represents a significant change in practice for entities that currently expense the costs of obtaining a contract and will be required to capitalise them under the new standard. In addition, this may be a change for entities that currently capitalise costs to obtain a contract, particularly if the amounts currently capitalised are not incremental and, therefore, would not be eligible for capitalisation under IFRS 15, unless they are explicitly chargeable to the customer regardless of whether the contract is obtained.

9.3.1.A *Would an entity capitalise commissions paid on contract modifications?*

An entity would capitalise commissions paid on contract modifications if they are incremental (i.e. they would not have been incurred if there had not been a modification) and recoverable. Contract modifications are accounted for in one of three ways: (1) as a separate contract; (2) as a termination of the existing contract and the creation of a new contract; or (3) as part of the existing contract (see 3.4 above for further requirements on contract modifications). In all three cases, commissions paid on contract modifications are incremental costs of obtaining a contract and should be capitalised if they are recoverable. In the first two cases, a new contract is created, so the costs of obtaining that contract would be incremental. The TRG agenda paper 23 noted that commissions paid on the modification of a contract that is accounted for as part of the existing contract are incremental costs even though they are not initial incremental costs.[106]

9.3.1.B Would fringe benefits on commission payments be included in the capitalised amounts?

Fringe benefits should be capitalised as part of the incremental cost of obtaining a contract if the additional costs are based on the amount of commissions paid and the commissions qualify as costs to obtain a contract. However, if the costs of fringe benefits would have been incurred regardless of whether the contract had been obtained (e.g. health insurance premiums), the fringe benefits should not be capitalised. That is, an entity cannot allocate to the commission (and, therefore, capitalise a portion of the costs of benefits) it would provide regardless of whether the commission was paid.[107]

9.3.1.C Must an entity apply the practical expedient to expense contract acquisition costs to all of its qualifying contracts across the entity or can it apply the practical expedient to individual contracts?

We believe the practical expedient to expense contract acquisition costs (that would, otherwise, be amortised over a period of one year or less) must be applied consistently to contracts with similar characteristics and in similar circumstances.

9.3.1.D How would an entity account for capitalised commissions upon a modification of the contract that is treated as the termination of an existing contract and the creation of a new contract?

We believe an asset recognised for incremental costs to obtain a contract that exists when the related contract is modified should be carried forward into the new contract, if the modification is treated as the termination of an existing contract and the creation of a new contract and the goods and services to which the original contract cost asset relates are part of the new contract. This is because the contract cost asset relates to goods and services that have not yet been transferred and the accounting for the modification is prospective. This conclusion is similar to the one reached by the FASB TRG members in relation to the accounting for contract assets upon a contract modification, as discussed at 10.1.1.E below.

The contract cost asset that remains on the entity's statement of financial position at the date of modification would continue to be evaluated for impairment in accordance with IFRS 15 (see 9.3.4 below). In addition, an entity should determine an appropriate amortisation period for the contract cost asset (see 9.3.3 below).

9.3.2 *Costs to fulfil a contract*

The standard divides contract fulfilment costs into two categories: (1) costs that give rise to an asset; and (2) costs that are expensed as incurred. When determining the appropriate accounting treatment for such costs, IFRS 15 makes it clear that any other applicable standards (e.g. IAS 2 – *Inventories*, IAS 16 or IAS 38) are considered first.

That is, if costs incurred in fulfilling a contract are within the scope of another standard, an entity accounts for those costs in accordance with those other standards. *[IFRS 15.95-96]*. If those other standards preclude capitalisation of a particular cost, then an asset cannot be recognised under IFRS 15.

If the costs incurred to fulfil a contract are not within the scope of another standard, an entity capitalises such costs only if they meet all of the following criteria: *[IFRS 15.95]*

(a) the costs relate directly to a contract or to an anticipated contract that the entity can specifically identify (e.g. costs relating to services to be provided under renewal of an existing contract or costs of designing an asset to be transferred under a specific contract that has not yet been approved);

(b) the costs generate or enhance resources of the entity that will be used in satisfying (or in continuing to satisfy) performance obligations in the future; and

(c) the costs are expected to be recovered.

Note that, when effective, IFRS 16 will consequentially amend paragraph 97(c) of IFRS 15 to include, as an additional example, 'right-of-use assets'.

When determining whether costs meet the criteria for capitalisation, an entity must consider its specific facts and circumstances. IFRS 15 states that costs can be capitalised even if the revenue contract with the customer is not finalised. However, rather than allowing costs to be related to any potential future contract, the standard requires that the costs be associated with a specifically anticipated contract.

The standard discusses and provides examples of costs that may meet the first criterion for capitalisation (i.e. costs that relate directly to the contract or a specifically anticipated contract) as follows: *[IFRS 15.97]*

(a) direct labour (e.g. salaries and wages of employees who provide the promised services directly to the customer);

(b) direct materials (e.g. supplies used in providing the promised services to a customer);

(c) allocations of costs that relate directly to the contract or to contract activities (e.g. costs of contract management and supervision, insurance and depreciation of tools and equipment used in fulfilling the contract);

(d) costs that are explicitly chargeable to the customer under the contract; and

(e) other costs that are incurred only because an entity entered into the contract (e.g. payments to subcontractors).

Significant judgement may be required to determine whether costs generate or enhance resources of the entity that will be used in satisfying performance obligations in the future. In the Basis for Conclusions, the IASB explained that the standard only results in the capitalisation of costs that meet the definition of an asset and precludes an entity from deferring costs merely to normalise profit margins throughout a contract (by allocating revenue and costs evenly over the contract term). *[IFRS 15.BC308]*.

For costs to meet the 'expected to be recovered' criterion, they need to be either explicitly reimbursable under the contract, or reflected through the pricing on the contract and recoverable through margin. If the costs incurred in fulfilling a contract do not give rise to an asset, based on the criteria above, they must be expensed as incurred. The standard provides some common examples of costs that must be expensed as incurred, as follows: *[IFRS 15.98]*

(a) general and administrative costs (unless those costs are explicitly chargeable to the customer under the contract, in which case an entity shall evaluate those costs in accordance with the above criteria for capitalising costs to fulfil a contract);

(b) costs of wasted materials, labour or other resources to fulfil the contract that were not reflected in the price of the contract;

(c) costs that relate to satisfied (or partially satisfied) performance obligations (i.e. costs that relate to past performance); and

(d) costs for which an entity cannot distinguish whether the costs relate to unsatisfied performance obligations or to satisfied (or partially satisfied) performance obligations.

If a performance obligation (or a portion of a performance obligation that is satisfied over time) has been satisfied, fulfilment costs related to that performance obligation (or portion thereof) can no longer be capitalised. Once an entity has begun satisfying a performance obligation that is satisfied over time, it would only capitalise costs that relate to future performance. If an entity is unable to determine whether certain costs relate to past or future performance and the costs are not eligible for capitalisation under other IFRSs, the costs are expensed as incurred.

The standard provides the following example that illustrates costs that are capitalised under other IFRSs, costs that meet the capitalisation criteria and costs that do not. *[IFRS 15.IE192-IE196]*.

Example 30.71: Costs that give rise to an asset

An entity enters into a service contract to manage a customer's information technology data centre for five years. The contract is renewable for subsequent one-year periods. The average customer term is seven years. The entity pays an employee a CU10,000 sales commission upon the customer signing the contract. Before providing the services, the entity designs and builds a technology platform for the entity's internal use that interfaces with the customer's systems. That platform is not transferred to the customer, but will be used to deliver services to the customer.

Incremental costs of obtaining a contract

In accordance with paragraph 91 of IFRS 15, the entity recognises an asset for the CU10,000 incremental costs of obtaining the contract for the sales commission because the entity expects to recover those costs through future fees for the services to be provided. The entity amortises the asset over seven years in accordance with paragraph 99 of IFRS 15, because the asset relates to the services transferred to the customer during the contract term of five years and the entity anticipates that the contract will be renewed for two subsequent one-year periods.

Costs to fulfil a contract

The initial costs incurred to set up the technology platform are as follows:

	CU
Design services	40,000
Hardware	120,000
Software	90,000
Migration and testing of data centre	100,000
Total costs	350,000

The initial setup costs relate primarily to activities to fulfil the contract but do not transfer goods or services to the customer. The entity accounts for the initial setup costs as follows:

(a) hardware costs – accounted for in accordance with IAS 16;

(b) software costs – accounted for in accordance with IAS 38; and

(c) costs of the design, migration and testing of the data centre – assessed in accordance with paragraph 95 of IFRS 15 to determine whether an asset can be recognised for the costs to fulfil the contract. Any resulting asset would be amortised on a systematic basis over the seven-year period (i.e. the five-year contract term and two anticipated one-year renewal periods) that the entity expects to provide services related to the data centre.

In addition to the initial costs to set up the technology platform, the entity also assigns two employees who are primarily responsible for providing the service to the customer. Although the costs for these two employees are incurred as part of providing the service to the customer, the entity concludes that the costs do not generate or enhance resources of the entity (see paragraph 95(b) of IFRS 15). Therefore, the costs do not meet the criteria in paragraph 95 of IFRS 15 and cannot be recognised as an asset using IFRS 15. In accordance with paragraph 98, the entity recognises the payroll expense for these two employees when incurred.

9.3.2.A Can an entity defer costs of a transferred good or service that would otherwise generate an up-front loss because variable consideration is fully or partially constrained?

An entity should not defer the costs of a transferred good or service when the application of the constraint on variable consideration results in an upfront loss, even if the entity ultimately expects to recognise a profit on that good or service, unless other specific requirements allow or require a deferral of those costs. The criteria in IFRS 15 must be met to capitalise costs to fulfil a contract, including the criterion that the costs must generate or enhance resources of the entity that will be used in satisfying performance obligations in the future. An entity recognises such costs when control of a good or service transfers to the customer. As such, the cost of those sales would not generate or enhance resources used to satisfy future performance obligations.

Consider the following example: An entity sells goods with a cost of CU500,000 for consideration of CU600,000. The goods have a high risk of obsolescence, which may require the entity to provide price concessions in the future, resulting in variable consideration (see 5.2.1.A above). The entity constrains the transaction price and concludes that it is highly probable that CU470,000 will not result in a significant revenue reversal, even though the vendor reasonably expects the contract to ultimately be profitable. When control transfers, the entity recognises revenue of CU470,000 and costs of CU500,000. It would not capitalise the loss of CU30,000 because the loss does not generate or enhance resources of the entity that will be used in satisfying performance obligations in the future.

9.3.2.B Accounting for fulfilment costs incurred prior to the contract establishment date that are outside the scope of another standard

How should an entity account for fulfilment costs incurred prior to the contract establishment date that are outside the scope of another standard (e.g. IAS 2)? Entities sometimes will begin activities on a specifically anticipated contract either (e.g. before agreeing to the contract with the customer, before the contract satisfies the criteria to be accounted for under IFRS 15).

At the March 2015 TRG meeting, the TRG members generally agreed that costs in respect of pre-contract establishment date activities that relate to a good or service that will transfer to the customer at or after the contract establishment date may be capitalised as costs to fulfil a specifically anticipated contract. However, the TRG members noted that such costs would still need to meet the other criteria in the standard to be capitalised (e.g. they are expected to be recovered under the anticipated contract).

Subsequent to capitalisation, costs that relate to goods or services that are transferred to the customer at the contract establishment date would be expensed immediately. Any remaining capitalised costs would be amortised over the period that the related goods or services are transferred to the customer.[108]

For requirements on recognising revenue for a performance obligation satisfied over time when activities are completed before the contract establishment date, see 7.2.4.F above.

9.3.3 Amortisation of capitalised costs

Any capitalised contract costs are amortised, with the expense recognised on a systematic basis that is consistent with the entity's transfer of the related goods or services to the customer. *[IFRS 15.99]*.

It is important to note that certain capitalised costs will relate to multiple goods and services (e.g. design costs to manufacture multiple distinct goods when design services are not a separate performance obligation) in a single contract, so the amortisation period could be the entire contract term). The amortisation period could also extend beyond a single contract if the capitalised costs relate to goods or services being transferred under multiple contracts or to a specifically anticipated contract, such as when the customer is expected to renew its current services contract for another term. *[IFRS 15.99]*. In these situations, the capitalised costs would be amortised over the expected period of benefit. The expected period of benefit may be the expected customer relationship period. To determine the appropriate amortisation period, an entity will need to evaluate the type of capitalised costs, what the costs relate to and the specific facts and circumstances of the arrangement. Entities are required to update the amortisation (as a change in accounting estimate in accordance with IAS 8) to reflect a significant change in the expected timing of transfer to the customer of the goods or services to which the asset relates. *[IFRS 15.100]*.

When evaluating whether the amortisation period for a sales commission extends beyond the contract period, an entity would also evaluate whether an additional commission is paid for subsequent renewals. In the Basis for Conclusions, the IASB explained that amortising the asset over a longer period than the initial contract would not be appropriate if an entity pays a commission on a contract renewal that is commensurate with the commission paid on the initial contract. In that case, the costs of obtaining the initial contract do not relate to the subsequent contract. *[IFRS 15.BC309]*. Judgement will be required to determine whether a renewal commission is commensurate with the commission paid on the initial contract.

An entity updates the amortisation period when there is a significant change in the expected timing of transfer to the customer of the goods or services to which the asset relates, as illustrated in the following example.

Example 30.72: Amortisation period

Entity A enters into a three-year contract with a new customer for transaction processing services. To fulfil the contract, Entity A incurred set-up costs of CU60,000, which it capitalised in accordance with paragraphs 95-98 of IFRS 15 and will amortise over the term of the contract.

At the beginning of the third year, the customer renews the contract for an additional two years. Entity A will benefit from the initial set-up costs during the additional two-year period. Therefore, it changes the remaining amortisation period from one year to three years and adjusts the amortisation expense in the period of the change and future periods in accordance with the requirements in IAS 8 for changes in accounting estimates. The disclosure requirements of IAS 8 related to changes in estimates are also applicable.

However, under IFRS 15, if Entity A had been in the position to anticipate the contract renewal at contract inception, Entity A would have amortised the set-up costs over the anticipated term of the contract including the expected renewal (i.e. five years).

9.3.3.A *Can an entity attribute the capitalised contract costs to the individual performance obligations in the contract to determine the appropriate amortisation period?*

We believe an entity can attribute the capitalised contract costs to the individual performance obligations in the contract to determine the appropriate amortisation period, but it is not required to do so. Paragraph 99 of IFRS 15 states that the asset recognised is amortised on a systematic basis 'that is consistent with the transfer to the customer of the goods or services to which the asset relates'. *[IFRS 15.99]*. An entity may meet this objective by allocating the capitalised costs to performance obligations on a relative basis (i.e. in proportion to the transaction price allocated to each performance obligation) to determine the period of amortisation.[109] An entity may also meet the objective by allocating specific capitalised costs to individual performance obligations when the costs relate specifically to certain goods or services. An entity should have objective evidence to support a conclusion that a specified amount of the costs relates to a specific performance obligation.

In addition, as discussed above, an entity that attributes capitalised contract costs to individual performance obligations will need to consider whether the amortisation period for some or all of the performance obligations should extend beyond the original contract (see 9.3.3 above).

9.3.3.B *Over what period should an entity amortise a sales commission (that is only paid once a threshold is met) that is determined to be an incremental cost to obtain a contract?*

The January 2015 TRG agenda paper 23 stated that two of the alternatives discussed would meet the objective of amortising the costs on a systematic basis that is consistent with the transfer to the customer of the goods or services to which the asset relates. However, either alternative should be applied consistently to similar circumstances. In one alternative, an entity allocated the capitalised costs to all of the contracts that cumulatively resulted in the threshold being met and amortised the costs over the expected customer relationship period of each of those contracts. In the other alternative, an entity allocated the capitalised costs to the contract that resulted in the threshold being met and amortised the costs over the expected customer relationship period of that contract. The TRG agenda paper noted that the second alternative may result in a counterintuitive answer if the commission paid upon obtaining the contract that resulted in the threshold being met was large in relation to the transaction price for only that contract. The TRG agenda paper did not contemplate all possible alternatives.[110]

9.3.3.C How should capitalised contract costs and its amortisation be presented in the statement of financial position and statement of profit and loss and other comprehensive income, respectively?

As discussed at 9.3.1 to 9.3.3 above, IFRS 15 requires incremental costs of obtaining a contract and certain costs to fulfil a contract to be recognised as an asset and that asset to be amortised on a systematic basis. Paragraph 128 of IFRS 15 requires separate disclosure of closing balances and the amount of amortisation and impairment losses recognised during the period (see 10.4.3 below). However, the standard is silent on the classification of that asset and the related amortisation.

Under current IFRS, IAS 2 includes the notion of work in progress (or 'inventory') of a service provider. However, this will be consequentially removed from IAS 2 and replaced with the relevant requirements in IFRS 15. Furthermore, while these capitalised cost assets are intangible, in nature, IAS 38 specifically excludes from its scope intangible assets arising from contracts with customers that are recognised in accordance with IFRS 15. *[IAS 38.3(i)]*. In the absence of a standard that specifically deals with classification and presentation of contract costs, management would need to apply the requirements in IAS 8 to select an appropriate accounting policy. *[IAS 8.10-12]*.

In developing such an accounting policy, we believe that costs to obtain a contract and costs to fulfil a contract need to be considered separately for the purpose of presentation in financial statements.

- Considering the nature of *costs to obtain a contract* and the lack of guidance in IFRS, we believe an entity may choose to present these costs as either:
  - a separate class of intangible assets in the statement of financial position and its amortisation in the same line item as amortisation of intangible assets within the scope of IAS 38 – this accounting treatment would be similar to the current practice of accounting for certain subscriber acquisitions costs in the telecommunications industry; or
  - a separate class of asset (similar in nature to work in progress, or 'inventory', of a service provider) in the statement of financial position and its amortisation within cost of goods sold, changes in contract costs or similar.
- In contrast, the nature of *costs to fulfil a contract* is such that they directly impact the entity's performance under the contract. Therefore, costs to fulfil a contract should be presented as a separate class of asset in the statement of financial position and its amortisation within cost of goods sold, changes in contract costs or similar.

  We do not believe it would be appropriate to analogise to the requirements for intangible assets in IAS 38. Instead, such costs are consistent in nature to costs incurred in the process of production, as is currently contemplated in IAS 2. That is, in nature, they are consistent with work in progress, or 'inventory', of a service provider. Furthermore, whether or not costs to fulfil a contract meet the criteria for capitalisation in paragraph 95 of IFRS 15 or are expensed as incurred, we believe that presentation of such costs in the statement of profit and loss and other comprehensive income needs to be consistent.

9.3.4 Impairment of capitalised costs

Any asset recorded by the entity is subject to an assessment of impairment at the end of each reporting period. This is because costs that give rise to an asset must continue to be recoverable throughout the contract (or period of benefit, if longer), in order to meet the criteria for capitalisation.

An impairment exists if the carrying amount of any asset(s) exceeds the amount of consideration the entity expects to receive in exchange for providing the associated goods and services, less the remaining costs that relate directly to providing those goods and services. Impairment losses are recognised in profit and loss. *[IFRS 15.101]*.

In July 2014, the TRG members generally agreed that an impairment test of capitalised contract costs should include future cash flows associated with contract renewal or extension periods, if the period of benefit of the costs under assessment is expected to extend beyond the present contract.[111] In other words, an entity should consider the total period over which it expects to receive economic benefits relating to the asset, for the purpose of both determining the amortisation period and estimating cash flows to be used in the impairment test. The question was raised because of an inconsistency within IFRS 15. IFRS 15 indicates that costs capitalised under the standard could relate to goods or services to be transferred under 'a specific anticipated contract' (e.g. goods or services to be provided under contract renewals and/or extensions). *[IFRS 15.99]*. The standard also indicates that an impairment loss would be recognised when the carrying amount of the asset exceeds the remaining amount of consideration expected to be received (determined by using principles in IFRS 15 for determining the transaction price, see 5 above). *[IFRS 15.101(a), 102]*. However, the requirements for measuring the transaction price in IFRS 15 indicate that an entity does not anticipate that the contract will be 'cancelled, renewed or modified' when determining the transaction price. *[IFRS 15.49]*. In some instances, excluding renewals or extensions would trigger an immediate impairment of a contract asset because the consideration an entity expects to receive would not include anticipated cash flows from contract extensions or renewal periods. However, the entity would have capitalised contract costs on the basis that they would be recovered over the contract extension or renewal periods.

When an entity determines the amount it expects to receive (see 5 above), the requirements for constraining estimates of variable consideration are not considered. That is, if an entity were required to reduce the estimated transaction price because of the constraint on variable consideration, it would use the unconstrained transaction price for the impairment test. *[IFRS 15.102]*. While unconstrained, this amount must be reduced to reflect the customer's credit risk before it is used in the impairment test.

However, before recognising an impairment loss on capitalised costs incurred to obtain or fulfil a contract, the entity will need to consider impairment losses recognised in accordance with another standard (e.g. IAS 36). After applying the impairment test to the capitalised costs, an entity includes the resulting carrying amount in the carrying amount of a cash-generating unit for purposes of applying the requirements in IAS 36. *[IFRS 15.103]*.

Under IFRS, IAS 36 permits the reversal of some or all of previous impairment losses on assets (other than goodwill) or cash-generating units if the estimates used to determine the assets' recoverable amount have changed. *[IAS 36.109-125]*. Consistent with IAS 36, IFRS 15 permits reversal of impairment losses when impairment conditions no longer exist or have improved. However, the increased carrying amount of asset must not exceed the amount that would have been determined (net of amortisation) if no impairment loss had been recognised previously. *[IFRS 15.104]*.

Under US GAAP, the reversal of previous impairment losses is prohibited. In US GAAP, the cost requirements that are equivalent to those within IFRS 15 are contained within ASC 340-40, *Other Assets and Deferred Costs – Contracts with Customers*, instead of ASC 606. In May 2016, the FASB proposed clarifying the inconsistency between ASC 640-40 and ASC 606 as discussed by the TRG (noted above in the context of IFRS 15) to make it clear that, when performing impairment testing, an entity should consider expected contract renewals and extensions. Furthermore, an entity should include both the amount of consideration it already has received, but has not recognised as revenue and the amount the entity expects to receive in the future. The FASB also proposed clarifying the interaction of the impairment testing in ASC 340-40 with other ASC topics (e.g. ASC 360) and the order of impairment testing. Comments were due by 2 July 2016. To finalise this change, the FASB will need to issue a final amendment. The IASB is not expected to propose a similar amendment to IFRS 15.

10 PRESENTATION AND DISCLOSURE

IFRS 15 provides explicit presentation and disclosure requirements, which are more detailed than under current IFRS.

The disclosure requirements discussed in the following sections are required on an ongoing basis. Disclosures required as part of the transition to IFRS 15 are discussed at 1.3 above.

For US GAAP preparers, the standard provides requirements on presentation and disclosure that apply to both public and non-public entities and provide some relief on disclosure requirements for non-public entities. The FASB's standard defines a public entity as one of the following:

- a public business entity, as defined;
- a not-for-profit entity that has issued, or is a conduit bond obligor for, securities that are traded, listed or quoted on an exchange or an over-the-counter market; or
- an employee benefit plan that files or furnishes financial statements with the SEC.

An entity that does not meet any of the criteria above is considered a non-public entity for purposes of the FASB's standard.

IFRS 15 does not differentiate between public and non-public entities. Therefore, an entity that applies IFRS 15 must apply all of its requirements.

10.1 Presentation requirements for contract assets and contract liabilities

The revenue model is based on the notion that a contract asset or contract liability is generated when either party to a contract performs, depending on the relationship between the entity's performance and the customer's payment. The standard requires that an entity present these contract assets or contract liabilities in the statement of financial position. *[IFRS 15.105]*.

When an entity satisfies a performance obligation by transferring a promised good or service, the entity has earned a right to consideration from the customer and, therefore, has a contract asset. When the customer performs first, for example, by prepaying its promised consideration, the entity has a contract liability. *[IFRS 15.106-107]*.

Contract assets may represent conditional or unconditional rights to consideration. The right would be conditional, for example, when an entity must first satisfy another performance obligation in the contract before it is entitled to payment from the customer. If an entity has an unconditional right to receive consideration from the customer, the contract asset is accounted for as a receivable and presented separately from contract assets. *[IFRS 15.105, BC323-BC324]*. A right is unconditional if nothing other than the passage of time is required before payment of that consideration is due. *[IFRS 15.108]*.

In the Basis for Conclusions on IFRS 15, the Board explains that in many cases an unconditional right to consideration (i.e. a receivable) arises when an entity satisfies a performance obligation, which could be before it invoices the customer (e.g. an unbilled receivable) if only the passage of time is required before payment of that consideration is due. It is also possible for an entity to have an unconditional right to consideration before it satisfies a performance obligation. *[IFRS 15.107, BC325]*.

In some industries, it is common for an entity to invoice its customers in advance of performance (and satisfaction of the performance obligation). For example, an entity that enters into a non-cancellable contract requiring payment a month before the entity provides the goods or services would recognise a receivable and an offsetting contract liability on the date when payment is due. This conclusion (i.e. that a receivable is recognised when payment is due) is based on paragraph IE200 in Example 38, Case B, of IFRS 15 (see Example 30.73 below). In this situation, revenue is not recognised until goods or services are transferred to the customer.

In the Basis for Conclusions, the Board noted that making the distinction between a contract asset and a receivable is important because doing so provides users of financial statements with relevant information about the risks associated with the entity's rights in a contract. Although both would be subject to credit risk, a contract asset is also subject to other risks (e.g. performance risk). *[IFRS 15.BC323]*.

Under the standard, entities are not required to use the terms 'contract asset' or 'contract liability', but must disclose sufficient information so that users of the financial statements can clearly distinguish between unconditional rights to consideration (receivables) and conditional rights to receive consideration (contract assets). *[IFRS 15.109]*. In addition, entities need consider the requirements in IAS 1 on classification of current assets and liabilities in their statement of financial position when determining whether their contract assets and contract liabilities need to be presented as current or non-current.

The standard provides the following example of presentation of contract balances. *[IFRS 15.IE198-IE200]*.

Example 30.73: Contract liability and receivable

Case A – Cancellable contract

On 1 January 20X9, an entity enters into a cancellable contract to transfer a product to a customer on 31 March 20X9. The contract requires the customer to pay consideration of CU1,000 in advance on 31 January 20X9. The customer pays the consideration on 1 March 20X9. The entity transfers the product on 31 March 20X9. The following journal entries illustrate how the entity accounts for the contract:

- The entity receives cash of CU1,000 on 1 March 20X9 (cash is received in advance of performance):

Cash	CU1,000	
Contract liability		CU1,000

- The entity satisfies the performance obligation on 31 March 20X9:

Contract liability	CU1,000	
Revenue		CU1,000

Case B – Non-cancellable contract

The same facts as in Case A apply to Case B except that the contract is non-cancellable. The following journal entries illustrate how the entity accounts for the contract:

- The amount of consideration is due on 31 January 20X9 (which is when the entity recognises a receivable because it has an unconditional right to consideration):

Receivable	CU1,000	
Contract liability		CU1,000

- The entity receives the cash on 1 March 20X9:

Cash	CU1,000	
Receivable		CU1,000

- The entity satisfies the performance obligation on 31 March 20X9:

Contract liability	CU1,000	
Revenue		CU1,000

If the entity issued the invoice before 31 January 20X9 (the due date of the consideration), the entity would not present the receivable and the contract liability on a gross basis in the statement of financial position because the entity does not yet have a right to consideration that is unconditional.

At the April 2016 FASB TRG meeting, the FASB staff provided an update on a question it had received from a preparer group regarding Case B of Example 38 in the standard (see Example 30.73 above). As noted in the extract above, this example indicates that an entity could not recognise a receivable until the date an invoice for a non-cancellable contract was due. However, the FASB staff explained that the standard requires any unconditional right to payment to be presented separately as a receivable. Furthermore, a right to consideration is unconditional if only the passage of time is required for payment of that consideration to be due. As such, the FASB staff indicated it would likely propose that the FASB issue a technical correction to clarify this in Example 38 of its standard. The IASB is not expected to propose a similar amendment to IFRS 15.

The standard includes another example of presentation of contract balances that illustrates when an entity has satisfied a performance obligation, but does not have an unconditional right to payment and, therefore, recognises a contract asset. *[IFRS 15.IE201-IE204]*.

Example 30.74: Contract asset recognised for the entity's performance

On 1 January 20X8, an entity enters into a contract to transfer Products A and B to a customer in exchange for CU1,000. The contract requires Product A to be delivered first and states that payment for the delivery of Product A is conditional on the delivery of Product B. In other words, the consideration of CU1,000 is due only after the entity has transferred both Products A and B to the customer. Consequently, the entity does not have a right to consideration that is unconditional (a receivable) until both Products A and B are transferred to the customer:

The entity identifies the promises to transfer Products A and B as performance obligations and allocates CU400 to the performance obligation to transfer Product A and CU600 to the performance obligation to transfer Product B on the basis of their relative stand-alone selling prices. The entity recognises revenue for each respective performance obligation when control of the product transfers to the customer.

The entity satisfies the performance obligation to transfer Product A:

Contract asset	CU400	
Revenue		CU400

The entity satisfies the performance obligation to transfer Product B and to recognise the unconditional right to consideration:

Receivable	CU1,000	
Contract asset		CU400
Revenue		CU600

After initial recognition, receivables and contract assets are subject to an impairment assessment in accordance with IFRS 9 or IAS 39 (the requirements in respect of impairment under those standards are discussed in Chapters 50 and 49, respectively). *[IFRS 15.107]*. In addition, if upon initial measurement there is a difference between the measurement of the receivable under IFRS 9 or IAS 39 and the corresponding amount of revenue, that difference will be presented immediately in profit or loss (e.g. as an impairment loss). *[IFRS 15.108]*. Since the initial measurement of a financial instrument is at fair value, there may be a number of reasons why such differences may arise (e.g. changes in the fair value of non-cash consideration not yet received). This will be the case when the difference is attributable to customer credit risk, rather than an implied price concession. Implied price concessions are deducted from the contract price to derive the transaction price, which is the amount recognised as revenue. Distinguishing between implied price concessions and expense due to customer credit risk will require judgement (see 5.2.1.A above). Impairment losses resulting from contracts with customers are presented separately from other impairment losses.

An entity could also have recognised other assets related to contracts with a customer (e.g. the incremental costs of obtaining the contract and other costs incurred that meet the criteria for capitalisation). The standard requires that any such assets be presented separately from contract assets and contract liabilities in the statement of financial position (assuming that they are material). These amounts are also assessed for impairment separately (see 9.3.4 above).

10.1.1 Implementation questions on presentation of contract assets and liabilities

10.1.1.A Determining the presentation of contract assets and liabilities for contracts that contain multiple performance obligations

At the October 2014 TRG meeting, the TRG members were asked how an entity would determine the presentation of contract assets and liabilities for contracts that contain multiple performance obligations. The TRG members generally agreed that contract assets and liabilities would be determined at the contract level and not at the performance obligation level. That is, an entity would not separately recognise an asset or liability for each performance obligation within a contract, but would aggregate them into a single contract asset or liability.[112]

This question arose in part because, under the standard, the amount and timing of revenue recognition is determined based on progress toward complete satisfaction of *each* performance obligation. Therefore, some constituents questioned whether an entity could have a contract asset and a contract liability for a single contract. An example is when the entity has satisfied (or partially satisfied) one performance obligation in a contract for which consideration is not yet due, but has received a prepayment for another unsatisfied performance obligation in the contract. The TRG members generally agreed that the discussion in the Basis for Conclusions was clear that contract asset or contract liability positions are determined for each contract on a net basis. This is because the rights and obligations in a contract with a customer are interdependent – the right to receive consideration from a customer depends on the entity's performance and, similarly, the entity performs only as long as the customer continues to pay. The Board decided that those interdependencies are best reflected by accounting and presenting contract assets or liabilities on a net basis. *[IFRS 15.BC317]*.

10.1.1.B Determining the presentation of two or more contracts that are required to be combined under the standards

At the October 2014 TRG meeting, the TRG members considered how an entity would determine the presentation of two or more contracts that are required to be combined under the standard. The TRG members generally agreed that the contract asset or liability would be combined (i.e. presented net) for different contracts with the same customer (or a related party of the customer) if an entity is otherwise required to combine those contracts under the standard (see 3.3 above for discussion of the criteria for combining contracts).[113] When two or more contracts are required to be combined under the standard, the rights and obligations in the individual contracts are interdependent. Therefore, as discussed at 10.1.1.A above, this interdependency is best reflected by combining the individual contracts as if they were a single contract. However, the TRG members acknowledged that this analysis may be operationally difficult for some entities because their systems may capture data at the performance obligation level in order to comply with the recognition and measurement aspects of the standard.

10.1.1.C Offsetting contract assets and liabilities against other statement of financial position items (e.g. accounts receivable)

At the October 2014 TRG meeting, the TRG members considered when an entity would offset contract assets and liabilities against other statement of financial position items (e.g. accounts receivable). The TRG members generally agreed that, because the standard does not provide requirements for offsetting, entities will need to apply the requirements of other standards to determine whether offsetting is appropriate (e.g. IAS 1, IAS 32 – *Financial Instruments: Presentation*).[114] For example, if an entity has a contract asset (or a receivable) and a contract liability from separate contracts with the same customer (that are not required to be combined under the standard), the entity will need to look to requirements outside IFRS 15 to determine whether offsetting is appropriate.

10.1.1.D Is a refund liability a contract liability (and, thus, subject to the presentation and disclosure requirements of a contract liability)?

We believe that a refund liability will not typically meet the definition of a contract liability. When an entity makes the conclusion that a refund liability is not a contract liability, it would present the refund liability separately from any contract liability (or asset) and it would not be subject to the disclosure requirements in paragraphs 116-118 of IFRS 15 discussed at 10.4.1 below.

When a customer pays consideration (or consideration is unconditionally due) and the entity has an obligation to transfer *goods or services* to the customer, the entity recognises a contract liability. When the entity expects to refund some or all of the *consideration* received (or receivable) from the customer, it recognises a refund liability. A refund liability generally does not represent an obligation to transfer goods or services in the future. Similar to receivables (which are considered a subset of contract assets), refund liabilities could be considered a subset of contract liabilities. We believe refund liabilities are also similar to receivables in that they should be extracted from the net contract position and presented separately (if material). This conclusion is consistent with the standard's specific requirement to present the corresponding asset for expected returns separately. *[IFRS 15.B25]*.

If an entity were to conclude, based on its specific facts and circumstances, that a refund liability did represent an obligation to transfer goods or services in the future, it would be a contract liability subject to the disclosure requirements in paragraphs 116-118 of IFRS 15. In addition, in that situation, the entity would present a single net contract liability or asset (i.e. including the refund liability) determined at the contract level, as discussed at 10.1.1.A above.

10.1.1.E Accounting for a contract asset that exists when a contract is modified if the modification is treated as the termination of an existing contract and the creation of a new contract

How would an entity account for a contract asset that exists when a contract is modified if the modification is treated as the termination of an existing contract and the creation of a new contract? The FASB TRG members generally agreed that a contract asset that exists when a contract is modified would be carried forward into the new contract if the modification is treated as the termination of an existing contract and the creation of a new contract.

Some stakeholders questioned the appropriate accounting for contract assets when this type of modification occurs because the termination of the old contract could indicate that any remaining balances associated with the old contract should be written off.

FASB TRG members generally agreed that it is appropriate to carry forward the related contract asset in such modifications because the asset relates to a right to consideration for goods and services that have already been transferred and are distinct from those to be transferred in the future. As such, the revenue recognised to date would not be reversed and the contract asset would continue to be realised as amounts become due from the customer and are presented as a receivable. The contract asset that remains on the entity's statement of financial position at the date of modification would continue to be subject to evaluation for impairment under IFRS 15.[115]

While the FASB TRG members did not discuss this point, we believe a similar conclusion would be appropriate when accounting for an asset created under IFRS 15, such as capitalised commissions which exists immediately before a contract modification, that is treated as if it were a termination of the existing contract and creation of a new contract. See 9.3.1.D above for further discussion.

10.1.1.F Determining when an entity has an unconditional right to payment if it has not transferred a good or service

The standard states in paragraph 108 of IFRS 15 that a receivable is an entity's right to consideration that is unconditional. We believe it may be difficult to assert that the entity has an unconditional right to payment when it has not transferred a good or service. *[IFRS 15.108]*.

An entity may enter into non-cancellable contracts that provide unconditional rights to payment from the customer for services that the entity has not yet completed providing or services it will provide in the near future (e.g. amounts invoiced in advance related to a service or maintenance arrangement). When determining whether it is acceptable (or required) to recognise accounts receivable and a corresponding contract liability, the contractual terms and specific facts and circumstances supporting the existence of an unconditional right to payment should be evaluated. Factors to consider include:

- Does the entity have a contractual (or legal) right to invoice and receive payment from the customer for services being provided currently (and not yet completed) or being provided in the near future (e.g. amounts invoiced in advance related to a service or maintenance arrangement)?
- Is the advance invoice consistent with the entity's normal invoicing terms?
- Will the entity commence performance within a relatively short time frame of the invoice date?
- Is there more than one year between the advance invoice and performance?

10.2 Other presentation considerations

The standard also changes the presentation requirements for products expected to be returned and for those that contain a significant financing component. See 5.4.1 and 5.5.3 above for presentation considerations related to rights of return and significant financing components, respectively. Also see 9.3.3.C above for presentation considerations related to contract cost assets arising from capitalised costs to obtain and fulfil a contract.

10.3 Disclosure objective and general requirements

In response to criticism that the current revenue recognition disclosures are inadequate, the Board sought to create a comprehensive and coherent set of disclosures. As a result, IFRS 15 described the overall objective of the disclosures, consistent with other recent standards, as detailed below.

The objective is for an entity to 'disclose sufficient information to enable users of financial statements to understand the nature, amount, timing and uncertainty of revenue and cash flows arising from contracts with customers'. To achieve that objective, an entity is required to disclose qualitative and quantitative information about all of the following: *[IFRS 15.110]*

(a) its contracts with customers (discussed further at 10.4.1 below);

(b) the significant judgements, and changes in the judgements, made in applying the standard to those contracts (discussed further at 10.4.2 below); and

(c) any assets recognised from the costs to obtain or fulfil a contract with a customer (discussed further at 10.4.3 below).

The standard also requires that an entity consider the level of detail necessary to satisfy the disclosure objective and how much emphasis to place on each of the various requirements. The level of aggregation or disaggregation of disclosures will require judgement. Entities are required to ensure that useful information is not obscured by either the inclusion of a large amount of insignificant detail or the aggregation of items that have substantially different characteristics. *[IFRS 15.111]*.

An entity does not need to disclose information in accordance with IFRS 15 if it discloses that information in accordance with another standard. *[IFRS 15.112]*.

As explained in the Basis for Conclusions, many preparers raised concerns that they would need to provide voluminous disclosures at a cost that may outweigh any potential benefits. *[IFRS 15.BC327, BC331]*. As summarised above, the Board clarified the disclosure objective and indicated that the disclosures described in the standard are not meant to be a checklist of minimum requirements. That is, entities do not need to include disclosures that are not relevant or are not material to them. In addition, the Board decided to require qualitative disclosures instead of tabular reconciliations for certain disclosures.

Entities should review their disclosures to determine whether they have met the standard's disclosure objective to enable users to understand the nature, amount, timing and uncertainty of revenue and cash flows arising from contracts with customers. For example, some entities may make large payments to customers that do not represent payment for a distinct good or service and therefore reduce the transaction price and affect the amount and timing of revenue recognised. Although there are no specific requirements in the standard to disclose balances related to consideration paid or payable to a customer, an entity may need to disclose qualitative and/or quantitative information about those arrangements to meet the objective of the IFRS 15 disclosure requirements in the standard if the amounts are material.

The disclosures are required for (and as at) each annual period for which a statement of comprehensive income and a statement of financial position are presented.

Certain interim revenue disclosures are also required for entities preparing interim financial statements. When it issued IFRS 15, the IASB amended IAS 34 – *Interim Financial Reporting* – to require disclosure of disaggregated revenue information. However, none of the other annual disclosures are required for interim financial statements (see Chapter 39 for further discussion on interim financial reporting). The required interim disclosures differ under IFRS and US GAAP. While the IASB requires only disaggregated revenue information to be disclosed for interim financial statements, the FASB requires the quantitative disclosures about revenue required for annual financial statements to also be disclosed in interim financial statements. As discussed more fully below, IFRS 15 significantly increases the volume of disclosures required in entities' financial statements, particularly annual financial statements. In addition, many are completely new requirements.

We believe entities may need to expend additional effort when initially preparing the required disclosures for their interim and annual financial statements. For example, entities operating in multiple segments with many different product lines may find it challenging to gather the data needed to provide the disclosures. As a result, entities will need to ensure that they have the appropriate systems, internal controls, policies and procedures in place to collect and disclose the required information. In light of the expanded disclosure requirements and the potential need for new systems to capture the data needed for these disclosures, entities may wish to prioritise this portion of their implementation efforts.

10.4 Specific disclosure requirements

10.4.1 Contracts with customers

The majority of the standard's disclosures relate to an entity's contracts with customers. These disclosures include disaggregation of revenue, information about contract asset and liability balances and information about an entity's performance obligations. To provide context for the disclosures, the Board decided to require entities to disclose the following amounts related to contracts with customers: *[IFRS 15.113, BC332]*

- Paragraph 113(a) of IFRS 15 requires an entity to disclose (or present in the statement of comprehensive income) the amount of revenue recognised from contracts with customers separately from other sources of revenue. For example, a large equipment manufacturer that both sells and leases its equipment should present (or disclose) amounts from these transactions separately.
- Paragraph 113(b) of IFRS 15 also requires an entity to disclose impairment losses from contracts with customers separately from other impairment losses if they are not presented in the statement of comprehensive income separately. As noted in the Basis for Conclusion, the Board felt that separately disclosing the impairment losses on contracts with customers will provide the most relevant information to users of financial statements. *[IFRS 15.BC334]*.

10.4.1.A Disaggregation of revenue

Entities will be required to disclose disaggregated revenue information to illustrate how the nature, amount, timing and uncertainty about revenue and cash flows are affected by economic factors. *[IFRS 15.114]*. This is the only disclosure requirement for IFRS preparers that is required in both an entity's interim and annual financial statements.

As noted above, an entity is required to separately disclose any impairment losses recognised in accordance with IFRS 9 or IAS 39 on receivables or contract assets arising from contracts with customers. However, entities are not required to further disaggregate such losses for uncollectible amounts.

While the standard does not specify precisely how revenue should be disaggregated, the application guidance suggests categories for entities to consider. The application guidance indicates that the most appropriate categories for a particular entity will depend on its facts and circumstances, but an entity should consider how it disaggregates revenue in other communications (e.g. press releases, other public filings) when determining which categories are most relevant and useful. These categories could include, but are not limited to: *[IFRS 15.B87-B89]*

- type of good or service (e.g. major product lines);
- geographical region (e.g. country or region);
- market or type of customer (e.g. government and non-government customers);
- type of contract (e.g. fixed-price and time-and-materials contracts);
- contract duration (e.g. short-term and long-term contracts);
- timing of transfer of goods or services (e.g. revenue from goods or services transferred to customers at a point in time and revenue from goods or services transferred over time); and
- sales channels (e.g. goods sold directly to consumers and goods sold through intermediaries).

As noted in the Basis for Conclusions, the Board decided not to prescribe a specific characteristic of revenue as the basis for disaggregation because it intended for entities to make this determination based on entity-specific and/or industry-specific factors that would be most meaningful for their businesses. The Board acknowledged that an entity may need to use more than one type of category to disaggregate its revenue. *[IFRS 15.B87, BC336]*.

Paragraph 112 of IFRS 15 clarifies that an entity does not have to duplicate disclosures required by another standard. *[IFRS 15.112]*. For example, an entity that provides disaggregated revenue disclosures as part of its segment disclosures, in accordance with IFRS 8 – *Operating Segments*, does not need to separately provide disaggregated revenue disclosures if the segment-related disclosures are sufficient to illustrate how the nature, amount, timing and uncertainty about revenue and cash flows from contracts with customer are affected by economic factors and are presented on a basis consistent with IFRS.

However, segment disclosures may not be sufficiently disaggregated to achieve the disclosure objectives of IFRS 15. The IASB noted in the Basis for Conclusions that segment disclosures on revenue may not always provide users of financial statements with enough information to help them understand the composition of revenue recognised in the period. *[IFRS 15.BC340]*. If an entity applies IFRS 8, paragraph 115 of IFRS 15 requires an entity to explain the relationship between the disaggregated revenue information and the segment information. *[IFRS 15.115]*. Users of the financial statements believe this information is critical to their ability to understand not only the composition of revenue, but also how revenue relates to other information provided in the segment disclosures. Entities can provide this information in a tabular or a narrative form.

The Board provided some examples of the disclosures for disaggregation of revenue, as follows. *[IFRS 15.IE210-IE211]*.

Example 30.75: Disaggregation of revenue – quantitative disclosure

An entity reports the following segments: consumer products, transportation and energy, in accordance with IFRS 8. When the entity prepares its investor presentations, it disaggregates revenue into primary geographical markets, major product lines and timing of revenue recognition (i.e. goods transferred at a point in time or services transferred over time).

The entity determines that the categories used in the investor presentations can be used to meet the objective of the disaggregation disclosure requirement in paragraph 114 of IFRS 15, which is to disaggregate revenue from contracts with customers into categories that depict how the nature, amount, timing and uncertainty of revenue and cash flows are affected by economic factors. The following table illustrates the disaggregation disclosure by primary geographical market, major product line and timing of revenue recognition, including a reconciliation of how the disaggregated revenue ties in with the consumer products, transportation and energy segments, in accordance with paragraph 115 of IFRS 15.

Segments	**Consumer products**	**Transport**	**Energy**	**Total**
	CU	CU	CU	CU
Primary geographical markets				
North America	990	2,250	5,250	8,490
Europe	300	750	1,000	2,050
Asia	700	260	–	960
	1,990	3,260	6,250	11,500
Major goods/service lines				
Office Supplies	600	–	–	600
Appliances	990	–	–	990
Clothing	400	–	–	400
Motorcycles	–	500	–	500
Automobiles	–	2,760	–	2,760
Solar Panels	–	–	1,000	1,000
Power Plant	–	–	5,250	5,250
	1,990	3,260	6,250	11,500
Timing of revenue recognition				
Goods transferred at a point in time	1,990	3,260	1,000	6,250
Services transferred over time	–	–	5,250	5,250
	1,990	3,260	6,250	11,500

10.4.1.B Contract balances

The Board noted in the Basis for Conclusions that users of the financial statements need to understand the relationship between the revenue recognised and changes in the overall balances of an entity's total contract assets and liabilities during a particular reporting period. *[IFRS 15.BC341]*. As a result, an entity is required to disclose: *[IFRS 15.116]*

- the opening and closing balances of receivables, contract assets and contract liabilities from contracts with customers, if not otherwise separately presented or disclosed;
- revenue recognised in the reporting period that was included in the contract liability balance at the beginning of the period; and
- revenue recognised in the reporting period from performance obligations satisfied (or partially satisfied) in previous periods (e.g. changes in transaction price).

In addition, an entity is required to explain how the timing of satisfaction of its performance obligations (see (a)(i) below at 10.4.1.C) relates to the typical timing of payment (see (a)(ii) below at 10.4.1.C) and the effect that those factors have on the contract asset and the contract liability balances. This explanation may use qualitative information. *[IFRS 15.117]*.

An entity is also required to provide an explanation of the significant changes in the contract asset and the contract liability balances during the reporting period. This explanation is required to include both qualitative and quantitative information. The standard identifies the following examples of changes in the entity's balances of contract assets and contract liabilities: *[IFRS 15.118]*

- changes due to business combinations;
- cumulative catch-up adjustments to revenue that affect the corresponding contract asset or contract liability, including adjustments arising from a change in the measure of progress, a change in an estimate of the transaction price (including any changes in the assessment of whether an estimate of variable consideration is constrained) or a contract modification;
- impairment of a contract asset;
- a change in the time frame for a right to consideration to become unconditional (i.e. for a contract asset to be reclassified to a receivable); and
- a change in the time frame for a performance obligation to be satisfied (i.e. for the recognition of revenue arising from a contract liability).

Entities are permitted to disclose information about contract balances, and changes therein, as they deem to be most appropriate, which would include a combination of tabular and narrative information. The IASB explained in the Basis for Conclusions that these disclosures are intended to provide financial statement users with information they requested on when contract assets are typically transferred to accounts receivable or collected as cash and when contract liabilities are recognised as revenue. *[IFRS 15.BC346]*.

In addition to the disclosures on contract balances and changes, the standard requires entities to disclose the amount of revenue recognised in the period that relates to amounts allocated to performance obligations that were satisfied (or partially satisfied) in previous periods (e.g. due to a change in transaction price or in estimates related to the constraint on revenue recognised). As noted in the Basis for Conclusions, the Board noted that this information is not required elsewhere in the financial statements and will provide relevant information about the timing of revenue recognised that was not a result of performance in the current period. *[IFRS 15.BC347]*.

The example below is an example of how an entity may fulfil these requirements.

Example 30.76: Contract asset and liability disclosures

Company A discloses trade receivables separately in the statement of financial position. To comply with the other disclosure requirements for contract assets and liabilities, Company A includes the following information in the notes to the financial statements:

	20X9	**20X8**	**20X7**
	CU	CU	CU
Contract asset	1,500	2,250	1,800
Contract liability	(200)	(850)	(500)

	20X9	**20X8**	**20X7**
	CU	CU	CU
Revenue recognised in the period from:			
Amounts included in contract liability at the beginning of the period	650	200	100
Performance obligations satisfied in previous periods	200	125	200

We receive payments from customers based on a billing schedule, as established in our contracts. Contract asset relates to our right to consideration for our completed performance under the contract. Accounts receivable are recognised when the right to consideration becomes unconditional. Contract liability relates to payments received in advance of performance under the contract. Contract liabilities are recognised as revenue as (or when) we perform under the contract. In addition, contract asset decreased in 20X9 due to a contract asset impairment of CU400 relating to the early cancellation of a contract with a customer.

Disclosing contract assets and liabilities and the revenue recognised from changes in contract liabilities and performance obligations satisfied in previous periods will likely be a change in practice for most entities. They will need to make sure they have appropriate systems, policies and procedures and internal controls in place to collect and disclose the required information.

For example, a sales-based or usage-based royalty received by the entity in reporting periods after it delivers a right-to-use licence of intellectual property represents revenue that the entity receives in subsequent periods that relates to the previously satisfied performance obligation. As such, it would be disclosed separately in accordance with paragraph 116(c) of IFRS 15.

10.4.1.C Performance obligations

To help users of financial statements analyse the nature, amount, timing and uncertainty about revenue and cash flows arising from contracts with customers, the Board decided to require disclosures about an entity's performance obligations. As noted in the Basis for Conclusions, current IFRS requires entities to disclose their accounting policies for recognising revenue, but users of financial statements had commented that many entities provide a 'boilerplate' description that does not explain how the policy relates to the contracts they enter into with customers. *[IFRS 15.BC354]*. To address this criticism, IFRS 15 requires an entity to provide more descriptive information about its performance obligations.

An entity is also required to disclose information about remaining performance obligations and the amount of the transaction price allocated to such obligations, including an explanation of when it expects to recognise the amount(s) in its financial statements.

Both quantitative and qualitative information are required, as follows: *[IFRS 15.119-120]*

(a) Information about its performance obligations, including a description of all of the following:
   - (i) when the entity typically satisfies its performance obligations (e.g. upon shipment, upon delivery, as services are rendered or upon completion of service), including when performance obligations are satisfied in a bill-and-hold arrangement;
   - (ii) the significant payment terms (e.g. when payment is typically due, whether the contract has a significant financing component, whether the consideration amount is variable and whether the estimate of variable consideration is typically constrained);
   - (iii) the nature of the goods or services that the entity has promised to transfer, highlighting any performance obligations to arrange for another party to transfer goods or services (i.e. if the entity is acting as an agent);
   - (iv) obligations for returns, refunds and other similar obligations; and
   - (v) types of warranties and related obligations.

(b) For remaining performance obligations:
   - (i) the aggregate amount of the transaction price allocated to the performance obligations that are unsatisfied (or partially unsatisfied) as of the end of the reporting period; and
   - (ii) an explanation of when the entity expects to recognise as revenue the amount disclosed in accordance with (b)(i) above. An entity discloses this in either of the following ways:
     - on a quantitative basis using the time bands that would be most appropriate for the duration of the remaining performance obligations; or
     - by using qualitative information.

In the Basis for Conclusions, the Board noted that many users of financial statements commented that information about the amount and timing of revenue that an entity expects to recognise from its existing contracts would be useful in their analyses of revenue, especially for long-term contracts with significant unrecognised revenue. *[IFRS 15.BC348]*. The Board also observed that a number of entities often voluntarily disclose such 'backlog' information. However, this information is typically presented outside the financial statements and may not be comparable across entities because there is no common definition of backlog. As summarised in the Basis for Conclusions, the Board's intention in including the disclosure requirements in paragraph 120 of

Chapter 30

IFRS 15 is to provide users of an entity's financial statements with additional information about the following: *[IFRS 15.BC350]*

- the amount and expected timing of revenue to be recognised from the remaining performance obligations in existing contracts;
- trends relating to the amount and expected timing of revenue to be recognised from the remaining performance obligations in existing contracts;
- risks associated with expected future revenue (e.g. uncertainties should an entity expect not to satisfy a performance obligation until a much later date); and
- the effect of changes in judgements or circumstances on an entity's revenue.

This disclosure can be provided on either a quantitative basis (e.g. amounts to be recognised in given time bands, such as between one and two years and between two and three years) or by disclosing a mix of quantitative and qualitative information. In addition, this disclosure would only include amounts related to performance obligations in the current contract. For example, expected contract renewals that have not been executed and are not material rights would not be performance obligations in the current contract. As such, an entity would not disclose amounts related to such renewals. However, if an entity concluded that expected contract renewals represented a material right to acquire goods or services in the future (and, therefore, was a separate performance obligation – see 4.6 above), the entity would include in its disclosure the consideration attributable to the material right for the options that have not yet been exercised (i.e. the unsatisfied performance obligation(s)).

The disclosure of the transaction price allocated to the remaining performance obligations does not include consideration that has been excluded from the transaction price. However, the standard requires entities to disclose qualitatively whether any consideration is not included in the transaction price and, therefore, is not included in the disclosure of the remaining performance obligations (e.g. variable consideration amounts that are constrained and, therefore, excluded from the transaction price).

The Board also provided a practical expedient under which an entity can decide not to disclose the amount of the remaining performance obligations for contracts with an original expected duration of less than one year or those that meet the requirements of the right to invoice practical expedient in paragraph B16 IFRS 15. As explained in 7.2.1.A above, the right to invoice practical expedient permits an entity that is recognising revenue over time to recognise revenue as invoiced if the entity's right to payment is an amount that corresponds directly with the value to the customer of the entity's performance to date. *[IFRS 15.121]*. For example, an entity is not required to make the disclosure for a three-year service contract under which it has a right to invoice the customer a fixed amount for each hour of service provided. If an entity uses this disclosure practical expedient, it will be required to qualitatively disclose that fact. *[IFRS 15.122]*.

The FASB proposed an additional practical expedient that would allow an entity not to disclose variable consideration allocated to performance obligations related to either: (a) sales-based or usage-based royalties on licences of intellectual property; or (b) variable consideration allocated entirely to a wholly unsatisfied performance obligation, or to a wholly unsatisfied promise to transfer a distinct good or service that forms part of a single performance obligation, when certain criteria are met. Comments were due 2 July 2016. To finalise this change, the FASB will need to issue a final amendment. The IASB is not expected to propose a similar practical expedient in IFRS 15.

The standard provides the following examples on various scenarios for these required disclosures. *[IFRS 15.IE212-IE219]*.

Example 30.77: Disclosure of the transaction price allocated to the remaining performance obligations

On 30 June 20X7, an entity enters into three contracts (Contracts A, B and C) with separate customers to provide services. Each contract has a two-year non-cancellable term. The entity considers the requirements in paragraphs 120-122 of IFRS 15 in determining the information in each contract to be included in the disclosure of the transaction price allocated to the remaining performance obligations at 31 December 20X7.

Contract A

Cleaning services are to be provided over the next two years typically at least once per month. For services provided, the customer pays an hourly rate of CU25.

Because the entity bills a fixed amount for each hour of service provided, the entity has a right to invoice the customer in the amount that corresponds directly with the value of the entity's performance completed to date in accordance with paragraph B16 of IFRS 15. Consequently, no disclosure is necessary if the entity elects to apply the practical expedient in paragraph 121(b) of IFRS 15.

Contract B

Cleaning services and lawn maintenance services are to be provided as and when needed with a maximum of four visits per month over the next two years. The customer pays a fixed price of CU400 per month for both services. The entity measures its progress towards complete satisfaction of the performance obligation using a time-based measure.

The entity discloses the amount of the transaction price that has not yet been recognised as revenue in a table with quantitative time bands that illustrates when the entity expects to recognise the amount as revenue. The information for Contract B included in the overall disclosure is as follows:

	20X8	**20X9**	**Total**
	CU	CU	CU
Revenue expected to be recognised on this contract as of 31 December 20X7	4,800(a)	2,400(b)	7,200

(a) CU4,800 = CU400 × 12 months.

(b) CU2,400 = CU400 × 6 months.

Contract C

Cleaning services are to be provided as and when needed over the next two years. The customer pays fixed consideration of CU100 per month plus a one-time variable consideration payment ranging from CU0-CU1,000 corresponding to a one-time regulatory review and certification of the customer's facility (i.e. a performance bonus). The entity estimates that it will be entitled to CU750 of the variable consideration. On the basis of the entity's assessment of the factors in paragraph 57 of IFRS 15, the entity includes its estimate of CU750 of variable consideration in the transaction price because it is highly probable that a significant reversal in the amount of cumulative revenue recognised will not occur. The entity measures its progress towards complete satisfaction of the performance obligation using a time-based measure.

The entity discloses the amount of the transaction price that has not yet been recognised as revenue in a table with quantitative time bands that illustrates when the entity expects to recognise the amount as revenue. The entity also includes a qualitative discussion about any significant variable consideration that is not included in the disclosure. The information for Contract C included in the overall disclosure is as follows:

	20X8	20X9	Total
	CU	CU	CU
Revenue expected to be recognised on this contract as of 31 December 20X7	1,575[(a)]	788[(b)]	2,363

(a) Transaction price = CU3,150 (CU100 × 24 months + CU750 variable consideration) recognised evenly over 24 months at CU1,575 per year.

(b) CU1,575 ÷ 2 = CU788 (i.e. for 6 months of the year).

In addition, in accordance with paragraph 122 of IFRS 15, the entity discloses qualitatively that part of the performance bonus has been excluded from the disclosure because it was not included in the transaction price. That part of the performance bonus was excluded from the transaction price in accordance with the requirements for constraining estimates of variable consideration.

The standard also provides an example of how an entity would make the disclosure required by paragraph 120(b) of IFRS 15 using qualitative information (instead of quantitatively, using time bands) as follows. *[IFRS 15.IE220-IE221]*.

Example 30.78: Disclosure of the transaction price allocated to the remaining performance obligations – qualitative disclosure

On 1 January 20X2, an entity enters into a contract with a customer to construct a commercial building for fixed consideration of CU10 million. The construction of the building is a single performance obligation that the entity satisfies over time. As of 31 December 20X2, the entity has recognised CU3.2 million of revenue. The entity estimates that construction will be completed in 20X3, but it is possible that the project will be completed in the first half of 20X4.

At 31 December 20X2, the entity discloses the amount of the transaction price that has not yet been recognised as revenue in its disclosure of the transaction price allocated to the remaining performance obligations. The entity also discloses an explanation of when the entity expects to recognise that amount as revenue. The explanation can be disclosed either on a quantitative basis using time bands that are most appropriate for the duration of the remaining performance obligation or by providing a qualitative explanation. Because the entity is uncertain about the timing of revenue recognition, the entity discloses this information qualitatively as follows:

> 'As of 31 December 20X2, the aggregate amount of the transaction price allocated to the remaining performance obligation is CU6.8 million and the entity will recognise this revenue as the building is completed, which is expected to occur over the next 12-18 months.'

10.4.1.D Use of the 'backlog' practical expedient when the criteria to use the 'right to invoice' practical expedient are not met

If an entity determines that it has not met the criteria to use the 'right to invoice' practical expedient (e.g. because there is a substantive contractual minimum payment or a volume discount), can the entity still use the disclosure practical expedient under which an entity can decide not to disclose the amount of transaction price allocated to remaining performance obligations? The TRG considered this question at the July 2015 TRG meeting.

The TRG members generally agreed that the standard is clear that an entity can only use the practical expedient to avoid disclosing the amount of the transaction price allocated to remaining performance obligations for contracts: (a) with an original expected duration of less than one year; or (b) that qualify for the 'right to invoice' practical expedient. *[IFRS 15.121]*. If a contract does not meet either of these criteria, an entity must disclose the information about remaining performance obligations that is required by Paragraph 120 of IFRS 15. *[IFRS 15.120]*. However, under these requirements, an entity is able to qualitatively describe any consideration that is not included in the transaction price (e.g. any estimated amount of variable consideration that is constrained).

Stakeholders had questioned whether an entity can still use this disclosure practical expedient if it determines that it has not met the criteria to use the right to invoice practical expedient (e.g. because there is a substantive contractual minimum payment or a volume discount).[116]

10.4.2 Significant judgements

The standard specifically requires disclosure of significant accounting estimates and judgements (and changes to those judgements) made in determining the transaction price, allocating the transaction price to performance obligations and determining when performance obligations are satisfied. *[IFRS 15.123]*.

IFRS currently has general requirements requiring disclosures about significant accounting estimates and judgements made by an entity. Because of the importance placed on revenue by users of financial statements, as noted in the Basis for Conclusion on IFRS 15, the Board decided to require specific disclosures about the estimates used and the judgements made in determining the amount and timing of revenue recognition. *[IFRS 15.BC355]*. These requirements exceed those in the general requirements for significant judgements and accounting estimates required by IAS 1 and discussed in more detail below. *[IAS 1.122-133]*.

10.4.2.A Determining the timing of satisfaction of performance obligations

IFRS 15 requires entities to provide disclosures about the significant judgements made in determining the timing of satisfaction of performance obligations. The disclosure requirements for performance obligations that are satisfied over time differ from those satisfied at a point in time, but the objective is similar – to disclose the judgements made in determining the timing of revenue recognition. Entities must disclose: *[IFRS 15.124]*

- the methods used to recognise revenue (e.g. a description of the output methods or input methods used and how those methods are applied); and
- an explanation of why the methods used provide a faithful depiction of the transfer of goods or services.

For performance obligations that are satisfied at a point in time, entities must disclose the significant judgements made in evaluating the point in time when the customer obtains control of the goods or services. *[IFRS 15.125]*.

When an entity has determined that a performance obligation is satisfied over time, IFRS 15 requires the entity to select a single revenue recognition method for each performance obligation that best depicts the entity's performance in transferring the goods or services. Entities must disclose the method used to recognise revenue.

For example, assume an entity enters into a contract to refurbish a multi-level building for a customer and the work is expected to take two years. The entity concludes that the promised refurbishment service is a single performance obligation satisfied over time and it decides to measure progress using a percentage of completion method, based on the costs incurred. The entity discloses the method used, how it has been applied to the contract and why the method selected provides a faithful depiction of the transfer of goods or services.

When an entity has determined that a performance obligation is satisfied at a point in time, the standard requires the entity to disclose the significant judgements made in evaluating when the customer obtains control of the promised goods or services. For example, an entity will need to consider the indicators of the transfer of control listed in paragraph 38 of IFRS 15 to determine when control transfers and disclose the significant judgements made in reaching that conclusion.

10.4.2.B Determining the transaction price and the amounts allocated to performance obligations

Entities often exercise significant judgement when estimating the transaction prices of their contracts, especially when those estimates involve variable consideration.

Furthermore, significant judgement may be required when allocating the transaction price, including estimating stand-alone selling prices; for example, entities will likely need to exercise judgement when determining whether a customer option gives rise to a material right (see 4.6 above) and in estimating the stand-alone selling price for those material rights.

Given the importance placed on revenue by financial statement users, the standard requires entities to disclose qualitative information about the methods, inputs and assumptions used in their annual financial statements for all of the following: *[IFRS 15.126, BC355]*

- determining the transaction price – includes, but is not limited to, estimating variable consideration, adjusting the consideration for the effects of the time value of money and measuring non-cash consideration;
- assessing whether an estimate of variable consideration is constrained;
- allocating the transaction price – includes estimating stand-alone selling prices of promised goods or services and allocating discounts and variable consideration to a specific part of the contract (if applicable); and
- measuring obligations for returns, refunds and other similar obligations.

Disclosing information about the methods, inputs and assumptions they use to determine and allocate the transaction price will be a change in practice for some entities. Entities with diverse contracts will need to ensure they have the processes and procedures in place to capture all of the different methods, inputs and assumptions used.

10.4.3 Assets recognised from the costs to obtain or fulfil a contract

As discussed at 9.3 above, the standard specifies the accounting for costs an entity incurs to obtain and fulfil a contract to provide goods and services to customers. IFRS 15 requires entities to disclose information about the assets recognised to help users understand the types of costs recognised as assets and how those assets are subsequently amortised or impaired. These disclosure requirements are: *[IFRS 15.127-128]*

- A description of:
  - (a) the judgements made in determining the amount of the costs incurred to obtain or fulfil a contract with a customer; and
  - (b) the method it uses to determine the amortisation for each reporting period;
- the closing balances of assets recognised from the costs incurred to obtain or fulfil a contract with a customer, by main category of asset (for example, costs to obtain contracts with customers, pre-contract costs and setup costs); and
- the amount of amortisation and any impairment losses recognised in the reporting period.

Entities will be required to disclose the judgements made in determining the amount of costs that were incurred to obtain or fulfil contracts with customers that meet the criteria for capitalisation, as well as the method the entity uses to amortise the assets recognised. For example, for costs to obtain a contract, an entity that capitalises commission costs upon the signing of each contract will need to describe the judgements used to determine the commission costs that qualified as costs incurred to obtain a contract with a customer, as well as the determination of the amortisation period. See the discussion at 9.3 above on the presentation requirements for contract cost assets.

10.4.4 Practical expedients

The standard allows entities to use several practical expedients. The standard requires entities to disclose their use of two practical expedients: (a) the practical expedient in paragraph 63 of IFRS 15 associated with the determination of whether a significant financing component exists (see 5.5 above); and (b) the expedient in paragraph 94 of IFRS 15 for recognising an immediate expense for certain incremental costs of obtaining a contract with a customer (see 9.3.1 above). *[IFRS 15.129]*.

10.5 Transition disclosure requirements

IFRS 15 requires retrospective application. However, the Board decided to allow either full retrospective adoption in which the standard is applied to all of the periods presented or a modified retrospective adoption. The transition disclosure requirements will differ for entities depending on the transition method selected. See 1.3 above for additional discussion on transition, including the disclosure requirements.

References

1 The FASB's standard defines a public entity as one of the following: A public business entity (as defined); A not-for-profit entity that has issued, or is a conduit bond obligor for, securities that are traded, listed or quoted on an exchange or an over-the-counter market; An employee benefit plan that files or furnishes financial statements with the US SEC.

2 *Speech by James V. Schnurr, 22 March 2016. Refer to the SEC website at http://www.sec.gov/news/speech/schnurr-remarks-12th-life-sciences-accounting-congress.html*

3 As originally issued, the standards under IFRS and US GAAP were identical except for these areas: (1) the Boards used the term 'probable' to describe the level of confidence needed when assessing collectability to identify contracts with customers, which will result in a higher threshold under US GAAP than under IFRS; (2) the FASB required more interim disclosures than the IASB; (3) the IASB allowed early adoption and the FASB did not; (4) the IASB allowed reversals of impairment losses and the FASB did not; and (5) the FASB provided relief for non-public entities relating to specific disclosure requirements and the effective date.

4 *Effective Date of IFRS 15*, September 2015.

5 *The FASB's amendments to its standard were effected through the following: ASU 2105-14, Revenue from Contracts with Customers (Topic 606): Deferral of the Effective Date; ASU 2016-08, Revenue from Contracts with Customers (Topic 606): Principal versus Agent Considerations (Reporting Revenue Gross versus Net); ASU 2016-10, Revenue from Contracts with Customers (Topic 606): Identifying Performance Obligations and Licensing (April 2016); and ASU 2016-12, Revenue from Contracts with Customer (Topic 606): Narrow-Scope Improvements and Practical Expedients (May 2016).*

6 *Proposed ASU, Technical Corrections and Improvements to Update No. 2014-09, Revenue from Contracts with Customers (Topic 606), issued 18 May 2016.*

7 The FASB's standard defines a public entity as one of the following: A public business entity (as defined); A not-for-profit entity that has issued, or is a conduit bond obligor for, securities that are traded, listed or quoted on an exchange or an over-the-counter market; An employee benefit plan that files or furnishes financial statements with the US SEC.

8 As defined in US GAAP in ASC 606-10-65-1(c)(2).

9 ESMA Public Statement: *Issues for consideration in implementing IFRS 15: Revenue from Contracts with Customers,* issued 20 July 2016.

10 ESMA Public Statement: *Issues for consideration in implementing IFRS 15: Revenue from Contracts with Customers,* issued 20 July 2016, paragraph 13.

11 TRG Agenda paper 17, *Application of IFRS 15 to permitted Islamic Finance Transactions,* dated 26 January 2015.

12 TRG Agenda paper 25, *January 2015 Meeting – Summary of Issues Discussed and Next Steps,* dated 30 March 2015.

13 FASB TRG Agenda paper 52, *Scoping Considerations for Financial Institutions,* dated 18 April 2016.

14 TRG Agenda paper 36, *Scope: Credit Cards,* dated 13 July 2015.

15 TRG Agenda paper 36, *Scope: Credit Cards,* dated 13 July 2015.

16 TRG Agenda paper 26, *Whether Contributions are Included or Excluded from the Scope,* dated 30 March 2015 and TRG Agenda paper 34, *March 2015 Meeting – Summary of Issues Discussed and Next Steps,* dated 13 July 2015.

17 TRG Agenda paper 47, *Whether Fixed Odds Wagering Contracts are Included or Excluded from the Scope of Topic 606,* dated 9 November 2015.

18 For US GAAP, the term 'probable' is defined in the master glossary of the US Accounting Standards Codification as 'the future event or events are likely to occur'.

19 TRG Agenda paper 25, *January 2015 Meeting – Summary of Issues Discussed and Next Steps,* dated 30 March 2015.

20 TRG Agenda paper 13, *Collectibility,* dated 26 January 2015.

21 TRG Agenda paper 13, *Collectibility,* dated 26 January 2015 and TRG Agenda paper 25, *January 2015 Meeting – Summary of Issues Discussed and Next Steps,* dated 30 March 2015.

22 TRG Agenda paper 10, *Contract enforceability and termination clauses,* dated 31 October 2014 and TRG Agenda paper 11, *October 2014 Meeting – Summary of Issues Discussed and Next Steps,* dated 26 January 2015.

23 TRG Agenda paper 48, *Customer options for additional goods and services,* dated 9 November 2015.
24 TRG Agenda paper 10, *Contract enforceability and termination clauses,* dated 31 October 2014.
25 Paragraph 47a of TRG Agenda paper 48, *Customer options for additional goods and services,* dated 9 November 2015.
26 TRG Agenda paper 25, *January 2015 Meeting – Summary of Issues Discussed and Next Steps,* dated 30 March 2015.
27 TRG Agenda paper 46, *Pre-Production Activities,* dated 9 November 2015.
28 TRG Agenda paper 16, *Stand-Ready Performance Obligations,* dated 26 January 2015.
29 TRG Agenda paper 16, *Stand-Ready Performance Obligations,* dated 26 January 2015.
30 TRG Agenda paper 48, *Customer options for additional goods and services,* dated 9 November 2015.
31 TRG Agenda paper 25, *January 2015 Meeting – Summary of Issues Discussed and Next Steps,* dated 30 March 2015.
32 TRG Agenda paper 48, *Customer options for additional goods and services,* dated 9 November 2015.
33 TRG Agenda paper 39, *Application of the Series Provision and Allocation of Variable Consideration,* dated 13 July 2015.
34 TRG Agenda paper 39, *Application of the Series Provision and Allocation of Variable Consideration,* dated 13 July 2015.
35 TRG Agenda paper 27, *Series of Distinct Goods or Services,* dated 30 March 2015.
36 TRG Agenda paper 27, *Series of Distinct Goods or Services,* dated 30 March 2015.
37 TRG Agenda paper 34, *March 2015 Meeting – Summary of Issues Discussed and Next Steps,* dated 13 July 2015.
38 TRG Agenda paper 27, *Series of Distinct Goods or Services,* dated 30 March 2015.
39 TRG Agenda paper 27, *Series of Distinct Goods or Services,* dated 30 March 2015 and TRG Agenda paper 34, *March 2015 Meeting – Summary of Issues Discussed and Next Steps,* dated 13 July 2015.
40 TRG Agenda paper 39, *Application of the Series Provision and Allocation of Variable Consideration,* dated 13 July 2015.
41 TRG Agenda paper 39, *Application of the Series Provision and Allocation of Variable Consideration,* dated 13 July 2015.
42 TRG Agenda paper 39, *Application of the Series Provision and Allocation of Variable Consideration,* dated 13 July 2015.
43 TRG Agenda paper 39, *Application of the Series Provision and Allocation of Variable Consideration,* dated 13 July 2015.
44 TRG Agenda paper 2, *Gross versus Net Revenue: Amounts Billed to Customers,* dated 18 July 2014.
45 FASB ASU 2016-08, *Revenue from Contracts with Customers (Topic 606): Principal versus Agent Considerations* (March 2016), paragraph BC38.
46 TRG Agenda paper 6, *Customer options for additional goods and services and nonrefundable upfront fees,* dated 31 October 2014 and TRG Agenda paper 11, *October 2014 Meeting – Summary of Issues Discussed and Next Steps,* dated 26 January 2015.
47 TRG Agenda paper 6, *Customer options for additional goods and services and nonrefundable upfront fees,* dated 31 October 2014 and TRG Agenda paper 11, *October 2014 Meeting – Summary of Issues Discussed and Next Steps,* dated 26 January 2015.
48 TRG Agenda paper 48, *Customer options for additional goods and services,* dated 9 November 2015.
49 TRG Agenda paper 48, *Customer options for additional goods and services,* dated 9 November 2015.
50 TRG Agenda paper 48, *Customer options for additional goods and services,* dated 9 November 2015.
51 TRG Agenda paper 48, *Customer options for additional goods and services,* dated 9 November 2015.
52 TRG Agenda paper 48, *Customer options for additional goods and services,* dated 9 November 2015.
53 TRG Agenda paper 48, *Customer options for additional goods and services,* dated 9 November 2015.
54 FASB TRG Agenda paper 54, *Considering Class of Customer When Evaluating Whether a Customer Option Gives Rise to a Material Right,* dated 18 April 2016.
55 TRG Agenda paper 32, *Accounting for a Customer's Exercise of a Material Right,* dated 30 March 2015.
56 TRG Agenda paper 32, *Accounting for a Customer's Exercise of a Material Right,* dated 30 March 2015.
57 TRG Agenda paper 34, *March 2015 Meeting – Summary of Issues Discussed and Next Steps,* dated 13 July 2015.
58 TRG Agenda paper 34, *March 2015 Meeting – Summary of Issues Discussed and Next Steps,* dated 13 July 2015.

59 TRG Agenda paper 32, *Accounting for a Customer's Exercise of a Material Right,* dated 30 March 2015.
60 TRG Agenda paper 5, *July 2014 Meeting – Summary of Issues Discussed and Next Steps,* originally dated 31 October 2014, reissued 18 March 2015.
61 TRG Agenda paper 39, *Application of the Series Provision and Allocation of Variable Consideration,* dated 13 July 2015.
62 TRG Agenda paper 38, *Portfolio Practical Expedient and Application of Variable Consideration Constraint,* dated 13 July 2015.
63 As defined in US GAAP in the master glossary of the Accounting Standards Codification.
64 TRG Agenda paper 38, *Portfolio Practical Expedient and Application of Variable Consideration Constraint,* dated 13 July 2015.
65 As discussed in ASC 605-25 and SEC Staff Accounting Bulletin Topic 13: *Revenue Recognition.*
66 TRG Agenda paper 14, *Variable Consideration,* dated 26 January 2015 and TRG Agenda paper 25, *January 2015 Meeting – Summary of Issues Discussed and Next Steps,* dated 30 March 2015.
67 TRG Agenda paper 38, *Portfolio Practical Expedient and Application of Variable Consideration Constraint,* dated 13 July 2015.
68 TRG Agenda paper 38, *Portfolio Practical Expedient and Application of Variable Consideration Constraint,* dated 13 July 2015.
69 TRG Agenda paper 35, *Accounting for Restocking Fees and Related Costs,* dated 13 July 2015.
70 TRG Agenda paper 35, *Accounting for Restocking Fees and Related Costs,* dated 13 July 2015.
71 Consistent with the discussions within TRG Agenda paper 30, *Significant Financing Components,* dated 30 March 2015.
72 TRG Agenda paper 30, *Significant Financing Components,* dated 30 March 2015.
73 TRG Agenda paper 34, *March 2015 Meeting – Summary of Issues Discussed and Next Steps,* dated 13 July 2015.
74 TRG Agenda paper 34, *March 2015 Meeting – Summary of Issues Discussed and Next Steps,* dated 13 July 2015.
75 TRG Agenda paper 30, *Significant Financing Components,* dated 30 March 2015.
76 TRG Agenda paper 30, *Significant Financing Components,* dated 30 March 2015 and TRG Agenda paper 34, *March 2015 Meeting – Summary of Issues Discussed and Next Steps,* dated 13 July 2015.
77 TRG Agenda paper 30, *Significant Financing Components,* dated 30 March 2015.
78 TRG Agenda paper 34, *March 2015 Meeting – Summary of Issues Discussed and Next Steps,* dated 13 July 2015.
79 TRG Agenda paper 30, *Significant Financing Components,* dated 30 March 2015 and TRG Agenda paper 34, *March 2015 Meeting – Summary of Issues Discussed and Next Steps,* dated 13 July 2015.
80 TRG Agenda paper 30, *Significant Financing Components,* dated 30 March 2015 and TRG Agenda paper 34, *March 2015 Meeting – Summary of Issues Discussed and Next Steps,* dated 13 July 2015.
81 TRG Agenda paper 28, *Consideration Payable to a Customer,* dated 30 March 2015, TRG Agenda paper 34, *March 2015 Meeting – Summary of Issues Discussed and Next Steps,* dated 13 July 2015 and TRG Agenda paper 37, *Consideration Payable to a Customer,* dated 13 July 2015.
82 TRG Agenda paper 28, *Consideration Payable to a Customer,* dated 30 March 2015, TRG Agenda paper 34, *March 2015 Meeting – Summary of Issues Discussed and Next Steps,* dated 13 July 2015 and TRG Agenda paper 37, *Consideration Payable to a Customer,* dated 13 July 2015.
83 TRG Agenda paper 37, *Consideration Payable to a Customer,* dated 13 July 2015.
84 TRG Agenda paper 44, *July 2015 Meeting – Summary of Issues Discussed and Next Steps,* dated 9 November 2015.
85 TRG Agenda paper 32, *Accounting for a Customer's Exercise of a Material Right,* dated 30 March 2015 and TRG Agenda paper 34, *March 2015 Meeting – Summary of Issues Discussed and Next Steps,* dated 13 July 2015.
86 TRG Agenda paper 39, *Application of the Series Provision and Allocation of Variable Consideration,* dated 13 July 2015.
87 TRG Agenda paper 39, *Application of the Series Provision and Allocation of Variable Consideration,* dated 13 July 2015.
88 TRG Agenda paper 31, *Allocation of the Transaction Price for Discounts and Variable Consideration,* dated 30 March 2015 and TRG Agenda paper 34, *March 2015 Meeting – Summary of Issues Discussed and Next Steps,* dated 13 July 2015.
89 TRG Agenda paper 43, *Determining When Control of a Commodity Transfers,* dated 13 July 2015.
90 TRG Agenda paper 40, *Practical Expedient for Measuring Progress toward Complete Satisfaction of a Performance Obligation,* dated 13 July 2015.

91 TRG Agenda paper 40, *Practical Expedient for Measuring Progress toward Complete Satisfaction of a Performance Obligation,* dated 13 July 2015.
92 TRG Agenda paper 40, *Practical Expedient for Measuring Progress toward Complete Satisfaction of a Performance Obligation,* dated 13 July 2015.
93 TRG Agenda paper 44, *July 2015 Meeting – Summary of Issues Discussed and Next Steps,* dated 9 November 2015.
94 TRG Agenda paper 16, *Stand-Ready Performance Obligations,* dated 26 January 2015 and TRG Agenda paper 25, *January 2015 Meeting – Summary of Issues Discussed and Next Steps,* dated 30 March 2015.
95 TRG Agenda paper 41, *Measuring progress when multiple goods or services are included in a single performance obligation,* dated 13 July 2015.
96 TRG Agenda paper 41, *Measuring progress when multiple goods or services are included in a single performance obligation,* dated 13 July 2015.
97 FASB TRG Agenda paper 53, *Evaluating How Control Transfers Over Time,* dated 18 April 2016.
98 TRG Agenda paper 40, *Practical Expedient for Measuring Progress toward Complete Satisfaction of a Performance Obligation,* dated 13 July 2015.
99 TRG Agenda paper 33, *Partial Satisfaction of Performance Obligations Prior to Identifying the Contract,* dated 30 March 2015.
100 TRG Agenda paper 34, *March 2015 Meeting – Summary of Issues Discussed and Next Steps,* dated 13 July 2015.
101 TRG Agenda paper 45, *Licences – Specific Application Issues About Restrictions and Renewals,* dated 9 November 2015.
102 FASB ASU 2016-10, *Revenue from Contracts with Customers (Topic 606): Identifying Performance Obligations and Licensing,* April 2016, paragraph BC71.
103 TRG Agenda paper 29, *Warranties,* dated 30 March 2015 and TRG Agenda paper 34, *March 2015 Meeting – Summary of Issues Discussed and Next Steps,* dated 13 July 2015.
104 TRG Agenda paper 23, *Incremental costs of obtaining a contract,* dated 26 January 2015.
105 TRG Agenda paper 23, *Incremental costs of obtaining a contract,* dated 26 January 2015.
106 TRG Agenda paper 23, *Incremental costs of obtaining a contract,* dated 26 January 2015.
107 TRG Agenda paper 23, *Incremental costs of obtaining a contract,* dated 26 January 2015.
108 TRG Agenda paper 33, *Partial Satisfaction of Performance Obligations Prior to Identifying the Contract,* dated 30 March 2015 and TRG Agenda paper 34, *March 2015 Meeting – Summary of Issues Discussed and Next Steps,* dated 13 July 2015.
109 TRG Agenda paper 23, *Incremental costs of obtaining a contract,* dated 26 January 2015.
110 TRG Agenda paper 23, *Incremental costs of obtaining a contract,* dated 26 January 2015.
111 TRG Agenda paper 4, *Impairment testing of capitalised contract costs,* dated 18 July 2014.
112 TRG Agenda paper 7, *Presentation of a contract as a contract asset or a contract liability,* dated 31 October 2014 and TRG Agenda paper 11, *October 2014 Meeting – Summary of Issues Discussed and Next Steps,* dated 26 January 2015.
113 TRG Agenda paper 7, *Presentation of a contract as a contract asset or a contract liability,* dated 31 October 2014 and TRG Agenda paper 11, *October 2014 Meeting – Summary of Issues Discussed and Next Steps,* dated 26 January 2015.
114 TRG Agenda paper 7, *Presentation of a contract as a contract asset or a contract liability,* dated 31 October 2014 and TRG Agenda paper 11, *October 2014 Meeting – Summary of Issues Discussed and Next Steps,* dated 26 January 2015.
115 FASB TRG Agenda paper 51, *Contract Asset Treatment in Contract Modifications,* dated 18 April 2016.
116 TRG Agenda paper 40, *Practical Expedient for Measuring Progress toward Complete Satisfaction of a Performance Obligation,* dated 13 July 2015.

Chapter 31 Income taxes

List of examples

Chapter 31 Income taxes

1 INTRODUCTION

1.1 The nature of taxation

Taxation has certain characteristics which set it apart from other business expenses and which might justify a different treatment, in particular:

- tax payments are not typically made in exchange for goods or services specific to the business (as opposed to access to generally available national infrastructure assets and services); and
- the business has no say in whether or not the payments are to be made.

1.2 Allocation between periods

The most significant accounting question which arises in relation to taxation is how to allocate tax expense between accounting periods. The recognition of transactions in the financial statements in a particular period is governed by the application of IFRS. However, the timing of the recognition of transactions for the purposes of measuring the taxable profit is governed by the application of tax law, which sometimes prescribes a treatment different from that used in the financial statements. The generally accepted view is that it is necessary for the financial statements to seek some reconciliation between these different treatments.

Accordingly IFRS requires an entity to recognise, at each reporting date, the tax consequences expected to arise in future periods in respect of the recovery of its assets and settlement of its liabilities recognised at that date. Broadly speaking, those tax consequences that are legal assets or liabilities at the reporting date are referred to as current tax. The other consequences, which are expected to become, or (more strictly) form part of, legal assets or liabilities in a future period, are referred to as deferred tax.

This is illustrated by Example 31.1, which considers the treatment of tax deductions received against the cost of property, plant and equipment (PP&E), and the further discussion in 1.2.1 and 1.2.2, below.

Example 31.1: PP&E attracting tax deductions in advance of accounting depreciation

An item of equipment is purchased on 1 January 2017 for €50,000 and is estimated to have a useful life of five years, at the end of which it will be scrapped. There is no change to the estimated residual amount of zero over the life of the equipment. The depreciation charge will therefore be €10,000 per year for five years.

The entity is tax-resident in a jurisdiction where the corporate tax rate is 30%. No tax deductions are given for depreciation charged in the financial statements. Instead, the cost may be deducted from taxes payable in the year that the asset is purchased. The entity's profit before tax, including the depreciation charge, for each of the five years ended 31 December 2017 to 31 December 2021 is €100,000. All components of pre-tax profit, other than the accounting depreciation, are taxable or tax-deductible.

The entity's tax computations for each year would show the following (all figures in €s)[1]:

	2017	2018	2019	2020	2021
Accounting profit	100,000	100,000	100,000	100,000	100,000
Accounting depreciation	10,000	10,000	10,000	10,000	10,000
Tax depreciation	(50,000)	–	–	–	–
Taxable profit	60,000	110,000	110,000	110,000	110,000
Tax payable @ 30%	18,000	33,000	33,000	33,000	33,000

1.2.1 No provision for deferred tax ('flow through')

If the entity in Example 31.1 above were to account only for the tax legally due in respect of each year ('current tax'), it would report the amounts in the table below in profit or loss. Accounting for current tax only is generally known as the 'flow through' method.

€s	2017	2018	2019	2020	2021	Total
Profit before tax	100,000	100,000	100,000	100,000	100,000	500,000
Current tax	18,000	33,000	33,000	33,000	33,000	150,000
Profit after tax	82,000	67,000	67,000	67,000	67,000	350,000
Effective tax rate (%)	18	33	33	33	33	30

The 'effective tax rate' in the last row of the table above is the ratio, expressed as a percentage, of the profit before tax to the charge for tax in the financial statements, and is regarded as a key performance indicator by many preparers and users of financial statements. As can be seen from the table above, over the full five-year life of the asset, the entity pays tax at the statutory rate of 30% on its total profits of €500,000, but with considerable variation in the effective rate in individual accounting periods.

The generally held view is that simply to account for the tax legally payable as above is distortive, and that the tax should therefore be allocated between periods. Under IAS 12 – *Income Taxes* – this allocation is achieved by means of deferred taxation (see 1.2.2 below).

However, the flow-through method attracts the support of a number of commentators. They argue that the tax authorities impose a single annual tax assessment on the entity based on its profits as determined for tax purposes, not on accounting profits. That assessment is the entity's only liability to tax for that period, and any tax to be assessed in future years is not a present liability as defined in the IASB's *Conceptual Framework.* Supporters of flow-through acknowledge the distortive effect of transactions such as that in Example 31.1 above, but argue that this is better remedied by disclosure than by creating what they see as an 'imaginary' liability for deferred tax.

1.2.2 Provision for deferred tax (the temporary difference approach)

The approach currently required by IAS 12 is known as the temporary difference approach, which focuses on the difference between the carrying amount of an asset or liability in the financial statements and the amount attributed to it for tax purposes, known as its 'tax base'.

In Example 31.1 above, the carrying value of the PP&E in the financial statements at the end of each reporting period is:

€s	2017	2018	2019	2020	2021
PP&E	40,000	30,000	20,000	10,000	–

If the tax authority were to prepare financial statements based on tax law rather than IFRS, it would record PP&E of nil at the end of each period, since the full cost of €50,000 was written off in 2017 for tax purposes. There is therefore a difference, at the end of 2017, of €40,000 between the carrying amount of €40,000 of the asset in the financial statements and its tax base of nil. This difference is referred to as a 'temporary' difference because, by the end of 2021, the carrying value of the PP&E in the financial statements and its tax base are both nil, so that there is no longer a difference between them.

As discussed in more detail later in this Chapter, IAS 12 requires an entity to recognise a liability for deferred tax on the temporary difference arising on the asset, as follows.

€s	2017	2018	2019	2020	2021
Net book value	40,000	30,000	20,000	10,000	–
Tax base	–	–	–	–	–
Temporary difference	40,000	30,000	20,000	10,000	–
Deferred tax[1]	12,000	9,000	6,000	3,000	–
Movement in deferred tax in period	12,000	(3,000)	(3,000)	(3,000)	(3,000)

1 Temporary difference multiplied by tax rate of 30%

IAS 12 argues that, taking the position as at 31 December 2017 as an example, the carrying amount of the PP&E of €40,000 implicitly assumes that the asset will ultimately be recovered or realised by a cash inflow of at least €40,000. Any tax that will be paid on that inflow represents a present liability. In this case, the entity pays tax at 30% and will be unable to make any deduction in respect of the asset for tax purposes in a future period. It will therefore pay tax of €12,000 (30% of €[40,000 – nil]) as the asset is realised. This tax is as much a liability as the PP&E is an asset, since it would be internally inconsistent for the financial statements simultaneously to represent that the asset will be recovered at €40,000 while ignoring the tax consequences of doing so. *[IAS 12.16]*.

The deferred tax liability is recognised in the statement of financial position and any movement in the deferred tax liability during the period is recognised as deferred tax income or expense in profit or loss, with the following impact:

€s	2017	2018	2019	2020	2021	Total
Profit before tax	100,000	100,000	100,000	100,000	100,000	500,000
Current tax	18,000	33,000	33,000	33,000	33,000	150,000
Deferred tax	12,000	(3,000)	(3,000)	(3,000)	(3,000)	–
Total tax	30,000	30,000	30,000	30,000	30,000	150,000
Profit after tax	70,000	70,000	70,000	70,000	70,000	350,000
Effective tax rate (%)	30	30	30	30	30	30

It can be seen that the effect of accounting for deferred tax is to present an effective tax rate of 30% in profit or loss for each period. As will become apparent later in the Chapter, there is some tension in practice between the stated objective of IAS 12 (to recognise the appropriate amount of tax assets and liabilities in the statement of financial position) and what many users and preparers see as the real objective of IAS 12 (to match the tax effects of a transaction with the recognition of its pre-tax effects in the statement of comprehensive income or equity).

This tension arises in part because earlier methods of accounting for income tax, which explicitly focused on tax income and expense ('income statement approaches') rather than tax assets and liabilities ('balance sheet approaches'), remain part of the professional 'DNA' of many preparers and users. Moreover, as will be seen later in the Chapter, a number of aspects of IAS 12 are difficult to reconcile to the purported balance sheet approach of the standard, because, in reality, they are relics of the now superseded income statement approaches.

1.3 The development of IAS 12

The current version of IAS 12 was published in October 1996, and has been amended by a number of subsequent pronouncements. IAS 12 is based on the same principles as the US GAAP guidance (FASB ASC Topic 740 – *Income Taxes*). However, there are important differences of methodology between the two standards which can lead to significant differences between the amounts recorded under IAS 12 and US GAAP. Some of the main differences between the standards are noted at relevant points in the discussion below.

In July 2000, the SIC issued an interpretation of IAS 12, SIC-25 – *Income Taxes – Changes in the Tax Status of an Entity or its Shareholders* (see 10.9 below).[2]

In March 2009 the IASB issued an exposure draft (ED/2009/2 – *Income Tax*) of a standard to replace IAS 12. This was poorly received by commentators and there is no prospect of a new standard in this form being issued in the foreseeable future. Nevertheless, the IASB continues to consider possible limited changes to IAS 12 with the aim of improving it or clarifying its existing provisions.

In December 2010, the IASB issued an amendment to IAS 12 – *Deferred Tax: Recovery of Underlying Assets*. The amendment addressed the measurement of deferred tax associated with non-depreciable revalued property, plant and equipment and investment properties accounted for at fair value (see 8.4.6 and 8.4.7 below).

In October 2015 the Interpretations Committee published a Draft Interpretation, DI/2015/1 – *Uncertainty over Income Tax Treatments,* on the recognition and measurement of uncertain tax treatments. At the time of writing, the responses to these proposals are being deliberated by the Committee. In January 2016 it issued *Recognition of Deferred Tax Assets for Unrealised Losses (Amendments to IAS 12)* – in relation to the recognition of deferred tax assets for losses on debt securities measured at fair value and related clarifications to the guidance on determining future taxable profits and applicable for annual periods beginning on or after 1 January 2017 (with earlier application permitted, provided that this fact is disclosed). These are discussed respectively at 9 and at 7.4.5 below.

1.3.1 References to income taxes in standards other than IAS 12

There are numerous references in other standards and interpretations to income taxes, the more significant of which are noted at relevant points in the discussion below. In particular, the requirements of IFRS for accounting for income taxes in interim financial statements are discussed in Chapter 39 at 9.5.

2 OBJECTIVE AND SCOPE OF IAS 12

2.1 Objective

The stated objective of IAS 12 is 'to prescribe the accounting treatment for income taxes. The principal issue in accounting for income taxes is how to account for the current and future tax consequences of:

(a) the future recovery (settlement) of the carrying amount of assets (liabilities) that are recognised in an entity's statement of financial position; and

(b) transactions and other events of the current period that are recognised in an entity's financial statements.' *[IAS 12 Objective]*.

IAS 12 requires this approach (the 'temporary difference approach') to be adopted, on the grounds that it is inherent in the recognition of an asset or liability that the reporting entity expects to recover or settle the carrying amount of that asset or liability. IAS 12 requires an entity to consider whether it is probable that recovery or settlement of that carrying amount will result in future tax payments larger (or smaller) than they would be if such recovery or settlement had no tax consequences. *[IAS 12.10, 16, 25]*. If it is probable that such a larger or smaller tax payment will arise, in most cases IAS 12 requires an entity to recognise a deferred tax liability or deferred tax asset. This is discussed further at 3 to 9 and 11 below.

IAS 12 also requires an entity to account for the tax consequences of transactions and other events in a manner consistent with the accounting treatment of the transactions and other events themselves. *[IAS 12 Objective]*. In other words:

- tax effects of transactions and other events recognised in profit or loss are also recognised in profit or loss;
- tax effects of transactions and other events recognised in other comprehensive income are also recognised in other comprehensive income;
- tax effects of transactions and other events recognised directly in equity are also recognised directly in equity; and
- deferred tax assets and liabilities recognised in a business combination affect:
  - the amount of goodwill arising in that business combination; or
  - the amount of the bargain purchase gain recognised.[3]

This is discussed in more detail at 10 and 12 below.

Finally the standard deals with:

- the recognition of deferred tax assets arising for unused tax losses or unused tax credits (see 7.4.6 below);
- the presentation of income taxes in financial statements (see 13 below); and
- the disclosure of information relating to income taxes (see 14 below).

IAS 12 requires an entity to account for the tax consequences of recovering assets or settling liabilities at their carrying amount in the statement of financial position, not for the total tax expected to be paid (which will reflect the amount at which the asset or liability is actually settled, not its carrying amount at the reporting date).

IAS 12 may require an entity to recognise tax even on an accounting transaction that is not itself directly taxable, where the transaction gives rise to an asset (or liability) whose recovery (or settlement) will have tax consequences. For example, an entity might revalue a property. If (as is the case in many tax jurisdictions) no tax is payable on the revaluation, one might conclude that it has no tax effect. However, this is not the correct analysis under IAS 12, which focuses not on whether the revaluation itself is directly taxed, but rather on whether the profits out of which the increased carrying value of the property will be recovered will be subsequently taxed. This is discussed further at 8.4 below.

2.2 Overview

The overall requirements of IAS 12 can be summarised as follows:

- determine whether a tax is an 'income tax' (see 4 below);
- recognise income tax due or receivable in respect of the current period (current tax), measured using enacted or substantively enacted legislation (see 5 below), and having regard to any uncertain tax treatments (see 9 below);
- determine whether there are temporary differences between the carrying amount of assets and liabilities and their tax bases (see 6 below), having regard to the expected manner of recovery of assets or settlement of liabilities (see 8 below);
- determine whether there are unused tax losses or investment tax credits;
- determine whether IAS 12 prohibits or restricts recognition of deferred tax on any temporary differences or unused tax losses or investment tax credits (see 7 below);
- recognise deferred tax on all temporary differences, unused tax losses or investment tax credits not subject to such a prohibition or restriction (see 7 below), measured using enacted or substantively enacted legislation (see 8 below), and having regard to:
  - the expected manner of recovery of assets and settlement of liabilities (see 8 below); and
  - any uncertain tax treatments (see 9 below);
- allocate any income tax charge or credit for the period to profit or loss, other comprehensive income and equity (see 10 below);
- present income tax in the financial statements as required by IAS 12 (see 13 below); and
- make the disclosures required by IAS 12 (see 14 below).

3 DEFINITIONS

IAS 12 uses the following terms with the meanings specified below. *[IAS 12.1, 2, 5]*.

Income taxes include all domestic and foreign taxes which are based on taxable profits. Income taxes also include taxes, such as withholding taxes, which are payable by a subsidiary, associate or joint arrangement on distributions to the reporting entity.

Accounting profit is profit or loss for a period before deducting tax expense.

Taxable profit (tax loss) is the profit (loss) for a period, determined in accordance with the rules established by the taxation authorities, upon which income taxes are payable (recoverable).

Tax expense (tax income) is the aggregate amount included in the determination of profit or loss for the period in respect of current tax and deferred tax.

Current tax is the amount of income taxes payable (recoverable) in respect of the taxable profit (tax loss) for a period.

Deferred tax liabilities are the amounts of income taxes payable in future periods in respect of *taxable temporary differences* (see below).

Deferred tax assets are the amounts of income taxes recoverable in future periods in respect of *deductible temporary differences* (see below), together with the carryforward of unused tax losses and tax credits.

Temporary differences are differences between the carrying amount of an asset or liability in the statement of financial position and its *tax base*. Temporary differences may be either:

- *taxable temporary differences*, which are temporary differences that will result in taxable amounts in determining taxable profit (tax loss) of future periods when the carrying amount of the asset or liability is recovered or settled; or
- *deductible temporary differences*, which are temporary differences that will result in amounts that are deductible in determining taxable profit (tax loss) of future periods when the carrying amount of the asset or liability is recovered or settled.

The *tax base* of an asset or liability is the amount attributed to that asset or liability for tax purposes.

4 SCOPE

IAS 12 should be applied in accounting for income taxes, defined as including:

- all domestic and foreign taxes which are based on taxable profits; and
- taxes, such as withholding taxes, which are payable by a subsidiary, associate or joint arrangement on distributions to the reporting entity. *[IAS 12.1-2]*.

IAS 12 does not apply to accounting for government grants, which fall within the scope of IAS 20 – *Accounting for Government Grants and Disclosure of Government Assistance*, or investment tax credits. However, it does deal with the accounting for any temporary differences that may arise from grants or investment tax credits. *[IAS 12.4]*.

A tax classified as an income tax is accounted for under IAS 12. Taxes other than income taxes are accounted for under IAS 37 – *Provisions, Contingent Liabilities and Contingent Assets* – and, in particular, IFRIC 21 – *Levies*. The classification of a tax as an income tax affects its accounting treatment in several key respects:

- *Deferred tax*

  IAS 12 requires an entity to account for deferred tax in respect of income taxes. IAS 37 has no equivalent requirement for other taxes, recognising only legal or constructive obligations.

- *Recognition and measurement*

  IAS 12 requires tax to be recognised and measured according to a relatively tightly-defined accounting model. IAS 37 requires a provision to be recognised only where it is more likely than not that an outflow of resources will occur as a result of a past obligating event, and measured at the best estimate of the amount expected to be paid.

- *Presentation*

  IAS 1 – *Presentation of Financial Statements* – requires income tax assets, liabilities, income and expense to be presented in separate headings in profit or loss and the statement of financial position. There is no requirement for separate presentation of other taxes, but neither can they be included within the captions for 'income taxes'.
- *Disclosure*

  IAS 12 requires disclosures for income taxes significantly more detailed than those required by IAS 37 for other taxes.

4.1 What is an 'income tax'?

This is not as clear as might be expected, since the definition is circular. Income tax is defined as a tax based on 'taxable profits', which are in turn defined as profits 'upon which income taxes are payable' (see 3 above).

It seems clear that those taxes that take as their starting profit the total net profit or loss before appropriations are income taxes. However, several jurisdictions raise 'taxes' on sub-components of net profit. These include:

- sales taxes;
- goods and services taxes;
- value added taxes;
- levies on the sale or extraction of minerals and other natural resources;
- taxes on certain goods as they reach a given state of production or are moved from one location to another; or
- taxes on gross production margins.

Taxes that are simply collected by the entity from one third party (generally a customer or employee) on behalf of another third party (generally local or national government) are generally not regarded as 'income taxes' for the purposes of IAS 12. This view is supported by the requirement of IAS 18 – *Revenue* – that taxes which are collected from customers by the entity on behalf of third parties do not form part of the entity's revenue, *[IAS 18.8]*, (and therefore, by implication, are not an expense of the entity either). IFRS 15 – *Revenue from Contracts with Customers* – similarly excludes such sales taxes from revenue. *[IFRS 15.47]*.

In cases where such taxes are a liability of the entity, they may often have some characteristics both of production or sales taxes (in that they are payable at a particular stage in the production or extraction process and may well be allowed as an expense in arriving at the tax on net profits) and of income taxes (in that they may be determined after deduction of certain allowable expenditure). This makes the classification of such taxes (as income taxes or not) difficult – see, for example, the discussion in Chapter 41 at 19.

In March 2006 the Interpretations Committee considered whether to give guidance on which taxes are within the scope of IAS 12. The Committee noted that the definition of 'income tax' in IAS 12 (i.e. taxes that are based on taxable profit) implies that:

- not all taxes are within the scope of IAS 12; but
- because taxable profit is not the same as accounting profit, taxes do not need to be based on a figure that is exactly accounting profit to be within the scope of IAS 12.

The latter point is also implied by the requirement in IAS 12 to disclose an explanation of the relationship between tax expense and accounting profit – see 14.2 below. *[IAS 12.81(c)]*. The Interpretations Committee further noted that the term 'taxable profit' implies a notion of a net rather than gross amount, and that any taxes that are not in the scope of IAS 12 are in the scope of IAS 37 (see Chapter 28).

The Interpretations Committee drew attention to the variety of taxes that exist across the world and the need for judgement in determining whether some taxes are income taxes. The Committee therefore believed that guidance beyond the observations noted above could not be developed in a reasonable period of time and decided not to take a project on this issue onto its agenda.[4]

The Interpretations Committee's deliberations reinforce the difficulty of formulating a single view as to the treatment of taxes. The appropriate treatment will need to be addressed on a case-by-case basis depending on the particular terms of the tax concerned and the entity's own circumstances.

Where a tax is levied on multiple components of net income, it is more likely that the tax should be viewed as substantially a tax on income and therefore subject to IAS 12. Even where such taxes are not income taxes, if they are deductible against current or future income taxes, they may nevertheless give rise to tax assets which do fall within the scope of IAS 12.

4.1.1 Levies

A number of governments have recently introduced levies on certain types of entity, particularly those in the financial services sector. In many cases the levies are expressed as a percentage of a measure of revenue or net assets, or some component(s) of revenue or net assets, at a particular date. Such levies are not income taxes and should be accounted for in accordance with IAS 37 and IFRIC 21 (see Chapter 28 at 6.8).

4.1.2 Hybrid taxes (including minimum taxes)

Some jurisdictions impose income taxes which are charged as a percentage of taxable profits in the normal way, but are subject to a requirement that a minimum amount of tax must be paid. This minimum may be an absolute amount or a proportion of one or more components of the statement of financial position – for example, total equity as reported in the financial statements, or total share capital and additional paid-in capital (share premium).

Such taxes raise the issue of how they should be accounted for. One view would be that the fixed minimum element is not an income tax and should be accounted for under IAS 37, but any excess above the fixed minimum element is an income tax which should be accounted for under IAS 12.

There is a logical elegance to this approach, but it has the significant practical disadvantage that the future rate of tax accounted for as income tax is unpredictable, as it will depend on the level of profit in future periods. Suppose for example that an entity is required to pay tax at 30% on its taxable profit, but subject to a minimum tax of €100,000 per year. If its taxable profits were €1 million, it would pay tax of €300,000 (€1,000,000 at 30%). Under this approach, this €300,000 would be accounted for as comprising a minimum (non-income) tax of €100,000 and income tax of €200,000. The effective rate of tax accounted for as income tax would be 20% (€200,000/€1,000,000). If, however, the entity's taxable profits were €2,000,000 it would pay tax of €600,000 (€2,000,000 at 30%). In this case, this €600,000 would be accounted for as comprising a minimum (non-income) tax of €100,000 and income tax of €500,000. The effective rate of tax accounted for as income tax would be 25% (€500,000/€2,000,000). This illustrates that, in order to calculate deferred income taxes for the purposes of IAS 12, any future income tax rate would be subject to constant re-estimation, even if the 'headline' rate were a known enacted rate.

Some therefore favour an alternative analysis which would be to consider the overall substance of the tax. Those who take this view would argue that, if it is apparent that the overall intention of the legislation is to levy taxes based on income, but subject to a floor, the tax should be accounted for as an income tax in its entirety, even if the floor would not be an income tax if considered in isolation.

In our view, either of these broad approaches can be adopted so long as it is applied consistently to all taxes of a similar nature in all periods. We would generally expect a common approach to be applied to the same tax in the same jurisdiction.

4.2 Withholding and similar taxes

As noted at 4.1 above, IAS 12 also includes in its scope those taxes, such as withholding taxes, which are payable by a subsidiary, associate or joint arrangement on distributions to the reporting entity. *[IAS 12.2]*. This gives rise to further questions of interpretation.

The most basic issue is what is meant by a 'withholding tax'. This is discussed at 10.3.2 and 10.3.4 below.

A second issue is whether the scope of IAS 12 covers only taxes on distributions from a subsidiary, associate or joint arrangement, or whether it extends to tax on distributions from other entities in which the reporting entity has an investment. Such an investment will typically be accounted for at fair value under IAS 39 – *Financial Instruments: Recognition and Measurement* – or, where applied, IFRS 9 – *Financial Instruments.*

The rationale for the treatment as income taxes of taxes payable by a subsidiary, associate or joint arrangement on distributions to the investor is discussed further at 7.5 below. Essentially, however, the reason for considering withholding taxes within the scope of income tax accounting derives from the accounting treatment of the investments themselves. The accounting treatment for such investments – whether by full consolidation or the equity method – results in the investor recognising profit that may be taxed twice: once as it is earned by the investee entity concerned, and again as that entity distributes the profit as dividend to the investor. IAS 12 ensures that the financial statements reflect both tax consequences.

Some argue that this indicates a general principle that an entity should account for all the tax consequences of realising the income of an investee as that income is recognised. On this analysis withholding taxes suffered on any investment income should be treated as income taxes. Others argue that the reference in IAS 12 to distributions from 'a subsidiary, associate or joint arrangement' should be read restrictively, and that no wider general principle is implied. In addition, because the amount of the tax relates to a single component of the investor entity's income, it can be argued that (without the specific reference to a 'withholding tax') such amounts are not within the scope of IAS 12 because they are not 'based on taxable profits', *[IAS 12.2]*, (see 4.1 above).

We believe that judgement is required to decide whether a tax deducted from investment income at the source of the income is a withholding tax in the scope of IAS 12. As well as the considerations noted above, the decision requires consideration of all the relevant facts and circumstances of the jurisdiction that levies the tax, especially the national tax legislation and the design of the investor entity. If it is determined that the tax withheld from investment income is within the scope of IAS 12, any non-refundable portion of such withholding taxes is recognised as a tax expense in the statement of comprehensive income. In addition, the entity should apply all the provisions of IAS 12 for current and deferred taxes, including recognition, measurement, presentation and disclosure.

Accordingly, an entity may determine that it should treat as income taxes the withholding taxes that could potentially be suffered on distributions from all investments, not just subsidiaries, associates and joint arrangements. Whether or not any tax liability is recognised will depend on an analysis of the facts and circumstances in each particular case, in particular whether the investment concerned is expected to be recovered through receipt of dividend income or through sale (see 8.4 below).

4.3 Investment tax credits

Investment tax credits are not defined in IAS 12, but for the purposes of the following discussion they are taken to comprise government assistance and incentives for specific kinds of business activity and investment delivered through the tax system. Investment tax credits can take different forms and be subject to different conditions. Sometimes a tax credit is given as a deductible expense in computing the entity's tax liability, and sometimes as a deduction from the entity's tax liability, rather than as a deductible expense. In some cases, the value of the credit is chargeable to income taxes and in others it is not.

Entitlement to receive investment tax credits can be determined in a variety of ways. Some investment tax credits may relate to direct investment in property, plant and equipment. Other entities may receive investment tax credits relating to research and development or other specific activities. Some credits may be realisable only through a reduction in current or future income taxes payable, while others may be settled directly in cash if the entity does not have sufficient income taxes payable to offset the credit within a certain period. Access to the credit may be limited according to total taxes paid (i.e. including taxes such as payroll and sales taxes remitted to government in addition to income taxes). There may be other conditions associated with receiving the investment tax credit, for example with respect to the conduct and continuing activities of the entity, and the credit may become repayable if ongoing conditions are not met.

As noted at 4 above, investment tax credits are not within the scope of IAS 12 (although any temporary differences that arise from them are in the scope of the standard). Moreover, government assistance that is either provided by way of a reduction in taxable income, or determined or limited according to an entity's income tax liability, is excluded from the scope of IAS 20. *[IAS 20.2]*. Conversely, government assistance that is not determined or limited by reference to an entity's liability to income taxes falls within the scope of IAS 20 and should therefore be accounted for as a government grant (see Chapter 26 at 2.3.1).

The fact that both IAS 20 and IAS 12 exclude from their scope those investment tax credits that are realisable only through a reduction in current or future income taxes payable does not prohibit an entity from applying either standard in accounting for such credits. Indeed, either IAS 12 or IAS 20 will generally provide an appropriate accounting framework, by analogy under the 'GAAP hierarchy' in IAS 8 – *Accounting Policies, Changes in Accounting Estimates and Errors* (see Chapter 3).

Which standard provides the better accounting model in a particular case is a matter of judgement. In our view, such a judgement would be informed by reference to the specific terms of the arrangement including the following factors:

Feature of credit	**Indicator of IAS 12 treatment**	**Indicator of IAS 20 treatment**
Method of realisation	Only available as a reduction in income taxes payable (i.e. benefit is forfeit if there are insufficient income taxes payable). However, the longer the period allowed for carrying forward unused credits, the less relevant this indicator becomes.	Directly settled in cash where there are insufficient taxable profits to allow credit to be fully offset, or available for set off against payroll taxes, sales taxes or amounts owed to government other than income taxes payable.
Number of conditions not related to tax position (e.g. minimum employment, manner of ongoing use of purchased assets)	None or few	Many
Restrictions as to nature of expenditure required to receive the grant	Broad criteria encompassing many different types of qualifying expenditure	Highly specific
Tax status of grant income	Not taxable	Taxable

In group accounts, in which entities from a number of different jurisdictions may be consolidated, it is desirable that each particular investment tax credit should be consistently accounted for, either as an IAS 12 income tax or as a government grant under IAS 20. However, the fact that judgment is required in making this determination may mean that predominant practice in a particular jurisdiction for a specific type of investment tax credit has evolved differently from predominant practice in another jurisdiction for a substantially similar credit. We believe that, in determining whether IAS 12 or IAS 20 should be applied, an entity should consider the following factors in the order listed below:

- the predominant local treatment for a specific credit in the relevant tax jurisdiction;
- if there is no predominant local treatment, the group-wide accounting policy for such a credit; and
- in the absence of a predominant local treatment or a group-wide accounting policy, the indicators listed in the table above should provide guidance.

This may occasionally mean that an entity operating in a number of territories adopts different accounting treatments for apparently similar arrangements in different countries, but it at least ensures a measure of comparability between different entities operating in the same tax jurisdiction. Similar considerations apply in determining the meaning of 'substantively enacted' legislation in different jurisdictions (see 5.1 below).

Where a tax credit is accounted for as an income tax, the incentive should be recognised as a reduction in current income tax (up to the amount of the incentive that has already been used) as soon as:

- there is reasonable assurance that the entity will comply with all the conditions of the tax credit; and
- the tax credit becomes allowable against the income tax liability of the current or preceding years.

A deferred tax asset will be recognised for any unused tax credits (up to the amount of incentive that has already been made available) to the extent that:

- there is reasonable assurance that the entity will comply with all the conditions of the tax credit; and
- it is probable that future taxable profit will be available against which the unused tax credits can be utilised.

Reasonable assurance requires persuasive evidence that each of the conditions that must be met will in fact be met.

For incentives related to the initial recognition of assets (i.e. not relating to items expensed for accounting purposes), it would also be acceptable, as an alternative to immediate recognition in profit or loss, to treat the tax credit as an adjustment to the tax base of the asset. If this alternative approach is taken, the initial recognition exception would apply to prohibit recognition of the excess of the tax base over the accounting carrying value. The subsequent accounting would then be similar to the accounting followed for a super-deductible asset. The treatment of super-deductible assets is discussed further at 7.2.6 below.

4.4 Interest and penalties

Many tax regimes provide for interest and/or penalties to be paid on late payments of tax. This raises the question of whether or not such penalties fall within the scope of IAS 12. The issue is primarily one of presentation in the income statement. If such penalties and interest fall within the scope of IAS 12, they are presented as part of tax expense. If they do not fall within the scope of IAS 12, they should be included within profit before tax.

Some argue that penalties and interest have the characteristics of tax – they are paid to the tax authorities under tax legislation and in many jurisdictions are not a tax-deductible expense. Others contend that penalties and interest are distinct from the main tax liability and should not therefore form part of tax expense. Those who hold this view would point out, for example, that under IFRS the unwinding of the discount on discounted items is generally accounted for separately from the discounted expense.

The Interpretations Committee considered this issue in June 2004. It decided not to add the issue to its agenda, given that the disclosure requirements of IAS 12 and IAS 1 provide adequate transparency of these items.[5] The reference to IAS 12 indicates that the Interpretations Committee at the very least does not consider it inappropriate to account for interest and penalties as income taxes under IAS 12. Moreover, in the exposure draft of a possible replacement for IAS 12 issued in 2009, the IASB proposed that an entity should make an accounting policy decision whether to classify interest and penalties payable to tax authorities as tax expense.[6]

In our view:

- Where interest and penalties are not deductible in determining taxable income, there are reasonable grounds for treating them as either part of the tax charge or as an expense in arriving at profit before tax. Entities should determine their accounting policy for such items and apply it consistently.
- Where interest and penalties are tax-deductible, we believe that it is more generally appropriate to treat them as an expense in arriving at profit before tax.

4.5 Effectively tax-free entities

In a number of jurisdictions, certain classes of entity are exempt from income tax, and accordingly are not within the scope of IAS 12.

However, a more typical, and more complex, situation is that tax legislation has the effect that certain classes of entities, whilst not formally designated as 'tax-free' in law, are nevertheless exempt from tax provided that they meet certain conditions that, in practice, they are almost certain to meet. A common example is that, in many jurisdictions, investment vehicles pay no tax, provided that they distribute all, or a minimum percentage, of their earnings to investors.

Accounting for the tax affairs of such entities raises a number of challenges, as discussed further at 8.5.1 below.

5 CURRENT TAX

Current tax is the amount of income taxes payable (recoverable) in respect of the taxable profit (tax loss) for a period. *[IAS 12.5]*.

Current tax for current and prior periods should, to the extent unpaid, be recognised as a liability. If the amount already paid in respect of current and prior periods exceeds the amount due for those periods, the excess should be recognised as an asset. *[IAS 12.12]*.

The benefit relating to a tax loss that can be carried back to recover current tax of a previous period should be recognised as an asset. When a tax loss is used to recover current tax of a previous period, an entity recognises the benefit as an asset in the period in which the tax loss occurs because it is probable that the benefit will flow to the entity and the benefit can be reliably measured. *[IAS 12.13-14]*.

Current tax should be measured at the amount expected to be paid to or recovered from the tax authorities by reference to tax rates and laws that have been enacted or substantively enacted by the end of the reporting period. *[IAS 12.46]*.

5.1 Enacted or substantively enacted tax legislation

IAS 12 requires current tax to be measured using tax rates or laws enacted 'or substantively enacted' at the end of the reporting period. The standard comments that, in some jurisdictions, announcements of tax rates (and tax laws) by the government have the substantive effect of actual enactment, which may follow the announcement by a period of several months. In these circumstances, tax assets and liabilities are measured using the announced tax rate (and tax laws). *[IAS 12.48]*.

IAS 12 gives no guidance as to how this requirement is to be interpreted in different jurisdictions and both the IASB and the Interpretations Committee have resisted various requests for it. In most jurisdictions, however, a consensus has emerged as to the meaning of 'substantive enactment' for that jurisdiction (see 5.1.1 below). Nevertheless, apparently similar legislative processes in different jurisdictions may give rise to different treatments under IAS 12. For example, in most jurisdictions, tax legislation requires the formal approval of the head of state in order to become law. However, in some jurisdictions the head of state has real executive power (and could potentially not approve the legislation), whereas in others the head of state has a more ceremonial role (and cannot practically fail to approve the legislation).

The view tends to be that in those jurisdictions where the head of state has executive power, legislation is not substantively enacted until actually enacted by the head of state. Where, however, the head of state's powers are more ceremonial, substantive enactment is generally regarded as occurring at the stage of the legislative process where no further amendment is possible.

This test of 'substantive enactment' is applied very strictly. IAS 10 – *Events after the Reporting Period* – identifies the enactment or announcement of a change in tax rates and laws after the end of the reporting period as an example of a non-adjusting event. *[IAS 10.22(h)]*. For example, an entity with a reporting period ending on 31 December issuing its financial statements on 20 April the following year would measure its tax assets and liabilities by reference to tax rates and laws enacted or substantively enacted as at 31 December even if these had changed significantly before 20 April. However, the entity would have to disclose the nature of those changes and provide an estimate of the financial effect of those changes if the impact is expected to be significant (see 14.2 below). *[IAS 10.21]*.

5.1.1 Meaning of substantive enactment in various jurisdictions

The following table summarises the meaning of 'substantive enactment' in various jurisdictions as generally understood in those jurisdictions.[7]

Country	Point of substantive enactment
United Kingdom	A Finance Bill has been passed by the House of Commons and is awaiting only passage through the House of Lords and Royal Assent. Alternatively, a resolution having statutory effect has been passed under the Provisional Collection of Taxes Act 1968.
Canada	If there is a majority government, substantive enactment generally occurs with respect to proposed amendments to the Federal Income Tax Act when detailed draft legislation has been tabled for first reading in Parliament. If there is a minority government, proposed amendments to the Federal Income Tax Act would not normally be considered to be substantively enacted until the proposals have passed the third reading in the House of Commons.
Australia	The Bill has passed through both Houses of Parliament (but before Royal Assent).
France	Signature of the legislation by the executive.
Germany	The Bundestag and Bundesrat pass the legislation.
Japan	The Diet passes the legislation.
United States	The legislation is signed by the President or there is a successful override vote by both houses of Congress.
South Africa	Changes in tax rates not inextricably linked to other changes in tax law are substantively enacted when announced in the Minister of Finance's Budget statement. Other changes in tax rates and tax laws are substantively enacted when approved by Parliament and signed by the President.

5.2 Uncertain tax treatments

In recording the 'amount expected to be paid or recovered' as required by IAS 12, the entity will need to have regard to any uncertain tax treatments. 'Uncertain tax treatment' (or 'uncertain tax position') is not defined in IAS 12, but is generally understood in practice to refer to an item, the tax treatment of which is unclear or is a matter of unresolved dispute between the reporting entity and the relevant tax authority. An uncertain tax treatment generally occurs where there is an uncertainty as to the meaning of the tax law, or to the applicability of the law to a particular transaction, or both.

Accounting for uncertain tax treatments is a particularly challenging aspect of accounting for tax. In October 2015, the Interpretations Committee issued DI/2015/1 – *Uncertainty over Income Tax Treatments*, as discussed at 9 below.

5.3 'Prior year adjustments' of previously presented tax balances and expense (income)

The determination of the tax liability for all but the most straightforward entities is a complex process. It may be several years after the end of a reporting period before the tax liability for that period is finally agreed with the tax authorities and settled. Therefore, the tax liability initially recorded at the end of the reporting period to which it relates is no more than a best estimate at that time, which will typically require revision in subsequent periods until the liability is finally settled.

Tax practitioners often refer to such revisions as 'prior year adjustments' and regard them as part of the overall tax charge or credit for the current reporting period whatever their nature. However, for financial reporting purposes, the normal provisions of IAS 8 (see Chapter 3) apply to tax balances and the related expense (income). Therefore, the nature of any revision to a previously stated tax balance should be considered to determine whether the revision represents:

- a correction of a material prior period error (in which case it should be accounted for retrospectively, with a restatement of comparative amounts and, where applicable, the opening balance of assets, liabilities and equity at the start of the earliest period presented); *[IAS 8.42]* or
- a refinement in the current period of an estimate made in a previous period (in which case it should be accounted for in the current period). *[IAS 8.36]*.

In some cases the distinction is clear. If, for example, the entity used an incorrect substantively enacted tax rate (see 5.1 above) to calculate the liability in a previous period, the correction of that rate would – subject to materiality – be a prior year adjustment. A more difficult area is the treatment of accounting changes to reflect the resolution of uncertain tax treatments (see 5.2 above). These have in practice almost always been treated as measurement adjustments in the current period. However, a view could be taken that the eventual denial, or acceptance, by the tax authorities of a position taken by the taxpayer indicates that one or other party (or both of them) were previously taking an erroneous view of the tax law. As with other aspects of accounting for uncertain tax treatments, this is an area where judgement may be required. The Draft Interpretation on uncertainty over income tax treatments suggests that entities would reassess judgements and estimates in response to a change in facts and circumstances, and that the financial effect would be recognised in the period of change[8] (see 9.5 below).

5.4 Intra-period allocation, presentation and disclosure

The allocation of current tax income and expense to components of total comprehensive income and equity is discussed at 10 below. The presentation and disclosure of current tax income expense and assets and liabilities are discussed at 13 and 14 below.

6 DEFERRED TAX – TAX BASES AND TEMPORARY DIFFERENCES

All deferred tax liabilities and many deferred tax assets represent the tax effects of temporary differences. Therefore, the first step in measuring deferred tax is to identify all temporary differences. The discussion in section 6 of this Chapter addresses only whether a temporary difference exists. It does not necessarily follow that deferred tax is recognised in respect of that difference, since there are a number of situations, discussed at 7 below, in which IAS 12 prohibits the recognition of deferred tax on a temporary difference.

Temporary differences are differences between the carrying amount of an asset or liability in the statement of financial position and its *tax base*. Temporary differences may be either:

- *taxable temporary differences*, which result in taxable amounts in determining taxable profit (tax loss) of future periods when the carrying amount of the asset or liability is recovered or settled; or
- *deductible temporary differences,* which result in amounts that are deductible in determining taxable profit (tax loss) of future periods when the carrying amount of the asset or liability is recovered or settled.

The *tax base* of an asset or liability is 'the amount attributed to that asset or liability for tax purposes'. *[IAS 12.5].*

In consolidated financial statements, temporary differences are determined by comparing the carrying amounts of an asset or liability in the consolidated financial statements with the appropriate tax base. The appropriate tax base is determined:

- in those jurisdictions in which a consolidated tax return is filed, by reference to that return; and
- in other jurisdictions, by reference to the tax returns of each entity in the group. *[IAS 12.11].*

As the definition of tax base is the one on which all the others relating to deferred tax ultimately depend, understanding it is key to a proper interpretation of IAS 12. A more detailed discussion follows at 6.1 and 6.2 below. However, the overall effect of IAS 12 can be summarised as follows:

A *taxable* temporary difference will arise when:

- *The carrying amount of an asset is higher than its tax base*

  For example, an item of PP&E is recorded in the financial statements at €8,000, but has a tax base of only €7,000. In future periods, tax will be paid on €1,000 more profit than will be recognised in the financial statements (since €1,000 of the remaining accounting depreciation is not tax-deductible).
- *The carrying amount of a liability is lower than its tax base*

  For example, a loan payable of €100,000 is recorded in the financial statements at €99,000, net of issue costs of €1,000 which have already been allowed for tax purposes (so that the loan is regarded as having a tax base of €100,000 – see 6.2.1.B below). In future periods, tax will be paid on €1,000 more profit than is recognised in the financial statements (since the €1,000 issue costs will be charged to the income statement but not be eligible for further tax deductions).

Conversely, a *deductible* temporary difference will arise when:

- *The carrying amount of an asset is lower than its tax base*

  For example, an item of PP&E is recorded in the financial statements at €7,000, but has a tax base of €8,000. In future periods, tax will be paid on €1,000 less profit than is recognised in the financial statements (since tax deductions will be claimed in respect of €1,000 more depreciation than is charged to the income statement in those future periods).

- *The carrying amount of a liability is higher than its tax base*

  For example, the financial statements record a liability for unfunded pension costs of €2 million. A tax deduction is available only as cash is paid to settle the liability (so that the liability is regarded as having a tax base of nil – see 6.2.2.A below). In future periods, tax will be paid on €2 million less profit than is recognised in the financial statements (since tax deductions will be claimed in respect of €2 million more expense than is charged to the income statement in those future periods).

This may be summarised in the following table.

Asset/liability	**Carrying amount higher or lower than tax base?**	**Nature of temporary difference**	**Resulting deferred tax (if recognised)**
Asset	Higher	Taxable	Liability
Asset	Lower	Deductible	Asset
Liability	Higher	Deductible	Asset
Liability	Lower	Taxable	Liability

6.1 Tax base

6.1.1 Tax base of assets

The tax base of an asset is the amount that will be deductible for tax purposes against any taxable economic benefits that will flow to an entity when it recovers the carrying amount of the asset. If those economic benefits will not be taxable, the tax base of the asset is equal to its carrying amount. *[IAS 12.7]*.

In some cases the 'tax base' of an asset is relatively obvious. In the case of a tax-deductible item of PP&E, it is the tax-deductible amount of the asset at acquisition less tax depreciation already claimed (see Example 31.1 at 1.2 above). Other items, however, require more careful analysis.

For example, an entity may have accrued interest receivable of €1,000 that will be taxed only on receipt. When the asset is recovered, all the cash received is subject to tax. In other words, the amount deductible for tax on recovery of the asset, and therefore its tax base, is nil. Another way of arriving at the same conclusion might be to consider the amount at which the tax authority would recognise the receivable in notional financial statements for the entity prepared under tax law. At the end of the reporting period the receivable would not be recognised in such notional financial statements, since the interest has not yet been recognised for tax purposes.

Conversely, an entity may have a receivable of €1,000 the recovery of which is not taxable. In this case, the tax base is €1,000 on the rule above that, where realisation of an asset will not be taxable, the tax base of the asset is equal to its carrying amount. This applies irrespective of whether the asset concerned arises from:

- a transaction already recognised in total comprehensive income and already subject to tax on initial recognition (e.g. in most jurisdictions, a sale);
- a transaction already recognised in total comprehensive income and exempt from tax (e.g. tax-free dividend income); or
- a transaction not affecting total comprehensive income at all (e.g. the principal of a loan receivable). *[IAS 12.7]*.

The effect of deeming the tax base of the €1,000 receivable to be equal to its carrying amount will be that the temporary difference associated with it is nil, and that no deferred tax is recognised in respect of it. This is appropriate given that, in the first case, the debtor represents a sale that has already been taxed and, in the second and third cases, the debtors represent items that are outside the scope of tax.

6.1.2 *Tax base of liabilities*

The tax base of a liability is its carrying amount, less any amount that will be deductible for tax purposes in respect of that liability in future periods. In the case of revenue which is received in advance, the tax base of the resulting liability is its carrying amount, less any amount of the revenue that will not be taxable in future periods. *[IAS 12.8]*.

As in the case of assets, the tax base of some items is relatively obvious. For example, an entity may have recognised a provision for environmental damage of CHF5 million, which will be deductible for tax purposes only on payment. The liability has a tax base of nil. Its carrying amount is CHF5 million, which is also the amount that will be deductible for tax purposes on settlement in future periods. The difference between these two (equal) amounts – the tax base – is nil. Another way of arriving at the same conclusion might be to consider the amount at which the tax authority would recognise the liability in notional financial statements for the entity prepared under tax law. At the end of the reporting period the liability would not be recognised in such notional financial statements, since the expense has not yet been recognised for tax purposes.

Likewise, if the entity records revenue of £1,000 received in advance that was taxed on receipt, its tax base is nil. Under the definition above, the carrying amount is £1,000, none of which is taxable in future periods. The tax base is the difference between the £1,000 carrying amount and the amount *not* taxed in future periods (£1,000) – i.e. nil.

Again, if we were to consider a notional statement of financial position of the entity drawn up by the tax authorities under tax law, this liability would not be included, since the relevant amount would, in the notional tax financial statements, have already been taken to income.

An entity may have a liability of (say) €1,000 that will attract no tax deduction when it is settled. In this case, the tax base is €1,000 (on the analogy with the rule in 6.1.1

above that where, realisation of an asset will not be taxable, the tax base of the asset is equal to its carrying amount). This applies irrespective of whether the liability concerned arises from:

- a transaction already recognised in total comprehensive income and already subject to a tax deduction on initial recognition (e.g. in most jurisdictions, the cost of goods sold or accrued expenses);
- a transaction already recognised in total comprehensive income and outside the scope of tax (e.g. non tax-deductible fines and penalties); or
- a transaction not affecting total comprehensive income at all (e.g. the principal of a loan payable). *[IAS 12.8]*.

This is appropriate given that, in the first case, the liability represents a cost that has already been deducted for tax purposes and, in the second and third cases, the liabilities represent items that are outside the scope of tax.

6.1.3 Assets and liabilities whose tax base is not immediately apparent

IAS 12 indicates that where the tax base of an asset or liability is not immediately apparent, it is helpful to consider the fundamental principle on which the standard is based: an entity should, with certain limited exceptions, recognise a deferred tax liability (asset) wherever recovery or settlement of the carrying amount of an asset or liability would make future tax payments larger (smaller) than they would be if such recovery or settlement were to have no tax consequences. *[IAS 12.10]*. In other words: provide for the tax that would be payable or receivable if the assets and liabilities in the statement of financial position were to be recovered or settled at book value.

The implication of this is that in the basic 'equation' of IAS 12, i.e.

carrying amount – tax base = temporary difference,

the true unknown is not in fact the temporary difference (as implied by the definitions of tax base and temporary difference) but the tax base (as implied by paragraph 10).

It will be apparent from the more detailed discussion at 6.2 below that this clarification is particularly relevant to determining the tax bases of certain financial liabilities, which often do not fit the general 'formula' of carrying amount less amount deductible on settlement.

6.1.4 Tax base of items not recognised as assets or liabilities in financial statements

Certain items are not recognised as assets or liabilities in financial statements, but may nevertheless have a tax base. Examples may include:

- research costs (which are required to be expensed immediately by IAS 38 – *Intangible Assets* – see Chapter 17);
- the cost of equity-settled share-based payment transactions (which under IFRS 2 – *Share-based Payment* – give rise to an increase in equity and not a liability – see Chapter 32); and
- goodwill deducted from equity under previous IFRS or national GAAP.

Where such items are tax-deductible, their tax base is the difference between their carrying amount (i.e. nil) and the amount deductible in future periods. *[IAS 12.9]*. This may seem somewhat contrary to the definition of tax base, in which it is inherent that, in order for an item to have a tax base, that item must be an asset or liability, whereas none of the items above was ever recognised as an asset.[9] The implicit argument is that all these items were initially (and very briefly) recognised as assets before being immediately written off in full.

Local tax legislation sometimes gives rise to liabilities that have a tax base but no carrying amount. For example, a subsidiary of the reporting entity may receive a tax deduction for a provision that has been recognised in the individual financial statements of that subsidiary prepared under local accounting principles. For the purposes of the entity's consolidated financial statements, however, the provision does not currently satisfy the recognition requirements of IAS 37, but is likely to do so in the future. In such situations we consider it appropriate to regard the tax deduction received as giving rise to a deferred tax liability in the consolidated financial statements (by virtue of there being a provision with a tax base but no carrying amount) in addition to the current tax income recorded for the subsidiary.

Similar situations may arise where local tax legislation permits deductions for certain expenditure determined according to tax legislation without reference to any financial statements. Again, in those cases where an equivalent amount of expenditure is likely to be recognised in the financial statements at a later date, we would regard it as appropriate to regard the tax deduction received as giving rise to a deferred tax liability in the consolidated financial statements.

6.1.5 Equity items with a tax base

The definition of 'tax base' refers to the tax base of an 'asset or liability'. This begs the question of whether IAS 12 regards equity items as having a tax base and therefore whether deferred tax can be recognised in respect of equity instruments (since deferred tax is the tax relating to temporary differences which, by definition, can only arise on items with a tax base – see above).

In February 2003 the Interpretations Committee considered this issue. It drew attention to the IASB's proposal at that time to amend the definition of 'tax base' so as to refer not only to assets and liabilities but also equity instruments as supporting the view that deferred tax should be recognised where appropriate on equity instruments. This was effectively the approach proposed in the exposure draft ED/2009/2 (see 1.3 above).[10]

An alternative analysis might be that equity items do not have a tax base, but that any tax effects of them are to be treated as items that are not recognised as assets or liabilities but nevertheless have a tax base (see 6.1.4 above).

Given the lack of explicit guidance in the current version of IAS 12 either analysis may be acceptable, provided that it is applied consistently. This is reflected in a number of the examples in the remainder of this Chapter.

6.1.6 Items with more than one tax base

Some assets and liabilities have more than one tax base, depending on the manner in which they are realised or settled. These are discussed further at 8.4 below.

6.1.7 Tax bases disclaimed or with no economic value

In some situations an entity may choose not to claim an available deduction for an item as part of an overall tax planning strategy. In other cases, a deduction available as a matter of tax law may have no real economic effect – for example because the deduction will increase a pool of brought forward tax losses which the entity does not expect to recover in the foreseeable future.

In our view, the fact that the entity chooses not to take advantage of a potential tax deduction, or that such a deduction would have no real economic effect in the foreseeable future, does not mean that the asset to which the deduction relates has no tax base. While such considerations will be relevant to determining whether a deductible temporary difference gives rise to a recoverable deferred tax asset (see 7.4 below), the tax base of an asset is determined by reference to the amount attributed to the item by tax law. *[IAS 12.5]*.

6.2 Examples of temporary differences

The following are examples of taxable temporary differences, deductible temporary differences and items where the tax base and carrying value are the same so that there is no temporary difference. They are mostly based on those given in IAS 12, *[IAS 12.17-20, 26, IE.A-C]*, but include several others that are encountered in practice. It will be seen that a number of categories of assets and liabilities may give rise to either taxable or deductible temporary differences.

A temporary difference will not always result in a deferred tax asset or liability being recorded under IAS 12, since the difference may be subject to other provisions of the standard restricting the recognition of deferred tax assets and liabilities, which are discussed at 7 below. Moreover, even where deferred tax is recognised, it does not necessarily create tax income or expense, but may instead give rise to additional goodwill or bargain purchase gain in a business combination, or to a movement in equity.

6.2.1 Taxable temporary differences

6.2.1.A Transactions that affect profit or loss

- *Interest received in arrears*

  An entity with a financial year ending on 31 December 2017 holds a medium-term cash deposit on which interest of €10,000 is received annually on 31 March. The interest is taxed in the year of receipt. At 31 December 2017, the entity recognises a receivable of €7,000 in respect of interest accrued but not yet received. The receivable has a tax base of nil, since its recovery has tax consequences and no tax deductions are available in respect of it. The temporary difference associated with the receivable is €7,000 (€7,000 carrying amount less nil tax base).

- *Sale of goods taxed on a cash basis*

  An entity has recorded revenue from the sale of goods of €40,000, together with a cost of the goods sold of €35,000, since the goods have been delivered. However, the transaction is taxed in the following financial year when the cash from the sale is collected.

  The entity will have recognised a receivable of €40,000 for the sale. The receivable has a tax base of nil, since its recovery has tax consequences and no tax deductions are available in respect of it. The temporary difference associated with the receivable is €40,000 (€40,000 carrying amount less nil tax base).

  There is also a deductible temporary difference of €35,000 associated with the (now derecognised) inventory, which has a carrying amount of zero but a tax base of €35,000 (since it will attract a tax deduction of €35,000 when the sale is taxed) – see 6.2.2.A below.

- *Depreciation of an asset accelerated for tax purposes*

  An entity with has an item of PP&E whose cost is fully tax deductible, but with deductions being given over a period shorter than the period over which the asset is being depreciated under IAS 16 – *Property, Plant and Equipment.* At the reporting date, the asset has been depreciated to £500,000 for financial reporting purposes but to £300,000 for tax purposes.

  Recovery of the PP&E has tax consequences since, although there is no deduction for accounting depreciation in the tax return, the PP&E is recovered through future taxable profits. There is a taxable temporary difference of £200,000 between the carrying value of the asset (£500,000) and its tax base (£300,000).

- *Capitalised development costs already deducted for tax*

  An entity incurred development costs of $1 million during the year ended 31 December 2017. The costs were fully deductible for tax purposes in the tax return for that period, but were recognised as an intangible asset under IAS 38 in the financial statements. The amount carried forward at 31 December 2017 is $800,000.

  Recovery of the intangible asset through use has tax consequences since, although there is no deduction for accounting amortisation in the tax return, the asset is recovered through future profits which will be taxed. There is a taxable temporary difference of $800,000 between the carrying value of the asset ($800,000) and its tax base (nil). Although the expenditure to create the asset is tax-deductible in the current period, its tax base is the amount deductible in *future* periods, which is nil, since all deductions were made in the tax return for 2017.

  A similar analysis would apply to prepaid expenses that have already been deducted on a cash basis in determining the taxable profit of the current or previous periods.

6.2.1.B Transactions that affect the statement of financial position

- *Non-deductible and partially deductible assets*

  An entity acquires a building for €1 million. Any accounting depreciation of the building is not deductible for tax purposes, and no deduction will be available for tax purposes when the asset is sold or scrapped.

  Recovery of the building, whether in use or on sale, nevertheless has tax consequences since the building is recovered through future taxable profits of €1 million. There is a taxable temporary difference of €1 million between the carrying value of the asset (€1 million) and its tax base of zero.

  A similar analysis applies to an asset which, when acquired, is deductible for tax purposes, but for an amount lower than its cost. The difference between the cost and the amount deductible for tax purposes is a taxable temporary difference.

- *Deductible loan transaction costs*

  A borrowing entity records a loan at £9.5 million, being the proceeds received of £10 million (which equal the amount due at maturity), less transaction costs of £500,000, which are deducted for tax purposes in the period when the loan was first recognised. For financial reporting purposes, IAS 39 requires the costs, together with interest and similar payments, to be accrued over the period to maturity using the effective interest method.

  Inception of the loan gives rise to a taxable temporary difference of £500,000, being the difference between the carrying amount of the loan (£9.5 million) and its tax base (£10 million). This tax base does not conform to the general definition of the tax base of a liability – i.e. the carrying amount, less any amount that will be deductible for tax purposes in respect of that liability in future periods (see 6.1.2 above).

  The easiest way to derive the correct tax base is to construct a notional statement of financial position prepared by the tax authorities according to tax law. This would show a liability for the full £10 million (since the amortisation of the issue costs that has yet to occur in the financial statements has already occurred in the notional tax authority financial statements). This indicates that the tax base of the loan is £10 million.

  A far simpler analysis for the purposes of IAS 12 might have been that the £9.5 million carrying amount comprises a loan of £10 million (with a tax base of £10 million, giving rise to temporary difference of zero) offset by prepaid transaction costs of £500,000 (with a tax base of zero, giving rise to a taxable temporary difference of £500,000). However, this is inconsistent with the analysis in IAS 39 that the issue costs are an integral part of the carrying value of the loan.

  The consequence of recognising a deferred tax liability in this case is that the tax deduction for the transaction costs is recognised in profit or loss, not on inception of the loan, but as the costs are recognised through the effective interest method in future periods.

- *Non-deductible loan transaction costs*

  As in the immediately preceding example, a borrowing entity records a loan at £9.5 million, being the proceeds received of £10 million (which equal the amount due at maturity), less transaction costs of £500,000. In this case, however, the transaction costs are not deductible in determining the taxable profit of future, current or prior periods. For financial reporting purposes, IAS 39 requires the costs to be accrued over the period to maturity using the effective interest method.

  Just as in the preceding example (and perhaps rather counter-intuitively, given that the costs are non-deductible) inception of the loan gives rise to a taxable temporary difference of £500,000, being the difference between the carrying amount of the loan (£9.5 million) and its tax base (£10 million). This is because a notional statement of financial position prepared by the tax authorities according to tax law would show a liability for the full £10 million, since the transaction costs would never have been recorded (as they never occurred for tax purposes).

- *Liability component of compound financial instrument*

  An entity issues a convertible bond for €5 million which, in accordance with the requirements of IAS 32 – *Financial Instruments: Presentation*, is analysed as comprising a liability component of €4.6 million and a residual equity component of €400,000. If the entity were to settle the liability for €4.6 million it would be liable to tax on €400,000 (€5 million less €4.6 million). Therefore the tax base of the liability is €5 million and there is a taxable temporary difference of €400,000 between this and the carrying amount of the liability component. This is discussed further at 7.2.8 below.

6.2.1.C Revaluations

- *Financial assets and property carried at valuation*

  An entity holds investments, accounted for at fair value through profit or loss, with a carrying amount of CHF2 million and an original cost (and tax base) of CHF1.3 million. There is a taxable temporary difference of CHF700,000 associated with the investments, being the amount on which the entity would pay tax if the investments were realised at their carrying value.

  A similar analysis would apply to investment property or PP&E carried at a value that exceeds cost, where no equivalent adjustment is made for tax purposes.

6.2.1.D Tax re-basing

- *Withdrawal of tax depreciation for classes of PP&E*

  An entity holds buildings with a carrying amount of £15 million and a tax base of £12 million, giving rise to a taxable temporary difference of £3 million. As part of a general fiscal reform package introduced by the government, future tax deductions for the buildings (their tax base) are reduced to £1 million. This increases the taxable temporary difference by £11 million to £14 million.

6.2.1.E Business combinations and consolidation

- *Fair value adjustments*

  Where the carrying amount of an asset is increased to fair value in a business combination, but no equivalent adjustment is made for tax purposes, a taxable temporary difference arises just as on the revaluation of an asset (see 6.2.1.C above).

- *Non-deductible or partially-deductible goodwill*

  Where goodwill is not deductible, or only partially deductible, in determining taxable profit there will be a taxable temporary difference between the carrying amount of the goodwill and its tax base, similar to that arising on a non-deductible or partially-deductible asset (see 6.2.1.B above).

- *Intragroup transactions*

  Although intragroup transactions are eliminated in consolidated financial statements, they may give rise to temporary differences. An entity in a group (A) might sell inventory with a cost and tax base of £1,000 to another group entity (B) for £900, which becomes the cost and tax base to B. If the carrying value in the consolidated financial statements remains £1,000 (i.e. the inventory is not actually impaired, notwithstanding the intragroup sale at a loss), a new taxable temporary difference of £100 emerges in the consolidated financial statements between the carrying value of £1,000 and the new tax base of £900.

- *Undistributed earnings of group investments*

  A parent entity P holds an investment in subsidiary S. Retained earnings of $1 million relating to S are included in the consolidated financial statements of P. S must pay a non-refundable withholding tax on any distribution of earnings to P. There is therefore a taxable temporary difference in the consolidated financial statements of $1 million associated with the net assets representing the retained earnings, since their recovery (in the form of distribution to the parent) has tax consequences, with no offsetting tax deductions.

  Similar temporary differences may arise on the retained earnings of branches, associates and joint arrangements.

6.2.1.F Foreign currency differences

- *Translation of foreign subsidiary to presentation currency*

  A UK entity acquires the equity of a French entity, which therefore becomes its subsidiary, for €10 million. For UK tax purposes, the tax base of the investment is £8 million (the spot-rate equivalent of €10 million at the date of acquisition). The presentation currency of the UK entity's consolidated financial statements is sterling.

  Between the date of acquisition and the first reporting date, the French entity makes no gains or losses, such that its net assets and goodwill as included in the consolidated financial statements, expressed in euros, remain €10 million. However, the exchange rate has moved, so that the sterling equivalent of €10 million at the reporting date, included in the consolidated statement of financial position, is £9 million.

  This gives rise to a £1 million taxable temporary difference between the £9 million carrying value of the investment and its £8 million tax base.

- *Functional currency different from currency used to compute tax*

  On 1 January 2017 an entity which, under IAS 21 – *The Effects of Changes in Foreign Exchange Rates*, has determined its functional currency as US dollars (see Chapter 15), purchases plant for $1 million, which will be depreciated to its estimated residual value of zero over 10 years. The entity is taxed in the local currency LC, and is entitled to receive tax deductions for the depreciation charged in the financial statements. The exchange rate is $1=LC2 at 1 January 2017 (so that the cost of the asset for local tax purposes is LC2 million). The exchange rate at 31 December 2017 is $1=LC2.5.

  At 31 December 2017 there is a taxable temporary difference of $180,000, being the difference between the net book value of the plant of $900,000 (cost $1,000,000 less depreciation $100,000) and its tax base of $720,000 (cost LC2,000,000 less depreciation LC200,000 = LC1,800,000 translated at year end rate of $1=LC2.5).

6.2.1.G Hyperinflation

A taxable temporary difference (similar to those in 6.2.1.F above) arises when non-monetary assets are restated in terms of the measuring unit current at the end of the reporting period under IAS 29 – *Financial Reporting in Hyperinflationary Economies* – but no equivalent adjustment is made for tax purposes.

6.2.2 Deductible temporary differences

6.2.2.A Transactions that affect profit of loss

- *Expenses deductible for tax on cash basis*

  An entity records a liability of €1 million for retirement benefit costs which are tax deductible only when paid. The tax base of the liability is zero, being its carrying amount (€1 million) less the amount deductible for tax purposes when the liability is settled (also €1 million). There is therefore a deductible temporary difference of €1 million (€1 million carrying amount less zero tax base) associated with the liability.

- *Depreciation of an asset delayed for tax purposes*

  An entity has an item of PP&E that originally cost £1 million. The cost is fully tax deductible, with deductions being given over a period longer than the period over which the asset is being depreciated under IAS 16. At the reporting date, the asset has been depreciated to £300,000 for financial reporting purposes but to only £500,000 for tax purposes.

  Recovery of the PP&E has tax consequences since, although there is no deduction for accounting depreciation in the tax return, the PP&E is recovered through future taxable profits of £300,000. There is a deductible temporary difference of £200,000 between the carrying value of the asset (£300,000) and its tax base (£500,000).

- *Sale of goods taxed on a cash basis*

  An entity has recorded revenue from the sale of goods of €40,000, together with a cost of the goods sold of €35,000, since the goods have been delivered.

However, the transaction is taxed in the following financial year when the cash from the sale is collected.

There is a deductible temporary difference of €35,000 associated with the (now derecognised) inventory, which has a carrying amount of zero but a tax base of €35,000 (since it will attract a tax deduction of €35,000 when the sale is taxed).

There is also a taxable temporary difference of €40,000 associated with the receivable (see 6.2.1.A above).

- *Write-down of asset not deductible for tax purposes until realised*

  An entity purchases inventory for $1,000, which is also its tax base. The inventory is later written down to a net realisable value of $800. However, no loss is recognised for tax purposes until the inventory is sold. There is a deductible temporary difference of $200 between the $800 carrying amount of the inventory and its $1,000 tax base.

- *Deferred income taxed on receipt*

  In the year ended 31 December 2016, an entity received €2 million, being 5 years' rent of an investment property received in advance. In the statement of financial position as at 31 December, €1,800,000 is carried forward as deferred income. However, the whole €2 million is taxed in the tax return for the period.

  There is a deductible temporary difference of €1,800,000 associated with the deferred income, being its carrying amount (€1,800,000), less its tax base of zero, computed as the carrying amount (€1,800,000) less the amount not taxable in future periods (also €1,800,000 since the income has already been taxed).

- *Deferred non-taxable income*

  An entity receives a non-taxable government grant of £1 million, of which £700,000 is carried forward in the statement of financial position as at the period end.

  There is a deductible temporary difference of £700,000 associated with the deferred income, being its carrying amount (£700,000), less its tax base of zero, computed as the carrying amount (£700,000) less the amount of income not taxable in future periods (also £700,000 since the income is tax free). In this case, while there is a deductible temporary difference, no deferred tax asset would be recognised, as discussed in Example 31.7 at 7.2.3. *[IAS 12.24, 33].*

6.2.2.B Transactions that affect the statement of financial position

- *Asset deductible for more than cost*

  An entity invests NOK10 million in PP&E for which tax deductions of NOK13 million may be claimed. There is a deductible temporary difference of NOK3 million between the NOK10 million carrying value of the PP&E and its tax base of NOK13 million.

6.2.2.C Revaluations

- *Financial assets and property carried at valuation*

  An entity holds investments, accounted for at fair value through profit or loss, with a carrying amount of CHF2 million and an original cost (and tax base) of CHF2.5 million. There is a taxable temporary difference of

CHF500,000 associated with the investments, being the amount for which the entity would receive a tax deduction if the investments were realised at their carrying value.

A similar analysis would apply to investment property or PP&E carried at a value below cost, where no equivalent adjustment is made for tax purposes.

6.2.2.D Tax re-basing

- *Indexation of assets for tax purposes*

  An entity acquires land for $5 million, which is also its tax base at the date of purchase. A year later, as part of a general fiscal reform package introduced by the government, future tax deductions for the land (its tax base) are increased to $6 million. This creates a deductible temporary difference of $1 million in respect of the land.

6.2.2.E Business combinations and consolidation

- *Fair value adjustments*

  Where a liability is recognised at fair value in a business combination, but the liability is deductible for tax purposes only on settlement, a deductible temporary difference arises similar to that arising on the initial recognition of a liability for an expense deductible for tax on a cash basis (see 6.2.2.A above).

- *Intragroup transactions*

  Although intragroup transactions are eliminated in consolidated financial statements, they may give rise to deductible temporary differences. An entity in a group (A) might sell inventory with a cost and tax base of £1,000 to another group entity (B) for £1,200, which becomes the cost and tax base to B. Since the carrying value in the consolidated financial statements remains £1,000, a new deductible temporary difference of £200 emerges in the consolidated financial statements between the carrying value of £1,000 and the new tax base of £1,200.

6.2.2.F Foreign currency differences

- *Translation of foreign subsidiary to presentation currency*

  A UK entity acquires the equity of a French entity, which therefore becomes its subsidiary, for €10 million. For UK tax purposes, the tax base of the investment is £8 million (the spot-rate equivalent of €10 million at the date of acquisition). The presentation currency of the UK entity's consolidated financial statements is sterling.

  Between the date of acquisition and the first reporting date, the French entity makes no gains or losses, such that its net assets and goodwill as included in the consolidated financial statements, expressed in euros, remain €10 million. However, the exchange rate has moved, so that the sterling equivalent of €10 million at the reporting date, included in the consolidated statement of financial position, is £7 million.

  This gives rise to a £1 million deductible temporary difference between the £7 million carrying value of the investment and its £8 million tax base.

- *Functional currency different from currency used to compute tax*

  On 1 January 2017 an entity which, under IAS 21 has determined its functional currency as US dollars (see Chapter 15), purchases plant for $1 million, which will be depreciated to its estimated residual value of zero over 10 years. The entity is taxed in the local currency LC, and is entitled to receive tax deductions for the depreciation charged in the financial statements. The exchange rate is $1=LC2 at 1 January 2017 (so that the cost of the asset for local tax purposes is LC2 million). The exchange rate at 31 December 2017 is $1=LC1.8.

  At 31 December 2017 there is a deductible temporary difference of $100,000, being the difference between the net book value of the plant of $900,000 (cost $1,000,000 less depreciation $100,000) and its tax base of $1,000,000 (cost LC2,000,000 less depreciation LC200,000 = LC1,800,000 translated at year end rate of $1=LC1.8).

6.2.3 Assets and liabilities with no temporary difference (because tax base equals carrying amount)

- *Liability for expense already deducted for tax*

  An entity accrues £200,000 for electricity costs in the year ended 31 March 2016. The expense is deductible for tax in that period. The temporary difference associated with the liability is zero. This is calculated as the carrying amount of £200,000 less the tax base of £200,000, being the carrying amount (£200,000) less amount deductible for tax in future periods (zero).

- *Liability for expense never deductible for tax*

  An entity accrues €400,000 for a fine for environmental pollution, which is not deductible for tax. The temporary difference associated with the liability is zero. This is calculated as the carrying amount of €400,000 less the tax base of €400,000, being the carrying amount (€400,000) less amount deductible for tax in future periods (zero).

- *Loan repayable at carrying amount*

  An entity borrows $2 million. This is the carrying amount of the loan on initial recognition, which is the same as the amount repayable on final maturity of the loan. The temporary difference associated with the liability is zero. This is calculated as the carrying amount of $2 million less the tax base of $2 million, being the carrying amount ($2 million) less amount deductible for tax in future periods (zero).

- *Receivable for non-taxable income*

  In its separate financial statements an entity records a receivable for a £1 million dividend due from a subsidiary accounted for at cost. The dividend is not taxable. Accordingly it gives rise to a temporary difference of zero, since the tax base of any asset, the recovery of the carrying amount of which is not taxable, is taken to be the same as its carrying amount.

7 DEFERRED TAX – RECOGNITION

7.1 The basic principles

7.1.1 Taxable temporary differences (deferred tax liabilities)

IAS 12 requires a deferred tax liability to be recognised in respect of all taxable temporary differences except those arising from:

- the initial recognition of goodwill; or
- the initial recognition of an asset or liability in a transaction that:
  - is not a business combination; and
  - at the time of the transaction, affects neither accounting profit nor taxable profit (tax loss).

These exceptions to the recognition principles do not apply to taxable temporary differences associated with investments in subsidiaries, branches and associates, and interests in joint arrangements, which are subject to further detailed provisions of IAS 12 (see 7.5 below). *[IAS 12.15]*.

Examples of taxable temporary differences are given in 6.2.1 above.

7.1.2 Deductible temporary differences (deferred tax assets)

IAS 12 requires a deferred tax asset to be recognised in respect of all deductible temporary differences to the extent that it is probable that taxable profit will be available against which the deductible temporary difference will be utilised except those arising from the initial recognition of an asset or liability in a transaction that:

- is not a business combination; and
- at the time of the transaction, affects neither accounting profit nor taxable profit (tax loss). *[IAS 12.24]*.

IAS 12 does not define 'probable' in this context. However, it is generally understood that, as in other IFRSs, it should be taken to mean 'more likely than not'. The exposure draft ED/2009/2 (see 1.3 above) effectively clarified that this is the intended meaning.[11]

These exceptions to the recognition principles do not apply to deductible temporary differences associated with investments in subsidiaries, branches and associates, and interests in joint arrangements, which are subject to further detailed provisions of IAS 12 (see 7.5 below).

Examples of deductible temporary differences are given in 6.2.2 above.

7.1.3 Interpretation issues

7.1.3.A Accounting profit

The provisions of IAS 12 summarised above refer to a transaction that affects 'accounting profit'. In this context 'accounting profit' clearly means any item recognised in total comprehensive income, whether recognised in profit or loss or in other comprehensive income.

7.1.3.B Taxable profit 'at the time of the transaction'

The provisions of IAS 12 summarised above also refer to a transaction which affects taxable profit 'at the time of the transaction'. Strictly speaking, no transaction affects taxable profit 'at the time of the transaction', since the taxable profit is affected only when the relevant item is included (some time later) in the tax return for the period. It is clear, however, that the intended meaning is that the transaction that gives rise to the initial recognition of the relevant asset or liability affects the current tax liability for the accounting period in which the initial recognition occurs.

Suppose that, in the year ended 31 December 2016, an entity received €2 million, being 5 years' prepaid rent of an investment property. In the statement of financial position as at 31 December, €1,800,000 is carried forward as deferred income. The whole €2 million is taxed on receipt and will therefore be included in the tax return for the period, which is not filed until 2017.

It could be argued that, in a literal legal sense, the transaction 'affects taxable profit' only in 2017. For the purposes of IAS 12, however, the transaction is regarded as affecting taxable profit during 2016 (since it affects the current tax for that period). This gives rise to the recognition, subject to the restrictions discussed at 7.4 below, of a deferred tax asset based on a deductible temporary difference of €1,800,000 (see 6.2.2.A above).

7.2 The initial recognition exception

The exceptions (summarised at 7.1 above) from recognising the deferred tax effects of certain temporary differences arising on the initial recognition of some assets and liabilities are generally referred to as the 'initial recognition exception' or 'initial recognition exemption', sometimes abbreviated to 'IRE'. 'Exception' is the more accurate description, since a reporting entity is required to apply it, rather than having the option to do so implicit in the term 'exemption'.

The initial recognition exception has its origins in the now superseded 'income statement' approaches to accounting for deferred tax. Under these approaches, deferred tax was not recognised on so-called 'permanent differences' – items of income or expense that appeared in either the financial statements or the tax return, but not in both. The majority of transactions to which the initial recognition exception applies would have been regarded as permanent differences under income statement approaches of accounting for deferred tax.

The purpose of the initial recognition exception is most easily understood by considering the accounting consequences that would follow if it did not exist, as illustrated in Example 31.2 below.

Example 31.2: Rationale for initial recognition exception

An entity acquires an asset for €1,000 which it intends to use for five years and then scrap (i.e. the residual value is nil). The tax rate is 40%. Depreciation of the asset is not deductible for tax purposes. On disposal, any capital gain would not be taxable and any capital loss would not be deductible.

Although the asset is non-deductible, its recovery has tax consequences, since it will be recovered out of taxable income of €1,000 on which tax of €400 will be paid. The tax base of the asset is therefore zero, and a temporary difference of €1,000 arises on initial recognition of the asset.

Absent the initial recognition exception, the entity would recognise a deferred tax liability of €400 on initial recognition of the asset, being the taxable temporary difference of €1,000 multiplied by the tax rate of 40%. A debit entry would then be required to balance the credit for the liability.

One possibility might be to recognise tax expense of €400 in the statement of total comprehensive income. This would be meaningless, since the entity has clearly not suffered a loss simply by purchasing a non-deductible asset in an arm's length transaction for a price that (economically) must reflect the asset's non-deductibility.

A second possibility would be to gross up the asset by €400 to €1,400. However, IAS 12 states that to make such adjustments to the carrying value of the asset would make the financial statements 'less transparent'. *[IAS 12.22(c)]*.

A third possibility (broadly the guidance provided under US GAAP) would be to gross up the asset to the amount that would rationally have been paid for it, had it been fully tax-deductible, and recognise a corresponding amount of deferred tax. As the asset is non-deductible, the €1,000 cost must theoretically represent the anticipated minimum *post*-tax return from the asset. In order to achieve a post-tax return of €1,000, an entity paying tax at 40% needs to earn pre-tax profits of €1,667 (€1,000/[1 – 0.4]). Therefore, the cost of an equivalent fully-deductible asset would, all else being equal, be €1,667. On this analysis, the entity would gross up the asset to €1,667 and recognise deferred tax of €667 (€1,667 @ 40%).

The fourth possibility, which is what is actually required by IAS 12, is not to provide for deferred tax at all, where to do so would lead to one of the three outcomes above. However, in cases where provision for the deferred tax on a temporary difference arising on initial recognition of an asset or liability would not lead to one of the outcomes above, the initial recognition exception does not apply. This is the case in a business combination or a transaction affecting taxable profit or accounting profit (or both).

- *Business combination*

  In a business combination, the corresponding accounting entry for a deferred tax asset or liability forms part of the goodwill arising or the bargain purchase gain recognised. No deferred tax income or expense is recorded.

- *Transaction affecting taxable profit or accounting profit*

  In a transaction affecting taxable profit or accounting profit (or both), the corresponding accounting entry for a deferred tax asset or liability is recorded as deferred tax income or expense.

  This ensures that the entity recognises all future tax consequences of recovering the assets, or settling the liabilities, recognised in the transaction. The effect of this on the statement of total comprehensive income is broadly to recognise items the tax effects of the various components of income and expenditure in the same period(s) in which those items are recognised for financial reporting purposes (as illustrated at 1.2.2 above).

In short, the initial recognition exception may simply be seen as the least bad of the four theoretically possible options for dealing with 'day one' temporary differences.

7.2.1 Acquisition of tax losses

The initial recognition exception applies only to deferred tax relating to temporary differences. It does not apply to tax assets, such as purchased tax losses, that do not arise from deductible temporary differences. The definition of 'deferred tax assets' (see 3 above) explicitly distinguishes between deductible temporary differences and unused losses and tax credits. *[IAS 12.5]*. There is therefore no restriction on the recognition of acquired tax losses other than the general criteria of IAS 12 for recognition of tax assets (see 7.4 below).

Under the general principles of IAS 12, acquired tax losses are initially recognised at the amount paid, subsequently re-assessed for recoverability (see 7.4.6 below) and re-measured accordingly (see 8 below). Changes in the recognised amount of acquired tax losses are generally recognised in profit or loss, on the basis that, as acquired losses, they do not relate to any pre-tax transaction previously accounted for by the entity (see 10 below). However, in some limited circumstances, changes to tax losses acquired as part of a business combination are required to be treated as an adjustment to goodwill (see 12.1.2 below).

7.2.2 Initial recognition of goodwill

7.2.2.A Taxable temporary differences

In many jurisdictions goodwill is not tax-deductible either as it is impaired or on ultimate disposal, such that it gives rise to a temporary difference equal to its carrying amount (representing its carrying amount less its tax base of zero).

It may well be that the shares in the acquired entity have a tax base equal to their cost so that, economically, an amount equal to the goodwill is deductible on disposal of those shares. However, accounting for the tax effects of the shares in an acquired subsidiary (or other significant group investment) is subject to separate provisions of IAS 12, which are discussed at 7.5 below.

The initial recognition exception for taxable temporary differences on goodwill prevents the grossing-up of goodwill that would otherwise occur. Goodwill is a function of all the net assets of the acquired business, including deferred tax. If deferred tax is provided for on goodwill, the goodwill itself is increased, which means that the deferred tax on the goodwill is increased further, which means that the goodwill increases again, and so on. Equilibrium is reached when the amount of goodwill originally recorded is grossed up by the fraction $1/(1 - t)$, where t is the entity's tax rate, expressed as a decimal fraction. For example, an entity that pays tax at 30% and recognises CU1,400 of goodwill before recognising deferred tax would (absent the initial recognition exception) increase the goodwill to CU2,000 and recognise a deferred tax liability of CU600 (which is 30% of the restated goodwill of CU2,000).

IAS 12 takes the view that this would not be appropriate, since goodwill is intended to be a residual arising after fair values have been determined for the assets and liabilities acquired in a business combination, and recognition of deferred tax would increase that goodwill. *[IAS 12.21]*.

7.2.2.B Deductible temporary differences

Where the carrying amount of goodwill arising in a business combination is less than its tax base, a deductible temporary difference arises. IAS 12 requires a deferred tax asset to be recognised in respect of any deductible temporary difference, to the extent that it is probable that taxable profit will be available against which the temporary difference could be utilised. *[IAS 12.32A]*. This contrasts with the prohibition against recognising a deferred tax liability on any *taxable* temporary difference on initial recognition of goodwill (see 7.2.2.A above). A more general discussion of the criteria in IAS 12 for assessing the recoverability of deferred tax assets may be found at 7.4 below.

IAS 12 gives no guidance on the method to be used in calculating the resulting deferred tax asset, which is not entirely straightforward, as illustrated by the following example.

Example 31.3: Deferred tax asset on initial recognition of goodwill

An entity that pays tax at 40% recognises, in the initial accounting for a business combination, goodwill of €1,000. Tax deductions of €1,250 are given for the goodwill over a 5 year period.

One approach would be to adopt an iterative method similar to that described at 7.2.2.A above, whereby recognition of a deferred tax asset on goodwill leads to a reduction of the goodwill, which in turn will lead to a further increase in the deferred tax asset, and so on. Equilibrium is reached when the goodwill is adjusted to an amount equal to $(g - bt)/(1 - t)$, where:

- g is the amount of goodwill originally recorded (before recognising a deferred tax asset);
- b is the tax base of the goodwill; and
- t is the tax rate, expressed as a decimal fraction.

Under this method, the entity would record goodwill of €833 (being [€1,000 – 0.4 × €1,250] ÷ 0.6) and a deferred tax asset of €167. This represents a deductible temporary difference of €417 (comprising the tax base of €1,250 less the adjusted carrying amount of €833), multiplied by the tax rate of 40%. On any subsequent impairment or disposal of the goodwill, the entity would report an effective tax rate of 40% (the statutory rate), comprised of pre-tax expense of €833 and tax income of €333 (the real tax deduction of €500 (€1,250 @ 40%), less the write-off of the deferred tax asset of €167).

An alternative approach might be to record a deferred tax asset based on the carrying amount of goodwill before calculating the deferred tax asset, and adjust the goodwill only once, rather than undertaking the iterative reduction in the goodwill described in the previous paragraph. In the example above this would lead to the entity recording a deferred tax asset of €100 (representing 40% of the deductible temporary difference of €250 between the tax base of the goodwill of €1,250 and its original carrying amount of €1,000) and goodwill of €900. On any subsequent impairment or disposal of the goodwill the entity would report an effective tax rate of 44% (higher than the statutory rate), comprised of pre-tax expense of €900 and tax income of €400 (the real tax deduction of €500 (€1,250 @ 40%), less the write-off of the deferred tax asset of €100).

7.2.2.C Tax deductible goodwill

Where goodwill is tax-deductible, new temporary differences will arise after its initial recognition as a result of the interaction between tax deductions claimed and impairments (if any) of the goodwill in the financial statements. These temporary differences do not relate to the initial recognition of goodwill, and therefore deferred tax should be recognised on them, as illustrated by Example 31.14 at 7.2.4.C below. *[IAS 12.21B]*.

7.2.3 Initial recognition of other assets and liabilities

Where a temporary difference arises on initial recognition of an asset or liability, its treatment depends on the circumstances which give rise to the recognition of the asset or liability.

If the temporary difference arises as the result of a business combination, deferred tax is recognised on the temporary difference with a corresponding adjustment to goodwill or any bargain purchase gain.

If the temporary difference arises in a transaction that gives rise to an accounting or taxable profit or loss, deferred tax is recognised on the temporary difference, giving rise to deferred tax expense or deferred tax income.

If the temporary difference arises in any other circumstances (i.e. neither in a business combination nor in a transaction that gives rise to an accounting or taxable profit or loss) no deferred tax is recognised. *[IAS 12.22]*.

The application of the initial recognition exception to assets and liabilities is illustrated in Examples 31.4 to 31.7 below.

Example 31.4: Non-deductible PP&E

An entity acquires a building for €1 million. Any accounting depreciation of the building is not deductible for tax purposes, and no deduction will be available for tax purposes when the asset is sold or demolished.

Recovery of the building, whether in use or on sale, has tax consequences since the building is recovered through future taxable profits of €1 million. There is a taxable temporary difference of €1 million between the €1 million carrying value of the asset and its tax base of zero.

Under the initial recognition exception, no deferred tax liability is provided for. The non-deductibility of the asset is reflected in an effective tax rate higher than the statutory rate (assuming that all other components of pre-tax profit are taxed at the statutory rate) as the asset is depreciated in future periods.

If the asset had been acquired as part of a larger business combination, the initial recognition would not have applied. Deferred tax of would have been provided for, with a corresponding increase in goodwill. As the asset is depreciated, the deferred tax liability is released to deferred tax income in the income statement, as illustrated in Example 31.1 above. This results in an effective tax rate equal to the statutory rate (assuming that all other components of pre-tax profit are taxed at the statutory rate).

Example 31.5: Inception of loan with tax-deductible issue costs

A borrowing entity records a loan at £9.5 million, being the proceeds received of £10 million (which equal the amount due at maturity), less transaction costs of £500,000, which are deducted for tax purposes in the period when the loan is first recognised. For financial reporting purposes, IAS 39 requires the costs, together with interest and similar payments, to be accrued over the period to maturity using the effective interest method.

Inception of the loan gives rise to a taxable temporary difference of £500,000, being the difference between the carrying amount of the loan (£9.5 million) and its tax base (£10 million). This analysis is explained in more detail at 6.2.1.B above.

Initial recognition of the transaction costs gives rise to no accounting loss (because they are included in the carrying amount of the loan). However, there is a tax loss (since the costs are included in the tax return for the period of inception). Accordingly, the initial recognition exception does not apply and a deferred tax liability is recognised on the taxable temporary difference of £500,000.

Example 31.6: Inception of loan with non-deductible issue costs

A borrowing entity records a loan at £9.5 million, being the proceeds received of £10 million (which equal the amount due at maturity), less transaction costs of £500,000, which are not deductible for tax purposes either in the period when the loan is first recognised or subsequently. For financial reporting purposes, IAS 39 requires the costs, together with interest and similar payments, to be accrued over the period to maturity using the effective interest method.

Inception of the loan gives rise to a taxable temporary difference of £500,000, being the difference between the carrying amount of the loan (£9.5 million) and its tax base (£10 million). This analysis is explained in more detail at 6.2.1.B above.

Initial recognition of the transaction costs gives rise to no accounting loss (because they are included in the carrying amount of the loan) or tax loss (because in this case there is no deduction for the issue costs). Accordingly, the initial recognition exception applies and no deferred tax liability is recognised.

If the same loan (including the unamortised transaction costs) had been recognised as part of a larger business combination, the initial recognition exception would not have applied. Deferred tax of would have been provided for recognised on the taxable temporary difference of £500,000, with a corresponding increase in goodwill (or decrease in any bargain purchase gain).

Example 31.7: Purchase of PP&E subject to tax-free government grant

An entity acquires an item of PP&E for €1 million subject to a tax free government grant of €350,000. The asset is also fully-tax deductible (at €1 million). IAS 20 permits the grant to be accounted for either as deferred income or by deduction from the cost of the asset. Whichever treatment is followed, a deductible temporary difference arises:

- If the grant is accounted for as deferred income, there is a deductible temporary difference between the liability of €350,000 and its tax base of nil (carrying amount €350,000 less amount not taxed in future periods, also €350,000).
- If the grant is accounted for as a reduction in the cost of the PP&E, there is a deductible temporary difference between the carrying amount of the PP&E (€650,000) and its tax base (€1 million).

IAS 12 emphasises that the initial recognition exception applies, and no deferred tax asset should be recognised. *[IAS 12.33]*.

7.2.4 Changes to temporary differences after initial recognition

The initial recognition exception applies only to temporary differences arising on initial recognition of an asset or liability. It does not apply to new temporary differences that arise on the same asset or liability after initial recognition. When the exception has been applied to the temporary difference arising on initial recognition of an asset or liability, and there is a different temporary difference associated with that asset or liability at a subsequent date, it is necessary to analyse the temporary difference at that date between:

- any amount relating to the original temporary difference (on which no deferred tax is recognised); and
- the remainder, which has implicitly arisen after initial recognition of the asset or liability (on which deferred tax is recognised).

IAS 12 does not set out comprehensive guidance to be followed in making this analysis, but it does give a number of examples, from which the following general principles may be inferred:

- the new temporary difference is treated as part of the temporary difference arising on initial recognition to the extent that any change from the original temporary difference is due to:
  - the write-down (through depreciation, amortisation or impairment) of the original carrying amount of an asset with no corresponding change in the tax base (see 7.2.4.A below); or
  - the increase in the original carrying amount of a liability arising from the amortisation of any discount recognised at the time of initial recognition of that liability, with no corresponding change in the tax base (see 7.2.4.A below);
- the new temporary difference is regarded as arising after initial recognition to the extent that any change from the original temporary difference is due to:
  - a change in the carrying value of the asset or liability, other than for the reasons set out above (see 7.2.4.B below); or
  - a change in the tax base due to items being recorded on the tax return (see 7.2.4.C below); and
- where the change in the temporary difference results from a change in the tax base due to legislative change, IAS 12 provides no specific guidance, and more than one treatment may be possible (see 7.2.4.D below).

7.2.4.A Depreciation, amortisation or impairment of initial carrying value

The following are examples of transactions where the initial temporary difference changes as the result of the amortisation of the original carrying amount, so that the adjusted temporary difference is regarded as part of the temporary difference arising on initial recognition, rather than a new difference.

Example 31.8: Impairment of non-deductible goodwill

Goodwill of £10 million (not tax-deductible) arose on a business combination in 2008. In accordance with IAS 12 no deferred tax liability was recognised on the taxable temporary difference of £10 million that arose on initial recognition of the goodwill. During the year ended 31 December 2017, following an impairment test, the carrying amount of the goodwill is reduced to £6 million.

No deferred tax is recognised on the new temporary difference of £6 million, because it is part of the temporary difference arising on the initial recognition of the goodwill. *[IAS 12.21A]*.

Example 31.9: Depreciation of non-deductible PP&E

During the year ended 31 March 2018 an entity acquires an item of PP&E for €1 million which it intends to use for 20 years, with no anticipated residual value. No tax deductions are available for the asset. In accordance with IAS 12 no deferred tax liability was recognised on the taxable temporary difference of €1 million that arises on initial recognition of the PP&E.

The entity's accounting policy is to charge a full year's depreciation in the year of purchase, so that the carrying amount of the asset at 31 March 2018 is €950,000. No deferred tax is recognised on the current temporary difference of €950,000, because it is part of the temporary difference arising on the initial recognition of the PP&E. *[IAS 12.22(c)]*.

Example 31.10: Amortisation of non-deductible loan issue costs

A borrowing entity records a loan at £9.5 million, being the proceeds received of £10 million (which equal the amount due at maturity), less transaction costs of £500,000, which are not deductible for tax purposes either in the period when the loan is first recognised or subsequently. For financial reporting purposes, IAS 39 requires the costs, together with interest and similar payments, to be accrued over the period to maturity using the effective interest method.

Inception of the loan gives rise to a taxable temporary difference of £500,000, being the difference between the carrying amount of the loan (£9.5 million) and its tax base (£10 million). This analysis is explained in more detail at 6.2.1.B above.

In accordance with IAS 12, no deferred tax liability was recognised on the taxable temporary difference of £10 million that arose on initial recognition of the loan.

One year later, the carrying amount of the loan is £9.7 million, comprising the proceeds received of £10 million (which equal the amount due at maturity), less unamortised transaction costs of £300,000. This gives rise to a new temporary difference of £300,000. No deferred tax is recognised on the current temporary difference, because it is part of the temporary difference arising on the initial recognition of the loan.

7.2.4.B Change in carrying value due to revaluation

As illustrated in Example 31.4 at 7.2.3 above, a temporary difference arises when a non tax-deductible asset is acquired. Where the asset is acquired separately (i.e. not as part of a larger business combination) in circumstances giving rise to neither an accounting nor a taxable profit or loss, no deferred tax liability is recognised for that temporary difference.

If such an asset is subsequently revalued, however, deferred tax is recognised on the new temporary difference arising as a result of the revaluation, since this does not arise on initial recognition of the asset, as illustrated in Examples 31.11 and 31.12.

Example 31.11: Revaluation of non-deductible asset (1)

On 1 January 2017 an entity paying tax at 30% acquires a non tax-deductible office building for €1,000,000 in circumstances in which IAS 12 prohibits recognition of the deferred tax liability associated with the temporary difference of €1,000,000.

Application of IAS 16 results in no depreciation being charged on the building.

On 1 January 2018 the entity revalues the building to €1,200,000. The temporary difference associated with the building is now €1,200,000, only €1,000,000 of which arose on initial recognition. Accordingly, the entity recognises a deferred tax liability based on the remaining temporary difference of €200,000 giving deferred tax expense at 30% of €60,000. This tax expense would be recognised in other comprehensive income (see 10 below).

Example 31.12: Revaluation of non-deductible asset (2)

On 1 January 2017 an entity paying tax at 30% acquires a non tax-deductible office building for €1,000,000 in circumstances in which IAS 12 prohibits recognition of the deferred tax liability associated with the temporary difference of €1,000,000. The building is depreciated over 20 years at €50,000 per year to a residual value of zero. The entity's financial year ends on 31 December.

At 1 January 2019, the carrying amount of the building is €900,000, and it is revalued upwards by €450,000 to its current market value of €1,350,000. As there is no change to the estimated residual value of zero, or to the life of the building, this will be depreciated over the next 18 years at €75,000 per year.

Following the revaluation, the temporary difference associated with the building is €1,350,000. Of this amount, only €900,000 arose on initial recognition, since €100,000 of the original temporary difference of €1,000,000 arising on initial recognition of the asset has been eliminated through depreciation of the asset (see 7.2.4.A above). The carrying amount (which equals the temporary difference, since the tax base is zero) and depreciation during the year ended 31 December 2019 may then be analysed as follows.

	Total carrying amount	*Arising on initial recognition*	*Arising on revaluation*
	€	€	€
1 January 2019	1,350,000	900,000	450,000
Depreciation[1]	75,000	50,000	25,000
31 December 2019	1,275,000	850,000	425,000

1 The depreciation is allocated pro-rata to the cost element and revalued element of the total carrying amount.

On 1 January 2019 the entity recognises a deferred tax liability based on the temporary difference of €450,000 arising on the revaluation (i.e. after initial recognition) giving a deferred tax expense of €135,000 (€450,000 @ 30%), recognised in other comprehensive income (see 10 below). This has the result that the effective tax rate shown in the financial statements for the revaluation is 30% (€450,000 gain with deferred tax expense of €135,000).

As can be seen from the table above, as at 31 December 2019, €425,000 of the total temporary difference arose after initial recognition. The entity therefore provides for deferred tax of €127,500 (€425,000 @ 30%), and deferred tax income of €7,500 (the reduction in the liability from €135,000 to €127,500) is recognised in profit or loss.

The deferred tax income can be explained as the tax effect at 30% of the €25,000 depreciation relating to the revalued element of the building (see table above).

7.2.4.C Change in tax base due to deductions in tax return

The following are examples of transactions where a new temporary difference emerges after initial recognition as the result of claiming tax deductions.

Example 31.13: Tax deduction for land

An entity that pays tax at 35% acquires land with a fair value of €5 million. Tax deductions of €100,000 per year may be claimed for the land for the next 30 years (i.e. the tax base of the land is €3 million). In accordance with IAS 12, no deferred tax liability is recognised on the taxable temporary difference of €2 million that arises on initial recognition of the land.

In the period in which the land is acquired, the entity claims the first €100,000 annual tax deduction, and the original cost of the land is not depreciated or impaired. The taxable temporary difference at the end of the period is therefore €2.1 million (cost €5.0 million less tax base €2.9 million). Of this, €2 million arose on initial recognition and no deferred tax is recognised on this. However, the remaining €100,000 of the gross temporary difference arose after initial recognition. Accordingly the entity recognises a deferred tax liability of €35,000 (€100,000 @ 35%).

The analysis if the land had been impaired would be rather more complicated. The general issue of the treatment of assets that are tax-deductible, but for less than their cost, is discussed at 7.2.6 below.

Example 31.14: Tax-deductible goodwill

On 1 January 2017 an entity with a tax rate of 35% acquires goodwill in a business combination with a cost of €1 million, which is deductible for tax purposes at a rate of 20% per year, starting in the year of acquisition.

During 2017 the entity claims the full 20% tax deduction and writes off €120,000 of the goodwill as the result of an impairment test. Thus at the end of 2017 the goodwill has a carrying amount of €880,000 and a tax base of €800,000. This gives rise to a taxable temporary difference of €80,000 that does not relate to the initial recognition of goodwill, and accordingly the entity recognises a deferred tax liability at 35% of €28,000.

If, during 2017, there had been no impairment of the goodwill, but the full tax deduction had nevertheless been claimed, at the end of the year the entity would have had goodwill with a carrying amount of €1 million and a tax base of €800,000. This would have given rise to a taxable temporary difference of €200,000 that does not relate to the initial recognition of goodwill, and accordingly the entity would have recognised a deferred tax liability at 35% of €70,000.

7.2.4.D Temporary difference altered by legislative change

Any change to the basis on which an item is treated for tax purposes alters the tax base of the item concerned. For example, if the government decides that an item of PP&E that was previously tax-deductible is no longer eligible for tax deductions, the tax base of the PP&E is reduced to zero. Under IAS 12, any change in tax base normally results in an immediate adjustment of any associated deferred tax asset or liability, and the recognition of a corresponding amount of deferred tax income or expense.

However, where such an adjustment to the tax base occurs in respect of an asset or liability for which no deferred tax has previously been recognised because of the initial recognition exception, the treatment required by IAS 12 is not entirely clear. The issue is illustrated by Example 31.15 below.

Example 31.15: Asset non-deductible at date of acquisition later becomes deductible

During the year ended 31 March 2018 an entity acquired an item of PP&E for €1 million which it intends to use for 20 years, with no anticipated residual value. No tax deductions were available for the asset. In accordance with IAS 12 no deferred tax liability was recognised on the taxable temporary difference of €1 million that arose on initial recognition of the PP&E.

During the year ended 31 March 2019, the government announces that it will allow the cost of such assets to be deducted in arriving at taxable profit. The deductions will be allowed in equal annual instalments over a 10-year period. As at 31 March 2019, the carrying amount of the asset and its tax base are both €900,000. The carrying amount is the original cost of €1 million less two years' depreciation at €50,000 per year. The tax base is the original cost of €1 million less one year's tax deduction at €100,000 per year.

Prima facie, therefore, there is no temporary difference associated with the asset. However, the treatment required by IAS 12 in Examples 31.13 and 31.14 above would lead to the conclusion that this temporary difference of nil should in fact be analysed into:

- a taxable temporary difference of €900,000 arising on initial recognition of the asset (being the €1 million difference arising on initial recognition less the €100,000 depreciation charged); and
- a deductible temporary difference of €900,000 arising after initial recognition (representing the fact that, since initial recognition, the government increased the tax base by €1 million which has been reduced to €900,000 by the €100,000 tax deduction claimed in the current period).

This analysis indicates that no deferred tax liability should be recognised on the taxable temporary difference (since this arose on initial recognition), but a deferred tax asset should be recognised on the deductible temporary difference of €900,000 identified above. A contrary view would be that this is inappropriate, since it is effectively recognising a gain on the elimination of an income tax liability that was never previously recognised.

As far as the tax income and expense in profit or loss is concerned, the difference between the two approaches is one of timing. Under the analysis that the overall temporary difference of zero should be 'bifurcated' into an amount arising on initial recognition and an amount arising later, the change in legislation reduces income tax expense and the effective tax rate in the year of change. Under the analysis that the net temporary difference of zero is considered as a whole, the reduction in income tax expense and the effective tax rate is recognised prospectively over the remaining life of the asset.

In our view, the first approach ('bifurcation') is more consistent with the balance sheet approach of IAS 12, but, in the absence of specific guidance in the standard, the second approach is acceptable.

7.2.5 Intragroup transfers of assets with no change in tax base

In many tax jurisdictions the tax deductions for an asset are generally related to the cost of that asset to the legal entity that owns it. However, in some jurisdictions, where an asset is transferred between members of the same group within that jurisdiction, the tax base remains unchanged, irrespective of the consideration paid.

Therefore, where the consideration paid for an asset in such a case differs from its tax base, a temporary difference arises in the acquiring entity's separate financial statements on transfer of the asset. The initial recognition exception applies to any such temporary difference. A further complication is that the acquiring entity acquires an asset that, rather than conforming to the fiscal norms of being either deductible for its full cost or not deductible at all, is deductible, but for an amount different from its cost. The treatment of such assets in the context of the initial recognition exception is discussed more generally at 7.2.6 below.

In the consolidated financial statements of any parent of the buying entity, however, there is no change to the amount of deferred tax recognised provided that the tax rate of the buying and selling entity is the same. Where the tax rate differs, the deferred tax will be remeasured using the buying entity's tax rate.

Where an asset is transferred between group entities and the tax base of the asset changes as a result of the transaction, there will be deferred tax income or expense in the consolidated financial statements. This is discussed further at 8.7 below.

7.2.6 Partially deductible and super-deductible assets

In many tax jurisdictions the tax deductions for an asset are generally based on the cost of that asset to the legal entity that owns it. However, in some jurisdictions, certain categories of asset are deductible for tax but for an amount either less than the cost of the asset ('partially deductible') or more than the cost of the asset ('super-deductible').

IAS 12 provides no specific guidance on the treatment of partially deductible and super-deductible assets acquired in a transaction to which the initial recognition exception applies. The issues raised by such assets are illustrated in Examples 31.16 and 31.17 below.

Example 31.16: Partially deductible asset

An entity acquires an asset with a cost of €100,000 and a tax base of €60,000 in a transaction where IAS 12 prohibits recognition of deferred tax on the taxable temporary difference of €40,000 arising on initial recognition of the asset. The asset is depreciated to a residual value of zero over 10 years, and qualifies for tax deductions of 20% per year over 5 years. The temporary differences associated with the asset over its life will therefore be as follows.

Year	*Carrying amount*	*Tax base*	*Temporary difference*
	€	€	€
0	100,000	60,000	40,000
1	90,000	48,000	42,000
2	80,000	36,000	44,000
3	70,000	24,000	46,000
4	60,000	12,000	48,000
5	50,000	–	50,000
6	40,000	–	40,000
7	30,000	–	30,000
8	20,000	–	20,000
9	10,000	–	10,000
10	–	–	–

These differences are clearly a function both of:

- the €40,000 temporary difference arising on initial recognition relating to the non-deductible element of the asset; and
- the emergence of temporary differences arising from the claiming of tax deductions for the €60,000 deductible element in advance of its depreciation.

Whilst IAS 12 does not explicitly mandate the treatment to be followed here, the general requirement to distinguish between these elements of the gross temporary difference (see 7.2.4 above) suggests the following approach.

If the total carrying amount of the asset is pro-rated into a 60% deductible element and a 40% non-deductible element, and deferred tax is recognised on the temporary difference between the 60% deductible element and its tax base, the temporary differences would be calculated as follows:

Year	*Carrying amount*	*40% non-deductible element*	*60% deductible element*	*Tax base*	*Temporary difference*
	a	b (40% of a)	c (60% of a)	d	c – d
0	100,000	40,000	60,000	60,000	–
1	90,000	36,000	54,000	48,000	6,000
2	80,000	32,000	48,000	36,000	12,000
3	70,000	28,000	42,000	24,000	18,000
4	60,000	24,000	36,000	12,000	24,000
5	50,000	20,000	30,000	–	30,000
6	40,000	16,000	24,000	–	24,000
7	30,000	12,000	18,000	–	18,000
8	20,000	8,000	12,000	–	12,000
9	10,000	4,000	6,000	–	6,000
10	–	–	–	–	–

Assuming that the entity pays tax at 30%, the amounts recorded for this transaction during year 1 (assuming that there are sufficient other taxable profits to absorb the tax loss created) would be as follows:

	€
Depreciation of asset	(10,000)
Current tax income[1]	3,600
Deferred tax charge[2]	(1,800)
Net tax credit	1,800
Post tax depreciation	(8,200)

1 €100,000 [cost of asset] × 60% [deductible element] × 20% [tax depreciation rate] × 30% [tax rate]

2 €6,000 [temporary difference] × 30% [tax rate] – brought forward balance [nil]

If this calculation is repeated for all 10 years, the following would be reported in the financial statements.

Year	*Depreciation*	*Current tax credit*	*Deferred tax (charge)/ credit*	*Total tax credit*	*Effective tax rate*
	a	b	c	d (=b+c)	e (=d/a)
1	(10,000)	3,600	(1,800)	1,800	18%
2	(10,000)	3,600	(1,800)	1,800	18%
3	(10,000)	3,600	(1,800)	1,800	18%
4	(10,000)	3,600	(1,800)	1,800	18%
5	(10,000)	3,600	(1,800)	1,800	18%
6	(10,000)	–	1,800	1,800	18%
7	(10,000)	–	1,800	1,800	18%
8	(10,000)	–	1,800	1,800	18%
9	(10,000)	–	1,800	1,800	18%
10	(10,000)	–	1,800	1,800	18%

This methodology has the result that the effective tax rate in each period corresponds to the effective tax rate for the transaction as a whole – i.e. cost of €100,000 attracting total tax deductions of €18,000 (€60,000 at 30%), an overall rate of 18%.

However, this approach cannot be said to be required by IAS 12 and other methodologies could well be appropriate, provided that they are applied consistently in similar circumstances.

Example 31.17: Super-deductible asset

The converse situation to that in Example 31.16 exists in some jurisdictions which seek to encourage certain types of investment by giving tax allowances for an amount in excess of the expenditure actually incurred. Suppose that an entity invests $1,000,000 in PP&E with a tax base of $1,200,000 in circumstances where IAS 12 prohibits recognition of deferred tax on the deductible temporary difference of $200,000 arising on initial recognition of the asset. The asset is depreciated to a residual value of zero over 10 years, and qualifies for five annual tax deductions of 20% of its deemed tax cost of $1,200,000.

The approach adopted in Example 31.16 considered the deductible and non-deductible elements separately and recognised deferred tax on the temporary difference between the deductible element and its tax base. If a similar approach is applied to the deductible 'cost' element and a 'super deduction' element, and deferred tax is recognised by reference to the deductible 'cost' element and its tax base, the temporary differences would arise as follows.

Year	*Book value* a	*Tax base* b	*'Super deduction' element* c (=2/12 of b)	*Cost element* d (=10/12 of b)	*Temporary difference* a – d
0	1,000,000	1,200,000	200,000	1,000,000	–
1	900,000	960,000	160,000	800,000	100,000
2	800,000	720,000	120,000	600,000	200,000
3	700,000	480,000	80,000	400,000	300,000
4	600,000	240,000	40,000	200,000	400,000
5	500,000	–	–	–	500,000
6	400,000	–	–	–	400,000
7	300,000	–	–	–	300,000
8	200,000	–	–	–	200,000
9	100,000	–	–	–	100,000
10	–	–	–	–	–

Assuming that the entity pays tax at 30%, the amounts recognised for this transaction during year 1 (assuming that there are sufficient other taxable profits to absorb the tax loss created) would be as follows:

	$
Depreciation of asset	(100,000)
Current tax income[1]	72,000
Deferred tax charge[2]	(30,000)
Net tax credit	42,000
Profit after tax	(58,000)

1 $1,200,000 [deemed tax cost of asset] × 20% [tax depreciation rate] × 30% [tax rate]

2 $100,000 [temporary difference] × 30% [tax rate] – brought forward balance [nil]

If this calculation is repeated for all 10 years, the following would be recognised in the financial statements.

Year	*Depreciation* a	*Current tax credit* b	*Deferred tax (charge)/ credit* c	*Total tax credit* d (=b+c)	*Effective tax rate* e (=d/a)
1	(100,000)	72,000	(30,000)	42,000	42%
2	(100,000)	72,000	(30,000)	42,000	42%
3	(100,000)	72,000	(30,000)	42,000	42%
4	(100,000)	72,000	(30,000)	42,000	42%
5	(100,000)	72,000	(30,000)	42,000	42%
6	(100,000)	–	30,000	30,000	30%
7	(100,000)	–	30,000	30,000	30%
8	(100,000)	–	30,000	30,000	30%
9	(100,000)	–	30,000	30,000	30%
10	(100,000)	–	30,000	30,000	30%

This accounting results in an effective 42% tax rate for this transaction being reported in years 1 to 5, and a rate of 30% in years 6 to 10, in contrast to the true effective rate of 36% for the transaction as a whole – i.e. cost of $1,000,000 attracting total tax deductions of $360,000 ($1,200,000 at 30%). This is because, whilst in the case of a partially deductible asset as in Example 31.16 above there is an accounting mechanism (i.e. depreciation) for allocating the non-deductible cost on a straight-line basis, in the present case of a super deductible asset there is no ready mechanism for spreading the additional $60,000 tax deductions on a straight-line basis.

In individual cases it might be possible to argue that the additional tax deductions had sufficient of the characteristics of a government grant (e.g. if it were subject to conditions more onerous that those normally associated with tax deductions in the jurisdiction concerned) to allow application of the principles of IAS 20 so as to allocate the additional tax deductions over the life of the asset (see 4.3 above). However, such circumstances are rare.

Again, as in Example 31.16 above, no single approach can be said to be required by IAS 12 and other methodologies could well be appropriate, provided that they are applied consistently in similar circumstances.

7.2.7 Transactions involving the initial recognition of an asset and liability

As noted at 7.2 above, the initial recognition exception is essentially a pragmatic remedy to avoid accounting problems that would arise without it, particularly in transactions where one asset is exchanged for another (such as the acquisition of PP&E for cash).

However, experience has shown that the exception creates new difficulties of its own. In particular, it does not deal adequately with transactions involving the initial recognition of an equal and opposite asset and liability which subsequently unwind on different bases. Examples of such transactions include:

- recording a liability for decommissioning costs, for which the corresponding debit entry is an increase in PP&E (see 7.2.7.A below); and
- the inception of a finance lease by a lessee, which involves the recording of an asset and a corresponding financial liability (see 7.2.7.B below).

7.2.7.A Decommissioning costs

The underlying issue is illustrated by the following example.

Example 31.18: Asset and liability giving rise to equal temporary differences on initial recognition

On 1 January 2017 an entity paying tax at 40% recognises a provision for the clean-up costs of a mine that will require expenditure of €10 million at the end of 2021. A tax deduction for the expenditure will be given when it is incurred (i.e. as a reduction in the current tax liability for 2021).

In accordance with IAS 37, this provision is discounted (at a rate of 6%) to €7.5m, giving rise to the following accounting entry (see Chapter 28 at 6.3):

	€m	€m
PP&E	7.5	
Provision for clean-up costs		7.5

On initial recognition, the tax base of the PP&E is nil, since no deductions are available and the €7.5 million carrying value of the asset is recovered through future taxable profits. The tax base of the provision is also nil (carrying amount of €7.5 million, less the amount deductible in future periods, also €7.5 million). Although deductions of €10 million are expected to be received in 2021 when the decommissioning costs are incurred, the tax base is determined by reference to the consequences of the liability being settled at its carrying amount of €7.5 million, which would result in a tax deduction of only €7.5 million.

There is therefore a taxable temporary difference of €7.5 million associated with the PP&E and a deductible temporary difference of the same amount associated with the provision. However, the initial recognition exception in IAS 12 prohibits recognition of deferred tax on either temporary difference.

Over the next five years an expense of €10 million (equivalent to the ultimate cash spend) will be recognised in profit or loss, comprising depreciation of the €7.5 million PP&E and accretion of €2.5 million finance costs on the provision. Given that this €10 million is fully tax-deductible, it would seem reasonable for the income statement to reflect €4 million of deferred tax credits over this period, giving rise to an effective tax rate of 40% in each period. However, the result is somewhat different.

Under the general approach of IAS 12 summarised at 7.2.4 above, the depreciation of the PP&E is regarded as reducing the temporary difference arising on initial recognition of the asset, and therefore gives rise to no tax effect. However, the accretion of €2.5 million finance costs on the provision gives rise to an additional temporary difference arising after initial recognition, requiring recognition of a deferred tax asset (assuming that the general recognition criteria for assets are met – see 7.4 below). This gives rise to the following overall accounting entries for the year ended 31 December 2017.

	€m	€m
2017		
Depreciation (€7.5m ÷ 5)	1.50	
PP&E		1.50
Finance cost (€7.5m × 6%)	0.45	
Provision for clean-up costs		0.45
Deferred tax (statement of financial position)	0.18	
Deferred tax (profit or loss) (40% × €0.45m)		0.18

If equivalent entries are made for the following periods, the following amounts will be included in subsequent income statements (all figures in € millions):

	2017	**2018**	**2019**	**2020**	**2021**	**Total**
Depreciation	1.50	1.50	1.50	1.50	1.50	7.50
Finance costs	0.45	0.47	0.50	0.53	0.55	2.50
Cost before tax	1.95	1.97	2.00	2.03	2.05	10.00
Current tax (income)					(4.00)	(4.00)
Deferred tax (income)/charge[1]	(0.18)	(0.19)	(0.20)	(0.21)	0.78	–
Cost after tax	1.77	1.78	1.80	1.82	(1.17)	6.00
Effective tax rate	9.2%	9.6%	10.0%	10.3%	157.1%	40.0%

1 In years 2017-2020 40% × finance cost for period. In 2021, reversal of cumulative deferred tax asset recognised in previous periods.

Absent the initial recognition exception, the entity would, on initial recognition of the provision and the addition to PP&E, establish a deferred tax asset of €3 million in respect of the provision (€7.5m @ 40%) and an equal liability in respect of the asset. This would result in the following amounts being included in subsequent income statements (all figures in € millions):

	2017	**2018**	**2019**	**2020**	**2021**	**Total**
Depreciation	1.50	1.50	1.50	1.50	1.50	7.50
Finance costs	0.45	0.47	0.50	0.53	0.55	2.50
Cost before tax	1.95	1.97	2.00	2.03	2.05	10.00
Current tax (income)					(4.00)	(4.00)
Deferred tax (income)/charge[1]	(0.78)	(0.79)	(0.80)	(0.81)	3.18	–
Cost after tax	1.17	1.18	1.20	1.22	1.23	6.00
Effective tax rate	40.0%	40.0%	40.0%	40.0%	40.0%	40.0%

1 In 2017, the net of the reduction in deferred tax liability in respect of PP&E €0.6m (€1.5m @ 40%) and increase in asset in respect of provision €0.18m (€0.45m @ 40%) – similarly for 2018-2020. The charge in 2021 represents the release of the remaining net deferred tax asset (equal to cumulative income statement credits in 2017-2020).

It is not clear that the accounting treatment strictly required by IAS 12, with its widely fluctuating effective tax rates, appropriately reflects the economic reality that all expenditure is ultimately eligible for tax deductions at the standard rate of 40%. Indeed, it could be argued that an appropriate result is achieved when the initial recognition exception is disregarded, as in the alternative treatment set out above. Such an approach, whereby the recognition of a decommissioning liability and its associated asset is treated as a single transaction that gives rise to both a taxable temporary difference (on the asset) and a deductible temporary difference (on the liability), is consistent with the underlying intention of the initial recognition exception (that the reporting entity should provide for deferred tax on initial recognition unless to do so would create an immediate net tax expense or credit in the statement of comprehensive income). That implied intention of the exception would not be breached by providing for deferred tax on initial recognition in such cases.

7.2.7.B Finance leases taxed as operating leases

In a number of jurisdictions, tax deductions are given for finance leases as if they were operating leases (i.e. on the basis of lease payments made). The total cost for both accounting and tax purposes is obviously the same over the period of the lease, but for accounting purposes the cost comprises depreciation of the asset together with finance costs on the lease liability, rather than the cash paid, which is treated as a movement in the statement of financial position. Application of the initial recognition exception separately to the recognition of the leased asset and the lease liability would lead to a result similar to that set out in the first table in Example 31.18 above, where the entity recognises neither a deferred tax asset for the temporary difference on the lease liability nor the corresponding deferred tax liability for the temporary difference on the leased asset.

As noted at 7.2.7.A above, an alternative would be to regard the asset and liability recognised at the inception of a finance lease (or on establishment of a decommissioning provision) as a single transaction that gives rise to both a taxable temporary difference (on the asset) and a deductible temporary difference (on the liability). The temporary differences are equal and opposite and presumably meet the criteria for offset in the standard (see 13.1.1 below), to give rise to a net temporary difference of zero. In this case, the initial recognition exemption does not apply because there is no net temporary difference. However, in subsequent periods the leased asset will most likely be amortised at a different rate to the underlying finance lease liability at which point a net deferred tax asset or liability will result. In these circumstances, the effective tax rate in the income statement reflects the statutory rate actually applicable to the transaction as a whole (as illustrated in the second table in Example 31.18 above).

The Interpretations Committee considered this issue on two occasions in 2005. *IFRIC Update* for April 2005 appeared to support the former view:

> 'The [Interpretations Committee] noted that initial recognition exemption applies to each separate recognised element in the [statement of financial position], and no deferred tax asset or liability should be recognised on the temporary difference existing on the initial recognition of assets and liabilities arising from finance leases or subsequently.'[12]

However, only two months later, the Committee added:

> 'The [Interpretations Committee] considered the treatment of deferred tax relating to assets and liabilities arising from finance leases.
>
> While noting that there is diversity in practice in applying the requirements of IAS 12 to assets and liabilities arising from finance leases, the [Interpretations Committee] agreed not to develop any guidance because the issue falls directly within the scope of the Board's short-term convergence project on income taxes with the FASB.'[13]

This appears to indicate that, whilst the Interpretations Committee regards the analysis that the asset and lease liability must be considered separately as consistent with the letter of IAS 12 as drafted, it accepts the alternative approach.

7.2.8 Initial recognition of compound financial instruments by the issuer

IAS 32 requires 'compound' financial instruments (those with both a liability feature and an equity feature, such as convertible bonds) to be accounted for by the issuer using so-called split accounting. This is discussed in more detail in Chapter 45 at 6, but in essence an entity is required to split the proceeds of issue of such an instrument (say €1 million) into a liability component, measured at its fair value based on real market rates for non-convertible debt rather than the nominal rate on the bond (say €750,000), with the balance being treated as an equity component (in this case €250,000).

Over the life of the instrument, the €750,000 carrying value of the liability element will be accreted back up to €1,000,000 (or such lower or higher sum as might be potentially repayable), so that the cumulative income statement interest charge will comprise:

(a) any actual cash interest payments made (which are tax-deductible in most jurisdictions); and

(b) the €250,000 accretion of the liability from €750,000 to €1,000,000 (which is not tax-deductible in most jurisdictions).

Where such an instrument is issued, IAS 12 requires the treatment in Example 31.19 to be adopted. *[IAS 12 IE Example 4]*.

Example 31.19: Compound financial instrument

An entity issues a zero-coupon convertible loan of €1,000,000 on 1 January 2018 repayable at par on 1 January 2021. In accordance with IAS 32, the entity classifies the instrument's liability component as a liability and the equity component as equity. The entity assigns an initial carrying amount of €750,000 to the liability component of the convertible loan and €250,000 to the equity component. Subsequently, the entity recognises the imputed discount of €250,000 as interest expense at the effective annual rate of 10% on the carrying amount of the liability component at the beginning of the year. The tax authorities do not allow the entity to claim any deduction for the imputed discount on the liability component of the convertible loan. The tax rate is 40%.

Temporary differences arise on the liability element as follows (all figures in € thousands).

	1.1.18	**31.12.18**	**31.12.19**	**31.12.20**
Carrying value of liability component[1]	750	825	908	1,000
Tax base	1,000	1,000	1,000	1,000
Taxable temporary difference	250	175	92	–
Deferred tax liability @ 40%	100	70	37	–

1 Balance carried forward at end of previous period plus 10% accretion of notional interest less repayments.

The deferred tax arising at 1 January 2018 is deducted from equity. Subsequent reductions in the deferred tax balance are recognised in the income statement, resulting in an effective tax rate of 40%. For example, in 2018, the entity will accrete notional interest of €75,000 (closing loan liability €825,000 less opening balance €750,000) with deferred tax income of €30,000 (closing deferred tax liability €70,000 less opening liability €100,000).

Whilst this treatment is explicitly required by IAS 12, its conceptual basis is far from clear, and causes some confusion in practice. In the first instance, it appears to contravene the prohibition on recognition of deferred tax on temporary differences arising on the initial recognition of assets and liabilities (other than in a business combination) that do not give rise to accounting or taxable profit or loss. IAS 12 argues that this temporary difference does not arise on initial recognition of a liability but as a result of the initial recognition of the equity component as a result of split accounting. *[IAS 12.23]*.

Even if this analysis is accepted, it remains unclear why the deferred tax should be deducted from equity. It may have been seen as an application of the general allocation principle of IAS 12 that the tax effects of transactions accounted for in equity should also be accounted for in equity – see 10 below. However, this would have been correct only if the accounting entry giving rise to the liability had been:

DR Equity	€750,000	
CR Liability		€750,000

The actual entry was:

DR Cash	€1,000,000	
CR Liability		€750,000
CR Equity		€250,000

Therefore, in fact the general allocation rule in IAS 12 would have required the deferred tax liability to be recognised as a charge to profit or loss. This would have resulted in a 'day one' tax expense, suggesting that that initial recognition exception ought, in principle, to have been applied here also.

The accounting treatment required by Example 31.19 above could be seen as no more than 'tax equalisation' accounting – i.e. the recognition of deferred tax of an amount that, when released to profit or loss, will yield an effective tax rate equivalent to the statutory rate. Some would question whether it is appropriate to represent as tax-deductible a charge to the income statement that in reality is not tax-deductible. Nevertheless, as noted above, this treatment is explicitly required by IAS 12.

7.2.9 Acquisition of subsidiary not accounted for as a business combination

Occasionally, an entity may acquire a subsidiary which is accounted for as the acquisition of an asset rather than as a business combination. This will most often be the case where the subsidiary concerned is a 'single asset entity' holding a single item of property, plant and equipment which is not considered to comprise a business. Where an asset is acquired in such circumstances, the initial recognition exception applies, as illustrated by the following example.

Example 31.20: Acquired subsidiary accounted for as asset purchase

An entity (P) acquires a subsidiary (S), whose only asset is a property, for $10 million. The transaction is accounted for as the acquisition of a property rather than as a business combination. The tax base of the property is $4 million and its carrying value in the financial statements of S (under IFRS) is $6 million. The taxable temporary difference of $2 million in the financial records of S arose after the initial recognition by S of the property, and accordingly a deferred tax liability of $800,000 has been recognised by S at its tax rate of 40%.

The question then arises as to whether any deferred tax should be recognised for the property in the financial statements of P.

Having determined that the acquisition does not constitute a business combination, the initial recognition exception applies to the entire $6 million difference between the carrying value of the property in the financial statements of P of $10 million and its tax base of $4 million, in exactly the same way as if the property had been legally acquired as a separate asset rather than through acquisition of the shares of S. *[IAS 12.15(b)]*. Therefore, no deferred tax is recognised by P in respect of the property at the time of its acquisition.

7.3 Assets carried at fair value or revalued amount

IAS 12 notes that certain IFRSs permit or require assets to be carried at fair value or to be revalued. These include: *[IAS 12.20]*

- IAS 16 – *Property, Plant and Equipment*;
- IAS 38 – *Intangible Assets*;
- IAS 39 – *Financial Instruments: Recognition and Measurement*; and
- IAS 40 – *Investment Property*.

This would also be the case for entities applying IFRS 9 – *Financial Instruments* – or *IFRS* 16 – *Leases*.[14]

In most jurisdictions, the revaluation or restatement of an asset does not affect taxable profit in the period of the revaluation or restatement. Nevertheless, the future recovery of the carrying amount will result in a taxable flow of economic benefits to the entity and the amount that will be deductible for tax purposes (i.e. the original tax base) will differ from the amount of those economic benefits.

The difference between the carrying amount of a revalued asset and its tax base is a temporary difference and gives rise to a deferred tax liability or asset. IAS 12 clarifies that this is the case even if:

- the entity does not intend to dispose of the asset. In such cases, the revalued carrying amount of the asset will be recovered through use and this will generate taxable income which exceeds the depreciation that will be allowable for tax purposes in future periods; or
- tax on capital gains is deferred if the proceeds of the disposal of the asset are invested in similar assets. In such cases, the tax will ultimately become payable on sale or use of the similar assets. *[IAS 12.20]*. A discussion of the accounting for deferred taxable gains can be found at 7.7 below.

In some jurisdictions, the revaluation or other restatement of an asset to fair value affects taxable profit (tax loss) for the current period. In such cases, the tax base of the asset may be raised by an amount equivalent to the revaluation gain, so that no temporary difference arises.

7.4 Restrictions on recognition of deferred tax assets

There is an essential difference between deferred tax liabilities and deferred tax assets. An entity's deferred tax liabilities will crystallise if the entity recovers its existing net assets at their carrying amount. However, in order to realise its net deferred tax assets in full, an entity must earn profits in excess of those represented by the carrying amount of its net assets in order to generate sufficient taxable profits against which the deductions represented by deferred tax assets can be offset. Accordingly IAS 12 restricts the recognition of deferred tax assets to the extent that it is probable that taxable profit will be available against which the underlying deductible temporary differences can be utilised. *[IAS 12.27]*.

7.4.1 Restrictions imposed by relevant tax laws

When an entity assesses whether a deductible temporary difference is capable of being utilised, it must consider whether tax law restricts the sources of taxable profits against which deductions for this type of temporary difference are permitted. If tax law imposes no such restrictions, an entity can assess a deductible temporary difference in combination with all its other deductible temporary differences. However, if tax law restricts the utilisation of losses to deduction against a specific type of income, the recovery of a deductible temporary difference is assessed in combination only with other deductible temporary differences of the appropriate type. *[IAS 12.27A]*.

7.4.2 Sources of 'probable' taxable profit – taxable temporary differences

Before considering forecasts of future taxable profits, an entity should look to the deferred tax liabilities it has already recognised at the reporting date as a source of probable taxable profits that would allow any deductible temporary differences to be utilised. IAS 12 states that it is 'probable' that there will be sufficient taxable profit if a deductible temporary difference can be offset against a taxable temporary difference (deferred tax liability) relating to the same tax authority and the same taxable entity which will reverse in the same period as the asset, or in a period into which a loss arising from the asset may be carried back or forward. In such circumstances, a deferred tax asset is recognised. *[IAS 12.28]*.

There is no need at this stage to estimate the future taxable profits of the entity. If there are sufficient taxable temporary differences to justify the recognition of a deferred tax asset for deductible temporary differences, then the asset is recognised. The only condition to apply, as noted at 7.4.1 above, is that any deferred tax liability used as the basis for recognising a deferred tax asset represents a future tax liability against which the deductible temporary difference can actually be offset under the relevant tax law. *[IAS 12.27A]*. For example, in a tax jurisdiction where revenue and capital items are treated separately for tax purposes, a deferred tax asset representing a capital loss cannot be recognised by reference to a deferred tax liability relating to tax allowances received on PP&E in advance of the related depreciation expense.

7.4.3 Sources of 'probable' taxable profit – estimates of future taxable profits

Estimates of future taxable profits are only required to justify the recoverability of those deductible temporary differences in excess of the amounts already 'matched' against deferred tax liabilities recognised at the reporting date in the manner described at 7.4.2 above. Where there are insufficient taxable temporary differences relating to the same tax authority to offset deductible temporary differences, a deferred tax asset should be recognised to the extent that:

- it is probable that in future periods there will be sufficient taxable profits:
  - relating to the same tax authority;
  - relating to the same taxable entity; and
  - arising in the same period as the reversal of the deductible temporary difference or in a period into which a loss arising from the deferred tax asset may be carried back or forward; or
- tax planning opportunities are available that will create taxable profit in appropriate periods – see 7.4.4 below. *[IAS 12.29]*.

Where an entity has a history of recent losses it should also consider the guidance in IAS 12 for recognition of such losses (see 7.4.6 below). *[IAS 12.31]*.

7.4.3.A Ignore the origination of new future deductible temporary differences

In assessing the availability of future taxable profits, an entity must ignore taxable amounts arising from deductible temporary differences expected to originate in future periods. This is because those new deductible differences will themselves require future taxable profit in order to be utilised. *[IAS 12.29(a)(ii)]*.

For example, suppose that in 2017 an entity charges £100 to profit or loss for which a tax deduction is not available until 2018, when the amount is settled. However, in 2018 a further £100 is expected to be charged to profit or loss, for which a deduction will be available in 2019, and so on for the foreseeable future. This will have the effect that, in 2017, the entity will pay tax on the £100 for which no deduction is made on the 2017 tax return. In the tax return for 2018, there will be a deduction for that £100, but this will be offset by the add-back in the same tax return for the equivalent £100 charged for accounting purposes in 2018. If this cycle of '£100 deduction less £100 add-back' is expected to be perpetuated in each tax return for the foreseeable future, there is never any real recovery of the tax paid on the £100 in 2017 and, in the absence of any other taxable profits, no deferred tax asset would be recognised.

7.4.3.B Ignore the reversal of existing deductible temporary differences

In 2016, the IASB added text to the standard to clarify that the estimate of probable future taxable profit should exclude the tax deductions resulting from the reversal of the deductible temporary differences that are themselves being assessed for recognition as an asset. *[IAS 12.29(a)(i)]*. This amendment was made following the IASB's deliberations on the recognition of deferred tax assets for unrealised losses, as discussed at 7.4.5 below. The effect of the amendment is to clarify that the measure of taxable profit used for assessing the utilisation of deductible temporary differences is different from the taxable profit on which income taxes are payable. *[IAS 12.BC56]*.

The former is calculated before any allowances or deductions arising from the reversal of deductible temporary differences. The latter is the amount determined after the application of all applicable tax laws that gives rise to an entity's liability to pay income tax. *[IAS 12.5]*.

7.4.4 Tax planning opportunities

'Tax planning opportunities' are actions that the entity would take in order to create or increase taxable income in a particular period before the expiry of a tax loss or tax credit carryforward. IAS 12 notes that, in some jurisdictions, taxable profit may be created or increased by:

- electing to have interest income taxed on either a received or receivable basis;
- deferring the claim for certain deductions from taxable profit;
- selling, and perhaps leasing back, assets that have appreciated but for which the tax base has not been adjusted to reflect such appreciation; and
- selling an asset that generates non-taxable income (such as, in some jurisdictions, a government bond) in order to purchase another investment that generates taxable income.

Where tax planning opportunities advance taxable profit from a later period to an earlier period, the utilisation of a tax loss or tax credit carryforward still depends on the existence of future taxable profit from sources other than future originating temporary differences. *[IAS 12.30]*.

The requirement to have regard to future tax planning opportunities applies only to the measurement of deferred tax assets. It does not apply to the measurement of deferred tax liabilities. Thus, for example, it would not be open to an entity subject to tax at 30% to argue that it should provide for deferred tax liabilities at some lower rate on the grounds that it intends to invest in assets attracting investment tax credits that will allow it to pay tax at that lower rate (see 8.4.1 below).

IAS 12 describes tax planning opportunities as actions that the entity 'would' take – not those it 'could' take. In other words, they are restricted to future courses of action that the entity would actually undertake to realise such a deferred tax asset, and do not include actions that are theoretically possible but practically implausible, such as the sale of an asset essential to the ongoing operations of the entity. Only if such actions are both capable of being taken and are intended to be taken by the entity can it be said that the resulting tax planning would give rise to a 'probable' future taxable profit.

Implementation of a tax planning opportunity may well entail significant direct costs or the loss of other tax benefits or both. Accordingly, any deferred tax asset recognised on the basis of a tax planning opportunity must be reduced by any cost of implementing that opportunity (measured, where applicable, on an after-tax basis).

Moreover, IAS 12 regards tax planning opportunities as a component of future net taxable profits. Thus, where a tax planning opportunity exists, but the entity is expected to remain loss-making (such that the opportunity effectively will simply reduce future tax losses), we believe that such an opportunity does not generally form the basis for recognising a deferred tax asset, except to the extent that it will create *net* future taxable profits (see also 7.4.6 below).

7.4.5 Unrealised losses on available-for-sale debt securities

In January 2016, the IASB issued *Recognition of Deferred Tax Assets for Unrealised Losses (Amendments to IAS 12).* These amendments concluded deliberations started by the Interpretations Committee in May 2010 on the recognition of deferred tax assets for unrealised losses, for example on debt instruments measured at fair value. *[IAS 12.BC1A].*

The Committee had been asked to provide guidance on how an entity determines whether to recognise a deferred tax asset under IAS 12 in the following circumstances: *[IAS 12.BC37]*

(a) the entity classifies a debt instrument as an available-for-sale financial asset under IAS 39 (or has a debt instrument measured at fair value under IFRS 9) and changes in market interest rates result in a decrease in the fair value of the debt instrument below its cost;

(b) it is probable that the issuer of the debt instrument will make all the contractual payments;

(c) the tax base of the debt instrument is its cost;

(d) tax law does not allow a loss to be deducted on a debt instrument until the loss is realised for tax purposes;

(e) the entity has the ability and intention to hold the debt instrument until the unrealised loss reverses (which may be at its maturity);

(f) tax law distinguishes between capital gains and losses and ordinary income tax losses. While capital losses can only be offset against capital gains, ordinary losses can be offset against both capital gains and ordinary income; and

(g) the entity has insufficient taxable temporary differences and no other probable taxable profits against which the entity can utilise those deductible temporary differences.

The Interpretations Committee had identified diversity in practice because of uncertainty about the application of some of the principles in IAS 12, in particular in relation to the following:

(a) The existence of a deductible temporary difference, when there are no tax consequences to the recovery of the principal on maturity; the holder of the debt instrument expects to hold it to maturity; and it is probable that the issuer will pay all the contractual cash flows. *[IAS 12.BC38, BC39]*.

(b) Whether it is appropriate for an entity to determine deductible temporary differences and taxable temporary differences on the basis of the asset's carrying amount when at the same time it assumes that the asset is recovered for more than its carrying amount for the purposes of estimating probable future taxable profit against which deductible temporary differences are assessed for utilisation. This question is relevant when taxable profit from other sources is insufficient for the utilisation of the deductible temporary differences arising when the asset is measured at fair value. *[IAS 12.BC38, BC47]*.

(c) Whether the estimate of probable future taxable profit should include or exclude the effects of reversing the deductible temporary differences that are being assessed for recognition as an asset. *[IAS 12.BC38, BC55]*.

(d) The basis for assessing the recoverability of deductible temporary differences, i.e. for each deductible temporary difference separately, or in combination with other deductible temporary differences. This question is relevant, for example, when tax law distinguishes capital gains and losses from other taxable gains and losses and capital losses can only be offset against capital gains. *[IAS 12.BC38, BC57]*.

Whilst the amendments to IAS 12 were framed around the above example of a fixed-rate debt instrument classified as available-for-sale, the Board noted that the principle on which the amendments are based is not limited to any specific type or class of assets. *[IAS 12.BC52]*. However, as noted at 7.4.5.B below, the IASB acknowledged the concerns raised by respondents that the amendments could be applied too broadly and highlighted the need for particular caution where assets are measured at fair value. In response to that concern, the Board noted that entities will need to have sufficient evidence on which to base their estimate of probable future taxable profit, including when that estimate involves the recovery of an asset for more than its carrying amount. *[IAS 12.BC53]*.

7.4.5.A *The existence of a deductible temporary difference*

Because, in the case of many debt instruments, the collection of the principle on maturity does not give rise to any liability for tax, some believed that the collection of the principal is a non-taxable event. Consequently, proponents of this view argued that a deductible temporary difference cannot exist when an entity asserts that the contractual payments will be received, because any difference between the debt instrument's carrying amount and its higher tax base results from a loss that the entity expects never to realise for tax purposes. *[IAS 12.BC40]*.

The IASB rejected this argument. IAS 12 already states that a deductible temporary difference arises if the tax base of an asset exceeds its carrying amount. *[IAS 12.20, 26(d)]*. The calculation of a temporary difference is based on the premise that the carrying amount of the asset will be recovered. *[IAS 12.5]*. The calculation of the temporary difference is not affected by possible future changes in the carrying amount of the asset. The Board considered that the economic benefit embodied in the related deferred tax asset results from the ability of the holder of the debt instrument to achieve future taxable gains in the amount of the deductible temporary difference without paying tax on those gains. This is the case where a previous impairment reverses, such that the entity recovers the original principal on the debt instrument. *[IAS 12.BC42-44]*. Accordingly, the amendments add an example after paragraph 26 of IAS 12 to illustrate how a deductible temporary difference exists under paragraph 26(d).

Example 31.21: Deductible temporary difference when the asset is valued below cost

At the beginning of Year 1, Entity A purchases for $1,000 a debt instrument with a nominal value of $1,000 payable at the end of Year 5 and with an interest rate of 2% payable at the end of each year. The effective interest rate is determined to be 2% and the debt instrument is measured at fair value.

At the end of year 2, market interest rates have increased to 5%, causing the fair value of the debt instrument to decrease to $918. It is probable that Entity A will collect all the contractual cash flows if it continues to hold the debt instrument.

Any gains or losses on the debt instrument are taxable or deductible only when realised. Gains or losses arising on the sale or maturity of the instrument are calculated for tax purposes as the difference between the amount collected and the original cost of the debt instrument. Accordingly, the tax base of the debt instrument is its original cost.

The Example concludes that the difference between the carrying amount of the debt instrument of $918 and its tax base of $1,000 gives rise to a deductible temporary difference of $82 at the end of Year 2, *[IAS 12.20, 26(d)]*, irrespective of whether Entity A expects to recover the carrying amount of the debt instrument by sale or by use, i.e. by holding it and collecting contractual cash flows, or a combination of both. Whether the asset is realised on sale or on maturity (i.e. through use), Entity A will obtain a tax deduction equivalent to the tax base of $1,000 in determining any resultant taxable profit.

7.4.5.B Recovering an asset for more than its carrying amount

The Board concluded that the estimate of probable future taxable profit may include the recovery of some of an entity's assets for more than their carrying amount, but only if there is sufficient evidence that it is probable that the entity will achieve this. In the case of a fixed-rate debt instrument measured at fair value, recovery for more than the carrying amount is probable if the entity expects to collect the contractual cash flows. *[IAS 12.29A]*.

The determination of temporary differences and the estimation of probable future taxable profit are two separate steps, and the IASB concluded that the carrying amount of an asset is relevant only to determining the temporary differences. *[IAS 12.BC49]*. Indeed, the Board identified scenarios where an inappropriate outcome can arise if the possibility of realising a profit in excess of the carrying amount were limited. For example, a profitable manufacturing company relies on a business model that involves the sale of inventories and the recovery of property, plant and equipment for amounts exceeding their cost. Therefore, where such assets are recorded using the cost model, it would be inconsistent to assume that the entity will only recover these assets for their carrying amount. *[IAS 12.BC50]*. Nevertheless, in response to concerns raised by respondents that the amendment could be applied inappropriately, the Board acknowledged the need for caution where assets are measured at fair value. The risk of arbitrary estimates of future taxable profit is reduced where entities rely on evidence, such as the existence of contractual cash flows and an expectation of their recovery. *[IAS 12.BC53]*. For example, it would not be appropriate to assume recovery greater than an asset's carrying amount at fair value on the basis of an arbitrary assertion that fair value will inevitably recover in line with a longer-term improvement in the related market for the asset in question.

7.4.5.C Excluding the reversal of existing deductible temporary differences

During its deliberations, the Interpretations Committee observed uncertainty about how entities should calculate the measure of taxable profit that is used for assessing the amounts available for the future utilisation of deductible temporary differences. In particular, there seemed to be diversity of opinion relating to whether entities should include or exclude deductions that will arise when those deductible temporary differences reverse. *[IAS 12.BC55]*. As discussed above at 7.4.3.B, the IASB concluded that the estimate of future taxable profit used to assess whether deductions can be utilised is not the same as 'taxable profit' (which is the amount determined after the application of all applicable tax laws that gives rise to an entity's liability to pay income tax. *[IAS 12.5]*).

Therefore, entities should exclude the effect of deductions arising from the reversal of the deductible temporary differences being assessed for recoverability, or they would be counted twice. *[IAS 12.29(a)(i), BC56]*.

7.4.5.D The basis for assessing the recoverability of deductible temporary differences

As noted at 7.4 above, IAS 12 restricts the recognition of deferred tax assets to the extent that it is probable that taxable profit will be available against which the underlying deductible temporary differences can be utilised. *[IAS 12.27]*.

The Board noted that this is a matter for tax law; that IAS 12 defines taxable profit by reference to the application of the rules determined by tax authorities; and that no deferred tax is recognised if the reversal of the temporary difference will not lead to tax deductions. *[IAS 12.BC58]*. Therefore, the assessment of whether a deductible temporary difference can be utilised considers on a combined basis all deductible temporary differences relating to the same taxation authority and same taxable entity that are treated in a similar way under tax law. However, if tax law offsets specific types of losses against particular categories of income (for example when tax law allows capital losses to be deducted only against capital gains) such temporary differences are segregated according to their treatment under the relevant tax law. *[IAS 12.BC59]*.

IAS 12 was amended to clarify that entities making the assessment of the availability of taxable profits against which a deductible temporary difference can be utilised should do so in combination with all other deductible temporary differences, unless tax law restricts the sources of taxable profits against which that deductible temporary difference can be utilised. Where restrictions exist, the assessment is made together only with deductible temporary differences recoverable from the same sources. *[IAS 12.27A]*.

The amendments to IAS 12 add an example to illustrate how these requirements are applied to debt instruments measured at fair value, on which Example 31.22 below is based. *[IAS 12 Example 7]*.

Example 31.22: Debt instruments measured at fair value

At 31 December 2017 an entity holds a portfolio of three debt instruments, which are measured at fair value through other comprehensive income:

Debt instrument (All amounts in €)	**Cost**	**Fair value**	**Contractual interest rate**
Debt instrument A	2,000,000	1,942,857	2.00%
Debt instrument B	750,000	778,571	9.00%
Debt instrument C	2,000,000	1,961,905	3.00%

All the debt instruments were acquired for their nominal value. All three debt instruments mature on 31 December 2018, on which date repayment of the nominal value is due. Interest is paid at the end of each year. When the instruments were acquired, the contractually fixed interest rates were equal to the relevant market rates. However, at December 2017 the market interest rate is 5%, resulting in the fair value of instruments A and C to be below their cost and the fair value of instrument B to be above its cost. It is probable that the entity would receive all the contractual cash flows if it continues to hold the debt instruments.

The entity expects to hold instruments A and B to maturity, collecting the cash flows as they fall due, and to sell instrument C in early 2018 for its fair value of €1,961,905.

The tax base of the debt instruments is cost, which is deductible either on maturity when the principal is paid or against any sale proceeds when the instruments are sold. Tax law specifies that gains (losses) on the debt instruments are taxable (deductible) only when realised. Tax law distinguishes ordinary gains and losses from capital gains and losses. Ordinary losses can be offset against both ordinary gains and capital gains. Capital losses can only be offset against capital gains. Capital losses can be carried forward for 5 years and ordinary losses can be carried forward for 20 years.

Ordinary gains are taxed at 30 per cent and capital gains are taxed at 10 per cent.

Tax law classifies interest income from the debt instruments as 'ordinary' and gains and losses arising on the sale of the debt instruments as 'capital'. Losses that arise if the issuer of the debt instrument fails to pay the principal on maturity are classified as ordinary by tax law.

In addition to the above, there are other taxable temporary differences of €50,000 and deductible temporary differences of €430,000 which are expected to reverse in ordinary taxable profit in 2018.

In summary, the following temporary differences are identified at 31 December 2017:

Temporary differences (All amounts in €)	**Carrying amount**	**Tax base**	**Taxable temporary differences**	**Deductible temporary differences**
Debt instrument A	1,942,857	2,000,000		57,143
Debt instrument B	778,571	750,000	28,571	
Debt instrument C	1,961,905	2,000,000		38,095
Other sources (not specified)			50,000	430,000
Total temporary differences			78,571	525.238
Expected to reverse in ordinary gains or losses			78,571	487,143
Expected to reverse as capital losses				38,095

The entity expects to report an ordinary tax loss of €200,000 for the year ending 31 December 2018. The deductible temporary difference on instrument C is classified as a capital loss because it is expected to be realised by sale. There are no other capital gains against which the entity could utilise capital losses in the current or future periods. What is the entity's deferred tax asset or liability as at 31 December 2017?

The entity assesses the availability of probable future taxable profits in two steps:

- Step 1: Determine the availability of taxable temporary differences at the reporting date. *[IAS 12.28]*.
- Step 2: Determine the availability of probable future taxable profits. *[IAS 12.29]*.

Step 1: Determine the availability of Taxable temporary differences at the reporting date

All of the taxable temporary differences are expected to reverse in ordinary gains or losses and should therefore be compared to the deductible temporary differences of €487,143 that are capable of being utilised against ordinary gains. Accordingly, a deferred tax asset of €78,571 is justified at this stage, with €408,572 (487,143 less 78,571) of deductible temporary differences remaining to be utilised against ordinary gains or losses.

Step 2: Determine the availability of probable future taxable profits

The fact pattern states that the entity expects to report an ordinary tax loss of €200,000 for 2018. As noted at 7.4.5.C above, this figure is the amount determined after the application of all applicable tax laws that gives rise to an entity's liability to pay income tax. In order to calculate the available profits against which the deductible temporary differences can be utilised, the effect of deductions arising from the reversal of the deductible temporary differences must be excluded. The gives a probable future taxable profit of €208,572, as follows:

Excluding the reversal of existing temporary differences	**Amount €**
Expected tax loss reported for 2018	(200,000)
Reversal of taxable temporary differences (ordinary gains and losses)	(78,571)
Reversal of deductible temporary differences (ordinary gains and losses)	487,143
Probable taxable profit for 2018 excluding the effect of reversals	208,572

Accordingly, the entity recognises a deferred tax asset in respect of deductible temporary differences of €287,143, comprising €78,571 justified by reference to taxable temporary differences existing at the reporting date and €208,572 expected to be utilised against probable taxable profits in 2018. All of these deductible temporary differences are expected to reverse in ordinary gains or losses, for which the applicable tax rate is 30%.

Therefore, at 31 December 2017, the entity reports a deferred tax liability of €23,571, a deferred tax asset of €86,143 and unrecognised deductible temporary differences of €238,095, as follows:

Temporary differences (All amounts in €)	**Amount**	**Tax rate**	**Deferred tax liability**	**Deferred tax asset**
Taxable temporary differences	78,571	30%	23,571	
Total deductible temporary differences	525.238			
Less: eligible for recognition	(287,143)	30%		86,143
Unrecognised	238,095			

The unrecognised deductible temporary differences comprise €38,095 expected to reverse in capital gains and losses and €200,000 (487,143 – 287,143) expected to reverse in ordinary gains and losses.

7.4.5.E Transitional relief on initial application of the amendments to IAS 12

The amendments described above apply retrospectively for annual periods beginning on or after 1 January 2017. Earlier application is permitted, provided that this fact is disclosed. However, on initial application of the amendment, an entity is not required to allocate the restatement of opening equity of the earliest period presented between retained earnings and other components of equity, provided that use of this relief is disclosed. *[IAS 12.98G]*.

7.4.6 Unused tax losses and unused tax credits

A deferred tax asset should be recognised for the carryforward of unused tax losses and unused tax credits to the extent that it is probable that future taxable profit will be available against which the unused tax losses and unused tax credits can be utilised. *[IAS 12.34]*.

The criteria for recognition are essentially the same as those for deductible temporary differences, as set out in 7.4.1 to 7.4.4 above, in particular that it is 'probable' that there will be sufficient taxable profit against which a deductible temporary difference can be utilised when there are sufficient taxable temporary differences relating to the same taxation authority and the same taxable entity which are expected to reverse in the same period as the asset, or in a period into which a loss arising from the asset may be carried back or forward. *[IAS 12.28]*.

However, IAS 12 emphasises that the existence of unused tax losses is strong evidence that taxable profits (other than those represented by deferred tax liabilities) may not be available. Therefore, an entity with a history of recent losses recognises a deferred tax asset arising from unused tax losses or tax credits only to the extent that: *[IAS 12.35]*

- it has sufficient taxable temporary differences; or
- there is other convincing evidence that sufficient taxable profit will be available against which the unused tax losses or unused tax credits can be utilised by the entity.

In May 2014, the Interpretations Committee confirmed that the consideration of available reversing taxable temporary differences is made independently of the assessment of an entity's expectations of future tax losses. Accordingly, a deferred tax asset is recognised for the carryforward of unused tax losses to the extent of the existing taxable temporary differences, of an appropriate type, that reverse in an appropriate period. The reversal of those taxable temporary differences enables the utilisation of the unused tax losses and justifies the recognition of deferred tax assets.[15]

In addition to the question noted above, the Interpretations Committee was asked to clarify how the guidance in IAS 12 is applied when tax laws limit the extent to which tax losses brought forward can be recovered against future taxable profits. In the tax systems considered for this issue, the amount of tax losses brought forward that can be recovered in each tax year is limited to a specified percentage of the taxable profits of that year.

In these circumstances, the Committee noted that the amount of deferred tax assets recognised from unused tax losses as a result of suitable existing taxable temporary differences should be restricted as specified by the tax law. This is because when the suitable taxable temporary differences reverse, the amount of tax losses that can be utilised by that reversal is reduced as specified by the tax law. Also, the Committee noted that in this case future tax losses are not considered.[16]

Consequently, the availability of future taxable profits is only required to be considered if the unused tax losses exceed the amount of suitable existing taxable temporary differences (after taking into account any restrictions). The Interpretations Committee also confirmed in May 2014 that an additional deferred tax asset is recognised only if the following requirements are met:[17] *[IAS 12.36]*

- the entity has sufficient taxable temporary differences relating to the same taxation authority and the same taxable entity, which will result in taxable amounts against which the unused tax losses or unused tax credits can be utilised before they expire;
- the entity will have taxable profits before the unused tax losses or unused tax credits expire;
- whether the unused tax losses result from identifiable causes which are unlikely to recur; and
- whether tax planning opportunities (see 7.4.4 above) are available to the entity that will create taxable profit in the period in which the unused tax losses or unused tax credits can be utilised.

To the extent that it is not probable that taxable profit will be available against which the unused tax losses or unused tax credits can be utilised, a deferred tax asset is not recognised. *[IAS 12.36]*. Additional disclosures are required when an entity recognises a deferred tax asset on the assumption that there will be future taxable profits available in excess of the amount of existing taxable temporary differences, and the entity has suffered a loss in either the current or preceding period in the tax jurisdiction to which the deferred tax asset relates (see 14.3 below). *[IAS 12.35]*.

Some have suggested that the IASB should set time limits on the foresight period used. We consider that such generalised guidance would be inappropriate, particularly in the context of an international standard, which must address the great variety of tax systems that exist worldwide, and which impose a wide range of restrictions on the carryforward of tax losses or tax credits. In any event, it may well be the case that a deferred tax asset recoverable in twenty years from profits from a currently existing long-term supply contract with a creditworthy customer may be more robust than one recoverable in one year from expected future trading by a start-up company.

7.4.7 Re-assessment of deferred tax assets

An entity must review its deferred tax assets, both recognised and unrecognised, at each reporting date.

7.4.7.A Previously recognised assets

An entity should reduce the carrying amount of a deferred tax asset to the extent that it is no longer probable that sufficient taxable profit will be available to enable the asset to be recovered. Any such reduction should be reversed if it subsequently becomes probable that sufficient taxable profit will be available. *[IAS 12.56]*.

7.4.7.B *Previously unrecognised assets*

An entity recognises a previously unrecognised deferred tax asset to the extent that it has become probable that sufficient taxable profit will be available to enable the asset to be recovered. For example, an improvement in trading conditions may make it more probable that the entity will be able to generate sufficient taxable profit in the future for the deferred tax asset to meet the recognition criteria. Special considerations apply when an entity re-appraises deferred tax assets of an acquired business at the date of the business combination or subsequently (see 12.1.2 below). *[IAS 12.37]*.

7.4.8 *Effect of disposals on recoverability of tax losses*

In consolidated financial statements, the disposal of a subsidiary may lead to the derecognition of a deferred tax asset in respect of tax losses because either:

- the entity disposed of had incurred those tax losses itself; or
- the entity disposed of was the source of probable future taxable profits against which the tax losses of another member of the group could be offset, allowing the group to recognise a deferred tax asset.

It is clear that, once the disposal has been completed, those tax losses will no longer appear in the disposing entity's statement of financial position. What is less clear is whether those tax losses should be derecognised before the disposal itself is accounted for – and if so, when. IAS 12 does not give any explicit guidance on this point, beyond the general requirement to recognise tax losses only to the extent that their recoverability is probable (see 7.4 above).

In our view, three broad circumstances need to be considered:

- the entity has recognised a deferred tax asset in respect of tax losses of the subsidiary to be disposed of, the recoverability of which is dependent on future profits of that subsidiary (see 7.4.8.A below);
- the entity has recognised a deferred tax asset in respect of tax losses of a subsidiary that is to remain in the group, the recoverability of which is dependent on future profits of the subsidiary to be disposed of (see 7.4.8.B below); and
- the entity has recognised a deferred tax asset in respect of tax losses of the subsidiary to be disposed of, the recoverability of which is dependent on future profits of one or more entities that are to remain in the group (see 7.4.8.C below).

7.4.8.A *Tax losses of subsidiary disposed of recoverable against profits of that subsidiary*

In this situation, we consider that the deferred tax asset for the losses should remain recognised until the point of disposal, provided that the expected proceeds of the disposal are expected at least to be equal to the total consolidated net assets of the entity to be disposed of, including the deferred tax asset. Whilst the group will no longer recover the tax losses through a reduction in its future tax liabilities, it will effectively recover their value through the disposal. Moreover, it would be expected that the disposal price would reflect the availability of usable tax losses in the disposed of entity, albeit that any price paid would reflect the fair value of such tax losses, rather than the undiscounted value required to be recorded by IAS 12 (see 8.6 below).

7.4.8.B Tax losses of retained entity recoverable against profits of subsidiary disposed of

In this case, we believe that IAS 12 requires the deferred tax asset to be derecognised once the disposal of the profitable subsidiary is probable (effectively meaning that the recoverability of losses by the retained entity is no longer probable). This derecognition threshold may be reached before the subsidiary to be disposed of is classified as held for sale under IFRS 5 – *Non-current Assets Held for Sale and Discontinued Operations* (see Chapter 4). This is because the threshold for derecognising the deferred tax asset under IAS 12 (i.e. that the sale of the subsidiary is probable) is lower than the threshold for accounting for the net assets of subsidiary under IFRS 5 (i.e. that the subsidiary is ready for sale, and the sale is highly probable).

7.4.8.C Tax losses of subsidiary disposed of recoverable against profits of retained entity

In this situation, we believe that more than one analysis is possible. One view would be that – as in 7.4.8.A above – a deferred tax asset for the losses should remain recognised until the point of disposal, provided that the expected proceeds of the disposal are expected at least to be equal to the total consolidated net assets of the entity to be disposed of, including the deferred tax asset. Another view would be that the asset should be derecognised. In contrast to the situation in 7.4.8.A, it is not the case that the losses are of any benefit to the acquiring entity (since they are recognised by virtue of the expected profits of other entities in the group which are not being sold. Rather, as in 7.4.8.B above, the likely separation of the subsidiary from the profits available in one or more retained entities means that the utilisation of those losses by the retained subsidiary is no longer probable. A third view would be that it is necessary to determine whether or not the losses would be of value to the acquirer. If so, they should continue to be recognised to the extent that they are being recovered by the disposing entity through the sales proceeds (as in 7.4.8.A above). If not, they should be derecognised on the grounds that they will not be recovered either through a reduction in future taxable profits of the disposing entity, or through sale (as in 7.4.8.B above).

7.5 'Outside' temporary differences relating to subsidiaries, branches, associates and joint arrangements

Investments in subsidiaries, branches and associates or interests in joint arrangements can give rise to two types of temporary difference:

- Differences between the tax base of the investment or interest – typically the original cost of the equity held in that investment or interest – and its carrying amount. 'Carrying amount' in this context means:
  - in separate financial statements, the carrying amount of the relevant investment or interest, and

- in financial statements other than separate financial statements, the carrying amount of the net assets (including goodwill) relating to the relevant investment or interest, whether accounted for by consolidation or equity accounting.

These differences are generally referred to in practice as 'outside' temporary differences, and normally arise in the tax jurisdiction of the entity that holds the equity in the investment or interest. Accordingly, in general they directly affect the taxable profit of the investor entity.

- In financial statements other than separate financial statements, differences between the tax bases of the individual assets and liabilities of the investment or interest and the carrying amounts of those assets and liabilities (as included in those financial statements through consolidation or equity accounting).

These differences are generally referred to in practice as 'inside' temporary differences. They normally arise in the tax jurisdiction of the investment or interest and affect the taxable profit of the investee entity.

This section is concerned with 'outside' temporary differences, the most common source of which is the undistributed profits of the investee entities, where distribution to the investor would trigger a tax liability. 'Outside' temporary differences may also arise from a change in the carrying value of an investment due to exchange movements, provisions, or revaluations; or from a change in the tax base of the investee in the jurisdiction of the investor.

The reversal of most 'inside' temporary differences is essentially inevitable as assets are recovered or liabilities settled at their carrying amount in the normal course of business. However, an entity may be able to postpone the reversal of some or all of its 'outside' differences more or less permanently. For example, if a distribution of the retained profits of a subsidiary would be subject to withholding tax, the parent may effectively be able to avoid such a tax by making the subsidiary reinvest all its profits into the business. IAS 12 recognises this essential difference in the nature of 'outside' and 'inside' temporary differences by setting different criteria for the recognition of 'outside' temporary differences.

7.5.1 Calculation of 'outside' temporary differences

As noted above, 'outside' temporary differences arise in both consolidated and separate financial statements and may well be different, due to the different bases used to account for subsidiaries, branches and associates or interests in joint arrangements in consolidated and separate financial statements. *[IAS 12.38]*. This is illustrated by Example 31.23 below.

Chapter 31

Example 31.23: Temporary differences associated with subsidiaries, branches, associates and joint arrangements

On 1 January 2017 entity H acquired 100% of the shares of entity S, whose functional currency is different from that of H, for €600m. The tax rate in H's tax jurisdiction is 30% and the tax rate in S's tax jurisdiction is 40%.

The fair value of the identifiable assets and liabilities (excluding deferred tax assets and liabilities) of S acquired by H is set out in the following table, together with their tax base in S's tax jurisdiction and the resulting temporary differences (all figures in € millions).

	Fair value	*Tax base*	*(Taxable)/ deductible temporary difference*
PP&E	270	155	(115)
Accounts receivable	210	210	–
Inventory	174	124	(50)
Retirement benefit obligations	(30)	–	30
Accounts payable	(120)	(120)	–
Fair value of net assets acquired excluding deferred tax	504	369	(135)
Deferred tax (135 @ 40%)	(54)		
Fair value of identifiable assets acquired and liabilities assumed	450		
Goodwill (balancing figure)	150		
Carrying amount	600		

No deferred tax is recognised on the goodwill, in accordance with the requirements of IAS 12 as discussed at 7.2.2.A above.

At the date of combination, the tax base, in H's tax jurisdiction, of H's investment in S is €600 million. Therefore, in H's jurisdiction, no temporary difference is associated with the investment, either in the consolidated financial statements of H (where the investment is represented by net assets and goodwill of €600 million), or in its separate financial statements, if prepared (where the investment is shown as an investment at cost of €600 million).

During 2017:

- S makes a profit after tax, as reported in H's consolidated financial statements, of €150 million, of which €80 million is paid as a dividend (after deduction of withholding tax) before 31 December 2017, leaving a net retained profit of €70 million.
- In accordance with IAS 21, H's consolidated financial statements record a loss of €15 million on retranslation to the closing exchange rate of S's opening net assets and profit for the period.
- In accordance with IAS 36 – *Impairment of Assets*, H's consolidated financial statements record an impairment loss of €10 million in respect of goodwill.

Thus in H's consolidated financial statements the carrying value of its investment in S is €645 million, comprising:

	€m
Carrying amount at 1.1.2017	600
Retained profit	70
Exchange loss	(15)
Impairment of goodwill	(10)
Carrying amount at 31.12.2017	645

7.5.1.A *Consolidated financial statements*

Assuming that the tax base in H's jurisdiction remains €600 million, there is a taxable temporary difference of €45 million (carrying amount €645m less tax base €600m) associated with S in H's consolidated financial statements. Whether or not any deferred tax is required to be provided for on this difference is determined in accordance with the principles discussed at 7.5.2 below. Any tax provided for would be allocated to profit or loss, other comprehensive income or equity in accordance with the general provisions of IAS 12 (see 10 below). In this case, the foreign exchange loss, as a presentational rather than a functional exchange difference, would be recognised in other comprehensive income (see Chapter 15 at 6.1), as would any associated tax effect. The other items, and their associated effects, would be recognised in profit or loss.

Irrespective of whether provision is made for deferred tax, H would be required to make disclosures in respect of this difference (see 14.2.2 below).

7.5.1.B *Separate financial statements*

The amount of any temporary difference in H's separate financial statements would depend on the accounting policy adopted in those statements. IAS 27 – *Separate Financial Statements* – allows entities the choice of accounting for investments in group companies at either cost (less impairment), using the equity method or at fair value – see Chapter 8 at 2. Suppose that, notwithstanding the impairment of goodwill required to be recognised in the consolidated financial statements, the investment in S taken as a whole is not impaired, and indeed its fair value at 31 December 2017 is €660 million.

If, in its separate financial statements, H accounts for its investment at cost of €600 million, there would be no temporary difference associated with S in H's separate financial statements, since the carrying amount and tax base of S would both be €600 million.

If, however, in its separate financial statements, H accounts for its investment at its fair value of €660 million, there would be a taxable temporary difference of €60 million (carrying amount €660m less tax base €600m) associated with S in H's separate financial statements. Whether or not any deferred tax is required to be provided for on this difference is determined in accordance with the principles discussed at 7.5.2 and at 7.5.3 below. Any tax provided for would be allocated to profit or loss, other comprehensive income or equity in accordance with the general provisions of IAS 12 (see 10 below). Irrespective of whether provision is made for deferred tax, H would be required to make disclosures in respect of this difference (see 14.2.2 below).

In August 2014, the IASB issued an amendment to IAS 27 – *Equity Method in Separate Financial Statements* (Amendments to IAS 27). The amendments introduced are mandatory for annual periods beginning on or after 1 January 2016. The amendments are to be applied retrospectively. *[IAS 27.18J]*. See Chapter 8 at 1.

The amendments to IAS 27 allow entities to use the equity method as described in IAS 28 – *Investments in Associates and Joint Ventures* – to account for investments in subsidiaries, joint ventures and associates in their separate financial statements. *[IAS 27.10(c)]*. Where the equity method is used, dividends from those investments are to be recognised as a reduction from the carrying value of the investment. *[IAS 27.12]*.

The same principles apply as those discussed above. Any difference between the carrying value of the entity's interest in its subsidiaries, joint ventures and associates, in this case determined using the equity method, and the tax base in the investor's jurisdiction gives rise to a temporary difference. Whether or not any deferred tax is required to be recognised on this difference is determined in accordance with the principles discussed at 7.5.2 below. Any tax provided for would be allocated to profit or loss, other comprehensive income or equity in accordance with the general provisions of IAS 12 (see 10 below).

7.5.2 Taxable temporary differences

IAS 12 requires a deferred tax liability to be recognised for all taxable temporary differences associated with investments (both domestic and foreign) in subsidiaries, branches and associates or interests in joint arrangements, unless:

(a) the parent, investor joint venturer or joint operator is able to control the timing of the reversal of the temporary difference; and

(b) it is probable that the temporary difference will not reverse in the foreseeable future. *[IAS 12.39]*.

IAS 12 does not currently define the meaning of 'probable' in this context. However, we consider that, as in other IFRSs, it should be taken to mean 'more likely than not'. IAS 12 also does not elaborate on the meaning of 'foreseeable'. In our view, the period used will be a matter of judgement in individual circumstances.

What this means in practice is best illustrated by reference to its application to the retained earnings of subsidiaries, branches and joint arrangements on the one hand, and those of associates on the other.

In the case of a subsidiary or a branch, the parent is able to control when and whether the retained earnings are distributed. Therefore, no provision need be made for the tax consequences of distribution of profits that the parent has determined will not be distributed in the foreseeable future. *[IAS 12.40]*. In the case of a joint arrangement, provided that the joint venturer or joint operator can control the distribution policy, similar considerations apply. *[IAS 12.43]*.

In the case of an associate, however, the investor cannot control the distribution policy. Therefore provision should be made for the tax consequences of the distribution of the retained earnings of an associate, except to the extent that there is a shareholders' agreement that those earnings will not be distributed.

Some might consider this a counter-intuitive result. In reality, it is extremely unusual for any entity (other than one set up for a specific project) to pursue a policy of full distribution. To the extent that it occurs at all, it is much more likely in a wholly-owned subsidiary than in an associate; and yet IAS 12 effectively treats full distribution by associates as the norm and that by subsidiaries as the exception. Moreover, it seems to ignore the fact that equity accounting was developed as a regulatory response to the perceived ability of investors in associates to exert some degree of control over the amount and timing of dividends from them.

In some jurisdictions, some or all of the temporary differences associated with such investments in subsidiaries, branches and associates or interests in joint arrangements are taxed on disposal of that investment or interest. Clearly, where the entity is contemplating such a disposal, it would no longer be able to assert that it is probable that the relevant temporary difference will not reverse in the foreseeable future.

The measurement of any deferred tax liability recognised is discussed at 8.4.9 below.

7.5.3 Deductible temporary differences

IAS 12 requires a deferred tax asset to be recognised for all deductible temporary differences associated with investments in subsidiaries, branches and associates or interests in joint arrangements, only to the extent that it is probable that:

(a) the temporary difference will reverse in the foreseeable future; and

(b) taxable profit will be available against which the temporary difference can be utilised. *[IAS 12.44]*.

IAS 12 does not define the meaning of 'probable' in this context. However, we consider that, as in other IFRS, it should be taken to mean 'more likely than not'.

The guidance discussed at 7.4 above is used to determine whether or not a deferred tax asset can be recognised for such deductible temporary differences. *[IAS 12.45]*.

Any analysis of whether a deductible temporary difference gives rise to an asset must presumably make the same distinction between controlled and non-controlled entities as is required when assessing whether a taxable temporary difference gives rise to a liability (see 7.5.2 above). This may mean, in practical terms, that it is never possible to recognise a deferred tax asset in respect of a non-controlled investment (such as an associate), unless either the investee entity is committed to a course of action that would realise the asset or, where the asset can be realised by disposal, that it is probable that the reporting entity will undertake such a disposal.

The measurement of any deferred tax asset recognised is discussed at 8.4.9 below.

7.5.4 Anticipated intragroup dividends in future periods

Under IAS 10 and IAS 18, a dividend may be recognised as a liability of the paying entity and revenue of the receiving entity only when it has been declared by the paying entity. This raises the question of when a reporting entity should account for the tax consequences of a dividend expected to be paid by a subsidiary out of its retained profits as at the reporting date.

7.5.4.A Consolidated financial statements of receiving entity

In our view, IAS 12 requires the group to make provision for the taxes payable on the retained profits of the group as at each reporting date based on the best evidence available to it at the reporting date. In other words, if in preparing its financial statements for 31 December 2017, an entity believes that, in order to meet the dividend expectations of its shareholders in 2018 and 2019, it will have to cause the retained earnings of certain overseas subsidiaries (as included in the group accounts at 31 December 2017) to be distributed, the group should provide for any tax consequences of such distributions in its consolidated financial statements for the period ended 31 December 2017.

It is not relevant that such dividends have not yet been recognised in the separate financial statements of the relevant members of the group. Indeed, such intragroup dividends will never be recognised in the group financial statements, as they will be eliminated on consolidation. What IAS 12 requires is a best estimate of the taxes ultimately payable on the net assets of the group as at 31 December 2017. However, for this reason it would not be appropriate to recognise any liability for the tax anticipated to be paid out of an intragroup dividend in a future period that is likely to be covered by profits made in *future* periods, since such profits do not form part of the net assets of the group as at 31 December 2017.

7.5.4.B Separate financial statements of paying entity

Irrespective of whether a provision is made in the consolidated financial statements for the tax effects of an expected future intragroup dividend of the retained earnings of a subsidiary, the paying subsidiary would not recognise a liability for the tax effects of any distribution in its individual or separate financial statements until the liability to pay the dividend was recognised in those individual or separate financial statements.

7.5.5 Unpaid intragroup interest, royalties, management charges etc.

It is common for groups of companies to access the earnings of subsidiaries not only through distribution by way of dividend, but also by levying charges on subsidiaries such as interest, royalties or general management charges for central corporate services. In practice, such charges are often not settled but left outstanding on the intercompany account between the subsidiary and the parent. In some jurisdictions such income is taxed only on receipt.

This has led some to argue that, where settlement of such balances is within the control of the reporting entity, and it can be demonstrated that there is no foreseeable intention or need to settle such balances, such balances are economically equivalent to unremitted earnings, so that there is no need to provide for the tax consequences of settlement.

In February 2003 the Interpretations Committee considered the issue and indicated that it believes that the exemption from provision for deferred taxes on 'outside' temporary differences arising from subsidiaries, branches, associates and interests in joint arrangements is intended to address the temporary differences arising from the undistributed earnings of such entities. The exception does not apply to the 'inside' temporary differences that exist between the carrying amount and the tax base of individual assets and liabilities within the subsidiary, branch, associate or interest in a joint arrangement. Accordingly, the Interpretations Committee concluded that a deferred tax liability should be provided for the tax consequences of settling unpaid intragroup charges.[18]

7.5.6 *Other overseas income taxed only on remittance*

In May 2007 the Interpretations Committee considered the more general issue of whether deferred taxes should be recognised in respect of temporary differences arising because foreign income is not taxable unless it is remitted to the entity's home jurisdiction.

The Interpretations Committee resolved not to add this issue to its agenda, but to draw it to the attention of the IASB. This decision reflected the status of the IASB's project on income taxes at that time – particularly the Board's decision to eliminate the notion of a 'branch'.[19]

7.6 'Tax-transparent' ('flow-through') entities

In many tax jurisdictions certain entities are not taxed in their own right. Instead the income of such entities is taxed in the hands of their owners as if it were income of the owners. An example might be a partnership which does not itself pay tax, but whose partners each pay tax on their share of the partnership's profits. Such entities are sometimes referred to as 'tax-transparent' or 'flow-through' entities.

The tax status of such an entity is of no particular relevance to the accounting treatment, in the investor's financial statements, of the current tax on the income of the entity. An investor in such an entity will determine whether the entity is a subsidiary, associate, joint arrangement, branch or a financial asset investment and account for it accordingly. The investor then accounts for its own current tax payable as it arises in the normal way.

The investor will also determine whether the basis on which the investment has been accounted for (e.g. through consolidation or equity accounting) has led to the recognition of assets or liabilities which give rise to temporary differences and recognise deferred tax on these in the normal way.

Finally, the investor will also determine whether there are 'outside' temporary differences associated with the investment as a whole and account for these as above.

Examples 31.24 and 31.25 illustrate the accounting treatment for, respectively, a consolidated and an equity-accounted tax-transparent entity.

Example 31.24: Tax-transparent entity (consolidated)

An entity (A) acquires 60% of a tax-transparent partnership (P) for $100 million in a transaction accounted for as a business combination. The aggregate fair value of the identifiable net assets of the partnership is $80 million and their tax base is $60m. A is directly liable to tax at 25% on 60% of the taxable profits of the partnership, in computing which it is entitled to offset 60% of the tax base of the assets. A elects to measure the non-controlling interest at its proportionate share of the net assets of the partnership.

The accounting entry to record the business combination is:

	$m	$m
Net assets	80	
Goodwill (balancing figure)	55	
Consideration paid		100
Deferred tax*		3
Non-controlling interest†		32

* In recovering the carrying value of the net assets ($80m), A will pay tax on 60% of $20m ($80m – $60m) = $12m at 25% = $3m.

† 40% of $80m.

Chapter 31

By contrast, if the partnership were a tax-paying entity, the accounting entry would be:

	$m	$m
Net assets	80	
Goodwill (balancing figure)	55	
Consideration paid		100
Deferred tax*		5
Non-controlling interest†		30

* In recovering the carrying value of the net assets ($80m), P will pay tax on $20m ($80m – $60m) at 25% = $5m.

† 40% of $75m (net assets excluding deferred tax $80m less deferred tax (as above) $5m).

Example 31.25: Tax-transparent entity (equity-accounted)

The facts are the same as in Example 31.24 above, except that, due to an agreement between A and the other partners, P is a jointly-controlled entity, rather than a subsidiary, of A, which accounts for P using the equity method. In this case it is less clear how to account for the deferred tax liability, which, it must be remembered, is not a liability of P, but of A and therefore does not form part of the net assets and goodwill underlying A's investment in P.

One analysis might be that the deferred tax relates to a temporary difference arising on the initial recognition of the investment in P in a transaction that gives rise to no accounting or taxable profit, and therefore is not recognised under the initial recognition exception (see 7.2.3 above). On this view, the initial accounting entry is simply:

	$m	$m
Investment in P	100	
Consideration		100

Another analysis might be that the true cost of the investment in P comprises both the consideration paid to the vendor and the assumption by A of the deferred tax liability associated with its share of the underlying assets (other than goodwill) of the investment. On this view the initial accounting entry is:

	$m	$m
Investment in P	103	
Deferred tax (see Example 31.24 above)		3
Consideration		100

This second method has the merit that it results in the same implied underlying goodwill as arises on full consolidation in Example 31.24 above: $103m – $48m [60% of $80m] = $55m. However, it does raise the issue of an apparent 'day one' impairment, as discussed in more detail at 12.3 below.

In our view, either analysis is acceptable so long as it is applied consistently.

Any income tax relating to a tax-transparent entity accounted for using equity accounting forms part of the investor's tax charge. It is therefore included in the income tax line in profit or loss and not shown as part of the investor's share of the results of the tax-transparent entity.

7.7 Deferred taxable gains

Some tax regimes mitigate the tax impact of significant asset disposals by allowing some or all of the tax liability on such transactions to be deferred, typically subject to conditions, such as a requirement to reinvest the proceeds from the sale of the asset disposed of in a similar 'replacement' asset. The postponement of tax payments achieved in this way may either be for a fixed period (e.g. the liability must be paid in any event no later than ten years after the original disposal) or for an indefinite period (e.g. the liability crystallises when, and only when, the 'replacement' asset is subsequently disposed of).

As noted at 7.3 above, IAS 12 makes it clear that the ability to postpone payment of the tax liability arising on disposal of an asset – even for a considerable period – does not extinguish the liability. In many cases, the effect of such deferral provisions in tax legislation is to reduce the tax base of the 'replacement' asset. This will increase any taxable temporary difference, or reduce any deductible temporary difference, associated with the asset.

8 DEFERRED TAX – MEASUREMENT

8.1 Legislation at the end of the reporting period

Deferred tax should be measured by reference to the tax rates and laws, as enacted or substantively enacted by the end of the reporting period, that are expected to apply in the periods in which the assets and liabilities to which the deferred tax relates are realised or settled. *[IAS 12.47]*.

When different tax rates apply to different levels of taxable income, deferred tax assets and liabilities are measured using the average rates that are expected to apply to the taxable profit (tax loss) of the periods in which the temporary differences are expected to reverse. *[IAS 12.49]*.

IAS 12 comments that, in some jurisdictions, announcements of tax rates (and tax laws) by the government have the substantive effect of actual enactment, which may follow the announcement by a period of several months. In these circumstances, tax assets and liabilities are measured using the announced tax rate (and tax laws). *[IAS 12.48]*.

IAS 12 gives no guidance as to how this requirement is to be interpreted in different jurisdictions and both the IASB and the Interpretations Committee have resisted various requests for it. In most jurisdictions, however, a consensus has emerged as to the meaning of 'substantive enactment' for that jurisdiction. Nevertheless, in practice apparently similar legislative processes in different jurisdictions may give rise to different treatments under IAS 12. For example, in most jurisdictions, tax legislation requires the formal approval of the head of state in order to become law. However, in some jurisdictions the head of state has real executive power (and could potentially not approve the legislation), whereas in others head of state has a more ceremonial role (and cannot practically fail to approve the legislation).

The view tends to be that, in those jurisdictions where the head of state has executive power, legislation is not substantively enacted until actually enacted by the head of state. Where, however, the head of state's powers are more ceremonial, substantive enactment is generally regarded as occurring at the stage of the legislative process where no further amendment is possible.

Some examples of the interpretation of 'substantive enactment' in particular jurisdictions are given at 5.1.1 above.

8.2 Uncertain tax treatments

'Uncertain tax treatment' (or 'uncertain tax position') is not a defined term in IAS 12, but is generally understood in practice to refer to an item the tax treatment of which is unclear or is a matter subject to an unresolved dispute between the reporting entity and the relevant tax authority. An uncertain tax treatment generally occurs where there is an uncertainty as to the meaning of the tax law, or to the applicability of the law to a particular transaction, or both.

Accounting for uncertain tax treatments is a particularly challenging aspect of accounting for tax. In October 2015, the Interpretations Committee issued DI/2015/1 – *Uncertainty over Income Tax Treatments*, as discussed further at 9 below.

8.3 'Prior year adjustments' of previously presented tax balances and expense (income)

This is discussed in the context of current tax at 5.3 above. The comments there apply equally to adjustments to deferred tax balances and expense (income). Accordingly, for accounting purposes, the normal provisions of IAS 8 apply, which require an entity to determine whether the revision represents a correction of a material prior period error or a refinement in the current period of an earlier estimate.

8.4 Expected manner of recovery of assets or settlement of liabilities

Deferred tax should be measured by reference to the tax consequences that would follow from the manner in which the entity expects, at the end of the reporting period, to recover or settle the carrying amount of the asset or liability to which it relates. *[IAS 12.51]*.

8.4.1 *Tax planning strategies*

As discussed at 7.4.4 above, IAS 12 allows tax planning strategies to be taken into account in determining whether a deferred tax asset may be recognised. This raises the question of the extent to which tax planning strategies may be taken into account more generally in applying IAS 12.

For example, some jurisdictions may offer incentives in the form of a significantly reduced tax rate for entities that undertake particular activities, or invest in particular plant, property and equipment, or create a certain level of employment.

Some argue that, where an entity has the ability and intention to undertake transactions that will lead to its being taxed at a lower rate, it may take this into account in measuring deferred tax liabilities relating to temporary differences that will reverse in future periods when the lower rate is expected to apply.

We do not agree that this is appropriate. IAS 12's references to tax planning opportunities are purely in the context of determining whether a deferred tax asset should be recognised. Such opportunities do not impact on the measurement of deferred tax until the entity has undertaken them, or is at least irrevocably committed to doing so.

8.4.2 *Carrying amount*

IAS 12 requires an entity to account for the tax consequences of recovering an asset or settling a liability at its *carrying amount*, and not, for example, the tax that might arise on a disposal at the current estimated fair value of the asset. This is illustrated by the example below.

Example 31.26: Measurement of deferred tax based on carrying amount of asset

During 2011 an entity, which has an accounting date of 31 December and pays tax at 40%, purchased a business and assigned €3 million of the purchase consideration to goodwill. The goodwill originally had a tax base of €3 million, deductible only on disposal of the goodwill. Thus there was no temporary difference on initial recognition of the goodwill (and, even if there had been, no deferred tax would have been recognised under the initial recognition exception – see 7.2.2 above). During 2012 the entity disposed of another business giving rise to a taxable gain of €500,000. The tax law of the relevant jurisdiction allowed the gain to be deferred by deducting it from the tax base of the goodwill, which therefore became €2.5 million.

Since IFRS prohibits the amortisation of goodwill, but instead requires it to be measured at cost less impairment, in our view IAS 12 effectively requires any deferred tax to be measured at the amount that would arise if the goodwill were sold at its carrying amount. At the end of 2012, the goodwill was still carried at €3 million. The decrease in the tax base during the period through deferral of the taxable gain gave rise to a taxable temporary difference of €500,000 (€3 million carrying amount less €2.5 million tax base), which, since it arose *after* the initial recognition of the goodwill (see 7.2.4 above), gave rise to the recognition of a deferred tax liability of €200,000 (€500,000 @ 40%).

During 2013, the acquired business suffered a severe downturn in trading, such that the goodwill of €3 million was written off in its entirety. This gave rise to a deductible temporary difference of €2.5 million (carrying amount of zero less €2.5 million tax base). The deferred tax liability of €200,000 recognised at the end of 2012 was released. However, no deferred tax asset was recognised since it did not meet the criteria in IAS 12 for recognition of tax assets, since there was no expectation of suitable taxable profits sufficient to enable recovery of the asset (see 7.4 above).

During 2017, a new trading opportunity arises in the acquired business, with the result that, at the end of 2017, the value of the goodwill of that business is once more €3 million. However, in accordance with IAS 36, which prohibits the reinstatement of previously impaired goodwill (see Chapter 20 at 6.3), no accounting adjustment is made to the carrying value of goodwill.

If the goodwill were disposed of for its current fair value of €3 million, tax of €200,000 would arise. However, the entity recognises no deferred tax liability at the end of 2017, since IAS 12 requires the entity to recognise the tax (if any) that would arise on disposal of the goodwill for its *carrying amount* of zero. If the asset were sold for zero, a tax loss of €2.5 million would arise but, in accordance with the general provisions of IAS 12 discussed at 7.4 above, a deferred tax asset could be recognised in respect of this deductible temporary difference only if there were an expectation of suitable taxable profits sufficient to enable recovery of the asset.

This may mean that any deferred tax asset or liability recognised under IAS 12 will reflect the expected manner of recovery or settlement, but not the expected amount of recovery or settlement, where this differs from the current carrying amount.

8.4.3 Assets and liabilities with more than one tax base

IAS 12 notes that, in some jurisdictions, the manner in which an entity recovers (settles) the carrying amount of an asset (liability) may affect either or both of:

(a) the tax rate applicable when the entity recovers (settles) the carrying amount of the asset (or liability); and

(b) the tax base of the asset (or liability).

In such cases, an entity should measure deferred tax assets and liabilities using the tax rate and the tax base that are consistent with the expected manner of recovery or settlement. *[IAS 12.51A]*.

Assets which are treated differently for tax purposes depending on whether their value is recovered through use or sale are commonly referred to as 'dual-based assets'. The basic requirements of IAS 12 for dual-based assets can be illustrated with a simple example.

Example 31.27: Calculation of deferred tax depending on method of realisation of asset

A building, which is fully tax-deductible, originally cost €1 million. At the end of the reporting period it is carried at €1,750,000, but tax allowances of €400,000 have been claimed in respect of it. If the building were sold the tax base of the building would be €1.5 million due to inflation-linked increases in its tax base.

Any gain on sale (calculated as sale proceeds less tax base of €1.5 million) would be taxed at 40%. If the asset is consumed in the business, its depreciation will be charged to profits that are taxed at 30%. If the intention is to retain the asset in the business, it will be recovered out of future income of €1.75 million, on which tax of €345,000 will be paid, calculated as:

	€000
Gross income	1,750
Future tax allowances for asset (£1m less £400,000 claimed to date)	(600)
	1,150
Tax at 30%	345

If, however, the intention is to sell the asset, the required deferred tax liability is only €100,000 calculated as:

	€000
Sales proceeds	1,750
Tax base	(1,500)
	250
Tax at 40%	100

8.4.4 Determining the expected manner of recovery of assets

Example 31.27 above, like the various similar examples in IAS 12, assumes that an asset will either be used in the business or sold. In practice, however, many assets are acquired, used for part of their life and then sold before the end of that life. This is particularly the case with long-lived assets such as property. We set out below the approach which we believe should be adopted in assessing the manner of recovery of:

- depreciable PP&E, investment properties and intangible assets (see 8.4.5 below);
- non-depreciable PP&E, investment properties and intangible assets (see 8.4.6 and 8.4.7 below); and
- other assets and liabilities (see 8.4.8 below).

8.4.5 Depreciable PP&E and intangible assets

Depreciable PP&E and investment properties are accounted for in accordance with IAS 16. Amortisable intangibles are accounted for in accordance with IAS 38. IAS 16 and IAS 38, which are discussed in detail in Chapters 17 and 18, require the carrying amount of a depreciable asset to be separated into a 'residual value' and a 'depreciable amount'.

'Residual value' is defined as:

> '... the estimated amount that an entity would currently obtain from disposal of the asset, after deducting the estimated costs of disposal, if the asset were already of the age and condition expected at the end of its useful life'

and 'depreciable amount' as:

> '... the cost of an asset, or other amount substituted for cost, less its residual value'. *[IAS 16.6, IAS 38.8]*.

It is inherent in the definitions of 'residual value' and 'depreciable amount' that, in determining residual value, an entity is effectively asserting that it expects to recover the depreciable amount of an asset through use and its residual value through sale. If the entity does not expect to sell an asset, but to use and scrap it, then the residual value (i.e. the amount that would be obtained from sale) must be nil.

Accordingly, we believe that, in determining the expected manner of recovery of an asset for the purposes of IAS 12, an entity should assume that, in the case of an asset accounted for under IAS 16 or IAS 38, it will recover the residual value of the asset through sale and the depreciable amount through use. This view is reinforced by the Basis for Conclusions on IAS 12 which notes that 'recognition of depreciation implies that the carrying amount of a depreciable asset is expected to be recovered through use to the extent of its depreciable amount, and through sale at its residual value'. *[IAS 12.BC6]*.

Such an analysis is also consistent with the requirement of IAS 8 to account for similar transactions consistently (see Chapter 3 at 4.1.4). This suggests that consistent assumptions should be used in determining both the residual value of an asset for the purposes of IAS 16 and IAS 38 and the expected manner of its recovery for the purposes of IAS 12.

The effect of this treatment is as follows.

Example 31.28: Dual-based asset

As part of a business combination an entity purchases an opencast mine to which there is assigned a fair value of €10 million. The tax system of the jurisdiction where the mine is located provides that, if the site is sold (with or without the minerals *in situ*), €9 million will be allowed as a deduction in calculating the taxable profit on sale. The profit on sale of the land is taxed as a capital item. If the mine is exploited through excavation and sale of the minerals, no tax deduction is available.

The entity intends fully to exploit the mine and then to sell the site for retail development. Given the costs that any developer will need to incur in preparing the excavated site for development, the ultimate sales proceeds are likely to be nominal. Thus, for the purposes of IAS 16, the quarry is treated as having a depreciable amount of €10 million and a residual value of nil.

On the analysis above, there is a taxable temporary difference of €10 million associated with the depreciable amount of the asset (carrying amount of €10 million less tax base in use of nil), and a deductible temporary difference of €9 million associated with the residual value (carrying amount of nil less tax base on disposal of €9 million).

The entity will therefore provide for a deferred tax liability on the taxable temporary difference. Whether or not a deferred tax asset is recognised in respect of the deductible temporary difference will be determined in accordance with the criteria discussed in 7.4 above. In some tax regimes, capital profits and losses are treated more or less separately from revenue profits and losses to a greater or lesser degree, so that it may be difficult to recognise such an asset due to a lack of suitable taxable profits.

However, we acknowledge that this is not the only interpretation of IAS 12 adopted in practice. For example, BHP Billiton indicates that, where an asset has only a capital gains tax base deductible on sale, it computes deferred tax based on that tax base irrespective of the expected manner of recovery of the asset.

Extract 31.1: BHP Billiton plc (2014)

7.1.6 Notes to the Financial Statements [extract]

1 Accounting policies [extract]

Taxation [extract]

The amount of deferred tax recognised is based on the expected manner and timing of realisation or settlement of the carrying amount of assets and liabilities, with the exception of items that have a tax base solely derived under capital gains tax legislation, using tax rates enacted or substantively enacted at period end. To the extent that an item's tax base is solely derived from the amount deductible under capital gains tax legislation, deferred tax is determined as if such amounts are deductible in determining future assessable income.

If applied to the fact pattern in Example 31.28 above, this treatment would result in the recognition of a deferred tax liability on a taxable temporary difference of €1 million (i.e. the extent to which the capital gains tax base does not exceed the carrying amount). An argument for this treatment would be that disposal of the mine will attract a deduction of €9 million, and – at the time of initial acquisition – the entity could dispose of the asset in such a way as to recover the full potential tax deduction. If the mine were immediately disposed of for that amount, the deduction would be fully recovered. As the mine is depleted, its carrying amount will fall below its tax base, giving rise to a gradually increasing deductible temporary difference. It may well not be possible to recognise a deferred tax asset on this difference for all the reasons set out in Example 31.28.

In our view, the difficulty with this treatment is that, as BHP Billiton acknowledges in explaining its accounting policy, it effectively provides for the tax consequences of recovery of the asset in a single sale transaction, although it appears more likely that it will in fact be recovered through ongoing extraction over an extended period, with no current tax deductions for the depletion cost. This is difficult to reconcile to:

- the requirement of IAS 12 to have regard to the expected manner of recovery of the mine in determining its tax base, and
- the overall objective of IAS 12 to 'account for the current and future tax consequences of ... the future recovery (settlement) of the carrying amount of assets (liabilities) that are recognised in an entity's statement of financial position' (see 2.1 and 8.4.2 above).

8.4.6 Non-depreciable PP&E and intangible assets

During 2009 and 2010 the IASB received representations from various entities and bodies that it was often difficult and subjective to determine the manner of recovery of certain categories of asset for the purposes of IAS 12. This was particularly the case for investment properties accounted for at fair value under IAS 40 which are often traded opportunistically, without a specific business plan, but yield rental income until disposed of. In many jurisdictions rental income is taxed at the standard rate, while gains on asset sales are tax-free or taxed at a significantly lower rate. The principal difficulty was that the then extant guidance (SIC-21 – *Income Taxes – Recovery of Revalued Non-Depreciable Assets*) effectively required entities to determine what the residual amount of the asset would be if it were depreciated under IAS 16 rather than accounted for at fair value,[20] which many regarded as an exercise divorced from commercial reality.

To deal with these concerns, in December 2010 the IASB amended IAS 12 so as to give more specific guidance on determining the expected manner of recovery for non-depreciable assets measured using the revaluation model in IAS 16 (see 8.4.6.A below) and for investment properties measured using the fair value model in IAS 40 (see 8.4.7 below). As noted at 8.4.6.B below, an indefinite-life intangible asset (that is not amortised because its useful economic life cannot be reliably determined) is not the same as a non-depreciable asset to which this amendment would apply.

8.4.6.A PP&E accounted for using the revaluation model

IAS 16 allows property, plant and equipment (PP&E) to be accounted for using a revaluation model under which PP&E is regularly revalued to fair value (see Chapter 18 at 6). IAS 12 clarifies that where a non-depreciable asset is revalued, any deferred tax on the revaluation should be calculated by reference to the tax consequences that would arise if the asset were sold at book value irrespective of the basis on which the carrying amount of the asset is measured. *[IAS 12.51B]*. The rationale for this treatment is that, in accounting terms, the asset is never recovered through use, as it is not depreciated. *[IAS 12.BC6]*.

IAS 12 clarifies that these requirements are subject to the general restrictions on the recognition of deferred tax assets (see 7.4 above). *[IAS 12.51E]*.

An issue not explicitly addressed in IAS 12 is whether the term 'non-depreciable' asset refers to an asset that is not currently being depreciated or to one that does not have a limited useful life. This is explored further in the discussion of non-amortised intangible assets immediately below.

8.4.6.B Non-amortised or indefinite life intangible assets

Under IAS 38 an intangible asset with an indefinite life is not subject to amortisation.

The analysis at 8.4.5 and 8.4.6.A above would appear to lead to the conclusion that, where an intangible asset is not amortised, any deferred tax related to that asset should be measured on an 'on sale' basis. IAS 12 requires tax to be provided for based on the manner in which the entity expects to recover the 'carrying amount' of its assets. In this case it could be argued that if the asset is not amortised under IAS 38, the financial statements are asserting that the carrying amount is never recovered through use.

However, an alternative analysis would be that the fact that an intangible asset is not being amortised does not of itself indicate that the expected manner of recovery is by sale. Rather, an intangible asset is regarded as having an indefinite life when it is determined that there is no foreseeable limit to the period over which the asset is expected to generate net cash inflows for the entity. *[IAS 38.88]*. This could still indicate an expectation of recovery through use.

This question was considered by the Interpretations Committee, which issued in July 2016 a tentative agenda decision indicating its preference for the latter analysis, as follows:[21]

- an indefinite life intangible asset *is not* a non-depreciable asset as envisaged by paragraph 51B of IAS 12. This is because a non-depreciable asset has an unlimited (or infinite) life. IAS 38 is clear that the term 'indefinite' does not mean 'infinite'. *[IAS 38.91]*. Consequently, the requirements in paragraph 51B of IAS 12 do not apply to indefinite life intangible assets;
- the reason for not amortising an indefinite life intangible asset is not because there is no consumption of the future economic benefits embodied in the asset. When the IASB amended IAS 38 in 2004, it observed that an indefinite life intangible asset is not amortised because there is no foreseeable limit on the period during which the entity expects to consume the future economic benefits embodied in the asset and, hence, amortisation over an arbitrarily determined maximum period would not be representationally faithful; *[IAS 38.BC74]*
- the fact that an entity does not amortise an indefinite life intangible asset does not necessarily mean that its carrying amount will be recovered only through sale and not through use. An entity recovers the carrying amount of an asset in the form of economic benefits that flow to the entity in future periods, which could be through use or sale of the asset; and
- accordingly, an entity should determine its expected manner of recovery of the carrying value of the indefinite life intangible asset in accordance with the requirements in paragraphs 51 and 51A of IAS 12 (as discussed at 8.4.3 above) and reflect the tax consequences that follow from that expected manner of recovery.

8.4.7 Investment properties

IAS 40 allows investment properties to be accounted for at fair value (see Chapter 19 at 6). IAS 12 requires any deferred tax asset or liability associated with such a property to be measured using a rebuttable presumption that the carrying amount of the investment property will be recovered through sale. *[IAS 12.51C]*. The same rebuttable presumption is used when measuring any deferred tax asset or liability associated with an investment property acquired in a business combination if the entity intends to adopt the fair value model in accounting for the property subsequently. *[IAS 12.51D]*.

The presumption is rebutted if the investment property is depreciable and the entity's business model is to consume substantially all the economic benefits embodied in the investment property over time, rather than through sale. The Interpretations Committee has clarified that the presumption can be rebutted in other circumstances, provided that sufficient evidence is available to support that rebuttal. However, the Committee neither gave any indication of, nor placed any restriction on, what those other circumstances might be.[22] If the presumption is rebutted, the entity applies the normal requirements of IAS 12 for determining the manner of recovery of assets (see 8.4.1 to 8.4.5 above). *[IAS 12.51C]*.

IAS 12 clarifies that these requirements are subject to the general restrictions on the recognition of deferred tax assets (see 7.4 above). *[IAS 12.51E]*.

8.4.8 *Other assets and liabilities*

In a number of areas of accounting IFRS effectively requires a transaction to be accounted for in accordance with an assumption as to the ultimate settlement of that transaction that may not reflect the entity's expectation of the actual outcome.

For example, if the entity enters into a share-based payment transaction with an employee that gives the employee the right to require settlement in either shares or cash, IFRS 2 requires the transaction to be accounted for on the assumption that it will be settled in cash, however unlikely this may be. IAS 19 – *Employee Benefits* – may assert that an entity has a surplus on a defined benefit pension scheme on an accounting basis, when in reality it has a deficit on a funding basis. Similarly, if an entity issues a convertible bond that can also be settled in cash at the holder's option, IAS 32 requires the bond to be accounted for on the assumption that it will be repaid, however probable it is that the holders will actually elect for conversion. It may well be that such transactions have different tax consequences depending on the expected manner of settlement, as illustrated in Example 31.29 below.

Example 31.29: Convertible bond deductible if settled

An entity issues a convertible bond for €1 million. After three years, the holders can elect to receive €1.2 million or 100,000 shares of the entity. If the bond were settled in cash, the entity would receive a tax deduction for the €200,000 difference between its original issue proceeds and the amount payable on redemption. If the bond is converted, no tax deduction is available.

Under IAS 32, the bond would be accreted from €1 million to €1.2 million over the three year issue period. The tax base remains at €1 million throughout, so that a deductible temporary difference of €200,000 emerges over the issue period. It is assumed that the deferred tax asset relating to this difference would meet the recognition criteria in IAS 12 (see 7.4 above).

For various reasons, it is extremely unlikely that the bond will be redeemed in cash.

Example 31.29 raises the issue of whether any deferred tax asset should be recognised in respect of the €200,000 temporary difference.

One view would be that no deferred tax asset should be recognised on the basis that there is no real expectation that the transaction will be settled in cash, thus allowing the entity to claim a tax deduction. The contrary view would be that the underlying rationale of IAS 12 is that, in order for the financial statements to be internally consistent, the tax effects of recognised assets and liabilities must also be recognised (see 2.1 above). Accordingly, a deferred tax asset should be recognised.

8.4.9 *'Outside' temporary differences relating to subsidiaries, branches, associates and joint arrangements*

In this section, an 'outside' temporary difference means a difference between the tax base in the jurisdiction of the investor of an investment in a subsidiary, associate or branch or an interest in a joint arrangement and carrying amount of that investment or interest (or the net assets and goodwill relating to it) included in the financial statements. Such differences, and the special recognition criteria applied to them by IAS 12, are discussed in more detail at 7.5 above.

Where deferred tax is recognised on such a temporary difference, the question arises as to how it should be measured. Broadly speaking, investors can realise an investment in one of two ways – either indirectly (by remittance of retained earnings or capital) or directly (through sale of the investment to a third party or by receiving residual assets upon liquidation of the associate). In many jurisdictions, the two means of realisation have very different tax consequences.

The entity should apply the general rule (discussed in more detail above) that, where there is more than one method of recovering an investment, the entity should measure any associated deferred tax asset or liability by reference to the tax consequences associated with the expected manner of recovery of the investment. *[IAS 12.51A]*. In other words, to the extent that the investment is expected to be realised through sale, the deferred tax is measured according to the tax rules applicable on sale, but to the extent that the temporary difference is expected to be realised through a distribution of earnings or capital, the deferred tax is measured according to the tax rules applicable on distribution. In its decision in March 2015 not to take a question on this matter to its agenda, the Interpretations Committee confirmed this view. Accordingly, if one part of the temporary difference is expected to be received as dividends, and another part is expected to be recovered upon sale or liquidation (for example, an investor has a plan to sell the investment later and expects to receive dividends until the sale of the investment), different tax rates would be applied to the parts of the temporary difference in order to be consistent with the expected manner of recovery.[23]

Where the expected manner of recovery is through distribution, there may be tax consequences for more than one entity in the group. For example, the paying company may suffer a withholding tax on the dividend paid and the receiving company may suffer income tax on the dividend received. In such cases, provision should be made for the cumulative effect of all tax consequences. As discussed further at 10.3.3 below, a withholding tax on an intragroup dividend is not accounted for in the consolidated financial statements as a withholding tax (i.e. within equity), but as a tax expense in profit or loss, since the group is not making a distribution but transferring assets from a group entity to a parent of that entity.

8.4.10 'Single asset' entities

In many jurisdictions it is common for certain assets (particularly properties) to be bought and sold by transferring ownership of a separate legal entity formed to hold the asset (a 'single asset' entity) rather than the asset itself.

A 'single asset' entity may be formed for a number of reasons. For example, the insertion of a 'single asset' entity between the 'real' owner and the property may limit the 'real' owner's liability for obligations arising from ownership of the property. More pertinent to the current discussion, it may also provide shelter from tax liabilities arising on disposal of the property since, in many jurisdictions, the sale of shares is taxed at a lower rate than the sale of property.

This raises the question whether, in determining the expected manner of recovery of an asset for the purposes of IAS 12, an entity may have regard to the fact that an asset held by a 'single asset' entity can be disposed of by disposing of the shares of the entity rather than the asset itself.

The Interpretations Committee has discussed this matter on a number of occasions since September 2011. In May 2012, the Committee noted the following significant diversity in practice:[24]

- some preparers recognise deferred tax on both the asset within, and the shares of, the 'single asset' entity;
- some preparers recognise tax on the shares only; and
- some preparers provide deferred tax on the difference between the asset within the entity and the tax base of its shares, using the tax rate applicable to a disposal of the shares.

The Interpretations Committee noted that current IAS 12 requires the parent to recognise deferred tax on both the asset within, and the shares of, the 'single asset' entity, if tax law considers the asset and the shares as two separate assets and if no specific exemptions in IAS 12 apply. At that time, the Committee asked its staff to undertake more research with the possible outcome of an amendment to IAS 12 addressing this specific type of transaction. Such an amendment would, in the Committee's view, be beyond the scope of the Annual Improvements project.[25]

Following further deliberations, the Interpretations Committee decided in July 2014 not to take the issue onto its agenda but instead to recommend to the IASB that it should analyse and assess the concerns raised about the current requirements in IAS 12 in its research project on Income Taxes. In issuing its agenda decision, the Committee noted that:[26]

a) paragraph 11 of IAS 12 requires the entity to determine temporary differences in the consolidated financial statements by comparing the carrying amounts of assets and liabilities in the consolidated financial statements with the appropriate tax base. In the case of an asset or a liability of a subsidiary that files separate tax returns, this is the amount that will be taxable or deductible on the recovery (settlement) of the asset (liability) in the tax returns of the subsidiary; and

b) the requirement in paragraph 11 of IAS 12 is complemented by the requirement in paragraph 38 of IAS 12 to determine the temporary difference related to the shares held by the parent in the subsidiary by comparing the parent's share of the net assets of the subsidiary in the consolidated financial statements, including the carrying amount of goodwill, with the tax base of the shares for purposes of the parent's tax returns.

The Interpretations Committee also noted that these paragraphs require a parent to recognise both the deferred tax related to the asset inside and the deferred tax related to the shares, if:[27]

a) tax law attributes separate tax bases to the asset inside and to the shares;

b) in the case of deferred tax assets, the related deductible temporary differences can be utilised as specified in paragraphs 24 to 31 of IAS 12; and

c) no specific exceptions in IAS 12 apply.

Accordingly, in determining the expected manner of recovery of an asset for the purposes of IAS 12, the entity should have regard to the asset itself and the shares.

8.4.11 Change in expected manner of recovery of an asset or settlement of a liability

A change in the expected manner recovery of an asset or settlement of a liability should be dealt with as an item of deferred tax income or expense for the period in which the change of expectation occurs, and recognised in profit or loss or in other comprehensive income or movements in equity for that period as appropriate (see 10 below).

This may have the effect, in certain situations, that some tax consequences of a disposal transaction are recognised before the transaction itself. For example, an entity might own an item of PP&E which has previously been held for use but which the entity now expects to sell. In our view, any deferred tax relating to that item of PP&E should be measured on a 'sale' rather than a 'use' basis from that point, even though the disposal itself, and any related current tax, will not be accounted for until the disposal occurs. As noted at 7.4.8 above, which discusses the effect of disposals on the recoverability of tax losses, the change in measurement will be required even if the asset does not yet meet the criteria for being classified as held for sale in IFRS 5 (see Chapter 4 at 2.1.2). This is because those criteria set a higher hurdle for reclassification ('highly probable') than the reference in IAS 12 to the entity's expected manner of recovery of an asset.

8.5 Different tax rates applicable to retained and distributed profits

In some jurisdictions, the rate at which tax is paid depends on whether profits are distributed or retained. In other jurisdictions, distribution may lead to an additional liability to tax, or a refund of tax already paid. IAS 12 requires current and deferred taxes to be measured using the rate applicable to undistributed profits until a liability to pay a dividend is recognised, at which point the tax consequences of that dividend should also be recognised, as illustrated in Example 31.30 below. *[IAS 12.52A, 52B]*.

Example 31.30: Different tax rates applicable to retained and distributed profits

An entity operates in a jurisdiction where income taxes are payable at a higher rate on undistributed profits (50%) with an amount being refundable when profits are distributed. The tax rate on distributed profits is 35%. At the end of the reporting period, 31 December 2017, the entity does not recognise a liability for dividends proposed or declared after the end of the reporting period. As a result, no dividends are recognised in the year 2017. Taxable income for 2017 is €100,000. Net taxable temporary differences have increased during the year ended 31 December 2017 by €40,000.

The entity recognises a current tax liability and a current income tax expense of €50,000 (€100,000 taxable profit @ 50%). No asset is recognised for the amount potentially recoverable as a result of future dividends. The entity also recognises a deferred tax liability and deferred tax expense of €20,000 (€40,000 @ 50%) representing the income taxes that the entity will pay when it recovers or settles the carrying amounts of its assets and liabilities based on the tax rate applicable to undistributed profits.

Subsequently, on 15 March 2018 the entity declares, and recognises as a liability, dividends of €10,000 from previous operating profits. At that point, the entity recognises the recovery of income taxes of €1,500 (€10,000 @ [50% – 35%]), representing the refund of tax due in respect of the dividends recognised as a liability, as a current tax asset and as a reduction of current income tax expense for the year ended 31 December 2018.

8.5.1 Effectively tax-free entities

In a number of jurisdictions certain types of entity, typically investment vehicles, are generally exempt from corporate income tax provided that they fulfil certain criteria, which generally include a requirement to distribute all, or a minimum percentage, of their annual income as a dividend to investors. This raises the question of how such entities should measure income taxes.

One view would be that, under the basic principle set out above, such an entity has a liability to tax at the normal rate until the dividend for a year becomes a liability. The liability for a dividend for an accounting period typically arises after the end of that period (as in Example 31.30 above). Under this analysis, therefore, such an entity would be required, at each period end, to record a liability for current tax at the standard corporate rate. That liability would be released in full when the dividend is recognised as a liability in the following period. This would mean that, on an ongoing basis, the income statement would show a current tax charge or credit comprising:

- a charge for a full liability for the current period; and
- a credit for the reversal of the corresponding liability for the prior period.

In addition, deferred tax would be recognised at the standard tax rate on all temporary differences.

A second view would be that the provisions of IAS 12 regarding different tax rates for distributed and undistributed tax rates are intended to apply where the only significant factor determining the differential tax rate is the retention or distribution of profit. By contrast, the tax status of an investment fund typically depends on many more factors than whether or not profits are distributed, such as restrictions on its activities, the nature of its investments and so forth. On this view, the analysis would be that such an entity can choose to operate within one of two tax regimes (a 'full tax' regime or a 'no tax' regime), rather than that it operates in a single tax regime with a dual tax rate depending on whether profits are retained or distributed.

The IASB previously appeared to regard IAS 12 as favouring the first analysis, while accepting that the resulting accounting treatment – a cycle of raising full tax provisions and then reversing them – does not reflect economic reality. Accordingly, the exposure draft ED/2009/2 proposed that the measurement of tax assets and liabilities should include the effect of expected future distributions, based on the entity's past practices and expectations of future distributions.[28] Following the withdrawal of the exposure draft, the IASB intends to consider this issue further. However, no formal decision has been taken, nor proposals issued for comment.

8.5.2 Withholding tax or distribution tax?

In practice, it is sometimes difficult to determine whether a particular transaction should be accounted for under the provisions of IAS 12 relating to different tax rates for distributed and undistributed profits, or in accordance with the provisions of the standard relating to withholding taxes.

The classification can significantly affect tax expense, because IAS 12 requires a withholding tax to be accounted for as a deduction from equity, whereas a higher tax rate for distributed profits is typically accounted for as a charge to profit or loss.

This issue is discussed further at 10.3 below.

8.6 Discounting

IAS 12 prohibits discounting of deferred tax, on the basis that:

- it would be unreasonable to require discounting, given that it requires scheduling of the reversal of temporary differences, which can be impracticable or at least highly complex; and
- it would be inappropriate to permit discounting because of the lack of comparability between financial statements in which discounting was adopted and those in which it was not. *[IAS 12.53, 54]*.

Moreover, IAS 12 notes that when deferred tax is recognised in relation to an item that is itself discounted (such as a liability for post-employment benefits or a finance lease liability), the deferred tax, being based on the carrying amount of that item, is also effectively discounted. *[IAS 12.55]*.

8.7 Unrealised intragroup profits and losses in consolidated financial statements

As noted at 6.2.1 and 6.2.2 above, an unrealised intragroup profit or loss eliminated on consolidation will give rise to a temporary difference where the profit or loss arises on a transaction that alters the tax base of the item(s) subject to the transaction. Such an alteration in the tax base creates a temporary difference because there is no corresponding change in the carrying amount of the assets or liabilities in the consolidated financial statements, due to the intragroup eliminations.

IAS 12 does not specifically address the measurement of such items. However, IAS 12 generally requires an entity, in measuring deferred tax, to have regard to the expected manner of recovery or settlement of the tax. It would generally be consistent with this requirement to measure deferred tax on temporary differences arising from intragroup transfers at the tax rates and laws applicable to the 'transferee' company rather than those applicable to the 'transferor' company, since the 'transferee' company will be taxed when the asset or liability subject to the transfer is realised or sold.

This interpretation is indirectly confirmed by the fact that under current US GAAP deferred tax on such intragroup temporary differences is measured using the 'transferor' company's tax rate and law as an explicit exception to the general application of the temporary difference approach, implying that, absent such an exception, the 'transferee' company's tax rate and laws apply. In January 2015, the FASB issued an Exposure Draft of an amendment to remove this exception, in a manner that is intended to 'align the recognition of income tax consequences of intra-entity asset transfers with International Financial Reporting Standards (IFRS). Specifically, IAS 12, Income Taxes, requires recognition of current and deferred income taxes resulting from an intra-entity asset transfer when the transfer occurs'.[29]

There are some jurisdictions where the tax history of an asset or liability subject to an intragroup transfer remains with the 'transferor' company. In such cases, the general principles of IAS 12 should be used to determine whether any deferred tax should be measured at the tax rate of the 'transferor' or the 'transferee' company.

The effect of the treatment required by IAS 12 is that tax income or expense may be recognised on transactions eliminated on consolidation, as illustrated by Examples 31.31 and 31.32.

Example 31.31: Elimination of intragroup profit (1)

H, an entity taxed at 30%, has a subsidiary S, which is taxed at 34%. On 15 December 2017 S sells inventory with a cost of €100,000 to H for €120,000, giving rise to a taxable profit of €20,000 and tax at 34% of €6,800. If H were preparing consolidated financial statements for the year ended 31 December 2017, the profit made by S on the sale to H would be eliminated.

Under IAS 12, a deferred tax asset would be recognised on the unrealised profit of €20,000, based on H's 30% tax rate, i.e. €6,000. The additional €800 tax actually paid by S would be recognised in profit or loss for the period ended 31 December 2017, the accounting entry being:

	DR	CR
	€	€
Current tax (profit or loss)	6,800	
Current tax (statement of financial position)		6,800
Deferred tax (statement of financial position)	6,000	
Deferred tax (profit or loss)		6,000

The net €800 tax charge to profit or loss (current tax charge €6,800 less deferred tax credit €6,000) reflects the fact that, by transferring the inventory from one tax jurisdiction to another with a lower tax rate, the group has effectively denied itself a tax deduction of €800 (i.e. €20,000 at the tax rate differential of 4%) for the inventory that would have been available had the inventory been sold by S, rather than H, to the ultimate third party customer.

Example 31.32: Elimination of intragroup profit (2)

H, an entity taxed at 34%, has a subsidiary S, which is taxed at 30%. On 15 December 2017 S sells inventory with a cost of €100,000 to H for €120,000, giving rise to a taxable profit of €20,000 and tax at 30% of €6,000. If H were preparing consolidated financial statements for the year ended 31 December 2017, the profit made by S on the sale to H would be eliminated.

In this case, the consolidated financial statements would record current tax paid by S of €6,000 and a deferred tax asset measured at H's effective tax rate of 34% of €6,800, giving rise to the following entry:

	DR	CR
	€	€
Current tax (profit or loss)	6,000	
Current tax (statement of financial position)		6,000
Deferred tax (statement of financial position)	6,800	
Deferred tax (profit or loss)		6,800

In this case there is a net €800 tax credit to profit or loss (current tax charge €6,000 less deferred tax credit €6,800). This reflects the fact that, by transferring the inventory from one tax jurisdiction to another with a higher tax rate, the group has put itself in the position of being able to claim a tax deduction for the inventory of €800 (i.e. €20,000 at the tax rate differential of 4%) in excess of that which would have been available had the inventory been sold by S, rather than H, to the ultimate third party customer.

8.7.1 *Intragroup transfers of goodwill and intangible assets*

It is common in some jurisdictions to sell goodwill and intangible assets from one entity in a group to another in the same group, very often in order either to increase tax deductions on an already recognised asset or to obtain deductions for a previously unrecognised asset. This raises the issue of how the tax effects of such transactions should be accounted for in the financial statements both of the individual entities concerned and in the consolidated financial statements, as illustrated by Example 31.33 below.

Example 31.33: Intragroup transfer of goodwill

A parent company P has two subsidiaries – A, which was acquired some years ago and B, which was acquired during the period ended 31 December 2016 at a cost of €10 million. For the purposes of this discussion, it is assumed that B had negligible identifiable assets and liabilities. Accordingly, P recorded goodwill of €10 million in its consolidated financial statements.

During 2017, B sells its business to A for its then current fair value of €12.5 million. As the goodwill inherent in B's business was internally generated, it was not recognised in the financial statements of B. Hence, the entire consideration of €12.5 million represents a profit to B, which is subject to current tax at 20% (i.e. €2.5 million). However, as a result of this transaction, A will be entitled to claim tax deductions (again at 20%) for its newly-acquired goodwill of €12.5 million. The deductions will be received in ten equal annual instalments from 2017 to 2026. For the purposes of this discussion, it is assumed that A will have sufficient suitable taxable profits to be able to recover these deductions in full.

8.7.1.A *Individual financial statements of buyer*

The buyer (A) accounts for the acquisition of B's business. As the business still has negligible identifiable assets and liabilities, this gives rise to goodwill of €12.5 million within A's own financial statements. A has acquired an asset for €12.5 million with a tax base of the same amount. There is therefore no temporary difference (and thus no deferred tax) to be accounted for in the financial statements of A.

8.7.1.B *Individual financial statements of seller*

As described above, the individual financial statements of the seller (B) reflect a profit of €12.5 million and current tax of €2.5 million.

8.7.1.C *Consolidated financial statements*

In the consolidated financial statements of P, the sale of the business from B to A will be eliminated on consolidation. However, the €2.5 million current tax suffered by B will be reflected in the consolidated financial statements, since this is a transaction with a third party (the tax authority), not an intragroup transaction. The question is what, if any, deferred tax arises as the result of this transaction.

One analysis would be that the tax base of consolidated goodwill has effectively been increased from nil to €12.5 million. Compared to its carrying amount of €10 million, this creates a deductible temporary difference of €2.5 million on which a deferred tax asset at 20% (€500,000) may be recognised. It could also be argued that there is an analogy here with the general treatment of deferred tax on intragroup profits and losses eliminated on consolidation (see Examples 31.31 and 31.32 above).

Under this analysis, the consolidated income statement would show a net tax charge of €2.0 million (€2.5 million current tax expense arising in B, less €0.5 million deferred tax income arising on consolidation). However, this is arguably inconsistent with the fact that the entity is not in an overall tax-paying position (since it has incurred a current tax loss of €2.5 million, but expects to receive tax deductions of the same amount over the next ten years). Clearly, there is an economic loss since the entity has effectively made an interest free loan equal to the current tax paid to the tax authority, but this is not relevant, since tax is not measured on a discounted basis under IAS 12 (see 8.6 above).

An alternative analysis might therefore be to argue that the goodwill reflected in the consolidated statement of financial position still has no tax base. Rather, the tax base attaches to the goodwill recognised in the separate financial statements of A, which is eliminated on consolidation, and therefore has no carrying amount in the consolidated financial statements. Thus, applying the general principle illustrated in Examples 31.31 and 31.32 above, there is a deductible temporary difference of €12.5 million, being the difference between the carrying value of the goodwill (zero in the *consolidated* statement of financial position) and its tax base (€12.5 million). Alternatively, as noted at 6.1.4 above, certain items may have a tax base, but no carrying amount, and thus give rise to deferred tax.

This analysis would allow recognition of a deferred tax asset of €2.5 million on a temporary difference of €12.5 million, subject to the recognition criteria for deferred tax assets. This would result in a net tax charge of nil (€2.5 million current tax expense arising in B less €2.5 million deferred tax income arising on consolidation).

In our view, there are arguments for either analysis and entities need to take a view on their accounting policy for such transactions and apply it consistently.

8.7.1.D *When the tax base of goodwill is retained by the transferor entity*

In May 2014, the Interpretations Committee considered another example involving the internal reorganisation of a previously acquired business, as set out in Example 31.34 below.[30]

Example 31.34: Intragroup transfer of goodwill when tax base is retained by transferor

A parent company, H, recognised goodwill that had resulted from the acquisition of a group of assets (Business C) that meets the definition of a business in IFRS 3 – *Business Combinations.* Entity H subsequently recorded a deferred tax liability relating to goodwill deducted for tax purposes. Against this background, Entity H effects an internal reorganisation in which:

- Entity H set up a new wholly-owned subsidiary (Subsidiary A);
- Entity H transfers Business C, including the related (accounting) goodwill to Subsidiary A;
- However, for tax purposes, the (tax) goodwill is retained by Entity H and not transferred to Subsidiary A.

How should Entity H calculate deferred tax following this internal reorganisation transaction in its consolidated financial statements in accordance with IAS 12?

The Interpretations Committee noted that when entities in the same consolidated group file separate tax returns, separate temporary differences will arise in those entities. Consequently, when an entity prepares its consolidated financial statements, deferred tax balances would be determined separately for those temporary differences, using the applicable tax rates for each entity's tax jurisdiction. *[IAS 12.11]*.

The Interpretations Committee also noted that when calculating the deferred tax amount for the consolidated financial statements:

(a) the amount used as the carrying amount by the 'receiving' entity (in this case, Subsidiary A that receives the (accounting) goodwill) for an asset or a liability is the amount recognised in the consolidated financial statements; and

(b) the assessment of whether an asset or a liability is being recognised for the first time for the purpose of applying the initial recognition exception (see 7.2 above) is made from the perspective of the consolidated financial statements.

The Interpretations Committee noted that transferring the goodwill to Subsidiary A would not meet the initial recognition exception in the consolidated financial statements. Consequently, deferred tax would be recognised in the consolidated financial statements for any temporary differences arising in each separate entity by using the applicable tax rates for each entity's tax jurisdiction (subject to meeting the recoverability criteria for recognising deferred tax assets described at 7.4 above).

To the extent that there is a temporary difference between the carrying amount of the investment in Subsidiary A and the tax base of the investment (a so-called 'outside basis difference') in the consolidated financial statements, deferred tax for such a temporary difference would also be recognised subject to the limitations and exceptions discussed at 7.5.2 and 7.5.3 above.

The Interpretations Committee also noted that transferring assets between the entities in the consolidated group would affect the consolidated financial statements in terms of recognition, measurement and presentation of deferred tax, if the transfer affects the tax base of assets or liabilities, or the tax rate applicable to the recovery or settlement of those assets or liabilities. Such a transfer could also affect:

(a) the recoverability of any related deductible temporary differences and thereby affect the recognition of deferred tax assets; and

(b) the extent to which deferred tax assets and liabilities of different entities in the group are offset in the consolidated financial statements.

9 UNCERTAIN TAX TREATMENTS

The terms 'uncertain tax treatment' or 'uncertain tax position' refer to an item, the tax treatment of which is either unclear or is a matter of unresolved dispute between the reporting entity and the relevant tax authority. Uncertain tax treatments generally occur where there is an uncertainty as to the meaning of the law, or to the applicability of the law to a particular transaction, or both. For example, the tax legislation may allow the deduction of research and development expenditure, but there may be disagreement as to whether a specific item of expenditure falls within the definition of eligible research and development costs in the legislation. In some cases, it may not be clear how tax law applies to a particular transaction, if at all. In other situations, a tax return might have been submitted to the tax authorities, who are yet to opine on the treatment of certain transactions, or may even have indicated that they disagree with the entity's interpretation of tax law.

Estimating the outcome of an uncertain tax treatment is often one of the most complex and subjective areas in accounting for tax. However, IAS 12 does not specifically address the measurement of uncertain tax treatments, which are therefore implicitly subject to the general requirement of the standard to measure current tax at the amount expected to be paid or recovered, *[IAS 12.46]*, (see 5 above).

Uncertain liabilities are generally accounted for under IAS 37. However, IAS 37 does not apply to income taxes (see Chapter 28 at 2.2.1.B). Therefore, whilst an entity might have chosen to apply IAS 37 to the measurement of uncertain tax treatments by applying the 'GAAP hierarchy' in IAS 8 (see Chapter 3 at 4.3), it has never been required to do so and, as a result, a number of methodologies for accounting for uncertain tax treatments are seen in practice. In 2014, the Interpretations Committee was asked to consider the interaction between IAS 12 and IAS 37 in the situation where entities are required to make payments on account to the tax authorities before an uncertain tax treatment is resolved (see 9.7 below). The Committee concluded that IAS 12, not IAS 37, provides the relevant guidance on the recognition of current tax.[31] It then embarked on a project to give guidance on the recognition and measurement of income tax assets and liabilities in these circumstances, in particular in relation to how probability and detection risk should be reflected.[32]

In October 2015, the Committee issued DI/2015/1 – *Uncertainty over Income Tax Treatments*. The period for comments ended on 19 January 2016 and as at the time of writing, the IASB is analysing feedback with a view to determining the project direction towards the end of 2016.[33] If implemented, it is expected that an entity would apply the Interpretation retrospectively, with the option to recognise the cumulative effect of initially applying the Interpretation in retained earnings at the start of the reporting period in which an entity first applies the Interpretation. However, full retrospective application to each reporting period presented, in accordance with IAS 8, would be permitted if the entity has the information necessary to do so and this information is available without the use of hindsight. The entity should disclose which method of transition it has applied.[34]

9.1 Scope of DI/2015/1 and definitions used

The Draft Interpretation applies to the determination of taxable profit (tax loss), tax bases, unused tax losses, unused tax credits and tax rates, in circumstances in which there is uncertainty over income tax treatments that affects the application of IAS 12. Whilst the above items are determined in accordance with the Draft Interpretation if there is uncertainty over income tax treatments, the existing requirements of IAS 12 are not changed.[35]

The following issues are addressed by the Draft Interpretation:[36]

a) whether an entity should consider uncertain tax treatments collectively;

b) the assumptions an entity should make about the examination of tax treatments by taxation authorities;

c) how an entity should determine taxable profit (tax loss), tax bases, unused tax losses, unused tax credits and tax rates; and

d) how an entity should consider changes in facts and circumstances.

Accounting for interest and penalties is excluded from the scope of the Draft Interpretation on the basis that the Committee had not identified any current evidence of significant diversity in practice.[37]

The Draft Interpretation uses the following terms in addition to those listed at 3 above and defined in IAS 12:[38]

- *tax treatment* refers to the treatments used or planned to be used in the entity's income tax filings;
- *taxation authority* is the body or bodies that make a decision about whether tax treatments are acceptable under the law. This might include a court;
- *uncertain tax treatment* is a tax treatment over which there is uncertainty concerning its acceptance under the law by the taxation authority. An entity's decision not to submit any tax filing in one tax jurisdiction or not to include specific income in taxable profits would also be an uncertain tax treatment, if its acceptability is unclear under the law.

9.2 Whether to consider uncertain tax treatments collectively (unit of account)

A key input to any estimation process is to determine the unit of account for uncertain tax treatments. In practice this might be an entire tax computation, individual uncertain treatments, or a group of related uncertain treatments (e.g. all positions in a particular tax jurisdiction, or all positions of a similar nature or relating to the same interpretation of tax legislation). This choice of unit of account is particularly important where an entity will only recognise tax treatments that are more-likely-than-not to be confirmed, as illustrated by Example 31.35 below.

Example 31.35: Uncertain tax treatments – importance of the unit of account

An entity has submitted a tax return indicating a current tax liability of £2.5 million. This £2.5 million includes the tax effect of a deduction disputed by the tax authority, the tax effect of which is £500,000. In other words, if the tax authority's challenge is sustained the entity's tax liability will in fact be £3 million. The entity has received advice that the tax authority is extremely unlikely (say 10%) to sustain its challenge.

If the entity regards the unit of account as the tax return as a whole, it is clearly more likely than not that the tax return will result in a payment of tax. Based on the advice the entity has received, there is a 90% probability that the liability will be £2.5 million and 10% probability that the liability will be £3 million. It would therefore record a current tax liability of £2.55 million (£2.5m × 0.9 + £3.0m × 0.1). This could equally have been calculated as £2.5m × 1 + £0.5m × 0.1 (i.e. the £2.5 million on the submitted return that is certain to be paid, with a 10% probability that an additional £500,000 will be paid).

If, however, the entity regards its unit of account as the disputed deduction, it would not recognise any liability for this at all, based on the advice received that the probability of the tax authority's challenge being sustained is only 10%. It would therefore recognise a current tax liability of only £2.5 million (i.e. the undisputed amount of the tax return).

The Interpretations Committee concluded that the selection of unit of account is a matter for judgement that could affect the amount of a tax liability or asset unless expected values are always used.[39] The Draft Interpretation would require that entities determine whether they consider tax uncertainties separately or grouped together on the basis of which approach provides a better prediction of the resolution of the uncertainty. For example, if the entity prepares and supports tax treatments as a group or if the entity expects the taxation authority to assess items collectively during a tax examination, it would be appropriate to consider those uncertain tax treatments together.[40] This implies that material tax uncertainties would be considered separately if there was no such inter-dependency as to the expected outcome.

9.3 Assumptions about the examination of tax treatments ('detection risk')

'Detection risk' is a term commonly used to refer to the likelihood that the taxation authority examines the amounts reported to it by the entity. The Interpretations Committee was informed that there are diverse views on whether such detection risk should be reflected in the measurement of tax assets and liabilities arising from uncertain tax treatments. It concluded that in cases where the taxation authority has a right to examine amounts reported to it, the entity should assume that it will do so; and that when it performs those examinations, the taxation authority will have full knowledge of all relevant information.[41]

The Committee noted that this position is consistent with the requirement in paragraphs 46 and 47 of IAS 12 to measure the amount of a tax liability or asset based on the tax laws that have been enacted or substantively enacted at the reporting date.[42] Indeed, in many jurisdictions, the tax law imposes a legal obligation on an entity operating in that jurisdiction to disclose its full liability to tax, or to assess its own liability to tax, and to make all relevant information available to the taxation authorities. In such a tax jurisdiction it might be difficult, as a matter of corporate governance, for an entity to record in its financial statements an amount calculated on the basis that the taxation authority will not become aware of a particular treatment which the entity has a legal obligation to disclose to that authority.

9.4 Determining an uncertain tax treatment or group of tax treatments

A variety of methodologies for determining uncertain tax treatments under IAS 12 have been applied in practice, including a weighted average probability of outcomes, the most likely single outcome and an 'all or nothing approach' (i.e. no liability is recognised for an uncertain tax treatment with a probability of occurrence below the selected recognition threshold and a full liability for a position with a probability of occurrence above the threshold).

The Interpretations Committee proposes that entities first consider whether or not it is probable that a taxation authority will accept an uncertain tax treatment or group of uncertain tax treatments.[43] If the entity concludes that it is probable that the taxation authority will accept the tax treatment used or planned to be used in its tax filings, the entity determines its tax position on that basis.[44] This is consistent with the requirement that current tax is measured at the amount expected to be paid or recovered from the taxation authorities, *[IAS 12.46]*, and that deferred tax is measured using the rates and tax laws expected to apply when the related asset is realised or liability is settled. *[IAS 12.47]*.

If the entity concludes that acceptance of the uncertain tax treatment by the taxation authorities is not probable, it should apply one of the following two methods for reflecting the effect of uncertainty in its estimate of the amount it expects to pay or recover from the tax authorities:[45]

(a) the most likely amount – the single most likely amount in a range of possible outcomes; or

(b) the expected value – the sum of the probability-weighted amounts in a range of possible outcomes.

The entity is required to use the method that it concludes will provide the better prediction of the resolution of the uncertainty. The Draft Interpretation suggests that the most likely amount may be a better method if the outcomes are binary (for example where an item might be deductible or disallowed for tax purposes) or are concentrated on one value (that is clearly more likely that the alternative outcomes). The expected value method may be more appropriate if possible outcomes are widely dispersed with low individual probabilities (where a number of individual but related uncertainties have been combined into a single unit of account).[46]

The Draft Interpretation provides three examples to illustrate how an entity might apply its requirements based on the limited facts presented, as follows:

- when one tax treatment is considered independently and when the most likely amount is used to reflect the effect of uncertainty tax[47] (Example 31.36 below);
- when multiple tax treatments are considered collectively and when the expected value is used to reflect the effect of uncertainty[48] (Example 31.37 below); and
- when a deferred tax asset is recognised and measured based on the most likely amount for a tax base that reflects the effect of uncertainty[49] (Example 31.38 below).

In all of these examples, the entities have assumed that the taxation authority will examine the amounts reported to them and have full knowledge of all relevant information, as discussed at 9.3 above.[50]

Example 31.36: Treatment considered independently, most likely amount is used

Entity A has an unresolved dispute over whether a specific item should be deductible in determining the taxable profit for a specific period. A tax investigator did not accept this tax treatment but the entity appealed against this to the court, which makes a final decision on the acceptability under the tax law. Entity A noted that this uncertain tax treatment affects neither accounting for deferred tax nor tax rates and it concluded that it is probable that the taxation authority will accept the other tax treatments used in its tax filing. Entity A has no similar disputes and it therefore decides that this tax treatment should be considered independently. If the taxation authority does not accept the tax treatment (i.e. if the court's final decision does not accept the tax treatment), the taxable profit for the specific period will increase by $100. At the end of the reporting period, Entity A determines that it is not probable that the taxation authority will accept the tax treatment on the basis of an evaluation of all available evidence and that the most likely amount (an additional $100 of taxable profit) will provide the better prediction of the resolution of the uncertainty. Entity A therefore recognises and measures a current tax liability based on a taxable profit that includes $100 in addition to the amount reported in its tax filing.

Example 31.37: Multiple treatments, expected value method

Entity B's tax filing included a number of deductions related to transfer pricing. The taxation authority in its jurisdiction may challenge those tax treatments. Entity B notes that the taxation authority's decision on one transfer pricing matter would affect, or be affected by, the other transfer pricing matters. Entity B determines that the tax treatments should be considered collectively, because it concludes that this will provide the best prediction of the resolution of the uncertainty. At the end of the reporting period, Entity B concludes, on the basis of an evaluation of all available evidence, that it is not probable that the taxation authority will accept all of the tax treatments. Entity B notes that this group of uncertain tax treatments affect neither accounting for deferred tax nor tax rates and it concludes that it is probable that the taxation authority will accept the other tax treatments used in its tax filing.

Entity B estimates the probabilities of what would be added to the taxable profits, as follows:

	Estimate outcome	Probability	Expected value
Outcome 1	–	5%	–
Outcome 2	200	5%	10
Outcome 3	400	20%	80
Outcome 4	600	20%	120
Outcome 5	800	30%	240
Outcome 6	1,000	20%	200
		100%	650

Entity B observes that the possible outcomes are widely dispersed and notes that the most likely amount of £800 does not provide the better prediction of the resolution of the uncertainty. Entity B therefore concludes that the expected value (£650) would provide the better prediction of the resolution of the uncertainty. Consequently, Entity B adds £650 to the amount of the taxable profit in its tax filing. Entity B notes that the tax treatments may affect income taxes for other tax jurisdictions. It also notes that the relevant tax rules indicate that this particular tax jurisdiction's decision would not affect decisions to be made by taxation authorities in other tax jurisdictions, in respect of these tax treatments. Consequently, Entity B considers tax treatments in income taxes separately for these other tax jurisdictions.

Example 31.38: Treatment relates to deferred tax asset, most likely amount is applied

Entity C acquired a separately identifiable intangible asset for £100 that has an indefinite life and is, therefore, not amortised in accordance with IAS 38 Intangible Assets. It is certain that the full amount of the intangible asset is deductible for tax purposes, but the timing of deductibility (i.e. period of amortisation under the tax law) is uncertain. Entity C has no similar intangible assets and it therefore decides that this tax treatment should be considered independently.

Entity C deducted £100 from taxable income for tax purposes for Year 1. At the end of Year 1, Entity C concludes, on the basis of an evaluation of all available evidence (e.g. information about disputes for other entities' similar transactions), that it is not probable that this tax treatment will be accepted, although Entity C believes that the entity's interpretation of the tax law could be appropriate and therefore retains the amounts reported to the taxation authorities in the tax return. Consequently, Entity C uses the most likely amount, rather than the amount to be used in its tax filings, to reflect the uncertainty in determining the tax base, because Entity C concluded that this amount would provide the better prediction of the resolution of uncertainty.

Entity C observes that the most likely amount that the taxation authority will accept as the deductible amount for Year 1 will be £10. Consequently, the most likely amount for the corresponding tax base for the intangible asset will be £90. At the end of Year 1, Entity C recognises and measures a deferred tax liability by applying the relevant requirements in IAS 12, based on the amount of the temporary difference between the carrying amount of the intangible asset in its financial statements and the most likely amount of the tax base (i.e. the difference between £100 and £90).

Entity C also concludes that it should reflect the effect of the uncertainty in determining the taxable profit for Year 1, because this uncertain tax treatment also affects the taxable profit. Entity C recognises and measures a current tax liability, based on the estimates and judgements that are consistent with those made for deferred tax accounting. Entity C therefore recognises and measures a current tax liability in accordance with IAS 12, based on the taxable profit that includes £90, in addition to the amount in its tax filing. (This is because Entity C deducted £100 from taxable income for Year 1, whereas the most likely amount was £10. Entity C concluded that it is not probable that the tax treatment will be accepted.)

Where the uncertain tax treatment affects both current tax and deferred tax, an entity is required to make estimates and judgements on a consistent basis.[51]

9.5 Consideration of changes in facts and circumstances

The Draft Interpretation will require an entity to reassess its conclusions about the acceptability of tax treatments or its estimates of the effect of uncertainty, or both if facts and circumstances change. In such a situation, the entity would reflect this change in its determination of the taxable profit (tax loss), tax bases, unused tax losses, unused tax credits and tax rates, in the period of the change.[52]

The Application Guidance in Appendix A to the Draft Interpretation describes the application of this requirement in the context of the taxation authorities' rights to examine tax treatments as discussed at 9.3 above.

(a) Where applicable laws and regulations impose a time limit on or after which the taxation authority is no longer able to challenge an entity's tax treatments (sometimes referred to as a statute of limitations), an entity shall reflect this change of circumstances when these rights expire.[53]

(b) Before the rights to examination expire, an entity shall also consider the following guidance about the results of examinations by taxation authorities:

  (i) if taxation authorities retain the right to re-examine the amounts even after a previous examination, an entity shall continue to assume that the taxation authorities will exercise that right and have full knowledge of all relevant information when making those additional examinations;[54]

  (ii) the results of any examination by taxation authorities are new facts and circumstances and they may affect an entity's conclusions about the acceptability of tax treatments and its estimates of the effect of uncertainty. This can also be the case when an entity becomes aware that the taxation authority has challenged a similar tax treatment with another entity that the taxation authority had previously accepted for the reporting entity;[55]

  (iii) if a taxation authority explicitly accepts an entity's tax treatment during an examination for a specific period, this explicit acceptance is a new fact for tax treatments within the scope of the examination (tax treatments for the specific period) and may affect similar tax treatments for other periods;[56] and

  (iv) implicit acceptance of an entity's tax treatment should be treated with some caution. For example, the taxation authority may review the entity's tax filing that includes tax treatments for a specific period, and it may be silent about those tax treatments. This implicit acceptance is a new fact for tax treatments within the scope of the examination (for example, tax treatments for the specific period). However, it may still not be appropriate to regard this implicit acceptance as a new fact for similar tax treatments that are not within the scope of the examination (for example, similar tax treatments for other periods).[57] This is because the implicit acceptance does not necessarily mean that the taxation authority has a specific view for such tax treatments.[58]

9.6 Disclosures relating to uncertain tax treatments

The Draft Interpretation does not propose any new disclosures. Instead it reminds entities of existing disclosure requirements that may be relevant in these circumstances:

- to disclose judgements made in the process of applying the entity's accounting policies in accordance with paragraph 122 of IAS 1 (see Chapter 3 at 5.1.1.B). Such judgements might include the decision to consider uncertain tax treatments individually or collectively (see 9.2 above); the determination as to whether acceptance by the taxation authorities is probable; or the decision to apply the 'most likely amount' or 'expected value' method to reflect uncertainty (see 9.4 above);[59]
- to disclose information about the assumptions the entity makes and other estimates used in determining taxable profit or loss, tax bases, unused tax losses, unused tax credits and tax rates. The requirement to disclose is considered in accordance with paragraphs 125 to 129 of IAS 1 regarding the sources of estimation uncertainty[60] (see Chapter 3 at 5.2.1); and
- to provide information about tax-related contingencies where the entity is unable to determine that acceptance by the taxation authorities is probable.[61]

As discussed at 9.4 above, when an entity determines that it is probable that a taxation authority will accept the tax treatment used or planned to be used in its tax filings, it determines its tax position on that basis.[62] In that case, there is no need to reflect uncertainty in the measurements used in the financial statements and accordingly there is no tax-related contingency to disclose.[63]

As noted above, uncertain tax treatments generally relate to the estimate of the entity's liability for current tax. Any amount recognised for an uncertain current tax treatment should therefore normally be classified as current tax, and presented (or disclosed) as current or non-current in accordance with the general requirements of IAS 1 (see Chapter 3 at 3.1.1).

However, there are circumstances where an uncertain tax treatment affects the tax base of an asset or liability and therefore relates to deferred tax. For example, there might be doubt as to the amount of tax depreciation that can be deducted in respect of a particular asset, which in turn would lead to doubt as to the tax base of the asset. There may sometimes be an equal and opposite uncertainty relating to current and deferred tax. For example, there might be uncertainty as to whether a particular item of income is taxable, but – if it is – any tax payable will be reduced to zero by a loss carried forward from a prior period. As discussed at 13.1.1.C below, it is not appropriate to offset current and deferred tax items.

9.7 Recognition of an asset for payments on account

IAS 12 requires that the liability for current tax is recorded after deducting payments made, and states that if the amount already paid exceeds the tax liability for current and past periods, an asset is recognised for the excess. *[IAS 12.12]*.

In some jurisdictions, entities are required to make payments to the tax authorities before an uncertain tax treatment is resolved. If an entity considers its liability to be lower than the assessment made by the tax authorities, it would record an asset for a payment in excess of its estimated liability for current tax, but recovery of that excess would be contingent upon the successful resolution of the uncertainty.

In these circumstances, some had argued that the 'virtually certain' threshold in IAS 37 should be applied before allowing recognition of such a 'contingent' asset. *[IAS 37.35]*. Others argue that the requirement in IAS 12 to measure current tax assets at the amount expected to be recovered from the tax authorities requires only a 'probable' assessment of recovery to be sufficient for recognising an asset. *[IAS 12.46]*. As a result, there has been diversity in the approach used to determine whether an asset should be recognised for the amount potentially recoverable from the tax authority.

In 2014 the Interpretations Committee considered a request to clarify the criteria under which a tax asset would be recognised in these circumstances. In the situation described by the submitter, the entity expects, but is not certain, to recover some, or all, of the amount paid. The Interpretations Committee noted that:

a) paragraph 12 of IAS 12 provides guidance on the recognition of current tax assets and current tax liabilities. In particular, it states that:
   i) current tax for current and prior periods shall, to the extent unpaid, be recognised as a liability; and
   ii) if the amount already paid in respect of current and prior periods exceeds the amount due for those periods, the excess shall be recognised as an asset.
b) in the specific fact pattern described in the submission, an asset is recognised if the amount of cash paid (which is a certain amount) exceeds the amount of tax expected to be due (which is an uncertain amount);
c) the timing of payment should not affect the amount of current tax expense recognised.

The Interpretations Committee acknowledged that the reference to IAS 37 in paragraph 88 of IAS 12 in respect of tax-related contingent liabilities and contingent assets may have been understood by some to mean that IAS 37 applied to the recognition of such items. However, the Interpretations Committee noted that this paragraph provides guidance only on disclosures required for such items. Accordingly, the Interpretations Committee determined that IAS 12, not IAS 37, provides the relevant guidance on recognition, as described above.[64]

10 ALLOCATION OF TAX CHARGE OR CREDIT

Current and deferred tax is normally recognised as income or an expense in the profit or loss for the period, except to the extent that it arises from:

- an item that has been recognised directly outside profit or loss, whether in the same period or in a different period (see 10.1 to 10.7 below);
- a share-based payment transaction (see 10.8 below); or
- a business combination (see 12 below). *[IAS 12.57, 58, 68A-68C]*.

Where a deferred tax asset or liability is remeasured subsequent to its initial recognition, the change should be accounted for in profit or loss, unless it relates to an item originally recognised outside profit or loss, in which case the change should also be accounted for outside profit or loss. Such remeasurement might result from:

- a change in tax law;
- a re-assessment of the recoverability of deferred tax assets (see 7.4 above); or
- a change in the expected manner of recovery of an asset or settlement of a liability (see 8.4.11 above). *[IAS 12.60].*

Whilst IAS 12 as drafted refers only to remeasurement of 'deferred' tax, it seems clear that these principles should also be applied to any remeasurement of current tax.

Any current tax or deferred tax on items recognised outside profit or loss, whether in the same period or a different period, is also recognised directly outside profit or loss. Such items include:

- revaluations of property, plant and equipment under IAS 16 (see 10.1 below);
- retrospective restatements or retrospective applications arising from corrections of errors and changes in accounting policy under IAS 8 (see 10.2 below);
- exchange differences arising on translation of the financial statements of a foreign operation under IAS 21 (see 7.5 above); and
- amounts taken to equity on initial recognition of a compound financial instrument by its issuer (so-called 'split accounting') under IAS 32 (see 7.2.8 above). *[IAS 12.61A, 62, 62A].*

IAS 12 acknowledges that, in exceptional circumstances, it may be difficult to determine the amount of tax that relates to items recognised in other comprehensive income and/or equity. In these cases a reasonable pro-rata method, or another method that achieves a more appropriate allocation in the circumstances, may be used. IAS 12 gives the following examples of situations where such an approach may be appropriate:

- there are graduated rates of income tax and it is impossible to determine the rate at which a specific component of taxable profit (tax loss) has been taxed;
- a change in the tax rate or other tax rules affects a deferred tax asset or liability relating (in whole or in part) to an item that was previously recognised outside profit or loss; or
- an entity determines that a deferred tax asset should be recognised, or should no longer be recognised in full, and the deferred tax asset relates (in whole or in part) to an item that was previously recognised outside profit or loss. *[IAS 12.63].*

IAS 12 requires tax relating to items not accounted for in profit or loss, whether in the same period or a different period, to be recognised:

- in other comprehensive income, if it relates to an item accounted for in other comprehensive income; and
- directly in equity, if it relates to an item accounted for directly in equity. *[IAS 12.61A].*

This requirement to have regard to the previous history of a transaction in accounting for its tax effects is commonly referred to as 'backward tracing'.

10.1 Revalued and rebased assets

Where an entity depreciates a revalued item of PP&E, it may choose to transfer the depreciation in excess of the amount that would have arisen on a historical cost basis from revaluation surplus to retained earnings. In such cases, the relevant portion of any deferred tax liability recognised on the revaluation should also be transferred to retained earnings. A similar treatment should be adopted by an entity which has a policy of transferring revaluation gains to retained earnings on disposal of a previously revalued asset. *[IAS 12.64]*.

When an asset is revalued for tax purposes and that revaluation is related to an accounting revaluation of an earlier period, or to one that is expected to be carried out in a future period, the tax effects of both the asset revaluation and the adjustment of the tax base are credited or charged to equity in the periods in which they occur.

However, if the revaluation for tax purposes is not related to an accounting revaluation of an earlier period, or to one that is expected to be carried out in a future period, the tax effects of the adjustment of the tax base are recognised in profit or loss. *[IAS 12.65]*. For example, when tax law gives additional deductions to reflect the indexation of assets for tax purposes (see 6.2.2.D above) the tax base of the asset changes without any corresponding change to the asset's carrying amount in the financial statements. Because the carrying amount has not changed, there is no gain or loss in relation to indexation in profit and loss or in other comprehensive income. Accordingly, the effect of the change in tax base is recorded in profit or loss. *[IAS 12.65]*.

10.1.1 Non-monetary assets with a tax base determined in a foreign currency

Another example arises when the tax base of a non-current asset is determined in a foreign currency. This can be the case in oil and gas producing entities that have a functional currency of US dollars but operate (and are accountable for income taxes) in various local jurisdictions under different currencies (see Chapter 41 at 9.1).

IAS 12 notes that in this situation the entity measures its non-monetary asset using its functional currency as at the date of purchase. The tax base (denominated in local currency) is retranslated to determine the temporary difference (on a functional currency basis) as at each reporting date. Because this retranslation has no effect on carrying values recognised in the financial statements, there is no corresponding gain or loss against which the tax can be allocated. As a result, the movement in deferred tax is recorded in profit or loss. *[IAS 12.41]*.

In 2015, the Interpretations Committee considered a submission that requested confirmation as to whether deferred taxes arising from the effect of exchange rate changes on the tax bases of non-current assets are recognised through profit or loss. The Committee completed its deliberations in January 2016 and, in noting the requirement in paragraph 41 of IAS 12, determined that:[65]

- deferred tax does not arise from a transaction or event that is recognised outside profit or loss and is therefore charged or credited to profit or loss in accordance with paragraph 58 of IAS 12;
- such a deferred tax charge or credit would be presented with other deferred taxes, instead of with foreign exchange gains or losses, in the statement of profit or loss; and
- paragraph 79 of IAS 12 requires the disclosure of the major components of tax expense (income). When changes in the exchange rate are the cause of a major component of the deferred tax charge or credit, an explanation of this in accordance with paragraph 79 of IAS 12 would help explain the tax expense (income) to the users of the financial statements.

In the light of the existing IFRS requirements the Interpretations Committee determined that neither an Interpretation nor an amendment to a Standard was necessary.[66]

10.2 Retrospective restatements or applications

IAS 8 requires retrospective restatements or retrospective applications arising from corrections of errors and changes in accounting policy to be accounted for by adjusting the amounts presented in the financial statements of comparative periods and restating the opening balances of assets, liabilities and equity for the earliest prior period presented.

Because IAS 12 requires tax relating to an item that has been recognised outside profit or loss to be treated in the same way, any tax effect of a retrospective restatement or retrospective application on the opening comparative statement of financial position is dealt with as an adjustment to equity also. *[IAS 12.58]*.

However, the fact that IAS 12 states that tax arising in a different period, but relating to a transaction or event arising outside profit or loss should also be recognised in other comprehensive income or equity (as applicable) is taken by some to mean that any subsequent remeasurement of tax originally recognised in equity as part of a prior year adjustment should be accounted for in equity also. In our view, such an assertion fails to reflect the true nature of retrospective application, which is defined in IAS 8 as the application of a new accounting policy 'to transactions, other events or conditions *as if that policy had always been applied*' (our emphasis). *[IAS 8.5]*. This is illustrated by Example 31.39 below.

Example 31.39: Remeasurement of deferred tax liability recognised as the result of retrospective application

An entity's date of transition to IFRS was 1 January 2004. As a result of the adoption of IAS 37, its first IFRS financial statements (prepared for the year ended 31 December 2005) showed an additional liability for environmental rectification costs of €5 million as an adjustment to opening reserves, together with an associated deferred tax asset at 40% of €2 million.

The environmental liability does not change substantially over the following accounting periods, but during the year ended 31 December 2017 the tax rate falls to 30%. This requires the deferred tax asset to be remeasured to €1.5 million giving rise to tax expense of €500,000. Should this expense be recognised in profit or loss for the period or in equity?

If read in isolation, IAS 12 could be construed as requiring this expense to be accounted for in equity, as being a remeasurement of an amount originally recognised in equity. However, as discussed above, IAS 8 defines retrospective application as the application of a new accounting policy 'to transactions, other events or conditions as if that policy had always been applied'. If the entity had presented comparative information for all periods since it first commenced business, rather than present a single 'catch up' adjustment at the start of the earliest period presented, the charge for environmental costs (and all the related deferred tax) would have been reflected in profit or loss in previous periods. It is therefore clear that the tax relates to a transaction which would have been recognised in profit or loss on a full retrospective application of IFRS, and that the tax expense arising from a change in tax rate should be treated in the same way.

10.3 Dividends and transaction costs of equity instruments

10.3.1 Dividend subject to differential tax rate

In some jurisdictions, the rate at which tax is paid depends on whether profits are distributed or retained. In other jurisdictions, distribution may lead to an additional liability to tax, or a refund of tax already paid. IAS 12 requires current and deferred taxes to be measured using the rate applicable to undistributed profits until a liability to pay a dividend is recognised, at which point the tax consequences of that dividend should also be recognised. This is discussed further at 8.5 above.

Where taxes are remeasured on recognition of a liability to pay a dividend, the difference should normally be recognised in profit or loss rather than directly in equity, even though the dividend itself is recognised directly in equity under IFRS. IAS 12 takes the view that any additional (or lower) tax liability relates to the original profit now being distributed rather than to the distribution itself. Where, however, the dividend is paid out of profit arising from a transaction that was originally recognised in other comprehensive income or equity, the adjustment to the tax liability should also be recognised in other comprehensive income or equity. *[IAS 12.52B]*.

10.3.2 Dividend subject to withholding tax

Where dividends are paid by the reporting entity subject to withholding tax, the withholding tax should be included as part of the dividend charged to equity. *[IAS 12.65A]*.

This provision of IAS 12 proves somewhat problematic in practice. There may be little economic difference, from the paying entity's perspective, between a requirement to pay a 5% 'withholding tax' on all dividends and a requirement to pay an additional 5% 'income tax' on distributed profit. Yet, the accounting treatment varies significantly depending on the analysis. If the tax is considered a withholding tax, it is treated as a deduction from equity in all circumstances. If, however, it is considered as an additional income tax, it will generally be treated as a charge to profit or loss (see 10.3.1 above). This distinction therefore relies on a clear definition of withholding tax, which IAS 12 unfortunately does not provide.

IAS 12 describes a withholding tax as a 'portion of the dividends [paid] to taxation authorities on behalf of shareholders'. *[IAS 12.65A]*. However, this begs the question whether the determination of whether or not the tax is paid 'on behalf of shareholders' should be made by reference to the characterisation of the tax:

- in the paying entity's tax jurisdiction – in which case, there is the problem noted above that one jurisdiction's 'additional distribution tax' may be economically identical to another jurisdiction's 'withholding tax'; or
- in the receiving entity's tax jurisdiction – in which case there would be the problem that the tax on a dividend paid to one shareholder is a 'withholding tax' (because credit is given for it on the shareholder's tax return) but the tax on a dividend paid to another shareholder the same time is not (because no credit is given for it on that shareholder's tax return).

This distinction is also relevant in accounting for dividend income that has been subject to withholding tax, as discussed at 10.3.4 below.

10.3.3 Intragroup dividend subject to withholding tax

Where irrecoverable withholding tax is suffered on intragroup dividends, the withholding tax does not relate to an item recognised in equity in the consolidated financial statements (since the intragroup dividend to which it relates has been eliminated in those financial statements). The tax should therefore be accounted for in profit or loss for the period.

10.3.4 Incoming dividends

IAS 12 does not directly address the treatment of incoming dividends on which tax has been suffered (i.e. whether they should be shown at the amount received, or gross of withholding tax together with a corresponding tax charge). As discussed at 4.2 above, we believe that judgement is required to determine whether a tax deducted from investment income at the source of the income is a withholding tax in the scope of IAS 12.

As well as the considerations discussed at 4.2, it is noted at 10.3.2 above that an entity paying dividends that are subject to withholding tax would record the gross value of the distribution in equity, on the basis that the withholding tax is regarded as an amount paid to the tax authorities 'on behalf of shareholders'. *[IAS 12.65A]*. If it is determined from the point of view of the recipient of the dividend that a particular withholding tax is an income tax in the scope of IAS 12, it would therefore be consistent with this treatment to show dividends (and other investment income subject to withholding taxes) gross of withholding taxes and to recognise any non-refundable portion of such withholding taxes as a tax expense in the statement of comprehensive income.

Some jurisdictions also give tax deductions for the 'underlying' tax suffered on dividends received. This is based on the concept that the dividend has been paid out of profits already subject to tax, so that to tax the full amount received again would amount to a punitive double taxation of the underlying profits. In our view, such underlying tax (which would form part of the tax charge, not the dividend, of the paying company) is not directly paid on behalf of the shareholder, and accordingly incoming dividends should not be grossed up for underlying tax.

10.3.5 Tax benefits of distributions and transaction costs of equity instruments

IAS 32 as originally issued required distributions to shareholders and transaction costs of equity instruments to be accounted for in equity net of any related income tax benefit (see Chapter 45 at 8.2).

Annual Improvements to IFRSs 2009-2011 Cycle, issued in May 2012, amended IAS 32 so as to remove the reference to income tax benefit. This means that all tax effects of equity transactions are allocated in accordance with the general principles of IAS 12. Unfortunately, it is not entirely clear how IAS 12 requires the tax effects of certain equity transactions to be dealt with, as illustrated by Example 31.40 below.

Example 31.40: Tax deductible distribution on equity instrument

An entity paying tax at 25% has issued a capital instrument that is treated as equity for accounting purposes (because distributions are discretionary), but as debt for tax purposes (i.e. all distributions are tax deductible). The entity makes a distribution of €1 million and is able to claim a tax deduction of €250,000. There no restrictions on the recoverability of that deduction for tax purposes.

Some take the view that the tax deduction clearly relates to the distribution, which was accounted for in equity, and that the deduction should therefore be credited to equity.

Others take the view that the provisions of IAS 12 regarding differential tax rates for retained and distributed profits (see 8.5 above) apply. They argue that, in most cases, the amount distributed is part of an accumulation of retained earnings originally accounted for in profit or loss. The tax deduction for the distribution means that those profits have effectively been taxed at a lower rate than would have been the case if the profits had been retained. Accordingly, under the general rule in IAS 12, the effect of that rate benefit should be accounted for in profit or loss.

Those who believe that the tax deduction should be accounted for in equity argue that the provisions of IAS 12 regarding differential tax rates for retained and distributed profits (see 8.5 above) do not apply, as there is no difference to the headline tax rate applied to the taxable profits of the entity as a whole. Instead, the treatment of the distribution as an expense for tax purposes simply reduces the amount of taxable profit to be taxed at the single headline rate.

Those who believe that the tax deduction should be credited to profit or loss counter that the reference in paragraph 52A of IAS 12 to taxes 'payable at a higher or lower rate', should be interpreted as including a higher or lower effective rate, as well as a higher or lower headline rate.

This question has been considered by the Interpretations Committee, which observed that the circumstances to which the requirements in paragraph 52B of IAS 12 apply are unclear. Nonetheless, the Interpretations Committee decided that the applicability of the requirements in paragraph 52B relating to the presentation of any income tax consequences of dividends should not be limited to only those circumstances described in paragraph 52A (i.e. circumstances in which there are different tax rates for distributed and undistributed profits). Consequently, the Interpretations Committee decided to propose an amendment to IAS 12 to clarify that the presentation requirements in paragraph 52B of IAS 12 apply to all payments on financial instruments classified as equity that are distributions of profits, and are not limited to the circumstances described in paragraph 52A of IAS 12.[67]

At its meeting in June 2016, the IASB agreed with the Interpretations Committee's conclusion and tentatively decided to include the proposed amendment in the next cycle of annual improvements (2015–2017). Additionally, the Board tentatively decided that an entity should apply the proposed amendment retrospectively and early application should be permitted.[68]

Until such an amendment is made to the standard, we believe that either view continues to be acceptable, provided that it is applied consistently.

10.4 Gains and losses reclassified ('recycled') to profit or loss

Several IFRSs (notably IAS 21 and IAS 39) require certain gains and losses that have been accounted for outside profit or loss to be reclassified ('recycled') to profit or loss at a later date when the assets or liabilities to which they relate are realised or settled. Whilst IAS 12 requires any tax consequences of the original recognition of the gains or losses outside profit or loss also to be accounted for outside profit or loss, it is silent on the treatment to be adopted when the gains or losses are reclassified. In our view, any tax consequences of reclassified gains or losses originally recognised outside profit or loss should also be reclassified through profit or loss in the same period as the gains or losses to which they relate. Indeed, such reclassification is often an automatic consequence of the reversal of previously recognised deferred tax income or expense and its 're-recognition' as current tax income or expense, as illustrated in Example 31.41.

Example 31.41: Tax on reclassified ('recycled') items

On 1 January 2017 an entity purchases for €2,000 an equity security that it classifies as available-for-sale ('AFS'). At 31 December 2017 it restates the security to its fair value of €2,400, which was also its fair value on 1 May 2018. On 1 July 2018 it disposes of the investment for €2,100.

The entity's tax rate for 2017 is 40% and for 2018 35%. The change of rate was made in legislation enacted (without previous substantive enactment) on 1 May 2018. The entity is subject to tax on disposal of the investment (based on disposal proceeds less cost) in the period of disposal.

The accounting entries for this transaction would be as follows:

	€	€
1 January 2017		
AFS asset	2,000	
Cash		2,000
31 December 2017		
AFS asset [€2,400 – €2,000]	400	
Deferred tax (statement of financial position) [€400 @ 40%]		160
Other comprehensive income ('OCI')		240
Recognition of increase in value of asset, and related deferred tax		
1 May 2018		
Deferred tax (statement of financial position) [€400 @ (35% – 40%)]	20	
OCI		20
Remeasurement of deferred tax (no change in the fair value of the AFS asset since 31 December 2017)		
1 July 2018		
Cash	2,100	
OCI (reclassification of €400 (before tax) credited 31.12.16)	400	
AFS asset		2,400
Profit on disposal of AFS asset [cash €2,100 less original cost €2,000]		100
Deferred tax (statement of financial position)	140	
Deferred tax income (OCI)		140
Current tax (profit or loss)	35	
Current tax (statement of financial position) [35% of €100 pre-tax profit]		35

10.5 Gain/loss in profit or loss and loss/gain outside profit or loss offset for tax purposes

It often happens that a gain or loss accounted for in profit or loss can be offset for tax purposes against a gain or loss accounted for in other comprehensive income (or an increase or decrease in equity). This raises the question of how the tax effects of such transactions should be accounted for, as illustrated by Example 31.42 below.

Example 31.42: Loss in other comprehensive income and gain in profit or loss offset for tax purposes

During the year ended 31 December 2017, an entity that pays tax at 35% makes a taxable profit of €50,000 comprising:

- €80,000 trading profit less finance costs accounted for in profit or loss; and
- €30,000 foreign exchange losses accounted for in other comprehensive income ('OCI').

Should the total tax liability of €17,500 (35% of €50,000) be presented as either:

(a) a charge of €17,500 in profit or loss; or

(b) a charge of €28,000 (35% of €80,000) in profit or loss and a credit of €10,500 (35% of €30,000) in OCI?

In our view, (b) is the appropriate treatment, since the amount accounted for in OCI represents the difference between the tax that would have been paid absent the exchange loss accounted for in OCI and the amount actually payable. This indicates that this is the amount that, in the words of paragraph 61A of IAS 12, 'relates to' items that are recognised outside profit or loss.

Similar issues may arise where a transaction accounted for outside profit or loss generates a suitable taxable profit that allows recognition of a previously unrecognised tax asset relating to a transaction previously accounted for in profit or loss, as illustrated by Example 31.43 below.

Example 31.43: Recognition of deferred tax asset in profit or loss on the basis of tax liability accounted for outside profit or loss

An entity that pays tax at 30% has brought forward unrecognised deferred tax assets (with an indefinite life) totalling £1 million, relating to trading losses accounted for in profit or loss in prior periods. On 1 January 2017 it invests £100,000 in government bonds, which it holds until they are redeemed for the same amount on maturity on 31 December 2020. For tax purposes, any gain made by the entity on disposal of the bonds can be offset against the brought forward tax losses. The tax base of the bonds remains £100,000 at all times.

The entity elects to account for the bonds as available-for-sale and therefore carries them at fair value (see Chapter 49 at 2.4). Over the period to maturity the fair value of the bonds at the end of each reporting period (31 December) is as follows:

	£000
2017	110
2018	115
2019	120
2020	100

Under IAS 39 the movements in value would all be accounted for in other comprehensive income ('OCI') – see Chapter 49 at 2.4. Taken in isolation, the valuation gains in 2017 to 2019 would give rise to a deferred tax liability (at 30%) of £3,000 (2017), £4,500 (2018) and £6,000 (2019). However, these liabilities arise from taxable temporary differences that can be offset against the losses brought forward (see 7.4 above), and accordingly the (equal and opposite) deferred tax liability and deferred tax asset are offset in the statement of financial position (see 13.1.1 below). This raises the question as to whether there should be either:

(a) no tax charge or credit in either profit or loss or OCI in any of the periods affected; or

(b) in each period, a deferred tax charge in OCI (in respect of the taxable temporary difference arising from valuation gains on the bonds) and deferred tax income in profit or loss (representing the recognition of the previously unrecognised deferred tax asset).

In our view, the treatment in (b) should be followed. The fact that no deferred tax is presented in the statement of financial position arises from the offset of a deferred tax asset and deferred tax liability – it does not imply that there is no deferred tax. Moreover, although the recognition of the deferred tax asset is possible only as the result of the recognition of a deferred tax liability arising from a transaction accounted for in OCI, the asset itself relates to a trading loss previously accounted for in profit or loss. Accordingly, the deferred tax credit arising from the recognition of the asset is properly accounted for in profit or loss.

10.6 Discontinued operations

IAS 12 does not explicitly address the allocation of income tax charges and credits between continuing and discontinued operations. However, that some allocation is required is implicit in the requirement of paragraph 33(b)(ii) of IFRS 5 to disclose how much of the single figure post-tax profit or loss of discontinued operations disclosed in the statement of comprehensive income is comprised of 'the related income tax expense' (see Chapter 4). *[IFRS 5.33(b)(ii)]*. In our view, the provisions of IAS 12 for the allocation of tax income and expense between profit or loss, other comprehensive income and equity also form a basis for allocating tax income and expense between continuing and discontinued operations, as illustrated by Examples 31.44 to 31.46 below.

Example 31.44: Profit in continuing operations and loss in discontinued operations offset for tax purposes

Entity A, which pays tax at 25%, has identified an operation as discontinued for the purposes of IFRS 5. During the period the discontinued operation incurred a loss of £2 million and the continuing operations made a profit of £10 million. The net £8 million profit is fully taxable in the period, and there is no deferred tax income or expense. In our view, the tax expense should be allocated as follows:

	£m	£m
Current tax expense (continuing operations)[1]	2.5	
Current tax income (discontinued operation)[2]		0.5
Current tax liability[3]		2.0

1 Continuing operations profit £10m @ 25% = £2.5m

2 Discontinued operations loss £2m @ 25% = £0.5m.

3 Net taxable profit £8m @ 25% = £2.0m

The tax allocated to the discontinued operation represents the difference between the tax that would have been paid absent the loss accounted for in discontinued operations and the amount actually payable.

Example 31.45: Taxable profit on disposal of discontinued operation reduced by previously unrecognised tax losses

Entity B disposes of a discontinued operation during the current accounting period. The disposal gives rise to a charge to tax of €4 million. However, this is reduced to zero by offset against brought forward tax losses, which relate to the continuing operations of the entity, and for which no deferred tax asset has previously been recognised.

In our view, even though there is no overall tax expense, this should be reflected for financial reporting purposes as follows:

	€m	€m
Current tax expense (discontinued operation)	4.0	
Current tax income (continuing operations)		4.0

Chapter 31

This allocation reflects that fact that, although the transaction that allows recognition of the brought forward tax losses is accounted for as a discontinued operation, the losses themselves arose from continuing operations. This is essentially the same analysis as is used in Example 31.43 above (where a deferred tax liability recognised in other comprehensive income gives rise to an equal deferred tax asset recognised in profit or loss).

Example 31.46: Taxable profit on disposal of discontinued operation reduced by previously recognised tax losses

Entity B disposes of a discontinued operation during the current accounting period. The disposal gives rise to a charge to tax of €4 million. However, this is reduced to zero by offset against brought forward tax losses, which relate to the entity's continuing operations, and for which a deferred tax asset has previously been recognised.

In our view, even though there is no overall tax expense, this should be reflected for financial reporting purposes as follows:

	€m	€m
Current tax expense (discontinued operation)	4.0	
Deferred tax expense (continuing operations)	4.0	
Current tax income (continuing operations)		4.0
Deferred tax asset (statement of financial position)		4.0

This allocation reflects that fact that, although the transaction that allows recognition of the brought forward tax losses is accounted for as a discontinued operation, the losses themselves arose from continuing operations. This is essentially the same analysis as is used in Example 31.45 above.

10.7 Defined benefit pension plans

IAS 19 requires an entity, in accounting for a defined benefit post-employment benefit plan, to recognise actuarial gains and losses relating to the plan in full in other comprehensive income ('OCI'). At the same time, a calculated current (and, where applicable, past) service cost and net interest on the net defined benefit liability or asset are recognised in profit or loss – see Chapter 33 at 10.

In many jurisdictions, tax deductions for post-employment benefits are given on the basis of cash contributions paid to the plan fund (or benefits paid when a plan is unfunded).

This significant difference between the way in which defined plans are treated for tax and financial reporting purposes can make the allocation of tax deductions for them between profit or loss and OCI somewhat arbitrary, as illustrated by Example 31.47 below.

Example 31.47: Tax deductions for defined benefit pension plans

At 1 January 2017 an entity that pays tax at 40% has a fully-funded defined benefit pension scheme. During the year ended 31 December 2017 it records a total cost of €1 million, of which €800,000 is allocated to profit or loss and €200,000 to other comprehensive income ('OCI'). In January 2018 it makes a funding payment of €400,000, a tax deduction for which is received through the current tax charge for the year ended 31 December 2018.

Assuming that the entity is able to recognise a deferred tax asset for the entire €1 million charged in 2017, it will record the following entry for income taxes in 2017.

	€	€
Deferred tax asset [€1,000,000 @ 40%]	400,000	
Deferred tax income (profit or loss) [€800,000 @ 40%]		320,000
Deferred tax income (OCI) [€200,000 @ 40%]		80,000

When the funding payment is made in January 2018, the accounting deficit on the fund is reduced by €400,000. This gives rise to deferred tax expense of €160,000 (€400,000 @ 40%), as some of the deferred tax asset as at 31 December 2017 is released, and current tax income of €160,000 is recorded. The difficulty is how to allocate this movement in the deferred tax asset between profit or loss and OCI, as it is ultimately a matter of arbitrary allocation as to whether the funding payment is regarded as making good (for example):

- €400,000 of the €800,000 deficit previously accounted for in profit or loss;
- the whole of the €200,000 of the deficit previously accounted for in OCI and €200,000 of the €800,000 deficit previously accounted for in profit or loss; or
- a pro-rata share of those parts of the total deficit accounted for in profit or loss and OCI.

Indeed, for an entity that has adopted the transitional provision of IFRS 1 – *First-time Adoption of International Financial Reporting Standards* – that allows all cumulative actuarial gains and losses to be recognised on transition to IFRS, it may be impossible to determine how much of the portion of those cumulative gains and losses that arose before transition to IFRS would have been accounted for in profit or loss, and how much in OCI.

In the example above, the split is of relatively minor significance, since the entity was able to recognise 100% of the potential deferred tax asset associated with the pension liability. This means that, as the scheme is funded, there will be an equal and opposite amount of current tax income and deferred tax expense. The only real issue is therefore one of presentation, namely whether the gross items comprising this net nil charge are disclosed within the tax charge in profit or loss or in OCI.

In other cases, however, there might be an amount of net tax income or expense that needs to be allocated. Suppose that, as above, the entity recorded a pension cost of €1 million in 2017 but determined that the related deferred tax asset did not meet the criteria for recognition under IAS 12. In 2018, the entity determines that an asset of €50,000 can be recognised in view of the funding payments and taxable profits anticipated in 2018 and later years. This results in a total tax credit of €210,000 (€160,000 current tax, €50,000 deferred tax) in 2018, raising the question of whether it should be allocated to profit or loss, to OCI, or allocated on a pro-rata basis. This question might also arise if, as the result of newly enacted tax rates, the existing deferred tax balance were required to be remeasured.

In our view, these are instances of the exceptional circumstances envisaged by IAS 12 when a strict allocation of tax between profit or loss and OCI is not possible (see 10 above). Accordingly, any reasonable method of allocation may be used, provided that it is applied on a consistent basis.

One approach might be to compare the funding payments made to the scheme in the previous few years with the charges made to profit or loss under IAS 19 in those periods. If, for example, it is found that the payments were equal to or greater than the charges to profit or loss, it might reasonably be concluded that the funding payments have 'covered' the charge recognised in profit or loss, so that any surplus or deficit on the statement of financial position is broadly represented by items that have been accounted for in OCI.

However, a surplus may also arise from funding the scheme to an amount greater than the liability recognised under IAS 19 (for example under a minimum funding requirement imposed by local legislation or agreed with the pension fund trustees). In this case, the asset does not result from previously recognised income but from a reduction in another asset (i.e. cash). The entity should assess the expected manner of recovery of any asset implied by the accounting treatment of the surplus – i.e. whether it has been recognised on the basis that it will be 'consumed' (resulting in an accounting expense) or refunded to the entity in due course. The accounting treatment of refunds is discussed further in Chapter 33, and at 10.7.1 below.

The entity will account for the tax consequences of the expected manner of recovery implied by the accounting treatment. Where it is concluded that the asset will be 'consumed' (resulting in accounting expense), the entity will need to determine whether such an expense is likely to be recognised in profit or loss or in OCI in a future period.

10.7.1 Tax on refund of pension surplus

In some jurisdictions, a pension fund may be permitted or required to make a refund to the sponsoring employee of any surplus in the fund not required to settle the known or anticipated liabilities of the fund. It may be that such a refund is subject to tax. IFRIC 14 – *IAS 19 – The Limit on a Defined Benefit Asset, Minimum Funding Requirements and their Interaction* – requires any asset recorded in respect of such a refund to be shown net of any tax other than an income tax (see Chapter 33). In determining whether such a tax is an income tax of the entity, the general principles at 4.1 above should be applied. Relevant factors may include:

- whether tax is levied on the pension fund or the sponsoring entity; and
- whether tax is levied on the gross amount of the refund in all cases, or has regard to the sponsoring entity's other taxable income, or the amount of tax deductions received by the sponsoring entity in respect of contributions to the fund.

10.8 Share-based payment transactions

The accounting treatment of share-based payment transactions, some knowledge of which is required to understand the discussion below, is dealt with in Chapter 32.

In many tax jurisdictions, an entity receives a tax deduction in respect of remuneration paid in shares, share options or other equity instruments of the entity. The amount of any tax deduction may differ from the related remuneration expense, and may arise in a later accounting period. For example, in some jurisdictions, an entity may recognise an expense for employee services in accordance with IFRS 2 (based on the fair value of the award at the date of grant), but not receive a tax deduction until the share options are exercised (based on the intrinsic value of the award at the date of exercise).

As noted at 6.1.4 above, IAS 12 effectively considers the cumulative expense associated with share-based payment transactions as an asset that has been fully expensed in the financial statements in advance of being recognised for tax purposes, thus giving rise to a deductible temporary difference. *[IAS 12.68A, 68B]*.

If the tax deduction available in future periods is not known at the end of the period, it should be estimated based on information available at the end of the period. For example, if the tax deduction will be dependent upon the entity's share price at a future date, the measurement of the deductible temporary difference should be based on the entity's share price at the end of the period. *[IAS 12.68B]*.

10.8.1 Allocation of tax deduction between profit or loss and equity

Where the amount of any tax deduction (or estimated future tax deduction) exceeds the amount of the related cumulative remuneration expense, the current or deferred tax associated with the excess should be recognised directly in equity. *[IAS 12.68C]*. This treatment is illustrated by Example 31.48 below.

Example 31.48: Tax deductions for share-based payment transactions – allocation to profit or loss and equity

At the start of year 1, an entity with a tax rate of 40% grants options, which vest at the end of year 3 and are exercised at the end of year 5. Tax deductions are received at the date of exercise of the options, based on their intrinsic value at the date of exercise. Details of the expense recognised for employee services received and consumed in each accounting period, the number of options expected to vest by the entity at each year-end during the vesting period and outstanding after the end of the vesting period, and the intrinsic value of the options at each year-end, are as follows:

Year	*IFRS 2 expense for period* £	*Cumulative IFRS 2 expense* £	*Number of options*	*Intrinsic value per option* £	*Total intrinsic value* £
1	188,000	188,000	50,000	5	250,000
2	185,000	373,000	45,000	8	360,000
3	190,000	563,000	40,000	13	520,000
4		563,000	40,000	17	680,000
5		563,000	40,000	20	800,000

The tax base of, and the temporary difference and deferred tax asset associated with, the employee services is calculated as follows. Since the book value of the employee services is in all cases zero, the temporary difference associated with the services is at all times equal to their tax base as set out below.

Year	*Intrinsic value (see table above)* £	*Expired portion of vesting period* [1]	*Tax base (and temporary difference)* £	*Tax asset* [2] £	*Tax income* [3] £
	a	b	c = a × b	40% of c	
1	250,000	1/3	83,333	33,333	33,333
2	360,000	2/3	240,000	96,000	62,667
3	520,000	3/3	520,000	208,000	112,000
4	680,000	3/3	680,000	272,000	64,000
5	800,000	3/3	800,000	320,000	48,000

1 The expired portion of the vesting period is consistent with that used to calculate the cumulative charge employee costs under IFRS 2 (see Chapter 32).

2 Deferred tax asset in years 1 to 4 and current tax asset in year 5.

3 Year-on-year increase in asset.

By comparing the 'Cumulative IFRS 2 expense' column in the first table with the 'Tax base (and temporary difference)' column in the second table it can be seen that in years 1 to 3 the expected tax deduction is lower than the cumulative expense charged, and is therefore dealt with entirely in profit or loss. However in years 4 and 5 the expected (and in year 5 the actual) tax deduction is higher than the cumulative expense charged. The tax relating to the cumulative expense charged is dealt with in profit or loss, and the tax relating to the excess of the tax-deductible amount over the amount charged in profit or loss is dealt with in equity as follows:

	DR	CR
Year 1		
Deferred tax (statement of financial position)	33,333	
Deferred tax (profit or loss)		33,333
Year 2		
Deferred tax (statement of financial position)	62,667	
Deferred tax (profit or loss)		62,667
Year 3		
Deferred tax (statement of financial position)	112,000	
Deferred tax (profit or loss)		112,000
Year 4		
Deferred tax (statement of financial position)	64,000	
Deferred tax (profit or loss)[1]		17,200
Equity		46,800
Year 5		
Deferred tax (profit or loss)	225,200	
Deferred tax (equity)	46,800	
Deferred tax (statement of financial position)		272,000
Current tax (statement of financial position)	320,000	
Current tax (profit or loss)[2]		225,200
Current tax (equity)		94,800

1 Cumulative tax credit to profit or loss restricted to 40% of cumulative expense of £563,000 = £225,200. Amount credited in years 1 to 3 is £(33,333 + 62,667 + 112,000) = £212,000. Therefore amount recognised in profit or loss is £(225,200 – 212,000) = £17,200.

2 Current tax credit in profit or loss is restricted to £225,200 as explained in note 1 above. The £48,000 net increase in total cumulative tax income since year 4 (£320,000 – £272,000) is dealt with entirely in equity (current tax income €94,800 less deferred tax charge €46,800).

Example 31.48 above is based on Example 5 in the illustrative examples accompanying IAS 12 (as inserted by IFRS 2). However, the example included in IAS 12 states that the cumulative tax income is based on the number of options 'outstanding' at each period end. This would be inconsistent with the methodology in IFRS 2 (see Chapter 32), which requires the share-based payment expense during the vesting period to be based on the number of options expected to vest (as that term is defined in IFRS 2), not the total number of options outstanding, at the period end. It would only be once the vesting period is complete that the number of options outstanding becomes relevant. We assume that this is simply a drafting slip by the IASB.

IAS 12 asserts that the allocation of the tax deduction between profit or loss and equity illustrated in Example 31.48 is appropriate on the basis that the fact that the tax deduction (or estimated future tax deduction) exceeds the amount of the related cumulative remuneration expense 'indicates that the tax deduction relates not only to remuneration expense but also to an equity item.' *[IAS 12.68C]*.

However, some (including the IASB itself in the exposure draft that preceded IFRS 2) take the view that any tax deductions in excess of the amount charged to profit or loss relate to an increase in the fair value of the award from the date of grant to the date of exercise, which, under the 'grant date measurement' model in IFRS 2, is not recognised in equity, or indeed anywhere in the financial statements. The 'excess' tax deduction therefore does not meet the criteria for recognition in equity in IAS 12, and would (on application of the normal rules in IAS 12) be accounted for in profit or loss by default.

The treatment required by IFRS 2 seems to have been adopted for consistency with US GAAP. However, as the IASB acknowledges, while the final cumulative allocation of tax between profit or loss and equity is broadly consistent with that required by US GAAP, the basis on which it is measured and reported at reporting dates before exercise date is quite different. *[IFRS 2.BC311-BC329]*.

10.8.2 Determining the tax base

IAS 12 does not specify exactly how the tax base of a share-based payment transaction is to be determined. However, Example 5 in the illustrative examples accompanying IAS 12 (the substance of which is reproduced at 10.8.1 above) calculates the tax base as:

- the amount that would be deductible for tax if the event triggering deduction occurred at the end of the reporting period; multiplied by
- the expired portion of the vesting period at the end of the reporting period.

IFRS 2 treats certain share-based payment awards as, in effect, a parcel of a number of discrete awards, each with a different vesting period. This may be the case where an award is subject to graded vesting, has been modified, or has separate equity and liability components (see Chapter 32). In order to determine the tax base for such an award, it is necessary to consider separately the part, or parts, of the award with the same vesting period, as illustrated in Example 31.49 below.

Example 31.49: Tax deductions for share-based payment transactions – 'multi-element' awards

An entity awards 550 free shares to an employee, with no conditions other than continuous service. 100 shares vest after one year, 150 shares after two years and 300 shares after three years. Any shares received at the end of years 1 and 2 have vested unconditionally.

At the date the award is granted, the fair value of a share delivered in one year's time is €3.00; in two years' time €2.80; and in three years' time €2.50.

Under IFRS 2, the analysis is that the employee has simultaneously received an award of 100 shares vesting over one year, an award of 150 shares vesting over two years and an award of 300 shares vesting over 3 years (see Chapter 32 at 6.2.2). This would be accounted for as follows (assuming that the award was expected to vest in full at each reporting date and did actually vest in full – see Chapter 32):

Year	Calculation of cumulative expense	Cumulative expense (€)	Expense for period (€)
1	[100 shares × €3.00] + [150 shares × €2.80 × 1/2] + [300 shares × €2.50 × 1/3]	760	760
2	[100 shares × €3.00] + [150 shares × €2.80 × 2/2] + [300 shares × €2.50 × 2/3]	1,220	460
3	[100 shares × €3.00] + [150 shares × €2.80 × 2/2] + [300 shares × €2.50 × 3/3]	1,470	250

The entity receives a tax deduction at 30% for the awards based on the fair value of the shares delivered. The fair value of a share at the end of years 1, 2 and 3 is, respectively, €3.60, €2.00 and €6.00.

At the end of year 1, a current tax deduction of €108 (100 shares × €3.60 @ 30%) is receivable in respect of the 100 shares that vest. The tax base of the shares expected to vest in years 2 and 3 is calculated by reference to the year-end share price of €3.60 as:

- in respect of the 150 shares expected to vest at the end of year 2, €270 (150 shares × €3.60 × 1/2). This will give rise to a deferred tax asset of €81 (€270 @ 30%); and
- in respect of the 300 shares expected to vest at the end of year 3, €360 (300 shares × €3.60 × 1/3). This will give rise to a deferred tax asset of €108 (€360 @ 30%).

The total deferred tax asset at the end of year is therefore €189 (€81 + €108).

At the end of year 2, a current tax deduction of €90 is receivable in respect of the 150 shares that vest (150 shares × €2.00 @ 30%). The tax base of the shares expected to vest in year 3 is calculated by reference to the year-end share price of €2.00 as €400 (300 shares × €2.00 × 2/3). This gives rise to a deferred tax asset of €120 (€400 @ 30%).

At the end of year 3, a current tax deduction of €540 (300 shares × €6.00 @ 30%) is receivable in respect of the 300 shares that vest.

When an award has multiple elements that vest at different times, the question arises as to whether the unit of account for applying the 'cap' on recognition of the tax benefit in profit or loss is the award as a whole or each element separately accounted for. In our view, the determination needs to be made for each element of the award separately. This is similar to our analysis at 10.7.3 below (multiple awards outstanding) and 10.7.4 below (awards for which a tax deduction is received on exercise which are exercised at different times).

Based on the information above, the total current and deferred tax income or expense (i.e. before allocation to profit or loss and equity) at the ends of years 1 to 3 would be as follows, assuming in each case that there is no restriction on the recognition of tax assets (see 7.4 above).

Year	*Current tax asset and income* €	*Deferred tax asset* €	*Deferred tax income/ (expense)* €
1	108	189	189
2	90	120	(69)
3	540	–	(120)

The required accounting entries for income taxes are as follows:

	DR	CR
Year 1		
Current tax (statement of financial position)	108	
Current tax (profit or loss)		90
Current tax (equity)[1]		18
Deferred tax (statement of financial position)	189	
Deferred tax (profit or loss) (€63 + €75 – see below)		138
Deferred tax (equity)[2] (€18 + €33 – see below)		51

1 The current tax deduction relates to the 100 shares vesting in year 1, for which the charge to profit or loss is €300 (100 shares × €3.00). The tax deduction accounted for in profit or loss is therefore restricted to 30% of €300 = €90. The balance of €18 is credited to equity, and relates to the €0.60 difference between the grant date fair value of a 'Year 1' share at grant (€3.00) and at vesting (€3.60) – 100 shares × €0.60 = €60 @ 30% = €18.

2 The total deferred tax income of €189 represents:

- €81 (see above) in respect of the 150 shares expected to vest in year 2, for which the charge to profit or loss is €210 (150 shares × €2.80 × 1/2). The tax deduction accounted for in profit or loss is restricted to 30% of €210 = €63, with the balance of €18 credited to equity; and
- €108 (see above) in respect of the 300 shares expected to vest in year 3, for which the expected charge to profit or loss is €250 (300 shares × €2.50 × 1/3). The tax deduction accounted for in profit or loss is therefore restricted to 30% of €250 = €75, with the balance of €33 credited to equity.

	DR	CR
Year 2		
Current tax (statement of financial position)	90	
Current tax (profit or loss)[3]		90
Deferred tax (profit or loss)[4]	18	
Deferred tax (equity)[4]	51	
Deferred tax (statement of financial position)[4]		69

3 The current tax deduction relates to the 150 shares vesting in year 2, for which the cumulative charge to profit or loss is €420 (150 shares × €2.80). The cumulative tax deduction accounted for in profit or loss would therefore be restricted to 30% of €420 = €126. The entire amount of current tax deduction received (€90) is therefore credited to profit or loss.

4 At the end of year 2, the deferred tax relates to the 300 shares expected to vest at the end of year 3, which has been measured based on the year end share price of €2.00. This is lower than the share price on which the IFRS 2 charge has been based. Therefore there is no requirement to allocate any deferred tax to equity, and the balance of deferred tax in equity is reduced to nil. The balance of the total €69 movement in the deferred tax balance is allocated to profit or loss.

The net tax credit in profit or loss in year 2 of €72 (current tax credit €90, less deferred tax charge €18) can be seen as representing:

Credit relating to IFRS 2 expense recognised in the period[5]	105
Charge relating to remeasurement of prior year deferred tax[6]	(33)
Total	72

5 In this case the tax credit recognised in profit or loss is not the 'expected' credit of €138 (IFRS 2 charge of €460 @ 30%). This is because the current tax deduction for the shares vesting in year 2 and the deferred tax deduction for the shares expected to vest in year 3 are based on the year-end share price of €2.00, which is lower than the share values used to calculate the IFRS 2 charge (€2.80 and €2.50). During the year, an IFRS 2 expense has been recognised for 75 'whole share equivalents' in respect of the shares vesting in year 2 (150 shares × 1/2) and 100 'whole share equivalents' in respect of the shares expected to vest in year 3 (300 shares × 1/3), a total of 175 'whole share equivalents'. Accordingly the credit for the year is €105 (175 × €2.00 × 30%).

6 In year 1 the deferred tax credit (based on the year 1 year end share price of €3.60) recognised in profit of loss in respect of the shares expected to vest in years 2 and 3 was €138. If this had been based on the year 2 year end share price of €2.00 this would have been only €105. [150 × 1/2 × €2.00] + [300 × 1/3 × €2.00] = €350 × 30% = €105. €138 – €105 = €33.

	DR	CR
Year 3		
Current tax (statement of financial position)	540	
Current tax (profit or loss)		225
Current tax (equity)[7]		315
Deferred tax (profit or loss)	120	
Deferred tax (statement of financial position)[8]		120

7 The current tax deduction relates to the 300 shares vesting in year 1, for which the cumulative charge to profit or loss is €750 (300 shares × €2.50). The tax deduction accounted for in profit or loss is therefore restricted to 30% of €750 = €225.

8 The deferred tax asset, all of which was – on a cumulative basis – recognised in profit or loss, is derecognised in profit or loss.

The net tax credit in profit or loss in year 3 of €105 (current tax credit €225, less deferred tax charge €120) can be seen as representing:

Credit relating to IFRS 2 expense recognised in the period[9]	75
Credit relating to remeasurement of prior year deferred tax[10]	30
Total	105

9 €250 @ 30%.

10 The opening balance deferred tax asset of €120 is based on the year 2 share price of €2.00. If this had been based on the year 3 share price of €6.00 it would have been €360. However, the amount recognised in profit or loss would have been restricted to €150 – 30% of the cumulative expense at the end of year 2 of €500 (300 shares × €2.50 × 2/3). €150 – €120 = €30.

10.8.3 Allocation when more than one award is outstanding

As noted above, IAS 12 requires that, 'where the amount of any tax deduction ... exceeds the amount of the related cumulative remuneration expense, the current or deferred tax associated with the excess should be recognised directly in equity'. Some have therefore argued that, as drafted, IAS 12 requires the cumulative expense for all outstanding share schemes to be compared in aggregate with the aggregate tax deduction for all share schemes. Others argue that the comparison should be made for each scheme separately. The effect of each treatment is illustrated in Example 31.50 below.

Example 31.50: Tax deductions for share-based payment transactions – more than one award

An entity that pays tax at 30% has two outstanding share schemes, Scheme A and Scheme B. The entity receives tax deductions for share-based payment transactions based on their intrinsic value at the date of exercise.

At the end of the reporting period, the cumulative expense charged for each scheme is £1 million. Scheme A has a negative intrinsic value at the end of the reporting period, and is not expected to recover its value to the extent that employees will exercise their options. Accordingly no deferred tax asset is recognised for Scheme A. Scheme B has an intrinsic value of £1.5 million. The entity will therefore record a deferred tax asset of £450,000 (30% of £1.5 million), subject to the recognition criteria for deferred tax assets being satisfied.

Those who argue that comparison of share-based payment expense to tax deduction should be made on an aggregated basis would conclude that, because the cumulative potential tax deduction of £1.5 million (which relates only to Scheme B) is lower than the cumulative aggregate expense for both Scheme A and Scheme B (£2 million), the deferred tax income should be recognised entirely in profit or loss.

However, those who argue that comparison of share-based payment expense to tax deduction should be made on a discrete basis for each scheme would conclude that, because the cumulative tax deduction for Scheme B (£1.5 million) is higher than the cumulative aggregate expense for Scheme B (£1 million), only £300,000 of the deferred tax income (30% of £1 million) should be recognised in profit or loss, with the remaining £150,000 recognised in equity.

In our view, the comparison must be made on a discrete scheme-by-scheme basis. As noted at 10.8.2 above, it is clear from IAS 12 and the Basis for Conclusions to IFRS 2 that the IASB's intention was to exclude from profit or loss any tax deduction that is effectively given for the growth in fair value of an award that accrues after grant date. *[IAS 12.68C, IFRS 2.BC311-BC329]*. This can be determined only on an award-by-award basis. Moreover, IAS 12 requires the amount of any tax deduction to be accounted for in equity when it 'exceeds the amount of the *related* cumulative remuneration expense'. In Example 31.50 above, the tax deduction on Scheme B cannot, in our view, be said to be 'related' to the remuneration expense for Scheme A. Accordingly, the expense relating to Scheme A is not relevant for determining the amount of tax income relating to Scheme B that is required to be accounted for in equity.

It may also be that what is regarded as a single scheme may need to be further sub-divided for the purposes of the comparison for reasons such as the following:

- where the same award is made to regular employees and also to top management, the fair value of the options granted to each population may nevertheless be different for the purposes of IFRS 2 given different exercise behaviours (see Chapter 32 at 8.5.2.A);
- an award is made to employees which attracts tax deductions in more than one tax jurisdiction; or
- an award is made in the same tax jurisdiction to employees in different entities, not all of which are able to recognise a deferred tax asset.

10.8.4 Staggered exercise of awards

The example in IAS 12, the substance of which is included in Example 31.48 at 10.8.1 above, addresses a situation in which all vested awards are exercised simultaneously. In practice, however, vested awards are often exercised at different dates.

Once an award under a given scheme has vested, and different awards in that scheme are exercised at different times, the question arises as to whether the 'cap' on recognition of the tax benefit in profit or loss should be calculated by reference to the cumulative expense recognised in respect of the total number of awards vested, or in respect only of as yet unexercised vested awards. In our view, where a tax deduction is received on exercise, the calculation must be undertaken by reference to the cumulative expense recognised for outstanding unexercised options. This is illustrated by Example 31.51 below.

Example 31.51: Tax deductions for share-based payment transactions – staggered exercise of award

At the start of year 1, an entity with a tax rate of 40% grants 20 options each to 5 employees. The options have a fair value of €5 and vest at the end of year 2. The options vest in full. 25 are exercised at the end of year 3 and 75 at the end of year 6. The entity is able to support the view that any deferred tax asset arising before exercise will be recoverable, and may therefore be recognised in full.

Tax deductions are given in the year of exercise, based on the intrinsic value of the options at the date of exercise. The intrinsic value of options at the end of each reporting period is as follows:

Year	*Intrinsic value per option*
	€
1	3
2	8
3	8
4	1
5	7
6	6

On the basis of the information above:

- there would be an IFRS 2 charge of €250 in years 1 and 2 (20 options × 5 employees × €5 × 1/2 (portion of vesting period)
- current and deferred tax assets should be recognised at the end of each period as follows:

Current tax

Year	*Number of options exercised*	*Intrinsic value per option*	*Total intrinsic value*	*Tax effect at 40%*
		€	€	€
3	25	8	200	80
6	75	6	450	180

Deferred tax

Year	*Number of options outstanding*	*Temporary difference per option*	*Total temporary difference*	*Tax effect at 40%*
		€	€	€
1	100	1.5[1]	150	60
2	100	8	800	320
3	75	8	600	240
4	75	1	75	30
5	75	7	525	210
6	–	6	–	–

1 Intrinsic value €3 × 1/2 (expired portion of vesting period).

The required accounting entries for income taxes are as follows

	DR	CR
	€	€
Year 1		
Deferred tax (statement of financial position)	60	
Deferred tax (profit or loss)[1]		60
Year 2		
Deferred tax (statement of financial position)[2]	260	
Deferred tax (profit or loss)[3]		140
Deferred tax (equity)		120
Year 3		
Deferred tax (profit or loss)[4]	50	
Deferred tax (equity)	30	
Deferred tax (statement of financial position)[5]		80
Current tax (statement of financial position)[6]	80	
Current tax (profit or loss)[4]		50
Current tax (equity)		30

Year 4		
Deferred tax (profit or loss)[7]	120	
Deferred tax (equity)	90	
Deferred tax (statement of financial position)[8]		210
Year 5		
Deferred tax (statement of financial position)[9]	180	
Deferred tax (profit or loss)[10]		120
Deferred tax (equity)		60
Year 6		
Deferred tax (profit or loss)[11]	150	
Deferred tax (equity)	60	
Deferred tax (statement of financial position)		210
Current tax (statement of financial position)[12]	180	
Current tax (profit or loss)[13]		150
Current tax (equity)		30

1 The cumulative tax income is based on expected deductions of €150, which is less than the cumulative IFRS 2 charge of €250 (see above).

2 Year 2 year-end balance of €320 (see table above), less €60 recognised at end of year 1 = €140.

3 Cumulative deferred tax recognised in profit or loss must not exceed 40% × €500 (cumulative IFRS 2 charge) = €200. This limits the credit for year 2 to €200 less the €60 credited in year 1 = €140.

4 Reversal of deferred tax income previously recognised in profit or loss for the 25 options exercised: 25 × €5 [IFRS 2 charge per option] × 40% = €50. This also represents the limit on the amount of current tax deduction that can be recognised in profit or loss.

5 Year 3 year-end balance of €240 (see table above), less €320 recognised at end of year 2 = €80.

6 25 options × €8 intrinsic value × 40% = €80.

In years 4 to 6, the amount of tax recognised in profit or loss is restricted by the cumulative IFRS 2 expense of €375 for the 75 options left outstanding (75 options × €5).

7 Cumulative (maximum) tax deduction already recognised in profit or loss is €375 @ 40% = €150. This needs to be reduced to €30 (year end deferred tax balance), giving rise to a charge of €150 – €30 = €120. This can be seen as representing the fact that, at the start of the period a cumulative potential tax deduction of €5 per award had been recognised in profit or loss. At the end of the period it is expected that deductions of only €1 per award will be available. Therefore there is a loss to be recognised in profit or loss of 75 awards × (€5 – €1) × 40% = €120.

8 Year 4 year-end balance of €30 (see table above), less €240 recognised at end of year 3 = €(210).

9 Year 5 year-end balance of €210 (see table above), less €30 recognised at end of year 4 = €180.

10 Cumulative maximum tax deduction that can be recognised in profit or loss is €150 (see note 7). €30 cumulative deduction is brought forward, so that credit for period is limited to €150 – €30 = €120.

11 Reversal of deferred tax previously recognised. The amount previously taken to profit or loss was limited to €150 (see notes 7 and 9).

12 75 options × €6 × 40% = €180.

13 Deduction restricted to €375 [IFRS 2 charge] × 40% = €150.

Chapter 31

It will be noted that the cumulative effect of the above entries in profit or loss is as follows (tax income in brackets):

Year	*Deferred tax*	*Current tax*	*Total*
	€	€	€
1	(60)		(60)
2	(140)		(140)
3	50	(50)	–
4	120		120
5	(120)		(120)
6	150	(150)	–
		Total	(200)

The cumulative effect of the above entries in equity is as follows (tax income in brackets):

Year	*Deferred tax*	*Current tax*	*Total*
	€	€	€
1			–
2	(120)		(120)
3	30	(30)	–
4	90		90
5	(60)		(60)
6	60	(30)	30
		Total	(60)

The overall effect is to take credit in profit or loss for the lower of total tax deductions actually received of €260 (€80 in year 3 and €180 in year 6) and the tax deductions on the IFRS 2 expense of €200 (40% of €500). The excess tax deductions of €60 are recognised in equity.

10.8.5 Replacement awards in a business combination

IFRS 3 contains some detailed provisions on the treatment of share-based payment awards issued by an acquirer to replace awards made by the acquired entity before the business combination occurred. These are discussed in Chapter 32 at 11.

IFRS 3 amended IAS 12 to include an illustrative example for the treatment of tax deductions on such replacement awards, the substance of which is reproduced as Example 31.52 below. *[IAS 12 IE Example 6].*

Example 31.52: Deferred tax on replacement share-based awards in a business combination

On 1 January 2017 Entity A acquired Entity B. A paid cash consideration of €400 million to the former owners of B. At the acquisition date B had outstanding fully-vested employee share options with a fair value of €100 million. As part of the business combination B's outstanding share options are replaced by fully vested share options of A (replacement awards) with a market-based measure of €100 million and an intrinsic value of €80 million. In accordance with IFRS 3, the replacement awards are part of the consideration transferred for B (see Chapter 32 at 11).

A tax deduction will be given only when the options are exercised, based on the intrinsic value of the options at that date. A's tax rate is 40%.

A recognises a deferred tax asset of €32 million (intrinsic value of €80m × 40%) on the replacement awards at the acquisition date (see 10.8.1 above). IAS 12 does not indicate the calculation if only part of the fair value of the award were regarded as part of the consideration transferred. However, it would be consistent with the general approach indicated at 10.8.2 above to calculate the tax base of the award by adjusting the intrinsic value by the ratio of the expired vesting period at acquisition to the total vesting period of the award (as determined for the purposes of IFRS 3 – see Chapter 32 at 11).

A measures the identifiable net assets obtained in the business combination (excluding deferred tax assets and liabilities) at €450 million, with a combined tax base of €300 million, giving rise to a taxable temporary difference at the acquisition date of €150 million, on which deferred tax at 40% of €60 million is recognised. Goodwill is calculated as follows:

	€m
Cash consideration	400
Replacement options	100
Total consideration	500
Identifiable net assets (excluding deferred tax)	(450)
Deferred tax asset	(32)
Deferred tax liability	60
Goodwill	78

Reductions in the carrying amount of goodwill are not deductible for tax purposes. In accordance with the initial recognition exception in IAS 12 (see 7.2 above), A recognises no deferred tax liability for the taxable temporary difference associated with the goodwill recognised in the business combination. The accounting entry for the business combination is therefore as follows:

	DR €m	CR €m
Goodwill	78	
Identifiable net assets	450	
Deferred tax asset	32	
Cash		400
Equity		100
Deferred tax liability		60

On 31 December 2017 the intrinsic value of the replacement awards is €120 million, in respect of which A recognises a deferred tax asset of €48 million (€120 m at 40%). This gives rise to deferred tax income of €16 million (€48 million recognised at 31 December 2017 less €32 million arising on acquisition). IAS 12 notes, somewhat redundantly, that this amount is credited to 'deferred tax income', but with no indication as to whether the amount should be recognised in profit or loss or in equity. In our view, the general principles of IAS 12 regarding tax deductions on share-based payment transactions suggest that the entire amount is recognised in equity. This is because the consolidated financial statements of A have never recognised any expense for the award in profit or loss (since it is attributed fully to the consideration transferred). Therefore none of the tax deductions can be recognised in profit or loss either.

10.8.6 Share-based payment transactions subject to transitional provisions of IFRS 1 and IFRS 2

IFRS 1 and IFRS 2 provide, respectively, first-time adopters and existing IFRS preparers with some transitional exemptions from accounting for share-based payment transactions. The accounting treatment of the tax effects of transactions to which these exemptions have been applied is discussed in Chapter 5 at 7.4.2. Whilst that discussion specifically addresses the tax effects of transactions subject to the exemption for first-time adopters of IFRS, it is equally applicable to the tax effects of transactions subject to the exemptions in IFRS 2 for existing IFRS preparers.

10.9 Change in tax status of entity or shareholders

Sometimes there is a change in an entity's tax assets and liabilities as a result of a change in the tax status of the entity itself or that of its shareholders. SIC-25 clarifies that the effect of such a change should be recognised in profit or loss except to the extent that it involves a remeasurement of tax originally accounted for in other comprehensive income or in equity, in which case the change should also be dealt with in, respectively, other comprehensive income or equity. *[SIC-25.4]*.

10.10 Previous revaluation of PP&E treated as deemed cost on transition to IFRS

In some cases IFRS 1 allows an entity, on transition to IFRS, to treat the carrying amount of property, plant, and equipment (PP&E) revalued under its pre-transition GAAP as a deemed cost for the purposes of IFRS (see Chapter 5 at 5.5).

Where an asset is carried at deemed cost on transition to IFRS, but the tax base of the asset remains at original cost (or an amount based on original cost), the pre-transition revaluation will give rise to a temporary difference (typically, a taxable temporary difference) associated with the asset. IAS 12 requires deferred tax to be recognised on any such temporary difference at transition.

If, after transition, the deferred tax is required to be remeasured (e.g. because of a change in tax rate, or a re-basing of the asset for tax purposes), and the asset concerned was revalued outside profit or loss under pre-transition GAAP, the question arises as to whether the resulting deferred tax income or expense should be recognised in, or outside, profit or loss. This is discussed in Chapter 5 at 7.4.1.

10.11 Disposal of an interest in a subsidiary that does not result in a loss of control

A decrease in a parent's ownership interest in a subsidiary that does not result in a loss of control is accounted for in the consolidated financial statements as an equity transaction, i.e. a transaction with owners in their capacity as owners. *[IFRS 10.23]*. In these circumstances, the carrying amounts of the controlling and non-controlling interests are adjusted to reflect the changes in their relative interests in the subsidiary. 'The entity shall recognise directly in equity any difference between the amount by which the non-controlling interests are adjusted and the fair value of the consideration paid or received, and attribute it to the owners of the parent.' *[IFRS 10.B96]*. In other words, no changes in a subsidiary's assets (including goodwill) and liabilities are recognised in a transaction in which a parent increases or decreases its ownership interest in a subsidiary that it already controls. *[IFRS 10.BCZ173]*. Increases or decreases in the ownership interest in a subsidiary do not result in the recognition of a gain or loss. Accounting for disposals of interests that do not result in a loss of control is discussed in Chapter 7 at 3.3.

As the transaction is accounted for as an equity transaction, which does not affect profit or loss in the consolidated financial statements, one might assume that the full amount of any tax effect should also be recognised in equity. *[IAS 12.58(a)]*. However, this is not the case to the extent that any adjustment to non-controlling interests relates to the post acquisition profit of the subsidiary, which was previously recognised in the consolidated income statement, as illustrated in Example 31.53 below.

Example 31.53: Tax effect of a disposal of an interest in a subsidiary that does not result in a loss of control

A parent owns 100% of the equity shares of a subsidiary and presents the investment at a cost of $1,000,000 in its separate financial statements. To date, the parent had not recognised deferred taxation, as it considered it probable that the temporary difference would not reverse in the foreseeable future. At the end of the reporting period, the subsidiary's post acquisition profit and net asset value recognised in the parent's consolidated financial statements are $500,000 and $1,500,000 respectively. The parent agrees to dispose of a 20% interest in the subsidiary for a cash consideration of $1,400,000 (the 'Transaction').

It is assumed that the tax base of the investment in the subsidiary is the same as its original cost of $1,000,000. The taxable gain is calculated on the same basis as the gain recognised in the separate financial statements and the applicable tax rate is 25%.

The parent recognises a gain of $1,200,000 (i.e. $1,400,000 – [$1,000,000 × 20%]) in its separate financial statements and is liable for a current tax of $300,000 (i.e. $1,200,000 × 25%).

The Transaction does not result in the parent losing control of the subsidiary and it is accounted for in equity in the consolidated financial statements of the parent. The parent recognises non-controlling interests of $300,000 (i.e. $1,500,000 × 20%) and credits equity for $1,100,000, being the difference between the consideration of $1,400,000 and the non-controlling interests of $300,000, in the consolidated financial statements of the parent.

What are the current and deferred tax effects in the consolidated financial statements if:

(a) the transaction is not completed until after the end of the reporting period; or

(b) the transaction is completed at the end of the reporting period?

If the transaction is not completed until after the end of the reporting period, no current tax is recognised. However, as the parent intends to recover 20% of its investment in the subsidiary through sale, it must recognise a deferred tax liability for the temporary difference associated with its investment in the subsidiary that is expected to reverse in the foreseeable future. *[IAS 12.39]*. Its carrying value in the consolidated financial statements is $1,500,000 and its tax base is $1,000,000. Accordingly, deferred tax of $25,000 (i.e. [$1,500,000 – $1,000,000] × 20% × 25%) should be recognised in profit or loss in the consolidated financial statements. This deferred tax would reverse through profit or loss upon disposal, because it relates to the post acquisition profit recognised in an earlier period. *[IAS 12.58]*.

If the transaction is completed at the end of the reporting period, the consolidated financial statements would include a current tax charge of $300,000 on the taxable gain on sale recorded by the subsidiary. Whilst the transaction is recorded in equity, because there is no loss of control, the entity does not recognise all of this tax directly in equity because only $1,100,000 out of the total taxable gain of $1,200,000 was taken to non-controlling interests in equity. *[IAS 12.58(a)]*. Therefore, $275,000 (i.e. $1,100,000 × 25%) is recognised directly in equity because it arises from the equity transaction. *[IAS 12.61A(b)]*. The remaining current tax of $25,000 (i.e. [$1,500,000 – $1,000,000] × 20% × 25%) relates to the post acquisition profit of the subsidiary, and is recognised in the consolidated income statement.

11 CONSOLIDATED TAX RETURNS AND OFFSET OF TAXABLE PROFITS AND LOSSES WITHIN GROUPS

In some jurisdictions one member of a group of companies may file a single tax return on behalf of all, or some, members of the group. In other jurisdictions, it is possible for one member of a group to transfer tax losses to one or more other members of the group in order to reduce their tax liabilities. In some groups a company whose tax liability is reduced by such an arrangement may be required to make a payment to the member of the group that pays tax on its behalf, or transfers losses to it, as the case may be. In other groups no such charge is made.

Such transactions raise the question of the appropriate accounting treatment in the separate financial statements of the group entities involved – in particular, whether the company benefiting from such an arrangement should reflect income (or more likely a capital contribution) from another member of the group equal to the tax expense mitigated as a result of the arrangement.

Some argue that the effects of such transactions should be reflected in the separate financial statements of the entities involved, as is required by some national standards (e.g. those of the US and Australia). Others argue that, except to the extent that a management charge is actually made (see 11.1 below), there is no need to reflect such transactions in the separate financial statements of the entities involved. Those that take this view point out that it is inconsistent to require companies to show a capital contribution for tax losses ceded to them without charge, unless all other intragroup transactions are also restated on arm's-length terms – which would be somewhat radical. Moreover, IAS 24 – *Related Party Disclosures* – merely requires disclosure of the actual terms of such transactions, not that they be remeasured, either for financial reporting or disclosure purposes, on the same basis as a similar notional arm's length transaction (see Chapter 37).

IAS 12 is silent on the issue and, in our view, neither approach can be said to either be prohibited or required. Accordingly, either approach may be adopted on a consistent basis.

The (now withdrawn) exposure draft of a standard to replace IAS 12 published in March 2009 (see 1.3 above) proposed that each entity within a group filing a consolidated tax return should recognise an appropriate share of the total tax liability shown in the return.

11.1 Payments for intragroup transfer of tax losses

Where one member of a group transfers tax losses to another member of the group, the entity whose tax liability is reduced may be required, as matter of group policy, to pay an amount of compensation to the member of the group that transfers the losses to it. Such payments are known by different terms in different jurisdictions, but are referred to in the discussion below as 'tax loss payments'.

Tax loss payments are generally made in an amount equal to the tax saved by the paying company. In some cases, however, payment may be made in an amount equal to the nominal amount of the tax loss, which will be greater than the amount of tax saved. This raises the question of how such payments should be accounted for.

The first issue is whether such payments should be recognised:

- in total comprehensive income; or
- as a distribution (in the case of a payment from a subsidiary to a parent) or a capital contribution (in the case of a payment from a parent to a subsidiary).

The second issue is, to the extent that the payments are accounted for in total comprehensive income, whether they should be classified as:

- income tax, allocated between profit or loss, other comprehensive income or equity (see 10 above). The argument for this treatment is that the payments made or received are amounts that would otherwise be paid to or received from (or offset against an amount paid to) a tax authority; or
- operating income or expense in profit or loss (on the grounds that, as a matter of fact, the payments are not made to or received from any tax authority).

IAS 12 is silent on these issues. However, there is a long-standing practice in many jurisdictions that such payments are treated as if they were income taxes. We believe that this practice is appropriate to the extent that the intragroup payment is for an amount up to the amount of tax that would otherwise have been paid by the paying company. Where a tax loss payment is made in excess of this amount, we consider that it is more appropriate to account for the excess not as an income tax but as either:

- a distribution or capital contribution (as applicable); or
- operating income or expense (as applicable).

The chosen treatment should be applied consistently.

12 BUSINESS COMBINATIONS

Additional deferred tax arises on business combinations as a result of items such as:

- the application of IAS 12 to the assets and liabilities of the acquired business in the consolidated financial statements, when it has not been applied in the separate financial statements of that business;
- where the acquired entity already applies IAS 12 in its own financial statements, the recognition in the fair value exercise of deferred tax in respect of assets and liabilities of the acquired entity where no deferred tax is provided in those financial statements. This may be the case where a temporary difference arose on initial recognition of an asset or liability in the acquired entity's own financial statements. Deferred tax would then be recognised in the acquirer's consolidated financial statements, because, in those statements, the difference arises on initial recognition in a business combination (see 7.2 above); and
- adjustments made to measure the assets and liabilities of the acquired business fair value, with consequential changes in the temporary differences associated with those assets and liabilities.

Any deferred tax assets or liabilities on temporary differences that arise on a business combination affect the amount of goodwill or bargain purchase gain. *[IAS 12.66]*. Example 31.23 at 7.5.1 above illustrates the application of this principle.

12.1 Measurement and recognition of deferred tax in a business combination

IFRS 3 generally requires assets acquired and liabilities assumed in a business combination to be:

- recognised only to the extent that they were assets or liabilities of the acquired entity at the date of acquisition; *[IFRS 3.10]* and
- measured at fair value. *[IFRS 3.18]*.

These provisions of IFRS 3 are discussed in more detail in Chapter 9 at 5. As exceptions to this general principle, IFRS 3 requires an acquirer to:

- recognise and measure a deferred tax asset or liability arising from the assets acquired and liabilities assumed in a business combination 'in accordance with IAS 12'; *[IFRS 3.24]* and
- account for the potential tax effects of temporary differences and carryforwards of an acquiree that exist at the acquisition date or arise as a result of the acquisition 'in accordance with IAS 12'. *[IFRS 3.25]*.

There are essentially two reasons underlying these exceptions. The first is that IAS 12 does not purport to measure future tax at fair value, but at an amount based on a prescribed model that takes no account of the time value of money. Secondly, and more subtly, IAS 12 requires a number of questions of both recognition and measurement to be resolved by reference to management's plans and expectations – in particular, the expected manner of recovery of assets (see 8.4 above) or the likelihood of recovering deferred tax assets (see 7.4 above). The expectations and plans of the acquirer may well differ from those of the acquired entity. For example, the acquired entity might have assessed, for the purposes of IAS 12, that an asset would be recovered through use, whereas the acquirer assesses it as recoverable through sale. The exceptions made by IFRS 3 allow the deferred tax recognised in a business combination to reflect the expectations of the acquirer rather than those of the acquiree.

Areas that give rise to particular difficulties of interpretation are:

- determining the manner of recovery of assets and settlement of liabilities at the date of the business combination (see 12.1.1 below); and
- deferred tax assets (see 12.1.2 below).

12.1.1 Determining the manner of recovery of assets and settlement of liabilities

As discussed at 8.4 above, IAS 12 requires deferred tax to be measured at an amount that reflects the tax consequences that would follow from the manner in which the entity expects to recover its assets or settle its liabilities. The expected manner of recovery or settlement may affect both the tax base of an asset or liability and the tax rate to be applied to any temporary difference arising.

As further noted above, the acquirer's assessment of the manner of recovery for the purposes of IAS 12 may well differ from that of the acquired entity. For example, the acquired entity might have intended to recover an asset through use, whereas the acquirer intends to sell it. In such a case, in our view, the requirement of IFRS 3 to recognise and measure deferred tax in accordance with IAS 12 has the effect that the expectations of the acquirer are used to determine the tax base of an item and the measurement of any deferred tax associated with the item.

12.1.1.A Changes in tax base consequent on the business combination

In some jurisdictions, a business combination may provide the opportunity to revise the tax base of an asset to an amount equal to the fair value assigned to it in accounting for the business combination. Most significantly, this may include the ability to create a tax base for an intangible asset or goodwill which may have had no tax base at all for the acquiree.

In some cases, the increase (as it generally is) in tax base may be more or less automatic. In others, the taxpayer may be required to make a formal claim or election for the increase to the tax authority. Sometimes further restructuring may be required – for example, it may be necessary for the business of the acquired entity to be transferred to another entity in the acquirer's group in the same tax jurisdiction.

An increase in a tax base that requires action by the relevant entity after the acquisition (such as making a claim or election or undertaking a restructuring) occurs after the business combination. However, some hold the view that the ability to increase a tax base following a business combination is a benefit that is taken into account by an informed buyer in negotiating the purchase price. Accordingly, it is argued, the increase is most appropriately reflected by adjusting the tax base of assets acquired as at the date of the business combination as if the increase had occurred at that date. This reduces any deferred tax liability and, therefore, reduces any goodwill (or increases any 'bargain purchase' gain).

Those who support this view note that, if the increase in tax base is accounted for only when it legally occurs in the post-combination period, the net effect is to increase goodwill and reduce post-combination tax expense when in reality the entity may have done little more than fill in a form. It might also be difficult to sustain the higher carrying amount of goodwill arising from this treatment.

We believe that it is generally appropriate to anticipate an increase to a tax base that legally occurs following a business combination in accounting for the business combination where the increase:

- is automatic or requires only a notification to the tax authority;
- requires an application the tax authority that is not normally refused for transactions of a comparable nature; or
- is contingent on some post-acquisition restructuring, where this can be done without substantial difficulty.

Conversely, we believe that it would not generally be appropriate to account for an increase in a tax base until it occurs where the increase:

- relies on 'bespoke' tax planning that may be challenged by the tax authority;
- requires an application to the tax authority that in practice is frequently and successfully challenged for transactions of a comparable nature; or
- is contingent on some post-acquisition restructuring, where this will involve a substantial process, such as obtaining approval from regulators, unions, pension fund trustees etc.

12.1.2 Deferred tax assets arising on a business combination

12.1.2.A Assets of the acquirer

If, as a result of a business combination, the acquiring entity is able to recognise a previously unrecognised tax asset of its own (e.g. unused tax losses), the recognition of the asset is accounted for as income, and not as part of the accounting for the business combination. *[IAS 12.67]*.

12.1.2.B Assets of the acquiree

It may be the case that deferred tax assets of an acquired entity do not meet the recognition criteria of IAS 12 from the perspective of the acquired entity, but do meet the criteria from the perspective of the acquirer. In such cases, the general principles of IAS 12 require the acquirer's perspective to be applied as at the date of the business combination.

The potential benefit of the acquiree's income tax loss carryforwards or other deferred tax assets may not satisfy the criteria for separate recognition when a business combination is initially accounted for but may be realised subsequently. Any changes in recognised deferred tax assets of an acquired entity are accounted for as follows:

- Acquired deferred tax benefits recognised within the measurement period (see Chapter 9 at 5.6.2) that result from new information about facts and circumstances that existed at the acquisition date are applied to reduce the carrying amount of any goodwill related to that acquisition. If the carrying amount of that goodwill is zero, any remaining deferred tax benefits are recognised in profit or loss.
- All other acquired deferred tax benefits realised are recognised in profit or loss (or outside profit or loss if IAS 12 so requires – see 10 above). *[IAS 12.68]*.

12.1.3 Deferred tax liabilities of acquired entity

IAS 12 contains no specific provisions regarding the recognition of a deferred tax liability of an acquired entity after the date of the original combination. The recognition of such liabilities should therefore be accounted for in accordance with the normal rules of IAS 12 (i.e. in the period in which the liability arises), unless either:

- the recognition of the liability occurs within the provisional measurement period for the business combination and reflects new information about facts and circumstances that existed at the acquisition date, in which case the acquisition date value of the liability is retrospectively adjusted – see Chapter 9 at 12; or
- the failure to recognise the liability at the time of the combination was an error, in which case the provisions of IAS 8 should be applied – see Chapter 3 at 4.6.

12.2 Tax deductions for replacement share-based payment awards in a business combination

IFRS 3 contains some guidance on the treatment of tax deductions for share-based payment transactions made by an acquirer as a replacement for awards made by the acquired entity before the business combination. This is discussed in more detail at 10.8.5 above.

12.3 Apparent immediate impairment of goodwill created by deferred tax

The requirement of IAS 12 to recognise deferred tax on all temporary differences arising on net assets acquired in a business combination leads to the creation of goodwill which, on a literal reading of IAS 36 may then be required to be immediately impaired, as illustrated by Example 31.54 below.

Example 31.54: Apparent 'day one' impairment arising from recognition of deferred tax in a business combination

Entity A, which is taxed at 40%, acquires Entity B for €100m in a transaction that is a business combination. The fair values and tax bases of the identifiable net assets of Entity B are as follows:

	Fair value €m	*Tax base* €m
Brand name	60	–
Other net assets	20	15

This will give rise to the following consolidation journal:

	€m	€m
Goodwill (balance)	46	
Brand name	60	
Other net assets	20	
Deferred tax[1]		26
Cost of investment		100

1 40% of (€[60m + 20m] – €15m)

The fair value of the consolidated assets of the subsidiary (excluding deferred tax) and goodwill is now €126m, but the cost of the subsidiary is only €100m. Clearly €26m of the goodwill arises solely from the recognition of deferred tax. However, IAS 36, paragraph 50, explicitly requires tax to be excluded from the estimate of future cash flows used to calculate any impairment. This raises the question of whether there should not be an immediate impairment write-down of the assets to €100m. In our view, this cannot have been the intention of IAS 36 (see the further discussion in Chapter 20 at 5.2.1).

12.4 Tax deductions for acquisition costs

12.4.1 Business combinations accounted for under 'old' IFRS 3

The discussion in this section is relevant to business combinations to which the current version of IFRS 3 (as revised in January 2008) is not applied. The current version of IFRS 3 generally requires transaction costs to be recognised as an expense, so that any tax deduction for those costs would be allocated to profit or loss, in accordance with the general principles discussed at 10 above. However, the previous version of IFRS 3 ('old IFRS 3') permitted certain acquisition costs to be treated as part of the consideration of the business.

In some jurisdictions, tax deductions are given for certain costs of an acquisition which, in the consolidated financial statements prepared under old IFRS 3, are effectively subsumed into the carrying amount of goodwill. This raises the question of how the effects of the tax deductions should be accounted for, as illustrated by Example 31.55 below.

Example 31.55: Tax deduction for acquisition costs under 'old' IFRS 3

Entity A, which pays tax at 40%, acquired 100% of Entity B for €1,000,000 on 1 January 2009. In addition A bore transaction costs, such as professional fees, of €50,000 so that the total purchase price recorded by A for B was €1,050,000. The transaction costs were deductible for tax purposes in the year ended 31 December 2009, so that A received a current tax credit of €20,000 as a result of the transaction costs.

The tax base of the investment in B is €1,000,000, and, if it were sold, any gain arising would be taxable.

In the separate financial statements of A, the carrying amount of the investment in B is €1,050,000. In the consolidated financial statements of A, the net assets of and goodwill of B are carried at €1,050,000 (i.e. the transaction costs represent €50,000 of the goodwill recognised).

A has received a tax deduction of €20,000 (€50,000 @ 40%) in the period and so must record current tax income of this amount.

The issue then arises as to how to deal with the taxable temporary difference of €50,000 associated with the carrying amount of the net assets and goodwill of the investment (cost €1,050,000 less tax base €1,000,000).

Although the transaction costs have been subsumed within the cost of acquisition (and therefore within goodwill) under 'old' IFRS 3, this temporary difference did not arise on the initial recognition of goodwill. It resulted from the claim for a tax deduction relating to the transaction costs that had been included in a tax return after the acquisition date. Whilst deferred tax is not recognised where it arises from the initial recognition of goodwill, *[IAS 12.15(a)]*, deferred tax assets and liabilities for temporary differences relating to goodwill are required to be recognised to the extent that they do not arise from the initial recognition of goodwill. *[IAS 12.21B]*.

12.4.2 Business combinations accounted for under 'new' IFRS 3

Under the current version of IFRS 3 transaction costs are required to be expensed. However, in a number of jurisdictions, transaction costs are regarded as forming part of the cost of the investment, with the effect that a tax deduction for them is given only when the investment is subsequently sold or otherwise disposed of, rather than at the time that the costs are charged to profit or loss.

In such jurisdictions, there will be a deductible 'outside' temporary difference (see 7.5 above) between the carrying value of the net assets and goodwill of the acquired entity in the consolidated financial statements (which will exclude transaction costs) and tax base of the investment in the entity (which will include transaction costs). Whether or not a deferred tax asset is recognised in respect of such a deductible temporary difference will be determined in accordance with the general provisions of IAS 12 for deductible temporary differences (see 7.5.3 above).

In the separate financial statements of the acquirer, there may be no temporary difference where the transaction costs are, under IAS 27, included in the cost of the investment.

13 PRESENTATION

13.1 Statement of financial position

Tax assets and liabilities should be shown separately from other assets and liabilities and current tax should be shown separately from deferred tax on the face of the statement of financial position. Where an entity presents current and non-current assets and liabilities separately, deferred tax should not be shown as part of current assets or liabilities. *[IAS 1.54-56]*.

13.1.1 Offset

13.1.1.A Current tax

Current tax assets and liabilities should be offset if, and only if, the entity:

- has a legally enforceable right to set off the recognised amounts; and
- intends either to settle them net or simultaneously. *[IAS 12.71]*.

These restrictions are based on the offset criteria in IAS 32. Accordingly, while entities in many jurisdictions have a right to offset current tax assets and liabilities, and the tax authority permits the entity to make or receive a single net payment, IAS 12 permits offset in financial statements only where there is a positive intention for simultaneous net settlement. *[IAS 12.72]*.

The offset restrictions also have the effect that, in consolidated financial statements, a current tax asset of one member of the group may be offset against a current tax liability of another only if the two group members have a legally enforceable right to make or receive a single net payment and a positive intention to recover the asset or settle the liability simultaneously. *[IAS 12.73]*.

13.1.1.B Deferred tax

Deferred tax assets and liabilities should be offset if, and only if:

- the entity has a legally enforceable right to set off current tax assets and liabilities; and
- the deferred tax assets and liabilities concerned relate to income taxes raised by the same taxation authority on either:
  - the same taxable entity; or
  - different taxable entities which intend, in each future period in which significant amounts of deferred tax are expected to be settled or recovered, to settle their current tax assets and liabilities either on a net basis or simultaneously. *[IAS 12.74]*.

The offset criteria for deferred tax are less clear than those for current tax. The position is broadly that, where in a particular jurisdiction current tax assets and liabilities relating to future periods will be offset, deferred tax assets and liabilities relating to that jurisdiction and those periods must be offset (even if the deferred tax balances actually recognised in the statement of financial position would not satisfy the criteria for the offset of current tax).

IAS 12 suggests that this slightly more pragmatic approach was adopted in order to avoid the detailed scheduling of the reversal of temporary differences that would be necessary to apply the same criteria as for current tax. *[IAS 12.75].*

However, IAS 12 notes that, in rare circumstances, an entity may have a legally enforceable right of set-off, and an intention to settle net, for some periods but not for others. In such circumstances, detailed scheduling may be required to establish reliably whether the deferred tax liability of one taxable entity in the group will result in increased tax payments in the same period in which a deferred tax asset of a second taxable entity in the group will result in decreased payments by that second taxable entity. *[IAS 12.76].*

13.1.1.C Offset of current and deferred tax

IAS 12 contains no provisions allowing or requiring the offset of current tax and deferred tax. Also, as noted at 13.1 above, IAS 1 requires tax assets and liabilities to be shown separately from other assets and liabilities and current tax to be shown separately from deferred tax on the face of the statement of financial position. *[IAS 1.54(n), 54(o)].* Accordingly, in our view, current and deferred tax may not be offset against each other and should always be presented gross.

13.2 Statement of comprehensive income

The tax expense (or income) related to profit or loss from ordinary activities should be presented as a component of profit or loss in the statement of comprehensive income. *[IAS 12.77].*

The results of discontinued operations should be presented on a post-tax basis. *[IFRS 5.33].*

The results of equity-accounted entities should be presented on a post-tax basis. *[IAS 1.IG6].* Any income tax relating to a 'tax-transparent' equity-accounted entity (see 7.6 above) forms part of the investor's tax charge. It is therefore included in the income tax line in profit or loss and not shown as part of the investor's share of the results of the tax-transparent entity.

Components of other comprehensive income may be presented either:

- net of related tax effects; or
- before related tax effects with one amount shown for the total income tax effects relating to the items that might be reclassified subsequently to profit and loss and another amount shown for the total income tax effects relating to those items that will not be subsequently reclassified to profit and loss. *[IAS 1.91].*

IAS 12 notes that, whilst IAS 21 requires certain exchange differences to be recognised within income or expense, it does not specify where exactly in the statement of comprehensive income they should be presented. Accordingly, exchange differences relating to deferred tax assets and liabilities may be classified as deferred tax expense (or income), if that presentation is considered to be the most useful to users of the financial statements. *[IAS 12.78].* IAS 12 makes no reference to the treatment of exchange differences on current tax assets and liabilities but, presumably, the same considerations apply.

13.3 Statement of cash flows

Cash flows arising from taxes on income are separately disclosed and classified as cash flows from operating activities, unless they can be specifically identified with financing and investing activities. *[IAS 7.35]*.

IAS 7 – *Statement of Cash Flows* – notes that, whilst it is relatively easy to identify the expense relating to investing or financing activities, the related tax cash flows are often impracticable to identify. Therefore, taxes paid are usually classified as cash flows from operating activities. However, when it is practicable to identify the tax cash flow with an individual transaction that gives rise to cash flows that are classified as investing or financing activities, the tax cash flow is classified as an investing or financing activity as appropriate. When tax cash flows are allocated over more than one class of activity, the total amount of taxes paid is disclosed. *[IAS 7.36]*.

14 DISCLOSURE

IAS 12 imposes extensive disclosure requirements as follows.

14.1 Components of tax expense

The major components of tax expense (or income) should be disclosed separately. These may include:

(a) current tax expense (or income);

(b) any adjustments recognised in the period for current tax of prior periods;

(c) the amount of deferred tax expense (or income) relating to the origination and reversal of temporary differences;

(d) the amount of deferred tax expense (or income) relating to changes in tax rates or the imposition of new taxes;

(e) the amount of the benefit arising from a previously unrecognised tax loss, tax credit or temporary difference of a prior period that is used to reduce current tax expense;

(f) the amount of the benefit from a previously unrecognised tax loss, tax credit or temporary difference of a prior period that is used to reduce deferred tax expense;

(g) deferred tax expense arising from the write-down, or reversal of a previous write-down, of a deferred tax asset; and

(h) the amount of tax expense (or income) relating to those changes in accounting policies and errors which are included in the profit or loss in accordance with IAS 8 because they cannot be accounted for retrospectively (see Chapter 3 at 4.7). *[IAS 12.79-80]*.

14.2 Other disclosures

The following should also be disclosed separately: *[IAS 12.81]*

(a) the aggregate current and deferred tax relating to items that are charged or credited to equity;

(b) the amount of income tax relating to each component of other comprehensive income;

(c) an explanation of the relationship between tax expense (or income) and accounting profit in either or both of the following forms:
  (i) a numerical reconciliation between tax expense (or income) and the product of accounting profit multiplied by the applicable tax rate(s), disclosing also the basis on which the applicable tax rate(s) is (are) computed; or
  (ii) a numerical reconciliation between the average effective tax rate (i.e. tax expense (or income) divided by accounting profit), *[IAS 12.86]*, and the applicable tax rate, disclosing also the basis on which the applicable tax rate is computed;

  This requirement is discussed further at 14.2.1 below.

(d) an explanation of changes in the applicable tax rate(s) compared to the previous accounting period;

(e) the amount (and expiry date, if any) of deductible temporary differences, unused tax losses, and unused tax credits for which no deferred tax asset is recognised in the statement of financial position;

(f) the aggregate amount of temporary differences associated with investments in subsidiaries, branches and associates and interests in joint arrangements, for which deferred tax liabilities have not been recognised;

  This is discussed further at 14.2.2 below.

(g) in respect of each type of temporary difference, and in respect of each type of unused tax losses and unused tax credits:
  (i) the amount of the deferred tax assets and liabilities recognised in the statement of financial position for each period presented;
  (ii) the amount of the deferred tax income or expense recognised in profit or loss, if this is not apparent from the changes in the amounts recognised in the statement of financial position;

  The analysis in (ii) will be required, for example, by any entity with acquisitions and disposals, or deferred tax accounted for in other comprehensive income or equity, since this will have the effect that the year-on-year movement in the statement of financial position is not solely due to items recognised in profit or loss;

(h) in respect of discontinued operations, the tax expense relating to:
  (i) the gain or loss on discontinuance; and
  (ii) the profit or loss from the ordinary activities of the discontinued operation for the period, together with the corresponding amounts for each prior period presented;

(i) the amount of income tax consequences of dividends to shareholders of the entity that were proposed or declared before the financial statements were authorised for issue, but are not recognised as a liability in the financial statements.

  Further disclosures are required in respect of the tax consequences of distributing retained earnings, which are discussed at 14.4 below;

(j) if a business combination in which the entity is the acquirer causes a change in the amount of a deferred tax asset of the entity (see 12.1.2 above), the amount of that change; and

(k) if the deferred tax benefits acquired in a business combination are not recognised at the acquisition date, but are recognised after the acquisition date (see 12.1.2 above), a description of the event or change in circumstances that caused the deferred tax benefits to be recognised.

Tax-related contingent liabilities and contingent assets (such as those arising from unresolved disputes with taxation authorities) are disclosed in accordance with IAS 37 (see Chapter 28 at 7). *[IAS 12.88]*.

Significant effects of changes in tax rates or tax laws enacted or announced after the reporting period on current and deferred tax assets and liabilities are disclosed in accordance with IAS 10 (see Chapter 36 at 2). *[IAS 12.88]*.

14.2.1 Tax (or tax rate) reconciliation

IAS 12 explains that the purpose of the tax reconciliation required by (c) above is to enable users of financial statements to understand whether the relationship between tax expense (or income) and accounting profit is unusual and to understand the significant factors that could affect that relationship in the future. The relationship may be affected by the effects of such factors as:

- revenue and expenses that are outside the scope of taxation;
- tax losses; and
- foreign tax rates. *[IAS 12.84]*.

Accordingly, in explaining the relationship between tax expense (or income) and accounting profit, an entity should use an applicable tax rate that provides the most meaningful information to the users of its financial statements.

Often, the most meaningful rate is the domestic rate of tax in the country in which the entity is domiciled. In this case, the tax rate applied for national taxes should be aggregated with the rates applied for any local taxes which are computed on a substantially similar level of taxable profit (tax loss). However, for an entity operating in several jurisdictions, it may be more meaningful to aggregate separate reconciliations prepared using the domestic rate in each individual jurisdiction. *[IAS 12.85]*. Where this latter approach is adopted, the entity may need to discuss the effect of significant changes in either tax rates, or the mix of profits earned in different jurisdictions, in order to satisfy the requirement of IAS 12 to give an explanation of changes in the applicable tax rate(s) compared to the previous accounting period – see item (d) at 14.2 above.

Example 31.56 illustrates how the selection of the applicable tax rate affects the presentation of the numerical reconciliation.

Example 31.56: Alternative presentations of tax reconciliation

In 2017 an entity has accounting profit of €3,000m (2016: €2,500m) comprising €1,500m (2016: €2,000m) in its own jurisdiction (country A) and €1,500m (2016: €500m) in country B. The tax rate is 30% in country A and 20% in country B. In country B, expenses of €200m (2016: €100m) are not deductible for tax purposes. There are no other differences between accounting profit and profit that is subject to current tax, or on which deferred tax has been provided for under IAS 12.

Thus the accounting tax charge in the financial statements for each period will be as follows:

	2017 €m	2016 €m
Country A		
€1,500m/€2,000m @ 30%	450	600
Country B		
€[1,500 + 200]m/€[500 + 100]m @ 20%	340	120
Total tax charge	790	720

Reconciliation based on A's domestic tax rate

If the entity presents a tax reconciliation based on its own (i.e. country A's) domestic tax rate, the following presentation would be adopted.

	2017 €m	2016 €m
Accounting profit	3,000	2,500
Tax at domestic rate of 30%	900	750
Effect of:		
Expenses not deductible for tax purposes[1]	60	30
Overseas tax rates[2]	(170)	(60)
Tax expense	790	720

1 €200m/€100m @ 30%

2 B's taxable profit €1,700m/€600m @ (20% – 30%)

Reconciliation based on each jurisdiction's tax rate

If the entity presents a tax reconciliation based on each jurisdiction's domestic tax rate, the following presentation would be adopted.

	2017 €m	2016 €m
Accounting profit	3,000	2,500
Tax at domestic rates applicable to individual group entities[1]	750	700
Effect of:		
Expenses not deductible for tax purposes[2]	40	20
Tax expense	790	720

1 2017: A = €450m [€1,500m @ 30%], B = €300m [€1,500m @ 20%], total €750m
2016: A = €600m [€2,000m @ 30%], B = €100m [€500m @ 20%], total €700m

2 €200m/€100m @ 20%

14.2.2 Temporary differences relating to subsidiaries, associates, branches and joint arrangements

IAS 12 requires an entity to disclose the gross temporary differences associated with subsidiaries, associates, branches and joint arrangements, as opposed to the unrecognised deferred tax on those temporary differences – see (f) under 14.2 above.

IAS 12 clarifies that this approach is adopted because it would often be impracticable to compute the amount of unrecognised deferred tax. Nevertheless, where practicable, entities are encouraged to disclose the amounts of the unrecognised deferred tax liabilities because financial statement users may find such information useful. *[IAS 12.87]*.

14.3 Reason for recognition of certain tax assets

Separate disclosure is required of the amount of any deferred tax asset that is recognised, and the nature of the evidence supporting its recognition, when:

(a) utilisation of the deferred tax asset is dependent on future profits in excess of those arising from the reversal of deferred tax liabilities; and

(b) the entity has suffered a loss in the current or preceding period in the tax jurisdiction to which the asset relates. *[IAS 12.82]*.

In effect these disclosures are required when the entity has rebutted the presumption inherent in the recognition rules of IAS 12 that tax assets should not normally be recognised in these circumstances (see 7.4 above).

14.4 Dividends

As discussed at 8.5 above, where there are different tax consequences for an entity depending on whether profits are retained or distributed, tax should be measured at the rates applicable to retained profits except to the extent that there is a liability to pay dividends at the end of the reporting period, where the rate applicable to distributed profits should be used.

Where such differential tax rates apply, the entity should disclose the nature of the potential income tax consequences that would arise from a payment of dividends to shareholders. It should quantify the amount of potential income tax consequences that is practicably determinable and disclose whether there are any potential income tax consequences that are not practicably determinable. *[IAS 12.82A]*. This will include disclosure of the important features of the income tax systems and the factors that will affect the amount of the potential income tax consequences of dividends. *[IAS 12.87A]*.

The reason for this rather complicated requirement is that, as IAS 12 acknowledges, it can often be very difficult to quantify the tax consequences of a full distribution of profits (e.g. where there are a large number of overseas subsidiaries). Moreover, IAS 12 concedes that there is a tension between, on the one hand, the exemption from disclosing the deferred tax associated with temporary differences associated with subsidiaries and other investments (see 14.2.2 above) and, on the other hand, this requirement to disclose the tax effect of distributing undistributed profits – in some cases they could effectively be the same number.

However, to the extent that any liability can be quantified, it should be disclosed. This may mean that consolidated financial statements will disclose the potential tax effect of distributing the earnings of some, but not all, subsidiaries, associates, branches and joint arrangements.

IAS 12 emphasises that, in an entity's separate financial statements, this requirement applies only to the undistributed earnings of the entity itself and not those of any of its subsidiaries, associates, branches and joint arrangements. *[IAS 12.87A-87C]*.

14.5 Example of disclosures

Examples of many of the disclosures required under IAS 12 are given by BP p.l.c.

Extract 31.2: BP p.l.c. (2014)

Notes on financial statements [extract]

7. Taxation

Tax on profit

			$ million
	2014	2013	2012
Current tax			
Charge for the year	**4,444**	5,724	6,664
Adjustment in respect of prior years	**48**	61	252
	4,492	5,785	6,916
Deferred tax			
Origination and reversal of temporary differences in the current year	**(3,194)**	529	67
Adjustment in respect of prior years	**(351)**	149	(103)
	(3,545)	678	(36)
Tax charge on profit	**947**	6,463	6,880

In 2014, the total tax credit recognized within other comprehensive income was $1,481 million (2013 $1,374 million charge and 2012 $270 million credit). See Note 30 for further information. The total tax charge recognized directly in equity was $36 million (2013 $33 million credit and 2012 $6 million credit).

For information on significant estimates and judgements made in relation to taxation see Income taxes within Note 1.

Reconciliation of the effective tax rate

The following table provides a reconciliation of the UK statutory corporation tax rate to the effective tax rate of the group on profit before taxation. With effect from 1 April 2014 the UK statutory corporation tax rate reduced from 23% to 21% on profits arising from activities outside the North Sea. For 2014, the items presented in the reconciliation are distorted as a result of the tax credits related to the impairment losses recognized in the year, and the effect of the impairment losses on the profit for the year. In order to provide a more meaningful analysis of the effective tax rate for 2014, the table also presents separate reconciliations for the group excluding the effects of the impairment losses, and for the effects of the impairment losses in isolation. For 2013 and 2012, the effective tax rate is not affected significantly by impairment losses. See Note 3 for further information.

					$ million
	2014 excluding impairments	**2014 impacts of impairments**	**2014**	2012	2012
Profit (loss) before taxation	**13,166**	**(8,216)**	**4,950**	30,221	18,131
Tax charge (credit) on profit or loss	**5,036**	**(4,089)**	**947**	6,463	6,880
Effective tax rate	**38%**	**50%**	**19%**	21%	38%

			% of profit before taxation		
UK statutory corporation tax rate	**21**	**21**	**21**	23	24
Increase (decrease) resulting from					
UK supplementary and overseas taxes at higher or lower rates[a]	**17**	**34**	**(11)**	4	12
Tax reported in equity-accounted entities	**(5)**	**–**	**(14)**	(2)	(5)
Adjustments in respect of prior years	**(2)**	**–**	**(6)**	1	1
Movement in deferred tax not recognized	**4**	**(3)**	**17**	2	2
Tax incentives for investment	**(4)**	**–**	**(10)**	(2)	(2)
Gulf of Mexico oil spill non-deductible costs	**–**	**–**	**1**	–	8
Permanent differences relating to disposals[b]	**(1)**	**–**	**(1)**	(8)	–
Foreign exchange	**4**	**–**	**10**	2	(1)
Items not deductible for tax purposes	**4**	**(2)**	**12**	1	2
Other	**–**	**–**	**–**	–	(3)
Effective tax rate	**38**	**50**	**19**	21	38

a For 2014 excluding impairments, jurisdictions which contribute significantly to this item are Angola, with an applicable statutory tax rate of 50%, Trinidad, with an applicable statutory tax rate of 55% and the US with an applicable federal tax rate of 35%. For 2014, impairment charges have generated losses on which tax credits arise, mainly in Norway and the UK North Sea, with applicable statutory tax rates of 78% and 62% respectively. For 2013 and 2012, jurisdictions which contribute significantly are Angola, the UK and Trinidad with rates as disclosed above.

b For 2013, this relates to the non-taxable gain on disposal of our investment in TNK-BP.

Legislation to reduce the UK supplementary charge tax rate applicable to profits arising in the North Sea is expected to be enacted in 2015. The evaluation of the effect of this change for BP has not yet been completed.

Deferred tax					$ million
		Income statement		Balance sheet	
	2014	2013	2012	**2014**	2013
Deferred tax liability					
Depreciation	**(2,178)**	(474)	(75)	**29,062**	31,551
Pension plan surpluses	**(272)**	(691)	–	**–**	284
Other taxable temporary differences	**(1,278)**	(199)	(2,239)	**2,445**	3,653
	(3,728)	(1,364)	(2,314)	**31,507**	35,488
Deferred tax asset					
Pension plan and other post-retirement benefit plan deficits	**492**	787	(33)	**(2,761)**	(2,026)
Decommissioning, environmental and other provisions	**52**	1,385	1,872	**(11,237)**	(11,301)
Derivative financial instruments	**166**	30	(7)	**(575)**	(579)
Tax credits	**589**	(174)	1,802	**(298)**	(888)
Loss carry forward	**(1,397)**	(343)	(911)	**(3,848)**	(2,585)
Other deductible temporary differences	**281**	357	(445)	**(1,204)**	(1,655)
	183	2,042	2,278	**(19,923)**	(19,034)
Net deferred tax charge (credit) and net deferred tax liability	**(3,545)**	678	(36)	**11,584**	16,454
Of which – deferred tax liabilities				**13,893**	17,439
– deferred tax assets				**2,309**	985

The recognition of deferred tax assets of $1,467 million (2013 $67 million), in entities which have suffered a loss in either the current or preceding period, is supported by forecasts which indicate that sufficient future taxable profits will be available to utilize such assets.

		$ million
Analysis of movements during the year in the net deferred tax liability	**2014**	2013
At 1 January	**16,454**	14,369
Exchange adjustments	**122**	43
Charge (credit) for the year on profit	**(3,545)**	678
Charge (credit) for the year in other comprehensive income	**(1,563)**	1,397
Charge (credit) for the year in equity	**36**	(33)
Acquisitions	**80**	–
At 31 December	**11,584**	16,454

A summary of temporary differences, unused tax credits and unused tax losses for which deferred tax has not been recognized is shown in the table below.

		$ billion
At 31 December	**2014**	2013
Unused tax losses[a]	**2.1**	1.8
Unused tax credits	**20.1**	18.0
of which – arising in the UK[b]	**18.0**	16.3
– arising in the US[c]	**2.0**	1.7
Deductible temporary differences[d]	**17.9**	11.2
Taxable temporary differences associated with investments in subsidiaries and equity-accounted entities[e]	**1.0**	1.1

a Substantially all the tax losses have no fixed expiry date.

b The UK unused tax credits arise predominantly in overseas branches of UK entities based in jurisdictions with high tax rates. No deferred tax asset has been recognized on these tax credits as they are unlikely to have value in the future; UK taxes on these overseas branches are largely mitigated by double tax relief on the overseas tax. These tax credits have no fixed expiry date.

c The US tax credits expire 10 years after generation and will all expire in the period 2015-2023.

d Deductible temporary differences of $1.0 billion are expected to expire in the period 2015-2021, the remainder do not have an expiry date.

e An amendment has been made to the comparative amount.

			$ billion
Impact of previously unrecognized deferred tax or write-down of deferred tax assets on current year tax charge	**2014**	2013	2012
Current tax benefit relating to the utilization of previously unrecognized tax credits	**0.2**	0.2	0.4
Deferred tax benefit relating to the recognition of previously unrecognized tax credits	**–**	0.2	0.1
Deferred tax expense arising from the write-down of a previously recognized deferred tax asset	**0.2**	–	–

14.6 Discontinued operations – interaction with IFRS 5

IFRS 5 requires the post-tax results of discontinued operations to be shown separately on the face of the statement of comprehensive income (and any separate income statement presenting the components of profit or loss). This may be done by giving the results of discontinued operations after those of continuing operations. This is discussed further in Chapter 4.

The definitions of income tax, tax expense and taxable profit in IAS 12 (see 3 above) do not distinguish between the results of continuing and discontinued operations, or the tax on those results. Thus, as drafted, IAS 12 applies not only to the tax income or expense on continuing operations (i.e. the amount shown in the 'tax line' in the income statement) but also to any tax income or expense relating to the results of discontinued operations separately disclosed after those of continuing operations.

However, IFRS 5 clarifies that items accounted for under that standard are not subject to the disclosure requirements of other standards, other than:

- specific disclosures in respect of non-current assets (or disposal groups) classified as held for sale or discontinued operations; or
- disclosures about the measurement of assets and liabilities within a disposal group that are not within the scope of the measurement requirements of IFRS 5, where such disclosures are not already provided in the other notes to the financial statements. *[IFRS 5.5B]*.

References

1 Throughout this Chapter, the tax treatment described in examples is purely illustrative, and does not necessarily relate to a specific provision of tax law in a jurisdiction using the currency in the example.
2 SIC-25, *Income Taxes – Changes in the Tax Status of an Entity or its Shareholders*, SIC, July 2000.
3 For transactions not accounted for under IFRS 3 – *Business Combinations* – as revised in January 2008: 'the amount of any excess of the acquirer's interest in the net fair value of the acquiree's identifiable assets, liabilities and contingent liabilities over the cost of the combination'.
4 *IFRIC Update*, March 2006.
5 *IFRIC Update*, June 2004.
6 ED/2009/2 *Income Tax*, IASB, March 2009, para. 39.
7 Based on a summary in *IASB Update*, February 2005.
8 DI/2015/1 *Uncertainty over Income Tax Treatments*, IASB, October 2015, para. 18.
9 In some cases research and share-based payment costs may be included as part of the cost of other assets, such as inventories or PP&E.
10 ED/2009/2, Appendix A, definition of 'tax basis'.
11 ED/2009/2, paras. 20 and 23.
12 *IFRIC Update*, April 2005.
13 *IFRIC Update*, June 2005.
14 IFRS 16 – *Leases*, Appendix D, Amendments to other Standards, IASB, January 2016.
15 *IFRIC Update*, May 2014.
16 *IFRIC Update*, May 2014.
17 *IFRIC Update*, May 2014.
18 *IFRIC Update*, February 2003.
19 *IFRIC Update*, May 2007. The IFRIC made its decision based on the then current of IAS 12, which referred to 'joint ventures' rather than 'joint arrangements'.
20 SIC-21, Income Taxes – *Recovery of Non-Depreciable Assets*, SIC, July 2000, para. 4.
21 *IFRIC Update*, July 2016.
22 *IFRIC Update*, November 2011.
23 *IFRIC Update*, March 2015.
24 *IFRIC Update*, May 2012.
25 *IFRIC Update*, May 2012.
26 *IFRIC Update*, July 2014.
27 *IFRIC Update*, July 2014.
28 ED/2009/2, paras. 27(d), B31-B32.
29 Proposed Accounting Standards Update, Income Taxes (Topic 740) – *Intra-Entity Asset Transfers, File Reference No. 2015-200*, FASB, January 2015, p.1.
30 *IFRIC Update*, May 2014.
31 *IFRIC Update*, July 2014.
32 *IFRIC Update*, July 2014.
33 *IASB Work Plan – as at 20 July 2016*, Maintenance of IFRS Standards, Narrow-scope amendments and IFRIC Interpretations, – Uncertainty over Income Tax Treatments, IASB.
34 DI/2015/1, paras. B2, B3.
35 DI/2015/1, paras. 8, 9.
36 DI/2015/1, para. 10.
37 DI/2015/1, para. BC9.
38 DI/2015/1, paras. 5, 6.

39 DI/2015/1, para. BC10.
40 DI/2015/1, paras. 11, 12.
41 DI/2015/1, para. 13.
42 DI/2015/1, para. BC12.
43 DI/2015/1, para. 14.
44 DI/2015/1, para. 15.
45 DI/2015/1, para. 16.
46 DI/2015/1, para. 16.
47 DI/2015/1, para. IE2.
48 DI/2015/1, paras. IE3-IE7.
49 DI/2015/1, paras. IE8-IE12.
50 DI/2015/1, para. IE1.
51 DI/2015/1, para. 17.
52 DI/2015/1, para. 18.
53 DI/2015/1, para. A2.
54 DI/2015/1, para. A3.
55 DI/2015/1, para. A4.
56 DI/2015/1, para. A5.
57 DI/2015/1, para. A6.
58 DI/2015/1, para. BC30.
59 DI/2015/1, para. 19.
60 DI/2015/1, para. 20.
61 DI/2015/1, para. 21.
62 DI/2015/1, para. 15.
63 DI/2015/1, para. 21.
64 *IFRIC Update*, July 2014.
65 *IFRIC Update*, January 2016.
66 *IFRIC Update*, January 2016.
67 *IFRIC Update*, March 2016.
68 *IASB Update*, June 2016.

Chapter 32 Share-based payment

Chapter 32

List of examples

Chapter 32 Share-based payment

1 INTRODUCTION

1.1 Background

Share-based payment is one of the most controversial projects so far tackled by the IASB. Most share-based payment transactions undertaken by entities are awards of shares and options as remuneration to employees, in particular senior management and directors. In a number of countries, shares and options now comprise the greatest element of the total remuneration package of senior personnel, a trend encouraged by the current consensus that it is a matter of good corporate governance to promote significant long-term shareholdings by senior management, so as to align their economic interests with those of shareholders.

One advantage of shares and options as remuneration is that they need not entail any cash cost to the entity. If an executive is entitled under a bonus scheme to a free share, the entity can satisfy this award simply by printing another share certificate, which the executive can sell, so that the cash cost of the award is effectively borne by shareholders rather than by the entity itself. However, this very advantage was the source of the controversy surrounding share-based remuneration.

Investors became increasingly concerned that share-based remuneration was resulting in a significant cost to them, through dilution of their existing shareholdings. As a result, there emerged an increasing consensus among investors that awards of shares and share options should be recognised as a cost in the financial statements.

The opposing view, held by most entities, was that the financial statements were simply reflecting the economic reality that such awards are ultimately a cost to other shareholders and not to the entity. Another powerful argument for those opposed to expensing options was to point out that some patently successful companies, particularly in the new technology sector, would never have shown a profit if they had been required to book an accounting expense for options.

The strength of feeling amongst opponents of expensing share-based remuneration was graphically illustrated in the early 1990s when the FASB in the United States attempted to issue an accounting standard requiring options to be expensed, only to be forced into a partial climb-down by an unprecedented political campaign. As a result, the US standard issued by the FASB at that stage, FAS 123 – *Accounting for Stock-Based Compensation,* was a compromise which required the fair value of shares or options issued to employees to be disclosed, but merely recommended, without requiring, those fair values to be expensed in the financial statements. Eventually, however, in December 2004, following the issue of IFRS 2 – *Share-based Payment* – earlier that year (see 1.2 below), the FASB issued FASB ASC 718 – *Compensation – Stock Compensation* (formerly FAS 123(R) – *Share-Based Payment*) – which requires the fair value of share awards to be expensed.

1.2 Development of IFRS 2

In November 2002, the IASB issued an exposure draft ED 2 – *Share-based Payment* – proposing that share-based payments for goods and services should be expensed. The exposure draft proved highly controversial. Those who supported it in principle nevertheless had concerns on nearly every detail of the accounting treatment proposed, in particular the fact that it did not permit any 'truing up', i.e. reversing any expense previously charged for an award that never actually crystallises. More fundamentally, many questioned whether there yet existed a methodology sufficiently robust for valuing shares and share options subject to the restrictions and performance conditions typically associated with employee share awards. There also remained a significant minority who still questioned the whole principle of expensing options and other share awards.

Despite these comments, the IASB finalised its proposals with the publication of IFRS 2 on 19 February 2004, although some significant changes had been necessary to the prohibition on 'truing up' in the ED. In particular, IFRS 2 requires an expense to be recognised only for awards that vest (or are considered by IFRS 2 to vest), but (in the case of awards settled in shares) based on their fair value at the date of grant. Nevertheless, IFRS 2 remains contentious: for example, there is still only limited provision for 'truing up', with the result that significant costs can potentially be recognised for awards that ultimately have no value to their recipients, and give rise to no dilution of the interests of other shareholders. Some commentators continue to question whether existing option valuation models can produce a reliable valuation of employee share awards.

The IASB has issued the following amendments to the original version of IFRS 2:

- *Vesting Conditions and Cancellations,*[1] issued in January 2008 ('the January 2008 amendment'). Entities are required to apply IFRS 2 as modified by this amendment for periods beginning on or after 1 January 2009; *[IFRS 2.62]*
- *Group Cash-settled Share-based Payment Transactions,*[2] issued in June 2009 ('the June 2009 amendment'). Entities are required to apply IFRS 2 as modified by this amendment for periods beginning on or after 1 January 2010; *[IFRS 2.63]*
- *Improvements to IFRSs,* issued in April 2009 ('the April 2009 amendment'). This made a minor amendment to the scope of IFRS 2, as discussed at 2.2.3.D below;
- *Annual Improvements to IFRSs 2010-2012 Cycle,* issued in December 2013, which made amendments to the definitions in Appendix A of IFRS 2 relating to vesting conditions. Entities are required to apply these amendments prospectively to share-based payment transactions with a grant date on or after 1 July 2014 although earlier application is permitted. *[IFRS 2.63B]*. These amendments are discussed at 3 and at 7.4.1.A below; and

- *Classification and Measurement of Share-based Payment Transactions,*[3] issued in June 2016 ('the June 2016 amendments'). Entities are required to apply these amendments for accounting periods beginning on or after 1 January 2018 although earlier application is permitted. Application is generally on a prospective basis and subject to specific transitional provisions which are covered in more detail in the later sections dealing with the amendments and at 16.2 below. The narrow-scope amendments address the following three topics:
  - treatment of vesting and non-vesting conditions in the measurement of a cash-settled share-based payment (see 9.3.2 below);
  - classification of share-based payment transactions with a net settlement feature for withholding tax obligations (see 14.3.1 below); and
  - accounting for a modification of a share-based payment that changes its classification from cash-settled to equity-settled (see 9.4.2.A below).

There have also been two interpretations of IFRS 2 by the IFRS Interpretations Committee, IFRIC 8 – *Scope of IFRS 2* – and IFRIC 11 – *IFRS 2 – Group and Treasury Share Transactions*, but these were incorporated into IFRS 2 as part of the June 2009 amendment and the separate interpretations withdrawn. *[IFRS 2.64]*.

Revision of, and amendments to, IFRS 3 – *Business Combinations* – in 2008 and 2010 respectively, led to consequential amendments to IFRS 2. The revised and amended IFRS 3 provides guidance on the replacement of share-based payment awards in a business combination (see 11 below).

IFRS 2 is supplemented by implementation guidance. However, as noted above the first paragraph of the implementation guidance, this 'accompanies, but is not part of, IFRS 2'.

1.2.1 IFRS 2 research project

In May 2015, the IASB announced the commencement of a research project into certain aspects of IFRS 2.[4]

The objectives of the project were:

- to identify whether it is IFRS 2 that is causing perceived complexity in accounting for share-based payment arrangements and, if it is, to identify the most common areas of complexity; and
- to analyse why IFRS 2 has attracted so many interpretation requests.

In November 2015 the IASB considered a staff report which included an analysis of application issues and their causes, an analysis of the two measurement models in IFRS 2 (equity-settled and cash-settled) and various approaches for moving the project forward.[5] The staff report observed that, on the basis of research and outreach performed, the complexity of applying IFRS 2 in practice has two main causes: the complexity of share-based payment arrangements themselves and use of the grant date fair value measurement model.[6]

The record of the IASB's meeting in May 2016 refers back to the November 2015 meeting. Following an update on feedback received by its staff since November 2015, the IASB decided:

- not to perform any further research on this topic;
- that there is no need to seek feedback on that decision or on the staff's findings; and
- that there is no need to publish a formal research paper or discussion paper summarising the research performed as part of this project but the staff will consider how best to make the work performed visible and retrievable.[7]

1.3 Scope of the chapter and referencing convention

This chapter generally discusses the requirements of IFRS 2 for accounting periods beginning on or after 1 January 2017 and reflects the amendments to the original version of IFRS 2 referred to at 1.2 above that are effective (without early adoption) as at that date. This amended version of IFRS 2 is referred to as 'IFRS 2' throughout the chapter. A detailed discussion of the application of earlier versions of the standard can be found in *International GAAP 2016* and prior editions.

1.4 Overall approach of IFRS 2

IFRS 2 is a complex standard, in part because its overall accounting approach is something of a hybrid. Essentially the total cost (i.e. measurement) of an award is calculated by determining whether the award is a liability or an equity instrument, using criteria somewhat different from those in IAS 32 – *Financial Instruments: Presentation* (see 1.4.1 below), but then applying the measurement principles generally applicable to liabilities or equity instruments under IAS 32 and IAS 39 – *Financial Instruments: Recognition and Measurement*. However the periodic allocation (i.e. recognition) of the cost[8] is determined using something closer to a straight-line accruals methodology, which would not generally be used for financial instruments.

This inevitably has the result that, depending on its legal form, a transaction of equal value to the recipient can result in several different potential charges in profit or loss for the entity, causing some to call into question the comparability of the information provided. Moreover, IFRS 2 is in many respects a rules-based 'anti-avoidance' standard, which often requires an expense to be recorded for transactions that either have no ultimate value to the counterparty or to which, in some cases, the counterparty actually has no entitlement at all.

IFRS 2 has an unusually long Basis for Conclusions – longer in fact than the standard and implementation guidance combined, highlighting some of the controversy in the development of the standard.

1.4.1 Classification differences between IFRS 2 and IAS 32/IAS 39

As noted above, not only are there differences between the accounting treatment of liabilities or equity under IFRS 2 as compared with that under IAS 32 and IAS 39, but the classification of a transaction as a liability or equity transaction under IFRS 2 may differ from that under IAS 32.

The most important difference between IAS 32 and IFRS 2 is that a transaction involving the delivery of equity instruments within the scope of IFRS 2 is always accounted for as an equity transaction, whereas a similar transaction within the scope of IAS 32 might well be classified as a liability if the number of shares to be delivered varies.

The IASB offers some (pragmatic rather than conceptual) explanation for these differences in the Basis for Conclusions to IFRS 2. First, it is argued that to apply IAS 32 to share option plans would mean that a variable share option plan (i.e. one where the number of shares varied according to performance) would give rise to a more volatile (and typically greater) cost than a fixed plan (i.e. one where the number of shares to be awarded is fixed from the start), even if the same number of shares was ultimately delivered under each plan, which would have 'undesirable consequences'. *[IFRS 2.BC109].* Second, it is argued that this is just one of several inconsistencies between IAS 32 and IFRS 2 to be addressed in the round as part of the IASB's review of the definitions of liabilities and equity (which is an ongoing research project). *[IFRS 2.BC110].*

2 THE OBJECTIVE AND SCOPE OF IFRS 2

Section 2 sets out the objective of IFRS 2 (see 2.1 below) and then considers the scope of the standard in the following sub-sections:

- definitions in IFRS 2 relevant to the scope of the standard (see 2.2.1 below);
- transactions and arrangements within the scope of IFRS 2 (see 2.2.2 below) including arrangements within a group and with shareholders (see 2.2.2.A below);
- transactions outside the scope of IFRS 2 (see 2.2.3 below); and
- application of the scope requirements to a number of situations frequently encountered in practice (see 2.2.4 below).

Further details of the transactions and arrangements discussed are given at the start of each sub-section.

2.1 Objective

The objective of IFRS 2 is 'to specify the financial reporting by an entity when it undertakes a share-based payment transaction. In particular, it requires an entity to reflect in its profit or loss and financial position the effects of share-based payment transactions, including expenses associated with transactions in which share options are granted to employees'. *[IFRS 2.1].*

2.2 Scope

2.2.1 Definitions

The following definitions from Appendix A to IFRS 2 are relevant to the scope of IFRS 2.

A *share-based payment arrangement* is 'an agreement between the entity (or another group entity or any shareholder of any group entity) and another party (including an employee) that entitles the other party to receive

(a) cash or other assets of the entity for amounts that are based on the price (or value) of equity instruments (including shares or share options) of the entity or another group entity, or

(b) equity instruments (including shares or share options) of the entity or another group entity,

provided the specified vesting conditions, if any, are met.'

A *share-based payment transaction* is 'a transaction in which the entity

(a) receives goods or services from the supplier of those goods or services (including an employee) in a share-based payment arrangement, or

(b) incurs an obligation to settle the transaction with the supplier in a share-based payment arrangement when another group entity receives those goods or services.'

An *equity-settled share-based payment transaction* is 'a share-based payment transaction in which the entity

(a) receives goods or services as consideration for its own equity instruments (including shares or share options), or

(b) receives goods or services but has no obligation to settle the transaction with the supplier.'

A *cash-settled share-based payment transaction* is 'a share-based payment transaction in which the entity acquires goods or services by incurring a liability to transfer cash or other assets to the supplier of those goods or services for amounts that are based on the price (or value) of equity instruments (including shares or share options) of the entity or another group entity'.

A *group entity* in the four definitions above means any parent, subsidiary, or subsidiary of any parent, of the entity and is based on the definition of 'group' in Appendix A to IFRS 10 – *Consolidated Financial Statements* – as 'a parent and its subsidiaries'. *[IFRS 2.63A, BC22E]*.

An *equity instrument* is 'a contract that evidences a residual interest in the assets of an entity after deducting all of its liabilities'.

An *equity instrument granted* is 'the right (conditional or unconditional) to an equity instrument of the entity conferred by the entity on another party, under a share-based payment arrangement'.

A *share option* is 'a contract that gives the holder the right, but not the obligation, to subscribe to the entity's shares at a fixed or determinable price for a specified period of time'. *[IFRS 2 Appendix A]*.

It will be seen from these definitions that IFRS 2 applies not only to awards of shares and share options but also to awards of cash (or other assets) of a value equivalent to the value, or a movement in the value, of a particular number of shares. Such cash awards may arise in a number of situations. For example:

- an entity may wish to extend its share scheme to the employees of overseas subsidiaries in jurisdictions where it may be difficult, or even illegal, to trade in the entity's shares, or where delivering shares would not give the same tax benefits to employees as would apply in the parent's own jurisdiction; or
- the entity may not wish to dilute existing shareholdings by significant share awards to employees.

In such cases, the employees may instead be offered cash equivalent to the value of the shares that they would otherwise have obtained.

2.2.2 *Transactions within the scope of IFRS 2*

Subject to the exceptions noted at 2.2.3 below, IFRS 2 must be applied to all share-based payment transactions, including:

(a) equity-settled share-based payment transactions (discussed at 4 to 8 below);

(b) cash-settled share-based payment transactions (discussed at 9 below); and

(c) transactions where either the entity or the supplier of goods or services can choose whether the transaction is to be equity-settled or cash-settled (discussed at 10 below). *[IFRS 2.2]*.

Whilst the boundaries between these types of transaction are reasonably self-explanatory, there may be transactions – as discussed in more detail at 9 and 10 below – that an entity may intuitively regard as equity-settled which are in fact required to be treated as cash-settled under IFRS 2.

Although IFRS 2 was primarily a response to concerns over share-based remuneration, its scope is not restricted to transactions with employees. For example, if an external supplier of goods or services, including another group entity, is paid in shares or share options, or cash of equivalent value, IFRS 2 must be applied. Goods include:

- inventories;
- consumables;
- property, plant and equipment;
- intangibles; and
- other non-financial assets. *[IFRS 2.5]*.

It will be seen that 'goods' do not include financial assets, which raises some further issues (see 2.2.3.F below).

The scope of IFRS 2 extends to:

- group share schemes and certain transactions with shareholders (see 2.2.2.A below);
- transactions with employee benefit trusts and similar vehicles (see 2.2.2.B below);
- transactions where the identifiable consideration received appears to be less than the consideration given (see 2.2.2.C below);
- 'all employee' share plans (see 2.2.2.D below); and
- vested transactions (see 2.2.2.E below).

2.2.2.A Group schemes and transactions with group shareholders: scope issues

The definitions of 'share-based payment arrangement' and 'share-based payment transaction' at 2.2.1 above have the effect that the scope of IFRS 2 is not restricted to transactions where the reporting entity acquires goods or services in exchange for its own equity instruments (or cash or other assets based on the cost or value of those equity instruments). Within a group of companies it is common for one member of the group (typically the parent) to have the obligation to settle a share-based payment transaction in which services are provided to another member of the group (typically a subsidiary). This transaction is within the scope of IFRS 2 for the entity receiving the services (even though it is not a direct party to the arrangement between its parent and its employee), the entity settling the transaction and the group as a whole.

Accordingly, IFRS 2 requires an entity to account for a transaction in which it either:

- receives goods or services when another entity in the same group (or a shareholder of any group entity) has the obligation to settle the share-based payment transaction, or
- has an obligation to settle a share-based payment transaction when another entity in the same group receives the goods or services

unless the transaction is clearly for a purpose other than payment for goods or services supplied to the entity receiving them. *[IFRS 2.3A]*.

Moreover, the definitions of 'equity-settled share-based payment transaction' and 'cash-settled share-based payment transaction' have the effect that the analysis of the transaction as equity-settled or cash-settled (and its accounting treatment) may differ when viewed from the perspective of the entity receiving the goods or services, the entity settling the transaction and the group as a whole. *[IFRS 2.43A]*.

We consider below seven scenarios, based on the simple structure in Figure 32.1 below. These scenarios are by no means exhaustive, but cover the situations most commonly seen in practice.

The accounting treatment of group share schemes is discussed in more detail at 12 below.

Figure 32.1: Scope of IFRS 2

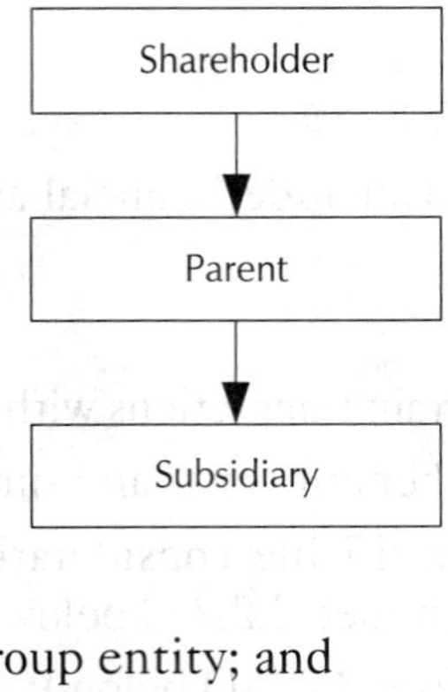

The scenarios assume that:

- the shareholder is not a group entity; and
- the subsidiary is directly owned by the parent company (see 12.2.1 below in relation to intermediate parent companies).

Scenario	Who grants the award?	Which entity receives the goods or services?	Who settles the award?	On which entity's shares is the award based?	Award settled in shares or cash?
1	Parent	Subsidiary	Parent	Parent	Shares
2	Shareholder	Subsidiary	Shareholder	Parent	Shares
3	Subsidiary	Subsidiary	Subsidiary	Parent	Shares
4	Subsidiary	Subsidiary	Subsidiary	Subsidiary	Shares
5	Parent	Subsidiary	Parent	Subsidiary	Shares
6	Parent	Subsidiary	Parent	Parent	Cash
7	Shareholder	Subsidiary	Shareholder	Parent	Cash

Scenario 1

Parent awards equity shares in Parent to employees of Subsidiary in exchange for services to Subsidiary. Parent settles the award with the employees of Subsidiary. *[IFRS 2.43B-43C, B52(a), B53-B54]*.

Consolidated financial statements of Parent

Under the definition of 'share-based payment transaction', 'the entity [i.e. the Parent group] ... receives goods or services ... in a share-based payment arrangement ...'. A share-based payment arrangement includes 'an agreement between the entity ... and another party (including an employee) that entitles the other party to receive ... equity instruments ... of the entity ...'.

The transaction is classified as an equity-settled transaction because it is settled in an equity instrument of the group.

Separate financial statements of Parent

Under the definition of 'share-based payment transaction', the 'entity [i.e. the Parent as a single entity] ... incurs an obligation to settle the transaction with the supplier in a share-based payment arrangement when another group entity receives those goods or services'.

The transaction is classified as an equity-settled transaction because it is settled in an equity instrument of Parent.

Subsidiary

Under the definition of 'share-based payment transaction', 'the entity [i.e. Subsidiary] ... receives goods or services ... in a share-based payment arrangement ...'. A 'share-based payment arrangement' includes 'an agreement between ... another group entity [i.e. Parent] ... and another party (including an employee) that entitles the other party to receive ... equity instruments of ... another group entity'.

The transaction is classified as an equity-settled transaction because Subsidiary 'has no obligation to settle the transaction with the supplier'.

Even if Subsidiary is not a party to the agreement with its employees, it nevertheless records a cost for this transaction. In effect, the accounting treatment is representing that Subsidiary has received a capital contribution from Parent, which Subsidiary has then 'spent' on employee remuneration. This treatment is often referred to as 'push-down' accounting – the idea being that a transaction undertaken by one group entity (in this case, Parent) for the benefit of another group entity (in this case, Subsidiary) is 'pushed down' into the financial statements of the beneficiary entity.

Scenario 2

Shareholder awards equity shares in Parent to employees of Subsidiary in exchange for services to Subsidiary. Shareholder settles the award with the employees of Subsidiary. *[IFRS 2.B48(b)]*.

Consolidated financial statements of Parent

Under the definition of 'share-based payment transaction', 'the entity [i.e. the Parent group] ... receives goods or services ... in a share-based payment arrangement'. A 'share-based payment arrangement' includes 'an agreement between ... any shareholder ... and another party (including an employee) that entitles the other party to receive ... equity instruments (including shares or share options) of the entity...'.

The transaction is classified as an equity-settled transaction, because the Parent group 'has no obligation to settle the transaction with the supplier'.

Separate financial statements of Parent

Scenario 2 is not within the scope of IFRS 2 for the separate financial statements of Parent, because Parent (as a separate entity) receives no goods or services, nor does it settle the transaction.

Subsidiary

Under the definition of 'share-based payment transaction', 'the entity [i.e. Subsidiary] ... receives goods or services ... in a share-based payment arrangement'. A 'share-based payment arrangement' includes 'an agreement between ... any shareholder of any group entity [i.e. Shareholder] ... and another party (including an employee) that entitles the other party to receive equity instruments of ... another group entity [i.e. Parent]'.

The transaction is classified as an equity-settled transaction, because Subsidiary 'has no obligation to settle the transaction with the supplier'.

IFRS 2 explicitly does not address the accounting treatment for such a transaction within the financial statements of a shareholder that is not a group entity. *[IFRS 2.BC22G]*. We discuss at 12.9 below the accounting treatment of such transactions in the financial statements of a shareholder that is an investor in a joint venture or associate.

Scenario 3

Subsidiary awards equity shares in Parent to employees of Subsidiary in exchange for services to Subsidiary. Subsidiary settles the award with the employees of Subsidiary. *[IFRS 2.43B, B52(b), B55]*.

Consolidated financial statements of Parent

Under the definition of 'share-based payment transaction', 'the entity [i.e. the Parent group] ... receives goods or services ... in a share-based payment arrangement'. A 'share-based payment arrangement' includes 'an agreement between the entity ... and another party (including an employee) that entitles the other party to receive ... equity instruments (including shares or share options) of the entity'.

The transaction is classified as an equity-settled transaction, because the Parent group 'receives goods or services as consideration for its own equity instruments (including shares or share options)...'.

Separate financial statements of Parent

Scenario 3 is not within the scope of IFRS 2 for the separate financial statements of Parent, because Parent (as a separate entity) receives no goods or services, nor does it settle the transaction.

Subsidiary

Under the definition of 'share-based payment transaction', 'the entity [i.e. Subsidiary] ... receives goods or services ... in a share-based payment arrangement'. A 'share-based payment arrangement' includes 'an agreement between ... [a] group entity [i.e. Subsidiary] ... and another party (including an employee) that entitles the other party to receive equity instruments of ... another group entity [i.e. Parent]'.

The transaction is classified as a cash-settled transaction because Subsidiary has the obligation to settle the award with equity instruments issued by Parent – i.e. a financial asset in Subsidiary's separate financial statements – rather than with Subsidiary's own equity instruments.

However, for the approach in this Scenario to apply, it must be the case that Subsidiary grants the award as a principal rather than as agent for Parent. If Subsidiary appears to be granting an award but is really doing so only on the instructions of Parent, as will generally be the case in certain jurisdictions, then the approach in Scenario 1 above is more likely to apply. This is discussed in more detail at 12.2.5.B below.

Scenario 4

Subsidiary awards equity shares in Subsidiary to employees of Subsidiary in exchange for services to Subsidiary. Subsidiary settles the award with the employees of Subsidiary. *[IFRS 2.43B, B49].*

Consolidated financial statements of Parent

Under the definition of 'share-based payment transaction', 'the entity [i.e. the Parent group] ... receives goods or services ... in a share-based payment arrangement'. A share-based payment arrangement includes 'an agreement between the entity ... and another party (including an employee) that entitles the other party to receive ... equity instruments ... of the entity ...'.

The transaction is classified as an equity-settled transaction, because it is settled in an equity instrument of the group. In the consolidated financial statements of Parent, shares of Subsidiary not held by Parent are a non-controlling (minority) interest, classified as equity (see Chapter 7 at 4).

Subsidiary

Under the definition of 'share-based payment transaction', 'the entity [i.e. Subsidiary] ... receives goods or services ... in a share-based payment arrangement'.

The transaction is classified as an equity-settled transaction, because it is settled in an equity instrument of Subsidiary.

Scenario 5

Parent awards equity shares in Subsidiary to employees of Subsidiary in exchange for services to Subsidiary. Parent settles the award with the employees of Subsidiary. *[IFRS 2.43B-43C, B50]*.

Consolidated financial statements of Parent

Under the definition of 'share-based payment transaction', 'the entity [i.e. the Parent group] ... receives goods or services ... in a share-based payment arrangement'. A share-based payment arrangement includes 'an agreement between the entity ... and another party (including an employee) that entitles the other party to receive ... equity instruments of the entity ...'.

The transaction is classified as an equity-settled transaction, because it is settled in an equity instrument of the group. In the consolidated financial statements of Parent, shares of Subsidiary not held by Parent are a non-controlling (minority) interest, classified as equity (see Chapter 7 at 4).

Separate financial statements of Parent

Under the definition of 'share-based payment transaction', the 'entity [i.e. the Parent as a single entity] ... incurs an obligation to settle the transaction with the supplier in a share-based payment arrangement when another group entity [i.e. Subsidiary] receives those goods or services'. The transaction is a share-based payment arrangement for Subsidiary (see below) and the consolidated financial statements of Parent (see above).

For Parent, the transaction is classified as a cash-settled transaction, because it is settled not in an equity instrument issued by Parent, but in an equity instrument issued by a subsidiary and held by Parent – i.e. a financial asset in Parent's separate financial statements.

Subsidiary

Under the definition of 'share-based payment transaction', 'the entity [i.e. Subsidiary] ... receives goods or services ... in a share-based payment arrangement'. A 'share-based payment arrangement' includes 'an agreement between ... another group entity [i.e. Parent] ... and another party (including an employee) that entitles the other party to receive equity instruments of the entity...'.

The transaction is classified as an equity-settled transaction, because Subsidiary 'has no obligation to settle the transaction with the supplier'.

Scenario 6

Parent awards cash based on the value of shares in Parent to employees of Subsidiary in exchange for services to Subsidiary. Parent settles the award with the employees of Subsidiary. *[IFRS 2.43C, B56-B58]*.

Consolidated financial statements of Parent

Under the definition of 'share-based payment transaction', 'the entity [i.e. the Parent group] ... receives goods or services ... in a share-based payment arrangement'. A 'share-based payment arrangement' includes 'an agreement between the entity ... and another party (including an employee) that entitles the other party to receive ... cash ... of the entity ... based on the price (or value) of equity instruments ... of the entity ...'.

The transaction is classified as a cash-settled transaction, because it is settled in cash of the group.

Separate financial statements of Parent

Under the definition of 'share-based payment transaction', the 'entity [i.e. the Parent as a single entity] ... incurs an obligation to settle the transaction with the supplier in a share-based payment arrangement when another group entity [i.e. Subsidiary] receives those goods or services'.

The transaction is classified as a cash-settled transaction, because it is settled in cash of Parent.

Subsidiary

IFRS 2 contains detailed guidance for the accounting treatment of such transactions by the employing subsidiary (see 12 below), from which it may reasonably be inferred that the IASB intended them to be in the scope of IFRS 2 for the subsidiary.

However, this is strictly not the case when the drafting of IFRS 2 is examined closely. In order to be a share-based payment *transaction* (and therefore in the scope of IFRS 2) for the reporting entity, a transaction must also be a share-based payment *arrangement*. A share-based payment arrangement is defined as one in which the counterparty receives (our emphasis added):

- equity of the entity *or any other group entity*, or
- cash or other assets *of the entity*.

As drafted, the definition has the effect that a transaction settled in equity is in the scope of IFRS 2 for a reporting entity, whether the equity used to settle is the entity's own equity or that of another group entity. Where a transaction is settled in cash, however, the definition has the effect that a transaction is in the scope of IFRS 2 for a reporting entity only when that entity's own cash (or other assets) is used in settlement, and not when another group entity settles the transaction.

However, given the guidance referred to above in IFRS 2 for the accounting treatment for the reporting entity of transactions settled in cash by another group entity, we believe that the exclusion of such transactions from the definition of 'share-based payment arrangement' should be disregarded as an unfortunate drafting slip.

The transaction is classified as an equity-settled transaction by Subsidiary, because Subsidiary 'has no obligation to settle the transaction with the supplier'.

Scenario 7

Shareholder awards cash based on the value of shares in Parent to employees of Subsidiary in exchange for services to Subsidiary. Shareholder settles the award with the employees of Subsidiary.

For the reasons set out in Scenario 6 above, this transaction is not strictly in the scope of IFRS 2 as drafted either for the consolidated financial statements of Parent or for the separate financial statements of Parent or Subsidiary. As noted in Scenario 6 above, the definition of 'share-based payment arrangement' as drafted excludes any arrangement that is settled in cash by a party other than the reporting entity. Moreover, whilst IFRS 2 gives detailed guidance that effectively appears to 'over-ride' the definition in respect of a transaction settled by another group entity (see Scenario 6 above), there is no such over-riding guidance in respect of a transaction settled in cash by a non-group shareholder.

Nevertheless, we believe that the transaction should be treated as within the scope of IFRS 2 for the consolidated financial statements of Parent and the separate financial statements of Subsidiary. One of the original objectives of the project that led to the issue of the June 2009 amendment to IFRS 2 was to address a concern that, as originally issued, IFRS 2 did not require an entity to account for a cash-settled share-based payment transaction settled by an external shareholder.

In addition to the accounting treatment under IFRS 2, the group entities in this Scenario would need to consider the requirements of IAS 24 – *Related Party Disclosures* – as any payments by a shareholder would potentially need to be disclosed (see Chapter 37).

2.2.2.B Transactions with employee benefit trusts and similar vehicles

In some jurisdictions, it is common for an entity to establish a trust to hold shares in the entity for the purpose of satisfying, or 'hedging' the cost of, share-based awards to employees. In such cases, it is often the trust, rather than any entity within the legal group, that actually makes share-based awards to employees.

A sponsoring employer (or its wider group) will need to assess whether it controls the trust in accordance with the requirements of IFRS 10 and therefore whether the trust should be consolidated (see 12.3 below and Chapter 6).

Awards by employee benefit trusts and similar vehicles are within the scope of IFRS 2, irrespective of whether or not the trust is consolidated, since:

- where the trust is consolidated, it is an award by a group entity; and
- where the trust is not consolidated, it is an award by a shareholder.

2.2.2.C *Transactions where the identifiable consideration received appears to be less than the consideration given*

A share-based payment transaction as defined (see 2.2.1 above) involves the receipt of goods or services by the reporting entity. Nevertheless, IFRS 2 also applies to share-based payment transactions where no specifically identifiable goods or services have been (or will be) received. *[IFRS 2.2]*.

IFRS 2 asserts that, if the identifiable consideration received (if any) appears to be less than the fair value of consideration given, the implication is that, in addition to the identifiable goods and services acquired, the entity must also have received some unidentifiable consideration equal to the difference between the fair value of the share-based payment and the fair value of any identifiable consideration received. Accordingly, the cost of the unidentified consideration must be accounted for in accordance with IFRS 2. *[IFRS 2.13A]*.

For example, if an entity agrees to pay a supplier of services with a clearly identifiable market value of £1,000 by issuing shares with a value of £1,500, IFRS 2 requires the entity to recognise an expense of £1,500. This is notwithstanding the normal requirement of IFRS 2 that an equity-settled share-based payment transaction with a non-employee be recognised at the fair value of the goods or services received (see 5.1 and 5.4 below).

This requirement was introduced by IFRIC 8 (since incorporated into IFRS 2). The reason for the change is alluded to in an illustrative example. *[IFRS 2.IG5D, IG Example 1]*. As part of general economic reforms in South Africa, under arrangements generally referred to as black economic empowerment or 'BEE' (discussed further at 15.5 below), various entities issued or transferred significant numbers of shares to bodies representing historically disadvantaged communities. Some held that these transactions did not fall within the scope of IFRS 2 as originally drafted because the entities concerned were not purchasing goods or services. Rather, BEE arrangements were simply meant to replicate a transfer of shares from one group of shareholders to another. Accordingly, it was argued, such transactions did not fall within the scope of IFRS 2, since it is intrinsic to the definition of a 'share-based payment transaction' (see 2.2.1 above) that goods or services are received.

IFRS 2 rejects this argument. It effectively takes the view that, since the directors of an entity would not issue valuable consideration for nothing, something must have been received. *[IFRS 2.BC18C]*. IFRS 2 suggests that a transfer of equity under BEE and similar schemes is made 'as a means of enhancing [the entity's] image as a good corporate citizen'. *[IFRS 2 IG Example 1]*.

There seems little doubt that this aspect of IFRS 2 is in part an 'anti-avoidance' measure. As discussed in 4 to 8 below, the general measurement rule in IFRS 2 is that share-based payment transactions with employees are measured by reference to the fair value of the consideration given and those with non-employees by reference to the fair value of the consideration received. We argue at 5.2.2 below that the requirement to measure transactions with employees by reference to the consideration given is essentially an anti-avoidance provision. It prevents entities from recognising a low cost for employee share options on the grounds that little incremental service is provided for them beyond that already provided for cash-based remuneration. The changes introduced by IFRIC 8 removed the potential for a similar abuse in accounting for transactions with non-employees.

Nevertheless, the IASB acknowledges that there may be rare circumstances in which a transaction may occur in which no goods or services are received by the entity. For example, a principal shareholder of an entity, for reasons of estate planning, may transfer shares to a relative. In the absence of indications that the relative has provided, or is expected to provide, goods or services to the entity in exchange for the shares, such a transfer would be outside the scope of IFRS 2. *[IFRS 2.BC18D]*.

See also the discussions at 2.2.3.A below relating to transactions with shareholders in their capacity as such and at 2.2.4.K below relating to dual pricing on a share issue.

2.2.2.D 'All employee' share plans

Many countries encourage wider share-ownership by allowing companies to award a limited number of free or discounted shares to employees without either the employee or the employer incurring tax liabilities which would apply if other benefits in kind to an equivalent value were given to employees.

Some national accounting standards exempt some such plans from their scope, to some extent as the result of local political pressures. Prior to issuing IFRS 2, the IASB received some strong representations that IFRS should give a similar exemption, on the grounds that not to do so would discourage companies from continuing with such schemes.

The IASB concluded that such an exemption would be wrong in principle and difficult to draft in practice. By way of concession, the Basis for Conclusions hints that if the IFRS 2 charge for such schemes is (as asserted by some of the proponents of an exemption) *de minimis*, then there would be no charge under IFRS 2 anyway, since, like all IFRSs, it applies only to material items. *[IFRS 2.BC8-17]*. However, our experience is that, in many cases, the charge is material.

2.2.2.E Vested transactions

Once a transaction accounted for under IFRS 2 has vested in the counterparty (see 3 below), it does not necessarily cease to be in the scope of IFRS 2 just because the entity has received the goods or services required for the award to vest. This is made clear by the numerous provisions of IFRS 2 referring to the accounting treatment of vested awards.

Once equity shares have been unconditionally delivered or beneficially transferred to the counterparty (e.g. as the result of the vesting of an award of ordinary shares, or the exercise of a vested option over ordinary shares), the holder of those shares will often be in exactly the same position as any other holder of ordinary shares and the shares will generally be accounted for under IAS 32 and IAS 39 rather than IFRS 2.

If, however, the holder of a share or vested option enjoys rights not applicable to all holders of that class of share, such as a right to put the share or the option to the entity for cash, the share or option might still remain in the scope of IFRS 2 as long as any such rights continue to apply. The same is true of modifications made after vesting which add such rights to a vested share or option or otherwise alter the life of the share-based payment transaction. The special terms or rights will often be linked to the holder's employment with the entity but could also apply to an arrangement with a non-employee.

The significance of this is that issued equity instruments and financial liabilities not within the scope of IFRS 2 would typically fall within the scope of IAS 32 and IAS 39, which might require a significantly different accounting treatment from that required by IFRS 2. See, for example:

- the discussion at 2.2.4.B below of the treatment in consolidated financial statements of an award with a right to put the share to the parent entity;
- the discussion at 2.2.4.G below which highlights that a share option with a foreign currency strike price is accounted for as an equity instrument under IFRS 2, but as a liability under IAS 32 and IAS 39; and
- the discussion at 10.1.6 below of the treatment of convertible instruments issued in exchange for goods and services and accounted for under IFRS 2 rather than under IAS 32 and IAS 39.

2.2.3 *Transactions not within the scope of IFRS 2*

The following transactions are outside the scope of IFRS 2:

- transactions with shareholders as a whole and with shareholders in their capacity as such (see 2.2.3.A below);
- transfers of assets in certain group restructuring arrangements (see 2.2.3.B below);
- business combinations (see 2.2.3.C below);
- combinations of businesses under common control and the contribution of a business to form a joint venture (see 2.2.3.D below); and
- transactions in the scope of IAS 32 – *Financial Instruments: Presentation* – and IAS 39 – *Financial Instruments: Recognition and Measurement* (see 2.2.3.E below).

In addition, the scope exemptions in IFRS 2 combined with those in IAS 32 and IAS 39 appear to have the effect that there is no specific guidance in IFRS for accounting for certain types of investment when acquired in return for shares (see 2.2.3.F below).

As noted at 2.2.2.D above, there is no exemption from IFRS 2 for share schemes aimed mainly at lower- and middle-ranking employees, referred to in different jurisdictions by terms such as 'all-employee share schemes', 'employee share purchase plans' and 'broad-based plans'.

2.2.3.A *Transactions with shareholders in their capacity as such*

IFRS 2 does not apply to transactions with employees (and others) purely in their capacity as shareholders. For example, an employee may already hold shares in the entity as a result of previous share-based payment transactions. If the entity then raises funds through a rights issue, for example, whereby all shareholders (including the employee) can acquire additional shares for less than the current fair value of the shares, such a transaction is not a share-based payment transaction for the purposes of IFRS 2. *[IFRS 2.4]*.

2.2.3.B Transfer of assets in group restructuring arrangements

In some group restructuring arrangements, one entity will transfer a group of net assets, which does not meet the definition of a business, to another entity in return for shares. Careful consideration of the precise facts and circumstances is needed in order to determine whether, for the separate or individual financial statements of any entity affected by the transfer, such a transfer falls within the scope of IFRS 2. If the transfer is considered primarily to be a transfer of goods by their owner in return for payment in shares then, in our view, this should be accounted for under IFRS 2. However, if the transaction is for another purpose and is driven by the group shareholder in its capacity as such, the transaction may be outside the scope of IFRS 2 (see 2.2.3.A above). Accounting for intra-group asset transfers in return for shares is considered further in Chapter 8 at 4.4.1.

2.2.3.C Business combinations

IFRS 2 does not apply to share-based payments to acquire goods (such as inventories or property, plant and equipment) as part of a business combination to which IFRS 3 applies.

However, the Interpretations Committee has clarified that in a reverse acquisition involving an entity that does not constitute a business (i.e. an asset acquisition or the provision of a service), IFRS 2 rather than IFRS 3 is likely to apply (see Chapter 9 at 14.8).[9]

Transactions in which equity instruments are issued to acquire goods as part of the net assets in a business combination are outside the scope of IFRS 2 but equity instruments granted to the employees of the acquiree in their capacity as employees (e.g. in return for continued service following the business combination) are within its scope, as are the cancellation, replacement or modification of a share-based payment transaction as the result of a business combination or other equity restructuring (see 11 and 12.8 below). *[IFRS 2.5]*.

Thus, if a vendor of an acquired business remains as an employee of that business following the business combination and receives a share-based payment for transferring control of the entity and for remaining in continuing employment, it is necessary to determine how much of the share-based payment relates to the acquisition of control (which forms part of the cost of the combination, accounted for under IFRS 3) and how much relates to the provision of future services (which is a post-combination operating expense accounted for under IFRS 2). Guidance on this issue is given in IFRS 3 – see Chapter 9 at 11.2 – and there is discussion of related issues at 2.2.4.B below.

2.2.3.D Common control transactions and formation of joint arrangements

IFRS 2 also does not apply to a combination of entities or businesses under common control (see Chapter 10), or the contribution of a business on the formation of a joint venture as defined by IFRS 11 – *Joint Arrangements* (see Chapter 12). *[IFRS 2.5]*.

The exemption for common control combinations took effect for annual periods beginning on or after 1 July 2009. *[IFRS 2.61]*. The exemption based on IFRS 11 takes effect from the date of application of that standard. *[IFRS 2.63A]*.

It should be noted that the contribution of non-financial assets (which do not constitute a business) to a joint venture in return for shares is within the scope of IFRS 2 and the assets should be accounted for at fair value in accordance with IFRS 2 (see 2.2.2 above).

IFRS 2 does not directly address other types of transactions involving joint ventures or transactions involving associates, particularly arrangements relating to the employees of associates or joint ventures. These are discussed further at 12.9 below.

2.2.3.E Transactions in the scope of IAS 32 and IAS 39

IFRS 2 does not apply to transactions within the scope of IAS 32 or IAS 39 (see Chapter 43). For example, if an entity enters into a share-based payment transaction to purchase a commodity surplus to its production requirements or with a view to short-term profit taking, the contract is treated as a financial instrument under IAS 32 and IAS 39 rather than a share-based payment transaction under IFRS 2. *[IFRS 2.6]*.

Some practical examples of scope issues involving IFRS 2 and IAS 32 / IAS 39 are discussed at 2.2.4 below.

2.2.3.F Transactions in financial assets outside the scope of IAS 32 and IAS 39

As noted at 2.2.2 above, IFRS 2 applies to share-based payment transactions involving goods or services, with 'goods' defined so as to exclude financial assets, presumably on the basis that these fall within IAS 32 and IAS 39. However, investments in subsidiaries, associates and joint ventures in the separate financial statements of the investing entity are financial assets as defined in IAS 32 (and hence outside the scope of IFRS 2), but are outside the scope of IAS 39 where the entity chooses to account for them at cost (see Chapter 8 at 2.1 and Chapter 43 at 3.1).

Moreover, IFRS has no general requirements for accounting for the issue of equity instruments. Rather, consistent with the position taken by the *Conceptual Framework* that equity is a residual rather than an item 'in its own right', the amount of an equity instrument is normally measured by reference to the item (expense or asset) in consideration for which the equity is issued, as determined in accordance with IFRS applicable to that other item.

This means that, when (as is commonly the case) an entity acquires an investment in a subsidiary, associate or joint venture in return for the issue of equity instruments, there is no explicit guidance in IFRS as to the required accounting in the separate financial statements of the investor, and in particular as to how the 'cost' of such an item is to be determined. This is discussed further in Chapter 8 at 2.1.1.A.

2.2.4 Some practical applications of the scope requirements

This section addresses the application of the scope requirements of IFRS 2 to a number of situations frequently encountered in practice:

- remuneration in non-equity shares and arrangements with put rights over equity shares (see 2.2.4.A below);
- the treatment in the consolidated accounts of the parent of an equity-settled award of a subsidiary with a put option against the parent (see 2.2.4.B below);
- an increase in the counterparty's ownership interest with no change in the number of shares held (see 2.2.4.C below);
- awards for which the counterparty has paid 'fair value' (see 2.2.4.D below);
- a cash bonus which depends on share price performance (see 2.2.4.E below);
- cash-settled awards based on an entity's 'enterprise value' or other formula (see 2.2.4.F below);
- awards with a foreign currency strike price (see 2.2.4.G below);
- holding own shares to satisfy or 'hedge' awards (see 2.2.4.H below);
- shares or warrants issued in connection with a financial liability (see 2.2.4.I below);
- options over puttable instruments classified as equity under the specific exception in IAS 32 in the absence of other equity instruments (see 2.2.4.J below); and
- special discounts to certain categories of investor on a share issue (see 2.2.4.K below).

The following aspects of the scope requirements are covered elsewhere in this chapter:

- employment taxes on share-based payment transactions (see 14 below); and
- instruments such as limited recourse loans and convertible bonds that sometimes fall within the scope of IFRS 2 rather than IAS 32/IAS 39 because of the link both to the entity's equity instruments and to goods or services received in exchange. Convertible bonds are discussed at 10.1.6 below and limited recourse loans at 15.2 below.

2.2.4.A *Remuneration in non-equity shares and arrangements with put rights over equity shares*

A transaction is within the scope of IFRS 2 only where it involves the delivery of an equity instrument, or cash or other assets based on the price or value of an 'equity instrument', in return for goods or services (see 2.2.1 above).

In some jurisdictions, there can be fiscal advantages in giving an employee, in lieu of a cash payment, a share that carries a right to a 'one-off' dividend, or is mandatorily redeemable, at an amount equivalent to the intended cash payment. Such a share would almost certainly be classified as a liability under IAS 32 (see Chapter 45). Payment in such a share would not fall in the scope of IFRS 2 since the consideration paid by the entity for services received is a financial liability rather than meeting the definition of an equity instrument (see the definitions in 2.2.1 above).

If, however, the amount of remuneration delivered in this way were equivalent to the value of a particular number of equity instruments issued by the entity, then the transaction would be in scope of IFRS 2 as a cash-settled share-based payment transaction, since the entity would have incurred a liability (i.e. by issuing the redeemable shares) for an amount based on the price of its equity instruments.

Similarly, if an entity grants an award of equity instruments to an employee together with a put right whereby the employee can require the entity to purchase those shares for an amount based on their fair value, both elements of that transaction are in the scope of IFRS 2 as a single cash-settled transaction (see 9 below). This is notwithstanding the fact that, under IAS 32, the share and the put right might well be analysed as a single synthetic instrument and classified as a liability with no equity component (see Chapter 45).

Differences in the classification of instruments between IFRS 2 and IAS 32 are discussed further at 1.4.1 above.

Put options over instruments that are only classified as equity in limited circumstances (in accordance with paragraphs 16A to 16B of IAS 32) are discussed at 2.2.4.J below.

2.2.4.B *Equity-settled award of subsidiary with put option against the parent – treatment in consolidated accounts of parent*

It is sometimes the case that a subsidiary entity grants an award over its own equity instruments and, either on the same date or later, the parent entity separately grants the same counterparty a put option to sell the equity instruments of the subsidiary to the parent for a cash amount based on the fair value of the equity instruments. Accounting for such an arrangement in the separate financial statements of the subsidiary and the parent will be determined in accordance with the general principles of IFRS 2 (see 2.2.2.A above). However, IFRS 2 does not explicitly address the accounting treatment of all such arrangements in the parent's consolidated financial statements.

In our view, the analysis differs according to whether the put option is granted during or after the vesting period and whether it relates to ordinary shares or to share options.

If the put option is granted during the vesting period (whether at the same time as the grant of the equity instruments or later), the two transactions should be treated as linked and accounted for in the consolidated financial statements as a single cash-settled transaction from the date the put option is granted. This reflects the fact that this situation is similar in group terms to a modification of an award to add a cash-settlement alternative – see 10.1.4 below.

If the put option is only granted once the equity instruments have vested, the accounting will depend on whether the equity instruments in the original share-based payment transaction are unexercised options or whether they are ordinary shares.

If they are unexercised options, the vested options remain within the scope of IFRS 2 until they are exercised (see 2.2.2.E above) and, in this case, the put option should be treated as a linked transaction. Its effect in group terms is to modify the original award from an equity- to a cash-settled transaction until final settlement date.

However, if the equity instruments are fully vested ordinary shares (whether free shares or shares from the exercise of options), rather than unexercised options, they are generally no longer within the scope of IFRS 2 as they are no different from any other ordinary shares issued by the subsidiary. In such cases, the parent entity will need to evaluate whether or not the grant of the put option, as a separate transaction which modifies the terms of certain of the subsidiary's equity instruments, falls within the scope of IFRS 2. For example, the addition of a condition that relates to one shareholder of a subsidiary might indicate that it continues to be appropriate to account for the arrangement in accordance with the requirements of IFRS 2. By contrast, a modification to an entire class of shares would generally not be within the scope of IFRS 2.

A similar analysis is required in a situation where an individual sells a controlling interest in an entity for fair value and put and call options are granted over the individual's remaining non-controlling interest or over shares in the acquirer which have been given to the individual in return for the business acquired. To the extent that the exercise price of the call option depends on the fulfilment of a service condition in the period following the acquisition of the controlling interest, it is likely that the arrangement will fall within the scope of IFRS 2 with any payments contingent on future services recognised as compensation costs.

Put options over non-controlling interests that do not fall within the scope of IFRS 2 are addressed in Chapter 7 at 5.2.

2.2.4.C Increase in ownership interest with no change in number of shares held

An increasingly common arrangement, typically found in entities with venture capital investors, is one where an employee (often part of the key management) subscribes initially for, say, 1% of the entity's equity with the venture capitalist holding the other 99%. The employee's equity interest will subsequently increase by a variable amount depending on the extent to which certain targets are met. This is achieved not by issuing new shares but by cancelling some of the venture capitalist's shares. In our view, such an arrangement falls within the scope of IFRS 2 as the employee is rewarded with an increased equity stake in the entity if certain targets are achieved. The increased equity stake is consistent with the definition in Appendix A of IFRS 2 of an equity instrument as 'a contract that evidences a residual interest...' notwithstanding the fact that no additional shares are issued.

In such arrangements, it is often asserted that the employee has subscribed for a share of the equity at fair value. However, the subscription price paid must represent a fair value using an IFRS 2 valuation basis in order for there to be no additional IFRS 2 expense to recognise (see 2.2.4.D below).

2.2.4.D Awards for which the counterparty has paid 'fair value'

In certain situations, such as where a special class of share is issued, the counterparty might be asked to subscribe a certain amount for the share which is agreed as being its 'fair value' for taxation or other purposes. This does not mean that such arrangements fall outside the scope of IFRS 2, either for measurement or disclosure purposes, if the arrangement meets the definition of a share-based payment transaction. In many cases, the agreed 'fair value' will be lower than a fair value measured in accordance with IFRS 2 because it will reflect the impact of service and non-market performance vesting conditions which are excluded from an IFRS 2 fair value. This is addressed in more detail at 15.4.5 below.

2.2.4.E Cash bonus dependent on share price performance

An entity might agree to pay its employees a €100 cash bonus if its share price remains at €10 or more over a given period. Intuitively, this appears to be within the scope of IAS 19 – *Employee Benefits* – rather than that of IFRS 2 because the employee is not being given cash of equivalent value to a particular number of shares. However, it could be argued that it does fall within the scope of IFRS 2 on the basis that the entity has incurred a liability, and the amount of that liability is 'based on' the share price (in accordance with the definition of a cash-settled share-based payment transaction) – it is nil if the share price is below €10 and €100 if the share price is €10 or more. In our view, either interpretation is acceptable.

2.2.4.F Cash-settled awards based on an entity's 'enterprise value' or other formula

As noted at 2.2.1 above, IFRS 2 includes within its scope transactions in which the entity acquires goods or services by incurring a liability 'based on the price (or value) of equity instruments (including shares or share options) of the entity or another group entity'. Employees of an unquoted entity may receive a cash award based on the value of the equity of that entity. Such awards are typically, but not exclusively, made by venture capital investors to the management of entities in which they have invested and which they aim to sell in the medium term. Further discussion of the accounting implications of awards made in connection with an exit event may be found at 15.4 below.

More generally, where employees of an unquoted entity receive a cash award based on the value of the equity, there is no quoted share price and an 'enterprise value' has therefore to be calculated as a surrogate for it. This begs the question of whether such awards are within the scope of IFRS 2 (because they are based on the value of the entity's equity) or that of IAS 19.

In order for an award to be within the scope of IFRS 2, any calculated 'enterprise value' must represent the fair value of the entity's equity. Where the calculation uses techniques recognised by IFRS 2 as yielding a fair value for equity instruments (as discussed at 8 below), we believe that the award should be regarded as within the scope of IFRS 2.

Appendix B of IFRS 2 notes that an unquoted entity may have calculated the value of its equity based on net assets or earnings (see 8.5.3.B below). *[IFRS 2.B30]*. In our view, this is not intended to imply that it is always appropriate to do so, but simply to note that it may be appropriate in some cases.

Where, for example, the enterprise value is based on a constant formula, such as a fixed multiple of earnings before interest, tax, depreciation and amortisation ('EBITDA'), in our view it is unlikely that this will represent a good surrogate for the fair value of the equity on an ongoing basis, even if it did so at the inception of the transaction. It is not difficult to imagine scenarios in which the fair value of the equity of an entity could be affected with no significant change in EBITDA, for example as a result of changes in interest rates and effective tax rates, or a significant impairment of assets. Alternatively, there might be a significant shift in the multiple of EBITDA equivalent to fair value, for example if the entity were to create or acquire a significant item of intellectual property.

For an award by an individual entity, there is unlikely to be any significant difference in the cost ultimately recorded under IFRS 2 or IAS 19. However, the disclosure requirements of IFRS 2 are more onerous than those of IAS 19. In a group situation where the parent entity grants the award to the employees of a subsidiary, the two standards could result in different levels of expense in the books of the subsidiary because IAS 19, unlike IFRS 2, does not require the employing subsidiary to recognise an expense for a transaction which it has no direct obligation to settle and for which the parent does not allocate the cost (see Chapter 33 at 2.2.2).

The accounting treatment of awards based on the 'market price' of an unquoted subsidiary or business unit raises similar issues to those discussed in this section, as discussed more fully at 6.3.8 below.

2.2.4.G Awards with a foreign currency strike price

Many entities award their employees options with a foreign currency strike price. This will arise most commonly in a multinational group where employees of overseas subsidiaries are granted options on terms that they can pay the option strike price in their local currency. They may also arise where an entity, which has a functional currency different from that of the country in which it operates (e.g. an oil company based in the United Kingdom with a functional currency of United States dollars), grants its UK-based employees options with a strike price in pounds sterling, which is a foreign currency from the perspective of the currency of the financial statements.

Under IAS 32, as currently interpreted, such an award could not be regarded as an equity instrument because the strike price to be tendered is not a fixed amount of the reporting entity's own currency (see Chapter 45 at 5.2.3). However, under IFRS 2, as discussed at 2.2.1 above, equity instruments include options, which are defined as the right to acquire shares for a 'fixed *or determinable* price'. Moreover, it is quite clear from the Basis for Conclusions in IFRS 2 that an award which ultimately results in an employee receiving equity is equity-settled under IFRS 2 whatever its status under IAS 32 might be (see 1.4.1 above). Thus an option over equity with a foreign currency strike price is an equity instrument if accounted for under IFRS 2.

The fair value of such an award should be assessed at grant date and, where the award is treated as equity-settled, should not subsequently be revised for foreign exchange movements (on the basis that the equity instrument is a non-monetary item translated using the exchange rate at the date when the fair value was measured). This applies to the separate financial statements of a parent or subsidiary entity as well as to consolidated financial statements. Where the award is treated as cash-settled, however, the periodic reassessment through profit or loss of the fair value of the award required by IFRS 2 will also need to take into account any exchange difference arising from the requirements of IAS 21 – *The Effects of Changes in Foreign Exchange Rates.*

2.2.4.H Holding own shares to satisfy or 'hedge' awards

Entities often seek to hedge the cost of share-based payment transactions, most commonly by buying their own equity instruments in the market. For example, an entity could grant an employee options over 10,000 shares and buy 10,000 of its own shares into treasury at the date that the award is made. If the award is share-settled, the entity will deliver the shares to the counterparty. If it is cash-settled, it can sell the shares to raise the cash it is required to deliver to the counterparty. In either case, the cash cost of the award is capped at the market price of the shares at the date the award is made, less any amount paid by the employee on exercise. It could of course be argued that such an arrangement is not a true hedge at all. If the share price goes down so that the option is never exercised, the entity is left holding 10,000 of its own shares that cost more than they are now worth.

Whilst these strategies may provide a hedge of the cash cost of share-based payment transactions that are eventually exercised, they will not have any effect in hedging the charge to profit or loss required by IFRS 2 for such transactions. This is because purchases and sales of own shares are accounted for as movements in equity and are therefore never included in profit or loss (see 4.1 below). In any event, IAS 39 does not recognise a hedge of, or using, own equity as a valid hedging relationship (see Chapter 52).

The illustrative examples of group share schemes at 12.4 and 12.5 below show the interaction of the accounting required for a holding of own shares and the requirements of IFRS 2.

2.2.4.I Shares or warrants issued in connection with a financial liability

As noted at 2.2.3.E above, IFRS 2 does not apply to transactions within the scope of IAS 32 and IAS 39. However, if shares or warrants are granted to the lender by the counterparty as part of a financing arrangement, the measurement of those shares or warrants might fall within the scope of IFRS 2. The determination of the relevant standard is likely to require significant judgement based on the precise terms of individual transactions. If the shares or warrants are considered to be in lieu of a cash fee for services provided by the lender then IFRS 2 is likely to be the appropriate standard, but if the shares or warrants are considered instead to be part of the overall return to the lender then IAS 32 and IAS 39 are more likely to apply.

2.2.4.J Options over puttable instruments classified as equity under specific exception in IAS 32

Some entities, such as certain types of trust, issue tradable puttable instruments that are classified as equity instruments rather than as a financial liability because the entity has no other equity instruments. This classification is based on a specific exception in IAS 32 that makes it clear that such instruments are not equity instruments for the purposes of IFRS 2. *[IAS 32.16A-16B, 96C]*. However, should options over such instruments granted to employees – and allowing them to obtain the instruments at a discount to the market price – be treated as cash-settled awards under IFRS 2 or are they outside the scope of IFRS 2 and within that of IAS 19?

The entity has no equity apart from the instruments classified as such under the narrow exception in IAS 32 and, in the absence of equity, the entity cannot logically issue equity instruments in satisfaction of an award to employees nor can it pay cash based on the price or value of its equity instruments. In our view, paragraph 96C of IAS 32 should be interpreted as meaning that, for the purposes of IFRS 2, such awards are not share-based payments and the appropriate standard is IAS 19 rather than IFRS 2.

Those who take the view that such options could be cash-settled share-based payments seem to rely more on the general IAS 32 definition of equity than on the more specific requirements of paragraph 96C of IAS 32 (that 'these instruments should not be considered as equity instruments under IFRS 2'). We believe that the more specific guidance should take precedence over the general definition.

2.2.4.K Special discounts to certain categories of investor on a share issue

In the context of a flotation or other equity fundraising, an entity might offer identical shares at different prices to institutional investors and to individual (retail) investors. Should the additional discount given to one class of investor be accounted for under IFRS 2 as representing unidentified goods or services received or receivable?

The Interpretations Committee was asked to clarify the accounting treatment in this area. The request submitted to the Committee referred to the fact that the final retail price could differ from the institutional price because of:

- an unintentional difference arising from the book-building process; or
- an intentional difference arising from a retail discount given by the issuer of the equity instruments as indicated in the prospectus.

For example, a discount to the institutional investor price might need to be offered to encourage retail investors to buy shares in order to meet the requirements of a particular stock exchange for an entity to have a minimum number of shareholders.

The Interpretations Committee considered whether the discount offered to retail investors in the above example involves the receipt of identifiable or unidentifiable goods or services from the retail shareholder group and, therefore, whether the discount is a share-based payment transaction within the scope of IFRS 2.

IFRS 2 was specifically amended for situations where the identifiable consideration received by the entity appears to be less than the fair value of the equity instruments granted (see 2.2.2.C above). *[IFRS 2.2, 13A]*. The Interpretations Committee noted that the application of this guidance requires judgement and consideration of the specific facts and circumstances of each transaction.

In the circumstances underlying the submission to the Interpretations Committee, the Committee observed that the entity issues shares at two different prices to two different groups of investors for the purpose of raising funds. Any difference in price between the two groups appears to relate to the existence of different markets – one accessible only to retail investors and the other accessible only to institutional investors – rather than to the receipt of additional goods or services. The only relationships involved are those between the investors and the investee entity and the investors are acting in their capacity as shareholders.

The Interpretations Committee therefore observed that the guidance in IFRS 2 is not applicable because there is no share-based payment transaction.

A distinction was drawn between the example above and a situation considered by the Interpretations Committee in 2013 (accounting for reverse acquisitions that do not constitute a business – see 2.2.3.C above). In the latter situation, a stock exchange listing received by the accounting acquirer was considered to be a service received from the accounting acquiree and to represent the difference between the fair value of the equity instruments issued and the identifiable net assets acquired. Hence an IFRS 2 expense would be required in order to recognise this difference. In the situation relating to retail and institutional investors considered above, however, there is no service element and the difference in prices for the two different types of investor is due solely to an investor-investee relationship rather than to unidentifiable goods or services received from the investors.

At its July 2014 meeting the Interpretations Committee decided not to add this matter to its agenda on the basis that sufficient guidance exists without further interpretation or the need for an amendment to a standard.[10]

In other situations, an entity might voluntarily offer a discount to one class of investor, e.g. to an institution underwriting the share issue. In our view, this type of discount is likely to require an IFRS 2 expense to be recognised unless there is evidence that separate prices, and therefore different fair values, are required for each category of investor.

However, in some cases – such as the example above where an institution provides underwriting services – it might be possible to conclude that any additional cost under IFRS 2 is actually a cost of issuing the equity instruments and should therefore be debited to equity rather than to profit or loss.

Similar considerations to those discussed in this section apply when, in advance of an IPO, a private company issues convertible instruments at a discount to their fair value in order both to attract key investors and to boost working capital. There is further discussion on convertible instruments at 10.1.6 below.

3 GENERAL RECOGNITION PRINCIPLES

The recognition rules in IFRS 2 are based on a so-called 'service date model'. In other words, IFRS 2 requires the goods or services received or acquired in a share-based payment transaction to be recognised when the goods are acquired or the services rendered. *[IFRS 2.7]*. For awards to employees (or others providing similar services), this contrasts with the measurement rules, which normally require a share-based payment transaction to be measured as at the date on which the transaction was entered into, which may be some time before or after the related services are received – see 4 to 7 below.

Where the goods or services received or acquired in exchange for a share-based payment transaction do not qualify for recognition as assets they should be expensed. *[IFRS 2.8]*. The standard notes that typically services will not qualify as assets and should therefore be expensed immediately, whereas goods will generally be recognised initially as assets and expensed later as they are consumed. However, some payments for services may be capitalised (e.g. as part of the cost of PP&E, intangible assets or inventories) and some payments for goods may be expensed immediately (e.g. where they are for items included within development costs written off as incurred). *[IFRS 2.9]*.

The corresponding credit entry is, in the case of an equity-settled transaction, an increase in equity and, in the case of a cash-settled transaction, a liability (or decrease in cash or other assets). *[IFRS 2.7]*.

The primary focus of the discussion in the remainder of this chapter is the application of these rules to transactions with employees. The accounting treatment of transactions with non-employees is addressed further at 5.1 and 5.4 below.

3.1 Vesting conditions

Under IFRS 2, the point at which a cost is recognised for goods or services depends on the concept of 'vesting'. The following definitions in Appendix A to IFRS 2 are relevant.

A share-based payment to a counterparty is said to *vest* when it becomes an entitlement of the counterparty. Under IFRS 2, a share-based payment arrangement vests when the counterparty's entitlement is no longer conditional on the satisfaction of any vesting conditions. *[IFRS 2 Appendix A]*.

A *Vesting condition* is a condition that determines whether the entity receives the services that entitle the counterparty to receive cash, other assets or equity instruments of the entity, under a share-based payment arrangement. A vesting condition is either a service condition or a performance condition. *[IFRS 2 Appendix A]*.

A *service condition* is a vesting condition that requires the counterparty to complete a specified period of service during which services are provided to the entity. If the counterparty, regardless of the reason, ceases to provide service during the vesting period, it has failed to satisfy the condition. A service condition does not require a performance target to be met. *[IFRS 2 Appendix A]*. For example, if an employee is granted a share option with a service condition of remaining in employment with an entity for three years, the award vests three years after the date of grant if the employee is still employed by the entity at that date.

A *performance condition* is a vesting condition that requires:

(a) the counterparty to complete a specified period of service (i.e. a service condition); the service requirement can be explicit or implicit; and

(b) specified performance target(s) to be met while the counterparty is rendering the service required in (a).

The period of achieving the performance target(s):

(a) shall not extend beyond the end of the service period; and

(b) may start before the service period on the condition that the commencement date of the performance target is not substantially before the commencement of the service period.

A performance target is defined by reference to:

(a) the entity's own operations (or activities) or the operations or activities of another entity in the same group (i.e. a non-market condition); or

(b) the price (or value) of the entity's equity instruments or the equity instruments of another entity in the same group (including shares and share options) (i.e. a market condition).

A performance target might relate either to the performance of the entity as a whole or to some part of the entity (or part of the group), such as a division or individual employee. *[IFRS 2 Appendix A]*.

The definition of a *market condition* is included at 6.3 below.

In order for a condition to be a vesting condition – rather than a 'non-vesting' condition (see 3.2 below) – there must be a service requirement and any additional performance target must relate to the entity or to some part of the entity or group. Thus a condition that an award vests if, in three years' time, earnings per share has increased by 10% and the employee is still in employment, is a performance condition. If, however, the award becomes unconditional in three years' time if earnings per share has increased by 10%, irrespective of whether the employee is still in employment, that condition is not a performance condition but a non-vesting condition because there is no associated service requirement.

The different types of performance condition and the related accounting requirements are discussed more fully at 6 below. The distinction between vesting and non-vesting conditions is discussed at 3.2 below.

The accounting treatment in a situation where the counterparty fails to meet a service condition – a situation now explicitly covered by the definition of a service condition above – is considered in more detail at 7.4.1.A below.

In addition to the general discussion throughout Section 3, specific considerations relating to awards that vest on a flotation or change of control (or similar exit event) are addressed at 15.4 below.

The definitions of 'vesting condition', 'service condition' and 'performance condition' reproduced above reflect the amendments in the IASB's *Annual Improvements to IFRSs 2010-2012 Cycle* aimed at clarifying the distinction between different types of condition attached to a share-based payment. The amended definitions took effect prospectively for share-based payment transactions with a grant date on or after 1 July 2014, with earlier application permitted.

3.1.1 'Malus' clauses and clawback conditions

Whether as a result of an entity's own decision or in response to regulatory requirements, an increasing number of share-based payment awards include conditions that mean that the awards will only vest if there is no breach of any 'malus' clause on the part of the employee and/or the entity. Often these or other provisions are put in place to allow an entity to claw back vested awards from employees should any wrongdoing or underperformance be identified.

The impact of such clauses on the accounting treatment required by IFRS 2 depends on the precise terms of a particular arrangement. Aspects of arrangements that entities will need to consider include the following:

- whether the terms are sufficiently clear at the inception of the arrangement that there can still be a grant in IFRS 2 terms (see 5.3 below for further discussion of the requirements relating to grant date);
- whether the malus clause relates only to the actions of the individual employee (so-called 'at fault' malus) and whether the relevant period for consideration of the condition is limited to the vesting period or extends over a longer period;
- whether the malus clause relates only to the overall performance of the entity (so-called 'not at fault' malus) and, again, the applicable period during which the clause may be invoked; and
- whether the associated clawback arrangements are clear or depend on further decisions by the entity at the time the relevant 'malus' clause is invoked.

Broadly, it is likely to be the case that there will be a grant at inception provided the terms of the malus and clawback arrangements are sufficiently clear for there to be a shared understanding of the arrangements by both parties.

If the employee's ultimate entitlement to an award depends on satisfaction of an 'at fault' malus clause, this is generally likely to be taken into account as part of any service vesting condition. If the condition extends beyond the usual vesting date of the award and the employee breaches the condition after the end of the vesting period, the vested awards will be treated as a cancellation under IFRS 2 (but there would be no impact on the expense already recognised for a vested award).

Depending on the precise terms, the assessment of a 'not at fault' malus clause is likely to require greater judgement. To the extent that the entity's overall performance formed part of the conditions on which the award would vest, it seems appropriate to treat the condition as part of a performance vesting condition. To the extent that a 'not at fault' malus clause could result in the clawback of an award after the end of the vesting period, there would need to be an assessment of how the identified fault or wrongdoing interacted with the position of the entity as previously determined at the end of the vesting period. The fault might relate solely to a situation that should have prevented the original vesting of the award (for example, a restatement of accounts relating to the vesting period) or it might be a more general condition relating to the ongoing performance of the entity.

If the condition extended beyond the service period, the entity would need to consider whether the award had a non-vesting condition from inception (see 3.2 below). However, given the nature of the condition, in our view it would be unlikely that there would be a significant reduction, if any, in the fair value of the award as a consequence of the non-vesting condition.

3.2 Non-vesting conditions (conditions that are neither service conditions nor performance conditions)

3.2.1 Background

Some share-based payment transactions, particularly those with employees, require the satisfaction of conditions that are neither service conditions nor performance conditions. For example, an employee might be given the right to 100 shares in three years' time, subject only to the employee not working in competition with the reporting entity during that time. An undertaking not to work for another entity does not 'determine whether the entity receives ... services' – the employee could sit on a beach for three years and still be entitled to collect the award. Accordingly, such a condition is not regarded as a vesting condition for the purposes of IFRS 2, but is instead referred to as a 'non-vesting condition'. The accounting treatment of non-vesting conditions is discussed in detail at 6.4 below.

IFRS 2 does not explicitly define a 'non-vesting condition' (see 3.2.2 below), but uses the term to describe a condition that is neither a service condition nor a performance condition. Sometimes the condition will be wholly within the control of the counterparty and unconnected with the delivery of services, such as a requirement to save (see below). However, the identification of such conditions is not always straightforward.

The concept of a 'non-vesting condition', like much of IFRS 2 itself, had its origins as an anti-avoidance measure. It arose from a debate on how to account for employee share option schemes linked to a savings contract. In some jurisdictions, options are awarded to an employee on condition that the employee works for a fixed minimum period and, during that period, makes regular contributions to a savings account, which is then used to exercise the option. The employee is entitled to withdraw from the savings contract before vesting, in which case the right to the award lapses.

Entities applying IFRS 2 as originally issued almost invariably treated an employee's obligation to save as a vesting condition. If the employee stopped saving this was treated as a failure to meet a vesting condition and accounted for as a forfeiture, with the reversal of any expense so far recorded (see 6.1 and 6.2 below).

Some saw in this a scope for abuse of the general principle of IFRS 2 that, if a share-based payment transaction is cancelled, any amount not yet expensed for it is immediately recognised in full (see 7.4 below). The concern was that, if such a plan were 'out of the money', the employer, rather than cancel the plan (and thereby trigger an acceleration of expense) would 'encourage' the employee to stop saving (and thereby create a reversal of any expense already charged).

The broad effect of the January 2008 amendment to IFRS 2 (see 1.2 above) was to remove this perceived anomaly from the standard.

However, following the publication of the January 2008 amendment, it became apparent that the concept of the 'non-vesting' condition was not clear. This resulted in differing views on the appropriate classification of certain types of condition depending on whether or not they were considered to be measures of the entity's performance or activities and hence performance vesting conditions.

The Interpretations Committee took a number of the above issues onto its agenda as part of a wider project on vesting and non-vesting conditions. Where the issues were not addressed through the IASB's *Annual Improvements to IFRSs 2010-2012 Cycle*, there is further discussion at 3.4 below.

3.2.2 Defining a non-vesting condition

As noted at 3.1 above, IFRS 2 defines a *vesting* condition as a condition that determines whether the entity receives the services that entitle the counterparty to receive payment in equity or cash. Performance conditions are those that require the counterparty to complete a specified period of service and specified performance targets to be met (such as a specified increase in the entity's profit over a specified period of time).

The Basis for Conclusions to IFRS 2 adds that the feature that distinguishes a performance condition from a non-vesting condition is that the former has an explicit or implicit service requirement and the latter does not. *[IFRS 2.BC171A]*.

In issuing its *Annual Improvements to IFRSs 2010-2012 Cycle* in December 2013 the IASB considered whether a definition of 'non-vesting condition' was needed. It decided that 'the creation of a stand-alone definition ... would not be the best alternative for providing clarity on this issue'. *[IFRS 2.BC364]*. Instead, it sought to provide further clarification in the Basis for Conclusions to IFRS 2, as follows:

'...the Board observed that the concept of a non-vesting condition can be inferred from paragraphs BC170-BC184 of IFRS 2, which clarify the definition of vesting conditions. In accordance with this guidance it can be inferred that a non-vesting condition is any condition that does not determine whether the entity receives the services that entitle the counterparty to receive cash, other assets or equity instruments of the entity under a share-based payment arrangement. In other words, a non-vesting condition is any condition that is not a vesting condition.' *[IFRS 2.BC364]*.

Although it is stated that the Basis for Conclusions does not form part of IFRS 2, the IASB nonetheless appears to rely on users of the standard referring to the Basis for Conclusions in order to 'infer' the definition of a non-vesting condition.

A performance metric may be a non-vesting condition rather than a vesting condition in certain circumstances. For a condition to be a performance vesting condition, it is not sufficient for the condition to be specific to the performance of the entity. There must also be an explicit or implied service condition that extends to the end of the performance period. For example, a condition that requires the entity's profit before tax or its share price to reach a minimum level, but without any requirement for the employee to remain in employment throughout the performance period, is not a performance condition but a non-vesting condition.

Specific examples of non-vesting conditions given by IFRS 2 include:

- a requirement to make monthly savings during the vesting period;
- a requirement for a commodity index to reach a minimum level;
- restrictions on the transfer of vested equity instruments; or
- an agreement not to work for a competitor after the award has vested – a 'non-compete' agreement (see 3.2.3 below). *[IFRS 2.BC171B, IG24]*.

The IASB has also clarified in the Basis for Conclusions to IFRS 2 that a condition related to a share market index target (rather than to the specific performance of the entity's own shares) is a non-vesting condition because a share market index reflects not only the performance of an entity but also that of other entities outside the group. Even where an entity's share price makes up a substantial part of the share market index, the IASB confirmed that this would still be a non-vesting condition because it reflects the performance of other, non-group, entities. *[IFRS 2.BC354-BC358]*.

Thus, whilst conditions that are not related to the performance of the entity are always, by their nature, non-vesting conditions, conditions that relate to the performance of the entity may or may not be non-vesting conditions depending on whether there is also a requirement for the counterparty to render service.

As noted at 3.1 above, the definition of a performance vesting condition was clarified and expanded in the IASB's *Annual Improvements.* The amended definition includes wording intended to clarify the extent to which the period of achieving the performance target(s) needs to coincide with the service period and states that this performance period:

(a) shall not extend beyond the end of the service period; and

(b) may start before the service period on the condition that the commencement date of the performance target is not substantially before the commencement of the service period.

During the process of finalising the amended definition, the IASB moved away from a requirement for the duration of the performance condition to fall wholly within the period of the related service requirement. In response to comments on the draft version of the *Annual Improvements,* the Board decided to clarify that the start of the period of achieving the performance target could be before the start of the service period, provided that the commencement date of the performance target was not substantially before the commencement of the service period. As stated in the definition above, however, the performance period cannot extend beyond the end of the service period.

It is interesting to note that, in the US, the EITF also considered the question of non-coterminous service and performance conditions but, unlike the IASB, reached the conclusion that a performance target that affects the vesting of a share-based payment and that could be achieved after the requisite service period is a performance condition and does not need to be reflected in the fair value of the award at grant date.[11] This was on the premise that the original definition of a performance condition in ASC 718 requires only a specified period of service. Before finalising the amendments to IFRS 2, the IASB specifically reconfirmed its own decision against the background of the US decision.[12] This will therefore be an area of difference between IFRS and US GAAP.

The late adjustment by the IASB will go some way towards removing an issue that is extremely common in practice, particularly with awards made to employees under a single scheme but at various times. The IASB cites the example of an earnings per share target as one of the areas in which respondents to the draft definitions observed that there could be a problem in practice, noting that the measure of earnings per share growth set as a performance target could often be that between the most recently published financial statements at grant date and those before the vesting date. *[IFRS 2.BC341]*. However, notwithstanding the amended definition, there clearly remains an element of judgement in the interpretation of 'substantially' as used in the definition.

There is further discussion of the accounting treatment of non-vesting conditions at 6.4 below.

3.2.3 Non-compete agreements

In some jurisdictions it is relatively common to have a non-compete clause in share-based payment arrangements so that if the counterparty starts to work for a competitor within a specified timescale, i.e. he breaches the non-compete provision, he is required to return the shares (or an equivalent amount of cash) to the entity. Generally, a non-compete provision is relevant once an individual has ceased employment with the entity and so no future service is expected to be provided to the entity. However, the non-compete provision is often found in share-based payment awards entered into while the individual is still an employee of the entity and when there is no current intention for employment to cease. There are two divergent views on how such non-compete arrangements should be accounted for under IFRS 2.

The Basis for Conclusions to IFRS 2 states that 'a share-based payment vests when the counterparty's entitlement to it is no longer conditional on future service or performance conditions. Therefore, conditions such as non-compete provisions and transfer restrictions, which apply after the counterparty has become entitled to the share-based payment, are not vesting conditions.' *[IFRS 2.BC171B]*.

One view is that, under the current definitions in the standard, this means that all non-compete agreements should be treated as non-vesting conditions with the condition reflected in the grant date fair value. Another reading of paragraph BC171B is that in some situations such arrangements meet the definition of a vesting condition and this allows any IFRS 2 expense to be reversed should the condition not be met. This view is explained further below. The lack of clarity in the standard as currently drafted means that there is diversity in practice. The issue has been referred to the Interpretations Committee and to the IASB.

Those who take the view that a non-compete arrangement is not always a non-vesting condition read paragraph BC171B as distinguishing between non-compete clauses which apply after the counterparty has become entitled to an award (a non-vesting condition) and those that, by implication, apply before the counterparty has become entitled to an award (a vesting condition). Broadly, therefore, if an employee has been given shares at the start of a non-compete period he is entitled to them (a non-vesting condition), but if the shares are retained by the entity or held in escrow, the employee is not entitled to the shares until the end of the non-compete period (a vesting condition).

This view may be difficult to reconcile with IFRS 2 as currently drafted because:

- it requires the reference to 'entitlement' to an award to be read as including a contingent obligation to forfeit the share, which is not in accordance with the general approach of IFRS 2; and
- it requires the words 'which apply after the counterparty has become entitled to the share-based payment' to be read with an implied emphasis on the word 'after', so as to distinguish it from an implied (unstated) alternative scenario in which the conditions apply *before* the counterparty becomes entitled to the share-based payment. A more natural reading is perhaps to consider these words as describing all non-compete agreements and transfer restrictions.

The classification of a non-compete provision remains a potential agenda item for the IASB (see 3.4 below).

3.3 Vesting period

The *vesting period* is the period during which all the specified vesting conditions of a share-based payment arrangement are to be satisfied. *[IFRS 2 Appendix A]*. This is not the same as the exercise period or the life of the option, as illustrated by Example 32.1 below.

Example 32.1: Meaning of 'vesting period' – award with vesting conditions only

An employee is awarded options that can be exercised at any time between three and ten years from the date of the award, provided the employee remains in service for at least three years from the date of the award. For this award, the vesting period is three years; the exercise period is seven years; and the life of the option is ten years. However, as discussed further in 8 below, for the purposes of calculating the fair value of the award under IFRS 2, the life of the award is taken as the period ending with the date on which the counterparty is most likely actually to exercise the option, which may be some time before the full ten year life expires.

It is also important to distinguish between vesting conditions and other restrictions on the exercise of options and/or trading in shares, as illustrated by Example 32.2 below.

Example 32.2: Meaning of 'vesting period' – award with vesting and non-vesting conditions

An employee is awarded options that can be exercised at any time between five and ten years from the date of the award, provided the employee remains in service for at least three years from the date of the award. In this case, the vesting period remains three years as in Example 32.1 above, provided that the employee's entitlement to the award becomes absolute at the end of three years – in other words, the employee does not have to provide any services to the entity in years 4 and 5. The restriction on exercise of the award in the period after vesting is a non-vesting condition, which would be reflected in the original valuation of the award at the date of grant (see 4, 5 and 8 below).

The accounting implications of vesting conditions, non-vesting conditions and vesting periods for equity-settled transactions are discussed in 4 to 7 below and for cash-settled transactions in 9 below.

3.4 Vesting and non-vesting conditions: issues referred to the Interpretations Committee and the IASB

In January 2010 the Interpretations Committee added to its agenda a request for clarification of the following:

- the basis on which vesting conditions, especially performance conditions, can be distinguished from non-vesting conditions, especially the distinction between a service condition, a performance condition and a non-vesting condition; and
- the interaction of multiple conditions.

The amendments to IFRS 2 published in December 2013 as part of the IASB's *Annual Improvements to IFRSs 2010-2012 Cycle* were intended to address the first bullet point together with related application issues that had been raised with the Interpretations Committee (see 3.1 and 3.2 above).

In addition to considering matters subsequently addressed by the IASB in the *Annual Improvements*, the Interpretations Committee tentatively decided at its meetings in July and September 2010[13] that a non-compete provision should be presumed to be a 'contingent feature' – a term not defined in IFRS 2.[14]

The Interpretations Committee subsequently concluded that the classification of a non-compete provision and the question of how to account for the interaction of multiple vesting conditions should be referred to the IASB.[15] In September 2011 the IASB agreed that these issues should be considered as future agenda items.[16]

The IASB has since launched and concluded a research project into IFRS 2 (see 1.2.1 above). Both the conclusions relating to this project and the IASB's draft work plan resulting from the 2015 Agenda Consultation seem to indicate that further discussion of these IFRS 2 matters by the IASB is unlikely – even though the issues continue to result in some diversity in practice (see also 3.2.3 above and 6.3.6 to 6.3.7 below).[17]

4 EQUITY-SETTLED TRANSACTIONS – OVERVIEW

4.1 Summary of accounting treatment

The detailed provisions of IFRS 2 are complex, but their key points can be summarised as follows.

(a) All equity-settled transactions are measured at fair value. However, transactions with employees are normally measured using a 'grant date model' (i.e. the transaction is recorded at the fair value of the equity instrument at the date when it is originally granted), whereas transactions with non-employees are normally measured using a 'service date model' (i.e. the transaction is recorded at the fair value of the goods or services received at the date they are received). As noted in 3 above, all transactions, however *measured*, are *recognised* using a 'service date model' (see 5 below).

(b) Where an award is made subject to future fulfilment of conditions, a 'market condition' (i.e. one related to the market price of the entity's equity instruments) or a 'non-vesting condition' (i.e. one that is neither a service condition nor a performance condition) is taken into account in determining the fair value of the award. However, the effect of conditions other than market or non-vesting conditions is ignored in determining the fair value of the award (see 3 above and 6 below).

(c) Where an award is made subject to future fulfilment of vesting conditions, its cost is recognised over the service period during which the conditions are fulfilled (see 3 above and 6 below). The corresponding credit entry is recorded within equity (see 4.2 below).

(d) Until an equity instrument has vested (i.e. the entitlement to it is no longer conditional on future service) any amounts recorded are in effect contingent and will be adjusted if more or fewer awards vest than were originally anticipated to do so. However, an equity instrument awarded subject to a market condition or a non-vesting condition is considered to vest irrespective of whether or not that market or non-vesting condition is fulfilled, provided that all other vesting conditions (if any) are satisfied (see 6 below).

(e) No adjustments are made, either before or after vesting, to reflect the fact that an award has no value to the person entitled to it e.g. in the case of a share option, because the option exercise price is above the current market price of the share (see 6.1.1 and 6.1.3 below).

(f) If an equity instrument is cancelled, whether by the entity or the counterparty (see (g) below) before vesting, any amount remaining to be expensed is charged in full at that point (see 7.4 below). If an equity instrument is modified before vesting (e.g. in the case of a share option, by changing the performance conditions or the exercise price), the financial statements must continue to show a cost for at least the fair value of the original instrument, as measured at the original grant date, together with any excess of the fair value of the modified instrument over that of the original instrument, as measured at the date of modification (see 7.3 below).

(g) Where an award lapses during the vesting period due to a failure by the counterparty to satisfy a non-vesting condition within the counterparty's control, or a failure by the entity to satisfy a non-vesting condition within the entity's control, the lapse of the award is accounted for as if it were a cancellation (see (f) above and 6.4.3 below).

(h) In determining the cost of an equity-settled transaction under IFRS 2, whether the entity satisfies its obligations under the transaction with a fresh issue of shares or by purchasing own shares in the financial markets is completely irrelevant to the charge in profit or loss, although there is clearly a difference in the cash flows. Where own shares are purchased, they are accounted for as treasury shares under IAS 32 (see 2.2.4.H above and Chapter 45 at 9). *[IFRS 2.BC330-333]*.

The requirements summarised in (d) to (g) above can have the effect that IFRS 2 requires a cost to be recorded for an award that ultimately has no value to the counterparty, because the award either does not vest or vests but is not exercised. These rather counter-intuitive requirements of IFRS 2 are in part 'anti-abuse' provisions to prevent entities from applying a 'selective' grant date model, whereby awards that increase in value after grant date remain measured at grant date while awards that decrease in value are remeasured. This is discussed further in the detailed analysis at 5 to 7 below.

4.2 The credit entry

As noted at (c) in the summary in 4.1 above, the basic accounting entry for an equity-settled share-based payment transaction is: debit profit or loss for the period (employee costs), credit equity.

IFRS 2 does not prescribe the component of equity to which the credit should be taken. The IASB presumably adopted this non-prescriptive approach so as to ensure there was no conflict between, on the one hand, the basic requirement of IFRS 2 that there should be a credit in equity and, on the other, the legal requirements of various jurisdictions as to exactly how that credit should be allocated within equity. Depending on the requirements of the particular jurisdiction, it might be appropriate to take the credit to retained earnings or to a separate component of equity or entities may be able to make a policy choice.

Occasionally there will be a credit to profit or loss (see for instance Example 32.11 at 6.2.4 below) and a corresponding reduction in equity.

In some arrangements the share-based payment transaction will be settled in equity instruments of a subsidiary of the reporting entity. This is most commonly the case where the subsidiary is partly-owned with traded shares held by external shareholders. In the consolidated financial statements, the question arises as to whether the credit entry for such transactions should be presented as a non-controlling interest (NCI) or as part of the equity attributable to the shareholders of the parent. This is discussed further in Chapter 7 at 4.5.

5 EQUITY-SETTLED TRANSACTIONS – COST OF AWARDS

5.1 Cost of awards – overview

The general measurement rule in IFRS 2 is that an entity must measure the goods or services received, and the corresponding increase in equity, directly, at the fair value of the goods or services received, unless that fair value cannot be estimated reliably. If the fair value of the goods or services received cannot be estimated reliably, the entity must measure their value, and the corresponding increase in equity, indirectly, by reference to the fair value of the equity instruments granted. *[IFRS 2.10]*. 'Fair value' is defined as the amount for which an asset could be exchanged, a liability settled, or an equity instrument granted could be exchanged, between knowledgeable, willing parties in an arm's length transaction. *[IFRS 2 Appendix A]*. IFRS 2 has its own specific rules in relation to determining the fair value of share-based payments which differ from the more general fair value measurement requirements in IFRS 13 – *Fair Value Measurement* (see 5.5 below). *[IFRS 2.6A]*.

On their own, the general measurement principles of IFRS 2 would suggest that the reporting entity must determine in each case whether the fair value of the equity instruments granted or that of the goods or services received is more reliably determinable. However, IFRS 2 goes on to clarify that:

- in the case of transactions with employees, the fair value of the equity instruments must be used (see 5.2 below), except in those extremely rare cases where it is not possible to measure this fair value reliably, when the intrinsic value of the equity instruments may be used instead (see 5.5 below); but
- in the case of transactions with non-employees, there is a rebuttable presumption that the fair value of the goods or services provided is more reliably determinable (see 5.4 below).

Moreover, transactions with employees are measured at the date of grant (see 5.2 below), whereas those with non-employees are measured at the date when goods or services are received (see 5.4 below).

The overall position can be summarised by the following matrix.

Counterparty	**Measurement basis**	**Measurement date**	**Recognition date**
Employee	Fair value of equity instruments awarded	Grant date	Service date
Non-employee	Fair value of goods or services received	Service date	Service date

The Basis for Conclusions addresses the issue of why the accounting treatment for apparently identical transactions should, in effect, depend on the identity of the counterparty.

The main argument put forward to justify the approach adopted for transactions with employees is essentially that, once an award has been agreed, the value of the services provided pursuant to the transaction does not change significantly with the value of the award. *[IFRS 2.BC88-96]*. However, some might question this proposition, on the grounds that employees are more likely to work harder when the value of their options is rising than when it has sunk irretrievably.

As regards transactions with non-employees, the IASB offers two main arguments for the use of measurement at service date.

The first is that, if the counterparty is not firmly committed to delivering the goods or services, the counterparty would consider whether the fair value of the equity instruments at the delivery date is sufficient payment for the goods or services when deciding whether to deliver the goods or services. This suggests that there is a high correlation between the fair value of the equity instruments at the date the goods or services are received and the fair value of those goods or services. *[IFRS 2.BC126]*. This argument is clearly vulnerable to the challenge that it has no relevance where (as would more likely be the case) the counterparty is firmly committed to delivering the goods or services.

The second is that non-employees generally provide services over a short period commencing some time after grant date, whereas employees generally provide services over an extended period beginning on the grant date. This leads to a concern that transactions with non-employees could be entered into well in advance of the due date for delivery of goods or services. If an entity were able to measure the expense of such a transaction at the grant date fair value, the result, assuming that the entity's share price rises, would be to understate the cost of goods and services delivered. *[IFRS 2.BC126-127]*.

The true reason for the IASB's approach may have been political as much as theoretical. One effect of a grant date measurement model is that, applied to a grant of share options that is eventually exercised, it 'freezes' the accounting cost at the (typically) lower fair value at the date of grant. This excludes from the post-grant financial statements the increased cost and volatility that would be associated with a model that constantly remeasured the award to fair value until exercise date. The IASB might well have perceived it as a marginally easier task to persuade the corporate sector of the merits of a 'lower cost, zero volatility' approach as opposed to a 'fair value at exercise date' model (such as is used for cash-settled awards – see 9 below).

The price to be paid in accounting terms for the grant date model is that, when an award falls in value after grant date, it continues to be recognised at its higher grant date value. It is therefore quite possible that, during a period of general economic downturn, financial statements will show significant costs for options granted in previous years, but which are currently worthless. This could well lead to (in fact, sometimes groundless) accusations of rewarding management for failure.

5.2 Transactions with employees

These will comprise the great majority of transactions accounted for under IFRS 2, and include all remuneration in the form of shares, share options and any other form of reward settled in equity instruments of the entity or a member of its group.

5.2.1 Who is an 'employee'?

Given the difference between the accounting treatment of equity-settled transactions with employees and that of those with non-employees, it is obviously important for IFRS 2 to define what is meant by employees. In fact IFRS 2 strictly refers to 'employees and others providing similar services' *[IFRS 2.11]*, who are defined as individuals who render personal services to the entity and either:

(a) the individuals are regarded as employees for legal or tax purposes;

(b) the individuals work for the entity under its direction in the same way as individuals who are regarded as employees for legal or tax purposes; or

(c) the services rendered are similar to those rendered by employees.

The term encompasses all management personnel, i.e. those persons having authority and responsibility for planning, directing and controlling the activities of the entity, including non-executive directors. *[IFRS 2 Appendix A]*.

The implication of (a) and (b) above is that it is not open to an entity to argue that an individual who is not an employee as a matter of law is therefore automatically a non-employee for the purposes of IFRS 2.

The implication of (b) and (c) above is that, where a third party provides services pursuant to a share-based payment transaction that could be provided by an employee (e.g. where an external IT consultant works alongside an in-house IT team), that third party is treated as an employee rather than a non-employee for the purposes of IFRS 2.

Conversely, however, where an entity engages a consultant to undertake work for which there is not an existing in-house function, the implication is that such an individual is not regarded as an employee. In other words, in our view, the reference in (c) to 'services ... similar to those rendered by employees' is to services rendered by employees that the entity actually has, rather than to employees that the entity might have if it were to recruit them. Otherwise, the distinction in IFRS 2 between employees and non-employees would have no effect, since it would always be open to an entity to argue that it could employ someone to undertake any task instead of engaging a contractor.

Exceptionally there might be cases where the same individual is engaged in both capacities. For example, a director of the entity might also be a partner in a firm of lawyers and be engaged in that latter capacity to advise the entity on a particular issue. It might be more appropriate to regard payment for the legal services as made to a non-employee rather than to an employee.

Related questions of interpretation arise where an award is made to an employee of an associate or a joint venture (see 12.9 below).

The effect of a change of status from employee to non-employee (or *vice versa*) is addressed at 5.4.1 below.

5.2.2 *Basis of measurement*

As noted above, IFRS 2 requires equity-settled transactions with employees to be measured by reference to the fair value of the equity instruments granted at 'grant date' (see 5.3 below). *[IFRS 2.11]*. IFRS 2 asserts that this approach is necessary because shares, share options and other equity instruments are typically only part of a larger remuneration package, such that it would not be practicable to determine the value of the work performed in consideration for the cash element of the total package, the benefit-in-kind element, the share option element and so on. *[IFRS 2.12]*.

In essence, this is really an anti-avoidance provision. The underlying concern is that, if an entity were able to value options by reference to the services provided for them, it might assert that the value of those services was zero, on the argument that its personnel are already so handsomely rewarded by the non-equity elements of their remuneration package (such as cash and health benefits), that no additional services are (or indeed could be) obtained by granting options.

5.3 Grant date

As noted above, IFRS 2 requires equity-settled transactions with employees to be accounted for at fair value at grant date, defined as 'the date at which the entity and another party (including an employee) agree to a share-based payment arrangement, being when the entity and the counterparty have a shared understanding of the terms and conditions of the arrangement'. *[IFRS 2 Appendix A]*.

The determination of grant date is critical to the measurement of equity-settled share-based transactions with employees, since grant date is the date at which such transactions must be measured (see 5.2 above).

In practice, it is not always clear when a mutual understanding of the award (and, therefore, grant date) has occurred. Issues of interpretation can arise as to:

- how precise the shared understanding of the terms of the award must be; and
- exactly what level of communication between the reporting entity and the counterparty is sufficient to ensure that there is the appropriate degree of agreement and 'shared understanding'.

As a consequence, the determination of the grant date is often difficult in practice. We discuss the following issues in more detail in the sections below:

- basic determination of grant date (see 5.3.1 below);
- the communication of awards to employees and the rendering of services in advance of grant date (see 5.3.2 below);
- awards where the exercise price depends on a formula or on a future share price (see 5.3.3 below);
- awards where the exercise price is paid in shares (see 5.3.4 below);
- an award of equity instruments to a fixed monetary value (see 5.3.5 below);
- awards over a fixed pool of shares (including 'last man standing' arrangements) (see 5.3.6 below);
- awards with multiple service and performance periods (see 5.3.7 below);
- awards subject to modification or discretionary re-assessment by the entity after the original grant date (see 5.3.8 below);
- mandatory or discretionary awards to 'good leavers' (see 5.3.9 below); and
- shares issued by special purpose acquisition companies (see 5.3.10 below).

The grant date for 'matching' awards (i.e. arrangements where an additional award of shares is granted to match an initial cash bonus or award of shares) is discussed at 15.1 below.

5.3.1 Determination of grant date

IFRS 2 and the accompanying implementation guidance emphasise that a grant occurs only when all the conditions are known and agreed by the parties to the arrangement and any required approval process has been completed. Thus, for example, if an entity makes an award 'in principle' to an employee of options whose terms are subject to review or approval by a remuneration committee or the shareholders, 'grant date' is the later date when the necessary formalities have been completed. *[IFRS 2 Appendix A, IG1-3]*.

The implementation guidance to IFRS 2 emphasises that the word 'agree' is 'used in its usual sense, which means that there must be both an offer and an acceptance of that offer'. Therefore, there cannot be a grant unless an offer by one party has been accepted by the other party. The guidance notes that agreement will be explicit in some cases (e.g. if an agreement has to be signed), but in others it might be implicit, such as when an employee starts to deliver services for the award. *[IFRS 2.IG2]*.

The counterparty's agreement to an offer might be particularly difficult to determine when it is implicit rather than explicit. For example, if an award required both the rendering of service and a subscription payment (other than a minimal one) by the employee, it is likely that the employee's agreement, and hence the grant date of the award, would coincide with the payment date – provided this occurs shortly after the offer date. If, however, the employee had the choice at the offer date of deferring payment until a much later date and could therefore decide whether the entity's subsequent performance justified his payment, then it is more likely that grant date would be the date on which the services commenced. Determination of when the counterparty has agreed to an offer will often be an area of judgement that depends on the precise facts and circumstances of a particular situation.

The implementation guidance to IFRS 2 further notes that employees may begin rendering services in consideration for an award before it has been formally ratified. For example, a new employee might join the entity on 1 January 2017 and be granted options relating to performance for a period beginning on that date, but subject to formal approval by the remuneration committee at its quarterly meeting on 15 March 2017. In that case, the entity would typically begin expensing the award from 1 January 2017 based on a best estimate of its fair value, but would subsequently adjust that estimate so that the ultimate cost of the award was its actual fair value at 15 March 2017. *[IFRS 2.IG4]*. This reference to formal approval could be construed as indicating that, in fact, IFRS 2 requires not merely that there is a mutual understanding of the award (which might well have been in existence since 1 January 2017), but also that the entity has completed all processes necessary to make the award a legally binding agreement.

In practice, many situations are much less clear-cut than the examples given in the implementation guidance. For example, if a remuneration committee has discretion over some aspects of an award and whether it vests, does that mean that there is not a shared understanding until the vesting date? Similarly, does the counterparty need to have full quantification of every aspect of an award (performance targets, exercise price, etc.) or would an understanding of the formula for calculating performance or price be sufficient?

Some of these practical interpretation issues are considered further in the sections below.

5.3.2 Communication of awards to employees and services in advance of grant date

As discussed at 5.3.1 above, the implementation guidance to IFRS 2 indicates that, in order for a grant to have been made, there must not merely be a mutual understanding of the terms – including the conditions attached to the award as discussed further in the sections that follow – but there must also be a legally enforceable arrangement. Thus, if an award requires board or shareholder approval for it to be legally binding on the reporting entity, for the purposes of IFRS 2 it has not been granted until such approval has been given, even if the terms of the award are fully understood at an earlier date. However, if services are effectively being rendered for an award from a date earlier than the grant date as defined in IFRS 2, the cost of the award should be recognised over a period starting with that earlier date. *[IFRS 2.IG4]*. In our view, this approach applies in situations where there is a constructive obligation or a valid expectation of an award but where the precise terms and conditions of an award have yet to be confirmed as well as to situations where formal approval does not take place until a later date.

The implications of this requirement are illustrated in Example 32.3 below for a situation where formal approval of an award is delayed. It is important, however, to retain a sense of proportion. In cases where the share price is not particularly volatile, whether the grant date is, say, 1 January or 1 April may not make a great difference to the valuation of the award, particularly when set beside the range of acceptable valuations resulting from the use of estimates in the valuation model.

Example 32.3: Determination of grant date

Scenario 1

On 1 January 2017 an entity advises employees of the terms of a share award designed to reward performance over the three years ended 31 December 2019. The award is subject to board approval, which is given on 1 March 2017. Grant date is 1 March 2017. However, the cost of the award would be recognised over the three year period beginning 1 January 2017, since the employees would have effectively been rendering service for the award from that date.

Scenario 2

On 1 January 2017 an entity's board resolves to implement a share scheme designed to reward performance over the three years ended 31 December 2019. The award is notified to employees on 1 March 2017. Grant date is again 1 March 2017. *Prima facie*, in this case, the cost of the award would be recognised over the two years and ten months period beginning 1 March 2017, since the employees could not be regarded as rendering service in January and February for an award of which they were not aware at that time.

However, if a similar award is made each year, and according to a similar timescale, there might be an argument that, during January and February 2017, employees are rendering service for an award of which there is high expectation, and that the cost should therefore, as in Scenario 1, be recognised over the full three year period. The broader issue of the accounting treatment for awards of which there is a high expectation is addressed in the discussion of matching share awards at 15.1 below.

Scenario 3

On 1 January 2017 an entity advises employees of the terms of a share award designed to reward performance over the three years ended 31 December 2019. The award is subject to board approval, which is given on 1 March 2017. However, in giving such approval, the Board makes some changes to the performance conditions as originally communicated to employees on 1 January. The revised terms of the award are communicated to employees on 1 April 2017. Grant date is 1 April 2017. However, the cost of the award would be recognised over the three year period beginning 1 January 2017, since the employees would have effectively been rendering service for the award from that date.

Examples of situations where an employee might render service in advance of the IFRS 2 grant date because the precise conditions of an award are outstanding are considered at 5.3.3 to 5.3.7 and at 15.4.1 below.

5.3.3 Exercise price or performance target dependent on a formula or future share price

Some share plans define the exercise price not in absolute terms, but as a factor of the share price. For example, the price might be expressed as:

- a percentage of the share price at exercise date; or
- a percentage of the lower of the share price at grant date and at exercise date.

The effect of this is that, although the actual exercise price is not known until the date of exercise, both the entity and the counterparty already have a shared understanding of how the price will be calculated and it is possible to estimate the outcome on an ongoing basis without the need for additional approval or inputs.

A similar approach might be applied in the setting of performance targets i.e. they are set by reference to a formula rather than in absolute terms and so do not require further input by the entity or its remuneration committee, for example.

In order for there to be a shared understanding and a grant date, the formula or method of determining the outcome needs to be sufficiently clear and objective to allow both the entity and the counterparty to make an estimate of the outcome of the award during the vesting period. Accordingly, in our view, grant date is the date on which the terms and conditions (including the formula for calculating the exercise price or performance target) are determined sufficiently clearly and agreed by the entity and the counterparty, subject to the matters discussed at 5.3.2 above.

5.3.4 Exercise price paid in shares (net settlement of award)

Some share awards allow the exercise price to be paid in shares. In practical terms, this means that the number of shares delivered to the counterparty will be the total 'gross' number of shares awarded less as many shares as have, at the date of exercise, a fair value equal to the strike price.

In our view, this situation is analogous to that in 5.3.3 above in that, whilst the absolute 'net' number of shares awarded will not be known until the date of exercise, the basis on which that 'net' number will be determined is established in advance. Accordingly, in our view, grant date is the date on which the terms and conditions (including the ability to surrender shares to a fair value equal to the exercise price) are determined and agreed by the entity and the counterparty, subject to the matters discussed at 5.3.2 above.

Such a scheme could be analysed as a share-settled share appreciation right (whereby the employee receives shares to the value of the excess of the value of the shares given over the exercise price), which is treated as an equity-settled award under IFRS 2.

Awards settled in shares net of a cash amount to meet an employee's tax obligation are considered further at 14.3 below.

5.3.5 Award of equity instruments to a fixed monetary value

Some entities may grant employees awards of shares to a fixed value. For example, an entity might award as many shares as are worth €100,000, with the number of shares being calculated by reference to the share price as at the vesting date. The number of shares ultimately received will not be known until the vesting date. This begs the question of whether such an award can be regarded as having been granted until that date, on the argument that it is only then that the number of shares to be delivered – a key term of the award – is known, and therefore there cannot be a 'shared understanding' of the terms of the award until that later date.

In our view, however, this situation is analogous to those in 5.3.3 and 5.3.4 above. Although the absolute number of shares awarded will not be known until the vesting date, the basis on which that number will be determined is established in advance in a manner sufficiently clear and objective to allow an ongoing estimate by the entity and by the counterparty of the number of awards expected to vest. Accordingly, in our view, grant date is the date on which the terms and conditions are determined sufficiently clearly and agreed by the entity and the counterparty, subject to the matters discussed at 5.3.2 above.

The measurement of such awards raises further issues of interpretation, which we discuss at 8.10 below.

5.3.6 Awards over a fixed pool of shares (including 'last man standing' arrangements)

An award over a fixed pool of shares is sometimes granted to a small group of, typically senior, employees. Such awards might involve an initial allocation of shares to each individual but also provide for the redistribution of each employee's shares to the other participants should any individual leave employment before the end of the vesting period. This is often referred to as a 'last man standing' arrangement.

The accounting requirements of IFRS 2 for such an arrangement are unclear. In the absence of specific guidance, several interpretations are possible and we believe that an entity may make an accounting policy choice, provided that choice is applied consistently to all such arrangements.

The first approach is based on the view that the unit of account is all potential shares to be earned by the individual employee and that, from the outset, each employee has a full understanding of the terms and conditions of both the initial award and the reallocation arrangements. This means that there is a grant on day one with each individual's award being valued on the basis of:

- that employee's initial allocation of shares; plus
- an additional award with a non-vesting condition relating to the potential reallocation of other participants' shares.

Under this approach, the departure of an employee will be accounted for as a forfeiture and any cost reversed as the service condition will not have been met (see 6.1.2 below), but the redistribution of that individual's shares to the other employees will have no accounting impact. This approach is likely to result in a total expense that is higher than the number of shares awarded multiplied by the grant date price per share.

The second approach, which we believe is consistent with US GAAP, also considers the individual employee's award to be the unit of account. Under this approach, there is an initial grant to all the employees and it is only these awards for which the fair value is measured at the date of the initial grant. Any subsequent reallocations of shares should be accounted for as a forfeiture of the original award and a completely new grant to the remaining employees. This approach accounts only for the specific number of shares that have been allocated to the individual employee as at the end of each reporting period. No account is taken in this approach of shares that might be allocated to the individual employee in the future due to another employee's forfeiture, even though the reallocation formula is known to the individual employees at the initial grant date.

A third view, which takes a pragmatic approach in the light of the issues arising from the two approaches outlined above, is to account for the award on the basis of the total pool of shares granted rather than treating the individual employee as the unit of account. In our view this approach is likely to be materially acceptable for many arrangements where the pool of shares relates to the same small number of participants from the outset. Under this approach, the fair value of the total pool of shares is measured at the grant date (day one) with the non-vesting condition effectively ignored for valuation purposes. Subsequent forfeitures and reallocations would have no effect on the accounting.

There is a distinction between the 'last man standing' arrangement described above and a situation where an entity designates a fixed pool of shares to be used for awards to employees but where the allocation of leavers' shares is discretionary rather than pre-determined. In this situation, the valuation of the initial award would not take account of any potential future reallocations. If an employee left employment during the vesting period, that individual's award would be accounted for as a forfeiture and any reallocation of that individual's shares would be accounted for as a new grant with the fair value determined at the new grant date (i.e. a similar accounting treatment to that in approach two above).

A further type of award relating to a fixed pool of shares is one where an entity makes an award over a fixed number or percentage of its shares to a particular section of its workforce, the final allocation of the pool being made to those employed at the vesting date. In such an arrangement, some employees will typically join and leave the scheme during the original vesting period which will lead to changes in each employee's allocation of shares. Although employees are aware of the existence, and some of the terms, of the arrangement at the outset, the fact that there is no objective formula (see 5.3.3 to 5.3.5 above) for determining the number of shares that each individual will ultimately receive means that there is no grant under IFRS 2 until the date of final allocation. However, because the employees render service under the arrangement in advance of the grant date – either from day one or from a later joining date – the entity should estimate the fair value of the award to each individual from the date services commence and expense this over the full service period of the award with a final truing up of the expense to the fair value of the award at the eventual grant date (see 5.3.2 above).

This has the effect that, where an entity decides to set aside a bonus pool of a fixed amount of cash, say £1 million, with the allocation to individual employees to be made at a later date, there is a known fixed cost of £1 million. However, where an entity decides to set aside a bonus pool of a fixed number of shares, with the allocation to individual employees to be made at a later date, the final cost is not determined until the eventual grant date.

5.3.7 Awards with multiple service and performance periods

Entities frequently make awards that cover more than one reporting period, but with different performance conditions for each period, rather than a single cumulative target for the whole vesting period. In such cases, the grant date may depend on the precision with which the terms of the award are communicated to employees, as illustrated by Example 32.4 below.

Example 32.4: Awards with multiple service and performance periods

Scenario 1

On 1 January 2017, the entity enters into a share-based payment arrangement with an employee. The employee is informed that the maximum potential award is 40,000 shares, 10,000 of which will vest on 31 December 2017, and 10,000 more on each of 31 December 2018, 31 December 2019 and 31 December 2020. Vesting of each tranche of 10,000 shares is conditional on:

(a) the employee having been in continuous service until 31 December of the relevant year; and

(b) revenue targets for each of those four years, as communicated to the employee on 1 January 2017, having been attained.

In this case, the terms of the award are clearly understood by both parties at 1 January 2017, and this is therefore the grant date under IFRS 2 (subject to issues such as any requirement for later formal approval – see 5.3 to 5.3.2 above). The cost of the award would be recognised using a 'graded' vesting approach – see 6.2.2 below.

Scenario 2

On 1 January 2017, the entity enters into a share-based payment arrangement with an employee. The employee is informed that the maximum potential award is 40,000 shares, 10,000 of which will vest on 31 December 2017, and 10,000 more on each of 31 December 2018, 31 December 2019 and 31 December 2020. Vesting of each tranche of 10,000 shares is conditional on:

(a) the employee having been in continuous service until 31 December of the relevant year; and

(b) revenue targets for each of those four years, to be communicated to the employee on 1 January of each year in respect of that year only, having been attained.

In this case, in our view, as at 1 January 2017, there is a clear shared understanding only of the terms of the first tranche of 10,000 shares that will potentially vest on 31 December 2017. There is no clear understanding of the terms of the tranches potentially vesting in 2018 to 2020 because their vesting depends on revenue targets for those years which have not yet been set.

Accordingly, each of the four tranches of 10,000 shares has a separate grant date (and, therefore, a separate measurement date) – i.e. 1 January 2017, 1 January 2018, 1 January 2019 and 1 January 2020 – and a vesting period of one year from the relevant grant date.

A variation on the above two scenarios which is seen quite frequently in practice is an award where the target is quantified for the first year and the targets for subsequent years depend on a formula-based increase in the year 1 target. The formula is set at the same time as the year 1 target. Whether the accounting treatment for scenario 1 above or scenario 2 above is the more appropriate in such a situation is, in our view, a matter of judgement depending on the precise terms of the arrangement (see 5.3.3 above).

5.3.8 Awards subject to modification by entity after original grant date

As noted at 5.3.1 above, some employee share awards are drafted in terms that give the entity discretion to modify the detailed terms of the scheme after grant date. Some have questioned whether this effectively means that the date originally determined as the 'grant date' is not in fact the grant date as defined in IFRS 2, on the grounds that the entity's right to modify means that the terms are not in fact understood by both parties in advance.

In our view, this is very often not an appropriate analysis. If it were, it could also mean that, in some jurisdictions, nearly all share-based awards to employees would be required to be measured at vesting date, which clearly was not the IASB's intention.

However, the assessment of whether or not an intervention by the entity after grant date constitutes a modification is often difficult. Some situations commonly encountered in practice are considered in the sections below. See also the discussion at 3.1.1 above relating to the clawback of awards.

5.3.8.A Significant equity restructuring or transactions

Many schemes contain provisions designed to ensure that the value of awards is maintained following a major capital restructuring (such as a share split or share consolidation – see 7.8 below) or a major transaction with shareholders as a whole (such as the insertion of a new holding company over an existing group (see 12.8 below), a major share buyback or the payment of a special dividend). These provisions will either specify the adjustments to be made in a particular situation or, alternatively, may allow the entity to make such discretionary adjustments as it sees fit in order to maintain the value of awards. In some cases the exercise of such discretionary powers may be relatively mechanistic (e.g. the adjustment of the number of shares subject to options following a share split). In other cases, more subjectivity will be involved (e.g. in determining whether a particular dividend is a 'special' dividend for the purposes of the scheme).

In our view, where the scheme rules specify the adjustments to be made or where there is a legal requirement to make adjustments in order to remedy any dilution that would otherwise arise, the implementation of such adjustments would not result in the recognition of any incremental IFRS 2 fair value. This assumes that the adjustment would simply operate on an automatic basis to put the holders of awards back to the position that they would have been in had there not been a restructuring and hence there would be no difference in the fair value of the awards before and after the restructuring (or other specified event).

However, where there is no such explicit requirement in the scheme rules or under relevant legislation, we believe that there should be a presumption that the exercise of the entity's discretionary right to modify is a 'modification' as defined in IFRS 2. In such a situation, the fair values before and after the modification may differ and any incremental fair value should be expensed over the remaining vesting period (see 7.3 below).

5.3.8.B Interpretation of general terms

More problematic might be the exercise of any discretion by the entity or its remuneration committee to interpret the more general terms of a scheme in deciding whether performance targets have been met and therefore whether, and to what extent, an award should vest. Suppose, for example, that an entity makes an award to its executives with a market performance condition based on total shareholder return (TSR) with a maximum payout if the entity is in the top quartile of a peer group of 100 entities (i.e. it is ranked between 1 and 25 in the peer group).

It might be that the entity is ranked 26 until shortly before the end of the performance period, at which point the entity ranked 25 suddenly announces that it is in financial difficulties and ceases trading shortly afterwards. This then means that the reporting entity moves up from 26 to 25 in the rankings. However, the entity might take the view that, in the circumstances, it could not be considered as having truly been ranked 25 in the peer group, so that a maximum payout is not justified.

In this case, the entity's intervention might be considered to be a modification. However, as the effect would be to reduce the fair value of the award, it would have no impact on the accounting treatment (see 7.3.2 below).

If such an intervention were not regarded as a modification, then the results might be different depending on the nature of the award. Where an award is subject to a market condition, as here, or to a non-vesting condition, an expense might well have to be recognised in any event, if all the non-market vesting conditions (e.g. service) were satisfied – see 6.3 and 6.4 below.

However, suppose that the award had been based on a non-market performance condition, such as an EPS target, which was met, but only due to a gain of an unusual, non-recurring nature, such as the revaluation of PP&E for tax purposes, giving rise to a deferred tax credit. The remuneration committee concludes that this should be ignored, with the effect that the award does not vest. If this is regarded as the exercise of a pre-existing right to ensure that the award vests only if 'normal' EPS reaches a given level, then there has been no modification. On this analysis, the award has not vested, and any expense previously recognised would be reversed. If, however, the committee's intervention is regarded as a modification, it would have no impact on the accounting treatment in this case, as the effect would be to reduce the fair value of the award and this would be ignored under the general requirements of IFRS 2 relating to modifications (see 7.3.2 below).

5.3.8.C Discretion to make further awards

Some schemes may give the entity the power to increase an award in circumstances where the recipient is considered to have delivered exceptional performance, or some such similar wording. In our view, unless the criteria for judging such exceptional performance are so clear as to be, in effect, performance conditions under IFRS 2, the presumption should be that any award made pursuant to such a clause is granted, and therefore measured, when it is made. We note at 15.1 below that there may be circumstances where an award described as 'discretionary' may not truly be so, since the entity has created an expectation amounting to a constructive obligation to make the award. However, we believe that it would be somewhat contradictory to argue that such expectations had been created in the case of an award stated to be for (undefined) exceptional performance only.

5.3.9 'Good leaver' arrangements

In some jurisdictions it is common for awards to contain a so-called 'good leaver' clause. A 'good leaver' clause is one which makes provision for an employee who leaves employment before the end of the full vesting period of the award to receive some or all of the award on leaving (see 5.3.9.A below).

In other cases, the original terms of an award will either make no reference to 'good leavers' or will not be sufficiently specific to allow the accounting treatment on cessation of employment to be an automatic outcome of the original terms of the scheme. In such cases, and where awards are made to leavers on a fully discretionary basis, the approach required by IFRS 2 differs from that required where the original terms are clear about 'good leaver' classification and entitlement (see 5.3.9.B below).

It is also increasingly common in some jurisdictions to see awards which allow the majority of participants, rather than just a few specified categories of 'good leaver', to retain all or part of an award if they leave employment during the vesting period (see 5.3.9.C below).

We refer throughout this section on 'good leavers' to an employee leaving employment, but similar considerations apply when an individual automatically becomes entitled to an award before the end of the original vesting period due to other reasons specified in the terms of the agreement, e.g. attaining a certain age or achieving a specified length of service, even if the individual remains in employment after the relevant date. In these situations, the date of full entitlement is the date on which any services – and therefore expense recognition – cease for IFRS 2 purposes.

Arrangements for a good leaver to receive all, or part, of an award on leaving employment should be distinguished from a situation where an employee leaves with no award and where forfeiture accounting is likely to apply (see 7.4.1.A below).

5.3.9.A Provision for 'good leavers' made in original terms of award

In some cases the types of person who are 'good leavers' may be explicitly defined in the original terms of the arrangement (common examples being persons who die or reach normal retirement age before the end of the full vesting period, or who work for a business unit that is sold or closed during the vesting period). In other cases, the entity may have the discretion to determine on a case-by-case basis whether a person should be treated as a 'good leaver'.

In addition, some schemes may specify the entitlement of a 'good leaver' on leaving (e.g. that the leaver receive a portion of the award pro-rata to the extent that the performance conditions have been met), whereas others leave the determination of the award to the entity at the time that the employee leaves.

Whichever situation applies, any expense relating to an award to a good leaver must be fully recognised by the leaving date because, at that point, the good leaver ceases to provide any services to the entity and any remaining conditions attached to the award will be treated as non-vesting rather than vesting conditions (see 3.2 above).

In our view, an award which vests before the end of the original vesting period due to the operation of a 'good leaver' clause is measured at the original grant date only where – under the rules of the scheme as understood by both parties at the original grant date – the award is made:

- to a person clearly identified as a 'good leaver'; and
- in an amount clearly quantified or quantifiable.

Where, as outlined above, the rules of the scheme make clear the categories of 'good leaver' and their entitlement, the entity should assess at grant date how many good leavers there are likely to be and to what extent the service period for these particular individuals is expected to be shorter than the full vesting period. The grant date fair value of the estimated awards to good leavers should be separately determined, where significant, and the expense relating to good leavers recognised over the expected reduced vesting period between grant date and leaving employment. In this situation the entity would re-estimate the number of good leavers and adjust the cumulative expense at each reporting date. This would be a change of estimate rather than a modification of the award as it would all be in accordance with the original terms and would require no discretionary decisions on the part of the entity. We would not generally expect an entity to have significant numbers of good leavers under such an arrangement.

It is important to draw a clear distinction between the IFRS 2 accounting on a straight line basis over a reduced vesting period in the above case and that on a graded vesting basis in a situation of broader entitlement as outlined at 5.3.9.C below.

5.3.9.B Discretionary awards to 'good leavers'

5.3.9.A above discusses awards where the arrangements for leavers are clear as at the original grant date of the award. However, where – as is more usually the case – the entity determines only at the time that the employee leaves either that the employee is a 'good leaver' or the amount of the award, grant date or modification date (see further below) should be taken as the later of the date on which such determination is made, or the date on which the award is notified to the employee. This is because the employee had no clear understanding at the original grant date of an automatic entitlement to equity instruments other than through full vesting of the award at the end of the full service period.

In our view, an entity should assess the appropriate accounting treatment based on the particular facts and circumstances and the extent to which the discretionary award is linked to the original award. The discretionary award at the time of leaving is considered to be either a modification of an original award in the employee's favour (for example, where vesting conditions are waived to allow an individual to keep an award) or the forfeiture of the original award and the granting of a completely new award on a discretionary basis (see 7.3 and 7.5 below).

In some cases, a good leaver will be allowed, on a discretionary basis, to keep existing awards that remain subject to performance conditions established at the original grant date. In this situation, any conditions that were previously treated as vesting conditions will become non-vesting conditions following the removal of the service requirement (see 3.1 and 3.2 above). This will be the case whether the discretionary arrangement is accounted for as the forfeiture of the old award plus a new grant or as a modification of the original award.

The non-vesting conditions will need to be reflected in the measurement of the fair value of the award as at the date of modification or new grant (although the non-vesting conditions alone will not result in any incremental fair value). Any fair value that is unrecognised as at the date of the good leaver ceasing employment will need to be expensed immediately as there is no further service period over which to recognise the expense.

There is further discussion of modifications at 7.3 below and of replacement and ex gratia awards granted on termination of employment at 7.5 below.

5.3.9.C Automatic full or pro rata entitlement on leaving employment

In some jurisdictions it is becoming increasingly common for entities to establish schemes where a significant number of the participants will potentially leave employment before the end of the full vesting period and will be allowed to keep a *pro rata* share of the award. This gives rise to a much broader category of employee than the small number of good leavers that one would generally expect under a scheme where 'good leaver' refers only to employees who die, retire or work for a business unit that is sold or closed (see 5.3.9.A above).

The substance of an arrangement where significant numbers of employees are expected to leave with a *pro rata* entitlement is that the entire award to all participants vests on a graded basis over the vesting period as a whole. So, for example, an arrangement that gives employees 360 shares at the end of three years but, whether under the rules of the scheme or by precedent, allows the majority of leavers to take a *pro rata* share – based on the number of months that have elapsed – at their date of departure, should be treated as vesting at the rate of 10 shares per month for all employees. Such an arrangement should be accounted for using the graded vesting approach illustrated at 6.2.2 below.

Some take the view that the situation outlined in the previous paragraph does not require graded vesting and that a straight-line approach may be taken because the award only vests *pro rata* if an employee leaves. Supporters of this view argue that the requirement to leave employment in order to receive the award before the end of the full vesting period is itself a substantive condition over and above the requirement to provide ongoing service. If an employee remains in employment the award only vests on completion of three years' service and there is no earlier entitlement on a *pro rata* basis. Although this treatment has some appeal, in our view it is difficult to reconcile to the standard and is not therefore an appropriate alternative accounting treatment to the graded approach outlined above.

In other cases, rather than just a *pro rata* apportionment, any good leaver will be allowed to keep the entire award regardless of when they leave employment. If this is the case, and in substance there is no required minimum service period attached to the award, then the award should be treated as immediately vested in all employees and fully expensed at the grant date.

5.3.10 Special purpose acquisition companies ('SPACs')

An increasing number of IPOs and trade sales are being achieved through the medium of special purpose acquisition companies ('SPACs'). The detailed features of SPACs may vary, but common features tend to be:

- The SPAC is established by a small number of founders, typically with expertise in selecting attractive targets for flotation or sale. The founder shares contain a term to the effect that, if a target is eventually identified and floated or sold, the holders of the founder shares will receive a greater proportion of any proceeds than other shareholders at the time of flotation.
- At a later date, other (non-founder) shareholders invest. This is frequently achieved by an IPO of the SPAC. It is typically the case that, if a specific target is not identified and agreed by a required majority of non-founder shareholders, within a finite timescale, the other (non-founder) shareholders will have their funds returned.
- The SPAC seeks a target which is then approved (or not, as the case may be) by the required majority of non-founder shareholders.

The three stages outlined above have given rise to three interpretations as to the grant date for IFRS 2 purposes.

The first view is that there is no shared understanding until the specific target is identified and agreed (the third stage above). Holders of this view argue that the substance of the founder shareholders' interest is economically equivalent to an award of shares in any target finally approved. Therefore, until the target is finally approved, there is no clarity as to the nature and value of the award to the founder shareholders.

The second view is that a shared understanding occurs at the point at which the non-founder shareholders invest (i.e. the second stage above). Holders of this view argue that a share-based payment can only occur when there has been a transfer of value from the non-founder shareholders to the founder shareholders and this cannot occur until there are some non-founder shareholders in place. However, once those non-founder shareholders are in place, there is a shared understanding that – if a transaction is subsequently approved – there will be a benefit for founder shareholders.

The third view is that a shared understanding occurs on the issue of the founder shares (i.e. the first stage above). Holders of this view argue that at that point there is a shared understanding that there will be a benefit for founder shareholders if non-founder shareholders are subsequently introduced and a transaction is subsequently approved. The benefit for founder shareholders consists both in seeking further investors and in identifying a suitable target. The founder shareholders will be actively rendering service towards these goals from the outset.

The IFRS Interpretations Committee has conducted some initial outreach research into how SPACs are currently treated in practice, but the question has not been formally discussed to date. Until such time as additional guidance is given, it seems that the diversity in practice outlined above will remain and entities should use judgement to determine an appropriate grant date based on the specific terms of the arrangement.

5.4 Transactions with non-employees

In accounting for equity-settled transactions with non-employees, the entity must adopt a rebuttable presumption that the value of the goods or services received provides the more reliable indication of the fair value of the transaction. The fair value to be used is that at the date on which the goods are obtained or the services rendered. *[IFRS 2.13]*. This implies that, where the goods or services are received on a number of dates over a period, the fair value at each date should be used, although in the case of a relatively short period there may be no great fluctuation in fair value.

If 'in rare cases' the presumption is rebutted, the entity may use as a surrogate measure the fair value of the equity instruments granted, but as at the date when the goods or services are received, not the original grant date. However, where the goods or services are received over a relatively short period where the share price does not change significantly, an average share price can be used in calculating the fair value of equity instruments granted. *[IFRS 2.13, IG5, IG6-7]*.

5.4.1 *Effect of change of status from employee to non-employee (or vice versa)*

IFRS 2 does not give specific guidance on how to account for an award when the status of the counterparty changes from employee to non-employee (or *vice versa*) but, in all other respects, the award remains unchanged. In our view, the accounting following the change of status will depend on the entity's assessment of whether or not the counterparty is performing the same or similar services before and after the change of status.

If it is concluded that the counterparty is providing the same or similar services before and after the change of status, the measurement approach remains unchanged.

However, if the services provided are substantially different, the accounting following the change of status will be determined by the counterparty's new status, as follows:

- For a change from non-employee to employee status, the expense for periods following the change should be measured as if the award had been granted at the date of change of status. This revised measurement only applies to the expense for the portion of the award that vests after the change of status and there is no effect on the expense recognised in prior periods.
- For a change from employee to non-employee status, the expense for periods following the change should be measured on the basis of the fair value of the counterparty's services as they are received – if this is reliably determinable. Otherwise, the fair value used is that of the equity instruments granted but measured at the date the services are received (see 5.4 above). There is no effect on the expense recognised in prior periods.

If the status of the counterparty changes and the terms of the award are modified in order to allow the award to continue to vest, the modification and change of status should be assessed in accordance with the general principles in IFRS 2 relating to the modification of awards (see 7.3 below).

5.5 Determining the fair value of equity instruments

As discussed in 5.2 to 5.4 above, IFRS 2 requires the following equity-settled transactions to be measured by reference to the fair value of the equity instruments issued rather than that of the goods or services received:

- all transactions with employees (except where it is impossible to determine fair value – see below); and
- transactions with non-employees where, in rare cases, the entity rebuts the presumption that the fair value of goods or services provided is more reliably measurable.

There will also be situations where the identifiable consideration received (if any) from non-employees appears to be less than the fair value of consideration given. In such cases, the cost of the unidentifiable goods or services received, if any, must be accounted for in accordance with IFRS 2 by determining the fair value of the equity instruments. This requirement is discussed at 2.2.2.C above.

For all transactions measured by reference to the fair value of the equity instruments granted, IFRS 2 requires fair value to be measured at the 'measurement date' – i.e. grant date in the case of transactions with employees and service date in the case of transactions with non-employees. *[IFRS 2 Appendix A]*. Fair value should be based on market prices if available. *[IFRS 2.16]*. In the absence of market prices, a valuation technique should be used to estimate what the market price would have been on the measurement date in an arm's length transaction between informed and willing parties. The technique used should be a recognised technique and incorporate all factors that would be taken into account by knowledgeable and willing market participants. *[IFRS 2.17]*.

Appendix B to IFRS 2 contains more detailed guidance on valuation, which is discussed at 8 below. *[IFRS 2.18]*. IFRS 2 also deals with those 'rare' cases where it is not possible to value equity instruments reliably, where an intrinsic value approach may be used. This is more likely to apply in the case of awards of options rather than those of shares, and is discussed further at 8.8 below.

IFRS 2 rather confusingly states that the fair value of equity instruments granted must take into account the terms and conditions on which they were granted, but this requirement is said to be 'subject to the requirements of paragraphs 19-22'. *[IFRS 2.16]*. When those paragraphs are consulted, however, a somewhat different picture emerges, since they draw a distinction between:

- non-vesting conditions (i.e. those that are neither service conditions nor performance conditions);
- vesting conditions which are market conditions (i.e. those related to the entity's share price); and
- other vesting conditions (i.e. service and non-market performance conditions).

These are discussed in more detail at 6.2 to 6.4 and at 8 below, but the essential difference is that, while non-vesting conditions and market conditions must be taken into account in any valuation, other vesting conditions must be ignored. *[IFRS 2.19-21A]*. As we explain in the more detailed discussion later, these essentially arbitrary distinctions originated in part as anti-avoidance measures.

The 'fair value' of equity instruments under IFRS 2 therefore takes account of some, but not all, conditions attached to an award rather than being a 'true' fair value.

The approach to determining the fair value of share-based payments continues to be that specified in IFRS 2 and share-based payments fall outside the scope of IFRS 13 which applies more generally to the measurement of fair value under IFRSs (see Chapter 14). *[IFRS 2.6A]*.

5.5.1 Reload features

A 'reload feature' is a feature in a share option that provides for an automatic grant of additional share options (reload options) whenever the option holder exercises previously granted options using the entity's shares, rather than cash, to satisfy the exercise price. *[IFRS 2 Appendix A]*. IFRS 2 requires reload features to be ignored in the initial valuation of options that contain them. Instead any reload option should be treated as if it were a newly granted option when the reload conditions are satisfied. *[IFRS 2.22]*. This is discussed further at 8.9 below.

6 EQUITY-SETTLED TRANSACTIONS – ALLOCATION OF EXPENSE

6.1 Overview

Equity-settled transactions, particularly those with employees, raise particular accounting problems since they are often subject to vesting conditions (see 3.1 above) that can be satisfied only over an extended vesting period. This raises the issue of whether a share-based payment transaction should be recognised:

- when the relevant equity instrument is first granted;
- when it vests;
- during the vesting period; or
- during the life of the option.

An award of equity instruments that vests immediately is presumed, in the absence of evidence to the contrary, to relate to services that have already been rendered, and is therefore expensed in full at grant date. *[IFRS 2.14]*. This may lead to the immediate recognition of an expense for an award to which the employee may not be legally entitled for some time, as illustrated in Example 32.5.

Example 32.5: Award with non-vesting condition only

An entity grants a director share options, exercisable after three years provided the director does not compete with the reporting entity for a period of at least three years. The 'non-compete' clause is considered to be a non-vesting condition (see 3.2 above and 6.4 below). As this is the only condition to which the award is subject, the award has no vesting conditions and therefore vests immediately. The fair value of the award at the date of grant, including the effect of the 'non-compete' clause, is determined to be €150,000. Accordingly, the entity immediately recognises a cost of €150,000.

This cost can never be reversed, even if the director goes to work for a competitor and loses the award. This is discussed more fully at 3.2.3 above and at 6.1.2 and 6.4 below.

Where equity instruments are granted subject to vesting conditions (as in many cases they will be, particularly where payments to employees are concerned), IFRS 2 creates a presumption that they are a payment for services to be received in the future, during the 'vesting period', with the transaction being recognised during that period, as illustrated in Example 32.6. *[IFRS 2.15]*.

Example 32.6: Award with service condition only

An entity grants a director share options on condition that the director remain in employment for three years. The requirement to remain in employment is a service condition, and therefore a vesting condition, which will take three years to fulfil. The fair value of the award at the date of grant, ignoring the effect of the vesting condition, is determined to be €300,000. The entity will record a cost of €100,000 a year in profit or loss for three years, with a corresponding increase in equity.

In practice, the calculations required by IFRS 2 are unlikely to be as simple as that in Example 32.6. In particular:

- the final number of awards that vest cannot be known until the vesting date (because employees may leave before the vesting date, or because relevant performance conditions may not be met); and/or
- the length of the vesting period may not be known in advance (since vesting may depend on satisfaction of a performance condition with no, or a variable, time-limit on its attainment).

In order to deal with such issues, IFRS 2 requires a continuous re-estimation process as summarised in 6.1.1 below.

6.1.1 The continuous estimation process of IFRS 2

The overall objective of IFRS 2 is that, at the end of the vesting period, the cumulative cost recognised in profit or loss (or, where applicable, included in the carrying amount of an asset), should represent the product of:

- the number of equity instruments that have vested, or would have vested, but for the failure to satisfy a market condition (see 6.3 below) or a non-vesting condition (see 6.4 below); and
- the fair value (excluding the effect of any non-market vesting conditions, but including the effect of any market conditions or non-vesting conditions) of those equity instruments at the date of grant.

It is essential to appreciate that the 'grant date' measurement model in IFRS 2 seeks to capture the value of the contingent right to shares promised at grant date, to the extent that that promise becomes (or is deemed by IFRS 2 to become – see 6.1.2 below) an entitlement of the counterparty, rather than the value of any shares finally delivered. Therefore, if an option vests, but is not exercised because it would not be in the counterparty's economic interest to do so, IFRS 2 still recognises a cost for the award.

In order to achieve this outcome, IFRS 2 requires the following process to be applied:

(a) at grant date, the fair value of the award (excluding the effect of any service and non-market performance vesting conditions, but including the effect of any market performance conditions or non-vesting conditions) is determined;

(b) at each subsequent reporting date until vesting, the entity calculates a best estimate of the cumulative charge to profit or loss at that date, being the product of:

  (i) the grant date fair value of the award determined in (a) above;

  (ii) the current best estimate of the number of awards that will vest (see 6.1.2 below); and

  (iii) the expired portion of the vesting period;

(c) the charge (or credit) to profit or loss for the period is the cumulative amount calculated in (b) above less the amounts already charged in previous periods. There is a corresponding credit (or debit) to equity *[IFRS 2.19-20]*;

(d) once the awards have vested, no further accounting adjustments are made to the cost of the award, except in respect of certain modifications to the award – see 7 below; and

(e) if a vested award is not exercised, an entity may (but need not) make a transfer between components of equity – see 6.1.3 below.

The overall effect of this process is that a cost is recognised for every award that is granted, except when it is forfeited, as that term is defined in IFRS 2 (see 6.1.2 below). *[IFRS 2.19]*.

6.1.2 Vesting and forfeiture

In normal English usage, and in many share scheme documents, an award is described as 'vested' when all the conditions needed to earn it have been met, and as 'forfeited' where it lapses before vesting because one or more of the conditions has not been met.

IFRS 2 uses the term 'forfeiture' in a much more restricted sense to mean an award that does not vest in IFRS 2 terms. This is a particularly complex aspect of IFRS 2, which is discussed in more detail at 6.2 to 6.4 below. Essentially:

- where an award is subject only to vesting conditions other than market conditions, failure to satisfy any one of the conditions is treated as a forfeiture by IFRS 2;
- where an award is subject to both
  - vesting conditions other than market conditions, and
  - market conditions and/or non-vesting conditions,

  failure to satisfy any one of the vesting conditions other than market conditions is treated as a forfeiture by IFRS 2. Otherwise (i.e. where all the vesting conditions other than market conditions are satisfied), the award is deemed to vest by IFRS 2 even if the market conditions and/or non-vesting conditions have not been satisfied; and
- where an award is subject only to non-vesting conditions, it is always deemed to vest by IFRS 2.

Where an award has been modified (see 7.3 below) so that different vesting conditions apply to the original and modified elements of an award, forfeiture will not apply to the original award if the service and non-market performance conditions attached to that element have been met. This will be the case even if the service and non-market performance conditions attached to the modified award have not been met and so the modified award is considered to have been forfeited (resulting in the reversal of any incremental expense relating to the modification). Examples 32.22 and 32.23 at 7.3 below illustrate this point.

As a result of the interaction of the various types of condition, the reference in the summary at 6.1.1 above to the 'best estimate of the number of awards that will vest' really means the best estimate of the number of awards for which it is expected that all service and non-market vesting conditions will be met.

In practice, however, it is not always clear how that best estimate is to be determined, and in particular what future events may and may not be factored into the estimate. This is discussed further at 6.2 to 6.4 and at 7.6 below.

6.1.3 Accounting after vesting

Once an equity-settled transaction has vested (or, in the case of a transaction subject to one or more market or non-vesting conditions, has been treated as vested under IFRS 2 – see 6.1.2 above), no further accounting entries are made to reverse the cost already charged, even if the instruments that are the subject of the transaction are subsequently forfeited or, in the case of options, are not exercised. However, the entity may make a transfer between different components of equity. *[IFRS 2.23]*. For example, an entity's accounting policy might be to credit all amounts recorded for share-based transactions to a separate reserve such as 'Shares to be issued'. Where an award lapses after vesting, it would then be appropriate to transfer an amount equivalent to the cumulative cost for the lapsed award from 'Shares to be issued' to another component of equity.

This prohibition against 'truing up' (i.e. reversing the cost of vested awards that lapse) is controversial, since it has the effect that a cost is still recognised for options that are never exercised, typically because they are 'underwater' (i.e. the current share price is lower than the option exercise price), so that it is not in the holder's interest to exercise the option. Some commentators have observed that an accounting standard that can result in an accounting cost for non-dilutive options does not meet the needs of those shareholders whose concerns about dilution were the catalyst for the share-based payment project in the first place (see 1.1 above).

The IASB counters such objections by pointing out that the treatment in IFRS 2 is perfectly consistent with that for other 'contingent' equity instruments, such as warrants, that ultimately result in no share ownership. Where an entity issues warrants for valuable consideration such as cash and those warrants lapse unexercised, the entity recognises no gain under IFRS. *[IFRS 2.BC218-221]*.

6.2 Vesting conditions other than market conditions

6.2.1 *Awards with service conditions*

Most share-based payment transactions with employees are subject to explicit or implied service conditions. The application of the general periodic allocation principles discussed in 6.1 above to awards subject only to service conditions is illustrated by Examples 32.7 and 32.8 below. *[IFRS 2.IG11]*.

Example 32.7: Award with no change in the estimate of number of awards vesting

An entity grants 100 share options to each of its 500 employees. Vesting is conditional upon the employees working for the entity over the next three years. The entity estimates that the fair value of each share option is €15. The entity's best estimate at each reporting date is that 20% of the original 500 employees will leave during the three year period and therefore forfeit their rights to the share options.

If everything turns out exactly as expected, the entity will recognise the following amounts during the vesting period for services received as consideration for the share options.

Year	Calculation of cumulative expense	Cumulative expense (€)	Expense for period‡ (€)
1	50,000 options × 80%* × €15 × 1/3†	200,000	200,000
2	50,000 options × 80% × €15 × 2/3	400,000	200,000
3	50,000 options × 80% × €15 × 3/3	600,000	200,000

* The entity expects 20% of employees to leave and therefore only 80% of the options to vest.

† The vesting period is 3 years, and 1 year of it has expired.

‡ In each case the expense for the period is the difference between the calculated cumulative expense at the beginning and end of the period.

Example 32.8: Award with re-estimation of number of awards vesting due to staff turnover

As in Example 32.7 above, an entity grants 100 share options to each of its 500 employees. Vesting is conditional upon the employee working for the entity over the next three years. The entity estimates that the fair value of each share option is €15.

In this case, however, 20 employees leave during the first year, and the entity's best estimate at the end of year 1 is that 15% of the original 500 employees will have left before the end of the vesting period. During the second year, a further 22 employees leave, and the entity revises its estimate of total employee departures over the vesting period from 15% to 12% of the original 500 employees. During the third year, a further 15 employees leave. Hence, a total of 57 employees (20 + 22 + 15) forfeit their rights to the share options during the three year period, and a total of 44,300 share options (443 employees × 100 options per employee) finally vest.

The entity will recognise the following amounts during the vesting period for services received as consideration for the share options.

Year	Calculation of cumulative expense	Cumulative expense (€)	Expense for period (€)
1	50,000 options × 85% × €15 × 1/3	212,500	212,500
2	50,000 options × 88% × €15 × 2/3	440,000	227,500
3	44,300 options × €15 × 3/3	664,500	224,500

Note that in Example 32.8 above, the number of employees that leave during year 1 and year 2 is not directly relevant to the calculation of cumulative expense in those years, but would naturally be a factor taken into account by the entity in estimating the likely number of awards finally vesting.

6.2.2 *Equity instruments vesting in instalments ('graded' vesting)*

An entity may make share-based payments that vest in instalments (sometimes referred to as 'graded' vesting). For example, an entity might grant an employee 600 options, 100 of which vest if the employee remains in service for one year, a further 200 after two years and the final 300 after three years. In today's more mobile labour markets, such awards are increasingly favoured over awards which vest only on an 'all or nothing' basis after an extended period.

IFRS 2 requires such an award to be treated as three separate awards, of 100, 200 and 300 options, on the grounds that the different vesting periods will mean that the three tranches of the award have different fair values. *[IFRS 2.IG11]*. This may well have the effect that compared to the expense for an award with a single 'cliff' vesting, the expense for an award vesting in instalments will be for a different amount in total and require accelerated recognition of the expense in earlier periods, as illustrated in Example 32.9 below.

Example 32.9: Award vesting in instalments ('graded' vesting)

An entity is considering the implementation of a scheme that awards 600 free shares to each of its employees, with no conditions other than continuous service. Two alternatives are being considered:

- All 600 shares vest in full only at the end of three years.
- 100 shares vest after one year, 200 shares after two years and 300 shares after three years. Any shares received at the end of years 1 and 2 would have vested unconditionally.

The fair value of a share delivered in one year's time is €3; in two years' time €2.80; and in three years' time €2.50.

For an employee that remains with the entity for the full three year period, the first alternative would be accounted for as follows:

Year	Calculation of cumulative expense	Cumulative expense (€)	Expense for period (€)
1	600 shares × €2.50 × 1/3	500	500
2	600 shares × €2.50 × 2/3	1,000	500
3	600 shares × €2.50 × 3/3	1,500	500

For the second alternative, the analysis is that the employee has simultaneously received an award of 100 shares vesting over one year, an award of 200 shares vesting over two years and an award of 300 shares vesting over 3 years. This would be accounted for as follows:

Year	Calculation of cumulative expense	Cumulative expense (€)	Expense for period (€)
1	[100 shares × €3.00] + [200 shares × €2.80 × 1/2] + [300 shares × €2.50 × 1/3]	830	830
2	[100 shares × €3.00] + [200 shares × €2.80 × 2/2] + [300 shares × €2.50 × 2/3]	1,360	530
3	[100 shares × €3.00] + [200 shares × €2.80 × 2/2] + [300 shares × €2.50 × 3/3]	1,610	250

At first sight, such an approach seems to be taking account of non-market vesting conditions in determining the fair value of an award, contrary to the basic principle of paragraph 19 of IFRS 2 (see 6.1.1 above). However, it is not the vesting conditions that are being taken into account *per se*, but the fact that the varying vesting periods will give rise to different lives for the award (which are required to be taken into account – see 7.2 and 8 below).

Provided all conditions are clearly understood at the outset, the accounting treatment illustrated in Example 32.9 would apply even if the vesting of shares in each year also depended on a performance condition unique to that year (e.g. that profit in that year must reach a given minimum level), as opposed to a cumulative performance condition (e.g. that profit must have grown by a minimum amount by the end of year 1, 2 or 3). This is because there is a service condition covering a longer period. In other words, an award that vests at the end of year 3 conditional on profitability in year 3 is also conditional on the employee providing service for three years from the date of grant in order to be eligible to receive the award. This is discussed further at 5.3.7 above.

The accounting treatment illustrated in Example 32.9 is the only treatment for graded vesting permitted under IFRS 2. This contrasts with US GAAP[18] which permits, for awards with graded vesting where vesting depends solely on a service condition, a policy choice between the approach illustrated above and a straight-line recognition method.

6.2.3 *Transactions with variable vesting periods due to non-market performance vesting conditions*

An award may be made with a vesting period of variable length. For example, an award might be contingent upon achievement of a particular performance target (such as achieving a given level of cumulative earnings) within a given period, but vesting immediately once the target has been reached. Alternatively, an award might be contingent on levels of earnings growth over a period, but with vesting occurring more quickly if growth is achieved more quickly. Also some plans provide for 're-testing', whereby an original target is set for achievement within a given vesting period, but if that target is not met, a new target and/or a different vesting period are substituted.

In such cases, the entity needs to estimate the length of the vesting period at grant date, based on the most likely outcome of the performance condition. Subsequently, it is necessary continuously to re-estimate not only the number of awards that will finally vest, but also the date of vesting, as shown by Example 32.10. *[IFRS 2.15(b), IG12]*. This contrasts with the treatment of awards with market conditions and variable vesting periods, where the initial estimate of the vesting period may not be revised (see 6.3.4 below).

Example 32.10: Award with non-market vesting condition and variable vesting period

At the beginning of year 1, the entity grants 100 shares each to 500 employees, conditional upon the employees remaining in the entity's employment during the vesting period. The shares will vest:

- at the end of year 1 if the entity's earnings increase by more than 18%;
- at the end of year 2 if the entity's earnings increase by more than an average of 13% per year over the two year period; or
- at the end of year 3 if the entity's earnings increase by more than an average of 10% per year over the three year period.

The award is estimated to have a fair value of $30 per share at grant date. It is expected that no dividends will be paid during the whole three year period.

By the end of the first year, the entity's earnings have increased by 14%, and 30 employees have left. The entity expects that earnings will continue to increase at a similar rate in year 2, and therefore expects that the shares will vest at the end of year 2. The entity expects, on the basis of a weighted average probability, that a further 30 employees will leave during year 2, and therefore expects that an award of 100 shares each will vest for 440 (500 – 30 – 30) employees at the end of year 2.

By the end of the second year, the entity's earnings have increased by only 10% and therefore the shares do not vest at the end of that year. 28 employees have left during the year. The entity expects that a further 25 employees will leave during year 3, and that the entity's earnings will increase by at least 6%, thereby achieving the average growth of 10% per year necessary for an award after 3 years, so that an award of 100 shares each will vest for 417 (500 – 30 – 28 – 25) employees at the end of year 3.

By the end of the third year, a further 23 employees have left and the entity's earnings have increased by 8%, resulting in an average increase of 10.67% per year. Therefore, 419 (500 – 30 – 28 – 23) employees receive 100 shares at the end of year 3.

The entity will recognise the following amounts during the vesting period for services received as consideration for the shares:

Year	Calculation of cumulative expense	Cumulative expense ($)	Expense for period ($)
1	440 employees × 100 shares × $30 × 1/2*	660,000	660,000
2	417 employees × 100 shares × $30 × 2/3*	834,000	174,000
3	419 employees × 100 shares × $30	1,257,000	423,000

* The entity's best estimate at the end of year 1 is that it is one year through a two year vesting period and at the end of year 2 that it is two years through a three year vesting period.

It will be noted that in Example 32.10, which is based on IG Example 2 in the implementation guidance to IFRS 2, it is assumed that the entity will pay no dividends (to any shareholders) throughout the maximum possible three year vesting period. This has the effect that the fair value of the shares to be awarded is (some might say, rather too conveniently) equivalent to their market value at the date of grant.

If dividends were expected to be paid during the vesting period, this would no longer be the case. Employees would be better off if they received shares after two years rather than three, since they would have a right to receive dividends from the end of year two. In practice, an entity is unlikely to suspend dividend payments in order to simplify the calculation of its share-based payment expense, and it is unfortunate that IG Example 2 is not more realistic. *[IFRS 2 IG Example 2]*.

One solution might be to use the approach in IG Example 4 in the implementation guidance to IFRS 2 (the substance of which is reproduced as Example 32.12 at 6.2.5 below). That Example deals with an award whose exercise price is either CHF12 or

CHF16, dependent upon various performance conditions. Because vesting conditions other than market conditions must be ignored in determining the value of an award, the approach is in effect to treat the award as the simultaneous grant of two awards, whose value, in that case, varies by reference to the different exercise prices. *[IFRS 2 IG Example 4]*.

The same principle could be applied to an award of shares that vests at different times according to the performance conditions, by determining different fair values for the shares (in this case depending on whether they vest after one, two or three years). The cumulative charge during the vesting period would be based on a best estimate of which outcome will occur, and the final cumulative charge would be based on the grant date fair value of the actual outcome (which will require some acceleration of expense if the actual vesting period is shorter than the previously estimated vesting period).

Such an approach appears to be taking account of non-market vesting conditions in determining the fair value of an award, contrary to the basic principle of paragraph 19 of IFRS 2 (see 6.1.1 above). However, it is not the vesting conditions that are being taken into account *per se*, but the fact that the varying vesting periods will give rise to different lives for the award (which are required to be taken into account – see 7.2 and 8 below). That said, the impact of the time value of the different lives on the fair value of the award will, in many cases, be insignificant and it will therefore be a matter of judgement as to how precisely an entity switches from one fair value to another.

Economically speaking, the entity in Example 32.10 has made a single award, the true fair value of which must be a function of the weighted probabilities of the various outcomes occurring. However, under the accounting model for share-settled awards in IFRS 2, the probability of achieving non-market performance conditions is not taken into account in valuing an award. If this is required to be ignored, the only approach open is to proceed as in Example 32.10 above and treat the arrangement as if it consisted of the simultaneous grant of three awards.

Some might object that this methodology is not relevant to the award in Example 32.10 above, since it is an award of shares rather than, in the case of Example 32.12 (see 6.2.5 below), an award of options. However, an award of shares is no more than an award of options with an exercise price of zero. Moreover, the treatment outlined in the previous paragraph is broadly consistent with the rationale given by IFRS 2 for the treatment of an award vesting in instalments (see 6.2.2 above).

In Example 32.10 above, the vesting period, although not known, is at least one of a finite number of known possibilities. The vesting period for some awards, however, may be more open-ended, such as is frequently the case for an award that vests on a trade sale or flotation of the business. Such awards are discussed further at 15.4 below.

6.2.4 Transactions with variable number of equity instruments awarded depending on non-market performance vesting conditions

More common than awards with a variable vesting period are those where the number of equity instruments awarded varies, typically increasing to reflect the margin by which a particular minimum target is exceeded. In accounting for such awards, the entity must continuously revise its estimate of the number of shares to be awarded, as illustrated in Example 32.11 below (which is based on IG Example 3 in the implementation guidance to IFRS 2). *[IFRS 2 IG Example 3]*.

Example 32.11: Award with non-market performance vesting condition and variable number of equity instruments

At the beginning of year 1, an entity grants an option over a variable number of shares (see below), estimated to have a fair value at grant date of £20 per share under option, to each of its 100 employees working in the sales department. The share options will vest at the end of year 3, provided that the employees remain in the entity's employment, and provided that the volume of sales of a particular product increases by at least an average of 5% per year. If the volume of sales of the product increases by an average of between 5% and 10% per year, each employee will be entitled to exercise 100 share options. If the volume of sales increases by an average of between 10% and 15% each year, each employee will be entitled to exercise 200 share options. If the volume of sales increases by an average of 15% or more, each employee will be entitled to exercise 300 share options.

By the end of the first year, seven employees have left and the entity expects that a total of 20 employees will leave by the end of year 3. Product sales have increased by 12% and the entity expects this rate of increase to continue over the next two years, so that 80 employees will be entitled to exercise 200 options each.

By the end of the second year, a further five employees have left. The entity now expects only three more employees to leave during year 3, and therefore expects a total of 15 employees to have left during the three year period. Product sales have increased by 18%, resulting in an average of 15% over the two years to date. The entity now expects that sales will average 15% or more over the three year period, so that 85 employees will be entitled to exercise 300 options each.

By the end of year 3, a further seven employees have left. Hence, 19 employees have left during the three year period, and 81 employees remain. However, due to trading conditions significantly poorer than expected, sales have increased by a 3 year average of only 12%, so that the 81 remaining employees are entitled to exercise only 200 share options.

The entity will recognise the following amounts during the vesting period for services received as consideration for the options.

Year	Calculation of cumulative expense	Cumulative expense (£)	Expense for period (£)
1	80 employees × 200 options × £20 × 1/3	106,667	106,667
2	85 employees × 300 options × £20 × 2/3	340,000	233,333
3	81 employees × 200 options × £20	324,000	(16,000)

This Example reinforces the point that, under the methodology in IFRS 2, it is quite possible for an equity-settled transaction to give rise to a credit to profit or loss for a particular period during the period to vesting.

6.2.5 Transactions with variable exercise price due to non-market performance vesting conditions

Another mechanism for delivering higher value to the recipient of a share award so as to reflect the margin by which a particular target is exceeded might be to vary the exercise price depending on performance. IFRS 2 requires such an award to be dealt with, in effect, as more than one award. The fair value of each award is determined, and the cost during the vesting period based on the best estimate of which award will actually vest, with the final cumulative charge being based on the actual outcome. *[IFRS 2.IG12, IG Example 4]*.

This is illustrated in Example 32.12 below.

Example 32.12: Award with non-market performance vesting condition and variable exercise price

An entity grants to a senior executive 10,000 share options, conditional upon the executive's remaining in the entity's employment for three years. The exercise price is CHF40. However, the exercise price drops to CHF30 if the entity's earnings increase by at least an average of 10% per year over the three year period.

On grant date, the entity estimates that the fair value of the share options, with an exercise price of CHF30, is CHF16 per option. If the exercise price is CHF40, the entity estimates that the share options have a fair value of CHF12 per option. During year 1, the entity's earnings increased by 12%, and the entity expects that earnings will continue to increase at this rate over the next two years. The entity therefore expects that the earnings target will be achieved, and hence the share options will have an exercise price of CHF30.

During year 2, the entity's earnings increased by 13%, and the entity continues to expect that the earnings target will be achieved. During year 3, the entity's earnings increased by only 3%, and therefore the earnings target was not achieved. The executive completes three years' service, and therefore satisfies the service condition. Because the earnings target was not achieved, the 10,000 vested share options have an exercise price of CHF40.

The entity will recognise the following amounts during the vesting period for services received as consideration for the options.

Year	Calculation of cumulative expense	Cumulative expense (CHF)	Expense for period (CHF)
1	10,000 options × CHF16 × 1/3	53,333	53,333
2	10,000 options × CHF16 × 2/3	106,667	53,334
3	10,000 options × CHF12	120,000	13,333

At first sight this may seem a rather surprising approach. In reality, is it not the case that the entity in Example 32.12 has made a single award, the fair value of which must lie between CHF12 and CHF16, as a function of the weighted probabilities of either outcome occurring? Economically speaking, this is indeed the case. However, under the accounting model for equity-settled share-based payments in IFRS 2, the probability of achieving non-market performance conditions is not taken into account in valuing an award. If this is required to be ignored, the only approach open is to proceed as above.

6.3 Market conditions

6.3.1 *What is a 'market condition'?*

Following the amendments to IFRS 2 as part of the *Annual Improvements to IFRSs 2010-2012 Cycle*, a market condition is defined as follows:

'A performance condition upon which the exercise price, vesting or exercisability of an equity instrument depends that is related to the market price (or value) of the entity's equity instruments (or the equity instruments of another entity in the same group), such as:

(a) attaining a specified share price or a specified amount of intrinsic value of a share option; or

(b) achieving a specified target that is based on the market price (or value) of the entity's equity instruments (or the equity instruments of another entity in the same group) relative to an index of market prices of equity instruments of other entities.

'A market condition requires the counterparty to complete a specified period of service (i.e. a service condition); the service requirement can be explicit or implicit.' *[IFRS 2 Appendix A]*.

A market condition is a type of performance condition and the above definition should be read together with the definition of a performance condition (see 3.1 above). If there is no service requirement, the condition will be a non-vesting condition rather than a performance vesting condition (see 3.2 above).

The 'intrinsic value' of a share option means 'the difference between the fair value of the shares to which the counterparty has the (conditional or unconditional) right to subscribe or which it has the right to receive, and the price (if any) the counterparty is (or will be) required to pay for those shares'. *[IFRS 2 Appendix A]*. In other words, an option to acquire for $8 a share with a fair value of $10 has an intrinsic value of $2. A performance condition based on the share price and one based on the intrinsic value of the option are effectively the same, since the values of each will obviously move in parallel.

An example of a market condition is a condition based on total shareholder return (TSR). TSR is a measure of the increase or decrease in a given sum invested in an entity over a period on the assumption that all dividends received in the period had been used to purchase further shares in the entity. The market price of the entity's shares is an input to the calculation.

However, a condition linked to a purely internal financial performance measure such as profit or earnings per share is not a market condition. Such measures will affect the share price, but are not directly linked to it, and hence are not market conditions.

A condition linked to a general market index is a non-vesting condition rather than a market condition (see 3.2 above and 6.4 below). For example, suppose that an entity engaged in investment management and listed only in London grants options to an employee responsible for the Far East equities portfolio. The options have a condition linked to movements in a general index of shares of entities listed in Hong Kong, so as to compare the performance of the portfolio of investments for which the employee is responsible with that of the overall market in which they are traded. That condition would not be regarded as a market condition under IFRS 2, because even though it relates to the performance of a market, the reporting entity's own share price is not relevant to the satisfaction of the condition.

However, if the condition were that the entity's own share price had to outperform a general index of shares of entities listed in Hong Kong, that condition would be a market condition because the reporting entity's own share price is then relevant to the satisfaction of the condition.

6.3.2 Summary of accounting treatment

The key feature of the accounting treatment of an equity-settled transaction subject to a market condition is that the market condition is taken into account in valuing the award at the date of grant, but then subsequently ignored, so that an award is treated as vesting irrespective of whether the market condition is satisfied, provided that all service and non-market performance vesting conditions are satisfied. *[IFRS 2.21, IG13]*. This can have rather controversial consequences, as illustrated by Example 32.13.

Example 32.13: Award with market condition

An entity grants an employee an option to buy a share on condition of remaining in employment for three years and the share price at the end of that period being at least €7. At the end of the vesting period, the share price is €6.80. The share price condition is factored into the initial valuation of the option, and the option is considered to vest provided that the employee remains for three years, irrespective of whether the share price does in fact reach €7.

Therefore, IFRS 2 sometimes treats as vesting (and recognises a cost for) awards that do not actually vest in the natural sense of the word. See also Example 32.15 at 6.3.4 below.

This treatment is clearly significantly different from that for transactions involving a non-market vesting condition, where no cost would be recognised where the conditions were not met. The Basis for Conclusions indicates that the IASB accepted this difference for two main reasons:

(a) it was consistent with the approach in the US standard FAS 123; and

(b) in principle, the same approach should have been adopted for all performance conditions. However, whereas market conditions can be readily incorporated into the valuation of options, other conditions cannot. *[IFRS 2.BC183-184]*.

The methodology prescribed by IFRS 2 for transactions with a vesting condition other than a market condition is therefore to determine the fair value of the option ignoring the condition and then to multiply that fair value by the estimated (and ultimately the actual) number of awards expected to vest based on the likelihood of that non-market vesting condition being met. It is interesting to note, however, that the January 2008 amendment to IFRS 2 (see 1.2 above) had the effect that certain conditions previously regarded as non-market vesting conditions (and therefore 'impossible' to incorporate in the determination of fair value) became non-vesting conditions (and therefore required to be incorporated in the determination of fair value)!

One of the reasons for adoption of this approach under US GAAP (not referred to in the Basis for Conclusions in IFRS 2) was as an 'anti-avoidance' measure. The concern was that the introduction of certain market conditions could effectively allow for the reversal of the expense for 'underwater' options (i.e. those whose exercise price is higher than the share price such that it is not in the holder's interest to exercise the option) for which all significant vesting conditions had been satisfied, contrary to the general principle in US GAAP (and IFRS 2) that no revisions should be made to the expense for an already vested option.

For example, an entity could grant an employee an option, when the share price is £10, exercisable at £10, provided that a certain sales target had been met within one year. If the target were achieved, IFRS 2 would require an expense to be recognised even if the share price at the end of the year were only £8, so that the employee would not rationally exercise the option. If, however, the performance conditions were that (a) the sales target was achieved and (b) the share price was at least £10.01, the effect would be (absent specific provision for market conditions) that the entity could reverse any expense for 'underwater' options.

It appears that it may be possible to soften the impact of IFRS 2's rules for market conditions relatively easily by introducing a non-market vesting condition closely correlated to the market condition. For instance, the option in Example 32.13 above could be modified so that exercise was dependent not only upon the €7 target share price and continuous employment, but also on a target growth in earnings per share. Whilst there would not be a perfect correlation between earnings per share and the share price, it would be expected that they would move roughly in parallel, particularly if the entity has historically had a fairly consistent price/earnings ratio. Thus, if the share price target were not met, it would be highly likely that the earnings per share target would not be met either. This would allow the entity to show no cumulative cost for the option, since only one (i.e. not *all*) of the non-market related vesting conditions would have been met.

Similarly, entities in sectors where the share price is closely related to net asset value (e.g. property companies and investment trusts) could incorporate a net asset value target as a non-market performance condition that would be highly likely to be satisfied only if the market condition was satisfied.

The matrices below illustrate the interaction of market conditions and vesting conditions other than market conditions. Matrix 1 summarises the possible outcomes for an award with the following two vesting conditions:

- the employee remaining in service for three years ('service condition'); and
- the entity's total shareholder return ('TSR') relative to that of a peer group being in the top 10% of its peer group at the end of the period ('TSR target').

Matrix 1

	Service condition met?	**TSR target met?**	**IFRS 2 expense?**
1	Yes	Yes	Yes
2	Yes	No	Yes
3	No	Yes	No
4	No	No	No

It will be seen that, to all intents and purposes, the 'TSR target met?' column is redundant, as this market condition is not relevant to whether or not the award is treated as vesting by IFRS 2. The effect of this is that the entity would recognise an expense for outcome 2, even though no awards truly vest.

Matrix 2 summarises the possible outcomes for an award with the same conditions as in Matrix 1, plus a requirement for earnings per share to grow by a general inflation index plus 10% over the period ('EPS target').

Matrix 2

	Service condition met?	TSR target met?	EPS target met?	IFRS 2 expense?
1	Yes	Yes	Yes	Yes
2	Yes	No	Yes	Yes
3	Yes	Yes	No	No
4	Yes	No	No	No
5	No	Yes	Yes	No
6	No	No	Yes	No
7	No	Yes	No	No
8	No	No	No	No

Again it will be seen that, to all intents and purposes, the 'TSR target met?' column is redundant, as this market condition is not relevant to whether or not the award is treated as vesting by IFRS 2. The effect of this is that the entity would recognise an expense for outcome 2, even though no awards truly vest. However, no expense would be recognised for outcome 4, which is, except for the introduction of the EPS target, equivalent to outcome 2 in Matrix 1, for which an expense is recognised. This illustrates that the introduction of a non-market vesting condition closely related to a market condition may mitigate the impact of IFRS 2.

Examples of the application of the accounting treatment for transactions involving market conditions are given in 6.3.3 to 6.3.5 below.

6.3.3 *Transactions with market conditions and known vesting periods*

The accounting for such transactions is essentially the same as that for transactions without market conditions but with a known vesting period, except that adjustments are made to reflect the changing probability of the achievement of the non-market vesting conditions only, as illustrated by Example 32.14 below. *[IFRS 2.19-21, IG13, IG Example 5].*

Example 32.14: Award with market condition and fixed vesting period

At the beginning of year 1, an entity grants to 100 employees 1,000 share options each, conditional upon the employees remaining in the entity's employment until the end of year 3. However, the share options cannot be exercised unless the share price has increased from €50 at the beginning of year 1 to more than €65 at the end of year 3.

If the share price is above €65 at the end of year 3, the share options can be exercised at any time during the next seven years, i.e. by the end of year 10. The entity applies a binomial option pricing model (see 8 below), which takes into account the possibility that the share price will exceed €65 at the end of year 3 (and hence the share options vest and become exercisable) and the possibility that the share price will not exceed €65 at the end of year 3 (and hence the options will be treated as having vested under IFRS 2 but will never be exercisable – as explained below). It estimates the fair value of the share options with this market condition to be €24 per option.

IFRS 2 requires the entity to recognise the services received from a counterparty who satisfies all other vesting conditions (e.g. services received from an employee who remains in service for the specified service period), irrespective of whether that market condition is satisfied. It makes no difference whether the share price target is achieved, since the possibility that the share price target might not be achieved has already been taken into account when estimating the fair value of the share options at grant date. However, the options are subject to another condition (i.e. continuous employment) and the cost recognised should be adjusted to reflect the ongoing best estimate of employee retention.

By the end of the first year, seven employees have left and the entity expects that a total of 20 employees will leave by the end of year 3, so that 80 employees will have satisfied all conditions other than the market condition (i.e. continuous employment).

By the end of the second year, a further five employees have left. The entity now expects only three more employees will leave during year 3, and therefore expects that a total of 15 employees will have left during the three year period, so that 85 employees will have satisfied all conditions other than the market condition.

By the end of year 3, a further seven employees have left. Hence, 19 employees have left during the three year period, and 81 employees remain. However, the share price is only €60, so that the options cannot be exercised. Nevertheless, as all conditions other than the market condition have been satisfied, a cumulative cost is recorded as if the options had fully vested in 81 employees.

The entity will recognise the following amounts during the vesting period for services received as consideration for the options (which in economic reality do not vest).

Year	Calculation of cumulative expense	Cumulative expense (€)	Expense for period (€)
1	80 employees × 1,000 options × €24 × 1/3	640,000	640,000
2	85 employees × 1,000 options × €24 × 2/3	1,360,000	720,000
3	81 employees × 1,000 options × €24	1,944,000	584,000

6.3.4 *Transactions with variable vesting periods due to market conditions*

Where a transaction has a variable vesting period due to a market condition, a best estimate of the most likely vesting period will have been used in determining the fair value of the transaction at the date of grant. IFRS 2 requires the expense for that transaction to be recognised over an estimated expected vesting period consistent with the assumptions used in the valuation, without any subsequent revision. *[IFRS 2.15(b), IG14]*.

This may mean, for example, that, if the actual vesting period for an employee share option award turns out to be longer than that anticipated for the purposes of the initial valuation, a cost is nevertheless recorded in respect of all employees who reach the end of the *anticipated* vesting period, even if they do not reach the end of the *actual* vesting period, as shown by Example 32.15 below, which is based on IG Example 6 in the implementation guidance in IFRS 2. *[IFRS 2 IG Example 6]*.

Example 32.15: Award with market condition and variable vesting period

At the beginning of year 1, an entity grants 10,000 share options with a ten year life to each of ten senior executives. The share options will vest and become exercisable immediately if and when the entity's share price increases from £50 to £70, provided that the executive remains in service until the share price target is achieved.

The entity applies a binomial option pricing model, which takes into account the possibility that the share price target will be achieved during the ten year life of the options, and the possibility that the target will not be achieved. The entity estimates that the fair value of the share options at grant date is £25 per option. From the option pricing model, the entity determines that the most likely vesting period is five years. The entity also estimates that two executives will have left by the end of year 5, and therefore expects that 80,000 share options (10,000 share options × 8 executives) will vest at the end of year 5.

Throughout years 1 to 4, the entity continues to estimate that a total of two executives will leave by the end of year 5. However, in total three executives leave, one in each of years 3, 4 and 5. The share price target is achieved at the end of year 6. Another executive leaves during year 6, before the share price target is achieved.

Paragraph 15 of IFRS 2 requires the entity to recognise the services received over the expected vesting period, as estimated at grant date, and also requires the entity not to revise that estimate. Therefore, the entity recognises the services received from the executives over years 1-5. Hence, the transaction amount is ultimately based on 70,000 share options (10,000 share options × 7 executives who remain in service at the end of year 5). Although another executive left during year 6, no adjustment is made, because the executive had already completed the expected vesting period of 5 years.

The entity will recognise the following amounts during the initial expected five year vesting period for services received as consideration for the options.

Year	Calculation of cumulative expense	Cumulative expense (£)	Expense for period (£)
1	8 employees × 10,000 options × £25 × 1/5	400,000	400,000
2	8 employees × 10,000 options × £25 × 2/5	800,000	400,000
3	8 employees × 10,000 options × £25 × 3/5	1,200,000	400,000
4	8 employees × 10,000 options × £25 × 4/5	1,600,000	400,000
5	7 employees × 10,000 options × £25	1,750,000	150,000

IFRS 2 does not specifically address the converse situation, namely where the award actually vests before the end of the anticipated vesting period. In our view, where this occurs, any expense not yet recognised at the point of vesting should be immediately accelerated. We consider that this treatment is most consistent with the overall requirement of IFRS 2 to recognise an expense for share-based payment transactions 'as the services are received'. *[IFRS 2.7]*. It is difficult to regard any services being received for an award after it has vested.

Moreover, the prohibition in IFRS 2 on adjusting the vesting period as originally determined refers to 'the estimate of the expected vesting period'. In our view, the acceleration of vesting that we propose is not the revision of an estimated period, but the substitution of a known vesting period for an estimate.

Suppose in Example 32.15 above, the award had in fact vested at the end of year 4. We believe that the expense for such an award should be allocated as follows:

Year	Calculation of cumulative expense	Cumulative expense (£)	Expense for period (£)
1	8 employees × 10,000 options × £25 × 1/5	400,000	400,000
2	8 employees × 10,000 options × £25 × 2/5	800,000	400,000
3	8 employees × 10,000 options × £25 × 3/5	1,200,000	400,000
4	8 employees × 10,000 options × £25 × 4/4	2,000,000	800,000

6.3.5 *Transactions with multiple outcomes depending on market conditions*

In practice, it is very common for an award subject to market conditions to give varying levels of reward that increase depending on the extent to which a 'base line' market performance target has been met. Such an award is illustrated in Example 32.16 below.

Example 32.16: Award with market conditions and multiple outcomes

At the beginning of year 1, the reporting entity grants an employee an award of shares that will vest on the third anniversary of grant if the employee is still in employment. The number of shares depends on the share price achieved at the end of the three-year period. The employee will receive:

- no shares if the share price is below €10.00
- 100 shares if the share price is in the range €10.00 – €14.99
- 150 shares if the share price is in the range €15.00 – €19.99
- 180 shares if the share price is €20.00 or above.

In effect the entity has made three awards, which need to be valued as follows:

(a) 100 shares if the employee remains in service for three years and the share price is in the range €10.00 – €14.99

(b) 50 (150 – 100) shares if the employee remains in service for three years and the share price is in the range €15.00 – €19.99; and

(c) 30 (180 – 150) shares if the employee remains in service for three years and the share price is €20.00 or more.

Each award would be valued, ignoring the impact of the three-year service condition but taking account of the share price target. This would result in each tranche of the award being subject to an increasing level of discount to reflect the relative probability of the share price target for each tranche of the award being met. All three awards would then be expensed over the three-year service period, and forfeited only if the awards lapsed as a result of the employee leaving during that period.

It can be seen that the (perhaps somewhat counterintuitive) impact of this is that an equity-settled share-based payment where the number of shares increases in line with increases in the entity's share price may nevertheless have a fixed grant date value irrespective of the number of shares finally awarded.

6.3.6 Transactions with independent market conditions, non-market vesting conditions or non-vesting conditions

6.3.6.A Independent market and non-market vesting conditions

The discussion at 6.3.2 above addressed the accounting treatment of awards with multiple conditions that must all be satisfied, i.e. a market condition *and* a non-market vesting condition. However, it is increasingly common for entities to make awards with multiple conditions, only one of which need be satisfied, i.e. the awards vest on satisfaction of either a market condition *or* a non-market vesting condition. IFRS 2 provides no explicit guidance on the treatment of such awards, which is far from clear, as illustrated by Example 32.17 below.

Example 32.17: Award with independent market conditions and non-market vesting conditions

An entity grants an employee 100 share options that vest after three years if the employee is still in employment and the entity achieves either:

- cumulative total shareholder return (TSR) over three years of at least 15%, or
- cumulative profits over three years of at least £200 million.

The fair value of the award, ignoring vesting conditions, is £300,000. The fair value of the award, taking account of the TSR condition, but not the other conditions, is £210,000.

In our view, the entity has, in effect, simultaneously issued two awards – call them 'A' and 'B' –which vest as follows:

A on achievement of three years' service plus minimum TSR,

B on achievement of three years' service plus minimum earnings growth.

If the conditions for both awards are simultaneously satisfied, one or other effectively lapses.

It is clear that award A, if issued separately, would require the entity to recognise an expense of £210,000 if the employee were still in service at the end of the three year period. It therefore seems clear that, if the employee does remain in service, there should be a charge of £210,000 irrespective of whether the award actually vests. It would be anomalous for the entity to avoid recording a charge that would have been recognised if the entity had made award A in isolation simply by packaging it with award B.

If in fact the award vested because the earnings condition, but not the market condition, had been satisfied, it would then be appropriate to recognise a total expense of £300,000.

During the vesting period, we believe that the entity should make an assessment at each reporting date of the basis on which the award is expected to vest. It should assess the probability, as at that date, of the award vesting by virtue of the earnings condition, but not the TSR condition, being satisfied. Assume (for example) that the entity assesses at the end of year 1 that the award is likely to vest by virtue of the TSR condition, and at the end of year 2 that it is likely to vest by virtue of the earnings condition, and that the award actually does not vest, but the employee remains in service. This would give rise to annual expense as follows:

Year	Calculation of cumulative expense	Cumulative expense (£)	Expense for period (£)
1	210,000 × 1/3	70,000	70,000
2	300,000 × 2/3	200,000	130,000
3	210,000 × 3/3	210,000	10,000

We believe that ongoing reassessment during the vesting period is most consistent with the general approach of IFRS 2 to awards with a number of possible outcomes (see 10 below).

Of course, as for other awards, the accounting treatment would also require an assessment of whether or not the employee was actually going to remain in service.

A further question that arises is how the award should be accounted for if both conditions are satisfied. It would clearly be inappropriate to recognise an expense of £510,000 (the sum of the separate fair values of the award) – this would be double-counting, because the employee receives only one package of 100 options. However, should the total expense be taken as £210,000 or £300,000? In our view, it is appropriate to recognise a cost of £300,000 since the non-market vesting condition has been satisfied.

Ultimately, this is an issue which only the IASB can solve, since it arises from the inconsistent treatment by IFRS 2 of awards with market conditions and those with non-market conditions. As noted at 3.4 above, the IASB agreed in September 2011 to consider the interaction of multiple vesting conditions as a future agenda item but had not done so as at the time of writing and does not appear to have this matter on its agenda following its IFRS 2 research project.[19]

6.3.6.B *Independent market conditions and non-vesting conditions*

Arrangements are also seen where a share-based payment transaction vests on the satisfaction of either a market condition or a non-vesting condition.

In our view, an entity granting an award on the basis of a service condition (and any other non-market vesting conditions) plus either a market condition or a non-vesting condition should measure the fair value of the award at grant date taking into account both the probability of meeting the market condition and the probability of meeting the non-vesting condition. The fact that there are two alternative conditions on which the award might vest means that, unless the two conditions are perfectly correlated, the grant date fair value of such an award will be higher than that of an award where there is only one possible basis on which the award might vest. Irrespective of whether the market condition and/or the non-vesting conditions are met, the entity will recognise the grant date fair value provided all other service and non-market vesting conditions are met (i.e. the expense recognition is consistent with that of any award with market and/or non-vesting conditions).

6.3.7 *Transactions with hybrid or interdependent market conditions and non-market vesting conditions*

Awards may sometimes have a performance condition which depends simultaneously on a market element and a non-market element, sometimes known as 'hybrid' conditions. Examples of such conditions include:

- a particular price-earnings (PE) ratio (calculated by reference to share price, a market condition, and earnings, a non-market vesting condition); and
- a maximum level of discount of market capitalisation (a market condition) below net asset value (a non-market vesting condition).

Such awards are rather curious, in the sense that these ratios may remain fairly constant irrespective of the underlying performance of the entity, so that a performance condition based on them is arguably of limited motivational value.

In our view, in contrast to our suggested treatment of awards with independent market and non-market vesting conditions discussed at 6.3.6.A above, awards with interdependent market and non-market vesting conditions must be accounted for entirely as awards with market conditions. These awards contain at least one element that meets the definition of a market condition but which cannot be completely split from the non-market element for separate assessment. An indicator such as the PE ratio, or discount of market capitalisation below net asset value, is a market condition as defined since it is 'related to the market price ... of the entity's equity instruments' (see 6.3.1 above).

6.3.8 *Awards based on the market value of a subsidiary or business unit*

Awards with a market condition are usually based on the market price or value of the (typically quoted) equity instruments of the parent entity. However, a group might consider the parent's share price to be a somewhat blunt instrument for measuring the performance of the employees of a particular subsidiary or business unit. Indeed, it is not difficult to imagine situations in which a particular subsidiary might perform well but the parent's share price might be dragged down by other factors, or conversely where the parent's share price might rise notwithstanding poor results for that subsidiary.

Accordingly, entities are increasingly implementing share-based remuneration schemes which aim to reward employees by reference to the 'market' value of the equity of the business unit for which they work. The detail of such schemes varies, but the general effect is typically as follows:

- at grant date, the employee is allocated a (real or notional) holding in the equity of the employing subsidiary, the market value of which is measured at grant date; and
- the employee is granted an award of as many shares of the listed parent as have a value, at a specified future date (often at, or shortly after, the end of the vesting period but sometimes at a later date), equal to the increase over the vesting period in the market value of the employee's holding in the equity of the employing subsidiary.

Some take the view that such a scheme contains a market condition, since it depends on the fair value of the subsidiary's shares, with the result that the grant date fair value per share:

- reflects this market condition (see 6.3.2 above); and
- is fixed, irrespective of how many parent company shares are finally issued, since the entity has effectively issued a market-based award with multiple outcomes based on the market value of the equity of a subsidiary (see 6.3.5 above).

In our view, however, the treatment of such schemes under IFRS 2 is not as straightforward as suggested by this analysis. A fundamental issue is whether any award dependent on the change in value of the equity of an unquoted entity contains a market condition at all. IFRS 2 defines a market condition (see 6.3.1 above) as one dependent on the 'market price (or value)' of the entity's equity. *Prima facie*, if there is no market, there is no market price or value.

Notwithstanding the absence of a market, some argue that there are generally accepted valuation techniques for unquoted equities which can yield a fair value as a surrogate for market value. The difficulty with that argument, in our view, is that the IASB refers in the definition of 'market condition' to 'market price (or value)' and not to 'fair value'. The latter term is, of course, used extensively elsewhere in IFRS 2, which suggests that the IASB does not see the two terms as equivalent. This concern is reinforced by that fact that, even though it does not apply to the measurement of awards accounted for under IFRS 2, the 'valuation hierarchy' in IFRS 13 gives a quoted market price as the preferred (but not the only) method of arriving at fair value (see Chapter 14 at 16).

An entity implementing such an award must therefore make an assessment, in any particular situation, of whether the basis on which the subsidiary equity is valued truly yields a 'market price (or value)' or merely a fair value according to a valuation model.

Furthermore, in order for there to be a market condition, as defined in IFRS 2, there needs to be a specified performance target. It is not always clear in such situations that there is such a target if the various outcomes depend on an exchange of shares regardless of the level of market price or value achieved by the subsidiary.

If it is considered that there is no market condition within the arrangement and there is simply an exchange of shares – in effect, using one entity's shares as the currency for the other – then the arrangement might nonetheless be viewed as containing a non-vesting condition (similar to when an arrangement depends on the performance of an index, for example (see 3.2 above and 6.4 below)). Like a market condition, a non-vesting condition would be taken into account in determining the fair value of the award and would result in a fixed grant date fair value irrespective of the number of shares finally delivered.

6.3.8.A Awards with a condition linked to flotation price

The situations discussed above and at 2.2.4.F above relate to ongoing conditions linked to the calculated value of an unlisted entity's equity instruments and therefore differ from those where the condition is linked to the market price at which a previously unlisted entity floats. On flotation there is clearly a market and a market price for the entity's equity instruments and the achievement of a specific price on flotation would, in our view, be a market condition when accompanied by a corresponding service requirement (see 15.4 below).

6.4 Non-vesting conditions

The accounting treatment for awards with non-vesting conditions has some similarities to that for awards with market conditions in that:

- the fair value of the award at grant date is reduced to reflect the impact of the condition; and
- an expense is recognised for the award irrespective of whether the non-vesting condition is met, provided that all vesting conditions (other than market conditions) are met. *[IFRS 2.21A]*.

However, the accounting for non-vesting conditions differs from that for market conditions as regards the timing of the recognition of expense if the non-vesting condition is not satisfied (see 6.4.3 below).

6.4.1 Awards with no conditions other than non-vesting conditions

The effect of the treatment required by IFRS 2 is that any award that has only non-vesting conditions (e.g. an option award to an employee that may be exercised on a trade sale or IPO of the entity, irrespective of whether the employee is still in employment at that time) must be expensed in full at grant date. This is discussed further at 3.2 above and at 15.4 below, and illustrated in Example 32.5 at 6.1 above.

6.4.2 Awards with non-vesting conditions and variable vesting periods

IFRS 2 does not explicitly address the determination of the vesting period for an award with a non-vesting condition but a variable vesting period (e.g. an award which delivers 100 shares when the price of gold reaches a given level, but without limit as to when that level must be achieved, so long as the employee is still in employment when the target is reached). However, given the close similarity between the required treatment for awards with non-vesting conditions and that for awards with market conditions, we believe that entities should follow the guidance in the standard for awards with market conditions and variable vesting periods (see 6.3.4 above).

6.4.3 Failure to meet non-vesting conditions

As noted above, the accounting for non-vesting conditions differs from that for market conditions as regards the timing of the recognition of expense if the non-vesting condition is not satisfied. The treatment depends on the nature of the non-vesting condition, as follows:

- if a non-vesting condition within the control of the counterparty (e.g. making monthly savings in an SAYE scheme or holding a specified number of shares in a matching share arrangement) is not satisfied during the vesting period, the failure to satisfy the condition is treated as a cancellation (see 7.4 below), with immediate recognition of any expense for the award not previously recognised *[IFRS 2.28A, IG24]*;
- if a non-vesting condition within the control of the entity (e.g. continuing to operate the scheme) is not satisfied during the vesting period, the failure to satisfy the condition is treated as a cancellation (see 7.4 below), with immediate recognition of any expense for the award not previously recognised *[IFRS 2.28A, IG24]*; but
- if a non-vesting condition within the control of neither the counterparty nor the entity (e.g. a financial market index reaching a minimum level) is not satisfied, there is no change to the accounting and the expense continues to be recognised over the vesting period, unless the award is otherwise treated as forfeited by IFRS 2. *[IFRS 2.BC237A, IG24]*. In our view, the reference to the vesting period would include any deemed vesting period calculated as described in 6.4.2 above.

If an award is forfeited due to a failure to satisfy a non-vesting condition after the end of the vesting period (e.g. a requirement for an employee not to work for a competitor for a two year period after vesting), no adjustment is made to the expense previously recognised, consistent with the general provisions of IFRS 2 for accounting for awards in the post-vesting period (see 6.1.3 above). This would be the case even if shares previously issued to the employee were required to be returned to the entity on forfeiture (see 3.1.1 and 3.2.3 above for further discussion of clawback arrangements and non-compete arrangements respectively).

7 EQUITY-SETTLED TRANSACTIONS – MODIFICATION, CANCELLATION AND SETTLEMENT

7.1 Background

It is quite common for equity instruments to be modified or cancelled before or after vesting. Typically this is done where the conditions for an award have become so onerous as to be virtually unachievable, or (in the case of an option) where the share price has fallen so far below the exercise price of an option that it is unlikely that the option will ever be 'in the money' to the holder during its life. In such cases, an entity may take the view that the equity awards are so unattainable as to have little or no motivational effect, and accordingly replace them with less onerous alternatives. Conversely, and more rarely, an entity may make the terms of a share award more onerous (possibly because of shareholder concern that targets are insufficiently demanding). In addition an entity may 'settle' an award, i.e. cancel it in return for cash or other consideration.

A target entity might also modify existing share-based payment arrangements in the period leading up to a business combination. In this situation, it needs to be determined whether the guidance in IFRS 2 is applicable or whether the modification is being made for the benefit of the acquirer or the combined entity, in which case the guidance in IFRS 3 is likely to apply (see 11.2 below).

IFRS 2 contains detailed provisions for modification, cancellation and settlement. Whilst these provisions (like the summary of them below) are framed in terms of share-based payment transactions with employees, they apply to transactions with parties other than employees that are measured by reference to the fair value of the equity instruments granted (see 5.4 above). In that case, however, all references to 'grant date' should be taken as references to the date on which the third party supplied goods or rendered service. *[IFRS 2.26]*.

In the discussion below, any reference to a 'cancellation' is to any cancellation, whether instigated by the entity or the counterparty. As well as more obvious situations where an award is cancelled by either the entity or the counterparty, cancellations include:

- a failure by the entity to satisfy a non-vesting condition (see 6.4.3 above) within the control of the entity; and
- a failure by the counterparty to satisfy a non-vesting condition (see 6.4.3 above) within the control of the counterparty. *[IFRS 2.28A, IG24]*.

The discussion below is not relevant to cancellations and modifications of those equity-settled transactions that are (exceptionally) accounted for at intrinsic value (see 8.8 below).

The basic principles of the rules for modification, cancellation and settlement, which are discussed in more detail at 7.3 and 7.4 below, can be summarised as follows.

- As a minimum, the entity must recognise the amount that would have been recognised for the award if it remained in place on its original terms. *[IFRS 2.27]*.
- If the value of an award to an employee is reduced (e.g. by reducing the number of equity instruments subject to the award or, in the case of an option, by increasing the exercise price), there is no reduction in the cost recognised in profit or loss. *[IFRS 2.27, B42, B44]*.
- However, where the effect of the modification, cancellation or settlement is to increase the value of the award to an employee (e.g. by increasing the number of equity instruments subject to the award or, in the case of an option, by reducing the exercise price), the incremental fair value must be recognised as a cost. The incremental fair value is the difference between the fair value of the original award and that of the modified award, both measured at the date of modification. *[IFRS 2.27, B43]*.

It might be thought that, when an award has been modified, and certainly when it has been cancelled altogether, it no longer exists, and that it is therefore not appropriate to recognise any cost for it. However, such a view would be consistent with a vesting date measurement model rather than with the grant/service date measurement model of IFRS 2. Under the IFRS 2 model, the value of an award at grant date or service date cannot be changed by subsequent events.

Another reason given for the approach in IFRS 2 is that if entities were able not to recognise the cost of modified or cancelled options they would in effect be able to apply a selective form of 'truing up', whereby options that increased in value after grant would remain 'frozen' at their grant date valuation under the general principles of IFRS 2, whilst options that decreased in value could be modified or cancelled after grant date and credit taken for the fall in value. *[IFRS 2.BC222-237]*.

7.2 Valuation requirements when an award is modified, cancelled or settled

These provisions have the important practical consequence that, when an award is modified, cancelled or settled, the entity must obtain a fair value not only for the modified award, but also for the original award, updated to the date of modification. If the award had not been modified, there would have been no need to obtain a valuation for the original award after the date of grant.

Any modification of a performance condition clearly has an impact on the 'real' value of an award but it may have no direct effect on the value of the award for the purposes of IFRS 2. As discussed at 6.2 to 6.4 above, this is because market vesting conditions and non-vesting conditions are taken into account in valuing an award whereas non-market vesting conditions are not. Accordingly, by implication, a change to a non-market performance condition will not necessarily affect the expense recognised for the award under IFRS 2.

For example, if an award is contingent upon sales of a given number of units and the number of units required to be sold is decreased, the 'real' value of the award is clearly increased. However, as the performance condition is a non-market condition, and therefore not relevant to the original determination of the value of the award, there is no incremental fair value required to be accounted for by IFRS 2. However, if the change in the condition results in an increase in the estimated number of awards expected to vest, the change of estimate will give rise to an accounting charge (see 6.1 to 6.4 above).

If an award is modified by changing the service period, the situation is somewhat more complex. A service condition does not of itself change the fair value of the award for the purposes of IFRS 2, but a change in service period may well indirectly change the life of the award, which is relevant to its value (see 8 below). Similar considerations apply where performance conditions are modified in such a way as to alter the anticipated vesting date.

The valuation requirements relating to cancelled and settled awards are considered further at 7.4 below.

7.3 Modification

When an award is modified, the entity must as a minimum recognise the cost of the original award as if it had not been modified (i.e. at the original grant date fair value, spread over the original vesting period, and subject to the original vesting conditions).

This applies unless the award does not vest because of failure to satisfy a vesting condition (other than a market condition) that was specified at grant date. *[IFRS 2.27, B42-43]*.

In addition, a further cost must be recognised for any modifications that increase the fair value of the award. This additional cost is spread over the period from the date of modification until the vesting date of the modified award, which might not be the same as that of the original award. Where a modification is made after the original vesting period has expired, and is subject to no further vesting conditions, any incremental fair value should be recognised immediately. *[IFRS 2.27, B42-43]*.

Whether a modification increases or decreases the fair value of an award is determined as at the date of modification, as illustrated by Example 32.18. *[IFRS 2.27, B42-44]*.

Example 32.18: Does a modification increase or decrease the value of an award?

At the beginning of year 1, an entity granted two executives, A and B, a number of options worth $100 each.

At the beginning of year 2, A's options are modified such that they have a fair value of $85, their current fair value being $80. This is treated as an increase in fair value of $5 (even though the modified award is worth less than the original award when first granted). Therefore an additional $5 of expense would be recognised in respect of A's options.

At the beginning of year 3, B's options are modified such that they have a fair value of $120, their current fair value being $125. This is treated as a reduction in fair value of $5 (even though the modified award is worth more than the original award when first granted). However, there is no change to the expense recognised for B's options as IFRS 2 requires the entity to recognise, as a minimum, the original grant date fair value of the options (i.e. $100).

This treatment ensures that movements in the fair value of the original award are not reflected in the entity's profit or loss, consistent with the treatment of other equity instruments under IFRS.

IFRS 2 provides further detailed guidance on this requirement as discussed below.

7.3.1 Modifications that increase the value of an award

7.3.1.A Increase in fair value of equity instruments granted

If the modification increases the fair value of the equity instruments granted, (e.g. by reducing the exercise price or changing the exercise period), the incremental fair value, measured at the date of modification, must be recognised over the period from the date of modification to the date of vesting for the modified instruments, as illustrated in Example 32.19 below. *[IFRS 2.B43(a), IG15, IG Example 7]*.

Example 32.19: Award modified by repricing

At the beginning of year 1, an entity grants 100 share options to each of its 500 employees. Each grant is conditional upon the employee remaining in service over the next three years. The entity estimates that the fair value of each option is €15.

By the end of year 1, the entity's share price has dropped, and the entity reprices its share options. The repriced share options vest at the end of year 3. The entity estimates that, at the date of repricing, the fair value of each of the original share options granted (i.e. before taking into account the repricing) is €5 and that the fair value of each repriced share option is €8.

40 employees leave during year 1. The entity estimates that a further 70 employees will leave during years 2 and 3, so that there will be 390 employees at the end of year 3 (500 – 40 – 70).

During year 2, a further 35 employees leave, and the entity estimates that a further 30 employees will leave during year 3, so that there will be 395 employees at the end of year 3 (500 – 40 – 35 – 30).

During year 3, 28 employees leave, and hence a total of 103 employees ceased employment during the original three year vesting period, so that, for the remaining 397 employees, the original share options vest at the end of year 3.

IFRS 2 requires the entity to recognise:

- the cost of the original award at grant date (€15 per option) over a three year vesting period beginning at the start of year 1, plus
- the incremental fair value of the repriced options at repricing date (€3 per option, being the €8 fair value of each repriced option less the €5 fair value of the original option) over a two year vesting period beginning at the date of repricing (end of year 1).

This would be calculated as follows:

Year	Calculation of cumulative expense Original award (a)	Modified award (b)	Cumulative expense (€) (a+b)	Expense for period (€)
1	390 employees × 100 options × €15 × 1/3		195,000	195,000
2	395 employees × 100 options × €15 × 2/3	395 employees × 100 options × €3 × 1/2	454,250	259,250
3	397 employees × 100 options × €15	397 employees × 100 options × €3	714,600	260,350

In effect, IFRS 2 treats the original award and the incremental value of the modified award as if they were two separate awards.

A similar treatment to that in Example 32.19 above is adopted where the fair value of an award subject to a market condition has its value increased by the removal or mitigation of the market condition. *[IFRS 2.B43(c)]*. Where a vesting condition other than a market condition is changed, the treatment set out in 7.3.1.C below is adopted. IFRS 2 does not specifically address the situation where the fair value of an award is increased by the removal or mitigation of a non-vesting condition. It seems appropriate, however, to account for this increase in the same way as for a modification caused by the removal or mitigation of a market condition – i.e. as in Example 32.19 above.

7.3.1.B Increase in number of equity instruments granted

If the modification increases the number of equity instruments granted, the fair value of the additional instruments, measured at the date of modification, must be recognised over the period from the date of modification to the date of vesting for the modified instruments. If there is no further vesting period for the modified instruments, the incremental cost should be recognised immediately. *[IFRS 2.B43(b)]*.

7.3.1.C Removal or mitigation of non-market vesting conditions

Where a vesting condition, other than a market condition, is modified in a manner that is beneficial to the employee, the modified vesting condition should be taken into account when applying the general requirements of IFRS 2 as discussed in 6.1 to 6.4 above – in other words, the entity would continuously estimate the number of awards likely to vest and/or the vesting period. *[IFRS 2.B43(c)]*. This is consistent with the general principle of IFRS 2 that vesting conditions, other than market conditions, are not taken into account in the valuation of awards, but are reflected by recognising a cost for those instruments that ultimately vest on achievement of those conditions. See also the discussion at 7.2 above.

IFRS 2 does not provide an example that addresses this point specifically, but we assume that the intended approach is as in Example 32.20 below. In this Example, the entity modifies an award in a way that is beneficial to the employee even though the modification does not result in any incremental fair value. The effect of the modification is therefore recognised by basing the expense on the original grant date fair value of the awards and an assessment of the extent to which the modified vesting conditions will be met.

Example 32.20: Modification of non-market performance condition in employee's favour

At the beginning of year 1, the entity grants 1,000 share options to each member of its sales team, with exercise conditional upon the employee remaining in the entity's employment for three years, and the team selling more than 50,000 units of a particular product over the three year period. The fair value of the share options is £15 per option at the date of grant.

At the end of year 1, the entity estimates that a total of 48,000 units will be sold, and accordingly records no cost for the award in year 1.

During year 2, there is so severe a downturn in trading conditions that the entity believes that the sales target is too demanding to have any motivational effect, and reduces the target to 30,000 units, which it believes is achievable. It also expects 14 members of the sales team to remain in employment throughout the three year performance period. It therefore records an expense in year 2 of £140,000 (£15 × 14 employees × 1,000 options × 2/3). This cost is based on the originally assessed value of the award (i.e. £15) since the performance condition was never factored into the original valuation, such that any change in performance condition likewise has no effect on the valuation and does not result in any incremental fair value.

By the end of year 3, the entity has sold 35,000 units, and the share options vest as the modified performance condition has been met. Twelve members of the sales team have remained in service for the three year period. The entity would therefore recognise a total cost of £180,000 (12 employees × 1,000 options × £15), giving an additional cost in year 3 of £40,000 (total charge £180,000, less £140,000 charged in year 2).

The difference between the accounting consequences for different methods of enhancing an award could cause confusion in some cases. For example, it may sometimes not be clear whether an award has been modified by increasing the number of equity instruments or by lowering the performance targets, as illustrated in Example 32.21.

Example 32.21: Increase in number of equity instruments or modification of vesting conditions?

An entity grants a performance-related award which provides for different numbers of options to vest after 3 years, depending on different performance targets as follows:

Profit growth	Number of options
5%-10%	100
10%-15%	200
over 15%	300

During the vesting period, the entity concludes that the criteria are too demanding and modifies them as follows:

Profit growth	Number of options
5%-10%	200
over 10%	300

This raises the issue of whether the entity has changed:

(a) the performance conditions for the vesting of 200 or 300 options; or

(b) the number of equity instruments awarded for achieving 5%-10% or over 10% growth.

In our view, the reality is that the change is to the performance conditions for the vesting of 200 or 300 options, and should therefore be dealt with as in 7.3.1.C, rather than 7.3.1.B, above. Suppose, however, that the conditions had been modified as follows:

Profit growth	Number of options
5%-10%	200
10%-15%	300
over 15%	400

In that case, there has clearly been an increase in the number of equity instruments subject to an award for an increase of over 15% growth, which would have to be accounted for as such (i.e. under 7.3.1.B, rather than 7.3.1.C, above). In such a case, it seems more appropriate also to deal with the changes to the lower bands as changes to the number of shares awarded rather than as changes to the performance conditions.

7.3.2 Modifications that decrease the value of an award

This type of modification does not occur very often, as the effect would be somewhat demotivating and, in some cases, contrary to local labour regulations. However, there have been occasional examples of an award being made more onerous – usually in response to criticism by shareholders that the original terms were insufficiently demanding.

The general requirement of IFRS 2 (as outlined at 7.3 above) is that, where an award is made more onerous (and therefore less valuable), the financial statements must still recognise the cost of the original award. This rule is in part an anti-avoidance measure since, without it, an entity could reverse the cost of an out-of-the-money award by modifying it so that it was unlikely to vest (for example, by adding unattainable performance conditions) rather than cancelling the award and triggering an acceleration of expense as in 7.1 above.

7.3.2.A Decrease in fair value of equity instruments granted

If the modification decreases the fair value of the equity instruments granted (e.g. by increasing the exercise price or reducing the exercise period), the decrease in value is effectively ignored and the entity continues to recognise a cost for services as if the awards had not been modified. *[IFRS 2.B44(a)]*. This approach applies to reductions in the fair value of an award by the addition of a market condition or by making an existing market condition more onerous. *[IFRS 2.B44(c)]*. Although IFRS 2 has no specific guidance on the point, we assume that reductions in the fair value resulting from the addition or amendment of a non-vesting condition are similarly ignored.

7.3.2.B *Decrease in number of equity instruments granted*

If the modification reduces the number of equity instruments granted, IFRS 2 requires the reduction to be treated as a cancellation of that portion of the award (see 7.4 below). *[IFRS 2.B44(b)]*. Essentially this has the effect that any previously unrecognised cost of the cancelled instruments is immediately recognised in full, whereas the cost of an award whose value is reduced by other means continues to be spread in full over the remaining vesting period.

In situations where a decrease in the number of equity instruments is combined with other modifications so that the total fair value of the award remains the same or increases, it is unclear whether IFRS 2 requires an approach based on the value of the award as a whole or, as in the previous paragraph, one based on each equity instrument as the unit of account. This is considered further at 7.3.4 below.

7.3.2.C *Additional or more onerous non-market vesting conditions*

Where a non-market vesting condition is modified in a manner that is not beneficial to the employee, again it is ignored and a cost recognised as if the original award had not been modified, as shown by Example 32.22 (which is based on IG Example 8 in the implementation guidance to IFRS 2). *[IFRS 2.B44(c), IG15, IG Example 8]*.

Example 32.22: Award modified by changing non-market performance conditions or service conditions

At the beginning of year 1, the entity grants 1,000 share options to each member of its sales team, conditional upon the employee remaining in the entity's employment for three years, and the team selling more than 50,000 units of a particular product over the three year period. The fair value of the share options is £15 per option at the date of grant. During year 2, the entity believes that the sales target is insufficiently demanding and increases it to 100,000 units. By the end of year 3, the entity has sold 55,000 units, and the modified share options are forfeited. Twelve members of the sales team have remained in service for the three year period.

On the basis that the original target would have been met, and twelve employees would have been eligible for awards, the entity would recognise a total cost of £180,000 (12 employees × 1,000 options × £15) in accordance with the minimum cost requirements of paragraph 27 of IFRS 2. The cumulative cost in years 1 and 2 would, as in the Examples above, reflect the entity's best estimate of the *original* 50,000 unit sales target being achieved at the end of year 3. If, conversely, sales of only 49,000 units had been achieved, any cost booked for the award in years 1 and 2 would have been reversed in year 3, since the original target of 50,000 units would not have been met.

It is noted in IG Example 8 that the same accounting result would have occurred if the entity had increased the service requirement rather than modifying the performance target. Because such a modification would make it less likely that the options would vest, which would not be beneficial to the employees, the entity would take no account of the modified service condition when recognising the services received. Instead, it would recognise the services received from the twelve employees who remained in service for the original three year vesting period. Other modifications to vesting periods are discussed below.

7.3.3 Modifications with altered vesting period

As noted at 7.3.1 above, where an award is modified so that its value increases, IFRS 2 requires the entity to continue to recognise an expense for the grant date fair value of the unmodified award over its *original* vesting period, even where the vesting period of the modified award is longer. This appears to have the effect that an expense may need to be recognised for awards that do not actually vest, as illustrated by Example 32.23 (which is based on Example 32.19 above).

Example 32.23: Award modified by reducing the exercise price and extending the vesting period

At the beginning of year 1, an entity grants 100 share options to each of its 500 employees, with vesting conditional upon the employee remaining in service over the next three years. The entity estimates that the fair value of each option is €15.

By the end of year 1, the entity's share price has dropped, and the entity reprices its share options. The repriced share options vest at the end of year 4. The entity estimates that, at the date of repricing, the fair value of each of the original share options granted (i.e. before taking into account the repricing) is €5 and that the fair value of each repriced share option is €7.

40 employees leave during year 1. The entity estimates that a further 70 employees will leave during years 2 and 3, and a further 25 employees during year 4, such that there will be 390 employees at the end of year 3 (500 – 40 – 70) and 365 (500 – 40 – 70 – 25) at the end of year 4.

During year 2, a further 35 employees leave, and the entity estimates that a further 30 employees will leave during year 3 and 30 more in year 4, such that there will be 395 employees at the end of year 3 (500 – 40 – 35 – 30) and 365 (500 – 40 – 35 – 30 – 30) at the end of year 4.

During year 3, 28 employees leave, and hence a total of 103 employees ceased employment during the original three year vesting period, so that, for the remaining 397 employees, the original share options would have vested at the end of year 3. The entity now estimates that only a further 20 employees will leave during year 4, leaving 377 at the end of year 4. In fact 25 employees leave, so that 372 satisfy the criteria for the modified options at the end of year 4.

In our view IFRS 2 requires the entity to recognise:

- the cost of the original award at grant date (€15 per option) over a three year vesting period beginning at the start of year 1, based on the ongoing best estimate of, and ultimately the actual, number of employees at the end of the *original three year* vesting period;
- the incremental fair value of the repriced options at repricing date (€2 per option, being the €7 fair value of each repriced option less the €5 fair value of the original option) over a three year vesting period beginning at the date of repricing (*end* of year one), but based on the ongoing best estimate of, and ultimately the actual, number of employees at the end of the *modified four year* vesting period.

This would be calculated as follows:

Year	Calculation of cumulative expense Original award	 Modified award	Cumulative expense (€)	Expense for period (€)
1	390 employees × 100 options × €15 × 1/3		195,000	195,000
2	395 employees × 100 options × €15 × 2/3	365 employees × 100 options × €2 × 1/3	419,333	224,333
3	397 employees × 100 options × €15	377 employees × 100 options × €2 × 2/3	645,767	226,434
4	397 employees × 100 options × €15	372 employees × 100 options × €2	669,900	24,133

It may seem strange that a cost is being recognised for the original award in respect of the 25 employees who leave during year 4, who are never entitled to anything. However, in our view, this is consistent with:

- the overall requirement of IFRS 2 that the minimum cost of a modified award should be the cost that would have been recognised if the award had not been modified; and
- IG Example 8 in IFRS 2 (the substance of which is reproduced in Example 32.22 above) where an expense is clearly required to be recognised to the extent that the original performance conditions would have been met if the award had not been modified.

Moreover, as Examples 32.22 and 32.23 illustrate, the rule in IFRS 2 requiring recognition of a minimum expense for a modified award (i.e. as if the original award had remained in place) applies irrespective of whether the effect of the modification is that an award becomes less valuable to the employee (as in Example 32.22) or more valuable to the employee (as in Example 32.23).

Where a modified vesting period is shorter than the original vesting period, all of the expense relating to both the original and modified elements of the award should, in our view, be recognised by the end of the modified vesting period as no services will be rendered beyond that point. In this type of modification – as distinct from a change of estimate where there is a variable vesting period (see 6.2.3 above) – we believe that an entity has an accounting policy choice between retrospective and prospective adjustment of the vesting period as at the modification date. The overall expense recognised between grant date and vesting date will be the same in both cases, but there will be timing differences in the recognition of the expense, with retrospective accounting resulting in a higher expense as at the modification date itself.

7.3.4 Modifications that reduce the number of equity instruments granted but maintain or increase the value of an award ('value for value' exchanges and 'give and take' modifications)

As discussed at 7.3.2.B above, cancellation accounting has to be applied to a reduction in the number of equity instruments when a modification reduces both the number of equity instruments granted and the total fair value of the award. *[IFRS 2.B44(b)]*. This approach is consistent with the fact that part of the award has been removed without compensation to the employee. However, a modification of this kind is rarely seen in practice because of the demotivating effect and, in some jurisdictions, a requirement to pay compensation to the counterparty. An entity is more likely to modify an award so that the overall fair value remains the same, or increases, even if the number of equity instruments is reduced. These types of modification, sometimes known as 'value for value' exchanges or 'give and take' modifications, are considered below.

Where an entity reduces the number of equity instruments but also makes other changes so that the total fair value of the modified award remains the same as that of the original award as at the modification date or exceeds it, it is unclear whether the unit of account for accounting purposes should be an individual equity instrument or the award as a whole. Examples 32.24 and 32.25 below illustrate the two situations and the two approaches.

Example 32.24: Modification where number of equity instruments is reduced but total fair value of award is unchanged

At the beginning of year 1, an entity granted an employee 200 share options with a grant date fair value of £9 and a vesting period of three years. During years 1 and 2, the entity recognises a cumulative expense of £1,200 (200 × £9 × 2/3). At the end of year 2 the exercise price of the options is significantly higher than the market price and the options have a fair value of £5 per option. On this date, the entity modifies the award and exchanges the 200 underwater options for 100 'at the money' options with a fair value of £10 each. The total fair value of the new awards of £1,000 (100 × £10) equals the total fair value of the awards exchanged (200 × £5), as measured at the modification date.

View 1 is that the unit of account is an individual option. Taking this approach, the decrease in the number of options from 200 to 100 will be accounted for as a cancellation with an acceleration at the modification date of any unexpensed element of the grant date fair value of 100 options (i.e. recognition of an additional amount of £300 (100 × £9 × 1/3)) The grant date fair value of the remaining 100 options continues to be recognised over the remainder of the vesting period together with their incremental fair value following the modification. Therefore, in year 3, there would be an expense of £300 (for the remaining grant date fair value) plus £500 (100 × (£10 – £5)) for the incremental fair value of 100 options. In total, therefore, an expense of £2,300 is recognised.

View 2 is that the total number of options exchanged is the more appropriate unit of account. In this case, the cancellation of the original options and the grant of replacement options are accounted for as one modification. There would therefore be no acceleration of expense in respect of the reduction in the number of options from 200 to 100 and the grant date fair value of the original award would continue to be recognised over the vesting period. In this case, the total expense recognised would be £1,800 (200 × £9).

Example 32.25: Modification where number of equity instruments is reduced but total fair value of award is increased

At the beginning of year 1, an entity granted to its employees 1,000 share options with an exercise price equal to the market price of the shares at grant date. There is a two year vesting period and the grant date fair value is £10 per option. The entity's share price has declined significantly so that the share price is currently significantly less than the exercise price. At the end of year 1, the entity decides to reduce the exercise price of the options and, as part of the modification, it also reduces the number of options from 1,000 to 800. At the date of modification, the fair value of the original options is £7 per option and that of the modified options £11 per option.

View 1 is that the unit of account is an individual option. Taking this approach, the decrease in the number of options from 1,000 to 800 will be accounted for as a cancellation of 200 options with an acceleration at the modification date of any remaining grant date fair value relating to those 200 options. The total expense recognised in year 1 is £6,000 ((800 × £10 × ½) + (200 × £10)). The grant date fair value of the remaining 800 options continues to be recognised over the remainder of the vesting period together with the incremental fair value of those options as measured at the modification date. In total the entity will recognise an expense of £13,200 (original grant date fair value of £10,000 (1,000 × £10) plus incremental fair value of £3,200 (800 × £(11 – 7)).

View 2 is that the unit of account is the total number of options as there are linked modifications forming one package. In this case, the incremental fair value is calculated as the difference between the total fair value before and after the modification. In total the entity will recognise an expense of £11,800 (original grant date fair value of £10,000 (1,000 × £10) plus incremental fair value on modification of £1,800 ((800 × £11) – (1,000 × £7)).

In both Examples above, the first view is based on paragraph B44(b) of IFRS 2 which states that 'if the modification reduces the number of equity instruments granted to an employee, that reduction shall be accounted for as a cancellation of that portion of the grant, in accordance with the requirements of paragraph 28'. This is perhaps further supported by paragraph B43(a) which, in providing guidance on accounting for a modification that increases the fair value of an equity instrument, appears only to refer to individual equity instruments when it states that 'the incremental fair value granted' in a modification is 'the difference between the fair value of the modified equity instrument and that of the original equity instrument, both estimated as at the date of modification'. *[IFRS 2.B43-44]*.

The second view is based on the overriding requirement in paragraph 27 of IFRS 2 for the grant date fair value of the equity instruments to be recognised unless the awards do not vest due to a failure to meet a vesting condition (other than a market condition). This requirement is applicable even if the award is modified after the grant date. The same paragraph also requires an entity to recognise the effect of modifications 'that increase the total fair value of the share-based payment arrangement or are otherwise beneficial to the employee'. This reference to 'total fair value' supports the view that the total award is the unit of account and is reiterated in paragraphs B42 and B44 which provide guidance, respectively, for situations where the total fair value decreases or increases as a consequence of the modification of an award. Supporters of view 2 further consider that, in contrast to the cancellation accounting approach that is required in the very specific case where part of the award is, in effect, settled for no consideration (see 7.3.2.B above), a modification that reduces the number of equity instruments but maintains or increases the overall fair value of the award clearly provides the counterparty with a benefit. As a consequence, it is considered that no element of the grant date fair value should be accelerated as a cancellation expense. *[IFRS 2.27, B42, B44]*.

Given the lack of clarity in IFRS 2, we believe that an entity may make an accounting policy choice as to whether it considers the unit of account to be an individual equity instrument or an award as a whole. However, once made, that accounting policy choice should be applied consistently to all modifications that reduce the number of equity instruments but maintain or increase the overall fair value of an award. Whichever policy is chosen, the general requirements of IFRS 2 will still need to be applied in order to determine whether or not the amendments to the arrangement are such that it is appropriate to treat the changes as a modification (in IFRS 2 terms) rather than as a completely new award (see 7.4.2 and 7.4.4 below).

7.3.5 Modification of award from equity-settled to cash-settled (and vice versa)

Occasionally an award that was equity-settled when originally granted is modified so as to become cash-settled, or an originally cash-settled award is modified so as to become equity-settled. Such modifications are discussed at 9.4 below.

7.4 Cancellation and settlement

Where an award is cancelled or settled (i.e. cancelled with some form of compensation), other than by forfeiture for failure to satisfy the vesting conditions:

(a) if the cancellation or settlement occurs during the vesting period, it is treated as an acceleration of vesting, and the entity recognises immediately the amount that would otherwise have been recognised for services received over the remainder of the vesting period;

(b) where the entity pays compensation for a cancelled award:

   (i) any compensation paid up to the fair value of the award at cancellation or settlement date (whether before or after vesting) is accounted for as a deduction from equity, as being equivalent to the redemption of an equity instrument;

   (ii) any compensation paid in excess of the fair value of the award at cancellation or settlement date (whether before or after vesting) is accounted for as an expense in profit or loss; and

   (iii) if the share-based payment arrangement includes liability components, the fair value of the liability is remeasured at the date of cancellation or settlement. Any payment made to settle the liability component is accounted for as an extinguishment of the liability; and

(c) if the entity grants new equity instruments during the vesting period and, on the date that they are granted, identifies them as replacing the cancelled or settled instruments, the entity is required to account for the new equity instruments as if they were a modification of the cancelled or settled award. Otherwise it accounts for the new instruments as an entirely new award. *[IFRS 2.28, 29].*

The treatment of the cancelled or settled award in (a) above is similar, in its effect on profit or loss, to the result that would have occurred if:

- the fair value of the equity instruments issued had been recorded in full at grant date with a corresponding debit to a prepayment for 'services to be rendered';
- the prepayment were written off on a periodic basis until cancellation or settlement; and
- any remaining prepayment at the date of cancellation or settlement were written off in full.

It should be noted that the calculation of any additional expense in (b) above depends on the fair value of the award at the date of cancellation or settlement, not on the cumulative expense already charged. This has the important practical consequence that, when an entity pays compensation on cancellation or settlement of an award, it must obtain a fair value for the original award, updated to the date of cancellation or settlement. If the award had not been cancelled or settled, there would have been no need to obtain a valuation for the original award after the date of grant.

These requirements raise some further detailed issues of interpretation on a number of areas, as follows:

- the distinction between 'cancellation' and 'forfeiture' (see 7.4.1 below);
- the distinction between 'cancellation' and 'modification' (see 7.4.2 below);
- the calculation of the expense on cancellation (see 7.4.3 below); and
- replacement awards (see 7.4.4 and 7.5 below).

7.4.1 Distinction between cancellation and forfeiture

The above provisions of IFRS 2 apply when an award of equity instruments is cancelled or settled 'other than a grant cancelled by forfeiture when the vesting conditions are not satisfied'. *[IFRS 2.28]*. The significance of this is that the terms of many share-based awards provide that they are, or can be, 'cancelled', in a legal sense, on forfeiture. IFRS 2 is clarifying that, where an award is forfeited (within the meaning of that term in IFRS 2 – see 6.1.2 above), the entity should apply the accounting treatment for a forfeiture (i.e. reversal of expense previously recognised), even if the award is legally cancelled as a consequence of the forfeiture.

7.4.1.A Termination of employment by entity

Based on the guidance in paragraph 28 of IFRS 2 referred to at 7.4.1 above, it might not be immediately clear in some cases whether cancellation or forfeiture has occurred, particularly where options lapse as the result of a termination of employment by the entity. For example, an entity might grant options to an employee on 1 January 2016 on condition of his remaining in employment until at least 31 December 2018. During 2017, however, economic conditions require the entity to make a number of its personnel, including that employee, redundant, as a result of which his options lapse. Is this lapse a forfeiture or a cancellation for the purposes of IFRS 2?

The uncertainty arises because it could be argued either that the employee will be unable to deliver the services required in order for the options to vest (suggesting a forfeiture) or that the options lapse as a direct result of the employer's actions (suggesting a cancellation).

The IASB noted that there was no guidance on this question in IFRS 2 and addressed this by including a new definition of 'service condition' in IFRS 2 as part of its *Annual Improvements to IFRSs 2010-2012 Cycle* (see 3.1 above). The definition includes the following guidance:

'... If the counterparty, regardless of the reason, ceases to provide service during the vesting period, it has failed to satisfy the condition. ...' *[IFRS 2 Appendix A]*.

Therefore, application of the amended version of IFRS 2 (to grants on or after 1 July 2014) requires any termination of employment to be accounted for as a forfeiture rather than as a cancellation.

7.4.1.B Surrender of award by employee

It is sometimes the case that an employee, often a member of senior management, will decide – or be encouraged by the entity – to surrender awards during the vesting period. The question arises as to whether this should be treated as a cancellation or forfeiture for accounting purposes. IFRS 2 allows forfeiture accounting, and the consequent reversal of any cumulative expense, only in situations where vesting conditions are not satisfied. A situation where the counterparty voluntarily surrenders an award, and therefore the opportunity to meet the vesting conditions, is a decision within the control of the counterparty rather than a failure to satisfy a vesting condition and should be accounted for as a cancellation rather than as a forfeiture.

In its amendment of IFRS 2 (as discussed at 7.4.1.A above), we do not believe that the IASB's intention was to allow an employee to 'fail' to meet a service condition by voluntarily surrendering an award. Such an action should therefore continue to be treated as a cancellation rather than as a forfeiture.

7.4.2 Distinction between cancellation and modification

One general issue raised by IFRS 2 is where the boundary lies between 'modification' of an award in the entity's favour and outright cancellation of the award. As a matter of legal form, the difference is obvious. However, if an entity were to modify an award in such a way that there was no realistic chance of it ever vesting (for example, by introducing a requirement that the share price increase 1,000,000 times by vesting date), some might argue that this amounts to a *de facto* cancellation of the award. The significance of the distinction is that, whereas the cost of a 'modified' award continues to be recognised on a periodic basis over the vesting period (see 7.3 above), the remaining cost of a cancelled award is recognised immediately.

7.4.3 Calculation of the expense on cancellation

The basic accounting treatment for a cancellation and settlement is illustrated in Example 32.26 below.

Example 32.26: Cancellation and settlement – basic accounting treatment

At the start of year 1 an entity grants an executive 30,000 options on condition that she remain in employment for three years. Each option is determined to have a fair value of $10.

At the end of year 1, the executive is still in employment and the entity charges an IFRS 2 expense of $100,000 (30,000 × $10 × 1/3). At the end of year 2, the executive is still in employment. However, the entity's share price has suffered a decline which the entity does not expect to have reversed by the end of year 3, such that the options, while still 'in the money' now have a fair value of only $6. Moreover, the entity is under pressure from major shareholders to end option schemes with no performance criteria other than continuing employment.

Accordingly, the entity cancels the options at the end of year 2 and in compensation pays the executive $6.50 per option cancelled, a total payment of $195,000 (30,000 options × $6.50).

IFRS 2 first requires the entity to record a cost as if the options had vested immediately. The total cumulative cost for the award must be $300,000 (30,000 options × $10). $100,000 was recognised in year 1, so that an additional cost of $200,000 is recognised.

As regards the compensation payment, the fair value of the awards cancelled is $180,000 (30,000 options × $6.00). Accordingly, $180,000 of the payment is accounted for as a deduction from equity, with the remaining payment in excess of fair value, $15,000, charged to profit or loss.

The net effect of this is that an award that ultimately results in a cash payment to the executive of only $195,000 (i.e. $6.50 per option) has resulted in a total charge to profit or loss of $315,000 (i.e. $10.50 per option, representing $10 grant date fair value + $6.50 compensation payment – $6.00 cancellation date fair value).

Example 32.26 illustrates the basic calculation of the cancellation 'charge' required by IFRS 2. In more complex situations, however, the amount of the 'charge' may not be so clear-cut, due to an ambiguity in the drafting of paragraph 28(a) of the standard, which reads as follows:

> 'the entity shall account for the cancellation or settlement as an acceleration of vesting, and shall therefore recognise immediately the amount that would otherwise have been recognised for services received over the remainder of the vesting period.' *[IFRS 2.28(a)]*.

There is something of a contradiction within this requirement as illustrated by Example 32.27.

Example 32.27: Cancellation and settlement – best estimate of cancellation expense

At the beginning of year 1, entity A granted 150 employees an award of free shares, with a grant date fair value of £5, conditional upon continuous service and performance targets over a 3-year period from grant date. The number of shares awarded varies according to the extent to which targets (all non-market vesting conditions) have been met, and could result in each employee still in service at the end of year 3 receiving a minimum of 600, and a maximum of 1,000 shares.

Half way through year 2 (i.e. 18 months after grant date), A is acquired by B, following which all of A's share awards are cancelled. At the time of the cancellation, 130 of the original 150 employees were still in employment. At that time, it was A's best estimate that, had the award run to its full term, 120 employees would have received 900 shares each. Accordingly the cumulative expense recognised by A for the award as at the date of takeover would, under the normal estimation processes of IFRS 2 discussed at 6.1 to 6.4 above, be £270,000 (900 shares × 120 employees × £5 × 18/36).

How should A account for the cancellation of this award?

The opening phrase of paragraph 28(a) – 'the entity shall account for the cancellation ... as an acceleration of vesting' – suggests that A should recognise a cost for all 130 employees in service at the date of cancellation. However, the following phrase – '[the entity] shall therefore recognise immediately the amount that would otherwise have been recognised for services received over the remainder of the vesting period' – suggests that the charge should be based on only 120 employees, the best estimate, as at the date of cancellation of the number of employees in whom shares will finally vest. In our view, either reading of paragraph 28(a) is possible.

There is then the issue of the number of shares per employee that should be taken into account in the cancellation charge. Should this be 1,000 shares per employee (the maximum number that could vest) or 900 shares per employee (the number expected by the entity at the date of cancellation actually to vest)?

In our view, it is unclear from the standard whether the intention was that the cancellation charge should be based on the number of shares considered likely, as at the date of cancellation, to vest for each employee (900 shares in this example) or whether it should be based on the maximum number of shares (1,000 shares in this example). Given the lack of clarity, in our view an entity may make an accounting policy choice.

In extreme cases, the entity's best estimate, as at the date of cancellation, might be that no awards are likely to vest. In this situation, no cancellation expense would be recognised. However, there would need to be evidence that this was not just a rather convenient assessment made as at the date of cancellation. Typically, the previous accounting periods would also have reflected a cumulative IFRS 2 expense of zero on the assumption that the awards would never vest.

An effect of these requirements is that IFRS 2 creates an accounting arbitrage between an award that is 'out of the money' but not cancelled (the cost of which continues to be spread over the remaining period to vesting) and one which is formally cancelled (the cost of which is recognised immediately). Entities might well prefer to opt for cancellation so as to create a 'one-off' charge to earnings rather than continue to show, particularly during difficult trading periods, significant periodic costs for options that no longer have any real value. However, such early cancellation of an award precludes any chance of the cost of the award being reversed through forfeiture during, or at the end of, the vesting period if the original vesting conditions are not met.

7.4.4 Replacement awards

The required accounting treatment of replacement awards, whilst generally clear, nevertheless raises some issues of interpretation. Most of this sub-section addresses the replacement of unvested awards but the treatment of vested awards is addressed at 7.4.4.C below.

7.4.4.A Designation of award as replacement award

Whether or not an award is a 'replacement' award (and therefore recognised at only its incremental, rather than its full, fair value) is determined by whether or not the entity designates it as such on the date that it is granted. In other words, the accounting treatment effectively hinges on declared management intent, notwithstanding the IASB's systematic exclusion of management intent from many other areas of financial reporting. The Basis for Conclusions does not really explain the reason for this approach, which is also hard to reconcile with the fact that the value of an award is unaffected by whether, or when, the entity declares it to be a 'replacement' award for the purposes of IFRS 2. Presumably, the underlying reason is to prevent a retrospective, and possibly opportunistic, assertion that an award that has been in issue for some time is a replacement for an earlier award.

Entities need to ensure that designation occurs on grant date as defined by IFRS 2 (see 5.3 above). For example, if an entity cancels an award on 15 March 2017 and notifies an employee in writing on the same day of its intention to ask the remuneration committee to grant replacement options at its meeting on 15 May 2017, such notification (although formal and in writing) may not strictly meet IFRS 2's requirement for designation on grant date (i.e. 15 May 2017). However, in our view, what is important is that the entity establishes a clear link between the cancellation of the old award and the granting of a replacement award even if there is later formal approval of the replacement award following the communication of its terms to the counterparty at the same time as the cancellation of the old award.

As drafted, IFRS 2 gives entities an apparently free choice to designate any newly granted awards as replacement awards. In our view, however, such designation cannot credibly be made unless there is evidence of some connection between the cancelled and replacement awards. This might be that the cancelled and replacement awards involve the same counterparties, or that the cancellation and replacement are part of the same arrangement.

7.4.4.B Incremental fair value of replacement award

Where an award is designated as a replacement award, it must be recognised, over its vesting period, at its incremental fair value. This is the difference between the fair value of the replacement award and the 'net fair value' of the cancelled or settled award, both measured at the date on which the replacement awards are granted. The net fair value of the cancelled or settled award is the fair value of the award, immediately before cancellation, less any compensation payment that is accounted for as a deduction from equity. *[IFRS 2.28(c)]*. Thus the 'net fair value' of the original award can never be less than zero (since any compensation payment in excess of the fair value of the cancelled award would be accounted for in profit or loss, not in equity – see Example 32.26 at 7.4.3 above).

There is some confusion within IFRS 2 as to whether a different accounting treatment is intended to result from, on the one hand, modifying an award and, on the other hand, cancelling it and replacing it with a new award on the same terms as the modified award. This is explored in the discussion of Example 32.28 below, which is based on the same fact pattern as Example 32.19 at 7.3.1.A above.

Example 32.28: Is there an accounting arbitrage between modification and cancellation of an award?

At the beginning of year 1, an entity grants 100 share options to each of its 500 employees. Each grant is conditional upon the employee remaining in service over the next three years. The entity estimates that the fair value of each option is €15.

By the end of year 1, the entity's share price has dropped. The entity cancels the existing options and issues options which it identifies as replacement options, which also vest at the end of year 3. The entity estimates that, at the date of cancellation, the fair value of each of the original share options granted is €5 and that the fair value of each replacement share option is €8.

40 employees leave during year 1. The entity estimates that a further 70 employees will leave during years 2 and 3, so that there will be 390 employees at the end of year 3 (500 – 40 – 70).

During year 2, a further 35 employees leave, and the entity estimates that a further 30 employees will leave during year 3, so that there will be 395 employees at the end of year 3 (500 – 40 – 35 – 30).

During year 3, 28 employees leave, and hence a total of 103 employees ceased employment during the original three year vesting period, so that, for the remaining 397 employees, the replacement share options vest at the end of year 3.

The intention of the IASB appears to have been that the arrangement should be accounted for in exactly the same way as the modification in Example 32.19 above, since the Basis for Conclusions to IFRS 2 notes:

> '...the Board saw no difference between a repricing of share options and a cancellation of share options followed by the granting of replacement share options at a lower exercise price, and therefore concluded that the accounting treatment should be the same.' *[IFRS 2.BC233]*.

However, it is not clear that this intention is actually reflected in the drafting of IFRS 2, paragraph 28 of which reads as follows:

> 'If a grant of equity instruments is cancelled or settled during the vesting period (other than a grant cancelled by forfeiture when the vesting conditions are not satisfied):
>
> (a) the entity shall account for the cancellation or settlement as an acceleration of vesting, and shall therefore recognise immediately the amount that otherwise would have been recognised for services received over the remainder of the vesting period.
>
> (b) any payment made to the employee on the cancellation or settlement of the grant shall be accounted for as the repurchase of an equity interest, i.e. as a deduction from equity, except to the extent that the payment exceeds the fair value of the equity instruments granted, measured at the repurchase date. Any such excess shall be recognised as an expense....
>
> (c) if new equity instruments are granted to the employee and, on the date when those new equity instruments are granted, the entity identifies the new equity instruments granted as replacement equity instruments for the cancelled equity instruments, the entity shall account for the granting of replacement equity instruments in the same way as a modification of the original grant of equity instruments, in accordance with paragraph 27 and the guidance in Appendix B ...'. *[IFRS 2.28]*.

As a matter of natural construction, paragraph (a) requires the cancellation of the existing award to be treated as an acceleration of vesting – explicitly and without qualification. In particular there is no rider to the effect that the requirement of paragraph (a) is to be read as 'subject to paragraph (c) below'.

Paragraph (c) requires any 'new equity instruments' granted to be accounted for in the same way as a modification of the original grant of equity instruments. It does not require this treatment for the cancellation of the *original* instruments, because this has already been addressed in paragraph (a).

Moreover, in order to construe paragraphs (a) and (c) in a manner consistent with the Basis for Conclusions to the standard, it would be necessary to read paragraph (c) as effectively superseding paragraph (a). However, for this to be a valid reading, it would also be necessary to read paragraph (b) as also superseding paragraph (a), and this would produce a manifestly incorrect result, namely that, if an award is cancelled *and settled*, there is no need ever to expense any part of the cancelled award not yet expensed at the date of cancellation.

The application of, firstly, the main text of IFRS 2 and, secondly, the Basis for Conclusions to IFRS 2 to the entity in Example 32.28 is set out below.

The main text in IFRS 2 appears to require the entity to recognise:

- The entire cost of the original options at the end of year 1 (since cancellation has the effect that they are treated as vesting at that date), based on the 390 employees expected at that date to be in employment at the end of the vesting period. This is not the only possible interpretation of the requirement of paragraph 28(a) – see below and the broader discussion in Example 32.27 at 7.4.3 above.
- For the options replacing the 390 cancelled awards, the incremental fair value of the replacement options at repricing date (€3 per option, being the €8 fair value of each replacement option less the €5 fair value of each cancelled option) over a two year vesting period beginning at the date of cancellation (end of year 1), based on the (at first estimated and then actual) number of employees at the end of year 3 (i.e. the final number could be less than the estimate of 390).
- For any additional replacement options (i.e. replacement options awarded in excess of the 390 × 100 options that were expected to vest at cancellation date), the full incremental fair value at repricing date (being the €8 fair value of each replacement option) over a two year vesting period beginning at the repricing date (end of year 1). The expense is based on the (at first estimated and then actual) number of employees in excess of 390 at the end of year 3.

This would be calculated as follows:

Year	Calculation of cumulative expense Original award	 Replacement award	Cumulative expense (€)	Expense for period (€)
1	390 employees × 100 options × €15	–	585,000	585,000
2	390 employees × 100 options × €15	390 employees × 100 options × €3 × 1/2 5 employees × 100 options × €8 × 1/2	645,500	60,500
3	390 employees × 100 options × €15	390 employees × 100 options × €3 7 employees × 100 options × €8	707,600	62,100

By contrast, the accounting treatment implied by the Basis for Conclusions is as follows (see Example 32.19 above):

Year	Calculation of cumulative expense Original award (a)	Modified award (b)	Cumulative expense (€) (a+b)	Expense for period (€)
1	390 employees × 100 options × €15 × 1/3	–	195,000	195,000
2	395 employees × 100 options × €15 × 2/3	395 employees × 100 options × €3 × 1/2	454,250	259,250
3	397 employees × 100 options × €15	397 employees × 100 options × €3	714,600	260,350

It will be seen that both the periodic allocation of expense and the total expense differ under each interpretation. This is because, under the first interpretation, the cost of the original award is accelerated at the end of year 1 for all 390 employees expected at that date to be in employment at the end of the vesting period, whereas under the second interpretation a cost is recognised for the 397 employees whose awards finally vest. The difference between the two total charges of €7,000 (€714,600 – €707,600) represents 397 – 390 = 7 employees @ €1,000 [100 options × €10[€15 + €3 – €8]] each = €7,000.

We believe that either interpretation is valid, and an entity should adopt one or other consistently as a matter of accounting policy.

In Example 32.28 above, we base the cancellation calculations on 390 employees (the number expected to be employed at the end of the vesting period as estimated at the cancellation date) rather than on 460 employees (the number in employment at the cancellation date). As discussed in Example 32.27 at 7.4.3 above, either approach may be adopted but the selected approach should be applied consistently.

The Examples considered above involve a relatively straightforward fact pattern where, as at the date of cancellation and replacement, there was an amount to accelerate in respect of the cancelled awards and an incremental fair value associated with the replacement awards. In other scenarios, the two accounting outcomes might result in greater divergence. For example, if the cancelled awards were expected never to vest, because performance conditions had become unachievable and this had been the conclusion for some time (see 7.4.3 above), the cancelled awards might have a value of zero on a cancellation basis and the full value of the replacement awards would be recognised. If modification accounting were applied, however, the entity would have to recognise the grant date fair value of the cancelled awards plus any incremental value of the replacement awards over the fair value of the cancelled awards as at cancellation date. The latter approach might result in a significantly higher cost.

The discussion above relates to situations in which awards are cancelled and replaced for reasons other than expected, or actual, failure by the counterparty to meet a service condition. Changes to awards in contemplation, or as a consequence, of cessation of employment are considered at 5.3.9.B above and at 7.5 and 7.6 below.

7.4.4.C Replacement of vested awards

The rules for replacement awards summarised in paragraph (c) at 7.4 above apply 'if a grant of equity instruments is cancelled or settled during the vesting period ...'. *[IFRS 2.28]*. However, if the original award has already vested when a replacement award is granted, there is no question of accelerating the cost of the cancelled award, as it has already been recognised in full during the vesting period. The issue is rather the treatment of the new award itself. IFRS 2 does not explicitly address this point but it appears that such a replacement award should be treated in the same way as a completely new award. In other words, its full fair value should be recognised immediately or, if there are any vesting conditions for the replacement award, over its vesting period.

By contrast, the rules for modification of awards discussed in 7.3 above apply whether the award has vested or not. Paragraphs 26 and 27 of IFRS 2 (modifications) are not restricted to events 'during the vesting period' in contrast to paragraph 28 (cancellation and settlement, including replacement awards), which is restricted to events 'during the vesting period'. *[IFRS 2.26-28]*.

This has the effect that the accounting cost of modifying an already vested award (i.e. the incremental fair value of the modified award) may, at first sight, appear to be lower than the cost of cancelling and replacing it, which requires the full fair value of the new award to be expensed. However, the full fair value of the new replacement award will be reduced by the fair value of the cancelled award that the employee has surrendered as part of the consideration for the new award. This analysis will, in many cases, produce an accounting outcome similar to that of the modification of an unvested award.

7.5 Replacement and ex gratia awards on termination of employment

When an employee's employment is terminated during the vesting period of an award of shares or options, the award will typically lapse in consequence. It is common in such situations, particularly where the employee was part of the senior management, for the entity to make an alternative award, or to allow the employee to retain existing awards, as part of the package of benefits agreed with the employee on termination of employment.

Generally, such an award is an *ex gratia* award – in other words, it is a discretionary award to which the outgoing employee had no legal entitlement under the terms of the original award. However, a number of plan rules set out, in a 'good leaver' clause (see 5.3.9 above), the terms on which any *ex gratia* award may be made, usually by applying a formula to determine, or limit, how much of the original award can be considered to have vested.

In many cases the award will be made on a fully vested basis, i.e. the employee has full entitlement without further conditions needing to be fulfilled. In other cases, however, an employee will be allowed to retain awards that remain subject to the fulfilment of the original conditions (other than future service). Whichever form the award takes, in IFRS 2 terms it will be treated as vesting at the date of termination of employment because any remaining conditions will be accounted for as non-vesting conditions in the absence of an explicit or implied service condition (see 3.2 above).

As discussed at 7.4.1.A above, IFRS 2 as amended by the *Annual Improvements to IFRSs 2010-2012 Cycle* requires an entity to apply forfeiture (rather than cancellation) accounting to awards that lapse if an employee is unable to satisfy a service condition for any reason. In amending the standard to make clear that forfeiture accounting applied to the termination of employment, the IASB did not specifically address the accounting for any replacement or *ex gratia* awards on termination of employment.

If the original award is accounted for as a forfeiture and any previously recognised cost reversed in anticipation of the employee's expected departure, it perhaps follows that any replacement award will be treated as a completely new award and recognised and measured based on its own grant date. However, the standard is not clear and there might be situations where entities consider it more appropriate to apply modification accounting (recognising the original grant date fair value of the award that would otherwise be forfeited on its original terms (because the service condition would not be met) plus the incremental value of the modified terms). In the absence of clarity in IFRS 2, we believe that judgement will be required based on the specific facts and circumstances and the extent to which the changes to the arrangements are considered to be a waiver of existing conditions in connection with the cessation of employment rather than introduction of a discretionary replacement arrangement on completely new terms.

Example 32.29: Replacement award on termination of employment

On 1 January 2016, an executive is granted the right to 10,000 free shares on condition of remaining in service until 31 December 2018. The fair value of the award at grant date is £2.00 per share.

On 31 December 2017, the executive's employment is terminated and he therefore loses his right to any shares. However, as *ex gratia* (voluntary) compensation, the remuneration committee awards him 6,667 shares vesting immediately. At 31 December 2017, the share price was £4.00, and the fair value of the original award was £3.60 per share. (This is lower than the current share price because the holder of a share is entitled to receive any dividends paid during 2018, whereas the holder of an unvested right to a share is not – see 8.5.4 below.)

This raises the question of how the *ex gratia* award of 6,667 shares should be accounted for. The factors to be considered in determining the grant date in such cases are discussed further at 5.3.9 above. For the purposes of this Example, it is assumed that the replacement award is treated as having been granted, or the original award is treated as having been modified, on 31 December 2017 rather than the terms being in place as at 1 January 2016.

Where the lapse is treated as a forfeiture, the entity:

- reverses the cost already booked for the award of £13,333 (10,000 shares × £2 × 2/3); and
- recognises the cost of the *ex gratia* award (at the fair value at that award's grant date) of £26,668 (6,667 shares × £4)

This results in a net charge on termination of £13,335.

If the lapse is treated as a modification of the original award, the entity:

- accelerates the cost not yet booked for the original award of £6,667 (10,000 shares × £2 = £20,000, less £13,333 already recognised – see above) as there is no future service period; and
- treats the *ex gratia* award as a replacement award at incremental value. The fair value of the replacement award of £26,668 (6,667 shares × £4 – see above) is compared to the fair value of the original award of £36,000 (10,000 shares × £3.60). Since the fair value of the replacement award is less than that of the original award, there is no incremental cost required to be recorded under IFRS 2.

This results in a net charge on termination of £6,667.

Example 32.29 assumes that the entity treats the entire award as the unit of account. An entity that has made a policy choice to base its modification accounting on an individual share or option as the unit of account (see further discussion at 7.3.4 above) will have a different accounting outcome.

7.6 Entity's plans for future modification or replacement of award – impact on estimation process at reporting date

As discussed at 6.1.1 and 6.1.2 above, IFRS 2 requires an entity to determine a cumulative IFRS 2 charge at each reporting date by reference to the 'best available estimate' of the number of awards that will vest (within the special meaning of that term in IFRS 2).

In addition to the normal difficulties inherent in any estimation process, it is not entirely clear which anticipated future events should be taken into account in the IFRS 2 estimation process and which should not, as illustrated by Example 32.30 below.

Example 32.30: Estimation of number of awards expected to vest – treatment of anticipated future events

At the beginning of year 1, an entity granted an award of 1,000 shares to each of its 600 employees at a particular manufacturing unit. The award vests on completion of three years' service. As at the end of year 1, the entity firmly intends to close the unit, and terminate the employment of employees, as part of a rationalisation programme. This closure would occur part way through year 2. The entity has not, however, announced its intentions or taken any other steps so as to allow provision for the closure under IAS 37 – *Provisions, Contingent Liabilities and Contingent Assets* (see Chapter 28 at 6.1).

Under the original terms of the award, the award would lapse on termination of employment. However, the entity intends to compensate employees made redundant by changing the terms of their award so as to allow full vesting on termination of employment.

What is the 'best estimate', as at the end of year 1, of the number of awards expected to vest? Specifically should the entity:

(a) ignore the intended closure altogether, on the grounds that there is no other recognition of it in the financial statements;

(b) take account of the impact of the intended closure on vesting of the current award, but ignore the intended future change to the terms of the award to allow vesting; or

(c) take account of both the intended closure and the intended change to the terms of the award?

In our view, there is no basis in IFRS 2 for accounting for an anticipated future change to the terms of an award. The entity must account for awards in issue at the reporting date, not those that might be in issue in the future. Accordingly we do not consider approach (c) above to be appropriate if any change to the issued awards was simply an intention.

Equally, we struggle to support approach (a) above. IFRS 2 requires the entity to use its 'best available estimate' and its best available estimate as at the end of year 1 must be that the unit will be closed, and the employees' employment terminated, in year 2. This view is supported by the fact that, unlike IAS 36 – *Impairment of Assets* (see Chapter 20) and IAS 37 – *Provisions, Contingent Liabilities and Contingent Assets* (see Chapter 28), IFRS 2 does not explicitly prohibit an entity from taking account of the consequences of reorganisations and similar transactions to which it is not yet committed.

Accordingly, we believe that approach (b) should be followed under IFRS 2.

The entity's best estimate at the end of year 1 must be that none of the awards currently in place will vest (because all the employees will be made redundant and so will not meet the service condition before the end of the vesting period). It therefore applies forfeiture accounting at the end of year 1 and reverses any cost previously recorded for the award.

When the terms of the award are changed at the time of the redundancy in year 2 to allow full vesting, the entity will either recognise the full cost of the new award (as all cost relating to the original award has been reversed) or will treat the revised arrangement as a modification of the original award that is beneficial to the employee. In effect, the modification approach is based on a view that the original award is not now going to lapse because it will be modified before employment ceases and the forfeiture crystallises. In our view, in the absence of clarity in IFRS 2, the entity should assess the more appropriate approach based on the particular facts and circumstances. Either approach will have what many may see as the less than ideal result that the entity will recognise a credit in profit or loss in year 1 and an expense in year 2, even though there has been no change in management's best estimate of the overall outcome. This follows from the analysis, discussed above, that we do not believe that the entity can account in year 1 for the award on the basis of what its terms may be in year 2.

The best estimate is made as at each reporting date. A change in estimate made in a later period in response to subsequent events affects the accounting expense from that later period only (i.e. there is no restatement of earlier periods presented).

7.7 Two awards running 'in parallel'

In some jurisdictions, it is not readily possible formally to cancel or modify an award. This may be because formal cancellation or modification triggers either a legal requirement for the entity to pay compensation to the holder, or adverse tax consequences for the holder. In such cases, where an award has become unattractive (for example, because it is 'out-of-the-money'), the entity may issue a second award rather than cancel or modify the original award. The second award cannot be designated as a replacement award, because the original award is still in place. The entity therefore has two awards running 'in parallel'.

However, a mechanism is then put in place to ensure that the employee can receive only one award. For instance, if the original award were 1,000 options, it might be replaced with a second award of 1,000 options, but on condition that, if options under one award are exercised, the number of options exercisable under the other award is correspondingly reduced, so that no more than 1,000 options can be exercised in total.

The accounting for such arrangements is discussed in Example 32.31 below.

Example 32.31: Two option awards running in parallel

At the beginning of year 1, an entity granted 1,000 A options to an employee, subject to non-market vesting conditions. The grant date fair value of an A option was €50.

As at the beginning of year 2, the entity's share price is significantly below the exercise price of an A option, which now has a fair value of €5. Without modifying or cancelling the A options, the entity awards the employee 1,000 new B options. The B options are subject to non-market vesting conditions different in nature from, and more onerous than, those applicable to the A options, but have a lower exercise price. The terms of the B options include a provision that for every A option that is exercised, the number of B options that can be exercised is reduced by one, and *vice versa.* The fair value of a B option at the beginning of year 2 is €15.

Clearly, the employee will exercise whichever series of options, A or B, has the higher intrinsic value. There are four possible outcomes:

1. Neither the A options nor the B options vest.
2. Only the A options vest.
3. Only the B options vest.
4. Both the A options and B options vest and the employee must choose which to exercise. Rationally, the employee would exercise the B options as they have the lower exercise price.

In our view, the B options are most appropriately accounted for as if they were a modification of the A options. In substance the A options have been modified by adding alternative non-market vesting conditions with a different option exercise price.

On the date of the substantive modification, the entity estimates the fair value of both the original and modified options and calculates the incremental fair value of the modification. As only one series of options can be exercised, we believe that the most appropriate treatment is to account for whichever award the entity believes, at each reporting date, is more likely to be exercised. This is analogous to the accounting treatment we suggest in Example 32.12 at 6.2.5 above and in Example 32.17 at 6.3.6 above.

If the entity believes that neither award will vest, any expense previously recorded would be reversed.

If the entity believes that only the A options will vest, it will recognise expense based on the grant date fair value of the A options (€50 each).

If the entity believes that only the B options will vest, it will recognise expense based on:

(a) the grant date fair value of the A options (€50 each) over the original vesting period of the A options, plus

(b) the incremental fair value of the B options, as at their grant date (€10 each, being their €15 fair value less the €5 fair value of an A option), over the vesting period of the B options.

If the entity believes that both the A options and B options will vest, it follows the accounting treatment of outcome 3 above (i.e. vesting of the B options). This is because the employee will either choose the B options or, if the employee decides to choose the A options, the entity has to expense both the value of the A options and the incremental value of the B options because that incremental value relates to a vested award.

The entity revises the assessment at each reporting date and at the end of the vesting period when the actual outcome is known, so that the cumulative expense is based on the actual outcome.

Other types of arrangement with multiple outcomes are illustrated, for example, at 6.2.5 above and at 10.3 and 15.4 below.

7.8 Share splits and consolidations

It is common for an entity to divide its existing equity share capital into a larger number of shares (share splits) or to consolidate its existing share capital into a smaller number of shares (share consolidations). The impact of such splits and consolidations is not specifically addressed in IFRS 2, and a literal application of IFRS 2 could lead to some rather anomalous results.

Suppose that an employee has options over 100 shares in the reporting entity, with an exercise price of £1. The entity undertakes a '1 for 2' share consolidation – i.e. the number of shares in issue is halved such that, all other things being equal, the value of one share in the entity after the consolidation is twice that of one share before the consolidation.

IFRS 2 is required to be applied to modifications to an award arising from equity restructurings. *[IFRS 2.BC24]*. In many cases, a share scheme will provide for automatic adjustment so that, following the consolidation, the employee holds options over only 50 shares with an exercise price of £2. As discussed at 5.3.8.A above, all things being equal, it would be expected that the modified award would have the same fair value as the original award and so there would be no incremental expense to be accounted for.

However, it may be that the scheme has no such provision for automatic adjustment, such that the employee still holds options over 100 shares. The clear economic effect is that the award has been modified, since its value has been doubled. It could be argued that, on a literal reading of IFRS 2, no modification has occurred, since the employee holds options over 100 shares at the same exercise price before and after the consolidation. The Interpretations Committee discussed this issue at its July and November 2006 meetings but decided not to take it onto its agenda because it 'was not a normal commercial occurrence and ... unlikely to have widespread significance'.[20] This decision was re-confirmed by the Interpretations Committee in March 2011.[21] In our view, whilst it seems appropriate to have regard to the substance of the transaction, and treat it as giving rise to a modification, it can be argued that IFRS 2 as drafted does not require such a treatment, particularly given the decision of the Interpretations Committee not to discuss the issue further.

Sometimes, the terms of an award give the entity discretion to make modifications at a future date in response to more complex changes to the share structure, such as those arising from bonus issues, share buybacks and rights issues where the effect on existing options may not be so clear-cut. These are discussed further at 5.3.8.A above.

8 EQUITY-SETTLED TRANSACTIONS – VALUATION

8.1 Introduction

The IASB provides some guidance on valuation in Appendix B to the standard, which we summarise and elaborate upon below. The guidance is framed in terms of awards to employees which are valued at grant date, but many of the general principles are equally applicable to awards to non-employees valued at service date. *[IFRS 2.B1]*.

As discussed in more detail at 4 to 7 above, IFRS 2 requires a 'modified grant-date' approach, under which the fair value of an equity award is estimated on the grant date without regard to the possibility that any service conditions or non-market performance vesting conditions will not be met. Although the broad intention of IFRS 2 is to recognise the cost of the goods or services to be received, the IASB believes that, in the case of services from employees, the fair value of the equity instruments awarded is more readily determinable than the fair value of the services received.

As noted at 5.1 above, IFRS 2 defines fair value as 'the amount for which an asset could be exchanged, a liability settled, or an equity instrument granted could be exchanged, between knowledgeable, willing parties in an arm's length transaction'.

IFRS 2 requires fair value to be based on the market price of the equity instruments, where available, or calculated using an option-pricing model. While fair value may be readily determinable for awards of shares, market quotations are not available for long-term, non-transferable share options because these instruments are not generally traded.

As discussed further at 8.2.2 below, the fair value of an option at any point in time is made up of two basic components – intrinsic value and time value. Intrinsic value is the greater of (a) the market value of the underlying share less the exercise price of the option and (b) zero.

Time value reflects the potential of the option for future gain to the holder, given the length of time during which the option will be outstanding, and possible changes in the share price during that period. Because market price information is not normally available for an employee share option, the IASB believes that, in the absence of such information, the fair value of a share option awarded to an employee generally must be estimated using an option-pricing model. *[IFRS 2.BC130]*. This is discussed further at 8.3 below.

The discussion below aims to provide guidance on the valuation of options and similar awards under IFRS 2; it is not intended to provide detailed instructions for constructing an option pricing model.[22]

The approach to determining the fair value of share-based payments continues to be that specified in IFRS 2 as share-based payments fall outside the scope of IFRS 13 which applies more generally to the measurement of fair value under IFRSs (see Chapter 14). *[IFRS 2.6A]*.

8.2 Options

8.2.1 *Call options – overview*

Before considering the features of employee share options that make their valuation particularly difficult, a general overview of call options may be useful.

Call options give the holder the right, but not the obligation, to buy the underlying shares at a specified price (the 'exercise' or 'strike' price) on, or before, a specified date. Share-based payments take the form of call options over the underlying shares.

Options are often referred to as American or European. American options can be exercised at any time up to the expiry date, whereas European options can be exercised only on the expiry date itself.

The terms of employee options commonly have features of both American and European options, in that there is a period, generally two or three years, during which the option cannot be exercised (i.e. the vesting period). At the end of this period, if the options vest, they can be exercised at any time up until the expiry date. This type of option is known as a Window American option or Bermudan option.

A grant of shares is equivalent to an option with an exercise price of zero and will be exercised regardless of the share price on the vesting date. Throughout the discussion below, any reference to share options therefore includes, to the extent applicable, share grants or zero strike price options. There is further discussion of grants of free shares at 8.7.1 below.

8.2.2 *Call options – valuation*

As noted in 8.1 above, option value consists of intrinsic value and time value. For a call option, intrinsic value is the greater of:

- the share price less the exercise price, and
- zero.

Figure 32.2 below sets out the intrinsic value (or payoff) for a call option with an exercise price of $5.00.

Figure 32.2: Intrinsic value of a call option

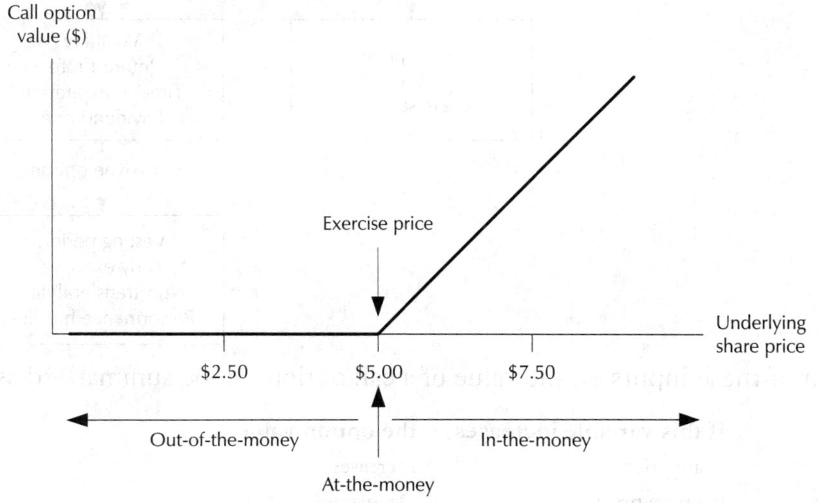

A call option is said to be 'in-the-money' when the share price is above the exercise price of the option and 'out-of-the-money' when the share price is less than the exercise price. An option is 'at-the-money' when the share price equals the exercise price of the option.

The time value of an option arises from the time remaining to expiry. As well as the share price and the exercise price, it is impacted by the volatility of the share price, time to expiry, dividend yield and the risk-free interest rate and the extent to which it is in- or out-of-the-money. For example, when the share price is significantly less than the exercise price, the option is said to be 'deeply' out-of-the-money. In this case, the fair value consists entirely of time value, which decreases the more the option is out-of-the-money.

The main inputs to the value of a simple option are:

- the exercise price of the option;
- the term of the option;
- the current market price of the underlying share;
- the expected future volatility of the price of the underlying share;
- the dividends expected to be paid on the shares during the life of the option (if any); and
- the risk-free interest rate(s) for the expected term of the option.

Their effect on each of the main components of the total value (intrinsic value and time value) is shown in Figure 32.3 below.

Figure 32.3: Determinants of the fair value of a call option

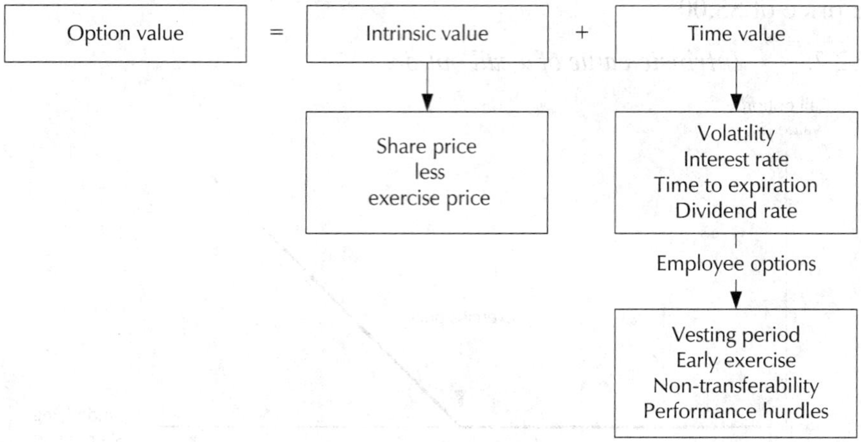

The effect of these inputs on the value of a call option can be summarised as follows:

If this variable increases,	**the option value ...**
Share price	Increases
Exercise price	Decreases
Volatility	Increases
Time to expiry	Usually increases*
Interest rate	Increases
Dividend yield/payout	Decreases

* When there is a dividend yield and the option is considerably in-the-money, an option may have a zero or negative time value. In this case, as the time to expiry increases, a European call option will reduce in value and an American call option will stay constant in value.

The factors to be considered in estimating the determinants of an option value in the context of IFRS 2 are considered in more detail at 8.5 below.

8.2.3 Factors specific to employee share options

In addition to the factors referred to in 8.2.2 above, employee share options are also affected by a number of specific factors that can affect their true economic value. These factors, not all of which are taken into account for IFRS 2 valuation purposes (see 8.4 and 8.5 below), include the following:

- non-transferability (see 8.2.3.A below);
- continued employment requirement (see 8.2.3.B below);
- vesting and non-vesting conditions (see 8.2.3.C below);
- periods during which holders cannot exercise their options – referred to in various jurisdictions as 'close', 'restricted' or 'blackout' periods (see 8.2.3.D below);
- limited ability to hedge option values (see 8.2.3.E below); and
- dilution effects (see 8.2.3.F below).

8.2.3.A *Non-transferability*

Holders of freely-traded share options (i.e. those outside a share-based payment transaction) can choose to 'sell' their options (typically by writing a call option on the same terms) rather than exercise them. By contrast, employee share options are generally non-transferable, leading to early (and sub-optimal) exercise of the option. This will lower the value of the options.

8.2.3.B *Continued employment requirement*

Holders of freely-traded share options can maintain their positions until they wish to exercise, regardless of other circumstances. In contrast, employee share options cannot normally be held once employment is terminated. If the options have not vested, they will be lost. If the options have vested, the employee will be forced to exercise the options immediately or within a short timescale, or forfeit them altogether, losing all time value. This will lower the value of the options.

8.2.3.C *Vesting and non-vesting conditions*

Holders of freely-traded share options have an unconditional right to exercise their options. In contrast, employee share options may have vesting and non-vesting conditions attached to them, which may not be met, reducing their value. This is discussed in more detail in 8.4 below.

Although a non-market vesting condition reduces the 'true' fair value of an award, it does not directly affect its valuation for the purposes of IFRS 2 (see 6.2 above). However, non-market vesting conditions may indirectly affect the value. For example, when an award vests on satisfaction of a particular target rather than at a specified time, its value may vary depending on the assessment of when that target will be met, since that may influence the expected life of the award, which is relevant to its fair value under IFRS 2 (see 6.2.3 and 8.2.2 above and 8.5.1 below).

8.2.3.D *Periods during which exercise is restricted*

Holders of traded American or Bermudan share options can exercise at any time during the exercisable window. In contrast, employees may be subject to 'blackout' periods in which they cannot exercise their options, for example to prevent insider trading. While this could conceivably make a significant impact if the shares were significantly mis-priced in the market, in an efficient market blackout periods will only marginally decrease the value.

8.2.3.E *Limited ability to hedge option values*

In the case of traded share options, it is reasonable to justify the theoretical valuation on the basis that, for any other value, arbitrage opportunities could arise through hedging. In contrast, employee share options are usually awarded only in relatively small amounts, and the employees are usually subject to restrictions on share trading (especially short selling the shares, as would be required to hedge an option). When considered in combination with the non-transferability of the options (see 8.2.3.A above), this means that exercising the options is the only way to remove exposure to fluctuations in value, which lowers the value of the options.

8.2.3.F Dilution effects

When third parties write traded share options, the writer delivers shares to the option holder when the options are exercised, so that the exercise of the traded share options has no dilutive effect. By contrast, if an entity writes share options to employees and, when those share options are exercised, issues new shares (or uses shares previously repurchased and held in treasury) to settle the awards, there is a dilutive effect. As the shares will be issued at the exercise price rather than the current market price at the date of exercise, this actual or potential dilution may reduce the share price, so that the option holder does not make as large a gain as would arise on the exercise of similar traded options which do not dilute the share price.

8.3 Selection of an option-pricing model

Where, as will almost always be the case, there are no traded options over the entity's equity instruments that mirror the terms of share options granted to employees, IFRS 2 requires the fair value of options granted to be estimated using an option-pricing model. The entity must consider all factors that would be considered by knowledgeable, willing market participants in selecting a model. *[IFRS 2.B4-5]*.

The IASB decided that it was not necessary or appropriate to prescribe the precise formula or model to be used for option valuation. It notes that there is no particular option pricing model that is regarded as theoretically superior to the others, and there is the risk that any model specified might be superseded by improved methodologies in the future. *[IFRS 2.BC131]*.

The three most common option-pricing methodologies for valuing employee options are:

- the Black-Scholes-Merton formula (see 8.3.1 below);
- the binomial model (see 8.3.2 below); and
- the Monte Carlo Simulation (see 8.3.3 below).

It is important to understand all the terms and conditions of a share-based payment arrangement, as this will influence the choice of the most appropriate option pricing model.

IFRS 2 names the Black-Scholes-Merton formula and the binomial model as examples of acceptable models to use when estimating fair value *[IFRS 2.BC152]*, while noting that there are certain circumstances in which the Black-Scholes-Merton formula may not be the most appropriate model (see 8.3.1 below). Moreover, there may be instances where, due to the particular terms and conditions of the share-based payment arrangement, neither of these models is appropriate, and another methodology is more appropriate to achieving the intentions of IFRS 2. A model commonly used for valuing more complex awards is Monte Carlo Simulation (often combined with the Black-Scholes-Merton formula or the binomial model). This can deal with the complexities of a plan such as one with a market condition based on relative total shareholder return (TSR), which compares the return on a fixed sum invested in the entity to the return on the same amount invested in a peer group of entities.

8.3.1 *The Black-Scholes-Merton formula*

The Black-Scholes-Merton methodology is commonly used for assessing the value of a freely-traded put or call option. In recent years the formula has been further developed to allow the incorporation of static dividends on shares. The assumptions underlying the Black-Scholes-Merton formula are as follows:

- the option can be exercised only on the expiry date (i.e. it is a European option);
- there are no taxes or transaction costs and no margin requirements;
- the volatility of the underlying asset is constant and is defined as the standard deviation of the continuously compounded rates of return on the share over a specified period;
- the risk-free interest rate is constant over time;
- short selling is permitted;
- there are no risk-free arbitrage opportunities;
- there are log normal returns (i.e. the continuously compounded rate of return is normally distributed); and
- security trading is continuous.

The main limitation of the Black-Scholes-Merton methodology is that it only calculates the option price at one point in time. It does not consider the steps along the way when there could be a possibility of early exercise of an American option (although as discussed at 8.4 below this can be partially mitigated by using an assumed expected term as an input to the calculation).

The Black-Scholes-Merton formula is an example of a closed-form model, which is a valuation model that uses an equation to produce an estimated fair value. The formula is as shown in Figure 32.4 below.

Figure 32.4: The Black-Scholes-Merton formula

$$c = S_0 e^{-qT} N(d_1) - K e^{-rT} N(d_2)$$

Where :

$$d_1 = \frac{\ln(S_0 / K) + (r - q + \sigma^2 / 2)T}{\sigma\sqrt{T}}$$

$$d_2 = d_1 - \sigma\sqrt{T}$$

c =	price of a written call
S_0 =	price of the underlying share
N =	the cumulative probability distribution function for a standardised normal distribution
q =	dividend yield (continuously compounded)
K =	call option exercise price
r =	the continuously compounded risk-free rate
σ =	annualised volatility of the underlying share
T =	time to expiry (in years)

Note: 'e' represents the mathematical constant, the base of the natural logarithm (2.718282...), and 'ln' is the natural logarithm of the indicated value

Whilst the Black-Scholes-Merton formula is complex, its application in practice is relatively easy. It can be programmed into a spreadsheet, and numerous programs and calculators exist that use it to calculate the fair value of an option. As a result, the formula is used widely by finance professionals to value a large variety of options. However, a number of the assumptions underlying the formula may be better suited to valuing short-term, exchange-traded share options rather than employee share options.

The attributes of employee share options that render the Black-Scholes-Merton formula less effective as a valuation technique include:

- *Long term to expiry*

  The formula assumes that volatility, interest rates and dividends are constant over the life of the option. While this may be appropriate when valuing short-term options, the assumption of constant values is less appropriate when valuing long-term options.

- *Non-transferability and early exercise*

  The formula assumes a fixed maturity/exercise date. While IFRS 2 provides for the use of an 'expected term' in place of the contractual life to reflect the possibility of early exercise resulting from the non-transferability of employee share options or other reasons (see 8.5 below), this may not adequately describe early exercise behaviour.

- *Vesting conditions and non-vesting conditions*

  The formula does not take into account any market-based vesting conditions or non-vesting conditions.

- *Blackout periods*

  As the formula assumes exercise on a fixed date, and does not allow earlier exercise, it does not take into consideration any blackout periods (see 8.2.3.D above).

In summary, application of the Black-Scholes-Merton formula is relatively simple, in part because many of the complicating factors associated with the valuation of employee share options cannot be incorporated into it directly and, therefore, must be derived outside of the formula (e.g. the input of an expected term).

IFRS 2 states that the Black-Scholes-Merton formula may not be appropriate for long-lived options which can be exercised before the end of their life and which are subject to variation in the various inputs to the model over the life of the option. However, IFRS 2 suggests that the Black-Scholes-Merton formula may give materially correct results for options with shorter lives and with a relatively short exercise period. *[IFRS 2.B5]*.

The development of appropriate assumptions for use in the Black-Scholes-Merton formula is discussed at 8.5 below.

As noted above, the Black-Scholes-Merton formula is an example of a closed form model that is not generally appropriate for awards that include market performance conditions. However, in certain circumstances it may be possible to use closed form solutions other than the Black-Scholes-Merton formula to value options where, for example, the share price has to reach a specified level for the options to vest. These other solutions are beyond the scope of this chapter.

8.3.2 The binomial model

The binomial model is one of a subset of valuation models known as lattice models, which adopt a flexible, iterative approach to valuation that can capture the unique aspects of employee share options. A binomial model produces an estimated fair value based on the assumed changes in prices of a financial instrument over successive periods of time. In each time period, the model assumes that at least two price movements are possible. The lattice represents the evolution of the value of either a financial instrument or a market variable for the purpose of valuing a financial instrument.

The concepts that underpin lattice models and the Black-Scholes-Merton formula are the same, but the key difference between a lattice model and a closed-form model is that a lattice model is more flexible. The valuations obtained using the Black-Scholes-Merton formula and a lattice model will be very similar if the lattice model uses identical assumptions to the Black-Scholes-Merton calculation (e.g. constant volatility, constant dividend yields, constant risk-free rate, the same expected life). However, a lattice model can explicitly use dynamic assumptions regarding the term structure of volatility, dividend yields, and interest rates.

Further, a lattice model can incorporate assumptions about how the likelihood of early exercise of an employee share option may increase as the intrinsic value of that option increases, or how employees may have a high tendency to exercise options with significant intrinsic value shortly after vesting.

In addition, a lattice model can incorporate market conditions that may be part of the design of an option, such as a requirement that an option is only exercisable if the underlying share price reaches a certain level (sometimes referred to as 'target share price' awards). The Black-Scholes-Merton formula is not generally appropriate for awards that have a market-based performance condition because it cannot handle that additional complexity.

Most valuation specialists believe that lattice models, through their versatility, generally provide a more accurate estimate of the fair value of an employee share option with market performance conditions or with the possibility of early exercise than a value based on a closed-form Black-Scholes-Merton formula. As a general rule, the longer the term of the option and the higher the dividend yield, the larger the amount by which the binomial lattice model value may differ from the Black-Scholes-Merton formula value.

To implement the binomial model, a 'tree' is constructed the branches (or time steps) of which represent alternative future share price movements over the life of the option. In each time step over the life of the option, the share price has a certain probability of moving up or down by a certain percentage amount. It is important to emphasise the assumption, in these models, that the valuation occurs in a risk-neutral world, where investors are assumed to require no extra return on average for bearing risks and the expected return on all securities is the risk free interest rate.

To illustrate how the binomial model is used, Example 32.32 below constructs a simple binomial lattice model with a few time steps. The valuation assumptions and principles will not differ in essence from those in a Black-Scholes-Merton valuation except that it will allow for early exercise of the option. The relevant difference between the two models is the specification of a very small number of time steps, for illustrative purposes, in the binomial lattice model (see also 8.3.2.A below). We discuss below how the model can be augmented for a more complex set of assumptions.

Example 32.32: Binomial model

A share option is issued with an exercise price of $10, being the share price on the grant date. This Example assumes a constant volatility (50%) and risk-free rate (5% continuously compounded) although, as discussed later, those static assumptions may not be appropriate when valuing a long-term share option. It is also assumed that: the grantor pays dividends with a yield of 2% (continuously compounded) on its shares; the term of the option is five years; and each branch of the tree represents a length of time of one year.

At t = 0 (the grant date), the model is started at the grant date share price ($10 in this Example). At each node (the base of any price time step), two possible price changes (one increase and one decrease) are computed based on the volatility of the shares. The two new share prices are computed as follows:

The up-node price utilises the following formula:

$$u = e^{\sigma\sqrt{dt}} = e^{0.5*\sqrt{1}} = 1.6487$$

Where:

σ = annualised volatility of the underlying share

dt = period of time between nodes

The down-node is the inverse of the up-node:

$$d = \frac{1}{u} = \frac{1}{1.6487} = 0.6065$$

The probability of each upward and downward price movement occurring is calculated from:

- the probability of an upward movement in price:

$$p = \frac{e^{(r-q)dt} - d}{u - d} = \frac{e^{(.05-.02)*1} - 0.6065}{1.6487 - 0.6065} = 0.4068$$

Where:

r = continuously compounded risk free rate

q = dividend yield (continuously compounded)

dt = period of time between nodes

- the probability of a downward movement in price:

$$= 1 - p = 1 - 0.4068 = 0.5932$$

Using the above price multiples, the price tree can then be constructed as shown diagrammatically below – each rising node is built by multiplying the previous price by 'u' and each falling node is similarly calculated by multiplying the previous price by 'd'.

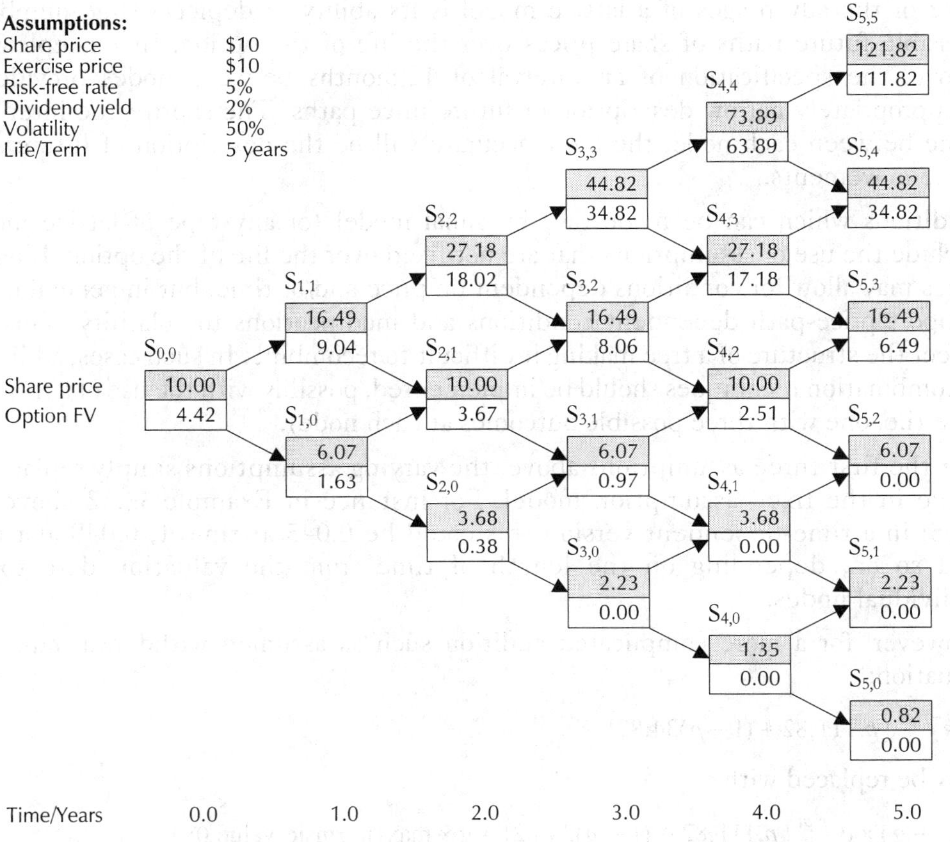

To calculate the option value:

- The option payoffs at the final time node (time 5 above) must be calculated. This is the share price less the exercise price, or zero if the payoff is negative.
- Then the option values must be calculated at the previous time point (time 4 above). This is done by calculating the expected value of the option for the branch paths available to the particular node being valued discounted at the risk-free rate. For example, for $S_{4,4}$ in the chart above the option value is the probability of going to node $S_{5,5}$ multiplied by the option value at that node plus the probability of going to node $S_{5,4}$ multiplied by the option value at that node, all discounted at the risk-free rate):

  $$= e^{-r.dt}\{p.111.82 + (1 - p)34.82\} = 0.95\{0.4068 \times 111.82 + 0.5932 \times 34.82\} = 62.92$$

  This would be the value at node $S_{4,4}$ if the option were European and could not be exercised earlier. As the binomial model can allow for early exercise, the option value at node $S_{4,4}$ is the greater of the option value just calculated and the intrinsic value of the option which is calculated the same way as the end option payoff. In this case, as the intrinsic value is $63.89 ($73.89 – $10.00), the node takes the value of $63.89.
- The previous steps are then repeated throughout the entire lattice (i.e. for all nodes at time 4, then all nodes at time 3, etc.) until finally the option value is determined at time 0 – this being the binomial option value of $4.42.
- Additionally, if there is a vesting period during which the options cannot be exercised, the model can be adjusted so as not to incorporate the early exercise condition stipulated in the previous point and allow for this only after the option has vested and has the ability to be exercised before expiry.

One of the advantages of a lattice model is its ability to depict a large number of possible future paths of share prices over the life of the option. In Example 32.32 above, the specification of an interval of 12 months between nodes provides an inappropriately narrow description of future price paths. The shorter the interval of time between each node, the more accurate will be the description of future share price movements.

Additions which can be made to a binomial model (or any type of lattice model) include the use of assumptions that are not fixed over the life of the option. Binomial trees may allow for conditions dependent on price and/or time, but in general do not support price-path dependent conditions and modifications to volatility. This may affect the structure of a tree making it difficult to recombine. In such cases, additional recombination techniques should be implemented, possibly with the use of a trinomial tree (i.e. one with three possible outcomes at each node).

For the first three assumptions above, the varying assumptions simply replace the value in the fixed assumption model. For instance in Example 32.32 above r = 0.05; in a time-dependent version this could be 0.045 at time 1, 0.048 at time 2 and so on, depending on the length of time from the valuation date to the individual nodes.

However, for a more complicated addition such as assumed withdrawal rates, the equation:

$$= e^{-r.dt}\{p.111.82 + (1-p)34.82\}$$

may be replaced with

$$= (1-g) \times e^{-r.dt}\{p.111.82 + (1-p)34.82\} + g \times \max(\text{intrinsic value}, 0)$$

where 'g' is the rate of employee departure, on the assumption that, on departure, the option is either forfeited or exercised. As with the other time and price dependent assumptions, the rate of departure could also be made time or price dependent (i.e. the rate of departure could be assumed to increase as the share price increases, or increase as time passes, and so forth).

8.3.2.A Lattice models – number of time steps

When performing a lattice valuation, a decision must be taken as to how many time steps to use in the valuation (i.e. how much time passes between each node). Generally, the greater the number of time steps, the more accurate the final value. However, as more time steps are added, the incremental increase in accuracy declines. To illustrate the increases in accuracy, consider the diagram below, which values the option in Example 32.32 above as a European option. In this case, the binomial model has not been enhanced to allow for early exercise (i.e. the ability to exercise prior to expiry).

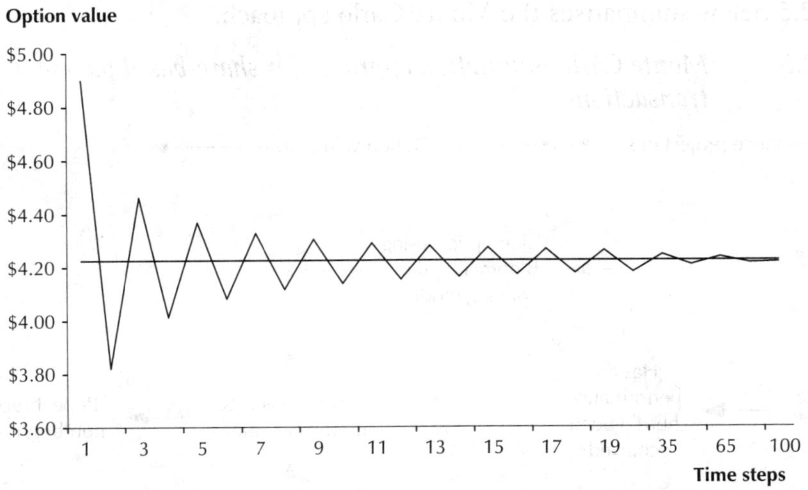

Whilst the binomial model is very flexible and can deal with much more complex assumptions than the Black-Scholes-Merton formula, there are certain complexities it cannot handle, which can best be accomplished by Monte Carlo Simulation – see 8.3.3 below.

The development of appropriate assumptions for use in a binomial model is discussed at 8.5 below.

In addition to the binomial model, other lattice models such as trinomial models or finite difference algorithms may be used. Discussion of these models is beyond the scope of this chapter.

8.3.3 Monte Carlo Simulation

In order to value options with market-based performance targets where the market value of the entity's equity is an input to the determination of whether, or to what extent, an award has vested, the option methodology applied must be supplemented with techniques such as Monte Carlo Simulation.

TSR compares the return on a fixed sum invested in the entity to the return on the same amount invested in a peer group of entities. Typically, the entity is then ranked in the peer group and the number of share-based awards that vest depends on the ranking. For example, no award might vest for a low ranking, the full award might vest for a higher ranking, and a pro-rated level of award might vest for a median ranking.

The following table gives an example of a possible vesting pattern for such a scheme, with a peer group of 100 entities.

Ranking in peer group	Percentage vesting
Below 50	0%
50	50%
51-74	50% plus an additional 2% for each increase of 1 in the ranking
75 or higher	100%

Figure 32.5 below summarises the Monte Carlo approach.

Figure 32.5: Monte Carlo Simulation approach for share-based payment transactions

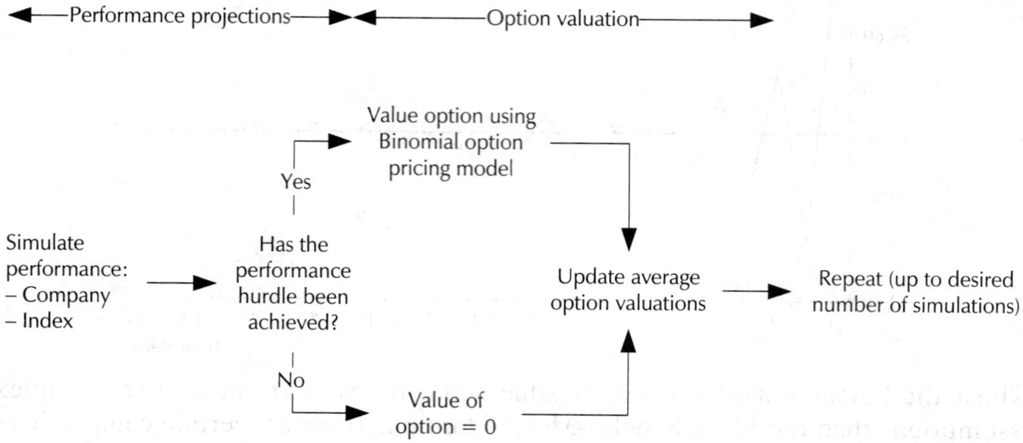

The valuation could be performed using either:

- a binomial valuation or the Black-Scholes-Merton formula, dependent on the results of the Monte Carlo Simulation; or
- the Monte Carlo Simulation on its own.

The framework for calculating future share prices uses essentially the same underlying assumptions as lie behind Black-Scholes-Merton and binomial models – namely a risk-neutral world and a log normal distribution of share prices.

For a given simulation, the risk-neutral returns of the entity and those of the peer group or index are projected until the performance target is achieved and the option vests. At this point, the option transforms into a 'vanilla' equity call option that may be valued using an option pricing model. This value is then discounted back to the grant date so as to give the value of the option for a single simulation.

When the performance target is not achieved and the option does not vest, a zero value is recorded. This process is repeated thousands or millions of times. The average option value obtained across all simulations provides an estimate of the value of the option, allowing for the impact of the performance target.

8.4 Adapting option-pricing models for share-based payment transactions

Since the option-pricing models discussed in 8.3 above were developed to value freely-traded options, a number of adjustments are required in order to account for the restrictions usually attached to share-based payment transactions, particularly those with employees. The restrictions not accounted for in these models include:

- non-transferability (see 8.4.1 below); and
- vesting conditions, including performance targets, and non-vesting conditions that affect the value for the purposes of IFRS 2 (see 8.4.2 below).

8.4.1 Non-transferability

As noted at 8.2.3.A above, employee options and other share-based awards are almost invariably non-transferable, except (in some cases) to the employee's estate in the event of death in service. Non-transferability often results in an option being exercised early (i.e. before the end of its contractual life), as this is the only way for the employee to realise its value in cash. Therefore, by imposing the restriction of non-transferability, the entity may cause the effective life of the option to be shorter than its contractual life, resulting in a loss of time value to the holder. *[IFRS 2.BC153-169]*.

One aspect of time value is the value of the right to defer payment of the exercise price until the end of the option term. When the option is exercised early because of non-transferability, the entity receives the exercise price much earlier than it otherwise would. Therefore, as noted by IFRS 2, the effective time value granted by the entity to the option holder is less than that indicated by the contractual life of the option.

IFRS 2 requires the effect of early exercise as a result of non-transferability and other factors to be reflected either by modelling early exercise in a binomial or similar model or by using expected life rather than contractual life as an input into the option-pricing model. This is discussed further at 8.5.1 below.

Reducing the time to expiry effectively reduces the value of the option. This is a simplified way of reducing the value of the employee stock option to reflect the fact that employees are unable to sell their vested options, rather than applying an arbitrary discount to take account of non-transferability.

8.4.2 Treatment of vesting and non-vesting conditions

Many share-based payment awards to employees have vesting and non-vesting conditions attached to them which must be satisfied before the award can be exercised. It must be remembered that a non-market vesting condition, while reducing the 'true' fair value of an award, does not directly affect its valuation for the purposes of IFRS 2 (see 6.2 above). However, non-market vesting conditions may indirectly affect the value. For example, when an award vests on satisfaction of a particular target rather than at a specified time, its value may vary depending on the assessment of when that target will be met, since that may influence the expected life of the award, which is relevant to its fair value under IFRS 2 (see 6.2.3 and 8.2.2 above and 8.5 below).

8.4.2.A Market-based performance measures and non-vesting conditions

As discussed at 6.3 and 6.4 above, IFRS 2 requires market-based vesting conditions and non-vesting conditions to be taken into account in estimating the fair value of the options granted. Moreover, the entity is required to recognise a cost for an award with a market condition or non-vesting condition if all the non-market vesting conditions attaching to the award are satisfied regardless of whether the market condition or non-vesting condition is satisfied. This means that a more sophisticated option pricing model may be required.

8.4.2.B Non-market vesting conditions

As discussed at 6.2 above, IFRS 2 requires non-market vesting conditions to be ignored when estimating the fair value of share-based payment transactions. Instead, such vesting conditions are taken into account by adjusting the number of equity instruments included in the measurement of the transaction (by estimating the extent of forfeiture based on failure to vest) so that, ultimately, the amount recognised is based on the number of equity instruments that eventually vest.

8.5 Selecting appropriate assumptions for option-pricing models

IFRS 2 notes that, as discussed at 8.2.2 above, option pricing models take into account, as a minimum:

- the exercise price of the option;
- the life of the option (see 8.5.1 and 8.5.2 below);
- the current price of the underlying shares;
- the expected volatility of the share price (see 8.5.3 below);
- the dividends expected on the shares (if appropriate – see 8.5.4 below); and
- the risk-free interest rate for the life of the option (see 8.5.5 below). *[IFRS 2.B6]*.

Of these inputs, only the exercise price and the current share price are objectively determinable. The others are subjective, and their development will generally require significant analysis. The discussion below addresses the development of assumptions for use both in a Black-Scholes-Merton formula and in a lattice model.

IFRS 2 requires other factors that knowledgeable, willing market participants would consider in setting the price to be taken into account, except for those vesting conditions and reload features that are excluded from the measurement of fair value – see 5 and 6 above and 8.9 below. Such factors include:

- restrictions on exercise during the vesting period or during periods where trading by those with inside knowledge is prohibited by securities regulators; or
- the possibility of the early exercise of options (see 8.5.1 below). *[IFRS 2.B7-9]*.

However, the entity should not consider factors that are relevant only to an individual employee and not to the market as a whole (such as the effect of an award of options on the personal motivation of an individual). *[IFRS 2.B10]*.

The objective of estimating the expected volatility of, and dividends on, the underlying shares is to approximate the expectations that would be reflected in a current market or negotiated exchange price for the option. Similarly, when estimating the effects of early exercise of employee share options, the objective is to approximate the expectations about employees' exercise behaviour that would be developed by an outside party with access to detailed information at grant date. Where (as is likely) there is a range of reasonable expectations about future volatility, dividends and exercise behaviour, an expected value should be calculated, by weighting each amount within the range by its associated probability of occurrence. *[IFRS 2.B11-12]*.

Such expectations are often based on past data. In some cases, however, such historical information may not be relevant (e.g. where the business of the entity has changed significantly) or even available (e.g. where the entity is unlisted or newly listed). An entity should not base estimates of future volatility, dividends or exercise behaviour on historical data without considering the extent to which they are likely to be reasonably predictive of future experience. *[IFRS 2.B13-15]*.

8.5.1 Expected term of the option

IFRS 2 allows the estimation of the fair value of an employee share award to be based on its expected life, rather than its maximum term, as this is a reasonable means of reducing the value of the award to reflect its non-transferability.

Option value is not a linear function of option term. Rather, value increases at a decreasing rate as the term lengthens. For example, a two year option is worth less than twice as much as a one year option, if all other assumptions are equal. This means that to calculate a value for an award of options with widely different individual lives based on a single weighted average life is likely to overstate the value of the entire award. Accordingly, assumptions need to be made as to what exercise or termination behaviour an option holder will exhibit. Considerations include:

- vesting period – the expected term of the option must be at least as long as its vesting period. The length of time employees hold options after they vest may vary inversely with the length of the vesting period;
- past history of employee exercise and termination patterns for similar grants (adjusted for current expectations) – see 8.5.2 below;
- expected volatility of the underlying share – on average, employees tend to exercise options on shares with higher volatility earlier;
- periods during which exercise may be precluded and related arrangements (e.g. agreements that allow for exercise to occur automatically during such periods if certain conditions are satisfied);
- employee demographics (age, tenure, sex, position etc.); and
- time from vesting date – the likelihood of exercise typically increases as time passes.

As discussed at 8.4 above, IFRS 2 notes that the effect of early exercise can be reflected:

- in a pricing model such as the Black-Scholes-Merton formula, by treating the expected, rather than the contractual, life of the option as an input to the model (see 8.5.1.A below); or
- by using contractual life as an input to a binomial or similar model. *[IFRS 2.B16-17]*.

8.5.1.A Expected term under the Black-Scholes-Merton formula

An estimate of expected term based on the types of inputs described above can be used in the Black-Scholes-Merton formula as well as a lattice model. However, the formula requires only a single expected term to be used. This is one of the reasons why the Black-Scholes-Merton formula may provide a higher valuation for the same options than a lattice model.

The difference in value that arises from using only a single expected term results, in part, from the convex shape of a typical option valuation curve, as illustrated below.

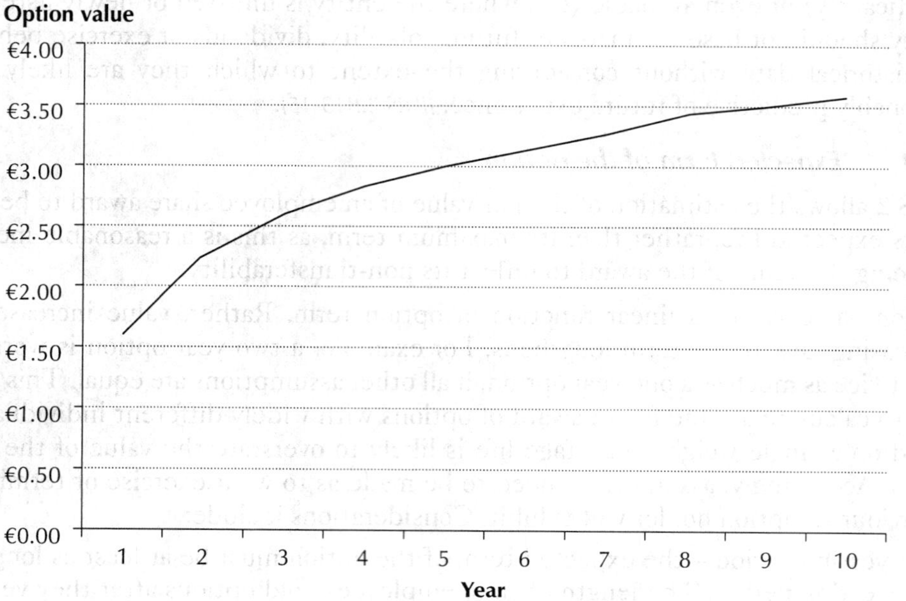

It is assumed, for the purposes of this illustration, that an at-the-money option on a €10 share with a 10-year contractual term is equally likely to be exercised at the end of each year beginning with year two. An average expected term of six years [(2+3+4+...10)/9] would be used in a Black-Scholes-Merton calculation giving a fair value of €3.10 for the option. If, instead, nine separate valuations were performed, each with a different expected term corresponding to each of the possible terms (from two to ten years), the average of those valuations (also calculated using the Black-Scholes-Merton formula) would be €2.9854. The latter amount is lower than €3.10 because of the convex shape of the valuation curve, reflecting the fact that the value increases at a decreasing rate as the term lengthens. Therefore, the value of the share option with an average expected term of six years will exceed the value derived from averaging the separate valuations for each potential term.

In a lattice model, exercise can occur at any time based on the rules specified in the model regarding exercise behaviour. The lattice model can therefore be thought of as analogous to the calculation in the above example in which the fair value was calculated as the average of the valuations from periods two to ten. In contrast, the Black-Scholes-Merton valuation allows only a single expected term to be specified. Therefore, it is analogous to the valuation described in the above example based on a single average expected term of six years.

Therefore, even if the expected term derived from a lattice model were used as an input in the Black-Scholes-Merton formula (and all other inputs were identical), the two models would give different values.

To mitigate the impact of the convex shape of the valuation curve, an entity with a broad-based share option plan might consider stratifying annual awards into different employee groups for the purposes of estimating the expected option lives (see 8.5.2 below).

Determining a single expected term can be quite challenging, particularly for an entity seeking to base its estimate on the periods for which previously granted options were outstanding, which would have been highly dependent on the circumstances during those periods. For example, if the entity's share price had increased significantly during the option period (as would be the case for share options granted by certain entities at the beginning of a bull market), it is likely that employees would have exercised options very soon after vesting. Alternatively, if options were granted at the end of a bull market and the share price declined significantly after the grant date, it is likely that the options would be exercised much later (if at all). These relationships would exist because, as discussed previously, the extent to which an option is in-the-money has a significant impact on exercise behaviour. Accordingly, deriving a single expected term in these situations involves considerable judgement.

8.5.2 Exercise and termination behaviour

IFRS 2 notes that employees often exercise options early for a number of reasons, most typically:

- restrictions on transferability mean that this is the only way of realising the value of the option in cash;
- aversion to the risk of not exercising 'in the money' options in the hope that they increase in value; or
- in the case of leavers, a requirement to exercise, or forfeit, all vested options on or shortly after leaving (see 8.5.2.B below).

Factors to consider in estimating early exercise include:

(a) the length of the vesting period, because the share option cannot be exercised until the end of the vesting period. Hence, determining the valuation implications of expected early exercise is based on the assumption that the options will vest;

(b) the average length of time similar options have remained outstanding in the past;

(c) the price of the underlying shares. Experience may indicate that employees tend to exercise options when the share price reaches a specified level above the exercise price;

(d) the employee's level within the organisation. For example, experience might indicate that higher-level employees tend to exercise options later than lower-level employees (see also 8.5.2.A below); and

(e) the expected volatility of the underlying shares. On average, employees might tend to exercise options on highly volatile shares earlier than on shares with low volatility. *[IFRS 2.B18]*.

In addition, the pattern of terminations of employment after vesting may be relevant (see 8.5.2.B below).

In our view, past exercise behaviour should generally serve as the starting point for determining expected exercise behaviour. That behaviour should be analysed, correlated to the factors above, and extrapolated into the future. However, significant changes in the underlying share price or in other salient characteristics of the entity, changes in option plans, tax laws, share price volatility and termination patterns may indicate that past exercise behaviour is not indicative of expected exercise behaviour. The expected life may also be estimated indirectly, by using a modified option pricing model to compute an option value, an input to which is an assumption that the options will be expected to be exercised when a particular share price is reached.

Some entities, including recently listed entities, or entities for which all outstanding grants have been out-of-the-money for a long period, may simply not be able to observe any exercise behaviour or may not possess enough history to perform a reasonable analysis of past exercise behaviour. In these cases, in our view, entities may have to look to the exercise history of employees of similar entities to develop expectations of employee exercise behaviour. At present there is only limited publicly-available information about employee exercise patterns, but valuation professionals and human resource consultants may have access to relevant data, which we expect to become more broadly available in the future.

In the absence of extensive information regarding exercise behaviour, another solution could be to use a midpoint assumption – i.e. selecting as the expected date of exercise the midpoint between the first available exercise date (the end of the vesting period) and the last available exercise date (the contracted expiry date). However, this should be undertaken only when the entity is satisfied that this does not lead to a material misstatement. It is also plausible to assume exercise at the earliest possible time or to undertake a reasonable analysis of past behaviour and set up the amount of intrinsic value which, when exceeded, will trigger exercise of the option.

8.5.2.A Grouping employees with homogeneous exercise behaviour

IFRS 2 emphasises that the estimated life of an option is critical to its valuation. Therefore, where options are granted to a group of employees, it will generally be necessary to ensure that either:

(a) all the employees are expected to exercise their options within a relatively narrow time-frame; or

(b) if not, that the group is divided into sub-groups of employees who are expected to exercise their options within a similar relatively narrow time-frame.

IFRS 2 suggests that it may become apparent that middle and senior management tend to exercise options later than lower-level employees, either because they choose to do so, or because they are encouraged or compelled to do so as a result of required minimum levels of ownership of equity instruments (including options) among more senior employees. *[IFRS 2.B19-21]*.

8.5.2.B Post-vesting termination behaviour

Most employee share options provide that, if employment is terminated, the former employee typically has only a short period (e.g. 90 days from the date of termination of employment) in which to exercise any vested options, the contractual expiry of which would otherwise be some years away. Accordingly, an entity should look at its prior termination patterns, adjust those patterns for future expectations and incorporate those expected terminations into a lattice model as expected early exercises.

Patterns of employee turnover are not necessarily linear and may be a non-linear function of a variety of factors, such as:

- employee demographics (age, sex, tenure, position, etc.);
- path of share price – for example, if options are deeply out-of-the-money, they may have little retention value and more employees may leave than if the options were at- or in-the-money; and
- economic conditions and other share prices.

8.5.3 *Expected volatility of share price*

Expected volatility is a measure of the amount by which a price is expected to fluctuate during a period. Share price volatility has a powerful influence on the estimation of the fair value of an option, much of the value of which is derived from its potential for appreciation. The more volatile the share price, the more valuable the option. It is therefore essential that the choice of volatility assumption can be properly supported.

IFRS 2 notes that the measure of volatility used in option pricing models is the annualised standard deviation of the continuously compounded rates of return on the share over a period of time. Volatility is typically expressed in annualised terms that are comparable regardless of the time period used in the calculation (for example, daily, weekly or monthly price observations).

The expected annualised volatility of a share is the range within which the continuously compounded annual rate of return is expected to fall approximately two-thirds of the time. For example, to say that a share with an expected continuously compounded rate of return of 12% has a volatility of 30% means that the probability that the rate of return on the share for one year will be between minus 18% (12% – 30%) and 42% (12% + 30%) is approximately two-thirds. If the share price is €100 at the beginning of the year, and no dividends are paid, the year-end share price would be expected to be between €83.53 (€100 × $e^{-0.18}$) and €152.20 (€100 × $e^{0.42}$) approximately two-thirds of the time.

The rate of return (which may be positive or negative) on a share for a period measures how much a shareholder has benefited from dividends and appreciation (or depreciation) of the share price. *[IFRS 2.B22-24]*.

IFRS 2 gives examples of factors to consider in estimating expected volatility including the following *[IFRS 2.B25]*:

- *Implied volatility from traded share options*

  Implied volatility is the volatility derived by using an option pricing model with the traded option price (if available) as an input and solving for the volatility as the unknown on the entity's shares. It may also be derived from other traded instruments of the entity that include option features (such as convertible debt).

  Implied volatilities are often calculated by analysts and reflect market expectations for future volatility as well as imperfections in the assumptions in the valuation model. For this reason, the implied volatility of a share may be a better measure of prospective volatility than historical volatility (see below). However, traded options are usually short-term, ranging in general from one month to two years. If the expected lives are much longer than this, both the implied and historical volatilities will need to be considered.

- *Historical volatility*

  It may be relevant to consider the historical volatility of the share price over the most recent period that is generally commensurate with the expected term of the option (taking into account the remaining contractual life of the option and the effects of expected early exercise). However, this assumes that past share price behaviour is likely to be representative of future share price behaviour. Upon any restructuring of an entity, the question of whether or not past volatility will be likely to predict future volatility would need to be reassessed.

  The historical volatilities of similar entities may be relevant for newly listed entities, unlisted entities or entities that have undergone substantial restructuring (see 8.5.3.A to 8.5.3.C below).

- *The length of time the entity's shares have been publicly traded*

  A newly listed entity might have a high historical volatility, compared with similar entities that have been listed longer. Further guidance for newly listed entities is given in 8.5.3.A below.

- *'Mean-reverting tendency'*

  This refers to the tendency of volatility to revert to its long-term average level, and other factors indicating that expected future volatility might differ from past volatility. For example, if an entity's share price was extraordinarily volatile for some identifiable period of time because of a failed takeover bid or a major restructuring, that period could be disregarded in computing historical average annual volatility. However, an entity should not exclude general economic factors such as the effect of an economic downturn on share price volatility.

- *Appropriate and regular intervals for price observations*

  The price observations should be consistent from period to period. For example, an entity might use the closing price for each week or the opening price for the week, but it should not use the closing price for some weeks and the opening price for other weeks. Also, the price observations should be expressed in the same currency as the exercise price. In our view, at least thirty observations are generally required to calculate a statistically valid standard deviation. Our experience has been that, in general, it is more appropriate to make such observations daily or weekly rather than monthly.

8.5.3.A *Newly listed entities*

As noted under 'Historical volatility' at 8.5.3 above, an entity should consider the historical volatility of the share price over the most recent period that is generally commensurate with the expected option term. If a newly listed entity does not have sufficient information on historical volatility, it should compute historical volatility for the longest period for which trading activity is available. It should also consider the historical volatility of similar entities. For example, an entity that has been listed for only one year and grants options with an average expected life of five years might consider the historical volatility of entities in the same industry, which are of a similar size and operate similar businesses, for the first six years in which the shares of those entities were publicly traded. *[IFRS 2.B26]*.

8.5.3.B *Unlisted entities*

An unlisted entity will have neither historical nor current market information to consider when estimating expected volatility. IFRS 2 suggests that, in some cases, an unlisted entity that regularly issues options or shares might have set up an internal market for its shares. The volatility of those share prices could be considered when estimating expected volatility. Alternatively, if the entity has based the value of its shares on the share prices of similar listed entities, the entity could consider the historical or implied volatility of the shares of those similar listed entities. *[IFRS 2.B27-29]*.

If the entity has not used a valuation methodology based on the share prices of similar listed entities, the entity could derive an estimate of expected volatility consistent with the valuation methodology used. For example, the entity might consider it appropriate to value its shares on a net asset or earnings basis if this approximates to the fair value of the equity instruments, in which case it could consider the expected volatility of those net asset values or earnings. *[IFRS 2.B30]*.

8.5.3.C *Listed entities that have undergone significant restructuring*

An issue not specifically addressed by IFRS 2 is the approach required in the case of an entity that has been listed for some time but which has recently undergone significant restructuring or refocusing of the business (e.g. as a result of acquisitions, disposals or refinancing). In such cases, it may well be appropriate to adopt the approach advocated for newly listed entities in 8.5.3.A above.

8.5.3.D *Expected volatility under the Black-Scholes-Merton formula*

In calculating the fair value of a share option using the Black-Scholes-Merton formula, a single expected volatility assumption must be used. That amount should be based on the volatility expected over the expected term of the option. Frequently, expected volatility is based on observed historical share price volatility during the period of time equal to the expected term of the option and ending on the grant date. Implied volatilities (i.e. volatilities implied by actual option prices on the entity's shares observed in the market) also may be considered in determining the expected volatility assumption (see 8.5.3 above).

When developing an expected volatility assumption, current and historical implied volatilities for publicly traded options and historical realised share volatilities should be considered for shares of the grantor and shares of other entities in the grantor's industry and comparable entities.

The volatility of a market index will not generally provide an appropriate input as the diversified nature of the index tends to produce a lower volatility figure than that applicable to individual shares.

8.5.3.E Expected volatility under lattice models

Expected volatility is more accurately taken into account by lattice models than by the Black-Scholes-Merton formula, because lattice models can accommodate dynamic assumptions regarding the term structure and path-dependence of volatility. For example, there is evidence that volatility during the life of an option depends on the term of the option and, in particular, that short-term options often exhibit higher volatility than similar options with longer terms. Additionally, volatility is path-dependent, in that it is often lower (higher) after an increase (decrease) in share price.

An entity that can observe sufficiently extensive trading of options over its shares may decide, when developing a term structure of expected volatility, to place greater weight on current implied volatilities than on historical observed and implied volatilities. It is likely that current implied volatilities are better indicators of the expectations of market participants about future volatility.

8.5.4 Expected dividends

The valuation of an award of options depends on whether or not the holder is entitled to dividends or dividend equivalents (whether in the form of cash payments or reductions in the exercise price) before the award is ultimately exercised. *[IFRS 2.B31-32, B34]*. The accounting treatment of awards that entitle the holder to dividends before exercise is discussed further at 15.3 below.

Dividends paid on the underlying share will impact the share option value – the higher the expected dividend yield (i.e. dividend per share ÷ share price), the lower the option value. Option holders generally do not have dividend rights until they actually exercise the options and become shareholders. All other things being equal, a share option for a share yielding a high dividend is less valuable than one for a share yielding a low dividend.

Where employees are entitled to dividends or dividend equivalents, the options granted should be valued as if no dividends will be paid on the underlying shares, so that the input for expected dividends (which would otherwise reduce the valuation of an option) is zero. Conversely, where employees are not entitled to dividends or dividend equivalents, the expected dividends should be included in the application of the pricing model. *[IFRS 2.B31-32, B34]*.

While option pricing models generally call for an expected dividend yield, they may be modified to use an expected dividend amount rather than a yield. Where an entity uses expected payments rather than expected yields, it should consider its historical pattern of increases in dividends. For example, if an entity's policy has generally been to increase dividends, its estimated option value should not assume a fixed dividend amount throughout the life of the option unless there is evidence to support that assumption. *[IFRS 2.B35]*.

Determination of the expected dividends over the expected term of the option requires judgement. Generally, the expected dividend assumption should be based on current expectations about an entity's anticipated dividend policy. For example, an entity that has demonstrated a stable dividend yield in past years, and has indicated no foreseeable plans to change its dividend policy, may simply use its historical dividend yield to estimate the fair value of its options. If an entity has never paid a dividend, but has publicly announced that it will begin paying a dividend yielding 2% of the current share price, it is likely that an expected dividend yield of 2% would be assumed in estimating the fair value of its options.

Generally assumptions about expected dividends should be based on publicly available information. Thus, an entity that does not pay dividends and has no plans to do so should assume an expected dividend yield of zero. However, an emerging entity with no history of paying dividends might expect to begin paying dividends during the expected lives of its employee share options. Such entities could use an average of their past dividend yield (zero) and the mean dividend yield of a comparable peer group of entities. *[IFRS 2.B36]*.

8.5.4.A Expected dividends under the Black-Scholes-Merton formula

Closed-form option-pricing models generally call for a single expected dividend yield as an input. That input should be determined based on the guidance at 8.5.4 above.

8.5.4.B Expected dividends under the binomial model and other lattice models

Lattice models can be adapted to use an expected dividend amount rather than a dividend yield, and therefore can also take into account the impact of anticipated dividend changes. Such approaches might better reflect expected future dividends, since dividends do not always move in a fixed fashion with changes in the entity's share price. This may be a time- or price-dependent assumption, similar to those described in the discussion of the binomial model at 8.3.2 above. Expected dividend estimates in a lattice model should be determined based on the general guidance above. Additionally, when the present value of dividends becomes significant in relation to the share price, standard lattice models may need to be amended.

8.5.5 Risk-free interest rate

Typically, the risk-free interest rate is the implied yield currently available on zero-coupon government issues of the country in whose currency the exercise price is expressed, with a remaining term equal to the expected term of the option being valued (based on the remaining contractual life of the option and taking into account the effects of expected early exercise). It may be necessary to use an appropriate substitute, if no such government issues exist, or where the implied yield on zero-coupon government issues may not be representative of the risk-free interest rate (for example, in high inflation economies). An appropriate substitute should also be used if market participants would typically determine the risk-free interest rate by using that substitute. *[IFRS 2.B37]*.

The risk-free interest rate will not have an impact on most free share grants unless the counterparty is not entitled to dividends during the vesting period and the fair value of the grant has been reduced by the present value of the dividends. Otherwise, grants of free shares have an exercise price of zero and therefore involve no cash outflow for the holder.

8.5.5.A Risk-free interest rate under the Black-Scholes-Merton formula

The Black-Scholes-Merton formula expressed at 8.3.1 above uses a continuously compounded interest rate, which means that any interest rate calculated or obtained needs to be in this format. The continuously compounded interest rate is given by the formula:

$$\text{continuously compounding rate} = \ln(1 + \text{annual rate}),$$

where ln represents a natural logarithm. For example, a 7.79% annual effective rate results in a continuously compounded rate of 7.50%:

$$7.50\% = \ln(1 + 0.0779)$$

8.5.5.B Risk-free interest rate under binomial and other lattice models

At each node in the lattice, the option values in the lattice should be discounted using an appropriate forward rate as determined by a yield curve constructed from the implied yield on zero coupon government bond issues. In stable economies this will have minimal impact and it is therefore likely that a flat risk-free rate that is consistent with the expected life assumption will be a reasonable estimate for this input.

8.6 Capital structure effects and dilution

Typically, traded share options are written by third parties, not the entity issuing the shares that are the subject of the option. When these share options are exercised, the writer delivers to the option holder shares acquired from existing shareholders. Hence the exercise of traded share options has no dilutive effect. By contrast, when share options written by the entity are exercised, new shares may be issued (either in form or in substance, if shares previously repurchased and held in treasury are used), giving rise to dilution. This actual or potential dilution may reduce the share price, so that the option holder does not make as large a gain on exercise as on exercising an otherwise similar traded option that does not dilute the share price. *[IFRS 2.B38-39]*.

Whether or not this has a significant effect on the value of the share options granted depends on various factors, such as the number of new shares that will be issued on exercise of the options compared with the number of shares already issued. Also, if the market already expects that the option grant will take place, the market may have already factored the potential dilution into the share price at the date of grant. However, the entity should consider whether the possible dilutive effect of the future exercise of the share options granted might have an impact on their estimated fair value at grant date. Option pricing models can be adapted to take into account this potential dilutive effect. *[IFRS 2.B40-41]*.

In practice, in our view, it is unlikely that a listed entity would be required to make such an adjustment unless it makes a very large, unanticipated grant of share options.

Indeed, even in that case, if the potential dilution is material and is not already incorporated into the share price, it would be expected that the announcement of the grant would cause the share price to decline by a material amount. Unlisted entities should consider whether the dilutive impact of a very large option grant is already incorporated into the estimated share price used in their option-pricing model. If that is not the case, some adjustment to the fair value may be appropriate.

8.7 Other awards requiring the use of option valuation models

As noted at 8.1 above, the discussion in 8.3 to 8.5 above may well be relevant to share-based payments other than options. These include, but are not restricted to:

- awards of shares (see 8.7.1 below);
- non-recourse loans (see 8.7.2 below);
- share appreciation rights (SARs) (see 8.7.3 below); and
- performance rights (see 8.7.4 below).

8.7.1 Shares

IFRS 2 requires shares granted to employees to be valued at their market price (where one exists) or an estimated market value (where the shares are not publicly traded), in either case adjusted to take account of the terms and conditions on which the shares were granted, other than those vesting conditions that IFRS 2 requires to be excluded in determining the grant date fair value (see 6.2 above). *[IFRS 2.B2]*.

For example, the valuation should take account of restrictions on the employee's right:

- to receive dividends in the vesting period (see below); or
- to transfer shares after vesting, but only to the extent that such restrictions would affect the price that a knowledgeable and willing market participant would pay for the shares. Where the shares are traded in a deep and liquid market, the effect may be negligible.

The valuation should not, however, take account of restrictions on transfer or other restrictions that exist during the vesting period and which stem from the existence of vesting conditions. *[IFRS 2.B3]*.

Whether dividends should be taken into account in measuring the fair value of shares depends on whether the counterparty is entitled to dividends or dividend equivalents (which might be paid in cash) during the vesting period. When the grant date fair value of shares granted to employees is estimated, no adjustment is required if the employees are entitled to receive dividends during the vesting period (as they are in no different a position in this respect than if they already held shares). However, where employees are not entitled to receive dividends during the vesting period, the valuation should be reduced by the present value of dividends expected to be paid during the vesting period. *[IFRS 2.B31, B33-34]*. The basis on which expected dividends during the vesting period might be determined is discussed in the context of the impact of expected dividends on the fair value of share options at 8.5.4 above.

The accounting treatment of awards which give the right to receive dividends or dividend equivalents during the vesting period is discussed further at 15.3 below.

8.7.2 Non-recourse loans

Non-recourse loans are loans granted by an entity to the employee to allow the employee to buy shares, and are discussed in more detail at 15.2 below. Generally, however, the loan is interest-free, with the dividends received on the purchased shares being used to repay the loan. The loan acts like an option, in that, at the point in time when the holder decides to sell the shares to repay the loan, if the shares are worth less than the loan, the remaining part of the loan is forgiven, with the effect that, just as in the case of an option, the holder bears no risk of ownership.

8.7.3 Share appreciation rights (SARs)

A share appreciation right (SAR) is a grant whereby the employee will become entitled either to shares or, more commonly, to a future cash payment based on the increase in the entity's share price from a specified level over a period of time (see further discussion at 9 below on cash-settled awards). This essentially has the same payoff as a call option, except the award is generally cash- rather than equity-settled.

8.7.4 Performance rights

A performance right is the right to acquire further shares after vesting, upon certain criteria being met. These criteria may include certain performance conditions which can usually be modelled with either a Black-Scholes-Merton formula or a binomial lattice model or a Monte Carlo Simulation depending on the nature of the conditions attached to the rights. Such awards may be structured as matching share awards, as discussed in more detail at 15.1 below.

8.8 Awards whose fair value cannot be measured reliably

IFRS 2 acknowledges that there may be rare cases where it is not possible to determine the fair value of equity instruments granted. In such cases, the entity is required to adopt a method of accounting based on the intrinsic value of the award (i.e. the price of the underlying share less the exercise price, if any, for the award). This is slightly puzzling in the sense that, for unlisted entities, a significant obstacle to determining a reliable fair value for equity instruments is the absence of a market share price, which is also a key input in determining intrinsic value. In fact, the intrinsic value model is arguably more onerous than the fair value model since, as discussed further in 8.8.1 and 8.8.2 below, it requires intrinsic value to be determined not just once, but at initial measurement date and each subsequent reporting date until exercise.

8.8.1 Intrinsic value method – the basic accounting treatment

Under the intrinsic value method:

(a) the entity measures the intrinsic value of the award at each reporting date between grant date and settlement (whether through exercise, forfeiture or lapse);

(b) at each reporting date during the vesting period the cumulative expense should be determined as the intrinsic value of the award at that date multiplied by the expired portion of the vesting period, with all changes in the cumulative expense recognised in profit or loss; and

(c) once options have vested, all changes in their intrinsic value until settlement should be recognised in profit or loss. *[IFRS 2.24(a)]*.

The cumulative expense during the vesting period, like that for awards measured at fair value, should always be based on the best estimate of the number of awards that will actually vest (see 6 above). However, the distinction between market vesting conditions, non-market vesting conditions and non-vesting conditions that would apply to equity-settled awards measured at fair value (see 6.1 to 6.4 above) does not apply in the case of awards measured at intrinsic value. *[IFRS 2.24(b)]*. In other words, where an award measured at intrinsic value is subject to a market condition or non-vesting condition that is not met, there is ultimately no accounting expense for that award. This is consistent with a model requiring constant remeasurement.

The cost of awards measured at intrinsic value is ultimately revised to reflect the number of awards that are actually exercised. However, during the vesting period the cost should be based on the number of awards estimated to vest and thereafter on the number of awards that have vested. In other words, any post-vesting forfeiture or lapse should not be anticipated, but should be accounted for as it occurs. *[IFRS 2.24(b)]*.

Example 32.33 illustrates the intrinsic value method.

Example 32.33: Intrinsic value method

At the beginning of year 1, an entity grants 1,000 share options to 50 employees.

The share options will vest at the end of year 3, provided the employees remain in service until then. The options can be exercised at the end of year 4, and then at the end of each subsequent year up to and including year 10. The exercise price, and the entity's grant date share price, is €60. At the date of grant, the entity concludes that it cannot estimate reliably the fair value of the share options granted.

At the end of year 1, the entity estimates that 80% of the share options will vest. At the end of year 2, the entity revises its estimate of the number of share options that it expects will vest to 86%.

During the vesting period, a total of seven employees leave, so that 43,000 share options vest.

The intrinsic value of the options, and the number of share options exercised during years 4-10, are as follows:

Year	Intrinsic value €	Number exercised
1	3	
2	5	
3	15	
4	28	6,000
5	40	8,000
6	30	5,000
7	36	9,000
8	45	8,000
9	48	5,000
10	55	2,000

The expense recognised under IFRS 2 will be as follows. In the period up to vesting the 'cumulative expense' methodology used in the examples at 6.1 to 6.4 above can be adopted to derive the expense for each period:

Year	Calculation of cumulative expense	Cumulative expense (€)	Expense for period (€)
1	50,000 options × €3 × 80% × 1/3	40,000	40,000
2	50,000 options × €5 × 86% × 2/3	143,333	103,333
3	43,000 options × €15	645,000	501,677

In years 4 to 10 it is more straightforward to calculate the expense directly. Since all options exercised during each year are exercised at the end of that year, the annual expense can be calculated as the change in intrinsic value during each year of the options outstanding at the *start* of the year.

Year		Expense for period (€)
4	43,000 options × €(28 – 15)	559,000
5	43,000 – 6,000 = 37,000 options × €(40 – 28)	444,000
6	37,000 – 8,000 = 29,000 options × €(30 – 40)	(290,000)
7	29,000 – 5,000 = 24,000 options × €(36 – 30)	144,000
8	24,000 – 9,000 = 15,000 options × €(45 – 36)	135,000
9	15,000 – 8,000 = 7,000 options × €(48 – 45)	21,000
10	7,000 – 5,000 = 2,000 options × €(55 – 48)	14,000

If, more realistically, the options had been exercisable, and were exercised, at other dates, it would have been necessary to record as an expense for those options the movement in intrinsic value from the start of the year until exercise date. For example, if the 6,000 options in year 4 had been exercised during the year when the intrinsic value was €20, the expense for that period would have been €511,000 comprising €481,000 change in value for the options outstanding at the end of year [37,000 options × €(28 – 15)] and €30,000 change in value of options exercised during the period [6,000 options × €(20 – 15)].

8.8.2 Modification, cancellation and settlement

The methodology of the intrinsic value method has the effect that modification or cancellation is dealt with automatically, and the rules for modification and cancellation of awards measured at fair value (see 7 above) therefore do not apply. *[IFRS 2.25]*.

Where an award accounted for at intrinsic value is settled in cash, the following provisions apply, which are broadly similar to the rules for settlement of awards accounted for at fair value.

If settlement occurs before vesting, the entity must treat this as an acceleration of vesting and 'recognise immediately the amount that would otherwise have been recognised for services received over the remainder of the vesting period'. *[IFRS 2.25(a)]*. The wording here is the same as that applicable to settlement of awards accounted for at fair value, which we discuss in more detail at 7.4.3 above.

Any payment made on settlement must be deducted from equity, except to the extent that it is greater than the intrinsic value of the award at settlement date. Any such excess is accounted for as an expense. *[IFRS 2.25(b)]*.

8.9 Awards with reload features

Some share options contain a reload feature (see 5.5.1 above). Reloads commonly provide that, where an exercise price is satisfied in shares of the issuing entity rather than cash, there is a new grant of at-the-money options over as many shares as are equal to the exercise price of the exercised option. For example, if there were 100 options with an exercise price of $10, and the new share price were $15, 67 options (€1,000 ÷ €15) would be re-issued.

Even though the reload feature (i.e. the possibility that additional options would be issued in the future) is a feature of the original option, and can be readily incorporated into the valuation of the original option using a lattice model, the IASB concluded that the fair value of a reload feature should not be incorporated into the estimate of the fair value of the award at grant date. As a result, subsequent grants of reload awards under the reload feature would be accounted for as new awards and measured on their respective grant dates. *[IFRS 2.BC188-192]*.

On the assumption that the exercise price of an award is at least the share price at grant date, the grant-date fair value of the reload award will generally be greater than the incremental value of the reload feature as at the date the original award was granted. This is because the reload award will only be granted if the original option is in-the-money and is exercised. As a result, the award would have increased in the period between the original grant date and the reload grant date, and the higher share price would be used to value the reload grant. However, from the perspective of the aggregate compensation cost, this result is mitigated by the fact that, as the value of the underlying share increases, fewer shares must be tendered to satisfy the exercise price requirement of the exercised option and, therefore, fewer reload options will be granted (as above when only 67 options are re-issued for the 100 originally issued).

If the reload feature were incorporated into the valuation of the original grant, then not only would a lower price be used, but the valuation would consider the possibility that the original option would never be exercised and, therefore, that the reload options would not be granted. Under the approach in IFRS 2, if the original award expires unexercised, no compensation cost results from the reload feature, so that the compensation cost is lower than would be the case if the value of the reload feature were incorporated into the measurement of the original award. Effectively, the approach in IFRS 2 incorporates subsequent share price changes into the valuation of a reload award.

8.10 Awards of equity instruments to a fixed monetary value

Entities may make an award of shares to a fixed monetary value (see 5.3.5 above). This is commonly found as part of a matching share award where an employee may be offered the choice of receiving cash or shares of an equivalent value, or a multiple of that value (see 15.1 below).

IFRS 2 does not address directly the valuation of such awards. Intuitively, it might seem obvious that an award which promises (subject to vesting conditions) shares to the value of €10,000 must have a grant date fair value of €10,000, adjusted for the time value of money, together with market conditions and non-vesting conditions. However, matters are not so clear-cut, as Example 32.34 illustrates:

Example 32.34: Award of shares to a fixed monetary value

At the beginning of year 1 the reporting entity grants:

- to Employee A an award of 1,000 shares subject to remaining in employment for three years; and
- to Employee B €10,000 subject to remaining in employment for three years, to be paid in as many shares as are (at the end of year 3) worth €10,000.

Both awards vest, and the share price at the end of year 3 is €10, so that both employees receive 1,000 shares.

The IFRS 2 charge for A's award is clearly 1000 × the fair value as at the beginning of year 1 of a share deliverable in three years' time. What is the charge for B's award? A number of potential alternatives exist including:

- the number of shares actually delivered multiplied by the fair value at the grant date (start of year 1);
- an amount based on a grant date estimate of the number of shares (which is not subsequently revisited due to the existence of a market condition);
- €10,000, adjusted for the time value of money.

The Basis for Conclusions to IFRS 2 creates some confusion over this point. Paragraphs BC106 to BC118 discuss in general terms why IFRS 2 adopts a definition of equity instrument different from that in IAS 32. Paragraphs BC107 to BC109 particularly note that the IASB did not believe it appropriate that a fixed-cost award and a variable-cost award ultimately delivered in shares should be classified, and measured, (as would be the case under IAS 32) as, respectively, equity and a liability. *[IFRS 2.BC106-118]*.

Whilst the primary focus of the discussion in the Basis for Conclusions is whether variable equity-settled awards should be liabilities (as they would be under IAS 32) or equity (as they are under IFRS 2), the reference to measurement as well as classification of awards can be read as meaning that the IASB believed that two awards that ultimately deliver 1,000 shares (as in Example 32.34 above) should have the same grant date fair value.

Some argue that an award of shares to a given monetary amount contains a market condition, since the number of shares ultimately delivered (and therefore vesting) depends on the market price of the shares on the date of delivery. This allows the award to be valued at a fixed amount at grant date. We acknowledge that a literal reading of the definition of 'market condition' in IFRS 2 supports this view, but question whether this can really have been intended. In our view, the essential feature of a share-based payment transaction subject to a market condition must be that the employee's ultimate entitlement to the award depends on the share price rather than the share price simply being used to determine the number of shares.

In our view, the principal question is whether the measurement under IFRS 2 should be based on the overall award or on each share or share equivalent making up the award. In the absence of clear guidance in IFRS 2 as to the appropriate unit of account, entities may take a number of views on how to value awards of shares to a given value, but should adopt a consistent approach for all such awards.

9 CASH-SETTLED TRANSACTIONS

Throughout the discussion in this section, 'cash' should be read as including 'other assets' in accordance with the definition of a cash-settled share-based payment transaction (see 2.2.1 above).

9.1 Scope of requirements

Cash-settled share-based payment transactions include transactions such as:

- share appreciation rights (SARs), where employees are entitled to a cash payment equivalent to the gain that would have arisen from a holding of a particular number of shares from the date of grant to the date of exercise; or
- phantom options, where employees are entitled to a cash payment equivalent to the gain that would have been made by exercising options at a notional price over a notional number of shares and then selling the shares at the date of exercise. *[IFRS 2.31]*.

However, IFRS 2 looks beyond the simple issue of whether an award entitles an employee to receive instruments that are in form shares or options to the terms of those instruments. For example, an award of shares or options over shares whose terms provide for their redemption either mandatorily according to their terms (e.g. on cessation of employment) or at the employee's option would be treated as a cash-settled, not an equity-settled, award under IFRS 2. *[IFRS 2.31]*. This is consistent with the fact that IAS 32 would regard a share with these terms as a financial liability rather than an equity instrument of the issuer (see Chapter 45 at 4).

In some cases the boundary between equity-settled and cash-settled schemes may appear somewhat blurred, so that further analysis may be required to determine whether a particular arrangement is equity-settled or cash-settled. Some examples of such arrangements are discussed at 9.2 below.

9.2 What constitutes a cash-settled award?

There are a number of possible circumstances in which, on, or shortly after, settlement of an equity-settled award either:

- the entity incurs a cash outflow equivalent to that that would arise on cash-settlement (e.g. because it purchases shares in the market at fair value to deliver to counterparties); or
- the counterparty receives a cash inflow equivalent to that that would arise on cash-settlement (e.g. because the shares are sold in the market for cash on behalf of the counterparty).

Such situations raise the question of whether such schemes are in fact truly equity-settled or cash-settled.

Examples of relatively common mechanisms for delivering the cash-equivalent of an equity-settled award to employees are discussed below. It emerges from the analysis below that, in reality, IFRS 2 is driven by questions of form rather than substance. To put it rather crudely, what matters is often not so much whether the entity has written a cheque for the fair value of the award, but rather the name of the payee on the cheque.

The significance of this is that the analysis affects the profit or loss charge for the award, as illustrated by Example 32.35 below.

Example 32.35: Equity-settled award satisfied with market purchase of treasury shares

An entity awards an employee a free share with a fair value at grant date of £5 which has a fair value of £8 at vesting. At vesting the entity purchases a share in the market for £8 for delivery to the employee. If the scheme were treated as cash-settled, there would be a charge to profit or loss of £8 (the fair value at vesting date – see 9.3 below). If it were treated as equity-settled (as required in this case by IFRS 2), profit or loss would show a charge of only £5 (the fair value at grant date), with a further net charge of £3 in equity, comprising the £8 paid for the share accounted for as a treasury share (see Chapter 45 at 9) less the £5 credit to equity (being the credit entry corresponding to the £5 charge to profit or loss – see 4.2 above).

The analyses below all rely on a precise construction of the definition of a cash-settled share-based payment transaction, i.e. one 'in which the entity acquires goods or services *by incurring a liability to transfer cash or other assets to the supplier of those goods or services* for amounts that are based on the price (or value) of the entity's shares or other equity instruments of the entity' (emphasis added). *[IFRS 2 Appendix A]*. Thus, if the entity is not actually required – legally or constructively – to pay cash to the *counterparty*, there is no cash-settled transaction under IFRS 2, even though the arrangement may give rise to an external cash flow and, possibly, a liability under another standard.

9.2.1 Economic compulsion for cash settlement (including unlisted company schemes)

Some share-based payment awards, particularly when made by unlisted entities, might appear to be equity-settled in form but, in our view, will need to be accounted for as cash-settled awards under IFRS 2. This reflects either specific arrangements put in place for the employees to sell their shares or, more generally, the illiquid market in the shares which, in the absence of compelling evidence to the contrary, is likely to result in a cash payment by the entity to the counterparty at some stage.

This is similar to the assessment for awards where the agreement states that entities have a choice of settlement in equity or cash (see 10.2.1.A below).

9.2.2 Market purchases of own equity used to satisfy awards

It is common for an entity to choose to settle equity-settled transactions using shares previously purchased in the market rather than by issuing new shares. This does not mean that the transaction is cash-settled, since there is no obligation to deliver cash to the counterparty. *[IFRS 2.B48-49]*.

The purchase of own shares is accounted for in accordance with the provisions of IAS 32 relating to treasury shares and other transactions over own equity (see Chapter 45 at 9).

A question sometimes asked is whether the entity should recognise some form of liability to repurchase its own equity in situations where the entity has a stated policy of settling equity-settled transactions using previously purchased treasury shares. In our view, the normal provisions of IAS 32 apply. For example, a public commitment to settle equity-settled transactions by purchasing treasury shares is no different in substance to a commitment to a share buyback programme. There would be no question under IAS 32 of recognising a liability to repurchase own equity on the basis merely of a declared intention. It is only when the entity enters into a forward contract or a call option with a third party that some accounting recognition of a future share purchase may be required.

9.2.3 Market purchases of own equity following equity-settlement of award

An entity might sometimes make a market purchase of its own shares shortly after issuing a similar number of shares in settlement of an equity-settled transaction. This raises the question of whether such a scheme would be considered as in substance cash-settled.

In our view, further enquiry into the detailed circumstances of the market purchase is required in order to determine the appropriate analysis under IFRS 2.

Broadly speaking, so long as there is no obligation (explicit or implicit) for the entity to settle in cash with the counterparty, such market purchase arrangements will not require a scheme to be treated as cash-settled under IFRS 2. This will be the case even where the entity, as a means of managing the dilutive impact on earnings per share of equity-settlement, routinely buys back shares broadly equivalent to the number issued in settlement.

However, in our view, there might be situations in which post-settlement market share purchases are indicative of an obligation to the counterparty, such that treatment as a cash-settled scheme would be appropriate.

For example, the shares might be quoted in a market which is not very deep, or in which the entity itself is a major participant. If the entity were to create an expectation by employees that any shares awarded can always be liquidated immediately, because the entity will ensure that there is sufficient depth in the market to do so, it could well be appropriate to account for such a scheme as cash-settled. The treatment of schemes in which the entity has a choice of settlement, but has created an expectation of cash-settlement, provides a relevant analogy (see 10.2.1 below).

A more extreme example of such a situation would be where the entity has arranged for the shares delivered to the counterparty to be sold on the counterparty's behalf by a broker (see 9.2.4 below), but has at the same time entered into a contract to purchase those shares from the broker. In that situation, in our view, the substance is that:

- the entity has created an expectation by the counterparty of a right to receive cash; and
- the broker is no more than an agent paying that cash to the counterparty on behalf of the entity.

Accordingly, it would be appropriate to account for such an arrangement as a cash-settled award.

In a situation where the entity had pre-arranged to purchase some, but not all, the shares from the broker, in our view it would generally be appropriate to treat the award as cash-settled only to the extent of the shares subject to the purchase agreement.

9.2.4 Arrangements to sell employees' shares including 'broker settlement'

Many recipients of share awards, particularly employees in lower and middle ranking positions within an entity, do not wish to become long-term investors in the entity and prefer instead to realise any equity-settled awards in cash soon after receipt. In order to facilitate this, the entity may either sell the shares in the market on the employees' behalf or, more likely, arrange for a third party broker to do so.

Such an arrangement (sometimes referred to as 'broker settlement') does not of itself create a cash-settled award, provided that the entity has not created any obligation to provide cash to the employees. If, however, the entity has either created an expectation among employees that it will step in to make good any lack of depth in the market, or has indeed itself contracted to repurchase the shares in question, that may well mean that analysis as a cash-settled scheme is more appropriate (see also 9.2.3 above).

Broker settlement arrangements may raise a general concern that an entity may be masking what are really issues of shares to raise cash to pay its employees as sales of shares on behalf of employees. If an entity were simply to issue shares (or reissue treasury shares) for cash, and then use that cash to pay an employee's salary, the normal accounting treatment for such a transaction would be to credit equity with the proceeds of issue or reissue of shares, and to charge the payment to the employee to profit or loss.

By contrast, a sale of shares on behalf of an employee is undertaken by the entity as agent and does not give rise to an increase in equity and an expense, although an expense will be recognised for the award of shares under IFRS 2. However, the entity may enter into much the same transaction with a broker whether it is selling shares on its own behalf or on behalf of its employees. The challenge is therefore for the entity to be able to demonstrate the true economic nature of the transaction.

For this reason, some take the view that a sale of shares can be regarded as part of a broker settlement arrangement only if the shares are first legally registered in the name of the employee. Whilst we understand the concerns that lie behind this view, we nevertheless question whether legal registration is necessary to demonstrate the substance of a broker settlement arrangement. For example, suppose that 100 shares vest in each of 10 employees who all express a wish that the entity sell the shares on their behalf, and the entity then sells 1,000 treasury shares on behalf of the employees, but without first re-registering title to the shares to the employees. We do not believe that the entity should automatically be precluded from regarding this as a broker settlement arrangement, particularly where the treasury shares are held not by the entity directly but through an employee benefit trust or similar vehicle (see 12.3 below) that is permitted to hold or sell shares only for the benefit of employees.

By contrast, the entity might regularly purchase and sell treasury shares, but identify some of the sales as being undertaken on behalf of employees only after they have occurred. Such an arrangement, in our view, is more difficult to construe as a true broker-settlement arrangement.

Where shares are sold on behalf of an employee, they will typically attract transaction costs, such as brokerage fees or taxes. If such costs are borne by the entity, they should, in our view, be included within profit or loss as an additional component of employment costs, rather than deducted from equity as a cost of a transaction in own shares.

This highlights a commercial disadvantage of broker settlement arrangements. The entity may have to:

- purchase shares in the market (incurring transaction costs) on behalf of an employee who does not want them and then sell them back into the market on the employee's behalf (incurring more transaction costs); or
- sell shares in the market (incurring transaction costs) on behalf of an employee who does not want them and then buy them back in the market on behalf of another employee who does want them (incurring more transaction costs).

In order to avoid this, entities may try to structure arrangements with their brokers involving back-to-back sale and purchase contracts, under which shares are never physically delivered, but the entity makes a cash payment to the broker in purported settlement of the purchase by the broker of shares on behalf of the entity and the broker passes it on to the employee in purported settlement of the sale of the shares by the broker on behalf of the employee.

In our view, such arrangements cannot be seen as equity-settled transactions with broker settlement, but must be regarded as cash-settled share-based payment transactions, using the broker as paying agent.

Related issues are raised by the 'drag along' and 'tag along' rights that are often a feature of awards designed to reward employees for a successful flotation or other exit event (see 15.4.6 below).

9.3 Required accounting

9.3.1 Basic accounting treatment

It is clear that the ultimate cost of a cash-settled transaction must be the actual cash paid to the counterparty, which will be the fair value at settlement date. Moreover, the cumulative cost recognised until settlement is clearly a liability, not a component of equity.

The periodic determination of this liability is as follows:

- at each reporting date between grant and settlement the fair value of the award is determined in accordance with the specific requirements of IFRS 2;
- during the vesting period, the liability recognised at each reporting date is the IFRS 2 fair value of the award at that date multiplied by the expired portion of the vesting period;
- from the end of the vesting period until settlement, the liability recognised is the full fair value of the liability at the reporting date.

All changes in the liability are recognised in profit or loss for the period. *[IFRS 2.30-33, IG Example 12]*. Where the cost of services received in a cash-settled transaction is recognised in the carrying amount of an asset (e.g. inventory) in the entity's statement of financial position, the carrying amount of the asset is not adjusted for changes in the fair value of the liability. *[IFRS 2.IG19]*.

The fair value of the liability should be determined, initially and at each reporting date until it is settled, by applying an option pricing model, taking into account the terms and conditions on which the cash-settled transaction was granted, and the extent to which the employees have rendered service to date. *[IFRS 2.33]*. It should be noted that IFRS 2 uses the term 'share appreciation rights' when referring to measurement of the liability but this should clearly be read as including any cash-settled share-based payment transaction. Indeed, this wider reading has been confirmed as part of the amendments to IFRS 2 issued in June 2016 (see 9.3.2.C below) and paragraph 31 of IFRS 2 has been amended accordingly.

This has the effect that, although the liability will ultimately be settled at its then intrinsic value, its measurement at reporting dates before settlement is based on its fair value. During the exposure period of ED 2, a number of respondents suggested that, for reasons of consistency and simplicity of calculation, cash-settled transactions should be measured at intrinsic value throughout their entire life. The IASB, while accepting these merits of the intrinsic value approach, rejected it on the basis that, since it does not include a time value, it is not an adequate measure of either the liability or the cost of services consumed. *[IFRS 2.BC246-251]*.

As noted at 5.5 above, the approach to determining the fair value of share-based payments continues to be that specified in IFRS 2 as share-based payments fall outside the scope of IFRS 13 which applies more generally to the measurement of fair value under IFRSs (see Chapter 14). *[IFRS 2.6A]*.

9.3.2 *Application of the accounting treatment*

The treatment required by IFRS 2 for cash-settled transactions is illustrated by Example 32.36 (which is based on IG Example 12 in the implementation guidance accompanying IFRS 2). *[IFRS 2 IG Example 12]*. Entities should also consider the amendment to IFRS 2 relating to the measurement of cash-settled share-based payment transactions (see 9.3.2.C below).

Example 32.36: Cash-settled transaction

An entity grants 100 cash share appreciation rights (SARs) to each of its 500 employees, on condition that the employees remain in its employment for the next three years. The SARs can be exercised on the third, fourth and fifth anniversary of the grant date.

During year 1, 35 employees leave. The entity estimates that a further 60 will leave during years 2 and 3 (i.e. the award will vest in 405 employees).

During year 2, 40 employees leave and the entity estimates that a further 25 will leave during year 3 (i.e. the award will vest in 400 employees).

During year 3, 22 employees leave, so that the award vests in 403 employees. At the end of year 3, 150 employees exercise their SARs (leaving 253 employees still to exercise).

Another 140 employees exercise their SARs at the end of year 4, leaving 113 employees still to exercise, who do so at the end of year 5.

The entity estimates the fair value of the SARs at the end of each year in which a liability exists as shown below. The intrinsic values of the SARs at the date of exercise (which equal the cash paid out) at the end of years 3, 4 and 5 are also shown below.

Year	Fair value	Intrinsic value
	£	£
1	14.40	
2	15.50	
3	18.20	15.00
4	21.40	20.00
5		25.00

The entity will recognise the cost of this award as follows:

Year	Calculation of liability	Calculation of cash paid	Liability (£)	Cash paid (£)	Expense for period (£)*
1	405 employees × 100 SARs × £14.40 × 1/3		194,400	–	194,400
2	400 employees × 100 SARs × £15.50 × 2/3		413,333	–	218,933
3	253 employees × 100 SARs × £18.20	150 employees × 100 SARs × £15.00	460,460	225,000	272,127
4	113 employees × 100 SARs × £21.40	140 employees × 100 SARs × £20.00	241,820	280,000	61,360
5	–	113 employees × 100 SARs × £25.00	–	282,500	40,680

* Liability at end of period + cash paid in period – liability at start of period

The accounting treatment for cash-settled transactions is therefore (despite some similarities in the methodology) significantly different from that for equity-settled transactions. An important practical issue is that, for a cash-settled transaction, the entity must determine the fair value at each reporting date and not merely at grant date (and at the date of any subsequent modification or settlement) as would be the case for equity-settled transactions. However, as Example 32.36 shows, it is not generally necessary, although arguably required by IFRS 2, to determine the fair value of a cash-settled transaction at grant date, at least to determine the expense under IFRS 2. However, for entities subject to IAS 33 – *Earnings per Share* – the grant date fair value may be required in order to make the disclosures required by that standard – see Chapter 35 at 6.4.2.

IFRS 2 raises some issues of interpretation on detailed aspects of the methodology such as:

- determining the vesting period (see 9.3.2.A below);
- periodic allocation of cost (see 9.3.2.B below);
- treatment of non-market vesting conditions (see 9.3.2.C below);
- treatment of market conditions and non-vesting conditions (see 9.3.2.D below); and
- treatment of modification, cancellation and settlement (see 9.3.2.E below).

9.3.2.A Determining the vesting period

The rules for determining vesting periods are the same as those applicable to equity-settled transactions, as discussed in 6.1 to 6.4 above. Where an award vests immediately, IFRS 2 creates a presumption that, in the absence of evidence to the contrary, the award is in respect of services that have already been rendered, and should therefore be expensed in full at grant date. *[IFRS 2.32]*.

Where cash-settled awards are made subject to vesting conditions (as in many cases they will be, particularly where payments to employees are concerned), IFRS 2 creates a presumption that they are a payment for services to be received in the future, during the 'vesting period', with the transaction being recognised during that period, as illustrated in Example 32.36 above. *[IFRS 2.32]*.

9.3.2.B Periodic allocation of cost

IFRS 2 states that the required treatment for cash-settled transactions is simply to measure the fair value of the liability at each reporting date *[IFRS 2.30]*, which might suggest that the *full* fair value, and not just a time-apportioned part of it, should be recognised at each reporting date – as would be the case for any liability that is a financial instrument and measured at fair value under IAS 39.

However, the standard goes on to clarify that the liability is to be measured at an amount that reflects 'the extent to which employees have rendered service to date', and the cost is to be recognised 'as the employees render service'. *[IFRS 2.32-33]*. This, together with IG Example 12 in IFRS 2 (the substance of which is reproduced as Example 32.36 above), indicates that a spreading approach is to be adopted.

9.3.2.C Non-market vesting conditions

As currently drafted, IFRS 2 does not specifically address the impact of vesting conditions in the context of cash-settled transactions – the provisions of IFRS 2 relating to vesting conditions are to be found in paragraphs 19 to 21, all of which fall under the main heading 'Equity-settled share-based payment transactions' immediately before paragraph 10. However, the IASB has published an amendment to IFRS 2 in respect of the treatment of vesting conditions applicable to cash-settled share-based payment transactions (see further below).

Where there is a service vesting condition, IG Example 12 in IFRS 2 (broadly reproduced as Example 32.36 above) clearly indicates that, during the period to vesting, the liability should be estimated on the basis of the current best estimate of the number of awards that will vest, this estimate being made exactly as for an equity-settled transaction. Therefore, as confirmed by the amendment to IFRS 2 discussed below, IFRS 2 does not require the probability of achieving a service condition to be directly reflected in the fair value of a cash-settled award but, instead, requires this to be taken into account in estimating the expense, as for an equity-settled award.

Where a cash-settled award has non-market performance conditions, it is unclear in IFRS 2, as currently drafted, whether an entity should:

- analogise to the treatment of service periods in IG Example 12 (see Example 32.36 above), basing the liability until vesting date on the current best estimate of the outcome of those conditions; or
- reflect the estimated outcome of the conditions other than service as part of the fair value calculation.

Both approaches have been used in practice and, in view of the diversity of interpretation, in June 2016 the IASB published an amendment to IFRS 2 to clarify how vesting and non-vesting conditions should be treated in the measurement of cash-settled share-based payment transactions.[23] The amendments change the standard to make clear that:

- market performance conditions and non-vesting conditions should be taken into account when estimating the fair value of a cash-settled share-based payment both at grant date and at subsequent remeasurement dates;
- vesting conditions (other than market conditions) should not be taken into account in estimating the fair value of a cash-settled share-based payment. Instead, as for equity-settled share-based payment transactions, such conditions should be taken into account in the measurement of the liability incurred by adjusting the number of awards that are expected to vest. This estimate should be revised, if necessary, whenever the liability is remeasured between grant date and vesting date; and
- on a cumulative basis, the amount ultimately recognised for goods or services received as consideration for the cash-settled share-based payment will be equal to the cash that is paid.

The amendments also include an additional example for the implementation guidance to IFRS 2 to illustrate the accounting treatment of a cash-settled award with a non-market performance condition (Example 12A).

The amendment applies to accounting periods beginning on or after 1 January 2018 although earlier application is permitted, if disclosed. The transitional provisions relating to application of the amendment are set out at 16.2 below. Until the amendment is applied, either reading of IFRS 2, as currently drafted, remains possible. However, in light of the amendment to the standard and the IASB's discussions in finalising the amendment, as a minimum those entities without an existing policy for the valuation of cash-settled share-based payment transactions should have regard to the requirements of the amended standard when selecting an accounting policy.

9.3.2.D *Market conditions and non-vesting conditions*

There is no specific guidance in IFRS 2, as currently drafted, as to whether a distinction is to be drawn between the treatment of non-vesting conditions and market conditions and that of other non-market vesting conditions, as would be the case for an equity-settled transaction (see 6.2 to 6.4 above).

As discussed at 9.3.2.C above, this is addressed in the IASB's amendment to IFRS 2.

Under both the current and amended versions of the standard, market performance conditions and non-vesting conditions should be taken into account in measuring the fair value of the cash-settled share-based payment. There will be no ultimate cost for an award subject to a market condition or non-vesting condition that is not satisfied as any liability would be reversed. This is different from the accounting model for equity-settled transactions with market conditions or non-vesting conditions, which can result in a cost being recognised for awards subject to a market or non-vesting condition that is not satisfied (see 6.3 and 6.4 above).

9.3.2.E Modification, cancellation and settlement

IFRS 2 provides no specific guidance on modification, cancellation and settlement of cash-settled awards. However, as cash-settled awards are accounted for using a full fair value model no such guidance is needed. It is clear that:

- where an award is modified, the liability recognised at and after the point of modification will be based on its new fair value, with the effect of any movement in the liability recognised immediately;
- where an award is cancelled the liability will be derecognised, with a credit immediately recognised in profit or loss; and
- where an award is settled, the liability will be derecognised, and any gain or loss on settlement immediately recognised in profit or loss.

9.4 Modification of award from equity-settled to cash-settled or from cash-settled to equity-settled

An entity will sometimes modify the terms of an award in order to change the manner of settlement. In other words, an award that at grant date was equity-settled is modified so as to become cash-settled, or *vice versa.*

IFRS 2 provides no explicit guidance on such modifications. However, we believe that it is possible to arrive at a reasonable approach by analogy to the provisions of IFRS 2 in respect of:

- the modification of equity-settled awards during the vesting period (see 7.3 above);
- the addition of a cash-settlement alternative to an equity-settled award after grant date (see 10.1.4 below);
- the settlement of equity-settled awards in cash (see 7.4 above); and
- the settlement in equity of awards where the entity has a choice of settlement, but where the awards have been accounted for as cash-settled during the vesting period (see 10.2 below).

As a result of the lack of guidance in IFRS 2 and resultant diversity in accounting practice, the IASB has issued an amendment to clarify the accounting treatment of modifications that change the classification of an award from cash-settled to equity-settled. This amendment is discussed at 9.4.2.A below.

9.4.1 Equity-settled award modified to cash-settled award

This section focuses on accounting for a change of settlement method rather than on the accounting treatment of other modifications to an equity-settled award that might be made at the same time as the change of settlement method (see 7.3 above).

Drawing on the principles within the guidance referred to at 9.4 above, we suggest that entities generally select one of the two approaches discussed below to account for the modification of an award from equity-settled to cash-settled during the vesting period. The first approach is based more closely on the IFRS 2 treatment for the modification of an equity-settled award (see 7.3 above) and the second on that for the repurchase or settlement in cash of an equity instrument (see 7.4 above).

Both approaches take into account IG Example 9 in the implementation guidance to IFRS 2 (see 10.1.4 below) which shows the recognition of an expense for the post-modification remeasurement of the cash-settlement alternative in addition to an expense for the full grant date fair value of the equity-settled arrangement. Although this Example reflects a choice of settlement by the counterparty, rather than the elimination of a method of settlement (as is the case in a modification from equity-settlement to cash-settlement), we believe that an analogy may be drawn between the two situations because the addition of a cash alternative for the counterparty effectively results in the award being treated as cash-settled from the date of modification.

The two approaches are discussed in more detail below and illustrated in Example 32.37. In our view, either approach is acceptable in the absence of clear guidance in IFRS 2 but the choice of approach should be applied consistently to all such modifications.

Both approaches require the recognition, as a minimum, of an IFRS 2 expense which comprises the following elements:

- the grant date fair value of the original equity-settled award (see 7.3 above); plus
- any incremental fair value arising from the modification of that award (see 7.1 above); plus
- any remeasurement of the liability between its fair value at the modification date and the amount finally settled (see 10.1.4 below).

Over the vesting period as a whole, both approaches result in the same total IFRS 2 expense and liability/cash settlement amount with the net overall difference between the two being an adjustment to equity. However, the timing of recognition of any incremental fair value arising on modification will differ under the two approaches, as explained below.

Approach 1

- At the date of modification a liability is recognised based on the fair value of the cash-settled award as at that date and the extent to which the vesting period has expired.
- The entire corresponding debit is taken to equity. Any incremental fair value of the cash-settled award over that of the equity-settled award as at the modification date will be expensed over the period from the date of modification to the date of settlement of the cash-settled award (i.e. no expense is recognised at the date of modification).
- The total fair value of the cash-settled award is remeasured through profit or loss on an ongoing basis between the date of modification and the date of settlement.

As Approach 1 is based on the accounting treatment for a modification of an equity-settled award, no incremental fair value is recognised as an expense at the modification date. This means that, in cases where the fair value of the modified award is higher at the date of modification than that of the original award, the reduction in equity at the date of modification will be higher than the proportionate fair value at that date of the original equity-settled award. This situation reverses over the remainder of the vesting period when an expense (and corresponding credit to equity) will be recognised for the incremental fair value of the modified award.

Approach 2

- As for Approach 1, at the date of modification a liability is recognised based on the fair value of the cash-settled award as at that date and the extent to which the vesting period has expired.
- Unlike Approach 1, the corresponding debit is taken to equity only to the extent of the fair value of the original equity-settled award as at the date of modification. Any incremental fair value of the cash-settled award over the equity-settled award as at the modification date is expensed immediately on modification to the extent that the vesting period has expired. The remainder of any incremental value is expensed over the period from the date of modification to the date of settlement.
- As for Approach 1, the total fair value of the cash-settled award is remeasured through profit or loss on an ongoing basis between the date of modification and the date of settlement.

Approach 2 is based on the accounting treatment for the repurchase of an equity instrument where a reduction in equity up to the fair value of the equity instrument is recognised as at the date of repurchase with any incremental fair value of the repurchase arrangement being treated as an expense. Whilst Approach 2 avoids the potential problem of an immediate reduction in equity in excess of the fair value of the equity-settled award, its settlement approach could be seen as diverging from the basic IFRS 2 treatment for the modification of an equity-settled award where none of the incremental fair value arising on a modification is expensed at the date of modification.

As noted at the start of this section, the Approaches outlined above are based on the specific principles referred to at 9.4 above. In the absence of clear guidance in the standard, other interpretations of the appropriate expense and equity adjustment are also possible, although these will sometimes result in a higher expense through profit or loss than the two Approaches above. For example, in relation to the cash-settled award, the Approaches outlined above expense only the difference between the final settlement amount and the full fair value of the liability at the modification date, with the remainder adjusted through equity. An alternative view follows the accounting treatment for cash-settled awards which would lead to the recognition of an expense for the entire remeasurement of the liability from the amount recognised for a part-vested award at modification date to the amount finally settled.

As part of its discussions in developing the amendment to IFRS 2 for modifications from cash-settled to equity-settled (see 9.4.2 below), the IASB decided that existing implementation guidance in IFRS 2 could be applied by analogy to other types of modification. As an example of this, it states in paragraph BC237K of the amended Basis for Conclusions that IG Example 9 illustrates a grant of shares to which a cash settlement alternative is subsequently added. It appears therefore that the IASB sees this illustrative example as sufficient guidance for accounting for a modification from equity-settled to cash-settled. As noted above, the approach in IG Example 9 has been considered within our two suggested accounting approaches and is also discussed further in the context of Example 32.37 below.

Example 32.37: Modification of equity-settled award to cash-settled award

A Modified award with same fair value as original award

On 1 January 2017 an entity granted an equity-settled award, with a fair value at that date of €500, and vesting if the employee is still in service on 31 December 2020. On 1 January 2019, the award is modified so as to become cash-settled, but its terms are otherwise unchanged. The fair value at that date of both alternatives is €150. The liability is actually settled for €180 on 31 December 2020.

	Approach 1			Approach 2		
	Expense	Equity	Liability	Expense	Equity	Liability
	€	€	€	€	€	€
Two years ended 31.12.2018	250	(250)	–	250	(250)	–
1.1.2019 – modification	–	75	(75)	–	75	(75)
Two years ended 31.12.2020	280	(175)	(105)	280	(175)	(105)
Totals	530	(350)	(180)	530	(350)	(180)

During 2017 and 2018 the entity recognises a cumulative expense of €250, being the proportion of the grant date fair value of the equity-settled award of €500 attributable to 2/4 of the vesting period.

At 1 January 2019, it is necessary to recognise a liability of €75 (€150 × 2/4 – see 9.3.2 above). The full amount of this liability is recognised as a reduction in equity under both Approaches as there is no difference between the fair value of the original and modified awards as at the modification date.

As the award is continuing, there is no acceleration at the modification date of the as yet unrecognised amount of the grant date fair value of the original award (€250, being €500 × 2/4), as would occur in an immediate settlement (see 7.4 above).

During 2019 and 2020 (the period from modification to settlement date), the entity recognises an increase of €105 in the fair value of the liability (€180 – €75). During this period it also recognises employee costs totalling €280, being the remaining grant date fair value of €250 (€500 total less €250 expensed prior to modification) plus the post-modification remeasurement of the liability of €30 (€180 – €150). The balance of €175 is credited to equity.

In total the entity recognises an expense of €530, being the original grant date fair value of the equity-settled award of €500 plus the post-modification remeasurement of the liability of €30. This adjustment of €30 is consistent with the approach taken in IG Example 9 in the implementation guidance to IFRS 2 (see 10.1.4 and Example 32.41 below).

Scenario E below considers a situation where the awards have the same fair value as at the date of modification but this fair value is higher than the original grant date fair value of the equity-settled award.

B Modified award with greater fair value than original award

On 1 January 2017 an entity granted an equity-settled award, with a fair value at that date of €500, and vesting if the employee is still in service on 31 December 2020. On 1 January 2019, the award is modified so as to become cash-settled, with other modifications meaning that the new award has a higher fair value than the original award. At that date, the fair value of the original award is €150, but that of the cash-settled replacement award is €170. The liability is actually settled for €200 on 31 December 2020.

	Approach 1			Approach 2		
	Expense	Equity	Liability	Expense	Equity	Liability
	€	€	€	€	€	€
Two years ended 31.12.2018	250	(250)	–	250	(250)	–
1.1.2019 – modification	–	85	(85)	10	75	(85)
Two years ended 31.12.2020	300	(185)	(115)	290	(175)	(115)
Totals	550	(350)	(200)	550	(350)	(200)

Chapter 32

During 2017 and 2018 the entity recognises a cumulative expense of €250, being the proportion of the grant date fair value of the equity-settled award of €500 attributable to 2/4 of the vesting period.

At 1 January 2019, it is necessary to recognise a liability of €85 (€170 × 2/4 – see 9.3.2 above). Under Approach 1 the difference between the fair value of the original equity-settled award and the modified award (€20 in total) is not recognised immediately as an expense but is spread over the remainder of the vesting period (i.e. starting from the date of modification). The liability of €85 is therefore recognised as a reduction in equity. Under Approach 2, the difference between the fair value of the original equity-settled award and the modified award is expensed immediately to the extent that the vesting period has already expired (€20 × 2/4) with the remainder being expensed in the post-modification period.

As the award is continuing, there is no acceleration at the modification date of the as yet unrecognised amount of the grant date fair value of the original award (€250, being €500 × 2/4) as would occur in an immediate settlement (see 7.4 above).

During 2019 and 2020 (the period from modification to settlement date), the entity recognises an increase of €115 in the fair value of the liability (€200 – €85). During this period, under Approach 1 it also recognises employee costs totalling €300, being the remaining grant date fair value of €250 (€500 total less €250 expensed prior to modification) plus the incremental modification fair value of €20 (€170 – €150) plus the remeasurement of the liability of €30 (€200 – €170) between modification date and settlement date. The balance of €185 is credited to equity. For Approach 2, the expense and the credit to equity during this period are €10 less than under Approach 1 because a proportionate amount of the incremental fair value was expensed immediately at the modification date.

In total the entity recognises an expense of €550, being the original grant date fair value of the equity-settled award of €500 plus the incremental fair value of €20 arising on modification of the award plus the post-modification remeasurement of the liability of €30. This remeasurement adjustment of €30 is consistent with the approach taken in IG Example 9 in the implementation guidance to IFRS 2 (see 10.1.4 and Example 32.41 below).

C Modified award with lower fair value than original award

On 1 January 2017 an entity granted an equity-settled award, with a fair value at that date of €500, and vesting if the employee is still in service on 31 December 2020. On 1 January 2019, the award is modified so as to become cash-settled, with other modifications meaning that the new award has a lower fair value than the original award. At that date, the fair value of the original award is €150, but that of the cash-settled replacement award is €130. The liability is actually settled for €180 on 31 December 2020.

	Approach 1			Approach 2		
	Expense	Equity	Liability	Expense	Equity	Liability
	€	€	€	€	€	€
Two years ended 31.12.2018	250	(250)	–	250	(250)	–
1.1.2019 – modification	–	65	(65)	–	65	(65)
Two years ended 31.12.2020	300	(185)	(115)	300	(185)	(115)
Totals	550	(370)	(180)	550	(370)	(180)

During 2017 and 2018 the entity recognises a cumulative expense of €250, being the proportion of the grant date fair value of the equity-settled award of €500 attributable to 2/4 of the vesting period.

At 1 January 2019, it is necessary to recognise a liability of €65 (€130 × 2/4 – see 9.3.2 above). The full amount of this liability is recognised as a reduction in equity under both Approaches as the fair value of the modified award is lower than that of the original award. No gain is recognised for the reduction in fair value consistent with the general principle in IFRS 2 that the cost recognised for an equity-settled award must be at least the grant date fair value of the award.

As the award is continuing, there is no acceleration at the modification date of the as yet unrecognised amount of the grant date fair value of the original award (€250, being €500 × 2/4) as would occur in an immediate settlement (see 7.4 above).

During 2019 and 2020 (the period from modification to settlement date), the entity recognises an increase of €115 in the fair value of the liability (€180 – €65). During this period it also recognises employee costs totalling €300, being the remaining grant date fair value of €250 (€500 total less €250 expensed prior to modification) plus the remeasurement of the liability of €50 (€180 – €130) between modification date and settlement date. The balance of €185 is credited to equity.

In total the entity recognises an expense of €550, being the original grant date fair value of the equity-settled award of €500 plus the post-modification remeasurement of the liability of €50. This adjustment of €50 is consistent with the approach taken in IG Example 9 in the implementation guidance to IFRS 2 (see 10.1.4 and Example 32.41 below).

Whilst the overall liability in Scenario C is the same as that in Scenario A above, the total expense and overall net credit to equity are higher even though the cash-settled award had a lower fair value at the modification date than that in Scenario A. This might appear illogical but is consistent with the approach in IG Example 9 and the requirement to recognise, as a minimum, the grant date fair value of the original equity-settled award together with any post-modification change in the fair value of the liability.

D Modified award with greater fair value than original award but settled for less than modification date fair value

On 1 January 2017 an entity granted an equity-settled award, with a fair value at that date of €500, and vesting if the employee is still in service on 31 December 2020. On 1 January 2019, the award is modified so as to become cash-settled, with other modifications meaning that the new award has a higher fair value than the original award. At that date, the fair value of the original award is €150, but that of the cash-settled replacement award is €170. The liability is actually settled for €125 on 31 December 2020.

	Approach 1			Approach 2		
	Expense	Equity	Liability	Expense	Equity	Liability
	€	€	€	€	€	€
Two years ended 31.12.2018	250	(250)	–	250	(250)	–
1.1.2019 – modification	–	85	(85)	10	75	(85)
Two years ended 31.12.2020	225	(185)	(40)	215	(175)	(40)
Totals	475	(350)	(125)	475	(350)	(125)

During 2017 and 2018 the entity recognises a cumulative expense of €250, being the proportion of the grant date fair value of the equity-settled award of €500 attributable to 2/4 of the vesting period.

At 1 January 2019, it is necessary to recognise a liability of €85 (€170 × 2/4 – see 9.3.2 above). Under Approach 1 the difference between the fair value of the original equity-settled award and the modified award (€20 in total) is not recognised immediately as an expense but is spread over the remainder of the vesting period (i.e. starting from the date of modification). The liability of €85 is therefore recognised as a reduction in equity. Under Approach 2, the difference between the fair value of the original equity-settled award and the modified award is expensed immediately to the extent that the vesting period has already expired (€20 × 2/4) with the remainder being expensed in the post-modification period.

As the award is continuing, there is no acceleration at the modification date of the as yet unrecognised amount of the grant date fair value of the original award (€250, being €500 × 2/4) as would occur in an immediate settlement (see 7.4 above).

During 2019 and 2020 (the period from modification to settlement date), the entity recognises an increase of €40 in the fair value of the liability (€125 – €85). During this period, under Approach 1 it also recognises employee costs totalling €225, being the remaining grant date fair value of €250 (€500 total less €250 expensed prior to modification) plus the incremental modification fair value of €20 less a reduction of €45 (€170 – €125) in the fair value of the liability since modification date. The balance of €185 is credited to equity. For Approach 2, the expense and the credit to equity during this period are €10 less than under Approach 1 because a proportionate amount of the incremental fair value was expensed immediately at the modification date.

In total the entity recognises an expense of €475, being the original grant date fair value of the equity-settled award of €500 plus the incremental fair value of €20 arising on modification of the award less the post-modification remeasurement of the liability of €45. This remeasurement adjustment of €45 is consistent with the approach taken in IG Example 9 in the implementation guidance to IFRS 2 (see 10.1.4 and Example 32.41 below).

E Modified award with same fair value as original award but where modification date fair value is higher than original grant date fair value

On 1 January 2017 an entity granted an equity-settled award, with a fair value at that date of €500, and vesting if the employee is still in service on 31 December 2020. On 1 January 2019, the award is modified so as to become cash-settled, but its terms are otherwise unchanged. The fair value of the award at that date on both an equity-settled basis and a cash-settled basis is €800. The liability is actually settled for €700 on 31 December 2020.

	Approach 1			Approach 2		
	Expense	Equity	Liability	Expense	Equity	Liability
	€	€	€	€	€	€
Two years ended 31.12.2018	250	(250)	–	250	(250)	–
1.1.2019 – modification	–	400	(400)	–	400	(400)
Two years ended 31.12.2020	300		(300)	300		(300)
Totals	550	150	(700)	550	150	(700)

During 2017 and 2018 the entity recognises a cumulative expense of €250, being the proportion of the grant date fair value of the equity-settled award of €500 attributable to 2/4 of the vesting period.

At 1 January 2019, it is necessary to recognise a liability of €400 (€800 × 2/4 – see 9.3.2 above). The full amount of this liability is recognised as a reduction in equity under both Approaches as there is no difference between the fair value of the original and modified awards as at the modification date.

As the award is continuing, there is no acceleration at the modification date of the as yet unrecognised amount of the grant date fair value of the original award (€250, being €500 × 2/4), as would occur in an immediate settlement (see 7.4 above).

During 2019 and 2020 (the period from modification to settlement date), the entity recognises a net increase of €300 in the fair value of the liability (€700 – €400). During this period it also recognises employee costs totalling €300, being the remaining modification date fair value of the cash-settled award (€800 × 2/4) plus the post-modification remeasurement of the liability of €(100) (€800 – €700).

In total the entity recognises an expense of €550. This expense reflects half of the grant date fair value of the original equity-settled award and half of the modification date fair value of the cash-settled award. As the award had increased in value between grant date and modification date, the requirement of paragraph 27 of IFRS 2 to recognise, as a minimum, the original grant date fair value of the equity-settled award (€250) has been met. The overall expense also reflects, in accordance with the requirements for cash-settled share-based payments, the remeasurement of the liability between modification and settlement. In our view, this is consistent with the approach taken in IG Example 9 in the implementation guidance to IFRS 2 (see 10.1.4 and Example 32.41 below).

Some take the view that the approach in IG Example 9 would lead to a total expense of €400 in the example above, rather than €550 (being the original grant date fair value of €500 plus the remeasurement of the liability of €100 in the period following the modification). The difference of €150 would be debited to equity in the two years following modification. In other words, in recognising an expense for the cash-settled award during the vesting period after the modification date, no account is taken of the fact that the fair value of the arrangement *increased* between the original grant date and the modification date.

IG Example 9 illustrates a situation where there is a *decrease* in the fair value between original grant date and modification date. As a result, that Example expenses the grant date fair value of the original equity-settled award (plus the remeasurement of the liability) in order to meet the minimum expense requirements of paragraph 27 of IFRS 2. In a situation such as that outlined in Scenario E above, it does not seem appropriate, in our view, to limit the post-modification expense for the cash-settled award to an amount based on the original grant date fair value of the equity-settled award (€150) rather than applying cash-settled accounting to the element of the award for which services are delivered in years 3 and 4 and recognising a corresponding expense of €300.

9.4.2 Cash-settled award modified to equity-settled award

As currently drafted, IFRS 2 does not contain specific guidance for modifications from cash-settlement to equity-settlement and there has been diversity in the accounting treatment seen in practice. As a consequence, this matter was taken onto the agenda of the Interpretations Committee and then referred to the IASB. In June 2016 the IASB published an amendment to IFRS 2 to clarify how such modifications should be treated (see 9.4.2.A below).

Using the current version of the standard, we believe that it is appropriate to draw on the guidance for the settlement in equity of awards where there is a choice of settlement, but which have been accounted for as cash-settled during the vesting period (see 10.1.3.B and 10.2 below). Essentially, IFRS 2 requires the liability in such cases to be remeasured to fair value at the date of settlement and transferred to equity. Any excess of the fair value of the equity instruments used to settle the award over the fair value of the liability is recognised in profit or loss. This principle can be adapted to the modification of an award from cash- to equity-settlement so that, in effect, the original cash-settled award is treated as having been cancelled and replaced with an equity-settled award.

Within this overall methodology, we believe that there are two approaches for the recognition of any incremental fair value of the equity-settled award as measured at the date of modification. The incremental fair value may be recognised either:

- immediately in profit or loss for the vested portion of the award (an approach that follows more closely the requirements of settlement accounting); or
- over the remaining vesting period (an approach that combines settlement accounting with the spreading approach applied when an equity-settled award is modified – see 7.3 above).

The previous paragraph refers to *incremental* fair value arising on the modification. This is because the guidance in IFRS 2 for the settlement in equity of awards with a choice of settlement only leads to the recognition through profit or loss of an increase in fair value (i.e. a debit) and does not recognise a decrease in fair value (i.e. a credit). However, the amendment to IFRS 2 (see 9.4.2.A below) recognises any difference between the fair value of the cancelled liability and the replacement equity-settled award – whether a debit or a credit – in profit or loss. In view of the IASB's guidance in this area, we consider the immediate recognition of a credit also to be an acceptable approach (under the current version of IFRS 2) in a situation where the fair value of the modified award is lower than that of the original cash-settled award as at the date of modification. This is illustrated in Scenario C of Example 32.38 below.

With the exception of situations where a credit is recognised immediately in profit or loss at the date of modification, the two approaches outlined above result in the same total expense and credit to equity by the end of the vesting period and differ only in the timing of recognition of part of the expense. Example 32.38 below illustrates the two approaches. Given the lack of clarity in the current version of the standard, we believe that entities currently have an accounting policy choice. However, in selecting a policy, entities should take into consideration the fact that the IASB's amendment to IFRS 2 adopts the first approach based on settlement accounting (see 9.4.2.A below).

Example 32.38: Modification of cash-settled award to equity-settled award (pre-amendment to IFRS 2)

A Modified award with same fair value as original award

In this situation there is no difference between accounting alternatives 1 and 2.

At the beginning of year 1 an entity granted a cash-settled award, vesting over four years. At the beginning of year 3, the award is modified so as to become equity-settled, but its terms are otherwise unchanged. The fair value of both alternatives at the date of modification is €150.

By the end of year 2, the entity will have recognised a liability of €75 (€150 × 2/4 – see 9.3.2 above). At the date of modification this is transferred to equity in order to recognise the equity-settled award. As there is no difference between the fair value of the original cash-settled award and the modified award, no further expense is recognised:

		€	€
Modification date (start of year 3)	Liability	75	
	Equity		75

The remainder of the fair value of the equity-settled award, measured as at the date of modification, of €75 (€150 – €75) is recognised in profit or loss over the remaining vesting period, with a corresponding credit to equity:

		€	€
Years 3 and 4 (total)	Employee costs	75	
	Equity		75

B Modified award with greater fair value than original award

At the beginning of year 1 an entity granted a cash-settled award, vesting over four years. At the beginning of year 3, the award is modified so as to become equity-settled. At the date of modification, the fair value of the original award is €150, but that of the equity-settled replacement award is €190.

Accounting alternative 1: immediate recognition of increase in fair value as an expense

By the end of year 2, the entity will have recognised a liability of €75 (€150 × 2/4 – see 9.3.2 above). At the date of modification, this is transferred to equity as part of the recognition of the equity-settled award. The fair values of the original and modified awards, to the extent that they have vested, must be compared. These are respectively €75 (€150 × 2/4) and €95 (€190 × 2/4). The increase in value of €20 is recognised immediately as an expense at the date of modification, with a corresponding credit to equity:

		€	€
Modification date (start of year 3)	Employee costs	20	
	Liability	75	
	Equity		95

The remainder of the fair value of the equity award, measured as at the date of modification, of €95 (€190 – €95) is recognised in profit or loss over the remaining two year vesting period from the date of modification (as in A above):

		€	€
Years 3 and 4 (total)	Employee costs	95	
	Equity		95

Accounting alternative 2: recognition of increase in fair value as an expense over the remainder of the vesting period

By the end of year 2, the entity will have recognised a liability of €75 (€150 × 2/4 – see 9.3.2 above). At the date of modification, this is transferred to equity as part of the recognition of the equity-settled award. The fair values of the original and modified awards, to the extent that they have vested, must be compared. These are respectively €75 (€150 × 2/4) and €95 (€190 × 2/4). The liability of €75 is transferred to equity at the date of modification and the increase in value of €20 is recognised as an expense over the remaining two year vesting period, with a corresponding credit to equity (together with the remainder of the cost of the equity-settled award of €95 (€190 × 2/4)):

		€	€
Modification date (start of year 3)	Liability	75	
	Equity		75
Years 3 and 4 (total)	Employee costs	115	
	Equity		115

C *Modified award with lower fair value than original award*

If the view is taken that there is no incremental fair value to be recognised because the equity-settled award has a lower fair value than the cash-settled award then there is no difference between accounting alternatives 1 and 2 because there is no profit or loss impact arising from the modification.

However, if the approach in the IASB's amendment is followed as a third possible approach, an immediate credit will be recognised in profit or loss (see 9.4.2.A below).

At the beginning of year 1 an entity granted a cash-settled award, vesting over four years. At the beginning of year 3, the award is modified so as to become equity-settled. At the date of modification, the fair value of the original award is €150, but that of the equity-settled replacement award is only €130.

By the end of year 2, the entity will have recognised a liability and employee costs of €75 (€150 × 2/4 – see 9.3.2 above). The fair values of the original and modified awards, to the extent that they have vested, are compared as at the date of modification. These are respectively €75 (€150 × 2/4) and €65 (€130 × 2/4). Although the fair value of the modified award is lower than that of the original award, no gain is recognised unless an entity follows the approach in the amendment to IFRS 2.

		€	€
Modification date (start of year 3)	Liability	75	
	Equity		75

The alternative approach, as suggested by the IASB's discussions and amendment to IFRS 2, results in the following:

		€	€
Modification date (start of year 3)	Liability	75	
	Employee costs		10
	Equity		65

Whichever approach is taken to the modification date accounting, the remainder of the fair value of the equity award, measured as at the date of modification, of €65 (€130 × 2/4) is recognised in profit or loss over the remaining two year vesting period from the date of modification:

		€	€
Years 3 and 4 (total)	Employee costs	65	
	Equity		65

9.4.2.A Modification that changes the classification of an award from cash-settled to equity-settled: amendment to IFRS 2

As noted at 9.4.2 above, in June 2016 the IASB published an amendment to IFRS 2 to provide guidance in situations where the terms and conditions of a cash-settled award are modified so that it becomes equity-settled.[24]

The amendment is mandatory for accounting periods beginning on or after 1 January 2018 (with earlier adoption permitted) but applies only to modifications that occur on or after the date that an entity first applies the amendment. The transitional provisions relating to this amendment are discussed at 16.2 below.

The amendment adds guidance to Appendix B to IFRS 2. A new paragraph B44A states that the transaction will be accounted for as equity-settled from the date of the modification and specifically:

- the equity-settled share-based payment transaction is measured by reference to the modification date fair value of the equity instruments granted at that date;
- the equity-settled share-based payment transaction is recognised in equity on the modification date to the extent to which goods or services have been received;
- the liability for the cash-settled share-based payment transaction as at the modification date is derecognised on that date; and
- any difference between the carrying amount of the liability derecognised and the amount recognised in equity on the modification date is recognised immediately in profit or loss.

Paragraph B44B states that if the vesting period is extended or shortened as a result of the modification, the modified vesting period is reflected in applying the requirements above. The amendment also clarifies that the requirements apply even if the modification takes place after the vesting period.

The amendment further clarifies in a new paragraph B44C that the requirements of paragraphs B44A and B44B apply if a cash-settled share-based payment is cancelled or settled (other than by forfeiture when vesting conditions are not satisfied) and equity instruments are designated as a replacement for the cancelled or settled share-based payment. In order to qualify as a replacement, the equity instruments must be designated as such on the grant date.

As part of the amendment, IG Example 12C has been added to the implementation guidance in IFRS 2 and forms the basis of Example 32.39 below.

The accounting treatment required by the amendment is consistent with Alternative 1 in Scenario B in Example 32.38 above for an arrangement where the modification of a cash-settled award results in an equity-settled award with a higher fair value. The impact on modifications where the equity-settled award has a lower fair value, including the immediate recognition of a credit in profit or loss, is illustrated in Scenario C in Example 32.38 above.

The IASB notes in paragraph BC237H of its Basis for Conclusions on the amendment that the immediate recognition in profit or loss of any difference between the derecognised liability and the amount recognised in equity is consistent with how cash-settled share-based payments are measured in accordance with paragraph 30 of IFRS 2.

It also observes that the approach is consistent with the requirements for the extinguishment of a financial liability (fully or partially by the issue of equity instruments) in IFRS 9 – *Financial Instruments* – and in IFRIC 19 – *Extinguishing Financial Liabilities with Equity Instruments.*

Example 32.39: Modification of cash-settled award to equity-settled award (application of June 2016 amendment)

At the beginning of year 1 an entity grants 100 cash-settled share appreciation rights (SARs) to each of 100 employees on condition that they remain in the entity's service for four years.

At the end of year 1 each SAR has an estimated fair value of €10 and at the end of year 2 €12.

At the end of year 2 the entity cancels the SARs and, in their place, grants 100 share options to each employee on condition that each remains in service for two years, i.e. the original service period is unchanged. At the date of grant, the fair value of each share option is €13.20. All of the employees are expected to meet the service condition.

In years 1 and 2 the entity recognises a cash-settled share-based payment expense of €25,000 and €35,000 respectively, based on the fair value of the SARs at each reporting date and the extent to which the vesting period has been completed. At the modification date, the requirements of paragraph B44A are applied as follows:

		€	€
Modification date (end of year 2)	Equity		66,000
	Liability	60,000	
	Profit or loss	6,000	

The entity compares the fair value of the equity award, measured as at the date of modification, of €66,000 (€132,000 × 2/4) with the fair value of the liability for the cash-settled award of €60,000 (€120,000 × 2/4) at the same date. The difference of €6,000 is recognised immediately in profit or loss.

The remainder of the equity-settled share-based payment, as measured at the modification date, is recognised in profit or loss during years 3 and 4.

10 TRANSACTIONS WITH EQUITY AND CASH ALTERNATIVES

It is common for share-based payment transactions (particularly those with employees) to provide either the entity or the counterparty with the choice of settling the transaction either in shares (or other equity instruments) or in cash (or other assets). The general principle of IFRS 2 is that a transaction with a cash alternative, or the components of that transaction, should be accounted for:

(a) as a cash-settled transaction if, and to the extent that, the entity has incurred a liability to settle in cash or other assets; or

(b) as an equity-settled transaction if, and to the extent that, no such liability has been incurred. *[IFRS 2.34]*.

More detailed guidance is provided as to how that general principle should be applied to transactions:

- where the counterparty has choice of settlement (see 10.1 below); and
- where the entity has choice of settlement (see 10.2 below).

Rather than providing either the entity or the counterparty with a choice between settlement in equity or in cash, some transactions offer no choice but instead require an arrangement that will generally be equity-settled to be settled in cash in certain specific and limited circumstances (awards with contingent cash settlement). This type of arrangement is considered in more detail at 10.3 below.

Some awards offer an equity alternative and a cash alternative where the cash alternative is not based on the price or value of the equity instruments. These arrangements are considered at 10.4 below.

A common type of arrangement in practice is the 'matching' award where an employee is offered a share award or a cash alternative to 'match' a share award or a cash bonus earned during an initial period. This type of arrangement is addressed at 15.1 below.

10.1 Transactions where the counterparty has choice of settlement in equity or in cash

Where the counterparty has the right to elect for settlement in either shares or cash, IFRS 2 regards the transaction as a compound transaction to which split accounting must be applied. The general principle is that the transaction must be analysed into a liability component (the counterparty's right to demand settlement in cash) and an equity component (the counterparty's right to demand settlement in shares). *[IFRS 2.35]*. Once split, the two components are accounted for separately. The methodology of split accounting required by IFRS 2 is somewhat different from that required by IAS 32 for issuers of other compound instruments (see Chapter 45 at 6).

A practical issue is that, where a transaction gives the counterparty a choice of settlement, it will be necessary to establish a fair value for the liability component both at grant date and at each subsequent reporting date until settlement. By contrast, in the case of transactions that can be settled in cash only, no fair value is required at grant date for IFRS 2 accounting purposes, but a fair value is required at each subsequent reporting date until settlement (see 9 above). However, for entities subject to IAS 33, the grant date fair value is required in order to make the disclosures required by that standard – see Chapter 35 at 6.4.2.

Sections 10.1.1 to 10.1.3 below consider in more detail the accounting treatment required by IFRS 2 for transactions where the counterparty has a settlement choice. In addition, the following specific situations are discussed:

- the addition of a cash-settlement alternative after the grant date (see 10.1.4 below);
- arrangements where the counterparty is given a choice to cover more or less remote contingencies e.g. restrictions or limits on the issue of shares in a particular jurisdiction (see 10.1.5 below);
- the issue of convertible bonds in return for goods or services (see 10.1.6 below).

10.1.1 Transactions in which the fair value is measured directly

Transactions with non-employees are normally measured by reference to the fair value of goods and services supplied at service date (i.e. the date at which the goods or services are supplied) – see 4 and 5 above.

Accordingly where an entity enters into such a transaction where the counterparty has choice of settlement, it determines the fair value of the liability component at service date. The equity component is the difference between the fair value (at service date) of the goods or services received and the fair value of the liability component. *[IFRS 2.35]*.

10.1.2 Transactions in which the fair value is measured indirectly – including transactions with employees

All other transactions, including those with employees, are measured by reference to the fair value of the instruments issued at 'measurement date', being grant date in the case of transactions with employees and service date in the case of transactions with non-employees *[IFRS 2 Appendix A]* – see 4.1 and 5.1 above.

The fair value should take into account the terms and conditions on which the rights to cash or equity instruments were issued. *[IFRS 2.36]*. IFRS 2 does not elaborate further on this, but we assume that the IASB intends a reporting entity to apply:

- as regards the equity component of the transaction, the provisions of IFRS 2 relating to the impact of terms and conditions on the valuation of equity-settled transactions (see 4 to 6 above); and
- as regards the liability component of the transaction, the provisions of IFRS 2 relating to the impact of terms and conditions on the valuation of cash-settled transactions (see 9.3 above).

The entity should first measure the fair value of the liability component and then that of the equity component. The fair value of the equity component must be reduced to take into account the fact that the counterparty must forfeit the right to receive cash in order to receive shares. The sum of the two components is the fair value of the whole compound instrument. *[IFRS 2.37]*. IG Example 13 in IFRS 2 (the substance of which is reproduced as Example 32.40 below) suggests that this may be done by establishing the fair value of the equity alternative and subtracting from it the fair value of the liability component. This approach may be appropriate in a straightforward situation involving ordinary shares and cash, as illustrated in the Example in the implementation guidance, but will not necessarily be appropriate in more complex situations that include, for example, the likelihood of options being exercised.

In many share-based payment transactions with a choice of settlement, the value to the counterparty of the share and cash alternatives is equal. The counterparty will have the choice between (say) 1,000 shares or the cash value of 1,000 shares. This will mean that the fair value of the liability component is equal to that of the transaction as a whole, so that the fair value of the equity component is zero. In other words, the transaction is accounted for as if it were a cash-settled transaction.

However, in some jurisdictions it is not uncommon, particularly in transactions with employees, for the equity-settlement alternative to have more value (as in Example 32.40 below). For example, an employee might be able to choose at vesting between the cash value of 1,000 shares immediately or 2,000 shares (often subject to further conditions such as a minimum holding period, or a further service period). In such cases the equity component will have an independent value. *[IFRS 2.37]*. Such schemes are discussed in more detail at 15.1 below.

10.1.3 Accounting treatment

10.1.3.A During vesting period

Having established a fair value for the liability and equity components as set out in 10.1.1 and 10.1.2 above, the entity accounts for the liability component according to the rules for cash-settled transactions (see 9 above) and for the equity component according to the rules for equity-settled transactions (see 4 to 8 above). *[IFRS 2.38]*.

Example 32.40 below illustrates the accounting treatment for a transaction with an employee (as summarised in 10.1.2 above) where the equity component has a fair value independent of the liability component.

Example 32.40: Award with employee choice of settlement with different fair values for cash-settlement and equity-settlement

An entity grants to an employee an award with the right to choose settlement in either:

- 1,000 phantom shares, i.e. a right to a cash payment equal to the value of 1,000 shares, or
- 1,200 shares.

Vesting is conditional upon the completion of three years' service. If the employee chooses the share alternative, the shares must be held for three years after vesting date.

At grant date, the entity estimates that the fair value of the share alternative, after taking into account the effects of the post-vesting transfer restrictions, is €48 per share. The fair value of the cash alternative is estimated as:

	€
Grant date	50
Year 1	52
Year 2	55
Year 3	60

The grant date fair value of the equity alternative is €57,600 (1,200 shares × €48). The grant date fair value of the cash alternative is €50,000 (1,000 phantom shares × €50). Therefore the fair value of the equity component excluding the right to receive cash is €7,600 (€57,600 – €50,000). The entity recognises a cost based on the following amounts.

	Equity component			Liability component		
Year	Calculation of cumulative expense	Cumulative expense (€)	Expense for year (€)	Calculation of cumulative expense	Cumulative expense (€)	Expense for year (€)
1	€7,600 × 1/3	2,533	2,533	1,000 phantoms × €52 × 1/3	17,333	17,333
2	€7,600 × 2/3	5,066	2,533	1,000 phantoms × €55 × 2/3	36,667	19,334
3	€7,600	7,600	2,534	1,000 phantoms × €60	60,000	23,333

This generates the following accounting entries.

	€	€
Year 1		
Profit or loss (employment costs)	19,866	
Liability		17,333
Equity		2,533
Year 2		
Profit or loss (employment costs)	21,867	
Liability		19,334
Equity		2,533
Year 3		
Profit or loss (employment costs)	25,867	
Liability		23,333
Equity		2,534

The above Example is based on IG Example 13 in IFRS 2, in which the share price at each reporting date is treated as the fair value of the cash alternative. As discussed more fully at 9 above, the fair value of a cash award is not necessarily exactly the same as the share price as it will depend on the terms and conditions of the award, a point reinforced by IG Example 12 in IFRS 2 (the basis for Example 32.36 at 9.3.2 above). Accordingly, in adapting IG Example 13 as Example 32.40 above, we have deliberately described the numbers used in respect of the liability component as 'fair value' and not as the 'share price'. *[IFRS 2 IG Example 13]*.

Example 32.40 also ignores the fact that transactions of this type often have different vesting periods for the two settlement alternatives. For instance, the employee might have been offered:

(a) the cash equivalent of 1,000 shares in three years' time subject to performance conditions; or

(b) subject to the performance criteria in (a) above being met over three years, 3,000 shares after a further two years' service.

IFRS 2 offers no guidance as to how such transactions are to be accounted for. Presumably, however, the equity component would be recognised over a five year period and the liability component over a three year period. This is considered further in the discussion of 'matching' share awards at 15.1 below.

10.1.3.B Settlement

At the date of settlement, the liability component is restated to fair value through profit or loss. If the counterparty elects for settlement in equity, the restated liability is transferred to equity as consideration for the equity instruments issued. If the liability is settled in cash, the cash is obviously applied to reduce the liability. *[IFRS 2.39-40]*. In other words, if the transaction in Example 32.40 above had been settled in shares the accounting entry would have been:

	€	€
Liability*	60,000	
Equity†		60,000

* There is no need to remeasure the liability in this case as it has already been stated at fair value at vesting date, which is the same as settlement date.

† The precise allocation of this amount within equity, and its impact on distributable reserves, will depend on a number of factors, including jurisdictional legal requirements, which are not discussed here.

If the transaction had been settled in cash the entry would simply have been:

	€	€
Liability	60,000	
Cash		60,000

If the transaction is settled in cash, any amount taken to equity during the vesting period (€7,600 in Example 32.40 above) is not adjusted. However, the entity may transfer it from one component of equity to another (see 4.2 above). *[IFRS 2.40]*.

10.1.4 Transactions with cash-settlement alternative for employee introduced after grant date

Such transactions are not specifically addressed in the main body of IFRS 2. However, IG Example 9 in the implementation guidance does address this issue, in the context of the rules for the modification of awards (discussed at 7.3 and 9.4 above). The substance of this example is reproduced as Example 32.41 below. *[IFRS 2 IG Example 9]*.

Example 32.41: Award with employee cash-settlement alternative introduced after grant

At the beginning of year 1, the entity grants 10,000 shares with a fair value of $33 per share to a senior executive, conditional upon the completion of three years' service. By the end of year 2, the fair value of the award has dropped to $25 per share. At that date, the entity adds a cash alternative to the grant, whereby the executive can choose whether to receive 10,000 shares or cash equal to the value of 10,000 shares on vesting date. The share price is $20 on vesting. The implementation guidance to IFRS 2 proposes the following approach.

For the first two years, the entity would recognise an expense of $110,000 per year, (representing 10,000 shares × $33 × 1/3), giving rise to the cumulative accounting entry by the end of year 2:

	$	$
Profit or loss (employee costs)	220,000	
Equity		220,000

The addition of a cash alternative at the end of year 2 constitutes a modification of the award, but does not increase the fair value of the award at the date of modification, which under either settlement alternative is $250,000 (10,000 shares × $25), excluding the effect of the non-market vesting condition as required by IFRS 2.

The fact that the employee now has the right to be paid in cash requires the 'split accounting' treatment set out in 10.1.2 above. Because of the requirement, under the rules for modification of awards (see 7.3 above), to recognise at least the fair value of the original award, the total fair value of the equity alternative of the award is deemed to remain $330,000. This is then reduced (in accordance with the rules in 10.1.2 above) to reflect the fact that the equity-settlement option would entail the sacrifice of the cash-settled option (modification date fair value $250,000), giving an implied value for the equity-settlement option of $80,000 ($330,000 – $250,000).

The award is now 2/3 through its vesting period, implying that the cumulative amount accounted for in equity should be only $53,333 ($80,000 × 2/3), as opposed to the $220,000 that has actually been accounted for in equity. Accordingly, the difference of $166,667 is transferred from equity to liabilities, the entry being:

	$	$
Equity	166,667	
Liability		166,667

The $166,667 carrying amount of the liability can be seen as representing 2/3 of the $250,000 fair value of the liability component at modification date.

From now on, the accounting for the equity component will be based on this implied value of $80,000. This results in the following accounting entry for the expense in year 3.

	$	$
Profit or loss	60,000*	
Liability		33,333†
Equity		26,667‡

* Balancing figure.

† Carried forward liability $200,000 (10,000 shares × year 3 fair value $20) less the brought forward liability $166,667.

‡ $80,000 equity component (as determined above) × 1/3.

This results in a total cumulative expense for the award of $280,000 ($220,000 for years 1 and 2 and $60,000 for year 3), which represents the actual cash liability at the end of year 3 of $200,000 plus the $80,000 deemed excess of the fair value of the equity component over the liability component at the end of year 2.

The $280,000 expense could also be analysed (as is done by the implementation guidance to IFRS 2 itself), as representing the grant date fair value of the award ($330,000) less the movement in the fair value of the liability alternative ($50,000, representing the fair value of $250,000 at the end of year 2 less the fair value of $200,000 at vesting). The implementation guidance may have adopted this approach to support an argument that this methodology does not breach the fundamental principle of the modification rules for equity-settled transactions that the minimum expense recognised for a modified award should be the expense that would have been recognised had the award not been modified (see 7.3 above).

IG Example 9 only illustrates a situation where the grant date fair value of the equity-settled award exceeds the modification date fair value of both the equity and cash alternatives and the settlement date value of the cash alternative. In Example 32.37 at 9.4.1 above we consider alternative scenarios, including one where the modification date fair value exceeds the grant date fair value.

10.1.5 'Backstop' cash settlement rights

Some schemes may provide cash settlement rights to the holder so as to cover more or less remote contingencies. For example, an employee whose nationality and/or country of permanent residence is different from the jurisdiction of the reporting entity may be offered the option of cash settlement in case unforeseen future events make the transfer of equity from the entity's jurisdiction, or the holding or trading of it in the employee's country, inconvenient or impossible.

If the terms of the award provide the employee with a general right of cash-settlement, IFRS 2 requires the award to be treated as cash-settled. This is the case even if the right of cash settlement is extremely unlikely to be exercised (e.g. because it would give rise to adverse tax consequences for the employee as compared with equity settlement). If, however, the right to cash-settlement is exercisable only in specific circumstances, a more detailed analysis may be required (see 10.3 below).

10.1.6 Convertible bonds issued to acquire goods or services

In some jurisdictions entities issue convertible bonds to employees or other counterparties in exchange for goods or services. When this occurs, the bond will generally be accounted for under IFRS 2 rather than IAS 32 since it falls within the scope of IFRS 2 as a transaction 'in which the entity receives or acquires goods or services and the terms of the arrangement provide either the entity or the supplier of those goods or services with a choice of whether the entity settles the transaction in cash (or other assets) or by issuing equity instruments' (see 2.2.1 and 2.2.2 above). *[IFRS 2.2(c)]*.

As noted at 10.1 above, the methodology for splitting such an instrument into its liability and equity components under IFRS 2 differs from that under IAS 32. Moreover, under IAS 32 a convertible instrument is (broadly) recognised at fair value on the date of issue, whereas under IFRS 2 the fair value is accrued over time if the arrangement includes the rendering of services.

It is therefore possible that, if an entity has issued to employees convertible bonds that have also been issued in the market, the accounting treatment of the bonds issued to employees will differ significantly from that of the bonds issued in the market.

Where a convertible instrument is issued to an employee, the IFRS 2 expense will be based on the fair value of the instrument. If an entity issues a convertible instrument in return for an asset, for example a property, the entity will initially recognise a liability component at fair value and an equity component based on the difference between the fair value of the asset and the fair value of the liability component. *[IFRS 2.35]*. If the fair value of the asset were lower than the fair value of the instrument as a whole then, in our view, the entity should also recognise the shortfall in accordance with the requirements of IFRS 2 for unidentified goods or services. *[IFRS 2.13A]*. In the case of the acquisition of an asset, it is possible that this additional debit could be capitalised as part of the cost of the asset under IAS 16 – *Property, Plant and Equipment* – but in other cases it would be expensed.

After the initial accounting outlined above, the question arises as to whether the subsequent accounting for the convertible instrument should be in accordance with IFRS 2 or IAS 39. In our view, the instrument should generally continue to be accounted for under IFRS 2 until shares or cash are delivered to the counterparty. However, if the instrument were freely transferable prior to conversion or settlement then a switch to IAS 39 might be appropriate following transfer to a different counterparty (if considered practical to apply) – see also the discussion at 2.2.2.E above.

10.2 Transactions where the entity has choice of settlement in equity or in cash

The accounting treatment for transactions where the entity has choice of settlement is quite different from transactions where the counterparty has choice of settlement, in that:

- where the counterparty has choice of settlement, a liability component and an equity component are identified (see 10.1 above); whereas
- where the entity has choice of settlement, the accounting treatment is binary – in other words the whole transaction is treated either as cash-settled or as equity-settled, depending on whether or not the entity has a present obligation to settle in cash, *[IFRS 2.41]*, determined according to the criteria discussed in 10.2.1 below.

10.2.1 *Transactions treated as cash-settled*

IFRS 2 requires a transaction to be treated as a liability (and accounted for using the rules for cash-settled transactions discussed in 9 above) if:

(a) the choice of settlement has no commercial substance (for example, because the entity is legally prohibited from issuing shares);

(b) the entity has a past practice or stated policy of settling in cash; or

(c) the entity generally settles in cash whenever the counterparty asks for cash settlement. *[IFRS 2.41-42]*.

These criteria are fundamentally different from those in IAS 32 for derivatives over own shares (which is what cash-settled share-based payment transactions are) not within the scope of IFRS 2. IAS 32 rejects an approach based on past practice or intention and broadly requires all derivatives over own equity that could result in an exchange by the reporting entity of anything other than a fixed number of shares for a fixed amount of cash to be treated as giving rise to a financial liability (see Chapter 45 at 4).

An important practical effect of the IFRS 2 criteria is that some schemes that may appear at first sight to be equity-settled may in fact have to be treated as cash-settled. For example, if an entity has consistently adopted a policy of granting *ex gratia* cash compensation to all those deemed to be 'good' leavers (or all 'good' leavers of certain seniority) in respect of partially vested share options, such a scheme may well be treated as cash-settled for the purposes of IFRS 2 to the extent to which there are expected to be such 'good' leavers during the vesting period. 'Good leaver' arrangements are also discussed at 5.3.9 above.

Another common example is that an entity may have a global share scheme with an entity option for cash settlement which it always exercises in respect of awards to employees in jurisdictions where it is difficult or illegal to hold shares in the parent. Such a scheme should be treated as a cash-settled scheme in respect of those jurisdictions. It would, however, in our view, be appropriate to account for the scheme in other jurisdictions as equity-settled (provided of course that none of the criteria in (a) to (c) above applied in those jurisdictions).

Where an entity has accounted for a transaction as cash-settled, IFRS 2 gives no specific guidance as to the accounting treatment on settlement, but it is clear from other provisions of IFRS 2 that the liability should be remeasured to fair value at settlement date and:

- if cash-settlement occurs, the cash paid is applied to reduce the liability; and
- if equity-settlement occurs, the liability is transferred into equity (see 10.1.3.B above).

10.2.1.A *Economic compulsion for cash settlement (including unlisted entity awards with a presumption of cash settlement)*

Some awards may nominally give the reporting entity the choice of settling in cash or equity, while in practice giving rise to an economic compulsion to settle only in cash. In addition to the examples mentioned at 10.2.1 above, this will often be the case where an entity that is a subsidiary or owned by a small number of individuals, such as members of the same family, grants options to employees. In such cases there will normally be a very strong presumption that the entity will settle in cash in order to avoid diluting the existing owners' interests. Similarly, where the entity is not listed, there is little real benefit for an employee in receiving a share that cannot be realised except when another shareholder wishes to buy it or there is a change in ownership of the business as a whole. In our view, such schemes are generally most appropriately accounted for as cash-settled schemes from inception. In any event, once the scheme has been operating for a while, it is likely that there will be a past practice of cash settlement such that the scheme is required to be treated as a liability under the general provisions of IFRS 2 summarised above.

A similar conclusion is often reached even where the terms of the agreement do not appear to offer the entity a choice of settling the award in cash but it has established a constructive obligation or a past practice of so doing (see 9.2.1 above).

10.2.2 Transactions treated as equity-settled

A transaction not meeting the criteria in 10.2.1 above to be treated as cash-settled should be accounted for as an equity-settled transaction using the rules for such transactions discussed in 4 to 8 above. *[IFRS 2.43]*.

However, when the transaction is settled the following approach is adopted:

(a) subject to (b) below:
 (i) if the transaction is cash-settled, the cash is accounted for as a deduction from equity; or
 (ii) if the transaction is equity-settled, there is a transfer from one component of equity to another (if necessary); and

(b) if the two methods of settlement are of different fair value at the date of settlement, and the entity chooses the method with the higher fair value, the entity recognises an additional expense for the excess fair value of the chosen method. *[IFRS 2.43]*.

This is illustrated in Examples 32.42 and 32.43 below.

Example 32.42: Settlement of transaction treated as equity-settled where fair value of cash settlement exceeds fair value of equity settlement

An entity has accounted for a share-based payment transaction where it has the choice of settlement as an equity-settled transaction, and has recognised a cumulative expense of £1,000 based on the fair value at grant date.

At settlement date the fair value of the equity-settlement option is £1,700 and that of the cash-settlement option £2,000. If the entity settles in equity, no further accounting entry is required by IFRS 2. However, either at the entity's discretion or in compliance with local legal requirements, there may be a transfer within equity of the £1,000 credited to equity during the vesting period.

If the entity settles in cash, the entity must recognise an additional expense of £300, being the difference between the fair value of the equity-settlement option (£1,700) and that of the cash-settlement option (£2,000). The accounting entry is:

	£	£
Profit or loss (employee costs)	300	
Equity	1,700	
Cash		2,000

Example 32.43: Settlement of transaction treated as equity-settled where fair value of equity settlement exceeds fair value of cash settlement

As in Example 32.42, an entity has accounted for a share-based payment transaction where it has the choice of settlement as an equity-settled transaction, and has recognised a cumulative expense of £1,000 based on the fair value at grant date.

In this case, however, at settlement date the fair value of the equity-settlement option is £2,000 and that of the cash-settlement option £1,700. If the entity chooses to settle in equity, it must recognise an additional expense of £300, being the difference between fair value of the equity-settlement option (£2,000) and that of the cash-settlement option (£1,700). The accounting entry is:

	£	£
Profit or loss (employee costs)	300	
Equity		300

No further accounting entry is required by IFRS 2. However, either at the entity's discretion or in compliance with local legal requirements, there may be a transfer within equity of the £1,300 credited during the vesting period and on settlement.

If the entity settles in cash, no extra expense is recognised, and the accounting entry is:

	£	£
Equity	1,700	
Cash		1,700

It can be seen in this case that, if the transaction is settled in equity, an additional expense is recognised. If, however, the transaction had simply been an equity-settled transaction (i.e. with no cash alternative), there would have been no additional expense on settlement and the cumulative expense would have been only £1,000 based on the fair value at grant date.

10.2.3 Change in entity's settlement policy or intention leading to change in classification of award after grant date

IFRS 2 does not specify whether a transaction where the entity has a choice of settlement in equity or cash should be assessed as equity-settled or cash-settled only at the inception of the transaction or also at each reporting date until it is settled.

However, in describing the accounting treatment IFRS 2 states several times that the accounting depends on whether the entity '*has a present obligation* to settle in cash'. In our view, this suggests that IFRS 2 intends the position to be reviewed at each reporting date and not just considered at the inception of the transaction.

IFRS 2 does not specify the accounting treatment to be followed if such a change in classification is considered appropriate following a change in the entity's policy or intention. In our view, however, the most appropriate treatment is to account for such a change as if it were a modification of the manner of settlement of the award (see 9.4 above). In this situation, the entity is able to choose the manner of settlement which, in substance, is the same as choosing to modify the manner of settlement of an award which does not already give the entity a choice. These situations are distinct from those where the manner of settlement depends on the outcome of a contingent event outside the entity's control (see 10.3 below).

10.3 Awards requiring cash settlement in specific circumstances (awards with contingent cash settlement)

Rather than giving either the entity or the counterparty a general right to choose between equity- or cash-settlement, some awards require cash settlement in certain specific and limited circumstances but otherwise will be equity-settled. These arrangements are referred to by IAS 32 as contingent settlement provisions and are driven by the occurrence or non-occurrence of specific outcomes rather than by choice (see Chapter 45 at 4.3). In the absence of specific guidance in IFRS 2, questions then arise as to whether such an award should be accounted for as equity-settled or cash-settled and whether this should be re-assessed on an ongoing basis during the vesting period. This is a subject that has been considered by both the Interpretations Committee and the IASB and their discussions are considered further at 10.3.6 below.

In the sections below we consider:

- three different approaches to the assessment of awards with contingent cash settlement (see 10.3.1 to 10.3.3 below);
- awards that require cash settlement on a change of control (see 10.3.4 below); and
- the accounting treatment for changes in the manner of settlement where the award is contingent on future events (see 10.3.5 and 10.3.6 below).

10.3.1 Analysis 1 – Treat as cash-settled if contingency is outside entity's control

One approach might be to observe that the underlying principle that determines whether an award is accounted for as equity-settled or cash-settled under IFRS 2 appears to be whether the reporting entity can unilaterally avoid cash-settlement (see 10.1 and 10.2 above). Thus, any award where the counterparty has a right to cash-settlement is treated as a liability in any event, irrespective of the probability of cash-settlement, since there is nothing that the entity could do to prevent cash-settlement. However, an award where the choice of settlement rests with the entity is accounted for as a liability only where the entity's own actions have effectively put it in a position where it has no real choice but to settle in cash.

This analysis would lead to the conclusion that it is first necessary to consider whether the event that requires cash-settlement is one over which the entity has control. If the event, however improbable, is outside the entity's control, then under this analysis the award should be treated as cash-settled. However, if the event is within the entity's control, the award should be treated as cash-settled only if the entity has a liability by reference to the criteria summarised in 10.1 and 10.2 above.

Whilst, in our view, this analysis is an acceptable accounting approach, the analysis does not seem entirely satisfactory. For example, in a number of jurisdictions, it is common for an equity-settled share-based payment award to contain a provision to the effect that, if the employee dies in service, the entity will pay to the employee's estate the fair value of the award in cash. The analysis above would lead to the conclusion that the award must be classified as cash-settled, on the basis that it is beyond the entity's control whether or not an employee dies in service. This seems a somewhat far-fetched conclusion, and is moreover inconsistent with the accounting treatment that the entity would apply to any other death-in-service benefit under IAS 19. IAS 19 would generally require the entity to recognise a liability for such a benefit based on an actuarial estimate (see Chapter 33 at 3.6), rather than on a presumption that the entire workforce will die in service.

10.3.2 Analysis 2 – Treat as cash-settled if contingency is outside entity's control and probable

It was presumably considerations such as those above that led the FASB staff to provide an interpretation[25] of the equivalent provisions of FASB ASC 718 – *Compensation – Stock Compensation* (formerly FAS 123(R) – *Share-Based Payment*) regarding awards that are cash-settled in certain circumstances. This interpretation states that a cash settlement feature that can be exercised only upon the occurrence of a contingent event that is outside the employee's control does not give rise to a liability until it becomes probable that that event will occur.[26]

In our view, an approach based on the probability of a contingent event that is outside the control of both the counterparty and the entity is also acceptable under IFRS and is frequently applied in practice. The implied rationale (by reference to IFRS literature) is that:

- IFRS 2 clearly notes a number of inconsistencies between IFRS 2 and IAS 32 (see 1.4.1 above) and so there is no requirement to follow IAS 32 in respect of contingent cash settlement arrangements; and
- it is therefore appropriate to have regard to the principles of IAS 37 in determining whether an uncertain future event gives rise to a liability. IAS 37 currently requires a liability to be recognised only when it is probable (i.e. more likely than not) to occur (see Chapter 28).

The impact of Analysis 1 and Analysis 2 can be illustrated by reference to an award that requires cash-settlement in the event of a change of control of the entity (see 10.3.4 below).

10.3.3 Analysis 3 – Treat as two mutually exclusive awards and determine cash and equity elements based on probability of contingency

A third approach – not specifically addressed in the discussions of the Interpretations Committee and the IASB (see 10.3.6 below) but which is sometimes seen in practice in accounting for an arrangement with two potential outcomes from grant date – is one that treats the arrangement as two mutually exclusive awards, one equity-settled and one cash-settled. In our view, this approach is also acceptable under IFRS 2 as currently drafted but will need to be re-assessed on application of the IASB's recent amendment relating to cash-settled share-based payments (see further below).

Under this approach:

- the cash-settled award always has a fair value and a corresponding liability is recognised over the vesting period. The fair value of the liability depends on the likelihood of cash-settlement and the liability will reduce to nil at the end of the vesting period if the award is finally settled in equity; and
- the equity-settled alternative is only recognised if it is considered to be probable and no amount is ultimately recognised if the contingent event happens and the award is finally settled in cash.

In effect, this approach treats the settlement method as a non-market vesting condition. During the vesting period, this approach is likely to result in an expense that exceeds the total value of the award because a fair value is recognised for the cash-settled award until such time as an award is finally settled in equity rather than cash. If the award is finally settled in equity there will be a credit to profit or loss on the release of any liability for cash-settlement.

As referred to above, the amendment to IFRS 2 relating to the measurement of cash-settled awards (see 9.3.2.C above) clarifies that non-market vesting conditions attached to cash-settled awards should be treated in the same way as those attached to equity-settled awards. Following application of the amendment, an entity will be required to ignore the likelihood of cash settlement when estimating the fair value of the liability and recognise a liability only if cash settlement is probable.

10.3.4 Application of Analysis 1 and Analysis 2 to awards requiring cash settlement on a change of control

It is not uncommon for the terms of an award to provide for compulsory cash-settlement by the entity if there is a change of control of the reporting entity. Such a provision ensures that there is no need for any separate negotiations to buy out all employee options, so as to avoid non-controlling interests arising in the acquired entity when equity-settled awards are settled after the change of control.

The question of whether or not a change of control is within the control of the entity is a matter that has been the subject of much discussion in the context of determining the classification of certain financial instruments by their issuer, and is considered more fully in Chapter 45 at 4.3.

If the facts and circumstances of a particular case indicate that a change of control is within the entity's control, the conclusion under either Analysis 1 or Analysis 2 above would be that the award should be treated as cash-settled only if the entity has a liability by reference to the criteria summarised in 10.2.1 above.

If, however, the change of control is not considered to be within the control of the reporting entity, the conclusion will vary depending on whether Analysis 1 or Analysis 2 is followed. Under Analysis 1, an award requiring settlement in cash on a change of control outside the control of the entity would be treated as cash-settled, however unlikely the change of control may be. Under Analysis 2 however, an award requiring settlement in cash on a change of control outside the control of the entity would be treated as cash-settled only if a change of control were probable.

A difficulty with Analysis 2 is that it introduces rather bizarre inconsistencies in the accounting treatment for awards when the relative probability of their outcome is considered. As noted at 10.1.5 above, an award that gives the counterparty an absolute right to cash-settlement is accounted for as a liability, however unlikely it is that the counterparty will exercise that right. Thus, under this approach, the entity could find itself in the situation where it treats:

- as a liability: an award with an unrestricted right to cash-settlement for the counterparty, where the probability of the counterparty exercising that right is less than 1%; but

- as equity: an award that requires cash settlement in the event of a change of control which is assessed as having a 49% probability of occurring.

In our view, an entity may adopt either of these accounting treatments, or indeed that suggested by Analysis 3, but should do so consistently and state its policy for accounting for such transactions if material.

In selecting an accounting policy, an entity should however take note of the IASB's recent discussions on whether an approach based on the 'probable' outcome should be applied or whether an approach based on the accounting treatment for a compound instrument should be used (see 10.3.6 below).

There is further discussion at 15.4 below of awards that vest or are exercisable on a flotation or change of control, including the question of whether a cash-settlement obligation rests with the entity itself or with other parties involved in the change of control (see 15.4.6 below).

10.3.5 Accounting for change in manner of settlement where award is contingent on future events outside the control of the entity and the counterparty

When, under Analysis 2 and Analysis 3 above, the manner of settlement of an award changes solely as a consequence of a re-assessment of the probability of a contingent event, there is neither settlement of the award nor modification of its original terms (see 10.3.5.A below for discussion of awards that have also been modified). The award is such that there have been two potential outcomes, one equity-settled and one cash-settled, running in parallel since grant date.

At each reporting date the entity should assess which outcome is more likely and account for the award on an equity- or cash-settled basis accordingly. In our view, any adjustments to switch between the cumulative cash-settled award and the cumulative equity-settled award should be taken to profit or loss in the current period. This is similar to the approach for an award with multiple independent vesting conditions (see 6.3.6 above).

Taking the approach that the two outcomes have both been part of the arrangement from grant date, the fair value of the equity-settled award would be measured only at the original grant date and would not be remeasured at the date of change in settlement method. As the cash-settled award would be remeasured on an ongoing basis, a switch in the manner of settlement during the period until the shares vest or the award is settled in cash could give rise to significant volatility in the cumulative expense. At the date of vesting or settlement, however, the cumulative expense will equate to either the grant date fair value of the equity-settled approach or the settlement value of the cash-settled approach depending on whether or not the contingent event has happened.

The situation discussed in this section (i.e. an arrangement with two potential outcomes from grant date because the manner of settlement is not within the control of either the entity or the counterparty) is not the same as an award where the manner of settlement is entirely within the entity's control. Where the entity has such control and therefore a choice of settlement, a change in the manner of settlement would be treated as a modification with a potential catch-up adjustment through equity (see 9.4 and 10.2.3 above).

As noted at 10.3.6 below, discussions by the Interpretations Committee indicated a preference for treating an award as equity-settled or cash-settled in its entirety rather than as a compound instrument, but subsequent discussions by the IASB were divided.

10.3.5.A Distinction between re-assessment of settlement method and modification of terms of award

Some awards include arrangements for contingent cash-settlement if an event outside the control of the entity and the counterparty, such as some forms of exit, has not happened within a certain timescale. During the initial period of such an arrangement there might be an expectation that the exit (or other event) will take place. In this case, the award would be treated as equity-settled using an approach based on the probability of this outcome, as outlined above. However, if it is decided, close to the end of the period during which equity-settlement would apply, to modify the terms of the award so that this period is extended, the entity needs to re-assess the arrangement on both its original and modified terms.

It might therefore be the case that cash-settlement under the original terms of the award becomes the more likely outcome for a short time and that the entity has to switch the award from an equity-settled to a cash-settled basis in line with the guidance at 10.3.5 above. If a modification is then made to extend the period during which the award can be equity-settled and hence the settlement in cash once again becomes less likely, the entity should then switch again to an equity-settled basis of accounting using modification accounting (see 9.4.2 above).

10.3.6 Manner of settlement contingent on future events: possible future developments

Following an earlier request to the Interpretations Committee for clarification on how share-based payment transactions should be classified and measured if the manner of settlement is contingent on either:

- a future event that is outside the control of both the entity and the counterparty; or
- a future event that is within the control of the counterparty,

the IASB agreed that transactions in which the manner of settlement is contingent on future events should be considered together with other issues relating to IFRS 2 (see 3.4 above).[27]

Prior to discussion by the IASB, the Interpretations Committee discussed the matter again in May 2013, noting that paragraph 34 of IFRS 2 requires an entity to account on a cash-settled basis if, and to the extent that, the entity has incurred a liability to settle in cash or other assets. However, it was further noted that IFRS 2 only provides guidance where the entity or the counterparty has a choice of settlement and not where the manner of settlement is contingent on a future event that is outside the control of both parties. The Interpretations Committee also observed that it was unclear which other guidance within IFRS and the Conceptual Framework would provide the best analogy to this situation. It was concluded that there was significant diversity in practice.[28]

In September 2013, the Interpretations Committee noted that the results of additional outreach indicated that shared-based payment transactions in which the manner of settlement is contingent on a future event within the control of the counterparty (but not the entity) are not significantly widespread and so the Committee decided not to add this element of the original submission to its agenda.[29]

The Interpretations Committee also returned to the question of accounting when the manner of settlement is contingent on a future event that is outside the control of both the entity and the counterparty. It was noted that such arrangements are settled either in cash or in equity instruments in their entirety and that neither party to the arrangement has control over the manner of settlement. Accordingly, the Committee observed that the share-based payment should be classified as either equity-settled or cash-settled in its entirety depending on which outcome is probable.

The Interpretations Committee also discussed the accounting for a change in classification of the transaction arising from a change in the more likely settlement method. A majority of the Committee thought that there should be a cumulative adjustment recorded at the time of the change of classification, in such a way that the cumulative cost would be the same as if the change of classification had occurred at the inception of the arrangement (see 10.3.5 above). The Committee decided to recommend that the IASB make a narrow-scope amendment to IFRS 2 based on the approach above.[30]

The IASB discussed these recommendations in February 2014. Some IASB members expressed concern over use of a 'probable' approach for deciding the classification of a share-based payment. They took the view that such share-based payment transactions were similar to those in which the counterparty has a choice of settlement method because the entity does not have the unconditional right to avoid delivering cash or other assets. Therefore they considered that such arrangements should be accounted for, by analogy, in accordance with the compound instrument approach set out in paragraphs 35 to 40 of IFRS 2, noting that this would also be consistent with the requirements for contingent settlement provisions in IAS 32.[31]

The topic was discussed again by the IASB in April 2014 when, notwithstanding the diversity in practice, the Board decided not to propose an amendment to IFRS 2 for this issue. Some IASB members were concerned that the suggested amendment would introduce a principle for distinguishing between a liability and equity in IFRS 2 that would be inconsistent with the requirements of IAS 32 and also noted that the definition of a liability is being discussed as part of the Conceptual Framework project (see Chapter 2).[32]

10.4 Cash settlement alternative not based on share price or value

Some awards may provide a cash-settlement alternative that is not based on the share price. For example, an employee might be offered a choice between 500 shares or €1,000,000 on the vesting of an award. Whilst an award of €1,000,000, if considered in isolation, would obviously not be a share-based payment transaction, it nevertheless falls within the scope of IFRS 2, rather than – say – IAS 19, if it is offered as an alternative to a transaction that is within the scope of IFRS 2. The Basis for Conclusions to IFRS 2 states that the cash alternative may be fixed or variable and, if variable, may be determinable in a manner that is related, or unrelated, to the price of the entity's shares. *[IFRS 2.BC256]*.

11 REPLACEMENT SHARE-BASED PAYMENT AWARDS ISSUED IN A BUSINESS COMBINATION

11.1 Background

It is frequently the case that an entity (A) acquires another (B) which, at the time of the business combination, has outstanding employee share options or other share-based awards. If no action were taken by A, employees of B would be entitled, once any vesting conditions had been satisfied, to shares in B. This is not a very satisfactory outcome for either party: A now has non-controlling (minority) shareholders in subsidiary B, which was previously wholly-owned, and the employees of B are the owners of unmarketable shares in an effectively wholly-owned subsidiary.

The obvious solution, adopted in the majority of cases, is for some mechanism to be put in place such that the employees of B end up holding shares in the new parent A. This can be achieved, for example, by:

- A granting the employees of B options over the shares of A in exchange for the surrender of their options over the shares of B; or
- changing the terms of the options so that they are over a special class of shares in B which are mandatorily convertible into shares of A.

This raises the question of how such a substitution transaction should be accounted for in the consolidated financial statements of A (the treatment in the single entity financial statements of B is discussed at 11.4 below).

IFRS 3 addresses the accounting treatment required in a business combination where an acquirer:

- replaces acquiree awards on a mandatory basis (see 11.2.1 below);
- replaces acquiree awards on a voluntary basis, even if the acquiree awards would not expire as a consequence of the business combination (see 11.2.2 below); or
- does not replace acquiree awards (see 11.3 below).

Section 11 relates only to business combinations. Share-based payment arrangements in the context of group reorganisations are addressed at 12.8 below.

11.2 Replacement awards in business combinations accounted for under IFRS 3

A more comprehensive discussion of the requirements of IFRS 3 may be found in Chapter 9.

IFRS 3 requires an acquirer to measure a liability or an equity instrument related to the replacement of an acquiree's share-based payment awards in accordance with IFRS 2, rather than in accordance with the general principles of IFRS 3. References to the 'fair value' of an award in the following discussion therefore mean the fair value determined under IFRS 2, for which IFRS 3 uses the term 'market-based measure'. The fair value measurement is to be made as at the acquisition date determined in accordance with IFRS 3. *[IFRS 3.30]*.

IFRS 3 notes that a transaction entered into by or on behalf of the acquirer or primarily for the benefit of the acquirer or the combined entity, rather than that of the acquiree (or its former owners) before the combination, is likely to be a transaction separate from the business combination itself. This includes a transaction that remunerates employees or former owners of the acquiree for future services. *[IFRS 3.52]*. Target entities will therefore need to consider carefully whether any modifications to existing share-based payment arrangements in the period leading up to the business combination are straightforward modifications by the target entity for its own benefit or that of its owners at the time (and hence fully within the scope of IFRS 2) or whether the changes need to be assessed under the guidance in IFRS 3 because they are for the benefit of the acquirer or the combined entity. The indicators in paragraph B50 of IFRS 3 should be used to determine when the modification should be measured and recognised.

The Application Guidance in Appendix B to IFRS 3 and the illustrative examples accompanying the standard explain how the general principle of paragraph 52 is to be applied to replacement share-based payment transactions. Essentially, however, IFRS 3 appears to view an exchange of share options or other share-based payment awards in conjunction with a business combination as a form of modification (see 7.3 above). *[IFRS 3.B56]*.

11.2.1 Awards that the acquirer is 'obliged' to replace

Where the acquirer is 'obliged' to replace the acquiree awards (see below), either all or a portion of the fair value of the acquirer's replacement awards forms part of the consideration transferred in the business combination. *[IFRS 3.B56]*.

IFRS 3 regards the acquirer as 'obliged' to replace the acquiree awards if the acquiree or its employees have the ability to enforce replacement, for example if replacement is required by:

- the terms of the acquisition agreement;
- the terms of the acquiree's awards; or
- applicable laws or regulations.

The required treatment of replacement awards may be summarised as follows:

(a) at the date of acquisition, the fair values of the replacement award and the original award are determined in accordance with IFRS 2;

(b) the amount of the replacement award attributable to pre-combination service (and therefore included as part of the consideration transferred for the business) is determined by multiplying the fair value of the original award by the ratio of the vesting period completed, as at the date of the business combination, to the greater of:

  - the total vesting period, as determined at the date of the business combination (being the period required to satisfy all vesting conditions, including conditions added to, or removed from, the original award by the replacement award); and
  - the original vesting period; and

(c) any excess of the fair value of the replacement award over the amount determined in (b) above is recognised as a post-combination remuneration expense, in accordance with the normal principles of IFRS 2 (see 3 to 7 above). *[IFRS 3.B57-59]*.

The requirements summarised in (a) to (c) above have the effect that any excess of the fair value of the replacement award over the original award is recognised as a post-combination remuneration expense. The requirement in (b) above has the effect that, if the replacement award requires service in the period after the business combination, an IFRS 2 cost is recognised in the post-combination period, even if the acquiree award being replaced had fully vested at the date of acquisition. It also has the effect that if a replacement award requires no service in the post-combination period, but the acquiree award being replaced would have done so, a cost must be recognised in the post-combination period. *[IFRS 3.B59]*.

There is no specific guidance in IFRS 3 on how and when to recognise the post-combination remuneration expense in the consolidated financial statements of the acquirer. In our view, the expense should be recognised over the post-combination vesting period of the replacement award in accordance with the general principles of IFRS 2 (see 6.2 to 6.4 above).

The portions of the replacement award attributable to pre- and post-combination service calculated in (b) and (c) above are calculated, under the normal principles of IFRS 2, based on the best estimate of the number of awards expected to vest (or to be treated as vesting by IFRS 2). Rather than being treated as adjustments to the consideration for the business combination, any changes in estimates or forfeitures occurring after the acquisition date are reflected in remuneration cost for the period in which the changes occur in accordance with the normal principles of IFRS 2. Similarly, the effects of other post-acquisition events, such as modifications or the outcome of performance conditions, are accounted for in accordance with IFRS 2 as part of the determination of the remuneration expense for the period in which such events occur. *[IFRS 3.B60]*. The application of these requirements is discussed in more detail at 11.2.3 below.

The requirements above to split an award into pre-combination and post-combination portions apply equally to equity-settled and cash-settled replacement awards. All changes after the acquisition date in the fair value of cash-settled replacements awards and their tax effects (recognised in accordance with IAS 12 – *Income Taxes*) are recognised in the post-combination financial statements when the changes occur. *[IFRS 3.B61-62]*. IFRS 3 does not specify where in the income statement any changes in the pre-combination element of a cash-settled award should be reflected and, in the absence of clear guidance, an entity will need to consider whether this is remuneration expense or whether it is closer to a change in a liability for contingent consideration.

The treatment of the income tax effects of replacement share-based payment transactions in a business combination is discussed further in Chapter 31 at 10.8.5.

11.2.1.A *Illustrative examples of awards that the acquirer is 'obliged' to replace*

IFRS 3 provides some examples in support of the written guidance summarised above, the substance of which is reproduced as Examples 32.44 to 32.47 below. *[IFRS 3.IE61-71]*. These deal with the following scenarios.

Is post-combination service required for the replacement award?	Has the acquiree award being replaced vested before the combination?	Example
Not required	Vested	32.44
Not required	Not vested	32.45
Required	Vested	32.46
Required	Not vested	32.47

In all the examples, it is assumed that the replacement award is equity-settled.

Example 32.44: Replacement award requiring no post-combination service replacing vested acquiree award

Entity A acquires Entity B and issues replacement awards with a fair value at the acquisition date of €1.1 million for awards of Entity B with a fair value at the acquisition date of €1.0 million. No post-combination services are required for the replacement awards and Entity B's employees had rendered all of the required service for the acquiree awards as of the acquisition date.

The amount attributable to pre-combination service, and therefore included in the consideration transferred in the business combination, is the fair value of Entity B's awards at the acquisition date (€1.0 million). The amount attributable to post-combination service is €0.1 million, the difference between the total value of the replacement awards (€1.1 million) and the portion attributable to pre-combination service (€1.0 million). Because no post-combination service is required for the replacement awards, Entity A immediately recognises €0.1 million as remuneration cost in its post-combination financial statements.

Example 32.45: Replacement award requiring no post-combination service replacing unvested acquiree award

Entity A acquires Entity B and issues replacement awards with a fair value at the acquisition date of €1.0 million for awards of Entity B also with a fair value at the acquisition date of €1.0 million. When originally granted, the awards of Entity B had a vesting period of four years and, as of the acquisition date, the employees of Entity B had rendered two years' service. The replacement award vests in full immediately.

The portion of the fair value of the replacement awards attributable to pre-combination services is the fair value of the award of Entity B being replaced (€1 million) multiplied by the ratio of the pre-combination vesting period (two years) to the greater of the total vesting period (now two years) and the original vesting period of Entity B's award (four years). Thus, €0.5 million (€1.0 million × 2/4 years) is attributable to pre-combination service and therefore included in the consideration transferred for the acquiree. The remaining €0.5 million is attributable to post-combination service, but, because no post-combination service is required for the replacement award to vest, Entity A recognises the entire €0.5 million immediately as remuneration cost in the post-combination financial statements.

Example 32.46: Replacement award requiring post-combination service replacing vested acquiree award

Entity A acquires Entity B and issues replacement awards with a fair value at the acquisition date of €1.0 million for awards of Entity B also with a fair value at the acquisition date of €1.0 million. The replacement awards require one year of post-combination service. The awards of Entity B being replaced had a vesting period of four years. As of the acquisition date, employees of Entity B holding unexercised vested awards had rendered a total of seven years of service since the grant date.

Even though the Entity B employees have already rendered all of the service for their original awards, Entity A attributes a portion of the replacement award to post-combination remuneration cost, because the replacement awards require one year of post-combination service. The total vesting period is five years – the vesting period for the original Entity B award completed before the acquisition date (four years) plus the vesting period for the replacement award (one year). The fact that the employees have rendered seven years of service in total in the pre-combination period is not relevant to the calculation because only four years of that service were necessary in order to earn the original award.

The portion attributable to pre-combination services equals the fair value of the award of Entity B being replaced (€1 million) multiplied by the ratio of the pre-combination vesting period (four years) to the total vesting period (five years). Thus, €0.8 million (€1.0 million × 4/5 years) is attributed to the pre-combination vesting period and therefore included in the consideration transferred in the business combination. The remaining €0.2 million is attributed to the post-combination vesting period and is recognised as remuneration cost in Entity A's post-combination financial statements in accordance with IFRS 2, over the remaining one year vesting period.

Example 32.47: Replacement award requiring post-combination service replacing unvested acquiree award

Entity A acquires Entity B and issues replacement awards with a fair value at the acquisition date of €1.0 million for awards of Entity B also with a fair value at the acquisition date of €1.0 million. The replacement awards require one year of post-combination service. When originally granted, the awards of Entity B being replaced had a vesting period of four years and, as of the acquisition date, the employees had rendered two years' service.

The replacement awards require one year of post-combination service. Because employees have already rendered two years of service, the total vesting period is three years. The portion attributable to pre-combination services equals the fair value of the award of Entity B being replaced (€1 million) multiplied by the ratio of the pre-combination vesting period (two years) to the greater of the total vesting period (three years) or the original vesting period of Entity B's award (four years). Thus, €0.5 million (€1.0 million × 2/4 years) is attributable to pre-combination service and therefore included in the consideration transferred for the acquiree. The remaining €0.5 million is attributable to post-combination service and therefore recognised as remuneration cost in Entity A's post-combination financial statements, over the remaining one year vesting period.

11.2.2 Acquiree awards that the acquirer is not 'obliged' to replace

IFRS 3 notes that, in some situations, acquiree awards may expire as a consequence of a business combination. In such a situation, the acquirer might decide to replace those awards even though it is not obliged to do so. It might also be the case that the acquirer decides voluntarily to replace awards that would not expire and which it is not otherwise obliged to replace.

Following the May 2010 amendment to IFRS 3 there is no difference in the basic approach to accounting for a replacement award that the acquirer is obliged to make and one that it makes on a voluntary basis (i.e. the approach is as set out at 11.2.1 above). In other words, the accounting is based on the fair value of the replacement award at the date of acquisition, with an apportionment of that amount between the cost of acquisition and post-acquisition employment expense.

However, in situations where the acquiree awards would expire as a consequence of the business combination if they were not voluntarily replaced by the acquirer, none of the fair value of the replacement awards is treated as part of the consideration transferred for the business (and therefore included in the computation of goodwill), but the full amount is instead recognised as a remuneration cost in the post-combination financial statements. The IASB explains that this is because the new award by the acquirer can only be for future services to be provided by the employee as the acquirer has no obligation to the employee in respect of past services. *[IFRS 3.B56, BC311B]*.

11.2.3 Accounting for changes in vesting assumptions after the acquisition date

Whilst the requirements outlined at 11.2.1 above to reflect changes in assumptions relating to the post-acquisition portion of an award through post-combination remuneration appear consistent with the general principles of IFRS 2 and IFRS 3, the application of the requirements to the pre-combination portion is less straightforward.

Paragraph B60 of IFRS 3 appears to require all changes to both the pre- and post-combination portions of the award to be reflected in post-combination remuneration expense. *[IFRS 3.B60]*. This could lead to significant volatility in post-combination profit or loss as a consequence of forfeitures, or other changes in estimates, relating to awards accounted for as part of the consideration for the business combination.

An alternative approach relies on a combination of paragraphs B60 and B63(d). Whilst paragraph B60 is clear that no adjustment can be made to the purchase consideration, paragraph B63(d) refers to IFRS 2 providing 'guidance on subsequent measurement and accounting for *the portion of replacement share-based payment awards ... that is attributable to employees' future services'* (emphasis added). *[IFRS 3.B60, B63(d)]*. Supporters of this view therefore argue that the remeasurement requirements of paragraph B60 apply only to the portion of the replacement award that is attributed to future service and that the award should be split into two parts:

- a pre-combination element that is treated as if it were vested at the acquisition date and then accounted for in the same way as other contingent consideration settled in equity; and
- a post-combination portion that is treated as a new award and reflects only the employees' post-combination service.

A further alternative approach is based on the guidance in paragraph B59 of IFRS 3 which states that 'the acquirer attributes any excess of the market-based measure of the replacement award over the market-based measure of the acquiree award to post-combination service and recognises that excess as remuneration cost in the post-combination financial statements'. *[IFRS 3.B59]*. As for the second approach above, the pre-combination element is considered to be fixed and cannot be reversed. However, any subsequent changes in assumptions that give rise to an incremental expense over the amount recognised as pre-combination service should be recognised as part of the post-combination remuneration expense.

Whilst the second and third approaches above are more consistent with the general requirement under IFRS 2 that vested awards should not be adjusted, the first approach, based on paragraph B60, is arguably the most obvious reading of IFRS 3 as currently drafted. In the absence of clear guidance in the standard, we believe that an entity may make an accounting policy choice between the three approaches but, once chosen, the policy should be applied consistently.

The three approaches are illustrated in Example 32.48 below.

Example 32.48: Accounting for post-acquisition changes in estimates relating to replacement awards

Entity A grants an award of 1,000 shares to each of two employees. The award will vest after three years provided the employees remain in service. At the end of year 2, Entity A is acquired by Entity B which replaces the award with one over its own shares but otherwise on the same terms. The fair value of each share at the date of acquisition is €1. At this date, Entity B estimates that one of the two employees will leave employment before the end of the remaining one year service period.

At the date of acquisition, Entity B recognises €667 (1 employee × 1,000 shares × €1 × 2/3) as part of the consideration for the business combination and expects to recognise a further €333 as an expense through post-acquisition profit or loss (1 × 1,000 × €1 × 1/3).

However, if the estimates made as at the date of the acquisition prove to be inaccurate and either both employees leave employment during year 3, or both remain in employment until the vesting date, there are three alternative approaches to the accounting as explained above:

- Approach 1 – all changes in estimates are reflected in post-acquisition profit or loss (drawing on paragraph B60 of IFRS 3);
- Approach 2 – changes to the estimates that affect the amount recognised as part of the purchase consideration are not adjusted for and changes affecting the post-acquisition assumptions are adjusted through post-acquisition profit or loss (drawing on paragraph B63(d) of IFRS 3); or
- Approach 3 – the amount attributable to pre-combination service, and treated as part of the business combination, is fixed and cannot be reversed. However, any changes in assumptions that give rise to an additional cumulative expense are reflected through post-acquisition profit or loss (drawing on paragraph B59 of IFRS 3).

Using the fact pattern above, and assuming that both employees leave employment in the post-acquisition period, the three alternative approaches would give rise to the following entries in accounting for the forfeitures:

- Approach 1 – a credit of €667 to post-acquisition profit or loss to reflect the reversal of the amount charged to the business combination. In addition to this, any additional expense that had been recognised in the post-acquisition period would be reversed.
- Approaches 2 and 3 – the reversal through post-acquisition profit or loss of any additional expense that had been recognised in the post-acquisition period.

If, instead, both employees remained in employment in the post-acquisition period and both awards vested, the three alternative approaches would give rise to the following entries:

- Approach 1 – an expense of €1,333 through post-acquisition profit or loss to reflect the remaining €333 fair value of the award to the employee who was expected to remain in service plus €1,000 for the award to the employee who was not expected to remain in service.
- Approach 2 – an expense of €666 (2 × €333) through post-acquisition profit or loss for the remaining 1/3 of the acquisition date fair value of the two awards. There is no adjustment to the business combination or to post-acquisition profit or loss for the €667 pre-acquisition element of the award that, as at the acquisition date, was not expected to vest.
- Approach 3 – an expense of €1,333 through post-acquisition profit or loss to reflect the remaining €333 fair value of the award to the employee who was expected to remain in service plus €1,000 for the award to the employee who was not expected to remain in service.

11.3 Acquiree award not replaced by acquirer

It may occasionally happen that the acquirer does not replace awards of the acquiree at the time of the acquisition. This might be the case where the acquired subsidiary is only partly-owned and is itself listed.

IFRS 3 distinguishes between vested and unvested share-based payment transactions of the acquiree that are outstanding at the date of the business combination but which the acquirer chooses not to replace.

If vested, the outstanding acquiree share-based payment transactions are treated by the acquirer as part of the non-controlling interest in the acquiree and measured at their IFRS 2 fair value at the date of acquisition.

If unvested, the outstanding share-based payment transactions are fair valued in accordance with IFRS 2 as if the acquisition date were the grant date. The fair value should be allocated to the non-controlling interest in the acquiree on the basis of the ratio of the portion of the vesting period completed to the greater of:

- the total vesting period; and
- the original vesting period of the share-based payment transactions.

The balance is treated as a post-combination remuneration expense in accordance with the general principles of IFRS 2. *[IFRS 3.B62A-B62B]*. Forfeitures in the post-combination period will need to be assessed in accordance with the approaches set out at 11.2.3 above.

11.4 Financial statements of the acquired entity

The replacement of an award based on the acquiree's equity with one based on the acquirer's equity is, from the perspective of the acquired entity, a cancellation and replacement, to be accounted for in accordance with the general principles of IFRS 2 for such transactions (see 7.4 above). However, in addition to considerations about whether this is accounted for as a separate cancellation and new grant or as a modification of the original terms, the acquiree needs to take into account its new status as a subsidiary of the acquirer.

If the acquirer is responsible for settling the award in its own equity with the acquiree's employees, the acquiree will continue to account for the award on an equity-settled basis. If, however, the acquiree is responsible for settling the award with shares of the acquirer, then the acquiree would have to switch from an equity-settled basis of accounting to a cash-settled basis of accounting (see 2.2.2.A and 9.4.1 above).

Even if the acquiree continues to account for the award on an equity-settled basis, the share-based payment expense recorded in the consolidated financial statements (based on fair value at the date of the business combination) will generally not be the same as that in the financial statements of the acquired entity (based on fair value at the date of original grant plus any incremental value granted at the date of acquisition, if modification accounting is applied). The exact timing of the recognition of the expense in the financial statements of the acquired entity after the date of cancellation and replacement will depend on its interpretation of the requirements of IFRS 2 for the cancellation and replacement of options (see Example 32.28 at 7.4.4.B above).

12 GROUP SHARE SCHEMES

In this section we consider various aspects of share-based payment arrangements operated within a group and involving several legal entities. The focus of the section is on the accounting by the various parties involved and includes several comprehensive illustrative examples. The main areas covered are as follows:

- typical features of a group share scheme (see 12.1 below);
- a summary of the accounting treatment of group share schemes (see 12.2 below);
- employee benefit trusts ('EBTs') and similar vehicles (see 12.3 below);
- an example of a group share scheme (based on an equity-settled award satisfied by a market purchase of shares) illustrating the accounting by the different entities involved (see 12.4 below);
- an example of a group share scheme (based on an equity-settled award satisfied by a fresh issue of shares) illustrating the accounting by the different entities involved (see 12.5 below);
- an example of a group cash-settled transaction where the award is settled by an entity other than the one receiving goods or services (see 12.6 below);
- the accounting treatment when an employee transfers between group entities (see 12.7 below); and
- group reorganisations (see 12.8 below).

Whilst associates and joint arrangements accounted for as joint ventures do not meet the definition of group entities, there will sometimes be share-based payment arrangements that involve the investor or venturer and the employees of its associate or joint venture. These arrangements are discussed at 12.9 below.

12.1 Typical features of a group share scheme

In this section we use the term 'share scheme' to encompass any transaction falling within the scope of IFRS 2, whether accounted for as equity-settled or cash-settled.

It is common practice for a group to operate a single share scheme covering several subsidiaries. Depending on the commercial needs of the entity, the scheme might cover all group entities, all group entities in a particular country or all employees of a particular grade throughout a number of subsidiaries.

The precise terms and structures of group share schemes are so varied that it is rare to find two completely identical arrangements. From an accounting perspective, however, group share schemes can generally be reduced to a basic prototype, as described below, which will serve as the basis of the discussion.

A group scheme typically involves transactions by several legal entities:

- the parent, over whose shares awards are granted;
- the subsidiary employing an employee who has been granted an award ('the employing subsidiary'); and
- the trust that administers the scheme. Such trusts are known by various names in different jurisdictions, but, for the sake of convenience, in this section we will use the term 'EBT' ('employee benefit trust') to cover all such vehicles by whatever name they are actually known. The accounting treatment of transactions with EBTs is discussed at 12.3 below.

In practice, it might not always be a simple assessment to determine which entity is receiving an employee's services and which entity is responsible for settling the award. For example, the scheme may be directed by a group employee services entity or an individual might be a director of the parent as well as providing services to other operating entities within the group.

Where an employee services company is involved it will be necessary to evaluate the precise group arrangements in order to decide whether that entity is, in substance, the employer or whether the entity or entities to which it makes a recharge for an individual's services should be treated as the employer(s). It will also often be the case that the services company is simply administering the arrangements on behalf of the parent entity. Where an individual provides services to more than one group entity, an assessment will need to be made as to which entity or entities are receiving the individual's services in return for the award. This will depend on the precise facts and circumstances of a particular situation.

A share-based award is often granted to an employee by the parent, or a group employee services entity, which will in turn have an option exercisable against the EBT for the shares that it may be required to deliver to the employee. Less commonly, the trustees of the EBT make awards to the employees and enter into reciprocal arrangements with the parent.

If the parent takes the view that it will satisfy any awards using existing shares it will often seek to fix the cash cost of the award by arranging for the EBT to purchase in the market, on the day that the award is made, sufficient shares to satisfy all or part of the award. This purchase will be funded by external borrowings, a loan from the parent, a contribution from the employing subsidiary, or some combination. The cash received from the employee on exercise of the option can be used by the EBT to repay any borrowings.

If the parent takes the view that it will satisfy the options with a fresh issue of shares, these will be issued to the EBT, either:

(a) at the date on which the employee exercises his option (in which case the EBT will subscribe for the new shares using the cash received from the employee together with any non-refundable contribution made by the employing subsidiary – see below). Such arrangements are generally referred to as 'simultaneous funding';

(b) at some earlier date (in which case the EBT will subscribe for the new shares using external borrowings, a loan from the parent or a contribution from the employing subsidiary, or some combination. The cash received from the employee on exercise of the option may then be used by the EBT to repay any borrowings). Such arrangements are generally referred to as 'pre-funding'; or

(c) some shares will be issued before the exercise date as in (b) above, and the balance on the exercise date as in (a) above.

As noted in (a) above, the employing subsidiary often makes a non-refundable contribution to the EBT in connection with the scheme, so as to ensure that employing subsidiaries bear an appropriate share of the overall cost of a group-wide share scheme.

12.2 Accounting treatment of group share schemes – summary

12.2.1 *Background*

From a financial reporting perspective, it is generally necessary to consider the accounting treatment in:

- the group's consolidated financial statements;
- the parent's separate financial statements; and
- the employing subsidiary's financial statements.

We make the assumption throughout Section 12 that the subsidiary is directly owned by the parent company. In practice, there will often be one or more intermediate holding companies between the ultimate parent and the subsidiary. The intermediate parent company generally will not be the entity granting the award, receiving the goods or services or responsible for settling the award. Therefore, under IFRS 2, we believe that there is no requirement for the intermediate company to account for the award in its separate or individual financial statements (although it might choose to recognise an increase in its investment in the subsidiary and a corresponding capital contribution from the ultimate parent in order for the transaction to be reflected throughout the chain of companies).

The accounting entries to be made in the various financial statements will broadly vary according to:

- whether the award is satisfied using shares purchased in the market or a fresh issue of shares;
- whether any charge is made to the employing subsidiary for the cost of awards to its employees;
- whether an employee benefit trust (EBT) is involved. The accounting treatment of transactions undertaken with and by EBTs is discussed in more detail at 12.3 below; and
- the tax consequences of the award. However, for the purposes of the discussion and illustrative examples below, tax effects are ignored, since these will vary significantly by jurisdiction. A more general discussion of the tax effects of share-based payment transactions may be found at 14 below and in Chapter 31 at 10.8.

12.2.2 *Scope of IFRS 2 for group share schemes*

By virtue of the definition of 'share-based payment transaction' (see 2.2.1 and 2.2.2.A above), a group share-based payment transaction is in the scope of IFRS 2 for:

- the consolidated financial statements of the group (the accounting for which follows the general principles set out in 3 to 10 above);
- the separate or individual financial statements of the entity in the group that receives goods or services (see 12.2.3 below); and
- the separate or individual financial statements of the entity in the group (if different from that receiving the goods or services) that settles the transaction with the counterparty. This entity will typically, but not necessarily, be the parent (see 12.2.4 below).

IFRS 2 provides further guidance on the application of its general principles to:

- transactions settled in the equity of the entity, or in the equity of its parent (see 12.2.5 below); and
- cash-settled transactions settled by a group entity other than the entity receiving the goods or services (see 12.2.6 below).

Section 2.2.2.A above considers seven scenarios commonly found in practice and outlines the approach required by IFRS 2 in the consolidated and separate or individual financial statements of group entities depending on whether the award is settled in cash or shares and which entity grants the award, has the obligation to settle the award and receives the goods or services.

It is common practice in a group share scheme to require each participating entity in the group to pay a charge, either to the parent or to an EBT, in respect of the cost of awards made under the scheme to employees of that entity. This is generally done either as part of the group's cash-management strategy, or in order to obtain tax relief under applicable local legislation. The amount charged could in principle be at the discretion of the group, but is often based on either the fair value of the award at grant date or the fair value at vesting, in the case of an award of free shares, or exercise, in the case of an award of options.

IFRS 2 does not directly address the accounting treatment of such intragroup management charges and other recharge arrangements, which is discussed further at 12.2.7 below. *[IFRS 2.B45-46]*.

Worked examples illustrating how these various principles translate into accounting entries are given at 12.4 to 12.6 below.

12.2.3 Entity receiving goods or services

The entity in a group receiving goods or services in a share-based payment transaction determines whether the transaction should be accounted for, in its separate or individual financial statements, as equity-settled or cash-settled. It does this by assessing the nature of the awards granted and its own rights and obligations. *[IFRS 2.43A]*.

The entity accounts for the transaction as equity-settled when either the awards granted are the entity's own equity instruments, or the entity has no obligation to settle the share-based payment transaction. Otherwise, the entity accounts for the transaction as cash-settled. Where the transaction is accounted for as equity-settled it is remeasured after grant date only to the extent permitted or required by IFRS 2 for equity-settled transactions generally, as discussed at 3 to 6 above. *[IFRS 2.43B]*.

IFRS 2 notes that a possible consequence of these requirements is that the amount recognised by the entity may differ from the amount recognised by the consolidated group or by another group entity settling the share-based payment transaction. *[IFRS 2.43A]*. This is discussed further at 12.6 below.

The cost recognised by the entity receiving goods or services is always calculated according to the principles set out above, regardless of any intragroup recharging arrangement. *[IFRS 2.43D, B45]*. The accounting for such arrangements is discussed at 12.2.7 below.

12.2.4 Entity settling the transaction

A group entity which settles a share-based payment transaction in which another group entity receives goods or services accounts for the transaction as an equity-settled share-based payment transaction only if it is settled in the settling entity's own equity instruments. Otherwise, the transaction is accounted for as cash-settled. *[IFRS 2.43C]*.

IFRS 2 specifies only the credit entry – the classification of the transaction as equity- or cash-settled, and its measurement. IFRS 2 does not specify the debit entry, which is therefore subject to the general requirement of IFRS 2 that a share-based payment transaction should normally be treated as an expense, unless there is the basis for another treatment under other IFRS (see 3 above).

In our view, the settling entity is not always required to treat the transaction as an expense:

- Where the settling entity is a parent (direct or indirect) of the entity receiving the goods or services and is accounting for the transaction as equity-settled, it will generally account for the settlement under IAS 27 – *Separate Financial Statements* – as an addition to the cost of its investment in the employing subsidiary (or of that holding company of the employing subsidiary which is the settling entity's directly-held subsidiary). *[IFRS 2.B45]*. It may then be necessary to review the carrying value of that investment to ensure that it is not impaired.
- Where the settling entity is a parent (direct or indirect) of the entity receiving the goods or services and is accounting for the transaction as cash-settled (whereas the subsidiary will be accounting for the transaction as equity-settled), in our view it has an accounting policy choice for the treatment of the remeasurement of the cash-settled liability. Either:
    - it accounts for the entire award as part of the contribution to the subsidiary and therefore as an addition to the cost of its investment in the employing subsidiary (or of that holding company of the employing subsidiary which is the settling entity's directly-held subsidiary); or
    - after the initial capitalisation of the grant date fair value of the liability, it remeasures the liability through profit or loss.

  Whichever policy is chosen, it may then be necessary to review the carrying value of the investment to ensure that it is not impaired.
- In other cases (i.e. where the settling entity is a subsidiary (direct or indirect) or fellow subsidiary of the entity receiving the goods or services), it should treat the settlement as a distribution, and charge it directly to equity. Whether or not such a settlement is a legal distribution is a matter of law in the jurisdiction concerned.

We adopt the approach of full capitalisation by the parent entity in the worked examples set out in 12.4 to 12.6 below.

12.2.5 Transactions settled in equity of the entity or its parent

12.2.5.A Awards settled in equity of subsidiary

Where a subsidiary grants an award to its employees and settles it in its own equity, the subsidiary accounts for the award as equity-settled.

The parent accounts for the award as equity-settled in its consolidated financial statements. In its separate financial statements, the parent is not required by IFRS 2 to account for the award. In both cases, the transaction may have implications for other aspects of the financial statements, since its settlement results in the partial disposal of the subsidiary (see Chapter 7).

Where the parent settles the award, it accounts for the transaction as equity-settled in its consolidated financial statements. In its separate financial statements, however, it accounts for the award as cash-settled, since it is settled not in its own equity, but in the equity of the subsidiary. From the perspective of the parent's separate financial statements, the equity of a subsidiary is a financial asset. *[IFRS 2.B50]*.

12.2.5.B Awards settled in equity of the parent

Where the parent grants an award directly to the employees of a subsidiary and settles it in its own equity, the subsidiary accounts for the award as equity-settled, with a corresponding increase in equity as a contribution from the parent. *[IFRS 2.B53]*.

The parent accounts for the award as equity-settled in both its consolidated and separate financial statements. *[IFRS 2.B54]*.

Where a subsidiary grants an award of equity in its parent to its employees and settles the award itself, it accounts for the award as cash-settled, since it is settled not in its own equity, but in the equity of its parent. From the perspective of the subsidiary's separate or individual financial statements, the equity of the parent is a financial asset. *[IFRS 2.B55]*.

This requirement potentially represents something of a compliance burden. For the purposes of the parent's consolidated financial statements the fair value of the award needs to be calculated once, at grant date. For the purposes of the subsidiary's financial statements, however, IFRS 2 requires the award to be accounted for as cash-settled, with the fair value recalculated at each reporting date.

It is, however, important to note that IFRS 2 requires this accounting treatment only for a subsidiary that 'grants' such an award. *[IFRS 2.B52, headings to B53 & B55]*. In some jurisdictions it is normal for grants of share awards to be made by the parent, or an employee service company or EBT, rather than by the subsidiary, although the subsidiary may well make recommendations to the grantor of the award as to which of its employees should benefit.

In those cases, the fact that the subsidiary may communicate the award to the employee does not necessarily mean that the subsidiary itself has granted the award. It may simply be notifying the employee of an award granted by another group entity. In that case the subsidiary should apply the normal requirement of IFRS 2 to account for the award as equity-settled.

12.2.6 Cash-settled transactions not settled by the entity receiving goods or services

IFRS 2 considers arrangements in which the parent has an obligation to make cash payments to the employees of a subsidiary linked to the price of either:

- the subsidiary's equity instruments, or
- the parent's equity instruments.

In both cases, the subsidiary has no obligation to settle the transaction and therefore accounts for the transaction as equity-settled, recognising a corresponding credit in equity as a contribution from its parent.

The subsidiary then subsequently remeasures the cost of the transaction only for any changes resulting from non-market vesting conditions not being met in accordance with the normal provisions of IFRS 2 discussed at 3 to 6 above. IFRS 2 points out that this will differ from the measurement of the transaction as cash-settled in the consolidated financial statements of the group. *[IFRS 2.B56-57].*

In both cases, the parent has an obligation to settle the transaction in cash. Accordingly, the parent accounts for the transaction as cash-settled in both its consolidated and separate financial statements. *[IFRS 2.B58].*

The requirement for the subsidiary to measure the transaction as equity-settled is somewhat controversial. The essential rationale for requiring the subsidiary to record the cost of a share-based payment transaction settled by its parent is to reflect that the subsidiary is effectively receiving a capital contribution from its parent.

The IASB specifically considered whether it would be more appropriate to measure that contribution by reference to the cash actually paid by the parent, but concluded that the approach adopted in IFRS 2 better reflects the perspective of the subsidiary as a separate reporting entity. An accounting treatment based on the cash paid by the parent would, in the IASB's view, reflect the perspective of the parent rather than that of the subsidiary. *[IFRS 2.BC268H-268K].*

12.2.7 Intragroup recharges and management charges

As noted at 12.2.2 above, IFRS 2 does not deal specifically with the accounting treatment of intragroup recharges and management charges that may be levied within the group on the subsidiary that receives goods or services, the consideration for which is equity instruments or cash provided by another group entity.

The timing of the recognition of intercompany recharges was considered by the Interpretations Committee in 2013 (see 12.2.7.A below).

The accounting requirements of IFRS 2 for group share schemes derive from IFRIC 11 (now incorporated within IFRS 2 – see 1.2 above), which was based on an exposure draft (D17) published in 2005.

D17 proposed that any such payment made by a subsidiary should be charged directly to equity, on the basis that it represents a return of the capital contribution recorded as the credit to equity required by IFRS 2 (see 12.2.3 and 12.2.6 above) up to the amount of that contribution, and a distribution thereafter.[33]

In our view, whilst IFRS 2 as currently drafted does not explicitly require this treatment, this is likely to be the more appropriate analysis for most cases where the amount of the recharge or management charge to a subsidiary is directly related to the value of the share-based payment transaction. Indeed, the only alternative, 'mechanically' speaking, would be to charge the relevant amount to profit or loss. This would result in a double charge (once for the IFRS 2 charge, and again for the management charge or recharge) which we consider to be not only less desirable an approach for most entities, but also less appropriate in cases where the amounts are directly related. Accordingly, in the examples at 12.4 to 12.6 below, we apply the treatment originally proposed in D17 to any payments made by the subsidiary for participation in the group scheme.

Many intragroup recharge arrangements are based directly on the value of the underlying share-based payment – typically at grant date, vesting date or exercise date. In other cases, a more general management charge might be levied that reflects not just share-based payments but also a number of other arrangements or services provided to the subsidiary by the parent. Where there is a more general management charge of this kind, we believe that it is more appropriate for the subsidiary to recognise a double charge to profit or loss (once for the IFRS 2 charge, and again for the management charge) rather than debiting the management charge to equity as would be the case for a direct recharge.

IFRS 2 also does not address how the parent should account for a recharge or management charge received. In our view, to the extent that the receipt represents a return of a capital contribution made to the subsidiary, the parent may choose whether to credit:

- the carrying amount of its investment in the subsidiary; or
- profit or loss (with a corresponding impairment review of the investment).

Even if part of the recharge received is credited to the carrying amount of the investment, any amount received in excess of the capital contribution previously debited to the investment in subsidiary should be accounted for as a distribution from the subsidiary and credited to the income statement of the parent. Where applicable, the illustrative examples at 12.4 to 12.6 below show the entire amount as a credit to the income statement of the parent rather than part of the recharge being treated as a credit to the parent's investment in its subsidiary.

The treatment of a distribution from a subsidiary in the separate financial statements of a parent is more generally discussed in Chapter 8 at 2.4.

A further issue that arises in practice is the timing of recognition of the recharge by the parties to the arrangement. The treatment adopted might depend to some extent on the precise terms and whether there are contractual arrangements in place, but two approaches generally result in practice:

- to account for the recharge when it is actually levied or paid (which is consistent with accounting for a distribution); or
- to accrue the recharge over the life of the award or the recharge agreement even if, as is commonly the case, the actual recharge is only made at vesting or exercise date.

An entity should choose the more appropriate treatment for its particular circumstances. The first approach is often the more appropriate in a group context where recharge arrangements might be rather informal and therefore not binding until such time as a payment is made. It is also consistent with the overall recognition of the arrangement through equity. The second approach, which is likely to be the more appropriate approach when a liability is considered to exist in advance of the payment date, is closer to the accounting treatment of a provision or financial liability but, unlike the requirements of IAS 37 or IAS 39, reflects changes in the recognised amount through equity rather than profit or loss and builds up the recharge liability over the life of the award rather than recognising the liability in full when a present obligation has been identified.

Whichever accounting treatment is adopted, any adjustments to the amount to be recognised as a recharge, whether arising from a change in the IFRS 2 expense or other changes, should be recognised in the current period and previous periods should not be restated.

Where applicable, the examples at 12.4 to 12.6 below illustrate the first of the two treatments outlined above and recognise the recharge only when it becomes payable at the date of exercise.

12.2.7.A Timing of recognition of intercompany recharges: discussion by the IFRS Interpretations Committee

In January 2013 the Interpretations Committee discussed whether a subsidiary's liability to pay to its parent the settlement value of share-based payments to the subsidiary's employees should be recognised by the subsidiary from the grant date of the award or only at the date of settlement of the award.

While outreach conducted by the Interpretations Committee suggested that there is diversity in practice (as indicated at 12.2.7 above), the Interpretations Committee concluded in May 2013 that the topic could not be restricted to recharges relating to share-based payments and therefore decided not to add this issue to its agenda.[34]

12.3 Employee benefit trusts ('EBTs') and similar arrangements

12.3.1 Background

For some time entities have established trusts and similar arrangements for the benefit of employees. These are known by various names in different jurisdictions, but, for the sake of convenience, in this section we will use the term 'EBT' ('employee benefit trust') to cover all such vehicles by whatever name they are actually known.

The commercial purposes of using such vehicles vary from employer to employer, and from jurisdiction to jurisdiction, but may include the following:

- An EBT, in order to achieve its purpose, needs to hold shares that have either been issued to it by the entity or been bought by the EBT on the open market. In some jurisdictions, the direct holding of shares in an entity by the entity itself is unlawful.
- In the case of longer-term benefits the use of an EBT may 'ring fence' the assets set aside for the benefit of employees in case of the insolvency of the entity.
- The use of an EBT may be necessary in order to achieve a favourable tax treatment for the entity or the employees, or both.

The detailed features of an EBT will again vary from entity to entity, and from jurisdiction to jurisdiction, but typical features often include the following:

- The EBT provides a warehouse for the sponsoring entity's shares, for example by acquiring and holding shares that are to be sold or transferred to employees in the future. The trustees may purchase the shares with finance provided by the sponsoring entity (by way of cash contributions or loans), or by a third-party bank loan, or by a combination of the two. Loans from the entity are usually interest-free. In other cases, the EBT may subscribe directly for shares issued by the sponsoring entity or acquire shares in the market.
- Where the EBT borrows from a third party, the sponsoring entity will usually guarantee the loan, i.e. it will be responsible for any shortfall if the EBT's assets are insufficient to meet its debt repayment obligations. The entity will also generally make regular contributions to the EBT to enable the EBT to meet its interest payments, i.e. to make good any shortfall between the dividend income of the EBT (if any) and the interest payable. As part of this arrangement the trustees may waive their right to dividends on the shares held by the EBT.
- Shares held by the EBT are distributed to employees through an employee share scheme. There are many different arrangements – these may include:
  - the purchase of shares by employees when exercising their share options under a share option scheme;
  - the purchase of shares by the trustees of an approved profit-sharing scheme for allocation to employees under the rules of the scheme; or
  - the transfer of shares to employees under some other incentive scheme.
- The trustees of an EBT may have a legal duty to act at all times in accordance with the interests of the beneficiaries under the EBT. However, most EBTs (particularly those established as a means of remunerating employees) are specifically designed so as to serve the purposes of the sponsoring entity, and to ensure that there will be minimal risk of any conflict arising between the duties of the trustees and the interest of the entity.

12.3.2 Accounting for EBTs

Historically, transactions involving EBTs were accounted for according to their legal form. In other words, any cash gifted or lent to the EBT was simply treated as, respectively, an expense or a loan in the financial statements of the employing entity.

However, this treatment gradually came to be challenged, not least by some tax authorities who began to question whether it was appropriate to allow a corporate tax deduction for the 'expense' of putting money into an EBT which in some cases might remain in the EBT for some considerable time (or even be lent back to the entity) before being actually passed on to employees. Thus, the issue came onto the agenda of the national standard setters.

The accounting solution proposed by some national standard setters, such as those in the United States and the United Kingdom, was to require a reporting entity to account for an EBT as an extension of the entity. The basis for this treatment was essentially that, as noted at 12.3.1 above, EBTs are specifically designed to serve the purposes of the sponsoring entity, and to ensure that there will be minimal risk of any conflict arising between the duties of the trustees and the interest of the entity, suggesting that they are under the *de facto* control of the entity.

Unlike the approach required by some national standard setters, IFRS does not mandate the treatment of an EBT as an extension of the sponsoring entity in that entity's separate financial statements and the accounting treatment in the separate entity is therefore less clear under IFRS (see 12.3.4 below). If an entity does not treat the EBT as an extension of itself in its own financial statements it will need to assess for its consolidated IFRS financial statements whether the EBT should be consolidated as a separate vehicle. This assessment will be based on the control criteria set out in IFRS 10, as discussed in more detail in Chapter 6. However, in summary, the entity will need to decide whether:

- it has power over the EBT;
- it has exposure, or rights, to variable returns from its involvement with the EBT; and
- it has the ability to use its power over the EBT to affect the amount of the sponsoring entity's returns.

Paragraphs BC70 to BC74 of the Basis for Conclusions to IFRS 2 are clearly written on the assumption that the trust referred to in paragraph BC70 is being included in the financial statements of the reporting entity. This suggests that the IASB regards the consolidation of such vehicles as normal practice. *[IFRS 2.BC70-74]*.

In addition to a decision as to whether it is appropriate to consolidate an EBT, reporting entities also need to make an assessment as to the level within a group at which the EBT should be consolidated i.e. whether the EBT is controlled by a sponsoring entity at a sub-group level or whether just by the ultimate parent entity. In many cases, an EBT holding shares in the ultimate parent entity will be considered to be under the control of that entity but there will be exceptions in some group scenarios. The discussion below generally assumes that the reporting entity is the sponsoring entity of the EBT and consolidates an EBT holding the reporting entity's own shares.

Consolidation of an EBT will have the following broad consequences for the consolidated financial statements of the reporting entity:

- Until such time as the entity's own shares held by the EBT vest unconditionally in employees:
  - any consideration paid for the shares should be deducted in arriving at shareholders' equity in accordance with IAS 32 (see Chapter 45 at 9); and
  - the shares should be treated as if they were treasury shares when calculating earnings per share under IAS 33 (see Chapter 35 at 3.2).
- Other assets and liabilities (including borrowings) of the EBT should be recognised as assets and liabilities in the consolidated financial statements of the sponsoring entity.
- No gain or loss should be recognised in profit or loss on the purchase, sale, issue or cancellation of the entity's own shares, as required by IAS 32. Although not explicitly required by IFRS, we suggest that entities show consideration paid or

received for the purchase or sale of the entity's own shares in an EBT separately from other purchases and sales of the entity's own shares in the reconciliation of movements in shareholders' equity. This may be particularly relevant for entities in jurisdictions that distinguish between 'true' treasury shares (i.e. those legally held by the issuing entity) and those accounted for as such under IFRS (such as those held by an EBT).

- Any dividend income arising on own shares should be excluded in arriving at profit before tax and deducted from the aggregate of dividends paid and proposed. In our view, the deduction should be disclosed if material.
- Finance costs and any administration expenses should be charged as they accrue and not as funding payments are made to the EBT.

The discussion above, and in the remainder of Section 12, focuses on arrangements where the EBT holds unallocated shares of the reporting entity and/or shares that have been allocated to employees in connection with share awards but where the awards have not yet vested. It should be noted that there will also be situations in practice in which an EBT reaches the stage where, or is designed so that, it only holds shares to which employees have full entitlement (i.e. the shares are fully vested). In this situation the shares are beneficially owned and controlled by the individual employees but might remain in trust for tax or other reasons in the period following vesting. Where an EBT does not hold any unvested shares and there are no other assets or liabilities in the EBT over which the entity continues to exercise control, there will be nothing left in the EBT to be consolidated.

12.3.3 *Illustrative Examples – awards satisfied by shares purchased by, or issued to, an EBT*

The following Examples assume that the EBT is consolidated in accordance with IFRS 10 and show the interaction of the requirements of IFRS 10 with those of IFRS 2. Example 32.49 illustrates the treatment where an award is satisfied using shares previously purchased in the market. Example 32.50 illustrates the treatment where freshly issued shares are used.

Example 32.49: Interaction of IFRS 10, IAS 32 and IFRS 2 (market purchase)

On 1 January in year 1, the EBT of ABC plc made a market purchase of 100,000 shares of ABC plc at £2.50 per share. These were the only ABC shares held by the EBT at that date.

On 1 May in the same year, ABC granted executives options over between 300,000 and 500,000 shares at £2.70 per share, which will vest at the end of year 1, the number vesting depending on various performance criteria. It is determined that the cost to be recognised in respect of this award under IFRS 2 is 15p per share.

Four months later, on 1 September, the EBT made a further market purchase of 300,000 shares at £2.65 per share.

At the end of year 1, options vested over 350,000 shares and were exercised immediately.

The accounting entries for the above transaction required by IFRS 10, IAS 32 and IFRS 2 in the consolidated financial statements of ABC would be as follows. It should be noted that all these pronouncements require various entries to be recorded in 'equity'. Thus, some variation may be found in practice as to the precise characterisation of the reserves, depending on local legal requirements and other 'traditions' in national GAAP which are retained to the extent that they do not conflict with IFRS.

	£	£
1 January		
Own shares (equity)	250,000	
Cash		250,000
To record purchase of 100,000 £1 shares at £2.50/share		
1 May – 31 December		
Profit or loss	52,500	
Equity†		52,500
To record cost of vested 350,000 options at 15p/option		
1 September		
Own shares (equity)	795,000	
Cash		795,000
To record purchase of 300,000 £1 shares at £2.65/share		
31 December		
Cash	945,000	
Equity†[1]		945,000
Receipt of proceeds on exercise of 350,000 options at £2.70/share		
Equity†	914,375	
Own shares (equity)[2]		914,375
Release of shares from EBT to employees		

1 This reflects the fact that the entity has had an increase in resources as a result of a transaction with an owner, which gives rise to no gain or loss and is therefore credited direct to equity.

2 It is necessary to transfer the cost of the shares 'reissued' by the EBT out of own shares, as the deduction for own shares would otherwise be overstated. The total cost of the pool of 400,000 shares immediately before vesting was £1,045,000 (£250,000 purchased on 1 January and £795,000 purchased on 1 September), representing an average cost per share of £2.6125. £2.6125 × 350,000 shares = £914,375.

† We recommend that, subject to any local legal restrictions, these amounts should all be accounted for in the same component of equity.

Example 32.49 illustrates the importance of keeping the accounting treatment required by IAS 32 for the cost of the shares completely separate from that for the cost of the award required by IFRS 2. In cash terms, ABC has made a 'profit' of £30,625, since it purchased 350,000 shares with a weighted average cost of £914,375 and issued them to the executives for £945,000. However, this 'profit' is accounted for entirely within equity, whereas a calculated IFRS 2 cost of £52,500 is recognised in profit or loss.

Example 32.50: Interaction of IFRS 10, IAS 32 and IFRS 2 (fresh issue of shares)

On 1 January in year 1, the EBT of ABC plc subscribed for 100,000 £1 shares of ABC plc at £2.50 per share, paid for in cash provided by ABC by way of loan to the EBT. Under local law, these proceeds must be credited to the share capital account up to the par value of the shares issued, with any excess taken to a share premium account (additional paid-in capital). These were the only ABC shares held by the EBT at that date.

On 1 May in the same year, ABC granted executives options over between 300,000 and 500,000 shares at £2.70 per share, which will vest at the end of year 1, the number vesting depending on various performance criteria. It is determined that the cost to be recognised in respect of this award is 15p per share.

Four months later, on 1 September, the EBT subscribed for a further 300,000 shares at £2.65 per share, again paid for in cash provided by ABC by way of loan to the EBT.

At the end of year 1, options vested over 350,000 shares and were exercised immediately.

The accounting entries for the above transaction required by IFRS 10, IAS 32 and IFRS 2 in the consolidated financial statements of ABC would be as follows. It should be noted that all these pronouncements require various entries to be recorded in 'equity'. Thus, some variation may be found in practice as to the precise characterisation of the reserves, depending on local legal requirements and other 'traditions' in national GAAP which are retained to the extent that they do not conflict with IFRS.

	£	£
1 January		
Equity†1	250,000	
Share capital		100,000
Share premium		150,000
To record issue of 100,000 £1 shares to EBT at £2.50/share		
1 May – 31 December		
Profit or loss	52,500	
Equity†		52,500
To record cost of vested 350,000 options at 15p/option		
1 September		
Equity†1	795,000	
Share capital		300,000
Share premium		495,000
To record issue of 300,000 £1 shares at £2.65/share		
31 December		
Cash	945,000	
Equity2†		945,000
Receipt of proceeds on exercise of 350,000 options at £2.70/share		

1 This entry is required to reconcile the requirement of local law to record an issue of shares with the fact that, in reality, there has been no increase in the resources of the reporting entity. All that has happened is that one member of the reporting group (the EBT) has transferred cash to another (the parent entity). In our view, this amount should not necessarily be accounted for within any 'Own shares reserve' in equity if such a reserve is generally restricted to shares acquired from third parties.

2 This reflects the fact that the entity has had an increase in resources as a result of a transaction with an owner, which gives rise to no gain or loss and is therefore credited direct to equity.

† We recommend that, subject to any local legal restrictions, these amounts should all be accounted for in the same component of equity.

12.3.4 Separate financial statements

As noted at 12.3.2 above, in contrast to some national GAAPs, where an EBT is treated as a direct extension of the parent entity, such that the assets and liabilities of the EBT are included in both the separate and consolidated financial statements of the parent, under IFRS the accounting model is *prima facie* to treat the EBT as a separate group entity.

This means that the separate financial statements of the employing entity must show transactions and balances with the EBT rather than the transactions, assets and liabilities of the EBT. This raises some accounting problems, for some of which IFRS currently provides no real solution, as illustrated by Example 32.51 below. This has led the Interpretations Committee and others to discuss whether the 'separate entity' approach to accounting for EBTs is appropriate (see further discussion below).

Example 32.51: EBTs in separate financial statements of sponsoring entity

An entity lends its EBT €1 million which the EBT uses to make a market purchase of 200,000 shares in the entity. In the separate financial statements of the EBT the shares will be shown as an asset. In the consolidated financial statements, the shares will be accounted for as treasury shares, by deduction from equity.

In the separate financial statements of the entity, on the basis that the EBT is a separate entity, like any other subsidiary, the normal accounting entry would be:

	€	€
Loan to EBT	1,000,000	
Cash		1,000,000

The obvious issue with this approach is that it is, in economic substance, treating the shares held by the EBT (represented by the loan to the EBT) as an asset of the entity, whereas, if they were held directly by the entity, they would have to be accounted for as treasury shares, by deduction from equity. If the share price falls such that the EBT has no means of repaying the full €1,000,000, *prima facie* this gives rise to an impairment of the €1,000,000 loan. Again, however, this seems in effect to be recognising a loss on own equity.

Suppose now that employees are granted options over the shares with an exercise price of zero, which have a value under IFRS 2 of €1,200,000. The entity will therefore book an expense of €1,200,000 under IFRS 2. When the options are exercised, the shares are delivered to employees. At that point the €1,000,000 loan to the EBT clearly becomes irrecoverable (as it has no assets), and must be written off. Normally, the write-off of an investment or loan is an expense required to be recognised in profit or loss. However, to recognise the €1,000,000 investment write-off as an expense as well as the €1,200,000 IFRS 2 charge would clearly be a form of double counting.

Some suggest that a solution to this problem is to say that the entity has effectively bought a gross-settled call option over its own shares from the EBT, whereby it can require the EBT to deliver 200,000 shares in return for a waiver of its €1,000,000 loan. Thus the accounting for the settlement of the call over the shares is as for any other gross-settled purchased call option over own equity under IAS 32 – see Chapter 45 at 11.2.1.

	€	€
Own shares (deduction from equity)	1,000,000	
Loan to EBT		1,000,000

When the shares are delivered to employees (some milliseconds later), the entry is:

	€	€
Other component of equity	1,000,000	
Own shares (deduction from equity)		1,000,000

At its meetings in May and July 2006, the Interpretations Committee discussed whether the EBT should be treated as an extension of the sponsoring entity, such as a branch, or as a separate entity. The Interpretations Committee decided to explore how specific transactions between the sponsor and the EBT should be treated in the sponsor's separate or individual financial statements and whether transactions between the EBT and the sponsor's employees should be attributed to the sponsor.

Interestingly, the Interpretations Committee fell short of dismissing the 'extension of the parent company' approach and has not since revisited this topic other than to re-confirm in March 2011 that it had not become aware of additional concerns or of diversity in practice and hence it did not think it necessary for this to be considered for the IASB's agenda. In our view, whilst any requirement to consolidate EBTs under IFRS 10 could be argued to give a clear steer towards treating the EBT as a separate entity, until there is any final clarification of this issue, it appears acceptable to treat an EBT as an extension of, or agent for, the sponsoring entity in that entity's separate financial statements. This treatment would result in outcomes essentially the same as those in Examples 32.49 and 32.50 above, while avoiding the problems highlighted in Example 32.51 above.

12.3.5 Financial statements of the EBT

The EBT may be required to prepare financial statements in accordance with requirements imposed by local law or by its own trust deed. The form and content of such financial statements are beyond the scope of this chapter.

12.4 Illustrative example of group share scheme – equity-settled award satisfied by market purchase of shares

The discussion in 12.4.1 to 12.4.3 below is based on Example 32.52 and addresses the accounting treatment for three distinct aspects of a group share scheme – a share-based payment arrangement involving group entities (see 12.2 above), the use of an EBT (see 12.3 above) and a group recharge arrangement (see 12.2.7 above).

This illustrative example treats the recharge by the parent to the subsidiary as an income statement credit in the individual accounts of the parent and recognises the recharge when it is paid. In some situations, entities might consider it appropriate to apply alternative accounting treatments (see 12.2.7 above).

Example 32.52: Group share scheme (market purchase of shares)

On 1 July 2017 an employee of S Limited, a subsidiary of the H plc group, is awarded options under the H group share scheme over 3,000 shares in H plc at £1.50 each, exercisable between 1 July 2020 and 1 July 2023, subject to a service condition and certain performance criteria being met in the three years ending 30 June 2020.

H plc is the grantor of the award, and has the obligation to settle it. On 1 January 2018, in connection with the award, the H plc group EBT purchases 3,000 shares at the then prevailing market price of £2.00 each, funded by a loan from H plc. On exercise of the option, S Limited is required to pay the differential between the purchase price of the shares and the exercise price of the option (50p per share) to the EBT.

For the purposes of IFRS 2, the options are considered to have a fair value at grant date of £1 per option. Throughout the vesting period of the option, H takes the view that the award will vest in full.

The option is exercised on 1 September 2022, at which point the EBT uses the option proceeds, together with the payment by S Limited, to repay the loan from H plc.

H plc and its subsidiaries have a 31 December year end.

12.4.1 Consolidated financial statements

So far as the consolidated financial statements are concerned, the transactions to be accounted for are:

- the purchase of the shares by the EBT and their eventual transfer to the employee; and
- the cost of the award.

Transactions between H plc or S Limited and the EBT are ignored since, in this Example, the EBT is consolidated (see 12.3 above). The accounting entries required are set out below. As in other examples in this chapter, where an entry is shown as being made to equity the precise allocation to a particular component of equity will be a matter for local legislation and, possibly, local accounting 'tradition', to the extent that this is not incompatible with IFRS.

		£	£
y/e 31.12.2017	Profit or loss (employee costs)*	500	
	Equity		500
1.1.2018	Own shares (equity)	6,000	
	Cash		6,000
y/e 31.12.2018	Profit or loss (employee costs)*	1,000	
	Equity		1,000
y/e 31.12.2019	Profit or loss (employee costs)*	1,000	
	Equity		1,000
y/e 31.12.2020	Profit or loss (employee costs)*	500	
	Equity		500
1.9.2022	Cash (option proceeds)†	4,500	
	Equity‡	1,500	
	Own shares (equity)**		6,000

* Total cost £3,000 (3000 options × £1) spread over 36 months. Charge for period to December 2017 is 6/36 × £3,000 = £500, and so on. In practice, where options are granted to a group of individuals, or with variable performance criteria, the annual charge will be based on a continually revised cumulative charge (see further discussion at 6.1 to 6.4 above).

† 3,000 options at £1.50 each.

‡ This reflects the fact that the overall effect of the transaction for the group *in cash terms* has been a 'loss' of £1,500 (£6,000 original cost of shares less £4,500 option proceeds received). However, under IFRS this is an equity transaction, not an expense.

** £6,000 cost of own shares purchased on 1 January 2018 now transferred to the employee. In practice, it is more likely that the appropriate amount to be transferred would be based on the weighted average price of shares held by the EBT at the date of exercise, as in Example 32.49 at 12.3.3 above. In such a case there would be a corresponding adjustment to the debit to equity marked with ‡ above.

12.4.2 Parent

The parent has to consider the accounting treatment of the EBT (i.e. whether it is accounted for as a separate entity or an extension of the parent – see 12.3 above). This gives two possible accounting treatments:

- EBT treated as separate entity (see 12.4.2.A below); and
- EBT treated as extension of parent (see 12.4.2.B below).

We also discuss, at 12.4.2.C below, the accounting implications if the parent, rather than – as in Example 32.52 – a subsidiary, is the employing entity.

12.4.2.A EBT treated as separate entity

The parent accounts for the share-based payment transaction under IFRS 2 as an equity-settled transaction, since the parent settles the award by delivering its own equity instruments to the employees of the subsidiary (see 12.2.4 above). However, as discussed at 12.2.4 above, instead of recording a cost, as in its consolidated financial statements, the parent records an increase in the carrying value of its investment in subsidiary. It might then be necessary to consider whether the ever-increasing investment in subsidiary is supportable or is in fact impaired. As this is a matter to be determined in the light of specific facts and circumstances, it is not considered in this example. Any impairment charge would be recorded in profit or loss.

In addition to accounting for the share-based payment transaction, the parent records its transactions with the EBT and the purchase of shares.

This gives rise to the following entries:

		£	£
y/e 31.12.2017	Investment in subsidiary*	500	
	Equity		500
1.1.2018	Loan to EBT	6,000	
	Cash		6,000
y/e 31.12.2018	Investment in subsidiary*	1,000	
	Equity		1,000
y/e 31.12.2019	Investment in subsidiary*	1,000	
	Equity		1,000
y/e 31.12.2020	Investment in subsidiary*	500	
	Equity		500
1.9.2022	Cash	6,000	
	Loan to EBT		6,000

* Total increase in investment £3,000 (3000 shares × £1 fair value of each option) recognised over 36 months. Increase during period to December 2017 is 6/36 × £3,000 = £500, and so on. In practice, where options were granted to a group of individuals, or with variable performance criteria, the annual adjustment would be based on a continually revised cumulative adjustment (see further discussion at 6.1 to 6.4 above).

12.4.2.B EBT treated as extension of the parent

The parent accounts for the share-based payment transaction under IFRS 2 as an equity-settled transaction, since the parent settles the award by delivering its own equity instruments to the employees of the subsidiary (see 12.2.4 above). However, as discussed at 12.2.4 above, instead of recording a cost, as in its consolidated financial statements, the parent records an increase in the carrying value of its investment in subsidiary. It might then be necessary to consider whether the ever-increasing investment in subsidiary is supportable or is in fact impaired. As this is a matter to be determined in the light of specific facts and circumstances, it is not considered in this example. Any impairment charge would be recorded in profit or loss.

In addition to accounting for the share-based payment transaction, the parent records the transactions of the EBT and the purchase of shares.

This gives rise to the following entries:

		£	£
y/e 31.12.2017	Investment in subsidiary*	500	
	Equity		500
1.1.2018	Own shares (equity)	6,000	
	Cash		6,000
y/e 31.12.2018	Investment in subsidiary*	1,000	
	Equity		1,000
y/e 31.12.2019	Investment in subsidiary*	1,000	
	Equity		1,000
y/e 31.12.2020	Investment in subsidiary*	500	
	Equity		500
1.9.2022	Cash†	6,000	
	Equity‡	1,500	
	Profit or loss§		1,500
	Own shares** (equity)		6,000

* Total increase in investment £3,000 (3000 shares × £1 fair value of each option) spread over 36 months. Increase during period to December 2017 is 6/36 × £3,000 = £500, and so on. In practice, where options were granted to a group of individuals, or with variable performance criteria, the annual adjustment would be based on a continually revised cumulative adjustment (see further discussion at 6.1 to 6.4 above).

† £4,500 option exercise proceeds from employee plus £1,500 contribution from S Limited.

‡ This is essentially a balancing figure representing the fact that the entity is distributing own shares with an original cost of £6,000, but has treated £1,500 of the £6,000 of the cash it has received as income (see § below) rather than as payment for the shares.

§ The £1,500 contribution by the subsidiary to the EBT has been treated as a distribution from the subsidiary (see 12.2.7 above) and recorded in profit or loss. It might then be necessary to consider whether, as a result of this payment, the investment in the subsidiary had become impaired (see Chapter 8 at 2.4). As this is a matter to be determined in the light of specific facts and circumstances, it is not considered in this example. Any impairment charge would be recorded in profit or loss.

** £6,000 cost of own shares purchased on 1 January 2018 now transferred to employee. In practice, it is more likely that the appropriate amount to be transferred would be based on the weighted average price of shares held by the EBT at the date of exercise, as in Example 32.49 at 12.3.3 above.

12.4.2.C Parent company as employing company

If, in Example 32.52, the employing entity were the parent rather than the subsidiary, it would record an expense under IFRS 2. It would also normally waive £1,500 of its £6,000 loan to the EBT (i.e. the shortfall between the original loan and the £4,500 option proceeds received from the employee).

If the EBT is treated as an extension of the parent, the accounting entries for the parent would be the same as those for the group, as set out in 12.4.1 above.

If the EBT is treated as a separate entity, the accounting entries might be as follows:

		£	£
y/e 31.12.2017	Profit or loss*	500	
	Equity		500
1.1.2018	Loan to EBT	6,000	
	Cash		6,000
y/e 31.12.2018	Profit or loss*	1,000	
	Equity		1,000
y/e 31.12.2019	Profit or loss*	1,000	
	Equity		1,000
y/e 31.12.2020	Profit or loss*	500	
	Equity		500
1.9.2022	Own shares (Equity)†	1,500	
	Cash	4,500	
	Loan to EBT		6,000
	Equity	1,500	
	Own shares (Equity)		1,500

* Total cost £3,000 (3000 options × £1) spread over 36 months. Charge for period to December 2017 is 6/36 × £3,000 = £500, and so on. In practice, where options were granted to a group of individuals, or with variable performance criteria, the annual charge would be based on a continually revised cumulative charge (see further discussion at 6.1 to 6.4 above).

† This takes the approach of treating the parent as having a gross-settled purchased call option over its own equity (see Example 32.51 at 12.3.4 above), under which it can acquire 3,000 own shares from the EBT for the consideration of the waiver of £1,500 of the original £6,000 loan. The £4,500 cash inflow represents the £4,500 option exercise proceeds received by the EBT from the employee, which is then used to pay the balance of the original £6,000 loan.

12.4.3 *Employing subsidiary*

The employing subsidiary is required to account for the IFRS 2 expense and the contribution to the EBT on exercise of the award. This gives rise to the accounting entries set out below. The entries to reflect the IFRS 2 expense are required by IFRS 2 (see 12.2.3 above). The contribution to the EBT is treated as a distribution (see 12.2.7 above).

		£	£
y/e 31.12.2017	Profit or loss*	500	
	Equity		500
y/e 31.12.2018	Profit or loss*	1,000	
	Equity		1,000
y/e 31.12.2019	Profit or loss*	1,000	
	Equity		1,000
y/e 31.12.2020	Profit or loss*	500	
	Equity		500
1.9.2022	Equity†	1,500	
	Cash		1,500

* Total cost £3,000 (3000 options × £1) spread over 36 months. Charge for period to December 2017 is 6/36 × £3,000 = £500, and so on. In practice, where options were granted to a group of individuals, or with variable performance criteria, the annual charge would be based on a continually revised cumulative charge (see further discussion at 6.1 to 6.4 above).

† This should be treated as a reduction of whatever component of equity was credited with the £3,000 quasi-contribution from the parent in the accounting entries above.

12.5 Illustrative example of group share scheme – equity-settled award satisfied by fresh issue of shares

Such schemes raise slightly different accounting issues. Again, these are most easily illustrated by way of an example. The discussion in 12.5.1 to 12.5.3 below is based on Example 32.53. As with Example 32.52 at 12.4 above, this section addresses the accounting treatment for three distinct aspects of a group share scheme – a share-based payment arrangement involving group entities (see 12.2 above), the use of an EBT (see 12.3 above) and a group recharge arrangement (see 12.2.7 above).

This illustrative example treats the recharge by the parent to the subsidiary as an income statement credit in the individual accounts of the parent and recognises the recharge when it is paid. In some situations, entities might consider it appropriate to apply alternative accounting treatments (see 12.2.7 above).

Example 32.53: Group share scheme (fresh issue of shares)

On 1 July 2017 an employee of S Limited, a subsidiary of the H plc group, is awarded options under the H group share scheme over 3,000 shares in H plc at £1.50 each, exercisable between 1 July 2020 and 1 July 2023, subject to a service condition and certain performance criteria being met in the three years ending 30 June 2020. The fair value of the options on 1 July 2017 is £1 each.

H plc grants the award and has the obligation to settle it.

When preparing accounts during the vesting period H plc and its subsidiaries assume that the award will vest in full. The options are finally exercised on 1 September 2022, at which point H plc issues 3,000 new shares to the EBT at the then current market price of £3.50 for £10,500. The EBT funds the purchase using the £4,500 option proceeds received from the employee together with £6,000 contributed by S Limited, effectively representing the fair value of the options at exercise date (3,000 × [£3.50 – £1.50]). H plc and its subsidiaries have a 31 December year end.

12.5.1 Consolidated financial statements

The consolidated financial statements need to deal with:

- the charge required by IFRS 2 in respect of the award; and
- the issue of shares.

Transactions between H plc or S Limited and the EBT are ignored since, in this Example, the EBT is consolidated (see 12.3 above). The accounting entries required are set out below. As in other examples in this chapter, where an entry is shown as being made to equity, the precise allocation to a particular component of equity will be a matter for local legislation and, possibly, local accounting 'tradition', to the extent that this is not incompatible with IFRS.

		£	£
y/e 31.12.2017	Profit or loss*	500	
	Equity		500
y/e 31.12.2018	Profit or loss*	1,000	
	Equity		1,000
y/e 31.12.2019	Profit or loss*	1,000	
	Equity		1,000
y/e 31.12.2020	Profit or loss*	500	
	Equity		500
1.9.2022	Cash	4,500	
	Equity†		4,500

* Total cost £3,000 (3000 options × £1) spread over 36 months. Charge for period to December 2017 is 6/36 × £3,000 = £500, and so on. In practice, where options were granted to a group of individuals, or with variable performance criteria, the annual charge would be based on a continually revised cumulative charge (see further discussion at 6.1 to 6.4 above).

† From the point of view of the consolidated group, the issue of shares results in an increase in net assets of only £4,500 (i.e. the exercise price received from the employee), since the £6,000 contribution from the employing subsidiary to the EBT is an intragroup transaction. However, it may be that, in certain jurisdictions, the entity is required to increase its share capital and share premium (additional paid in capital) accounts by the £10,500 legal consideration for the issue of shares. In that case, this entry would be expanded as below, which effectively treats the £6,000 consideration provided from within the group as a bonus issue.

		£	£
1.9.2022	Cash	4,500	
	Other equity	6,000	
	Share capital/premium		10,500

12.5.2 Parent

The parent has to consider the accounting treatment of the EBT (i.e. whether it is accounted for as a separate entity or an extension of the parent – see 12.3 above). This gives two possible accounting treatments:

- EBT treated as separate entity (see 12.5.2.A below); and
- EBT treated as extension of parent (see 12.5.2.B below).

We also discuss, at 12.5.2.C below, the accounting implications if the parent, rather than – as in Example 32.53 – a subsidiary, is the employing entity.

12.5.2.A EBT treated as separate entity

The parent accounts for the share-based payment transaction under IFRS 2 as an equity-settled transaction, since the parent settles the award by delivering its own equity instruments to the employees of the subsidiary (see 12.2.4 above). However, as discussed at 12.2.4 above, instead of recording a cost, as in its consolidated financial statements, the parent records an increase in the carrying value of its investment in subsidiary. It might then be necessary to consider whether the ever-increasing investment in subsidiary is supportable or is in fact impaired. As this is a matter to be determined in the light of specific facts and circumstances, it is not considered in this example. Any impairment charge would be recorded in profit or loss.

In addition to accounting for the share-based payment transaction, the parent records its transactions with the EBT and the issue of shares.

		£	£
y/e 31.12.2017	Investment in subsidiary*	500	
	Equity		500
y/e 31.12.2018	Investment in subsidiary*	1,000	
	Equity		1,000
y/e 31.12.2019	Investment in subsidiary*	1,000	
	Equity		1,000
y/e 31.12.2020	Investment in subsidiary*	500	
	Equity		500
1.9.2022	Cash†	10,500	
	Share capital/premium		10,500

* Total increase in investment £3,000 (3000 shares × £1 fair value of each option), recognised over 36 months. Increase in period to December 2017 is 6/36 × £3,000 = £500, and so on. In practice, where options were granted to a group of individuals, or with variable performance criteria, the annual adjustment would be based on a continually revised cumulative adjustment (see further discussion at 6.1 to 6.4 above).

† £4,500 option exercise proceeds from employee plus £6,000 contribution from the subsidiary.

12.5.2.B EBT treated as extension of parent

The parent accounts for the share-based payment transaction under IFRS 2 as an equity-settled transaction, since the parent settles the award by delivering its own equity instruments to the employees of the subsidiary (see 12.2.4 above). However, as discussed at 12.2.4 above, instead of recording a cost, as in its consolidated financial statements, the parent records an increase in the carrying value of its investment in subsidiary. It might then be necessary to consider whether the ever-increasing investment in subsidiary is supportable or is in fact impaired. As this is a matter to be determined in the light of specific facts and circumstances, it is not considered in this example. Any impairment charge would be recorded in profit or loss.

In addition to accounting for the share-based payment transaction, the parent records the transactions of the EBT and the issue of shares.

		£	£
y/e 31.12.2017	Investment in subsidiary*	500	
	Equity		500
y/e 31.12.2018	Investment in subsidiary*	1,000	
	Equity		1,000
y/e 31.12.2019	Investment in subsidiary*	1,000	
	Equity		1,000
y/e 31.12.2020	Investment in subsidiary*	500	
	Equity†		500
1.9.2022	Cash†	10,500	
	Equity‡	6,000	
	Profit or loss**		6,000
	Share capital/premium		10,500

* Total increase in investment £3,000 (3000 shares × £1 fair value of each option) spread over 36 months. Increase during period to December 2017 is 6/36 × £3,000 = £500, and so on. In practice, where options were granted to a group of individuals, or with variable performance criteria, the annual adjustment would be based on a continually revised cumulative adjustment (see further discussion at 6.1 to 6.4 above).

† £4,500 option exercise proceeds from employee plus £6,000 contribution from the subsidiary.

‡ This assumes that local law requires the entity to record share capital and share premium (additional paid-in capital) of £10,500, as in 12.5.2.A above. However, IFRS *prima facie* requires the £6,000 cash received by the EBT from the subsidiary to be treated as income (see ** below) rather than as part of the proceeds of the issue of shares. In order, in effect, to reconcile these conflicting analyses, £6,000 of the £10,500 required by law to be capitalised as share capital and share premium has been treated as an appropriation out of other equity.

** The £6,000 contribution by the subsidiary to the EBT has been treated as a distribution from the subsidiary (see 12.2.7 above) and recorded in profit or loss. It might then be necessary to consider whether, as a result of this payment, the investment in the subsidiary had become impaired (see Chapter 8 at 2.4). As this is a matter to be determined in the light of specific facts and circumstances, it is not considered in this Example. Any impairment charge would be recorded in profit or loss.

12.5.2.C *Parent company as employing company*

If, in Example 32.53, the employing entity were the parent rather than the subsidiary, it would clearly have to record an expense under IFRS 2. It would also have to fund the £6,000 shortfall between the option exercise proceeds of £4,500 and the £10,500 issue proceeds of the shares.

If the EBT is treated as an extension of the parent, the accounting entries for the parent would be the same as those for the group, as set out in 12.5.1 above.

In our view, the treatment in 12.5.1 above may also be appropriate for this specific transaction, even where the EBT is treated as a separate entity. The issue of shares requires the parent company to fund the EBT with £6,000 which immediately returns it to the parent, along with the £4,500 received from the employee, in exchange for an issue of shares. Whilst this 'circulation' of the £6,000 might have some significance for legal purposes it is, economically speaking, a non-transaction that could be ignored for accounting purposes under IFRS. It might, however, be relevant, under local law, to the amount of equity shown as share capital and share premium (additional paid-in capital), in which case the expanded entry in 12.5.1 above would be appropriate.

Where, however, the EBT is treated as a separate entity, and the cash used to subscribe for the shares arises from a prior transaction, such as an earlier loan to the EBT, matters are more complicated. Suppose that, during the life of the award under discussion, the company were to advance £50,000 to the EBT for general funding purposes. At that point it would clearly record the entry:

	£	£
Loan to EBT	50,000	
Cash		50,000

Suppose that, on exercise of the option, the EBT were to use some of that cash to fund the parent's 'top up' for the share issue. This effectively impairs the loan by £6,000 and leaves a 'missing debit' indicated by '?' in the journal below:

	£	£
Cash	10,500	
?	6,000	
Loan to EBT		6,000
Share capital/premium		10,500

This looks very much like an impairment loss on the loan required to be reported in profit or loss. On the other hand, it does not resemble a loss in any conventional sense. This suggests that another analysis may be possible.

Example 32.51 at 12.3.4 above addresses the situation where an EBT is pre-funded to enable it to buy the reporting entity's own shares in the market, and those shares are finally delivered to the entity for distribution to employees. Example 32.51 suggests that this could be construed as the execution of a gross-settled purchased call option by the entity.

If that analogy is extended, the present situation could be construed as comprising a back-to-back:

- gross-settled purchased call option (whereby the entity can require the EBT to provide 3,000 shares in return for waiver of £6,000 of its outstanding loan to the EBT), which triggers the exercise of
- a gross-settled written call option (whereby the EBT can require the entity to issue 3,000 fresh shares for £10,500 to the EBT, so that it can satisfy its obligations to the entity under the purchased call).

If these two call options are accounted for under IAS 32 (see Chapter 45 at 11.2), the write-off of the loan to the EBT can be effectively charged to equity, as follows:

	£	£
Cash	10,500	
Share capital/premium		10,500
Exercise by EBT of written call		
Own shares (Equity)	6,000	
Loan to EBT		6,000
Exercise by entity of purchased call		
Equity (other)	6,000	
Own shares (Equity)		6,000
Issue of shares to employee		

12.5.3 *Employing subsidiary*

The employing subsidiary is required to account for the IFRS 2 expense and the contribution to the EBT on exercise of the award. This gives rise to the accounting entries set out below. The entries to reflect the IFRS 2 expense are required by IFRS 2 (see 12.2.3 above). The contribution to the EBT is treated as a distribution (see 12.2.7 above).

		£	£
y/e 31.12.2017	Profit or loss*	500	
	Equity		500
y/e 31.12.2018	Profit or loss*	1,000	
	Equity		1,000
y/e 31.12.2019	Profit or loss*	1,000	
	Equity		1,000
y/e 31.12.2020	Profit or loss*	500	
	Equity		500
1.9.2022	Equity†	6,000	
	Cash		6,000

* Total cost £3,000 (3000 options × £1) spread over 36 months. Charge for period to December 2017 6/36 × £3,000 = £500, and so on. In practice, where options were granted to a group of individuals, or with variable performance criteria, the annual charge would be based on a continually revised cumulative charge (see further discussion at 6.1 to 6.4 above).

† £3,000 of this payment should be treated as a reduction of whatever component of equity was credited with the £3,000 quasi-contribution from the parent in the accounting entries above. The remaining £3,000 would be treated as a distribution and charged to any appropriate component of equity.

12.6 Illustrative example – cash-settled transaction not settled by the entity receiving goods or services

The discussion in 12.6.1 to 12.6.3 below is based on Example 32.54.

Example 32.54: Cash-settled scheme not settled by receiving entity

On 1 July 2017 an employee of S Limited, a subsidiary of the H plc group, is awarded a right, exercisable between 1 July 2020 and 1 July 2023, to receive cash equivalent to the value of 3,000 shares in H plc at the date on which the right is exercised. Exercise of the right is subject to a service condition and certain performance criteria being met in the three years ending 30 June 2020. The cash will be paid to the employee not by S, but by H. Throughout the vesting period of the award, H and S take the view that it will vest in full.

The award does in fact vest, and the right is exercised on 1 September 2022.

The fair value of the award (per share-equivalent) at various relevant dates is as follows:

Date	Fair value
	£
1.7.2017	1.50
31.12.2017	1.80
31.12.2018	2.70
31.12.2019	2.40
31.12.2020	2.90
31.12.2021	3.30
1.9.2022	3.50

If the award had been equity-settled (i.e. the employee had instead been granted a right to 3,000 free shares), the grant date fair value of the award would have been £1.50 per share.
H plc and its subsidiaries have a 31 December year end.

12.6.1 *Consolidated financial statements*

The group has entered into a cash-settled transaction which is accounted for using the methodology discussed at 9.3 above. This gives rise to the following accounting entries:

		£	£
y/e 31.12.2017	Profit or loss*	900	
	Liability		900
y/e 31.12.2018	Profit or loss*	3,150	
	Liability		3,150
y/e 31.12.2019	Profit or loss*	1,950	
	Liability		1,950
y/e 31.12.2020	Profit or loss*	2,700	
	Liability		2,700
y/e 31.12.2021	Profit or loss*	1,200	
	Liability		1,200
y/e 31.12.2022	Profit or loss*	600	
	Liability		600
1.9.2022	Liability	10,500	
	Cash		10,500

* Charge for period to 31 December 2017 is 6/36 × 3000 × £1.80 [reporting date fair value] = £900. Charge for year ended 31 December 2018 is 18/36 × 3000 × £2.70 = £4,050 less £900 charged in 2017 = £3,150 and so on (refer to Example 32.36 at 9.3.2 above). In practice, where options were granted to a group of individuals, or with variable performance criteria, the annual charge would be based on a continually revised cumulative charge (see further discussion at 9 above).

12.6.2 *Parent company*

The parent accounts for the share-based payment transaction under IFRS 2 as a cash-settled transaction, since the parent settles the award by delivering cash to the employees of the subsidiary (see 12.2.4 above). However, as discussed at 12.2.4 above, instead of recording a cost, as in its consolidated financial statements, the parent treats the debit entry (including, as a matter of accounting policy choice, any remeasurement of the liability) as an increase in the carrying value of its investment in subsidiary. It might then be necessary to consider whether the ever-increasing investment in subsidiary is supportable or is in fact impaired. As this is a matter to be determined in the light of specific facts and circumstances, it is not considered in this example. Any impairment charge would be recorded in profit or loss.

This would result in the following accounting entries.

		£	£
y/e 31.12.2017	Investment in subsidiary*	900	
	Liability		900
y/e 31.12.2018	Investment in subsidiary*	3,150	
	Liability		3,150
y/e 31.12.2019	Investment in subsidiary*	1,950	
	Liability		1,950
y/e 31.12.2020	Investment in subsidiary*	2,700	
	Liability		2,700
y/e 31.12.2021	Investment in subsidiary*	1,200	
	Liability		1,200
y/e 31.12.2022	Investment in subsidiary*	600	
	Liability		600
1.9.2022	Liability	10,500	
	Cash		10,500

* Increase in investment to 31 December 2017 is 6/36 × 3000 × £1.80 [reporting date fair value] = £900. Increase for year ended 31 December 2018 is 18/36 × 3000 × £2.70 = £4,050 less £900 charged in 2017 = £3,150 and so on (refer to Example 32.36 at 9.3.2 above). In practice, where options were granted to a group of individuals, or with variable performance criteria, the annual charge would be based on a continually revised cumulative charge (see further discussion at 9 above).

Where the parent entity was also the employing entity (and therefore receiving goods or services), it would apply the same accounting treatment in its separate financial statements as in its consolidated financial statements (see 12.6.1 above).

12.6.3 Employing subsidiary

The employing subsidiary accounts for the transaction as equity-settled, since it receives services, but incurs no obligation to its employees (see 12.2.3 and 12.2.6 above). This gives rise to the following accounting entries.

		£	£
y/e 31.12.2017	Profit or loss*	750	
	Equity		750
y/e 31.12.2018	Profit or loss*	1,500	
	Equity		1,500
y/e 31.12.2019	Profit or loss*	1,500	
	Equity		1,500
y/e 31.12.2020	Profit or loss*	750	
	Equity		750

* Charge for period to 31 December 2017 is 6/36 × 3000 × £1.50 [grant date fair value] = £750, and so on. In practice, where options were granted to a group of individuals, or with variable performance criteria, the annual charge would be based on a continually revised cumulative charge (see further discussion at 6.1 to 6.4 above).

The effect of this treatment is that, while the group ultimately records a cost of £10,500, the subsidiary records a cost of only £4,500.

However, there may be cases where the subsidiary records a higher cost than the group. This would happen if, for example:

- the award vests, but the share price has fallen since grant date, so that the value of the award at vesting (as reflected in the consolidated financial statements) is lower than the value at grant (as reflected in the subsidiary's financial statements); or
- the award does not actually vest because of a failure to meet a market condition and/or a non-vesting condition (so that the cost is nil in the consolidated financial statements) but is treated by IFRS 2 as vesting in the subsidiary's financial statements, because it is accounted for as equity-settled (see 6.3 and 6.4 above).

12.7 Employee transferring between group entities

It is not uncommon for an employee to be granted an equity-settled share-based payment award while in the employment of one subsidiary in the group, but to transfer to another subsidiary in the group before the award is vested, but with the entitlement to the award being unchanged.

In such cases, each subsidiary measures the services received from the employee by reference to the fair value of the equity instruments at the date those rights to equity instruments were originally granted, and the proportion of the vesting period served by the employee with each subsidiary. *[IFRS 2.B59]*. In other words, for an award with a three-year vesting period granted to an employee of subsidiary A, who transfers to subsidiary B at the end of year 2, subsidiary A will (cumulatively) record an expense of 2/3, and subsidiary B 1/3, of the fair value at grant date. However, any subsidiary required to account for the transaction as cash-settled in accordance with the general principles discussed at 12.2 above accounts for its portion of the grant date fair value and also for any changes in the fair value of the award during the period of employment with that subsidiary. *[IFRS 2.B60]*.

After transferring between group entities, an employee may fail to satisfy a vesting condition other than a market condition, for example by leaving the employment of the group. In this situation each subsidiary adjusts the amount previously recognised in respect of the services received from the employee in accordance with the general principles of IFRS 2 (see 6.1 to 6.4 above). *[IFRS 2.B61]*. This imposes upon the original employing entity the rather curious burden of tracking the service record of its former employees, where the accounting impact is expected to be significant.

12.8 Group reorganisations

Following a group reorganisation, such as the insertion of a new parent entity above an existing group, share-based payment arrangements with employees are often amended or replaced so that they relate to the shares of the new parent. Group reorganisations of entities under common control are not within the scope of IFRS 3 and so the requirements set out at 11 above are not directly applicable.

In some cases, the terms and conditions of a share-based payment arrangement will contain provisions relating to restructuring transactions (see 5.3.8.A above) so that the application of any changes is not necessarily considered to be a modification in IFRS 2 terms. Where no such provision is made, the situation is less clear-cut.

In our view, in the consolidated financial statements, such changes to share-based payments would generally be construed as a cancellation and replacement to which modification accounting could be applied (see 7.4.4 above). However, in most cases, the changes made to the share-based payment awards following a group reorganisation are likely to be such that there is no incremental fair value arising from the cancellation and replacement, the intention being simply to replace like with like.

A subsidiary receiving the services of employees but with no obligation to settle the amended award would continue to apply equity-settled accounting in its own financial statements and, as for the consolidated financial statements, would strictly account for the changes as a cancellation and replacement of the original award. The accounting consequences would be more complicated if the subsidiary itself had an obligation to settle the award in the shares of its new parent, when previously it had had to settle in its own shares, as this would mean a change from equity-settled to cash-settled accounting (see 9.4 above). However, we would expect this to be a rare occurrence in practice (see 12.2.5.B above in relation to the grantor of an award in a situation involving parent and subsidiary entities).

The new parent entity becomes a party to the share-based payment arrangements for the first time and, assuming it has no employees of its own but is considered to have granted and to have the obligation to settle the awards, needs to account for the awards to the employees of its subsidiaries (see 12.2.4 and 12.2.5 above). The requirements of IFRS 2 in this situation are unclear and one could argue:

- either that this is a new award by the parent and so should be valued as at the date of the new award; or
- in accordance with the general principle that there is no overall change as a consequence of a reorganisation of entities under common control, that the parent should use the same (original grant date) fair value as the subsidiary.

In our view, either approach is acceptable provided it is applied consistently.

12.9 Share-based payments to employees of joint ventures or associates

The majority of share-based payment transactions with employees involve payments to employees of the reporting entity or of another entity in the same group. Occasionally, however, share-based payments may be made to employees of significant investees of the reporting entity such as joint ventures or associates. For example, if one party to a joint venture is a quoted entity and the other not, it might be commercially appropriate for the quoted venturer to offer payments based on its quoted shares to employees of the joint venture, while the unquoted party contributes to the venture in other ways.

Such arrangements raise some questions of interpretation of IFRS 2, as illustrated by Example 32.55 below. References to an associate in the example and discussions below should be read as also referring to a joint venture.

Example 32.55: Share-based payment to employees of associate

At the beginning of year 1, an entity grants an award of free shares with a fair value at that date of €600,000 to employees of its 40% associate. The shares vest over a three-year period. It is assumed throughout the vesting period of the award that it will vest in full, which is in fact the case.

12.9.1 Financial statements of the associate or joint venture

For the financial statements of the associate, the transaction does not strictly fall within the scope of IFRS 2. In order for a transaction to be in the scope of IFRS 2 for a reporting entity, it must be settled in the equity of the entity itself, or that of another member of the same group. A group comprises a parent and its subsidiaries (see Chapter 6 at 2.3), and does not include associates.

Nevertheless, we believe that it would be appropriate for the associate to account for the transaction as if it did fall within the scope of IFRS 2 by applying the 'GAAP hierarchy' in IAS 8 – *Accounting Policies, Changes in Accounting Estimates and Errors* (see Chapter 3 at 4.3). The investor has effectively made a capital contribution to the associate (in the form of the investor's own equity), no less than if it made a capital contribution in cash which was then used to pay employees of the associate.

If the investor in the associate had instead granted an award settled in the equity of the associate, the transaction would have been in the scope of IFRS 2 for the associate, as being the grant of an award over the equity of the reporting entity by a shareholder of that entity (see 2.2.2.A above).

If the award is, or is treated as being, within the scope of IFRS 2 for the associate, the following entries are recorded:

		€000	€000
Year 1	Employee costs†	200	
	Equity		200
Year 2	Employee costs	200	
	Equity		200
Year 3	Employee costs	200	
	Equity		200

† Grant date fair value of award €600,000 × 1/3. The credit to equity represents a capital contribution from the investor.

12.9.2 Consolidated financial statements of the investor

The investor has entered into a share-based payment transaction since it has granted an award over its equity to third parties (the employees of the associates) in exchange for their services to a significant investee entity. However, employees of an associate are not employees of a group entity and are therefore not employees of the investor's group.

The issue for IFRS 2 purposes is, therefore, whether the award should be regarded as being made to persons providing similar services to employees (and therefore measured at grant date) or to persons other than employees or those providing similar services to employees (and therefore measured at service date) – see 5.2 to 5.4 above.

In our view, it is more appropriate to regard such awards as made to persons providing similar services to employees and therefore measured at grant date.

There are then, we believe, two possible approaches to the accounting. In our view, in the absence of clear guidance in the standard, an entity should choose the more appropriate approach based on the specific circumstances.

In any event, the investor's consolidated financial statements must show a credit to equity of €200,000 a year over the vesting period. The accounting issue is the analysis of the corresponding debit.

It seems clear that the investor must as a minimum recognise an annual cost of €80,000 (40% of €200,000), as part of its 'one-line' share of the result of the associate. The issue then is whether it should account for the remaining €120,000 as a further cost or as an increase in the cost of its investment in its associate.

The argument for treating the €120,000 as an expense is that the associate will either have recorded nothing or, as set out in 12.9.1 above, an entry that results in no net increase in the equity of the associate. Therefore there has been no increase in the investor's share of the net assets of the associate, and there is no basis for the investor to record an increase in its investment. This is broadly the approach required under US GAAP (although US GAAP requires the associate itself to recognise the expense and a corresponding capital contribution).

It may be possible to conclude in some situations that the €120,000 is an increase in the cost of the investment in associate. IAS 28 – *Investments in Associates and Joint Ventures* – defines the equity method of accounting as (emphasis added):

> 'a method of accounting whereby the investment is *initially recognised at cost and adjusted thereafter* for the post-acquisition change in the investor's share of the investee's net assets'. *[IAS 28.3]*.

For example, there may be cases where another shareholder has made, or undertaken to make, contributions to the associate that are not reflected in its recognised net assets (such as an undertaking to provide knowhow or undertake mineral exploration).

Where an entity takes the view that the €120,000 is an increase in the cost of its investment, it is essential to ensure that the resulting carrying value of the investment is sustainable. This may be the case if, for example:

- the fair value of the investment in the associate exceeds its carrying amount; or
- the investor has agreed to enter into the transaction while another major shareholder has agreed to bear equivalent costs.

In other circumstances, the carrying amount of the investment may not be sustainable, and the investor may need to recognise an impairment of its investment in accordance with IAS 36 (see Chapter 20).

12.9.3 Separate financial statements of the investor

The discussion below assumes that the investor accounts for its investment in the associate at cost in its separate financial statements (see Chapter 8).

The issues here are much the same as in 12.9.2 above. The investor has clearly entered into a share-based payment transaction since it has granted an award over its equity to third parties (the employees of the associates) in exchange for their services to a significant investee entity. As in 12.9.2 above, we believe that this is most appropriately characterised as a transaction with persons providing similar services to employees and therefore measured at its grant date fair value.

In any event, the investor's separate financial statements must show a credit to equity of €200,000 a year over the vesting period but, as in 12.9.2 above, the analysis of the debit entry is more complex.

13 DISCLOSURES

IFRS 2 requires three main groups of disclosures, explaining:

- the nature and extent of share-based payment arrangements (see 13.1 below);
- the valuation of share-based payment arrangements (see 13.2 below); and
- the impact on the financial statements of share-based payment transactions (see 13.3 below).

All of the disclosure requirements of IFRS 2 are subject to the overriding materiality considerations of IAS 1 – *Presentation of Financial Statements* (see Chapter 3 at 4.1.5). However, depending on the identity of the counterparty and whether, for example, the individual is a member of key management, it will be necessary to assess whether an arrangement is material by nature even if it is immaterial in monetary terms.

13.1 Nature and extent of share-based payment arrangements

IFRS 2 requires an entity to 'disclose information that enables users of the financial statements to understand the nature and extent of share-based payment arrangements that existed during the period'. *[IFRS 2.44]*.

In order to satisfy this general principle, the entity must disclose at least:

(a) a description of each type of share-based payment arrangement that existed at any time during the period, including the general terms and conditions of each arrangement, such as vesting requirements, the maximum term of options granted, and the method of settlement (e.g. whether in cash or equity). An entity with substantially similar types of share-based payment arrangements may aggregate this information, unless separate disclosure of each arrangement is necessary to satisfy the general principle above;

(b) the number and weighted average exercise prices of share options for each of the following groups of options:
   (i) outstanding at the beginning of the period;
   (ii) granted during the period;
   (iii) forfeited during the period;
   (iv) exercised during the period;
   (v) expired during the period;
   (vi) outstanding at the end of the period; and
   (vii) exercisable at the end of the period;

(c) for share options exercised during the period, the weighted average share price at the date of exercise. If options were exercised on a regular basis throughout the period, the entity may instead disclose the weighted average share price during the period; and

(d) for share options outstanding at the end of the period, the range of exercise prices and weighted average remaining contractual life. If the range of exercise prices is wide, the outstanding options must be divided into ranges that are meaningful for assessing the number and timing of additional shares that may be issued and the cash that may be received upon exercise of those options. *[IFRS 2.45]*.

The reconciliation in (b) above should, in our view, reflect all changes in the number of equity instruments outstanding. In addition to awards with a grant date during the period, the reconciliation should include subsequent additions to earlier grants e.g. options or shares added to the award in recognition of dividends declared during the period (where this is part of the original terms of the award), and changes to the number of equity instruments as a result of demergers, share splits or consolidations and other similar changes.

The following extract from the financial statements of Dairy Crest Group plc shows additional awards from the reinvestment of dividends within the reconciliation of outstanding awards.

Extract 32.1: Dairy Crest Group plc (2016)

Notes to the financial statements [extract]

26 Share based payment plans [extract]

[...]

The number of share options and weighted average exercise price for each of the principal schemes is set out as follows:

	LTAP*	TIA*	DBP*	LTISP*	Sharesave Scheme	
	number	number	number	number	number	weighted average exercise price (pence)
Options outstanding at 1 April 2015	716,937	240,623	68,934	196,737	3,119,443	319.3
Options granted during the year	264,779	–	–	–	–	–
Reinvested dividends	38,490	11,935	2,189	8,902	–	–
Options exercised during the year	–	–	–	(71,738)	(1,771,686)	285.9
Options forfeited during the year	(142,375)	–	–	(2,332)	(355,957)	351.9
Options outstanding at 31 March 2016	**877,831**	**252,558**	**71,123**	**131,569**	**991,800**	**367.8**
Exercisable at 31 March 2016	**63,640**	**–**	**–**	**131,569**	**579,195**	**–**

[...]

*The weighted average exercise price for LTAP, TIA, DBP and LTISP options is nil.

As drafted, the requirements in (b) to (d) above appear to apply only to share options. However, since there is little distinction in IFRS 2 between the treatment of an option with a zero exercise price and the award of a free share, in our view the disclosures should not be restricted to awards of options.

13.2 Valuation of share-based payment arrangements

IFRS 2 requires an entity to 'disclose information that enables users of the financial statements to understand how the fair value of the goods or services received, or the fair value of the equity instruments granted, during the period was determined'. *[IFRS 2.46]*.

As drafted, this requirement, and some of the detailed disclosures below, appears to apply only to equity-settled transactions. However, it would be anomalous if detailed disclosures were required about the valuation of an award to be settled in shares, but not one to be settled in cash. In our view, therefore, the disclosures apply both to equity-settled and to cash-settled transactions.

If the entity has measured the fair value of goods or services received as consideration for equity instruments of the entity indirectly, by reference to the fair value of the equity instruments granted (i.e. transactions with employees and, in exceptional cases only, with non-employees), the entity must disclose at least the following:

(a) for share options granted during the period, the weighted average fair value of those options at the measurement date and information on how that fair value was measured, including:
   - (i) the option pricing model used and the inputs to that model, including the weighted average share price, exercise price, expected volatility, option life, expected dividends, the risk-free interest rate and any other inputs to the model, including the method used and the assumptions made to incorporate the effects of expected early exercise;
   - (ii) how expected volatility was determined, including an explanation of the extent to which expected volatility was based on historical volatility; and
   - (iii) whether and how any other features of the option grant were incorporated into the measurement of fair value, such as a market condition;

(b) for other equity instruments granted during the period (i.e. other than share options), the number and weighted average fair value of those equity instruments at the measurement date, and information on how that fair value was measured, including:
   - (i) if fair value was not measured on the basis of an observable market price, how it was determined;
   - (ii) whether and how expected dividends were incorporated into the measurement of fair value; and
   - (iii) whether and how any other features of the equity instruments granted were incorporated into the measurement of fair value;

(c) for share-based payment arrangements that were modified during the period:
   - (i) an explanation of those modifications;
   - (ii) the incremental fair value granted (as a result of those modifications); and
   - (iii) information on how the incremental fair value granted was measured, consistently with the requirements set out in (a) and (b) above, where applicable. *[IFRS 2.47]*.

These requirements can be seen to some extent as an anti-avoidance measure. It would not be surprising if the IASB had concerns that entities might seek to minimise the impact of IFRS 2 by using unduly pessimistic assumptions that result in a low fair value for share-based payment transactions, and the disclosures above seem designed to deter entities from doing so. However, these disclosures give information about other commercially sensitive matters. For example, (a)(i) above effectively requires disclosure of future dividend policy for a longer period than is generally covered by such forecasts. Entities may need to consider the impact on investors and analysts of dividend yield assumptions disclosed under IFRS 2.

In our view, it is important for entities, in making these disclosures, to ensure that any assumptions disclosed, particularly those relating to future performance, are consistent with those used in other areas of financial reporting that rely on estimates of future events, such as the impairment of property, plant and equipment, intangible assets and goodwill, income taxes (recovery of deferred tax assets out of future profits) and pensions and other post-retirement benefits.

If the entity has measured a share-based payment transaction directly by reference to the fair value of goods or services received during the period, the entity must disclose how that fair value was determined (e.g. whether fair value was measured at a market price for those goods or services). *[IFRS 2.48]*.

As discussed in 5.4 above, IFRS 2 creates a rebuttable presumption that, for an equity-settled transaction with a counterparty other than an employee, the fair value of goods and services received provides the more reliable basis for assessing the fair value of the transaction. Where the entity has rebutted this presumption, and has valued the transaction by reference to the fair value of equity instruments issued, it must disclose this fact, and give an explanation of why the presumption was rebutted. *[IFRS 2.49]*.

13.3 Impact of share-based payment transactions on financial statements

IFRS 2 requires an entity to 'disclose information that enables users of the financial statements to understand the effect of share-based payment transactions on the entity's profit or loss for the period and on its financial position.' *[IFRS 2.50]*.

In order to do this, it must disclose at least:

(a) the total expense recognised for the period arising from share-based payment transactions in which the goods or services received did not qualify for recognition as assets and hence were recognised immediately as an expense, including separate disclosure of that portion of the total expense that arises from transactions accounted for as equity-settled share-based payment transactions;

(b) for liabilities arising from share-based payment transactions:

   (i) the total carrying amount at the end of the period; and

   (ii) the total intrinsic value at the end of the period of liabilities for which the counterparty's right to cash or other assets had vested by the end of the period (e.g. vested share appreciation rights). *[IFRS 2.51]*.

The disclosures section of IFRS 2 has a final paragraph requiring an entity to disclose additional information about its share-based payments should the information requirements set out above and at 13.1 and 13.2 above be insufficient to meet the general disclosure principles of the standard. *[IFRS 2.52]*.

As part of the June 2016 amendments to IFRS 2 (applicable for accounting periods beginning on or after 1 January 2018), the IASB has expanded this general disclosure requirement in paragraph 52 by including awards with a net settlement feature for withholding tax obligations (see 14.3.1 below) as an example of where additional disclosure might be appropriate. Where the information is considered necessary for the purposes of informing the users of the financial statements about the future cash flow effects of the share-based payment arrangement, the amendment indicates that the entity should disclose the estimated expected payment to the tax authority.

13.4 Example of IFRS 2 disclosures

An example of many of the disclosures required by IFRS 2 may be found in the financial statements of Aviva plc for the year ended 31 December 2015.

Extract 32.2: Aviva plc (2015)

Notes to the consolidated financial statements [extract]

31 – Group's share plans

This note describes various equity compensation plans operated by the Group, and shows how the Group values the options and awards of shares in the Company. [...]

(a) Description of the plans

The Group maintains a number of active share option and award plans and schemes (the Group's share plans). These are as follows:

(i) Savings-related options

These are options granted under the tax-advantaged save as you earn (SAYE) share option scheme in the UK and Irish revenue-approved SAYE share option scheme in Ireland. The SAYE allows eligible employees to acquire options over the Company's shares at a discount of up to 20% of their market value at the date of grant.

Options are normally exercisable during the six-month period following either the 3rd, 5th or 7th anniversary of the start of the relevant savings contract, subject to a statutory savings limit, currently £500 per month. From 2012, only 3 and 5 year contracts have been offered and Aviva's current policy is to apply a savings limit of £250 per month in the UK and €500 per month in Ireland.

(ii) Aviva long-term incentive plan awards

These awards have been made under the Aviva long-term incentive plan 2011 (LTIP), and are described in section (b) below and in the directors' remuneration report.

(iii) Aviva annual bonus plan awards

These awards have been made under the Aviva annual bonus plan 2011 (ABP), and are described in section (b) below and in the directors' remuneration report.

(iv) Aviva recruitment and retention share plan awards

These are conditional awards granted under the Aviva recruitment and retention share award plan (RRSAP) in relation to the recruitment or retention of senior managers excluding executive directors. The awards vest in tranches on various dates and vesting is conditional upon the participant being employed by the Group on the vesting date and not having served notice of resignation. Some awards can be subject to performance conditions. If a participant's employment is terminated due to resignation or dismissal, any tranche of the award which has vested within the 12 months prior to the termination date will be subject to clawback and any unvested tranches of the award will lapse in full.

(v) Aviva Investors long-term incentive plan awards

These awards have been made under the Aviva Investors Holdings Limited 2009 Long Term Incentive Plan (AI LTIP), a long-term profit sharing arrangement for key Aviva Investors' employees. Awards will vest on the 3rd anniversary of grant, subject to achieving performance conditions.

(vi) Aviva Investors deferred share award plan awards

These awards have been made under the Aviva Investors Deferred Share Award Plan (AI DSAP), where employees can choose to have the deferred element of their bonus deferred into awards over Aviva shares. The awards vest in three equal tranches on the 2nd, 3rd and 4th year following the year of grant.

(vii) The Aviva Chief Financial Officer Award 2014

Awards were granted to Tom Stoddard under the Aviva Chief Financial Officer Award 2014 (Aviva CFO Award) following his recruitment to compensate Mr Stoddard for the loss from his previous employer, on a like for like basis. The awards are described in section (b) below and in the directors' remuneration report. No further awards will be made under this plan.

No new Aviva plc ordinary shares will be issued to satisfy awards made under plans iv, v, vi or vii.

(b) Outstanding options and awards

(i) Share options

At 31 December 2015, options to subscribe for ordinary shares of 25 pence each in the Company were outstanding as follows:

Aviva savings related share option scheme	Option price p	Number of shares	Normally exercisable	Option price p	Number of shares	Normally exercisable
	410	36,354	2015	268	3,051,213	2016 or 2018
	316	157,482	2016	312	2,221,690	2016 or 2018
	310	289,794	2015 or 2017	419	2,518,442	2017 or 2019
	266	1,762,817	2015 or 2017	380	7,456,710	2018 or 2020

Aviva Ireland savings related share option scheme (in euros)	Option price c	Number of shares	Normally exercisable	Option price c	Number of shares	Normally exercisable
	374	2,128	2015	369	93,649	2016 or 2018
	304	111,470	2016	527	81,430	2017 or 2019
	336	69,802	2015 or 2017	518	299,418	2018 or 2020

The following table summarises information about options outstanding at 31 December 2015:

Range of exercise prices	Outstanding options Number	Weighted average remaining contractual life Years	Weighted average exercise price p
£2.66 – £3.65	7,760,045	2	283.21
£3.66 – £4.64	10,392,354	4	389.86
£4.65 – £5.63	–	–	–

The comparative figures as at 31 December 2014 were:

Range of exercise prices	Outstanding options Number	Weighted average remaining contractual life Years	Weighted average exercise price p
£2.66 – £3.65	13,176,872	2	280.26
£3.66 – £4.64	4,031,026	4	418.85
£4.65 – £5.63	33,636	–	563.00

(ii) Share awards

At 31 December 2015, awards issued under the Company's executive incentive plans over ordinary shares of 25 pence each in the Company were outstanding as follows:

Aviva long-term incentive plan 2011	Number of shares	Year of vesting
	9,627,862	2016
	7,628,744	2017
	9,113,030	2018

Aviva annual bonus plan 2011	Number of shares	Year of vesting
	3,045,795	2016
	2,305,523	2017
	2,932,551	2018

Aviva recruitment and retention share award plan	Number of shares	Year of vesting
	830,806	2016
	879,867	2017
	106,838	2018
	3,992	2019

Aviva Investors Holdings Limited 2009 long-term incentive plan	Number of shares	Year of vesting
	346,677	2016

Aviva Investors deferred share award plan	Number of shares	Year of vesting
	37,053	2016
	37,053	2017
	11,571	2018

The Aviva Chief Financial Officer Award 2014	Number of shares	Year of vesting
	47,151	2016
	98,232	2017

The vesting of awards under the ABP is subject to the attainment of performance conditions as described in the directors' remuneration report.

No performance conditions are attached to the awards under the ABP, AI DSAP, Aviva CFO Award or some of the awards under the RRSAP except as outlined below. Under the RRSAP, some shares are subject to the attainment of the same performance conditions that apply to the LTIP grants as follows.

- 321,330 of the shares which vest in 2016 are linked to the same performance conditions that apply to the 2013 grant.
  - 96,238 of the shares which vest in 2016 are subject to the performance conditions relating to the performance of the participant's previous employer.
- 561,887 of the shares which vest in 2017 are linked to the same performance conditions that apply to the 2014 grant
  - 22,222 of the shares which vest in 2017 are subject to the performance conditions relating to the performance of the participant's previous employer.
- 39,349 of the shares which vest in 2018 are linked to the same performance conditions that apply to the 2015 grant.
  - 22,222 of the shares which vest in 2018 are subject to the performance conditions relating to the performance of the participant's previous employer.

These performance conditions are as outlined in the relevant year's directors' remuneration report.

The vesting of the awards under the AI LTIP are subject to Aviva Investors Holdings Limited achieving a return on capital employed (ROCE) of 27% per annum over a three year performance period.

Shares which do not vest will lapse.

(iii) Shares to satisfy awards and options

New issue shares are now generally used to satisfy all awards and options granted under plans that have received shareholder approval and where local regulations permit. Further details are given in note 32.

(c) Movements in the year

A summary of the status of the option plans as at 31 December 2014 and 2015, and changes during the years ended on those dates, is shown below.

	2015		2014	
	Number of options	**Weighted average exercise price p**	Number of options	Weighted average exercise price p
Outstanding at 1 January	**17,241,534**	**313.21**	20,069,848	286.18
Granted during the year	**7,810,302**	**380.00**	3,994,548	419.00
Exercised during the year	**(5,011,905)**	**275.90**	(4,626,781)	282.30
Forfeited during the year	**(323,950)**	**341.43**	(1,028,382)	277.24
Cancelled during the year	**(1,446,795)**	**401.38**	(490,267)	298.10
Expired during the year	**(116,787)**	**383.40**	(677,432)	412.83
Outstanding at 31 December	**18,152,399**	**344.27**	17,241,534	313.21
Exercisable at 31 December	**1,146,249**	**278.53**	2,277,929	283.83

(d) Expense charged to the income statement

The total expense recognised for the year arising from equity compensation plans was as follows:

	2015 £m	2014 £m
Equity-settled expense	**40**	39
Cash-settled expense	**8**	1
Total (note 10b)	**48**	40

(e) Fair value of options and awards granted after 7 November 2002

The weighted average fair values of options and awards granted during the year, estimated by using the Binomial option pricing model and Monte Carlo Simulation model, were £0.88 and £4.49 *(2014: £1.47 and £4.19)* respectively.

(i) Share options

The fair value of the options was estimated on the date of grant, based on the following weighted average assumptions:

Weighted average assumption	2015	2014
Share price	**453p**	524p
Exercise price	**380p**	419p
Expected volatility	**26%**	32%
Expected life	**3.69 years**	3.73 years
Expected dividend yield	**3.99%**	2.91%
Risk-free interest rate	**0.94%**	1.42%

The expected volatility used was based on the historical volatility of the share price over a period equivalent to the expected life of the option prior to its date of grant. The risk-free interest rate was based on the yields available on UK government bonds as at the date of grant. The bonds chosen were those with a similar remaining term to the expected life of the options. 5,011,905 options granted after 7 November 2002 were exercised during the year *(2014: 4,626,781)*.

(ii) Share awards

The fair value of the awards was estimated on the date of grant based on the following weighted average assumptions:

Weighted average assumption	2015	2014
Share price	**560p**	484p
Expected volatility[1]	**25%**	33%
Expected volatility of comparator companies' share price[1]	**22%**	29%
Correlation between Aviva and comparator competitors' share price[1]	**44%**	58%
Expected life[1]	**2.85 years**	2.83 years
Expected dividend yield[2]	**3.20%**	2.94%
Risk-free interest rate[1]	**0.56%**	0.75%

[1] For awards with market-based performance conditions.

[2] The majority of awards with market based performance conditions include additional shares being provided to employees equal to dividend rights before vesting. As a result, no dividend yield assumption is required on these awards.

The expected volatility used was based on the historical volatility of the share price over a period equivalent to the expected life of the share award prior to its date of grant. The risk-free interest rate was based on the yields available on UK government bonds as at the date of grant. The bonds chosen were those with a similar remaining term to the expected life of the share awards.

Depending on the precise regulatory requirements of a particular jurisdiction, it might be possible to meet some of the IFRS 2 disclosure requirements by means of a cross-reference between the financial statements and other parts of an annual report published together with the financial statements, such as a management commentary or statutory remuneration report (as in the case of Aviva plc above). However, even where such an approach is permissible, care needs to be taken to ensure that any such cross-reference is clear and specific and that all of the relevant IFRS 2 requirements have been addressed as these requirements vary depending on when an award was granted. For example, detailed fair value information for an equity-settled award is generally required only in the year of grant (and as comparative information in the following period(s)), whereas the conditions attached to an award are required to be disclosed in every period in which that award is outstanding.

14 TAXES RELATED TO SHARE-BASED PAYMENT TRANSACTIONS

14.1 Income tax deductions for the entity

In many jurisdictions entities are entitled to receive income tax deductions for share-based payment transactions. In many, if not most, cases the tax deduction is given for a cost different to that recorded under IFRS 2. For example, some jurisdictions give a tax deduction for the fair or intrinsic value of the award at the date of exercise; others may give a tax deduction for amounts charged to a subsidiary by its parent or a trust controlled by the parent in respect of the cost of group awards to the employees of that subsidiary. In either case, both the amount and timing of the expense for tax purposes will be different from the amount and timing of the expense required by IFRS 2.

The particular issues raised by share-based payment transactions are addressed in IAS 12 and discussed further in Chapter 31 at 10.8.

14.2 Employment taxes of the employer

In many jurisdictions, an employing entity is required to pay employment taxes or social security contributions on share options and other share-based payment transactions with employees, just as if the employees had received cash remuneration. This raises the question of how such taxes should be accounted for.

14.2.1 Applicable standard

The choice of accounting method does not affect the total expense ultimately recognised (which must always be the tax actually paid), but rather its allocation to different accounting periods. IFRS is unclear as to which standard should be applied in accounting for such employment taxes. Some consider that such taxes are most appropriately accounted for under IAS 37 (see 14.2.1.A below), others favour IFRS 2 (see 14.2.1.B below) or IAS 19 (see 14.2.1.C below). A reporting entity may therefore choose what it considers an appropriate policy for employment taxes in its particular circumstances.

Such taxes do not fall within the scope of IAS 39 since, like income taxes, they are not contractual liabilities (see Chapter 43 at 2.2.1).

14.2.1.A IAS 37

Some consider that, for the reasons set out in 14.2.1.B and 14.2.1.C below, employment taxes of the employer do not fall within the scope of IFRS 2 or of IAS 19.

Accordingly, since the amount ultimately payable is uncertain, the most appropriate standard to apply is IAS 37.

Where IAS 37 is applied, the entity will recognise a provision for the employment tax in accordance with the provisions of IFRIC 21 – *Levies* – which requires identification of the activity that triggers the payment, as identified by the legislation (see Chapter 28 at 3.1 and 6.8). However, there is some room for discussion as to what constitutes the activity that triggers the payment. Is it:

- the granting of the award;
- the consumption of services received from employees;
- the event (typically exercise) that gives rise to a real tax liability; or
- the vesting of the award?

Entities applying IAS 37 need therefore to consider the appropriate treatment of employment taxes in the light of IFRIC 21.

14.2.1.B IFRS 2

Some argue that, since the employment taxes are a payment of an amount of cash typically directly linked to the share price, they should be accounted for as a cash-settled share-based payment transaction under IFRS 2. This would require the taxes to be measured at each reporting date at fair value, multiplied by the expired vesting period of the award to which they relate (see 9.3.1 above).

A difficulty with this analysis is that IFRS 2 defines a cash-settled share-based payment transaction as one in which the entity incurs a liability to the 'supplier of ... goods or services'. The liability for such employment taxes is clearly due to the tax authorities, not to the supplier of goods and services (i.e. the employee). This leads some who support the application of IFRS 2 to accept that IFRS 2 is not directly applicable, but to argue that it is nevertheless the most appropriate standard to apply under the 'GAAP hierarchy' in IAS 8 (see Chapter 3 at 4.3). The objective of IFRS 2 (see 2.1 above) states that the standard is intended to apply to 'expenses associated with transactions in which share options are granted to employees'. However, the standard contains no explicit provisions relevant to this objective.

14.2.1.C IAS 19

Some argue that such payments are more appropriately accounted for under IAS 19 (see Chapter 33). Again the difficulty is that IAS 19 defines employee benefits as 'all forms of consideration given by an entity in exchange for service rendered by employees or for the termination of employment' *[IAS 19.8]*, which would appear to rule out payments to the tax authority, but for the fact that IAS 19 refers to social security contributions as a component part of short-term employee benefits. *[IAS 19.9(a)]*. However, many share-based payment transactions would, if they were within the scope of IAS 19, be classified as long-term benefits. That brings the added complication that IAS 19 would require the employment taxes due on long-term benefits to be accounted for, like the benefits themselves, using the projected unit credit method, which seems an unduly complex approach in the circumstances.

In some situations the entity may require employees to discharge any liability for employment taxes. The accounting issues raised by such arrangements are discussed at 14.2.2 and 14.3 below.

14.2.2 Recovery of employer's taxes from employees

As discussed at 14.2 above, in some jurisdictions employers are required to pay employment taxes on share-based payment transactions. This detracts from one of the key attractions for an employer of a share-based payment transaction, namely that it entails no cash cost. This is particularly the case where the tax payable is based on the fair value of the award at vesting, where the employer's liability is potentially unlimited.

Accordingly, employers liable to such taxes are increasingly making it a condition of receiving a share-based award that the employee bear all or some of the employer's cash cost of any related employment taxes. This may be done in a number of ways, including:

- direct payment to the entity;
- authorising the entity to deduct the relevant amount from the employee's salary; or
- surrendering as many shares to the entity as have a fair value equal to the tax liability.

The accounting treatment of schemes where the recovery of the employer's tax cost from the employee is made through surrendering of a number of shares with an equivalent value is similar to that discussed at 14.3 below for the recovery of the employee's taxes.

Where the scheme requires direct cash reimbursement by employees of the cost of the employer's taxes, different considerations apply, as illustrated by Example 32.56 below.

Example 32.56: Recovery of employment tax on share-based payment from employee

At the beginning of year 1, an entity granted an executive an award of free shares with a fair value of €100,000 on condition that the executive remain in employment for three years. In the jurisdiction concerned, an employment tax at the rate of 12% is payable by the employer when the shares vest, based on their fair value at the date of vesting. As a condition of obtaining the shares on vesting, the executive is required to pay cash equal to the tax liability to the employer.

When the shares vest at the end of year 3, their fair value is €300,000, on which employment taxes of €36,000 are due. The executive pays this amount to the entity.

In our view, this arrangement can be construed in one of two ways, with somewhat different accounting outcomes:

- View 1: The executive's obligation to make whole the employer's tax liability means that this is, economically, not an award of free shares, but an option to acquire the shares for an exercise price equivalent to 12% of their market value at the date of exercise. The employer's tax liability is a separate transaction.
- View 2: The executive's obligation to make whole the employer's tax liability should be accounted for as such, separately from the share-based payment transaction.

In our view, either approach may be adopted, so long as it is applied consistently as a matter of accounting policy. The essential differences between View 1 and View 2, as illustrated below, are that:

- under View 1 the reimbursement received from the employee is credited to equity, whereas under View 2 it is credited to profit or loss; and
- under View 1, the IFRS 2 charge is lower than under View 2 reflecting the fact that under View 1 the award is construed as an option, not an award of free shares.

View 1 Reimbursement treated as exercise price

On this analysis, the award is construed as an option to acquire shares with an exercise price of 12% of the fair value, at vesting, of the shares. The grant date fair value of the award construed as an option is €88,000. The entity would process the following accounting entries (on a cumulative basis).

	€000	€000
Employee costs*	88	
Equity		88
Employee costs†	36	
Cash		36
Cash§	36	
Equity		36

* IFRS 2 charge.

† Employment taxes (12% of €300,000).

§ The receipt of cash from the employee to reimburse the tax is treated as the receipt of the exercise price for an option and credited to equity.

View 2 Reimbursement treated separately from the IFRS 2 charge

On this analysis, the award is construed as an award of free shares, with a grant date fair value of €100,000. The reimbursement is accounted for as such, giving rise to a credit to profit or loss. The entity would process the following accounting entries (on a cumulative basis).

	€000	€000
Employee costs*	100	
Equity		100
Employee costs†	36	
Cash		36
Cash§	36	
Employee costs		36

* IFRS 2 charge.

† Employment taxes (12% of €300,000).

§ The receipt of cash from the employee to reimburse the tax is treated as a reduction in employee costs.

It will be seen that View 1 results in a total employee expense of €124,000, while View 2 results in a total employee expense of €100,000.

14.2.3 Holding of own shares to 'hedge' tax liabilities

As noted at 14.2 above, in many jurisdictions, an award of shares or options to an employee also gives rise to an employment tax liability for the employer, often related to the fair value of the award when it vests or, in the case of an option, is exercised. Employers may hold their own shares in order to hedge this liability (in an economic sense, if not under the criteria in IAS 39 – see 2.2.4.H above), and later sell as many shares as are needed to raise proceeds equal to the tax liability.

These are two separate transactions. The purchase and sale of own shares are treasury share transactions accounted for in accordance with IAS 32 (see Chapter 45 at 9). The accounting treatment of the employment tax liability is discussed at 14.2.1 above.

14.3 Sale or surrender of shares by employee to meet employee's tax liability ('sell to cover')

In some jurisdictions, an award of shares or options to an employee gives rise to a personal tax liability for the employee, often related to the fair value of the award when it vests or, in the case of an option, is exercised. In order to meet this tax liability, employees may wish to sell as many shares as are needed to raise proceeds equal to the tax liability (sometimes described as 'sell to cover').

This *in itself* does not, in our view, require the scheme to be considered as cash-settled, any more than if the employee wished to liquidate the shares in order to buy a car or undertake home improvements. However, if the manner in which the cash is passed to the employee gives rise to a legal or constructive obligation for the employer, then the scheme might well be cash-settled (see 9.2.2 to 9.2.4 above), to the extent of any such obligation.

In some jurisdictions where employees must pay income tax on share awards, the tax is initially collected from (and is a legal liability of) the employer, but with eventual recourse by the tax authorities to the employee for tax not collected from the employer. Such tax collection arrangements mean that even an equity-settled award results in a cash cost for the employer for the income tax.

In such a situation, the employer may require the employee, as a condition of taking delivery of any shares earned, to indemnify the entity against the tax liability, for example by:

- direct payment to the entity;
- authorising the entity to deduct the relevant amount from the employee's salary; or
- surrendering as many shares to the entity as have a fair value equal to the tax liability.

If the entity requires the employee to surrender the relevant number of shares, in our view it is appropriate – under IFRS 2 as currently drafted – to treat the scheme as cash-settled to the extent of the indemnified amount, as explained in Example 32.57 below. This view has been confirmed by the IASB in discussions relating to its recent amendment to IFRS 2.

The amendment makes an exception to the current requirements of IFRS 2. Following adoption of the amendment, net-settled arrangements meeting certain specified criteria will be accounted for as equity-settled in their entirety. However, the amendment is narrow in scope and the current requirement to assess whether an arrangement has an equity-settled element and a cash-settled element will continue to be relevant in many cases. The amendment is discussed further at 14.3.1 below.

The following example illustrates the current requirements of IFRS 2.

Example 32.57: Surrendering of vested shares by employee to indemnify liability of entity to pay employee's tax liability (net settlement)

An entity operates in a jurisdiction where the personal tax rate is 40%, and free shares are taxed at their fair value on vesting. The entity grants an award of 100 free shares with a grant date fair value of £3 each. The fair value at vesting date is £5, so that the employee's tax liability (required to be discharged in the first instance by the employer) is £200 (40% of £500). The award is to be satisfied using treasury shares with an original cost of £2.50 per share.

If the employee were required to surrender the 40 shares needed to settle the tax liability, in our view the substance of the transaction is that, at grant date, the entity is making an award of only 60 shares (with a grant date fair value of £3 each) and is bearing the cost of the employment tax itself. On this analysis, the entity will have recorded the following entries by the end of the vesting period:

	£	£
Employee costs	180	
Equity		180
Employee costs	200	
Employment tax liability		200

The award is then satisfied by delivery of 60 treasury shares (with a cost of £2.50 each) to the employee:

	£	£
Equity	150	
Treasury shares		150

The entity might well then sell the 40 shares 'surrendered' by the employee in order to raise the cash to pay the tax, but this would be accounted for as an increase in equity on the reissue of treasury shares, not as income (see 14.2.3 above).

If, however, the employee has a free choice as to how to indemnify the employer rather than being required to surrender shares, the employer will have recorded the following entries by the end of the vesting period:

	£	£
Employee costs	300	
Equity		300
Receivable from employee	200	
Employment tax liability		200

The award is then satisfied by delivery of shares to the employee, and the employee indicates that he wishes to surrender 40 shares to discharge his obligation to the employer under the indemnity arrangement. The entity then receives 40 shares from the employee in settlement of the £200 receivable from him.

In practice, this would almost certainly be effected as a net delivery of 60 shares, but in principle there are two transactions, a release of 100 treasury shares, with a cost of £2.50 each, to the employee:

	£	£
Equity	250	
Treasury shares		250

and the re-acquisition of 40 of those shares at £5 each from the employee:

	£	£
Treasury shares	200	
Receivable from employee		200

The entity then settles the tax liability:

	£	£
Employment tax liability	200	
Cash		200

Even in this case, however, some might take the view that the substance of the arrangement is that the employee has the right to put 40 shares to the employer, and accordingly 40% of the award should be accounted for as cash-settled, resulting in essentially the same accounting as when the employee is required to surrender 40 shares, as set out above. An entity should therefore make a careful assessment of the appropriate accounting treatment based on the terms of a particular arrangement.

14.3.1 *Share-based payments with a net settlement feature for withholding tax obligations: amendment to IFRS 2 (accounting periods beginning on or after 1 January 2018)*

In 2010 the Interpretations Committee began to discuss the classification of a share-based payment transaction in which an entity withholds a specified portion of shares that would otherwise be issued to the counterparty at the date of exercise or vesting. The shares are withheld in return for the entity settling the counterparty's tax liability relating to the share-based payment. The question asked was whether the portion of the share-based payment that is withheld should be classified as cash-settled or equity-settled in a situation where, in the absence of the net settlement feature, the award would be treated in its entirety as equity-settled?

Having concluded that the issue is widespread and causes significant diversity in practice, the Interpretations Committee decided to recommend that the IASB issue an amendment to IFRS 2 to add specific guidance for certain types of share-based payment transaction with a net settlement feature.[35]

In November 2014 the IASB published a draft amendment to IFRS 2 to add an exception to the standard in the case of specific types of share-based payment transactions with a net settlement feature. The final version of the amendment was published in June 2016.[36]

The amendment adds several new paragraphs to IFRS 2. A new paragraph 33E states that 'tax laws or regulations may oblige an entity to withhold an amount for an employee's tax obligation associated with a share-based payment and transfer that amount, normally in cash, to the tax authority on the employee's behalf. To fulfil this obligation, the terms of the share-based payment arrangement may permit or require the entity to withhold the number of equity instruments equal to the monetary value of the employee's tax obligation from the total number of equity instruments that otherwise would have been issued to the employee upon exercise (or vesting) of the share-based payment (i.e. the share-based payment arrangement has a "net settlement feature")'.

If a transaction meeting the above criteria would have been classified entirely as equity-settled were it not for this net settlement feature, then the exception in paragraph 33F (also discussed in paragraph BC255G of the Basis for Conclusions) specifies that it should be accounted for as equity-settled in its entirety (rather than being divided into an equity-settled portion and a cash-settled portion as discussed at 14.3 above).[37]

Paragraph 33G of the amended standard requires an entity applying the exception to account for the withholding of shares to fund the payment to the tax authority as a deduction from equity (in accordance with paragraph 29 of IFRS 2). However, the deduction from equity may only be made up to the fair value at the net settlement date of the shares withheld. If the payment exceeds this fair value, the excess is expensed through profit or loss.

The amendment also specifies in paragraph 33H(b) that if the entity withholds any equity instruments in excess of the employee's tax obligation associated with the share-based payment (i.e. the entity withholds an amount of shares that exceeds the monetary value of the employee's tax obligation), then the excess shares should be accounted for as a cash-settled share-based payment when this amount is paid in cash (or other assets) to the employee. In other words, such shares are treated as a separate cash-settled share-based payment and fully recognised as an expense (rather than as a deduction from equity) as at the date of settlement.

To illustrate the additional paragraphs in the standard, the IASB has added a new example to the implementation guidance accompanying IFRS 2 (IG Example 12B). The substance of this example is reproduced as Example 32.58 below.

The amendment also introduces an example of additional disclosures that an entity might need to make in respect of the future cash payment to the tax authorities in situations where the exception is applied in accounting for a share-based payment transaction (see 13.3 above).

The IASB notes in paragraph BC255J of the amended Basis for Conclusions that the exception is designed to alleviate the operational difficulties, and any associated undue cost, encountered by entities when they are required, under the requirements of IFRS 2, to divide a share-based payment transaction into an equity-settled element and a cash-settled element (see 14.3 above).

However, at the same time, the IASB made it very clear during its discussions that the amendment only addresses the narrow situation where the net settlement arrangement is designed to meet an entity's obligation under tax laws or regulations to withhold a certain amount to meet the counterparty's tax obligation associated with the share-based payment and transfer the amount in cash to the taxation authorities. This point is incorporated into the final amendments to IFRS 2 with the addition of the following guidance in paragraph 33H(a):

'The exception in paragraph 33F does not apply to:

(a) a share-based payment arrangement with a net settlement feature for which there is no obligation on the entity under tax laws or regulations to withhold an amount for an employee's tax obligation associated with that share-based payment; [...]'.

Other types of arrangement that are commonly seen in practice might appear similar in substance to the legal or regulatory obligation covered by the amendment. For example, the terms of a share-based payment arrangement might require the counterparty to forfeit sufficient shares to meet the tax liability or the counterparty might have some choice over whether or not shares are withheld and/or directly sold in order to raise cash to settle the tax liability (as discussed at 14.3 above). However, unless the arrangements for net settlement are put in place to meet the entity's obligation under tax laws or regulations as described above, the exception introduced by the amendment will not apply as the extract above makes clear. Therefore careful analysis of such arrangements will continue to be required to determine whether part of the award should be treated as cash-settled or whether it is appropriate to apply the exception and treat the entire arrangement as equity-settled.

Example 32.58: Share-based payment transactions with a net settlement feature for withholding tax obligations (application of June 2016 amendment)

On 1 January 2018 an entity grants an award of 100 shares to an employee. The award is conditional upon the completion of four years' service which the employee is expected to achieve.

The employee's tax obligation of 40% is based on the fair value of the shares at vesting date. Tax law in the entity's jurisdiction requires the entity to withhold an amount for an employee's tax obligation associated with a share-based payment and transfer that amount in cash to the tax authority on behalf of the employee.

The terms and conditions of the share-based payment arrangement require the entity to withhold shares from the settlement of the award to the employee in order to settle the employee's tax obligation. Accordingly, the entity settles the transaction on a net basis by withholding the number of shares with a fair value equal to the monetary value of the employee's tax obligation and issuing the remaining shares to the employee at the end of the vesting period.

The fair value at grant date is £2 per share and at 31 December 2021 £10 per share.

The fair value of the shares on the vesting date is £1,000 (100 × £10) and therefore the employee's tax obligation is £400 (100 × £10 × 40%). Accordingly, on the vesting date, the entity issues 60 shares to the employee, withholds 40 shares from the employee and pays £400 (the fair value of the shares withheld) in cash to the tax authority on the employee's behalf. In effect, it is as if the entity issued 100 vested shares to the employee and then repurchased 40 of them at fair value.

Accounting during the vesting period and on recognition and settlement of the tax obligation

Over the four-year vesting period, the entity recognises a cumulative IFRS 2 expense of £200 (£50 per annum) with a corresponding credit to equity. This is calculated as 100 shares × £2 grant date fair value.

	£	£
Employee costs	200	
Equity		200

At the date of vesting the tax liability is recognised and subsequently paid:

	£	£
Equity	400	
Tax liability		400
Tax liability	400	
Cash		400

The example in the implementation guidance also notes that the entity should consider disclosing at each reporting date an estimate of the expected tax payment (see 13.3 above).

15 OTHER PRACTICAL ISSUES

We discuss below the following aspects of the practical application of IFRS 2:

- matching share awards (see 15.1 below);
- loans to employees to purchase shares (limited recourse and full recourse loans) (see 15.2 below);
- awards entitled to dividends during the vesting period (see 15.3 below);
- awards vesting or exercisable on a flotation (or trade sale or other change of control) (see 15.4 below); and
- arrangements under South African black economic empowerment ('BEE') legislation and similar arrangements (see 15.5 below).

15.1 Matching share awards (including deferred bonuses delivered in shares)

As noted in the discussion at 10.1.2 above, the rules in IFRS 2 for awards where there is a choice of equity- or cash-settlement do not fully address awards where the equity and cash alternatives may have significantly different fair values and vesting periods. In some jurisdictions, an increasingly popular type of scheme giving rise to such issues is a matching share award.

Under a matching share award, the starting point is usually that an employee is awarded a bonus for a one year performance period. At the end of that period, the employee may then be either required or permitted to take all or part of that bonus in shares rather than cash. To the extent that the employee takes shares rather than cash, the employing entity may then be required or permitted to make a 'matching' award of an equal number of shares (or a multiple or fraction of that number). The matching award will typically vest over a longer period.

Whilst such schemes can appear superficially similar, the accounting analysis under IFRS 2 may vary significantly, according to whether:

- the employee has a choice, or is required, to take some of the 'base' bonus in shares and whether any such shares have to be retained by the employee in order for the matching shares to vest; and/or
- the employer has a choice, or is required, to match any shares taken by the employee.

Examples 32.59 to 32.63 below set out an analysis of the five basic variants of such schemes, as summarised in the following matrix.

Employee's taking shares required or discretionary?	**Employer's matching required or discretionary?**	**Example**
Required	Required	32.59
Required	Discretionary	32.60
Discretionary	No provision for matching award	32.61
Discretionary	Required	32.62
Discretionary	Discretionary	32.63

A requirement for the employee to retain a base shareholding for the duration of the matching arrangement is a non-vesting condition and this is considered at the end of 15.1 (following Example 32.63).

Example 32.59: Mandatory investment by employee of cash bonus into shares with mandatory matching award by employer

On 1 January 2017 an employee is told that he is to participate in a bonus scheme which will pay £1,000 if certain performance criteria are met for the year ended 31 December 2017 and he remains in service. The bonus will be paid on 1 January 2018. 50% will be paid in cash and the employee will be required to invest the remaining 50% in as many shares as are worth £500 at 1 January 2018. Thus, if the share price were £2.50, the employee would receive £500 cash and 200 shares. These shares are fully vested.

If this first award is achieved, the entity is required to award an equal number of additional shares ('matching shares') – in this example 200 shares – conditional upon the employee remaining in service until 31 December 2019. The award of any matching shares will be made on 1 January 2018.

Annual bonus

The 50% of the bonus paid in cash is outside the scope of IFRS 2 and within that of IAS 19 (see Chapter 33). The 50% of the annual bonus settled in shares is an equity-settled share-based payment transaction within the scope of IFRS 2, since there is no discretion over the manner of settlement. The measurement date for this element of the bonus is 1 January 2017 and the vesting period is the year ended 31 December 2017, since all vesting conditions have been met as at that date. Notwithstanding that the two legs of the award strictly fall within the scope of two different standards, the practical effect will be to charge an expense over the year ended 31 December 2017.

Matching shares

The terms of the award of 200 matching shares have the effect that the entity has committed, as at 1 January 2017, to award shares with a value of £500 as at 1 January 2018, subject to satisfaction of:

- a performance condition relating to the year ended 31 December 2017; and
- a service condition relating to the three years ended 31 December 2019.

Those terms are understood by all parties at 1 January 2017, which is therefore the measurement date. The fact that the matching award is not formally made until 1 January 2018 is not relevant, since there has been a binding commitment to make the award, on terms understood both by the entity and the employee, since 1 January 2017 (see 5.3 above).

The vesting period is the three years ended 31 December 2019. As at 31 December 2017 only one of the vesting conditions (i.e. the performance condition) has been met. The further vesting condition (i.e. the service condition) is not met until 31 December 2019.

The discussion in 8.10 above is relevant to the valuation of the equity elements of the award.

Example 32.60: Mandatory investment by employee of cash bonus into shares with discretionary matching award by employer

On 1 January 2017 an employee is told that he is to participate in a bonus scheme which will pay £1,000 if certain performance criteria are met for the year ended 31 December 2017. The bonus will be paid on 1 January 2018. 50% will be paid in cash and the employee will be required to invest the remaining 50% in as many shares as are worth £500 at 1 January 2018. Thus, if the share price were £2.50, the employee would receive £500 cash and 200 shares. These shares are fully vested.

If this first award is achieved, the entity has the discretion, but not the obligation, to award an equal number of additional shares ('matching shares') – in this case 200 shares – conditional upon the employee remaining in service until 31 December 2019. The award of any matching shares will be made on 1 January 2018.

Annual bonus

The 50% of the bonus paid in cash is outside the scope of IFRS 2 and within that of IAS 19 (see Chapter 33). The 50% of the annual bonus settled in shares is an equity-settled share-based payment transaction within the scope of IFRS 2, since there is no discretion over the manner of settlement. The measurement date for this element of the bonus is 1 January 2017 and the vesting period is the year ended 31 December 2017, since all vesting conditions have been met as at that date. Notwithstanding that the two legs of the award strictly fall within the scope of two different standards, the practical effect will be to charge an expense over the year ended 31 December 2017.

Matching shares

In our view, it is necessary to consider whether the entity's discretion is real or not, this being a matter for judgement in the light of individual facts and circumstances.

In some cases the entity's discretion to make awards may be more apparent than real. For example, the awards may simply be documented as 'discretionary' for tax and other reasons. It may also be that the entity has consistently made matching awards to all eligible employees (or all members of a particular class of eligible employees), so that it has no realistic alternative but to make matching awards if it wants to maintain good staff relations. In such cases, it may be helpful to consider what the accounting for the 'matching' award would be if it were a pure cash award falling within the scope of IAS 19:

> 'An entity may have no legal obligation to pay a bonus. Nevertheless, in some cases, an entity has a practice of paying bonuses. In such cases, the entity has a constructive obligation because the entity has no realistic alternative but to pay the bonus. The measurement of the constructive obligation reflects the possibility that some employees may leave without receiving a bonus.' *[IAS 19.21]*.

This is discussed further in Chapter 33 at 12.3.

In making the determination of whether a constructive obligation would exist under IAS 19, it would be necessary to consider past data (e.g. the percentage of employees who have received matching awards having received the original award).

If it is concluded that the entity does not have a constructive obligation to make a matching award, the accounting treatment would follow the legal form of the transaction. On this view, the grant date (and therefore measurement date) would be 1 January 2018, and the vesting period two years from 1 January 2018 to 31 December 2019.

If it is concluded that the entity does have a constructive obligation to make a matching award, the effect is that the matching award of shares is equivalent to the mandatory matching award in Example 32.59 above, and should therefore be accounted for in the same way – i.e. the measurement date is 1 January 2017 and the vesting period is the three years ended 31 December 2019.

The discussion in 8.10 above is relevant to the valuation of the matching equity award.

Example 32.61: Discretionary investment by employee of cash bonus into shares with no matching award

On 1 January 2017 an employee is told that he is to participate in a bonus scheme which will pay £1,000 if certain performance criteria are met for the year ended 31 December 2017. The bonus will be paid on 1 January 2018. 50% will be paid in cash and the employee will be permitted, but not required, to invest the remaining 50% in as many shares as are worth £500 at 1 January 2018. Thus, if the share price were £2.50, the employee could choose to receive either (a) £1,000 or (b) £500 cash and 200 shares. Any shares received are fully vested.

The 50% of the bonus automatically paid in cash is outside the scope of IFRS 2 and within that of IAS 19 (see Chapter 33).

The 50% of the bonus that may be invested in shares falls within the scope of IFRS 2 as a share-based payment transaction in which the terms of the arrangement provide the counterparty with the choice of settlement. This is the case even though the value of the alternative award is always £500 and does not depend on the share price (see 10.4 above).

The measurement date of the award is 1 January 2017 and the vesting period is the year ended 31 December 2017. The methodology set out in IFRS 2 for awards where the counterparty has a choice of settlement would lead to recognition over the vesting period of a liability component of £500 and an equity component of zero (see 10.1.2 above). If in fact the employee took shares at vesting, the £500 liability would be transferred to equity.

Example 32.62: Discretionary investment by employee of cash bonus into shares with mandatory matching award by employer

On 1 January 2017 an employee is told that he is to participate in a bonus scheme which will pay £1,000 if certain performance criteria are met for the year ended 31 December 2017. The bonus will be paid on 1 January 2018. 50% will be paid in cash and the employee will be permitted, but not required, to invest the remaining 50% in as many shares as are worth £500 at 1 January 2018. Thus, if the share price were £2.50, the employee could choose to receive either (a) £1,000 or (b) £500 cash and 200 shares.

If the employee elects to reinvest the bonus in shares, the shares are not fully vested unless the employee remains in service until 31 December 2019. However, if the employee elects to receive 50% of the bonus in shares, the entity is required to award an equal number of additional shares ('matching shares'), in this case 200 shares, also conditional upon the employee remaining in service until 31 December 2019. The award of any matching shares will be made on 1 January 2018.

The 50% of the bonus automatically paid in cash is outside the scope of IFRS 2 and within that of IAS 19 (see Chapter 33).

The 50% of the bonus that may be invested in shares falls within the scope of IFRS 2 as a share-based payment transaction in which the terms of the arrangement provide the counterparty with the choice of settlement. This is the case even though the value of the alternative award is always £500 and does not depend on the share price (see 10.4 above).

The mandatory nature of the matching shares means that the award is a share-based payment transaction, entered into on (and therefore measured as at) 1 January 2017, in which the terms of the arrangement provide the counterparty with a choice of settlement between:

- at 1 January 2018: cash of £500, subject to performance in the year ended 31 December 2017; or
- at 31 December 2019: shares with a value of £1,000 as at 1 January 2018, subject to:
  - (i) performance in the year ended 31 December 2017; and
  - (ii) service during the three years ended 31 December 2019.

The equity component as calculated in accordance with IFRS 2 will have a value in excess of zero (see 10.1.2 above). The measurement date of the equity component is 1 January 2017. However, as discussed at 10.1.3.A above, IFRS 2 does not specify how to deal with a transaction where the counterparty has the choice of equity- or cash-settlement but the liability and equity components have different vesting periods. In our view it is appropriate to recognise the liability and equity components independently over their different vesting periods, i.e. in this case:

- for the liability component (i.e. the fair value of the cash alternative), the year ended 31 December 2017;
- for the equity component (i.e. the excess of the total fair value of the award over the fair value of the cash alternative), the three years ended 31 December 2019.

Thus, at the end of the year ended 31 December 2017, the entity will have recorded an IFRS 2 expense together with a corresponding:

- liability for the cost of the portion of the annual award that the employee may take in cash or equity (the liability component referred to above);
- credit to equity, for one-third of the cost of the matching award (the equity component referred to above).

If the employee decides to take shares, the entity would simply transfer the amount recorded as a liability to equity and recognise the remaining cost of the matching shares over the following two years.

If, however, the employee elects to take cash, the position is more complicated. Clearly, the main accounting entry is to reduce the liability, with a corresponding reduction in cash, when the liability is settled. However, this raises the question of what is to be done with the one-third cost of the matching award already recognised in equity and the remaining, as yet unrecognised, two-thirds cost.

An election by the employee for cash at the end of 2017 should be treated as a cancellation of the matching award, due to the employee's failure to fulfil a non-vesting condition (i.e. not taking the cash alternative) for the matching award – see 3.2 and 6.4 above. Therefore the one-third cost that had already been expensed would not be reversed and the remaining two-thirds of the matching award not yet recognised would be recognised immediately, resulting in an expense for an award that does not actually crystallise.

The analysis above assumes that the equity award either vests or is cancelled because the employee decides to take the cash award. An alternative outcome would be that the employee chooses the equity-settled award but then fails to meet the three year service condition attached to that award. This would result in forfeiture of the equity-settled award and the reversal of any expense previously recognised for the equity component. However, this raises a question about the treatment of the amount for the cash component that was credited to equity when the employee chose the equity award rather than the cash award. In our view, there are two alternative approaches:

- The employee's decision to invest 50% of the bonus into the share award is similar to the employee making a non-refundable deposit for the shares and so it is appropriate to leave this amount in equity and not reverse it through profit or loss as part of the forfeiture accounting for the equity award.
- The reclassification of £500 from liability to equity is part of the consideration for the forfeited equity instruments and relates to past service rendered in connection with the equity component of the award and so it is appropriate to reverse this amount through profit or loss as part of the forfeiture.

In our view, either approach is acceptable but should be applied consistently.

Example 32.63: Discretionary investment by employee of cash bonus into shares with discretionary matching award by employer

On 1 January 2017 an employee is told that he is to participate in a bonus scheme which will pay £1,000 if certain performance criteria are met for the year ended 31 December 2017. The bonus will be paid on 1 January 2018. 50% will be paid in cash and the employee will be permitted, but not required, to invest the remaining 50% in as many shares as are worth £500. Thus, if the share price were £2.50, the employee could choose to receive either (a) £1,000 or (b) £500 cash and 200 shares. Any shares received under this part of the arrangement are fully vested.

If the employee elects to receive shares, the entity has the discretion, but not the obligation, to award additional shares ('matching shares') – in this case 200 shares – conditional upon the employee remaining in service until 31 December 2019. The award of any matching shares will be made on 1 January 2018.

The 50% of the bonus automatically paid in cash is outside the scope of IFRS 2 and within that of IAS 19 (see Chapter 33).

The 50% of the bonus that may be invested in shares falls within the scope of IFRS 2 as a share-based payment transaction in which the terms of the arrangement provide the counterparty with the choice of settlement. This is the case even though the value of the alternative award is always £500 and does not depend on the share price (see 10.4 above).

It is in our view necessary, as discussed in Example 32.60 above, to consider whether the entity's discretion to make an award of matching shares is real or not, this being a matter for judgement in the light of individual facts and circumstances.

If it is determined that the entity is effectively obliged to match any share award taken by the employee, then the award should be analysed as giving the employee the choice of settlement between:

- at 1 January 2018: cash of £500, subject to performance in the year ended 31 December 2017; or
- at 1 January 2018 shares with a value of £500 at 1 January 2018 subject to performance in the year ended 31 December 2017; and, at 31 December 2019: the same number of shares again subject to (i) performance in the year ended 31 December 2017 and (ii) service during the three years ended 31 December 2019.

In this case the grant date (and therefore measurement date) of all the equity awards would be taken as 1 January 2017. As regards the award due to vest on 1 January 2018, this would be split into its equity and liability components, and in this case the equity component would have a value of zero (since the two components are essentially worth the same amount of £500). Thus the entity would accrue a liability over the year to 31 December 2017. The matching share award would be expensed over the three years ending on 31 December 2019.

Thus, at the end of the year ended 31 December 2017, the entity will have recorded an IFRS 2 expense together with a corresponding:

- liability for the cost of the portion of the annual award that the employee may take in cash or equity (the liability component); and
- credit to equity for one-third of the cost of the matching award (the equity component).

If the employee decides to take shares at 1 January 2018, the entity would simply transfer the amount recorded as a liability to equity and recognise the remaining cost of the matching shares over the following two years.

If, however, the employee elects to take cash, the position is more complicated. Clearly, the main accounting entry is to reduce the liability, with a corresponding reduction in cash, when the liability is settled. However, this raises the question of what is to be done with the one-third cost of the matching award already recognised in equity and the remaining, as yet unrecognised, two-thirds cost.

As in Example 32.62 above, an election by the employee for cash at the end of 2017 should be treated as a cancellation of the matching award, due to the employee's failure to fulfil a non-vesting condition (i.e. not taking the cash alternative) for the matching award – see 3.2 and 6.4 above. Therefore the one-third cost that had already been expensed would not be reversed and the remaining two-thirds of the matching award not yet recognised would be recognised immediately, resulting in an expense for an award that does not actually crystallise.

If it is concluded that the entity has genuine discretion to make a matching award, the analysis is somewhat different.

The portion of the annual award that may be taken in shares should be analysed as giving the employee the choice, at 1 January 2018, between cash of £500 and shares worth £500 (the number of shares being determined by reference to the share price at that date). This would be split into its equity and liability components, and in this case the equity component would have a value of zero (since the two components are essentially worth the same). Thus the entity would accrue a liability over the year to 31 December 2017. If the employee elected to receive shares, this liability would be transferred to equity.

Any matching share award would be treated as being granted on, and measured as at, 1 January 2018. The cost would be recognised over the two years ended 31 December 2019.

The discussion in 8.10 above is relevant to the valuation of the matching equity award.

Example 32.62 above discusses the accounting treatment in a situation where the employee fails to meet the service condition.

If, as is often the case in practice, the employee had to retain his original holding of shares and complete a further period of service in order for the matching award to vest, the requirement to retain the original shares would be treated as a non-vesting condition and taken into account in the grant date fair value of the matching award (see 6.4 above). Failure to meet this non-vesting condition, by disposing of the shares whilst remaining in employment during the matching period, would be treated as a cancellation of the matching award as holding the shares is a condition within the employee's control (see 6.4.3 above).

15.2 Loans to employees to purchase shares (limited recourse and full recourse loans)

In some jurisdictions, share awards to employees are made by means of so-called 'limited recourse loan' schemes. The detailed terms of such schemes vary, but typical features include the following:

- the entity makes an interest-free loan to the employee which is immediately used to acquire shares to the value of the loan on behalf of the employee;
- the shares may be held by the entity, or a trust controlled by it (see 12.3 above), until the loan is repaid;
- the employee is entitled to dividends, except that these are treated as paying off some of the outstanding loan;
- within a given period (say, five years) the employee must either have paid off the outstanding balance of the loan, at which point the shares are delivered to the employee, or surrendered the shares. Surrender of the shares by the employee is treated as discharging any outstanding amount on the loan, irrespective of the value of the shares.

The effect of such an arrangement is equivalent to an option exercisable within five years with a strike price per share equal to the share price at grant date less total dividends since grant date – a view reinforced by the Interpretations Committee.[38] There is no real loan at the initial stage. The entity has no right to receive cash or another financial asset, since the loan can be settled by the employee returning the (fixed) amount of equity 'purchased' at grant date.

Indeed, the only true cash flow in the entire transaction is any amount paid at the final stage if the employee chooses to acquire the shares at that point. The fact that the strike price is a factor of the share price at grant date and dividends paid between grant date and the date of repayment of the 'loan' is simply an issue for the valuation of the option.

The arrangement is valued using an option-pricing model and the fair value is based on the employee's implicit right to buy the shares at a future date rather than being the share price at grant date (the face value of the loan).

The loan arrangement might have a defined period during which the employee must remain in service (five years in the example above) and during which there might also be performance conditions to be met. Where this is the case, the IFRS 2 expense will be recognised by the entity over this period. However, where, as is frequently the case, such an award is subject to no future service or performance condition, i.e. the 'option' is, in effect, immediately exercisable by the employee should he choose to settle the 'loan', IFRS 2 requires the cost to be recognised in full at grant date (see 6.1 above).

There are also some arrangements where the loan to the employee to acquire the shares is a full recourse loan (i.e. it cannot be discharged simply by surrendering the shares and there can be recourse to other assets of the employee). However, the amount repayable on the loan is reduced not only by dividends paid on the shares, but also by the achievement of performance targets, such as the achievement of a given level of earnings.

The appropriate analysis of such awards is more difficult, as they could be viewed in two ways:

- either the employer has made a loan (which the employee has chosen to use to buy a share), accounted for under IAS 39, and has then entered into a performance-related cash bonus arrangement with the employee, accounted for under IAS 19; or
- the transaction is a share option where the strike price varies according to the satisfaction of performance conditions and the amount of dividends on the shares, accounted for under IFRS 2.

The different analyses give rise to potentially significantly different expenses. This will particularly be the case where one of the conditions for mitigation of the amount repayable on the loan is linked to the price of the employer's equity. As this is a market condition, the effect of accounting for the arrangement under IFRS 2 may be that an expense is recognised in circumstances where no expense would be recognised under IAS 19.

Such awards need to be carefully analysed, in the light of their particular facts and circumstances, in order to determine the appropriate treatment. Factors that could suggest that IFRS 2 is the more relevant standard would, in our view, include:

- the employee can use the loan only to acquire shares;
- the employee cannot trade the shares until the loan is discharged; or
- the entity has a practice of accepting (e.g. from leavers) surrender of the shares as full discharge for the amount outstanding on the loan and does not pursue any shortfall between the fair value of the shares and the amount owed by the employee. This would tend to indicate that, in substance, the loan is not truly full recourse.

15.3 Awards entitled to dividends during the vesting period

Some awards entitle the holder to receive dividends on unvested shares (or dividend equivalents on options) during the vesting period.

For example, in some jurisdictions, entities make awards of shares that are regarded as fully vested for the purposes of tax legislation (typically because the employee enjoys the full voting and dividend rights of the shares), but not for accounting purposes (typically because the shares are subject to forfeiture if a certain minimum service period is not achieved). In practice, the shares concerned are often held by an EBT until the potential forfeiture period has expired.

Another variant of such an award that is sometimes seen is where an entity grants an employee an option to acquire shares in the entity which can be exercised immediately. However, if the employee exercises the option but leaves within a certain minimum period from the grant date, he is required to sell back the share to the entity (typically either at the original exercise price, or the lower of that price or the market value of the share at the time of the buy-back – see also the discussions at 15.4.5 below).

Such awards do not fully vest for the purposes of IFRS 2 until the potential forfeiture or buy-back period has expired. The cost of such awards should therefore be recognised over this period.

This raises the question of the accounting treatment of any dividends paid to employees during the vesting period. Conceptually, it could be argued that such dividends cannot be dividends for financial reporting purposes since the equity instruments to which they relate are not yet regarded as issued for financial reporting purposes (and would be excluded from the number of shares in issue for the purposes of IAS 33). This would lead to the conclusion that dividends paid in the vesting period should be charged to profit or loss as an employment cost.

However, the charge to be made for the award under IFRS 2 will already take account of the fact that the recipient is entitled to receive dividends during the vesting period. If the recipient is not entitled to receive dividends during the vesting period a discount would be reflected in the fair value of the award; if the recipient is entitled to dividends, no such adjustment is made (see 8.5.4 above). Thus, it could be argued that also to charge profit or loss with the dividends paid is a form of double counting. Moreover, whilst the relevant shares may not have been fully issued for financial reporting purposes, the basic IFRS 2 accounting does build up an amount in equity over the vesting period. It could therefore be argued that – conceptually, if not legally – any dividend paid relates not to an issued share, but rather to the equity instrument represented by the cumulative amount that has been recorded for the award as a credit to equity, and can therefore appropriately be shown as a deduction from equity.

However, this argument is valid only to the extent that the credit to equity represents awards that are expected to vest. It cannot apply to dividends paid to employees whose awards are either known not to have vested or treated as expected not to vest when applying IFRS 2 (since there is no credit to equity for these awards). Accordingly, we believe that the most appropriate approach is to analyse the dividends paid so that, by the date of vesting, cumulative dividends paid on awards treated by IFRS 2 as vested are deducted from equity and those paid on awards treated by IFRS 2 as unvested are charged to profit or loss. The allocation for periods prior to vesting should be based on a best estimate of the final outcome, as illustrated by Example 32.64 below.

Example 32.64: Award with rights to receive (and retain) dividends during vesting period

An entity grants 100 free shares to each of its 500 employees. The shares are treated as fully vested for legal and tax purposes, so that the employees are eligible to receive any dividends paid. However, the shares will be forfeited if the employee leaves within three years of the award being made. Accordingly, for the purposes of IFRS 2, vesting is conditional upon the employee working for the entity over the next three years. The entity estimates that the fair value of each share (including the right to receive dividends during the IFRS 2 vesting period) is €15. Employees are entitled to retain any dividend received even if the award does not vest.

20 employees leave during the first year, and the entity's best estimate at the end of year 1 is that 75 employees will have left before the end of the vesting period. During the second year, a further 22 employees leave, and the entity revises its estimate of total employee departures over the vesting period from 75 to 60. During the third year, a further 15 employees leave. Hence, a total of 57 employees (20 + 22 + 15) forfeit their rights to the shares during the three year period, and a total of 44,300 shares (443 employees × 100 shares per employee) finally vest.

The entity pays dividends of €1 per share in year 1, €1.20 per share in year 2, and €1.50 in year 3.

Under IFRS 2, the entity will recognise the following amounts during the vesting period for services received as consideration for the shares.

Year	Calculation of cumulative expense	Cumulative expense (€)	Expense for period (€)
1	100 shares × 425 employees × €15 × 1/3	212,500	212,500
2	100 shares × 440 employees × €15 × 2/3	440,000	227,500
3	100 shares × 443 × €15 × 3/3	664,500	224,500

On the assumption that all employees who leave during a period do so on the last day of that period (and thus receive dividends paid in that period), in our view the dividends paid on the shares should be accounted for as follows:

		€	€
Year 1	Profit or loss (employee costs)[1]	7,500	
	Equity[1]	42,500	
	Cash[2]		50,000
Year 2	Profit or loss (employee costs)[3]	3,300	
	Equity[3]	54,300	
	Cash[4]		57,600
Year 3	Profit or loss (employee costs)[5]	1,590	
	Equity[5]	67,110	
	Cash[6]		68,700

1 20 employees have left and a further 55 are anticipated to leave. Dividends paid to those employees (100 shares × 75 employees × €1 = €7,500) are therefore recognised as an expense. Dividends paid to other employees are recognised as a reduction in equity.

2 100 shares × 500 employees × €1.

3 22 further employees have left and a further 18 are anticipated to leave. The cumulative expense for dividends paid to leavers and anticipated leavers should therefore be €10,800 (100 shares × 20 employees × €1 = €2,000 for leavers in year 1 + 100 shares × 40 employees × [€1 + €1.20] for leavers and anticipated leavers in year 2 = €8,800). €7,500 was charged in year 1, so the charge for year 2 should be €10,800 – €7,500 = €3,300. This could also have been calculated as charge for leavers and expected leavers in current year €4,800 (100 shares × 40 [22 + 18] employees × €1.20) less reversal of expense in year 1 for reduction in anticipated final number of leavers €1,500 (100 shares × 15 [75 – 60] employees × €1.00). Dividends paid to other employees are recognised as a reduction in equity.

4 100 shares × 480 employees in employment at start of year × €1.20.

5 15 further employees have left. The cumulative expense for dividends paid to leavers should therefore be €12,390 (€2,000 for leavers in year 1 (see 3 above) + 100 shares × 22 employees × [€1 + €1.20] = €4,840 for leavers in year 2 + 100 shares × 15 employees × [€1 + €1.20 + €1.50] = €5,550 for leavers in year 3). A cumulative expense of €10,800 (see 3 above) was recognised by the end of year 2, so the charge for year 3 should be €12,390 – €10,800 = €1,590. This could also have been calculated as charge for leavers in current year €2,250 (100 shares × 15 employees × €1.50) less reversal of expense in years 1 and 2 for reduction in final number of leavers as against estimate at end of year 2 €660 (100 shares × 3 [60 – 57] employees × [€1.00 + €1.20]). Dividends paid to other employees are recognised as a reduction in equity.

6 100 shares × 458 employees in employment at start of year × €1.50.

15.4 Awards vesting or exercisable on an exit event or change of control (flotation, trade sale etc.)

Entities frequently issue awards connected to a significant event such as a flotation, trade sale or other change of control of the business. It may be that an award that would otherwise be equity-settled automatically becomes cash-settled if such an event crystallises (as discussed at 10.3 above).

However, it may also be the case that an award vests only on such an event, which raises various issues of interpretation, as discussed below.

The sections below should be read together with the more general discussions elsewhere in this chapter (as referred to in the narrative below) on grant date, vesting period and vesting and non-vesting conditions. References to flotation should be read as also including other exit events.

15.4.1 Grant date

Sometimes such awards are structured so that they will vest on flotation or so that they will vest on flotation subject to further approval at that time. For awards in the first category, grant date as defined in IFRS 2 will be the date on which the award is first communicated to employees (subject to the normal requirements of IFRS 2 relating to a shared understanding, offer and acceptance, as discussed at 5.3 above). For awards in the second category, grant date will be at or around the date of flotation, when the required further approval is given.

This means that the IFRS 2 cost of awards subject to final approval at flotation will generally be significantly higher than that of awards that do not require such approval. Moreover, as discussed further at 5.3.2 above, it may well be the case that employees begin rendering service for such awards before grant date (e.g. from the date on which the entity communicates its intention to make the award in principle). In that case, the entity would need to make an initial estimate of the value of the award for the purpose of recognising an expense from the date services have been provided, and continually re-assess that value up until the actual IFRS 2 grant date. As with any award dependent on a non-market vesting condition, an expense would be recognised only to the extent that the award is considered likely to vest. The classification of a requirement to float as a non-market vesting condition is discussed further at 15.4.3 below.

15.4.2 Vesting period

Many awards that vest on flotation have a time limit – in other words, the award lapses if flotation has not occurred on or before a given future date. In principle, as discussed at 6.2.3 above, when an award has a variable vesting period due to a non-market performance condition, the reporting entity should make a best estimate of the likely vesting period at each reporting date and calculate the IFRS 2 charge on the basis of that best estimate.

In practice, the likely timing of a future flotation is notoriously difficult to assess months, let alone years, in advance. In such cases, it would generally be acceptable simply to recognise the cost over the full potential vesting period until there is real clarity that a shorter period may be more appropriate. However, in making the assessment of the likelihood of vesting, it is important to take the company's circumstances into account. The likelihood of an exit event in the short- to medium-term is perhaps greater for a company owned by private equity investors seeking a return on their investment than for a long-established family-owned company considering a flotation.

It is worth noting that once an exit event becomes likely, the IFRS 2 expense will in some cases need to be recognised over a shorter vesting period than was originally envisaged as the probability of the exit event occurring will form the basis at the reporting date of the estimate of the number of awards expected to vest (see also the discussion at 6.2.3 and 7.6 above).

This contrasts with the US GAAP approach where, in practice, an exit event that is a change in control or an initial public offering is only recognised when it occurs. In a situation where a change in control or an initial public offering occurs shortly after the reporting date, it is therefore possible that the expense will need to be recognised in an earlier period under IFRS than under US GAAP.

15.4.3 Is flotation or sale a vesting condition or a non-vesting condition?

There was debate in the past about whether a requirement for a flotation or sale to occur in order for an award to vest was a vesting condition or a non-vesting condition. The argument for it being a non-vesting condition was that flotation or sale may occur irrespective of the performance of the entity. The counter-argument was essentially that the price achieved on flotation or sale, which typically affects the ultimate value of the award (see 15.4.4 below), reflects the performance of the entity and is therefore a non-market performance condition (provided there is an associated service condition – see further below).

As part of its wider project on vesting and non-vesting conditions, the Interpretations Committee reached a tentative decision in July 2010 that a condition requiring an initial public offering (IPO) or a change of control should be deemed to be a performance vesting condition rather than a non-vesting condition. This was subsequently reflected in general terms through the IASB's amendments to the definition of a performance condition in the *Annual Improvements to IFRSs 2010-2012 Cycle* (see 3.1 and 3.2 above). The amendments were intended, *inter alia*, to make clear that a requirement for flotation or sale (with an associated service condition) is a performance condition rather than a non-vesting condition on the basis that the flotation or sale condition is by reference to the entity's own operations.

The amendments also make it clear that a performance target period cannot extend beyond the end of the associated service period in order for the definition of a performance vesting condition to be met (see 3.2.2 above). Therefore, the flotation or sale condition will be treated as a non-vesting condition, rather than as a vesting condition, if the service period is not at least as long as the duration of the flotation or sale condition.

Even though the condition is deemed to relate to the entity's own operations and therefore generally classified as a performance condition, it will sometimes be concluded that fulfilment of the condition is outside the control of both the entity and the counterparty. The settlement of an award in equity or cash might depend on the outcome of the condition i.e. there might be either cash- or equity-settlement that is entirely contingent on the exit event. Such contingent arrangements are discussed at 10.3 above.

15.4.4 Awards requiring achievement of a minimum price on flotation or sale

Some awards with a condition dependent on flotation (or another similar event) vest only if a minimum price per share is achieved. For example, an entity might grant all its employees share options, the vesting of which is conditional upon a flotation or sale of the shares at a price of at least €5 per share within five years, and the employee still being in employment at the time of the flotation or sale.

Taken alone, the requirement for a flotation or sale to occur is a non-market performance condition (see further below and at 15.4.3 above). However, if a minimum market price has to be achieved, the question arises as to whether, in addition to the service requirement, such an award comprises:

- a single market performance condition (i.e. float or sell within five years at a share price of at least €5); or
- two conditions:
  - a market performance condition (share price at time of flotation or sale of at least €5); and
  - a non-market performance condition (flotation or sale achieved within five years).

The significance of this is the issue discussed at 6.3 above, namely that an expense must always be recognised for all awards with a market condition, if *all* the non-market vesting conditions are satisfied, even if the market condition is not. In either case, however, there is a market condition which needs to be factored into the valuation of the award.

If the view is that 'flotation or sale at €5 within five years' is a single market condition, the entity will recognise an expense for the award for all employees still in service at the end of the five year period, since the sole non-market vesting condition (i.e. service) will have been met. Note that this assumes that the full five-year period is considered the most likely vesting period at grant date (see 6.3.4 and 15.4.2 above).

If, on the other hand, the view is that 'flotation or sale within five years' and 'flotation or sale share price €5' are two separate conditions, and no flotation or sale occurs, no expense will be recognised since the performance element of the non-market vesting condition (i.e. 'flotation or sale within five years') has not been satisfied. However, even on this second analysis, if a sale or flotation is achieved at a price less than €5, an expense must be recognised, even though the award does not truly vest, since the non-market condition (i.e. 'flotation or sale within five years' with its associated service requirement) will have been met.

In our view, the appropriate analysis is to regard 'flotation or sale within five years' and 'flotation or sale share price €5' as two separate conditions.

The example above assumes that there is a service condition equal in duration to the other conditions attached to the award and hence the analysis above only considers vesting conditions. If the fact pattern were such that there was no service condition, or a service condition that was of a shorter duration than the other conditions, then those conditions would need to be treated as non-vesting conditions rather than as performance vesting conditions (see 3.1 and 3.2 above).

15.4.5 Awards 'purchased for fair value'

As noted at 2.2.4.D above, entities that are contemplating a flotation or trade sale may invite employees to subscribe for shares (often a special class of share) for a relatively nominal amount. In the event of a flotation or trade sale occurring, these shares may be sold or will be redeemable at a substantial premium. It is often argued that the initial subscription price paid represents the fair value of the share at the time, given the inherent high uncertainty as to whether a flotation or trade sale will in fact occur.

The premium paid on the shares in the event of a flotation or trade sale will typically be calculated in part by reference to the price achieved. The question therefore arises as to whether such awards fall within the scope of IFRS 2. It might be argued for example that, as the employee paid full fair value for the award at issue, there has been no share-based payment and, accordingly, the instrument should be accounted for under IAS 32 and IAS 39.

In our view, in order to determine whether the arrangement falls within the scope of IFRS 2, it is necessary to consider whether the award has features that would not be expected in 'normal' equity transactions – in particular, a requirement for the holder of the shares to remain in employment until flotation or sale and/or individual buyback arrangements. If this is the case, regardless of the amount subscribed, the terms suggest that the shares are being awarded in connection with, and in return for, employee services and hence that the award is within the scope of IFRS 2. This may mean that, even if the award has no material fair value once the subscription price has been taken into account (and therefore gives rise to no IFRS 2 expense), it may be necessary to make the disclosures required by IFRS 2.

Moreover, even if the amount paid by the employees can be demonstrated to be fair value for tax or other purposes, that amount would not necessarily constitute fair value under IFRS 2. Specifically, a 'true' fair value would take into account non-market vesting conditions (such as a requirement for the employee to remain in employment until flotation or a trade sale occurs). However, a valuation for IFRS 2 purposes would not take such conditions into account (see 5.5 and 6.2.1 above) and would therefore typically be higher than the 'true' fair value.

If the arrangement relates to a special class of share rather than ordinary equity shares, the underlying shares might well be classified as a liability rather than as equity under IAS 32. However, if the redemption amount is linked to the flotation price of the 'real' equity, the arrangement will be a cash-settled share-based payment transaction under IFRS 2 (see 2.2.4.A above).

It is common in such situations for the cost of satisfying any obligations to the special shareholders to be borne by shareholders rather than by the entity itself. This raises a number of further issues, which are discussed at 2.2.2.A above and at 15.4.6 below.

The approach outlined in this section, i.e. that there will generally be no additional IFRS 2 expense to recognise when the counterparty subscribes for a share at fair value, is the approach most commonly applied in practice by entities accounting under IFRS. In this type of arrangement, the subscription price, or market value if lower, is often refundable to employees who leave employment before the shares vest. In such cases, subscription amounts paid by the counterparty for the shares are generally classified as a liability by the entity until such time as the shares finally vest (at which point the cash paid will be treated as the proceeds of issuing shares).

However, this is not the only approach seen in practice. US GAAP, for example, requires in certain circumstances the recognition of an expense (representing the amount potentially at risk) in cases where an employee subscribes for a share at fair value but risks forfeiting some, or all, of the price paid for that share, together with any subsequent increases in value, should he fail to fulfil the service condition. In determining whether an expense must be recognised for the amount risked by the employee, an entity applying US GAAP must establish that there is a clear business purpose for the employee taking such a risk. In our view, in the absence of specific guidance, the recognition of such an expense is not a requirement based on IFRS 2 as currently drafted.

15.4.6 *'Drag along' and 'tag along' rights*

An increasingly common form of award is for the management of an entity to be allowed to acquire a special class of equity at fair value (as in 15.4.5 above), but (in contrast to 15.4.5 above) with no redemption right on an exit event. However, rights are given:

- to any buyer of the 'normal' equity also to buy the special shares (sometimes called a 'drag along' right);
- to a holder of the special shares to require any buyer of the 'normal' equity also to buy the special shares (sometimes called a 'tag along' right).

Such schemes are particularly found in entities where the 'normal' equity is held by a provider of venture capital, which will generally be looking for an exit in the medium term.

It may well be that, under the scheme, the entity itself is required to facilitate the operation of the drag along or tag along rights, which may involve the entity collecting the proceeds from the buyer and passing them on to the holder of the special shares.

This raises the issue of whether such an arrangement is equity-settled or cash-settled. The fact that, in certain circumstances, the entity is required to deliver cash to the holder of a share suggests that the arrangement is an award requiring cash settlement in specific circumstances, the treatment of which is discussed at 10.3 above.

However, if the terms of the award are such that the entity is obliged to pass on cash to the holder of the share only if, and to the extent that, proceeds are received from an external buyer, in our view, the arrangement may be economically no different to the broker settlement arrangements typically entered into by listed entities, as discussed at 9.2.4 above. This could allow the arrangement to be regarded as equity-settled because the entity's only involvement as a principal is in the initial delivery of shares to employees, provided that consideration is given to all the factors (discussed at 9.2.4 above) that could suggest that the scheme is more appropriately regarded as cash-settled.

In making such an assessment, care needs to be taken to ensure that the precise facts of the arrangement are considered. For example, a transaction where the entity has some discretion over the amount of proceeds attributable to each class of shareholder might indicate that it is inappropriate to treat the entity simply as an agent in the cash payment arrangement. It might also be relevant to consider the extent to which, under relevant local law, the proceeds received can be 'ring fenced' so as not to be available to settle other liabilities of the entity.

It is also the case that arrangements that result in employees obtaining similar amounts of cash can be interpreted very differently under IFRS 2 depending on how the arrangement is structured and whether, for example:

- the entity is required to pay its employees cash on an exit (having perhaps held shares itself via a trust and those shares having been subject to 'drag along' rights); or
- the employees themselves have held the right to equity shares on a restricted basis with vesting – and 'drag along' rights – taking effect on a change of control and the employees receiving cash for their shares.

The appropriate accounting treatment in such cases requires a significant amount of judgement based on the precise facts and circumstances.

15.5 South African black economic empowerment ('BEE') and similar arrangements

As part of general economic reforms in South Africa, arrangements – commonly referred to as black economic empowerment or 'BEE' deals – have been put in place to encourage the transfer of equity, or economic interests in equity, to historically disadvantaged individuals. Similar arrangements have also been put in place in other jurisdictions. These arrangements are intended to give disadvantaged individuals, or entities controlled by disadvantaged individuals, a means of meaningful participation in the economy.

An entity can enhance its BEE status in a number of ways (through employment equity, skills development or preferential procurement policies to name but a few). This section focuses on BEE deals involving transfers of equity instruments, or interests in equity instruments, to historically disadvantaged individuals at a discount to fair value.

Such transfers have generally been concluded at a discount to the fair value of the equity instruments concerned, even where the fair value takes into account any restrictions on these equity instruments. As a result of having empowered shareholders, the reporting entity is able to claim its 'BEE credentials', thus allowing the reporting entity greater business opportunities in the South African economy. These arrangements raise a number of practical issues of interpretation, and indeed led to the scope of IFRS 2 being extended to include transactions where the consideration received appears less than the consideration given, as discussed further at 2.2.2.C above.

The goods or services received from the disadvantaged people or entities controlled by them in return for the equity instruments may or may not be specifically identifiable. As explained in guidance issued by the South African Institute of Chartered Accountants (SAICA),[39] it is therefore the case that IFRS 2 applies to the accounting for BEE transactions where the fair value of cash and other assets received is less than the fair value of equity instruments granted to the BEE partner, i.e. to the BEE equity credentials.

BEE deals are typically complex and their specific structures and terms may vary considerably. However, they do exhibit certain features with some regularity, as discussed below.

Typically BEE arrangements have involved the transfer of equity instruments to:

- empowerment companies controlled by prominent BEE qualifying individuals;
- BEE qualifying employees of the reporting entity; or
- beneficiaries in the BEE qualifying communities in which the entity operates.

The arrangements generally lock the parties in for a minimum specified period and if they want to withdraw they are able to sell their interest only to others with qualifying BEE credentials, usually with the lock-in provision also transferred to the buyer.

Generally these individuals have not been able to raise sufficient finance in order to purchase the equity instruments. Accordingly, the reporting entity often facilitates the transaction and assists the BEE party in securing the necessary financing.

A BEE arrangement often involves the creation of a trust or corporate entity, with the BEE party holding beneficial rights in the trust which in turn holds equity instruments of the reporting entity (or a member of its group).

The awards made by the trust may be in the form of:

- the equity instruments originally transferred to the trust;
- units in the trust itself, usually with a value linked in some way to the value of the equity instruments of the reporting entity originally transferred to the trust; or
- payments made from the proceeds (dividends received, sale of equity instruments etc.) that the trust generates.

The accounting issues arising from such schemes include:

- the nature of the trust (specifically, whether it meets the criteria for consolidation by the reporting entity);
- whether any charge arises under IFRS 2 and, if so, the grant date and therefore, under a grant date model, the amount of the charge; and
- whether awards are equity-settled or cash-settled.

15.5.1 Nature of the trust

The first issue to consider in any accounting analysis is whether any trust to which the equity instruments of the reporting entity have been transferred meets the requirements for consolidation by the reporting entity under IFRS 10 (see Chapter 6). Factors that may indicate that the trust should be consolidated include:

- the reporting entity is involved in the design of the trust and the trust deed at inception, the intention being that the design is such that the desired BEE credentials are obtained;
- the potential beneficiaries of the trust are restricted to persons in the employment of, or otherwise providing services to, the reporting entity;
- the reporting entity has a commitment to ensure that the trust operates as designed in order to maintain its BEE credentials;
- the reporting entity has the right to control (on 'autopilot' or otherwise), or does in practice control, the management of the trust; or
- the relevant activities of the trust are to service the loan and to make distributions to the beneficiaries in line with the trust deed,

but all the IFRS 10 control criteria will need to be assessed.

The generic form of a BEE arrangement normally requires the reporting entity either to finance the acquisition of the shares by the trust or to provide cross guarantees to the financiers of the trust. Alternative methodologies that have been employed include capital enhancements created in the trust by the sale of equity instruments at a severely discounted amount.

When the reporting entity finances the arrangement, the finance is generally interest-free or at a lower than market interest rate. The debt is serviced with the dividends received and, at the end of the repayment period, any outstanding balance can be treated in various ways; refinanced or waived by the reporting entity, or settled by the return of a number of shares equal to the outstanding value.

In summary, the BEE party generally injects only a notional amount of capital into the trust, which obtains financing to acquire the shares in the reporting entity and uses the dividend cash flows to service the debt it has raised. In such generic schemes, the BEE party faces a typical option return profile: the maximum amount of capital at risk is notional and the potential upside increase in value of the shares of the reporting entity accrues to the BEE party through the party's beneficial rights in the trust.

15.5.2 Measurement and timing of the accounting cost

If the analysis under 15.5.1 above is that the trust should be consolidated, the transfer of equity instruments to that entity is essentially the same as a transfer of own equity to an employee benefit trust, as discussed at 12.3 above. Such a transfer, considered alone, is an intra-entity transaction and therefore does not give rise to a charge under IFRS 2. The equity instruments held by the trust are therefore treated as treasury shares, and no non-controlling interests are recognised.

It is only when the trust itself makes an award to a third party that a charge arises, which will be measured at the time at which the grant to the third party occurs. In a rising stock market this will lead to a higher charge than would have occurred had there been a grant, as defined in IFRS 2, on the date that the equity instruments were originally transferred to the trust. Generally, the value of the award is based on an option pricing model and the BEE party is treated as the holder of an option.

Where the trust is not consolidated, the presumption will be that the transfer of equity instruments to the trust crystallises an IFRS 2 charge at the date of transfer. However, it is important to consider the terms of the transaction in their totality. For example, if the entity has the right to buy back the equity instruments at some future date, the benefit transferred may in fact be an economic interest in the equity instruments for a limited period. This may, depending on the method used to determine the buy-back price, influence the measurement of any IFRS 2 charge (which would normally be based on the presumption that the benefits of a vested share had been passed in perpetuity).

Some have sought to argue that BEE credentials result in the recognition of an intangible asset rather than an expense. In order to be recognised as an asset, an entity must have control over the resource as a result of a past event. Paragraphs 13 and 16 of IAS 38 – *Intangible Assets* – indicate that control over an intangible asset may be evidenced in two ways:

- as legal rights that are enforceable by law; or
- as exchange transactions for the same or similar non-contractual customer relationships.

In BEE transactions, a contract is usually entered into with a BEE partner. The contract between the entity and the BEE partner may include a contractual lock-in period or a clause that only allows the transfer of such equity instruments to another BEE partner, usually with the lock-in provision also transferred to the buyer. However, the contract does not provide the entity with legal rights that give it the power to obtain the future economic benefits arising from the BEE transaction, nor the ability to restrict the access of others to those benefits. Therefore BEE credentials do not qualify for recognition of intangible assets and the difference between the fair value of the award and the consideration received should be expensed. This is consistent with guidance issued by SAICA.[40]

An issue to be considered in determining the timing of the IFRS 2 expense is that many BEE transactions require the BEE party to be 'locked into' the transaction for a pre-determined period. During this period the BEE party or trust is generally prohibited from selling or transferring the equity instruments. As no specific performance is generally required during this period, it is not considered part of the vesting period (see 3.3 and 6.1 above). Rather, the post-vesting restrictions would be taken into account in calculating the fair value of the equity instruments (see 8.4.1 above). This is illustrated in the following example (based in part on Example 5 in the SAICA guidance).

Example 32.65: Receipt of BEE credentials with no service or performance condition

Entity A grants shares with a fair value of $1,000,000 to a BEE consortium for no consideration. As a result of the BEE ownership entity A obtains BEE credentials. The BEE consortium are entitled to the shares immediately and not required to perform any services to entity A nor are any performance conditions required to be met. However in order to secure the BEE credentials, the consortium may not sell their shares for a period of 7 years from grant date.

In this transaction shares have been issued at a discount to fair value in return for BEE credentials and would fall into the scope of IFRS 2. As there is neither a service nor a performance condition, the fair value of the shares given should be expensed at grant date. The restriction on the transfer of the shares would be treated as a post-vesting restriction and taken into account when estimating the fair value of the equity instruments granted. If the shares in this example were listed, the listed price would not necessarily be the fair value as the fair value would need to be adjusted for the restriction of transfer.

15.5.3 Classification of awards as equity- or cash-settled

Certain schemes, particularly where the reporting entity is not listed, give the BEE party the right to put the shares back to the entity (or another group entity) after a certain date. This is often done to create liquidity for the BEE parties, should they decide to exit the scheme. Such a feature would require the scheme to be classified as cash-settled (see 9.1 above).

Similarly, where the BEE transaction is facilitated through a trust, the trust may have granted awards to beneficiaries in the form of units in the trust. The trustees may have the power to reacquire units from beneficiaries in certain circumstances (e.g. where the beneficiaries are employees, when they leave the employment of the entity). Where the trust does not have sufficient cash with which to make such payments, the reporting entity may be obliged, legally or constructively, to fund them.

Such arrangements may – in their totality – create a cash-settled scheme from the perspective of the reporting entity. In analysing a particular scheme, it should be remembered that, under IFRS 2, cash-settled schemes arise not only from legal liabilities, but also from constructive or commercial liabilities (e.g. to prevent a former employee having rights against what is essentially an employee trust) – see 10.2 above.

Finally, a transaction may be structured in such a way that the trust holds equity instruments of the reporting entity for an indefinite period. Dividends received by the trust may be used to fund certain expenses in a particular community in which the reporting entity operates (e.g. tuition fees for children of the reporting entity's employees or the costs of certain community projects). The scheme may even make provision for the shares to be sold after a certain period with the eventual proceeds being distributed amongst members of the community.

In such a case it is necessary to consider the nature of the distribution requirement and whether or not the reporting entity (through the trust) has a legal or constructive obligation under the scheme to make cash payments based on the price or value of the shares held by the trust. Where there is such an obligation, the arrangement would be classified as a cash-settled scheme. If however the trust merely acts as a conduit through which:

- dividend receipts by the trust are paid out to beneficiaries with the shares never leaving the trust; or
- proceeds from the sale of shares are distributed to beneficiaries,

the precise terms of the arrangement should be assessed to determine whether or not the arrangement meets the definition of a cash-settled share-based payment (see 15.4.6 above for a discussion of similar considerations in the context of 'drag along' and 'tag along' rights).

Any dividend payments by the Group for the period that the trust is consolidated should be treated as an equity distribution or as an expense, as appropriate, in accordance with the principles discussed at 15.3 above.

16 FIRST-TIME ADOPTION AND TRANSITIONAL PROVISIONS

16.1 First-time adoption provisions

The requirements of IFRS 1 – *First-time Adoption of International Financial Reporting Standards* – in relation to share-based payment arrangements are discussed in Chapter 5 at 5.3. However, one provision may remain relevant for entities that have already adopted IFRS and would no longer generally be considered 'first-time adopters'.

IFRS 1 does not require an entity to account for equity-settled transactions:

- granted on or before 7 November 2002; or
- granted after 7 November 2002 but vested before the later of the date of transition to IFRS and 1 January 2005.

However, where such an award is modified, cancelled or settled, the rules regarding modification, cancellation and settlement (see 7 above) apply in full unless the modification occurred before the date of transition to IFRS. *[IFRS 1.D2]*. The intention of this provision is to prevent an entity from avoiding the recognition of a cost for a new award by structuring it as a modification to an earlier award not in the scope of IFRS 2.

There is slight ambiguity on this point in the wording of IFRS 1, paragraph D2 of which refers only to the *modification* of such awards. However, paragraph D2 also requires an entity to apply 'paragraphs 26-29' of IFRS 2 to 'modified' awards. Paragraphs 26-29 deal not only with modification but also with cancellation and settlement, and indeed paragraphs 28 and 29 are not relevant to *modification* at all. This makes it clear, in our view, that the IASB intended IFRS 1 to be applied not only to the modification but also to the cancellation and settlement of such awards.

16.2 Transitional provisions for June 2016 amendments

As noted at 1.2 above, in June 2016 the IASB amended IFRS 2 in three areas:

- treatment of vesting and non-vesting conditions in the measurement of a cash-settled share-based payment (see 9.3.2 above);
- classification of share-based payment transactions with a net settlement feature for withholding tax obligations (see 14.3.1 above); and
- modification of a share-based payment from cash-settled to equity-settled (see 9.4.2.A above).

Paragraph 63D of the amended standard states that the amendments are applicable for accounting periods beginning on or after 1 January 2018 with earlier application permitted provided it is disclosed.

The amendments have detailed transitional provisions. These begin by stating that prior periods should not be restated when an entity first applies the amendments (although an entity may elect to apply them retrospectively subject to certain conditions – see below).

A new paragraph 59A specifies that if an entity does not elect to apply the amendments retrospectively it should apply them as follows:

- the amendment relating to modifications of awards from cash-settled to equity-settled applies only to modifications that occur on or after the date that an entity first applies the amendments;
- the amendment relating to the treatment of vesting and non-vesting conditions in a cash-settled award applies to share-based payment transactions that are unvested at the date that an entity first applies the amendments and to share-based payment transactions with a grant date on or after that date of first application. For unvested share-based payment transactions with a grant date prior to the date of initial application, the entity should remeasure the liability at the date it first applies the amendment. The effect of the remeasurement should be recognised in opening retained earnings, or other component of equity, of the reporting period in which the amendment is first applied;
- the amendment relating to awards with a net settlement feature for withholding tax obligations applies to share-based payment transactions that are unvested (or vested but unexercised) at the date the amendments are first applied and to share-based payment transactions with a grant date on or after that date of first application. For unvested (or vested but unexercised) share-based payment transactions (or components thereof) that were previously classified as cash-settled but are now classified as equity-settled in accordance with the amendments, the carrying value of the liability should be reclassified to equity at the date on which the amendments are first applied.

Notwithstanding the requirements set out above, paragraph 59B states that the amendments may be applied retrospectively, subject to the existing transitional provisions set out in IFRS 2, in accordance with the requirements of IAS 8, if, and only if, it is possible to do so without hindsight. If retrospective application is elected, it must be applied to all three areas covered by the June 2016 amendments.

References

1 *Amendment to International Financial Reporting Standards: IFRS 2 Share-based Payment – Vesting Conditions and Cancellations*, IASB, January 2008 ('January 2008 amendment').
2 *Group Cash-settled Share-based Payment Transactions, Amendments to IFRS 2*, IASB, June 2009 ('June 2009 amendment').
3 *Classification and Measurement of Share-based Payment Transactions, Amendments to IFRS 2*, IASB, June 2016 ('June 2016 amendments').
4 *IASB Update,* May 2015.
5 *IASB Update,* November 2015.
6 Agenda Paper 16, IASB, November 2015.
7 *IASB Update,* May 2016.
8 For convenience, throughout this chapter we refer to the recognition of a cost for share-based payments. In some cases, however, a share-based payment transaction may initially give rise to an asset (e.g. where employee costs are capitalised as part of the cost of PP&E or inventories).
9 *IFRIC Update*, March 2013.
10 *IFRIC Update*, July 2014.
11 Accounting Standards Update 2014-12, FASB, *Accounting for Share-Based Payments When the Terms of an Award Provide That a Performance Target Could Be Achieved after the Requisite Service Period (Topic 718).*
12 *IASB Update*, November 2013.
13 *IFRIC Update*, July 2010 and September 2010.
14 'Contingent feature' is not a defined term in IFRS 2 but is used in the September 2011 IASB Agenda Paper 7D (para. 49) to refer to a condition not currently defined in IFRS 2.
15 *IFRIC Update*, November 2010 and March 2011.
16 *IASB Update*, September 2011.
17 *IASB Update*, May 2016.
18 FASB ASC 718 – *Compensation – Stock Compensation* (formerly FAS123(R), *Share-Based Payment*), FASB, December 2004, [20-55-25].
19 *IASB Update*, September 2011 and IASB Agenda Paper 7D September 2011 para. 57 et seq.
20 *IFRIC Update*, July 2006.
21 *IFRIC Update*, March 2011.
22 More detailed guidance on this may be found in a publication such as Options, Futures, and Other Derivatives, John C. Hull.
23 *Classification and Measurement of Share-based Payment Transactions, Amendments to IFRS 2,* IASB, June 2016.
24 *Classification and Measurement of Share-based Payment Transactions, Amendments to IFRS 2,* IASB, June 2016.
25 FASB Staff Position 123(R)-4, *Classification of Options and Similar Instruments Issued as Employee Compensation That Allow for Cash Settlement upon the Occurrence of a Contingent Event.*
26 FASB ASC 718 – *Compensation – Stock Compensation* (formerly FAS123(R), *Share-Based Payment*), FASB, December 2004, para. 32, footnote 18a.
27 *IASB Update*, September 2011.
28 *IFRIC Update*, May 2013.
29 *IFRIC Update*, September 2013.
30 *IFRIC Update*, September 2013.
31 *IASB Update*, February 2014.
32 *IASB Update*, April 2014.
33 D17 – *IFRS 2 – Group and Treasury Share Transactions*, IASB, 2005, para. IE5.
34 *IFRIC Update*, May 2013.
35 *IFRIC Update*, March 2013.
36 *Classification and Measurement of Share-based Payment Transactions, Amendments to IFRS 2,* IASB, June 2016.
37 *Classification and Measurement of Share-based Payment Transactions, Amendments to IFRS 2,* IASB, June 2016.
38 *IFRIC Update*, November 2005.
39 Financial Reporting Guide 2 – *Accounting for Black Economic Empowerment (BEE) Transactions*, Accounting Practices Committee (APC) of SAICA, December 2012.
40 Financial Reporting Guide 2 – *Accounting for Black Economic Empowerment (BEE) Transactions*, Accounting Practices Committee (APC) of SAICA, December 2012.

References

1 [illegible] International [illegible] Accounting Standard [illegible] IFRS 2 Share-based Payment [illegible] Vesting Conditions and Cancellations, IASB, January 2008 ([illegible] 2008 amendment).
2 Group Cash-settled Share-based Payment Transactions Amendments to IFRS 2, IASB, June 2009 (June 2009 amendment).
3 Classification and Measurement of Share-based Payment Transactions Amendments to IFRS 2, IASB, June 2016 ([illegible] 2016 amendment).
4 IASB Update, May 2013.
5 IASB Update, November 2013.
6 Agenda Paper 4C, IASB, November 2013.
7 IASB Update, May 2016.
8 For convenience, throughout this chapter we refer to the recognition of a cost for share-based payments. In some cases, however, [illegible] share-based payment transaction may initially give rise to an asset (e.g. where employee costs are capitalised as part of the cost of PP&E or inventories).
9 IFRIC Update, March 2011.
10 IFRIC Update, July 2015.
11 Accounting Standards Update 2014-12, FASB: Accounting for Share-Based Payments When the Terms of an Award Provide That a Performance Target Could be Achieved after the Requisite Service Period (Topic 718).
12 IASB Update, November 2015.
13 IFRIC Update, July 2010 and November 2010.
14 'Contingent feature' is not a defined term in IFRS 2 but is used in the September 2011 IASB Agenda Paper 7E [illegible] [illegible] condition not currently defined in IFRS 2.
15 IFRIC Update, November 2010 and [illegible] 2011.
16 IASB Update, September 2014.
17 IASB Update, May 2016.
18 FASB ASC 718 – Compensation – Stock Compensation (formerly FAS 123(R) Share-Based Payment), [illegible] December 2004 [illegible].
19 IASB Update, September 2011 and IASB Agenda Paper 7E September 2011 paras 57 [illegible].
20 IFRIC Update, [illegible] 2006.
21 IFRIC Update, [illegible] 2014.
22 More detailed [illegible] can be found in [illegible] Options, Futures and Other Derivatives, John C. Hull.
23 Classification and Measurement of Share-based Payment Transactions Amendments to IFRS 2, IASB, June 2016.
24 Classification and Measurement of Share-based Payment Transactions Amendments to IFRS 2, IASB, June 2016.
25 [illegible] Staff Position 123(R)-4, Classification of [illegible] [illegible] [illegible] Contingent Event.
26 FASB ASC 718 – Compensation – Stock Compensation (formerly FAS 123(R) Share-Based Payment), FASB, December 2004 [illegible].
27 IASB Update, [illegible] 2015.
28 IFRIC Update, May 2015.
29 IFRIC Update, September 2015.
30 IFRIC Update, September 2015.
31 IASB Update, February 2014.
32 IASB Update, April 2014.
33 [illegible] IFRS 2 – Group and Treasury Share Transactions, [illegible] 2006 [illegible].
34 IFRIC Update, March [illegible].
35 IFRIC Update, March [illegible].
36 Classification and Measurement of Share-based Payment Transactions Amendments to IFRS 2, IASB, June 2016.
37 Classification and Measurement of Share-based Payment Transactions Amendments to IFRS 2, IASB, June 2016.
38 IFRIC Update, November [illegible].
39 Financial Reporting Guide [illegible] (Black Economic Empowerment) [illegible] Transactions, Accounting Practices Committee (APC) of SAICA, December 2012.
40 Financial Reporting Guide [illegible] for Black Economic Empowerment (BEE) Transactions, Accounting Practices Committee (APC) of SAICA, December 2012.

Chapter 33 Employee benefits

List of examples

Chapter 33 Employee benefits

1 INTRODUCTION

This Chapter deals with IAS 19 – *Employee Benefits* – as published in June 2011 (and amended in November 2013 as discussed at 7.6.1 below and in September 2014 as discussed in 7.6 below). *[IAS 19.172]*. Predecessors of this standard are discussed in earlier editions of International GAAP.

Employee benefits typically form a very significant part of any entity's costs, and can take many and varied forms. Accordingly, IFRS devotes considerable attention to them in two separate standards. IFRS 2 – *Share-based Payment* – which is discussed in Chapter 32. All other employee benefits are dealt with in IAS 19.

Many issues raised in accounting for employee benefits can be straightforward, such as the allocation of wages paid to an accounting period, and are generally dealt with by IAS 19 accordingly. In contrast, accounting for the costs of retirement benefits in the financial statements of employers presents one of the most difficult challenges in the whole field of financial reporting. The amounts involved are large, the timescale is long, the estimation process is complex and involves many areas of uncertainty which have to be made the subject of assumptions. Furthermore, the complexities for an International Standard are multiplied by the wide variety of arrangements found in different jurisdictions.

2 OBJECTIVE AND SCOPE OF IAS 19

2.1 Objective

IAS 19 sets out its objective as follows:

'The objective of this Standard is to prescribe the accounting and disclosure for employee benefits. The Standard requires an entity to recognise:

(a) a liability when an employee has provided service in exchange for employee benefits to be paid in the future; and

(b) an expense when the entity consumes the economic benefit arising from service provided by an employee in exchange for employee benefits.' *[IAS 19.1]*.

This provides the first glimpse of the direction taken by the standard. Driven by the focus on assets and liabilities in the IASB's *Conceptual Framework*, it approaches the issues from the perspective of the statement of financial position.

2.2 Scope

Section 2.2.1 below deals with the general scope of the standard. The issue of employee benefits settled not by the employing entity but by a shareholder or other member of a group is discussed at 2.2.2 below.

2.2.1 General scope requirements of IAS 19

As its name suggests, IAS 19 is not confined to pensions and other post-retirement benefits, but rather addresses all forms of consideration (apart from share-based payments which are dealt with by IFRS 2 and discussed in Chapter 32) given by an employer in exchange for service rendered by employees or for the termination of employment. *[IAS 19.2, 8]*. In particular, in addition to post-retirement benefits employee benefits include: *[IAS 19.5]*

(a) short-term benefits, including wages and salaries, paid annual leave, bonuses, benefits in kind, etc. The accounting treatment of these is discussed at 12 below;

(b) long-term benefits, such as long-service leave, long-term disability benefits, long-term bonuses, etc. These are to be accounted for in a similar way to post-retirement benefits by using actuarial techniques and are discussed at 13 below; and

(c) termination benefits. These are to be provided for and expensed when the employer becomes committed to the redundancy plan, on a similar basis to that required by IAS 37 – *Provisions, Contingent Liabilities and Contingent Assets* – for provisions generally, and are discussed at 14 below.

The standard addresses only the accounting by employers, and excludes from its scope reporting by employee benefit plans themselves. These are dealt with in IAS 26 – *Accounting and Reporting by Retirement Benefit Plans*. *[IAS 19.3]*. The specialist nature of these requirements puts them beyond the scope of this book.

The standard makes clear it applies widely and in particular to benefits:

(a) provided to all employees (whether full-time, part-time, permanent, temporary or casual staff and specifically including directors and other management personnel); *[IAS 19.7]*

(b) however settled, including payments in cash or goods or services, whether paid directly to employees, their spouses, children or other dependants or any other party (such as insurance companies); *[IAS 19.6]* and

(c) however provided, including:

   (i) under formal plans or other formal agreements between an entity and individual employees, groups of employees or their representatives;

   (ii) under legislative requirements, or through industry arrangements, whereby entities are required to contribute to national, state, industry or other multi-employer plans; or

(iii) by those informal practices that give rise to a constructive obligation, that is where the entity has no realistic alternative but to pay employee benefits. An example of a constructive obligation is where a change in the entity's informal practices would cause unacceptable damage to its relationship with employees. *[IAS 19.4]*.

The standard does not define the term 'employee'. However, it is clear from the reference in (a) above to 'full-time, part-time, permanent, casual or temporary staff' and specifically including directors and other management personnel that the term is intended to apply widely. In particular, it is not necessary for there to be a contract of employment in order for an individual to be considered an employee for IAS 19 purposes. In our view, the standard applies to anyone who is in substance an employee, and that will be a matter of judgement in light of all the facts and circumstances.

2.2.2 *Employee benefits settled by a shareholder or another group entity*

In some circumstances, employee benefits may be settled by a party other than the entity to which services were rendered by employees. Examples would include a shareholder or another entity in a group of entities under common control.

IAS 19 is silent on whether, and if so how, an entity receiving employee services in this way should account for them. IFRS 2, on the other hand, devotes quite some detail to this topic for employee services within its scope.

An entity could make reference to the hierarchy in IAS 8 – *Accounting Policies, Changes in Accounting Estimates and Errors* (discussed in Chapter 3 at 4.3) when deciding on an accounting policy under IAS 19. Accordingly, these provisions of IFRS 2 could be applied by analogy to transactions within the scope of IAS 19.

The relevant requirements of IFRS 2 are discussed in Chapter 32 at 2.2.2.A and at 12.

3 PENSIONS AND OTHER POST-EMPLOYMENT BENEFITS – DEFINED CONTRIBUTION AND DEFINED BENEFIT PLANS

3.1 The distinction between defined contribution plans and defined benefit plans

IAS 19 draws the important distinction between defined contribution plans and defined benefit plans. The determination is made based on the economic substance of the plan as derived from its principal terms and conditions. *[IAS 19.27]*. The approach it takes is to define defined contribution plans, with the defined benefit plans being the default category. The relevant terms defined by the standard are as follows: *[IAS 19.8]*

'*Post-employment benefits* are employee benefits (other than termination benefits and short-term employee benefits) that are payable after the completion of employment'.

'*Post-employment benefit plans* are formal or informal arrangements under which an entity provides post-employment benefits for one or more employees'.

'*Defined contribution plans* are post-employment benefit plans under which an entity pays fixed contributions into a separate entity (a fund) and will have no legal or constructive obligation to pay further contributions if the fund does not hold sufficient assets to pay all employee benefits relating to employee service in the current and prior periods'.

'*Defined benefit plans* are post-employment benefit plans other than defined contribution plans'.

IAS 19 applies to all post-employment benefits (whether or not they involve the establishment of a separate entity to receive contributions and pay benefits) which include, for example, retirement benefits such as pensions; and post-employment life assurance or medical care. *[IAS 19.26]*. A less common benefit is the provision of services.

Under defined benefit plans the employer's obligation is not limited to the amount that it agrees to contribute to the fund. Rather, the employer is obliged (legally or constructively) to provide the agreed benefits to current and former employees. Examples of defined benefit schemes given by IAS 19 are: *[IAS 19.29]*

(a) plans where the benefit formula is not linked solely to the amount of contributions and requires the entity to provide further contributions if assets are insufficient to meet the benefits in the plan formula;

(b) guarantees, either directly or indirectly through a plan, of a specified return on contributions; and

(c) those informal practices that give rise to a constructive obligation, such as a history of increasing benefits for former employees to keep pace with inflation even where there is no legal obligation to do so.

The most significant difference between defined contribution and defined benefit plans is that, under defined benefit plans, some actuarial risk or investment risk falls, in substance, on the employer. This means that if actuarial or investment experience is worse than expected, the employer's obligation may be increased. *[IAS 19.30]*. Consequently, because the employer is in substance underwriting the actuarial and investment risks associated with the plan, the expense recognised for a defined benefit plan is not necessarily the amount of the contribution due for the period. *[IAS 19.56]*. Conversely, under defined contribution plans the benefits received by the employee are determined by the amount of contributions paid (either by the employer, the employee or both) to the benefit plan or insurance company, together with investment returns, and hence actuarial and investment risk fall in substance on the employee. *[IAS 19.28]*.

3.2 Insured benefits

One factor that can complicate making the distinction between defined benefit and defined contribution plans is the use of external insurers. IAS 19 recognises that some employers may fund their post-employment benefit plans by paying insurance premiums and observes that the benefits insured need not have a direct or automatic relationship with the entity's obligation for employee benefits. However, it makes clear that post-employment benefit plans involving insurance contracts are subject to the same distinction between accounting and funding as other funded plans. *[IAS 19.47]*.

Where insurance premiums are paid to fund post-employment benefits, the employer should treat the plan as a defined contribution plan unless it has (either directly or indirectly through the plan) a legal or constructive obligation to:

(a) pay the employee benefits directly when they fall due; or

(b) pay further amounts if the insurer does not pay all future employee benefits relating to employee service in the current and prior periods.

If the employer has retained such a legal or constructive obligation it should treat the plan as a defined benefit plan. *[IAS 19.46]*. In setting out how to apply defined benefit accounting, however, the standard refers to slightly different criteria to determine whether a legal or constructive obligation is retained. Rather than referring to 'either directly or indirectly through the plan', paragraph 48 of IAS 19 refers to '... the entity (either directly, indirectly through the plan, *through the mechanism for setting future premiums or through a related party relationship with the insurer*) retains a legal or constructive obligation ...' (emphasis added). *[IAS 19.48]*. In our view, this asymmetry is most likely a drafting error and the additional text applies in both instances.

In cases where such obligations are retained by the employer, it recognises its rights under a 'qualifying insurance policy' as a plan asset and recognises other insurance policies as reimbursement rights. *[IAS 19.48]*. Plan assets are discussed at 6 below.

By way of final clarification, the standard notes that where an insurance policy is in the name of a specified plan participant or a group of plan participants and the employer does not have any legal or constructive obligation to cover any loss on the policy, the employer has no obligation to pay benefits to the employees and the insurer has sole responsibility for paying the benefits. In that case, the payment of fixed premiums under such contracts is, in substance, the settlement of the employee benefit obligation, rather than an investment to meet the obligation. Consequently, the employer no longer has an asset or a liability. Accordingly, it should treat the payments as contributions to a defined contribution plan. *[IAS 19.49]*. The important point here is that employee entitlements will be of a defined benefit nature unless the employer has no obligation whatsoever to pay them should the insurance fail or otherwise be insufficient.

The analysis that is given in the standard of insured plans, which is described above, along with the definition of defined benefit and defined contribution plans seems comprehensive at first glance. However, there will be circumstances where the distinction may not be so apparent and careful analysis may be required. For example, it is possible that an employer buys insurance on a regular basis (say annually), retaining no further obligation in respect of the benefits insured, but has an obligation (legal or constructive) to keep doing so in the future. In such a scenario, the employer may be exposed to future actuarial variances reflected in a variable cost of purchasing the required insurance in future years (for example, due to changing mortality estimates by the insurer).

Another scenario would be where each year the employee earns an entitlement to a pension of (say) 2% of that year's (i.e. current as opposed to final) salary and the employer purchases each year an annuity contract to commence on the date of retirement.

In our view, the standard is not entirely clear as to the nature of such an arrangement. On the one hand, it could be argued that it is a defined contribution plan because the definition of defined contribution plans is met when:

- 'fixed' payments are paid to a separate fund; and
- the employer is not obliged to pay further amounts if the fund has insufficient assets to pay the benefits relating to employee service in the *current and prior periods.*

Further, as noted above the standard considers the payment of 'fixed' premiums to purchase insurance specific to an employee (or group thereof) with no retention of risk in respect of the insured benefits to be a defined contribution arrangement.

On the other hand, it could be argued that this is a defined benefit plan on the grounds that:

- the premiums of future years are not 'fixed' in any meaningful sense (certainly not in the same way as an intention simply to pay a one-off contribution of a given % of salary);
- the standard acknowledges that one factor that can mean insured arrangements are defined benefit in nature is when the employer retains an obligation indirectly through the mechanism for setting future premiums; *[IAS 19.48]* and
- the standard observes that under defined benefit plans '... actuarial risk (that benefits will cost more than expected) and investment risk fall, in substance, on the entity. If actuarial or investment experience are worse than expected, the entity's obligation may be increased'. *[IAS 19.30]*.

Much would seem to depend on just what 'fixed' means in such circumstances. Although not expressly addressed by the standard, in our view such arrangements will very likely be defined benefit in nature, albeit with regular (and perhaps only partial) settlement and, if so, should be accounted for as such. This is because the employer has retained actuarial risks by committing to pay whatever it takes in future years to secure the requisite insurance. Naturally, for any schemes that are determined to be defined benefit plans, the next step would be to see whether the frequent settlement renders the output of the two accounting models materially the same. That would depend, *inter alia*, on the attribution of the benefit to years of service and the impact of an unwinding discount.

The wide variety of possible arrangements in practice mean that careful consideration of individual circumstances will be required to determine the true substance of such arrangements.

3.3 Multi-employer plans

3.3.1 *Multi-employer plans other than plans sharing risks between entities under common control*

3.3.1.A *The treatment of multi-employer plans*

Multi-employer plans, other than state plans (see 3.4 below), under IAS 19 are defined contribution plans or defined benefit plans that:

(a) pool assets contributed by various entities that are not under common control; and

(b) use those assets to provide benefits to employees of more than one entity, on the basis that contribution and benefit levels are determined without regard to the identity of the entity that employs the employees. *[IAS 19.8]*.

Accordingly, they exclude group administration plans, which simply pool the assets of more than one employer, for investment purposes and the reduction of administrative and investment costs, but keep the claims of different employers segregated for the sole benefit of their own employees. The standard observes that group administration plans pose no particular accounting problems because information is readily available to treat them in the same way as any other single employer plan and because they do not expose the participating employers to actuarial risks associated with the current and former employees of other entities. Accordingly, the standard requires group administration plans to be classified as defined contribution plans or defined benefit plans in accordance with the terms of the plan (including any constructive obligation that goes beyond the formal terms). *[IAS 19.38]*.

The standard gives a description of one example of a multi-employer scheme as follows:

(a) the plan is financed on a pay-as-you-go basis: contributions are set at a level that is expected to be sufficient to pay the benefits falling due in the same period; and future benefits earned during the current period will be paid out of future contributions; and

(b) employees' benefits are determined by the length of their service and the participating entities have no realistic means of withdrawing from the plan without paying a contribution for the benefits earned by employees up to the date of withdrawal. Such a plan creates actuarial risk for the entity: if the ultimate cost of benefits already earned at the end of the reporting period is more than expected, it will be necessary for the entity either to increase its contributions or persuade employees to accept a reduction in benefits. Therefore, such a plan is a defined benefit plan. *[IAS 19.35]*.

A multi-employer plan should be classified as either a defined contribution plan or a defined benefit plan in accordance with its terms in the normal way (see 3.1 above) *[IAS 19.32]*. If a multi-employer plan is classified as a defined benefit plan, IAS 19 requires that the employer should account for its proportionate share of the defined benefit obligation, plan assets and costs associated with the plan in the same way as for any other defined benefit plan (see 5-11 below). *[IAS 19.33, 36]*.

The standard does, however, contain a practical exemption if insufficient information is available to use defined benefit accounting. This could be the case, for example, where:

(a) the entity does not have access to information about the plan that satisfies the requirements of the standard; or

(b) the plan exposes the participating entities to actuarial risks associated with the current and former employees of other entities, with the result that there is no consistent and reliable basis for allocating the obligation, plan assets and cost to individual entities participating in the plan. *[IAS 19.36]*.

In such circumstances, an entity should account for the plan as if it were a defined contribution plan and make the disclosures set out at 15.2.4 below. *[IAS 19.36]*.

The standard notes that there may be a contractual agreement between the multi-employer plan and its participants that determines how the surplus in the plan will be distributed to the participants (or the deficit funded). In these circumstances, an entity participating in such a plan, and accounting for it as a defined contribution plan (as described above), should recognise the asset or liability arising from the contractual agreement and the resulting income or expense in profit or loss. *[IAS 19.37]*. The standard illustrates this with an example of an entity participating in a multi-employer defined benefit plan which it accounts for as a defined contribution plan because no IAS 19 valuations are prepared. A non-IAS 19 funding valuation shows a deficit of CU100 million in the plan. The plan has agreed under contract a schedule of contributions with the participating employers in the plan that will eliminate the deficit over the next five years. The entity's total contributions to eliminate the deficit under the contract are CU8 million. IAS 19 requires the entity to recognise immediately a liability for the contributions adjusted for the time value of money and an equal expense in profit or loss. The important point here is that the standard makes clear that 'defined contribution accounting' is not the same as cash accounting. Extra payments to make good a deficit should be provided for immediately when they are contracted for.

3.3.1.B What to do when 'sufficient information' becomes available

As discussed above, IAS 19 requires a multi-employer defined benefit plan to be treated for accounting purposes as a defined contribution plan when insufficient information is available to use defined benefit accounting. The standard does not address the accounting treatment required when that situation changes because sufficient information becomes available in a period. Two possible approaches present themselves:

(a) an immediate charge/credit to profit or loss equal to the deficit/surplus; or

(b) an actuarial gain or loss recognised on other comprehensive income.

Arguments in favour of (a) would be that *for accounting purposes* the scheme was a defined contribution scheme. Accordingly, starting defined benefit accounting is akin to introducing a new scheme. The defined benefit obligation recognised is essentially a past service cost. In addition, as discussed at 3.3.1.A above, the standard clarifies that while defined contribution accounting is being applied an asset or liability should be recognised where there is a contractual arrangement to share a surplus or fund a deficit. The receipt of full information could be considered to represent such an arrangement and hence require full recognition in the statement of financial position with an equivalent entry in profit or loss.

Arguments for (b) would be that the scheme has not changed and that defined contribution accounting was a proxy (and best available estimate) for what the defined benefit accounting should have been. Accordingly, any change to that estimate due to the emergence of new information is an actuarial variance which is recognised in other comprehensive income.

Given the ambiguity of the standard either approach is acceptable if applied consistently.

3.3.1.C Withdrawal from or winding-up of a multi-employer scheme

IAS 19 requires the application of IAS 37 to determine when to recognise and how to measure a liability relating to the withdrawal from, or winding-up of, a multi-employer scheme. *[IAS 19.39]*.

3.3.2 Defined benefit plans sharing risks between entities under common control

IAS 19 provides that defined benefit plans that share risks between various entities under common control, for example a parent and its subsidiaries, are not multi-employer plans. *[IAS 19.40]*.

The test, described earlier, for allowing a defined benefit multi-employer plan to be accounted for as a defined contribution plan is that insufficient information is available. By completely excluding entities that are under common control from the definition of multi-employer plans the standard is essentially saying that for these employers sufficient information is deemed always to be available – at least for the plan as a whole. The standard requires an entity participating in such a plan to obtain information about the plan as a whole measured in accordance with IAS 19 on the basis of assumptions that apply to the plan as a whole. *[IAS 19.41]*. Whilst a subsidiary may not be in a position to demand such information (any more than participants in schemes described at 3.3.1 above), the standard is essentially saying that the parent must make the information available if it wants the subsidiary to be able to comply with IAS 19.

The standard then goes on to specify the accounting treatment to be applied in the individual financial statements of the participating entities. The standard states: 'If there is a contractual agreement or stated policy for charging to individual group entities the net defined benefit cost for the plan as a whole measured in accordance with this Standard, the entity shall, in its separate or individual financial statements, recognise the net defined benefit cost so charged. If there is no such agreement or policy, the net defined benefit cost shall be recognised in the separate or individual financial statements of the group entity that is legally the sponsoring employer for the plan. The other group entities shall, in their separate or individual financial statements, recognise a cost equal to their contribution payable for the period'. *[IAS 19.41]*. This seems to raise more questions than it answers. For example, it provides no clarity on what is meant by:

- the 'net defined benefit cost ... measured in accordance with [IAS 19]'. In particular, are actuarial gains and losses part of this 'net cost'?
- an entity that 'is legally the sponsoring employer for the plan'. The pan-jurisdictional scope of IFRS makes such a determination particularly difficult. Furthermore, it suggests that there is only one such legal sponsor – which may not be the case in practice.

A further difficulty with these provisions of the standard is whether it is ever likely in practice that entities would be charged an amount based on the 'defined benefit cost measured in accordance with [IAS 19]'. Naturally, situations vary not just across, but also within, individual jurisdictions. However, it is typically the case that funding valuations will not be on an IAS 19 basis, so that any amounts 'charged' will not be measured in accordance with IAS 19. Indeed, as discussed at 3.3.1 above, the standard gives non-IAS 19 funding valuations in a multi-employer plan as a reason why sufficient information to allow defined benefit accounting is not available.

Some further insight as to the IASB's intentions can be found in the Basis for Conclusions to the standard.

'The Board noted that, if there were a contractual agreement or stated policy on charging the net defined benefit cost to group entities, that agreement or policy would determine the cost for each entity. If there is no such contractual agreement or stated policy, the entity that is the sponsoring employer bears the risk relating to the plan by default. The Board therefore concluded that a group plan should be allocated to the individual entities within a group in accordance with any contractual agreement or stated policy. If there is no such agreement or policy, the net defined benefit cost is allocated to the sponsoring employer. The other group entities recognise a cost equal to any contribution collected by the sponsoring employer. This approach has the advantages of (a) all group entities recognising the cost they have to bear for the defined benefit promise and (b) being simple to apply'. *[IAS 19.BC48-49]*.

This analysis is particularly noteworthy in these respects:

(a) there is no mention of amounts charged being measured in accordance with IAS 19. Indeed, the third sentence refers to *any* such agreement or stated policy;

(b) the focus is not on 'amounts charged' but rather an 'allocation' of the scheme across entities;

(c) references are to a 'sponsoring employer' crucially not a *legally* sponsoring employer. The term is slightly clarified by the explanation that a sponsoring employer is one that by default bears the 'risks relating to the plan'; and

(d) the discussion of employers other than the sponsoring employer is explicitly by reference to 'amounts collected'.

Given the ambiguities in the standard we expect that, for entities applying IFRS at an individual company level, there may well be divergent treatments in practice.

The standard makes clear that, for each individual group entity, participation in such a plan is a related party transaction. Accordingly, the disclosures set out at 15.2.5 below are required. *[IAS 19.42]*.

3.4 State plans

IAS 19 observes that state plans are established by legislation to cover all entities (or all entities in a particular category, for example a specific industry) and are operated by national or local government or by another body (for example an autonomous agency created specifically for this purpose) which is not subject to control or influence by the reporting entity. *[IAS 19.44]*. The standard requires that state plans be accounted for in the same way as for a multi-employer plan (see 3.3.1 above). *[IAS 19.43]*. It goes on to note that it is characteristic of many state plans that:

- they are funded on a pay-as-you-go basis with contributions set at a level that is expected to be sufficient to pay the required benefits falling due in the same period; and
- future benefits earned during the current period will be paid out of future contributions.

Nevertheless, in most state plans, the entity has no legal or constructive obligation to pay those future benefits: its only obligation is to pay the contributions as they fall due and if the entity ceases to employ members of the state plan, it will have no obligation to pay the benefits earned by its own employees in previous years. For this reason, the standard considers that state plans are normally defined contribution plans. However, in cases when a state plan is a defined benefit plan, IAS 19 requires it to be treated as such as a multi-employer plan. *[IAS 19.45]*.

Some plans established by an entity provide both compulsory benefits which substitute for benefits that would otherwise be covered under a state plan and additional voluntary benefits. IAS 19 clarifies that such plans are not state plans. *[IAS 19.44]*.

3.5 Plans that would be defined contribution plans but for the existence of a minimum return guarantee

It is common in some jurisdictions for the employer to make contributions to a defined contribution post-employment benefit plan and to guarantee a minimum level of return on the assets in which the contributions are invested. In other words, the employee enjoys upside risk on the investments but has some level of protection from downside risk.

The existence of such a guarantee means the arrangement fails to meet the definition of a defined contribution plan (see 3.1 above) and accordingly is a defined benefit plan. Indeed, the standard is explicit as it uses plans which guarantee a specified return on contributions as an example of a defined benefit arrangement. *[IAS 19.29(b)]*. The somewhat more difficult issue is how exactly to apply defined benefit accounting to such an arrangement, as this would require projecting forward future salary increases and investment returns, and discounting these amounts at corporate bond rates. Although this approach is clearly required by the standard, some consider it to be inappropriate in such circumstances. This issue was debated by the Interpretations Committee, which published a draft interpretation on 8 July 2004 entitled D9 – *Employee Benefit Plans with a Promised Return on Contributions or Notional Contributions*. The approach taken in D9 was to distinguish two different types of benefits:

(a) a benefit of contributions or notional contributions plus a guarantee of a fixed return (in other words, benefits which can be estimated without having to make an estimate of future asset returns); and

(b) a benefit that depends on future asset returns.

For benefits under (a) above, it was proposed that the defined benefit methodology in IAS 19 be applied as normal. In summary, that meant:

- calculating the benefit to be paid in the future by projecting forward the contributions or notional contributions at the guaranteed fixed rate of return;
- allocating the benefit to periods of service;
- discounting the benefits allocated to the current and prior periods at the rate specified in IAS 19 to arrive at the plan liability, current service cost and net interest; and
- recognising any remeasurements in accordance with the entity's accounting policy (note that there is no longer an accounting policy choice under IAS 19 and remeasurements must be recorded in other comprehensive income).

For benefits covered by (b) above, it was proposed that the plan liability should be measured at the fair value, at the end of the reporting period, of the assets upon which the benefit is specified (whether plan assets or notional assets). No projection forward of the benefits would be made, and discounting of the benefit would not therefore be required.

D9 suggested that plans with a combination of a guaranteed fixed return and a benefit that depends on future asset returns should be accounted for by analysing the benefits into a fixed component and a variable component. The defined benefit asset or liability that would arise from the fixed component alone would be measured and recognised as described above. The defined benefit asset (or liability) that would arise from the variable component alone would then be calculated as described above and compared to the fixed component. An additional plan liability would be recognised to the extent that the asset (or liability) calculated for the variable component is smaller (or greater) than the asset (or liability) recognised in respect of the fixed component.

The great complexity of these provisions was not wholeheartedly supported by respondents to the document. Also, many commentators pointed out that the proposals effectively re-wrote, rather than interpreted, the standard (as drafted at the time). In August 2005, the Interpretations Committee announced the withdrawal of D9, observing the following: 'The staff found the fixed/variable and modified fixed/variable approaches inadequate to give a faithful representation of the entity's obligation for more complex benefit structures. They believed that some aspects of the fixed/variable approach in D9 were not fully consistent with IAS 19. ... The staff ... recommended that the correct treatment for D9 plans should be determined as part of an IASB project.'

The Interpretations Committee was asked in 2012 whether the revisions to IAS 19 in 2011 affect the accounting for these types of employee benefits and concluded they do not.[1]

The Interpretations Committee re-opened its examination of the subject and spent some time considering the issue. In May 2014, it decided not to proceed with the issue, stating the following: 'In the Interpretations Committee's view, developing accounting requirements for these plans would be better addressed by a broader consideration of accounting for employee benefits, potentially through the research agenda of the IASB. The Interpretations Committee acknowledged that reducing diversity in practice in the short term would be beneficial. However, because of the difficulties encountered in progressing the issues, the Interpretations Committee decided to remove the project from its agenda. The Interpretations Committee notes the importance of this issue because of the increasing use of these plans. Consequently, the Interpretations Committee would welcome progress on the IASB's research project on post-employment benefits'.[2]

What this means is that the current text of IAS 19 applies. Accordingly, the projected unit credit method will need to be applied to such benefits as it is to other defined benefit arrangements.

3.6 Death-in-service benefits

The provision of death-in-service benefits is a common part of employment packages (either as part of a defined benefit plan or on a standalone basis). We think it is regrettable that IAS 19 provides no guidance on how to account for such benefits, particularly as E54 (the exposure draft preceding an earlier version of IAS 19) devoted considerable attention to the issue.[3] IAS 19 explains the removal of the guidance as follows: 'E54 proposed guidance on cases where death-in-service benefits are not insured externally and are not provided through a post-employment benefit plan. IASC concluded that such cases will be rare. Accordingly, IASC deleted the guidance on death-in-service benefits.' *[IAS 19.BC253]*.

In our view, this misses the point – E54 also gave guidance on cases where the benefits *are* externally insured and where they are provided through a post-employment benefit plan. In our view, the proposals in E54 had merit, and it is worth reproducing them here.

> 'An enterprise should recognise the cost of death-in-service benefits ... as follows:
>
> (a) in the case of benefits insured or re-insured with third parties, in the period in respect of which the related insurance premiums are payable; and
>
> (b) in the case of benefits not insured or re-insured with third parties, to the extent that deaths have occurred before the end of the reporting period.
>
> 'However, in the case of death-in-service benefits provided through a post-employment benefit plan, an enterprise should recognise the cost of those benefits by including their present value in the post-employment benefit obligation.
>
> 'If an enterprise re-insures a commitment to provide death-in-service benefits, it acquires a right (to receive payments if an employee dies in service) in exchange for an obligation to pay the premiums.
>
> 'Where an enterprise provides death-in-service benefits directly, rather than through a post-employment benefit plan, the enterprise has a future commitment to provide death-in-service coverage in exchange for employee service in those same future periods (in the same way that the enterprise has a future commitment to pay salaries if the employee renders service in those periods). That future commitment is not a present obligation and does not justify recognition of a liability. Therefore, an obligation arises only to the extent that a death has already occurred by the end of the reporting period.
>
> 'If death-in-service benefits are provided through a pension plan (or other post-employment plan) which also provides post-employment benefits to the same employee(s), the measurement of the obligation reflects both the probability of

a reduction in future pension payments through death in service and the present value of the death-in-service benefits (see [E-54's discussion of mutual compatibility of actuarial assumptions]).

'Death-in-service benefits differ from post-employment life insurance because post-employment life insurance creates an obligation as the employee renders services in exchange for that benefit; an enterprise accounts for that obligation in accordance with [the requirements for defined benefit plans]. Life insurance benefits that are payable regardless of whether the employee remains in service comprise two components: a death-in-service benefit and a post-employment benefit. An enterprise accounts for the two components separately.'

We suggest that the above may continue to represent valid guidance to the extent it does not conflict with extant IFRS. In particular, an appropriate approach could be that:

- death-in-service benefits provided as part of a defined benefit post-employment plan are factored into the actuarial valuation. In this case any insurance cover should be accounted for in accordance with the normal rules of IAS 19 (see 6 below). An important point here is that insurance policies for death-in-service benefits typically cover only one year, and hence will have a low or negligible fair value. As a result, it will not be the case that the insurance asset is equal and opposite to the defined benefit obligation;
- other death-in-service benefits which are externally insured are accounted for by expensing the premiums as they become payable; and
- other death-in-service benefits which are not externally insured are provided for as deaths in service occur.

The first bullet is particularly important. The measure of the post-employment benefit (like a pension) will be reduced to take account of expected deaths in service. Accordingly, it would be inappropriate to ignore the death in service payments that would be made. The question that arises is how exactly to include those expected payments. This raises the same issue as disability benefits (discussed at 13.2.2 below), i.e. what to do with the debit entry. However, IAS 19 has no explicit special treatment for death-in-service benefits comparable to that for disability benefits. Given the absence of specific guidance, the requirement is to apply the projected unit credit method to death in service benefits. As the benefit is fully vested, an argument could be made that the expected benefit should be accrued fully (on a discounted basis). Another approach would be to build up the credit entry in the statement of financial position over the period to the expected date of death.

An alternative approach could be to view death-in-service benefits as being similar to disability benefits. Proponents of this view would argue that the recognition requirements for disability benefits (discussed at 13.2.2 below) could also be applied to death-in-service.

In January 2008, the Interpretations Committee published its agenda decision explaining why it decided not to put death-in-service benefits onto its agenda.[4] In the view of the Interpretations Committee, 'divergence in this area was unlikely to be significant. In addition, any further guidance that it could issue would be application guidance on the use of the Projected Unit Credit Method'. In our view, the second reason seems more credible than the first.

As part of its analysis, the 'rejection notice' sets out some of the Interpretations Committee's views on the subject. It observes the following:

(a) in some situations, IAS 19 requires these benefits to be attributed to periods of service using the Projected Unit Credit Method;

(b) IAS 19 requires attribution of the cost of the benefits until the date when further service by the employee will lead to no material amount of further benefits under the plan, other than from further salary increases;

(c) the anticipated date of death would be the date at which no material amount of further benefit would arise from the plan; and

(d) using different mortality assumptions for a defined benefit pension plan and an associated death-in-service benefit would not comply with the requirement of IAS 19 to use actuarial assumptions that are mutually compatible.

Points (a) to (c) above support the analysis that a provision should be built up gradually from the commencement of employment to the expected date of death. They also suggest that making an analogy to the specific rules in the standard on disability may not be appropriate. In addition, point (c) is simply re-iterating a clear requirement of the standard. The above agenda decision of the Interpretations Committee is not as helpful as we would have liked. The use of the phrase 'in some situations' in point (a) above leaves uncertain just what those circumstances may be. In September 2007, the Interpretations Committee published a tentative agenda decision which said '[i]f these benefits are provided as part of a defined benefit plan, IAS 19 requires them to be attributed to periods of service using the Projected Unit Credit Method'.[5] At the following meeting the Interpretations Committee discussed the comment letters received which noted that it could be argued that such attribution would be required only if the benefits were dependent on the period of service. No decision was reached on the final wording of the rejection notice because 'IFRIC ... was unable to agree on wording for its agenda decision'.[6]

Given the lack of explicit guidance on death-in-service benefits in IAS 19 itself, and given the Interpretations Committee's decision not to address the matter, it seems likely that practice will be mixed.

4 DEFINED CONTRIBUTION PLANS

4.1 Accounting requirements

4.1.1 General

Accounting for defined contribution plans (see 3 above) is straightforward under IAS 19 because, as the standard observes, the reporting entity's obligation for each period is determined by the amounts to be contributed for that period. Consequently, no actuarial assumptions are required to be made to measure the obligation or the expense and there is no possibility of any actuarial gain or loss to the reporting entity. Moreover, the obligations are measured on an undiscounted basis, except where they are not expected to be settled wholly before twelve months after the end of the period in which the employees render the related service. *[IAS 19.50]*. Where discounting is required, the discount rate should be determined in the same way as for defined benefit plans, which is discussed at 7.6 below. *[IAS 19.52]*. In general, though, it would seem unlikely for a defined contribution scheme to be structured with such a long delay between the employee service and the employer contribution.

IAS 19 requires that, when an employee has rendered service during a period, the employer should recognise the contribution payable to a defined contribution plan in exchange for that service:

(a) as a liability (accrued expense), after deducting any contribution already paid. If the contribution already paid exceeds the contribution due for service before the end of the reporting period, the excess should be recognised as an asset (prepaid expense) to the extent that the prepayment will lead to, for example, a reduction in future payments or a cash refund; and

(b) as an expense, unless another IFRS requires or permits its capitalisation. *[IAS 19.51]*.

As discussed at 3.3.1.A above, IAS 19 requires multi-employer defined benefit plans to be accounted for as defined contribution plans in certain circumstances. The standard makes clear that contractual arrangements to make contributions to fund a deficit should be fully provided for (on a discounted basis) even if they are to be paid over an extended period. *[IAS 19.37]*.

4.1.2 Defined contribution plans with vesting conditions

In February 2011, the Interpretations Committee received a request seeking clarification on the effect that vesting conditions have on the accounting for defined contribution plans. The Interpretations Committee was asked whether contributions to such plans should be recognised as an expense in the period for which they are paid or over the vesting period. In the examples given in the submission, the employee's failure to meet a vesting condition could result in the refund of contributions to, or reductions in future contributions by, the employer.

The Interpretations Committee decided not to add the issue to its agenda, noting that there is no significant diversity in practice in respect of the effect that vesting conditions have on the accounting for defined contribution post-employment benefit plans, nor does it expect significant diversity in practice to emerge in the future.

Explaining its decision, the Interpretations Committee observed that each contribution to a defined contribution plan is to be recognised as an expense or recognised as a liability (accrued expense) over the period of service that obliges the employer to *pay* this contribution to the defined contribution plan. This period of service is distinguished from the period of service that entitles an employee to *receive* the benefit from the defined contribution plan (i.e. the vesting period). Refunds are recognised as an asset and as income when the entity/employer becomes entitled to the refunds, e.g. when the employee fails to meet the vesting condition.[7]

5 DEFINED BENEFIT PLANS – GENERAL

The standard notes that accounting for defined benefit plans is complex because actuarial assumptions are required to measure both the obligation and the expense, and there is a possibility of actuarial gains and losses. Moreover, the obligations are measured on a discounted basis because they may be settled many years after the employees render the related service. *[IAS 19.55]*. Also, IAS 19 makes clear that it applies not just to unfunded obligations of employers but also to funded plans. The details of pension scheme arrangements vary widely from jurisdiction to jurisdiction and, indeed, within them. Frequently though, they involve some entity or fund, separate from the employer, to which contributions are made by the employer (and sometimes employees) and from which benefits are paid. Typically, the employer (through either legal or constructive obligations) essentially underwrites the fund in the event that the assets in the fund are insufficient to pay the required benefits. This is the key feature which means such an arrangement is a defined benefit plan (see 3 above). *[IAS 19.56]*.

In addition to specifying accounting and disclosure requirements, IAS 19 summarises the steps necessary to apply its rules, to be applied separately to each separate plan, as follows:

(a) determining the deficit or surplus by:
  - (i) using an actuarial technique, the projected unit credit method, to make a reliable estimate of the ultimate cost to the entity of the benefit that employees have earned in return for their service in the current and prior periods. This requires an entity to determine how much benefit is attributable to the current and prior periods and to make estimates (actuarial assumptions) about demographic variables (such as employee turnover and mortality) and financial variables (such as future increases in salaries and medical costs) that will affect the cost of the benefit;
  - (ii) discounting that benefit in order to determine the present value of the defined benefit obligation and the current service cost; and
  - (iii) deducting the fair value of any plan assets from the present value of the defined benefit obligation.

(b) determining the amount of the net defined benefit liability (asset) as the amount of the deficit or surplus determined in (a), adjusted for any effect of limiting a net defined benefit asset to the asset ceiling;

(c) determining amounts to be recognised in profit or loss:
  - (i) current service cost;
  - (ii) any past service cost and gain or loss on settlement;
  - (iii) net interest on the net defined benefit liability (asset); and

(d) determining the remeasurements of the net defined benefit liability (asset), to be recognised in other comprehensive income, comprising:
  - (i) actuarial gains and losses;
  - (ii) return on plan assets, excluding amounts included in net interest on the net defined benefit liability (asset); and
  - (iii) any change in the effect of the asset ceiling, excluding amounts included in net interest on the net defined benefit liability (asset). *[IAS 19.57]*.

Retirement benefits will often be very significant in the context of an employer's financial statements. Therefore, the standard encourages, but does not require involvement of a qualified actuary in the measurement of all material post-employment benefit obligations. *[IAS 19.59]*. However, the standard acknowledges that in some circumstances estimates, averages and computational shortcuts may provide a reliable approximation. *[IAS 19.60]*. These steps are discussed in further detail in the sections 7.5 and 7.6 below.

6 DEFINED BENEFIT PLANS – PLAN ASSETS

6.1 Definition of plan assets

IAS 19 provides the following definitions relating to plan assets:

'*Plan assets* comprise:

(a) assets held by a long-term employee benefit fund; and

(b) qualifying insurance policies.' *[IAS 19.8]*.

'Plan assets exclude unpaid contributions due from the reporting entity to the fund, as well as any non-transferable financial instruments issued by the entity and held by the fund. Plan assets are reduced by any liabilities of the fund that do not relate to employee benefits for example, trade and other payables and liabilities resulting from derivative financial instruments.' *[IAS 19.114]*.

'*Assets held by a long-term employee benefit fund* are assets (other than non-transferable financial instruments issued by the reporting entity) that:

(a) are held by an entity (a fund) that is legally separate from the reporting entity and exists solely to pay or fund employee benefits; and

(b) are available to be used only to pay or fund employee benefits, are not available to the reporting entity's own creditors (even in bankruptcy), and cannot be returned to the reporting entity, unless either:

    (i) the remaining assets of the fund are sufficient to meet all the related employee benefit obligations of the plan or the reporting entity; or

    (ii) the assets are returned to the reporting entity to reimburse it for employee benefits already paid.'

Whilst non-transferable financial instruments issued by the employer are excluded from the definition of plan assets, plans can, and do, own transferrable instruments issued by the employer (such as listed shares and bonds) and these would qualify as plan assets.

'A *qualifying insurance policy* is an insurance policy issued by an insurer that is not a related party (as defined in IAS 24 – *Related Party Disclosures*) of the reporting entity, if the proceeds of the policy:

(a) can be used only to pay or fund employee benefits under a defined benefit plan; and

(b) are not available to the reporting entity's own creditors (even in bankruptcy) and cannot be paid to the reporting entity, unless either:

(i) the proceeds represent surplus assets that are not needed for the policy to meet all the related employee benefit obligations; or

(ii) the proceeds are returned to the reporting entity to reimburse it for employee benefits already paid.' *[IAS 19.8]*.

A footnote to this definition clarifies that a qualifying insurance policy is not necessarily an insurance contract as defined in IFRS 4 – *Insurance Contracts.*

IFRS 4 further mentions insurance contracts in the context of pensions. It discusses insurance policies issued by an insurer to a pension plan covering employees of the insurer or another entity consolidated in the same financial statements as the insurer. In such circumstances, IFRS 4 provides that the contract will generally be eliminated from the financial statements. The financial statements will:

- include the full amount of the pension obligation under IAS 19, with no deduction for the plan's rights under the contract;
- not include a liability to policyholders under the contract; and
- include the assets backing the contract. *[IFRS 4.IG2. E1.21]*.

6.2 Measurement of plan assets

IAS 19 requires plan assets to be measured at their fair value, *[IAS 19.113]*, which is defined as the price that would be received to sell an asset or paid to transfer a liability in an orderly transaction between market participants at the measurement date. *[IAS 19.8]*. This is the same definition as is used in IFRS 13 – *Fair Value Measurement* (see Chapter 14).

The fair value of any plan assets is deducted from the present value of the defined benefit obligation in determining the deficit or surplus – see 8 below. *[IAS 19.113]*.

6.3 Qualifying insurance policies

Where plan assets include qualifying insurance policies that exactly match the amount and timing of some or all of the benefits payable under the plan, the fair value of those insurance policies is deemed to be the present value of the related obligations, subject to any reductions required if the amounts receivable under the insurance policies are not recoverable in full. *[IAS 19.115]*.

6.4 Reimbursement rights

Some employers may have in place arrangements to fund defined benefit obligations which do not meet the definition of qualifying insurance policies above but which do provide for another party to reimburse some or all of the expenditure required to settle a defined benefit obligation. In such a case, the expected receipts under the arrangement are not *classified* as plan assets under IAS 19 (and hence they are not presented as part of a net pension asset/liability – see 8 below). Instead, the employer should recognise its right to reimbursement as a separate asset, but only when it is virtually certain that another party will reimburse some or all of the expenditure required to settle a defined benefit obligation. The asset should be measured at fair value and, in all other respects, it should be treated in the same way as a plan asset. In particular, changes in fair value are disaggregated and accounted for in the same way as plan assets – see 10.2 below. In profit or loss, the expense relating to a defined benefit plan may be presented net of the amount recognised for a reimbursement. *[IAS 19.116-118]*.

As is the case for qualifying insurance policies, for reimbursement rights that exactly match the amount and timing of some or all of the benefits payable fair value is determined as the present value of the related obligation, subject to any reduction required if the reimbursement is not recoverable in full. *[IAS 19.119]*.

6.5 Contributions to defined benefit funds

Contributions to defined benefit plans under IAS 19 are a movement between line items in the statement of financial position – the reduction in cash for the employer being reflected by an increase in the plan assets. Perhaps because of this straightforward accounting, the standard provides no guidance on contributions, which it implicitly deals with as always being in the form of cash.

Although contributions are very commonly in cash, there is no reason why an employer could not contribute any other assets to a defined benefit plan and that raises the question of how to account for the disposal – particularly so, since from the point of transfer the assets will be measured at fair value under IAS 19. In our view, such a transfer of a non-cash asset should be treated as a disposal, with proceeds equal to the fair value of the asset. That would give rise to gains and losses in profit or loss (unless the asset in question was already carried at fair value) and, for certain assets (such as available for sale securities), the reclassification into profit or loss of amounts previously recognised in other comprehensive income.

6.6 Longevity swaps

In August 2014, the Interpretations Committee received a request to clarify the accounting for longevity swaps. A longevity swap transfers the risk of members living longer (or shorter) than expected from the pension scheme to an external party.

In response to a request to clarify the measurement of longevity swaps held by an entity's defined benefit plan, the Interpretations Committee discussed whether an entity should:

(a) account for a longevity swap as a single instrument and measure its fair value as part of plan assets in accordance with paragraphs 8 and 113 of IAS 19 and IFRS 13, with changes in fair value being recorded in other comprehensive income; or

(b) split longevity swaps into two components.

The two components in (b) would be a 'fixed leg' and a 'variable leg'. The variable leg is thought to represent a qualifying insurance policy and is measured at the present value of the related obligation in accordance with paragraph 115 of IAS 19.

The fixed leg comprises a series of fixed payments to be made in return for the receipt of the variable leg receipts. If the two legs are considered separately, an appropriate accounting policy would need to be applied to the fixed leg. Two possibilities were discussed by the Interpretations Committee as follows. It would initially be measured at fair value with subsequent accounting either:

- if part of plan assets, at fair value with changes being included in other comprehensive income in accordance with paragraph 57(d) of IAS 19; or
- if a financial liability at amortised cost using the effective interest rate with interest recognised in profit and loss.

The Interpretations Committee noted that when such transactions take place, the predominant practice is to account for a longevity swap as a single instrument and measure it at fair value as part of plan assets.

The Interpretations Committee decided not to add this issue to its agenda as it did not expect diversity to develop in the application of IAS 19.[8]

7 DEFINED BENEFIT PLANS – PLAN LIABILITIES

7.1 Legal and constructive obligations

IAS 19 refers to the liabilities of defined benefit plans as the present value of defined benefit obligations, which it defines as '... the present value, without deducting any plan assets, of expected future payments required to settle the obligation resulting from employee service in the current and prior periods'. *[IAS 19.8]*.

The obligations should include not only the benefits set out in the plan, but also any constructive obligations that arise from the employer's informal practices which go beyond the formal plan terms, and should where relevant include an estimate of expected future salary increases (taking into account inflation, seniority, promotion and other relevant factors, such as supply and demand in the employment market). *[IAS 19.61, 87-90]*.

A constructive obligation exists where a change in the employer's informal practices would cause unacceptable damage to its relationship with employees and which therefore leaves the employer with no realistic alternative but to pay those employee benefits. *[IAS 19.61]*. The term constructive obligation is not defined by IAS 19; however, as can be seen from the above it is very similar to the meaning of the term as used in IAS 37 where it is defined as follows:

'A constructive obligation is an obligation that derives from an entity's actions where:

(a) by an established pattern of past practice, published policies or a sufficiently specific current statement, the entity has indicated to other parties that it will accept certain responsibilities; and

(b) as a result, the entity has created a valid expectation on the part of those other parties that it will discharge those responsibilities.' *[IAS 37.10]*.

However, IAS 19 goes on to add a further nuance. The standard observes that it is usually difficult to cancel a retirement benefit plan (without payment) whilst still retaining staff, and in light of this it requires that reporting entities assume (in the absence of evidence to the contrary) any currently promised benefits will continue for the remaining working lives of employees. *[IAS 19.62]*. In our view, this is a somewhat lower hurdle, and could bring into the scope of defined benefit accounting promises which are (strictly) legally unenforceable and which would not necessarily be considered constructive obligations under IAS 37.

An employer's obligations (legal or constructive) may also extend to making changes to benefits in the future. The standard requires all such effects to be built into the computation of the obligation and gives the following examples of what they might comprise:

(a) a past history of increasing benefits, for example, to mitigate the effects of inflation, and no indication that this practice will change in the future;

(b) the entity is obliged, either by the formal terms of the plan (or a further constructive obligation) or by legislation to use any surplus in the plan for the benefit of plan participants; or

(c) benefits vary in response to a performance target or other criteria. For example, the terms of the plan may state that it will pay reduced benefits or require additional contributions from employees if the plan assets are insufficient. The measurement of the obligation reflects the best estimate of the effect of target or other criteria. *[IAS 19.88]*.

By contrast, any other future changes in the obligation (i.e. where no legal or constructive obligation previously existed) will be reflected in future current service costs, future past service costs or both (discussed at 10.1 below). *[IAS 19.89]*.

IAS 19 also deals with the situation where the level of defined benefits payable by a scheme varies with the level of state benefits. When this is the case a best estimate of any changes in state benefit should be factored into the actuarial computations only if they are enacted by the end of the reporting period or are predictable based on past history or other evidence. *[IAS 19.87, 95]*.

Some defined benefit plans limit the contributions that an entity is required to pay. The ultimate cost of the benefits takes account of the effect of a limit on contributions. The effect of a limit on contributions is determined over the shorter of the estimated life of the entity and the estimated life of the plan. *[IAS 19.91]*.

7.2 Contributions by employees and third parties

The standard notes that some defined benefit plans require employees or third parties to contribute to the cost of the plan. Contributions by employees reduce the cost of the benefits to the entity. The standard requires an entity to 'consider' whether third-party contributions reduce the cost of the benefits to the entity, or are a reimbursement right (discussed at 6.4 above). Contributions by employees or third parties are either set out in the formal terms of the plan (or arise from a constructive obligation that goes beyond those terms), or are discretionary. IAS 19 requires discretionary contributions by employees or third parties to be accounted for as a reduction in service cost when they are paid to the plan. *[IAS 19.92]*.

The standard draws a distinction between non-discretionary contributions from employees or third parties set out in the formal terms of the plan which are 'linked to service' and those which are not. Such contributions not dependent upon years of service reduce remeasurements of the net defined benefit liability (asset). An example given by the standard is if the contributions are required to reduce a deficit arising from losses on plan assets or actuarial losses. *[IAS 19.93]*.

For contributions which are linked to service, the standard states that they reduce the service cost as follows:

- if the amount of the contributions is dependent on the number of years of service (e.g. contributions that increase with years of service), they should be attributed to periods of service using the same attribution method required for the gross benefit (i.e. either using the plan's contribution formula or on a straight-line basis – see 7.3 below); or
- if the amount of the contributions is independent of the number of years of service (e.g. contributions that are a fixed percentage of salary), they are permitted to be recognised as a reduction of the service cost in the period in which the related service is rendered. Examples of contributions that are independent of the number of years of service include those that are a fixed percentage of the employee's salary, a fixed amount throughout the service period or dependent on the employee's age. *[IAS 19.93]*.

Application guidance is given in Appendix A to the standard in the form of the following flow chart.

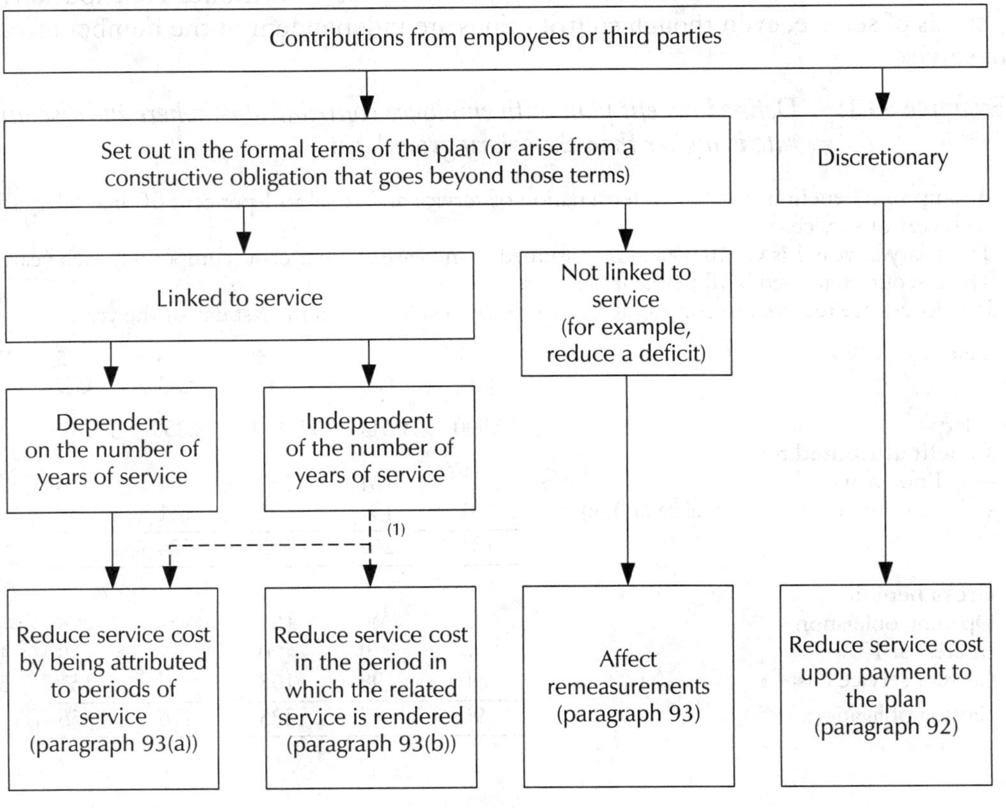

(1) This dotted arrow means that an entity is permitted to choose either accounting

Regrettably, the standard does not explain the 'mechanics' of an attribution which is required where contributions are linked to service.

In particular, it is unclear how to treat employee contributions made over the service period. As shown in Example 33.2 at 7.3 below, the projected unit credit method requires the net benefit to be expressed as a single net sum as at the date of retirement. Example 33.2 illustrates post-employment benefit payments being discounted to their present value as at the retirement date using the IAS 19 discount rate (discussed at 7.6 below). On the same principle, therefore, employee contributions made over the period of employment would logically need to be inflated to be expressed in the 'time value' as at retirement. However, IAS 19 does not indicate what rate should be used for this purpose.

We note, in this regard, that when the Interpretations Committee discussed the matter in November 2012, it considered a Staff Paper which touched on the matter. The numerical examples appended to the paper expressed the 'future value' of in-service employee contributions as at the date of retirement using the IAS 19 discount rate.[9] The content of the third example in this Staff Paper is reflected in the example set out below. This example pre-dates the amendments to IAS 19 in respect of employee contributions and therefore, we assume, that under the current standard that the entity has made an accounting policy choice to attribute contributions to periods of service, even though contributions are independent of the number of years of service.

Example 33.1: Defined benefit plan with employee contributions, where the discount rate is higher than the salary growth rate

A lump sum benefit is payable on termination of service and equal to 1 per cent of final salary for each year of service.
The salary in year 1 is CU10,000 and is assumed to increase at 7 per cent (compound) each year.
The discount rate used is 10 per cent per year.
Employees are required to contribute 0.5% of salary each year, on the last day of the year.

Year	1	2	3	4	5	**Total**
	CU	CU	CU	CU	CU	
Salary	10,000	10,700	11,449	12,250	13,108	
Benefit attributed to:						
– Prior years	–	131	262	393	524	
– Current year (1% of final salary) (a)	131	131	131	131	131	
	131	262	393	524	655	
Gross benefit						
Opening obligation	–	90	197	325	476	
Interest at 10%	–	9	20	32	48	109
Current service cost	90	98	108	119	131	546
Closing obligation	90	197	325	476	655	

Year	1 CU	2 CU	3 CU	4 CU	5 CU	Total
Employee contributions						
Actual contributions	(50)	(54)	(57)	(61)	(66)	(288)
Projected total contributions ('gross') (b)	(73)	(71)	(69)	(67)	(66)	(346)
Attributed contributions ('gross') (c)	(69)	(69)	(69)	(69)	(70)	(346)
Attributed contributions ('discounted')						
Opening	–	(47)	(104)	(172)	(251)	
Interest at 10%	–	(5)	(11)	(17)	(25)	(58)
Negative benefit (d)	(47)	(52)	(57)	(62)	(70)	(288)
Closing	(47)	(104)	(172)	(251)	(346)	
Benefit including effect of contributions						
Opening obligation	–	93	202	330	480	
Interest at 10% (e)	–	9	20	32	48	109
Net current service cost – current service cost less negative benefit (f)	43	46	51	57	61	258
Actual contributions	50	54	57	61	66	288
Closing	93	202	330	480	655	
Net benefit (gross benefit minus projected total contribution) is attributed to each year using the discount rate						
Current service cost (f)	43	46	51	57	61	258

(a) Straight-lined per paragraph 70
(b) Future-valued contributions (e.g. for Year 1, value of contribution paid at end of year 1 at end of year 5 using discount rate of 10% will be CU50 × 1.1^4 = CU73)
(c) Straight-lined to be on the same basis with the attributed benefit
(d) Present value of attributed contributions
(e) Includes rounding difference of (1) in Year 4
(f) Present value of gross benefit minus present value of projected total contributions

Journal entries (for Year 1)
To recognise net service cost
  Dr Service cost 43
  Cr Defined obligation 43
To reflect employee contributions
  Dr Plan asset 50
  Cr Defined benefit obligation 50

The standard notes that changes in employee or third-party contributions dependent on number of years of service result in:

(a) current and past service cost if the changes are not set out in the formal terms of the plan and do not arise from a constructive obligation; or
(b) actuarial gains and losses if the changes in contributions are set out in the formal terms of the plan or arise from a constructive obligation. *[IAS 19.94]*.

7.3 Actuarial methodology

IAS 19 notes that the ultimate cost of a defined benefit plan may be influenced by many variables, such as final salaries, employee turnover and mortality, employee contributions and medical cost trends. The ultimate cost of the plan is uncertain and this uncertainty is likely to persist over a long period of time. In order to measure the present value of the post-employment benefit obligations and the related current service cost, it is necessary:

- to apply an actuarial valuation method;
- to attribute benefit to periods of service; and
- to make actuarial assumptions. *[IAS 19.66]*.

These steps are discussed in the following sections.

Plan obligations are to be measured using the projected unit credit method, *[IAS 19.67]*, (sometimes known as the accrued benefit method pro-rated on service or as the benefit/years of service method). This method sees each period of service as giving rise to an additional unit of benefit entitlement and measures each unit separately to build up the final obligation. *[IAS 19.68]*. This actuarial method also determines the current service cost and any past service cost. *[IAS 19.67]*. IAS 19 provides a simple example of what this entails as follows: *[IAS 19.68]*

Example 33.2: The projected unit credit method

A lump sum benefit is payable on termination of service and equal to 1% of final salary for each year of service. The salary in year 1 is 10,000 and is assumed to increase at 7% (compound) each year. The discount rate used is 10% per year. The following table shows how the obligation builds up for an employee who is expected to leave at the end of year 5, assuming that there are no changes in actuarial assumptions. For simplicity, this example ignores the additional adjustment needed to reflect the probability that the employee may leave the entity at an earlier or later date.

Year	*1*	*2*	*3*	*4*	*5*
Benefit attributed to:					
– prior years	–	131	262	393	524
– current year (1% of final salary)	131	131	131	131	131
– current and prior years	131	262	393	524	655
Opening obligation	–	89	196	324	476
Interest at 10%	–	9	20	33	48
Current service cost	89	98	108	119	131
Closing obligation	89	196	324	476	655

Note:
– The opening obligation is the present value of benefit attributed to prior years.
– The current service cost is the present value of benefit attributed to the current year.
– The closing obligation is the present value of benefit attributed to current and prior years.

As can be seen in this simple example, the projected unit credit method produces a figure for current service cost and interest cost (and, although not illustrated here, would where appropriate produce a figure for past service cost). These cost components are discussed at 10 below.

This example from the standard contains no underlying workings or proofs. The most useful would be as follows:

Final salary at year 5 (10,000 compounded at 7%)	$10{,}000 \times (1 + 0.07)^4 = 13{,}100$
1% of final salary attributed to each year	131
Expected final benefit	5 years × 1% × 131,000 = 655
Current service cost, being present value of 131 discounted at 10%: e.g.	
Year 1	$131 \times (1 + 0.1)^{-4} = 89$
Year 2	$131 \times (1 + 0.1)^{-3} = 98$
Closing obligation, being years served multiplied by present value of 131: e.g.	
Year 3	$3 \text{ years} \times 131 \times (1 + 0.1)^{-2} = 324$

7.4 Attributing benefit to years of service

The projected unit credit method requires benefits to be attributed to the current period (in order to determine current service cost) and the current and prior periods (in order to determine the present value of defined benefit obligations). IAS 19 requires benefits to be attributed to the periods in which the obligation to provide post-employment benefits arises. That is taken to be when employees render services in return for post-employment benefits which an entity expects to pay in future reporting periods. The standard takes the view that actuarial techniques allow an entity to measure that obligation with sufficient reliability to justify recognition of a liability. *[IAS 19.71]*.

In applying the projected unit credit method, IAS 19 normally requires benefits to be attributed to periods of service under the plan's benefit formula (as is the case in Example 33.2 above). If, however, an employee's service in later years will lead to a materially higher level of benefit, the benefit should be attributed on a straight-line basis from:

(a) the date when service by the employee first leads to benefits under the plan; until

(b) the date when further service by the employee will lead to no material amount of further benefits under the plan, other than from further salary increases. *[IAS 19.70]*.

The standard considers that this requirement is necessary because the employee's service throughout the entire period will ultimately lead to benefit at that higher level. *[IAS 19.73]*.

The standard explains that employee service gives rise to an obligation under a defined benefit plan even if the benefits are conditional on future employment (in other words they are not vested). *[IAS 19.70]*. Employee service before the vesting date is considered to give rise to a constructive obligation because, at each successive period end, the amount of future service that an employee will have to render before becoming entitled to the benefit is reduced. In measuring its defined benefit obligation, an entity should consider the probability that some employees may not satisfy any vesting requirements. Similarly, although certain post-employment benefits, such as post-employment medical benefits, become payable only if a specified event occurs when an employee is no longer employed, an obligation is considered to be created when the employee renders service that will provide entitlement to the benefit if the specified event occurs. The probability that the specified event will occur affects the measurement of the obligation, but does not determine whether for accounting purposes the obligation exists. [IAS 19.72].

The obligation is considered to increase until the date when further service by the employee will lead to no material amount of further benefits, and accordingly all benefit should be attributed to periods ending on or before that date. [IAS 19.73].

IAS 19 illustrates the attribution of benefits to service periods with a number of worked examples as follows: [IAS 19.71-74]

Example 33.3: Attributing benefits to years of service

1. *A defined benefit plan provides a lump-sum benefit of 100 payable on retirement for each year of service.*

   A benefit of 100 is attributed to each year. The current service cost is the present value of 100. The present value of the defined benefit obligation is the present value of 100, multiplied by the number of years of service up to the end of the reporting period.

   If the benefit is payable immediately when the employee leaves the entity, the current service cost and the present value of the defined benefit obligation reflect the date at which the employee is expected to leave. Thus, because of the effect of discounting, they are less than the amounts that would be determined if the employee left at the end of the reporting period.

2. *A plan provides a monthly pension of 0.2% of final salary for each year of service. The pension is payable from the age of 65.*

   Benefit equal to the present value, at the expected retirement date, of a monthly pension of 0.2% of the estimated final salary payable from the expected retirement date until the expected date of death is attributed to each year of service. The current service cost is the present value of that benefit. The present value of the defined benefit obligation is the present value of monthly pension payments of 0.2% of final salary, multiplied by the number of years of service up to the end of the reporting period. The current service cost and the present value of the defined benefit obligation are discounted because pension payments begin at the age of 65.

3. *A plan pays a benefit of 100 for each year of service. The benefits vest after ten years of service.*

   A benefit of 100 is attributed to each year. In each of the first ten years, the current service cost and the present value of the obligation reflect the probability that the employee may not complete ten years of service.

4. *A plan pays a benefit of 100 for each year of service, excluding service before the age of 25. The benefits vest immediately.*

   No benefit is attributed to service before the age of 25 because service before that date does not lead to benefits (conditional or unconditional). A benefit of 100 is attributed to each subsequent year.

5. *A plan pays a lump-sum benefit of 1,000 that vests after ten years of service. The plan provides no further benefit for subsequent service.*

   A benefit of 100 (1,000 divided by ten) is attributed to each of the first ten years. The current service cost in each of the first ten years reflects the probability that the employee may not complete ten years of service. No benefit is attributed to subsequent years.

6. *A plan pays a lump-sum retirement benefit of 2,000 to all employees who are still employed at the age of 55 after twenty years of service, or who are still employed at the age of 65, regardless of their length of service.*

   For employees who join before the age of 35, service first leads to benefits under the plan at the age of 35 (an employee could leave at the age of 30 and return at the age of 33, with no effect on the amount or timing of benefits). Those benefits are conditional on further service. Also, service beyond the age of 55 will lead to no material amount of further benefits. For these employees, the entity attributes benefit of 100 (2,000 divided by twenty) to each year from the age of 35 to the age of 55.

For employees who join between the ages of 35 and 45, service beyond twenty years will lead to no material amount of further benefits. For these employees, the entity attributes benefit of 100 (2,000 divided by twenty) to each of the first twenty years.

For an employee who joins at the age of 55, service beyond ten years will lead to no material amount of further benefits. For this employee, the entity attributes benefit of 200 (2,000 divided by ten) to each of the first ten years.

For all employees, the current service cost and the present value of the obligation reflect the probability that the employee may not complete the necessary period of service.

7. *A post-employment medical plan reimburses 40% of an employee's post-employment medical costs if the employee leaves after more than ten and less than twenty years of service and 50% of those costs if the employee leaves after twenty or more years of service.*

   Under the plan's benefit formula, the entity attributes 4% of the present value of the expected medical costs (40% divided by ten) to each of the first ten years and 1% (10% divided by ten) to each of the second ten years. The current service cost in each year reflects the probability that the employee may not complete the necessary period of service to earn part or all of the benefits. For employees expected to leave within ten years, no benefit is attributed.

8. *A post-employment medical plan reimburses 10% of an employee's post-employment medical costs if the employee leaves after more than ten and less than twenty years of service and 50% of those costs if the employee leaves after twenty or more years of service.*

   Service in later years will lead to a materially higher level of benefit than in earlier years. Therefore, for employees expected to leave after twenty or more years, the entity attributes benefit on a straight-line basis under paragraph 68 of the standard. Service beyond twenty years will lead to no material amount of further benefits. Therefore, the benefit attributed to each of the first twenty years is 2.5% of the present value of the expected medical costs (50% divided by twenty).

   For employees expected to leave between ten and twenty years, the benefit attributed to each of the first ten years is 1% of the present value of the expected medical costs. For these employees, no benefit is attributed to service between the end of the tenth year and the estimated date of leaving.

   For employees expected to leave within ten years, no benefit is attributed.

9. *Employees are entitled to a benefit of 3% of final salary for each year of service before the age of 55.*

   Benefit of 3% of estimated final salary is attributed to each year up to the age of 55. This is the date when further service by the employee will lead to no material amount of further benefits under the plan. No benefit is attributed to service after that age.

None of the illustrations above are controversial. The following points of note are brought out in the above:

- the scenarios in 3 and 5 are economically identical, and are attributed to years of service accordingly. In each case benefits only vest after ten years, however an obligation is to be built up over that period rather than at the end; and
- example 8 illustrates that accruing a 10% benefit over a period of 20 years of service which jumps to 50% once 20 years have been completed is an example of service in later years leading to a materially higher level of benefit. Accordingly, the obligation is to be built-up on a straight-line basis over 20 years.

As regards example 9, the standard explains that where the amount of a benefit is a constant proportion of final salary for each year of service, future salary increases will affect the amount required to settle the obligation that exists for service before the end of the reporting period, but do not create an additional obligation. Therefore:

(a) for the purpose of allocating benefits to years of service, salary increases are not considered to lead to further benefits, even though the amount of the benefits is dependent on final salary; and

(b) the amount of benefit attributed to each period should be a constant proportion of the salary to which the benefit is linked. *[IAS 19.74]*.

7.5 Actuarial assumptions

The long timescales and numerous uncertainties involved in estimating obligations for post-employment benefits require many assumptions to be made when applying the projected unit credit method. These are termed actuarial assumptions and comprise:

(a) demographic assumptions about the future characteristics of current and former employees (and their dependants) who are eligible for benefits and deal with matters such as:

  (i) mortality, both during and after employment;

  (ii) rates of employee turnover, disability and early retirement;

  (iii) the proportion of plan members with dependants who will be eligible for benefits; and

  (iv) claim rates under medical plans; and

(b) financial assumptions, dealing with items such as:

  (i) the discount rate;

  (ii) future salary and benefit levels, excluding the cost of benefits that will be met by the employees;

  (iii) in the case of medical benefits, future medical costs, including claim handling costs, which the standard describes as costs that will be incurred in processing and resolving claims, including legal and adjuster's fees; and

  (iv) taxes payable by the plan on contributions relating to service before the reporting date or on benefits resulting from that service. *[IAS 19.76]*.

The requirements of IAS 19 in this regard are set out below, with the exception of the discount rate which is discussed at 7.6 below.

The standard requires that actuarial assumptions be unbiased (that is, neither imprudent nor excessively conservative), mutually compatible and represent the employer's best estimates of the variables that will determine the ultimate cost of providing post-employment benefits. *[IAS 19.75-77]*. Actuarial assumptions are mutually compatible if they reflect the economic relationships between factors such as inflation, rates of salary increase and discount rates. For example, all assumptions which depend on a particular inflation level (such as assumptions about interest rates and salary and benefit increases) in any given future period should assume the same inflation level in that period. *[IAS 19.78]*.

The financial assumptions must be based on market expectations at the end of the reporting period, for the period over which the obligations are to be settled. *[IAS 19.80]*.

The standard requires that a defined benefit obligation be measured on a basis that reflects:

(a) the benefits set out in the terms of the plan (or resulting from any constructive obligation that goes beyond those terms) at the end of the reporting period;

(b) any estimated future salary increases that affect the benefits payable;

(c) the effect of any limit on the employer's share of the cost of the future benefits; and

(d) contributions from employees or third parties that reduce the ultimate cost to the entity of those benefits. *[IAS 19.87]*.

Regarding mortality, the standard requires assumptions to be a best estimate of the mortality of plan members both during and after employment. *[IAS 19.81]*. In particular, expected changes in mortality should be considered, for example by modifying standard mortality tables with estimates of mortality improvements. *[IAS 19.82]*.

Assumptions about medical costs should take account of inflation as well as specific changes in medical costs (including technological advances, changes in health care utilisation or delivery patterns, and changes in the health status of plan participants). *[IAS 19.96-97]*. The standard provides a quite detailed discussion of the factors that should be taken into account in making actuarial assumptions about medical costs, in particular:

(a) measuring post-employment medical benefits requires assumptions about the level and frequency of future claims, and the cost of meeting them. An employer should make such estimates based on its own experience, supplemented where necessary by historical data from other sources (such as other entities, insurance companies and medical providers); *[IAS 19.97]*

(b) the level and frequency of claims is particularly sensitive to the age, health status and sex of the claimants, and may also be sensitive to their geographical location. This means that any historical data used for estimating future claims need to be adjusted to the extent that the demographic mix of the plan participants differs from that of the population used as the basis for the historical data. Historical data should also be adjusted if there is reliable evidence that historical trends will not continue; *[IAS 19.98]* and

(c) estimates of future medical costs should take account of any contributions that claimants are required to make based on the terms (whether formal or constructive) of the plan at the end of the reporting period. The treatment of contributions by employees and third parties is discussed at 7.2 above.

Clearly, the application of actuarial techniques to compute plan obligations is a complex task, and it seems likely that few entities would seek to prepare valuations without the advice of qualified actuaries. However, IAS 19 only encourages, but does not require that an entity take actuarial advice. *[IAS 19.59]*.

However sophisticated actuarial projections may be, reality will (apart from the most simple scenarios) always diverge from assumptions. This means that when a surplus or deficit is estimated, it will almost certainly be different from the predicted value based on the last valuation. These differences are termed actuarial gains and losses. The standard observes that actuarial gains and losses result from increases or decreases in the present value of a defined benefit obligation because of changes in actuarial assumptions and experience adjustments (see 10.3.1 below). Causes of actuarial gains and losses could include, for example:

(a) unexpectedly high or low rates of employee turnover, early retirement or mortality or of increases in salaries, benefits (if the formal or constructive terms of a plan provide for inflationary benefit increases) or medical costs;
(b) differences between the actual return on plan assets and amounts included as part of net interest in profit or loss;
(c) the effect of changes to assumptions concerning benefit payment options;
(d) the effect of changes in estimates of future employee turnover, early retirement or mortality or of increases in salaries, benefits (if the formal or constructive terms of a plan provide for inflationary benefit increases) or medical costs; and
(e) the effect of changes in the discount rate. *[IAS 19.128]*.

Actuarial gains and losses are discussed further at 10.3.1 below.

7.6 Discount rate

Due to the long timescales involved, post-employment benefit obligations are discounted. The whole obligation should be discounted, even if part of it is expected to be settled within twelve months of the end of the reporting period. *[IAS 19.69]*. The standard requires that the discount rate reflect the time value of money but not the actuarial or investment risk. Furthermore, the discount rate should not reflect the entity-specific credit risk borne by the entity's creditors, nor should it reflect the risk that future experience may differ from actuarial assumptions. *[IAS 19.84]*. The discount rate should reflect the estimated timing of benefit payments. For example, an appropriate rate may be quite different for a payment due in, say, ten years as opposed to one due in twenty. The standard observes that in practice, an acceptable answer can be obtained by applying a single weighted average discount rate that reflects the estimated timing and amount of benefit payments and the currency in which the benefits are to be paid. *[IAS 19.85]*. The standard does not preclude the use of a more granular approach in discounting cash flows at different periods along the yield curve. Nor does it preclude the use of different discount rates for different classes of participant in the interest of achieving a more precise measure of the defined benefit obligation than the computational shortcut which is seemingly allowed by the standard. An example of where discount rates may vary by class or participant is where there are both active and pensioner members, discount rates will vary by each of these classes purely as a result of their ages and the resultant timing of outflows associated to these classes.

IAS 19 also stipulates that the discount rate (and other financial assumptions) should be determined in nominal (stated) terms, unless estimates in real (inflation-adjusted) terms are more reliable, for example, in a hyper-inflationary economy (see Chapter 16 for a discussion of IAS 29 – *Financial Reporting in Hyperinflationary Economies*), or where the benefit is index-linked and there is a deep market in index-linked bonds of the same currency and term. *[IAS 19.79]*.

The basic part of this requirement – that a nominal rate be used – is consistent with the definition of the present value of a defined benefit obligation in that it should be

'... the present value ... of expected future payments required to settle the obligation ...' (see 7.1 above). In other words, as the future cash flows are stated at the actual amounts expected to be paid, the rate used to discount them should reflect that and not be adjusted to remove the effects of expected inflation. In contrast, the reference to the use of index-linked bonds seems to allow taking account of inflation through the discount rate (which would require expressing cash flows in current prices). This approach seems to be in conflict with the definition of the obligation. However, in practice few index-linked corporate bonds exist (so it may be quite rare to have a deep market in them) and a more reliable approach may often be to take account of inflation via the projected cash flows.

The Interpretations Committee in July 2013 discussed whether the rate should be pre- or post-tax. It observed that the discount rate used to calculate a defined benefit obligation should be a pre-tax discount rate and decided not to add this issue to its agenda.[10]

7.6.1 *High quality corporate bonds*

The rate used should be determined 'by reference to' the yield (at the end of the reporting period) on high quality corporate bonds of currency and term consistent with the liabilities. For currencies in which there is no deep market in such bonds, the yields on government bonds should be used instead (see 7.6.2 below). *[IAS 19.83]*.

IAS 19 does not explain what is meant by the term 'high quality'. In practice it is considered, rightly in our view, to mean either: bonds rated AA, bonds rated AA or higher by Standard and Poor's, or an equivalent rating from another rating agency.

The requirement that the rate be determined 'by reference to' high quality bond rates is an important one.

The standard gives an example of this in the context of the availability of bonds with sufficiently long maturities. It notes that in some cases, there may be no deep market in bonds with a sufficiently long maturity to match the estimated maturity of all the benefit payments. In such cases, the standard requires the use of current market rates of the appropriate term to discount shorter-term payments, and estimation of the rate for longer maturities by extrapolating current market rates along the yield curve. It goes on to observe that the total present value of a defined benefit obligation is unlikely to be particularly sensitive to the discount rate applied to the portion of benefits that is payable beyond the final maturity of the available corporate or government bonds. *[IAS 19.86]*.

In November 2013, the Interpretations Committee was asked whether corporate bonds with a rating lower than 'AA' can be considered to be 'high quality corporate bonds' ('HQCB').

The Interpretations Committee decided not to add the item to its agenda as issuing additional guidance or changing the requirements would be too broad for it to achieve in an efficient manner. The Interpretations Committee recommended that the IASB should address the issue as part of its research project on discount rates.[11] The Interpretations Committee reported this conclusion to the IASB at its December 2013 meeting. The IASB noted that no further work is currently planned on the issue of determining the discount rate for post-employment benefit obligations.[12]

The key observations of the Interpretations Committee were as follows.

- IAS 19 does not specify how to determine the market yields on HQCB, and in particular what grade of bonds should be designated as high quality.
- That 'high quality' as used in IAS 19 reflects an absolute concept of credit quality and not a concept of credit quality that is relative to a given population of corporate bonds, which would be the case, for example, if the paragraph used the term 'the highest quality'. Consequently, the concept of high quality should not change over time. Accordingly, a reduction in the number of HQCB should not result in a change to the concept of high quality. The Committee does not expect that an entity's methods and techniques used for determining the discount rate so as to reflect the yields on HQCB will change significantly from period to period.
- IAS 19 already contains requirements if the market in HQCB is no longer deep or if the market remains deep overall, but there is an insufficient number of HQCB beyond a certain maturity.
- Typically, the discount rate will be a significant actuarial assumption to be disclosed with sensitivity analyses under IAS 19.

As required by IAS 1 – *Presentation of Financial Statements* (see Chapter 3 at 5.1.1.B), disclosure is required of the judgements that management has made in the process of applying the entity's accounting policies and that have the most significant effect on the amounts recognised in the financial statements and that typically the identification of the HQCB population used as a basis to determine the discount rate requires the use of judgement, which may often have a significant effect on the entity's financial statements.

In June 2005, the Interpretations Committee considered the question – when there is no deep market in high quality corporate bonds in a country, whether the discount rate could be determined by reference to a synthetically constructed equivalent instead of using the yield on government bonds? At this time IAS 19 referred to 'countries' where there was no deep market rather than 'currencies'. The Interpretations Committee did not add the issue onto its agenda and concluded that the standard 'is clear that a synthetically constructed equivalent to a high quality corporate bond by reference to the bond market in another country may not be used to determine the discount rate'. The Interpretations Committee further observed that the reference to 'in a country' could reasonably be read as including high quality corporate bonds that are available in a regional market to which the entity has access, provided that the currency of the regional market and the country were the same (e.g. the euro). This would not apply if the country currency differed from that of the regional market.[13]

It is more than a little difficult to know what to make of those observations. Without a proper and detailed fact pattern one cannot know the details of the question being addressed and quite what a 'synthetically constructed equivalent' actually means. Whilst that may well be the case, there is no reason why employee benefits could not be denominated in another currency. In our view, it would have been more helpful if the Interpretations Committee had progressed to a formal interpretation to explore how and to what extent observed bond yields could form a starting point to extrapolate a discount rate. Whilst it would be wrong to understate the liabilities of the plan by using an inappropriately high rate (say, because the only relevant bonds in issue are not 'high quality'), it would be equally wrong, in our view, to overstate them by using the default rate of government debt when a reliable rate could be estimated by reference to market yields. Indeed, the standard suggests this in its discussion of actuarial assumptions in general, requiring that they be unbiased, that is neither imprudent nor excessively conservative. *[IAS 19.75, 77]*.

7.6.2 No deep market

In currencies where there is no deep market deep market in high quality corporate bonds, the market yields (at the end of the reporting period) on government bonds shall be used. *[IAS 19.83]*.

7.7 Frequency of valuations

When it addresses the frequency of valuations, IAS 19 does not give particularly prescriptive guidance. Rather, its starting point is simply to require that the present value of defined benefit obligations, and the fair value of plan assets, should be determined frequently enough to ensure that the amounts recognised in the financial statements do not differ materially from the amounts that would be determined at the end of the reporting period. *[IAS 19.58]*. An argument could be launched that without a full valuation as at the end of the reporting period to compare with, it cannot be possible to know whether any less precise approach is materially different. However, it is reasonably clear that the intention of the standard is not necessarily to require full actuarial updates as at the reporting date. This is because the standard goes on to observe that for practical reasons a detailed valuation may be carried out before the end of the reporting period and that if such amounts determined before the end of the reporting period are used, they should be updated to take account of any material transactions or changes in circumstances up to the end of the reporting period. *[IAS 19.59]*. Much may depend on what is considered to be a 'material change', however it is expressly to include changes in market prices (hence requiring asset values to be those at the end of the reporting period) and interest rates, as well as financial actuarial assumptions. *[IAS 19.59, 80]*.

In this regard, it is also worth noting the observation in the standard that '[i]n some cases, estimates, averages and computational shortcuts may provide a reliable approximation of the detailed computations illustrated in this Standard'. *[IAS 19.60]*. It should be remembered, though, that it is the amounts in the financial statements which must not differ materially from what they would be based on a valuation at the end of the reporting period. For funded schemes, the net surplus or deficit is usually the difference between two very large figures – plan assets and plan liabilities. Such a net item is inevitably highly sensitive, in percentage terms, to a given percentage change in the gross amounts.

In summary, a detailed valuation will be required on an annual basis, but not necessarily as at the end of the reporting period. A valuation undertaken other than as at the end of the reporting period will need to be updated as at the end of the reporting period to reflect *at least* changes in financial assumptions, asset values and discount rates. The need for updates in respect of other elements of the valuation will depend on individual circumstances.

8 DEFINED BENEFIT PLANS – TREATMENT OF THE PLAN SURPLUS OR DEFICIT IN THE STATEMENT OF FINANCIAL POSITION

8.1 Net defined benefit liability (asset)

IAS 19 defines the net defined benefit liability or asset as the deficit or surplus in the plan adjusted for any effect of the asset ceiling (see 8.2 below).

The deficit or surplus is the present value of the defined benefit obligation (see 7 above) less the fair value of the plan assets (if any) (see 6 above).

The standard requires that the net defined benefit liability (asset) be recognised in the statement of financial position at each reporting period. *[IAS 19.63].*

8.2 Restriction of assets to their recoverable amounts

The net defined benefit balance determined under IAS 19 may be an asset. The standard asserts that an asset may arise (that is, an asset measured on the basis of IAS 19) where a defined benefit plan has been 'over-funded' or when actuarial gains have arisen. The standard justifies the recognition of an asset in such cases because:

(a) the entity controls a resource, which is the ability to use the surplus to generate future benefits;

(b) that control is a result of past events (contributions paid by the entity and service rendered by the employee); and

(c) future economic benefits are available to the entity in the form of a reduction in future contributions or a cash refund, either directly to the entity or indirectly to another plan in deficit; the present value of those benefits is described as the asset ceiling. *[IAS 19.8, 65].*

In practice, pension plans tend to be funded on a significantly more prudent basis than would be the case if a surplus or deficit was measured in accordance with IAS 19. In particular, the discount rate used for funding purposes is typically lower than the rate required by the standard. For this reason, an IAS 19 valuation may produce a surplus, when for funding purposes there is a deficit.

When there is a surplus in a defined benefit plan, the standard requires the net asset recognised to be restricted to the lower of the surplus in the plan and the asset ceiling discounted using the same discount rate used for determining the defined benefit obligation (see 7.6 above). *[IAS 19.8, 64, IFRIC 14.1].*

Any adjustment required by the ceiling test is accounted for in other comprehensive income (see 10.3 below).

This limitation has proved quite problematic in practice and as a result was considered by the Interpretations Committee, initially in the context of statutory minimum funding requirements ('MFR'). This resulted in the publication, in July 2007, of

IFRIC 14 – *IAS 19 – The Limit on a Defined Benefit Asset, Minimum Funding Requirements and their Interaction.* Whilst dealing with the interaction of the asset ceiling with MFR, IFRIC 14 also deals more generally with the restriction of an asset on recoverability grounds. *[IFRIC 14.1-3, 6]*. Subsequently, IFRIC 14 was amended to deal with pre-paid MFR – see 8.2.3 below. It should also be noted that the IASB has published an exposure draft of proposed amendments to IAS 19 and IFRIC 14 which addresses whether other parties' (for example pension trustees) power to enhance benefits for plan members or wind up a plan affects the availability of a refund (see 16.2.2 below).

The Interpretations Committee notes that MFR exist in many countries and normally stipulate a minimum amount or level of contribution that must be made to a plan over a given period. Therefore, a minimum funding requirement may limit an entity's ability to reduce future contributions. *[IFRIC 14.2]*.

In addition, the limit on the measurement of a defined benefit asset may cause a minimum funding requirement to be onerous. Normally, a requirement to make contributions to a plan would not affect the measurement of the defined benefit asset or liability. This is because the contributions, once paid, will become plan assets and so the additional net liability is nil. However, a minimum funding requirement may give rise to a liability if the required contributions will not be available to the entity once they have been paid. *[IFRIC 14.3]*.

The issues addressed by IFRIC 14 are: *[IFRIC 14.6]*

- when refunds or reductions in future contributions should be regarded as available in accordance with the definition of the asset ceiling (discussed at 8.2.1 and 8.2.2 below);
- how a minimum funding requirement might affect the availability of reductions in future contributions (discussed at 8.2.3 below); and
- when a minimum funding requirement might give rise to a liability (discussed at 8.2.4 below).

8.2.1 IFRIC Interpretation 14 – general requirements concerning the limit on a defined benefit asset

IFRIC 14 clarifies that economic benefits, in the form of refunds or reduced future contributions, are available if they can be realised by the entity at some point during the life of the plan or when the plan liabilities are settled. In particular, such economic benefits may be available even if they are not realisable immediately at the end of the reporting period. *[IFRIC 14.8]*.

Furthermore, the benefit available does not depend on how the entity intends to use the surplus. The entity should determine the maximum economic benefit that is available from refunds, reductions in future contributions or a combination of both. However, economic benefits should not be recognised from a combination of refunds and reductions in future contributions based on assumptions that are mutually exclusive. *[IFRIC 14.9]*. Perhaps unnecessarily, the interpretation requires the availability of a refund or a reduction in future contributions to be determined in accordance with the terms and conditions of the plan and any statutory requirements in the jurisdiction of the plan. *[IFRIC 14.7]*.

The interpretation observes that an unconditional right to a refund can exist whatever the funding level of a plan at the end of the reporting period. The interpretation further states that benefits are available as a refund only if the entity has an unconditional right to a refund:

(a) during the life of the plan, without assuming that the plan liabilities must be settled in order to obtain the refund; or

(b) assuming the gradual settlement of the plan liabilities over time until all members have left the plan; or

(c) assuming the full settlement of the plan liabilities in a single event (i.e. as a plan wind-up).

However, if the right to a refund of a surplus depends on the occurrence or non-occurrence of one or more uncertain future events not wholly within an entity's control, the entity does not have an unconditional right and should not recognise an asset. *[IFRIC 14.11-12]*.

The economic benefit available as a refund should be measured as the amount of the surplus at the end of the reporting period (being the fair value of the plan assets less the present value of the defined benefit obligation) that the entity has a right to receive as a refund, less any associated costs. For example, if a refund would be subject to a tax other than income tax of the reporting entity, it should be measured net of the tax. *[IFRIC 14.13]*. Tax on defined benefit pension plans is discussed further in Chapter 31 at 10.7.

In measuring the amount of a refund available when the plan is wound up (point (c) above), the costs to the plan of settling the plan liabilities and making the refund should be included. For example, a deduction should be made for professional fees if these are paid by the plan rather than the entity, and the costs of any insurance premiums that may be required to secure the liability on wind-up. *[IFRIC 14.14]*.

It is usually the case that the trustees of a pension fund are independent of the entity. Trustees may have a variety of powers to influence a surplus in a plan. For example:

- setting the investment strategy whereby assets with lower risk and lower return would erode a surplus over time; or the purchase of assets in the form of insurance policies matching all or some of the cash outflows of the plan; or
- full or partial settlement of liabilities; or the improvement of benefits under the plan.

IFRIC 14 makes it clear that for future benefit improvements made by the employer and actuarial gains and losses, the existence of an asset at the end of the reporting period is not affected by possible future changes to the amount of the surplus. If future events occur that change the amount of the surplus, their effects are recognised when they occur. *[IFRIC 14.BC10]*.

The standard is also clear that if the right to a refund of a surplus depends on the occurrence or non-occurrence of one or more uncertain future events that are not wholly within an entity's control, the entity does not have an unconditional right and should not recognise a surplus. *[IFRIC 14.11-12]*.

However neither IAS 19 nor IFRIC 14 address the question of whether the entity's right to a refund of a surplus which depends on the occurrence or non-occurrence of uncertain future events means that no surplus should be recognised in any scenario where trustees have the power to 'spend' a surplus.

As noted above, the IASB has published an exposure draft of proposed amendments to IFRIC 14 which addresses whether the power of other parties (for example pension trustees) to enhance benefits for plan members or wind up a plan affects the availability of a refund (see 16.2.2 below). This exposure draft was issued as a response to two requests to the Interpretations Committee, suggesting that there is diversity in practice in this area. In the Basis for Conclusions on the exposure draft the IASB noted that paragraph BC10 of IFRIC 14 had not specifically addressed the circumstances in which trustees have such unconditional powers. The exposure draft proposes that the amount of the surplus that the entity recognises as an asset on the basis of a future refund shall not include amounts that other parties can use for other purposes that affect the benefits for plan members, for example by enhancing those benefits without the entity's consent. Until the issue is clarified through the amendment to the standard and interpretation we expect diversity in practice to continue in this area.

If the amount of a refund is determined as the full amount or a proportion of the surplus, rather than a fixed amount, an entity should make no adjustment for the time value of money, even if the refund is realisable only at a future date. *[IFRIC 14.15]*.

8.2.2 Economic benefits available as reduced future contributions when there are no minimum funding requirements for future service

IFRIC 14 addresses separately cases where there are minimum funding requirements relating to benefits to be awarded in future periods in exchange for services to be rendered in those periods, and cases where there are no such funding requirements.

This section deals with the situation where there are no such funding requirements. The implications of future service minimum funding requirements are discussed at 8.2.3 below.

IFRIC 14 requires that the economic benefit available by way of reduced future contributions be determined as the future service cost to the entity for each period over the shorter of the expected life of the plan and the expected life of the entity. The future service cost to the entity excludes amounts that will be borne by employees. *[IFRIC 14.16]*.

Future service costs should be determined using assumptions consistent with those used to determine the defined benefit obligation and with the situation that exists at the end of the reporting period as determined by IAS 19. Accordingly, no future changes to the benefits to be provided by a plan should be assumed until the plan is amended, and a stable workforce in the future should be assumed unless the entity makes a reduction in the number of employees covered by the plan. In the latter case, the assumption about the future workforce should include the reduction. The present value of the future service cost should be determined using the same discount rate as that used in the calculation of the defined benefit obligation (discount rates are discussed at 7.6 above). *[IFRIC 14.17]*.

8.2.3 IFRIC Interpretation 14 – the effect of a minimum funding requirement on the economic benefit available as a reduction in future contributions

IFRIC 14 defines minimum funding requirements as 'any requirements to fund a post-employment or other long-term defined benefit plan'. *[IFRIC 14.5]*. This is clearly quite a wide definition encompassing more than just statutory regimes.

Some minimum funding arrangements require periodic reappraisal (for example, every three years). Should such an arrangement cover a longer period, all payments over this longer period constitute the minimum funding requirement, not just the three years until the next reappraisal. In its March 2015 meeting the Interpretations Committee, following a request for clarification, discussed whether an entity should assume that the minimum funding requirement for contributions to cover future services (see below) would continue over the estimated life of the pension plan. The Interpretations Committee tentatively decided not to add this issue to its agenda as it believed that sufficient guidance existed and that neither an Interpretation nor an amendment to the standard was necessary.[14] In its July 2015 meeting, the Interpretations Committee noted that the entity should assume a continuation of existing funding principals because[15]:

- For any factors not specified by the minimum funding basis (for example, the period to continue the plan is not specified by the existing funding principles), the assumptions for determining future service costs and those used to estimate the future minimum funding requirement contributions for future service must be consistent. This is because the Interpretation requires an entity to use assumptions that are consistent with those used to determine the defined benefit obligation and with the situation that exists at the end of the reporting period. *[IFRIC 14.17, 21]*
- The estimate should not include changes to the funding principles to determine contributions for future service, if such changes require future negotiations with pension trustees. *[IFRIC 14.21, BC30]*.

The interpretation requires any minimum funding requirement at a given date to be analysed into contributions that are required to cover: *[IFRIC 14.18]*

(a) any existing shortfall for past service on the minimum funding basis. These contributions do not affect future contributions for future service. However, they may give rise to a liability under IFRIC 14 (see 8.2.4 below); *[IFRIC 14.19]* and

(b) future service.

If there is a minimum funding requirement for contributions relating to future service, the economic benefit available as a reduction in future contributions is the sum of: *[IFRIC 14.20]*

(a) any amount that reduces future minimum funding requirement contributions for future service because the entity made a pre-payment (that is, it paid the amount before being required to do so); and

(b) the estimated future service cost in each period (as discussed at 8.2.2 above) less the estimated minimum funding requirement contributions that would be required for future service in those periods if there were no pre-payment as described in (a).

The future minimum funding contributions required in respect of future service should be calculated:

- taking into account the effect of any existing surplus on the minimum funding requirement basis but excluding the pre-payment discussed in (a) immediately above;
- using assumptions consistent with the minimum funding requirement basis. For any factors not specified by the minimum funding requirement, the assumptions used should be consistent with those used to determine the defined benefit obligation and with the situation that exists at the end of the reporting period as determined by IAS 19;
- including any changes expected as a result of the entity paying the minimum contributions when they are due;
- excluding the effect of expected changes in the terms and conditions of the minimum funding basis that are not substantively enacted or contractually agreed at the end of the reporting period. *[IFRIC 14.21]*.

If the future minimum funding contribution required in respect of future service exceeds the future IAS 19 service cost in any given period, the present value of that excess reduces the amount of the asset available as a reduction in future contributions. However, the amount of the asset available as a reduction in future contributions can never be less than zero. *[IFRIC 14.22]*.

The mechanics of the above requirements are illustrated in the following two examples based on the illustrative examples accompanying IFRIC 14. *[IFRIC 14.IE9-IE27]*. Example 33.4 also illustrates the requirement in certain circumstances to recognise an additional liability for future MFR payments in respect of past service (discussed at 8.2.4 below).

Example 33.4: Deficit-clearing future minimum funding requirements when refunds are not available

An entity has a funding level on the minimum funding requirement basis (which is measured on a different basis from that required under IAS 19) of 95% in Plan C. Under the minimum funding requirements, the entity is required to pay contributions to increase the funding level to 100% over the next three years. The contributions are required to make good the deficit on the minimum funding requirement basis (shortfall) and to cover future service.

Plan C also has an IAS 19 surplus at the end of the reporting period of €50m, which cannot be refunded to the entity under any circumstances. There are no unrecognised amounts.

The nominal amounts of the minimum funding contribution requirements in respect of the shortfall and the future IAS 19 service cost for the next three years are set out below.

Year	Total minimum funding contribution requirement	Minimum contributions required to make good the shortfall	Minimum contributions required to cover future accrual
	€m	€m	€m
1	135	120	15
2	125	112	13
3	115	104	11

The entity's present obligation in respect of services already received includes the contributions required to make good the shortfall but does not include the minimum contributions required to cover future service.

The present value of the entity's obligation, assuming a discount rate of 6% per year, is approximately 300, calculated as follows:

€120m/(1.06) + €112m /(1.06)^2 + €104m/(1.06)^3

When these contributions are paid into the plan, the IAS 19 surplus (i.e. the fair value of assets less the present value of the defined benefit obligation) would, other things being equal, increase from €50m to €350m. However, the surplus is not refundable although an asset may be available as a future contribution reduction.

As noted above, the economic benefit available as a reduction in future contributions is the present value of:

- the future service cost in each year to the entity; less
- any minimum funding contribution requirements in respect of the future accrual of benefits in that year

over the expected life of the plan.

The amounts available as a future contribution reduction are set out below.

	IAS 19 service cost	Minimum contributions required to cover future accrual	Amount available as contribution reduction
Year	€m	€m	€m
1	13	15	(2)
2	13	13	0
3	13	11	2
4+	13	9	4

Assuming a discount rate of 6%, the economic benefit available as a future contribution reduction is therefore equal to:

€(2)m/(1.06) + €0m/(1.06)^2 + €2m/(1.06)^3 + €4m/(1.06)^4 + €4m/(1.06)^5 + €4m/(1.06)^6 .... = €56m.

The asset available from future contribution reductions is accordingly limited to €56m.

As discussed at 8.2.4 below, IFRIC 14 requires the entity to recognise a liability to the extent that the additional contributions payable will not be fully available. Therefore, the effect of the asset ceiling is to reduce the defined benefit asset by €294m (€50m + €300m – €56m).

As discussed at 10.3 below, the effect of the asset ceiling is part of remeasurements and the €294m is recognised immediately in other comprehensive income and the entity recognises a net liability of €244m. No other liability is recognised in respect of the obligation to make contributions to fund the minimum funding shortfall.

When the contributions of €300m are paid into the plan, the net asset will become €56m (€300m – €244m).

Example 33.5: Effect of a prepayment when a minimum funding requirement exceeds the expected future service charge

An entity is required to fund Plan D so that no deficit arises on the minimum funding basis. The entity is required to pay minimum funding requirement contributions to cover the service cost in each period determined on the minimum funding basis.

Plan D has an IAS 19 surplus of 35 at the beginning of 2015. This example assumes that the discount rate is 0%, and that the plan cannot refund the surplus to the entity under any circumstances but can use the surplus for reductions of future contributions.

The minimum contributions required to cover future service are €15 for each of the next five years. The expected IAS 19 service cost is €10 in each year.

The entity makes a prepayment of €30 at the beginning of 2015 in respect of years 2015 and 2016, increasing its surplus at the beginning of 2015 to €65. That prepayment reduces the future contributions it expects to make in the following two years, as follows:

Year	IAS 19 service cost (€)	Minimum funding requirement contribution: Before pre-payment (€)	After pre-payment (€)
2015	10	15	0
2016	10	15	0
2017	10	15	15
2018	10	15	15
2019	10	15	15
Total	50	75	45

At the beginning of 2015, the economic benefit available as a reduction in future contributions is the sum of:

- 30, being the prepayment of the minimum funding requirement contributions; and
- nil. The estimated minimum funding requirement contributions required for future service would be 75 if there was no prepayment. Those contributions exceed the estimated future service cost (50); therefore the entity cannot use any part of the surplus of 35.

Assuming a discount rate of 0%, the present value of the economic benefit available as a reduction in future contributions is equal to 30. Accordingly, the entity recognises an asset of 30 (because this is lower than the IAS 19 surplus of 65).

Two points worth noting in Example 33.5 above are as follows. The first is that, if IFRIC 14 did not allow the recognition of such prepayments, the full surplus of €65 would have been written off. The second is that, in the fact pattern of the question, it is unnecessary to know that the surplus before the prepayment was €35. This is because any surplus (other than the prepayment of MFR) would not be recognised because refunds are not available and future MFR exceeds future service costs.

8.2.4 *IFRIC Interpretation 14 – when a minimum funding requirement may give rise to a liability*

If there is an obligation under a minimum funding requirement to pay contributions to cover an existing shortfall on the minimum funding basis in respect of services already received, the entity should determine whether the contributions payable will be available as a refund or reduction in future contributions after they are paid into the plan. *[IFRIC 14.23]*. Recovery through reduced future contributions is discussed at 8.2.2 and 8.2.3 above.

If a surplus is recoverable by way of a refund (see 8.2.1 above), a minimum funding requirement to cover a shortfall in respect of past services will neither restrict an IAS 19 asset nor trigger the recognition of a liability as it will be recoverable with any refund. IFRIC 14 illustrates this by way of an example upon which the following is based. *[IFRIC 14.IE1-2]*.

Example 33.6: Effect of the minimum funding requirement when there is an IAS 19 surplus and the minimum funding contributions payable are fully refundable to the entity

An entity has a funding level on the minimum funding requirement basis (which is measured on a different basis from that required under IAS 19) of 82% in Plan A. Under the minimum funding requirements, the entity is required to increase the funding level to 95% immediately. As a result, the entity has a statutory obligation at the end of the reporting period to contribute €200m to

Plan A immediately. The plan rules permit a full refund of any surplus to the entity at the end of the life of the plan. The year-end valuations for Plan A are set out below.

	€million
Fair value of assets	1,200
Present value of defined benefit obligation under IAS 19	(1,100)
Surplus	100
Defined benefit asset (before consideration of the minimum funding requirement)	100

Payment of the contributions of €200m will increase the IAS 19 surplus from €100m to €300m. Under the rules of the plan this amount will be fully refundable to the entity with no associated costs. Therefore, no liability is recognised for the obligation to pay the contributions and the net defined benefit asset will be recognised at €100m.

To the extent that the contributions payable will not be available after they are paid into the plan, a liability should be recognised when the obligation arises. The liability should reduce the net defined benefit asset or increase the net defined benefit liability so that no gain or loss is expected to result from the effect of the asset ceiling when the contributions are paid. *[IFRIC 14.24]*.

IFRIC 14 illustrates this by way of an example upon which the following is based. *[IFRIC 14.IE3-8]*.

Example 33.7: Effect of a minimum funding requirement when there is an IAS 19 deficit and the minimum funding contributions payable would not be fully available

An entity has a funding level on the minimum funding requirement basis (which is measured on a different basis from that required under IAS 19) of 77% in Plan B. Under the minimum funding requirements, the entity is required to increase the funding level to 100% immediately. As a result, the entity has a statutory obligation at the end of the reporting period to pay additional contributions of €300m to Plan B. The plan rules permit a maximum refund of 60% of the IAS 19 surplus to the entity and the entity is not permitted to reduce its contributions below a specified level which happens to equal the IAS 19 service cost. The year-end valuations for Plan B are set out below.

	€million
Fair value of assets	1,000
Present value of defined benefit obligation under IAS 19	(1,100)
Deficit	(100)

The payment of €300m would change the IAS 19 deficit of €100m to a surplus of €200m. Of this €200m, 60% (€120m) is refundable. Therefore, of the contributions of €300m, €100m eliminates the IAS 19 deficit and €120m (60% of €200m) is available as an economic benefit. The remaining €80m (40% of €200m) of the contributions paid is not available to the entity. As discussed above, IFRIC 14 requires the entity to recognise a liability to the extent that the additional contributions payable are not available to it. Accordingly, the net defined benefit liability is €180m, comprising the deficit of €100m plus the additional liability of €80m. No other liability is recognised in respect of the statutory obligation to pay contributions of €300m. When the contributions of €300m are paid, the net asset will be €120m. If the entity were required to achieve a 100% funding position at some point in the future, but not immediately, the present value of its contributions over this period would be used in the calculation above.

9 DEFINED BENEFIT PLANS – PRESENTATION OF THE NET DEFINED BENEFIT LIABILITY (ASSET)

Neither IAS 19 nor IAS 1 specifies where in the statement of financial position a net asset or net liability in respect of a defined benefit plan should be presented, nor whether such balances should be shown separately on the face of the statement of financial position or only in the notes – this is left to the discretion of the reporting entity subject to the general requirements of IAS 1 discussed in Chapter 3 at 3.1. If the format of the statement of financial position distinguishes current assets and liabilities from non-current ones, the question arises as to whether this split needs also to be made for pension balances. IAS 19 does not specify whether such a split should be made, on the grounds that it may sometimes be arbitrary. *[IAS 19.133, BC200]*.

Employers with more than one plan may find that some are in surplus while others are in deficit. IAS 19 contains offset criteria closely modelled on those in IAS 32 – *Financial Instruments: Presentation*. *[IAS 19.132]*. An asset relating to one plan may only be offset against a liability relating to another plan when there is a legally enforceable right to use a surplus in one plan to settle obligations under the other plan, and the employer intends to settle the obligations on a net basis or realise the surplus and settle the obligation simultaneously. *[IAS 19.131]*. We believe that these offset criteria are unlikely to be met in practice.

10 DEFINED BENEFIT PLANS – TREATMENT IN PROFIT OR LOSS AND OTHER COMPREHENSIVE INCOME

IAS 19 identifies three components of annual pension cost as follows:

(a) service cost (see 10.1 below);

(b) net interest on the net defined benefit liability (asset) (see 10.2 below); and

(c) remeasurements of the net defined benefit liability (see 10.3 below). *[IAS 19.120]*.

Of these, (a) and (b) are recognised in profit or loss and (c) is recognised in other comprehensive income. This is unless another standard requires or permits the costs to be included in the cost of an asset, for example IAS 2 – *Inventories* – and IAS 16 – *Property, Plant and Equipment*. Where the post-employment benefit costs are included in the cost of an asset the appropriate proportion of *all* the above items must be included. *[IAS 19.121]*. There is no guidance in the standard as to what an 'appropriate' proportion of these items might be, although both IAS 2 and IAS 16 are clear that only those costs which are directly attributable to the asset qualify for capitalisation. It is not necessarily the case that the appropriate proportion will be the same for all of the components and judgement will be required in deciding how much of each item can meaningfully be said to relate to the production of an asset.

Remeasurements recognised in other comprehensive income should not be reclassified to profit and loss in a subsequent period. The standard notes that those amounts may be transferred within equity. *[IAS 19.122]*.

The standard states that it does not specify how an entity should present service cost and net interest on the net defined benefit liability or asset. These components are accounted for in accordance with IAS 1 (see Chapter 3 at 3.2). *[IAS 19.134]*.

10.1 Service cost

Service cost comprises:

(a) current service cost – the increase in the present value of the defined benefit obligation resulting from employee service in the current period;

(b) past service cost – which is the change in the present value of the defined benefit obligation for employee service in prior periods, resulting from a plan amendment (the introduction or withdrawal of, or changes to, a defined benefit plan) or a curtailment (a significant reduction by the entity in the number of employees covered by a plan); and

(c) any gain or loss on settlement – being the difference, at the date of settlement, between the present value of the defined benefit obligation being settled and the settlement price, including any plan assets transferred and any payments made directly by the entity in connection with the settlement. *[IAS 19.8, 109]*.

The current service cost should be determined using the projected unit credit method. *[IAS 19.67]*. The basic computation is illustrated in Example 33.2 at 7.3 above.

Past service costs and settlements are discussed in sections 10.1.1 and 10.1.2 below.

Before determining past service cost, or a gain or loss on settlement, the net defined benefit liability (asset) should be remeasured using the current fair value of plan assets and current actuarial assumptions (including current market interest rates and other current market prices) reflecting the benefits offered under the plan before the plan amendment, curtailment or settlement. *[IAS 19.99]*.

There is no need to distinguish between past service cost resulting from a plan amendment, past service cost resulting from a curtailment and a gain or loss on settlement if these transactions occur together. In some cases, a plan amendment occurs before a settlement, such as when an entity changes the benefits under the plan and settles the amended benefits later. In those cases an entity recognises past service cost before any gain or loss on settlement. *[IAS 19.8, 100]*.

A settlement occurs together with a plan amendment and curtailment if a plan is terminated with the result that the obligation is settled and the plan ceases to exist. However, the termination of a plan is not a settlement if the plan is replaced by a new plan that offers benefits that are, in substance, the same. *[IAS 19.101]*.

10.1.1 Past service cost

Past service cost is the change in the present value of the defined benefit obligation resulting from a plan amendment or curtailment. *[IAS 19.8, 102]*.

Past service costs should be recognised at the earlier of the date when:

(a) the plan amendment or curtailment occurs; and

(b) the entity recognises related restructuring costs in accordance with IAS 37 (discussed in Chapter 28 at 6.1). *[IAS 19.8, 103].*

A plan amendment occurs when an entity introduces, or withdraws, a defined benefit plan or changes the benefits payable under an existing defined benefit plan. *[IAS 19.8, 104].*

A curtailment occurs when an entity significantly reduces the number of employees covered by a plan. A curtailment may arise from an isolated event, such as the closing of a plant, discontinuance of an operation or termination or suspension of a plan. *[IAS 19.8, 105].*

Past service cost may be either positive (when benefits are introduced or changed so that the present value of the defined benefit obligation increases) or negative (when benefits are withdrawn or changed so that the present value of the defined benefit obligation decreases). *[IAS 19.8, 106].*

Where an entity reduces benefits payable under an existing defined benefit plan and, at the same time, increases other benefits payable under the plan for the same employees, the entity treats the change as a single net change. *[IAS 19.8, 107].*

Past service cost excludes:

(a) the effect of differences between actual and previously assumed salary increases on the obligation to pay benefits for service in prior years (there is no past service cost because actuarial assumptions allow for projected salaries, accordingly the effect of any such difference is an actuarial gain or loss – see 7.5 above);

(b) under- and over-estimates of discretionary pension increases when an entity has a constructive obligation to grant such increases (there is no past service cost because actuarial assumptions allow for such increases, accordingly the effect of any such under- or over-estimate is an actuarial gain or loss – see 7.5 above);

(c) estimates of benefit improvements that result from actuarial gains or from the return on plan assets that have been recognised in the financial statements if the entity is obliged, by either the formal terms of a plan (or a constructive obligation that goes beyond those terms) or legislation, to use any surplus in the plan for the benefit of plan participants, even if the benefit increase has not yet been formally awarded (the resulting increase in the obligation is an actuarial loss and not past service cost, see 7.5 above); and

(d) the increase in vested benefits (that is, those not conditional on future employment) when, in the absence of new or improved benefits, employees complete vesting requirements (there is no past service cost because the estimated cost of benefits was recognised as current service cost as the service was rendered, accordingly the effect of any such increase is an actuarial gain or loss, see 7.5 above). *[IAS 19.108].*

10.1.2 Settlements

IAS 19 defines a settlement as a transaction that eliminates all further legal or constructive obligations for part or all of the benefits provided under a defined benefit plan, other than a payment of benefits to, or on behalf of, employees that is set out in the terms of the plan and included in the actuarial assumptions. *[IAS 19.8]*.

A settlement occurs when an employer enters into a transaction that eliminates all further legal or constructive obligations for part or all of the benefits provided under a defined benefit plan (other than a payment of benefits to, or on behalf of, employees in accordance with the terms of the plan and included in the actuarial assumptions). For example, a one-off transfer of significant employer obligations under the plan to an insurance company through the purchase of an insurance policy (often referred to as a buy-out) is a settlement; a lump sum cash payment, under the terms of the plan, to plan participants in exchange for their rights to receive specified post-employment benefits is not. *[IAS 19.111]*.

In other words, settlement occurs at the point of absolute risk extinguishment.

The interaction between the asset ceiling and past service cost or a gain or loss on settlement is discussed further at 16.2.2 below.

IAS 19 observes that an employer may acquire an insurance policy to fund some or all of the employee benefits relating to employee service in the current and prior periods. The acquisition of such a policy is *not a settlement* if the employer retains a legal or constructive obligation to pay further amounts if the insurer does not pay the employee benefits specified in the insurance policy (often referred to as a buy-in). *[IAS 19.112]*. However, the acquisition of an insurance policy will mean an entity has an asset which needs to be measured at fair value. As discussed at 6.2 above, certain insurance policies are valued at an amount equal to the present value of the defined benefit obligation which they match. The cost of buying such a policy will typically greatly exceed its subsequent carrying amount. That raises the question of how to treat the resultant debit entry. One view might be that the loss is, in substance, very similar to a settlement loss and should be recognised in profit or loss. This treatment may be appropriate, for example, if the purchase of the insurance is in anticipation of full settlement with the insurer at a later date. Another view is that because the loss results from exchanging one plan asset for another it is an actuarial loss. The typical bid-offer spread in quoted investments results in the same type of actuarial loss, albeit typically less significant. In our view, either approach is acceptable if applied consistently and, where material, disclosed.

The following extract from IHG plc illustrates a buy-in which has occurred in one financial period and followed by a buy-out in the following financial period. As the policy was structured so as to enable the plan to move to a buy-out, and the intention was to proceed on that basis, the buy-in transaction was accounted for as a settlement with the loss arising recorded in the income statement.

Extract 33.1: InterContinental Hotels Group PLC (2014)

Notes to the Group Financial Statements [extract]

25. Retirement benefits [extract]

UK [extract]

Historically UK retirement and death in service benefits have been provided for eligible employees in the UK principally by the InterContinental Hotels UK Pension Plan, which has both defined benefit and defined contribution sections. The defined benefit section was subject to a buy-in transaction on 15 August 2013 whereby the assets of the plan were invested in a bulk purchase annuity policy with the insurer Rothesay Life under which the benefits payable to defined benefit members became fully insured. On 31 October 2014, the plan completed the move to a full buy-out of the defined benefit section, following which Rothesay Life has become fully and directly responsible for the pension obligations. On completion of the buy-out, the defined benefit assets (comprising the Rothesay Life insurance policy) and matching defined benefit liabilities were derecognised from the Group Statement of financial position.

US and other [extract]

In respect of the defined benefit plans, the amounts recognised in the Group income statement, in administrative expenses, are:

	Pension plans											
	UK			US and other			Post-employment benefits			Total		
	2014 $m	2013 $m	2012 $m	**2014 $m**	2013 $m	2012 $m	**2014 $m**	2013 $m	2012 $m	**2014 $m**	2013 $m	2012 $m
Current service cost	**–**	2	5	**1**	1	1	**–**	–	–	**1**	3	6
Past service cost	**–**	–	–	**–**	1	–	**–**	–	–	**–**	1	–
Net interest expense	**2**	–	1	**3**	3	3	**1**	1	1	**6**	4	5
Administration costs	**3**	1	1	**–**	1	1	**–**	–	–	**3**	2	2
Operating profit before exceptional items	**5**	3	7	**4**	6	5	**1**	1	1	**10**	10	13
Exceptional items:												
Settlement cost	**6**	147	–	**–**	–	–	**–**	–	–	**6**	147	–
	11	150	7	**4**	6	5	**1**	1	1	**16**	157	13

[...]

The settlement cost in 2013 resulted from the buy-in transaction described on the previous page and comprised a past service cost of $5m relating to additional benefits secured by the transaction, the $137m difference between the cost of the insurance policy and the accounting value of the liabilities secured and transaction costs of $5m. As the policy was structured to enable the plan to move to a buy-out and the intention was to proceed on that basis, the buy-in transaction was accounted for as a settlement with the loss arising recorded in the income statement. The full buy-out was completed on 31 October 2014.

10.2 Net interest on the net defined benefit liability (asset)

Net interest on the net defined benefit liability (asset) is the change during the period in the net defined benefit liability (asset) that arises from the passage of time. *[IAS 19.8]*. It is determined by multiplying the net defined benefit liability (asset) by the discount rate (see 7.6 above), both as determined at the start of the annual reporting period, taking account of any changes in the net defined benefit liability (asset) during the period as a result of contribution and benefit payments. *[IAS 19.123]*.

In our view, the requirement to take account of payments to and from the fund should also apply to other significant changes in the net defined benefit liability, for example settlements and curtailments. This is currently being discussed by the Interpretations Committee (see 16.2.1 below).

As the net item in the statement of financial position is comprised of two or three separate components (the defined benefit obligation, plan assets and the asset ceiling), the net interest is made up of interest unwinding on each of these components in the manner described above. *[IAS 19.124]*. Although, computationally, the net interest is so composed, for the purposes of presentation in profit or loss it is a single net amount.

Interest on plan assets calculated as described above will not, other than by coincidence, be the same as the actual return on plan assets. The difference is a remeasurement recognised in other comprehensive income (see 10.3.2 below). *[IAS 19.125]*.

Similarly, the difference in the asset ceiling between the start and end of the period is unlikely to equal the interest on this component described above. The difference between the total change in the effect of the asset ceiling and the interest effect is accounted for as a remeasurement in other comprehensive income. *[IAS 19.126]*.

10.3 Remeasurements

Remeasurements of the net defined benefit liability (asset) comprise:

(a) actuarial gains and losses;

(b) the return on plan assets, excluding amounts included in net interest on the net defined benefit liability (asset); and

(c) any change in the effect of the asset ceiling (see 8.2 above), excluding amounts included in net interest on the net defined benefit liability (asset). *[IAS 19.8, 127]*.

10.3.1 Actuarial gains and losses

Actuarial gains and losses are changes in the present value of the defined benefit obligation resulting from: experience adjustments (the effects of differences between the previous actuarial assumptions and what has actually occurred); and the effects of changes in actuarial assumptions. *[IAS 19.8]*. These can result, for example, from:

(a) unexpectedly high or low rates of: employee turnover, early retirement, mortality, increases in salaries or benefits, or medical costs (if the formal or constructive terms of the plan provide for inflationary benefits);

(b) the effect of changes to assumptions concerning benefit payment options;

(c) the effect of changes in estimates of: future employee turnover, early retirement or mortality or of increases in salaries, benefits (if the formal or constructive terms of the plan provide for inflationary benefit increases) or medical costs; and

(d) the effect of changes in the discount rate. *[IAS 19.128]*.

Actuarial gains and losses do not include changes in the present value of the defined benefit obligation because of the introduction, amendment, curtailment or settlement of the defined benefit plan, or changes to the benefits payable under the defined benefit plan. Such changes result in past service cost or gains or losses on settlement (see 10.1.1 and 10.1.2 above). *[IAS 19.129]*.

10.3.2 The return on plan assets, excluding amounts included in net interest on the net defined benefit liability (asset)

The return on plan assets is interest, dividends and other income derived from the plan assets, together with realised and unrealised gains on the assets, less

- any costs of managing plan assets; and
- any tax payable by the plan itself, other than tax included in the actuarial assumptions used to measure the present value of the defined benefit obligation.

Other administration costs are not deducted from the return on plan assets, as discussed further at 11 below. *[IAS 19.130]*.

11 DEFINED BENEFIT PLANS – COSTS OF ADMINISTERING EMPLOYEE BENEFIT PLANS

Some employee benefit plans incur costs as part of delivering employee benefits. The costs are generally more significant for post-retirement benefits such as pensions. Examples of costs include actuarial valuations, audits and the costs of managing any plan assets.

IAS 19 deals with some costs, as discussed below, but is silent on others.

The following costs are required to be factored into the measurement of the defined benefit obligation as part of the actuarial assumptions (see 7.5 above):

- in the case of medical benefits, future medical costs, including claim handling costs (i.e. the costs that will be incurred in processing and resolving claims, including legal and adjuster's fees); and
- taxes payable by the plan on contributions relating to service before the reporting date or on benefits resulting from that service. *[IAS 19.76(b)]*.

The following costs (and no others) are deducted from the return on plan assets (see 10.3.2 above):

- the costs of managing the plan assets; and
- any tax payable by the plan itself, other than tax included in the actuarial assumptions used to measure the defined benefit obligation. *[IAS 19.130]*.

As discussed at 10.2 above, net interest on the net liability or asset is reported in the income statement. This is a wholly computed amount which is uninfluenced by actual asset returns; the difference between actual asset returns and the credit element of the net interest amount forms part of remeasurements reported in other comprehensive income.

So, although not expressed in these terms, costs of administering plan assets and the tax mentioned above are reported in other comprehensive income.

The standard is silent on the treatment of any other costs of administering employee benefit plans. However, the Basis for Conclusions on IAS 19 contains the following: 'the Board decided that an entity should recognise administration costs when the administration services are provided. This practical expedient avoids the need to attribute costs between current and past service and future service'. *[IAS 19.BC127]*. The Board may well have taken that decision, however it did not include such a requirement in the standard.

In our view, such an approach is certainly an acceptable way to account for costs not dealt with in the standard; however other approaches could be acceptable, for example, in relation to closed schemes as discussed below. Entities need, in compliance with IAS 8, to develop an accounting policy in light of the standard not dealing with these costs. However, IAS 1 is clear that such costs would not be reported in other comprehensive income. *[IAS 1.88]*.

One alternative to simple accruals-accounting as costs are incurred could be relevant to closed plans, where employees are no longer exchanging services for defined benefits. In this situation, it is clear that any and all future costs of administering the plan relate to past periods and no attribution is necessary. An entity with such an arrangement may select a policy of full provision of all costs of 'running-off' the plan (apart from those specifically dealt with by the standard).

12 SHORT-TERM EMPLOYEE BENEFITS

Short-term employee benefits are employee benefits (other than termination benefits) that are expected to be settled wholly before twelve months after the end of the annual reporting period in which the employees render the related service. *[IAS 19.8]*.

The standard states that reclassification is not necessary if an entity's expectation of the timing of settlement changes temporarily. However, if the characteristics of the benefit change (such as a change from a non-accumulating benefit to an accumulating benefit) or if a change in expectations of the timing of settlement is not temporary, then the entity considers whether the benefit still meets the definition of short-term employee benefits. *[IAS 19.10]*.

They can include:

- wages, salaries and social security contributions;
- paid annual leave and paid sick leave;
- profit-sharing and bonuses; and
- non-monetary benefits (such as medical care, housing, cars and free or subsidised goods or services) for current employees. *[IAS 19.9]*.

12.1 General recognition criteria for short-term employee benefits

An entity should recognise the undiscounted amount of short-term benefits attributable to services that have been rendered in the period as an expense, unless another IFRS requires or permits the benefits to be included in the cost of an asset. This may particularly be the case under IAS 2 (see Chapter 22 at 3) and IAS 16 (see

Chapter 18 at 4). Any difference between the amount of cost recognised and cash payments made should be treated as a liability or prepayment as appropriate. *[IAS 19.11]*. There are further requirements in respect of short-term paid absences and profit-sharing and bonus plans as detailed below.

12.2 Short-term paid absences

These include absences for vacation (holiday), sickness and short-term disability, maternity or paternity leave, jury service and military service. These can either be accumulating or non-accumulating absences. *[IAS 19.14]*. Accumulating absences are those that can be carried forward and used in future periods if the entitlement in the current period is not used in full. They can be either vesting entitlements (which entitle employees to a cash payment in lieu of absences not taken on leaving the entity) or non-vesting entitlements (where no cash compensation is payable). Non-accumulating absences are those where there is no entitlement to carry forward unused days. An obligation arises as employees render service that increases their entitlement to future paid absences. *[IAS 19.15]*.

12.2.1 Accumulating absences

The cost of accumulating paid absences should be recognised when employees render the service that increases their entitlement to future paid absences. No distinction should be made between the recognition of vesting and non-vesting entitlements (see 12.2 above), on the basis that the liability arises as services are rendered in both cases. However, the measurement of non-vesting entitlements should take into account the possibility of employees leaving before receiving them. *[IAS 19.15]*.

The cost of accumulating paid absences should be measured as the additional amount that the entity expects to pay as a result of the unused entitlement that has accumulated at the end of the reporting period. *[IAS 19.16]*. In the case of unused paid sick leave, provision should be made only to the extent that it is expected that employees will use the sick leave in subsequent periods. The standard observes that in many cases, it may not be necessary to make detailed computations to estimate that there is no material obligation for unused paid absences. For example, IAS 19 considers it unlikely that a sick leave obligation will be material unless if there is a formal or informal understanding that unused paid sick leave may be taken as paid vacation. *[IAS 19.17]*.

The standard provides an example to illustrate the requirements for accumulating paid absences upon which the following is based: *[IAS 19.17]*

Example 33.8: Accumulating paid absences

An entity has 100 employees, who are each entitled to five working days of paid sick leave for each year. Unused sick leave may be carried forward for one calendar year. Sick leave is taken first out of the current year's entitlement and then out of any balance brought forward from the previous year (a LIFO basis). At 31 December 2015, the average unused entitlement is two days per employee. The entity expects, based on past experience which is expected to continue, that 92 employees will take no more than five days of paid sick leave in 2016 and that the remaining eight employees will take an average of six and a half days each.

The entity expects that it will pay an additional 12 days of sick pay as a result of the unused entitlement that has accumulated at 31 December 2015 (one and a half days each, for eight employees). Therefore, the entity recognises a liability equal to 12 days of sick pay.

12.2.2 Non-accumulating paid absences

The cost of non-accumulating absences should be recognised as and when they arise, on the basis that the entitlement is not directly linked to the service rendered by employees in the period. This is commonly the case for sick pay (to the extent that unused past entitlement cannot be carried forward), maternity or paternity leave and paid absences for jury service or military service. *[IAS 19.13(b), 18]*.

12.3 Profit-sharing and bonus plans

An entity should recognise the expected cost of profit-sharing and bonus payments when and only when:

- the entity has a present legal or constructive obligation to make such payments as a result of past events; and
- a reliable estimate of the obligation can be made. *[IAS 19.19]*.

The above are discussed in turn at 12.3.1 and 12.3.2 below. Statutory profit-sharing arrangements based on taxable profit are discussed at 12.3.3.

12.3.1 Present legal or constructive obligation

A present obligation exists when, and only when, the entity has no realistic alternative but to make the payments. *[IAS 19.19]*. IAS 19 clarifies that where a profit-sharing plan is subject to a loyalty period (i.e. a period during which employees must remain with the entity in order to receive their share), a constructive obligation is created as employees render service that increases the amount to be paid if they remain in service until the end of the specified period. However, the possibility of employees leaving during the loyalty period should be taken into account in measuring the cost of the plan. *[IAS 19.20]*. The standard illustrates the approach as follows:

Example 33.9: Profit sharing and bonus plans

A profit-sharing plan requires an entity to pay a specified proportion of its net profit for the year to employees who serve throughout the year. If no employees leave during the year, the total profit-sharing payments for the year will be 3% of profit. The entity estimates that staff turnover will reduce the payments to 2.5% of profit.

The entity recognises a liability and an expense of 2.5% of net profit.

It is worth noting that in the scenario above, when an entity prepares its accounts for the year it will no longer be uncertain whether all eligible employees become entitled to the bonus, as that is determined at the year-end. That means the reduction in the accrual from 3% to 2.5% should be an observable fact not an 'estimate'.

In our view, the standard is ambiguous regarding the period over which the expense of profit-sharing arrangements should be recognised where the amount paid is calculated by reference to the profit for a period, but payment is conditional upon the employee remaining in service beyond the end of that period. In particular, the requirement to recognise a cost over the period during which '... employees render service that increases the amount to be paid if they remain in service until the end of the specified period' could be read in two ways depending on the view taken as to what is the reference point in relation to which the amount paid increases.

One interpretation would be that the employee would receive nothing if he were to leave before the end of the additional service period. On this view, the cost would be recognised over not just the year in which it is 'earned', but over the longer period to when the employee has an unconditional right.

An alternative interpretation would be that, as the profit share is determined by reference to profit for a particular financial year, the amount of the bonus to be received stops increasing once the profit for the financial year stops increasing. Under this view, the cost of the bonus would all be recognised during that financial year.

In our opinion, either view is acceptable if applied consistently.

The standard also states that where an entity has a practice of paying bonuses, it has a constructive obligation to pay a bonus, even though there may be no legal obligation for it to do so. Again, however, in measuring the cost, the possibility of employees leaving before receiving a bonus should be taken into account. *[IAS 19.21]*.

12.3.2 *Reliable estimate of provision*

A reliable estimate of a legal or constructive obligation under a profit-sharing or bonus plan can be made when and only when:

- the formal terms of the plan contain a formula for determining the amount of the benefit;
- the entity determines the amounts to be paid before the financial statements are authorised for issue; or
- past practice gives clear evidence of the amount of the entity's constructive obligation. *[IAS 19.22]*.

IAS 19 states that an obligation under a profit-sharing or bonus plan must be accounted for as an expense and not a distribution of profit, since it results from employee service and not from a transaction with owners. *[IAS 19.23]*. Where profit-sharing and bonus payments are not expected to be settled wholly before twelve months after the end of the annual reporting period in which the employees render the related service, they should be accounted for as other long-term employee benefits (see 13 below). *[IAS 19.24]*.

12.3.3 *Statutory profit-sharing based on taxable profit.*

In November 2010, the Interpretations Committee was asked to clarify how to account for a particular statutory employee benefit whereby 10% of taxable profit is shared with employees. In particular, the request sought clarification as to whether analogy could be made to IAS 12 – *Income Taxes* – to account for temporary differences between accounting and taxable profit which would reverse in the future.

The Interpretations Committee thought that such an approach was not acceptable. It decided not to add the item to its agenda saying '[t]he Committee noted that the statutory employee profit-sharing arrangement described in the request should be accounted for in accordance with IAS 19, and that IAS 19 provides sufficient guidance on amounts that should be recognised and measured, with the result that significantly divergent interpretations are not expected in practice. Consequently, the Committee decided not to add this issue to its agenda'.[16]

13 LONG-TERM EMPLOYEE BENEFITS OTHER THAN POST-EMPLOYMENT BENEFITS

13.1 Meaning of other long-term employee benefits

These are all employee benefits other than post-employment benefits and termination benefits. *[IAS 19.8]*. They include the following if not expected to be settled wholly before twelve months after the end of the annual reporting period in which the employees rendered the related service:

- long-term paid absences such as long-service or sabbatical leave;
- jubilee or other long-service benefits;
- long-term disability benefits;
- profit-sharing and bonuses; and
- deferred remuneration. *[IAS 19.153]*.

13.2 Recognition and measurement

For such benefits IAS 19 requires a simplified version of the accounting treatment required in respect of defined benefit plans (which is discussed in detail at 5 above). The amount recognised as a liability for other long-term employee benefits should be the net total, at the end of the reporting period, of the present value of the defined benefit obligation and the fair value of plan assets (if any) out of which the obligations are to be settled directly. The net total of the following amounts should be recognised in profit or loss, except to the extent that another IFRS requires or permits their inclusion in the cost of an asset:

(a) service cost;

(b) net interest on the net defined benefit liability (asset); and

(c) remeasurements of the net defined benefit liability (asset).

In other words, all assets, liabilities, income and expenditure relating to such benefits should be accounted for in the same way, and subject to the same restrictions on the recognition of assets and income, as those relating to a defined benefit pension plan (see 8.1 and 8.2 above), except that remeasurements are recognised in profit or loss. *[IAS 19.155-156]*.

The standard explains the use of this simplified approach by asserting that the measurement of other long-term employee benefits is not usually subject to the same degree of uncertainty as that of post-employment benefits. *[IAS 19.154]*.

An illustration of the methodology to calculate the defined benefit obligation, service and interest costs is given in Example 33.2 at 7.3 above.

13.2.1 Attribution to years of service

Long-term employee benefit arrangements will typically have conditions attached to secure their vesting.

IAS 19 is unclear on the attribution of long-term remuneration to the years of service over which they are earned.

Consider an award made at the start of the year for a fixed cash payment. A third of the payment vests on each of the first, second and third anniversaries of the grant for employees still employed at each vesting date.

One interpretation would be that the 'benefit formula' attributes a third of the award to each year and that each of the three income statements will bear one third of the expense.

An alternative view is that there are three distinct awards with the same grant date, but with durations of one, two and three years. This pattern of vesting is sometimes described as 'graded vesting' and is discussed, in relation to share-based payments, in Chapter 32 at 6.2.2 and illustrated in Example 32.9.

In our view, either approach is acceptable if applied consistently.

13.2.2 Long-term disability benefit

Where long-term disability benefit depends on the length of service of the employee, an obligation arises as the employee renders service, which is to be measured according to the probability that payment will be required and the length of time for which payment is expected to be made. If, however, the level of benefit is the same for all disabled employees regardless of years of service, the expected cost is recognised only when an event causing disability occurs. *[IAS 19.157]*.

It is not clear why this distinction is made, since in principle both types of benefit are equally susceptible to actuarial measurement. If anything the cost of benefits applicable to all employees regardless of service is probably easier to quantify actuarially. Given that an exposure to disability benefits which grows with years of service is fully provided for (actuarially) as it grows over time, it would seem logical for full provision to be made immediately for an exposure which comes into being (in full) on the day the employee commences employment. The problem with such an approach would be what to do with the debit entry. It would not represent an asset as envisaged in the *Conceptual Framework*, which would tend to imply an instant charge to profit or loss. This may have been the reason for the Board to make the exception and link the recognition to the actual disability event. These issues are similar to those surrounding death-in-service benefits discussed at 3.6 above.

14 TERMINATION BENEFITS

Termination benefits are employee benefits payable as a result of either:

- an entity's decision to terminate an employee's employment before the normal retirement date; or
- an employee's decision to accept an offer of benefits in exchange for the termination of employment. *[IAS 19.8]*.

They are accounted for differently from other employee benefits because the event that gives rise to an obligation for them is the termination of employment rather than the rendering of service by the employee. *[IAS 19.159]*.

Termination benefits do not include employee benefits resulting from termination of employment at the request of the employee without an entity's offer, or as a result of mandatory retirement requirements, because those benefits are post-employment benefits. Some entities provide a lower level of benefit for termination of employment at the request of the employee (in substance, a post-employment benefit) than for termination of employment at the request of the entity. The difference between the benefit provided for termination of employment at the request of the employee and a higher benefit provided at the request of the entity is a termination benefit. *[IAS 19.160]*.

The form of the employee benefit does not determine whether it is provided in exchange for service or in exchange for termination of the employee's employment. Termination benefits are typically lump sum payments, but sometimes also include:

- enhancement of post-employment benefits, either indirectly through an employee benefit plan or directly; and
- salary until the end of a specified notice period if the employee renders no further service that provides economic benefits to the entity. *[IAS 19.161]*.

Indicators that an employee benefit is provided in exchange for services include the following:

- the benefit is conditional on future service being provided (including benefits that increase if further service is provided); and
- the benefit is provided in accordance with the terms of an employee benefit plan. *[IAS 19.162]*.

Some termination benefits are provided in accordance with the terms of an existing employee benefit plan. For example, they may be specified by statute, employment contract or union agreement, or may be implied as a result of the employer's past practice of providing similar benefits. As another example, if an entity makes an offer of benefits available for more than a short period, or there is more than a short period between the offer and the expected date of actual termination, an entity should consider whether it has established a new employee benefit plan and hence whether the benefits offered under that plan are termination benefits or post-employment benefits. Employee benefits provided in accordance with the terms of an employee benefit plan are termination benefits if they both result from an entity's decision to terminate an employee's employment and are not conditional on future service being provided. *[IAS 19.163]*. Benefits payable to incentivise employees to remain in service with the entity until the end of the termination period (referred to as stay bonuses) are not termination benefits because they are dependent on service being provided. These would be accounted for as either a short-term or long-term employee benefit as appropriate (see 12 and 13 above).

14.1 Statutory termination indemnities

Some employee benefits are provided regardless of the reason for the employee's departure. The payment of such benefits is certain (subject to any vesting or minimum service requirements) but the timing of their payment is uncertain. Although such benefits are described in some jurisdictions as termination indemnities or termination gratuities, they are post-employment benefits rather than termination benefits, and an entity accounts for them as post-employment benefits. *[IAS 19.164]*.

14.2 Recognition

An entity should recognise termination benefits as a liability and an expense at the earlier of the following dates:

- when it can no longer withdraw the offer of those benefits; and
- when it recognises costs for a restructuring that is within the scope of IAS 37 and involves the payment of termination benefits (discussed in Chapter 28 at 6.1). *[IAS 19.165].*

For termination benefits payable as a result of an employee's decision to accept an offer of benefits in exchange for the termination of employment, the time when an entity can no longer withdraw the offer of termination benefits is the earlier of:

- when the employee accepts the offer; and
- when a restriction (e.g. a legal, regulatory or contractual requirement or other restriction) on the entity's ability to withdraw the offer takes effect. This would be when the offer is made, if the restriction existed at the time of the offer. *[IAS 19.166].*

For termination benefits payable as a result of an entity's decision to terminate an employee's employment, the entity can no longer withdraw the offer when the entity has communicated to the affected employees a plan of termination meeting all of the following criteria:

- actions required to complete the plan indicate that it is unlikely that significant changes to the plan will be made;
- the plan identifies the number of employees whose employment is to be terminated, their job classifications or functions and their locations (but the plan need not identify each individual employee) and the expected completion date; and
- the plan establishes the termination benefits that employees will receive in sufficient detail that employees can determine the type and amount of benefits they will receive were their employment to be terminated. *[IAS 19.167].*

The standard notes that when an entity recognises termination benefits, it may also have to account for a plan amendment or a curtailment of other employee benefits (discussed at 10.1.1 above). *[IAS 19.168].*

14.3 Measurement

IAS 19 requires that on initial recognition and subsequent remeasurement, termination benefits should be measured in accordance with the nature of the employee benefit. If the termination benefits are an enhancement to post-employment benefits, the entity applies the requirements for post-employment benefits. Otherwise:

- if the termination benefits are expected to be settled wholly before twelve months after the end of the annual reporting period in which the termination benefit is recognised, the requirements for short-term employee benefits should be applied (discussed at 12 above); and
- if the termination benefits are not expected to be settled wholly before twelve months after the end of the annual reporting period, the requirements for other long-term employee benefits should be applied (discussed at 13 above). *[IAS 19.169].*

Because termination benefits are not provided in exchange for service, the standard notes that its rules relating to the attribution of the benefit to periods of service are not relevant (discussed at 7.4 above). *[IAS 19.170]*.

IAS 19 illustrates the accounting for termination benefits with an example.

Example 33.10: Termination benefits

Background

As a result of a recent acquisition, an entity plans to close a factory in ten months and, at that time, terminate the employment of all of the remaining employees at the factory. Because the entity needs the expertise of the employees at the factory to complete some contracts, it announces a plan of termination as follows.

Each employee who stays and renders service until the closure of the factory will receive on the termination date a cash payment of $30,000. Employees leaving before closure of the factory will receive $10,000.

There are 120 employees at the factory. At the time of announcing the plan, the entity expects 20 of them to leave before closure. Therefore, the total expected cash outflows under the plan are $3,200,000 (i.e. 20 × $10,000 + 100 × $30,000). As required by the standard, the entity accounts for benefits provided in exchange for termination of employment as termination benefits and accounts for benefits provided in exchange for services as short-term employee benefits.

Termination benefits

The benefit provided in exchange for termination of employment is $10,000. This is the amount that an entity would have to pay for terminating the employment regardless of whether the employees stay and render service until closure of the factory or they leave before closure. Even though the employees can leave before closure, the termination of all employees' employment is a result of the entity's decision to close the factory and terminate their employment (i.e. all employees will leave employment when the factory closes). Therefore the entity recognises a liability of $1,200,000 (i.e. 120 × $10,000) for the termination benefits provided in accordance with the employee benefit plan at the earlier of when the plan of termination is announced and when the entity recognises the restructuring costs associated with the closure of the factory.

Benefits provided in exchange for service

The incremental benefits that employees will receive if they provide services for the full ten-month period are in exchange for services provided over that period. The entity accounts for them as short-term employee benefits because the entity expects to settle them before twelve months after the end of the annual reporting period. In this example, discounting is not required, so an expense of $200,000 (i.e. $2,000,000 ÷ 10) is recognised in each month during the service period of ten months, with a corresponding increase in the carrying amount of the liability.

15 DISCLOSURE REQUIREMENTS

15.1 Defined contribution plans

IAS 19 requires the disclosure of the expense recognised for defined contribution plans. It also notes that IAS 24 requires disclosure of the contributions in respect of key management personnel. *[IAS 19.53, 54]*.

15.2 Defined benefit plans

IAS 19 requires extensive disclosure in relation to defined benefit plans, as set out below.

The standard requires an entity to disclose information that:

(a) explains the characteristics of its defined benefit plans and risks associated with them;

(b) identifies and explains the amounts in its financial statements arising from its defined benefit plans; and

(c) describes how its defined benefit plans may affect the amount, timing and uncertainty of the entity's future cash flows. *[IAS 19.135]*.

To achieve the above, the standard sets out a long and detailed list of narrative and numerical disclosure requirements (considered further below).

The Board also noted that entities must comply with the general materiality requirements of IAS 1 (discussed in Chapter 3 at 4.1.5), including the requirement to disclose additional information if necessary, and that the financial statements need not contain disclosures that are not material. *[IAS 19.BC209]*.

One of the Board's objectives in regard to disclosure was to ensure that financial statements provide relevant information that is not obscured by excessive detail. *[IAS 19.BC207]*.

These references to excessive detail and non-disclosure of immaterial items suggest the Board is expecting entities to apply judgement regarding the level of detail to be provided rather than giving everything set out in the standard.

To meet the objectives above, the standard requires consideration of all the following:

(a) the level of detail necessary to satisfy the disclosure requirements;

(b) how much emphasis to place on each of the various requirements;

(c) how much aggregation or disaggregation to undertake; and

(d) whether users of financial statements need additional information to evaluate the quantitative information disclosed. *[IAS 19.136]*.

If the disclosures provided in accordance with the requirements of IAS 19 and other IFRSs are insufficient to meet the objectives above, an entity should disclose additional information necessary to meet those objectives. For example, an entity may present an analysis of the present value of the defined benefit obligation that distinguishes the nature, characteristics and risks of the obligation. Such a disclosure could distinguish:

(a) between amounts owing to active members, deferred members, and pensioners;

(b) between vested benefits and accrued but not vested benefits; and

(c) between conditional benefits, amounts attributable to future salary increases and other benefits. *[IAS 19.137]*.

An assessment should be made as to whether all or some disclosures should be disaggregated to distinguish plans or groups of plans with materially different risks. For example, an entity may disaggregate disclosure about plans showing one or more of the following features:

(a) different geographical locations;

(b) different characteristics such as flat salary pension plans, final salary pension plans or post-employment medical plans;

(c) different regulatory environments;

(d) different reporting segments; and

(e) different funding arrangements (e.g. wholly unfunded, wholly funded or partly funded). *[IAS 19.138]*.

15.2.1 Characteristics of defined benefit plans and risks associated with them

IAS 19 requires disclosure of:

(a) information about the characteristics of its defined benefit plans, including:

 (i) the nature of the benefits provided by the plan (e.g. final salary defined benefit plan or contribution-based plan with guarantee);

 (ii) a description of the regulatory framework in which the plan operates, for example the level of any minimum funding requirements, and any effect of the regulatory framework on the plan, such as the asset ceiling;

 (iii) a description of any other entity's responsibilities for the governance of the plan, for example responsibilities of trustees or of board members of the plan; and

(b) a description of the risks to which the plan exposes the entity, focused on any unusual, entity-specific or plan-specific risks, and of any significant concentrations of risk. For example, if plan assets are invested primarily in one class of investments, e.g. property, the plan may expose the entity to a concentration of property market risk; and

(c) a description of any plan amendments, curtailments and settlements. *[IAS 19.139]*.

15.2.2 *Explanation of amounts in the financial statements*

The disclosures should provide a reconciliation from the opening balance to the closing balance for each of the following, if applicable:

(a) the net defined benefit liability (asset), showing separate reconciliations for:
   - (i) plan assets;
   - (ii) the present value of the defined benefit obligation; and
   - (iii) the effect of the asset ceiling; and

(b) any reimbursement rights. If there are reimbursement rights a description of the relationship between them and the related obligation should be given. *[IAS 19.140]*.

Each reconciliation listed in (a) and (b) above should show each of the following, if applicable:

(a) current service cost;

(b) interest income or expense (see 10.2 above);

(c) remeasurements of the net defined benefit liability (asset), showing separately:
   - (i) the return on plan assets, excluding amounts included in interest in (b) above;
   - (ii) actuarial gains and losses arising from changes in demographic assumptions;
   - (iii) actuarial gains and losses arising from changes in financial assumptions; and
   - (iv) changes in the effect of limiting a net defined benefit asset to the asset ceiling, excluding amounts included in interest in (b). There should also be disclosure of how the maximum economic benefit available was determined, i.e. whether those benefits would be in the form of refunds, reductions in future contributions or a combination of both;

(d) past service cost and gains and losses arising from settlements. Past service cost and gains and losses arising from settlements need not be distinguished if they occur together (see 10.1 above);

(e) the effect of changes in foreign exchange rates;

(f) contributions to the plan, showing separately those by the employer and by plan participants;

(g) payments from the plan, showing separately the amount paid in respect of any settlements; and

(h) the effects of business combinations and disposals. *[IAS 19.141]*.

The following extract from BT Group plc shows how they have presented the above reconciliations.

Extract 33.2: BT Group plc (2016)

Notes to the consolidated financial statements [extract]

19. Retirement benefit plans [extract]

Movements in defined benefit plan assets and liabilities

The table below shows the movements on the plan assets and liabilities in the year and indicates where they are reflected in the financial statements.

	Assets £m	Liabilities £m	Deficit £m
At 31 March 2014	40,133	(47,135)	(7,022)
Current service cost (including administrative expenses and PPF levy)	(42)	(254)	(296)
Interest on pension deficit	1,663	(1,955)	(292)
Past service credit	–	5	5
Included in the group income statement			**(583)**
Return on plan assets above the amount included in the group income statement[a]	3,083	–	3,083
Actuarial loss arising from changes in financial assumptions[b]	–	(4,703)	(4,703)
Actuarial gain arising from changes in demographic assumptions[b]	–	126	126
Actuarial gain arising from experience adjustments[c]	–	443	443
Included in the group statement of comprehensive income			**(1,051)**
Regular contributions by employer	178	–	178
Deficit contributions by employer	876	–	876
Included in the group cash flow statement			**1,054**
Contributions by employees	12	(12)	–
Benefits paid	(2,231)	2,231	–
Foreign exchange	(25)	44	19
Other movements			**19**
At 31 March 2015	**43,627**	**(51,210)**	**(7,583)**
Current service cost (including administration expenses and PPF levy)	(40)	(261)	(301)
Interest on pension deficit	1,406	(1,627)	(221)
Included in the group income statement			**(522)**
Return on plan assets below the amount included in the group income statement[a]	(423)	–	(423)
Actuarial gain arising from changes in financial assumptions[b]	–	255	255
Actuarial gain arising from demographic assumptions[b]	–	2	2
Actuarial gain arising from experience adjustments[c]	–	921	921
Included in the group statement of comprehensive income			**755**
Regular contributions by employer	226	–	226
Deficit contributions by employer	880	–	880
Included in the group cash flow statement			**1,106**
EEPS position at acquisition	585	(698)	(113)
Contributions by employees	10	(10)	–
Benefits paid	(2,321)	2,321	–
Foreign exchange	18	(43)	(25)
Other movements			**(138)**
At 31 March 2016	**43,968**	**(50,350)**	**(6,382)**

a	The total actual return on plan assets in 2015/16 was a gain of £983m (2014/15: £4,746m).
b	The actuarial gain or loss arises from changes in the assumptions used to value the defined benefit liabilities at the end of the year compared with the assumptions used at the start of the year. This includes both financial assumptions, which are based on market conditions at the year end, and demographic assumptions such as life expectancy.
c	The actuarial loss or gain arising from experience adjustments on defined benefit liabilities represents the impact on the liabilities of differences between actual experience during the year compared with the assumptions made at the start of the year. Such differences might arise, for example, from members choosing different benefit options at retirement, actual salary increases being different from those assumed or actual benefit increases being higher than the inflation assumption.

The fair value of the plan assets should be disaggregated into classes that distinguish the nature and risks of those assets, subdividing each class of plan asset into those that have a quoted market price in an active market (as defined in IFRS 13, see Chapter 14) and those that do not. For example, and considering the level of detail of disclosure, aggregation and emphasis discussed at 15.2 above, an entity could distinguish between:

(a) cash and cash equivalents;

(b) equity instruments (segregated by industry type, company size, geography etc.);

(c) debt instruments (segregated by type of issuer, credit quality, geography etc.);

(d) real estate (segregated by geography etc.);

(e) derivatives (segregated by type of underlying risk in the contract, for example, interest rate contracts, foreign exchange contracts, equity contracts, credit contracts, longevity swaps etc.);

(f) investment funds (segregated by type of fund);

(g) asset-backed securities; and

(h) structured debt. *[IAS 19.142]*.

The fair value of an entity's own transferable financial instruments held as plan assets, and the fair value of plan assets that are property occupied by, or other assets used by, the entity should be disclosed. *[IAS 19.143]*.

The following extract from Diageo plc illustrates how the plan assets may be disaggregated.

Extract 33.3: Diageo plc (2014)

OPERATING ASSETS AND LIABILITIES [extract]

13. POST EMPLOYMENT BENEFITS [extract]

(c) Investment and hedging strategy [extract]

	2014				2013 (restated)			
	United Kingdom £ million	**Ireland £ million**	**United States and other £ million**	**Total £ million**	United Kingdom **£ million**	Ireland **£ million**	United States and other **£ million**	Total **£ million**
Equities								
Quoted	**1,222**	**433**	**249**	**1,904**	1,289	468	315	2,072
Unquoted and private equity	**281**	**2**	**22**	**305**	299	2	23	324
Bonds								
Fixed-interest government	**319**	**64**	**36**	**419**	347	65	67	479
Inflation-linked government	**857**	**100**	**4**	**961**	684	203	3	890
Investment grade corporate	**835**	**362**	**210**	**1,407**	820	162	94	1,076
Non-investment grade	**224**	**12**	**11**	**247**	110	18	3	131
Loan securities	**469**	**143**	**–**	**612**	359	60	–	419
Repurchase agreements	**710**	**–**	**–**	**710**	553	–	–	553
Property – unquoted	**525**	**75**	**8**	**608**	484	72	9	565
Hedge funds	**202**	**127**	**–**	**329**	209	129	–	338
Interest rate and inflation swaps	**(295)**	**60**	**–**	**(235)**	(161)	55	–	(106)
Cash and other	**147**	**7**	**59**	**213**	230	43	68	341
Total bid value of assets	**5,496**	**1,385**	**599**	**7.480**	5,223	1,277	582	7,082

An entity should disclose the significant actuarial assumptions used to determine the present value of the defined benefit obligation. Such disclosure should be in absolute terms (e.g. as an absolute percentage, and not just as a margin between different percentages and other variables). When an entity provides disclosures in total for a grouping of plans, it should provide such disclosures in the form of weighted averages or relatively narrow ranges. *[IAS 19.144]*.

15.2.3 Amount, timing and uncertainty of future cash flows

An entity should disclose:

(a) a sensitivity analysis for each significant actuarial assumption as of the end of the reporting period, showing how the defined benefit obligation would have been affected by changes in the relevant actuarial assumption that were reasonably possible at that date;

(b) the methods and assumptions used in preparing the sensitivity analyses required by (a) and the limitations of those methods; and

(c) changes from the previous period in the methods and assumptions used in preparing the sensitivity analyses, and the reasons for such changes. *[IAS 19.145]*.

A description should be given of any asset-liability matching strategies used by the plan or the entity, including the use of annuities and other techniques, such as longevity swaps, to manage risk. *[IAS 19.146]*.

To provide an indication of the effect of the defined benefit plan on the entity's future cash flows, an entity should disclose:

(a) a description of any funding arrangements and funding policies that affect future contributions;

(b) the expected contributions to the plan for the next annual reporting period; and

(c) information about the maturity profile of the defined benefit obligation. This will include the weighted average duration of the defined benefit obligation and may include other information about the distribution of the timing of benefit payments, such as a maturity analysis of the benefit payments. *[IAS 19.147]*.

The following extract from BT Group plc illustrates the maturity profile of the defined benefit obligation.

Extract 33.4: BT Group plc (2016)

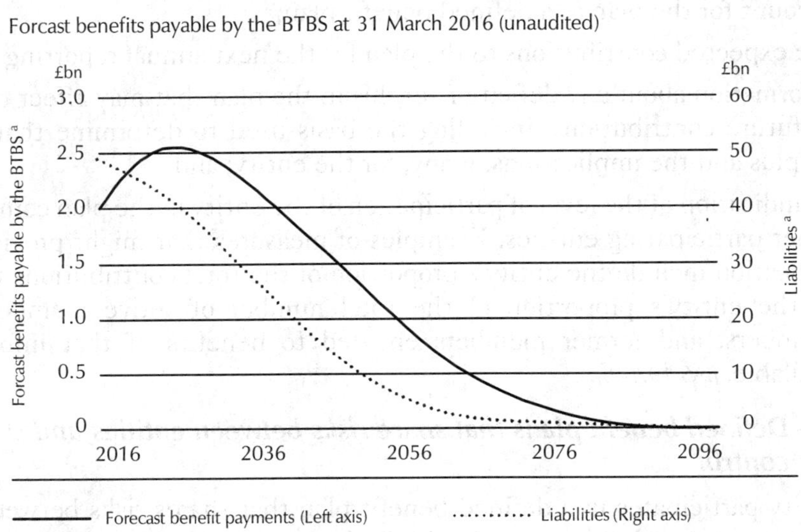

[a] Based on accrued benefits to date.

15.2.4 *Multi-employer plans*

If an entity participates in a multi-employer defined benefit plan, different disclosures are required depending upon how the arrangement is accounted for. These are discussed below.

15.2.4.A Plans accounted for as defined benefit plans

If an entity participates in a multi-employer defined benefit plan and accounts for it as such, it should make all the required disclosures discussed above. In addition, it should disclose:

(a) a description of the funding arrangements, including the method used to determine the entity's rate of contributions and any minimum funding requirements;

(b) a description of the extent to which the entity can be liable to the plan for other entities' obligations under the terms and conditions of the multi-employer plan;

(c) a description of any agreed allocation of a deficit or surplus on:

 (i) wind-up of the plan; or

 (ii) the entity's withdrawal from the plan. *[IAS 19.148]*.

15.2.4.B Plans accounted for as defined contribution plans

If an entity accounts for a multi-employer defined benefit plan as if it were a defined contribution plan, it should disclose the following, in addition to the information required by 15.2.4.A above and instead of the disclosures normally required for defined benefits and discussed in 15.2 to 15.2.3 above:

(a) the fact that the plan is a defined benefit plan;

(b) the reason why sufficient information is not available to enable the entity to account for the plan as a defined benefit plan;

(c) the expected contributions to the plan for the next annual reporting period;

(d) information about any deficit or surplus in the plan that may affect the amount of future contributions, including the basis used to determine that deficit or surplus and the implications, if any, for the entity; and

(e) an indication of the level of participation of the entity in the plan compared with other participating entities. Examples of measures that might provide such an indication include the entity's proportion of the total contributions to the plan or the entity's proportion of the total number of active members, retired members, and former members entitled to benefits, if that information is available. *[IAS 19.148]*.

15.2.5 Defined benefit plans that share risks between entities under common control

If an entity participates in a defined benefit plan that shares risks between entities under common control, the entity should disclose:

(a) the contractual agreement or stated policy for charging the net defined benefit cost or the fact that there is no such policy; and

(b) the policy for determining the contribution to be paid by the entity. *[IAS 19.149]*.

Further disclosures are required depending upon how the arrangement is accounted for. These are discussed below.

15.2.5.A Plans accounted for as defined benefit plans

If an entity participates in a defined benefit plan that shares risks between entities under common control and accounts for an allocation of the net defined benefit cost, it should also disclose all the information about the plan as a whole set out in 15.2 to 15.2.3 above. *[IAS 19.149]*.

15.2.5.B Plans accounted for as defined contribution plans

If an entity participates in a defined benefit plan that shares risks between entities under common control and accounts for the net contribution payable for the period, it should also disclose the information set out below. *[IAS 19.149]*.

The standard requires disclosure of information that:

(a) explains the characteristics of its defined benefit plans and risks associated with them;

(b) identifies and explains the amounts in its financial statements arising from its defined benefit plans; and

(c) describes how its defined benefit plans may affect the amount, timing and uncertainty of the entity's future cash flows.

To meet the objectives above, the standard requires consideration of all the following:

(a) the level of detail necessary to satisfy the disclosure requirements;

(b) how much emphasis to place on each of the various requirements;

(c) how much aggregation or disaggregation to undertake; and

(d) whether users of financial statements need additional information to evaluate the quantitative information disclosed. *[IAS 19.136]*.

If the disclosures provided in accordance with the requirements in IAS 19 and other IFRSs are insufficient to meet the objectives above, an entity should disclose additional information necessary to meet those objectives. For example, an entity may present an analysis of the present value of the defined benefit obligation that distinguishes the nature, characteristics and risks of the obligation. Such a disclosure could distinguish:

(a) between amounts owing to active members, deferred members, and pensioners;

(b) between vested benefits and accrued but not vested benefits; and

(c) between conditional benefits, amounts attributable to future salary increases and other benefits. *[IAS 19.137]*.

IAS 19 requires disclosure of:

(a) information about the characteristics of its defined benefit plans, including:

  (i) the nature of the benefits provided by the plan (e.g. final salary defined benefit plan or contribution-based plan with guarantee);

  (ii) a description of the regulatory framework in which the plan operates, for example the level of any minimum funding requirements, and any effect of the regulatory framework on the plan, such as the asset ceiling; and

  (iii) a description of any other entity's responsibilities for the governance of the plan, for example responsibilities of trustees or of board members of the plan;

(b) a description of the risks to which the plan exposes the entity, focused on any unusual, entity-specific or plan-specific risks, and of any significant concentrations of risk. For example, if plan assets are invested primarily in one class of investments, e.g. property, the plan may expose the entity to a concentration of property market risk; and

(c) a description of any plan amendments, curtailments and settlements.

The fair value of the plan assets should be disaggregated into classes that distinguish the nature and risks of those assets, subdividing each class of plan asset into those that have a quoted market price in an active market (as defined in IFRS 13, discussed in Chapter 14) and those that do not. For example, and considering the level of detail of disclosure, aggregation and emphasis discussed at 15.2 above, an entity could distinguish between:

(a) cash and cash equivalents;

(b) equity instruments (segregated by industry type, company size, geography etc.);

(c) debt instruments (segregated by type of issuer, credit quality, geography etc.);

(d) real estate (segregated by geography etc.);

(e) derivatives (segregated by type of underlying risk in the contract, for example, interest rate contracts, foreign exchange contracts, equity contracts, credit contracts, longevity swaps etc.);

(f) investment funds (segregated by type of fund);

(g) asset-backed securities; and

(h) structured debt. *[IAS 19.142]*.

The fair value of the entity's own transferable financial instruments held as plan assets, and the fair value of plan assets that are property occupied by, or other assets used by, the entity should be disclosed. *[IAS 19.143]*.

An entity should disclose the significant actuarial assumptions used to determine the present value of the defined benefit obligation. Such disclosure should be in absolute terms (e.g. as an absolute percentage, and not just as a margin between different percentages and other variables). When an entity provides disclosures in total for a grouping of plans, it shall provide such disclosures in the form of weighted averages or relatively narrow ranges.

To provide an indication of the effect of the defined benefit plan on the entity's future cash flows, an entity should disclose:

(a) a description of any funding arrangements and funding policy that affect future contributions; and

(b) the expected contributions to the plan for the next annual reporting period.

The information described in 15.2.5.A and 15.2.5.B must be presented in the entity's own accounts. The rest of the information discussed in this section may be disclosed by cross-reference to disclosures in another group entity's financial statements if:

(a) that group entity's financial statements separately identify and disclose the information required about the plan; and

(b) that group entity's financial statements are available to users of the financial statements on the same terms as the financial statements of the entity and at the same time as, or earlier than, the financial statements of the entity. *[IAS 19.150]*.

15.2.6 *Disclosure requirements in other IFRSs*

IFRIC 14 does not introduce any new disclosure requirements. However, it suggests that any restrictions on the current realisability of the surplus or a description of the basis used to determine the amount of the economic benefit available (see 8.2 above), may require disclosure under the provisions in IAS 1 about key sources of estimation uncertainty. *[IFRIC 14.10]*. These requirements are discussed in Chapter 3 at 5.2.1.

Where required by IAS 24 an entity discloses information about:

(a) related party transactions with post-employment benefit plans; and

(b) post-employment benefits for key management personnel. *[IAS 19.151]*.

Where required by IAS 37 an entity discloses information about contingent liabilities arising from post-employment benefit obligations. *[IAS 19.152]*.

15.3 Other employee benefits

IAS 19 has no specific disclosure requirements in respect of other types of employee benefits within its scope (i.e. short-term employee benefits, long-term employee benefits other than post-employment benefits and termination benefits) but contains reminders that:

- IAS 24 requires disclosure of employee benefits for key management personnel (see Chapter 37); and
- IAS 1 requires disclosure of employee benefits expense. *[IAS 19.25, 158, 171]*.

16 POSSIBLE FUTURE DEVELOPMENTS

16.1 IASB activities

As discussed at 1 above, the IASB published the current version of IAS 19 in June 2011 (with amendments in November 2013 and September 2014). This represented the first phase in what was originally to be a two phase project. The second phase was to be a comprehensive review of all aspects of the standard. The IASB is now considering a plan for a research project to review the accounting for post-employment benefits. The review will be broad-based, focusing on developing a model that provides sound financial reporting, from the perspective of the reporting entity, of plans that range from pure defined contribution to pure defined benefit. The IASB noted that there is a growing range of hybrid plan designs that incorporate features of both defined contribution and defined benefit plans. Such plans were not envisaged when IAS 19 was developed and are becoming problematic for IAS 19.[17]

16.2 Interpretations Committee activities

The Interpretations Committee is currently discussing two IAS 19/IFRIC 14 matters:

- remeasurements following a plan amendment, curtailment or settlement (see 16.2.1 below); and
- the availability of a refund from a defined benefit plan (see 16.2.2 below).

16.2.1 Remeasurements following a plan amendment, curtailment or settlement

In May 2014, the Interpretations Committee received a request to clarify the accounting treatment for issues related to the remeasurement of the net defined benefit liability in the event of a plan amendment or curtailment. It discussed two issues.

If a significant plan amendment or curtailment of a defined benefit plan occurs, should an entity:

- take account of the remeasurement of the net defined benefit liability at the event date when determining net interest for the post-event period; and
- revise any actuarial assumptions for the calculation of service cost and net interest in the post-event period?

The Interpretations Committee noted that paragraph BC64 of IAS 19 implies that an entity should not revise any assumptions for the calculation of service cost and net interest in the post-event period, even if a significant event or change to the pension plan occurs. However, the Interpretations Committee raised a concern that this would result in presenting current service cost and net interest in the post-event period, ignoring the effects of the significant event or change. The Interpretations Committee tentatively decided to develop an amendment to address this concern. It thought that updating the net defined benefit liability and any actuarial assumptions to determine current service cost and net interest in the post-event period if a significant event or change occurs would result in more relevant information.[18]

The Interpretations Committee reaffirmed this decision at its meeting in July 2014. The matter was proposed to the IASB as an annual improvement.[19]

During the drafting of this proposed amendment some of the members had questioned whether a significant market fluctuation occurring during an annual period also required the remeasurement of the net defined benefit liability when preparing annual financial statements. The matter was further discussed by the Interpretations Committee at its meeting in November 2014. The Interpretations Committee was concerned that addressing this issue might be too broad for it to deal with and could lead to a significant change in the application of IAS 19. Consequently, the Interpretations Committee agreed that the scope of its proposal should only cover situations resulting from a plan amendment, curtailment or settlement.[20]

In June 2015, the IASB published an exposure draft containing proposed amendments to IAS 19.[21] The exposure draft addresses the accounting when a plan amendment, curtailment or settlement occurs during a period with the following proposed guidance:

- When the net defined benefit liability (asset) is remeasured in accordance with paragraph 99 of IAS 19 (i.e. when a plan amendment, curtailment or settlement occurs):
  - the current service cost and the net interest for the period after the remeasurement are determined using the assumptions used for the remeasurement; and
  - an entity determines the net interest for the remaining period based on the remeasured net defined benefit liability (asset).

- The current service cost and the net interest in the current reporting period before a plan amendment, curtailment or settlement are not affected by, or included in, the past service cost or gain or loss on settlement.

It is proposed that these amendments should be applied retrospectively in accordance with IAS 8, except that an entity need not adjust the carrying amount of assets outside the scope of IAS 19 for changes in employee benefit costs that were included in the carrying amount of those assets before the beginning of the earliest comparative period presented in the financial statements in which these amendments first applied. Earlier application is permitted, but must be disclosed.

A summary of the feedback on the exposure draft was discussed by the Interpretations Committee in their July 2016 meeting, but no decisions were made at this date.[22] The Interpretations Committee deliberated the proposed amendments at their September 2016 meeting, taking into account the feedback received. The Interpretation Committee's recommendations will be taken to the Board at a future date. It is expected that the amendments will be issued in early 2017 with an effective date of 1 January 2019.

16.2.2 The availability of a refund from a defined benefit plan

At 8.2.1 above we discuss how certain powers of pension fund trustees (to set investment policy, for example) may influence the recognition of a net defined benefit asset by reference to refunds.

The Interpretations Committee received a similar question and, in May 2014, published a description of its initial discussion which is summarised below.

The Interpretations Committee discussed a question about whether an employer has an unconditional right to a refund of a surplus in the following circumstances:

- the trustee acts on behalf of the plan's members and is independent from the employer; and
- the trustee has discretion in the event of a surplus arising in the plan to make alternative use of that surplus by augmenting the benefits payable to members or by winding up the plan through purchase of annuities, or both.

The question discussed related to a plan that is closed to accrual of future benefits, such that there will be no future service costs, and so no economic benefit is available through a reduction in future contributions. The Interpretations Committee also noted that:

- the fact that an existing surplus at the balance sheet date could be decreased or extinguished by uncertain future events that are beyond the control of the entity is not relevant to the existence of the right to a refund;
- if the trustee can use a surplus by augmenting the benefits in the future, pursuant to the formal terms of a plan (or a constructive obligation that goes beyond those terms), this fact should be considered when the entity measures its defined benefit obligation; and
- the amount of surplus to be recognised could be zero, as a consequence of the measurement of the defined benefit obligation.[23]

The Interpretations Committee discussed the matter again at its meeting in July 2014 and considered the informal feedback received from the IASB members.

The Interpretations Committee noted the difficulty associated with assessing the consequences of the trustee's future actions and its effect on the entity's ability to estimate reliably the amount to be received. Consequently, a majority of Interpretations Committee members observed that no asset should be recognised in this circumstance.

However, some Interpretations Committee members were concerned about the consequences that this conclusion could have on the accounting for a minimum funding requirement and the consistency of this conclusion with the recognition and measurement requirements of IAS 19.

Consequently, the Interpretations Committee requested the staff to perform further analyses on the interaction of this tentative decision with the requirement to recognise an additional liability when a minimum funding requirement applies and the relationship with the general requirements of IAS 19.

In its meeting in September 2014, as a result of its detailed analysis, the Interpretations Committee noted that it believed that there would be no conflicts between its conclusion at the July 2014 meeting and the recognition and measurement requirements of IAS 19, as the application of the asset ceiling requirements is separate from the determination of a surplus (deficit) under IAS 19. It also noted that the conclusion should lead to consistent results when a minimum funding requirement exists.[24] The Interpretations Committee thought that the trustees' powers to buy annuities or make other investment decisions are different from their ability to use a surplus to enhance benefits (a pension promise). It also thought that an entity's ability to realise an economic benefit through a 'gradual settlement' is restricted if a trustee can decide at any time to make a full settlement (i.e. a plan wind-up), even though paragraph 14 of IFRIC 14 allows the assumption of a gradual settlement over time until all members have left the plan. The Committee proposed amendments to IFRIC 14 which are detailed below.

As a result of the discussions in the September 2014 meeting, the IASB has published an exposure draft which, if approved, will amend IFRIC 14 to require that, when an entity determines the availability of a refund from a defined benefit plan:

- The amount of the surplus that an entity recognises as an asset on the basis of a future refund should not include amounts that other parties (for example, the plan trustees) can use for other purposes without the entity's consent.
- An entity should not assume gradual settlement of the plan as the justification for the recognition of an asset, if other parties can wind up the plan without the entity's consent.
- Other parties' power to buy annuities as plan assets or make other investment decisions without changing the benefits for plan members does not affect the availability of a refund.

The exposure draft also proposes amending IFRIC 14 to confirm that when an entity determines the availability of a refund and a reduction in future contributions, the entity should take into account the statutory requirements that are substantively enacted, as well as the terms and conditions that are contractually agreed and any constructive obligations.

In addition, the exposure draft addresses the interaction between the asset ceiling and a past service cost or a gain or loss on settlement. It proposes amending IAS 19 to clarify that:

- the past service cost or gain or loss on settlement is measured and recognised in profit and loss in accordance with IAS 19; and
- changes in the effect of the asset ceiling are recognised in other comprehensive income, and are determined after the recognition of the past service cost or the gain or loss on settlement.

The transition requirements would be the same as those detailed above in 16.2.1.

A summary of the feedback on the exposure draft was discussed by the Interpretations Committee in their July 2016 meeting, but no decisions were made at this date.[25] The Interpretations Committee deliberated the proposed amendments at their September 2016 meeting, taking into account the feedback received. The Interpretation Committee's recommendations will be taken to the Board at a future date. It is expected that the amendments will be issued in early 2017 with an effective date of 1 January 2019 (early adoption permitted).

References

1 *IFRIC Update,* IFRS Interpretations Committee, September 2012.
2 *IFRIC Update*, May 2014.
3 E54 *Employee Benefits*, IASC, October 1996, paras. 17-21.
4 *IFRIC Update*, January 2008.
5 *IASB Update*, September 2007.
6 *IASB Update*, November 2007.
7 *IFRIC Update,* May 2011.
8 *IFRIC update*, November 2014.
9 Staff paper for the February 2013 IASB meeting, Agenda ref 9B, Appendix C-Staff paper for the November 2012 IFRS IC meeting, Appendix A, Examples 3-5.
10 *IFRIC Update*, July 2013.
11 *IFRIC Update*, November 2013.
12 *IASB Update*, December 2013.
13 *IFRIC Update*, June 2005.
14 *IFRIC Update*, March 2015.
15 *IFRIC Update*, July 2015.
16 *IFRIC Update*, November 2010.
17 *IASB Update*, September 2014.
18 *IFRIC Update*, May 2014.
19 *IFRIC Update*, July 2014.
20 *IFRIC Update*, November 2014.
21 *Exposure draft ED/2015/5: Remeasurement on a Plan Amendment, Curtailment of Settlement/Availability of a refund from a Defined Benefit Plan*, June 2015.
22 *IFRIC Update*, July 2016.
23 *IFRIC Update*, May 2014.
24 *IFRIC Update*, September 2014.
25 *IFRIC Update*, July 2016.

[illegible]

Chapter 34 Operating segments

List of examples

Chapter 34 Operating segments

1 INTRODUCTION

1.1 Background

IFRS 8 – *Operating Segments* – was published in November 2006. The Standard has been mandatory since 2009. *[IFRS 8.35]*.

In Europe, the introduction of IFRS 8 was controversial. Opponents shared concerns expressed in the dissenting opinions of two IASB members that the lack of a defined measure of segment profit or loss and the absence of any requirement for that measure to be consistent with the attribution of assets to reportable segments would encourage the proliferation of non-GAAP measures that could mislead users.[1] These concerns were raised in the European Parliament together with questions about the governance of the IASB, as a result of which the process to endorse IFRS 8 in the European Union was not completed until November 2007, a year after the Standard had been published.

During this period, the IFRS Foundation announced enhancements to oversight and due process to include a requirement for the IASB to conduct 'a review of issues identified as contentious as part of the consultation process related to all new IFRSs (including IFRS 8), major amendments to IFRSs and major IFRIC interpretations'. Such a review would be performed after at least two full years of implementation and be completed within three years of the pronouncement's effective date.[2] IFRS 8 was the first standard subject to a post-implementation review, which was completed in 2013 and is further discussed at 7 below.

1.2 The main features of IFRS 8

IFRS 8 is a disclosure standard. It specifies the way an entity should report information about its operating segments in annual financial statements and, as a consequential amendment to IAS 34 – *Interim Financial Reporting*, requires an entity to report selected information about its operating segments in interim financial reports (see Chapter 39 at 4.4). It also sets out requirements for related disclosures about an entity's products and services, geographical areas and major customers. *[IFRS 8.IN4]*. The disclosures required include:

- financial and descriptive information about the entity's reportable segments, which are operating segments above a certain size or (where specific criteria are met) aggregations of operating segments; *[IFRS 8.IN5]*
- segment revenues and a measure of profit or loss for each reportable segment, reconciled to the amounts disclosed in the entity's financial statements; *[IFRS 8.IN6]*
- a measure of segment assets, segment liabilities and particular income and expense items to the extent that such information is regularly provided to the chief operating decision maker of the entity, reconciled to the amounts disclosed in the entity's financial statements; *[IFRS 8.IN6]*
- unless the information is not available and the cost of its development would be excessive, information about the revenues derived from the entity's products and services (or groups of similar products and services), about the countries in which it earns revenues and holds assets, and about major customers, regardless of whether this information is used by management in making operating decisions; and *[IFRS 8.IN7]*
- descriptive information about the way that operating segments were determined, the products and services provided by the segments, differences between the measurements used in reporting segment information and those used in the entity's financial statements, and changes in the measurement of segment amounts from period to period. *[IFRS 8.IN8]*.

The process of identifying operating segments for external reporting purposes begins with the information used by the entity's chief operating decision maker to assess performance and to make decisions about future allocations of resources. *[IFRS 8.5]*. Entities applying IFRS 8 report on a single set of components according to the way that the business is sub-divided for management reporting purposes. *[IFRS 8.10]*.

If a component of an entity is managed as a separate segment, IFRS 8 requires it to be treated as such even if it sells exclusively or primarily to internal customers. *[IFRS 8.IN12]*.

IFRS 8 does not go so far as to require an entity to report all the information that is reviewed by the chief operating decision maker, recognising that such detail may not be useful to users of financial statements and could be cumbersome in its presentation. Instead it allows entities to aggregate components and to disclose information only for those segments that exceed certain quantitative criteria. *[IFRS 8.BC Appendix A 72]*.

Under IFRS 8, the amounts reported about identified segments are prepared according to the manner in which information is presented to the entity's chief operating decision maker. This can be different to the way that the entity applies its accounting policies used in the preparation of the financial statements under IFRSs. *[IFRS 8.IN13]*.

IFRS 8 requires an entity to describe the factors used to identify the entity's operating segments, including a description of the basis of organisation. This description would explain whether the organisation is structured according to products and services, geographical areas, regulatory environments or other factors and state whether operating segments have been aggregated for reporting purposes. In addition, the entity must describe the types of products and services from which each reportable segment derives its revenues. *[IFRS 8.IN15]*.

IFRS 8 specifies amounts which should be disclosed about each reportable segment, but only if those measures are included in the measure of profit or loss used by, or otherwise regularly provided to, the chief operating decision maker (see 5.2 below). *[IFRS 8.IN16]*. These specified amounts include a requirement to report separately interest revenue and interest expense by segment (but only if those measures are included in the measure of profit or loss used, or otherwise regularly provided to the by the chief operating decision maker) unless a majority of the segment's revenues is derived from interest and performance is assessed primarily on the basis of net interest revenue. *[IFRS 8.IN17]*.

Certain 'entity-wide disclosures' are also required to be provided under IFRS 8, even if the entity has only one reportable segment (see 6 below). Entity-wide information is disclosed for the entity as a whole about its products and services, geographical areas and major customers, regardless of the way the entity is organised and the information presented to the chief operating decision maker. *[IFRS 8.IN18]*. The amounts reported for this entity-wide information is based on the financial information used to produce the entity's financial statements. *[IFRS 8.32-33]*.

There is no 'competitive harm' exemption in IFRS 8 from the requirement to disclose segment information, or components of such information, for example on the grounds of commercial sensitivity, confidentiality or being otherwise detrimental to the entity's competitive position. *[IFRS 8.BC43-45]*.

These features are discussed in more detail in this chapter.

1.3 Terms used in IFRS 8

The following terms are used in IFRS 8 with the meanings specified:

Term	Meaning
Operating segment	A component of an entity: (a) that engages in business activities from which it may earn revenues and incur expenses (including revenues and expenses relating to transactions with other components of the same entity); (b) whose operating results are regularly reviewed by the entity's chief operating decision maker to make decisions about resources to be allocated to the segment and assess its performance; and (c) for which discrete financial information is available. *[IFRS 8.5, IFRS 8.Appendix A]*.
Chief operating decision maker	The function of allocating resources to and assessing the performance of the operating segments of an entity. This is not necessarily a manager with a specific title, but can be an entity's chief executive officer, chief operating officer, a group of executive directors or others. *[IFRS 8.7]*.
Segment manager	The function of being directly accountable to and maintaining regular contact with the chief operating decision maker to discuss operating activities, financial results, forecasts, or plans for the segment. *[IFRS 8.9]*.
Reportable segment	An operating segment or a group of two or more operating segments determined to be eligible for aggregation in accordance with IFRS 8.12; and which exceeds the quantitative thresholds in IFRS 8.13. *[IFRS 8.11]*.

Term	Meaning
Aggregation criteria	Two or more operating segments may be aggregated into a single operating segment if aggregation is consistent with the core principle of IFRS 8, they have similar economic characteristics, such as long-term average gross margins, and are similar in each of the following respects: (a) the nature of the products and services; (b) the nature of the production processes; (c) the type or class of customer for their products and services; (d) the methods used to distribute their products or provide their services; (e) if applicable, the nature of the regulatory environment, for example, banking, insurance or public utilities. *[IFRS 8.12]*.
Quantitative thresholds	Information about an operating segment that meets any of the following criteria: (a) its reported revenue, including both sales to external customers and intersegment sales or transfers, is 10% or more of combined revenue, internal and external, of all operating segments; or (b) its reported profit or loss is, in absolute terms, 10% or more of the greater of, in absolute amount: (i) the combined profit of all operating segments that did not report a loss; and (ii) the combined reported loss of all operating segments that reported a loss; or (c) its assets are 10% or more of the combined assets of all operating segments. *[IFRS 8.13]*.

1.4 Transitional provisions

There are no special arrangements for entities applying IFRS 8 for the first time, with the Standard requiring comparative information to be restated. Only where the necessary information is both unavailable and incapable of being developed without excessive cost is an entity exempt from full restatement. *[IFRS 8.36]*. Accordingly, an entity should ensure that internal reporting systems can provide the information needed to meet the disclosure requirements of IFRS 8 for all periods presented in its financial statements.

2 OBJECTIVE AND SCOPE OF IFRS 8

2.1 Objective

The objective of IFRS 8 is expressed as a 'core principle', being that an entity shall disclose information to enable users of its financial statements to evaluate the nature and financial effects of the business activities in which it engages and the economic environments in which it operates. *[IFRS 8.1]*.

2.2 Scope of IFRS 8

IFRS 8 applies to both the separate or individual financial statements of an entity and the consolidated financial statements of a group with a parent:

(a) whose debt or equity instruments are traded in a public market (a domestic or foreign stock exchange or an over-the-counter market, including local and regional markets); or

(b) that files, or is in the process of filing, its financial statements with a securities commission or other regulatory organisation for the purpose of issuing any class of instruments in a public market. *[IFRS 8.2]*.

The Board has confirmed that for consolidated financial statements, the above test is applied to the parent entity alone. *[IFRS 8.BC23]*. Therefore, IFRS 8 does not apply to a group headed by a parent that has no listed financial instruments, even if the group includes a subsidiary that has any of its equity or debt instruments traded in a public market. The scope of IAS 33 – *Earnings per Share* – is similarly defined. *[IFRS 8.BC23]*.

Of course, a subsidiary with publicly traded debt or equity instruments would be required to provide segment information under IFRS 8 in its own financial statements from its perspective as a reporting entity.

2.2.1 The meaning of 'traded in a public market'

The Standard describes a 'public market' as including a domestic or foreign stock exchange or an over-the-counter market, including local and regional markets, *[IFRS 8.2]*, but does not define what would make some markets 'public' and others not.

In our view, a market is 'public' when buyers and sellers (market participants) can transact with one another (directly; through agents; or in a secondary market) at a price determined in that market. A public market does not exist when the buyers and sellers can transact only with the entity itself (or an agent acting on its behalf). The requirement for an entity to list its securities on a stock exchange is not the sole factor determining whether the entity is in the scope of IFRS 8. Its securities must be *traded* in a public market meeting the criteria noted above.

Example 34.1: The meaning of 'public market' in the context of a fund

Many investment funds are listed on a public stock exchange for informational purposes, in particular to facilitate the valuation of portfolios by investors or because it is a requirement for the fund to be listed on a public stock exchange to make it eligible for investment by entities that are required to invest only in listed securities. However, in spite of such a listing, subscriptions and redemptions are handled by a fund administrator or a transfer agent (acting on behalf of the fund) and no transactions are undertaken on the public stock exchange. In addition, the prices for those transactions are determined by the fund agreement, such as on the basis of the fund's Net Asset Value, rather than the price quoted on the public stock exchange and determined by supply and demand.

In our view the debt or equity instruments of such entities are not traded in a public market and so the entity would not fall within the scope of IFRS 8. Nevertheless, regulators can mandate that funds provide segment information, or funds can voluntarily disclose segment information. In such cases, the funds need to comply with the requirements of IFRS 8

Such 'public markets' would include exchange markets, dealer markets, brokered markets, and principal-to-principal markets as described in IFRS 13 – *Fair Value Measurement* – and

Chapter 34

listed in that Standard as examples of markets in which fair value inputs might be observable (see Chapter 14 at 15.1). *[IFRS 13.B34]*.

2.2.2 *Consolidated financial statements presented with those of the parent*

When both the consolidated financial statements and the parent's separate or individual financial statements are contained in the same financial report, segment information is only required in the consolidated financial statements. *[IFRS 8.4]*.

2.2.3 *Entities providing segment information on a voluntary basis*

Entities for which IFRS 8 is not mandatory might still want to provide information about their business activities, for example about sales by segment, without triggering the need to comply fully with the Standard. The Board concluded that this would be acceptable, provided that such disclosure is not referred to as 'segment information'. *[IFRS 8.BC22]*. Consequently, entities giving information about segments on a voluntary basis cannot describe that information as 'segment information' unless it has been prepared in compliance with IFRS 8. *[IFRS 8.3]*.

3 IDENTIFYING A SINGLE SET OF OPERATING SEGMENTS

IFRS 8 adopts a 'bottom up' approach to determining the level of detail required for segment reporting in the notes to the financial statements. It requires the entity's revenue earning activities to be divided into operating segments (based on the same components used by management to run the business) and only allows that information to be aggregated for reporting purposes if specific criteria are met. This process can involve considerable judgement, as it may not always be immediately clear what activities are operating segments for the purposes of the Standard or which layer of the entity's organisational structure represents the level at which those activities are managed. This is particularly the case when management information is presented in a number of different ways (for example by product, by geographical market and by legal entity) or where management structures distinguish operational, strategic and oversight responsibilities.

Notwithstanding such difficulties, the requirement is to identify a single set of components as constituting the entity's operating segments. *[IFRS 8.8]*.

The process for determining operating segments is important not only to entities applying IFRS 8 for external reporting purposes, but also to entities implementing the requirements of IAS 36 – *Impairment of Assets* – for testing indefinite-lived intangible assets and goodwill for impairment. As such, the way that operating segments are defined and determined under IFRS 8 can affect the financial statements of entities to which the disclosure requirements in IFRS 8 do not apply, such as those without traded equity or debt. This is because the Standard on impairment, applicable to all entities, states that a group of cash-generating units (CGUs) for impairment testing purposes cannot be larger than an operating segment before aggregation (as determined below). *[IAS 36.80(b)]*. See Chapter 20 at 4.2.

3.1 Definition of an operating segment

An operating segment is defined as a component of an entity:

(a) that engages in business activities from which it may earn revenues and incur expenses (including revenues and expenses relating to transactions with other components of the same entity);

(b) whose operating results are regularly reviewed by the entity's chief operating decision maker to make decisions about resources to be allocated to the segment and assess its performance; and

(c) for which discrete financial information is available. *[IFRS 8.5]*.

This means that the determination of an entity's operating segments starts with the smallest components of the business for which information about profit is presented for use by the entity's chief operating decision maker (sometimes referred to as 'CODM').

3.1.1 Revenue earning business activities

A significant feature of an operating segment is the potential for revenue generation rather than actually earning revenues in the reporting period. Accordingly, a start-up operation can be treated as an operating segment while it has yet to earn revenues. *[IFRS 8.5]*.

However, not every part of an entity is necessarily an operating segment. For example, a corporate headquarters or a functional department (such as a centralised data processing centre) that either does not earn revenues or for which revenues are only incidental to the activities of the entity would not be an operating segment for the purposes of IFRS 8. Similarly, an entity's post-employment benefit plans would not be regarded as operating segments. *[IFRS 8.6]*.

3.1.2 'Chief operating decision maker' and 'segment manager'

Arguably the most important judgements made in implementing IFRS 8 relate to the identification of the entity's chief operating decision maker. The nature of what is ultimately disclosed in the financial statements about operating segments and the level of detail (or segmentation) required is directly related to the information regularly provided to the chief operating decision maker.

References in the standard to 'chief operating decision maker' are to the function of allocating resources and assessing performance of the operating segments and not to a manager with a specific title. Often the chief operating decision maker of an entity is its chief executive officer or chief operating officer (i.e. an individual), but the term could refer equally to a group of executive directors or others charged with that role. *[IFRS 8.7]*.

In Extract 34.1 below, the Go-Ahead Group identifies its Group Chief Executive as the chief operating decision maker:

Extract 34.1: The Go-Ahead Group plc (2015)

NOTES TO THE CONSOLIDATED FINANCIAL STATEMENTS [extract]

3. **SEGMENTAL ANALYSIS** [extract]

The information reported to the Group Chief Executive in his capacity as chief operating decision maker does not include an analysis of assets and liabilities and accordingly IFRS 8 does not require this information to be presented. Segment performance is evaluated based on operating profit or loss excluding amortisation of intangible assets, goodwill impairment and exceptional items.

The determination of chief operating decision maker will not be the same for all entities applying IFRS 8 and will depend upon the particular facts and circumstances applying to each entity. However, in stating that the term could apply to a group of executive directors or others, *[IFRS 8.7]*, the Standard is clear that the function of CODM is an executive role. The IFRS Interpretations Committee confirmed this view in 2011. While it observed that in practice the functions of CODM are sometimes carried out by multiple persons and that all such persons involved in those activities would be part of the CODM group, the Committee noted that the CODM would not normally include non-executive directors.[3] For example, an entity may have a single board of executive and non-executive directors which reviews the performance of individual business units, makes decisions about the operating budgets for those businesses and reviews significant applications for investment. In that case, the full board could be identified as the chief operating decision maker. However, if the entity also has a sub-committee of executive directors or another grouping of key management personnel (sometimes referred to as an 'operational board'), this smaller group of executives would be identified as the chief operating decision maker.

Essentially, the chief operating decision maker is found at the most senior executive decision-making level of an organisation and as such should be distinguished from higher levels of management fulfilling primarily an oversight or approval role and who, to reflect their non-executive function, are provided information at a more aggregated level as a matter of course. For example, in some jurisdictions, supervisory bodies may be part of an entity's governance structure and be entrusted with significant oversight responsibilities. This role may give the supervisory body significant veto rights and rights of approval. However, that supervision will not typically represent the level of decision-making implicit in the notion of the CODM.

In the extract below, ABB Ltd identifies as the CODM its Executive Committee, a group of senior executives which is headed by the Chief Executive Officer and is appointed by and reports to the Board of Directors.

Extract 34.2: ABB Ltd (2015)

Notes to the Consolidated Financial Statements [extract]

Note 23 Operating segment and geographic data [extract]

The Chief Operating Decision Maker (CODM) is the Company's Executive Committee. The CODM allocates resources to and assesses the performance of each operating segment using the information outlined below. The Company's operating segments consist of Discrete Automation and Motion, Low Voltage Products, Process Automation, Power Products and Power Systems. The remaining operations of the Company are included in Corporate and Other.

Another important distinction to be made is between chief operating decision maker and the function of 'segment manager'. The segment manager is accountable to and maintains regular contact with the chief operating decision maker to discuss operating activities, financial results, forecasts or plans for the segment. The chief operating decision maker may also fulfil the role of segment manager for some operating segments and a single segment manager may be responsible for more than one operating segment. *[IFRS 8.9]*. For example, if the CODM is a group of executives, members of that group may fulfil the role of segment manager for certain components of the entity.

Considerations of how components of the entity are managed are relevant to the identification of an entity's operating segments and not to how they might be reported in the financial statements. Accordingly, separate operating segments which otherwise meet the definition at 3.1 above are not aggregated into single reportable operating segments simply because they have a common segment manager. The Standard is clear that such segments are only aggregated into reportable operating segments if they exhibit similar long-term economic characteristics and are similar in respect of the qualitative criteria set out at 3.2.1 below. *[IFRS 8.12]*. In addition, because the oversight role of the CODM is separate from the operational role of the segment manager, it is possible that an entity could regard an investee accounted for by the equity method as an operating segment (see 3.1.5 below).

In practice, judgement is required to determine whether the component(s) for which a segment manager is held responsible represents one or more operating segments. For example, if targets are set by the CODM for the entire area of one segment manager's responsibility and the remuneration of that segment manager is based on the achievement of those targets, on an aggregated basis, this could support a determination that the area of responsibility is one operating segment in the absence of other evidence indicating that the CODM reviews the results of these components separately. Equally, whilst IFRS 8 states that segment managers will generally exist, their existence is an important indicator for identifying operating segments, but not a necessary condition. The key determinant is based on the activity of the CODM with respect to the internally reported results of that component.

A common situation in practice is that detailed financial information is provided or available to the chief operating decision maker on a regular basis about various levels of management and operational activity within an entity. In these circumstances, the interplay between the three criteria at 3.1 above becomes very important, as the existence of more detailed internal reporting could otherwise lead to a determination that there are more operating segments. If the three criteria apply to more than one set of components of an entity, but there is only one set that has segment managers, generally the set of components with segment managers constitutes the operating segments. *[IFRS 8.8]*.

Example 34.2: Identifying operating segments – CODM and segment manager

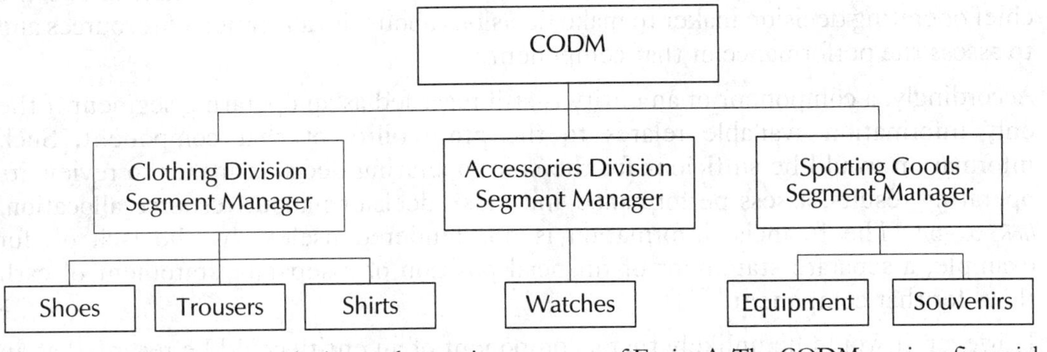

The diagram above sets out the internal reporting structure of Entity A. The CODM receives financial information about the entity's operations, the most detailed of which (including revenue and operating profit) relates to the six business units (Shoes, Trousers, Shirts, Watches, Equipment and Souvenirs). However, these units do not have their own segment manager. Instead, the six business units are grouped into three divisions (Clothing, Accessories and Sporting Goods), each of which has a segment manager who reports directly to the CODM. The three divisions report financial information to the CODM who uses it to assess performance and allocate resources.

In this case, the entity decides that the operating segments as defined in IFRS 8 comprise the three divisions as opposed to the six business units, because only the divisions have segment managers.

Proper application of the requirements of IFRS 8 requires a clear understanding of what information is given to the chief operating decision maker and how the CODM uses that information, in conjunction with the segment managers. In the above example, the fact that the CODM receives detailed financial information about activities below the divisional level could raise doubts about the determination that the divisions represent the entity's operating segments, rather than the business units. In these circumstances, entities would be required to demonstrate that:

- the more detailed information is not used by the CODM to assess performance and allocate resources.
- segment managers operate only at the divisional level and are not, in effect, managers for each of the business units in their division. As noted above, components otherwise meeting the characteristics of an operating segment under IFRS 8 are not combined simply because they share a segment manager.

It might be evident from the records of the discussions between segment managers and the CODM that results are monitored at divisional rather than at business unit level. It might equally be clear from the records of board meetings that more detailed information is not referred to by the CODM in its deliberations. However, there is evidence that when regulators and other enforcement agencies assess the quality of an entity's compliance with IFRS 8, they adopt the presumption that the CODM uses whatever detailed information is provided to him/her on a regular basis for decision-making and assessment purposes.

3.1.3 *Availability of discrete financial information*

As noted above, a component of an entity can only be regarded as an operating segment if discrete financial information is available about that component. *[IFRS 8.5(c)]*. This requirement relates solely to the existence of discrete information that allows the chief operating decision maker to make decisions about the allocation of resources and to assess the performance of that component.

Accordingly, a component of an entity is still regarded as an operating segment if the only information available relates to the profitability of that component. Such information would be sufficient for the chief operating decision maker to review its operating results, assess performance and make decisions about resource allocation. *[IFRS 8.5(b)]*. The financial information is not rendered useless by the lack of, for example, a separate statement of financial position or a separate statement of cash flows for that component.

However, it would be unlikely that a component of an entity could be regarded as an operating segment solely because the chief operating decision maker receives information about revenue from that component. Without a measure of the component's operating results it would be difficult to make meaningful assessments of the effect of allocating more or less resource to that activity. As such, information on revenue alone would have limited value in decision making. Therefore, the search for an entity's operating segments starts with the smallest components of the business for which a measure of profitability is provided to the entity's CODM.

3.1.4 *When a single set of components is not immediately apparent*

For many entities, the search for operating segments is concluded after applying the three criteria listed at 3.1 above.

However, in cases where a single set of operating segments cannot be identified clearly by applying the above criteria, for example in an entity where its business activities are reported internally and assessed in a variety of ways, IFRS 8 states that other factors should be considered, including the nature of the business activities of each component, the existence of a manager responsible for it, and the information presented to the board of directors. *[IFRS 8.8]*. Therefore, if an entity's activities are reported internally in a number of different ways, each with their own set of business components as defined above, but there is only one set to which segment managers are assigned, then that will comprise the operating segments to report in the financial statements for IFRS 8 purposes. *[IFRS 8.9]*. For example, if an entity's board of directors manages its business using information on revenues and costs analysed both by product grouping as well as by geographical market, but the management structure operates only on geographical lines, then the financial statements would include segmental information on a geographical basis.

A single set of operating segments must be identified, even where two or more sets of components of an entity are managed in a matrix structure, for example where financial information is available and performance is assessed and segment managers assigned not only on the basis of product and service lines worldwide but also by geographical area irrespective of products and service lines. In that situation the choice of a single set of components is a matter of judgement, made by reference to the core principle of the Standard as set out at 2.1 above. *[IFRS 8.10]*. This requirement is different to FASB ASC Topic 280 and ED 8, which proposed that in such circumstances operating segments be drawn up on product and service lines.[4] The IASB agreed with respondents to the exposure draft that a default position mandating the use of components based on products and services was inconsistent with a management approach founded on what is important to the chief operating decision maker. *[IFRS 8.BC27]*.

3.1.5 *An equity accounted investment can be an operating segment*

The definition of an operating segment focuses on the review of its operating results by the entity's chief operating decision maker and the assessment of its performance and the allocation of resources to it by the CODM. *[IFRS 8.5(b)]*. This raises the question of whether the reporting entity needs to have control over the activities conducted in what otherwise would meet the definition of an operating segment, or whether it is sufficient that the CODM reviews its results and this review influences decisions about investment in those activities. In our view, control over the activities in which the entity is investing is not a requirement.

The core principle of IFRS 8 requires the disclosure of information relating to the business activities in which an entity engages and the economic environments in which it operates. *[IFRS 8.1]*. No restriction is imposed according to the manner of that engagement, just the way in which the CODM makes decisions about allocating resources and assesses its performance.

For example, an equity method investee (i.e. associate or joint venture) could be considered an operating segment, if it meets the criteria in IFRS 8. The CODM may regularly review the operating results and performance of an equity method investee for the purposes of making additional investments or advances, evaluating financial performance or evaluating whether to retain its investment. The CODM is not required to be responsible for making decisions at the investee operating level that affect the investee's operations and performance in order for it to be identified as an operating segment. Further, the definition of an operating segment does not require that the revenue generating activities of the investee are included in the entity's revenue as reported in the IFRS financial statements. Segment performance could be measured by reference to the amounts included in the entity's IFRS financial statements or equally by reference to the financial information prepared by the investee itself. Any difference between the measures used by the CODM and the accounting treatment under IFRS would be reported as a reconciling item in the entity's disclosures under IFRS 8 (see 5.6 below).

This view is consistent with the disclosure requirements of IFRS 8, which require the entity's share of the profits and losses of equity accounted associates and joint ventures and the amount of investment in equity accounted investees to be presented, if those amounts are included in the measures reviewed by the CODM of segment profit or loss and segment assets respectively (see 5.3 and 5.4 below). *[IFRS 8.23(g), IFRS 8.24(a)]*.

3.2 Identifying externally reportable segments

Having identified a single set of internal operating segments, the Standard describes how reportable segments are determined. As a minimum an entity must separately disclose information on reportable segments above a certain size (see 3.2.2 below). In addition, a previously identified reportable segment continues to be disclosed separately in the current period if management judges it to be of continuing significance, even if it no longer satisfies the quantitative thresholds. *[IFRS 8.17]*.

Thereafter, an entity is only compelled to give information on other segments (either individually or in certain circumstances on a combined basis) if the unallocated element is too large (see 3.2.4 below).

The implementation guidance to IFRS 8 includes a diagram illustrating how to apply the main provisions of the Standard for identifying reportable segments, which is reproduced below:

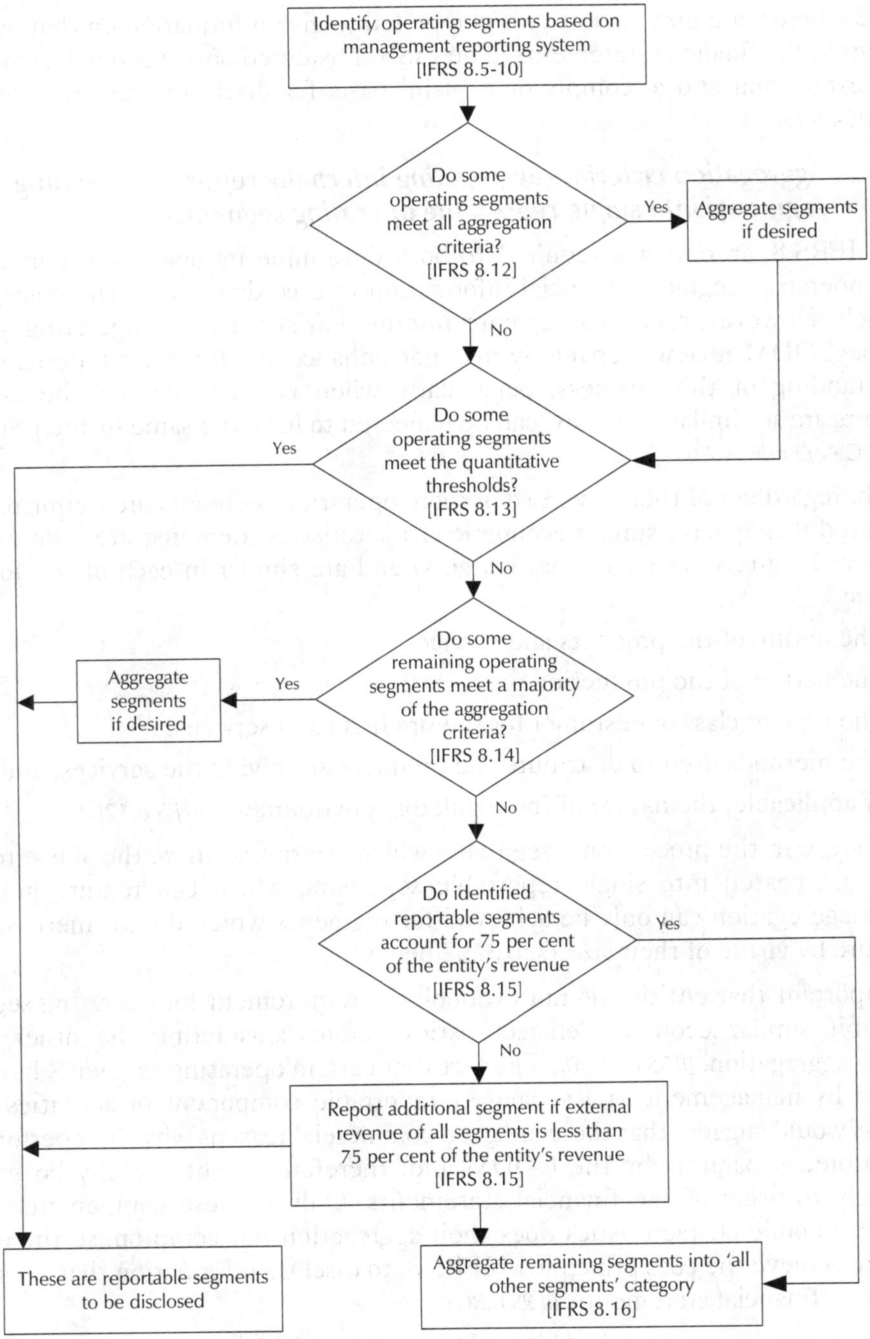

As indicated in the implementation guidance, the diagram is a visual supplement to the IFRS. It should not be interpreted as altering or adding to any requirements of the IFRS nor should it be regarded as a substitute for its requirements. *[IFRS 8.IG7]*.

IFRS 8 does not permit the omission of segment information when management believe that its disclosure is commercially sensitive or potentially detrimental to the entity's competitive position. If the criteria for separate disclosure described at 3.2.2

and 3.2.4 below are met, an entity is compelled to give information on that operating segment in the financial statements. The IASB considered both a general 'competitive harm' exemption and a 'comply or explain' basis for disclosure and rejected both. *[IFRS 8.BC43-45]*.

3.2.1 Aggregation criteria – aggregating internally reported operating segments into single reportable operating segments

Under IFRS 8, an entity is required to both determine its operating segments and report operating segment financial information in accordance with the management approach. However, reporting separate information about every operating segment that the CODM reviews separately may not enhance the financial statement user's understanding of the business, particularly when two or more of the operating segments are so similar that they 'can be expected to have the same future prospects.' *[IFRS 8.BC Appendix A.73]*.

As such, regardless of their size, two or more operating segments are permitted to be aggregated if they have similar economic characteristics (demonstrated, for example, by similar long-term average gross margins) and are similar in each of the following respects:

(a) the nature of the products and services;

(b) the nature of the production processes;

(c) the type or class of customer for the products and services;

(d) the methods used to distribute the products or provide the services; and

(e) if applicable, the nature of the regulatory environment. *[IFRS 8.12]*.

At this stage in the process only segments which are similar in *all* the above respects can be aggregated into single reportable segments, which can require judgment. Further aggregation can only be achieved for segments which do not merit separate disclosure by virtue of their size (see 3.2.2 below).

It is important that entities do not overlook the requirement for operating segments to exhibit similar economic characteristics before considering the other factors allowing aggregation. *[IFRS 8.BC30]*. The fact that certain operating segments have been selected by management as a separately reportable component of activities in the business would suggest that there are good commercial reasons why their performance is monitored separately by the CODM and, therefore, might usefully be reported separately to users of the financial statements. Only if those components exhibit similar economic characteristics does their aggregation not compromise the entity's ability to achieve the core principle of IFRS 8, to disclose information that is useful to users of its financial statements. *[IFRS 8.BC32]*.

There is a certain presumption inherent in any standard on segment reporting that investors would prefer information on a more disaggregated basis. As a result, it may be questioned whether it is consistent with the objective and basic principles of IFRS 8 for a company to report just one reportable segment or a limited number of reportable segments, especially if such reportable segments are inconsistent with an entity's basic organisational structure. Companies that choose to aggregate operating segments should be prepared to explain why an operating segment is important enough to be individually reported to the CODM, but similar enough to other segments to be aggregated when reported to investors.

In assessing whether the aggregation criteria are met, it is important to note that the aggregation criteria are tests, not indicators, of similarity between operating segments. Each of the criteria must be met for aggregation to be permitted:

(a) *The nature of the products and services.* Similar products or services generally will have similar purposes or end uses. Thus, they may be similar types and degrees of risk and similar opportunities for growth. We believe that it often will be appropriate to evaluate the similarity of products or services based on the range of activities of the organisation. For example, for a large, diversified organisation, which includes a consumer products division, all consumer products might be viewed as having a similar nature, whereas the nature of products sold by a consumer products company might be distinguished more narrowly, such as foods versus beverages.

(b) *The nature of the production processes.* A similar production process might be demonstrated by the sharing of common or interchangeable production facilities, equipment, labour force or service group and by using similar raw materials in the production process. Likewise, similarity in the nature and type of labour or amounts of capital required also may be indicative of a similar production process. The nature of the production process of two different products may be similar, even if the products do not function similarly. Consider the following example:

Example 34.3: Similar production process

Assume that Life Co., a life sciences company manufactures various pharmaceutical products for commercial sale. These products include cold medicines and diet pills. Each product is manufactured through the same production process, even though the products have different applications. Both products consist of various chemical compounds that are mixed together in batches to create the end product. Both products undergo quality control testing in order to confirm the efficacy of the product. Both products also use the same manufacturing equipment for parts of the production process. Thus, Life Co. concludes that for the purposes of the segment aggregation criteria, the production processes are similar, despite the differences in the applications of the end products.

(c) *The type or class of customer for their products and services.* Factors to consider in evaluating whether the type or class of customer are similar include: (1) the region or geography in which the products and services are marketed; (2) the methods used to market the products or services, including the use of a common or interchangeable sales force; and (3) the nature or type of customer including the industries in which the customers may operate. Consider the following example:

Example 34.4: Type and class of customer

Market Co., a diversified clothing manufacturer has two operating segments, Retail and Wholesale. Retail primarily markets its products to consumers through electronic and print advertising. In contrast, Wholesale principally markets its products through a network of sales representatives who call upon the distributors to purchase the products. In considering the type or class of customer, Market Co. concludes that the type and class of customer are not similar for the two operating segments based upon the distinction between retail and wholesale as well as the primary marketing methods for its products. As such, aggregation of the two operating segments would not be permitted.

(d) *The methods used to distribute their products or provide their services.* The determination of whether two methods of distribution are similar will depend on the structure of a particular company. Consider the following examples:

Example 34.5: Retail outlets and internet distribution

Software Co., a software retailer, has two operating segments: Retail, which distributes its products through retail outlets, and Internet, which distributes its products through a website on the internet. In evaluating whether these operating segments can be aggregated, Software Co., might conclude that the methods to distribute its products are not similar because Retail and Internet distribute products through different distribution channels.

(e) *If applicable, the nature of the regulatory environment,* for example, banking, insurance, or public utilities. Entities that operate within certain industries may be subject to regulatory requirements that are promulgated by a government agency. Sometimes two operating segments may produce the same product through the same production process, but because of differences in the class of customer and the regulatory environment, the operating segments should not be aggregated. For example, it may not be appropriate for an entity to aggregate an operating segment that produces a product under government contracts together with an operating segment that produces the same product for commercial purposes.

Some entities are comprised of operating segments that operate within different regulatory environments. We believe that the nature of the regulatory environments in which two or more operating segments operate can be regarded as similar, even if the regulatory bodies are not the same.

The following example illustrates how the management of an entity has interpreted these requirements. However, any judgments to be made will be specific to the entity and the environment in which it operates and in different circumstances some of the characteristics considered will be relatively more or less relevant than others.

Example 34.6: Aggregating internally reported operating segments with similar characteristics into a single reportable operating segment

In the information presented to the executive directors, a single-product company has identified seven components of its business that are internally reported operating segments, Africa, Australia and Pacific, France, Germany, Italy, UK and Ireland and USA. The company dominates its markets in Australia and Pacific and in Germany and consequently enjoys superior operating profits. Its other markets are fragmented, competition is greater and therefore historic and expected margins are lower. Can any segments be aggregated for external reporting purposes?

Management has considered each of the criteria set out in paragraph 12 of IFRS 8 to determine whether the economic characteristics of these separate operating segments are similar, including competitive and operating risks, currency risks and political conditions, as well as current performance and future trading prospects In these circumstances, management decided that it would not combine operating segments with different underlying currency risks and regulatory environments. That left only France, Germany and Italy as candidates for combination, since they all operate within the Euro zone. However, Germany has not been included in a larger reportable segment because, whilst similar in all other ways, its long-term financial performance is not expected to be comparable to France and Italy, as evidenced by its superior operating profits. On this basis, management decided to aggregate only its operations in France and Italy for external segment reporting purposes.

As can be seen in the above example, operating segments trading in clearly different economic environments (for example with unrelated functional currencies) should not be aggregated for segment reporting purposes (unless they are so small as to fall within the 'all other segments' category discussed at 3.2.4 below). The Standard states that the existence of similar long-term average gross margins would be a positive indicator. *[IFRS 8.12]*. This implies that operating segments should not be aggregated if their long-term average gross margins are significantly different, even if they are similar in all the other respects noted above. While IFRS 8 includes long-term gross margin as an example of similar economic characteristics, if the CODM uses a different measure of profit or loss (e.g. EBITDA) to assess performance and allocate resources to each operating segment, that measure of profit or loss should also be considered when assessing whether operating segments possess similar economic characteristics. In addition, if other economic measures are provided to the CODM, the similarities of those economic measures should also be considered. For example, if the CODM uses sales metrics, return on investment, or other standard industry measures, those metrics may also be relevant in determining economic similarity.

In assessing whether long-term average gross margins (or the appropriate measure of operating performance used by the CODM to assess performance and allocate resources, such as EBITDA) of operating segments are sufficiently similar, companies should look to past and present performance as indicators that segments are expected to have the same future prospects. In other words, if operating segments do not currently have similar gross margins and sales trends but are expected to have similar long-term average gross margins and sales trends, it may be appropriate to aggregate the two operating segments (provided all other criteria are met). Conversely, if operating segments happen to have similar gross margins or sales trends in a given year but it is not expected that the similar gross margins or sales trends will continue in the future, the operating segments should not be aggregated for the current-year segment disclosures just because current economic measures happen to be similar. It follows that operating segments that have been profitable over the longer term should not be combined with segments that over the longer term have been consistently loss-making.

IFRS 8 does not define the term 'similar' and does not provide guidance about what is similar for aggregation purposes. As the above discussion indicates, the determination of whether two or more operating segments are similar requires judgment and is dependent on the individual facts and circumstances.

In a response to a submission, the Interpretations Committee has acknowledged that IFRS 8 could usefully include further guidance on the meaning of 'similar economic characteristics' and the criteria for identifying similar segments listed in (a) to (e) above.[5] In a move to improve the Standard in this area, the IASB decided to enhance the disclosures on the aggregation of segments but not to add any further guidance at that time (see 5.1.1 below). However, the IASB intends to include further examples of similar economic characteristics a result of the Post-implementation Review (see 7 below).

3.2.2 Quantitative thresholds – operating segments which are reportable because of their size

IFRS 8 includes a number of quantitative measures for determining whether information on the identified operating segments should be reported separately. Accordingly, an operating segment (or combination of segments meeting the qualitative criteria for aggregation described at 3.2.1 above) merits separate disclosure if it meets any of the following thresholds:

(a) its reported revenue (including both sales to external customers and intersegment sales or transfers) is 10% or more of the combined revenue (internal and external) of all operating segments; or

(b) its reported profit or loss is, in absolute terms, 10% or more of the greater of:
   (i) the combined profit of all operating segments that did not report a loss; or
   (ii) the combined loss of all operating segments that reported a loss; or

(c) its assets are 10% or more of the combined assets of all operating segments. *[IFRS 8.13]*.

The definition of an operating segment includes a component of an entity earning revenues and incurring expenses relating to transactions with other components of the same entity. *[IFRS 8.5]*. Therefore an entity would have to report separately information on an operating segment that exceeds the above criteria, even if that segment earns a majority of its revenues from transactions with other components of the same entity.

Example 34.7: Identifying reportable segments using the quantitative thresholds

An entity divides its business into 9 operating units for internal reporting purposes and presents information to the Chief Operating Decision Maker as follows:

	Unit 1 £000	Unit 2 £000	Unit 3 £000	Unit 4 £000	Unit 5 £000	Unit 6 £000	Unit 7 £000	Unit 8 £000	Unit 9 £000	Total £000
Revenue:										
External	34,000	3,000	15,000	30,000	35,000	35,000	77,500	55,500	25,000	310,000
Internal	35,000	34,000	12,500	2,200	0	1,500	7,800	2,300	0	95,300
Total	69,000	37,000	27,500	32,200	35,000	36,500	85,300	57,800	25,000	405,300
Profit/(loss)	21,500	24,500	(4,500)	2,300	10,000	7,500	3,500	35,000	(21,250)	78,550
Assets	12,250	77,800	25,000	24,000	40,000	7,730	145,000	55,000	4,300	391,080

Assuming that none are eligible for aggregation under the qualitative aggregation criteria set out at 3.2.1 above, which units are required to be reported as operating segments in the entity's financial statements?

Applying the above quantitative thresholds, Units 1, 2, 5, 7, 8 and 9 should be identified as reportable segments, as follows:

- A Unit whose internal and external revenue is 10% or more of the total revenue of all segments is a reportable segment. On this criterion Unit 1 (17%), Unit 7 (21%) and Unit 8 (14%) are reportable segments.
- A Unit is a reportable segment if its profit or loss, in absolute terms, is 10% or more of the greater of the combined profits of all profitable segments or the combined losses of all segments in loss. The combined profit of all profitable segments is £104.3m, which is greater than the total of £25.75m for segments in loss. On this basis, Unit 1 (21%), Unit 2 (23%), Unit 8 (34%) and the loss-making Unit 9 (20%) are reportable segments.

- A Unit is also a reportable segment if the measure of assets reported to the chief operating decision maker is 10% or more of the total reported measure of assets of all segments. On this test, Unit 5 (10%) joins the list of reportable segments, with Unit 2 (20%), Unit 7 (37%) and Unit 8 (14%) having been already identified under other criteria.

Only those segments that have similar economic characteristics (demonstrated, for example, by similar long-term average gross margins) and are similar in all of the qualitative criteria set out at 3.2.1 above could be combined into a larger segment for reporting purposes.

Even if an internally reported operating segment falls below all of the quantitative thresholds, it may still be considered as reportable, and separately disclosed, if management believes information about the segment would be useful to users of the financial statements. *[IFRS 8.13]*. Where information about segment assets is not disclosed under IFRS 8 because it is not provided regularly to the CODM, *[IFRS 8.23]*, it would be appropriate to ignore criterion (c) above for determining the reportable segments.

3.2.3 *Combining small operating segments into a larger reportable segment*

Operating segments which individually fall below the size criteria may be combined with other small operating segments into a single larger reporting segment provided that:

(a) the operating segments being combined have similar economic characteristics; and

(b) they share a majority (rather than all) of the criteria listed at 3.2.1 above. *[IFRS 8.14]*.

For the avoidance of doubt, if an entity proposes to combine a small operating segment with one that exceeds any of the quantitative thresholds, they must share all of the criteria described at 3.2.1 above. The requirement that combining segments must demonstrate similar economic characteristics applies to combinations of both larger and smaller operating segments into reportable segments, without exception. Therefore, irrespective of their size, operating segments cannot be combined if they do not meet the criteria in 3.2.1 above.

3.2.4 *'All other segments'*

At this stage the entity has been divided into a single set of components, based on the elements reported to the chief operating decision maker. Components (operating segments) have been combined where permitted by the Standard and the entity has identified a number of individual operating segments or groups of operating segments that are required to be disclosed separately in the financial statements because each exceeds the quantitative thresholds for a reportable segment. The entity may then be left with a number of operating segments which have not been identified as being reportable, as well as other business activities that are not an operating segment or part of an operating segment.

Information about other business activities and operating segments that are not reportable should be combined and disclosed in a separate category for 'all other segments'. *[IFRS 8.16]*. However, this residual category cannot be too large. If total external revenue for the operating segments already reported separately is less than 75% of the entity's revenue, the entity should identify additional operating segments for external reporting until the 75% target is reached. In this situation segments would have to be reported separately even if they fall below the quantitative thresholds described at 3.2.2 above and are not otherwise regarded as being significant. *[IFRS 8.15]*.

There is no requirement to identify as a reportable segment the next largest internally reported operating segment. The choice of additional reporting segments is aimed simply to reach the 75% threshold, as illustrated below.

Example 34.8: Reaching the threshold of 75% of external revenue

In Example 34.7 above, Units 1, 2, 5, 7, 8 and 9 were identified as reportable segments. The total external revenue attributable to these reportable segments is £230m. This is only 74.2% of total external revenues and therefore less than the required 75% of total external revenue of £310m.

The entity is therefore required to identify additional segments as reportable segments, even if they do not meet the quantitative thresholds at 3.2.2 above. Entities that have numerous operating segments often will have latitude in selecting operating segments to meet the 75% test. In this case, Unit 3, with external revenue of £15m (4.8%), Unit 4's external revenue of £30m (9.7%) and Unit 6's external revenue of £35m (11.3%) would each take the total above the required 75%. The entity can choose to present any of these as a reportable segment, leaving the others to be combined to form the item for 'all other segments'.

The 'all other segments' category must be presented separately from other reconciling items. *[IFRS 8.16]*. This raises the question whether headquarters, treasury and similar central functions (sometimes referred to as 'corporate items') should be included in 'all other segments' or in the reconciliation. In practice, the headquarters activities and its related accounting effects will not always be allocated to the operating segments for internal reporting purposes. The description of 'all other segments' refers to 'other business activities and operating segments'. *[IFRS 8.16]*. It could be argued that central functions are not business activities, but support functions which should be part of the reconciliation. On the other hand, they could be regarded as incidental business activities. There is no guidance to suggest that either presentation is ruled out by the Standard.

3.2.5 A 'practical limit' for the number of reported operating segments

IFRS 8 states that there may be a practical limit to the number of separately reportable segments beyond which segment information may become too detailed. Without prescribing such a limit, it suggests that an entity expecting to disclose more than 10 separate reportable segments should consider whether the practical limit has been reached. *[IFRS 8.19]*.

3.2.6 Restatement of segments reported in comparative periods

When an operating segment is identified for the first time as a reportable segment in accordance with the thresholds at 3.2.2 above, the prior period segment data that is presented for comparative purposes should be restated to reflect the newly reportable segment regardless of whether it would have satisfied the quantitative thresholds in the prior period. Only if the necessary information is not available and the cost to develop it would be excessive would prior periods not be restated. *[IFRS 8.18]*.

4 MEASUREMENT

For an entity that does not present IFRS-compliant financial information to its chief operating decision maker, the measurement regime in IFRS 8 means that the values disclosed for segment revenue, profit or loss, and (when reported) assets or liabilities could be very different to those reported elsewhere in the financial statements. For example, management might include gains on sale of property, plant and equipment in its measure of segment revenue but not be permitted to do so in its financial statements. *[IAS 16.68]*.

There is no requirement in IFRS 8 for segment information to be prepared in conformity with the accounting policies used to present the financial statements of the consolidated group or entity. IFRS 8 requires amounts reported to be the same as those measures used by the chief operating decision maker for determining resource allocation and for assessing performance. *[IFRS 8.25]*. This requirement is interpreted strictly. For example, unless adjustments and eliminations made in preparing the financial statements are reflected in the information used by the chief operating decision maker, an entity is prohibited from restating reported segment profit or loss for those adjustments and eliminations. In addition, the Standard prohibits any further allocation of revenues, expenses and gains and losses in determining segment profit or loss unless that measure is used by the chief operating decision maker. *[IFRS 8.25]*. IFRS 8 does not require symmetry between the revenues and expenses included in segment result and the assets and liabilities allocated to segments; it simply requires disclosure of the nature and effect of any asymmetrical allocations to reportable segments, for example when depreciation expense is reflected in segment profit or loss, but the related depreciable assets are not allocated to that segment. *[IFRS 8.27(f)]*. Only those assets and liabilities taken into account by the chief operating decision maker will be included in assets and liabilities reported for that segment. *[IFRS 8.25]*.

The amounts presented for segment revenue, profit or loss, assets and liabilities need bear no relationship to the values reported elsewhere in the financial statements, if the *only* measure of each that is used by the chief operating decision maker is not prepared in accordance with the entity's accounting policies or even under IFRS. *[IFRS 8.26]*. However, there is a constraint on this otherwise 'free-for-all', since in those cases where a number of measures of segment profit or loss, assets or liabilities are used by the chief operating decision maker, an entity is required to select for its segment disclosures the measurements that are most consistent with those used in preparing the financial statements. *[IFRS 8.26]*. A key judgement that can significantly affect the segment disclosures reported in the financial statements arises when an entity seeks to distinguish information used by the chief operating decision maker for determining resource allocation and for assessing performance from other information and supporting detail which is regularly provided. Whether, for example, it is appropriate to ignore IFRS-compliant measures provided to the chief operating decision maker on the basis that they are not used for determining resource allocation and for assessing performance depends on the facts and circumstances supporting that assertion. Nevertheless, it might be appropriate to apply a rebuttable presumption that management effort is not normally wasted in providing the chief operating decision maker with information that is not used.

Instead of defining the elements of segment information to be disclosed and requiring that they be prepared under the same policies and principles applied in producing the financial statements, IFRS 8 requires an entity to explain how it has measured segment profit or loss and segment assets and liabilities for each reportable segment and to reconcile this to the information reported under IFRS. *[IFRS 8.27-28]*. These requirements are discussed at 5.5 and 5.6 below.

5 INFORMATION TO BE DISCLOSED ABOUT REPORTABLE SEGMENTS

IFRS 8 establishes a general principle for an entity to disclose information to enable users of its financial statements to evaluate the nature and financial effects of the types of business activities in which the entity engages and the economic environments in which it operates. *[IFRS 8.20]*. This principle is met by disclosing the following information for each period for which a statement of comprehensive income or separate income statement is presented:

(a) general information on segments identified for reporting;

(b) reported segment profit or loss, including information about specified revenues and expenses included in reported segment profit or loss, segment assets and segment liabilities (if reported to the CODM) and the basis of measurement; and

(c) reconciliations of the totals of segment revenues, reported segment profit or loss, segment assets, segment liabilities and other material segment items to the corresponding entity amounts in the financial statements. *[IFRS 8.21]*.

Reconciliations of amounts reported in the statement of financial position for reportable segments are required as at each date for which a statement of financial position is presented. *[IFRS 8.21]*.

These requirements are addressed in more detail below and the information described therein should be given separately for each segment determined to be reportable using the process set out at 3.2 above. *[IFRS 8.11]*.

As discussed at 3.1.2 above, the identification of the chief operating decision maker can be a critical judgment in applying IFRS 8 because of its potential impact on what information is considered for disclosure. However, there is no explicit requirement in the Standard to identify the CODM. When in 2011, the Interpretations Committee and the IASB considered a request to amend the Standard to require disclosure, they decided to defer this issue until the completion of the Post-implementation Review of IFRS 8 rather than through an interpretation or annual improvement.[6] As part of that exercise, the IASB intends to require disclosure of the nature of the CODM. The results of the Post-implementation Review are discussed at 7 below. In our view, it would be good practice to disclose the individual or group identified as CODM (see examples at 3.1.2 above).

5.1 General information about reportable segments

The factors used to identify reportable segments should be described. This would include an explanation of the entity's basis of organisation, for example whether management has chosen to organise the entity by different products and services, by geographical area, by regulatory environment or by applying a combination of factors.

The description would also indicate whether operating segments have been aggregated. The general information on reportable segments would include a description of the types of products and services from which each reportable segment derives its revenues. *[IFRS 8.22]*. The disclosures should also include a description of the sources of the revenue classified in the 'all other segments' category. *[IFRS 8.16]*.

In Extract 34.3 below, Daimler describes how its activities have been segmented into its principal business activities and specific product lines.

Extract 34.3: Daimler AG (2015)

NOTES TO THE CONSOLIDATED FINANCIAL STATEMENTS [extract]

33. Segment reporting [extract]

Reportable segments

The reportable segments of the Group are Mercedes-Benz Cars, Daimler Trucks, Mercedes-Benz Vans, Daimler Buses and Daimler Financial Services. The segments are largely organized and managed separately according to nature of products and services provided, brands, distribution channels and profile of customers.

The vehicle segments develop and manufacture passenger cars, trucks, vans and buses. The Mercedes-Benz Cars segment comprises premium vehicles of the Mercedes-Benz brand and small cars under the smart brand, as well as the service brand Mercedes me. Daimler Trucks distributes its trucks under the brand names Mercedes-Benz, Freightliner, FUSO, Western Star, Thomas Built Buses and BharatBenz. The vans of the Mercedes-Benz Vans segment are primarily sold under the brand name Mercedes-Benz and also under the Freightliner brand. Daimler Buses sells completely built-up buses under the brand names Mercedes-Benz and Setra. In addition, Daimler Buses produces and sells bus chassis. The vehicle segments also sell related spare parts and accessories.

The Daimler Financial Services segment supports the sales of the Group's vehicle segments worldwide. Its product portfolio mainly comprises tailored financing and leasing packages for customers and dealers. The segment also provides services such as fleet management, the brokering of automotive insurance, banking services and various innovative mobility services (under the brands moovel and car2go.

5.1.1 Disclosure of how operating segments are aggregated

IFRS 8 requires disclosure of the judgements made by management in applying the aggregation criteria in the Standard. This includes a brief description of the operating segments that have been aggregated in this way and the economic indicators that were considered in determining that the aggregated operating segments share similar economic characteristics. *[IFRS 8.22(aa)]*. The aggregation criteria are discussed at 3.2.1 above.

Amcor Limited describes the basis for aggregating three smaller operating segments into its Amcor Flexibles reporting segment in the following extract.

Extract 34.4: Amcor Limited (2015)

Notes to the Financial Statements [extract]

1.3 **Segment Performance** [extract]

Amcor is a global market leader in its industry with the following operational structure and reportable segments:

Reportable Segment	Operations
Amcor Rigid Plastics	Manufactures rigid plastic containers for a broad range of predominantly beverage and food products, including carbonated soft drinks, water, juices, sports drinks, milk-based beverages, spirits and beer, sauces, dressings, spreads and personal care items and plastic caps for a wide variety of applications.
Amcor Flexibles	This reporting segment represents the aggregation of three operating segments of which each manufactures flexible and film packaging for their respective industries. The operating segments are: • Amcor Flexibles Europe & Americas which provides packaging for the food and beverage industry including confectionery, coffee, fresh food and dairy, pet food packaging, champagne and wine closures and medical packaging for the pharmaceutical sector. • Amcor Tobacco Packaging which manufactures flexible packaging for specialty folding cartons for tobacco packaging and other industries. • Amcor Flexibles Asia Pacific which provides packaging for the food and beverage industry including confectionery, coffee, fresh food and dairy and packaging for the pharmaceutical and home and personal care. These operating segments share similar characteristics as they are engaged in the printing and packaging of fast moving consumer products. Management believe that it is appropriate to aggregate these three operating segments as one reporting segment due to the similarities in the nature of each operating segment.
Other/Investments	This segment holds the Group's equity accounted investments in the associate AMVIG Holdings Limited (AMVIG) and the joint venture Discma AG (Discma). AMVIG is principally involved in the manufacture of tobacco packaging while Discma's operations primarily relate to the development and licensing of packaging product innovations. This segment also includes the Corporate function of the Group.

5.2 A measure of segment profit or loss, total assets and total liabilities

For each reportable segment, an entity is required to disclose a measure of profit or loss for each segment. An entity is also required to disclose a measure of total assets and total liabilities for each reportable segment, but only if such amounts are regularly provided to the chief operating decision maker. *[IFRS 8.23]*. This 'measure' means segment profit or loss and segment assets and liabilities as defined in the information used by the chief operating decision maker.

5.2.1 Other measures of segment performance

Entities typically use not only a measure of profit or loss, but also a combination of different financial and non-financial key performance indicators to assess performance of their operating segments and allocate resources to them. Examples include key measures based on capital invested like return on capital employed (ROCE), free cash flow or orders on hand. Since these are not measures of profit or loss, they would not need to be disclosed. However, the Standard does not prohibit their disclosure.

Siemens includes measures of new orders and free cash flow in its segment information as shown in Extract 34.5 below.

Extract 34.5: Siemens AG (2015)

B.6 Notes to Consolidated Financial Statements [extract]
NOTE 28 Segment information [extract]

	Orders[1]		Free cash flow	
	Fiscal year		Fiscal year	
(in millions of €)	*2015*	*2014*	2015	2014
Power and Gas	*15,666*	*13,996*	1,331	1,517
Wind Power and Renewables	*6,136*	*7,759*	389	552
Energy Management	*12,956*	*11,210*	691	(105)
Building Technologies	*6,099*	*5,587*	546	544
Mobility	*10,262*	*9,280*	118	353
Digital Factory	*10,014*	*9,233*	1,840	1,454
Process Industries and Drives	*9,337*	*9,968*	496	732
Healthcare	*13,349*	*12,126*	2,048	1,927
Industrial Business	***83,819***	***79,158***	**7,460**	**6,975**
Financial Services (SFS)	*1,048*	*937*	884	522
Reconciliation to Consolidated Financial Statements	*(2,527)*	*(2,438)*	(3,359)	(2,219)
Siemens (continuing operations)	**82,340**	**77,657**	**4,984**	**5,278**

1 This supplemental information on Orders is provided on a voluntary basis. It is not part of the Consolidated Financial Statements subject to the audit opinion.

5.3 Disclosure of other elements of revenue, income and expense

The following items should also be disclosed about each reportable segment if the specified amounts are included in the measure of segment profit or loss reviewed by the chief operating decision maker or are otherwise regularly provided in respect of those segments to the chief operating decision maker (even if not included in that measure of segment profit or loss):

(a) revenues from external customers;

(b) revenues from transactions with other operating segments of the same entity;

(c) interest revenue;

(d) interest expense;

(e) depreciation and amortisation;

(f) material items of income and expense disclosed in accordance with paragraph 97 of IAS 1 – *Presentation of Financial Statements*;

(g) the entity's interest in the profit or loss of associates and joint ventures accounted for by the equity method;

(h) income tax expense or income; and

(i) material non-cash items other than depreciation and amortisation. *[IFRS 8.23]*.

Interest revenue should be reported separately from interest expense for each reportable segment unless a majority of the segment's revenues are from interest and the chief operating decision maker relies primarily on net interest revenue to assess the performance of the segment and make decisions on the allocation of resources to it. In that case, the entity can report net interest revenue or expense for the segment provided that it discloses it has done so. *[IFRS 8.23]*.

Where the measure of segment profit or loss is determined after deducting depreciation and amortisation, these amounts will have to be disclosed separately for purposes of segment reporting, even if they are not separately reported to the CODM.

It can be seen that whilst IFRS 8 indicates the line items of income or expense or other information that might merit disclosure by segment, what an entity actually reports in its financial statements is determined by the line items used by the chief operating decision maker to define segment profit or loss and segment assets or liabilities, together with the other information otherwise regularly provided to the chief operating decision maker. *[IFRS 8.23-24]*. This means that different entities (even those with very similar activities) will make different disclosures, depending on what information is provided to the chief operating decision maker. Indeed, what is disclosed by one entity for each of its reportable segments might vary because, for example, the result of one segment is determined after deducting interest whilst that of other segments is drawn before interest; or because the information provided to the chief operating decision maker about one segment includes equity-accounted associates but for other segments does not. As such the disclosures made by an entity are tailored according to exactly what appears in the information presented to the chief operating decision maker.

Statoil provides segment disclosures based on its internal management reporting, with reportable segments determined based on differences in the nature of their operations, products and services, as follows:

Extract 34.6: Statoil ASA (2015)

8.1 Notes to the Consolidated financial statements [extract]

3 **Segments** [extract]

Segment data for the years ended 31 December 2015, 2014 and 2013 is presented below... [extract]

(in NOK billion)	Development and Production Norway	Development and Production International	Marketing, Midstream and Processing	Other	Eliminations	Total
Full year 2015						
Revenues third party and other income	(0.9)	15.3	465.5	3.1	–	483.1
Revenues inter-segment	140.4	53.9	1.5	0.0	(195.7)	(0.0)
Net income (loss) from equity accounted investments	0.0	(0.8)	0.4	0.0	–	(0.3)
Total revenues and other income	139.5	68.4	467.4	3.2	(195.7)	482.8
Purchases [net of inventory variation]	(0.0)	(0.1)	(406.5)	(0.0)	195.4	(211.2)
Operating and SG&A expenses	(25.8)	(27.3)	(37.6)	(2.8)	1.5	(91.9)
Depreciation, amortisation and net impairment losses	(51.4)	(81.6)	0.4	(1.1)	0.0	(133.8)
Exploration expenses	(4.6)	(26.3)	0.0	0.0	0.0	(31.0)
Net operating income	57.6	(66.9)	23.7	(0.8)	1.2	14.9
Additions to PP&E, intangibles and equity accounted investments	50.6	65.4	7.3	2.2	0.0	125.5
Balance sheet information						
Equity accounted investments	0.0	2.9	1.9	2.4	–	7.3
Non-current segment assets	244.1	330.1	49.2	6.1	–	629.5
Non-current assets, not allocated to segments						82.0
Total non-current assets						718.7

5.4 Additional disclosures relating to segment assets

If any of the following items are either included in the measure of segment assets reviewed by the chief operating decision maker or otherwise regularly provided in respect of those segments (whether included in segment assets or not), an entity should also disclose for each segment:

(a) the investment in equity-accounted associates and joint ventures; and

(b) total expenditures for additions to non-current assets other than financial instruments, deferred tax assets, post-employment benefit assets and rights arising under insurance contracts. *[IFRS 8.24]*.

5.5 Explanation of the measurements used in segment reporting

As noted at 4 above, instead of prescribing how an entity should calculate the amounts reported in its segmental disclosures, IFRS 8 requires an entity to explain how its measures of segment profit or loss, segment assets and segment liabilities have been determined. As a minimum, the following information is required:

(a) the basis of accounting for any transactions between reportable segments;

(b) if not apparent from the required reconciliations (see 5.6 below), the nature of any differences between the measurement of total reported segment profit or loss and the entity's profit or loss before income taxes and discontinued operations;

(c) the nature of any differences between the measurements of total reported segment assets and the entity's assets, if not apparent from the required reconciliations;

(d) the nature of any differences between the measurements of total reported segment liabilities and the entity's liabilities, if not apparent from the required reconciliations;

(e) the nature of any changes from prior periods in the measurement methods used to determine segment profit or loss, including the financial effect, if any, of those changes; and

(f) the nature and effect of any asymmetrical allocations to reportable segments, such as where depreciation is included in segment profit but the related property, plant and equipment is not included in segment assets. *[IFRS 8.27]*.

The kind of disclosures in (b), (c) and (d) above that are necessary for an understanding of the reported segment information could relate to the accounting policies used, including policies for the allocation of centrally incurred costs in arriving at segment profit or loss and for the allocation of jointly used assets and liabilities in determining segment assets and segment liabilities. *[IFRS 8.27]*. Other examples might include the use of previous local GAAP numbers, where internal reporting does not reflect the entity's move to IFRS, or the use of budgeted figures, for example when applying budgeted or constant foreign currency rates.

In Extract 34.7 below, Daimler confirms that segment information is prepared using the same accounting policies as the IFRS financial statements, describes how 'EBIT' is the measure of segment profit or loss and explains how segment assets and liabilities are determined.

Extract 34.7: Daimler AG (2015)

NOTES TO THE CONSOLIDATED FINANCIAL STATEMENTS [extract]

33. Segment reporting [extract]

Management and reporting system

The Group's management reporting and controlling systems principally use accounting policies that are the same as those described in Note 1 in the summary of significant accounting policies according to IFRS.

The Group measures the performance of its operating segments through a measure of segment profit or loss which is referred to as "EBIT" in our management and reporting system.

EBIT comprises gross profit, selling and general administrative expenses, research and non-capitalized development costs, other operating income/expense, and our share of profit/loss from equity-method investments, net, as well as other financial income/expense, net. Although amortization of capitalized borrowing costs is included in cost of sales, it is not included in EBIT.

Intersegment revenue is generally recorded at values that approximate third-party selling prices.

Segment assets principally comprise all assets. The industrial business segments' assets exclude income tax assets, assets from defined benefit pension plans and other post-employment benefit plans, and certain financial assets (including liquidity).

Segment liabilities principally comprise all liabilities. The industrial business segments' liabilities exclude income tax liabilities, liabilities from defined benefit pension plans and other post-employment benefit plans, and certain financial liabilities (including financing liabilities).

Daimler Financial Services' performance is measured on the basis of return on equity, which is the usual procedure in the banking business.

The residual value risks associated with the Group's operating leases and finance lease receivables are generally borne by the vehicle segments that manufactured the leased equipment. Risk sharing is based on agreements between the respective vehicle segments and Daimler Financial Services; the terms vary by vehicle segment and geographic region.

Non-current assets consist of intangible assets, property, plant and equipment and equipment on operating leases.

Capital expenditures for intangibles assets and property, plant and equipment reflect the cash effective additions to these property, plant and equipment and intangible assets as far as they do not relate to capitalized borrowing costs, goodwill and finance leases.

Depreciation and amortization may also include impairments as far as they do not relate to goodwill impairment as per IAS 36.

Amortization of capitalized borrowing costs is not included in the amortization of intangible assets or depreciation of property, plant and equipment since it is not considered as part of EBIT.

In its 2015 financial statements, HOCHTIEF provided an explanation of the basis of accounting for transactions between reportable segments.

Extract 34.8: HOCHTIEF Aktiengesellschaft (2015)

Notes to the Consolidated Financial Statements [extract]

36. Segment reporting [extract]

HOCHTIEF's structure reflects the operating focus of our business as well as the Group's presence in key national and international regions and markets. Segmental reporting in the HOCHTIEF Group is based on the Group's divisional operations. The breakdown mirrors the Group's internal reporting systems.

The Group's reportable segments* (divisions) are as follows:

HOCHTIEF Americas encompasses the construction activities of operational units in the USA and Canada

HOCHTIEF Asia Pacific pools the construction activities and contract mining in the Asia-Pacific region

HOCHTIEF Europe brings together the core business in Europe as well as selected other regions and designs, develops, builds, operates, and manages real estate and infrastructure.

The Corporate Headquarters/Consolidation unit comprises Corporate Headquarters, other activities not assigned to separately listed divisions, including management of financial resources and insurance activities, plus consolidation effects. Insurance activities are managed from Corporate Headquarters under the responsibility of HOCHTIEF Insurance Broking and Risk Management Solutions GmbH with various companies in Luxembourg, including Builders Reinsurance S.A. The HOCHTIEF insurance companies primarily provide mainly reinsurance offerings for builders' risk, subcontractor default, third-party liability, and workers's compensation insurance.

Explanatory notes to the segmental data [extract]

Intersegment sales represent revenue generated between divisions. They are transacted on an arm's length basis. External sales mainly comprise revenue recognized using the percentage-of-completion method in the mainstream construction business, construction management, and contract mining, in the amount of EUR 17,965,879 thousand (2014: EUR 18,448,153 thousand). The sum of external sales and intersegment sales gives total sales revenue for each division.

5.6 Reconciliations

Reconciliations are required of all the following:

(a) the total of revenue from reportable segments to the entity's revenue;

(b) the total profit or loss for reportable segments to the entity's profit or loss before income taxes and discontinued operations. Where items such as income taxes have been allocated to arrive at segment profit or loss, the reconciliation can be made to the entity's profit or loss after those items;

(c) if segment assets are reported (see 5.2 above), the total of the reportable segments' assets to the entity's assets;

(d) if segment liabilities are reported (see 5.2 above), the total of reportable segments' liabilities to the entity's liabilities; and

(e) for every other material item of information the entity chooses to give in its segment information, the total of each item from all reportable segments to the corresponding amount for the entity. *[IFRS 8.28]*.

In each of the above reconciliations an entity must separately identify and describe all material reconciling items. For example, when reconciling segment profit or loss to the entity's profit or loss before income taxes and discontinued operations, each material adjustment arising from differences in accounting policies would have to be separately identified and described. *[IFRS 8.28]*. In addition, IFRS 8 requires information about the 'all other segments' category to be shown separately from other reconciling items. *[IFRS 8.16]*.

National Australia Bank evaluates the performance of operating segments on the basis of cash earnings. This post-tax measure of the profit or loss of reportable segments is reconciled to the consolidated financial statements as follows:

Extract 34.9: National Australia Bank Limited (2015)

Notes to the financial statements [extract]

2 Segment information [extract]

Reconciliations between reportable segment information and statutory results [extract]

The tables below reconcile the information in the segment tables presented above, which have been prepared on a cash earnings basis, to the relevant statutory information presented in the Financial Report. In addition to the sum of the reportable segments, the cash earnings basis includes the segments that do not meet the threshold to be reportable segments and intra group eliminations. The NAB Wealth adjustment represents a reallocation of the income statement of the NAB Wealth business prepared on a cash earnings basis into the appropriate statutory income statement lines.

[...]

	Group	
	2015[1] **$m**	2015[1] $m
Cash earnings		
Group cash earnings[2]	**5,839**	5,055
Non-cash earnings items (after tax):		
Distributions	**175**	180
Treasury shares	**4**	(43)
Fair value and hedge ineffectiveness	**497**	83
Life insurance economic assumption variation	**13**	(20)
Amortisation of acquired intangible assets	**(94)**	(74)
Sale and demerger transaction costs	**(77)**	–
Net profit/loss attributable to discontinued operations[3]	**(19)**	114
Net profit attributable to owners of NAB	**6,338**	5,295

[1] *[...]*
[2] *Includes eliminations and distributions*
[3] *[...]*

5.7 Restatement of previously reported information

Entities may need to change their organisation to respond to their business needs. This may have an impact on the entity's segment reporting. IFRS 8 provides explicit guidance if such a change in the organisation changes the composition of its reportable segments. However, it does not explicitly address any changes that impact reportable segments, such as a change in segment measures. This is discussed further below.

5.7.1 Changes in organisation structure

When an entity changes its organisational structure in a manner that causes a change in the composition of its reportable segments, corresponding amounts for earlier periods should be restated unless the information is not available and the cost to develop it would be excessive. This requirement also applies to the presentation of segment information in respect of interim periods. *[IFRS 8.29]*.

The exemption from restatement on grounds of excessive cost is applied to each individual item of disclosure. *[IFRS 8.29]*. This means that an entity should restate its comparative information for all the items it can, even if this results in some comparative information not being presented or restated, such as inter-segment revenues. When the composition of reportable segments has changed, an entity should disclose whether the corresponding items of segment information have been restated. *[IFRS 8.29]*.

Where corresponding information is not restated to reflect the new composition of reportable segments, the segment information for the current period should be presented on both the old and the new bases of segmentation. Only if the necessary information were unavailable and the cost of developing it excessive would an entity not have to show current information on the old basis of segmentation. *[IFRS 8.30]*. In our view, given the importance of comparable segment information in particular in years of changing segmentation, the 'excessive cost' criterion represents a high hurdle to overcome.

If an entity decides to change its organisational structure during the reporting period, the fact that this requirement applies equally to interim periods *[IFRS 8.29]* indicates that information presented at the reporting date is also restated to reflect the new basis of segmentation, even though for part of the annual reporting period the entity was managed and monitored on the old basis.

The following extract illustrates that changes in the composition of operating segments can often be combined with a review of other aspects of segment reporting, such as a review of performance measures:

Extract 34.10: Nestlé S.A. (2015)

Notes [extract]

1. Accounting Policies [extract]

Changes in presentation – Analyses by segment [extract]

The scope of the operating segments has been modified following the changes in management responsibilities as from 1 January 2015. Zone Europe has been renamed Zone Europe, Middle East and North Africa (EMENA) and now includes the Maghreb, the Middle East, the North East Africa region, Turkey and Israel, which were formerly included in Zone Asia, Oceania and Africa. Zone Asia, Oceania and Africa has been renamed Zone Asia, Oceania and sub-Saharan Africa (AOA). Nestlé Nutrition now includes Growing-Up Milks business formerly included in the geographic Zones. Finally, Other businesses now includes the Bübchen business, formerly included in Nestlé Nutrition.

The amount of segment assets is no longer disclosed. Segment assets are not included in the measures used for allocating resources and assessing segment performance. The Group discloses on a voluntary basis invested capital (as defined in Note 3) as well as goodwill and intangible assets by segment for consistency with long-standing practice. Goodwill and intangible assets are not included in invested capital since the amounts recognised are not comparable between segments due to differences in the intensity of acquisition activity and changes in accounting standards which were applicable at various points in time when the Group undertook significant acquisitions.

Information by product has been modified following the main transfer of Growing-Up Milks business in Milk products and Ice cream to Nutrition and Health Science.

Sales and non-current assets in Switzerland and countries which individually represent at least 10% of the Group sales or 10% of the Group non-current assets are disclosed separately, instead of the top ten countries and Switzerland.

In addition, intangible assets are attributed to the country of their legal owner rather than being allocated to the countries of the affiliated companies using these assets. Finally, goodwill items which were presented as part of unallocated items are attributed to the countries of the affiliated companies where the related acquired business is operated.

2014 comparative information has been restated.

Segment information may also change as a result of the disposal of an entire reportable segment or a component of it which qualifies under IFRS 5 – *Non-current Assets Held for Sale and Discontinued Operations* – as a discontinued operation. The presentation of discontinued operations is governed by IFRS 5. The requirements of other standards do not apply to discontinued operations, unless they specify disclosures applicable to them. *[IFRS 5.5B]*. Since IFRS 8 does not refer to discontinued operations, entities are not required to include them in their segment disclosures. This would be the case even if the CODM continued to monitor the discontinued operation until disposal. Nevertheless, an entity would not be prohibited from disclosing such information if it wished, on the basis that the requirements of IFRS 8 relate to the measures reported to the CODM without any adjustments being made in preparing the entity's IFRS financial statements. *[IFRS 8.25]*.

5.7.2 Changes in segment measures

When an entity changes any of its segment measures, including the definition of segment profit, or changes the allocation of income, expenses, assets or liabilities to segments, without a change to the composition of its reportable segments, the general principles of IAS 1 for changes in presentation or classification of items apply. Therefore, comparative information would be restated, unless this is impracticable. *[IAS 1.41]*.

In 2013, Deutsche Telekom changed the allocation of some of its activities for purposes of its segment reporting:

Extract 34.11: Deutsche Telekom AG (2013)

Notes to the consolidated financial statements [extract]

32. SEGMENT REPORTING [extract]

Since January 1, 2013, the tasks and functions of Group Technology including the Global Network Factory, which was previously part of Group Headquarters & Group Services, have been reported under the Europe operating segment. Group Technology's tasks include the efficient and customer-oriented provision of technologies, platforms, and services for mobile and fixed-network communications. The Global Network Factory designs and operates a worldwide network, which allow us to offer customers voice and data communication. The change was made to improve the way in which these units can be managed. Comparative figures have been adjusted retrospectively.

5.8 Disclosure of commercially sensitive information

The criteria for determining the externally reportable segments, as discussed at 3.2 above, attempt to define which internally reported operating units can be combined, which must be reported separately and which are included in an unallocated reconciling item. The interaction between these criteria, in particular with the requirement that segments cannot be combined if they exhibit different long-term financial performance, leaves entities open to the risk of having to disclose information that management would be concerned about sharing with competitors, customers, suppliers or employees.

However, IFRS 8 does not permit the omission of segment information when management believes that its disclosure is commercially sensitive or potentially detrimental to the entity's competitive position. Indeed, IAS 1 requires an entity not only to present information in a manner that provides relevant, reliable, comparable and understandable information, but also to provide *additional* disclosures if compliance with an individual standard is insufficient to enable users to understand the entity's financial position and financial performance. *[IAS 1.17]*. The only justification for failing to meet these requirements is if disclosure would be so misleading that it would conflict with the objective of financial statements set out in the IASB's *Conceptual Framework*. *[IAS 1.19]*.

Given that the objective of IFRS 8 is to disclose information to help users of financial statements evaluate the nature and financial effects of the entity's business activities and the economic environments in which it operates, *[IFRS 8.1]*, this possibility would seem to be remote. The IASB rejected similar concerns raised by respondents to ED 8, noting that entities would be unlikely to suffer competitive harm from the required disclosures since most competitors have sources of detailed information about an entity other than its financial statements. *[IFRS 8.BC44]*. This concern was raised again by respondents to the post-implementation review. However, the IASB continues to reject such a limitation, because it would provide a means for broad-based non-compliance with the standard.[7]

6 ENTITY-WIDE DISCLOSURES FOR ALL ENTITIES

In addition to disclosing segment information derived from the formats and measurements presented to the chief operating decision maker, IFRS 8 requires certain entity-wide disclosures about products and services, geographical areas and major customers. The information described below is required even if the entity has only a single reportable segment, but need not be repeated if already provided as part of the disclosures on reportable segments set out above. *[IFRS 8.31]*. The amounts reported about products and services and about geographical areas in these entity-wide disclosures are measured using the same accounting policies and estimates as the entity's financial statements (i.e. IFRS amounts). *[IFRS 8.32-33]*. As such, the amounts disclosed in this part of the segment disclosures might well be different to the information already provided in other segment information, which might not be measured in accordance with IFRS (see 4 above).

Exemption from the requirements set out at 6.1 and 6.2 below is offered if the necessary information is unavailable and the cost to develop it would be excessive. If disclosure is not made on these grounds, that fact should be stated. *[IFRS 8.32-33]*. Some respondents to ED 8 expressed concern that the basis of this exemption was inconsistent with the test of impracticability in IAS 1, which makes no allowance for the cost of compliance. *[IAS 1.7]*. However, the IASB did not see any merit in divergence from FASB ASC Topic 280 in this respect and therefore retained the exemption from disclosure if the necessary information were unavailable and the cost of developing it excessive. *[IFRS 8.BC46-47]*.

This exemption is not available in respect of the disclosures about major customers set out at 6.3 below.

6.1 Information about products and services

An entity should report revenues from external customers for each product and service or for each group of similar products and services, measuring revenues on the same basis as the entity's financial statements. *[IFRS 8.32]*.

In Extract 34.6 above, Statoil provides segment information based on its internal management reporting, with reportable segments relating to domestic, North American and international development and production activities; marketing, processing and renewable energy; and other activities. Accordingly, it also discloses external revenues by product group (and combines it with a geographical analysis of revenue), as follows:

Extract 34.12: Statoil ASA (2015)

4 Financial review [extract]

4.1.3 Segment performance and analysis[extract]

The following tables show total revenues by geographic area. [extract]

2015 Total revenues and other income by geographic area (in NOK billion)	Crude oil	Gas	NGL	Refined Products	Other	Total sales
Norway	182.4	86.9	39.8	45.4	15.7	370.1
US	29.9	9.1	4.3	12.8	7.7	63.8
Sweden	0.0	0.0	0.0	14.2	1.0	15.2
Denmark	0.0	0.0	0.0	14.1	0.1	14.1
Other	10.8	3.6	0.1	0.0	5.4	19.8
Total revenues (excluding net income (loss) from equity accounted investments) and other income	223.1	99.6	44.2	86.5	29.8	483.1

6.2 Information about geographical areas

IFRS 8 requires disclosure of the following geographical information:

(a) revenues from external customers, analysed between amounts attributed to the entity's country of domicile and the total of those attributed to all foreign countries; and

(b) non-current assets other than financial instruments, deferred tax assets, post-employment benefit assets and rights arising under insurance contracts, analysed between assets located in the entity's country of domicile and the total of those located in all foreign countries. *[IFRS 8.33]*.

In addition, if revenues from external customers or assets attributed to an individual foreign country are material, separate disclosure of that country's revenues or assets is required. *[IFRS 8.33]*. The Standard does not indicate what might be regarded as 'material', but given the criteria for a reportable segment and a major customer for reporting purposes (see 3.2.2 above and 6.3 below respectively) it would seem appropriate to consider the need for separate disclosure in respect of a foreign country accounting for more than 10% of total external revenues or more than 10% of total non-current assets.

Disclosure of the above information would be required even if the entity's segment reporting is already based on geography and it is determined that individual operating segments include a number of countries. Thus, an entity may need to provide additional information on revenue or non-current assets by country that is not disclosed in the segment information used by the chief operating decision maker.

The basis on which revenues from external customers are attributed to individual countries should be disclosed. An entity can elect to provide, in addition to the information required above, subtotals of geographical information about groups of countries. *[IFRS 8.33]*. In Extract 34.13 below, BAE Systems provides this more detailed level of disclosure and goes on to reconcile the measure of total segment assets to the amounts shown on the statement of financial position, even though such a reconciliation is not required for this entity-wide disclosure.

Extract 34.13: BAE Systems plc (2015)

Notes to the group accounts [extract]

17. Geographical analysis of assets

Analysis of non-current assets by geographical location

Asset location	Notes	**2015 £m**	2014 £m
UK		**2,537**	2,505
Rest of Europe		**538**	546
US		**8,635**	8,444
Saudi Arabia		**349**	316
Australia		**406**	469
Rest of Asia and Pacific		**1**	2
Africa, and Central and South America		**–**	2
Non-current segment assets		**12,466**	12,284
Retirement benefit surpluses	20	**193**	162
Other financial assets	13	**159**	74
Tax		**989**	1,334
Inventories	15	**726**	690
Current trade and other receivables	12	**2,940**	2,850
Cash (as defined by the Group)[1]	24	**2,590**	2,318
Assets held for sale		**20**	76
Consolidated total assets		**20,083**	19,788

[1] Includes cash and cash equivalents (note 16) and debt-related derivative financial instrument assets (note 13).

6.3 Information about major customers

IFRS 8 also requires an entity to give disclosures indicating the extent of its reliance on its major customers. If revenues from a single external customer account for 10% or more of the entity's total revenues, the entity should disclose:

(a) that fact;

(b) the total amount of revenues from each such customer; and

(c) the identity of the reportable segment or segments reporting the revenues. *[IFRS 8.34]*.

Disclosure is not required of the name of each major customer, nor the amounts of revenue reported in each segment for that customer. *[IFRS 8.34]*. However, the disclosure must be provided if it relates only to one segment.

Roche elects to provide the customers' names in the following extract.

Extract 34.14: Roche Holding Ltd (2015)

Notes to the Roche Group Consolidated Financial Statements [extract]

2. **Operating segment information** [extract]

Major customers

In total three US national wholesale distributors represent just over a quarter of the Group's revenues in 2015. The three US national wholesale distributors are AmerisourceBergen Corp. with CHF 5 billion (2014: CHF 5 billion); McKesson Corp. with CHF 6 billion (2014: CHF 5 billion) and Cardinal Health, Inc. with CHF 4 billion (2014: CHF 3 billion). Approximately 93% of these revenues were in the Pharmaceuticals operating segment, with the residual in the Diagnostics segment.

6.3.1 *Customers known to be under common control*

For the purposes of the above disclosures, a group of entities known to a reporting entity to be under common control are to be considered a single customer. *[IFRS 8.34]*.

However, judgement is required to assess whether a government (including government agencies and similar bodies whether local, national or international), and entities known to the reporting entity to be under the control of that government are considered a single customer. The assessment of whether entities should be regarded as a single customer for these purposes should take into account the extent of economic integration between those entities. *[IFRS 8.34]*. The standard does not include any further guidance on the factors relevant to determining the extent of economic integration.

BAE Systems identifies revenues from three principal governments.

Extract 34.15: BAE Systems plc (2015)

Notes to the Group accounts [extract]

1. **Segmental analysis** [extract]

Revenue by major customer

Revenue from the Group's three principal customers, which individually represent over 10% of total revenue, is as follows:

	2015	2014
	£m	£m
UK Ministry of Defence[1]	**4,838**	4,230
US Department of Defense	**3,838**	3,655
Kingdom of Saudi Arabia Ministry of Defence and Aviation	**3,582**	3,124

1. Includes £1.4bn (2014 £1.1bn) generated under the Typhoon work share agreement with Eurofighter Jagdflugzeug GmbH.

Revenue from the UK Ministry of Defence and the US Department of Defense was generated by the five principal reporting segments. Revenue from the Kingdom of Saudi Arabia Ministry of Defence and Aviation was generated by the Platforms & Services (UK) and Platforms & Services (International) reporting segments.

In its segment disclosures made under FASB ASC Topic 280, Lockheed Martin provides more detailed information about customer revenues by segment as well as total revenues for foreign governments and commercial customers.

Extract 34.16: Lockheed Martin Corporation (2015)

Notes to Consolidated Financial Statements [extract]

Note 5 – Information on Business Segments [extract]

Selected Financial Data by Business Segment [extract]

Net Sales by Customer Category [extract]

Net sales by customer category were as follows (in millions):

	2015	2014	2013
U.S. Government			
Aeronautics	**$ 11,195**	$ 10,704	$ 11,025
Information Systems & Global Solutions	**4,990**	5,204	5,823
Missiles and Fire Control	**4,150**	4,509	4,069
Mission Systems and Training	**6,961**	6,752	7,132
Space Systems	**8,845**	8,921	9,124
Total U.S. Government net sales	**$ 36,141**	$ 36,090	$ 37,173
International (a)			
Aeronautics	**$ 4,328**	$ 4,183	$ 3,078
Information Systems & Global Solutions	**520**	401	262
Missiles and Fire Control	**2,449**	2,421	2,535
Mission Systems and Training	**2,016**	1,921	1,792
Space Systems	**218**	89	101
Total international net sales	**$ 9,531**	$ 9,015	$ 7,768
U.S. Commercial and Other			
Aeronautics	**$ 47**	$ 33	$ 20
Information Systems & Global Solutions	**86**	49	30
Missiles and Fire Control	**171**	162	191
Mission Systems and Training	**114**	59	113
Space Systems	**42**	192	63
Total U.S. commercial and other net sales	**$ 460**	$ 495	$ 417
Total net sales	**$ 46,132**	$ 45,600	$ 45,358

(a) International sales include foreign military sales contracted through the U.S. Government, direct commercial sales with international governments and commercial and other sales to international customers.

7 RESULTS OF THE POST-IMPLEMENATION REVIEW OF IFRS 8

As noted at 1.1 above, IFRS 8 is the first standard to have been subject to a post-implementation review (PIR), which was added to the IASB's due process by the Trustees in 2007. The first phase of the PIR consisted of an initial assessment of the issues related to IFRS 8 and consultation with interested parties to establish the objective and scope of the review. As a second step of the PIR, the IASB issued in July 2012 its first due process document, *Request for Information – Post-implementation Review: IFRS 8 Operating Segments*, which was intended to formally gather information from the various groups of IASB's constituents about their experience with implementing IFRS 8.[8]

The Request for Information included open questions which focused not only on those aspects of IFRS 8 which had been considered to be the benefits of the new segment approach but also on the aspects of the Standard that were considered to be controversial when it was issued, including the effects of:

- using the management perspective;
- using non-IFRS measurements in segment reporting;
- using internally-reported line items;
- the IFRS 8 disclosures on the role of preparers and investors; and
- the implementation of IFRS 8 on preparers and investors.

In July 2013, the IASB issued its *Report and Feedback Statement – Post-implementation Review: IFRS 8 Operating Segments*, which summarised the PIR process, the feedback received and conclusions reached by IASB.[9] The IASB found that preparers generally think that the standard works well. While auditors, accounting firms, standard-setters and regulators were generally supportive of the Standard, some improvements were suggested for its application. In contrast, feedback from investor groups was mixed. Some investors prefer to have segment information based on the measures used by management, especially where this is consistent with information in the management commentary and in presentations to analysts. In some cases, investors expressed concern that a process based on the management perspective allowed segments to be presented in a way that obscures the entity's true management structure (often as a result of concerns about commercial sensitivity) or to mask loss-making activities within individual segments.[10]

Based on all of the feedback, the IASB concluded that the benefits of applying the Standard were largely as expected and that overall the Standard achieved its objectives and has improved financial reporting. The IASB noted the concerns raised by some investors but concluded that they do not suggest significant failings in the Standard and therefore do not warrant a revision of the principles underlying IFRS 8.[11]

However, the IASB acknowledged that some issues could be considered for improvement and warrant further investigation and can be classified as requests for implementation guidance and requests for improved disclosures.

Requests for implementation guidance included:[12]

- clarification of the concept of the chief operating decision maker; and
- guidance on how reconciliations should be presented.

Requests for improved disclosures included:[13]

- the provision of additional periods of comparative information in the event of a reorganisation;
- the introduction of defined line items of segmental disclosure to provide some degree of comparability between entities;
- measures to prevent inappropriate aggregation of segments, including guidance on the nature of 'similar economic characteristics'; and
- reconciliations being prepared on a segment-by-segment basis, where reconciling items can be allocated on a systematic basis.

In 2015, after due consideration of the above issues, the IASB tentatively decided to propose a narrow-scope amendment to IFRS 8, as follows:[14]

- to emphasise that the appropriate application of IFRS 8 facilitates consistent description of the entity across presentations to investors, the management commentary and operating segments disclosures, and that this consistency increases the information value of each form of reporting;
- to clarify that the CODM includes both individuals and committees and that the CODM is a function that makes operating decisions;
- to require disclosure of the nature of the entity's CODM;
- to provide additional guidance about the type of information that is most useful to investors (e.g. information about non-cash expenses, non-recurring items and other line items that affect future cash flows);and
- to extend the number of examples of similar economic characteristics contained in paragraph 12 of IFRS 8; and
- to require more explanation of reconciling and unallocated items.

Whilst the IASB concluded that it was not necessary to extend the requirements of IFRS 8 regarding the presentation of comparative information in the event of a reorganisation (see 5.7.1 above), the Board tentatively agreed to amend IAS 34 to require that an entity present all restated interim comparative periods for the preceding year as part of its first interim report following a reorganisation.[15] At the time of writing, the IASB plans to issue an Exposure Draft in the second half of 2016.[16]

References

1 IFRS 8 D01-D04.

2 Press Release, *Summary of the IASC Foundation Trustees meeting 2 and 3 July 2007, Madrid,* IFRS Foundation, 18 July 2007.

3 *IFRIC Update*, July 2011, p.5.

4 ED 8, *Operating Segments*, IASB, January 2006.

5 *IFRIC Update*, September 2011, p.5.

6 *IASB Update*, September 2011, p.15.

7 Report and Feedback Statement *Post-implementation Review: IFRS 8 Operating Segments*, July 2013, p.19.

8 Request for Information *Post-implementation Review: IFRS 8 Operating Segments*, Introduction, p.4.

9 Report and Feedback Statement *Post-implementation Review: IFRS 8 Operating Segments*, July 2013.

10 Report and Feedback Statement, p.5.

11 Report and Feedback Statement, p.6.

12 Report and Feedback Statement, p.7.

13 Report and Feedback Statement, p.7.

14 *IASB Update*, May 2015, pp.7-8.

15 *IASB Update*, May 2015, p.8.

16 *IASB Work Plan – as at 20 July 2016*, Maintenance of IFRS Standards, Narrow-scope amendments and IFRIC Interpretations, Clarifications to IFRS 8 Arising from the Post-implementation Review, IASB.

Chapter 35 Earnings per share

List of examples

Chapter 35 Earnings per share

1 INTRODUCTION

Earnings per share (EPS) is one of the most widely quoted statistics in financial analysis. It came into great prominence in the US during the late 1950s and early 1960s due to the widespread use of the price earnings ratio (PE) as a yardstick for investment decisions. As a result, standard setters in some jurisdictions (notably the US and the UK) have had rules on EPS for many years. However, it was not until 1997 that an international accounting standard on the subject was published.

IAS 33 – *Earnings per Share* – was introduced for accounting periods beginning on or after 1 January 1998. In December 2003, as part of the improvements project, the IASB updated IAS 33 to provide more detailed guidance in some complex areas. There have been no substantive changes since. The requirements of IAS 33 are discussed at 2 to 7 below, and the standard's illustrative examples of particular issues are included in the text of the chapter, whilst its comprehensive worked example is included as an Appendix.

1.1 Definitions

IAS 33 defines a number of its terms and these are dealt with in the text of this chapter where appropriate. One term which is particularly pervasive is 'fair value'. This term is defined and explained in IFRS 13 – *Fair Value Measurement* – and is discussed in Chapter 14. *[IAS 33.8]*. However, in the context of share-based payments the term fair value has the meaning used in IFRS 2 – *Share-based Payment.* The relevance of share-based payment to EPS is discussed at 6.4.5 below; IFRS 2 is discussed in Chapter 32. *[IAS 33.47A]*.

2 OBJECTIVE AND SCOPE OF IAS 33

2.1 Objective

IAS 33 sets out its objective as follows: 'to prescribe principles for the determination and presentation of earnings per share, so as to improve performance comparisons between different entities in the same reporting period and between different reporting periods for the same entity. Even though earnings per share data have limitations because of the different accounting policies that may be used for determining "earnings", a consistently determined denominator enhances financial reporting. The focus of this Standard is on the denominator of the earnings per share calculation.' *[IAS 33.1]*.

The standard requires the computation of both basic and diluted EPS, explaining the objective of each as follows:

- the objective of basic earnings per share information is to provide a measure of the interests of each ordinary share of a parent entity in the performance of the entity over the reporting period; *[IAS 33.11]* and
- the objective of diluted earnings per share is consistent with that of basic earnings per share – to provide a measure of the interest of each ordinary share in the performance of an entity – while giving effect to all dilutive potential ordinary shares outstanding during the period. *[IAS 33.32]*.

The underlying logic here is that EPS, including diluted EPS, should be an historical performance measure. This impacts particularly on the reporting of diluted EPS, in steering it away from an alternative purpose: to warn of potential future dilution. Indeed the tension between these differing objectives is evident in the standard. As discussed more fully at 6.4.6 below, IAS 33 sets out a very restrictive regime for including certain potentially dilutive shares in the diluted EPS calculation. Yet diluted EPS is only to take account of those potential shares that would dilute earnings from *continuing* operations (see 6.3.1 below) which seems to have more of a forward looking 'warning signal' flavour. Discontinued operations are discussed in Chapter 4.

2.2 Scope

IAS 33 applies to:

(a) the separate or individual financial statements of an entity:

  (i) whose ordinary shares or potential ordinary shares are traded in a public market (a domestic or foreign stock exchange or an over-the-counter market, including local and regional markets); or

  (ii) that files, or is in the process of filing, its financial statements with a securities commission or other regulatory information for the purpose of issuing ordinary shares in a public market; and

(b) the consolidated financial statements of a group with a parent:

  (i) whose ordinary shares or potential ordinary shares are traded in a public market (a domestic or foreign stock exchange or an over-the-counter market, including local and regional markets); or

  (ii) that files, or is in the process of filing, its financial statements with a securities commission or other regulatory information for the purpose of issuing ordinary shares in a public market. *[IAS 33.2]*.

IAS 33 also applies to any other entity that discloses earnings per share. *[IAS 33.3]*. Where both the parent's consolidated and separate financial statements are presented, the standard only requires consolidated earnings per share to be given. If the parent chooses to present EPS data based on its separate financial statements the standard requires that the disclosures be restricted to the face of the parent-only statement of comprehensive income (or separate income statement) and not be included in the consolidated financial statements. *[IAS 33.4]*.

In January 2014, the IASB published IFRS 14 – *Regulatory Deferral Accounts.* This standard allows a first-time adopter within its scope to continue to account for regulatory deferral account balances in its first IFRS financial statements in accordance with its previous GAAP when it adopts IFRS. The standard introduces limited changes to some previous GAAP accounting practices for regulatory deferral account balances, which are primarily related to the presentation of these accounts. For entities applying IFRS 14 certain additional EPS disclosures are required. This is discussed in Chapter 5 at 5.23.

3 THE BASIC EPS

IAS 33 requires the computation of basic EPS for the profit or loss (and, if presented, the profit or loss from continuing operations) attributable to ordinary equity holders. *[IAS 33.9]*. It defines, or rather describes, basic earnings per share in the following manner: 'Basic earnings per share shall be calculated by dividing profit or loss attributable to ordinary equity holders of the parent entity (the numerator) by the weighted average number of ordinary shares outstanding (the denominator) during the period.' *[IAS 33.10]*.

3.1 Earnings

The starting point for determining the earnings figure to be used in the basic EPS calculation (both for total earnings and, if appropriate, earnings from continuing operations) is the net profit or loss for the period attributable to ordinary equity holders. *[IAS 33.12]*. This will, in accordance with IAS 1 – *Presentation of Financial Statements* – include all items of income and expense, including, dividends on preference shares classified as liabilities and tax and is stated after the deduction of non-controlling interests. *[IAS 33.13, A1]*. This is then adjusted for the after-tax amounts of preference dividends, differences arising on the settlement of preference shares, and other similar effects of preference shares classified as equity. *[IAS 33.12]*. These adjustments are discussed at 5.2 below.

3.2 Number of shares

An ordinary share is defined as 'an equity instrument that is subordinate to all other classes of equity instruments'. *[IAS 33.5]*. 'Equity instrument' has the same meaning as in IAS 32 – *Financial Instruments: Presentation* – that is 'any contract that evidences a residual interest in the assets of an entity after deducting all of its liabilities'. *[IAS 33.8, IAS 32.11]*. IAS 33 goes on to observe that ordinary shares participate in profit for the period only after other types of share such as preference shares have participated. *[IAS 33.6]*. The standard also clarifies that there may be more than one class of ordinary share and requires the computation and presentation of EPS for each class that has a different right to share in profit for the period. *[IAS 33.6, 66]*. In practice, it is usually straightforward to determine which instruments are ordinary shares for EPS purposes. The treatment of different classes of shares is discussed at 5.4 below.

The basic rule in IAS 33 is that all outstanding ordinary shares are brought into the basic EPS computation – time-weighted for changes in the period (changes in ordinary shares are discussed at 4 below). *[IAS 33.19]*. There are three exceptions to this:

- ordinary shares that are issued as partly paid are included in the weighted average as a fraction of a share based on their dividend participation relative to fully paid shares (so if although only partly paid, they ranked equally for dividends they would be included in full); *[IAS 33.A15]*
- treasury shares, which are presented in the financial statements as a deduction from equity, are not considered outstanding for EPS purposes for the period they are held in treasury. Although not stated explicitly in the standard itself, this requirement is clearly logical (as although the shares are still legally in issue, they are accounted for as if redeemed) and is illustrated in one of the examples appended to the standard (see Example 35.1 at 4.1 below); *[IAS 33.IE2]* and
- shares that are contingently returnable (that is, subject to recall) are not treated as outstanding until they cease to be subject to recall, and hence are excluded from basic EPS until that time. *[IAS 33.24]*.

The standard contains some specific guidance on when newly issued ordinary shares should be considered outstanding. In general, shares are to be included from the date consideration is receivable (considered by the standard generally to be the date of their issue), for example: *[IAS 33.21]*

- shares issued in exchange for cash are included when cash is receivable;
- shares issued on the voluntary reinvestment of dividends on ordinary or preference shares are included when the dividends are reinvested;
- shares issued as a result of the conversion of a debt instrument to ordinary shares are included as of the date interest ceases accruing;
- shares issued in place of interest or principal on other financial instruments are included as of the date interest ceases accruing;
- shares issued in exchange for the settlement of a liability of the entity are included as of the settlement date;
- shares issued as consideration for the acquisition of an asset other than cash are included as of the date on which the acquisition is recognised;
- shares issued in exchange for the rendering of services to the entity are included as the services are rendered; and
- shares that will be issued upon the conversion of a mandatorily convertible instrument are included in the calculation of basic earnings per share from the date the contract is entered into. *[IAS 33.23]*.

Most of these provisions are straightforward, however some are worthy of note.

Shares issued in exchange for services will be accounted for in accordance with IFRS 2, with a charge to income matched by a credit to equity. IAS 33 has some guidance on the inclusion of such potential shares in *diluted* EPS (see 6.4.5 below); however there is no further elaboration of the meaning of 'included as the services are rendered'. What seems to be implicit in the phrase is that the shares concerned vest unconditionally as services are rendered. On that basis, clearly it would be appropriate to include shares in basic EPS as entitlement to them vests, notwithstanding that the actual issue of shares may be at a different time. However, a very common form of share-based remuneration involves entitlement to shares vesting at the end of an extended period conditional on future events (typically continued employment and sometimes specific future performance). Such arrangements are clearly conditionally issuable shares and should be excluded from basic EPS until vesting. Indeed, when discussing employee share schemes in the context of diluted EPS the standard is explicit, as follows. 'Employee share options with fixed or determinable terms and non-vested ordinary shares are treated as options in the calculation of diluted earnings per share, even though they may be contingent on vesting. They are treated as outstanding on the grant date. Performance-based employee share options are treated as contingently issuable shares because their issue is contingent upon satisfying specified conditions in addition to the passage of time.' *[IAS 33.48]*. Contingently issuable shares are discussed at 6.4.6 below.

In respect of the final bullet point, the standard does not define what a mandatorily convertible instrument is. One view would be that the requirement to account for the shares in EPS from inception must mean it refers to instruments where the proceeds also are received at inception. On that basis, it would exclude a forward contract for the issue of shares which (as required by the first bullet above) would increase the denominator of basic EPS only from the time the cash is receivable. Similarly, in the reverse situation of a forward contract to redeem ordinary shares the shares would only be removed from basic EPS when the consideration becomes payable. Another view would be that all binding agreements to issue or redeem ordinary shares should be reflected in basic EPS when the entity becomes party to the arrangement. A further possible complexity is the question of whether or not a symmetrical treatment for the issue and redemption of shares should be applied for EPS purposes. Whilst that certainly seems logical, it is not beyond question in all circumstances particularly given the asymmetrical accounting treatment for certain derivatives over own shares required by IAS 32 (discussed in Chapter 45 at 5).

More generally, the standard goes on to say the timing of inclusion is determined by the attaching terms and conditions, and also that due consideration should be given to the substance of any contract associated with the issue. *[IAS 33.21]*. Ordinary shares that are issuable on the satisfaction of certain conditions (contingently issuable shares) are to be included in the calculation of basic EPS only from the date when all necessary conditions have been satisfied; in effect when they are no longer contingent. *[IAS 33.24]*. This provision is interpreted strictly, as illustrated in Example 7 appended to the standard (see Example 35.14 at 6.4.6.A below). In that example earnings in a year, by meeting certain thresholds, would trigger the issue of shares. Because it is not certain that the condition is met until the last day of the year (when earnings become known with certainty) the new shares are excluded from basic EPS until the following year. Where shares will be issued at some future date (that is, solely after the passage of time) they are not considered contingently issuable by IAS 33, as the passage of time is a certainty. *[IAS 33.24]*. In principle, this would seem to mean that they should be included in basic EPS from the agreement date. However, careful consideration of the individual facts and circumstances would be necessary.

The calculation of the basic EPS is often simple but a number of complications can arise; these may be considered under the following two headings:

(a) changes in ordinary shares outstanding; and

(b) matters affecting the numerator.

These are discussed in the next two sections.

4 CHANGES IN OUTSTANDING ORDINARY SHARES

Changes in ordinary shares outstanding can occur under a variety of circumstances, the most common of which are dealt with below. Whenever such a change occurs during the accounting period, an adjustment is required to the number of shares in the EPS calculation for that period; furthermore, in certain situations the EPS for previous periods will also have to be recalculated.

4.1 Weighted average number of shares

Implicit in the methodology of IAS 33 is a perceived correlation between the capital of an entity (or rather the income-generating assets it reflects) and earnings. Accordingly, to compute EPS as a performance measure requires adjusting the number of shares in the denominator to reflect any variations in the period to the capital available to generate that period's earnings. The standard observes that using the weighted average number of ordinary shares outstanding during the period reflects the possibility that the amount of shareholders' capital varied during the period as a result of a larger or smaller number of shares being outstanding at any time. The weighted average number of ordinary shares outstanding during the period is the number of ordinary shares outstanding at the beginning of the period, adjusted by the number of ordinary shares bought back or issued during the period multiplied by a time-weighting factor. The time-weighting factor is the number of days that the shares are outstanding as a proportion of the total number of days in the period; IAS 33 notes that a reasonable approximation of the weighted average is adequate in many circumstances. *[IAS 33.20]*. Computation of a weighted average number of shares is illustrated in the following example: *[IAS 1.IE2]*

Example 35.1: Calculation of weighted average number of shares

		Shares issued	*Treasury shares**	*Shares outstanding*
1 January 2017	Balance at beginning of year	2,000	300	1,700
31 May 2017	Issue of new shares for cash	800	–	2,500
1 December 2017	Purchase of treasury shares for cash	–	250	2,250
31 December 2017	Balance at year end	2,800	550	2,250

Calculation of weighted average:

(1,700 × 5/12) + (2,500 × 6/12) + (2,250 × 1/12) = 2,146 shares *or*

(1,700 × 12/12) + (800 × 7/12) – (250 × 1/12) = 2,146 shares

* Treasury shares are equity instruments reacquired and held by the issuing entity itself or by its subsidiaries.

The use of a weighted average number of shares is necessary because the increase in the share capital would have affected earnings only for that portion of the year during which the issue proceeds were available to management for use in the business.

4.2 Purchase and redemption of own shares

An entity may, if it is authorised to do so by its constitution and it complies with any relevant legislation, purchase or otherwise redeem its own shares. Assuming this is done at fair value, then the earnings should be apportioned over the weighted average share capital in issue for the year. This was illustrated in Example 35.1 above in relation to the purchase of treasury shares. If, on the other hand, the repurchase is at significantly more than market value then IAS 33 requires adjustments to be made to EPS for periods before buy-back. This is discussed at 4.3.5 below.

4.3 Changes in ordinary shares without corresponding changes in resources

IAS 33 requires the number of shares used in the calculation to be adjusted (for all periods presented) for any transaction (other than the conversion of potential ordinary shares) that changes the number of shares outstanding without a corresponding change in resources. *[IAS 33.26]*. This is also to apply when some, but not all, such changes have happened after the year-end but before the approval of the financial statements.

The standard gives the following as examples of changes in the number of ordinary shares without a corresponding change in resources:

(a) a capitalisation or bonus issue (sometimes referred to as a stock dividend);

(b) a bonus element in any other issue, for example a bonus element in a rights issue to existing shareholders;

(c) a share split; and

(d) a reverse share split (share consolidation). *[IAS 33.27]*.

Another example not mentioned by the standard would be any bonus element in a buy-back, such as a put warrant involving the repurchase of shares at significantly more than their fair value. The adjustments required to EPS for each of these is discussed below.

As noted above, IAS 33 requires retrospective adjustment for all such events that happen in the reporting period. However, it only requires restatement for those in (a), (c) and (d) if they happen after the year-end but before the financial statements are authorised for issue. *[IAS 33.64]*.

4.3.1 Capitalisation, bonus issue, share split and share consolidation

4.3.1.A Capitalisation, bonus issues and share splits

A capitalisation or bonus issue or share split has the effect of increasing the number of shares in issue without any inflow of resources, as further ordinary shares are issued to existing shareholders for no consideration. Consequently, no additional earnings will be expected to accrue as a result of the issue. The additional shares should be treated as having been in issue for the whole period and also included in the EPS calculation of all earlier periods presented so as to give a comparable result. For example, on a two-for-one bonus issue, the number of ordinary shares outstanding before the issue is multiplied by three to obtain the new total number of ordinary shares, or by two to obtain the number of additional ordinary shares. *[IAS 33.28]*.

The EPS calculation involving a bonus issue is illustrated in the following example. *[IAS 33.IE3]*.

Example 35.2: A bonus issue

Profit attributable to ordinary equity holders of the parent entity 2016	€180
Profit attributable to ordinary equity holders of the parent entity 2017	€600
Ordinary shares outstanding until 30 September 2017	200
Bonus issue 1 October 2017	2 ordinary shares for each ordinary share outstanding at 30 September 2017
	200 × 2 = 400
Basic earnings per share 2017	$\frac{€600}{(200+400)} = €1.00$
Basic earnings per share 2016	$\frac{€180}{(200+400)} = €0.30$

Because the bonus issue was without consideration, it is treated as if it had occurred before the beginning of 2016, the earliest period presented.

Again, although the standard is silent on the matter, we believe that any financial ratios disclosed for earlier periods, which are based on the number of equity shares at a year-end (e.g. dividend per share) should also be adjusted in a similar manner.

4.3.1.B Stock dividends

Stock or scrip dividends refer to the case where an entity offers its shareholders the choice of receiving further fully paid up shares in the company as an alternative to receiving a cash dividend. It could be argued that the dividend foregone represents payment for the shares, usually at fair value, and hence no restatement is appropriate. Alternatively, the shares could be viewed as being, in substance, bonus issues which require the EPS for the earlier period to be adjusted. IAS 33 seems to suggest the latter view, as it notes that capitalisation or bonus issues are sometimes referred to as stock dividends. However, entities often refer to these arrangements as dividend reinvestment plans which suggests the acquisition of new shares for valuable consideration.

In our view, this distinction should be a factual one. If an entity (say, through proposal and subsequent approval by shareholders) has a legal obligation to pay a dividend in cash or, at the shareholder's option, shares then the cash payment avoided if the stock dividend is taken up is consideration for the shares. This may be equivalent to an issue at fair value or it may contain some bonus element requiring retrospective adjustment of EPS. In practice the fair value of shares received as a stock dividend alternative may exceed the cash alternative; this is often referred to as an enhanced stock dividend. In these cases IAS 33 requires a bonus element to be identified, and prior EPS figures restated accordingly. This is essentially the same as adjustments for the bonus element in a rights issue, discussed at 4.3.3 below.

Furthermore, in this scenario, during the period between the obligation coming into existence and its settlement (in cash or shares) it could be argued to represent a written call option and hence potentially affect diluted EPS (see 6.4.2.B below). Given that the standard is silent on this aspect of some stock dividends we do not believe that such an approach was intended. In any event, we generally do not believe the effect on diluted EPS would be significant. Conversely, if the entity issues new shares *instead of* a dividend it would be a bonus issue requiring full retrospective adjustment to EPS.

4.3.1.C Share consolidations

Occasionally, entities will consolidate their equity share capital into a smaller number of shares. Such a consolidation generally reduces the number of shares outstanding without a corresponding outflow of resources, and this would require an adjustment to the denominator for periods before the consolidation. *[IAS 33.29]*.

4.3.2 Share consolidation with a special dividend

Share consolidations as discussed at 4.3.1.C above normally do not involve any outflow of funds from the entity. However, entities may return surplus cash to their shareholders by paying special dividends accompanied by a share consolidation, the purpose of which is to maintain the value of each share following the payment of the dividend. This issue is specifically addressed by IAS 33. The normal rule of restating the outstanding number of shares for all periods for a share consolidation is not applied when the overall effect is a share repurchase at fair value because in such cases the reduction of shares *is* the result of a corresponding reduction in resources. In such cases the weighted average number of shares is adjusted for the consolidation from the date the special dividend is recognised. *[IAS 33.29]*.

4.3.3 Rights issue

A rights issue is a popular method through which entities are able to access the capital markets for further capital. Under the terms of such an issue, existing shareholders are given the opportunity to acquire further shares in the entity on a pro-rata basis to their existing shareholdings.

The 'rights' shares will usually be offered either at the current market price or at a price below that. In the former case, the treatment of the issue for EPS purposes is as discussed in 4.1 above. However, where the rights price is at a discount to market it is not quite as straightforward, since the issue is equivalent to a bonus issue (see 4.3.1 above) combined with an issue at full market price. In such cases, IAS 33 requires an adjustment to the number of shares outstanding before the rights issue to reflect the bonus element inherent in it. *[IAS 33.26-27]*.

The bonus element of the rights issue available to all existing shareholders is given by the following adjustment factor, sometimes referred to as the bonus fraction: *[IAS 33.A2]*

$$\frac{\text{Fair value per share immediately before the exercise of rights}}{\text{Theoretical ex-rights fair value per share}}$$

The fair value per share immediately before the exercise of rights is the *actual* price at which the shares are quoted inclusive of the right to take up the future shares under the rights issue. Where the rights are to be traded separately from the shares the fair value used is the closing price on the last day on which the shares are traded inclusive of the right. *[IAS 33.A2]*.

The 'ex-rights fair value' is the *theoretical* price at which the shares would be expected to be quoted, other stock market factors apart, after the rights issue shares have been issued. It is calculated by adding the aggregate fair value of the shares immediately before the exercise of the rights to the proceeds from the exercise, and dividing by the number of shares outstanding after the exercise. *[IAS 33.A2]*. The EPS calculation involving a rights issue is illustrated in the following example. *[IAS 33.IE4]*.

Example 35.3: Rights issue at less than full market price

		2015	2016	2017
Profit attributable to ordinary equity holders of the parent entity		€1,100	€1,500	€1,800

Shares outstanding before rights issue	500 shares
Rights issue	One new share for each five outstanding shares (100 new shares total) Exercise price: €5.00 Date of rights issue: 1 January 2016 Last date to exercise rights: 1 March 2016
Market price of one ordinary share immediately before exercise on 1 March 2016	€11.00
Reporting date	31 December

Calculation of theoretical ex-rights value per share

$$\frac{\text{Fair value of all outstanding shares before the exercise of rights} + \text{Total amount received from exercise of rights}}{\text{Number of shares outstanding before exercise} + \text{Number of shares issued in the exercise}} =$$

$$\frac{(€11.00 \times 500\text{ shares}) + (€5.00 \times 100\text{ shares})}{500\text{ shares} + 100\text{ shares}}$$

Theoretical ex-rights value per share = €10.00

Calculation of adjustment factor

$$\frac{\text{Fair value per share before exercise of rights}}{\text{Theoretical ex-rights value per share}} = \frac{€11.00}{€10.00} = 1.10$$

Calculation of basic earnings per share

	2015	2016	2017
2015 basic EPS as originally reported:			
€1,100 ÷ 500 shares =	€2.20		
2015 basic EPS restated for rights issue:			
€1,100 ÷ (500 shares × 1.1) =	€2.00		
2016 basic EPS including effects of rights issue:			
$\dfrac{€1{,}500}{(500 \times 1.1 \times 2/12) + (600 \times 10/12)} =$		€2.54	
2017 basic EPS:			
€1,800 ÷ 600 shares =			€3.00

Rather than multiplying the denominator by 11/10ths, the previous year's EPS (and any EPS disclosures in a historical summary) could alternatively be arrived at by multiplying the original EPS by 10/11ths.

During the period that the rights are outstanding they represent, strictly speaking, a written call option over the entity's shares which could have implications for diluted EPS (see 6.4.2 below).

It is possible that shares could be issued as a result of open offers, placings and other offerings of equity shares not made to existing shareholders, at a discount to the market price. In such cases it would be necessary to consider whether the issue contained a bonus element, or rather simply reflected differing views on the fair value of the shares. In our opinion the latter is a more realistic alternative. Accordingly the shares should be dealt with on a weighted average basis without calculating any bonus element when computing the EPS.

4.3.4 B share schemes

One method by which some entities have returned capital to shareholders is the so-called 'B share scheme'. These schemes involve issuing 'B shares' (usually undated preference shares with low or zero coupons) to existing shareholders, either as a bonus issue or via a share split. These are then repurchased for cash and cancelled, following which the ordinary shares are consolidated. The overall effect is intended to be the same as a repurchase of ordinary shares at fair value, and accordingly no retrospective adjustment to EPS is necessary, assuming that the intention is achieved. *[IAS 33.29]*.

4.3.5 Put warrants priced above market value

As noted at 4.3 above, an example of a change in the number of shares outstanding without a corresponding change in resources not mentioned by the standard would be any bonus element in a buy-back, such as a put warrant involving the repurchase of shares at significantly more than their fair value. The accounting requirements for such instruments are discussed in Chapter 45 at 5.

IAS 33 does not give an illustrative calculation for a put warrant at significantly more than fair value, but it does for the more familiar rights issue (which are discussed at 4.3.3 above). In a rights issue new shares are issued at a discount to market value, whereas with put warrants shares are bought back at a premium to market value. In both cases the remaining shares are viewed as being devalued for the purposes of comparing EPS over time. Applying the logic of adjusting EPS when there is a change in the number of shares without a corresponding change in resources would seem to require that put warrants are treated as a reverse rights issue. This would mean calculating a similar 'adjustment factor', and applying it to the number of shares outstanding before the transaction. The difference in the calculation would be that the number of shares issued and the consideration received for them would be replaced by negative amounts representing the number of shares put back to the entity and the amount paid for them.

An illustration of what this might entail is as follows:

Example 35.4: Put warrants priced above market value

The following example takes the same scenario as Example 35.3 above (a rights issue), altered to illustrate a put warrant scheme. In that example the shares are issued at a discount of €6.00 to the €11.00 market price on a one for five basis two months into the year. Reversing this would give a put warrant to sell shares back to the company at a €6 premium, again on a one for five basis. All other details have been left the same for comparability, although in reality the rising earnings following a rights issue may well become falling earnings after a buy-back. The calculation would then become:

Calculation of theoretical ex-warrant value per share

$$\frac{\text{fair value of all outstanding shares before the exercise of warrants} - \text{total amount paid on exercise of warrants}}{\text{shares outstanding before exercise} - \text{shares cancelled in the exercise}} =$$

$$\frac{(€11 \times 500) - (€17 \times 100)}{500 - 100} = €9.50$$

Calculation of adjustment factor

$$\frac{\text{Fair value per share before exercise of warrants}}{\text{Theoretical ex - warrant value per share}} = \frac{€11}{€9.5} = 1.16$$

Calculation of basic earnings per share

	2015	2016	2017
	€	€	€
2015 EPS as originally reported: €1,100 ÷ 500 shares =	2.20		
2015 EPS restated for warrants: €1,100 ÷ (500 shares × 1.16) =	1.90		
2016 EPS including effects of warrants: $\frac{€1{,}500}{(500 \times 1.16 \times 2/12) + (400 \times 10/12)} =$		3.49	
2017 basic EPS: €1,800 ÷ 400 shares =			3.49

Whilst the above seems a sensible interpretation of the requirements, as the procedure is not specified there may be scope for other interpretations.

4.4 Options exercised during the year

Shares issued as a result of options being exercised should be dealt with on a weighted average basis in the basic EPS. *[IAS 33.38]*. Furthermore, options that have been exercised during the year will also affect diluted EPS calculations. If the options in question would have had a diluting effect on the basic EPS had they been exercised at the beginning of the year, then they should be considered in the diluted EPS calculation as explained in 6.4.2 below, but on a weighted average basis for the period up to the date of exercise. The exercise of options is a 'conversion of potential ordinary shares'. The standard excludes such conversions from the general requirement (see 4.3 above) to adjust prior periods' EPS when a change in the number of shares happens without a corresponding change in resources. *[IAS 33.26]*.

4.5 Post balance sheet changes in capital

The EPS figure should not reflect any changes in the capital structure occurring after the reporting period, but before the financial statements are authorised for issue, which was effected for fair value. This is because any proceeds received from the issue were not available for use during the period. However, EPS for all periods presented should be adjusted for any bonus element in certain post year-end changes in the number of shares, as discussed at 4.3 above. When this is done that fact should be disclosed. *[IAS 33.64]*.

4.6 Issue to acquire another business

4.6.1 Acquisitions

As a result of a share issue to acquire another business, funds or other assets will flow into the reporting entity and extra profits will be expected to be generated. When calculating EPS, it should be assumed that the shares were issued on the acquisition date (even if the actual date of issue is later), since this will be the date from which the results of the newly acquired business are recognised. *[IAS 33.21(f), 22]*.

4.6.2 Reverse acquisitions

Reverse acquisition is the term used to describe a business combination whereby the legal parent entity after the combination is in substance the acquired and not the acquiring entity (discussed in Chapter 9 at 14). IAS 33 is silent on the subject; however, an appendix to IFRS 3 – *Business Combinations* – contains a discussion of the implications for EPS of such transactions. Following a reverse acquisition the equity structure appearing in the consolidated financial statements will reflect the equity of the legal parent, including the equity instruments issued by it to effect the business combination. *[IFRS 3.B25]*.

For the purposes of calculating the weighted average number of ordinary shares outstanding during the period in which the reverse acquisition occurs:

(a) the number of ordinary shares outstanding from the beginning of that period to the acquisition date shall be computed on the basis of the weighted average number of ordinary shares of the legal acquiree (accounting acquirer) outstanding during the period multiplied by the exchange ratio established in the merger agreement; and

(b) the number of ordinary shares outstanding from the acquisition date to the end of that period shall be the actual number of ordinary shares of the legal acquirer (the accounting acquiree) outstanding during that period. *[IFRS 3.B26]*.

The basic EPS disclosed for each comparative period before the acquisition date is calculated by dividing the profit or loss of the legal subsidiary attributable to ordinary shareholders in each of those periods by the legal acquiree's historical weighted average number of ordinary shares outstanding multiplied by the exchange ratio established in the acquisition agreement *[IFRS 3.B27]*.

IFRS 3 presents an illustrative example of a reverse acquisition, including the EPS calculation, see Chapter 9 at 14.5.

4.6.3 Establishment of a new parent undertaking

Where a new parent entity is established by means of a share for share exchange and its consolidated financial statements have been presented as a continuation of the existing group (discussed in Chapter 10 at 4.2.1), the number of shares taken as being in issue for both the current and preceding periods would be the number of shares issued by the new parent entity. However, EPS calculations for previous periods in the new parent entity's financial statements would have to reflect any changes in the number of outstanding ordinary shares of the former parent entity that may have occurred in those periods, as illustrated in the example below:

Example 35.5: Calculation of EPS where a new holding company is established

Entity A has been established as the newly formed parent entity of Entity B in a one for one share exchange on 30 June 2017. At that date, Entity B has 1,000,000 €1 ordinary shares in issue. Previously, on 30 June 2016 Entity B had issued 200,000 €1 ordinary shares for cash at full market price. Both entities have a 31 December year-end and the trading results of Entity B are as follows:

	2017 €	2016 €
Profit for equity shareholders after taxation	500,000	300,000

The earnings per share calculation of Entity A is shown below:

	2017		2016
Number of equity shares		$800{,}000 \times \frac{6}{12} =$	400,000
		$1{,}000{,}000 \times \frac{6}{12} =$	500,000
	1,000,000		900,000
EPS	$\frac{500{,}000}{1{,}000{,}000} = €0.50$		$\frac{300{,}000}{900{,}000} = €0.33$

If, in the above example, the share exchange did not take place on a one for one basis, but Entity A issued three shares for every one share held in Entity B, then the number of shares issued by Entity B in 2016 would have to be apportioned accordingly before carrying out the weighted average calculation. The earnings per share calculation would, therefore, have been as follows:

	2017		2016
Number of equity shares			
		$2{,}400{,}000 \times \frac{6}{12} =$	1,200,000
		$3{,}000{,}000 \times \frac{6}{12} =$	1,500,000
	3,000,000		2,700,000
EPS	$\frac{500{,}000}{3{,}000{,}000} = €0.17$		$\frac{300{,}000}{2{,}700{,}000} = €0.11$

4.7 Adjustments to EPS in historical summaries

In order to ensure comparability of EPS figures, the previously published EPS figures for all periods presented in IFRS financial statements should be adjusted for subsequent changes in capital not involving full consideration at fair value (apart from the conversion of potential ordinary shares) in the manner described in 4.3 above Often entities will include EPS figures in historical summaries (typically five years) in the analyses and discussions accompanying (but not part of) the financial statements. We believe that all such analyses need similar adjustments in order to be meaningful. We also believe that the resultant figures should be described as restated.

5 MATTERS AFFECTING THE NUMERATOR

5.1 Earnings

The earnings figure on which the basic EPS calculation is based should be the consolidated net profit or loss for the year after tax, non-controlling interests and after adjusting for returns to preference shareholders that are not already included in net profit (as will be the case for preference shares classified as liabilities under IAS 32).

5.2 Preference dividends

The adjustments to net profit attributable to ordinary shareholders in relation to returns to preference shareholders should include:

- the after-tax amount of any preference dividends on non-cumulative preference shares declared in respect of the period; *[IAS 33.14(a)]*
- the after-tax amount of the preference dividends for cumulative preference shares required for the period, whether or not the dividends have been declared. This does not include the amount of any preference dividends for cumulative preference shares paid or declared during the current period in respect of previous periods; *[IAS 33.14(b)]*
- any original issue discount or premium on increasing rate preference shares which is amortised to retained earnings using the effective interest method. Increasing rate preference shares are those that provide: a low initial dividend to compensate an entity for selling them at a discount; or an above-market

dividend in later periods to compensate investors for purchasing them at a premium (see Example 35.6 below); *[IAS 33.15]*

- the excess of the fair value of the consideration paid to shareholders over the carrying amount of the preference shares when the shares are repurchased under an entity's tender offer to the holders. As this represents a return to the holders of the shares (and a charge to retained earnings for the entity) it is deducted in calculating profit or loss attributable to ordinary equity holders of the parent entity; *[IAS 33.16]*
- the excess of the fair value of the ordinary shares or other consideration paid over the fair value of the ordinary shares issuable under the original conversion terms when early conversion of convertible preference shares is induced through favourable changes to the original conversion terms or the payment of additional consideration. This is a return to the preference shareholders, and accordingly is deducted in calculating profit or loss attributable to ordinary equity holders of the parent entity; *[IAS 33.17]* and
- any excess of the carrying amount of preference shares over the fair value of the consideration paid to settle them. This reflects a gain to the entity and is added in calculating profit or loss attributable to ordinary equity holders. *[IAS 33.18]*.

The computation of EPS involving increasing rate preference shares is illustrated in the following example. *[IAS 33.IE1]*.

Example 35.6: Increasing rate preference shares

Entity D issued non-convertible, non-redeemable class A cumulative preference shares of €100 par value on 1 January 2017. The class A preference shares are entitled to a cumulative annual dividend of €7 per share starting in 2020. At the time of issue, the market rate dividend yield on the class A preference shares was 7 per cent a year. Thus, Entity D could have expected to receive proceeds of approximately €100 per class A preference share if the dividend rate of €7 per share had been in effect at the date of issue.

In consideration of the dividend payment terms, however, the class A preference shares were issued at €81.63 per share, i.e. at a discount of €18.37 per share. The issue price can be calculated by taking the present value of €100, discounted at 7 per cent over a three-year period. Because the shares are classified as equity, the original issue discount is amortised to retained earnings using the effective interest method and treated as a preference dividend for earnings per share purposes. To calculate basic earnings per share, the following imputed dividend per class A preference share is deducted to determine the profit or loss attributable to ordinary equity holders of the parent entity:

Year paid	Carrying amount of class A preference shares 1 January	Imputed dividend [1]	Carrying amount of class A preference shares 31 December [2]	Dividend
	€	€	€	€
2017	81.63	5.71	87.34	–
2018	87.34	6.12	93.46	–
2019	93.46	6.54	100.00	–
Thereafter:	100.00	7.00	107.00	(7.00)

[1] at 7% of the carrying amount

[2] This is before dividend payment.

5.3 Retrospective adjustments

Where comparative figures have been restated (for example, to correct a material error or as a result of a change in accounting policy), earnings per share for all periods presented should also be restated. *[IAS 33.64]*.

5.4 Participating equity instruments and two class shares

As noted at 3.2 above, IAS 33 envisages entities having more than one class of ordinary shares and requires the calculation and presentation of EPS for each such class. *[IAS 33.66]*. Although perhaps not exactly obvious from the definition, some instruments that have a right to participate in profits are viewed by the standard as ordinary shares. The standard observes that the equity of some entities includes:

(a) instruments that participate in dividends with ordinary shares according to a predetermined formula (for example, two for one) with, at times, an upper limit on the extent of participation (for example, up to, but not beyond, a specified amount per share); and

(b) a class of ordinary shares with a different dividend rate from that of another class of ordinary shares but without prior or senior rights. *[IAS 33.A13]*.

Whilst category (a) could encompass some participating preference shares (as illustrated in Example 35.7 below), not all participating preference shares would necessarily be treated as ordinary shares for EPS purposes. This is because the participation features of some instruments could mean that they are not subordinate to all other classes of equity instrument. The meaning of ordinary shares for EPS purposes is discussed at 3.2 above.

To calculate basic (and diluted) earnings per share:

(a) profit or loss attributable to ordinary equity holders of the parent entity is adjusted (a profit reduced and a loss increased) by the amount of dividends declared in the period for each class of shares and by the contractual amount of dividends (or interest on participating bonds) that must be paid for the period (for example, unpaid cumulative dividends);

(b) the remaining profit or loss is allocated to ordinary shares and participating equity instruments to the extent that each instrument shares in earnings as if all of the profit or loss for the period had been distributed. The total profit or loss allocated to each class of equity instrument is determined by adding together the amount allocated for dividends and the amount allocated for a participation feature; and

(c) the total amount of profit or loss allocated to each class of equity instrument is divided by the number of outstanding instruments to which the earnings are allocated to determine the earnings per share for the instrument.

For the calculation of diluted earnings per share, all potential ordinary shares assumed to have been issued are included in outstanding ordinary shares. *[IAS 33.A14]*. This is discussed at 6.4 below.

Participating equity instruments and two-class ordinary shares are illustrated with the following example. *[IAS 33.IE11]*.

Example 35.7: Participating equity instruments and two-class ordinary shares

Profit attributable to equity holders of the parent entity	€100,000
Ordinary shares outstanding	10,000
Non-convertible preference shares	6,000
Non-cumulative annual dividend on preference shares (before any dividend is paid on ordinary shares)	€5.50 per share

After ordinary shares have been paid a dividend of €2.10 per share, the preference shares participate in any additional dividends on a 20:80 ratio with ordinary shares (i.e. after preference and ordinary shares have been paid dividends of €5.50 and €2.10 per share, respectively, preference shares participate in any additional dividends at a rate of one-fourth of the amount paid to ordinary shares on a per-share basis).

Dividends on preference shares paid	€33,000	(€5.50 per share)
Dividends on ordinary shares paid	€21,000	(€2.10 per share)

Basic earnings per share is calculated as follows:

	€	€
Profit attributable to equity holders of the parent entity		100,000
Less dividends paid:		
Preference	33,000	
Ordinary	21,000	
		(54,000)
Undistributed earnings		46,000

Allocation of undistributed earnings:
Allocation per ordinary share = A
Allocation per preference share = B; B = 1/4 A

(A 10,000) + (1/4 A 6,000) = €46,000
A = €46,000 ÷ (10,000 + 1,500)
A = €4.00
B = 1/4 A
B = €1.00

Basic per share amounts:

	Preference shares	*Ordinary shares*
Distributed earnings	€5.50	€2.10
Undistributed earnings	€1.00	€4.00
Totals	€6.50	€6.10

NB. This example does not illustrate the classification of the components of convertible financial instruments as liabilities and equity or the classification of related interest and dividends as expenses and equity as required by IAS 32.

It is worth noting that this calculation provided by the standard does not follow the procedure specified by IAS 33. As noted above, the method outlined by the standard is to allocate dividends and then all remaining profits to the different classes of share then divide this by the number of shares in each class. The above example computes dividends and then remaining profit on a per-share basis and then combines them.

5.5 Other bases

It is not uncommon for entities to supplement the EPS figures required by IAS 33 by voluntarily presenting additional amounts per share. For additional *earnings* per share amounts, the standard requires:

(a) that the denominator used should be that required by IAS 33;

(b) that basic and diluted amounts be disclosed with equal prominence and presented in the notes;

(c) an indication of the basis on which the numerator is determined, including whether amounts per share are before or after tax; and

(d) if the numerator is not reported as a line item in the statement of comprehensive income or separate statement of profit or loss, a reconciliation between it and a line item that is reported in the statement of comprehensive income. *[IAS 33.73, 73A]*.

In September 2007 the IASB indicated that it intended to modify IAS 33 to prohibit the presentation of alternative EPS figures on the face of the statement of comprehensive income as part of the annual improvements project. *[IAS 1.BC103]*. However, that project was ultimately finalised without addressing this issue. As a result, alternative EPS figures may be (and, in practice, are[1]) presented on the face of the statement of comprehensive income (or separate income statement) as well as in the notes, provided that basic and diluted amounts are similarly disclosed with equal prominence.

6 DILUTED EARNINGS PER SHARE

6.1 The need for diluted EPS

The presentation of basic EPS seeks to show a performance measure, by computing how much profit an entity has earned for each of the shares in issue for the period. Entities often enter into commitments to issue shares in the future which would result in a change in basic EPS. IAS 33 refers to such commitments as potential ordinary shares, which it defines as 'a financial instrument or other contract that may entitle its holder to ordinary shares'. *[IAS 33.5]*.

Examples of potential ordinary shares given by IAS 33 are:

(a) financial liabilities or equity instruments, including preference shares, that are convertible into ordinary shares;

(b) options and warrants (whether accounted for under IAS 32 or IFRS 2);

(c) shares that would be issued upon the satisfaction of conditions resulting from contractual arrangements, such as the purchase of a business or other assets. *[IAS 33.7]*.

When potential shares are actually issued, the impact on basic EPS will be two-fold. First, the number of shares in issue will change; second, profits could be affected, for example by lower interest charges or the return made on cash inflows. Scenarios whereby such an adjustment to basic EPS is unfavourable are described by the standard as dilution, defined as 'a reduction in earnings per share or an increase in loss per share resulting from the assumption that convertible instruments are converted, that options or warrants are exercised, or that ordinary shares are issued upon the satisfaction of specified conditions'. *[IAS 33.5]*. This potential fall in EPS is quantified by computing diluted EPS, and as a result:

(a) profit or loss attributable to equity holders is increased by the after-tax amount of dividends and interest recognised in the period in respect of the dilutive potential ordinary shares and is adjusted for any other changes in income or expense that would result from the conversion of the dilutive potential ordinary shares; and

(b) the weighted average number of ordinary shares outstanding is increased by the weighted average number of additional ordinary shares that would have been outstanding assuming the conversion of all dilutive potential ordinary shares. *[IAS 33.32]*.

6.2 Calculation of diluted EPS

IAS 33 requires a diluted EPS figure to be calculated for the profit or loss attributable to ordinary equity holders of the parent and, if presented, profit or loss from continuing operations attributable to them. *[IAS 33.30]*. For these purposes, the profit or loss attributable to ordinary equity holders and the weighted average number of shares outstanding should be adjusted for the effects of all potential ordinary shares. *[IAS 33.31]*. In calculating diluted EPS, the number of shares should be that used in calculating basic EPS, plus the weighted average number of shares that would be issued on the conversion of all the dilutive potential ordinary shares into ordinary shares. As is the case for outstanding shares in the basic EPS calculation, potential ordinary shares should be weighted for the period they are outstanding. *[IAS 33.36, 38]*. Accordingly, potential ordinary shares:

- should be deemed to have been converted into ordinary shares at the beginning of the period or, if not in existence at the beginning of the period, the date of their issue; *[IAS 33.36]*
- which are cancelled or allowed to lapse should be included only for the period they are outstanding; and
- which convert into ordinary shares during the period are included up until the date of conversion (from which point they will be included in the basic EPS). *[IAS 33.38]*.

The number of dilutive potential ordinary shares should be determined independently for each period presented, and not subsequently revisited. In particular, prior periods' EPS are not restated for changes in assumptions about the conversion of potential shares into shares. IAS 33 also stresses that the number of dilutive potential ordinary shares included in the year-to-date period is not a weighted average of the dilutive potential ordinary shares included in each interim computation. *[IAS 33.37, 65]*.

6.2.1 *Diluted earnings*

The earnings figure should be that used for basic EPS adjusted to reflect any changes that would arise if the potential shares outstanding in the period were actually issued. Adjustment is to be made for the post-tax effects of:

(a) any dividends or other items related to dilutive potential ordinary shares deducted in arriving at the earnings figure used for basic EPS;

(b) any interest recognised in the period related to dilutive potential ordinary shares; and

(c) any other changes in income or expense that would result from the conversion of the dilutive potential ordinary shares. *[IAS 33.33]*.

These adjustments will also include any amounts charged in accordance with the effective interest method prescribed by IAS 39 – *Financial Instruments: Recognition and Measurement* – as a result of allocating transaction costs, premiums or discounts over the term of the instrument. *[IAS 33.34]*. Instruments with a choice of settlement method may also require adjustments to the numerator as discussed at 6.2.2 below.

The standard notes that certain earnings adjustments directly attributable to the instrument could also affect other items of income or expense which will need to be accounted for. For example, the lower interest charge following conversion of convertible debt could lead to higher charges under profit sharing schemes. *[IAS 33.35]*.

No imputed earnings are taken into account in respect of the proceeds to be received on exercise of share options or warrants. The effect of such potential ordinary shares on the diluted EPS is reflected in the computation of the denominator. This is discussed at 6.4.2 below.

6.2.2 *Diluted number of shares*

IAS 33 discusses a number of specific types of potential ordinary shares and how they should be brought into the calculation; these are discussed at 6.4 below.

More generally, the standard also discusses scenarios where the method of conversion or settlement of potential ordinary shares is at the discretion of one of the parties, as follows:

(a) the number of shares that would be issued on conversion should be determined from the terms of the potential ordinary shares. When more than one basis of conversion exists, the calculation should assume the most advantageous conversion rate or exercise price from the standpoint of the holder of the potential ordinary shares; *[IAS 33.39]*

(b) when an entity has issued a contract that may be settled in shares or cash at its option, it should presume that the contract will be settled in shares. The resulting potential ordinary shares would be included in diluted earnings per share if the effect is dilutive. *[IAS 33.58]*. When such a contract is presented for accounting purposes as an asset or a liability, or has an equity component and a liability component, the numerator should be adjusted for any changes in profit or loss that would have resulted during the period if the contract had been classified wholly as an equity instrument. That adjustment is similar to the adjustments discussed at 6.2.1 above; *[IAS 33.59]* and

(c) for contracts that may be settled in ordinary shares or cash at the holder's option, the more dilutive of cash settlement and share settlement should be used in calculating diluted earnings per share. *[IAS 33.60]*.

An example of an instrument covered by (b) above is a debt instrument that, on maturity, gives the issuer the unrestricted right to settle the principal amount in cash or in its own ordinary shares (see Example 35.10 at 6.4.1.A below). An example of an instrument covered by (c) is a written put option that gives the holder a choice of settling in ordinary shares or cash. *[IAS 33.61]*.

In our view, the requirements of the standard in (b) and (c) above relating to settlement options are somewhat confused. In particular they seem to envisage a binary accounting model based on the strict legal form of settlement (cash or shares). However, IAS 32 sets out rules for *three* different settlement methods – net cash, net shares and gross physical settlement (discussed in Chapter 45 at 5). One consequence of the above is that, if taken literally, the numerator is only required to be adjusted to remove items of income or expense arising from a liability when there is a choice of settlement method. However, mandatory net share settlement also gives rise to a liability and income/expense under IAS 32. In our view any such income statement items should be removed for diluted EPS purposes.

6.3 Dilutive potential ordinary shares

Only those potential shares whose issue would have a dilutive effect on EPS are brought into the calculation. Potential ordinary shares are 'antidilutive' when their conversion to ordinary shares would increase earnings per share or decrease loss per share. *[IAS 33.5, 43]*. The calculation of diluted earnings per share should not assume conversion, exercise, or other issue of potential ordinary shares that would have an antidilutive effect on earnings per share. *[IAS 33.43]*. The standard gives detailed guidance for determining which potential shares are deemed to be dilutive, and hence brought into the diluted EPS calculation. This guidance covers the element of profit which needs to be diluted to trigger inclusion, and the sequence in which potential shares are tested to establish cumulative dilution. Each is discussed below.

6.3.1 Dilution judged by effect on profits from continuing operations

Potential ordinary shares are only to be treated as dilutive if their conversion to ordinary shares would decrease earnings per share or increase loss per share from *continuing* operations. The 'control number' that this focuses on is therefore the net result from continuing operations, which is the net profit or loss attributable to the parent entity, after deducting items relating to preference shares (see 5.2 above) and after excluding items relating to discontinued operations. *[IAS 33.42]*. The same denominator is required to be used to compute diluted EPS from continuing operations and total diluted EPS. Determining which potential shares are to be included by reference to their impact on continuing EPS can produce some slightly curious results for total EPS. For example, it is possible to exclude instruments which would dilute basic EPS (but not continuing EPS), and include items which are anti-dilutive as regards total profit. This latter point is acknowledged by the standard as follows.

> 'To illustrate the application of the control number notion ... assume that an entity has profit from continuing operations attributable to the parent entity of CU 4,800, a loss from discontinued operations attributable to the parent entity of (CU 7,200), a loss attributable to the parent entity of (CU 2,400),

and 2,000 ordinary shares and 400 potential ordinary shares outstanding. The entity's basic earnings per share is CU 2.40 for continuing operations, (CU 3.60) for discontinued operations and (CU 1.20) for the loss. The 400 potential ordinary shares are included in the diluted earnings per share calculation because the resulting CU 2.00 earnings per share for continuing operations is dilutive, assuming no profit or loss impact of those 400 potential ordinary shares. Because profit from continuing operations attributable to the parent entity is the control number, the entity also includes those 400 potential ordinary shares in the calculation of the other earnings per share amounts, even though the resulting earnings per share amounts are antidilutive to their comparable basic earnings per share amounts, i.e. the loss per share is less [(CU 3.00) per share for the loss from discontinued operations and (CU 1.00) per share for the loss].' *[IAS 33.A3]*.

6.3.2 *Dilution judged by the cumulative impact of potential shares*

Where an entity has a number of different potential ordinary shares, in deciding whether they are dilutive (and hence reflected in the calculation), each issue or series of potential ordinary shares is to be considered in sequence from the most to the least dilutive. Only those potential shares which produce a cumulative dilution are to be included. This means that some potential shares which would dilute basic EPS if viewed on their own may need to be excluded. This results in a diluted EPS showing the maximum overall dilution of basic EPS. The standard observes that options and warrants should generally be included first as they do not affect the numerator in the diluted EPS calculation (but see the discussion at 6.4.2 below). *[IAS 33.44]*. The way this is to be done is illustrated in the following example. *[IAS 33.IE9]*.

Example 35.8: Calculation of weighted average number of shares: determining the order in which to include dilutive instruments

Earnings	€
Profit from continuing operations attributable to the parent entity	16,400,000
Less dividends on preference shares	(6,400,000)
Profit from continuing operations attributable to ordinary equity holders of the parent entity	10,000,000
Loss from discontinued operations attributable to the parent entity	(4,000,000)
Profit attributable to ordinary equity holders of the parent entity	6,000,000

Ordinary shares outstanding	2,000,000
Average market price of one ordinary share during year	€75.00

Potential Ordinary Shares

Options	100,000 with exercise price of €60
Convertible preference shares	800,000 shares with a par value of €100 entitled to a cumulative dividend of €8 per share. Each preference share is convertible to two ordinary shares.
5% convertible bonds	Nominal amount €100,000,000. Each €1,000 bond is convertible to 20 ordinary shares. There is no amortisation of premium or discount affecting the determination of interest expense.
Tax rate	40%

Increase in Earnings Attributable to Ordinary Equity Holders on Conversion of Potential Ordinary Shares

	Increase in earnings €	Increase in number of ordinary shares	Earnings per incremental share €
Options			
Increase in earnings	Nil		
Incremental shares issued for no consideration			
100,000 × (€75 – €60) ÷ €75 =		20,000	Nil
Convertible preference shares			
Increase in earnings			
€800,000 × 100 × 0.08 =	6,400,000		
Incremental shares			
2 × 800,000 =		1,600,000	4.00
5% convertible bonds			
Increase in earnings			
€100,000,000 × 0.05 × (1 – 0.40) =	3,000,000		
Incremental shares			
100,000 × 20 =		2,000,000	1.50

The order in which to include the dilutive instruments is therefore:

(1) Options
(2) 5% convertible bonds
(3) Convertible preference shares

Calculation of Diluted Earnings per Share

	Profit from continuing operations attributable to ordinary equity holders of the parent entity (control number) €	Ordinary shares	Per share €	
As reported	10,000,000	2,000,000	5.00	
Options	–	20,000		
	10,000,000	2,020,000	4.95	Dilutive
5% convertible bonds	3,000,000	2,000,000		
	13,000,000	4,020,000	3.23	Dilutive
Convertible preference shares	6,400,000	1,600,000		
	19,400,000	5,620,000	3.45	Antidilutive

Because diluted earnings per share is increased when taking the convertible preference shares into account (from €3.23 to €3.45), the convertible preference shares are antidilutive and are ignored in the calculation of diluted earnings per share. Therefore, diluted earnings per share for profit from continuing operations is €3.23:

	Basic EPS €		Diluted EPS €	
Profit from continuing operations attributable to ordinary equity holders of the parent entity	5.00		3.23	
Loss from discontinued operations attributable to ordinary equity holders of the parent entity	(2.00)	(a)	(0.99)	(b)
Profit attributable to ordinary equity holders of the parent entity	3.00	(c)	2.24	(d)

(a) (€4,000,000) ÷ 2,000,000 = (€2.00)
(b) (€4,000,000) ÷ 4,020,000 = (€0.99)
(c) €6,000,000 ÷ 2,000,000 = €3.00
(d) (€6,000,000 + €3,000,000) ÷ 4,020,000 = €2.24

This example does not illustrate the classification of the components of convertible financial instruments as liabilities and equity or the classification of related interest and dividends as expenses and equity as required by IAS 32.

6.4 Particular types of dilutive instruments

6.4.1 Convertible instruments

In order to secure a lower rate of interest, entities sometimes attach benefits to loan stock, debentures or preference shares in the form of conversion rights. These permit the holder to convert his holding in whole or part into equity capital. The right is normally exercisable between specified dates. The ultimate conversion of the instrument will have the following effects:

(a) there will be an increase in earnings by the amount of the interest (or items relating to preference shares) no longer payable. As interest is normally allowable for tax purposes, the effect on earnings may be net of a tax deduction relating to some or all of the items; and

(b) the number of ordinary shares in issue will increase. The diluted EPS should be calculated assuming that the instrument is converted into the maximum possible number of shares. *[IAS 33.49]*.

Convertible preference shares will be antidilutive whenever the amount of the dividend on such shares declared in or accumulated for the current period per ordinary share obtainable on conversion exceeds basic earnings per share. Similarly, convertible debt will be antidilutive whenever its interest (net of tax and other changes in income or expense) per ordinary share obtainable on conversion exceeds basic earnings per share. *[IAS 33.50]*.

6.4.1.A Convertible debt

The EPS calculation for convertible bonds is illustrated in the following example: *[IAS 33.IE6]*

Example 35.9: Treatment of convertible bonds in diluted EPS calculations

Profit attributable to ordinary equity holders of the parent entity	€1,004
Ordinary shares outstanding	1,000
Basic earnings per share	€1.00
Convertible bonds	100
Each block of 10 bonds is convertible into three ordinary shares	
Interest expense for the current year relating to the liability component of the convertible bonds	€10
Current and deferred tax relating to that interest expense	€4

Note: the interest expense includes amortisation of the discount arising on initial recognition of the liability component (see IAS 32).

Adjusted profit attributable to ordinary equity holders of the parent entity	€1,004 + €10 – €4 = €1,010
Number of ordinary shares resulting from conversion of bonds	30
Number of ordinary shares used to calculate diluted earnings per share	1,000 + 30 = 1,030
Diluted earnings per share	€1,010 ÷ 1,030 = €0.98

This example does not illustrate the classification of the components of convertible financial instruments as liabilities and equity or the classification of related interest and dividends as expenses and equity as required by IAS 32.

Chapter 35

As discussed at 6.2.2 above, the standard also discusses the impact on diluted EPS of different settlement options. As discussed earlier, we believe this should be taken to mean that for diluted EPS purposes earnings should be adjusted to remove any items that arose from an instrument being classified as an asset or liability rather than equity. The standard illustrates settlement options with the following example. *[IAS 33.IE8]*.

Example 35.10: Convertible bonds settled in shares or cash at the issuer's option

An entity issues 2,000 convertible bonds at the beginning of Year 1. The bonds have a three-year term, and are issued at par with a face value of €1,000 per bond, giving total proceeds of €2,000,000. Interest is payable annually in arrears at a nominal annual interest rate of 6 per cent. Each bond is convertible at any time up to maturity into 250 common shares. The entity has an option to settle the principal amount of the convertible bonds in ordinary shares or in cash.

When the bonds are issued, the prevailing market interest rate for similar debt without a conversion option is 9 per cent. At the issue date, the market price of one common share is €3. Income tax is ignored.

Profit attributable to ordinary equity holders of the parent entity Year 1	€1,000,000
Ordinary shares outstanding	1,200,000
Convertible bonds outstanding	2,000
Allocation of proceeds of the bond issue:	
Liability component	* €1,848,122
Equity component	€151,878
	€2,000,000

The liability and equity components would be determined in accordance with IAS 32. These amounts are recognised as the initial carrying amounts of the liability and equity components. The amount assigned to the issuer conversion option equity element is an addition to equity and is not adjusted.

* This represents the present value of the principal and interest discounted at 9% – €2,000,000 payable at the end of three years; €120,000 payable annually in arrears for three years.

Basic earnings per share Year 1:

$$\frac{€1,000,000}{1,200,000} = €0.83 \text{ per ordinary share}$$

Diluted earnings per share Year 1:

It is presumed that the issuer will settle the contract by the issue of ordinary shares. The dilutive effect is therefore calculated in accordance with paragraph 59 of the Standard.

$$\frac{€1,000,000 + €166,331^{(a)}}{1,200,000 + 500,000^{(b)}} = €0.69 \text{ per ordinary share}$$

(a) Profit is adjusted for the accretion of €166,331 (€1,848,122 × 9%) of the liability because of the passage of time.

(b) 500,000 ordinary shares = 250 ordinary shares × 2,000 convertible bonds

6.4.1.B Convertible preference shares

The rules for convertible preference shares are very similar to those detailed above in the case of convertible debt, i.e. dividends and other returns to preference shareholders are added back to earnings used for basic EPS and the maximum number of ordinary shares that could be issued on conversion should be used in the calculation.

As discussed at 5.2 above, one possible return to preference shareholders is a premium payable on redemption or induced early conversion in excess of the original terms. IAS 33 notes that the redemption or induced conversion of convertible preference shares may affect only a portion of the previously outstanding convertible preference shares. In such cases, the standard makes clear that any excess consideration is attributed to those shares that are redeemed or converted for the purpose of determining whether the remaining outstanding preference shares are dilutive. In other words, the shares redeemed or converted are considered separately from those shares that are not redeemed or converted. *[IAS 33.51]*.

6.4.1.C *Participating equity instruments and two class shares with conversion rights*

The treatment for basic EPS of participating equity instruments and two class shares is discussed at 5.4 above. When discussing these instruments the standard observes that when calculating diluted EPS:

- conversion is assumed for those instruments that are convertible into ordinary shares if the effect is dilutive;
- for those that are not convertible into a class of ordinary shares, profit or loss for the period is allocated to the different classes of shares and participating equity instruments in accordance with their dividend rights or other rights to participate in undistributed earnings. *[IAS 33.A14]*.

What the standard seems to be hinting at here, without directly addressing, is how to present EPS for two or more classes of ordinary shares (say, class A and class B) when one class can convert into another (say, class B can convert into class A). In this scenario, in our view the basic EPS for each class should be calculated based on profit entitlement (see 5.4 above). For diluted EPS it would be necessary to attribute to class A the profits attributed to class B in the basic EPS – if the overall effect were dilutive to class A, conversion should be assumed.

6.4.2 *Options, warrants and their equivalents*

6.4.2.A *The numerator*

IAS 33 contains detailed guidance on the treatment for diluted EPS purposes of options, warrants and their equivalents which it defines as 'financial instruments that give the holder the right to purchase ordinary shares'. *[IAS 33.5]*. However, it was largely written before the significant developments in accounting for such instruments (IFRS 2 and IAS 32). As a result, individual facts and circumstances must be considered and judgment is required in some circumstances to address the dilutive effects on EPS.

IAS 33 clearly states that 'Options and warrants ... do not affect the numerator of the calculation' *[IAS 33.44]* and this text was added in 2003 as part of the improvements project, so clearly drafted against the back drop of the impending move to expensing share-based payments and also the (then) recent changes to IAS 32 regarding accounting for derivatives over an entity's own shares. As regards employee share options in particular, neither IAS 33 (as updated by IFRS 2) nor the worked example appended to it (see Example 35.13 at 6.4.5 below) make reference to removing either some or all the charge when computing diluted EPS. However, this seems to sit somewhat awkwardly (particularly for options outside the scope of IFRS 2) with the general requirement for calculating diluted EPS that earnings be adjusted for the effects of 'any other changes in income or expense that would result from the conversion of the dilutive potential ordinary shares'. *[IAS 33.33]*. Furthermore, IAS 33 explicitly requires an adjustment to the numerator in some circumstances:

(a) as discussed at 6.2.2 above, adjustment to the numerator may be required for a contract (which could include options and warrants) that may be settled in ordinary shares or cash at the entity's option when such a contract is presented for accounting purposes as an asset or a liability, or has an equity component and a liability component. In such a case, the standard requires that 'the entity shall adjust the numerator for any changes in profit or loss that would have resulted during the period if the contract had been classified wholly as an equity instrument'. For contracts that may be settled in ordinary shares or cash at the holder's option, 'the more dilutive of cash settlement and share settlement shall be used in calculating diluted earnings per share'; *[IAS 33.59-60]*

(b) where an option agreement requires or permits the tendering of debt in payment of the exercise price (and, if the holder could choose to pay cash, that tendering debt is more advantageous to him) the numerator should be adjusted for the after tax amount of any such debt assumed to be tendered (see 6.4.2.E below); *[IAS 33.A7]* and

(c) where option proceeds are required to be applied to redeem debt or other instruments of the entity (see 6.4.2.F below). *[IAS 33.A9]*.

For situations covered by (b) and (c) above the specific requirements of the standard for adjusting the numerator should be followed. In other circumstances, the interaction of these complex and conflicting requirements with each other and with IFRS 2 and IAS 32 lead to the following requirements when computing the numerator for diluted EPS:

(a) for instruments accounted for under IAS 32:
  - (i) for a contract classified wholly as an equity instrument, no adjustment to the numerator will be necessary; and
  - (ii) for a contract not classified wholly as an equity instrument, the numerator should be adjusted for any changes in profit or loss that would have resulted if it had been classified wholly as an equity instrument; and

(b) for instruments accounted for under IFRS 2:
  - (i) for those treated as equity-settled, the IFRS 2 charge should *not* be adjusted for; and
  - (ii) for those treated as cash-settled, the numerator should be adjusted for any changes in profit or loss that would have resulted if the instrument had been classified wholly as an equity instrument.

In respect of (b), part (i) is supported by the IASB's view regarding share-based payments as follows.

'Some argue that any cost arising from share-based payment transactions is already recognised in the dilution of earnings per share (EPS). If an expense were recognised in the income statement, EPS would be "hit twice".

However, the Board noted that this result is appropriate. For example, if the entity paid the employees in cash for their services and the cash was then returned to the entity, as consideration for the issue of share options, the effect on EPS would be the same as issuing those options direct to the employees.

The dual effect on EPS simply reflects the two economic events that have occurred: the entity has issued shares or share options, thereby increasing the number of shares included in the EPS calculation – although, in the case of options, only to the extent that the options are regarded as dilutive – and it has also consumed the resources it received for those options, thereby decreasing earnings. ...

In summary, the Board concluded that the dual effect on diluted EPS is not double-counting the effects of a share or share option grant – the same effect is not counted twice. Rather, two different effects are each counted once.' *[IFRS 2.BC54-BC57]*.

As for part (ii) of (b) above, this is the explicit requirement of IAS 33 when the entity can choose cash or share settlement. It is also implicit in the requirement of the standard that for contracts that may be settled in ordinary shares or cash at the holder's option, the more dilutive of cash settlement and share settlement should be used in calculating diluted earnings per share. This would also explain why IFRS 2 requires the computation of grant date fair values for cash-settled share-based payments when that information is not actually required for accounting purposes (see Chapter 32 at 9.3.2).

6.4.2.B Written call options

Entities may issue options or warrants which give holders the right to subscribe for shares at fixed prices on specified future dates. If the options or warrants are exercised then:

(a) the number of shares in issue will be increased; and

(b) funds will flow into the company and these will produce income.

For calculating diluted EPS, IAS 33 requires the exercise of all dilutive options and warrants to be assumed. *[IAS 33.45]*. Options and warrants are considered dilutive when they would result in the issue of ordinary shares for less than the average market price of ordinary shares during the period. The amount of the dilution is taken to be the average market price of ordinary shares during the period minus the issue price. *[IAS 33.46]*.

Under IAS 33 the effects of such potential ordinary shares on the diluted EPS are reflected in the computation of the denominator using a method sometimes called the 'treasury stock method'.

For this purpose, the weighted average number of shares used in calculating the basic EPS is increased, but not by the full number of shares that would be issued on exercise of the instruments. To determine how many additional shares to include in the denominator, the assumed proceeds from these issues are to be treated as having been received in exchange for:

- a certain number of shares at their average market price for the period (i.e. no EPS impact); and
- the remainder for no consideration (i.e. full dilution). *[IAS 33.45-46]*.

This means that the excess of the total number of potential shares over the number that could be issued at their average market price for the period out of the issue proceeds is included within the denominator; the calculation is illustrated as follows: *[IAS 33.IE5]*

Example 35.11: Effects of share options on diluted earnings per share

Profit attributable to ordinary equity holders of the parent entity for year	€1,200,000
Weighted average number of ordinary shares outstanding during year	500,000 shares
Average market price of one ordinary share during year	€20.00
Weighted average number of shares under option during year	100,000 shares
Exercise price for shares under option during year	€15.00

Calculation of earnings per share

	Earnings	*Shares*	*Per share*
Profit attributable to ordinary equity holders of the parent entity for year	€1,200,000		
Weighted average shares outstanding during year		500,000	
Basic earnings per share			€2.40
Weighted average number of shares under option		100,000	
Weighted average number of shares that would have been issued at average market price: (100,000 × €15.00) ÷ €20.00	*	(75,000)	
Diluted earnings per share	€1,200,000	525,000	€2.29

* Earnings have not increased because the total number of shares has increased only by the number of shares (25,000) deemed to have been issued for no consideration.

The number of shares viewed as fairly priced (and hence neither dilutive nor antidilutive) for this purpose is calculated on the basis of the average price of the ordinary shares during the reporting period. *[IAS 33.46]*. The standard observes that, in theory, calculating an average share price for the period could include every market transaction in the shares. However, it notes that as a practical matter an average (weekly or monthly) will usually be adequate. *[IAS 33.A4]*. The individual prices used should generally be the closing market price unless prices fluctuate widely, in which case the average of high and low prices may be more representative. Whatever method is adopted, it should be used consistently unless it ceases to yield a representative price. For example, closing prices may have been used consistently in a series of relatively stable periods then a change to high/low average could be appropriate when prices begin to fluctuate more widely. *[IAS 33.A5]*.

The shares would be deemed to have been issued at the beginning of the period or, if later, the date of issue of the warrants or options. Options which are exercised or lapse in the period are included for the portion of the period during which they were outstanding. *[IAS 33.36, 38]*.

Although the standard seems to require that the fair value used should be the average for the reporting period for all outstanding options or warrants, in our view, for instruments issued, lapsed or exercised during the period a credible case could be made for using an average price for that part of the reporting period that the instrument was outstanding. Indeed, this view is supported by the comprehensive example included in the standard (see the appendix to this chapter), where in computing the number of warrants to be included in calculating the diluted EPS for the full year, the average price used was not that for the full year, but only for the period that the warrants were outstanding.

One practical problem with this requirement is that the average market price of ordinary shares for the reporting period may not be available. Examples would include an entity only listed for part of the period, or an unlisted entity giving voluntary disclosures. In such cases estimates of the market price would need to be made.

6.4.2.C *Written put options and forward purchase agreements*

Contracts that require the entity to repurchase its own shares, such as written put options and forward purchase contracts, should be reflected in the calculation of diluted earnings per share if the effect is dilutive. If these contracts are 'in the money' during the period (i.e. the exercise or settlement price is above the average market price for that period), IAS 33 requires the potential dilutive effect on EPS to be calculated as follows:

- it should be assumed that at the beginning of the period sufficient ordinary shares are issued (at the average market price during the period) to raise proceeds to satisfy the contract;
- the proceeds from the issue are then assumed to be used to satisfy the contract (i.e. to buy back ordinary shares); and
- the incremental ordinary shares (the difference between the number of ordinary shares assumed issued and the number of ordinary shares received from satisfying the contract) should be included in the calculation of diluted earnings per share. *[IAS 33.63]*.

The standard illustrates this methodology as follows: '... assume that an entity has outstanding 120 written put options on its ordinary shares with an exercise price of CU 35. The average market price of its ordinary shares for the period is CU 28. In calculating diluted earnings per share, the entity assumes that it issued 150 shares at CU 28 per share at the beginning of the period to satisfy its put obligation of CU 4,200. The difference between the 150 ordinary shares issued and the 120 ordinary shares received from satisfying the put option (30 incremental ordinary shares) is added to the denominator in calculating diluted earnings per share.' *[IAS 33.A10]*.

6.4.2.D Options over convertible instruments

Although not common, it is possible that an entity grants options or warrants to acquire not ordinary shares directly but other instruments convertible into them (such as convertible preference shares or debt). In this scenario, IAS 33 sets a dual test:

- exercise is assumed whenever the average prices of both the convertible instrument and the ordinary shares obtainable upon conversion are above the exercise price of the options or warrants; but
- exercise is not assumed unless conversion of similar outstanding convertible instruments, if any, is also assumed. *[IAS 33.A6]*.

6.4.2.E Settlement of option exercise price with debt or other instruments of the entity

The standard notes that options or warrants may permit or require the tendering of debt or other instruments of the entity (or its parent or a subsidiary) in payment of all or a portion of the exercise price. In the calculation of diluted earnings per share, those options or warrants have a dilutive effect if (a) the average market price of the related ordinary shares for the period exceeds the exercise price or (b) the selling price of the instrument to be tendered is below that at which the instrument may be tendered under the option or warrant agreement and the resulting discount establishes an effective exercise price below the market price of the ordinary shares obtainable upon exercise. In the calculation of diluted EPS, those options or warrants should be assumed to be exercised and the debt or other instruments assumed to be tendered. If tendering cash is more advantageous to the option or warrant holder and the contract permits it, tendering of cash should be assumed. Interest (net of tax) on any debt assumed to be tendered is added back as an adjustment to the numerator. *[IAS 33.A7]*.

Similar treatment is given to preference shares that have similar provisions or to other instruments that have conversion options that permit the investor to pay cash for a more favourable conversion rate. *[IAS 33.A8]*.

6.4.2.F Specified application of option proceeds

IAS 33 observes that the underlying terms of certain options or warrants may require the proceeds received from the exercise of those instruments to be applied to redeem debt or other instruments of the entity (or its parent or a subsidiary). In which case it requires that in 'the calculation of diluted earnings per share, those options or warrants are assumed to be exercised and the proceeds applied to purchase the debt at its average market price rather than to purchase ordinary shares. However, the excess proceeds received from the assumed exercise over the amount used for the assumed purchase of debt are considered (i.e. assumed to be used to buy back ordinary shares) in the diluted earnings per share calculation. Interest (net of tax) on any debt assumed to be purchased is added back as an adjustment to the numerator.' *[IAS 33.A9]*.

6.4.3 *Purchased options and warrants*

IAS 33 states that a holding by an entity of options over its own shares will always be antidilutive because:

- put options would only be exercised if the exercise price were higher than the market price; and
- call options would only be exercised if the exercise price were lower than the market price.

Accordingly, the standard requires that such instruments are not included in the calculation of diluted EPS. *[IAS 33.62].*

However, depending upon the settlement mechanism and the share price at the beginning and end of the period, the option could have resulted in a gain being reported (see Chapter 45 at 5). It is therefore possible that the removal of any such gain from the numerator could have a greater dilutive effect than the reduction in the denominator and hence render the option dilutive. In that circumstance, the option should be included in the diluted EPS calculation.

6.4.4 *Partly paid shares*

As noted at 3 above, shares issued in partly paid form are to be included in the basic EPS as a fraction of a share, based on dividend participation. As regards diluted EPS they are to be treated, to the extent that they are not entitled to participate in dividends, as the equivalent of options or warrants. The unpaid balance is assumed to represent proceeds used to purchase ordinary shares. The number of shares included in diluted earnings per share is the difference between the number of shares subscribed and the number of shares assumed to be purchased. *[IAS 33.A16].* The mechanics of this treatment are not further spelt out in the standard, but the phrase 'treated as a fraction of an ordinary share' is not repeated. Instead, it is 'the number of shares subscribed' which the standard says should be compared to the number assumed purchased to measure dilution. However, 'the number of shares subscribed' is not defined. Whilst this could be read to mean that the remaining unpaid consideration is to be treated as the exercise price for options over *all* of the shares issued in partly paid form, we believe the better interpretation is that the unpaid capital should be viewed as the exercise price for options over the proportion of the shares not reflected in the basic EPS. This would mean that if the average share price for the period were the same as the total issue price, then no dilution would be reported. Furthermore, an issue of partly paid shares, say 50% paid with 50% dividend entitlement is economically identical to an issue of half the quantity as fully paid (with full dividend entitlement) and a forward contract for the remaining half. In that scenario, the issued shares would be incorporated into the basic and diluted EPS in full from the date of issue. The forward contract would be included in diluted EPS calculation by comparing the contracted number of shares with the number of shares that could be bought out of proceeds based on the average share price for the period. In our view, these economically identical transactions should produce the same diluted EPS – that would be achieved by interpreting 'the number of shares subscribed' as the number *economically* subscribed, i.e. the proportion of part-paid shares not already included in basic EPS.

An illustration of what the calculation would look like is as follows:

Example 35.12: Partly paid shares

Capital structure

Issued share capital as at 31 December 2016:
2,000,000 ordinary shares of 10c each

Issued on 1 January 2017:
500,000 part paid ordinary shares of 10c each. Full consideration of 50c per share (being fair value at 1 January 2017) paid up 50% on issue. Dividend participation 50% until fully paid. New shares remain part paid at 31 December 2017.

Average fair value of one ordinary share for the period 60c.

Trading results

Net profit attributable to ordinary shareholders for the year ended 31 December 2017: €100,000.

Computation of basic and diluted EPS

	Net profit attributable to ordinary shareholders €	*Ordinary shares* No.	*Per share*
Fully paid shares		2,000,000	
Partly paid shares (1)		250,000	
Basic EPS	100,000	2,250,000	4.44c
Dilutive effect of partly paid shares (2)		41,667	
Diluted EPS	100,000	2,291,667	4.36c

(1) 50% dividend rights for 500,000 shares.

(2) Outstanding consideration of €125,000 (500,000 × 25c), using fair value of 60c this equates to 208,333 shares, hence the number of dilutive shares deemed issued for free is 41,667 (250,000 – 208,333).

The example assumes the fair value of the shares over the year is higher than the issue price, which explains why some extra shares are included in the diluted EPS. If the average fair value remained at the issue price of 50c then no additional shares would be included for diluted EPS.

6.4.5 Share-based payments

Share options and other incentive schemes are a common feature of employee remuneration, and can come in many forms. For diluted EPS purposes, IAS 33 identifies two categories and specifies the diluted EPS treatment for each. The categories are:

(a) performance-based employee share options; and

(b) employee share options with fixed or determinable terms and non-vested ordinary shares. *[IAS 33.48]*.

Before moving on to the diluted EPS treatment, it is worth noting an issue that arises from the way IAS 33 phrases this categorisation and subsequent guidance. Although not clearly stated in the standard, we believe all schemes should be treated as either category (a) or category (b). Any arrangements where entitlement is subject to future performance would fall into category (a) with category (b) being the default for all other arrangements.

Schemes in the first category are to be treated as contingently issuable shares (see 6.4.6 below) because their issue is contingent upon satisfying specified conditions in addition to the passage of time. *[IAS 33.48]*.

Those in the second category are to be treated as options (see 6.4.2 above). They should be regarded as outstanding from the grant date, even if they vest, and hence can be realised by the employees, at some later date. *[IAS 33.48]*. An example would be an unexpired loyalty period. This means that some shares may be included in diluted EPS which never, in fact, get issued to employees because they fail to remain with the company for this period. Furthermore, for share options and other share-based payment arrangements to which IFRS 2 applies, the proceeds figure to be used in calculating the dilution under such schemes should include the fair value (as determined in accordance with IFRS 2) of any goods or services to be supplied to the entity in the future under the arrangement. *[IAS 33.47A]*. An example illustrating the latter point is as follows: *[IAS 33.IE5A]*.

Example 35.13: Determining the exercise price of employee share options

Weighted average number of unvested share options per employee	1,000
Weighted average amount per employee to be recognised over the remainder of the vesting period for employee services to be rendered as consideration for the share options, determined in accordance with IFRS 2	€1,200.00
Cash exercise price of unvested share options	€15.00
Calculation of adjusted exercise price	
Fair value of services yet to be rendered per employee:	€1,200.00
Fair value of services yet to be rendered per option: (€1,200 ÷ 1,000)	€1.20
Total exercise price of share options: (€15.00 + €1.20)	€16.20

Whilst the standard requires that the additional deemed proceeds is the *fair value* of goods or services yet to be received, the example clarifies that it is the IFRS 2 expense yet to be charged to income.

What this requirement seeks to reflect is that for such options the issuer will receive not just the cash proceeds (if any) under the option when it is exercised but also valuable goods and services over its life. This will result in the dilutive effect of the options increasing over time as the deemed proceeds on exercise of the options reduces.

6.4.6 Contingently issuable shares

IAS 33 contains considerable detailed guidance, including a numerical worked example, on contingently issuable shares. Contingently issuable ordinary shares are defined as 'ordinary shares issuable for little or no cash or other consideration upon satisfaction of specified conditions in a contingent share agreement.' A contingent share agreement is defined by the standard as 'an agreement to issue shares that is dependent on the satisfaction of specified conditions.' *[IAS 33.5]*. The basic rule is that the number of contingently issuable shares to be included in the diluted EPS calculation is 'based on the number of shares that would be issuable if the end of the period were the end of the contingency period'. *[IAS 33.52]*. This requirement to look at the status of the contingency at the end of the reporting period, rather than to consider the most likely outcome, seems to have the overall result of *reducing* the amount of dilution disclosed.

The discussions in the standard cover three broad categories: earnings-based contingencies, share price-based contingencies, and other contingencies. These are discussed in turn below.

Chapter 35

The number of shares contingently issuable may depend on future earnings and future prices of the ordinary shares. In such cases, the standard makes clear that the number of shares included in the diluted EPS calculation is based on both conditions (i.e. earnings to date and the current market price at the end of the reporting period). In other words, contingently issuable shares are not included in the diluted EPS calculation unless both conditions are met. *[IAS 33.55]*.

6.4.6.A Earnings-based contingencies

The standard discusses the scenario where shares would be issued contingent upon the attainment or maintenance of a specified amount of earnings for a period. In such a case the standard requires that 'if that amount has been attained at the end of the reporting period but must be maintained beyond the end of the reporting period for an additional period, then the additional ordinary shares are treated as outstanding, if the effect is dilutive, when calculating diluted earnings per share. In that case, the calculation of diluted earnings per share is based on the number of ordinary shares that would be issued if the amount of earnings at the end of the reporting period were the amount of earnings at the end of the contingency period'. *[IAS 33.53]*. As a result, earnings-based contingencies need to be viewed as an absolute cumulative hurdle which either is met or not met at the reporting date. Often, such contingencies may be contractually expressed in terms of *annual* performance over a number of years, say an average of €1million profit per year for three years. In our view, 'the attainment or maintenance of a specified amount of earnings for a period' in this scenario would mean generating a total of €3million of profits. If that is achieved by the end of a reporting period, the shares are outstanding for diluted EPS purposes and included in the computation if the effect is dilutive. It could, perhaps, be argued that the potential shares should be considered outstanding if profits of €1million were generated at the end of the first year. However, the requirement that the calculation be 'based on the number of ordinary shares that would be issued if the amount of earnings at the end of the reporting period were the amount of earnings at the end of the contingency period' means that the test must be: would shares be issued if the current earnings of €1million were all the profits earned by the end of the three year contingency period? In this example the answer is no, as that amount of earnings would fall short of averaging €1million per year. The standard then notes that, because earnings may change in a future period, the calculation of basic EPS does not include such contingently issuable shares until the end of the contingency period because not all necessary conditions have been satisfied. *[IAS 33.53]*.

An earnings-based contingency is illustrated in the following example: *[IAS 33.IE7]*

Example 35.14: Contingently issuable shares

Ordinary shares outstanding during 2017:	1,000,000 (there were no options, warrants or convertible instruments outstanding during the period)

An agreement related to a recent business combination provides for the issue of additional ordinary shares based on the following conditions:

	5,000 additional ordinary shares for each new retail site opened during 2017
	1,000 additional ordinary shares for each €1,000 of consolidated profit in excess of €2,000,000 for the year ended 31 December 2017

Retail sites opened during the year:	one on 1 May 2017 one on 1 September 2017
Consolidated year-to-date profit attributable to ordinary equity holders of the parent entity:	€1,100,000 as of 31 March 2017 €2,300,000 as of 30 June 2017 €1,900,000 as of 30 September 2017 (including a €450,000 loss from a discontinued operation) €2,900,000 as of 31 December 2017

Basic earnings per share

	First quarter	*Second quarter*	*Third quarter*	*Fourth quarter*	*Full year*
Numerator (€)	1,100,000	1,200,000	(400,000)	1,000,000	2,900,000
Denominator:					
Ordinary shares outstanding	1,000,000	1,000,000	1,000,000	1,000,000	1,000,000
Retail site contingency	–	3,333 (a)	6,667 (b)	10,000	5,000 (c)
Earnings contingency (d)	–	–	–	–	–
Total shares	1,000,000	1,003,333	1,006,667	1,010,000	1,005,000
Basic earnings per share (€)	1.10	1.20	(0.40)	0.99	2.89

(a) 5,000 shares × 2/3
(b) 5,000 shares + (5,000 shares × 1/3)
(c) (5,000 shares × 8/12) + (5,000 shares × 4/12)
(d) The earnings contingency has no effect on basic earnings per share because it is not certain that the condition is satisfied until the end of the contingency period. The effect is negligible for the fourth-quarter and full-year calculations because it is not certain that the condition is met until the last day of the period.

Diluted earnings per share

	First quarter	*Second quarter*	*Third quarter*	*Fourth quarter*	*Full year*
Numerator (€)	1,100,000	1,200,000	(400,000)	1,000,000	2,900,000
Denominator:					
Ordinary shares outstanding	1,000,000	1,000,000	1,000,000	1,000,000	1,000,000
Retail site contingency	–	5,000	10,000	10,000	10,000
Earnings contingency	– (e)	300,000 (f)	– (g)	900,000 (h)	900,000 (h)
Total shares	1,000,000	1,305,000	1,010,000	1,910,000	1,910,000
Diluted earnings per share (€)	1.10	0.92	(0.40) (i)	0.52	1.52

(e) Year-to-date profits do not exceed €2,000,000 at 31 March 2017. The Standard does not permit projecting future earnings levels and including the related contingent shares.
(f) [(€2,300,000 – €2,000,000) ÷ 1,000] × 1,000 shares = 300,000 shares.
(g) Year-to-date profit is less than €2,000,000.
(h) [(€2,900,000 – €2,000,000) ÷ 1,000] × 1,000 shares = 900,000 shares.
(i) Because the loss during the third quarter is attributable to a loss from a discontinued operation, the antidilution rules do not apply. The control number (i.e. profit or loss from continuing operations attributable to the equity holders of the parent entity) is positive. Accordingly, the effect of potential ordinary shares is included in the calculation of diluted earnings per share.

This example from IAS 33 illustrates *quarterly* financial reporting. However, the principles are the same whether the reporting period is illustrated as three months or one year. The example does illustrate that the earnings target is a cumulative hurdle

Chapter 35

over the entire contingency period (four reporting periods in the example) rather than including potential shares based on the assumption that the level of quarterly profit would be maintained for the four quarters.

The standard only discusses earnings criteria based on *absolute* measures; in the example above a cumulative profit in excess of €2,000,000. In our experience such criteria are rare. In practice criteria are often phrased in terms of *relative* performance against an external benchmark. Examples would be earnings growth targets of inflation plus 2% or EPS growth being in the top quartile of a group of competitors. For contingencies such as these it is impossible to establish an absolute target in order to ask whether it is met at the period end. For example, consider the earnings contingency in IAS 33, discussed above, to achieve profits in excess of €2,000,000 over four quarters. If this instead required the profits to be €2,000,000 adjusted in line with inflation, it would be impossible to know how many shares would be issued if the cumulative profit at the end of the second quarter of €2,300,000 were the amount of earnings at the end of the contingency period. Until the end of the year the absolute level of profit required would be unknown; it would be more or less than €2,000,000 depending on the level of inflation or deflation over the period.

There would seem to be (at least) two different ways of interpreting the requirements of IAS 33 in such a scenario, each resulting in a different diluted EPS figure. One approach would be to consider such criteria as being based on 'a condition other than earnings or market price'. That would mean (as discussed at 6.4.6.C below) that the number of shares brought into diluted EPS would be based on the status of the condition at the end of the reporting period. *[IAS 33.56]*. So, if the target was earnings for the year in excess of €2,000,000 adjusted in line with inflation and at the end of the second quarter inflation had been 4%, then the target would become €2,080,000 and hence 220,000 shares would be included for diluted EPS for the second quarter. An alternative approach would be to regard it as an earnings-based contingency and make an assumption as to future inflation over the contingency period. This would allow a cumulative hurdle to be calculated and compared with actual earnings to date. So if at the end of the second quarter it was estimated that the annual inflation for the year was 5%, then the target would become €2,100,000 and hence 200,000 shares would be included for diluted EPS for the second quarter. Given the lack of clarity in the standard, it seems likely that either of the above approaches may be selected in practice.

6.4.6.B Share price-based contingencies

The provisions here are more straightforward. In these cases, if the effect is dilutive, the calculation of diluted EPS is based on the number of shares that would be issued if the market price at the end of the reporting period were the market price at the end of the contingency period. If the condition is based on an average of market prices over a period of time that extends beyond the end of the reporting period, the average for the period of time that has lapsed should be used. Again the standard explains that, because the market price may change in a future period, the calculation of basic earnings per share does not include such contingently issuable ordinary shares until the end of the contingency period because not all necessary conditions have been satisfied. *[IAS 33.54]*.

6.4.6.C *Other contingencies*

The requirement regarding contingencies not driven by earnings or share price is as follows: 'assuming that the present status of the condition remains unchanged until the end of the contingency period, the contingently issuable ordinary shares are included in the calculation of diluted earnings per share according to the status at the end of the reporting period.' *[IAS 33.56]*.

The standard illustrates the 'other contingency' rules by the example of shares being issued depending upon the opening of a specified number of retail sites, and such a contingency is included in the numerical example in the standard (see Example 35.14 above). As is the case for earnings-based contingencies discussed above, it would seem that such conditions are always deemed to be expressed as a cumulative hurdle which may or may not be met by the end of the reporting period. Accordingly, the required treatment would be the same if the condition had been expressed in terms of achieving a certain average annual level of shop openings.

6.4.7 *Potential ordinary shares of investees*

A subsidiary, joint venture or associate may issue to parties other than the parent or investors with joint control of, or significant influence over the investee potential ordinary shares that are convertible into either ordinary shares of the subsidiary, joint venture or associate, or ordinary shares of the parent or investors with joint control of, or significant influence over the investee (the reporting entity). If these potential ordinary shares of the subsidiary, joint venture or associate have a dilutive effect on the basic EPS of the reporting entity, they should be included in the calculation of diluted earnings per share. *[IAS 33.40]*.

The standard requires that such potential ordinary shares should be included in the calculation of diluted EPS as follows:

(a) instruments issued by a subsidiary, joint venture or associate that enable their holders to obtain ordinary shares of the subsidiary, joint venture or associate should be included in calculating the diluted EPS data of the subsidiary, joint venture or associate. Those EPS are then included in the reporting entity's EPS calculations based on the reporting entity's holding of the instruments of the subsidiary, joint venture or associate; and

(b) instruments of a subsidiary, joint venture or associate that are convertible into the reporting entity's ordinary shares should be considered among the potential ordinary shares of the reporting entity for the purpose of calculating diluted EPS. Similarly, options or warrants issued by a subsidiary, joint venture or associate to purchase ordinary shares of the reporting entity should be considered among the potential ordinary shares of the reporting entity in the calculation of consolidated diluted EPS. *[IAS 33.A11]*.

For the purpose of determining the EPS effect of instruments issued by a reporting entity that are convertible into ordinary shares of a subsidiary, joint venture or associate, the standard requires that the instruments are assumed to be converted and the numerator (profit or loss attributable to ordinary equity holders of the parent entity) adjusted as necessary in accordance with the normal rules (see 6.2.1 above). In addition to those adjustments, the numerator is adjusted for any change in the profit or loss recorded by the reporting entity (such as dividend income or equity method income) that is attributable to the increase in the number of ordinary shares of the subsidiary, joint venture or associate outstanding as a result of the assumed conversion. The denominator of the diluted EPS calculation is not affected because the number of ordinary shares of the reporting entity outstanding would not change upon assumed conversion. *[IAS 33.A12]*.

The computation under (a) above is illustrated in the following example. *[IAS 33.IE10]*.

Example 35.15: Warrants issued by a subsidiary

Parent:	
Profit attributable to ordinary equity holders of the parent entity	€12,000 (excluding any earnings of, or dividends paid by, the subsidiary)
Ordinary shares outstanding	10,000
Instruments of subsidiary owned by the parent	800 ordinary shares 30 warrants exercisable to purchase ordinary shares of subsidiary 300 convertible preference shares
Subsidiary:	
Profit	€5,400
Ordinary shares outstanding	1,000
Warrants	150, exercisable to purchase ordinary shares of the subsidiary
Exercise price	€10
Average market price of one ordinary share	€20
Convertible preference shares	400, each convertible into one ordinary share
Dividends on preference shares	€1 per share

No inter-company eliminations or adjustments were necessary except for dividends.
For the purposes of this illustration, income taxes have been ignored.

Subsidiary's earnings per share

Basic EPS €5.00 calculated: $\dfrac{€5{,}400^{(a)} - €400^{(b)}}{1{,}000^{(c)}}$

Diluted EPS €3.66 calculated: $\dfrac{€5{,}400^{(d)}}{1{,}000 + 75^{(e)} + 400^{(f)}}$

(a) Subsidiary's profit.
(b) Dividends paid by subsidiary on convertible preference shares.
(c) Subsidiary's ordinary shares outstanding.
(d) Subsidiary's profit attributable to ordinary equity holders (€5,000) increased by €400 preference dividends for the purpose of calculating diluted earnings per share.
(e) Incremental shares from warrants, calculated: [(€20 – €10) ÷ €20] × 150.
(f) Subsidiary's ordinary shares assumed outstanding from conversion of convertible preference shares, calculated: 400 convertible preference shares × conversion factor of 1.

Consolidated earnings per share

Basic EPS €1.63 calculated: $\dfrac{€12{,}000^{(g)} + €4{,}300^{(h)}}{10{,}000^{(i)}}$

Diluted EPS €1.61 calculated: $\dfrac{€12{,}000 + €2{,}928^{(j)} + €55^{(k)} + €1{,}098^{(l)}}{10{,}000}$

(g) Parent's profit attributable to ordinary equity holders of the parent entity.
(h) Portion of subsidiary's profit to be included in consolidated basic earnings per share, calculated: (800 × CU 5.00) + (300 × €1.00)
(i) Parent's ordinary shares outstanding.
(j) Parent's proportionate interest in subsidiary's earnings attributable to ordinary shares, calculated: (800 ÷ 1,000) × (1,000 shares × €3.66 per share)
(k) Parent's proportionate interest in subsidiary's earnings attributable to warrants, calculated: (30 ÷ 150) × (75 incremental shares × €3.66 per share)
(l) Parent's proportionate interest in subsidiary's earnings attributable to convertible preference shares, calculated: (300 ÷ 400) × (400 shares from conversion × €3.66 per share)

This example does not illustrate the classification of the components of convertible financial instruments as liabilities and equity or the classification of related interest and dividends as expenses and equity as required by IAS 32.

6.4.8 *Contingently issuable potential ordinary shares*

The standard requires that contingently issuable potential ordinary shares (other than those covered by a contingent share agreement, such as contingently issuable convertible instruments) to be included in the diluted EPS calculation as follows:

(a) determine whether the potential ordinary shares may be assumed to be issuable on the basis of the conditions specified for their issue in accordance with the provisions of the standard for contingent ordinary shares (see 6.4.6 above); and
(b) if those potential ordinary shares should be reflected in diluted EPS, determine their impact on the calculation of diluted earnings per share by following the provisions of the standard for that type of potential ordinary share.

However, exercise or conversion is not to be assumed for the purpose of calculating diluted earnings per share unless exercise or conversion of similar outstanding potential ordinary shares that are not contingently issuable is assumed. *[IAS 33.57]*.

7 PRESENTATION, RESTATEMENT AND DISCLOSURE

7.1 Presentation

As discussed in Chapter 3 at 3.2.1, IAS 1 requires that all items of income and expense be presented either:

(a) in a single statement of profit or loss and comprehensive income; or
(b) in two separate statements:
    (i) a statement of profit or loss; and
    (ii) a statement, beginning with profit or loss, presenting items of other comprehensive income. *[IAS 1.10A]*.

If the approach in (b) is followed, the separate statement of profit or loss must be displayed immediately before the statement of comprehensive income. *[IAS 1.10A]*.

If (a) is adopted, the EPS presentational requirements below apply to that single statement. If (b) is chosen, the requirements apply to the separate statement of profit or loss only and not the separate statement of comprehensive income. *[IAS 33.4A, 67A, 68A]*.

IAS 33 requires the presentation of basic and diluted EPS (with equal prominence and even if the amounts are negative – i.e. a loss per share) for each period for which a statement of comprehensive income (or separate income statement) is presented. *[IAS 33.66, 69]*. This is required for the profit or loss attributable to ordinary equity holders for:

(a) overall profit;

(b) profit or loss from continuing operations; and

(c) profit or loss from discontinued operations, if any. *[IAS 33.66, 68]*.

In the case of (a) and (b), separate figures are required for each class of ordinary shares with a different right to share in profits for the period. The figures for (a) and (b) must be displayed on the face of the statement. *[IAS 33.66]*. Those for (c) may be either on the face or in the notes. *[IAS 33.68]*. The standard states that if diluted EPS is given for at least one period it must be given for all periods presented. IAS 33 notes that if basic and diluted EPS are equal, dual presentation can be accomplished in one line in the statement. *[IAS 33.67]*.

Regarding (c), the wording of the standard is not very clear. In particular, if an entity has more than one discontinued operation it does not specify whether separate EPS disclosures are required for each or whether one aggregate figure is needed. The wording leans to the former, as it uses the singular – 'An entity that reports a discontinued operation shall disclose the basic and diluted amounts per share for the discontinued operation ...'. However, IFRS 5 – *Non-current Assets Held for Sale and Discontinued Operations* – only requires the statement of comprehensive income (or separate income statement) to identify the total result from all discontinued operations. *[IFRS 5.33]*. In light of this, we believe aggregate figures are acceptable.

7.2 Restatement

IAS 33 contains requirements to restate prior periods' EPS for events that change the number of shares outstanding without a corresponding change in resources. Additionally it specifies circumstances when EPS should not be restated.

Basic and diluted EPS for all periods presented should be adjusted for:

- events (other than the conversion of potential ordinary shares) which change the number of ordinary shares without a corresponding change in resources (discussed at 4.3 above); *[IAS 33.26, 64]*
- the effects of errors and adjustments resulting from changes in accounting policies accounted for retrospectively (see 5.3 above); *[IAS 33.64]* and
- the effects of group reorganisations that are accounted for as a pooling of interests (discussed at 4.6 above).

No adjustment should be made:

- to basic or diluted EPS when a share consolidation is combined with a special dividend where the overall commercial effect is that of a share repurchase at fair value (discussed at 4.3.2 above); *[IAS 33.29]*

- to previously reported diluted EPS due to changes in the prices of ordinary shares which would have given a different dilutive effect for options and warrants; *[IAS 33.47]*
- to prior period diluted EPS as a result of a contingency period coming to an end without the conditions attaching to contingently issuable shares being met; *[IAS 33.52]* or
- to prior period diluted EPS for changes in the assumptions used in the calculations or for the conversion of potential ordinary shares into ordinary shares. *[IAS 33.65]*.

7.3 Disclosure

IAS 33 requires disclosure of the following:

(a) the amounts used as the numerators in calculating basic and diluted EPS, and a reconciliation of those amounts to profit or loss attributable to the parent entity for the period. The reconciliation should include the individual effect of each class of instruments that affects EPS;

(b) the weighted average number of ordinary shares used as the denominator in calculating basic and diluted earnings per share, and a reconciliation of these denominators to each other. The reconciliation should include the individual effect of each class of instruments that affects EPS;

(c) instruments (including contingently issuable shares) that could potentially dilute basic EPS in the future, but were not included in the calculation because they were antidilutive for the period(s) presented; and

(d) a description of ordinary share transactions or potential ordinary share transactions (other than those accounted for in EPS for the year – see 4.3 above – in which case that fact should be stated), that occur after the end of the reporting period and that would have changed significantly the number of ordinary shares or potential ordinary shares outstanding at the end of the period if those transactions had occurred before the end of the reporting period. *[IAS 33.70]*.

Examples of transactions in (d) include:

(a) an issue of shares for cash;

(b) an issue of shares when the proceeds are used to repay debt or preference shares outstanding at the end of the reporting period;

(c) the redemption of ordinary shares outstanding;

(d) the conversion or exercise of potential ordinary shares outstanding at the end of the reporting period into ordinary shares;

(e) an issue of options, warrants, or convertible instruments; and

(f) the achievement of conditions that would result in the issue of contingently issuable shares.

The standard observes that EPS amounts are not adjusted for such transactions occurring after the reporting period because such transactions do not affect the amount of capital used to produce profit or loss for the period. *[IAS 33.71]*. Changes in ordinary shares are discussed at 4 above.

The standard observes that financial instruments and other contracts generating potential ordinary shares may incorporate terms and conditions that affect the measurement of basic and diluted earnings per share. These terms and conditions may determine whether any potential ordinary shares are dilutive and, if so, the effect on the weighted average number of shares outstanding and any consequent adjustments to profit or loss attributable to ordinary equity holders. The disclosure of the terms and conditions of such financial instruments and other contracts is encouraged by IAS 33, if not otherwise required by IFRS 7 – *Financial Instruments: Disclosures* (discussed in Chapter 54). *[IAS 33.72]*.

8 APPENDIX

Reproduced below is the comprehensive worked example in IAS 33 of the computation and presentation of EPS. *[IAS 33.IE12]*. It illustrates four quarters and then the full year, but the principles and calculations would be the same whatever the length of the periods considered.

CALCULATION AND PRESENTATION OF BASIC AND DILUTED EARNINGS PER SHARE (COMPREHENSIVE EXAMPLE)

This example illustrates the quarterly and annual calculations of basic and diluted earnings per share in the year 20X1 for Company A, which has a complex capital structure. The control number is profit or loss from continuing operations attributable to the parent entity. Other facts assumed are as follows:

Average market price of ordinary shares: The average market prices of ordinary shares for the calendar year 20X1 were as follows:

First quarter	CU 49
Second quarter	CU 60
Third quarter	CU 67
Fourth quarter	CU 67

The average market price of ordinary shares from 1 July to 1 September 20X1 was CU 65.

Ordinary shares: The number of ordinary shares outstanding at the beginning of 20X1 was 5,000,000. On 1 March 20X1, 200,000 ordinary shares were issued for cash.

Convertible bonds: In the last quarter of 20X0, 5 per cent convertible bonds with a principal amount of CU 12,000,000 due in 20 years were sold for cash at CU 1,000 (par). Interest is payable twice a year, on 1 November and 1 May. Each CU 1,000 bond is convertible into 40 ordinary shares. No bonds were converted in 20X0. The entire issue was converted on 1 April 20X1 because the issue was called by Company A.

Convertible preference shares: In the second quarter of 20X0, 800,000 convertible preference shares were issued for assets in a purchase transaction. The quarterly dividend on each convertible preference share is CU 0.05, payable at the end of the quarter for shares outstanding at that date. Each share is convertible into one ordinary share. Holders of 600,000 convertible preference shares converted their preference shares into ordinary shares on 1 June 20X1.

Warrants: Warrants to buy 600,000 ordinary shares at CU 55 per share for a period of five years were issued on 1 January 20X1. All outstanding warrants were exercised on 1 September 20X1.

Options: Options to buy 1,500,000 ordinary shares at CU 75 per share for a period of 10 years were issued on 1 July 20X1. No options were exercised during 20X1 because the exercise price of the options exceeded the market price of the ordinary shares.

Tax rate: The tax rate was 40 per cent for 20X1.

20X1	*Profit (loss) from continuing operations attributable to the parent entity* (a) *CU*	*Profit (loss) attributable to the parent entity CU*	
First quarter	5,000,000	5,000,000	
Second quarter	6,500,000	6,500,000	
Third quarter	1,000,000	(1,000,000)	(b)
Fourth quarter	(700,000)	(700,000)	
Full year	11,800,000	9,800,000	

(a) This is the control number (before adjusting for preference dividends).

(b) Company A had a CU 2,000,000 loss (net of tax) from discontinued operations in the third quarter.

First Quarter 20X1

Basic EPS calculation	*CU*	
Profit from continuing operations attributable to the parent entity	5,000,000	
Less: preference shares dividends	(40,000)	(c)
Profit attributable to ordinary equity holders of the parent entity	4,960,000	

Dates	*Shares Outstanding*	*Fraction of period*	*Weighted-average shares*
1 January 28 February	5,000,000	2/3	3,333,333
Issue of ordinary shares on 1 March	200,000		
1 March 31 March	5,200,000	1/3	1,733,333
Weighted-average shares			5,066,666
Basic EPS			**CU 0.98**

(c) 800,000 shares × CU 0.05

Diluted EPS calculation			
Profit attributable to ordinary equity holders of the parent entity			CU 4,960,000
Plus: profit impact of assumed conversions			
Preference share dividends	CU 40,000	(d)	
Interest on 5% convertible bonds	CU 90,000	(e)	
Effect of assumed conversions			CU 130,000
Profit attributable to ordinary equity holders of the parent entity including assumed conversions			CU 5,090,000
Weighted-average shares			5,066,666
Plus: incremental shares from assumed conversions			
Warrants	0	(f)	
Convertible preference shares	800,000		
5% convertible bonds	480,000		
Dilutive potential ordinary shares			1,280,000
Adjusted weighted-average shares			6,346,666
Diluted EPS			**CU 0.80**

(d) 800,000 shares × CU 0.05

(e) (CU 12,000,000 × 5%) ÷ 4; less taxes at 40%

(f) The warrants were not assumed to be exercised because they were antidilutive in the period (CU 55 [exercise price] > CU 49 [average price]).

Chapter 35

Second Quarter 20X1

Basic EPS calculation			*CU*	
Profit from continuing operations attributable to the parent entity			6,500,000	
Less: preference shares dividends			(10,000)	(g)
Profit attributable to ordinary equity holders of the parent entity			6,490,000	

Dates	*Shares outstanding*	*Fraction of period*	*Weighted-average shares*
1 April	5,200,000		
Conversion of 5% bonds on 1 April	480,000		
1 April - 31 May	5,680,000	2/3	3,786,666
Conversion of preference shares on 1 June	600,000		
1 June - 30 June	6,280,000	1/3	2,093,333
Weighted-average shares			5,880,000
Basic EPS			**CU 1.10**

(g) 200,000 shares × CU 0.05

Diluted EPS calculation			
Profit attributable to ordinary equity holders of the parent entity			CU 6,490,000
Plus: profit impact of assumed conversions			
Preference share dividends	CU 10,000	(h)	
Effect of assumed conversions			CU 10,000
Profit attributable to ordinary equity holders of the parent entity including assumed conversions			CU 6,500,000
Weighted-average shares			5,880,000
Plus: incremental shares from assumed conversions			
Warrants	50,000	(i)	
Convertible preference shares	600,000	(j)	
Dilutive potential ordinary shares			650,000
Adjusted weighted-average shares			6,530,000
Diluted EPS			**CU 1.00**

(h) 200,000 shares × CU 0.05

(i) CU 55 × 600,000 = CU 33,000,000; CU 33,000,000 ÷ CU 60 = 550,000; 600,000 – 550,000 = 50,000 shares *or* [(CU 60 – CU 55) ÷ CU 60] × 600,000 shares = 50,000 shares

(j) (800,000 shares × 2/3) + (200,000 shares × 1/3)

Third Quarter 20X1

Basic EPS calculation	*CU*
Profit from continuing operations attributable to the parent entity	1,000,000
Less: preference shares dividends	(10,000)
Profit from continuing operations attributable to ordinary equity holders of the parent entity	990,000
Loss from discontinued operations attributable to the parent entity	(2,000,000)
Loss attributable to ordinary equity holders of the parent entity	(1,010,000)

Dates	*Shares outstanding*	*Fraction of period*	*Weighted-average shares*
1 July - 31 August	6,280,000	2/3	4,186,666
Exercise of warrants on 1 September	600,000		
1 September - 30 September	6,880,000	1/3	2,293,333
Weighted-average shares			6,480,000

Basic EPS	
Profit from continuing operations	**CU 0.15**
Loss from discontinued operations	**(CU 0.31)**
Loss	**(CU 0.16)**

Diluted EPS calculation			
Profit from continuing operations attributable to ordinary equity holders of the parent entity			CU 990,000
Plus: profit impact of assumed conversions			
Preference shares dividends	CU 10,000		
Effect of assumed conversions			CU 10,000
Profit from continuing operations attributable to ordinary equity holders of the parent entity including assumed conversions			CU 1,000,000
Loss from discontinued operations attributable to the parent entity			(CU 2,000,000)
Loss attributable to ordinary equity holders of the parent entity including assumed conversions			(CU 1,000,000)
Weighted-average shares			6,480,000
Plus: incremental shares from assumed conversions			
Warrants	61,538	(k)	
Convertible preference shares	200,000		
Dilutive potential ordinary shares			261,538
Adjusted weighted-average shares			6,741,538
Diluted EPS			
Profit from continuing operations			**CU 0.15**
Loss from discontinued operations			**(CU 0.30)**
Loss			**(CU 0.15)**

(k) [(CU 65 – CU 55) ÷ CU 65] × 600,000 = 92,308 shares; 92,308 × 2/3 = 61,538 shares

Note: The incremental shares from assumed conversions are included in calculating the diluted per-share amounts for the loss from discontinued operations and loss even though they are antidilutive. This is because the control number (profit from continuing operations attributable to ordinary equity holders of the parent entity, adjusted for preference dividends) was positive (i.e. profit, rather than loss).

Fourth Quarter 20X1	
Basic and diluted EPS calculation	*CU*
Loss from continuing operations attributable to the parent entity	(700,000)
Add: preference shares dividends	(10,000)
Loss attributable to ordinary equity holders of the parent entity	(710,000)

Dates	*Shares outstanding*	*Fraction of period*	*Weighted-average shares*
1October - 31 December	6,880,000	3/3	6,880,000
Weighted-average shares			6,880,000
Basic and diluted EPS			
Loss attributable to ordinary equity holders of the parent entity			**(CU 0.10)**

Note: The incremental shares from assumed conversions are not included in calculating the diluted per-share amounts because the control number (loss from continuing operations attributable to ordinary equity holders of the parent entity adjusted for preference dividends) was negative (i.e. a loss, rather than profit).

Full Year 20X1

Basic EPS calculation	*CU*
Profit from continuing operations attributable to the parent entity	11,800,000
Less: preference shares dividends	(70,000)
Profit from continuing operations attributable to ordinary equity holders of the parent entity	11,730,000
Loss from discontinued operations attributable to the parent entity	(2,000,000)
Profit attributable to ordinary equity holders of the parent entity	9,730,000

Dates	*Shares Outstanding*	*Fraction of period*	*Weighted-average shares*
1 January - 28 February	5,000,000	2/12	833,333
Issue of ordinary shares on 1March	200,000		
1 March - 31 March	5,200,000	1/12	433,333
Conversion of 5% bonds on 1April	480,000		
1 April - 31 May	5,680,000	2/12	946,667
Conversion of preference shares on 1June	600,000		
1 June - 31 August	6,280,000	3/12	1,570,000
Exercise of warrants on 1September	600,000		
1 September - 31 December	6,880,000	4/12	2,293,333
Weighted-average shares			6,076,667
Basic EPS			
Profit from continuing operations			**CU 1.93**
Loss from discontinued operations			**(CU 0.33)**
Profit			**CU 1.60**

Diluted EPS calculation			
Profit from continuing operations attributable to ordinary equity holders of the parent entity			CU 11,730,000
Plus: profit impact of assumed conversions			
Preference share dividends	CU 70,000		
Interest on 5% convertible bonds	CU 90,000	(l)	
Effect of assumed conversions			CU 160,000
Profit from continuing operations attributable to ordinary equity holders of the parent entity including assumed conversions			CU 11,890,000
Loss from discontinued operations attributable to the parent entity			(CU 2,000,000)
Profit attributable to ordinary equity holders of the parent entity including assumed conversions			CU 9,890,000
Weighted-average shares			6,076,667
Plus: incremental shares from assumed conversions			
Warrants	14,880	(m)	
Convertible preference shares	450,000	(n)	
5% convertible bonds	120,000	(o)	
Dilutive potential ordinary shares			584,880
Adjusted weighted-average shares			6,661,547
Diluted EPS			
Profit from continuing operations			**CU 1.78**
Loss from discontinued operations			**(CU 0.30)**
Profit			**CU 1.48**

(l) (CU 12,000,000 × 5%) ÷ 4; less taxes at 40%

(m) [(CU 57.125* – CU 55) ÷ CU 57.125] × 600,000 = 22,320 shares; 22,320 × 8/12 = 14,880 shares
* The average market price from 1 January 20X1 to 1 September 20X1

(n) (800,000 shares × 5/12) + (200,000 shares × 7/12)

(o) 480,000 shares × 3/12

The following illustrates how Company A might present its earnings per share data in its statement of comprehensive income. Note that the amounts per share for the loss from discontinued operations are not required to be presented on the face of the statement of comprehensive income.

	For the year ended 20X1
	CU
Earnings per ordinary share	
Profit from continuing operations	1.93
Loss from discontinued operations	(0.33)
Profit	1.60
Diluted earnings per ordinary share	
Profit from continuing operations	1.78
Loss from discontinued operations	(0.30)
Profit	1.48

The following table includes the quarterly and annual earnings per share data for Company A. The purpose of this table is to illustrate that the sum of the four quarters' earnings per share data will not necessarily equal the annual earnings per share data. The Standard does not require disclosure of this information.

	First quarter *CU*	*Second quarter* *CU*	*Third quarter* *CU*	*Fourth quarter* *CU*	*Full year* *CU*
Basic EPS					
Profit (loss) from continuing operations	0.98	1.10	0.15	(0.10)	1.93
Loss from discontinued operations	–	–	(0.31)	–	(0.33)
Profit (loss)	0.98	1.10	(0.16)	(0.10)	1.60
Diluted EPS					
Profit (loss) from continuing operations	0.80	1.00	0.15	(0.10)	1.78
Loss from discontinued operations	–	–	(0.30)	–	(0.30)
Profit (loss)	0.80	1.00	(0.15)	(0.10)	1.48

This example does not illustrate the classification of the components of convertible financial instruments as liabilities and equity or the classification of related interest and dividends as expenses and equity as required by IAS 32.

References

1 See, for example, the 2015 Annual Report and Accounts of Meggitt PLC.

Chapter 36 Events after the reporting period

List of examples

Chapter 36 Events after the reporting period

1 INTRODUCTION

IAS 10 – *Events after the Reporting Period* – deals with accounting for, and disclosure of, events after the reporting period, which are defined as 'those events, favourable and unfavourable, that occur between the end of the reporting period and the date when the financial statements are authorised for issue'. *[IAS 10.2, 3]*. Therefore, the definition includes all events occurring between those dates – irrespective of whether they relate to conditions that existed at the end of the reporting period. The principal issue is determining which events after the reporting period to reflect in the financial statements.

The following timeline of an entity with a 31 December year-end illustrates events after the end of the reporting period that are within the scope of IAS 10:

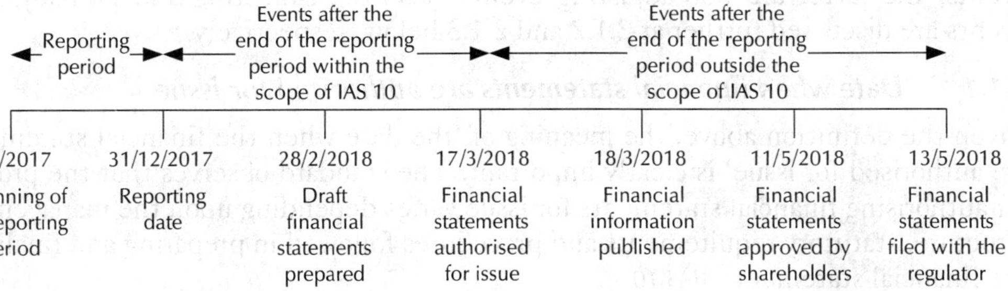

The financial statements of an entity present, among other things, an entity's financial position at the end of the reporting period. Therefore, it is appropriate to adjust the financial statements for all events that offer greater clarity concerning the conditions that existed at the end of the reporting period, that occur prior to the date the financial statements are authorised for issue. The standard requires entities to adjust the amounts recognised in the financial statements for 'adjusting events' that provide evidence of conditions that existed at the end of the reporting period. *[IAS 10.3(a), 8]*. An entity does not recognise in the financial statements those events that relate to conditions that arose after the reporting period ('non-adjusting events'). However, if non-adjusting events are material (that is, non-disclosure of the event could influence the economic decisions that users make on the basis of the financial statements), the standard requires certain disclosures about them. *[IAS 10.3(b), 10, 21]*.

One exception to the general rule of the standard for non-adjusting events is when the going concern basis becomes inappropriate. This is treated as an adjusting event. *[IAS 10.1, 14]*.

The requirements of IAS 10 and practical issues resulting from these requirements are dealt with at 2 and 3 below.

2 REQUIREMENTS OF IAS 10

2.1 Objective, scope and definitions

The objective of IAS 10 is to prescribe:

- when an entity should adjust its financial statements for events after the reporting period; and
- the required disclosures about the date when the financial statements were authorised for issue and about events after the reporting period.

The standard does not permit an entity to prepare its financial statements on a going concern basis if events after the reporting period indicate that the going concern assumption is not appropriate. *[IAS 10.1]*. This requirement is discussed further at 2.2.2 below. The going concern basis is discussed in Chapter 3 at 4.1.2.

IAS 10 defines events after the reporting period as 'those events, favourable and unfavourable, that occur between the end of the reporting period and the date when the financial statements are authorised for issue'. *[IAS 10.3]*. This definition therefore includes events that provide additional evidence about conditions that existed at the end of the reporting period, as well as those that do not. The former are adjusting events, the latter are non-adjusting events. *[IAS 10.3]*. Adjusting and non-adjusting events are discussed further at 2.1.2 and 2.1.3 below, respectively.

2.1.1 Date when financial statements are authorised for issue

Given the definition above, the meaning of 'the date when the financial statements are authorised for issue' is clearly important. The standard observes that the process for authorising financial statements for issue varies depending upon the management structure, statutory requirements and procedures followed in preparing and finalising the financial statements. *[IAS 10.4]*.

The standard identifies two particular instances of the different meaning of 'authorised for issue' as follows:

(a) An entity may be required to submit its financial statements to its shareholders for approval (as in France, for example) after the financial statements have been issued. In such cases, the financial statements are authorised for issue on the date of issue, not the date when shareholders approve them. *[IAS 10.5]*.

(b) The management of an entity may be required to issue its financial statements to a supervisory board (made up solely of non-executives) for approval. Such financial statements are authorised for issue when management authorises them for issue to the supervisory board. *[IAS 10.6]*.

These two meanings are illustrated by the following two examples, which are based on the illustrative examples contained in IAS 10. *[IAS 10.5-6]*.

Example 36.1: Financial statements required to be approved by shareholders

The management of an entity completes draft financial statements for the year to 31 December 2017 on 28 February 2018. On 17 March 2018, the board of directors reviews the financial statements and authorises them for issue. The entity announces its profit and certain other financial information on 18 March 2018. The financial statements are made available to shareholders and others on 1 April 2018. The shareholders approve the financial statements at their annual meeting on 11 May 2018 and the approved financial statements are then filed with a regulatory body on 13 May 2018.

The financial statements are authorised for issue on 17 March 2018 (date of board authorisation for issue).

Example 36.2: Financial statements required to be approved by supervisory board

On 17 March 2018, the management of an entity authorises for issue to its supervisory board financial statements for the year to 31 December 2017. The supervisory board consists solely of non-executives and may include representatives of employees and other outside interests. The supervisory board approves the financial statements on 25 March 2018. The financial statements are made available to shareholders and others on 1 April 2018. The shareholders approve the financial statements at their annual meeting on 11 May 2018 and the financial statements are filed with a regulatory body on 13 May 2018.

The financial statements are authorised for issue on 17 March 2018 (date of management authorisation for issue to the supervisory board).

An uncommon, but possible, situation that may occur is that the financial statements are changed after they are authorised for issue to the supervisory board. The following example illustrates such a situation.

Example 36.3: Financial statements required to be approved by supervisory board – changes are made by supervisory board

Same facts as in Example 36.2 above, except that the supervisory board reviews the financial statements on 25 March 2018 and proposes changes to certain note disclosures. The management of the entity incorporates the suggested changes and re-authorises those financial statements for issue to the supervisory board on 27 March 2018. The supervisory board then approves the financial statements on 30 March 2018.

The financial statements are authorised for issue on 27 March 2018 (date of management re-authorisation for issue to the supervisory board).

A fourth example illustrates when the entity releases preliminary information, but not complete financial statements, before the date of the authorisation for issue.

Example 36.4: Release of financial information before date of authorisation for issue

The management of an entity completes the primary financial statements (e.g. statement of financial position, statement of comprehensive income, cash flow statement) for the year to 31 December 2017 on 21 January 2018, but has not yet completed the explanatory notes. On 26 January 2018, the board of directors (which includes management and non-executives) reviews the primary financial statements and authorises them for public media release. The entity announces its profit and certain other financial information on 28 January 2018. On 11 February 2018, management issues the financial statements (with full explanatory notes) to the board of directors, which approves the financial statements for filing on 18 February 2018. The entity files the financial statements with a regulatory body on 21 February 2018.

The financial statements are authorised for issue on 18 February 2018 (date the board of directors, approves the financial statements for filing).

Example 36.4 illustrates that events after the reporting period include all events up to the date when the financial statements are authorised for issue, even if those events occur after the public announcement of profit or of other selected financial information. *[IAS 10.7]*. Accordingly, the information in the financial statements might differ from the equivalent information in a preliminary announcement. As governance structures vary by jurisdiction, entities may be allowed to organise their procedures differently and adjust the financial reporting process accordingly.

An example of a company which is required to submit its financial statements to its shareholders for approval is Holcim Ltd, as illustrated in the following extract:

Extract 36.1: Holcim Ltd (2014)

Notes to the consolidated financial statements [extract]

43 Authorization of the financial statements for issuance

The consolidated financial statements were authorized for issuance by the Board of Directors of Holcim Ltd on February 20, 2015, and are subject to shareholder approval at the annual general meeting of shareholders scheduled for April 13, 2015.

As discussed above, an entity may be required to issue its financial statements to a supervisory board (made up solely of non-executives) for approval. For such instances, the phrase 'made up solely of non-executives' is not defined by the standard, although it contemplates that a supervisory board may include representatives of employees and other outside interests. However, it seems to draw a distinction between those responsible for the executive management of an entity (and the preparation of its financial statements) and those in a position of high-level oversight (including reviewing and approving the financial statements). This situation seems to describe the typical two-tier board system seen in some jurisdictions (for example, Germany). An example of a company with this structure is Bayer AG, as illustrated in the following extract.

Extract 36.2: Bayer Aktiengesellschaft (2015)

Combined Management Report [extract]

16. Corporate Governance Report [extract]

16.2 Governance [extract]

SUPERVISORY BOARD: OVERSIGHT AND CONTROL FUNCTIONS

The role of the 20-member Supervisory Board is to oversee and advise the Board of Management. Under the German Codetermination Act, half of the Supervisory Board's members are elected by the stockholders, and half by the company's employees. The Supervisory Board is directly involved in decisions on matters of fundamental importance to the company, regularly conferring with the Board of Management on the company's strategic alignment and the implementation status of the business strategy.

The Chairman of the Supervisory Board coordinates its work and presides over the meetings. Through regular discussions with the Board of Management, the Supervisory Board is kept constantly informed about business policy, corporate planning and strategy. The Supervisory Board approves the annual budget and financial framework. It also approves the financial statements of Bayer AG and the consolidated financial statements of the Bayer Group, along with the combined management report, taking into account the reports by the auditor.

2.1.1.A Re-issuing financial statements

IFRSs do not address whether and how an entity may amend its financial statements after they have been authorised for issue. Generally, such matters are dealt with in local laws or regulations.

If an entity re-issues financial statements (whether to correct an error or to include events that occurred after the financial statements were originally authorised for issue), there is a new date of authorisation for issue. The financial statements should then appropriately reflect all adjusting events, by updating the amounts recognised in the financial statements, and non-adjusting events, through additional disclosure, up to the new date of authorisation for issue.

However, in certain circumstances, the re-issuing of previously issued financial statements is required by local regulators particularly for inclusion in public offering and similar documents. Consequently, in November 2012, the Interpretations Committee was asked to clarify the accounting implications of applying IAS 10 when previously issued financial statements are re-issued in connection with an offering document.[1]

The issue arose in jurisdictions in which securities laws and regulatory practices require an entity to re-issue its previously issued annual financial statements in connection with an offering document, when the most recently filed interim financial statements reflect matters that are accounted for retrospectively under the applicable accounting standards. In these jurisdictions, securities law and regulatory practices do not require or permit the entity, in its re-issued financial statements, to recognise events or transactions that occur between the time the financial statements were first authorised for issuance and the time the financial statements are re-issued, unless the adjustment is required by national regulation. Instead, security and regulatory practices require the entity to recognise in its re-issued financial statements only those adjustments that would ordinarily be made to the comparatives in the following year's financial statements. These adjustments would include, for example, adjustments for changes in accounting policy that are applied retrospectively, but would not include changes in accounting estimates.[2]

Accordingly, in January 2013, the Interpretations Committee was asked about the date of authorisation required by IAS 10 when considered within the context of re-issuing previously issued financial statements in connection with an offering document.[3]

In May 2013, the Interpretations Committee responded that:

- the scope of IAS 10 is the accounting for, and disclosure of, events after the reporting period and that the objective of this Standard is to prescribe:
  - (a) when an entity should adjust its financial statements for events after the reporting period; and
  - (b) the disclosures that an entity should give about the date when the financial statements were authorised for issue and about events after the reporting period;
- financial statements prepared in accordance with IAS 10 should reflect all adjusting and non-adjusting events up to the date that the financial statements were authorised for issue; and
- IAS 10 does not address the presentation of re-issued financial statements in an offering document when the originally issued financial statements have not been withdrawn, but the re-issued financial statements are provided either as supplementary information or a re-presentation of the original financial statements in an offering document in accordance with regulatory requirements.

Chapter 36

The Interpretations Committee decided not to add this issue to its agenda on the basis of the above and because the issue arises in multiple jurisdictions, each with particular securities laws and regulations which may dictate the form for re-presentations of financial statements.[4]

2.1.2 Adjusting events

Adjusting events are 'those that provide evidence of conditions that existed at the end of the reporting period.' *[IAS 10.3(a)]*.

Examples of adjusting events are as follows:

(a) the settlement after the reporting period of a court case that confirms that the entity had a present obligation at the end of the reporting period. In this situation, an entity adjusts any previously recognised provision related to this court case in accordance with IAS 37 – *Provisions, Contingent Liabilities and Contingent Assets* – or recognises a new provision. Mere disclosure of a contingent liability is not sufficient because the settlement provides additional evidence of conditions that existed at the end of the reporting period that would give rise to a provision in accordance with IAS 37 (see Chapter 28 at 3.1.1 and 3.2.1);

(b) the receipt of information after the reporting period indicating that an asset was or was not impaired at the end of the reporting period, or that the amount of a previously recognised impairment loss for that asset needs to be adjusted. For example:

  (i) the bankruptcy of a customer that occurs after the reporting period usually confirms that a loss existed at the end of the reporting period on a trade receivable and that the entity needs to adjust the carrying amount of the trade receivable[5] (this is discussed further at 3.3 below); and

  (ii) the sale of inventories after the reporting period may give evidence about their net realisable value at the end of the reporting period;

(c) the determination after the reporting period of the cost of assets purchased, or the proceeds from assets sold, before the end of the reporting period;

(d) the determination after the reporting period of the amount of profit-sharing or bonus payments, if the entity had a present legal or constructive obligation at the end of the reporting period to make such payments as a result of events before that date; and

(e) the discovery of fraud or errors that show that the financial statements are incorrect (see 3.5 below). *[IAS 10.9]*.

In addition, IAS 33 – *Earnings per Share* – requires an adjustment to earnings per share for certain share transactions after the reporting period (such as bonus issues, share splits or share consolidations as discussed in Chapter 35 at 4.5) even though the transactions themselves are non-adjusting events (see 2.1.3 below). *[IAS 10.22]*.

2.1.3 *Non-adjusting events*

The standard states that non-adjusting events are 'those that are indicative of conditions that arose after the reporting period'. *[IAS 10.3(b)]*.

As examples of non-adjusting events, the standard gives the following events after the reporting period:

(a) a major business combination (IFRS 3 – *Business Combinations* – requires specific disclosures in such cases, see Chapter 9 at 16.1.2) or disposing of a major subsidiary;

(b) announcing a plan to discontinue an operation;

(c) major purchases of assets, classification of assets as held for sale in accordance with IFRS 5 – *Non-current Assets Held for Sale and Discontinued Operations*, other disposals of assets, or expropriation of major assets by government (see Chapter 4 at 5.1 for certain disclosures that are required to be made);

(d) the destruction of a major production plant by a fire;

(e) announcing, or commencing the implementation of, a major restructuring (discussed in Chapter 28 at 6.1);

(f) major ordinary share transactions and potential ordinary share transactions (although as noted at 2.1.2 above, some transactions in ordinary shares are adjusting events for the purposes of computing earnings per share);

(g) abnormally large changes in asset prices or foreign exchange rates;

(h) changes in tax rates or the enactment or announcement of tax laws that significantly affect current and deferred tax assets and liabilities (discussed in Chapter 31 at 8.1);

(i) entry into significant commitments or contingent liabilities, for example, by issuing significant guarantees;

(j) start of major litigation arising solely out of events that occurred after the reporting period;

(k) a decline in fair value of investments; and

(l) a declaration of dividends to holders of equity instruments (as defined in IAS 32 – *Financial Instruments: Presentation* – discussed in Chapter 45 at 8). *[IAS 10.11, 12, 22]*.

The reference in (a) and (c) above to asset disposals as examples of non-adjusting events is not quite the whole story as they may indicate an impairment of assets, which may be an adjusting event. In addition, (b) and (e) above regarding announcements of plans to discontinue an operation or to restructure a business, respectively, may also lead to an impairment charge (see Chapter 20 at 2.3.1).

For declines in fair value of investments, as in (k) above, the standard notes that the decline in fair value does not *normally* relate to the condition of the investments at the end of the reporting period, but reflects circumstances that arose subsequently. Therefore, in those circumstances the amounts recognised in financial statements for the investments are not adjusted. Similarly, the standard states that an entity does not update the amounts disclosed for the investments as at the end of the reporting period, although it may need to give additional disclosure, if material, as discussed at 2.3 below. *[IAS 10.11]*.

However, the assertion that a decline in fair value of investments does not *normally* relate to conditions at the end of the reporting period is similar wording to that used for bankruptcy and the sale of inventories (see 2.1.2(b) above). Therefore, it requires an assessment of the circumstances in order to determine which conditions actually existed at the end of the reporting period – although this can be difficult in practice, particularly when fraud is involved (see 3.5 below).

In respect of dividend declarations, as in (l) above, dividends are only recognised as a liability if declared on or by the end of the reporting period. If an entity declares dividends to holders of equity instruments (as defined in IAS 32) after the reporting period, the entity shall not recognise those dividends as a liability at the end of the reporting period. *[IAS 10.13]*. While an entity may have a past practice of paying dividends, such dividends are not declared and, therefore, not recognised as an obligation. *[IAS 10.BC4]*.

As a consequential amendment to IAS 10, the definition of 'declared' in this context was moved to IFRIC 17 – *Distributions of Non-cash Assets to Owners*. IFRIC 17 did not change the principle regarding the appropriate timing for the recognition of dividends payable. *[IFRIC 17.BC18-20]*. It states that an entity recognises a liability to pay a dividend when the dividend is appropriately authorised and is no longer at the discretion of the entity, which is the date:

- when declaration of the dividend, e.g. by management or the board of directors, is approved by the relevant authority, e.g. the shareholders, if the jurisdiction requires such approval; or
- when the dividend is declared, e.g. by management or the board of directors, if the jurisdiction does not require further approval. *[IFRIC 17.10]*.

In many jurisdictions, the directors may keep discretion to cancel an interim dividend until such time as it is paid. In this case, the interim dividend is not declared (within the meaning described above), and is, therefore, not recognised until paid. Final dividends proposed by directors, in many jurisdictions, are only binding when approved by shareholders in general meeting or by the members passing a written resolution. Therefore, such a final dividend is only recognised as a liability when declared, i.e. approved by the shareholders at the annual general meeting or through the passing of a resolution by the members of an entity.

IAS 10 contains a reminder that an entity discloses dividends, both proposed and declared after the reporting period but before the financial statements are authorised for issue, in the notes to the financial statements in accordance with IAS 1 – *Presentation of Financial Statements* (see Chapter 3 at 5.5). *[IAS 10.13]*.

Similar issues arise regarding the declaration of dividends by subsidiaries, associates and other equity investments. Although IAS 10 does not specifically address such items, IAS 18 – *Revenue* – requires a shareholder to recognise dividends when the shareholder's right to receive payment is established. *[IAS 18.30(c)]*. Similarly, IAS 27 – *Separate Financial Statements* – contains this general principle in recognising in an entity's separate financial statements those dividends received from subsidiaries, joint ventures or associates when its right to receive the dividend is established (see Chapter 8 at 2.4.1). *[IAS 27.12]*. Accordingly, a shareholder does not recognise such dividend income until the period in which the dividend is declared.

2.2 The treatment of adjusting events

2.2.1 Events requiring adjustment to the amounts recognised, or disclosures, in the financial statements

IAS 10 requires that the amounts recognised in the financial statements be adjusted to take account of an adjusting event. *[IAS 10.8]*.

The standard also notes that an entity may receive information after the reporting period about conditions existing at the end of the reporting period relating to disclosures made in the financial statements but not affecting the amounts recognised in them. *[IAS 10.20]*. In such cases, the standard requires the entity to update the disclosures that relate to those conditions for the new information. *[IAS 10.19]*.

For example, evidence may become available after the reporting period about a contingent liability that existed at the end of the reporting period. In addition to considering whether to recognise or change a provision under IAS 37, IAS 10 requires an entity to update its disclosures about the contingent liability for that evidence. *[IAS 10.20]*.

2.2.2 Events indicating that the going concern basis is not appropriate

If management determines after the reporting period (but before the financial statements are authorised for issue) either that it intends to liquidate the entity or to cease trading, or that it has no realistic alternative but to do so, the financial statements should not be prepared on the going concern basis. *[IAS 10.14]*.

Deterioration in operating results and financial position after the reporting period may indicate a need to consider whether the going concern assumption is still appropriate. If the going concern assumption is no longer appropriate, the standard states that the effect is so pervasive that it results in a fundamental change in the basis of accounting, rather than an adjustment to the amounts recognised within the original basis of accounting. *[IAS 10.15]*. As discussed in Chapter 3 at 4.1.2, IFRS contains no guidance on this 'fundamental change in the basis of accounting'. Accordingly, entities will need to consider carefully their individual circumstances to arrive at an appropriate basis.

The standard also contains a reminder of the specific disclosure requirements under IAS 1:

(a) when the financial statements are not prepared on a going concern basis, that fact should be disclosed, together with the basis on which the financial statements have been prepared and the reason why the entity is not regarded as a going concern; or

(b) when management is aware of material uncertainties related to events or conditions that may cast significant doubt upon the entity's ability to continue as a going concern, disclosure of those uncertainties should be made. *[IAS 10.16, IAS 1.25]*.

While IFRSs are generally written from the perspective that an entity is a going concern, they are also applicable when another basis of accounting is used to prepare financial statements. Various IFRSs acknowledge that financial statements may be prepared on either a going concern basis or an alternative basis of accounting. *[IAS 1.25, IAS 10.14, Framework 4.1]*. Such IFRSs do not specifically exclude the application of IFRS when an alternative basis of accounting is used. As a result, financial statements prepared on a 'non-going concern' basis of accounting may be described as complying with IFRS as long as that other basis of preparation is sufficiently described in accordance with paragraph 25 of IAS 1.

When an entity prepares financial statements on a basis other than a going concern basis, certain deviations from specific sections or paragraphs of IFRSs may be appropriate. Significant judgement may be involved in determining the appropriate degree of deviation from IFRSs based on the facts and circumstances that is acceptable whilst still meeting the requirement to 'present fairly' the financial statements using the stated basis of preparation. Adequate disclosure as required under (a) above, including disclosure of individual accounting policies used, is important in such circumstances to allow users of financial statements to understand how the financial statements have been prepared. *[IAS 1.117(b)]*. Further considerations on disclosures relating to accounting policies are discussed in Chapter 3 at 5.1.

In some circumstances, an entity preparing IFRS financial statements may use US GAAP as an analogy (specifically ASU 2013-07 – *Liquidation Basis of Accounting*, codified in ASC 205-30). However, we believe that using this analogy to ASC 205 and describing the resulting liquidation basis financial statements as IFRS compliant would be appropriate only when liquidation is imminent and the likelihood is remote that the entity will return from liquidation.

Regarding the requirement in (b) above, the events or conditions requiring disclosure may arise after the reporting period. *[IAS 10.16(b)]*.

2.3 The treatment of non-adjusting events

IAS 10 prohibits the adjustment of amounts recognised in financial statements to reflect non-adjusting events. *[IAS 10.10]*. It indicates that if non-adjusting events are material, non-disclosure could influence the economic decisions of users of the financial statements. Accordingly, an entity should disclose the following for each material category of non-adjusting event: *[IAS 10.21]*

(a) the nature of the event; and

(b) an estimate of its financial effect, or a statement that such an estimate cannot be made.

To illustrate how these requirements have been applied in practice, examples of disclosures for certain types of non-adjusting events are given below.

Possibly the non-adjusting events that appear most regularly in financial statements are the acquisition/disposal of a non-current asset, such as an investment in a subsidiary or a business, subsequent to the end of the reporting period. Extract 36.3 contains an example of the disclosures required for 2.1.3(a) above related to a business combination:

Extract 36.3: AstraZeneca PLC (2015)

Notes to the Group Financial Statements [extract]

30. Subsequent events

On 2 February 2016, AstraZeneca completed an agreement to invest in a majority equity stake in Acerta Pharma B.V. (Acerta), a privately owned biopharmaceutical company based in the Netherlands and US. The transaction provides AstraZeneca with a potential best-in-class irreversible oral Bruton's tyrosine kinase (BTK) inhibitor, acalabrutinib (ACP-196), currently in Phase III development for B-cell blood cancers and in Phase I/II clinical trials in multiple solid tumours.

Under the terms of the agreement, AstraZeneca has acquired 55% of the issued share capital of Acerta for an upfront payment of $2.5bn. A further payment of $1.5bn will be paid either on receipt of the first regulatory approval for acalabrutinib for any indication in the US, or the end of 2018, depending on which is first. The agreement also includes options which, if exercised, provide the opportunity for Acerta shareholders to sell, and AstraZeneca to buy, the remaining 45% of shares in Acerta. The options can be exercised at various points in time, conditional on the first approval of acalabrutinib in both the US and Europe and when the extent of the commercial opportunity has been fully established, at a price of approximately $3bn net of certain costs and payments incurred by AstraZeneca and net of agreed future adjusting items, using a pre-agreed pricing mechanism. Acerta has approximately 150 employees.

AstraZeneca's 55% holding is a controlling interest and Acerta's combination of intangible product rights with an established workforce and their operating processes requires that the transaction is accounted for as a business combination in accordance with IFRS 3. Acerta's results and net assets will be consolidated into the Company's results from 2 February 2016.

Given the close proximity of the completion of the transaction to the date the Financial Statements were approved, the accounting entries for this transaction have not yet been determined. Our provisional assessment of the fair values of the assets and liabilities acquired will be completed in 2016.

Extract 36.4 contains examples of the disclosures required for abnormally large changes after the reporting period in foreign exchange rates as described at 2.1.3(g) above:

> *Extract 36.4: UBS AG (2014)*
>
> **Financial information** [extract]
> **Notes to the UBS AG consolidated financial statements** [extract]
> **Additional information** [extract]
> **37. Events after the reporting period**
>
> On 15 January 2015, the Swiss National Bank (SNB) discontinued the minimum targeted exchange rate for the Swiss franc versus the euro, which had been in place since September 2011. At the same time, the SNB lowered the interest rate on deposit account balances at the SNB that exceed a given exemption threshold by 50 basis points to negative 0.75%. It also moved the target range for three-month LIBOR to between negative 1.25% and negative 0.25%, (previously negative 0.75% to position 0.25%). These decisions resulted in a considerable strengthening of the Swiss franc against the euro, US dollar, British pound, Japanese yen and several other currencies, as well as a reduction in Swiss franc interest rates. As of 28 February 2015, the Swiss franc exchange rate was 0.95 to the US dollar, 1.07 to the euro, 1.47 to the British pound and 0.80 to 100 Japanese yen. Volatility levels in foreign currency exchange and interest rates also increased.
>
> A significant portion of the equity of UBS's foreign operations is denominated in US dollar, euros, British pounds and other foreign currencies. The appreciation of the Swiss franc would have led to an estimated decline in total equity of approximately CHF 1.2 billion or 2% when applying currency translation rates as of 28 February 2015 to the reported balances as of 31 December 2014. This includes a reduction in recognized deferred tax assets, mainly related to the US, of approximately CHF 0.4 billion (of which CHF 0.2 billion relates to temporary differences deferred tax assets) which would be recognized in *Other comprehensive income*.
>
> On a fully applied basis for Swiss systemically relevant banks (SRB), UBS AG would have experienced the following approximate declines in its capital balances when applying currency translation rates as of 28 February 2015 to the reported balances as of 31 December 2014: CHF 0.5 billion or 2% in fully applied common equity tier 1 (CET 1) capital and CHF 0.8 billion or 2% in fully applied total capital.
>
> In aggregate, UBS AG did not experience negative revenues in its trading businesses in connection with the SNB announcement. However, the portion of operating income denominated in non-Swiss franc currencies is greater than the portion of operating expenses denominated in non-Swiss franc currencies. Therefore, appreciation of the Swiss franc against other currencies generally has an adverse effect on earnings in the absence of any mitigating actions.
>
> In addition to the estimated effects from changes in foreign currency exchange rates, UBS AG's equity and capital are affected by changes in interest rates. In particular, the calculation of its net defined benefit assets and liabilities is sensitive to the assumptions applied. Specifically, the changes in applicable discount rate and interest rate related assumptions for its Swiss pension plan during January and February would have reduced equity and fully applied Swiss SRB CET 1 capital by around CHF 0.7 billion. Also, the persistently low interest rate environment would continue to have an adverse effect on replication portfolios, and net interest income would further decrease.
>
> Furthermore, the stronger Swiss franc may have a negative impact on the Swiss economy, which, given its reliance on exports, could impact some of the counterparties within UBS AG's domestic lending portfolio and lead to an increase in the level of credit loss expenses in future periods.

It is important to note that the list of examples of non-adjusting events in IAS 10, and summarised at 2.1.3 above, is not an exhaustive one; IAS 10 requires disclosure of any material non-adjusting event.

2.3.1 Declaration to distribute non-cash assets to owners

There are specific disclosure requirements when an entity declares a dividend to distribute a *non-cash asset* to owners after the end of a reporting period but before the financial statements are authorised for issue. IFRIC 17 requires an entity in such cases to disclose:

(a) the nature of the asset to be distributed;

(b) the carrying amount of the asset to be distributed as of the end of the reporting period; and

(c) the fair value of the asset to be distributed as of the end of the reporting period, if it is different from its carrying amount, and the following information about the method(s) used to measure that fair value: *[IFRIC 17.17]*

 (i) the level of the fair value hierarchy within which the fair value measurement is categorised (Level 1, 2 or 3); *[IFRS 13.93(b)]*

 (ii) for fair value measurement categorised within Level 2 and Level 3 of the fair value hierarchy, a description of the valuation technique(s) and the inputs used in the fair value measurement. If there has been a change in valuation technique (e.g. changing from a market approach to an income approach or the use of an additional valuation technique), the entity should disclose that change and the reason(s) for making it. For fair value measurement categorised within Level 3 of the fair value hierarchy, quantitative information about the significant unobservable inputs used in the fair value measurement should be provided. An entity is not required to create quantitative information to comply with this disclosure requirement if quantitative unobservable inputs are not developed by the entity when measuring fair value (e.g. when an entity uses prices from prior transactions or third-party pricing information without adjustment). However, when providing this disclosure the quantitative unobservable inputs that are significant to the fair value measurement and are reasonably available to the entity should not be ignored; *[IFRS 13.93(d)]*

 (iii) for fair value measurement categorised within Level 3 of the fair value hierarchy, a description of the valuation processes used by the entity (including, for example, how an entity decides its valuation policies and procedures and analyses changes in fair value measurements from period to period); *[IFRS 13.93(g)]* and

 (iv) if the highest and best use of the non-financial asset differs from its current use, an entity should disclose that fact and why the non-financial asset is being used in a manner that differs from its highest and best use. *[IFRS 13.93(i)]*.

In the case of (c) above, any quantitative disclosures are required to be presented in a tabular format, unless another format is more appropriate. *[IFRS 13.99]*. Fair value measurement is further discussed in Chapter 14.

2.3.2 *Breach of a long-term loan covenant and its subsequent rectification*

When an entity breaches a provision of a long-term loan arrangement on or before the end of the reporting period with the effect that the liability becomes payable on demand, it classifies the liability as current in its statement of financial position. *[IAS 1.74]*. This may also give rise to going concern uncertainties (see 2.2.2 above).

It is not uncommon that such covenant breaches are subsequently rectified; however, a subsequent rectification is not an adjusting event and therefore does not change the classification of the liability in the statement of financial position from current to non-current.

IAS 1 requires disclosure of the following remedial arrangements if such events occur between the end of the reporting period and the date the financial statements are authorised for issue:

- refinancing on a long-term basis;
- rectification of a breach of a long-term loan arrangement; and
- the granting by the lender of a period of grace to rectify a breach of a long-term loan arrangement ending at least twelve months after the reporting period (see Chapter 3 at 5.5). *[IAS 1.76]*.

2.4 Other disclosure requirements

The disclosures required in respect of non-adjusting events are discussed at 2.3 above. As IAS 10 only requires consideration to be given to events that occur up to the date when the financial statements are authorised for issue, it is important for users to know that date, since the financial statements do not reflect events after that date. *[IAS 10.18]*. Accordingly, it requires disclosure of the date the financial statements were authorised for issue. Furthermore, it requires disclosure of who authorised the financial statements for issue and, if the owners of the entity or others have the power to amend them after issue, disclosure of that fact is needed. *[IAS 10.17]*. In practice, this information can be presented in a number of ways:

(a) on the face of a primary statement (for example, entities that are required to have the statement of financial position signed could include the information at that point);

(b) in the note dealing with other IAS 10 disclosures or another note (such as the summary of significant accounting policies); or

(c) in a separate statement such as a statement of directors' responsibilities for the financial statements (that is, outside of the financial statements as permitted in certain jurisdictions).

Strictly speaking, this information is required to be presented within the financial statements. So, if (c) were chosen, either the whole report would need to be part of the financial statements or the information could be incorporated into them by way of a cross-reference.

The financial statements should also disclose new standards that are issued but are not yet effective for the entity (see Chapter 3 at 5.1.2.C). *[IAS 8.30]*.

3 PRACTICAL ISSUES

The standard alludes to practical issues such as those discussed below. It states that a decline in fair value of investments after the reporting period does not *normally* relate to conditions at the end of the reporting period and therefore would be a non-adjusting event (see 2.1.3 above). At the same time, the standard asserts that the bankruptcy of a customer that occurs after the reporting period would *usually* be an adjusting event (see 2.1.2(b)(i) above). Judgement of the facts and circumstances is required to determine whether an event that occurs after the reporting period provides evidence about a condition that existed at the end of the reporting period, or whether the condition arose subsequent to the reporting period.

In April 2015 the IFRS Transition Resource Group for Impairment of Financial Instruments (ITG) discussed whether, and if so, how to incorporate events and forecasts that occur between the reporting date and the date the financial statements are authorised for issue, when applying the impairment requirements of IFRS 9 – *Financial Instruments* – at the reporting date. The ITG noted that if new information becomes available between the reporting date and the date of signing the financial statements, an entity needs to apply judgement, based on the specific facts and circumstances, to determine whether it is an adjusting or non-adjusting event in accordance with IAS 10. This is further discussed in Chapter 50 at 5.4.8.C. The case of the insolvency of a debtor is discussed at 3.3 below.

3.1 Valuation of inventory

The sale of inventories after the reporting period is normally a good indicator of their net realisable value (NRV) at that date. IAS 10 states that such sales 'may give evidence about their net realisable value at the end of the reporting period'. *[IAS 10.9(b)(ii)]*. However, in some cases, NRV decreases because of conditions that did not exist at the end of the reporting period.

Therefore, the problem is determining why NRV decreased. Did it decrease because of circumstances that existed at the end of the reporting period, which subsequently became known, or did it decrease because of circumstances that arose subsequently? A decrease in price is merely a response to changing conditions so it is important to assess the reasons for these changes.

Some examples of changing conditions are as follows:

(a) Price reductions caused by a sudden increase in cheap imports

Whilst it is arguable that the 'dumping' of cheap imports after the reporting period is a condition that arises subsequent to that date, it is more likely that this is a reaction to a condition that already existed such as overproduction in other parts of the world. Thus, it might be more appropriate in such a situation to adjust the value of inventories based on its subsequent NRV.

(b) Price reductions caused by increased competition

The reasons for price reductions and increased competition do not generally arise overnight but normally occur over a period. For example, a competitor may have built up a competitive advantage by investing in machinery that is more efficient. In these circumstances, it is appropriate for an entity to adjust the valuation of its inventories because its own investment in production machinery is inferior to its competitor's and this situation existed at the end of the reporting period.

(c) Price reductions caused by the introduction of an improved competitive product

It is unlikely that a competitor developed and introduced an improved product overnight. Therefore, it is correct to adjust the valuation of inventories to their NRV after that introduction because the entity's failure to maintain its competitive position in relation to product improvements existed at the end of the reporting period.

Competitive pressures that caused a decrease in NRV after the reporting period are generally additional evidence of conditions that developed over a period and existed at the end of the reporting period. Consequently, their effects normally require adjustment in the financial statements.

However, for certain types of inventory, there is clear evidence of a price at the end of the reporting period and it is inappropriate to adjust the price of that inventory to reflect a subsequent decline. An example is inventories for which there is a price on an appropriate commodities market. In addition, inventory may be physically damaged or destroyed after the reporting period (e.g. by fire, flood, or other disaster). In these cases, the entity does not adjust the financial statements. However, the entity may be required to disclose the subsequent decline in NRV of the inventories if the impact is material (see 2.3 above).

3.2 Percentage of completion estimates

Events after the reporting period frequently give evidence about the profitability of construction contracts (or other contracts for which revenue is recognised using percentage of completion) that are in progress at the end of the reporting period.

IAS 11 – *Construction Contracts* – requires an assessment to be made of the outcome of a contract, as of the end of the reporting period, to recognise revenue and expenses under the percentage of completion method (see Chapter 23 at 3). *[IAS 11.22]*. In such an assessment, consideration should be given to events that occur after the reporting period and a determination should be made as to whether they are adjusting or non-adjusting events for which the financial effect is included in the percentage of completion calculation.

3.3 Insolvency of a debtor

The insolvency of a debtor or inability to pay debts usually builds up over a period. Consequently, if a debtor has an amount outstanding at the end of the reporting period and this amount is written off because of information received after the reporting period, the event is normally adjusting. IAS 10 states that the bankruptcy of a customer that occurs after the reporting period usually confirms that a loss existed at the end of the reporting period. *[IAS 10.9(b)(i)]*. If, however, there is evidence to show that the insolvency of the debtor resulted solely from an event occurring after the reporting period, then the event is a non-adjusting event. However, if the impact is material, the entity may be required to disclose the impact of the debtor's default (see 2.3 above).

3.4 Valuation of investment property at fair value and tenant insolvency

The fair value of investment property reflects, among other things, the quality of tenants' covenants and the future rental income from the property. If a tenant ceases to be able to meet its lease obligations due to insolvency after the reporting period, an entity considers how this event is reflected in the valuation at the end of the reporting period.

IAS 40 – *Investment Property* – requires the fair value of investment property, when measured in accordance with IFRS 13 – *Fair Value Measurement*, to reflect, among other things, rental income from current leases and other assumptions that market participants would use when pricing investment property under current market conditions. *[IAS 40.40]*. In addition, professional valuations generally reference the state of the market at the date of valuation without the use of hindsight. Consequently, the insolvency of a tenant is not *normally* an adjusting event to the fair value of the investment property because the investment property still holds value in the market. However, it would generally be indicative of an adjusting event for any rent receivable from that tenant.

This conclusion is consistent with the treatment of investment property measured using the alternative cost model. IAS 10 states that a decline in fair value of investments after the reporting period and before the date the financial statements are authorised for issue is a non-adjusting event, as the decline does not *normally* relate to a condition at the end of the reporting period (see 2.1.3 above). This decline in fair value, however, may be required to be disclosed if material (see 2.3 above).

3.5 Discovery of fraud after the reporting period

When fraud is discovered after the reporting date the implications on the financial statements should be considered. In particular, it should be determined whether the fraud is indicative of a prior period error, and that financial information should be restated, or merely a change in estimate requiring prospective adjustment. Application of the IAS 8 – *Accounting Policies, Changes in Accounting Estimates and Errors* – definitions of a 'prior period error' and a 'change in accounting estimate' (see Chapter 3) in the case of a fraud is judgemental. The facts and circumstances are evaluated to determine if the discovery of the fraud resulted from a previous failure to use, or misuse of, reliable information; or from new information. If the fraud meets the definition of a prior period error, the fraud would be an adjusting event as it relates to conditions that existed at the end of the reporting period. However, if the fraud meets the definition of a change in estimate, the application of IAS 10 is required to determine whether financial information is required to be adjusted, or whether disclosure is sufficient. The facts and circumstances are evaluated to determine if the discovery of the fraud provides evidence of circumstances that existed at the end of the reporting period or circumstances that arose after that date. Determining this is a complex task and requires judgement and careful consideration of the specifics to each case.

References

1 *IFRIC Update*, November 2012.
2 *IFRIC Update*, January 2013.
3 *IFRIC Update*, January 2013.
4 *IFRIC Update*, May 2013.
5 IFRS 9 – *Financial Instruments* issued in July 2014 amended the wording of paragraph 9(b)(i) of IAS 10. The amended paragraph states that 'the bankruptcy of a customer that occurs after the reporting period usually confirms that the customer was credit-impaired at the end of the reporting period'. Entities should apply the amendment when they apply IFRS 9 but no later than for periods beginning on or after 1 January 2018.

Chapter 37 Related party disclosures

List of examples

Chapter 37 Related party disclosures

1 INTRODUCTION

Related party relationships and transactions between related parties are a normal feature of commerce and business. Many entities carry on their business activities through subsidiaries, joint ventures, and associates and there are inevitably transactions between these parties. The entity has the ability to affect the financial and operating policies of the investee. *[IAS 24.5]*. It is also common for entities under common control, which are not a group for financial reporting purposes, to transact with each other. These are matters addressed by IAS 24 – *Related Party Disclosures.*

1.1 The related party issue

The problems posed by related party relationships and transactions are described in IAS 24 as follows:

> 'A related party relationship could have an effect on the profit or loss and financial position of an entity. Related parties may enter into transactions that unrelated parties would not. For example, an entity that sells goods to its parent at cost might not sell on those terms to another customer. In addition, transactions between related parties may not be made at the same amounts as between unrelated parties.
>
> The profit or loss and financial position of an entity may be affected by a related party relationship even if related party transactions do not occur. The mere existence of the relationship may be sufficient to affect the transactions of the entity with other parties. For example, a subsidiary may terminate relations with a trading partner on acquisition by the parent of a fellow subsidiary engaged in the same activity as the former trading partner. Alternatively, one party may refrain from acting because of the significant influence of another – for example, a subsidiary may be instructed by its parent not to engage in research and development.' *[IAS 24.6-7]*.

1.2 Possible solutions

1.2.1 Remeasurement of related party transactions at fair values

One solution to the problems posed by related party relationships and transactions is to adjust the financial statements to value related party transactions as if they occurred with an independent third party and recognise any such transactions at an arm's length price. However, the consensus for over thirty years is that it is often impossible to establish what would have been the terms of any non-arm's length transaction had it been negotiated on an arm's length basis. This is because no comparable transactions may have taken place and, in any event, the transaction might never have taken place at all if it had been negotiated using different values.

1.2.2 Disclosure of transactions

Because of this problem, accounting standards internationally require disclosure of related party transactions and relationships, rather than adjustment of the financial statements. This approach is adopted by the IASB in IAS 24 which is a disclosure standard. IAS 24 does not establish any recognition or measurement requirements. Related party transactions are accounted for in accordance with the requirements of the IFRS applicable to the transaction. The disclosures required by IAS 24 are in addition to those required by other IFRSs. For example, a loan to a related party will also be subject to the disclosure requirements of IFRS 7 – *Financial Instruments: Disclosures.*

The purpose of presenting the disclosures required by IAS 24 is to give users of the financial statements information about transactions, outstanding balances, including commitments, and relationships with related parties that may affect their assessment of an entity's operations, including assessments of the risks and opportunities facing an entity. *[IAS 24.8].*

2 REQUIREMENTS OF IAS 24

2.1 Objective and scope

2.1.1 Objective

IAS 24 states that its objective 'is to ensure that an entity's financial statements contain the disclosures necessary to draw attention to the possibility that its financial position and profit or loss may have been affected by the existence of related parties and by transactions and outstanding balances, including commitments, with such parties'. *[IAS 24.1].*

Accordingly, IAS 24 requires disclosure of related party transactions and outstanding balances, including commitments, together with the names of any parties who control the reporting entity.

2.1.2 *Scope*

IAS 24 applies in:

(a) identifying related party relationships and transactions;

(b) identifying outstanding balances, including commitments, between an entity and its related parties;

(c) identifying the circumstances in which disclosure of the items in (a) and (b) is required; and

(d) determining the disclosures to be made about those items. *[IAS 24.2]*.

The standard explicitly requires disclosure of related party relationships, transactions and outstanding balances, including commitments, in both the consolidated and separate financial statements of a parent or investors with joint control of, or significant influence over, an investee presented in accordance with IFRS 10 – *Consolidated Financial Statements* – or IAS 27 – *Separate Financial Statements*. *[IAS 24.3]*.

All entities within a group that prepare their financial statements under IFRS must disclose related party transactions and outstanding balances with other entities in the group in the entity's own financial statements. *[IAS 24.4]*. There are no disclosure exemptions for subsidiaries, or for parent companies that produce separate financial statements even where those separate financial statements are issued with the consolidated financial statements of the group of which they are a part. The IASB considers that the financial statements of an entity that is part of a consolidated group may include the effects of extensive intragroup transactions. Therefore, it concluded that the disclosures required by IAS 24 are essential to understanding the financial position and financial performance of such an entity and should be required for separate financial statements presented in accordance with IAS 27. The IASB also believes that disclosure of intragroup transactions is essential because external users of the financial statements need to be aware of the interrelationships between related parties, including the level of support provided by related parties, to assist in their economic decisions. *[IAS 24.BC16-17]*.

The standard notes that 'intragroup related party transactions and outstanding balances are eliminated in the preparation of consolidated financial statements of the group'. *[IAS 24.4]*. This implies that disclosure of such transactions and balances is not required in the group's consolidated financial statements since, so far as those financial statements are concerned, such items do not exist. However, transactions and balances between an investment entity and those of its subsidiaries, held as part of an investment portfolio that are measured at fair value through profit or loss and not consolidated in accordance with IFRS 10 should be disclosed in the consolidated financial statements. *[IAS 24.4]*.

2.2 Identification of a related party and related party transactions

A related party is defined as 'a person or entity that is related to the entity that is preparing its financial statements (the "reporting entity")'. *[IAS 24.9]*.

The standard contains a multi-part definition of 'related party' and the following are considered to be related parties of the reporting entity:

- certain persons or a close member of that person's family (see 2.2.1 below);
- entities that are members of the same group (see 2.2.2 below);
- entities that are associates or joint ventures (see 2.2.3 below);
- entities that are joint ventures of the same third party (see 2.2.4 below);
- entities that are joint ventures and associates of the same third entity (see 2.2.5 below);
- post-employment benefit plans (see 2.2.6 below);
- entities under control or joint control of certain categories of persons or close members of such a person's family (see 2.2.7 below);
- entities under significant influence of certain categories of persons or close members of such a person's family (see 2.2.8 below);
- entities, or any member of the group of which they are a part, that provide key management personnel services (see 2.2.9 below); and
- government-related entities (see 2.2.10 below).

The standard emphasises that attention should be directed to the substance of the relationship and not merely the legal form. *[IAS 24.10].*

A related party transaction is a transfer of resources, services or obligations between a reporting entity and a related party, regardless of whether a price is charged. *[IAS 24.9].*

2.2.1 *Persons or close members of a person's family that are related parties*

A person or close member of that person's family is related to a reporting entity if that person:

(i) has control or joint control over the reporting entity;

(ii) has significant influence over the reporting entity; or

(iii) is a member of the key management personnel of the reporting entity or of a parent of the reporting entity. *[IAS 24.9].*

Close members of a family of a person are defined as 'those family members who may be expected to influence, or be influenced by, that person in their dealings with the entity' and include:

(a) that person's children and spouse or domestic partner;

(b) children of that person's spouse or domestic partner; and

(c) dependants of that person or that person's spouse or domestic partner. *[IAS 24.9].*

The Interpretations Committee confirmed in May 2015 – see below – that the definition appears to provide no scope to argue that there are circumstances in which the specific family members described in (a) to (c) above are not related parties. Dependants are not limited to children and may include other relatives depending on the facts and circumstances.

In May 2015, the Interpretations Committee discussed a request to clarify whether the definition of close members of a person's family should include a person's parents.

Local regulations in some jurisdictions include the parents of a person within the definition of 'close members of the family of a person'. The Interpretations Committee observed that the definition of close members of the family of a person:

- is expressed in a principle-based manner and involves the use of judgement to determine whether members of the family of a person (including that person's parents) are related parties or not; and
- includes a list of family members that are always considered close members of the family of a person.

The Interpretations Committee further noted that the list of family members that are always considered 'close members' is non-exhaustive and does not preclude other family members from being considered as close members of the family of a person. Consequently, other family members, including parents or grandparents, could qualify as close members of the family depending on the assessment of specific facts and circumstances. Therefore, the Interpretations Committee determined that neither an Interpretation nor an amendment to the Standard was necessary and therefore decided not to add this issue to its agenda.[1]

IAS 24 does not elaborate on the meaning of 'may be expected to influence, or be influenced by, that person'. A narrow interpretation is that the standard explicitly mentions only those instances where such influence is expected without doubt. Thus, a relationship with, for example, siblings or relatives that are even more distant would need to be assessed to determine whether there is evidence of sufficient influence. A broader interpretation would support the fact that the mere existence of the family relationship is sufficient to trigger the disclosure requirements included in IAS 24.

Relationships involving a person or close family members as investors are illustrated in the following examples, which are based on illustrative examples published by the IASB, which accompany, but are not part of IAS 24.

Example 37.1: Person as investor

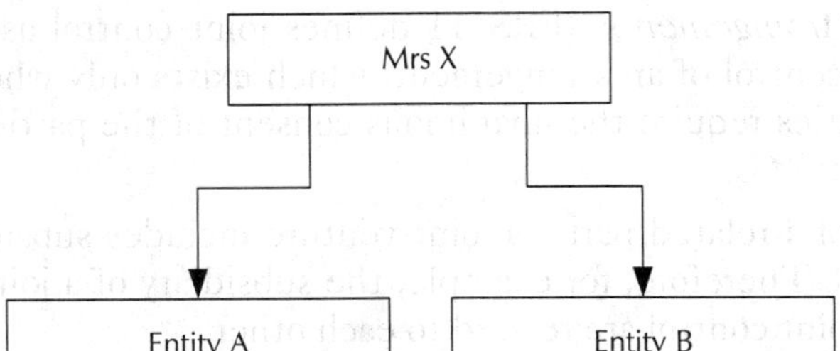

Mrs X has an investment in Entity A and Entity B.

For Entity A's financial statements, if Mrs X controls or jointly controls Entity A, Entity B is related to Entity A when Mrs X has control, joint control or significant influence over Entity B.

For Entity B's financial statements, if Mrs X controls or jointly controls Entity A, Entity A is related to Entity B when Mrs X has control, joint control or significant influence over Entity B. If Mrs X has significant influence over both Entity A and Entity B, Entities A and B are not related to each other.

If Mrs X is a member of the key management personnel of both Entity A and Entity B, Entities A and B are not, in the absence of any other indicator of a related party relationship, related to each other (see 2.3 below).

Example 37.2: Close members of the family holding investments

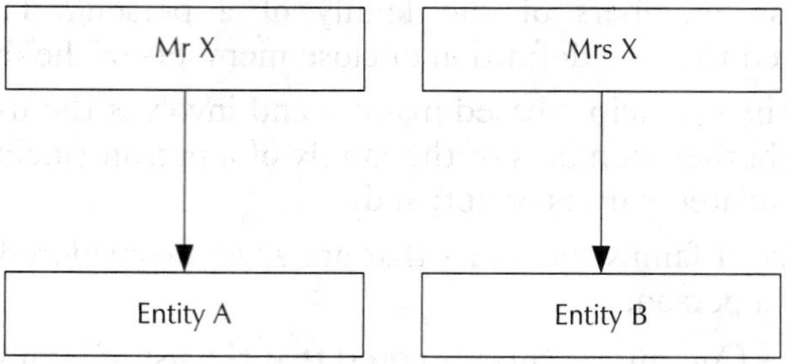

Mr X is the spouse of Mrs X. Mr X has an investment in Entity A and Mrs X has an investment in Entity B.

For Entity A's financial statements, if Mr X controls or jointly controls Entity A, Entity B is related to Entity A when Mrs X has control, joint control or significant influence over Entity B.

For Entity B's financial statements, if Mr X controls or jointly controls Entity A, Entity A is related to Entity B when Mrs X has control, joint control or significant influence over Entity B.

If Mr X has significant influence (but not control or joint control) over Entity A and Mrs X has significant influence (but not control or joint control) over Entity B, Entities A and B are not related to each other (see 2.3 below).

If Mr X is a member of the key management personnel of Entity A and Mrs X is a member of the key management personnel of Entity B, Entities A and B are not related to each other (see 2.3 below).

2.2.1.A Control

The definition of 'control' in IAS 24 is a cross-reference to the definition in IFRS 10. IFRS 10 states that 'an investor controls an investee when the investor is exposed, or has rights, to variable returns from its involvement with the investee and has the ability to affect those returns through its power over the investee'. *[IFRS 10 Appendix A]*.

2.2.1.B Joint control

The definition of 'joint control' in IAS 24 is a cross-reference to the definition in IFRS 11 – *Joint Arrangements*. IFRS 11 defines joint control as 'the contractually agreed sharing of control of an arrangement, which exists only when decisions about the relevant activities require the unanimous consent of the parties sharing control'. *[IFRS 11 Appendix A]*.

In the definition of a related party, a joint venture includes subsidiaries of the joint venture. *[IAS 24.12]*. Therefore, for example, the subsidiary of a joint venture and the investor who has joint control are related to each other.

2.2.1.C Significant influence

The definition of 'significant influence' in IAS 24 is a cross-reference to the definition in IAS 28 – *Investments in Associates and Joint Ventures*. IAS 28 defines significant influence as 'the power to participate in the financial and operating policy decisions of the investee but is not control or joint control of those policies'. *[IAS 28.3]*.

In the definition of a related party, an associate includes subsidiaries of the associate. Therefore, for example, the subsidiary of an associate and the investor who has significant influence over the associate are related to each other. *[IAS 24.12]*.

2.2.1.D *Key management personnel*

'Key management personnel' are those persons with authority and responsibility for planning, directing and controlling the activities of an entity, directly or indirectly, including any director (whether executive or otherwise) of that entity. *[IAS 24.9]*.

A related party includes all key management personnel of a reporting entity and of a parent of the reporting entity. This means that all key management personnel of all parents (i.e. the immediate parent, any intermediate parent and the ultimate parent) of a reporting entity are related parties of the reporting entity.

Some entities may have more than one level of key management. For example, some entities may have a supervisory board, whose members have responsibilities similar to those of non-executive directors, as well as a board of directors that sets the overall operating strategy. All members of either board will be considered to be key management personnel.

The definition of key management personnel is not restricted to directors. It also includes other individuals with authority and responsibility for planning, directing and controlling the activities of an entity. The main intention of the definition is presumably to ensure that transactions with persons with responsibilities similar to those of directors, and the compensation paid to such persons, do not escape disclosure simply because they are not directors. Otherwise, there would be an obvious loophole in the standard. For example, in some jurisdictions, a chief financial officer or a chief operating officer may not be directors but could meet the definition of key management personnel. Other examples of the type of persons who are not directors but may meet the definition of key management personnel include a divisional chief executive or a director of a major trading subsidiary of the entity, but not of the entity itself, who nevertheless participates in the management of the reporting entity. A reference to individuals who are not directors in a reporting entity's business review or management discussion and analysis might indicate that those persons are considered to be key management personnel. One might argue that, if the individual was truly part of the 'key management' of the group, he or she would be on the parent entity's board. However, this view is inconsistent with the view of the IASB that 'key management' may be found outside the boardroom.

'Key management personnel' are normally employees of the reporting entity (or of another entity in the same group). However, the definition does not restrict itself to employees. Therefore, seconded staff and persons engaged under management or outsourcing contracts may also have a level of authority or responsibility such that they are 'key management personnel'.

The definition of key management personnel refers to 'persons'. In some jurisdictions, the term 'person' includes both a 'corporate person' and a 'natural person'. Additionally, in some jurisdictions, a corporate entity must by law have the authority and responsibility for planning, directing and controlling the activities of an investment fund for the benefit of the fund's investors in accordance with the fund's constitution and relevant statutes (i.e. the corporate entity is the body acting as key management personnel). IAS 24 clarifies that if a reporting entity receives key management personnel services from another entity (described as a 'management entity') the disclosure requirements for key management personnel compensation (see 2.2.9 below) do not apply to the compensation paid or payable by the management entity to the management entity's employees or directors. *[IAS 24.17A]*. Instead, overall amounts incurred by the reporting entity for provision of key management personnel services by the separate management entity are disclosed. *[IAS 24.18A]*.

2.2.2 *Entities that are members of the same group*

'An entity is related to a reporting entity if:

(i) The entity and the reporting entity are members of the same group (which means that each parent, subsidiary and fellow subsidiary is related to the others).' *[IAS 24.9(b)]*.

IAS 24 does not define group, parent and subsidiary. However, these terms are defined in IFRS 10 as follows:

- a group is 'a parent and its subsidiaries';
- a parent is 'an entity that controls one or more entities'; and
- a subsidiary as 'an entity that is controlled by another entity'. *[IFRS 10 Appendix A]*.

Therefore, all entities controlled by the same ultimate parent are related parties. This would include entities where the reporting entity holds less than a majority of the voting rights but which are subsidiaries as defined in IFRS 10. There are no exceptions to this rule.

Example 37.3: Entities that are members of the same group

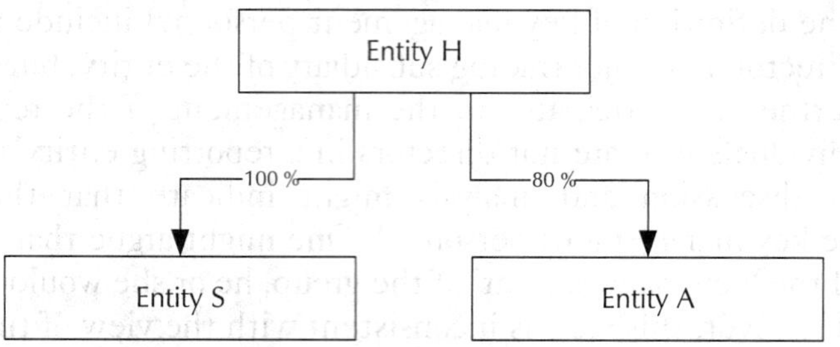

Entities H, S and A are all related parties to each other as they are members of the same group. Both Entity S and Entity A are subsidiaries of Entity H.

Related party disclosures will be required in the financial statements of Entity S in respect of transactions with Entities H and A, in the financial statements of Entity A in respect of transactions with Entities H and S and in the separate financial statements of Entity H in respect of transactions with Entities S and A.

2.2.3 *Entities that are associates or joint ventures*

'An entity is related to a reporting entity if:

...

(ii) One entity is an associate or joint venture of the other entity (or an associate or joint venture of a member of a group of which the other entity is a member).' *[IAS 24.9(b)]*.

IAS 24 does not define associate or joint venture. However, these terms are defined in IAS 28 and IFRS 11.

IAS 28 defines an associate as 'an entity over which the investor has significant influence'. *[IAS 28.2]*.

IFRS 11 defines a joint venture as 'a joint arrangement whereby the parties that have joint control of the arrangement have rights to the net assets of the arrangement'. *[IFRS 11 Appendix A]*.

Any entity that a reporting entity determines is an associate under IAS 28 or a joint venture under IFRS 11 is a related party. This requirement further applies to investments in associates or joint ventures held by a venture capital organisation, mutual fund, unit trust or similar entity, even where the investment is accounted for at fair value through profit or loss or held for trading under IAS 39 – *Financial Instruments: Recognition and Measurement* – rather than under the equity method. Likewise, any reporting entity that is an associate or joint venture of another entity must treat that investor entity as a related party.

As noted above, in the definition of a related party, an associate includes subsidiaries of the associate and a joint venture includes subsidiaries of the joint venture. Therefore, for example, an associate's subsidiary and the investor that has significant influence over the associate are related to one another. *[IAS 24.12]*.

The definition also means that an associate of a reporting entity's parent is also a related party of the reporting entity.

However, the definition does not cause investors in a joint venture or an associate to be related to each other (see 2.3 below). Investors in joint operations (as defined in IFRS 11) are also not related to each other.

The application of these requirements is illustrated in the example below, which is based on an illustrative example accompanying IAS 24.

Example 37.4: Associates of the reporting entity's group that are related parties

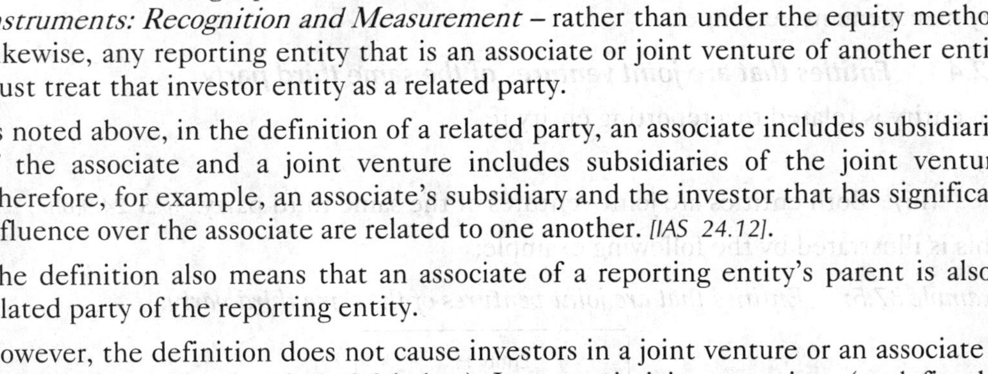

In Parent's separate financial statements, Associates 1, 2 and 3 are related parties. For Parent's consolidated financial statements, Associates 1, 2 and 3 are related to the group.

For Subsidiary A's financial statements, Associates 1, 2 and 3 are related parties. For Subsidiary B's consolidated or separate financial statements, Associates 1, 2 and 3 are related parties. For Subsidiary C's financial statements, Associates 1, 2 and 3 are related parties.

For the financial statements of Associates 1, 2 and 3, Parent and Subsidiaries A, B and C are related parties. Associates 1, 2 and 3 are not related to each other.

Chapter 37

2.2.3.A Joint operations

IAS 24 defines 'joint ventures' of the reporting entity as related parties. The definition of a joint venture in IFRS 11 excludes joint operations, so that an investment in a joint operation is not a related party.

A share in a joint operation can be seen as being part of the entity itself, since IFRS 11 refers to the recognition by a joint operator of its assets, revenue, liabilities and expenses. *[IFRS 11.20]*. Thus, a transaction with a joint operation is either a transaction by the reporting entity with itself or a transaction with the other joint operator which would not be a related party unless it otherwise met the related party definition in IAS 24 for some other reason (e.g. because it was an entity controlled by a member of key management personnel).

2.2.4 Entities that are joint ventures of the same third party

'An entity is related to a reporting entity if:

...

(iii) Both entities are joint ventures of the same third party.' *[IAS 24.9(b)]*.

This is illustrated by the following example:

Example 37.5: Entities that are joint ventures of the same third party

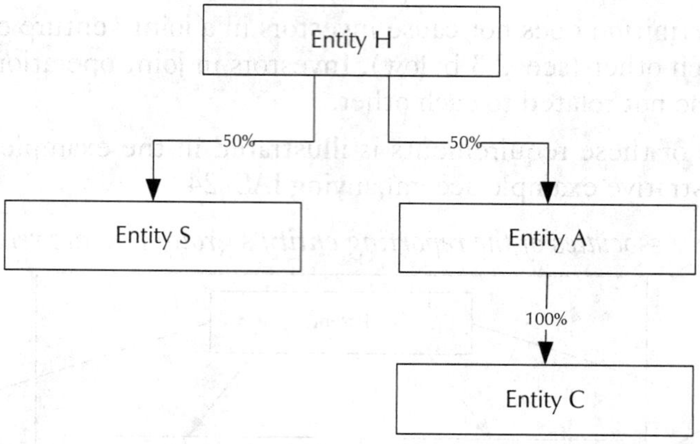

In this example, Entities S and A are joint ventures of Entity H and are therefore related parties. Entity C, as a subsidiary of Entity A, is also a related party of Entity H and Entity S.

If, however, Entities S and A were only associates (rather than joint ventures) of the same third party then they would not be related parties. In the Basis for Conclusions to IAS 24, it was explained that a distinction was made between joint ventures and associates because the IASB considered that 'significant influence' was not as close a relationship as control or joint control. *[IAS 24.BC19(a)]*.

As noted above, in the definition of a related party, a joint venture includes subsidiaries of the joint venture. Therefore, for example, a joint venture's subsidiary and the investor that has joint control over the joint venture are related to each other. *[IAS 24.12]*.

2.2.5 *Entities that are joint ventures and associates of the same third entity*

'An entity is related to a reporting entity if:

...

(iv) One entity is a joint venture of a third entity and the other entity is an associate of the third entity.' *[IAS 24.9(b)].*

This definition treats joint ventures in a similar manner to subsidiaries as illustrated in Examples 37.3 and 37.5 above and therefore an associate and a joint venture are related parties where they share the same investor. This is illustrated in the example below:

Example 37.6: Entities that are joint ventures and associates of the same third entity

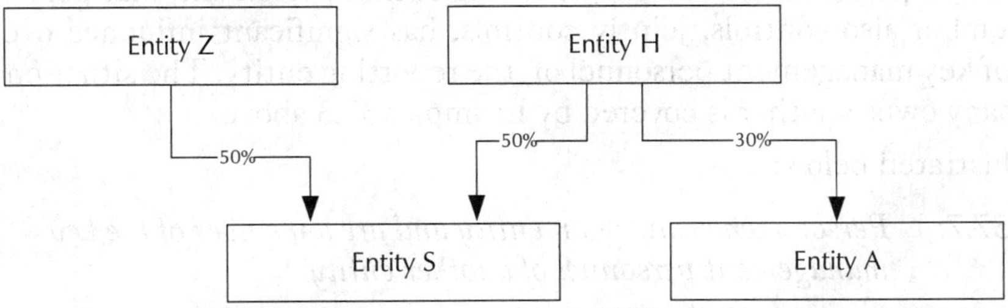

Entity S is a joint venture of Entity H and Entity A is an associate of Entity H. Therefore, Entities S and A are related parties.

However, Entities Z and H are not related parties (see 2.3 below).

2.2.6 *Post-employment benefit plans*

'An entity is related to a reporting entity if:

...

(v) The entity is a post-employment benefit plan for the benefit of employees of either the reporting entity or an entity related to the reporting entity. If the reporting entity is itself such a plan, the sponsoring employers are also related to the reporting entity.' *[IAS 24.9(b)].*

The standard does not indicate why a post-employment benefit plan is a related party of the entity. Presumably, the reason for including this category is that an entity sponsoring a post-employment benefit plan generally has at least significant influence over the plan.

The definition is quite wide-ranging and includes post-employment benefit plans of any entity related to the reporting entity. This includes, for example, post-employment benefit plans of an associate or joint venture of the reporting entity or a post-employment benefit plan of an associate of the reporting entity's parent.

Sponsoring employers are also related parties of a post-employment benefit plan.

2.2.7 Entities under control or joint control of certain persons or close members of their family

'An entity is related to a reporting entity if:

...

(vi) The entity is controlled or jointly controlled by a person or close member of that person's family who has control or joint control over the reporting entity, has significant influence over the reporting entity or is a member of key management personnel of the reporting entity.' *[IAS 24.9]*.

This is intended to cover situations in which an entity is controlled or jointly controlled by a person or close family member of that person and that person or close family member also controls, jointly controls, has significant influence over, or is a member of key management personnel of, the reporting entity. The situation whereby one company owns another is covered by Example 37.3 above.

This is illustrated below:

Example 37.7: Persons who control an entity and are a member of the key management personnel of another entity

Mrs X has a 100% investment in Entity A and is a member of the key management personnel of Entity S. Entity M has a 100% investment in Entity S.

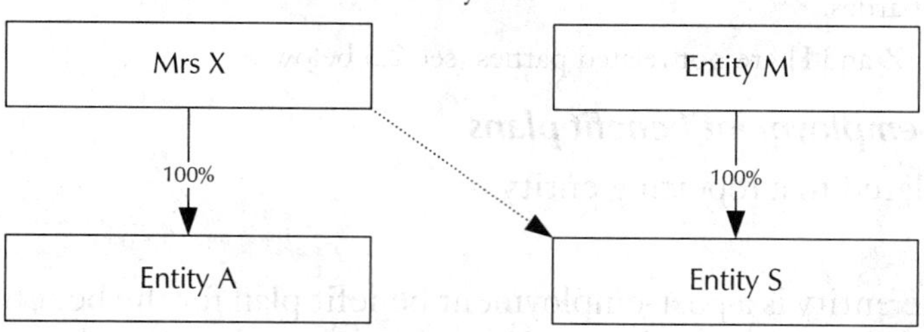

For Entity S's financial statements, Entity A is related to Entity S because Mrs X controls Entity A and is a member of the key management personnel of Entity S.

For Entity S's financial statements, Entity A is also related to Entity S if Mrs X is a member of the key management personnel of Entity M and not of Entity S.

This outcome would be the same if Mrs X has joint control over Entity A (if Mrs X only had significant influence over Entity A and not control or joint control then Entities A and S would not be related parties).

For Entity A's financial statements, Entity S is related to Entity A because Mrs X controls Entity A and is a member of Entity S's key management personnel. This outcome would be the same if Mrs X has joint control over Entity A and would further be the same if Mrs X is a member of the key management personnel of Entity M rather than Entity S (see 2.2.8 below). Note that Entity A and Entity M would also be related parties in this instance.

For Entity M's consolidated financial statements, Entity A is a related party of the Group if Mrs X is a member of the key management personnel of the Group.

2.2.8 *Entities under significant influence of certain persons or close members of their family*

'An entity is related to a reporting entity if:

...

(vii) A person or a close family member of that person who has control or joint control over the reporting entity has significant influence over the entity or is a member of the key management personnel of the entity (or of a parent of the entity).' *[IAS 24.9(b)].*

This is the reciprocal of 2.2.7 and is illustrated in Example 37.7 above.

Entities that are significantly influenced by the same person or close member of that person's family or who simply share the same key management personnel are not related parties in the absence of any control or joint control by those persons (see 2.3 below).

2.2.9 *Entities, or any member of the group of which they are a part, that provide key management personnel services*

'An entity is related to a reporting entity if:

...

(viii) The entity, or any member of a group of which it is a part, provides key management personnel services to the reporting entity or to the parent of the reporting entity.' *[IAS 24.9(b)].*

This is intended to cover situations in which an entity (described as a 'management entity'), or a member of its group, provides key management personnel services to the reporting entity (see 2.6 and 2.8 below). It applies to the provision of key management personnel services by the separate management entity. Staff acting for the management entity that are responsible for planning, directing and controlling the activities of the reporting entity are not considered to be key management personnel of the reporting entity. It is not necessary to look through the management entity to determine natural persons as key management personnel.

Example 37.8: Entities that provide key management personnel services to a reporting entity

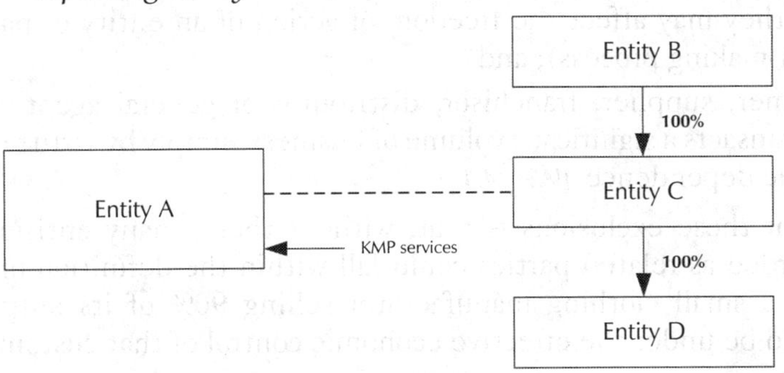

Entity C provides key management personnel services to Entity A. For Entity A's financial statements, Entities B, C and D are all related parties. However, Entity A is not a related party of Entities B, C and D (i.e. the related party relationship between the management entity and the reporting entity is not symmetrical).

2.2.10 Government-related entities

A 'government-related entity' is an entity that is controlled, jointly controlled or significantly influenced by a government. *[IAS 24.9]*.

'Government' in this context refers to government, government agencies and similar bodies whether local, national or international. *[IAS 24.9]*. This is the same as the definition used in IAS 20 – *Accounting for Government Grants and Disclosure of Government Assistance*. The Board decided that it would not provide a more comprehensive definition or additional guidance on how to determine what is meant by 'government'. In the Board's view, a more detailed definition could not capture every conceivable government structure across every jurisdiction. In addition, judgement is required by a reporting entity when applying the definition because every jurisdiction has its own way of organising government-related activities. *[IAS 24.BC41]*. This implies that there may well be diversity in practice across different jurisdictions in defining what is meant by 'government'.

Where an entity is controlled, jointly controlled or significantly influenced by a government then relationships, transactions and outstanding balances, including commitments, with that government are related party transactions. Similarly, transactions and outstanding balances, including commitments, with other entities controlled, jointly controlled or significantly influenced by that government are related party transactions.

Related party transactions with government-related entities are subject to certain disclosure exemptions. These are discussed at 2.9 below.

2.3 Parties that are not related parties

Having included such a detailed definition of related parties, the standard clarifies that the following are not related parties:

- two entities simply because they have a director or other member of key management personnel in common or because a member of key management personnel of one entity has significant influence over the other entity;
- two venturers simply because they share joint control over a joint venture;
- providers of finance, trade unions, public utilities and departments and agencies of, a government that do not control, jointly control or significantly influence the reporting entity, simply by virtue of their normal dealings with the entity (even though they may affect the freedom of action of an entity or participate in its decision-making process); and
- a customer, supplier, franchisor, distributor or general agent with whom an entity transacts a significant volume of business, simply by virtue of the resulting economic dependence. *[IAS 24.11]*.

The reason for these exclusions is that, without them, many entities that are not normally regarded as related parties could fall within the definition of related party. For example, a small clothing manufacturer selling 90% of its output to a single customer could be under the effective economic control of that customer.

These exclusions are effective only where these parties are 'related' to the reporting entity simply because of the relationship noted above. If there are other reasons why a party is a related party, the exclusions do not apply. Consider the following examples:

- A water company that supplies the reporting entity is not a related party if the only link between the two is the supply of water. If, however, the water company is also an associate of the reporting entity, the exclusion does not apply; the two are related parties, and the transactions relating to the supply of water are disclosed if material.
- Two investors in the same entity are not related parties simply because one holds a controlling interest and the other shareholder (not in the group) holds a non-controlling interest in a subsidiary of the group. Even if the investor holding the non-controlling interest exercises significant influence over the subsidiary, provided it is not otherwise related to the controlling investor, it is not normally a related party of the controlling investor. However, the non-controlling investor might have significant influence over the group if the subsidiary was significant to the group in which case the group, including the controlling investor and the non-controlling investor are related parties.
- Two entities are not related parties simply because they share common key management personnel. However, if the common member of key management personnel exerts control or joint control over one or more of the entities then they are related parties. See 2.2.7 or 2.2.8 above.
- An administrator, custodian, broker and fund manager of the same fund are not related parties, to each other or to the fund to which they provide services simply because they each provide services to the fund, even if any of the parties are economically dependent upon the income from such services. However, any such party could meet the definition of 'key management personnel' of the fund if it provides key management personnel services (see 2.2.9 above). In addition, any shared ownership (e.g. control, joint control, or significant influence) between such parties should be evaluated to determine if the parties are related.

An interest in an unconsolidated structured entity as defined by IFRS 12 – *Disclosure of Interests in Other Entities* – held by a reporting entity does not make the structured entity a related party to the reporting entity unless it would otherwise meet the definition of a related party (e.g. because the structured entity is an associate of the reporting entity).

2.4 Disclosure of controlling relationships

IAS 24 asserts that, in order to enable users of financial statements to form a view about the effects of related party relationships on an entity, it is appropriate to disclose the related party relationship when control exists, irrespective of whether there have been transactions between the related parties. *[IAS 24.14]*. Accordingly, the standard requires an entity to disclose:

- the name of its parent and, if different;
- the ultimate controlling party.

If neither the entity's parent nor the ultimate controlling party produces consolidated financial statements available for public use, the name of the next most senior parent that does so must also be disclosed. *[IAS 24.13]*.

The 'next most senior parent' is the first parent in the group above the immediate parent that produces consolidated financial statements available for public use. *[IAS 24.16]*. Consequently, in some circumstances, an entity may need to disclose the names of three parents.

The use of the word 'party' means that the disclosure applies to both individuals and to entities. Disclosure must be made even if the parent or ultimate controlling party does not prepare financial statements. In the situation when the ultimate controlling party is an individual, rather than an entity, the reporting entity is likely to have to disclose the name of the next most senior parent in addition since the individual undoubtedly does not produce financial statements for public use. IAS 1 – *Presentation of Financial Statements* – also requires disclosure of the 'ultimate parent' of the group. *[IAS 1.138(c)]*. This is not necessarily synonymous with the 'ultimate controlling party' where that party is an individual. This is illustrated in the example below.

Example 37.9: Disclosure of parent, ultimate parent and ultimate controlling party

Entity S is controlled by Entity P which in turn is controlled by Entity H which in turn is controlled by Entity Y. The ultimate controlling party of Entity Y is Mr A. Entities P and Y do not produce consolidated financial statements available for public use.

The group structure is illustrated as follows:

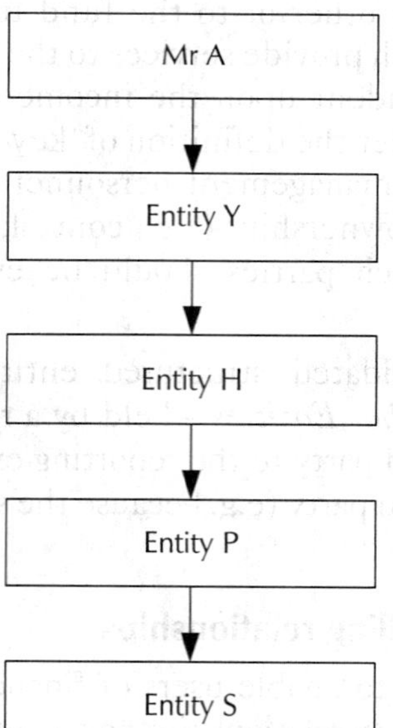

For Entity S's financial statements, IAS 24 requires disclosure of Entity P (the parent), Entity H (the next most senior parent that produces consolidated financial statements available for public use) and Mr A (the ultimate controlling party). In addition, IAS 1 requires disclosure of Entity Y (the ultimate parent of the group).

For Entity P's financial statements, IAS 24 requires disclosure of Entity H (the parent) and Mr A (the ultimate controlling party). In addition, IAS 1 requires disclosure of Entity Y (the ultimate parent of the group).

For Entity H's financial statements, IAS 24 requires disclosure of Entity Y (the parent) and Mr A (the ultimate controlling party). IAS 1 does not require any additional disclosure.

For Entity Y, IAS 24 requires disclosure of Mr A (ultimate controlling party). IAS 1 does not require any additional disclosure.

The ultimate controlling party could be a group of individuals or entities acting together. IAS 24 is silent on the issue of individuals or entities acting together to exercise joint control. However, IFRS 3 – *Business Combinations* – states that a group of individuals can be regarded as a controlling party when, as a result of contractual arrangements, they collectively have the power to govern that entity's financial and operating policies so as to obtain benefits from its activities. *[IFRS 3.B2]*. In such circumstances, these entities or individuals should be identified as the controlling party. Where there is no such contractual arrangement, IFRS is silent on whether a group of individuals acting in an informal way could be considered to be the ultimate controlling party of an entity. However, as discussed at 2.2 above, IAS 24 emphasises that attention should be directed to the substance of any related party relationship and not merely the legal form. It is likely that such an informal arrangement would at least give such individuals acting collectively significant influence over the reporting entity and as such, those individuals would be related parties to the reporting entity under IAS 24.

The standard also clarifies that the requirement to disclose related party relationships between a parent and its subsidiaries is in addition to the disclosure requirements of IAS 27 and IFRS 12. *[IAS 24.15]*. IFRS 12 requires an entity to disclose information to enable users to understand the composition of a group – see Chapter 13 at 4.1.

2.5 Disclosable transactions

A related party transaction is defined as 'a transfer of resources, services or obligations between a reporting entity and a related party, regardless of whether a price is charged.' *[IAS 24.9]*. Read literally, this definition requires many transactions to be disclosed more than once. For example, if an entity buys goods on credit from a related party and pays for them 30 days later, both the original purchase and the final payment represent a 'transfer of resources ... between a reporting entity and a related party' and, therefore on a literal reading, are required to be separately disclosed. However, we doubt that this reading is the IASB's intention, and the nature of the disclosures required by IAS 24 seems to support this view. This definition also appears to exclude those commitments which do not transfer resources.

The definition of a related party transaction implies that transactions are disclosable only for the period in which parties are related. For example, where a reporting entity has disposed of a subsidiary during the reporting period, only transactions with the subsidiary up to the date of disposal are related party transactions in the financial statements of the reporting entity. Similarly, if a person became a member of key management personnel of a reporting entity during a reporting period, no disclosure is required of any remuneration paid to that person before that person's appointment as key management personnel.

There is no requirement in IAS 24 to disclose information about related party transactions in one comprehensive note. However, it may be more useful to users of the financial statements to present information this way.

IAS 1 requires that, except where a standard permits otherwise (which IAS 24 does not), comparative information in respect of the previous period must be disclosed for all amounts reported in the current period's financial statements. *[IAS 1.38]*.

2.5.1 Materiality

In determining whether an entity discloses related party transactions in financial statements, the general concept of materiality is applied. IAS 24 does not refer specifically to materiality since this requirement is in IAS 1, which states that 'an entity need not provide a specific disclosure required by an IFRS if the information is not material.' *[IAS 1.31]*. Omissions or misstatements of items are material within IAS 1 'if they could, individually or collectively, influence the economic decisions that users make on the basis of the financial statements. Materiality depends on the size and nature of the omission or misstatement judged in the surrounding circumstances. The size or nature of the item, or a combination of both, could be the determining factor.' *[IAS 1.7]*.

This may have the effect that any related party transaction whose disclosure is considered sensitive (for tax reasons perhaps) is by definition material because it is expected by the reporting entity to influence a user of the financial statements. Therefore, it may not be possible to avoid disclosing such items on the grounds that they are quantitatively immaterial. In addition, a transaction conducted at advantageous terms to either the related party or the reporting entity is more likely to be material than one conducted at arm's length. Since IAS 24 requires disclosure of related party transactions irrespective of whether consideration is received, disclosure cannot be avoided on the argument that, since there is no consideration, the transaction must be immaterial.

2.6 Disclosure of key management personnel compensation

IAS 24 requires disclosure of key management personnel compensation.

There is no requirement in IAS 24 to disclose individual key management personnel compensation. Instead, the standard requires an entity to disclose key management personnel compensation in total and for each of the following categories:

- short-term employee benefits;
- post-employment benefits;
- other long-term benefits;
- termination benefits; and
- share-based payment. *[IAS 24.17]*.

In certain jurisdictions, some of the key management personnel compensation disclosures are similar to the disclosures required by local law or other regulations and it might therefore be possible to give some of the disclosures by means of a cross-reference to other parts of the Annual Report, such as a directors' remuneration report. However, care should be taken that all of the IAS 24 requirements have been addressed. If the remuneration report does not give the information required by IAS 24 because, for example, it requires disclosure of the number of shares granted rather than the share-based payment compensation, additional disclosures must be made to comply with IAS 24.

IAS 24 (see 2.2.9 above) clarifies that where an entity obtains key management personnel services from another entity ('management entity') it is not required to apply the requirements above to the compensation paid or payable by the management entity to the management entity's employees or directors. *[IAS 24.17A]*.

2.6.1 Compensation

'Compensation' includes all employee benefits (as defined in IAS 19 – *Employee Benefits*) including employee benefits to which IFRS 2 – *Share-based Payment* – applies. Employee benefits are all forms of consideration given by an entity, or on behalf of the entity, in exchange for services rendered to the entity. Employee benefits also include such consideration paid on behalf of the entity in respect of the entity. *[IAS 24.9]*. Therefore, the compensation disclosed by an entity in its financial statements is that which is for services to that entity, irrespective of whether it is paid by the reporting entity or by another entity or individual on behalf of the reporting entity.

Under IAS 24, compensation includes:

(a) short-term employee benefits, such as wages, salaries and social security contributions, paid annual leave and paid sick leave, profit-sharing and bonuses (if payable within twelve months of the end of the period) and non-monetary benefits (such as medical care, housing, cars and free or subsidised goods or services) for current employees;

(b) post-employment benefits such as pensions, other retirement benefits, post-employment life insurance and post-employment medical care;

(c) other long-term employee benefits, including long-service leave or sabbatical leave, jubilee or other long-service benefits, long-term disability benefits and, if they are not payable wholly within twelve months after the end of the reporting period, profit-sharing, bonuses and deferred compensation;

(d) termination benefits; and

(e) share-based payment. *[IAS 24.9]*.

It is unclear from the standard the basis on which the amount for each of the categories above is determined. There are alternative views that the disclosure is the amount:

- paid or payable by the entity (or on its behalf);
- recognised as an expense under the relevant standard by the entity (or on its behalf);
- attributed to the benefit for tax purposes;
- due under contract by the entity (or due on its behalf); or
- determined on some other basis.

In the Basis for Conclusions accompanying the standard, the IASB noted that the guidance on compensation in IAS 19 is sufficient to enable an entity to disclose the relevant information, which suggests that the IASB is expecting the amounts to be based on the expense recognised under the relevant standards. *[IAS 24.BC10]*. It is helpful to remember that the definition of compensation states that 'employee benefits are all forms of consideration paid, payable or provided by the entity, or on behalf of the entity in exchange for services rendered...'. *[IAS 24.9]*.

Issues relating to each of the categories are discussed below.

For an illustrative example of the disclosure of key management personnel compensation, see Extract 37.1 at 2.6.9 below.

2.6.2 Short-term employee benefits

As indicated at 2.6.1 above, these include wages, salaries and social security contributions, paid annual leave and paid sick leave, profit-sharing and bonuses (if expected to be settled wholly before twelve months after the end of the reporting period). Most of these should not cause difficulty, since the expense for such items under IAS 19 is generally equivalent to the amount payable for the period. However, there are instances when adjustments are necessary. For example, if the total expense under IAS 19 for a profit-sharing plan includes a deduction for anticipated staff turnover, this deduction may need to be adjusted in determining the amount disclosed for key management personnel. That is, the turnover rate for staff as a whole is likely different from the turnover rate for key management personnel, and the deduction should be adjusted accordingly for disclosure purposes.

Non-monetary benefits (such as medical care, housing, cars and free or subsidised goods or services) must also be included within the amount disclosed for short-term employee benefits. *[IAS 24.9]*. In some cases, these might have been provided at no direct cost to the entity. In such circumstances it would appear reasonable to either attribute a value for non-monetary benefits (for example, the attributable tax benefit), so as to describe them quantitatively, or to describe such benefits qualitatively.

2.6.3 Post-employment benefits

As indicated at 2.6.1 above, these include pensions, other retirement benefits, post-employment life insurance and post-employment medical care. The inclusion of this category suggests that amounts are disclosed while members of key management are providing services. If amounts were only disclosed when the benefits are payable, then in many cases there would be no disclosure since the individuals would no longer be members of key management.

For defined contribution plans, it seems appropriate that the amount included is based on the total expense recognised under IAS 19, which is the equivalent of the contributions payable to the plan for service rendered in the period.

The main issue related to defined benefit plans is to determine an appropriate calculation for the disclosable amount for the period. IAS 24 is silent on how the disclosable amount should be determined. Normally, for defined benefit plans, the expense recognised under IAS 19 differs from the contributions payable to the plan. Disclosing the contributions payable usually does not reflect the benefits provided by the entity in exchange for the services rendered, particularly when the entity is benefitting from a contribution holiday. One approach to determine the disclosable amount would be to include an amount based on the total IAS 19 expense recognised in total comprehensive income. The total amounts recognised under IAS 19 for defined benefit plans includes items such as interest, actuarial remeasurement gains and losses and the effects of curtailments and settlements. This approach requires an apportionment of the total expense to the extent that it relates to the individuals concerned. Another approach would be to determine the disclosable amount based only on the current service cost and, when applicable, past service cost related to those individuals on the grounds that the other items relate more to the overall plan than to the individuals. An entity should adopt a consistent accounting policy for determining the amounts disclosed.

2.6.4 *Other long-term benefits*

As indicated at 2.6.1 above, these include long-service leave or sabbatical leave, jubilee or other long-service benefits, long-term disability benefits and, if they are not expected to be settled wholly before twelve months after the end of the reporting period, profit sharing, bonuses and deferred compensation. Since the accounting for such items under IAS 19 is on a similar basis to that for post-employment benefits similar issues to those discussed at 2.6.3 above are applicable.

2.6.5 *Termination benefits*

These should not cause difficulty, since an entity generally recognises such items, particularly for key management personnel, in line with the recognition criteria included in IAS 19.

2.6.6 *Share-based payment transactions*

This category includes share options, share awards or cash-settled awards granted in return for service by the members of key management. Such compensation is accounted for under IFRS 2. For equity-settled share based payment transactions, such as share options or share awards, IFRS 2 broadly requires measurement of their fair value at grant date, and that expense is recognised over the period that employees render services. For cash-settled share-based payment transactions, IFRS 2 requires measurement and recognition based on the cash ultimately paid.

IAS 24 does not specify a basis on which the compensation disclosed should be determined. One basis would be to disclose an amount based on the expense under IFRS 2. Another basis would be to disclose amounts based on the fair value that the individual received (based on the value of the shares at date of vesting, or at date of exercise of share options or the cash that is ultimately payable) rather than over the period of the service. An entity should adopt a consistent accounting policy for determining the amounts disclosed.

2.6.7 *Reporting entity part of a group*

One additional practical difficulty for an entity in a group is that the disclosure of its key management personnel compensation is for the services rendered to the reporting entity. Accordingly, where key management personnel of the reporting entity also provide services to other entities within the group, an apportionment of the compensation is necessary. Likewise, where the reporting entity receives services from key management personnel that are also key management personnel of other entities within the group, the reporting entity may have to impute the compensation received. Such apportionments and allocations required judgement and an assessment of the time commitment involved.

2.6.8 *Key management personnel compensated by other entities*

A reporting entity also applies the principles set out in 2.6.7 above to situations in which the other entity is a third party, outside of the group, but is a related party.

2.6.9 Illustrative disclosure of key management personnel compensation

An example of the disclosure of key management personnel compensation can be found in the financial statements of BP p.l.c.

Extract 37.1: BP p.l.c. (2015)

Notes on financial statements [extract]

33. Remuneration of senior management and non-executive directors [extract]

Remuneration of directors and senior management

			$ million
	2015	2014	2013
Total for senior management and non-executive directors			
Short-term employee benefits	**33**	34	36
Pensions and other post-retirement benefits	**4**	3	3
Share-based payments	**36**	34	43
Total	**73**	71	82

Senior management comprises members of the executive team, see pages 60-61 for further information.

Short-term employee benefits

These amounts comprise fees and benefits paid to the non-executive chairman and non-executive directors, as well as salary, benefits and cash bonuses for senior management. Deferred annual bonus awards, to be settled in shares, are included in share-based payments. There was no compensation for loss of office included in Short-term employee benefits in 2015 (2014 $1.5 million and 2013 $3 million).

Pensions and other post-retirement benefits

The amounts represent the estimated cost to the group of providing pensions and other post-retirement benefits to senior management in respect of the current year of service measured in accordance with IAS 19 'Employee Benefits'.

Share-based payments

This is the cost to the group of senior management's participation in share-based payment plans, as measured by the fair value of options and shares granted, accounted for in accordance with IFRS 2 'Share-based Payments'.

2.7 Disclosure of other related party transactions, including commitments

IAS 24 requires an entity that has had related party transactions during the periods covered by its financial statements to disclose the nature of the related party relationship as well as information about those transactions and outstanding balances, including commitments, necessary for users to understand the potential effect of the relationship on the financial statements. *[IAS 24.18]*.

2.7.1 Related party transactions requiring disclosure

IAS 24 gives the following as examples of transactions to be disclosed, if they are with a related party. The list is not intended to be exhaustive:

- purchases or sales of goods (finished or unfinished);
- purchases or sales of property and other assets;
- rendering or receiving of services;
- leases;
- transfers of research and development;
- transfers under licence agreements;

- transfers under finance arrangements (including loans and equity contributions in cash or in kind);
- provisions of guarantees or collateral;
- commitments to do something if a particular event occurs or does not occur in the future, including executory contracts (recognised and unrecognised); and
- settlement of liabilities on behalf of the entity or by the entity on behalf of that related party. *[IAS 24.21]*.

The standard does not contain any exemptions based on the nature of the transaction. Consequently, related party transactions include transactions such as dividend payments and the issue of shares under rights issues to major shareholders or key management personnel (i.e. those that fall within the definition of related parties), even where they participate on the same basis as other shareholders. However, for dividend payments, a preparer might conclude that no additional disclosures are necessary beyond those required by IAS 1, to explain the potential effect of the relationship on the financial statements. *[IAS 1.137]*.

The standard also includes transactions with those individuals identified as related parties where their dealings with the entity are in a private capacity, rather than in a business capacity.

Participation by a parent or subsidiary in a defined benefit plan that shares risks between group entities is a transaction between related parties (see Chapter 33 at 3.3.2). *[IAS 24.22]*.

As indicated at 2.5 above, disclosure is required irrespective of whether or not consideration is received, which means that the standard applies to gifts of assets or services and to asset swaps. Common examples of such transactions which may occur within a group include:

- administration by an entity of another entity within a group (or of its post-employment benefit plan) free of charge;
- transfer of tax assets from one member of a group to another without payment;
- rent-free accommodation or the loan of assets at no charge; or
- guarantees by directors of bank loans to the entity.

2.7.1.A Aggregation of items of a similar nature

Presumably in order to minimise the volume of disclosures, IAS 24 permits aggregation of items of a similar nature, except when separate disclosure is necessary for an understanding of the effects of the related party transactions on the financial statements of the entity. *[IAS 24.24]*. The standard does not expand on this requirement, but it seems appropriate that, for example, purchases or sales of goods with other subsidiaries within a group can be aggregated, but any purchases or sales of property, plant, and equipment or of intangible assets with such entities are shown as a separate category. However, the level of aggregation is limited by the separate disclosure of transactions with particular categories of related parties (see 2.7.2 below).

2.7.1.B Commitments

'Commitments' are not defined in IFRS. However, IAS 39 (IFRS 9 – *Financial Instruments*) describes a firm commitment as 'a binding agreement for the exchange of a specified quantity of resources at a specified price on a specified future date or dates'. *[IAS 39.9, IFRS 9 Appendix A]*. IFRS 12 states that the commitments relating to joint ventures are those that may give rise to a future outflow of cash or other resources. *[IFRS 12.B18]*.

IAS 24 specifically mentions executory contracts (recognised and unrecognised) as commitments requiring disclosure. Executory contracts are excluded from the scope of IAS 37 – *Provisions, Contingent Liabilities and Contingent Assets* – unless they are onerous to the reporting entity. An executory contract is a contract under which neither party has performed any of its obligations or both parties have partially performed their obligations to an equal extent. *[IAS 37.3]*. An example of an executory contract would be a contract to buy an asset at a future date where neither the transfer of the asset nor the payment of consideration has occurred.

The words 'commitments to do something if a particular event occurs or does not occur in the future' can potentially have a wide application. One obvious type of arrangement to which this applies would be some form of commitment by a subsidiary to its parent to undertake certain trading or research and development activities.

With respect to the type of transaction that the IASB is expecting to be disclosed, IFRS 12 provides a list of illustrative but not exhaustive examples of the type of unrecognised commitments that could relate to joint ventures. Some of these examples could apply equally to other related party arrangements. IFRS 12 clarifies that the commitments required to be disclosed under IAS 24 in respect of joint ventures include an entity's share of commitments made jointly with other investors with joint control of a joint venture. *[IFRS 12.B18]*.

IFRS 12 provides the following illustrations of commitments relating to joint ventures that would typically be disclosable under paragraph 18 of IAS 24 and could apply equally to other related party arrangements:

- unrecognised commitments to contribute funding or resources as a result of, for example:
  - the constitution or acquisition agreements of a joint venture (that, for example, require an entity to contribute funds over a specific period);
  - capital intensive projects undertaken by a joint venture;
  - unconditional purchase obligations, comprising procurement of equipment, inventory or services that an entity is committed to purchasing from, or on behalf of, a joint venture;
  - unrecognised commitments to provide loans or other financial support to a joint venture;
  - unrecognised commitments to contribute resources to a joint venture, such as assets or services; and

- other non-cancellable unrecognised commitments relating to a joint venture.
- unrecognised commitments to acquire another party's ownership interest (or a portion of that ownership interest) in a joint venture if a particular event occurs or does not occur in the future. *[IFRS 12.B19-20].*

Provisions of guarantees, which are a form of commitment, require separate disclosure. Disclosure of commitments to purchase property, plant and equipment and intangible assets in aggregate is required separately by IAS 16 – *Property, Plant and Equipment* – and IAS 38 – *Intangible Assets* – respectively. *[IAS 16.74(c), IAS 38.122(e)].*

2.7.2 Disclosures required for related party transactions, including commitments

The standard states that, at a minimum, the disclosures must include:

(a) the amount of the transactions;

(b) the amount of outstanding balances, including commitments, and:

  (i) their terms and conditions, including whether they are secured, and the nature of the consideration to be provided in settlement; and

  (ii) details of any guarantees given or received;

(c) provisions for doubtful debts related to the amount of outstanding balances; and

(d) the expense recognised during the period in respect of bad or doubtful debts due from related parties. *[IAS 24.18].*

The standard gives no exemption from disclosure on the grounds of sensitivity or confidentiality. However, since there is no requirement to disclose the name of a related party, this lack of exemption is likely to be less of a concern.

The requirement in (b) above could be read literally as requiring outstanding balances and commitments to be amalgamated into a single balance. However, commitments such as executory contracts do not give rise to outstanding balances. In practice, narrative disclosure of the terms and conditions of material commitments will be necessary.

There is no requirement to disclose individually significant transactions. However, as discussed at 2.9 below, there is such a requirement for transactions with government-related entities where a reporting entity has decided to apply the disclosure exemption. One IASB member dissented from the decision not to require all entities to provide information about each individually significant transaction for all related parties. *[IAS 24.DO1].*

The disclosures are made separately for each of the following categories:

(a) the parent;

(b) entities with joint control of, or significant influence over, the entity;

(c) subsidiaries;

(d) associates;

(e) joint ventures in which the entity is a joint venturer;

(f) key management personnel of the entity or its parent; and

(g) other related parties. *[IAS 24.19].*

In our view the references in (a) and (f) above to 'the parent' should be read as including all parents of the entity, i.e. its immediate parent, any intermediate parent, and the ultimate parent. In the context of the financial statements of an entity within a group, it is insufficient to disclose related party transactions for a single category of 'group companies'. Separate categories are required for parent(s), subsidiaries and 'other related parties'.

IAS 24 does not identify fellow subsidiaries as a separate category of related party, and they are therefore included within the category 'other related parties'. However, a preparer might wish to consider separate disclosure of transactions with fellow subsidiaries if this would provide useful information to users of the subsidiary's financial statements.

The classification of amounts payable to, and receivable from, related parties in the different categories is an extension of the disclosure requirement in IAS 1 for an entity to present information either in the statement of financial position or in the notes. *[IAS 1.78(b)]*. The categories are extended to provide a more comprehensive analysis of related party balances and apply to related party transactions. *[IAS 24.20]*.

Outstanding balances with key management personnel would include unpaid bonuses or liabilities under cash-settled share-based payment transactions.

IAS 24 discourages an entity from disclosing that transactions are on normal commercial terms or on an arm's length basis, by stating that such disclosures 'are made only if such terms can be substantiated.' *[IAS 24.23]*. This wording implies a rebuttable presumption that related party transactions are not on an arm's length basis unless the reporting entity can demonstrate otherwise. To substantiate that related party transactions are on an arm's length basis an entity would need to be satisfied that a transaction with similar terms and conditions could be obtained from an independent third party.

The company financial statements of J Sainsbury plc provide the following disclosures of related party relationships with subsidiaries and joint ventures.

Extract 37.2: J Sainsbury plc (2016)

Notes to the financial statements [extract]

37 Related party transactions [extract]

Company [extract]

a) Subsidiaries

The Company enters into loans with its subsidiaries at both fixed and floating rates of interest on a commercial basis. Hence, the Company incurs interest expense and earns interest income on these loans and advances. The Company also received dividend income from its subsidiaries during the financial year. The amounts outstanding are unsecured and settled in cash.

Transactions with subsidiaries

	2016 £m	2015 £m
Repayment of floating rate subordinated dated/undated loan capital from Sainsbury's Bank[1]	**–**	60
Investment in Sainsbury's Bank	**(137)**	(59)
Loans and advances given to, and dividend income received from subsidiaries		
Loans and advances given	**17**	229
Loans and advances repaid by subsidiaries	**(122)**	(45)
Interest income received in respect of interest bearing loans and advances	**222**	201
Dividend income received	**5,556**	252
Loans and advances received from subsidiaries		
Loans and advances received	**(299)**	(275)
Loans and advances repaid	**49**	21
Loan settlement in the year attributable to liquidations	**4,306**	–
Interest expense paid in respect of interest bearing loans and advances	**(47)**	(56)

[1] The £60 million dated subordinated loan capital was repaid in December 2014.

Year-end balances arising from transactions with subsidiaries

	2016 £m	2015 £m
Receivables		
Loans and advances due from subsidiaries	**2,720**	2,758
Payables		
Loans and advances due to subsidiaries	**(817)**	(5,201)

b) Joint ventures and associates

Transactions with joint ventures and associates
For the 52 weeks to 12 March 2016, the Company entered into transactions with joint ventures and associates as set out below.

	2016 £m	2015 £m
Investment in joint ventures	**(15)**	(12)

Year-end balances arising from transactions with joint ventures and associates

	2016 £m	2015 £m
Payables		
Loans due to joint ventures	**(5)**	(5)

Chapter 37

The financial statements of British Sky Broadcasting Group plc illustrate the disclosure of transactions with a party controlled by a close family member of key management.

Extract 37.3: British Sky Broadcasting Group plc (2014)

Notes to the consolidated financial statements [extract]

28. Transactions with related parties and major shareholders [extract]

c) Other transactions with related parties [extract]

A close family member of one Director of the Company runs Freud Communications Limited ("Freud"), which has provided external support to the press and publicity activities of the Group. During the year the Group incurred expenditure amounting to £1 million (2013: £1 million) with Freud. At 30 June 2014 there was £1 million (2013: less than £1 million) due to Freud.

The financial statements of BP p.l.c. illustrate the disclosure of commitments to related parties:

Extract 37.4: BP p.l.c. (2015)

Notes on financial statements [extract]

12 Capital commitments

Authorized future capital expenditure for property, plant and equipment by group companies for which contracts had been signed at 31 December 2015 amounted to $10,379 million (2014 $14,590 million – amended from $15,635 million previously disclosed). BP's share of capital commitments of joint ventures amounted to $586 million (2014 $369 million).

16 Investments in associates [extract]

BP has commitments amounting to $11,446 million (2014 $6,946 million), primarily in relation to contracts with its associates for the purchase of transportation capacity.

2.8 Disclosure of expense incurred with management entity

As discussed at 2.2.9 above disclosure of amounts incurred by the entity for the provision of key management personnel services by a separate management entity is required. *[IAS 24.18A]*.

2.9 Disclosures with government-related entities

IAS 24 provides an exemption from the disclosure requirements of paragraph 18, discussed at 2.7.2 above, in relation to related party transactions and outstanding balances, including commitments, with:

(a) a government that has control or joint control of, or significant influence over, the reporting entity; and

(b) another entity that is a related party because the same government has control or joint control of, or significant influence over, both the reporting entity and the other entity. *[IAS 24.25]*.

This wording implies that a reporting entity is related to an entity that is significantly influenced by a government that also has significant influence over the reporting entity. However, the definition of a related party does not include entities that are subject to significant influence from the same entity, but are not otherwise related parties as defined in IAS 24 (see 2.2.3 above).

The application of the disclosure exemption is illustrated in the example below, which is based on an illustrative example accompanying IAS 24.

Example 37.10: Application of the disclosure exemption for government-related entities

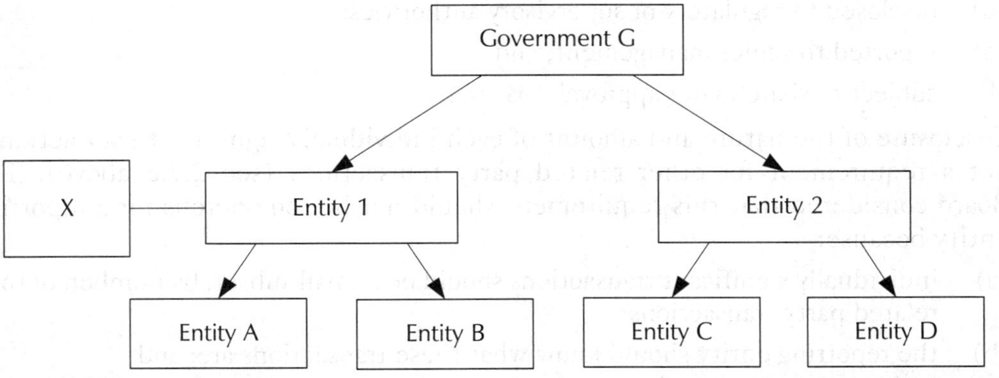

Government G directly or indirectly controls Entities 1 and 2 and Entities A, B, C and D. Person X is a member of the key management personnel of Entity 1.

For Entity A's financial statements the exemption applies to: (a) transactions with Government G which is the government that ultimately controls Entity A; and (b) transactions with Entities 1, 2, B, C and D which are related entities because they are controlled by the same government as A, i.e.: Government G.

The exemption does not apply to transactions with Person X because Person X is not controlled by Government G.

The use of the disclosure exemption is conditional on the reporting entity making the following disclosures about the transactions and related outstanding balances with the government-related entities:

(a) the name of the government and the nature of its relationship with the reporting entity (i.e. control, joint control or significant influence);

(b) the following information in sufficient detail to enable users of the entity's financial statements to understand the effect of related party transactions on its financial statements:

  (i) the nature and amount of each individually significant transaction; and

  (ii) for other transactions that are collectively, but not individually, significant, a qualitative or quantitative indication of their extent. Types of transactions include those discussed at 2.7.1 above. *[IAS 24.26]*.

The wording above does not explicitly mention 'commitments' when referring to transactions. However, given that IAS 24 describes a commitment as a form of transaction (see 2.7.1 above), disclosure of individually and collectively significant commitments with government-related entities is required.

In using its judgement to determine the level of detail to be disclosed in accordance with the requirements in (b) above, a reporting entity considers the closeness of the

Chapter 37

related party relationship and other factors relevant in establishing the level of significance of the transaction such as whether it is:

(a) significant in terms of size;

(b) carried out on non-market terms;

(c) outside normal day-to-day business operations, such as the purchase and sale of businesses;

(d) disclosed to regulatory or supervisory authorities;

(e) reported to senior management; and

(f) subject to shareholder approval. *[IAS 24.27]*.

Disclosure of the nature and amount of each individually significant transaction is not a requirement for other related party transactions (see 2.7.2 above). The Board considered that this requirement should not be too onerous for a reporting entity because:

(a) individually significant transactions should be a small subset, by number, of total related party transactions;

(b) the reporting entity should know what these transactions are; and

(c) reporting such items on an exceptional basis takes into account cost-benefit considerations. *[IAS 24.BC45]*.

The Board also considered that more disclosure of individually significant transactions would better meet the objective of IAS 24 because this approach focuses on transactions that, through their nature or size, are of more interest to users and are more likely to be affected by the related party relationship. *[IAS 24.BC46]*. In response to concerns about whether a reporting entity would be able to identify whether the counterparty to such transactions was a government-related entity, the Board concluded that 'management will know, or will apply more effort in establishing, who the counterparty to an individually significant transaction is and will have, or be able to obtain, background information on the counterparty'. *[IAS 24.BC47-48]*.

One Board member disagreed with the decision to give a disclosure exemption for government-related parties in IAS 24. That same member also disagreed with the decision not to require all entities to provide information about individually significant transactions with a related party. *[IAS 24.DO1]*.

Extract 37.5 below from the financial statements of The Royal Bank of Scotland Group plc illustrates disclosure summarising the types of transactions with government-controlled entities that are related parties and details of an individually material transaction.

Extract 37.5: The Royal Bank of Scotland Group plc (2015)

Notes on the consolidated accounts [extract]

39 Related parties [extract]

UK Government

On 1 December 2008, the UK Government through HM Treasury became the ultimate controlling party of The Royal Bank of Scotland Group plc. The UK Government's shareholding is managed by UK Financial Investments Limited, a company wholly owned by the UK Government. As a result, the UK Government and UK Government controlled bodies became related parties of the Group. During 2015, all of the B shares held by the UK Government were converted into ordinary shares of £1 each and the Dividend Access Share Retirement Agreement was agreed between RBS and HM Treasury (see Note 24 on page 325).

The Group enters into transactions with many of these bodies on an arm's length basis. Transactions include the payment of: taxes principally UK corporation tax (page 292) and value added tax;

national insurance contributions; local authority rates; and regulatory fees and levies (including the bank levy (page 282) and FSCS levies (page 334) together with banking transactions such as loans and deposits undertaken in the normal course of banker-customer relationships.

The following are other illustrations of the type of disclosures required for transactions with government-related entities based on examples in the standard:

Example 37.11: Individually significant transaction carried out on non-market terms

On 15 January 2017 the company sold a 10-hectare piece of land to an entity controlled by Government G for €5,000,000. On 31 December 2017 a plot of land in a similar location, of similar size and with similar characteristics, was sold for €3,000,000. There had not been any appreciation or depreciation of the land in the intervening period. See Note X for disclosure of government assistance as required by IAS 20.

Example 37.12: Individually significant transaction because of size of transaction

In the year ended 31 December 2017 Government G provided the company with a loan equivalent to 50% of its funding requirement, repayable in quarterly instalments over the next five years. Interest is charged on the loan at a rate of 5%, which is comparable to that charged on the company's external bank loans.

Example 37.13: Collectively significant transactions

The company's significant transactions with Government G and other entities controlled, jointly controlled or significantly influenced by Government G are a large portion of its sales of goods and purchases of raw materials [alternatively – about 50% of its sales of goods and services and about 35% of its purchases of raw materials].

The company also benefits from guarantees by Government G of the company's bank borrowing. See Note X of the financial statements for disclosure of government assistance as required by IAS 20.

In Example 37.13 above, either a qualitative or a quantitative disclosure is permitted for transactions that are collectively but not individually significant.

References

1 *IFRIC Update*, May 2015, IASB.

Chapter 37

Chapter 38 Statement of cash flows

List of examples

Chapter 38

Chapter 38 Statement of cash flows

1 INTRODUCTION

A statement of cash flows provides useful information about an entity's activities in generating cash to repay debt, distribute dividends, or reinvest to maintain or expand operating capacity; about its financing activities, both debt and equity; and about its investing or spending of cash. This information, when combined with information in the rest of the financial statements, is useful in assessing factors that may affect the entity's liquidity, financial flexibility, profitability, and risk.

IAS 7 – *Statement of Cash Flows* – specifies how entities report information about the historical changes in cash and cash equivalents and has a relatively flexible approach, which allows it to be applied by all entities regardless of their business activities, including financial institutions. This flexibility can be seen, for example, in the way entities can determine their own policy for the classification of interest and dividend cash flows, provided they are separately disclosed and this is applied consistently from period to period (see 4.4.1 below). It can also accommodate the need of entities to provide additional information specific to their circumstances and indeed encourages additional disclosures. In addition, IAS 7 is based on a relatively straightforward principle, that only transactions which require the use of cash or cash equivalents should be included in the statement of cash flows (see 5.4 below).

1.1 Terms used in IAS 7

The following terms are used in IAS 7 with the meanings specified: *[IAS 7.6]*

Cash comprises cash on hand and demand deposits.

Cash equivalents are short-term, highly liquid investments that are readily convertible to known amounts of cash and which are subject to an insignificant risk of changes in value.

Cash flows are inflows and outflows of cash and cash equivalents.

Operating activities are the principal revenue-producing activities of the entity and other activities that are not investing or financing activities.

Investing activities are the acquisition and disposal of long-term assets and other investments not included in cash equivalents.

Financing activities are activities that result in changes in the size and composition of the contributed equity and borrowings of the entity.

2 OBJECTIVE AND SCOPE OF IAS 7

2.1 Objective

The objective of IAS 7 is to require entities to provide information about historical changes in cash and cash equivalents in a statement which classifies cash flows during the period from operating, investing and financing activities. The standard aims to give users of financial statements a basis to evaluate the entity's ability to generate cash and cash equivalents and its needs to utilise those cash flows. *[IAS 7 Objective]*. The historical cash flow information is often used as an indicator of the amount, timing and certainty of future cash flows. It is also useful in examining the relationship between profitability and net cash flow and the impact of changing prices. *[IAS 7.5]*.

2.2 Scope

IAS 7 applies to all entities, regardless of size, operations, ownership structure or industry, and therefore includes wholly owned subsidiaries and banks, insurance entities and other financial institutions. There are no exemptions from the standard. Users of an entity's financial statements are interested in how the entity generates and uses cash and cash equivalents regardless of the nature of the entity's activities and irrespective of whether cash can be viewed as the product of the entity, as may be the case with a financial institution. All entities need cash to conduct their operations, to pay their obligations, and to provide returns to their investors. Accordingly, all entities are required to present a statement of cash flows. *[IAS 7.3]*. In particular, a statement of cash flows is required to make up a complete set of a parent entity's separate financial statements in accordance with IFRS, *[IAS 1.10]*, even if the separate financial statements are presented together with consolidated financial statements which include a statement of cash flows.

3 CASH AND CASH EQUIVALENTS

Since the objective of a statement of cash flows is to provide an analysis of changes in cash and cash equivalents, the definitions of cash and cash equivalents at 1.1 above are essential to its presentation. It is also important to understand the reporting entity's cash management policies, especially when considering whether balances that are not obviously cash on hand and demand deposits should be classified as cash equivalents, as the standard states that cash equivalents are held for the purpose of meeting short-term cash commitments rather than for investment or other purposes. *[IAS 7.7]*. Cash management includes the investment of cash in excess of immediate needs into cash equivalents, *[IAS 7.9]*, such as short-term investments. For short term investments to qualify as a cash equivalent, they must be:

- highly liquid;
- readily convertible into known amounts of cash; and
- subject to insignificant risk of changes in value. *[IAS 7.6]*.

Having determined that such highly liquid investments are equivalent to cash, a statement of cash flows under IAS 7 excludes movements between cash on hand and cash equivalents because these are components of an entity's cash management, rather than part of its operating, investing and financing activities. *[IAS 7.9]*. However, as shown below, the definition of cash equivalents can cause some difficulty in practice.

3.1 Policy for determining components of cash equivalents

Because an entity's cash management policies are an important factor in determining cash equivalents, not all investments that appear to satisfy the definition at 1.1 above are required to be classified as such. However, regardless of an entity's cash management policies and practices, an investment can only be classified within cash equivalents if all of the criteria in the definition are satisfied (see 3.2 below).

In view of the variety of cash management practices and banking arrangements around the world, entities are required to disclose the policy adopted in determining the composition of cash and cash equivalents. *[IAS 7.46]*. Changes in that policy, such as a reclassification of financial instruments previously considered as being part of an entity's investment portfolio, should be reported under IAS 8 – *Accounting Policies, Changes in Accounting Estimates and Errors*. *[IAS 7.47]*. This would require comparatives to be restated and additional disclosures given, including the reasons for the change in policy.

The inclusion or exclusion of a certain type of investment in cash equivalents gives rise to a change in policy if an entity reclassified investments already held at the beginning of the current period or if it makes a different classification of new investments held for the same purposes as those in the prior period. On the contrary, a new investment in the current period (even in a type of investment previously classified otherwise) which is included in or excluded from cash equivalents according to the reason for holding that investment under the entity's cash management practices, is not considered a change in policy.

VTech Holdings disclosed its policy to include short-term investments and bank overdrafts as components of cash equivalents.

Extract 38.1: VTech Holdings Limited (2015)

Notes to the Financial Statements [extract]

Principal Accounting Policies [extract]

O Cash and Cash Equivalents

Cash and cash equivalents comprise cash on hand, demand deposits with banks and other financial institutions, short-term highly liquid investments that are readily convertible into known amounts of cash and which are subject to an insignificant risk of changes in value and which have a maturity of three months or less at acquisition. Bank overdrafts that are repayable on demand and form an integral part of the Group's cash management are also included as a component of cash and cash equivalents for the purpose of statement of cash flows.

Lufthansa disclosed not only the required policy for determining cash and cash equivalents (as defined in IAS 7) but also elected to disclose all the assets used by the entity to manage its liquidity.

Extract 38.2: Deutsche Lufthansa AG (2015)

Notes to the consolidated cash flow statement [extract]

The cash flow statement shows how cash and cash equivalents have changed over the reporting period at the Lufthansa Group. In accordance with IAS 7, cash flows are divided into cash flows from operating activities, from investing activities and from financing activities. The cash and cash equivalents shown in the cash flow statement comprise the balance sheet items bank balances and cash-in-hand, without fixed-term deposits with terms of three to twelve months, amounting to EUR 103m (previous year: EUR 125m). The amount of liquidity in the broader sense is reached by adding short-term securities.

3.2 Components of cash and cash equivalents

3.2.1 Demand deposits and short-term investments

In defining 'cash', IAS 7 does not explain what is meant by 'demand deposits', perhaps because the term is commonly understood as amounts that can be withdrawn on demand, without prior notice being required or a penalty being charged (for example, by an additional fee or forfeiture of interest). In any event, the distinction is largely irrelevant because amounts not classified as demand deposits may qualify as cash equivalents and end up being treated in the same way. Thus, whether or not an amount meets the definition of a cash equivalent may become the more important determination.

Cash equivalents are held for the purpose of meeting short-term cash commitments rather than for investment or other purposes. For an investment to qualify as a cash equivalent it must be readily convertible to a known amount of cash and be subject to an insignificant risk of changes in value. Normally only an investment with a short maturity of, say, three months or less from the date of acquisition qualifies as a cash equivalent. Equity investments are excluded unless they are cash equivalents in substance. IAS 7 provides an example of such an instrument, being redeemable preference shares acquired within a short period of their maturity and with a specified redemption date. *[IAS 7.7]*.

When the standard refers to a 'known amount of cash' it means that the amount should be known or determinable at the date on which the investment is acquired. Accordingly, traded commodities, such as gold bullion, would not be eligible for inclusion in cash equivalents because the proceeds to be realised from such an investment is determined at the date of disposal rather than being known or determinable when the investment is made.

3.2.2 *Money market funds*

Entities commonly invest in money market funds such as an open-ended mutual fund that invests in certificates of deposit, commercial paper, treasury bills, bankers' acceptances and repurchase agreements and other money market instruments. An investment in a money market fund aims to provide investors with low-risk, low-return investment while preserving the value of the assets and maintaining a high level of liquidity. The question then arises as to whether investments in such funds can be classified as cash equivalents.

In most cases, a money market fund investment is quoted in an active market and, as such, could be regarded as highly liquid. However, this is not enough to meet the definition of a cash equivalent. The short-term and highly liquid investment must be readily convertible into known amounts of cash which are subject to an insignificant risk of changes in value. *[IAS 7.6]*. The Interpretations Committee considered the issue in July 2009 and confirmed that the amount of cash that will be received must be known at the time of the initial investment. Accordingly, investments in shares or units of money market funds cannot be considered as cash equivalents simply because they are convertible at any time at the then market price in an active market. The Interpretations Committee also confirmed that an entity would have to satisfy itself that any investment was subject to an insignificant risk of change in value for it to be classified as a cash equivalent.[1]

Therefore in assessing whether the change in value of an investment in a money market fund can be regarded as insignificant, an entity has to conclude that the range of possible returns is very small. This evaluation is made at the time of acquiring the investment and will involve consideration of factors such as the maturity of the investment (for example a maturity of less than 90 days); the credit rating of the fund (for example AAA or an equivalent highest rating); the nature of the investments held by the fund (i.e. not subject to volatility); the extent of diversification in the portfolio (which is expected to be very high); and any mechanisms by the fund to guarantee returns (for example by reference to short-term money market interest rates).

Investments are often held for purposes other than to act as a ready store of value that can be quickly converted into cash when needed to meet short-term cash commitments. It is therefore important to understand why the entity invested in a particular money market fund when determining whether classification as a cash equivalent is appropriate. This approach is illustrated by Henkel AG in Extract 38.3 below.

> *Extract 38.3: Henkel AG &Co. KGaA (2014)*
> **Notes to the consolidated financial statements** [extract]
> **8 Cash and cash equivalents**
> Recognized under cash and cash equivalents are liquid funds, sight deposits and other financial assets with an original term of not more than three months. In accordance with IAS 7, also recognized under cash equivalents are shares in money market funds which, due to their first-class credit rating and investment in extremely short-term money market securities, undergo only minor value fluctuations and can be readily converted within one day into known amounts of cash. Utilized bank overdrafts are recognized in the statement of financial position as liabilities to banks.

3.2.3 Investments with maturities greater than three months

The longer the term of the investment, the greater the risk that a change in market conditions (such as interest rates) can have an effect on its value that is other than insignificant. For this reason, IAS 7 excludes most equity investments from cash equivalents and restricts the inclusion of other investments to those with a short maturity of, say, three months or less from the date of their acquisition by the entity. *[IAS 7.7]*.

Similarly, an investment with a term on acquisition of, say, nine months is not reclassified as a cash equivalent from the date on which there is less than three months remaining to its maturity. If such reclassifications were permitted, the statement of cash flows would have to reflect movements between investments and cash equivalents. This would be misleading because no actual cash flows would have occurred.

The criteria explained above are guidelines, not rules, and a degree of common sense should be used in their application. In the final analysis, cash equivalents are held for the purpose of meeting short-term cash commitments and amounts should be included in cash equivalents only if they can be regarded as being nearly as accessible as cash and essentially as free from exposure to changes in value as cash.

For example, an entity might justify including in cash equivalents a fixed deposit with an original term longer than three months if it effectively functions like a demand deposit. Typically, a fixed deposit will carry a penalty charge for withdrawal prior to maturity. A penalty will usually indicate that the investment is held for investment purposes rather than the purpose of meeting short-term cash needs. However, some fixed deposits still offer interest at a prevailing demand deposit rate in the event of early withdrawal, with any penalty limited to the entity being required to forego the incremental higher interest that it would have received if the deposit were held to maturity. In this case, it may be arguable that there is effectively no significant penalty for early withdrawal, as the entity receives at least the same return that it otherwise would have in a demand deposit arrangement. Where an entity does assert that this type of investment is held for meeting short-term cash needs and classifies the investment as a cash equivalent, the accrual of interest receivable should be on a consistent basis. In this example, the entity is asserting that it is likely to withdraw the deposit should the need arise, and therefore should consider accruing interest receivable at the demand deposit rate, as this reflects the extent to which the receipt of revenue is probable.

3.2.4 *Bank overdrafts*

Although bank borrowings are generally considered to be financing activities, there are circumstances in which bank overdrafts repayable on demand are included as a component of cash and cash equivalents. This is in cases where the use of short-term overdrafts forms an integral part of an entity's cash management practices. Evidence supporting such an assertion would be that the bank balance often fluctuates from being positive to overdrawn. *[IAS 7.8]*.

3.3 Reconciliation with items in the statement of financial position

The amount shown alongside the caption in the statement of financial position for 'cash and cash equivalents' will not always be a reliable guide for IAS 7 purposes. Many entities present the components of cash and cash equivalents separately on the face of the statement of financial position, such as 'cash and bank balances' and 'short-term bank deposits'. Additionally, some entities may include bank overdrafts in cash and cash equivalents for cash flow purposes, but, if no legal right of set-off exists, will present bank overdrafts separate from cash in the statement of financial position as financial liabilities. *[IAS 32.42]*.

The standard requires an entity to disclose the components of cash and cash equivalents and to present a reconciliation to the statement of financial position, *[IAS 7.45]*, which means that any difference between 'cash and cash equivalents' for IAS 7 purposes and presentation in the statement of financial position will be evident in the notes to the financial statements.

Schiphol Group provides a reconciliation of the components of cash and cash equivalents, which includes cash held for sale.

Extract 38.4: Schiphol Group (2015)

Consolidated statement of cash flow for 2015 [extract]
(in thousands of euros)

	2015	2014
Cash from continuing operations	394,045	177,663
Cash equivalents presented as other receivable	40,000	–
Cash held for sale	3,263	5,590
	437,308	183,253

3.4 Restrictions on the use of cash and cash equivalents

The amount of significant cash and cash equivalent balances that is not available for use by the group should be disclosed, together with a commentary by management to explain the circumstances of the restriction. *[IAS 7.48]*. Examples include cash and cash equivalents held by a subsidiary operating under exchange controls or other legal restrictions that prevent their general use by the parent or other subsidiaries. *[IAS 7.49]*.

Chapter 38

The nature of the restriction must also be assessed to determine if the balance is ineligible for inclusion in cash equivalents because the restriction results in the investment ceasing to be highly liquid or readily convertible. For example, where an entity covenants to maintain a minimum level of cash or deposits as security for certain short-term obligations, and provided that no amounts are required to be designated for that specific purpose, such balances could still be regarded as cash equivalents, albeit subject to restrictions, as part of a policy of managing resources to meet short-term commitments.

However, an entity may be required formally to set aside cash, for example as a result of a regulated minimum cash balance or by way of a deposit into an escrow account, as part of a specific project or transaction, such as the acquisition or construction of a property. In such circumstances, it is necessary to consider the terms and conditions relating to the account and the conditions relating to both the entity's and the counterparty's access to the funds within it to determine whether it is appropriate for the deposit to be classified in cash equivalents.

In Extract 38.5 below, Lloyds Banking Group has various restricted cash balances. The Bank is required to exclude from cash and cash equivalents the mandatory reserve deposits held with local central banks because these amounts are not available to finance the entity's day-to-day operations. Conversely, certain balances held by its life fund subsidiaries do still meet the definition of cash and cash equivalents, and the Group is only required to disclose the restrictions thereon.

Extract 38.5: Lloyds Banking Group plc (2015)

Notes to the Consolidated Financial Statements [extract]

Note 54: CONSOLIDATED CASH FLOW STATEMENT [extract]

(D) Analysis of cash and cash equivalents as shown in the balance sheet

	2015 £m	2014 £m	2013 £m
Cash and balances at central banks	**58,417**	50,492	49,915
Less: mandatory reserve deposits[1]	**(941)**	(980)	(937)
	57,476	49,512	48,978
Loans and advances to banks	**25,117**	26,155	25,365
Less: amounts with a maturity of three months or more	**(10,640)**	(10,520)	(7,546)
	14,477	15,635	17,819
Total cash and cash equivalents	**71,953**	65,147	66,797

[1] Mandatory reserve deposits are held with local central banks in accordance with statutory requirements; these deposits are not available to finance the Group's day-to-day operations.

Included within cash and cash equivalents at 31 December 2015 is £13,545 million (2014: £12,855 million; 2013: £14,058 million) held within the Group's life funds, which is not immediately available for use in the business.

Similarly, in the following extract, InterContinental Hotels Group includes certain amounts of restricted cash, which are pledged as collateral to insurance companies for risks retained by the group, in loans and receivables within 'Other financial assets' on the statement of financial position, rather than in cash and cash equivalents.

Extract 38.6: InterContinental Hotels Group PLC (2015)

Notes to the Group Financial Statements [extract]

15. **Other financial assets** [extract]

Trade deposits and loans include a deposit of $37m made in 2011 to a hotel owner in connection with the renegotiation of a management contract. The deposit is non-interest-bearing and repayable at the end of the management contract, and is therefore held at its discounted value of $14m (2014: $13m); the discount unwinds to the income statement within 'financial income' over the period to repayment.

Restricted funds comprise cash held in bank accounts which is pledged as collateral to insurance companies for risks retained by the Group and other amounts held in escrow.

In the exposure draft ED/2014/6 – *Disclosure Initiative – Proposed amendments to IAS 7*, issued in December 2014, the IASB noted that additional restrictions, such as financial disincentives to utilising certain cash balances, or other considerations may be relevant to understanding the liquidity of the entity, as they affect the decision to utilise cash and cash equivalents. The example is given of tax liabilities that would arise on the repatriation of foreign cash and cash equivalent balances. The exposure draft proposes that where such matters exist, they should be disclosed. In October 2015, the IASB decided not to include disclosures relating to such disincentives in the amendments to IAS 7, but rather to review them as part of a broader investigation into liquidity disclosures.[2] Nevertheless, entities might want to consider making additional disclosures where such restrictions or disincentives exist.

4 CLASSIFICATION IN THE STATEMENT OF CASH FLOWS

The statement of cash flows reports inflows and outflows of cash and cash equivalents during the period classified under:

- operating activities;
- investing activities; and
- financing activities. *[IAS 7.10].*

This classification is intended to allow users to assess the impact of these three types of activity on the financial position of the entity and the amount of its cash and cash equivalents. Whilst not stated explicitly in the standard, the presentation of operating, investing and financing cash flows usually follows this sequence in practice, and a total net cash flow for each standard heading should be shown. Comparative figures are required for all items in the statement of cash flows and the related notes. *[IAS 1.38].*

The components of cash flows are classified as operating, investing or financing activities in a manner which is most appropriate to the business of the entity. *[IAS 7.11].* For example, the purchase of investments is likely to be classified as an operating cash flow for a financial institution, but as an investing cash flow for a manufacturer. Additionally, a single transaction may comprise elements of differently classified cash flows. For example, when repayments on a loan include both interest and capital, the element reflecting the interest expense may be included in either operating activities or financing activities (see 4.4.1 below) whereas the capital repayment must be classified as a financing cash flow. *[IAS 7.12].*

The format of the statement of cash flows is illustrated in Extract 38.7. As permitted by the standard, AstraZeneca has included interest paid under operating activities, interest received under investing activities and dividends paid under financing activities.

Extract 38.7: AstraZeneca PLC (2015)

Consolidated Statement Of Cash Flows

for the year ended 31 December

	Notes	**2015 $m**	2014 $m	2013 $m
Cash flows from operating activities				
Profit before tax		**3,069**	1,246	3,267
Finance income and expense	3	**1,029**	885	445
Share of after tax losses of joint ventures	10	**16**	6	–
Depreciation, amortisation and impairment		**2,852**	3,282	4,583
Decrease/(increase) in trade and other receivables		**152**	311	(383)
(Increase)/(decrease) in inventories		**(315)**	108	135
Increase in trade and other payables and provisions		**114**	2,089	414
Gains on disposal of intangible assets	2	**(961)**	–	–
Non-cash and other movements		**(782)**	865	258
Cash generated from operations		**5,174**	8,792	8,719
Interest paid		**(496)**	(533)	(475)
Tax paid		**(1,354)**	(1,201)	(844)
Net cash inflow from operating activities		**3,324**	7,058	7,400
Cash flows from investing activities				
Upfront payments on business acquisitions	24	**(2,446)**	(3,804)	(1,158)
Payment of contingent consideration on business acquisitions	18	**(579)**	(657)	–
Purchase of property, plant and equipment		**(1,328)**	(1,012)	(742)
Disposal of property, plant and equipment		**47**	158	69
Purchase of intangible assets		**(1,460)**	(1,740)	(1,316)
Disposal of intangible assets		**1,130**	–	35
Purchase of non-current asset investments		**(57)**	(130)	(91)
Disposal of non-current asset investments		**93**	59	38
Movement in short-term investments and fixed deposits		**283**	34	130
Payments to joint ventures	10	**(45)**	(70)	–
Interest received		**123**	140	114
Payments made by subsidiaries to non-controlling interests		**–**	(10)	(10)
Payments received by subsidiaries from non-controlling interests		**–**	–	42
Net cash outflow from investing activities		**(4,239)**	(7,032)	(2,889)
Net cash (outflow)/inflow before financing activities		**(915)**	26	4,511
Cash flows from financing activities				
Proceeds from issue of share capital		**43**	279	482
Repayment of obligations under finance leases		**(42)**	(36)	(27)
Issue of loans		**5,928**	919	–
Repayment of loans		**(884)**	(750)	–
Dividends paid		**(3,486)**	(3,521)	(3,461)
Hedge contracts relating to dividend payments		**(51)**	(14)	(36)
Payments to acquire non-controlling interest		**–**	(102)	–
Movement in short-term borrowings		**(630)**	520	(5)
Net cash inflow /(outflow) from financing activities		**878**	(2,705)	(3,047)

Net (decrease)/increase in cash and cash equivalents in the period		**(37)**	(2,679)	1,464
Cash and cash equivalents at the beginning of the period		**6,164**	8,995	7,596
Exchange rate effects		**(76)**	(152)	(65)
Cash and cash equivalents at the end of the period	16	**6,051**	6,164	8,995

Having reviewed a variety of requests received from constituents for further guidance on the classification of cash flows, the Interpretations Committee and the IASB have observed that the primary principle for classification of cash flows should be in accordance with the nature of the activity in a manner that is most appropriate to the business of the entity (see 4.4.10 below).[3]

4.1 Cash flows from operating activities

Operating activities are defined as 'the principal revenue-producing activities of the entity and other activities that are not investing or financing activities'. *[IAS 7.6]*. The standard states that the value of information on operating cash flows is twofold. It provides a key indicator of the extent to which the entity has generated sufficient cash flows from its operations to repay debt, pay dividends and make investments to maintain and increase its operating capability, without recourse to external sources of financing. Also, information about the components of historical operating cash flows may assist in the process of forecasting future operating cash flows, when used in conjunction with other financial statement information. *[IAS 7.13]*.

Cash flows from operating activities generally result from transactions and other events that enter into the determination of profit or loss. Examples include:

(a) cash receipts from the sale of goods and the rendering of services;

(b) cash receipts from royalties, fees, commissions and other revenue;

(c) cash payments to suppliers for goods and services;

(d) cash payments to and on behalf of employees;

(e) cash receipts and cash payments of an insurance entity for premiums and claims, annuities and other policy benefits;

(f) cash payments or refunds of income taxes unless they can be specifically identified with financing and investing activities; and

(g) cash receipts and payments from contracts held for dealing or trading purposes (see 4.4.9 below regarding the allocation of cash flows on derivative contracts). *[IAS 7.14]*.

This section is also a 'default category' for any cash flows that do not meet the criteria of investing or financing cash flows. For example, as discussed at 6.3.1 below, acquisition-related costs in a business combination that have to be recognised as an expense, *[IFRS 3.53]*, would also be classified as operating cash flows because there is no related asset that would justify classification as an investing cash flow. *[IAS 7.16]*.

When an entity holds securities and loans for dealing or trading purposes they are similar to inventory acquired specifically for resale. Therefore, any related cash flows are classified as operating activities. Similarly, cash advances and loans made by financial institutions are usually classified as operating activities, since they relate to the main revenue-generating activity of that entity (see 7.1 below). *[IAS 7.15]*.

The proceeds from the sale of property, plant and equipment, which are usually included in cash flows from investing activities, are an example of an item that enters into the determination of profit or loss that is *not* usually an operating cash flow. *[IAS 7.14]*. However, the proceeds from sales of assets previously held for rental purposes are classified as cash flows from operating activities if the entity routinely sells such assets in its ordinary course of business. Similarly, cash payments to manufacture or acquire property, plant and equipment held for rental to others, and that are routinely sold in the ordinary course of business after rental, are also classified as cash flows from operating activities (see 4.4.5 below). *[IAS 7.14]*.

Cash flows from operating activities may be reported on a gross or net basis, also known as the direct and indirect methods. *[IAS 7.18]*.

4.1.1 The direct method

Under the direct method, major classes of gross cash receipts and gross cash payments are disclosed. *[IAS 7.18]*. IAS 7 encourages entities to use the direct method, on the grounds that it provides information which may be useful in estimating future cash flows and which is not available under the indirect method. *[IAS 7.19]*.

Under the direct method, information about major classes of gross cash receipts and payments may be obtained either:

(a) from the accounting records of the entity (essentially based on an analysis of the cash book); or

(b) by adjusting sales, cost of sales (interest and similar income and interest expenses and similar charges for a financial institution) and other items recognised in profit or loss for:

 (i) changes during the period in inventories and operating receivables and payables;

 (ii) other non-cash items; and

 (iii) other items for which the cash effects are investing or financing cash flows. *[IAS 7.19]*.

The direct method statement of cash flows should include the same disclosures of gross cash receipts and gross cash payments irrespective of which approach has been used to determine their value. There is no requirement for entities using the approach described in (b) above to present a reconciliation showing the adjustments made between, for example, revenue in the statement of comprehensive income and cash receipts from customers.

African Rainbow Minerals Limited is an example of an entity using the direct method for presenting its cash flows from operating activities, as illustrated in Extract 38.8 below.

Extract 38.8: African Rainbow Minerals Limited (2015)

Statements of Cash Flows [extract]
for the year ended 30 June 2015

	Group	
	F2015 Rm	F2014 Rm
Cash flows from operating activities		
Cash receipts from customers	**11 093**	9 950
Cash paid to suppliers and employees	**(8 585)**	(7 877)
Cash generated from operations	**2 508**	2 073
Interest received	**120**	99
Interest paid	**(109)**	(113)
Dividends received	**1**	1
Dividends received from joint venture	**1 500**	1 750
Dividend paid to non-controlling interest – Impala Platinum	**(277)**	(236)
Dividend paid	**(1 302)**	(1 102)
Taxation paid	**(386)**	(395)
Net cash inflow from operating activities	**2 055**	**2 077**

4.1.2 *The indirect method*

The indirect method arrives at the same value for net cash flows from operating activities, but does so by working back from amounts reported in the statement of comprehensive income. There are two approaches for presenting the net cash flows from operating activities when using the indirect method. The most common approach adjusts reported profit or loss for the effects of:

(a) changes in inventories and operating receivables and payables during the period;

(b) non-cash items such as depreciation, provisions, deferred taxes, unrealised foreign currency gains and losses, and undistributed profits of associates; and

(c) all other items for which the cash effects are investing or financing cash flows. *[IAS 7.20]*.

Chapter 38

Anheuser-Busch InBev has used this adjusted profit approach to present its indirect method statement of cash flows, as illustrated in Extract 38.9 below.

Extract 38.9: Anheuser-Busch InBev NV/SA (2015)

Consolidated Cash Flow Statement [extract]
For the year ended 31 December

Million US dollar	**2015**	**2014**
Operating activities		
Profit	9 867	11 302
Depreciation, amortization and impairment	3 153	3 353
Impairment losses on receivables, inventories and other assets	64	108
Additions/(reversals) in provisions and employee benefits	324	(85)
Net finance cost	1 453	1 319
Loss/(gain) on sale of property, plant and equipment and intangible assets	(189)	4
Loss/(gain) on sale of subsidiaries, associates and assets held for sale	(362)	(219)
Equity-settled share-based payment expense	221	249
Income tax expense	2 594	2 499
Other non-cash items included in the profit	(389)	(190)
Share of result of associates	(10)	(9)
Cash flow from operating activities before changes in working capital and use of provisions	**16 726**	**18 331**
Decrease/(increase) in trade and other receivables	(138)	(371)
Decrease/(increase) in inventories	(424)	(354)
Increase/(decrease) in trade and other payables	2 348	1 540
Pension contributions and use of provisions	(449)	(458)
Cash generated from operations	**18 063**	**18 688**
Interest paid	(1 943)	(2 476)
Interest received	334	273
Dividends received	22	30
Income tax paid	(2 355)	(2 371)
Cash flow from operating activities	**14 121**	**14 144**

Alternatively, the indirect method of presentation can show separately revenues and expenses, adjusted for non-cash, investing or financing items, making up operating profit before working capital changes. *[IAS 7.20]*. An example of this rarely used alternative is given at the end of Appendix A to IAS 7.

When an entity adopts the adjusted profit approach to presenting net cash flows from operating activities under the indirect method, the reconciliation should start either with profit or loss before tax (as in Extract 38.7 above) or profit or loss after tax (as in Extract 38.9 above). Any other basis, such as EBITDA, EBIT, or profit or loss excluding non-controlling interests, does not meet the requirement in IAS 7 for 'adjusting profit or loss', *[IAS 7.20]*, which includes 'all items of income and expense in a period'. *[IAS 1.88]*.

To obtain the information on working capital movements for the indirect method, the figures in the statement of financial position have to be analysed according to the three standard headings of the statement of cash flows. Thus, the reconciliation of profit or loss to cash flow from operating activities will include, not the increase or decrease in all receivables or payables, but only in respect of those elements thereof that relate to operating activities. For example, amounts owed in respect of the acquisition of property, plant and equipment (other than assets held for rental and subsequent sale), intangible assets, or non-operational investments will be excluded from the movement in payables included in this reconciliation. Although this may not present practical difficulties in the preparation of a single-entity statement of cash flows, it is important that sufficient information is collected from subsidiaries for preparing the group statement of cash flows.

Furthermore, when a group has made an acquisition of a subsidiary during the year, the change in working capital items will have to be split between the increase due to the acquisition (to the extent that the purchase consideration was settled in cash, this will be shown under investing activities) and the element related to post-acquisition operating activities which will be shown in the reconciliation.

4.2 Cash flows from investing activities

Investing activities are defined as 'the acquisition and disposal of long-term assets and other investments not included in cash equivalents'. *[IAS 7.6]*. This separate category of cash flows allows users of the financial statements to understand the extent to which expenditures have been made for resources intended to generate future income and cash flows. Cash flows arising from investing activities include:

(a) payments to acquire, and receipts from the sale of, property, plant and equipment, intangibles and other long-term assets (including payments and receipts relating to capitalised development costs and self-constructed property, plant and equipment);

(b) payments to acquire, and receipts from the sale of, equity or debt instruments of other entities and interests in jointly controlled entities (other than payments and receipts for those instruments considered to be cash equivalents or those held for dealing or trading purposes);

(c) advances and loans made to, and repaid by, other parties (other than advances and loans made by a financial institution); and

(d) payments for, and receipts from, futures contracts, forward contracts, option contracts and swap contracts, except when the contracts are held for dealing or trading purposes, or the cash flows are classified as financing activities (see 4.4.9 below regarding allocation of cash flows on derivative contracts). *[IAS 7.16]*.

Only expenditures that result in a recognised asset in the statement of financial position are eligible for classification as investing activities. *[IAS 7.16]*. Therefore, cash flows relating to costs recognised as an expense cannot be classified within investing activities. As a result, payments including those for exploration and evaluation activities and for research and development that are recognised as an asset are classified as investing cash flows, while entities that recognise such expenditures as an expense would classify the related payments as operating cash flows.

This requirement was added in response to submissions made to the Interpretations Committee about the classification of expenditure incurred with the aim of generating future revenues, but that may not always result in the recognition of an asset. Examples included exploration and evaluation expenditure, advertising and promotional activities, staff training, and research and development. *[IAS 7.BC3]*. It has been effective since 1 January 2010. *[IAS 7.56]*. The IASB believes that the change better aligns the classification of investing cash flows with the presentation in the statement of financial position; reduces divergence in practice and, therefore, results in financial statements that are easier for users to understand. *[IAS 7.BC7]*. It does not seem unreasonable that recurrent expenditure on items such as research and expensed mining costs should be classified as operating cash flows. However, application to other items that do not give rise to an asset in the statement of financial position, such as acquisition-related costs (discussed at 6.3.1 below) and the settlement of contingent consideration in a business combination (discussed at 6.3.3 below) may prove to be more complicated.

Since the implementation of this change, the Interpretations Committee and the IASB has discussed its application in practice, as some users appear to have given precedence to the classification of cash flows consistently with the classification of the related item in the statement of financial position *[IAS 7.BC7]* (sometime referred to as the 'cohesiveness principle') over the objective in the standard to classify cash flows in accordance with the nature of the activity giving rise to the cash flow. *[IAS 7.11]*. In discussion, the IASB agreed that the primary principle for the classification of cash flows should be in accordance with the nature of the activity, and that the requirement for the recognition of an asset should be read as a constraint on the application of the primary principle, rather than as a competing principle.[4]

Major classes of gross receipts and gross payments arising from investing activities are reported separately, except for those items that IAS 7 permits to be reported on a net basis, as discussed at 5.2 below. *[IAS 7.21]*.

4.3 Cash flows from financing activities

Financing activities are defined as those 'activities that result in changes in the size and composition of the contributed equity and borrowings of the entity'. *[IAS 7.6]*. The standard states that this information is useful in predicting claims on future cash flows by providers of capital to the entity. *[IAS 7.17]*. However, it would seem more likely that information on financing cash flows would indicate the extent to which the entity has had recourse to external financing to meet its operating and investing needs in the period. The disclosure of the value and maturity of the entity's financial liabilities would contribute more to predicting future claims on cash flows.

Cash flows arising from financing activities include:

(a) proceeds from issuing shares or other equity instruments;

(b) payments to owners to acquire or redeem the entity's shares;

(c) proceeds from issuing, and outflows to repay, debentures, loans, notes, bonds, mortgages and other short or long-term borrowings; and

(d) payments by a lessee for the reduction of the outstanding liability relating to a finance lease (or relating to all leases requiring the recognition of a lease liability under IFRS 16 – *Leases*). *[IAS 7.17]*.

In consolidated financial statements, financing cash flows will include those arising from changes in ownership interests in a subsidiary that do not result in a loss of control (see 6.2 below). *[IAS 7.42A]*.

Major classes of gross receipts and gross payments arising from financing activities should be reported separately, except for those items that can be reported on a net basis, as discussed at 5.2 below. *[IAS 7.21]*.

Disclosure requirements in respect of changes in liabilities arising from financing activities are discussed at 5.5 below.

4.4 Allocating items to operating, investing and financing activities

Sometimes it is not clear how cash flows should be classified between operating, investing and financing activities. IAS 7 provides additional guidance on the classification of certain transactions, including interest, dividends and income taxes, while other questions are not addressed explicitly in the standard. These, as well as some common areas where judgement may be required to classify cash flows, are discussed below.

4.4.1 *Interest and dividends*

An entity is required to disclose separately cash flows from interest and dividends received and paid, and their classification as either operating, investing or financing activities should be applied in a consistent manner from period to period. *[IAS 7.31]*. For a financial institution, interest paid and interest and dividends received are usually classified as operating cash flows. However, IAS 7 notes that there is no consensus on the classification of these cash flows for other entities and suggests that:

- interest paid may be classified under either operating or financing activities; and
- interest received and dividends received may be included in either operating or investing cash flows. *[IAS 7.33]*.

The standard allows dividends paid to be classified as a financing cash flow (because they are a cost of obtaining financial resources) or as a component of cash flows from operating activities. *[IAS 7.34]*.

In Extract 38.7 at 4 above, AstraZeneca has included interest paid under operating activities, interest received under investing activities and dividends paid under financing activities, as permitted by the standard. A different treatment is adopted by Anheuser-Busch InBev in Extract 38.9 at 4.1.2 above, where interest paid, interest received and dividends received are all disclosed as operating cash flows.

All of these treatments are equally acceptable. Nevertheless, it could be argued that entities which do not include interest or dividends received within revenue should not include interest or dividends in operating cash flows, because cash flows from operating activities are primarily derived from the principal revenue-producing activities of the entity, *[IAS 7.14]*, and the amount of cash flows arising from operating activities is intended to be a key indicator of the extent to which the operations of the entity have generated sufficient cash flows to repay loans, pay dividends and make new investments without recourse to external sources of financing. *[IAS 7.13]*. On this basis, where management does not consider these items as part of the operating profit of the entity, interest paid would be a financing cash flow and interest and dividends received classified as investing cash flows. *[IAS 7.33]*. Such entities would also treat dividends paid as a financing cash flow, because they are a cost of obtaining financial resources. *[IAS 7.34]*. In addition, the standard requires the total amount of interest paid during the period to be disclosed in the statement of cash flows, whether it has been recognised as an expense or capitalised as part of the cost of an asset in accordance with IAS 23 – *Borrowing Costs*. *[IAS 7.32]*. A literal reading of this requirement might suggest that interest paid should be presented as a single figure under operating or financing activities. However, it would also seem appropriate to include the cash outflow relating to capitalised borrowing costs under investing activities, provided that when this is done, the total amount of interest paid is also disclosed, either on the face of the statement of cash flows or in the notes. The Interpretations Committee tried to address this apparent inconsistency between paragraph 16 of IAS 7 and paragraphs 32 to 33 of IAS 7 in May 2011. They had initially recommended that the IASB amend IAS 7 through the annual improvements process to clarify that interest payments capitalised under IAS 23 should be classified in a manner consistent with the classification of the underlying asset to which those payments were capitalised.[5] This proposed amendment was issued for public consultation under the exposure draft *Annual Improvements to IFRSs 2010-2012 Cycle*.[6]

However, in response to concerns raised by respondents to the proposed amendments about the difficulty of implementation, the Committee recommended that the IASB refrain from making the proposed changes. The IASB agreed and decided in April 2013 not to finalise the proposed amendment.[7]

4.4.2 Taxes on income

Cash flows arising from taxes on income should be separately disclosed within operating cash flows unless they can be specifically identified with investing or financing activities. *[IAS 7.35]*.

Whilst it is possible to match elements of tax expense to transactions for which the cash flows are classified under investing or financing activities; taxes paid are usually classified as cash flows from operating activities, because it is often impracticable to match tax cash flows with specific elements of tax expense. Also, those tax cash flows may arise in a different period from the underlying transaction. *[IAS 7.36]*. This is the presentation adopted by Anheuser-Busch InBev in Extract 38.9 at 4.1.2 above. However, when it is practicable to make this determination, the tax cash flow is identified as an investing or financing activity in accordance with the individual transaction that gives rise to such cash flows. In cases where tax cash flows are allocated over more than one class of activity, the entity should disclose the total amount for taxes paid. *[IAS 7.36]*.

4.4.3 Sales taxes and other non-income tax cash flows

Although it provides guidance on the treatment of taxes on income, IAS 7 does not specifically address the treatment of cash flows relating to other taxes, such as value added tax (VAT) or other sales taxes and duty. The Interpretations Committee has considered whether it should add the question about VAT to its agenda and decided that it was not appropriate to develop an interpretation. Instead, it suggested that the issue of cash flows relating to VAT be considered by the IASB in its review of IAS 7 as part of the project on Financial Statement Presentation.

In explaining why it would not add this question to its agenda, the Interpretations Committee noted that 'IAS 7 does not explicitly address the treatment of VAT' and added that 'while different practices may emerge, they are not expected to be widespread'.[8]

Therefore, it seems that entities can choose to disclose VAT receipts and VAT payments separately in the statement of cash flows or as part of the related cash inflows and outflows. Given the availability of alternative treatments, the Interpretations Committee noted that it would be appropriate in complying with IAS 1 – *Presentation of Financial Statements* – for entities to disclose whether cash flows are presented inclusive or exclusive of related VAT.[9] We believe that the same principles should be applied for other non-income taxes.

4.4.4 Cash flows from factoring of trade receivables and supply-chain financing

Another question not explicitly addressed in the standard is the classification of cash receipts from the factoring of trade receivables and deferred cash payments to suppliers through supply-chain financing.

In the case of debt factoring, an entity aims to provide cash flow from trade receivables more quickly than would arise from normal collection from customers, generally by transferring rights over those receivables to a financial institution. In our view, the classification of the cash receipt from the financial institution depends on whether the transfer results in derecognition of the trade receivables, or to the continued recognition of the trade receivables and the recognition of a financial liability for the funding received from the factoring entity. The characteristics determining which of these accounting treatments would be appropriate are discussed in Chapter 51 at 4.5 and 5.

Only to the extent that the factoring arrangement results in the derecognition of the original trade receivable would it be appropriate to regard the cash receipt in the same way as any other receipt from the sale of goods and rendering of services and classify it in operating activities. *[IAS 7.14(a)]*. In cases where the trade receivable is not derecognised and a liability is recorded, the nature of the arrangement is a borrowing secured against trade receivables and accordingly we believe that the cash receipt from factoring should be treated in the same way as any short-term borrowing and included in financing activities. *[IAS 7.17(c)]*. The later cash inflow from the customer for settlement of the trade receivable would be included in operating cash flows and the reduction in the liability to the financial institution would be a financing outflow. Following the principle in IAS 39 – *Financial Instruments: Recognition and Measurement* – for the disclosure of income and expenditure relating to a transferred asset that continues to be recognised, *[IAS 39.36]*, these two amounts would not be netted off in the statement of cash flows. However, it would be acceptable for the entity to disclose the net borrowing receipts from, and repayments to, the financial institution, if it was determined that these relate to advances made for and the repayment of short-term borrowings such as those which have a maturity period of three months or less. *[IAS 7.23]*. In some cases, the factoring arrangement requires customers to remit cash directly to the financial institution. When the transfer does not give rise to derecognition of the trade receivable by the reporting entity, we believe that entity can apply either of the following ways to depict the later satisfaction of the debt by the customer:

(a) as a non-cash transaction. No cash flows would be reported at the time of the ultimate derecognition of the trade receivable and the related factoring liability; or

(b) as a transaction in which the factoring entity collects the receivable as agent of the entity and then draws down amounts received in settlement of the entity's liability to the financial institution. In this case the entity would report an operating cash inflow from the customer and a financing cash outflow to the financial institution.

In the case of supply-chain financing or reverse factoring arrangements, typically a purchaser aims to defer cash flows through an arrangement with a financial intermediary, see Chapter 51 at 6.5. In this scenario cash outflows would arise on the settlement of the debt payable to the intermediary. An entity would need to consider whether these cash flows are operating or financing in nature, and would reach this conclusion based on factors similar to those considered for deferred payments, as discussed at 5.4.1 below.

4.4.5 Property, plant and equipment held for rental

Payments to acquire and receipts from the sale of, property, plant and equipment are usually included in investing cash flows; however, this is not always the case.

A number of entities routinely sell assets that were previously held for rental, for example, car rental companies that acquire vehicles with the intention of holding them as rental cars for a limited period and then selling them. IAS 16 – *Property, Plant and Equipment* – requires an entity, that, in its ordinary course of business, routinely sells items of property, plant and equipment that it has held for rental to others, to classify gains on the sale of such property, plant and equipment as revenue. *[IAS 16.68A]*. Accordingly, the proceeds from the sale of such assets are classified as cash flows from operating activities, as are cash payments to manufacture or acquire property, plant and equipment held for rental to others and routinely sold in the ordinary course of business. *[IAS 7.14]*.

The requirement to classify payments for such property, plant and equipment held for rental under operating cash flows is intended to avoid initial expenditure on purchases of assets being classified as investing activities, while inflows from sales are recorded within operating activities. However, this means that management will need to determine, at the time of acquisition or manufacture, which of the assets that it intends to rent out will be ultimately held for sale in the ordinary course of business.

4.4.6 Cash flows for service concession arrangements

Because a cash flow is only classified in investing activities if it results in a recognised asset in the statement of financial position, a question arises regarding the classification of the cash inflows and outflows of the operator of a service concession arrangement that is within the scope of IFRIC 12 – *Service Concession Arrangements*.

IFRIC 12 features two possible accounting models – the intangible asset model or the financial asset model. Under both models, the service element relating to the construction of the infrastructure asset is accounted for in accordance with IAS 11 – *Construction Contracts* – and the revenue recognised gives rise to an intangible or a financial asset, in the form of a receivable, respectively. It is unclear whether cash flows incurred in the construction or upgrade phase should always be regarded as operating cash flows, because they relate to the provision of construction services; or whether they are more accurately classified as investing activities.

In the case of an arrangement under the intangible asset model, the cash flows incurred during construction or upgrading could be classified in investing activities as they relate to the acquisition of an intangible that will generate future income and cash flows. Once the operating phase is reached, the inflows received would be most appropriately be classified in operating activities as most operating and maintenance costs are likely to be executory and will be accounted for as incurred.

On the other hand, when the financial asset model applies, cash inflows may considered to be deferred payments and therefore represent the provision of financing to the grantor. In a corollary of the discussion on deferred payments at 5.4 below, where the time value of money is significant to the transaction, the transaction may be tantamount to providing a loan, and the repayment of such an instrument would be considered an investing cash flow (or potentially split between investing and operating cash flows for the capital and interest components respectively, depending on the policy of the entity).

Since there is no specific guidance relating to the classification of cash flows for service concession arrangements, current practice is mixed and therefore either treatment can be applied. IFRIC 12 is discussed in more detail in Chapter 27.

4.4.7 Treasury shares

Treasury shares are an entity's own equity instruments that are acquired and held by the entity, a subsidiary or other members of the consolidated group. The consideration paid or received for treasury shares is recognised directly in equity and not as a movement in investments. *[IAS 32.33]*. As such, it should be clear that payments and receipts to acquire or issue treasury shares should be classified within financing activities. *[IAS 7.17]*. Even where such treasury shares are acquired by the entity as part of an equity-settled share-based payment transaction, the cash outflow should be classified under financing activities. Whilst cash payments to and on behalf of employees are classified under operating activities, *[IAS 7.14]*, the acquisition of treasury shares does not settle a transaction between the entity and its employees. An equity-settled share-based payment transaction is completed when the entity transfers its equity instruments to employees in consideration for the services received.

When a cash payment is made by a subsidiary to its parent or a trust that holds treasury shares as part of an equity-settled share-based payment arrangement, the payment should be accounted for as a deduction from equity in the separate financial statements of the subsidiary, on the grounds that the payment does not settle the transaction with the employees, but is effectively a distribution to the parent or the trust (see Chapter 32 at 12.4.3 and 12.5.3). Having regarded this as a distribution, it follows that the cash flow should be classified as either operating or financing, according to the entity's policy on dividends as discussed at 4.4.1 above.

4.4.8 Cash flows related to the costs of a share issue

Costs directly related to the issue of shares are required to be deducted from equity. *[IAS 32.35]*. As the costs reduce the amount of the proceeds received from the share issue, they should be classified as a financing cash flow. *[IAS 7.17(c)]*. However, where a proposed share issue is cancelled, there would be no proceeds from the issue to record and the related expenses would be included in profit and loss rather than equity. As such, the definition of a financing cash flow would not be met, and the transaction costs would be classified in operating cash flows.

4.4.9 Cash flows on derivative contracts

Payments and receipts relating to derivative contracts can be classified within operating, investing or financing in different circumstances. Where the contract is held for dealing or trading purposes, the cash flows are classified under operating activities. *[IAS 7.14]*. IAS 7 requires that payments for, and receipts from, futures contracts, forward contracts, option contracts and swap contracts are classified as cash flows from investing activities, except when the contracts are held for dealing or trading purposes, or the cash flows are classified as financing activities. *[IAS 7.16]*.

The standard adds that when a contract is accounted for as a hedge of an identifiable position, the cash flows of the contract are classified under the same heading as the cash flows of the position being hedged. *[IAS 7.16]*. An example is an interest rate swap. An entity wishing to convert an existing fixed rate borrowing into a floating rate equivalent could enter into an interest rate swap under which it receives interest at fixed rates and pays at floating rates. All the cash flows under the swap should be reported under the same cash flow heading as interest paid (i.e. as financing activities or operating activities, in accordance with the entity's determined policy, as discussed at 4.4.1 above), because they are equivalent to interest or are hedges of interest payments.

The standard suggests that receipts and payments on contracts might be included in financing cash flows; but, except for the text on contracts accounted for as hedges of an identifiable position, gives no indication of the circumstances under which such a classification would be appropriate. *[IAS 7.16]*.

So how should an entity classify the cash flows from a derivative contract that is considered by management as part of a hedging relationship, but for which the entity elects not to apply hedge accounting (taking all movements to profit or loss) or for which hedge accounting is not permitted under IAS 39 or IFRS 9 – *Financial Instruments*? Consider the following example.

Example 38.1: Cash flows from derivatives not qualifying for hedge accounting

Company A has the euro as its functional currency. On 1 January 2015, it sells goods to a US customer for which it charges US$1,000,000. The spot exchange rate on this date is 1:1 and it recognises revenue of €1,000,000. Payment is due to be received on 30 June 2015. A enters into a forward contract to exchange US$1,000,000 for €1,095,000 on 30 June 2015. It does not designate it as a hedge because the effects of movements on the contract and those of retranslating the receivable will already offset in profit or loss. On 30 June 2015 the exchange rate is such that A receives the equivalent of €1,200,000 from its customer and pays €105,000 on the forward contract.

Taken literally, IAS 7 would suggest that the receipt from the customer of €1,200,000 is classified as an operating cash inflow; but, because the forward contract is not held for dealing or trading purposes and is not accounted for as a hedge of an identifiable position, the €105,000 cash outflow on the forward contract cannot be classified under operating activities. As such, the €105,000 would have to appear in investing or possibly financing cash flows. However, had the entity elected to apply hedge accounting, the standard would require the €105,000 to be included in operating cash flows.

This example highlights a current deficiency in IAS 7; its terminology was never updated or refined when IAS 39 was issued. This deficiency is acknowledged by the IASB when it discusses, in the implementation guidance to IAS 39, the classification of cash flows from hedging instruments. *[IAS 39.IG.G.2]*. Therefore, in our opinion, since the IASB has not reflected the requirements of IAS 39 in the text of IAS 7, it does not require the treatment of cash flows 'when a contract is accounted for as a hedge of an identifiable position', *[IAS 7.16]*, to be restricted only to those hedging relationships that either are designated as hedges under IAS 39 or would otherwise qualify for hedge accounting had they been so designated. Accordingly, in Example 38.1 above, entity A would include the payment on the forward contract in cash flows from operating activities.

4.4.10 Classification of cash flows – future developments

Over the years, the Interpretations Committee has received several requests from constituents for guidance on the classification of cash flows for a variety of transactions. In attempting to determine an appropriate guiding principle for classification, the Committee noted that two alternative classification principles had been applied in the past to support its conclusions whether to issue an agenda decision or to propose an improvement to IAS 7:

(a) classification according to the nature of the activity to which the cash flows relate; and

(b) consistency with the classification of the related or underlying item in the statement of financial position (otherwise referred to as the cohesiveness principle).

The Committee observed that in some circumstances the application of the cohesiveness principle could lead to transactions being split into operating, investing or financing components.

The Committee decided that the primary principle behind the classification of cash flows in IAS 7 should be in accordance with the nature of the activity that is most appropriate to the business of the entity, according to the IAS 7 definitions of operating, investing and financing activities.[10] However, after discussing several fact patterns, they also noted that the existing guidance did not lead to consistent application of the principle.[11]

Consequently, the Committee directed the staff to consider how the descriptions of operating, investing and financing cash flows could be clarified to promote more consistent application and to consider the relevance of other factors such as the identity of the counterparty or the timing of cash flows to their classification.[12]

Based on these discussions, the Committee concluded that a project to clarify the application of the primary principle by modifying the current definitions in IAS 7 would be too broad. In addition, the Committee determined that since it could not take a holistic approach in clarifying the classification of cash flows, amendments to IAS 7 should not be made on a piecemeal basis, for example in response to specific requests made by submitters on classification of cash flows for particular transactions.[13] The IASB agreed.[14]

Subsequently, the IASB has included the general requirements of IAS 7 within the scoping of its Disclosure Initiative research projects, and the proposed changes to this and a number of other standards are currently under discussion. The results of this research are expected to form the basis of a Discussion Paper and ultimately an amendment to requirements relating to cash flow statements.

5. OTHER CASH FLOW PRESENTATION ISSUES

5.1 Exceptional and other material cash flows

IAS 1 prohibits the presentation of extraordinary items either on the face of the statement of comprehensive income, the separate income statement (if presented) or in the notes. *[IAS 1.87]*. Consequently, IAS 7 does not refer to extraordinary items.

As regards exceptional and other material cash flows, IAS 1 requires the nature and amount of material items of income and expense to be disclosed separately, *[IAS 1.97]*. It also requires additional line items, headings and sub-totals to be presented on the face of the statement of financial position when this is relevant to an understanding of the entity's financial position. *[IAS 1.55]*. Therefore, although IAS 7 is silent on the matter, it would be appropriate for material cash flows or cash flows relating to material items in the statement of comprehensive income to be presented as separate line items on the face of the statement of cash flows, provided that they remain classified according to their nature as either operating, investing or financing cash flows.

If items are described as 'exceptional' cash flows, the entity's statement of accounting policies should explain the circumstances under which an item would be classified as exceptional and the notes to the financial statements should include an appropriate description of the nature of the amounts so treated.

5.2 Gross or net presentation of cash flows

In general, major classes of gross receipts and gross payments should be reported separately. *[IAS 7.21]*. Operating, investing or financing cash flows can be reported on a net basis if they arise from:

(a) cash flows that reflect the activities of customers rather than those of the entity and are thereby made on behalf of customers; or

(b) cash flows that relate to items in which the turnover is quick, the amounts are large, and the maturities are short. *[IAS 7.22]*.

Examples of cash receipts and payments that reflect the activities of customers rather than those of the entity include the acceptance and repayment of demand deposits by a bank, funds held for customers by an investment company and rents collected on behalf of, and paid over to, the owners of properties. *[IAS 7.23]*. Other transactions where the entity is acting as an agent or collector for another party would be included in this category, such as the treatment of cash receipts and payments relating to concession sales.

Examples of cash receipts and payments in which turnover is quick, the amounts are large and the maturities are short include advances made for and the repayment of:

(a) principal amounts relating to credit card customers;

(b) the purchase and sale of investments; and

(c) other short-term borrowings, such as those with a maturity on draw down of three months or less. *[IAS 7.23A]*.

An example noted in IAS 20 – *Accounting for Government Grants and Disclosure of Government Assistance* – where gross presentation is deemed appropriate for major classes of cash flows is the receipt of government grants, which 'are often disclosed as separate items in the statement of cash flows regardless of whether or not the grant is deducted from the related asset for presentation purposes in the statement of financial position'. *[IAS 20.28]*.

See 7.2 below for the gross or net presentation of cash flows for financial institutions.

5.3 Foreign currency cash flows

IAS 21 – *The Effects of Changes in Foreign Exchange Rates* – excludes from its scope the translation of cash flows of a foreign operation and the presentation of foreign currency cash flows in a statement of cash flows. *[IAS 21.7]*. Nevertheless, IAS 7 requires foreign currency cash flows to be reported in a manner consistent with IAS 21. *[IAS 7.27]*. Accordingly, cash flows arising from transactions in a foreign currency should be reported in an entity's functional currency in the statement of cash flows by applying the exchange rate in effect at the date of the cash flow. *[IAS 7.25]*. Similarly, the cash flows of a foreign subsidiary should be translated using the exchange rates prevailing at the dates of the cash flows. *[IAS 7.26]*.

For practical reasons, an entity can apply a rate that approximates the actual rate on the date of the cash flow (such as a weighted average for a period) but, like IAS 21, translation using the exchange rate as at the end of the reporting period is not permitted. *[IAS 7.27]*. The requirements for entities falling within the scope of IAS 29 – *Financial Reporting in Hyperinflationary Economies* – are discussed in Chapter 16.

Unrealised gains and losses arising from exchange rate movements on foreign currency cash and cash equivalents are not cash flows. However, it is necessary to include these exchange differences in the statement of cash flows in order to reconcile the movement in cash and cash equivalents at the beginning and end of the period. The effect of exchange rate movements on cash and cash equivalents is presented as a single amount at the foot of the statement of cash flows, separately from operating, investing and financing cash flows and includes the differences, if any, had those cash flows been reported at end of period exchange rates. *[IAS 7.28]*.

5.3.1 Entities applying the direct method

When an entity enters into a transaction denominated in a foreign currency, there are no consequences for the statement of cash flows until payments are received or made. The receipts and payments will be recorded in the entity's accounting records at the exchange rate prevailing at the date of payment and these amounts should be reflected in the statement of cash flows. *[IAS 7.25]*.

The consolidated statement of cash flows prepared under the direct method uses the foreign currency financial statements of each foreign subsidiary as the starting point. This means that cash flows are measured first in the functional currency of the subsidiary and then retranslated into the currency in which the consolidated financial statements are presented.

5.3.2 Entities applying the indirect method

Under the indirect method, profit or loss is adjusted for the effects of transactions of a non-cash nature, any deferrals of operating cash receipts or payments and income or expenses associated with investing or financing cash flows. *[IAS 7.18]*. Exchange differences will be included in profit or loss when the settled amount differs from the amount recorded at the date of the transaction. Likewise, if the transaction remains unsettled at the reporting date, exchange differences will also be taken to profit or loss on the retranslation of the unsettled monetary items at closing rates. Entities must therefore determine what adjustments should be made to ensure that foreign currency items are only included in the statement of cash flows to the extent that cash flows have occurred.

5.3.2.A Foreign currency operating transactions settled in the period

Where the exchange differences relate to operating items such as sales or purchases of inventory by an entity, no further adjustments need to be made when the indirect method of calculating the cash flow from operating activities is used. For example, if a sale transaction and cash settlement take place in the same period, the operating profit will include both the amount recorded at the date of sale and the amount of the exchange difference on settlement, the combination of which gives the amount of the actual cash flow.

5.3.2.B Unsettled foreign currency operating transactions

Similarly, where an exchange difference has been recognised on an unsettled balance relating to operating activities no reconciling item is needed. This is because the movement in the related receivable or payable included in the reconciliation to operating profit will incorporate the exchange gain or loss. Adjusting profit for the movement on the receivable or payable will eliminate the effect of movements in exchange rates since the date of the transaction.

5.3.2.C Determining the value of non-operating cash flows

Any exchange difference arising on a settled transaction relating to non-operating cash flows will give rise to an adjustment between reported profit and the cash flow from operating activities.

For example, the foreign currency purchase of property, plant and equipment would be recorded initially at the rate prevailing on the date of the transaction. The difference on payment of the foreign currency payable would be taken to the statement of comprehensive income as an exchange gain or loss. If left unadjusted in the statement of cash flows, the investing cash flow for the asset purchase would be recorded at the historical rate, rather than at the exchange rate prevailing at the date of settlement. This difference needs to be taken into account in calculating the cash flow to be shown under the relevant classification, in this case investing cash flows, which would otherwise be recorded at the amount shown in the note of the movements in property, plant and equipment.

5.3.2.D The indirect method and foreign subsidiaries

Entities should take care when applying the indirect method at the 'more consolidated level' as described at 6.1 below when there are foreign subsidiaries. If the translated financial statements are used, exchange differences will be included in the movements between the opening and closing group balance sheets. For example, an increase in inventories held by a US subsidiary from \$240 to \$270 during the year will be reported as an unchanged amount of £150 if the opening exchange rate of £1=\$1.60 becomes £1=\$1.80 by the year-end. In these circumstances an entity should take the functional currency financial statements of the foreign subsidiary as the starting point. The \$30 increase in inventories can then be translated at the average exchange rate.

5.4 Non-cash transactions and transactions on deferred terms

Non-cash transactions only ever appear in a statement of cash flows as adjustments to profit or loss for the period when using the indirect method of presenting cash flows from operating activities as discussed at 4.1.2 above. Investing and financing transactions that do not involve cash or cash equivalents are always excluded from the statement of cash flows. Disclosure is required elsewhere in the financial statements in order to provide all relevant information about these investing and financing activities. *[IAS 7.43]*. Examples of such non-cash transactions include the conversion of debt to equity; acquiring assets by assuming directly related liabilities or by means of a finance lease (or by means of any lease requiring the recognition of a lease liability under IFRS 16); and issuing equity as consideration for the acquisition of another entity. *[IAS 7.44]*. Similarly, asset exchange transactions and the issue of bonus shares out of retained earnings are disclosed as non-cash transactions. Extract 38.10 below shows the disclosures made by China Mobile Limited.

Extract 38.10: China Mobile Limited (2015)

CONSOLIDATED STATEMENT OF CASH FLOWS
for the year ended 31 December 2014 [extract]
Significant non-cash transactions [extract]

The Group recorded payables of RMB125,210,000,000 (2014: RMB120,327,000,000) to equipment suppliers as at 31 December 2015 for additions of construction in progress during the year then ended.

On 31 October 2015, the Group completed the transfer of its telecommunications towers and related assets to China Tower Corporation Limited ("China Tower"). In addition to 45,151,000,000 equity shares at a par value of RMB1 per share issued to the Group by China Tower to pay the consideration, China Tower would also pay cash consideration of RMB57,585,000,000. In February 2016, China Tower has paid RMB5,000,000,000, and the remaining balance of cash consideration is deferred and will be settled before 31 December 2017.

5.4.1 Asset purchases on deferred terms

The purchase of assets on deferred terms can be a complicated area because it may not be clear whether the associated cash flows should be classified under investing activities, as capital expenditure, or within financing activities, as the repayment of borrowings. In the US, FASB ASC Topic 230 – *Statement of Cash Flows* – takes the line that only advance payments, the down payment or other amounts paid at or near to the time of purchase of property, plant and equipment and other productive assets are investing cash flows; and, incurring directly related debt to the seller is a financing transaction with subsequent payments of principal on that debt classified as financing cash flows.[15] This treatment also appears to be implicit in IAS 7.

Where an entity acquires an asset under a finance lease (or under any lease requiring the recognition of a lease liability under IFRS 16), the acquisition of the asset is clearly a non-cash transaction, *[IAS 7.44]*, and the payments to reduce the outstanding liability relating to a finance lease are clearly financing cash flows. *[IAS 7.17]*. Because payments of deferred amounts do not result in recognition of an asset, but rather a reduction of a liability, they would not meet the definition of investing cash flows. However, as discussed at 4.4.10 above, the Interpretations Committee and the IASB have affirmed in 2013 their position that in determining the classification of cash flows, the nature of the activity is still the primary principle to be considered.[16] Accordingly, the classification of the payment comes down to a judgement as to whether its nature relates to the acquisition of an asset or the repayment of a liability.

In our view, in cases where financing is provided by the seller of the asset, the acquisition and financing should be treated as a non-cash transaction and disclosed accordingly. Subsequent payments to the seller are then included in financing cash flows. Nevertheless, if the period between acquisition and payment is not significant, the existence of credit terms should not be interpreted as changing the nature of the cash payment from investing to financing. The period between acquisition and payment would be regarded as significant if it gave rise to the seller recognising imputed interest under IAS 18 – *Revenue* (see Chapter 29 at 3.5), *[IAS 18.11]*, or under IFRS 15 – *Revenue from Contracts with Customers* (see Chapter 30 at 5.5.1). *[IFRS 15.60-65]*. Therefore, the settlement of a short-term payable for the purchase of an asset is an investing cash flow, whereas payments to reduce the liability relating to a lease or other finance provided by the seller for the purchase of an asset should be included in financing cash flows.

5.4.2 *Asset disposals on deferred terms*

It follows that the derecognition of property, plant and equipment by the lessor under a finance lease or another arrangement determined to be the provision of finance by the vendor would be disclosed as a non-cash transaction. Receipts to reduce the receivable from the purchaser would be investing cash flows, but described as the repayment of advances and loans rather than the proceeds on sale of property, plant and equipment. *[IAS 7.16]*.

It should be noted that, just as in the case of the factoring of trade receivables (see 4.4.4 above), the proceeds received by the seller in a sale and leaseback transaction is classified as a financing cash flow if the related asset is not derecognised.

5.5 Changes in liabilities arising from financing activities

In January 2016, the IASB amended IAS 7 to require disclosures that enable users of financial statements to evaluate changes in liabilities arising from financing activities, including both changes arising from cash flows and non-cash changes. *[IAS 7.44A]*. This amendment was in response to feedback from users, who highlighted that understanding an entity's cash flows is critical to their analysis and that there is a need for improved disclosures about an entity's debt, including changes in debt during the reporting period. *[IAS 7.BC9]*. Liabilities arising from financing activities are liabilities for which cash flows were, or future cash flows will be, classified in the statement of cash flows as cash flows from financing activities (see 4.3 above). In addition, financial asset related cash flows which will be included in cash flows from financing activities (such as assets that hedge liabilities arising from financing activities), should also be included in the scope of this disclosure. *[IAS 7.44C]*.

The following changes should be disclosed to explain the movements in these instruments:

(a) changes from financing cash flows;

(b) changes arising from obtaining or losing control of subsidiaries or other businesses;

(c) the effect of changes in foreign exchange rates;

(d) changes in fair values; and

(e) other changes. *[IAS 7.44B]*.

The standard suggests that these disclosures could be presented in the form of a reconciliation of the opening and closing balances in the statement of financial position for liabilities arising from financing activities. Where such a reconciliation is presented, sufficient information should be provided to enable the link of items included in the reconciliation to the statement of financial position and the statement of cash flows. *[IAS 7.44C]*. If an entity provides the disclosure required by paragraph 44A in combination with disclosures of changes in other assets and liabilities, it should disclose the changes in liabilities arising from financing activities separately from changes in those other assets and liabilities. *[IAS 7.44E]*.

5.6 Voluntary disclosures

IAS 7 encourages the disclosure of additional cash flow related information that may help users better understand the financial position of the entity, including a commentary by management, as follows:

(a) the amount of undrawn borrowing facilities that may be available for future operating activities and to settle capital commitments, indicating any restrictions on the use of these facilities;

(b) the aggregate amount of cash flows that represent increases in operating capacity separately from those cash flows that are required to maintain operating capacity (see 5.6.1 below); and

(c) the amount of the cash flows arising from the operating, investing and financing activities of each reportable segment (as defined in IFRS 8 – *Operating Segments*) (see 5.6.2 below). *[IAS 7.50]*.

5.6.1 Cash flows to increase and maintain operating capacity

IAS 7 does not contain any guidance as to how to distinguish cash flows for expansion from cash flows for maintenance in relation to the voluntary disclosure referred to under (b) above. The standard merely states that this information is useful in helping the user to determine whether the entity is investing adequately in the maintenance of its operating capacity or whether it may be sacrificing future profitability for the sake of current liquidity and distributions to owners. *[IAS 7.51]*.

Hongkong Land Holdings distinguishes renovations expenditure from developments capital expenditure in its analysis of investing cash flows.

Extract 38.11: Hongkong Land Holdings Ltd (2015)

Consolidated Cash Flow Statement [extract]
for the year ended 31st December 2015

	2015 US$m	2015 US$m
Investing activities		
Major renovations expenditure	**(57.8)**	(37.8)
Developments capital expenditure	**(152.3)**	(136.6)
Investments in and loans to associates and joint ventures	**(255.8)**	(215.6)
Advances and repayments from associates and joint ventures	**390.9**	478.2
Payment of deposit for a joint venture	**(70.9)**	–
Cash flows from investing activities	**(145.9)**	88.2

5.6.2 Segment cash flow disclosures

Disclosure of segmental cash flows is encouraged because it reveals the availability and variability of cash flows in each segment and allows users to better understand the relationship between the cash flows of the business as a whole and those of its component parts. *[IAS 7.52]*.

IAS 7 contains an example of the segmental disclosure advocated under (c) at 5.6 above.[17] However, this example simply reports the operating, investing and financing cash flows of its two segments with no reconciliation of the total to the statement of cash flows. In practice it might be difficult to allocate financing cash flows across the entity's reportable segments, given that this is not how treasury functions tend to operate.

A.P. Møller – Mærsk provides an analysis of operating cash flows and capital expenditure (part of its investing cash flows) by reportable segment. The entity does not disclose financing cash flows by reportable segment (comparative information is provided in the financial statements but is not reproduced here).

Extract 38.12: A.P. Møller – Mærsk A/S (2015)

Notes to the consolidated financial statements [extract]

NOTE 1 SEGMENT INFORMATION [extract]

AMOUNTS IN USD MILLION

2015	Maersk Line	Maersk Oil	APM Terminals	Maersk Drilling	Maersk Tankers
Cash flow from operating activities	3,271	1,768	874	1,283	291
Cash flow used for capital expenditure	–2,143	–2,017	–774	–854	–185

	Maersk Supply Service	Svitzer	Damco	Total reportable segments
Cash flow from operating activities	250	138	127	8,002
Cash flow used for capital expenditure	–206	–152	6	–6,325

6 ADDITIONAL IAS 7 CONSIDERATIONS FOR GROUPS

IAS 7 does not distinguish between single entities and groups, and there are no specific requirements as to how an entity should prepare a consolidated statement of cash flows. In the absence of specific requirements, cash inflows and outflows would be treated in the same way as income and expenses under IFRS 10 – *Consolidated Financial Statements*. Applying these principles, the statement of cash flows presented in consolidated financial statements should reflect only the flows of cash and cash equivalents into and out of the group, i.e. consolidated cash flows are presented as those of a single economic entity. *[IFRS 10 Appendix A]*. On the same basis, the cash flows of a consolidated subsidiary should be included in the consolidated statement of cash flows for the same period as its results are reported in the consolidated statement of comprehensive income, i.e. from the date the group gains control until the date it loses control. *[IFRS 10.B88]*.

Cash flows that are internal to the group (such as payments and receipts for intra-group sales, management charges, dividends, interest and financing arrangements) should be eliminated. *[IFRS 10.B86]*. However, transactions with non-controlling interests as well as with associates, joint ventures and unconsolidated subsidiaries would not be eliminated and are discussed in greater detail below.

6.1 Preparing a consolidated statement of cash flows

In principle, the group statement of cash flows should be built up from those prepared by individual subsidiaries with intra-group cash flows being eliminated as part of the aggregation process. This would generally be the case for entities presenting operating cash flows under the direct method, where information on gross cash receipts and payments has been obtained from each group entity's accounting records.

In practice, however, it may be possible to prepare a statement of cash flows at a more consolidated level, by starting with the disclosures in the consolidated statement of comprehensive income and statement of financial position and then applying the adjustments reflected as part of the financial statements consolidation process, together with information provided on external cash flows by individual subsidiaries. Thus, an entity adopting the direct method could use this information to derive the value of the major classes of gross cash receipts and gross cash payments. *[IAS 7.19]*. An entity presenting operating cash flows under the indirect method would use this information to calculate the values for movements in inventories, operating receivables and payables and other non-cash items that appear in the reconciliation of consolidated profit or loss to the group's cash flow from operating activities. *[IAS 7.20]*.

Cash flows from investing and financing activities could similarly be derived from a reconciliation of the relevant headings in the consolidated statement of comprehensive income to statement of financial position movements. However, for this to be possible, subsidiaries would have to provide supplementary information (as part of internal group reporting) to prevent gross cash flows from being netted off and to ensure that the cash flows are shown under the correct classifications. In particular, detailed information about receivables and payables would be essential to ensure that the movements in operating, investing and financing receivables and payables are identified.

6.2 Transactions with non-controlling interests

Dividends paid to non-controlling interest holders in subsidiaries are included under cash flows from financing activities or operating activities, in accordance with the entity's determined policy for dividends paid (see 4.4.1 above).

IFRS 10 requires entities to distinguish between transactions that give rise to a change in control and those that do not, because a transaction when there is no change in control is effectively one with the owners in their capacity as owners. *[IFRS 10.BCZ168]*. Changes in ownership interests in a subsidiary that do not result in a loss of control are therefore accounted for as equity transactions, and the resulting cash flows are classified in the same way as other transactions with owners. *[IAS 7.42B]*. Accordingly, IAS 7 requires that cash flows arising from changes in ownership interests in a subsidiary that occur after control is obtained, but do not give rise to a loss of control are classified as cash flows from financing activities. *[IAS 7.42A]*.

6.3 Acquisitions and disposals

An entity should present separately within investing activities the aggregate cash flows arising from obtaining or losing control of subsidiaries or other businesses. *[IAS 7.39]*. For transactions involving obtaining or losing control of subsidiaries or other businesses during the period, disclosure is also required, in aggregate, of each of the following:

(a) the total consideration paid or received;

(b) the portion of the consideration consisting of cash and cash equivalents;

(c) the amount of cash and cash equivalents in the subsidiaries or other businesses over which control is obtained or lost; and

(d) the amount of the assets and liabilities, other than cash or cash equivalents, in the subsidiaries or other businesses over which control is obtained or lost, summarised by each major category. *[IAS 7.40]*.

Cash flows arising from changes in ownership interests in a subsidiary that do not result in a loss of control are classified as financing cash flows (see 6.2 above). *[IAS 7.42A]*.

The aggregate amount of cash paid or received as consideration is reported in the statement of cash flows net of cash and cash equivalents acquired or disposed of. *[IAS 7.42]*. The cash flow effects of losing control are not deducted from those of gaining control. *[IAS 7.41]*. This implies that entities should present one analysis for all acquisitions and another for all disposals, such as that presented by Naspers, shown in Extract 38.13 below.

Extract 38.13: Naspers Limited (2016)

Consolidated statement of cash flows [extract]
for the year ended 31 March 2016

	31 March 2016 US$'m	31 March 2015 US$'m
Cash flows from investing activities [extract]		
Acquisitions of subsidiaries and businesses, net of cash acquired	**(1 231)**	(41)
Disposals of subsidiaries and businesses	**282**	158

Notes to the consolidated annual financial statements [extract]
for the year ended 31 March 2016

34. ACQUISITIONS OF SUBSIDIARIES AND BUSINESSES [extract]

	31 March 2016 US$'m	31 March 2015 US$'m
Carrying values of assets and liabilities:		
property, plant and equipment	**6**	11
other intangible assets	**812**	46
net current assets	**33**	–
deferred taxation	**(159)**	(14)
long-term liabilities	**–**	(2)
	692	41
Non-controlling interests	**(210)**	(4)
Derecognition of equity-accounted investments	**(97)**	(6)
Remeasurement of previously held interest	**(348)**	(3)
Option obligations raised in acquisitions	**(24)**	–
Remeasurment of acquiree share-based payment awards	**(22)**	–
Goodwill	**1 260**	105
Purchase consideration	**1 251**	133
Settlement of loans as part of purchase agreement	**(17)**	–
Settled through the issuance of equity instruments of the group	**–**	(70)
Settled through contribution of business	**–**	(16)
Amount to be settled in future	**–**	(7)
Settlement of amounts owing in respect of prior-year purchases	**22**	1
Net cash in subsidiaries and businesses acquired	**(25)**	–
Net cash outflow from acquisitions of subsidiaries and businesses	**1 231**	41

35. DISPOSALS OF SUBSIDIARIES AND BUSINESSES [extract]

	31 March 2016	
	2016 US$'m	**2015 US$'m**
Carrying values of assets and liabilities:		
property, plant and equipment	3	51
disposal groups classified as held for sale	160	–
goodwill	7	84
other intangible assets	4	25
net current assets	4	38
deferred taxation	–	(4)
long-term liabilities	(1)	(70)
foreign currency translation reserve realised	2	17
	179	141
Non-controlling interests	(1)	(12)
Existing control business combination reserve	4	–
Remeasurement of retained interest	–	1
Profit on sale	105	101
Selling price	**287**	231
Net cash in subsidiaries and businesses disposed of	(4)	(28)
Shares received as settlement	–	(45)
Amounts to be received in the future	(1)	–
Net cash inflow from disposals of subsidiaries and businesses	**282**	158

6.3.1 *Acquisition-related costs*

IFRS 3 – *Business Combinations* – requires acquisition-related costs (other than those costs relating to the issue of equity or debt securities) to be recognised as an expense in the period in which the costs are incurred and the services are received. *[IFRS 3.53]*. As discussed at 4.2 above, the IASB amended the definition of investing activities in IAS 7, whereby 'only expenditures that result in a recognised asset in the statement of financial position' give rise to investing cash flows. *[IAS 7.16]*. As a result, cash flows relating to acquisition costs recognised as an expense would have to be classified within operating activities.

6.3.2 *Deferred and other non-cash consideration*

Not all acquisitions or disposals of businesses are satisfied in full by the exchange of cash. Any non-cash consideration, such as shares issued by either party or amounts to be paid or received by the entity at a later date, is not included in the amount presented under investing activities. *[IAS 7.43]*. Instead, the non-cash element of the acquisition or disposal is disclosed; and in acquisitions where the deferred element of the consideration is regarded as the provision of finance by the vendor, its settlement is classified as a financing cash flow. This is explained in more detail at 5.4 above.

6.3.3 *Contingent consideration*

6.3.3.A Business combinations

When a business combination agreement allows for adjustments to the cost of the combination that are contingent on one or more future events, IFRS 3 requires the acquirer to recognise the acquisition-date fair value of the contingent consideration

[IFRS 3.39] and classify an obligation to pay the contingent consideration as a liability or as equity in accordance with the provisions of IAS 32 – *Financial Instruments: Presentation*. *[IFRS 3.40]*. Changes resulting from events after the acquisition date, such as meeting a performance target, are *not* reflected by adjusting the recorded cost of the business combination. Instead, any payment or receipt in excess of the carrying amount of the related liability or asset is recognised in profit or loss. *[IFRS 3.58]*.

The primary principle for the classification of cash flows should be the nature of the activity giving rise to the cash flow, according to the definitions of operating, investing and financing activities in the Standard (see 4.4.10 above). This might imply that all payments relating to a business combination should be classified as investing cash flows. However, as discussed at 4.2 above, the definition of investing activities states that only expenditures that result in a recognised asset are eligible for classification as investing activities. *[IAS 7.16]*. This raises the question of how an entity should classify cash payments for any contingent consideration in excess of the amount that was recorded on the acquisition date (and thereby included in the carrying value of the acquired assets including goodwill). When the final value of the contingent consideration is dependent upon meeting performance targets after the acquisition date, it could be considered that the nature of activity giving rise to the incremental payment is the earning of revenues and profits in the period after the business combination. Accordingly, cash payments in excess of the acquisition-date fair value of the contingent consideration would be classified as cash flows from operating activities.

In most circumstances, cash payments up to the amount recognised for the acquisition-date fair value of the contingent consideration would be classified in investing activities, on the basis that these are cash flows arising from obtaining or losing control of subsidiaries. *[IAS 7.39]*. However, to the extent that an element of the contingent consideration payment represents a provision of finance by the seller, it may qualify to be included in financing activities (see 5.4.1 above). Judgement is required to determine whether the terms of the arrangement indicate that any of the amount attributed to the acquisition date fair value of the contingent consideration represents the provision of finance by the vendor.

In our view, if the period between acquisition and payment is not significant, it would not be appropriate to regard any of the payment as a financing cash flow. On the other hand, if the period of deferral is significant, payments to reduce this liability could be regarded as financing cash flows. However, the greater the extent to which the actual value of the contingent consideration payable depends on factors other than the time value of money, such as future business performance, the more difficult it would be to identify a financing element.

6.3.3.B Asset acquisitions outside of business combinations

The purchase price of intangible assets or tangible assets acquired outside of a business combination often includes contingent consideration as well. The appropriate disclosure of the cash payment of that contingent consideration will depend on the facts and circumstances of the transaction. The classification in the statement of cash flow should follow the accounting treatment adopted in the statement of financial position and statement of comprehensive income with regard to changes in the fair value of that contingent consideration.

6.3.4 Settlement of amounts owed by the acquired entity

A question that sometimes arises is how to treat a payment made by the acquirer to settle amounts owed by a new subsidiary, either to take over a loan that is owed to the vendor by that subsidiary or to extinguish an external borrowing.

Payments made to acquire debt instruments of other entities are normally included under investing activities. *[IAS 7.16]*. Therefore, the payment to the vendor is classified under the same cash flow heading irrespective of whether it is regarded as being part of the purchase consideration or the acquisition of a debt. This presentation can be contrasted with the repayment of external debt by the new subsidiary, using funds provided by the parent, which is a cash outflow from financing activities. *[IAS 7.17]*.

6.3.5 Settlement of intra-group balances on a demerger

A similarly fine distinction might apply on the demerger of subsidiaries. These sometimes involve the repayment of intra-group indebtedness out of the proceeds from external finance raised by the demerged subsidiary. If the external funding is raised immediately prior to the subsidiary leaving the group, it is strictly a financing inflow in the consolidated statement of cash flows, being cash proceeds from issuing short or long-term borrowings. *[IAS 7.17]*. If the subsidiary both raises the external funding and repays the intra-group debt after the demerger, the inflow is shown in the consolidated statement of cash flows under investing activities, being a cash receipt from the repayment of advances and loans made to other parties. *[IAS 7.16]*.

6.4 Cash flows of subsidiaries, associates and joint ventures

6.4.1 Investments in associates and joint ventures

Changes in cash and cash equivalents relating to associates or joint ventures accounted for under the equity or cost method will impact the entity's statement of cash flows only to the extent of the cash flows between the group and the investee. *[IAS 7.37]*. The same concept would apply to associates or joint ventures carried at fair value as allowed by IAS 28 – *Investments in Associates and Joint Ventures* (discussed in Chapter 11). Examples include cash dividends received and loans advanced or repaid. *[IAS 7.37]*. Cash flows in respect of an entity's investment in an equity accounted associate or joint venture would also be presented. *[IAS 7.38]*.

Cash dividends received from equity accounted associates and joint ventures would be classified as operating or investing activities in accordance with the entity's determined policy for other dividends received (see 4.4.1 above). Where the net cash inflow from operating activities is determined using the indirect method, the group's share of profits or losses from equity-accounted investments will appear as a non-cash reconciling item in the cash flow statement (see 4.1.2 above).

Chapter 38

6.4.2 Cash flows of joint operations

IAS 7 does not specifically deal with the treatment of the cash flows of joint operations. However, following the guidance of IFRS 11 – *Joint Arrangements* – all transactions should be reflected in the accounts of the joint operators financial results to the extent of its interests in those transactions. *[IFRS 11.20]*. Therefore the cash flows of the joint arrangement are already included in the operator's financial statements and no additional adjustments are required to reflect the activities of the joint operation.

The treatment of cash flows for the acquisition and disposal of a joint operation is less clear as there is an argument for presentation either as a single net cash flow in investing activities (as is required for the cost of a business combination, discussed at 6.3 above); or as separate cash flows, classified according to the nature of the underlying assets and liabilities acquired. The IASB issued an amendment to IFRS 11, effective from 1 January 2016, *[IFRS 11.C1AA]*, which requires an entity to determine whether the activity undertaken by a joint operation constitutes a business as defined in IFRS 3 and to apply business combination or asset acquisition accounting in accordance with that analysis. *[IFRS 11.21A]*. Whilst this amendment does not change the requirements of IAS 7, it would be appropriate to apply a similar approach, with acquisitions and disposals of operations meeting the definition of a business giving rise to a single investing cash flow, and acquisitions and disposals of operations not regarded as a business giving rise to cash flows according to the nature of the assets and liabilities acquired. However, other approaches would be acceptable.

6.4.3 Cash flows in investment entities

IAS 7 does not address the treatment of subsidiaries held at fair value in an investment entity. As these investments are accounted for at fair value through profit or loss in accordance with IFRS 9 (or IAS 39 if IFRS 9 is not yet applied), the related cash flows would be treated consistently with cash flows from joint ventures and associates discussed at 6.4.1 above.

The disclosures required by an investment entity on the acquisition of subsidiaries are less than those required for other entities. Investment entities need only disclose the total consideration paid or received and the portion of the consideration consisting of cash and cash equivalents are required to be disclosed. *[IAS 7.40-40A]*.

6.5 Cash flows in separate financial statements

6.5.1 Cash flows of subsidiaries, associates and joint ventures

IAS 7 addresses the treatment of cash flows of associates, joint ventures and subsidiaries accounted for by use of the cost method, restricting its reporting in the statement of cash flows to the cash flows between itself and the investee, for example, to dividends and advances as discussed in 6.4.1 above. *[IAS 7.37]*. This treatment would also be applied to associates, joint ventures and subsidiaries held at fair value in separate financial statements if the election is made to account for these fair value through profit or loss in accordance with IFRS 9 (or IAS 39 if IFRS 9 is not yet applied), as allowed by IAS 27 – *Separate Financial Statements* – and discussed in Chapter 8.

6.5.2 *Group treasury arrangements*

Some groups adopt treasury arrangements under which cash resources are held centrally, either by the parent company or by a designated subsidiary company. Any excess cash is transferred to the designated group entity. In some cases a subsidiary might not even have its own bank account, with all receipts and payments being made directly from centrally controlled funds. Subsidiaries record an intercompany receivable when otherwise they would have held cash and bank deposits at each period end. A question that arises is whether or not a statement of cash flows should be presented when preparing the separate financial statements of such a subsidiary given that there is no cash or cash equivalents balance held at each period end and, for some entities, at any time during the year. In our view, the preparation of the statement of cash flows should be based upon the actual cash flows during the period regardless of cash and cash equivalents balance held directly by the entity.

Where no cash flows through an entity, but rather all transactions flow through another group company, the entity should still record receipts from debtors and payments to suppliers, albeit with an associated deposit to or withdrawal from a balance with another group company. Just as a bank processes payments and receipts as agent for the account holder, so the group treasury function acts as agent for the entity, and these transactions should be reflected in a statement of cash flows. This approach is consistent with the requirements in IAS 7 that all entities should prepare a statement of cash flows which forms an integral part of the financial statements. *[IAS 7.1]*.

Where the subsidiary makes net deposits of funds to, or net withdrawals of funds from the designated group entity during the reporting period, a further question arises as to how movements should be presented in the subsidiary's statement of cash flows. Normally these transactions give rise to intercompany balances. Therefore, the net deposits or net withdrawals should be shown as investing activities or financing activities, respectively.

In extremely rare cases the intercompany balances may meet the definition of cash equivalents and be regarded as short-term highly liquid investments that are readily convertible into known amounts of cash and are subject to insignificant risk of changes in value. However, in most cases such funds are transferred to the designated group entity for an indeterminate term and the fact that both the subsidiary and designated group entity are controlled by the parent company makes it difficult to conclude that the subsidiary could demand repayment of amounts deposited independently of the wishes of the parent company.

7 ADDITIONAL IAS 7 CONSIDERATIONS FOR FINANCIAL INSTITUTIONS

IAS 7 applies to banks, insurance entities and other financial institutions. Nevertheless, there are some differences in its application as compared to entities that are not financial institutions. For example, in considering the components of cash and cash equivalents, banks would not usually have borrowings with the characteristics of an overdraft, and cash for their purposes should normally include cash and balances at central banks, together with loans and advances to other banks repayable on demand.

Allianz discloses such items as components of its cash and cash equivalents, as shown in Extract 38.14 below.

Extract 38.14: Allianz SE (2015)

NOTES TO THE CONSOLIDATED BALANCE SHEETS [extract]

7 – Cash and cash equivalents

CASH AND CASH EQUIVALENTS

€ MN as of 31 December	2015	2014
Balances with banks payable on demand	7,764	6,657
Balances with central banks	388	397
Cash on hand	225	184
Treasury bills, discounted treasury notes, similar treasury securities, bills of exchange and checks	6,465	6,625
Total	**14,842**	**13,863**

IAS 7 contains a number of additional provisions affecting the preparation of statements of cash flow by financial institutions. These are covered in broad outline below.

7.1 Operating cash flows

Cash advances and loans made by financial institutions are usually classified as operating activities (and not as investing activities, as they are for other entities) since they relate to a financial institution's main revenue-producing activity. *[IAS 7.15, 16(e)]*. Similarly, receipts from the repayment of loans and advances would be included in operating cash flows. *[IAS 7.16(f)]*.

Interest paid and interest and dividends received are usually classified as operating cash flows for a financial institution. *[IAS 7.33]*.

For an insurance entity, cash receipts and cash payments for premiums and claims, annuities and other policy benefits would be included in its operating cash flows. *[IAS 7.14(e)]*.

Under the direct method of reporting operating cash flows, a financial institution that does not obtain information from its accounting records can derive the disclosures for major classes of gross cash receipts and payments by adjusting interest and similar income and interest expense and similar charges and other items recognised in profit or loss for:

(a) changes during the period in operating receivables and payables;

(b) other non-cash items; and

(c) other items for which the cash effects are investing or financing cash flows. *[IAS 7.19]*.

Where an insurance entity presents its operating cash flows using the direct method, it should separately disclose cash flows arising from insurance contracts. *[IFRS 4.37(b)]*. Comparative information is required. *[IFRS 4.42]*.

Subject to the differences noted above, the principles for a financial institution presenting operating cash flows under the indirect method are the same as those discussed at 4.1.2 above for other entities.

7.2 Reporting cash flows on a net basis

Cash flows from each of the following activities of a financial institution may be reported on a net basis:

(a) cash receipts and payments for the acceptance and repayment of deposits with a fixed maturity date;

(b) the placement of deposits with and withdrawal of deposits from other financial institutions; and

(c) cash advances and loans made to customers and the repayment of those advances and loans. *[IAS 7.24]*.

8 REQUIREMENTS OF OTHER STANDARDS

8.1 Cash flows of discontinued operations

IFRS 5 – *Non-current Assets Held for Sale and Discontinued Operations* – requires an entity to disclose the net cash flows attributable to the operating, investing and financing activities of discontinued operations. These disclosures can be presented either on the face of the statement of cash flows or in the notes. Disclosure is not required for disposal groups that are newly acquired subsidiaries which are classified as held for sale on acquisition in accordance with IFRS 5. *[IFRS 5.33(c)]*. The general presentation requirements of IFRS 5 are dealt with in Chapter 4.

In the example below, Netcare Limited elected to show the cash flows of discontinued operations on the face of the statement of cash flows, as well as in the note. Over and above this, the entity has elected to include additional disclosures by splitting cash flows in respect of interest and tax paid into those relating to continuing and discontinued operations. In the notes to the financial statements, Netcare Limited further analyses these cash flows by separate major business line.

Extract 38.15: Netcare Limited (2012)

GROUP STATEMENT OF CASH FLOWS [extract]
for the year ended 30 September

Rm	2012	2011
Cash generated from operations	5 193	5 572
Interest paid	(1 976)	(1 836)
Continuing operations	(1 959)	(1 817)
Discontinued operations	(17)	(19)
Taxation paid	(740)	(674)
Continuing operations	(720)	(658)
Discontinued operations	(20)	(16)
Capital reductions paid		(83)
Ordinary dividends paid	(694)	(553)
Ordinary dividends paid by subsidiaries	(4)	(3)
Preference dividends paid	(46)	(47)
Distributions to beneficiaries of the HPFL trusts	(43)	(47)
Net cash from operating activities	1 690	2 329
Continuing operations	1 646	2 285
Discontinued operations	44	44

NOTES TO THE GROUP ANNUAL FINANCIAL STATEMENTS [extract]

12.1 Discontinued operations [extract]

Rm	**Care**	**Transform**	**Total**
2012			
Cash flows from operating activities	**17**	**27**	**44**
Cash flows from investing activities	**(3)**	**(7)**	**(10)**
2011			
Cash flows from operating activities	39	5	44
Cash flows from investing activities	(3)	(8)	(11)
Cash flows from financing activities	(14)	3	(11)

8.2 Cash flows arising from insurance contracts

IFRS 4 – *Insurance Contracts* – requires that where an insurance entity presents its operating cash flows using the direct method, it should separately disclose cash flows arising from insurance contracts. *[IFRS 4.37(b)]*. Comparative information is required. *[IFRS 4.42]*.

8.3 Cash flows arising from the exploration of mineral resources

In a similar vein, IFRS 6 – *Exploration for and Evaluation of Mineral Resources* – requires that an entity discloses the amounts of operating and investing cash flows arising from the exploration for and evaluation of mineral resources. *[IFRS 6.24(b)]*. The requirements of IFRS 6 are discussed in Chapter 41. The requirement for investing cash flows to give rise to the recognition of an asset, discussed at 4.2 above, is particularly relevant to entities applying IFRS 6.

8.4 Cash flows arising from interests in subsidiaries, joint ventures and associates

IFRS 12 – *Disclosure of Interests in Other Entities* – requires an entity to disclose in its consolidated financial statements summarised financial information about the cash flows for each subsidiary that has non-controlling interests that are material to the entity. *[IFRS 12.B10(b)]*. These amounts are stated before inter-company eliminations. *[IFRS 12.B11]*.

In addition, for each material joint venture and associate an entity is also required to disclose dividends received from the joint venture or associate *[IFRS 12.B12(a)]* and, for joint ventures, the amount of cash and cash equivalents. *[IFRS 12.B13(a)]*. IFRS 12 is discussed in more detail in Chapter 13.

References

1 *IFRIC Update*, July 2009, p.3.
2 *IASB Update*, October 2015, p.5.
3 *IASB Update*, April 2013, p.13.
4 *IASB Update*, April 2013, p.13.
5 *IFRIC Update*, May 2011, p.4.
6 ED 2012/1, *Annual Improvements to IFRSs 2010-2012 Cycle*, IASB, May 2012, p.36.
7 *IASB Update*, April 2013, p.12.
8 *IFRIC Update*, August 2005, p.5.
9 *IFRIC Update*, August 2005, p.5.
10 *IFRIC Update*, March 2012, p.7.
11 *IFRIC Committee meeting agenda item 3, July 2012*, p.7.
12 *IFRIC Update*, July 2012, p.6.
13 *IFRIC Update*, March 2013, p.7.
14 *IASB Update*, April 2013, p.13.
15 FASB Accounting Standards Codification (ASC) Topic *Statement of Cash Flows*, 230-10-45-13, (Formerly SFAS 95, *Statement of Cash Flows, FASB, November 1987*, para. 17, footnote).
16 *IASB Update*, April 2013, p.13.
17 IAS 7, *Statement of Cash Flows*, IASB, Appendix A, part D. *Segment Information*.

Chapter 39 Interim financial reporting

List of examples

Chapter 39 Interim financial reporting

1 INTRODUCTION

One of the major issues in interim financial reporting is whether the interim period is a discrete period, or whether an interim period is an instalment of the full year. Under the first approach, an entity uses the same accounting policies and principles for annual financial statements as for interim periods. Under the second approach, the purpose of the interim report is to give investors, analysts and other users a better guide to the outcome of the full year, which requires modifications to the policies and principles used in annual financial reporting. The former approach is generally referred to as the 'discrete' approach, and the latter as the 'integral' approach.

The integral approach is not clearly defined, but implies deferring or accruing items of income or expense in order to present measures of performance for that interim period that are more indicative of the expected outcome for the year as a whole. Critics say that this approach obscures the results of the interim period. Proponents say that such modifications prevent distortion; an interim period is a more artificial interval than a financial year, and that to report transactions outside of the context of the annual operating cycle for which they are incurred could potentially present a misleading picture.

In practice, the distinction between discrete and integral approaches is less clear-cut than the description above suggests. IAS 34 – *Interim Financial Reporting* – requires an entity to use a 'year-to-date' approach, *[IAS 34.28]*, which is largely based on the requirement to report the entity's financial position as at the interim reporting date, but for which certain estimates and measurements are based on the expected financial position of the entity at year-end. However, the standard does not allow such estimates and measurements to amount to smoothing. For example, the estimate of tax expense for an interim period is based on actual profits earned as at the interim reporting date and not the expected tax expense for the year divided by the number of interim reporting periods, as discussed at 9.5 below.

The extent of disclosures in interim reports raises similar questions as to the purpose. If interim reporting is simply a more frequently published version of annual reporting, then the form and content of the interim report should be the same. However, if interim reporting is only an instalment of a longer period, then a reporting package that highlights changes in circumstances during an interim period makes more sense than an update of all the disclosures in an entity's annual financial statements. IAS 34 allows an entity to include either a complete set of financial statements or a condensed version in the interim report. *[IAS 34.4]*. While some jurisdictions require the complete form and even an audit of the interim report, current practice under IFRS favours the condensed version. The differences between full and condensed interim financial statements are discussed at 3 below.

There is no requirement for entities that prepare annual financial statements in conformity with IFRS to prepare interim financial statements in accordance with IAS 34. *[IAS 34.2]*. Historically, interim reporting was the prerogative of capital markets and regulators and IAS 34 leaves governments, securities regulators, stock exchanges and others to determine which entities report interim information, how often and how soon after the reporting period. *[IAS 34.1]*. Accordingly, adherence to local regulatory or legal requirements in interim financial reports is required.

Nevertheless, governments and regulators are increasingly referring to IAS 34 as they establish or revise their own requirements for interim financial reporting.

1.1 Definitions

The standard defines an interim period as 'a financial reporting period shorter than a full financial year.' *[IAS 34.4]*.

The term 'interim financial report' means a financial report for an interim period that contains either a complete set of financial statements (as described in IAS 1 – *Presentation of Financial Statements*) or a set of condensed financial statements as described in IAS 34 (see 3.2 below). *[IAS 34.4]*.

2 OBJECTIVE AND SCOPE OF IAS 34

2.1 Objective

The stated objective of the standard is 'to prescribe the minimum content of an interim financial report and to prescribe the principles for recognition and measurement in complete or condensed financial statements for an interim period. Timely and reliable interim financial reporting improves the ability of investors, creditors, and others to understand an entity's capacity to generate earnings and cash flows and its financial condition and liquidity.' *[IAS 34 Objective]*.

2.2 Scope

IAS 34 does not prescribe which entities are required to publish interim financial reports, how often, or how soon after the end of an interim period. The standard notes that governments, securities regulators, stock exchanges, and accountancy bodies often require entities whose debt or equity securities are publicly traded to publish interim financial reports. Therefore, in the absence of any specific regulatory requirement (or obligation of the entity, for example, by covenant), entities are not required to publish interim financial information in a form that complies with IAS 34. Instead, IAS 34 only applies if an entity either elects or is required to publish an interim financial report in accordance with IFRS. *[IAS 34.1]*. Accordingly, if an entity's interim financial report states that it complies with IFRS, then the requirements of IAS 34 must be met in full. *[IAS 34.3]*.

The decision to present interim financial reports in accordance with IFRS operates independently of the annual financial statements. Hence, entities may still prepare annual financial statements conforming to IFRS even if their interim financial statements do not comply with IAS 34. *[IAS 34.2]*.

Nevertheless, the IASB encourages publicly traded entities to issue interim financial reports that conform to the recognition, measurement and disclosure principles set out in IAS 34. Those entities are specifically encouraged: *[IAS 34.1]*

(a) to provide interim financial reports at least as of the end of the first half of their financial year; and

(b) to make their interim financial reports available not later than 60 days after the end of the interim period.

However, since an entity can only describe an interim financial report as complying with IFRS if it meets all of the requirements of IAS 34, *[IAS 34.3]*, an entity that applies all IFRS recognition and measurement requirements in its interim financial report, but does not include all the required disclosures may not describe the interim financial report as complying with IFRS.

As shown in the Extract below, Peel Hotels PLC disclosed that its interim financial statements for the period ended 16 August 2015 were not prepared in accordance with IAS 34.

Extract 39.1: Peel Hotels PLC (interim ended August 2015)

NOTES TO THE INTERIM RESULTS [extract]

1. **Basis of Accounting** [extract]

The interim financial information has been prepared on the basis of the recognition and measurement requirements of adopted IFRSs as at 16 August 2015 that are effective (or available for early adoption) at 31 January 2016. Based on these adopted IFRSs, the Directors have applied the accounting policies, which they expect to apply when the annual IFRS financial statements are prepared for the year ending 31 January 2016.

The group has chosen not to adopt IAS 34 (Interim Financial Statements) in preparing these interim financial statements and therefore the interim financial information is not in full compliance with International Financial Reporting Standards.

The group's accounting policies remain as stated in the group's full annual accounts for the year ended 1 February 2015.

3 COMPONENTS, FORM AND CONTENT OF AN INTERIM FINANCIAL REPORT UNDER IAS 34

The standard does not prohibit or discourage an entity from: *[IAS 34.7]*

- publishing a complete set of financial statements (as described in IAS 1) in its interim financial report, rather than condensed financial statements and selected explanatory notes; or
- including in condensed interim financial statements more than the minimum line items or selected explanatory notes as set out in IAS 34.

The recognition and measurement guidance in the standard, together with the note disclosures required by the standard, apply to both complete and condensed financial statements presented for an interim period. *[IAS 34.7]*.

3.1 Complete set of interim financial statements

An entity that publishes a complete set of financial statements in its interim financial report should include the following components, as required in IAS 1: *[IAS 34.5]*

(a) a statement of financial position as at the end of the interim period;

(b) a statement of profit or loss and other comprehensive income for the period;

(c) a statement of changes in equity for the period;

(d) a statement of cash flows for the period;

(e) notes, comprising a summary of significant accounting policies and other explanatory information;

(f) comparative information in respect of the preceding period for each of the statements listed at (a) to (d) above, and for all amounts reported in the current period's financial statements (unless specifically exempted by another IFRS); as well as (if relevant to understanding the current period's financial statements) comparative information for narrative and descriptive information; *[IAS 1.38, 38A]* and

(g) a statement of financial position as at the beginning of the preceding period (without a requirement for related notes) when: *[IAS 1.40A-40D]*

  (i) an accounting policy has been applied retrospectively; or

  (ii) a retrospective restatement has been made; or

  (iii) items have been reclassified,

  and the effect of such retrospective application on the information presented in that statement of financial position is material.

Entities may use alternative titles for the above statements other than those stated above. For example, an entity may use the title 'statement of comprehensive income' instead of 'statement of profit or loss and other comprehensive income'. *[IAS 34.5]*. Also an entity can refer to the 'statement of financial position' as 'balance sheet'.

If an entity publishes a complete set of financial statements in its interim financial report, the form and content of those statements should conform to the requirements of IAS 1. *[IAS 34.9]*. These requirements are discussed in Chapter 3 at 3. In addition, the entity should disclose the information specifically required by IAS 34 for interim financial reports as well as those required by other IFRSs (particularly those discussed at 4 below). *[IAS 34.7]*.

3.2 Condensed interim financial statements

In the interest of timeliness, cost, and avoiding repetition of previously reported information, an entity might be required to or elect to give less information at interim dates as compared with its annual financial statements. *[IAS 34.6]*. The standard defines the minimum content of an interim report, as including condensed financial statements and selected notes, as follows: *[IAS 34.6, 8]*

(a) a condensed statement of financial position;

(b) a condensed statement or condensed statements of profit or loss and other comprehensive income;

(c) a condensed statement of changes in equity;

(d) a condensed statement of cash flows; and

(e) selected explanatory notes.

Consistent with the standard's requirements for accounting policies (see 8.1 below), an entity would only depart from using the same presentation as in its most recent annual financial statements if it had determined that the format will change in its next annual financial statements. *[IAS 34.28]*.

The condensed statement of profit or loss and other comprehensive income referred to at (b) above should be presented using the same format as the entity's annual financial statements. Accordingly, if an entity presents a separate statement of profit or loss in its annual financial statements, then it should present a separate statement in the interim financial report as well. Similarly, if a combined statement of profit or loss and other comprehensive income is presented in the annual financial statements, the same format must be adopted in the interim financial report. *[IAS 34.8A]*.

As a minimum, the condensed financial statements should include each of the headings and subtotals that were included in the entity's last annual financial statements. *[IAS 34.10]*. However, the condensed financial statements do not need to look exactly like the year-end financial statements. Whilst IAS 34 requires 'headings and subtotals' to be the same, there is no similar requirement for the 'line items' under those headings referred to in IAS 1. *[IAS 1.54, 82]*.

A literal reading could mean that an entity is only required to present non-current assets, current assets, etc., on an interim statement of financial position. However, one of the purposes of an interim report is to help the users of the financial statements to understand the changes in financial position and performance of the entity since the previous annual reporting period. *[IAS 34.15]*. To that end, IAS 34 also requires additional line items or notes to be included if their omission makes the condensed financial statements misleading. *[IAS 34.10]*. In addition, the overriding goal of IAS 34 is to ensure that the interim report includes all information necessary to understand the financial position and the performance during the interim period. *[IAS 34.25]*. Therefore, the aggregation of information to this extent would be inconsistent with the objectives of IAS 34 and judgement is required to determine which line items provide useful information for decision-makers, and are presented, accordingly.

Inclusion of most of the line items in the annual financial statements has the benefit of providing the most information to help users of the financial statements understand the changes since the previous year-end. Nonetheless, entities may aggregate line items used in the annual financial statements, if doing so does not render the information misleading or prevent users of the financial statements from performing meaningful trend analysis. In response to a submission relating to the presentation and content of the condensed statement of cash flows, the Interpretations Committee expressed a view that a three-line condensed statement of cash flows showing only a total for each of operating, investing and financing cash flows would generally not meet the requirements of IAS 34 as set out above.[1]

Consideration should also be given to regulatory requirements, for example, where a regulator requires an entity to present certain line items using some form of materiality criteria (e.g. in terms of amount, percentage relative to headings, or percentage change from prior periods). Entities may apply similar measures of materiality as a guide for determining which line items to present separately, even where there is no regulatory requirement.

The following example illustrates one possible way in which an entity might choose to combine line items presented separately in the annual financial statements when preparing a condensed set of interim financial statements. However, such presentation is at the discretion of management, based on facts and circumstances, including materiality (as noted above), regulatory environment, and the overarching goal of IAS 34 to provide relevant information. *[IAS 34.25]*. Accordingly, other presentations may be appropriate.

Example 39.1: Presenting the same headings and sub-totals in condensed interim financial statements

Statement of financial position	*Annual financial statements*	*Condensed interim financial statements*
Assets		
Non-current assets		
Intangible assets	●	●
Property, plant and equipment	●	●
Deferred tax assets	●	●
Investments in associates	○	
Available-for-sale financial assets	○	
Other non-current assets	○	○
Total non-current assets	●	●
Current assets		
Inventories	○	
Trade and other receivables	●	●
Current income tax assets	○	
Other current assets	○	○
Cash and cash equivalents	●	●
Total current assets	●	●
Total assets	●	●

Liabilities		
Current liabilities		
Trade and other payables	●	●
Current income tax liabilities	○	
Borrowings	●	●
Provisions for other liabilities	○	
Other current liabilities	○	○
Total current liabilities	●	●
Non-current liabilities		
Borrowings	●	●
Pension obligations	●	●
Deferred tax liabilities	●	●
Other non-current liabilities	○	○
Provisions for other liabilities	○	
Total non-current liabilities	●	●
Total liabilities	●	●
Equity		
Share capital	●	●
Other reserves	●	●
Retained earnings	●	●
Total equity	●	●

● Included same line item in annual and interim financial statements
○ Denotes line items that have been combined in the interim financial statements

Statement of profit or loss and other comprehensive income	*Annual financial statements*	*Condensed interim financial statements*
Sale of goods	○	
Rendering of services	○	
Total revenue	○	○
Cost of goods	●	●
Cost of services	●	●
Gross profit	●	●
Selling costs	○	
General and administrative costs	○	
Other operating expenses	○	
Total operating expenses	○	○
Operating profit	●	●
Finance costs	●	●
Share of profit of associates	●	●
Profit before tax	●	●
Income tax expense	●	●
Profit for the period	●	●

	Annual financial statements	*Condensed interim financial statements*
Other comprehensive income to be reclassified to profit or loss in subsequent periods		
Translation of foreign operations	○	
Net gain on hedge of net investment	○	
Related income tax expense	○	
Net other comprehensive income to be reclassified to profit or loss in subsequent periods	○	○
Other comprehensive income that will not be reclassified subsequently to profit or loss		
Actuarial losses on defined benefit plans	○	
Related income tax credit	○	
Net other comprehensive income that will not be reclassified subsequently to profit or loss	○	○
Total other comprehensive income	●	●
Comprehensive income for the period	●	●

● Included same line item in annual and interim financial statements
○ Denotes line items that have been combined in the interim financial statements

Statement of cash flows	*Annual financial statements*	*Condensed interim financial statements*
Operating activities		
Profit before tax	●	●
Non-cash adjustments:		
Depreciation and amortisation	○	
Gain on disposal of property	○	
Finance cost	○	
Share of net profit of associate	○	
Movements in pensions	○	
Total non-cash adjustments	●	○
Working capital adjustments:		
Trade and other receivables	○	
Inventories	○	
Trade and other payables	○	
Total working capital adjustments	●	○
Net cash flows generated from operations	●	●
Income taxes paid	●	●
Acquisition expenses paid	●	●
Net cash flows from operating activities	●	●
Investing activities		
Interest received	●	●
Proceeds from sale of property	●	●
Purchases of property	●	●
Purchase of intangible assets	●	●
Proceeds from sale of available-for-sale financial assets	●	●
Net cash flows from investing activities	●	●

Financing activities		
Proceeds from borrowings	•	•
Repayment of borrowings	•	•
Interest paid	•	•
Dividends paid	•	•
Net cash flows from financing activities	•	•
Net increase in cash and cash equivalents	•	•
Net foreign exchange difference	•	•
Cash and cash equivalents at beginning of year	•	•
Cash and cash equivalents at end of year	•	•

• Included same line item in annual and interim financial statements
o Denotes line items that have been combined in the interim financial statements

For reasons of space, a statement of changes in equity is not presented in this example.

3.3 Requirements for both complete and condensed interim financial information

The general principles for preparing annual financial statements are equally applicable to condensed interim financial statements. These principles include fair presentation, going concern, the accrual basis of accounting, materiality and aggregation, and offsetting. *[IAS 1.4, 15-35]*. (See Chapter 3 at 4.1).

Furthermore, the following requirements apply irrespective of whether an entity provides complete or condensed financial statements for an interim period:

- if applicable, basic and diluted earnings per share should be presented on the face of the statement that presents items of profit or loss for an interim period. *[IAS 34.11]*. If the entity presents items of profit or loss in a separate statement in its annual financial statements, it should present basic and diluted earnings per share on the face of that separate statement in the interim financial report; *[IAS 34.11A]* and
- if the last annual financial statements were consolidated financial statements, the interim financial report should also be prepared on a consolidated basis. *[IAS 34.14]*.

If the entity's last annual financial report included the parent's separate financial statements and consolidated financial statements, IAS 34 neither requires nor prohibits the inclusion of the parent's separate financial statements in the interim financial report. *[IAS 34.14]*.

3.4 Management commentary

A management commentary is not explicitly required by IAS 34, but frequently included by entities in their interim financial reports along with the interim financial statements. In most cases the requirement for a narrative review comes from local stock market regulations and the entities should, therefore, follow the relevant guidance issued by those regulators.

IAS 34 allows information required under the standard to be presented outside the interim financial statements, i.e. in other parts of interim financial report. Thus some of the required disclosures may be included in a management commentary (see 4.2.1 below). The standard itself does not establish specific requirements for the content of a management commentary beyond what should be contained in (or cross-referred from) the interim financial statements.

4 DISCLOSURES IN CONDENSED FINANCIAL STATEMENTS

IAS 34 combines a number of disclosure principles:

- Entities should provide information about events and transactions in the interim period that are significant to an understanding of the changes in financial position and performance since the last annual reporting period. In this context it is not necessary to provide relatively insignificant updates to information reported in the last annual financial statements (see 4.1 below). *[IAS 34.15, 15A]*.
- In addition to information to explain significant changes since the last annual reporting period, a number of specific disclosures are required to be given, if not disclosed elsewhere in the interim financial report. *[IAS 34.16A]*. In this case the decision to disclose is subject to a materiality assessment (see 4.2 below).
- The materiality assessment for disclosure is based on the interim period by itself, to ensure all information is provided that is relevant to understanding the entity's financial position and its performance during the interim period (further discussed at 6 below). *[IAS 34.25]*.

Overall, applying those disclosure principles requires the exercise of judgement by the entity regarding what information is significant or relevant. The practice of interim reporting confirms that entities take advantage of that room for judgement, both for disclosures provided in the notes to the financial statements and outside.

4.1 Significant events and transactions

IAS 34 presumes that users of an entity's interim financial report also have access to its most recent annual financial report. *[IAS 34.15A]*. On that basis, an interim financial report should explain events and transactions that are significant to an understanding of the changes in financial position and performance of the entity since the previous annual reporting period and provide an update to the relevant information included in the financial statements of the previous year. *[IAS 34.15, 15C]*. The inclusion of only selected explanatory notes is consistent with the purpose of an interim financial report, to update the latest complete set of annual financial statements. Accordingly, condensed financial statements avoid duplicating previously reported information and focus on new activities, events, and circumstances. *[IAS 34.6]*.

The standard requires disclosure of following events and transactions in interim financial reports, if they are significant: *[IAS 34.15B]*

(a) write-down of inventories to net realisable value and the reversal of such a write-down;

(b) recognition of a loss from the impairment of financial assets, property, plant, and equipment, intangible assets, or other assets, and the reversal of such an impairment loss;

(c) reversal of any provisions for the costs of restructuring;

(d) acquisitions and disposals of items of property, plant, and equipment;

(e) commitments for the purchase of property, plant, and equipment;

(f) litigation settlements;

(g) corrections of prior period errors;

(h) changes in the business or economic circumstances that affect the fair value of the entity's financial assets and financial liabilities, whether those assets or liabilities are recognised at fair value or amortised cost;

(i) any loan default or breach of a loan agreement that is not remedied on or before the end of the reporting period;

(j) related party transactions;

(k) transfers between levels of the fair value hierarchy used in measuring the fair value of financial instruments;

(l) changes in the classification of financial assets as a result of a change in the purpose or use of those assets; and

(m) changes in contingent liabilities or contingent assets.

The standard specifies that the above list of events and transactions is not exhaustive and the interim financial report should explain any additional events and transactions that are significant to an understanding of changes in the entity's financial position and performance. *[IAS 34.15, 15B]*. Therefore, when information relating to items not on the above list changes significantly, an entity should still provide disclosure in the interim financial statements, in sufficient detail to explain the nature of the change and any changes in estimates. This would apply, for example, when the values of non-financial assets and liabilities that are measured at fair value change significantly.

As discussed at 4.2.1 below, the IASB has considered questions around the delineation of the interim financial statements within an interim financial report and decided to amend paragraph 16A of the standard to require a cross-reference from the interim financial statements when information required by the Standard is presented elsewhere in the interim financial report. In our view, the IASB's acceptance of cross-referencing as a means of bringing information required by paragraph 16A into the condensed financial statements suggests that preparers of the interim financial report should also provide such a cross-reference where the information required above about significant events and transactions is given outside the interim financial statements.

4.1.1 Relevance of other standards in condensed financial statements

Whilst other standards specify disclosures required in a complete set of financial statements, if an entity's interim financial report includes only condensed financial statements as described in IAS 34, then the disclosures required by those other standards are not mandatory. However, if disclosure is considered to be necessary in the context of an interim report, those other standards provide guidance on the appropriate disclosures for many of these items. *[IAS 34.15C]*.

In practice, entities exercise judgement to determine whether including the disclosures required by other standards are material to an understanding of the entity and will provide a benefit to users of the interim financial statements. *[IAS 34.25]*. For example, the existence of acquisitions and disposal of items of property plant and equipment does not automatically require the interim report to include a reconciliation of the carrying amount at the beginning and end of the interim period. *[IAS 16.73(e)]*. In many cases, a narrative disclosure would be sufficient, and in some cases, the change may be immaterial, and therefore no disclosures are required. However, in an interim period with material changes, as for instance when assets are acquired by purchase, obtained in a business combination, and transferred to a disposal unit as well as sold in the normal course of business, such a reconciliation could be judged to be an appropriate way of presenting this information in the interim financial statements.

An issue arises on initial adoption of IFRS 9 – *Financial Instruments* – on the extent of required disclosures in interim reports in the year of initial application (see 12.2 below).

4.2 Other disclosures required by IAS 34

In addition to disclosing significant events and transactions as discussed at 4.1 above, IAS 34 requires an entity to include the following information in the notes to its interim financial statements if not disclosed elsewhere in the interim financial report: *[IAS 34.16A]*

(a) a statement that the same accounting policies and methods of computation are followed in the interim financial statements as in the most recent annual financial statements or, if those policies or methods have changed, a description of the nature and effect of the change;

(b) explanatory comments about the seasonality or cyclicality of interim operations;

(c) the nature and amount of items affecting assets, liabilities, equity, net income, or cash flows that are unusual because of their nature, size, or incidence;

(d) the nature and amount of changes in estimates of amounts reported in prior interim periods of the current year or changes in estimates of amounts reported in prior years;

(e) issues, repurchases, and repayments of debt and equity securities;

(f) dividends paid (aggregate or per share) separately for ordinary shares and other shares;

(g) certain segment disclosures required by IFRS 8 – *Operating Segments* – as discussed at 4.4 below;

(h) events after the interim period that are not reflected in the financial statements for the interim period;

(i) the effect of changes in the composition of the entity during the interim period, including business combinations, obtaining or losing control of subsidiaries and long-term investments, restructurings, and discontinued operations. For business combinations, the entity should disclose the information required under IFRS 3 – *Business Combinations* (see Chapter 9 at 16);

(j) for financial instruments, certain fair value disclosures required by IFRS 7 – *Financial Instruments: Disclosures* – and IFRS 13 – *Fair Value Measurement* – as discussed at 4.5 below; and

(k) for entities becoming, or ceasing to be, investment entities, as defined in IFRS 10 – *Consolidated Financial Statements*, the disclosures in IFRS 12 – *Disclosure of Interests in Other Entities* – as required by paragraph 9B of that standard (see Chapter 13 at 4.6.2). *[IAS 34.16A(k)]*.

This information is disclosed on a financial year-to-date basis. *[IAS 34.16A]*. However, the requirement in item (i) above for disclosures of business combinations applies not only for those effected during the current interim period, but also to business combinations after the reporting period but before the interim financial report is authorised for issue. *[IFRS 3.59(b), IFRS 3.B66]*. An entity is not required to provide all of the disclosures for business combinations after the reporting period, if the accounting for the business combination is incomplete as at the date on which the financial statements are authorised for issue. In this case, the entity should state which disclosures cannot be made and the reasons why they cannot be made. *[IFRS 3.B66]*.

IFRS 3 requires disclosures in aggregate for business combinations effected during the reporting period that are individually immaterial. *[IFRS 3.B65]*. However, materiality is assessed for the interim period financial data, *[IAS 34.23]*, which implies that IAS 34 may require detailed disclosures on business combinations that are material to an interim period, even if they could be aggregated for disclosure purposes in the annual financial statements.

The list above also requires disclosure of the effect of changes in the composition of the entity arising from disposals, discontinued operations and restructurings in the interim period. *[IAS 34.16A(i)]*.

If an entity has operations that are discontinued or disposed of during an interim period, these operations should be presented separately in the condensed interim statement of comprehensive income following the principles set out in IFRS 5 – *Non-current Assets Held for Sale and Discontinued Operations*. In addition if an entity has non-current assets or a disposal group classified as held for sale or distribution at the end of the interim reporting period, then these should be measured in accordance with the requirements of IFRS 5 and presented separately from other assets and liabilities in the condensed interim statement of financial position.

An entity contemplating a significant restructuring that will have an impact on its composition should follow the guidance in IAS 37 – *Provisions, Contingent Liabilities and Contingent Assets* – for the recognition of any restructuring cost, *[IAS 37.71]*, and IAS 19 – *Employee Benefits* – for termination benefits. *[IAS 19.165(b)]*. In subsequent interim periods any significant changes to provisions will require disclosure. *[IAS 34.15B(c)]*.

The inclusion of the above disclosure requirements among the items required by the standard to be given 'in addition to disclosing significant events and transactions', *[IAS 34.16A]*, distinguishes them from the items listed at 4.1 above, which are disclosed to update information presented in the most recent annual financial report. *[IAS 34.15]*. Therefore, disclosure of the above information is required for each interim reporting period, subject only to a materiality assessment in relation to that interim report, i.e.

an entity could consider it unnecessary to disclose the above information on the grounds that it is not relevant to an understanding of its financial position and performance in that specific interim period. *[IAS 34.25]*. In making that judgement care would need to be taken to ensure any omitted information would not make the interim financial report incomplete and therefore misleading.

In summary, the 'selected explanatory notes' *[IAS 34.8(e)]* required under IFRSs for interim financial reporting are extensive. For example, the disclosures are significant for business combinations, segments, and the recognition and reversal of impairments of assets. See Chapter 9 at 16; 4.4 below and 4.3.2 below respectively.

4.2.1 *Location of the specified disclosures in an interim financial report*

IAS 34 defines an 'interim financial report' as 'a financial report containing either a complete set of financial statements... or a set of condensed financial statements... for an interim period.' *[IAS 34.4]*. Therefore, since an interim financial report *contains* the interim financial statements, it is clear that these are two different concepts. Accordingly, an entity is not required to disclose the information listed at 4.2 above in the interim financial statements themselves (but rather, might include the disclosures in the management commentary), as long as a cross-reference is provided from the financial statements to the location of the information included in another part of the interim financial report. *[IAS 34.16A]*.

Additionally, for a cross-reference to be acceptable, the information given 'elsewhere in the interim financial report' needs to both satisfy the disclosure requirements in IFRSs and be available on the same terms as the interim financial statements, i.e. users should have access to the referenced material (for example, the management commentary or a risk report) on the same basis and at the same time as they have for accessing the condensed financial statements from which the reference is made.

The cross-reference should identify the specific part that includes the required disclosure to allow the reader to easily navigate within the interim financial report.

4.3 Illustrative examples of disclosures

The extracts below show examples of disclosures required by IAS 34.

4.3.1 *Inventory write-down and reversals*

In the extract below, BP discloses write downs of its inventories and reversals in the current and corresponding periods. *[IAS 34.15B(a)]*.

Extract 39.2: BP p.l.c. (interim ended June 2016)

Notes [extract]

10. Inventory valuation

A provision of $689 million was held at 30 June 2016 ($677 million at 31 March 2016 and $590 million at 30 June 2015) to write inventories down to their net realizable value. The net movement charged to the income statement during the second quarter 2016 was $12 million (first quarter 2016 was a credit of $616 million and second quarter 2015 was a credit of $210 million).

4.3.2 *Impairment*

In Extract 39.3 below, as part of its note on intangible assets, Roche discloses the impairment charges on its intangible assets during the reporting period and provides a breakdown by division and further background to those impairments. *[IAS 34.15B(b)]*.

Extract 39.3: Roche Holding Ltd (interim ended June 2016)

Notes to the Roche Group Interim Consolidated Financial Statements [extract]

8. Intangible assets [extract]

Impairment charges – 2016 [extract]

Pharmaceuticals Division. Impairment charges totalling CHF377 million were recorded which related to:

- A delay in the development of the compound acquired as part of the Trophos acquisition following regulatory feedback (CHF187 million). The asset concerned, which was not yet being amortised, was written down to its estimated recoverable value of CHF291 million.
- A portfolio reassessment of one compound (CHF162 million). The asset concerned, which was not yet being amortised, was fully written down.
- A decision to stop development of one compound (CHF28 million). The asset concerned, which was not yet being amortised, was fully written down.

4.3.3 *Reversal of restructuring provisions*

Among the various items that have impacted its other operating income for the period, Deutsche Post DHL AG provides the following narrative to explain the reversal of a restructuring provision. *[IAS 34.15B(c)]*.

Extract 39.4: Deutsche Post DHL (interim ended September 2014)

Selected Explanatory Notes [extract]

Basis of preparation [extract]

Income Statement Disclosures [extract]

5 Other operating income [extract]

Income from the reversal of provisions increased mainly because of a change in the assessment of settlement payment obligations assumed in the context of the restructuring measures in the USA. The probability that this obligation will occur has declined to the point where the provision was reversed and the potential obligation disclosed as a contingent liability in the amount of €125 million. [...]

4.3.4 *Acquisition and disposal of property, plant and equipment*

In Extract 39.5 below, Wilmington meets the requirement to disclose additions and disposals of items of property, plant and equipment in the interim period, *[IAS 34.15B(d)]*, in a note reconciling the movements, in aggregate, in property, plant and equipment; intangible assets; and goodwill. In addition, Wilmington provides information about movements in the comparative periods (not reproduced here).

Extract 39.5: Wilmington plc (interim ended December 2015)

Notes to the Financial Results [extract]

13. **Goodwill, Intangible assets and Property, plant and equipment** [extract]

	Goodwill £'000	Intangible assets £'000	Property, plant and equipment £'000
At 30 June 2014 (audited)	76,855	28,746	5,727
[...]			
Closing net book amount as at 30 June 2015 (audited)	77,063	23,636	4,841
Acquisitions (provisional)	4,718	4,718	–
Additions	217	472	290
Disposals	–	–	(7)
Exchange translation differences	469	377	5
Depreciation of property, plant and equipment	–	–	(447)
Amortisation of publishing rights, titles and benefits	–	(3,011)	–
Amortisation of computer software	–	(512)	–
Closing net book amount as at 31 December 2015 (unaudited)	82,467	25,680	4,682

4.3.5 Capital commitments

In a brief descriptive note, Deutsche Lufthansa discloses its commitments for capital expenditure. *[IAS 34.15B(e)]*.

Extract 39.6: Deutsche Lufthansa AG (interim ended March 2016)

Interim financial statements [extract]

Notes [extract]

4) **Contingencies and events after the balance sheet date** [extract]

[...] At the end of March 2016, there were order commitments of EUR 15.8bn for capital expenditure on property, plant and equipment and intangible assets. As of 31 December 2015, the order commitments came to EUR 16.5bn. [...]

4.3.6 Litigation settlements

UBS provides details about significant litigation in its interim report. The extract below illustrates its disclosure about related settlements. *[IAS 34.15B(f)]*.

Extract 39.7: UBS Group AG (interim ended June 2016)

Notes to the UBS AG interim consolidated financial statements [extract]

Note 16 **Provisions and contingent liabilities** [extract]

b) **Litigation, regulatory and similar matters** [extract]

5. Foreign exchange, LIBOR, and benchmark rates and other trading practices
LIBOR and other benchmark-related civil litigation:

A number of putative class actions and other actions are pending in, or expected to be transferred to, the federal courts in New York against UBS and numerous other banks on behalf of parties who transacted in certain interest rate benchmark-based derivatives. Also pending are actions asserting losses related to various products whose interest rate was linked to USD LIBOR, including adjustable rate mortgages, preferred and debt securities, bonds pledged as collateral, loans, depository accounts, investments and other interest-bearing instruments. All of the complaints allege manipulation, through various means, of various benchmark interest rates including USD LIBOR, Euroyen TIBOR, Yen LIBOR, EURIBOR, CHF LIBOR, GBP LIBOR or USD ISDAFIX rates, and seek unspecified compensatory and other damages under varying legal theories. [...]

With respect to additional matters and jurisdictions not encompassed by the settlements and order referred to above, our balance sheet at 31 March 2016 reflected a provision in an amount that UBS believes to be appropriate under the applicable accounting standard. [...]

4.3.7 Correction of prior period errors

In Extract 39.8 below, euromicron provides the following narrative disclosures to accompany a detailed tabular presentation (not reproduced here) that explain the effect on the comparative information of adjustments made to correct errors discovered between the issue of the previous interim financial statements and the annual report for the 2014 year-end. *[IAS 34.15B(g)]*.

Extract 39.8: euromicron AG (interim ended June 2015)

INTERIM CONSOLIDATED FINANCIAL STATEMENTS [extract]

NOTES [extract]

Corrections according to IAS 8 [extract]

During the preparation of IFRS interim financial statements for euromicron AG as of June 30, 2015 adjustments were required of the comparative figures for the respective period of the previous year (period from January 01 to June 30, 2014). These will be presented below. They relate to the presentation of individual items in the income statement, the statement of cash flows and the statement of changes in equity for the respective half-year of the previous year. The presented corrections do not necessitate any change to the balance sheet, since the balance as of December 31, 2014 is shown as the comparative information in the half-year financial statements dated June 30, 2015 and all items in it are accurately presented.

1. Due to the correction of errors in accordance with IAS 8 in the valuation of projects in previous periods in the IFRS 2014 consolidated financial statements, subsequent adjustments were made in the IFRS half-year financial statements dated June 30, 2015, relating to the comparative disclosures for the respective half-year of the previous year from January 01 to June 30, 2014. These subsequent adjustments comprise sales, cost of materials, personnel expenses and other operating expenses in the first half-year of 2014 for the projects affected by the corrections. In addition, income taxes were also affected. Because of the adjustments made in these half-year financial statements dated June 30, 2015 the effects from the subsequent corrections, which were recorded in the profit/loss of the fourth quarter of 2014, but relate to the first and second quarter of 2014, are now recognized in the correct period in the profit/loss for the first half-year of 2014. The audited and published consolidated financial statements 2014 are not affected, since the corrections only relate to the comparative figures for the respective quarters of 2014 and are fully eliminated by the end of fiscal year 2014 ("change adaptation in 2014 IAS 8 Correction Project Review"). [...]

> In the present half-year financial statements dated June 30, 2015 the comparative figures for the period from January 01 to June 30, 2014 were adjusted for all disclosures relating to the figures in the income statement. The adjustments in accordance with IAS 8 are also indicated in the statement of changes in equity and the statement of cash flows.
>
> The follow tables show the impact of the corrections on the comparative figures reported in the financial statements dated June 30, 2015 for the period January 01, to June 30, 2014 as well as the impact on the comparative figures for the second quarter of 2014 (period of April 01, to June 30, 2014). These figures are referenced at various points in the half-year financial statements: [...]

4.3.8 Changes in circumstances affecting fair values

In their half-yearly interim report for 2016, Rolls-Royce Holdings plc describes the effect of changes in financial markets following the result of the UK Referendum on its membership of the European Union. *[IAS 34.15B(h)]*.

> *Extract 39.9: Rolls-Royce Holdings plc (interim ended June 2016)*
>
> **Chief Executive's Review** [extract]
> **Performance in the first six months of 2016** [extract]
>
> Since the EU referendum vote at the end of June, the value of sterling relative to the US dollar fell significantly. As a result, we have recognised a £2.2bn non-cash mark-to-market valuation adjustment for our US dollar hedge book. Reported revenue of £6,462m (2015: £6,370m) was unaffected by this; however the valuation adjustment was the principle reason for reported financing costs being £(2,386)m (2015: £(69)m) and reported loss before tax being £(2,150)m (2015: £310m profit).

4.3.9 Default or breach of loan covenants not remedied before the end of interim period

In Extract 39.10 below, Hellenic Company for Telecommunications and Telematic Applications S.A. (Forthnet S.A.) discusses breaches of loan covenants. *[IAS 34.15B(i)]*. The existence of breaches or defaults that have not been remedied by the end of the reporting period will merit disclosure about management's assessment of the entity's ability to continue as a going concern. This is discussed at 8.1.3 and illustrated for Forthnet S.A. in Extract 39.10 below.

> *Extract 39.10: Forthnet S.A. (interim ended September 2015)*
>
> **Notes to the Interim Financial Statements (Unaudited)** [extract]
> **3 GOING CONCERN** [extract]
>
> As at September 30, 2015, Forthnet S.A. and Forthnet Media S.A. continue not to meet certain financial covenants under their respective bond loans (see Note 18). Specifically, the Group was not in compliance with its Net Debt to Total Equity, the Net Debt to Normalised EBITDA and the Normalised EBITDA to Total Interest ratios for the existing bond loans ("EBL") and its new bond loans ("NBL") and has not made contractual payments of €180.0 million through the date that the financial statements were authorized for issue. Accordingly, as at September 30, 2015, the Group has retained the classification of all outstanding balances of such bond loans amounting to €324.7 million and €100.0 million for the Group and Company, respectively, as current. The classification of the outstanding balances of the bond loans as current has, among others, led to the Group's and the Company's current liabilities exceeding their current assets by approximately €402.0 and €41.5 million, respectively, as at September 30, 2015. [...]

4.3.10 *Related party transactions*

In Extract 39.11 below, Deutsche Bank discloses related party transactions. *[IAS 34.15B(j)]*.

Extract 39.11: Deutsche Bank Aktiengesellschaft (interim ended March 2016)

Other Financial Information (unaudited) [extract]

Related Party Transactions

Parties are considered to be related if one party has the ability to directly or indirectly control the other party or exercise significant influence over the other party in making financial or operational decisions. The Group's related parties include:

- key management personnel, close family members of key management personnel and entities which are controlled, significantly influenced by, or for which significant voting power is held by key management personnel or their close family members,
- subsidiaries, joint ventures and associates and their respective subsidiaries, and
- post-employment benefit plans for the benefit of Deutsche Bank employees.

Transactions with Key Management Personnel

Key management personnel are those persons having authority and responsibility for planning, directing and controlling the activities of Deutsche Bank Group, directly or indirectly. The Group considers the members of the Management Board as currently mandated and the Supervisory Board of the parent company to constitute key management personnel for purposes of IAS 24. Among the Group's transactions with key management personnel as of March 31, 2016, were loans and commitments of €11 million and deposits of €8 million. As of December 31, 2015, there were loans and commitments of €11 million and deposits of €8 million among the Group's transactions with key management personnel. In addition, the Group provides banking services, such as payment and account services as well as investment advice, to key management personnel and their close family members.

Transactions with Subsidiaries, Associates and Joint Ventures

Transactions between Deutsche Bank AG and its subsidiaries meet the definition of related party transactions. If these transactions are eliminated on consolidation, they are not disclosed as related party transactions. Transactions between the Group and its associated companies and joint ventures and their respective subsidiaries also qualify as related party transactions.

Loans issued and guarantees granted

	Associated companies and other related parties	
in € m.	Mar 31, 2016	Dec 31, 2015
Loans outstanding, beginning of period	**396**	321
Loans issued during the period	92	464
Loan repayments during the period	64	376
Changes in the group of consolidated companies	0	(31)
Exchange rate changes/other	0	18
Loans outstanding, end of period[1]	**425**	396
Other credit risk related transactions:		
Allowance for loan losses	1	1
Provision for loan losses	0	0
Guarantees and commitments	263	263

1 Loans past due were €8 million as of March 31, 2016, and €4 million as of December 31, 2015. For the above loans, the Group held collateral of €78 million and €69 million as of March 31, 2016 and December 31, 2015, respectively.

Chapter 39

Deposits received

in € m.	Associated companies and other related parties Mar 31, 2016	Dec 31, 2015
Deposits, beginning of period	**162**	128
Deposits received during the period	75	326
Deposits repaid during the period	119	295
Changes in the group of consolidated companies	0	(0)
Exchange rate changes/other	(1)	2
Deposits, end of period	**115**	162

Other transactions

Trading assets and positive market values from derivative financial transactions with associated companies amounted to €39 million as of March 31, 2016, and €32 million as of December 31, 2015. Trading liabilities and negative market values from derivative financial transactions with associated companies were €0 million as of March 31, 2016, and €0 million as of December 31, 2015.

Transactions with Pension Plans

The Group has business relationships with a number of its pension plans pursuant to which it provides financial services to these plans, including investment management. Pension funds may hold or trade Deutsche Bank AG shares or securities. As of March 31, 2016, transactions with these plans were not material for the Group.

4.3.11 Transfers between different levels of fair value hierarchy

Detailed reconciliation is provided by HSBC in the extract below relating to fair value measurements in level 3 of the fair value hierarchy. The reconciliation, among other items, includes transfer of items in and out of level 3. *[IAS 34.15B(k)]*. The same level of detail is provided for the comparative periods from 1 July 2014 to December 2014 and 1 January 2014 to 30 June 2014, but for reasons of space is not reproduced below.

Extract 39.12: HSBC Holdings plc (interim ended June 2015)

Notes on the Financial Statements (unaudited) (continued) [extract]
8 – Fair values of financial instruments carried at fair value [extract]
Movement in Level 3 financial instruments

	Assets				Liabilities		
	Available for sale $m	Held for trading $m	Designated at fair value through profit or loss $m	Derivatives $m	Held for trading $m	Designated at fair value through profit or loss $m	Derivatives $m
At 1 January 2015	4,988	6,468	726	2,924	6,139	–	1,907
Total gains/(losses) recognised in profit or loss	(17)	(14)	(19)	344	(223)	(1)	(467)
– trading income /(expense) excluding net interest income	–	(14)	–	344	(223)	–	(467)
– net income/ (expense) from other financial instruments designated at fair value	–	–	(19)	–	–	(1)	–

– gains less losses from financial investments	(29)	–	–	–	–	–	–
– loan impairment charges and other credit risk provisions	12	–	–	–	–	–	–
Total gains/(losses) recognised in other comprehensive income[1]	72	(6)	(9)	5	(20)	(1)	1
– available for sale investments: fair value gains	70	–	–	–	–	–	–
– exchange differences	2	(6)	(9)	5	(20)	(1)	1
Purchases	342	435	165	–	–	9	–
New issuances	–	–	–	–	863	–	–
Sales	(420)	(1,134)	(46)	–	(10)	(2)	–
Settlements	(15)	(90)	(72)	43	(681)	–	41
Transfers out	(1,257)	(31)	(272)	(312)	(889)	–	(52)
Transfers in	314	112	–	64	126	–	13
At 30 June 2015	**4,007**	**5,740**	**473**	**3,068**	**5,305**	**5**	**1,443**

[...]

1 Included in 'Available-for-sale investments: fair value gains/(losses)' and 'Exchange differences' in the consolidated statement of comprehensive income.

Transfers between levels of the fair value hierarchy are deemed to occur at the end of the reporting period. Movements in available-for-sale assets are mainly driven by sales of private equity investments and the transfer out of Level 3 of legacy credit assets following greater price certainty. Purchases and sales in trading assets reflect origination and sell-down of syndicated loans. [...]

4.3.12 Changes in classification of financial assets arising from changes in use

In the Extract below, Deutsche Bank discloses changes in classification of certain financial assets due to a change in purpose or use. *[IAS 34.15B(l)]*.

Extract 39.13: Deutsche Bank Aktiengesellschaft (interim ended March 2016)

Information on the Consolidated Balance Sheet (unaudited) [extract]

Amendments to IAS 39 and IFRS 7, "Reclassification of Financial Assets" [extract]

Under the amendments to IAS 39 and IFRS 7, issued in October 2008, certain financial assets were reclassified in the second half of 2008 and the first quarter 2009 from the financial assets at fair value through profit or loss and the available for sale classifications into the loans classification. No reclassifications have been made since the first quarter 2009.

The Group identified assets, eligible under the amendments, for which at the reclassification date it had a clear change of intent and ability to hold for the foreseeable future rather than to exit or trade in the short term. The reclassifications were made at the fair value of the assets at the reclassification date.

[...]

Carrying values and fair values by asset type of assets reclassified in 2008 and 2009

In € m.	Mar 31, 2016 Carrying value	Mar 31, 2016 Fair value	Dec 31, 2015 Carrying value	Dec 31, 2015 Fair value
Trading assets reclassified to loans:				
Securitization assets	1,147	1,039	1,382	1,346
Debt securities	255	264	396	405
Loans	814	784	916	857
Total trading assets reclassified to loans	**2,216**	**2,087**	2,695	2,608
Financial assets available for sale reclassified to loans:				
Securitization assets	1,262	1,176	1,540	1,470
Debt securities	0	0	168	179
Total financial assets available for sale reclassified to loans	**1,262**	**1,176**	1,708	1,648
Total financial assets reclassified to loans	**3,478**[1]	**3,263**	4,403[1]	4,256

1 There is an associated effect on the carrying value from effective fair value hedge accounting for interest rate risk to the carrying value of the reclassified assets shown in the table above. This effect increases carrying value by €4 million and decreases by €3 million as at March 31, 2016 and December 31, 2015, respectively.

4.3.13 Contingent liabilities

In the Extract below, Downer discloses changes in its contingent liabilities during the interim period in the notes to the condensed consolidated half-year financial report. *[IAS 34.15B(m)].*

Extract 39.14: Downer EDI Limited (interim ended December 2015)

Condensed consolidated financial report for the half-year ended 31 December 2015 [extract]

D5 Contingent liabilities [extract]

vi) Ground subsidence at the Waratah Train Maintenance Centre located on Manchester Road, Auburn ('AMC') has been identified. The design and construction of the AMC formed part of the Waratah Train Project, with Reliance Rail contracting Downer to design and build the AMC. In turn, Downer subcontracted this work to John Holland Pty Ltd. The design and construction of the areas in which subsidence has been observed formed part of the subcontractor's design and construct obligations. Investigations into the causes of the subsidence, the cost of remediation and operational impacts are ongoing. While it is too early to reliably estimate the total cost of the remediation, in the opinion of the Directors, there is no material exposure to either Downer EDI Rail Pty Limited or Downer EDI PPP Maintenance Pty Limited arising from the subsidence, based on the fact that there are a rangeof recovery options being pursued.

vii) On 27 February 2014, the Group announced that the IMF (Australia) Ltd (IMF) funded shareholder class action had been settled ('First Class Action').

Slater & Gordon has also advised that it reserves its position in relation to a second claim arising out of the second impairment to the Waratah Train Project announced on 27 January 2011, although no basis for this position has been provided.

On 27 March 2014, Downer was served with a second class action claim alleging breaches of Downer's continuous disclosure obligations in connection with the Group's $190 million impairment to the Waratah Train Project announced on 1 June 2010 i.e. based on the same events as the First Class Action ("Second Class Action").

The Second Class Action has been commenced in the Victorian Supreme Court with a hearing commencing in February 2016.

4.3.14 Accounting policies and methods of computation

In the Extract below, BNP discloses changes to the accounting policies applied in the current interim period. *[IAS 34.16A(a)]*. Using the guidance in IAS 8 – *Accounting Policies, Changes in Accounting Estimates and Errors*, BNP provides comprehensive quantitative information for the first-time adoption of IFRIC 21 – *Levies*. Refer to 9.7.5 below for a further discussion of the application of IFRIC 21 in interim financial reporting.

Extract 39.15: BNP Paribas Fortis SA (interim ended June 2015)

Notes to the Consolidated Interim Financial Statements [extract]

2 **Retrospective impact of the IFRIC 21 interpretation** [extract]

As of 1 January 2015, BNP Paribas Fortis has applied the IFRIC 21 "Levies" interpretation in the consolidated financial statements. As this interpretation has a retrospective effect, the comparative financial statements as at 1 January, 30 June and 31 December 2014 have been restated.

The IFRIC 21 interpretation provides guidance on the timing for recognising levies that are accounted for in accordance with IAS 37 "Provisions, Contingent Liabilities and Contingent Assets". These levies are mainly classified as other operating expenses in the profit and loss account. Income taxes and equivalent taxes that are within the scope of IAS 12 "Income Taxes" are excluded from the scope of this interpretation. The obligating event that gives rise to the recognition of a levy which is within the scope of IFRIC 21 is the activity that triggers the payment of the levy, as identified by the legislation. Thus, some levies which were previously recognised progressively over the fiscal year (such as Financial Stability Contributions, Deposit Guarantee Schemes, Subscription Tax and the "Contribution Sociale de Solidarité" in France), have to be accounted for as at 1 January in their entirety. The European Single Resolution fund is applied as from 1 January 2015 and has no retrospective impact for the year 2014. [...]

Profit and loss account

As regards the profit and loss account for the first half of 2014, the application of IFRIC 21 led to a EUR 128 million rise in other operating expenses, as well as an increase of EUR 42 million in the associated deferred tax gains. The following table shows impacts on profit and loss account for the first half of 2014 according the IFRIC 21 interpretation

In millions of euros	First half 2014 as published	First half 2014 restated IFRIC 21	IFRIC 21 adjustments
Commission expense	(389)	(390)	(1)
REVENUES	**3,453**	**3,452**	**(1)**
Other operating expense	(819)	(947)	(128)
GROSS OPERATING INCOME	**1,260**	**1,131**	**(129)**
OPERATING INCOME	**1,100**	**971**	**(129)**
Share of earnings of associates	81	79	(2)
PRE-TAX INCOME	**1,183**	**1,052**	**131**
Corporate income tax	(334)	(292)	42
NET INCOME BEFORE DISCONTINUED OPERATIONS	**849**	**760**	**(89)**
NET INCOME	**849**	**760**	**(89)**
Net income attributable to minority interests	195	193	(2)
NET INCOME ATTRIBUTABLE TO EQUITY HOLDERS	**654**	**567**	**(87)**

4.3.15 Seasonality or cyclicality of operations

Extract 39.16 below shows how Ardagh Packaging discloses the effects of seasonality in its interim report. *[IAS 34.16A(b)]*.

Extract 39.16: Ardagh Packaging Holdings Limited (interim ended March 2016)

Notes to the Unaudited Condensed Consolidated Interim Financial Statements [extract]

12. Seasonality of operations [extract]

The Group's revenue and cash flows are both subject to seasonal fluctuations. Demand for our glass products is typically strongest during the summer months and in the period prior to December because of the seasonal nature of beverage consumption. Demand for our metal products is largely related to agricultural harvest periods. The investment in working capital for Glass Packaging North America and Glass Packaging Europe typically peaks in the first quarter. The investment in working capital for Metal Packaging generally builds over the first three quarters of the year, in line with the seasonal pattern, and then unwinds in the fourth quarter, with the calendar year-end being the low point. The Group manages the seasonality of working capital by supplementing operating cash flows with drawings under our securitisation and revolving credit facilities.

4.3.16 Amounts that are unusual because of their nature, size or incidence

Pinafore discloses the nature and effects of unusual items in Extract 39.17 below by identifying 'restructuring costs' and a 'gain on disposals and on the exit of businesses' not identified as discontinued operations. In addition, quantitative information is provided about the allocation of 'restructuring costs' and 'disposals and exit of businesses' to regions, the corporate level and discontinued operations. *[IAS 34.16A(c)]*. Refer to Extract 39.23 for another example illustrating disclosures about restructuring activities.

Extract 39.17: Pinafore Holdings B.V. and Subsidiaries (interim ended March 2014)

CONDENSED CONSOLIDATED INCOME STATEMENT (Unaudited) [extract]

	Note	**Q1 2014** $ million	Q1 2013* $ million
Continuing operations			
Sales	2	**763.8**	744.6
Cost of sales		**(477.0)**	(472.1)
Gross profit		**286.8**	272.5
Distribution costs		**(81.8)**	(80.6)
Administrative expenses		**(113.7)**	(122.4)
Transaction costs		**(5.7)**	–
Impairments		**–**	(0.4)
Restructuring costs	3	**(8.0)**	(5.8)
Net gain on disposals and on the exit of businesses	3	**4.2**	0.2
Operating profit		**81.8**	63.5

[...]

* Re-presented for discontinued operations (see note 6)

NOTES TO THE CONDENSED CONSOLIDATED FINANCIAL STATEMENTS [extract]

3. RESTRUCTURING INITIATIVES [extract]

Restructuring costs of $8.0 million (Q1 2013: $5.8 million) were recognized in Q1 2014, including $6.8 million in relation to the closure of the Ashe County plant within Gates North America. Also recognized during Q1 2014 were costs of $1.0 million in relation to the closure of the London corporate center and the transfer of the majority of those functions to the Group's corporate headquarters in Denver, Colorado.

Restructuring costs incurred in Q1 2013 included $3.3 million in relation to the closure of the London corporate center and the transfer of the majority of those functions to the Group's corporate headquarters in Denver, Colorado and costs of $0.7 million incurred in relation to the closure of the Charleston plant. [...]

4.3.17 Changes in estimates

In the Extract below, Greentech Energy Systems discloses the nature and amounts of changes in estimates of amounts that resulted in a material effect on the current interim period. *[IAS 34.16A(d)]*.

Extract 39.18: Greentech Energy System A/S (interim ended September 2015)

Notes [extract]

1. Accounting policies [extract]

Critical choices and judgments in the accounting policies and critical accounting estimates [extract]

The Group regularly reviews the useful life of its assets in order to bring it into line with the technical and economic measurements, taking into consideration their technological capacity and regulatory frameworks. In Q1 2015, based on a study performed by an independent advisor, Greentech has changed the useful life of its operating wind farms from 20 to 25 years, with effect from 1 January 2015 (see note 3).

[...]

3. Intangible assets, property, plant and equipment [extract]

Starting from January 2015, Greentech has changed the useful life of the wind farms from 20 to 25 years (see note 1), following to a technical study performed by an independent technical advisor. This useful life applies to tangible and intangible assets and the estimated impact of this change on the profit/loss before taxes was approximately EUR 3.3M over the Q1-Q3 period in 2015 (of which 2.2M in H1 2015) and of EUR 4.5M on a yearly basis, considering the current installed capacity.

4.3.18 *Issues, repurchases and repayments of debt and equity securities*

Extract 39.19 below illustrates the disclosure of material changes in borrowings. *[IAS 34.16A(e)]*.

Extract 39.19: OSRAM Licht Group (interim ended June 2015)

Notes to the Condensed Interim Consolidated Financial Statements [extract]

5 | Financial Instruments [extract]

The reduction in loans from banks from €181.8 million as of September 30, 2014, to €97.3 million as of June 30, 2015, is due in particular to the repayment in full of the syndicated term loan totaling €140.0 million. In this context, the unamortized portion of the transaction costs in the amount of €1.7 million was recognized as interest expense using the effective interest rate method. This was partially offset by the drawdown of a €50.0 million tranche under the loan agreement with the European Investment Bank that was entered into in the first quarter of fiscal 2015.

4.3.19 *Dividends paid for each class of share*

In the Extract below, ASML Holding discloses dividends paid during the interim period. *[IAS 34.16A(f)]*.

Extract 39.20: ASML Holding N.V. (interim ended July 2016)

Notes to the Consolidated Condensed Interim Financial Statements [extract]

Note 12 Dividends and Share Buybacks [extract]

As part of our financing policy, we aim to pay an annual dividend that will be stable or growing over time. [...]

In the AGM of April 29, 2016, a dividend of EUR 1.05 per ordinary share of EUR 0.09 nominal value was adopted for 2015. As a result, a total dividend of EUR 445.9 million was paid to our shareholders on May 17, 2016.

4.3.20 *Events after the interim reporting date*

In the Extract below, Ferratum reports the issuance of a bond after the interim period. *[IAS 34.16A(h)]*.

Extract 39.21: Ferratum Group (interim ended June 2015)

IFRS unaudited condensed interim consolidated financial statements [extract]

Significant events after the reporting date

In July 2015, Ferratum Bank Plc, a subsidiary of Ferratum Oyj (ISIN: FI4000106299, WKN: A1W9NS; together with its consolidated subsidiaries hereinafter "Ferratum Group" or "Ferratum"), successfully placed a bond with institutional investors in Germany and other EU countries. The bank has placed an issue volume of EUR 20 million with a denomination of EUR 100,000 as the first tranche under a total bond issue program of EUR 30 million. The bond is guaranteed by Ferratum Oyj. The bond is admitted for trading on the EU-regulated European Wholesale Securities Market ("EWSM") in Malta. Furthermore, the bond has also been co-listed on the Frankfurt Stock Exchange in the open market segment (Freiverkehr). The bond has a coupon of 4.90% per annum and matures after 18 months. The interest payments are due on July 21, 2016, and January 21, 2017.

The bond issue will allow Ferratum to further optimize its financing structure and replace expiring financings. This refinancing is part of a regular adjustment of corporate financing where a certain volume is now shifted to the level of our bank and thus sustainably improves Ferratum's financing structure. It strengthens Ferratum Bank and its ability to enter the deposit business.

Although not a requirement under IAS 34, it is useful to disclose the date on which the interim financial statements are authorised for issue as it helps the users to better understand the context of any disclosure of events after the interim reporting date. *[IAS 10.17]*.

4.3.21 Changes in the composition of the entity

The notion of changes in the composition of the entity is broadly defined to include acquisitions, restructurings and discontinued operations. *[IAS 34.16A(i)]*.

In the Extract below, Deutsche Bank discloses the effects of finalising the acquisition accounting during the interim period. This disclosure about the change in the nature of their interest in Xchanging Transaction Bank is accompanied by other disclosures required by IFRS 3 for business combinations, which are not included here.

Extract 39.22: Deutsche Bank Aktiengesellschaft (interim ended June 2014)

Consolidated financial statements [extract]
Other Financial Information (unaudited) [extract]

Business Combinations

Xchanging Transaction Bank

On September 2, 2013, Deutsche Bank AG announced that it completed the purchase of the remaining 51% of the shares in its joint venture Xchanging etb GmbH ("Xetb"), which is the holding company of Xchanging Transaction Bank GmbH ("XTB"). The purchase price paid for the step-acquisition consists of a base component of €41 million, subject to certain adjustments. Of that amount, €36 million was paid as cash consideration by the acquirer. The remaining €5 million was paid by XTB to the seller, Xchanging plc., in the course of closing the transaction, which resulted in a reduction of the acquired net assets.

The acquisition accounting was finalized in the second quarter 2014, resulting in a net increase of the purchase consideration paid and a corresponding increase of goodwill recognized of €1 million each. Accordingly, the final amount of goodwill originating from the transaction amounted to €38 million, which has been allocated to PBC (€25 million), GTB (€6 million), CB&S (€5 million) and DeAWM (€2 million). The reconciliation of the total purchase consideration and the opening balance sheet as of the acquisition date were as follows: [...]

Chapter 39

In the Extract below, Roche discloses extensive information on its ongoing significant restructuring activities. In addition, further break-downs of the type of costs incurred and information about the classification of depreciation, amortisation and impairment and of other costs in the income statement is provided (not reproduced here).

Extract 39.23: Roche Holding Ltd (interim ended June 2015)

Notes to the Roche Group Interim Consolidated Financial Statements [extract]

6. Global restructuring plans

During the six months ended 30 June 2015 the Group continued with the implementation of several major global restructuring plans initiated in prior years, notably the programme to address long-term profitability in the Diabetes Care business in the Diagnostics Division.

Global restructuring plans: costs incurred in millions of CHF

	Diagnostics[1)]	Site consolidation[2)]	Other plans[3)]	Total
Six months ended 30 June 2015				
Global restructuring costs				
– Employee-related costs	20	35	47	102
– Site closure costs	1	25	–	26
– Divestment of products and businesses[12]	–	–	23	23
– Other reorganisation expenses	95	–	21	116
Total global restructuring costs	**116**	**60**	**91**	**267**

1) Includes the Diabetes Care 'Autonomy and Speed' restructuring plan.
2) Includes closure of the Nutley site and associated infrastructure and environmental remediation costs.
3) Includes plans for Pharmaceuticals Division research and development strategic realignment and InterMune integration.

Diagnostics Division

On 26 September 2013 Roche Diabetes Care announced the 'Autonomy and Speed' initiative which will enable the business to focus on Diabetes Care specific requirements, speed up processes and decision-making and drive efficiencies. During the six months ended 30 June 2015 total costs of 74 million Swiss francs were incurred, mainly for consultancy and IT-related costs as well as employee-related costs. Spending on other smaller plans within the Division was 42 million Swiss francs and included costs related to IT projects and the restructuring of the former Applied Science business. [...]

In the Extract below, Fortum describes the impact of its significant divestments. In addition, the company discloses quantitative information about the results of discontinued for the current and prior interim periods as well as net cash flows attributable to the discontinued operations (not reproduced here).

Extract 39.24: Fortum Corporation (interim ended June 2015)

Notes to the condensed consolidated interim financial statements [extract]

6. Discontinued operations [extract]

In March 2015 Fortum signed a binding agreement to sell the Swedish Distribution business. The transaction was completed in June 2015. In 2014 Fortum divested both the Finnish and Norwegian Distribution operations. For information regarding the divestments see Note 7.

After the divestment of the Swedish Distribution business Fortum does not have any distribution operations and therefore Distribution segment has been treated as discontinued operations since the first quarter 2015 according to IFRS 5 Non-current Assets held for Sale and Discontinued operations. [...]

Discontinued operations include the distribution operations in Fortum, including sales gains from the divestment of Swedish operations in June 2015 and Finnish and Norwegian distribution operations in 2014, and effects from internal sales and purchases have also been included. The net financial costs allocated to discontinued operations are based on the fact that the financing activities and risk management have been centralised on group level and subsidiaries have been funded with intra-group loans. No corporate overhead costs have been allocated to the discontinued operations. The assets relating to Distribution businesses have continued to be depreciated until the businesses were disposed.

4.4 Segment information

If an entity is required to disclose segment information in its annual financial statements, certain segment disclosures are required in its interim financial report. IFRS 8 is discussed in more detail in Chapter 34.

An entity applying IFRS 8 in its annual financial statements should include the following information in its interim financial report about its reportable segments: *[IAS 34.16A(g)]*

(a) segment revenues from external customers (if included in the measure of segment profit or loss reviewed by or otherwise regularly provided to the chief operating decision maker);

(b) intersegment revenues (if included in the measure of segment profit or loss reviewed by or otherwise regularly provided to the chief operating decision maker);

(c) a measure of segment profit or loss;

(d) a measure of total assets and liabilities for a particular reportable segment if such amounts are regularly provided to the chief operating decision maker and if there has been a material change from the amount disclosed in the last annual financial statements for that reportable segment;

(e) a description of differences in the basis of segmentation or in the basis of measurement of segment profit or loss from the last annual financial statements; and

(f) a reconciliation of the total profit or loss for reportable segments to the entity's profit or loss before income taxes and discontinued operations. However, if an entity allocates such items as income taxes to arrive at segment profit or loss, the reconciliation can be to the entity's profit or loss after those items. The entity should separately identify and describe all material reconciling items.

In Extract 39.25 below, Daimler discloses segment revenues and segment profit or loss in its interim financial report for the second quarter of 2016. Presumably, information required by (d) above is not included because it is not applicable for the periods presented. In addition, the reconciliation to group figures is also provided for the full first half of 2015 (not reproduced here).

Extract 39.25: Daimler AG (interim ended June 2016)

Notes to the Unaudited Interim Consolidated Financial Statements [extract]

20. Segment reporting [extract]

Segment information for the three-month periods ended June 30, 2016 and June 30, 2015 is as follows:

E.24

Segment reporting for the three-month periods ended June 30

In millions of euros	Mercedes-Benz Cars	Daimler Trucks	Mercedes-Benz Vans	Daimler Buses	Daimler Financial Services	Total segments	Recon-ciliation	Daimler Group
Q2 2016								
External revenue	**21,235**	**8,274**	**3,295**	**1,104**	**4,708**	**38,616**	**–**	**38,616**
Intersegment revenue	**887**	**392**	**146**	**18**	**306**	**1,749**	**–1,749**	**–**
Total revenue	**22,122**	**8,666**	**3,441**	**1,122**	**5,014**	**40,365**	**–1,749**	**38,616**
Segment profit (EBIT)	1,410	621	401	88	479	2,999	259	3,258
Thereof share of profit/loss from equity-method investments	120	9	10	–	–1	138	12	150
Thereof profit/loss from compounding and changes in discount rates of provisions for other risks	–35	–12	–3	–2	–	–52	–	–52

Reconciliation. Reconciliation of the total segments' profit (EBIT) to profit before income taxes is as shown in table ↗ E.26.

The reconciliation comprises corporate items for which headquarters is responsible. Transactions between the segments are eliminated in the context of consolidation.

Share of profit from equity-method investments in the first quarter of 2016 primarily comprises an impairment of the investment in BAIC Motor of €244 million. It also includes the proportionate share in the results of BAIC Motor (Q2 2016: €11 million; Q2 2015: €24 million and Q1-2 2016: €27 million; Q1-2 2015: €65 million). Other corporate items include the gain of €605 million recognized in connection with the contribution of the shares of Renault and Nissan, which was previously presented under other comprehensive income. The second quarter of 2016 also includes expenses of €400 million in connection with legal proceedings. Furthermore, the item includes losses from currency transactions which are not allocated to business operations (Q2 2016: €19 million, Q2 2015: €0 million and Q1-2 2016: €241 million, Q1-2 2015: €43 million).

E.26

Reconciliation to Group figures [extract]

In millions of euros	**Q2 2016**	Q2 2015
Total segments' profit (EBIT)	**2,999**	3,645
Share of profit from equity-method investments	**12**	25
Other corporate items	**225**	41
Eliminations	**22**	7
Group EBIT	**3,258**	3,718
Amortization of capitalized borrowing costs[1]	**–3**	–3
Interest income	**71**	36
Interest expense	**–150**	–126
Profit before income taxes	**3,176**	3,625

1 Amortization of capitalized borrowing costs is not considered in internal performance measure "EBIT," but is included in cost of sales.

4.5 Fair value disclosures for financial instruments

IAS 34 requires that an entity should include the following in its interim financial report in relation to financial instruments: *[IAS 34.16A(j)]*:

(a) disclosures to help users of the financial statements assess the valuation techniques and inputs used to develop the fair value measurements used for financial instruments in the statement of financial position and, for financial instruments measured using unobservable inputs, the effect of those measurements on profit or loss or other comprehensive income in the period *[IFRS 13.91]* (see Chapter 14 at 20.1);

(b) certain disclosures for fair value measurements that are *recognised* in the statement of financial position after initial recognition, including the carrying amount, categorisation within the fair value hierarchy and additional disclosures for those not classified as level 1 (see Chapter 14 at 20.3); *[IFRS 13.93]*

(c) accounting policy disclosures relating to how the entity has determined appropriate classes of financial assets and liabilities for which information about fair value measurement is given; how it determined when transfers between levels of the fair value hierarchy have occurred; and how the entity has measured any groups of financial assets and liabilities managed on the basis of its net exposure (see Chapter 14 at 20.1.2.A and 20.2); *[IFRS 13.94-96]*

(d) disclosures regarding liabilities measured at fair value and issued with an inseparable third-party credit enhancement (see Chapter 14 at 20.5); *[IFRS 13.98]* and

(e) disclosures about fair value required by IFRS 7, including for each class of financial asset and financial liability a comparison between fair value and carrying amount, unless the carrying amount is a reasonable approximation of the fair value, *[IFRS 7.25, 26, 29a]*, and disclosures relating to the deferral and subsequent recognition of gains and losses arising when fair value is determined using unobservable inputs or when the fair value cannot be determined reliably (see Chapter 54 at 4.5). *[IFRS 7.28, 7.29b, 30]*.

Quantitative disclosures would normally be given in a tabular format unless another format is more appropriate. *[IFRS 13.99]*. In respect of (a) above, the entity should assess whether the disclosures are sufficient to meet the disclosure objectives of IFRS 13. This requires judgements to be made about the level of detail; how much emphasis to place on each of the various requirements; and level of aggregation or disaggregation. If necessary, additional information should be given in order to meet those objectives (see Chapter 14 at 20.1). *[IFRS 13.92]*.

The Extract below from the half-year financial report of Slater and Gordon illustrates the valuation techniques used, fair value hierarchy and recurring level 3 fair value disclosures.

Extract 39.26: Slater and Gordon Limited (Half-Year ended December 2015)

Notes to Financial Statements [extract]

Note 13. Fair Value Measurements [extract]

i) Fair value hierarchy [Extract]

31 December 2015 **Recurring Fair Value Measurements**	**Level 1** **$'000**	**Level 2** **$'000**	**Level 3** **$'000**	**Total** **$'000**
Financial liabilities				
Derivative financial instruments – interest rate swaps	–	2,000	–	2,000
Contingent consideration	–	–	3,111	3,111
	–	2,000	3,111	5,111

30 June 2015 **Recurring Fair Value Measurements**	**Level 1** **$'000**	**Level 2** **$'000**	**Level 3** **$'000**	**Total** **$'000**
Financial liabilities				
Derivative financial instruments – interest rate swaps	–	1,621	–	1,621
Contingent consideration	–	–	6,089	6,089
	–	1,621	6,089	7,710

ii) Valuation techniques and inputs used in Level 2 and 3 fair value measurements

The fair value of the interest rate swaps is measured with reference to market data which can be used to estimate future cash flows. The key input into this valuation is the interest rate swap revaluation statement as provided by Westpac Banking Corporation and National Australia Bank.

The fair value of contingent consideration payable in a business combination is measured with reference to current fee and performance forecasts which can be used to estimate future cash flows. The key inputs into this valuation are the estimated future cash flows and the average discount rate of 9.2% used to determine the present value of the future cash flows.

iii) Reconciliation of recurring Level 3 fair value movements

	31 Dec 2015 **$'000**	**30 Jun 2015** **$'000**
Contingent Consideration		
Opening balance	6,089	7,927
Acquisitions	–	4,185
Payments	(3,195)	(1,865)
Adjustment to contingent consideration	–	(4,983)
Interest	217	378
Foreign exchange differences	–	447
Closing balance	3,111	6,089

There has been no change in the range of undiscounted contingent consideration outcomes during the period.

iv) Sensitivity analysis for recurring Level 3 fair value measurements

A reasonable movement in the unobservable inputs would not significantly impact the fair value of contingent consideration as at the end of the reporting period and therefore not impact profit after tax and equity.

4.6 Disclosure of compliance with IFRS

If an interim financial report complies with the requirements of IAS 34, this fact should be disclosed. Furthermore, an interim financial report should not be described as complying with IFRS unless it complies with all the requirements of International Financial Reporting Standards, *[IAS 34.19]*, a requirement similar to that found in IAS 1. *[IAS 1.16]*. Therefore, an entity would only provide a statement of compliance with IFRS (as opposed to IAS 34 alone) in its interim report if it prepared a complete set of interim financial statements.

Extract 39.27: BMW AG (interim ended March 2016)

Condensed Notes to the Group Financial Statement to 31 March 2016 [extract]
Accounting Principles and Policies [extract]
1 Basis of preparation [extract]

The Group Financial Statements of BMW AG at 31 December 2015 were drawn up in accordance with International Financial Reporting Standards (IFRSs), as applicable in the European Union (EU) at that date. The Interim Group Financial Statements (Interim Report) at 31 March 2016, which have been prepared in accordance with International Accounting Standard (IAS) 34 (Interim Financial Reporting), have been drawn up using, in all material respects, the same accounting methods as those utilised in the 2015 Group Financial Statements. The BMW Group applies the option of publishing condensed group financial statements. All Interpretations issued by the International Financial Reporting Interpretations Committee (IFRIC) which were mandatory at 31 March 2016 have been applied. The Interim Report also complies with German Accounting Standard No. 16 (GAS 16) – Interim Financial Reporting – issued by the German Accounting Standards Committee e.V. (GASC).

When entities either choose or are required by local regulations to meet other requirements in addition to IAS 34, the statement of compliance can be more complicated. In the extract above, BMW simply adds a statement confirming its compliance with the specific German Accounting Standard on interim reporting. Additional complexity can arise when the entity seeks to meet the requirements of its (IFRS-based) local GAAP as well as IFRS as issued by the IASB. Extract 39.28 below shows how the dual listed BHP Billiton disclosed compliance with IFRS, IFRS as endorsed by the EU, Australian Accounting Standards and the requirements of the Financial Conduct Authority in the UK.

Extract 39.28: BHP Billiton plc (interim ended December 2015)

Notes to the Financial Information [extract]
1. **Accounting policies** [extract]

This general purpose financial report for the half year ended 31 December 2015 is unaudited and has been prepared in accordance with IAS 34 "Interim Financial Reporting" as issued by the International Accounting Standards Board (IASB), IAS 34 "Interim Financial Reporting" as adopted by the EU, AASB 134 "Interim Financial Reporting" as issued by the Australian Accounting Standards Board (AASB) and the Disclosure and Transparency Rules of the Financial Conduct Authority in the United Kingdom and the Australian Corporations Act 2001 as applicable to interim financial reporting.

The extract above also highlights a compliance issue for adopters of IFRS-based standards, such as entities in Australia and the European Union. Because of the time taken to secure local endorsement of IFRS issued by the IASB, an entity may not be able to state at a particular reporting date that the financial statements comply with both IFRS as issued by the IASB and IFRS as endorsed locally.

For example, when the Interpretations Committee issues an interpretation that is effective before the end of the interim reporting period, entities may choose not to comply with IAS 34 in their interim financial statements rather than risk applying an interpretation in their full year financial statements that is not yet locally endorsed. Alternatively, an entity may publish interim financial information prepared under locally endorsed IFRS, for example, IFRS as adopted by the European Union. In such cases, the basis of preparation should state that IAS 34 is being applied in this context.

5 PERIODS FOR WHICH INTERIM FINANCIAL STATEMENTS ARE REQUIRED TO BE PRESENTED

Irrespective of whether an entity presents condensed or complete interim financial statements, the components of its interim reports should include information for the following periods: *[IAS 34.20]*

(a) statements of financial position as of the end of the current interim period and a comparative statement of financial position as of the end of the immediately preceding year;

(b) statements of profit or loss and other comprehensive income for the current interim period and cumulatively for the current year-to-date, with comparative statements of profit or loss and other comprehensive income for the comparable interim periods (current and year-to-date) of the immediately preceding year;

(c) statements of changes in equity cumulatively for the current year-to-date period, with a comparative statement for the comparable year-to-date period of the immediately preceding year; and

(d) statements of cash flows cumulatively for the current year-to-date, with a comparative statement for the comparable year-to-date period of the immediately preceding year.

An interim report may present for each period either a single statement of 'profit or loss and other comprehensive income', or separate statements of 'profit or loss' and 'comprehensive income'. *[IAS 1.10A, IAS 34.20(b)]*. The condensed statement of comprehensive income referred to at (b) above should be presented in a manner consistent with the entity's annual financial statements. Accordingly, if the entity presents a separate statement for items of profit or loss in its annual financial statements, it should present a separate condensed statement of profit or loss in the interim financial report. *[IAS 34.8A]*.

If an entity's business is highly seasonal, then the standard encourages reporting additional financial information for the twelve months up to the end of the interim period, and comparative information for the prior twelve-month period, in addition to the financial statements for the periods set out above. *[IAS 34.21]*.

The standard does not require an entity to present a statement of financial position as at the end of the comparable interim period. However, in practice many entities reporting under IFRS disclose this information, either on a voluntary basis, or due to local regulations. Similarly, many entities also present the income statement for the immediately preceding full year. Such presentation is allowed under IAS 34, but any additional information included in the interim financial statements should be prepared and presented in compliance with the standard.

The examples below illustrate the periods that an entity is required and encouraged to disclose under IAS 34. *[IAS 34.22, Illustrative examples, part A].*

Example 39.2: Entity publishes interim financial reports half-yearly

If an entity's financial year ends on 31 December (calendar year), it should present the following financial statements (condensed or complete) in its half-yearly interim financial report as of 30 June 2017:

Half-yearly interim report	*End of the current interim period*	*End of the comparative interim period*	*Immediately preceding year-end*
	30/6/2017	30/6/2016	31/12/2016
Statement of financial position	●		●
Statement(s) of profit or loss and other comprehensive income			
– Current period and year-to-date (6 months) ending	●	●	
– 12 months ending	○	○	
Statement of changes in equity			
– Year-to date (6 months) ending	●	●	
– 12 months ending	○	○	
Statement of cash flows			
– Year-to-date (6 months) ending	●	●	
– 12 months ending	○	○	

● Required ○ Disclosure encouraged if the entity's business is highly seasonal

If an entity publishes a separate interim financial report for the final interim period (i.e. second half of its financial year), it presents the following financial statements (condensed or complete) in its second half-yearly interim financial report as of 31 December 2017:

Second half-yearly interim report	*End of the current interim period*	*End of the comparative interim period*
	31/12/2017	31/12/2016
Statement of financial position	●	●
Statement(s) of profit or loss and other comprehensive income		
– Current period (6 months) ending	●	●
– Year-to-date (12 months) ending	●	●
Statement of changes in equity		
– Year-to-date (12 months) ending	●	●
Statement of cash flows		
– Year-to-date (12 months) ending	●	●

● Required

Chapter 39

Example 39.3: Entity publishes interim financial reports quarterly

If an entity's financial year ends on 31 December (calendar year), it should present the following financial statements (condensed or complete) in its quarterly interim financial reports for 2017:

First quarter interim report	*End of the current interim period*	*End of the comparative interim period*	*Immediately preceding year-end*
	31/3/2017	31/3/2016	31/12/2016
Statement of financial position	●		●
Statement(s) of profit or loss and other comprehensive income			
– Current period and year-to-date (3 months) ending	●	●	
– 12 months ending	○	○	
Statement of changes in equity			
– Year-to-date (3 months) ending	●	●	
– 12 months ending	○	○	
Statement of cash flows			
– Year-to-date (3 months) ending	●	●	
– 12 months ending	○	○	

● Required ○ Disclosure encouraged if the entity's business is highly seasonal

Second quarter interim report	*End of the current interim period*	*End of the comparative interim period*	*Immediately preceding year-end*
	30/6/2017	30/6/2016	31/12/2016
Statement of financial position	●		●
Statement(s) of profit or loss and other comprehensive income			
– Current period (3 months) ending	●	●	
– Year-to-date (6 months) ending	●	●	
– 12 months ending	○	○	
Statement of changes in equity			
– Year-to-date (6 months) ending	●	●	
– 12 months ending	○	○	
Statement of cash flows			
– Year-to-date (6 months) ending	●	●	
– 12 months ending	○	○	

● Required ○ Disclosure encouraged if the entity's business is highly seasonal

Third quarter interim report	*End of the current interim period* 30/9/2017	*End of the comparative interim period* 30/9/2016	*Immediately preceding year-end* 31/12/2016
Statement of financial position	•		•
Statement(s) of profit or loss and other comprehensive income			
– Current period (3 months) ending	•	•	
– Year-to-date (9 months) ending	•	•	
– 12 months ending	○	○	
Statement of changes in equity			
– Year-to-date (9 months) ending	•	•	
– 12 months ending	○	○	
Statement of cash flows			
– Year-to-date (9 months) ending	•	•	
– 12 months ending	○	○	

• Required ○ Disclosure encouraged if the entity's business is highly seasonal

If an entity publishes a separate interim financial report for the final interim period (i.e. fourth quarter of its financial year), it presents the following financial statements (condensed or complete) in its fourth quarter interim financial report as of 31 December 2017:

Fourth quarter interim report	*End of the current interim period* 31/12/2017	*End of the comparative interim period* 31/12/2016
Statement of financial position	•	•
Statement(s) of profit or loss and other comprehensive income		
– Current period (3 months) ending	•	•
– Year-to-date (12 months) ending	•	•
Statement of changes in equity		
– Year-to-date (12 months) ending	•	•
Statement of cash flows		
– Year-to-date (12 months) ending	•	•

• Required

5.1 Other comparative information

For entities presenting condensed financial statements under IAS 34, there is no explicit requirement that comparative information be presented in the explanatory notes. Nevertheless, where an explanatory note is required by the standard (such as for inventory write-downs, impairment provisions, segment revenues etc.) or otherwise determined to be needed to provide useful information about changes in the financial position and performance of the entity since the end of the last annual reporting period, *[IAS 34.15]*, it would be appropriate to provide information for each period presented. However, in certain cases it would be unnecessary to provide comparative information where this repeats information that was reported in the notes to the most recent annual financial statements. *[IAS 34.15A]*. For example it would only be necessary to provide information about business combinations in a comparative period when there is a revision of previously disclosed fair values. Refer to Extract 39.22 above.

For entities presenting complete financial statements, whilst IAS 34 sets out the periods for which components of the interim report are included, it is less clear how these rules interact with IAS 1's requirement to report comparative information for all amounts in the financial statements. *[IAS 1.38]*. In our view, a complete set of interim financial statements that contains a statement of compliance under IAS 1 should meet the requirements of IAS 1 in full, irrespective of any apparent contradiction with IAS 34, as shown in the example below.

Example 39.4: Disclosing movements on non-current assets in a complete set of interim financial statements

An entity preparing complete IFRS financial statements is required to reconcile the carrying amount at the beginning and end of the period showing movements during that period for both intangible assets and property, plant and equipment. *[IAS 38.118, IAS 16.73]*. Therefore, an entity presenting complete IFRS financial statements for the six months ended 30 June 2017 would disclose the movements in intangible assets and in property, plant and equipment between 1 January 2017 and 30 June 2017. In our view, the requirement for comparatives in IAS 1 requires the entity to reconcile movements during the comparative interim period, between 1 January 2016 and 30 June 2016, even though the entity is not required to present a statement of financial position as at 30 June 2016 (as shown in Example 39.2 above).

In addition to presenting comparative information for the corresponding interim period, it is suggested that entities preparing a complete set of interim financial statements also include information for the previous full year, such as the required comparative information for the current interim period and reconciliations to the previous year-end statement of financial position. In Example 39.4 above, this requirement could be achieved by reconciling movements in non-current assets during the second six months of the previous year (between 1 July 2016 and 31 December 2016).

If an entity presents complete financial statements and restates comparative information (e.g. following a change in accounting policy, correction of an error, or reclassification) and this restatement is material, then the entity should present a third statement of financial position at the beginning of the earliest comparative period in its interim financial reporting accordance with IAS 1. *[IAS 1.10(f)]*. No such requirement applies in the case of an entity preparing a condensed set of interim financial statements, *[IAS 1.BC33]*, however, additional disclosures are required in the case of correction of prior period errors, *[IAS 34.15B(g)]* (see 4.3.7 above), or when accounting policies are changed, *[IAS 34.16A(a)]* (see 4.3.14 above).

5.2 Length of interim reporting period

IAS 34 does not limit interim reporting to quarterly or half-yearly periods; an interim period may be any period shorter than a full year. *[IAS 34.4]*. In the extract below Bossard AG presented its interim report for a four-month interim period under IAS 34. This was acceptable under local regulation, but not a common practice. Since then the company has changed to the local minimum requirement of half-year interim reporting.

Extract 39.29: Bossard Holding AG (interim ended April 2008)

Notes to the Consolidated Financial Statements [extract]

Basis for the Preparation of the Consolidated Financial Statements (2) [extract]

The unaudited, consolidated interim financial statements for the first four months of 2008 were prepared in accordance with the International Financial Reporting Standards (IFRS) "Interim Financial Reporting IAS 34".

The consolidated financial statements of the Bossard Group are based on the financial statements of the individual Group companies at April 30, 2008 prepared in accordance with uniform accounting policies. The consolidated financial statements have been prepared under the historical cost convention except for the revaluation of certain financial assets and liabilities at market value, in accordance with International Financial Reporting Standards (IFRS), including International Accounting Standards (IAS) and interpretations issued by the International Accounting Standards Board (IASB). They are prepared in accordance with Swiss law and the listing rules of the Swiss Exchange SWX.

5.3 Change in financial year-end

The requirement in IAS 34 to present a comparative statement of profit or loss and other comprehensive income 'for the comparable interim periods (current and year-to-date) of the immediately preceding financial year', *[IAS 34.20]*, can give rise to diversity in practice in the case of an entity that changes its annual financial reporting date. For example, an entity changing its reporting date from 31 December to 31 March would change its half-yearly reporting date from 30 June to 30 September and therefore present its first half-yearly report after its new annual reporting date for the six month period from 1 April to 30 September. A 'comparable' comparative interim period in this scenario could be taken to mean the six months ended 30 September in the prior year, as illustrated in example 39.5 below.

Example 39.5: Entity changes financial year-end

If an entity changes its financial year-end from 31 December (calendar year) to 31 March, and first reflects the change in its annual financial statements for the period ended 31 March 2017. It determines that the requirement for comparable comparative information in IAS 34 requires it to present the following financial statements (condensed or complete) in its half-yearly interim financial report for the six months ending 30 September 2017:

Half-yearly interim report	*End of the current interim period*	*End of the comparative interim period*	*Immediately preceding year-end*
	30/9/2017	30/9/2016	31/03/2017
Statement of financial position	●		●
Statement(s) of profit or loss and other comprehensive income			
– Current period and year-to-date (6 months) ending	●	●	
– 12 months ending	○	○	
Statement of changes in equity			
– Year-to date (6 months) ending	●	●	
– 12 months ending	○	○	
Statement of cash flows			
– Year-to-date (6 months) ending	●	●	
– 12 months ending	○	○	

● Required ○ Disclosure encouraged if the entity's business is highly seasonal

The entity in the example above did not show information for the half-year ended 30 June 2016 as the comparative period, notwithstanding the fact that this period would have been the reporting date for the last published half-yearly report.

Other interpretations of IAS 34 in this regard are also possible. As illustrated in the Extract below, Sirius Minerals changed its annual financial reporting period-end from March to December, which resulted in the company reporting on a shorter (nine-month) annual financial period ended 31 December 2015. For its next set of condensed interim financial statements (for the six months ended 30 June 2016), Sirius presented comparative information for the first six-months of the previous annual financial period, being the six-months ended 30 September 2015. The company have also included information for the previous annual reporting period (in this case the shortened nine-month period ended 31 December 2015), in common with many UK reporters who present comparative information for the previous annual reporting period in addition to the information required by IAS 34.

Extract 39.30: Sirius Minerals Plc (interim ended June 2016)

Basis of Preparation [extract]

The condensed interim unaudited consolidated financial statements for the six-month period ended 30 June 2016 have been prepared in accordance with the Disclosure and Transparency Rules of the Financial Conduct Authority and with IAS 34 'Interim Financial Reporting' as adopted by the European Union ("EU"). As a result of changing the accounting reference date, from 31 March to 31 December, these financial statements should be read in conjunction with the condensed financial

> statements for the six-month period ended 30 September 2015 which have been prepared in accordance with IFRSs as adopted by the EU. Comparability with the current period is maintained due to the low seasonality of the Group's operations.
>
> The accounting policies applied are consistent with those of the Group financial statements for the nine-month period ended 31 December 2015, which have also been voluntarily included in these financial statements for reference.

Given the lack of clarity in IAS 34 as to the meaning of 'comparable' in the case where the current financial year runs for a period that is different to 'the immediately preceding financial year', *[IAS 34.20]*, there are arguments to support each of the interpretations illustrated in Example 39.5 and Extract 39.30 above.

In the Extract above, Sirius Minerals notes that it has considered seasonality of its operations in determining whether the information presented for a prior interim period is comparable. The implication is that had it determined that operations were seasonal, the entity might have reported a different comparative period (perhaps for the six months ended 30 June 2015). As noted at 5 above and illustrated in Example 39.2, in cases where the entity's business is highly seasonal, IAS 34 encourages the reporting of additional financial information for the twelve months up to the end of the interim period, and comparative information for the prior twelve-month period, in addition to the financial statements for the periods set out above. *[IAS 34.21]*.

5.4 Comparatives following a financial period longer than a year

The discussion at 5.3 above demonstrates that when an entity changes its annual reporting date, the determination of comparative periods in the interim financial statements could be interpreted differently without definitive guidance in IAS 34.

Another situation where confusion may be caused by the requirement to present comparative information for 'the *comparable* interim periods (current and year-to-date) of the immediately preceding financial year', *[IAS 34.20]*, arises when the previous annual financial statements related to a period other than twelve months. This situation is not uncommon for a newly incorporated entity, which might have either a shorter or a longer reporting period in its first financial year.

Consider an entity that has a long initial accounting period of eighteen months and that is required to prepare interim financial reports on a quarterly basis. Accordingly, it would have *six* 'quarters' in its first financial reporting period and in line with the requirements of IAS 34, the entity would present statements of profit or loss and other comprehensive income, changes in equity and cash flows for each three month period and cumulatively for the year-to-date. In the next financial year, however, the previously published year-to-date amounts would no longer be comparable. The following example illustrates this situation.

Example 39.6: Disclosing comparatives in interim financial statements when the preceding financial year covers a longer period

An entity's financial year-end is 31 December and it issues quarterly interim financial statements. It was incorporated on 1 July 2015 and prepared its first set of financial statements for a period of eighteen months to 31 December 2016. In this period, the entity prepared interim financial statements under IAS 34 for each of the three month periods ended 30 September 2015, 31 December 2015, 31 March 2016, 30 June 2016, 30 September 2016 and 31 December 2016. Each interim report contained information for the three month period and the year-to-date, which started on 1 July 2015.

In the next year, a twelve month annual reporting period, the entity is preparing its interim financial report for the three months (and half-year) ending 30 June 2017. Accordingly, it presents statements of profit or loss and other comprehensive income, changes in equity and cash flows for the three month period from 1 April 2017 to 30 June 2017 and for the year-to-date (from 1 January 2017 to 30 June 2017). Under IAS 34, the entity is also required to present comparative statements of profit or loss and other comprehensive income, cash flows, and changes in equity for the comparable interim periods in the preceding financial year. However, in its interim report for the three months ended 30 June 2016, i.e. in the prior year, the entity had presented information for the three month period from 1 April 2016 to 30 June 2016 as well as for the year-to-date period, from 1 July 2015 to 30 June 2016, which was then a period of twelve months.

The entity determines that the year-to-date comparative statements would cover the same period in the preceding year as the current year, which in this case would be for the three month period from 1 April 2016 to 30 June 2016 and for the six-month period from 1 January 2016 to 30 June 2016.

It should be noted in the above example that none of the interim financial statements issued in the entity's first (eighteen month) reporting period would contain comparative information. In particular, no comparatives would be required for the three month periods ended 30 September 2016 and 31 December 2016 because the corresponding periods in the preceding *calendar* year (i.e. 30 September 2015 and 31 December 2015) actually form part of the same (eighteen month) financial period and therefore comparatives from a preceding financial reporting period did not exist.

5.5 When the comparative period is shorter than the current period

The same considerations apply when determining the comparable comparative period in the following circumstances when a newly incorporated entity's first financial year was short.

Example 39.7: Disclosing comparatives in interim financial statements when the preceding financial year covers a shorter period

An entity was incorporated on 17 December 2016 and its equity shares were admitted to trading on a recognised stock market in April 2017. It determined that its annual reporting date will be 30 June each year and issues its first set of annual financial statements for the period ended 30 June 2017.

In compliance with the rules of the stock market, the entity issues its first half-yearly report for the six months ended 31 December 2017. This begs the question whether the comparative period for this interim would be the short period from 17 December 2016 (i.e. the date of incorporation) to 31 December 2016 or the first six months following the entity's incorporation, from 17 December 2016 to 16 June 2017.

As in Example 39.6 above, the entity could determine that the period-to-date comparative statements would cover the same period in the preceding annual reporting period as the current year, which in this case would be from 17 December 2016 to 31 December 2016. The entity should provide sufficient disclosure to explain the particular circumstances and the limited comparability with the current period.

6 MATERIALITY

In making judgements on recognition, measurement, classification, or disclosures in interim financial reports, the overriding goal in IAS 34 is to ensure that an interim financial report includes all information relevant to understanding an entity's financial position and performance during the interim period. *[IAS 34.25]*. The standard draws from IAS 1 and IAS 8, which define an item as material if its omission or misstatement could influence the economic decisions of users of the financial statements but do not contain quantitative guidance on materiality. *[IAS 34.24]*. IAS 34 requires materiality to be assessed based on the interim period financial data. *[IAS 34.23]*.

Therefore, decisions on the recognition and disclosure of unusual items, changes in accounting policies or estimates, and errors are based on materiality in relation to the interim period figures to determine whether non-disclosure is misleading. *[IAS 34.25]*.

Neither the previous year's financial statements nor any expectations of the financial position at the current year-end are relevant in assessing materiality for interim reporting. However, the standard adds that interim measurements may rely on estimates to a greater extent than measurements of annual financial data. *[IAS 34.23]*.

7 DISCLOSURE IN ANNUAL FINANCIAL STATEMENTS

An estimate of an amount reported in an interim period can change significantly during the remainder of the year. An entity that does not present a separate interim financial report for its final interim period should disclose the nature and amount of significant changes in estimates in a note to the annual financial statements for that year. *[IAS 34.26]*. This disclosure requirement is intended to be narrow in scope, relating only to the change in estimate, and does not create a requirement to include additional interim period financial information in the annual financial statements. *[IAS 34.27]*.

The requirement to disclose significant changes in estimates since the previous interim reporting date is consistent with IAS 8 and paragraph 16A(d) of IAS 34. These standards require disclosure of the nature and the amount of a change in estimate that has a material effect in the current reporting period or is expected to have a material effect in subsequent periods. IAS 34 cites changes in estimate in the final interim period relating to inventory write-downs, restructurings, or impairment losses recognised in an earlier interim period as examples of items that are required to be disclosed. *[IAS 34.27]*.

8 RECOGNITION AND MEASUREMENT

The recognition and measurement requirements in IAS 34 arise mainly from the requirement to report the entity's financial position as at the interim reporting date, but also requires certain estimates and measurements to take into account the expected financial position of the entity at year-end, where those measures are determined on an annual basis (as in the case of income taxes). Many preparers misinterpret this approach as representing some form of hybrid of the discrete and integral methods to interim financial reporting. This can cause confusion in application and can lead to the accusation that IAS 34 seems internally inconsistent.

In requiring the year-to-date to be treated as a discrete period, IAS 34 prohibits the recognition or deferral of revenues and costs for interim reporting purposes unless such recognition or deferral is appropriate at year-end. As with a set of annual financial statements complying with IAS 8, IAS 34 requires changes in estimates and judgements reported in previous interim periods to be revised prospectively, whereas changes in accounting policies and errors are required to be recognised by prior period adjustment. However, IAS 34 allows looking beyond the interim reporting period, for example in estimating the tax rate to be applied on earnings for the period, when a year-to-date approach does not.

The recognition and measurement requirements of IAS 34 apply regardless of whether an entity presents a complete or condensed set of financial statements for an interim period, *[IAS 34.7]*, and are discussed below.

8.1 Same accounting policies as in annual financial statements

The principles for recognising assets, liabilities, income and expenses for interim periods are the same as in the annual financial statements. *[IAS 34.29]*. Accordingly, an entity uses the same accounting policies in its interim financial statements as in its most recent annual financial statements, adjusted for accounting policy changes that will be reflected in the next annual financial statements. However, IAS 34 also states that the frequency of an entity's reporting (annual, half-yearly or quarterly) do not affect the measurement of its annual results. To achieve that objective, measurements for interim reporting purposes are on a year-to-date basis. *[IAS 34.28]*.

8.1.1 Measurement on a year-to-date basis

Measurement on a year-to-date basis acknowledges that an interim period is a part of a full year and allows adjustments to estimates of amounts reported in prior interim periods of the current year. *[IAS 34.29]*.

Still, the principles for recognition and the definitions of assets, liabilities, income, and expenses for interim periods are the same as in annual financial statements. *[IAS 34.29, 31]*. Therefore, for assets, the same tests of future economic benefits apply at interim dates as at year-end. Costs that, by their nature, do not qualify as assets at year-end, do not qualify for recognition at interim dates either. Similarly, a liability at the end of an interim reporting period must represent an existing obligation at that date, just as it must at the end of an annual reporting period. *[IAS 34.32]*. Under IAS 34, as under the IASB's *Conceptual Framework*, an essential characteristic of income and expenses is that the related inflows and outflows of assets and liabilities have already occurred. If those inflows or outflows have occurred, the related income and expense are recognised; otherwise they are not recognised. *[IAS 34.33]*.

The standard lists several circumstances that illustrate these principles:

- inventory write-downs, impairments, or provisions for restructurings are recognised and measured on the same basis as at a year-end. Except for reversals of certain impairments (see 9.2 below), later changes in the original estimate are recognised in the subsequent interim period, either by recognising additional accruals or reversals of the previously recognised amount; *[IAS 34.30(a)]*
- costs that do not meet the definition of an asset at the end of an interim period are not deferred in the statement of financial position, either to await information on whether it meets the definition of an asset, or to smooth earnings over interim periods within a year. *[IAS 34.30(b)]*. For example, costs incurred in acquiring an intangible asset before the recognition criteria are met are expensed under IAS 38 – *Intangible Assets*. Only those costs incurred after the recognition criteria are met can be recognised as an asset; there is no reinstatement as an asset in a later period of costs previously expensed because the recognition criteria were not met at that time; *[IAS 38.71]* and
- income tax expense is 'recognised in each interim period based on the best estimate of the weighted-average annual income tax rate expected for the full financial year. Amounts accrued for income tax expense in one interim period may have to be adjusted in a subsequent interim period of that financial year if the estimate of the annual income tax rate changes'. *[IAS 34.30(c)]*.

Another example would be acquisition costs (excluding debt or share issue costs) incurred in relation to a business combination, which are required to be accounted as expenses in the periods in which the costs are incurred and the services are received. *[IFRS 3.53]*. Such costs would not qualify for deferral at an interim reporting date, even if the business combination to which the costs relate had not been completed until after the interim reporting date.

The year-to-date approach differs from the discrete approach in that the financial position and performance at each reporting date are evaluated not as an isolated period but as part of a cumulative period that builds up to a full year, whose results should not be influenced by interim reporting practices. Amounts reported for previous interim periods are not retrospectively adjusted, and therefore year-to-date measurements may involve changes in estimates of amounts reported in previous interim periods of the current year. As discussed at 4.2 and 7 above, IAS 34 requires disclosure of the nature and amount of material changes in previously reported estimates in the interim financial report and when separate interim financial report is not presented for the final interim period, in the full year financial statements. *[IAS 34.16A(d), 26, 34-36]*. However, the principle that the results of the full year should not be influenced by interim reporting practices, has been challenged, as the IASB and Interpretations Committee have identified and tried to resolve certain conflicts between IAS 34 and other standards, as discussed at 9.2 below.

8.1.2 New accounting pronouncements and other changes in accounting policies

As noted above, under IAS 34, an entity uses the same accounting policies in its interim financial statements as in its most recent annual financial statements, adjusted for accounting policy changes that will be in the next annual financial statements, and to determine measurements for interim reporting purposes on a year-to-date basis. *[IAS 34.28]*.

Unless transition rules are specified by a new standard or interpretation, IAS 34 requires a change in accounting policy to be reflected by: *[IAS 34.43]*

(a) restating the financial statements of prior interim periods of the current year and the comparable interim periods of any prior financial years that will be restated in the annual financial statements under IAS 8; or

(b) when it is impracticable to determine the cumulative effect at the beginning of the year of applying a new accounting policy to all prior periods, adjusting the financial statements of prior interim periods of the current year and comparable interim periods of prior years to apply the new accounting policy prospectively from the earliest date practicable.

Therefore, regardless of when in a financial year an entity decides to adopt a new accounting policy, it has to be applied from the beginning of the current year. *[IAS 34.44]*. For example, if an entity that reports on a quarterly basis decides in its third quarter to change an accounting policy, it must restate the information presented in earlier quarterly financial reports to reflect the new policy as if it had been applied from the start of the annual reporting period.

8.1.2.A New pronouncements becoming mandatory during the current year

One objective of the year-to-date approach is to ensure that a single accounting policy is applied to a particular class of transactions throughout a year. *[IAS 34.44]*. To allow accounting policy changes as of an interim date would mean applying different accounting policies to a particular class of transactions within a single year. This would make interim allocation difficult, obscure operating results, and complicate analysis and understandability of the interim period information. *[IAS 34.45]*.

Accordingly, when preparing interim financial information, consideration is given to which new standards and interpretations are mandatory in the next (current year) annual financial statements. The entity generally adopts these standards in all interim periods during that year.

For example, IFRS 15 – *Revenue from Contracts with Customers* – is mandatory for annual periods beginning on or after 1 January 2018. *[IFRS 15.C1]*. Therefore, an entity with a 31 December year-end would have to apply the standard in its half-yearly report for the six months ending 30 June 2018.

As discussed in 8.1.2.B below, a change in accounting policy would require a restatement of prior comparative financial statements, except for new accounting standards that have specific application and transition requirements during the financial year. *[IAS 34.43]*. For example, IFRIC 18 – *Transfers of Assets from Customers* – was applied prospectively to transfers of assets received from customers *on or after* 1 July 2009, which was a departure from the Interpretations Committee's and IASB's normal practice of issuing standards to be applied for annual periods beginning on or after a certain date. Thus, in this circumstance, an entity could have used two different accounting policies during a financial year.

An added complication arises for entities incorporated in jurisdictions which apply a locally endorsed version of IFRS, such as in the European Union, when the IASB issues a new standard or interpretation that is not yet endorsed as at the end of the interim reporting period. For example, as noted at 4.4 above, an entity applying IFRS 8 should disclose the specified segment information in its interim financial reports. In its interim report for the six months ended 30 June 2007, Deutsche Bank stated its intention to apply IFRS 8 in its next IFRS annual financial statements. However, because the European Union had not yet endorsed the standard as at the end of the interim reporting period, it included the disclosures required by both IFRS 8 and IAS 14 – *Segment Reporting* – as explained in the Extract below.

Extract 39.31: Deutsche Bank Aktiengesellschaft (interim ended June 2007)

Basis of Preparation [extract]

The consolidated interim financial statements were prepared in accordance with IFRS issued and effective at December 31, 2006, which were unchanged at 30 June 2007. The segment information presented in this Report is based on IFRS 8, "Operating Segments," with a reconciliation to IAS 14, "Segment Reporting". IFRS 8, whilst approved by the IASB, has yet to be endorsed by the EU. On this basis, the Group presents the accounting policies that are expected to be adopted when the Group prepares its first annual financial statements under IFRS.

8.1.2.B Voluntary changes of accounting policy

An entity can also elect at any time during a year to apply a new standard or interpretation before it becomes mandatory, or otherwise decide to change an accounting policy voluntarily. However, before voluntarily changing an accounting policy, consideration should be given to the interaction of the requirements of IAS 1 and IAS 8, which only permit an entity to change an accounting policy if the information results in information that is 'more reliable and more relevant' to the users of the financial statements. *[IAS 8.14(b)]*.

When it is concluded that a voluntary change in accounting policy is permitted and appropriate, its effect is generally reflected in the first interim report the entity presents after the date on which the entity changed its policy. Under IAS 8, a change in accounting policy is reflected by retrospective application, with restatement of prior period financial data as far back as is practicable. However, if the cumulative amount of the adjustment relating to financial years is impracticable to determine, then under IAS 8, the new policy is applied prospectively from the earliest date practicable. *[IAS 34.44]*. An entity is generally not permitted to reflect the effect of a change in accounting policy from a later date than the beginning of the current year, such as at the start of the most recent interim period in which the decision was made to change the policy. To allow two different accounting policies to be applied to a particular class of transactions within a single year would make interim allocations difficult, obscure operating results, and complicate analysis and understandability of the interim period information. *[IAS 34.45]*. The restatement of information reported in previous interim periods is also discussed at 11 below.

One exception to this principle of retrospective adjustment of earlier interim periods is when an entity changes from the cost model to the revaluation model under IAS 16 – *Property, Plant and Equipment* – or IAS 38. These are not changes in accounting policy that are covered by IAS 8 in the usual manner, but instead required to be treated as a revaluation in the period. *[IAS 8.17]*. Therefore, the general requirements of IAS 34 do not over-ride the specific requirements of IAS 8 to treat such changes prospectively.

However, to avoid using two differing accounting policies for a particular class of assets in a single financial year, consideration should be given to changing from the cost model to the revaluation model at the beginning of the financial year. Otherwise, an entity will end up depreciating assets based on cost for some interim periods and based on the revalued amounts for later interim periods.

8.1.2.C New pronouncements becoming mandatory in future annual reporting periods

There is no requirement in IAS 34 for a condensed set of financial statements to include disclosures about standards and interpretations that take effect in future annual reporting periods. However, when an entity preparing a complete set of interim financial statements has not applied a new IFRS that has been issued but is not yet effective, it should disclose:

(a) that fact; and

(b) known or reasonably estimable information relevant to assessing the possible impact that application of the new IFRS will have on the financial statements in the period of initial application. *[IAS 8.30]*.

In producing the above disclosure, the standard requires that an entity should consider disclosing:

(a) the title of the new IFRS;

(b) the nature of the impending change or changes in accounting policy;

(c) the date by which application of the IFRS is required;

(d) the date as at which it plans to apply the IFRS initially; and

(e) either:

  (i) a discussion of the impact that initial application of the IFRS is expected to have on the entity's financial statements; or

  (ii) if that impact is not known or reasonably estimable, a statement to that effect. *[IAS 8.31]*.

8.1.3 Change in going concern assumption

Another situation in which an entity applies different accounting policies in its interim financial statements as compared to its most recent annual financial statements is when the going concern assumption is no longer appropriate.

Although IAS 34 does not specifically address the issue of going concern, the general requirements of IAS 1 apply to both a complete set and to condensed interim financial statements. *[IAS 1.4]*. IAS 1 states that when preparing financial statements, management assesses an entity's ability to continue as a going concern, and that the financial statements are prepared on a going concern basis unless management either intends to liquidate the entity or cease trading, or has no realistic alternative but to do so. *[IAS 1.25]*. The going concern assessment is discussed in more detail in Chapter 3 at 4.1.2.

Under IAS 1, the assessment is made based on all available information about the future, which at a minimum is twelve months from the *end of the reporting period*. *[IAS 1.26]*. Therefore, with respect to interim reporting under IAS 34, the minimum period for management's assessment is also at least twelve months from the interim reporting date; it is not limited, for example, to one year from the date of the most recent annual financial statements.

Example 39.8: Going concern assessment

An entity's financial year-end is 31 December (calendar year) and its annual financial statements as of 31 December 2016 are prepared on a going concern basis. In assessing the going concern assumption as at 31 December 2016, management considered all future available information through to 31 December 2017.

In preparing its quarterly interim financial statements (condensed or complete) as at 31 March 2017, management should evaluate all future available information to at least 31 March 2018.

If management becomes aware, in making its assessment, of material uncertainties related to events or conditions that may cast significant doubt upon the entity's ability to continue as a going concern, the entity should disclose those uncertainties. If the entity does not prepare financial statements on a going concern basis, it should disclose that fact, together with the basis on which it prepared the financial statements and the reason why the entity is not regarded as a going concern. *[IAS 1.25]*.

8.1.4 Voluntary changes in presentation

In some cases, the presentation of the interim financial statements might be changed from that used in prior interim reporting periods. However, before changing the presentation used in its interim report from that of previous periods, management should consider the interaction of the requirements of IAS 34 to include in a set of condensed financial statements the same headings and sub-totals as the most recent annual financial statements, *[IAS 34.10]*, and to apply the same accounting policies as the most recent or the next annual financial report, *[IAS 34.28]*, and the requirements of IAS 1 as they will relate to those next annual financial statements. IAS 1 states that an entity should retain the presentation and classification of items in the financial statements, unless it is apparent following a significant change in the nature of operations or a review of the financial statements that another presentation is more appropriate, or unless the change is required by IFRS. *[IAS 1.45]*.

If a presentation is changed, the entity should also reclassify comparative amounts for both earlier interim periods of the current financial year and comparable periods in prior years. *[IAS 34.43(a)]*. In such cases, an entity should disclose the nature of the reclassifications, the amount of each item (or class of items) that is reclassified, and the reason for the reclassification. *[IAS 8.29]*.

8.2 Seasonal businesses

Some entities do not earn revenues or incur expenses evenly throughout the year, for example, agricultural businesses, holiday companies, domestic fuel suppliers, or retailers who experience peak demand at Christmas. The financial year-end is often chosen to fit their annual operating cycle, which means that an individual interim period would give little indication of annual performance and financial position.

An extreme application of the integral approach would suggest that they should predict their annual results and contrive to report half of that in the half-year interim financial statements. However, this approach does not portray the reality of their business in individual interim periods, and is, therefore, not permitted under the year-to-date approach adopted in IAS 34. *[IAS 34.28]*.

8.2.1 Revenues received seasonally, cyclically, or occasionally

The standard prohibits the recognition or deferral of revenues that are received seasonally, cyclically, or occasionally at an interim date, if recognition or deferral would not be appropriate at year-end. *[IAS 34.37]*. Examples of such revenues include dividend revenue, royalties, government grants, and seasonal revenues of retailers; such revenues are recognised when they occur. *[IAS 34.38]*.

IAS 34 also requires an entity to explain the seasonality or cyclicality of its business and the effect on interim reporting (see 4.3.15 above). *[IAS 34.16A(b)]*. If businesses are highly seasonal, IAS 34 encourages reporting of additional information for the twelve months up to the end of the interim period and comparatives for the prior twelve-month period (see 5 above). *[IAS 34.21]*.

8.2.2 Costs incurred unevenly during the year

IAS 34 prohibits the recognition or deferral of costs for interim reporting purposes if recognition or deferral of that type of cost is inappropriate at year-end, *[IAS 34.39]*, which is based on the principle that assets and liabilities are recognised and measured using the same criteria as at year-end. *[IAS 34.29, 31]*. This principle prevents smoothing of costs in seasonal businesses. Furthermore, the recognition of assets or liabilities at the interim date would not be appropriate if they would not qualify for recognition at the end of an annual reporting period. *[IAS 34. 32]*.

For direct costs, this approach has limited consequences, as the timing of recognising these costs and the related revenues is usually similar. However, for indirect costs, the consequences may be greater, depending on which standard an entity follows.

For example, manufacturing entities that use fixed production overhead absorption rates recognise an asset in respect of attributable overheads based on the normal capacity of the production facilities in accordance with IAS 2 – *Inventories*. Any variances and unallocated overheads are expensed. *[IAS 2.13]*. Construction contractors that use the percentage of completion method may recognise as an asset indirect contract costs that are attributable to contract activity in general, if it is probable that they will be recovered. *[IAS 11.27]*. IAS 11 – *Construction Contracts* – does not provide any guidance on how to determine if it is probable that a cost will be recovered when it relates to contract activity in general.

The implications are unclear for professional service companies that recognise revenue under IAS 18 – *Revenue* – using the percentage of completion method. On one hand, IAS 18 refers to IAS 11, *[IAS 18.21]*, implying that such entities can defer costs and the related variances at the end of an interim reporting period, even though they may not be constructing an asset and are therefore not technically within the scope of IAS 11. On the other hand, service providers might also follow the guidance in IAS 2, which also gives guidance for the cost of inventories of a service provider, and which results in expensing such costs and variances at the end of the reporting period. *[IAS 2.19]*. The circumstances in which IFRS 15 allows an asset to be recognised in relation to costs incurred to fulfil a contract are discussed in Chapter 30 at 9.3. However, these are issues that an entity would also face at the end of an annual reporting period. What is clear is that an entity should not diverge from these requirements just because information is being prepared for an interim period.

9 EXAMPLES OF THE RECOGNITION AND MEASUREMENT PRINCIPLES

Part B of the illustrative examples accompanying the standard provides several examples that illustrate the recognition and measurement principles in interim financial statements. *[IAS 34.40]*. In addition, the Interpretations Committee addressed one particular conflict between IAS 34 and other standards, in the reversal of impairment losses for goodwill, investments in an equity instruments classified as available-for-sale and financial assets carried at cost when it issued IFRIC 10 – *Interim Financial Reporting and Impairment* – in July 2006. These examples are discussed below.

9.1 Property, plant and equipment and intangible assets

9.1.1 Depreciation and amortisation

Depreciation and amortisation for an interim period is based only on assets owned during that interim period and does not consider asset acquisitions or disposals planned for later in the year. *[IAS 34.B24]*.

An entity applying a straight-line method of depreciation (amortisation) does not allocate the depreciation (amortisation) charge between interim periods based on the level of activity. However, under IAS 16 and IAS 38 an entity may use a 'unit of production' method of depreciation, which results in a charge based on the expected use or output (see Chapter 18 at 5.6.2). An entity can only apply this method if it most closely reflects the expected pattern of consumption of the future economic benefits embodied in the asset. The chosen method should be applied consistently from period to period unless there is a change in the expected pattern of consumption of those future economic benefits. *[IAS 16.62, IAS 38.98]*. Therefore, an entity cannot apply a straight-line method of depreciation in its annual financial statements, while allocating the depreciation charge to interim periods using a 'unit of production' based approach.

9.1.2 Impairment of assets

IAS 36 – *Impairment of Assets* – requires an entity to recognise an impairment loss if the recoverable amount of an asset declines below its carrying amount. *[IAS 34.B35]*. An entity should apply the same impairment testing, recognition, and reversal criteria at an interim date as it would at year-end. *[IAS 34.B36]*.

However, IAS 34 states that an entity is not required to perform a detailed impairment calculation at the end of each interim period. Rather, an entity should perform a review for indications of significant impairment since the most recent year-end to determine whether such a calculation is needed. *[IAS 34.B36]*. Nevertheless, the standard does not exempt an entity from performing impairment tests at the end of its interim periods. For example, an entity that recognised an impairment charge in the immediately preceding year, may find that it needs to update its impairment calculations at the end of subsequent interim periods because impairment indicators remain. There is also no exemption under IFRIC 10 for the assessment of goodwill impairment (see 9.2 below).

9.1.3 Recognition of intangible assets

An entity should apply the same IAS 38 definitions and recognition criteria for intangible assets in an interim period as in an annual period. Therefore, costs incurred before the recognition criteria are met should be recognised as an expense. *[IAS 34.B8]*. Expenditures on intangibles that are initially expensed under IAS 38 cannot be reinstated and recognised as part of the cost of an intangible asset subsequently (e.g. in a later interim period). *[IAS 38.71]*. Furthermore, 'deferring' costs as assets in an interim period in the hope that the recognition criteria will be met later in the year is not permitted. Only costs incurred after the specific point in time at which the criteria are met should be recognised as part of the cost of an intangible asset. *[IAS 34.B8]*.

9.1.4 Capitalisation of borrowing costs

An entity that recognises finance expenses in the cost of a qualifying asset under IAS 23 – *Borrowing Costs* – should determine the amount to be capitalised from the actual finance cost during the period (when funds are specifically borrowed) *[IAS 23.12]* or, when the asset is funded out of general borrowings, by applying a capitalisation rate equal to the weighted-average of the finance costs attributable to actual borrowings outstanding during the period *[IAS 23.14]* (see Chapter 21 at 5.2 and 5.3). For interim financial reporting, measurement should be made on a year-to-date basis, *[IAS 34.28]*, regardless of how often the entity issues interim reports during a year. For example, an entity that issues quarterly interim reports would have to revise its estimated capitalisation rate in successive quarters during the same year for changes in actual year-to-date borrowings and finance costs. As required in IAS 34, the cumulative effect of changes in the estimated capitalisation rate should be recognised in the current quarter and not retrospectively. *[IAS 34.36]*.

9.2 Reversal of impairment losses recognised in a previous interim period (IFRIC 10)

The two requirements in IAS 34, to apply the same accounting policies in interim financial reports as are applied for the annual financial statements, and to use year-to-date measurements for interim reporting purposes, do not sit easily together when considering the reversal of certain impairments.

As discussed at 9.1.2 above, the requirement to use the same accounting policies means that an entity should apply the same impairment testing, recognition, and reversal criteria at the end of an interim period as it would at year-end. *[IAS 34.B36]*. In applying the same reversal criteria at the end of an interim period, the following requirements are significant: *[IFRIC 10.4-6]*

- IAS 36 prohibits the reversal in a subsequent period of an impairment loss recognised for goodwill; *[IAS 36.124]*
- an impairment loss recognised in profit or loss for an investment in an equity instrument classified under IAS 39 – *Financial Instruments: Recognition and Measurement* – as available for sale cannot be reversed through profit or loss; *[IAS 39.69]* and
- IAS 39 also prohibits the reversal of an impairment loss relating to an unquoted equity instrument carried at cost because its fair value cannot be reliably measured, or to a derivative asset that is linked to and must be settled by such an unquoted equity instrument. *[IAS 39.66]*.

However, the use of year-to-date measurements implies that the calculation of impairments as at interim reporting dates in the same annual reporting period should be based on conditions as at the end of each interim period and determined independently of assessments at earlier interim dates. Applying this requirement of IAS 34 would lead to reversals of previously reported impairments if conditions change and justify a higher carrying value for the related asset.

Whilst it may be unlikely for the conditions causing an impairment of goodwill at an interim date to reverse before year-end, IFRIC 10 states that the specific requirements of the standards noted above take precedence over the more general statement in IAS 34. *[IFRIC 10.BC9]*. As such, IFRIC 10 prohibits the reversal of an impairment loss recognised in a previous interim period for goodwill or an investment in either an equity instrument or a financial asset carried at cost. *[IFRIC 10.8]*.

Thus, in the albeit unlikely event that the conditions mentioned above do reverse in successive interim periods, there can be situations where two entities facing an identical set of circumstances, yet with different frequency of interim reporting, could end up reporting different annual results. Consider the following example:

Example 39.9: Impact of IFRIC 10 on results due to differences in frequency of interim financial reporting

Entity A, reporting quarterly, and entity B, reporting six-monthly, are otherwise identical, having financial years ending on 31 December and holding an investment in equity instruments of Company X. As at 31 March, the fair value of the investment in X has declined significantly below cost. However, the decline has reversed in full before the end of June. In its interim financial statements for the 1st Quarter, entity A recognises an impairment loss on its investment in X based on the significant decline in its fair value below cost. At the end of 2nd Quarter, following the guidance in IFRIC 10, entity A cannot reverse the impairment that it recognised in 1st Quarter to reflect the recovery in the value of the investment.

By contrast, entity B does not recognise any impairment in its investment in entity X in its interim financial statements for half year ended 30 June. Consequently, the entities would report different annual results for the year ended 31 December due to an impairment recognised in an interim period by entity A but not by entity B.

In July 2014, the IASB issued the final version of IFRS 9, which *inter alia* amends IFRIC 10 (see 12.2 below). This amendment should be applied in tandem with the adoption of IFRS 9 and deletes references to equity instruments and financial assets carried at cost. *[IFRS 9.C51]*. With the adoption of IFRS 9, the Interpretation will be relevant only to the treatment of impairment losses on goodwill.

IFRIC 10 should not be applied by analogy to derive a general principle that the specific requirements of a standard take precedence over the year-to-date approach in IAS 34. *[IFRIC 10.9]*.

9.3 Employee benefits

9.3.1 Employer payroll taxes and insurance contributions

If employer payroll taxes or contributions to government-sponsored insurance funds are assessed on an annual basis, the employer's related expense should be recognised in interim periods using an estimated average annual effective rate, even if it does not reflect the timing of payments. A common example contained in Appendix B to IAS 34 is employer payroll tax or insurance contribution subject to a certain maximum level of earnings per employee. Higher income employees would reach the maximum income before year-end, and the employer would make no further payments for the remainder of the year. *[IAS 34.B1]*.

9.3.2 Year-end bonuses

The nature of year-end bonuses varies widely. Some bonus schemes only require continued employment whereas others require certain performance criteria to be attained on a monthly, quarterly, or annual basis. Payment of bonuses may be purely discretionary, contractual or based on years of historical precedent. *[IAS 34.B5]*. A bonus is recognised for interim reporting only if: *[IAS 34.B6]*

(a) the entity has a present legal or constructive obligation to make such payments as a result of past events; and

(b) a reliable estimate of the obligation can be made.

A present obligation exists only when an entity has no realistic alternative but to make the payments. *[IAS 19.19]*. IAS 19 gives guidance on accounting for profit sharing and bonus plans (see Chapter 33 at 12.3).

In recognising a bonus at an interim reporting date, an entity should consider the facts and circumstances under which the bonus is payable, and determine an accounting policy that recognises an expense reflecting the obligation on the basis of the services received to date. Several possible accounting policies are illustrated in Example 39.10 below.

Example 39.10: Measuring interim bonus expense

An entity pays an annual performance bonus if earnings exceed £10 million, under which 5% of any earnings in excess over £10 million will be paid up to a maximum of £500,000. Earnings for the six months ended 30 June 2017 are £7 million, and the entity expects earnings for the full year ended 31 December 2017 to be £16 million.

The following table shows various accounting policies and the expense recognised thereunder in the interim financial statements for the six months ended 30 June 2017.

	Expense (£)
Method 1 – constructive obligation exists when earnings target is met	Nil
Method 2 – assume earnings for remainder of year will be same	200,000
Method 3 – proportionate recognition based on full-year estimate	131,250
Method 4 – one-half recognition based on full-year estimate	150,000

Method 1 is generally not appropriate, as this method attributes the entire bonus to the latter portion of the year, whereas employees provided services during the first six months to towards earning the bonus. Likewise, Method 2 is generally not appropriate, as the expense of £200,000 [(£14 million – £10 million) × 5%] assumes that the employees will continue to provide services in the latter half of the year to achieve the bonus target, but does not attribute any services to that period.

In contrast to Methods 1 and 2, Method 3 illustrates an accounting policy whereby an estimate is made of the full-year expense and attributed to the period based on the proportion of that bonus for which employees have provided services at 30 June 2017. The amount recognised is calculated as (£7 million ÷ £16 million) × [5% × (£16 million – £10 million)].

Similar to Method 3, Method 4 also takes the approach of recognising an expense based on the full year estimate, but allocates that full-year estimate equally to each period (which is similar to the approach used for share-based payment transactions). The amount recognised is calculated as [50% × 5% × (£16 million – £10 million)].

In addition to Methods 3 and 4, which might be appropriate, depending on the facts and circumstances, an entity might determine another basis on which to recognise bonus that considers both the constructive obligation that exists as of 30 June 2017, and the services performed to date, which is also appropriate.

9.3.3 Pensions

Pension costs for an interim period are calculated on a year-to-date basis using the actuarially determined pension cost rate at the end of the prior year, adjusted for significant market fluctuations and for significant one-off events, such as plan amendments, curtailments and settlements. *[IAS 34.B9]*.

In the absence of such significant market fluctuations and one-off events, the estimate of the actuarial liabilities is rolled forward in the scheme based on assumptions as at the beginning of the year and adjusted for significant changes in the membership of the scheme. If there are significant changes to pension arrangements during the interim period (such as changes resulting from a material business combination or from a major redundancy programme) consideration should be given to obtaining a new actuarial valuation of scheme liabilities. Similarly, if there are significant market fluctuations, such as those arising from changes in corporate bond markets, the validity of the assumptions in the last actuarial estimate, such as the discount rate applied to scheme liabilities, should be reviewed and revised as appropriate. Since the revised version of IAS 19 became effective on 1 January 2013, entities are required to recognise the full defined benefit obligation as liability. With this approach it is more likely than under the previous corridor approach that changes in market conditions may have a significant effect on the pension liability.

In Extract 39.32 Bayer discloses changes in the discount rates used for pension obligations. In normal circumstances, companies would not necessarily go through the full process of measuring pension liabilities at interim reporting dates, but rather would look to establish a process to assess the impact of any changes in underlying parameters (e.g. through extrapolation). If, for example, the discount rate estimated based on circumstances prevalent at the half-year interim reporting date has changed, the following 'rule of thumb' may help assess the impact on the pension obligation:

- Estimated change in DBO (%) = [Change in the discount rate (basis points) × duration of the pension obligation (in years)] / 100

(Note: Basis points = 0.01%)

As with all approximations, the appropriateness in the circumstances should be considered.

Extract 39.32: Bayer AG (interim ended June 2016)

Interim Group Management Report [extract]
ASSET AND CAPITAL STRUCTURE [extract]

[...] The net defined benefit liability for post-employment benefits increased by €0.5 billion overall in the second quarter of 2016 to €13.8 billion, due mainly to an effect of €0.8 billion resulting from the decrease in long-term capital market interest rates for high-quality corporate bonds in Germany, the United Kingdom and the United States and to a contribution of €0.3 billion to Bayer Pension Trust e.V.

Condensed Consolidated Interim Financial Statements as of June 30, 2016 [extract]
Notes [extract]
Changes in underlying parameters [extract]

Changes in the underlying parameters relate primarily to currency exchange rates and the interest rates used to calculate pension obligations [...]

The most important interest rates used to calculate the present value of pension obligations are given below:

Discount Rate for Pension Obligations			**Table 33**
%	**Dec. 31, 2015**	**March 31, 2016**	**June 30, 2016**
Germany	2.40	1.70	1.50
United Kingdom	3.80	3.45	2.80
United States	4.00	3.50	3.20

9.3.4 *Vacations, holidays, and other short-term paid absences*

IAS 19 distinguishes between accumulating and non-accumulating paid absences. *[IAS 19.13]*. Accumulating paid absences are those that are carried forward and can be used in future periods if the current period's entitlement is not used in full. IAS 19 requires an entity to measure the expected cost of and obligation for accumulating paid absences at the amount the entity expects to pay as a result of the unused entitlement that has accumulated at the end of the reporting period (see Chapter 33 at 12.2.1). IAS 34 requires the same principle to be applied at the end of interim reporting periods. Conversely, an entity should not recognise an expense or liability for non-accumulating paid absences at the end of an interim reporting period, just as it would not recognise any at the end of an annual reporting period. *[IAS 34.B10]*.

9.4 Inventories and cost of sales

9.4.1 Inventories

The recognition and measurement principles of IAS 2 are applied in the same way for interim financial reporting as for annual reporting purposes. At the end of a financial reporting period an entity would determine inventory quantities, costs, and net realisable values. However, IAS 34 does comment that to save cost and time, entities often use estimates to measure inventories at interim dates to a greater extent than at annual reporting dates. *[IAS 34.B25].*

Net realisable values are determined using selling prices and costs to complete and dispose at the end of the interim period. A write-down should be reversed in a subsequent interim period only if it would be appropriate to do so at year-end (see Chapter 22 at 3.4). *[IAS 34.B26].*

9.4.2 Contractual or anticipated purchase price changes

Both the payer and the recipient of volume rebates, or discounts and other contractual changes in the prices of raw materials, labour, or other purchased goods and services should anticipate these items in interim periods if it is probable that these have been earned or will take effect. However, discretionary rebates and discounts should not be recognised because the resulting asset or liability would not meet the recognition criteria in the IASB's *Conceptual Framework. [IAS 34.B23].*

9.4.3 Interim period manufacturing cost variances

Price, efficiency, spending, and volume variances of a manufacturing entity should be recognised in profit or loss at interim reporting dates to the same extent that those variances are recognised at year-end. It is not appropriate to defer variances expected to be absorbed by year-end, which could result in reporting inventory at the interim date at more or less than its actual cost. *[IAS 34.B28].* See 8.2.2 above for a discussion on this topic as it applies to costs incurred by service providers.

9.5 Taxation

Taxation is one of the most difficult areas of interim financial reporting, primarily because IAS 34 does not clearly distinguish between current income tax and deferred tax, referring only to 'income tax expense.' This causes tension between the approach for determining the expense and the asset or liability in the statement of financial position. In addition, the standard's provisions combine terminology, suggesting an integral approach with guidance requiring a year-to-date basis to be applied. The integral method is used in determining the effective income tax rate for the whole year, but that rate is applied to year-to-date profit in the interim financial statements. In addition, under a year-to-date basis, the estimated rate is based on tax rates and laws that are enacted or substantively enacted by the end of the interim period. Changes in legislation expected to occur before the end of the current year are not recognised in preparing the interim financial report. The assets and liabilities in the statement of financial position, at least for deferred taxes, are derived solely from a year-to-date approach, but sometimes the requirements of the standard are unclear, as discussed below.

9.5.1 Measuring interim income tax expense

IAS 34 states that income tax expense should be accrued using the tax rate applicable to expected total annual earnings, by applying the estimated weighted-average annual effective income tax rate to pre-tax income for the interim period. *[IAS 34.30(c), B12]*. However, this is not the same as estimating the total tax expense for the year and allocating a proportion of that to the interim period (even though it might sometimes appear that way), as demonstrated in the discussion below.

Because taxes are assessed on an annual basis, using the integral approach to determine the annual effective income tax rate and applying it to year-to-date actual earnings, it is consistent with the basic concept in IAS 34, that the same recognition and measurement principles apply in interim financial reports as in annual financial statements. *[IAS 34.B13]*.

In estimating the weighted-average annual income tax rate, an entity should consider the progressive tax rate structure expected for the full year's earnings, including changes in income tax rates scheduled to take effect later in the year that are enacted or substantively enacted as at the end of the interim period. *[IAS 34.B13]*. This situation is illustrated in Example 39.11 below. *[IAS 34.B15]*.

Example 39.11: Measuring interim income tax expense

An entity reporting quarterly expects to earn 10,000 pre-tax each quarter and operates in a jurisdiction with a tax rate of 20% on the first 20,000 of annual earnings and 30% on all additional earnings. Actual earnings match expectations. The following table shows the income tax expense reported each quarter:

	Pre-tax earnings	Effective tax rate	Tax expense
First quarter	10,000	25%	2,500
Second quarter	10,000	25%	2,500
Third quarter	10,000	25%	2,500
Fourth quarter	10,000	25%	2,500
Annual	40,000		10,000

10,000 of tax is expected to be payable for the full year on 40,000 of pre-tax income (20,000 @ 20% + 20,000 @ 30%), implying an average annual effective income tax rate of 25% (10,000 / 40,000).

In the above example, it might look as if the interim income tax expense is calculated by dividing the total expected tax expense for the year (10,000) by the number of interim reporting periods (4). However, this is only the case in this example because profits are earned evenly over each quarter. The expense is actually calculated by determining the effective annual income tax rate and multiplying that rate to year-to-date earnings, as illustrated in Example 39.12 below. *[IAS 34.B16]*.

Example 39.12: Measuring interim income tax expense – quarterly losses

An entity reports quarterly, earns 15,000 pre-tax profit in the first quarter but expects to incur losses of 5,000 in each of the three remaining quarters (thus having zero income for the year), and operates in a jurisdiction in which its standard statutory annual income tax rate is 20%. The following table shows the income tax expense reported each quarter:

	Pre-tax earning	Effective tax rate	Tax expense
First quarter	15,000	20%	3,000
Second quarter	(5,000)	20%	(1,000)
Third quarter	(5,000)	20%	(1,000)
Fourth quarter	(5,000)	20%	(1,000)
Annual	0		0

The above example shows how an expense is recognised in periods reporting a profit and a credit is recognised when a loss is incurred. This result is very different from allocating a proportion of the expected total income tax expense for the year, which in this case is zero.

If an entity operates in a number of tax jurisdictions, or where different income tax rates apply to different categories of income (such as capital gains or income earned in particular industries), the standard requires that to the extent practicable, an entity: *[IAS 34.B14]*

- estimates the average annual effective income tax rate for each taxing jurisdiction separately and apply it individually to the interim period pre-tax income of each jurisdiction; and
- applies different income tax rates to each individual category of interim period pre-tax income.

This means that the entity should perform the analysis illustrated in Example 39.12 above for each tax jurisdiction and arrive at an interim tax charge by applying the tax rate for each jurisdiction to actual earnings from each jurisdiction in the interim period. However, the standard recognises that, whilst desirable, such a degree of precision may not be achievable in all cases and allows using a weighted-average rate across jurisdictions or across categories of income, if such rate approximates the effect of using rates that are more specific. *[IAS 34.B14]*.

Example 39.13: Measuring interim tax expense – many jurisdictions

An entity operates in 3 countries, each with its own tax rates and laws. In order to determine the interim tax expense, the entity determines the effective annual income tax rate for each jurisdiction and applies those rates to the actual earnings in each jurisdiction, as follows:

(All values in €)	Country A	Country B	Country C	Total
Expected annual tax rate	25%	40%	20%	
Expected annual earnings	300,000	250,000	200,000	750,000
Expected annual tax expense	75,000	100,000	40,000	215,000
Actual half-year earnings	140,000	80,000	150,000	370,000
Interim tax expense	35,000	32,000	60,000	127,000

By performing a separate analysis for each jurisdiction, the entity determines an interim tax expense of €127,000, giving an effective average tax rate of 34.3% (€127,000 ÷ €370,000). Had the entity used a weighted-average rate across jurisdictions, using the expected annual earnings, it would have determined an effective tax rate of 28.7% (€215,000 ÷ €750,000), resulting in a tax expense for the interim period of €106,190 (370,000 @ 28.7%). Whether the difference of nearly €21,000 lies within the range for a reasonable approximation is a matter of judgement.

9.5.2 Changes in the effective tax rate during the year

9.5.2.A Enacted changes for the current year that apply after the interim reporting date

As noted above, the estimated income tax rate applied in the interim financial report should reflect changes that are enacted or substantively enacted as at the end of the interim reporting period, but scheduled to take effect later in the year. *[IAS 34.B13]*. IAS 12 – *Income Taxes* – acknowledges that in some jurisdictions, announcements by government have substantively the same effect as enactment. *[IAS 12.48]*. Accordingly, an entity should determine the date on which a change in tax rate or tax law is substantively enacted based on the specific constitutional arrangements of the jurisdiction.

For example, assume that the 30% tax rate (on earnings above 20,000) in Example 39.11 was substantively enacted as at the second quarter reporting date and applicable before year-end. In that case, the estimated income tax rate for interim reporting would be the same as the estimated average annual effective income tax rate computed in that example (i.e. 25%) after considering the higher rate, even though the entity's earnings are not above the required threshold at the half-year.

If legislation is enacted only after the end of the interim reporting period but before the date of authorisation for issue of the interim financial report, its effect is disclosed as a non-adjusting event. *[IAS 10.22(h)]*. Under IAS 10 – *Events after the Reporting Period* – estimates of tax rates and related assets or liabilities are not revised. *[IAS 10.10]*.

9.5.2.B Changes to previously reported estimated income tax rates for the current year

IAS 34 requires an entity to re-estimate at the end of each interim reporting period the estimated average annual income tax rate on a year-to-date basis. *[IAS 34.B13]*. Accordingly, the amounts accrued for income tax expense in one interim period may have to be adjusted in a subsequent interim period if that estimate changes. *[IAS 34.30(c)]*. IAS 34 requires disclosure in interim financial statements of material changes in estimates of amounts reported in an earlier period or, in the annual financial statements, of material changes in estimates of amounts reported in the latest interim financial statements. *[IAS 34.16A(d), 26]*.

Accordingly, just as the integral approach does not necessarily result in a constant tax charge in each interim reporting period, it also does not result in a constant effective tax rate when circumstances change. In 2015, Coca-Cola HBC described how its tax rate is estimated in the following interim report.

Extract 39.33: Coca-Cola Hellenic Bottling Company S.A. (interim ended July 2015)

Selected explanatory notes to the condensed consolidated interim financial statements (unaudited) [extract]

9. Tax

The Group's effective tax rate for 2015 may differ from the theoretical amount that would arise using the weighted average tax rate applicable to profits of the consolidated entities, as a consequence of a number of factors, the most significant of which are the application of statutory tax rates of the countries in which the Group operates, the non-deductibility of certain expenses, non-taxable income and one off tax items.

Example 39.14: Changes in the effective tax rate during the year

Taking the fact pattern in Example 39.11 above, an entity reporting quarterly expects to earn 10,000 pre-tax each quarter; from the start of the third quarter the higher rate of tax on earnings over 20,000 increases from 30% to 40%. Actual earnings continue to match expectations. The following table shows the income tax expense reported in each quarter:

	Period pre-tax earnings	Pre-tax earnings: year to date	Effective tax rate	Tax expense: year to date	Period tax expense
First quarter †	10,000	10,000	25%	2,500	2,500
Second quarter †	10,000	20,000	25%	5,000	2,500
Third quarter	10,000	30,000	30%	9,000	4,000
Fourth quarter	10,000	40,000	30%	12,000	3,000
Annual	40,000				12,000

† As previously reported from Example 39.11 using an effective tax rate of 25%.

The increase in the tax rate means that 12,000 of tax is expected to be payable for the full year on 40,000 of pre-tax income (20,000 @ 20% + 20,000 @ 40%), implying an average annual effective income tax rate of 30% (12,000 / 40,000). With cumulative pre-tax earnings of 30,000 as at the end of the third quarter, the estimated tax liability is 9,000, requiring a tax expense of 4,000 (9,000 – 2,500 – 2,500) to be recognised during that quarter. In the final quarter, earnings of 10,000 results in a tax charge of 3,000, using the revised effective rate of 30%.

9.5.2.C Enacted changes applying only to subsequent years

In many jurisdictions, tax legislation is enacted that takes effect not only after the interim reporting date but also after year-end. Such circumstances are not addressed explicitly in the standard. As IAS 34 does not clearly distinguish between current income tax and deferred tax, combined with the different approaches taken in determining the expense recognised in profit or loss compared to the statement of financial position, these issues can lead to confusion in this situation.

On the one hand, the standard states that the estimated income tax rate for the interim period includes enacted or substantively enacted changes scheduled to take effect later in the year. *[IAS 34.B13]*. This implies that the effect of changes that do not take effect in the current year is ignored in determining the appropriate rate for current tax. On the other hand, IAS 34 also requires that the principles for recognising assets, liabilities, income, and expenses for interim periods are the same as in the annual financial statements. *[IAS 34.29]*. In annual financial statements, deferred tax is measured at the tax rates expected to apply to the period when the asset is realised or the liability is settled, based on tax rates (and tax laws) enacted or substantively enacted by the end of the reporting period, as required by IAS 12. *[IAS 12.47]*. Therefore, an entity should recognise the effect of a change applying to future periods if enacted by the end of the interim reporting period.

These two requirements seem to be mutually incompatible. IAS 34 makes sense only in the context of calculating the effective *current* tax rate on income earned in the period. Once a deferred tax asset or liability is recognised, it should be measured under IAS 12. Therefore, an entity should recognise an enacted change applying to future years in measuring deferred tax assets and liabilities as at the end of the interim reporting period. One way to treat the cumulative effect to date of this remeasurement is to recognise it in full, by a credit to profit or loss or to other comprehensive income, depending on the nature of the temporary difference being remeasured, in the period during which the tax legislation is enacted, in a similar way to the treatment shown in Example 39.14 above, and as illustrated in Example 39.15 below.

Example 39.15: Enacted changes to tax rates applying after the current year

An entity reporting half-yearly operates in a jurisdiction subject to a tax rate of 30%. Legislation is enacted during the first half of the current year, which reduces the tax rate to 28% on income earned from the beginning of the entity's next financial year. Based on a gross temporary difference of 1,000, the entity reported a deferred tax liability in its most recent annual financial statements of 300 (1,000 @ 30%). Of this temporary difference, 200 is expected to reverse in the second half of the current year and 800 in the next financial year. Assuming that no new temporary differences arise in the current period, what is the deferred tax balance at the interim reporting date?

Whilst the entity uses an effective tax rate of 30% to determine the tax expense relating to income earned in the period, it should use a rate of 28% to measure those temporary differences expected to reverse in the next financial year. Accordingly, the deferred tax liability at the half-year reporting date is 284 (200 @ 30% + 800 @ 28%).

Alternatively, if the effective *current* tax rate is not distinguished from the measurement of deferred tax, it could be argued that IAS 34 allows the reduction in the deferred tax liability of 16 (300 – 284) to be included in the estimate of the effective income tax rate for the year. Approach 2 in Example 39.18 below applies this argument. In our view, because IAS 34 does not distinguish between current and deferred taxes, either approach would be acceptable provided that is applied consistently.

9.5.3 Difference in financial year and tax year

If an entity's financial year and the income tax year differ, the income tax expense for the interim periods of that financial year should be measured using separate weighted-average estimated effective tax rates for each of the income tax years applied to the portion of pre-tax income earned in each of those income tax years. *[IAS 34.B17]*. In other words, an entity should compute a weighted-average estimated effective tax rate for each income tax year, rather than for its financial year.

Example 39.16: Difference in financial year and tax year [IAS 34.B18]

An entity's financial year ends 30 June and it reports quarterly. Its taxable year ends 31 December. For the financial year that begins 1 July 2016 and ends 30 June 2017, the entity earns 10,000 pre-tax each quarter.

The estimated average annual income tax rate is 30% in the income tax year to 31 December 2016 and 40% in the year to 31 December 2017.

Quarter ending	Pre-tax earnings	Effective tax rate	Tax expense
30 September 2016	10,000	30%	3,000
31 December 2016	10,000	30%	3,000
31 March 2017	10,000	40%	4,000
30 June 2017	10,000	40%	4,000
Annual	40,000		14,000

9.5.4 Tax loss and tax credit carrybacks and carryforwards

Appendix B to IAS 34 repeats the requirement in IAS 12 that for carryforwards of unused tax losses and tax credits, a deferred tax asset should be recognised to the extent that it is probable that future taxable profit will be available against which the unused tax losses and unused tax credits can be utilised. In assessing whether future taxable profit is available, the criteria in IAS 12 are applied at the interim date. If these criteria are met as at the end of the interim period, the effect of the tax loss carryforwards is included in the estimated average annual effective income tax rate. *[IAS 34.B21]*.

Example 39.17: Tax loss carryforwards expected to be recovered in the current year *[IAS 34.B22]*

An entity that reports quarterly has unutilised operating losses of 10,000 for income tax purposes at the start of the current financial year for which a deferred tax asset has not been recognised. The entity earns 10,000 in the first quarter of the current year and expects to earn 10,000 in each of the three remaining quarters. Excluding the effect of utilising losses carried forward, the estimated average annual income tax rate is 40%. Including the carryforward, the estimated average annual income tax rate is 30%. Accordingly, tax expense is determined by applying the 30% rate to earnings each quarter as follows:

	Pre-tax earnings	Effective tax rate	Tax expense
First quarter	10,000	30%	3,000
Second quarter	10,000	30%	3,000
Third quarter	10,000	30%	3,000
Fourth quarter	10,000	30%	3,000
Annual	40,000		12,000

This result is consistent with the general approach for measuring income tax expense in the interim report, in that any entitlement for relief from current tax due to carried forward losses is determined on an annual basis. Accordingly, its effect is included in the estimate of the average annual income tax rate and not, for example, by allocating all of the unutilised losses against the earnings of the first quarter to give an income tax expense of zero in the first quarter and 4,000 thereafter.

In contrast, the year-to-date approach of IAS 34 means that the benefits of a tax loss carryback are recognised in the interim period in which the related tax loss occurs, *[IAS 34.B20]*, and are not included in the assessment of the estimated average annual tax rate, as shown in Example 39.12 above. This approach is consistent with IAS 12, which requires the benefit of a tax loss that can be carried back to recover current tax already incurred in a previous period to be recognised as an asset. *[IAS 12.13]*. Therefore, a corresponding reduction of tax expense or increase of tax income is also recognised. *[IAS 34.B20]*.

Where previously unrecognised tax losses are expected to be utilised in full in the current year, it seems intuitive to recognise the recovery of those carried forward losses in the estimate of the average annual tax rate, as shown in Example 39.16 above. Where the level of previously unrecognised tax losses exceeds expected taxable profits for the current year, a deferred tax asset should be recognised for the carried forward losses that are now expected to be utilised, albeit in future years.

The examples in IAS 34 do not show how such a deferred tax asset is created in the interim financial report. In our view, two approaches are acceptable, as shown in Example 39.18 below.

Example 39.18: Tax loss carryforwards in excess of current year expected profits

An entity that reports half-yearly has unutilised operating losses of 75,000 for income tax purposes at the start of the current financial year for which no deferred tax asset has been recognised. At the end of its first interim period, the entity reports a profit before tax of 25,000 and expects to earn a profit of 20,000 before tax in the second half of the year. The entity reassesses the likelihood of generating sufficient profits to utilise its carried forward tax losses and determines that the IAS 12 recognition criteria for a deferred tax asset are satisfied for the full amount of 75,000. Excluding the effect of utilising losses carried forward, the estimated average annual income tax rate is the same as the enacted or substantially enacted rate of 40%.

As at the end of the current financial year the entity expects to have unutilised losses of 30,000 (75,000 carried forward less current year pre-tax profits of 45,000). Using the enacted rate of 40%, a deferred tax asset of 12,000 is recognised at year-end. How is this deferred tax asset recognised in the interim reporting periods?

Approach 1

Under the first approach, the estimate of the average annual effective tax rate includes only those carried forward losses expected to be utilised in the current financial year and a separate deferred tax asset is recognised for those carried forward losses now expected to be utilised in future annual reporting periods.

In the fact pattern above, using 45,000 of the carried forward tax losses gives an average effective annual tax rate of nil, as follows:

Estimation of the annual effective tax rate – Approach 1

Expected annual tax expense before utilising losses carried forward (45,000 @ 40%)	18,000
Tax benefit of utilising carried forward tax losses (45,000 @ 40%)	(18,000)
Expected annual tax expense before the effect of losses carried forward to future annual periods	0
Expected annual effective tax rate	0%
Effect of tax losses carried forward to future periods (75,000 – 45,000 @ 40%)	(12,000)
Tax income to be recognised in the interim period	(12,000)

The remaining tax losses give rise to a deferred tax asset of 12,000, which is recognised in full at the half-year, to give reported profits after tax as follows:

	First half-year	*Second half-year*	*Annual*
Profit before income tax	25,000	20,000	45,000
Income tax (expense)/credit			
– at expected annual effective rate	0	0	0
– recognition of deferred tax asset	12,000	0	12,000
Net profit after tax	37,000	20,000	57,000

Approach 2

Under the second approach, the estimate of the average annual effective tax rate reflects the expected recovery of all the previously unutilised tax losses from the beginning of the period in which the assessment of recoverability changed. In the fact pattern above, recognition of the unutilised tax losses gives an average effective annual tax rate of –26.67%, as follows:

Estimation of the annual effective tax rate – Approach 2

Expected annual tax expense before utilising losses carried forward (45,000 @ 40%)	18,000
Tax benefit of recognising unutilised tax losses (75,000 @ 40%)	(30,000)
Expected annual tax credit after recognising unutilised tax losses	(12,000)
Expected annual effective tax rate (–12,000 ÷ 45,000)	–26.67%

This approach results in reported profits after tax as follows:

	First half-year	*Second half-year*	*Annual*
Profit before income tax	25,000	20,000	45,000
Income tax (expense)/credit – at expected annual effective rate	6,667	5,333	12,000
Net profit after tax	31,667	25,333	57,000

Approach 1 is consistent with the requirements of IAS 12 as it results in recognising the full expected deferred tax asset as soon as it becomes 'probable that taxable profit will be available against which the deductible temporary difference can be utilised'. *[IAS 12.24]*. However, given that IAS 34 does not specifically address this situation, and is unclear about whether the effective tax rate reflects changes in the assessment of the recoverability of carried forward tax losses, we also believe that Approach 2 is acceptable.

9.5.5 *Tax credits*

IAS 34 also discusses in more detail the treatment of tax credits, which may for example be based on amounts of capital expenditures, exports, or research and development expenditures. Such benefits are usually granted and calculated on an annual basis under tax laws and regulations and therefore are reflected in the estimated annual effective income tax rate used in the interim report. However, if tax benefits relate to a one-time event, they should be excluded from the estimate of the annual rate and deducted separately from income tax expense in that interim period. Occasionally, some tax credits are more akin to a government grant, which are recognised in the interim period in which they arise. *[IAS 34.B19]*.

In Extract 39.34 below, Inmarsat explains the reasons for a decrease in the effective tax rate in the interim period and the effect of related one-off tax credits.

> *Extract 39.34: Inmarsat plc (interim ended June 2015)*
>
> **Interim Management Report** [extract]
> **Income tax expense**
>
> The tax charge for the first half 2015 was $34.3m, an increase of $2.7m, compared with the first half 2014. Included within the tax charge are non-recurring adjustments which, for the half year ended 30 June 2015, resulted in a tax charge of $0.2m compared to a tax credit of $0.6m for the half year ended 30 June 2014. If the effects of the above adjustments are removed, the effective tax rate for the half year ended 30 June 2015 was 20.7%, compared with 19.1% for the half year ended 30 June 2014.
>
> This difference largely arises as, in the half year ended 30 June 2015, the Group has both tax due in jurisdictions where the statutory tax rate is higher than the UK as well as non-UK losses arising in other jurisdictions for which no benefit is recognised. For the half year ended 30 June 2014, the Group was able to offset losses previously unrecognised against tax due in non UK jurisdictions which reduced the effective tax rate.

9.6 Foreign currency translation

9.6.1 *Foreign currency translation gains and losses*

An entity measures foreign currency translation gains and losses for interim financial reporting using the same principles that IAS 21 – *The Effects of Changes in Foreign Exchange Rates* – requires at year-end (see Chapter 15). *[IAS 34.B29]*. An entity should use the actual average and closing foreign exchange rates for the interim period (i.e. it may not anticipate changes in foreign exchange rates for the remainder of the current year in translating at an interim date). *[IAS 34.B30]*. Where IAS 21 requires translation adjustments to be recognised as income or expense in the period in which they arise, the same approach should be used in the interim report. An entity should not defer some foreign currency translation adjustments at an interim date, even if it expects the adjustment to reverse before year-end. *[IAS 34.B31]*.

9.6.2 *Interim financial reporting in hyperinflationary economies*

Interim financial reports in hyperinflationary economies are prepared using the same principles as at year-end. *[IAS 34.B32]*. IAS 29 – *Financial Reporting in Hyperinflationary Economies* – requires that the financial statements of an entity that reports in the currency of a hyperinflationary economy be stated in terms of the measuring unit current at the end of the reporting period, and the gain or loss on the net monetary position be included in net income. In addition, comparative financial data reported for prior periods should be restated to the current measuring unit (see Chapter 16). *[IAS 34.B33]*. As shown in Examples 39.2 and 39.3 above, IAS 34 requires an interim report to contain many components, which are all restated at every interim reporting date.

The measuring unit used is the same as that as of the end of the interim period, with the resulting gain or loss on the net monetary position included in that period's net income. An entity may not annualise the recognition of gains or losses, nor may it estimate an annual inflation rate in preparing an interim financial report in a hyperinflationary economy. *[IAS 34.B34]*.

IAS 29 applies from the beginning of the reporting period in which an entity identifies the existence of hyperinflation in the country in whose currency it reports. *[IAS 29.4]*. Accordingly, for interim reporting purposes, IAS 29 should be applied from the beginning of the interim period in which the hyperinflation is identified. The Interpretations Committee has clarified that adoption of IAS 29 should be fully retrospective, by applying its requirements as if the economy had always been hyperinflationary (see Chapter 16 at 9). *[IFRIC 7.3]*.

It is less obvious though, as to how a parent, which does not operate in a hyperinflationary economy, should account for the restatement of a subsidiary that operates in an economy that becomes hyperinflationary in the current reporting period when incorporating it within its consolidated financial statements.

This issue has been clarified by paragraph 42(b) of IAS 21 which specifically prohibits restatement of comparative figures when the reporting currency is not hyperinflationary. This means that when the financial statements of a hyperinflationary subsidiary are translated into the non-hyperinflationary reporting currency of the parent, the comparative amounts are not adjusted.

Notwithstanding the above, some argue that in interim period reports of the subsequent year, the parent should adjust its comparative information for the corresponding interim periods which are part of the (first) full financial year affected by hyperinflation. This is because comparative interim information had been part of the full year financial statements, which were adjusted for hyperinflation.

In our view, the parent is allowed, but not required, to adjust the comparative interim information that relates to the first full financial year affected by hyperinflation, as illustrated in the example below:

Example 39.19: Accounting by the parent when a hyperinflationary subsidiary first applies IAS 29

A parent with 31 December year-end owns a subsidiary, whose functional currency is considered hyperinflationary from 31 July 2016 onwards. In preparing its interim consolidated financial statements for the quarter ended 31 March 2017, the parent consolidates this subsidiary in both the current and comparative interim periods.

In our view the parent is allowed, but not required, to adjust the comparative interim information (for the quarter ended 31 March 2016) in its 31 March 2017 interim financial report.

Whilst IAS 34 and IAS 29 are silent on the matter, a consequence of this approach suggests that when an economy stops being hyperinflationary, the entity should stop applying the requirements of IAS 29 during that interim period. However, in practice, it is difficult to determine when an economy stops being hyperinflationary. The characteristics indicating restored confidence in an economy (such as the population ceasing to store wealth in a more stable foreign currency) change gradually as sufficient time elapses to indicate that the three-year cumulative inflation rate is likely to stay below 100%. When the exit from hyperinflation can reasonably be identified, an entity should stop applying IAS 29 in that interim period. Prior interim periods should not be restated; instead, the entity should treat the amounts expressed in the measuring unit current as at the end of the previous reporting period as the basis for the carrying amounts in its subsequent interim reports, *[IAS 29.38]*, (see Chapter 16 at 10.2).

9.7 Provisions, contingencies and accruals for other costs

9.7.1 Provisions

IAS 34 requires an entity to apply the same criteria for recognising and measuring a provision at an interim date as it would at year-end. *[IAS 34.B4]*. Hence, an entity should recognise a provision when it has no realistic alternative but to transfer economic benefits because of an event that has created a legal or constructive obligation. *[IAS 34.B3]*. The standard emphasises that the existence or non-existence of an obligation to transfer benefits is a question of fact, and does not depend on the length of the reporting period. *[IAS 34.B4]*.

The obligation is adjusted upward or downward at each interim reporting date, if the entity's best estimate of the amount of the obligation changes. The standard states that any corresponding loss or gain should normally be recognised in profit or loss. *[IAS 34.B3]*. However, an entity applying IFRIC 1 – *Changes in Existing Decommissioning, Restoration and Similar Liabilities* – might instead need to adjust the carrying amount of the corresponding asset rather than recognise a gain or loss. *[IFRIC 1.4-6]*.

9.7.2 Other planned but irregularly occurring costs

Many entities budget for costs that they expect to incur irregularly during the year, such as advertising campaigns, employee training and charitable contributions. Even though these costs are planned and expected to recur annually, they tend to be discretionary in nature. Therefore, it is generally not appropriate to recognise an obligation at the end of an interim financial reporting period for such costs that are not yet incurred, as they do not meet the definition of a liability. *[IAS 34.B11]*.

As discussed at 8.2.2 above, IAS 34 prohibits the recognition or deferral of costs incurred unevenly throughout the year at the interim date if recognition or deferral would be inappropriate at year-end. *[IAS 34.39]*. Accordingly, such costs should be recognised as they are incurred and an entity should not recognise provisions or accruals in the interim report to adjust these costs to their budgeted amount.

Extract 39.35: Coca-Cola Hellenic Bottling Company S.A. (interim ended July 2015)

Selected explanatory notes to the condensed consolidated interim financial statements (unaudited) [extract]

1. Accounting policies [extract]

Basis of preparation [extract]

Operating results for the first half of 2015 are not indicative of the results that may be expected for the year ending 31 December 2015 because of business seasonality. Business seasonality results from higher unit sales of the Group's products in the warmer months of the year. The Group's methods of accounting for fixed costs such as depreciation and interest expense are not significantly affected by business seasonality.

Costs that are incurred unevenly during the financial year are anticipated or deferred in the interim report only if it would also be appropriate to anticipate or defer such costs at the end of the financial year.

9.7.3 *Major planned periodic maintenance or overhaul*

The cost of periodic maintenance, a planned major overhaul, or other seasonal expenditures expected to occur after the interim reporting date should not be recognised for interim reporting purposes unless an event before the end of the interim period causes the entity to have a legal or constructive obligation. The mere intention or necessity to incur expenditures in the future is not sufficient to recognise an obligation as at the interim reporting date. *[IAS 34.B2]*. Similarly, an entity may not defer and amortise such costs if they are incurred early in the year, but do not satisfy the criteria for recognition as an asset as at the interim reporting date.

9.7.4 *Contingent lease payments*

Contingent lease payments can create legal or constructive obligations that are recognised as liabilities. If a lease includes contingent payments based on achieving a certain level of annual sales (or annual use of the asset), an obligation can arise in an interim period before the required level of annual sales (or usage) is achieved. If the entity expects to achieve the required level of annual sales (or usage), it should recognise a liability as it has no realistic alternative but to make the future lease payment. *[IAS 34.B7]*.

Where entities apply IFRS 16 – *Leases* – the terminology used in illustrative example B7 of IAS 34 is changed from 'contingent' to 'variable' lease payments.[2]

9.7.5 *Levies charged by public authorities*

When governments or other public authorities impose levies on entities in relation to their activities, as opposed to income taxes, it is not always clear when the liability to pay a levy arises and a provision should be recognised. In May 2013, the Interpretations Committee issued Interpretation 21 – *Levies*. The scope of the Interpretation is limited to provisions within the scope of IAS 37 and specifically need not be applied to emissions trading schemes. *[IFRIC 21.2, 6]*.

The Interpretation requires that for an activity within its scope, an entity should recognise a liability for a levy only when the activity that triggers payment, as identified by the relevant legislation, occurs *[IFRIC 21.8]*. The Interpretation states that neither a constructive nor a present obligation arises as a result of being economically compelled to continue operating; or from any implication of continuing operations in the future arising from the use of the going concern assumption in the preparation of financial statements (see Chapter 28 at 6.8). *[IFRIC 21.9-10]*.

The Interpretation states that the same recognition principles should be applied in the interim financial statements. Therefore, a liability for any levy expense should not be anticipated if there is no present obligation to pay the levy at the end of the interim reporting period. Similarly, a liability should not be deferred if a present obligation to pay the levy exists at the end of the interim period. *[IFRIC 21.31]*.

This is relatively simple when a levy is triggered on a specific day or when a specific event occurs. When a levy is triggered progressively, for example as the entity generates revenues, the levy is accrued over time. At any time in the year, the entity would have a present obligation to pay an amount of levy that would be based on revenues generated to that date and recognises a liability and an expense on that basis. *[IFRIC 21.11]*.

The following examples illustrate the above principles in a number of scenarios and demonstrate how the appropriate accounting treatment has to reflect the specific facts and circumstances that apply in determining an entity's obligation to pay the levy in line with the relevant legislation.

When the legislation provides that a levy is triggered by an entity operating in a market only at the end of the annual reporting period, no liability is recognised until the last day of the annual reporting period. No amount is recognised before that date in anticipation of the entity still operating in the market. This means that in the interim financial reports for that year, no liability for the levy expense is recognised. Only if the entity reports for the last quarter of that year would the expenditure appear in an interim report. *[IFRIC 21.IE.1 Example 2]*.

If a levy is triggered in full as soon as the entity commences generating revenues, the liability is recognised in full on the first day that the entity commences generating revenue. In this case, the entity does not defer any expense and amortise this amount over the year or otherwise allocate it to subsequent interim periods. The example below illustrates this situation. *[IFRIC 21.IE.1 Example 2]*.

Example 39.20: A levy is triggered in full as soon as the entity generates revenue

An entity has a calendar year end. In accordance with legislation, a levy is triggered in full as soon as the entity generates revenue in 2017. The amount of the levy is determined by reference to revenue generated by the entity in 2017. The entity generated revenue in 2016 and starts to generate revenue in 2017 on 3 January 2017.

In this example, the liability is recognised in full on 3 January 2017 because the obligating event, as identified by the legislation, is the first generation of revenue in 2017. The generation of revenue in 2017 is necessary, but not sufficient, to create a present obligation to pay a levy. Before 3 January 2017, the entity has no obligation. In other words, the activity that triggers the payment of the levy as identified by the legislation is the first generation of revenue at a point in time in 2017.

The generation of revenues in 2017 is not the activity that triggers the payment of the levy. The amount of revenue generated in 2017 only affects the measurement of the liability.

In the interim financial report, because the liability is recognised in full on 3 January 2017, the expense is recognised in full in the first interim period of 2017. The expense should not be deferred until subsequent interim periods and shall not be anticipated in previous interim periods.

Another situation is when a levy is triggered in full as soon as the entity generates revenue from an activity above a certain annual threshold is illustrated in the following example. *[IFRIC 21.IE.1 Example 4]*.

Example 39.21: A levy is triggered in full as soon as the entity generates revenue from a certain activity above an annual threshold, which is reduced pro rata when the entity ceases participation in that activity during the year

A bank has a calendar year end. In accordance with legislation, a bank levy is triggered only if the bank generated revenue above the annual threshold of CU10 million in 2017. The amount of the levy payable is calculated based on 0.1% of the annual threshold of CU10 million and is assessed as at 31 December every year. i.e. Annual revenue below CU10 million attracts no levy and revenue of at least CU10 million attracts a levy of CU10,000 (0.1% × CU10 million). However, if the bank ceases operations during the year, the annual threshold of CU10 million will then be reduced *pro rata*, based on the number of days the bank was in operation during the year and the levy payable will then be based on 0.1% of the pro-rated annual threshold.

The owners of the bank ceased operation with effect from 1 July 2017. As at 31 March 2017 and 30 June 2017, the revenue generated amounted to CU4 million and CU8 million, respectively.

In this example, the liability is recognised in the interim financial report as follows:

31 March 2017:	Nil
30 June 2017:	Nil
30 September 2017:	CU5,000 (CU10 million × (6/12 months) × 0.1%)
31 December 2017:	CU5,000 (CU10 million × (6/12 months) × 0.1%)

Based on discussions by the IFRS Interpretations Committee during their March 2015 meeting, the threshold for determining the entity's liability would only be reduced (or pro-rated) if, and only if, the entity stops the relevant activity before the end of the annual assessment period.[3] This means that the pro-rated annual threshold would only apply from the date the entity stops the relevant activity in the market.

At 31 March 2017 and 30 June 2017, the bank has not ceased operations and the annual threshold remains at CU10 million. Since the revenue generated as at 31 March 2017 and 30 June 2017 did not meet the annual threshold, no liability is recognised under IFRIC 21 on both dates.

In contrast, the bank ceased operation from 1 July 2017. Hence, the annual threshold would have been pro-rated and reduced to CU5 million at that date.

For the quarters as at 30 September and 31 December 2017 a liability of CU5,000 should thus be recognised accordingly.

In many countries, property taxes are levied by municipalities or other local government bodies on the owner of a property. Such taxes are relevant and may be material to entities in certain sectors (e.g. real estate). Even within a single jurisdiction, there could be several different property tax mechanisms. Generally, each property tax arrangement must be assessed on its own merits. To facilitate such assessments, we have explored some illustrative fact patterns of property tax mechanisms in the following examples:

Example 39.22: A levy is triggered in full as soon as the entity holds the property at a specified date

In accordance with the legislation, property tax is imposed on the registered owner of the property as at 1 April each year. The amount payable is calculated based on 0.1% of the appraised value estimated by the tax authorities as at 1 April each year. Payments are to be made in arrears in instalments on June, September, December and March month-end dates and any unpaid instalments remain as the liability of the registered owner of the property as at 1 April.

The law also states that if the property is sold during the year, there will be no refund from the government to the seller. The new property owner will only be liable to pay the property tax on 1 April of the coming year, subsequent to the date of purchase.

An entity has a calendar year-end and prepares quarterly interim financial reports. It holds a property as at 1 April 2017, which has an appraised value of CU50 million. On 30 June 2017, it sold the property to another entity.

In this example, the liability is recognised in the interim financial report as follows:

31 March 2017:	Nil, since the obligating event is not until 1 April, assuming that all previous year instalments have been paid on time
1 April 2017:	CU50,000 (CU million × 0.1%), i.e. the liability is recognised in full

For the subsequent interim period's reports as at 30 June, 30 September and 31 December, the liability recognised in the statement of financial position would be CU50,000 less the instalment payments made during the year.

If in a variation to the above fact pattern, the seller is able to obtain a refund of a proportionate share of the paid property tax (i.e. CU 37,500) from the buyer of the property and this refund will form part of the sales price of the property based on the sales contract between the buyer and the seller, it would not change the accounting under IFRIC 21.

Yet another situation arises where a levy is triggered progressively.

Example 39.23: A levy is triggered progressively as the entity holds the asset through a specified period of time

In accordance with the legislation, property tax is imposed on the registered owner of the property as at 1 April each year. The amount payable is calculated based on 0.1% of the appraised value estimated by the tax authorities as at 1 April each year. Payments are to be made in instalments at every March, June, September and December month-end.

The law does not explicitly state that the property tax relate to a period of time. However, if the property is sold during the year, the amount of property tax will be pro-rated for the period from 1 April to the date of sale, and any excess will be refunded to the entity by the government. The new property owner will only be liable to pay the property tax upon the date of purchase, for the period from the date of purchase.

An entity has a calendar year-end and prepares quarterly interim financial reports. It holds a property as at 1 April 2017 to 31 March 2018, which has an appraised value of CU50 million as at 1 April 2017. Prior to 1 April 2017 the entity did not hold any property. For simplicity, assume that the appraised value does not change year on year.

In this example, although the law does not explicitly state that the property tax relates to the entity holding the property over a period of time, it is evident that the obligating event occurs rateably over the 12-month period from 1 April to 31 March. This is because the law allows for a pro-rated refund to be given to the entity for the period whereby the entity no longer holds the property. This implies that it is a time-based progressive levy.

As such, the levy is triggered over a 12-month period and the liability is recognised rateably over the 12-month period. In contrast with Example 39.22, it is not the ownership of the property at a specified date that is the obligating even. Rather, it is the continued holding of the property throughout the period that gives rise to the obligating event.

As such, the liability is recognised in the interim report as follows:

31 March 2017:	Nil
30 June 2017:	CU12,500 (CU50,000 divided by 4), less any instalment payments made
30 September 2017	CU25,000 (cumulative portion of the prior quarter and current quarter), less any instalment payments made
31 December 2017	CU37,500 (cumulative portion of the prior two quarters and current quarter), less any instalment payments made
31 March 2018	CU50,000 (cumulative portion of the prior three quarter and current quarter), less any instalment payments made

The impact on interim reports for the various types of levies is summarised below:

Illustrative examples	Obligating event	Recognition of liability in interim reports
Levy triggered progressively as revenue is generated in specified period	Generation of revenue in the specified period	Recognise progressively based on revenue generated
Levy triggered in full as soon as revenue is generated in one period, based on revenues from a previous period	First generation of revenue in subsequent period	Recognise only if first revenue generated in interim period
Levy triggered in full if entity operates as a bank at the end of the annual reporting period	Operating as a bank at the end of the reporting period	Recognise only if interim period includes the last day of the annual reporting period specified in the legislation. Otherwise, a provision would not be permitted to be recognised in interim reports
Levy triggered if revenues are above a minimum specified threshold (e.g. when a certain level of revenue has been achieved)	Reaching the specified minimum threshold	Recognise only where the minimum threshold has been met or exceeded during the interim period. Otherwise, a provision would not be permitted to be recognised in interim reports

These requirements provide a clear demonstration of what is meant by the concept of the 'year-to-date' basis in IAS 34 and discussed at 8 above.

9.8 Earnings per share

Earnings per share (EPS) in an interim period is computed in the same way as for annual periods. However, IAS 33 – *Earnings per Share* – does not allow diluted EPS of a prior period to be restated for subsequent changes in the assumptions used in those EPS calculations. *[IAS 33.65]*. This approach might be perceived as inconsistent to the year-to-date approach which should be followed for computing EPS for an interim period. For example, if an entity, reporting quarterly, computes diluted EPS in its first quarter financial statements, it cannot restate the reported diluted EPS subsequently for any changes in the assumptions used. However, following a year-to-date approach, the entity should consider the revised assumptions to compute the diluted EPS for the six months in its second quarter financial statements, which, in this case would not be the sum of its diluted EPS for first quarter and the second quarter.

10 USE OF ESTIMATES

IAS 34 requires that the measurement procedures followed in an interim financial report should be designed to ensure that the resulting information is reliable and that all material financial information that is relevant to an understanding of the financial position or performance of the entity is appropriately disclosed. Whilst estimation is necessary in both interim and annual financial statements, the standard recognises that preparing interim financial reports generally requires greater use of estimates than at year-end. *[IAS 34.41]*. Because the standard accepts a higher degree of estimation by the entity, the measurement of assets and liabilities at an interim date may involve less use of outside experts in determining amounts for items such as provisions, contingencies, pensions or non-current assets revalued at fair values. Reliable measurement of such amounts may simply involve updating the previously reported year-end position. The procedures may be less rigorous than those at year-end. The example below is based on Appendix C to IAS 34. *[IAS 34.42]*.

Example 39.24: Use of estimates

Inventories	Full stock-taking and valuation procedures may not be required for inventories at interim dates, although it may be done at year-end. It may be sufficient to make estimates at interim dates based on sales margins.
Classifications of current and non-current assets and liabilities	Entities may do a more thorough investigation for classifying assets and liabilities as current or non-current at annual reporting dates than at interim dates.
Provisions	Determining the appropriate provision (such as a provision for warranties, environmental costs, and site restoration costs) may be complex and often costly and time-consuming. Entities sometimes engage outside experts to assist in the annual calculations. Making similar estimates at interim dates often entails updating of the prior annual provision rather than the engaging of outside experts to do a new calculation.
Pensions	IAS 19 requires an entity to determine the present value of defined benefit obligations and the fair value of plan assets at the end of each reporting period and encourages an entity to involve a professionally qualified actuary in measurement of the obligations. As discussed at 9.3.3 above, market values of plan assets as at the interim reporting date should be available without recourse to an actuary, and reliable measurement of defined benefit obligations for interim reporting purposes can often be extrapolated from the latest actuarial valuation.
Income taxes	Entities may calculate income tax expense and deferred income tax liability at annual dates by applying the tax rate for each individual jurisdiction to measures of income for each jurisdiction. Paragraph 14 of Appendix B (see 9.5.1 above) acknowledges that while that degree of precision is desirable at interim reporting dates as well, it may not be achievable in all cases, and a weighted-average of rates across jurisdictions or across categories of income is used if it is a reasonable approximation of the effect of using more specific rates.
Contingencies	The measurement of contingencies may involve the opinions of legal experts or other advisers. Formal reports from independent experts are sometimes obtained for contingencies. Such opinions about litigation, claims, assessments, and other contingencies and uncertainties may or may not also be needed at interim dates.
Revaluations and fair value accounting	IAS 16 allows an entity to choose as its accounting policy the revaluation model whereby items of property, plant and equipment are revalued to fair value. Similarly, IAS 40 – *Investment Property* – requires an entity to measure the fair value of investment property. An entity should revalue at the end of the interim reporting period, but may choose not to rely on professionally qualified valuers to the extent that is required at year-end.

Intercompany reconciliations	Some intercompany balances that are reconciled on a detailed level in preparing consolidated financial statements at year-end might be reconciled at a less detailed level in preparing consolidated financial statements at an interim date.
Specialised industries	Because of complexity, costliness, and time, interim period measurements in specialised industries might be less precise than at year-end. An example is calculation of insurance reserves by insurance companies.

Attention is given to items that are recognised at fair value. Although an entity is not required to use professionally qualified valuers at interim reporting dates, and may only update the previous year-end position, the entity is required to recognise impairments in the proper interim period.

11 RESTATEMENT OF PREVIOUSLY REPORTED INTERIM PERIODS

As discussed at 8.1 above, an entity should apply the same accounting policies as applied in the most recent annual financial statements as adjusted for accounting policy changes that are to be reflected in the next annual financial statements. *[IAS 34.28]*. One objective of IAS 34's rules on the adoption of new accounting policies is to ensure that a single accounting policy is applied to a particular class of transactions throughout the year. Another objective is to ensure consistency with IAS 8, under which a change in accounting policy is adopted retrospectively and prior period financial data are restated as far back as practicable. *[IAS 34.44]*.

In the absence of any specified transitional provisions in a new IFRS or interpretation, IAS 34 requires a change in accounting policy to be reflected: *[IAS 34.43]*

(a) by restating the financial statements of prior interim periods of the current year, and the comparable interim periods of any prior years that will be restated in the annual financial statements under IAS 8; or

(b) when it is impracticable to determine the cumulative effect at the beginning of the year of applying a new accounting policy to all prior periods, by:

   (i) adjusting the financial statements of prior interim periods of the current year; and

   (ii) applying the new accounting policy prospectively from the earliest date practicable in comparable interim periods of prior years.

IAS 1 states that application of a requirement is 'impracticable' when the entity cannot apply it after making every reasonable effort to do so. *[IAS 1.7]*.

Therefore, as discussed at 8.1.2 above, a new accounting policy has to be applied from the beginning of the current year (regardless of when in a financial year an entity decides to adopt that policy) and prior interim periods are restated unless it is impracticable to do so. *[IAS 34.44]*. Disclosures regarding the restatement can be presented on the face of the financial statements or disclosed in the notes to the financial statements. If an entity prepares a complete set of interim financial statements, it should present a third statement of financial position. *[IAS 34.5(f)]*. (See 3.1 above).

12 EFFECTIVE DATES AND TRANSITIONAL RULES

12.1 First-time presentation of interim reports complying with IAS 34

IAS 34 does not contain any general transitional rules. Therefore, an existing IFRS reporting entity must apply the requirements of IAS 34 in full and without any transitional relief when it first chooses (or is required) to publish an interim financial report prepared under IFRS.

For example, an entity that has already published annual financial statements prepared under IFRS and either chooses (or is required) to prepare interim financial reports in compliance with IAS 34 must present all the information required by the standard for the current interim period, cumulatively for the current year-to-date, and for comparable periods (current and year-to-date) of the preceding year. *[IAS 34.20]*. The absence of any transitional provisions requires such entities to restate previously reported interim financial information to comply with IAS 34 and to present information relating to comparative interim periods, such as in respect of segment disclosures or in relation to asset write-downs and reversals thereof, which might not previously have been reported.

12.1.1 Condensed financial statements in the year of incorporation or when an entity converts from its local GAAP to IFRS

The standard defines 'interim period' as a financial reporting period shorter than a full financial year, *[IAS 34.4]*, and requires the format of condensed financial statements for an interim period to include each of the headings and subtotals that were included in the entity's most recent annual financial statements. *[IAS 34.10]*.

However, IAS 34 provides no guidance for an entity that either is required or chooses to issue interim financial statements before it has prepared a set of IFRS compliant annual financial statements. This situation might arise in the entity's first year of its existence or in the year in which the entity converts from its local GAAP to IFRS. Whilst the standard does not prohibit the entity from preparing a condensed set of interim financial statements, it does not specify how an entity would interpret the minimum disclosure requirements of IAS 34 when there are no annual financial statements to refer to.

The entity should consider making additional disclosures to recognise that a user of this first set of interim financial statements does not have the access otherwise assumed by the standard to the most recent annual financial report of the entity. Accordingly, the explanation of significant events and transactions and changes in financial position in the period should be more detailed than the update normally expected in IAS 34. *[IAS 34.15]*. In the absence of any specific regulatory requirements to which the entity is subject, the following are examples of additional considerations that would apply:

- since it is not possible to make a statement that the same accounting policies and methods of computation have been applied, *[IAS 34.16A(a)]*, the entity should disclose all those accounting policies and methods of computation in the same level of detail as it would in a set of annual financial statements. When the entity issues interim reports on a quarterly basis, the first quarter interim report should provide the abovementioned details; subsequent quarterly reports could refer to the details included in the first quarter report;

- similarly, the disclosure of the nature and amount of changes in estimates of amounts reported in prior periods will have to go into more detail than just the changes normally required to be disclosed; *[IAS 34.16A(d)]*
- mere disclosure of transfers between levels of the fair value hierarchy used in measuring the fair value of financial instruments, *[IAS 34.15B(k)]*, would not be meaningful unless put in the context of how those fair values are determined (e.g. methods used, any assumptions applied) and providing a detailed classification of all such financial instrument measurements using fair value hierarchy, based on the significance of the inputs used;
- rather than disclosing changes in the basis of segmentation or in the basis of measurement of segment profit and loss, *[IAS 34.16A(g)(v)]*, a full description will be necessary, as will the disclosure of segment assets and liabilities, *[IAS 34.16A(g)(iv)]*, where such information is required to be disclosed in the annual financial statements; *[IAS 34.16A(g)]*
- more extensive disclosure than simply the changes since the last report date will be required for contingent liabilities and contingent assets; *[IAS 34.15B(m)]* and
- in the absence of a complete set of annual financial statements complying with IFRS, the entity should include each of the headings and subtotals in the condensed financial statements that it would expect to include in its first financial statements prepared under IFRS.

Entities that have converted from local GAAP to IFRS and have not yet presented IFRS annual financial statements are subject to additional requirements under IFRS 1 – *First-time Adoption of International Financial Reporting Standards* – when presenting interim reports in accordance with IAS 34. Such requirements are discussed in detail in Chapter 5 at 6.6.

12.2 Consequential amendments to IFRIC 10 when first adopting IFRS 9

As discussed at 9.2 above, the IASB issued IFRS 9 in November 2009 (subsequently expanded and amended in October 2010), which made amendments to IFRIC 10. The amendment deletes references to equity instruments and financial assets carried at cost. With the adoption of IFRS 9, such financial assets would not be carried at cost and as a consequence, the determination of impairment and related reversals would not be relevant for such instruments in this context.

These amendments should be applied concurrently with the adoption of IFRS 9, which is mandatory for annual periods beginning on or after 1 January 2018 *[IFRS 9.7.1.1]*. The transitional arrangements for the adoption of IFRS 9 are discussed in Chapter 47 at 10.

12.3 Consequential amendments to IFRS 7 when first adopting IFRS 9

As discussed at 9.2. above, the IASB issued IFRS 9 in November 2009 (subsequently expanded and amended in October 2010), which made amendments to IFRS 7 that specify required classification and measurement disclosures in the year of initial application of IFRS 9. *[IFRS 7.42I]*. These amendments refer to 'the reporting period' rather than 'the annual period'. This begs the question whether these disclosure requirements would need to be met in full in any interim report in the period when first adopting IFRS 9. In our view, the reference to 'reporting period' should be interpreted as the first annual period in which IFRS 9 is adopted. For this reason, the nature and extent of disclosures about this change in accounting in interim reports for that period are subject to the same judgment as applied for other changes (see 4.2 above).

The transitional arrangements for the adoption of IFRS 9 are discussed in Chapter 47 at 10.

12.4 Consequential amendments to IAS 34 when first adopting IFRS 15

The IASB made the following consequential amendments to IAS 34 when it issued IFRS 15:

- the list of significant events and transactions for which disclosure would be required under paragraph 15B (see 4.1 above) is amended in paragraph 15B(b) to add impairment losses related to assets arising from contracts with customers; and
- paragraph 16A(l) is added to the list of other disclosures specified by IAS 34 (see 4.2 above) to require the disaggregation of revenue from contracts with customers into the categories required by paragraph 114 of IFRS 15 and sufficient information to be given to explain the relationship between these categories and revenues reported by segment (as required by paragraph 115 of IFRS 15). These requirements are discussed in Chapter 30 at 9.3.1.A.

These amendments should be applied concurrently with the adoption of IFRS 15, which is mandatory for annual periods beginning on or after 1 January 2018. *[IFRS 15.C1]*.

References

1 *IFRIC Update*, March 2014, p.7.
2 IFRS 16, Illustrative Examples, Appendix, Amendments to guidance on other Standards, IASB, January 2016.
3 *IFRIC Update*, March 2014, pp.5-6.

Chapter 40 Agriculture

List of examples

Chapter 40 Agriculture

1 INTRODUCTION

IAS 41 – *Agriculture* – prescribes the accounting treatment for most agricultural activity, from the initial recognition of a biological asset to the harvest of agricultural produce.

Practical difficulties may arise when determining which assets are within the scope of the standard, particularly for arrangements that involve leases or concessions. However, it is the standard's application of the fair value model that can be the most challenging and contentious.

IAS 41 applies to some, but not all biological assets. For assets that are in-scope, IAS 41 requires the application of the fair value model to animals and plant life alike, with limited relief. Under this approach, a market price for an animal or part-grown crop is presumed to exist (or is presumed to be reliably measureable if there is no such market price) and the animal or part-grown crop must be valued at this price in the entity's financial statements. The fair value model is applied to all biological assets that are in-scope, regardless of whether they are consumed as part of the agricultural activity (consumable biological assets) or not (bearer biological assets).

In June 2014 the IASB issued *Agriculture: Bearer Plants* (Amendments to IAS 16 – *Property, Plant and Equipment* – and IAS 41). These amendments became effective for annual periods beginning on or after 1 January 2016. Early adoption was permitted, provided that fact was disclosed (see 6 below for further discussion on transition). This chapter discusses the requirements of IAS 41, as amended, along with the requirements for bearer plants under IAS 16.

The amendments changed the accounting requirements for biological assets that meet the definition of bearer plants (e.g. fruit trees – see 2.2.1.A and 2.3.3 below):

- bearer plants, as defined, are now within the scope of IAS 16 and are subject to all of the requirements therein. This includes the ability to choose between the cost model and revaluation model for subsequent measurement (see 3.2.3.A below);
- agricultural produce growing on bearer plants (e.g. fruit growing on a tree) remain within the scope of IAS 41 (see 3.2.3.B below); and

- government grants relating to bearer plants are now accounted for in accordance with IAS 20 – *Accounting for Government Grants and Disclosure of Government Assistance*, instead of in accordance with IAS 41 (see 3.3 below).

The bearer plants amendments did not change the disclosure requirements in IAS 16 or IAS 41.

The amendments were intended to address concerns about the cost, complexity and reliability of a fair value model in the absence of observable markets. However, there may still be a number of challenges in practice, for example:

- initial scoping considerations due to the definition of a bearer plant (see 2.2.1.A below);
- identifying the costs that should be capitalised under IAS 16; and
- tracking bearer plants and unharvested agricultural produce separately.

As discussed at 3.2.3.A below, the requirements give entities the option to continue measuring their bearer plants at fair value by applying a revaluation model under IAS 16. However, fair value changes are recognised in other comprehensive income, rather than profit or loss.

In addition, the amendments did not entirely alleviate the need to measure fair value or eliminate the volatility in profit or loss as produce growing on a bearer plant and agricultural produce is still measured at fair value. Furthermore, since appropriate fair value measurement methodologies (e.g. discounted cash flow techniques) are needed to measure the fair value of these assets separately from the bearer plants on which they are growing, the measurement of these assets may be complex and subjective (see 3.2.3.B below).

2 OBJECTIVE, DEFINITIONS AND SCOPE

2.1 Objective

The stated objective of IAS 41 is to 'prescribe the accounting treatment and disclosures related to agricultural activity'. *[IAS 41 Objective]*.

2.2 Definitions

2.2.1 Agriculture-related definitions

IAS 41 defines *agricultural activity* as 'the management by an entity of the biological transformation and harvest of biological assets for sale or for conversion into agricultural produce or into additional biological assets'. *[IAS 41.5]*.

The standard states that 'agricultural activity' covers a wide range of activities, e.g. 'raising livestock, forestry, annual or perennial cropping, cultivating orchards and plantations, floriculture, and aquaculture (including fish farming)'. *[IAS 41.6]*. Nevertheless, these agricultural activities have certain common features:

'(a) *Capability to change.* Living animals and plants are capable of biological transformation;

(b) *Management of change.* Management facilitates biological transformation by enhancing, or at least stabilising, conditions necessary for the process to take place (for example, nutrient levels, moisture, temperature, fertility, and light). Such management distinguishes agricultural activity from other activities. For example, harvesting from unmanaged sources (such as ocean fishing and deforestation) is not agricultural activity; and

(c) *Measurement of change.* The change in quality (for example, genetic merit, density, ripeness, fat cover, protein content, and fibre strength) or quantity (for example, progeny, weight, cubic metres, fibre length or diameter, and number of buds) brought about by biological transformation or harvest is measured and monitored as a routine management function.' *[IAS 41.6]*.

Biological transformation under IAS 41 'comprises the processes of growth, degeneration, production, and procreation that cause qualitative or quantitative changes in a biological asset'. *[IAS 41.5]*. The standard explains that biological transformation results in the following types of outcomes:

'(a) asset changes through (i) growth (an increase in quantity or improvement in quality of an animal or plant), (ii) degeneration (a decrease in the quantity or deterioration in quality of an animal or plant), or (iii) procreation (creation of additional living animals or plants); or

(b) production of agricultural produce such as latex, tea leaf, wool, and milk.' *[IAS 41.7]*.

IAS 41 defines the following additional terms that are used throughout the standard: *[IAS 41.5]*

- A *biological asset* is a living animal or plant.
- A *group of biological assets* is an aggregation of similar living animals or plants.
- *Agricultural produce* is the harvested product of the entity's biological assets.
- *Harvest* is the detachment of produce from a biological asset or the cessation of a biological asset's life processes.
- *Costs to sell* are the incremental costs directly attributable to the disposal of an asset excluding finance costs and income taxes.

The standard provides examples to illustrate the above definitions. In addition to providing these examples, the standard notes that some of the plants mentioned in the table may meet the definition of bearer plants and, therefore, be within the scope of IAS 16. However, the produce growing on such plants is within the scope of IAS 41 (see 2.2.1.A and 2.3.3 below). The following table is based on those examples, but has been modified to provide examples of possible bearer plants and produce growing on those plants: *[IAS 41.4]*

Biological assets that may meet the definition of a bearer plant	Biological assets (including produce growing on a bearer plant)	Agricultural produce	Products that are the result of processing after harvest
	Sheep	Wool	Yarn, carpet
	Trees in a timber plantation	Felled trees	Logs, lumber
	Dairy cattle	Milk	Cheese
	Pigs	Carcass	Sausages, cured hams
Cotton plants	Growing plants	Harvested cotton	Thread, clothing
Sugar-cane roots	Sugarcane	Harvested cane	Sugar
Tobacco plants	Leaves on the tobacco plants	Picked leaves	Cured tobacco
Tea bushes	Leaves on the tea bushes	Picked leaves	Tea
Grape vines	Grapes on the vines	Picked grapes	Wine
Fruit trees	Fruit on the trees	Picked fruit	Processed fruit
Oil palms	Growing fruit	Picked fruit	Palm oil
Rubber trees	Latex	Harvested latex	Rubber products

2.2.1.A Definition of bearer plants

A bearer plant is defined as 'a living plant that:

- is used in the production or supply of agricultural produce;
- is expected to bear produce for more than one period; and
- has a remote likelihood of being sold as agricultural produce, except for incidental scrap sales'. *[IAS 41.5]*.

All of the above criteria need to be met for a plant to be considered a bearer plant.

The definition captures plants that would intuitively be considered to be bearers, for instance, grape vines. Some plants that may appear to be consumable, such as the root systems of perennial plants (e.g. sugar cane, bamboo or asparagus), but due to the perennial nature of their root systems, they are expected to meet the definition of a bearer plant.

Annual crops and other plants that are held solely to be harvested as agricultural produce (e.g. many traditional arable crops such as maize, wheat and soya, as well as trees grown for lumber), are explicitly excluded from the definition of a bearer plant. In addition, plants that have a dual use (i.e. plants cultivated to bear agricultural produce, but for which there is more than remote likelihood that the plant itself will be harvested and sold as agricultural produce, beyond incidental scrap sales) are not bearer plants. *[IAS 41.5A]*. This may be the case when, for example, an entity holds rubber trees to sell both the latex as agricultural produce and the trees as lumber.

Bearer animals, like bearer plants, may be held solely for the produce that they bear. However, bearer animals have been explicitly excluded from the bearer plants amendments and will continue to be accounted for under IAS 41 on the basis that the measurement model would become more complex if applied to such assets.

Determining whether an asset meets the definition of a bearer plant may not be entirely intuitive. Careful assessment will, therefore, be important. We believe that judgement will be needed in the following areas:

- *Used in the production or supply of agricultural produce*

  Judgement may be needed to determine whether a plant is used in the production or supply of agricultural produce, rather than consumed in the process. For example, some plants that are generally thought of as consumable are harvested twice, but with the first harvest having the principal purpose of improving the yield of the second harvest. It is not clear whether the fact that there are two harvests would be sufficient to make these plants bearer assets.

  For certain plants, new produce may be capable of being grown from various parts of the plant (e.g. pineapples). For others, the plant itself may be cut back and re-grown. For example, after a harvest of bananas, the banana plant may be cut down to its base and re-grown the next year to produce more bananas. In such situations, judgement may be needed to determine which part of the plant might be the bearer plant (e.g. the banana palm or the base).

- *Expected to bear produce for more than one period*

  The definition of a bearer plant requires that a plant be expected to bear produce for more than one period. It would seem appropriate to think of an annual period in this context. However, the standard does not use this term, so an entity needs to consider if an interim period, a season or a production cycle (i.e. through to harvest) might also be appropriate.

- *Incidental scrap sales*

  Whether the likelihood of the plant being sold as agricultural produce is remote will also be a matter of judgement. However, it is intended to be a high hurdle. The standard does allow for the fact that there may be some 'incidental scrap sales', but this term is not defined.

  The standard notes that bearer plants might be cut down and sold as scrap, (e.g. for firewood) at the end of their productive life and states that 'such incidental scrap sales would not prevent the plant from satisfying the definition of a bearer plant'. *[IAS 41.5B]*. However, it is reasonably evident that such sales would be 'incidental'. Since no further guidance is given in the standard, entities will need to apply judgement in determining what constitutes 'scrap sales' (e.g. would it include ad-hoc sales before the productive life has ended, such as selling trees removed while thinning?). Furthermore, the standard does not clarify at what level sales cease to be incidental and whether this is a qualitative or quantitative assessment. Therefore, judgement may be needed.

In addition to the considerations above, an entity may also need to reassess whether a plant meets the definition of a bearer plant after initial recognition. If a plant initially meets the definition of a bearer plant, but this subsequently changes, would IAS 41 then apply instead of IAS 16? The bearer plants amendments do not address this question or specify how to transfer such assets between IAS 16 and IAS 41 (or *vice versa*). Once again, management will need to apply judgement in developing an accounting policy in these situations.

2.2.2 *General definitions*

IAS 41 defines the general terms it uses throughout the standard as follows: *[IAS 41.8]*

- *Carrying amount* is the amount at which an asset is recognised in the statement of financial position.
- Government grants are as defined in IAS 20 (see Chapter 26).

With the introduction of IFRS 13 – *Fair Value Measurement*, the definitions of fair value and active market were deleted from IAS 41. IFRS 13 defines fair value as 'the price that would be received to sell an asset or paid to transfer a liability in an orderly transaction between market participants at the measurement date'. *[IFRS 13.9]*. Measuring fair value in accordance with IFRS 13 is discussed further at 4 below and in Chapter 14.

2.3 Scope

IAS 41 applies to most biological assets, agricultural produce at the point of harvest and government grants involving biological assets measured at fair value less costs to sell. However, to be within the scope of IAS 41, these items must relate to agricultural activity. *[IAS 41.1]*. As discussed at 2.2.1 above, agricultural activity refers to 'the management by an entity of the biological transformation and harvest of biological assets for sale or for conversion into agricultural produce or into additional biological assets'. *[IAS 41.5]*. It is important to note that this definition does not focus on the primary purpose of holding such assets or the number of sales that may result. In fact, the definition refers to 'sale *or* conversion'; therefore, an entity need not intend to sell the biological assets or agricultural produce in order for the entity to be undertaking agricultural activity. Furthermore, the standard contemplates an entity applying IAS 41 to assets that it will use itself; the Basis for Conclusions refers, as an example, to an entity accounting for trees as biological assets within IAS 41 when it intends to use the harvested logs in the construction of a building for its own use. *[IAS 41.B8]*.

IAS 41 explicitly excludes the following assets from its scope: *[IAS 41.2]*

- bearer plants (see 2.2.1.A above), which are within the scope of IAS 16, however, produce growing on a bearer plant is still within the scope of IAS 41;
- government grants that relate to bearer plants, to which IAS 20 applies;
- land related to agricultural activity, which should be accounted for under either IAS 16 or IAS 40 – *Investment Property*; and *[IAS 41.B55-B57]*
- intangible assets related to agricultural activity, for instance the costs of developing new disease resistant crops, which should be accounted for under IAS 38 – *Intangible Assets*. *[IAS 41.B58-B60]*.

2.3.1 *Biological assets outside the scope of IAS 41*

Biological assets may be outside the scope of IAS 41 when they are not used in agricultural activity. For example, animals in a zoo (or game park) that does not have an active breeding programme and rarely sells any animals or animal products would be outside the scope of the standard. Another example is activities in the pharmaceutical industry that involve the culture of bacteria. Such activity would not fall within the scope of IAS 41. While the bacteria may be considered a biological asset, the development of a culture by a pharmaceutical company would not constitute agricultural activity.

Biological assets outside the scope of IAS 41 will normally fall within the scope of either IAS 16 or IAS 2 – *Inventories.*

2.3.2 *Agricultural produce before and after harvest*

IAS 41 only applies to agricultural produce (i.e. harvested produce) at the point of harvest; not prior or subsequent to harvest. Under IAS 41, unharvested agricultural produce is considered to be part of the biological asset from which it will be harvested. Therefore, before harvest, agricultural produce should not be accounted for separately from the biological asset from which it comes. For example, milk is accounted for as part of the dairy cow right up to the moment at which the cow is milked.

Subsequent to harvest, agricultural produce is accounted for under IAS 2 or another standard, if applicable. *[IAS 41.3]*. Under IAS 2, agricultural produce is initially recognised as inventory at its fair value less costs to sell, which becomes its cost for IAS 2 purposes. *[IAS 41.B45]*.

2.3.3 *Bearer plants and produce growing on a bearer plant*

IAS 41 explicitly excludes bearer plants (see 2.2.1.A above) from its scope; instead IAS 16 applies to these assets. However, the produce growing on a bearer plant remains within the scope of IAS 41. *[IAS 41.2(b)]*.

Entities will need to carefully assess which of its plants meet the definition of a bearer plant. This is because the scope exclusion, while focused on the definition of a bearer plant, also affects the accounting treatment for the produce growing on a bearer plant and any related government grants (see 3.3 below).

Bearer plants and their agricultural produce are considered to be two separate assets for accounting purposes (i.e. two units of account), with different measurement models being applied under different standards (see 3.2.3 below for further discussion).

In developing the requirements for bearer plants, the Board noted that bearer plants are held by an entity solely to grow produce over their productive life, similar to plant and equipment and, therefore, do not directly affect the entity's future cash flows. As a result, it decided that bearer plants should be treated as property, plant and equipment in accordance with IAS 16. However, the IASB believes that 'the same argument is not true for the produce growing on the bearer plants that is undergoing biological transformation until it is harvested (for example, grapes growing on a grape vine). The Board observed that the produce is a consumable biological asset growing on the bearer plant and the growth of the produce directly increases the expected revenue from the sale of the produce. Consequently, fair value measurement of the growing produce provides useful information to users of financial statements about future cash flows that an entity is expected to realise'. *[IAS 41.BC4B]*. The Board also indicated that such produce ultimately has a market value on its own, whereas the bearer plants on which they grow generally do not. As such, the Board decided that produce growing on a bearer plant should remain within the scope of IAS 41, which is expected to keep consistency between produce growing in the ground and produce growing on a bearer plant. *[IAS 41.BC4A-BC4D]*.

2.3.4 Products that are the result of processing after harvest

IAS 41 does not deal with the processing of agricultural produce after harvest. The standard makes it clear that, even if the processing is considered 'a logical and natural extension of agricultural activity, and the events taking place ... bear some similarity to biological transformation, such processing is not included within the definition of agricultural activity'. *[IAS 41.3]*. For example, the process of brewing beer – in which yeast (a fungus) converts sugars into alcohol – would not meet the definition of agricultural activity in the standard. Similarly, cheese production would fall outside the definition of agricultural activity.

2.3.5 Leases of biological assets (excluding bearer plants)

Leases involving biological assets are common in many jurisdictions, for example, the leasing of a sheep farm, where the lessee rents the farm, including the land, sheep and other assets, tends the sheep and sells the wool.

Whether or not a leased biological asset (other than a leased bearer plant) is within the scope of IAS 41 will depend on the specific facts and circumstances of each arrangement. Currently, a key determinant is the classification of such leases as either a finance lease or operating lease under IAS 17 – *Leases* (see Chapter 24 for a discussion regarding leases). *[IAS 41.B82(n)]*.

For finance leases of biological assets (excluding bearer plants):

- The lessee initially recognises the leased biological asset under IAS 17. Subsequently, the lessee measures and presents it under IAS 41 (for measurement purposes the leased biological asset is outside the scope of IAS 17). The lessee accounts for the lease liability in accordance with IAS 17. The lessee makes disclosures both under IAS 41 and IAS 17. *[IAS 41.B82(n)]*.
- The lessor accounts for the net investment in the lease (i.e. the lease receivable, not the biological asset) in accordance with IAS 17.

For operating leases of biological assets (excluding bearer plants):

- The lessee accounts for the lease (i.e. the expensed lease payments, not the biological asset) in accordance with IAS 17.
- The lessor measures and presents the leased biological asset under IAS 41 (for measurement purposes the leased biological asset is outside the scope of IAS 17). The lessor accounts for other rights and obligations under the lease (e.g. lease income) in accordance with IAS 17. The lessor makes disclosures both under IAS 41 and IAS 17. *[IAS 41.B82(n)]*.

Such lease arrangements may include the land to which the asset is attached. Any leased land would need to be separately accounted for under the relevant standard, for example IAS 16 or IAS 40, as it is explicitly excluded from the scope of IAS 41 (see 2.3 above).

In the example above, where the sheep are leased under an operating lease, the arrangement would be within the scope of IAS 41. Therefore, the lessor must account for the leased sheep (excluding any related land and other assets) under IAS 41 – both upon initial recognition and subsequently – at fair value less costs to sell. It is worth noting that, unless specifically excluded from its scope, IAS 41 applies to all biological assets when they relate to agricultural activity. *[IAS 41.1]*. In this case, the wool is the agricultural produce. The sheep are being managed to produce that wool, albeit by the lessee and not the lessor. Since IAS 41 does not specify who must do the managing, the definition of agricultural activity is met.

The IASB, jointly with the US FASB, has concluded its project on lease accounting and issued IFRS 16 – *Leases* (see Chapter 25), which will replace IAS 17 and related Interpretations. IFRS 16 is effective for periods beginning on or after 1 January 2019, with early adoption permitted in certain circumstances. When effective, IFRS 16 will exclude from its scope lessee accounting for leases of biological assets within the scope of IAS 41.[1] However, lessor accounting for leases of biological assets, including those within the scope of IAS 41, will be in the scope of IFRS 16.

2.3.6 *Concessions*

A concession typically involves a government, or other controlling authority, granting land to an entity, but requiring that the land be used for a specific purpose, for example, growing certain crops for a minimum period of time.

The treatment of each concession will be dependent on the specific facts and circumstances. However, if the concession requires an entity to undertake agricultural activity, as defined in IAS 41 (see 2.2.1 above), the biological assets (other than bearer plants) and agriculture produce will be within the scope of IAS 41. The grant received may also be within the scope of the standard. However, the land granted would be within the scope of IAS 16 or IAS 40. The discussion at 3.3 below addresses the treatment of government grants related to biological assets (other than bearer plants).

3 RECOGNITION AND MEASUREMENT PRINCIPLES

3.1 Recognition

An entity recognises a biological asset (including produce growing on a bearer plant) or agricultural produce that is within the scope of IAS 41 only when: *[IAS 41.10]*

(a) it controls the asset as a result of past events;

(b) it is probable that future economic benefits associated with the asset will flow to the entity; and

(c) the fair value or cost of the asset can be measured reliably.

Considerations for the recognition of produce growing on a bearer plant are discussed at 3.2.3.B below.

3.1.1 Control

In agricultural activity, an entity may evidence control by, for example, 'legal ownership of cattle and the branding or otherwise marking of the cattle on acquisition, birth, or weaning'. *[IAS 41.11]*.

3.2 Measurement

3.2.1 Biological assets within the scope of IAS 41

3.2.1.A Initial and subsequent measurement

A biological asset (including produce growing on a bearer plant) that is within the scope of IAS 41 (i.e. excluding bearer plants, which are now scoped out of the standard) is measured on initial recognition and at the end of each reporting period at its fair value less costs to sell, unless an entity can demonstrate at initial recognition that fair value cannot be measured reliably. *[IAS 41.12]*. In the latter case, the entity measures the biological asset at historic cost less any accumulated depreciation and any accumulated impairment losses (see 3.2.5 below), unless fair value becomes reliably measureable.

3.2.1.B Subsequent expenditure

IAS 41 does not prescribe how an entity should account for subsequent expenditure in relation to biological assets, because the (then) IASC believed this to be unnecessary with a fair-value-based measurement approach. *[IAS 41.B62]*.

Such expenditure may be expensed as incurred or capitalised as additions to the related biological asset. However, under the fair value model, the biological asset will be re-measured at the end of each reporting period. As such, any amounts capitalised will only result in a reallocation between expenses and the fair value gain or loss for the biological asset. Therefore, an entity's policy in relation to subsequent expenditure will have no effect on its equity or net profit or loss, although it will affect:

- the reconciliation of changes in the carrying amount of biological assets;
- the classification of the expenditure in the income statement as either an expense or as part of the net gain or loss on biological assets; and
- the presentation of investments in biological assets in the statement of cash flows.

In our view, an entity should select an accounting policy for subsequent expenditure that is broadly consistent with the principles in other standards, such as IAS 16 and IAS 38. For example, in the case of livestock, an entity may expense maintenance costs, such as routine vaccinations, while treating costs that increase the originally expected yield of the asset as capital expenditure. For example, an entity must consider whether it is appropriate to add costs that improve initially anticipated yields (such as additional vaccinations or feed supplements) to the carrying value of the asset. However, such additions would be adjusted at each period end when the biological asset concerned is revalued to its new fair value. Judgement may be required to determine whether costs that take place after maturity (e.g. vaccinations or feed supplements) would be maintenance costs or improvements.

3.2.2 *Agricultural produce*

Agricultural produce harvested from an entity's biological assets should initially 'be measured at its fair value less costs to sell at the point of harvest'. *[IAS 41.13]*. The standard presumes that an entity can always reliably measure this amount and hence does not permit valuation at historical cost. *[IAS 41.32, B43]*.

The value resulting from initial measurement is subsequently used as cost in applying IAS 2 (if the agricultural produce is to be sold), IAS 16 (if harvested logs are used for the construction of a building) or other applicable IFRSs. *[IAS 41.13, B8]*.

An important reason for requiring agricultural produce at the point of harvest to be measured at fair value was to ensure that the basis of measurement would be consistent with that of biological assets and to avoid inconsistent and distorted reporting of current period performance upon harvest of agricultural produce. *[IAS 41.B42]*.

3.2.3 *Requirements for produce growing on a bearer plant*

3.2.3.A *Requirements for bearer plants in the scope of IAS 16*

Bearer plants are subject to all of the recognition and measurement requirements in IAS 16 (see Chapter 18), including the following (see Figure 40.1 below):

- before maturity, bearer plants must be measured at their accumulated cost, similar to the accounting treatment for a self-constructed item of plant and equipment before it is available for use; and
- after the bearer plant is mature, entities have a policy choice to measure the bearer plants using either the cost model or the revaluation model:
  - if the revaluation model is selected, revaluations will need to take place with sufficient regularity to ensure the carrying amount does not differ materially from the asset's fair value had it been measured at the end of the reporting period;
  - entities following either model need to determine the useful life of the bearer plant in order to depreciate it. The useful life needs to be re-evaluated each year; and
  - unlike biological assets within the scope of IAS 41, items of property, plant and equipment within the scope of IAS 16 are not scoped out of IAS 36 – *Impairment of Assets*. Entities, therefore, need to assess whether there are indicators that a bearer plant is impaired at the end of each reporting period. If such indicators exist, an impairment loss will be recognised if the carrying value is higher than the bearer asset's recoverable amount (being the higher of the asset's fair value less costs of disposal and its value in use).

The requirements for bearer plants do not completely eliminate volatility in profit or loss, as entities still need to recognise any changes in the fair value of agricultural produce growing on the bearer plant, as discussed at 3.2.3.B below.

Figure 40.1: Measurement requirements for bearer plants (assuming fair value can be reliably measured)

At initial recognition	• Measured *separately* from any related agricultural produce (i.e. two units of account). • Measured at cost, accumulated until maturity.

Subsequent measurement requirements	• Measured *separately* from any related agricultural produce (i.e. two units of account).
	• Measured at:
	  • cost, less any subsequent accumulated depreciation and impairment, with changes recognised in profit or loss; or
	  • fair value at each revaluation date, less any subsequent accumulated depreciation and impairment. Revaluation adjustments (and impairment, to the extent it reverses previous revaluation increases) recognised in other comprehensive income; all other changes recognised in profit or loss.

IAS 16 is written with property, plant and equipment in mind. As such, entities may need to use judgement to apply its requirement to bearer plants and we note the following areas for consideration.

(a) Unit of account for bearer plants

IAS 16 does not specify the unit of account for bearer plants. Therefore, entities will need to use judgement in light of the general requirements of IAS 16 (see Chapter 18) and may need to consider that IAS 41 will apply to each item of produce growing on a bearer plant.

The Basis for Conclusions to IAS 16 notes that 'IAS 16 does not prescribe the unit of measure, or the extent to which items can be aggregated and treated as a single item of property, plant and equipment. Consequently, applying the recognition criteria in IAS 16 to bearer plants will require judgement. This would give an entity flexibility, depending on its circumstances, to decide how to aggregate individual plants for the purpose of determining a measurable unit of bearer plants'. *[IAS 16.BC81].*

(b) Determining when a bearer plant is mature

IAS 16 requires an entity to determine when a bearer plant reaches maturity – that is, when it is in the 'location and condition necessary for it to be capable of operating in the manner intended by management'. *[IAS 16.16(b)].* This determination is important because it is when an entity must cease capitalising costs as part of the initial cost of the asset. The requirements for bearer plants seem to assume that the point in time when a plant is capable of producing (which is referred to as 'maturity') marks a distinct end to all bearer plants' biological transformation. However, the life cycles of plants can vary widely and it may be difficult, in practice, to identify when maturity has been reached.

Determining at what stage during biological transformation a bearer plant would be considered mature could, therefore, be challenging. Alternatives could include: when the bearer plant is capable of producing its first crop; when the produce is expected to be of sufficient quality to be sold (e.g. macadamia trees start producing fruit after 3-4 years, but only reach commercial levels when the trees are 7 years old); or when the growth phase of biological transformation is complete for the bearer plant (and is thereafter expected to degenerate or for its productive capacity to decline).

The Board decided not to provide specific application guidance for bearer plants. As such, entities will need to apply judgement to determine when a bearer plant is mature for accounting purposes. In reaching its decision not to provide additional guidance, the IASB noted that options, such as those listed above, would have needed further defining and could have led to interpretive issues. Furthermore, 'a similar scenario arises for a factory or retail outlet that is not yet capable of operating at full capacity and did not think that this was a major issue in practice'. *[IAS 16.BC82]*. Entities should, therefore, carefully consider the requirements of IAS 16, including those related to sales prior to an item of property, plant and equipment being available for use (see Chapter 18).

(c) Determining initial cost for bearer plants (prior to maturity)

IAS 16 requires that bearer plants be 'accounted for in the same way as self-constructed items of property, plant and equipment before they are in the location and condition necessary to be capable of operating in the manner intended by management. Consequently, references to "construction" ... should be read as covering activities that are necessary to cultivate the bearer plants before they are in the location and condition necessary to be capable of operating in the manner intended by management'. *[IAS 16.22A]*.

While IAS 16 provides guidance (see Chapter 18) that entities will need to consider for bearer plants, there are differences between traditional plant and equipment and biological assets. As such, entities will need to apply judgement in determining which costs can be capitalised. For example, as a plant is growing, an entity will incur costs related to water, fertiliser, greenhouses, etc. The entity will need to assess whether these costs are directly attributable to the bearer plant reaching maturity.

Another example is the cost of abnormal amounts of wasted material, labour and other resources. IAS 16 does not permit these costs to be included in the cost of a self-constructed asset. *[IAS 16.22]*. Entities will need to determine what constitutes a normal level of wastage means for bearer plants. For example, many bearers will die before maturity (e.g. due to disease or adverse weather) and will be subject to planned thinning. Whether either or both of these will be normal wastage will require judgement.

(d) Costs incurred after maturity

A number of costs, such as fertilising, pruning and thinning are incurred after maturity and can improve the quality of the produce or extend the productive life of a bearer plant. Entities will need to use judgement to determine whether these costs are maintenance costs or are considered to be improvements.

In addition, many costs incurred after maturity will be incurred to benefit both the bearer plant and the produce growing on the bearer plant. Entities will also need to carefully consider the basis on which to allocate costs between a bearer plant and the produce growing on a bearer plant when the costs are incurred in relation to both assets (e.g. fertilising costs).

(e) Depreciation and impairment considerations

As discussed at 3.2.5.B below, entities will need to carefully consider an appropriate depreciation rate for their bearer plants. The model in IAS 16 generally assumes that improvements in productivity and quality of produce do not occur after maturity without additional expenditure to improve the asset. However, many plants mature with age and cultivation. As discussed at 2.2.1 above, biological transformation continues after a bearer plant begins to produce and includes degeneration. *[IAS 41.5, 7]*. A decline in productivity might, therefore, occur only at the end of a plant's productive life, which differs from wear and tear on an item of machinery.

Applying the requirements of IAS 36 to a bearer plant may also be challenging. For example, an individual bearer plant may not generate its own cash inflows and may, therefore, need to be tested for impairment as part of a cash generating unit. In addition, the produce growing on a bearer plant is treated as a separate asset from the bearer plant and, because it is measured at fair value less costs to sell on an ongoing basis, under IAS 41, it is excluded from the scope of IAS 36. When testing the bearer plant for impairment, entities will need to determine whether or not it can include the produce currently growing on the bearer plant in its impairment assessment.

(f) Revaluation model in IAS 16

IAS 16 permits an entity, after initial recognition to apply the revaluation model. However, this is not the same as applying the fair value model in IAS 41. The former is one that recognises valuation adjustments in other comprehensive income as a form of capital maintenance; the latter is a model that recognises valuation adjustment in the income statement as part of periodic performance. In addition, unlike the model in IAS 41, if the revaluation model is applied under IAS 16 entities will be required to:

- depreciate bearer plants between revaluations, with the depreciation expense recognised in profit or loss;
- identify appropriate indicators of impairment for bearer plants in accordance with IAS 36, and to assess annually whether indicators exist. If they do, then those bearer plants should be tested for impairment (as discussed above); and
- maintain cost records for each bearer plant so as to separately track impairment that is recognised in profit or loss and impairment that is recognised in other comprehensive income.

Furthermore, an entity will be unable to recognise increases in fair value that arise from a bearer plant's biological transformation in profit or loss, during the periods in which it is held and used. Since bearer plants are considered property, plant and equipment, the sale of a bearer plant will result in a gain or loss on disposal, while revenue will only be recognised in relation to sales of agricultural produce.

Despite these challenges, entities may elect to measure their bearer plants using the revaluation model to ensure consistency with the produce growing on them or because the fair value information is useful. That is, a change in the productive capacity of a bearer plant, or a change in the prices for the future output of a bearer plant, can provide useful information.

3.2.3.B *Requirements for agricultural produce growing on bearer plants*

As noted at 3.2.3.A above, IAS 16 and IAS 41 require an entity to recognise a bearer plant separately from produce growing on it from the time it exists until the point of harvest.

Produce growing on a bearer plant remains within the scope of IAS 41 and is measured at fair value less costs to sell, with changes recognised in profit or loss as the produce grows. In the IASB's view, this requirement will ensure that produce growing in the ground as an annual crop (e.g. wheat) and produce growing on a bearer biological asset (e.g. grapes) are accounted for consistently. *[IAS 41.BC4D]*. As a result, changes in the fair value of such agricultural produce will continue to be recognised in profit or loss at the end of each reporting period.

Figure 40.2: Measurement requirements for agricultural produce growing on bearer plants

At the end of each reporting period prior to harvest	Measured *separately* from the bearer plant at fair value less costs to sell.
At the point of harvest	Measured *separately* from the bearer plant at fair value less costs to sell (i.e. no change from previous requirements).

(a) Determining when agricultural produce exists

As discussed at 3.1 above, paragraph 10 of IAS 41 provides criteria for recognising biological assets and agricultural produce. *[IAS 41.10]*. However, since produce growing on a plant is not acquired, but grown, it may be difficult to determine when that produce exists and can be recognised for accounting purposes. Would an entity, for example, wait for physical evidence, e.g. blossom on a tree? If so, how would this be done when the produce is within the bearer plant and not visible, such as with maple or rubber trees? Entities may also need to check their procedures for ensuring that sufficient information is gathered, i.e. identify each item of produce growing on a bearer plant when it is at the right stage of development to be recognised. The key question when assessing the recognition criteria (see 3.1 above) may be whether it is probable that future economic benefits will flow to the entity. At such an early stage of development, it may be difficult to determine for each item of produce growing on the bearer plant. However, historical information about similar bearer plants and their produce may be of help.

Determining when produce on a bearer plant exists is important as it affects when an entity should recognise and initially measure fair value less costs to sell. This, in turn, determines when an entity should assess whether it is able to measure produce at fair value reliably (or otherwise apply the measurement exception discussed at 3.2.5 below).

(b) Applying the requirements for biological assets to produce growing on a bearer plant

IAS 41 does not explicitly address the accounting for produce growing on a bearer plant. Instead, the standard says that 'produce growing on bearer plants is a biological asset'. *[IAS 41.5C]*. Therefore, an entity is required to apply the accounting required for other biological assets to such produce. This has a number of consequences, including the following:

- The unit of account is each item of produce, not the produce growing on each plant as a group. However, while the unit of account is the individual item, an entity is permitted to group these together for measurement purposes (see 4.2.2 below).
- Each item of produce growing on a bearer plant must be measured at fair value less costs to sell from the time it is recognised until the point of harvest, unless the measurement exception for biological assets for which the fair value cannot be reliably measured at initial recognition is applicable (see 3.2.5 below).

  The fair value less costs to sell may initially be negligible. That is, a market participant acquiring the bearer plant would only pay a negligible amount for the produce in the early stages of development because they would want to be compensated for the costs they would need to incur to continue growing the produce through to harvest and for risks, such as crop failure or price falls during the maturation period. Furthermore, cost to sell will need to be deducted from the fair value of the asset. As discussed at 3.2.3.A above, entities will also need to carefully consider which costs relate to a bearer plant and which relate to the produce growing on the bearer plant.

  The different stages of maturity of the produce and the allocation of the costs related to both the bearer plants and to the produce may make valuing the produce on its own challenging. Measuring fair value for produce growing on a bearer plant will also have the same challenges as measuring part-grown biological assets and those that are physically attached to land (as discussed at 4.7 and 4.6.2.A below, respectively).
- The disclosure requirements that apply to biological assets also apply to produce growing on a bearer plant (see 5 below). Some of the required disclosures may be challenging for entities. For example, paragraph 46 of IAS 41 requires an entity to disclose non-financial measures or estimates of physical quantities for each group of biological assets. *[IAS 41.46]*. While entities may gather such information for management reporting purposes, entities need to ensure that information is available for produce growing on bearer plants separately from the bearer plants on which they are growing.

3.2.4 Gains and losses

IAS 41 requires gains and losses arising on the initial recognition of a biological asset (including produce growing on a bearer plant) at fair value less costs to sell to be included in profit or loss for the period in which they arise. *[IAS 41.26]*. The standard warns that '[a] loss may arise on initial recognition of a biological asset, because costs to sell are deducted in determining fair value less costs to sell of a biological asset.' On the other hand, a gain may arise on the initial recognition of a biological asset (e.g. when a calf is born). *[IAS 41.27]*.

Subsequent to initial recognition, reported gains or losses essentially represent the difference between two fair values. As such, the standard effectively decouples profit recognition from a sales transaction. One consequence of this approach is to anticipate some of the profit that will be realised, often by a matter of years for long-term crops, such as trees.

The implications for initial recognition of agricultural produce are similar – an entity may need to recognise a gain or loss on agricultural produce upon harvesting, if the fair value of the harvested produce is different from the pre-harvest valuation. *[IAS 41.29]*. The standard requires that '[a] gain or loss arising on initial recognition of agricultural produce at fair value less costs to sell ... be included in profit or loss for the period in which it arises'. *[IAS 41.28]*.

3.2.5 *Inability to measure fair value reliably*

3.2.5.A *Rebutting the presumption*

Under IAS 41, there is a presumption that the fair value of all biological assets (including produce growing on a bearer plant) can be measured reliably. This presumption can only be rebutted on initial recognition for a biological asset (*not* agricultural produce). In our view, such a rebuttal will be rare, as to be able to do so, an entity must demonstrate both of the following:

(a) quoted market prices for the biological asset (including produce growing on a bearer plant) are not available; and

(b) alternative fair value measurements for the biological asset are determined to be clearly unreliable. *[IAS 41.30]*.

Since IAS 41 requires that the fair value of a biological asset (including produce growing on a bearer plant) be measured in accordance with IFRS 13 (see Chapter 14), an entity would need to consider the requirements of that standard in order to determine whether fair value can be reliably measured.

In relation to (a) above, it is important to note that IAS 41 does not restrict the criteria to quoted prices in an *active* market. Therefore, in order to rebut the presumption, an entity would need to determine that quoted prices in both active and inactive markets are unavailable for the asset.

If an entity is able to determine that quoted prices for the asset are unavailable, it would still need to determine that all other methods for measuring fair value are *clearly* unreliable before it can rebut the presumption. This is not the same identifying that a fair value measurement is complex and/or subjective. That is, measuring fair value often involves estimation and significant judgement, but this does not mean that it is automatically unreliable. Furthermore, the requirement is for the measurements to be 'clearly unreliable', which is arguably a higher hurdle than 'unreliable'.

Determining that alternative fair value measurements are clearly unreliable would likely include, but not be limited to, considering the reliability of the following factors:

- Estimates of quantities on hand and the stage of development – while estimates are often required of quantities on hand (including current stage of biological transformation and anticipated yields for future agricultural produce), the mere fact that estimates are used is not sufficient to demonstrate that fair value is unreliable. Rather, an entity would need to demonstrate that their estimates of the quantity and current state of their biological assets are often incorrect. This may be challenging for entities to demonstrate if the underlying information is regularly used by management to make decisions about future operations of the business.
- Prices for the asset in a future state (e.g. for the mature biological asset or the agricultural produce that will ultimately be harvested).
- Price for similar assets that can be used as an input into the fair value measurement – this could include plants and animals that are similar to the asset held by the entity or the ultimate agricultural produce that will result from managing the biological transformation of the asset held by the entity.
- Cash flow projections for the asset.
- The replacement cost of the asset.

Entities may also need to consider whether other entities (within a country or globally) are able to demonstrate that fair value can be reliably measured for the same or similar assets.

An entity that previously measured a biological asset at its fair value less costs to sell cannot revert to a cost-based measurement in a later period, even if a fair value can no longer be measured reliably. *[IAS 41.31]*. The standard assumes that reliable estimates of fair value would rarely, if ever, cease to be available. *[IAS 41.B36]*. Section 4.7 below discusses in more detail some of the practical problems associated with determining fair value in the absence of a market price.

If it becomes possible at a later date to measure the fair value of a biological asset reliably, the entity is required to apply the fair value model to that asset from that date onwards. *[IAS 41.30]*. In developing the standard, the (then) IASC noted in this respect that 'in agricultural activity, it is likely that fair value becomes measurable more reliably as biological transformation occurs and that fair value measurement is preferable to cost in those cases'. Therefore, the IASC 'decided to require fair value measurement once fair value becomes reliably measurable'. *[IAS 41.B35]*.

IAS 41 presumes that the fair value of a non-current biological asset that 'meets the criteria to be classified as held for sale (or is included in a disposal group that is classified as held for sale) in accordance with IFRS 5 – *Non-current Assets Held for Sale and Discontinued Operations*' can always be measured reliably. *[IAS 41.30]*.

In situations where the cost model is initially applied and then fair value becomes reliably measurable, a question that sometimes arises is whether acquisition-related transaction costs (i.e. those that have been incurred by the entity on purchasing the asset) that have been capitalised can be taken into account when subsequently measuring the fair value component of 'fair value less costs to sell'. Fair value is a market-based measure and is defined in IFRS 13 as an exit price.

The objective is to measure the price that would be obtained in a transaction between market participants to sell an asset; not the costs each party would incur in order to transact – those costs reflect the characteristics of the transaction and not of the asset being hypothetically sold. It would, therefore, be inappropriate to include acquisition-related transaction costs, particularly since a seller would not incur such costs. In addition, as discussed at 4.6.4.A below, IFRS 13 specifically states that transaction costs that would be incurred in a transaction to sell an asset are not part of fair value (that is, they are not added to, or deducted from, the exit price used to measure fair value). *[IFRS 13.25]*. However, IAS 41 requires 'costs to sell' to be deducted from fair value, measured in accordance with IFRS 13, before recognition in the financial statements leading to a lower valuation than a pure IFRS 13 valuation.

3.2.5.B The cost model

If on initial recognition an entity rebuts the presumption and demonstrates that fair value cannot be measured reliably, it applies the cost model to the biological asset (including produce growing on a bearer plant), i.e. the asset is measured at cost less any accumulated depreciation and any accumulated impairment losses. *[IAS 41.30]*.

When determining cost, accumulated depreciation and accumulated impairment losses an entity needs to consider the requirements of IAS 2, IAS 16 and IAS 36. *[IAS 41.33]*. IAS 41 provides no further guidance on the application of the cost model or the extent to which entities should consider the requirements of these standards.

Both IAS 2 and IAS 16 establish frameworks within which to determine cost. The nature of the biological asset may be helpful when determining which approach to use. Consumable biological assets that are to be harvested as agricultural produce or sold as biological assets, for example livestock to be slaughtered or held for sale, fish in farms or crops to be harvested, may be more consistent with inventories accounted for in accordance with IAS 2. Bearer biological assets, such as dairy cows may be more consistent with plant and equipment accounted for in accordance with IAS 16. When the IASB issued the bearer plants amendments, it noted that, although bearer plants are dissimilar in form to plant and machinery, similarities in how they are used supported accounting for them in the same way. *[IAS 16.BC67]*.

The nature of the biological asset may also be helpful in determining when to commence depreciation and the useful life of the asset. Paragraph 53 of IAS 16 requires depreciation to commence when an asset is available for use. *[IAS 16.53]*. Determining when a biological asset is available for use may be more obvious in relation to bearer biological assets. For example, a cow may be considered available for use as soon as it is sufficiently mature to produce milk. However, for consumable biological assets defining when an asset is available for use is less clear because the period between these assets reaching maturity and being sold or harvested is typically short.

The last component of the cost model is the assessment of impairment in accordance with IAS 36. That standard requires an entity to determine the recoverable amount of an asset or cash-generating unit (CGU) and compare it to its carrying amount in order to determine whether the asset or CGU is impaired. Recoverable amount is defined by IAS 36 as the higher of either the value in use or fair value less costs of disposal of the asset or CGU (IAS 36 is discussed in Chapter 20). Entities that have demonstrated that fair value cannot be reliably determined for a biological asset should be careful to apply a consistent approach when determining the recoverable amount of an asset. As such, using a value in use approach to determine recoverable amount will be required, possibly at the CGU level. Even in this situation, entities may need to carefully consider whether information used to measure value in use could be used to measure the fair value of the biological asset.

An entity that uses the reliability exception (and, therefore, applies the cost model) is required to disclose certain additional information in its financial statements. This is discussed further at 5.3 below. *[IAS 41.B37].*

3.3 Government grants

Government grants involving biological assets that are within the scope of IAS 41 (i.e. excluding bearer plants, which are specifically scoped out of IAS 41) are only accounted for under IAS 20 if the biological asset is 'measured at its cost less any accumulated depreciation and any accumulated impairment losses' as discussed at 3.2.5 above (see Chapter 26 for a discussion of government grants). *[IAS 41.37-38].* IAS 41 applies to government grants relating to all other biological assets (including produce growing on a bearer plant) accounted for at fair value less costs to sell.

What is not clear is whether government grants that relate to both a bearer plant and the produce growing on that bearer plant would be within the scope of either IAS 20 or IAS 41. Entities will need to use judgement in relation to such grants.

Under IAS 20, government grants are either:

- recognised as deferred income and then recognised in profit or loss on a systematic basis over the useful life of the asset; or
- deducted in calculating the carrying amount of the asset and then recognised in profit or loss over the life of a depreciable asset as a reduced depreciation expense.

Under IAS 41, an unconditional government grant related to a biological asset that is 'measured at its fair value less costs to sell shall be recognised in profit or loss when, and only when, the government grant becomes receivable'. *[IAS 41.34].* An entity is, therefore, not permitted under IAS 41 to deduct a government grant from the carrying amount of the related asset. This would be inconsistent with a 'fair value model in which an asset is measured and presented at its fair value' because the entity would recognise even conditional government grants in income immediately. *[IAS 41.B66].*

Any conditional government grant related to a biological asset measured at its fair value less costs to sell – including government grants that require an entity not to engage in a specified agricultural activity – are only recognised when the conditions attaching to the grant are met. *[IAS 41.35].* IAS 41 permits an entity to recognise a government grant as income only to the extent that it: (i) has met the terms and conditions of the grant; and (ii) has no obligation to return the grant. The following example, which is derived from IAS 41, illustrates how an entity should apply these requirements. *[IAS 41.36].*

Example 40.1: Conditional government grants

A government grant requires an entity to farm in a particular location for five years and requires the entity to return the entire government grant if it farms for less than five years. The government grant is not recognised as income until the five years have passed.

A government grant allows part of the government grant to be retained based on the passage of time. The entity recognises the government grant as income on a time proportion basis.

4 MEASURING FAIR VALUE LESS COSTS TO SELL

4.1 The interaction between IAS 41 and IFRS 13

IFRS 13 specifies how to measure fair value. However, it does not specify what must be measured at fair value or when a fair value measurement must be performed. Therefore, an entity applies IAS 41 to determine what to measure at fair value less costs to sell and when to measure fair value (i.e. the measurement date). The entity then applies IFRS 13 to measure 'fair value', taking into consideration the specific requirements in IAS 41 (see 4.5 below). 'Costs to sell', measured in accordance with IAS 41, are then deducted.

As discussed at 5 below, disclosures in relation to the fair value measurement will need to be prepared in accordance with IFRS 13 and also IAS 41, to the extent that it requires additional agriculture-specific disclosures.

The following sections consider further the interaction between IFRS 13 and IAS 41 and highlight some of the key requirements of IFRS 13 relating to biological assets and agricultural produce, comparing them to the previous requirements in IAS 41. See Chapter 14 for a discussion regarding the requirements of IFRS 13.

4.2 Establishing what to measure

4.2.1 *Unit of account*

The unit of account identifies what is being measured for financial reporting purposes, i.e. the level of aggregation (or disaggregation) for presentation and disclosure purposes. For example, whether the information presented and disclosed in the financial statements is for an individual asset or for a group of assets.

The unit of account in IAS 41 is the individual biological asset or agricultural produce. For example, the standard applies to the individual trees in a forest, not the forest as a whole. As discussed at 4.2.2 below, the standard does permit grouping of assets. This is intended to facilitate measuring fair value, but this does not change the unit of account.

4.2.2 *Grouping of assets*

IAS 41 states that '[t]he fair value measurement of a biological asset or agricultural produce may be facilitated by grouping biological assets or agricultural produce according to significant attributes; for example, by age or quality. An entity selects the attributes corresponding to the attributes used in the market as a basis for pricing'. *[IAS 41.15]*.

For example, when undertaking a valuation of livestock, an entity may group each of the animals in the herd based on factors such as species, age, weight and the expected yield.

4.3 When to measure fair value

In order to apply the requirements of IFRS 13, an entity needs to determine when to measure fair value, i.e. the measurement date. IFRS 13 relies on the standard that requires, or permits, the fair value measurement to specify this date, i.e. IAS 41 for biological assets (including produce growing on a bearer plant) and agricultural produce.

As discussed at 3.2.1.A above, biological assets within the scope of IAS 41 are required to be measured at fair value less costs to sell at initial recognition and subsequently, on a recurring basis, at the end of each reporting period.

The fair value less costs to sell of agricultural produce is measured on the date that it is harvested (see 3.2.2 above).

4.4 Determining costs to sell

Costs to sell are defined in IAS 41 as 'the incremental costs directly attributable to the disposal of an asset, excluding finance costs and income taxes'. *[IAS 41.5]*.

Therefore, of all the costs that are necessary for a sale to occur, costs to sell include those that would otherwise not arise. However, costs already included within the fair value measurement, such as transportation costs, should be excluded from costs to sell. Examples of costs to sell could include brokers' and dealers' commissions, levies by regulatory agencies and commodity exchanges, transfer taxes and duties. *[IAS 41.BC3, B22]*.

4.5 Measuring fair value: IAS 41-specific requirements

4.5.1 Use of external independent valuers

IAS 41 does not require an entity to use an external independent valuer to determine the value of biological assets. In fact, the Board rejected a proposal to require external independent valuations because they are 'not commonly used for certain agricultural activity and it would be burdensome to require an external independent valuation. The Board believes that it is for entities to decide how to determine fair value reliably, including the extent to which independent valuers need to be involved'. *[IAS 41.B33]*. Furthermore, the Board also noted that requiring the disclosure of the extent to which the carrying amount of biological assets reflects a valuation by an external independent valuer would not be appropriate for the same reasons. *[IAS 41.B81]*.

4.5.2 Obligation to re-establish a biological asset after harvest

It is common in certain industries, particularly where a biological asset is physically attached to land, for an entity to have an obligation to re-establish a biological asset after harvest. The standard gives the example of an entity that has an obligation to replant the trees in forest after harvest.

IAS 41 does not permit an entity to include the costs of re-establishing a biological asset after harvest when using estimated future cash flows to measure fair value. *[IAS 41.22]*. This is consistent with the unit of account being the individual biological asset (see 4.2.1 above). For example, an entity that owns a forest might consider its intention, or obligation, to replace its trees in the future if it were measuring the fair value of the forest as a whole. However, the entity would be required by IAS 41 to measure the individual trees that are actually planted in the forest on the measurement date. It would be inconsistent to consider replanting, since removal of an existing tree (in order to plant a new tree) would be the end of that asset's useful life.

The Interpretations Committee considered such obligations in May 2004 and confirmed its previous decisions that if an entity has an obligation to re-establish a biological asset after harvest, that obligation is attached to the land and does not affect the fair value of the biological assets currently growing on the land.

The problem of how to account for an obligation to replant was considered by the Board in 2007. Circumstances can arise where an entity is legally obliged (whether by law or contract) to replant a biological asset after harvest. The interaction of the fair value measurement basis of IAS 41, the prohibition on including the replanting costs in determining that fair value in paragraph 22 of IAS 41 and the potential recognition of a provision for the cost of replanting in accordance with IAS 37 – *Provisions, Contingent Liabilities and Contingent Assets* – when the biological asset is harvested, could lead to a net expense being recognised at the point of harvest.

Even in situations where there is a legal obligation to replant, an entity cannot consider replanting when measuring the fair value of a biological asset.

4.5.3 Forward sales contracts

When an entity enters into a contract to sell its biological assets (including produce growing on a bearer plant) or agricultural produce at a future date, the standard does not permit it to measure those assets at the contracted price, stating that 'the fair value ... is not adjusted because of the existence of a contract'. *[IAS 41.16]*.

The (then) IASC considered whether it should require sales contracts to be measured at fair value, but concluded that no solution would be practicable without a complete review of the accounting for commodity contracts that are not in the scope of IAS 39 – *Financial Instruments: Recognition and Measurement*. *[IAS 41.B50-B54]*.

It follows from this that if an entity engaged in agricultural activity enters into forward sales contracts for its produce it will need to consider whether such contracts are within the scope of IAS 39. Paragraph 5 of IAS 39 states 'this standard shall be applied to those contracts to buy or sell a non-financial item that can be settled net in cash or another financial instrument, or by exchanging financial instruments, as if the contracts were financial instruments, with the exception of contracts that were entered into and continue to be held for the purpose of receipt or delivery of a non-financial item in accordance with the entity's expected purchase, sale or usage requirements'. *[IAS 39.5]*. Accordingly, an agricultural commodity sales contract will be accounted for under IAS 39 by an entity which intends to net settle that contract even if it is also a producer of the underlying agricultural produce. Conversely, a farmer who intends to settle a forward sales contract for barley by physical delivery would not account for the contract under IAS 39, but would treat it as an executory contract. This issue is discussed further in Chapter 43.

4.5.4 Onerous contracts

Although a forward sales contract scoped out of IAS 39 (see 4.5.3 above) is treated as an executory contract, IAS 41 notes that if the contracted price is lower than the fair value of the assets, the contract for the sale of a biological asset (including produce growing on a bearer plant) or agricultural produce may be an onerous contract, as defined in IAS 37, and if so, should be accounted for under that standard *[IAS 41.16]* (the accounting for onerous contracts is dealt with in Chapter 28).

However, IAS 41 provides no further guidance on the subject of when such a contract becomes onerous. The standard is also silent on what this might mean, given the fact that IAS 37 defines an onerous contract as 'a contract in which the unavoidable costs of meeting the obligations under the contract exceed the economic benefits expected to be received under it'. *[IAS 41.B50-B54]*. In other words, a contract that is not loss-making, but that has a contract price lower than the fair value of the produce concerned, is not automatically defined as onerous by IAS 37, yet seems to be regarded as onerous under IAS 41.

Nevertheless, it is our view that a contract to sell a biological asset at an amount that is below its fair value less costs to sell (and, therefore, its carrying amount) should be regarded as onerous under IAS 37.

4.5.5 *Financing cash flows and taxation*

IAS 41 does not permit an entity to include any cash flows for financing an asset or tax cash flows when using estimated future cash flows to measure fair value. *[IAS 41.22]*.

The exclusion of taxation is likely to be practically challenging if an entity uses an income approach to measure fair value. Valuers typically prepare post-tax calculations, discounting post-tax cash flows using a post-tax discount rate. If this approach is used to derive a pre-tax equivalent fair value, entities will need to ensure the assumptions related to tax are not entity-specific. As discussed at 4.6 below, IFRS 13 requires that assumptions used to measure fair value reflect what market participants would consider.

4.6 Measuring fair value: overview of IFRS 13's requirements

4.6.1 *The fair value measurement framework*

The objective of a fair value measurement is 'to estimate the price at which an orderly transaction to sell the asset or to transfer the liability would take place between market participants at the measurement date under current market conditions'. *[IFRS 13.B2]*. In order to measure the fair value of a biological asset or agricultural produce, an entity needs to determine all of the following:

(a) the particular asset that is the subject of the measurement (consistent with its unit of account – see 4.2 above);

(b) the valuation premise that is appropriate for the measurement (consistent with its highest and best use – see 4.6.2 below);

(c) the principal market (or in the absence of a principal market, the most advantageous market) for the asset or liability (see 4.6.3 below); and

(d) the valuation technique(s) appropriate for the measurement, considering the availability of data with which to develop inputs that represent the assumptions that market participants would use when pricing the asset and the level of the fair value hierarchy within which the inputs are categorised (see 4.6.3 and 4.6.4 below). *[IFRS 13.B2]*.

4.6.2 *Highest and best use and valuation premise*

IFRS 13 requires that the fair value of non-financial assets, such as biological assets and agricultural produce, take into account 'a market participant's ability to generate economic benefits by using the asset in its *highest and best use* or by selling it to another market participant that would use the asset in its highest and best use'. *[IFRS 13.27]*.

The objective in determining highest and best use is to identify the use by market participants that would maximise the value of the asset, either on its own or with other assets and/or liabilities. Therefore, in order to determine the highest and best use of a non-financial asset, an entity needs to make the assessment from the perspective of market participants (see 4.6.3 below).

Importantly, IFRS 13 starts with the presumption that the highest and best use is an asset's current use. Alternative uses are not considered unless market or other factors suggest that market participants would use that asset differently to maximise the value of that asset. *[IFRS 13.29]*. If such factors exist, an entity would only consider those alternative uses that are physically possible, legally permissible and financially feasible. *[IFRS 13.28]*. Appropriately determining an asset's highest and best use is a critical step and can have significant implications on the measurement of fair value. Therefore, this assessment should be based on the weight of evidence available. Careful consideration will be needed to ensure consistent assumptions regarding the principal market (or in the absence of a principal market, the most advantageous market) and the participants in that market, since highest and best use is determined from the market participants' perspective.

Determining highest and best use is discussed further in Chapter 14. As discussed at 5.2 below, additional disclosures are required if an entity determines that the highest and best use of a non-financial asset is different from its current use.

Dependent on its highest and best use, the fair value of the non-financial asset will either be measured based on the value it would derive on a stand-alone basis or in combination with other assets or other assets and liabilities (known as the valuation premise). *[IFRS 13.31]*. For example, as discussed at 4.6.2.A below, the highest and best use of a biological asset might be in combination with the land to which it is physically attached.

Even in situations where the valuation premise of a biological asset (including produce growing on a bearer plant) is 'in combination with other assets and/or liabilities', the objective of a fair value measurement is still to measure the price to sell the biological asset, not the combined group. IFRS 13 assumes that the market participants that would purchase the biological asset would use it in combination with those other assets and/or liabilities. That is, if the market participants already had those other assets and/or liabilities, what price would the market participants pay to acquire the biological asset? In reality, sales are unlikely to be structured in this way. Entities might need to sell the 'other assets and/or liabilities' in order to sell the biological asset (particularly if they are physically attached, as is discussed at 4.6.2.A below). However, regardless of how an entity might structure an actual sale, IFRS 13 contemplates a hypothetical sale and specifically states that, when the highest and best use is the use of the asset in combination with other assets and/or liabilities, a fair value measurement assumes that the market participant acquiring the asset already holds the complementary assets and the associated liabilities. *[IFRS 13.32]*.

In practice, an entity may need to measure the price to sell the biological asset by measuring the price for the combined assets and/or liabilities and then allocating that fair value to the various components. IFRS 13 does not specify which allocation approaches can or cannot be used. Therefore, an entity must use its judgement to select the most appropriate technique. Even if this approach is used, the objective is to measure the fair value of the biological asset assuming it is sold consistent with its unit of account, which for a biological asset is the individual asset. *[IFRS 13.32]*. This is discussed further at 4.6.2.A below.

4.6.2.A Biological assets attached to land

IAS 41 observes that biological assets are often physically attached to land, for example, crops growing in a field. In many cases, there will be no separate market for biological assets in their current condition and location. The objective of a fair value measurement is to determine the price for the asset in its current form. However, as discussed at 4.7 below (see also Chapter 14 at 5.2), if no market exists for an biological asset in its current form, but there is a market for the converted or transformed asset, an entity would adjust the price that would be received for the converted or transformed asset for the costs a market participant would incur to re-condition the asset (after acquiring the asset in its current condition) and the compensation they would expect for the effort in order to measure fair value.

IFRS 13 does not require a market to be observable or active in order to measure fair value. However, it is clear that, if there is a principal market for the asset, the fair value measurement represents the price in that market at the measurement date (regardless of whether that price is directly observable or estimated using another valuation technique). This price must be used even if a price in a different market is potentially more advantageous. *[IFRS 13.18]*. While the price need not be observable to measure fair value, the standard does require an entity to prioritise observable inputs in the principal (or in the absence of a principal market, the most advantageous) market over unobservable inputs. *[IFRS 13.67]*.

If an income approach (such as a discounted cash flow approach) is used to measure the biological asset (excluding the land) and the land, to which the asset is physically attached, is owned by the entity, care is needed to ensure that fair value measurement is not overstated. This is because land owned by the entity would not derive any expected cash outflows. It is, therefore, common for entities to include a notional rental charge for the land, reflecting what would be paid to rent the land, using market participant assumptions.

IAS 41 suggests that where there is no separate market for biological assets in their current form and they are physically attached to land, an active market might exist for the combined assets, i.e. for the biological assets, land and land improvements. If this is the case, an entity could use the information regarding the combined assets to determine the fair value of the biological assets. *[IAS 41.25]*. Similar considerations will also be relevant for produce growing on a bearer plant, which will likely have no separate market in its current form and are physically attached to the bearer plant and, in turn, to the land.

IFRS 13 defines an active market as 'a market in which transactions for the asset or liability take place with sufficient frequency and volume to provide pricing information on an ongoing basis'. *[IFRS 13 Appendix A]*. Whether such a market exists for the combined assets is a matter of judgement, taking into consideration all the relevant facts and circumstances. However, an entity should have sufficient evidence to support such an assumption.

Importantly, the unit of account established by IAS 41 is an individual asset (see 4.2.1 above). Therefore, if fair value is measured for the combined assets, the total fair value would need to be allocated to each component in order to derive the fair value for the biological asset or produce growing on a bearer plant (as is illustrated by Figure 40.3 below). As discussed at 4.6.2 above, IFRS 13 does not provide guidance on how to perform such an allocation. IAS 41 suggests the use of the residual method as one possible way to allocate the fair value between the biological assets and the land. However, this might be difficult to apply in practice, as illustrated in Example 40.2 below. Therefore, entities will need to apply judgement when determining the appropriate allocation.

Example 40.2: Assets attached to land

Entity A acquired a 10-hectare vineyard on 1 January 2017 for CU1,200. The purchase price of the vineyard was attributed as follows:

1 January 2017	*CU*
Purchase price	1,200
Land	(780)
Vineyard improvements	(130)
Grape vines	(255)
Grapes growing on the vines	35

At the end of its financial year Entity A needs to determine the fair value of the grapes growing on the vines in accordance with IAS 41 and invites two equally skilled professional valuers to determine their value.

31 December 2017	*Valuer 1* *CU*	*Valuer 2* *CU*
Fair value of an average 10-hectare vineyard	1,105	1,100
Adjustment for soil and climatic conditions	135	150
Estimated fair value of Entity A's vineyard	1,240	1,250
Fair value of the land	(830)	(825)
Fair value of vineyard improvements	(135)	(125)
Fair value of grape vines	(245)	(250)
Grapes growing on the vines	30	50

Valuer 1 and Valuer 2 make a virtually identical assessment of the market values of the vineyard, the land, vineyard improvements and the grape vines. Nevertheless, because the value of grapes growing on the vines is calculated by subtracting all the other known elements from the total value of the vineyard, a noticeable difference arises in the valuation of the grapes growing on the vines. In a similar vein, entities that use only one valuer need to be aware that even small changes in assumptions from period-to-period could have a significant impact on the valuation of biological assets or plants growing on a bearer plant and, therefore, reported profits or losses. For this reason, IFRS 13 requires extensive disclosures about assumptions used in determining fair value.

In April 2012, the Interpretations Committee received a request to clarify the use of the residual approach, as discussed in paragraph 25 of IAS 41 (in light of the requirement in IFRS 13 to measure the fair value of non-financial assets based on their highest and best use). Specifically, the Committee was asked to consider the situation where a biological asset was physically attached to land and no separate market for the biological asset existed in its current condition and location. The submitter of the request assumed entities would apply paragraph 25 of IAS 41, measure the biological asset and land on a combined basis and use the residual approach to derive a fair value for the biological asset. The submitter was concerned about situations where the highest and best use of the biological asset is in combination with the land, but the value of the land could be higher if measured assuming some alternative use (such as property development). In these circumstances, the allocated fair value of the biological asset might be nil or negligible. The fact pattern was further complicated because it was assumed the land to which the biological asset was attached was measured using the cost model in accordance with IAS 16.[2]

The Committee elected not to take the issue onto its agenda, but noted that, in the development of IFRS 13, the IASB had considered the situation where the highest and best use of an asset in a group of assets is different from its current use. However, 'IFRS 13 does not explicitly address the accounting implications if those circumstances arise and the fair value measurement of the asset based on its highest and best use assumes that other assets in the group need to be converted or destroyed'. The Committee also observed that this issue may affect non-financial assets within the scope of other standards, not just those within the scope of IAS 41.[3] The Committee asked the IASB to provide clarification of the accounting requirements for the issues it had considered. However, as outreach indicated the issue was not widespread, in May 2013, the IASB decided it could, instead, be considered for review in the Post-Implementation Review of IFRS 13.[4]

Determining the highest and best use of an asset requires judgement (see 4.6.2 above), but an entity should start with the presumption that the highest and best use is an asset's current use. As discussed above, paragraph 25 of IAS 41 is only relevant where there is no separate market for a biological asset or produce growing on a bearer plant in its current form and it (or the bearer plant on which it grows) is physically attached to land. In addition, that paragraph suggests an active market may exists for the combined assets (e.g. land and biological asset) and, therefore, that an observable price in that market for the assets (on a combined basis) could be used to derive fair value for the biological asset. *[IAS 41.25]*. Selecting appropriate valuation techniques with which to measure fair value in accordance with IFRS 13 requires judgement. Some might use the residual approach to do this, as indicated in the submission. However, paragraph 25 of IAS 41 does not require the use of the residual approach; it is only mentioned as an example. The IASB reaffirmed this when they considered this matter in May 2013. They also noted that IFRS 13 encourages the use of multiple valuation techniques, where appropriate.[5]

The outcome from a fact pattern, such as the one the Committee discussed, may be somewhat counterintuitive. However, the fact that the fair value of the land, in that situation, would not be recognised in the financial statements is, in our view, irrelevant to the measurement of fair value. The objective of a fair value measurement does not change regardless of whether it is recognised or unrecognised.

Figure 40.3: Applying paragraph 25 of IAS 41 to measure the fair value of a biological asset

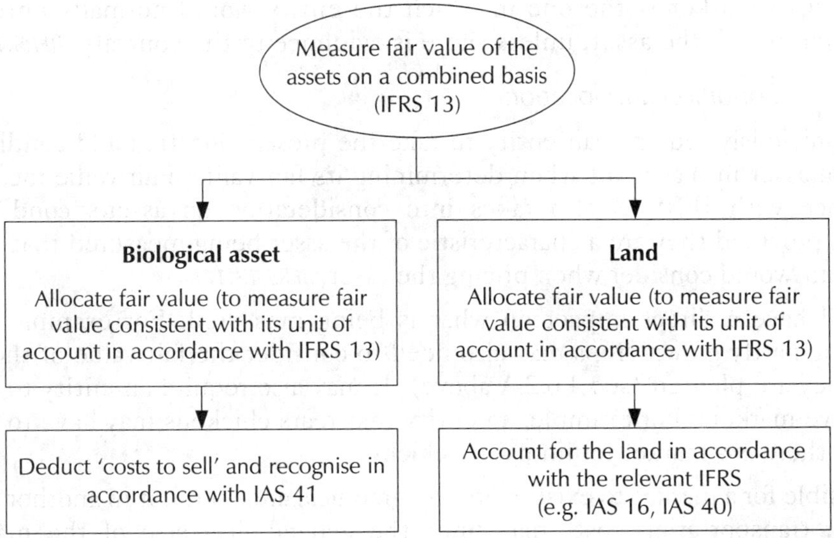

4.6.3 *Selecting appropriate assumptions*

Selecting the appropriate assumption with which to measure the fair value of biological assets and agricultural produce can often be difficult. According to IFRS 13, an entity should select assumptions that:

- market participants would use, i.e. they are not entity-specific;
- are consistent with the unit of account and characteristics of the asset, including an asset's condition and location and any restrictions on the use or sale of the asset;
- are consistent with an orderly transaction to sell the asset in the principal market, or in the absence of a principal market, the most advantageous market; and
- maximise the use of observable inputs and minimise the use of unobservable inputs (based on the fair value hierarchy, see Chapter 14).

Focusing on market participant assumptions is consistent with the previous requirements in IAS 41. However, IFRS 13 clarifies that the transaction to sell the asset would be between market participants, not between the entity and a market participant. In addition, assumptions should reflect those that market participants generally would assume, not those of a particular market participant. In order to select the appropriate assumptions, an entity would identify characteristics of market participants. At a minimum, IFRS 13 assumes that market participants will be independent of each other, knowledgeable about the asset, able and willing to enter into a transaction for the asset. *[IFRS 13 Appendix A]*. An entity need not identify specific market participants, but needs to identify the distinguishing characteristics of market participants. *[IFRS 13.23]*.

Identifying the appropriate market participants (or their characteristics) depends on the principal market for the asset or, in the absence of a principal market, the most advantageous market (see Chapter 14 for further discussion). *[IFRS 13.23]*.

IAS 41 previously referred to the most relevant market, typically the market the entity would normally transact in. There is a general presumption in IFRS 13 that the principal market is the one in which the entity would normally enter into a transaction to sell the asset, unless there is evidence to the contrary. *[IFRS 13.17]*.

4.6.3.A Condition and location

IAS 41 previously required an entity to take the present location and condition of a biological asset into account when determining its fair value. Fair value measured in accordance with IFRS 13 also takes into consideration an asset's condition and location, provided they are a characteristic of the asset being measured that a market participant would consider when pricing the asset. *[IFRS 13.11]*.

This will have a direct impact on what is being measured. For example, entities measuring partly grown crops may also need to consider the fair value of the land in which they are planted (see 4.6.2.A above). It may also require an entity to consider alternative markets. For example, an entity that rears chickens may have to consider whether there is a market for immature chicks.

It is possible for a market to exist in one geographical area, but not in another area. For example, transportation costs may limit the geographical size of the market for agricultural produce significantly, possibly to the point where a local cooperative or factory is the only buyer.

If no market exists for an asset in its current form, but there is a market for the converted or transformed asset, an entity adjusts the fair value for the costs a market participant would incur to re-condition the asset (after acquiring the asset in its current condition) and the compensation they would expect for the effort.

If the location of a biological asset or agricultural produce would require it to be transported to the market in order to sell it, transportation costs would be deducted from the market price in order to measure fair value, consistent with the previous requirements in IAS 41. Given the logistical problems and generally high costs of transporting living animals and plants, there could be many different fair values for identical biological assets depending on their location.

4.6.4 Valuation techniques in IFRS 13

IFRS 13 does not limit the types of valuation techniques an entity might use to measure fair value. However, it does require the valuation techniques to be consistent with one of three approaches: the market approach, the income approach or the cost approach. *[IFRS 13.62]*.

Unlike the previous requirements in IAS 41, IFRS 13 does not prioritise the use of one valuation technique over another, or require the use of only one technique. Instead, IFRS 13 establishes a hierarchy for the inputs used in those valuation techniques, requiring an entity to maximise observable inputs and minimise the use of unobservable inputs (this is discussed further in Chapter 14 at 16). *[IFRS 13.74]*.

Previously, IAS 41 provided a hierarchy of valuation techniques for determining the fair value of a biological asset or agricultural produce:

(a) *An active market existed* – the quoted price in that market was the appropriate basis for determining the fair value of that asset.

(b) *No active market existed* – if an active market did not exist an entity used one or more of the following *market-determined prices or values* to estimate fair value: *[IAS 41(2012).18]*

   (i) the most recent market transaction price, provided the economic circumstances had not significantly changed;

   (ii) market prices for similar assets with adjustments to reflect differences; and

   (iii) sector benchmarks.

   Where no active market existed, an entity was required by IAS 41 to use all available market-determined prices or values since otherwise there was 'a possibility that entities may opt to use present value of expected net cash flows from the asset even when useful market-determined prices or values are available'. *[IAS 41.B30]*.

(c) *No active market existed and no market-based information was available* – only if an active market did not exist and there was no market-based information available on which to base an estimate of fair value, could an entity estimate fair value using a *discounted cash flows* method or *cost as an approximation of fair value. [IAS 41(2012).20, 24]*.

The approach in IFRS 13 is generally consistent with previous requirements in IAS 41. For example, the best indication of fair value is still a quoted price in an active market. In addition, the use of techniques previously required by IAS 41 would be consistent with the approaches permitted by IFRS 13. However, since multiple techniques should be used, when applicable, under IFRS 13, judgement is needed to select the techniques that are appropriate in the circumstances. *[IFRS 13.63]*. Selecting appropriate valuation techniques is discussed further in Chapter 14 at 14.

4.6.4.A *Cost as an approximation of fair value*

The definition of fair value in IFRS 13 is not significantly different from the previous definition in IAS 41, which was, 'the amount for which an asset could be exchanged, or a liability settled, between knowledgeable, willing parties in an arm's length transaction'. *[IAS 41(2012).8]*. However, IFRS 13 clarifies that fair value is a current exit price, not an entry price. Therefore, while exit and entry prices may be identical in many situations, the transaction price (an entry price) is not presumed to represent the fair value of an asset or liability measured in accordance with IFRS 13 on its initial recognition. *[IFRS 13.57-59]*.

IAS 41 indicates that cost may sometimes approximate fair value. The standard gives two situations where this might occur: *[IAS 41.24]*

- when little biological transformation has taken place since cost was initially incurred – seedlings planted immediately prior to the end of a reporting period and newly acquired livestock are given as examples; or
- when the impact of the biological transformation on price is not expected to be material – for example, during the initial phase of growth for a pine plantation with a 30-year production cycle.

Even in such situations, the objective is still to measure fair value in accordance with IFRS 13. Therefore, as with an entry price on initial recognition, an entity cannot presume that cost approximates fair value. Instead, it should ensure cost is materially consistent with a current exit price for the asset. For example, entities would need to carefully consider which costs could be included in the entry price. IFRS 13 specifically states that transaction costs are not part of fair value (that is, they are not added to or deducted from the exit price), *[IFRS 13.25]*, therefore, we would not expect an entity to deduct such costs from the entry price – particularly as 'costs to sell' are deducted from fair value before being recognised in the financial statements. Nor would we expect entities applying a fair value model to include acquisition-related transaction costs within an entry price used to approximate fair value.

4.7 The problem of measuring fair value for part-grown biological assets

Entities may be required to measure their biological assets part way through the transformation process, particularly when the time to harvest is greater than 12 months. In these circumstances, there may not be an active market for the asset in its current condition and location. In the absence of an active market, preparers often use a discounted cash flow model to estimate fair value.

In these situations, a common question is whether an entity can take into consideration the future biological transformation when estimating the fair value of a biological asset.

As discussed at 4.6.3.A above, IFRS 13 makes it clear that the fair value of an asset considers characteristics of an asset, such as its current condition and location. An entity must consider this objective in determining an appropriate discount rate and estimating its future cash flows, which must be based on assumptions market participants would use. Therefore, if a market participant would consider the potential for future growth, the related cash flows and risks from additional biological transformation should be included in determining the appropriate fair value.

IFRS 13 is clear that, if there is a principal market for the asset or liability, the fair value measurement shall represent the price in that market at the measurement date (regardless of whether that price is directly observable or estimated using another valuation technique). The price in the principal market must be used even if the price in a different market is potentially more advantageous. *[IFRS 13.18]*. Since an entity can consider the expected cash flows the asset can generate in its principal market, the entity is not permitted to use available prices in other active markets for part-grown biological assets. Even in situations where there is no principal market, once the most advantageous market has been selected, an entity would not look to other markets for available prices or use prices in the most advantageous market if market participants would not consider them.

The original version of IAS 41 had caused confusion in this area, as it had required that the estimation of future cash flows 'exclude any increases in value from additional biological transformation and future activities of the entity'. *[IAS 41(2008).21]*. This seemed to suggest that the value of immature biological assets should be based on values in their current condition, rather than recognising that part of the value must logically lie in their potential, given appropriate husbandry, to grow to full size. The IASB amended IAS 41 to clarify that entities should consider the risks associated with cash flows from additional biological transformation in determining the cash flows, the discount rate or some combination of the two provided a market participant would take the additional biological transformation into consideration.

While paragraph 21 of IAS 41 was subsequently deleted by the introduction of IFRS 13, this clarification is consistent with the requirements in that standard and is helpful in understanding its requirements in situations where prices are available in an active market for part-grown biological assets, but that market is not the principal market (or in the absence of a principal market, the most advantageous market).

This issue is illustrated by an extract from (the former) CESR's database of enforcement decisions published in April 2007 (Decision ref. EECS/0407-11) in relation to the fair value measurement requirements in IAS 41 (prior to the issuance of IFRS 13). Norwegian fish farmers had developed a practice of recording live immature fish at cost on the basis that they were unable to value them reliably in accordance with paragraph 30 of IAS 41. The Norwegian regulator took the view that slaughtered fish sold whole and gutted should be considered the same as live salmon under paragraph 18(b) of the 2012 version of IAS 41 (IAS 41(2012)) and that it was possible to value the live immature fish based on the market price for slaughtered fish of the same size. Smaller fish are sold on the market because they are harvested with mature fish, however their value per kilo is significantly below that of mature fish and the Norwegian fish farming entities did not, therefore, believe that it was appropriate to use their market price as a basis for fair value. The regulator's decision was appealed to the Norwegian Ministry of Finance and the database reports the conclusion as follows:

> 'The Ministry of Finance upheld the decision of the enforcer, with some adjustments and additions. Most significantly, the final ruling upholds the enforcer's decision that slaughtered salmon which is sold whole and gutted is in an accounting sense to be considered as a similar asset of live salmon, according to IAS 41.18(b) and that this also applies to so-called immature farmed salmon. Hence, the observable prices of slaughtered salmon shall be used as a basis for determining the fair value of live immature salmon. The key amendment to the decision made by the Ministry of Finance is that it added certain comments relating to how the term "adjustments to reflect differences" in IAS 41.18(b) was to be applied. The adjustments should reflect the differences between the price of an immature salmon and the hypothetical market price in an active market for live immature salmon.'

As a result of this decision, the Norwegian entities were required to record immature salmon at fair value, rather than at cost, by making appropriate adjustments to available market prices for similar sized slaughtered fish.

While IFRS 13 has now replaced the requirements in paragraph 18(b) of IAS 41(2012) to which this decision related, the same approach could be used when measuring fair value in accordance with that standard. IFRS 13 prioritises the use of observable inputs for identical or similar items when measuring fair value. Therefore, in situations where an active market does not exist for the asset in its current form, entities might use prices for similar assets, for which observable prices do exist, as an input into the fair value measurement.

As discussed in the Norwegian salmon example above and in Chapter 14 at 5.2.1, an entity would need to identify any differences between the asset being measured at fair value and similar asset (e.g. a converted or transformed asset), for which observable market prices are available. The entity would then adjust the similar asset's market price for the costs a market participant would incur (after acquiring the asset in its current condition) and the compensation they would expect for the effort. Such adjustments could affect the categorisation of the fair value measurement as a whole within the fair value hierarchy. Categorisation within the hierarchy is done for disclosure purposes as it affects how much information must be disclosed about the fair value measurement (see 5.2 below). IFRS 13 requires that, '[i]f an observable input requires an adjustment using an unobservable input and that adjustment results in a significantly higher or lower fair value measurement, the resulting measurement would be categorised within Level 3 of the fair value hierarchy'. *[IFRS 13.75]*. Categorisation within IFRS 13's fair value hierarchy is discussed further at 16 in Chapter 14.

5 DISCLOSURE

5.1 General

5.1.1 Statement of financial position

IAS 1 – *Presentation of Financial Statements* – requires biological assets (including produce growing on a bearer plant) to be presented separately on the face of an entity's statement of financial position (see Chapter 3). *[IAS 1.54]*. Agricultural produce after the point of harvest should be accounted for under IAS 2. That standard does not require agricultural produce to be disclosed separately on the face of the statement of financial position (see Chapter 22). The following example, which is derived from the Illustrative Examples to IAS 41, illustrates the requirement to disclose biological assets in the statement of financial position. *[IAS 41.IE1]*.

Example 40.3: Presentation of biological assets in the statement of financial position

The statement of financial position below illustrates how a dairy farming business might present biological assets in its statement of financial position.

XYZ Dairy Ltd.
Statement of financial position

ASSETS	**31 December 20X1**	**31 December 20X0**
Non-current assets		
Dairy livestock – immature *	52,060	47,730
Dairy livestock – mature *	372,990	411,840
Subtotal – biological assets	425,050	459,570
Property, plant and equipment	1,462,650	1,409,800
Total non-current assets	**1,887,700**	**1,869,370**
Current assets		
Inventories	82,950	70,650
Trade and other receivables	88,000	65,000
Cash	10,000	10,000
Total current assets	**180,950**	**145,650**
Total assets	**2,068,650**	**2,015,020**

EQUITY AND LIABILITIES		
Equity		
Issued capital	1,000,000	1,000,000
Retained earnings	902,828	865,000
Total equity	**1,902,828**	**1,865,000**
Current liabilities		
Trade and other payables	165,822	150,020
Total current liabilities	**165,822**	**150,020**
Total equity and liabilities	**2,068,650**	**2,015,020**

* An entity is encouraged, but not required, to provide a quantified description of each group of biological assets, distinguishing between consumable and bearer biological assets or between mature and immature biological assets, as appropriate. An entity discloses the basis for making any such distinctions. (Bearer biological assets are those assets that self-regenerate, e.g. cows that bear calves).

5.1.1.A *Current versus non-current classification*

IAS 1 requires an asset to be classified as current when: *[IAS 1.66]*

(a) the entity expects to sell, consume or realise the asset in its normal operating cycle;

(b) the asset is primarily for trading purposes;

(c) the entity expects to realise the asset within 12 months after the reporting period; or

(d) the asset is cash or a cash equivalent (as defined in IAS 7 – *Statement of Cash Flows*, see Chapter 38), unless it is restricted from being exchanged or used to settle a liability for at least twelve months after the reporting period.

If these criteria are not met, the asset is classified as non-current.

The classification of agricultural produce is usually consistent with an entity's assessment for its inventories, i.e. typically classified as a current asset because it will be sold, consumed or realised as part of the normal operating cycle.

The classification of biological assets (including produce growing on a bearer plant) typically varies based on the nature of the biological asset and the time it takes to mature.

For consumable biological assets that only have one harvest, classification will depend on when the asset will be harvested and sold. For example, livestock held for slaughter would likely be realised within 12 months after the end of the reporting period or as part of the normal operating cycle, and therefore would be classified as a current asset. Trees in a forest usually take more than 20 years to mature. Therefore, forests are usually classified as non-current.

Bearer biological assets, such as dairy cows or animals used for breeding, are often classified as non-current. Such assets usually provide multiple harvests, which may extend beyond one accounting period. Therefore, in order to classify the asset appropriately, an entity would need to consider the period over which it will derive future economic benefits from the asset, which is likely to be when the biological asset will be sold, replaced or removed. This is essentially consistent with determining the useful life of an item of property, plant and equipment in accordance with IAS 16.

In situations where biological assets are classified as non-current, there is some debate about whether a portion should be classified as current. Some believe that, particularly for bearer biological assets, the asset should be classified as non-current, consistent with the classification of property, plant and equipment under IAS 16. In this situation, an entity would probably only classify the asset as current when it is held for sale in accordance with IFRS 5 (see Chapter 4). Others argue that, since the unit of account in IAS 41 is the individual asset (see 4.2.1 above), a portion of a group of biological assets could be classified as current. The current portion would be comprised of biological assets that will be removed permanently (e.g. sold, up-rooted or otherwise removed) within 12 months after the end of the reporting period. Determining such a split may be more obvious for consumable biological assets with only one harvest, for example, the trees in a forest an entity expects to harvest within 12 months of the end of the reporting period. For other biological assets, care is needed to ensure that it is the final removal of the biological asset itself that is considered and not its agricultural produce. An example of the final removal of such biological assets include dairy cows in a herd that an entity sells for slaughter. Regardless of which approach is used, an entity should be consistent from period to period across all similar types of biological assets. An entity should also assess whether its policy for classifying, or not classifying, a portion of its biological assets as current should be disclosed (see Chapter 3 for further discussion).

Produce growing on a bearer plant (e.g. grapes on a vine) is accounted for in accordance with IAS 41, separately from the bearer plant (which is within the scope of IAS 16, see 3.2.3 above). As a result, entities need to consider the appropriate classification of any produce growing on a bearer plant. Produce growing on a bearer plant will likely be a current asset, unless it takes more than a year to mature.

5.1.2 *Income statement*

IAS 1 is silent on the presentation of gains and losses on biological assets (including produce growing on a bearer plant) and agricultural produce in the income statement. IAS 41 requires that an entity disclose 'the aggregate gain or loss arising during the current period on initial recognition of biological assets and agricultural produce and from the change in fair value less costs to sell of biological assets'. *[IAS 41.40]*. The standard only requires disclosure of the aggregate gain or loss; it does not require or encourage disaggregating the gain or loss. *[IAS 41.B78-B79]*. Example 1 of the Illustrative Examples to IAS 41 illustrates gains on biological assets and agricultural produce presented near the top of the income statement, although it is not entirely clear from the example whether losses on biological assets should be presented in the same position or elsewhere in the income statement. *[IAS 41.IE1]*.

The extract below is from the combined and consolidated financial statements of Mondi Limited. The Mondi Limited group recognised changes in fair value less costs to sell in profit or loss, but did not separately disclose that amount on the face of the financial statements. Instead, as is illustrated below, the change in the fair value less costs to sell of biological assets was separately disclosed in the notes to the financial statements.

Extract 40.1: Mondi Limited (2015)

Notes to the combined and consolidated financial statements for the year ended 31 December 2015 [extract]

34 Accounting policies [extract]

Non-current non-financial assets excluding goodwill, deferred tax and net retirement benefits asset [extract]

Agriculture – Owned forestry assets (note 13)

Owned forestry assets are measured at fair value, calculated by applying the expected selling price, less costs to harvest and deliver, to the estimated volume of timber on hand at each reporting date. The estimated volume of timber on hand is determined based on the maturity profile of the area under afforestation, the species, the geographic location and other environmental considerations and excludes future growth. The product of these is then adjusted to present value by applying a market related pre tax discount rate.

Changes in fair value are recognised in the combined and consolidated income statement within other net operating expenses. At point of felling, the carrying value of forestry assets is transferred to inventory.

Directly attributable costs incurred during the year of biological growth and investments in standing timber are capitalised and presented within cash flows from investing activities.

13 Forestry assets

€ million	**2015**	2014
At 1 January	235	233
Capitalised expenditure	38	35
Acquisition of assets	3	2
Fair value gains	40	34
Disposal of assets	(1)	(13)
Felling costs	(51)	(54)
Reclassified to assets held for sale (see note 25)	–	(11)
Currency movements	(45)	9
At 31 December	**219**	235
Comprising		
Mature	139	148
Immature	80	87
Total forestry assets	**219**	235

The Group has approximately 154,000 hectares (2014: 164,000 hectares) of owned and leased land under afforestation, all of which is in South Africa.

Mature forestry assets are those plantations that are harvestable, while immature forestry assets have not yet reached that stage of growth. Timber is harvested according to a rotation plan, once trees reach maturity. This period ranges from 6.5 to 14.5 years for both years presented, depending on species, climate and location.

The fair value of forestry assets is a level 3 measure in terms of the fair value measurement hierarchy (see note 30b) and this category is consistent with prior years. The fair value of forestry assets is calculated on the basis of future expected net cash flows arising on the Group's owned forestry assets, discounted based on a pre tax yield on long-term bonds over the last five years.

The following assumptions have a significant impact on the valuation of the Group's forestry assets:

- The net selling price, which is defined as the selling price less the costs of transport, harvesting, extraction and loading. The net selling price is based on third-party transactions and is influenced by the species, maturity profile and location of timber. In 2015, the net selling price used ranged from the South African rand equivalent of €9 per tonne to €33 per tonne (2014: €10 per tonne to €35 per tonne) with a weighted average of €20 per tonne (2014: €22 per tonne).

Chapter 40

- The conversion factor used to convert hectares of land under afforestation to tonnes of standing timber, which is dependent on the species, the maturity profile of the timber, the geographic location, climate and a variety of other environmental factors. In 2015, the conversion factors ranged from 8.9 to 25.2 (2014: 8.8 to 25.2).
- The discount rate of 15.2% (2014: 10.6%) based on a pre tax yield from long-term South African government bonds matching the average age of the timber and adjusted for the risks associated with forestry assets.

The valuation of the Group's forestry assets is determined in rand and converted to euro at the closing exchange rate on 31 December of each year.

The reported value of owned forestry assets would change as follows should there be a change in these underlying assumptions:

€ million	**2015**
Effect of €1/tonne increase in net selling price	11
Effect of 1% increase in conversion factor (hectares to tonnes)	2
Effect of 1% increase in discount rate	(2)
Effect of 1% increase in EUR/ZAR exchange rate	(2)

IAS 41 is not clear about how gains should be presented in the income statement. IAS 1 prohibits offsetting of income and expenses in the income statement. *[IAS 1.32]*. Therefore, if the sale of biological assets or agricultural produce meets the definition of revenue under IAS 18 – *Revenue* (and IFRS 15 – *Revenue from Contracts with Customers*, when effective), i.e. it results in a gross inflow of economic benefits during the period arising from the ordinary activities of the entity, it should be presented on a gross basis in the income statement. However, if sales of non-current biological assets are incidental to the main revenue-generating activities of the entity they should be presented on a net basis. *[IAS 1.34]*. However, under IAS 41 the gross margin on agricultural produce sold shortly after harvest may be negligible, as the produce may have been previously carried at a valuation near to its sales price.

5.1.3 Groups of biological assets

The standard requires an entity to provide a narrative or quantitative description of each group of biological assets. *[IAS 41.41,42]*. An entity is encouraged to provide 'a quantified description of each group of biological assets, distinguishing between consumable and bearer biological assets or between mature and immature biological assets, as appropriate'. *[IAS 41.43]*. The standard suggests that an entity may separately disclose the carrying amounts of: *[IAS 41.43,44]*

- consumable biological assets (i.e. assets that are to be harvested as agricultural produce, sold as biological assets or produce growing on a bearer plant); and
- bearer biological assets (i.e. assets that are not consumable, but rather are self-regenerating).

The standard continues by suggesting that an entity 'may further divide those carrying amounts between mature and immature assets. These distinctions provide information that may be helpful in assessing the timing of future cash flows'. *[IAS 41.43]*. Mature biological assets are defined by the standard as those assets 'that have attained harvestable specifications (for consumable biological assets) or are able to sustain regular harvests (for bearer biological assets)'. *[IAS 41.45]*. If an entity makes such distinctions, it should disclose the basis for making those distinctions. *[IAS 41.43]*.

5.1.4 Other disclosures

If not disclosed elsewhere in information published with the financial statements, an entity is required to describe:

'(a) the nature of its activities involving each group of biological assets; and

(b) non-financial measures or estimates of the physical quantities of:

  (i) each group of the entity's biological assets at the end of the period; and

  (ii) output of agricultural produce during the period'. *[IAS 41.46]*.

In addition, an entity shall disclose the following information:

(a) the existence and carrying amounts of biological assets whose title is restricted, and the carrying amounts of biological assets pledged as security for liabilities; *[IAS 41.49]*

(b) the amount of commitments for the development or acquisition of biological assets; *[IAS 41.49]*

(c) financial risk management strategies related to agricultural activity; *[IAS 41.49]*

(d) a reconciliation of changes in the carrying amount of biological assets between the beginning and the end of the current period, which includes: *[IAS 41.50]*

  (i) the gain or loss arising from changes in fair value less costs to sell;

  (ii) increases due to purchases;

  (iii) decreases attributable to sales and biological assets classified as held for sale (or included in a disposal group that is classified as held for sale) in accordance with IFRS 5;

  (iv) decreases due to harvest;

  (v) increases resulting from business combinations;

  (vi) net exchange differences arising on the translation of financial statements into a different presentation currency, and on the translation of a foreign operation into the presentation currency of the reporting entity; and

  (vii) other changes.

Fair value measurement disclosures are discussed at 5.2 below.

The standard also encourages, but does not require, an entity 'to disclose, by group or otherwise, the amount of change in fair value less costs to sell included in profit or loss due to physical changes and due to price changes', because this information is 'useful in appraising current period performance and future prospects, particularly when there is a production cycle of more than one year'. *[IAS 41.51, B74-B77]*. IAS 41 notes that physical change itself can be broken down further into growth, degeneration, production and procreation, but the standard does not specifically encourage disclosure of this information. *[IAS 41.52]*. The following example, which is derived from the standard, explains how an entity should go about separating the effect of physical changes from those of price changes. *[IAS 41.IE2]*.

Example 40.4: Physical change and price change

A herd of ten 2-year-old animals was held at 1 January 2017. One animal aged 2½ years was purchased on 1 July 2017 for CU108, and one animal was born on 1 July 2017. No animals were sold or disposed of during the period. Per-unit fair values less costs to sell were as follows:

	1/1/2017	*1/7/2017*	*31/12/2017*
Newborn animal	–	CU70	CU72
½ year old animal	–	–	CU80
2 year old animal	CU100	–	CU105
2½ year old animal	–	CU108	CU111
3 year old animal	–	–	CU120

Fair value less costs to sell of herd at 1 January 2017:			
	(10 × CU100) =		CU1,000
Purchase on 1 July 2017:			
	(1 × CU108) =		CU108
Increase in fair value less costs to sell due to price change:			
	10 × (CU105 – CU100) =	CU50	
	1 × (CU111 – CU108) =	CU3	
	1 × (CU72 – CU70) =	CU2	
			CU55
Increase in fair value less costs to sell due to physical change:			
	10 × (CU120 – CU105) =	CU150	
	1 × (CU120 – CU111) =	CU9	
	1 × (CU80 – CU72) =	CU8	
	1 × CU70 =	CU70	
			CU237
Fair value less costs to sell of herd at 31 December 2017:			
	11 × CU120 =	CU1,320	
	1 × CU80 =	CU80	
			CU1,400

In January 2012, the Interpretations Committee considered a request for clarification in relation to paragraph 51 of IAS 41. The submitter was concerned that this paragraph may be contributing to an unacceptable application of the market approach to valuing biological assets. To remedy this, the submitter suggested that the disclosure be amended as part of annual improvements so that it would only be encouraged when the entity's biological assets are at the same level of biological transformation as those quoted in an active market. However, the Committee did not believe an amendment was needed, noting that paragraph 51 of IAS 41 addresses disclosures, not measurement. The Committee also pointed out that the requirements for measuring fair value are set out in IFRS 13, which is not affected by paragraph 51 of IAS 41.[6]

In addition to the above required and encouraged disclosures, the standard notes that agricultural activity is 'often exposed to climatic, disease and other natural risks. If an event occurs that gives rise to a material item of income or expense, the nature and amount of that item are disclosed in accordance with IAS 1' (see Chapter 3). For example, an entity may need to disclose events such as 'an outbreak of a virulent disease, a flood, a severe drought or frost, and a plague of insects'. *[IAS 41.53]*.

Many of the uncertainties and judgements inherent in the valuations that have to be made under IAS 41 are very clearly explained in the financial statements of Sappi Limited, as shown in the following extract.

Extract 40.2: Sappi Limited (2015)

notes to the group annual financial statements
for the year ended September 2015 [extract]

2 Accounting Policies [extract]

2.3 Critical accounting policies and key sources of estimation uncertainty [extract]

2.3.5 Plantations

Plantations are stated at fair value less estimated cost to sell at the harvesting stage and is a Level 3 measure in terms of the fair value measurement hierarchy as established by IFRS 13 Fair Value Measurement. The group uses the income approach in determining fair value as it believes that this method yields the most appropriate valuation.

In arriving at plantation fair values, the key assumptions are estimated prices less cost of delivery, discount rates, and volume and growth estimations. All changes in fair value are recognised in the period in which they arise.

The impact of changes in estimated prices, discount rates and, volume and growth assumptions may have on the calculated fair value and other key financial information on plantations is disclosed in note 11.

- **Estimated prices less cost of delivery**

The group uses a 12 quarter rolling historical average price to estimate the fair value of all immature timber and mature timber that is to be felled in more than 12 months from the reporting date. Twelve quarters is considered a reasonable period of time after taking the length of the growth cycle of the plantations into account. Expected future price trends and recent market transactions involving comparable plantations are also considered in estimating fair value.

Mature timber that is expected to be felled within 12 months from the end of the reporting period are valued using unadjusted current market prices. Such timber is expected to be used in the short term and consequently, current market prices are considered an appropriate reflection of fair value.

The fair value is derived by using the prices as explained above and reduced by the estimated cost of delivery. Cost of delivery includes all costs associated with getting the harvested agricultural produce to the market, including harvesting, loading, transport and allocated fixed overheads.

- **Discount rate**

The discount rate used is the applicable pre-tax weighted average cost of capital of the business unit.

- **Volume and growth estimations and cost assumptions**

The group focuses on good husbandry techniques which include ensuring that the rotation of plantations is met with adequate planting activities for future harvesting. The age threshold used for quantifying immature timber is dependent on the rotation period of the specific timber genus which varies between 8 and 18 years. In the Southern African region, softwood less than eight years and hardwood less than five years are classified as immature timber.

Trees are generally felled at the optimum age when ready for intended use. At the time the tree is felled, it is taken out of plantations and accounted for under inventory and reported as a depletion cost (fellings).

Depletion costs include the fair value of timber felled which is determined on the average method, plus amounts written off against standing timber to cover loss or damage caused by fire, disease and stunted growth. These costs are accounted for on a cost per metric ton allocation method multiplied by unadjusted current market prices. Tons are calculated using the projected growth to rotation age and are extrapolated to current age on a straight-line basis.

The group has projected growth estimation over a period of 8 to 18 years per rotation. In deriving this estimate, the group established a long-term sample plot network which is representative of the species and sites on which trees are grown and the measured data from these permanent sample plots were used as input into the group's growth estimation. Periodic adjustments are made to existing models for new genetic material.

The group directly manages plantations established on land that is either owned or leased from third parties. Indirectly managed plantations represent plantations established on land held by independent commercial farmers where Sappi provides technical advice on the growing and tendering of trees.

The associated costs for managing plantations are recognised as silviculture costs in cost of sales (see note 4).

11 Plantations [extract]

Sappi manages the establishment, maintenance and harvesting of its plantations on a compartmentalised basis. These plantations are comprised of pulpwood and sawlogs and are managed to ensure that the optimum fibre balance is supplied to its paper and pulping operations in Southern Africa.

The group manages its plantations on a rotational basis. As such, increases by means of growth are negated by fellings, for the group's own use or for external sales, over the rotation period.

The group manages plantations on land that the group owns, as well as on land that the group leases. The group discloses both of these as directly managed plantations. With regard to indirectly managed plantations, the group has several different types of agreements with many independent farmers. The terms of the agreements depend on the type and specific needs of the farmer as well as the areas planted and range in duration from one to more than 20 years. In certain circumstances, the group provides loans to farmers that are disclosed as other non-current assets on the group balance sheet (these loans are considered, individually and in aggregate, immaterial to the group).

If the group provides seedlings, silviculture and/or technical assistance, the costs are expensed when incurred by the group.

The group is exposed to financial risks arising from climatic changes, disease and other natural risks such as fire, flooding and storms as well as human-induced losses arising from strikes, civil commotion and malicious damage. These risks are covered by an appropriate level of insurance as determined by management. The plantations have an integrated management system that complies with FSC™ standards.

Plantations are stated at fair value less estimated cost to sell at the harvesting stage and is a Level 3 measure in terms of the fair value measurement hierarchy as established by IFRS 13 *Fair Value Measurement* which is consistent with the prior year.

The fair value of plantations has been calculated using a real pre-tax discount rate of 9.32%. The group currently values approximately 30 million tons of timber using selling prices and delivery costs that are benchmarked against industry norms. The average annual growth is measured at approximately 18 tons of timber per hectare while immature timber comprise approximately 100,000 hectares of plantations. As changes to estimated prices, the discount rate, costs to sell, and volume and growth assumptions applied in the valuation of immature timber may impact the calculated fair value, the group has calculated the sensitivity of a change in each of these assumptions as tabled below:

US$ million	**2015**	2014	2013
Market price changes			
1% increase in market prices	**2**	2	2
1% decrease in market prices	**(2)**	(2)	(2)
Discount rate (for immature timber)			
1% increase in rate	**(2)**	(2)	(3)
1% decrease in rate	**2**	2	3
Volume assumption			
1% increase in estimate of volume	**4**	4	5
1% decrease in estimate of volume	**(4)**	(4)	(5)
Costs to sell			
1% increase in costs to sell	**(1)**	(2)	(2)
1% decrease in costs to sell	**1**	2	2
Growth assumptions			
1% increase in rate of growth	**1**	1	2
1% decrease in rate of growth	**(1)**	(1)	(2)

5.2 Fair value measurement disclosures

IFRS 13 specifies the disclosures that are required for fair value measurements of biological assets and agricultural produce. Prior to the introduction of IFRS 13, IAS 41 required an entity to disclose:

(a) the methods and significant assumptions applied in determining the fair value of each group of agricultural produce at the point of harvest and each group of biological assets; *[IAS 41(2012).47]* and

(b) the fair value less costs to sell of agricultural produce harvested during the period, determined at the point of harvest. *[IAS 41(2012).48]*.

While these requirements have now been removed from IAS 41, they are subsumed within the disclosure requirements in IFRS 13. That standard requires substantially more information to be disclosed about fair value measurements, for example:

- the classification of a fair value measurement within the fair value hierarchy, i.e. Level 1, 2 or 3, and, for recurring fair value measurements, any transfers between levels in the hierarchy;
- a detailed reconciliation of movements for fair value measurements classified within Level 3 of the hierarchy, along with narrative sensitivity analysis; and
- the highest and best use of a non-financial asset if it differs from its current use, including why the non-financial asset is being used in a manner that differs from its highest and best use. *[IFRS 13.93]*.

The following extract illustrates fair value disclosures for biological assets, as do the extracts at 5.1.2 and 5.1.4 above.

Chapter 14 at 20 discusses IFRS 13's disclosure requirements in more detail.

Extract 40.3: Marine Harvest ASA (2014)

MARINE HARVEST GROUP / FINANCIAL STATEMENTS AND NOTES [extract]

NOTE 6 / BIOLOGICAL ASSETS [extract]

VALUATION OF BIOLOGICAL ASSETS

Biological assets are, in accordance with IAS 41, measured at fair value, unless the fair value cannot be measured reliably. Broodstock, smolt and live fish below 1 kilogram are measured at cost less impairment losses, as the fair value cannot be measured reliably.

Biomass beyond this is measured at fair value in accordance with IFRS 13, and the measurement is categorized into Level 3 in the fair value hierarchy, as the input is primarily unobservable. Live fish over 4 kilograms are measured to full net value, while a proportionate expected net profit at harvest is incorporated for live fish between 1 and 4 kilograms. The valuation is completed for each business unit based on a model and basis for assumptions supplied by corporate. All assumptions are subject to quality assurance and analysis on a monthly basis from a corporate level.

The valuation is based on an income approach and takes into consideration unobservable input based on biomass in sea for each seawater site, estimated growth rate on site level, mortality in the business unit, quality of the fish going forward, costs and market price. Special assessment is performed for sites with high/low performance due to disease or other special factors. The market prices are set for each business unit, and are derived from observable market prices (when available), achieved prices and development in contract prices.

ASSUMPTIONS USED FOR DETERMINING FAIR VALUE OF LIVE FISH

The estimated fair value of biomass will always be based on uncertain assumptions, even though the company has built substantial expertise in assessing these factors. Estimates are applied to the following factors: biomass volume, the quality of the biomass, the size distribution and market prices.

Biomass volume: The biomass volume is in itself an estimate based on the number of smolt put to sea, the estimated growth from the time of stocking, estimated mortality based on observed mortality in the period etc. The uncertainty with regards to biomass volume is normally low.

The uncertainty will, however, be higher if an incident has resulted in mass mortality, especially early in the cycle, or if the health status restricts handling the fish. If the total biomass at sea was 1% higher than our estimates, this would result in an increase in the valuation of NOK 59.9 million.

The quality of the biomass: The quality of the biomass can be difficult to assess prior to harvesting, if the reason for downgrading is related to muscle quality (e.g. the effect of Kudoa in Canada). In Norway downgraded fish is normally priced based on standard rates of deduction compared to a Superior quality fish. For fish classified as ordinary grade the standard rate of reduction is NOK 1.50 - NOK 2.00 per kilogram gutted weight. For fish classified as production grade the standard rate of reduction is NOK 5.00 to NOK 15.00 per kilogram gutted weight depending on the reason for downgrading. In other countries the price deductions related to quality are not as standardized. The quality of harvested fish has been good in 2014. A 1% change from Production grade to Superior quality would result in a change of NOK 21.3 million in the valuation.

The size distribution: Fish in sea grows at different rates and even in a situation with good estimates for the average weight of the fish there can be considerable spread in the quality and weight of the fish. The size distribution affects the price achieved for the fish as each size category of fish is priced separately in the market. When estimating the biomass value a normal size distribution is applied.

Market price: The market price assumption is very important for the valuation and even minor changes in the market price will give significant changes in the valuation. The methodology used for establishing the market price is explained in note 2. A NOK 1.00 increase in the market price would result in an increase in the valuation of NOK 188.2 million.

Valuation of biological assets is affected by the market prices of fish. The market price risk is reduced through fixed price/volume customer contracts and financial contracts as well as our downstream integration as explained in note 13.

RECONCILIATION OF CHANGES IN CARRYING AMOUNT OF BIOLOGICAL ASSETS (NOK million) [extract]	**2014**	**2013**
Carrying amount as of 01.01	9 536.6	6 207.9
Cost to stock	10 277.8	8 540.8
Fair value adjustment on biological assets	5 007.7	6 118.3
Fair value uplift on harvested fish	–5 518.5	–4 323.7
Mortality for fish in sea	–310.9	–158.4
Cost of harvested fish	–9 635.7	–7 419.4
Assets acquired – continued operations	168.4	338.9
Currency translation differences	488.6	232.2
Total carrying amount of biological assets as of 31.12	**10 014.0**	**9 536.6**

PRICE SENSITIVITIES EFFECT ON FAIR VALUE (SALMON ONLY) AT YEAR-END (NOK million)	Price +1 NOK	Biomass +1% LWT	Quality +1% SUP
Marine Harvest Norway	117.9	43.1	7.3
Marine Harvest Chile	33.3	2.6	3.9
Marine Harvest Canada	19.6	9.5	4.1
Marine Harvest Scotland	13.5	3.0	4.5
Marine Harvest Faroe Islands	0.1	0.1	–
Marine Harvest Ireland	3.8	1.6	1.5
Total price sensitivities effect on fair value	**188.2**	**59.9**	**21.3**

5.3 Additional disclosures if fair value cannot be measured reliably

If an entity rebuts the presumption that fair value can be reliably measured on initial recognition of a biological asset (including produce growing on a bearer plant) and measures the asset at its cost less any accumulated depreciation and any accumulated impairment losses it is required to disclose the following information:

(a) if the entity holds such assets at the end of the period: *[IAS 41.54]*
   - (i) a description of the biological assets;
   - (ii) an explanation of why fair value cannot be measured reliably;
   - (iii) if possible, the range of estimates within which fair value is highly likely to lie;
   - (iv) the depreciation method used;
   - (v) the useful lives or the depreciation rates used; and
   - (vi) the gross carrying amount and the accumulated depreciation (aggregated with accumulated impairment losses) at the beginning and end of the period;

(b) if the entity held such assets at any point during the current period: *[IAS 41.55]*
   - (i) any gain or loss recognised on disposal of such biological assets;
   - (ii) the reconciliation required by paragraph 50 of IAS 41 (see 5.1.4 above) shall disclose amounts related to such biological assets separately;
   - (iii) that reconciliation shall include the following amounts included in profit or loss related to those biological assets:
     - impairment losses;
     - reversals of impairment losses; and
     - depreciation;

(c) if the entity held such assets and their fair value became reliably measurable during the current period: *[IAS 41.56]*
   - (i) a description of the biological assets;
   - (ii) an explanation of why fair value has become reliably measurable; and
   - (iii) the effect of the change.

5.4 Government grants

An entity that has received government grants related to agricultural activity covered by IAS 41 is required to disclose the following information:

'(a) the nature and extent of government grants recognised in the financial statements;

(b) unfulfilled conditions and other contingencies attaching to government grants; and

(c) significant decreases expected in the level of government grants.' *[IAS 41.57]*.

6 TRANSITION AND EFFECTIVE DATE

6.1 Transition and effective date for the bearer plants amendments

In June 2014, the IASB issued the bearer plants amendments, which changed the accounting requirements for biological assets that meet the definition of bearer plants (e.g. fruit trees). The amendments were effective for annual periods beginning on or after 1 January 2016, with early adoption permitted. If an entity early adopted the amendments, it was required to disclose that fact. *[IAS 41.62]*.

Entities were permitted to apply the amendments on a fully retrospective basis or elect to measure a bearer plant at its fair value at the beginning of the earliest period presented in the first financial statements in which the amendments were first applied. If the latter option was selected, the fair value would be used as its deemed cost at that date. Any difference between the previous carrying amount and fair value would be recognised in retained earnings. *[IAS 16.81M]*.

In the reporting period in which the bearer plants amendments were first applied, an entity was generally required to disclose certain information in accordance with IAS 8 – *Accounting Policies, Changes in Accounting Estimates and Errors*. *[IAS 41.62]*. For the bearer plants amendments, the IASB provided relief. For example, the quantitative information required by paragraph 28(f) of IAS 8 (i.e. the amount of the adjustment arising from adopting the amendments for each financial statement line item affected and the impact of basic and diluted earnings per share if IAS 33 – *Earnings per Share* – applies to the entity) need not be disclosed for the current period. *[IAS 8.28(f)]*. However, entities were required to disclose this information for each prior period presented. *[IAS 41.63]*.

References

1 See paragraph 3(b) of IFRS 16.

2 Agenda Paper 13, *Valuation of biological assets using a residual method*, IFRS Interpretations Committee Meeting, May 2012.

3 *IFRIC Update*, March 2013.

4 *IASB Update*, May 2013.

5 *IASB Update*, May 2013.

6 *IFRIC Update*, January 2012.

Chapter 41 Extractive industries

List of examples

Chapter 41 Extractive industries

1 INTRODUCTION AND BACKGROUND

1.1 Defining extractive industries

'Extractive industries' were defined in the IASC's Issues Paper – *Extractive Industries* (IASC issues paper) published in November 2000 as 'those industries involved in finding and removing wasting natural resources located in or near the earth's crust'.[1] However, this chapter adopts a slightly narrower focus and concentrates on the accounting issues that affect mining companies and oil and gas companies. The IASC issues paper was prepared by the IASC as part of its original project on 'extractive industries' which was led by an IASC Steering Committee on Extractive Industries. This paper considered a broad range of issues including reserves and resources estimation, historical and valuation based concepts of measurement of resources related assets, treatment of removal and restoration costs, impairment, revenue, inventories and arrangements to share risks and costs. While it was non-authoritative this paper is referred to throughout this chapter where relevant as it provided a broad range of information on the common practices observed in the extractive industries and the common terms used.

IFRSs currently use the term 'minerals' and 'mineral assets' when referring to the extractive industries as a whole. This is used as a collective term to include both mining and oil and gas reserves and resources. In contrast, a distinction between the two industries was introduced in the Extractive Activities DP (discussed below at 1.3), where the term 'minerals' has been used to refer to the mining sector and the term 'oil and gas' has been used to refer to the oil and gas sector.

For the purposes of this chapter, consistency with the current wording in IFRSs will be maintained and therefore, unless stated otherwise, 'minerals' and 'mineral assets' will encompass both mining and oil and gas.

Historically the IASB and its predecessor, the IASC, have avoided dealing with specific accounting issues in the extractive industries by excluding minerals and mineral products/reserves from the scope of their accounting standards. Currently, minerals and mineral products/reserves are excluded at least in part from the scope of the following standards:

- IAS 2 – *Inventories*; [IAS 2.3(a), 4]
- IAS 16 – *Property, Plant and Equipment*; [IAS 16.3(d)]
- IAS 17 – *Leases*; [IAS 17.2(a)]
- IFRS 16 – *Leases*; [IFRS 16.3(a)]
- IAS 18 – *Revenue*; [IAS 18.6(h)]. Note: Minerals and mineral products/reserves are not scoped out of IFRS 15 – *Revenue from Contracts with Customers* – see 12.7 below for more details on IFRS 15;
- IAS 38 – *Intangible Assets*; [IAS 38.2(c)]
- IAS 40 – *Investment Property*; [IAS 40.4(b)] and
- IFRIC 4 – *Determining whether an Arrangement contains a Lease*. [IFRIC 4.4].

While these standards exclude 'minerals' from their scope, the exact wording of the scope exclusions differs between standards – see 3.1.1 below for more information. In addition, although minerals and mineral products/reserves themselves are excluded from the scope of many standards, assets used for the exploration, development and extraction of minerals are covered by existing IFRSs.

Many of the financial reporting issues that affect entities that operate in the extractive industries are a result of the environment in which they operate. Specific accounting issues arise because of the uncertainties involved in mineral exploration and extraction, the wide range of risk sharing arrangements, and government involvement in the form of mandatory participations and special tax regimes. At the same time, however, some of the business arrangements that are aimed at mitigating certain risks give rise to financial reporting complications. The financial reports of these entities need to reflect the risks and rewards to which they are exposed. In many cases, there are legitimate differences of opinion about how an entity should account for these matters.

The IASC's Issues Paper identified the following characteristics of activities in the extractive industries, which are closely related to the financial reporting issues that are discussed in this chapter:

- *High risks* – In the extractive industries there is a high risk that the amounts spent in finding new mineral resources will not result in additional commercially recoverable reserves. In financial reporting terms this means that it can remain uncertain for a long period whether or not certain expenditures give rise to an asset. Further risks exist in relation to production (i.e. quantities actually produced may differ considerably from those previously estimated) and price (i.e. commodity prices are often volatile).
- *Little relationship between risks and rewards* – In the extractive industries a small expenditure may result in finding mineral deposits with a value of many times the amount of the expenditure. Conversely, large expenditures can frequently result in little or no future production. This has given rise to different approaches in financial reporting that can be broadly categorised as follows: (1) expense all expenditures as the future benefits are too uncertain, (2) capitalise some or all expenditures as the cumulative expenditures may be matched to the cumulative benefits, or (3) recognise the minerals asset found at fair value.

- *Long lag between expenditure and production* – Exploration and/or development may take years to complete. During this period it is often far from certain that economic benefits will be derived from the costs incurred.
- *High costs of individual projects* – The costs of individual projects can be very high (e.g. offshore oil and gas projects and deep mining projects). Exploration expenditures that are carried forward pending the outcome of mineral acquisition and development projects may be highly significant in relation to the equity and the total assets of an entity.
- *Unique cost-sharing arrangements* – High costs and high risks, as discussed above, often lead entities in the extractive industries to enter into risk-sharing arrangements (e.g. joint arrangements, farm-out arrangements, carried interest arrangements, oilfield services arrangements and contract mining). These types of arrangements, which are much more common in the extractive industries than elsewhere, often give rise to their own financial reporting issues.
- *Intense government oversight and regulation* – The regulation of the extractive industries ranges from 'outright governmental ownership of some (especially petroleum) or all minerals to unusual tax benefits or penalties, price controls, restrictions on imports and exports, restrictions on production and distribution, environmental and health and safety regulations, and others'. Governments may also seek to charge an economic rent for resources extracted. These types of government involvement give rise to financial reporting issues, particularly when the precise nature of the government involvement is not obvious.
- *Scarce non-replaceable assets* – Mineral reserves are unique and scarce resources that an entity may not be able to replace in any location or in any form.
- *Economic, technological and political factors* – While these factors are not unique to the extractive industries, the IASC's Issues Paper argues that they tend to have a greater impact on the extractive industries because:
  '(a) fluctuating market prices for minerals (together with floating exchange rates) have a direct impact on the economic viability of reserves and mineral properties. A relatively small percentage change in long-term prices can change decisions on whether or when to explore for, develop, or produce minerals;
  (b) there is a sharp impact from cost changes and technological developments. Changes in costs and, probably more significantly, changes in technology can significantly change the economic viability of particular mineral projects; and
  (c) in almost every country, mineral rights are owned by the state. In those countries where some mineral rights are privately owned, public reliance on adequate sources of minerals for economic and defence purposes often leads to governmental regulations and control. At other times, governmental policies may be changed to levy special taxes or impose governmental controls on the extractive industries.'

While it may be the case that the above factors affect the extractive industries more than others, to the extent that they also arise in the pharmaceutical, bio-technology, agricultural and software industries some of these risks give rise to further financial reporting issues. However, those industries are not affected by the combination of these circumstances to the same extent as is the case with the extractive industries. It is a combination of these factors, a lack of specific guidance in IFRSs and a long history of industry practice and guidance from previous GAAPs that have given rise to a range of accounting practices in the extractive industries.

There is as yet no IFRS that addresses all of the specific issues of the extractive industries although attempts to devise such a standard commenced quite some time ago. Furthermore, these draft proposals to date would not have addressed many of these specific issues that affect the extractive industries.

1.1.1 Definition of key terms

The most important terms and abbreviations used are defined in this chapter when discussed or in the glossary at 21 below. However, alternative or more detailed definitions of financial reporting terms, and of mining and oil and gas technical terms and abbreviations, can be found in the following publications:

- *Issues Paper Extractive Industries*, IASC, November 2000;
- *Petroleum Resources Management System*, Society of Petroleum Engineers, 2007;
- *The Australasian Code for Reporting of Exploration Results, Mineral Resources and Ore Reserves* (the JORC Code), Australasian Joint Ore Reserves Committee (the JORC Committee); and
- The former UK Oil Industry Accounting Committee Statement of Recommended Practice (OIAC SORP) (see 1.4 below).

1.2 The development of IFRS 6 – *Exploration for and Evaluation of Mineral Resources*

In December 2004, the IASB issued IFRS 6 – *Exploration for and Evaluation of Mineral Resources* – which addresses the accounting for one particular aspect of the extractive industries – being exploration and evaluation ('E&E') activities. IFRS 6 was issued as a form of interim guidance to clarify the application of IFRSs and the IASB's *Conceptual Framework* to E&E activities and to provide temporary relief from existing IFRSs in some areas. The IASB decided to develop IFRS 6 because mineral rights and mineral resources are outside the scope of IAS 16 and IAS 38, E&E expenditures are significant to entities engaged in extractive activities, and there were different views on how these expenditures should be accounted for under IFRSs. Other standard-setting bodies have had diverse accounting practices for E&E assets which often differed from practices in other sectors with analogous expenditures. *[IFRS 6.IN1]*.

One of the IASB's goals in developing IFRS 6 was to avoid unnecessary disruption for both users and preparers. The Board therefore proposed to limit the need for entities to change their existing accounting policies for E&E assets. As a result, IFRS 6 defines what E&E expenditures are, makes limited improvements to existing accounting practices for E&E expenditures, such as specifying when entities need to assess E&E assets for impairment in accordance with IAS 36 – *Impairment of Assets,* and requires certain disclosures.

E&E expenditures are 'expenditures incurred by an entity in connection with the exploration for and evaluation of mineral resources before the technical feasibility and commercial viability of extracting a mineral resource are demonstrable'. E&E assets are 'exploration and evaluation expenditures recognised as assets in accordance with the entity's accounting policy'. *[IFRS 6 Appendix A]*.

The IFRS Interpretations Committee ('the Interpretations Committee') has noted that the effect of the limited scope of IFRS 6 is to grant relief only to policies in respect of E&E activities, and that this relief did not extend to activities before or after the E&E phase. The Interpretations Committee confirmed that the scope of IFRS 6 limited the relief from the hierarchy to policies applied to E&E activities only and that there is no basis for interpreting IFRS 6 as granting any additional relief in areas outside its scope.

The detailed requirements of IFRS 6 are discussed at 3 below.

1.3 April 2010 Discussion Paper: Extractive Activities

In April 2010, as part of the long running project of trying to progress the issue of extractive industries accounting, the IASB published the staff Discussion Paper – *Extractive Activities* (the DP). The DP was developed by a research team comprising members of the Australian, Canadian, Norwegian and South African accounting standard-setters.[2] Although the IASB has discussed the project team's findings, the DP only reflects the views of the project team. The Board did not express any preliminary views or make any tentative decisions on the DP and, due to other standard-setting priorities, has put the project on hold (see 1.3.6 below for a status update).

The DP addressed some of the financial reporting issues associated with exploring for and finding minerals, oil and natural gas deposits, developing those deposits and extracting the minerals, oil and natural gas. These were collectively referred to as 'extractive activities' or, alternatively, as 'upstream activities'.[3] The aim of the project was to create a single accounting and disclosure model that would only apply to upstream extractive activities in both the minerals and oil and gas industries. This represented a change from IFRS 6, which currently includes exploration and evaluation activities relating to minerals, oil, natural gas and similar non-regenerative resources within its scope. The project team decided against a broader scope in the DP as this would result in the need to develop additional definitions, accounting models and disclosures.[4]

The DP concluded that there were similarities in the main business activities, and the geological and other risks and uncertainties of both the minerals and oil and gas industries.[5] There were also similarities in the definitions of reserves and resources used by the Committee for Mineral Reserves International Reporting Standards (CRIRSCO) and the Society of Petroleum Engineers Oil and Gas Reserves Committee (SPE OGRC).[6] The DP therefore proposed that there should be a single accounting and disclosure model that applies to all extractive activities (as defined, see 1.1 above).

While it has been generally acknowledged that the issues addressed in the DP are important, a significant number of respondents to the DP commented that the scope of the DP did not address many of the more complex accounting issues where practice is diverse and greater consistency is required.

These issues included:

- the lack of guidance on complex areas such as farm-out and farm-in transactions (see 6.2); and
- accounting for production sharing and royalty agreements (see 5.3 and 5.7).

The main proposals in the DP have been summarised briefly below.

1.3.1 Definitions of reserves and resources

The DP explored a number of alternatives for defining reserves and resources. The definition used is 'reserves and resources are either the most significant assets or amongst the most significant assets for most entities engaged in extractive activities. Assessing the financial position and performance of an entity engaged in extractive activities in order to make economic decisions therefore requires an understanding of the entity's minerals or oil and gas reserves and resources, which are the source of future cash flows'.[7]

This chapter considers the definitions of reserves and resources that should be used in financial reporting. See 2 below for further discussion.

1.3.2 Asset recognition

The DP proposed that legal rights (i.e. exploration rights and extraction rights) should form the basis of a minerals asset or oil and gas asset. An asset should be recognised when the legal rights are acquired. Associated with these legal rights is information about the (possible) existence of minerals or oil and gas, the extent and characteristics of the deposit, and the economics of their extraction. The project team believed that rights and information associated with minerals or oil and gas properties satisfy the asset recognition criteria. While such information does not represent a separate asset, the project team proposed that information obtained from subsequent exploration and evaluation activities and development works would be treated as enhancements of the asset represented by the legal rights.

When considering the appropriate unit of account (see 4 below), the DP proposed that the geographical boundary of the unit of account would be defined initially on the basis of the exploration rights held. As exploration, evaluation and development activities took place, the unit of account would contract progressively until it became no greater than a single area, or group of contiguous areas, for which the legal rights were held and which are managed separately and would be expected to generate largely independent cash flows.

1.3.3 Asset measurement

The DP considered both current value (e.g. fair value) and historical cost as potential measurement bases for minerals and oil and gas assets. Based on their findings, and taking the views of users and preparers into account, the project team concluded that minerals and oil and gas assets should be measured at historical cost and that detailed disclosures should be provided to enhance the relevance of the financial statements.

The project team acknowledged that its choice of historical cost as the measurement basis was based to a large extent on doing the 'least harm'.

In relation to impairment, it was considered that the IAS 36 impairment testing model was not feasible for exploration properties. Therefore, the DP concluded that exploration properties should only be tested for impairment whenever, in management's judgement, there is evidence that suggests that there is a high likelihood that the carrying amount of an exploration asset will not be recovered in full. This would require management to apply a separate set of indicators to such properties in order to assess whether their continued recognition as assets would be justified. In addition, further disclosures would be required in respect of the impairment of exploration properties due to the fact that management may take different views on the exploration properties. These would include separate presentation of exploration properties, the factors that led to an impairment being recognised, and management's view as to why the remaining value of the asset or the other exploration assets is not impaired. This impairment assessment would need to be conducted separately for each exploration property.

1.3.4 Disclosure

The DP proposed extensive disclosures aimed at ensuring users of financial reports could evaluate:

- the value attributable to an entity's minerals or oil and gas assets;
- the contribution of those assets to current period financial performance; and
- the nature and extent of risks and uncertainties associated with those assets.

The DP proposed detailed disclosures about the quantities of reserves and resources, and production revenues and costs. If the assets are measured at historical cost then detailed information should be disclosed about their current value and how it was determined. If, instead, the assets are measured at fair value then detailed information should be disclosed about that fair value and how it was determined.

It is noted that a number of the proposed disclosures differ from US GAAP. These include disclosures of:

- key reserve estimate assumptions and sensitivity analysis (not required by US GAAP); and
- proved and probable reserves (US GAAP only requires proved reserves, with an option to disclose probable reserves).

1.3.5 Publish What You Pay proposals

A coalition of non-governmental organisations has promoted, and continues to promote, a campaign called Publish What You Pay (PWYP), proposing that entities undertaking extractive activities should be required to disclose, in their financial reports, the payments they make to each host government. Furthermore, PWYP recommended that its disclosure proposals should be incorporated into an eventual IFRS for extractive activities. Given this, a section in the DP was dedicated to the PWYP proposals. The DP acknowledged that the disclosure of payments made to governments provides information that would be of use to capital providers in making their investment and lending decisions, but noted that providing this information might be difficult and costly for some entities.

These proposals were partially in response to a perception that in certain countries some mining companies and oil and gas companies are not paying their 'fair share' in exchange for extracting scarce natural resources. In addition, there has been and continues to be increasing political pressure to expand the disclosure of payments to governments by entities within extractive industries as a means of reducing corruption by shining a light on these payments. As well as the proposals made in the DP, there are also increasing calls for transparency in the reporting of taxes and other payments to governments. This has led to a variety of transparency or publish what you pay types of initiatives being introduced in different jurisdictions around the world (e.g. US, Europe, UK, Canada, Australia, to name just a few), however these are outside the scope of IFRS and are governed by specific legislation.

1.3.6 Status of Extractive Activities project

As part of the IASB's 2011 agenda consultation process, the Extractive Activities project was included in the list of projects to be considered for inclusion on the IASB's active agenda for the following three years. After the outreach was completed, the IASB decided that this project would not be added to their active agenda. Instead, it became one of the four longer-term research projects, was combined with intangible assets and research and development activities, and was assigned as low. Since this date, it has remained inactive and the IASB has not received strong demand to recommence any active research on this project. Given this, it is unlikely that there will be any significant developments on this project in the near term.

1.4 Status of the Statement of Recommended Practice, UK Oil Industry Accounting Committee, June 2001 (OIAC SORP)

The Oil Industry Accounting Committee (OIAC), based in the United Kingdom, had previously developed a Statement of Recommended Practice (SORP) titled *Accounting for Oil and Gas Exploration, Development, Production and Decommissioning Activities*, which was updated and adopted by the UK Accounting Standards Board (ASB) in 2001.

The main function of the OIAC SORP had been to set out best practice in relation to activities in the oil and gas industry that were not covered directly by the main body of UK accounting standards. However, as much of the OIAC SORP has now been superseded by subsequent changes to accounting standards, the OIAC has concluded that the SORP is no longer applicable in directing best practice guidance. From 1 January 2015, non-listed UK entities moved to new accounting standards – FRS 100 – *Application of Financial Reporting Requirements*, FRS 101 – *Reduced Disclosure Framework*, and FRS 102 – *The Financial Reporting Standard applicable in the UK and Republic of Ireland*, and therefore were required by FRS 101 and FRS 102 to apply IFRS 6. As such, there is no intention to further update the SORP for future industry developments or changes in accounting standards. The ASB has indicated it will continue to provide the OIAC SORP as a reference document, but it will primarily be for educational purposes, will not carry the authoritative accounting weight it did previously, and will not be reviewed or endorsed by the UK Financial Reporting Council (UK FRC). In future OIAC may, when considered necessary, issue guidance notes addressing industry specific accounting matters under IFRS and UK GAAP but these will not be endorsed by the UK FRC.

Given the long history of companies in certain jurisdictions looking to the OIAC SORP for guidance for oil and gas accounting and reporting, and the lack of definitive guidance elsewhere, the SORP is likely to continue to be a valuable source of industry guidance e.g. reserves reporting (see 2.4.1). However, we highlight the importance of having to overlay IFRS pronouncements and guidance as and when they are available. Throughout this chapter the OIAC SORP will be referred to as the 'former OIAC SORP' because it has been decommissioned.

1.5 Guidance under national accounting standards

Entities complying with IFRSs do not have a free hand in selecting accounting policies – indeed the very purpose of a body of accounting literature is to restrict such choices. IAS 8 – *Accounting Policies, Changes in Accounting Estimates and Errors* – makes it clear that when a standard or an interpretation specifically applies to a transaction, other event or condition, the accounting policy or policies applied to that item should be determined by applying the standard or interpretation and considering any relevant implementation guidance issued by the IASB. *[IAS 8.7]*.

However, in the extractive industries there are many circumstances where a particular event, transaction or other condition is *not* specifically addressed by IFRS. When this is the case, IAS 8 sets out a hierarchy of guidance to be considered in the selection of an accounting policy (see Chapter 3 at 4.3).

The primary requirement of the standard is that management should use its judgement in developing and applying an accounting policy that results in information that is both relevant and reliable. *[IAS 8.10]*.

In making the judgement, management *should* refer to, and consider the applicability of, the following sources in descending order:

(a) the requirements in standards and interpretations dealing with similar and related issues; and

(b) the definitions, recognition criteria and measurement concepts for assets, liabilities, income and expenses in the *Conceptual Framework*. *[IAS 8.11]*.

Management may also take into account the most recent pronouncements of other standard-setting bodies that use a similar conceptual framework to develop accounting standards, other accounting literature and accepted industry practices, to the extent that these do not conflict with the sources in (a) and (b) above. *[IAS 8.12]*.

The stock exchanges in Australia, Canada, South Africa, the United Kingdom and the United States have historically been home to the majority of the listed mining companies and oil and gas companies. Consequently, it is organisations from those countries that have been the most active in developing both reserves and resources measurement standards and accounting standards specifically for companies engaged in extractive activities. In developing an accounting policy for an issue that is not specifically dealt with in IFRSs, an entity operating in an extractive industry may find it useful to consider accounting standards developed in these countries. It should be noted, however, that the requirements in such guidance were developed under national accounting standards and may contradict specific requirements and guidance in IFRSs that deals with similar and related issues.

1.6 Upstream versus downstream activities

Upstream activities in the extractive industries are defined as 'exploring for, finding, acquiring, and developing mineral resources up to the point that the reserves are first capable of being sold or used, even if the enterprise intends to process them further'.[8] *Downstream activities* are 'the refining, processing, marketing, and distributing of petroleum, natural gas, or mined mineral (other than refining or processing that is necessary to make the minerals that have been mined or extracted capable of being sold)'.[9]

Thus, activities that are required to make the product saleable or usable are generally considered to be upstream activities. For example, the removal of water to produce dry gas would be an upstream activity, because otherwise the gas cannot be sold at all. However, refining crude oil is considered to be a downstream activity, because crude oil can be sold.

This chapter focuses on upstream activities in the extractive industries as they are primarily affected by the issues discussed above. However, downstream activities are discussed to the extent that they give rise to issues that are unique to the extractive industries (e.g. provisional pricing clauses) or are subject to the same issues as upstream activities (e.g. production sharing contracts).

1.6.1 Phases in upstream activities

Although there is not a universally accepted classification of upstream activities in the extractive industries, the IASC Issues Paper identified the following eight phases which other authors also commonly identify:[10]

(a) *Prospecting* – Prospecting involves activities undertaken to search for an area of interest, a geologic anomaly or structure that may warrant detailed exploration.[11] Prospecting is undertaken typically before mineral rights in the area have been acquired, and if the prospecting results are negative the area of prospecting generally will be abandoned and no mineral rights acquired.[12] However, sometimes it will be necessary to acquire a prospecting permit as the prospecting activities require access to the land to carry out geological and geophysical tests.[13]

(b) *Acquisition of mineral rights* – The acquisition phase involves the activities related to obtaining legal rights to explore for, develop, and/or produce wasting resources on a mineral property.[14] Legal rights may be acquired in a number of ways as discussed at 5 below.

(c) *Exploration* – Exploration is the detailed examination of a geographical area of interest that has shown sufficient mineral-producing potential to merit further exploration, often using techniques that are similar to those used in the prospecting phase.[15] In the mining sector, exploration usually involves taking cores for analysis, sinking exploratory shafts, geological mapping, geochemical analysis, cutting drifts and crosscuts, opening shallow pits, and removing overburden in some areas.[16] In the oil and gas sector, exploration involves techniques such as shooting seismic, core drilling, and ultimately the drilling of an exploratory well to determine whether oil and gas reserves do exist.[17]

(d) *Appraisal or evaluation* – This involves determining the technical feasibility and commercial viability of mineral deposits that have been found through exploration.[18] This phase typically includes:[19]

- (i) detailed engineering studies and drilling of additional wells by oil and gas companies to determine how the reservoir can best be developed to obtain maximum recovery;
- (ii) determination by mining companies of the volume and grade of deposits through drilling of core samples, trenching, and sampling activities in an area known to contain mineral resources;
- (iii) examination and testing by mining companies of extraction methods and metallurgical or treatment processes;
- (iv) surveying transportation and infrastructure requirements;
- (v) conducting market and finance studies; and
- (vi) making detailed economic evaluations to determine whether development of the reserves is commercially justified.

(e) *Development* – Development is the establishment of access to the mineral reserve and other preparations for commercial production. In the mining sector, development includes sinking shafts and underground drifts, making permanent excavations, developing passageways and rooms or galleries, building roads and tunnels, and advance removal of overburden and waste rock.[20] In the oil and gas sector the development phase involves gaining access to, and preparing, well locations for drilling, constructing platforms or preparing drill sites, drilling wells, and installing equipment and facilities.[21]

(f) *Construction* – Construction involves installing facilities, such as buildings, machinery and equipment to extract, treat, and transport minerals.[22]

(g) *Production* – The production phase involves the extraction of the natural resources from the earth and the related processes necessary to make the produced resource marketable or transportable.[23]

(h) *Closure and decommissioning* – Closure means ceasing production, removing equipment and facilities, restoring the production site to appropriate conditions after operations have ceased and abandoning the site.[24]

The above phases are not necessarily discrete sequential steps. Instead, the phases often overlap or take place simultaneously. Nevertheless, they provide a useful framework for developing accounting policies in the extractive industries. Accounting for expenditures depends very much on the phase during which they are incurred; for example, as discussed further below, costs incurred in the prospecting phase cannot be recognised as assets, whereas most costs incurred in the construction phase should be capitalised.

2 MINERAL RESERVES AND RESOURCES

As noted in 1.1 above, IFRSs currently use the term 'minerals' and 'mineral assets' when referring to the extractive industries as a whole. This is used as a collective term to include both mining and oil and gas reserves and resources. For the purposes of this chapter, consistency with the current wording in IFRSs will be maintained and therefore, unless stated otherwise, 'minerals' and 'mineral assets' will encompass both mining and oil and gas.

This section discusses in some detail the underlying principles used by entities to estimate the quantity of recoverable mineral reserves and resources for both mining and oil and gas, that the entity owns or has a right to extract. At the commercial level, these estimates are considered of paramount importance by stakeholders in making investment decisions and are also fundamental in accounting for mining activities and oil and gas activities.

The importance of estimating resources and reserves is matched by the difficulty in doing so, both technically and methodologically. For example, there is no firm consensus amongst regulators and the industries on which commodity prices should be used in reserves estimation (i.e. historical, spot or forward-looking). We therefore aim to provide an introduction to this subject, and to explain the main methods used to arrive at reserve estimates, including the valuation methods used once quantities of reserves have been estimated. In our view, without a sound grasp of this aspect, it is difficult to make an informed judgement as to how to account for mineral reserves.

Mineral reserves are often the most valuable assets of mining companies and oil and gas companies and mineral reserve estimates are a very important part of the way these companies report to their stakeholders. However, in an entity's financial statements, assets relating to mineral resources reserves are generally measured under IFRSs at their historical cost which, other than by coincidence, will not be their market value. Currently, IFRSs do not require disclosure of reserves, though certain national standards (e.g. US GAAP) and stock exchange regulators (e.g. US Securities and Exchange Commission (SEC), Australian Stock Exchange (ASX), Toronto Stock Exchange, Johannesburg Stock Exchange (JSE) to name just a few) do. Having said this, there are variances in what is required and what categories are disclosed, including differences between mining and oil and gas. Other regulators are considering introducing disclosure requirements, for example, the Securities Commission of Malaysia (SC) is considering the implementation of reserves disclosure requirements for oil and gas companies as it embarks on listing improvement initiatives relating to the oil and gas industry.

Notwithstanding there are no specific disclosure requirements in IFRSs, detailed reserve estimates are required in order to apply historical cost accounting under IFRS in:

- deciding whether to capitalise E&E costs (see 3.2 below);
- calculating the annual depreciation, depletion and amortisation charge under the units of production method (see 16.1.3 below);

- calculating deferred stripping cost adjustments (applicable to mining companies only – see 15.5 below);
- determining impairment charges and reversals under IAS 36 (see 11 below);
- determining whether a gain or loss should be recognised on transactions such as asset swaps, carried interest arrangements and farm-in or farm-out arrangements (see 6 below);
- determining the fair value of acquired mineral reserves and resources when applying the purchase method of accounting under IFRS 3 – *Business Combinations* (see 8 below); and
- estimating the timing of decommissioning or restoration activities (see 10 below).

Reserves reporting in the mining sector and oil and gas sector have been under development since the beginning of the twentieth century. However, reserve estimation techniques in the mining sector and oil and gas sector have developed largely independently as a result of the different nature of the reserves involved. Therefore, the terminology and definitions used in the oil and gas sector and mining sector are discussed separately at 2.2 and 2.3 below respectively. Disclosure is discussed at 2.4 below.

The international efforts to harmonise reserve estimation and reporting are discussed below.

2.1 International harmonisation of reserve reporting

The project team concluded in the Extractive Activities DP (see 1.3 above) that the nature and extent of the similarities between the CRIRSCO Template (mining) and the PRMS reserve and resource definitions (oil and gas) indicate that these definitions are capable of providing a platform for setting comparable accounting and disclosure requirements for both mining and oil and gas activities. Therefore they recommended that the CRIRSCO template and the PRMS definitions of reserves and resources are suitable to use in a future IFRS for Extractive Activities. Nonetheless, there is some tension between the definition of an asset in the IASB's *Conceptual Framework* and the assumptions underlying the reserves and resources definitions.[25] The points of tension highlighted in the DP include:

- the CRIRSCO Template and the PRMS both make use of entity-specific assumptions that are applied to derive a reserve or resource estimate, whereas IFRS typically requires that estimates should make use of economic assumptions that reflect market-based evidence, where available;
- the CRIRSCO Template and the PRMS require that certain conditions must exist before a resource can be converted into a reserve. In contrast, management's intentions are not a feature of the Conceptual Framework's definition of an asset.

While the DP recommended the use of the CRIRSCO Template and PRMS, it also recommended that the alternative option of using the *United Nations Framework Classification for Fossil Energy and Mineral Resources* (UNFC) should be reconsidered if an Extractive Activities project is added to the IASB's active agenda.[26]

Chapter 41

In 2009, the SEC revised its oil and gas reserves estimation and disclosure requirements. The primary objectives of the final rule – *Modernization of Oil and Gas Reporting (Release No. 33-8995)* were to increase the transparency and information value of reserve disclosures and improve comparability among oil and gas companies, including comparability between domestic registrants and foreign private issuers. Although the SEC has revised its oil and gas requirements, a similar revision process has not been undertaken for mineral reserves. As a result, despite calls from both the CRIRSCO and the Society for Mining, Metallurgy and Exploration (SME) to consider the need for convergence given the increasing overlap between oil and gas and mining in such areas as tar sands and oil shales, no progress has been made in achieving convergence between the SEC requirements and the various other requirements. Key differences that still remain include:

- the SEC does not allow the term 'resources' to be used in reports;
- the SEC states that final or bankable feasibility studies need to be completed before new greenfield reserves can be declared; and
- the SEC requirement for mining companies to use three year trailing average rather than forward-looking commodity prices in reserve estimation under SEC Industry Guide 7.

2.2 Petroleum reserve estimation and reporting

The '*SPE/WPC/AAPG/SPEE Petroleum Resources Management System*' (SPE-PRMS), which was published in 2007, is the leading framework for the estimation and reporting of petroleum reserves and resources. It was prepared by the Oil and Gas Reserves Committee of the Society of Petroleum Engineers (SPE) and reviewed and sponsored by the World Petroleum Council (WPC), the American Association of Petroleum Geologists (AAPG) and the Society of Petroleum Evaluation Engineers (SPEE). The definitions and guidelines in the SPE-PRMS, which are internationally used within the oil and gas sector, deal with:[27]

- classification and categorisation of resources;
- evaluation and reporting; and
- estimation of recoverable quantities.

Most of the major regulatory agencies have developed disclosure guidelines that impose classification rules similar to, but not directly linked to, the SPE-PRMS, and most typically mandate disclosure of only a subset of the total reserves and resources defined in the SPE-PRMS. For example, the SEC specifies that only Proved Reserves should be disclosed,[28] but now allows for optional disclosure of probable reserves.

2.2.1 *Basic principles and definitions*

The following diagram summarises the SPE-PRMS resources classification system:[29]

Figure 41.1

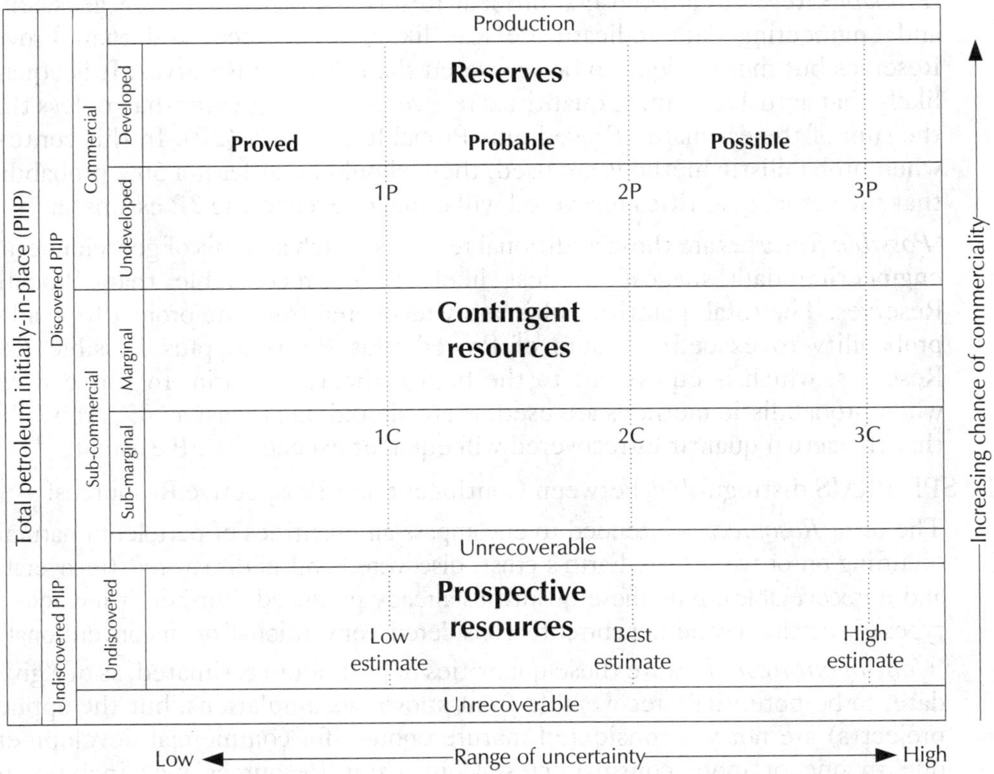

The *range of uncertainty* reflects a range of estimated quantities potentially recoverable, while the vertical axis represents the *chance of* commerciality (and project maturity), that is, the chance that the project will be developed and reach commercial producing status.[30]

The SPE-PRMS defines proved, probable and possible reserves as follows:

- '*Reserves* are those quantities of petroleum anticipated to be commercially recoverable by application of development projects to known accumulations from a given date forward under defined conditions. Reserves must further satisfy four criteria: they must be discovered, recoverable, commercial, and remaining (as of the evaluation date) based on the development project(s) applied. Reserves are further categorized in accordance with the level of certainty associated with the estimates and may be sub-classified based on project maturity and/or characterized by development and production status.'[31]
- '*Proved Reserves* are those quantities of petroleum, which, by analysis of geoscience and engineering data, can be estimated with reasonable certainty to be commercially recoverable, from a given date forward, from known reservoirs and under defined economic conditions, operating methods, and government regulations. If deterministic methods are used, the term reasonable certainty is intended to express a high degree of confidence that the quantities will be recovered. If probabilistic methods are used, there should be at least a 90% probability that the quantities actually recovered will equal or exceed the estimate.'[32]

- '*Probable Reserves* are those additional Reserves which analysis of geoscience and engineering data indicate are less likely to be recovered than Proved Reserves but more certain to be recovered than Possible Reserves. It is equally likely that actual remaining quantities recovered will be greater than or less than the sum of the estimated Proved plus Probable Reserves (2P). In this context, when probabilistic methods are used, there should be at least a 50% probability that the actual quantities recovered will equal or exceed the 2P estimate.'[33]
- '*Possible Reserves* are those additional reserves which analysis of geoscience and engineering data suggest are less likely to be recoverable than Probable Reserves. The total quantities ultimately recovered from the project have a low probability to exceed the sum of Proved plus Probable plus Possible (3P) Reserves, which is equivalent to the high estimate scenario. In this context, when probabilistic methods are used, there should be at least a 10% probability that the actual quantities recovered will equal or exceed the 3P estimate.'[34]

The SPE-PRMS distinguishes between Contingent and Prospective Resources:

- The term *Resources* is intended to encompass all quantities of petroleum naturally occurring on or within the Earth's crust, discovered and undiscovered (recoverable and unrecoverable), plus those quantities already produced. Further, it includes all types of petroleum whether currently considered 'conventional' or 'unconventional'.[35]
- '*Contingent Resources* are those quantities of petroleum estimated, as of a given date, to be potentially recoverable from known accumulations, but the applied project(s) are not yet considered mature enough for commercial development due to one or more contingencies. Contingent Resources may include, for example, projects for which there are currently no viable markets, or where commercial recovery is dependent on technology under development, or where evaluation of the accumulation is insufficient to clearly assess commerciality. Contingent Resources are further categorized in accordance with the level of certainty associated with the estimates and may be sub-classified based on project maturity and/or characterized by their economic status.'[36]
- '*Prospective Resources* are those quantities of petroleum estimated, as of a given date, to be potentially recoverable from undiscovered accumulations by application of future development projects. Prospective Resources have both an associated chance of discovery and a chance of development. Prospective Resources are further subdivided in accordance with the level of certainty associated with recoverable estimates assuming their discovery and development and may be sub-classified based on project maturity.'[37]

Total petroleum initially-in-place is that quantity of petroleum that is estimated to exist originally in naturally occurring accumulations. *Discovered Petroleum Initially-in-Place* is that quantity of petroleum that is estimated, as of a given date, to be contained in known accumulations prior to production. *Undiscovered Petroleum Initially-in-Place* is that quantity of petroleum estimated, as of a given date, to be contained within accumulations yet to be discovered.[38]

Production is the cumulative quantity of petroleum that has been recovered at a given date. *Unrecoverable* is that portion of Discovered or Undiscovered Petroleum Initially-in-Place quantities which is estimated, as of a given date, not to be recoverable by future development projects. A portion of these quantities may become recoverable in the future as commercial circumstances change or technological developments occur; the remaining portion may never be recovered due to physical/chemical constraints represented by subsurface interaction of fluids and reservoir rocks.[39]

2.2.2 *Classification and categorisation guidelines*

The SPE-PRMS provides guidance on classifying resources depending on the relative maturity of the development projects being applied to yield the recoverable quantity estimates, as follows:[40]

Figure 41.2

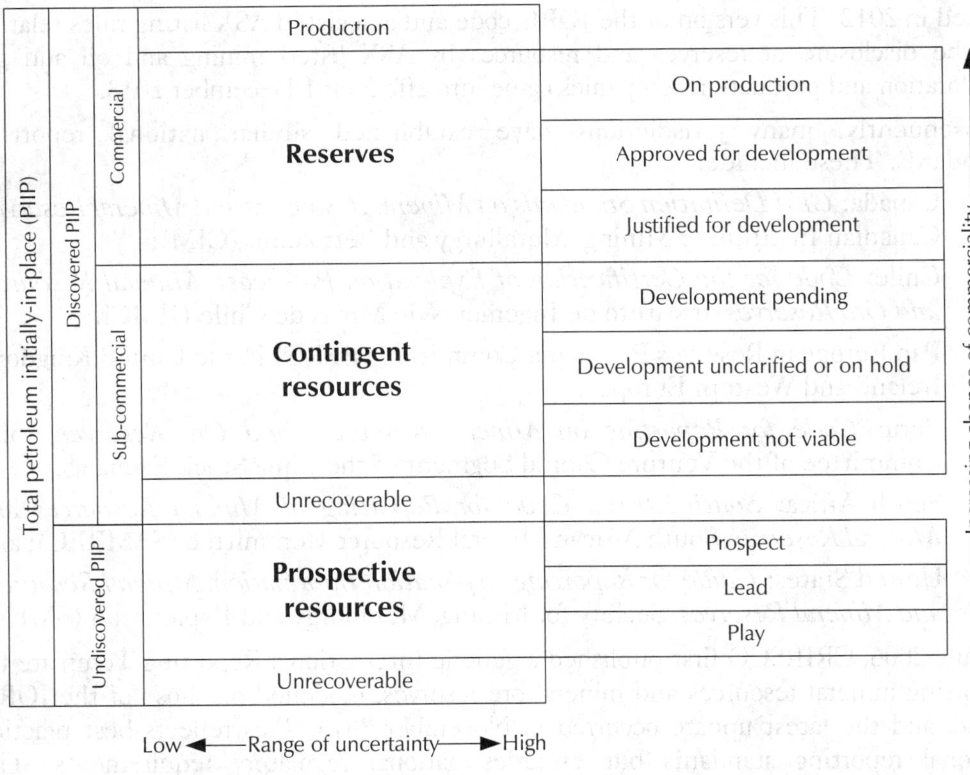

Project maturity may be indicated qualitatively by allocation to classes and sub-classes and/or quantitatively by associating a project's estimated chance of reaching producing status.

The SPE-PRMS also provides guidance on categorising resources, depending on the associated degrees of uncertainty, into the following cumulative categories:[41]

- proved, probable and possible (1P, 2P and 3P) for reserves;
- low, best and high (1C, 2C and 3C) for contingent resources; and
- low estimate, best estimate and high estimate for prospective resources.

Additionally, guidance is provided on categorisation of reserves and resources related to incremental projects, such as workovers, infill drilling and improved recovery.

To promote consistency in project evaluations and reporting, the SPE-PRMS provides guidelines on the economic assumptions that are to be used, measurement of production, and resources entitlement and recognition,[42] and also provides guidance on the analytical procedures, and on the deterministic and probabilistic methods to be used.

2.3 Mining resource and reserve reporting

The *Australasian Code for Reporting of Exploration Results, Mineral Resources and Ore Reserves* (JORC Code) is prepared by the Joint Ore Reserves Committee (JORC) of the Australasian Institute of Mining and Metallurgy, Australian Institute of Geoscientists and Minerals Council of Australia. The JORC was established in 1971, the first edition of the JORC Code was published in 1989,[43] with the most recent edition of the JORC Code issued in 2012. This version of the JORC code and associated ASX listing rules relating to the disclosure of reserves and resources by ASX listed mining and oil and gas exploration and production companies came into effect on 1 December 2013.

Subsequently, many jurisdictions have established similar national reporting standards. These include:

- Canada: *CIM Definition Standards on Mineral Resources and Mineral Reserves*, Canadian Institute of Mining, Metallurgy and Petroleum (CIM);
- Chile: *Code for the Certification of Exploration Prospects, Mineral Resources and Ore Reserves*, Instituto de Ingenieros de Minas de Chile (IIMCh);
- Pan European Reserves Reporting Committee (PERC) in the United Kingdom, Ireland and Western Europe;
- Peru: *Code for Reporting on Mineral Resources and Ore Reserves*, Joint Committee of the Venture Capital Segment of the Lima Stock Exchange;
- South Africa: *South African Code for Reporting of Mineral Resources and Mineral Reserves*, South African Mineral Resource Committee (SAMREC); and
- United States: *Guide for Reporting Exploration Information, Mineral Resources and Mineral Reserves*, Society for Mining, Metallurgy and Exploration (SME).

In July 2006, CRIRSCO first published a generic International Reporting Template for reporting mineral resources and mineral ore reserves, modelled on those of the JORC Code, and the latest update occurred in November 2013. This reflects best practice national reporting standards but excludes national regulatory requirements. The template serves as a guide to national standard-setters that do not have a reporting standard or who want to revise their existing standard to an internationally acceptable form.[44] 'The system is primarily targeted at establishing international best practice standards for regulatory and public disclosures and combines the basic components of a number of national reporting codes and guidelines that have been adopted in similar forms by all the major agencies [other than] the SEC. The classification is applied, with small modifications or extensions, by most mining companies for the purpose of internal resource management.'[45]

In the United States, public disclosures of mineral resources and mineral reserves are regulated by the SEC, which does not recognise the CRIRSCO guidelines. Unsurprisingly, some of the SEC requirements (Industry Guide 7) for public release of information are materially different from those applicable in other countries.[46] The SEC's Industry Guide 7 is discussed at 2.4.2 below.

2.3.1 CRIRSCO International Reporting Template (November 2013)

Set out below are the main requirements of the CRIRSCO International Reporting Template (CRIRSCO Template) to the extent that they are relevant to financial reporting by mining companies.

2.3.1.A Scope

The main principles governing the operation and application of the CRIRSCO Template are transparency, materiality and competence. These are aimed at ensuring that the reader of a public report is provided with:[47]

- sufficient information that is clear and unambiguous (transparency);
- a report that contains all relevant information which investors and their professional advisers would reasonably require and would reasonably expect to find, to be able to form a reasoned and balanced judgement about the Exploration Results, Mineral Resources or Mineral Reserves being reported (materiality); and
- information that is based on work that is the responsibility of suitably qualified and experienced persons who are subject to an enforceable professional code of ethics and rules of conduct (competence).

A *public report* is a report 'prepared for the purpose of informing investors or potential investors and their advisors on Exploration Results, Mineral Resources or Mineral Reserves. They include, but are not limited to, annual and quarterly company reports, press releases, information memoranda, technical papers, website postings and public presentations'.[48] The CRIRSCO Template is applicable to all solid minerals, including diamonds, other gemstones, industrial minerals, stone and aggregates, and coal.[49] The CRIRSCO Template provides supplementary rules on reporting related to coal, diamonds and industrial minerals, due to the special nature of those types of deposit.

A public report should be prepared by a *competent person*, defined in the CRIRSCO Template as '... a minerals industry professional (NRO to insert appropriate membership class and organisation including Recognised Professional Organisations) with enforceable disciplinary processes including the powers to suspend or expel a member'.[50] (Note that NRO stands for 'national representative organisations').

2.3.1.B Reporting terminology

The general relationship between Exploration Results, Mineral Resources and Mineral Reserves can be summarised in the following diagram:[51]

Figure 41.3

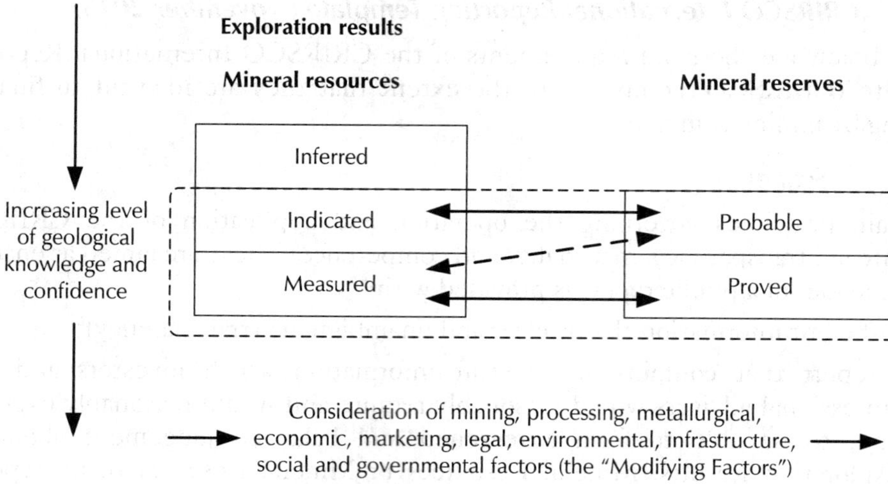

The terms in the above diagram are defined as follows.

Exploration Results include data and information generated by mineral exploration programmes that might be of use to investors but which do not form part of a declaration of Mineral Resources or Mineral Reserves.[52] The CRIRSCO Template specifically requires that any information relating to Exploration Results be expressed in such a way that it does not unreasonably imply that potentially economic mineralisation has been discovered.[53]

A *Mineral Resource* is a concentration or occurrence of solid material of economic interest in or on the Earth's crust in such form, grade, quality and quantity that there are reasonable prospects for eventual economic extraction. The location, quantity, grade, continuity and other geological characteristics of a Mineral Resource are known, estimated or interpreted from specific geological evidence and knowledge, including sampling. Mineral Resources are sub-divided, in order of increasing geological confidence, into Inferred, Indicated and Measured categories:[54]

- 'An *Inferred Mineral Resource* is that part of a Mineral Resource for which quantity and grade or quality are estimated on the basis of limited geological evidence and sampling. Geological evidence is sufficient to imply but not verify geological and grade or quality continuity. An Inferred Resource has a lower level of confidence than that applying to an Indicated Mineral Resource and must not be converted to a Mineral Reserve. It is reasonably expected that the majority of Inferred Mineral Resources could be upgraded to Indicated Mineral Resources with continued exploration.'[55]

- 'An *Indicated Mineral Resource* is that part of a Mineral Resource for which quantity, grade or quality, densities, shape and physical characteristics are estimated with sufficient confidence to allow the application of Modifying Factors in sufficient detail to support mine planning and evaluation of the economic viability of the deposit. Geological evidence is derived from adequately detailed and reliable exploration, sampling and testing and is sufficient to assume geological and grade or quality continuity between points of observation. An Indicated Mineral Resource has a lower level of confidence than that applying to a Measured Mineral Resource and may only be converted to a Probable Mineral Reserve.'[56]
- 'A *Measured Mineral Resource* is that part of a Mineral Resource for which quantity, grade or quality, densities, shape and physical characteristics are estimated with confidence to allow the application of Modifying Factors to support detailed mine planning and final evaluation of the economic viability of the deposit. Geological evidence is derived from detailed and reliable exploration, sampling and testing and is sufficient to confirm geological and grade or quality continuity between points of observation. A Measured Mineral Resource has a higher level of confidence than that applying to either an Indicated Mineral Resource or an Inferred Mineral Resource. It may be converted to a Proved Mineral Reserve or to a Probable Mineral Reserve.'[57]
- 'Modifying factors are considerations used to convert Mineral Resources to Mineral Reserves. These include, but are not restricted to, mining, processing, metallurgical, infrastructure, economic, marketing, legal, environmental, social and governmental factors.'[58]
- 'A *Mineral Reserve* is the economically mineable part of a Measured and/or Indicated Mineral Resource. It includes diluting materials and allowances for losses, which may occur when the material is mined or extracted and is defined by studies at Pre-Feasibility or Feasibility level as appropriate that include application of Modifying Factors. Such studies demonstrate that, at the time of reporting, extraction could reasonably be justified.'[59]
- 'A *Probable Mineral Reserve* is the economically mineable part of an Indicated, and in some circumstances, a Measured Mineral Resource. The confidence in the Modifying Factors applying to a Probable Mineral Reserve is lower than that applying to a Proved Mineral Reserve. A Probable Mineral Reserve has a lower level of confidence than a Proved Mineral Reserve but is of sufficient quality to serve as the basis for a decision on the development of the deposit.'[60]
- 'A *Proved Mineral Reserve* is the economically mineable part of a Measured Mineral Resource. A Proved Mineral Reserve implies a high degree of confidence in the Modifying Factors. A Proved Mineral Reserve represents the highest confidence category of reserve estimate.'[61]

The CRIRSCO Template contains more detailed guidance on how a competent person should decide on mineral resource and mineral reserve classification and contains a checklist and guideline for the preparation of public reports.

2.4 Disclosure of mineral reserves and resources

Mineral reserves and resources are a significant element in communications by mining companies and oil and gas companies to their stakeholders. IFRS requires an entity to provide 'additional disclosures when compliance with the specific requirements in IFRSs is insufficient to enable users to understand the impact of particular transactions, other events and conditions on the entity's financial position and financial performance'. *[IAS 1.17(c)]*. Therefore, although IFRS does not specifically require it, disclosures regarding mineral resources and reserves will generally be necessary under IFRS to provide users with the information they need to understand the entity's financial position and performance.

As noted in 2 above, entities have to use reserves data and sometimes resources data for a number of accounting purposes and the methodology should be consistent with the definitions in the IFRS *Conceptual Framework* for asset recognition. We believe that users of the financial statements need to be able to identify the methodology used to estimate reserves and resources in order to understand an entity's financial statements. If management uses proved reserves for investment appraisal and uses these same reserves for depreciation and impairment calculations, this should be clearly identified in the reserves disclosure. Conversely, if management uses different reserves and/or resources definitions for different purposes, that should be made clear in the financial statements.

In the absence of guidance under IFRS, entities not subject to the requirements of a national regulator may wish to use the disclosure requirements of other standard-setters as a starting point in developing their own policies. The sections below discuss the disclosure requirements of several standard-setters for mineral reserve and resource quantities for oil and gas companies and mining companies (see 2.4.1 and 2.4.2 respectively below) and reserve values (see 2.4.3 below).

However, while disclosure of information about mineral reserves and resources is clearly very useful, users of financial statements should be aware that there are many differences between different jurisdictions or even within those jurisdictions. Therefore, comparisons between entities may be difficult or even impossible. In particular, the following aspects are important:

- *Proven and probable reserves* – The definition of reserves can vary greatly, e.g. the former OIAC SORP permitted disclosure of either 'proven and probable' or 'proved developed and undeveloped' reserves, whereas Accounting Standards Codification (ASC) Topic 932-235-50 – *Extractive Activities – Oil and Gas – Notes to Financial Statements – Disclosure* – requires disclosure of 'proved reserves, proved developed reserves and proved undeveloped reserves';[62]
- *Commodity price* – The quantity of economically recoverable reserves may depend to a large extent on the price assumptions that an entity uses. Differences often arise because the entity:
  - uses its own long-term price assumption which, for example, was permitted under the former OIAC SORP;
  - is required to use 12-month average prices, which is required by the SEC Release No. 33-8995 in the oil and gas sector; or

  - is required to use a three year trailing average, which is required to comply with the SEC's Industry Guide 7 in the mining sector;
- *Royalties* – Royalties payable in-kind to the government or legal owner of the mineral rights may or may not be included in reserves;
- *Non-controlling interests* – Generally 'reserves' include all reserves held by the parent and its consolidated subsidiaries. While in many jurisdictions mining companies and oil and gas companies are required to disclose the reserves attributable to significant non-controlling interests, this is not always required;
- *Associates, joint arrangements and other investments* – An entity may have economic ownership of reserves through investments in associates and joint arrangements, equity interests (see 7 below) or royalty yielding contracts (see 5.7 below). Such reserves are generally not included in consolidated reserves, but may need to be disclosed separately; and
- *Production sharing contracts and risk service contracts* (see 5.3 and 5.5.1 respectively below) – Frequently the mining company or oil and gas company does not legally own the mineral reserves and resources in the ground, i.e. the government retains legal ownership. A significant amount of judgement concerning the nature of the rights and economic interests of the entity may be required to determine whether the entity is the economic owner of any reserves or resources. Depending on the reserve reporting framework that the entity is subject to, such 'economic' reserves may or may not be included in reserves or resources.

In addition to those matters set out above, there may be other differences in the reserves definition and disclosure requirements in different jurisdictions of which users of IFRS financial statements should be aware. Such differences may affect IFRS financial reporting directly.

2.4.1 Oil and gas sector

Many oil and gas companies are required to disclose information about reserve quantities in accordance with the rules and requirements of the stock exchange on which they are listed. However, those oil and gas companies that are not subject to the specific disclosure requirements of a stock exchange or other local regulator should consider the need to disclose reserves and resources information to provide users with the information they need to understand the entity's financial position and performance.

Companies may continue to consider disclosing the information previously required under the former OIAC SORP or the US ASC 932-235-50, or could look to the example disclosures contained in the 2010 DP at 1.3.4 above.

2.4.2 Mining sector

Many mining companies are required to disclose information about reserve quantities in accordance with the rules and requirements of the stock exchange on which they are listed. However, those mining companies that are not subject to the specific disclosure requirements of a stock exchange or other local regulator may wish to consider disclosing the information required under the US Securities and Exchange Commission's Industry Guide 7 – *Description of Property by Issuers Engaged or to Be Engaged in Significant Mining Operations* (SEC Industry Guide 7).

Mining companies that are subject to the SEC rules and regulations need to understand not only the content of Industry Guide 7, but also the current interpretation of this content by the SEC's staff. While many of the definitions may seem familiar, the SEC staff's interpretations may differ considerably from those of regulators in other countries.[63] Refer to SEC Industry Guide 7 sections I-III for details.

2.4.3 Disclosure of the value of reserves

As part of its work on the Extractive Activities DP (see 1.3.4 above) the IASB staff considered whether a disclosure-focused approach might be appropriate in an extractive industries financial reporting standard. It is in this context that the DP noted that, given the near unanimity of the feedback from users on the lack of relevance of either historical cost or current value accounting for reserves and resources, a disclosure-focused approach needed to be considered as one alternative in the discussion paper.[64]

One of the key issues to consider before developing a disclosure-focused approach is whether or not disclosure of the value of mineral reserves should be a requirement. A secondary issue is whether the mineral reserves should be disclosed at their fair value or at a standardised measure of value, similar to the requirement under ASC 932-235-50 which is based on discounted cash net cash flows.

This disclosure requirement is not uncontroversial, as the 'standardized measure of oil and gas' (often abbreviated to SMOG) does not represent the market value of an entity's proved reserves. However, the standardised measure of the value of oil and gas reserves greatly reduces the impact of management's opinion about future development on the value calculated, e.g. the method prescribes the discount rate and commodity price to be used. While this may not take into account relevant insights that management may have, the advantage is that comparability of the disclosures between entities is increased. As illustrated in Extract 41.1, some companies caution against over-reliance on these disclosures.

Extract 41.1: BP p.l.c. (2015)

Supplementary information on oil and natural gas (unaudited) [extract]

Standardized measure of discounted future net cash flows and changes therein relating to proved oil and gas reserves [extract]

The following tables set out the standardized measure of discounted future net cash flows, and changes therein, relating to crude oil and natural gas production from the group's estimated proved reserves. This information is prepared in compliance with FASB Oil and Gas Disclosures requirements.

Future net cash flows have been prepared on the basis of certain assumptions which may or may not be realized. These include the timing of future production, the estimation of crude oil and natural gas reserves and the application of average crude oil and natural gas prices and exchange rates from the previous 12 months. Furthermore, both proved reserves estimates and production forecasts are subject to revision as further technical information becomes available and economic conditions change. BP cautions against relying on the information presented because of the highly arbitrary nature of the assumptions on which it is based and its lack of comparability with the historical cost information presented in the financial statements.

It is clear that reaching agreement as to what constitutes useful and relevant disclosures about the value of mineral reserves is not straightforward and will be controversial. Still, in September 2008, the Board indicated support for the Extractive Activities DP to propose the disclosure of 'a current value measurement, such as a standardised measure of discounted cash flows, and the key assumptions necessary for a user to make use of that measurement'. This would not be disclosed if the minerals or oil and gas assets are measured on the balance sheet at fair value or some other current value measurement. In that case, an entity would provide disclosures similar to those required in the US (by ASC 820-10-50-1, 2, 3 – *Fair Value Measurements and Disclosures*).'[65] Accordingly, the DP concluded that:

- if the assets are measured at historical cost then detailed information should be disclosed about their current value (either fair value or standardised measure) and how it was determined;
- if, instead, the assets are measured at fair value then detailed information should be disclosed about that fair value and how it was determined.

2.4.3.A ASC 932-235-50 – disclosure of standardised measure of oil and gas

All entities engaged in significant oil and gas producing activities that report under US GAAP are required by ASC 932-235-50 to disclose a standardised measure of discounted future net cash flows relating to proved oil and gas reserve quantities. There may also be non-US GAAP oil and gas companies who, while they are not subject to these specific disclosure requirements, still elect to refer to these when determining the reserves and resources information to provide to their users. ASC 932-235-50 is highly prescriptive and should be reviewed directly in full to ensure compliance with its requirements.

3 IFRS 6 – EXPLORATION FOR AND EVALUATION OF MINERAL RESOURCES

3.1 Objective and scope

The IASB's objective in developing IFRS 6, as noted at 1.2 above, was restricted to making limited improvements to existing accounting practices for exploration and evaluation (E&E) expenditures. E&E expenditures are 'expenditures incurred by an entity in connection with the exploration for and evaluation of mineral resources before the technical feasibility and commercial viability of extracting a mineral resource are demonstrable', while E&E assets are 'exploration and evaluation expenditures recognised as assets in accordance with the entity's accounting policy'. *[IFRS 6 Appendix A]*.

IFRS 6 is limited to specifying the financial reporting for the exploration for and evaluation of mineral resources, which the standard defines as 'the search for mineral resources, including minerals, oil, natural gas and similar non-regenerative resources after the entity has obtained legal rights to explore in a specific area, as well as the determination of the technical feasibility and commercial viability of extracting the mineral resource'. *[IFRS 6.1, Appendix A]*. The standard also specifies when entities need to assess E&E assets for impairment in accordance with IAS 36 and requires certain disclosures.

An entity may not apply IFRS 6 to expenditures incurred before the exploration for and evaluation of mineral resources (e.g. expenditures incurred before the entity has obtained the legal rights to explore a specific area such as prospecting and acquisition of mineral rights) or after the technical feasibility and commercial viability of extracting a mineral resource are demonstrable (e.g. development, construction, production and closure). *[IFRS 6.5]*. Furthermore, it deals only with E&E expenditures and does not provide guidance on other sector-specific issues that may arise during the E&E phase.

Equipment used in the E&E phase, e.g. property, plant and equipment and any other intangibles, such as software, are not in the scope of IFRS 6, instead, they are in the scope of IAS 16 or IAS 38.

3.1.1 Scope exclusions in other standards relating to the extractive industries

In the Basis for Conclusions on IFRS 6 the IASB confirmed that 'even though no IFRS has addressed extractive activities directly, all IFRSs (including International Accounting Standards and Interpretations) are applicable to entities engaged in the exploration for and evaluation of mineral resources that make an unreserved statement of compliance with IFRSs in accordance with IAS 1'. *[IFRS 6.BC6]*. However, certain aspects of activities that occur in the extractive industries that fall outside the scope of IFRS 6 are excluded from the scope of other standards.

Various standards exclude 'minerals' from their scope, but the exact wording of the scope exclusions differs from standard to standard. Therefore, it would be incorrect to conclude that the same aspects of the extractive industries' activities are excluded from the scope of these standards:

- IAS 2 – does not apply to the measurement of minerals and mineral products, 'to the extent that they are measured at net realisable value in accordance with well-established practices in those industries'. *[IAS 2.3(a), 4]*. The practice of measuring minerals and mineral products inventories at net realisable value is, in reality, relatively rare in many areas of the extractive industries.
- IAS 16 – does not apply to 'mineral rights and mineral reserves such as oil, natural gas and similar non-regenerative resources'. *[IAS 16.3(d)]*. In addition, the standard does not apply to 'the recognition and measurement of exploration and evaluation assets'. *[IAS 16.3(c)]*. Equipment used in extracting reserves is within the scope of IAS 16.
- IAS 17 – does not apply to 'leases to explore for or use minerals, oil, natural gas and similar non-regenerative resources'. *[IAS 17.2(a)]*. However, leases of assets used for exploration or evaluation activities are in the scope of IAS 17.
- IFRS 16 – does not apply to 'leases to explore for or use minerals, oil, natural gas and similar non-regenerative resources'. *[IFRS 16.3(a)]*. However, leases including leases of right-of-use assets in a sublease of assets used for exploration or evaluation activities are in the scope of IFRS 16.

- IAS 18 – does not deal with revenue arising from 'the extraction of mineral ores'; *[IAS 18.6(h)]*. Note: As mentioned earlier, minerals and mineral products/reserves are not scoped out of IFRS 15 – see 12.7 below for more details on IFRS 15.
- IAS 38 – does not apply to 'expenditure on the exploration for, or development and extraction of, minerals, oil, natural gas and similar non-regenerative resources' or to the recognition and measurement of E&E assets. *[IAS 38.2(c)-(d)]*.
- IAS 40 – does not apply to 'mineral rights and mineral reserves such as oil, natural gas and similar non-regenerative resources'. *[IAS 40.4(b)]*.
- IFRIC 4 – does not apply to arrangements that are, or contain, leases excluded from the scope of IAS 17. *[IFRIC 4.4]*.

3.2 Recognition of exploration and evaluation assets

3.2.1 Developing an accounting policy under IFRS 6

When developing its accounting policy for E&E expenditures, IFRS 6 requires an entity recognising E&E assets to apply paragraph 10 of IAS 8. *[IFRS 6.6, BC19]*. Hence management should use its judgement in developing and applying an accounting policy that results in information that is relevant and reliable. *[IAS 8.10]*. However, IFRS 6 does provide an exemption from paragraphs 11 and 12 of IAS 8, *[IFRS 6.7, BC17]*, which 'specify sources of authoritative requirements and guidance that management is required to consider in developing an accounting policy for an item if no IFRS applies specifically to that item' (the so-called 'GAAP hierarchy', see Chapter 3 at 4.3). In developing such a policy, IFRS 6 imposes a number of significant constraints on an entity's choice of accounting policy because:

- an entity needs to specify which expenditures are recognised as E&E assets and apply that accounting policy consistently (see 3.3.1 below); *[IFRS 6.9]*
- expenditures related to the development of mineral resources should not be recognised as E&E assets (see 3.3.1 below); *[IFRS 6.10]* and
- the requirement to apply IAS 16, IAS 38 and IAS 36 after the E&E phase affects the choice of accounting policies during the E&E phase. In January 2006 the IFRIC clarified that 'it was clear that the scope of IFRS 6 consistently limited the relief from the hierarchy to policies applied to E&E activities and that there was no basis for interpreting IFRS 6 as granting any additional relief in areas outside its scope'.[66] For example, an entity may be able to apply the full cost method of accounting (see 3.2.4 below) during the E&E phase, but it will not be able to apply that policy after the E&E phase.

The IASB believed that waiving these requirements in IFRS 6 would 'detract from the relevance and reliability of an entity's financial statements to an unacceptable degree'. *[IFRS 6.BC23]*.

3.2.2 Options for an exploration and evaluation policy

Entities active in the extractive industries have followed, and continue to follow, a large variety of accounting practices for E&E expenditure, which range 'from deferring on the balance sheet nearly all exploration and evaluation expenditure to recognising all such expenditure in profit or loss as incurred'. *[IFRS 6.BC17]*. As mentioned earlier,

IFRS 6 provides an exemption from paragraphs 11 and 12 of IAS 8. The inference from this is that the standard 'grandfathers' all existing practices by not requiring these to have any authoritative basis. The Basis for Conclusions states that 'the Board decided that an entity could continue to follow the accounting policies that it was using when it first applied the IFRS's requirements, provided they satisfy the requirements of paragraph 10 of IAS 8 ... with some exceptions ...'. *[IFRS 6.BC22]*. These exceptions in IFRS 6, described above, have a rather more profound impact than may be obvious at first sight and, in fact, instead of allowing previous national GAAP accounting policies, IFRS 6 effectively prohibits many of them.

There are several methods adopted by oil and gas companies (and modified by some mining companies) to account for E&E costs. These include successful efforts, full cost and area of interest accounting. These methods have evolved through the use of previous GAAPs and industry practice. While these terms and methods (or similar methods) are commonly used in the sector, none of these is specifically referred to in IFRS.

We explore below each of these methods and consider to what extent they are compliant with the requirements of IFRS.

3.2.3 Successful efforts method

The successful efforts methods that have been developed by different accounting standard-setters are generally based on the successful efforts concept as set out in US GAAP, under which generally only those costs that lead directly to the discovery, acquisition, or development of specific, discrete mineral resources and reserves are capitalised and become part of the capitalised costs of the cost centre. Costs that when incurred fail to meet this criterion are generally charged to expense in the period they are incurred. Some interpretations of the successful efforts concept allow entities to capitalise the cost of unsuccessful development wells.[67]

Under the successful efforts method an entity will generally consider each individual mineral lease, concession, or production sharing contract as a cost centre.

When an entity applies the successful efforts method under IFRS, it will need to account for prospecting costs incurred before the E&E phase under IAS 16 or IAS 38. As economic benefits are highly uncertain at this stage of a project, prospecting costs will typically be expensed as incurred. Costs incurred to acquire undeveloped mineral rights, however, should be capitalised under IFRS if an entity expects an inflow of future economic benefits.

To the extent that costs are incurred within the E&E phase of a project, IFRS 6 does not prescribe any recognition and measurement rules. Therefore, it would be acceptable for such costs to be recorded as assets and written off when it is determined that the costs will not lead to economic benefits or to be expensed as incurred if the outcome is uncertain. Deferred costs of an undeveloped mineral right may be depreciated over some determinable period, subject to an impairment test each period with the amount of impairment charged to expense, or an entity may choose to carry forward the deferred costs of the undeveloped mineral right until the entity determines whether the property contains mineral reserves.[68] However, E&E assets should no longer be classified as such when the technical feasibility and commercial viability of extracting mineral resources are demonstrable. *[IFRS 6.17]*. At that time the asset should be tested for impairment under IAS 36, reclassified in the statement of financial position and accounted for under IAS 16 or IAS 38. If it is determined that no commercial reserves are present, then the costs capitalised should be expensed. Costs incurred after the E&E phase should be accounted for in accordance with the applicable IFRSs (i.e. IAS 16 and IAS 38).

It is worth noting that with the emergence of unconventional resource E&E projects, such as shale, coal seam and tight oil or gas, the potential timeframe to determine the technical feasibility and commercial viability of a resource can be considerably longer than that of a conventional resource. This is primarily due to the scale of work required to determine the technical feasibility and commercial viability of these more complex and/or less accessible resources in a higher cost environment. Such feasibility determinations may include the drilling and analysing of a significant number of wells over an extended period of time. As such, the overall success of a drilling campaign targeting unconventional resources may not be determined until completion of the campaign – as opposed to the more common well by well basis that is often the case for conventional projects.

Therefore, the costs incurred on unconventional projects over an extended E&E campaign, may be carried forward under existing policies adopted, including capitalisation under a successful efforts policy that permits such treatment, until such time as the broader resource body is deemed to be either successful or unsuccessful.

The essence of most successful efforts approaches is that costs are capitalised pending evaluation, and this would be acceptable under IFRS.

The following extract from the financial statements of Premier Oil illustrates a typical successful efforts method accounting policy applied under IFRS.

Extract 41.2: Premier Oil plc (2015)

ACCOUNTING POLICIES [extract]

For the year ended 31 December 2015

Oil and gas assets [extract]

The Company applies the successful efforts method of accounting for exploration and evaluation ('E&E') costs, having regard to the requirements of IFRS 6 – 'Exploration for and Evaluation of Mineral Resources'.

(a) Exploration and evaluation assets

Under the successful efforts method of accounting, all licence acquisition, exploration and appraisal costs are initially capitalised in well, field or specific exploration cost centres as appropriate, pending determination. Expenditure incurred during the various exploration and appraisal phases is then written off unless commercial reserves have been established or the determination process has not been completed.

Pre-licence costs

Costs incurred prior to having obtained the legal rights to explore an area are expensed directly to the income statement as they are incurred.

Exploration and evaluation costs

Costs of E&E are initially capitalised as E&E assets. Payments to acquire the legal right to explore, costs of technical services and studies, seismic acquisition, exploratory drilling and testing are capitalised as intangible E&E assets.

Tangible assets used in E&E activities (such as the Group's vehicles, drilling rigs, seismic equipment and other property, plant and equipment used by the Company's exploration function) are classified as property, plant and equipment. However, to the extent that such a tangible asset is consumed in developing an intangible E&E asset, the amount reflecting that consumption is recorded as part of the cost of the intangible asset. Such intangible costs include directly attributable overhead, including the depreciation of property, plant and equipment utilised in E&E activities, together with the cost of other materials consumed during the exploration and evaluation phases.

E&E costs are not amortised prior to the conclusion of appraisal activities.

Treatment of E&E assets at conclusion of appraisal activities

Intangible E&E assets related to each exploration licence/prospect are carried forward, until the existence (or otherwise) of commercial reserves has been determined subject to certain limitations including review for indications of impairment. If commercial reserves have been discovered, the carrying value, after any impairment loss, of the relevant E&E assets, is then reclassified as development and production assets, once a field development plan has been approved or a gas sales agreement has been signed. If, however, commercial reserves have not been found, the capitalised costs are charged to expense after conclusion of appraisal activities.

(b) Development and production assets

Development and production assets are accumulated generally on a field-by-field basis and represent the cost of developing the commercial reserves discovered and bringing them into production, together with the E&E expenditures incurred in finding commercial reserves transferred from intangible E&E assets, as outlined in accounting policy (a) on the previous page.

The cost of development and production assets also includes the cost of acquisitions and purchases of such assets, directly attributable overheads, finance costs capitalised, and the cost of recognising provisions for future restoration and decommissioning.

> **Depreciation of producing assets**
>
> The net book values of producing assets are depreciated generally on a field-by-field basis using the unit-of-production method by reference to the ratio of production in the year and the related commercial (proved and probable) reserves of the field, taking into account future development expenditures necessary to bring those reserves into production.
>
> Producing assets are generally grouped with other assets that are dedicated to serving the same reserves for depreciation purposes, but are depreciated separately from producing assets that serve other reserves.
>
> Pipelines are depreciated on a unit-of-throughput basis.

3.2.4 Full cost method

The full cost method under most national GAAPs required all costs incurred in prospecting, acquiring mineral interests, exploration, appraisal, development, and construction to be accumulated in large cost centres, e.g. individual countries, groups of countries, or the entire world.[69] However, although an entity is permitted by IFRS 6 to develop an accounting policy without reference to other IFRSs or to the hierarchy, as described at 3.2.1 above, IFRS 6 cannot be extrapolated or applied by analogy to permit application of the full cost method outside the E&E phase. This was confirmed by the Interpretations Committee in January 2006.[70]

There are several other areas in which application of the full cost method under IFRS is restricted because:

- IFRS 6 requires E&E assets to be classified as tangible or intangible assets according to the nature of the assets. *[IFRS 6.15]*. In other words, even when an entity accounts for E&E costs in relatively large pools, it will still need to distinguish between tangible and intangible assets.
- While the full cost method under most national GAAPs requires the application of some form of 'ceiling test', IFRS 6 requires – when impairment indicators are present – an impairment test to be performed in accordance with IAS 36 (although in accordance with IFRS 6, E&E assets can be allocated to CGUs or groups of CGUs (which may include producing CGUs), provided certain criteria are met – see 3.5.2 below for further information).
- Once the technical feasibility and commercial viability of extracting mineral resources are demonstrable, IFRS 6 requires E&E assets to be tested for impairment under IAS 36 and reclassified in the statement of financial position and accounted for under IAS 16 or IAS 38. *[IFRS 6.17]*. This means that it is not possible to account for successful and unsuccessful projects within one cost centre or pool.

For these reasons it is not possible to apply the full cost method of accounting under IFRS without making very significant modifications in the application of the method. An entity might want to use the full cost method as its starting point in developing its accounting policy for E&E assets under IFRS. However, it will rarely be appropriate to describe the resulting accounting policy as a 'full cost method' because key elements of the full cost method are not permitted under IFRS.

In July 2009, the IASB published an amendment to IFRS 1 – *Additional Exemptions for First-time Adopters (Amendments to IFRS 1)*, which introduced a first-time adoption exemption for first-time adopters that accounted under their previous GAAP for 'exploration and development costs for oil and gas properties in the development or production phases ... in cost centres that include all properties in a large geographical area' (i.e. the full cost method).[71] Under the exemption, a first-time adopter may elect to measure oil and gas assets at the date of transition to IFRSs on a deemed cost basis (see Chapter 5 at 5.5.3), but does not permit continued application of the previous GAAP accounting policy.

3.2.5 Area-of-interest method

The area-of-interest method is an accounting concept by which 'costs incurred for individual geological or geographical areas that have characteristics conducive to containing a mineral reserve are deferred as assets pending determination of whether commercial reserves are found. If the area of interest is found to contain commercial reserves, the accumulated costs are capitalised. If the area is found to contain no commercial reserves, the accumulated costs are charged to expense.'[72]

Some consider the area-of-interest method to be a version of the successful efforts method that uses an area-of-interest, rather than an individual licence, as its unit of account. Others believe that the area-of-interest method is more akin to the full cost method applied on an area-of-interest basis.[73] 'Under the area-of-interest concept, all costs identified with an area of interest would be deferred and capitalised if commercial reserves are later determined to exist in the area. However, costs incurred up to the point that an area of interest is identified (prospecting costs) are often charged to expense by those who consider that they are applying the area-of-interest concept. Costs of individual unsuccessful activities incurred on a specific area of interest, such as drilling an exploratory well that finds no reserves, are accumulated as part of the total cost of the area of interest.'[74]

While IFRS 6 will often not permit all aspects of an area-of-interest method defined by a national GAAP, an entity that uses relatively small areas of interest may be able to implement the method in a meaningful way under IFRS. The area-of-interest method is more common in the mining sector than in the oil and gas sector. Still, there are some entities that apply the method to oil and gas activities.

Extract 41.3: BHP Billiton plc (2015)

43 Significant accounting policies [extract]

(f) Exploration and evaluation expenditure

Exploration and evaluation activity involves the search for mineral and petroleum resources, the determination of technical feasibility and the assessment of commercial viability of an identified resource. Exploration and evaluation activity includes:

- researching and analysing historical exploration data;
- gathering exploration data through topographical, geochemical and geophysical studies;
- exploratory drilling, trenching and sampling;
- determining and examining the volume and grade of the resource;
- surveying transportation and infrastructure requirements;
- conducting market and finance studies.

Administration costs that are not directly attributable to a specific exploration area are charged to the income statement. Initial payments for the acquisition of intangible lease assets are capitalised and amortised over the term of the permit.

Exploration and evaluation expenditure (including amortisation of capitalised licence and lease costs) is charged to the income statement as incurred except in the following circumstances, in which case the expenditure may be capitalised:

- In respect of minerals activities:
  - The exploration and evaluation activity is within an area of interest which was previously acquired as an asset acquisition or in a business combination and measured at fair value on acquisition; or
  - The existence of a commercially viable mineral deposit has been established.
- In respect of petroleum activities:
  - The exploration and evaluation activity is within an area of interest for which it is expected that the expenditure will be recouped by future exploitation or sale; or
  - Exploration and evaluation activity has not reached a stage which permits a reasonable assessment of the existence of commercially recoverable reserves.

Capitalised exploration and evaluation expenditure considered to be a tangible asset is recorded as a component of property, plant and equipment at cost less impairment charges. Otherwise, it is recorded as an intangible asset (such as certain licence and lease arrangements). In determining whether the purchase of an exploration licence or lease is an intangible asset or a component of property, plant and equipment, consideration is given to the substance of the item acquired not its legal form. Licences or leases purchased, which allow exploration over an extended period of time, meet the definition of an intangible exploration lease asset where they cannot be reasonably associated with a known resource (minerals) or reserves (petroleum). All capitalised exploration and evaluation expenditure is monitored for indications of impairment. When a potential impairment is indicated, assessment is performed for each area of interest in conjunction with the group of operating assets (representing a cash-generating unit) to which the exploration is attributed. Exploration areas in which reserves have been discovered but require major capital expenditure before production can begin, are continually evaluated to ensure that commercial quantities of reserves exist or to ensure that additional exploration work is under way or planned. To the extent that capitalised expenditure is no longer expected to be recovered, it is charged to the income statement.

44 Application of accounting estimates, assumptions and judgements [extract]

Application of critical accounting policies and estimates [extract]

Exploration and evaluation expenditure

The Group's accounting policy for exploration and evaluation expenditure results in certain items of expenditure being capitalised for an area of interest where it is considered likely to be recoverable by future exploitation or sale or where the activities have not reached a stage which permits a reasonable assessment of the existence of reserves. This policy requires management to make certain estimates and assumptions as to future events and circumstances, in particular whether an economically viable extraction operation can be established. Any such estimates and assumptions may change as new information becomes available. If, after having capitalised the expenditure under the policy, a judgement is made that recovery of the expenditure is unlikely, the relevant capitalised amount will be written off to the income statement.

3.2.6 Changes in accounting policies

The standard permits a change in an entity's accounting policies for E&E expenditures only if 'the change makes the financial statements more relevant to the economic decision-making needs of users and no less reliable, or more reliable and no less relevant to those needs'. *[IFRS 6.13, BC49]*. In making such a change, an entity should judge the relevance and reliability using the criteria in IAS 8. The entity should justify the change by demonstrating that the change 'brings its financial statements closer to meeting the criteria in IAS 8, but the change need not achieve full compliance with those criteria'. *[IFRS 6.14]*.

3.3 Measurement of exploration and evaluation assets

IFRS 6 draws a distinction between measurement at recognition (i.e. the initial recognition of an E&E asset on acquisition) and measurement after recognition (i.e. the subsequent treatment of the E&E asset).

The standard requires that upon initial recognition, E&E assets should be measured at cost, *[IFRS 6.8]*, which is the same as the initial recognition requirements found in IAS 16, *[IAS 16.15]*, and IAS 38. *[IAS 38.24]*. Therefore, the question arises as to what may be included in the cost of an item. The standard contains considerable guidance on this matter, under the heading 'Elements of cost of exploration and evaluation assets' (see also 3.3.1 below).

After initial recognition IFRS 6 allows one of two alternatives to be chosen as the accounting policy for E&E assets that it must apply consistently to all E&E assets. The first is the 'cost model' whereby the item is carried at cost less impairment. *[IFRS 6.12]*. Entities that apply the 'cost model' should therefore develop an accounting policy within the constraints of IFRS 6 (see 3.2.1 above). As a result, an entity will either develop an accounting policy based on the successful efforts type of method or area-of-interest type of method (see 3.2.3 and 3.2.5 above) – that requires capitalisation of E&E costs pending evaluation; or develop a policy similar to the full cost type of method, which capitalises all E&E costs (successful and unsuccessful), although it is not possible to continue using this method outside the E&E phase (see 3.2.4 above).

The alternative is the 'revaluation model', which is not defined in IFRS 6 itself. Instead, the standard requires an entity to classify E&E assets as tangible or intangible assets (see 3.4 below) and apply the IAS 16 revaluation model to the tangible assets and the IAS 38 revaluation model to the intangible assets (see Chapter 18 at 6 and Chapter 17 at 8.2). *[IFRS 6.12]*. Practically what this means is that E&E classified as intangible assets may not be revalued, since the IAS 38 revaluation model may only be applied to intangible assets that are traded in an active market. *[IAS 38.72, 75, IFRS 6.BC29-BC30]*.

3.3.1 Types of expenditure in the exploration and evaluation phase

The standard requires an entity to determine an accounting policy specifying which expenditures are recognised as E&E assets and apply the policy consistently. Such an accounting policy should take into account the degree to which the expenditure can be associated with finding specific mineral resources. Types of expenditure include:

(a) acquisition of rights to explore;

(b) topographical, geological, geochemical and geophysical studies;

(c) exploratory drilling;

(d) trenching;

(e) sampling; and

(f) activities in relation to evaluating the technical feasibility and commercial viability of extracting a mineral resource. *[IFRS 6.9]*.

This list is not intended to be exhaustive.

In permitting geological and geophysical costs (G&G costs) to be included in the initial measurement of E&E assets, IFRS differs from US GAAP – ASC 932 – *Extractive Activities – Oil and Gas*, which does not permit capitalisation of G&G costs,[75] and may differ from the requirements under other national standards.

IFRS 6 allows an accounting policy choice as to how to treat expenditures on administration and other general overhead costs; however, the chosen policy should be consistent with one of the treatments available under other IFRSs, i.e. expense or capitalise. *[IFRS 6.BC28]*. This is because there are inconsistencies between IAS 16 (which does not allow such costs to be capitalised), IAS 2 (which requires capitalisation of production overheads but not general administration) and IAS 38 (which only allows capitalisation if directly attributable to bringing the asset into use, otherwise capitalisation is prohibited).

Expenditures related to the development of mineral resources should not be recognised as E&E assets. Instead, the IASB's *Conceptual Framework* and IAS 38 should be applied in developing guidance on accounting for such assets. *[IFRS 6.10]*. IFRS does not define 'development of mineral resources', but notes that 'development of a mineral resource once the technical feasibility and commercial viability of extracting the mineral resource had been determined was an example of the development phase of an internal project'. *[IFRS 6.BC27]*. While this is not a full definition, in practice this means that until a feasibility study is complete and a development is approved, accumulated costs are considered E&E assets and are accounted for under IFRS 6. The timing of transferring expenditure from the exploration phase to the development phase is discussed in further detail at 3.4.1 below.

The standard specifically requires the application of IAS 37 – *Provisions, Contingent Liabilities and Contingent Assets* – to any obligations for removal and restoration that are incurred during a particular period as a consequence of having undertaken the exploration for and evaluation of mineral resources. *[IFRS 6.11]*. Although IFRS 6 did not make a corresponding amendment to the scope of IFRIC 1 – *Changes in Existing Decommissioning, Restoration and Similar Liabilities* – which applies to such liabilities when they are recognised in property, plant and equipment under IAS 16, we believe that the interpretation should also be applied in relation to E&E assets. However, if the E&E costs were originally expensed, then the future costs of any related removal and restoration obligations should also be expensed.

The extract below from Xstrata illustrates a typical accounting policy for E&E assets for a mining company.

Extract 41.4: Glencore Xstrata plc (2015)

Notes to the financial statements [extract]

1. ACCOUNTING POLICIES [extract]

Exploration and evaluation expenditure

Exploration and evaluation expenditure relates to costs incurred in the exploration and evaluation of potential mineral and petroleum resources and includes costs such as exploration and production licences, researching and analysing historical exploration data, exploratory drilling, trenching, sampling and the costs of pre-feasibility studies. Exploration and evaluation expenditure for each area of interest, other than that acquired from another entity, is charged to the consolidated statement of income as incurred except when the expenditure is expected to be recouped from future exploitation or sale of the area of interest and it is planned to continue with active and significant operations in relation to the area, or at the reporting period end, the activity has not reached a stage which permits a reasonable assessment of the existence of commercially recoverable reserves, in which case the expenditure is capitalised. As the intangible component (i.e. licences) represents an insignificant and indistinguishable portion of the overall expected tangible amount to be incurred and recouped from future exploitation, these costs along with other capitalised exploration and evaluation expenditure are recorded as a component of property, plant and equipment. Purchased exploration and evaluation assets are recognised at their fair value at acquisition.

As the capitalised exploration and evaluation expenditure asset is not available for use, it is not depreciated. All capitalised exploration and evaluation expenditure is monitored for indications of impairment. Where a potential impairment is indicated, an assessment is performed for each area of interest or at the CGU level. To the extent that capitalised expenditure is not expected to be recovered it is charged to the consolidated statement of income.

Administration costs that are not directly attributable to a specific exploration area are charged to the consolidated statement of income. Licence costs paid in connection with a right to explore in an existing exploration area are capitalised and amortised over the term of the permit.

The extract below from BP illustrates an accounting policy for E&E assets for an oil and gas company.

Extract 41.5: BP p.l.c. (2015)

Notes on financial statements [extract]

1. Significant accounting policies, judgements, estimates and assumptions [extract]

Oil and natural gas exploration, appraisal and development expenditure

Oil and natural gas exploration, appraisal and development expenditure is accounted for using the principles of the successful efforts method of accounting as described below.

Licence and property acquisition costs

Exploration licence and leasehold property acquisition costs are capitalized within intangible assets and are reviewed at each reporting date to confirm that there is no indication that the carrying amount exceeds the recoverable amount. This review includes confirming that exploration drilling is still under way or planned or that it has been determined, or work is under way to determine, that the discovery is economically viable based on a range of technical and commercial considerations, and sufficient progress is being made on establishing development plans and timing. If no future activity is planned, the remaining balance of the licence and property acquisition costs is written off. Lower value licences are pooled and amortized on a straight-line basis over the estimated period of exploration. Upon recognition of proved reserves and internal approval for development, the relevant expenditure is transferred to property, plant and equipment.

> **Exploration and appraisal expenditure**
>
> Geological and geophysical exploration costs are recognized as an expense as incurred. Costs directly associated with an exploration well are initially capitalized as an intangible asset until the drilling of the well is complete and the results have been evaluated. These costs include employee remuneration, materials and fuel used, rig costs and payments made to contractors. If potentially commercial quantities of hydrocarbons are not found, the exploration well costs are written off as a dry hole. If hydrocarbons are found and, subject to further appraisal activity, are likely to be capable of commercial development, the costs continue to be carried as an asset. If it is determined that development will not occur then the costs are expensed.
>
> Costs directly associated with appraisal activity undertaken to determine the size, characteristics and commercial potential of a reservoir following the initial discovery of hydrocarbons, including the costs of appraisal wells where hydrocarbons were not found, are initially capitalized as an intangible asset. When proved reserves of oil and natural gas are determined and development is approved by management, the relevant expenditure is transferred to property, plant and equipment.

3.3.2 *Capitalisation of borrowing costs in the exploration and evaluation phase*

IAS 23 – *Borrowing Costs* – requires capitalisation of borrowing costs that are directly attributable to the acquisition, construction or production of a 'qualifying asset' as part of the cost of that asset. *[IAS 23.8]*. An E&E asset will generally meet the definition of a qualifying asset as it 'necessarily takes a substantial period of time to get ready for its intended use or sale'. *[IAS 23.5]*. However, IAS 23 requires capitalisation of borrowing costs only when it is probable that they will result in future economic benefits to the entity and the costs can be measured reliably. *[IAS 23.9]*. Unlike IAS 23, IFRS 6 permits capitalisation of E&E assets even when it is not probable that they will result in future economic benefits. Unless an entity's E&E project has resulted in the classification of mineral resources as proven or probable, it is unlikely that future economic benefits from that project can be considered probable. In these circumstances, it is consistent with the requirements of IFRS 6 and IAS 23 to capitalise an E&E asset but not capitalise borrowing costs in respect of it.

3.4 Presentation and classification

E&E assets should be classified consistently as either tangible or intangible assets in accordance with the nature of the assets acquired. *[IFRS 6.15]*. For example, drilling rights should be presented as intangible assets, whereas vehicles and drilling rigs are tangible assets. A tangible asset that is used in developing an intangible asset should still be presented as a tangible asset. However, to the 'extent that a tangible asset is consumed in developing an intangible asset, the amount reflecting that consumption is part of the cost of the intangible asset'. For example, the depreciation of a drilling rig would be capitalised as part of the intangible E&E asset that represents the costs incurred on active exploration projects. *[IFRS 6.16, BC33]*.

3.4.1 *Reclassification of E&E assets*

E&E assets should no longer be classified as such when 'technical feasibility and commercial viability of extracting a mineral resource are demonstrable'.

Determining when technical feasibility and commercial viability have been demonstrated may involve significant judgement, particularly in relation to complex assets or projects where feasibility assessment may be ongoing over an extended period of time: for example Liquefied Natural Gas (LNG) projects, unconventional assets, large scale, technically challenging projects, or where significant upfront investment in long lead items is required.

A final investment decision being approved is often a common signal that technical feasibility and commercial viability have been determined. However, absent this, other factors may also need to be considered, such as the booking of significant quantities of commercial reserves, approval of budgeted expenditure to commence commercial development activities or the actual commencement of expenditure on development activities. It should be noted that both technical feasibility and commercial viability must be demonstrated before an asset can be transferred out of E&E. Activities that occur prior to this point which are aimed at assessing the viability of a resource, may still be regarded as E&E in nature and must be accounted for accordingly.

Before reclassification, E&E assets should be assessed for impairment individually or as part of a cash-generating unit and any impairment loss should be recognised. *[IFRS 6.17]*.

3.5 Impairment

As E&E assets do not generate cash inflows and there is insufficient information about the mineral resources in a specific area for an entity to make reasonable estimates of an E&E asset's recoverable amount, it is not possible to estimate either fair value less costs of disposal ('FVLCD') or value in use ('VIU'), the two measures of recoverable amount in IAS 36. Therefore under IFRS 6, the assessment of impairment should be triggered by changes in facts and circumstances. However once an entity had determined that there is an impairment trigger for an E&E asset, IAS 36 should be used to measure, present and disclose that impairment in the financial statements. This is subject to the special requirements with respect to the level at which impairment is assessed. *[IFRS 6.BC37]*.

IFRS 6 makes two important modifications to IAS 36:

- it defines separate impairment testing 'triggers' for E&E assets; and
- it allows groups of cash-generating units to be used in impairment testing. *[IFRS 6.18-20]*.

3.5.1 Impairment testing 'triggers'

E&E assets should be assessed for impairment when facts and circumstances suggest that the carrying amount of an E&E asset may exceed its recoverable amount. *[IFRS 6.18]*. Under IFRS 6 one or more of the following facts and circumstances could indicate that an impairment test is required. The list is not intended to be exhaustive:

(a) the period for which the entity has the right to explore in the specific area has expired during the period or will expire in the near future, and is not expected to be renewed;

(b) substantive expenditure on further exploration for and evaluation of mineral resources in the specific area is neither budgeted nor planned;

(c) exploration for and evaluation of mineral resources in the specific area have not led to the discovery of commercially viable quantities of mineral resources and the entity has decided to discontinue such activities in the specific area; and

(d) sufficient data exist to indicate that, although a development in the specific area is likely to proceed, the carrying amount of the E&E asset is unlikely to be recovered in full from successful development or by sale. *[IFRS 6.20]*.

Finding that an exploratory or development well does not contain oil or gas in commercial quantities (i.e. finding a 'dry hole') is not listed in IFRS 6 as an impairment indicator. If finding a dry hole marks the end of budgeted or planned exploration activity, indicator (b) above would require impairment testing under IAS 36. Similarly, if the dry hole led to a decision that activities in the area would be discontinued, indicator (c) would require that an impairment test be performed, and indicator (d) requires an entity to do an impairment test if it is unlikely that it will recover the E&E costs from successful development or sale. However, absent one of these indicators being met, drilling a dry hole would not necessarily trigger an impairment test. For example, if the first well in a 3 well campaign is a dry hole, but the entity still intends to drill the remaining 2 wells, an impairment trigger may not be met.

3.5.2 *Specifying the level at which E&E assets are assessed for impairment*

When deciding the level at which E&E assets should be assessed, rather than introduce a special cash-CGU for E&E assets, IFRS 6 allows CGUs to be aggregated in a way consistent with the approach applied to goodwill in IAS 36. *[IFRS 6.BC40-BC47]*. Therefore, an entity should determine an accounting policy for allocating E&E assets to CGUs or to CGU groups for the purpose of assessing them for impairment. *[IFRS 6.21]*. Each CGU or group of CGUs to which an E&E asset is allocated should not be larger than an operating segment (which is smaller than a reportable segment) determined in accordance with IFRS 8 – *Operating Segments*. *[IFRS 6.21]*. See also Chapter 20 at 4.2.4.

Hence, the level identified by an entity for the purposes of testing E&E assets for impairment may be comprised of one or more CGUs. *[IFRS 6.22]*.

3.5.3 Cash-generating units comprising successful and unsuccessful E&E projects

IFRS 6 does not specifically address whether successful and unsuccessful E&E projects can be combined in a single CGU (which will occur under full cost accounting and may occur under area of interest accounting). There are some issues to consider before doing this:

- Regardless of whether there is an impairment trigger (see 3.5.1 above), IFRS 6 requires E&E assets to be tested for impairment before reclassification when the technical feasibility and commercial viability of extracting a mineral resource are demonstrable. *[IFRS 6.17]*. That means that the successful conclusion of a small E&E project and its reclassification out of E&E would result in an impairment test of a much larger CGU and possible recognition of an impairment loss on that larger CGU.
- Successful E&E projects should be reclassified as tangible or intangible assets under IAS 16 and IAS 38, respectively. *[IFRS 6.15]*. Therefore, a CGU comprising both successful and unsuccessful E&E projects would be subject to the impairment triggers in both IFRS 6 and IAS 36. This would significantly increase the frequency of impairment testing. *[IFRS 6.20, IAS 36.8-17]*.
- An entity should carefully consider the consequences of including several E&E projects in a CGU, because the unsuccessful conclusion of one project would usually trigger an impairment test of the entire CGU. *[IFRS 6.20]*.

3.5.4 Order of impairment testing

CGUs often contain other assets as well as E&E assets. When developing IFRS 6, ED 6 specifically stated that such other assets should be tested for impairment first, in accordance with IAS 36, before testing the CGU inclusive of the E&E assets.[76] However, IFRS 6 does not specifically address this topic. Despite this, we believe that as the impairment test is completed in accordance with IAS 36, and a similar approach is adopted as that applied to goodwill, the order of the impairment testing as set out in IAS 36 would apply. That is, an entity would test the underlying assets/CGU without the E&E assets first, recognise any write down (if applicable) and then test the CGU/CGU group with the E&E assets allocated.

3.5.5 Additional considerations if E&E assets are impaired

In some circumstances an entity that recognises an impairment of an E&E asset must also decide whether or not to derecognise the asset because no future economic benefits are expected, as illustrated in Example 41.1 below.

Example 41.1: Impairment losses on E&E assets

Entity A's exploration activity in a specific area does not discover oil and/or gas resources. Therefore, A recognises an impairment of the cash-generating unit and derecognises the related E&E assets.

Entity B's exploration activity in a specific area leads to the discovery of a significant quantity of resources, but these are located in a complex reservoir. Therefore, at present the costs of extraction of the discovered resources do not justify the construction of the required infrastructure. Nevertheless, B's management believes that the surrounding area has strong potential to yield other discoveries on other geological structures and it is considered possible that the required infrastructure will be constructed in the future, although at this stage management has no plans to undertake further exploration activity. Entity B recognises an impairment of the E&E assets, but since it expects future economic benefits the related E&E assets are not derecognised.

If an entity concludes that production is not technically feasible or commercially viable, that provides evidence that the related E&E asset needs to be tested for impairment. It is also possible that such evidence may indicate that no future economic benefits are expected from such assets and therefore any remaining assets should be derecognised. When considering the two examples above, in Entity A's situation, no oil and/or gas resources were discovered and based on current plans, no future economic benefits were expected from the related E&E assets so they were derecognised. Whereas in Entity B's situation, while oil and/or gas resources were discovered, extraction was not commercially viable at this stage. So while an impairment was recognised, the remaining assets were not derecognised as management did expect future economic benefits to flow from such assets.

Although IFRS 6 does not specifically deal with derecognition of E&E assets, the entity should derecognise the E&E asset because the asset is no longer in the exploration and evaluation phase and hence outside the scope of IFRS 6 and other asset standards such as IAS 16 and IAS 38 would require derecognition under those circumstances. Once derecognised, the costs of an E&E asset that have been written off cannot be re-recognised as part of a new E&E asset, so unlike an impairment, the write off is permanent.

3.5.6 *Income statement treatment of E&E write downs – impairment or exploration expense*

In some circumstances, it may be unclear whether an E&E asset is impaired, or whether a write off of unsuccessful exploration is required. In an unconventional project, or in circumstances where costs have been carried forward for some time pending determination of technical feasibility and commercial viability, judgement will be required in concluding on the most appropriate income statement presentation. Key considerations may include whether the objectives of drilling or other expenditure programs have been met, whether the indicative impairment triggers in IFRS 6 have been met, and management's future intentions for the asset.

3.5.7 *Reversal of impairment losses*

Any impairment loss on an E&E asset recognised in accordance with IFRS 6 needs to be reversed if there is evidence that the loss no longer exists or has decreased. The entity must apply the requirements specified in IAS 36 for reversing an impairment loss (see Chapter 20 at 6). *[IFRS 6.BC48, IAS 36.109-123]*.

3.6 Disclosure

To identify and explain 'the amounts recognised in its financial statements arising from the exploration for and evaluation of mineral resources', *[IFRS 6.23]*, an entity should disclose:

(a) its accounting policies for exploration and evaluation expenditures including the recognition of exploration and evaluation assets; and

(b) the amounts of assets, liabilities, income and expense and operating and investing cash flows arising from the exploration for and evaluation of mineral resources. *[IFRS 6.24]*.

The extract below from Tullow Oil's 2015 financial statements illustrates the disclosures required by IFRS 6.

Extract 41.6: Tullow Oil plc (2015)

GROUP INCOME STATEMENT [extract]
YEAR ENDED 31 DECEMBER 2015

	Notes	2015 $m	2014 $m
Continuing activities			
Sales revenue	2	**1,606.6**	2,212.9
Cost of sales	4	**(1,015.3)**	(1,116.7)
Gross Profit		**591.3**	1,096.2
Administrative expenses	4	**(193.6)**	(192.4)
Restructuring cost	4	**(40.8)**	
Loss on disposal	9	**(56.5)**	(482.4)
Goodwill impairment	10	**(53.7)**	(132.8)
Exploration costs written off	11	**(748.9)**	(1,657.3)
Impairment of property, plant and equipment, net	12	**(406.0)**	(595.9)
Provision for onerous service contracts	23	**(185.5)**	–
Operating loss	4	**(1,093.7)**	(1,964.6)
(Loss)/gain on hedging instruments	21	**(58.8)**	50.8
Finance revenue	2	**4.2**	9.6
Finance costs	5	**(149.0)**	(143.2)
Loss from continuing activities before tax		**(1,297.3)**	(2,047.4)
Income tax credit	6	**260.4**	407.5
Loss for the year from continuing activities		**(1,036.9)**	(1,639.9)
Attributable to:			
Owners of the Company		**(1,034.8)**	(1,555.7)
Non-controlling interest	26	**(2.1)**	(84.2)
		(1,036.9)	(1,639.9)
Loss per ordinary share from continuing activities	8	**¢**	¢
Basic		**(113.6)**	(170.9)
Diluted		**(113.6)**	(170.9)

GROUP BALANCE SHEET [extract]
AS AT 31 DECEMBER 2015

	Notes	2015 $m	2014 $m
ASSETS			
Non-current assets			
Goodwill	10	**164.0**	217.7
Intangible exploration and evaluation assets	11	**3,400.0**	3,660.8
Property, plant and equipment	12	**5,204.4**	4,887.0
Investments	13	**1.0**	1.0
Other non-current assets	14	**223.4**	119.7
Derivative financial instruments	21	**218.7**	193.9
Deferred tax assets	24	**295.3**	255.0
		9,506.8	9,335.1

GROUP CASH FLOW STATEMENT [extract]
YEAR ENDED 31 DECEMBER 2015

	Notes	2015 $m	2014 $m
Cash flows from investing activities			
Proceeds from disposals	9	**55.8**	21.3
Purchase of intangible exploration and evaluation assets		**(647.6)**	(1,255.1)
Purchase of property, plant and equipment		**(1,464.8)**	(1,098.3)
Interest received		**4.2**	4.6
Net cash used in investing activities		**(2,052.4)**	(2,327.5)

ACCOUNTING POLICIES [extract]
YEAR ENDED 31 DECEMBER 2015

(l) Exploration, evaluation and production assets

The Group adopts the successful efforts method of accounting for exploration and evaluation costs. Pre-licence costs are expensed in the period in which they are incurred. All licence acquisition, exploration and evaluation costs and directly attributable administration costs are initially capitalised in cost centres by well, field or exploration area, as appropriate. Interest payable is capitalised insofar as it relates to specific development activities.

These costs are then written off as exploration costs in the income statement unless commercial reserves have been established or the determination process has not been completed and there are no indications of impairment.

All field development costs are capitalised as property, plant and equipment. Property, plant and equipment related to production activities is amortised in accordance with the Group's depletion and amortisation accounting policy.

Cash consideration received on farm-down of exploration and evaluation assets is credited against the carrying value of the asset.

NOTES TO GROUP FINANCIAL STATEMENTS [extract]
YEAR ENDED 31 DECEMBER 2015
Note 11. Intangible exploration and evaluation assets [extract]

	Notes	2015 $m	2014 $m
At 1 January		**3,660.8**	4,148.3
Additions	1	**626.3**	1,405.5
Disposals	9	**(5.2)**	(26.8)
Amounts written-off		**(748.9)**	(1,657.3)
Amounts written-off previously classified as held for sale		**–**	(5.1)
Write-off associated with Norway contingent consideration provision	23	**–**	(88.8)
Net transfer to assets held for sale	18	**–**	(13.8)
Transfer to property, plant and equipment	12	**(63.6)**	–
Currency translation adjustments		**(69.4)**	(101.2)
At 31 December		**3,400.0**	3,660.8

An entity should treat E&E assets as a separate class of assets and make the disclosures required by IAS 16 and IAS 38 for tangible E&E assets and intangible E&E assets, respectively. *[IFRS 6.25, BC53]*.

3.6.1 Statement of cash flows

IAS 7 – *Statement of Cash Flows* – states that only expenditures that result in a recognised asset in the statement of financial position are eligible for classification as investing activities. *[IAS 7.16]*. The IASB specifically notes that 'the exemption in IFRS 6 applies only to recognition and measurement of exploration and evaluation assets, not to the classification of related expenditures in the statement of cash flows'. *[IFRS 6.BC23B]*. This means that an entity that expenses E&E expenditure will not be able to classify the associated cash flows as arising from investing activities.

4 UNIT OF ACCOUNT

One of the key issues in the development of accounting standards and in the selection of accounting policies by preparers, is deciding the level at which an entity should separately account for assets, i.e. what is the 'unit of account'? The definition of the unit of account has significant accounting consequences, as can be seen in the example below.

Example 41.2: Unit of account – dry well

An oil and gas company concludes, based on a number of exploration wells, that oil and gas reserves are present. However, it needs to drill a number of delineation wells to determine the amount of reserves present in the field. The first delineation well that is drilled is a dry hole, i.e. no reserves are found.

There are two ways of looking at the cost of drilling the dry hole:

- the dry hole provides important information about the extent of the oil and gas reserves present in the oil field and should therefore be capitalised as part of the larger oil field; or
- the dry hole will not produce oil in the future and in the absence of future economic benefits the costs should be expensed immediately.

This example suggests that assets or actions that have no value or meaning at one level may actually be valuable and necessary at another level.

The unit of account plays a significant role in:

(1) recognition and derecognition of assets;

(2) determining the rate of depreciation or amortisation;

(3) deciding whether or not certain costs should be capitalised;

(4) undertaking impairment testing;

(5) determining the substance of transactions;

(6) application of the measurement model subsequent to recognition of the asset; and

(7) determining the level of detail of the disclosures required.

The decisions about the unit of account will consider, *inter alia*, cost/benefits and materiality, whether the items are capable of being used separately, their useful economic lives, whether the economic benefits that the entity will derive are separable and the substance of the transaction. To some degree the choice of the unit of account will depend on industry practice, as discussed below.

In Example 41.2 above, an individual dry hole might not be considered a separate asset because individual wells are typically not capable of being used separately, their economic benefits are inseparable, the wells are similar in nature and the substance of the matter can only be understood at the level of the project as a whole. However, in concluding on whether to capitalise or expense the cost of the individual dry hole as set out in Example 41.2 above, an entity will consider its specific accounting policy and its definition of the unit of account. This is discussed further at 4.1 below.

4.1 Unit of account in the extractive industries

In the extractive industries the definition of the unit of account is particularly important in deciding whether or not certain costs may be capitalised, determining the rate of depreciation and in impairment testing. Historically entities in the extractive industries have accounted for preproduction costs using methods such as:

- successful efforts method;
- area-of-interest method; and
- full cost method.

These are discussed further at 3.2.3 – 3.2.5 above. A key issue under each of these methods is determining the appropriate unit of account, which is referred to in the industry as the 'cost centre' or 'pool'. In practice, entities would define their cost centres along geographical, political or legal boundaries or align them to the operating units in their organisation. The IASC's Issues Paper listed the following, commonly used, cost centres that have been used pre-IFRS:[77]

(a) the world;

(b) each country or group of countries in which the entity operates;

(c) each contractual or legal mineral acquisition unit, such as a lease or production sharing contract;

(d) each area of interest (geological feature, such as a mine or field, that lends itself to a unified exploration and development effort);

(e) geological units other than areas of interest (such as a basin or a geologic province); or

(f) the entity's organisational units.

IFRS does not provide industry specific guidance on determining appropriate units of account for the extractive industries. Nevertheless, we believe that in determining the unit of account an entity should take the legal rights (see (c) above) as its starting point and apply the criteria discussed above to assess whether the unit of account should be larger or smaller. The other cost centres listed above might result in a unit of account that is unjustifiably large when viewed in the light of the factors influenced by the unit of account as set out at 4 above.

The definition of 'unit of account' was considered in the Extractive Activities DP (see 1.3 above). While the DP would not need to be considered in the context of the IAS 8 hierarchy, it did draw attention to the fact that the selection of an appropriate unit of account might need to take into account the stage of the underlying activities. In particular, the DP proposed that '...the geographical boundary of the unit of account would be defined initially on the basis of the exploration rights held. As exploration, evaluation and development activities take place, the unit of account would contract progressively until it becomes no greater than a single area, or group of contiguous areas, for which the legal rights are held and which is managed separately and would be expected to generate largely independent cash flows'. The DP's view was that the components approach in IAS 16 would apply to determine the items that should be accounted for as a single asset. However, the DP suggested that an entity may decide to account for its assets using a smaller unit of account.

The thinking underlying the above proposal in the DP would be relevant in the following types of situations:

- Certain transactions in the extractive industries (e.g. carried interests arrangements) result in the creation of new legal rights out of existing legal rights. Whenever this is the case, an entity needs to assess whether such transactions give rise to new units of account. If so, the accounting policies should be applied to those new units of account rather than the previous unit/s of account.
- When an entity acquires a business that owns reserves and resources, it needs to consider whether it should define the unit of account at the level of the licence or separate ore zones or reservoirs within the licence.

Determining the unit of account is an area that requires a significant amount of judgement, which may need to be disclosed under IAS 1 – *Presentation of Financial Statements* – together with other judgements that management has made in the process of applying the entity's accounting policies and that have the most significant effect on the amounts recognised in the financial statements. *[IAS 1.122]*.

As the prevalence of unconventional oil and gas projects increases, the determination of the unit of account is becoming an increasingly common topic. With unconventional programs, the objectives of individual wells or drilling campaigns may differ to those for a conventional drilling program. It may be that the drilling of each well provides important information about the extent of the oil and gas reserves present in the oil and gas field, but multiple wells need to be drilled before a decision can be made regarding success. So unlike conventional oil and gas projects, concluding whether a well cost should be capitalised may not be possible on an individual well basis immediately after each well is drilled. In these circumstances, an entity may determine that the costs of an individual well should be carried forward pending further analysis.

5 LEGAL RIGHTS TO EXPLORE FOR, DEVELOP AND PRODUCE MINERAL PROPERTIES

An entity can acquire legal rights to explore for, develop and produce wasting resources on a mineral property by:[78]

(a) purchasing of minerals (i.e. outright ownership);

(b) obtaining a lease or concession (see 5.2 below);

(c) entering into a production-sharing contract or production-sharing agreement (see 5.3 below);

(d) entering into a pure-service contract (see 5.4 below);

(e) entering into a service contract (also called a service agreement or risk service contract) (see 5.5.1 below);

(f) entering into a joint operating agreement (see 5.6 below); and

(g) retaining an overriding royalty or other royalty interest subsequent to sale of an interest (see 5.7 below).

Although many of these are more commonly encountered in the oil and gas sector, which is reflected in many of the examples and illustrations below, they are not restricted to this sector and mining companies can and do enter into similar arrangements.

The IASC Issues Paper noted that 'in the mining sector, rights to explore for, develop, and produce minerals are often acquired by purchase of either the mineral rights alone (which does not include ownership of the land surface) or by purchase of both mineral rights and surface rights. In other cases, they are acquired through a right to mine contract, which grants the enterprise the rights to develop and mine the property and may call for a payment at the time the contract becomes effective and subsequent periodic payments. In the mining sector, rights to explore, develop, and produce minerals may also be acquired by mineral leases from private owners or from the government.'[79]

In the oil and gas sector entities usually obtain the rights to explore for, develop, and produce oil and gas through mineral leases, concession agreements, production-sharing contracts, or service contracts.[80] Arrangements similar to production sharing contracts are also becoming more common in the mining sector. The type of legal arrangement used depends to a large extent on the legal framework of the country and market practice. The main features of each of these legal rights to access mineral reserves and resources, except for the outright ownership of minerals, are discussed below.

The extract below from the financial statements of TOTAL illustrates the different types of legal arrangements that an oil and gas company may enter into to secure access to mineral reserves and resources.

Extract 41.7: TOTAL S.A. (2015)

Business overview [extract]

2. Upstream segment [extract]

2.1. Exploration & Production [extract]

2.1.5. Contractual framework of activities [extract]

Licenses, permits and contracts governing the Group's ownership of oil and gas interests have terms that vary from country to country and are generally granted by or entered into with a government entity or a state-owned company and are sometimes entered into with private owners. These agreements usually take the form of concessions or production sharing contracts.

In the framework of oil concession agreements, the oil company owns the assets and the facilities and is entitled to the entire production. In exchange, the operating risks, costs and investments are the oil company's responsibility and it agrees to remit to the relevant host country, usually the owner of the subsoil resources, a production-based royalty, income tax, and possibly other taxes that may apply under local tax legislation.

The production sharing contract ("PSC") involves a more complex legal framework than the concession agreement: it defines the terms and conditions of production sharing and sets the rules governing the cooperation between the company or consortium in possession of the license and the host country, which is generally represented by a state-owned company. The latter can thus be involved in operating decisions, cost accounting and production allocation. The consortium agrees to undertake and finance all exploration, development and production activities at its own risk. In exchange, it is entitled to a portion of the production, known as "cost oil", the sale of which is intended to cover its incurred expenses (capital and operating costs). The balance of production, known as "profit oil", is then shared in varying proportions, between the company or consortium, on the one hand, and with the host country or the state-owned company, on the other hand.

Today, concession agreements and PSCs coexist, sometimes in the same country or even on the same block. Even though there are other contractual models, TOTAL's license portfolio is comprised mainly of concession agreements.

On most licenses, the partners and authorities of the host country, often assisted by international accounting firms, perform joint venture and PSC cost audits and ensure the observance of contractual obligations.

In some countries, TOTAL has also signed contracts called "risked service contracts", which are similar to PSCs. However, the profit oil is replaced by a defined cash monetary remuneration, agreed by contract, which depends notably on field performance parameters such as the amount of barrels produced.

Oil and gas exploration and production activities are subject to authorization granted by public authorities (licenses), which are granted for specific and limited periods of time and include an obligation to relinquish a large portion, or the entire portion in case of failure, of the area covered by the license at the end of the exploration period.

TOTAL pays taxes on income generated from its oil and gas production and sales activities under its concessions, PSCs and risked service contracts, as provided for by local regulations. In addition, depending on the country, TOTAL's production and sales activities may be subject to a number of other taxes, fees and withholdings, including special petroleum taxes and fees. The taxes imposed on oil and gas production and sales activities are generally substantially higher than those imposed on other industrial or commercial businesses.

5.1 How does a mineral lease work?

In most countries the government owns all minerals and rights over those minerals, but in some other countries minerals and mineral rights can also be directly owned by individuals. While these contracts are negotiated individually, and therefore each may be different, they typically share a large number of common features, which are discussed below:

(a) the *owner/lessor* of the mineral rights retains a *royalty interest*, which entitles it to a specified percentage of the mineral produced. The lessor is normally only required to pay for its share of the severance taxes and the costs of getting the production into a marketable state, but not for any exploration and development costs. The *royalty* is either payable in cash or payable in kind. Although the lessor is normally not interested in receiving its royalty in kind, the option of receiving the royalty in kind is often included for tax purposes;

(b) the lessee obtains a *working interest* under the mineral lease, which entitles it to explore for, develop, and produce minerals from the property at its cost. The working interest can be held by more than one party, in which case a *joint operating agreement* needs to be executed (see 5.6 below);

(c) upon signing of the mineral lease agreement the lessee typically pays the lessor a *lease bonus* or *signature bonus*, which is a one-off upfront payment in exchange for the lessor's signing of the mineral lease agreement;

(d) it is in the lessor's interest for the lessee to explore the property as quickly as possible. To ensure that the lessee does not delay exploration and development unnecessarily, the following terms are typically included:
- most mineral leases define a *primary term* during which the lessee is required to commence drilling;
- normally the lessee has a *drill or exploration obligation* that must be met within a certain period. However, by paying *delay rentals* the lessee can defer commencement of drilling or exploration; and
- the mineral lease will remain in force once the obligatory drilling/exploration programme has been completed successfully and production commences, but the lease will be cancelled if activities are suspended for a prolonged period;

(e) most mineral leases provide that the lessee and the lessor have the right to assign their interest to another party without approval from the owner/lessor. This means that both the lessee and the lessor can create new rights out of existing rights (see 5.7 below);

(f) under many oil and gas lease contracts the lessee can be required to pay *shut-in royalties* when a successful well capable of commercial production has been completed, but production has not commenced within a specified time; and

(g) the lessor is typically not entitled to royalties on any minerals consumed in producing further minerals from a property.

5.2 Concessionary agreements (concessions)

Concessionary agreements or concessions are mineral leases 'under which the government owning mineral rights grants the concessionaire the right to explore, develop, and produce the minerals'.[81] However, unlike a production sharing contract (see 5.3 below), under a concessionary agreement, the extractive industries company retains title to the assets constructed during the term of the concession. Furthermore, the company bears all the risks and there is no profit sharing arrangement with the government. Rather, the government is entitled to a royalty computed in much the same way as a royalty under lease contracts.[82] In addition, depending on the country's fiscal policies, the government will typically also collect taxes such as duties, severance or production taxes, and income taxes.

In some jurisdictions, the government may retain the option to participate in the project as a working interest owner in the property. In this case, the company initially holds 100% of the working interest. If the project is successful and reserves are found, the national oil company or entity representing the government becomes a working interest owner and will pay for its proportionate share of the investment.

5.3 Traditional production sharing contracts

A production sharing contract (PSC) or production sharing arrangement (PSA) is a contract between a national oil company (NOC) or the government of a host country and a contracting entity (contractor) to carry out oil and gas exploration and production activities in accordance with the terms of the contract, with the two parties sharing mineral output.[83] While these arrangements have historically been more commonly found in the oil and gas sector, similar types of arrangements do exist in the mining sector.

In such countries the ownership of the mineral reserves and resources in the ground does not pass to the contractor. Instead, the contractor is permitted to recover its costs and share in the profits from the exploration and production activities. Although the precise form and content of a PSC may vary, the following features are likely to be encountered in traditional oil and gas PSCs:[84]

(a) the government retains ownership of the reserves and resources and grants the contractor the right to explore for, develop, and produce the reserves;

(b) the government is often directly involved in the operation of the property, either by way of an *operating committee* that comprises representatives of the contractor and the government or NOC, or by requiring the contractor to submit its annual work programme and corresponding annual budget to the government or NOC for approval. The contractor is responsible to the NOC for carrying out operations in accordance with contract terms;

(c) upon signing of the PSC the contractor pays the government a *signature bonus*, which is a one-off upfront payment in exchange for the government's signing of the PSC;

(d) the contractor pays the government a *production bonus* upon commencement of production and when the average production over a given period first exceeds a threshold level;

(e) the government is entitled to a *royalty payment* that is calculated as a percentage of the net production (i.e. net of petroleum lost, flared or re-injected) and which is payable in kind or in cash at the option of the government. The royalty rate applicable is not necessarily a fixed percentage, but may depend on the production volume or destination of the production (e.g. different rates may apply to crude oil and gas that is exported);

(f) the contractor provides all financing and technology necessary to carry out operations and pays all of the costs specified;

(g) the contractor is typically required to bear all of the risks related to exploration and, perhaps, development (i.e. the government does not have a working interest during the exploration and development phases);

(h) the contractor is frequently required to provide infrastructure, such as streets, electricity, water systems, roads, hospitals, schools, and other items during various phases of activities. Additionally, the contract customarily requires the contractor to provide specified training of personnel. Infrastructure and training costs may or may not be recoverable from future production by the contractor;[85]

(i) the contractor may have a *domestic market obligation* that requires them to meet, as a priority, the needs of domestic oil and/or gas consumption in the host country. Alternatively, the contractor may be required to sell oil and/or gas to the NOC at the official oil or gas price;

(j) the contractor is normally committed to completing a *minimum work programme* in each of the phases of the project, which generally needs to be completed within a specified period. If the work is not performed, the contract may require the unspent amount to be paid in cash to the government;

(k) a PSC normally requires *relinquishment* of a certain percentage of the original contract area by the end of the initial term of the exploration period. A further reduction is typically required by the end of the exploration period. The government can negotiate a new contract with another party for the continued exploration of the surrendered acreage. Any data and information relating to the surrendered area often becomes the exclusive property of the government;

(l) equipment that is acquired for the development and production activities normally becomes the property of the government or NOC;

(m) operating costs and specified exploration and development costs are recoverable out of *cost recovery oil*, which is a specified percentage of production revenues after the royalty payment each year. The PSC specifies whether particular types of cost are recoverable or non-recoverable. Recoverable costs not recovered by the contractor in the current period can be carried forward to the following reporting period for recovery purposes;

(n) revenues remaining after royalty and cost recovery are called *profit oil*. Profit oil is split between the government and the contractor on a predetermined basis;

(o) many PSCs provide that the income tax to which the contractor is subject is deemed to have been paid to the government as part of the payment of profit oil (see 19.2 below); and

(p) some PSCs give the contractor the right to set up a decommissioning reserve fund which enables the contractor to recover the costs associated with future decommissioning and site restoration. In cases where the PSC terminates before the end of the life of the field, the government is typically responsible for decommissioning and site restoration.

Even in situations where the provisions of a PSC are fairly straightforward at first sight, it may be rather complicated to calculate the entitlement of each of the parties involved as is illustrated in the example below.

Example 41.3: Production sharing contract

An oil and gas company (contractor) entered into a PSC that includes the following terms:

- the oil and gas company pays for all exploration costs;
- the government is entitled to:
  - 15% royalty on the production;
  - severance tax of USD 2.50 per barrel;
  - USD 5 million production bonus when average production first exceeds 25,000 barrels per day; and
  - 10% of the profit oil;
- operating expenses are recoverable before exploration costs;
- development costs are recoverable after exploration costs;
- cost recovery oil is capped at 45% of the annual production; and
- the national oil company (NOC) and the contractor have a 51% and 49% working interest, respectively.

How should the production be allocated between parties, assuming the following for 2016?

- annual production in 2016 is 10 million barrels;
- recoverable operating costs in 2016 are USD 25 million;
- the average oil price in 2016 is USD 100/barrel (this amount is used to convert any amount calculated in monetary units i.e. USD, back into volumetric units i.e. barrels of oil);
- during 2016 average production exceeded 25,000 barrels per day for the first time;
- unrecovered exploration costs at the beginning of 2016 were USD 180 million; and
- unrecovered development costs at the beginning of 2016 were USD 275 million.

		Barrels	Contractor (49%)	NOC (51%)	Government
			bbls	bbls	bbls
Production in 2016	a	10,000,000			
Royalty 15% of 10,000,000 =	b	1,500,000			1,500,000
Severance tax 10,000,000 × $2.50 ÷ $100 =	c	250,000			250,000
Cost oil					
Operating costs $25,000,000 ÷ $100 =	d	250,000	122,500	127,500	
Exploration cost $180,000,000 ÷ $100 =	e	1,800,000	1,800,000		
Development cost $275,000,000 ÷ $100, but capped at 2,450,000	f	2,450,000	1,200,500	1,249,500	
Total cost oil 45% of 10,000,000 =	g	4,500,000			
Production bonus $5,000,000 ÷ $100 =	h	50,000			50,000
Profit oil: a – b – c – g – h =	i	3,700,000			

Government profit oil					
10% of 3,700,000 =	j	370,000			370,000
Working interest in profit oil					
3,700,000 – 370,000 =	k	3,330,000	1,631,700	1,698,300	
Total		10,000,000	4,754,700	3,075,300	2,170,000
Unrecovered development costs					
$275,000,000 –					
(2,450,000 × $100) =		$30,000,000	$14,700,000	$15,300,000	

The above example illustrates not only that calculating an entity's share in the production of the current period requires a detailed knowledge of the PSC's provisions, but also that calculating the contractor's share of the remaining reserves requires a number of assumptions.

The reserves and production that the parties are entitled to varies depending on the oil price. Had the average oil price in 2016 been $50/barrel the parties' entitlements would have been as follows: Contractor 5,540,400 barrels, NOC 2,019,600 barrels and Government 2,440,000 barrels. The quantity of reserves and production attributable to each of the parties often reacts to changes in oil prices in ways that, at first, might seem counterintuitive.

It is important to note that the type and nature of contracts emerging continue to evolve. New contracts have some attributes of PSCs, but do differ from the traditional PSC. We discuss these in more detail at 5.5 below.

5.4 Pure-service contracts

A pure-service contract is an agreement between a contractor and a host government that typically covers a defined technical service to be provided or completed during a specific period of time. The service company investment is typically limited to the value of equipment, tools, and personnel used to perform the service. In most cases, the service contractor's reimbursement is fixed by the terms of the contract with little exposure to either project performance or market factors. Payment for services is normally based on daily or hourly rates, a fixed turnkey rate, or some other specified amount. Payments may be made at specified intervals or at the completion of the service. Payments, in some cases, may be tied to the field performance, operating cost reductions, or other important metrics.

The risks of the service company under this type of contract are usually limited to non-recoverable cost overruns, losses owing to client breach of contract, default, or contractual dispute. Such a contract is generally considered to be a services contract that gives rise to revenue from the rendering of services and not income from the production of mineral. Therefore, the minerals produced are not included in the normal reserve disclosures of the contractor,[86] and the contractor bears no risk if reserves are not found. It is worth noting that such contracts do need to be assessed for embedded leases in accordance with the requirements of IFRIC 4. See 17.1 below for more information. As noted above with respect to PSCs, the type and nature of contracts continue to evolve. These new contracts also have some attributes of services contracts, but do differ from pure-service contracts. We discuss these in more detail at 5.5 below.

5.5 Evolving contractual arrangements

The type and nature of contracts emerging continues to evolve. New contracts have some attributes of PSCs, but do differ from the traditional PSC. As these contractual arrangements evolve, determining the accounting implications of these contracts is becoming increasingly complex. This not only has an impact on the accounting for such contracts but also on whether, and the extent to which, the contractor entity is able to recognise reserves in relation to its interests in mineral volumes arising from these contracts.

Each contractual arrangement needs to be analysed carefully to determine whether reserves recognition in relation to these contractual interests in mineral volumes is appropriate. Such an analysis would include, at a minimum:

- the extent of risk to which the contractor party is exposed, including exploration and/or development risk;
- the structure of the contractor's reimbursement arrangements and whether it is subject to performance/reservoir risk or price risk; and
- the ability for the contractor to take product in-kind, rather than a cash reimbursement only.

Other facts and circumstances may also be relevant in reaching the final assessment. Given the varying terms and conditions that exist within these contracts and the fact that they are continuing to change/evolve, each contract will need to be individually analysed and assessed in detail.

5.5.1 Risk service contracts

An example of a contractual arrangement that has continued to evolve is a risk service contract (RSC). Unlike pure-service contracts, under a RSC (also called risked service agreement or at-risk service contract), a fee is not certain: an entity (contractor) agrees to explore for, develop, and produce minerals on behalf of a host government, but the contractor is at risk for the amount spent on exploration and development costs. That is, if no minerals are found in commercial quantities, no fee is paid.[87] Although a RSC does not result in the contractor's ownership of the minerals in place, the contractor may be at risk for the costs of exploration and may have economic interest in those minerals. The IASC Issues Paper noted that in the case of RSCs:[88]

- the fee may be payable in cash or in minerals produced;
- the contract may call for the contractor to bear all or part of the costs of exploration that are usually recoverable, in whole or in part, from production. If there is no production, there is no recovery; and
- the contract may also give the contractor the right to purchase part of the minerals produced.

As noted in Extract 41.7 above from TOTAL's financial statements, RSCs are similar to PSCs in a number of respects. Although the precise form and content of a RSC may vary, the following features are common:

(a) the repayment of expenses and the compensation for services are established on a monetary basis;

(b) an RSC is for a limited period, after which the government or national oil company will take over operations;

(c) under an RSC the contractor does not obtain ownership of the mineral reserves or production;

(d) the contractor is normally required to carry out a minimum amount of work in providing the contracted services;

(e) the fee that is payable to the contractor covers its capital expenditure, operating costs and an agreed-upon profit margin; and

(f) ownership of the assets used under the contract passes to the government when the contractor has been reimbursed for its costs.

The SPE's *Guidelines for the Evaluation of Petroleum Reserves and Resources* notes in connection with RSCs that 'under the existing regulations, it may be more difficult for the contractor to justify reserves recognition, and special care must be taken in drafting the agreement. If regulations are satisfied, reserves equivalent to the value of the cost-recovery-plus-revenue-profit split are normally reported by the contractor.'[89]

The nature and terms and conditions of these RSCs continue to change over time. Therefore each contract will need to be analysed in detail to determine how it should be accounted for.

5.6 Joint operating agreements

When several entities are involved in a joint arrangement (e.g. joint ownership of a property, production sharing contract or concession) they will need to enter into some form of joint operating agreement (JOA). A JOA is a contract between two or more parties to a joint arrangement that sets out the rights and obligations to operate the property. Typically, a JOA designates one of the working interest owners as the operator and it governs the operations and sharing of costs between parties. A JOA does not override, but instead builds upon, the contracts that are already in place (such as production sharing contracts). In fact, many production sharing contracts require the execution of a JOA between the parties. A JOA may give rise to a joint arrangement under IFRS 11 – *Joint Arrangements* (see 7.1 below).

5.7 Different types of royalty interests

Mining companies and oil and gas companies frequently enter into royalty arrangements with owners of mineral rights (e.g. governments or private land owners). These royalties are often payable upon the extraction and/or sale of minerals. The royalty payments may be based on a specified rate per unit of the commodity (e.g. tonne or barrel) or the entity may be obliged to dispose of all of the relevant production and pay over a specified proportion of the aggregate proceeds of sale, often after deduction of certain extraction costs.

There are also other types of arrangements, which may be referred to as royalty payments/arrangements, but may potentially represent a different type of arrangement. Under these arrangements the royalty holder may have retained (or obtained) a more direct interest in the underlying production and may undertake mineral extraction and sale arrangements independently. We discuss these further below.

5.7.1 Working interest and basic royalties

As discussed at 5.1 above, under a mineral lease the owner/lessor of the mineral rights retains a *basic royalty* interest (or non-operating interest), which entitles it to a specified percentage of the mineral produced, while the lessee obtains a *working interest* (or operating interest) under the mineral lease, which entitles it to explore for, develop, and produce minerals from the property.

If the owner of a working interest cannot fund or does not wish to bear the risk of exploration, development or production from the property, it may be able to – if this is permitted by the underlying lease – sell the working interest or to create new types of interest out of its existing working interest. By creating new types of non-operating interests, the working interest owner is able to raise financing and spread the risk of the development. The original working interest holder may either:

- retain the new non-operating interest and transfer the working interest (i.e. the rights and obligations for exploring, developing and operating the property); or
- carve out and transfer a new non-operating interest to another party, while retaining the working interest.

The following non-operating interests are commonly created in practice:[90]

- overriding royalties (see 5.7.2 below);
- production payment royalties (see 5.7.3 below); and
- net profits interests (see 5.7.4 below).

5.7.2 Overriding royalties

An *overriding royalty* is very similar to a basic royalty, except that the former is created out of the operating interest and if the operating interest expires, the overriding royalty also expires.[91] An overriding royalty owner bears only its share of production taxes and sometimes of the costs incurred to get the product into a saleable condition.

5.7.3 Production payment royalties

A *production payment royalty* is the right to recover a specified amount of cash or a specified quantity of minerals, out of the working interest's share of gross production. For example, the working interest holder may assign a production payment royalty to another party for USD 12 million, in exchange for a repayment of USD 15 million plus 12% interest out of the first 65% of the working interest holder's share of production. Production payments that are specified as a quantity of minerals are often called volumetric production payments or VPPs.

5.7.4 Net profits interests

A *net profits interest* is similar to an overriding royalty. However, the amount to be received by the royalty owner is a share of the net proceeds from production (as defined in the contract) that is paid solely from the working interest owner's share. The owner of a net profits interest is not liable for any expenses.

5.7.5 Revenue and royalties: gross or net?

Many mineral leases, concession agreements and production sharing contracts require the payment of a royalty to the original owner of the mineral reserves or the government. The current accounting treatment for government and other royalties payable is diverse. Under IAS 18 it is not entirely clear whether revenue should be presented net of royalty payments or not. Historically, many companies have presented revenue net of those royalties that are paid in kind. This is on the basis that the entity has no legal right to the royalty product and, hence, never receives any inflow of economic benefits from those volumes. *[IAS 18.8]*. However, when the entity is required to sell the physical product in the market and remit the net proceeds (after deduction of certain costs incurred) to the royalty holder, it may be exposed to the risks and rewards of ownership to such an extent that it is appropriate to present revenue on a gross basis and include the royalty payment within cost of sales or taxes (depending on how the royalty is calculated).

Extracts 41.8 and 41.9 below, from the financial statements of Premier Oil and BHP Billiton respectively, illustrate typical accounting policies for royalties under IFRS.

Extract 41.8: Premier Oil plc (2015)

ACCOUNTING POLICIES [extract]

For the year ended 31 December 2015

Royalties

Royalties are charged as production costs to the income statement in the year in which the related production is recognised as income.

Extract 41.9: BHP Billiton plc (2015)

43 Significant accounting policies

(d) Sales revenue [extract]

Revenue is not reduced for royalties and other taxes payable from the Group's production.

Extract 41.10 below, from the financial statements of Statoil, illustrates some of the complications that may arise in determining revenue when an entity sells product on behalf of the government.

> *Extract 41.10: Statoil ASA (2015)*
>
> **Notes to the Consolidated financial statements** [extract]
>
> **2 Significant accounting policies** [extract]
>
> **Transactions with the Norwegian State** [extract]
>
> Statoil markets and sells the Norwegian State's share of oil and gas production from the Norwegian continental shelf (NCS). The Norwegian State's participation in petroleum activities is organised through the State's direct financial interest (SDFI). All purchases and sales of the SDFI's oil production are classified as *Purchases [net of inventory variation]* and *Revenues,* respectively. Statoil sells, in its own name, but for the Norwegian State's account and risk, the State's production of natural gas. These sales and related expenditures refunded by the Norwegian State, are presented net in the Consolidated financial statements.
>
> **Critical accounting judgements and key sources of estimation uncertainty** [extract]
>
> **Revenue recognition – gross versus net presentation of traded SDFI volumes of oil and gas production**
>
> As described under Transactions with the Norwegian State above, Statoil markets and sells the Norwegian State's share of oil and gas production from the NCS. Statoil includes the costs of purchase and proceeds from the sale of the SDFI oil production in *Purchases [net of inventory variation]* and *Revenues*, respectively. In making the judgement, Statoil considered the detailed criteria for the recognition of revenue from the sale of goods and, in particular, concluded that the risk and reward of the ownership of the oil had been transferred from the SDFI to Statoil.
>
> Statoil sells, in its own name, but for the Norwegian State's account and risk, the State's production of natural gas. These gas sales, and related expenditures refunded by the State, are shown net in Statoil's Consolidated financial statements. In making the judgement, Statoil considered the same criteria as for the oil production and concluded that the risk and reward of the ownership of the gas had not been transferred from the SDFI to Statoil.

The SPE-PRMS (see 2.2 above) notes that 'royalty volumes should be deducted from the lessee's entitlement to resources. In some agreements, royalties owned by the host government are actually treated as taxes to be paid in cash. In such cases, the equivalent royalty volumes are controlled by the contractor who may (subject to regulatory guidance) elect to report these volumes as reserves and/or contingent resources with appropriate offsets (increase in operating expense) to recognize the financial liability of the royalty obligation.'[92]

For a discussion on the potential impact of IFRS 15 see 12.7.7.B below.

6 RISK-SHARING ARRANGEMENTS

As discussed at 1.1 above, the high costs and high risks in the extractive industries often lead entities to enter into risk-sharing arrangements. The following types of risk-sharing arrangements are discussed in this chapter:

- carried interests (see 6.1 below);
- farm-ins and farm-outs (see 6.2 below);
- asset swaps (see 6.3 below);
- unitisations (see 15.4 below);
- investments in subsidiaries, joint arrangements and associates (see 7 below);
- production sharing contracts (see 5.3 above), which result in a degree of risk sharing with local governments; and
- risk service contracts (see 5.5.1 above).

6.1 Carried interests

Carried interests often arise when a party in an arrangement is either unable or unwilling to bear the risk of exploration or is unable or unwilling to fund its share of the cost of exploration or development. A carried interest is an agreement under which one party (the carrying party) agrees to pay for a portion or all of the pre-production costs of another party (the carried party) on a licence in which both own a portion of the working interest.[93] In effect, commercially, the carried party is trading a share of any production to which it is entitled in the future in exchange for the carrying party funding one or more phases of the project. In other words, the parties create a new interest out of an existing working interest. If the project is unsuccessful then the carrying party will not be reimbursed for the costs that it has incurred on behalf of the carried party. If the project is successful then the carrying party will be reimbursed either in cash out of proceeds of the share of production attributable to the carried party, or by receiving a disproportionately high share of the production until the carried costs have been recovered.[94]

6.1.1 Types of carried interest arrangements

Carried interest arrangements tend to fall into one of the following two categories:

- *Financing-type arrangements* – The carrying party provides funding to the carried party and receives a lender's return on the funds provided, while the right to additional production acts as a security that underpins the arrangement; or
- *Purchase/sale-type arrangement* – The carried party effectively sells an interest or a partial interest in a project to the carrying party. The carrying party will be required to fund the project in exchange for an increased share of any proceeds if the project succeeds, while the carried party retains a much reduced share of any proceeds.

In practice, however, it is not always easy to determine in which category a particular carried interest arrangement falls, as is illustrated in the example below.

Example 41.4: Carried interests (1)

Scenario 1

The carrying party has proposed a $10 million project, which has a very high chance of succeeding. The carried party, which is unable to fund its share of the project, agrees that the carrying party is entitled to recover its cost plus 7% interest by giving it a disproportionately high share of the production. If the production from this project is insufficient to repay the initial investment, the carried party should reimburse the carrying party out of its share of production from other fields within the same licence.

Scenario 2

The carrying party has proposed a project that may cost up to $6 million, the outcome of which is uncertain. The carried party, which is unwilling to participate in the project, agrees that the carrying party is entitled to all production from the project until it has recovered three times its initial investment.

Scenario 3

The carrying party has proposed a project that may cost up to $5 million, which has a good chance of succeeding. The carrying party has a 60% interest in the licence and the carried party holds the remaining 40%. The carried party, which is unable to fund its share of the project, agrees that the carrying party is entitled to an additional 25% of the production until the carrying party has recovered its costs plus a 20% return.

When entering into a carried interest arrangement, an entity must assess whether the arrangement is a financing-type arrangement or purchase/sale-type arrangement. Some of the indicators that a carried interest arrangement should be accounted for as a financing-type arrangement are that:

- the carried party is unable to fund its share of the project;
- the risks associated with the development are not significant, i.e. financing-type arrangements will be more common in the development stage; and
- the carrying party receives a return that is comparable to a lender's rate of return.

Indicators that a carried interest arrangement should be treated as a purchase/sale-type arrangement include:

- the carrying party and carried party have genuinely different opinions about the chances of success of the project, and the carried party could fund its share of the project if it wanted to;
- there are significant uncertainties about the outcome of the project. Purchase/sale-type arrangements are therefore more common in the E&E phase;
- the arrangement gives the carrying party voting rights in the project;
- there are significant uncertainties about the costs of the project, perhaps because it involves use of a new technology or approach;
- the carrying party could lose all of its investment or possibly earn a return significantly in excess of a lender's rate of return; and
- the carrying party can only recover its investment from the project that is subject to the arrangement and there is no recourse to other assets or interests of the carried party.

In Example 41.4 above, scenario 1 has the characteristics of a financing-type arrangement, while scenario 2 has those of a purchase/sale-type arrangement. However, when an arrangement (such as scenario 3) has financing-type and purchase/sale-type characteristics (e.g. as a result of the relative bargaining strength of the parties), an entity will need to analyse the arrangement carefully and exercise judgement in developing an appropriate accounting policy.

The following types of carried interest arrangements are discussed below:

- carried interest arrangements in the E&E phase (see 6.1.2 below);
- financing-type carried interest arrangements in the development phase (see 6.1.3 below); and
- purchase/sale-type carried interest arrangements in the development phase (see 6.1.4 below).

6.1.2 *Carried interest arrangements in the E&E phase*

While IFRS 6 should be applied to accounting for E&E expenditures, the standard does not address other aspects of accounting by entities engaged in the exploration for and evaluation of mineral resources. *[IFRS 6.4]*. That leaves unanswered the question of whether carried interest arrangements can ever fall within the scope of IFRS 6. In the case of a purchase/sale-type carried interest arrangement the transaction, at least in economic terms, leads to the acquisition of an E&E asset by the carrying party and a disposal by the carried party. Therefore, we believe that purchase/sale-type carried interest arrangements in the E&E phase would fall within the scope of IFRS 6. Hence an entity has two options: either to develop an accounting policy under IAS 8 as discussed at 6.1.4 below, or, on transition to IFRS or first application under IFRS, to develop an accounting policy under IFRS 6 that is based on a previous national GAAP that contains such guidance. In practice this usually means that:

- the carrying party accounts for its expenditures under a carried interest arrangement in the same way as directly incurred E&E expenditure (see 3.2 and 3.3 above); and
- the carried party would not record expenditure incurred by the carrying party on its behalf subsequent to the arrangement commencing. However, the carried party may need to recognise a loss when the terms of the transaction indicate that the existing carrying value of the asset is impaired. Alternatively, to the extent that an arrangement is favourable, the carried party would – depending on its accounting policy – recognise the gain either in profit or loss or as a reduction in the carrying amount of the E&E asset.

On the other hand, a finance-type carried interest arrangement (which is generally not as common in the E&E phase) that has no significant impact on the risks and rewards that an entity derives from the underlying E&E working interest, may be more akin to a funding arrangement. As IFRS 6 deals only with accounting for E&E expenditures and assets, it is a matter of judgement whether or not the accounting for finance-type carried interest arrangements is considered to be outside the scope of IFRS 6. If an arrangement is considered to be outside the scope of IFRS 6, it might be appropriate to account for it in the same way as finance-type carried interest arrangements that relate to projects that are not in the E&E phase (see 6.1.3 below).

6.1.3 Financing-type carried interest arrangements in the development phase

As financing-type carried interest arrangements do not result in the transfer of the economic risks and rewards of the underlying working interest between parties, such arrangements are not accounted for as a sale (purchase) by the carried party (carrying party). Instead these arrangements are in effect secured borrowings in which the underlying asset is used as collateral that provides an identifiable stream of cash flows.

These arrangements are most appropriately accounted for as giving rise to a financial asset for the carrying party and a financial liability for the carried party.

The carried party will continue to recognise the expenditure incurred in relation to its full share of the working interest prior to the execution of the carried interest arrangement, and a corresponding financial liability for the amount that it is expected to reimburse to the carrying party as the pre-production costs being met by the carrying party are incurred, irrespective of whether it is a non-recourse arrangement or not. The liability is accounted for as a loan at amortised cost under IAS 39 – *Financial Instruments: Recognition and Measurement*, which means that the carried party should accrete interest on the liability and reduce the loan to the extent the carrying party recovers its costs. It should be noted, however, that the application of the effective interest rate method under IAS 39 requires adjustment of the carrying amount when the entity revises its estimates of the payments to be made. *[IAS 39.AG8]*.

Conversely the carrying party should recognise a financial asset for the amount that it expects to recover as a reimbursement as the pre-production costs (which are being met by the carrying party) are incurred. Classification of this financial asset as a loan or receivable under IAS 39 is only possible when the carrying party expects to recover substantially all of its entire investment. *[IAS 39.9]*. This should normally be the case in financing-type carried interest arrangements.

This approach to accounting for carried interest arrangements might not be appropriate if there were more than an insignificant transfer of risk (without necessarily resulting in a purchase/sale-type carried interest arrangement). The transfer of risk would suggest that:

- the carried party should recognise a provision under IAS 37 rather than a liability under IAS 39; and
- the carrying party should account for its right to receive reimbursement as an available-for-sale investment under IAS 39 or a reimbursement right under IAS 37.

Under IFRS 9 – *Financial Instruments* – an entity would need to determine the classification of the financial asset based on an assessment of the entity's business model for managing financial assets and the contractual cash flow characteristics of the financial assets. See Chapter 47 at 2 for more information. Any financial liability would likely be measured at amortised cost unless it meets the definition of a derivative or was designated at fair value through profit or loss. See Chapter 47 at 3 for more information.

6.1.4 Purchase/sale-type carried interest arrangements in the development phase

The accounting suggested in this section for the carried party is the same as that set out in paragraph 155 of the former OIAC SORP, which stated that the disposal should be accounted for in accordance with the entity's normal accounting policy.

Historically, some entities have accounted for these types of transactions on a cash basis, i.e. the carried party does nothing and the carrying party accounts for its actual cash outlays. It is hard to see how this can be justified under IFRS.

In purchase/sale-type carried interest arrangements, the carried party effectively sells part of its interest in a project to the carrying party. For example, the carried party may sell part of its interest in the mineral reserves to the carrying party which, in exchange, is obliged to fund the remaining costs of developing the field. Consequently, the arrangement has two elements, the purchase/sale of mineral reserves and the funding of developments costs, which should be accounted for in accordance with their substance. Therefore, the carried party should:

- derecognise the part of the asset that it has sold to the carrying party, consistent with the derecognition principles of IAS 16 or IAS 38. *[IAS 16.67, IAS 38.112]*. Determining the amount to be derecognised may require a considerable amount of judgement depending on how the interest sold is defined;
- recognise the consideration received or receivable from the carrying party;
- recognise a gain or loss on the transaction for the difference between the net disposal proceeds and the carrying amount of the asset disposed of. Recognition of a gain would be appropriate only when the value of the consideration can be determined reliably. If not, then the carried party should account for the consideration received as a reduction in the carrying amount of the underlying assets. (NOTE: These requirements relate to IAS 18, for details of the potential impact of IFRS 15 see 12.7 below and Chapter 30); and
- test the retained interest for impairment if the terms of the arrangement indicate that the retained interest may be impaired.

In accounting for its purchase the carrying party should:

- recognise an asset that represents the underlying (partially) undeveloped interest acquired at cost in accordance with the principles of IAS 16 or IAS 38. *[IAS 16.15, IAS 38.21]*. Cost is defined in these standards as 'the amount of cash or cash equivalents paid or the fair value of the other consideration given to acquire an asset at the time of its acquisition or construction or, where applicable, the amount attributed to that asset when initially recognised in accordance with the specific requirements of other IFRSs'; *[IAS 16.6, IAS 38.8]* and
- recognise a liability for the obligation to make defined payments on behalf of the carried party, which relate to the carried party's share of future investments.

The application of this approach is illustrated in Example 41.5 below.

Example 41.5: Carried interests (2)

An oil and gas company is developing an oil field. Assume that the company did not capitalise any E&E costs in relation to the field, but that by 1 January 2016 it had capitalised $250 million of costs in relation to the construction of property, plant and equipment. To complete the development of the oil field and bring it to production a further investment in property, plant and equipment of $350 million is required in the first half of 2016.

At 1 January 2016, the oil and gas company (the carried party) enters into a purchase/sale-type carried interest arrangement with a carrying party, which will fund the entire $350 million required for the further development of the field. Upon entering into the carried interest arrangement the carried party's entitlement to oil is expected to be reduced from 15,000,000 barrels of oil to 9,000,000 barrels of oil, i.e. its interest in the oil field and the related property, plant and equipment has been reduced to 60% (9,000,000 ÷ 15,000,000). In practice, calculating the portion of the interest sold may require a considerable amount of judgement (e.g. in scenario 2 in Example 41.4 above it would not be straightforward to calculate the portion of the interest sold).

Both parties believe that the fair value of the oil field and related property, plant and equipment will be $1 billion once the remaining investment of $350 million has been made. Consequently, the fair value of the oil field and related property, plant and equipment at 1 January 2016 is $650 million ($1 billion – $350 million).

The fair value of the interest acquired (which comprises a portion of the oil field and a portion of the related property, plant and equipment) by the carrying party is $260 million (40% × $650 million). In exchange for its interest, the carrying party will pay $50 million in cash and undertakes to pay the remaining investments related to the carried party's interest.

The carried party accounts for the transaction as follows:

	$	$
Cash received from the carrying party	50	
Capital calls to be paid by the carrying party (60% × $350 million =) †	210	
Property, plant and equipment (40% × $250 million =)		100
Gain on sale (40% × ($650 million – $250 million) =)		160

† *The carried party has obtained the commitment from the carrying party to make certain payments on its behalf.*

If the carried party had recognised a loss on the interest sold, it would need to perform an impairment test on the interest retained.

The carrying party accounts for the transaction as follows:

	$	$
Assets acquired ($50 million + $210 million =) †	260	
Cash paid to the carried party		50
Capital calls payable on behalf of the carried party (60% × $350 million =) ‡		210

† *As discussed above, the cost of property, plant and equipment is defined as the fair value of the consideration. In an arm's length transaction the fair value of property, plant and equipment acquired is normally equal to the fair value of the consideration paid. The fair value of the portion of the oil field and the portion of the related property, plant and equipment acquired is (40% × $650 million =) $260 million.*

‡ *The carrying party has assumed a liability to make these payments on behalf of the carried party. The carrying party will also be required to pay (40% × $350 million =) $140 million for its own share of the future investments, but that amount is only recognised as a liability upon recognition of the related property, plant and equipment.*

The receivable recognised by the carried party and the corresponding liability recognised by the carrying party are reduced over the course of the construction of the assets to which they relate. The carrying party reduces the liability as it funds the carried party's share of the investment and the carried party recognises its share of the assets being constructed while reducing the balance of the receivable.

6.2 Farm-ins and farm-outs

A farm-out (from the viewpoint of the transferor) or a farm-in (from the viewpoint of the transferee) was defined in the former OIAC SORP as 'the transfer of part of an oil and gas interest in consideration for an agreement by the transferee (farmee) to meet, absolutely, certain expenditure which would otherwise have to be undertaken by the owner (farmor).'[95] Farm-in transactions generally occur in the exploration or development phase and are characterised by the transferor (i.e. farmor) giving up future economic benefits, in the form of reserves, in exchange for a (generally) permanent reduction in future funding obligations.

Under a carried interest arrangement, the carried party transfers a *portion* of the risks and rewards of a property, in exchange for a funding commitment from the carrying party. Under a farm-in arrangement the farmor transfers all the risks and rewards of a *proportion* (i.e. a straight percentage) of a property, in exchange for a commitment from the farmee to fund certain expenditures. Therefore, a farm-out represents the complete disposal of a *proportion* of a property and is similar to purchase/sale-type carried interest arrangements as discussed at 6.1.4 above.

The following types of farm-in arrangements are separately discussed below:

- farm-in arrangements in the E&E phase (see 6.2.1 below); and
- farm-in arrangements outside the E&E phase (see 6.2.2 below).

6.2.1 Farm-in arrangements in the E&E phase

IFRS 6 deals only with accounting for E&E expenditures and does not address other aspects of accounting by entities engaged in the exploration for and evaluation of mineral resources. *[IFRS 6.4]*. That leaves open the question of whether farm-in arrangements can ever fall within the scope of IFRS 6. However, as a farm-in arrangement leads to the acquisition of an E&E asset by the farmee and a disposal by the farmor, we believe that a farm-in arrangement would fall within the scope of IFRS 6. Hence an entity has two options: either to develop an accounting policy under IAS 8 as discussed at 6.2.2 below; or to develop an accounting policy under IFRS 6. In practice many entities use the second option and apply an accounting policy to farm-in arrangements that is based on a previous national GAAP.

Accounting policies for farm-in arrangements in the E&E phase that are based on an entity's previous national GAAP will often require that:

- the farmee recognises its expenditure under the arrangement in respect of its own interest and that retained by the farmor, as and when the costs are incurred. The farmee accounts for its expenditures under a farm-in arrangement in the same way as directly incurred E&E expenditure; and
- the farmor accounts for the farm-out arrangement as follows:
  - the farmor does not record any expenditure made by the farmee on its behalf;
  - the farmor does not recognise a gain or loss on the farm-out arrangement, but rather redesignates any costs previously capitalised in relation to the whole interest as relating to the partial interest retained; and
  - any cash consideration received is credited against costs previously capitalised in relation to the whole interest with any excess accounted for by the farmor as a gain on disposal.

If an entity applies its previous GAAP accounting policy in respect of farm-in arrangements, we would expect the entity also to make the farm-in disclosures required by its previous GAAP.

6.2.2 Farm-in arrangements outside the E&E phase: accounting by the farmee

A farm-in represents the complete acquisition of a *proportion* of a property. The accounting for such an arrangement will depend on whether the entity is farming into an asset or into an arrangement that is considered a business (and which is a joint operation), or whether the farm-in results in the arrangement becoming a joint operation.

6.2.2.A Farming into an asset

Where a farmee farms into an asset, regardless of whether it is a joint operation or results in the formation of a joint operation, it should recognise an asset that represents the underlying (partially) undeveloped interest acquired at cost in accordance with IAS 16 or IAS 38, *[IAS 16.15, IAS 38.21]*, and recognise a liability that reflects obligations to fund the farmor's share of the future investment from which the farmee itself will not derive any future economic benefits.

Farm-in arrangements can be structured in numerous ways, some requiring payment of a fixed monetary amount while others are more flexible and state, for example, that capital expenditures over the next five years will be paid for by the farmee regardless of what those amounts may be. Accounting for these arrangements is uncertain.

In some cases, the liability may meet the definition of a financial liability under IAS 32 – *Financial Instruments: Presentation* – and should be accounted for in accordance with IAS 39/IFRS 9. In other scenarios, such as the latter example above (i.e. where the farmee pays all capital expenditure incurred over a five year period, regardless of the amount), the liability may meet the definition of a provision under IAS 37 as the timing and amount of the liability are uncertain. *[IAS 37.10]*. If an entity concludes that IAS 37 applies, then there can be some debate as to when a provision should be recognised as that standard is not clear.

The issue of contingent consideration in the context of the acquisition of assets has been discussed by the Interpretations Committee but they were unable to reach consensus on whether IAS 37 or IAS 39 applies. Hence, different treatments will continue to be encountered in practice. See 8.4 below for further discussion on this issue and an update on current status.

An arrangement involving a farm-in into an asset is illustrated below in the extract from Newcrest's 2009 financial statements.

Extract 41.11: Newcrest Mining Limited (2009)

29. Interests in Unincorporated Joint Venture Assets [extract]

(b) Acquisition of Interest in the Morobe Mining Joint Venture [extract]

During the year Newcrest acquired a 50% interest in the Papua New Guinea (PNG) gold assets of Harmony Gold Mining Ltd (Harmony) via unincorporated joint venture structures. The joint venture assets comprise:

– The Hidden Valley mining operation, a gold and silver project, expected to produce over 250,000 ounces of gold and 4 million ounces of silver per annum over a 14-year mine life;
– The highly-prospective Wafi-Golpu gold-copper deposit and its surrounding exploration tenements; and
– Extensive exploration tenements in the Morobe province of PNG.

The acquisition of the interest in the joint ventures comprised two stages:

– In the first stage, which was completed on 7 August 2008, Newcrest acquired an initial 30.01% interest for cash consideration of US$228.0 million (A$249.4 million) consisting of an initial payment of US$180.0 million together with a reimbursement to Harmony of US$48.0 million in project expenditure incurred between 1 January 2008 and 7 August 2008.
– The second stage represented a farm-in commitment for the remaining 19.99% interest. In this stage, Newcrest solely funded all project expenditure up to 30 June 2009 which totalled US$297.7 million (A$420.8 million).

6.2.2.B *Farming into a business which is a joint operation or results in the formation of a joint operation*

Where a farmee farms into a project that is considered to be a business (as defined in IFRS 3) which is either a joint operation or results in the formation of a joint operation, historically there has been some diversity in how this was to be accounted for. Some have applied the business combination principles in IFRS 3 and other standards and some have applied the asset acquisition accounting principles (as discussed above at 6.2.2.A).

This issue was resolved by the IASB issuing an amendment to IFRS 11 which was effective for annual reporting periods commencing on or after 1 January 2016. This amendment requires that where an entity acquires an interest in a joint operation which constitutes a business, the business combination accounting principles of IFRS 3 and other standards must be applied. See Chapter 12 at 8.3.1 for further discussion on this. These requirements will include such interests acquired through a farm-in.

6.2.3 *Farm-in arrangements outside the E&E phase: accounting by the farmor*

In accounting for a farm-in arrangement the farmor should:

- derecognise the proportion of the asset that it has sold to the farmee, consistent with the principles of IAS 16 or IAS 38; *[IAS 16.67, IAS 38.112]*
- recognise the consideration received or receivable from the farmee, which represents the farmee's obligation to fund the capital expenditure in relation to the interest retained by the farmor;
- recognise a gain or loss on the transaction for the difference between the net disposal proceeds and the carrying amount of the asset disposed of. *[IAS 16.71, IAS 38.113]*. Recognition of a gain would be appropriate only when the value of the consideration can be determined reliably. If not, then the carried party should account for the consideration received as a reduction in the carrying amount of the underlying assets; and
- test the retained interest for impairment if the terms of the arrangement indicate that the retained interest may be impaired.

Under IAS 16, IAS 38 and IAS 18, the consideration receivable on disposal of an item of property, plant and equipment or an intangible asset is recognised initially at its fair value by the farmor. However, if 'payment for the item is deferred, the consideration received is recognised initially at the cash price equivalent. The difference between the nominal amount of the consideration and the cash price equivalent is recognised as interest revenue in accordance with IAS 18 reflecting the effective yield on the receivable.' *[IAS 16.72, IAS 38.116]*.

Under IFRS 15, the consideration to be included in the gain/loss arising from the disposal and hence the receivable that is recognised, is the amount the entity expects to be entitled in exchange for disposing of the interest in the property, plant and equipment. See Chapter 30 at 5 and 5.2 for more information.

Any part of the consideration that is receivable in the form of cash will meet the definition of a financial asset under IAS 32 and should be accounted for in accordance with IAS 39, *[IAS 32.11]*, either at amortised cost or fair value depending on the nature of the receivable or how the farmor designates the receivable. See Chapter 47 at 2 for more information on classifying a financial asset under IFRS 9.

The extract below describes the farm-in transactions of Harmony Gold.

Extract 41.12: Harmony Gold Mining Company Limited (2009)

Directors' report [extract]

Disposals [extract]

Sale of interest in PNG to Newcrest

During the year, the group sold 50% of its interest in its PNG assets in Morobe Province to Newcrest. This took place in three stages, with the disposal of 30.01% for US$229 million (stage one) being completed on 31 July 2008. Stages two and three were completed by the end of quarters three and four of the financial year respectively with Newcrest having earned in a further 10% and 9.99% respectively in each of these stages.

Notes to the group financial statements [extract]

6 Profit of sale of property, plant and equipment [extract]

Included in the total for 2009 is R931 million (US$111.9 million) profit on sale of 50% of Harmony's gold and copper assets in Morobe Province, Papua New Guinea, to Newcrest Mining Limited (Newcrest) in terms of the Master Purchase and Farm-in agreement. The sale was concluded in three stages. On 31 July 2008, stage 1, being the sale of an initial 30.1% participating interest in the assets, was concluded at a profit of R416 million (US$57.9 million). The remaining 19.99% interest was sold in two further stages, resulting in a profit of R439 million (US$44.6 million) for the 10% interest of stage 2 and a profit of R76 million (US$9.9 million) for the 9.99% interest of stage 3. These stages were completed on 27 February 2009 and 30 June 2009 respectively. Refer to note 23.

23 Investment in joint venture [extract]

a) Papua New Guinea (PNG) Partnership agreement (50%)

On 22 April 2008, Morobe Consolidated Goldfields Limited and WafiMining Limited, subsidiaries of Harmony Australia, entered into a Master Purchase and Farm-in Agreement with Newcrest. This agreement provided for Newcrest to purchase a 30.01% participating interest (stage 1) and a further farm-in of an additional 19.99% participating interest in Harmony's PNG gold and copper assets, giving them a 50% interest. The total value of the transaction was estimated at US$530 million.

On 16 July 2008, the conditions to the Master Purchase and Farm-in agreement were finalised, which included regulatory and statutory approvals by the PNG Government. Stage 1 completion took place on 31 July 2008, and a total consideration of R1 792 million (US$229.8 million) was received on 7 August 2008, of which R390 million (US$50 million) was placed in a jointly controlled escrow account. This amount was subsequently released to Harmony following confirmation of approval of an exploration licence during September 2008 by the PNG mining authorities.

Harmony recognised a profit of R416 million (US$58 million) on the completion of stage 1, which represented a sale of a 30.01% undivided interest of Harmony's PNG gold and copper assets and liabilities comprising the joint venture.

During the farm-in period, Harmony agreed to transfer a further 19.99% interest to Newcrest in consideration for an agreement by Newcrest to meet certain expenditure which would otherwise have to be undertaken by Harmony. The interest to be transferred were conditional on the level of capital expenditures funded by Newcrest at certain milestones, and by the end of February 2009, Newcrest acquired another 10% through the farm-in arrangement. The final 9.99% was acquired by 30 June 2009.

At the date of completion of each party's obligations under the farm-in arrangement, Harmony derecognised the proportion of the mining assets and liabilities in the joint venture that it had sold to Newcrest, and recognised its interest in the capital expenditure at fair value. The difference between the net disposal proceeds and the carrying amounts of the asset disposed of during the farm-in arrangement amounted to a gain of R515 million (US$54 million), which has been included in the consolidated income statements for 2009.

6.3 Asset swaps

Asset exchanges are transactions that have challenged standard-setters for a number of years. For example, an entity might swap certain intangible assets that it does not require or is no longer allowed to use for those of a counterparty that has other surplus assets. It is not uncommon for entities to exchange assets as part of their portfolio and risk management activities or simply to meet demands of competition authorities.

The key accounting issues that need to be addressed are:

- whether such an exchange should give rise to a profit when the fair value of the asset received is greater than the carrying value of the asset given up; and
- whether the exchange of similar assets should be recognised.

In the extractive industries an exchange of assets could involve property, plant and equipment (PP&E), intangible assets, investment property or E&E assets, which are in the scope of IAS 16, IAS 38, IAS 40 and IFRS 6, respectively. Hence there are three possible types of exchanges (which will be discussed below), those involving:

(a) only E&E assets;

(b) only PP&E, intangible assets and/or investment property; and

(c) a combination of E&E assets, PP&E, intangible assets and/or investment property.

6.3.1 E&E assets

Accounting for E&E assets, and therefore also accounting for swaps involving only E&E assets, falls within the scope of IFRS 6. *[IFRS 6.3]*. As that standard does not directly address accounting for asset swaps, it is necessary to consider its hierarchy of guidance in the selection of an accounting policy. IFRS 6 does not require an entity to look at other standards and interpretations that deal with similar issues, or the guidance in the IASB's *Conceptual Framework*. *[IFRS 6.7]*. Instead, it allows entities to develop their own accounting policies, or use the guidance issued by other standard-setters, thereby effectively allowing entities to continue using accounting policies that they applied under their previous national GAAP. Therefore, many entities, especially those which consider that they can never determine the fair value of E&E assets reliably, have selected an accounting policy under which they account for E&E assets obtained in a swap transaction at the carrying amount of the asset given up. An alternative approach, which is also permitted under IFRS 6, would be to apply an accounting policy that is based on the guidance in other standards as discussed below.

6.3.2 PP&E, intangible assets and investment property

Three separate international accounting standards contain virtually identical guidance on accounting for exchanges of assets: IAS 16, IAS 38 and IAS 40. These standards require the acquisition of PP&E, intangible assets or investment property, as the case may be, in exchange for non-monetary assets (or a combination of monetary and non-monetary assets) to be measured at fair value. The cost of the acquired asset is measured at fair value unless:

(a) the exchange transaction lacks 'commercial substance'; or

(b) the fair value of neither the asset received nor the asset given up is reliably measurable. *[IAS 16.24, IAS 38.45, IAS 40.27]*.

For more information, see Chapter 18 at 4.4 (PP&E), Chapter 17 at 4.7 (intangible assets) and Chapter 19 at 4.6 (investment properties).

6.3.3 Exchanges of E&E assets for other types of assets

An entity that exchanges E&E assets for PP&E, intangible assets or investment property needs to apply an accounting treatment that meets the requirements of IFRS 6 and those of IAS 16, IAS 38 or IAS 40. As discussed above, exchanges involving PP&E, intangible assets and investment property that have commercial substance should be accounted for at fair value. Since this treatment is also allowed under IFRS 6, an entity that exchanges E&E assets for assets within the scope of IAS 16, IAS 38 or IAS 40 should apply an accounting policy that complies with the guidance in those standards.

7 INVESTMENTS IN THE EXTRACTIVE INDUSTRIES

Extractive industries are characterised by the high risks associated with the exploration for and development of mineral reserves and resources. To mitigate those risks, industry participants use a variety of ownership structures that are aimed at sharing risks, such as joint investments through subsidiaries, joint arrangements, associates or equity interests. IFRS defines each of these as follows:

- *subsidiaries* – entities controlled by the reporting entity. Sometimes entities in the extractive industries do not own 100% of these subsidiaries, and there can often be significant non-controlling shareholders that share in some of the risk and rewards. Accounting for non-controlling interests is discussed in detail in Chapter 7 at 4. Furthermore, the existence of put and/or call options over non-controlling interests may transfer some of the risks between the parent entity and the non-controlling shareholders. This issue is discussed in detail in Chapter 7 at 5;
- *joint arrangements* – contractual arrangements of which two or more parties have joint control (see 7.1 below);
- *undivided interests* – participations in projects which entitle the reporting entity only to a share of the production or use of an asset, and do not of themselves give the entity any form of control, joint control or significant influence (see 7.2 below);
- *associates* – entities that, while not controlled or jointly controlled by the reporting entity, are subject to significant influence by it (see Chapter 11 at 4); and
- *equity interests* – entities over which the reporting entity cannot exercise any control, joint control or significant influence (see Chapter 46, 47 and 48).

7.1 Joint arrangements

Joint arrangements have always been, and continue to be, a common structure in the extractive industries. Such arrangements are used to bring in partners to source new projects, combine adjacent mineral licences, improve utilisation of expensive infrastructure, attract investors and help manage technical or political risk or comply with local regulations. The majority of entities operating in the extractive industries are party to at least one joint arrangement. However, not all arrangements that are casually described as 'joint arrangements' or 'joint ventures' meet the definition of a joint arrangement under IFRS.

Accounting for joint arrangements is governed by IFRS 11. Given the prevalence of joint arrangements in the extractive industries, careful analysis of IFRS 11, in conjunction with the requirements of IFRS 10 – *Consolidated Financial Statements* (see Chapter 6) and IFRS 12 – *Disclosure of Interests in Other Entities* (see Chapter 13) is required. Chapter 12 contains a full discussion on IFRS 11 and its requirements and therefore while some specific areas for extractives companies to consider are set out below, this section should be read in conjunction with that chapter.

We also discuss some issues relating to the acquisition of interests in joint operations (see 8.3 below).

A joint arrangement in the scope of IFRS 11 is an arrangement over which two or more parties have joint control. *[IFRS 11.4]*. (See 7.1.1 below for further discussion on the definition of joint control). Under IFRS 11, there are two types of joint arrangements – 'joint operations' and 'joint ventures'.

Joint operation: a joint arrangement whereby the parties that have joint control of the arrangement have rights to the assets, and obligations for the liabilities, relating to the arrangement. *[IFRS 11 Appendix A]*.

Joint venture: a joint arrangement whereby the parties that have joint control of the arrangement have rights to the net assets of the arrangement. *[IFRS 11 Appendix A]*.

Classification between these two types of arrangements is based on the rights and obligations that arise from the contractual arrangement. An entity will need to have a detailed understanding of the specific rights and obligations of each of its arrangements to be able to determine the impact of this new standard.

Since IFRS 11's issuance, the Interpretations Committee has been discussing various implementation issues particularly when it comes to classifying a joint arrangement that is structured through a separate vehicle. In March 2015, the Interpretations Committee issued an agenda decision dealing with a range of issues, including:

- how and why particular facts and circumstances create rights and obligations;
- implication of 'economic substance'; and
- application of 'other facts and circumstances' to specific fact patterns:
  - output sold at a market price;
  - financing from a third party;
  - nature of output (i.e. fungible or bespoke output); and
  - determining the basis for 'substantially all of the output'.

This agenda decision includes a number of fact patterns which may be relevant for extractive industries, including (for example) the impact on agreements to purchase a joint arrangement's output. See Chapter 12 at 5.4.3 for further discussion.

7.1.1 Assessing joint control

Joint control is defined as '...the contractually agreed sharing of control of an arrangement which exists only when the decisions about the relevant activities require the unanimous consent of the parties sharing control'. *[IFRS 11.7, Appendix A]*. IFRS 11 describes the key aspects of joint control as follows:

- *Contractually agreed* – contractual arrangements are usually, but not always, written, and set out the terms of the arrangements. *[IFRS 11.5(a), B2]*.
- *Control and relevant activities* – IFRS 10 describes how to assess whether a party has control, and how to identify the relevant activities, which are described in more detail in Chapter 6 at 3 and 4.1. Some of the aspects of 'relevant activities' and 'control' that are most relevant to extractives arrangements are discussed at 7.1.1.A and 7.1.2 below, respectively. *[IFRS 11.8, B5]*.
- *Unanimous consent* – means that any party (with joint control) can prevent any of the other parties, or a group of the parties, from making unilateral decisions about the relevant activities without its consent. *[IFRS 11.B9]*. Joint control requires sharing of control or collective control by two or more parties. Some of the aspects of 'unanimous consent' for extractives arrangements are discussed at 7.1.1.B below.

For more information on assessing joint control see Chapter 12 at 4.

7.1.1.A Relevant activities

Relevant activities are those activities of the arrangement which significantly affect the returns of the arrangement. Determining what these are for each arrangement may require significant judgement.

Examples of decisions about relevant activities include, but are not limited to:

- Establishing operating and capital decisions of the arrangement including budgets – for an arrangement in the extractive industries, this may include approving the operating and/or capital expenditure programme for the next year; and
- Appointing and remunerating a joint arrangement's key management personnel or service providers and terminating their services or employment – for example, appointing a contract miner or oil field services provider to undertake operations.

For more information on identifying relevant activities, see Chapter 12 at 4.1.

7.1.1.B Meaning of unanimous consent

Unanimous consent means that any party with joint control can prevent any of the other parties, or a group of parties, from making unilateral decisions about relevant activities.

For further discussion on unanimous consent, see Chapter 12 at 4.3.

In some extractive industries operations, decision-making may vary over the life of the project, e.g. during the exploration and evaluation phase, the development phase or the production phase. For example, it may be agreed at the time of initially entering the contractual arrangement that during the exploration and evaluation phase, one party to the arrangement may be able to make all of the decisions, whereas once the project enters the development phase, decisions may then require unanimous consent. To determine whether the arrangement is jointly controlled, it will be necessary to decide (at the point of initially entering the contractual arrangement, and subsequently, should facts and circumstances change) which of these activities, e.g. exploration and evaluation and/or development, most significantly affect the returns of the arrangement. This is because the arrangement will only be considered to be a joint arrangement if those activities which require unanimous consent are the ones that most significantly affect the returns. This will be a highly judgemental assessment.

For further information on the impact of different decision-making arrangements over various activities, see Chapter 12 at 4.1.

7.1.2 Determination of whether a manager of a joint arrangement has control

It is common in the extractive industries for one of the parties to be appointed as the operator or manager of the joint arrangement. The manager is frequently referred to as the operator, but as IFRS 11 uses the terms 'joint operation' and 'joint operator' with specific meanings, to avoid confusion we refer to such a party as the manager. The other parties to the arrangement may delegate some of the decision-making rights to this manager. In many instances, it is considered that the manager does not control the joint arrangement, but simply carries out the decisions of the parties under the joint venture (or operating) agreement (JOA), i.e. the manager acts as an agent. This view is based on the way in which these roles are generally established and referred to, or perceived, in the industries. Under IFRS 11, consideration is given to whether the manager actually controls the arrangement. This is because when decision-making rights have been delegated, IFRS 10 describes how to assess whether the decision-maker is acting as a principal or an agent, and therefore, which party (if any) has control.

Careful consideration of the following will be required:

- Scope of the manager's decision-making authority;
- Rights held by others (e.g. protective rights and removal rights);
- Exposure to variability in returns through the remuneration of the manager; and
- Variable returns held through other interests (e.g. direct investments by the manager in the joint arrangement).

Of these factors, rights held by others and variable returns held through other interests will be particularly relevant for mining companies and oil and gas companies. Each of the above is discussed in Chapter 6 at 6 in more detail.

It is important to note that assessing whether an entity is a principal or an agent will require consideration of all factors collectively. See Chapter 6 at 6.1 for more details regarding the principal versus agent requirements.

Where it is determined that a manager is acting as a principal and therefore controls an arrangement, the impact of this will depend upon the rights and obligations conveyed by the arrangement (see 7.1.2.A and 7.1.2.B below for further discussion on this issue). Where it is determined that the manager is acting as an agent, the manager would only recognise its own interests in the joint arrangement (the accounting for which will depend upon whether it is a joint operation or joint venture) and its operator/management fee.

7.1.2.A Implications of controlling a joint operation

While the principal versus agent assessment may lead to a conclusion that an manager has control, if the joint arrangement is a joint operation, and each party has specific rights to, and obligations for, the underlying assets and liabilities of the arrangement by virtue of the contract, then the manager does not control anything over and above its own direct interest in those assets and liabilities. Therefore, it still only recognises its interest in those assets and liabilities conveyed to it by the contractual arrangement. This accounting applies regardless of whether the arrangement is in a separate vehicle or not, as the contractual terms are the primary determinant of the accounting. Note that IFRS 11 defines a separate vehicle as 'a separately identifiable financial structure, including separate legal entities or entities recognised by statute, regardless of whether those entities have a legal personality.' *[IFRS 11 Appendix A]*. To explain this further, it is worth considering the two types of joint arrangements contemplated by IFRS 11 – one that is not structured through a separate vehicle (e.g. a contract alone) and one that is structured through a separate vehicle.

No separate vehicle: Even if the manager 'controlled' the arrangement, there is really nothing for it to control. This is because each party would continue to account for its rights and obligations arising from the contract, e.g. it would apply IAS 16 to account for its rights to any tangible assets, IAS 38 to account for its rights to any intangible assets or IAS 39 to account for its obligations for any financial liabilities etc. Additionally, the consolidation requirements of IFRS 10 would not apply as they only apply to entities and, in most circumstances, a contract does not create an entity.

Separate vehicle: If a manager controls an arrangement structured through a separate vehicle, e.g. a company or trust, one may consider that an entity would automatically look to IFRS 10 and consolidate the arrangement and account for the interests of the other parties as non-controlling interests. However, in such situations, a contract may exist which gives other parties to the arrangement direct rights to, and obligations for, the underlying assets and liabilities of that arrangement. Therefore, this requires consideration of the impact of such an arrangement on the separate financial statements of the joint operation.

Given this, the rights and obligations arising from the contractual arrangement should be accounted for first. That is, each party to the arrangement should recognise its respective share of the assets and liabilities (applying each IFRS as appropriate, e.g. IAS 16, IAS 38, IAS 39 etc.).

To the extent that the parties to the arrangement have specific rights to the assets, or obligations for the liabilities, from the perspective of the separate vehicle, this means that the rights to, and obligations for, its assets and liabilities have been contracted out to other parties (i.e. the parties to the contractual arrangement) and therefore there may be no assets or liabilities remaining in the separate vehicle to recognise.

Consequently, from the perspective of the manager of the joint arrangement, who may be considered to control the separate vehicle, it would initially account for its and other parties' rights and obligations arising from the contract, and then when it looks to consolidate the separate vehicle, there may be nothing left to consolidate, as the separate vehicle may effectively be empty. However, this would only apply where the separate vehicle was an entity as IFRS 10 only applies to entities.

The above analysis demonstrates that where parties to an arrangement genuinely have contractual rights to, and obligations for, the underlying assets and liabilities of the arrangement, concluding that a manager controls the arrangement does not change the accounting for either the manager or the non-operator parties. However, the disclosure requirements would likely differ, since IFRS 12 does not apply to joint arrangements in which a party does not have joint control, unless that party has significant influence. The disclosure requirements of IFRS 12 are discussed in Chapter 13.

7.1.2.B Implications of controlling a joint venture

If a manager has control of a joint venture which was structured through a separate vehicle which is considered to be an entity, the manager would have to consolidate the separate vehicle and recognise any non-controlling interest(s). However, if the joint venture is structured through a separate vehicle that is not an entity, IFRS 10 would not apply, and the manager would apply the relevant IFRSs.

7.1.3 Parties to a joint arrangement without joint control or control

The accounting treatment of an interest in a contractual arrangement that does not give rise to joint control or control depends on the rights and obligations of the party.

7.1.3.A Joint operations

In some cases, a mining company or oil and gas company may be involved in a joint operation, but it does not have joint control or control of that arrangement. Similar to the situation discussed above at 7.1.2.A, effectively, if the joint arrangement is a joint operation, and the party has rights to the assets and obligations for the liabilities relating to that joint operation, it does not matter whether the parties to that joint arrangement have control, joint control or not – the accounting is the same as that for a joint operation under IFRS 11, which is discussed in more detail in Chapter 12 at 6.4. *[IFRS 11.23]*. However, the disclosure requirements would likely differ, since IFRS 12 does not apply to joint arrangements in which a party does not have joint control, unless that party has significant influence. The disclosure requirements of IFRS 12 are discussed in Chapter 13.

If the party does *not* have rights to the assets and obligations for the liabilities relating to the joint operation, it accounts for its interest in the joint operation in accordance with other applicable IFRSs. *[IFRS 11.23]*. For example, if it:

(a) has significant influence over a separate vehicle which is an entity – apply IAS 28 – *Investments in Associates and Joint Ventures*;

(b) has significant influence over a separate vehicle which is not an entity – apply other applicable IFRSs;

(c) does not have significant influence over a separate vehicle – account for that interest as a financial asset under IAS 39 or IFRS 9; or

(d) has an interest in an arrangement without a separate vehicle – apply other applicable IFRSs.

7.1.3.B Joint ventures

In some cases, a mining company or oil and gas company may be involved in a joint venture, but it does not have joint control or control of that arrangement. In this instance it would account for its interest as follows:

(a) significant influence over a separate vehicle which is an entity – still apply IAS 28 *[IFRS 11.25]*, however, the disclosure requirements differ for an associate versus a joint venture (see Chapter 13 at 5);

(b) significant influence over a separate vehicle which is not an entity – apply other applicable IFRSs; or

(c) does not have significant influence over a separate vehicle – account for that interest as a financial asset under IAS 39 at fair value through profit or loss or other comprehensive income, unless the investment was held for trading. See Chapter 47 for a detailed analysis of the impact of IFRS 9. *[IFRS 11.25, C14]*.

7.1.4 Managers of joint arrangements

It is clear that a participant in a joint operation is required to recognise its rights to the assets, and its obligations for the liabilities (or share thereof), of the joint arrangement. Therefore it is important that an entity fully understands what these rights and obligations are and how these may differ between the parties.

See 7.1.2 above for a discussion of the principal versus agent assessment that needs to be considered when an entity is appointed as manager of a joint arrangement and what impact that assessment might have on the manager's accounting.

7.1.4.A Reimbursements of costs

A manager often carries out activities on behalf of the joint arrangement on a no gain, no loss basis. Generally, these activities can be identified separately and are carried out by the manager in its capacity as an agent for the joint arrangement, which is effectively the principal in those transactions. The manager receives reimbursement of direct costs recharged to the joint arrangement. Such recharges are reimbursements of costs that the manager incurred as an agent for the joint arrangement and therefore have no effect on profit or loss in the statement of comprehensive income (or income statement) of the manager.

In many cases, a manager also incurs certain general overhead expenses in carrying out activities on behalf of the joint arrangement. As these costs can often not be specifically identified, many joint operating agreements allow the manager to recover the general overhead expenses incurred by charging an overhead fee that is based on a fixed percentage of the total costs incurred for the year. Although the purpose of this recharge is very similar to the reimbursement of direct costs, the manager is not acting as an agent in this case. Therefore, the manager should recognise the general overhead expenses and the overhead fee in profit or loss in its statement of comprehensive income (or income statement) as an expense and income, respectively.

7.1.4.B *Direct legal liability for costs incurred and contracts entered into*

The manager of a joint arrangement may have a direct legal liability to third party creditors in respect of the entire balance arising from transactions related to the joint arrangement, e.g. suppliers, lessors etc.[96] IFRS prohibits the offsetting of such liabilities against the amounts recoverable from the other joint arrangement participants. *[IAS 1.32, IAS 32.42]*. The manager may therefore need to recognise and/or disclose, for example, some of the leases or supply arrangements that it has entered into on behalf of the joint arrangement, as if it entered into these in its own name.

7.1.4.C *Joint and several liability*

It is also possible that there may be liabilities in the arrangement where the obligation is joint and several. That is, an entity is not only responsible for its proportionate share, but it is also liable for the other party's or parties' share(s) should it/they be unable or unwilling to pay. A common example of this in the extractives industries is restoration, rehabilitation and decommissioning obligations.

In these instances, each party not only takes up its proportionate share of the decommissioning/restoration obligation, it is also required to assess the likelihood that the other party/ies will not be able or willing to meet their share. The facts and circumstances would need to be assessed in each case, and any additional liability and disclosures would be accounted for, and disclosed, in accordance with IAS 37.

Any increase in the provision would be accounted for under IFRIC 1, if it related to a restoration or decommissioning liability that had both been included as part of an asset measured in accordance with IAS 16 and measured as a liability in accordance with IAS 37 (see Chapter 28 at 6.3.1 and 6.3.2 for more details). Such an addition to the asset would also require an entity to consider whether this is an indication of impairment of the asset as a whole, and if so, would need to test for impairment in accordance with IAS 36. Increases that do not meet the requirements of IFRIC 1 would be recognised in profit or loss.

7.1.5 *Non-operators of joint arrangements*

For expenses and liabilities incurred by the manager directly in its own name which it recharges to the non-operators, the non-operator entities would be required to recognise an amount payable to the operator for such amounts. These would be recognised as a financial instrument under IAS 32 and IAS 39/IFRS 9 or potentially a provision under IAS 37 and not under the standard which relates to the type of cost being reimbursed. For example, the non-operator's share of employee entitlements relating to the manager's employees who work on the joint project would not be recognised as an employee benefit under IAS 19 – *Employee Benefits*. In addition, the related disclosure requirements of IAS 19 would not apply, instead the disclosure requirements of other standards, e.g. IFRS 7 – *Financial Instruments: Disclosures* – would apply. Expenses and liabilities incurred by the manager jointly on behalf of all of the parties to the arrangement would have to be recognised directly by each of the non-operator parties in proportion to their respective interests in the arrangement.

7.2 Undivided interests

Undivided interests are usually subject to joint control (see Chapter 12 at 4.4.1) and can, therefore, be accounted for as joint operations. However, some JOAs do not establish joint control but are, instead, based on some form of supermajority voting whereby a qualified majority (e.g. 75%) of the participants can approve decisions. This situation usually arises when the group of participants is too large for joint control to be practical or when the main investor wants to retain a certain level of influence.

Where joint control does not exist, such undivided interests cannot be accounted for as joint operations in the scope of IFRS 11. Instead, the appropriate accounting treatment by the investor depends on the nature of the arrangement:

- If the investor has rights to the underlying asset then the arrangement should be accounted for as a tangible or intangible asset under IAS 16 or IAS 38, respectively. The investor's proportionate share of the operating costs of the asset (e.g. repairs and maintenance) should be accounted for in the same way as the operating costs of wholly owned assets; or
- If the investor is entitled only to a proportion of the cash flows generated by the asset then its investment will generally meet the definition of a financial asset under IAS 32. As the investor is exposed to risks other than credit risk, such investments do not meet the definition of 'loans and receivables' under IAS 39 and should, instead, be classified as either 'at fair value through profit or loss' or 'available for sale'. *[IAS 39.9]*. See Chapter 47 at 2 for a detailed analysis of the impact of IFRS 9 on the classification of this investment.

With respect to such undivided interests, entities also enter into arrangements in which they buy and sell parts of undivided assets, e.g. carried interests (see 6.1 above) and farm-in arrangements outside the E&E phase (see 6.2.2 and 6.2.3 above). Although neither IAS 16 nor IAS 38 addresses part-disposals of undivided assets, it is industry practice to apply the principles in those standards when the vendor disposes of these interests in circumstances in which it can demonstrate that it neither controls nor jointly controls the whole of the original asset. In these circumstances, the principles of IAS 16 and IAS 38 are applied and the entity derecognises part of the asset, having calculated an appropriate carrying value for the part disposed of, and a gain or loss on disposal. See Chapter 17 at 9.5 and Chapter 18 at 7.3.

8 ACQUISITIONS

8.1 Business combinations versus asset acquisitions

When an entity acquires an asset or a group of assets, careful analysis is required to identify whether what is acquired constitutes a business or represents only an asset or group of assets. Accounting for business combinations is discussed in detail in Chapter 9.

8.1.1 *Differences between asset purchase transactions and business combinations*

The reason it is important to distinguish between an asset acquisition and a business combination is because the accounting consequences are significantly different. The main differences between accounting for an asset acquisition and a business combination can be summarised as follows:

- goodwill or a bargain purchase (also sometimes referred to as negative goodwill) only arise in business combinations;
- assets and liabilities are accounted for at fair value in a business combination, while they are assigned a carrying amount based on their relative fair values in an asset acquisition;
- transaction costs should be recognised as an expense under IFRS 3, but can be capitalised on an asset acquisition; and
- in an asset acquisition no deferred tax will arise in relation to acquired assets and assumed liabilities as the initial recognition exception for deferred tax under IAS 12 – *Income Taxes* – applies.

8.1.2 *Definition of a business*

A business is defined in IFRS 3 as 'an integrated set of activities and assets that is capable of being conducted and managed for the purpose of providing a return in the form of dividends, lower costs or other economic benefits directly to investors or other owners, members or participants.' *[IFRS 3 Appendix A]*. Specifically IFRS 3: *[IFRS 3.BC18]*

- requires the integrated set of activities and assets to be 'capable' of being conducted and managed for the purpose of providing a return in the form of dividends, lower costs or other economic benefits directly to investors or other owners, members or participants. The focus on the capability to achieve the purposes of the business helps avoid the unduly restrictive interpretations that existed under the former guidance;
- clarifies the meaning of the terms 'inputs', 'processes' and 'outputs', which helps eliminate the need for extensive detailed guidance and the misinterpretations that sometimes stem from such guidance;
- clarifies that inputs and processes applied to those inputs are essential and that although the resulting outputs are normally present, they need not be present; and
- clarifies that a business need not include all of the inputs or processes that the seller used in operating that business if a market participant is capable of continuing to produce outputs, which helps avoid the need for extensive detailed guidance and assessments about whether a missing input or process is minor.

As discussed in Chapter 9 at 3.2.1, we believe that, in most cases, the acquired set of activities and assets must have at least some inputs and processes in order to be considered a business. If an acquirer obtains control of an input or set of inputs without any processes, we think it is unlikely that the acquired input(s) would be considered a business, even if a market participant had all the processes necessary to operate the input(s) as a business. The definition of a business under IFRS 3 is discussed in more detail in Chapter 9 at 3.2.

Determining whether a particular set of integrated activities and assets is a business will often require a significant amount of judgement, particularly for oil and gas companies and mining companies as illustrated in Example 41.6 below.

Example 41.6: Definition of a business under IFRS 3

Oil and gas company C acquires a single oil exploration area where there are active exploration activities underway, oil has been found and the company is close to declaring reserves but implementation of the development plan has not yet commenced.

This may be a business under IFRS 3 as assets and processes have been acquired and a market participant is capable of producing outputs by integrating these with its own inputs and processes.

Mining company D acquires a development stage mine, including all inputs (i.e. employees, mineral reserve and property, plant and equipment) and processes (i.e. exploration and evaluation processes e.g. active drilling programmes etc.) that are required to generate output.

This meets the definition of a business under IFRS 3 because it includes inputs and processes even though there are currently no outputs.

Oil and gas company E acquires a group of pipelines (or a fleet of oil or gas tankers) used for transporting gas on behalf of customers and the employees responsible for operational, maintenance and administrative tasks transfer to the buyer.

This meets the definition of a business under IFRS 3 because it includes inputs, processes and outputs.

Mining company F acquires a mine that was abandoned 10 years ago. There are no activities currently occurring at the mine. The company plans to perform new geological and geophysical survey to determine whether sufficient economic reserves are present.

The abandoned mine does not meet the definition of a business because there are no processes acquired in addition to the assets purchased.

Oil and gas company G acquires a producing oil field, but the seller's on-site staff will *not* transfer to the buyer. Instead, oil and gas company G will enter into maintenance and oil field services contracts with different contractors.

A business need not include all of the inputs or processes that the seller used in operating that business if market participants are capable of continuing to produce outputs. If market participants can easily outsource processes to contractors then the oil field would be a business under IFRS 3.

In June 2016, in response to stakeholder concerns raised during the post implementation review of IFRS 3, the IASB proposed amendments that clarify how to apply the definition of a business in IFRS 3. The proposed amendments aim to provide additional guidance to help distinguish between the acquisition of a business and the acquisition of a group of assets. See Chapter 9 at 3.2.6 for more information.

8.2 Business combinations

8.2.1 Goodwill in business combinations

Prior to the adoption of IFRS, many mining companies and oil and gas companies assumed that the entire consideration paid for upstream assets should be allocated to the identifiable net assets acquired, i.e. any excess of the consideration transferred over the fair value of the identifiable net assets (excluding mineral reserves and resources) acquired would then have been included within mineral reserves and resources acquired and goodwill would not generally be recognised. However, goodwill could arise as a result of synergies, overpayment by the acquirer, or when IFRS requires that acquired assets and/or liabilities are measured at an amount that is not fair value (e.g. deferred taxation). Therefore, it is unlikely to be appropriate for mining companies or oil and gas companies to simply assume that goodwill would never arise in a business combination and that any differential automatically goes to mineral reserves and resources. Mineral reserves and resources and any exploration potential (if relevant) acquired should be valued separately and any excess of the consideration transferred over and above the supportable fair value of the identifiable net assets (which include mineral reserves, resources and acquired exploration potential), should be allocated to goodwill.

By virtue of the way IFRS 3 operates, if an entity were simply to take any excess of the consideration transferred over the fair value of the identifiable net assets acquired to mineral reserves and resources, they may end up having to allocate significantly larger values to minerals reserves and resources than expected. This is because, under IFRS 3, an entity is required to provide for deferred taxation on the temporary differences relating to all identifiable net assets acquired (including mineral reserves and resources), but not on temporary differences related to goodwill. Therefore, if any excess was simply allocated to mineral reserves and resources, to the extent that this created a difference between the carrying amount and the tax base of the mineral reserves and resources, IAS 12 would give rise to a deferred tax liability on the temporary difference, which would create a further excess. This would then result in an iterative calculation in which the deferred tax liability recognised would increase the amount attributed to mineral reserves and resources, which would in turn give rise to an increase in the deferred tax liability (see Chapter 31 at 7.2.2). Given the very high marginal tax rates to which extractive activities are often subject (i.e. tax rates of 60 to 80% are not uncommon) the mineral reserves and resources might end up being grossed up by a factor of 2.5 to 5 (i.e. 1/(1 – 60%) = 2.5). Such an approach would only be acceptable if the final amount allocated to mineral reserves and resources remained in the range of fair values determined for those mineral reserves and resources. If not, such an approach would lead to excessive amounts being allocated to mineral reserves and resources which could not be supported by appropriate valuations.

The extract below from Glencore Xstrata's financial statements illustrates a typical accounting policy for business combinations in which excess consideration transferred is treated as goodwill.

Extract 41.13: Glencore Xstrata plc (2015)

Notes to the financial statements [extract]

1. ACCOUNTING POLICIES [extract]

Business combinations and goodwill [extract]

Acquisitions of subsidiaries and businesses are accounted for using the acquisition method of accounting. The cost of the acquisition is measured at fair value, which is calculated as the sum of the acquisition date fair values of the assets transferred, liabilities incurred to the former owners of the acquiree and the equity interests issued in exchange for control of the acquiree. The identifiable assets, liabilities and contingent liabilities ("identifiable net assets") are recognised at their fair value at the date of acquisition. Acquisition related costs are recognised in the consolidated statement of income as incurred.

[...]

Where the fair value of consideration transferred for a business combination exceeds the fair values attributable to Glencore's share of the identifiable net assets, the difference is treated as purchased goodwill.

8.2.2 Impairment of assets and goodwill recognised on acquisition

There are a number of circumstances in which the carrying amount of assets and goodwill acquired as part of a business combination and as recorded in the consolidated accounts, may be measured at a higher amount through recognition of notional tax benefits, also known as tax amortisation benefits (i.e. the value has been grossed up on the assumption that its carrying value is deductible for tax) or deferred tax (which can increase goodwill as described above). Application of IAS 36 to goodwill which arises upon recognition of deferred tax liabilities in a business combination is discussed in Chapter 20 at 5.2.1.

8.2.3 Value beyond proven and probable reserves (VBPP)

In the mining sector specifically, the 'value beyond proven and probable reserves' (VBPP) is defined as the economic value of the estimated cash flows of a mining asset beyond that asset's proven and probable reserves.

While this term is specifically relevant to the mining sector by virtue of specific guidance in US GAAP, the concept may be equally relevant to the oil and gas sector, i.e. the economic value of an oil and gas licence/area beyond the proven and probable reserves.

For mining companies, there are various situations in which mineralisation and mineral resources might not be classified as proven or probable:

- prior to the quantification of a resource, a mining company may identify mineralisation following exploration activities. However, it may be too early to assess if the geology and grade is sufficiently expansive to meet the definition of a resource;
- Acquired Exploration Potential (AEP) represents the legal right to explore for minerals in a particular property, occurring in the same geological area of interest;
- carrying out the required assessments and studies to obtain classification of mineral reserves can be very costly. Consequently, these activities are often deferred until they become necessary for the planning of future operations. Significant mineral resources are often awaiting the initiation of this process; and
- if an entity acquires a mining company at a time when commodity prices are particularly low, the mineral resources owned by the acquiree may not meet the definition of proven or probable reserves because extraction might not be commercially viable.

While the above types of mineralisation and mineral resources cannot be classified as proven or probable, they will often be valuable because of the future potential that they represent (i.e. reserves may be proven in the future and commodity price increases may make extraction commercially feasible).

IFRS 3 requires that an acquirer recognises the identifiable assets acquired and liabilities assumed that meet the definitions of assets and liabilities at the acquisition date. *[IFRS 3.11]*.

While the legal or contractual rights that allow an entity to extract minerals are not themselves tangible assets, the mineral reserves concerned clearly are. The legal or contractual rights – that allow an entity to extract mineral reserves and resources – acquired in business combinations should be recognised, without exception, at fair value.

An entity that acquires mineral reserves and resources that cannot be classified as proven or probable, should account for the VBPP as part of the value allocated to mining assets, to the extent that a market participant would include VBPP in determining the fair value of the asset, rather than as goodwill.[97] In practice, the majority of mining companies treat mining assets, the related mineral reserves and resources and licences as tangible assets on the basis that they relate to minerals in the ground, which are themselves tangible assets. However, some entities present the value associated with E&E assets as intangible assets.

AEP would often be indistinguishable from the value of the mineral licence to which it relates. Therefore, the classification of AEP may vary depending on how an entity presents its mining assets and licences. If an entity presents them as tangible assets, they may be likely to treat AEP (or its equivalent), where applicable, as forming part of mineral properties, and hence AEP would be classified as a tangible asset. For an entity that classifies some of its mineral assets as intangible assets, e.g. E&E assets, then they may classify AEP as an intangible also.

Determining the fair value of VBPP requires a considerable amount of expertise. An entity should not only take account of commodity spot prices but also consider the effects of anticipated fluctuations in the future price of minerals, in a manner that is consistent with the expectations of a market participant. An entity should consider all available information including current prices, historical averages, and forward pricing curves and maximise the use of observable inputs. Those market participant assumptions typically are consistent with the acquiring entity's operating plans for developing and producing minerals. However entities need to undertake steps to demonstrate this is true (to ensure compliance with the requirements of IFRS 13 – *Fair Value Measurement*). The potential upside associated with mineral resources that are not classified as reserves can be much larger than the downward risk. A valuation model that only takes account of a single factor, such as the spot price, historical average or a single long-term price, without considering other information that a market participant would consider, would generally not be able to reflect the upward potential that determines much of the value of VBPP. Consequently, an entity may need to apply option valuation techniques in measuring VBPP.

There are commonly considered to be three categories of VBPP, including:

- mineral resources not yet tested for economic viability;
- early mineralisation; and
- acquired exploration potential.

The CRIRSCO reporting standards consider the geological definition of mineral resources that have not yet been tested for economic viability, which is the first category of VBPP. Valuation techniques used for this category include:

- probability weighted discounted-cash flows;
- resource reserve conversion adjustment;
- comparable transactions; and
- option valuation.

In relation to early mineralisation, the second category of VBPP, while it may represent a discovery, its true value will be determined by further appraisal/evaluation activities to confirm whether a resource exists. This category of VBPP is often grouped with the next (and final) category, being AEP, even though it has a higher intrinsic value, and is valued using:

- cost based methods;
- budgeted expenditure methods;
- comparable sales;
- farm in/out values; or
- sophisticated option pricing.

In relation to AEP, the basis for its valuation varies from studying historic cost to the use of sophisticated option valuation techniques.

As VBPP does not provide current economic benefits, there is no need to allocate its cost against current revenue and hence no need for amortisation or depreciation. However, as part of the process of completing the acquisition accounting, an entity should form a view about how that value will ultimately be ascribed to future discoveries and converted into proven and probable reserves and then ultimately depreciated. Such methodologies might include a per unit (e.g. tonnes/ounces) basis or possibly an area (e.g. acreage) basis. VBPP would need to be tested for impairment under IAS 36 if, depending on the classification of VBPP, there is an indicator of impairment under that standard or IFRS 6. The VBPP may ultimately be impaired because it may never be converted into proven or probable reserves, but impairment may not be confirmed until the entity is satisfied that the project will not continue.

An impairment of VBPP should be recognised if its book value exceeds the higher of fair value less costs of disposal and value in use. In practice, there may not be a convenient method to determine the value in use. Hence, impairment testing will often need to rely on an approach based on fair value less costs of disposal.

Extract 41.14 below illustrates that AngloGold Ashanti does not subsume the 'value beyond proven and probable reserves' in goodwill but instead recognises it as part of the value ascribed to mineral resources.

Extract 41.14: AngloGold Ashanti Limited (2015)

GROUP – NOTES TO THE FINANCIAL STATEMENTS [extract]

For the year ended 31 December

1 ACCOUNTING POLICIES [extract]

1.3 SUMMARY OF SIGNIFICANT ACCOUNTING POLICIES [extract]

Intangible assets [extract]

Acquisition and goodwill arising thereon

Where an investment in a subsidiary, joint venture or an associate is made, any excess of the consideration transferred over the fair value of the attributable Mineral Resource including value beyond Proven and Probable Ore Reserves, exploration properties and net assets is recognised as goodwill. Goodwill in respect of subsidiaries is disclosed as goodwill.

Goodwill relating to subsidiaries is tested annually for impairment and carried at cost less accumulated impairment losses. Gains and losses on the disposal of an entity include the carrying amount of goodwill relating to the entity sold. Goodwill is allocated to cash-generating units for the purpose of impairment testing.

8.3 Acquisition of an interest in a joint operation that is a business

One area where there has historically been a lack of clarity is how to account for acquisitions of interests in joint operations (under IFRS 11) which constitute businesses. However, an amendment to IFRS 11 has been made by the IASB to clarify this, which applies prospectively to acquisitions that occur on or after 1 January 2016. The amendment states that where an entity is acquiring an interest in a joint operation that is a business as defined in IFRS 3, it should apply, to the extent of its share in accordance with paragraph 20 of IFRS 11, all of the principles of business combinations accounting in IFRS 3, and in other IFRSs, that do not conflict with IFRS 11. In addition, the entity should disclose the information that is required in those IFRSs in relation to business combinations. However, if an entity acquires an interest in a (group of) asset(s) that is (are) not a business as defined in IFRS 3 then it should apply the guidance on asset acquisitions that IFRS already provides. *[IFRS 11.BC45I].*

The requirements apply to the acquisition of an initial interest in a joint operation or where the acquisition leads to the formation of a joint operation that constitute a business, and also to the acquisition of additional interests in a joint operation to the extent that joint control is maintained. The amendment also makes it clear that any previously held interest in the joint operation would not be remeasured if the joint operator acquires an additional interest while retaining joint control.

Until these new requirements become effective, the accounting method selected by an entity should be appropriate based on the facts and circumstances of the transaction.

See Chapter 12 at 8.3.1.B for further discussion on this.

In addition to the matters outlined above, there are a number of additional issues which have been raised in relation to joint operations. These include:

- **A passive investor in a joint operation becomes a joint operator:** In this situation, the issue is whether a previously held interest in the assets and liabilities of a joint operation that is a business is remeasured to fair value when the investor's acquisition of an additional interest results in the investor becoming a joint operator (i.e. assumes joint control) in that joint operation. The Interpretations Committee considered this issue recently and tentatively decided that the previously held interest in this situation should not be remeasured. The IASB agreed with this decision and an exposure draft has been issued proposing to amend IFRS 11 to reflect this conclusion (see Chapter 12 at 8.3.1.B for further discussion on this).
- **Obtaining control over a joint operation:** Where a party obtains control over a joint operation where it previously held an interest in the assets and liabilities immediately before the acquisition date, either as a joint operator or as a party that participates in a joint operation but does not have joint control, it is required to apply the business combination achieved in stages accounting requirements in IFRS 3, if the acquiree meets the definition of a business (see Chapter 9 at 3.2). However, it had not previously been clear, when this acquisition related to a joint operation that was not structured through a separate vehicle, whether the previously held interest in the assets and liabilities of the joint operation should be remeasured to fair value at the date when control is obtained. As a result, diversity had existed. This diversity arose because of differing

interpretations of the term 'equity interests' and whether this included interests in the assets and liabilities of a joint operation. This issue was raised with the Interpretations Committee who agreed that this issue was not covered by current standards and proposed that these interests should be remeasured to fair value at the date of obtaining control. The IASB agreed with this and an exposure draft has been issued proposing an amendment to IFRS 3 to reflect this conclusion (see Chapter 12 at 8.3.2 for more information).

8.4 Asset acquisitions

The acquisition of an asset, group of assets or an entity that does not constitute a business is not a business combination. In such cases the acquirer should identify and recognise the individual identifiable assets acquired and liabilities assumed. The cost of the acquisition should be allocated to the individual identifiable assets acquired and liabilities assumed on the basis of their relative fair values at the date of purchase. Such a transaction or event does not give rise to goodwill. *[IFRS 3.2(b)]*.

Any difference between the carrying amount of the assets and liabilities thus recognised and their tax base would not give rise to a recognised deferred tax asset or liability under IAS 12 as it would fall within the initial recognition exception under that standard (see Chapter 31 at 7.2). *[IAS 12.15, 24]*.

8.4.1 Asset acquisitions and conditional purchase consideration

When an asset or a group of assets/net assets that do not constitute a business are acquired, they are required to be accounted for at cost. There are various standards in which 'cost' is defined, with those of most relevance to the acquisition of an asset being IAS 16, IAS 38 and IAS 40. Cost is defined in those standards as 'the amount of cash or cash equivalents paid or the fair value of the other consideration given to acquire an asset at the time of its acquisition or construction or, where applicable, the amount attributed to that asset when initially recognised in accordance with the specific requirements of other IFRSs, e.g. IFRS 2 – *Share-based Payment*'. *[IAS 16.6, IAS 38.8, IAS 40.5]*. Amounts capitalised under IFRS 6 are also required to be measured initially at cost. *[IFRS 6.8]*.

These requirements sometimes give rise to issues in situations where the purchase price is conditional upon certain events or facts. These issues can best be illustrated by an example.

Example 41.7: Asset acquisitions with a conditional purchase price

Scenario 1

Entity A agrees to buy a group of assets from Entity B which does not constitute a business for a total purchase price of $15 million. However, the purchase contract provides a formula for adjusting the purchase price upward or downward based on the report of a surveyor on the existence and quality of the assets listed in the contract.

Scenario 2

Entity C agrees to buy an exploration licence and several related assets from Entity D which do not constitute a business for a total purchase price of $35 million. However, Entity C would only be allowed to extract minerals in excess of 20 million barrels (or tonnes), upon payment of an additional consideration transferred of $12 million.

In scenario 1, we believe Entity A would be required to account for the fair value of the consideration transferred as determined at the date of acquisition. In contrast to the treatment under IFRS 3, there is no purchase price allocation or measurement period under IAS 16. However, suppose that three weeks after the initial accounting the surveyor reports that at the date of acquisition a number of assets listed in the contract were not present or were of inferior quality, the purchase price is therefore adjusted downwards to $14.5 million. Rather than recognising a profit arising from this adjustment, the entity should adjust the cost of the asset as the surveyor's report provides evidence of conditions that existed at the date of acquisition. *[IAS 10.3(a)]*.

In scenario 2 above, Entity C pays an additional $12 million in exchange for additional rights to extract minerals in excess of 20 million barrels (or tonnes) agreed upon in the initial transaction. At the date that Entity C purchases the additional rights it accounts for this as an additional asset acquisition. In more complicated scenarios, however, it might be necessary to assess whether the first and second acquisition should be accounted for together.

It is clear from the above two scenarios that changes in the facts and circumstances can have a significant effect on the accounting for conditional purchase consideration.

When considering asset acquisitions with contingent consideration, several issues need to be addressed. These include:

- how and when the contingent element should be accounted for, i.e. when a liability should be recognised and how it should be measured;
- whether the initial cost of the asset acquired includes an amount relating to the contingent element; and
- how the remeasurement (if any) of any liability recognised in relation to the contingent element should be accounted for. Should it be recognised as an adjustment to the cost of the asset acquired, or should it be recognised in profit or loss?

IAS 32 (as currently worded) is clear that the purchase of goods on credit gives rise to a financial liability when the goods are delivered (see Chapter 43 at 2.2.6) and that a contingent obligation to deliver cash meets the definition of a financial liability (see Chapter 43 at 2.2.3). Consequently, it would seem that given the current requirements of IFRS, a financial liability arises on the outright purchase of an item of property, plant and equipment or an intangible asset if the purchase contract requires the subsequent payment of contingent consideration, for example amounts based on the performance of the asset. Further, because there is currently no exemption from applying IAS 39 and IFRS 9 to such contracts, one might expect that such a liability would be accounted for in accordance with IAS 39 or IFRS 9, i.e. any measurement changes to that liability would flow through profit or loss. This would be consistent with the accounting treatment for contingent consideration arising from a business combination under IFRS 3 (see Chapter 43 at 3.7.1.A). However, this is not necessarily clear and for this reason the issue of how to account for contingent consideration in the acquisition of an item of PP&E was taken to the Interpretations Committee. See below for further discussion of this issue.

The current definition of cost in IAS 16 and IAS 38 requires the cost of an asset on the date of purchase to include the fair value of the consideration given (if a reliable estimate can be made), such as an obligation to pay a contingent price. Based on our experience and the level of diversity of views identified as part of the Interpretations Committee's considerations of this, not all would agree that all contingent payments are for the original asset and, indeed, the circumstances of a particular contract might support this. In addition to this issue, there is the issue of how to account for the remeasurement of the liability and whether changes should be recognised in profit or loss, or included as an adjustment to the cost of the asset.

In practice, contracts can be more complex than suggested above and often give rise to situations where the purchaser can influence or control the crystallisation of the contingent payments, e.g. where the contingent payments are dependent on the purchaser's future actions – such as those that take the form of production-based royalties. These complexities can raise broader questions about the nature of the obligations and, as in the case of royalty-based contingent payments, the appropriate accounting standard to apply initially, as well as how to account for subsequent adjustments to any liability that may have been recognised. To date, these complexities and lack of clarity as to the appropriate accounting have led to various treatments, including:

- the cost of the asset does not initially include any amount relating to the contingent element. Any subsequent payments made in relation to the contingent element are either adjusted against the cost of the asset (once paid) or recognised in profit or loss as incurred;
- the cost of the asset includes an estimate of the contingent consideration at the date of purchase. Subsequent changes in the liability relating to the contingent consideration are then recognised in profit or loss; or
- the cost of the asset includes an estimate of the contingent consideration at the date of purchase. Subsequent changes in the liability relating to the contingent consideration that do not reflect the passage of time are adjusted against the cost of the asset.

The first approach (which is relatively common in the extractive industries) considers that the applicable standard is IAS 37, and applies the concepts of obligating events, probability, contingencies and not providing for future operations. This means that nothing relating to the contingent payment is recognised at the date of purchase. The second approach applies the methodology in IFRS 3, while the third is based on the principles of IFRIC 1.[98]

Given this divergence in practice, this issue was referred to the Interpretations Committee in January 2011. The Committee and the IASB have discussed this issue for a number of years since this date. They had been attempting to clarify how the initial recognition and subsequent changes in relation to such contingent consideration should be recognised but did not conclude.

Until the Interpretations Committee and/or IASB progress this issue and the matter is resolved, an entity must capitalise expenditure that meets the definition of an asset, although it may choose not to recognise these costs until incurred. For other variable costs, it has the option to either:

(i) not capitalise on initial recognition and expense variable payments; or

(ii) capitalise them at their fair value on initial recognition and recognise the changes in contingent consideration in profit or loss or as an asset if certain conditions are met.

The accounting policy must be applied consistently.

For further information on this issue see Chapter 17 at 4.5, Chapter 18 at 4.1.9 and Chapter 43 at 3.8.

8.4.2 Accounting for land acquisitions

Obtaining the legal rights to explore for, develop and produce minerals can be achieved in a number of ways, as outlined at 5 above. One of these ways is through the outright purchase of the minerals and the land on, or under, which the minerals are located. In undertaking such a transaction, it is not uncommon for an entity to pay an amount in excess of the intrinsic value of the land itself. In such a situation, an entity needs to ensure it appropriately allocates the purchase price between the fair value of the land and the fair value of the mineral or surface mining rights acquired. The amount allocated to land will be capitalised and not depreciated, whereas the amount allocated to the minerals or surface mining rights will form part of the total cost of mining assets and will ultimately be depreciated on a units of production basis over the economically recoverable reserves to which it relates.

9 FUNCTIONAL CURRENCY

9.1 Determining functional currency

Determining functional currency correctly is important because it will, for example, affect volatility of revenue and operating profit resulting from exchange rate movements, determine whether transactions can be hedged or not and influence the identification of embedded currency derivatives. The movements may give rise to temporary differences that affect profit or loss. *[IAS 12.41]*. While under IAS 21 – *The Effects of Changes in Foreign Exchange Rates* – an entity can select any presentation currency, it does not have a free choice in determining its functional currency. Choice of functional currency is discussed in detail in Chapter 15 at 4; below is a summary of the application of the requirements to the extractive industries.

IAS 21 requires an entity to determine separately the functional currency of each entity within a consolidated group. There is no concept of the functional currency of the group, only a presentation currency. Therefore, the functional currency of an operating subsidiary may differ from that of the group's parent and/or foreign sales company to which it sells its production. The factors taken into account in determining functional currency may differ for operating companies and for group entities that are financing or intermediate holding companies (see Chapter 15 at 4.2). IAS 21 requires an entity to consider the following factors in determining its functional currency:

(a) the currency that mainly influences sales prices for goods and services (this will often be the currency in which sales prices for its goods and services are denominated and settled);

(b) the currency of the country whose competitive forces and regulations mainly determine the sales prices of its goods and services; and

(c) the currency that mainly influences labour, material and other costs of providing goods or services (this will often be the currency in which such costs are denominated and settled). *[IAS 21.9]*.

While the currency referred to under (a) above will often be the currency in which sales prices for its goods and services are denominated and settled, this is not always the case. The US dollar is used for many commodities as the contract or settlement currency in transactions (e.g. iron ore, oil), but the pricing of transactions is often driven by factors completely unrelated to the US dollar or the US economy (e.g. it may be influenced more by demand from the local economy or other economies such as China).

As the extractive industries are international, it is often difficult to determine the currency of the country whose competitive forces and regulations mainly determine the sales prices of its goods and services. Therefore, factor (b) above will often prove to be inconclusive when a particular product is produced in many different countries.

It will generally be fairly straightforward to identify the currency that mainly influences an entity's key inputs (i.e. factor (c) above). In developing countries an entity will often need to import a significant proportion of its key inputs (e.g. fuel, equipment and expatriate workers) and even local inputs in an economy with a high inflation rate will often be linked to the US dollar. In such a case, the local currency is less likely to be the main currency that influences an entity's key inputs. In most developed countries, however, the inputs tend to be denominated in the local currency, although some inputs (e.g. major items of equipment) may be denominated in another currency. As the extractive industries are capital intensive, the cost of equipment often far exceeds the operating expenses incurred. Equipment is often purchased in US dollars.

When the factors (a) to (c) above are mixed, as they often are in practice, and the functional currency is not obvious, management should use 'its judgement to determine the functional currency that most faithfully represents the economic effects of the underlying transactions, events and conditions'. *[IAS 21.12]*. If the above factors are inconclusive then an entity should also consider the following secondary factors:

- the currency in which funds from financing activities (i.e. issuing debt and equity instruments) are generated;
- the currency in which receipts from operating activities are usually retained; and
- the functional currency of the reporting entity that has the foreign operation as its subsidiary, branch, associate or joint venture. *[IAS 21.10, 11]*.

After considering both the primary and secondary factors the functional currency may not be obvious because, for example, revenue is denominated in US dollars while virtually all expenses are denominated in the local currency. In that situation management may conclude that revenue, while denominated in US dollars, is in fact influenced by a basket of currencies. It is therefore possible that companies operating in a similar environment can reach different conclusions about their functional currency. Even in developed countries there is a general bias towards the US dollar as the functional currency.

Although local statutory and tax requirements should be ignored in determining the functional currency, there may be a requirement to keep two sets of accounting records when an entity concludes that its local currency is not its functional currency.

The extract below from Rio Tinto illustrates a typical currency translation accounting policy of a mining company.

Extract 41.15: Rio Tinto plc (2015)

Notes to the 2015 financial statements [extract]

1 Principal accounting policies [extract]

(d) Currency translation

The functional currency for each entity in the Group, and for joint arrangements and associates, is the currency of the primary economic environment in which that entity operates. For many entities, this is the currency of the country in which they are located. Transactions denominated in other currencies are converted to the functional currency at the exchange rate ruling at the date of the transaction. Monetary assets and liabilities denominated in foreign currencies are retranslated at year-end exchange rates. The Group's accounting policies for derivative financial instruments and hedge accounting are explained in more detail in note 1(p)(iii).

The Group's financial statements are presented in US dollars, as that presentation currency most reliably reflects the global business performance of the Group as a whole. On consolidation, income statement items for each entity are translated from the functional currency into US dollars at average rates of exchange where the average is a reasonable approximation of rates prevailing on the transaction date. Balance sheet items are translated into US dollars at period-end exchange rates.

Exchange differences arising on the translation of the net assets of entities with functional currencies other than the US dollar are recognised directly in the currency translation reserve. These translation differences are shown in the statement of comprehensive income, with the exception of translation adjustments relating to Rio Tinto Limited's share capital which are shown in the statement of changes in equity.

Where an intragroup balance is, in substance, part of the Group's net investment in an entity, exchange gains and losses on that balance are taken to the currency translation reserve.

Except as noted above, or in note 1(p) below relating to derivative contracts, all other exchange differences are charged or credited to the income statement in the year in which they arise.

9.2 Changes in functional currency

IAS 21 requires management to use its judgement to determine the entity's functional currency so that it most faithfully represents the economic effects of the underlying transactions, events and conditions that are relevant to the entity. Note that IAS 21 requires the functional currency to be determined by reference to factors that exist *during* the reporting period. Therefore, an entity should ignore future developments in its business, no matter how likely those developments are. For example, even if an entity is convinced that in three years' time it will have revenues that will be denominated in

US dollars, this is not a factor to be considered in determining its functional currency today. This is particularly relevant for entities in the extractive industries given the nature of their operations. For example, a company may conclude that during the development phase of the project the local currency is its functional currency but that once production and sales commence the US dollar will become its functional currency. Alternatively, exposure to a particular currency may increase during a period.

This is illustrated in the extract below from Woodside Petroleum's 2010 financial statements.

Extract 41.16: Woodside Petroleum Ltd (2010)

Overview

CHIEF FINANCIAL OFFICER'S REPORT [extract]

Funding our growth plans and sustaining superior shareholder returns [extract]

US dollar functional currency implemented

With approximately 90% of revenue and more than 90% of debt denominated in US dollars, Woodside's directors adopted a US dollar functional currency and presentation currency for the purpose of all financial reporting, effective 1 January 2010. This change provides shareholders with a more accurate reflection of the company's underlying performance, while increasing comparability of our financial results with those of our industry peers.

The one-off impacts of this change are highlighted in the Notes to the Financial Report.

Notes to and forming part of the Financial Report continued [extract]

For the year ended 31 December 2010

1. Summary of significant accounting policies (continued) [extract]

(a) Basis of preparation (continued) [extract]

Change in functional and presentation currency

An entity's functional currency is the currency of the primary economic environment in which the entity operates. Woodside Petroleum Ltd has experienced a period of sustained growth in US dollar revenue streams and in the period up to 31 December 2009 increased its US dollar debt levels significantly. Consequently, the company announced on 22 March 2010 that the directors had determined that the functional currency of the company and all its subsidiaries is US dollars. The change in functional currency has been applied prospectively with effect from 1 January 2010 in accordance with the requirements of the Accounting Standards.

Following the change in functional currency, Woodside Petroleum Ltd has elected to change its presentation currency from Australian dollars to US dollars. The directors believe that changing the presentation currency to US dollars will enhance comparability with its industry peer group, the majority of which report in US dollars. The change in presentation currency represents a voluntary change in accounting policy, which has been applied retrospectively.

To give effect to the change in functional currency, the assets and liabilities of entities with an Australian dollar functional currency at 31 December 2009 were converted into US dollars at a fixed exchange rate on 1 January 2010 of US$1:A$1.1193 and the contributed equity, reserves and retained earnings were converted at applicable historical rates. In order to derive US dollar comparatives (presentation currency), the Australian dollar functional currency assets and liabilities at 31 December 2009 were converted at the spot rate of US$1:A$1.1193 on the reporting date; revenue and expenses for the year ended 31 December 2009 were converted at the average exchange rate of US$1:A$1.261 for the reporting period, or at the exchange rates ruling at the date of the transaction to the extent practicable, and equity balances were converted at applicable historical rates.

The above stated procedures resulted in a foreign currency translation reserve of US$594 million on 1 January 2009. Earnings per share for 2009 has also been restated in US dollars to reflect the change in the presentation currency (refer to Note 5).

Once the functional currency is determined, the standard allows it to be changed only if there is a change in those underlying transactions, events and conditions. For example, a change in the currency that mainly influences the sales prices of goods and services may lead to a change in an entity's functional currency. *[IAS 21.36]*.

The extract below, from Angel Mining plc's financial statements, provides an example of a change in conditions that resulted in a change in functional currency. Accounting for a change in functional currency is discussed in Chapter 15 at 5.5.

Extract 41.17: Angel Mining plc (2010)

Notes to the financial statements
Year ended 28 February 2010 [extract]
1a. Basis of preparation – Change in functional currency

Previously, the directors considered the functional currency of the Company to be Sterling. In light of developments within the Company's operations and the nature of its funding, the directors have reassessed the functional currency of the Company and concluded that the currency of the primary economic environment in which Angel Mining operates is now the US dollar. The date of change from Sterling to US dollars has been taken as 1 March 2009. The key factors influencing this decision include the following:

(i) During the year, the Company acquired the Nalunaq license and mining assets. This will be the first producing mine for the Company. The consideration for these assets was paid in US dollars;

(ii) During the year, the Company sourced plant, machinery and employees with technical skills on a global basis. A significant proportion of these costs were based in US dollars. In prior years, the Company's costs had been incurred primarily in Sterling;

(iii) The Company's primary form of finance during the period was the long term and short term debt facilities provided by FBC. These facilities are all based in US dollars. During prior periods, the Company had been more heavily dependent upon equity finance which was denominated in Sterling;

(iv) The vast majority of the forms of finance which the Company has been pursuing and is likely to pursue going forward are US dollar based;

(v) Commencing during the year, one of the largest consumables used by the Company in its operations in Greenland was diesel fuel. Although the Company pays for its diesel in Danish Kroner, the price of diesel is determined globally and priced in US dollars; and

(vi) The resources that the Company is working to exploit are global commodities which are always priced in US dollars. When the Company begins producing, all its revenues will be dollar based.

The change in the Company's functional currency has been accounted for prospectively from 1 March 2009 in accordance with IAS 21. This change constituted a prospective change in accounting policy. The financial statements for 2009 have been prepared using Sterling as the functional currency and US dollars as the presentational currency.

The change in the presentational currency from Sterling to US dollar is and therefore is applied retrospectively in accordance with IAS 8 'Accounting Policies, Changes in Accounting Estimates and Errors' and therefore require comparative information to be restated and consequently, a third balance sheet is required to be presented in the financial statements.

The impact of this change in presentational currency for 2009, is as follows:

(i) The assets and liabilities for both the Group and the Company at 28 February 2009 have been translated using the closing rate for the same date of $1.426/£;

(ii) The consolidated income statement for 2009 has been translated using the average rate for the year ended 28 February 2009 of $1.771/£ on the basis that this average rate approximates the exchange rates on the dates of transactions; and

The resulting gain on retranslation from average to closing rate has been recognised in the consolidated statement of comprehensive income.

Chapter 41

10 DECOMMISSIONING AND RESTORATION/REHABILITATION

The operations of entities engaged in extractive industries can have a significant impact on the environment. Decommissioning or restoration activities at the end of a mining or oil and gas operation may be required by law, the terms of mineral licences or an entity's stated policy and past practice. The associated costs of decommissioning, remediation or restoration can be significant. The accounting treatment for such costs is therefore critical. Different terms may be used, often interchangeably, to essentially refer to the same activity, e.g. restoration, remediation and rehabilitation. In this section we shall use the words decommissioning and restoration.

Accounting for decommissioning and restoration costs is governed by the requirements of IAS 37 and IFRIC 1. The discussion below should be read in conjunction with Chapter 18 (Property, Plant and Equipment) at 4.3, Chapter 28 (Provisions, Contingent Liabilities and Contingent Assets) and Chapter 31 (Income Taxes) at 7.2.7.A. Some of the specific issues to consider with respect to such provisions are listed below:

- Initial recognition – see 10.1.1 below;
- Initial measurement – see 10.1.2 below;
- Discount rates – see Chapter 28 at 4.3;
- Decommissioning or restoration costs incurred in the production phase – see 10.1.3 below;
- Changes in decommissioning and restoration/rehabilitation costs – see Chapter 28 at 6.3.1 and 6.3.2;
- Treatment of foreign exchange differences – see 10.2 below;
- Accounting for deferred taxes – see Chapter 31 at 7.2.7.A;
- Indefinite life assets – see 10.3 below; and
- Funds established or put aside to meet a decommissioning or restoration obligation – see Chapter 28 at 6.3.3.

10.1 Recognition and measurement issues

10.1.1 Initial recognition

Initial recognition of a decommissioning or restoration provision only on commencement of commercial production is generally not appropriate under IFRS, because the obligation to remove facilities and to restore the environment typically arises during the development/construction of the facilities, with some further obligations arising during the production phase. Therefore, a decommissioning or restoration provision should be recognised during the development or construction phase (see 1.6.1 above) of the project, i.e. before any production takes place, and should form part of the cost of the assets acquired or constructed. It may also be necessary to recognise a further decommissioning or restoration provision during the production phase (see 10.1.3 below).

While the damage caused in the exploration phase may generally be immaterial, an entity should recognise a decommissioning or restoration provision where the damage is material and the entity will be required to carry out remediation. The accounting for such a provision will depend on how the related E&E costs have been accounted for. If the E&E costs are capitalised, the associated decommissioning costs should also be capitalised. However, if the E&E costs are expensed, any associated decommissioning or restoration costs should also be expensed.

Finally, even if decommissioning and restoration were not planned to take place in the foreseeable future (for example because the related assets are continually renewed and replaced), IAS 37 would still require a decommissioning or restoration provision to be recognised. However, in these cases the discounted value of the obligation may be comparatively insignificant.

10.1.2 Measurement of the liability

Measurement of a decommissioning or restoration provision requires a significant amount of judgement because:

- the amount of remedial work required will depend on the scale of the operations. In the extractives industries the environmental damage may vary considerably depending on the type and development of the project;
- the amount of remedial work further depends on environmental standards imposed by local regulators, which may vary over time;
- detailed decommissioning and remedial work plans will often not be developed until fairly shortly before closure of the operations;
- it may not always be clear which costs are directly attributable to decommissioning or restoration (e.g. security costs, maintenance cost, ongoing environmental monitoring and employee termination costs);
- the timing of the decommissioning or restoration depends on when the fields or mines cease to produce at economically viable rates, which depends upon future commodity prices and reserves; and
- the actual decommissioning or restoration work will often be carried out by specialised contractors, the cost of which will depend on future market prices for the necessary remedial work.

Many of the uncertainties above can only be finally resolved towards the end of the production phase, shortly before decommissioning and restoration are to take place. A significant increase in the decommissioning or restoration provision resulting from revised estimates would result in recognition of an additional asset. However, as IFRIC 1 specifically states that any addition to an asset as a result of an increase in a decommissioning or restoration provision is considered to be a trigger for impairment testing, a significant increase in a decommissioning or restoration provision close to the end of the production phase may lead to an immediate impairment of that additional asset. Conversely, a decrease in the decommissioning or restoration provision could exceed the carrying amount of the related asset, in which case the excess should be recognised as a gain in profit or loss.

10.1.3 Decommissioning or restoration costs incurred in the production phase

IAS 16 considers the initial estimate of the costs of dismantling and removing the item and restoring the site on which it is located to be part of the cost of an item of property, plant and equipment. *[IAS 16.16(c)]*. However, an entity should apply IAS 2 to the costs of obligations for dismantling, removing and restoring the site on which an item is located that are incurred during a particular period as a consequence of having used the item to produce inventories during that period. *[IAS 16.18]*. That means that such additional decommissioning or restoration costs resulting from production activities should be included in the cost of inventories, *[IAS 2.10]*, while decommissioning costs resulting from the construction of assets during the production phase should be accounted for as discussed above.

An entity that incurs abnormal amounts of costs (e.g. costs of remediation of soil contamination from oil spills or overflowing of a tailings pond) should not treat these as part of the cost of inventories under IAS 2, but expense them immediately. *[IAS 2.16]*.

10.2 Treatment of foreign exchange differences

In most cases it will be appropriate for the exchange differences arising on provisions to be taken to profit or loss in the period they arise. However, it may be that an entity has recognised a decommissioning provision under IAS 37 and capitalised it as part of the initial cost of an asset under IAS 16. One practical difficulty with decommissioning provisions recognised under IAS 37 is that due to the long period over which the actual cash outflows will arise, an entity may not know the currency in which the transaction will actually be settled. Nevertheless, if it is determined that it is expected to be settled in a foreign currency it will be a monetary item. The main issue then is what should happen to any exchange differences.

As discussed in Chapter 28 at 6.3, IFRIC 1 applies to any decommissioning or similar liability that has been both included as part of an asset and measured as a liability in accordance with IAS 37. IFRIC 1 requires, *inter alia*, that any adjustment to such a provision resulting from changes in the estimated outflow of resources embodying economic benefits (e.g. cash flows) required to settle the obligation should not be taken to profit or loss as it occurs, but should be added to or deducted from the cost of the asset to which it relates. Therefore, the requirement of IAS 21 to take the exchange differences arising on the provision to profit or loss in the period in which they arise conflicts with this requirement in IFRIC 1. It is our view that IFRIC 1 is the more relevant pronouncement for decommissioning purposes, therefore we consider that this type of exchange difference should not to be taken to profit or loss, but dealt with in accordance with IFRIC 1.

10.3 Indefinite life assets

While the economic lives of oil fields and mines are finite, certain infrastructure assets (e.g. pipelines and refineries) are continually being repaired, replaced and upgraded. While individual parts of such assets may not have an indefinite economic life, these assets may occupy a particular site for an indefinite period.

Regardless of whether or not the related asset has an indefinite life, the decommissioning provision will normally meet the criteria relating to the recognition of a provision as set out in IAS 37.14(a) and (b), in that an entity will have a present obligation and it will be probable that an outflow of resources will be required to settle the obligation. With respect to the final criterion in paragraph (c), while it might seem that a reliable estimate of the decommissioning provision cannot be made if the underlying asset has an indefinite life, 'indefinite' does not mean that the asset has an infinite life but that the life is long and has not yet been determined. IAS 37 presumes that:

> 'Except in extremely rare cases, an entity will be able to determine a range of possible outcomes and can therefore make an estimate of the obligation that is sufficiently reliable to use in recognising a provision.' *[IAS 37.25]*.

Therefore, it should be extremely rare for an entity to conclude that it cannot make a reliable estimate of the amount of the obligation. Even if an entity did conclude in an extremely rare case that no reliable estimate could be made, there would still be a contingent liability and the following disclosures would be required:

- a brief description of the nature of the contingent liability; and
- where practicable:
  - an estimate of its financial effect, measured under paragraphs 36-52 of IAS 37;
  - an indication of the uncertainties relating to the amount or timing of any outflow; and
  - the possibility of any reimbursement. *[IAS 37.26, 86]*.

Finally, it should be noted that the discounted value of decommissioning costs that will only be incurred far into the future may be relatively insignificant.

11 IMPAIRMENT OF ASSETS

The following issues require additional attention when a mining company or oil and gas company applies the impairment testing rules under IFRS:

- impairment indicators (see 11.1 below);
- identifying cash-generating units (see 11.2 below);
- projections of cash flows (see 11.4.2 and 11.5.1 below);
- cash flows from mineral reserves and resources and the appropriate discount rate (see 11.4.2.A below);
- commodity price assumptions (see 11.4.3 and 11.5.2 below).
- future capital expenditure (see 11.4.4 and 11.5.3 below);
- foreign currency cash flows (see 11.4.5 and 11.5.4 below); and
- consistency in cash flows and carrying amount of CGU (see 11.4.1 below).

The general requirements of IAS 36 are covered in Chapter 20.

11.1 Impairment indicators

Impairment indicators applicable to assets of mining companies and oil and gas companies are found in two places, IFRS 6 and IAS 36. IFRS 6 describes a number of situations in which an entity should test E&E assets for impairment, discussed at 3.5.1 above, while an entity should apply the impairment indicators in IAS 36 to assets other than E&E assets. The lists of impairment indicators in IFRS 6 and IAS 36 are not exhaustive. Entities operating in the extractive industries may also consider carrying out an impairment test in the following situations:[99]

- declines in prices of products or increases in production costs;
- governmental actions, such as new environmental regulations, imposition of price controls and tax increases;
- actual production levels from the cost centre or cost pool are below forecast and/or there is a downward revision in production forecasts;
- serious operational problems and accidents;
- capitalisation of large amounts of unsuccessful pre-production costs in the cost centre;
- decreases in reserve estimates;
- increases in the anticipated period over which reserves will be produced;
- substantial cost overruns during the development and construction phases of a field or mine; and
- adverse drilling results.

The extract below shows BHP Billiton's accounting policy for impairment testing.

Extract 41.18: BHP Billiton plc (2015)

7.1.6 Notes to Financial Statements [extract]

43 Significant accounting policies [extract]

(f) Exploration and evaluation expenditure [extract]

Capitalised exploration and evaluation expenditure considered to be a tangible asset is recorded as a component of property, plant and equipment at cost less impairment charges. Otherwise, it is recorded as an intangible asset (such as certain licence and lease arrangements). In determining whether the purchase of an exploration licence or lease is an intangible asset or a component of property, plant and equipment, consideration is given to the substance of the item acquired not its legal form. Licences or leases purchased, which allow exploration over an extended period of time, meet the definition of an intangible exploration lease asset where they cannot be reasonably associated with a known resource (minerals) or reserves (petroleum). All capitalised exploration and evaluation expenditure is monitored for indications of impairment. When a potential impairment is indicated, assessment is performed for each area of interest in conjunction with the group of operating assets (representing a cash-generating unit) to which the exploration is attributed. Exploration areas in which reserves have been discovered but require major capital expenditure before production can begin, are continually evaluated to ensure that commercial quantities of reserves exist or to ensure that additional exploration work is under way or planned. To the extent that capitalised expenditure is no longer expected to be recovered, it is charged to the income statement.

(g) Impairment and reversal of impairment of non-current assets

Formal impairment tests are carried out annually for goodwill. In addition, formal impairment tests for all assets are performed when there is an indication of impairment. The Group conducts an internal review of asset values annually, which is used as a source of information to assess for any indications of impairment or reversal of previously recognised impairment losses. External factors, such as changes in expected future prices, costs and other market factors, are also monitored to assess for indications of impairment or reversal of previously recognised impairment losses. If any such indication exists, an estimate of the asset's recoverable amount is calculated, being the higher of fair value less direct costs of disposal and the asset's value in use.

If the carrying amount of the asset exceeds its recoverable amount, the asset is impaired and an impairment loss is charged to the income statement so as to reduce the carrying amount in the balance sheet to its recoverable amount. A reversal of a previously recognised impairment loss is limited to the lesser of the amount that would not cause the carrying amount to exceed (a) its recoverable amount; or (b) the carrying amount that would have been determined (net of depreciation) had no impairment loss been recognised for the asset or cash-generating unit.

Fair value is determined as the amount that would be obtained from the sale of the asset in an orderly transaction between market participants. Fair value for mineral assets is generally determined as the present value of the estimated future cash flows expected to arise from the continued use of the asset, including any expansion prospects, and its eventual disposal, using assumptions that an independent market participant may take into account. These cash flows are discounted at an appropriate rate to arrive at a net present value of the asset.

Value in use is determined as the present value of the estimated future cash flows expected to arise from the continued use of the asset in its present form and its eventual disposal. Value in use is determined by applying assumptions specific to the Group's continued use and cannot take into account future development. These assumptions are different to those used in calculating fair value and consequently the value in use calculation is likely to give a different result (usually lower) to a fair value calculation.

In testing for indications of impairment and performing impairment calculations, assets are considered as collective groups and referred to as cash-generating units. Cash-generating units are the smallest identifiable group of assets, liabilities and associated goodwill that generate cash inflows that are largely independent of the cash inflows from other assets or groups of assets.

The impairment assessments are based on a range of estimates and assumptions, including:

Estimates/assumptions:		*Basis:*
• Future production	–	proved and probable reserves, resource estimates and, in certain cases, expansion projects
• Commodity prices	–	forward market and contract prices, and longer-term price protocol estimates
• Exchange rates	–	current (forward) market exchange rates
• Discount rates	–	cost of capital risk-adjusted appropriate to the resource

11.2 Identifying cash-generating units (CGUs)

An entity is required under IAS 36 to test individual assets for impairment. However, if it is not possible to estimate the recoverable amount of an individual asset then an entity should determine the recoverable amount of the CGU to which the asset belongs. *[IAS 36.66]*. A CGU is defined by the standard as the smallest identifiable group of assets that generates cash inflows that are largely independent of the cash inflows from other assets or groups of assets. *[IAS 36.6]*. See Chapter 20 at 4.1 for further discussion about how an entity should determine its CGUs.

In determining appropriate CGUs, mining companies and oil and gas companies may need to consider some of the following issues:

(a) active markets for intermediate products (see 11.2.1 below);

(b) external users of the processing assets (see 11.2.2 below);

(c) fields or mines that are operated as one 'complex' through the use of shared infrastructure (see 11.2.3 below); and

(d) stand-alone fields or mines that operate on a portfolio basis (see 11.2.4 below).

These issues are discussed further below.

11.2.1 Markets for intermediate products

In vertically integrated operations the successive stages of the extraction and production process are often considered to be one CGU as it is not possible to allocate net cash inflows to individual stages of the process. This is common in some mining operations. However, if there is an active market for intermediate commodities (e.g. bauxite, alumina and aluminium) then a vertically integrated mining company needs to consider whether its smelting and refining operations are part of the same CGU as its mining operations. If there is an active market for the output produced by an asset or group of assets, the assets concerned are identified as a separate CGU, even if some or all of the output is used internally. If extraction and smelting or refining are separate CGUs and the cash inflows generated by the asset or each CGU are based on internal transfer pricing, the best estimate of an external arm's length transaction price should be used in estimating the future cash flows to determine the asset's or CGU's VIU. *[IAS 36.70]*. See Chapter 20 at 4.1.

11.2.2 External users of processing assets

When an entity is able to derive cash inflows from its processing assets (e.g. smelting or refining facilities) under tolling arrangements (see 18 below), the question arises as to whether or not those processing assets are a separate CGU. If an entity's processing assets generate significant cash inflows from arrangements with third parties then those assets are likely to be a separate CGU.

11.2.3 Shared infrastructure

When several fields or mines share infrastructure (e.g. pipelines to transport gas or oil onshore, railways, ports or refining and smelting and other processing facilities) the question arises as to whether the fields or mines and the shared infrastructure should be treated as a single CGU. Treating the fields or mines and the shared infrastructure as part of the same CGU is not appropriate under the following circumstances:

(a) if the shared infrastructure is relatively insignificant;

(b) if the fields or mines are capable of selling their product without making use of the shared infrastructure;

(c) if the shared infrastructure generates substantial cash inflows from third parties as well as the entity's own fields or mines; or

(d) if the shared infrastructure is classified as a corporate asset, which is defined under IAS 36 as 'assets other than goodwill that contribute to the future cash flows of both the cash-generating unit under review and other cash-generating units'. *[IAS 36.6]*. In that case, the entity should apply the requirements in IAS 36 regarding corporate assets, which are discussed in Chapter 20 at 4.3.2.

However, if none of the conditions under (a) to (d) above apply then it may be appropriate to treat the fields or mines and the shared infrastructure as one CGU.

Any shared infrastructure that does not belong to a single CGU but relates to more than one CGU still need to be considered for impairment purposes. It is considered that there are two ways to do this and an entity should use the method most appropriate. Shared infrastructure can be allocated to individual CGUs or the CGUs can be grouped together to test the shared assets (similar to the way corporate assets are tested – see commentary above).

Under the first approach, the shared assets should be allocated to each individual CGU or group of CGUs on a reasonable and consistent basis. The cash flows associated with the shared assets, such as fees from other users and expenditure, should be allocated similarly and should form part of the cash flows of the individual CGU. Under the second approach, the group of CGUs that benefit from the shared assets are grouped together with the shared assets to test the shared assets for impairment.

11.2.4 Fields or mines operated on a portfolio basis

Mining companies and oil and gas companies sometimes operate a 'portfolio' of similar mines or fields, which are completely independent from an operational point of view. However, IAS 36 includes the following illustrative example. *[IAS 36 IE Example 1C]*.

Example 41.8: Single product entity

Entity M produces a single product and owns plants A, B and C. Each plant is located in a different continent. A produces a component that is assembled in either B or C. The combined capacity of B and C is not fully utilised. M's products are sold worldwide from either B or C. For example, B's production can be sold in C's continent if the products can be delivered faster from B than from C. Utilisation levels of B and C depend on the allocation of sales between the two sites.

Although there is an active market for the products assembled by B and C, cash inflows for B and C depend on the allocation of production across the two sites. It is unlikely that the future cash inflows for B and C can be determined individually. Therefore, it is likely that B and C together are the smallest identifiable group of assets that generates cash inflows that are largely independent.

The same rationale could also be applied by a mining company that, for example, operates two coal mines on a portfolio basis, or an oil and gas company that, for example, operates two fields within the one PSC and the entitlement to revenue is dependent on production of, the revenue earned and costs incurred across the PSC, not on a field by field basis. However, judgement needs to be exercised before concluding that it is appropriate to treat separate fields or mines as one CGU, particularly when the production costs of the output of fields or mines differ considerably. This is because there may be a desire to combine them into one CGU, so that the higher cost fields or mines are protected by the headroom of the lower cost fields or mine, thereby avoiding a recognition of an impairment charge. Therefore, to be able to combine on a portfolio basis, a mining company or oil and gas company would have to be able to demonstrate that the future cash inflows for the individual mines or fields cannot be determined individually and therefore, the combined group represents the smallest identifiable group of assets that generates cash inflows that are largely independent.

11.3 Basis of recoverable amount – value-in-use or fair value less costs of disposal

The standard requires the carrying amount of an asset or CGU to be compared with its recoverable amount, which is the higher of fair value less costs of disposal (FVLCD) and value-in-use (VIU). *[IAS 36.18]*. If either the FVLCD or the VIU is higher than the carrying amount, no further action is necessary as the asset is not impaired. *[IAS 36.19]*. Recoverable amount is calculated for an individual asset, unless that asset does not generate cash inflows that are largely independent of those from other assets or groups of assets. *[IAS 36.22]*.

At 11.4 and 11.5 below we further consider the practical and technical aspects associated with the calculation of VIU and FVLCD respectively for mining companies and oil and gas companies.

11.4 Calculation of VIU

IAS 36 defines VIU as the present value of the future cash flows expected to be derived from an asset or CGU. *[IAS 36.6]*. Estimating the VIU of an asset/CGU involves estimating the future cash inflows and outflows that will be derived from the use of the asset and from its ultimate disposal in its current condition, and discounting them at an appropriate rate. *[IAS 36.31]*. There are complex issues involved in determining the cash flows and choosing a discount rate and often there is no agreed methodology to follow. IAS 36 contains detailed and explicit requirements concerning the data to be assembled to calculate VIU that can best be explained and set out as a series of steps. The steps in the process are:

- Step 1: Dividing the entity into CGUs (see 11.2 above);
- Step 2: Allocating goodwill to CGUs or CGU groups (see Chapter 20 at 4.2);
- Step 3: Identifying the carrying amount of CGU assets (see 11.4.1 below);
- Step 4: Estimating the future pre-tax cash flows of the CGU under review (see 11.4.2 – 11.4.5 below);
- Step 5: Identifying an appropriate discount rate and discounting the future cash flows (see Chapter 20 at 4.5 and below at 11.4.2.A);
- Step 6: Comparing carrying value with VIU (assuming FVLCD is lower than carrying value) and recognising impairment losses (see Chapter 20 at 6.1 and 6.2).

11.4.1 Consistency in cash flows and book values attributed to the CGU

An essential requirement of impairment testing under IAS 36 is that the recoverable amount of a CGU must be determined in the same way as for an individual asset and its carrying amount must be determined on a basis that is consistent with the way in which its recoverable amount is determined. *[IAS 36.74, 75]*.

The carrying amount of a CGU includes only those assets that can be attributed directly, or allocated on a reasonable and consistent basis. These must be the assets that will generate the future cash inflows used in determining the CGU's VIU. It does not include the carrying amount of any recognised liability, unless the recoverable amount of the cash-generating unit cannot be determined without taking it into account.

For practical reasons the entity may determine the recoverable amount of a CGU after taking into account assets and liabilities such as receivables or other financial assets, trade payables, pensions and other provisions that are outside the scope of IAS 36 and not part of the CGU. *[IAS 36.79]*. If the cash flows of a CGU are determined taking into account these sorts of items, then it is essential that cash flows and assets and liabilities within CGUs are prepared on a consistent basis.

Specific issues mining companies and oil and gas companies will need to consider are:

- environmental provisions and similar provisions and liabilities (see 11.4.1.A below); and
- working capital such as trade debtors, trade payables and inventories (see Chapter 20 at 4.3.1.C for further discussion).

11.4.1.A Environmental provisions and similar provisions and liabilities

IAS 36 requires the carrying amount of a liability to be excluded from the carrying amount of a CGU unless the recoverable amount of the CGU cannot be determined without consideration of that liability *[IAS 36.76, 78]*. This typically applies when the asset/CGU cannot be separated from the associated liability. See Chapter 20 at 4.3.1.A for further discussion of some of the practical challenges associated with this.

11.4.2 Projections of cash flows

IAS 36 requires that in calculating VIU an entity base its cash flow projection on the most recent financial budgets/forecasts approved by management, excluding any estimated future cash inflows or outflows expected to arise from future restructurings or from improving or enhancing the asset's performance. The assumptions used to prepare the cash flows should be reasonable and supportable, which can best be achieved by benchmarking against market data or performance against previous budgets. These projections cannot cover a period in excess of five years, unless a longer period can be justified. *[IAS 36.33(b)]*. Entities are permitted to use a longer period if they are confident that their projections are reliable, based on past experience. *[IAS 36.35]*.

In practice, most production or mining/field plans will cover a period of more than five years and hence management will typically make financial forecasts for a corresponding period. The use of such longer term forecasts may be appropriate where it is based on proved and probable reserves and expected annual production rates. Assumptions as to the level of reserves expected to be extracted should be consistent with the latest estimates prepared by reserve engineers; annual production rates should be consistent with those for a certain specified preceding period, e.g. five years; and price and cost assumptions should be consistent with the final period of specific assumptions.

11.4.2.A Cash flows from mineral reserves and resources and the appropriate discount rate

As discussed at 2.2 and 2.3 above, a significant amount of work is required before an entity can conclude that its mineral resources should be classified as mineral reserves. In practice, an entity may not have formally completed all of the detailed work that is

Chapter 41

required in order to designate mineral resources as mineral reserves. IAS 36 requires the cash flow projection used in calculating the VIU of assets to be based on 'reasonable and supportable assumptions that represent management's best estimate of the range of economic conditions that will exist over the remaining useful life of the asset'. *[IAS 36.33(a)]*. Therefore, while ordinarily the starting point for the calculation of VIU would be based upon the mineral reserves recorded, it may sometimes be appropriate under IAS 36 to take into account mineral resources that have not formally been designated as mineral reserves. However an entity would need to adjust the discount rate it uses in its VIU calculation for the additional risks associated with mineral resources for which the future cash flow estimates have not been adjusted. *[IAS 36.55]*. If the risks have been factored into the future cash flow estimates modelled, an entity should be aware not to also adjust for this risk via the discount rate applied.

The requirements of IAS 36 for determining an appropriate discount rate are discussed in detail in Chapter 20 at 4.5.

11.4.3 Commodity price assumptions

Forecasting commodity prices is never straightforward, because it is not usually possible to know whether recent changes in commodity prices are a temporary aberration or the beginning of a longer-term trend. Management usually takes a longer term approach to estimates of commodity prices for internal management purposes but these are not always consistent with the VIU rules. Given the long life of most mines and oil fields, an entity should not consider price levels only for the past three or four years. Instead, it should consider historical price levels for longer periods and assess how these prices are influenced by changes in underlying supply and demand levels.

For actively traded commodities, there are typically forward price curves available and in such situations, these provide a reference point for forecast price assumptions.

The commodity assumptions need to match the profile of the life of the mine or oil field. Spot prices and forward curve prices (where they are available as at the impairment testing date) are more relevant for shorter life mines and oil fields, while long-term price assumptions are more relevant for longer life mines and oil fields. Forecast prices (where available) should be used for the future periods covered by the VIU calculation. Where the forward price curve does not extend far enough into the future, the price at the end of the forward curve is generally held steady, or is often dropped to a longer term average price (in real terms), where appropriate.

The future cash flows relating to the purchase or sale of commodities might be known from forward purchase or sales contracts. Use of these contracted prices in place of the spot price or forward curve price for the contracted volumes will generally be acceptable. However, it is possible that some of these forward contracts might be accounted for as derivatives contracts at fair value in accordance with IAS 39, and therefore the related assets or liabilities will be recognised in the statement of financial position. Such balances would be excluded from the IAS 36 impairment test. Given this, the cash flow projections prepared for the purposes of the IAS 36 impairment test should exclude the pricing terms associated with these forward contracts.

The commodity price is a key assumption in calculating the VIU of any mine or oil field. Only in the context of impairment testing of goodwill and indefinite life intangible assets does IAS 36 specifically require disclosure of:

(i) a description of each key assumption on which management has based its cash flow projections for the period covered by the most recent budgets/forecasts. Key assumptions are those to which the unit's (group of units') recoverable amount is most sensitive; and

(ii) a description of management's approach to determining the value(s) assigned to each key assumption, whether those value(s) reflect past experience or, if appropriate, are consistent with external sources of information, and, if not, how and why they differ from past experience or external sources of information. *[IAS 36.134(d)(i)-(ii), 134(e)(i)-(ii)].*

In practice, considerable differences may exist between entities in their estimates of future commodity prices. Therefore, we recommend disclosure of the actual commodity prices used in calculating the VIU of any mine or oil field that does not have any goodwill or indefinite life intangibles allocated to it, even though this is not specifically required by IAS 36 as these would generally be considered a significant judgement or estimate and hence would require disclosure under IAS 1. *[IAS 1.122, 125].* A possible approach to such disclosures is illustrated in the following extract from the financial statements of BP.

Extract 41.19: BP p.l.c. (2015)

Notes on financial statements [extract]

1.Significant accounting policies, judgements, estimates and assumptions [extract]

Impairment of property, plant and equipment, intangible assets, and goodwill [extract]

Significant estimate or judgement: recoverability of asset carrying values [extract]

[...]

Market prices used for the first five years of both value-in-use and fair value less costs of disposal impairment tests performed at year end are shown in the table below:

					as at 31 December 2015
Price assumptions for the first five years	**2016**	**2017**	**2018**	**2019**	**2020**
Brent oil price ($/bbl)	**40**	**47**	**52**	**54**	**56**
Henry Hub natural gas price ($/mmBtu)	**2.38**	**2.76**	**2.90**	**3.03**	**3.18**
					as at 31 December 2014
	2015	2016	2017	2018	2019
Brent oil price ($/bbl)	61	69	73	76	77
Henry Hub natural gas price ($/mmBtu)	3.11	3.53	3.82	4.00	4.15

[...]

For value-in-use calculations relating to Upstream assets, prices for oil and natural gas used for future cash flow calculations are based on market prices for the first five years (consistent with those shown in the table above) and the group's flat nominal long-term price assumptions thereafter. As at 31 December 2015, the group's long-term flat nominal price assumptions were $90 per barrel for Brent and $6.50/mmBtu for Henry Hub (2014 $90 per barrel and $6.50/mmBtu). These long-term price assumptions are subject to periodic review.

The extract below illustrates a similar type of disclosure by Newcrest Mining from its 30 June 2015 financial statements, in this case as part of the key assumption disclosures within its impairment disclosures.

Extract 41.20: Newcrest Mining Limited (2015)

Notes to the Consolidated Financial Statements [extract]

For the year ended 30 June 2015

19. IMPAIRMENT CHARGES AND REVERSALS

(a) Impairment and Impairment Reversal Testing [extract]

ii) Key Assumptions [extract]

The table below summarises the key assumptions used in the 2015 end of year carrying value assessments, and for comparison also provides the equivalent assumptions used in 2014:

[extract]	2015			2014	
Assumptions	**2016**	**2017**	**Long term (2018+)**	**2015-2020**	**Long term (2021+)**
Gold (US$ per ounce)	$1,100	$1,200	$1,250	$1,300	$1,300
Copper (US$ per pound)	$2.40	$2.70	$3.00	$3.00	$3.00

Commodity prices and exchange rates estimation approach

Commodity price and foreign exchange rates are estimated with reference to external market forecasts and reviewed at least annually. The rates applied have regard to observable market data including spot and forward values, and to market analysis including bank analyst estimates.

Metal prices

Newcrest has reduced its US dollar gold price estimates for both the short term (2016 and 2017) and long-term (2018+) compared to 2014, reflecting a sustained reduction in the US dollar gold price during the 2015 calendar year and Newcrest's analysis of observable market data for future periods.

The reduced gold price assumptions has primarily impacted the Fair Values of Newcrest's non-Australian CGUs which all have a US dollar functional currency, contributing to the impairments recognised at 30 June 2015 at Hidden Valley and West Africa. The impact of the reduced gold price assumptions on the valuation of Lihir was offset by lower AUD:USD and USD:PGK rates (detailed further below). Newcrest's Australian assets all have an Australian dollar functional currency, with the impact of the lower US dollar gold price estimates mitigated by lower AUD:USD exchange rate estimates (detailed further below).

11.4.4 Future capital expenditure

When determining VIU, although the standard permits an entity to take account of cash outflows required to make an asset ready for use, i.e. those relating to assets under construction, *[IAS 36.42]*, it does not allow inclusion of cash outflows relating to future enhancements of an asset's performance or capacity to which an entity is not committed. *[IAS 36.44]*. This may have a significant impact on relatively new assets and on fields or mines that will be developed over time. Note that while enhancement capital expenditure may not be recognised, routine or replacement capital expenditure necessary to maintain the function or current performance of the asset or assets in the CGU has to be included. Entities must therefore distinguish between maintenance and enhancement expenditure. This distinction may not be easy to draw in practice but, for example, an anticipated increase in mineral reserves as a consequence of incurring future capital expenditure may be an indicator that the expenditure is enhancement expenditure.

11.4.5 Foreign currency cash flows

An entity in the extractive industries will often sell its product in a currency that is different from the one in which it incurs its production costs (e.g. silver production may be sold in US dollars while production costs may be incurred in pesos). In such situations, impairment testing and calculating VIU under IAS 36 require that the foreign currency cash flows should first be estimated in the currency in which they will be generated and then discounted using a discount rate appropriate for that currency. An entity should translate the present value calculated in the foreign currency using the spot exchange rate at the date of the VIU calculation. *[IAS 36.54]*. This is to avoid the problems inherent in using forward exchange rates, which are based on differential interest rates. Using such forward rates would result in double-counting the time value of money, first in the discount rate and then in the forward rate. *[IAS 36.BCZ49]*.

This requirement, however, is more complex than it may initially appear. Effectively, this method requires an entity to perform separate impairment tests for cash flows generated in different currencies, but make them consistent with one another so that the combined effect is meaningful. This can be a difficult exercise to undertake. Many different factors need to be considered, including relative inflation rates and relative interest rates, as well as appropriate discount rates for the currencies in question. Because of this, the possibility for error is significant, given this, it is important for entities to seek input from experienced valuers who will be able to assist them in dealing with these challenges.

11.5 Calculation of FVLCD

FVLCD is the price that would be received to sell an asset or paid to transfer a liability in an orderly transaction between market participants at the measurement date, less the costs of disposal. *[IAS 36.6]*. FVLCD is less restrictive in its application than VIU and can be easier to work with, which may be why some entities choose to use this approach for impairment testing purposes. While IAS 36 does not impose any restrictions on how an entity determines the FVLCD, there are specific requirements in IFRS 13 as to how to determine fair value. IFRS 13 is discussed in more detail in Chapter 14.

The concept of fair value in IFRS 13 is explicitly an exit price notion. FVLCD, like fair value, is not an entity-specific measurement, but is focused on market participants' assumptions for a particular asset or liability. Under IFRS 13 entities have to consider the highest and best use (from a market participant perspective) to which the asset could be put. However, it is generally presumed that an entity's current use of those mining or oil and gas assets or CGUs would be its highest and best use (unless market or other factors suggest that a different use by market participants would maximise the value of the asset).

IFRS 13 does not limit or prioritise the valuation technique(s) an entity might use to measure fair value. An entity may use any valuation technique, or multiple techniques, as long as it is consistent with one of three valuation approaches: market approach, income approach and cost approach and is appropriate for the type of asset/CGU being measured at fair value. However, IFRS 13 does focus on the type of inputs to be used and requires an entity to maximise the use of relevant observable inputs and minimise the use of the unobservable inputs.

Historically, many mining companies and oil and gas companies have calculated FVLCD using a discounted cash flow (DCF) valuation technique. This approach differs from VIU in a number of ways. One of the key differences is that FVLCD would require an entity to use assumptions that a market participant would be likely to take into account rather than entity-specific assumptions. For example, as mining sector and oil and gas sector market participants invest for the longer term, they would not restrict themselves to a limited project time horizon. Therefore, the cash flow forecasts included in a FVLCD calculation may cover a longer period than may be used in a VIU calculation. Moreover, market participants would also likely take into account future expansionary capital expenditure related to subsequent phases in the development of a mining property in a FVLCD calculation, whereas this is not permitted in a VIU calculation. Having said this, some of the issues discussed above for a VIU calculation also need to be considered for a FVLCD calculation which uses a DCF model (we discuss some of these further below). As illustrated in Extract 41.18 at 11.1 above, BHP Billiton uses this approach in determining the FVLCD for its mineral assets.

11.5.1 Projections of cash flows

As required by IFRS 13, the assumptions and other inputs used in a FVLCD DCF model is required to maximise the use of observable market inputs. These should be both realistic and consistent with what a typical market participant would assume.

11.5.2 Commodity price assumptions

Similar to a VIU calculation, commodity price is a key assumption in calculating the FVLCD of any mine or oil field when using a DCF model, and therefore similar issues as those discussed for a VIU calculation (see 11.4.3 above) apply. On the same basis, while the specific disclosure requirements relating to price assumptions in IAS 36 technically only apply in the context of impairment testing of CGUs to which goodwill and indefinite life intangible assets are allocated, because there can be considerable differences between entities in their estimates of future commodity prices, we recommend additional disclosures be provided. For example, an entity may wish to disclose the actual commodity prices used in calculating the FVLCD of any mine or oil field, as these would generally be considered a significant judgement or estimate and hence would require disclosure under IAS 1. *[IAS 1.122, 125]*.

11.5.3 Future capital expenditure

There are no restrictions similar to those applicable to a VIU calculation when determining FVLCD provided that it can be demonstrated that a market participant would be willing to attribute some value to the future enhancement and that the requirements of IFRS 13 have been complied with. IFRS 13 is discussed in more detail in Chapter 14.

The treatment of future capital expenditure is discussed in more detail in Chapter 20 at 4.4.1.A.

11.5.4 Foreign currency cash flows

For FVLCD calculations, the requirements relating to foreign currency are not specified other than they must reflect what a market participant would use when valuing the asset or CGU. In practice, entities that use a DCF analysis when calculating FVLCD will incorporate a forecast for exchange rates into their calculations rather than using the spot rate. A key issue in any forecast is the assumed timeframe over which the exchange rate may return to lower levels. This assumption is generally best analysed in conjunction with commodity prices in order to ensure consistency in the parameters used, i.e. a rise in prices will usually be accompanied by a rise in currency.

11.6 Low mine or field profitability near end of life

While mining companies and oil and gas companies would like to achieve steady profitability and returns over the life of a project, it is not uncommon to see profitability declining over the life of a mine or field. From an economic perspective, a mining company or oil and gas company will generally continue to extract minerals as long as the cash inflows from the sale of minerals exceed the cash cost of production.

From a mining perspective, most mine plans aim to maximise the net present value of mineral reserves by first extracting the highest grade ore with the lowest production costs. Consequently, in most mining operations, the grade of the ore mined steadily declines over the life of the mine which results in a declining annual production, while the production costs per volume of ore, e.g. tonne, gradually increases as it becomes more difficult to extract the ore. From an oil and gas perspective, both oil and gas may be produced from the same wells but ordinarily oil generates greater revenue per barrel of oil equivalent sold relative to gas. As the oil is often produced in greater quantities first, this means that the oil and gas operation is often more profitable in the earlier years relative to later years.

Consequently, where there is a positive net cash flow, a mining company or oil and gas company will continue to extract minerals even if it does not fully recover the depreciation of its property, plant and equipment and mineral reserves, as is likely to occur towards the end of the mine or field life. In part this is the result of the depreciation methods applied:

- the straight-line method of depreciation allocates a relatively high depreciation charge to periods with a low annual production;
- a units of production method based on the quantity of ore extracted allocates a relatively high depreciation charge to production of lower grade ore;
- a units of production method based upon the quantity of petroleum product produced in total terms allocates an even depreciation charge per barrel of oil equivalent, whereas the revenue earned varies; and
- a units of production method based on the quantity of minerals produced allocates a relatively high depreciation charge to production of minerals that are difficult to recover.

Each of these situations is most likely to occur towards the end of the life of a mine or field. It is possible the methods of depreciation most commonly used in each of the sectors do not allocate a sufficiently high depreciation charge to the early life of a project when production is generally most profitable. An entity should therefore be mindful of the fact that relatively small changes in facts and circumstances can lead to an impairment of assets.

Following on from this, the impairment tests in the early years of the life of a mine or field will often reveal that the project is cash flow positive and is able to produce a recoverable amount that is sufficient to recoup the carrying value of the project, i.e. the project is not impaired. However, when the impairment tests are conducted in later years, while the mine or field may still be cash flow positive, i.e. the expected cash proceeds from the future sale of minerals still exceed the expected future cash costs of production and hence management will continue with the mining or oil and gas operations, as margins generally reduce towards the end of mine or field life, the impairment tests may not produce a recoverable amount sufficient to recoup the remaining carrying value of the mine or field. Therefore, it will need to be impaired.

It is possible, when preparing the impairment models for a mine or field, for an entity to identify when (in the future) the remaining net cash inflows may no longer be sufficient to recoup the remaining carrying value, that is when compared to the way in which the assets are expected to be depreciated over the remaining useful life. However, provided the recoverable amount as at the date of the impairment test exceeds the carrying amount of the mine or field, there is no requirement to recognise any possible future impairment. It is only when the recoverable amount actually falls below the carrying amount that an impairment must be recognised.

12 REVENUE RECOGNITION

Each of the sub-sections below considers some of the specific revenue recognition issues faced by mining companies and oil and gas companies under the current requirements as set out in IAS 18 (see Chapter 29 for more details) and other relevant standards and the Conceptual Framework. The requirements of IFRS 15, which is effective for annual reporting periods beginning on or after 1 January 2018 (see Chapter 30 for a detailed discussion), and the potential impact on mining companies and/or oil and gas companies, have been considered further at 12.7 below.

12.1 Revenue in the development phase

Under IAS 16, the cost of an item of property, plant and equipment includes any costs directly attributable to bringing the asset to the location and condition necessary for it to be capable of operating in the manner intended by management. *[IAS 16.16(b)]*. During the development/construction of an asset, an entity may generate some revenue. The current treatment of such revenue depends on whether it is considered incidental or integral to bringing the asset itself into the location and condition necessary for it to be capable of operating in the manner intended by management.

If the asset is *already in* the location and condition necessary for it to be capable of being used in the manner intended by management, then IAS 16 requires capitalisation to cease and depreciation to start. *[IAS 16.20]*. In these circumstances, all income earned from using the asset must be recognised as revenue in profit or loss and the related costs of the activity should include an element of depreciation of the asset.

12.1.1 Incidental revenue

During the construction of an asset, an entity may enter into incidental operations that are not, in themselves, necessary to bring the asset itself into the location and condition necessary for it to be capable of operating in the manner intended by management. The standard gives the example of income earned by using a building site as a car park prior to starting construction. An extractives example may be income earned from leasing out the land surrounding the mine site or an onshore gas field to a local farmer to run his sheep on. Because incidental operations such as these are not necessary to bring an item to the location and condition necessary for it to be capable of operating in the manner intended by management, the income and related expenses of incidental operations are recognised in profit or loss and included in their respective classifications of income and expense. *[IAS 16.21]*. Such incidental income is not offset against the cost of the asset.

12.1.2 Integral to development

The directly attributable costs of an item of property, plant and equipment include the costs of testing whether the asset is functioning properly, after deducting the net proceeds from selling any items produced while bringing the asset to that location and condition. *[IAS 16.17(e)]*. The standard gives the example of samples produced when testing equipment.

There are other situations in which income may be generated wholly and necessarily as a result of the process of bringing the asset to the location and condition for its intended use. The extractive industries are highly capital intensive and there are many instances where income may be generated prior to the commencement of production. Some mining examples include:

- During the evaluation phase, i.e. when the technical feasibility and commercial viability are being determined, an entity may 'trial mine', to determine which method would be the most profitable and efficient in the circumstances, and which metallurgical process is the most efficient. Ore mined through trial mining may be processed and sold during the evaluation phase.
- As part of the process of constructing a deep underground mine, the mining operation may extract some saleable 'product' during the construction of the mine e.g. sinking shafts to the depth where the main ore-bearing rock is located.
- At the other end of the spectrum, income may be earned from the sale of product from 'ramping up' the mine to production at commercial levels.

Some oil and gas examples include:

- Onshore wells are frequently placed on long-term production test as part of the process of appraisal and formulation of a field development plan. Test production may be sold during this time.

Some interpret IAS 16's requirement quite narrowly as only applying to income earned from actually 'testing' the asset, while others interpret it more broadly to include other types of pre-commissioning or production testing revenue.

We have noted in practice that some income may be generated wholly and necessarily as a result of activities that are part of the process of bringing the asset into the location and condition for its intended use, i.e. the activities are integral to the construction or development of the mine or field. Some consider that as IAS 16 makes it clear that income generated from incidental operations is to be taken to revenue, *[IAS 16.21]*, but does not explicitly specify the treatment of integral revenue, it could be interpreted that income earned from activities that are integral to the development of the mine or field should be credited to the cost of the mine or field. This is because the main purpose of the activities is the development of the mine or field, not the production of ore or hydrocarbons. The income earned from production is an unintended benefit.

In our experience, practice in accounting for pre-commissioning or test production revenue varies. These various treatments have evolved as a result of the way in which the relatively limited guidance in IFRS has been interpreted and applied. In some instances, this has also been influenced by approaches that originated in previous and other GAAPs, where guidance was/is somewhat clearer.

The key challenge with this issue is usually not how to measure the revenue but how entities view this revenue and, more significantly, how to distinguish those costs that are directly attributable to developing the operating capability of the mine or field from those that represent the cost of producing saleable material. It can be extremely difficult to apportion these costs. Consequently, there is a risk of misstatement of gross profits if these amounts are recorded as revenue and the amount of costs included in profit or loss as cost of goods sold is too low or too high.

Other GAAPs have either previously provided or continue to provide further guidance that has influenced some of the approaches adopted under IFRS. For example, the now superseded Australian GAAP (AGAAP) standard on extractive industries[100] and the old UK guidance for the oil and gas industry (the former OIAC SORP)[101] provided more specific guidance. The former clearly required, and the latter recommended, that any proceeds earned from the sale of product obtained during the exploration, evaluation or development phases should be treated in the same manner as the proceeds from the sale of product in the production phase, i.e. recognised in profit or loss as part of income.

AGAAP required the estimated cost of producing the quantities concerned to be deducted from the accumulated costs of such activities and included as part of costs of goods sold.[102] By contrast, the former OIAC SORP was more specific and stated that an amount equivalent to the revenues should be both charged to cost of sales and credited against appraisal costs to record a zero net margin on such production.[103]

The various practices that are currently adopted and accepted in practice include:

- all pre-commissioning/test production revenue is considered integral to the development of the mine or field and is therefore credited to the asset in its entirety;
- only revenue genuinely earned from the testing of assets, e.g. product processed as a result of testing the processing plant and associated facilities, is credited to the associated asset, with all other revenue being recognised in profit or loss; or
- all pre-commissioning or test production revenue is recognised in profit or loss.

For entities that recognise pre-commissioning or test production revenue in profit or loss, various approaches have been observed in practice to determine the amount to be included in cost of goods sold and include:

- an amount equivalent to the revenues is charged to cost of sales and credited against the asset to record a zero net margin on such production (similar to the guidance in the former OIAC SORP);

- a standard or expected cost of production is ascribed to the volumes produced, e.g. weighted average cost per tonne/barrel based on actual results over a historical period, e.g. the last two or three years; or for new mines or fields, the expected cost per tonne/bbl as set out in the business, mine or field plan, producing a standard margin;
- recognising only the incremental cost of processing the product; or
- recognising nothing in cost of goods sold.

The net effect of all of these approaches is that any excess of the total cost incurred over the amount recognised in profit or loss as cost of goods sold, is effectively capitalised as part of the asset. Note that the first approach, where cost of goods sold is recognised at the same amount as the revenue, produces the same net balance sheet and profit or loss result as if the revenue had been credited to the asset in its entirety.

While diverse treatments may have been adopted and accepted in practice to date, it is unlikely the third and fourth cost of goods sold approaches would be appropriate because they would not provide a fair reflection of the cost to produce the saleable product.

There is a significant degree of divergence as to how entities account for pre-commissioning revenue. Significant judgement will also be required to determine when the asset is in the location and condition to be capable of operating as intended by management, i.e. when it is ready for its intended use. In the absence of specific guidance this divergence will continue. However, capitalisation (including recognising income as a credit to the cost of the asset) is to cease when the asset is ready for its intended use, regardless of whether or not it is achieving its targeted levels of production or profitability, or even operating at all.

12.1.2.A Future developments

One aspect of accounting for revenue in the development phase was referred to the Interpretations Committee in July 2014 and has been considered several times since this date. This concerned the cost of testing and the associated revenue; specifically whether the amount by which the net proceeds received exceed the cost of testing should be recognised in profit or loss or as a deduction from the cost of property, plant and equipment.

While a number of different aspects of this issue have been considered over the past few years, at its March 2016 meeting, the Interpretations Committee discussed the following approaches for the recognition of proceeds from selling items produced before the item of property, plant and equipment (PPE) is capable of operating as intended by management, including:

- restricting the amount of proceeds that an entity deducts from the cost of PPE to only those proceeds arising from testing activities, and clarifying that the net proceeds deducted should not exceed the costs of testing included as part of the cost of PPE; and
- prohibiting the deduction of any proceeds from the cost of PPE.

The Interpretations Committee tentatively decided to propose a narrow-scope amendment to IAS 16 to prohibit the deduction of proceeds from selling items produced before the item of PPE is capable of operating as intended by management from the cost of PPE (i.e. the second approach listed above).

At its September 2016 meeting, the following was discussed and proposed:

- Items produced by an item of PPE before it is available for use are likely to be output from an entity's ordinary activities and hence any revenue generated from selling such items would be in the scope of IFRS 15.
- An entity would account for the cost of selling such items in accordance with IAS 2.
- Additional disclosure requirements were not necessary as the disclosure requirements of IFRS 15 and IAS 2 were considered sufficient, i.e. if revenue and cost of output produced while making PPE available for use has a material effect on the profitability of the entity and/or trend information, entities would: a) consider revenue from sale of that output as a category for disclosure of disaggregated revenue; *[IFRS 15.114]* and b) disclose the accounting policy adopted in measuring the output, the carrying amount of the output in inventory (if any), and the cost of the output recognised as an expense. *[IAS 2.36]*.
- Prospective application of the proposed amendments to items of PPE made available for use from the beginning of the earliest comparative period when first applying the amendments, as the benefits of retrospective application were considered to be outweighed by the costs.

While this tentative decision seems to provide clarity as to the treatment of revenue in the development phase (i.e. it will all be recognised as a credit in profit or loss), and it states that the related costs should be determined in accordance with IAS 2, there is still a lack of clarity on exactly how these costs should be determined. For example, when determining the cost of inventory, ordinarily a portion of depreciation of the processing plant and other equipment used to convert the inventory into the finished product is allocated as part of the cost of that inventory. However, when it comes to inventory produced and processed before these items of PPE are available for use, these assets will not have commenced depreciation and therefore there is no depreciation to be allocated. It is unclear whether this is the intention of the tentative decision, or whether some depreciation should be imputed to the cost of the inventory.

For those entities that currently recognise pre-commissioning or test production revenue in profit or loss, the various approaches that have been observed in practice to determine the amount to be included in cost of goods sold are discussed at 12.1.2 above. Similar issues and considerations are likely to continue to arise and will require entities to exercise judgement. As noted above, the Interpretations Committee are suggesting that entities will use their disclosures to clarify their approach to revenue from testing and the determination of cost of goods sold.

With respect to this issue, IFRS 15 does not necessarily provide any further specific guidance. This is because IFRS 15 focuses on revenue from contracts from customers, how it should be measured, when it should be recognised and what should be disclosed, whereas this issue relates to where revenue should be recognised (i.e. in profit or loss or as a credit to the related asset). As noted above, the Interpretations Committee considers this revenue could be the output of an entity's ordinary activities and hence in the scope of IFRS 15, but it will be the amendment to IAS 16 that will now make it clear that this revenue cannot be recognised against the asset.

Entities should continue to monitor the discussions of the Interpretations Committee on this topic.

12.2 Sale of product with delayed shipment

From time to time, an entity may enter into a sales arrangement where the purchaser pays a significant portion of the final estimated purchase price but then requests delayed shipment, for example, because of limited storage space. These sales can sometimes also be referred to as 'in store sales' or 'bill-and-hold' sales. We see this more commonly in the mining sector.

Revenue can be recognised in relation to such sales if it is probable delivery will be made and if: a) the product is specifically identified as belonging to the purchaser; b) it is available for immediate delivery; and c) is held at the purchaser's risk. In many cases, the product is usually physically segregated from other product and is clearly marked as belonging to the purchaser and hence it is therefore not available for sale to other parties. In addition, acknowledgement of the arrangement by both the mining entity and purchaser must be evidenced in the form of a formal agreement between the parties and the usual payment terms apply, and there are no terms relating to the right/obligation to repurchase the product.

For a discussion on the potential impact of IFRS 15 see 12.7.9 below.

12.3 Exchanges of inventories

Under IAS 18, when goods or services are exchanged or swapped for goods or services that are of a similar nature and value, the exchange is not regarded as a transaction that generates revenue. This can occur with commodities like oil or gas and sometimes coal, where suppliers exchange or swap inventories in various locations to fulfil demand on a timely basis in a particular location. However, when goods are sold in exchange for dissimilar goods, the exchange is regarded as a transaction that generates revenue. *[IAS 18.12]*.

Accounting for exchanges of inventories requires a degree of judgement particularly:

- when the inventories exchanged are not identical (e.g. swaps of slightly different products, possibly with an adjustment for the difference in quality); or
- there is some past practice of settling net in cash.

Furthermore, any receivable or payable balance does not entirely meet the definition of inventory in IAS 2 but is instead a non-monetary receivable or payable. The product receivable or payable is normally recorded at cost within current assets or liabilities.

For a discussion on the potential impact of IFRS 15 see 12.7.2 below.

> *Extract 41.21: TOTAL S.A. (2015)*
>
> **Notes to the Consolidated Financial Statements – Note 1** [extract]
>
> **D) Sales and revenues from sales** [extract]
>
> **(i) Sales of goods** [extract]
>
> Exchanges of crude oil and petroleum products within normal trading activities do not generate any income and therefore these flows are shown at their net value in both the statement of income and the balance sheet.

12.4 Overlift and underlift (oil and gas)

In jointly owned oil and gas operations it is often not practical for each participant to take in kind or to sell its exact share of production during a period. In most periods some participants in the jointly owned operations will be in an overlift position (i.e. they have taken more product than their proportionate entitlement) while other participants may be in an underlift position (i.e. they have taken less product than their proportionate entitlement). Such lifting imbalances are usually settled in one of three ways:[104]

- in future periods the owner in an underlift position may sell or take product in excess of their normal entitlement, while the owner in an overlift position will sell or take less product than the normal entitlement;
- cash balancing may be used, whereby the overlift party will make a cash payment to the underlift party for the value of the imbalance volume; or
- if the co-owners have joint ownership interests in other properties, they may agree to offset balances in the two properties to the extent possible.

The two methods of accounting for underlifts and overlifts under current accounting standards that are commonly used in the oil and gas sector are (a) the sales method and (b) the entitlements method.[105]

12.4.1 Sales method

Under the *sales method*, revenue is the value of what a participant sells or the value of all product that has been transferred to its downstream activity.[106] Although revenue arising from the extraction of mineral ores is outside the scope of IAS 18, *[IAS 18.6(h)]*, the sales method is similar to the revenue recognition approach in IAS 18. This is because revenue is only recognised when an entity has transferred ownership of the goods and the amount of revenue can be measured reliably.

A drawback of the sales method is that when an imbalance occurs it gives rise to a mismatch between expenses and revenue. This mismatch arises because the participants' share of expenses for the period is often equal to its ownership percentage, while its revenues are based on actual sales. There are two approaches commonly observed in practice to dealing with the effects of such mismatches:

(a) *Accrue or defer expenses* – With this approach, an overlift participant would accrue for future expenses that are not matched by corresponding future revenues. Conversely, an underlift participant would defer expenses and match them against future catch-up production. Therefore, an overlift liability would be accounted for as accrued production costs, while an underlift asset would be accounted for as a prepaid cost at the lower of the amount of accrued production costs or net realisable value. However, as IFRS does not require matching of revenue and expenses, it seems that accrued (deferred) expenses would not meet the definition of a liability (asset) under the IASB's *Conceptual Framework*; or

(b) *No adjustment* – Not accounting for the effects of imbalances has been justified on the grounds that operating costs for the period should be expensed as incurred because they relate to the period's production activity and not to the revenues recognised.[107]

12.4.2 Entitlements method

Under the *entitlements method*, net revenue reflects the participant's share of production regardless of which participant has actually made the sale and invoiced the production. This is achieved by applying one of the following approaches in dealing with imbalances between actual sales and entitlements:[108]

(a) *Adjusting revenue* – The excess of product sold during the period over the participant's ownership share of production from the property is recognised by the overlift party as a liability and not as revenue.[109] Conversely, the underlift party would recognise an underlift asset and report corresponding revenue. As the participant's share of expenses for the period is generally equal to its ownership percentage, there is no need to make any further adjustments;[110] or

(b) *Adjusting cost of sales* – This version of the entitlements method, which is the recommended approach under the former OIAC SORP, requires the cost of sales to be adjusted to take account of an asset or liability that reflects the lifting imbalance. If the adjustments are recorded at the market value of the product then it results in recognition of gross profit on an entitlements basis, while at the same time permitting revenues to be shown at the actual invoiced amount.

It is important for an entity to define clearly the measurement point for determining its 'share of production' and to apply that definition consistently. While it is possible to measure production at the well head, in practice production is often measured at the point where product is transferred into a pipeline or from a floating production, storage and offloading (FPSO) vessel into a ship.

12.4.3 Settlement

When the entitlements method is used (see 12.4.2 above), the agreement with the other joint venture parties may allow for the overlift or underlift to be settled either in cash or by physical settlement. The accounting may be different depending on the specific terms of the agreement. Possible outcomes are discussed below.

12.4.3.A Cash balancing

If participants have the right to settle imbalances on a cash basis then an underlift asset (overlift liability) clearly meets the definition of a financial asset (financial liability) under IFRS and should be accounted for under IAS 39. Depending on the designation of the financial asset or financial liability, it should be measured either at amortised cost or at fair value. The fair value in such cases would equal the cash settlement amount that participants are entitled to or required to pay.

12.4.3.B Physical settlement

If settlement of imbalances takes place physically by adjusting future liftings or providing a quantity of product from another source, it is not immediately obvious at what value the asset or liability should be recognised.

An overlift liability generally meets the definition of a provision under IAS 37 as the timing and amount of the settlement are uncertain and are not payable in cash but in kind. In applying IAS 37 the amount recognised as a provision should be 'the best estimate of the expenditure required to settle the present obligation at the end of the reporting period', *[IAS 37.36]*, which is 'the amount that an entity would rationally pay to settle the obligation at the end of the reporting period'. *[IAS 37.37]*.

An underlift asset that gives an entity the right to receive a quantity of product from another party is equivalent to a prepaid commodity purchase (and also similar to product borrowing). Therefore, it is reasonable to account for such underlift assets in the same way and apply the guidance in IAS 2 by analogy. Therefore, an underlift asset can be measured either at the lower of cost or net realisable value or at net realisable value in accordance with well-established industry practice. *[IAS 2.3(a), 9]*.

12.4.4 Facility imbalances

Imbalances that are similar to overlifts and underlifts can also arise on facilities such as pipelines when a venturer delivers more or less product into a pipeline than it takes out in the same period. The resulting accounting issues arising are similar to those concerning overlifts and underlifts.

12.4.5 Overlift and underlift in practice

IFRS does not currently address accounting for underlifts and overlifts directly; hence an entity that applied the hierarchy in IAS 8 could consider guidance from a number of sources: *[IAS 8.12]*

- under US GAAP, ASC 932-10-S99-5 – *Extractive Activities – Oil and Gas – Overall – SEC Materials – General* – does not express a preference for the sales method or the entitlements method. In practice, it seems that of those companies that apply the sales method under US GAAP a large majority do not make adjustments for operating expenses related to imbalances;[111] and
- the former OIAC SORP recommended that entities apply the entitlements method and adjust cost of sales for the effect of underlifts and overlifts.

As illustrated in the extracts below, in practice both the entitlements method and the sales method are used under IFRS.

For a discussion on the potential impact of IFRS 15 see 12.7.3 below.

Extract 41.22: BG Group plc (2015)

Principal accounting policies [extract]

Revenue recognition [extract]

Revenue associated with E&P sales (of natural gas, crude oil and petroleum products) is recorded when title passes to the customer. Revenue from the production of natural gas and oil in which BG Group has an interest with other producers is recognised based on the Group's working interest and the terms of the relevant production sharing contracts (entitlement method).

Extract 41.23: Statoil ASA (2015)

8.1 Notes to the Consolidated financial statements [extract]

8.1.2 Significant accounting policies [extract]

Revenue recognition

Revenues associated with sale and transportation of crude oil, natural gas, petroleum products and other merchandise are recognised when risk passes to the customer, which is normally when title passes at the point of delivery of the goods, based on the contractual terms of the agreements.

Revenues from the production of oil and gas properties in which Statoil shares an interest with other companies are recognised on the basis of volumes lifted and sold to customers during the period (the sales method). Where Statoil has lifted and sold more than the ownership interest, an accrual is recognised for the cost of the overlift. Where Statoil has lifted and sold less than the ownership interest, costs are deferred for the underlift.

Revenue is presented net of customs, excise taxes and royalties paid in-kind on petroleum products. Revenue is presented gross of in-kind payments of amounts representing income tax.

Sales and purchases of physical commodities, which are not settled net, are presented on a gross basis as *Revenues* and *Purchases [net of inventory variation]* in the statement of income. Activities related to trading and commodity-based derivative instruments are reported on a net basis, with the margin included in *Revenues*.

12.5 Forward-selling contracts to finance development

Mineral and oil and gas exploration and development are highly capital intensive businesses and different financing methods have arisen. In recent years, obtaining financing for these major projects has become increasingly difficult, as equity markets have become tighter and loan financing more difficult to obtain. Some increasingly common structured transactions continue to emerge which involve the owner of the mineral interests, or oil and gas interests, i.e. a mining entity or oil and gas entity (the producer), selling a specified volume of future production from a specified property/field to a third party 'investor' for cash. Such arrangements can be referred to as streaming arrangements.

A common example in the mining sector might be a precious metal streaming arrangement where a bulk commodity producer (e.g. a copper producer who has a mine that also produces precious metals as a by-product) enters into an arrangement with a streaming company (the investor). Here the producer receives an upfront cash payment and (usually) an ongoing predetermined per ounce payment for part or all of the by-product precious metal (the commodity) production – ordinarily gold and/or silver, which is traded on an active market. By entering into these contracts, the mining entity is able to access funding by monetising the non-core precious metal, while the investor receives the future production of precious metals without having to invest directly in, or operate, the mine.

We also note that similar types of arrangements are increasingly being used in the oil and gas sector as a source of funding.

These arrangements can take many forms and accounting for such arrangements can be highly complex. In many situations there is no specific guidance for accounting for these types of arrangements under IFRS.

12.5.1 Accounting by the producer

Generally, the accounting for these arrangements by the producer is either:

- a financial liability (i.e. debt) in accordance with IAS 39/IFRS 9, when the arrangement establishes a contractual obligation for the producer to deliver cash or another financial asset in the future;
- a sale of a mineral interest (under IAS 16 or IAS 38) and a contract to provide services such as extraction, refining, etc., in accordance with IAS 18, when the arrangement effectively transfers the risks and economic benefits of ownership from the producer to the investor and there is an obligation to provide future extraction services; or
- a commodity contract, which is outside the scope of IAS 39/IFRS 9 and in the scope of IAS 18. This would only occur when the arrangement is an executory contract to deliver an expected amount of the commodity in the future to the investor from the producer's own operation (i.e. it meets the 'own-use' exemption). If the commodity contract does not meet the own-use exemption, the arrangement will be in scope of IAS 39/IFRS 9.

Note that the potential impact of IFRS 15 on these types of arrangements has been considered at 12.7.10 below.

In each classification, the producer must assess and determine whether the arrangement contains separable embedded derivatives. That is, the producer would need to determine whether the arrangement contains a component or terms which had the effect that some of the cash flows of the combined instrument (being the arrangement) vary in a similar way to a stand-alone derivative (i.e. an embedded derivative).

When determining the accounting for such arrangements, the following matters would be taken into consideration:

- **Financial liability:** A key factor in determining whether the contract is a financial liability is whether the contract establishes a contractual obligation for the producer to make payments in cash or another financial asset, *[IAS 32.11, IAS 32.16(a)]* – that is, whether the arrangement has more of the characteristics of debt.
- **Sale of a mineral interest and a contract to provide extraction services:** When the nature of the arrangement indicates that the investor's investment is more akin to an equity interest in the project (rather than debt), this may indicate that the producer has essentially sold an interest in a property to the investor in return for the advance. In such a situation, the arrangement would likely be considered (fully or partially) as a sale of a mineral interest. In some instances, some of the upfront payment may also relate to an extraction services contract representing the producer's obligation to extract the investor's share of the future production.

  To apply this accounting, an entity would have to be able to demonstrate that the criteria in relation to the sale of an asset in IAS 16 and IAS 18 have been satisfied; that the investor bears the risks and economic benefits of ownership related to the output (a mineral interest); and agrees to pay for a portion or all of the production costs of extracting and/or refining its new mineral interest to the producer. Some of the relevant risks include:

  - production risk (which party bears the risk the project will be unable to produce output or will have a production outage);
  - resource risk (which party bears the risk the project has insufficient reserves to repay the investor); and
  - price risk (which party bears the risk the price of the output will fluctuate).

  The entity would also need to determine whether it is required to provide future extraction services under IAS 18, and if so, it would need to defer part of the advanced payment until those services were provided. See 12.7.10 below for the potential impact of IFRS 15.
- **Commodity contract:** A producer and an investor may agree to enter such an arrangement where both parties have an expectation of the amount of the commodity to be delivered under the contract at inception (for example, based on the reserves) and that there may or may not be additional resources. On the basis that the reserves will be delivered under the contract (and the contract cannot be net settled in cash), the advance would be considered a deposit for the commodity to be delivered at a future date. In this case, the arrangement is a commodity contract that falls outside the scope of IAS 39/IFRS 9, but only if the contract will always be settled through the physical delivery of the commodity which has been extracted by the producer as part of its own operations (i.e. it meets the 'own-use exemption' discussed at 13.1 below). *[IAS 32.8, IAS 39.5, IFRS 9.2.4]*.

  To determine if the own-use exemption applies and continues to apply, the key tests are whether the contract will always be settled through the physical

Chapter 41

delivery of a commodity (that is, not in cash and would not be considered to be capable of net settlement in cash), and that the commodity will always be extracted by the producer as part of its own operations. This means that there is no prospect of the producer settling part, or the entire advance, by purchasing the commodity on the open market or from a third party.

As noted above, regardless of the classification, each contract would still need to be assessed for the existence of any embedded derivatives.

Whether the arrangement constitutes debt, a sale of mineral interest and a contract to provide services or a forward sale of a commodity, is subject to significant judgement.

12.5.2 Accounting by the investor

From the investor's perspective, where the accounting becomes more complex is where the investor has acquired a right to receive cash, some quantity or value of a particular commodity, or the option to choose one or the other, or some combination of both. From the investor's perspective, there are generally four common accounting outcomes that are frequently observed:

- acquisition of a mineral interest (under the principles of IAS 16 or IAS 38) and potentially a prepayment in relation to future services such as extraction, refining, etc., in accordance with IAS 38 – this would occur when the arrangement effectively transfers the risks and economic benefits of ownership from the producer to the investor and there is a right to receive future extraction services;
- commodity contract, which is outside the scope of IAS 39/IFRS 9 and in the scope of IAS 38 – this would only occur when the arrangement is an executory contract to receive an expected amount of the commodity in the future from the producer and its meets the 'own-use' exemption for the investor. If the commodity contract does not meet the own-use exemption, the arrangement will be in scope of IAS 39/IFRS 9;
- a financial asset (i.e. a receivable or some sort of other financial asset) in accordance with IAS 39/IFRS 9 – this would occur when the arrangement establishes a contractual right to receive cash or another financial asset in the future; or
- a mix of all three.

The accounting implications of each for the investor, from a profit or loss perspective, can be significantly different.

For both the producer and the investor, each arrangement will have very specific facts and circumstances that will need to be understood and assessed, as different accounting treatments may apply in certain circumstances. Understanding the economic motivations and outcomes for both the producer and the investor and the substance of the arrangement are necessary to ensure a robust and balanced accounting conclusion can be reached. In many cases, the route to determining the classification will be a non-linear and iterative process.

12.6 Trading activities

Many mining and metals and oil and gas companies engage in trading activities (e.g. crude oil cargos or coal) and they may either take delivery of the product or resell it without taking delivery. Even when an entity takes physical delivery and becomes the legal owner of a commodity, it may still only be as part of its trading activities. Such transactions do not fall within the normal purchase and sales exemption (see 13.1 below) when 'for similar contracts, the entity has a practice of taking delivery of the underlying and selling it within a short period after delivery for the purpose of generating a profit from short-term fluctuations in price or dealer's margin'. *[IAS 32.9(c), IAS 39.6(c), IFRS 9.2.6(c)]*. Where the entity has a practice of settling similar physical commodity-based contracts net in cash, these contracts also do not fall within the normal purchase and sales exemption. *[IAS 32.9(b), IAS 39.6(b), IFRS 9.2.6(b)]*. In that case, the purchase and sales contracts should be accounted for as derivatives within the scope of IAS 39/IFRS 9.

The extract below from the financial statements of BP illustrates an accounting policy that an entity can apply in accounting for trading activities.

Extract 41.24: BP p.l.c. (2015)

Notes on financial statements [extract]

1. Significant accounting policies, judgements, estimates and assumptions [extract]

Revenue [extract]

Revenue arising from the sale of goods is recognized when the significant risks and rewards of ownership have passed to the buyer, which is typically at the point that title passes, and the revenue can be reliably measured.

Revenue is measured at the fair value of the consideration received or receivable and represents amounts receivable for goods provided in the normal course of business, net of discounts, customs duties and sales taxes.

Physical exchanges are reported net, as are sales and purchases made with a common counterparty, as part of an arrangement similar to a physical exchange. Similarly, where the group acts as agent on behalf of a third party to procure or market energy commodities, any associated fee income is recognized but no purchase or sale is recorded. Additionally, where forward sale and purchase contracts for oil, natural gas or power have been determined to be for trading purposes, the associated sales and purchases are reported net within sales and other operating revenues whether or not physical delivery has occurred.

12.7 Impact of IFRS 15

IFRS 15 is the new revenue standard that is effective for annual reporting periods commencing on or after 1 January 2018. While, in general, the accounting for many common types of arrangements in the extractive industries may not be significantly impacted by the new standard, some arrangements may have different patterns of revenue recognition. Given this, entities will still need to evaluate how IFRS 15 affects specific contracts and their financial reporting processes overall. Extractive industries companies will need to change how they evaluate many of their transactions, even if the amount of revenue they report may not change significantly, or at all. Changes may also be required to processes and information systems to capture information needed to apply the standard and make the required disclosures.

While the requirements of the IFRS 15 model are discussed in detail in Chapter 30, some of the key aspects of IFRS 15 that are particularly relevant to mining companies and oil and gas companies include:

- Embedded derivatives in commodity arrangements (see 12.7.1 below).
  - Provisionally priced contracts (see 12.7.1.A below).
- Inventory exchanges with the same counterparty (see 12.7.2 below).
- Overlift and underlift and production imbalances (see 12.7.3 below).
- Production sharing contracts/arrangements (PSCs) (see 12.7.4 below).
- Royalty income (see 12.7.5 below).
  - Royalty arrangements with collaborative partners (see 12.7.5.A below).
  - Royalty arrangements with customers (see 12.7.5.B below).
  - Royalty arrangements and the sale of non-financial items (see 12.7.5.C below).
- Modifications to commodity-based contracts (see 12.7.6 below).
- Principal versus agent considerations in commodity-based contracts (see 12.7.7 below).
  - Relationships with joint arrangement partners (see 12.7.7.A below).
  - Royalty payments (see 12.7.7.B below).
- Shipping (see 12.7.8 below).
- Sale of product with delayed shipment (see 12.7.9 below).
- Forward-selling contracts to finance development (streaming arrangements) (see 12.7.10 below).
- Gold bullion sales (mining only) (see 12.7.11 below).
- Repurchase agreements (see 12.7.12 below).
- Multi-period commodity-based sales contracts (see 12.7.13 below).
- Take-or-pay contracts (see 12.7.14 below).

12.7.1 Embedded derivatives in commodity arrangements

IFRS 15 states that if a contract is partially within scope of this standard and partially in the scope of another standard, entities will first apply the separation and measurement requirements of the other standard(s). *[IFRS 15.7]*. Therefore, to the extent that there is an embedded derivative contained within a revenue contract, e.g. provisional pricing mechanisms (discussed in more detail at 12.7.1.A below), diesel price linkage in a crude oil contract, or oil price linkage in a gas sales contract, these will continue to be assessed and accounted for in accordance with IAS 39 and IFRS 9.

Under IAS 39 and IFRS 9, if a feature of a revenue contract is considered to be an embedded derivative that is not closely related to a non-financial host contract; both standards require the embedded derivative to be separated from the host contract. If it is closely related, it is not required to be separated. In the event that the embedded derivative is considered to be closely related to the non-financial host contract, once transfer of the product has occurred and the entity has an unconditional right to receive cash and the host contract becomes a financial asset (i.e. a receivable), the accounting changes.

Under IAS 39, the embedded derivative is no longer considered to be closely related. Therefore, at this point, the embedded derivative must be separated from the host financial receivable and measured at fair value until settlement occurs. Under IFRS 9, embedded derivatives will no longer be separated from a host financial receivable, because the receivable will fail the contractual cash flows test. As a consequence, the whole receivable will have to be subsequently measured at fair value from the date of recognition of that receivable. See Chapter 47 at 2 for more information on the classification of financial assets under IFRS 9.

The treatment of the embedded derivatives under both IAS 39 and IFRS 9 is not expected to change as a result of IFRS 15. Revenue within the scope of IFRS 15 will be recognised when control passes to the customer and will be measured at the amount to which the entity expects to be entitled. Any subsequent movements in the embedded derivative (under IAS 39) or the receivable (under IFRS 9) would be recognised in profit or loss. However, what might change under IFRS 15 is the presentation of such fair value movements, depending on where such movements are currently being presented. We discuss this in relation to provisionally priced sales at 12.7.1.A below.

12.7.1.A Provisionally priced contracts

Sales contracts for certain commodities (e.g. copper and oil) often provide for provisional pricing at the time of shipment. The final sales price is often based on the average market prices during a subsequent period (the 'quotational period' or 'QP'), the price on a fixed date after delivery or the amount subsequently realised by another party (e.g. the smelter or refiner, net of tolling charges).

As discussed at 13.2.2 below, under current IFRS, if these price adjustment features meet the definition of an embedded derivative, they are separated from the contract and accounted for under IAS 39 from the date of delivery. As also discussed at 13.2.2 below, under IFRS 9, the key change is that these QP pricing exposures will no longer be separated from the host financial receivable. Instead, the entire receivable will be measured at fair value from the date of delivery.

From a revenue recognition perspective, currently under IAS 18, revenue is initially recognised at the estimated fair value of the total consideration received or receivable when the product is delivered, which is usually when it passes the ship's rail. This fair value is estimated by reference to forward market prices. Under IFRS 15, revenue will be recognised when control passes to the customer and will be measured at the amount to which the entity expects to be entitled, being the estimate of the price expected to be received at the end of the QP. *[IFRS 15.47]*.

So, provided an entity determines that control is considered to pass to the customer at the same point (i.e. the point of delivery), there will be no change under IFRS 15 from current IFRS for the revenue initially recognised upon delivery. The exception may be if shipping is considered to be a separate performance obligation. See 12.7.8 below for further discussion.

The key change for these arrangements will be the presentation of any subsequent movements in the embedded derivative or fair value movements in the receivable. Similar to current practice under IAS 18, IFRS 15 does not address the presentation of subsequent movements in profit or loss relating to embedded derivatives or any fair value movements in receivables. Likewise, IAS 39 and IFRS 9 do not specify where such movements should be presented in profit or loss.

In issuing IFRS 15, the IASB only addressed a subset of total revenue (i.e. revenue from contracts with customers). That is, transactions outside the scope of IFRS 15 might result in the recognition of revenue. However, while IFRS 15 does not specifically prohibit movements in the fair value of an embedded derivative or the fair value movement of a receivable from being described as revenue, it does specifically require an entity to disclose revenue from contracts with customers separately from its other sources of revenue, either in the statement of comprehensive income or in the notes. *[IFRS 15.113]*. Therefore entities that recognise such movements as part of revenue but do not currently track these separately, will now need to do so for disclosure purposes. For some, this may require changes to systems and processes.

12.7.2 Inventory exchanges with the same counterparty

Mining companies and oil and gas companies may exchange inventory with other entities in the same line of business, which is often referred to as 'loans/borrows'. This can occur with commodities such as oil, uranium, coal or certain concentrates, for which suppliers exchange or swap inventories in various locations to supplement current production, to facilitate more efficient management of capacity and/or to help achieve lower transportation costs.

While both IAS 18 and IFRS 15 scope out certain non-monetary exchanges, the specific wording used in the two standards differs. IAS 18 uses the words 'similar in nature and value' *[IAS 18.12]*, whereas IFRS 15 uses the words 'exchanges between entities in the same line of business to facilitate sales to customers or potential customers'. *[IFRS 15.5(d)]*. While we understand the IASB did not necessarily expect or intend the treatment of inventory exchanges to change as a result of IFRS 15, the difference in wording does create some uncertainty as to whether this requirement can be interpreted and applied in the same way as current IFRS. In particular, whether some transactions that are currently treated as exchanges of dissimilar goods (and, hence, revenue-generating) may now not be considered to be revenue-generating if the entities are in the same line of business and the exchange is intended to facilitate sales to customers or potential customers.

Furthermore, while the scope section of IFRS 15 makes it clear that such inventory exchanges do not result in revenue generation, it does not provide application guidance on how the transactions between the two parties would be accounted for and no other specific requirements exist within IFRS. Given the lack of clarity, the current diversity in accounting practice may continue.

12.7.3 Overlift and underlift and production imbalances

Section 12.4 above sets out the two methods of accounting for underlifts and overlifts that are commonly used in the oil and gas sector under current accounting standards. These are the sales method and the entitlements method. Under current accounting standards and practices, revenue under the sales method is the value of what a participant sells or the value of all product that has been transferred to its downstream activity. Under the entitlements method, net revenue reflects the participant's share of production regardless of whether the participant, or one of its joint venture partners, has actually made the sale and invoiced the production. If an entity sells more or less than its entitlement, it recognises the overlift or underlift as payables or receivables, respectively, to the other joint venture partners.

Current IFRS does not address accounting for underlifts and overlifts directly; hence an entity that applied the hierarchy in IAS 8 may have considered guidance from the following sources: *[IAS 8.12]*

- under US GAAP, ASC 932-10-S99-5 – *Extractive Activities – Oil and Gas – Overall – SEC Materials – General* – does not express a preference for the sales method or the entitlements method; and
- the former OIAC SORP, which recommended that entities apply the entitlements method and adjust cost of sales for the effect of underlifts and overlifts.

Recent developments challenge the extent to which this hierarchy of guidance remains relevant. The first of these relates to some US GAAP guidance. The SEC announced in March 2016 it has rescinded its guidance that provided US GAAP upstream oil and gas entities with the choice to use either the sales method or entitlements method to account for production and sales imbalances (e.g. gas imbalances), effective upon adoption of the US GAAP equivalent to IFRS 15 (ASC 606).[112] The SEC staff indicated it would not challenge entities that continue to apply the sales method but did not say whether it would continue to consider the entitlements method acceptable once the new revenue standard was adopted. This is relevant because this rescindment will remove one source of accounting literature and accepted industry practice that has been observed in determining that the entitlements method is acceptable under IFRS. Secondly, the decommissioning of the former OIAC SORP (see 1.4 above), coupled with the need to overlay IFRS pronouncements and guidance where available, means the guidance set out in the former OIAC SORP may now be less relevant.

Entities will need to consider the facts and circumstances to determine whether, and if so how, revenue recognition using either the sales or entitlements methods could be considered consistent with the requirements of IFRS 15.

12.7.4 Production sharing contracts/arrangements (PSCs)

These arrangements are discussed more generally at 5.3 above. We believe it is necessary to consider whether such contracts are within the scope of IFRS 15. That is, whether the relationship between the government entity and the contracting enterprise (i.e. the mining company or oil and gas company) represents one between a customer and a supplier. IFRS 15 defines a customer as 'a party that has contracted with an entity to obtain goods or services that are an output of the entity's ordinary activities in exchange for consideration'. See Chapter 30 at 2.2 for details. *[IFRS 15 Appendix A]*.

Currently, there are no specific requirements within IFRS governing the accounting for PSCs, which has resulted in accounting approaches that have evolved over time. These contracts are generally considered to be more akin to working interest relationships than pure services contracts. This is because the contracting enterprise assumes risks associated with performing the exploration, development and production activities and receives a share (and often a greater share) of future production as specified in the contract. Under current IFRS, when an entity determines it has an interest in the mineral rights themselves, revenue is recognised only when the mining company or oil and gas company receives its share of the extracted minerals under the PSC and sells those volumes to third-party customers. In other arrangements, the entity's share of production is considered a fee for services (e.g. construction, development and/or operating services) which is recognised as the services are rendered to the national government entity.

IFRS 15 notes that, in certain transactions, while there may be payments between parties in return for what appears to be goods or services of the entity, a counterparty may not always be a 'customer' of the entity. Instead, the counterparty may be a collaborator or partner that shares the results from the activity or process (such as developing an asset in a collaboration arrangement) rather than to obtain the output of the entity's ordinary activities. Generally, contracts with collaborators or partners are not within the scope of the standard, except as discussed below. *[IFRS 15.6]*.

The IASB decided not to provide additional application guidance for determining whether certain revenue generating collaborative arrangements are in the scope of the standard. In the Basis for Conclusions to IFRS 15, it explains that it would not be possible to provide application guidance that applies to all collaborative arrangements. *[IFRS 15.BC54]*.

In determining whether the contract between a government entity and a contracting enterprise is within the scope of the standard, an entity must look to the definition of a customer and what constitutes its 'ordinary activities'. It may be that certain parts of the PSC relationship involve the contracting enterprise and the national government entity acting as collaborators (and, hence, that part of the arrangement would be outside the scope of IFRS 15), while for other parts of the arrangement the two parties may act as supplier and customer. The latter will be within the scope of IFRS 15 and an analysis of the impact of the requirements will be necessary. See Chapter 30 at 2.3.

12.7.5 Royalty income

Entities in the extractive industries sometimes enter into arrangements whereby they may receive some form of royalty income. This may arise when they sell some or all their interest in a mining project or oil and gas project and in return agree to accept a future royalty amount which may be based on production and/or payable in cash or in kind. Alternatively, the acquiring entity may pay a net profit interest, that is, a percentage of the net profit (calculated using an agreed formula) generated by the interest sold. There may be other types of arrangements where the mining company or oil and gas company grants another entity a right in return for other types of payments – for example streaming arrangement (see 12.5 above and 12.7.10 below for more detail).

Under current IFRS, accounting for mineral rights and mineral reserves is scoped out of a number of standards including IAS 18, IAS 16 and IAS 38. Consequently, diverse practice has emerged in the accounting for such transactions.

With respect to these royalty arrangements, these can take a number of different forms and different accounting approaches have emerged. These may include:

- **Future receipt is solely dependent on production:** For some arrangements, the future royalty stream is solely dependent on future production, such that, if there is no future production, no royalty income will be received.

  We observe that, in some instances, the inflows (i.e. the royalty income) and the associated royalty receivable, are only recognised once the related mineral is extracted and the royalty is due, rather than when the interest in the project is originally sold. When such royalty receipts occur, they are often disclosed as either revenue or other income.

  An alternate approach observed is that the sale of the mineral interest is considered to create a contractual right to receive these royalty amounts (i.e. a contractual right to receive cash). Therefore, such royalty amounts (and, hence, the related receivable) would be recognised at fair value at the date of disposal and included in the calculation of the gain or loss on sale. Further divergence exists as to how subsequent movements in the receivable are recognised in profit or loss (i.e. as revenue or as other gains/losses).

- **Minimum additional amount due, but timing linked to production:** In other arrangements, the entity may be entitled to receive a certain additional (minimum) amount of cash regardless of the level of production, but the timing of receipt is linked to future production. This type of arrangement is considered to establish a contractual right to receive cash at the point when the disposal transaction occurs. Therefore, an entity recognises a receivable and the associated income when the arrangement is entered into and this will form part of the gain or loss on sale of the mineral interest.

Under IFRS 15, the impact will depend on whether the royalty arrangement is considered to arise from a collaborative arrangement, in the context of a supplier-customer relationship, or from the sale of a non-financial asset.

12.7.5.A Royalty arrangements with collaborative partners

As discussed at 12.7.4 above, IFRS 15 only addresses contracts with customers for goods or services provided in the ordinary course of an entity's business, it does not apply to arrangements between collaborative partners. *[IFRS 15.6]*. Where royalties are received by an entity as part of such an arrangement, they will generally not be in the scope of IFRS 15, unless the collaborator or partner meets the definition of a customer for some, or all, aspects of the arrangement. See 12.7.5.B below.

12.7.5.B Royalty arrangements with customers

Unlike current IFRS, IFRS 15 does not scope out revenue from the extraction of minerals. Therefore, regardless of the type of product being sold, if the counterparty to the contract is determined to be a customer, then the contract will be in scope of IFRS 15.

If a royalty arrangement is considered to be a supplier-customer relationship (and, hence, is in scope), mining companies and oil and gas companies may face a number of challenges in applying the standard to these arrangements. These may include identifying the performance obligations, determining the transaction price (e.g. if consideration is variable and dependent upon actions by the customer, which would be the case for the future extraction of minerals), applying the constraint on variable consideration, and reallocating the transaction price when and if there is a change in the transaction price. See Chapter 30 for more details on these requirements.

When considering the accounting for such royalties, IFRS 15 contains specific requirements that apply to licences of intellectual property, which may appear similar to some types of royalty arrangements in extractives industries. However, it is important to note that these requirements only apply to licences of intellectual property and not all sales-based or usage-based royalties. So, the general requirements applicable to variable consideration, including those relating to the constraint, will need to be considered (see Chapter 30 at 5.2 for further discussion).

12.7.5.C Royalty arrangements and the sale of non-financial items

If the royalty arrangement is not considered to relate to a contract with a customer nor to a collaborative arrangement, but instead, relates to the sale of a non-financial asset (e.g. an interest in a mining project or oil and gas project), IFRS 15 may still require some changes. This is because the existing requirements for the recognition and measurement of a gain or loss on the transfer of some non-financial assets that are not the output of an entity's ordinary operations (e.g. property, plant and equipment in the scope of IAS 16), have been amended to now refer to the requirements of IFRS 15.

Specifically, these changes require an entity to:

- Determine the date of disposal and, therefore, the date of derecognition (i.e. the date control transfers to the acquirer) (see Chapter 30 at 7.3 for more detail).
- Measure the consideration to be included in the calculation of the gain or loss arising from disposal including any variable consideration requirements (see Chapter 30 at 5 for more detail).
- Recognise any subsequent changes to the estimated amount of consideration (see Chapter 30 at 5.2.4, 5.9 and 6.5 for more detail).

Mineral rights and mineral reserves (and, hence, the associated capitalised costs) are outside the scope of both IAS 16 and IAS 38. However, in selecting an accounting policy for the disposal of these assets, in practice, most entities look to the principles of these two standards. Therefore, these requirements are likely to be applied by analogy to arrangements in which an entity sells all (or part) of its mining properties or oil and gas properties and some of the consideration comprises a royalty-based component.

There is also a lack of clarity as to how to apply the requirements of IFRS 15 to such arrangements where, by virtue of the royalty rights, the vendor is considered to have retained an interest in the mineral property. This may impact what is recognised or derecognised from the balance sheet in terms of mineral assets and/or financial assets, and also the gain/loss that is recognised in profit or loss.

12.7.6 Modifications to commodity-based contracts

Mining entities and oil and gas entities frequently enter into long-term arrangements for the sale, transportation or processing of commodities. Over time these contractual arrangements may be amended to effect changes in tenure, volume, price, or delivery point, for example. This may take the form of amendments, new tranches under existing agreements, or, new contractual arrangements. IFRS 15 contains requirements on how to account for changes to a contract depending on whether the change is considered to be a contract modification, a new contract, or a combination of both. Further guidance on contract modifications is set out in Chapter 30 at 3.4.

12.7.7 Principal versus agent considerations in commodity-based contracts

When identifying performance obligations, there may be some arrangements for which an entity needs to determine whether it is acting as principal or agent. This will be important as it affects the amount of revenue the entity recognises. That is, when the entity is the principal in the arrangement, the revenue recognised is the gross amount to which the entity expects to be entitled. When the entity is the agent, the revenue recognised is the net amount the entity is entitled to retain in return for its services as the agent. The entity's fee or commission may be the net amount of consideration that the entity retains after paying the other party the consideration received in exchange for the goods or services to be provided by that party. See Chapter 30 at 4.4 for more information on the principal versus agent indicators.

12.7.7.A Relationships with joint arrangement partners

It is not uncommon for valid vendor-customer relationships to exist alongside joint arrangement/collaborator contracts such as joint operating agreements or production sharing contracts. The manager of a joint arrangement may have a vendor-customer contract to purchase volumes produced by the non-operating parties. The manager would then on sell the product to third parties, and depending on the specific contract terms, could be acting as the principal in the onward sale, or as agent that is selling on behalf of the other joint arrangement partners.

Similarly, an entity with a gathering station or processing plant could purchase commodities from other parties with tenements or fields in the same region at the point of entry into the plant. Both the seller and purchaser would have to consider whether the purchaser is a principal or an agent in the onward sale to the third-party customer and account for the revenue accordingly.

12.7.7.B Royalty payments

As discussed at 5.7.5 above, mining companies and oil and gas companies frequently enter into a range of different royalty arrangements with owners of mineral rights (e.g. governments or private land owners) and at times, the treatment under current standards is diverse. It is unclear whether, and how, such arrangements may be impacted by IFRS 15.

In situations where the royalty holder retains or obtains a direct interest in the underlying production, it may be that the relationship between the mining company or oil and gas company and the royalty holder is more like a collaborative arrangement (and, hence, is not within the scope of IFRS 15). See 12.7.4 above for further discussion.

If these royalty payments are in scope, the requirements relating to principal versus agent in IFRS 15 will be helpful in assessing how these royalty payments should be presented. Specifically, an entity will need to determine whether it obtains control of all of the underlying minerals once extracted, sells the product to its customers and then remits the proceeds to the royalty holder. If so, the mining company or oil and gas company will be considered to be acting as the principal and, hence, would recognise the full amount as revenue with any payments to the royalty holder being recognised as part of cost of goods sold (or possibly as an income tax, depending on the nature of the royalty payment – see 19 below for further discussion on determining when an arrangement is an income tax). Where the entity does not obtain control over those volumes, it may be acting as the royalty holder's agent and extracting the minerals on its behalf.

The principal versus agent assessment under IFRS 15 is discussed in more detail in Chapter 30 at 4.4 and the issue of how sales (and other similar) taxes should be accounted for are discussed in Chapter 30 at 5.1.

12.7.8 Shipping

Given the location of the commodities produced in the mining sector and oil and gas sector, they generally have to be shipped to the customer. Such transportation may occur by road, rail or sea. The terms associated with shipping can vary depending on the method of shipping and the contract.

With respect to the potential impact of IFRS 15, there are a number of factors to consider in relation to shipping terms linked to customer contracts which are set out below at 12.7.8.A-12.7.8.B.

12.7.8.A Identification of performance obligations

Since the issuance of IFRS 15, there has been some debate as to whether shipping represents a separate performance obligation. The issue was raised with the joint Transition Resources Group (TRG) and was also considered by the IASB and US FASB. The US FASB decided to amend their standard to allow US GAAP entities to elect to account for shipping and handling activities performed after the control of a good has been transferred to the customer as a fulfilment cost (i.e. an expense). Without such an accounting policy choice, a US GAAP entity that has shipping arrangements after the customer has obtained control may determine that the act of shipping is a performance obligation under the standard. The IASB has not permitted a similar policy choice IFRS 15.

Given this, mining companies and oil and gas companies will need to consider the requirements of IFRS 15 to determine whether shipping is a separate performance obligation. It is likely that any shipping services provided to a customer after the customer obtains control over a good will represent a separate performance obligation. If this is the case, the transaction price for that contract will need to be allocated to the various performance obligations including shipping. Revenue will then be recognised when the goods are delivered and when the shipping services have been provided, either at a point in time or over time.

12.7.8.B Satisfaction of performance obligations – control assessment

Under IFRS 15, an entity recognises revenue only when it satisfies a performance obligation by transferring control of a promised good or service to the customer and control may be transferred over time or at a point in time. See Chapter 30 at 7 for more information.

With the change from a risk and reward model under IAS 18 to a control model under IFRS 15, entities will need to carefully re-examine the terms of their contracts, including shipping terms, in light of the indicators of control, to assess whether this will impact the timing of revenue recognition.

It is also worth noting that there may be some shipping arrangements where title to the goods must pass to the carrier during transportation, but the related contract includes a clause that requires the carrier to sell the goods back to the mining company or oil and gas company at the same or another specified price. We discuss the impact of repurchase clauses at 12.7.12 below.

12.7.9 Sale of product with delayed shipment

A mining company or oil and gas company may enter into a sales contract whereby the purchaser pays a significant portion (or all) of the final estimated purchase price, but then requests delayed shipment, for example, because of limited storage space. These sales can sometimes be referred to as 'in-store sales', or more generally as 'bill-and-hold arrangements'.

Under the current guidance provided in the Illustrative Examples to IAS 18, revenue is recognised when the buyer takes title, provided that: it is probable the delivery will be made; the product is on hand, it is specifically identified as belonging to the purchaser and is ready for delivery; the purchaser specifically acknowledges the deferred delivery instructions; and the usual payment terms apply. *[IAS 18.IE1]*.

The application guidance in IFRS 15 specifically addresses bill-and-hold arrangements and the requirements are similar to those in IAS 18. IFRS 15 states that an entity will need to determine when it has satisfied its performance obligation to transfer a product by evaluating when a customer obtains control of that product (see Chapter 30 at 7 for more information on transfer of control). In addition to applying these general requirements, an entity must also meet the criteria to be able to demonstrate control has passed for a bill-and-hold arrangement. *[IFRS 15.B79-82]*. See Chapter 30 at 7.6 for more information.

IFRS 15 also states that even if an entity recognises revenue for the sale of a product on a bill-and-hold basis, it will also need to consider whether it has remaining performance obligations (e.g. for custodial services or security services) to which the entity will need to allocate a portion of the transaction price. *[IFRS 15.B82]*. See Chapter 30 at 7.6 for more information.

12.7.10 Forward-selling contracts to finance development (streaming arrangements)

As discussed at 12.5 above, owners of mineral interests, or oil and gas interests, i.e. a mining entity or oil and gas entity (the producer), may enter arrangements whereby they sell a specified volume of future production from a specified property/field to a third party (the investor) for cash. Such arrangements are often referred to as streaming arrangements.

These arrangements can take many forms and accounting for such arrangements can be highly complex. There is no specific guidance for accounting for these types of arrangements under IFRS. Generally, the accounting for these arrangements by the producer is either:

(a) a financial liability (i.e. debt) in accordance with IAS 39 or IFRS 9;

(b) a sale of a mineral interest and a contract to provide services such as extraction, refining, etc.; or

(c) a commodity contract, which is outside the scope of IAS 39 and IFRS 9, representing an executory contract to deliver an expected amount of the commodity in the future.

The potential implications of IFRS 15 need to be considered in light of the latter two scenarios.

12.7.10.A Sale of a mineral interest with a contract to provide services

The requirements of IFRS 15 will need to be considered with both aspects of this accounting approach. The amount paid by the investor will need to be allocated between the sale of the mineral interest and the provision of future extraction services.

For the portion allocated to the sale of the mineral interest, the issues discussed at 12.7.5.C above will need to be considered.

For the portion allocated to the future extraction services, the following provisions of IFRS 15 will need to be considered:

- the identification of performance obligations, i.e. future extraction services (see Chapter 30 at 4);
- the determination of the transaction price and whether it contains a significant financing component (see Chapter 30 at 5);
- the allocation of the transaction price to those performance obligations (see Chapter 30 at 6); and
- whether the performance obligations are satisfied over time or at a point in time (see Chapter 30 at 7).

Given the period over which these extraction services are to be provided may extend for quite some time into the future and/or may change (particularly if they relate to the remaining life of the mine or field), this may lead to some complexity in the accounting.

12.7.10.B Commodity contract – forward sale of future production

Under this accounting approach, the mining company or oil and gas company has effectively pre-sold its future production and the investor has made an upfront payment for some or all of these volumes. The issues to be considered under IFRS 15 will be the same as those relating to the provision of future extraction services (see 12.7.10.A above).

12.7.11 Gold bullion sales (mining only)

Under IFRS 15, revenue is recognised only when the identified performance obligation is satisfied by transferring the promised good or service to the customer. A good or service is transferred when the customer obtains control of that good or service.

When mining companies sell gold bullion, there is generally a period of time (usually a matter of days) between when the bullion leaves the mine site with the security shipper and when the gold is credited to the metal account of the customer. In the intervening period, the gold bullion is sent to the refinery where it is refined, 'out turned', and, finally, transferred or credited to the customer's metal account.

For some entities, revenue is currently being recognised on such gold bullion sales when the bullion leaves the mine site with the security shipper. This is on the basis that the risks and rewards associated with ownership of the bullion have passed. At the time when the gold bullion leaves the mine site, given the way these transactions are commonly structured, the customer may not control the bullion and the IFRS 15 indicators that control has transferred may not be present. That is, the customer may not have the ability to direct the use of, or receive the benefit from, the gold bullion. Instead, these indicators may only be present when the gold bullion is actually credited to the customer's metal account.

12.7.12 Repurchase agreements

Some agreements in the extractive industries include repurchase provisions, either as part of a sales contract or as a separate contract, that relates to the goods in the original agreement or similar goods (e.g. tolling, processing or shipping agreements). The application guidance to IFRS 15 clarifies the types of arrangements that qualify as repurchase agreements. The repurchased asset may be the asset that was originally sold to the customer, an asset that is substantially the same as that asset or another asset of which the asset that was originally sold is a component. *[IFRS 15.B64]*.

IFRS 15 specifically notes that repurchase agreements generally come in three forms:

- an entity's obligation to repurchase the asset (a forward);
- an entity's right to repurchase the asset (a call option); or
- an entity's obligation to repurchase the asset at the customer's request (a put option). *[IFRS 15.B65]*.

Where a repurchase agreement exists, this may change whether and when revenue is recognised. See Chapter 30 at 7.4 for more details on repurchase agreements.

12.7.13 Multi-period commodity-based sales contracts

In the extractive industries, entities commonly enter into long-term (multi-period) commodity-based sales contracts. There are a range of different issues to be considered to determine the potential impact of IFRS 15.

12.7.13.A Identify the contract

Judgement will need to be applied when identifying the contract for these long-term arrangements. A contract is an agreement between two or more parties that creates enforceable rights and obligations. *[IFRS 15 Appendix A]*. Entities will need to determine what the enforceable part of the contract is. That is, whether there is a specified minimum the customer must buy (e.g. in take-or-pay contracts – see 12.7.14 below), whether it is the overall agreement, sometimes referred to as the master services agreement, or whether it is each purchase order. See Chapter 30 at 3 for more details.

12.7.13.B Identify the performance obligations

The next step is to identify all the promised goods or services within the contract to determine which will be treated as separate performance obligations. Chapter 30 at 4.2 explores in detail the requirements for determining whether a good or service is distinct, whether the transfer of a good or service represents a separate performance obligation and/or whether (and when) they need to be bundled.

During the development of the standard, some respondents thought it was unclear whether a three-year service or supply contract would be accounted for as a single performance obligation or a number of performance obligations covering smaller time periods (e.g. yearly, quarterly, monthly, daily) or individual units such as ounces, tonnes or barrels.

The standard clarifies that even if a good or service is determined to be distinct, if that good or service is part of a series of goods and services that are substantially the same and have the same pattern of transfer, that series of goods or services is treated as a single performance obligation. However, before such a treatment can be applied, specific criteria must be met. See Chapter 30 at 4.2.2 for further discussion and guidance.

Given the nature of these multi-period commodity-based sales arrangements, each unit (e.g. each metric tonne (mt) of coal or each barrel of oil), would likely be a distinct good and therefore, each unit would represent a separate performance obligation that is satisfied at a point in time. Because such goods are satisfied at a point in time, they would not meet the criteria to be considered a series of distinct goods that would have to be treated as a single performance obligation.

In addition, any option for additional goods or services will need to be evaluated to determine if those goods or services should be considered a separate performance obligation. See Chapter 30 at 4.6 for further discussion.

12.7.13.C Determine the transaction price

The transaction price is the amount of consideration to which an entity expects to be entitled in exchange for transferring promised goods or services to a customer, excluding amounts collected on behalf of third parties (e.g. some sales taxes). When determining the transaction price, an entity should consider the effects of all of the following:

- variable consideration (including any related constraint);
- a significant financing component (i.e. the time value of money);
- non-cash consideration; and
- consideration payable to a customer.

In many cases, the transaction price is readily determinable because the entity will receive payment at or near the same time as it transfers the promised good or service and the price is fixed for the minimum committed purchases. However, determining the transaction price may be more challenging when it is variable in amount, when payment is received at a time that is different from when the entity provides the goods or services and the effect of the time value of money is significant to the contract, or when payment is in a form other than cash. See Chapter 30 at 5 for more information.

For a fixed price contract, this step will be relatively straightforward. For variable price contracts, determining the transaction price may appear to be significantly more complex than for a fixed price contract. Many commodity sales contracts contain market- or index-based pricing terms that create variable consideration. After separating out any parts of the transaction price that are within the scope of another standard (e.g. IAS 39 or IFRS 9 – see 12.7.1 above), an entity will need determine whether it should partially or fully constrain the portion of the variable transaction price. Chapter 30 at 5.2 discusses variable consideration and, in particular, the requirements relating to the constraint.

12.7.13.D Allocate the transaction price

The next step is to allocate the transaction price to the performance obligations, generally in proportion to their stand-alone selling prices (i.e. on a relative stand-alone selling price basis), with two exceptions relating to the allocation of variable consideration and discounts. See Chapter 30 at 6 for detail. With commodity-based sales contracts, there are a number of things to consider depending on whether the transaction price is variable (or contains a variable component), fixed and/or whether there is a discount. Some factors to consider with variable and fixed consideration are discussed below while the allocation of a discount is discussed in Chapter 30 at 6.4.

(a) Variable consideration

If certain criteria are met, an entity will need to allocate variable consideration (e.g. the market- or index-based price) to one or more, but not all, performance obligations (i.e. the distinct commodities transferred in that period) or distinct goods or services in a series (where relevant), instead of using the relative stand-alone selling price allocation approach to allocate variable consideration proportionately to all performance obligations. See Chapter 30 at 6.3 for detail on these criteria.

(b) Fixed consideration

Entities that have fixed-price commodity-based sales contracts that call for deliveries over multiple periods will need to determine the stand-alone selling price of the performance obligations to allocate the transaction price if they do not qualify to be combined into a single performance obligation as a series of distinct goods (discussed further at 12.7.13.B above). IFRS 15 states that the stand-alone selling price is the price at which an entity would sell a promised good or service separately to a customer. *[IFRS 15 Appendix A]*. This is best evidenced by the observable price of a good or service when the entity sells it separately in similar circumstances and to similar customers. In other cases, it must be estimated. Estimating the stand-alone selling price may require judgement in long-term fixed-price commodity-based sales contracts, particularly when forward prices are available for the commodity being sold in a location with an active market.

If stand-alone selling prices are not directly observable, entities should consider all information (including market conditions, entity-specific factors and information about the customer or class of customer) that is reasonably available to determine the stand-alone selling price for each performance obligation. An entity may consider a number of factors in making this estimate, such as the forward curve, spot prices, expectations of market supply and demand shifts that are not represented in the forward curve or spot prices and expected transportation and storage capacity constraints that lead to premiums or discounts. Entities should maximise the use of observable inputs and apply similar estimation methods consistently in similar circumstances. The standard sets out a number of different approaches for doing this. See Chapter 30 at 6 for further discussion.

12.7.13.E Recognise revenue

Finally, an entity will recognise revenue once each performance obligation is satisfied which will occur when control of the good transfers to the customer. As discussed earlier, for long-term commodity-based sales arrangement, the performance obligations are likely to be satisfied at a point in time. See Chapter 30 at 7 for more information on how to determine when a performance obligation is satisfied. The precise timing of when control transfers to a customer may be impacted by the shipping terms associated with each contract. See 12.7.8 above for further discussion on shipping.

12.7.14 Take-or-pay contracts

A take-or-pay contract is a specific type of long-term commodity-based sales agreement between a customer and a supplier in which the pricing terms are set for a specified minimum quantity of a particular good or service. The customer must pay the minimum amount as per the contract, even if it does not take the volumes. There may also be options for additional volumes in excess of the minimum.

We discuss some of the broader accounting considerations associated with these contracts further at 17.2 below. When it comes to the potential impact of IFRS 15, in addition to the issues outlined at 12.7.13 above, the matters outlined below may also need to be considered.

12.7.14.A Volumes paid for, but not taken

A feature unique to take-or-pay contracts is the terms relating to payments made for volumes not taken, as explained further at 17.2.1 below. The requirements of IFRS 15 may result in different accounting considerations and possibly different conclusions depending on the specific facts and circumstances of each arrangement.

(a) Payments cannot be applied to future volumes

If payments received for unused volumes cannot be applied to future volumes, the seller has no obligation to deliver the unused volumes in the future. Such amounts can generally only be recognised as revenue once the seller's obligations no longer exist (i.e. once the customer's right to volumes has expired unused).

For most take-or-pay contracts, such an assessment may only be possible at the end of a pre-defined period (e.g. the end of each contract year). This is because the customer's rights have technically not expired and the entity is still obliged to deliver volumes if the customer requests them, until the end of the stated period. This treatment is consistent with current practice.

The standard does, however, consider whether it may be possible to recognise revenue in relation to a customer's unexercised rights earlier through the requirements relating to breakage. This is discussed in more detail at 12.7.14.B below.

(b) Payments can be applied to future volumes

If payments received for unused volumes can be applied to future volumes, the seller has received consideration in advance for some future unsatisfied performance obligations (i.e. the delivery of the unused volumes at some point in the future). This amount represents a contract liability.

In this situation an entity will need to determine how such future volumes can be taken. That is, whether the timing of the future transfer of those volumes is at the discretion of the customer or is determined by the entity itself. This determination will be important as it may require an assessment of the time value of money (i.e. the existence of a significant financing component). See Chapter 30 at 5.5 for further discussion. It will also be necessary for an entity to understand whether the customer is likely to take its unused volumes as this may require an assessment of the requirements relating to unexercised customer rights or breakage (see 12.7.14.B below for further information). This could impact the amount and timing of revenue recognised.

Such determinations will need to be made in light of the contract terms and an assessment of the expected customer behaviours. For example, such an assessment may involve considering whether the make-up volumes:

- will be the first volumes taken at the start of the following period;
- can only be taken after the minimum volumes have been satisfied in the following periods; or
- can only be taken after a certain amount of time or at the end of the contract period.

12.7.14.B Breakage (customers' unexercised rights)

The standard requires that when an entity receives consideration that is attributable to a customer's unexercised rights, the entity is to recognise a contract liability equal to the amount prepaid by the customer (because the entity has not yet satisfied the performance obligations to which the payment relates). However, IFRS 15 discusses the situation where, in certain industries, customers may pay for goods or services in advance, but may not ultimately exercise all of their rights to these goods or services – either because they choose not to or are unable to. IFRS 15 refers to these unexercised rights as 'breakage'. *[IFRS 15.B44-47]*.

IFRS 15 states that when an entity expects to be entitled to a breakage amount, the expected breakage will be recognised as revenue in proportion to the pattern of rights exercised by the customer. Otherwise, breakage amounts will only be recognised when the likelihood of the customer exercising its right becomes remote. See Chapter 30 at 7.10 for more information.

This may apply to take-or-pay contracts, for which payments are received in relation to make-up volumes and the customer's rights remain unexercised. Such breakage provisions may be applicable if:

- a customer is unable to use the make-up volumes in other areas of its own operations;
- a customer is unable to store the make-up volumes and use them after the take-or-pay contract has expired;
- a customer is unable to take delivery of the make-up volumes and sell them into the market; or
- there are limitations (physical or contractual) that prevent the customer from taking all of the make-up volumes.

For take-or-pay contracts, this may mean that an entity may be able to recognise revenue in relation to breakage amounts in an earlier period, provided it can demonstrate it is not required to constrain its estimate of breakage. This could potentially occur in several ways:

- At contract inception, the mining entity or oil and gas entity may be able to reliably estimate the amount of breakage and would include that amount in the transaction price and allocate that to expected actual usage.
- If the entity cannot estimate an amount of breakage, it will recognise the revenue associated with those unexercised rights when it becomes remote that they will be exercised. This could occur during a make-up period after the initial term of the contract or when the deficiency make-up period expires outright (which would be consistent with current accounting).

It is also possible that, given the nature of these arrangements and the inherent uncertainty in being able to predict a customer's behaviour, it may be difficult to satisfy the requirements relating to constraint because the entity's experience may not be predictive of the outcome at this level of certainty (i.e. highly probable).

13 FINANCIAL INSTRUMENTS

13.1 Normal purchase and sales exemption

Contracts to buy or sell non-financial items generally do not meet the definition of a financial instrument because the contractual right of one party to receive a non-financial asset or service and the corresponding obligation of the other party do not establish a present right or obligation of either party to receive, deliver or exchange a financial asset. For example, contracts that provide for settlement only by the receipt or delivery of non-financial items (e.g. forward purchase of oil or a forward purchase of copper) are not financial instruments. However, some of these contracts are traded in a standardised form on organised markets in the same way as derivative financial instruments. The parties buying and selling the contract are, in effect, trading the underlying commodity. The ability to buy or sell a commodity contract for cash does not alter the characteristics of the contract and make it into a financial instrument. Nevertheless, some contracts to buy or sell non-financial items that can be settled net or by exchanging financial instruments, or in which the non-financial item is readily convertible to cash, are within the scope of the IAS 32 and IAS 39/IFRS 9 as if they were financial instruments. *[IAS 32.8, IAS 32.AG20]*.

IAS 32, IAS 39/IFRS 9 should generally be applied to those contracts to buy or sell a non-financial item that can be settled net as if the contracts were financial instruments, whether this be in cash, another financial instrument, or by exchanging financial instruments, unless the contracts were entered into and continue to be held for the purpose of the receipt or delivery of a non-financial item in accordance with the entity's expected purchase, sale or usage requirements. *[IAS 32.8, IAS 39.5, IFRS 9.2.4]*.

There are various ways in which a contract to buy or sell a non-financial item can be settled net, including:

(a) the terms of the contract permit either party to settle it net;

(b) the ability to settle the contract net is not explicit in its terms, but the entity has a practice of settling similar contracts net (whether with the counterparty, by entering into offsetting contracts or by selling the contract before its exercise or lapse);

(c) for similar contracts, the entity has a practice of taking delivery of the underlying and selling it within a short period after delivery for the purpose of generating a profit from short-term fluctuations in price or dealer's margin; and

(d) the non-financial item that is the subject of the contract is readily convertible to cash, e.g. precious metals or base metals quoted on the London Metal Exchange are considered to be readily convertible to cash. *[IAS 32.9, IAS 39.6]*.

There is no further guidance in IAS 39/IFRS 9 explaining what is meant by 'readily convertible to cash'. Typically, a non-financial item would be considered readily convertible to cash if it consists of largely fungible units and quoted spot prices are available in an active market that can absorb the quantity held by the entity without significantly affecting the price. Further discussion on the net settlement criteria can be found in Chapter 43 at 4.1.

Commodity-based contracts that are excluded from IAS 32 and IAS 39/IFRS 9 are contracts that were entered into and continue to be held for the purpose of the receipt or delivery of a non-financial item in accordance with the entity's expected purchase, sale or usage requirements. Contracts that fall within this exemption, which is known as the 'normal purchase or sale exemption', 'executory contract exemption' or 'own-use exemption', are accounted for as executory contracts. An entity recognises such contracts in its statement of financial position only when one of the parties meets its obligation under the contract to deliver either cash or a non-financial asset. *[Framework.4.46]*.

The IASB views the practice of settling net or taking delivery of the underlying and selling it within a short period after delivery as an indication that the contracts are not normal purchases or sales. Therefore, contracts to which (b) or (c) apply cannot be subject to the normal purchase or sale exception. Other contracts that can be settled net are evaluated to determine whether this exemption can actually apply. *[IAS 32.9, IAS 39.6, BC24, IFRS 9.2.6, BCZ2.18]*.

A written option to buy or sell a non-financial item that can be settled net in cash or another financial instrument, or by exchanging financial instruments, in accordance with (a) or (d) should be accounted for under IAS 39/IFRS 9 and does not qualify for use of the normal purchase or sale exemption. *[IAS 32.10, IAS 39.7, BC24, IFRS 9.2.7, BCZ2.18]*.

The conditions associated with the use of the normal purchase or sale exemption often pose problems for mining companies and oil and gas companies because, historically, they have settled many purchase and sales contracts on a net basis.

A further problem may arise when a mining company or oil and gas company holds a written option for the purpose of the receipt or delivery of a non-financial item in accordance with the entity's expected purchase, sale or usage requirements – because IAS 39 would require such contracts to be accounted for as derivative financial instruments.

Finally, from time to time mining companies and oil and gas companies may need to settle contracts for the sale of commodities on a net basis because of operational problems. Such a situation may mean that the company would usually need to treat those contracts as derivative financial instruments under IAS 39 as they may now have a practice of settling net under (b) or (c) above. Where this situation is caused by a unique event beyond management's control, a level of judgement will be required to determine whether that would prevent the company from applying the own use exemption to similar contracts. This should be assessed on a case by case basis.

Judgement will also be required as to what constitutes 'similar contracts'. The definition of similar contracts in IAS 39/IFRS 9, *[IAS 39.6, IFRS 9.2.4]*, considers the intended use for such contracts. This means that contracts identical in form may be dissimilar due to their intended use, e.g. own purchase requirements versus proprietary trading. If the intended use is for normal purchase or sale, such an intention must be documented at inception of the contract. A history of regular revisions of expected purchase or sale requirements could impair the ability of a company to distinguish identical contracts as being dissimilar.

The IFRS 9 requirements in relation to own use contracts are the same as IAS 39 except for the following amendment. IFRS 9 introduces a fair value option for own use contracts. At the inception of a contract, an entity may make an irrevocable designation to measure an own use contract at fair value through profit or loss (the 'fair value option') even if it was entered into for the purpose of the receipt or delivery of a non-financial item in accordance with the entity's expected purchase, sale or usage requirement. However, such designation is only allowed if it eliminates or significantly reduces an accounting mismatch that would otherwise arise from not recognising that contract because it is excluded from the scope of IFRS 9. *[IFRS 9.2.5]*.

See Chapter 43 at 4 for more information on the normal purchase and sales exemption.

The extract below from AngloGold Ashanti's 2008 financial statements illustrates how this could affect an entity's reported financial position. (Note that in October 2010, AngloGold Ashanti removed the last of its gold hedging instruments and long-term sales contracts.)

Extract 41.25: AngloGold Ashanti Limited (2008)

Risk management and internal controls [extract]

Risks related to AngloGold Ashanti's operations [extract]

A significant number of AngloGold Ashanti's forward sales contracts are not treated as derivatives and fair valued on the financial statements as they fall under the normal purchase sales exemption. Should AngloGold Ashanti fail to settle these contracts by physical delivery, then it may be required to account for the fair value of a portion, or potentially all of, the existing contracts in the financial statements. This could adversely affect AngloGold Ashanti's reported financial condition.

13.2 Embedded derivatives

A contract that qualifies for the normal purchase and sale exemption still needs to be assessed for the existence of embedded derivatives. An embedded derivative is a component of a hybrid or combined instrument that also includes a non-derivative host contract; it has the effect that some of the cash flows of the combined instrument vary in a similar way to a stand-alone derivative. In other words, it causes some or all of the cash flows that otherwise would be required by the contract to be modified according to a specified interest rate, financial instrument price, commodity price, foreign exchange rate, index of prices or rates, credit rating or credit index, or other underlying variable (provided in the case of a non-financial variable that the variable is not specific to a party to the contract). *[IAS 39.10, IFRS 9.4.3.1]*.

The detailed requirements regarding the separation of embedded derivatives and the interpretation and application of those requirements under IAS 39 and IFRS 9 are discussed in Chapter 44. A number of issues related to embedded derivatives that are of particular importance to the extractive industries are discussed at 13.2.1 to 13.2.4 below.

13.2.1 Foreign currency embedded derivatives

The most common embedded derivatives in the extractive industries are probably foreign currency embedded derivatives which arise when a producer of minerals sells these in a currency that is not the functional currency of any substantial party to the contract, the currency in which the price of the related commodity is routinely denominated in commercial transactions around the world or a currency that is commonly used in contracts to purchase or sell non-financial items in the economic environment in which the transaction takes place. *[IAS 39.AG33(d), IFRS 9.B4.3.8(d)]*. A more detailed analysis of these requirements can be found in Chapter 44 at 5.2.1.

13.2.2 Provisionally priced contracts

As discussed above at 12.7.1.A, sales contracts for certain commodities (e.g. copper and oil) often provide for provisional pricing at the time of shipment, with final pricing based on the average market price for a particular future period, i.e. the 'quotational period'.

Price adjustment features contained in non-cancellable contracts that are based on quoted market prices for a date subsequent to the date of shipment or delivery (e.g. the spot price three weeks after shipment or the average spot price for the month of shipment) are considered to be embedded derivatives.

Under IAS 39, these embedded derivatives require separation because the forward price at which the contract is to be settled is not closely related to the spot price. *[IAS 39.11, AG30(e)]*. The non-financial contract for the sale or purchase of the product, e.g. copper or oil, at a future date would be treated as the host contract, while the exposure to the price movements from the date of sale to the end of the quotational period would be treated as an embedded derivative.

If the contract is cancellable without penalty before delivery, the price adjustment feature does not meet the definition of a derivative because there is no contractual obligation until delivery takes place.

If the contract is not cancellable, there will be a contractual obligation, but until delivery, the embedded derivative would be considered to be closely related to the host commodity contract and does not need to be recorded separately.

When the embedded derivative is separated from the host contract, the host contract will normally meet the revenue recognition criteria of IAS 18 – in particular the requirement that revenue can be measured reliably and that significant risks and rewards have passed to the customer – at the date that the product is delivered. *[IAS 18.14]*.

Changes in the fair value of the embedded derivative from initial recognition at delivery date should be recognised in profit or loss for the period. While gains or losses from embedded derivatives should normally be presented together with those from other derivatives, many companies include adjustments of provisionally priced contracts within revenue, presumably on the grounds of materiality or as a matter of industry practice.

Antofagasta is an example of a mining company that discloses the effects of provisional pricing in its financial statements in considerable detail, including the quantities of minerals that are subject to provisional prices.

Extract 41.26: Antofagasta plc (2015)

Notes to the financial statements [extract]

2 Principal accounting policies continued [extract]

f) Revenue recognition [extract]

Revenue represents the value of goods and services supplied to third parties during the year. Revenue is measured at the fair value of consideration received or receivable, and excludes any applicable sales tax.

A sale is recognised when the significant risks and rewards of ownership have passed. This is generally when title and any insurance risk has passed to the customer, and the goods have been delivered to a contractually agreed location or when any services have been provided.

Revenue from mining activities is recorded at the invoiced amounts with an adjustment for provisional pricing at each reporting date, as explained below. For copper and molybdenum concentrates, which are sold to smelters and roasting plants for further processing, the invoiced amount is the market value of the metal payable by the customer, net of deductions for tolling charges. Revenue includes amounts from the sale of by-products. Copper and molybdenum concentrate sale agreements and copper cathode sale agreements generally provide for provisional pricing of sales at the time of shipment, with final pricing based on the monthly average London Metal Exchange ("LME") copper price or the monthly average market molybdenum price for specified future periods. This normally ranges from one to five months after delivery to the customer. Such a provisional sale contains an embedded derivative which is required to be separated from the host contract. The host contract is the sale of metals contained in the concentrate or cathode at the provisional invoice price less tolling charges deducted, and the embedded derivative is the forward contract for which the provisional sale is subsequently adjusted. At each reporting date, the provisionally priced metal sales together with any related tolling charges are marked-to-market, with adjustments (both gains and losses) being recorded in revenue in the consolidated income statement and in trade debtors in the balance sheet. Forward prices at the period end are used for copper concentrate and cathode sales, while period-end average prices are used for molybdenum concentrate sales due to the absence of a futures market.

[...]

5 Revenues [extract]

Copper and molybdenum concentrate sale agreements and copper cathode sale agreements generally provide for provisional pricing of sales at the time of shipment, with final pricing being based on the monthly average London Metal Exchange copper price or monthly average molybdenum price for specified future periods. This normally ranges from one to five months after shipment to the customer. The provisional pricing mechanism within the sale agreements is an embedded derivative under IFRS. Gains and losses from the marking-to-market of open sales are recognised through adjustments to revenue in the income statement and to trade debtors in the balance sheet. The Group determines mark-to-market prices using forward prices at each period end for copper concentrate and cathode sales, and period-end month average prices for molybdenum concentrate sales due to the absence of a futures market in the market price references for that commodity in the majority of the Group's contracts.

[...]

Copper and molybdenum concentrate sales are stated net of deductions for tolling charges, as shown in the tables below.

For the year ended 31 December 2015	Los Pelambres Copper concentrate $m	Centinela Copper concentrate $m	Centinela Copper cathodes $m	Michilla Copper cathodes $m
Provisionally invoiced gross sales	2,001.6	805.8	443.4	173.3
Effects of pricing adjustments to previous year invoices				
Reversals of mark-to-market adjustments at the end of the previous year	45.5	19.6	1.4	0.4
Settlement of sales invoiced in the previous year	(100.4)	(49.8)	(5.6)	(2.3)
Total effect of adjustments to previous year invoices in the current year	(54.9)	(30.2)	(4.2)	(1.9)
Effects of pricing adjustments to current year invoices				
Settlement of sales invoiced in the current year	(126.7)	(47.6)	(7.1)	(2.6)
Mark-to-market adjustments at the end of the current year	(14.5)	(6.2)	0.2	0.1
Total effect of adjustments to current year invoices	(141.2)	(53.8)	(6.9)	(2.5)
Total pricing adjustments	(196.1)	(84.0)	(11.1)	(4.4)
Realised gains on commodity derivatives	–	–	–	–
Revenue before deducting tolling charges	1,805.5	721.8	432.3	168.9
Tolling charges	(198.8)	(95.2)	–	–
Revenue net of tolling charges	1,606.7	626.6	432.3	168.9

[NOTE: 31 December 2014 comparatives were provided in a subsequent table – these have not be illustrated here]

(i) Copper concentrate

The typical period for which sales of copper concentrate remain open until settlement occurs is a range of approximately three to five months from shipment date.

At 31 December 2015 sales totalling 184,400 tonnes remained open as to price, with an average mark-to-market price of $2.13/lb compared with an average provisional invoice price of $2.18/lb.

At 31 December 2014 sales totalling 199,200 tonnes remained open as to price, with an average mark-to-market price of $2.86/lb compared with an average provisional invoice price of $3.01/lb.

(ii) Copper cathodes

The typical period for which sales of copper cathodes remain open until settlement occurs is approximately one month from shipment date.

At 31 December 2015, sales totalling 7,700 tonnes remained open as to price, with an average mark-to-market price of $2.13/lb compared with an average provisional invoice price of $2.12/lb.

At 31 December 2014, sales totalling 13,800 tonnes remained open as to price, with an average mark-to-market price of $2.88/lb compared with an average provisional invoice price of $2.94/lb.

See 12.7.1.A above for a discussion of the potential impact of IFRS 15.

Under IFRS 9, these embedded derivatives will no longer be separated from the receivables to which they relate. This is because these receivables will fail the contractual cash flows test and therefore will need to be measured at fair value through profit or loss in their entirety. See Chapter 47 at 2 for more information on the classification of financial assets.

13.2.3 Long-term supply contracts

Long-term supply contracts sometimes contain embedded derivatives because of a desire to shift certain risks between contracting parties or as a consequence of existing market practices. The fair value of embedded derivatives in long-term supply contracts can be highly material to the entities involved. For example, in the mining sector electricity purchase contracts sometimes contain price conditions based on the commodity that is being sold, which provides an economic hedge for the mining company. While the electricity price component (if fixed) would meet the definition of an embedded derivative, it would be considered closely related to the host contract and hence would not have to be separated. However, the linkage to the commodity price would be unlikely to be considered closely related and would likely have to be separately accounted for as an embedded derivative. In the oil and gas sector the sales price of gas is at times based on that of electricity, which provides an economic hedge for the utility company that purchases the gas, and would also likely represent an embedded derivative that has to be separately accounted for. See Chapter 44 at 5.2.2 for further discussion.

As can be seen in the following extract from BHP Billiton's 2007 financial statements, the pricing terms of embedded derivatives in purchase (sales) contracts often match those of the product that the entity sells (purchases).

Extract 41.27: BHP Billiton plc (2007)

Notes to Financial Statements [extract]
28 Financial instruments [extract]

Embedded derivatives

Derivatives embedded in host contracts are accounted for as separate derivatives when their risks and characteristics are not closely related to those of the host contracts or have intrinsic value at inception and the host contracts are not carried at fair value. These embedded derivatives are measured at fair value with gains or losses arising from changes in fair value recognised in the income statement.

Contracts are assessed for embedded derivatives when the Group becomes a party to them, including at the date of a business combination. Host contracts which incorporate embedded derivatives are entered into during the normal course of operations and are standard business practices in the industries in which the Group operate.

The following table provides information about the principal embedded derivatives contracts:

	Maturity date 2007	2006	Volume 2007	2006		Exposure price
Commodity Price Swaps						
Electricity purchase arrangement (a)	31 Dec 2024	31 Dec 2024	240,000	240,000	MWh	Aluminium
Electricity purchase arrangement (a)	30 June 2020	30 June 2020	576,000	576,000	MWh	Aluminium
Gas sales (b)	31 Dec 2013	31 Dec 2013	1,195,572	1,428,070	'000 therms	Electricity

Commodity Price Options						
Finance lease of plant and equipment (b)	31 Dec 2018	30 Dec 2018	38.5	39.5	mmboe	Crude Oil
Copper concentrate purchases and sales (b)	31 Dec 2007	31 Dec 2006	52	41	'000 tonnes	Copper
Lead concentrate purchases and sales (b)	31 Dec 2007	1 January 2007	11	67	'000 tonnes	Lead
Zinc concentrate purchases and sales (b)	31 Dec 2007	2 January 2007	51	6	'000 tonnes	Zinc
Silver concentrate sales (b)	31 Dec 2007	–	4,604	–	'000 ounces	Silver

(a) The volumes shown in these contracts indicate a megawatt volume per hour for each hour of the contract.

(b) The volumes shown in these contracts indicate the total volumes for the contract.

13.2.4 *Development of gas markets*

Where there is no active local market in gas, market participants often enter into long-term contracts that are priced on the basis of a basket of underlying factors, such as oil prices, electricity prices and inflation indices. In the absence of an active market in gas, such price clauses are not considered to give rise to embedded derivatives because there is no accepted benchmark price for gas that could have been used instead.

An entity that applies IAS 39 is required to assess whether an embedded derivative is required to be separated from the host contract and accounted for as a derivative when the entity first becomes a party to the contract. *[IAS 39.11]*. Under IFRIC 9 – *Reassessment of Embedded Derivatives* – subsequent reassessment is generally prohibited. *[IFRIC 9.7]*. Similar requirements have been included in IFRS 9. *[IFRS 9.B4.3.11]*. See Chapter 44 at 7 for more information. Therefore, in the case of gas, when an active market subsequently develops, an entity is not permitted to separate embedded derivatives from existing gas contracts, unless there is a change in the terms of the contract that significantly modifies the cash flows that otherwise would be required under the contract. However, if the entity enters into a new gas contract with exactly the same terms and conditions, it would be required to separate embedded derivatives from the new gas contract.

Judgement is required in determining whether there is an active market in a particular geographic region and the relevant geographic market for any type of commodity. Where no active market exists consideration should be given to the industry practice for pricing such commodity-based contracts. A pricing methodology that is consistent with industry practice would generally not be considered to contain embedded derivatives.

The extract below from BP shows the company's approach to embedded derivatives before and after the development of an active gas trading market in the UK, and demonstrates that the fair value of embedded derivatives in long-term gas contracts can be quite significant.

Extract 41.28: BP p.l.c. (2014)

Notes on financial statements [extract]

28. Derivative financial instruments [extract]

Embedded derivatives [extract]

The group is a party to certain natural gas contracts containing embedded derivatives. Prior to the development of an active gas trading market, UK gas contracts were priced using a basket of available price indices, primarily relating to oil products, power and inflation. After the development of an active UK gas market, certain contracts were entered into or renegotiated using pricing formulae not directly related to gas prices, for example, oil product and power prices. In these circumstances, pricing formulae have been determined to be derivatives, embedded within the overall contractual arrangements that are not clearly and closely related to the underlying commodity. The resulting fair value relating to these contracts is recognized on the balance sheet with gains or losses recognized in the income statement.

[...]

The commodity price embedded derivatives relate to natural gas contracts and are categorized in level 2 and 3 of the fair value hierarchy. The contracts in level 2 are valued using inputs that include price curves for each of the different products that are built up from active market pricing data. Where necessary, the price curves are extrapolated to the expiry of the contracts (the last of which is in 2018) using all available external pricing information; additionally, where limited data exists for certain products, prices are interpolated using historic and long-term pricing relationships.

[...]

The following table shows the changes during the year in the net fair value of embedded derivatives, within level 3 of the fair value hierarchy.

		$ million
	2014	2013
	Commodity price	Commodity price
Net fair value of contracts at 1 January	**(379)**	(1,112)
Settlements	**24**	316
Gains recognized in the income statement	**219**	142
Transfers out of level 3	**–**	258
Exchange adjustments	**10**	17
Net fair value of contracts at 31 December	**(126)**	(379)

The amount recognized in the income statement for the year relating to level 3 embedded derivatives still held at 31 December 2014 was a $220 million gain (2013 $67 million gain related to derivatives still held at 31 December 2013).

13.3 Volume flexibility in supply contracts

It is not uncommon for other sales contracts, such as those with large industrial customers, to contain volume flexibility features. For example, a supplier might enter into a contract requiring it to deliver, say, 100,000 units at a given price as well as giving the counterparty the option to purchase a further 20,000 units at the same price. Often such a supply contract will be readily convertible to cash as parties to the contract can settle the contract on a net basis, as discussed at 13.1 above. For example, precious metals or base metals quoted on the London Metal Exchange or oil contracts are considered to be readily convertible to cash, whereas bulk materials without spot prices (e.g. coal and iron) are generally not considered to be readily convertible to cash.

However, with increasing levels of liquidity in certain commodities, this view may need to be reconfirmed/rechallenged before concluding that this remains the case.

If the customer has access to markets for the non-financial item and, following the guidance of the Interpretations Committee the supplier might consider such a contract to be within the scope of IAS 39/IFRS 9 as it contains a written option (see Chapter 43 at 4.2.3). However, some would say that the supplier could split the contract into two separate components for accounting purposes: a forward contract to supply 100,000 units (which may qualify as a normal sale and so meet the recognition exemption) and a written option to supply 20,000 units (which would not). Arguments put forward include:

- the parties could easily have entered into two separate contracts, a forward contract and a written option; and
- it is appropriate to analogise to the requirements for embedded derivatives and separate a written option from the normal forward sale or purchase contract because it is not closely related.

Some contracts, however, contain operational volume tolerances such as, in the case of certain oil purchase and sale contracts, a volume that is plus or minus a certain (often quite small) percentage of the stated quantity. These tolerances relate to physical changes in the volume during transportation caused by, for example, evaporation. The optionality within the contract typically cannot be monetised by either party but, instead is a practical requirement of the contract. In such cases, the optionality would not be considered a separate derivative within the scope if IAS 39/IFRS 9. In other cases, however, the volume tolerance may be greater than that which is required for practical reasons. This optionality may give one party the ability to benefit from changing underlying prices and could be considered a separate derivative. Judgement is required in assessing the nature of these volume tolerances.

This issue is discussed in more detail in Chapter 43 at 4.2.4 and 4.2.5.

13.4 Hedging sales of metal concentrate (mining)

In the mining sector certain commodities are often sold in the form of a concentrate that comprises two or more metals and impurities. These concentrates are the output of mines and are sold and shipped to smelters for treatment and refining in order to extract the metals in their pure form from the concentrate (or, alternatively, the concentrate may be sold to traders who will subsequently sell and ship to smelters). The metal content of concentrate varies depending on the mine and grade of ore being mined. The sales proceeds of concentrate are typically determined as the total of the payments for the actual content of each of the metals contained in a given concentrate shipment and they reflect the condition in which the metal is sold (i.e. unrefined, still being dissolved in concentrate). Typical pricing formulas are based on the price for dissolved metal off the quoted price for refined metal (e.g. the London Metal Exchange (LME)), with deductions for amounts that reflect the fact that the metal sold is not treated and/or refined. Actual deductions may vary by contract but typically comprise treatment and refining charges, price participation clauses, transportation, impurity penalties, etc.

If an entity hedges the price risk of only one of the metals in the concentrate, the question arises whether, for hedge accounting purposes under IAS 39, the entity can designate as the hedged item, the sale of that individual metal, or instead, the sale of the concentrate as a whole. Paragraph 82 of IAS 39 requires that a non-financial asset is 'designated as a hedged item (a) for foreign currency risks, or (b) in its entirety for all risks, because of the difficulty of isolating and measuring the appropriate portion of the cash flows or fair value changes attributable to specific risks other than foreign currency risks'. *[IAS 39.82]*.

The terms and conditions of each sales contract need to be considered carefully in determining whether individual metals or only the concentrate as a whole can be designated as a hedged item. If each of the metals contained in the concentrate is sold at a price that is determined independently of the price of any other metal in the concentrate and any deductions relate specifically to each metal and there are no other deductions that would need to be allocated to the different metals then, for the purposes of hedge accounting under IAS 39, we believe that each metal may be viewed as a transaction in its own right instead of a risk-component of the sale of the concentrate as a whole.

Consequently, in these circumstances, the sale of each individual metal can be hedged separately. The price of each individual metal is the total price established under the sales contract for that metal, i.e. including the adjustments of the market price for refined metal for the various deductions and charges. This means that the entity is hedging the price for the unrefined metal that is dissolved in the concentrate, e.g. LME, less the various charges and deductions. This could lead to some hedge ineffectiveness. Designating only the part of the price that is linked to the market price for refined metal, e.g. the LME part of the pricing formula, would constitute the designation of a risk component of a non-financial item that is prohibited by IAS 39 (even if the pricing of the metal is separate). *[IAS 39.82]*.

This approach is conceptually no different from hedging the contents of a box that contains a number of non-financial assets, each of which is priced at fair value and itemised separately on the invoice. The approach clearly differs from hedging jet fuel with crude oil based derivatives because in that case, the underlying of the hedging instruments, being crude oil, could only be a risk component of the jet fuel (for which IAS 39 prohibits designation as the hedged item on a risk components basis) but not a separate content of a box that you can take out (like the individual metal that is extracted from the concentrate). *[IAS 39.82]*.

Under IFRS 9, the considerations relating to hedging metal in concentrate will change. This is because IFRS 9 now permits an entity to designate a risk component of a non-financial item as the hedged item in a hedging relationship, provided the risk component is separately identifiable and reliably measurable. See Chapter 53 at 3.4 for more information on the new IFRS 9 hedge accounting requirements and hedging of risk components. These considerations also apply from the perspective of an entity that purchases metals in the form of a concentrate.

14 INVENTORIES

Inventories should be measured at the lower of cost and net realisable value under IAS 2. However, IAS 2 does not apply to the measurement of minerals and mineral products, to the extent that they are measured at net realisable value in accordance with well-established practices in those industries. *[IAS 2.3(a)]*. There is also an exception for commodity broker traders who measure their inventories at fair value less costs to sell. When such inventories are measured at fair value less costs to sell, changes in fair value less costs to sell are recognised in profit or loss in the period of the change. *[IAS 2.3(b)]*. This is discussed further at 14.4 below.

Various cost methods are acceptable under IFRS and include specific identification, weighted average costs, or first-in first-out (FIFO). Last-in first-out (LIFO) is not permitted under IFRS.

Issues that mining companies and oil and gas companies commonly face in relation to inventory include:

- point of recognition (14.1 below);
- cost absorption in the measurement of inventory;
- method of allocating costs to inventory, e.g. FIFO or weighted average;
- determination of joint and by-products and measurement consequences (see 14.2 below);
- accounting for core inventories (see 14.3 below); and
- measuring inventory at fair value (see 14.4 below).

Additional issues relating to inventory for mining companies include:

- accounting for stockpiles of long-term, low grade ore (see 14.5 below); and
- heap leaching (see 14.6 below).

14.1 Recognition of work in progress

Determining when to start recognising inventory is more of an issue for mining companies than oil and gas companies. Inventory is recognised when it is probable that future economic benefits will flow to the entity and the asset has a cost or value than can be reliably measured.

Oil and gas companies often do not separately report work-in-progress inventories of either oil or gas. As is noted in the IASC Issues Paper 'the main reason is that, at the point of their removal from the earth, oil and gas frequently do not require processing and they may be sold or may be transferred to the enterprise's downstream operations in the form existing at the time of removal, that is, they are immediately recognised as finished goods. Even if the oil and gas removed from the earth require additional processing to make them saleable or transportable, the time required for processing is typically minimal and the amount of raw products involved in the processing at any one time is likely to be immaterial.'[113] However, if more than an insignificant quantity of product is undergoing processing at any given point in time then an entity may need to disclose work-in-progress under IAS 2. *[IAS 2.8, 37]*.

For mining companies, it has become accepted practice to recognise work-in-progress at the point at which ore is broken and the entity can make a reasonable assessment of quantity, recovery and cost.[114]

Extract 41.29 from the financial statements of Harmony Gold Mining illustrates the need for judgement in determining when work-in-progress can be recognised.

Extract 41.29: Harmony Gold Mining Company Limited (2015)

NOTES TO THE GROUP FINANCIAL STATEMENTS [extract]

for the years ended 30 June 2015

21 INVENTORIES [extract]

ACCOUNTING POLICY

Inventories, which include bullion on hand, gold-in-process, gold in lock-up, ore stockpiles and consumables, are measured at the lower of cost and net realisable value. Net realisable value is assessed at each reporting date and is determined with reference to relevant market prices.

The cost of bullion, gold-in-process and gold in lock-up is determined by reference to production cost, including amortisation and depreciation at the relevant stage of production. Ore stockpiles are valued at average production cost. Stockpiles and gold in lock-up are classified as non-current assets where the stockpile exceeds current processing capacity and where a portion of static gold in lock-up is expected to be recovered more than 12 months after balance sheet date.

Gold in-process inventories represent materials that are currently in the process of being converted to a saleable product. In-process material is measured based on assays of the material fed to process and the projected recoveries at the respective plants. In-process inventories are valued at the average cost of the material fed to process attributable to the source material coming from the mine or stockpile plus the in-process conversion costs, including the applicable depreciation relating to the process facility, incurred to that point in the process. Gold in-process includes gold in lock-up which is generally measured from the plants onwards. Gold in lock-up is expected to be extracted when plants are demolished at the end of their useful lives, which is largely dependent on the estimated useful life of the operations feeding the plants. Where mechanised mining is used in underground operations, in-progress material is accounted for at the earliest stage of production when reliable estimates of quantities and costs are capable of being made. At the group's open pit operations, gold in-process represents production in broken ore form.

Consumables are valued at weighted average cost value after appropriate allowances for slow moving and redundant items.

Measurement issues can arise in relation to work-in-progress for concentrators, smelters and refineries, where significant volumes of product can be located in pipes or vessels, with no uniformity of grade. Work-in-progress inventories may also be in stockpiles, for example underground, where it is more difficult to measure quantities.

Processing varies in extent, duration and complexity depending on the type of mineral and different production and processing techniques that are used. Therefore, measuring work-in-progress, as it moves through the various stages of processing, is difficult and determining the quantities of work-in-progress may require a significant degree of estimation. Practice varies in this area, which is a reflection of the genuine differences mining companies face in their ability to assess mineral content and predict production and processing costs.

Extract 41.30 below from the financial statements of Anglo American Platinum illustrates the complexity involved in making such estimates.

Extract 41.30: Anglo American Platinum Limited (2015)

SIGNIFICANT ACCOUNTING PRINCIPLES [extract]

FOR THE YEAR ENDED 31 DECEMBER 2015

Critical accounting estimates [extract]

Metal inventory

Work in progress metal inventory is valued at the lower of net realisable value and the average cost of production or purchase less net revenue from sales of other metals in the ratio of the contribution of these metals to gross sales revenue. Production costs are allocated to platinum, palladium, rhodium and nickel (joint products) by dividing the mine output into total mine production costs, determined on a 12-month rolling average basis. The quantity of ounces of joint products in work in progress is calculated based on the following factors:

- The theoretical inventory at that point in time which is calculated by adding the inputs to the previous physical inventory and then deducting the outputs for the inventory period.
- The inputs and outputs include estimates due to the delay in finalising analytical values.
- The estimates are subsequently trued up to the final metal accounting quantities when available.
- The theoretical inventory is then converted to a refined equivalent inventory by applying appropriate recoveries depending on where the material is within the production pipeline. The recoveries are based on actual results as determined by the inventory count and are in line with industry standards.

Other than at the precious metal refinery, an annual physical count of work in progress is done, usually around February of each year. The precious metal refinery is subject to a physical count usually every five years. The annual physical count is limited to once per annum due to the dislocation of production required to perform the physical inventory count and the in-process inventories being contained in tanks, pipes and other vessels. Once the results of the physical count are finalised, the variance between the theoretical count and actual count is investigated and recorded. Thereafter the physical quantity forms the opening balance for the theoretical inventory calculation. Consequently, the estimates are refined based on actual results over time. The nature of the production process inherently limits the ability to precisely measure recoverability levels. As a result, the metallurgical balancing process is constantly monitored and the variables used in the process are refined based on actual results over time.

Ore in circuit for a mining company at the end of a reporting period can be very difficult to measure as it is generally not easily accessible. The value of materials being processed should therefore be estimated based on inputs, throughput time and ore grade. The significance of the value of ore in circuit will depend on the type of commodity being processed. For example, precious metals producers may have a material value in process at reporting period end.

14.2 Sale of by-products and joint products

In the extractive industries it is common for more than one product to be extracted from the same reserves, e.g. copper is often found together with gold and silver and oil, gas and gas liquids are commonly found together. Products produced at the same time are classified as joint products or by-products and are usually driven by the importance of the different products to the viability of the mine or field. The same commodity may be treated differently based on differing grades and quantities of products. In most cases where more than one product is produced there is a clear distinction between the main product and the by-products. In other cases the distinction may not be as clear.

The decision as to whether these are joint products or whether one is a by-product, is important, as it impacts the way in which costs are allocated. This decision may also affect the classification of sales of the various products.

14.2.1 By-products

A by-product is a secondary product obtained during the course of production or processing, having relatively small importance when compared with the principal product or products.

IAS 2 prescribes the following accounting for by-products:

> '...When the costs of conversion of each product are not separately identifiable, they are allocated between the products on a rational and consistent basis. The allocation may be based, for example, on the relative sales value of each product either at the stage in the production process when the products become separately identifiable, or at the completion of production. Most by-products, by their nature, are immaterial. When this is the case, they are often measured at net realisable value and this value is deducted from the cost of the main product. As a result, the carrying amount of the main product is not materially different from its cost.' *[IAS 2.14]*.

By-products that are significant in value should be accounted for as joint products as discussed at 14.2.2 below. Where they are not significant, sales of by-products are often treated as a negative cost, i.e. credited against cost of goods sold.

The extract below from AngloGold Ashanti's financial statements illustrates how insignificant by-products for a mining company are deducted from costs of sales and how significant by-products are accounted for separately within inventories.

Extract 41.31: AngloGold Ashanti Limited (2015)

GROUP – NOTES TO THE FINANCIAL STATEMENTS [extract]

For the year ended 31 December

1 ACCOUNTING POLICIES [extract]

1.3 SUMMARY OF SIGNIFICANT ACCOUNTING POLICIES [extract]

Inventories [extract]

Inventories are valued at the lower of cost and net realisable value after appropriate allowances for redundant and slow moving items. Cost is determined on the following bases:

[...]

- by-products, which include uranium oxide and sulphuric acid, are valued using an average total production cost method. By-products are classified as a non-current asset where the by-products on hand exceed current processing capacity; [...]

Revenue recognition [extract]

Revenue is recognised at the fair value of the consideration received or receivable to the extent that it is probable that economic benefits will flow to the group and revenue and costs can be reliably measured. The following criteria must also be present:

[...]

- where a by-product is not regarded as significant, revenue is credited against cost of sales, when the significant risks and rewards of ownership of the products are transferred to the buyer. [...]

Although IAS 2 does not require extensive disclosures in respect of by-products, if amounts are material, disclosure of the following information, which many extractives companies provide on a voluntary basis, will greatly assist users:

- accounting policies applied to by-products;
- line items in the primary financial statements in which revenues and carried amounts have been disclosed;
- quantities of by-products sold; and
- average prices of by-products sold.

14.2.2 Joint products

Joint products are two or more products produced simultaneously from a common raw material source, with each product having a significant relative sales value. One joint product cannot be produced without the other and the products cannot be identified separately until a certain production stage, often called the 'split-off point', is reached. Joint products are very common in both the oil and gas sector (e.g. crude oil when run through a refinery produces a variety of products) and the mining sector.

Joint products, by definition, are all significant in value and require that an entity allocate on a rational and consistent basis the costs of conversion that are not separately identifiable for each product. The IASC Issues Paper outlined two approaches that have found acceptance in practice:[115]

(a) *allocation on the basis of physical characteristics* – In the oil and gas sector, entities often combine quantities of oil and gas based on their relative energy content (i.e. 6,000 cubic feet of gas is roughly equal in energy to one barrel of oil). This method, however, does not take account of the fact that, for example, gas is cheaper per unit of energy than oil because the latter is more difficult to transport; and

(b) *allocation on the basis of relative values* – This approach is more common in the mining sector where often it is not possible to identify a relevant physical characteristic that can be used to combine quantities of different products. The drawback of this method is that it results in very similar profit margins for each of the joint products, which may not be reflective of the underlying economic reality (i.e. one of the joint products, if mined in isolation, might have a completely different profit margin).

Although it should be kept in mind that neither method is perfect, both approaches are currently permitted under IFRS. It is true also that whichever method is selected, it is unlikely to have a material effect on reported profit overall. The extract below illustrates the application of approach (b) by Anglo American.

Extract 41.32: Anglo American plc (2015)

FINANCIAL STATEMENTS AND OTHER FINANCIAL INFORMATION

NOTES TO THE FINANCIAL STATEMENTS [extract]

ADDITIONAL DISCLOSURES

39. ACCOUNTING POLICIES [extract]

39q. Inventories

Inventory and work in progress are measured at the lower of cost and net realisable value. The production cost of inventory includes an appropriate proportion of depreciation and production overheads. Cost is determined on the following basis:

- Raw materials and consumables are measured at cost on a first in, first out (FIFO) basis or a weighted average cost basis.
- Work in progress and finished products are measured at raw material cost, labour cost and a proportion of manufacturing overhead expenses.
- Metal and coal stocks are included within finished products and are measured at average cost.

At precious metals operations that produce 'joint products', cost is allocated amongst products according to the ratio of contribution of these metals to gross sales revenues.

14.3 Core inventories

In certain industries, for example the petrochemical sector, certain processes or storage arrangements require a core of inventory to be present in the system at all times in order for it to function properly. For example, in order for a crude oil refining process to take place, the plant must contain a certain minimum quantity of oil. This oil can only be taken out once the plant is abandoned and could then only be sold as sludge. Similarly, underground gas storage caves are filled with gas; but a substantial part (in some instances 25%) of that gas can never be sold as its function is to pressurise the cave, thereby allowing the remaining 75% to be extracted. Even though the gas will be turned around on a continuing basis, at any one time 25% of it will never be available to sell and cannot be recouped from the cave. Finally, long distance pipelines contain a significant volume of gas that keeps them operational.

Similar examples of core inventories exist in the mining sector where certain processes or processing facilities require a core or minimum amount of inventory to be present in the system at all times. These may include:

- potlines in the aluminium industry;
- blast furnaces in the steel industry;
- electrowinning plants; or
- carbon in leach processing in the gold industry.

The key issue with such minimum amounts of inventory is whether they should be accounted for as inventory in accordance with IAS 2 or as PP&E in accordance with IAS 16. It is our view that if an item of inventory is not held for sale or consumed in a production process, but is necessary to the operation of a facility during more than one operating cycle, and its cost cannot be recouped through sale (or is significantly impaired), this item of inventory should be accounted for as an item of property, plant and equipment under IAS 16 rather than as inventory under IAS 2. This applies even if the part of inventory that is deemed to be an item of PP&E cannot be separated physically from the rest of inventory.

These matters will always involve the exercise of judgement, however, in the above instances, we consider that:

- the deemed PP&E items do not meet the definition of inventories;
- although it is not possible to physically separate the chemicals involved into inventory and PP&E categories, there is no accounting reason why one cannot distinguish between identical assets with different uses and therefore account for them differently. Indeed, IAS 2 does envisage such a possibility when discussing different cost formulas; *[IAS 2.25]*
- the deemed PP&E items are necessary to bring another item of PP&E to the condition necessary for it to be capable of operating in the manner intended by management. This meets the definition of the costs of PP&E in IAS 16 upon initial recognition; *[IAS 16.16(b)]* and
- recognising these items as inventories would lead to an immediate loss because these items cannot be sold or consumed in a production process, or during the process of rendering services. This does not properly reflect the fact that the items are necessary to operate another asset over more than one operating cycle.

By contrast, core inventory that is not necessary to operate the asset and that is recoverable (e.g. gas in a pipeline) is considered to be held for sale or to be consumed in the production process or process of rendering services. Therefore such gas is accounted for as inventory.

The issue of core inventories or 'minimum fill' was considered by the Interpretations Committee in March and July 2014. The staff paper considered by the Interpretations Committee proposed that base or cushion gas in storage facilities (required to maintain adequate cavern pressure) and pipeline fill (i.e. the minimum volume of oil or gas to be kept in a pipeline to ensure its operability) should be accounted for as property, plant and equipment under IAS 16 where the carrying amount was not considered recoverable through sale or consumption in the production process (which is consistent with our views above). After consideration of this issue, the Interpretations Committee noted that, although there was diversity in practice between industries, there was no, or only limited, diversity in practice within the industries for which the issue is significant (including extractive industries). Given there was not sufficient diversity within industry, they decided not to continue with the development of an interpretation, and to remove this item from its agenda.

The extract below from the financial statements of Engie SA shows how cushion gas is accounted for as a tangible asset that is depreciated over its economic life.

Extract 41.33: Engie SA (2015)

Notes to the consolidated financial statements [extract]

NOTE 1 ACCOUNTING STANDARDS AND METHODS[extract]

1.4 Accounting methods [extract]

1.4.5 Property, plant and equipment [extract]

1.4.5.1 Initial recognition and subsequent measurement [extract]

Cushion gas

"Cushion" gas injected into underground storage facilities is essential for ensuring that reservoirs can be operated effectively, and is therefore inseparable from these reservoirs. Unlike "working" gas which is included in inventories, cushion gas is reported in property, plant and equipment. [...]

1.4.10 Inventories [extract]

Gas inventories

Gas injected into underground storage facilities includes working gas which can be withdrawn without adversely affecting the operation of the reservoir and cushion gas which is inseparable from the reservoirs and essential for their operation (see 1.4.5.1).

Working gas is classified in inventory and measured at weighted average purchase cost upon entering the transportation network regardless of its source, including any regasification costs.

Group inventory outflows are valued using the weighted average unit cost method.

An impairment loss is recognized when the net realizable value of inventories is lower than their weighted average cost.

14.4 Carried at fair value

As noted earlier, inventories should be measured at the lower of cost and net realisable value under IAS 2. However, IAS 2 does not apply to the measurement of minerals and mineral products, to the extent that they are measured at net realisable value in accordance with well-established practices in those industries. *[IAS 2.3(a)]*. There is also an exception for commodity broker traders who measure their inventories at fair value less costs to sell. When such inventories are measured at fair value less costs to sell, changes in fair value less costs to sell are recognised in profit or loss in the period of the change. *[IAS 2.3(b)]*.

An extractives company that wishes to use the exemption relating to minerals and mineral products outlined above would need to demonstrate that valuation at net realisable value was a well-established practice in its industry, which may be difficult to do for base metals inventory.

The commodity broker trader exemption above is commonly used by companies that engage in commodity trading. The extract below from the financial statements of BP illustrates a typical accounting policy for an oil and gas company that makes use of this exemption.

An integrated oil company can include exploration, production, refinement and distribution along with a trading operation. In such cases, inventory held by the trading organisation may have originated from the entities own production. Where this has occurred it will be necessary to ensure the inventory that came from the entity's own production is valued at cost or net realisable value rather than fair value.

Extract 41.34: BP p.l.c. (2015)

Notes on financial statements [extract]

1. Significant accounting policies, judgements, estimates and assumptions [extract]

Inventories

[...]

Inventories held for trading purposes are stated at fair value less costs to sell and any changes in fair value are recognized in the income statement.

Supplies are valued at the lower of cost on a weighted average basis and net realizable value.

14.5 Stockpiles of low grade ore (mining)

Mining companies often stockpile low grade ore that cannot be economically processed at current market prices or to give priority to the processing of higher grade ore. Low grade ore stockpiles may not be processed for many years until market prices or technology have improved or until no higher grade ore remains available. Extract 41.35 below from AngloGold Ashanti illustrates that stockpiles of low grade ore may be held for many years.

Mineralised waste that is stockpiled in the hope, but without the expectation, that it may become economical to process in the future should be accounted in the same way as overburden and other waste materials (see 15.5 below). Low grade ore that is stockpiled with the expectation that it will be processed in the future should be accounted for in the same way as high grade ore. However, if the cost of the low grade ore exceeds its net realisable value, an entity should recognise an impairment charge that it might need to reverse at some point in the future if (and when) commodity prices were to increase.

If and when processing of low grade ore becomes economically viable and management intends to process the stockpile in the future, the ore is often presented as non-current inventory under IAS 2. Such stockpiles should be measured at the lower of cost and net realisable value. *[IAS 2.9, 30]*. In allocating production costs to the low grade ore stockpile and in subsequently assessing net realisable value, an entity should be mindful that:

(1) the commodity price at the reporting date may not be representative of the price that can realistically be expected to prevail when the ore is expected to be processed. The assumptions as to the long-term commodity prices used in the estimate of the sales proceeds and the expected timing of realisation, should generally be consistent with those used in the Life of Mine Plan and other models that would be used for valuation and impairment purposes;

(2) the costs of processing may change in the future because of inflation, technological changes and new environmental regulations; and

(3) the time value of money reduces the net realisable value. Therefore, application of a discount factor to the future cash flows associated with the sales proceeds and conversion costs may be appropriate to reflect the time value of money. The net realisable value of a stockpile which is not expected to be sold for a very long period of time, determined based on the discounted future cash flows, will typically be very low.

The extract below shows how AngloGold Ashanti accounts for ore stockpiles.

Extract 41.35: AngloGold Ashanti Limited (2015)

GROUP – NOTES TO THE FINANCIAL STATEMENTS [extract]
For the year ended 31 December
1 ACCOUNTING POLICIES [extract]
1.2 SIGNIFICANT ACCOUNTING JUDGEMENTS AND ESTIMATES [extract]
Stockpiles and metal in process

Costs that are incurred in or benefit the production process are accumulated as stockpiles, metals in process and ore on leach pads. Net realisable value tests are performed at least annually and represent the estimated future sales price of the product, based on prevailing and long-term metals prices, less estimated costs to complete production and bring the product to sale.

Stockpiles and underground metals in process are measured by estimating the number of tonnes added and removed from the stockpile and from underground, the number of contained ounces based on assay data, and the estimated recovery percentage based on the expected processing method. Stockpile and underground ore tonnages are verified by periodic surveys.

Although the quantities of recoverable metal are reconciled by comparing the grades of ore to the quantities of metal actually recovered (metallurgical balancing), the nature of the process inherently limits the ability to precisely monitor recoverability levels. As a result, the metallurgical balancing process is constantly monitored and engineering estimates are refined based on actual results over time.

Variations between actual and estimated quantities resulting from changes in assumptions and estimates that do not result in write-downs to net realisable value are accounted for on a prospective basis.

The carrying amount of inventories (excluding finished goods and mine operating supplies) for the group at 31 December 2015 was $393m (2014: $1,106m; 2013: $1,125m).

1.3 SUMMARY OF SIGNIFICANT ACCOUNTING POLICIES [extract]
Inventories [extract]

Inventories are valued at the lower of cost and net realisable value after appropriate allowances for redundant and obsolete items. Cost is determined on the following bases:

[...]

- ore stockpiles are valued at the average moving cost of mining and stockpiling the ore. Stockpiles are classified as a non-current asset where the stockpile exceeds current processing capacity;

The extract below illustrates the disclosure of an impairment of stockpiled ore (in 2008) and then disclosures relating to the reversal of impairment of stockpiled ore.

Extract 41.36: Kazakhmys PLC (2008 and 2010)

Notes to the consolidated financial statements [extract]

7. IMPAIRMENT LOSSES – 2008 [extract]

(d) Kazakhmys Copper and MKM inventories

Impairment of inventories includes an amount of $73 million and $15 million in respect of Kazakhmys Copper and MKM, respectively. For Kazakhmys Copper, the impairment primarily relates to the impairment of stockpiled ore which is not going to be processed in the foreseeable future as its processing is uneconomic at current commodity price levels. Within MKM, a provision has been recognised to record inventory at the lower of cost and net realisable value. This primarily relates to finished goods held in stock at the end of the year which have been written down reflecting the fall in copper price in December.

> **8. IMPAIRMENT LOSSES – 2010** [extract]
> **(b) Kazakhmys Copper inventories**
> Included within the provisions against inventories is an impairment loss of $15 million relating to general slow moving inventory, and a reversal of a previous impairment against certain stockpiled ore of $18 million. In 2008, it was envisaged that the stockpiled ore would not be processed in the future as this would have been uneconomic at the prevailing commodity prices. However, during 2010 certain of these stockpiles were processed and the previous impairment reversed.

14.6 Heap leaching (mining)

Heap leaching is a process which may be used for the recovery of metals from low grade ore. The crushed ore is laid on a slightly sloping, impermeable pad and leached by uniformly trickling a chemical solution through the heaps to be collected in ponds. The metals are subsequently extracted from the pregnant solution. Although heap leaching is one of the lowest cost methods of processing, recovery rates are relatively low.

Despite the estimation and measurement challenges associated with heap leaching, ore loaded on heap leach pads is usually recognised as inventory. An entity that develops an accounting policy for heap leaching needs to consider the following:

- the metal recovery factor is relatively low and will vary depending on the metallurgical characteristics of the material on the heap leach pad. The final (actual) recovery is therefore unknown until leaching is complete. Therefore, an entity will need to estimate the quantity of recoverable metal on each of its heap leach pads, based on laboratory test work or historical ore performance;
- the assayed head grade of ore added to the heap;
- the ore stockpiles on heap leach pads are accounted for as inventories that are measured at cost under IAS 2. As the valuable metal content is leached from these ore stockpiles, the cost basis is depleted based upon expected grades and recovery rates. The depletion charge should be accounted as the cost of production of work in progress or finished goods;
- the level at which the heap leach pads are measured – that is, whether they are measured separately, in groups or in total. The preferred approach is to consider each pad separately (where possible) because this reduces the expected volatility in ore type to more manageable levels; and
- ore stockpiles on heap leach pads from which metals are expected to be recovered in a period longer than 12 months are generally classified as non-current assets.

The extracts below from the financial statements of AngloGold Ashanti and Goldcorp illustrate the issues that an entity will need to consider in developing an accounting policy for heap leaching.

Extract 41.37: AngloGold Ashanti Limited (2015)

GROUP – NOTES TO THE FINANCIAL STATEMENTS [extract]
For the year ended 31 December 2015

1.3 SUMMARY OF SIGNIFICANT ACCOUNTING POLICIES [extract]
Inventories [extract]

Inventories are valued at the lower of cost and net realisable value after appropriate allowances for redundant and obsolete items. Cost is determined on the following bases:

[...]

- heap leach pad materials are measured on an average total production cost basis. The cost of materials on the leach pad from which metals are expected to be recovered in a period longer than 12 months is classified as a non-current asset.

Extract 41.38: Goldcorp (2015)

Notes to the Consolidated Financial Statements
For the Years Ended December 31, 2015 and 2014 [extract]
3. SUMMARY OF SIGNIFICANT ACCOUNTING POLICIES [extract]
(m) Inventories and stockpiled ore [extract]

Finished goods, work-in-process, heap leach ore and stockpiled ore are measured at the lower of weighted average cost and net realizable value. Net realizable value is calculated as the estimated price at the time of sale based on prevailing and long-term metal prices less estimated future costs to convert the inventories into saleable form and estimated costs to sell. [...]

Ore extracted from the mines is stockpiled and subsequently processed into finished goods (gold and by-products in doré or concentrate form). Costs are included in work-in-process inventory based on current costs incurred up to the point prior to the refining process, including applicable depreciation and depletion of mining interests, and removed at the weighted average cost per recoverable ounce of gold. The average costs of finished goods represent the average costs of work-in-process inventories incurred prior to the refining process, plus applicable refining costs.

The recovery of gold and by-products from certain oxide ore is achieved through a heap leaching process at the Peñasquito and Los Filos mines. Under this method, ore is stacked on leach pads and treated with a chemical solution that dissolves the gold contained within the ore. The resulting pregnant solution is further processed in a plant where the gold is recovered. Costs are included in heap leach ore inventory based on current mining and leaching costs, including applicable depreciation and depletion of mining interests, and removed from heap leach ore inventory as ounces of gold are recovered at the weighted average cost per recoverable ounce of gold on the leach pads. Estimates of recoverable gold on the leach pads are calculated based on the quantities of ore placed on the leach pads (measured tonnes added to the leach pads), the grade of ore placed on the leach pads (based on assay data), and a recovery percentage (based on ore type).

15 PROPERTY, PLANT AND EQUIPMENT

15.1 Major maintenance and turnarounds / renewals and reconditioning costs

Some assets (e.g. refineries, smelters and gas processing plants) require major maintenance at regular intervals, which is often described as an overhaul or turnaround in the oil and gas sector and renewal or reconditioning in the mining sector. When an entity incurs further costs in relation to an item of PP&E, IAS 16 requires it to determine the nature of the costs. Where such costs provide access to future economic benefits they should be capitalised. Costs of day-to-day servicing (e.g. costs of labour and consumables, and possibly the cost of small parts) should be expensed as incurred. *[IAS 16.12]*. If the costs relate to the replacement of a part of the entire asset then the entity derecognises the carrying amount of the part that is replaced and recognises the cost of the replacement part. *[IAS 16.13]*. However, the part need not represent a physical part of the asset.

When a major inspection, renewal or reconditioning project is performed, its cost should be recognised in the carrying amount of the item of property, plant and equipment and any remaining carrying amount of the cost of the previous inspection/renewal (which will be distinct from physical parts) is derecognised. This is not affected by whether the entity identified the cost of the previous inspection when the item was acquired or constructed. *[IAS 16.14]*. See Chapter 18 at 3.3.2.

Subsequent costs that meet the recognition criteria should therefore be capitalised even if the costs incurred merely restore the assets to their original standard of performance. However, under IAS 37 an entity cannot provide for the costs of planned future maintenance (e.g. turnarounds, renewals/reconditions) as is illustrated by Example 41.9, based on Example 11A in IAS 37. *[IAS 37 Appendix C]*.

Example 41.9: Refurbishment costs – no legislative requirement

A furnace has a lining that needs to be replaced every five years for technical reasons. At the end of the reporting period, the lining has been in use for three years.

Under IAS 37 no provision should be recognised as there is no present obligation. The cost of replacing the lining is not recognised because, at the end of the reporting period, no obligation to replace the lining exists independently of the company's future actions – even the intention to incur the expenditure depends on the company deciding to continue operating the furnace or to replace the lining. Instead of a provision being recognised, the depreciation of the lining takes account of its consumption, i.e. it is depreciated over five years. The re-lining costs then incurred are capitalised with the consumption of each new lining shown by depreciation over the subsequent five years.

Even a legal requirement to refurbish does not make the costs of a turnaround/renewal a liability under IAS 37, because no obligation exists independently of the entity's future actions – the entity could avoid the future overhaul expenditure by its future actions, for example by selling the refinery or the asset that is being renewed/reconditioned. *[IAS 37 IE Example 11B]*.

The extract below from BP illustrates a typical accounting policy for repairs, maintenance and inspection costs under IFRS.

> *Extract 41.39: BP p.l.c. (2015)*
>
> **Notes on financial statements** [extract]
>
> **1. Significant accounting policies, judgements, estimates and assumptions** [extract]
>
> **Property, plant and equipment** [extract]
>
> Expenditure on major maintenance refits or repairs comprises the cost of replacement assets or parts of assets, inspection costs and overhaul costs. Where an asset or part of an asset that was separately depreciated is replaced and it is probable that future economic benefits associated with the item will flow to the group, the expenditure is capitalized and the carrying amount of the replaced asset is derecognized. Inspection costs associated with major maintenance programmes are capitalized and amortized over the period to the next inspection. Overhaul costs for major maintenance programmes, and all other maintenance costs are expensed as incurred.

Turnarounds/renewals can have a considerable impact on financial performance because of additional costs incurred and lower revenues. Therefore, fairly detailed information is generally disclosed about turnaround costs incurred in the past and turnarounds planned in the future.

> *Extract 41.40: BP p.l.c. (2012)*
>
> **Business review: Group overview** [extract]
>
> **Our performance** [extract]
>
> **Safety** [extract]
>
> We continued our programme of major upstream turnarounds, with 30 turnarounds completed in 2012. We expect to carry out up to 22 further turnarounds in 2013.
>
> **Downstream** [extract]
>
> Refinery operations were strong this year, with Solomon refining availability of 94.8%. (See refining availability on page 74.) Utilization rates were at 88% despite a relatively high level of turnaround activity in 2012.
>
> **Business review: BP in more depth** [extract]
>
> **Profit or loss for the year** [extract]
>
> Compared with 2010, in 2011 there were higher realizations, higher earnings from equity-accounted entities, a higher refining margin environment and a stronger supply and trading contribution, partly offset by lower production volumes, rig standby costs in the Gulf of Mexico, higher costs related to turnarounds, higher exploration write-offs, and negative impacts of increased relative sweet crude prices in Europe and Australia, primarily caused by the loss of Libya production and the weather-related power outages in the US.
>
> **Risk factors** [extract]
>
> **Strategic and commercial risks** [extract]
>
> **Major project delivery – our group plan depends upon successful delivery of major projects, and failure to deliver major projects successfully could adversely affect our financial performance.**
>
> Successful execution of our group plan depends critically on implementing the activities to deliver the major projects over the plan period. Poor delivery of any major project that underpins production or production growth and/or any other major programme designed to enhance shareholder value, including maintenance turnaround programmes, could adversely affect our financial performance. Successful project delivery requires, among other things, adequate engineering and other capabilities and therefore successful recruitment and development of staff is central to our plans.

15.2 Well workovers and recompletions (oil and gas)

Well workovers or recompletions are often required when the producing oil sands become clogged and production declines or other physical or mechanical problems arise.[116] Workover costs that relate to the day-to-day servicing of the wells (i.e. primarily the costs of labour and consumables, and possibly the cost of small parts) should be expensed as incurred. However, as discussed at 15.1 above, costs incurred to restore a well to its former level of production should be capitalised under IFRS, but an entity should derecognise any relevant previously capitalised well completion costs. However, to the extent that an entity can forecast future well workovers, it will need to depreciate the original well completion costs over a shorter economic life. Conversely, if an entity unexpectedly incurs well workover costs, it may need to consider whether those additional costs result in the need to perform an impairment test.

15.3 Care and maintenance

At certain times, a mining operation, gas plant or other substantial component of operations may be suspended because of a change in circumstances, which may include a weakening of global demand for the commodity, lower prices, higher costs, changes in demand for processing, changes in exchange rates or changes in government policy. Such changes mean that continuing with production or further development becomes uneconomical. Instead of permanently shutting down and abandoning the mine or plant, the operations and development are curtailed and the mine, plant or operation is placed on 'care and maintenance'. This can happen either in the development phase or the production phase.

A decision to put an asset such as a mine or gas plant on care and maintenance would be an indicator of impairment (see 11.1 above). An impairment test would need to be conducted and if the recoverable amount of the CGU is less than the carrying amount, an impairment loss would need to be recognised.

While the asset remains in care and maintenance, expenditures are still incurred but usually at a lower rate than when the mine or gas plant is operating. A lower rate of depreciation for tangible non-current assets is also usually appropriate due to reduced wear and tear. Movable plant and machinery would generally be depreciated over its useful life. Management should consider depreciation to allow for deterioration. Where depreciation for movable plant and machinery had previously been determined on a units of production basis, this may no longer be appropriate.

Management should also ensure that any assets for which there are no longer any future economic benefits, i.e. which have become redundant, are written off.

The length of the closure and the associated care and maintenance expenditure may be estimated for depreciation and impairment purposes. However, it is not appropriate to recognise a provision for the entire estimated expenditure relating to the care and maintenance period. All care and maintenance costs are to be expensed as incurred.

Development costs amortised or depreciated using the units of production method would no longer be depreciated. Holding costs associated with such assets should be expensed in profit or loss in the period they are incurred. These may include costs such as security costs and site property maintenance costs.

The costs associated with restarting a mine or gas plant which had previously been on care and maintenance should only be capitalised if they improve the asset beyond its original operating capabilities. Entities will need to exercise significant judgement when performing this assessment.

15.4 Unitisations and redeterminations

15.4.1 Unitisations

A unitisation arrangement is 'an agreement between two parties each of which owns an interest in one or more mineral properties in an area to cross-assign to one another a share of the interest in the mineral properties that each owns in the area; from that point forward they share, as agreed, in further costs and revenues related to the properties'.[117] The parties pool their individual interests in return for an interest in the overall unit, which is then operated jointly to increase efficiency.[118] Once an area is subject to an unitisation arrangement, the parties share costs and production in accordance with their percentages established under the unitisation agreement. The unitisation agreement does not affect costs and production associated with non-unitised areas within the original licences, which continue to fall to the original licensees.[119]

IFRS does not specifically address accounting for a unitisation arrangement. Therefore, the accounting for such an arrangement depends on the type of asset that is subject to the arrangement. If the assets subject to the arrangement were E&E assets, then the transaction would fall within the scope of IFRS 6, which provides a temporary exemption from IAS 8 (see 3.2.1 above). An entity would be permitted to develop an accounting policy for unitisation arrangements involving E&E assets that is not based on IFRS. However, unitisations are unlikely to occur in the E&E phase when technical feasibility and commercial viability of extracting a mineral resource are not yet demonstrable.

For unitisations that occur outside the E&E phase, as there is no specific guidance in IFRS, an entity will need to develop an accounting policy in accordance with the IAS 8 hierarchy. The first step in developing an accounting policy for unitisations is setting criteria for determining which assets are included within the transaction. Particularly important is the assessment as to whether the unitisation includes the mineral reserves themselves or not. The main reason for not including the mineral reserves derives from the fact that they are subject to redetermination (see 15.4.2 below).

The example below, which is taken from the IASC's Issues Paper, illustrates how a unitisation transaction might work in practice.

Example 41.10: Unitisation[120]

Entities E and F have carried out exploration programs on separate properties owned by each in a remote area near the Antarctic Circle. Both entities have discovered petroleum reserves on their properties and have begun development of the properties. Because of the high operating costs and the need to construct support facilities, such as pipelines, dock facilities, transportation systems, and warehouses, the entities decide to unitise the properties, which mean that they have agreed to combine their properties into a single property. A joint operating agreement is signed and entity F is chosen as operator of the combined properties. Relevant data about each entity's properties and costs are given as follows:

Party E

Prospecting costs incurred prior to property acquisition	€8,000,000
Mineral acquisition costs	€42,000,000
Geological and geophysical exploration costs (G&G)	€12,000,000
Exploratory drilling costs:	
Successful	€16,000,000
Unsuccessful	€7,000,000
Development costs incurred	€23,000,000
Estimated reserves, agreed between parties (in barrels)	30,000,000

Party F

Prospecting costs incurred prior to property acquisition	€3,000,000
Mineral acquisition costs	€31,000,000
Geological and geophysical exploration costs (G&G)	€17,000,000
Exploratory drilling costs	
Successful	€24,000,000
Unsuccessful	€4,000,000
Development costs incurred	€36,000,000
Estimated reserves, agreed between parties (in barrels)	70,000,000

Ownership ratio in the venture is to be based on the relative quantity of agreed-upon reserves contributed by each party (30% to E and 70% to F). The parties agree that there should be an equalisation between them for the value of pre-unitisation exploration and development costs that directly benefit the unit, but not for other exploration and development costs. That is, there will be a cash settlement between the parties for the value of assets (other than mineral rights) or services that each party contributes to the unitisation. This is done so that the net value contributed by each party for the specified expenditures will equal that venturer's share of the total value of such expenditures at the time unitisation is consummated. Thus, the party contributing a value less than that party's share of ownership in the total value of those costs contributed by all the parties will make a cash payment to the other party so that each party's net contribution will equal that party's share of total value. The agreed amounts of costs to be equalised that are contributed by E and F are:

Expenditures made by:	**E**	**F**	**Total**
	€	€	€
Successful exploratory drilling	12,000,000	12,000,000	24,000,000
Development costs	18,000,000	30,000,000	48,000,000
Geological and geophysical exploration	4,000,000	14,000,000	18,000,000
Total expenditure	34,000,000	56,000,000	90,000,000

As a result of this agreement, F is obliged to pay E the net amount of €7,000,000 to equalise exploration and development costs. This is made up of the following components:

(a) €4,800,000 excess of value of exploratory drilling received by F (€16,800,000 = 70% × €24,000,000) in excess of value for successful exploratory drilling contributed (€12,000,000); plus

(b) €3,600,000 excess of value of development costs received by F in the unit (€33,600,000 = 70% × €48,000,000) in excess of the value of development costs contributed by F (€30,000,000); and less

(c) €1,400,000 excess of value of G&G costs contributed by F (€14,000,000) over the value of the share of G & G costs owned by F after unitisation (€12,600,000 = 70% × €18,000,000).

Although the reserves are unitised in the physical sense (i.e. each party will end up selling oil or gas that physically came out of the reserves of the other party), in volume terms the parties remain entitled to a quantity of reserves that is equal to that which they contributed. However, the timing of production and the costs to produce the reserves may be impacted by the unitisation agreement. The example below explains this in more detail.

Example 41.11: Reserves contributed in an unitisation

Entities A and B enter into a unitisation agreement and contribute Licences A and B, respectively. The table below shows the initial determination, redetermination and final determination of the reserves in each of the fields.

	Initial determination		Redetermination		Final determination	
	mboe		mboe		mboe	
Licence A	20	40.0%	19	37.3%	21	38.9%
Licence B	30	60.0%	32	62.7%	33	61.1%
	50	100.0%	51	100.0%	54	100.0%

Although Licences A and B were unitised, ultimately Entity A will be entitled to 21 mboe and Entity B will be entitled to 33 mboe, which is exactly the same quantity that they would have been entitled to had there been no unitisation.

To the extent that the unitisation of the mineral reserves themselves lacks commercial substance (see 6.3.2 above), it may be appropriate to exclude the mineral reserves in accounting for an unitisation. Where the unitisation significantly affects the risk and timing of the cash flows or the type of product (e.g. an unitisation could lead to an exchange of, say, gas reserves for oil reserves) there is likely to be substance to the unitisation of the reserves.

If the assets subject to the unitisation arrangement are not E&E assets, or not only E&E assets, then it is necessary to develop an accounting policy in accordance with the requirements of IAS 8. Unitisation arrangements generally give rise to joint control over the underlying assets or entities:

(a) if the unitisation arrangement results in joint control over a joint venture then the parties should apply IFRS 11 (see Chapter 12) and IAS 28 (see Chapter 11) and provide the relevant disclosures in accordance with the requirements contained in IFRS 12 (see Chapter 13); or

(b) if the unitisation arrangement gives rise to a joint operation or results in a swap of assets that are not jointly controlled, then each of the parties should account for the arrangement as an asset swap (see 6.3 above).

Under both (a) and (b) above, a party to an unitisation agreement would report a gain (or loss) depending on whether the fair value of the interest received is higher (or lower) than the carrying amount of the interest given up.

15.4.2 Redeterminations

The percentage interests in an unitisation arrangement are based on estimates of the relative quantities of reserves contributed by each of the parties. As field life progresses and production experience is gained, many unitisation agreements require the reserves to be redetermined, which often leads the parties to conclude that the recoverable reserves in one or perhaps both of the original properties are not as previously estimated. Unitisation agreements typically require one or more 'redeterminations' of percentage interests once better reservoir information becomes available. In most cases, the revised percentage interests are deemed to be effective from the date of the original unitisation agreement, which means that adjustments are required between the parties in respect of their relative entitlements to cumulative production and their shares of cumulative costs.[121]

Unitisation agreements normally set out when redeterminations need to take place and the way in which adjustments to the percentage interests should be effected. The former OIAC SORP described the process as follows:

'(a) Adjustments in respect of cumulative "capital" costs are usually made immediately following the redetermination by means of a lump sum reimbursement, sometimes including an "interest" or uplift element to reflect related financing costs.

(b) Adjustments to shares of cumulative production are generally effected prospectively. Participants with an increased share are entitled to additional "make-up" production until the cumulative liftings are rebalanced. During this period adjusted percentage interests are applied to both production entitlement and operating costs. Once equity is achieved the effective percentage interests revert to those established by the redetermination.'[122]

An adjustment to an entity's percentage interest due to a redetermination is not a prior period error under IFRS. *[IAS 8.5]*. Instead, the redetermination results from new information or new developments and therefore should be treated as a change in an accounting estimate. Accordingly, a redetermination should not result in a fully retrospective adjustment.

Redeterminations give rise to some further accounting issues which are discussed below.

15.4.2.A Redeterminations as capital reimbursements

Under many national GAAPs, redeterminations are accounted for as reimbursement of capital expenditure rather than as sales/purchases of a partial interest. Given that this second approach could result in the recognition of a gain upon redetermination, followed by a higher depreciation charge per barrel, it has become accepted industry practice that redeterminations should be accounted for as reimbursements of capital expenditure under IFRS. Both approaches are illustrated in Example 41.12 below.

In addition a redetermination gives rise to a number of questions, for example, how should the entities account for:

- the adjustment of their share in the remaining reserves;
- the 'make-up' oil obligation; and
- their revised shares in the decommissioning liabilities.

The 'make-up' oil obligation and the revised shares in the decommissioning liabilities are discussed further following the example below.

Example 41.12: Redetermination (1)

Entities A and B have a 10% and 90% percentage interest in a unitised property, respectively. On 1 January 2016, after three years of operations, their interests in the property are redetermined. The relevant data about each entity's interest in the property are as follows:

	A	B	Total
Percentage interest after initial determination	10%	90%	100%
Percentage interest after redetermination	8%	92%	100%
Initial reserves at 1/1/2013 (million barrels of oil equivalent)	100 mboe	900 mboe	1000 mboe
Total production from 2013 to 2015	30 mboe	270 mboe	300 mboe
Remaining reserves at 31/12/2015 before redetermination	70 mboe	630 mboe	700 mboe
Reserves after redetermination at 1/1/2016	56 mboe	644 mboe	700 mboe
'Make-up' oil: 300 mboe × (10% – 8%) =	–6 mboe	6 mboe	–
Total entitlement at 1/1/2016	50 mboe	650 mboe	700 mboe
	$	$	$
Exploration and development asset at 1/1/2013	400	3,600	4,000
Units of production depreciation:			
$400 ÷ 100 mboe × 30 mboe =	120		120
$3,600 ÷ 900 mboe × 270 mboe =		1,080	1,080
Exploration and development asset at 31/12/2015 before redetermination	280	2,520	2,800

	A	B	Total
Total investment based on 'initial determination': A: 10% of $4,000 = $400 and B: 90% of $4,000 = $3,600	400	3,600	4,000
Total investment based on redetermination: A: 8% of $4,000 = $320 and B: 92% of $4,000 = $3,680	320	3,680	4,000
Reimbursement of exploration and development costs	80	–80	–
Decommissioning asset at 1/1/2013	100	900	1,000
Units of production depreciation:			
$100 ÷ 100 mboe × 30 mboe =	30		30
$900 ÷ 900 mboe × 270 mboe =		270	270
Decommissioning asset at 31/12/2015 before redetermination	70	630	700
Decommissioning provision at 1/1/2013	100	900	1,000
Accreted interest from 1/1/2013 to 31/12/2015	20	180	200
Decommissioning provision at 31/12/2015 before redetermination	120	1,080	1,200
Reduction in decommissioning provision	–24	24	–
Decommissioning provision at 1/1/2016: A: 8% of $1,200 = $96 and B: 92% of $1,200 = $1,104	96	1,104	1,200

There are different ways in which an entity might interpret the effect of a redetermination on the exploration and development asset:

(a) Reimbursement of capital expenditure; or

(b) Sale/purchase of a partial interest.

Reimbursement of capital expenditure

Under this approach, the redetermination is treated as a reimbursement of capital expenditure and the 'make-up' oil is accounted for prospectively. This would lead entity A to make the following journal entries:

	$	$
Dr Cash	80	
Cr Exploration and development asset		80

The reimbursement of exploration and development costs is accounted for as a reduction in the exploration and development asset.

The overall impact on the statement of financial position of both Entities A and B is summarised in the table below:

	A $	**B** $	**Total** $
Exploration and development asset at 31/12/2015 before redetermination	280	2,520	2,800
Reimbursement of exploration and development costs	–80	80	–
Exploration and development asset at 1/1/2016 after redetermination	200	2,600	2,800

Before the redetermination both A and B would record depreciation of the exploration and development asset of $4/barrel (i.e. A: $400 ÷ 100 mboe = $4/barrel and B: $3,600 ÷ 900 mboe = $4/barrel). After the redetermination the depreciation of the exploration and development asset is still $4/barrel for both A and B (i.e. A: $200 ÷ 50 mboe = $4/barrel and B: $2,600 ÷ 650 mboe = $4/barrel).

Sale/purchase of a partial interest

The second approach, which is sometimes advocated, is to treat the redetermination as the equivalent of a sale or purchase of part of an interest.

	$	$
Dr Cash	80	
Cr Exploration and development asset: (8% – 10%) ÷ 10% × $280 =		56
Cr Gain on disposal of exploration and development asset		24

The reimbursement of exploration and development costs is accounted for as a partial disposal of the exploration and development asset.

However, Entity B will treat its entire payment of $80 to Entity A as the cost of the additional 2% interest that it 'acquired' in the redetermination. The overall impact on the statement of financial position of both Entities A and B is summarised in the table below:

	A $	**B** $	**Total** $
Exploration and development asset at 31/12/2015 before redetermination	280	2,520	2,800
Reimbursement of exploration and development costs	–56	80	–
Exploration and development asset at 1/1/2016 after redetermination	224	2,600	2,824

After the redetermination the depreciation of exploration and development asset for Entity A is ($224 ÷ 50 mboe =) $4.48/barrel and for Entity B is ($2,600 ÷ 650 mboe =) $4/barrel.

15.4.2.B 'Make-up' oil

As indicated in Example 41.12 above, Entity B would be entitled to 6 mboe of 'make-up' oil out of Entity A's share of the production. This raises the question whether Entity A should recognise a liability for the 'make-up' oil and whether Entity B should recognise an asset for the 'make-up' oil that it is entitled to.

'Make-up' oil is in many ways comparable to an overlift or underlift of oil, because after the redetermination it appears that Entity A is effectively in an overlift position (i.e. it has sold more product than its proportionate share of production) while Entity B is in an underlift position (i.e. it has sold less product than its proportionate share of production).

IFRS does not directly address accounting for underlifts and overlifts (as discussed at 12.4 above) or accounting for 'make-up' oil following a redetermination. Consequently, an entity that is entitled to receive or is obliged to pay 'make-up' oil will need to apply the hierarchy in IAS 8 to develop an accounting policy. Therefore, an entity might develop either an accounting policy that is:

(a) similar to the 'entitlements method' (see 12.4.2 above) and account for a 'make-up' oil asset or liability that is similar to an underlift asset or and overlift liability; or

(b) based on the accounting standards of another standard-setter with a similar conceptual framework, such as US GAAP or UK GAAP, in which case the entity would not recognise an asset or liability and account for the 'make-up' oil prospectively.

Under many unitisation agreements, entities are required to give up oil only to the extent that there is production from the underlying field. Proponents of method (b) believe that in the absence of future production, Entity A would have no obligation to deliver oil or make another form of payment to the other parties under the unitisation agreement. In those cases, the 'make-up' oil obligation would not meet the definition of financial liability under IAS 32 or that of a provision under IAS 37. It may also be considered that Entity B cannot recognise an asset, because its right to 'make-up' oil only arises because of a future event (i.e. the future production of oil).

15.4.2.C Decommissioning provisions

Another effect of a redetermination is that it may increase or decrease an entity's share of the decommissioning liability in relation to the project, as illustrated in the example below.

Example 41.13: Redetermination (2)

Assuming the same facts as in Example 41.12 above, how should Entities A and B account for the change in the decommissioning provision?

Under IFRIC 1 the change in a decommissioning provision should be added to, or deducted from, the cost of the related asset in the current period. However, if a decrease in the liability exceeds the carrying amount of the asset, the excess should be recognised immediately in profit or loss. *[IFRIC 1.5]*.

This would lead Entities A and B to make the following journal entries:

	$	$
Entity A		
Dr Decommissioning provision	24	
Cr Decommissioning asset		24
Entity B		
Dr Decommissioning asset	24	
Cr Decommissioning provision		24

The decommission asset is adjusted in accordance with IFRIC 1 for the change in the decommissioning provision.

If Entity A had recognised a gain of $24 upon the reduction of the decommissioning liability, this would have resulted in an increase in the depreciation of the decommissioning asset from ($100 ÷ 100 mboe =) $1/barrel to ($70 ÷ 50 mboe =) $1.40/barrel. The IFRIC 1 approach avoids this although it increases the depreciation of the decommissioning asset slightly to ($56 ÷ 50mboe =) $1.12/barrel, as the decommissioning provision is also affected by the accretion of interest. Nevertheless, the approach required by IFRIC 1 is largely consistent with the treatment of a redetermination as a reimbursement of capital expenditure in Example 41.12 above.

15.5 Stripping costs in the production phase of a surface mine (mining)

In surface mining operations it is necessary to remove overburden and other waste materials to gain access to ore from which minerals can be extracted – this is also referred to as stripping. IFRIC 20 – *Stripping Costs in the Production Phase of a Surface Mine* – specifies how stripping costs incurred during the production phase of a surface mine are to be accounted for. IFRIC 20 considers the different types of stripping costs encountered in a surface mining operation. These costs are separated into those incurred in the development phase of the mine (i.e. pre-production) and those that are incurred in the production phase. *[IFRIC 20.2, 3]*. For these purposes, the mine is considered to be an asset that is separate from the mineral rights and mineral reserves, which are outside the scope of IAS 16. *[IAS 16.3(d)]*.

15.5.1 Scope of IFRIC 20

Generally, those costs incurred in the development phase of a mine would be capitalised as part of the depreciable cost of building, developing and constructing the mine, under the principles of IAS 16. Ultimately, these capitalised costs are depreciated or amortised on a systematic basis, usually by using the units of production method, once production commences. The stripping costs incurred in the development phase of a mine are not considered by IFRIC 20.

Instead, the interpretation applies to all waste removal (stripping) costs incurred during the production phase of a surface mine (production stripping costs). *[IFRIC 20.2]*. It does not apply to oil and natural gas extraction and underground mining activities. Also, it does not address the question of whether oil sands extraction is considered to be a surface mining activity and therefore whether it is in scope or not. *[IFRIC 20.BC4]*.

Despite the importance of the term 'production phase', this is not defined in the Interpretation, or elsewhere in IFRS. The determination of the commencement of the production phase not only affects stripping costs, but also affects many other accounting issues in the extractive industries, described in more detail below. These include the cessation of the capitalisation of other costs, including borrowing costs, the commencement of depreciation or amortisation (see 16 below), and the treatment of certain pre-production revenues (see 12.1 above).

Stripping activity undertaken during the production phase may create two benefits (1) the extraction of ore (inventory) in the current period and (2) improved access to the ore body to be mined in a future period. Where the benefits are realised in the form of inventory produced, the production stripping costs are to be accounted for in accordance with IAS 2. Where the benefits are improved access to ore to be mined in the future, these costs are to be recognised as a non-current asset, if the required criteria are met (see 15.5.2 below). The Interpretation refers to this non-current asset as the 'stripping activity asset'. *[IFRIC 20.8]*.

15.5.2 Recognition criteria – stripping activity asset

IFRIC 20 states that an entity must recognise a stripping activity asset if, and only if, all of the following criteria are satisfied:

(a) it is probable that the future economic benefit (improved access to the ore body) associated with the stripping activity will flow to the entity;

(b) the entity can identify the component of the ore body for which access has been improved; and

(c) the costs relating to the stripping activity associated with that component can be measured reliably. *[IFRIC 20.9]*.

Instead of being a separate asset, the stripping activity asset is to be accounted for as an addition to, or as an enhancement of, an existing asset. This means that the stripping activity asset will be accounted for as part of an existing asset. *[IFRIC 20.10]*. IFRIC 20 does not specify whether the stripping activity asset is a tangible or intangible asset. Instead, it simply states that it should be classified as tangible or intangible according to the nature of the existing asset of which it is part – so it will depend upon whether an entity classifies its mine assets as tangible or intangible.

The Interpretation considers that the stripping activity asset might add to or improve a variety of existing assets, such as, the mine property (land), the mineral deposit itself, an intangible right to extract the ore or an asset that originated in the mine development phase. *[IFRIC 20.BC10]*. In most instances, entities classify their producing mine assets as tangible assets; therefore, it is likely that the stripping activity assets will also be classified as tangible assets.

15.5.3 Initial recognition

The stripping activity asset is to be initially measured at cost. This will be the accumulation of costs directly incurred to perform the stripping activity that benefits the identified component of ore, plus an allocation of directly attributable overhead costs. *[IFRIC 20.12]*. Examples of the types of costs expected to be included as directly attributable overhead costs are items such as salary costs of the mine supervisor overseeing that component of the mine, and an allocation of rental costs of any equipment hired specifically to perform the stripping activity. *[IFRIC 20.BC12]*.

Some incidental operations may take place at the same time as the production stripping activity that are not necessary for the production stripping activity to continue as planned. The costs associated with these incidental operations are not to be included in the cost of the stripping activity asset. *[IFRIC 20.12]*. An example provided in the Interpretation is the building of an access ramp in the area in which the production stripping activity is taking place. These ancillary costs must be recognised as assets or expensed in accordance with other IFRSs.

15.5.3.A *Allocating costs between inventory and the stripping activity asset*

If the costs of waste removal can be directly allocated between inventory and the stripping activity asset, then the entity should allocate those costs accordingly. However, it may be difficult in practice to identify these costs separately, particularly if inventory is produced at the same time as access to the ore body is improved. This is likely to be very common in practice. Where this is the case, the Interpretation permits an entity to use an allocation approach that is based on a relevant production measure as this is considered to be a good indicator of the nature of benefits that are generated for the activity taking place in the mine. *[IFRIC 20.13]*.

The Interpretation provides a (non-exhaustive) list of some of the possible metrics that could be used to determine the appropriate allocation basis. These include:

- cost of inventory produced compared with expected cost;
- volume of waste extracted compared with expected volume, for a given volume of ore production; and
- mineral content of the ore extracted compared with expected mineral content to be extracted, for a given quantity of ore produced. *[IFRIC 20.13]*.

An allocation basis which uses sales value or relative sales value is not acceptable. *[IFRIC 20.BC15]*.

The production measure is calculated for each identified component of the ore body. Application of this allocation methodology effectively involves a comparison of the expected level of activity for that component with the actual level of activity for the same component, to identify when additional activity may have occurred and may be creating a future benefit. See 15.5.3.B below for further discussion about how to determine a component.

Where the actual level of activity exceeds the expected level of activity, the waste removal activity incurred at the expected level and its associated costs would then form part of the cost of inventory produced in that period. Any excess of actual activity over the expected level (and the associated costs of such excess activity) needs to be considered to determine whether it represents a stripping activity asset.

It is important to note that where actual stripping levels exceed those expected for the identified component, this will not automatically result in the recognition of a stripping activity asset. An entity will need to assess whether the removal of such additional waste has actually resulted in a future economic benefit, i.e. improved access to future ore. If not, such costs should not be capitalised as an asset, but instead should be recognised in profit or loss in the period incurred. For example, the mining of an unexpected fault or dyke should not be capitalised but instead expensed as incurred.

Where actual waste removal activity is less than the expected level of activity, only the actual waste removed and its associated costs, not the expected costs, will form part of the cost of inventory produced in that period. This is because continuing to recognise waste costs at the expected level would require an entity to recognise a deferred stripping liability. This is not permitted under IFRIC 20 or generally under IFRS because, in the absence of a legal or constructive obligation to continue to mine the deposit, such costs would not satisfy the criteria to be recognised as a liability.

It is worth noting that while some of the allocation approaches set out in the Interpretation are similar to the life-of-mine average strip ratio approach used by many entities prior to the introduction of IFRIC 20, there are differences.

The key difference is that the level at which the expected level of activity is to be determined when calculating the relevant production measure is likely to be lower than that was previously used for the life-of-mine average strip ratio approach. The life-of-mine average strip ratio approach used the entire ore body, whereas IFRIC 20 requires this to be determined for each component of the ore body, which is expected to be a subset of the ore body. See 15.5.3.B below for further discussion about how to determine a component.

The other difference relates to the way in which any stripping activity asset is recognised in profit or loss. Under the life-of-mine average stripping ratio approach, a portion of the deferred stripping asset was recognised in profit or loss when the actual stripping ratio fell below the expected average life-of-mine strip ratio. Under IFRIC 20 however, the stripping activity asset is to be depreciated or amortised over the useful life of the identified component of the ore body that becomes more accessible. The units of production (UOP) method is to be used unless another method is more appropriate. *[IFRIC 20.15]*.

It is important to note that the calculation of the expected production measure for each component will need to be reviewed and updated if there are material changes to the mine plan for that component (for example due to differences in actual versus budgeted performance or changes in future mining plans resulting from other factors, e.g. changes in commodity prices or increases in costs). Should these changes impact the expected production measure for the remaining life of the component, then the IFRIC 20 calculations will need to be updated and applied on a prospective basis. The calculation of the expected production measures will also be required if and when new components commence production.

Example 41.14: Allocating costs between inventory and the stripping activity asset

Scenario A – actual performance measure exceeds the expected performance measure

The following example illustrates how an entity would allocate costs between inventory and the stripping activity asset where the actual performance measure exceeds the expected performance measure for a component in a particular period.

Assume Entity A has a mine which comprises two separate pits which are accessing the one ore body. For the purposes of IFRIC 20, each pit is identified as a component. Pit 1 has a total life of three years and at reporting period end, has been in production for one year. Pit 2 has a total life of five years but production has not yet commenced.

At the commencement of production from pit 1, the company has forecast the following mining and stripping activity:

Expected ore to be extracted over the 3 years	1,000 tonnes
Expected volume of waste to be extracted over the 3 years	3,000 tonnes

During the current period, the following had occurred in relation to the production from pit 1:

Cost incurred for mining activity	\$13,000,000 (a)
Actual tonnes of ore removed	100 tonnes (b)
Actual tonnes of waste removed	1,200 tonnes (c)
Average cost per tonne in year 1 = (a) / [(b)+(c)]	\$10,000

The company determined that it is not practically possible to identify separately what portion of the waste removal costs leads to the extraction of inventory and what portion to improved access to future ore. This is because these two activities were occurring simultaneously as there were multiple shovels in operation in multiple parts of the component and a single haulage fleet was used.

Given this, the company has decided that it will allocate costs by comparing the actual volume of waste and ore extracted (the actual strip ratio) in the period with the expected volume of waste and ore (expected strip ratio) for the life of the component i.e. for pit 1.

The allocation of the actual waste removal costs incurred will involve the following steps:

Step 1: Calculate the expected strip ratio for pit 1

Expected volume of waste to be extracted / expected volume of ore to be extracted

= 3,000 tonnes / 1,000 tonnes

= 3.00 (expected strip ratio)

This means that for every 1 tonne of ore extracted over the life of pit 1, the company expects (on average) to remove 3 tonnes of waste.

Step 2: Calculate the additional waste extracted compared to the expected waste extracted for the actual volume of ore extracted

Actual volume of ore extracted × expected strip ratio

= 100 tonnes × 3 tonnes

= 300 tonnes

Actual volume of waste extracted in year 1 = 1,200 tonnes

Additional waste extracted in year 1 = actual waste extracted less expected waste to be extracted

= 1,200 tonnes – 300 tonnes

= 900 tonnes of additional waste was extracted

Step 3: Allocate mining costs between inventory and the stripping activity asset

Stripping activity asset

Additional waste tonnes removed × cost per tonne

= 900 tonnes × $10,000

= $9,000,000

Inventory

Total mining costs incurred less costs allocated to the stripping activity asset

= $13,000,000 – $9,000,000

= $4,000,000

This comprises:

(1) The cost of extracting the inventory tonnes

= 100 × $10,000

= $1,000,000

Plus:

(2) The cost of waste removal allocated directly to inventory (which was allocated at the expected level of 3:1)

= 300 tonnes × $10,000

= $3,000,000

Scenario B – actual strip ratio is less than the expected strip ratio

Assume the same basic fact pattern as per Scenario A above, but with different actual mining results for pit 1 in the current period:

Cost incurred for mining activity	$13,000,000 (a)
Actual tonnes of ore removed	1,200 tonnes (b)
Actual tonnes of waste removed	100 tonnes (c)
Average cost per tonne in year 1 = (a) / [(b)+(c)]	$10,000

The allocation of the actual waste removal costs incurred will involve the following steps:

Step 1: Calculate the expected strip ratio for pit 1

Expected volume of waste to be extracted / expected volume of ore to be extracted

= 3,000 tonnes / 1,000 tonnes

= 3.00 (expected strip ratio)

This means that for every 1 tonne of ore extracted over the life of pit 1, the company expects (on average) to remove 3 tonnes of waste.

Step 2: Calculate the additional waste extracted compared to the expected waste extracted for the actual volume of ore extracted

Actual volume of ore extracted × expected strip ratio

= 1,200 tonnes × 3 tonnes

= 3,600 tonnes

Actual volume of waste extracted in year 1 = 100 tonnes

During the current period the actual strip ratio was only 0.0833. As this is less than the expected strip ratio, as explained above, there is no additional waste removed during the period.

Step 3: Allocate mining costs between inventory and the stripping activity asset

Stripping activity asset

As the actual strip ratio was below the expected strip ratio, no additional waste was removed during the period; therefore there is no amount to be added to the stripping activity asset.

Inventory

As the actual amount of waste removed during the current period is less than the expected level of waste for the life of the component, and there is no amount to be allocated to the stripping activity asset, then the total mining costs for the period will be allocated to inventory.

= $13,000,000

This comprises:

(1) The cost of extracting the inventory tonnes

= 1,200 × $10,000

= $12,000,000

Plus:

(2) The cost of waste removal allocated directly to inventory (which is allocated based on the actual waste tonnes removed during the period)

= 100 tonnes × $10,000

= $1,000,000

15.5.3.B Identifying the component of the ore body

Identifying the various components of the ore body is one of the critical steps in applying IFRIC 20. This is necessary for several reasons:

(a) production stripping costs can only be capitalised as an asset if the component of the ore body for which access has been improved, can be identified;

(b) to allocate stripping activity costs between inventory and the stripping activity asset, an entity needs to determine the expected level of activity for each component of the mine; and

(c) the stripping activity asset is required to be depreciated or amortised on a systematic basis, over the expected useful life of the identified component of the ore body that becomes more accessible as a result of the stripping activity.

The Interpretation provides limited guidance on how to identify components, although it does appear a component is expected to be a subset of the whole ore body. This view is supported in several parts of IFRIC 20.

- A 'component' refers to the specific volume of the ore body that is made more accessible by the stripping activity; the identified component of the ore body would typically be a subset of the total ore body of the mine; and a mine may have several components, which are identified during the mine planning stage. *[IFRIC 20.BC8]*.
- The depreciation or amortisation requirements state that the expected useful life of the identified component of the ore body that is used to depreciate or amortise the stripping activity asset will differ from the expected useful life that is used to depreciate or amortise the mine itself and the related life-of-mine assets, unless the stripping activity provides improved access to the whole of the ore body. *[IFRIC 20.BC17]*.

In practice, the identification of components of an ore body is a complex process which requires a significant amount of management judgement. While it is considered that an entity's mine plan will provide the information required allowing these judgements to be made with reasonable consistency, this may not be a straightforward exercise, and it will be particularly challenging for the more complex mines. This is because ore bodies vary significantly in shape and size and are more haphazard than often illustrated in simple examples. Management may identify components in a number of different ways. These could include identifying discrete components in the mine plan, such as phases, sections, push backs, cutbacks, lay backs, blocks, etc.; examining annual production plans; or examining push back campaigns. Whatever approach is adopted, it is essential that the components are recognisable to those who are responsible for mine planning as they will be the ones who will need to track progress as ore is removed and will need to update the assessment of components should the mine plan change. Given this, practice has revealed that when identifying the components of an ore body, it is essential that input is obtained from those who best understand the mine plan, i.e. the mining engineers and operational personnel.

The identification of components will need to be reassessed and updated (if necessary) whenever there are material changes to the mine plan. Given this, an entity will need to establish systems, processes, procedures and controls to ensure it is able to identify when material changes to the mine plan have occurred that would require the IFRIC 20 calculations to be updated. Identification of components will also be required when an entity commences production on a new component of the ore body or in relation to a new ore body.

15.5.4 Subsequent measurement

After initial recognition, the stripping activity asset must be carried at its cost or revalued amount less depreciation or amortisation and less impairment losses, in the same way as the existing asset of which it is a part. *[IFRIC 20.14]*. The stripping activity asset is to be depreciated or amortised on a systematic basis, over the expected useful life of the identified component of the ore body that becomes more accessible as a result of the stripping activity. *[IFRIC 20.15]*.

The units of production method is effectively required to be applied unless another method is more appropriate. *[IFRIC 20.15]*. The expected useful life of the identified component that is used to depreciate or amortise the stripping activity asset will differ from the expected useful life that is used to depreciate or amortise the mine itself and the related life-of-mine assets, unless the stripping activity provides improved access to the whole of the ore body (this is expected to be rare). *[IFRIC 20.16]*.

Consistent with the units of production method used for other mining assets, the calculation of the units of production rate will be completed when a stripping activity asset is first recognised. It will then need to be reviewed (and if necessary, updated) at the end of each reporting period, or when the mine plan changes. The new units of production rate will be applied prospectively.

Given the depreciation or amortisation of the stripping activity asset represents the consumption of the benefits associated with the stripping activity asset, and those benefits are realised by the extraction of the ore to which the stripping activity asset relates (i.e. the ore for which access was improved by the removal of this waste in prior periods), this depreciation or amortisation effectively represents part of the cost of extracting that ore in future periods. In accordance with IAS 2, such costs should be included in the cost of that subsequent ore. This effectively means that the depreciation or amortisation of the stripping activity asset should be recapitalised as part of the cost of the inventory produced in those subsequent periods. Once the inventory is sold, those costs will be recognised in profit or loss as part of cost of goods sold.

15.5.5 Disclosures

IFRIC 20 has no specific disclosure requirements. However, the general disclosure requirements of IAS 1 are relevant, e.g. the requirements to disclose significant accounting policies, *[IAS 1.117]*, and significant judgements, estimates and assumptions. *[IAS 1.125]*. For many entities, it is likely that the accounting policy for stripping costs would be considered a significant accounting policy which would therefore warrant disclosure, as would the judgements, estimates and assumptions they make when applying this policy.

The extract below from Rio Tinto illustrates an IFRIC 20 accounting policy disclosure.

Extract 41.41: Rio Tinto plc (2015)

Notes to the 2015 financial statements [extract]

1 Principal accounting policies [extract]

(h) Deferred stripping (note 14)

In open pit mining operations, overburden and other waste materials must be removed to access ore from which minerals can be extracted economically. The process of removing overburden and waste materials is referred to as stripping. During the development of a mine (or pit), before production commences, stripping costs are capitalised as part of cost of construction of the mine (or pit) and are subsequently amortised over the life of the mine (or pit) on a units of production basis.

In order for production phase stripping costs to qualify for capitalisation as a stripping activity asset, three criteria must be met:

- it must be probable that there will be an economic benefit in a future accounting period because the stripping activity has improved access to the orebody; and
- it must be possible to identify the "component" of the orebody for which access has been improved; and
- it must be possible to reliably measure the costs that relate to the stripping activity.

A "component" is a specific section of the orebody that is made more accessible by the stripping activity. It will typically be a subset of the larger orebody that is distinguished by a separate useful economic life (for example, a pushback).

Production phase stripping can give rise to two benefits: the extraction of ore in the current period and improved access to ore which will be extracted in future periods. When the cost of stripping which has a future benefit is not distinguishable from the cost of producing current inventories, the stripping costs is allocated to each of these activities based on a relevant production measure using a life-of-component strip ratio. The ratio divides the tonnage of waste mined for the component for the period either by the quantity of ore mined for the component or by the quantity of minerals contained in the ore mined for the component. In some operations, the quantity of ore is a more appropriate basis for allocating costs, particularly where there are significant by-products. Stripping costs for the component are deferred to the extent that the current period ratio exceeds the life of component ratio. The stripping activity asset is depreciated on a "units of production" basis based on expected production of either ore or contained minerals over the life of the component unless another method is more appropriate.

The life-of-component ratios are based on the ore reserves of the mine (and for some mines, other mineral resources) and the annual mine plan; they are a function of the mine design and therefore changes to that design will generally result in changes to the ratios. Changes in other technical or economic parameters that impact the ore reserves (and for some mines, other mineral resources) may also have an impact on the life-of-component ratios even if they do not affect the mine design. Changes to the ratios are accounted for prospectively.

It may be the case that subsequent phases of stripping will access additional ore and that these subsequent phases are only possible after the first phase has taken place. Where applicable, the Group considers this on a mine-by-mine basis. Generally, the only ore attributed to the stripping activity asset for the purposes of calculating a life-of-component ratio, and for the purposes of amortisation, is the ore to be extracted from the originally identified component.

Where a mine operates several open pits that are regarded as separate operations for the purpose of mine planning, initial stripping costs are accounted for separately by reference to the ore from each separate pit. If, however, the pits are highly integrated for the purpose of mine planning, the second and subsequent pits are regarded as extensions of the first pit in accounting for stripping costs. In such cases, the initial stripping (i.e. overburden and other waste removal) of the second and subsequent pits is considered to be production phase stripping.

The Group's judgment as to whether multiple pit mines are considered separate or integrated operations depends on each mine's specific circumstances.

The following factors would point towards the initial stripping costs for the individual pits being accounted for separately:

- If mining of the second and subsequent pits is conducted consecutively with that of the first pit, rather than concurrently.
- If separate investment decisions are made to develop each pit, rather than a single investment decision being made at the outset.
- If the pits are operated as separate units in terms of mine planning and the sequencing of overburden removal and ore mining, rather than as an integrated unit.
- If expenditures for additional infrastructure to support the second and subsequent pits are relatively large.
- If the pits extract ore from separate and distinct orebodies, rather than from a single orebody.

If the designs of the second and subsequent pits are significantly influenced by opportunities to optimise output from the several pits combined, including the co-treatment or blending of the output from the pits, then this would point to treatment as an integrated operation for the purposes of accounting for initial stripping costs. The relative importance of each of the above factors is considered in each case.

Deferred stripping costs are included in "Mining properties and leases" within "Property, plant and equipment" or within "Investments in equity accounted units", as appropriate. Amortisation of deferred stripping costs is included in "Depreciation of property, plant and equipment" within "Net operating costs" or in "Share of profit after tax of equity accounted units", as appropriate.

Critical accounting policies and estimates [extract]

(vi) Deferral of stripping costs (note 14)

Stripping of waste materials takes place throughout the production phase of a surface mine or pit. The identification of components within a mine and of life of component strip ratios is dependent on an individual mine's design. Changes to that design may introduce new components and/or change the life of component strip ratios. Changes in other technical or economic parameters that impact ore reserves may also have an impact on the life of component strip ratios, even if they do not affect the mine's design. Changes to the life of component strip ratios, are accounted for prospectively.

The Group's judgment as to whether multiple pit mines are considered separate or integrated operations determines whether initial stripping of a pit is deemed to be pre-production or production phase stripping and, therefore, the amortisation base for those costs. The judgment depends on each mine's specific circumstances and the analysis requires judgment: another mining company could make a different judgement even where the fact pattern appears to be similar.

14 Property, plant and equipment [extract]

(a) At 31 December 2015, the net book value of capitalised production phase stripping costs totalled US$1,923 million, with US$1,464 million within Property, plant and equipment and a further US$459 million within Investments in equity accounted units (2014 total of US$1,816 million with US$1,373 million in Property, plant and equipment and a further US$443 million within Investment in equity accounted units). During the year the capitalisation of US$455 million was partly offset by depreciation of US$266 million. Depreciation of deferred stripping costs of US$173 million (2014: US$84 million, 2013 US$70 million) is included within "Depreciation for the year".

16 DEPRECIATION, DEPLETION AND AMORTISATION (DD&A)

16.1 Requirements under IAS 16 and IAS 38

The main types of depreciable assets of mining companies and oil and gas companies are property, plant and equipment, intangible assets and mineral reserves, although the exact titles given to these types of assets may vary.

While 'mineral rights and expenditure on the exploration for, or development and extraction of, minerals, oil, natural gas and similar non-regenerative resources' are outside the scope of IAS 16 and IAS 38, any items of property, plant and equipment (PP&E) and other intangible assets that are used in the extraction of mineral reserves should be accounted for under IAS 16 and IAS 38. *[IAS 16.2, 3, IAS 38.2]*.

For items of PP&E, various descriptions are used for such assets which can include producing mines, mine assets, oil and gas assets, producing properties. Whatever the description given, IAS 16 requires depreciation of an item of PP&E over its useful life. Depreciation is required to be calculated separately for each part (often referred to as a 'component'), of an item of PP&E with a cost that is significant in relation to the total cost of the item, unless the item can be grouped with other items of PP&E that have the same useful life and depreciation method. *[IAS 16.43, 45]*.

The guidance in IAS 16 relating to parts of an asset does not apply directly to intangible assets as IAS 38 does not apply a 'parts' approach, or to mineral rights, but we believe that entities should use the general principles for determining an appropriate unit of account that are outlined at 4 above. IAS 16's general requirements are described in Chapter 18 and IAS 38 is addressed in Chapter 17.

16.1.1 Mineral reserves

In the absence of a standard or an interpretation specifically applicable to mineral reserves and their related expenditures, which are technically outside the scope of IAS 16 and IAS 38, management needs to develop an accounting policy for the depreciation or amortisation of mineral reserves in accordance with the hierarchy in IAS 8, taking into account the requirements and guidance in Standards and Interpretations dealing with similar and related issues and the definitions, recognition criteria and measurement concepts for assets, liabilities, income and expenses in the *Conceptual Framework*. *[IAS 8.11]*. In practice, an entity will generally develop an accounting policy that is based on the depreciation and amortisation principles in IAS 16 and IAS 38, which deal with similar and related issues.

16.1.2 Assets depreciated using the straight-line method

The straight-line method of depreciation is generally preferred in accounting for the depreciation of property, plant and equipment. The main practical advantages of the straight-line method are considered to be its simplicity and the fact that its results are often not materially different from the units of production method if annual production is relatively constant.[123] In general, the straight-line method is considered to be preferable for:

- assets whose loss in value is more closely linked to the passage of time than to the quantities of minerals produced (e.g. front-end loaders that are used in stripping overburden and production of minerals);
- assets that are unrelated to production and that are separable from the field or mine (e.g. office buildings);
- assets with a useful life that is either much longer (e.g. offshore platforms) or much shorter (e.g. drill jumbos) than that of the field or mine in which they are used;
- assets used in fields or mines whose annual production is relatively constant. However, if assets are used in fields or mines that are expected to suffer extended outages, due to weather conditions or periodic repairs and maintenance, then the straight-line method may be less appropriate; and
- assets that are used in more than one field or mine (e.g. service trucks).

If the production of a field or mine drops significantly towards the end of its productive life, then the straight-line method may result in a relatively high depreciation charge per unit of production in these latter years. In those cases, an entity may need to perform an impairment test on the assets involved.

The extract below indicates the assets to which BHP Billiton applies the straight-line method.

Extract 41.42: BHP Billiton plc (2015)

Notes to Financial Statements [extract]

43 Significant accounting policies [extract]

(e) Depreciation of property, plant and equipment

The carrying amounts of property, plant and equipment are depreciated to their estimated residual value over the estimated useful lives of the specific assets concerned, or the estimated life of the associated mine, field or lease, if shorter. Estimates of residual values and useful lives are reassessed annually and any change in estimate is taken into account in the determination of remaining depreciation charges. Depreciation commences on the date of commissioning. The major categories of property, plant and equipment are depreciated on a unit of production and/or straight-line basis using estimated lives indicated below. However, where assets are dedicated to a mine, field or lease and are not readily transferable, the below useful lives are subject to the lesser of the asset category's useful life and the life of the mine, field or lease:

• Buildings	–	25 to 50 years
• Land	–	not depreciated
• Plant and equipment	–	3 to 30 years straight-line
• Mineral rights and petroleum interests	–	based on reserves on a unit of production basis
• Capitalised exploration, evaluation and development expenditure	–	based on reserves on a unit of production basis

16.1.3 Assets depreciated using the units of production method

When it comes to assets relating to mineral reserves, the units of production method is the most common method applied. 'The underlying principle of the units of production method is that capitalised costs associated with a cost centre are incurred to find and develop the commercially producible reserves in that cost centre, so that each unit produced from the centre is assigned an equal amount of cost.'[124] The units of production method thereby effectively allocates an equal amount of depreciation to each unit produced, rather than an equal amount to each year as under the straight-line method.

When the level of production varies considerably over the life of a project (e.g. the production of oil fields is much higher in the periods just after the start of production than in the final periods of production), depreciation based on a units of production method will produce a more equal cost per unit from year to year than straight-line methods. Under the straight-line method the depreciation charge per unit in the early years of production could be much less than the depreciation per unit in later years. 'That factor, coupled with the fact that typically production costs per unit increase in later years, means that the profitability of operations would be distorted if the straight-line method is used, showing larger profits in early years and lower profits in later years of the mineral resource's life. The higher cost per unit in later years is, in part, due to fewer units being produced while many production costs remain fixed and, in part, a result of many variable costs per unit increasing over time because reserves may be harder to extract, there may be greater equipment repairs, and similar other factors.'[125] Nevertheless, even under the units of production method, profitability often drops significantly towards the end of the productive life of a field or mine. When this happens an entity will need to carry out an impairment test and may need to recognise an impairment charge (see 11 above).

In general, the units of production method is considered to be preferable for:

- assets used in fields or mines whose annual production may vary considerably over their useful economic life;
- assets whose loss in value is more closely linked to the quantities of minerals produced than to the passage of time (e.g. draglines used in the extraction of mineral ore);
- assets that are used in production or that are inseparable from the field or mine (e.g. wells and well heads);
- assets with a useful life that is the same as that of the field or mine in which they are used; and
- assets that are used in only one field or mine (e.g. overland conveyor belts).

Extract 41.42 above and Extract 41.43 below indicate the classes of asset to which BHP Billiton and Lonmin, respectively, apply the units of production method.

Extract 41.43: Lonmin Plc (2015)

Notes to the Accounts [extract]

1 Statement on accounting policies [extract]

Intangible assets

Intangible assets, other than goodwill, acquired by the Group have finite useful lives and are measured at cost less accumulated amortisation and accumulated impairment losses. Where amortisation is charged on these assets, the expense is taken to the income statement through operating costs.

Amortisation of mineral rights is provided on a 'units of production' basis over the remaining life of mine to residual value (20 to 40 years).

All other intangible assets are amortised over their useful economic lives subject to a maximum of 20 years and are tested for impairment at each reporting date when there is an indication of a possible impairment.

Property, plant and equipment [extract]

Depreciation

Depreciation is provided on a straight-line or units of production basis as appropriate over their expected useful lives or the remaining life of the mine, if shorter, to residual value. The life of mine is based on proven and probable reserves. The expected useful lives of the major categories of property, plant and equipment are as follows:

	Method	Rate	
Shafts and underground	Units of production	2.5%-5.0% per annum	20-40 years
Metallurgical	Straight line	2.5%-7.1% per annum	14-40 years
Infrastructure	Straight line	2.5%-2.9% per annum	35-40 years
Other plant and equipment	Straight line	2.5%-50.0% per annum	2-40 years

No depreciation is provided on surface mining land which has a continuing value and capital work in progress. Residual values and useful lives are re-assessed annually and if necessary changes are accounted for prospectively.

The practical application of the units of production method gives rise to the following issues that require entities to exercise a considerable degree of judgement in determining the:

(a) units of production formula (see 16.1.3.A below);

(b) reserves base (see 16.1.3.B below);

(c) unit of measure (see 16.1.3.C below); and

(d) joint and by-products (see 16.1.3.D below).

As discussed at 16.1.3.B below, the asset base that is subject to depreciation should be consistent with the reserves base that is used, which may require an entity to exclude certain costs from (or include future investments in) the depreciation pool.

16.1.3.A Units of production formula

There are a number of different ways in which an entity could calculate a depreciation charge under the units of production method. The most obvious of these is probably the following formula:

$$\text{Depreciation charge for the period} = \text{Current period's production} \times \frac{\text{Cost of the asset at the beginning of the period} - \text{Cumulative depreciation and impairment at the beginning of the period}}{\text{Opening reserves estimated at the beginning of the period}}$$

The reserves estimate used in the above formula is the best estimate of the reserves at the beginning of the period, but by the end of the period a revised and more accurate estimate is often available. Therefore, it may be considered that in order to take into account the most recent information, the opening reserves should be calculated by adding the 'closing reserves estimated at the end of the period' to the 'current period's production'. However, reserves estimates might change for a number of reasons:

(a) more detailed knowledge about existing reserves (e.g. detailed engineering studies or drilling of additional wells which occurred after the commencement of the period);

(b) new events that affect the physical quantity of reserves (e.g. major fire in a mine); and

(c) changes in economic assumptions (e.g. higher commodity prices).

It is generally not appropriate to take account of these events retrospectively. For example, changes in reserves estimates that result from events that took place after the end of the reporting period (such as those under (b) and (c)) are non-adjusting events that should be accounted for prospectively in accordance with IFRS. *[IAS 8.32-38, IAS 10.3]*. Changes in reserves estimates that result from new information or new developments which do not offer greater clarity concerning the conditions that existed at the end of the reporting period (such as those under (a)) are not considered to be corrections of errors; instead they are changes in accounting estimates that should be accounted for prospectively under IFRS. *[IAS 8.5, 32-38]*.

Determining whether actual changes in reserves estimates should be treated as adjusting or non-adjusting events will depend upon the specific facts and circumstances and may require significant judgement.

Usually, an entity will continue to invest during the year in assets in the depreciation pool (see 16.1.3.B below for a discussion of 'depreciation pools') that are used to extract minerals. This raises the question as to whether or not assets that were used for only part of the production during the period should be depreciated on a different basis. Under the straight-line method, an entity will generally calculate the depreciation of asset additions during the period based on the assumption that they were added (1) at the beginning of the period, (2) in the middle of the period or (3) at the end of the period. While method (2) is often the best approximation, methods (1) and (3) are generally not materially different when the accounting period is rather short (e.g. monthly or quarterly reporting) or when the level of asset additions is relatively low compared to the asset base.

The above considerations explain why the units of production formula that is commonly used in the extractive industries is slightly more complicated than the formula given above:

$$\text{Depreciation charge for the period} = \text{Current period's production} \times \frac{\text{Cost of the asset at the end of the period} - \text{Cumulative depreciation and impairment at the beginning of the period}}{\text{Closing reserves estimated at the end of the period} + \text{Current period's production}}$$

This units of production formula is widely used in the oil and gas sector by entities that apply US GAAP or did apply the former OIAC SORP. In the mining sector, however, both the first and the second units of production formulae are used in practice.

16.1.3.B Reserves base

An important decision in applying the units of production method is selecting the reserves base that will be used. The following reserves bases could in theory be used:

(a) proved developed reserves (see (a) below);

(b) proved developed and undeveloped reserves (see (b) below);

(c) proved and probable reserves (see (c) below);

(d) proved and probable reserves and a portion of resources expected to be converted into reserves (see (d) below); and

(e) proved, probable and possible reserves.

The term 'possible reserves', which is used in the oil and gas sector, is associated with a probability of only 10% (see 2.2.1 above). Therefore, it is generally not considered acceptable to include possible reserves within the reserves base in applying the units of production method.

It is important that whatever reserves base is chosen the costs applicable to that category of reserves are included in the depreciable amount to achieve a proper matching of costs and production.[126] For example, 'if the cost centre is not fully developed ... there may be costs that do not apply, in total or in part, to proved developed reserves, which may create difficulties in matching costs and reserves. In addition, some reserve categories will require future costs to bring them to the point where production may begin.'[127]

IFRS does not provide any guidance on the selection of an appropriate reserves base or cost centre (i.e. unit of account) for the application of the units of production method. The relative merits for the use of each of the reserves bases listed under (a) to (c) above are discussed in detail below.

(a) Proved developed reserves

Under some national GAAPs that have accounting standards for the extractive industries, an entity is required to use proved developed reserves as its reserves base for the depreciation of certain types of assets. An entity would therefore calculate its depreciation charge on the basis of actual costs that have been incurred to date. However, the cost centre frequently includes capitalised costs that relate to undeveloped reserves. To calculate the depreciation charge correctly, it will be necessary to exclude a portion of the capitalised costs from the depreciation calculation. Example 41.15 below, which is taken from the IASC's Issues Paper, illustrates how this might work.

Example 41.15: Exclusion of capitalised costs relating to undeveloped reserves[128]

In an offshore oil and gas field a platform may be constructed from which 20 development wells will be drilled. The platform's cost has been capitalised as a part of the total cost of the cost centre. If only 5 of the 20 wells have been drilled, it would be inappropriate to depreciate that portion of platform costs, as well as that portion of all other capitalised costs, that are deemed to be applicable to the 15 wells not yet drilled. Only 5/20ths of the platform costs would be subject to depreciation in the current year, while 15/20ths of the platform costs (those applicable to the 15 undrilled wells) would be withheld from the depreciable amount. The costs withheld would be transferred to the depreciable amount as the additional wells are drilled. In lieu of basing the exclusion from depreciation on the number of wells, the exclusion (and subsequent transfer to depreciable amount) could be based on the quantity of reserves developed by individual wells compared with the estimated total quantity of reserves to be developed.

Similarly, an appropriate portion of prospecting costs, mineral acquisition costs, exploration costs, appraisal costs, and future dismantlement, removal, and restoration costs that have been capitalised should be withheld from the depreciation calculation if proved developed reserves are used as the reserves base and if there are undeveloped reserves in the cost pool.[129]

By withholding some of the costs from the depreciation pool, an entity is able to achieve a better matching of the costs incurred with the benefits of production. This is particularly important in respect of pre-development costs, which provide future economic benefits in relation to reserves that are not yet classified as 'proved developed'.

However, excluding costs from the depreciation pool may not be appropriate if it is not possible to determine reliably the portion of costs to be excluded or if the reserves that are not 'proved developed' are highly uncertain. It may not be necessary to exclude any costs at all from the depreciation pool if those costs are immaterial, which is sometimes the case in mining operations.

As illustrated in Extract 41.44, Royal Dutch Shell, in reporting under IFRS, applies the units of production method based on proved developed reserves.

Extract 41.44: Royal Dutch Shell plc (2015)

NOTES TO THE CONSOLIDATED FINANCIAL STATEMENTS [extract]

2 KEY ACCOUNTING POLICIES, JUDGEMENTS AND ESTIMATES [extract]

Property, plant and equipment and intangible assets [extract]

DEPRECIATION, DEPLETION AND AMORTISATION [extract]

Property, plant and equipment related to hydrocarbon production activities generally are depreciated on a unit-of-production basis over the proved developed reserves of the field concerned. Assets whose useful lives differ from the lifetime of the field are depreciated applying a straight-line method. Rights and concessions in respect of proved properties are depleted on the unit-of-production basis over the total proved reserves of the relevant area. Where individually insignificant, unproved properties may be grouped and depreciated based on factors such as the average concession term and past experience of recognising proved reserves. [...]

(b) Proved developed and undeveloped reserves

Another approach that is common under IFRS is to use 'proved developed and undeveloped reserves' as the reserves base for the application of the units of production method. This approach reflects the fact that it is often difficult to allocate costs that have already been incurred between developed and undeveloped reserves and has the advantage that it effectively straight-lines the depreciation charge per unit of production across the different phases of a project. For example, if the depreciation cost in phase 1 of the development is $24/barrel and the depreciation cost in phase 2 of the development could be $18/barrel, an entity that uses proved developed and undeveloped reserves as its reserves base might recognise depreciation of, say, $22/barrel during phase 1 and phase 2.

Application of this approach is complicated by the fact that phase 1 of the project will start production before phase 2 is completed. To apply the units of production method on the basis of proved developed and undeveloped reserves, the entity would need to forecast the remaining investment related to phase 2. The approach does not appear unreasonable at first sight, given that the proved reserves are reasonably certain to exist and 'the costs of developing the proved undeveloped reserves will be incurred in the near future in most situations, the total depreciable costs can also be estimated with a high degree of reliability'.[130] Nevertheless, the entity would therefore define its cost pool (i.e. unit of account) as including both assets that it currently owns and certain future investments. Although there is no specific precedent within IFRS for using such a widely defined unit of account, such an approach is not prohibited, while in practice it has gained a broad measure of acceptance within the extractive industries.

(c) Proved and probable reserves

The arguments in favour of using 'proved and probable reserves' as the reserves base in applying the units of production method are similar to those discussed at (b) above. The IASC's Issues Paper summarised the arguments in favour of this approach as follows:

> 'Proponents of [using "proved and probable reserves" as the reserve base] use the same arguments given for including proved undeveloped reserves and related future costs in calculating depreciation. They point out that in a cost centre in which development has only begun a large part of capitalised prospecting, mineral acquisition, exploration, and appraisal costs may apply to probable reserves. Often in this situation there are large quantities of probable reserves, lacking only relatively minor additional exploration and/or appraisal work to be reclassified as proved reserves. They argue that, in calculating depreciation, it would be possible to defer all costs relating to the probable reserves if either proved developed reserves only, or all proved reserves, were to be used as the quantity on which depreciation is based. They contend that using probable and proved reserves in the reserve base and including in the depreciable costs any additional costs anticipated to explore and develop those reserves provides more relevant and reliable information.'[131]

The main drawbacks of this approach are that estimates of probable reserves are almost certainly different from actual reserves that will ultimately be developed and estimates of the costs to complete the development are likely to be incorrect because of the potentially long time scales involved.[132] Nevertheless, this approach has also found a considerable degree of acceptance under IFRS among mining companies and oil and gas companies that were permitted to apply the approach under their national GAAP before (e.g. UK GAAP). Both Tullow Oil and Anglo American apply this approach, as illustrated in Extracts 41.45 and 41.46 below.

Extract 41.45: Tullow Oil plc (2015)

ACCOUNTING POLICIES [extract]

YEAR ENDED 31 DECEMBER 2015

(m) Commercial reserves

Commercial reserves are proven and probable oil and gas reserves, which are defined as the estimated quantities of crude oil, natural gas and natural gas liquids which geological, geophysical and engineering data demonstrate with a specified degree of certainty to be recoverable in future years from known reservoirs and which are considered commercially producible. There should be a 50 per cent statistical probability that the actual quantity of recoverable reserves will be more than the amount estimated as proven and probable reserves and a 50 per cent statistical probability that it will be less.

(n) Depletion and amortisation – discovery fields [extract]

All expenditure carried within each field is amortised from the commencement of production on a unit of production basis, which is the ratio of oil and gas production in the period to the estimated quantities of commercial reserves at the end of the period plus the production in the period, generally on a field-by-field basis or by a group of fields which are reliant on common infrastructure. Costs used in the unit of production calculation comprise the net book value of capitalised costs plus the estimated future field development costs required to recover the commercial reserves remaining. Changes in the estimates of commercial reserves or future field development costs are dealt with prospectively.

Extract 41.46: Anglo American plc (2015)

NOTES TO THE FINANCIAL STATEMENTS

ADDITIONAL DISCLOSURES [extract]

39. ACCOUNTING POLICIES [extract]

39g. Property, plant and equipment [extract]

Depreciation of property, plant and equipment

Mining properties are depreciated to their residual values using the unit of production method based on Proved and Probable Ore Reserves and, in certain limited circumstances, other Mineral Resources included in the Life of Mine Plan. These other Mineral Resources are included in depreciation calculations where, taking into account historic rates of conversion to Ore Reserves, there is a high degree of confidence that they will be extracted in an economic manner. This is the case principally for diamond operations, where depreciation calculations are based on Diamond Reserves and Diamond Resources included in the Life of Mine Plan. This reflects the unique nature of diamond deposits where, due to the difficultly in estimating grade, Life of Mine Plans frequently include significant amounts of Indicated or Inferred Resources.

(d) Proved and probable reserves and a portion of resources expected to be converted into reserves (mining entities only)

We observe in practice that some mining entities adopt a slightly different approach when depreciating some of their mining assets. They use proven and probable reserves and a portion of resources expected to be converted into reserves. Such an approach tends to be limited to mining companies where the type of mineral and the characteristics of the ore body indicate that there is a high degree of confidence that those resources will be converted into reserves. For example, this is very common for underground operations that only perform infill drilling just prior to production commencing. This is done so that capital is not spent too early before it is really needed.

Such resources can comprise measured, indicated and inferred resources, and even exploration potential. Determining which of those have a high degree of confidence of being extracted in an economic manner will require judgement. Such an assessment will take into account the specific mineralisation and the 'reserves to resource' conversion that has previously been achieved for a mine.

Such an approach is generally justified on the basis that it helps to ensure the depreciation charges reflect management's best estimate of the useful life of the assets and provides greater accuracy in the calculation of the consumption of future economic benefits.

Anglo American applies this approach, as illustrated in Extract 41.46 above, as does Rio Tinto, as illustrated in Extract 41.47 below.

Extract 41.47: Rio Tinto plc (2015)

Notes to the 2015 financial statements [extract]

1 Principal accounting policies [extract]

(i) Depreciation and impairment (notes 13 and 14) [extract]

Depreciation of non-current assets [extract]

Units of production basis

For mining properties and leases and certain mining equipment, consumption of the economic benefits of the asset is linked to production. Except as noted below, these assets are depreciated on a units of production basis.

In applying the units of production method, depreciation is normally calculated based on production in the period as a percentage of total expected production in current and future periods based on ore reserves and, for some mines, other mineral resources. Other mineral resources may be included in depreciation calculations in limited circumstances and where there is a high degree of confidence that they can be extracted economically. This would be the case when the other mineral resources do not yet have the status of ore reserves merely because the necessary detailed evaluation work has not yet been performed and the responsible technical personnel agree that inclusion of a proportion of measured and indicated resources is appropriate based on historical reserve conversion rates.

Other mineral resources would usually only be included in unit of production calculations where there are very large areas of contiguous mineralisation, for which the economic viability is not sensitive to likely variations in grade, as may be the case for certain iron ore, bauxite and industrial minerals deposits. The required level of confidence is unlikely to exist for minerals that are typically found in low-grade ore (compared with the above), such as copper or gold. In these cases, specific areas of mineralisation have to be evaluated in considerable detail before their economic status can be predicted with confidence.

Where measured and indicated resources are used in the calculation of depreciation for infrastructure, primarily rail and port, which will benefit current and future mines, then the measured and indicated resources may relate to mines which are currently in production or to mines where there is a high degree of confidence that they will be brought into production in the future. The quantum of mineral resources is determined taking into account future capital costs as required by the Joint Ore Reserves Committee (JORC) code. The depreciation calculation, however, does not take into account future development costs for mines which are not yet in production. Measured and indicated resources are currently incorporated into depreciation calculations in the Group's Australian iron ore business.

An entity preparing its financial statements under IFRS will need to choose between using 'proved developed reserves', 'proved developed and undeveloped reserves', 'proved and probable reserves' and, for mining entities in relation to certain mines, 'proved and probable reserves and a portion of resources expected to be converted into reserves' as its reserves base. Each of these approaches is currently acceptable under IFRS. Preparers of financial statements should, however, be aware of the difficulties that exist in ensuring that the reserves base and the costs that are being depreciated correspond. Users of financial statements need to understand that comparability between entities reporting under IFRS may sometimes be limited and need to be aware of the impact that each of the approaches has on the depreciation charge that is reported. Given this, detailed disclosures are essential.

16.1.3.C Unit of measure

Under the units of production method, an entity assigns an equal amount of cost to each unit produced. Determining the appropriate unit by which to measure production requires a significant amount of judgement. An entity could measure the units of production by reference to physical units or, when different minerals are produced in a common process, cost could be allocated between the different minerals on the basis of their relative sales prices.

(a) Physical units of production method

If an entity uses the physical units of production method, each physical unit of reserves (such as barrels, tonnes, ounces, gallons, and cubic metres) produced is assigned a *pro rata* portion of undepreciated costs less residual value.

Example 41.16: Physical units of production method[133]

If an entity produces 100 units during the current period and the estimated remaining commercial reserves at the end of the period are 1,900 units, the units available would be 2,000. The fractional part of the depreciable basis to be charged to depreciation expense would be 100/2,000. Therefore, if the depreciable basis was 5,000 monetary units, the depreciation for the period would be 250 monetary units.

In applying the physical units of production method a mining company needs to decide whether to use either the quantity of ore produced or the quantity of mineral contained in the ore as the unit of measure.[134] Similarly, an oil and gas company needs to decide whether to use either the volume of hydrocarbons or the volume of hydrocarbons plus gas, water and other materials. When mining different grades of ore, a mining company's gross margin on the subsequent sale of minerals will fluctuate far less when it uses the quantity of minerals as its unit of measure. While a large part of the wear and tear of equipment used in mining is closely related to the quantity of ore produced, the economic benefits are more closely related to the quantity of mineral contained in the ore. Therefore, both approaches are currently considered to be acceptable under IFRS.

(b) Revenue-based units of production method

Another possible approach in applying the units of production method that may have been used by some entities previously is to measure the units produced based on the gross selling price of mineral.[135] However, this approach is no longer permitted. This is because as part of the 2011-2013 cycle of annual improvements the IASB approved an amendment to IAS 16 and IAS 38 to clarify that a revenue-based depreciation or amortisation method would not be appropriate.

16.1.3.D Joint and by-products

In the extractive industries it is common for more than one product to be extracted from the same reserves (e.g. copper mines often produce gold and silver; lead and zinc are often found together; and many oil fields produce both oil and gas). When the ratio between the joint products or between the main product and the by-products is stable, this does not pose any complications. Also, if the value of the by-products is immaterial then it will often be acceptable to base the depreciation charge on the main product. In other cases, however, it will be necessary to define a unit of measure that takes into account all minerals produced. The IASC's Issues Paper listed the following approaches in defining conversion factors for calculating such a unit of measure:[136]

'(a) physical characteristics:
 (i) based on volume: such as barrels, litres, gallons, thousand cubic feet or cubic metres;
 (ii) based on weight: such as tonnes, pounds, and kilograms; or
 (iii) based on energy content (British thermal units) of oil and gas;
(b) gross revenues for the period in relation to estimated total gross revenues of the current period and future periods (more commonly seen in the mining sector); and
(c) net revenues for the period in relation to total net revenues of the current and future periods'.

Calculation of a conversion factor based on volume or weight has the benefit of being easy to apply and can lead to satisfactory results if the relative value of the products is fairly stable. For example, some mining companies that produce both gold and silver from the same mines express their production in millions of ounces of silver equivalent. This is calculated as the sum of the ounces of silver produced plus their ounces of gold produced multiplied by some ratio of the gold price divided by the silver price. For example, if the gold price was $900 and the silver price was $12, this would provide a ratio of 1/75 – so the quantity of gold would be multiplied by 75 to determine the equivalent ounces of silver. However these ratios can change depending on the relationship between gold and silver.

Calculation of a conversion factor based on other physical characteristics is quite common in the oil and gas sector. Typically production and reserves in oil fields are expressed in millions of barrels of oil equivalent (mmboe), which is calculated by dividing the quantity of gas expressed in thousands of cubic feet by 6 and adding that to the quantity of oil expressed in barrels. This conversion is based on the fact that one barrel of oil contains as much energy as 6,000 cubic feet of gas. While this approach is commonly used, it is important to recognise two limiting factors: the actual energy conversion factor will not always be 1:6 but may vary between 1:5½ to 1:6½ and the market price of gas per unit of energy (typically BTU) is often lower than that of oil because of government price controls and the need for expensive infrastructure to deliver gas to end users.

An approach that is commonly used (more so in the mining sector than the oil and gas sector) in calculating a conversion factor when joint products are extracted, is to base it on gross revenues. As discussed at 16.1.3.C above, the main drawback of this method is that it requires an entity to forecast future commodity prices. Despite this drawback, there will be situations where no other viable alternative exists for calculating an appropriate conversion factor.

Finally, it is possible to calculate a conversion factor based on net revenue after deducting certain direct processing costs. An argument in favour of this method is that gross revenues do not necessarily measure the economic benefits from an asset. However, taken to an extreme this argument would lead down a path where no depreciation is charged in unprofitable years, which is clearly not an acceptable practice.

Accounting for the sale of joint products and by-products is addressed at 14.2 above.

16.2 Block caving – depreciation, depletion and amortisation (mining)

Given the nature of mining operations, determining the appropriate unit of account has always been a matter requiring considerable judgement for mining entities. See 4 above for further discussion. This issue is particularly relevant when assessing how to account for new mining techniques. For example, block cave mining is one such mining technique that is being increasingly proposed or used for a number of deposits worldwide.

Block cave mining is a mass mining method that allows for the bulk mining of large, relatively lower grade, ore bodies for which the grade is consistently distributed throughout. The word 'block' refers to the layout of the mine – which effectively divides the ore body into large sections, with areas that can be several thousand square metres in size. This approach adopts a mine design and process which involves the creation of an undercut by fracturing the rock section underneath the block through the use of blasting. This blasting destroys the rock's ability to support the block above. Caving of the rock mass then occurs under the natural forces of gravity (which can be in the order of millions of tonnes), when a sufficient amount of rock has been removed underneath the block. The broken ore is then removed from the base of the block. This mine activity occurs without the need for drilling and blasting, as the ore above continues to fall while the broken ore beneath is removed. Broken ore is removed from the area at the extraction level through the use of a grid of draw points. These effectively funnel the broken ore down to a particular point so that it can be collected and removed for further processing.

Block caving has been applied to large scale extraction of various metals and minerals, sometimes in thick beds of ore but more usually in steep to vertical masses. Examples of block caving operations include Northparkes (Australia), Palabora (South Africa), Questa Mine (New Mexico) and Freeport (Indonesia).[137]

Block cave mining does require substantial upfront development costs, as initial underground access followed by large excavations (undercutting), must be completed to gain access and initially 'undermine' the block that is to cave. In addition, large underground and above ground haulage and milling infrastructure must be constructed to extract and then process the ore that a successful cave will generate.

One of the key issues to be addressed is how these substantial upfront development costs, in addition to the ongoing development costs associated with each block (i.e. to extend the undercutting beneath each new block and construct the draw points for each block) should be treated for depreciation or amortisation.

Generally these costs are depreciated or amortised on a units of production basis – therefore in determining useful life, it is necessary to determine what the appropriate reserves base should be for each of these different types of costs. For example, in relation to the costs associated with initially going underground and constructing the main haulage tunnel which will be used to access and extract the reserves from the entire ore body, the useful life associated with such assets may be the reserves of the entire ore body.

In relation to the costs associated in constructing the milling infrastructure, it is possible that such assets may be used to process ore from multiple ore bodies. Therefore, the useful life of such assets may be the reserves of multiple ore bodies. However, this will depend upon the specific facts and circumstances of the particular development.

For those costs associated with each individual block, e.g. the undercutting costs directly attributable to each block and the costs associated in constructing the draw points for that block, the appropriate reserves base may potentially only be those to be extracted from that particular block, which may only be a component of the entire ore body.

The approach adopted by each entity will be determined by the specific facts and circumstances of each mine development, such as the nature of the block cave mining technique employed and how the associated assets will be used. Such an assessment will require entities to exercise considerable judgement. Appropriate disclosures are recommended where significant judgements and estimates are considered material.

17 LONG-TERM CONTRACTS AND LEASES

Given the nature of the extractive industries, mining companies and oil and gas companies regularly enter into a wide range of long-term contracts. These may relate to the provision of services or the sale of goods. There are a number of potential issues to be addressed when considering the accounting for these arrangements, these are discussed below.

17.1 Embedded leases

IFRIC 4 notes that there are arrangements that do not take the legal form of a lease but that convey rights to use items for agreed periods of time in return for a payment or series of payments. *[IFRIC 4.1]*.

The Interpretation focuses on the accounting implications of the following, all of which are forms of arrangements found in the extractive industries and in all of which an entity (the supplier) conveys a right to use an asset to another entity (the purchaser), together with related services or outputs:

- outsourcing arrangements;
- arrangements where suppliers of network capacity enter into contracts to provide purchasers with rights to capacity; and
- take-or-pay and similar contracts, in which purchasers must make specified payments regardless of whether they take delivery of the contracted products or services (e.g. where purchasers are committed to acquiring substantially all of the output of a supplier's power generator). *[IFRIC 4.1]*. See 17.2 below.

Other types of agreements common in the extractive industries and which would need to be assessed for the existence of embedded leases include:

- service arrangements – such as contract mining services arrangements or oilfield services arrangements;
- throughput arrangements (which may take the form of a take-or-pay arrangement);
- tolling contracts (see 18 below);
- contractor facilities located on the mining company's or oil and gas company's property;
- energy-related or utility contracts, e.g. gas, electricity, telecommunications, water; or
- transportation/freight services contracts.

IFRIC 4 specifies that one of these types of arrangements (or part thereof) could be within the scope of IAS 17 if it met the definition of a lease, e.g. if it conveyed to the lessee the right to use an asset for an agreed period of time in return for a payment or series of payments. *[IFRIC 4.BC2]*. IAS 17 applies to the lease element of the arrangement notwithstanding the related services or outputs because IAS 17 applies to 'agreements that transfer the right to use assets even though substantial services by the lessor may be called for in connection with the operation or maintenance of such assets.' *[IAS 17.3]*. This is regardless of the fact that the arrangement is not described as a lease and is likely to grant rights that are significantly different from those in a formal lease agreement. The detailed requirements of IFRIC 4 are discussed in Chapter 24 at 2.1. Note that the requirements of IFRS 16 have not been considered in this chapter but a detailed analysis of the impact of this new standard can be found at Chapter 25.

Engie SA has an accounting policy addressing IFRIC 4.

Extract 41.48: Engie SA (2015)

NOTES TO THE CONSOLIDATED FINANCIAL STATEMENTS [extract]

NOTE 1 ACCOUNTING STANDARDS AND METHODS [extract]

1.4 Accounting methods [extract]

1.4.9 Leases [extract]

1.4.9.3 Accounting for arrangements that contain a lease

IFRIC 4 deals with the identification of services and take-or-pay sales or purchasing contracts that do not take the legal form of a lease but convey rights to customers/suppliers to use an asset or a group of assets in return for a payment or a series of fixed payments. Contracts meeting these criteria should be identified as either operating leases or finance leases. In the latter case, a finance receivable should be recognized to reflect the financing deemed to be granted by the Group where it is considered as acting as lessor and its customers as lessees.

The Group is concerned by this interpretation mainly with respect to:

- some energy purchase and sale contracts, particularly where the contract conveys to the purchaser of the energy an exclusive right to use a production asset;
- certain contracts with industrial customers relating to assets held by the Group.

17.2 Take-or-pay contracts

A 'take-or-pay' contract is a specific type of long-term commodity-based sales agreement between a customer and a supplier in which the pricing terms are set for a specified minimum quantity of a particular good or service. The customer must pay the minimum amount as per the contract, even if it does not take the volumes. There may also be options for additional volumes in excess of the minimum. Take-or-pay contracts for the supply of gas are particularly common, because entities developing gas fields need to make very significant investments in infrastructure such as pipelines, liquefaction plants and shipping terminals, to make transport of gas to the end-consumer economically viable. In order to raise the funds to finance such investments, it is crucial to know that there is a profitable market for the gas, as it cannot easily be diverted and sold in an alternative market or to an alternative customer.

While take-or-pay contracts perhaps most commonly involve the supply of gas, they can also include other arrangements such as contracts for pipeline capacity or LNG regasification facilities. Take-or-pay contracts also are used in the mining sector, e.g. with some coal contracts, though less frequently than in the oil and gas sector. Often take-or-pay contracts permit the purchaser to recover payments for quantities not taken, by allowing the purchaser to take more than the minimum in later years and to apply the previously paid-for undertake amount towards the cost of product taken in the later years.[138]

The following issues need to be considered in accounting for take-or-pay contracts:

- *Structured entities* – If a take-or-pay contract transfers the majority of the risks and rewards from the development of a mine or gas field to the customer, it is necessary to consider whether the entity developing the gas field has, in effect, become a structured entity of that customer and therefore, the customer needs to consider the level of influence it has over that mining entity or oil and gas entity (see Chapter 6 at 4.4.1);
- *Embedded leases* – Take-or-pay contracts are often for a very significant portion of the output of the gas field that it relates to. Therefore, as illustrated in Extract 41.48 above, the operator and customer need to consider whether the take-or-pay contract contains a lease of the related assets (see 17.1 above);
- *Embedded derivatives* – As illustrated in Extract 41.49 below, the price of gas sold under take-or-pay contracts is often based on a 'basket' of fuel prices and/or inflation price indices. If there is an active market for gas then this often means that an embedded derivative needs to be separated from the underlying host take-or-pay contract (see 13.2 above);
- *Guarantees* – Lenders are often willing to provide funding for the development of a gas field only if the operator can present a solid business case, which includes a 'guaranteed' stream of revenue from a reputable customer. In such cases, the take-or-pay contract acts as a form of credit enhancement or possibly as a guarantee. The operator and customer may need to consider whether the take-or-pay arrangement includes a guarantee that should be accounted for such under IAS 39 (see Chapter 43 at 3.4);
- *Make-up product and undertake* – A customer that fails to take the specified volume during the period specified must nevertheless pay for the agreed-volume. However, a take-or-pay contract sometimes permits the customer to take an equivalent amount of production (makeup product) at a later date after the payment for the guaranteed amount has been made (see 12.7.14 above and 17.2.1 below).

Extract 41.49 below from the financial statements of Engie SA gives an overview of some of these important terms and conditions that exist in take-or-pay contracts.

Extract 41.49: Engie SA (2015)

2015 Registration Document

2 Risk factors [extract]

2.3 Operating risks[extract]

2.3.1 Purchases and sales [extract]

2.3.1.1 Purchase and sale of natural gas

The Group has established a portfolio composed in part of long-term, take-or-pay contracts (see Section 1.3.1.6.1 "Central Western Europe").

In case of major gas supply interruption (for example, due to an interruption of Russian deliveries or an interruption of transit in Ukraine) or an interruption of LNG supply (for example, from Yemen or Egypt) , the replacement cost for gas, including transportation, could be higher and affect the Group's margins. To mitigate this risk, the Group has a number of tools for flexibility and modulation (flexibility in long-term contracts, storage and regasification capacity, and purchasing in the marketplaces) as well as a diversified portfolio.

Prices of long-term purchase contracts (partially indexed to the price indices of oil products) may be decorrelated from selling prices or prices in the gas markets. This spread might have a significant impact on the Group's results. Long-term contracts include price adjustment clauses, so that the economic balance between producer and buyer can be altered. The Group's buy/sell margin may therefore change according to price adjustments in LNG or gaseous gas contracts and the state of the gas market in general.

Negotiations in recent years have led to the integration of market indices in long-term contracts and/or the reduction of the difference between the contract price and market price. They have also led to an increased frequency in price revisions.

1 Presentation of the Group [extract]

1.3 Description of business lines in 2015 [extract]

1.3.1 Energy Europe business line [extract]

1.3.1.6 Description of activities [extract]

1.3.1.6.1 Central Western Europe [extract]

Long-term gas contracts [extract]

OSS purchases natural gas under long-term contracts from its main suppliers. The aim of the supply strategy is to ensure the competitiveness of the portfolio and security of supply to the Group's customers, mainly through geographical diversification of resources and constant adaptation of the portfolio to the market situation.

In line with market practice, the long-term procurement contracts contain volume clauses: minimum volumes to be taken in a period (take-or-pay), transfer of withdrawals to a later period (make-up), or deduction of volumes withdrawn against a prior period (carry forward).

The contracts contain clauses that enable periodic revision of prices according to changes in the market, either on a regular basis or by way of exception. The parties are then required to negotiate in good faith and may, in the event of disagreement, revert to arbitration.

In 2015, EMT continued to renegotiate contracts with its main suppliers to adapt these contracts to new market conditions. As of December 31, 2015, over 60% of the long-term contract portfolio volumes in Europe were indexed to the price of gas sold on the spot market.

17.2.1 Make-up product and undertake

Under some take-or-pay arrangements, a customer who is required to pay for the product not taken will often have no right of future recovery. The customer should recognise an expense equal to the payment made, while the operator recognises the same amount as revenue. However, if the substance of the relationship between the operator and customer is such that a renegotiation of the arrangement is probable then it may be more appropriate for the operator to recognise the penalty payment as deferred revenue. The customer, however, should still recognise an expense in this case as it does not have a legal right to receive reimbursement or makeup product.[139]

The accounting is different when a customer that is required to pay for product not taken has a right to take makeup product in the future.

In this case, the operator would recognise deferred revenue equal to the amount paid for the 'undertake' as it represents an obligation to provide the product in the future. The operator only recognises revenue in accordance with IAS 18 once the make-up product has been taken by the customer. *[IAS 18.14(a)]*. Only once the make-up period has expired or it is clear that the purchaser has become unable to take the product, would the liability be eliminated and revenue recognised.[140] For a discussion on the potential impacts of IFRS 15 see 12.7.14 above.

From the customer's perspective, it would normally recognise a prepaid amount representing the make-up product that it is entitled to receive in the future. However, if the customer is entitled to more make-up product than it can sell, it may need to recognise an impairment charge.

Extract 41.50 below illustrates how Tullow Oil as an operator accounts for undertakes.

Extract 41.50: Tullow Oil plc (2015)

ACCOUNTING POLICIES [extract]

Year ended 31 December 2015

(g) Revenue [extract]

Sales revenue represents the sales value, net of VAT of the Group's share of liftings in the year together with tariff income. Revenue is recognised when goods are delivered and title has passed.

Revenues received under take-or-pay sales contracts in respect of undelivered volumes are accounted for as deferred income.

18 TOLLING ARRANGEMENTS

In the mining sector it is common for entities to provide raw material to a smelter or refiner for further processing. If the raw material is sold to the smelter or refiner and the relevant criteria are satisfied, the mining company recognises revenue in accordance with IAS 18. However, under a 'tolling' arrangement a mining company generally supplies, without transferring ownership, raw material to a smelter or refiner which processes it for a fee and then returns the finished product to the customer. Alternatively, the mining company may sell the raw material to the smelter or refiner, but is required to repurchase the finished product. In the latter two situations, no revenue should be recognised when the raw material is shipped to the smelter or refiner as there has not been a transfer of the risks and rewards.

An entity should carefully assess the terms and conditions of its tolling arrangements to determine:

- when it is appropriate to recognise revenue;
- whether those arrangements contain embedded leases that require separation under IFRIC 4 (see 17.1 above);
- whether the tolling arrangement is part of a series of transactions with a joint arrangement; and
- whether the toll processing entity is a structured entity that requires consolidation under IFRS 10 (see Chapter 6 at 4.4.1 for more information).

Extract 41.51 below describes a tolling arrangement between Norsk Hydro and one of its joint arrangements.

Extract 41.51: Norsk Hydro ASA (2013)

Notes to the consolidated financial statements [extract]

Note 26 – Investments in jointly controlled entities [extract]

Aluminium Norf GmbH (Alunorf) located in Germany is the world's largest rolling mill and is owned by Hydro and Hindalco Industries (50 percent each). Alunorf produces flat rolled products from raw material from the partners based on a tolling arrangement. Sales from Alunorf to Hydro amounted to NOK 1,499 million in 2013 and NOK 1,423 million in 2012. Hydro's capital and financing commitments are regulated in the Joint Venture agreement. Alunorf has investment commitments amounting to NOK 444 million as of December 31, 2013. Hydro's financing commitment based on its interest is NOK 189 million as of December 31, 2013. Alunorf is part of Rolled Products.

For a discussion on the potential impacts of IFRS 15 on repurchase agreements see 12.7.12 above.

19 TAXATION

As mentioned at 1.1 above, one of the characteristics of the extractive industries is the intense government involvement in their activities, which ranges from 'outright governmental ownership of some (especially petroleum) or all minerals to unusual tax benefits or penalties, price controls, restrictions on imports and exports, restrictions on production and distribution, environmental and health and safety regulations, and others'.[141]

Mining companies and oil and gas companies typically need to make payments to governments in their capacity as:

- owner of the mineral resources;
- co-owner or joint arrangement partner in the projects;
- regulator of, among other things, environmental matters and health and safety matters; and
- tax authority.

The total payment to a government is often described as the 'government take'. This includes fixed payments or variable payments that are based on production, revenue, or a net profit figure; and which may take the form of fees, bonuses, royalties or taxes.

Determining whether a payment to government meets the definition of income tax is not straightforward.

IAS 12 should be applied in accounting for income taxes, defined as including:

(a) all domestic and foreign taxes which are based on taxable profits; and

(b) taxes, such as withholding taxes, which are payable by a subsidiary, associate or joint arrangements on distributions to the reporting entity. *[IAS 12.1-2]*.

As discussed in Chapter 31 at 4.1, it is not altogether clear what an income tax actually is. In the extractive industries the main problem with the definition in IAS 12 occurs when:

(a) a government raises 'taxes' on sub-components of net profit (e.g. net profit before financing costs or revenue minus allowed costs); or

(b) there is a mandatory government participation in certain projects that entitle the government to a share of profits as defined in a joint operating agreement.

A considerable amount of judgement is required to determine whether a particular arrangement falls within the definition of 'income tax' under IAS 12 or whether it is another form of government take. From a commercial perspective the overall share of the economic benefits that the government takes is much more important than the distinction between its different forms. In practice, most governments receive benefits from extractive activities in several different ways, as discussed below. Governments can choose any of these methods to increase or decrease their share of the benefits.

However, the distinction is crucial given the considerable differences in the accounting treatments and disclosures that apply to income taxes, other taxes, fees and government participations. For example, it will affect where these amounts are presented in the profit or loss, e.g. in operating costs or income tax expense; and it will determine whether deferred tax balances are required to be recognised and the related disclosures provided.

19.1 Excise duties, production taxes and severance taxes

Excise duties, production taxes and severance taxes result in payments that are due on production (or severance) of minerals from the earth. Depending on the jurisdiction and the type of mineral involved, they are calculated:

(a) as a fixed amount per unit produced;

(b) as a percentage of the value of the minerals produced; or

(c) based on revenue minus certain allowable costs.

19.1.1 Production-based taxation

If the tax is based on a fixed amount per unit produced or as a percentage of the value of the minerals produced, then it will not meet the definition of an income tax under IAS 12. In these cases the normal principles of liability recognition under IAS 37 apply in recognising the tax charge.

Another issue that arises is whether these taxes are, in effect, collected by the entity from customers on behalf of the taxing authority, as an agent. In other cases, the taxpayer's role is more in the nature of principal than agent. The regulations differ significantly from one country to another. The practical accounting issue that arises concerns the interpretation of paragraph 8 of IAS 18; should excise duties, production taxes and severance taxes be deducted from revenue (net presentation) or included in the production costs and, therefore, revenue (gross presentation)? *[IAS 18.8]*.

The appropriate accounting treatment will depend on the particular circumstances. In determining whether gross or net presentation is appropriate, the entity needs to consider whether it is acting in a manner similar to that of an agent or principal. For further discussion of principal versus agent under IAS 18 see Chapter 29 at 3.3 and under IFRS 15 see 12.7.7 above and Chapter 30 at 4.4.

Given that excise duties, production taxes and severance taxes are aimed at taxing the production of minerals rather than the sale of minerals, they are considered to be a tax on extractive activities rather than a tax collected by a mining company or oil and gas company on behalf of the government. Based on this, the tax should be presented as a production cost.

However, it may be considered that when the excise duty, production tax or severance tax is payable in kind, that the mining company or oil and gas company never receives any of the benefits associated with the production of the associated minerals. Hence, it would be more appropriate to present revenue net of the production or severance tax as it is in substance the same as a royalty payment. For this reason, revenue is generally presented net of excise duties, as illustrated by Extract 41.52 below from the financial statements of Royal Dutch Shell.

> *Extract 41.52: Royal Dutch Shell plc (2015)*
>
> **NOTES TO THE CONSOLIDATED FINANCIAL STATEMENTS** [extract]
>
> **2 KEY ACCOUNTING POLICIES, JUDGEMENTS AND ESTIMATES** [extract]
>
> **Revenue recognition** [extract]
>
> Revenue from sales of oil, natural gas, chemicals and other products is recognised at the fair value of consideration received or receivable, after deducting sales taxes, excise duties and similar levies, when the significant risks and rewards of ownership have been transferred, which is when title passes to the customer. For sales by Upstream operations this generally occurs when product is physically transferred into a vessel, pipe or other delivery mechanism; for sales by refining operations, it is either when product is placed onboard a vessel or offloaded from the vessel, depending on the contractually agreed terms; and for wholesale sales of oil products and chemicals it is either at the point of delivery or the point of receipt, depending on contractual conditions.

19.1.2 Petroleum revenue tax (or resource rent tax)

Determining whether a petroleum revenue tax (or resource rent tax) is a production- or profit-based tax is often not straightforward. Example 41.17 below describes the petroleum revenue tax in the United Kingdom.

Example 41.17: Petroleum revenue tax[142]

Petroleum revenue tax (PRT) is a special tax that seeks to tax a high proportion of the economic rent (super-profits) from the exploitation of the UK's oil and gas. PRT is a cash-based tax that is levied on a field-by-field basis: in general, the costs of developing and running a field can only be set against the profits generated by that field. Any losses, e.g. arising from unused expenditure relief, can be carried back or forward within the field indefinitely. There is also a range of reliefs, including:

- oil allowance – a PRT-free slice of production;
- supplement – a proxy for interest and other financing costs;
- Tariff Receipts Allowance (TRA) – participators owning assets, for example pipelines, relating to one field will sometimes allow participators from other fields to share the use of the asset in return for the payment of tariffs, and TRA relieves some of the tariffs received from PRT;
- exemption from PRT for gas sold to British Gas under a pre-July 1975 contract; and
- cross-field relief for research expenditure.

PRT is currently charged at 50% on profits after these allowances. For a limited period, safeguard relief then applies to ensure that PRT does not reduce the annual return in the early years of production of a field to below 15% of the historic capital expenditure on the field.

PRT was abolished on 16 March 1993 for all fields given development consent on or after that date. This was part of a package of PRT reforms which also included the reduction of the rate of PRT from 75 per cent to 50 per cent and the abolition of PRT relief for Exploration and Appraisal (E&A) expenditure.

The UK PRT is similar to an income tax in that the tax is a percentage of revenue minus certain costs. However, there are also a number of other features that are not commonly found in income taxes or in some other resource rent taxes:

- the oil allowance is a physical quantity of oil that is PRT exempt in each field, subject to a cumulative maximum over the life of the field; and
- the tax is levied on individual oil fields rather than the entity owning the oil field as a whole.

There are many different types of petroleum revenue taxes (or resource rent taxes) around the world, some of which are clearly not income taxes, while others have some of the characteristics of an income tax. In determining whether a particular production tax meets the definition of an income tax under IAS 12, an entity will need to assess whether or not the tax is based on (or closely enough linked to) net profit for the period. If it does not meet the definition of an income tax, an entity should develop an accounting policy under the hierarchy in IAS 8.

Practice is mixed, which means that while some entities may treat a particular petroleum revenue tax (or resource rent tax) as an income tax under IAS 12 and hence provide for current and deferred taxes (see Extract 41.53 below), others may consider the same tax to be outside the scope of IAS 12.

Extract 41.53: Woodside Petroleum Ltd (2015)

NOTES TO THE FINANCIAL STATEMENTS A: Earnings for the year [extract]

for the year ended 31 December 2015

A.4 Taxes [extract]

Key estimates and judgements [extract]

(a) Income tax classification [extract]

[...] PRRT is considered, for accounting purposes, to be an income tax.

As illustrated in Extract 41.54 below, BHP Billiton assesses resource rent taxes and royalties individually to determine whether they meet the definition of an income tax or not.

> *Extract 41.54: BHP Billiton plc (2015)*
>
> **7.1.6 Notes to Financial Statements** [extract]
>
> **43 Significant accounting policies** [extract]
>
> **(i) Taxation** [extract]
>
> Royalties and resource rent taxes are treated as taxation arrangements when they have the characteristics of a tax. This is considered to be the case when they are imposed under government authority and the amount payable is calculated by reference to revenue derived (net of any allowable deductions) after adjustment for temporary differences. For such arrangements, current and deferred tax is provided on the same basis as described above for other forms of taxation. Obligations arising from royalty arrangements that do not satisfy these criteria are recognised as current provisions and included in expenses.

19.2 Grossing up of notional quantities withheld

Many production sharing contracts provide that the income tax to which the contractor is subject is deemed to have been paid to the government as part of the payment of profit oil to the government or its representative (e.g. the designated national oil company) (see 5.3 above). This raises the question as to whether an entity should be presenting current and deferred taxation arising from such 'notional' income tax, which is only deemed to have been paid, on a net or a gross basis.

Example 41.18: Grossing up of notional quantities withheld

Entity A is the operator of an oil field that produces 10 million barrels of oil per year. Under the production sharing contract between entity A and the national government, entity A and the government are entitled to 4,000,000 and 6,000,000 barrels of oil, respectively. The production sharing contract includes the following clause:

> 'The share of the profit petroleum to which the government is entitled in any calendar year in accordance with the production sharing contract shall be deemed to include a portion representing the corporate income tax imposed upon and due by entity A, and which will be paid directly by the government on behalf of entity A to the appropriate tax authorities.'

Assuming the following facts, how should entity A account for the income tax that it is deemed to have paid in 2016:

- the normal corporate income tax rate in the country in which entity A operates is 40%;
- entity A made a net profit of USD 30 million in 2016; and
- the average oil price during the year was USD 50/barrel.

Gross presentation

Entity A's profit after 40% corporate income tax was USD 30 million. Therefore, its profit before tax would have been USD 50 million (i.e. USD 30 million ÷ (100% – 40%)). In other words, the government is deemed to have paid corporate income tax of USD 20 million on behalf of entity A. Therefore, the government is deemed to have taken 400,000 barrels (i.e. USD 20 million ÷ USD 50/barrel) out of entity A's share of the production. Hence, entity A's share of production before corporate income tax was 4,400,000 barrels (i.e. 4,000,000 barrels + 400,000 barrels).

Net presentation

Under the net presentation approach, entity A ignores the corporate income tax that was deemed to have been paid by the government because it is not a transaction that entity A was party to *or* because the deemed transaction did not actually take place.

The disadvantage of presenting such tax on a gross basis is that the combined production attributed to the entity and that attributable to the government exceeds the total quantity of oil that is actually produced (i.e. in the above example the government and entity A would report a combined production of 10.4 million barrels whereas actual production was only 10 million barrels). Similarly, if the reserves were to be expressed on the same basis as revenues, the reserves reported by the entity would include oil reserves that it would not actually be entitled to.

On the other hand, if the host country has a well-established income tax regime that falls under the authority of the ministry of finance and the production sharing contract requires an income tax return to be filed, then the entity would have a legal liability to pay the tax until the date on which the national oil company or the ministry responsible for extractive activities (e.g. the ministry of mines, industry and energy) pays the tax on its behalf. In such cases it may be appropriate to present revenue and income tax on a gross basis.

20 EVENTS AFTER THE REPORTING PERIOD

20.1 Reserves proven after the reporting period

IAS 10 – *Events after the Reporting Period* – distinguishes between two types of events:

- adjusting events after the reporting period being those that provide evidence of conditions that existed at the end of the reporting period ; and
- non adjusting events after the reporting period being those that are indicative of conditions that arose after the reporting period. *[IAS 10.3]*.

This raises the question as to how an entity should deal with information regarding mineral reserves that it obtains after the end of its reporting period, but before its financial statements are authorised for issue i.e. finalised. For example, suppose that an entity concludes after the year-end that its remaining mineral reserves at that date were not 10 million barrels (or tonnes) but only 8 million barrels (or tonnes). As discussed at 16.1.3.A above, a company needs to assess whether such a change in mineral reserves should be treated as an adjusting event in accordance with IAS 10 (i.e. the new estimate provides evidence of conditions that existed previously) or as a change in estimate in accordance with IAS 8 (i.e. the new estimate resulted from new information or new developments).

20.2 Business combinations – application of the acquisition method

If the initial accounting for a business combination can be determined only provisionally by the end of the period in which the combination is effected – because either the fair values to be assigned to the acquiree's identifiable assets, liabilities or contingent liabilities or the fair value of the combination can be determined only provisionally – the acquirer should account for the combination using those provisional values. Where, as a result of completing the initial accounting within 12 months from the acquisition date, adjustments to the provisional values have been found to be necessary, IFRS 3 requires them to be recognised from the acquisition date. *[IFRS 3.45]*. Specifically IFRS 3 states that the provisional values are to be retrospectively adjusted to reflect new information obtained about facts and circumstances that existed as at the acquisition date and, if known, would have affected the measurement of the amounts recognised as at that date. This raises the question of how an entity should account for new information that it receives regarding an acquiree's reserves before it has finalised its acquisition accounting.

Example 41.19: Acquisition of an entity that owns mineral reserves

Entity A acquires Entity B for €27 million at 31 October 2015. At the time it assigned the following fair values to the acquired net assets:

	€ million
Mineral reserves (assuming reserves of 10 million barrels)	10
Other net assets acquired	5
Goodwill	12
Consideration transferred	27

At 30 June 2016, after conducting a drilling programme which commenced in March 2016, Entity A obtains information about the reserves (as at 30 June 2016), which when added to the production for the period (i.e. from 31 October 2015 to 30 June 2016) reveals that the mineral reserves at the date of acquisition were not 10 million barrels, as previously thought, but were only 8 million barrels.

Can Entity A revise its initial acquisition accounting to reflect the fact that the mineral reserves are only 8 million barrels, rather than 10 million?

The answer to this question is not straightforward and it is a matter of significant judgement which needs to be made based on the facts and circumstances of each individual situation.

IFRS 3 requires assets acquired and liabilities assumed to be measured at fair value as at the acquisition date. It then defines fair value as: the amount for which an asset could be exchanged, or a liability settled, between knowledgeable, willing parties in an arm's length transaction. The challenge with the new information obtained about the mineral reserves in Example 41.19 above is determining whether it provided new information about facts and circumstances that existed as at the acquisition date or whether it resulted from events that occurred after the acquisition date. As discussed in 16.1.3.A above, it is difficult to determine exactly what causes a reserve estimate to change, i.e. whether the facts and circumstances existed at acquisition date or whether it was due to new events.

In Example 41.19 above, the new reserves information arose as a result of a drilling programme that commenced five months after the acquisition date and it is not entirely clear why the reserves estimate changed. One may therefore conclude that as entity A should be valuing the mineral reserves acquired on the basis of information that a knowledgeable, willing party *would and could* reasonably have been expected to use in an arm's length transaction at 31 October 2015, that this new information should not have an impact on the provisional accounting. This is on the basis that this new information was not available at acquisition date and could not reasonably have been expected to be considered as part of the acquisition.

Similarly, if entity A had concluded at 30 June 2016 that its internal long-term oil price assumption was $80/barrel instead of $60/barrel that would not have any effect on the acquisition accounting. Entity A should be valuing the mineral reserves on the basis of information that a knowledgeable, willing party *would* have used in an arm's length transaction at 31 October 2015; this may, of course, have been neither $80 nor $60.

The conclusion may differ however, if the drilling programme had been completed and the information was available at acquisition date, but due to the pressures of completing the transaction, entity A had not been able to assess fully or take into account all of this information e.g. it had not had time to properly analyse all of the information available in the data room. In this instance, it would be appropriate to adjust the provisional accounting.

20.3 Completion of E&E activity after the reporting period

As discussed at 3.5.1 above, IFRS 6 requires E&E assets to be tested for impairment when exploration for and evaluation of mineral resources in the specific area have not led to the discovery of commercially viable quantities of mineral resources and the entity has decided to discontinue its activities in the specific area. *[IFRS 6.20]*. An entity that concludes, after its reporting period, that an exploration and evaluation project is unsuccessful, should account for this conclusion as:

- a *non-adjusting event* if the conclusion is indicative of conditions that arose after the reporting period, for example new information or new developments that did not offer greater clarity concerning the conditions that existed at the end of the reporting period (one possible example may be drilling that only commenced after reporting date). The new information or new developments are considered to be changes in accounting estimates under IAS 8. Also, based on the information that existed at the reporting period, the fair value less costs of disposal of the underlying E&E asset might well have been in excess of its carrying amount; *[IAS 8.5]*
- an *adjusting event* if the decision not to sanction the project for development was based on information that existed at the reporting date. Failure to use, or misuse of, reliable information that was available when financial statements for those periods were authorised for issue and could reasonably be expected to have been obtained and taken into account in the preparation and presentation of those financial statements, would constitute an error under IAS 8. *[IAS 8.5]*.

Evaluating whether information obtained subsequent to the reporting period but before the financial statements are authorised for issue is an adjusting or non-adjusting events may require significant judgement. The conditions should be carefully evaluated based on the facts and circumstances of each individual situation.

21 GLOSSARY

The glossary below defines some of the terms and abbreviations commonly used in the extractive industries.[143]

Abandon	To discontinue attempts to produce oil or gas from a well or lease, plug the reservoir in accordance with regulatory requirements and recover equipment.
Area-of-interest method	An accounting concept by which costs incurred for individual geological or geographical areas that have characteristics conducive to containing a mineral reserve are deferred as assets pending determination of whether commercial reserves are found. If the area of interest is found to contain commercial reserves, the accumulated costs are capitalised. If the area is found to contain no commercial reserves, the accumulated costs are charged to expense.
Barrels of oil equivalent (BOE)	Using prices or heating content, units of sulphur, condensate, natural gas and by products are converted to and expressed in equivalent barrels of oil for standard measurement purposes.
British Thermal Unit (BTU)	A measure of the amount of heat required to raise the temperature of one pound of water one degree Fahrenheit at the temperature at which water has its greatest density (39 degrees Fahrenheit).
Bullion	Metal in bars, ingots or other uncoined form.
Carried interest	An agreement by which an entity that contracts to operate a mineral property and, therefore, agrees to incur exploration or development costs (the carrying party) is entitled to recover the costs incurred (and usually an amount in addition to actual costs incurred) before the entity that originally owned the mineral interest (the carried party) is entitled to share in revenues from production.
Carried party	The party for whom funds are advances in a carried interest arrangement.
Carrying party	The party advancing funds in a carried interest agreement.
Concession	A contract, similar to a mineral lease, under which the government owning mineral rights grants the concessionaire the right to explore, develop, and produce the minerals.

Cost recovery oil	Oil revenue paid to an operating entity to enable that entity to recover its operating costs and specified exploration and development costs from a specified percentage of oil revenues remaining after the royalty payment to the property owner.
Customer smelter	A smelter which processes concentrates from independent mines. Concentrates may be purchased or the smelter may be contracted to do the processing for the independent company.
Delay rental	Annual payments by the lessee of a mineral property to the lessor until drilling has begun.
Delineation well	A well to define, or delineate, the boundaries of a reservoir.
Development well	A well drilled to gain access to oil or gas classified as proved reserves.
Downstream activities	The refining, processing, marketing, and distributing of petroleum, natural gas, or mined mineral (other than refining or processing that is necessary to make the minerals that have been mined or extracted capable of being sold).
Dry gas	Natural gas composed of vapours without liquids and which tends not to liquefy.
Dry hole	An exploratory or development well that does not contain oil or gas in commercial quantities.
Entitlements method	A method of revenue recognition by which a joint venturer records revenue based on the share of production for the period to which that venturer is entitled.
Exploratory well	A well drilled to find and produce oil or gas in an unproved area, to find a new reservoir in a field previously found to be productive of oil or gas in another reservoir, or to extend a known reservoir.
Farm out and farm in	An agreement by which the owner of operating rights in a mineral property (the farmor) transfers a part of that interest to a second party (the farmee) in return for the latter's paying all of the costs, or only specified costs, to explore the property and perhaps to carry out part or all of the development of the property if reserves are found.

Full cost method	An accounting concept by which all costs incurred in searching for, acquiring, and developing mineral reserves in a cost centre are capitalised, even though a specific cost clearly resulted from an effort that was a failure.
Geological and geophysical costs (G&G)	Costs of topographical, geological, geochemical, and geophysical studies.
Infill drilling	Technical and commercial analyses may support drilling additional producing wells to reduce the spacing beyond that utilised within the initial development plan. Infill drilling may have the combined effect of increasing recovery efficiency and accelerating production.
Joint operating agreement (JOA)	A contract between two parties to a sharing arrangement that sets out the rights and obligations to operate the property, if operating interests are owned by both parties after a sharing arrangement.
Overlift or underlift	Overlift is the excess of the amount of production that a participant in a joint venture has taken as compared to that participant's proportionate share of ownership in total production. Underlift is the shortfall in the amount of production that a participant in a joint venture has taken as compared to that participant's proportionate share of ownership in total production.
Production sharing contract (PSC)	A contract between a national oil company or the government of a host country and a contracting entity (contractor) to carry out oil and gas exploration and production activities in accordance with the terms of the contract, with the two parties sharing mineral output.
Profit oil	Revenue in excess of cost recovery oil and royalties.
Recompletion	The process of re-entering a previously completed well to install new equipment or to perform such services necessary to restore production.
Redetermination	A retroactive adjustment to the relative percentage interests of the participants in a field that is subject to an unitisation agreement.
Risk service contract	A contract by which an entity agrees to explore for, develop, and produce minerals on behalf of a host government in return for a fee paid by the host government.

Royalty	A portion of the proceeds from production, usually before deducting operating expenses, payable to a party having an interest in a lease.
Sales method	A method of revenue recognition by which a joint venturer records revenue based on the actual amount of product it has sold (or transferred downstream) during the period. No receivable or other asset is recorded for undertaken production (underlift) and no liability is recorded for overtaken production (overlift).
Stripping ratio	The ratio of tonnes removed as waste relative to the number of tonnes of ore removed from an open pit mine.
Successful efforts method	An accounting concept that capitalises only those upstream costs that lead directly to finding, acquiring and developing mineral reserves, while those costs that do not lead directly to finding, acquiring and developing mineral reserves are charged to expense.
Take-or-pay contracts	An agreement between a buyer and seller in which the buyer will still pay some amount even if the product or service is not provided. If the purchaser does not take the minimum quantity, payment is required for that minimum quantity at the contract price. Normally, deficiency amounts can be made up in future years if purchases are in excess of minimum amounts.
Unitisation	An agreement between two parties, each of which owns an interest in one or more mineral properties in an area, to cross-assign to one another a share of the interest in the mineral properties that each owns in the area; from that point forward they share, as agreed, in further costs and revenues related to the properties.
Upstream activities	Exploring for, finding, acquiring, and developing mineral reserves up to the point that the reserves are first capable of being sold or used, even if the entity intends to process them further.
Workovers	Major repairs, generally of oil and gas wells.

References

1 IASC Issues Paper, *Issues Paper Extractive Industries*, IASC, November 2000, 1.5.
2 Discussion Paper DP/2010/1, *Extractive Activities*, IASB, April 2010, P6.
3 DP/2010/1, 1.1.
4 DP/2010/1, 1.4-1.5.
5 DP/2010/1, 1.9.
6 DP/2010/1, 1.10.
7 DP/2010/2.1.
8 IASC Issues Paper, 1.16.
9 IASC Issues Paper, 1.18.
10 IASC Issues Paper, 2.3.
11 IASC Issues Paper, 2.5.
12 IASC Issues Paper, 2.6.
13 IASC Issues Paper, 2.10.
14 IASC Issues Paper, 2.12.
15 IASC Issues Paper, 2.24.
16 IASC Issues Paper, 2.26.
17 IASC Issues Paper, 2.27.
18 IASC Issues Paper, 2.29.
19 IASC Issues Paper, 2.29, 2.30.
20 IASC Issues Paper, 2.32.
21 IASC Issues Paper, 2.34.
22 IASC Issues Paper, 2.36.
23 IASC Issues Paper, 2.38.
24 IASC Issues Paper, 2.42.
25 Discussion Paper DP/2010/1, para. 2.48.
26 Discussion Paper DP/2010/1, para. 2.23.
27 SPE-PRMS, *Petroleum Resources Management Systems*, Society of Petroleum Engineers, 2007.
28 IASB Agenda Paper 13A, *Comparison of Petroleum and Minerals Reserves and Resource Classification Systems*, IASB, 22 June 2007, pp.3-4.
29 IASB Agenda Paper 13A, p.8 and SPE-PRMS, Figure 1-1.
30 SPE-PRMS, pp.2-3.
31 SPE-PRMS, pp.2-3.
32 SPE-PRMS, pp.10-11.
33 SPE-PRMS, pp.10-11.
34 SPE-PRMS, pp.10-11.
35 SPE-PRMS, pp.2-3.
36 SPE-PRMS, pp.2-3.
37 SPE-PRMS, pp.2-3.
38 SPE-PRMS, pp.2-3.
39 SPE-PRMS, pp.2-3.
40 SPE-PRMS, pp.6-9.
41 SPE-PRMS, pp.9-13.
42 SPE-PRMS, pp.13-19.
43 JORC Code, Australasian Code for Reporting of Exploration Results, Mineral Resources and Ore Reserves, Joint Ore Reserves Committee of the Australasian Institute of Mining and Metallurgy, Australian Institute of Geoscientists and Minerals Council of Australia (JORC), 2004, para. 1.
44 Weatherstone, p.5.
45 IASB Agenda Paper 13A, p.3.
46 J. M. Rendu, *Reporting Mineral Resources and Mineral Reserves in the United States of America – Technical and Regulatory Issues*, 20-25 August 2006, p.2.
47 CRIRSCO Template, *International Reporting Template for the public reporting of exploration results, mineral resources and mineral reserves*, CRIRSCO, November 2013, 3.
48 CRIRSCO Template, 4.
49 CRIRSCO Template, 5.
50 CRIRSCO Template, 8 and 11.
51 CRIRSCO Template, Figure 1.
52 CRIRSCO Template, 18.
53 CRIRSCO Template, 20.
54 CRIRSCO Template, 21.
55 CRIRSCO Template, 22.
56 CRIRSCO Template, 23.
57 CRIRSCO Template, 24.
58 CRIRSCO Template, 12.
59 CRIRSCO Template, 30.
60 CRIRSCO Template, 31.
61 CRIRSCO Template, 32.
62 Pre codification FAS 69, *Disclosures about Oil and Gas Producing Activities an amendment of FASB Statements 19, 25, 33, and 39*, FASB, November 1982, para. 10.
63 Rendu, pp.9 and 10.
64 IASB Agenda Paper 15C, *Possible principles for a historical cost accounting model that accompanies decision-useful disclosures of minerals and oil & gas reserves and resources*, IASB, 22 June 2007, 6.
65 *IASB Update*, September 2008, p.3.
66 *IFRIC Update*, January 2006, p.3.
67 IASC Issues Paper 4.18.
68 IASC Issues Paper 4.20.
69 IASC Issues Paper 4.45.
70 *IFRIC Update*, January 2006, p.3.

71 Amendments to IFRS 1, *Additional Exemptions for First-time Adopters*, IASB, July 2009, D8A.
72 IASC Issues Paper 4.16(b).
73 IASC Issues Paper 4.36.
74 IASC Issues Paper 4.39.
75 ASC 932-720-25-1, *Extractive Activities – Oil and Gas – Other Expenses – Recognition.*
76 ED 6, *Exploration for and Evaluation of Mineral Resources*, IASB, January 2004, 14.
77 IASC Issues Paper, 6.3.
78 IASC Issues Paper, 2.12.
79 IASC Issues Paper, 2.13.
80 IASC Issues Paper, 2.14.
81 IASC Issues Paper, 2.21.
82 IASC Issues Paper, 2.21.
83 IASC Issues Paper, Glossary.
84 IASC Issues Paper, 2.19.
85 IASC Issues Paper, 12.12(b).
86 IASC Issues Paper, 12.68.
87 IASC Issues Paper, 12.69.
88 IASC Issues Paper, 2.23.
89 *Guidelines for the Evaluation of Petroleum Reserves and Resources – A Supplement to the SPE/WPC Petroleum Reserves Definitions and the SPE/WPC/AAPG Petroleum Resources Definitions*, Society of Petroleum Engineers, 2001, p.120.
90 D. R. Jennings, J. B. Feiten and H. R. Brock, *Petroleum Accounting, Principles, Procedures, & Issues*, 5th edition, Professional Development Institute, Denton (Texas), pp.165-169.
91 IASC Issues Paper, 12.9.
92 SPE-PRMS, p.18.
93 Former Oil Industry Association Committee Statement of Recommended Practice *Accounting for Oil and Gas Exploration, Development, Production and Decommissioning Activities* (July 2001) "Former OIAC SORP" 149.
94 Former OIAC SORP 150.
95 Former OIAC SORP 16.
96 Former OIAC SORP para 144.
97 ASC 930-805-30-1 *Extractive Activities – Mining – Business Combinations – Initial Measurement* (pre-codification EITF 04-3, *Mining Assets: Impairment and Business Combinations*, EITF, March 2004).
98 *IFRIC Update*, January 2011.
99 IASC Issues Paper, 9.26.
100 AASB 1022 *Accounting for the Extractive Industries* (now superseded).
101 Former OIAC SORP.
102 AASB 1022 Accounting for the Extractive Industries (now superseded) para 62.
103 Former OIAC SORP) para 127.
104 IASC Issues Paper 10.27.
105 IASC Issues Paper 10.29, 10.32. Former OIAC SORP 114-121.
106 IASC Issues Paper 10.29.
107 IASC Issues Paper 10.29.
108 IASC Issues Paper 10.32.
109 IASC Issues Paper 10.32.
110 IASC Issues Paper 10.32.
111 IASC Issues Paper 10.29.
112 The SEC Observer comment to the Emerging Issues Task Force (EITF) on *Accounting for Gas-Balancing Arrangements* (formerly EITF 90-22) was codified in ASC 932-10-S99-5 and rescinded by FASB-ASU-2016-11 *Revenue Recognition* (Topic 605) and *Derivatives and Hedging* (Topic 815): Rescission of SEC Guidance Because of Accounting Standards Updates 2014-09 and 2014-16 Pursuant to Staff Announcements at the March 3, 2016 EITF Meeting.
113 IASC Issues Paper 11.17.
114 IASC Issues Paper 11.9-11.16.
115 IASC Issues Paper 7.61-7.68.
116 IASC Issues Paper 6.64.
117 IASC Issues Paper, 12.14.
118 Former OIAC SORP 175.
119 Former OIAC SORP 176.
120 IASC Issues Paper, 12.14.
121 Former OIAC SORP 177-178.
122 Former OIAC SORP 179-180.
123 IASC Issues Paper, 7.13.
124 IASC Issues Paper, 7.19.
125 IASC Issues Paper, 7.20.
126 IASC Issues Paper, 7.36.
127 IASC Issues Paper, 7.39.
128 IASC Issues Paper, 7.41.
129 IASC Issues Paper, 7.42.
130 IASC Issues Paper, 7.46.
131 IASC Issues Paper, 7.49.
132 IASC Issues Paper, 7.50.
133 IASC Issues Paper, 7.23.
134 IASC Issues Paper, 7.24.
135 IASC Issues Paper, 7.25.
136 IASC Issues Paper, 7.61.
137 Global infomine www.technology.infomine.com/reviews/Blockcaving (accessed 09/10/2015).
138 IASC Issues Paper, 10.26.
139 IASC Issues Paper, 10.23.
140 IASC Issues Paper, 10.24.
141 IASC Issues Paper, 1.27.
142 HM Revenue & Customs website, www.hmrc.gov.uk, *International – Taxation of UK oil production.*
143 IASC Issues Paper, Glossary of Terms.

Index of extracts from financial statements

Index of standards

Framework

IFRS 1

IFRS 2

IFRS 3 (2007)

IFRS 3

IFRS 4

IFRS 5

IFRS 6

IFRS 7 (2010)

IFRS 7

IFRS 8

IFRS 9 (2012)

IFRS 9 (2014)

IFRS 9

IFRS 10

IFRS 11

IFRS 12

IFRS 13

IFRS 14

IFRS 15

IFRS 16

IAS 1

IAS 2

IAS 7

IAS 10

IAS 11

IAS 12

IAS 16

IAS 17

IAS 18 (2008)

IAS 18

IAS 19

IAS 20

IAS 21

IAS 23

IAS 24

IAS 27 (2012)

IAS 27

IAS 28

IAS 29

IAS 32

IAS 33

IAS 34

IAS 36

IAS 37

IAS 38

IAS 39 (2012)

IAS 39

IAS 40

IAS 41 (2008)

IAS 41 (2012)

IAS 41

IFRIC 1

IFRIC 2

IFRIC 4

IFRIC 5

IFRIC 6

IFRIC 7

IFRIC 9

IFRIC 13

IFRIC 14

IFRIC 15

IFRIC 16

IFRIC 17

IFRIC 18

IFRIC 19

SIC 29

SIC 31

SIC 32

MC

Index

Notes

Notes

Notes

Notes

Notes